Edition 1

Retail Entertainment Data Publishing Limited
Paulton House, 8 Shepherdess Walk, London N1 7LB, UK
Tel: +44 (0)171 566 8216 Fax +44 (0)171 566 8259

Gramophone MusicMaster

EDITOR	Philippa Bunting
ASSISTANT EDITOR	Malcolm Walker
COMPILERS	Barbara Gavrielides Brian Godfrey Kathleen McSwiney Mark Walker Kathryn Wolfendale
SALES & MARKETING MANAGER	Brian Mulligan
SALES MANAGER	Marie-Clare Murray
PRODUCT MANAGER	Chris Spalding
PRODUCTION MANAGER	Keith Hawkins
PUBLISHING ASSISTANT	Becca Bailey
PUBLISHER	Brenda Daly

The Editor gratefully acknowledges the assistance given by John T. Hughes in the preparation of this publication

All enquiries:

Retail Entertainment Data Publishing Ltd.
Paulton House, 8 Shepherdess Walk, London N1 7LB, UK
Tel: +44 (0)171 566 8216 Fax: +44 (0)171 566 8259

Front Cover photograph supplied by The Image Bank, London, UK
Photograph by John Callanan

Database typeset by Barbers, Wrotham, Kent, UK

Printed and bound in Great Britain by BPC Wheatons Ltd., Exeter, Devon, UK

ISBN 0 904520 93 5

Recording and distributing companies reserve the right to withdraw any disc or cassette without giving previous notice, and although every effort is made to obtain the latest information for inclusion in this catalogue, no guarantee can be given that all the recordings listed are immediately available. Any difficulties should be referred to the issuing company concerned. The Publishers cannot accept responsibility for the consequences of any error. When ordering, purchasers are advised to quote all relevant information in addition to catalogue numbers.

Introduction

Since 1953 the Gramophone Classical Catalogue has been accepted as the ultimate authority on classical recordings. This first edition of the Gramophone Opera Catalogue is a product of the same extensive database and expertise that produces the Classical Catalogue.

Details of every currently available opera recording can be found in these pages: whether your interest is singers, composers, complete operas, or all three, the information is here. Fully cross-referenced indexes, designed for ease of use, provide the opera lover with everything he or she could want to know about recorded opera:

- Full cast details with their respective roles
- Number of acts
- Name of librettist
- English translations and nicknames
- Date and place of first performances
- Specific excerpts

A complete Artist index shows at a glance all available recordings by each featured singer.

The Titles index identifies works in the main Composer listing either by title or English translation.

This unrivalled wealth of detail, completely cross-referenced throughout makes the Gramophone Opera Catalogue the indispensable reference source for the collector of opera on CD.

Contents

How to use the catalogue

Title index

All titles, translations and nicknames found here are cross referenced to the Composer index.

Composer index

Works are listed in alphabetical order underneath each composer heading.

Each work title consists of:

- The full name of the opera, with any commonly used nickname or English translation
- The type of work (e.g.. 'opera seria'), number of acts, date and place of the first performance, name of librettist and any other relevant information
- A listing of arias, choruses and other contents

Recording information

- Complete opera recordings appear first in the listing, with full details of the cast and their respective roles
- Recitals or recordings of operatic highlights are listed below. Individual excerpts are specified, followed by abbreviated details of the featured artists (cross-referenced with the Artist index)
- Year of recording
- Record Company code cross-referenced to the Labels and Distributors index
- Number of discs in square brackets
- Date of review in Gramophone magazine
- Catalogue number, with recording format symbols

see the illustrated examples on adjoining page

Artist index

All artists who appear in the Composer index are listed alphabetically here and are cross-referenced with the works on which they perform, or the title and catalogue number of the relevant entry in the Concert index

Concert index

All recordings listed in the Composer index appear here, sorted numerically within each Record Company. Where applicable, abbreviated details of non-operatic works contained on recordings are noted, with any additional artists. These works or performers not associated with opera do not appear either in the Composer or Artist index.

Abbreviations used in this catalogue

This list will help identify terms presented in the abbreviated form throughout the catalogue as well as shortened names for many orchestras and ensembles.

Composer index examples

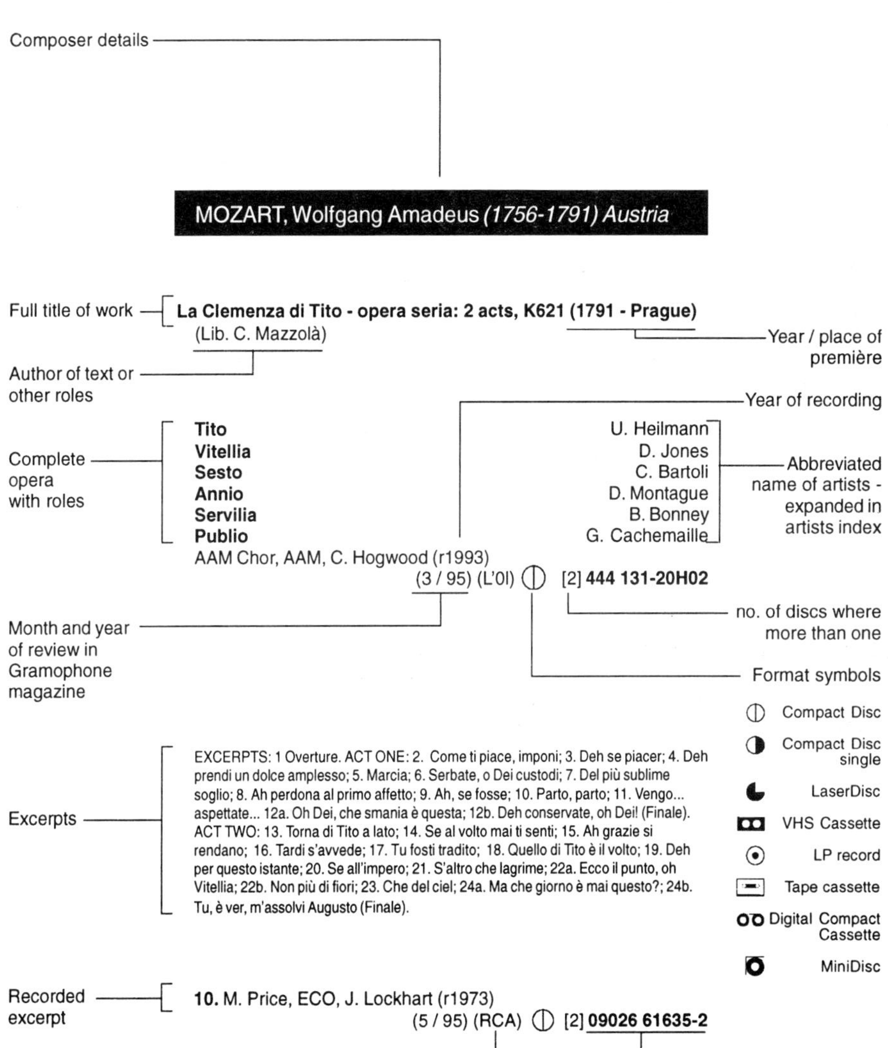

Composer details
MOZART, Wolfgang Amadeus *(1756-1791) Austria*
Full title of work
La Clemenza di Tito - opera seria: 2 acts, K621 (1791 - Prague)
(Lib. C. Mazzolà)
Year / place of première
Author of text or other roles
Year of recording
Complete opera with roles
Tito U. Heilmann
Vitellia D. Jones
Sesto C. Bartoli
Annio D. Montague
Servilia B. Bonney
Publio G. Cachemaille
Abbreviated name of artists - expanded in artists index
AAM Chor, AAM, C. Hogwood (r1993)
(3 / 95) (L'OI) [2] **444 131-20H02**
Month and year of review in Gramophone magazine
no. of discs where more than one
Format symbols
Compact Disc
Compact Disc single
LaserDisc
VHS Cassette
LP record
Tape cassette
Digital Compact Cassette
MiniDisc
Excerpts
EXCERPTS: 1 Overture. ACT ONE: 2. Come ti piace, imponi; 3. Deh se piacer; 4. Deh prendi un dolce amplesso; 5. Marcia; 6. Serbate, o Dei custodi; 7. Del più sublime soglio; 8. Ah perdona al primo affetto; 9. Ah, se fosse; 10. Parto, parto; 11. Vengo... aspettate... 12a. Oh Dei, che smania è questa; 12b. Deh conservate, oh Dei! (Finale). ACT TWO: 13. Torna di Tito a lato; 14. Se al volto mai ti senti; 15. Ah grazie si rendano; 16. Tardi s'avvede; 17. Tu fosti tradito; 18. Quello di Tito è il volto; 19. Deh per questo istante; 20. Se all'impero; 21. S'altro che lagrime; 22a. Ecco il punto, oh Vitellia; 22b. Non più di fiori; 23. Che del ciel; 24a. Ma che giorno è mai questo?; 24b. Tu, è ver, m'assolvi Augusto (Finale).
Recorded excerpt
10. M. Price, ECO, J. Lockhart (r1973)
(5 / 95) (RCA) [2] **09026 61635-2**
Abbreviated form of record company name
Catalogue number

Labels and **distributors** index

Alongside each catalogue number in the main indexes an abbreviated code denotes the issuing company of the recording. These labels and their various distributors are listed below.

An asterisk (*) against a distributor name indicates that the company may carry only selected items.

Price codes
Ⓕ Full price above £9·99
Ⓜ Medium price £6·99 - £9·99
Ⓑ Budget price £4·99 - £6·99
Ⓢ Super budget price below £4·99
All labels without a code are presumed to be Full price

Some label entries, displaced from their normal alphabetical positions, have been cross-referenced for ease of use.

Code	Label	Distributor
A		
ABBE	**Abbey Recording Co** *(Abbey Ⓜ, Alpha)*	Abbey Recording Co
ABBS	**Abbey Records** (SCS Music)	Conifer
ABCC	**ABC Classics**	Select
ACAD	**Academy Collection** Ⓜ	Terry Blood Distribution
ACCE	**Accent** *(Accent, Accent 2)*	Complete Record Co
ACCO	**Accord** (Musidisc)	Harmonia Mundi
ACNT	**Accento**	Accento
ACOU	**Acoustics Records**	Conifer
ACTA	**Acta Records**	Acta Records/Impetus
ADES	**Adès**	Harmonia Mundi
AETE	**Aeterna**	Complete Record Co
AL S	**Al Segno**	Koch International
ALBA	**Albany**	Albany Distribution
ALIE	**Alienor**	Harmonia Mundi
ALPH	**Alphée**	Discovery Records
ALTA	**Altarus**	Albany Distribution
ALTM	**Altamira Records**	Altamira Records
ALTN	**Alta Nova**	Michael G Thomas
ALTO	**Alto Records**	Complete Record Co
AMAT	**Amati**	Complete Record Co
AMBI	**Ambitus**	RRD (Distribution)
AMCA	**AmCam Recordings**	TradeLink Music Distribution
AMGR	**American Gramaphone**	New Note
AMIA	**Amiata**	Harmonia Mundi
AMON	**Amon Ra**	Harmonia Mundi/*CM
AMPH	**Amphion Sound Recordings** Ⓜ	Priory
ANDC	**André Charlin**	Discovery Records
ANDR	**Andromeda**	Kingdom
APPL	**Applecross**	Applecross
APR	**APR** Ⓜ	Harmonia Mundi/APR
ARAB	**Arabesque**	Seaford Music
ARC	**ARC Music**	ARC Music
ARCA	**Arcana**	Koch International
ARCL	**Arc of Light**	Sony Music Entertainment
ARCH	**Archiv Produktion** *(Archiv Produktion, Archiv Produktion Galleria Ⓜ)*	PolyGram Record Operations
ARCI	**Archiphon**	TradeLink Music Distribution
ARCO	**Arcobaleno**	Complete Record Co
AREM	**Arembe**	Arembe
ARGO	**Argo**	PolyGram Record Operations
ARHI	**Archive Documents**	Michael G Thomas
ARIO	**Arion**	Discovery Records
ARIS	**Arista**	BMG UK

Code	Label	Distributor
ARS	**Ars Produktion**	RRD (Distribution)
ARSC	**Ars Classicum** (Vox)	Complete Record Co
ARSM	**Ars Musici**	Vanderbeek and Imrie
ART	**Art and Music**	Priory
ARTI	**Artificial Eye**	FoxVideo Sales
AS D	**AS Discs**	Kingdom
ASPE	**Aspen Music**	Aspen/Impetus
ASTR	**Astrée Auvidis**	Harmonia Mundi
ASV	**ASV** *(ASV, COE, Gaudeamus, Musicmasters, White Line Ⓜ, Quicksilva Ⓢ)*	ASV/Koch International
ATHN	**Athene** (D&J Recording)	Albany Distribution
ATRI	**Atrium**	Discovery Records
ATS	**Arturo Toscanini Society**	Michael G Thomas
ATTA	**Attacca Babel**	Impetus
AUDI	**Audiofon**	APR
AUDP	**Audiophile Labs**	Sound and Media
AUVI	**Auvidis** *(Classique, Valois, Valois Biennnale de Lyon, Travelling)*	Harmonia Mundi

B

Code	Label	Distributor
B'NA	**B'nai Brith**	Jewish Music Distribution
BALK	**Balkanton** Ⓜ	Pinnacle/Impetus
BAND	**Bandleader**	Conifer
BATO	**Baton**	RRD (Distribution)
BAUE	**Michael Bauer Editions**	Impetus
BAY	**Bay Cities**	Albany Distribution
BAYE	**Bayer**	Priory
BAYR	**Concerto Bayreuth**	RRD (Distribution)
BBCR	**BBC Radio Classics**	Carlton/Complete Record Co
BEAG	**Bel Age**	Target
BEEC	**Sir Thomas Beecham Trust** Ⓜ	Beecham
BELA	**Belart** Ⓑ	Karussell/PolyGram Record Operations
BELL	**Belltree**	Dragonsfire
BERL	**Berlin Classics**	Complete Record Co
BETA	**Beta Productions**	Beta Productions
BEUL	**Beulah** Ⓜ	Priory/Beulah
BIDD	**Biddulph** Ⓜ	Biddulph
BIRM	**Birmingham Bach Choir**	Birmingham Bach Choir
BIS	**BIS**	Conifer
BITT	**Bitter and Twisted**	Impetus
BLOC	**Edition Block**	Impetus
BMS	**British Music Society**	British Music Society
BOGR	**Biographies in Music** (Lyric) Ⓜ	Complete Record Co
BONG	**Bongiovanni** *(Bongiovanni, Golden Age of Opera)*	Kingdom
BOST	**Boston Skyline**	Complete Record Co
BREW	**Brewhouse Music**	Complete Record Co
BRID	**Bridge**	Complete Record Co
BRIT	**British Music Label**	Kingdom/Forties Recording Co
BRM	**BRM**	Bosworth and Co
BUTT	**Butterfly Music** Ⓜ	RRD (Distribution)
BVHA	**BVHaast**	Cadillac

C

Code	Label	Distributor
CALA	**Cala**	Complete Record Co
CALC	**Calle Classics**	Complete Record Co
CALI	**Calig**	Priory

Code	Label	Distributor
CALL	**Calliope**	Harmonia Mundi
CAM	**CAM Productions**	Silver Sounds CD
CAMB	**Cambria**	RRD (Distribution)
CAME	**Camerata**	Impetus
CAMP	**Campion Records**	RRD (Distribution)
CNTO	**Cantoris**	*Koch International*
CANY	**Canyon Classics**	Complete Record Co
CANZ	**Canzone** (Kontrapunkt)	Impetus
CAPR	**Capriccio** *(Capriccio, Capella Edition)*	Target
CPRI	**Caprice** *(Caprice, Collector's Classics)*	*Complete Record Co*
CPRO	**Capriole** Ⓜ	*Manygate Marketing*
CAST	**Castle Vision**	BMG UK
CATE	**Cantate**	RRD (Distribution)
CATA	**Catalyst**	BMG UK
CAVA	**Cavalier** Ⓜ	Kingdom
CAVE	**Cavendish Cassettes** Ⓜ	Cavendish Distribution
CAW	**CAW Records**	Clive Wilkinson
CBC	**CBC Records** (*Musica Viva, SM5000, Perspective*)	Kingdom
CBS	**CBS** (Sony) (*CBS Masterworks, Masterworks Portrait* Ⓜ, *Digital Masters* Ⓜ, *Maestro* Ⓑ, Odyssey Ⓑ)	Sony Music Entertainment
CBS	**CBS** (France)	Discovery Records
CDM	**CdM Russian Season**	Harmonia Mundi
CEDI	**Cedille**	Seaford Music
CELE	**Celestial Harmonies**	Select
CENT	**Centaur**	Complete Record Co
EPM	**Classical Collector**	*Discovery Records*
CFP	**Classics for Pleasure** Ⓑ	Music for Pleasure
CFM	**Classic FM**	Complete Record Co
CGP	**Covent Garden Pioneer** *(video cassettes only)*	Covent Garden Pioneer FSP
CHAN	**Chandos** (*Chandos, Chaconne, Brass, New Direection, Collect* Ⓜ)	Chandos
CHAT	**Chatsworth**	Complete Record Co
CHES	**Chesky**	Complete Record Co
CHIE	**Chief**	Cadillac
CHNN	**Channel Classics** *(Channel Classics, Channel Crossings, Canal Grande* Ⓜ*)*	Select
CHNT	**Le Chant du Monde**	Harmonia Mundi
CHOI	**Choice Recordings**	Choice Recordings
CHOR	**Chorale Classics**	TSC Enterprises
CHRI	**Christophorus** *(Christophorus, Entree* Ⓜ*)*	Select
CHTI	**Chanticleer**	RRD (Distribution)
CIRR	**Cirrus** Ⓜ	Castle Communications
CLAD	**Claddagh**	*CM
CLAR	**Claremont** Ⓜ	Complete Record Co
CLAS	**Classic Studio**	RRD (Distribution)
CLAT	**Clarton**	Czech Music Enterpreises
CLAU	**Claudio**	Complete Record Co/Claudio
CLAV	**Claves** *(Claves, Favor* Ⓜ*)*	Complete Record Co
CLLE	**Collegium**	Koch International
CLOR	**Cleveland Orchestra** *(75th Anniversary CD Edition)*	Cleveland Orchestra
CLOU	**Cloud Nine Records**	Silva Screen
CLRI	**Clarinet Classics**	Select
CLTS	**Collets** Ⓜ	Complete Record Co
CMC	**Canadian Music Centre**	TradeLink Music Distribution
CNCE	**Concerto**	RRD (Distribution)
CNTE	**Canterino**	TradeLink Music Distribution
CNTI	**Continuum**	Select

Code	Label	Distributor
CNTO	**Cantoris**	Koch International
CNZO	**Canzone Italiana**	RRD (Distribution)
CLLE	***Collegium***	*Koch International*
COCE	**Consonance** Ⓜ/Ⓕ	Koch International
COLL	**Collins Classics** *(Collins Classics, 20th Century Plus, Quest* Ⓜ*)*	Conifer
COLO	**Colosseum**	Pinnacle
COLU	**Columbia**	Sony Music Entertainment
CONC	**Concert Artists**	Concert Artist/Fidelio
COND	**Condon Collection**	New Note
CONI	**Conifer Classics**	Conifer
CONN	**Connoisseur Society**	Harmony Records
CONS	**Consort**	Consort Records
COOP	**Co-operative Union**	Co-operative Union
DONE	**Donemus Composers' Voice**	Impetus
COPT	**Classical Options**	Target
CORO	**Coronata**	Presto Music
CPI	**CPI**	Quantum Audio
CPO	**CPO**	Koch International
CPRI	**Caprice** *(Caprice, Collector's Classics)*	Complete Record Co
CPRO	**Capriole** Ⓜ	Manygate Marketing
CRAM	**Cramer Music**	Priory/Cramer Music
CRD	**CRD**	Select
CRYS	**Crystal**	Impetus
CSTL	**Castle**	Castle Communications
CZEC	**Czech Radio**	Czech Music Enterpeises

D

Code	Label	Distributor
MDG	***Dabringhaus und Grimm***	*Koch International*
DACA	**Da Capo** (Marco Polo)	Select
DANA	**Danacord**	Discovery Records
DANI	**Danica**	RRD (Distribution)
DARM	**Darmo**	Darmo Records
DATU	**Datum**	Priory
DCB	**DCB Records**	DCB Records
DECC	**Decca Classics** *(Decca, New Line, Enterprise, Entartete Musik, The British Collection* Ⓜ*, Jubilee* Ⓜ*, Ovation* Ⓜ*, DDD Ovation* Ⓜ*, Double Decca* Ⓜ*, Grandi Voci* Ⓜ*, Grand Opera* Ⓜ*, Opera Gala* Ⓜ*, Serenata* Ⓜ*, Historic* Ⓜ*, Cinema Gala* Ⓜ*, 100 Best Tunes* Ⓜ*, World of . . .* Ⓜ*, Weekend* Ⓑ*, Headline* Ⓑ*)*	PolyGram Record Operations
DELL	**Dell'Arte**	Symposium Records
DELO	**Delos** *(3000 series, 1000 series* Ⓜ*)*	Conifer
DENO	**Denon** *(Denon, Aliare, Repertoire* Ⓜ*)*	Conifer
DERV	**Dervorguilla**	Harmonia Mundi
DG	**Deutsche Grammophon** *(DG, DG Galleria* Ⓜ*, 20th Century Classics* Ⓜ*, Dokumente* Ⓜ*, 3-D Classics* Ⓜ*,* Doubles Ⓜ*, Compact Editions* Ⓜ*, Compact Classics* Ⓑ*, Privilege* Ⓑ*, Classikon* Ⓑ*, Resonance* Ⓑ*)*	PolyGram Record Operations
DHM	**Deutsche Harmonia Mundi** *(Deutsche Harmonia Mundi, Editio Classica* Ⓜ*, Mozart Edition* Ⓑ*)*	BMG UK
DINE	**Dinemec Classics**	Scratch Records
DINT	**Discover International** Ⓢ/Ⓜ	Complete Record Co
DIVA	**Divas**	Divas
DIVE	**Divertimento**	RRD (Distribution)

Code	Label	Distributor
DIVI	**Divine Art**	Albany Distribution
DIVO	**Divox**	Complete Record Co
DIVU	**Divucsa**	Discovery Records
DONE	**Donemus Composers' Voice**	Impetus
DORE	**Doremi**	Priory
DORI	**Dorian**	Select
DORO	**Doron Music**	Discovery Records
DOYE	**Doyen Recordings**	Conifer
DPV	**De Plein Vent**	RRD (Distribution)
DRG	**DRG**	New Note
DUTT	**Dutton Laboratories** Ⓜ/Ⓕ	Complete Record Co
DYNA	**Dynamic** *(Dynamic, Il canale)*	Priory

E

Code	Label	Distributor
EAR	**Ear-Rational**	Impetus
EART	**Earthsounds**	Earthsounds
EBS	**EBS**	Kingdom
ECM	**ECM New Series**	New Note
EDA	**Edition Abseits**	RRD (Distribution)
EDEL	**Edelweiss**	Planetarium
EDIT	**Edit**	Czech Music Enterprises
EKLI	**Eklipse**	Parsifal Distribution
NONE	***Elektra Nonesuch***	*Warner Classics*
ELAN	**Elan**	Albany Distribution
ELCT	**Electrecord**	Priory
ELIT	**Elite Music**	Trittico
EMEC	**EMEC**	RRD (Distribution)
EMER	**Emergo Classics**	Complete Record Co
EMI	**EMI Classics** *(EMI, Reflexe, Studio* Ⓜ, *Digital DDD* Ⓜ, *Références* Ⓜ, *Great Recordings of the Century* Ⓜ, *Phoenixa* Ⓜ, *British Composers* Ⓜ, *L'Esprit français* Ⓜ, Klemperer Edition Ⓜ, Mozart Edition Ⓜ, Beecham Edition Ⓜ, Rouge et Noir Ⓜ, *Fun with Music* Ⓜ, *Miles of Music* Ⓜ*)*	EMI
EMIL	**EMI Laser** *(EMI Laser* Ⓑ, *EMI Mozart '91* Ⓑ*)*	Music for Pleasure
EMIN	**EMI Eminence** Ⓜ	Music for Pleasure
ENCO	**Encore**	Michael G Thomas
ENGL	**English Recording Co**	Complete Record Co
ENSA	**Ensayo**	Discovery Records
ENSB	**Ensemblegram**	Complete Record Co
ENSE	**Ensemble**	Kingdom
ENTP	**Enterprise**	Priory
ENTR	**Entr'acte** (Fifth Continent)	Silva Screen
EPIC	**Epic**	Sony Music Entertainment
EPM	**Classical Collector**	Discovery Records
ERAS	**Erasmus**	Impetus
ERAT	**Erato** *(Erato, MusiFrance, Bonsai* Ⓜ, *Emeraude* Ⓜ, *Libretto* Ⓜ, *Résidence* Ⓑ*)*	Warner Classics
ERIE	**Elysium Records**	RRD (Distribution)
ERMI	**Ermitage** Ⓜ	Target
ETCE	**Etcetera**	TradeLink Music Distribution
EUFO	**Eufoda**	Priory
EURO	**Eurodisc** *(Eurodisc, Mozart Year '91* Ⓑ*)*	BMG UK
EVEN	**Even Classics**	RRD (Distribution)
EVER	**Everest**	Complete Record Co

Code	Label	Distributor
EXTR	**Extraplatte**	Impetus
EYE	**Eye of the Storm**	Complete Record Co

F

Code	Label	Distributor
FACE	**Facet** (Delos) Ⓜ	Conifer
FAMO	**Famous and Fabulous**	Famous and Fabulous
FERM	**Fermate**	RRD (Distribution)
FEST	**Festivo**	Priory
FIDE	**Fidelio Classics**	Complete Record Co
FINL	**Finlandia**	Warner Classics
FIRS	**First Edition/Louisville**	Albany Distribution
FISH	**Fish Ear Records**	Fish Ear Communications
FLAM	**FlamencOVision**	Pinnacle
FLAP	**Flapper** (Pavilion)	Pinnacle
FLOA	**Floating Earth**	Complete Record Co
FLY	**Fly Records**	Bucks Music
FONE	**Fonè**	UK Distribution
FONI	**Fonitcetra** Ⓜ/Ⓕ	Target
FORL	**Forlane**	Target
FORT	**The Fourties**	RRD (Distribution)
FOUR	**Four Hands Music**	Priory
FOX	**20th Century Fox**	BMG UK
FOXG	**Foxglove Audio**	Complete Record Co
FOYE	**Foyer**	RRD (Distribution)
FRAG	**Fragile Records**	Pinnacle
FRST	**First Night Records**	Pinnacle
FSM	**FSM**	RRD (Distribution)
FY	**Fy Discovery Records**	
FYLK	**Fylkingen Records**	RER Megacorp

G

Code	Label	Distributor
GALA	**Gala** Ⓑ	Target
GALL	**Gallo**	RRD (Distribution)
GASP	**Gasparo**	Complete Record Co
GEES	**Geest**	Cadillac
GEGA	**Gega**	Impetus
GFON	**Gramofono 2000**	Complete Record Co
GHA	**GHA** Ⓜ/Ⓕ	Koch International
GIME	**Gimell**	Conifer
GIUL	**Giulia**	RRD (Distribution)
GLOB	**Globe**	Complete Record Co
GLOR	**Gloriae Dei Cantores**	Priory
GLOS	**Glossa**	Harmonia Mundi
GM R	**GM Recording**	Impetus
GNP	**GNP Crescendo Records**	Silva Screen
GOTH	**Gothic**	Gothic/Pro Organo
GRAS	**Grasmere**	Grasmere
GREA	**Great Hall**	Michael G Thomas
GREE	**Greentrax**	Conifer
GROS	**Grosvenor Nostalgia**	Grosvenor Nostalgia
GRP	**GRP**	New Note
GUIL	**Guild**	Guild

Code	Label	Distributor
H		
HANS	**Hänssler**	Select
HAPY	**Happy Days**	Conifer
HARM	**Harmonia Mundi** *(Harmonia Mundi, Musique d'abord Ⓜ, Plus Ⓑ)*	Harmonia Mundi
HATH	**Hat-Hut**	Harmonia Mundi
HEAR	**Hearts of Space**	Ultima Thule
HENE	**Heneghan and Lawson**	Heneghan and Lawson
HERA	**Herald**	Koch International
HERI	**Heritage Recordings**	Mirabilis
HISP	**Hispavox Zarzuela**	Discovery Records
HIST	**Historical Performers**	Kingdom
HLCN	**Helicon**	Helicon
HUNG	**Hungaroton**	Target
HUNT	**Hunter's Moon**	Symposium Records
HYPE	**Hyperion** *(Hyperion, Helios Ⓜ)*	Select
I		
IKON	**Ikon** *(Ikon Ⓜ, Neva Records)*	Priory
ILHA	**Ilha Formosa Records**	Seaford Music
IMG	**IMG Records**	Carlton/Complete Record Co
IMP	**IMP** *(IMP Masters Ⓕ, Red Label Ⓜ, Allegro Ⓜ, CDI Ⓜ, Duet Ⓜ, IMP Classics Ⓜ, Contour Classics Ⓜ, NTI Ⓜ, Discover the Classics Ⓑ, IMP Collectors Ⓑ, PWK Classics Ⓑ)*	Carlton/Complete Record Co
IMPE	**Imperial Sound**	Imperial Sound
INTD	**Intrada**	Silva Screen
INTU	**Intuition Records**	New Note
IRCC	**IRCC**	Parsifal Distribution
IRON	**Iron Needle**	Kingdom
ISIS	**Isis Records**	Complete Record Co
ITAL	**Italian Opera Rarities**	RRD (Distribution)
ITM	**ITM** *(jazz)*	Koch International
ITM	**ITM** *(other titles)*	TradeLink Music Distribution
J		
JADE	**Jade**	BMG UK
JARO	**Jaro**	New Note
JERU	**Jerusalem**	Jewish Music Distribution
JEWI	**Jewish Music Productions**	Jewish Music Distribution
JLR	**JLR**	KJ Associates
JMP	**JMP**	RRD (Distribution)
JMR	**John Marks Records**	May Audio Marketing
JMS	**Stafford**	Stafford
JOS	**JOS Records**	JOS Records
K		
KING	**Kingdom**	Kingdom
KINS	**Kingsway**	Complete Record Co
KLT	**KLT**	Kingdom
KLVI	**Klavier**	UK Distribution

Code	Label	Distributor
KOCH	**Koch International** *(Koch International Classics, Koch International Ⓜ, Koch Historic Ⓜ, Koch Treasure Ⓜ, Koch Praesent Ⓑ)*	Koch International
SCHW	***Koch Schwann***	*Koch International*
KONT	**Kontrapunkt**	Impetus
KOSS	**Koss Classics**	HW International
K617	**K617**	Discovery Records

L

Code	Label	Distributor
LAMM	**Lammas**	Lammas
LANS	**Lansdowne**	Lansdowne
LARG	**Largo Records**	Complete Record Co
LASE	**LaserLight** (Capriccio) Ⓢ	Target
L'EM	**L'Empreinte Digitale**	Harmonia Mundi
LEGA	**Legato Classics** (Lyric) *(Legato Classics, HRE Ⓜ, Standing Room Only Ⓜ)*	Complete Record Co
LEGE	**Legend**	Kingdom
LEO	**Leo Records**	Impetus
LHAL	**London Hall**	Impetus
LIBR	**Libra**	Griffin Soundalive
LIGI	**Ligia**	Discovery Records
LIND	**Lindenberg**	Priory
LINN	**Linn Records**	PolyGram Record Operations
LODI	**Lodia**	Lodia
LOND	**London** *(London, Jubilee Ⓜ)*	PolyGram Record Operations
LONG	**LongMan Records**	LongMan Records
L'OI	**L'Oiseau-Lyre** *(L'Oiseau-Lyre, Florilegium Ⓜ)*	PolyGram Record Operations
LORE	**LoreIt**	Complete Record Co
LOTO	**Lotos**	RRD (Distribution)
LOTU	**Lotus**	Impetus
LSO	**LSO Classic Masterpieces**	Carlton/Complete Record Co
LUNA	**Lunadisc**	Complete Record Co
LYCH	**Lyrichord**	CM Distribution
LYRC	**Lyric**	Complete Record Co
LYRI	**Lyrita**	Nimbus

M

Code	Label	Distributor
MAMI	**Master Mix**	New Note
MANC	**Manchester Camerata**	Camerata Productions
MAND	**Mandala**	Harmonia Mundi
MARC	**Marco Polo**	Select
MARQ	**Marquis**	Kingdom
MATE	**Materiali Sonari**	New Note
MATT	**Musica Attacca**	Musica Attacca
MAWS	**Mawsom and Wareham**	BMG UK
MAX	**Max Sound**	Max Sound
MAYA	**Maya Recordings**	Complete Record Co
MAYH	**Kevin Mayhew**	Priory
MCA	**MCA Records**	BMG UK
MCI	**Music Club International**	VCI Distribution
MDG	**Dabringhaus und Grimm**	Koch International
MEDI	**Medici-Whitehall**	Medici-Whitehall
MEL	**Mel Recordings**	Koch International
MELC	**Melcot**	Melcot
MELO	**Melodiya**	BMG UK
MEMO	**Memories** (Nuova Era) Ⓜ	Complete Record Co

Code	Label	Distributor
MERC	**Mercury** Ⓜ	PolyGram Record Operations
MERI	**Meridian** *(Meridian, Duo Ⓜ)*	Nimbus
MERL	**Merlin**	Merlin
METI	**Metier**	Albany/Metier Sound and Vision
METR	**Metronome**	Complete Record Co
MEZH	**Mezhdunarodnaya Kniga**	Complete Record Co
MFP	**Music for Pleasure**	Music for Pleasure
MGB	**Muzikszene Schweiz**	Complete Record Co
MILA	**Milan**	BMG UK
MIRA	**Mirabilis**	Albany Distribution
MITR	**Mitra**	Priory
MKI	**MKI Disques**	Priory
MMAS	**Music Masters** (UK)	Target
MMOI	**Memoir Classics**	Target
MNTA	**Montague Music**	Montague Music
MOBS	**Musical Observations**	Albany Distribution
MODE	**Mode Records**	Harmonia Mundi
MONR	**Monré Records**	Monré Records
MONT	**Montaigne** (Auvidis)	Harmonia Mundi
MOSC	**Musica Oscura**	Complete Record Co
MOTE	**Motette**	Priory
MOZA	**Mozart Edition**	Mozart Edition
MPHO	**Musicaphon**	RRD (Distribution)
MSCM	**Music Memoria**	Discovery Records
MSVE	**Musica Sveciae**	Complete Record Co
MSOU	**Mastersound** *(Mastersound, Fanfare, Profile Ⓜ)*	RRD (Distribution)
MULT	**Multisonic** Ⓜ/Ⓕ	Priory
MUSD	**Musidisc**	Harmonia Mundi
MUSI	**Music & Arts**	Harmonia Mundi
MUSM	**Music Masters** (US)	Nimbus

N

Code	Label	Distributor
NALB	**New Albion**	Harmonia Mundi
NATI	**Droffig** (National Trust)	Discovery Records
NAXO	**Naxos** Ⓢ	Select
NEW	**New World**	Harmonia Mundi
NEWP	**Newport Classic** *(Newport Classic, Newport Premier)*	RRD (Distribution)
NEWT	**New Tone**	Impetus
NIGH	**Nightingale Classics**	Koch International
NIMB	**Nimbus** *(Nimbus, Prima Voce Ⓜ)*	Nimbus
NMC	**NMC**	Complete Record Co
NMCL	**NM Classics**	Impetus
NONE	**Elektra Nonesuch**	Warner Classics
NORT	**Northeastern**	Priory
NOVA	**Novalis**	Albany Distribution
NOVL	**Novelbond**	Novelbond
NUOV	**Nuova Era** *(Nuova Era, Ancient Music)*	Complete Record Co
NYOS	**National Youth Orchestra of Scotland**	National Youth Orchestra of Scotland

O

Code	Label	Distributor
O111	**Opus 111**	Harmonia Mundi
ODE	**Ode** *(Ode, Manu Classic, Voyager)*	Discovery Records
OLYM	**Olympia** *(Olympia Ⓜ, Explorer)*	Priory
ONDI	**Ondine** *(Ondine, Octopus)*	Koch International

Code	Label	Distributor
ONGA	**Ongaku Records**	Quantum Audio
ONYX	**Onyx**	RRD (Distribution)
OPAL	**Opal** (Pavilion)	Harmonia Mundi
OPRA	**Opera Rara**	Opera Rara
TRES	***Opera Tres***	*Ashley Mark Publishing*
O111	***Opus 111***	*Harmonia Mundi*
OP3	**Opus 3**	May Audio Marketing/Pentacone
ORCH	**Orchid**	Complete Record Co
ORFE	**Orfeo**	Koch International
OTTA	**Ottavo**	Priory
OXRE	**OxRecs**	Priory/OxRecs

P

Code	Label	Distributor
PALL	**Palladio**	RRD (Distribution)
PAN	**Pan Classics**	Vanderbeek and Imrie
PANE	**Pantheon**	Kingdom
PANG	**Pangea**	Sony Music Entertainment
PANT	**Panton** Ⓜ	RRD (Distribution)
PART	**Partridge**	Seaford Music
PASP	**Past Perfect**	Terry Blood Distribution
PAUL	**Paula**	TradeLink Music Distribution
PAVA	**Pavane**	Kingdom
PAVR	**Pavarotti Collection**	RRD (Distribution)
PEAR	**Pearl** (Pavilion)	Harmonia Mundi
PHIL	**Philips Classics** *(Philips, Point Music, Insignia* Ⓜ, *Mozart Edition* Ⓜ, *Silver Line* Ⓜ, *Musica da Camara* Ⓜ, *Baroque Classics* Ⓜ, Duo Ⓜ, Solo Ⓜ, *Legendary Classics* Ⓜ, *HighTech* Ⓜ, *Laser Line* Ⓜ, *Concert Classics* Ⓑ*)*	PolyGram Record Operations
PHOE	**Phoenix** (USA)	Complete Record Co
PHOG	**Phonographe** (Nuova Era) Ⓜ	Complete Record Co
PP	***Pianissimo*** Ⓜ	*Albany Distribution*
PIER	**Pierre Verany** Ⓕ	Kingdom
PIER	**Pierre Verany Favourites** Ⓜ	Discovery Records
PION	**Pioneer**	VCI Distribution
PKO	**PKO**	RRD (Distribution)
PLAN	**Plant Life**	Sympoisum Records
PLAT	**Platz**	Conifer
PLDO	**Polydor**	PolyGram Record Operations
PNT	**Point Music**	PolyGram Record Operations
POIN	**Point Records**	RRD (Distribution)
POLS	**Polskie Nagrania** (Muza)	Priory
POLY	**Polyphonic**	Conifer/Polyphonic
PP	**Pianissimo** Ⓜ	Albany Distribution
PRAG	**Praga** Ⓕ/Ⓜ	Harmonia Mundi
PREA	**Preamble** (Fifth Continent)	Silva Screen
PREI	**Preiser**	Harmonia Mundi
PRES	**President**	President Records
PREZ	**Prezioso**	Priory
PRIO	**Priory**	Priory
PROD	**ProDigital Recordings**	Albany Distribution
PROM	**Prometheus Records**	Silva Screen
PROP	**Proprius**	May Audio Marketing
PROR	**Pro Organo**	Gothic/Pro Organo
PROU	**Proudsound**	Conifer
PYRA	**Pyramid Records** (USA)	Priory

Code	Label	Distributor
QUAN	**Quantum**	Discovery Records
QUIN	**Quintana**	Harmonia Mundi

R

Code	Label	Distributor
RADY	**Radio Years**	Complete Record Co
RCA	**RCA Victor** *(RCA, Red Seal, Gold Seal Ⓜ, Victrola Ⓑ, Silver Seal Ⓑ)*	BMG UK
RECO	**The Record Collector**	The Record Collector
RED	**Red Sky**	*CM
REDC	**Redcliffe Recordings**	Complete Record Co
REFE	**Reference Recordings**	May Audio Marketing
REGE	**Regent**	Regent
RELI	**Relief**	Albany Distribution
REM	**REM Editions**	Priory
REPL	**Replay Music**	RRD (Distribution)
RIBB	**Ribbonwood**	Discovery Records
RNCM	**RNCM**	Royal Northern College of Music
ROH	**Royal Opera House Records**	Conifer
ROMA	**Romantic Robot**	Romantic Robot
ROMO	**Romophone**	Complete Record Co
ROND	**Rondo**	RRD (Distribution)
RPO	**RPO**	Carlton/Complete Record Co
RSR	**RSR**	R. Smith and Co
RUSS	**Russian Disc**	Koch International

S

Code	Label	Distributor
SAGA	**Saga Classics** Ⓜ	Complete Record Co
SAIN	**Sain**	Sain
SAKK	**Sakkaris Records**	Pinnacle
SALA	**Salabert Actuels**	Harmonia Mundi
SALI	**Soundalive**	Koch International
SAYD	**Saydisc**	Harmonia Mundi/*CM
SCHW	**Koch Schwann** Ⓜ/Ⓕ *(Musica Mundi, Musica Sacra)*	Koch International
SCOM	**Scott Music**	Albany Distribution
SDBD	**Soundboard Records**	Soundboard Records
SEAV	**Seaview Music**	Seaview Music
SERE	**Serendipity**	Koch International
SHEF	**Sheffield Lab**	Quantum Audio
SIGN	**Signum**	TradeLink Music Distribution
SILO	**Silver Octopus**	Silver Octopus
SILV	**Silva Screen** (Silva Screen, Silva Classics, Silva Treasury Ⓜ)	Silva Screen/Conifer
SINE	**Sine Qua Non**	Sine Qua Non
SKAR	**Skarbo**	Discovery Records
SMIT	**Smithsonian Folkways**	Koch International
SMP	**SMP**	Priory
SOLE	**Solesmes**	Priory
SOLS	**Solstice**	Discovery Records
SOMM	**Somm Recordings**	Albany Distribution
SONP	**Sonpact**	Seaford Music
SONY	**Sony Classical** *(Sony Classical, Vivarte, Berlitz Passport, British Pageant Ⓜ, West End Ⓜ, Essential Classics Ⓑ)*	Sony Music Entertainment

Code	Label	Distributor
SOUT	**Southern Cross** (Fifth Continent)	Silva Screen
SPHE	**Sphemusations**	Sphemusations
SPRI	**Springthyme Records**	Springthyme Records
STAD	**The Strad**	The Strad
STAN	**Stanyan**	Conifer
STAR	**Start Classics**	Koch International
STDV	**Stradivarius**	Priory
STEN	**Stentor**	Mirabilis
STER	**Sterling**	Priory
STOC	**Stockhausen**	Stockhausen-Verlag
STOK	**Stokowski Society**	Stokowski Society
STRA	**Stradivari Classics**	Michèle International
STUD	**Studio SM**	Discovery Records
SUIT	**Suite**	RRD (Distribution)
SUMM	**Summit Records**	Kingdom
SUPR	**Supraphon**	Koch International
SUTT	**Sutton Sound**	Sutton Sound
SWIS	**Swiss Pan**	Vanderbeek and Imrie
SYMP	**Symposium**	Symposium Records
SYPH	**Symphonia**	Discovery Records
SYPY	**Symphony**	Target

T

Code	Label	Distributor
TAHR	**Tahra**	Priory
TAIZ	**Taizé** (Auvidis)	Harmonia Mundi
TALE	**Talent**	Seaford Music
TALL	**Tall Poppies**	Complete Record Co
TARA	**Tara**	*CM/Conifer
TELA	**Telarc**	Conifer
TELD	**Teldec Classics** *(Teldec Classics, Das Alte Werk, Reference Ⓜ, Viva Mozart Ⓜ, Digital Experience Ⓜ, Esprit Ⓑ)*	Warner Classics
TELS	**Telstar**	BMG UK
TEMP	**Tempo** (Auvidis)	Harmonia Mundi/Discovery Records
TER	**TER Classics**	Koch International
TEST	**Testament**	Complete Record Co
THIR	**Third Mind**	Third Mind Records
THOD	**Thodey**	Griffin Soundalive
THOR	**Thorofon**	RRD (Distribution)
TIMB	**Timbre Records**	Koch International
TIMP	**Timpani**	Discovery Records
TITA	**Titanic**	TradeLink Music Distribution/ Jewish Music Distribution
TMPL	**Temple Records**	Temple Records
TREM	**Tremula Records**	Symposium Records
TRES	**Opera Tres**	Ashley Mark Publishing
TRIN	**Tring International** Ⓢ	Tring International/Priory
TRIT	**Trittico**	Trittico
TROU	**Troubadisc**	Complete Record Co
TUDO	**Tudor**	TradeLink Music Distribution
TUXE	**Tuxedo Music**	TradeLink Music Distribution

U

Code	Label	Distributor
ULTP	**Ultraphon**	Koch International
ULTR	**Ultrasonic**	Ultrasonic

Code	Label	Distributor
UNIC	**Unicorn-Kanchana** *(Unicorn-Kanchana, Souvenir Ⓜ)*	Harmonia Mundi
UNIT	**United Recording**	Complete Record Co
UPBE	**Upbeat Records**	Target
USK	**Usk Recordings**	Complete Record Co

V

Code	Label	Distributor
VAI	**Video Artists International**	Parsifal Distribution
VANG	**Vanguard Classics** Ⓢ/Ⓜ	Complete Record Co
VARE	**Varèse-Sarabande**	Pinnacle
VERO	**Verona** Ⓑ	Complete Record Co
VIEW	**View Video**	Parsifal Distribution
VIRG	**Virgin Classics** *(Virgin Classics, Veritas, LCO, Duo Ⓜ, Virgo Ⓑ)*	EMI
VIR2	**Virgin Records**	EMI
VIRT	**Virtuosi Records**	Virtuosi Records
VITA	**Vital Communicxtions**	Vital Communications
VMM	**Vienna Modern Masters**	TradeLink Music Distribution
VOIC	**Voiceprint**	Voiceprint
VOIX	**Voix Celeste**	Voix Celeste
VOX	**Vox** *(Vox Turnabout Ⓑ, Vox Cum Laude Ⓜ, Vox Legends Ⓜ, Vox Box Ⓑ, Vox Unique Ⓜ, Allegretto Ⓑ)*	Complete Record Co

W

Code	Label	Distributor
WALH	**Walhall Records**	Parsifal Distribution
WALS	**Walsingham**	New Note
WCOU	**Watercourse**	Impetus
WEA	**WEA**	Warner Classics
WERG	**Wergo**	Harmonia Mundi
WIEN	**Wienerworld Classic**	PolyGram Record Operations
WOOD	**Woodmansterne**	Woodmansterne
WORK	**Work Music**, London	Harmonia Mundi

Y

Code	Label	Distributor
YELL	**Yellow Trail Records**	Ashley Mark Publishing
YORK	**York Ambisonic**	Target
YORR	**York Records**	York Records
YTV	**YTV**	YTV Enterprises

Z

Code	Label	Distributor
ZAPP	**Zappa Records**	Zappa Records
ZOPF	**Zopf**	PolyGram Record Operations

1

Code	Label	Distributor
10 R	**10 Records**	EMI

Record company names and addresses

Abbey Recording Company 1 Abbey Street, Eynsham, Oxford OX8 1HS.
Telephone/fax 01865 880240

Accento 61 Ravendale Road, London N16 6TJ.
Telephone 0181-800 4339
Fax 0181-800 3166

Acoustics Records PO Box 350, Reading, Berkshire RG6 2DQ. **Telephone** 01734 68615

Acta Records 28 Aylmer Road, London W12 9LQ.
Telephone 0171-740 1349

Aeterna 44 Tantallon Road, London SW12 8DG.
Telephone 0181-673 1901
Fax 0181-675 0927

Albany Distribution PO Box 13, Leominster HR6 87B.
Telephone 01568 614024
Fax 01568 610228

Albany Records (UK) PO Box 12, Carnforth, Lancashire LA5 9PD. **Telephone** 01524 735873
Fax 01524 736 448

Altamira Records 40 Hewitt Road, Hornsey, London N8 0BL.
Telephone 0181-341 5425
Fax 0181-347 5075

Altarus Records Easton Dene, Bailbrook Lane, Bath BA1 7AA.
Telephone 01225 852323
Fax 01225 852523

Amphion Sound Recordings Norton Lodge, 109 Beverly Road, Norton-on Derwent, Malton, North Yorkshire YO17 9PH.
Telephone 01653 698372

Anfield Music 276 Monument Road, Edgbaston, Birmingham B16 8XF. **Telephone** 0121-454 4671

Appian Publications & Recordings (APR) PO Box 1, Wark, Hexham, Northumberland NE48 3EW.
Telephone 01434 220627
Fax 0143 422 0627

Applecross Productions 92 Ritherdon Road, London SW17 8QH. **Telephone** 0181-542 7775
Fax 0181-542 8500

ARC Music PO Box 111, East Grinstead, West Sussex RH19 2YF.
Telephone 01342 312161
Fax 0342 315958

Arembe 84 Filsham Road, Hastings, Sussex TN38 0PG.
Telephone 01424 423260
Fax 01424 423260

Ashley Mark Publishing Olsover House, 43 Sackville Road, Newcastle-upon-Tyne NE6 5TA.
Telephone 0191-276 0448
Fax 0191-276 1623

Aspen Music 51 High Street, Wells-next-the-Sea, Norfolk NR23 1EN.
Telephone 01328 710552

ASV 1 Beaumont Avenue, London W14 9LP.
Telephone 0171-381 8747
Fax 0171-385 2653

Athene Records 7 Felden Street, London SW6 5AE.
Telephone 0171-736 9485
Fax 0171-371 7087

Bandleader Records 7 Garrick Street, London WC2E 9AR.
Telephone 0171-240 0658

Bath University Recordings c/o Music Office, Bath University, Building 1, East Room 21, Claverton Down, Bath BA2 7AY.
Telephone 01225 826431
Fax 01225 462508

Sir Thomas Beecham Trust Denton House, Denton, Harleston, Norfolk IP20 0AA.
Telephone 01986 788780

Beta Productions PO Box 309 Amersham, Buckinghamshire HP6 6DY.

Beulah The Signal Box, 1 Breach Road, Coalville, Leics LE67 3SB.
Telephone 01530 810828

Biddulph Recordings 34St George Street, Hanover Square, London W1R 0ND.
Telephone 0171-408 2458
Fax 0171-495 6501

Birmingham Bach Choir 16 Selwyn Road, Edgbaston, Birmingham B16 0SP.

Bitter and Twisted Records 22c Breakspars Road, London SE4 1UW.
Telephone 0181-691 8646

Terry Blood Distribution Unit 1, Rosevale Business Park, Newcastle-under-Lyme, Staffordshire ST5 7QT.
Telephone 01782 566566
Fax 01782 565400

BMG Classics Bedford House, 69-79 Fulham High Street, London SW6 3JW.
Telephone 0171-973 0011
Fax 0171-371 9571

BMG UK Lyng Lane, West Bromwich, West Midlands B70 7ST. **Telephone** 0121-500 5545

Bosworth and Co 14-18 Heddon Street, Regent Street, London W1R 8DP.
Telephone 0171-734 4961/2
Fax 0171-734 0475

Brewhouse Music Breeds Farm, 57 High Street, Wicken, Ely, Cambridgeshire CB7 5XR.
Telephone 01353 720309
Fax 01353 72 3364

British Music Society 7 Tudor Gardens, Upminster, Essex RM14 3DE.
Telephone 0171-454 6480

Bucks Music 1a Farm Place, London W8 7SX.
Telephone 0171-221 4275
Fax 0171-229 6893

Cadillac Distribution 61-71 Collier Street, London N1 9DF.
Telephone 0171-278 7391
Fax 0171-278 7394

Cala Records 17 Shakespeare Gardens, London N2 9LJ.
Telephone 0181-883 7306
Fax 0181-365 3388

Camerata Productions 30 Derby Road, Manchester M14 6UW.

Campion Records 13 Bank Square, Wilmslow, Cheshire SK9 1AN. **Telephone** 01625 527844
Fax 01625 536101

Cantoris Records 46 Bailgate, Lincoln LN1 3AP.
Telephone 01522 536981
Fax 01522 560550

Carlton Home Entertainment The Waterfront, Elstree Road, Elstree, Hertfordshire WD6 3BS.
Telephone 0181-207 6207
Fax 0181-207 5789

Castle Communications A29 Barwell Business Park, Leatherhead Road, Chessington, Surrey KT9 2NY.
Telephone 0181-974 1021
Fax 0181-974 2674

Cavendish Distribution *(ARTS Recordings)* 11 Wigmore Street, London W1H 9LA.
Telephone 0892 656298

CBS Records *see* Sony Music Entertainment

Chandos Records Chandos House, Commerce Way, Colchester, Essex CO2 8HQ.
Telephone 01206 794000
Fax 01206 794001

Choice Recordings 10a Morningside Place, Edinburgh EH10 5ER.
Telephone 0131-447 7122
Fax 0131-458 8641

Claddagh Records Dame House, Dame Street, Dublin 2, Eire. **Telephone** 010 353 1 778943

Clarinet Classics 77 St Albans Avenue, London E6 4HH.
Telephone 0181-472 2057

Classics for Pleasure EMI House, 43 Brook Green, London W6 7EF. **Telephone** 0171-605 5000
Fax 0171-650 5050

Claudio Records Studio 17, The Promenade, Peacehaven, Brighton BN9 8PU.
Telephone 01273 580250

Cleveland Orchestra (75th Anniversary CD Edition) Severance Hall, Cleveland, Ohio 44106 USA. **Telephone** 010 1 216 231 7300 *(for information)*
Cloud Nine Records 216 Royal College Street, London NW1 9LU. **Telephone** 0171-286 0705
CM Distribution 4 High Street, Starbeck, Harrogate, North Yorkshire HG2 7JU. **Telephone** 01423 888979/886696 **Fax** 01423 885761
Collegium Records PO Box 172, Whittlesford, Cambridge, CB2 4QZ. **Telephone** 01223 832474 **Fax** 01223 836723
Collins Classics Premier House, 10 Greycoat Place, London SW1P 1SB. **Telephone** 0171-222 1921 **Fax** 0171-222 1926
The Complete Record Co 12 Pepys Court, 84 The Chase, London SW4 0NF. **Telephone** 0171-498 9666 **Fax** 0171-498 1828
Concert Artist/Fidelio Twelve Tall Trees, Newmarket Road, Royston, Herts, SG8 7EG. **Telephone** 01763 246747
Conifer Records Claremont House, Horton Road, West Drayton, Middlesex UB7 8JL. **Telephone** 01895 447707 **Fax** 01895 420713
Consort Records 2 Salisbury Road, London W13 9TX. **Telephone** 0181-579 6283 **Fax** 0181-567 8824
Co-operative Union Holyoake House, Hanover Street, Manchester M6Q 0AS. **Telephone** 0161-832 4300 **Fax** 0161-831 7684
Covent Garden Pioneer FSP 100 Blythe Road, London W14 0HE. **Telephone** 0171-371 6191 **Fax** 0171-603 0668
Cramer Music 23 Garrick Street, London WC2E 9AX. **Telephone** 0171-240 1612 **Fax** 0171-240 2639
CRD PO Box 26, Stanmore, Middlesex HA7 4XB. **Telephone** 0181-958 7695 **Fax** 0181-958 1415
Czech Music Enterprises 5 Eversley Close, Rhyl, Clwyd LL18 4US. **Telephone** 01745 350645 **Fax** 01745 331331
Darmo Records Arvensis, Stour Lane, Stour Row, Shaftesbury, Dorset SP7 0QJ. **Telephone** 01747 838318
DCB Records The Cottage, Church Street, Fen Drayton, Cambridge CB4 5SG. **Telephone** 01954 231432
Decca Classics 1 Sussex Place, Hammersmith, London W6 9XS. **Telephone** 0181-910 5000 **Fax** 0181-748 4104
Dell'Arte Records PO Box 26, Hampton, Middlesex TW12 2NL. **Telephone** 0181-979 2479
Dervorguilla PO Box 363, Oxford OX1 4HB. **Telephone** 01865 725301 **Fax** 01865 271503
Deutsche Grammophon 1 Sussex Place, Hammersmith, London W6 9XS. **Telephone** 0181-910 5000 **Fax** 0181-748 4104
Discover International 1 Grange House, 229 Stoke Newington Church Street, London N16 9HL. **Telephone/fax** 0171-241 6459
Discovery Records The Old Church Mission Room, King's Corner, Pewsey, Wilts SN9 5BS. **Telephone** 01672 63931 **Fax** 01672 63934
Discurio 9 Gillingham Street, London SW1V 1HN. **Telephone** 0171-828 7963
Divas Records 20 Montpelier Street, Brighton BN1 3DJ. **Telephone/fax** 01273 327894
The Divine Art 31 Beach Road, South Shields, Tyne and Wear NE33 2QX. **Telephone** 0191-456 1837 **Fax** 0191-456 2954
Doremi London House, Suite 337, Old Court Place, London W8 4PL. **Telephone/fax** 0171-937 7171
Doyen Recordings Doyen House, 17 Coupland Close, Moorside, Oldham, Lancashire OL4 2TQ. **Telephone** 0161-628 3799 **Fax** 0161-628 3799
Dragonsfire 9 Hillside Road, Ashtead, Surrey KT2 1RZ. **Telephone** 01372 277703 **Fax** 01372 278406
Dutton Laboratories PO Box 576, Harrow, Middlesex HA3 6YW. **Telephone** 0181-421 1117 **Fax** 0181-421 2998
Earthsounds PO Box 1, Richmond, North Yorkshire DL10 5GB. **Telephone** 01748 825959
Eklipse Records 21-3 Cranley Gardens, London SW7 3BD. **Telephone** 0171-244 7358
EMI Records Customer Services EMI House, 43 Brook Green, London W6 7EF. **Telephone** 0171-605 5000 **Fax** 0171-605 5050
EMI Sales and Distribution Centre, Hermes Close, Tachbrook Park, Leamington Spa, Warwickshire, CV34 6RP. **Telephone** 01926 888888
English Recording Co 141 Abbeville Road, Clapham, London SW4 9JJ. **Telephone** 0171-622 8347 **Fax** 0171-720 4656
Erato Disques 46 Kensington Court, London W8 5DP. **Telephone** 0171-938 5542 **Fax** 0171-937 6645
Famous and Fabulous PO Box 1277, Chippenham, Wiltshire SN1S 3YZ. **Telephone** 01249 445400 **Fax** 01249 447691
First Night Records 2-3 Fitzroy Mews, London W1P 5DQ. **Telephone** 0171-383 7767 **Fax** 0171-383 3020
Fish Ear Communications PO Box 22, Teddington, Middlesex TW11 8PB.
FlamencOvision 54 Windsor Road, London N3 3SS. **Telephone** 0181-346 4500 **Fax** 0181-346 2488
Floating Earth Unit 14, 21 Wadsworth Road, Perivale, Middlesex UB6 7JD. **Telephone** 0181-997 4000 **Fax** 0181-998 5767
The Forties Recording Co 44 Challacombe, Furzton, Milton Keynes MK4 1DP. **Telephone** 01908 502836
Four Hands Music 15 Birchmead Close, St Albans, Herts AL3 6BS. **Telephone** 01727 58485 **Fax** 01727 51153
Foxglove Audio 10 Springwood Road, Little London, Rawden, West Yorkshire LS19 6BH. **Telephone** 01532 507282
FoxVideo Sales Twentieth Century House, 31-32 Soho Square, London W1V 6AP. **Telephone** 0171-753 8686
Gimell Records 4 Newtec Place, Magdalen Road, Oxford OX4 1RE. **Telephone** 01865 244557 **Fax** 01865 790472
Gothic/Pro Organo 4 Kendall Avenue, Sanderstead, Surrey CR2 0NH. **Telephone** 0181-660 4940
Grasmere Music 62 Pont Street Mews, Knightsbridge, London SW1X 0EF. **Telephone** 0171-584 9765 **Fax** 0171-823 7100
Griffin Church House, St Mary's Gate, 96 Church Street, Lancaster LA1 1TD. **Telephone** 01524 844399 **Fax** 01524 844335
Grosvenor Nostalgia Grosvenor Studios, 16 Birmingham Road, Birmingham B20 3NP.
Guild Records PO Box 5, Hadleigh, Ipswich, Suffolk IP7 6QF. **Telephone/fax** 01473 658026

Halcyon Submarine Records and Tapes, 13 Gardenia Road, Bush Hill Park, Enfield Road, Middlesex EN1 2JA.

Harmonia Mundi UK 19-21 Nile Street, London N1 7LL.
Telephone 0171-253 0863
Fax 0171-253 3237

Harmony Records Charborough Lodge, Charborough Park, Wareham BH20 7EL
Telephone/fax 01929 459589

Helicon Recordings PO Box 9, Hastings, E. Sussex, TN34 3JA.
Telephone 01424 422061

Heneghan and Lawson 15 Bradenham Place, Penarth, South Glamorgan CF6 2AG.
Telephone 01222 707202
Fax 01222 706735

Herald Audio Visual Publications The Studio, 29 Alfred Road, Farnham, Surrey GU9 8ND.
Telephone 01252 725349
Fax 01252 735567

Heritage Recordings 50 Bessborough Place, London SW1V 3SG.
Telephone 0171-828 1055

Hunters Moon Promotions Paget's Lane, Bubbenhall, Coventry, CV8 3BJ.
Telephone 01926 851325

HW International 167-171 Wiloughby Lane, Brantwood Industrial Area, London N17 0SB.
Telephone 0181-808 2222
Fax 0181-808 5599

Hyperion Records PO Box 25, Eltham, London SE9 1AX.
Telephone 0181-294 1166
Fax 0181-294 1161

Ikon Records Cathedral of the Assumption & All Saints, Ennismore Gardens, London, SW7 1NH.

Imperial Sound 16 Stonehill Road, London SW14 8RW.
Telephone 0181-876 3156

Impetus Distribution PO Box 1324, London W5 2ZU.
Telephone/fax 0181-998 6411

Isis Records 52 Argyle Street, Oxford OX4 1SS.
Telebphone/fax 01865 726553

Jewish Music Distribution PO Box 2268, Hendon, London NW4 3UW.

Jewish Music Productions 22 Gerard Road, Harrow, Middlesex HA1 2NE.
Telephone 0181-909 2445
Fax 0181-909 2445

JOS Records 2 Queen's Gate Place Mews, London SW7 5BQ.
Telephone/fax 0171-589 5318

Karussell PO Box 1425, Chancellor's House, 72 Chancellor's Road, Hammersmith, London W6 9QB.
Telephone 0181-910 5692
Fax 0181-910 5892

Kingdom Distribution 61 Collier Street, London N1 9BE.
Telephone 0171-713 7788
Fax 0171-713 0099

KJ Associates Fairwater, Childswickham Road, Broadway, Worcestershire WR12 7HA.
Telephone/fax 01386 852370

Koch International 24 Concord Road, London W3 0TH.
Telephone 0181-992 7177
Fax 0181-896 0817

Lammas Records 34 Carlisle Avenue, St Albans, Hertfordshire AL3 5LU.
Telephone/fax 01727 851553

Lansdowne CTS Studios Ltd, Engineers Way, Wembley, Middlesex HA9 0DR.

Libra Church Path, Hook, Nr Basingstoke, Hants RG27 9LZ.
Telephone 01256 762605

Linn Records Floors Road, Waterfoot, Eaglesham, Glasgow G76 0EP. **Telephone** 0141-644 5111
Fax 0141-644 4262

Lodia 2 Rugby Street, London WC1N 3QH.
Telephone/fax 0171-831 1910

LongMan Records PO Box 2649, Brighton, Sussex BN2 3PP.
Telephone 01273 383062

London Records 1 Sussex Place, Hammersmith, London W6 9XS. **Telephone** 0181-910 5000

Lyrita 99 Green Lane, Burnham, Slough, Bucks SL1 8EG.
Telephone 01628 604208

Manygate Marketing 13 Cotswold Mews, 12-16 Battersea High Street, London SW11 3JE.
Telephone 0171-223 7265
Fax 0171-585 2830

Mawson and Wareham Midgy Hall, Sharperton, Morpeth, Northumberland NE6S 7AS.

Max Sound 6 Stainbeck Lane, Leeds LS7 3QY.
Telephone 01532 694807

May Audio Marketing 83 Main Street, Burley–in-Wharfedale, West Yorkshire LS29 7BU.
Telephone 01943 864930
Fax 01943 863814

Kevin Mayhew Rattlesden , Bury St Edmunds, Suffolk IP30 0SZ.
Telephone 01449 737978
Fax 01449 737834

Medici-Whitehall
Telephone/fax 01483 272740

Melcot Music PO Box 2404, New Milton, Hampshire BH25 7XZ.
Telephone/fax 01425 611924

Memoir Records PO Box 66, Pinner, Middlesex HA5 2SA.
Fax 0181-866 7804

Meridian Records PO Box 317, Eltham, London SE9 4SF.
Telephone 0181-857 3213
Fax 0181-857 0731

Merlin Distribution Fifth Floor West, Enterprise House, Blyth Road, Hayes, Middlesex UB3 1DD.
Telephone 0181-561 9099
Fax 0181-573 1643

Metier Sound and Vision PO Box 270, Preston, Lancashire PR2 3LZ. **Telephone** 01772 866178

Metronome Productions Magdalen Studio, Chapel Lane, Farthingoe, Braekeley, Northamptonshire NN13 5PG.
Telephone 01295 710641
Fax 01295 710731

Michele International Michele House, The Acorn Centre, Roebuck Road, Hainault, Essex IG6 3TU. **Telephone** 0181-500 1819
Fax 0181-500 1745

Mirabilis Records Springwood Works, Water Street, Huddersfield, West Yorkshire HD1 4BB.
Telephone 01532 685123
Fax 01532 663069

Monré Records PO Box 234, Richmond, Surrey TW10 7XA.
Telephone/fax 01202 659199

Montague Music Courtyard Cottage, Southwick Hall, Peterborough PE8 5B7.
Telephone 01832 274790
Fax 0171-287 0377

Harold Moores Records and Video 2 Great Marlborough Street, London W1V 1DE.
Telephone 0171-439 9206

Mozart Edition 50 Potter Street, Northwood, Middlesex HA6 1QD.

Musica Attacca 46 Ravenscroft Road, Beckenham, Kent BR3 4TR.
Telephone 0181-778 8343
Fax 0181-659 1622

Music Collection International (MCI) Strand VCI House, Caxton Way, Watford, Hertfordshire.
Telephone 01923 55558
Fax 01923 816880

Music for Pleasure EMI House, 43 Brook Green, London W6 7EF.
Telephone 0171-605 5000
Fax 0171-650 5050

Music Masters (UK) The End House, Gurnells Road, Seer Green, Buckinghamshire HP9 2XJ.
Telephone 01494 672803
Fax 01494 678016

National Youth Orchestra of Scotland 13 Somerset Place, Glasgow G3 7JT.
Telephone 0141 332 8311
Fax 0141 332 3915

Naxos and Marco Polo UK PO Box 576, Sheffield, Yorkshire S10 1AY. **Telephone** 01142 678958
Fax 01142 671529

New Note Unit 2, Orpington Trading Estate, Sevenoaks Way, St Mary Cray, Orpington, Kent BR5 3SR. **Telephone** 01689 877884 **Fax** 01689 877891 *(dealers should contact Pinnacle)*
Nimbus Records Wyastone Leys, Monmouth, Gwent NP5 3SR. **Telephone** 01600 890682 **Fax** 01600 890779
NMC Francis House, Francis Street, London SW1P 1DE. **Telephone** 0171-828 3432 **Fax** 0171-828 3432
Nonesuch 46 Kensington Court, London W8 5DP. **Telephone** 0171-938 5542 **Fax** 0171-937 6645
Novelbond Soveriegn House, 212-224 Shaftesbury Avenue, London WC2H 8HQ.
Olympia Compact Discs 31 Warple Way, London W3 0RX. **Telephone** 0181-743 6767 **Fax** 0181-749 1300 *or* 0181-740 1300
Opera Rara 25 Compton Terrace, Canonbury, London N1 2UN. **Telephone** 0171-359 1777 **Fax** 0171-354 3942
OxRecs Magdalen Farm Cottage, Standlake, Witney,Oxon OX8 7RN. **Telephone** 01865 300347
Parsifal Distribution Bridge Studios, Suite No. 7, 318-326 Wandsworth Bridge Road, London SW6 2TZ. **Telephone** 0171-610 6725 **Fax** 0171-610 6729
Past Perfect Lower Farm Barns, Baunton Road, Bucknell, Oxon OX6 9LT. **Telephone** 01869 325052 **Fax** 01869 325072
Pavilion Records *(*Pearl) Sparrows Green, Wadhurst, East Sussex TN5 6SJ. **Telephone** 01892 783591 **Fax** 01892 784156
Pentacone 4 Cross Bank Road, Batley, West Yorkshire WF17 8PJ. **Telephone** 01924 445039
Philips Classics 1 Sussex Place, Hammersmith, London W6 9XS. **Telephone** 0181-910 5000 **Fax** 0181-748 4104
Pianissimo Ridgway Road, Pyrford, Woking, Surrey GU22 8PR. **Telephone** 01932 345371
Pinnacle Records Electron House, Cray Avenue, St Mary Cray, Orpington, Kent BR5 3RJ. **Telephone** 016898 70622 **Fax** 016898 78269
Planetarium Recordings 16 Wigmore Street, London W1H 9DE. **Telephone** 0171-636 5597 **Fax** 0171-636 5602
PolyGram Classics and Jazz 1 Sussex Place, Hammersmith, London W6 9XS. **Telephone** 0181-910 5000 **Fax** 0181-748 4104
PolyGram Record Operations PO Box 36, Clyde Works, Grove Road, Romford, Essex RM6 4QR. **Telephone** 0181-590 6044
Polyphonic Reproductions 77-79 Dudden Hill Lane, London NW10 1BD. **Telephone** 0181-459 6194/5 **Fax** 0181-451 6470
President Records Exmouth House, 11 Pine Street, London EC1R 0JH. **Telephone** 0171-837 5020 **Fax** 0171-837 4795
Presto Music 23 Portland Street, Royal Leamington Spa, CV32 5EZ. **Telephone** 01926 334834
Priory Records Unit 9b, Upper Wingbury Courtyard, Wingrave, near Aylesbury, Buckinghamshire HP22 4LW. **Telephone** 01296 682255 **Fax** 01296 682275
ProudSound 61 Iffley Road, Oxford OX4 1EB. **Telephone/fax** 01865 723764
Quantum Audio PO Box 26, Kilmarnock, Ayrshire KA1 1BA. **Telephone** 01563 71122
RCA Bedford House, 69-79 Fulham High Street, London SW6 3JW. **Telephone** 0171-973 0011 **Fax** 0171-371 9571
The Record Collector 111 Longshots Close, Broomsfield, Chelmsford, Essex CM1 5DU. **Telephone** 01245 441661 **Fax** 01245 443642
Redcliffe Recordings 68 Barrowgate Road, London W4 4QU. **Telephone** 0181-995 1223
Regent Records PO Box 528, Wolverhampton WV3 9YW. **Telephone** 01902 24377 **Fax** 01902 717661
RER Megacorp 46 The Gallop, Sutton, Surrey SMZ 5RY. **Telephone** 0181-770 2141 **Fax** 0181-642 6556
Romantic Robot 54 Deanscroft Avenue, London NW9 8EN. **Telephone** 0181-200 8870 **Fax** 0181-200 4075
Romophone PO Box 717, Oxford OX2 7YU. **Telephone** 01865 515353 **Fax** 01865 515335
Royal Northern College of Music 124 Oxford Road, Manchester M13 9RD. **Telephone** 0161-273 6283 **Fax** 0161-273 7611
RRD (Distribution) 13 Bank Square, Wilmslow, Cheshire SK9 1AN. **Telephone** 01625 549862 **Fax** 01625 536101
Rubini Records 45b Livingstone Road, Hove, Sussex BN3 2WN. **Telephone** 01273 726986
Sain (Recordiau) Llandwrog, Caernarfon, Gwynedd LL54 5TG. **Telephone** 01286 831111 **Fax** 01286 831497
Saydisc Chipping Manor, The Chipping, Wotton-under-Edge, Gloucester GL12 7AD. **Telephone** 01453 845036 **Fax** 01453 521056
Scratch Records Hatch Farm Studios, Unit 16, Hatch Farm, Chertsey Road, Addlestone Moor, Surrey KT15 2EH. **Telephone** 01932 828715 **Fax** 01932 828717
SCS Music 4 Newtec Place, Magdalen Road, Oxford OX4 1RE. **Telephone** 01865 790472 **Fax** 01865 790472
Seaford Music 24 Pevensey Road, Eastbourne, East Sussex BN21 3HP. **Telephone** 01323 732553 **Fax** 01323 417455
Seaview Music 42 Bateman Street, Cambridge CB2 1NA. **Telephone** 01223 415524 **Fax** 01223 415685
Select Music and Video Distributors 34a Holmethorpe Avenue, Holmethorpe Estate, Redhill, Surrey. **Telephone** 01737 760020 **Fax** 01737 766316
Silva Screen 261 Royal College Street, London NW1 9LU. **Telephone** 0171-284 0525 **Fax** 0171-482 2385
Silver Octopus 14 Alma Street, Buxton, Derbyshire SK17 7DY. **Telephone** 01298 26920 **Fax** 01298 72292
Silver Sounds CD Unit 7, Peerglow Estate, Queensway, Ponders End, Enfield, Middlesex EN3 4SN. **Telephone** 0181-364 7711 **Fax** 0181-805 1135
The Sine Qua Non Society The Old Forge, 2 Bridge Street, Hadleigh, Suffolk IP7 6B7. **Telephone** 01473 828494 **Fax** 01296 681989
R Smith and Co PO Box 367, Aylesbury, Buckinghamshire HP22 4LJ. **Telephone** 01296 68220
Somm Recordings 13 Riversdale Road, Thames Dutton, Surrey KT7 0QL. **Telephone** 0181-398 1586 **Fax** 0181-339 0981

Sony Music Entertainment 10 Great Marlborough Street, London W1V 2LP. **Telephone** 0171-911 8200 **Fax** 0171-911 8600

Sony Music Operations Rabans Lane, Aylesbury, Buckinghamshire HP19 3RT. **Telephone** 01296 395151

Sound and Media Unit 1, Mill Lane Trading Estate, Mill Lane, Purley Way, Croydon CR0 4AA. **Telephone** 0181-686 3636 **Fax** 0181-667 1388

Soundboard PO Box 5, Stanley, Co Durham DH9 7HR.

Sphemusations 12 Northfield Road, Onehouse, Stowmarket, Suffolk IP14 3HF. **Telephone** 01449 613388

Springthyme Records Balmalcolm House, Kingskettle, Fife KY7 7TJ. **Telephone** 01337 830773 **Fax** 01337 830431

J Martin Stafford 298 Blossomfield Road, Solihull, West Midlands B91 1TH. **Telephone** 0121-711 1975

Start Classics Suite 20a, Canada House, Blackburn Road, London NW6 1R2. **Telephone** 0171-625 7113 **Fax** 0171-624 3258

Stockhausen Verlag Kettenberg 15, 51515 Kürten, Germany.

Leopold Stokowski Society 12 Market Street, Deal, Kent CT14 6HS.

The Strad PO Box 500, Leicester LE99 0AA.

Sutton Sound 111a Westbourne Grove, London W2 4UW. **Telephone** 0171-262 9066

Symposium Records 5 High Street, Cromer, North Norfolk NR27 9HG. **Telephone/fax** 01263 511531

Target Records 23 Gardner Industrial Estate, Kent House Lane, Beckenham Lane, Kent BR3 1QZ. **Telephone** 0181-778 4040 **Fax** 0181-676 9949

Teldec Classics 46 Kensington Court, London W8 5DP. **Telephone** 0171-938 5542 **Fax** 0171-937 6645

Temple Records Shillinghill, Temple, by Gorebridge, Midlothian EH23 4SH. **Telephone** 0187 530328 **Fax** 0187 530392

Testament Records 14 Tootswood Road, Bromley, Kent BR2 0PD. **Telephone** 0181-464 5947 **Fax** 0181-464 5352

Thames Distribution Thames House, 63a Station Road, Hampton, Middlesex TW12 2BT. **Telephone** 0181-979 9033 **Fax** 0181-979 5055

Thats Entertainment Records 107 Kentish Town Road, London NW1 8PB. **Telephone** 0171-485 9593 **Fax** 0171-485 2282

Third Mind Records 15 Great Western Road, London W9 3NW. **Telephone** 0171-289 1021 **Fax** 0171-266 3202

Michael G Thomas 5a Norfolk Place, London W2 1QN. **Telephone** 0171-723 4935 / 01795 536074

Timbre Records 93 Brondesbury Road, London NW6 6RY. **Telephone** 0171-912 0043 **Fax** 0171-372 0784

Top Note Music 123 Crown Street, Aberdeen AB1 2HN. **Telephone** 01224 210259

TradeLink Music Distribution Eastwoods House, Church End, Potterspury, Northamptonshire NN12 7PX. **Telephone** 01908 543055 **Fax** 01908 543056

Tremula Records PO Box 1491, Windsor, Berkshire SL4 2PE. **Telephone** 01753 860522 **Fax** 01753 830957

Tring International Triangle Business Park, Wendover Road, Aylesbury, Bucks HP22 5BL. **Telephone** 01296 615800 **Fax** 01296 614250

Trittico Distributor 45 Argyll Road, London W8 7DA. **Telephone** 0171-937 2869 **Fax** 0171-938 1983

TSC Enterprises 5 Sanderson Street, Sheffield S9 2UA. **Telephone** 01142 442424 **Fax** 01142 434312

UK Distribution 23 Richings Way, Iver, Buckinghamshire SL0 9DA. **Telephone** 01753 652669 **Fax** 01753 654531

Ultima Thule 1 Conduit Street, Leicester LE2 0JN.

Ultrasonic Records 8 Church Studios, North Villas, London NW1 9AY. **Telephone** 0171-482 4868 **Fax** 0171-485 1819

Unicorn-Kanchana Records PO Box 339, London W8 7TJ. **Telephone** 0171-727 3881 **Fax** 0171-243 1701

The United Recording Company 17 Shakespeare Gardens, London N2 9LJ. **Telephone** 0181-883 7306 **Fax** 0181-365 3388

Upbeat Records Sutton Business Centre, Restmor Way, Wallington, Surrey SM6 7AH. **Telephone** 0181-773 1223 **Fax** 0181-647 5275

Usk Recordings 26 Caterham Road, London SE13 5AR. **Telephone/fax** 0181-318 2031

Vanderbeek and Imrie 15 Marvig, Lochs, Isle of Lewis PA86 9QP. **Telephone/fax** 01851 880216

VCI Distribution Caxton Way, Watford, Hertfordshire WD1 8UF. **Telephone** 01923 255558 **Fax** 01923 816880

Video Artists International 158 Linwood Plaza, Suite 301, Fort Lee, NJ 07024, USA. **UK Freephone** 0800 892931

Virgin Records Kensal House, 553-579 Harrow Road, London W10 4RH. **Telephone** 0181-964 6000 **Fax** 0181-964 6073

Virtuosi Records 38 York Street, London W1H 1FF.

Vital Communications 38 Nevil Road, Bishopston, Bristol BS7 9EH. **Telephone** 01179 422830 **Fax** 01179 247371

Voiceprint PO Box 5, Derwentside, Co Durham DH9 7HR. **Telephone** 0191-512 1103

Voix Celeste 18 Hill Close, Newmarket, Suffolk CB8 0NR. **Telephone** 01638 660531

Warner Classics 46 Kensington Court, London W8 5DP. **Telephone** 0171-938 5542 **Fax** 0171-937 6645

Westmoor Music Bay G-10, Wembley Commercial Centre, East Lane, Wembley, Middlesex HA9 7YH.

Clive Wilkinson 89 Beckfield Lane, Acomb, York YO2 5PW. **Telephone** 01904 794177

Woodmansterne Publications 2 Greenhill Crescent, Watford Business Park, Watford, Hertfordshire WD1 8RD. **Telephone** 01923 228236 **Fax** 01923 245788

York Ambisonic PO Box 66, Lancaster LA2 6HS. **Telephone** 01524 823020

York Records 30 Melbourne Street, York Y01 5AQ. **Telephone** 01904 634172

YTV Enterprises Television Centre, Kirkstall Road, Leeds LS3 1JS. **Telephone** 01132 438283

Zappa Records 102 Belsize Lane, London NW3 5BB. **Telephone** 0171-974 0283 **Fax** 0171-437 3531

Abbreviations

AAM Academy of Ancient Music
alphn alphorn
alto counter tenor/male alto
alto fl alto flute
alto sax alto saxophone
amplified pf amplified piano
AMTF American Music Theatre Festival
anon anonymous
archlte archlute
arr arranged
ASMF Academy of St Martin in the Fields
ATER Associazione Teatri Emilia Romagna
attrib attributed
b born
bamboo fl bamboo flute
bar baritone
bar hn baritone horn
bar sax baritone saxophone
baroque gtr baroque guitar
baroque vc baroque cello
baroque vn baroque violin
barrel org barrel organ
bass cl bass clarinet
bass fl bass flute
bass gtr bass guitar
bass tbn bass trombone
bass tpt bass trumpet
bass vn bass violin
bass-bar bass-baritone
basset cl basset clarinet
basset-hn basset-horn
BBC PO BBC Philharmonic Orchestra
BBC SO BBC Symphony Orchestra
bn bassoon
BNOC British National Opera Company
bp broadcast performance
BPDGB Barking Pumpkin Digital Gratification Band
BPO Berlin Philharmonic Orchestra
BRSO Bavarian Radio Symphony Orchestra
c circa (about)
cad cadenza
cath cathedral
CBSO City of Birmingham Symphony Orchestra
ch choir
chbr chamber
chor chorus
cl clarinet
clav clavichord
closed pf closed piano
CLS City of London Sinfonia
CO Chamber Orchestra
COE Chamber Orchestra of Europe
coll collected (by)
computer op computer operator
cond conductor
Cons Conservatoire
contr contralto (female alto)
cor ang cor anglais/english horn
cowhn cowhorn
cpsd composed
cpsr composer
cpted completed (by)
d died
db double bass
dbn double bassoon
dhp double harp
dig pf digital piano
dir director
dncr dancer
EBS English Baroque Soloists
ECCO European Community Chamber Orchestra
ECO English Chamber Orchestra
ECYO European Community Youth Orchestra
ed edited (by)/edition
elec electric/electronics
elec db electric double bass
elec gtr electric guitar
elec hpd electric harpsichord
elec kybd electric keyboard
elec org electric organ
elec pf electric piano
Eng English
ENO English National Opera
ens ensemble
EOG English Opera Group
exc excerpt
fest festival
fl flute
fl flourished
flugel hn flugel horn
FNO French National Orchestra
fp fortepiano
Fr French
FRNO French Radio National Orchestra
Ger German
glock glockenspiel
gtr guitar
harm harmonium
harmonic pf harmonic piano
hn horn
hp harp
hpd harpsichord
IMS International Musicians Seminar
inc music incidental music
inst instrument/instrumental
intro introduction
Ital Italian
jew's hp jew's harp
kybd(s) keyboard(s)
LCP London Classical Players
lib libretto
LJSO London Johann Strauss Orchestra
LMP London Mozart Players
LPO London Philharmonic Orchestra
LSC London Symphony Chorus
LSO London Symphony Orchestra

lte lute
lte-hpd lute-harpsichord
MCA Munich Capella Antiqua
medieval hp medieval harp
mez mezzo soprano
MIDI-hn MIDI-horn
MMF Maggio Musicale Fiorentino
mndl mandolin
movt movement
MS manuscript
narr narrator
nat national
Nat Op National Opera
NQHO New Queen's Hall Orchestra
NSO National Symphony Orchestra
NYO National Youth Orchestra of Great Britain
NYPO New York Philharmonic Orchestra
NYPSO New York Philharmonic Symphony Orchestra
NZBC New Zealand Broadcasting Corporation
ob oboe
ob d'amore oboe d'amore
ORBCB Orchestre Regional Bayonne-Côte Basque
op opus/opera
orch orchestra
org organ
orig original
ORR Orchestre Révolutionnaire et Romantique
OST Original Soundtrack
PAN Project Ars Nova
PAO Pro Arte Orchestra
PCA Pro Cantione Antiqua
perc percussion
perf performed/performance
pf piano
Philadelphia Philadelphia Orchestra
Philh Philharmonia Orchestra
picc piccolo
PJBE Philip Jones Brass Ensemble
PJWE Philip Jones Wind Ensemble
PO Philharmonic Orchestra
pp public performance
post hn post horn
prepared pf prepared piano
prod producer/film director
PSO Philharmonic Symphony Orchestra
pub published/publisher
QHLO Queen's Hall Light Orchestra
qnt quintet
qt quartet
r recorded
rad radio
RAHO Royal Albert Hall Orchestra
RCM Royal College of Music
RCS Royal Choral Society
rec recorder
rev revised
RLPO Royal Liverpool Philharmonic Orchestra
RMSM Royal Military School of Music
RNCM Royal Northern College of Music
ROHO Orchestra of the Royal Opera House, Covent Garden
RPO Royal Philharmonic Orchestra
RTE Eire Radio Telefis
ruined pf ruined piano
sax saxophone
sinf sinfonia
SABC South African Broadcasting Corporation
SCB Schola Cantorum Basiliensis
sngr singer
SNO Royal Scottish National Orchestra
sop soprano
sop sax soprano saxophone
sound proj sound projection
spkr speaker
SO Symphony Orchestra
sols soloists
Sp Spanish
square pf square piano
SRO Suisse Romande Orchestra
stgs strings
St Op State Opera
sym symphony
synth(s) synthesizer(s)
tangent pf tangent piano
tape op tape operator
tbn trombone
ten tenor
ten hn tenor horn
ten sax tenor saxophone
ten tuba tenor tuba
ten viol tenor viol
th theatre
timp timpani
tin fl tin flute
toy pf toy piano
tpt trumpet
trad traditional
trans transcribed/translated
traut trautonium
treb treble/boy soprano
treb viol treble viol
va viola
va bastarda viola bastarda
va d'amore viola d'amore
va da gamba viola da gamba
vars variations
vc cello
VCA Vienna Capella Academica
VCM Vienna Concentus Musicus
vib vibraphone
virg virginal
VJSO Vienna Johann Strauss Orchestra
vn violin
voc vocalist/voice
VPO Vienna Philharmonic Orchestra
wds words
wind hp wind harp
WNO Welsh National Opera
ww woodwind

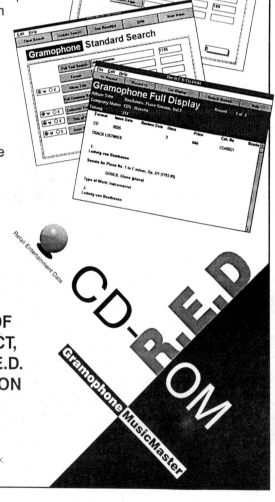

Gramophone Publications

Gramophone

Gramophone is the most influential record review magazine published today. Drawing on the skills of some of the world's most respected critics, ***Gramophone*** offers considered comment on more than 200 new recordings every month. In addition, there are in-depth interviews with today's leading performers and composers as well as surveys of recordings of specific works, artists and composers.

Gramophone is available at all good newsagents and record stores, or on subscription.

Single copy **£3·10** *UK annual subscription* **£34·10**

The Gramophone Classical Good CD Guide 1996

This indispensable guide is written by ***Gramophone***'s panel of distinguished reviewers and is acknowledged to be the finest publication of its kind. There are nearly 880 full reviews which are new to this edition. A major feature this year is the inclusion of a rating system, which highlights those releases which are considered to be recordings of particular distinction. Other new features include listings of the winners of *The Gramophone Awards* since their inception in 1977, together with a suggested basic library.

The Gramophone Classical Good CD Guide is available through all good book and record stores, or direct from the publishers, post free.

£15·99

The Gramophone Jazz Good CD Guide

The Gramophone Jazz Good CD Guide is the essential jazz companion. It contains over 1,600 reviews, recommending the best and most representative recordings by all the major jazz artists. This indispensable guide to jazz CDs includes a basic jazz library, highlighting recordings which have become cornerstones in the evolution of jazz.

The Gramophone Jazz Good CD Guide is available through all good book and record stores, or direct from the publishers, post free.

£15·99

International Classical Record Collector

Throughout the world there is a growing interest in recorded performances as they originally existed on cylinders, piano rolls, 78s and LPs, on shellac and on vinyl. Recognising this interest ***Gramophone*** has recently launched ***International Classical Record Collector***, a magazine which appeals to LP and CD reissue collectors, as well as audiophiles. ***ICRC*** covers all aspects of collecting classical music recordings from the past.

ICRC is published quarterly, in February, May, September and November. The magazine is available direct from the publishers and at selected record stores.

Single copy **£3·50** *UK annual subscription* **£14·00**

A few well-chosen words

Most of us can remember being read to – it is one of life's earliest luxuries – and it remains a pleasure in which we can indulge throughout our lives. *A few well-chosen words* is a new guide to some of the finest spoken word recordings. This unique book provides over 200 pages of reviews and recommendations for collectors, retailers, researchers and librarians. *A few well-chosen words* is available through selected record stores or direct from the publishers, post free.

£6·95

Order form overleaf

Order form

Or phone our credit card line 0181-907 4476

Gramophone Subscription

Please enter my subscription to ***Gramophone***, commencing with the issue dated:

Great Britain		£	Delivery	Europe		£	Delivery
☐ 1 year	Royal Mail	34·10	3-4 days	☐ 1 year	Surface	54·00	7-28 days
☐ 2 years	Royal Mail	68·20		☐ 2 years	Surface	108·00	
☐ 1 year	plus Index 73	8·00		☐ 1 year	plus Index 73	8·00	
☐ 2 years	plus Index 73+74	16·00		☐ 2 years	plus Index 73 and 74	16·00	
North America		**US $**	**Delivery**	**Rest of the World**		**£**	**Delivery**
☐ 1 year	Airspeeded	75·00	7-20 days	☐ 1 year	Airspeeded	71·95	7-21 days
☐ 2 years	Airspeeded	150·00		☐ 2 years	Airspeeded	143·90	
☐ 1 year	plus Index 73	12·90		☐ 1 year	plus Index 73	8·00	
☐ 2 years	plus Index 73+74	25·80		☐ 2 years	plus Index 73 and 74	16·00	

Other carriage rates are available on request

Gramophone magazine Single copies

☐ Great Britain £3·60 ☐ US $7·70 ☐ Overseas £4·75

The Gramophone Classical Good CD Guide 1996

☐ Great Britain £15·99 ☐ US $25·95 ☐ Overseas and Eire £15·99

The Gramophone Jazz Good CD Guide

☐ Great Britain £15·99 ☐ US $25·95 ☐ Overseas and Eire £15·99

A few well-chosen words

☐ Great Britain £6·95 ☐ US $13·95 ☐ Overseas £7·95

International Classical Record Collector Subscription

Please start my subscription with the Winter 1995 / Spring 1996 issue (delete as applicable)

☐ Great Britain £14·00 ☐ Europe £18·00 ☐ US $35·00 ☐ Rest of the World £20·00

International Classical Record Collector Single copy

Winter 1995 / Spring 1996 issue (delete as applicable)

☐ Great Britain £3·50 ☐ Europe £4·50 ☐ US $8·50 ☐ Rest of the World £5·00

Method of payment

☐ Cheque ☐ Sterling bank draft ☐ International Money Order

☐ British Postal Order ☐ Eurocheque ☐ Credit Card (see below)

I enclose a total payment of £ ______ or US $ (if resident in the USA) ______

Payment by credit card Please charge my

☐ Visa/Trustcard/Barclaycard ☐ Access/Mastercard/Eurocard

Total payment by credit card £ ______ or US $ (if resident in the USA) ______

Card number ☐☐☐☐☐☐☐☐☐☐☐☐☐☐☐☐

Expiry date ______

Signature ______ Date ______

Name ______

Address ______

______

Post/Zip code ______

Prices include postage and packing. Please allow 28 days for delivery in Great Britain. Please make cheques payable, and address all correspondence to: **Gramophone Publications Limited** 177-179 Kenton Road, Harrow, Middlesex, HA3 0HA, Great Britain. **Telephone** +44 (0)181-907 4476 **Fax** +44 (0)181-909 1893

OPCAT 1

Gramophone Publications

Titles index

Composer index

ABRAHAM, Paul *(1892–1960) Hungary*

Die **Blume von Hawaii– operetta: 3 acts (1931—Leipzig) (Lib. Grünwald, Löhner-Beda & Földes)**
H. Brauner, K. Equiluz, H. Winter, A. Niessner, Vienna Volksoper Chor, Vienna Volksoper Orch, J.L. Gruber (KOCH) Ⓓ **399 225**
Excs R. Schock, M. Schramm, L. Ebnet, F. Gruber, Günther Arndt Ch, Berlin SO, W. Schmidt-Boelcke (2/91) (EURO) Ⓓ **GD69024**

Viktoria und ihr Husar, 'Victoria and her Husar'– operetta: 3 acts (1930—Vienna) (Lib. A. Grünwald & Löhner-Beda)
Excs H. Brauner, K. Equiluz, H. Winter, A. Niessner, Vienna Volksoper Chor, Vienna Volksoper Orch, J.L. Gruber (KOCH) Ⓓ **399 225**
Excs R. Schock, M. Schramm, L. Ebnet, F. Gruber, Günther Arndt Ch, Berlin SO, W. Schmidt-Boelcke (2/91) (EURO) Ⓓ **GD69024**
Good night B. Weikl, Austrian RSO, K. Eichhorn (ORFE) Ⓓ **C077831A**

ADAM , Adolphe (Charles) *(1803–1856) France*

Le **chalet– opéra-comique: 1 act (1834—Paris) (Lib. Scribe & Mélesville)**
Arrêtons-nous ici P. Plançon, anon (r1904) (7/93) (NIMB) Ⓓ [2] **NI7840/1**
Vallons de l'Helvétie P. Plançon, anon (r1904) (12/94) (ROMO) Ⓓ [2] **82001-2**

Les **Pantins de Violette– operetta: 1 act (1856—Paris) (Lib. L. Battu)**
EXCERPTS: 1. Le chanson du canari.
1. S. Jo, ECO, R. Bonynge (r1993) (9/94) (DECC) Ⓓ **440 679-2DH**

Le **Postillon de Lonjumeau– opera: 3 acts, 1836 (Paris) (Lib. de Leuven and Brunswick)**
EXCERPTS: 1. Overture. ACT 1: 2. Le joli mariage!; 3. Quoi, tous les deux!; 4. Jeunes époux, voici l'heure fortunée; 5. Mes amis, écoutez l'histoire (Freunde, vernehmet die Geschichte); 6. A mes désirs, il faut te rendre. ACT 2: 7. Entr'acte (Vorspiel); 8. Je vais donc le revoir; 9. Ah! quel torment!; 10. Assis au pied d'un hêtre; 11. Oui, des choristes du théâtre; 12. Grâce au hasard; 13. Ah! quelle étonnante nouvelle! ACT 3: 14. Entr'acte; 15. Du vrai bonheur; 16. A la noblesse, je m'allie; 17. Pendu!; 18. A ma douleur soyez sensible.
5. H. Roswaenge, Berlin St Op Chor, Berlin St Op Orch, B. Seidler-Winkler (Ger: r1936) (MMOI) Ⓓ **CDMOIR405** (MMOI) ▭ **CMOIR405**
5. J. Schmidt, orch, O. Dobrindt (r1933: Ger) (EMI) Ⓓ [2] **CHS7 64673-2**
5. J. Schmidt, orch (Ger: r1933) (4/90) (EMI) Ⓓ **CDM7 69478-2**
5. H. Roswaenge, Berlin St Op Orch, B. Seidler-Winkler (r1936: Ger) (5/90) (PREI) Ⓓ **89018**
5. H. Roswaenge, orch (r1928: Ger) (2/92) (PREI) Ⓓ [2] **89201**
5. H.E. Groh, orch (Ger: r1932) (3/92) (PEAR) Ⓓ **GEMMCD9419**
5. H. Roswaenge, Berlin St Op Chor, Berlin St Op Orch, B. Seidler-Winkler (Ger: r1936) (10/92) (TEST) Ⓓ **SBT1005**
5. H. Roswaenge, Berlin St Op Orch, B. Seidler-Winkler (r1936: Ger) (4/95) (PREI) Ⓓ [2] **89209**

La **Poupée de Nuremberg– opera: 1 act (1852—Paris) (Lib. de Leuven and A. de Beauplan)**
Overture Munich RO, K. Redel (PIER) Ⓓ **PV786104**

Si j'étais roi, 'If I were King'– opera: 3 acts (1852—Paris) (Lib. Ennery and J. Brésil)
EXCERPTS: 1. Overture; 2. Chanson à boire; 3. Dans le sommeil; 4. De vos nobles aïeux.
Zéphoris A. Mallabrera
Néméa L. Berton
Le Roi R. Bianco
Kadour H. Médus
Piféar B. Alvi
Zélide A. Gabriel
Zizel P. Héral
Orch, Chor, R. Blareau (MUSD) Ⓓ [2] **20300-2**
Dans le sommeil A. Baugé, orch, G. Andolfi (r1936) (EMI) Ⓓ [2] **CZS5 68292-2**
1. Philh, A. Scholz (r1980) (ROSE) Ⓓ **3229**
1. Munich RO, K. Redel (PIER) Ⓓ **PV786104**
1. Detroit SO, P. Paray (r1960) (11/93) (MERC) Ⓓ **434 332-2MM**
2. G. Soulacroix, anon (r1904) (9/91) (SYMP) Ⓓ **SYMCD1089**
3. A. Baugé, orch (FORL) Ⓓ **UCD19022**
4. S. Jo, ECO, R. Bonynge (r1993) (9/94) (DECC) Ⓓ **440 679-2DH**

Le **Toréador– opera: 2 acts (1849—Paris) (Lib. T. Sauvage)**
EXCERPTS: 1. Ah, vous dirai-je, maman.
Coraline M. Mesplé
Tracolin R. Amade
Don Belflor C. Clavensy
ORTF Lyric Orch, E. Bigot (bp1963) (3/92) (MUSD) Ⓓ **20167-2**
1. E. Gruberová, Stuttgart RSO, K. Eichhorn (ORFE) Ⓓ **C072831A**
1. A. Galli-Curci, orch (r1921) (PEAR) Ⓓ **GEMMCD9450**
1. M. Korjus, Berlin RSO, J. Müller (r1934; Ger) (DANT) Ⓓ **LYS001**
1. M. Korjus, Berlin RO, J. Müller (Ger: r1934) (10/93) (PREI) Ⓓ **89054**
1. F. Hempel, orch (r1911) (3/94) (NIMB) Ⓓ **NI7849**
1. A. Galli-Curci, orch, J. Pasternack (r1921) (8/94) (ROMO) Ⓓ [2] **81004-2**

ADAMS, John *(b 1947) USA*

The **Death of Klinghoffer– opera: prologue & 2 acts (1991—Brussels) (Lib. A. Goodman)**
Leon Klinghoffer S. Sylvan
Omar S. Friedman
Captain J. Maddalena
First Officer T. Hammons
Molqi T.J. Young
Mamoud E. Perry
Marilyn Klinghoffer S. Nadler
London Op Chor, Lyon Op Orch, K. Nagano (3/93) (NONE) Ⓓ [2] **7559-79281-2**

Nixon in China– opera: 3 acts (1987—Houston) (Lib. A. Goodman)
Pat's Aria J. Gibson, M. Goldray, M. Riesman (r1992; arr sax & keybds) (6/93) (PNT) Ⓓ **434 873-2PTH**

ADORNO , Theodore Wiesengrund *(1903–1969) Germany*

Der **Schatz des Indianer-Joe– Singspiel (1932-33) (fragment only)**
EXCERPTS: 1. Totenlied auf den kater; 2. Hucks Auftrittslied.
M. Kiener, H. Neiser, Frankfurt Op Orch, G. Bertini (6/91) (WERG) Ⓓ **WER6173-2**

AGRICOLA , Johann Friedrich *(1720–1774) Germany*

Achille in Sciro– opera seria (1765—Berlin)
Del terreno, nel centro profondo J. Kowalski, Berlin CO, M. Pommer (9/88) (CAPR) Ⓓ **10 113** (9/88) (CAPR) ▭ **CC27 127**

ALBERT , Eugen (Francis Charles) d' *(1864–1932) Scotland/Germany*

Tiefland– opera: prologue & 2 acts (1903—Prague) (Lib. Lothar)
EXCERPTS: 1. Orchestral Prelude.
PROLOGUE: 2. Zwei Vaterunser bet'ich; 3. Wie ich nun gestern Abend (Träumzählung); 4. Du glabst am Ende, Weib und Glück sind eins?; 5. Ist Pedro nicht hier?; 6. Na, Mein Pedro, sag mir mal; 7. Hast du's gehört? Ich kreig und Weib; 8a. Meine Glücke zu!... 8b. Ich grüss noch einmal meine Berge; 9. Interlude. ACT 1: 10. Sag uns doch, ist ed wahr?; 11. Da bin ich!; 12. An einem Abend war's, der Mond ging auf; 13. Oh, sie ist fort!; 14. Sein bin ich, sein! Sein Eigentum!; 15. Er kommt! Wo kommt er? Wo?; 16. Da ist er, seht nur!; 17. Da bin ich Herr, da bin ich schon!; 18. Marta!—Tu mit mir, was di willst; 19. Er will kein Stutzer sein!; 20. Was suchst du noch, Moruccio?; 21a. Das Fest ist vorbei; 21b. Dor Tor ist zu; 21c. Mein Leben wagt' ich drum (Wofserzählung); 22a. Wind sind allein; 22b. Schau her, das ist ein Taler; 23. So nimm das Geld, ich schenk es dir. ACT 2: 24. Die Sterne gingen zur Ruh; 25. Da ist Marta. Nun will ich gehen; 26. Wo willst du hin?; 27. Ich weiss nicht, wer mein Vater dir; 28. So kamen wir denn eines Tags hierher; 29. Ich will vom Himmel Stärke dir erflehn; 30. Ei, so mürrisch, so verdreisslich!; 31. Da Essen ist da!; 32. Ja, du hast Furcht, ein Wicht bist du; 33. Ich soll dich töten?; 34. Was gibt es Neues?; 35. Hüll in die Mantille dich fester ein; 36. Was sagt der Mensch; 37. Was wollst Ihr, he?; 38. Nun hab' ich nichts als nich mehr auf der Welt; 39. Nun soll er kommen und idch nir entreissen!; 40. He, Burschen, her! Ihr Weiber kommt!.
2, 22b R. Tauber, orch (r1928) (PEAR) Ⓓ **GEMMCD9145**
2, 22b T. Ralf, Berlin St Op Orch, B. Seidler-Winkler (r1942) (10/94) (PREI) Ⓓ **89077**
8a, 8b, 21c J. Pölzer, R. Pauly, Vienna St Op Orch, K. Alwin (pp1933) (7/94) (SCHW) Ⓓ [2] **314512**
8b, 21c F. Völker, Berlin Staatskapelle, G. Steeger (r1940) (8/94) (PREI) Ⓓ **89070**
27. R. Tauber, orch (r1928) (7/89) (PEAR) Ⓓ **GEMMCD9327**

27. Leonie Rysanek, Philh, W. Schüchter (r1952)
(2/95) (EMI) ① **CDH5 65201-2**
35. E. Marton, R. Kollo, B. Weikl, Bavarian Rad Chor, Munich RO, M. Janowski
(3/89) (ACAN) ① **43 266**

Die **Toten Augen– opera: prologue & 1 act (1916—Dresden) (Lib. H H Ewers)**
Psyche wandelt durch Säulenhallen Lotte Lehmann, Berlin St Op Orch, F. Weissmann (r1933) (PEAR) ① **GEMMCD9410**
Psyche wandelt durch Säulenhallen Lotte Lehmann, orch (r1919)
(6/92) (PREI) ① [3] **89302**
Psyche wandelt durch Säulenhallen M. Reining, Vienna St Op Orch, R. Moralt (r1942)
(9/94) (PREI) ① **89065**

ALBINONI, Tomaso Giovanni *(1671–1751) Italy*

Il **Nascimento dell'Aurora– festa pastorale**

Dafne	J. Anderson
Zeffiro	M. Zimmermann
Flora	S. Klare
Apollo	S. Browne
Peneo	Y. Yamaj

Solisti Veneti, C. Scimone (r1983)
(7/95) (ERAT) ① [2] **4509-96374-2**

La **Statira– dramma per musica: 3 acts (1726—Rome) (Lib. Zeno and Pariati)**
Vien con nuova orribil guerra H. Field, J. Wallace, John Miller, Philh, S. Wright
(NIMB) ① **NI5123**

ALFANO, Franco *(1875–1954) Italy*

Risurrezione– dramma: 4 acts (1904—Turin) (Lib. C Hanau, after Tolstoy)

Katiusha Mikailovna	M. Olivero
Prince Dimitri	G. Gismondo
Simonson	A. Boyer
Matrena Pavlovna	A. Di Stasio
Anna	N. Condò
La Korableva	V. Magrini
Fedia	P. Pace
Head Warden	M. Stefanoni

Turin RAI Chor, Turin RAI Orch, E. Boncompagni (bp1971)
(10/93) (LYRC) ① [2] **SRO839**
Dio pietoso I. Tokody, orch, Anon (cond) (pp1991/2) (VAI) ① **VAIA1009**
Dio pietoso M. Garden, orch (r1926: Fr)
(8/93) (SYMP) ① **SYMCD1136**
Dio pietoso M. Garden, orch, Rosario Bourdon (r1926: 2 vers: Fr) (8/94) (ROMO) ① **81008-2**
Giunge il treno...Dio pietoso M. Freni, Venice La Fenice Orch, R. Abbado
(9/92) (DECC) ① **433 316-2DH**

ALMAN, Samuel *(1878–1947) England*

King Ahaz– opera (1912—London) (Lib. cpsr)
Excs H. Lawrence, C. Rosen, L. Berkman, A. Saunders (9/85) (JEWI) ▭ **BB 001**

ALONSO, Francisco *(1887–1948) Spain*

Coplas de Ronda– zarzuela (Lib. C Amiches & J de Lucia)
Bella niña de ojos negros P. Domingo, Madrid Zarzuela Chor, Madrid Rondalla Lírica, Madrid SO, M. Moreno-Buendia (r1987)
(1/89) (EMI) ① **CDC7 49148-2**

La **Parranda– zarzuela (Lib. F. Ardavín)**
En la huerta del Segura P. Domingo, Madrid Zarzuela Chor, Madrid Rondalla Lírica, Madrid SO, M. Moreno-Buendia (r1987)
(1/89) (EMI) ① **CDC7 49148-2**

ALWYN, William *(1905–1985) England*

Miss Julie– opera: 2 acts (1977—BBC Radio) (Lib. cpsr, after Strindberg)

Miss Julie	J. Gomez
Jean	B. Luxon
Kristin	D. Jones
Ulrik	J. Mitchinson

Philh, V. Tausky
(3/93) (LYRI) ① [2] **SRCD2218**

ANCELIN, Pierre *(b 1934) France*

Filius Hominis– opéra sacrée: 10 scenes (1989—Rome) (Text R. Cluzel)
Cpte R. Gilfry, M. Shearer, J. Topart, P. Lefebvre, Branco Krsmanovitch Chor, Lille Nat Orch, J-C. Casadesus (pp1989)
(CYBE) ① **CY853**

ANTHEIL, George (Johann Carl) *(1900–1959) USA*

Transatlantic– opera: 3 acts (1930—Frankfurt-am-Main) (Lib. cpsr)
EXCERPTS: 1. Tango.
1. M. Verbit (r1994; trans pf: M. Verbit)
(11/95) (ALBA) ① **TROY146-2**

APOLLONI, Giuseppe *(1822–1889) Italy*

L' **Ebreo– opera (1855—Venice)**
Si guerrieri...Fu Dio che disse A. DiGiorgio, orch (r1900s) (6/94) (IRCC) ① **IRCC-CD808**

ARENSKY, Anton Stepanovich *(1861–1906) Russia*

The **Dream on the Volga– opera: 4 acts, Op. 16 (1891—Moscow) (Lib. Ostrovsky)**
Cradle song E. Zbrueva, anon (r1903)
(6/93) (PEAR) ① [3] **GEMMCDS9004/6(2)**
Overture USSR SO, E. Svetlanov
(CLTS) ▭ **CML2026**

Raphael– opera: 1 act, Op. 37 (1894—Moscow) (Lib. A. Kryukov)
My heart trembles with passion L. Sobinov, orch (r1911)
(6/93) (PEAR) ① [3] **GEMMCDS9997/9(2)**

ARGENTO, Dominik *(b 1927) USA*

The **Dream of Valentino– opera (1993—Washington)**
EXCERPTS: 1. Tango.
1. Baltimore SO, D. Zinman (r1994)
(7/95) (ARGO) ① **444 454-2ZH**

ARIOSTI, Attilio (Malachia) *(1666–c1729) Italy*

Artaserse– opera: 3 acts (1724—London) (Lib. after Zeno & Pariati)
Fortunate passate mie pene A. Christofellis, Seicentonovecento Ens, F. Colusso (r1993/4)
(EMI) ① **CDC5 55250-2**

ARNE, Thomas Augustine *(1710–1778) England*

Artaxerxes– opera: 3 acts (1762 rev 1777—London) (Lib. cpsr, after Metastasio)
EXCERPTS: 1. The soldier tir'd of war's alarms; 2. Fair Aurora, prithee stay.
1. J. Sutherland, Orch, R. Bonynge
(VAI) ▭ **VAI69108**
1. J. Sutherland, Philomusica of London, Granville Jones (r1959)
(DECC) ① [2] **436 227-2DM2**
1. V. Masterson, R. Vignoles
(PEAR) ① **SHECD9590**
(7/86) (PEAR) ⊙ **SHE590**
1. B. Hoch, Hong Kong PO, K. Schermerhorn
(11/86) (IMP) ① **PCD827**
1. J. Sutherland, ROHO, F. Molinari-Pradelli
(1/90) (DECC) ① [2] **425 493-2DM2**

Love in a Village– ballad opera (1762—London) (Lib. T. Bickerstaffe)
EXCERPTS: 1. All I wish in her obtaining; 2. Begone, I agree; 3. Believe me, dear aunt; 4. Cease, gay seducers; 5. Go, naughty man; 6. In love should there meet; 7. In vain I every art essay; 8. My heart's own; 9. Oons, neighbour, never blush; 10. Since Hodge proves ungrateful; 12. Think, o my fairest; 13. The Traveller benighted; 14. Well come, let us hear; 15. When once love's subtle poison; 16. When we see a lover languish; 17. Whence can you inherit; 18. The World is a well-furnished table; 19. The Miller of Dee (traditional arr Arne).
13. J. Sutherland, Philomusica of London, Granville Jones (r1959)
(DECC) ① [2] **436 227-2DM2**
19. Broadside Band, J. Barlow (r1979)
(HARM) ① **HMA190 1039**
19. L. Skeaping, Broadside Band, J. Barlow (r1992; arr J. Barlow)
(6/93) (SAYD) ① **CD-SDL400**
(6/93) (SAYD) ▭ **CSDL400**

ARRIAGA (Y BALZOLA), Juan Crisóstomo (Jacobo Antonio) *(1806–1826) Spain*

Los **Esclavos felices– opera semiseria: 2 acts (1820—Bilbao) (Lib. Comella y Comella)**
EXCERPTS: 1. Overture.
1. Madrid Concerts Orch, J. Arámbarri
(GME) ① **GME225**
1. Concert des Nations, Capella Reial Instr Ens, J. Savall (r1994; rev Savall)
(10/95) (ASTR) ① **E8532**
1. Scottish CO, C. Mackerras (r1995)
(11/95) (HYPE) ① **CDA66800**

ASHLEY, Robert (Reynolds) *(b 1930) USA*

Improvement, 'Don Leaves Linda'– opera for television (Lib. cpsr)

Linda	J. Humbert
Don; Mr Payne; Linda's Companion	T. Buckner
Now Eleanor	J. La Barbara
Junior; Jr	S. Ashley
Doctor	A. Klein
Mr. Payne's Mother	A.X. Neuburg
Narrator	R. Ashley

Chor, T. Erbe, T. Hamilton
(NONE) ① [2] **7559-79289-2**

ATTERBERG, Kurt (Magnus) *(1887–1974) Sweden*

Fanal– opera: 3 acts (1934—Stockholm) (Lib cpsr, after Ritter & Welleminsky)
I männer över lag och rätt J. Björling, orch, N. Grevillius (r1935) (NIMB) ① **NI7835**
I männer över lag och rätt J. Björling, orch, N. Grevillius (r1935) (PEAR) ① **GEMMCD9043**

AUBER, Daniel-François-Esprit *(1782–1871) France*

Le **Cheval de bronze, '(The) Bronze Horse'– opéra-féerie: 3 acts (1835—Paris)**
EXCERPTS: 1. Overture.
1. Detroit SO, P. Paray
(MERC) ① **434 309-2MM**

Les **diamants de la couronne, 'Crown Diamonds'– opéra-comique: 3 acts (1841—Paris) (Lib. Scribe & V de Saint-Georges)**
EXCERPTS: ACT 1: 1. Overture.
Grand air L. Korsoff, orch (r1909)
(MSCM) ① **MM30221**
(MSCM) ▭ **MM040079**
1. Paris Cons, R. Leibowitz (r1960)
(CHES) ① **Chesky CD61**

Le **Domino noir, '(The) Black domino'– opéra-comique: 3 acts (1837)**
Je suis sauvée, enfin ... La belle Inès fait florès F. Révoil, orch (r1936)
(MSCM) ① **MM30221**
(MSCM) ▭ **MM040079**
Overture Black Dyke Mills Band, D. Hurst (arr brass band) (9/93) (CHAN) ① **CHAN4514**
(9/93) (CHAN) ▭ **BBTD4514**
Rondeau d'Angèle F. Révoil, orch, M. Cariven (r1935) (EMI) ① [2] **CZS5 68292-2**

Fra Diavolo– opéra-comique: 3 acts (1830—Paris) (Lib. Scribe)
EXCERPTS: 1. Overture; 2. ACT 1: Voyez sur cette roche. ACT 2: 3. Quel bonheur; 4. Agnès la jouvencelle. ACT 3: 5. O Sainte Vierge; 6. Pour toujours, disait-elle.

Fra Diavolo	N. Gedda
Zerline	M. Mesplé
Lorenzo	T. Dran

Lady Pamela J. Berbié
Lord Cockburn R. Corazza
Mathéo J. Bastin
Giacomo M. Trempont
Beppo M. Hamel
J Laforge Choral Ens, Monte Carlo PO, M. Soustrot (r1983/4)
(1/94) (EMI) Ⓓ [2] **CDS7 54810-2**
1. Detroit SO, P. Paray
(MERC) Ⓓ **434 309-2MM**
1. Berlin St Op Orch, O. Klemperer (r1929)
(2/89) (SYMP) Ⓓ **SYMCD1042**
3. J. Sutherland, Sydney Eliz Orch, R. Bonynge
(MCEG) ▣ **VVD780**
3. E. Berger, Berlin St Op Orch, L. Blech (Ger: r1934) (12/91) (PREI) Ⓓ **89035**
3. A. Nezhdanova, orch (r1910: Russ)
(6/93) (PEAR) Ⓓ [3] **GEMMCDS9007/9(2)**
3. A. Nezhdanova, orch (r1910; Russ)
(3/95) (NIMB) Ⓓ **NI7865**
4. N. Figner, anon (r1901: Russ)
(6/93) (PEAR) Ⓓ [3] **GEMMCDS9997/9(1)**
4. D. Yuzhin, anon (r1902: Russ)
(6/93) (PEAR) Ⓓ [3] **GEMMCDS9001/3(1)**
6. H. Roswaenge, Berlin St Op Orch, B. Seidler-Winkler (r1936: Ger) (5/90) (PREI) Ⓓ **89018**
6. H. Roswaenge, Berlin St Op Chor, Berlin St Op Orch, B. Seidler-Winkler (Ger: r1936)
(10/92) (TEST) Ⓓ **SBT1005**
6. H. Roswaenge, Berlin St Op Orch, B. Seidler-Winkler (r1936: Ger)
(4/95) (PREI) Ⓓ [2] **89209**

Gustav III– opéra-historique: 5 acts (1833—Paris)
Gustav L. Dale
Amélie R. Tawil
Ankastrom C. Treguier
Oscar B. Lafon
Arvedson V. Marestin
Ribbing R. Pujol
Dehorn G. Dubernet
Christian P. Foucher
Kaulbart; Armfelt; Valet; Chamberlain F. Leguérinel
Intermezzo Voc Ens, French Lyrique Orch, M. Swierczewski (pp1991)
(9/93) (ARIO) Ⓓ [3] **ARN368220**
Overture Stockholm PO, G. Rozhdestvensky (pp1976) (BIS) Ⓓ [8] **BIS-CD421/4(1)**

Manon Lescaut– opéra-comique: 3 acts (1856—Paris) (Lib. Scribe, after Prévost)
Manon Lescaut E. Vidal
Des Grieux A. Gabriel
Lescaut A. Cognet
Marquis R. Massis
Margueritte B. Lafon
Gervais A. Laiter
Zabi C. Estourelle
Renaud; Sergeant G. Dubernet
Durozeau D. Longuet
Madame Bancelin M-T. Orain
French Music Th Chor, Picardy Regional Orch, P. Fournillier (pp1990)
(CHNT) Ⓓ [2] **LDC278 1054/5**
C'est l'histoire amoureuse E. Gruberová, Tokyo PO, F. Haider (pp1993)
(NIGH) Ⓓ **NC090560-2**
C'est l'histoire amoureuse A. Galli-Curci, orch (r1917) (2/89) (PEAR) Ⓓ **GEMMCD9308**
C'est l'histoire amoureuse A. Galli-Curci, orch, J. Pasternack (r1917) (5/90) (NIMB) Ⓓ **NI7806**
(NIMB) ⊟ **NC7806**
C'est l'histoire amoureuse A. Galli-Curci, orch, J. Pasternack (r1917)
(3/94) (ROMO) Ⓓ [2] **81003-2**

La **Muette de Portici– opera: 5 acts (1828—Paris) (Lib. Scribe and Delavigne)**
EXCERPTS: 1. Overture; 2. Amis, la matinée; 3. Du pauvre seul ami fidèle!; 4. Voyez du haut ces rivages.
1. German Fest Orch, A. Scholz
(CAVA) Ⓓ **CAVCD018**
1. Sun Life Band, B. Hurdley (arr Winter)
(GRAS) Ⓓ **GRCD41**
1. Detroit SO, P. Paray
(MERC) Ⓓ **434 309-2MM**
1. Munich RO, K. Redel (PIER) Ⓓ **PV786104**
1. Luxembourg Rad & TV SO, L. de Froment
(FORL) Ⓓ **FF027**
1. Lamoureux Orch, I. Markevitch
(7/95) (DG) Ⓓ **447 406-2GOR**
2. E. Marcelin, orch (r1923)
(MSCM) Ⓓ **MM30377**
3. L. Slezak, orch (Ger: r1908)
(2/91) (PREI) Ⓓ **89020**

Zerline– opéra: 3 acts (1851—Paris)
EXCERPTS: ACT 1: 4. O Palerme! O Sicile!.
4. M. Horne, Monte Carlo PO, L. Foster (r1984)
(ERAT) Ⓓ **4509-98501-2**

AUDRAN, Edmond *(1840–1901) France*

Gillette de Narbonne– operetta: 3 acts (1882—Paris) (Lib. H Chivot & A Duru)
Chanson provençale F. Révoil, orch, M. Cariven (EMI) Ⓓ [2] **CZS5 68292-2**

La **Mascotte– operetta: 3 acts (1880—Paris) (Lib. H. Chivot and A. Duru)**
EXCERPTS: ACT 1: 1. La vendange est terminée...Vive le petite vin doux; 2. Un jour le diable ivre d'orgueil; 3a. On aime à voir; 3b. Les gens sensés et sages; 4. Ah! qu'il est beau!; 5. Je ne sais quoi; 6. Je sens lorsque je t'aperçois; 7. On sonne! O sonne! ACT 2: 8. Qu'elle est belle, qu'elle a de grâce; 9. Salut à vous, Seigneur...C'est moi, Saltarello; 10. Des courtisans; 11. Chasser le cerf...J'en suis tout à fait incapable; 12. Un jour, un brave capitaine. ACT 3: 13a. Ne tremblez-pas, braves gens; 13b. Le grand singe d'Amérique; 14. Je touche au but; 15. Eh! pourquoi donc crier ainsi; 16. Les envoyés du Paradis.
J'aim' bien mes dindons N. Vallin, A. Baugé, orch, G. Andolfi (r1934)
(EMI) Ⓓ [2] **CZS5 68292-2**
Les envoyés du paradis A. Baugé, orch, G. Andolfi (EMI) Ⓓ [2] **CZS5 68292-2**
16. A. Baugé, orch (r1930s)
(FORL) Ⓓ **UCD19022**

Miss Helyett– operetta: 3 acts (1890—Paris) (Wds. M. Boucheron)
Miss Helyett L. Dachary
Manuela Fernandez C. Collart
Señora Fernandez G. Ristori
Norette L. Arseguet
Paul A. Doniat
Pasteur Smithson D. Tirmont
Puycardas M. Hamel
James Richter R. Lenoty
Bacarel G. Rey
ORTF Lyric Chorale, ORTF Lyric Orch, M. Cariven (bp1963)
(11/93) (MUSD) Ⓓ [2] **20240-2**

La **Poupée– operetta: 4 acts (1896—Paris) (Lib. Ordonneau)**
P. Dawson, orch (r1929)
(PEAR) Ⓓ **GEMMCD9384**
Excs H. Hennetier, J. Peyron, R. Massard, Duvaleix, R. Lenoty, Génio, G. Ristori, P. Roi, J. Pruvost, French Rad Lyric Chor, French Rad Lyric Orch, M. Cariven (bp1958)
(11/93) (MUSD) Ⓓ [2] **20240-2**

BACH, Johann Christian *(1735–1782) Germany/Italy/England*

T Nos—C.S. Terry, J.C. Bach

Adriano in Siria– opera, T211 (1976—London) (Lib after Metastasio)
EXCERPTS: 1. Overture.
1. AAM, S. Standage (vn/dir) (r1993)
(12/93) (CHAN) Ⓓ **CHAN0540**

Catone in Utica– opera: 3 acts (Naples) (Lib after Metastasio)
EXCERPTS: 1. Overture; 2. Fiumicel che son de appena.
1. Hanover Band, A. Halstead (r1994)
(11/95) (CPO) Ⓓ **CPO999 129-2**
2. R. Sonnenschmidt, Sephira Ens (r1989)
(BAYE) Ⓓ **BR100083**

BALDUCCI, Giuseppe *(1796–?) Italy*

Tazia– dramma: 1 act (1826—Naples) (Lib. L. Ricciuti)
Che vedo!...Numa immenso...Non più veggio J. Rhys-Davies, P. Nilon, Philh, D. Parry
(8/95) (OPRA) Ⓓ [3] **ORCH104**

BALFE, Michael William *(1808–1870) Ireland*

The **Bohemian Girl– opera: 3 acts (1843—London) (Lib. A. Bunn, after Saint Georges)**
EXCERPTS: 1. Overture. ACT 1: 2. Up with the banner; 3. A soldier's life; 4. 'Tis sad to leave our fatherland; 5. In the gipsy's life you read; 6. Comrade, your hand; 7. Is no succour near at hand?; 8. What means this alarm?; 9. Waltz; 10. Down with the daring slave; 11. Galop; 12. What sounds break on the ear? ACT 2: 13. Silence, silence! The lady moon; 14. I dreamt I dwelt in marble halls; 15. The wound upon thy arm; 16. What is the spell hath yet effaced; 17. Listen, when I relate the hope of a Gipsy's fate; 18. In the gipsy's life you read; 19. 'Tis gone - the past was all a dream; 20. This is thy deed; 21b. Come with the gypsy bride; 22. Life itself is at the best; 23. My dear uncle, it delights me to see you; 24a. Whate'er the scenes; 24b. The heart bow'd down; 25. Hold! hold! ACT 3: 26a. Introduction; 26b. The past appears to me but a dream; 27. When other lips and other hearts; 28. Through the world wilt thou fly, love; 29. Welcome the present; 30. Through every hope be fled; 31. See at your feet a suppliant one; 32. When the fair land of Poland; 33. Let not the soul for sorrows grieve; 34. Oh! what full delight.
Arline N. Thomas
Thaddeus P. Power
Queen of the Gipsies B. Cullen
Count Arnheim J. Summers
Florestein T. German
RTE Phil Ch, Ireland National SO, R. Bonynge
(8/92) (ARGO) Ⓓ [2] **433 324-2ZH2**
14. J. Sutherland, LSO, R. Bonynge
(DECC) Ⓓ **425 850-2DWO**
(DECC) ⊟ **425 850-4DWO**
14. J. Sutherland, LSO, R. Bonynge
(DECC) Ⓓ **425 048-2DX**
(DECC) ⊟ **425 048-4DX**
14, 19. S. Murphy, WNO Orch, Julian Smith (r1992) (SONY) Ⓓ **474364-2**
24b C. Whitehill, orch (r1927)
(IRCC) Ⓓ **IRCC-CD810**
24b H. Scott, Orig Broadway Cast (r1913)
(5/94) (PEAR) Ⓓ [3] **GEMMCDS9059/61**
27. P. Power, Ireland National SO, R. Bonynge (r1991) (KIWI) Ⓓ **CDSLD-82**
27. H. Nash, orch (r1926)
(8/89) (PEAR) Ⓓ **GEMMCD9319**

Le **Puits d'amour– opéra-comique: 3 acts (1843—Paris) (Lib. E Scribe & A de Leuven)**
EXCERPTS: 1. Rèves d'amour, rêves de gloire.
1. S. Jo, ECO, R. Bonynge (r1993)
(9/94) (DECC) Ⓓ **440 679-2DH**

BARBER, Samuel *(1910–1981) USA*

Antony and Cleopatra– opera: 3 acts, Op. 40 (1966—New York) (Lib. Zeffirelli, after Shakespeare)
ACT ONE: 1. Prologue: From Alexandria; 2. These strong Egyptian fetters; 3. I am sick and sullen; 4. Orchestral Interlude; 5. Ah! Hail, Marcus Antonius!; 6. Give me some music; 7. The most infectious pestilence upon you!; 8. A sister I bequeath you; 9. When first she met Mark Antony; 10. Where's my serpent of old Nile? ACT TWO: 11. Contemning Rome, he has done all this; 12. Lord Alexas, sweet Alexas; 13. Hush, here come the Queen and Antony; 14. The night is shiny; 15a. Inside the tent; 15b. Oh take, oh take those lips away; 16. On to our ships; 17. Hark! the land bids me tread no more upon it; 18. Most kind ambassador; 19. Oh, bear me witness; 20. O sov'reign mistress of true melancholy; 21. Orchestral Interlude; 22. The last she spoke; 23. Where's Antony? ACT THREE: 24. O Charmian, I will never go from hence; 25. My lord, my lord! (On the death of Antony); 26. The breaking of so great a thing; 27. Prelude; 28. He words me, girls; 29. Here is a rural fellow; 30. Give me my robe; 31. Death of Cleopatra: She looks like sleep.
Antony J. Wells
Cleopatra E. Hinds
Caesar R. Grayson
Charmian K. Cowdrick
Iras J. Bunnell
Enobarbus E. Halfvarson

Maecenas M. Cleveland
Agrippa C. Damsel
A Messenger S. Cole
Eros D. Hickox
Dolabella D. Hamilton
Thidias K. Weaver
Westminster Ch, Spoleto Fest Orch, C. Badea
(NEW) Ⓓ [2] **NW322/4-2**
6, 30. L. Price, New Philh, T. Schippers (r1968)
(8/94) (RCA) Ⓓ **09026 61983-2**
6, 31. R. Alexander, Netherlands PO, E. de Waart (r1992) (6/93) (ETCE) Ⓓ **KTC1145**
25, 31. Cambridge Univ Chbr Ch, T. Brown (r1992) (11/93) (GAMU) Ⓓ **GAMCD535**
30. C. Vaness, NY Met Op Orch, J. Conlon (pp1991) (6/93) (RCA) Ⓓ **09026 61509-2**
30. L. Price, New Philh, T. Schippers (r1968)
(4/94) (RCA) Ⓓ [6] **09026 61580-2(7)**

A **Hand of Bridge– opera: 1 act, Op. 35 (1958—Spoleto)**
P. Neway, E. Alberts, W. Lewis, P. Maero, Sym of the Air, V. Golschmann
(8/92) (VANG) Ⓓ **08.4016.71**

Vanessa– opera: 4 acts, Op. 32 (1958—New York) (Lib. G Menotti)
EXCERPTS: ACT 1: 1. Portage crème aux perles; 2. No, I cannot understand; 3. Must the winter come so soon?; 4. Listen!...They are here; 5. Do not utter a word, Anatol; 6. Yes, I believe I shall love you; 7. Where are you? ACT 2: 8. And then?—He made me drink; 9. No, you are not as good a skater; 10. 'Under the willow tree...'; 11. Erika, I am so happy; 12. Our arms are entwined; 13. Did you hear her?; 14. Outside this house the world has changed; 15. Orchestral Interlude (Hymn). ACT 3: 16. The Count and Countess d'Albany; 17. I should never have been a doctor; 19. At last I found you; 20. Nothing to worry about. ACT 4: 21. Why did no one warm me?; 22. Why must the greatest sorrows; 23. There, look!; 24. Anatol, tell me the truth!; 25. Take me away; 26. Grandmother!—Yes, Erika; 27. Interlude; 28. By the time we arrive; 29. For every love there ia a last farewell; 30. And you, my friend; 31. To leave, to break (Quintet); 32. Goodbye, Erika.
Vanessa E. Steber
Erika R. Elias
The Old Baroness R. Resnik
Anatol N. Gedda
The Old Doctor G. Tozzi
Nicholas G. Cehanovsky
Footman R. Nagy
NY Met Op Chor, NY Met Op Orch, D. Mitropoulos
(7/90) (RCA) Ⓓ [2] **GD87899**
3. F. von Stade, NY Met Op Orch, J. Conlon (pp1991) (6/93) (RCA) Ⓓ **09026 61509-2**
3, 5. R. Alexander, Netherlands PO, E. de Waart (r1992) (6/93) (ETCE) Ⓓ **KTC1145**
5. L. Price, RCA Italiana Op Orch, F. Molinari-Pradelli (r1960s) (RCA) Ⓓ **09026 62596-2**
5. L. Price, RCA Italiana Op Orch, F. Molinari-Pradelli (12/92) (RCA) Ⓓ [4] **09026 61236-2**
10. Cambridge Univ Chbr Ch, T. Brown (r1992)
(11/93) (GAMU) Ⓓ **GAMCD535**
31. E. Steber, R. Elias, R. Resnik, N. Gedda, G. Tozzi, NY Met Op Orch, D. Mitropoulos (r1958)
(RCA) Ⓓ **09026 62689-2**
31. E. Steber, R. Elias, R. Resnik, N. Gedda, G. Tozzi, G. Cehanovsky, NY Met Op Orch, D. Mitropoulos (r1958)
(4/94) (RCA) Ⓓ [6] **09026 61580-2(5)**

BARBIERI , Francisco Asenjo *(1823–1894) Spain*

El **Barberillo de Lavapiès– zarzuela: 3 acts (1874—Madrid) (Lib. Larra)**
EXCERPTS: 1. Preludio: Dicen que en El Pardo; 2. Tirana: No hay que guitar; 3. Seguidillas manchegas: En el templo; 4. Canción de la paloma.
Paloma M.C. Ramirez
Marquesa del Bierzo D. Perez
Lamparilla L. Sagi-Vela
Don Luis de Haro F. Saura
Don Juan de Peralta R. Alonso
Don Pedro de Monforte L. Frutos
Madrid Coros Cantores, Spanish Lyric Orch, F. Moreno Torroba
(10/92) (HISP) Ⓓ **CDZ7 67454-2**
Canción de Paloma P. Lorengar, Seville SO, L.A. Garcia-Navarro (pp1991)
(RCA) Ⓓ **RD61191**
Canción de Paloma P. Lorengar, Seville SO, L.A. Garcia-Navarro (pp1991)
(RCA) OO **09026 61191-5**
Exc P. Perez Inigo, Madrid SO, E. G. Asensio (pp1991) (11/92) (IMP) Ⓓ **MCD45**
No hay que quitar los hilvanes J. Carreras, I. Rey, ECO, E. Ricci (r1994)
(2/95) (ERAT) Ⓓ **4509-95789-2**
(2/95) (ERAT) ▭ **4509-95789-4**
5. V. de los Angeles, Spanish Nat Orch, R. Frühbeck de Burgos (r1967)
(EMI) Ⓓ **CDM5 65579-2**

BARTÓK , Béla *(1881–1945) Hungary/USA*

Sz–numbers from A. Szöllösy's Bibliographie.... Bartók pub 1956

Duke Bluebeard's castle– opera: 1 act, Sz48 (Op. 11) (1918—Budapest) (Lib. B. Balázs)
Bluebeard M. Székely
Judith O. Szönyi
LSO, A. Dorati (r1962)
(7/93) (MERC) Ⓓ **434 325-2MM**
Bluebeard W. Berry
Judith C. Ludwig
LSO, I. Kertész (r1965)
(4/95) (DECC) Ⓓ **443 571-2DCS**
Bluebeard F. Struckmann
Judith K. Szendrényi
Frankfurt RSO, E. Inbal (r1992)
(10/95) (DENO) Ⓓ **CO-78932**
Figs. 81-2. Stockholm PO, A. Dorati (reh seq:r1982) (BIS) Ⓓ [8] **BIS-CD421/4(1)**

BAZIN, Francŏis (Emmanuel-Joseph) *(1816–1878) France*

Maître Pathelin– opéra comique: 3 acts (1856—Paris) (Lib. de Leuven and Langlé)
EXCERPTS: 1. Overture; 2. Pauvre avocat dans ton état; 3. Nous ferons ripaille; 4. Veux-te bien ranger la boutique; 5. Quel air de probité; 6. Quel triste sort; 7. Je pense a vous quand je m'éveille; 8. Je suis un avocat d'ithaque; 9. Quand on alliat te faire pendre; 10. C'est effroyable.
Guillemette C. Harbell
Bobinette M. Stiot
Angélique L. Felder
M. Pathelin B. Plantey
Charlot G. Friedmann
Josseaume M. Jarry
Le Bailli J. Peyron
Aignelet M. Hamel
French Rad Lyric Chor, French Rad Lyric Orch, J. Brebion (bp1971)
(4/94) (MUSD) Ⓓ [2] **202552**

Le **Voyage en Chine– opéra comique: 3 acts (1865—Paris) (Lib. E Labiche and A Delacour)**
EXCERPTS: 1. Overture. ACT 1: 2. Qu'a-t-elle donc?; 3. C'est jour de fête; 4. Je vous présente ici ma femme; 5. Ah! je vais donc la revoir; 6. Ah! quelle amusante folie; 7. C'est jour de fête. ACT 2: 8. Ah! quelle heureuse destinée; 9. Six cailloux, cinq cailloux; 10. Quel temps effroyable!; 11. Je suis breton; 12. Fille dénaturée. ACT 3: 13. Voguons, la mer est belle; 14. Quand le soleil sur notre monde; 15. En chine, en chine; 16. Faut-il hisser, capitaine.
Marie C. Collart
Henri de Kernoisan M. Sénéchal
Berthe L. Dachary
Pompéry A. Balbon
Madame Pompéry A. Martineau
Alidor de Rosenville G. Rey
Maurice Fréval R. Lenoty
Bonneteau Duvaleix
French Rad Lyric Chor, French Rad Lyric Orch, M. Cariven (bp1968)
(4/94) (MUSD) Ⓓ [2] **202552**

BEESON , Jack *(b 1921) USA*

Hello Out There– chamber opera: 1 act (1954—New York) (Wds. cpsr, after W. Saroyan)
Young man J. Reardon
Girl L. Gabriele
Husband M. Worden
Columbia CO, F. Waldman
(BAY) Ⓓ **BCD-1034**

BEETHOVEN, Ludwig van *(1770–1827) Germany*

Works without opus numbers are identified by Kinsky's Thematic Catalogue

Fidelio– opera: 2 acts, Op. 72 (1814—Vienna) (Lib. Sonnleithner and Treitschke)
EXCERPTS: 1. Overture; 2. ACT 1: Jetzt, Schätzchen, jetzt; 3. Oh, wär' ich schon; 4. Mir ist so wunderbar; 5. Hat man nicht auch Gold; 6. Gut, Söhnchen, gut; 7. March; 8. Ha! Welch ein Augenblick; 9. Jetzt, Alter; 10a. Abscheulicher!; 10b. Komm, Hoffnung; 11. O, welche Lust!; 12a. Nun sprecht, wie ging's?; 12b. Ach! Vater, eilt!. ACT 2: 13a. Gott! Welch Dunkel hier!; 13b. In des Lebens; 14a. Melodrama; 14b. Nur hurtig fort; 15. Euch werde Lohn; 16. Er sterbe!; 17. O, namen, namenlose Freude!; 18. Heil sei dem Tag; 19. Des besten Königs Wink und Wille; 20. Wer ein holdes Weib errungen.
Leonore E. Söderström
Florestan A. de Ridder
Pizarro R. Allman
Rocco C. Appelgren
Marzelline E. Gale
Jaquino I. Caley
Don Fernando M. Langdon
Prisoner I D. Johnston
Prisoner II R. Bryson
Glyndebourne Fest Chor, LPO, B. Haitink, P. Hall (pp1980)
(IMP) ▣ **SL2004**
Leonore G. Beňačková
Florestan J. Protschka
Pizarro M. Pederson
Rocco R. Lloyd
Marzelline M. McLaughlin
Jaquino N. Archer
Don Fernando H. Tschammer
Prisoner I L. Atkinson
Prisoner II M. Beesley
ROH Chor, ROHO, C. von Dohnányi, D. Bailey (pp)
(MCEG) ▣ **VVD951**
Leonore G. Beňačková
Florestan J. Protschka
Pizarro M. Pederson
Rocco R. Lloyd
Marzelline M. McLaughlin
Jaquino N. Archer
Don Fernando H. Tschammer
Prisoner I L. Atkinson
Prisoner II M. Beesley
ROH Chor, ROHO, C. von Dohnányi, D. Bailey
(PION) ◖ [2] **PLMCC00301**
Leonore J. Rutishauser
Florestan J. Stępień
Pizarro D. Washington
Rocco J. Ostapiuk
Marzelline M. Didusch
Jaquino E. Holland
Don Fernando A. Dymovski
Warsaw Nat Op Chor, Masurian PO, P. Kantschieder (r1990)
(SCHW) Ⓓ [2] **312942**
Leonore C. Ludwig
Florestan J. Vickers
Pizarro W. Berry
Rocco G. Frick
Marzelline I. Hallstein
Jaquino G. Unger
Don Fernando F. Crass
Prisoner I K. Wehofschitz
Prisoner II R. Wolansky
Philh Chor, Philh, O. Klemperer (r1962)
(EMI) Ⓓ [2] **CDS5 55170-2**
Leonore J. Altmeyer
Florestan S. Jerusalem
Pizarro S. Nimsgern
Rocco P. Meven
Marzelline C. Nossek
Jaquino R. Wohlers
Don Fernando T. Adam
Prisoner I K. König
Prisoner II F-P. Späthe
Leipzig Rad Chor, Berlin Rad Men's Chor, Leipzig Gewandhaus, K. Masur (r1980-1)
(RCA) Ⓓ [2] **74321 25278-2**
Leonore G. Jones
Florestan J. King
Pizarro T. Adam
Rocco F. Crass
Marzelline E. Mathis
Jaquino P. Schreier
Don Fernando M. Talvela

Prisoner I E. Büchner
Prisoner II G. Leib
Leipzig Rad Chor, Dresden St Op Chor, Staatskapelle Dresden, K. Böhm (r1969)
(DG) ⦶ [2] **445 448-2GX2**

Leonore H. Dernesch
Florestan P. Hofmann
Pizarro T. Adam
Rocco H. Sotin
Marzelline S. Ghazarian
Jaquino D. Kuebler
Don Fernando G. Howell
Prisoner I R. Johnson
Prisoner II P. Kraus
Chicago Sym Chor, Chicago SO, G. Solti (with dialogue)
(3/85) (DECC) ⦶ [2] **410 227-2DH2**

Leonore G. Janowitz
Florestan R. Kollo
Pizarro H. Sotin
Rocco M. Jungwirth
Marzelline L. Popp
Jaquino A. Dallapozza
Don Fernando D. Fischer-Dieskau
Prisoner I K. Terkal
Prisoner II A. Sramek
Vienna St Op Chor, VPO, L. Bernstein (with dialogue)
(6/87) (DG) ⦶ [2] **419 436-2GH2**

Leonore H. Dernesch
Florestan J. Vickers
Pizarro Z. Kélémen
Rocco K. Ridderbusch
Marzelline H. Donath
Jaquino H. Laubenthal
Don Fernando J. Van Dam
Prisoner I W. Hollweg
Prisoner II S.R. Frese
Berlin Deutsche Op Chor, BPO, H. von Karajan (with dialogue)
(4/88) (EMI) ⦶ [2] **CMS7 69290-2**

Leonore J. Norman
Florestan R. Goldberg
Pizarro E. Wlaschiha
Rocco K. Moll
Marzelline P. Coburn
Jaquino H-P. Blochwitz
Don Fernando A. Schmidt
Dresden St Op Chor, Staatskapelle Dresden, B. Haitink (r1989: with dialogue)
(1/91) (PHIL) ⦶ [2] **426 308-2PH2**

Leonore K. Flagstad
Florestan R. Maison
Pizarro F. Schorr
Rocco E. List
Marzelline M. Farell
Jaquino K. Laufkötter
Don Fernando A. Gabor
NY Met Op Chor, NY Met Op Orch, A. Bodanzky (pp1938: with recits!)
(5/91) (MUSI) ⦶ [2] **MACD-619**

Leonore R. Bampton
Florestan J. Peerce
Pizarro H. Janssen
Rocco S. Belarsky
Marzelline E. Steber
Jaquino J. Laderoute
Don Fernando N. Moscona
Chor, NBC SO, A. Toscanini (omits dialogue: bp1944/r1945)
(10/92) (RCA) ⦶ [2] **GD60273**

Leonore M. Mödl
Florestan W. Windgassen
Pizarro O. Edelmann
Rocco G. Frick
Marzelline S. Jurinac
Jaquino R. Schock
Don Fernando A. Poell
Prisoner I A. Hendriks
Prisoner II F. Bierbach
Vienna St Op Chor, VPO, W. Furtwängler (r1953: omits dialogue)
(5/93) (EMI) ⦶ [2] **CHS7 64496-2**

Leonore Leonie Rysanek
Florestan E. Haefliger
Pizarro D. Fischer-Dieskau
Rocco G. Frick
Marzelline I. Seefried
Jaquino F. Lenz
Don Fernando K. Engen
Bavarian St Op Chor, Bavarian St Orch, F. Fricsay (r1957: with dialogue)
(5/93) (DG) ⦶ [2] **437 345-2GDO2**

Leonore G. Schnaut
Florestan J. Protschka
Pizarro H. Welker
Rocco K. Rydl
Marzelline R. Ziesak
Jaquino U. Heilmann
Don Fernando T. Krause
Prisoner F. Struckmann
Vienna St Op Concert Ch, VPO, C. von Dohnányi (r1991: with dialogue)
(7/93) (DECC) ⦶ [2] **436 627-2DHO2**

Leonore K. Flagstad
Florestan J. Patzak
Pizarro P. Schoeffler
Rocco J. Greindl
Marzelline E. Schwarzkopf
Jaquino A. Dermota
Don Fernando H. Braun
Prisoner I H. Gallos
Prisoner II L. Pantscheff
Vienna St Op Chor, VPO, W. Furtwängler (pp1950: with dialogue)
(12/93) (EMI) ⦶ [2] **CHS7 64901-2**

Leonore H. Konetzni
Florestan T. Ralf
Pizarro P. Schoeffler
Rocco H. Alsen
Marzelline I. Seefried
Jaquino P. Klein
Don Fernando T. Neralič
Prisoner I H. Gallos
Prisoner II H. Schweiger
Vienna St Op Chor, Vienna St Op Orch, K. Böhm (pp1944: with dialogue)
(8/94) (PREI) ⦶ [2] **90195**

Leonore C. Margiono
Florestan P. Seiffert
Pizarro S. Leiferkus
Rocco L. Polgár
Marzelline B. Bonney
Jaquino D. van der Walt
Don Fernando B. Skovhus
Prisoner 1 R. Macias
Prisoner 2 R. Florianschütz
A. Schoenberg Ch, COE, N. Harnoncourt (r1994)
(10/95) (TELD) ⦶ [2] **4509-94560-2**

1. Octophoros (arr. Sedlak)
(ACCE) ⦶ **ACC48434D**
(ACCE) ⊟ **MC-ACC8434**

1. Slovak PO, S. Gunzenhauser
(NAXO) ⦶ **8 550072**

1. Berlin St Op Orch, A. von Zemlinsky
(SCHW) ⦶ **310037**

1. Staatskapelle Dresden, K. Böhm (r1969)
(DG) ⦶ **427 194-2GR**

1. BPO, H. von Karajan
(DG) ⦶ [2] **427 256-2GGA2**

1. Philadelphia, R. Muti
(EMI) ⦶ **CDC7 49490-2**

1. Budapest SO, T. Pál (LASE) ⦶ **15 622**
(LASE) ⊟ **79 622**

1. BPO, H. von Karajan
(DG) ⦶ [6] **429 089-2GSE6**

1. Philh, O. Klemperer (r1962)
(EMI) ⦶ **CDM7 63611-2**

1. VPO, C. Abbado
(DG) ⦶ [2] **429 762-2GH2**

1. Cleveland Orch, G. Szell
(SONY) ⦶ **SBK46533**
(SONY) ⊟ **SBT46533**

1. VPO, L. Bernstein
(DG) ⦶ [10] **435 091-2GCE10**

1. Cleveland Orch, G. Szell
(SONY) ⦶ [5] **SB5K48396**

1. Bamberg SO, E. Jochum
(RCA) ⦶ **09026 61212-2**
(RCA) ⊟ **09026 61212-4**

1. NBC SO, A. Toscanini (pp1939)
(RELI) ⦶ **CR1861**

1. BPO, H. von Karajan (r1985)
(DG) ⦶ **439 005-2GHS**

1. BPO, H. von Karajan (r1985)
(DG) **OO** **439 005-5GHS**

1. BPO, H. von Karajan (r1985)
(DG) ⦶ [6] **439 200-2GH6**

1. NY Harmonie Ens, S. Richman (r1992: arr W Sedlak) (MUSI) ⦶ **MACD-797**

1. Bavarian Nat Orch, F. Fricsay
(DG) ⦶ [2] **447 364-2GDB2**

1. BPO, H. von Karajan (r1965)
(8/85) (DG) ⦶ **415 276-2GH**

1. BPO, H. von Karajan
(8/87) (DG) ⦶ **419 051-2GGA**
(1/87) (DG) ⊟ **419 051-4GGA**

1. Philadelphia, R. Muti
(1/89) (EMI) ⦶ [6] **CDS7 49487-2**

1. VPO, L. Bernstein (pp1978)
(3/89) (DG) ⦶ [6] **423 481-2GX6**

1. Staatskapelle Dresden, K. Böhm
(12/91) (DG) ⦶ [2] **413 145-2GW2**

1. M. Arroyo, R. Sarfaty, N. di Virgilio, N. Scott, Juilliard Chor, NYPO, L. Bernstein (r1961)
(11/92) (SONY) ⦶ **SMK47518**

1. Leipzig Gewandhaus, K. Masur (r1973-4)
(5/94) (PHIL) ⦶ [2] **438 706-2PM2**

1. Staatskapelle Dresden, K. Böhm (r1969)
(4/95) (DG) ⦶ [2] **437 928-2GX2**

1. RPO, G. Herbig (r1994)
(6/95) (TRIN) ⦶ **TRP026**

1. BPO, R. Kempe (r c1958)
(11/95) (EMI) ⦶ [2] **CES5 68518-2**

1, 3, 4, 7, 8, 10a, 10b, 11, 13a, 13b, 16-18. D. Fischer-Dieskau, H. Sotin, R. Kollo, G. Janowitz, M. Jungwirth, L. Popp, A. Dallapozza, K. Terkal, A. Sramek, Vienna St Op Chor, VPO, L. Bernstein (r1978) (DG) ⦶ **445 461-2GMH**

1, 3-5, 8, 10a, 10b, 11, 13a, 13b, 16, 17, 20. H. Dernesch, J. Vickers, K. Ridderbusch, Z. Kélémen, J. van Dam, H. Donath, H. Laubenthal, W. Hollweg, S.R. Frese, Berlin Deutsche Op Chor, BPO, H. von Karajan (r1970)
(EMI) ⦶ **CDM7 63077-2**

1, 3-8, 10a, 11, 16-20. J. Norman, R. Goldberg, E. Wlaschiha, K. Moll, P. Coburn, H-P. Blochwitz, A. Schmidt, Dresden St Op Chor, Staatskapelle Dresden, B. Haitink (r1989)
(PHIL) ⦶ **438 496-2PH**

1, 4. H. Dernesch, H. Donath, H. Laubenthal, K. Ridderbusch, BPO, H. von Karajan (r1970)
(CFP) ⦶ **CD-CFP4656**
(CFP) ⊟ **TC-CFP4656**

1-7, 11, 15, 17. Amadeus Ens, J. Rudel (arr Sedlak: Wind Octet and Bass)
(MUSM) ⦶ [5] **67118-2**

3. P. Lorengar, Vienna St Op Orch, W. Weller (r1970) (DECC) ⦶ **443 931-2DM**

3. E. Schwarzkopf, Philh, A. Galliera (r1950)
(EMI) ⦶ **CDM5 65577-2**

3. E. Schwarzkopf, Philh, A. Galliera (r1950)
(4/92) (EMI) ⦶ [7] **CHS7 69741-2(4)**

3. I. Seefried, Bavarian St Orch, F. Fricsay (r1957) (9/93) (DG) ⦶ [2] **437 677-2GDO2**

4. P. Anders, T. Eipperle, M. Fuchs, G. Hann, Berlin RSO, A. Rother (bp1944)
(8/93) (ACAN) ⦶ **43 268**

4. E. Berger, H. Gottlieb, M. Wittrisch, W. Domgraf-Fassbaender, Berlin St Op Orch, F. Zweig (r1930s) (10/93) (NIMB) ⦶ **NI7848**

5. K. Moll, Munich RO, K. Eichhorn (r1981)
(ORFE) ⦶ **C009821A**

5. M. Salminen, Lahti SO, E. Klas
(8/92) (BIS) ⦶ **BIS-CD520**

6. C. Ludwig, E. Mathis, F. Crass, VPO, K. Böhm (pp1968) (ORFE) ⦶ **C365941A**

7. Budapest SO, T. Pál (LASE) ⦶ **15 510**
(LASE) ⊟ **79 510**

7. Banda Classica, C. Siegmann (arr Wenzel)
(SCHW) ⦶ **310110**

8. F. Schorr, orch (r1922) (PREI) ⦶ **89052**

8. N. Stanchiev, Bulgarian Nat Chor, Bulgarian RSO, E. Gracis (r1979) (FORL) ⦶ **UCD16651**

8. F. Schorr, New SO, A. Coates (r1930)
(9/91) (PEAR) ⦶ **GEMMCD9398**

8. P. Schoeffler, Vienna St Op Chor, Vienna St Op Orch, K. Böhm (r1944)
(4/92) (EMI) ⦶ [7] **CHS7 69741-2(4)**

9. J. Herrmann, K. Böhme, orch (r1943)
(PREI) ⦶ **89076**

10a, 10b R. Bampton, NBC SO, A. Toscanini (r1945) (RCA) ⦶ **GD60280**

10a, 10b H. Behrens, Chicago SO, G. Solti (r1979) (DECC) ⦶ **436 472-2DM**

10a, 10b K. Flagstad, Philadelphia, E. Ormandy (r1937) (IMP) ⦶ **GLRS105**

10a, 10b H. Wildbrunn, orch (r1922)
(PREI) ⦶ **89097**

10a, 10b K. Flagstad, Philadelphia, E. Ormandy (r1937) (SIMA) ⦶ [3] **PSC1821(2)**

10a, 10b F. Leider, orch, J. Barbirolli (r1928)
(2/90) (PREI) ⦶ **89004**

10a, 10b E. Schwarzkopf, Philh, H. von Karajan (r1954) (7/90) (EMI) ⦶ **CDH7 63201-2**

10a, 10b F. Leider, orch (r1921)
(5/91) (PREI) ⦶ [3] **89301**

10a, 10b K. Flagstad, Philadelphia, E. Ormandy (r1937) (2/92) (MMOI) ⦶ **CDMOIR408**

10a, 10b Lilli Lehmann, orch (r1907)
(7/92) (PEAR) ⦶ [3] **GEMMCDS9923(2)**

10a, 10b K. Flagstad, Philadelphia, E. Ormandy (r1937) (7/93) (NIMB) ⦶ **NI7847**

10a, 10b H. Konetzni, Berlin St Op Orch, H. Schmidt-Isserstedt (r1937)
(1/95) (PREI) ⦶ **90078**

10a, 10b R. Hunter, Tasmanian SO, D. Franks (r1989) (10/95) (ABCC) Ⓓ **8 7000 10**
10b Lotte Lehmann, orch, M. Gurlitt (r1927) (10/89) (NIMB) Ⓓ **NI7802** (NIMB) ▭ **NC7802**
11. Berlin Deutsche Op Chor, Berlin Deutsche Op Orch, G. Sinopoli (DG) OO **415 283-5GH**
11. R. Johnson, P. Kraus, Chicago Sym Chor, Chicago SO, G. Solti (r1979) (DECC) Ⓓ **433 443-2DA** (DECC) ▭ **433 443-4DA**
11. Vienna St Op Chor, VPO, L. Maazel (r1960s) (BELA) Ⓓ **450 117-2** (BELA) ▭ **450 117-4**
11. Chicago Sym Chor, Chicago SO, G. Solti (1979) (DECC) Ⓓ [2] **443 756-2DF2**
11. Berlin Deutsche Op Chor, Berlin Deutsche Op Orch, G. Sinopoli (10/85) (DG) Ⓓ **415 283-2GH**
11. F. Wunderlich, H.G. Nöcker, Stuttgart Rad Chor, Stuttgart RSO, A. Rischner (bp1957) (10/89) (ACAN) Ⓓ **43 267**
11. J.M. Ainsley, A. Miles, ROH Chor, ROHO, B. Haitink (12/89) (EMI) Ⓓ **CDC7 49849-2**
13a H. Roswaenge, Philh Hungarica, Z. Rozsnyai (pp1959) (PREI) Ⓓ **90103**
13a P. Seiffert, Munich RO, J. Kout (r1992-3) (RCA) Ⓓ **09026 61214-2**
13a H. Roswaenge, Berlin St Op Orch, B. Seidler-Winkler (r1938) (5/90) (PEAR) Ⓓ **GEMMCD9394**
13a H. Roswaenge, Berlin St Op Orch, B. Seidler-Winkler (r1938) (7/92) (PEAR) Ⓓ [3] **GEMMCDS9926(2)**
13a, 13b A. Dermota, Ljubljana RSO, S. Hubad (r1950s) (PREI) Ⓓ **90022**
13a, 13b P. Domingo, VPO, James Levine (DG) ◐ **072 187-1GH** (DG) ▣ **072 187-3GH**
13a, 13b H. Roswaenge, Berlin St Op Orch, B. Seidler-Winkler (r1938) (PREI) Ⓓ [2] **89211**
13a, 13b A. Piccaver, Berlin St Op Orch, J. Prüwer (r1930) (PREI) Ⓓ [2] **89217**
13a, 13b P. Domingo, VPO, James Levine (11/89) (DG) ◐ **072 110-1GH**
13a, 13b H. Roswaenge, Berlin St Op Orch, B. Seidler-Winkler (r1938) (5/90) (PREI) Ⓓ **89018**
13a, 13b F. Völker, Berlin Staatskapelle, A. Melichar (r1933) (8/94) (PREI) Ⓓ **89070**
13a, 13b, 17. P. Anders, W. Wegner, N German RSO, H. Schmidt-Isserstedt (bp1948) (8/93) (ACAN) Ⓓ **43 268**
13b K. Erb, orch (r1912) (PREI) Ⓓ **89095**
19, 20. R. Auvinen, S. Vihavainen, P. Lindroos, J. Silvasti, T. Krause, B. Rundgren, J. Hynninen, Savonlinna Op Fest Chor, Savonlinna Op Fest Orch, U. Söderblom (BIS) Ⓓ [2] **BIS-CD373/4**

Leonore– opera: 3 acts, Op. 72 (1805—Vienna) (Lib. J Sonnleither)
EXCERPTS: 1a. Leonore Overture No. 1, Op. 138; 1b. Leonore Overture No. 2; 1c. Leonore Overture No. 3. ACT 1:
1a Berlin RSO, R. Buckley (SCHW) Ⓓ [2] **314052**
1a BPO, R. Kubelík (BELA) Ⓓ **450 037-2** (BELA) ▭ **450 037-4**
1a South-West German RSO, M. Gielen (r1987) (INTE) Ⓓ **INT860 912**
1a BRSO, Colin Davis (r1985) (SONY) Ⓓ **SMK66927**
1a Concertgebouw, W. Mengelberg (r1931) (7/90) (SYMP) Ⓓ **SYMCD1078**
1a Philh, O. Klemperer (r1954) (8/92) (EMI) Ⓓ **CDM7 64143-2**
1a BBC SO, A. Toscanini (r1939) (5/94) (BIDD) Ⓓ [2] **WHL008/9**
1a-c BPO, H. von Karajan (DG) Ⓓ [2] **427 256-2GGA2**
1a-c Philh, O. Klemperer (r1963) (EMI) Ⓓ **CDM7 63611-2**
1a-c VPO, C. Abbado (DG) Ⓓ [2] **429 762-2GH2**
1a-c Leipzig Gewandhaus, K. Masur (r1973-4) (5/94) (PHIL) Ⓓ [2] **438 706-2PM2**
1a, 1b NBC SO, A. Toscanini (pp1939) (RELI) Ⓓ **CR1891**
1a, 1c Bamberg SO, E. Jochum (RCA) Ⓓ **09026 61212-2** (RCA) ▭ **09026 61212-4**
1b Danish RSO, F. Busch (r1950) (AS D) Ⓓ **AS311**
1b Bavarian St Orch, W. Sawallisch (ORFE) Ⓓ **C161871A**
1b Dresden PO, H. Kegel (LASE) Ⓓ **15 622** (LASE) ▭ **79 622**
1b Hamburg PO, G. Albrecht (pp1992) (ORFE) Ⓓ **C288921A**
1b BPO, W. Furtwängler (r1954) (EMI) Ⓓ [3] **CHS5 65513-2**
1b VPO, C. Abbado (9/89) (DG) Ⓓ [6] **427 306-2GH6**
1b Dresden PO, H. Kegel (10/90) (LASE) Ⓓ **15 523** (10/90) (LASE) ▭ **79 523**
1b BPO, E. Jochum (12/91) (DG) Ⓓ [2] **413 145-2GW2**
1b NBC SO, A. Toscanini (bp1939) (11/92) (RCA) Ⓓ **GD60267**
1b Chicago SO, F. Reiner (r1955) (12/92) (RCA) Ⓓ **09026 60962-2**
1b, 1c Philh, O. Klemperer (r1954) (4/92) (EMI) Ⓓ **CDM7 63855-2**
1c Slovak PO, S. Gunzenhauser (NAXO) Ⓓ **8 550072**
1c BPO, C. Abbado (DG) ▣ **072 124-3GH**
1c Staatskapelle Dresden, K. Böhm (r1969) (DG) Ⓓ **427 194-2GR**
1c(pt) Stockholm PO, W. Furtwängler (r1948: rehearsal seq) (BIS) Ⓓ [8] **BIS-CD421/4(1)**
1c(pt) Stockholm PO, E. Ormandy (r1949: rehearsal seq) (BIS) Ⓓ [8] **BIS-CD421/4(1)**
1c Czech PO, F. Vajnar (SUPR) Ⓓ **11 1118-2**
1c BPO, H. von Karajan (DG) Ⓓ [6] **429 089-2GSE6**
1c Czech PO, K. Ančerl (SUPR) Ⓓ **11 0572-2**
1c RPO, R. Leibowitz (CHES) Ⓓ **Chesky CD17**
1c NBC SO, A. Toscanini (bp1939) (RCA) Ⓓ **GD60255**
1c LPO, R. Armstrong (ACAD) Ⓓ **ACDM6** (ACAD) ▭ **MC-ACDM6**
1c Berlin St Op Orch, O. Klemperer (r1927) (SCHW) Ⓓ [2] **311162**
1c N German RSO, G. Wand (pp1990) (RCA) OO **09026 60755-5**
1c RPO, E. Bátiz (ASV) Ⓓ **CDQS6076** (ASV) ▭ **ZCQS6076**
1c BPO, H. von Karajan (r1985) (DG) OO **439 005-5GHS**
1c BPO, H. von Karajan (r1985) (DG) Ⓓ **439 005-2GHS**
1c Masurian PO, P. Kantschieder (r1990) (SCHW) Ⓓ **313242**
1c BPO, H. von Karajan (r1985) (DG) Ⓓ [6] **439 200-2GH6**
1c Stockholm PO, W. Furtwängler (r1948) (MUSI) Ⓓ **MACD-793**
1c LPO, A. Rahbari (r1993) (DINT) Ⓓ **DICD920114**
1c VPO, W. Furtwängler (pp1944) (PREI) Ⓓ **90251**
1c Staatskapelle Dresden, Colin Davis (r1993) (PHIL) Ⓓ [6] **446 067-2PH6**
1c BPO, H. von Karajan (4/87) (DG) Ⓓ **419 049-2GGA**
1c Cleveland Orch, C. von Dohnányi (r1986) (11/87) (TELA) Ⓓ **CD80145**
1c Philadelphia, R. Muti (1/89) (EMI) Ⓓ [6] **CDS7 49487-2**
1c VPO, L. Bernstein (pp1978) (3/89) (DG) Ⓓ [6] **423 481-2GX6**
1c NBC SO, A. Toscanini (bp1939) (5/90) (RCA) Ⓓ [5] **GD60324**
1c VPO, B. Walter (r1936) (1/91) (KOCH) Ⓓ **37011-2**
1c N German RSO, G. Wand (pp1990) (10/91) (RCA) Ⓓ **RD60755**
1c Philh, Vladimir Ashkenazy (12/91) (DECC) Ⓓ **430 721-2DM**
1c Staatskapelle Dresden, K. Böhm (12/91) (DG) Ⓓ [2] **413 145-2GW2**
1c VPO, W. Furtwängler (pp1944) (2/92) (DG) Ⓓ **435 324-2GWP**
1c VPO, W. Furtwängler (pp1944) (2/92) (DG) Ⓓ [12] **435 321-2GWP12**
1c National PO, L. Stokowski (4/92) (EMI) Ⓓ **CDM7 64140-2**
1c Chicago SO, G. Solti (4/92) (DECC) Ⓓ [6] **430 792-2DC6**
1c BPO, C. Abbado (pp1991) (5/92) (DG) Ⓓ **435 617-2GH** (5/92) (DG) ▭ **435 617-4GH**
1c NYPO, L. Bernstein (r1960) (11/92) (SONY) Ⓓ **SMK47521**
1c NBC SO, A. Toscanini (r1945) (11/92) (RCA) Ⓓ **GD60267**
1c BPO, F. Fricsay (r1958) (5/93) (DG) Ⓓ [2] **437 345-2GDO2**
1c VPO, B. Walter (r1936) (8/94) (PREI) Ⓓ **90157**
1c Staatskapelle Dresden, K. Böhm (r1969) (4/95) (DG) Ⓓ [2] **437 928-2GX2**
2. B. Martinů PO, P. Tiboris (r1994; ed Mahler) (ERIE) Ⓓ **GRK702**

BELLINI, Vincenzo (1801–1835) Italy

Adelson e Salvini– opera: 3 acts (1825—Naples) (Lib. A.L. Tottola)

Lord Adelson	F. Previati
Salvini	B. Williams
Nelly	A. Nafé
Bonifacio	A. Tomicich
Fanny	L. Rizzi
Madama Rivers	E. Jankovic
Struley	R. Coviello
Geronio	G. Tosi

Bellini Th Chor, Bellini Th Orch, A. Licata (pp1992) (2/94) (NUOV) Ⓓ [2] **7154/5**
Dopo l'oscuro nembo N. Focile, Philh, D. Parry (8/95) (OPRA) Ⓓ [3] **ORCH104**

Beatrice di Tenda– opera: 2 acts (1833—Venice) (Lib. F. Romani)
EXCERPTS: 1a. Prelude. ACT 1: 1b. Tu, signor, lasciar si presto; 1c. Ah! non pensar; 2a. Silenzio e notte intorno; 2b. Si rivale; 3a. Respiro io qui; 3b. Oh! mie fedeli!; 4a. Ma la sola, ahimè! son io; 4b. Ah! la pena in lor piombo; 5a. Tu qui, Filippo; 5b. E quali, spergiura; 5c. Qui di ribelli; 6. Lo vedeste?; 7a. Il mio dolore; 7b. Deh! se mi amast un giorno; 8a. Ciascun! non io; 8b. A ciuscun fidar vorrei; 9a. Parti: 9b. Vedi? Traditori!. ACT 2: 10. Lassa! e può il ciel; 11. Omai del suo destino; 12. Venga la rea...Di grave accusa il peso; 13. Orombello! oh, sciagurato; 14. Filippo!...Tu! ti appressa; 15a. Qui m'accolse oppresso; 15b. Non son io che la condanno; 16a. Ah! no, non sia la misera; 16b. Nulla io dissi; 16c. Angiol di pace; 17. Chi giunge?; 18a. Ah! se un urna; 18b. Ah! la morte a cui m'appresso.

Beatrice	M. Nicolesco
Orombello	V. La Scola
Filippo	P. Cappuccilli
Agnese	S. Toczyska
Anichino; Rizzardi	I. Zennaro

Prague Phil Chor, Monte Carlo Nat Op Orch, A. Zedda (r1986) (SONY) Ⓓ [3] **SM3K64539**

Beatrice	E. Gruberová
Orombello	D. Bernardini
Filippo	I. Morozov
Agnese	V. Kasarova
Anichino	B. Robinšak
Rizzardo	D. Sumegi

Vienna Jeunesse Ch, Austrian RSO, P. Steinberg (pp1992) (2/93) (NIGH) Ⓓ [2] **NC070560-2**

Beatrice	J. Sutherland
Orombello	L. Pavarotti
Filippo	C. Opthof
Agnese	J. Veasey
Anichino; Rizzardo	J. Ward

Ambrosian Op Chor, LSO, R. Bonynge (2/93) (DECC) Ⓓ [3] **433 706-2DMO3**

Bianca e Fernando– opera: 2 acts (1828—Genoa) (Lib. F. Romani, after Gilardoni)

Bianca	Y.O. Shin
Fernando	G. Kunde
Carlo	A. Tomicich
Filippo	H. Fu
Clemente	A. Caforio
Viscardo	S. Nigoghossian
Uggero	W. Coppola
Eloisa	E. Manhart

Bellini Th Chor, Bellini Th Orch, A. Licata (pp1991) (2/94) (NUOV) Ⓓ [2] **7076/7**
A tanto duol J. Pruett, RTBF SO, R. Zollman (r1990) (PRES) Ⓓ **PCOM1109**
Ove son?...Sorgi, o padre M. Freni, R. Scotto, National PO, L. Magiera (r1978) (DECC) Ⓓ **440 412-2DM**
Sorgi, o padre C. Muzio, orch (r1922) (5/90) (BOGR) Ⓓ [2] **BIM705-2**
Sorgi, o padre C. Muzio, orch (r1922) (1/94) (ROMO) Ⓓ [2] **81005-2**
Sorgio, o padren J. Bakker, K. Kusaka (r1990: arr D Miller) (PRES) Ⓓ **PCOM1109**

I Capuleti e i Montecchi– opera: 2 acts (1830—Venice) (Lib. F Romani)
EXCERPTS: 1a. Overture. ACT 1: 1b. Aggiorna

appena; 2a. E' serbata a questa acciaro; 2b. L'amo, ah, l'amo, e mi è più cara; 3. Se Romeo t'uccise un figlio; 4. La tremenda ultrice spada; 5a. Eccomi in lieta vesta; 5b. Oh! quante volte; 6. Si fuggire: a noi non resta; 7. Vieni, ah!, vieni, e in me riposa; 8. Lieta notte avventurosa; 9. Sorcorso, sostegno; 10. Se ogni speme è a nio rapita; 11. Morte io non tremo il sai; 12. Ah! non poss'io partire; 13. Solto! ad un sol mio grido; 14. Svena, ah! svena un disperato; 16. Sorgi, mio ben; 17a. Tu sola, o mia Giulietta; 17b. Deh! tu, deh!, tu, bell'anima.

Giulietta R. Scotto
Romeo G. Aragall
Tebaldo L. Pavarotti
Capellio G. Ferrin
Lorenzo A. Giacomotti
La Scala Chor, La Scala Orch, C. Abbado (pp1967)
(BUTT) Ⓓ [2] **BMCD012**
(BUTT) ⊟ [2] **BMK012**

Giulietta K. Ricciarelli
Romeo D. Montague
Tebaldo D. Raffanti
Capellio M. Lippi
Lorenzo A. Salvadori
Venice La Fenice Chor, Venice La Fenice Orch, B. Campanella (pp1991)
(3/92) (NUOV) Ⓓ [2] **7020/1**

Giulietta E. Gruberová
Romeo A. Baltsa
Tebaldo D. Raffanti
Capellio G. Howell
Lorenzo J. Tomlinson
ROH Chor, ROHO, R. Muti (pp1984)
(2/95) (EMI) Ⓓ [2] **CMS7 64846-2**

2a, 2b L. Pavarotti, G. Ferrin, A. Giacomotti, La Scala Chor, La Scala Orch, C. Abbado (pp1966)
(10/95) (RCA) Ⓓ **09026 68014-2**

3. M. Horne, Geneva Op Chor, SRO, H. Lewis
(DECC) Ⓓ **421 891-2DA**

3. B. Fassbaender, Stuttgart RSO, H. Graf
(11/86) (ORFE) Ⓓ **C096841A**

3. G. Fabbri, S. Cottone (two versions: r1903)
(12/89) (SYMP) Ⓓ **SYMCD1065**

5a, 5b R. Streich, Berlin Deutsche Op Orch, R. Peters (DG) Ⓓ [2] **435 748-2GDO2**

5a, 5b K. Battle, LPO, B. Campanella (r1991)
(DG) ⓞⓞ **435 866-5CH**

5a, 5b K. Battle, LPO, B. Campanella (r1991)
(12/93) (DG) Ⓓ **435 866-2GH**

5a, 5b M. Devia, Svizzera Italiana Orch, M. Rota (pp1992) (10/94) (BONG) Ⓓ **GB2513-2**

5b M. Mesplé, Paris Op Orch, G-F. Masini (r1974) (EMI) Ⓓ [2] **CZS7 67813-2**

5b K. Ricciarelli, Svizzera Italiana Orch, B. Amaducci (r1979) (ERMI) Ⓓ **ERM151**

5b M. Carosio, Philh, A. Fistoulari (r1951)
(4/92) (EMI) Ⓓ [7] **CHS7 69741-2(7)**

5b L. Orgonášová, Bratislava RSO, W. Humburg
(2/93) (NAXO) Ⓓ **8 550605**

6, 7. O. Stapp, I. Kirilová, Košice St PO, P. Vronský (OPUS) Ⓓ **9356 2047**

17b G. Simionato, Santa Cecilia Academy Orch, F. Ghione (r1954) (DECC) Ⓓ **440 406-2DM**

Norma– opera: 2 acts (1831—Milan) (Lib. F. Romani)

EXCERPTS: 1. Overture. ACT 1: 2. Ite sul colle, O Druidi; 3a. Svanir le voci!; 3b. Meco all'altar di Venere; 3c. Me protegge; 4a. Norma viene; 4b. Sediziose voci; 4c. Casta diva; 4d. Fine al rito; 4e. Ah! bello a me ritorna; 5. Sgombra è la sacra selva; 6a. Eccola! Va , mi lascia; 6b. Va, crudele; 7a. Vanne, e li cela entrambi; 7b. Oh, Rimembranza!; 7c. Sola, furtiva al tempio; 8a. Tremi tu? E per chi?...Oh, non tremare; 8b. Oh! Di qual sei tu vittima; 8c. Perfido!...Or basti. ACT 2: 9. Dormono entrambi; 10a. Me chiami, o Norma?; 10b. Mira, o Norma; 10c. Cedi! Deh, cedi!; 10d. Si, fino all'ore estreme; 11a. Non parti!; 11b. Guerrieri; 11c. Ah! del Tebro; 12. Ei tornerà; 13. Guerra, guerra!; 14a. In mia man; 14b. Ah! Crudele; 15a. All'ira vostra; 15b. Qual cor tradisti; 15c. Deh! Non volerli vittime.

Norma J. Sutherland
Adalgisa M. Elkins
Pollione R. Stevens
Oroveso C. Grant
Flavio T. Brown
Clothilde E. Piha
Australian Op Chor, Sydney Eliz Orch, R. Bonynge, S. Sequi (pp1978)
(VISI) ▣ **VVD1138**

Norma G. Cigna
Adalgisa E. Stignani
Pollione G. Breviario
Oroveso T. Pasero
Flavio E. Renzi
Clotilde A. Perris
Turin EIAR Chor, Turin EIAR Orch, V. Gui (pp1936)
(PEAR) Ⓓ [2] **GEMMCDS9422**

Norma J. Sutherland
Adalgisa M. Horne
Pollione John Alexander
Oroveso R. Cross
Flavio J. Ward
Clotilde Y. Minton
London Sym Chor, LSO, R. Bonynge
(DECC) Ⓓ [3] **425 488-2DM3**

Norma J. Sutherland
Adalgisa M. Horne
Pollione C. Bergonzi
Oroveso C. Siepi
Flavio R. MacWherter
Clotilde C. Ordassy
NY Met Op Chor, NY Met Op Orch, R. Bonynge (pp1970)
(MEMO) Ⓓ [2] **HR4216/7**

Norma M. Callas
Adalgisa E. Stignani
Pollione M. Filippeschi
Oroveso N. Rossi-Lemeni
Flavio P. Caroli
Clotilde R. Cavallari
La Scala Chor, La Scala Orch, T. Serafin (r1954)
(3/86) (EMI) Ⓓ [3] **CDS7 47304-8**

Norma J. Sutherland
Adalgisa M. Caballé
Pollione L. Pavarotti
Oroveso S. Ramey
Flavio K. Begley
Clotilde D. Montague
WNO Chor, WNO Orch, R. Bonynge
(4/88) (DECC) Ⓓ [3] **414 476-2DH3**

Norma M. Caballé
Adalgisa F. Cossotto
Pollione P. Domingo
Oroveso R. Raimondi
Flavio K. Collins
Clotilde E. Bainbridge
Ambrosian Op. Chor, LPO, C.F. Cillario
(7/88) (RCA) Ⓓ [3] **GD86502**

Norma M. Callas
Adalgisa C. Ludwig
Pollione F. Corelli
Oroveso N. Zaccaria
Flavio P. de Palma
Clotilde E. Vincenzi
La Scala Chor, La Scala Orch, T. Serafin (r1960)
(7/89) (EMI) Ⓓ [3] **CMS7 63000-2**

Norma R. Scotto
Adalgisa T. Troyanos
Pollione G. Giacomini
Oroveso P. Plishka
Flavio P. Crook
Clotilde A. Murray
Ambrosian Op Chor, National PO, James Levine (r1978)
(10/95) (SONY) Ⓓ [2] **SM2K35902**

Norma J. Eaglen
Adalgisa E. Mei
Pollione V. La Scola
Oroveso D. Kavrakos
Flavio E. Gavazzi
Clotilde C. Remigio
MMF Chor, MMF Orch, R. Muti (pp1994)
(10/95) (EMI) Ⓓ [3] **CDS5 55471-2**

Excs J. Sutherland, Orch, Anon (cond), D. Bailey (11/92) (DECC) ◐ **071 135-1DH**

1. Czech SO, A. Krieger (pp1991)
(IMP) Ⓓ **MCD42**

1. Philh, T. Serafin (r1961)
(EMI) Ⓓ [2] **CES5 68541-2**

1. Monte Carlo Nat Op Orch, L. Frémaux
(DG) Ⓓ [2] **447 364-2GDB2**

1. South-West German RSO, K. Arp (r1994)
(PIER) Ⓓ **PV730050**

2. F. Chaliapin, La Scala Orch, C. Sabajno (r1912) (PREI) Ⓓ **89030**

2. B. Christoff, Rome Op Chor, Rome Op Orch, V. Gui (r1955) (EMI) Ⓓ **CDH5 65500-2**

2. T. Pasero, orch, L. Molajoli (r1927)
(6/90) (PREI) Ⓓ **89010**

2. E. Pinza, NY Met Op Chor, NY Met Op Orch, G. Setti (r1927) (7/91) (MMOI) Ⓓ **CDMOIR404**
(MMOI) ⊟ **CMOIR404**

2. E. Pinza, NY Met Op Chor, NY Met Op Orch, G. Setti (r1927) (3/92) (PREI) Ⓓ **89050**

3a-c P. Domingo, P. Domingo jnr, Ambrosian Op Chor, National PO, E. Kohn
(11/90) (EMI) Ⓓ **CDC7 54053-2**

3b M. Gilion, orch (r c1909)
(BONG) Ⓓ **GB1076-2**

3b F. Merli, orch, L. Molajoli (r1935)
(PREI) Ⓓ **89091**

3b G. Lauri-Volpi, orch, Rosario Bourdon (r1928)
(9/90) (PREI) Ⓓ **89012**

3b G. Lauri-Volpi, orch, Rosario Bourdon (r1928)
(7/93) (NIMB) Ⓓ **NI7845**

3b G. Lauri-Volpi, orch, Rosario Bourdon (r1928)
(4/94) (RCA) Ⓓ [6] **09026 61580-2(3)**

4a, 13. Fiesole School of Music Female Chor, MMF Chor, MMF Orch, M. Arena
(ACAN) Ⓓ **43 540**

4b-d L. Price, B. Martinovich, Ambrosian Op Chor, Philh, H. Lewis (r1979)
(12/92) (RCA) Ⓓ [4] **09026 61236-2**

4b-d J. Sutherland, R. Cross, London Sym Chor, LSO, R. Bonynge
(2/93) (DECC) Ⓓ [3] **433 706-2DMO3**

4b-d, 7b, 8a, 10a-d, 13, 15b, 15c J. Sutherland, M. Horne, John Alexander, R. Cross, London Sym Chor, LSO, R. Bonynge
(DECC) Ⓓ **421 886-2DA**

4b-d, 15c L. Gencer, La Scala Orch, G. Gavazzeni (pp1965)
(MEMO) Ⓓ [2] **HR4239/40**

4b-e J. Sutherland, ROH Chor, London Sym Chor, F. Molinari-Pradelli (r1960)
(DECC) Ⓓ **440 404-2DM**

4b-e R. Ponselle, NY Met Op Chor, NY Met Op Orch, G. Setti (r1928/29)
(10/89) (NIMB) Ⓓ **NI7801**
(NIMB) ⊟ **NC7801**

4b-e J. Sutherland, ROH Chor, ROHO, F. Molinari-Pradelli
(1/90) (DECC) Ⓓ [2] **425 493-2DM2**

4b-e M. Callas, J. Mars, Paris Op Chor, Paris Op Orch, G. Sébastian (pp1958)
(11/91) (EMI) ◐ **LDB9 91258-1**
(11/91) (EMI) ▣ **MVC9 91258-3**

4b-e R. Ponselle, NY Met Op Chor, orch, G. Setti (r1928/9)
(11/94) (ROMO) Ⓓ [2] **81007-2**

4b-e, 10b-d R. Ponselle, M. Telva, NY Met Op Chor, NY Met Op Orch, G. Setti (r1928/9)
(1/89) (PEAR) Ⓓ [2] **GEMMCD9317**

4b, 4c M. Callas, La Scala Chor, La Scala Orch, T. Serafin (EMI) Ⓓ **CDC7 49502-2**

4b, 4c R. Ponselle, NY Met Op Chor, NY Met Op Orch, G. Setti (r1928/9)
(10/89) (NIMB) Ⓓ **NI7805**
(NIMB) ⊟ **NC7805**

4b, 4c R. Ponselle, NY Met Op Chor, NY Met Op Orch, G. Setti (r1928/9)
(1/90) (RCA) Ⓓ **GD87810**

4c M. Caballé, Barcelona SO, G. Navarro
(11/92) (RCA) ⊟ **09026 61204-4**

4c M. Caballé, Ambrosian Op Chor, LPO, C.F. Cillario (11/92) (RCA) ⊟ [2] **RK61044**

4c R. Ponselle, orch (r1919)
(PEAR) Ⓓ [2] **GEMMCDS9964**

4c J. Sutherland, London Sym Chor, LSO, R. Bonynge (DECC) Ⓓ **417 780-2DM**

4c M. Callas, Paris Op Chor, Paris Op Orch, G. Sébastian (pp1958) (MEMO) Ⓓ **HR4293/4**

4c J. Sutherland, LSO, London Sym Chor, R. Bonynge (DECC) Ⓓ **433 068-2DWO**
(DECC) ⊟ **433 068-4DWO**

4c M. Foley, Orch (r1949-53)
(ODE) Ⓓ **CDODE1062**

4c M. Callas, La Scala Chor, La Scala Orch, T. Serafin (EMI) Ⓓ **CDC7 54702-2**
(EMI) ⊟ **EL754702-4**

4c M. Caballé, Barcelona SO, G. Navarro
(RCA) ⓞⓞ **09026 61204-5**

4c J. Sutherland, C. Grant, Sydney Eliz Orch, R. Bonynge (DECC) ◐ **071 149-1DH**
(DECC) ▣ **071 149-3DH**

4c G. Simionato, Santa Cecilia Academy Chor, Santa Cecilia Academy Orch, A. Paoletti (r1961)
(DECC) Ⓓ **440 406-2DM**

4c M. Callas, La Scala Chor, La Scala Orch, T. Serafin (r1960) (EMI) Ⓓ **CDC5 55095-2**

4c E. Urbanová, Prague SO, J. Bělohlávek (r1993) (SUPR) Ⓓ **11 1851-2**

4c A. Cerquetti, MMF Chor, MMF Orch, G. Gavazzeni (r1956) (DECC) Ⓓ **440 411-2DM**

4c M. Caballé, LPO, C. F. Cillario (r1972)
(RCA) Ⓓ **74321 25817-2**
(RCA) ⊟ **74321 25817-4**

4c M. André, Toulouse Capitole Chor, Toulouse Capitole Orch, M. Plasson (arr tpt)
(1/89) (EMI) Ⓓ **CDC7 49219-2**

4c M. Callas, La Scala Orch, T. Serafin (2/90) (EMI) Ⓓ **CDM7 63182-2**
4c A. Patti, A. Barili (r1906) (4/90) (PEAR) Ⓓ **GEMMCD9312**
4c G. Cigna, orch, L. Molajoli (r1932) (11/90) (PREI) Ⓓ **89016**
4c G. Cigna, orch, L. Molajoli (r1932) (11/90) (LYRC) Ⓓ **SRO805**
4c M. de Macchi, anon (r1905) (11/92) (MEMO) Ⓓ [2] **HR4408/9(2)**
4c D. Giannini, La Scala Orch, C. Sabajno (r1931) (4/93) (PREI) Ⓓ **89044**
4c R. Raisa, orch (r1917) (1/94) (CLUB) Ⓓ **CL99-052**
4c T. Arkel, orch, C. Sabajno (r1905) (4/94) (EMI) Ⓓ [3] **CHS7 64860-2(1)**
4c I. Galante, Latvian Nat SO, A. Vilumanis (r1994) (11/95) (CAMP) Ⓓ **RRCD1335** (11/95) (CAMP) ▭ **RRMC8035**
4c-e R. Scotto, National PO, James Levine (SONY) Ⓓ **SBK46548** (SONY) ▭ **SBT46548**
4c-e M. Caballé, orch, C. F. Cillario (r1965) (RCA) Ⓓ **74321 24284-2** (RCA) ▭ **74321 24284-4**
4c, 4e I. Tokody, orch, Anon (cond) (pp1991/2) (VAI) Ⓓ **VAIA1009**
4c, 4e M. Callas, Turin RAI Orch, A. Basile (r1949) (FONI) Ⓓ **CDO104**
4c, 4e N. Ermolenko-Yuzhina, Moscow Imperial Op Chor, orch (r1909: Russ) (6/93) (PEAR) Ⓓ [3] **GEMMCDS9001/3(2)**
4c, 4e, 15b, 15c E. Burzio, orch (r1913) (1/91) (CLUB) Ⓓ [2] **CL99-587/8**
4c, 6b, 7b, 8a-c, 9, 10b, 13, 14a, 14b, 15c M. Callas, F. Corelli, C. Ludwig, N. Zaccaria, La Scala Chor, La Scala Orch, T. Serafin (r1960) (7/89) (EMI) Ⓓ **CDM7 63091-2**
5. I. Minghini-Cattaneo, La Scala Orch, C. Sabajno (r1929) (6/90) (PREI) Ⓓ **89008**
5, 10b G. Cigna, E. Stignani, EIAR Orch, V. Gui (r1937) (1/91) (PREI) Ⓓ **89014**
5, 6a, 6b M. Caballé, L. Pavarotti, P. Maag, R. Bonynge (r1984) (DECC) Ⓓ **443 928-2DM**
6a, 6b A. Baltsa, J. Carreras, LSO, P. Domingo (r1990-91) (SONY) Ⓓ **SK53968**
7a, 7b, 10a-d O. Stapp, I. Kirilová, Košice St PO, P. Vronský (OPUS) Ⓓ **9356 2047**
7b, 8a, 8b, 10a, 10b, 10d J. Sutherland, M. Horne, John Alexander, LSO, R. Bonynge (r1964) (10/93) (DECC) Ⓓ **436 303-2DA**
7c G. Russ, V. Guerrini, orch (r1913) (4/94) (EMI) Ⓓ [3] **CHS7 64860-2(2)**
10b J. Sutherland, M. Horne, Sydney Eliz Orch, R. Bonynge (MCEG) ▣ **VVD780**
10b J. Sutherland, M. Horne, NY Met Op Orch, R. Bonynge (pp1970) (MEMO) Ⓓ [2] **HR4392/3**
10b J. Zoon, H. de Vries, London Studio SO (arr Vrijens) (PHIL) Ⓓ **438 940-2PH**
10b J. Sutherland, M. Horne, LSO, R. Bonynge (r1964) (DECC) Ⓓ **436 315-2DA** (DECC) ▭ **436 315-4DA**
10b G. Groves, J. Watson, J. Partridge (r1994) (ASV) Ⓓ **CDWHL2088**
10b M. Caballé, S. Verrett, New Philh, A. Guadagno (RCA) Ⓓ **09026 62699-2** (RCA) ▭ **09026 62699-4**
10b R. Ponselle, M. Telva, NY Met Op Orch, G. Setti (r1929) (10/89) (NIMB) Ⓓ **NI7805** (NIMB) ▭ **NC7805**
10b J. Sutherland, M. Caballé, National PO, R. Bonynge (12/91) (DECC) Ⓓ **430 724-2DM**
10b G. Russ, V. Guerrini, orch (r1910) (11/92) (MEMO) Ⓓ [2] **HR4408/9(2)**
10b R. Ponselle, M. Telva, NY Met Op Chor, orch, G. Setti (r1929) (11/94) (ROMO) Ⓓ [2] **81007-2**
10b-10d M. Caballé, S. Verrett, New Philh, A. Guadagno (5/92) (RCA) Ⓓ **GD60818**
10d J. Sutherland, M. Horne, LSO, R. Bonynge (r1964) (DECC) Ⓓ **436 300-2DX** (DECC) ▭ **436 300-4DX**
11a Ambrosian Op Chor, LPO, C. F. Cillario (r1972) (RCA) Ⓓ **74321 24209-2**
11a E. Pinza, NY Met Op Chor, NY Met Op Orch, G. Setti (r1929) (9/93) (RCA) Ⓓ **09026 61245-2**
11c E. Pinza, Chor, orch, C. Sabajno (r1923) (2/89) (PEAR) Ⓓ **GEMMCD9306**
11c E. Pinza, NY Met Op Chor, NY Met Op Orch, G. Setti (r1929) (3/92) (PREI) Ⓓ **89050**
11c E. Pinza, NY Met Op Chor, NY Met Op Orch, G. Setti (r1929) (7/92) (PEAR) Ⓓ [3] **GEMMCDS9926(2)**
13. J. Sutherland, S. Ramey, WNO Chor, WNO Orch, R. Bonynge (r1980s) (BELA) Ⓓ **450 117-2** (BELA) ▭ **450 117-4**
14a G. Zenatello, E. Mazzoleni, orch (r1911) (5/94) (SYMP) Ⓓ **SYMCD1168**
14a G. Zenatello, E. Mazzoleni, orch (r1911) (5/94) (PEAR) Ⓓ [4] **GEMMCDS9074(1)**
14a, 14b, 15a-c M. Callas, M. Filippeschi, N. Rossi-Lemeni, La Scala Chor, La Scala Orch, T. Serafin (r1954) (2/90) (EMI) Ⓓ [4] **CMS7 63244-2**
15b(pt) G.B. de Negri, anon (r1902) (12/89) (SYMP) Ⓓ **SYMCD1065**

Pirata– opera seria: 2 acts (1827—Milan) (Lib. F. Romani)

EXCERPTS: 1. Overture. ACT 1: 2. Ciel! Qual procelle orribile; 3. Io vivi ancor!; 4. Nel furor delle tempeste; 5. Sorgete, è in me dover; 6. Lo sognai ferito; 7. Viva! Allegri!; 8. Ebben?; 9. Se in giorno; 10. Pietosa al padre!; 11. Bagnato dalle lagrime; 12. Più temuto, più splendido nome; 13. Sì vincemmo, e il pregio io sento; 14. Mi abbraccia, o donna; 15. Parlati ancora per poco; 16. Ebben: cominci, o barbara; 17. Ah! partiamo, i miei tormenti. ACT 2: 18. Che rechi tu?; 19. Tu m'apristi in cor ferita; 21. Lasciami, forma umana; 22. Vieni: cerchiam pe' mari; 23. Cedo al destino orribile; 24. Lasso! Perir così; 25. Giusto ciel!; 26. Tu vedrai la sventura; 27a. Oh! s'io potessi; 27b. Col sorriso d'innocenza.

Ernesto P. Cappuccilli
Imogene M. Caballé
Gualtiero F. Labò
Itulbo G. Baratti
Goffredo U. Trama
Adele F. Raffanelli
MMF Chor, MMF Orch, F. Capuana (pp1967) (MEMO) Ⓓ [2] **HR4186/7**

Ernesto P. Cappuccilli
Imogene M. Caballé
Gualtiero B. Marti
Itulbo G. Baratti
Goffredo R. Raimondi
Adele F. Raffanelli
Rome RAI Chor, Rome RAI Orch, G. Gavazzeni (r1970) (2/93) (EMI) Ⓓ [2] **CMS7 64169-2**

Ernesto C. Ego
Imogene M. Callas
Gualtiero P.M. Ferraro
Itulbo G. Peterson
Goffredo Chester Watson
Adele R. Sarfaty
American Op Soc Chor, American Op Soc Orch, N. Rescigno (pp1959) (1/94) (EMI) Ⓓ [2] **CMS7 64938-2**

1. Horreaux-Trehard Duo (arr 2 gtrs) (CALL) Ⓓ **CAL9218**
5, 6. M. Callas, M. Sinclair, A. Young, Philh Chor, Philh, A. Tonini (6/86) (EMI) Ⓓ **CDC7 47283-2**
5, 6, 27a, 27b M. Caballé, MMF Chor, MMF Orch, F. Capuana (pp1967) (MEMO) Ⓓ [2] **HR4279/80**
12. Rome RAI Chor, Rome RAI Orch, G. Gavazzeni (r1970) (EMI) Ⓓ [2] **CZS5 68559-2**
13. D. Hvorostovsky, Philh, I. Marin (r1992) (9/94) (PHIL) Ⓓ **434 912-2PH** (9/94) (PHIL) ▭ **434 912-4PH**
13, 19. M. Caballé, P. Cappuccilli, MMF Chor, MMF Orch, F. Capuana (pp1967) (MEMO) Ⓓ [2] **HR4273/4**
26. G. Morino, Warmia Nat PO, B. Amaducci (10/90) (NUOV) Ⓓ **6851**
27a, 27b M. Callas, Concertgebouw, N. Rescigno (pp1959) (EMI) Ⓓ **CDC7 49428-2**
27a, 27b M. Callas, N German RSO, N. Rescigno (pp1959) (MEMO) Ⓓ **HR4293/4**
27a, 27b M. Callas, Philh Chor, Philh, N. Rescigno (6/86) (EMI) Ⓓ **CDC7 47283-2**
27a, 27b M. Caballé, F. Raffanelli, G. Baratti, B. Marti, Rome RAI Chor, Rome RAI Orch, G. Gavazzeni (10/88) (EMI) Ⓓ **CDM7 69500-2**
27a, 27b M. Callas, Philh, N. Rescigno (2/90) (EMI) Ⓓ [4] **CMS7 63244-2**
27a, 27b M. Callas, Concertgebouw, N. Rescigno (pp1959) (1/94) (EMI) Ⓓ [2] **CMS7 64938-2**
27b M. Caballé, Rome RAI Orch, G. Gavazzeni (r1970) (EMI) Ⓓ **CDM5 65575-2**
27b L. Aliberti, Munich RO, L. Gardelli (11/86) (ORFE) Ⓓ **C119841A**

Puritani– opera: 3 acts (1835—Paris) (Lib. Pepoli)

EXCERPTS: 1a. Sinfonia; 1b. ACT 1: All'erta!; 2. O di Cromvel guerrieri; 3. A festa!; 4a. Or dove fuggo; 4b. Ah! per sempre; 4c. Bel sogno beato; 5a. O amato zio; 5b. O Ciel! E fia vero; 6. Ad Arturo onore; 7. A te, o cara; 8. Il rito augusto; 9. Son vergin vezzosa; 10a. Sulla verginea; 10b. Ferma invan; 11. Arturo! Tu ritorni; 12. Ma tu già mi fuggi. ACT 2: 13. Ah! dolor!; 14. Cinta di fiori; 15. E di morte; 16a. O rendetemi la speme; 16b. Qui la voce; 16c. Vien, diletto; 17a. Il rival salvar; 17b. Suoni la tromba. ACT 3: 18a. Son salvo; 18b. A una fonte; 19a. Son già lontani; 19b. Finì! Me lassa!; 19c. Nel mirarti un solo istante; 20. Vieni, fra queste braccia; 21a. Ascolta ancora; 21b. Credeasi, misera.

Elvira J. Sutherland
Arturo L. Pavarotti
Riccardo P. Cappuccilli
Giorgio N. Ghiaurov
Enrichetta A. Caminada
Gualtiero G. Luccardi
Bruno R. Cazzaniga
ROH Chor, LSO, R. Bonynge (4/89) (DECC) Ⓓ [3] **417 588-2DH3**

Elvira M. Callas
Arturo G. di Stefano
Riccardo R. Panerai
Giorgio N. Rossi-Lemeni
Bruno A. Mercuriali
Gualtiero C. Forti
Enrichetta A. Cattelani
La Scala Chor, La Scala Orch, T. Serafin (r1953) (4/89) (EMI) Ⓓ [2] **CDS7 47308-8**

Elvira M. Devia
Arturo W. Matteuzzi
Riccardo C. Robertson
Giorgio P. Washington
Enrichetta E. Jankovic
Gualtiero F. Federici
Catania Teatro Massimo Bellini Chor, Catania Teatro Massimo Bellini Orch, R. Bonynge (pp1989) (10/91) (NUOV) Ⓓ [3] **6842/4**

Elvira E. Gruberová
Arthuro J. Lavender
Riccardo E. Kim
Giorgio F.E. D'Artegna
Enrichetta K. Lytting
Gualtiero D. Siegele
Bruno C. Tuand
Bavarian Rad Chor, Munich RO, F. Luisi (pp1993) (12/94) (NIGH) Ⓓ [3] **NC070562-2**

Excs J. Sutherland, Orch, Anon (cond), D. Bailey (11/92) (DECC) ◖ **071 135-1DH**
4a C. Tagliabue, La Scala Orch, U. Berrettoni (r1946) (11/90) (PREI) Ⓓ **89015**
4a, 4b G. Taddei, Naples San Carlo Op Orch, U. Rapalo (PREI) Ⓓ **90020**
4a, 4b G. De Luca, orch (r1922) (PEAR) Ⓓ [3] **GEMMCDS9160(1)**
4a, 4b, 4c P. Cappuccilli, R. Cazzaniga, LSO, R. Bonynge (r1973) (DECC) Ⓓ **443 380-2DM**
4a, 4b, 17a, 17b S. Bruscantini, B. Giaiotti, Rome RAI Chor, Rome RAI Orch, R. Muti (pp1969) (MEMO) Ⓓ [2] **HR4300/1**
4b G. De Luca, orch (r1922) (1/92) (PREI) Ⓓ **89036**
4b M. Battistini, orch, C. Sabajno (r1911) (7/92) (PEAR) Ⓓ [3] **GEMMCDS9923(1)**
4b D. Hvorostovsky, Philh, I. Marin (r1992) (9/94) (PHIL) Ⓓ **434 912-2PH** (9/94) (PHIL) ▭ **434 912-4PH**
4c M. Battistini, orch (r1911) (PEAR) Ⓓ **GEMMCD9016**
7. G. di Stefano, M. Callas, N. Rossi-Lemeni, C. Forti, La Scala Chor, La Scala Orch, T. Serafin (r1953) (EMI) Ⓓ **CDC7 54016-2**
7. Alfredo Kraus, Milan RAI SO, A. Basile (pp1959) (MEMO) Ⓓ [2] **HR4233/4**
7. L. Pavarotti, M. Freni, B. Giaiotti, G. Antonini, Rome RAI Chor, Rome RAI Orch, R. Muti (pp1969) (BUTT) Ⓓ **BMCD015** (BUTT) ▭ **BMK015**
7. G. Lauri-Volpi, orch (r1930) (PEAR) Ⓓ **GEMMCD9129**
7. J. Sutherland, L. Pavarotti, G. Luccardi, N. Ghiaurov, ROH Chor, ROHO, R. Bonynge (7/86) (DECC) Ⓓ [2] **417 011-2DH2**

7. G. Sabbatini, Berlin RSO, R. Paternostro (10/89) (CAPR) ① 10 247
(10/89) (CAPR) ▭ CC27 247
7. Alfredo Kraus, M. Caballé, A. Ferrin, S. Elenkov, Ambrosian Op Chor, Philh, R. Muti (10/89) (EMI) ① CDM7 63104-2
7. G. Lauri-Volpi, orch (r1928) (10/89) (NIMB) ① NI7801
(NIMB) ▭ NC7801
7. M. Fleta, orch (r1923) (2/90) (PREI) ① 89002
7. G. Lauri-Volpi, orch, Rosario Bourdon (r1928) (9/90) (PREI) ① 89012
7. G. Morino, Warmia Nat PO, B. Amaducci (10/90) (NUOV) ① 6851
7. D. Borgioli, orch (r c1923) (12/90) (CLUB) ① CL99-014
7. A. Bonci, anon (r1905) (11/92) (MEMO) ① [2] HR4408/9(1)
7. G. Lauri-Volpi, orch (r1922) (7/93) (NIMB) ① NI7845
7. G. Lauri-Volpi, orch, Rosario Bourdon (r1928) (7/93) (NIMB) ① NI7845
7. A. Auger, R. Bunger, H. Lackner, Vienna Op Orch, N. Rescigno (r1969) (12/93) (DECC) ① 433 437-2DA
(DECC) ▭ 433 437-4DA
7. A. Bonci, anon (r1905) (4/94) (EMI) ① [3] CHS7 64860-2(1)
7. A. Pertile, La Scala Orch, C. Sabajno (r1930) (10/94) (PREI) ① 89072
7. A. Giorgini, orch (r1905) (4/95) (RECO) ① TRC3
7. M. Freni, L. Pavarotti, B. Giaiotti, chor, Rome SO, R. Muti (pp1969) (10/95) (RCA) ① 09026 68014-2
7, 18a, 18b R. Giménez, S.C. Dyson, Scottish Phil Sngrs, Scottish CO, M. Veltri (5/90) (NIMB) ① NI5224
(5/90) (NIMB) ▭ NC5224
7, 18a, 18b, 20, 21b M. Devia, W. Matteuzzi, C. Robertson, P. Washington, Catania Teatro Massimo Bellini Chor, Catania Teatro Massimo Bellini Orch, R. Bonynge (pp1989) (NUOV) ① 6892
9. A. Galli-Curci, orch (r1923) (PEAR) ① GEMMCD9450
9. E. Gruberová, V. Walterová, L.M. Vodička, P. Horáček, Smetana Th Chor, Czech PO, F. Haider (SUPR) ① 11 0345-2
9. J. Sutherland, ROHO, F. Molinari-Pradelli (DECC) ① 433 066-2DWO
(DECC) ▭ 433 066-4DWO
9. M. Caballé, J. Hamari, Alfredo Kraus, A. Ferrin, S. Elenkov, Ambrosian Op Chor, Philh, R. Muti (r1979) (EMI) ① CDM5 65575-2
9. M. André, Toulouse Capitole Orch, M. Plasson (arr tpt) (1/89) (EMI) ① CDC7 49219-2
9. L. Aliberti, Berlin RSO, R. Paternostro (10/89) (CAPR) ① 10 247
(10/89) (CAPR) ▭ CC27 247
9. A. Galli-Curci, orch, G. Polacco (r1923) (10/89) (NIMB) ① NI7801
(NIMB) ▭ NC7801
9. F. Toresella, anon (r1900) (12/89) (SYMP) ① SYMCD1065
9. J. Sutherland, ROHO, F. Molinari-Pradelli (1/90) (DECC) ① [2] 425 493-2DM2
9. L. Pons, Columbia SO, A. Kostelanetz (r1949) (7/90) (CBS) ① CD45694
9. Dilbèr, Estonia Op Orch, E. Klas (9/92) (ONDI) ① ODE768-2
9. A. Galli-Curci, orch, Rosario Bourdon (r1923) (8/94) (ROMO) ① [2] 81004-2
9, 16a-c J. Sutherland, M. Elkins, P. Duval, R. Capecchi, E. Flagello, MMF Chor, MMF Orch, R. Bonynge (2/93) (DECC) ① [3] 433 706-2DMO3
9, 16a-c, 20. M. Freni, L. Pavarotti, S. Bruscantini, B. Giaiotti, Rome RAI Chor, Rome RAI Orch, R. Muti (pp1969) (MEMO) ① [2] HR4277/8
13. Ambrosian Op Chor, Philh, R. Muti (r1979) (EMI) ① [2] CZS5 68559-2
14. E. Pinza, orch (r1924) (2/89) (PEAR) ① GEMMCD9306
14, 17a M. Pertusi, C. Alvarez, Bulgarian Nat Chor, Sofia PO, E. Tabakov (r1994) (CAPR) ① 10 704
16a-c M. Callas, Milan RAI SO, A. Simonetto (pp1956) (MEMO) ① HR4293/4
16a-c J. Sutherland, London Sym Chor, F. Molinari-Pradelli (r1960) (DECC) ① 440 404-2DM
16a-c M. Caballé, M. Manuguerra, A. Ferrin, Philh, R. Muti (10/88) (EMI) ① CDM7 69500-2
16a-c M. Freni, Rome Op Orch, F. Ferraris (10/89) (EMI) ① CDM7 63110-2
16a-c M. Callas, R. Panerai, N. Rossi-Lemeni, La Scala Chor, La Scala Orch, T. Serafin (r1953) (2/90) (EMI) ① [4] CMS7 63244-2
16a, 16b M. Callas, Turin RAI Orch, A. Basile (r1949) (SUIT) ① CDS1-5001
16a, 16b V. Zeani, A. Mongelli, A. Protti, Trieste Teatro Verdi Orch, F. M. Prandelli (pp1957) (BONG) ① GB1060-2
16a, 16b M. Callas, orch (r1949) (NIMB) ① NI7864
16a, 16b, 16c M. Callas, Turin RAI Orch, A. Basile (r1949) (FONI) ① CDO104
16b L. Aliberti, Munich RO, L. Gardelli (11/86) (ORFE) ① C119841A
16b A. Galli-Curci, orch (r1917) (2/89) (PEAR) ① GEMMCD9308
16b A. Galli-Curci, orch, J. Pasternack (r1917) (5/90) (NIMB) ① NI7806
(NIMB) ▭ NC7806
16b L. Orgonášová, Bratislava RSO, W. Humburg (2/93) (NAXO) ① 8 550605
16b M. Sembrich, orch (r1907) (7/93) (NIMB) ① [2] NI7840/1
16b M. Carosio, orch, A. Erede (r1948) (4/94) (EMI) ① [3] CHS7 64864-2(2)
16b, 16c A. Galli-Curci, orch, J. Pasternack (r1917) (3/94) (ROMO) ① [2] 81003-2
16b, 16c A. Galli-Curci, orch, J. Pasternack (r1920) (8/94) (ROMO) ① [2] 81004-2
16b, 16c M. Devia, Svizzera Italiana Orch, M. Rota (pp1992) (10/94) (BONG) ① GB2513-2
16c L. Tetrazzini, orch (r1912) (9/92) (EMI) ① [3] CHS7 63802-2(2)
16c L. Tetrazzini, orch (r1912) (9/92) (PEAR) ① GEMMCD9223
17a M. Biscotti, A. Silvestrelli, Berlin RSO, R. Buckley (SCHW) ① [2] 314052
17a P. Coni, R. Raimondi, Madrid SO, G.P. Sanzogno (pp1991) (IMP) ① [2] DPCD998
17a P. Coni, R. Raimondi, Madrid SO, G.P. Sanzogno (RNE) ① [2] 650004
17b P. Amato, M. Journet, orch (r1912) (PEAR) ① GEMMCD9104
18b A. Giorgini, orch (r1908) (4/95) (RECO) ① TRC3
19a L. Pavarotti, Catania Teatro Massimo Bellini Orch, A. Quadri (pp1968) (10/95) (RCA) ① 09026 62541-2
19b J. Sutherland, L. Pavarotti, ROHO, R. Bonynge (r1973) (DECC) ① 436 313-2DA
(DECC) ▭ 436 313-4DA
19b, 19c, 20. M. Callas, G. di Stefano, La Scala Orch, T. Serafin (10/88) (EMI) ① CDM7 69543-2
19c, 20. M. Callas, G. di Stefano, Mexico Palacio Orch, G. Picco (pp1952) (MEMO) ① HR4372/3
20. G. di Stefano, Turin RAI Orch, O. de Fabritiis (bp1953) (FONI) ① CDMR5003
20. F. Marconi, M. Galvany, orch (r1908) (10/90) (SYMP) ① SYMCD1069
20. D. Borgioli, E. Surinach, orch (r c1923) (12/90) (CLUB) ① CL99-014
21a C. Gonzales, E. Ferretti, M. Biscotti, A. Silvestrelli, Ernst-Senff Chbr Chor, Berlin RSO, R. Buckley (SCHW) ① [2] 314052

La **Sonnambula– opera: 2 acts (1831—Milan) (Lib. F. Romani)**

EXCERPTS - ACT 1: 1. Viva Amina!; 2. Tutto è gioia; 3. In Elvezia non v'ha rosa; 4a. Care compagne; 4b. A te, diletta tenera madre; 4c. Come per me sereno; 4d. Sovra il sen; 5. Io più di tutti, o Amina; 6a. Perdono, o mia diletta; 6b. Elvin, che rechi?; 6c. Prendi: l'anel ti dono; 6d. Ah! vorrei trovar parole; 7a. Qual rumore; 7b. Il mulino!; 7c. Vi ravviso, o luoghi ameni; 7d. Tu non sai con quei begli occhi; 8a. Contezza del paese avete voi, Signor; 8b. A fosco cielo, a notte bruna; 8c. Basta così; 9a. Elvino! E me tu lasci; 9b. Son geloso del zefiro errante; 10. Davver, non mi dispiace; 11. Che veggio?; 12. Osservate! L'uscio è aperto; 13. È menzogna; 14a. D'un pensiero e d'un accento; 14b. Non più nozze. ACT 2: 15. Qui la selva è più folta; 16a. Reggimi, o buono madre; 16b. Tutto è sciolto; 16c. Pasci il guardo e appaga l'alma; 17a. Viva il Conte!; 17b. Ah! perchè non posso odiarti; 18a. Lasciami: aver compreso; 18b. De'lieti auguri a voi son grata; 19a. Signor Conte, agli occhi miei; 19b. V'han certuni che dormendo; 19c. Piano, amici, non gridate; 20. Lisa mendace anch'essa!; 21a. Signor, che creder deggio?; 21b. Chi? Mira...ella stessa; 22a. Oh! se una volta sola; 22b. Ah! non credea mirarti; 22c. Ah! non giunge.

Amina	M. Devia
Elvino	L. Canonici
Rodolfo	A. Verducci
Lisa	E. Battaglia
Teresa	L. Musella
Alessio	G. Riva
Notary	V. Gattozzi

Como City Chor, Piacenza SO, M. Viotti (pp1988) (NUOV) ① [2] 6764/5

Amina	M. Callas
Elvino	N. Monti
Rodolfo	N. Zaccaria
Lisa	E. Ratti
Teresa	F. Cossotto
Alessio	G. Morresi
Notary	F. Ricciardi

La Scala Chor, La Scala Orch, A. Votto (r1957) (9/86) (EMI) ① [2] CDS7 47378-8

Amina	J. Sutherland
Elvino	L. Pavarotti
Rodolfo	N. Ghiaurov
Lisa	I. Buchanan
Teresa	D. Jones
Alessio	J. Tomlinson
Notary	P. de Palma

London Op Chor, National PO, R. Bonynge (4/87) (DECC) ① [2] 417 424-2DH2

Amina	J. Valásková
Elvino	J. Kundlák
Rodolfo	P. Mikuláš
Lisa	E. Antoličová
Teresa	J. Saparová
Alessio	J. Galla
Notary	V. Schrenkel

Slovak Phil Chor, Bratislava RSO, O. Lenárd (10/89) (OPUS) ① [2] 9356 1928/9
4a-c Dilbèr, Estonia Op Orch, E. Klas (9/92) (ONDI) ① ODE768-2
4a-d M. Callas, La Scala Orch, T. Serafin (r1955) (EMI) ① CDC5 55016-2
4a-d J. Sutherland, ROH Chor, ROHO, F. Molinari-Pradelli (1/90) (DECC) ① [2] 425 493-2DM2
4a-d M. Callas, La Scala Chor, La Scala Orch, A. Votto (r1957) (2/90) (EMI) ① [4] CMS7 63244-2
4a, 4b, 4c, 4d M. Devia, Svizzera Italiana Orch, M. Rota (pp1992) (10/94) (BONG) ① GB2513-2
4a, 6c, 7c, 9b, 13, 14a, 14b, 17b, 22a-c M. Devia, L. Canonici, A. Verducci, Como City Chor, Piacenza SO, M. Viotti (NUOV) ① 6887
4c L. Orgonášová, Bratislava RSO, W. Humburg (2/93) (NAXO) ① 8 550605
4c A. Galli-Curci, orch, J. Pasternack (r1920) (3/94) (ROMO) ① [2] 81003-2
4c, 4d L. Tetrazzini, orch (r1912) (9/92) (EMI) ① [3] CHS7 63802-2(2)
4c, 4d L. Tetrazzini, orch (r1912) (9/92) (PEAR) ① GEMMCD9223
4c, 4d, 22b A. Galli-Curci, orch (r1917-20) (2/89) (PEAR) ① GEMMCD9308
4c, 22b, 22c M. Callas, La Scala Orch, T. Serafin (r1955) (12/87) (EMI) ① CDC7 47966-2
4d A. Galli-Curci, orch, J. Pasternack (r1919) (5/90) (NIMB) ① NI7806
(NIMB) ▭ NC7806
4d A. Galli-Curci, orch, J. Pasternack (r1919) (3/94) (ROMO) ① [2] 81003-2
6a-c C. Valletti, La Scala Orch, L. Bernstein (pp1955) (MEMO) ① [2] HR4191/2
6b T. Dal Monte, T. Schipa, La Scala Chor, La Scala Orch, F. Ghione (r1933) (4/90) (EMI) ① CDH7 63200-2
6c T. Schipa, T. dal Monte, orch (r1933) (PEAR) ① GEMMCD9364
6c T. Schipa, T. dal Monte, orch, Anon (cond) (pp1933) (MEMO) ① [2] HR4220/1
6c F. Wunderlich, E. Köth, Munich RO, K. Eichhorn (Ger: bp) (DG) ① [5] 435 145-2GX5(1)
6c J. Zoon, H. de Vries, London Studio SO (arr Vrijens) (PHIL) ① 438 940-2PH
6c D. Borgioli, orch (r c1921) (PEAR) ① GEMMCD9091
6c T. Schipa, T. dal Monte, La Scala Chor, La Scala Orch, F. Ghione (r1933) (10/90) (MSCM) ① [2] MM30231
(MSCM) ▭ [2] MM40086
6c Ferruccio Tagliavini, EIAR Orch, U. Tansini (r1940) (3/94) (CENT) ① CRC2164
6c A. Giorgini, orch (r1905) (4/95) (RECO) ① TRC3

6c, 9b F. de Lucia, M. Galvany, anon (r1908)
(1/95) (SYMP) Ⓓ **SYMCD1149**
6c, 17b F. de Lucia, M. Galvany, anon (r1908)
(BONG) Ⓓ [2] **GB1064/5-2**
7b, 7c B. Christoff, Rome Op Chor, Rome Op Orch, V. Gui (r1955) (EMI) Ⓓ **CDH5 65500-2**
7b, 7c P. Plançon, anon (Fr: r1903)
(9/91) (PEAR) Ⓓ **GEMMCD9497**
7b, 7c P. Plançon, anon (r1903)
(12/94) (ROMO) Ⓓ [2] **82001-2**
7b, 7c P. Plançon, anon (r1903)
(1/95) (NIMB) Ⓓ **NI7860**
7c F. Chaliapin, La Scala Orch, C. Sabajno (r1912) (PREI) Ⓓ **89030**
7c A. Scotti, orch (r1906)
(PEAR) Ⓓ **GEMMCD9937**
7c F. Chaliapin, orch, Rosario Bourdon (r1927)
(12/89) (PEAR) Ⓓ **GEMMCD9314**
7c L. Sibiriakov, orch (r1911: Russ)
(6/93) (PEAR) Ⓓ [3] **GEMMCDS9007/9(2)**
7c T. Pasero, Rome Teatro Reale Orch, L. Ricci (r1943) (4/95) (PREI) Ⓓ **89074**
7c, 7d R. Arié, LSO, J. Krips (r1949)
(4/92) (EMI) Ⓓ [7] **CHS7 69741-2(7)**
7d T. Pasero, orch, L. Molajoli (r1928)
(6/90) (PREI) Ⓓ **89010**
9b T. Schipa, A. Galli-Curci, orch (r1923)
(PEAR) Ⓓ **GEMMCD9364**
9b A. Galli-Curci, T. Schipa, orch, Rosario Bourdon (r1923) (12/89) (RCA) Ⓓ **GD87969**
9b A. Galli-Curci, T. Schipa, orch, Rosario Bourdon (r1923) (5/90) (NIMB) Ⓓ **NI7806**
(NIMB) ▣ **NC7806**
9b T. Schipa, A. Galli-Curci, orch, Rosario Bourdon (r1923)
(10/90) (MSCM) Ⓓ [2] **MM30231**
(MSCM) ▣ [2] **MM40086**
9b A. Galli-Curci, T. Schipa, orch (r1923)
(3/94) (CONI) Ⓓ **CDHD201**
(3/94) (CONI) ▣ **MCHD201**
9b A. Galli-Curci, T. Schipa, orch, Rosario Bourdon (r1923)
(8/94) (ROMO) Ⓓ [2] **81004-2**
9b, 14a D. Borgioli, E. Surinach, orch (r c1923)
(12/90) (CLUB) Ⓓ **CL99-014**
11(pt) T. Pasero, G. Bernelli, Rome Teatro Reale Orch, L. Ricci (r1943)
(4/95) (PREI) Ⓓ **89074**
14a G. Pareto, G. Manuritta, chor, orch, C. Sabajno (r1924) (PEAR) Ⓓ **GEMMCD9117**
14a D. Borgioli, M. Gentile, G. Pedroni, I. Mannarini, La Scala Chor, orch, L. Molajoli (r1927) (PEAR) Ⓓ **GEMMCD9091**
14a, 22b T. dal Monte, A. Sinnone, Vienna St Op Chor, Vienna St Op Orch, G. del Campo (pp1935) (7/94) (SCHW) Ⓓ [2] **314512**
16b, 16c, 17b R. Giménez, S.C. Dyson, Scottish Phil Sngrs, Scottish CO, M. Veltri
(5/90) (NIMB) Ⓓ **NI5224**
(5/90) (NIMB) ▣ **NC5224**
17b C. Valletti, Orch, A. Basile (pp1955)
(MEMO) Ⓓ [2] **HR4191/2**
17b F. de Lucia, anon (r1908)
(1/95) (SYMP) Ⓓ **SYMCD1149**
22a-c K. Battle, R. Stene, R. Croft, M.S. Doss, LPO, B. Campanella (r1991)
(DG) OO **435 866-5CH**
22a-c K. Battle, R. Stene, R. Croft, M.S. Doss, LPO, B. Campanella (r1991)
(12/93) (DG) Ⓓ **435 866-2GH**
22b M. Callas, La Scala Orch, L. Bernstein (pp1955) (MEMO) Ⓓ **HR4293/4**
22b M. Mesplé, Paris Op Orch, G-F. Masini (r1974) (EMI) Ⓓ [2] **CZS7 67813-2**
22b M. Carosio, Turin RAI Orch, O. de Fabritiis (bp1953) (FONI) Ⓓ **CDMR5003**
22b A. Pendachanska, Sofia SO, M. Angelov (r1994) (CAPR) Ⓓ **10 706**
22b E. Gruberová, Munich RO, L. Gardelli
(11/86) (ORFE) Ⓓ **C101841A**
22b T. dal Monte, La Scala Orch, C. Sabajno (r1929) (2/90) (PREI) Ⓓ **89001**
22b A. Patti, A. Barili (r1906)
(4/90) (PEAR) Ⓓ **GEMMCD9312**
22b C. Muzio, orch, L. Molajoli (r1935)
(4/91) (NIMB) Ⓓ **NI7814**
(4/91) (NIMB) ▣ **NC7814**
22b A. Patti, A. Barili (r1906)
(7/92) (PEAR) Ⓓ [3] **GEMMCDS9923(1)**
22b L. Tetrazzini, orch, P. Pitt (r1909)
(9/92) (EMI) Ⓓ [3] **CHS7 63802-2(1)**
22b L. Tetrazzini, orch (r1911)
(9/92) (PEAR) Ⓓ **GEMMCD9223**
22b L. Tetrazzini, orch, P. Pitt (r1909)
(9/92) (PEAR) Ⓓ **GEMMCD9221**
22b A. Patti, A. Barili (r1906)
(7/93) (NIMB) Ⓓ [2] **NI7840/1**
22b A. Galli-Curci, orch, J. Pasternack (r1917)
(3/94) (ROMO) Ⓓ [2] **81003-2**
22b A. Galli-Curci, orch (r1917)
(3/94) (CONI) Ⓓ **CDHD201**
(3/94) (CONI) ▣ **MCHD201**
22b A. Patti, A. Barili (r1906)
(4/94) (EMI) Ⓓ [3] **CHS7 64860-2(1)**
22b T. dal Monte, La Scala Orch, C. Sabajno (r1929) (4/94) (EMI) Ⓓ [3] **CHS7 64864-2(1)**
22b, 22c M. Callas, La Scala Orch, A. Votto (r1957) (EMI) Ⓓ **CDC7 49502-2**
22b, 22c G. Pareto, orch (r1907)
(PEAR) Ⓓ **GEMMCD9117**
22b, 22c C. Studer, Munich RO, G. Ferro (r1989) (EMI) Ⓓ **CDC5 55350-2**
22b, 22c L. Aliberti, Munich RO, L. Gardelli
(11/86) (ORFE) Ⓓ **C119841A**
22b, 22c L. Tetrazzini, orch (r1911)
(10/90) (NIMB) Ⓓ **NI7808**
(10/90) (NIMB) ▣ **NC7808**
22b, 22c J. Sutherland, N. Monti, F. Corena, MMF Chor, MMF Orch, R. Bonynge
(2/93) (DECC) Ⓓ [3] **433 706-2DMO3**
22b, 22c S. Jo, Monte Carlo PO, P. Olmi (r1994)
(6/95) (ERAT) Ⓓ **4509-97239-2**
22c L. Tetrazzini, orch (r1911)
(10/89) (NIMB) Ⓓ **NI7801**
(NIMB) ▣ **NC7801**
22c M. Sembrich, orch (r1904)
(7/92) (PEAR) Ⓓ [3] **GEMMCDS9923(1)**
22c L. Tetrazzini, orch (r1911)
(9/92) (PEAR) Ⓓ **GEMMCD9224**
22c L. Tetrazzini, anon (r c1904)
(9/92) (PEAR) Ⓓ **GEMMCD9225**
22c L. Tetrazzini, orch (r1911)
(12/93) (NIMB) Ⓓ **NI7851**
22c M. Ivogün, orch (r1916)
(1/94) (CLUB) Ⓓ **CL99-020**
22c A. Galli-Curci, orch (r1924)
(3/94) (CONI) Ⓓ **CDHD201**
(3/94) (CONI) ▣ **MCHD201**
22c R. Peters, RCA SO, R. Cellini (r1958)
(4/94) (RCA) Ⓓ [6] **09026 61580-2(6)**
22c A. Galli-Curci, orch, Rosario Bourdon (r1924) (8/94) (ROMO) Ⓓ [2] **81004-2**

La **Straniera– opera seria: 2 acts (1829—Milan) (Lib. F. Romani)**

Serba, serba i tuoi segreti; Sono all'ara R. Scotto, Palermo Teatro Massimo Chor, Palermo Teatro Massimo Orch, N. Sanzogno (pp1968)
(MEMO) Ⓓ [2] **HR4291/2**
Un rittratto...Veggiam J. Sutherland, R. Conrad, LSO, R. Bonynge (r1963)
(DECC) Ⓓ **421 881-2DA**

Zaira– opera seria: 2 acts (1829—Milan) (Lib. F. Romani)

Zaira	K. Ricciarelli
Orosmane	S. Alaimo
Corasmino	R. Vargas
Nerestano	A. Papadjiakou
Fatima	S. Silbano
Meledor	R. de Candia
Lusignano	L. Roni
Castiglione	G.B. Palmieri

Catania Teatro Massimo Bellini Chor, Catania Teatro Massimo Bellini Orch, P. Olmi (pp1990)
(7/91) (NUOV) Ⓓ [2] **6982/3**
Amo ed amata in sono Y. Kenny, L. Davies, G. Mitchell Ch, Philh, D. Parry
(8/95) (OPRA) Ⓓ [3] **ORCH104**

BENATZKY, Ralph
(1884–1957)
Austria/Germany

Im weissen Rössl, 'White Horse Inn'– operetta: 3 acts (1930—Berlin) (some songs by Stolz & others; Lib Gilbert)

EXCERPTS: 1. Auf wiedersehen; 2. Mein Liebeslied muss ein Walzer sein (comp Stolz).

Josepha Vogelhuber	A. Rothenberger
Leopold Brandmeyer	P. Minich
Wilhelm Giesecke	B. Hoffmann
Ottilie	G. van Jüten
Dr. Otto Siedler	N. Orth
Sigismund Sülzheimer	P. Kraus
Klärchen	E. Schary
Emperor Franz Joseph II	H. Putz
Guide	W. Singh
House-boy	W. Mitteregger

Munich Children's Ch, Bavarian Rad Chor, Munich RO, W. Mattes (with dialogue)
(EMI) Ⓓ **CDM7 69217-2**

Excs H. Brauner, F. Loor, K. Equiluz, K. Terkal, A. Niessner, Vienna Volksoper Chor, F. Bauer-Theussl (KOCH) Ⓓ **399 225**
Excs E. Köth, I. Hallstein, R. Schock, P. Alexander, W. Hufnagel, chor, SO, J. Fehring
(2/91) (EURO) Ⓓ **GD69028**
1. J. Locke, orch, G. Scott-Wood (Eng: r1947)
(EMI) Ⓓ **CDP7 98844-2**
(EMI) ⊙ **GO2034**
2. M. Hill Smith, P. Morrison, Chandos Concert Orch, S. Barry (Eng)
(7/88) (CHAN) Ⓓ **CHAN8561**
(7/88) (CHAN) ▣ **LBTD019**

BENEDICT, Sir Julius
(1804–1885)
Germany/England

Lily of Killarney– opera: 3 acts (1862—London) (Lib. J Oxenford, after D Boucicault)

EXCERPTS—; 1. The moon hath raised her lamp above; 2. 'Tis charming girl I love; 3. I'm alone; 4. Eily Mavoureen.
1. Hilliard Ens, L-L. Kiesel
(12/91) (MERI) Ⓓ **DUOCD89009**
(12/91) (MERI) ▣ **KD89009**

BERG, Alban (Maria Johannes)
(1885–1935) Austria

Lulu– opera: 3 acts (1937—Zurich) (Wds. cpsr after Wedekind. Act 3 incomplete: cpted)

Lulu	T. Stratas
Dr Schön	F. Mazura
Alwa	K. Riegel
Countess Geschwitz	Y. Minton
Painter, Negro	R. Tear
Schigolch, Professor of Medicine, Police Officer	T. Blankenheim
Animal Tamer, Rodrigo	G. Nienstedt
Prince, Manservant, Marquis	H. Pampuch
Theatre Manager, Banker	J. Bastin
Dresser, High School Boy, Groom	H. Schwarz
Girl	J. Manning
Her Mother	U. Boese
Lady Artist	A. Ringart
Journalist	C. Meloni
Manservant	P-Y. Le Maigat

Paris Op. Orch, P. Boulez (r1979)
(11/86) (DG) Ⓓ [3] **415 489-2GH3**

Lulu	E. Lear
Dr Schön	D. Fischer-Dieskau
Alwa	D. Grobe
Countess Geschwitz	P. Johnson
Painter	L. Driscoll
Schigolch	J. Greindl
Professor of Medicine	W.W. Dicks
Animal Trainer; Rodrigo	G. Feldhoff
Prince	K-E. Mercker
Theatre Manager	L. Clam
Dresser	A. Oelke
High School Boy	B. Scherler

Berlin Deutsche Op Orch, K. Böhm
(1/93) (DG) Ⓓ [3] **435 705-2GX3**

Lulu	P. Wise
Dr Schön; Jack the Ripper	W. Schöne
Alwa	P. Straka
Countess Geschwitz	B. Fassbaender
Painter; Negro	G. Clark
Schigolch	H. Hotter
Professor of Medicine; Banker	E. Gutstein
Animal tamer; Athlete	B. Schwanbeck
Prince; Manservant; Marquis	S. Kale
Theatre Manager	B. Bakow
Dresser; High-School Boy; Groom	C. Clarey
Girl	C. Estourelle
Her Mother	L. Zannini
Lady Artist	M. Kobayashi
Journalist	F. Dudziak
Manservant	H. Hennequin

FNO, J. Tate (pp1991)
(1/93) (EMI) Ⓓ [3] **CDS7 54622-2**

Wozzeck– opera: 3 acts/15 scenes, Op. 7 (1925—Berlin) (Lib. Büchner)

Wozzeck	F. Grundheber
Marie	H. Behrens
Drum Major	W. Raffeiner
Andres	P. Langridge
Captain	H. Zednik
Doctor	A. Haugland

Margret A. Gonda
Vienna St Op Chor, Vienna St Op Orch, C. Abbado, B. Large
(PION) PLMCB00421
Wozzeck E. Waechter
Marie A. Silja
Drum-major H. Winkler
Andres H. Laubenthal
Captain H. Zednik
Doctor A. Malta
Margret G. Jahn
Vienna St Op Chor, VPO, C. von Dohnányi
(2/89) (DECC) ① [2] **417 348-2DH2**
Wozzeck F. Grundheber
Marie H. Behrens
Drum Major W. Raffeiner
Andres P. Langridge
Captain H. Zednik
Doctor A. Haugland
Margret A. Gonda
Vienna Boys' Ch, Vienna St Op Chor, VPO, C. Abbado (pp1987)
(2/89) (DG) ① [2] **423 587-2GH2**
Wozzeck D. Fischer-Dieskau
Marie E. Lear
Drum Major H. Melchert
Andres F. Wunderlich
Captain G. Stolze
Doctor K.C. Kohn
Margret A. Oelke
Berlin Deutsche Op Chor, Berlin Deutsche Op Orch, K. Böhm
(1/93) (DG) ① [3] **435 705-2GX3**
Excs H. Pilarczyk, LSO, A. Dorati (r1961)
(7/93) (MERC) ① **434 325-2MM**

BERGMAN, Erik (Valdemar) *(b 1911) Finland*

The **Singing Tree– opera: 2 acts, Op. 110 (1986-88—Helsinki) (Lib. B. Carpelan)**
King P. Lindroos
Witch C. Hellekant
Princess K. Hannula
Prince Hatt P. Salomaa
Fool S. Tiilikainen
Fruit Seller M. Wallén
Princess I A-L. Jakobson
Princess II M. Harju
Solo Voice I T-M. Tuomela
Solo Voice II E-K. Vilke
Solo Voice; Servant I T. Nyman
Servant II P. Lindroos
Dominante Ch, Tapiola Chbr Ch, Finnish Nat Op Orch, U. Söderblom (r1992)
(5/93) (ONDI) ① [2] **ODE794-2D**

BERIO, Luciano *(b 1925) Italy*

Laborintus II– opera (1965—Paris) (Wds. E. Sanguineti)
C. Legrand, J. Baucomont, C. Meunier, E. Sanguineti, Chorale Expérimentale, Musique Vivante Ens, L. Berio
(12/87) (HARM) ① **HMA190 764**

BERKELEY , Michael *(b 1948) England*

Baa Baa Black Sheep– opera: 3 acts (1993—Cheltenham) (Lib. D Marouf, after R Kipling)
Punch, Mowgli as a child M. Lorimer
Mowgli as a young man W. Dazeley
Judy, Grey Wolf A. Taylor-Morley
Father, Father Wolf, Messua's Husband G. Mosley
Mother, Mother Wolf, Messua E. Hulse
The Captain, Akela H. Newman
Auntirosa, Baldeo F. Kimm
Harry, Sheer Khan P. Sheffield
Bhini-in-the-garden, Baloo M. Holland
Meeta, Bagheera C. Bayley
Captain Sahib, Ka P. McCann
Priest B. Cookson
Op North Chor, English Northern Philh, P. Daniel (pp1993)
(4/95) (COLL) ① [2] **Coll7036-2**

BERLIOZ, (Louis-)Hector *(1803–1869) France*

Béatrice et Bénédict– opera: 2 acts (1862—Baden-Baden) (Lib. cpsr, after Shakespeare)
EXCERPTS: 1. Overture. ACT 1: 2. La More est en fuite; 3. Je vais le voir; 4. Comment le dédain pourrait-il mourir?; 5. Me marier? Dieu me pardonne!; 6. Mourez, tendres époux (épithalame); 7. Ah! je vais l'aimer; 8. Vous soupirez, madame? (nocturne); 9. Entr'acte. ACT 2: 10. Le vin de Syracuse; 11a. Non! que viens-je d'entendre?; 11b. Il m'en souvient; 12. Je vais d'un coeur aimant (trio); 13. Viens, de l'hyménée; 14. Dieu qui guidas nos bras; 15. Ici l'on voit Bénédict; 16. L'amour est un flambeau.
Béatrice J. Baker
Bénédict R. Tear
Héro C. Eda-Pierre
Ursule H. Watts
Claudio T. Allen
Somarone J. Bastin
Don Pedro R. Lloyd
Léonato R. Van Allan
John Alldis Ch, LSO, Colin Davis (with dialogue)
(9/87) (PHIL) ① [2] **416 952-2PH2**
Béatrice S. Graham
Bénédict J-L. Viala
Héro S. McNair
Ursule C. Robbin
Claudio G. Cachemaille
Somarone G. Bacquier
Don Pedro V. le Texier
Léonato P. Magnant
Lyon Op Chor, Lyon Op Orch, J. Nelson (with dialogue)
(6/92) (ERAT) ① [2] **2292-45773-2**
1. LPO, H. Harty (r1934)
(PEAR) ① **GEMMCD9485**
1. Sydney SO, R. Pickler
(CHAN) ① **CHAN6587**
1. San Diego SO, Y. Talmi (r1994)
(NAXO) ① **8 550999**
1. Hallé, J. Loughran (r1974)
(CFP) ① [2] **CD-CFPSD4751**
1. SNO, A. Gibson
(8/84) (CHAN) ① **CHAN8316**
1. Boston SO, C. Munch
(3/89) (RCA) ① **GD86805**
1. RPO, Y. Temirkanov
(11/92) (RCA) ① **09026 61203-2**
1. LSO, A. Previn
(3/93) (EMI) ① **CDM7 64630-2**
1. Boston SO, C. Munch (r1958)
(11/93) (RCA) ① **09026 61400-2**
1. Philh, J-P. Rouchon (r1993)
(8/94) (ASV) ① **CDDCA895**
1, 9. NYPO, P. Boulez (r1971)
(3/95) (SONY) ① [3] **SM3K64103**
8. A. Cantelo, H. Watts, LSO, Colin Davis (r1962) (DECC) ① **436 315-2DA**
(DECC) ▭ **436 315-4DA**
8. A. Cantelo, H. Watts, LSO, Colin Davis (r1962) (DECC) ① **443 335-2LRX**
(DECC) ▭ **443 335-4LRX**
10. J-P. Courtis, Lyon Nat Ch, Inst Ens, B. Tetu (r1988) (HARM) ① **HMP390 1293**

Benvenuto Cellini– opera: 2 acts (1838—Paris) (Lib. de Wailly and Barbier)
EXCERPTS: 1. Overture. ACT 1 SCENE 1: 2. Teresa...mais où peut-elle être?; 3. Tra la la la, De profundis!; 4a. Les belles fleurs!; 4b. Entre l'amour et le devoir; 5. O Teresa, vous que j'aime; 6. Ah! mourir, chère belle; 7. Ah! maître drôle, ah! libertin!. ACT 1 SCENE 2: 8a. Une heure encore; 8b. La gloire était ma seule idole; 9a. A boire, à boire; 9b. Si la terre aux beaux jours se couronne; 10. Que voulez-vous?; 11. Cette somme t'est due; 12. Ah! qui pourrait me résister?; 13. Vous voyer, j'espère; 14. Venez, venez, peuple de Rome. ACT 2 SCENE 1: 15. Ah, qu'est il devenu?; 16. Rosa purpurea; 17. Ma dague en main; 18. Ah! le ciel, cher époux; 19. Quand des sommets de la montagne; 20. Ah! je te trouve enfin; 21. Le Pape ici! de la prudence!; 22. Justice à nous; 23. Ah! ça, démon!; 24. Ah! maintainant de sa folle impudence. ACT 2 SCENE 2: 25. Tra la la...Mais qu'ai-je donc?; 26a. Seul pour lutter; 26b. Sur les monts; 27. Bienheureux les matelots; 28. Peuple ouvrier; 29. Du métal! du métal!.
Benvenuto Cellini N. Gedda
Balducci J. Bastin
Fieramosca R. Massard
Pope Clément VII R. Soyer
Francesco D. Blackwell
Bernadino R. Lloyd
Pompeo R. Herincx
Teresa C. Eda-Pierre
Innkeeper H. Cuénod
Ascanio J. Berbié
ROH Chor, BBC SO, Colin Davis
(1/89) (PHIL) ① [3] **416 955-2PH3**
1. Montpellier PO, C. Diederich
(FORL) ① **UCD16568**
1. Prague SO, Z. Fekete (SUPR) ① **11 1116-2**
1. CBSO, L. Frémaux (KLVI) ① **KCD11040**
1. LSO, A. Previn (r1974)
(EMI) ① **CDM7 64745-2**
1. San Diego SO, Y. Talmi (r1994)
(NAXO) ① **8 550999**
1. Hallé, J. Loughran (r1974)
(CFP) ① [2] **CD-CFPSD4751**
1. FNO, C. Munch (pp1966)
(11/88) (MONT) ① **MUN2011**
1. Baltimore SO, D. Zinman (r1987)
(12/88) (TELA) ① **CD80164**
1. Polish St PO, K. Jean
(1/91) (NAXO) ① **8 550231**
1. Brno St PO, P. Vronský
(10/91) (SUPR) ① **11 0388-2**
1. Toulouse Capitole Orch, M. Plasson
(2/92) (EMI) ① **CDC7 54237-2**
1. BPO, James Levine
(7/92) (DG) ① [2] **429 724-2GH2**
1. NYPO, L. Bernstein (r1960)
(11/92) (SONY) ① **SMK47525**
1. Strasbourg PO, A. Lombard
(6/93) (ERAT) ① **2292-45925-2**
1. Black Dyke Mills Band, G. Brand (arr F. Wright) (9/93) (RSR) ① **RSRD1002**
1. Boston SO, C. Munch (r1959)
(11/93) (RCA) ① **09026 61400-2**
1. San Francisco SO, P. Monteux (r1952)
(9/94) (RCA) ① [15] **09026 61893-2**
1. NYPO, P. Boulez (r1972)
(3/95) (SONY) ① [3] **SM3K64103**
8a, 8b P. Domingo, National PO, E. Kohn
(11/90) (EMI) ① **CDC7 54053-2**

Les **Troyens, '(The) Trojans'– opera: 5 acts (Acts 1-2: 1890; Acts 3-5: 1863—Acts 1-2: Karlsruhe; Acts 3-5: Paris) (Lib cpsr, after Virgil)**
PART I: LA PRISE DE TROIE. ACT 1: 1. Après dix ans; 2a. Les Grecs ont disparu!; 2b. Malheureux Roi!; 3a. Chorèbe! il faut qu'il; 3b. Reviens à toi, vierge adoré!; 3c. Si tu m'aimes, va-t-en; 4. Dieux protecteurs; 5. Combat de ceste et Pas de lutteurs; 6. Andromaque et son fils!; 7. Du peuple et des soldats, ô roi!; 8. Châtiment effroyable!; 9. Que la déesse nous protège; 10. Non, je ne verrai pas; 11a. Du roi des dieux, ô fille aimée (Trojan March); 11b. Arrêtez! Oui, la flamme! la hache!. ACT 2: 12a. Â lumière de Troie!; 12b. Ah!...fuis, fils de Vénus; 13. La ville ensanglantée; 14. Ah! Puissante Cybèle; 15a. Tous ne périront pas; 15b. O digne soeur d'Hector!; 16. Complices de sa gloire. PART 2: LES TROYENS À CARTHAGE. ACT 3: 17a. Prelude; 17b. De Carthage les cieux semblent bénir la fête; 18. Gloire à Didon; 19a. Nous avons vu finir; 19b. Chers Tyriens; 19c. Cette belle journée; 20. Entrée des constructeurs; 21. Entrée des matelots; 22. Entrée des laboureurs; 23. Peuple! tous les honneurs; 24a. Les chants joyeux; 24b. Sa voix fait naître dans mon sein; 25a. La porte du palais; 25b. Errante sur les mers; 26. Trojan March; 27. Auguste reine; 28. Reine, je suis Enée!. ACT 4: 29. Royal Hunt and Storm; 30a. Dites, Narbal; 30b. Pour de ce côte plus rien; 31. De quels revers; 32. Marche. BALLETS: 33a. Pas des Almées; 33b. Danse des Esclaves; 33c. Pas d'Esclaves nubiennes; 34. O blonde Cérès; 35a. Pardonne, Iopas; 35b. O pudeur! Tout conspire; 36a. Mais bannissons ces tristes souvenirs; 36b. Tout n'est que paix et charme; 37. Nuits d'ivresse! ACT 5: 38. Vallon sonore; 39. Préparez tout; 40. Par Bacchus! ils sont fous; 41a. Inutiles regrets!; 41b. Ah! quand viendra l'instant; 42. Encor ces voix!; 43. Debout, Troyens; 44. Errante sur tes pas; 45. Va, ma soeur, l'implorer; 46a. En mer, voyez!; 46b. Dieux immortels!; 47. Je vais mourir; 48. Adieu, fière cité; 49. Deiux de l'oubli; 50a. D'un malheureux amour; 50b. Mon souvenir vivra; 51. Quels cris!; 52a. Imprécation; 52b. Haine éternelle.

Dido R. Resnik
Aeneas R. Cassilly
Cassandra E. Steber
Choroebus M. Singher
Anna; Hecuba R. Sarfaty
Narbal J. Dennison
Pantheus; Trojan Soldier K. Smith
Ascanius F. Wyatt
Iopas W. Lewis
Priam; Mercury; Hector's Ghost; Choroebus's Ghost Chester Watson
Hylas; Helenus G. Peterson
American Op Soc Chor, American Op Soc Orch, R. Lawrence (pp1959/60)
(VAI) ① [3] **VAIA1006**

Dido J. Veasey
Aeneas J. Vickers
Cassandra B. Lindholm
Choroebus; Choroebus's Ghost P. Glossop
Anna H. Begg
Narbal R. Soyer
Pantheus A. Raffell
Ascanius A. Howells
Iopas I. Partridge
Priam; Mercury; Trojan Soldier P. Thau
Hecuba; Cassandra's Ghost E. Bainbridge
Hylas R. Davies
Priam's Ghost; Sentry I R. Herincx
Hector's Ghost; Sentry II D. Wicks
Helenus D. Lennox
Wandsworth Sch Boys' Ch, ROH Chor, ROHO, Colin Davis (r1969)
(12/86) (PHIL) ① [4] **416 432-2PH4**

Dido F. Pollet
Aeneas G. Lakes
Cassandra D. Voigt
Choroebus G. Quilico
Anna H. Perraguin
Narbal J-P. Courtis
Pantheus M. Philippe
Ascanius C. Dubosc
Iopas J-L. Maurette
Priam; Soldier I R. Schirrer
Hecuba C. Carlson
Hylas J. M. Ainsley
Hector's Ghost; Soldier II; Greek Captain M. Belleau
Sinon G. Cross
Mercury M. Beauchemin
Montreal Sym Chor, Montreal SO, C. Dutoit (r1993)
(12/94) (DECC) ① [4] **443 693-2DH4**

2a, 2b, 3a, 3b, 7, 10, 11b, 15a, 28, 36a, 36b, 37, 41a, 41b, 46a, 46b, 50a, 50b M. del Monaco, N. Rankin, G. Simionato, La Scala Orch, R. Kubelík (pp1960: Ital) (VAI) ① **VAIA1026**

2a, 2b, 10. M. Horne, Rome RAI Chor, Rome RAI Orch, G. Prêtre (pp1969) (MEMO) ① [2] **HR4392/3**

17a LSO, Colin Davis (12/86) (PHIL) ① **416 431-2PH**

17a San Francisco SO, P. Monteux (r1945) (9/94) (RCA) ① [15] **09026 61893-2**

17a, 29. San Diego Master Chorale, San Diego SO, Y. Talmi (r1994) (11/95) (NAXO) ① **8 553195**

29. Hallé, H. Harty (r1931) (PEAR) ① **GEMMCD9485**

29. Helsinki PO, S. Comissiona (PRO) ① **CDS580**

29. NSW Cons Op School, Sydney SO, R. Pickler (CHAN) ① **CHAN6587**

29. National PO, R. Bonynge (r1983) (DECC) ① **444 108-2DA**

29. Baltimore SO, D. Zinman (r1987) (12/88) (TELA) ① **CD80164**

29. ROH Chor, ROHO, B. Haitink (12/89) (EMI) ① **CDC7 49849-2**

29. RPO, K.H. Adler (pp1982) (8/91) (DECC) ① **430 716-2DM**
(8/91) (DECC) ▭ **430 716-4DM**

29. Boston SO, C. Munch (r1959) (11/93) (RCA) ① **09026 61400-2**

29. Paris Orch, D. Barenboim (r1976) (8/94) (SONY) ① **SBK53255**
(8/94) (SONY) ▭ **SBT53255**

29. Lyon Nat Orch, E. Krivine (r1993) (12/94) (DENO) ① **CO-78902**

29. NYPO, P. Boulez (r1971) (3/95) (SONY) ① [3] **SM3K64103**

41a, 41b G. Thill, chor, orch, E. Bigot (r1934) (MMOI) ① **CDMOIR405**
(MMOI) ▭ **CMOIR405**

41a, 41b J. Vickers, ROH Chor, ROHO, Colin Davis (PHIL) ① **442 602-2PM**
(PHIL) ▭ **442 602-4PM**

41a, 41b G. Thill, Orch, E. Bigot (r1934) (1/89) (EMI) ① **CDM7 69548-2**

47. F. Pollet, Montpellier PO, C. Diederich (r1989) (ERAT) ① **4509-98502-2**

47-49. J. Baker, B. Greevy, K. Erwen, G. Howell, Ambrosian Op Chor, LSO, A. Gibson (11/88) (EMI) ① **CDM7 69544-2**

48. G. Frozier-Marrot, orch (r1930) (MSCM) ① **MM30221**
(MSCM) ▭ **MM040079**

48. R. Gorr, Philh, L. Collingwood (r1958) (4/92) (EMI) ① [7] **CHS7 69741-2(3)**

BERNSTEIN, Leonard *(1918–1990) USA*

Candide– operetta: 2 acts (1956—New York) (Wds. various)

EXCERPTS—; 1. Overture. ACT 1: 2. The best of all possible worlds; 3. Oh, happy we; 4. Wedding Procession, Chorale and Battle Scene; 5. Candide begins her travels; 6. It must be so; 7. Lisbon Sequence; 8. Paris Waltz; 9. Glitter and be gay; 10. You were dead, you know; 11. Pilgrim's procession; 12. My Love; 13. I am easily assimilated (Buenos Aires); 14. Finale (Quartet). ACT 2: 15. Quiet; 16. The Ballade of Eldorado; 17. Bon Voyage; 18. Raft Sequence; 19. Venice Gambling Scene; 20. What's the use?; 21. The Venice Gavotte; 22. Return to Westphalia; 23. Make our garden grow. ADDITIONAL ITEM FOR LONDON PRODUCTION, 1959—; 24. We are women.

1. Czech PO, A. Copland (pp1973) (6/93) (ROMA) ① **RR1973**

1-3, 6-10, 12-17, 20, 21, 23. B. Cook, R. Rounseville, M. Adrian, W. Olvis, I. Pettina, G. Blackwell, T. Pyle, N. Roland, W. Chapman, R. Mesrobian, M. Beck Th Chor, M. Beck Th Orch, S. Krachmalnick (r1956) (SONY) ① **SK48017**

8. Scottish Op Orch, New Sadler's Wells Op Orch (TER) ① **CDVIR8315**

8. Hollywood Bowl SO, J. Mauceri (r1993) (6/94) (PHIL) ① **438 685-2PH**
(6/94) (PHIL) ▭ **438 685-4PH**

9. Orig Broadway Cast (r1956) (SONY) ① **SK53539**

9. M. Hill Smith, Scottish Op Orch, J. Brown (r1989-91) (10/91) (TER) ① **CDVIR8314**
(10/91) (TER) ▭ **ZCVIR8314**

9. S. Jo, Monte Carlo PO, P. Olmi (r1994) (6/95) (ERAT) ① **4509-97239-2**

Candide (opera house version)– comic operetta: 2 acts (1982—New York) (Wds. various)

EXCERPTS: 1. Overture. ACT 1: 2. Life is happiness indeed; 3. The Best of all possible worlds; 4. O happy we; 5. It must be so; 6. Fanfare, Chorale and Battle; 7. Glitter and be gay; 8. Dear boy; 9. Auto da Fé scene; 10. Candide's Lament; 12. I am easily assimilated; 13. Finale (Quartet). ACT 2: 14. To the New World; 15. My Love; 16. The Old Lady's Tale (Barcarolle); 17. Alleluia; 18. Sheep Song; 19. Governor's Waltz; 20. Bon Voyage; 21. Quiet; 22. What's the use; 23. Make our garden grow.

Candide D. Eisler
Cunegonde E. Mills
Pangloss; Voltaire; Businessman; Governor; Gambler II J. Langston
Maximilian S. Reeve
Paquette M. Clement
Old Lady J. Castle
Judge; First Gambler J. Billings
Grand Inquisitor; Pasha-Prefect J. Harrold
NYC Op Chor, NYC Op Orch, J. Mauceri (10/86) (NEW) ① [2] **NW340/1-2**
(10/86) (NEW) ▭ [2] **NWMC340/1**

5, 10. R. Alexander, T. Crone (2/87) (ETCE) ① **KTC1037**
(ETCE) ▭ **XTC1037**

23. P. Domingo, D. Graves, Rio de Janeiro Municipal Th Orch, J. DeMain (pp1992) (SONY) ◐ **SLV48362**
(SONY) ▣ **SHV48362**

Candide– comic operetta: 2 acts (1988 final version—Glasgow) (Wds. various)

EXCERPTS—ACT 1: 1. Overture; 1a. Westphalia chorale (wds. Bernstein/Wells); 2. Life is happiness indeed (wds. Sondheim); 3. The best of all possible worlds (wds. La Touche); 3a. Universal good (wds. Bernstein/Wells); 4. Oh, happy we (wds. Wilbur); 5. It must be so (wds. Wilbur); 6. Westphalia (wds. Bernstein/Wells); 6a. Battle music; 7. Candide's lament (wds. La Touche); 8. Dear Boy (wds. Wilbur); 9. Auto-da-fée (wds. La Touche/Wilbur); 10. Candide begins his travels; 10a. It must be me (wds. Wilbur); 11. The Paris waltz; 12. Glitter and be gay (wds. Wilbur); 13. You were dead, you know (wds. La Touche); 14. I am easily assimilated (wds. Bernstein); 15. Quartet finale (wds. Wilbur). ACT 2: 16. Universal good (wds. Bernstein/Wells); 17. My love (wds. Wilbur/La Touche); 18. We are women (wds. Bernstein); 19. The pilgrims' procession/Alleluia (wds. Wilbur); 20. Quiet (wds. Wilbur); 21. Introduction to Eldorado; 22. The ballad of Eldorado (wds. Hellman); 23. Words, words, words (wds. Bernstein); 24. Bon voyage (wds. Wilbur); 25. The kings' barcarolle (wds. Wilbur); 26. Money, money, money (wds. Wilbur); 27. What's the use (wds. Wilbur); 28. The Venice gavotte (wds. Wilbur/Parker); 29. Nothing more than this (wds. Bernstein); 30. Universal good (wds. Hellman/Bernstein); 31. Make our garden grow (wds. Wilbur).

Candide J. Hadley
Cunegonde J. Anderson
Dr Pangloss; Martin A. Green
Old Lady C. Ludwig
Governor; Vanderdendur; Ragotski N. Gedda
Paquette D. Jones
Maximilian; Captain; Jesuit Father K. Ollmann
Merchant; Inquisitor; Prince Charles Edward N. Jenkins
Junkman; Inquisitor; King Hermann Augustus R. Suart
Alchemist; Inquisitor; Sultan Achmet; Crook J. Treleaven
Doctor; Inquisitor; King Stanislaus L. Benson
Bear-Keeper; Inquisitor; Tsar Ivan C. Bayley
LSC, LSO, L. Bernstein, H. Burton (pp1989) (11/91) (DG) ▣ **072 423-3GH**

Candide J. Hadley
Cunegonde J. Anderson
Dr Pangloss; Martin A. Green
Old Lady C. Ludwig
Governor; Vanderdendur; Ragotski N. Gedda
Paquette D. Jones
Maximilian; Captain; Jesuit Father K. Ollmann
Merchant; Inquisitor; Prince Charles Edward N. Jenkins
Junkman; Inquisitor; King Hermann Augustus R. Suart
Alchemist; Inquisitor; Sultan Achmet; Crook J. Treleaven
Doctor; Inquisitor; King Stanislaus L. Benson
Bear-Keeper; Inquisitor; Tsar Ivan C. Bayley
LSC, LSO, L. Bernstein (8/91) (DG) ① [2] **429 734-2GH2**
(8/91) (DG) ▭ [2] **429 734-4GH2**

1. Orch, Anon Cond (pp1991) (MCI) ① **MCCD090**
(MCI) ▭ **MCTC090**

1. Empire Brass (r1992; arr. R. Smedvig) (1/94) (TELA) ① **CD80305**
(1/94) (TELA) ▭ **CS30305**

1, 12. T. Dahl, Calgary PO, M. Bernardi (r1992) (12/94) (CBC) ① **SMCD5125**

1, 15. E. Gruberová, Tokyo PO, F. Haider (pp1993) (NIGH) ① **NC090560-2**

1, 3, 3a, 4, 5, 7, 11-14, 17, 21, 22, 24, 27, 28, 31. N. Grace, M. Beudert, M. Hill Smith, A. Howard, M. Tinkler, B. Bottone, Scottish Op Chor, Scottish Op Orch, J. Brown (TER) ① **CDTEO1006**
(TER) ▭ **ZCTEO1006**

1, 3-5, 7, 11-14, 17, 21, 24, 27, 28, 31. N. Grace, M. Beudert, M. Hill Smith, A. Howard, M. Tinkler, G. Miles, B. Bottone, Scottish Op Chor, SNO, J. Brown (8/88) (TER) ① **CDTER1156**
(8/88) (TER) ▭ **ZCTER1156**

1, 4, 12, 14. J. Anderson, J. Hadley, C. Ludwig, LSO, L. Bernstein (r1989) (DG) ① **439 251-2GY**

1, 4, 12, 14. J. Anderson, J. Hadley, C. Ludwig, LSO, L. Bernstein (r1989) (DG) OO **439 251-5GY**

1-5, 6, 6a, 7, 9, 11, 12, 14, 17, 24, 27, 29, 31. J. Hadley, J. Anderson, C. Ludwig, A. Green, N. Gedda, D. Jones, K. Ollmann, LSC, LSO, L. Bernstein (r1989) (DG) OO **435 487-5GH**

1-5, 6, 6a, 7, 9, 11, 12, 14, 17, 24, 27, 29, 31. J. Hadley, J. Anderson, C. Ludwig, A. Green, N. Gedda, D. Jones, K. Ollmann, LSC, LSO, L. Bernstein (r1989) (DG) ① **435 487-2GH**
(DG) ▭ **435 487-4GH**

12. D. Upshaw, orch, E. Stern (r1993)
(12/94) (NONE) ① **7559-79345-2**
(NONE) ▭ **7559-79345-4**

31. Tanglewood Fest Chor, Boston Pops, J.T. Williams (SONY) ① **SK48224**

31. R. Fleming, J. Hadley, Collegiate Chorale, NY Met Op Orch, J. Conlon (pp1991)
(6/93) (RCA) ① **09026 61509-2**

A Quiet Place– opera: 3 acts (1983—Houston) (Lib. S. Wordsworth. Incorporating earlier 'Trouble)

What a movie W. White, Austrian RSO, L. Bernstein (r1986) (DG) ① **439 251-2GY**

What a movie W. White, Austrian RSO, L. Bernstein (r1986)
(DG) OO **439 251-5GY**

Trouble in Tahiti– opera: 7 scenes (1952—Waltham) (Lib. cpsr)

Cpte J. Reardon, J. Patrick, A. Butler, M. Clark, M. Brown, Columbia Wind Ens, L. Bernstein (r1973) (5/92) (SONY) ① [3] **SM3K47154**

West Side Story– musical show: 2 acts (1957—New York) (Book A. Laurents, lyrics S. Sondheim)

EXCERPTS: 1. Prologue. ACT 1: 2. Jet Song; 3. Something's coming; 4. The Dance at the Gym; 4a. Blues; 4b. Promenade; 4c. Mambo; 4d. Cha-Cha; 4e. Meeting; 4f. Jump; 5. Maria; 6. Tonight (Balcony scene); 7. America; 8. Cool; 9. One hand, one heart; 10. Tonight (Quintet); 11. The Rumble. ACT 2: 12. I feel pretty; 13a. Ballet sequence; 13b. transition to Scherzo; 13c. Scherzo; 13d. Somewhere; 13e. Procession and Nightmare; 14. Gee, Officer Krupke; 15. A boy like that/I have a love; 16. Taunting scene; 17. Finale. ADDITIONAL ITEMS FOR FILM VERSION—1960: 18. Overture; 19. End credits.

Maria K. Te Kanawa
Maria - dialogue N. Bernstein
Tony J. Carreras
Tony - dialogue A. Bernstein
Anita T. Troyanos
Off-stage voice M. Horne
Riff K. Ollmann
Rosalia L. Edeiken
Consuela S. Zambalis
Francisca A. Réaux
Action D. Livingstone
Diesel M. Nelson
Baby John S. Bogardus
A-rab P. Thom
Snowboy T. Lester
Bernardo R. Harrell

Broadway Chor, Broadway Orch, L. Bernstein (r1984)
(7/85) (DG) ▭ [2] **415 253-4GH2**

Maria K. Te Kanawa
Maria - dialogue N. Bernstein
Tony J. Carreras
Tony - dialogue A. Bernstein
Anita T. Troyanos
Off-stage voice M. Horne
Riff K. Ollmann
Rosalia L. Edeiken
Consuela S. Zambalis
Francisca A. Réaux
Action D. Livingstone
Diesel M. Nelson
Baby John S. Bogardus
A-rab P. Thom
Snowboy T. Lester
Bernardo R. Harrell

Broadway Chor, Broadway Orch, L. Bernstein (r1984)
(4/85) (DG) ① [2] **415 253-2GH2**

Maria M. Nixon
Tony J. Bryant
Riff R. Tamblyn

Orig Film Cast, J. Green (r1960)
(8/93) (SONY) ① **SK48211**
(8/93) (SONY) ▭ **ST48211**

Maria B. Bonney
Tony M. Ball
Anita L. Williams
Riff C. Howard
Rosalia M. Carewe
Consuela L. Gibson
Francisca J. O'Grady
Action D. Chessor
Diesel L. Benson
Baby John A. Busher
A-Rab J. Graeme
Bernardo M. Pearn

Royal Phil Chor, RPO, B. Wordsworth (r1993)
(10/93) (IMG) ① **IMGCD1801**
(10/93) (IMG) ▭ **IMGMC1801**

Maria T. Olafimihan
Tony P. Manuel
Anita C. O'Connor
Off-stage voice S. Burgess
Riff N. Warnford
Rosalia J. Paton
Consuela E. Stephenson
Francisca N. Carty
Action K. Daniels
Diesel M. Michaels
Baby John A. Sarple
A-rab A. Edmeads
Snowboy G. Stevens
Bernardo N. Ferranti

Chor, National SO, J.O. Edwards (r1993)
(2/94) (TER) ① [2] **CDTER2 1197**
(2/94) (TER) ▭ [2] **ZCTER2 1197**

Excs Stuttgart RSO, N. Marriner (pp1985)
(CAPR) ① **10 466**

Medley American Hn Qt (r1993; arr. W. Perkins)
(EBS) ① **EBS6038**

Medley Tetra (r1989-91: arr gtr qt: Storry)
(11/93) (CONI) ① **CDCF903**
(11/93) (CONI) ▭ **MCFC903**

Medley R. Stoltzman, LSO, E. Stern (r1993; arr Bennett: 'Variants')
(12/93) (RCA) ① **09026 61790-2**

1, 2, 4c, 5, 7, 8, 13c, 13d Netherlands Wind Ens, R. Dufallo (r1993: arr brass: E Crees)
(3/94) (CHAN) ① **CHAN9210**

1, 3, 4c, 5, 7, 8, 13c, 13d LSO Brass Ens, E. Crees (arr brass: Cress)
(1/92) (COLL) ① **Coll1288-2**

1, 3, 4, 7, 8, 13d HR-Brass, J. Whigham (r1991; arr Crees) (CAPR) ① **10 429**

1-3, 5-7, 11, 12, 13d, 15. D. Nettle, Richard Markham (r1988; arr Nettle & Markham: 2 pfs)
(IMP) ① **MCD76**

2, 3, 5-10, 12, 13d, 14-17. K. Te Kanawa, J. Carreras, T. Troyanos, K. Ollmann, M. Horne, Broadway Chor, Broadway Orch, L. Bernstein (r1984) (DG) ① **415 963-2GH**
(DG) ▭ **415 963-4GH**

2, 3, 5-10, 12, 13d, 14-17. K. Te Kanawa, J. Carreras, T. Troyanos, K. Ollmann, M. Horne, Broadway Chor, Broadway Orch, L. Bernstein (r1984) (DG) OO **415 963-5GH**

2, 3, 5, 7, 9, 10, 12, 15. K. Labèque, M. Labèque (arr Kostal) (1/90) (CBS) ▭ **40-45531**

2, 7. K. Labèque, M. Labèque (r1991;arr Kostal: 2 pfs) (SONY) ① **SK48381**
(SONY) ▭ **ST48381**

3. M. Patinkin, Orch, E. Stern (r1993; orch Troob, arr Ford)
(11/94) (NONE) ① **7559-79330-2**

3, 14. Orig Broadway Cast (r1957)
(SONY) ① **SK48201**
(SONY) ▭ **ST48201**

4c Empire Brass Qnt (r1991; arr Brass Ens)
(TELA) ① **CD80303**
(TELA) ▭ **CS30303**

5. Munich Brass (arr brass ens)
(ORFE) ① **C247911A**

5. NYPO, A. Kostelanetz
(SONY) ① **SBK39448**

5. Berlin Phil Vcs (TELD) ① **4509-92014-2**
(TELD) ▭ **4509-92014-4**

5. F. Araiza, Munich RSO, R. Weikert (arr Mattes) (3/93) (RCA) ① **09026 61163-2**

5. J. Hadley, NY Met Op Orch, J. Conlon (pp1991) (6/93) (RCA) ① **09026 61509-2**

5. P. Bertin, A. Scholl, D. Visse, F. Couturier (r1995: arr R Wagner)
(8/95) (HARM) ① **HMC90 1552**

5, 10. J. Carreras, P. Domingo, L. Pavarotti, MMF Orch, Rome Op Orch, Z. Mehta (pp1990)
(DECC) OO **430 433-5DH**

5, 10. J. Carreras, P. Domingo, L. Pavarotti, MMF Orch, Rome Op Orch, Z. Mehta (pp1990)
(10/90) (DECC) ① **430 433-2DH**
(10/90) (DECC) ▭ **430 433-4DH**

5, 13d J. Carreras, P. Domingo, L. Pavarotti, MMF Orch, Rome Op Orch, Z. Mehta (pp1990)
(DECC) ◐ **071 123-1DH**
(DECC) ▣ **071 123-3DH**

5-7, 12. J. Carreras, K. Te Kanawa, T. Troyanos, L. Edeiken, orch, chor, L. Bernstein (r1984)
(DG) ① **439 251-2GY**

5-7, 12. J. Carreras, K. Te Kanawa, T. Troyanos, L. Edeiken, orch, chor, L. Bernstein (r1984)
(DG) OO **439 251-5GY**

6. J. Carreras, R. Farnon Orch, R. Farnon (arr Farnon) (PHIL) ① **434 152-2PM**

6. K. Ricciarelli, J. Carreras, Orch, Anon Cond (pp1991) (MCI) ① **MCCD090**
(MCI) ▭ **MCTC090**

6. J. Carreras, R. Farnon Orch, R. Farnon (r1983: arr Farnon) (BELA) ① **450 059-2**
(BELA) ▭ **450 059-4**

6. Orig Broadway Cast (r1957)
(SONY) ① **SK53542**

6. V. Masterson, T. Allen, Philh, J.O. Edwards (r1990) (5/94) (TER) ① **CDVIR8317**
(5/94) (TER) ▭ **ZCVIR8317**

6. LPO Vcs, RPO Vcs, BBC SO Vcs, Philh Vcs, G. Simon (r1993; arr Balcombe)
(9/95) (CALA) ① **CACD0104**

6. S. Bullock, A. Davies, A. Bryn Parri (r1994)
(11/95) (SAIN) ① **SCDC2070**

6, 9, 12. K. Te Kanawa, J. Carreras, orch, L. Bernstein (r1984) (DECC) ① **440 280-2DH**
(DECC) ▭ **440 280-4DH**

7. Orig Broadway Cast (r1957)
(SONY) ① **SK53541**

7. B. Wand, G. Chakaris, chor, orch, J. Green (r1960) (SONY) ① [2] **SB2K64391**

7, 12, 13d Chee-Yun, A. Eguchi (arr vn/pf: Penaforte) (12/93) (DENO) ① **CO-75118**

9. L. Schouten, R. Ederveen (arr fl/hp)
(SAGA) ① **SCD9023**

10. J. Carreras, orch, R. Farnon
(PHIL) ① **416 973-2PM**
(PHIL) ▭ **416 973-4PM**

10. J. Carreras, Orch, R. Farnon
(PHIL) ① **432 692-2PH**
(PHIL) ▭ **432 692-4PH**

12. D. Upshaw, E. Stern, L. Stifelman (r1993: arr E Stern) (12/94) (NONE) ① **7559-79345-2**
(NONE) ▭ **7559-79345-4**

13b F. von Stade, Mormon Tabernacle Ch, Utah SO, J. Silverstein (arr D Cullen: pp1991)
(DECC) ① **436 284-2DH**

13d J. Norman, orch, L. Bernstein (r1984/93)
(DG) ① **439 251-2GY**

13d J. Norman, orch, L. Bernstein (r1984/93)
(DG) OO **439 251-5GY**

13d M. Horne, American Th Orch, P. Gemignani (r1993; arr D. Troob) (RCA) ① **09026 62647-2**

13d J. Lloyd Webber, RPO, N. Cleobury (arr vc)
(3/87) (PHIL) ① **416 698-2PH**

West Side Story– symphonic dances from musical show (1960)

1. Prologue; 2. Somewhere; 3. Scherzo; 4. Mambo; 5. Cha-Cha; 6. Meeting Scene; 7. 'Cool' Fugue; 8. Rumble; 9. Finale.

K. Labèque, M. Labèque, J-P. Drouet, S. Gualda, T. Gurtu (arr Kostal)
(1/90) (CBS) ▭ **40-45531**

C. Barbaosa-Lima, S. Isbin (arr 2 gtrs)
(CCOR) ① **CCD42012**
(CCOR) ▭ **CC2012**

RLPO, Carl Davis (CFP) ① **CD-CFP4601**
(CFP) ▭ **TC-CFP4601**

G. Pekinel, S. Pekinel, P. Sadlo (r1988; arr McKibbins/Philipps) (TELD) ① **4509-92143-2**

San Francisco SO, S. Ozawa (r1972)
(DG) ① **439 425-2GCL**
(DG) ▭ **439 425-4GCL**

Minnesota Orch, E. de Waart (r1990)
(VIRG) ① **CUV5 61194-2**

RCA Victor Orch, Robert Russell Bennett (r1959)
(RCA) ① **74321 24218-2**

Los Angeles PO, L. Bernstein (pp1982)
(8/83) (DG) ① **410 025-2GH**

D. Achatz (arr. piano)
(9/87) (BIS) ① **BIS-CD352**

San Francisco SO, S. Ozawa
(12/91) (DG) ① [2] **413 851-2GW2**

NYPO, L. Bernstein (r1961)
(5/92) (SONY) ① [3] **SM3K47154**

NYPO, L. Bernstein (r1959)
(11/92) (SONY) ① **SMK47529**

Hollywood Bowl Orch, J. Mauceri (r1992)
(1/94) (PHIL) ① **438 663-2PH**

1-4, 9. Los Angeles PO, L. Bernstein (r1982)
(DG) ① **439 251-2GY**

1-4, 9. Los Angeles PO, L. Bernstein (r1982)
(DG) OO **439 251-5GY**

4. NYPO, L. Bernstein (SONY) ① **SBK39448**

4. Baltimore SO, D. Zinman (r1994: 2 perfs)
(7/95) (ARGO) ① **444 454-2ZH**

BERTÉ, Heinrich *(1857–1924) Hungary*

Das **Dreimäderlhaus– operetta (1916—Vienna) (based on works by Schubert)**

Lied aus Wien B. Weikl, Austrian RSO, K. Eichhorn (ORFE) Ⓓ **C077831A**

Was macht glücklich E. Schumann, orch, W. Goehr (r1936) (ROMO) Ⓓ **81019-2**

Zu jeder Zeit; Nicht klagen R. Tauber, orch (r1926) (12/92) (NIMB) Ⓓ **NI7833**
(12/92) (NIMB) ▭ **NC7833**

BERWALD, Franz (Adolf) *(1796–1868) Sweden*

Estrella de Soria– opera: 3 acts (1862—Stockholm) (Lib. O Prechtler)

EXCERPTS: 1. Overture.

1. Stockholm PO, T. Mann (r1959: rehearsal sequence) (CPRI) Ⓓ [2] **CAP22032**

1. Gothenburg SO, T. Mann (r1941) (CPRI) Ⓓ [2] **CAP22032**

1. Stockholm PO, S. Broman (pp1968) (CPRI) Ⓓ [2] **CAP22032**

The **Queen of Golconda– opera: 3 acts (1868—Stockholm) (Lib. after J B C Vial & E G F de Favières)**

EXCERPTS: 1. Overture.

1. RPO, U. Björlin (r1976) (6/94) (EMI) Ⓓ **CDM5 65073-2**

BIBALO , Antonio *(b 1922) Norway/Italy*

Gespenster– music drama: 3 acts (1981) (based on Ibsen's play 'Ghosts')

Mrs. Alving E. Thallaug
Oswald K. M. Sandve
Pastor Manders T. Lindhjem
Carpenter A. Heggen
Regine Engstrand A-L. Berntsen
Bergen SO, K. Ingebretsen (AURO) Ⓓ [2] **ACD4982**

BIBER, Heinrich Ignaz Franz von *(1644–1704) Bohemia*

Arminio– opera: 3 acts (1691-2—Salzburg) (Lib. F M Raffaelini)

Giulia B. Schlick
Arminio G. Schwarz
Nerone G. Türk
Segesta X. Meijer
Tiberio G. Kenda
Calligola B. Landauer
Vitellio M. Forster
Germanico H. Oswald
Erchino O. Rastbichler
Claudia I. Troupova
Climmia R. Schwarzer
Seiano F. Mehltretter
Salzburg Hofmusik, W. Brunner (r1994) (6/95) (CPO) Ⓓ [3] **CPO999 258-2**

BILLI, Vincenzo *(1869–1938) Italy*

Tizianello– operetta

E canta il grillo T. Ruffo, orch (r1929) (2/93) (PREI) Ⓓ [3] **89303(2)**

BIRTWISTLE , Sir Harrison *(b 1934) England*

Punch and Judy– opera: 1 act (1968—Aldeburgh) (Lib. S. Pruslin)

Punch S. Roberts
Judy; Fortune-teller J. DeGaetani
Pretty Polly; Witch P. Bryn-Julson
Lawyer P. Langridge
Choregos; Jack Ketch D. Wilson-Johnson
Doctor J. Tomlinson
London Sinfonietta, D. Atherton (12/89) (ETCE) Ⓓ [2] **KTC2014**

BIZET, Georges (Alexandre César Léopold) *(1838–1875) France*

Carmen– opera: 4 acts (1875—Paris) (Lib. Meilhac and Halévy)

EXCERPTS; 1. Prelude; 2. ACT 1: Sur la place, chacun place; 3. Avec la garde montante; 4a. La cloche a sonné; 4b. La voilà!; 5. L'amour est un oiseau rebelle (Habanera); 6. Carmen! sur tes pas; 7. Parle-moi de ma mère!; 8. Au secours!; 9. Voyons, brigadier; 10a. Près des remparts de Séville (Séguidille); 10b. Voici l'ordre. ACT 2: 11a. Entr'acte; 11b. Les tringles des sistres (Gypsy Song); 11c. Danse bohemienne; 11d. Vous avez quelque chose; 12a. Vivat, vivat le torero!; 12b. Votre toast (Toreador's Song); 13. Nous avons en tête une affaire!; 14. Halte-là! Qui va là?; 15a. Je vais danser en votre honneur; 15b. Au quartier!; 15c. La fleur que tu m'avais jetée; 15d. Non! tu ne m'aimes pas!; 16. Holà! Carmen!. ACT 3: 17a. Entr'acte; 17b. Écoute compagnon; 17c. Notre métier est bon; 18a. Mêlons! Coupons! (Card Scene); 18b. Voyons, que j'essaie à mon tour; 18c. En vain, pour éviter; 19. Quant au douanier; 20. Je dis que rien ne m'épouvante(Micaëla's aria); 21. Je suis Escamillo. ACT 4: 22a. Entr'acte; 22b. A deux cuartos!; 23. Les voici; 24. Si tu m'aimes, Carmen; 25. C'est toi! (Finale).

Carmen A. Baltsa
Don José J. Carreras
Micaëla L. Mitchell
Escamillo S. Ramey
Frasquita M. Merritt
Mercédès D. Kesling
Dancaïre B. Hubbard
Remendado A. Laciura
Moralès V. Hartman
Zuniga A. Berberian
Lillas Pastia N. Castel
NY Met Op Ballet, NY Met Op Chor, NY Met Op Orch, James Levine, B. Large (DG) ◖ [2] **072 409-1GH2**
(DG) ▣ **072 409-3GH**

Carmen M. Ewing
Don José L. Lima
Micaëla L. Vaduva
Escamillo G. Quilico
Frasquita J. Howarth
Mércèdes J. Rigby
Dancaïre B. Caproni
Remendado F. Egerton
Moralès C. Booth-Jones
Zuniga R. Earle
ROH Chor, ROHO, Z. Mehta, B. Gavin (pp) (MCEG) ▣ **VVD950**

Carmen M. Ewing
Don José B. McCauley
Micaëla M. McLaughlin
Escamillo D. Holloway
Frasquita E. Collier
Mercédès J. Rigby
Dancaïre G. Sandison
Remendado P. Evangelides
Moralès M. Walker
Zuniga X. Depraz
Lillas Pastia F. Davià
Glyndebourne Fest Chor, LPO, B. Haitink, P. Hall (r1985: with dialogue) (CAST) ▣ **CVI2018**

Carmen M. Ewing
Don José L. Lima
Micaëla L. Vaduva
Escamillo G. Quilico
Frasquita J. Howarth
Mércèdes J. Rigby
Dancaïre B. Caproni
Remendado F. Egerton
Moralès C. Booth-Jones
Zuniga R. Earle
ROH Chor, ROHO, Z. Mehta, B. Gavin (PION) ◖ [2] **PLMCD00091**

Carmen G. Bumbry
Don José J. Vickers
Micaëla M. Freni
Escamillo K. Paskalis
Frasquita E. Lublin
Mercédès V. Cortez
Dancaïre M. Trempont
Remendado A. Voli
Moralès C. Meloni
Zuniga B. Gontcharenko
Lillas Pastia R. Outin
Guide L. Frémont
Petits Chanteurs à la Croix de Bois, Paris Op Chor, Paris Op Orch, R. Frühbeck de Burgos (r1969/70: with dialogue) (CFP) Ⓓ [2] **CD-CFPD4454**
(8/86) (CFP) ▭ [2] **TC-CFPD4454**

Carmen A. Moffo
Don José F. Corelli
Micaëla H. Donath
Escamillo P. Cappuccilli
Frasquita A. Auger
Mércèdes J. Berbié
Dancaïre J-C. Benoit
Remendado K-E. Mercker
Moralès B. McDaniel
Zuniga J. Van Dam
Schoenberg Boys' Ch, Berlin Deutsche Op Chor, Berlin Deutsche Op Orch, L. Maazel (r1970s) (RCA) Ⓓ [2] **74321 25279-2**

Carmen A. Baltsa
Don José J. Carreras
Micaëla K. Ricciarelli
Escamillo J. Van Dam
Frasquita C. Barbaux
Mercédès J. Berbié
Dancaïre G. Quilico
Remendado H. Zednik
Moralès M. Melbye
Zuniga A. Malta
Schöneberg Boys' Ch, Paris Op. Chor, BPO, H. von Karajan (r1982: with dialogue) (12/83) (DG) Ⓓ [3] **410 088-2GH3**

Carmen J. Migenes
Don José P. Domingo
Micaëla F. Esham
Escamillo R. Raimondi
Frasquita L. Watson
Mercédès S. Daniel
Dancaïre J-P. Lafont
Remendado G. Garino
Moralès F. Le Roux
Zuniga J.P. Bogart
Lillas Pastia J. Guiomar
Guide A. di Leo
French Rad Chor, FNO, L. Maazel (with dialogue) (9/85) (ERAT) Ⓓ [3] **2292-45207-2**

Carmen T. Troyanos
Don José P. Domingo
Micaëla K. Te Kanawa
Escamillo J. Van Dam
Frasquita N. Burrowes
Mércèdes J. Berbié
Dancaïre M. Roux
Remendado M. Sénéchal
Moralès T. Allen
Zuniga P. Thau
Lillas Pastia J. Loreau
Guide G. Berbié
John Alldis Ch, Haberdashers' Aske's Sch Ch, LPO, G. Solti (with dialogue) (9/85) (DECC) Ⓓ [3] **414 489-2DH3**

Carmen T. Berganza
Don José P. Domingo
Micaëla I. Cotrubas
Escamillo S. Milnes
Frasquita Y. Kenny
Mercédès A. Nafé
Dancaïre G. Sandison
Remendado G. Pogson
Moralès S. Harling
Zuniga R. Lloyd
Watson Coll Boys' Chor, Ambrosian Sngrs, LSO, C. Abbado (r1977: with dialogue) (2/88) (DG) Ⓓ [3] **419 636-2GH3**

Carmen V. de los Angeles
Don José N. Gedda
Micaëla J. Micheau
Escamillo E. Blanc
Frasquita D. Monteil
Mercédès M. Croisier
Mercédès M. Linval
Dancaïre J-C. Benoit
Remendado M. Hamel
Moralès B. Plantey
Zuniga X. Depraz
Petits Chanteurs de Versailles, French Rad Maîtrise, French Rad Chor, FRNO, T. Beecham (r1958/9: with recits) (6/88) (EMI) Ⓓ [3] **CDS7 49240-2**

Carmen L. Price
Don José F. Corelli
Micaëla M. Freni
Escamillo R. Merrill
Frasquita M. Linval
Mercédès G. Macaux

Dancaïre J-C. Benoit
Remendado M. Besançon
Moralès B. Demigny
Zuniga F. Schooten

Vienna Boys' Ch, Vienna St Op Chor, VPO, H. von Karajan (r1963: with recits)
(10/88) (RCA) ① [3] **GD86199**

Carmen R. Stevens
Don José J. Peerce
Micaëla L. Albanese
Escamillo R. Merrill
Frasquita P. Lenchner
Mercédès M. Roggero
Dancaïre G. Cehanovsky
Remendado A. de Paolis
Moralès H. Thompson
Zuniga O. Hawkins

NY Lycée Français Children's Ch, R. Shaw Chorale, RCA Victor Orch, F. Reiner (r1951; with recits)
(5/89) (RCA) ① [3] **GD87981**

Carmen J. Norman
Don José N. Shicoff
Micaëla M. Freni
Escamillo S. Estes
Frasquita G. Raphanel
Mercédès J. Rigby
Dancaïre F. Le Roux
Remendado G. Garino
Moralès N. Rivenq
Zuniga J-P. Courtis

French Rad Maîtrise, French Rad Chor, FNO, S. Ozawa (with dialogue)
(8/89) (PHIL) ① [3] **422 366-2PH3**

Carmen M. Horne
Don José J. McCracken
Micaëla A. Maliponte
Escamillo T. Krause
Frasquita C. Boky
Mercédès M. Baldwin
Dancaïre; Lillas Pastia R. Christopher
Remendado A. Velis
Moralès R. Gibbs
Zuniga D. Gramm

NY Met Op Children's Ch, Manhattan Op Chor, NY Met Op Orch, L. Bernstein (r1972: with dialogue)
(9/91) (DG) ① [3] **427 440-2GX3**

Carmen M. Callas
Don José N. Gedda
Micaëla A. Guiot
Escamillo R. Massard
Frasquita N. Sautereau
Mercédès J. Berbié
Dancaire J-P. Vauquelin
Remendado J. Pruvost
Remendado M. Maievski
Moralès C. Calès
Zuniga J. Mars

R. Duclos Ch, J. Pesneaud Children's Ch, Paris Op Orch, G. Prêtre (r1964: with recits)
(5/92) (EMI) ① [2] **CDS7 54368-2**

Carmen E. Destinn
Carmen O. Metzger
Don José K. Jörn
Micaëla M. Nast
Escamillo H. Bachmann
Frasquita M. Dietrich
Mercédès G. Parbs
Dancaïre J. Lieban
Remendado R. Krasa
Moralès; Zuniga F. Dahn

Berlin Court Op Chor, orch, B. Seidler-Winkler (r1908: Ger)
(12/94) (SUPR) ① [12] **11 2136-2(3)**

Carmen R. Resnik
Don José M. del Monaco
Micaëla J. Sutherland
Escamillo T. Krause
Frasquita G. Spanellys
Mercédès Y. Minton
Dancaïre J. Prudent
Remendado A. Hallett
Moralès C. Calès
Zuniga R. Geay

Geneva Grand Th Chor, SRO, T. Schippers (r1963)
(7/95) (DECC) ① [2] **443 871-2DF2**

Carmen S. Michel
Don José R. Jobin
Micaëla M. Angelici
Escamillo M. Dens
Frasquita G. Chellet
Mercédès R. Notti
Dancaïre J. Vieuille
Remendado F. Leprin
Moralès J. Thirache
Zuniga X. Smati

Paris Opéra-Comique Chor, Paris Opéra-Comique Orch, A. Cluytens (r1950: with dialogue)
(9/95) (EMI) ① [2] **CMS5 65318-2**

Carmen B. Uria-Monzon
Don José C. Papis
Micaëla L. Vaduva
Escamillo V. le Texier
Frasquita M. Castets
Mércèdes M. Olmeda
Dancaïre F. Leguérinel
Remendado T. Trégan
Moralès O. Lallouette
Zuniga L. Sarrazin
Lillas Pastia P. Renard

Bordeaux CNR Children's Ch, Bordeaux Th Chor, Bordeaux Aquitaine Orch, A. Lombard (r1994)
(10/95) (AUVI) ① [2] **V4734**

Excs J. Norman, N. Shicoff, S. Estes, FNO, S. Ozawa (PHIL) ▣ **070 118-3PH**
Excs P. Domingo (CAST) ▣ **CVI2021**
Excs J. Migenes, P. Domingo, R. Raimondi, F. Esham, S. Daniel, L. Watson, J.P. Bogart, F. Le Roux, French Rad. Chor, FNO, L. Maazel (ERAT) ⓞⓞ **2292-45209-5**
Excs J. Migenes, P. Domingo, R. Raimondi, F. Esham, S. Daniel, L. Watson, J.P. Bogart, F. Le Roux, French Rad. Chor, FNO, L. Maazel
(12/84) (ERAT) ① **2292-45209-2**
(ERAT) ▭ **2292-45209-4**
Excs T. Mazaroff, E. Réthy, E. Brems, A. Arnold, P. Pierotic, G. Monthy, D. Komarek, O. Levko-Antosch, M. Bokor, Vienna St Op Chor, Vienna St Op Orch, B. Walter (pp1937: Ger)
(2/95) (SCHW) ① [2] **314572**
Excs P. Gallois, London Fest Orch, R. Pople (r1993: arr fl: de Borne/Pierre)
(5/95) (DG) ① **445 822-2GH**
Fantasy A. Griminelli, Philh, L. Magiera (arr Guiot) (DECC) ⓞⓞ **436 320-5DH**
Fantasy M. Vengerov (r1990)
(CANY) ① **EC3655-2**
Fantasy A. Griminelli, Philh, L. Magiera (arr Guiot) (11/91) (DECC) ◐ **071 150-1DH**
(11/91) (DECC) ▣ **071 150-3DH**
Fantasy C. Arrau (r1928: arr Busoni)
(9/92) (PEAR) ① **GEMMCD9928**
Suite NBC SO, A. Toscanini (r1952: arr Toscanini) (RCA) ① [2] **GD60274**
1. LPO, G. Solti (DECC) ① **433 822-2DH**
(DECC) ▭ **433 822-4DH**
1. NY Met Op Orch, James Levine
(DECC) ◐ **071 142-1DH**
(DECC) ▣ **071 142-3DH**
1. Monte Carlo Nat Op Orch, L. Frémaux
(DG) ① [2] **447 364-2GDB2**
1. Vienna St Op Orch, B. Walter (pp1937)
(6/94) (SCHW) ① **314502**
1, 3, 5, 7, 10a, 11b, 12b, 15c, 18a, 20, 23, 25. M. Callas, N. Gedda, A. Guiot, R. Massard, N. Sautereau, J. Berbié, C. Calès, J. Mars, R Duclos Ch, J. Pesneaud Children's Ch, Paris Op. Orch, G. Prêtre (r1964)
(EMI) ① **CDM7 63075-2**
1-3, 5, 7, 10a, 11b, 11d, 12a, 12b, 15c, 18c, 22b, 25. A. Baltsa, J. Carreras, K. Ricciarelli, J. Van Dam, C. Barbaux, J. Berbié, G. Quilico, H. Zednik, M. Melbye, A. Malta, Paris Op. Chor, BPO, H. von Karajan (r1982)
(2/85) (DG) ① **413 322-2GH**
(10/84) (DG) ▭ **413 322-4GH**
1, 4a, 4b, 5, 10a, 11b, 12b, 13, 15b, 15c, 18a-c, 20, 25. R. Resnik, M. del Monaco, G. Spanellys, Y. Minton, T. Krause, J. Prudent, A. Hallett, J. Sutherland, Geneva Grand Th Chor, SRO, T. Schippers (1/92) (DECC) ① **433 626-2DSP**
(1/92) (DECC) ▭ **433 626-4DSP**
1, 4a, 4b, 5, 7, 10a, 11b, 12b, 15c, 20, 21, 23-25. T. Berganza, P. Domingo, S. Milnes, I. Cotrubas, Y. Kenny, A. Nafé, R. Lloyd, Watson Coll Boys' Chor, Ambrosian Sngrs, LSO, C. Abbado (r1977) (DG) ① **439 496-2GCL**
(DG) ▭ **439 496-4GCL**
1, 4a, 4b, 10a, 11-13, 15a-d, 17a, 18a, 20, 22a, 25. L. Price, F. Corelli, R. Merrill, M. Freni, M. Linval, G. Macaux, Vienna St Op Chor, VPO, H. von Karajan (RCA) ① **GD60190**
(RCA) ▭ **GK60190**
1, 4b, 5, 10a, 10b, 11b, 12a, 13, 15c, 15d, 18a-c, 20, 25. T. Troyanos, P. Domingo, J. van Dam, K. Te Kanawa, John Alldis Ch, LPO, G. Solti (r1975) (DECC) ① **436 310-2DA**
(DECC) ▭ **436 310-4DA**
1, 5, 10a, 11b, 12b, 13, 15c, 15d, 18a, 18c, 20, 25. J. Norman, M. Freni, N. Shicoff, S. Estes, G. Raphanel, J. Rigby, G. Garino, F. Le Roux, French Rad Chor, FNO, S. Ozawa
(PHIL) ① **426 040-2PH**
(PHIL) ▭ **426 040-4PH**
1, 5, 10a, 11b, 12b, 13, 15c, 15d, 18a, 18c, 20, 25. J. Norman, M. Freni, N. Shicoff, S. Estes, G. Raphanel, J. Rigby, G. Garino, F. Le Roux, French Rad Chor, FNO, S. Ozawa
(PHIL) ⓞⓞ **426 040-5PH**
1, 5, 10a, 17a M. Callas, ROHO, G. Prêtre (pp1962) (3/95) (EMI) ◐ **LDB4 91283-1**
(3/95) (EMI) ▣ **MVD4 91283-3**
3. J. Bálint, N. Mercz (r1992: arr fl/hp: Mercz)
(12/94) (NAXO) ① **8 550741**
4a ENON Chor, S. Westrop, J. Pryce-Jones
(12/85) (MAX) ▭ **MSCB3**
4a, 19, 23. L. Price, M. Linval, G. Macaux, Vienna St Op Chor, Vienna Boys' Ch, VPO, H. von Karajan (RCA) ① **GD60205**
4b, 5. R. Crespin, Geneva Grand Th Chor, SRO, A. Lombard (r1970/1) (DECC) ① **440 416-2DM**
4b, 10a, 15c J. Rhodes, A. Lance, Paris Op Orch, R. Benzi (r1959)
(10/94) (PHIL) ① [2] **442 272-2PM2**
5. M. Caballé, Philh, J. Collado
(11/92) (RCA) ▭ [2] **RK61044**
5. M. Callas, Paris Op Orch, G. Prêtre
(EMI) ① **CDC7 49502-2**
5. M. Callas, FRNO, G. Prêtre
(EMIL) ① **CDZ105**
5. M. Callas, Paris Cons, G. Prêtre
(CFP) ① **CD-CFP4277**
5. M. Horne, Vienna Op Orch, H. Lewis
(DECC) ① **433 064-2DWO**
5. E. Obraztsova, Czech SO, A. Krieger (pp1991) (IMP) ① **MCD42**
5. V. de los Angeles, FRN Chor, FRNO, T. Beecham (EMI) ① **CDM7 64359-2**
5. M. Mödl, Berlin City Op Orch, A. Rother (Ger: r1962) (PREI) ① **90136**
5. M. Callas, FRNO, G. Prêtre
(EMI) ① **CDC7 54702-2**
(EMI) ▭ **EL754702-4**
5. E. Obraztsova, Ambrosian Op Chor, Philh, G. Patanè (r1977) (CFP) ① **CD-CFP4602**
(CFP) ▭ **TC-CFP4602**
5. C. Powell, RPO, R. Stapleton (r1990)
(RPO) ① [2] **CDRPD9006**
(RPO) ▭ [2] **ZCRPD9006**
5. G. Simionato, Santa Cecilia Academy Orch, F. Previtali (r1956) (DECC) ① **440 406-2DM**
5. M. Horne, Vienna Op Orch, H. Lewis (r1967)
(DECC) ① **433 440-2DA**
(DECC) ▭ **433 440-4DA**
5. T. Troyanos, LPO, G. Solti (r1975)
(DECC) ① **440 947-2DH**
(DECC) ▭ **440 947-4DH**
5. T. Berganza, Cordoba Grand Th Chor, Seville SO, L. A. Garcia-Navarro
(RCA) ① **09026 61440-2**
(RCA) ▭ **09026 61440-4**
5. C. Powell, RPO, R. Stapleton (r1990)
(IMP) ① **PCDS23**
(IMP) ▭ **PCDSC23**
5. M. Davydova, anon (r1913: Russ)
(PEAR) ① [3] **GEMMCDS9111(2)**
5. L. Homer, anon (r1905)
(IRCC) ① **IRCC-CD810**
5. T. Troyanos, John Alldis Ch, LPO, G. Solti (r1975) (DECC) ① **443 378-2DM**
5. T. Berganza, Seville SO, G. Navarro
(RCA) ① **74321 25821-2**
(RCA) ▭ **74321 25821-4**
5. L. Price, VPO, H. von Karajan (r1963)
(RCA) ① **74321 24284-2**
(RCA) ▭ **74321 24284-4**
5. V. de los Angeles, FRNO, T. Beecham (r1958)
(EMI) ① **CDM5 65579-2**
5. J. Lloyd Webber, RPO, N. Cleobury (arr vc)
(3/87) (PHIL) ① **416 698-2PH**
5. C. Supervia, orch, G. Cloëz (r1930)
(10/89) (NIMB) ① **NI7801**
(NIMB) ▭ **NC7801**
5. I. Minghini-Cattaneo, orch, J. Barbirolli (Ital: r1929) (6/90) (PREI) ① **89008**
5. E. Teodorini, anon (r1903)
(5/91) (SYMP) ① **SYMCD1077**
5. J. Tourel, Philh, W. Susskind (r1951)
(4/92) (EMI) ① [7] **CHS7 69741-2(1)**
5. E. Calvé, anon (r1902)
(3/93) (SYMP) ① **SYMCD1100**
5. D. Soffel, Swedish CO, M. Liljefors (pp1986)
(4/93) (CPRI) ① **CAP21428**

15c M. Lorenz, Berlin St Op Orch, C. Schmalstich (Ger: r1928) (PREI) Ⓓ **89053**
15c P. Domingo, VPO, James Levine (DECC) ◐ **071 142-1DH** (DECC) ▣ **071 142-3DH**
15c J. Carreras, ROHO, J. Delacôte (EMI) Ⓓ **CDM7 64359-2**
15c J. Carreras, ROHO, J. Delacôte (EMI) Ⓓ **CDC7 54524-2**
15c J. Björling, B. Bokstedt (BLUE) Ⓓ **ABCD042**
15c E. Caruso, orch, W.B. Rogers (r1909) (RCA) Ⓓ **09026 61244-2**
15c N. Todisco, Verona Arena Orch, A. Guadagno (pp1992) (MCI) Ⓓ **MCCD099**
15c G. di Stefano, Zurich Tonhalle Orch, F. Patanè (r1958) (DECC) Ⓓ **440 403-2DM**
15c G. Di Stefano, Zurich Tonhalle Orch, F. Patanè (r1959) (BELA) Ⓓ **450 005-2** (BELA) ⊟ **450 005-4**
15c G. Nelepp, Bolshoi Th Orch, V. Nebolsin (r c1950: Russ) (PREI) Ⓓ **89081**
15c F. Corelli, VPO, H. von Karajan (RCA) Ⓓ **09026 61886-2** (RCA) ⊟ **09026 61886-4**
15c D. Smirnov, orch (r1912: Russ) (PEAR) Ⓓ **GEMMCD9106**
15c M. del Monaco, Milan SO, A. Quadri (r1951: Ital) (TEST) Ⓓ **SBT1039**
15c H. Roswaenge, Berlin St Op Orch, B. Seidler-Winkler (r1938: Ger) (PREI) Ⓓ [2] **89211**
15c R. Crooks, Berlin St Op Orch, C. Schmalstich (r1927: Ger) (PEAR) Ⓓ **GEMMCD9093**
15c P. Domingo, French Rad Chor, FNO, L. Maazel (ERAT) Ⓓ **4509-91715-2** (ERAT) ⊟ **4509-91715-4**
15c E. Scaramberg, anon (r1905) (SYMP) Ⓓ **SYMCD1173**
15c E. Caruso, orch (r1909) (ASV) Ⓓ **CDAJA5137** (ASV) ⊟ **ZCAJA5137**
15c P. Domingo, Los Angeles PO, C.M. Giulini (r1980) (DG) Ⓓ **445 525-2GMA** (DG) ⊟ **445 525-4GMA**
15c D. Borgioli, orch (r c1924: Ital) (PEAR) Ⓓ **GEMMCD9091**
15c F. Corelli, Milan RAI SO, O. de Fabritiis (bp1956: Ital) (FONI) Ⓓ **CDMR5014**
15c P. Franz, orch (r1911) (PREI) Ⓓ **89099**
15c F. de Lucia, anon (r1902: Ital) (BONG) Ⓓ [2] **GB1064/5-2**
15c B. Gigli, La Scala Orch, F. Ghione (r1935: Ital) (PEAR) Ⓓ [2] **GEMMCDS9176**
15c C. Kullman, orch, O. Dobrindt (r1932: Eng) (MMOI) Ⓓ **CDMOIR429**
15c F. Corelli, VPO, H. von Karajan (r1963) (RCA) Ⓓ **09026 62689-2**
15c R. Alagna, LPO, R. Armstrong (EMI) Ⓓ **CDC5 55540-2** (EMI) ⊟ **EL5 55540-4**
15c F. de la Mora, WNO Orch, C. Mackerras (r1994-5) (TELA) Ⓓ **CD80411**
15c L. Pavarotti, Vienna Volksoper Orch, L. Magiera (7/86) (DECC) Ⓓ [2] **417 011-2DH2**
15c P. Domingo, Los Angeles PO, C.M. Giulini (7/86) (DG) Ⓓ **415 366-2GH**
15c J. Björling, Hilversum RO, F. Weissmann (pp1939) (8/88) (BLUE) Ⓓ **ABCD006**
15c B. Gigli, La Scala Orch, F. Ghione (Ital: r1935) (9/88) (EMI) Ⓓ **CDH7 61051-2**
15c G. Thill, Orch, P. Gaubert (r1927) (1/89) (EMI) Ⓓ **CDM7 69548-2**
15c R. Tauber, orch (Ger: r1923) (7/89) (PEAR) Ⓓ **GEMMCD9327**
15c M. Fleta, orch (r1922: Ital) (2/90) (PREI) Ⓓ **89002**
15c H. Roswaenge, Berlin St Op Orch, B. Seidler-Winkler (Ger: r1938) (5/90) (PEAR) Ⓓ **GEMMCD9394**
15c H. Roswaenge, Berlin St Op Orch, B. Seidler-Winkler (r1938: Ger) (5/90) (PREI) Ⓓ **89018**
15c G. Lauri-Volpi, orch, Rosario Bourdon (r1930) (9/90) (PREI) Ⓓ **89012**
15c E. Caruso, anon (Ital: r1905) (12/90) (PEAR) Ⓓ [3] **EVC1(1)**
15c F. Ansseau, orch, P. Coppola (r1927) (1/91) (PREI) Ⓓ **89022**
15c E. Caruso, orch (r1909) (3/91) (PEAR) Ⓓ [3] **EVC2**
15c E. Caruso, orch (Ital: r1909) (3/91) (PEAR) Ⓓ [3] **EVC2**
15c F. Giraud, anon (Ital: r1904) (5/91) (SYMP) Ⓓ **SYMCD1077**
15c E. Caruso, orch, W.B. Rogers (r1909: 2 vers, Fr & Ital) (7/91) (RCA) Ⓓ [12] **GD60495(3)**
15c E. Caruso, anon (Ital: r1905) (7/91) (RCA) Ⓓ [12] **GD60495(1)**
15c A. Cortis, La Scala Orch, C. Sabajno (Ital: r1929) (10/91) (PREI) Ⓓ **89043**
15c G. Zenatello, orch, Rosario Bourdon (Ital: r1929) (11/91) (CLUB) Ⓓ **CL99-025**
15c G. Zenatello, orch, Rosario Bourdon (Ital: r1929) (11/91) (PREI) Ⓓ **89038**
15c H. Roswaenge, orch (r1928: Ger) (2/92) (PREI) Ⓓ [2] **89201**
15c R. Tauber, orch, N. Treep (bp1939) (2/92) (LYRC) Ⓓ [2] **SRO830**
15c C. Dalmores, orch (r1907) (7/92) (PEAR) Ⓓ [3] **GEMMCDS9924(1)**
15c Britannia Building Soc Band, H. Snell (r1990; arr Snell: brass band) (8/92) (DOYE) Ⓓ **DOYCD004** (DOYE) ⊟ **DOYMC004**
15c G. Thill, orch, P. Gaubert (r1927) (10/92) (TEST) Ⓓ **SBT1005**
15c R. Tauber, orch, K. Besl (Ger: r1923) (12/92) (NIMB) Ⓓ **NI7830** (12/92) (NIMB) ⊟ **NC7830**
15c G. Lauri-Volpi, orch, Rosario Bourdon (r1930) (7/93) (NIMB) Ⓓ **NI7845**
15c J. Björling, orch, N. Grevillius (r1938) (10/93) (NIMB) Ⓓ **NI7842**
15c J. Björling, orch, N. Grevillius (r1938) (10/93) (EMI) Ⓓ **CDH7 64707-2**
15c P. Domingo, LPO, G. Solti (r1975) (10/93) (DECC) Ⓓ **436 463-2DM** (10/93) (DECC) ⊟ **436 463-4DM**
15c A. Cortis, La Scala Orch, C. Sabajno (r1929: Ital) (3/94) (NIMB) Ⓓ **NI7850**
15c F. Corelli, VPO, H. von Karajan (r1963) (4/94) (RCA) Ⓓ [6] **09026 61580-2(7)**
15c G. Zenatello, orch (r1908: Ital) (5/94) (PEAR) Ⓓ [4] **GEMMCDS9073(1)**
15c G. Zenatello, orch (r1908: Ital) (5/94) (SYMP) Ⓓ **SYMCD1168**
15c G. Zenatello, orch, Rosario Bourdon (r1929: Ital) (5/94) (PEAR) Ⓓ [4] **GEMMCDS9074(2)**
15c G. Zenatello, orch (r1916: Ital) (5/94) (PEAR) Ⓓ [4] **GEMMCDS9074(1)**
15c P. Domingo, LSO, C. Abbado (r1977) (6/94) (BELA) Ⓓ **450 121-2** (6/94) (BELA) ⊟ **450 121-4**
15c J. Björling, orch, N. Grevillius (r1938) (9/94) (IMP) Ⓓ **GLRS103**
15c J. Björling, orch, N. Grevillius (r1938) (9/94) (CONI) Ⓓ **CDHD214** (9/94) (CONI) ⊟ **MCHD214**
15c L. David, anon (r1905) (12/94) (SYMP) Ⓓ **SYMCD1172**
15c J. Björling, orch, N. Grevillius (r1938) (12/94) (MMOI) Ⓓ **CDMOIR425**
15c F. de Lucia, orch (r1907: Ital) (1/95) (SYMP) Ⓓ **SYMCD1149**
15c J. Johnston, ROHO, M. Mudie (r1948: Eng) (4/95) (TEST) Ⓓ **SBT1058**
15c E. Caruso, orch (r1909) (7/95) (NIMB) Ⓓ **NI7866**
15c H. Nash, Liverpool PO, M. Sargent (r1944: Eng) (11/95) (PEAR) Ⓓ **GEMMCD9175**
15c A. Davies, A. Bryn Parri (r1994) (11/95) (SAIN) Ⓓ **SCDC2085**
15c B. Heppner, Munich RO, R. Abbado (r1993/4) (11/95) (RCA) Ⓓ **09026 62504-2**
15c, 15d, 25. P. Domingo, T. Troyanos, John Alldis Ch, LPO, G. Solti (r1975) (DECC) Ⓓ **440 410-2DM**
15c, 17a P. Dvorský, Bratislava RSO, O. Lenárd (5/92) (NAXO) Ⓓ **8 550343**
15c, 25. P. Domingo, V. Vergara, VPO, James Levine (DG) ◐ **072 187-1GH** (DG) ▣ **072 187-3GH**
15c, 25. P. Domingo, V. Vergara, VPO, James Levine (11/89) (DG) ◐ **072 110-1GH**
15c, 25. P. Domingo, T. Berganza, Ambrosian Sngrs, LSO, C. Abbado (5/93) (DG) Ⓓ **431 104-2GB**
15d T. Ralf, F. Beckmann, Berlin St Op Orch, B. Seidler-Winkler (r1942: Ger) (10/94) (PREI) Ⓓ **89077**
17a J. Stinton, A. Brewer (arr fl/hp) (COLL) Ⓓ **Coll1008-2**
17a FNO, L. Maazel (TELD) Ⓓ **4509-90055-2**
17a M. Beier, M. Eriksson (r1986) (DANA) Ⓓ **DACOCD306**
17a FRNO, T. Beecham (r1960) (CFP) Ⓓ **CD-CFP4659** (CFP) ⊟ **TC-CFP4659**
17a, 22a La Scala Orch, A. Guarnieri (r1927) (BONG) Ⓓ **GB1039-2**
18a M. Garden, orch (r1929) (PEAR) Ⓓ **GEMMCD9130**
18c M. Gay, orch (r1911) (7/92) (PEAR) Ⓓ [3] **GEMMCDS9924(2)**
18c M. Garden, orch (r1929) (8/93) (SYMP) Ⓓ **SYMCD1136**
18c M. Garden, orch, N. Shilkret (r1929) (8/94) (ROMO) Ⓓ **81008-2**
20. M. Major, NZ SO, P. Gamba (KIWI) Ⓓ **CDTRL075**
20. K. Te Kanawa, LPO, G. Solti (DECC) Ⓓ **433 064-2DWO**
20. K. Te Kanawa, LPO, G. Solti (r1975) (DECC) Ⓓ **436 300-2DX** (DECC) ⊟ **436 300-4DX**
20. L. Price, LSO, E. Downes (r1960s-70) (RCA) Ⓓ **09026 62596-2**
20. G. Farrar, orch (r1908) (NIMB) Ⓓ **NI7872**
20. P. Lorengar, Santa Cecilia Academy Orch, G. Patanè (r1966) (DECC) Ⓓ **443 931-2DM**
20. K. Te Kanawa, LPO, G. Solti (11/87) (DECC) Ⓓ **417 645-2DH**
20. M. Freni, La Scala Orch, A. Votto (10/89) (EMI) Ⓓ **CDM7 63110-2**
20. C. Muzio, orch (r1924) (5/90) (BOGR) Ⓓ [2] **BIM705-2**
20. E. Norena, orch, G. Cloëz (r1929) (3/91) (PREI) Ⓓ **89041**
20. Lotte Lehmann, orch (Ger: r1917) (6/92) (PREI) Ⓓ [3] **89302**
20. L. Tetrazzini, orch (Ital: r1911) (9/92) (EMI) Ⓓ [3] **CHS7 63802-2(1)**
20. L. Tetrazzini, orch (Ital: r1911) (9/92) (PEAR) Ⓓ **GEMMCD9222**
20. L. Tetrazzini, orch (Ital: r1914) (9/92) (PEAR) Ⓓ **GEMMCD9225**
20. L. Price, LSO, E. Downes (12/92) (RCA) Ⓓ [4] **09026 61236-2**
20. M. Caballé, New Philh, R. Giovaninetti (r1970) (5/93) (DG) Ⓓ **431 103-2GB**
20. I. Seefried, Vienna SO, F. Leitner (r1953) (9/93) (DG) Ⓓ [2] **437 677-2GDO2**
20. E. Eames, orch (r1906) (11/93) (ROMO) Ⓓ [2] **81001-2**
20. C. Muzio, orch (r1924) (1/94) (ROMO) Ⓓ [2] **81005-2**
20. M. Freni, VPO, H. von Karajan (r1963) (4/94) (RCA) Ⓓ [6] **09026 61580-2(8)**
20. E. Rethberg, orch (r1920: Ger) (7/94) (PREI) Ⓓ **89051**
20. P. Alarie, Lamoureux Orch, P. Dervaux (r1953) (11/94) (PHIL) Ⓓ [2] **438 953-2PM2**
20. C. Muzio, orch (r1918) (1/95) (ROMO) Ⓓ [2] **81010-2**
20. E. Eames, orch (r1906) (1/95) (NIMB) Ⓓ **NI7860**
20. E. Rethberg, Berlin SO, F. Weissmann (r1930: Ger) (10/95) (ROMO) Ⓓ [2] **81014-2**
20. I. Galante, Latvian Nat SO, A. Vilumanis (r1994) (11/95) (CAMP) Ⓓ **RRCD1335** (11/95) (CAMP) ⊟ **RRMC8035**
21. M. Journet, F. Ansseau, orch, P. Coppola (r1927) (PREI) Ⓓ **89021**
22a LSO, R. Frühbeck de Burgos (IMP) Ⓓ **PCDS012** (IMP) ⊟ **PCDSC012**
22a LSO, R. Frühbeck de Burgos (IMP) Ⓓ **PCDS014** (IMP) ⊟ **PCDSC014**
22a La Scala Orch, A. Toscanini (r1921) (NIMB) Ⓓ **NI7872**
22a Empire Brass (r1992; arr. R. Smedvig) (1/94) (TELA) Ⓓ **CD80305** (1/94) (TELA) ⊟ **CS30305**
22b, 23. Southend Boys' Ch, LSC, LSO, R. Hickox (r1987/8) (IMP) Ⓓ [3] **TCD1073**
22b, 23. Southend Boys' Ch, LSC, LSO, R. Hickox (4/89) (IMP) Ⓓ **PCD908**
23. Haberdashers' Aske's Sch Ch, ROH Chor, ROHO, B. Haitink (12/89) (EMI) Ⓓ **CDC7 49849-2**
24. M. Klose, M. Wittrisch, W. Grossmann, T. Gerson, S. Fischer, Berlin St Op Orch, F. Zweig (r1932: Ger) (7/95) (PREI) Ⓓ **89082**
25. N. Vallin, C. Friant, orch, G. Cloëz (r1927-32) (PEAR) Ⓓ **GEMMCD9948**
25. J. Rodgers, E. Barham, English Northern Philh, P. Daniel (r1992) (EMI) Ⓓ **CDC7 54785-2**
25. P. Domingo, D. Graves, Rio de Janeiro Municipal Th Chor, Rio de Janeiro Municipal Th Orch, J. DeMain (pp1992) (SONY) ◐ **SLV48362** (SONY) ▣ **SHV48362**

25. R. Resnik, M. del Monaco, Geneva Grand Th Chor, SRO, T. Schippers (r1963) (BELA) ① **450 006-2** (BELA) ▭ **450 006-4**
25. A. Baltsa, J. Carreras, Tallis Chbr Ch, LSO, P. Domingo (r1990-91) (SONY) ① **SK53968**
25. A. Pertile, A. Buades, La Scala Orch, L. Molajoli (Ital: r1932) (9/90) (PREI) ① **89007**
25. G. Zenatello, M. Gay, orch, Rosario Bourdon (Ital: r1930) (11/91) (CLUB) ① **CL99-025**
25. G. Zenatello, M. Gay, orch, Rosario Bourdon (Ital: r1930) (11/91) (PREI) ① **89038**
25. E. Leisner, H. Roswaenge, orch (r1928: Ger) (2/92) (PREI) ① [2] **89201**
25. E. Zbrueva, E. Witting, orch (r1911: Russ) (6/93) (PEAR) ① [3] **GEMMCDS9004/6(2)**
25. A. Davidov, E. Zbrueva, chor, orch (r1907: Russ) (6/93) (PEAR) ① [3] **GEMMCDS9007/9(1)**
25. G. Zenatello, M. Gay, chor, orch, Rosario Bourdon (r1930: Ital) (5/94) (PEAR) ① [4] **GEMMCDS9074(2)**

Carmen– concert suites from opera
SUITE NO 1: 1. Prelude, Act 1 (Les toréadors); 2. Entr'acte, Act 2 (Les dragons d'Alcala); 3. Entr'acte, Act 3 (Intermezzo); 4. Entr'acte, Act 4 (Aragonaise); 5. Séguedille, Act 1. SUITE NO. 2: 6. Avec la garde montante, Act 1; 7. Habanera, Act 1; 8. Danse bohème, Act 2; 9. Marche des Contrebandiers, Act 3; 10. Nocturne, Act 3 (Micaëla's aria); 11. Chanson de Toréador.
German Fest Orch, A. Scholz (CAVA) ① **CAVCD018**
Bamberg SO, G. Prêtre (EURO) ① **GD69322**
E. Glennie, LSO, B. Wordsworth, R. Greenberg (arr Shchedrin) (DECC) ◐ **071 121-1DH** (DECC) ▭ **071 121-3DH**
Montreal SO, C. Dutoit (DECC) ◯◯ **417 839-5DH**
Segovia Gtr Qt (r1992; arr gtr qt) (OTTA) ① **OTRC79239**
Ulster Orch, Y. P. Tortelier (r1989) (CHAN) ① **CHAN6600**
Lamoureux Concerts Orch, I. Markevitch (r1959) (BELA) ① **450 043-2** (BELA) ▭ **450 043-4**
Philh, I. Westrip (r1993) (IMP) ① **PCD1075**
Mexico City PO, E. Bátiz (ASV) ① **CDQS6133**
Montreal SO, C. Dutoit (6/88) (DECC) ① **417 839-2DH**
RPO, M. Ermler (r1993) (7/94) (TRIN) ① **TRP002** (TRIN) ▭ **MCTRP002**
Paris Orch, S. Bychkov (r1993) (12/94) (PHIL) ① **442 128-2PH** (12/94) (PHIL) ▭ **442 128-4PH**
Excs LSO, J. Mauceri (12/90) (DECC) ▭ **084 474-3**
Excs Slovak PO, A. Bramall (10/90) (NAXO) ① **8 550061**
Excs Budapest PO, J. Sándor (10/90) (LASE) ① **15 614** (10/90) (LASE) ▭ **79 614**
Excs Paris Bastille Orch, Myung-Whun Chung (11/91) (DG) ① **431 778-2GH**
Excs Malmö SO, J. DePreist (1/93) (BIS) ① **BIS-CD570**
1. LSO, R. Frühbeck de Burgos (IMP) ① **PCDS8** (IMP) ▭ **PCDSC8**
1. LSO, R. Frühbeck de Burgos (IMP) ① [3] **TCD1014**
1. LSO, R. Frühbeck de Burgos (IMP) ① **PCDS018** (IMP) ▭ **PCDSC018**
1. Mexico City PO, E. Bátiz (ASV) ① **CDQS6121**
1-11. Paris RSO, L. Bertrand (ROSE) ① **3201**
1, 2. Lamoureux Concerts Orch, A. Dorati (r1959) (10/94) (PHIL) ① [2] **442 272-2PM2**
1, 2, 3, 4. New Philh, I. Markevitch (r1960) (BELA) ① **461 001-2** (BELA) ▭ **461 001-4**
1, 3, 4, 6, 7. RPO, M. Reed (RPO) ① [2] **CDRPD9001** (RPO) ▭ [2] **ZCRPD9001**
1-4. Madrid SO, G.P. Sanzogno (pp1991) (IMP) ① [2] **DPCD998**
1-4. Madrid SO, G.P. Sanzogno (RNE) ① [2] **650004**
1-4. Paris Orch, D. Barenboim (r1972) (EMI) ① **CDM7 64869-2**
1-4. Luxembourg Rad & TV SO, L. de Froment (FORL) ① **FF028**
1-4. Bamberg SO, F. Leitner (r1950s) (DG) ① [2] **447 361-2GDB2**
1-4. LSO, C. Abbado (12/88) (DG) ① **423 472-2GGA**
1-4. FRNO, T. Beecham (r1958) (7/90) (EMI) ① **CDM7 63379-2**
1-4. BPO, H. von Karajan (8/91) (DG) ① **431 160-2GR**
1-4, 6, 8. LPO, T. Beecham (r1939) (6/94) (DUTT) ① **CDLX7003**
1-4, 6, 8, 9. Philadelphia, L. Stokowski (r1927) (8/95) (BIDD) ① **WHL012**
1-4, 7, 8. RPO, M. Reed (r1990) (RPO) ① **CDRPO5010**
1-5. Luxembourg Rad & TV SO, L. de Froment (FORL) ① **FF027**
1-5, 7. Paris Cons, R. Leibowitz (r1960) (CHES) ① **Chesky CD61**
1-5, 7. LSO, R. Frühbeck de Burgos (1/89) (IMP) ① **PCD905**
1-5, 7. Cincinnati SO, J. López-Cobos (11/90) (TELA) ① **CD80224**
1-6. Detroit SO, P. Paray (r1956) (8/93) (MERC) ① **434 321-2MM**
1-8. Philadelphia, E. Ormandy (SONY) ① **SBK48159**
1-8. LSO, N. Marriner (r1978) (PHIL) ① **446 198-2PM**
1-8. St. Louis SO, L. Slatkin (r1979) (10/84) (TELA) ① **CD80048**
1-8. NYPO, L. Bernstein (r1967) (11/92) (SONY) ① **SMK47531**
3. S. Kudo, R. Talitman (r1991) (DINT) ① **DICD920141**
4. LSO, R. Frühbeck de Burgos (IMP) ① **PCDS016** (IMP) ▭ **PCDSC016**
4. La Scala Orch, A. Toscanini (r1921) (11/92) (RCA) ① **GD60315**
6. LSO, R. Frühbeck de Burgos (IMP) ① **PCDS15** (IMP) ▭ **PCDSC15**
10. H. Britton (arr Britton) (ASV) ① **CDWHL2064** (ASV) ▭ **ZCWHL2064**
10. Stuttgart RSO, N. Marriner (r1987) (CFP) ① **CD-CFP4658** (CFP) ▭ **TC-CFP4658**
Fidelio Ens (arr Sheen) (GALL) ① **CD-674**

Djamileh– opera: 1 act (1872—Paris) (Wds. Gallet)
Djamileh L. Popp
Haroun F. Bonisolli
Splendiano J-P. Lafont
Merchant J. Pineau
Bavarian Rad Chor, Munich RO, L. Gardelli (r1983) (4/89) (ORFE) ① **C174881A**

Don Procopio– opera buffa: 2 acts (1906—Monte Carlo) (Lib. Cambiaggio)
1. LSO, R. Bonynge (r1971) (DECC) ① **444 111-2DA**

Ivan IV– opera: 5 acts (incomplete) (1946—Wurttemberg) (Lib. Leroy and Trianon)
Excs J. Micheau, H. Legay, M. Sénéchal, M. Roux, P. Savignol, L. Noguera, FRN Chor, FRNO, G. Tzipine (r1957) (4/89) (EMI) ① [2] **CMS7 69704-2**

La **Jolie Fille de Perth– concert suite from opera**
1. Prélude; 2. Sérénade; 3. Marche; 4. Danse Bohémienne.
Paris Orch, D. Barenboim (r1975) (EMI) ① **CDM7 64869-2**
Loire PO, M. Soustrot (PIER) ① **PV730022**
LSO, R. Benzi (r1965) (10/94) (PHIL) ① [2] **442 272-2PM2**
1, 3, 4. NZ SO, D. Johanos (r1994) (NAXO) ① **8 553027**
2. Mexico City PO, E. Bátiz (ASV) ① **CDQS6112**

La **Jolie fille de Perth, '(The) Fair Maid of Perth'– opera: 4 acts (1866—Paris) (Lib. Saint-Georges and Adenis, after Scott)**
EXCERPTS: 2. Quand la flamme de l'amour; 3. À la voix d'un amant fidèle (Sérénade); 4. Echo, viens sur l'air embaumé; 25. SUITE: 25a. Prelude; 25b. Aubade; 25c. Sérénade; 25d. Marche; 25e. Danse bohémienne.
Catherine J. Anderson
Henry Alfredo Kraus
The Duke G. Quilico
Ralph J. Van Dam
Simon G. Bacquier
Mab M. Zimmermann
French Rad Chor, French Rad New PO, G. Prêtre (2/88) (EMI) ① [2] **CDS7 47559-8**
2. M. Journet, orch, Rosario Bourdon (r1925) (PREI) ① **89021**
2. G. Souzay, New SO, P. Bonneau (r1956) (DECC) ① **440 419-2DM**
2. N. Ghiaurov, Bulgarian RSO, I. Marinov (r1970s) (FORL) ① **UCD16741**
2. M. Journet, SO, Rosario Bourdon (r1925) (1/94) (CLUB) ① **CL99-034**
3. H. Nash, orch, J. Batten (r1932: Eng) (ASV) ① **CDAJA5112** (ASV) ▭ **ZCAJA5112**
3. Alfredo Kraus, French Rad New PO, G. Prêtre (10/89) (EMI) ① **CDM7 63104-2**
3. H. Nash, orch, C. Raybould (r1932: Eng) (2/95) (DUTT) ① **CDLX7012**
3. H. Nash, orch, J. Batten (r1932: Eng) (11/95) (PEAR) ① **GEMMCD9175**
4. G. Catley, LSO, S. Robinson (r1949; Eng) (4/92) (EMI) ① [7] **CHS7 69741-2(1)**

Les **Pêcheurs de Perles, '(The) Pearl Fishers'– opera: 3 acts (1863—Paris) (Lib. Cormon and Carré)**
EXCERPTS: ACT 1: 1a. Sur la grève en feu; 1b. Mais qui vient là?; 2a. C'est toi; 2b. Au fond du temple saint; 3. Que vois-je?; 4. Sois la bienvenue; 5. Seule au milieu de nous; 6a. A cette voix; 6b. Je crois entendre encore; 7. Le ciel est bleu!; 8a. O Dieu Brahma; 8b. Dans le ciel sans voile. ACT 2: 9. L'ombre descend des cieux; 10a. Ma voilà seule dans la nuit; 10b. Comme autrefois; 11. De mon amie; 12a. Par cet étroit sentier; 12b. Ton coeur n'a pas compris le mien; 13. Ah! revenez à la raison (Finale). ACT 3: 14a. L'orage s'est calmé; 14b. O Nadir, tendre ami; 15a. Qu'ai-je vu?; 15b. Je frémis, je chancelle; 16. Entends au loin ce bruit; 17. Dès que le soleil; 18. Sombres divinités; 19. O lumière sainte.
Leïla J. Micheau
Nadir N. Gedda
Zurga E. Blanc
Nourabad J. Mars
Paris Opéra-Comique Chor, Paris Opéra-Comique Orch, P. Dervaux (r1960) (4/89) (EMI) ① [2] **CMS7 69704-2**
Leïla B. Hendricks
Nadir J. Aler
Zurga G. Quilico
Nourabad J-P. Courtis
Toulouse Capitole Chor, Toulouse Capitole Orch, M. Plasson (r1989) (1/90) (EMI) ① [2] **CDS7 49837-2**
Leïla I. Cotrubas
Nadir A. Vanzo
Zurga G. Sarabia
Nourabad R. Soyer
Paris Op Chor, Paris Op Orch, G. Prêtre (10/91) (CFP) ① [2] **CD-CFPD4721** (10/91) (CFP) ▭ [2] **TC-CFPD4721**
Leila A. Ruffini
Nadir G. Morino
Zurga B. Praticò
Nourabad E. Abumradi
Slovak Phil Chor, Italian International Orch, C. Piantini (pp1990) (10/91) (NUOV) ① [2] **6944/5**
Leïla P. Alarie
Nadir L. Simoneau
Zurga R. Bianco
Nourabad X. Depraz
E. Brasseur Ch, Lamoureux Concerts Orch, J. Fournet (r1953) (10/93) (PHIL) ① [2] **434 782-2PM2**
Leïla M. Angelici
Nadir H. Legay
Zurga M. Dens
Nourabad L. Noguera
Paris Opéra-Comique Chor, Paris Opéra-Comique Orch, A. Cluytens (r1954) (9/95) (EMI) ① [2] **CMS5 65266-2**
Non hai compreso F. de Lucia, J. Huguet, orch (r1906: Ital) (BONG) ① [2] **GB1064/5-2**
Prélude Mexico City PO, E. Bátiz (ASV) ① **CDQS6133**
2. B. Gigli, G. De Luca, orch (Ital: r1927) (CONI) ① **CDHD149** (CONI) ▭ **MCHD149**
2. L. de Luca, J. Borthayre, Paris Cons, A. Erede (DECC) ① **433 066-2DWO** (DECC) ▭ **433 066-4DWO**
2. B. Gigli, G. De Luca, orch, Rosario Bourdon (Ital: r1927) (9/88) (PEAR) ① **GEMMCD9316**

2a, 2b F. Wunderlich, H. Prey, Munich RO, H. Stein (Ger: bp) (DG) Ⓓ [5] **435 145-2GX5(1)**
2a, 2b G. Cross, G. Quilico, Montreal SO, C. Dutoit (r1993) (DECC) Ⓓ **440 947-2DH** (DECC) ▭ **440 947-4DH**
2a, 2b, 6a, 6b, 12a, 12b Alfredo Kraus, Milan RAI SO, A. La Rosa Parodi (Ital: pp1960) (MEMO) Ⓓ [2] **HR4233/4**
2b N. Gedda, E. Blanc, Paris Opéra-Comique Orch, P. Dervaux (EMI) Ⓓ **CDM7 69596-2**
2b N. Gedda, E. Blanc, Paris Opéra-Comique Orch, P. Dervaux (CFP) Ⓓ **CD-CFP9013** (CFP) ▭ **TC-CFP4498**
2b C. Bergonzi, D. Fischer-Dieskau, BRSO, J. López-Cobos (ORFE) Ⓓ **C028821A**
2b L. Pavarotti, N. Ghiaurov, National PO, R. Stapleton (DECC) Ⓓ **425 849-2DWO** (DECC) ▭ **425 849-4DWO**
2b B. Gigli, G. De Luca, orch, Rosario Bourdon (r1927: Ital) (NIMB) Ⓓ **NI7817** (NIMB) ▭ **NC7817**
2b G. Gudbjörnsson, J. Howard, RPO, M. Reed (pp1989) (RPO) Ⓓ [2] **CDRPD9001** (RPO) ▭ [2] **ZCRPD9001**
2b N. Gedda, E. Blanc, Paris Opéra-Comique Orch, P. Dervaux (EMI) Ⓓ [2] **CDEMTVD59** (EMI) ⊙ [2] **EMTVD59**
2b J. Luccioni, P. Deldi, orch (r1935) (MSCM) Ⓓ **MM30377**
2b M. Levin, Örebro CO, G.W. Nilson (arr Nilson) (BLUE) Ⓓ **ABCD038**
2b J. Oakman, S. Page, Czech PO, J. Bigg (with instr track for singing) (IMP) Ⓓ [2] **DPCD1015** (IMP) ▭ **CIMPCD1015**
2b N. Gedda, E. Blanc, Paris Opéra-Comique Orch, P. Dervaux (r1961) (CFP) Ⓓ **CD-CFP4602** (CFP) ▭ **TC-CFP4602**
2b E. Barham, A. Michaels-Moore, RPO, R. Stapleton (r1990) (RPO) Ⓓ [2] **CDRPD9006** (RPO) ▭ [2] **ZCRPD9006**
2b E. Barham, A. Michaels-Moore, English Northern Philh, P. Daniel (r1992) (EMI) Ⓓ **CDC7 54785-2**
2b J. Oakman, S. Page, Czech PO, J. Bigg (r1992) (IMP) Ⓓ **PCD1043**
2b G. Gudbjörnsson, J. Howard, RPO, M. Reed (pp1989) (RPO) Ⓓ **CDRPO5010**
2b B. Gigli, G. De Luca, orch (r1927: Ital) (IMP) Ⓓ **GLRS102**
2b L. de Luca, J. Borthayre, Paris Cons, A. Erede (BELA) Ⓓ **450 006-2** (BELA) ▭ **450 006-4**
2b J. Björling, R. Merrill, RCA Victor SO, R. Cellini (RCA) Ⓓ **09026 61440-2** (RCA) ▭ **09026 61440-4**
2b G. Gudbjörnsson, J. Howard, RPO, M. Reed (pp1989) (IMP) Ⓓ [3] **TCD1070**
2b L. Pavarotti, N. Ghiaurov, National SO, R. Stapleton (r1977) (DECC) Ⓓ [2] **443 585-2DF2** (DECC) ▭ [2] **433 585-4DWO2**
2b E. Caruso, M. Ancona, orch (r1907: Ital) (ASV) Ⓓ **CDAJA5137** (ASV) ▭ **ZCAJA5137**
2b E. Clément, M. Journet, orch (r1912) (PEAR) Ⓓ **GEMMCD9129**
2b P. Domingo, S. Milnes, LSO, A. Guadagno (RCA) Ⓓ **09026 62699-2** (RCA) ▭ **09026 62699-4**
2b J. Björling, R. Merrill, RCA Victor Orch, R. Cellini (r1951) (RCA) Ⓓ **74321 25817-2** (RCA) ▭ **74321 25817-4**
2b B. Gigli, G. De Luca, orch (r1927: Ital) (PEAR) Ⓓ [3] **GEMMCDS9160(2)**
2b T. Hampson, J. Hadley, WNO Orch, C. Rizzi (r1992) (TELD) Ⓓ **4509-98824-2**
2b T. Hampson, J. Hadley, WNO Orch, C. Rizzi (r c1989-94) (TELD) Ⓓ **4509-97463-2**
2b R. Hutt, H. Schlusnus, orch (r1921: Ger) (PREI) Ⓓ **89110**
2b P. Domingo, S. Milnes, LSO, A. Guadagno (r1970) (RCA) Ⓓ **09026 62595-2**
2b J. Björling, R. Merrill, RCA Victor SO, R. Cellini (2/89) (RCA) Ⓓ **GD87799** (RCA) ▭ **GK87799**
2b E. Barham, A. Michaels-Moore, RPO, R. Stapleton (10/90) (IMP) Ⓓ **MCD15** (10/90) (IMP) ▭ **MCC15**
2b E. Caruso, M. Ancona, orch, W.B. Rogers (Ital: r1907) (12/90) (PEAR) Ⓓ [3] **EVC1(2)**
2b D. Borgioli, B. Franci, orch (Ital: r c1923) (12/90) (CLUB) Ⓓ **CL99-014**
2b E. Caruso, M. Ancona, orch, W.B. Rogers (r1907: Ital) (7/91) (RCA) Ⓓ [12] **GD60495(2)**
2b B. Lazzaretti, R. Servile, Berlin RSO, H.M. Schneidt (5/92) (CAPR) Ⓓ **10 380**
2b R. Childs, N. Childs, Britannia Building Soc Band, G. Brand (pp1991: arr K Wilkinson) (8/92) (POLY) Ⓓ **QPRL049D** (8/92) (POLY) ▭ **CPRL049D**
2b B. Gigli, G. De Luca, orch, Rosario Bourdon (Ital: r1927) (6/93) (MMOI) Ⓓ **CDMOIR417**
2b J. Hadley, T. Hampson, WNO Orch, C. Rizzi (r1992) (11/93) (TELD) Ⓓ **9031-73283-2**
2b B. Gigli, G. De Luca, orch, Rosario Bourdon (r1927: Ital) (10/94) (PREI) Ⓓ **89073**
2b E. Caruso, M. Ancona, orch (r1907: Ital) (10/94) (NIMB) Ⓓ **NI7859**
2b L. Simoneau, R. Bianco, Lamoureux Concerts Orch, J. Fournet (r1953) (10/94) (PHIL) Ⓓ [2] **442 272-2PM2**
2b J. Lotrič, I. Morozov, Slovak RSO, J. Wildner (r1994) (2/95) (NAXO) Ⓓ **8 553030**
2b A. Giorgini, F. Federici, orch (r1909: Ital) (4/95) (RECO) Ⓓ **TRC3**
2b E. Clément, M. Journet, orch, Rosario Bourdon (r1912) (8/95) (ROMO) Ⓓ **82002-2**
2b E. Clément, M. Journet, orch, Rosario Bourdon (r1912) (8/95) (PEAR) Ⓓ **GEMMCD9161**
2b, 6b M. Wittrisch, G. Hüsch, Berlin St Op Orch, H.U. Müller (Ger: r1934) (PREI) Ⓓ **89024**
6a, 6b G. Anselmi, anon (r1907: Ital) (7/95) (SYMP) Ⓓ **SYMCD1170**
6a, 6b, 11. E. Caruso, F. Lapitino, orch, J. Pasternack (r1916) (10/91) (PEAR) Ⓓ [3] **EVC4(1)**
6b P. Domingo, Los Angeles PO, C.M. Giulini (DG) ▭ **419 091-4GW**
6b A. Vanzo, Paris Op Orch, G. Prêtre (EMI) Ⓓ **CDC7 54016-2**
6b B. Gigli, orch, Rosario Bourdon (r1929: Ital) (NIMB) Ⓓ **NI7817** (NIMB) ▭ **NC7817**
6b B. Gigli, orch, Rosario Bourdon (Ital: r1929) (CONI) Ⓓ **CDHD170**
6b T. Rossi, orch, M. Cariven (r1936) (FORL) Ⓓ **UCD19053**
6b D. Smirnov, orch (r1921: Ital) (PEAR) Ⓓ **GEMMCD9106**
6b P. Domingo, Los Angeles PO, C.M. Giulini (r1980) (DG) Ⓓ **445 525-2GMA** (DG) ▭ **445 525-4GMA**
6b B. Gigli, orch, Rosario Bourdon (r1929: Ital) (NIMB) Ⓓ **NI7864**
6b D. Borgioli, orch (r c1921: Ital) (PEAR) Ⓓ **GEMMCD9091**
6b T. Beltrán, RPO, R. Stapleton (r1994) (SILV) Ⓓ **SILKD6005** (SILV) ▭ **SILKC6005**
6b F. de Lucia, orch (r1917: Ital) (BONG) Ⓓ [2] **GB1064/5-2**
6b B. Gigli, orch, E. Goossens (r1931: Ital) (PEAR) Ⓓ [2] **GEMMCDS9176**
6b F. de la Mora, WNO Orch, C. Mackerras (r1994-5) (TELA) Ⓓ **CD80411**
6b B. Gigli, orch, E. Goossens (Ital: r1931) (9/88) (EMI) Ⓓ **CDH7 61051-2**
6b E. Caruso, S. Cottone (Ital: r1904) (5/89) (EMI) Ⓓ **CDH7 61046-2**
6b M. Fleta, orch (r1927: Ital) (2/90) (PREI) Ⓓ **89002**
6b B. Gigli, orch, Rosario Bourdon (Ital: r1929) (5/90) (PEAR) Ⓓ **GEMMCD9367**
6b D. Smirnov, orch (Ital: r1909) (7/90) (CLUB) Ⓓ **CL99-031**
6b G. Morino, Warmia Nat PO, B. Amaducci (Ital) (10/90) (NUOV) Ⓓ **6851**
6b B. Gigli, orch, Rosario Bourdon (Ital: r1929) (10/90) (RCA) Ⓓ **GD87811** (10/90) (RCA) ▭ **GK87811**
6b E. Caruso, S. Cottone (Ital: r1904) (12/90) (PEAR) Ⓓ [3] **EVC1(1)**
6b D. Borgioli, orch (Ital: r c1923) (12/90) (CLUB) Ⓓ **CL99-014**
6b E. Caruso, S. Cottone (Ital: r1904) (7/91) (RCA) Ⓓ [12] **GD60495(1)**
6b H.E. Groh, orch (Ger: r1932) (3/92) (PEAR) Ⓓ **GEMMCD9419**
6b N. Gedda, Philh, A. Galliera (r1953) (4/92) (EMI) Ⓓ [7] **CHS7 69741-2(5)**
6b A. Bonci, anon (Ital: r1906) (7/92) (PEAR) Ⓓ [3] **GEMMCDS9924(2)**
6b E. Caruso, anon (Ital: r1904) (11/92) (MEMO) Ⓓ [2] **HR4408/9(1)**
6b J. McCormack, orch (Ital: r1912) (5/93) (MMOI) Ⓓ **CDMOIR418**
6b L. Sobinov, orch (r1910: Russ) (6/93) (PEAR) Ⓓ [3] **GEMMCDS9997/9(2)**
6b B. Gigli, orch, E. Goossens (Ital: r1931) (6/93) (MMOI) Ⓓ **CDMOIR417**
6b A. Davidov, anon (r1901: Russ) (6/93) (PEAR) Ⓓ [3] **GEMMCDS9007/9(1)**
6b J. Björling, Stockholm Royal Op Orch, N. Grevillius (r1945) (10/93) (EMI) Ⓓ **CDH7 64707-2**
6b H. Nash, Liverpool PO, M. Sargent (r1944: Eng) (11/95) (PEAR) Ⓓ **GEMMCD9175**
6b, 11. E. Caruso, F. Lapitino, orch, J. Pasternack (r1916) (7/91) (RCA) Ⓓ [12] **GD60495(5)**
6b, 11. G. Lugo, orch, A. Wolff (r1932) (2/92) (PREI) Ⓓ **89034**
6b, 11. E. Caruso, orch (r1916) (10/94) (NIMB) Ⓓ **NI7859**
6b, 11. A. Giorgini, orch (r1908: Ital) (4/95) (RECO) Ⓓ **TRC3**
6, 11. E. Caruso, F. Lapitino, orch, J. Pasternack (r1916) (RCA) Ⓓ **09026 61244-2**
8a T. dal Monte, La Scala Orch, La Scala Chor, G. Nastrucci (r1929: Ital) (2/90) (PREI) Ⓓ **89001**
8a A. Nezhdanova, anon (r1907: Russ) (6/93) (PEAR) Ⓓ [3] **GEMMCDS9007/9(1)**
8a, 8b L. Tetrazzini, orch, P. Pitt (Ital: r1909) (9/92) (PEAR) Ⓓ **GEMMCD9222**
8a, 10b L. Tetrazzini, orch, P. Pitt (Ital: r1909) (9/92) (EMI) Ⓓ [3] **CHS7 63802-2(1)**
10. I. Cotrubas, Paris Op Orch, G. Prêtre (EMIN) Ⓓ **CD-EMX9519** (EMIN) ▭ **TC-EMX2099**
10. M. Mesplé, Paris Op Orch, J-P. Marty (r1968) (EMI) Ⓓ [2] **CZS7 67813-2**
10. K. Te Kanawa, ROHO, J. Tate (2/90) (EMI) Ⓓ **CDC7 49863-2**
10a, 10b R. Streich, Berlin Deutsche Op Orch, R. Peters (DG) Ⓓ [2] **435 748-2GDO2**
10a, 10b N. Vallin, orch, G. Cloëz (r c1931) (PEAR) Ⓓ **GEMMCD9948**
10a, 10b P. Lorengar, Santa Cecilia Academy Orch, G. Patanè (r1966) (DECC) Ⓓ **443 931-2DM**
10a, 10b M. Callas, Paris Cons, G. Prêtre (2/88) (EMI) Ⓓ **CDC7 49059-2**
10a, 10b M. Freni, La Scala Orch, A. Votto (10/89) (EMI) Ⓓ **CDM7 63110-2**
10a, 10b P. Alarie, Lamoureux Orch, P. Dervaux (r1953) (11/94) (PHIL) Ⓓ [2] **438 953-2PM2**
10b G. Bréjean-Silver, anon (r1905) (SYMP) Ⓓ **SYMCD1173**
10b G. Pareto, orch, P. Pitt (r1920: Ital) (PEAR) Ⓓ **GEMMCD9117**
10b R. Carteri, Milan RAI SO, O. de Fabritiis (bp1956: Ital) (FONI) Ⓓ **CDMR5014**
10b L. Pagliughi, orch (r c1938: Ital) (PEAR) Ⓓ [2] **GEMMCDS9180**
10b A. Galli-Curci, orch (r1921) (2/89) (PEAR) Ⓓ **GEMMCD9308**
10b T. dal Monte, La Scala Orch, C. Sabajno (r1929: Ital) (2/90) (PREI) Ⓓ **89001**
10b E. Berger, Berlin St Op Orch, L. Blech (Ger: r1934) (12/91) (PREI) Ⓓ **89035**
10b A. Noni, orch (Ital: r1951) (4/92) (EMI) Ⓓ [7] **CHS7 69741-2(7)**
10b L. Tetrazzini, orch, P. Pitt (Ital: r1909) (9/92) (PEAR) Ⓓ **GEMMCD9221**
10b A. Nezhdanova, U. Masetti (r1906: Russ) (6/93) (PEAR) Ⓓ [3] **GEMMCDS9007/9(1)**
10b A. Galli-Curci, orch (r1921) (8/94) (NIMB) Ⓓ **NI7852**
10b A. Galli-Curci, orch, J. Pasternack (r1921) (8/94) (ROMO) Ⓓ [2] **81004-2**
11. C. Watkinson, T. Crone (pp1982) (ETCE) Ⓓ **KTC1007** (8/83) (ETCE) ▭ **XTC1007**
11. G. di Stefano, Zurich Tonhalle Orch, F. Patanè (r1958) (DECC) Ⓓ **440 403-2DM**
11. F. de Lucia, anon (r1905: Ital) (BONG) Ⓓ [2] **GB1064/5-2**
12. R. Carteri, G. di Stefano, Milan SO, A. Tonini (Ital: r1957) (EMI) Ⓓ **CDM7 63105-2**
12. M. Mesplé, N. Gedda, Paris Op Orch, P. Dervaux (r1974) (EMI) Ⓓ [2] **CZS7 67813-2**
14a C. Tagliabue, orch, U. Berrettoni (Ital: r1946) (11/90) (PREI) Ⓓ **89015**
14a, 14b G. Laperrière, Three Rivers SO, G. Bellemare (r1992) (CBC) Ⓓ **SMCD5127**
14a, 14b G. Souzay, New SO, P. Bonneau (r1956) (DECC) Ⓓ **440 419-2DM**

BLACHER, Boris *(1903–1975)* *Germany*

Romeo und Juliet– chamber opera: 3 acts, Op. 22 (1943—Berlin) (Lib after Shakespeare)
So wilde Freude R. Klepper, E. Werba
(SCHW) ⌽ **314002**

BLEICHMAN, Julius Ivanovich *(1860–1910 or 1868–1909)* *Russia*

may be spelt Bleichmann

La **Princess lointaine– opera**
Love is a delightful dream A. Bogdanovich, anon (r1905)
(6/93) (PEAR) ⌽ [3] **GEMMCDS9007/9(1)**

BLITZSTEIN, Marc *(1905–1964) USA*

The **Magic Barrel– opera: 1 act (1963) (Lib. cpsr after Malamud)**
Then W. Sharp, S. Blier
(10/91) (KOCH) ⌽ **37050-2**

No for an Answer– opera: 2 acts (1938-40—New York) (Lib. cpsr)
In the clear; Penny Candy W. Sharp, S. Blier
(10/91) (KOCH) ⌽ **37050-2**
In the clear D. Upshaw, E. Stern (r1993: arr E Stern) (12/94) (NONE) ⌽ **7559-79345-2**
(NONE) ▭ **7559-79345-4**

Regina– opera: 3 acts (1946-49—New York) (Lib. cpsr after Hellmann)
Blues; What will it be for me K. Holvik, W. Sharp, S. Blier (10/91) (KOCH) ⌽ **37050-2**

BLODEK, Vilém *(1834–1874)* *Czechoslovakia*

In the Well– opera: 1 act (1867—Prague) (Lib. K. Sabina)
Intermezzo Czech PO, V. Neumann
(SUPR) ⌽ **11 1287-2**
Intermezzo Czech PO, V. Neumann
(9/90) (ORFE) ⌽ **C180891A**
The rising of the moon Prague CO, B. Novotný (r1993) (DENO) ⌽ **CO-78926**

BLOMDAHL, Karl-Birger *(1916–1968) Sweden*

Aniara– space opera: 2 acts (1959—Stockholm) (Lib. Lindegren)
EXCERPTS: 1. Start: Vintergatan; 2. Kristal.
1, 2. Hollywood Bowl Orch, J. Mauceri (r1994)
(PHIL) ⌽ **446 403-2PH**

BLOW, John *(1649–1708)* *England*

Venus and Adonis– masque (?1681—Oxford)
Cupid N. Argenta
Venus L. Dawson
Adonis S. Varcoe
Shepherdess E. van Evera
Shepherd I J.M. Ainsley
Shepherd II C. Daniels
Shepherd III Gordon Jones
Huntsman R. Covey-Crump
Chor, London Baroque, C. Medlam (r1987)
(9/88) (HARM) ⌽ **HMA190 1276**
Venus C. Bott
Adonis M. George
Cupid L. Crabtree
Shepherdess; Grace I J. Gooding
Shepherd I A. King
Shepherd II; Huntsman III; Grace III S. Grant
Shepherd III; Huntsman I; Grace II C. Robson
Huntsman II P. Agnew
Westminster Abbey Sch Chor, New London Consort, P. Pickett (r1992)
(7/94) (L'OI) ⌽ **440 220-2OH**
Suite Cambridge Baroque Camerata, J. Hellyer Jones (PLAN) ⌽ **PLCD076**

BOÏELDIEU, (François) Adrien *(1775–1834) France*

Angéla ou L'atelier de Jean Cousin– opéra-comique: 1 act (1814—Paris) (Lib. C. Montcloux d'Epinay)
Ma Fanchette est charmante J. Sutherland, M. Horne, R. Conrad, New SO, R. Bonynge (r1963)
(DECC) ⌽ **421 881-2DA**

Le **Calife de Bagdad, '(The) Caliph of Baghdad'– opéra-comique (1800—Paris) (Lib. Saint-Just)**
Isauun L. Dale
Zétulbé L. Mayo
Késie J. Michelini
Lémaïde C. Cheriez
Judge H. Rhys-Evans
Camerata de Provence Chor, Camerata de Provence Orch, A. de Almeida (r1992)
(9/94) (SONP) ⌽ **SPT93007**
Overture Munich RO, K. Redel
(PIER) ⌽ **PV786104**

La **Dame blanche– opéra-comique: 3 acts (1825—Paris) (Lib. Scribe)**
Gaveston A. Legros
Anna F. Louvay
Brown M. Sénéchal
Dickson A. Doniat
Jenny J. Berbié
Marguerite G. Baudoz
MacIrton P. Héral
Paris Sym Chor, Paris SO, P. Stoll
(11/90) (ACCO) ⌽ **22086-2**
Ah, quel plaisir E. Clément, anon (r1905)
(8/95) (ROMO) ⌽ **82002-2**
Overture Detroit SO, P. Paray (r1960)
(11/93) (MERC) ⌽ **434 332-2MM**
Rêverie de Georges Brown D. Devriès, orch, G. Cloëz (r1928) (9/94) (NIMB) ⌽ **NI7856**
Viens, gentille Dame F. Wunderlich, Bavarian St Orch, H. Müller-Kray (Ger)
(EMI) ⌽ [3] **CZS7 62993-2**
Viens, gentille dame H. Buff-Giessen, anon (r1905: Ger) (SYMP) ⌽ **SYMCD1085**
Viens, gentille dame H. Roswaenge, Berlin St Op Orch, F. Weissmann (Ger: r1928)
(5/90) (PEAR) ⌽ **GEMMCD9394**
Viens, gentille Dame H. Roswaenge, orch (r1928: Ger) (2/92) (PREI) ⌽ [2] **89201**

La **Fête du village voisin– opéra-comique: 3 acts (1816—Paris) (Lib. C Serwin)**
EXCERPTS: ACT 1: 1. Profitez de la vie (Boléro).
1. S. Jo, ECO, R. Bonynge (r1993)
(9/94) (DECC) ⌽ **440 679-2DH**

Les **Voitures Versées– opéra-comique: 1 act (1808—St Petersburg) (Lib. E. Dupaty)**
Mme de Melval C. Collart
Aurore L. Dachary
Elise D. Boursin
Agathe H. Hennetier
Eugénie C. Petit
Dormeuil A. Doniat
Le Rond B. Demigny
Florville A. Mallabrera
Armand J. Peyron
French Rad Lyric Orch, J. Brebion (bp1971)
(3/92) (MUSD) ⌽ **20152-2**

BOITO, Arrigo *(1842–1918)* *Italy*

Mefistofele– opera: prologue & 4 acts (1868—Milan) (Lib. cpsr)
EXCERPTS: PROLOGUE: 1. Prelude; 2. Ave Signor degli angeli; 3. Ave Signor! Perdona se il mio gergo; 4a. T'è noto Faust?; 4b. Siam nimbi; 4c. Salve Regina!. ACT 1: 5. Perchè di là?; 6. Al soave raggiar; 7. Sediam sovra quel sasso; 8. Dai campi, dai prati; 9a. Olà! chi urla?; 9b. Che baccano!; 10a. Sono lo spirito che nega; 10b. Strano figlio del Caos; 11a. Se tu mi doni; 11b. Fin da stanotte. ACT 2: 12. Cavaliero illustre e saggio; 13a. Dimmi se credi, Enrico; 13b. Colma il tuo cor; 14. Dio clemente (Walpurgis Night); 15a. Su, cammina; 15b. Folletto; 15c. Ascolta!; 16a. Popoli! E scettro e clamide; 16b. Ecco il mondo; 16c. Ah! su! riddiamo. ACT 3: 17. L'altra notte; 18. Dio di pietà!; 19. Lontano, lontano; 20. Sorge il dì!; 21. Spunta l'aurora pallida. ACT 4: 22. La luna immobile; 23. Ecco la notte del classico Sabba; 24. Danza; 25. Notte cupa, truce; 26. Forma ideal, purissima; 27. O incantesimo!. EPILOGUE: 28. Cammina, cammina; 29a. Ogni mortal; 29b. Giunto sul passo estremo; 30. Ave Signor.
Mefistofele S. Ramey
Faust D. O'Neil
Margherita; Elena G. Beňačková
Martha J. Christin
Wagner D. Harper
Pantalis E. Manhart
Nereo D. Wunsch
San Francisco Op Chor, San Francisco Op Orch, M. Arena, R. Carsen
(4/93) (MCEG) ▭ **VVD1089**
Mefistofele B. Christoff
Faust G. Prandelli
Margherita O. Moscucci
Martha A. Pini
Wagner P. de Palma
Rome Op Chor, Rome Op Orch, V. Gui (r c1955: omits Act 4)
(EMI) ⌽ [2] **CMS5 65655-2**
Mefistofele N. Ghiaurov
Faust L. Pavarotti
Margherita M. Freni
Elena M. Caballé
Martha N. Condò
Wagner P. de Palma
Pantalis D. Jones
Nereo R. Leggate
Trinity Boys' Ch, National PO, O. de Fabritiis
(12/85) (DECC) ⌽ [3] **410 175-2DH3**
Mefistofele S. Ramey
Faust P. Domingo
Margherita; Elena E. Marton
Martha T. Takács
Wagner S. Tedesco
Pantalis E. Farkas
Nereo A. Patak
Hungaroton Op Chor, Nyiregyházi Boys' Ch, Hungarian St Orch, G. Patanè
(4/91) (SONY) ⌽ [2] **S2K44983**
Mefistofele S. Ramey
Faust D. O'Neil
Margherita; Elena G. Beňačková
Martha J. Christin
Wagner D. Harper
Pantalis E. Manhart
Nereo D. Wunsch
San Francisco Op Chor, San Francisco Op Orch, M. Arena, R. Carsen (pp1989)
(4/93) (PION) ◖ **PLMCC00691**
Mefistofele C. Siep
Faust M. del Monaco
Margherita R. Tebald
Elena F. Cavall
Marta; Pantalis L. Daniel
Wagner; Nereo P. de Palma
Santa Cecilia Academy Chor, Santa Cecilia Academy Orch, T. Serafin (r1958)
(4/94) (DECC) ⌽ [2] **440 054-2DMO2**
1-4c J. Cheek, Morehouse-Spelman Chor, Callanwolde Young Sngrs, Atlanta Sym Chor, Atlanta SO, Robert Shaw
(9/85) (TELA) ⌽ [2] **CD80109**
1-4c N. Moscona, Columbus Boychoir, R. Shaw Chorale, NBC SO, A. Toscanini (bp1954)
(6/91) (RCA) ⌽ **GD60276**
2. J. Cheek, Morehouse-Spelman Chor, Morehouse-Spelman Chor, Atlanta Sym Chor, Atlanta SO, Robert Shaw (r1984)
(TELA) ⌽ **ECHOCD2**
3. F. Chaliapin, La Scala Orch, C. Sabajno (r1912) (PREI) ⌽ **89030**
3. B. Christoff, Philh, I. Dobroven (r1949)
(EMI) ⌽ **CDH5 65500-2**
3. E. Pinza, orch (r1924)
(2/89) (PEAR) ⌽ **GEMMCD9306**
3. F. Chaliapin, orch, Rosario Bourdon (r1927)
(12/89) (PEAR) ⌽ **GEMMCD9314**
3. F. Chaliapin, orch, V. Bellezza (pp1926)
(7/92) (PEAR) ⌽ [3] **GEMMCDS9925(2**
3. A. Didur, anon (r1906)
(7/92) (PEAR) ⌽ [3] **GEMMCDS9925(1**
3. J. Van Dam, Loire PO, M. Soustrot (r1992)
(8/93) (FORL) ⌽ **UCD1668**
3. A. Didur, anon (r1906)
(1/94) (CLUB) ⌽ **CL99-089**
3. F. Chaliapin, La Scala Orch, C. Sabajno (r1912) (4/94) (EMI) ⌽ [3] **CHS7 64860-2(2**
3, 10a C. Siepi, Santa Cecilia Academy Orch, T. Serafin (r1958) (DECC) ⌽ **440 418-2DM**
3, 10a, 10b, 16b T. Pasero, orch, L. Molajoli (r1927) (6/90) (PREI) ⌽ **8901**
3, 10, 16b N. de Angelis, orch, L. Molajoli (r1927) (7/92) (PREI) ⌽ **8904**

4c Ambrosian Op Chor, LSO, J. Rudel (r1973) (EMI) Ⓓ [2] **CZS5 68559-2**

8. P. Domingo, LSO, J. Rudel (EMI) Ⓓ **CDM7 63103-2**

8. L. Pavarotti, National PO, O. de Fabritiis (7/90) (DECC) Ⓓ [2] **425 681-2DM2** (7/90) (DECC) ▭ [2] **425 681-4DM2**

8. E. Caruso, S. Cottone (r1902) (7/90) (CLUB) Ⓓ **CL99-060**

8. F. Marconi, orch (r1908) (10/90) (SYMP) Ⓓ **SYMCD1069**

8. F. Marconi, S. Cottone (r1903) (10/90) (SYMP) Ⓓ **SYMCD1069**

8. G. Malipiero, orch, U. Berrettoni (r1940) (4/92) (EMI) Ⓓ [7] **CHS7 69741-2(7)**

8. B. Gigli, orch (r1921) (6/93) (MMOI) Ⓓ **CDMOIR417**

8. G. Zenatello, anon (r1906) (5/94) (PEAR) Ⓓ [4] **GEMMCDS9073(1)**

8. G. Zenatello, anon (r1906) (5/94) (SYMP) Ⓓ **SYMCD1168**

8. P. Domingo, LSO, J. Rudel (r1973) (6/94) (EMI) Ⓓ **CDC5 55017-2**

8. L. Escalais, anon (r1906: Fr) (12/94) (SYMP) Ⓓ **SYMCD1128**

8, 29a, 29b L. Pavarotti, National PO, O. de Fabritiis (r1979) (DECC) Ⓓ **440 400-2DM**

8, 29a, 29b, 30. G. di Stefano, C. Siepi, Santa Cecilia Academy Chor, Santa Cecilia Academy Orch, T. Serafin (r1958) (DECC) Ⓓ **440 403-2DM**

8, 29b B. Gigli, orch, Rosario Bourdon (r1927) (CONI) Ⓓ **CDHD170**

8, 29b B. Gigli, orch (r1927) (IMP) Ⓓ **GLRS102**

8, 29b F. de Lucia, orch (r1917) (BONG) Ⓓ [2] **GB1064/5-2**

8, 29b B. Gigli, orch, Rosario Bourdon (r1927) (9/88) (PEAR) Ⓓ **GEMMCD9316**

8, 29b E. Caruso, S. Cottone (r1902) (5/89) (EMI) Ⓓ **CDH7 61046-2**

8, 29b B. Gigli, orch (r1921) (5/90) (NIMB) Ⓓ **NI7807** (NIMB) ▭ **NC7807**

8(2 vers), 29b E. Caruso, S. Cottone (r1902) (12/90) (PEAR) Ⓓ [3] **EVC1(1)**

8(2 vers), 29b E. Caruso, S. Cottone (r1902) (7/91) (RCA) Ⓓ [12] **GD60495(1)**

8, 29b G. Zenatello, orch (r1908) (5/94) (PEAR) Ⓓ [4] **GEMMCDS9073(1)**

8, 29b A. Giorgini, orch (r c1913) (4/95) (RECO) Ⓓ **TRC3**

10. E. Pinza, orch, C. Sabajno (r1923) (2/89) (PEAR) Ⓓ **GEMMCD9306**

10a B. Christoff, Philh, N. Malko (r1949) (EMI) Ⓓ **CDH5 65500-2**

10a A. Didur, anon (r1901) (6/93) (PEAR) Ⓓ [3] **GEMMCDS9997/9(2)**

10a, 10b N. Ghiaurov, National PO, O. de Fabritiis (r1980) (DECC) Ⓓ **436 472-2DM**

10a, 10b A. Didur, S. Cottone (r1903) (6/93) (PEAR) Ⓓ [3] **GEMMCDS9997/9(2)**

10a, 10b A. Didur, orch (r1906) (1/94) (CLUB) Ⓓ **CL99-089**

10a, 10b, 16b T. Pasero, SO, D. Marzollo (r1944) (4/95) (PREI) Ⓓ **89074**

10a, 16b A. Didur, anon (r1900) (6/93) (PEAR) Ⓓ [3] **GEMMCDS9997/9(2)**

10a, 16b L. Sibiriakov, orch (r1908: Russ) (6/93) (PEAR) Ⓓ [3] **GEMMCDS9001/3(2)**

11a L. Sibiriakov, E. Vitting, orch (r1910: Russ) (PEAR) Ⓓ [3] **GEMMCDS9111(1)**

11b G. Zenatello, A. Didur, anon (r1906) (5/94) (PEAR) Ⓓ [4] **GEMMCDS9073(1)**

11b G. Zenatello, A. Didur, anon (r1906) (5/94) (SYMP) Ⓓ **SYMCD1168**

12. G. Cigna, I. Mannarini, P. Civil, T. Pasero, orch, L. Molajoli (r1932) (11/90) (PREI) Ⓓ **89016**

15a G. Mansueto, G. De Tura, chor, orch (r1909) (4/94) (EMI) Ⓓ [3] **CHS7 64860-2(2)**

16a N. de Angelis, orch, L. Molajoli (r1929) (7/92) (PREI) Ⓓ **89042**

16b A. Pirogov, Bolshoi Th Orch, S. Samosud (r c1950: Russ) (PREI) Ⓓ **89078**

17. I. Tokody, orch, Anon (cond) (pp1991/2) (VAI) Ⓓ **VAIA1009**

17. M. Freni, National PO, O. de Fabritiis (r1980) (DECC) Ⓓ **436 472-2DM**

17. R. Tebaldi, Santa Cecilia Academy Orch, T. Serafin (r1958) (DECC) Ⓓ **440 408-2DM**

17. M. Freni, National PO, O de Fabritiis (r1980) (DECC) Ⓓ **440 412-2DM**

17. C. Muzio, orch, L. Molajoli (r1935) (NIMB) Ⓓ **NI7864**

17. G. Farrar, orch (r1905) (IRCC) Ⓓ **IRCC-CD805**

17. M. Favero, orch (r1932) (BONG) Ⓓ **GB1078-2**

17. M. Caballé, LSO, J. Rudel (r1973) (EMI) Ⓓ **CDM5 65575-2**

17. M. Callas, Philh, T. Serafin (r1954) (11/86) (EMI) Ⓓ **CDC7 47282-2**

17. C. Muzio, orch, L. Molajoli (r1935) (10/89) (NIMB) Ⓓ **NI7802** (NIMB) ▭ **NC7802**

17. C. Muzio, orch (r1922) (5/90) (BOGR) Ⓓ [2] **BIM705-2**

17. G. Bellincioni, S. Cottone (r1903) (6/90) (SYMP) Ⓓ **SYMCD1073**

17. V. de los Angeles, Rome Op Orch, G. Morelli (r1954) (8/90) (EMI) Ⓓ **CDH7 63495-2**

17. K. Te Kanawa, LSO, Myung-Whun Chung (11/90) (EMI) Ⓓ **CDC7 54062-2**

17. E. Burzio, orch (r1913) (1/91) (CLUB) Ⓓ [2] **CL99-587/8**

17. C. Muzio, orch, L. Molajoli (r1935) (4/91) (NIMB) Ⓓ **NI7814** (4/91) (NIMB) ▭ **NC7814**

17. C. Ferrani, anon (r1902) (5/91) (SYMP) Ⓓ **SYMCD1077**

17. R. Tebaldi, Santa Cecilia Academy Orch, F. Molinari-Pradelli (8/91) (DECC) Ⓓ [2] **430 481-2DX2**

17. L. Price, RCA Italiana Op Orch, F. Molinari-Pradelli (12/92) (RCA) Ⓓ [4] **09026 61236-2**

17. R. Raisa, orch (r1924) (1/94) (CLUB) Ⓓ **CL99-052**

17. C. Muzio, orch (r1922) (1/94) (ROMO) Ⓓ [2] **81005-2**

17. P. Tassinari, La Scala Orch, F. Ghione (r1933) (4/94) (EMI) Ⓓ [3] **CHS7 64864-2(2)**

17. M. Freni, Ater Orch, L. Magiera (pp: Ital) (5/94) (DECC) Ⓓ [2] **443 018-2DF2**

17. C. Muzio, orch (r1917) (1/95) (ROMO) Ⓓ [2] **81010-2**

17. K. Vayne, orch (bp1958-9) (6/95) (PREI) Ⓓ **89996**

17. I. Galante, Latvian Nat SO, A. Vilumanis (r1994) (11/95) (CAMP) Ⓓ **RRCD1335** (11/95) (CAMP) ▭ **RRMC8035**

19. G. Farrar, anon (bp1935) (IRCC) Ⓓ **IRCC-CD805**

19. E. Clément, G. Farrar, orch, Rosario Bourdon (r1913) (8/95) (ROMO) Ⓓ **82002-2**

19. E. Clément, G. Farrar, orch, Rosario Bourdon (r1913) (8/95) (PEAR) Ⓓ **GEMMCD9161**

21. M. Favero, orch (r c1929) (BONG) Ⓓ **GB1078-2**

21. E. Burzio, orch (r c1907) (1/91) (CLUB) Ⓓ [2] **CL99-587/8**

21. T. Arkel, anon (r1903) (11/92) (MEMO) Ⓓ [2] **HR4408/9(1)**

25, 27. M. Caballé, L. Pavarotti, London Op Chor, National PO, O. de Fabritiis (r1982) (DECC) Ⓓ **443 928-2DM**

29a, 29b R. Alagna, LPO, R. Armstrong (EMI) Ⓓ **CDC5 55540-2** (EMI) ▭ **EL5 55540-4**

29b D. Smirnov, orch (r1909) (7/90) (CLUB) Ⓓ **CL99-031**

29b D. Borgioli, orch (r c1923) (12/90) (CLUB) Ⓓ **CL99-014**

29b G. Lauri-Volpi, orch (r1922) (7/93) (NIMB) Ⓓ **NI7845**

29b B. Gigli, orch, C. Sabajno (r1918) (4/94) (EMI) Ⓓ [3] **CHS7 64864-2(1)**

29b G. Zenatello, orch (r1908) (5/94) (SYMP) Ⓓ **SYMCD1168**

29b D. Smirnov, orch (r1910: Russ) (3/95) (NIMB) Ⓓ **NI7865**

Nerone– opera: 5 acts (1924—Milan) (Lib. cpsr)

EXCERPTS: ACT 1: 1. Canto d'amore, vola col vento; 2. Queste ed un lido fatal; 3. Se côlta (È il mio Nume l'adoro); 4. Padre Nostro; 5. Fanuèl!...Non t'alzar; 6. Gloria al tuo Dio (La Simonia); 7. Nessun ci segue?; 8. Egli è là; 9. Apollo torne. ACT 2: 10. Stupor! Portanto; 11. Tu qua ti nascondi; 12. Nell'antro ov'io m'ascondo tutto vedro2; 13. Ecco il magico specchio; 14. Ahimè! Non m'acciecar; 15. Ecco, la Dea si china; 16. Cieca la salma nell'error ripiomba; 17. Spiato son, là!... 18. Quesdta dagli angui amor. ACT 3: 19. E vedendo le turbe ad udir pronte; 20. A me i ligustri, a te gli allor; 21. Oh date a piene mani; 22. Di pace una dolente a lor favella; 23. Fanuèl, parla ti desta. Salvati per pietà; 24. Va guardingo, attento espolra; 25. Vivete in pace, in concento soave d'amor; 26. Qui sola resti? ACT 4: 27. Vittoria! Infamia! Morte!; 28. I verdi han vinto, è salva Roma; 29. Che vuoi dir? Una congiura; 30. Stande Vesta come la man che riscatta le vite; 31. E tu, non voli?; 32. Scendi, cerchiam fra i morti; 33. Ah! Non temer, son con te; 34. Fanuèl...Morirò?—Vivrai; 35. Sento che ascende (Laggiù tra i giunchi di Genezaret); 36. Quella che il mio truce Iddio ghermi sull'ara?.

Nerone	B. Prevedi
Simon Mago	A. Ferrin
Fanuèl; Dositeo	A. Cassis
Asteria	I. Ligabue
Rubria	R. Baldani
Tigellino	A. Zerbini
Gobrias	G. Corradi
Perside	A. Di Stasio
Cerinto	C. Vozza

Turin RAI Chor, Turin RAI Orch, G. Gavazzeni (bp1975) (ITAL) Ⓓ [2] **LO7704/5**

11, 12. M. Journet, orch (r1924) (4/94) (EMI) Ⓓ [3] **CHS7 64864-2(1)**

15. A. Pertile, orch (r1924) (4/94) (EMI) Ⓓ [3] **CHS7 64864-2(1)**

BONONCINI, Giovanni *(1670–1747) Italy*

Astarto– dramma per musica: 3 acts (1720—London) (Lib. Rolli, after Zeno & Pariati)

Mio caro ben J. Sutherland, R. Conrad, New SO, R. Bonynge (r1963) (DECC) Ⓓ **421 881-2DA**

Cefalo– pastorella: 1 act (1702—Berlin) (Lib. A Guridi)

EXCERPTS: 1a. Cintia, il tuo nome invòco; 1b. Sacro dardo, in te confido.

1a, 1b A. Monoyios, Berlin Barock Compagney (r1993) (10/95) (CAPR) Ⓓ **10 459**

Griselda– dramma per musica: 3 acts (1722—London) (Lib. Rolli)

Che giova fuggire J. Sutherland, LPO, R. Bonynge (r1966; ed Bonynge) (DECC) Ⓓ **421 881-2DA**

Che giova fuggire; Troppo è il dolore; Per la gloria d'adorarvi A. Christofellis, Inst Ens (r1985) (EMI) Ⓓ **CDC5 55259-2**

Per la gloria d'adorarvi L. Pavarotti, Bologna Teatro Comunale Orch, R. Bonynge (DECC) Ⓓ **425 037-2DM**

Per la gloria d'adoravi J. Carreras, ECO, V. Sutej (r1992; arr Agostinelli) (PHIL) OO **434 926-5PH**

Per la gloria J. Sutherland, Philomusica of London, Granville Jones (r1959) (DECC) Ⓓ [2] **436 227-2DM2**

Per la gloria d'adoravi J. Kowalski, Berlin CO, M. Pommer (9/88) (CAPR) Ⓓ **10 113** (9/88) (CAPR) ▭ **CC27 127**

Per la gloria d'adoravi J. Carreras, ECO, V. Sutej (r1992; arr Agostinelli) (6/93) (PHIL) Ⓓ **434 926-2PH**

Muzio Scevola– dramma per musica: 3 acts (1710—Vienna) (Lib. ?Stampaglia, after Minato)

EXCERPTS: 1. Pupille amate; 2. Come quando.

1, 2. J. Baird, F. Urrey, Brewer CO, R. Palmer (3/93) (NEWP) Ⓓ [2] **NPD85540**

Muzio Scevola (Act II)– dramma per musica: 3 acts (1721—London) (Lib. Rolli. Act 1 by Amadei; Act 3 by Handel)

EXCERPTS: 1. Overture; 2. Dolce pensier; 3. E pure in mezzo all'armi; 4. Si, t'ama, o cara.

1-4. J. Ostendorf, E. Mills, Brewer CO, R. Palmer (3/93) (NEWP) Ⓓ [2] **NPD85540**

Polifemo– dramma per musica: 1 act (1702—Berlin) (Lib. A Ariosti)

1a. Respira, alma, respira; 1b. Dove sei, dove t'ascondi; 2a. Non soffrir-a2, mai Circe; 2b. Pensiero di vendetta; 3. Voi del ciel numi clementi.

1a, 1b, 2a, 2b A. Monoyios, Berlin Barock Compagney (r1993) (10/95) (CAPR) Ⓓ **10 459**

3. J. Kowalski, Berlin CO, M. Pommer (9/88) (CAPR) Ⓓ **10 113** (9/88) (CAPR) ▭ **CC27 127**

Il Trionfo di Camilla– dramma per musica: 3 acts (1696—Naples) (Lib. S Stampiglia)

Pupille nere E. Pinza, F. Kitzinger (r1940) (9/93) (RCA) Ⓓ **09026 61245-2**

BORODIN, Alexander Porfir'yevich *(1833–1887)* *Russia*

Prince Igor– opera: prologue & 4 acts (1890—St Petersburg) (Lib. cpsr)
EXCERPTS—PROLOGUE: 1. Overture; 2. To the sun in his glory. ACT 1: 3. I hate a dreary life (Galitzky's Aria); 4. For long past (Yaroslavna's Aria). ACT 2: 5. The prairie floweret (Song of the Polovtsi maidens); 6. Dance of the Polovtsi maidens; 7. Daylight is fading (Vladimir's Aria); 8. Do you love? (Duet); 9. No sleep, no rest (Igor's Aria); 10. How goes it Prince? (Konchak's Aria); 11. Polovtsian Dances. ACT 3: 12. Polovtsian March. ACT 4: 13. I shed bitter tears (Yaroslavna's Lament).

Igor C. Chekerliski
Yaroslavna J. Wiener
Vladimir T. Todorov
Prince Galitsky; Khan Konchak B. Christoff
Konchakovna R. Penkova
Ovlur L. Mihailov
Skula A. Milkovsky
Eroshka K. Dulguerov
Sofia National Op Chor, Sofia National Op Orch, J. Semkow (omits Act 3)
(6/90) (EMI) Ⓓ [3] **CMS7 63386-2**

Igor B. Martinovich
Yaroslavna S. Evstatieva
Vladimir K. Kaludov
Prince Galitsky N. Ghiuselev
Khan Konchak N. Ghiaurov
Konchakovna A. Milcheva
Ovlur M. Popov
Skula S. Georgiev
Eroshka Anton Petkov
Sofia National Op Chor, Sofia Fest Orch, E. Tchakarov
(6/90) (SONY) Ⓓ [3] **S3K44878**
(6/90) (SONY) ⊟ [3] **S3T44878**

Igor S. Leiferkus
Yaroslavna A. Tomowa-Sintow
Vladimir A. Steblianko
Prince Galitsky N. Ghiuselev
Khan Konchak P. Burchuladze
Konchakovna E. Zaremba
Ovlur R. Leggate
Skula E. Garrett
Eroshka F. Egerton
Royal Ballet, ROH Chor, ROHO, B. Haitink, H. Burton (r1990)
(7/93) (DECC) ◐ [2] **071 421-1DH2**
(7/93) (DECC) ▣ [2] **071 421-3DH2**

Igor M. Kit
Yaroslavna G. Gorchakova
Vladimir G. Grigorian
Prince Galitsky V. Ognovenko
Khan Konchak B. Minzhilkiev
Konchakovna O. Borodina
Ovlur N. Gassiev
Skula G. Selezniev
Eroshka K. Pluzhnikov
Nurse E. Perlasova
Polovtsian Maiden T. Novikova
Kirov Th Chor, Kirov Th Orch, V. Gergiev (r1994)
(4/95) (PHIL) Ⓓ [3] **442 537-2PH3**

Excs P. Schoeffler, H. Braun, A. Dermota, A. Jerger, H. Alsen, E. Nikolaidi, D. Ilitsch, Vienna St Op Chor, Vienna St Op Orch, L. Ludwig (pp1941: Ger) (SCHW) Ⓓ [2] **314712**
Konchakovna's cavatina E. Zbrueva, orch (r1911)
(6/93) (PEAR) Ⓓ [3] **GEMMCDS9004/6(2)**
Suite M. Field, I. Boughton, BBC Sym Chor, Philh, G. Simon (r1992; orch Glazunov/Rimsky-Korsakov) (3/94) (CALA) Ⓓ **CACD1011**
(3/94) (CALA) ⊟ **CAMC1011**

1. BBC PO, E. Downes (IMP) Ⓓ **PCD1023**
1. Bolshoi Th Orch, A. Chistiakov (r1992)
(CDM) Ⓓ **LDC288 053**
1. BBC PO, E. Downes (IMP) Ⓓ [3] **TCD1070**
1. Philh, N. Malko (r1956) (TEST) Ⓓ **SBT1062**
1. BBC PO, E. Downes (r1990)
(IMP) Ⓓ **PCD2045**
1. Russian St SO, E. Svetlanov (r1992; orch Glazunov) (1/94) (RCA) Ⓓ **09026 61674-2**
1. Philh, C. Silvestri (r1959)
(11/94) (EMI) Ⓓ [2] **CZS5 68229-2**
1. Russian Nat Orch, M. Pletnev (orch Glazunov)
(12/94) (DG) Ⓓ **439 892-2GH**
(DG) ⊟ **439 892-4GH**
1. Hallé, L. Heward (r1942)
(2/95) (DUTT) Ⓓ **CDAX8010**
1, 11. Atlanta Sym Chor, Atlanta SO, Robert Shaw (r1978) (TELA) Ⓓ **CD80039**
1, 11. Paris Cons, R. Leibowitz (r1960)
(CHES) Ⓓ **Chesky CD61**
1, 11. Moscow RSO, V. Fedoseyev
(NOVA) Ⓓ **150 079-2**
1, 11. London Sym Chor, LSO, G. Solti (r1966)
(BELA) Ⓓ **450 017-2**
(BELA) ⊟ **450 017-4**
1, 11. RLPO, C. Mackerras (r1990; 1(orch Glazunov) (VIRG) Ⓓ **CUV5 61135-2**
1, 11. Boston Pops, A. Fiedler (r1957)
(RCA) Ⓓ **09026 68132-2**
1, 11. London Sym Chor, LSO, G. Solti (r1966: arr Rimsky-Korsakov)
(9/95) (DECC) Ⓓ **444 389-2DWO**
(DECC) ⊟ **444 389-4DWO**
1, 6, 11. Mexico St SO, E. Bátiz
(ASV) Ⓓ **CDQS6018**
(9/88) (ASV) ⊟ **ZCQS6018**
1, 6, 11. Gothenburg Sym Chor, Gothenburg SO, N. Järvi (9/92) (DG) Ⓓ [2] **435 757-2GH2**
1, 6, 11, 12. John Alldis Ch, National PO, L. Tjeknavorian (RCA) Ⓓ **VD60535**
(RCA) ⊟ **VK60535**
2, 5. Bulgarian Nat Ch, Sofia PO, R. Raichev
(FORL) Ⓓ **FF060**
3. A. Pirogov, Bolshoi Th Orch, A. Melik-Pashayev (r c1950) (PREI) Ⓓ **89078**
3. A. Pirogov, orch (r1938)
(PEAR) Ⓓ **GEMMCD9122**
3. N. Ghiaurov, Bulgarian RSO, V. Stefanov (r1970s) (FORL) Ⓓ **UCD16743**
3. A. Kipnis, Victor SO, N. Berezowski (r1945)
(9/92) (RCA) Ⓓ **GD60522**
3. L. Sibiriakov, orch (r1908)
(6/93) (PEAR) Ⓓ [3] **GEMMCDS9001/3(2)**
3. A. Jerger, Vienna St Op Chor, Vienna St Op Orch, L. Ludwig (pp1941: Ger)
(6/94) (SCHW) Ⓓ **314502**
3. N. Ghiaurov, London Sym Chor, LSO, E. Downes (r1965; orch Rimsky-Korsakov)
(9/95) (DECC) Ⓓ **444 389-2DWO**
(DECC) ⊟ **444 389-4DWO**
3, 10. P. Gluboky, Soviet Cinema Orch, E. Khachaturian (r1990)
(CDM) Ⓓ [2] **LDC288 005/6**
(CDM) ⊟ **KC488 005**
3, 10. B. Christoff, Philh, I. Dobroven (r1950)
(6/93) (EMI) Ⓓ **CDH7 64252-2**
4. N. Koshetz, orch (r1928)
(10/89) (NIMB) Ⓓ **NI7802**
(NIMB) ⊟ **NC7802**
4, 13. K. Vayne, anon (r1949)
(6/95) (PREI) Ⓓ **89996**
6. Philadelphia, L. Stokowski (r1937: arr Glazunov/Rimsky-Korsakov/Stokowski)
(11/94) (DUTT) Ⓓ **CDAX8009**
6, 11. Mexico St SO, E. Bátiz
(IMG) Ⓓ **IMGCD1610**
6, 11. Philh, H. von Karajan (EMIL) Ⓓ **CDZ101**
(EMIL) ⊟ **LZ101**
6, 11. LSO, Y. Ahronovitch (IMP) Ⓓ **PCD804**
6, 11. BPO, H. von Karajan
(4/87) (DG) Ⓓ **419 063-2GGA**
(DG) ⊟ **419 063-4GGA**
6, 11. LPO, W. Susskind
(11/87) (CFP) Ⓓ **CD-CFP9000**
7. B.S. Rosenberg, Budapest Concert Orch, J. Acs (pp1990) (OLYM) Ⓓ **OCD370**
7. J. Björling, orch, N. Grevillius (r1933: Swed)
(NIMB) Ⓓ **NI7835**
7. J. Björling, B. Bokstedt (BLUE) Ⓓ **ABCD042**
7. J. Björling, orch, N. Grevillius (r1933: Swed)
(PEAR) Ⓓ **GEMMCD9043**
7. D. Smirnov, orch, J. Harrison (r1923)
(PEAR) Ⓓ **GEMMCD9106**
7. W. Widdop, orch, L. Collingwood (r1926: Eng)
(PEAR) Ⓓ **GEMMCD9112**
7. J. Björling, orch, N. Grevillius (r1933: Swed)
(8/92) (BLUE) Ⓓ **ABCD016**
7. L. Sobinov, anon (r1901)
(6/93) (PEAR) Ⓓ [3] **GEMMCDS9997/9(1)**
7. D. Yuzhin, anon (r1902)
(6/93) (PEAR) Ⓓ [3] **GEMMCDS9001/3(1)**
7. D. Smirnov, orch, J. Harrison (r1923)
(6/93) (PEAR) Ⓓ [3] **GEMMCDS9004/6(1)**
7. J. Björling, orch, N. Grevillius (r1933: Swed)
(10/93) (EMI) Ⓓ **CDH7 64707-2**
7. C. Kullman, orch (Ger: r1935)
(11/93) (PREI) Ⓓ **89057**
7. W. Widdop, orch, L. Collingwood (r1926: Eng)
(5/94) (CLAR) Ⓓ **CDGSE78-50-52**
9. A. Safiulin, Soviet Cinema Orch, E. Khachaturian (r1990)
(CDM) Ⓓ [2] **LDC288 005/6**
(CDM) ⊟ **KC488 005**
9. A. Ivanov, Bolshoi Th Orch, A. Melik-Pashayev (r1951) (PREI) Ⓓ **89067**
9. M. Maksakov, anon (r1901)
(PEAR) Ⓓ [3] **GEMMCDS9111(2)**
9. H. Schlusnus, Berlin St Op Orch, A. Melichar (r1933: Ger) (PREI) Ⓓ [2] **89212**
9. H. Schlusnus, Berlin St Op Orch, A. Melichar (Ger: r c1931) (9/90) (PREI) Ⓓ **89006**
9. V. Kastorsky, orch (r1908)
(6/93) (PEAR) Ⓓ [3] **GEMMCDS9001/3(1)**
9. O. Kamionsky, anon (r1905)
(6/93) (PEAR) Ⓓ [3] **GEMMCDS9001/3(1)**
9. D. Hvorostovsky, Kirov Th Orch, V. Gergiev (r1993) (5/94) (PHIL) Ⓓ **438 872-2PH**
(5/94) (PHIL) ⊟ **438 872-4PH**
9, 10. K. Borg, Berlin RSO, H. Stein (r1963)
(12/94) (FINL) Ⓓ [3] **4509-95606-2**
10. F. Chaliapin, orch, A. Coates (r1927)
(6/88) (EMI) Ⓓ **CDH7 61009-2**
10. M. Reizen, Bolshoi Th Orch, A. Melik-Pashayev (r1951) (12/92) (PREI) Ⓓ **89059**
11. J. Björling, Stockholm Royal Op Orch, N. Grevillius (Swed: r1957) (RCA) ⊟ **GK85277**
11. Paris Cons, A. Cluytens (r1959)
(EMI) Ⓓ **CDM7 69110-2**
11. Ljubljana RSO, A. Nanut
(CAVA) Ⓓ **CAVCD003**
11. Chicago SO, D. Barenboim
(DG) Ⓓ **415 851-2GGA**
11. London Choral Soc, RPO, M. Reed (Eng:pp1989) (RPO) Ⓓ [2] **CDRPD9001**
(RPO) ⊟ [2] **ZCRPD9001**
11. RPO, A. Leaper (NAXO) Ⓓ **8 550501**
11. Monte Carlo Nat Op Orch, L. Frémaux
(BELA) Ⓓ **450 139-2**
(BELA) ⊟ **450 139-4**
11. LSO, A. Dorati (MERC) Ⓓ **434 308-2MM**
11. Chicago SO, S. Ozawa
(EMI) Ⓓ **CDC2 53045-2**
(EMI) ⊟ **EL2 53045-4**
11. T. Sporsén, Gothenburg Sym Chor, Gothenburg SO, N. Järvi
(DG) OO **429 984-5GH**
11. RPO, London Choral Soc, Scots Guards Band, Welsh Guards Band, M. Reed (pp1989)
(RPO) Ⓓ **CDRPO5009**
11. LSO, Y. Ahronovitch (r1985)
(IMP) Ⓓ **PCDS25**
(IMP) ⊟ **PCDSC25**
11. LSC, LSO, R. Hickox (r1987/8)
(IMP) Ⓓ [3] **TCD1070**
11. LSC, LSO, R. Hickox (r1987/8)
(IMP) Ⓓ [3] **TCD1073**
11. Russian Federation St SO, E. Svetlanov (r1992) (CANY) Ⓓ **EC3657-2**
11. Pittsburgh SO, W. Steinberg (r1958)
(EMI) Ⓓ **CDM5 65204-2**
11. Mexico St SO, E. Bátiz
(ASV) Ⓓ **CDQS6119**
11. Slovak PO, K. Redel (r1990)
(PIER) Ⓓ **PV730023**
11. Rhineland-Pfalz State PO, K. Redel (r1979)
(FORL) Ⓓ **FF058**
11. BBC SO, V. Tausky (pp1976)
(BBCR) Ⓓ **BBCRD9103**
11. Philh, L. von Matačić (r1958)
(EMI) Ⓓ [2] **CZS5 68550-2**
11. Stockholm PO, G. Rozhdestvensky (r1994)
(CHAN) Ⓓ **CHAN9386**
11. Beecham Choral Soc, RPO, T. Beecham (r1956) (9/87) (EMI) Ⓓ **CDC7 47717-2**
11. LSC, LSO, R. Hickox
(4/89) (IMP) Ⓓ **PCD908**
11. T. Sporsén, Gothenburg Sym Chor, Gothenburg SO, N. Järvi
(3/91) (DG) Ⓓ **429 984-2GH**
11. Slovak PO, D. Nazareth
(7/91) (NAXO) Ⓓ **8 550051**
11. Royal Phil Chor, WNO Chor, RPO, L. Stokowski (4/92) (DECC) Ⓓ **433 625-2DSP**
(4/92) (DECC) ⊟ **433 625-4DSP**
11. Glasgow CWS Band, R. Tennant (arr Snell)
(9/92) (DOYE) Ⓓ **DOYCD005**
(9/92) (DOYE) ⊟ **DOYMC005**
11. Black Dyke Mills Band, J. Watson (r1992: arr Huckridge) (9/93) (POLY) Ⓓ **QPRL053D**
(9/93) (POLY) ⊟ **CPRL053D**
11. NYPO, L. Bernstein (r1963)
(9/93) (SONY) Ⓓ **SMK47600**
11. Leeds Fest Chor, LPO, T. Beecham (r1934)
(6/94) (DUTT) Ⓓ **CDLX7003**

11. Chicago SO, F. Reiner (r1959) (8/94) (RCA) ① **09026 61958-2**
11. Paris Cons, C. Silvestri (r1961) (11/94) (EMI) ① [2] **CZS5 68229-2**
11. Philadelphia, L. Stokowski (r1937) (11/95) (BIDD) ① **WHL027**
11, Villagers' chorus Bolshoi Th Chor, Bolshoi Th Orch, A. Chistiakov (CDM) ① **LDC288 022**
11, Villagers' chorus, Be firm Countess Bolshoi Th Chor, Bolshoi SO, A. Lazarev (r1993) (5/94) (ERAT) ① **4509-91723-2**
11, 12. Philh, N. Malko (r1953) (TEST) ① **SBT1062**
11, 12. Kirov Th Chor, Kirov Th Orch, V. Gergiev (r1993) (4/94) (PHIL) ① **442 011-2PH** (4/94) (PHIL) ▭ **442 011-4PH**
12. LSO, A. Coates (r1932) (12/92) (KOCH) ① **37700-2**
12. Russian St SO, E. Svetlanov (r1992; orch Rimsky-Korsakov) (1/94) (RCA) ① **09026 61674-2**
12. LPO, T. Beecham (r1938) (6/94) (DUTT) ① **CDLX7003**
13. N. Davrath, Vienna St Op Orch, V. Golschmann (r1960s) (VANG) ① [2] **08.9081.72**

BÖRTZ, Daniel *(b 1943)* *Sweden*

The **Bacchae (Backanterna)– opera: 2 acts (1992—Stockholm) (Lib. I. Bergman)**

Meg Page	S. Lindenstrand
Teiresias	L. Andersson-Palme
Cadmos	S. Wahlund
Pentheus	P. Mattei
Agve	A. Soldh
Alfa	B. Lindholm
Beta	P. Hoffman
Gamma	C. Staern
Delta	E. Andreassen
Zeta	A-M. Mühle
Eta	K. Hammarström
Theta	A. Tomson
Lamda	E. Österberg
Xi	C. Morling
Rho	A. Fleetwood
Sigma	L. Hoel
Tau	H. Ströberg
Omega	I. Tobiasson
Soldier	C.M. Dellow
Herdsman	P. Mattsson
Messenger	P. Stormare

Stockholm Royal Op Chor, Stockholm Royal Orch, K. Ingebretsen (r1992) (CPRI) ① [2] **CAP22028**

BOTTACCHIARI, Ugo *(1879–1944) Italy*

L'**ombra– opera: 1 act (1899—Macerata) (Lib. Giogieri-Conti)**
O tu ch'el sai M. Favero, I. Ruotolo (r1946) (VAI) ① **VAIA1071**
O tu ch'el sai M. Favero, I. Ruotolo (r1946) (BONG) ① **GB1078-2**

BOTTESINI, Giovanni *(1821–1889) Italy*

Alì Babà– comic opera: 4 acts (1871)
Overture LSO, F. Petracchi (3/95) (ASV) ① **CDDCA907**

diavolo della notte– opera: 4 acts (1858)
Sinfonia LSO, F. Petracchi (3/95) (ASV) ① **CDDCA907**

Ero e Leandro– opera: 3 acts (1879—Turin) (Lib. A. Boito)
Prelude LSO, F. Petracchi (3/95) (ASV) ① **CDDCA907**
Romanza d'Ero A. Pinto, anon (r1902) (8/93) (SYMP) ① **SYMCD1111**
Splendi! erma facella A. Pinto, anon (r1902) (6/94) (IRCC) ① **IRCC-CD808**

BOUGHTON, Rutland *(1878–1960) England*

Bethlehem– choral drama (1915—Street) (Text cpsr, after Coventry Nativity Play)

Virgin Mary	H. Field
Gabriel	R. Bryan
Joseph	R. Bryson
Jem	R. Evans
Sym	J. Bowen
Dave	A. Peacock
Zarathustra	A. Opie
Nubar	J. MacDougall
Merlin	R. Van Allan
Believer	C. Seaton
Unbeliever	C. Campbell
Calchas	I. Boughton
Herod	G. Matheson-Bruce

Holst Sngrs, New London Children's Ch, CLS, A. Melville (r1993) (4/94) (HYPE) ① **CDA66690**

The **Immortal Hour– music drama: 2 acts (1914—Glastonbury) (Lib. F Macleod)**
EXCERPTS: 1. Introduction. ACT 1: 2. By dim moon-glimmering coasts and sad sea wastes; 3. Though you have travelled from one darkness of another; 4. Ye know not who I am; 5. I have come hither, led by dreams and visions; 6. Hail, Son of Shadow!; 7. I am old; more old more ancient; 8. Brother and kin to all the twilit gods; 9. Laugh not, ye outcasts of the invisible world; 10. Fair is the moonlight; 11. Hail, daughter of kings, and star among dreams; 12. Have you forgot the delicate smiling land; 13. I have forgotten all; 14. A king of men has wooed the Immortal Hour; 15. Led here by dreams; 16. I will go back to the Country of the Young; 17. Sir, I am glad; 18. I have come to this lone wood; 19. Look, O king!; 20. There is no backwrad way for such as I; 21. I have heard you calling, Dalua, Dalua!; 22. I've seen that man before who came tonight; 23. Yes, woman, yes, I know; 24. But sometimes...sometimes...Tell me: have you heard; 25. Good folk, I gave you greeting; 26. Good sir, you are most welcome; 27. At last I know why dreams have led me hither; 28. And your name, fair lord?; 29. Truly, I now know full well; 30. I, too, am lifted with the breath; 31. Who laughed?; 32. Dear Lord, sit here; 33. How beautiful they are (Unseen Voices). ACT 2: 34. By the Voice in the corries; 35. The The Bells of Youth are ringing; 36. But this was in the old, old far-off days; 37. Hail, Eochaidh, High King of Eire, hail!; 38. Green fire of Joy, green fire of Life; 39. Etain, speak, my Queen; 40. No, no, my Queen; 41. I, too, have heard strange, delicate music; 42. The Queen!; 43. Hail, Eochaidh, King of Eire!; 44. I am the king's first son; 45. Dagda, Lord of Thunder and Silence; 46. Fair lord, my thanks I give; 47. Have not great poets sung; 48. In the days of the Great Fires; 49. Hear us, Oengus, beautiful, terrible, Sun-Lord!; 50. But now, fair lord, tell me the boon you crave; 51. I have seen all things pass and all things go; 52. This nameless lord; 53. How beautiful they are (The Faery Song); 54. I have heard...I have dreamed that song; 55. I am a song in the Land of the Young; 56. I am a small leaf in a great wood; 57. O do not leave me, Star of my Desire!; 58. Hasten, lost love, found love!; 59. In the Land of Youth there are pleasant places; 60. They play with lances.

Dalua	R. Kennedy
A Spirit Voice	P. Taylor
Etain	Anne Dawson
Eochaidh	D. Wilson-Johnson
A Spirit Voice	V. Hill
Manus	R. Bryson
Maive	P. Taylor
An Old Bard	R. Bryson
Midir	M. Davies

G. Mitchell Ch, ECO, A. Melville (r1983) (8/87) (HYPE) ① [2] **CDA66101/2**
53. Webster Booth, J. Cockerill (r1939) (4/92) (EMI) ① [7] **CHS7 69741-2(2)**

BOURGAULT-DUCOUDRAY, Louis (Albert) *(1840–1910)* *France*

Thamara– opera: 2 acts (1891—Paris) (Lib. L. Gallet)
Belle d'une beauté fatale A. Affre, orch (r1907-8) (8/92) (IRCC) ① **IRCC-CD802**

BRAEIN, Edvard Fliflet *(1924–1976) Norway*

Anne Pedersdotter– opera: 4 acts (1971—Oslo) (Lib H. Kristiansen, after H. Wiers-Jensen)

Anne Pedersdotter	K. Ekeberg
Absalon Pedersøn Beyer	S. Carlsen
Merete Beyer	V. Hanssen
Martin Beyer	K. M. Sandve
Herlofs-Marte	R. Eriksen
Master Johannes	S. A. Thorsen
Master Laurentius	T. Stensvold
Master Olaus	C. Ehrstedt
Jens Schelderup	G. Oskarsson
David	A. Helleland
Bente	I. M. Brekke
Jørund	T. Gilje
Anfører	R. Nygård

Norwegian Nat Op Chor, Norwegian Nat Op Orch, P. Å. Andersson (r1991) (12/94) (SIMA) ① [2] **PSC3121**

BRANDL, Johann *(1835–1913) Austria*

Der **Liebe Augustin– operetta: 3 acts (1887—Vienna) (Lib. H. Klein)**
EXCERPTS: 1. Du alter Stephansturm (The Old Refrain).
1. J. McCormack, orch, W.B. Rogers (r1916) (BIDD) ① **LAB022**
1. M. Rabin, Hollywood Bowl SO, F. Slatkin (r1959: arr Kreisler) (EMI) ① [6] **CMS7 64123-2**
1. F. Kreisler, C. Lamson (r1924: arr Kreisler) (9/93) (BIDD) ① [2] **LAB068/9**
1. F. Kreisler, M. Raucheisen (r1930: arr Kreisler) (12/93) (EMI) ① **CDH7 64701-2**

BRAUNFELS, Walter *(1882–1954) Germany*

Verkündigung– opera: prologue & 4 acts, Op. 50 (1948—Cologne) (Lib. P Claudel)

Andreas Gradherz	S. Nimsgern
The mother	C. Rüggeberg
Violaine	A. Trauboth
Mara	C. Shirasaka-Teratani
Jakobäus	J. Bröcheler
Peter von Ulm	C. Bladin
Peter's assistant	C. Brüggemann
Angel	A. Kajiyama
Labourer	S. Sevenich
A woman	B. Dommer
Mayor of Rothenstein	R-D. Krüll

Cologne Sym Chor, Cologne SO, D.R. Davies (pp1992) (7/94) (EMI) ① [2] **CDS5 55104-2**

BRETAN, Nicolae *(1887–1968) Romania*

Arald– opera: 1 act (1982—Iaşi) (Lib. cpsr, after M. Eminescu)

Poet	D. Zancu
Seer	A. Agache
Arald, King of the Avares	I. Voineag
Maria, Empress	S. Şandru

Moldova PO, C. Mandeal (r1987) (10/95) (NIMB) ① **NI5424**

Golem– opera: 1 act (1923—Cluj) (Lib. cpsr, after I. Kaczév)

Golem	A. Agache
Rabbi Löw	T. Daróczi
Anna	S. Şandru
Baruch	D. Zancu

Chor, Moldova PO, C. Mandeal (r1987) (10/95) (NIMB) ① **NI5424**

BRETÓN, Tomás *(1850–1923) Spain*

La **Dolores– ópera: 3 acts (1895—Madrid)**
EXCERPTS: 1. Aragón la más famasa; 2. Di que es verdad que me llamas.
Jota Madrid SO, E.F. Arbós (r1928) (VAI) ① **VAIA1046**
Jota P. Domingo, Madrid SO, E. G. Asensio (pp1991) (11/92) (IMP) ① **MCD45**
1. P. Domingo, Madrid Zarzuela Chor, Madrid Rondalla Lírica, Madrid SO, M. Moreno-Buendia (r1987) (1/89) (EMI) ① **CDC7 49148-2**
P. Lorengar, P. Domingo, Austrian RSO, G. Navarro (SONY) ① **MK39210**

La **Verbena de La Paloma– sainte lírico: 1 act (1894—Madrid) (Lib. R de la Vega)**
EXCERPTS—; 1. El aceite de ricino; 2. El niño está dormido; 3. Seguidillas: Por ser la Virgen de la Paloma.

Susana	T. Tourné
Seña Rita; La cantaora	D. Ripolles
Tía Antonia	E. Garcia

Julián R. Cesari
Don Hilarión A.P. Bayod
Casta A. Armentia
Portera M. del Carmen Andres
Vecina M. del Pilar Alonso
Chula 1 J. Bermejo
Chula 2 A. Fernandez
Don Sebastián J. Portillo
Tabernero J.R. Henche
Sereno J.L. Cancela
Madrid Coros Cantores, Madrid Concerts Orch, F. Moreno Torroba
(10/92) (HISP) Ⓓ **CDZ7 67328-2**
Susana M. Bayo
Julian P. Domingo
Seña Rita R. Pierotti
Casta S. Tro
Don Hilarion R. Castejon
Don Sebastian J. Castejón
Tia Antonia A. M. Amengual
Cantaora Milagros Martin
Watchman E. Baquerizo
Madrid Comunidad Chor, Madrid SO, A. R. Marbà (r1994)
(9/95) (AUVI) Ⓓ **V4725**

BRIDGE , Frank *(1879–1941) England*

H—numbers used in Paul Hindmarsh's catalogue

The **Christmas Rose– opera: 3 scenes, H179 (1931—London) (Lib. M. Kemp-Welch and C. Cotterel)**
Miriam W. Eathorne
Reuben E. James
Shepherd I M. Davies
Shepherd II H. Herford
Shepherd III D. Wilson-Johnson
Chelsea Op Group Chor, Chelsea Op Group Orch, H. Williams
(PEAR) Ⓓ **SHECD9582**
(10/85) (PEAR) ⊙ **SHE582**

BRITTEN, (Edward) Benjamin (Lord Britten of Aldeburgh) *(1913–1976) England*

Albert Herring– chamber opera: 3 acts, Op. 39 (1947—Glyndebourne) (Lib. E Crozier, after G de Maupassant)
Albert Herring J. Graham-Hall
Lady Billows P. Johnson
Florence Pike F. Palmer
Mr Gedge D. Hammond-Stroud
Mr Budd R. Van Allan
Mr Upfold A. Oliver
Miss Wordsworth E. Gale
Mrs Herring P. Kern
Sid A. Opie
Nancy J. Rigby
Emmie M. Bovino
Cis B. Lord
Harry R. Peachey
LPO, B. Haitink, P. Hall (r1985)
(CAST) ▣ **CVI2051**
Albert Herring P. Pears
Lady Billows S. Fisher
Florence Pike J. Peters
Mr Gedge J. Noble
Mr Budd O. Brannigan
Mr Upfold E. Evans
Miss Wordsworth A. Cantelo
Mrs Herring S. Rex
Sid J. Ward
Nancy C. Wilson
Emmie S. Amit
Cis A. Pashley
Harry S. Terry
ECO, B. Britten
(6/89) (DECC) Ⓓ [2] **421 849-2LH2**

Billy Budd– opera: 4 acts, Op. 50 (1951—London) (Lib. E M Forster & E Crozier, after H Melville)
Billy Budd T. Allen
Captain Vere P. Langridge
Claggart R. Van Allan
Mr Redburn N. Howlett
Mr Flint P. Guy-Bromley
Mr. Ratcliffe C. Bayley
Red Whiskers E. Byles
Donald M. Richardson
Dansker J. Connell
Novice B. Banks
Squeak H. Milner
Bosun M. Rivers
1st Mate A. Cunningham
2nd Mate C. Ross
Maintop R. Reaville
Novice's Friend C. Booth-Jones
Arthur Jones R. Reaville
ENO Chor, ENO Orch, D. Atherton, T. Albery
(MCEG) ▣ **VVD545**
Billy Budd T. Uppman
Captain Vere P. Pears
Claggart F. Dalberg
Mr Redburn H. Alan
Mr Flint G. Evans
Mr Ratcliffe M. Langdon
Red Whiskers A. Marlowe
Donald B. Drake
Dansker I. Te Wiata
Novice W. McAlpine
Squeak D. Tree
Bosun Ronald Lewis
1st Mate R. Davies
2nd Mate H. Littlejohn
Maintop E. Jones
Novice's Friend J. Cameron
Arthur Jones A. Hobson
ROH Chor, ROHO, B. Britten (pp1951: four act vers)
(VAI) Ⓓ [3] **VAIA1034**
Interlude and Sea Shanties P. Glossop, D. Bowman, G. Dempsey, Ambrosian Op Chor, LSO, B. Britten (r1967)
(6/93) (DECC) Ⓓ **436 990-2DWO**
(6/93) (DECC) ⊡ **436 990-4DWO**

The **Burning Fiery Furnace– church parable: 1 act, Op. 77 (1966—Orford) (Lib. W Plomer)**
Nebuchadnezzar P. Pears
Astrologer B. Drake
Ananias J. Shirley-Quirk
Misael R. Tear
Azarias S. Dean
Herald P. Leeming
EOG Chor, EOG Orch, B. Britten (r1967)
(10/90) (DECC) Ⓓ **414 663-2LM**

Curlew River– church parable: 1 act, Op. 71 (1964—Orford) (Wds. W. Plomer)
Madwoman P. Pears
Ferryman J. Shirley-Quirk
Abbot H. Blackburn
Traveller B. Drake
Voice of the Spirit B. Webb
EOG Chor, EOG Orch, B. Britten
(9/89) (DECC) Ⓓ **421 858-2LM**
I come from the Westland B. Drake, EOG Orch, B. Britten, V. Tunnard (r1965)
(KIWI) Ⓓ **CDSLD-82**

Death in Venice– opera: 2 acts, Op. 88 (1973—Aldeburgh) (Lib. M Piper, after T Mann)
Gustav von Aschenbach R. Tear
Traveller; Elderly Fop; Hotel Manager; Players Leader A. Opie
Voice of Apollo M. Chance
English Clerk G. Finley
Hotel Porter C. Ventris
Glyndebourne Fest Chor, London Sinfonietta, Graeme Jenkins, S. Lawless (r1990)
(MCEG) ▣ **VVD847**
Gustav von Aschenbach P. Pears
Traveller; Elderly Fop; Old Gondolier J. Shirley-Quirk
Hotel Manager;Hotel Barber J. Shirley-Quirk
Leader of the Players J. Shirley-Quirk
Voice of Dionysus J. Shirley-Quirk
Voice of Apollo J. Bowman
Hotel Porter K. Bowen
English Clerk P. Leeming
Boy Player N. Williams
Girl Player P. MacKay
Strawberry Seller I. Saunders
EOG Chor, ECO, S. Bedford (r1974)
(5/90) (LOND) Ⓓ [2] **425 669-2LH2**

Death in Venice– concert suite from opera (arr S. Bedford)
Cpte ECO, S. Bedford
(1/86) (CHAN) Ⓓ **CHAN8363**

Gloriana– opera: 3 acts, Op. 53 (1953—London) (Lib. W. Plomer)
EXCERPTS: 13. Second Lute Song of the Earl of Essex; 17a. On rivalries 'tis safe for kings; 17b. O God, my King, sole ruler of the world.
Queen Elizabeth I Sarah Walker
Earl of Essex A. Rolfe Johnson
Countess of Essex J. Rigby
Lord Mountjoy N. Howlett
Lady Rich E. Vaughan
Sir Robert Cecil A. Opie
Sir Walter Raleigh R. Van Allan
Henry Cuffe M. Donnelly
ENO Chor, ENO Orch, M. Elder, C. Graham
(5/90) (MCEG) ▣ **VVD344**
Queen Elizabeth I J. Barstow
Earl of Essex P. Langridge
Countess of Essex D. Jones
Lord Mountjoy J. Summers
Sir Robert Cecil A. Opie
Lady Rich Y. Kenny
Sir Walter Raleigh R. Van Allan
Henry Cuffe B. Terfel
Lady in Waiting J. Watson
Blind ballad-singer W. White
Recorder of Norwich J. Shirley-Quirk
Spirit of the Masque J.M. Ainsley
Master of Ceremonies P. Hoare
WNO Chor, WNO Orch, C. Mackerras
(7/93) (ARGO) Ⓓ [2] **440 213-2ZHO2**
13. P. Pears, J. Bream (r1963-4)
(8/93) (RCA) Ⓓ [28] **09026 61583-2(5)**
13. P. Pears, J. Bream (r1963-4)
(9/94) (RCA) Ⓓ **09026 61601-2**
17a, 17b L. Price, Philh, H. Lewis (r1979)
(12/92) (RCA) Ⓓ [4] **09026 61236-2**

Gloriana– concert suite from opera, Op. 53a (arr cspr)
1. The Tournament; 2. The Lute Song; 3. The Courtly Dances; 4. Gloriana moritura.
LSO, S. Bedford (2/90) (COLL) Ⓓ **Coll1019-2**
RLPO, T. Yuasa (r1994)
(3/95) (EMIN) Ⓓ **CD-EMX2231**
BBC Northern SO, N. Del Mar (r1977)
(10/95) (BBCR) Ⓓ **BBCRD9129**
3. English SO, W. Boughton (NIMB) Ⓓ **NI5295**
3. RPO, A. Previn (10/87) (TELA) Ⓓ **CD80126**

The **Little Sweep– chamber opera: 1 act, Op. 45 (1949—Aldeburgh) (Lib. E Crozier: Act 3 o 'Let's Make An Opera')**
Sam D. Hemmings
Rowan J. Vyvyan
Miss Baggott N. Evans
Juliet Brook A. Cantelo
Black Bob; Tom T. Anthony
Clem; Alford P. Pears
Gay Brook M. Ingram
Sophie Brook Marilyn Baker
Johnny Crome R. Fairhurst
Hugh Crome L. Vaughan
Tina Crome G. Soskin
Alleyn's Sch Ch, EOG Orch, B. Britten (r1955)
(11/93) (LOND) Ⓓ **436 393-2LM**
Black Bob; Tom R. Lloyd
Clem; Alfred R. Tear
Sam S. Monck
Miss Baggott H. Begg
Juliet Brook C. Benson
Gay Brook C. Fordham
Sophie Brook C. Wearing
Rowan M. Wells
Johnny Crome D. Glick
Hugh Crome C. Huehns
Tina Crome K. Willis
J. Constable
F. Grier
T. Fry
Finchley Children's Music Group, King's College Ch, Medici Qt, P. Ledger (r1977)
(7/95) (EMI) Ⓓ **CDM5 65111-2**

A **Midsummer Night's Dream– opera: 3 acts, Op. 64 (1960—Aldeburgh) (Lib. cpsr & P. Pears, after Shakespeare)**
Oberon J. Bowman
Tytania I. Cotrubas
Lysander R. Davies
Demetrius D. Duesing
Hermia C. Buchan
Helena F. Lott
Theseus L. Visser
Hippolyta C. Powell
Bottom C. Appelgren
Quince R. Bryson
Flute P. Power
Snug A. Gallacher
Snout Adrian Thompson
Starveling D. Bell
Cobweb M. Warr
Peaseblossom S. Jones
Mustardseed J. Whiting
Moth S. King

Puck D. Nash
Glyndebourne Fest Chor, LPO, B. Haitink, P. Hall (r1981)
(CAST) ▣ **CVI2008**
Oberon A. Deller
Tytania E. Harwood
Lysander P. Pears
Demetrius T. Hemsley
Hermia J. Veasey
Helena H. Harper
Theseus J. Shirley-Quirk
Hippolyta H. Watts
Bottom O. Brannigan
Quince N. Lumsden
Flute K. Macdonald
Snug D. Kelly
Snout R. Tear
Starveling K. Raggett
Cobweb R. Dakin
Peaseblossom J. Prior
Mustardseed I. Wodehouse
Moth G. Clark
Puck S. Terry
Downside School Boys' Ch, Emanuel School Boys' Ch, LSO, B. Britten (r1966)
(5/90) (LOND) Ⓓ [2] **425 663-2LH2**
Oberon J. Bowman
Tytania L. Watson
Lysander J. Graham-Hall
Demetrius H. Herford
Hermia D. Jones
Helena J. Gomez
Theseus N. Bailey
Hippolyta P. Walker
Bottom D. Maxwell
Quince R. Bryson
Flute Adrian Thompson
Snug A. Gallacher
Snout R. Horn
Starveling R. Suart
Cobweb S. Hart
Peaseblossom G. Pierre
Mustardseed A. Mead
Moth N. Watson
Puck D. Fletcher
'rinity Boys' Ch, CLS, R. Hickox (r1990)
(8/93) (VIRG) Ⓓ [2] **VCD7 59305-2**

loye's Fludde– Chester miracle play, Op. 59 (1958—Orford) (Chester miracle play)
Noye O. Brannigan
Mrs Noye S. Rex
Sem D. Pinto
Ham D. Angadi
Jaffett S. Alexander
Voice of God T. Anthony
Mrs Sem C. Clack
Mrs Ham M-T. Pinto
Mrs Jaffett E. O'Donovan
hor, E. Suffolk Children's Orch, EOG Orch, N. del Mar (pp1961)
(11/93) (LOND) Ⓓ **436 397-2LM**
Noye D. Maxwell
Mrs Noye L. Ormiston
Sem A. Gallifant
Ham T. Lamb
Jaffett N. Berry
Voice of God R. Pasco
Mrs Sem C. Johnson
Mrs Ham P. Hewetson
Mrs Jaffett J. Brown
LS, R. Hickox (r1989)
(11/94) (VIRG) Ⓓ **CUV5 61122-2**
Noye, Noye, take thou thy company ... Sir! heare are lions T. Anthony, O. Brannigan, D. Pinto, D. Angadi, S. Alexander, C. Clack, M-T. Pinto, E. O'Donovan, E Suffolk Children's Orch, ECO, N. del Mar (pp1961)
(6/93) (DECC) Ⓓ **436 990-2DWO**
(6/93) (DECC) ⊟ **436 990-4DWO**

wen Wingrave– opera: 2 acts, Op. 85 (1971—BBC TV, London) (Lib. M. Piper, after H. James)
Owen Wingrave B. Luxon
Coyle J. Shirley-Quirk
Lechmere N. Douglas
Miss Wingrave S. Fisher
Mrs Coyle H. Harper
Mrs Julian J. Vyvyan
Kate J. Baker
General; Narrator P. Pears
Wandsworth Sch Boys' Ch, ECO, B. Britten (r1970)
(11/93) (LOND) Ⓓ [2] **433 200-2LHO2**

Paul Bunyan– operetta: prologue and 2 acts, Op. 17 (1941—New York) (Lib. W.H. Auden)
EXCERPTS: 1. Overture; 2. Lullaby of Dream Shadows; 3. Inkslinger's Love; 4. Song.
Narrator P. Wagner
Paul Bunyan J. Lawless
Johnny Inkslinger D. Dressen
Tiny E.C. Nelson
Slim C. Ware
1st Bad Cook V. Sutton
2nd Bad Cook M. Fristad
Hel Helson J. Bohn
Swede I P. Jorgenson
Swede II T. Dahl
Swede III T. Shaffer
Swede IV L. Weller
John Shears J. McKee
Western Union Boy J. Westbrock
Fido M. Jette
Moppet S. Herber
Poppet J. Hardy
Plymouth Music Series Chor, Plymouth Music Series Orch, P. Brunelle
(8/88) (VIRG) Ⓓ [2] **VCD7 59249-2**
(8/88) (VIRG) ⊟ [2] **VCD7 59249-4**
Blues Ens (r1992; arr Runswick: instr ens)
(9/93) (UNIC) Ⓓ **DKPCD9138**
Overture ECO, S. Bedford
(2/91) (COLL) Ⓓ **Coll1102-2**
1-4. D. Dressen, P. Forbes, B. Mills, A. Murgatroyd, Angus Smith, LP Ch, ECO, P. Brunelle (r1989) (VIRG) Ⓓ **VC5 45093-2**

Peter Grimes– opera: prologue & 3 acts, Op. 33 (1945—London) (Lib. M Slater, after G Crabbe's 'The Borough')
EXCERPTS: 1. Prologue; ACT 1; 2. Interlude (Dawn); 3. Oh, hang at open doors the net; 4. Good morning, good morning!; 5. I have to go from pub to pub; 6. Let her among you without fault; 7. And do you prefer the storm; 8. Picture what that day was like; 9. They listen to money; 10. What harbour shelters peace; 11. Interlude (Storm); 12a. Past time to close!; 12b. A joke's a joke; 13. We live and let live; 14. Now the Great Bear and Pleiades; 15. Old Joe has gone fishing. ACT 2: 16. Interlude (Sunday morning); 17. Glitter of waves; 18. Grimes is at his exercise; 19. We planned that our lives should have a new start; 20. From the gutter; 21. Passacaglia; 22. Go there!; 23. In dreams I've built myself some kindlier home; 24. The whole affair. ACT 3: 25. Interlude (Moonlight); 26a. Assign your prettiness to me; 26b. Mr Keene! Can you spare a moment; 27. Good night! It's time for bed; 28. Embroidery in childhood; 29. Mister Swallow; 30. Who holds himself apart; 31. Interlude; 32. Steady! There you are!; 33. Final Scene.
Grimes J. Vickers
Ellen Orford H. Harper
Balstrode N. Bailey
Auntie E. Bainbridge
Bob Boles J. Dobson
Swallow F. Robinson
Mrs Sedley P. Payne
Ned Keene P. Gelling
Rector J. Lanigan
Hobson J. Tomlinson
Niece I M. Hill Smith
Niece II A. Pashley
ROH Chor, ROHO, Colin Davis, E. Moshinsky
(CAST) ▣ **CVI2015**
Grimes P. Langridge
Ellen Orford J. Cairns
Balstrode A. Opie
Auntie A. Howard
Bob Boles A. Woodrow
Swallow A. Greenan
Mrs Sedley S. Gorton
Ned Keene R. Poulton
Rector E. Byles
Hobson M. Richardson
Niece I M. Bovino
Niece II S. Pring
ENO Chor, ENO Orch, D. Atherton, T. Albery, B. Gavin (pp1994)
(DECC) ▣ **071 428-3DH**
Grimes P. Pears
Ellen Orford C. Watson
Balstrode J. Pease
Auntie J. Watson
Bob Boles R. Nilsson
Swallow O. Brannigan
Mrs Sedley L. Elms
Ned Keene G. Evans
Rector J. Lanigan
Hobson D. Kelly
Niece I M. Studholme
Niece II I. Kells
ROH Chor, ROHO, B. Britten
(4/86) (DECC) Ⓓ [3] **414 577-2DH3**
Grimes J. Vickers
Ellen Orford H. Harper
Balstrode J. Summers
Auntie E. Bainbridge
Bob Boles J. Dobson
Swallow F. Robinson
Mrs Sedley P. Payne
Ned Keene T. Allen
Rector J. Lanigan
Hobson R. Van Allan
Niece I T. Cahill
Niece II A. Pashley
ROH Chor, ROHO, Colin Davis
(11/91) (PHIL) Ⓓ [2] **432 578-2PM2**
Grimes A. Rolfe Johnson
Ellen Orford F. Lott
Balstrode T. Allen
Auntie P. Payne
Bob Boles S. Kale
Swallow S. Dean
Mrs Sedley Sarah Walker
Ned Keene S. Keenlyside
Rector N. Jenkins
Hobson D. Wilson-Johnson
Niece I M. Bovino
Niece II G. Webster
ROH Chor, ROHO, B. Haitink (r1992)
(7/93) (EMI) Ⓓ [2] **CDS7 54832-2**
Grimes! Grimes! J. Vickers, H. Harper, J. Summers, ROH Chor, ROHO, Colin Davis
(PHIL) Ⓓ **442 602-2PM**
(PHIL) ⊟ **442 602-4PM**
2. ROHO, B. Britten (r1958)
(6/93) (DECC) Ⓓ **436 990-2DWO**
(6/93) (DECC) ⊟ **436 990-4DWO**
2, 11, 16, 21, 25. ROHO, B. Britten
(12/90) (LOND) Ⓓ **425 659-2LM**
6, 14, 16, 17, 23, 28, 31, 32. P. Pears, J. Cross, T. Culbert, BBC Th Chor, ROHO, R. Goodall (r1948) (2/94) (EMI) Ⓓ [2] **CMS7 64727-2**

The **Prodigal Son– church parable: 1 act, Op. 81 (1968) (Lib. W. Plomer)**
Tempter; Abbot P. Pears
Father J. Shirley-Quirk
Elder Son B. Drake
Younger Son R. Tear
EOG Chor, EOG Orch, B. Britten (r1969)
(9/90) (DECC) Ⓓ **425 713-2LM**

The **Rape of Lucretia– chamber opera: 2 acts, Op. 37 (1946—Glyndebourne) (Lib. R Duncan, after A Obey)**
Lucretia J. Rigby
Male Chorus A. Rolfe Johnson
Female Chorus K. Harries
Tarquinus R. Smythe
Collatinus R. Van Allan
Junius A. Opie
Lucia C. Pope
Bianca A-M. Owens
ENO Orch, L. Friend
(MCEG) ▣ **VVD617**
Lucretia J. Baker
Male Chorus P. Pears
Female Chorus H. Harper
Tarquinius B. Luxon
Collatinus J. Shirley-Quirk
Junius B. Drake
Lucia J. Hill
Bianca E. Bainbridge
ECO, B. Britten (r1970)
(5/90) (LOND) Ⓓ [2] **425 666-2LH2**
Abridged N. Evans, P. Pears, J. Cross, F. Sharp, N. Lumsden, D. Dowling, M. Ritchie, F. Nielsen, EOGCO, R. Goodall (r1947)
(2/94) (EMI) Ⓓ [2] **CMS7 64727-2**
Lucretia J. Rigby
Male Chorus N. Robson
Female Chorus C. Pierard
Tarquinius D. Maxwell
Collatinus A. Miles
Junius A. Opie
Lucia P. Rozario

Bianca A. Gunson
CLS, R. Hickox (r1993)
(3/94) (CHAN) ① [2] **CHAN9254/5**

The **Turn of the Screw– chamber opera: prologue and 2 acts, Op. 54 (1954—Venice) (Lib. M. Piper, after H. James)**

Prologue P. Langridge
Quint R. Tear
Governess H. Donath
Miles M. Ginn
Flora L. Watson
Mrs Grose A. June
Miss Jessel H. Harper
Guardian V. Müller
ROHO, Colin Davis, P. Weigl
(PHIL) ▭ **070 400-3PHE**

Prologue, Quint P. Pears
Governess J. Vyvyan
Miles D. Hemmings
Flora O. Dyer
Mrs Grose J. Cross
Miss Jessel A. Mandikian
EOG Orch, B. Britten (r1955)
(5/90) (LOND) ① [2] **425 672-2LH2**

Prologue; Quint P. Langridge
Governess F. Lott
Miles S. Pay
Flora E. Hulse
Mrs Grose P. Cannan
Miss Jessel N. Secunde
Aldeburgh Fest Ens, S. Bedford
(6/94) (COLL) ① [2] **Coll7030-2**

BROSCHI, Riccardo *(c1698–1756) Italy*

Artaserse– pasticcio (1734—London) (Lib. P Metastasio)
Se al labro mio A. Christofellis, Seicentonovecento Ens, F. Colusso (r1993/4)
(EMI) ① **CDC5 55250-2**

Merope– opera: 3 acts (1732)
Taccia il vento e la tempesta A. Christofellis, Inst Ens (r1987/8) (EMI) ① **CDC5 55259-2**

BRUCH, Max (Karl August) *(1838–1920) Germany*

Die **Loreley– romantic opera: 3 acts, Op. 16 (1863—Mannheim) (Lib. E Geibel)**
EXCERPTS: 1. Overture.
1. Rhenish PO, W. Balzer (r1984)
(EBS) ① **EBS6071**

BRUNEAU, (Louis Charles Bonaventure) Alfred *(1857–1934) France*

Messidor– opera: 3 acts (1897—Paris) (Lib. E Zola)
EXCERPTS: 1. Prelude to Act IV; 2. La légende de l'or (The Legend of Gold).
1, 2. Rhine State PO, J. Lockhart (r1989)
(MARC) ① **8 223498**

Naïs Micoulin– opera: 2 acts (1907—Monte Carlo) (Lib. cpsr, after E. Zola)
EXCERPTS: 1. Prélude, Act 4; 2. Ballet: 'La légende d'or'.
1. Rhine State PO, J. Lockhart (r1989)
(MARC) ① **8 223498**

Virginie– opera: 3 acts (1931—Paris) (Lib. H. Duvernois)
Quand j'avais la taille fine G. Féraldy, orch (r1931) (MSCM) ① **MM30221**
(MSCM) ▭ **MM040079**
Quand j'avais la taille fine; Ah! mon Dieu, quelle aventure! G. Féraldy, orch (r1931)
(8/92) (IRCC) ① **IRCC-CD802**

BUSONI, Ferruccio (Dante Michelangiolo Benvenuto) *(1866–1924) Italy/Germany*

Arlecchino, oder Die Fenster– opera: 1 act, Op. 50 (1917—Zurich) (Lib. cpsr)

Arlecchino K. Gester
Colombina E. Malbin
Ser Matteo del Sarto I. Wallace
Abbate Cospicuo G. Evans
Dottor Bombasto F. Ollendorff
Leandro M. Dickie
Glyndebourne Fest Orch, J. Pritchard (r1954)
(EMI) ① [2] **CMS5 65284-2**

Arlecchino E. T. Richter
Colombina S. Mentzer
Ser Matteo del Sarto T. Mohr
Abbate Cospicuo W. Holzmair
Dottor Bombasto P. Huttenlocher
Leandro S. Dahlberg
Lyon Op Chor, Lyon Op Orch, K. Nagano (r1992)
(11/93) (VIRG) ① [2] **VCD7 59313-2**

Arlecchino; Leandro R. Wörle
Colombina M. Bellamy
Ser Matteo del Sarto R. Pape
Abbate Cospicuo S. Lorenz
Dottor Bombasto P. Lika
Berlin RSO, G. Albrecht (r1992)
(11/94) (CAPR) ① **60 038**

Doktor Faust– poem for music: 6 sections (1925—Dresden) (Lib. cpsr: cpted/ed P. Jarnach)

Doktor Faust D. Fischer-Dieskau
Mephistopheles W. Cochran
Duke of Parma A. de Ridder
Duchess of Parma H. Hillebrecht
Wagner K.C. Kohn
Girl's brother; Scientist F. Grundheber
Lieutenant M. Schmidt
Jurist M. Rintzler
Theologian H. Sotin
Bavarian Rad Chor, BRSO, F. Leitner (r1969)
(8/89) (DG) ① [3] **427 413-2GC3**

Turandot– opera: 2 acts (1917—Zurich) (Lib. cpsr, after Gozzi)

Turandot M. Gessendorf
Kalaf S. Dahlberg
Altoum F-J. Selig
Adelma G. Sima
Barak F. Struckmann
Queen Mother A-M. Rodde
Truffaldino M. Schäfer
Pantalone M. Kraus
Tartaglia W. Holzmair
Lyon Op Chor, Lyon Op Orch, K. Nagano (r1991)
(11/93) (VIRG) ① [2] **VCD7 59313-2**

Turandot L. Plech
Kalaf J. Protschka
Altoum R. Pape
Adelma G. Schreckenbach
Barak F. Molsberger
Queen-Mother C. Lindsley
Truffaldino R. Wörle
Pantalone J.W. Prein
Tartaglia G. Schwarz
Berlin RIAS Chbr Ch, Berlin RSO, G. Albrecht (r1992)
(11/93) (CAPR) ① **60 039**

BUSSOTTI, Sylvano *(b 1931) Italy*

La **Passion selon Sade– chamber mystery-play: 1 act (1969—Stockholm) (Lib. L. Loulié)**
'O'—Atti Vocali (transcr Berberian)
C. Berberian (7/89) (WERG) ① **WER60054-50**

CABALLERO, Manuel Fernández *(1835–1906) Spain*

El **Dúo de la Africana– zarzuela: 1 act (1893—Madrid) (Lib. Echegaray)**
EXCERPTS: 1. Dúo-Jota.
1. J. Carreras, I. Rey, ECO, E. Ricci (r1994)
(2/95) (ERAT) ① **4509-95789-2**
(2/95) (ERAT) ▭ **4509-95789-4**
1, 2. P. Lorengar, P. Domingo, Austrian RSO, G. Navarro (SONY) ① **MK39210**

Gigantes y Cabezudos– zarzuela (1898—Madrid) (Lib. M. de Echegaray)
Esta es su carta V. de los Angeles, Spanish Nat Orch, R. Frühbeck de Burgos (r1967)
(EMI) ① **CDM5 65579-2**

CACCINI, Giulio *(c1545–1618) Italy*

Il **Rapimento di Cefalo– opera: prologue, 5 scenes & prologue (1600—Florence) (Lib. Chiabrera; collab with Venturi, Bati & Strozzi)**
EXCERPTS: 1. Caduca fiamma; 2. Muove sì dolce; 3. Qual trascorrendo; 4. Chi mi confort'ahime; 5. Ineffabile ardore (chorus); 6. Quand'il bell'anno (chorus).
2, 4. D. Thomas, A. Rooley (r1982)
(MOSC) ① **070974**

CAGE, John *(1912–1992) USA*

Europera 3– opera (1990)
Long Beach Op, A. Culver (pp1993)
(MODE) ① [2] **Mode38/9**

Europera 4– opera (1990)
Long Beach Op, A. Culver (r1993)
(MODE) ① [2] **Mode38/9**

CALLEJA, Rafael (Gómez) *(1874–1938) Spain*

Emigrantes– zarzuela: 1 act (1905—Madrid) (comp with Barrera)
Granadinas T. Schipa, orch, J. Pasternack (r1926) (NIMB) ① **NI7870**
Granadinas J. Carreras, ECO, E. Ricci (r1994)
(2/95) (ERAT) ① **4509-95789-2**
(2/95) (ERAT) ▭ **4509-95789-4**

CAMPANA, Fabio *(1819–1882) Italy*

Esmeralda– opera: 4 acts (1869—St Petersburg) (Lib. G T Cimino)
Piango ma questo lagrimar E. Foggi, anon (r1910s) (6/94) (IRCC) ① **IRCC-CD808**

CAMPRA, André *(1660–1744) France*

L' **Europe galante– opéra-ballet: prologue & 4 acts (1697—Paris)**
R. Yakar, M. Kweksilber, R. Jacobs, Petite Bande, G. Leonhardt (r1973)
(2/91) (DHM) ① [2] **GD77059**

Idoménée– tragédie lyrique: prologue and 5 acts (1712 (rev 1731) (Lib. A. Dachet)
EXCERPTS: 1. Ouverture. PROLOGUE: 2. Laissez nous sortir d'esclavage; 3. Quelle douce harmonie; 4. Sarabande; 5a. Chantez le dieu charmant; 5b. Air des Tritons; 6. Coulez Ruisseaux; 7. Jeunes Beautez. ACT ONE: 8. Venez, Gloire, Fierté; 9. Rassemblez les Troyens; 10. Marche; 11. Quittez vos fers; 12. Chantons, celebrons sa victoire; 13a. Rondeau; 13b. Tout se rend aux traits de la Beauté; 14. Seigneur, à tous les Grecs; 15. Son Pere ne vit plus!. ACT TWO: 16. O Dieux!; 17. Cessez de soulever les ondes; 18. La paix regne par tout; 19. Soyez témoins de mon inquiétude; 20. Il me fuit le Cruel!; 21. Vous, des tendres amours; 22. Nous obeissons à ta voix; 23. D'un amour qui s'éteint. ACT THREE: 24. Ne condamne point mes transports; 25. Je dois être jaloux; 26. Que d'immoler mon fils; 27. Votre bonté s'interesse pour moy; 28a. Symphonie; 28b. Je vois des Argiens; 29a. Premier & Deuxième Riguadons; 29b. Aimable espérance; 30. Allez, Prince, partez; 31. Je viens des vastes mers. ACT FOUR: 32. Espoir des Malheureux; 33. Princesse, à vos regards j'ose encore m'offrir; 34. Ciel! que vois-je!; 35. O Neptune, reçoy nos voeux; 36. Triomphez, remportez une immortelle gloire; 37. Musette; 38. Volez au son de nos musettes; 39. Riguadon. Menuets; 40. La Paix & les Plaisirs tranquiles; 41. Premier & Deuxième Passepieds; 42. Neptune a calmé sa colere. ACT FIVE: 43. Il est donc vray, Seigneur; 44. Ah! quel bonheur; 45. Peuples, pour la derniere fois; 46. Passacaille. Bourrées; 47. Gloire brillante, charmants plaisirs; 48. Je remets entre vos mains ces marques éclatantes; 49. Du Souverain des mers; 50. Quel feu dans mon sein se rallume!; 51. Quel pouvoir m'a conduit sur ce bord écarté?.
Idoménée B. Delétré

Electre S. Piau
Ilione M. Zanetti
Idamante J-P. Fouchécourt
Venus M. Boyer
Eole; Neptune; Jealousy; Nemesis J. Corréas
Arcas R. Dugay
Arbas; Protée J-C. Sarragosse
Cretan Girl M. Saint-Palais
1st Shepherd A. Pichard
2nd Shepherd; Trojan Girl A. Mopin
Arts Florissants Chor, Arts Florissants Orch, W. Christie (r1991)
(9/92) (HARM) ① [3] **HMC90 1396/8**
(9/92) (HARM) ▭ [3] **HMC40 1396/8**
1, 2, 11, 16, 19, 20, 25, 29a, 32, 34-39, 43, 44, 51. B. Delétré, S. Piau, M. Zanetti, J-P. Fouchécourt, M. Boyer, J. Corréas, R. Dugay, A. Pichard, A. Mopin, Arts Florissants Chor, Arts Florissants Orch, W. Christie (r1991)
(HARM) ① **HMC90 1506**

Tancrède– opera: prologue; 5 acts (1702—Paris) (Lib. Danchet, after Tasso)
Excs C. Dussaut, J. Bona, A. Arapian, Provence Instr Ens, Provence Vocal Ens, C. Zaffini
(PIER) ① **PV786111**

CARAFA DI COLOBRANO, Michele (Enrico-Francesco-Vincenzo-Aloisio-Paolo) *(1787–1872) Italy*

Gabriella di Vergy– opera: 2 acts (1816—Naples) (Lib. Tottola)
Ah! fermate...Raoul!...Perchè non chiusi al dì. Y. Kenny, P. Doghan, G. Mitchell Ch, Philh, D. Parry (r1987) (OPRA) ① **ORR201**
Ah! fermate...Raoul!...Perchè non chiusi al dì. Y. Kenny, P. Doghan, G. Mitchell Ch, Philh, D. Parry (r1987)
(10/90) (OPRA) ① [3] **ORCH103**

Le Nozze di Lammermoor– drama: 2 acts (1829—Paris) (Lib. L Balocchi)
D'un orribile tempesta S. McCulloch, T. Goble, I. Thompson, J. Viera, A. Thorburn, Philh, D. Parry (8/95) (OPRA) ① [3] **ORCH104**

CARVALHO, João de Sousa *(1742–1798) Portugal*

Testoride Argonauta– opera: 2 acts (1780—Lisbon) (Lib. Martinelli)
Icaro E. von Magnus
Testoride C. Rayam
Irene L. Meeuwsen
Leucippo D. Hennecke
Nicea L. Åkerlund
Clemencic Consort Baroque Orch, R. Clemenčić
(NUOV) ① [2] **6928/9**

CATALANI, Alfredo *(1854–1893) Italy*

Loreley– azione romantica: 4 acts (1890—Rome) (Lib. Zanardini. after D'Ormeville)
Amor, celeste abbrezza M. Freni, Venice La Fenice Orch, R. Abbado
(9/92) (DECC) ① **433 316-2DH**
Dance of the Water Nymphs La Scala Orch, A. Guarnieri (r1928) (BONG) ① **GB1039-2**
Danza delle Ondine P. Spada (arr pf)
(ASV) ① **CDDCA921**
Dove son? C. Muzio, orch (r1922)
(5/90) (BOGR) ① [2] **BIM705-2**
Dove son? C. Muzio, orch (r1922)
(1/94) (ROMO) ① [2] **81005-2**
Io stesso dunque Anna ... Fanciulla mesta P. Cappuccilli, La Scala Chor, La Scala Orch, G. Gavazzeni (pp1968)
(MEMO) ① [2] **HR4273/4**
Nel verde maggio B. Gigli, orch, Rosario Bourdon (r1923) (5/90) (NIMB) ① **NI7807**
(NIMB) ▭ **NC7807**
Vieni! Deh vien...Deh! ti rammenta F. Merli, B. Scacciati, orch, L. Molajoli (r1929)
(PREI) ① **89091**

La Wally– opera: 4 acts (1892—Milan) (Lib. Illica)
EXCERPTS: ACT 1: 1. Tr la la la...Bravo Gellner; 2. Un dì verso il Murzoll; 3a. S'ode echeggiar; 3b. Su per l'erto sentier; 4. Ma si direbbe; 5. Chi osò levar sul padre; 6. L'Hagenbach l'abborro; 7a. Sei tu che domandato hai; 7b. T'amo ben io; 8. Ebben?...Ne andrò lontana; 9. Ad ora così tarda. ACT 2: 10. Entro la folla che intorno s'aggira; 11. Suona la squilla mattutina; 12. No!...coll'amor tu non dei scherzar; 13. Eccola qua; 14. Finor non m'han baciata; 15a. Sei tu?...Son io; 15b. Cantava un dì mia nonna; 15c. Se tu, Wally, sapessi; 16. Che brami, Wally?; 17a. Già il canto fervido; 17b. No! parla! vo'saper. ACT 3: 18. Interlude and Orchestral Introduction; 19. Fa cor, Wally; 20. Non v'è maggior piacer; 21. Ebben...Dunque; 22. L'Hagenbach qui?; 23. Nè mai dunque avrò pace; 24. Buio è il sentier; 25. A me soccorso. ACT 4: 26. Orchestral Interlude; 27. Luogo sicura questo non è più; 28. Prendi, fanciul, e serbala; 29a. Eterne a me dintorno; 29b. Sì, come te, fanciulla del mio canto; 30a. Wally! Wally!...Come sei triste; 30b. Ah! sono, ahimè!; 30c. M'hai salvato...Quando a Sölden; 30d. Vieni, una placida vita.
Wally R. Tebaldi
Giuseppe Hagenbach M. del Monaco
Vincenzo Gellner P. Cappuccilli
Stromminger J. Diaz
Walter L. Marimpietri
Afra S. Malagù
Old Soldier A. Mariotti
Turin Lyric Chor, Monte Carlo Nat Op Orch, F. Cleva
(2/90) (DECC) ① [2] **425 417-2DM2**
Wally E. Marton
Stromminger F.E. d'Artegna
Vincenzo Gellner A. Titus
Giuseppe Hagenbach F. Araiza
Walter J. Kaufman
Afra B. Calm
Old Soldier M. Pertusi
Bavarian Rad Chor, Munich RO, P. Steinberg
(9/90) (EURO) ① [2] **RD69073**
7b R. Stracciari, orch (r1925)
(MSCM) ① [2] **MM30276**
7b R. Stracciari, orch (r1925)
(PEAR) ① **GEMMCD9178**
7b G. Bechi, La Scala Orch, U. Berrettoni (r1941) (PREI) ① **89995**
7b G. Bechi, La Scala Orch, U. Berrettoni (r1941) (2/90) (PREI) ① **89009**
8. N. Miricioiu, D. Harper (pp1985)
(ETCE) ▭ **XTC1041**
8. M. Callas, Philh, C.M. Giulini
(EMI) ① **CDM7 69596-2**
8. M. Callas, Philh, T. Serafin (r1954)
(EMI) ① **CDC7 49502-2**
8. R. Tebaldi, Rome RAI Orch, A. Basile (pp1960) (MEMO) ① [2] **HR4235/6**
8. M. Chiara, National PO, K.H. Adler
(DECC) ① **433 624-2DSP**
8. R. Tebaldi, Monte Carlo Nat Op Orch, F. Cleva (DECC) ① **433 822-2DH**
(DECC) ▭ **433 822-4DH**
8. R. Tebaldi, Monte Carlo Nat Op Orch, F. Cleva (DECC) ① **433 066-2DWO**
(DECC) ▭ **433 066-4DWO**
8. P. Lorengar, Seville SO, E. Colomer (pp1991)
(RCA) ① **RD61191**
8. P. Lorengar, Seville SO, E. Colomer (pp1991)
(RCA) **ᴏᴏ 09026 61191-5**
8. I. Tokody, orch, Anon (cond) (pp1991/2)
(VAI) ① **VAIA1009**
8. M. Callas, Philh, T. Serafin (r1954)
(EMI) ① **CDC7 54702-2**
(EMI) ▭ **EL754702-4**
8. K. Ricciarelli, Orch, Anon Cond (pp1991)
(MCI) ① **MCCD090**
(MCI) ▭ **MCTC090**
8. Daniel Smith, J. Still, Caravaggio Ens (arr bn/pf; r1993) (ASV) ① **CDWHL2078**
(ASV) ▭ **ZCWHL2078**
8. R. Tebaldi, Monte Carlo Nat Op Orch, F. Cleva (r1968) (DECC) ① **440 408-2DM**
8. R. Tebaldi, Monte Carlo Nat Op Orch, F. Cleva (r1968) (DECC) ① **433 440-2DA**
(DECC) ▭ **433 440-4DA**
8. M. Chiara, National PO, K. H. Adler
(BELA) ① **450 015-2**
(BELA) ▭ **450 015-4**
8. E. Marton, Munich RSO, P. Steinberg
(RCA) ① **09026 61440-2**
(RCA) ▭ **09026 61440-4**
8. D. Soviero, Cincinnati Pops, E. Kunzel (r1990)
(TELA) ① **CD80407**
8. K. Ricciarelli, Svizzera Italiana Orch, B. Amaducci (r1980) (ERMI) ① **ERM151**
8. R. Kabaivanska, Bulgarian RSO, V. Stefanov (r1970s) (FORL) ① **UCD16742**
8. V. de los Angeles, Rome Op Orch, G. Morelli (r1954) (EMI) ① **CDM5 65579-2**
8. G. Bumbry, Stuttgart RSO, S. Soltesz
(11/86) (ORFE) ① **C081841A**
8. M. Callas, Philh, T. Serafin (r1954)
(11/86) (EMI) ① **CDC7 47282-2**
8. C. Muzio, orch (r1920)
(5/90) (BOGR) ① [2] **BIM705-2**
8. N. Miricioiu, D. Harper (pp1985)
(5/90) (ETCE) ① **KTC1041**
8. V. de los Angeles, Rome Op Orch, G. Morelli (r1954) (8/90) (EMI) ① **CDH7 63495-2**
8. H. Spani, orch, C. Sabajno (r1928)
(9/90) (CLUB) ① [2] **CL99-509/10**
8. R. Tebaldi, Monte Carlo Nat Op Orch, F. Cleva (8/91) (DECC) ① [2] **430 481-2DX2**
8. L. Garrett, Philh, A. Greenwood (r1990-1)
(11/91) (SILV) ① **SONGCD903**
(11/91) (SILV) ▭ **SONGC903**
8. H. Spani, La Scala Orch, C. Sabajno (r1928)
(2/92) (MMOI) ① **CDMOIR408**
8. A. Marc, NZ SO, H. Wallberg
(6/92) (DELO) ① **DE3108**
(6/92) (DELO) ▭ **CS3108**
8. M. Gauci, Belgian Rad & TV Orch, A. Rahbari
(11/92) (NAXO) ① **8 550606**
8. H. Spani, La Scala Orch, C. Sabajno (r1928)
(12/92) (PREI) ① **89037**
8. J. Hammond, Philh, W. Susskind (r1949)
(12/92) (TEST) ① **SBT1013**
8. R. Pampanini, orch, L. Molajoli (r1927)
(8/93) (PREI) ① **89063**
8. R. Tebaldi, Monte Carlo Op Orch, F. Cleva (r1968) (10/93) (DECC) ① **436 461-2DM**
8. C. Muzio, orch (r1920)
(1/94) (ROMO) ① [2] **81005-2**
8. C. Muzio, orch (r1917)
(1/95) (ROMO) ① [2] **81010-2**
8, 23. M. Freni, Venice La Fenice Orch, R. Abbado (9/92) (DECC) ① **433 316-2DH**
23. G. Cigna, orch, L. Molajoli (r1932)
(11/90) (PREI) ① **89016**
23. G. Cigna, orch, L. Molajoli (r1932)
(11/90) (LYRC) ① **SRO805**

CAUDELLA, Eduard *(1841–1924) Romania*

Petru Rareş– opera: 3 acts (1889) (Lib. T. Rehbaum, after Gane)
Prelude Iaşi Moldova PO, I. Baciu
(ELCT) ① **ELCD104**

CAVALLI, (Pietro) Francesco *(1602–1676) Italy*

Calisto– opera: prologue & 3 acts (1652—Venice) (Lib. Faustini)
Calisto I. Cotrubas
Giove U. Trama
Mercurio P. Gottlieb
Endimione J. Bowman
Diana J. Baker
Linfea H. Cuénod
Satirino J. Hughes
Pane F. Davià
Silvano O. Brannigan
Giunone T. Kubiak
Natura M. Biggar
Eternità E. Hartle
Destino T. Cahill
Eco I. Brodie
Glyndebourne Fest Chor, LPO, R. Leppard (r1971: real. Leppard)
(DECC) ① [2] **436 216-2DMO2**
Calisto; Eternità M. Bayo
Giove M. Lippi
Mercurio S. Keenlyside
Endimione G. Pushee
Diana; Destino A. Mantovani
Giunone S. Theodoridou
Linfea G. Ragon
Pane; Natura B. Banks
Satirino; Furia D. Visse
Silvano D. Pittsinger
Furia J. Vindevogel
Concerto Vocale, R. Jacobs (r1994; realised Jacobs)
(9/95) (HARM) ① [3] **HMC90 1515/7**

Ardo, sospiro e piango F. Von Stade, Scottish CO, R. Leppard (r1984)
(ERAT) Ⓓ **4509-98504-2**

Didone– opera: prologue & 3 acts (1641—Venice) (Lib. Busenello)
L'alma fiacca svani F. Von Stade, Scottish CO, R. Leppard (r1984) (ERAT) Ⓓ **4509-98504-2**

Egisto– opera: prologue & 3 acts (1643—Venice) (Lib. Faustini)
Amor, che ti diè l'ali F. Von Stade, Scottish CO, R. Leppard (r1984) (ERAT) Ⓓ **4509-98504-2**

Giasone– opera: prologue and 3 acts (1649—Venice)
EXCERPTS: 1. Delizie contente.
Giasone M. Chance
Ercole; Giove H. van der Kamp
Besso; Volano M. Schopper
Isifile C. Dubosc
Oreste B. Delétré
Alinda; Amore A. Mellon
Medea G. Banditelli
Delfa; Eolo D. Visse
Egeo; Sole G. de Mey
Demo G. Fagotto
Concerto Vocale, R. Jacobs (r1988)
(7/89) (HARM) ▭ [3] **HMC40 1282/4**
1. C. Bartoli, G. Fischer
(12/92) (DECC) Ⓓ **436 267-2DH**
(12/92) (DECC) ▭ **436 267-4DH**

Orimonte– opera (1650—Venice) (Lib. Minato)
Numi ciechi più di me F. Von Stade, Scottish CO, R. Leppard (r1984)
(ERAT) Ⓓ **4509-98504-2**

L' **Ormindo– opera: 2 acts (1644—Venice) (Lib. G Faustini)**
EXCERPTS: 1. Sinfonia. ACT ONE: 2a. Miracolo d'amore; 2b. Quel che creduto io non avrei pur vidi; 2c. Huat, hanat, Ista; 2d. Perfidissimo Amida; 3. Verginella infelice; 4a. Se nel sen di giovinetti; 4b. Eccola appunto, Ormindo; 4c. Oh dell'anima mia; 5. Se del Perù le vene; 6a. Auree trecce inanellate; 6b. Dove, mia bella Aurora; 7. Volevo amar anch'io; 8. No, non vo' più amare. ACT TWO: 9. Che città; 10a. Quanto esclamasti; 10b. E' questo, s'io non erro; 10c. Che rimiro? Oh stupore; 11. Che dirà, che farà; 12. Ah pigri! Che tardate?; 13. In grembo al caro amato; 14a. Conosco gl'apparati; 14b. Ahi, spirò la mia vita; 14c. Son morti questi adulteri?; 14d. Un talamo ed un letto.
Ormindo J. Wakefield
Amida P-C. Runge
Nerillo I. Garcisanz
Sicle H. van Bork
Melide J. Allister
Erice H. Cuénod
Erisbe A. Howells
Mirinda J. Berbié
Ariadeno F. Davià
Osmano R. Van Allan
LPO, R. Leppard (r1968)
(9/95) (DECC) Ⓓ [2] **444 529-2DMO2**

Scipione affricano– opera: prologue & 3 acts (1664—Venice) (Lib. Minato)
Non è, non è crudel F. Von Stade, Scottish CO, R. Leppard (r1984) (ERAT) Ⓓ **4509-98504-2**

Xerse– opera: prologue & 3 acts (1654—Venice) (Lib. Minato)
Xerse R. Jacobs
Amastre J. Nelson
Arsamene J. Gall
Romilda I. Poulenard
Adelanta; Curiosity J. Feldman
Ariodante; Sesotre J. Elwes
Eumene; Architecture G. de Mey
Aristone; Scitalce R. Wistreich
Periarco; Painting J. Nirouët
Elviro; Poetry D. Visse
Clito; Music A. Mellon
Captain F. Fauché
Ens, R. Jacobs
(HARM) ▭ [4] **HMC40 1175/8**
La bellezza è un don fugace F. Von Stade, Scottish CO, R. Leppard (r1984)
(ERAT) Ⓓ **4509-98504-2**

CELLIER, Alfred *(1844–1891)* *England*

Dorothy– comedy opera: 3 acts (1886—London) (Lib. B C Stephenson)
Queen of my heart T. Burke, orch (r1932)
(PEAR) Ⓓ **GEMMCD9411**

CESTI, Antonio *(1623–1669)* *Italy*

Orontea– opera: 3 acts (1649—Venice) (Lib. G.A. Cicognini)
EXCERPTS: 1. Intorno all'idol mio.
Philosophy A. Bierbaum
Love C. Cadelo
Orontea H. Müller-Molinari
Ceronte G. Reinhart
Aristea G. de Mey
Alidoro R. Jacobs
Gelone G. Sarti
Corindo D. James
Silandra I. Poulenard
Giacinta J. Feldman
Baroque Instr Ens, R. Jacobs
(HARM) Ⓓ [3] **HMC90 1100/2**
1. D. Borgioli, anon (r c1941)
(PEAR) Ⓓ **GEMMCD9091**
1. C. Bartoli, G. Fischer
(12/92) (DECC) Ⓓ **436 267-2DH**
(12/92) (DECC) ▭ **436 267-4DH**
1. J. Baker, ASMF, N. Marriner
(1/93) (PHIL) Ⓓ **434 173-2PM**

CHABRIER , (Alexis-)Emmanuel *(1841–1894)* *France*

Briséïs, ou Les amants de Corinthe– drame lyrique: 1 act of unfinished opera (1888-91; perf 1897—Paris) (Lib. Mendès & Mikhaël, after Goethe)
Briséïs J. Rodgers
Hylas M. Padmore
Le Catéchiste S. Keenlyside
Stratoklès M. George
Thanastô K. Harries
Scottish Op Chor, BBC Scottish SO, J. Y. Ossonce (pp1994)
(8/95) (HYPE) Ⓓ **CDA66803**

Une **Éducation manquée– operetta: 1 act (1879—Paris) (Lib. E. Leterrier & A. Vanloo)**
Hélène L. Berton
Gontran J. Berbié
Pausanius J-C. Benoit
Paris Cons, J-C. Hartemann (r1965)
(EMI) Ⓓ **CDM5 65155-2**
Gontran C. Castelli
Hélène C. Collart
Pausanias X. Depraz
Orch, C. Bruck (with dialogue: r1950s)
(8/92) (CHNT) Ⓓ **LDC278 1068**
M. Delunsch, B. Desnoues, J-L. Georgel, Strasbourg Collegium Musicum Orch, R. Delage
(ARIO) Ⓓ **ARN68252**

L' **Étoile– opéra bouffe: 3 acts (1877—Paris) (Lib. Leterrier and Vanloo)**
Rondeau du colporteur; Romance de l'Étoile F. Révoil, orch, R. Desormière (r1934)
(EMI) Ⓓ [2] **CZS5 68292-2**

Fisch-Ton-Kan– operetta (1864—Paris) (Lib. P. Verlaine)
M. Delunsch, C. Mehn, F. Dudziak, J-L. Georgel, Vocal Ens, Strasbourg Collegium Musicum Orch, R. Delage (ARIO) Ⓓ **ARN68252**

Gwendoline– opera: 2 acts (1886—Brussels) (Lib. C. Mendes)
EXCERPTS: 1. Overture.
Blonde aux yeux de pervenche C. Castelli, H. Boschi (r1950s)
(8/92) (CHNT) Ⓓ **LDC278 1068**
Ne riez pas B. Hendricks, Toulouse Capitole Orch, M. Plasson
(2/91) (EMI) Ⓓ **CDC7 54004-2**
Overture Toulouse Capitole Orch, M. Plasson
(2/91) (EMI) Ⓓ **CDC7 54004-2**
1. Detroit SO, P. Paray (r1960)
(MERC) Ⓓ **434 303-2MM**
1. FNO, A. Jordan (r1982)
(ERAT) Ⓓ **4509-96370-2**
1. FRNO, T. Beecham (r1957)
(9/92) (EMI) Ⓓ **CDM7 63401-2**

Le **Roi malgré lui– opéra-comique: 3 acts (1887—Paris) (Lib. de Najac and Burani, rev Richepin)**
EXCERPTS: 1. Sextor des serves; 2. Chanson tzigane; 3. Danse slave; 4. Fête polonaise; 5. Beau pays (Romance du roi).
Minka B. Hendricks
Alexina I. Garcisanz
Henri de Valois G. Quilico
Comte de Nangis P. Jeffes
Duc de Fritelli J-P. Lafont
Lasky C. de Moor
Basile A. Battedou
Liancourt M. Shopland
D'Elboeuf A. Munier
Maugiron M. Sieyes
Villequier M. Walker
Caylus P. Bohée
Soldier P. Vilet
French Rad Chor, French Rad New PO, C. Dutoit
(ERAT) Ⓓ [2] **2292-45792-2**
Couplets du polonais; Couplets des Gondoles L. Fugère, orch (r1930)
(6/93) (SYMP) Ⓓ **SYMCD1125**
Fête polonaise; Danse slave Detroit SO, P. Paray (r1960) (MERC) Ⓓ **434 303-2MM**
Hélas, à l'esclavage C. Castelli, H. Boschi (r1950s) (8/92) (CHNT) Ⓓ **LDC278 1068**
Le polonais est triste et grave; Je suis du pays des gondoles L. Fugère, orch (r1930)
(9/91) (SYMP) Ⓓ **SYMCD1089**
3. FNO, A. Jordan (r1982)
(ERAT) Ⓓ **4509-96370-2**
3, 4. Toulouse Capitole Orch, M. Plasson (r1987)
(9/88) (EMI) Ⓓ **CDC7 49652-2**
4. Philh, I. Markevitch (r1954)
(TEST) Ⓓ **SBT1060**
4. Detroit SO, N. Järvi (r1992)
(8/94) (CHAN) Ⓓ **CHAN9227**
(8/94) (CHAN) ▭ **ABTD1604**
4. San Francisco SO, P. Monteux (r1947)
(9/94) (RCA) Ⓓ [15] **09026 61893-2**
5. G. Souzay, New SO, P. Bonneau (r1956)
(DECC) Ⓓ **440 419-2DM**

Vaucochard et Fils Ier– operetta (1864—Paris) (Lib. P Verlaine & L Viotti)
M. Delunsch, J-L. Georgel, F. Dudziak, Vocal Ens, Strasbourg Collegium Musicum Orch, R. Delage (ARIO) Ⓓ **ARN68252**

CHAILLEY , Jacques *(b 1910)* *France*

Thyl de Flandre– opera: 5 acts (1946-53—Brussels) (Lib. J. Bruyr)
Air de Katheline É. Norska, K. Bronk-Zdunowska (REM) Ⓓ **REM11036**

CHAPÍ (Y LORENTE), Ruperto *(1851–1909) Spain*

La **Bruja– comic opera: 3 acts (1887—Madrid) (Lib. M R Carrión)**
No extrañéis que se escapen P. Domingo, Madrid Zarzuela Chor, Madrid SO, M. Moreno-Buendia (r1987)
(1/89) (EMI) Ⓓ **CDC7 49148-2**

El tambor de Granaderos– zarzuela (1894—Madrid) (Lib. E. Sánchez Pastor)
Overture G. Pérez-Quer, D. Kassner (arr Pérez-Quer) (PRES) Ⓓ **PCOM1120**

Las **Hijas del Zebedeo– zarzuela: 2 acts (1889—Madrid) (Lib. Estremera)**
Al pensar en el dueño L. Tetrazzini, orch, P. Pitt (r1909)
(9/92) (EMI) Ⓓ [3] **CHS7 63802-2(1)**
Al penser en el dueño L. Tetrazzini, orch, P. Pitt (r1909) (9/92) (PEAR) Ⓓ **GEMMCD9222**
Carceleras V. de los Angeles, Sinfonia of London, R. Frühbeck de Burgos (orch Gamley)
(10/88) (EMI) Ⓓ **CDM7 69502-2**
Carceleras L. Tetrazzini, orch (r1911)
(9/92) (PEAR) Ⓓ **GEMMCD9223**

El **Milagro de la Virgen– zarzuela: 3 acts (1884—Madrid) (Lib. M. Pina Dominguez)**
Flores purisimas E. Caruso, G. Scognamiglio (r1914) (7/91) (RCA) Ⓓ [12] **GD60495(5)**

Flores purisimas E. Caruso, G. Scognamiglio (r1914) (10/91) (PEAR) ⓓ [3] **EVC3(1)**

El **Puñado de Rosas– zarzuela: 1 act (1902—Madrid) (Lib. Arniches & R. Asensio Más)**

Duo de Rosario y Pepe G. Sanchez, P. Domingo, Madrid SO, E. G. Asensio (pp1991) (11/92) (IMP) ⓓ **MCD45**

Romanza L. Bori, A. de Segurola, Victor Orch, W.B. Rogers (r1915) (ROMO) ⓓ [2] **81016-2**

La **Revoltosa– sainete lirico: 1 act (1897—Madrid) (Lib. F. Shaw and Silva)**

Mari Pepa T. Tourné
Soledad M. R. Gabriel
Chupitos A.M. Higueras
Felipe R. Cesari
Gorgonia M. Hernandez
Tiberio R. Diez
Cándido S. Garcia
Atenedoro A. Viñes
Madrid Coros Cantores, Madrid Concerts Orch, P. Sorozábal (10/92) (HISP) ⓓ **CDZ7 67328-2**

Porque de mis ojos L. Bori, A. de Segurola, Victor Orch, W.B. Rogers (r1915) (ROMO) ⓓ [2] **81016-2**

CHARPENTIER, Gustave *(1860–1950) France*

Louise– opera: 4 acts (1900—Paris) (Lib. cpsr)

EXCERPTS: 1. Prelude. ACT 1: 2a. O coeur ami! ô coeur promis!; 2b. Prêtez l'oreille; 3. Moi, je vous avais remarqué; 4. C'était mon adorée!; 5. Bonsoir! La soupe est prête?; 6. Une lettre?; 7. O mon enfant, ma Louise. ACT 2: 8. Prelude; 9. Dire qu'en c'moment y a des femmes; 10. Les bons lits! les belles robes!; 11. C'est ici? C'est là qu'elle travaille?; 12. Ella va paraître, ma joie, mon tourment!; 13. Bonjour! Bonjour! Comment vas-tu?; 14. Pourquoi te retourner?; 15. Laissez-moi, ah! de grâce!; 16. Marchand d'habits! avez-vous des habits à vendr'?; 17. Interlude; 18a. La! la! la! C'est énervant!; 18b. Oh! moi quand je suis dans la ruse; 19. Un!...Quell drôl' de fanfare!; 20. Dans la cité lointaine; 21. Qu'est-c' qui lui prend?. ACT 3: 22. Prelude; 23. Depuis le jour où je me suis donnée; 24. Louise!...Quelle belle vie!; 25. Ainsi tout enfant a le droit de choisir; 26. Julien! Louise!; 27. Ah! Prends-moi vite, vite; 28a. Ils sont là?; 28b. Choeur des gens de la butte; 29. Par Mercure aux pieds légers; 30. O jolie! Soeur choisie!; 31. Je ne viens pas en ennemie. ACT 4: 33a. Tu devrais te rapproacher de la fenêtre; 33b. Les pauvres gens peuvent-ils être heureux?; 34. Voir naître un enfant; 35. Louise! Louise! Quoi? Viens m'aider!; 36a. Bonsoir, père; 36b. Reste...repose-toi; 36c. L'enfant serait sage; 37. Tout être le droit de'être libre!; 38. Qu'il vienne vite, vite, mon bien-aimé; 39. Louise!...Louise!...

Louise I. Cotrubas
Julien P. Domingo
Father G. Bacquier
Mother J. Berbié
Noctambulist; King of Fools M. Sénéchal
Irma L. Guitton
Camille E. Manchet
Blanche L. Reid
Marguerite J. Jarvis
Gertrude S. Minty
Madeleine A. Butler
Suzanne M. Midgley
Elise; Coal Gatherer L. Richardson
Newspaper Girl; Urchin; Corn Girl P. Clark
Street Sweeper G. Jennings
Little Ragpicker P. Bartlett
Milkwoman M. Cable
Forewoman M. Dickinson
Apprentice Girl D. Murray
Ragpicker J. Noble
Junk Merchant; Watercress Vendor L. Fyson
Songwriter P. Bamber
Sculptor W. Mason
Poet V. Midgley
Student J. Lewington
Painter P. Halstead
1st Philosopher O. Broome
2nd Philosopher P. Bedford
Second-Hand Clothes Merchant N. Jenkins
1st Policeman; Apprentice E. Fleet
2nd Policeman M. Brown
Chairmender C. Parker
Artichoke Vendor J. Brown
Carrot Vendor M. Clark
Pea Vendor U. Connors
Bird-Seed Vendor A. MacGregor
Bohemian I. Thompson
Ambrosian Op Chor, New Philh, G. Prêtre (6/91) (SONY) ⓓ [3] **S3K46429**

Louise B. Monmart
Julien A. Laroze
Father L. Musy
Mother S. Michel
Noctambulist L. Rialland
King of Fools P. Giannotti
J. Fournet, Paris Opéra-Comique Chor, Paris Opéra-Comique Orch, J. Fournet (r1956) (9/94) (PHIL) ⓓ [3] **442 082-2PM3**

Louise B. Sills
Julien N. Gedda
Father J. Van Dam
Mother M. Dunn
Noctambulist; King of the Fools M. Hill
Irma E. Lublin
Maîtrise de la Résurrection, Paris Op Chor, Paris Op Orch, J. Rudel (r1977) (2/95) (EMI) ⓓ [3] **CMS5 65299-2**

Abridged: arr cpsr N. Vallin, G. Thill, A. Pernet, A. Lecouvreur, C. Gaudel, Rougel Chor, orch, E. Bigot (r1935) (NIMB) ⓓ **NI7829**

18b Y. Gall, orch (r1929) (MSCM) ⓓ **MM30221** (MSCM) ▭ **MM040079**

23. M. Caballé, Barcelona SO, C.F. Cillario (11/92) (RCA) ▭ [2] **RK61044**

23. K. Te Kanawa, LSO, J. Mauceri (12/90) (DECC) ▭ **084 474-3**

23. E. Steber, orch, H. Barlow (bp1949) (VAI) ▭ **VAI69102**

23. A. Moffo, Munich RO, K. Eichhorn (EURO) ⓓ **GD69113**

23. J. Sutherland, F. Corelli, R. Bonynge (DECC) ⓓ **433 064-2DWO**

23. M. Foley, Orch (r1949-53) (ODE) ⓓ **CDODE1062**

23. N. Vallin, orch, G. Cloëz (r c1927-32) (PEAR) ⓓ **GEMMCD9948**

23. M. Callas, FRNO, G. Prêtre (r1961) (EMI) ⓓ **CDC5 55016-2**

23. C. Muzio, orch (r1918) (PEAR) ⓓ **GEMMCD9143**

23. L. Price, RCA Italiana Op Orch, F. Molinari-Pradelli (r1960s) (RCA) ⓓ **09026 62596-2**

23. P. Lorengar, Santa Cecilia Academy Orch, G. Patanè (r1966) (DECC) ⓓ **443 931-2DM**

23. K. Te Kanawa, ROHO, J. Tate (r1988) (EMI) ⓓ **CDM5 65578-2**

23. G. Bumbry, Stuttgart RSO, S. Soltesz (11/86) (ORFE) ⓓ **C081841A**

23. M. Callas, FRNO, G. Prêtre (2/88) (EMI) ⓓ **CDC7 49059-2**

23. M. Freni, Rome Op Orch, F. Ferraris (10/89) (EMI) ⓓ **CDM7 63110-2**

23. M. Callas, FRNO, G. Prêtre (2/90) (EMIN) ⓓ **CD-EMX2123** (2/88) (EMIN) ▭ **TC-EMX2123**

23. K. Te Kanawa, ROHO, J. Tate (2/90) (EMI) ⓓ **CDC7 49863-2**

23. E. Steber, Philh, W. Susskind (r1947) (4/92) (EMI) ⓓ [7] **CHS7 69741-2(1)**

23. A. Marc, NZ SO, H. Wallberg (6/92) (DELO) ⓓ **DE3108** (6/92) (DELO) ▭ **CS3108**

23. K. Battle, M. Garrett (pp1991) (7/92) (DG) ⓓ **435 440-2GH**

23. L. Edvina, orch (r1919) (7/92) (PEAR) ⓓ [3] **GEMMCDS9925(1)**

23. L. Price, RCA Italiana Op Orch, F. Molinari-Pradelli (12/92) (RCA) ⓓ [4] **09026 61236-2**

23. M. Caballé, New Philh, R. Giovaninetti (r1970) (5/93) (DG) ⓓ **431 103-2GB**

23. M. Garden, orch (r1912) (8/93) (SYMP) ⓓ **SYMCD1136**

23. M. Garden, orch (r1926) (8/93) (SYMP) ⓓ **SYMCD1136**

23. N. Melba, G. Lapierre (r1913) (9/93) (RCA) ⓓ **09026 61412-2**

23. G. Moore, RCA SO, W. Pelletier (r1940) (4/94) (RCA) ⓓ [6] **09026 61580-2(4)**

23. M. Garden, orch, Rosario Bourdon (r1926: 2 vers) (8/94) (ROMO) ⓓ **81008-2**

23. M. Garden, J. Dansereau (r1927) (8/94) (ROMO) ⓓ **81008-2**

23. E. Mason, orch, F. Black (r1928) (8/94) (ROMO) ⓓ **81009-2**

23. A. Roocroft, LPO, F. Welser-Möst (10/94) (EMI) ⓓ **CDC5 55090-2** (10/94) (EMI) ▭ **EL5 55090-4**

23. M. Devia, Svizzera Italiana Orch, M. Rota (pp1992) (10/94) (BONG) ⓓ **GB2513-2**

23. C. Muzio, orch (r1918) (1/95) (ROMO) ⓓ [2] **81010-2**

23. N. Melba, orch, W.B. Rogers (r1913) (5/95) (ROMO) ⓓ [3] **81011-2(2)**

23. N. Melba, G. Lapierre (r1913) (5/95) (ROMO) ⓓ [3] **81011-2(2)**

26. P. Domingo, I. Cotrubas, New Philh, G. Prêtre (r1970s) (SONY) ⓓ **SMK39030**

34. L. Fugère, orch (r1928) (6/93) (SYMP) ⓓ **SYMCD1125**

36b M. Journet, orch, Rosario Bourdon (r1926) (PREI) ⓓ **89021**

36b M. Journet, SO, Rosario Bourdon (r1926) (1/94) (CLUB) ⓓ **CL99-034**

36b Vanni-Marcoux, orch (r1934) (1/94) (CLUB) ⓓ **CL99-101**

CHARPENTIER, Marc-Antoine *(1643–1704) France*

H–Numbers from H.W. Hitchcock's catalogue

Actéon– pastorale en musique, H481 (1683-85)

Actéon D. Visse
Diane A. Mellon
Junon G. Laurens
Arthébuze J. Feldman
Hyale F. Paut
Arts Florissants Voc Ens, Arts Florissants Instr Ens, W. Christie (HARM) ⓓ **HMA190 1095** (HARM) ▭ **HMA43 1095**

Andromède– tragédie, H504 (1682) (Lib. P. Corneille)

London Baroque, C. Medlam (r1986) (HARM) ⓓ **HMA190 1244**

Les **Arts Florissants– opera, H487 (1685-86)**

La Paix J. Feldman
La Musique A. Mellon
La Discorde G. Reinhart
La Poésie C. Dussaut
L'Architecture G. Laurens
La Peinture D. Visse
Un Guerrier P. Cantor
Arts Florissants Voc Ens, Arts Florissants Instr Ens, W. Christie (r1981) (12/87) (HARM) ⓓ **HMA190 1083** (HARM) ▭ **HMA43 1083**

Circé– intermèdes, H504 (1675) (Lib. T. Corneille and D. de Visé)

London Baroque, C. Medlam (r1986) (HARM) ⓓ **HMA190 1244**

La **Comtesse d'Escarbagnas/Le Mariage Forcé– ouverture/intermèdes nouveaux, H494 (1672) (Lib. Molière)**

D. Visse, M. Laplénie, P. Cantor, Arts Florissants Instr Ens, W. Christie (HARM) ⓓ **HMA190 1095** (HARM) ▭ **HMA43 1095**

Arts Florissants Voc Ens, Arts Florissants Instr Ens, W. Christie (HARM) ⓓ **HMP390 802**

David et Jonathas– tragédie en musique: prologue and 5 acts, H490 (1688)

David G. Lesne
Jonathas M. Zanetti
Saül J-F. Gardeil
Achis, Ghost of Samuel B. Delétré
Joabel J-P. Fouchécourt
La Pythonisse D. Visse
A Warrior R. Bischoff
Arts Florissants Voc Ens, Arts Florissants Instr Ens, W. Christie (12/88) (HARM) ▭ [2] **HMC40 1289/90**

David P. Esswood
Jonathas C. Alliot-Lugaz
Saül P. Huttenlocher
Achis R. Soyer
Joabel A. David
Ghost of Samuel P. Marinov
Joabel A. David
La Phythonisse R. Jacobs
A Warrior F. Le Roux
Lyon Enfants de la Cigale Ch, Lyon Lycée Musical Ch, Lyon Op Chor, English Bach Fest Baroque Orch, M. Corboz (ERAT) ⓓ [2] **2292-45162-2**

Overture; Prologue Arts Florissants Voc Ens, Arts Florissants Instr Ens, W. Christie
(HARM) ① **HMP390 802**

Médée– tragédie lyrique, H491 (1693) (Text P. Corneille)

Médée J. Feldman
Créon J. Bona
Créuse A. Mellon
Jason G. Ragon
Oronte P. Cantor
Nérine S. Boulin
Arts Florissants Chor, Arts Florissants Orch, W. Christie
(3/85) (HARM) ① [3] **HMC90 1139/41**

Médée L. Hunt
Créon B. Delétré
Créuese M. Zanetti
Jason M. Padmore
Oronte J-M. Salzmann
Nérine N. Rime
Arts Florissants Chor, Arts Florissants Orch, W. Christie (r1994)
(6/95) (ERAT) ① [3] **4509-96558-2**

Excs Arts Florissants Voc Ens, Arts Florissants Instr Ens, W. Christie (HARM) ① **HMP390 802**

CHAUSSON, (Amedée-)Ernest *(1855–1899) France*

Le **Roi Arthus– drama lyrique: 3 acts, Op. 23 (1903—Brussels) (Lib. cpsr)**

Arthus G. Quilico
Guenièvre T. Zylis-Gara
Lancelot G. Winbergh
Mordred R. Massis
Lyonnel G. Friedmann
Allan F. Loup
Merlin G. Cachemaille
Labourer T. Dran
Knight R. Schirrer
Squire A. Laiter
French Rad Chor, French Rad New PO, A. Jordan
(10/91) (ERAT) ① [3] **2292-45407-2**

CHERUBINI, Luigi (Carlo Zanobi Salvadore Maria) *(1760–1842) Italy*

Les **Abencérages– opera: 3 acts (1813—Paris) (Lib. V. J. E. de Jouy, after Chateaubriand)**
EXCERPTS: 1. Overture.
1. ASMF, N. Marriner
(9/92) (EMI) ① **CDC7 54438-2**

Ali-Baba, ou Les quarante voleurs– opera: prologue and 4 acts (1833—Paris) (Lib. Scribe and A. H. J. Mélesville)
Overture NBC SO, A. Toscanini (bp1949)
(RCA) ① **GD60278**
Speme non vè, tutto è perduto Alfredo Kraus, La Scala Orch, N. Sanzogno (pp1963)
(MEMO) ① [2] **HR4233/4**

Anacréon– opéra-ballet: 2 acts (1803—Paris) (Lib. C. R. Mendouze)
Overture NBC SO, A. Toscanini (bp1953)
(RCA) ① **GD60278**
Overture BPO, H. von Karajan
(EMI) ① **CDM7 64629-2**
Overture ASMF, N. Marriner
(9/92) (EMI) ① **CDC7 54438-2**
Overture Concertgebouw, W. Mengelberg (pp1943) (12/93) (ARHI) ① **ADCD111**
Overture Lamoureux Orch, I. Markevitch
(7/95) (DG) ① **447 406-2GOR**

Le **Crescendo– opera: 1 act (1810—Paris) (Lib. C. A. Sewin)**
Overture Tuscany Rad & TV Orch, D. Renzetti
(EURM) ① **350221**

Les **Deux journées– opera: 3 acts (Paris) (Lib. J. N. Bouilly)**
EXCERPTS: 1. Overture.
1. ASMF, N. Marriner
(9/92) (EMI) ① **CDC7 54438-2**

Elisa– opera: 2 acts (1794—Paris) (Lib. J. A. de R. Saint-Cyr)
Overture ASMF, N. Marriner
(9/92) (EMI) ① **CDC7 54438-2**

Faniska– opera: 3 acts (1806—Vienna) (Lib. J. Sonnenleithner)
Overture ASMF, N. Marriner
(9/92) (EMI) ① **CDC7 54438-2**

L' **Hôtellerie portugaise– opera: 1 act (1798—Paris) (Lib. E. Aignan)**
EXCERPTS: 1. Overture.
1. ASMF, N. Marriner
(9/92) (EMI) ① **CDC7 54438-2**

Ifigenia in Aulide– opera: 3 acts (1788—Turin) (Lib. Moretti)
Overture Tuscany Rad & TV Orch, D. Renzetti
(EURM) ① **350221**

Lodoïska– opera: 3 acts (1791—Paris)

Lodoïska M. Devia
Lysinka F. Pedaci
Floreski B. Lombardo
Titzikan T. Moser
Varbel A. Corbelli
Dourlinski W. Shimell
Altamoras M. Luperi
Talma D. Serraiocco
First Emissary P. Spina
Second Emissary E. Panariello
Third Emissary E. Capuano
First Tartar R. Cazzaniga
Second Tartar A. Bramante
La Scala Chor, La Scala Orch, R. Muti (pp1991)
(10/91) (SONY) ① [2] **S2K47290**

Miseri noi...Questo viaggio di piacere S. Bruscantini, Rome RAI Chor, Rome RAI Orch, O. de Fabritiis (pp1965)
(MEMO) ① [2] **HR4300/1**

Medea– opera: 3 acts (1797—Paris) (Lib. F.B. Hoffman)
ACT 1: 1a. Overture; 1b. Che? Quando già corona; 1c. Io cedo alla buona preghiera; 1d. O Amore, vieni a me; 1e. No, non temer; 2a. O bella Glauce; 2b. Colco! Pensier; 3a. Or che più non vedrò; 3b. Ah, già troppo turbò; 4a. Pronube dive; 4b. Signor! Ferma una donna; 5a. Qui tremar devi tu; 5b. Taci, Giason; 6a. Dei tuoi figli la madre; 6b. Son vane qui minacce; 7. Nemici senza cor. ACT 2: 8a. Introduction; 8b. Soffrir non posso; 9a. Data almen, per pietà; 9b. Medea! o Medea!; 10a. Solo un pianto; 10b. Creonte a me solo; 11a. Figli miei; 11b. Hai dato pronto ascolto; 12. Ah! Triste canto...Dio dell' Amor!. ACT 3: 13a. Introduction; 13b. Numi, venite a me; 14a. Del fiero duol; 14b. D'amore il raggio ancora; 15. E che? Io son Medea!.

Medea M. Callas
Jason M. Picchi
Glauce R. Scotto
Creon G. Modesti
Neris M. Pirazzini
Maidservant I L. Marimpietri
Maidservant II E. Galassi
Guard Captain A. Giacomotti
La Scala Chor, La Scala Orch, T. Serafin
(2/91) (EMI) ① [2] **CMS7 63625-2**

1a Tuscany Rad & TV Orch, D. Renzetti
(EURM) ① **350221**
1a NBC SO, A. Toscanini (bp1950)
(RCA) ① **GD60278**
1a Munich RO, K. Redel (PIER) ① **PV786104**
1a ASMF, N. Marriner
(9/92) (EMI) ① **CDC7 54438-2**
1c, 1d E. Gruberová, Munich RO, L. Gardelli
(11/86) (ORFE) ① **C101841A**
6a, 6b M. Horne, Monte Carlo PO, L. Foster (r1984: Fr) (ERAT) ① **4509-98501-2**
6a, 6b G. Bumbry, Stuttgart RSO, S. Soltesz
(11/86) (ORFE) ① **C081841A**
6a, 6b M. Callas, La Scala Orch, T. Serafin (r1955) (11/86) (EMI) ① **CDC7 47282-2**
6a, 6b M. Callas, La Scala Orch, T. Serafin (r1955) (2/90) (EMI) ① [4] **CMS7 63244-2**
9b, 10a F. Cossotto, Santa Cecilia Academy Orch, L. Gardelli (r1967)
(DECC) ① **443 378-2DM**
15. L. Gencer, Venice La Fenice Orch, C. Franci (pp1968) (MEMO) ① [2] **HR4239/40**

CHRISTINÉ, Henri *(1867–1941) Switzerland/France*

Phi-Phi– operetta: 3 acts (1918—Paris) (Lib. A. Willemetz & F. Solar)
EXCERPTS: 1. Overture. ACT 1: 2. Ensemble; 3. C'est une gamine charmante; 4. Maître, lorsque l'on a vingt ans; 5. Je conaais toutes les historiettes; 6. Vertu, Verturon, Verturonnette; 7. J'sortais des portes de Trézène; 8. Pour l'amour (Finale 1). ACT 2: 9. Ah! cher monsier!; 10. Prière à Pallas; 11. Tout tombe; 12. Ah! tais-toi! (Valse et Finale 2). ACT 3: 13. Duo des souvenirs; 14. Bien chapeautée; 15. Chanson des petits Païens; 16. Quintette; 17. Finale.
9. R. Crespin, Vienna Volksoper Orch, G. Sébastian (r1970/1) (DECC) ① **440 416-2DM**
13. B. Hendricks, G. Quilico, Lyon Op Orch, L. Foster (r1993) (6/95) (EMI) ① **CDC5 55151-2**

CHUECA, Federico *(1846–1908) Spain*

El **Bateo– zarzuela**
Prelude Madrid SO, E. G. Asensio (pp1991)
(11/92) (IMP) ① **MCD45**

La **Gran Vía– zarzuela (1886—Madrid) (Lib. F. Perez G: comp with Valverde)**
Schottisch del Eliseo Madrileño T. Verdera, Madrid SO, E. G. Asensio (pp1991)
(11/92) (IMP) ① **MCD45**

Los **Paraguas– zarzuela**
Mazurka G. Pérez-Quer, D. Kassner (arr Pérez-Quer) (PRES) ① **PCOM1120**

CHUKHADJIAN, Tigran *(1837–1898) Armenia*

may also be spelt Tchukhadzhan

Arshak II– opera (1868) (Lib. T. T'erzyan)
Arshak's arioso P. Lisitsian, Bolshoi Th Orch, A. Orlov (r1948) (8/93) (PREI) ① **89061**

CIAMPI, Vincenzo *(1719–1762) Italy*

Tre cicisbei ridicoli– opera (Lib. Contini)
Fanciullina H. Spani, orch, G. Nastrucci (r1929)
(9/90) (CLUB) ① [2] **CL99-509/10**

CILEA, Francesco *(1866–1950) Italy*

Adriana Lecouvreur– opera: 4 acts (1902—Milan) (Lib. Colautti, after Scribe and Legouvé)
EXCERPTS: 1. Introduction; 2. ACT 1: Per sembra più celeste!; 3a. Troppo, signori; 3b. Io son l'umile ancella; 4a. Adriana!; 4b. La dolcissimi effigie; 4c. Parliam di cosa lieta; 5a. Ecco il monologo; 5b. Bene! benissimo! ACT 2: 6a. Acerba voluttà; 6b. O vagabondo; 7. L'anima ho stanca; 8. Ma, dunque, è vero?; 9. Interlude; 10a. Non risponde; 10b. Sì, con l'ansia; 10c. Io son sua per l'amore. ACT 3: 11. Introduction; 12a. Madamigella; 12b. Il russo Méncikoff; 13. Ballet; 14. Giusto cielo! che feci in tal. ACT 4: 15. Intermezzo; 16. Poveri fiori; 17a. No, la mia fronte; 17b. No, più nobile; 17c. Il nostro amor; 18. Scostatevi, profani!.

Adriana R. Scotto
Maurizio P. Domingo
Michonnet S. Milnes
Princess de Bouillon E. Obraztsova
Prince de Bouillon G. Luccardi
Abbé de Chazeuil F. Andreolli
Jouvenot L. Watson
Dangeville A. Murray
Poisson; Major-domo P. Crook
Quinault P. Hudson
Ambrosian Op Chor, Philh, James Levine (r1977)
(3/90) (CBS) ① [2] **CD79310**

Adriana J. Sutherland
Maurizio C. Bergonzi
Michonnet L. Nucci
Princess de Bouillon C. Ciurca
Prince de Bouillon F.E. d'Artegna
Abbé de Chazeuil M. Sénéchal
Jouvenot F. Ginzer
Dangeville D. Stuart-Roberts
Poisson P. Bronder

Quinault B. Terfel
Major-Domo C. Cue
WNO Chor, WNO Orch, R. Bonynge (r1988)
(9/90) (DECC) Ⓓ [2] **425 815-2DH2**
Adriana R. Tebaldi
Maurizio M. del Monaco
Michonnet G. Fioravanti
Princess de Bouillon G. Simionato
Prince de Bouillon S. Maionica
Abbé de Chazeuil F. Ricciardi
Jouvenot D. Carral
Dangeville F. Cadoni
Poisson; Major-domo A. Mercuriali
Quinault G. Foiani
Santa Cecilia Academy Chor, Santa Cecilia Academy Orch, F. Capuana (r1961)
(8/91) (DECC) Ⓓ [2] **430 256-2DM2**
Eccoci soli alfin; 5a; So ch'ella dorme E. Bastianini, M. Olivero, F. Corelli, Naples San Carlo Op Chor, Naples San Carlo Op Orch, M. Rossi (pp1959) (MEMO) Ⓓ [2] **HR4400/1**
Excs J. Sutherland, Orch, Anon (cond), D. Bailey (11/92) (DECC) ● **071 135-1DH**
3a J. Hammond, Philh, W. Susskind (r1949) (12/92) (TEST) Ⓓ **SBT1013**
3a, 3b R. Tebaldi, Santa Cecilia Academy Orch, A. Erede (r1961) (DECC) Ⓓ **440 408-2DM**
3a, 3b M. Callas, Philh, T. Serafin (r1954) (EMI) Ⓓ **CDC5 55016-2**
3a, 3b K. Te Kanawa, LSO, Myung-Whun Chung (r1989) (EMI) Ⓓ **CDC5 55095-2**
3a, 3b R. Tebaldi, Santa Cecilia Academy Orch, A. Erede (8/91) (DECC) Ⓓ [2] **430 481-2DX2**
3a, 3b, 16. M. Freni, La Scala Orch, A. Votto (10/89) (EMI) Ⓓ **CDM7 63110-2**
3b M. Caballé, Barcelona SO, G-F. Masini (11/92) (RCA) ▭ [2] **RK61044**
3b K. Ricciarelli, Svizzera Italiana Orch, B. Amaducci (r1980) (ERMI) Ⓓ **ERM151**
3b J. Wiener-Chenisheva, Bulgarian Nat Op Orch, I. Marinov (r1970s) (FORL) Ⓓ **UCD16742**
3b G. Bumbry, Stuttgart RSO, S. Soltesz (11/86) (ORFE) Ⓓ **C081841A**
3b C. Muzio, orch (r1921) (5/90) (BOGR) Ⓓ [2] **BIM705-2**
3b A. Pandolfini, S. Cottone (r1903) (6/90) (SYMP) Ⓓ **SYMCD1073**
3b E. Burzio, orch (r c1906) (1/91) (CLUB) Ⓓ [2] **CL99-587/8**
3b A. Marc, NZ SO, H. Wallberg (6/92) (DELO) Ⓓ **DE3108**
(6/92) (DELO) ▭ **CS3108**
3b A. Pandolfini, anon (r1903) (11/92) (MEMO) Ⓓ [2] **HR4408/9(1)**
3b L. Price, RCA Italiana Op Orch, F. Molinari-Pradelli (12/92) (RCA) Ⓓ [4] **09026 61236-2**
3b C. Muzio, orch (r1921) (1/94) (ROMO) Ⓓ [2] **81005-2**
3b L. Garrett, RPO, P. Robinson (r1994) (4/95) (SILV) Ⓓ **SILKD6004**
(4/95) (SILV) ▭ **SILKC6004**
3b, 16. M. Callas, Philh, T. Serafin (r1954) (11/86) (EMI) Ⓓ **CDC7 47282-2**
3b, 16. G. Cigna, orch, L. Molajoli (r1932) (11/90) (PREI) Ⓓ **89016**
3b, 16. G. Cigna, orch, L. Molajoli (r1932) (11/90) (LYRC) Ⓓ **SRO805**
3b, 16. K. Te Kanawa, LSO, Myung-Whun Chung (11/90) (EMI) Ⓓ **CDC7 54062-2**
3b, 16, 18. J. Sutherland, A. Austin, J. Shaw, Sydney Eliz Orch, R. Bonynge (DECC) ● **071 149-1DH**
(DECC) ▣ **071 149-3DH**
4a, 4b F. Corelli, Naples San Carlo Op Orch, M. Rossi (pp1959; Ital) (MEMO) Ⓓ [2] **HR4204/5**
4a, 4b P. Domingo, R. Scotto, Philh, James Levine (r1970s) (SONY) Ⓓ **SMK39030**
4b M. del Monaco, R. Tebaldi, Santa Cecilia Academy Orch, F. Capuana (DECC) Ⓓ **433 067-2DWO**
(DECC) ▭ **433 067-4DWO**
4b C. Bergonzi, Santa Cecilia Academy Orch, G. Gavazzeni (r1957) (DECC) Ⓓ **436 314-2DA**
(DECC) ▭ **436 314-4DA**
4b P. Domingo, Berlin Deutsche Op Orch, N. Santi (TELD) Ⓓ **4509-96231-2**
(TELD) ▭ **4509-96231-4**
4b F. Corelli, Milan RAI SO, O. de Fabritiis (bp1956) (FONI) Ⓓ **CDMR5014**
4b A. Pertile, La Scala Orch, C. Sabajno (r1930) (10/94) (PREI) Ⓓ **89072**
4b, 7. L. Pavarotti, National PO, O. de Fabritiis (r1979) (DECC) Ⓓ **440 400-2DM**
4b, 7. M. del Monaco, Milan SO, T. Benintende-Neglia (r1952) (TEST) Ⓓ **SBT1039**
4b, 7. C. Bergonzi, Santa Cecilia Academy Orch, G. Gavazzeni (r1957) (DECC) Ⓓ **440 417-2DM**
4b, 7, 17b A. Giorgini, anon (r1904) (4/95) (RECO) Ⓓ **TRC3**
5a G. Taddei, Naples San Carlo Op Orch, U. Rapalo (PREI) Ⓓ **90020**
5a T. Gobbi, Philh, A. Erede (r1963) (10/89) (EMI) Ⓓ **CDM7 63109-2**
5b G. De Luca, F. Cilea (r1902) (PEAR) Ⓓ [3] **GEMMCDS9159(1)**
5b M. Sammarco, anon (r1905) (7/92) (PEAR) Ⓓ [3] **GEMMCDS9924(1)**
5b G. De Luca, F. Cilea (r1902) (8/93) (SYMP) Ⓓ **SYMCD1111**
6a L. Homer, orch (r1906) (IRCC) Ⓓ **IRCC-CD810**
7. P. Domingo, Philh, James Levine (SONY) Ⓓ **MDK47176**
(SONY) ▭ **MDT47176**
7. S. Islandi, Tivoli Concert Orch, S. Felumb (r1936) (4/92) (EMI) Ⓓ [7] **CHS7 69741-2(5)**
7. P. Domingo, New Philh, N. Santi (r1972) (4/94) (RCA) Ⓓ [6] **09026 61580-2(8)**
8. A. Stehle, E. Garbin, anon (r1904) (11/92) (MEMO) Ⓓ [2] **HR4408/9(1)**
8. R. Tebaldi, F. Corelli, SRO, A. Guadagno (r1972) (10/93) (DECC) Ⓓ **436 301-2DA**
10c G. Cigna, C. Elmo, EIAR Orch, U. Tansini (r1941) (11/90) (PREI) Ⓓ **89016**
15. BPO, H. von Karajan (10/87) (DG) Ⓓ [3] **419 257-2GH3**
15. Gothenburg SO, N. Järvi (6/90) (DG) Ⓓ **429 494-2GDC**
(6/90) (DG) ▭ **429 494-4GDC**
16. C. Muzio, orch (r1935) (PEAR) Ⓓ **GEMMCD9130**
16. K. Te Kanawa, LSO, Myung-Whun Chung (r1989) (EMI) Ⓓ **CDM5 65578-2**
16. E. Burzio, orch (r1913) (1/91) (CLUB) Ⓓ [2] **CL99-587/8**
16. C. Muzio, orch, L. Molajoli (r1935) (4/91) (NIMB) Ⓓ **NI7814**
(4/91) (NIMB) ▭ **NC7814**
16. M. Freni, Venice La Fenice Orch, R. Abbado (9/92) (DECC) Ⓓ **433 316-2DH**
16. L. Price, Philh, H. Lewis (r1977) (12/92) (RCA) Ⓓ [4] **09026 61236-2**
17b E. Caruso, F. Cilea (r1902) (5/89) (EMI) Ⓓ **CDH7 61046-2**
17b E. Caruso, F. Cilea (r1902) (12/90) (PEAR) Ⓓ [3] **EVC1(1)**
17b E. Caruso, F. Cilea (r1902) (7/91) (RCA) Ⓓ [12] **GD60495(1)**
17b G. Zenatello, orch (r1911) (5/94) (PEAR) Ⓓ [4] **GEMMCDS9073(2)**

L' **Arlesiana– opera: 4 acts (1902—Milan) (Lib. Colautti, after Scribe and Legouvé)**
EXCERPTS: 1. Prelude; 2a. E a te nè un bacio mai; 2b. Come due tizzi accesi; 3. O Dio, nessuno ancora!; 4a. Fra poco ei qui verrà; 4b. Buon dì; 5. Era un giorno di festa; 6. Mamma!; 7. Più di me stessa?; 8. Eccelente!; 9. La tua speranza; 10. Perchè state laggiù? ACT 2: 11a. Da quando il cerchi tu?; 11b. St qui. Stringi un po'; 12. Ehi! Come corre; 13. Vieni com me sui monti; 14. Quando la luce muor; 15. Portan tutti sul core; 16. E la solita storia; 17. Dormià quest'Innocente; 18. Se, come amo; 19. Nè te, nè alcuna!; 20. Sono respinta... 21. Perchè pianger così?; 22. Intermezzo. ACT 3: 23. Di gigli candidi; 24. O bella, allegra gioventù; 25. Farandole; 26. Non lo negar; 27. Bravi ragazzi miei; 28. Ah, finalmente!; 29. Ferve la danza; 30a. Cantano ancor laggiù; 30b. Esser madre è un inferno; 31. Che notte!... 32. Di scemi in casa non ce n'è più; 33. Già spunta il dì.
2a, 2b L. Pavarotti, Bologna Teatro Comunale Orch, L. Magiera (pp1991) (DECC) ● **071 140-1DH**
(DECC) ▣ **071 140-3DH**
2b G. Taddei, Naples San Carlo Op Orch, U. Rapalo (PREI) Ⓓ **90020**
2b T. Gobbi, La Scala Orch, U. Berrettoni (r1942) (PREI) Ⓓ **89995**
2b T. Gobbi, La Scala Orch, U. Berrettoni (r1942) (10/89) (EMI) Ⓓ **CDM7 63109-2**
2b T. Gobbi, La Scala Orch, U. Berrettoni (r1942) (12/93) (NIMB) Ⓓ **NI7851**
16. J. Carreras, MMF Orch, Rome Op Orch, Z. Mehta (pp1990) (DECC) ● **071 123-1DH**
(DECC) ▣ **071 123-3DH**
16. G. di Stefano, orch, A. Erede (r1947) (EMI) Ⓓ **CDM7 63105-2**
16. B. Gigli, Berlin St Op Orch, B. Seidler-Winkler (r1936) (NIMB) Ⓓ **NI7817**
(NIMB) ▭ **NC7817**
16. Alfredo Kraus, Milan RAI SO, A. Basile (pp1959) (MEMO) Ⓓ [2] **HR4233/4**
16. T. Schipa, orch, Anon (cond) (pp1927) (MEMO) Ⓓ [2] **HR4220/1**
16. J. Björling, MMF Orch, A. Erede (DECC) Ⓓ **433 069-2DWO**
(DECC) ▭ **433 069-4DWO**
16. J. Carreras, LSO, J. López-Cobos (PHIL) Ⓓ **434 152-2PM**
16. Alfredo Kraus, Madrid SO, G.P. Sanzogno (pp1991) (IMP) Ⓓ [2] **DPCD998**
16. Alfredo Kraus, Madrid SO, G.P. Sanzogno (RNE) Ⓓ [2] **650004**
16. J. Carreras, MMF Orch, Rome Op Orch, Z. Mehta (pp1990) (DECC) **ꝏ 430 433-5DH**
16. P. Domingo, LSO, N. Santi (r1971) (RCA) Ⓓ **09026 61356-2**
(RCA) ▭ **09026 61356-4**
16. A. Cupido, Verona Arena Orch, A. Guadagno (pp1992) (MCI) Ⓓ **MCCD099**
16. J. Vickers, Rome Op Orch, T. Serafin (r1961) (VAI) Ⓓ **VAIA1016**
16. J. Carreras, LSO, J. López-Cobos (r1979) (BELA) Ⓓ **450 059-2**
(BELA) ▭ **450 059-4**
16. J. Carreras, MMF Orch, Rome Op Orch, Z. Mehta (pp1990) (DECC) Ⓓ **440 947-2DH**
(DECC) ▭ **440 947-4DH**
16. J. Björling, MMF Orch, A. Erede (r1957) (DECC) Ⓓ **436 314-2DA**
(DECC) ▭ **436 314-4DA**
16. M. Lanza, C. Callinicos (pp1958) (RCA) Ⓓ **09026 61884-2**
(RCA) ▭ **09026 61884-4**
16. B. Gigli, Berlin St Op Orch, B. Seidler-Winkler (r1936) (PEAR) Ⓓ [2] **GEMMCDS9176**
16. R. Alagna, LPO, R. Armstrong (EMI) Ⓓ **CDC5 55540-2**
(EMI) ▭ **EL5 55540-4**
16. F. de la Mora, WNO Orch, C. Mackerras (r1994-5) (TELA) Ⓓ **CD80411**
16. J. Björling, Stockholm Concert Soc Orch, N. Grevillius (r1947) (10/88) (EMI) Ⓓ **CDH7 61053-2**
16. P. Dvorský, Bratislava RSO, Czech RSO, O. Lenárd (10/89) (OPUS) Ⓓ **9156 1824**
16. T. Schipa, orch, Rosario Bourdon (r1928) (12/89) (RCA) Ⓓ **GD87969**
16. B. Gigli, La Scala Orch, U. Berrettoni (r1941) (5/90) (EMI) Ⓓ **CDH7 61052-2**
16. T. Schipa, orch, Rosario Bourdon (r1927) (10/90) (MSCM) Ⓓ [2] **MM30231**
(MSCM) ▭ [2] **MM40086**
16. J. Carreras, MMF Orch, Rome Op Orch, Z. Mehta (pp1990) (10/90) (DECC) Ⓓ **430 433-2DH**
(10/90) (DECC) ▭ **430 433-4DH**
16. L. Pavarotti, RPO, K.H. Adler (pp1982) (8/91) (DECC) Ⓓ **430 716-2DM**
(8/91) (DECC) ▭ **430 716-4DM**
16. J. Björling, MMF Orch, A. Erede (r1957) (10/93) (DECC) Ⓓ **436 463-2DM**
(10/93) (DECC) ▭ **436 463-4DM**
16. Ferruccio Tagliavini, EIAR Orch, U. Tansini (r1940) (3/94) (CENT) Ⓓ **CRC2164**
16. L. Pavarotti, NYPO, L. Magiera (pp1993) (2/95) (DECC) Ⓓ **444 450-2DH**
(2/95) (DECC) ▭ **444 450-4DH**
16. Alfredo Kraus, WNO Orch, C. Rizzi (r1994) (8/95) (PHIL) Ⓓ **442 785-2PH**
(8/95) (PHIL) ▭ **442 785-4PH**
16. J. Björling, MMF Orch, A. Erede (r1959) (10/95) (DECC) Ⓓ **443 930-2DM**
30a, 30b M. Freni, Venice La Fenice Orch, R. Abbado (9/92) (DECC) Ⓓ **433 316-2DH**
30b C. Muzio, orch, L. Molajoli (r1935) (4/91) (NIMB) Ⓓ **NI7814**
(4/91) (NIMB) ▭ **NC7814**
30b R. Tebaldi, New Philh, O. de Fabritiis (8/91) (DECC) Ⓓ [2] **430 481-2DX2**

CIMAROSA, Domenico *(1749–1801) Italy*

Artemisia– opera: 3 acts (1801—Venice) (Lib. C Jamejo)
EXCERPTS: 1. Entro quest'anima.

1. A. Roocroft, ASMF, N. Marriner
(EMI) Ⓓ CDC5 55396-2
(EMI) ▭ EL5 55396-4

Chi dell'altrui si veste presto si spoglia– opera (1783—Naples) (Lib. G. Palomba)
Minestra ti chiedo S. Bruscantini, Naples Scarlatti Chor, Naples Scarlatti Orch, R. Muti (pp1968) (MEMO) Ⓓ [2] **HR4300/1**

I **due baroni di Rocca Azzurra– intermezzo in musica: 2 acts (1783—Rome) (Lib. Palomba)**
EXCERPTS: 1. Overture.
1. Haydn Philh, E. Rojatti (NUOV) Ⓓ **6726**

I **due supposti conti, ossia Lo sposo senza moglie– dramma giococo: 2 acts (1784—Milan) (Lib. A. Anelli)**
EXCERPTS: 1. Overture.
1. Haydn Philh, E. Rojatti (NUOV) Ⓓ **6726**

L' **Italiana in Londra– intermezzo in musica: 2 acts (1779—Rome) (Lib. ?Petrosellini)**
EXCERPTS: 1. Overture.
1. Haydn Philh, E. Rojatti (NUOV) Ⓓ **6726**

Il **matrimonio per raggiro (La donna bizzara)– opera: 2 acts (c1778-79—?Rome)**
EXCERPTS: 1. Overture.
1. NBC SO, A. Toscanini (bp1949)
(RCA) Ⓓ **GD60278**

Il **Matrimonio segreto– opera: 2 acts (1792—Vienna) (Lib. G. Bertati)**
EXCERPTS: 1. Overture.
Carolina A. Auger
Elisetta J. Varady
Geronimo D. Fischer-Dieskau
Fidalma J. Hamari
Paolino R. Davies
Count Robinson A. Rinaldi
ECO, D. Barenboim (r1975/6)
(8/93) (DG) Ⓓ [3] **437 696-2GX3**
1. NBC SO, A. Toscanini (bp1943)
(RCA) Ⓓ **GD60278**

CLEWING, Carl *(1884–1954) Germany*

Der **Singende Traum– operetta**
Alle Tage ist kein Sonntag F. Wunderlich, Berlin SO, G. Becker (EURO) Ⓓ **GD69018**
(EURO) ▭ **GK69018**

COCCHI, Gioacchino *(c1720–after 1788) Italy*

Per la patria– opera
M. Battistini, orch (r1911)
(2/92) (PREI) Ⓓ **89045**

COCCIA, Carlo *(1782–1873) Italy*

Clotilde– opera: 2 acts (1815—Venice) (Lib. Rossi)
Io servir! Oh avvilimento! E. Harrhy, J. Cashmore, Philh, D. Parry
(10/90) (OPRA) Ⓓ [3] **ORCH103**

Maria Stuart, Regina di Scozia– opera seria (1827—London) (Lib. Giannone)
Vieno, o Grande!...Ecco l'indegna B. Mills, J. Rhys-Davies, A. Mason, B. Ford, P. Nilon, I. Sharpe, C. Bayley, M. Glanville, A. Miles, G. Mitchell Ch, Philh, D. Parry
(8/95) (OPRA) Ⓓ [3] **ORCH104**

Rosmonda– melodramma serio: 2 acts (1829—Venice) (Lib. F Romani)
Perchè non ho del vento Y. Kenny, D. Montague, Philh, D. Parry (r1992)
(OPRA) Ⓓ **ORR201**
Volgon tre lune...Perchè non ho del vento? Y. Kenny, D. Montague, Philh, D. Parry
(8/95) (OPRA) Ⓓ [3] **ORCH104**

COCTEAU, Jean *(1889–1963) France*

Le **bel indifférent– monodrama (1940—Paris)**
E. Piaf, Inst Ens (r1953)
(10/94) (EMI) Ⓓ **CDM5 65156-2**

CONTI, Carlo *(1796–1868) Italy*

Giovanna Shore– melodramma serio: 3 acts (1829—Milan) (Lib. F Romani)
A che di fiore e lagrime M. Hill Smith, C. Bayley, A. Miles, Philh, D. Parry
(8/95) (OPRA) Ⓓ [3] **ORCH104**

COPLAND, Aaron *(1900–1990) USA*

The **Tender Land– opera: 2 acts (1954—New York) (Lib. H. Everett, after E. Johns)**
Laurie E. Comeaux
Ma Ross J. Hardy
Beth M. Jette
Grandpa Moss L. Lehr
Martin D. Dressen
Top J. Bohn
Mr Splinters V. Sutton
Mrs Splinters A. Smuda
Mr Jenks M. Fristad
Mrs Jenks S. Herber
Plymouth Music Series Chor, Plymouth Music Series Orch, P. Brunelle
(8/90) (VIRG) Ⓓ [2] **VCD7 59253-2**
(8/90) (VIRG) ▭ [2] **VCD7 59253-4**
The Promise of Living Tanglewood Fest Chor, Boston Pops, J.T. Williams
(SONY) Ⓓ **SK48224**
The Promise of Living Cincinnati Pops, E. Kunzel (10/87) (TELA) Ⓓ **CD80117**

The **Tender Land– concert suite from opera (1956)**
1. Introduction and Love Music; 2. Party Scene; 3. Finale: The Promise of Living.
Boston SO, A. Copland (r1959)
(RCA) Ⓓ **GD86802**
Boston SO, A. Copland (r1959)
(RCA) Ⓓ **09026 61505-2**
Phoenix SO, J. Sedares (r1991)
(4/92) (KOCH) Ⓓ **37092-2**

CORDELLA, Giacomo *(1786–1846 or 1847) Italy*

Lo **Sposo di provincia– commedia per musica: 2 acts (1821—Rome) (Lib. G Schmidt)**
Oh soave mia speranza N. Focile, F. Kimm, P. Nilon, Philh, D. Parry
(8/95) (OPRA) Ⓓ [3] **ORCH104**

CORGHI, Azio *(b 1937) Italy*

Divara—Wasser und Blut– opera: 3 act (1993—Münster) (Lib. cpsr & José Saramago)
Divara S. von der Burg
Jan van Leiden C. Krieg
Jan Matthys H. Hildmann
Bernhard Rothmann M. Holm
Bernd Knipperdollinck H. Fitz
Lame Man R. Schwarts
Hille Feiken E. L. Thingboe
Else Wandscherer S. McLeod
Mother G. Wunderer
Bishop Waldeck D. Midboe
Catholic Theologian M. Baba
Mayor G. Kiefer
Biblical Voice M. Coles
Trumpeter B. Trottmann
Münster City Th Chor, Münster SO, W. Humburg (r1993)
(10/95) (MARC) Ⓓ [2] **8 223706/7**

CORIGLIANO, John (Paul) *(b 1938) USA*

The **Ghosts of Versailles– opera buffa: 2 acts (Lib. W M Hoffman, after Beaumarchais)**
Marie Antoinette T. Stratas
Count Almaviva P. Kazaras
Countess Almaviva R. Fleming
Léon N. Rosenshein
Florestine T. Dahl
Marquis R. Drews
Cherubino S. Zambalis
Figaro G. Quilico
Susanna J. Christin
Beaumarchais H. Hagegård
Samira M. Horne
Louis XVI J. Courtney
Bégearss G. Clark
NY Met Op Ballet, NY Met Op Chor, NY Met Op Orch, James Levine, C. Graham (r1992)
(8/93) (DG) ◐ [2] **072 430-1GH2**
(8/93) (DG) ▣ **072 430-3GH**

CORNELIUS, (Carl August) Peter *(1824–1874) Germany*

Der **Barbier von Bagdad, '(The) Barber of Baghdad'– opera: 2 acts (1858—Weimar) (Lib. cpsr)**
EXCERPTS: 1. Overture; 2. Ach, das Leid hab' ich getragen; 3. Mein Sohn, sei Allahs Frieden; 4. O holdes Bild; 5. O wüsstest du, Verehter; 6. Salam aleikum; 7. Sanfter Schlummer; 8. So leb ich noch; 9. Vor deinem Fenster.
Abul Hassan O. Czerwenka
Margiana E. Schwarzkopf
Nureddin N. Gedda
Kalif H. Prey
Kadi G. Unger
Bostana G. Hoffman
Muezzin I E. Waechter
Muezzin II A. Jaresch
Muezzin III R. Christ
chor, Philh, E. Leinsdorf (r1956)
(EMI) Ⓓ [2] **CMS5 65284-2**
1. BPO, R. Strauss (r1928)
(KOCH) Ⓓ **37119-2**
2. H. Roswaenge, Berlin St Op Orch, B. Seidler-Winkler (r1939) (PREI) Ⓓ [2] **89211**
2. P. Seiffert, Munich RO, J. Kout (r1992-3)
(RCA) Ⓓ **09026 61214-2**
3. F. Wunderlich, K. Böhme, Stuttgart RSO, H. Müller-Kray (bp1957)
(10/89) (ACAN) Ⓓ **43 267**
4. M. Ivogün, K. Erb, orch (r1917)
(PREI) Ⓓ **89094**
4. H.E. Groh, E. Bettendorf, orch (r1933)
(3/92) (PEAR) Ⓓ **GEMMCD9419**
4. M. Ivogün, K. Erb, orch (r1917)
(1/94) (CLUB) Ⓓ **CL99-020**
4. H. Roswaenge, I. Roswaenge, Berlin St Op Orch, B. Seidler-Winkler (r1939)
(4/95) (PREI) Ⓓ [2] **89209**
5, 6. K. Moll, Munich RO, K. Eichhorn (r1981)
(ORFE) Ⓓ **C009821A**
7. H.E. Groh, orch (r1932)
(3/92) (PEAR) Ⓓ **GEMMCD9419**
8. A. Piccaver, orch (r1920)
(8/93) (PREI) Ⓓ **89060**
8, 9. F. Wunderlich, Bavarian St Orch, H. Müller-Kray (EMI) Ⓓ [3] **CZS7 62993-2**
9. M. Wittrisch, Berlin St Op Orch, C. Schmalstich (r1931) (PREI) Ⓓ **89024**

COWARD, Sir Noel (Pierce) *(1899–1973) England*

Bitter Sweet– operetta: 3 acts (1929—London) (Lib. cpsr)
EXCERPTS: ACT ONE: 1. Opening—That Wonderful Melody; 2. The Call of Life; 3. If You Could Only Come With Me; 4. I'll See You Again; 5. Polka; 6. What is Love?; 7. The Last Dance; 8. Finale. ACT TWO: 9. Opening Chorus: Life In the Morning; 10. Ladies of the Town; 11. If Love Were All; 12. Dear Little Café; 13. Bitter Sweet Waltz; 14. Officers' Chorus: We Wish to Order Wine; 15. Tokey; 16. Bonne nuit, merci; 17. Kiss Me. ACT THREE: 18. Ra-Ra-Ra-Boom-De-Ay; 19. Alas! The Time is Past; 20. We All Wear a Green Carnation; 21. Zigeuner; 22. Finale.
Marchioness of Shayne V. Masterson
Carl Linden M. Smith
Manon R. Ashe
August Lutte D. Maxwell
New Sadlers Wells Op Chor, New Sadlers Wells Op Orch, M. Reed (r1988)
(11/89) (TER) Ⓓ [2] **CDTER2 1160**
(11/89) (TER) ▭ **ZCTED 1160**
1, 3, 4, 6, 10-12, 14, 15, 17, 18, 20, 22. V. Masterson, R. Ashe, M. Smith, D. Maxwell, New Sadlers Wells Op Chor, New Sadlers Wells Op Orch, M. Reed (r1988) (TER) Ⓓ **CDTEO1001**
(TER) ▭ **ZCTEO1001**
4, 21. J. Sutherland, N. Coward, chor, orch, R. Bonynge (r1960s; arr Gamley)
(BELA) Ⓓ **450 014-2**
(BELA) ▭ **450 014-4**

12. London Concert Artists, J. Partridge (ASV) ① CDWHL2070 (ASV) ▭ ZCWHL2070
13. New Sadler's Wells Op Orch, M. Reed (TER) ① CDVIR8315

Operette– operetta (1938—London) (Lib. cpsr)
EXCERPTS: 1. Song of Joy; 2. The Stately Homes of England; 3. Where Are the Songs We Sung?; 4. Countess Mitzi; 5. Foolish Virgins; 6. Operette; 7. Model Maid; 8. Finale, Act 2; 9. Dearest Love.
3, 4, 9. J. Sutherland, chor, orch, R. Bonynge (r1960s; arr Gamley) (BELA) ① 450 014-2 (BELA) ▭ 450 014-4

CRUSELL, Bernhard Henrik *(1775–1838) Finland/Sweden*

Lilla Slafinnen– opera
From Ganges's beauteous strands I. Siebert, D. Klöcker, South-West German RSO, K. Donath (SCHW) ① 314018

CUI, César *(1835–1918) Russia*

Angelo– opera: 4 acts (1876—St Petersburg) (Lib. V Burenin, after V Hugo)
I live only for you L. Sobinov, anon (r1901) (6/93) (PEAR) ① [3] GEMMCDS9997/9(1)

A **feast in time of plague– opera: 1 act (1900—Moscow) (Lib. Pushkin)**
When powerful winter N. Shevelev, anon (r1901) (6/93) (PEAR) ① [3] GEMMCDS9007/9(2)

Le **Filibustier– opera: 3 acts (1894—Paris) (Lib. after J. Richepin)**
EXCERPTS: 1. Prelude.
1. Bratislava RSO, R. Stankovsky (r1992) (MARC) ① 8 223400

A **Prisoner in the Caucasus– opera: 3 acts (1883—St Petersburg) (Lib. V. Krilov, after Pushkin)**
Abubeker's aria I. Gryzunov, orch (r1910) (PEAR) ① [3] GEMMCDS9111(2)
Aria N. Shevelev, anon (r1901) (6/93) (PEAR) ① [3] GEMMCDS9007/9(2)

CUVILLIER, Charles *(19th–20th Cent) Belgium*

The **Lilac Domino– operetta (1914—New York) (English lyrics Harry B Smith)**
EXCERPTS: 1. The Lilac Domino.
1. E. Painter, Orig Broadway Cast (r1915) (5/94) (PEAR) ① [3] GEMMCDS9056/8

DARGOMIZHSKY , Alexander Sergeyevich *(1813–1869) Russia*

Rusalka– opera: 4 acts (1856—St Petersburg) (Lib. cpsr after Pushkin)
EXCERPTS: ACT 1: 1. Ah! you young girls are all the same (Miller's aria). ACT 2: 2. Slavonic Dance; 3. Gypsy Dance. ACT 3: 4. Once a husband asked his wife (Olga's aria); 5. Some unknown power (Prince's cavatina); 6. What does this mean? (Mad Scene and Death of Miller). ACT 4: 7. Natasha's aria; 8. Dance.
Ah! that time has passed M. Michailova, N. Bolshakov, L. Sibiriakov, anon (r1905) (PEAR) ① [3] GEMMCDS9111(2)
Be tender towards him M. Michailova, orch (r1908) (PEAR) ① [3] GEMMCDS9111(2)
Hark, the trumpets are sounding...Days of past enjoyment E. Zbrueva, orch (r1910) (6/93) (PEAR) ① [3] GEMMCDS9004/6(2)
Scene of the Miller and the Prince M. Reizen, G. Nelepp, Bolshoi Th Orch, V. Nebolsin (r1950) (2/95) (PREI) ① 89080
1. F. Chaliapin, LSO, M. Steinmann (r1931) (CONI) ① CDHD226 (CONI) ▭ MCHD226
1. A. Pirogov, Bolshoi Th Orch, V. Nebolsin (r c1950) (PREI) ① 89078
1. A. Kipnis, Victor SO, N. Berezowski (r1945) (9/92) (RCA) ① GD60522
1. M. Reizen, Bolshoi Th Orch, V. Nebolsin (r1948) (12/92) (PREI) ① 89059
1. L. Sibiriakov, orch (r1908) (6/93) (PEAR) ① [3] GEMMCDS9001/3(2)
1, 6. P. Gluboky, Soviet Cinema Orch, E. Khachaturian (r1990) (CDM) ① [2] LDC288 005/6 (CDM) ▭ KC488 005
1, 6. F. Chaliapin, G. Pozemkovsky, LSO, M. Steinmann (r1931) (6/88) (EMI) ① CDH7 61009-2
4. M. Michailova, orch (r1906) (PEAR) ① [3] GEMMCDS9111(2)
5. D. Smirnov, orch (r1913) (PEAR) ① GEMMCD9106
5. L. Sobinov, anon (r1901: 2 vers) (6/93) (PEAR) ① [3] GEMMCDS9997/9(1)
5. D. Smirnov, orch (r1913) (6/93) (PEAR) ① [3] GEMMCDS9004/6(1)
5. A. Bogdanovich, anon (r1903) (6/93) (PEAR) ① [3] GEMMCDS9007/9(1)

DAVID, Félicien(-César) *(1810–1876) France*

Lalla-Roukh– opéra-comique (1862—Paris) (Lib. H Lucas and M Carré, after T Moore)
Si vous ne savez plus aimer S. Petit-Renaux, orch (r1935) (MSCM) ① MM30221 (MSCM) ▭ MM040079

La **Perle du Brésil– opéra-comique: 1 act (c1857) (Lib. ?A. de Leuven)**
EXCERPTS: 1. Charmant oiseau.
Charmant oiseau R. Doria, Paris Sols Orch, J. Etcheverry (SYMP) ① SYMCD1103
1. F. Foster-Jenkins, C. McMoon (r c1944: arr voc/fl/pf) (RCA) ① GD61175
1. M. Michailova, anon (r1905: Russ) (PEAR) ① [3] GEMMCDS9111(1)
1. A. Galli-Curci, orch (r1912) (2/89) (PEAR) ① GEMMCD9308
1. L. Tetrazzini, orch (r1911) (9/92) (EMI) ① [3] CHS7 63802-2(1)
1. L. Tetrazzini, orch (r1911) (9/92) (PEAR) ① GEMMCD9224
1. L. Tetrazzini, orch (r1911) (9/92) (PEAR) ① GEMMCD9222
1. A. Nezhdanova, anon (r1907: Russ) (6/93) (PEAR) ① [3] GEMMCDS9007/9(1)
1. A. Galli-Curci, orch, J. Pasternack (r1917) (3/94) (ROMO) ① [2] 81003-2
1. A. Galli-Curci, orch (r1917) (8/94) (NIMB) ① NI7852
1. S. Jo, ECO, R. Bonynge (r1993) (9/94) (DECC) ① 440 679-2DH

DAVIS, Anthony *(b 1951) USA*

X: The Life and Times of Malcolm X– opera (1985—Philadelphia) (Lib. cpsr)

Malcolm	E. Perry
Street; Elijah	T.J. Young
Louise; Betty	P. Baskerville
Ella	H. Harris
Reginald	H. Perry
Social Worker; Reporter	C. Aaronson
Young Malcolm	T.D. Price
Preacher	R. Bazemore
Policeman; Reporter; Pilgrim	J. Daniecki
Policeman; Pilgrims	R. Edwards
Policeman; Pilgrims	R. Byrne

Episteme, St. Luke's Orch, W.H. Curry (r1992) (4/93) (GVIS) ① [2] R2-79470

DE KOVEN , (Henry Louis) Reginald *(1859–1920) USA*

Robin Hood– operetta (1890—Chicago) (Lib. Harry B. Smith)
EXCERPTS: 1. Song of Brown October Ale; 2. O Promise Me; 3. The Armorer's Song.
1. Cincinnati Uni Sngrs, Cincinnati Uni Th Orch, E. Rivers (r1978) (4/94) (NEW) ① 80221-2
2. J. B. Davis, Broadway Cast (r1898) (5/94) (PEAR) ① [3] GEMMCDS9050/2(1)
3. E. Cowles, Broadway Cast (r1906) (5/94) (PEAR) ① [3] GEMMCDS9050/2(1)

DE LARA, Isidore *(1858–1935) England*

Méssaline– opera (1899—Monte Carlo)
Dei del patrio suol F. Tamagno, anon (r1904) (4/94) (EMI) ① [3] CHS7 64860-2(2)
Elle m'avait pris A. Scotti, anon (r1902) (8/92) (IRCC) ① IRCC-CD802
O nuit d'amour A. Endrèze, orch, H. Defosse (r c1931) (11/92) (MSCM) ① MM30451
O nuit d'amour A. Scotti, anon (r1902) (3/93) (SYMP) ① SYMCD1100
Viens aimer A. Ghasne, orch (r1912) (9/91) (SYMP) ① SYMCD1089
Viens aimer A. Ghasne, orch (r1907) (8/92) (IRCC) ① IRCC-CD802

DEBUSSY, (Achille-)Claude *(1862–1918) France*

La **Chûte de la maison Usher– opéra: 2 scènes (incomplete) (1908-17) (Lib. cpsr after Poe)**

Lady Madeline	C. Barbaux
Doctor	F. Le Roux
Friend	P-Y. Le Maigat
Roderick	J-P. Lafont

Monte Carlo PO, G. Prêtre (r1983: cpted Allende-Blin) (9/93) (EMI) ① CDM7 64687-2

Pelléas et Mélisande– opera: 5 acts (1902—Paris) (Lib. Maeterlinck, abridged cpsr)
EXCERPTS: ACT 1 SCENE 1: 1. Je ne pourrai plus sortir de cette forêt; 2. Pourquoi pleures-tu?; 3. Je suis perdu aussi. SCENE 2: 4. Voici ce qu'il écrit à son frère Pelléas; 5. Qu'en dites-vous?; 6. Interlude. SCENE 3: 7. Il fait sombre dans les jardins; 8. Hoé! Hisse Hoé. ACT 2 SCENE 1: 9. Vous ne savez pas où je vous ai menée?; 10. C'est au bord d'une fontaine; 11. Interlude: SCENE 2: 12. Ah! Ah! Tout va bien; 13. Voyons, donne-moi ta main; 14. Interlude. SCENE 3: 15. Oui, c'est ici nous y sommes. ACT 3 SCENE 1: 16. Mes longs cheveux; 17. Je les tiens dans les mains; 18. Que faites-vous ici?. SCENE 2: 19. Prenez garde: par ici, par ici. SCENE 3: 20. Ah! je respire enfin; 21. Interlude; 22. Viens, nous allons nous asseoir ici; 23. Qu'ils s'embrassent, petit père? ACT 4 SCENE 1: 24. Où va-tu? SCENE 2: 25. Maintenant que le père de Pelléas; 26. Pelléas part ce soir; 27. Ne mettez pas ainsi votre main à la gorge; 28. Interlude. SCENE 3: 29. Oh! Cette pierre est lourde. SCENE 4: 30. C'est le dernier soir; 31. Nous sommes venus ici il y a bien longtemps; 32. In dirait que ta voix; 33. Quel est ce bruit? ACT 5: 34. Ce n'est pas de cette petite blessure; 35. Attention; je crois qu'elle s'éveille; 36. Mélisande, as-tu pitié de moi; 37. Non, non nous n'avons pas été coupables; 38. Qu'avez-vous fait?; 39. Qu'y a-t-il?; 40. Attention...attention.

Pelléas	C. Dormoy
Mélisande	M. Command
Golaud	G. Bacquier
Arkel	R. Soyer
Geneviève	J. Taillon
Yniold	M. Pouradier-Duteil
Doctor; Shepherd	X. Tamalet

Bourgogne Chor, Lyon Op Orch, S. Baudo (r1978) (EURO) ① [3] 353 266

Pelléas	R. Stilwell
Mélisande	F. von Stade
Golaud	J. Van Dam
Arkel	R. Raimondi
Geneviève	N. Denize
Yniold	C. Barbaux
Doctor; Shepherd	P. Thomas

Berlin Deutsche Op Chor, BPO, H. von Karajan (2/88) (EMI) ① [3] CDS7 49350-2

Pélleas	J. Jansen
Mélisande	M. Grancher
Golaud	M. Roux
Arkel	A. Vessières
Genevieve	S. Michel
Yniold	F. Ogéas
Doctor	M. Vigneron

FRN Chor, FNO, D-E. Inghelbrecht (pp1962) (8/88) (MONT) ① [3] TCE8710

Pelléas	J. Jansen
Mélisande	I. Joachim
Golaud	H. Etcheverry
Arkel	P. Cabanel
Geneviève	G. Cernay
Yniold	L.B. Sedira
Doctor	A. Narçon
Shepherd	E. Rousseau

Y. Gouverné Ch, SO, R. Desormière (r1941) (8/88) (EMI) ① [3] CHS7 61038-2

Pelléas	M. Walker
Mélisande	E. Manchet
Golaud	V. Le Texier
Arkel	P. Meven
Geneviève	C. Yahr

Yniold Anon (treb)
Doctor P. Le Hémonet
Nice Op Chor, Nice PO, J. Carewe
(8/89) (PIER) Ⓓ [2] **PV788093/4**

Pelléas D. Henry
Mélisande C. Alliot-Lugaz
Golaud G. Cachemaille
Arkel P. Thau
Geneviève C. Carlson
Yniold F. Golfier
Doctor; Shepherd P. Ens
Montreal Sym Chor, Montreal SO, C. Dutoit (r1990)
(3/91) (DECC) Ⓓ [2] **430 502-2DH2**

Pelléas E. Tappy
Mélisande R. Yakar
Golaud P. Huttenlocher
Arkel F. Loup
Geneviève J. Taillon
Yniold C. Alliot-Lugaz
Doctor; Shepherd M. Brodard
Monte Carlo Op Chor, Monte Carlo Nat Op Orch, A. Jordan
(12/91) (ERAT) Ⓓ [3] **2292-45684-2**

Pelléas F. Le Roux
Mélisande M. Ewing
Golaud J. Van Dam
Arkel; Shepherd J-P. Courtis
Geneviève C. Ludwig
Yniold P. Pace
Doctor R. Mazzola
Vienna St Op Chor, VPO, C. Abbado
(3/92) (DG) Ⓓ [2] **435 344-2GH2**

Pelléas G. Shirley
Mélisande E. Söderström
Golaud D. McIntyre
Arkel D. Ward
Geneviève Y. Minton
Yniold A. Britten
Doctor; Shepherd D. Wicks
ROH Chor, ROHO, P. Boulez
(4/92) (SONY) Ⓓ [3] **SM3K47265**

Pelléas N. Archer
Mélisande A. Hagley
Golaud D. Maxwell
Arkel K. Cox
Geneviève P. Walker
Yniold S. Burkey
Doctor; Shepherd P. Massocchi
WNO Chor, WNO Orch, P. Boulez, P. Stein
(6/94) (DG) ◖ [2] **072 431-1GH2**
(6/94) (DG) ▣ **072 431-3GH**

Pelléas J. Jansen
Mélisande V. de los Angeles
Golaud G. Souzay
Arkel P. Froumenty
Geneviève J. Collard
Yniold F. Ogéas
Doctor J. Vieuille
Raymond St Paul Chor, FRNO, A. Cluytens (r1956)
(6/95) (TEST) Ⓓ [3] **SBT3051**

Preludes and Interludes Cleveland Orch, E. Leinsdorf (r1946: ed/arr Leinsdorf)
(CLOR) Ⓓ [10] **TCO93-75**

Symphonic Suite Czech PO, S. Baudo (r1989: arr/ed M Constant) (SUPR) Ⓓ **11 1269-2**

1, 4, 9, 12, 16. M. Nespoulous, C. Croiza, A. Maguenat, H. Dufranne, A. Narçon, orch, G. Truc (r1928) (VAI) Ⓓ **VAIA1093**

4. S. Danco, A. Vessières, P. Mollet, SRO, E. Ansermet (pp1963) (1/93) (CASC) Ⓓ **VEL2010**

9, 12, 16(pt), 17, 20, 26(pt), 31, 33. Y. Brothier, C. Panzéra, Vanni-Marcoux, orch, P. Coppola (r1927) (VAI) Ⓓ **VAIA1093**

12. Vanni-Marcoux, orch, P. Coppola (r1927)
(PEAR) Ⓓ **GEMMCD9912**

15. M. Garden, C. Debussy (r1904)
(8/88) (EMI) Ⓓ [3] **CHS7 61038-2**

15 (pt) C. Panzéra, Y. Brothier, SO, P. Coppola (r1927) (3/93) (DANT) Ⓓ [2] **LYS003/4**

16. M. Garden, C. Debussy (r1904)
(10/92) (SYMP) Ⓓ **SYMCD1093**

25 (pt) Vanni-Marcoux, orch, P. Coppola (r1927)
(7/92) (PEAR) Ⓓ [3] **GEMMCDS9924(2)**

Rodrigue et Chimène– opera: 3 acts (1890-92) (Lib. C Mendès, after G de Castro & Corneille)

Rodrigue L. Dale
Chimène D. Brown
Iñez H. Jossoud
Hernan G. Ragon
Bermudo J-P. Fouchécourt
Don Diègue J. van Dam
Don Gomez J. Bastin
King V. le Texier
Don Juan d'Arcos J-L. Meunier
Don Pèdre de Terruel J. Delescluse
Lyon Op Chor, Lyon Op Orch, K. Nagano (r1993/4: recons R Langham Smith: orch E Denisov)
(10/95) (ERAT) Ⓓ [2] **4509-98508-2**

DELIBES, (Clément Philibert) Léo *(1836–1891) France*

Kassya– drame lyrique: 4 acts (1893—Paris) (Lib. H. Meilhac & Gille)

Trepak Bratislava RSO, O. Lenárd
(NAXO) Ⓓ **8 550080**

Lakmé– opera: 3 acts (1883—Paris) (Lib. Gondinet and Gille)

ACT 1: 1. Prelude; 2a. A l'heure accoutumée; 2b. Soyez trois fois bénis; 2c. Blanche Dourga; 3. Lakmé, c'est toi qui nous protèges!; 4a. Viens Mallika; 4b. Sous le dôme épais (Flower duet); 5. Ah! beaux faiseurs de systèmes; 6a. Prendre le dessin; 6b. Fantaisie aux divins mensonges; 7. O toi qui nous protèges; 8a. Les fleurs me paraissent plus belles; 8b. Pourquoi dans les grands bois; 9a. D'où viens-tu?; 9b. C'est le dieu de la jeunesse. ACT 2: 10. Danses; 11a. C'est un pauvre qui mendie; 11b. Lakmé, ton doux regard se voile; 12a. Par les dieux inspirée; 12b. Où va la jeune indoue (Bell Song); 12c. Là-bas dans la forêt plus sombre; 13a. Lakmé! c'est toi; 13b. Ah! c'est l'amour endormi; 14. Dans la forêt près de nous; 15. C'est pour admirer la déesse. ACT 3: 16. Entr'acte; 17. Sous le ciel tout étoilé; 18. Lakmé! Ah! viens dans la forêt profonde: 19. Tu m'as donné le plus doux rêve.

Lakmé M. Mesplé
Gérald C. Burles
Nilakantha R. Soyer
Mallika D. Millet
Fréderic J-C. Benoit
Ellen B. Antoine
Rose M. Linval
Mistress Bentson A. Disney
Hadji J. Peyron
Paris Opéra-Comique Chor, Paris Opéra-Comique Orch, A. Lombard (r1970)
(7/88) (EMI) Ⓓ [2] **CDS7 49430-2**

Lakmé J. Sutherland
Gérald A. Vanzo
Nilakantha G. Bacquier
Mallika J. Berbié
Fréderic C. Calès
Ellen G. Annear
Rose J. Clément
Mistress Bentson M. Sinclair
Hadji E. Belcourt
Monte Carlo Op Chor, Monte Carlo Op Orch, R. Bonynge
(12/89) (DECC) Ⓓ [2] **425 485-2DM2**

Excs J. Sutherland, Orch, Anon (cond), D. Bailey (11/92) (DECC) ◖ **071 135-1DH**

1, 4a, 6a, 8a, 9a, 11a, 12a, 13a, 17-19. M. Mesplé, D. Millet, C. Burles, R. Soyer, J-C. Benoit, Paris Opéra-Comique Chor, Paris Opéra-Comique Orch, A. Lombard (r1970)
(EMI) Ⓓ **CDM7 63447-2**
(EMI) ▭ **EG763447-4**

2c, 12b L. Tetrazzini, chor, orch (Ital: r1911)
(9/92) (EMI) Ⓓ [3] **CHS7 63802-2(1)**

2c, 12b L. Tetrazzini, chor, orch (Ital: r1911)
(9/92) (PEAR) Ⓓ **GEMMCD9222**

2c, 12b M. Korjus, Berlin St Op Orch, B. Seidler-Winkler (Ital: r1936) (10/93) (PREI) Ⓓ **89054**

4a J. Sutherland, M. Horne, Sydney Eliz Orch, R. Bonynge (MCEG) ▣ **VVD780**

4a E. Himy (arr Himy: pf) (BNL) Ⓓ **BNL112822**

4a, 4b M. Mesplé, D. Millet, Paris Opéra-Comique Orch, A. Lombard
(EMI) Ⓓ **CDM7 69596-2**

4a, 4b M. Mesplé, D. Millet, Paris Opéra-Comique Orch, A. Lombard
(CFP) Ⓓ **CD-CFP4582**
(CFP) ▭ **TC-CFP4582**

4a, 4b J. Sutherland, J. Berbié, Monte Carlo Nat Op Orch, R. Bonynge
(DECC) Ⓓ **433 066-2DWO**
(DECC) ▭ **433 066-4DWO**

4a, 4b V. Masterson, C. Powell, RPO, R. Stapleton (r1990) (RPO) Ⓓ [2] **CDRPD9006**
(RPO) ▭ [2] **ZCRPD9006**

4a, 4b J. Sutherland, J. Berbié, LSO, R. Bonynge (r1967) (DECC) Ⓓ **440 947-2DH**
(DECC) ▭ **440 947-4DH**

4a, 4b J. Sutherland, J. Berbié, Monte Carlo Nat Op Orch, R. Bonynge (r1967)
(DECC) Ⓓ **433 440-2DA**
(DECC) ▭ **433 440-4DA**

4a, 4b J. Sutherland, J. Berbié, Monte Carlo Nat Op Orch, R. Bonynge (r1967)
(DECC) Ⓓ **436 315-2DA**
(DECC) ▭ **436 315-4DA**

4a, 4b E. Eames, L. Homer, orch (r1908)
(11/93) (ROMO) Ⓓ [2] **81001-2**

4a, 4b A. Nezhdanova, E. Popello-Davidova, orch (r1910; Russ) (3/95) (NIMB) Ⓓ **NI7865**

4a, 4b, 5, 6a, 6b, 8a, 8b, 9a, 9b, 11a, 12b, 12c, 13a, 13b, 14, 17, 18, 19. J. Sutherland, A. Vanzo, G. Bacquier, J. Berbié, C. Calès, G. Annear, J. Clément, M. Sinclair, E. Belcourt, Monte Carlo Op Chor, Monte Carlo Op Orch, R. Bonynge (r1967)
(10/93) (DECC) Ⓓ **436 305-2DA**
(10/93) (DECC) ▭ **436 305-4DA**

4b M. Mesplé, D. Millet, Paris Opéra-Comique Orch, A. Lombard (CFP) Ⓓ **CD-CFP4613**
(CFP) ▭ **TC-CFP4613**

4b V. Masterson, C. Powell, RPO, R. Stapleton
(IMP) Ⓓ [3] **TCD1070**

4b L. Garrett, Philh, A. Greenwood (r1991)
(SILV) ◑ **SILVACD105**

4b L. Garrett, N. Raine (r1992; arr Raine)
(SILV) ◑ **SILVACD105**

4b G. Groves, J. Watson, J. Partridge (r1994)
(ASV) Ⓓ **CDWHL2088**

4b M. Mesplé, D. Millet, Paris Opéra-Comique Orch, A. Lombard (RCA) Ⓓ **74321 25817-2**
(RCA) ▭ **74321 25817-4**

4b V. Masterson, C. Powell, RPO, R. Stapleton
(10/90) (IMP) Ⓓ **MCD15**
(10/90) (IMP) ▭ **MCC15**

4b L. Garrett, Philh, A. Greenwood (r1990-1)
(11/91) (SILV) Ⓓ **SONGCD903**
(11/91) (SILV) ▭ **SONGC903**

4b A. Panina, M. Michailova, orch (r1911: Russ)
(6/93) (PEAR) Ⓓ [3] **GEMMCDS9001/3(2)**

4b L. Garrett, L. Christian, Philh, A. Greenwood
(10/93) (SILV) Ⓓ **FILMCD127**

4b, 8b J. Sutherland, H. Tourangeau, Sydney Eliz Orch, R. Bonynge
(DECC) ◖ **071 149-1DH**
(DECC) ▣ **071 149-3DH**

6a, 6b A. Austin, Australian Op & Ballet Orch, R. Bonynge (r1980) (KIWI) Ⓓ **CDSLD-82**

6a, 6b Alfredo Kraus, WNO Orch, C. Rizzi (r1994) (8/95) (PHIL) Ⓓ **442 785-2PH**
(8/95) (PHIL) ▭ **442 785-4PH**

6a, 6b, 9a, 9b, 19. P. Alarie, L. Simoneau, Lamoureux Orch, P. Dervaux (r1953)
(11/94) (PHIL) Ⓓ [2] **438 953-2PM2**

6b T. Schipa, orch (r1926)
(2/89) (PEAR) Ⓓ **GEMMCD9322**

6b E. Clément, orch (r c1911)
(8/95) (PEAR) Ⓓ **GEMMCD9161**

8a, 12b R. Streich, Berlin Deutsche Op Orch, R. Peters (DG) Ⓓ [2] **435 748-2GDO2**

8b L. Bori, orch (r1923)
(PEAR) Ⓓ **GEMMCD9458**

8b L. Bori, Victor Orch, Rosario Bourdon (r1923)
(ROMO) Ⓓ [2] **81016-2**

8b, 12b, 17. P. Alarie, Lamoureux Orch, A. Jouve (r1953)
(11/94) (PHIL) Ⓓ [2] **438 953-2PM2**

9a, 9b J. Anderson, Alfredo Kraus, Paris Op Orch, M. Veltri (pp1987)
(12/88) (EMI) Ⓓ **CDC7 49067-2**

9b M. Wittrisch, M. Korjus, Berlin St Op Orch, B. Seidler-Winkler (Ger: r1936) (PREI) Ⓓ **89024**

10. Bratislava RSO, O. Lenárd
(NAXO) Ⓓ **8 550081**

10, 16. Luxembourg Rad & TV SO, L. de Froment (r1992) (FORL) Ⓓ **FF044**

11b F. Chaliapin, orch, I.P. Arkadiev (Russian: r1908) (PREI) Ⓓ **89030**

11b T. Ruffo, orch (r1923)
(2/93) (PREI) Ⓓ [3] **89303(2)**

11b L. Sibiriakov, anon (r1905: Russ)
(6/93) (PEAR) Ⓓ [3] **GEMMCDS9001/3(2)**

12b J. Sutherland, ROHO, F. Molinari-Pradelli
(DECC) Ⓓ **417 780-2DM**

12b F. Foster-Jenkins, C. McMoon (r c1944)
(RCA) Ⓓ **GD61175**

12b M. Foley, Orch (r1949-53)
(ODE) Ⓓ **CDODE1062**

12b E. Gruberová, Tokyo PO, F. Haider (pp1993) (NIGH) Ⓓ **NC090560-2**

12b M. Callas, Philh, T. Serafin (r1954: Ital)
(EMI) Ⓓ **CDC5 55216-2**
(EMI) ▭ **EL555216-4**

12b M. André, Toulouse Capitole Orch, M. Plasson (arr tpt) (1/89) (EMI) Ⓓ **CDC7 49219-2**
12b L. Tetrazzini, orch (Ital: r1911) (10/90) (NIMB) Ⓓ **NI7808**
(10/90) (NIMB) ▣ **NC7808**
12b Dilbèr, Estonia Op Orch, E. Klas (9/92) (ONDI) Ⓓ **ODE768-2**
12b L. Tetrazzini, orch, P. Pitt (Ital: r1907) (9/92) (EMI) Ⓓ [3] **CHS7 63802-2(1)**
12b L. Tetrazzini, orch (Ital: r1911) (9/92) (PEAR) Ⓓ **GEMMCD9224**
12b L. Tetrazzini, orch, P. Pitt (Ital: r1907) (9/92) (PEAR) Ⓓ **GEMMCD9221**
12b A. Galli-Curci, orch, J. Pasternack (r1917) (3/94) (ROMO) Ⓓ [2] **81003-2**
12b A. Galli-Curci, orch (r1917) (8/94) (NIMB) Ⓓ **NI7852**
12b A. Nezhdanova, orch (r1912: Russ) (3/95) (NIMB) Ⓓ **NI7865**
12b, 12c E. Gruberová, Munich RO, G. Kuhn (EMIN) Ⓓ **CD-EMX9519**
(EMIN) ▣ **TC-EMX2099**
12b, 12c J. Sutherland, ROHO, F. Molinari-Pradelli (r1960) (DECC) Ⓓ **433 065-2DWO**
(DECC) ▣ **433 065-4DWO**
12b, 12c L. Pons, Orch, Rosario Bourdon (r1929) (MSCM) Ⓓ **MM30446**
12b, 12c L. Pons, orch, Rosario Bourdon (r1930) (RCA) Ⓓ **09026 61411-2**
12b, 12c J. Sutherland, ROHO, F. Molinari-Pradelli (r1960) (DECC) Ⓓ **443 377-2DM**
12b, 12c E. Gruberová, Munich RO, G. Kuhn (r c1980) (EMIN) Ⓓ **CD-EMX2234**
12b, 12c L. Pons, orch, American SO (r1930) (RCA) Ⓓ **74321 24284-2**
(RCA) ▣ **74321 24284-4**
12b, 12c M. Callas, Philh, T. Serafin (r1954) (11/86) (EMI) Ⓓ **CDC7 47282-2**
12b, 12c J. Sutherland, ROHO, F. Molinari-Pradelli (1/90) (DECC) Ⓓ [2] **425 493-2DM2**
12b, 12c L. Pons, orch, P. Cimara (r1944) (7/90) (CBS) Ⓓ **CD45694**
12b, 12c L. Pons, orch, Rosario Bourdon (r1930) (4/92) (MSOU) Ⓓ **DFCDI-111**
12b, 12c M. Devia, Svizzera Italiana Orch, M. Rota (pp1992) (10/94) (BONG) Ⓓ **GB2513-2**
12b, 12c T. Dahl, Calgary PO, M. Bernardi (r1992) (12/94) (CBC) Ⓓ **SMCD5125**
12b, 12c S. Jo, Monte Carlo PO, P. Olmi (r1994) (6/95) (ERAT) Ⓓ **4509-97239-2**
12b, 19. M. Mesplé, Paris Op Orch, J-P. Marty (r1968) (EMI) Ⓓ [2] **CZS7 67813-2**
18. J. McCormack, orch (r1910) (7/92) (PEAR) Ⓓ [3] **GEMMCDS9924(2)**

L' **Omelette à la Follembuche– opérette bouffe: 1 act (1859—Paris) (Lib. E. Labiche & M. Michel)**
Excs L. Dachary, C. Jacquin, J. Mollien, R. Lenoty, M. Pieri, ORTF Lyric Orch, J. Brebion (bp1973) (11/93) (MUSD) Ⓓ [2] **20239-2**

Le **roi l'a dit– opéra-comique: 3 acts (1873—Paris) (Lib. E. Gondinet)**
EXCERPTS: 1. Portons toujours des robes sombres.

Javotte	J. Micheau
Benoit	M. Sénéchal
Marquise	A. Martineau
Marquis	G. Wion
Miton	R. Lenoty
Philomène	G. Aurel
Chimène	G. Donnarieix
Agathe	A. Lequenne
Angélique	G. Parat
Pacôme	M. Le Breton
Merlussac	P. Saugey
Gautru	J. Scellier
Flarembel	J. Peyron
La Bluette	M. Hamel

French Rad Lyric Chor, French Rad Lyric Orch, A. Girard (bp1958) (11/93) (MUSD) Ⓓ [2] **20239-2**
1. Luxembourg Rad & TV SO, L. de Froment (r1992) (FORL) Ⓓ **FF044**
1. S. Jo, ECO, R. Bonynge (r1993) (9/94) (DECC) Ⓓ **440 679-2DH**

Les **serpent à plumes– farce: 1 act (1864—Paris) (Lib. P. Gille & Cham)**
Excs C. Harbell, M. Stiot, J. Peyron, R. Lenoty, B. Plantey, ORTF Lyric Orch, J. Brebion (bp1973) (11/93) (MUSD) Ⓓ [2] **20239-2**

DELIUS, Frederick (Theodore Albert) *(1862–1934) England*

RT—denotes Robert Threlfall's catalogue (1977)

Irmelin– opera: 3 acts, RT I/2 (1890-92 fp 1953—Oxford) (Lib. cpsr)
Away, far away to the woods J. Nolan, Elysian Sngrs, A. Ball, M. Greenall (r1992) (CNTI) Ⓓ **CCD1054**

Koanga– lyric drama: 3 acts, RT I/4 (1904—Elberfeld) (Lib, C F Keary, after G W Cable)
ACT 2; 1. La Calinda (choral dance); 2. 'Closing Scene' (ed/arr Beecham).
Creole dance A. Shulman, I. Brown (arr C. Palmer) (CNTI) Ⓓ **CCD1025**
1. ASMF, N. Marriner (r1979) (DECC) ▣ **433 870-4DWO**
1. Nova Scotia SO, G. Tintner (r1991: arr orch: Fenby) (CBC) Ⓓ **SMCD5134**
1. LPO, V. Handley (arr Fenby) (2/89) (CFP) Ⓓ **CD-CFP4304**
(2/89) (CFP) ▣ **TC-CFP40304**
1. ASMF, N. Marriner (arr Fenby) (8/89) (LOND) Ⓓ **421 390-2LM**
1. LPO, T. Beecham (arr Fenby: r1938) (11/90) (BEEC) Ⓓ **BEECHAM3**
1. K. Smith, P. Rhodes (trans Fenby: fl & pf) (1/91) (ASV) Ⓓ **CDDCA739**
1. LSO, B. Wordsworth (9/92) (COLL) Ⓓ **Coll1336-2**
1. Philh, G. Weldon (3/93) (EMIN) Ⓓ **CD-EMX2198**
1. Hallé, C. Lambert (r1941) (5/93) (TEST) Ⓓ **SBT1014**
1. ASMF, N. Marriner (r1977: arr Fenby) (4/94) (DECC) Ⓓ **440 323-2DWO**
(4/94) (DECC) ▣ **440 323-4DWO**
1. LPO, T. Beecham (r1938: arr Fenby) (6/94) (DUTT) Ⓓ **CDLX7003**
1. Northern Sinfonia, R. Hickox (r1985: arr Fenby) (7/94) (EMI) Ⓓ **CDM5 65067-2**
1. RPO, E. Fenby (r1981: arr Fenby) (8/95) (UNIC) Ⓓ **UKCD2073**
1. RPO, C. Seaman (r1994) (9/95) (TRIN) Ⓓ **TRP036**
1. R. Tear, Hallé, J. Barbirolli (r1968: arr Fenby) (10/95) (EMI) Ⓓ [2] **CMS5 65119-2**
1. NZ SO, M. Fredman (r1994: arr orch: Fenby) (10/95) (NAXO) Ⓓ **8 553001**
2. London Select Ch, LPO, T. Beecham (r1934) (10/94) (DUTT) Ⓓ **CDLX7011**
2. BBC Chor, RPO, T. Beecham (r1951) (11/94) (SONY) Ⓓ **SMK58934**

Margot la Rouge– drame lyrique: 1 act, RT I/7 (1902 fp 1981—BBC Radio 3) (Lib. Rosenval)
Prelude RPO, M. Davies (3/93) (EMIN) Ⓓ **CD-EMX2198**

A **Village Romeo and Juliet– lyric drama: 6 pictures, RT I/6 (1907—Berlin) (Lib. cpsr, after G Keller)**
EXCERPTS: SCENE 1: 1. Prelude; 2. A shame it is, to let such good land lie waste; 3. How strange the wind sounds; 4. 'Twixt us, methinks, will lie the bidding. SCENE 2: 5. Prelude; 6. Vreli!...Sali!; 7. Interlude—Prelude to Scene 3. SCENE 3: 8. I knew we'd meet again; 9. O Sali, I'm afraid!; 10. Shameless hussy! SCENE 4: 11. Prelude; 12. Ah, the night is approaching; 13. Dearest, I'll you no more; 14. The dream of Sali and Vrenchen (Wedding Scene); 15. Ah! it was a dream. SCENE 5: 16. Prelude; 17. O Sali, see what beautiful things!; 18. Well, well, gracious me, if it isn't Vreli Marti and Sali Manz; 19. Interlude—The Walk to the Paradise Garden. SCENE 6: 20. Dance along; 21. So you want to know, how the strife began; 22. 'Tis almost night; 23a. Come and live with us and taste the cream of life!; 23b. What say you, Vreli?; 24. Halleo! Halleo!; 25. See, the moonbeams kiss the woods.

Manz	B. Mora
Marti	S. Dean
Sali as a child	S. Linay
Sali	A. Davies
Vreli	H. Field
Dark Fiddler	T. Hampson
Gingerbread Woman	E. Dobie
Wheel of Fortune Woman; 3rd Woman	K. Barber
Cheap Jewellery Woman; 2nd Woman; Wild Girl	P.A. Caya
Showman; 3rd Bargee	V. Pirillo
Merry-Go-Round; Hunchbacked Bass Fiddler	R.L. Demers
Shooting Gallery Man; 2nd Bargee	J. Antoniou
Slim Girl	M. Venuti
Poor Horn Player	S. Lombana
1st Woman	A. Mellis
1st Bargee	D. McShane

A. Schoenberg Ch, Austrian RSO, C. Mackerras, P. Weigl
(DECC) ◐ **071 134-1DH**
(DECC) ▬ **071 134-3DH**

Manz	B. Mora
Marti	S. Dean
Sali as a child	S. Linay
Sali	A. Davies
Vreli	H. Field
Dark Fiddler	T. Hampson
Gingerbread Woman	E. Dobie
Wheel of Fortune Woman; 3rd Woman	K. Barber
Cheap Jewellery Woman; 2nd Woman; Wild Girl	P.A. Caya
Showman; 3rd Bargee	V. Pirillo
Merry-Go-Round; Hunchbacked Bass Fiddler	R.L. Demers
Shooting Gallery Man; 2nd Bargee	J. Antoniou
Slim Girl	M. Venuti
Poor Horn Player	S. Lombana
1st Woman	A. Mellis
1st Bargee	D. McShane

A. Schoenberg Ch, Austrian RSO, C. Mackerras (12/90) (ARGO) Ⓓ [2] **430 275-2ZH2**

Manz; 2nd Peasant	D. Dowling
Marti	F. Sharp
Sali as a child	M. Ritchie
Sali	R. Soames
Vreli	L. Dyer
Dark Fiddler	G. Clinton
Vreli as a child; Gingerbread Woman	D. Bond
Wheel of Fortune Woman; 1st Woman	M. Avis
Cheap Jewellery Woman; 2nd & 3rd Women; Wild Girl	G. Garside
Showman; Poor Horn Player	L. Strauss-Smith
Merry-Go-Round Man; 1st Peasant	D. Munro
Slim Girl	Marion Davies
Hunchbacked Bass-Fiddler	P. Hattey

Chor, RPO, T. Beecham (r1948) (11/92) (EMI) Ⓓ [2] **CMS7 64386-2**

Manz	D. Midhoe
Marti	A. Kovács
Sali as a child	A. Görner
Sali	K. Russ
Vrenchen as a child	A. Sikira
Vrenchen	E-C. Reimer
Dark Fiddler	K. Wallprecht
First Peasant	L. Kappaun
Second Peasant	K-P. Hallacker
First Woman	I. Schwarz
Second Woman	C. Forsén
Third Woman	A. Vogt
Gingerbread Woman	M. Koht
Wheel of Fortune Woman	C. Vincent
Cheap Jewellery Woman	I. Uhlemann
Showman	R. Klöpper
Merry-Go-Round-Man	H-J. Förter-Barth
Shooting Gallery Man	H. Hoffmann
Slim Girl	B. Bilandzija
Wild Girl	H. Fischer
Poor Horn Player	U. Köberle
Hunchbacked Bass Player	B. Gebhardt
First Bargeman	D. Henschel
Second Bargeman	J. Sabrowski
Third Bargeman	M. Fleitmann

Kiel Op Chor, Kiel PO, K. Seibel (r1994: Ger) (10/95) (CPO) Ⓓ [2] **CPO999 328-2**
1. Philh, O.A. Hughes (ASV) Ⓓ **CDQS6126**
1, 6, 7, 16-19. LPO, Carl Davis (arr D Matthews) (12/91) (VIRG) Ⓓ **VJ7 59654-2**
(12/91) (VIRG) ▣ **VJ7 59654-4**
14. Elysian Sngrs, M. Brafield, M. Greenall (r1992: arr E Fenby) (CNTI) Ⓓ **CCD1054**
19. LSO, J. Barbirolli (arr Beecham) (EMIL) Ⓓ **CDZ115**
19. RPO, M. Davies (r1971) (CFP) Ⓓ **CD-CFP4582**
(CFP) ▣ **TC-CFP4582**
19. LSO, J. Barbirolli (r1965) (EMI) Ⓓ **CDGO2039**
19. LSO, G. Toye (r1930) (BEUL) Ⓓ **2PD4**

19. ASMF, N. Marriner (BELA) Ⓓ **450 130-2**
(BELA) ▭ **450 130-4**
19. BBC SO, A. Davis
(TELD) Ⓓ **4509-96231-2**
(TELD) ▭ **4509-96231-4**
19. Nova Scotia SO, G. Tintner (r1991)
(CBC) Ⓓ **SMCD5134**
19. ASMF, N. Marriner (r1979)
(DECC) Ⓓ **443 334-2LRX**
(DECC) ▭ **443 334-4LRX**
19. Philh, O.A. Hughes (r1988)
(12/88) (ASV) Ⓓ **CDDCA627**
19. LPO, V. Handley (arr Beecham)
(2/89) (CFP) Ⓓ **CD-CFP4304**
(2/89) (CFP) ▭ **TC-CFP40304**
19. ASMF, N. Marriner (arr Beecham)
(5/89) (DECC) Ⓓ **417 778-2DM**
19. ASMF, N. Marriner (r1977: arr Beecham)
(8/89) (LOND) Ⓓ **421 390-2LM**
19. RPS Orch, T. Beecham (arr Beecham: r1927) (11/90) (BEEC) Ⓓ **BEECHAM3**
19. Desford Colliery Caterpillar Band, J. Watson (pp1991: trans brass: C Mowat)
(8/92) (POLY) Ⓓ **QPRL049D**
(8/92) (POLY) ▭ **CPRL049D**
19. LSO, B. Wordsworth
(9/92) (COLL) Ⓓ **Coll1336-2**
19. RPO, M. Davies (r1971)
(3/93) (EMIN) Ⓓ **CD-EMX2198**
19. BBC SO, A. Davis (r1992)
(1/94) (TELD) Ⓓ **4509-90845-2**
19. New SO, G. Toye (r1929)
(3/94) (DUTT) Ⓓ **CDAX8006**
19. ASMF, N. Marriner (r1977: arr Beecham)
(4/94) (DECC) Ⓓ **440 323-2DWO**
(4/94) (DECC) ▭ **440 323-4DWO**
19. RPO, N. del Mar (r1990)
(8/95) (UNIC) Ⓓ **UKCD2073**
19. Bournemouth SO, R. Hickox (r1994)
(9/95) (CHAN) Ⓓ **CHAN9355**
19. RPO, C. Seaman (r1994)
(9/95) (TRIN) Ⓓ **TRP036**
19. LSO, J. Barbirolli (r1966)
(10/95) (EMI) Ⓓ [2] **CMS5 65119-2**

DELLINGER, Rudolf *(1857–1910) Germany*

Don César– operetta: 3 acts (1885—Hamburg) (Lib. O. Walther, after Dumanoir and d'Ennery)
EXCERPTS: ACT 2: 1. Komm' herab, O Madonna Theresa.
1. J. Schmidt, chor, orch, F. Günther (r1936)
(EMI) Ⓓ [2] **CHS7 64676-2**

DIAZ DE LA PEÑA, Eugeno *(1837–1901) France*

Benvenuto Cellini– opera
De l'art splendeur immortelle G. De Luca, orch (r1924) (PEAR) Ⓓ [3] **GEMMCDS9160(2)**
De l'art splendeur immortelle G. De Luca, orch (r1924) (1/92) (PREI) Ⓓ **89036**

DIBDIN, Charles *(1745–1814) England*

The **Ephesian Matron; or The Widow's Tears– comic serenata (1769—London) (Wds. I. Bickerstaffe)**
Matron B. Mills
Maid J. Streeton
Centurion M. Padmore
Father A. Knight
Opera Restor'd, P. Holman (orch Fiske & Holman)
(5/93) (HYPE) Ⓓ **CDA66608**

DISTEL, Herbert *(20th cent)*

La **Stazione– experimental opera: 2 acts (1987-90)**
Cpte A. Schwarz, M. Meysenbug, F. Paternina, T. Fontana, V. Manzoni (r1987-90)
(HATH) Ⓓ **ARTCD6060**

DITTERSDORF, Carl Ditters von *(1739–1799) Austria*

Arcifanfano, re de' matti– opera (1777—Esterháza) (Lib. Goldini: Eng version—Auden & Kallman)
Gloriosa E. Steber
Garbata A. Russell
Semplicina P. Brooks
Sordidone J. McCollum
Furibondo H. Rehfuss
Arcifanfano David Smith
Malgoverno J. Sopher
Clarion Music Soc, N. Jenkins (pp 1965)
(VAI) Ⓓ [2] **VAIA 1010-2**

DONIZETTI, (Domenico) Gaetano (Maria) *(1797–1848) Italy*

L' **Ajo nell'imbarazzo– opera: 2 acts (1824—Rome) (Lib. J Ferretti; rev as 'Don Gregorio', 1826)**
Don Giulio A. Corbelli
Enrico P. Barbacini
Gilda L. Serra
Pippetto V. Gobbi
Don Gregorio E. Dara
Leonarda A. Haengel
Simone D. Menicucci
Turin Teatro Regio Orch, B. Campanella (pp1984)
(FONI) Ⓓ [2] **CDC81**

Alahor in Granata– opera: 2 acts (1836—Palermo) (Lib. M A)
Zobeida, il mira...Confusa è l'alma mia Y. Kenny, D. Jones, R. Smythe, J. Meek, C. McKerracher, G. Mitchell Ch, Philh, D. Parry (r1986/7) (OPRA) Ⓓ **ORR201**

Alfredo di grande– dramma: 2 acts (1823—Naples) (Lib. A L Tottola)
Che potrei dirti, o caro? L. Kitchen, T. Goble, D. Jones, B. McBride, D. Ashman, I. Platt, G. Mitchell Ch, D. Parry, D. Parry
(8/95) (OPRA) Ⓓ [3] **ORCH104**

Anna Bolena– opera: 2 acts (1830—Milan) (Lib. F. Romani)
EXCERPTS: 1. Overture. ACT 1: 2. Nè venne il re; 3. Ella di me, sollecita; 4a. Si taciturna e mesta; 4b. Deh! non voler costringere; 4c. Come, innocente giovane; 4d. Non v'ha sguardo; 5a. Oh! qual parlar fu il suo!; 5b. Ecco il re; 5c. Tremate voi?; 6a. Chi veggo?; 6b. Da quel dì che, lei perduta; 6c. Ah! così nei dì ridenti; 7a. Desta sì tosto; 7b. Voi Regina; 7c. Io senti sulla mia mano; 8a. È sgombra il loco; 8b. Ah! parea che per incanto; 9a. Odo rumor; 9b. Basta, tropp'oltre vai; 9c. S'ei t'abborre; 9d. Ah! per pietà del mio spavento; 10a. Alcun potrai; 10b. In separato carcere. ACT 2: 11. Dove mai ne andarono; 12a. Dio, che mi vedi in core; 12b. Sul suo capo aggravi un Dio; 13a. Ebben? dinanzi ai Giudici; 13b. Arresta Enrico; 14a. Sposa a Percy; 14b. Vieni, Seymour, tu sei Regina. SCENE 3: 15a. Tu pur dannato a morte; 15b. Vivi tu, te ne scongiuro; 16. Chi può vederla; 17a. Piangete voi?; 17b. Al dolce guidami; 17c. Qual mesto suon?; 17d. Cielo, a' miei lunghi spasimi; 17e. Coppia iniqua, l'estrema vendetta.
Anna Bolena M. Callas
Enrico VIII N. Rossi-Lemeni
Giovanna Seymour G. Simionato
Riccardo Percy G. Raimondi
Rochefort P. Clabassi
Smeton G. Carturan
Hervey L. Rumbo
La Scala Chor, La Scala Orch, G. Gavazzeni (pp1957)
(1/94) (EMI) Ⓓ [2] **CMS7 64941-2**
5a-c M. Horne, C. Cava, orch, H. Lewis (pp1966)
(MEMO) Ⓓ [2] **HR4392/3**
5a-c, 14b(pt) G. Simionato, P. Clabassi, Milan RAI Chor, Milan RAI SO, G. Gavazzeni (pp1958)
(MEMO) Ⓓ [2] **HR4386/7**
12a, 12b O. Stapp, I. Kirilová, Košice St PO, P. Vronský (OPUS) Ⓓ **9356 2047**
12a, 12b M. Caballé, S. Verrett, New Philh, A. Guadagno (5/92) (RCA) Ⓓ **GD60818**
14a, 14b S. Verrett, R. El Hage, RCA Italiana Op Orch, G. Prêtre (r1967)
(RCA) Ⓓ **09026 61457-2**
14a, 14b S. Verrett, RCA Italiana Op Orch, G. Prêtre (r1967) (RCA) Ⓓ **74321 24284-2**
(RCA) ▭ **74321 24284-4**
15b R. Vargas, ECO, M. Viotti
(11/92) (CLAV) Ⓓ **CD50-9202**
17a-e M. Caballé, Barcelona SO, C.F. Cillario
(11/92) (RCA) ▭ [2] **RK61044**
17a-e L. Gencer, Milan RAI SO, G. Gavazzeni (pp1958) (MEMO) Ⓓ [2] **HR4239/40**
17a-e E. Suliotis, Rome Op Orch, O. de Fabritiis (r1966) (DECC) Ⓓ **440 405-2DM**
17a-e M. Callas, M. Sinclair, J. Lanigan, D. Robertson, J. Rouleau, Philh Chor, Philh, N. Rescigno (6/86) (EMI) Ⓓ **CDC7 47283-2**
17a-e M. Callas, M. Sinclair, J. Lanigan, D. Robertson, J. Rouleau, Philh, N. Rescigno
(2/90) (EMI) Ⓓ [4] **CMS7 63244-2**
17a, 17b V. Zeani, Turin RAI Orch, F. Vernizzi (pp1958) (BONG) Ⓓ **GB1060-2**
17b K. Ricciarelli, Svizzera Italiana Orch, B. Amaducci (r1979) (ERMI) Ⓓ **ERM151**

L' **Assedio di Calais– opera: 3 acts (1836—Naples) (Lib. Cammarano)**
Eustachio C. du Plessis
Aurelio D. Jones
Edward III R. Smythe
Isabella E. Harrhy
Edmondo J. Treleaven
Incognito N. Bailey
Eleonora N. Focile
G. Mitchell Ch, Philh, D. Parry
(7/89) (OPRA) Ⓓ [2] **ORC009**
(7/89) (OPRA) ⊙ [3] **OR009**

Belisario– opera seria: 3 acts (1836—Venice) (Lib. S. Cammarano, after Marmontel)
Egli è spento L. Gencer, Venice La Fenice Orch, G. Gavazzeni (pp1969)
(MEMO) Ⓓ [2] **HR4239/40**
Liberi siete. Addio! J. Hadley, T. Hampson, WNO Orch, C. Rizzi (r1992)
(11/93) (TELD) Ⓓ **9031-73283-2**
Plauso! Voci di gioia...Sin la tromba M. Caballé, E. Mauro, LSO, C.F. Cillario
(11/92) (RCA) Ⓓ [2] **GD60941**

Il **Campanello di notte– opera: 1 act (1836—Naples) (Lib. cpsr, after Brunswick, Troin and Lhérie)**
Serafina A. Baltsa
Don Anibale Pistacchio E. Dara
Spiridione C. Gaifa
Madame Rosa B. Casoni
Enrico A. Romero
Vienna St Op Chor, Vienna SO, G. Bertini
(8/88) (CBS) Ⓓ **CD38450**

Caterina Cornaro– opera seria: prologue, 2 acts (1844—Naples) (Lib. Sacchero)
Caterina Cornaro M. Caballé
Gerardo J. Carreras
Lusignano L. Saccomani
Andrea Cornaro E. Serra
Mocenigo M. Mazzieri
Strozzi; Un cavaliere N. Williams
Matilde A. Edwards
LSC, LSO, C.F. Cillario (pp1972)
(FOYE) Ⓓ [2] **2-CF2048**
Da che sposa Caterina; Non turbati a questi accenti R. Bruson, Berlin RSO, R. Paternostro
(10/89) (CAPR) Ⓓ **10 247**
(10/89) (CAPR) ▭ **CC27 247**
Io trar non voglio C. Merritt, Munich RSO, J. Fiore (r1993) (9/94) (PHIL) Ⓓ **434 102-2PH**

Chiara e Serafina, ossia I pirati– melodramma semiserio: 2 acts (1822—Milan) (Lib. F Romani)
Tremante, smarrito Y. Kenny, L. Davies, Philh, D. Parry (8/95) (OPRA) Ⓓ [3] **ORCH104**

Il **diluvio universale– opera: 3 acts (1830—Naples) (Lib. D Gilardoni, after Byron)**
Non mi tradir speranza...Ah, non tacermi in core M. Elkins, Philh, J. Judd (r1979)
(9/94) (OPRA) Ⓓ **ORC004**

Dom Sébastien– opera: 5 acts (1843—Paris) (Lib. Scribe)
EXCERPTS: 1. Seul sur le terre (Deserto in terra); 2. O Lisbone, o ma patrie; 3. Ballet Music; 4. Que faire où cacher ma tristesse.
1. B.S. Rosenberg, Budapest Concert Orch, J. Acs (Ital: pp1990) (OLYM) Ⓓ **OCD370**
1. A. Cupido, Danish Rad Concert Orch, M. Elquist (Ital) (DENO) Ⓓ **CO-79785**
1. E. Caruso, orch (r1908: Ital)
(10/89) (NIMB) Ⓓ **NI7803**
(NIMB) ▭ **NC7803**
1. E. Caruso, orch (Ital: r1908)
(7/90) (CLUB) Ⓓ **CL99-060**
1 (2 vers) E. Caruso, orch (Ital: r1908)
(12/90) (PEAR) Ⓓ [3] **EVC1(2)**
1. E. Caruso, orch (r1908: Ital: 2 vers)
(7/91) (RCA) Ⓓ [12] **GD60495(2)**
1. A. Piccaver, orch (r1914: Ital)
(8/93) (PREI) Ⓓ **89060**

1. C. Merritt, Munich RSO, J. Fiore (r1993; Ital)
(9/94) (PHIL) ① **434 102-2PH**
1. Alfredo Kraus, WNO Orch, C. Rizzi (r1994; sung in Italian) (8/95) (PHIL) ① **442 785-2PH**
(8/95) (PHIL) ▭ **442 785-4PH**
2. A. Orda, Polish RSO, S. Rachoń (bp1964)
(SYMP) ① **SYMCD1117**
2. A. Granforte, orch, G.W. Byng (r1925: Ital)
(PREI) ① **89105**
2. M. Battistini, orch (r1906: Ital)
(PREI) ① **89995**
2. R. Bruson, Berlin RSO, R. Paternostro (Ital)
(10/89) (CAPR) ① **10 247**
(10/89) (CAPR) ▭ **CC27 247**
2. M. Battistini, orch (r1906: Ital)
(2/92) (PREI) ① **89045**
2. M. Battistini, orch, C. Sabajno (Ital: r1906)
(10/92) (NIMB) ① **NI7831**
(10/92) (NIMB) ▭ **NC7831**
2. D. Hvorostovsky, Philh, I. Marin (r1992)
(9/94) (PHIL) ① **434 912-2PH**
(9/94) (PHIL) ▭ **434 912-4PH**
4. M. Elkins, Philh, J. Judd (r1979)
(9/94) (OPRA) ① **ORC004**

Don Pasquale– opera: 3 acts (1843—Paris) (Lib. Ruffini and composer, after Anelli)

ACT 1: 1. Overture; 2. Son nov'ore; 3a. E' permesso?; 3b. Bella siccome un angelo; 4. Ah!...Un foco insolito; 5. Prender moglie?; 6. Sogno soave e casto; 7a. Quel guardo il cavaliere; 7b. So anch'io la virtù magica; 8a. Buone nuove, Norina; 8b. Pronto io son; 8c. Vado, corro; ACT 2: 9a. Povero Ernesto!; 9b. Cercherò lontana terra; 9c. E se fia; 10a. Quando avrete; 10b. Via, da bravo; 11. Fra da un parte etcetera; 12. Pria di partir, signore. 13. Siete marito e moglie. ACT 3: 14. I diamanti, presto; 15a. Vediamo: alla modista; 15b. Signorina, in tanta fretta; 15c. E' finita, Don Pasquale; 16. Che interminabile (Servants' Chorus); 17a. Siamo intesi; 17b. Don Pasquale...Cognato; 18a. Cheti, cheti immantinente; 18b. Aspetta, aspetta cara sposina; 19. Com' è gentil; 20. Tornami a dir (Notturno); 21a. Eccoli: attenti bene; 21b. Eccomi...A voi.

Don Pasquale G. Evans
Norina L. Watson
Ernesto R. Davies
Malatesta R. Smythe
Notary J. Dobson
WNO Chor, Welsh Philh, R. Armstrong, B. Coleman
(7/90) (IMP) ▣ **SL2007**

Don Pasquale E. Nesterenko
Norina L. Popp
Ernesto F. Araiza
Malatesta B. Weikl
Notary P. Lika
Bavarian Rad Chor, Munich RSO, H. Wallberg (r1979)
(EURO) ① [2] **352 884**

Don Pasquale S. Bruscantini
Norina M. Freni
Ernesto G. Winbergh
Malatesta L. Nucci
Notary G. Fabbris
Ambrosian Op Chor, Philh, R. Muti (r1982)
(8/88) (EMI) ① [2] **CDS7 47068-2**

Don Pasquale E. Dara
Norina L. Serra
Ernesto A. Bertolo
Malatesta A. Corbelli
Notary G. Pasella
Turin Teatro Regio Chor, Turin Teatro Regio Orch, B. Campanella (pp1988)
(5/89) (NUOV) ① [2] **6715/6**

Don Pasquale E. Badini
Norina A. Saraceni
Ernesto T. Schipa
Malatesta A. Poli
Notary G. Callegari
La Scala Chor, La Scala Orch, C. Sabajno (r1932)
(10/90) (MSCM) ① [2] **MM30231**
(MSCM) ▭ [2] **MM40086**

Don Pasquale G. Bacquier
Norina B. Hendricks
Ernesto L. Canonici
Malatesta G. Quilico
Notary R. Schirrer
Lyon Op Chor, Lyon Op Orch, G. Ferro
(11/90) (ERAT) ① **2292-45487-2**

Don Pasquale F. Corena
Norina G. Sciutti
Ernesto J. Oncina
Malatesta T. Krause
Notary A. Mercuriali
Vienna St Op Chor, Vienna St Op Orch, I. Kertész
(10/92) (DECC) ① [2] **433 036-2DM2**

Don Pasquale R. Capecchi
Norina B. Rizzoli
Ernesto P. Munteanu
Malatesta G. Valdengo
Notary C. Adorni
Naples San Carlo Op Chor, Naples San Carlo Op Orch, F. Molinari-Pradelli (r1955)
(10/94) (PHIL) ① [2] **442 090-2PM2**

Don Pasquale R. Bruson
Norina E. Mei
Ernesto F. Lopardo
Malatesta T. Allen
Notary A. Giacomotti
Bavarian Rad Chor, Munich RO, R. Abbado (r1993)
(12/94) (RCA) ① [2] **09026 61924-2**

Excs M. Freni, G. Winbergh, L. Nucci, S. Bruscantini, Philh, R. Muti
(EMI) ① **CDC7 54490-2**
1. Sydney Eliz Orch, R. Bonynge
(MCEG) ▣ **VVD780**
1. Sydney Eliz Orch, R. Bonynge
(DECC) ◐ **071 149-1DH**
(DECC) ▣ **071 149-3DH**
1. Philh, T. Serafin (r1961)
(EMI) ① [2] **CES5 68541-2**
1. South-West German RSO, K. Arp (r1994)
(PIER) ① **PV730050**
1. La Scala Orch, A. Toscanini (r1921)
(11/92) (RCA) ① **GD60315**
1(pt), 20. G. Groves, J. Watson, J. Partridge (r1994) (ASV) ① **CDWHL2088**
1-4, 6, 7a, 7b, 9b, 9c, 11-13, 15a-c, 18a, 18b, 19, 20, 21a, 21b E. Dara, L. Serra, A. Corbelli, A. Bertolo, Turin Teatro Regio Chor, Turin Teatro Regio Orch, B. Campanella (NUOV) ① **6766**
3b A. Scotti, orch (r1904)
(PEAR) ① **GEMMCD9937**
3b G. Laperrière, Three Rivers SO, G. Bellemare (r1992) (CBC) ① **SMCD5127**
3b G. De Luca, anon (r1902)
(PEAR) ① [3] **GEMMCDS9159(1)**
3b G. De Luca, anon (r1902)
(8/93) (SYMP) ① **SYMCD1111**
3b D. Hvorostovsky, Philh, I. Marin (r1992)
(9/94) (PHIL) ① **434 912-2PH**
(9/94) (PHIL) ▭ **434 912-4PH**
3b, 18a G. De Luca, F. Corradetti, anon (r1907)
(PEAR) ① [3] **GEMMCDS9159(1)**
4. M. Ivogün, orch (r1924)
(8/92) (NIMB) ① **NI7832**
(8/92) (NIMB) ▭ **NC7832**
4. A. Pini-Corsi, E. Badini, orch (r1906)
(4/94) (EMI) ① [3] **CHS7 64860-2(2)**
5, 6, 9a, 19, 20. T. Schipa, T. dal Monte, orch, Anon (cond) (pp1932/3)
(MEMO) ① [2] **HR4220/1**
6. T. Schipa, orch (r1926)
(PEAR) ① **GEMMCD9364**
6. D. Borgioli, orch (r1928)
(12/90) (CLUB) ① **CL99-014**
6. D. Borgioli, orch (r1928)
(4/94) (EMI) ① [3] **CHS7 64864-2(1)**
6. A. Giorgini, orch (r1905)
(4/95) (RECO) ① **TRC3**
6. G. Anselmi, anon (r1907)
(7/95) (SYMP) ① **SYMCD1170**
6, 20. D. Borgioli, A. Rettore, orch, L. Molajoli (r1928) (PEAR) ① **GEMMCD9091**
7a A. Panagulias, Miami SO, E. Kohn (pp1991)
(IMP) ① **MCD43**
7a M. Ivogün, orch (r1916: Ger)
(PREI) ① **89094**
7a G. Pareto, orch, P. Pitt (r1920)
(PEAR) ① **GEMMCD9117**
7a K. Battle, NY Met Op Orch, James Levine (pp1988) (DG) ① **445 552-2GMA**
(DG) ▭ **445 552-4GMA**
7a M. André, Toulouse Capitole Orch, M. Plasson (arr tpt)
(1/89) (EMI) ① **CDC7 49219-2**
7a A. Galli-Curci, orch, J. Pasternack (r1919)
(5/90) (NIMB) ① **NI7806**
(NIMB) ▭ **NC7806**
7a G. Pareto, orch (r1920)
(7/92) (PEAR) ① [3] **GEMMCDS9925(1)**
7a A. Galli-Curci, orch, J. Pasternack (r1919)
(3/94) (ROMO) ① [2] **81003-2**
7a, 7b L. Serra, Turin Teatro Regio Orch, B. Campanella (NUOV) ① **6820**
7a, 7b K. Battle, LPO, B. Campanella (r1991)
(DG) OO **435 866-5CH**
7a, 7b L. Aliberti, Munich RO, L. Gardelli
(11/86) (ORFE) ① **C119841A**
7a, 7b A. Galli-Curci, orch (r1919)
(2/89) (PEAR) ① **GEMMCD9308**
7a, 7b K. Battle, LPO, B. Campanella (r1991)
(12/93) (DG) ① **435 866-2GH**
8b, 8c L. Bori, G. De Luca, orch (r1921)
(PEAR) ① **GEMMCD9458**
8b, 8c G. De Luca, L. Bori, orch (r1921)
(PEAR) ① [3] **GEMMCDS9160(1)**
8b, 8c L. Bori, G. de Luca, Victor Orch, J. Pasternack (r1921) (ROMO) ① [2] **81016-2**
8b, 8c G. De Luca, L. Bori, orch (r1921)
(1/92) (PREI) ① **89036**
8b, 8c, 10b G. De Luca, A. Gonzaga, F. Corradetti, anon (r1907)
(PEAR) ① [3] **GEMMCDS9159(2)**
8c A. Scotti, M. Sembrich, orch (r1906)
(PEAR) ① **GEMMCD9937**
9a T. Beltrán, RPO, R. Stapleton (r1994)
(SILV) ① **SILKD6005**
(SILV) ▭ **SILKC6005**
9a-c R. Alagna, LPO, R. Armstrong
(EMI) ① **CDC5 55540-2**
(EMI) ▭ **EL5 55540-4**
9a-c R. Vargas, ECO, M. Viotti
(11/92) (CLAV) ① **CD50-9202**
9a-c, 19. R. Giménez, Scottish Phil Sngrs, Scottish CO, M. Veltri (5/90) (NIMB) ① **NI5224**
(5/90) (NIMB) ▭ **NC5224**
9a, 9b A. Cupido, Danish Rad Concert Orch, M. Elquist (DENO) ① **CO-79785**
9a, 9b L. Sobinov, orch (r1911: Russ)
(4/94) (EMI) ① [3] **CHS7 64860-2(2)**
15c(pt) E. Corsi, A. Pini-Corsi, orch (r1906)
(11/92) (MEMO) ① [2] **HR4408/9(1)**
16. Fiesole School of Music Female Chor, MMF Chor, MMF Orch, M. Arena (ACAN) ① **43 540**
16. ROH Chor, ROHO, L. Gardelli
(EMI) ① **CDM7 64356-2**
16. Ambrosian Op Chor, Philh, R. Muti (r1982)
(EMI) ① [2] **CZS5 68559-2**
19. L. Pavarotti, Ambrosian Sngrs, New Philh, L. Magiera (7/90) (DECC) ① [2] **425 681-2DM2**
(7/90) (DECC) ▭ [2] **425 681-4DM2**
19. E. Caruso, anon (r1905)
(12/90) (PEAR) ① [3] **EVC1(1)**
19. D. Borgioli, orch (r c1923)
(12/90) (CLUB) ① **CL99-014**
19. E. Caruso, anon (r1905)
(7/91) (RCA) ① [12] **GD60495(1)**
19. E. Caruso, anon (r1905)
(7/95) (NIMB) ① **NI7866**
19, 20. B. Hendricks, L. Canonici, Lyon Op Chor, Lyon Op Orch, G. Ferro
(ERAT) ① **4509-91715-2**
(ERAT) ▭ **4509-91715-4**
20. L. Serra, A. Bertolo, Turin Teatro Regio Chor, Turin Teatro Regio Orch, B. Campanella
(NUOV) ① **6905**
20. J. Sutherland, R. Conrad, LSO, R. Bonynge (r1963) (DECC) ① **421 881-2DA**
20. E. Berger, G. Sinimberghi, Berlin St Op Orch, E. Baltzer (r1939: Ger) (PREI) ① **89092**
20. L. Aliberti, G. Sabbatini, Berlin RSO, R. Paternostro (10/89) (CAPR) ① **10 247**
(10/89) (CAPR) ▭ **CC27 247**
20. T. Dal Monte, T. Schipa, La Scala Orch, F. Ghione (r1933) (4/90) (EMI) ① **CDH7 63200-2**
20. D. Borgioli, E. Surinach, orch (r c1923)
(12/90) (CLUB) ① **CL99-014**
20. E. Berger, G. Sinimberghi, Berlin Staatskapelle (r1939: Ger)
(10/93) (NIMB) ① **NI7848**
20. A. Galli-Curci, T. Schipa, orch, Rosario Bourdon (r1928) (3/94) (CONI) ① **CDHD201**
(3/94) (CONI) ▭ **MCHD201**
20. A. Galli-Curci, T. Schipa, orch, Rosario Bourdon (r1924)
(8/94) (ROMO) ① [2] **81004-2**
21b L. Aliberti, Berlin RSO, R. Paternostro
(10/89) (CAPR) ① **10 247**
(10/89) (CAPR) ▭ **CC27 247**

Il Duca d'Alba– opera: 4 acts (1882—Rome) (Lib. Scribe & Duveyier: score cpted Salvi etc)

EXCERPTS: 1a. Inosservato, penetrava; 1b. Angelo casto e bel; 2. Nei miei superbi gaudi.
1a, 1b A. Cupido, Danish Rad Concert Orch, M. Elquist (DENO) ① **CO-79785**
1a, 1b G. Morino, Warmia Nat PO, B. Amaducci
(10/90) (NUOV) ① **6851**
1a, 1b R. Vargas, ECO, M. Viotti
(11/92) (CLAV) ① **CD50-9202**

1b E. Caruso, orch (r1915)
(10/89) (NIMB) ① **NI7803**
(NIMB) ▭ **NC7803**
1b E. Caruso, orch, W.B. Rogers (r1915)
(7/91) (RCA) ① [12] **GD60495(5)**
1b E. Caruso, orch, W.B. Rogers (r1915)
(10/91) (PEAR) ① [3] **EVC3(2)**
1b C. Merritt, Munich RSO, J. Fiore (r1993)
(9/94) (PHIL) ① **434 102-2PH**
1b G. Anselmi, anon (r1909)
(7/95) (SYMP) ① **SYMCD1170**
2 (pt) L. Nucci, ECO, G-F. Masini (r1986)
(DECC) ① **443 380-2DM**
2. D. Hvorostovsky, Philh, I. Marin (r1992)
(9/94) (PHIL) ① **434 912-2PH**
(9/94) (PHIL) ▭ **434 912-4PH**

Elisabetta, o Il castello di Kenilworth– opera seria: 3 acts (1829—Naples) (Lib. Tottola, after Hugo)

Elisabetta M. Devia
Alberto J. Kundlák
Amelia D. Mazzola
Warney B. Anderson
Lambourne C. Striuli
Fanny C. Foti
Milan RAI Chor, Milan RAI SO, J. Latham-König (pp1989)
(FONI) ① [2] **RFCD2005**

L' **Elisir d'amore, 'Elixir of Love'– opera: 2 acts (1832—Milan) (Lib. Romani, after Scribe)**

EXCERPTS: 1a. Prelude. ACT 1: 1b. Bel conforto; 2. Quanto è bella; 3. Della crudele Isotta; 4. March; 5a. Come Paride vezzoso; 5b. Or se m'ami; 5c. Intanto, o mia ragazza; 6a. Una parola, Adina; 6b. Chiedi all'aura lusinghiera; 7. Che vuol dire codesta suonata?; 8a. Udite, o rustici; 8b. Ei move i paralitici; 9a. Ardir! Ha forse il cielo; 9b. Obbligato; 9c. Va, mortale fortunato; 10a. Caro elisir!; 10b. Chi è mai; 10c. Esulti pur la barbara; 10d. Tran, tran, tran, tran; 11a. Signor sargente; 11b. Adina, credimi. ACT 2: 12. Cantiamo, cantiam; 13a. Poichè cantar; 13b. La Nina Gondoliera; 13c. Io son ricco e tu sei bella; 14a. Cantiamo, cantiam; 14b. Le feste nuziali; 15a. La donna è un animale; 15b. Venti scudi; 16. Saria possibile?; 17. Dell'elisir mirabile; 18a. Come sen va contento!; 18b. Bella Adina; 18c. Quanto amore!; 19. Una furtiva lagrima; 20a. Eccola; 20b. Prendi...prendi, per me sei libero; 21. Alto! Fronte!; 22. Ei corregge ogni difetto; ADDITIONAL ARIA: 23. Nel dolce incanto.

Adina A. Scarabelli
Nemorino C. Merritt
Belcore A. Romero
Dulcamara S. Bruscantini
Giannetta B. Briscik
Parma Teatro Regio Chor, Toscanini SO, H. Soudant (pp1988)
(MEMO) ① [2] **DR3104/5**

Adina R. Grist
Nemorino L. Pavarotti
Belcore I. Wixell
Dulcamara S. Bruscantini
Giannetta S. Matsumoto
San Francisco Op Chor, San Francisco Op Orch, G. Patanè (pp1969)
(BUTT) ① [2] **BMCD006**
(BUTT) ▭ [2] **BMK006**

Adina L. Popp
Nemorino P. Dvorský
Belcore B. Weikl
Dulcamara E. Nesterenko
Giannetta E. Hobarth
Bavarian Rad Chor, Munich RO, H. Wallberg (r1982)
(RCA) ① [2] **74321 25280-2**

Adina R. Carteri
Nemorino L. Alva
Belcore R. Panerai
Dulcamara G. Taddei
Giannetta A. Vercelli
La Scala Chor, La Scala Orch, T. Serafin (r c1958)
(EMI) ① [2] **CMS5 65658-2**

Adina J. Sutherland
Nemorino L. Pavarotti
Belcore D. Cossa
Dulcamara S. Malas
Giannetta M. Casula
Ambrosian Sngrs, ECO, R. Bonynge
(6/86) (DECC) ① [2] **414 461-2DH2**

Adina K. Ricciarelli
Nemorino J. Carreras
Belcore L. Nucci
Dulcamara D. Trimarchi
Giannetta S. Rigacci
Turin RAI Chor, Turin RAI Orch, C. Scimone (r1984)
(6/86) (PHIL) ① [2] **412 714-2PH2**

Adina K. Battle
Nemorino L. Pavarotti
Belcore L. Nucci
Dulcamara E. Dara
Giannetta D. Upshaw
NY Met Op Chor, NY Met Op Orch, James Levine (r1989)
(2/91) (DG) ① [2] **429 744-2GH2**

Adina M. Devia
Nemorino R. Alagna
Belcore P. Spagnoli
Dulcamara B. Praticò
Giannetta F. Provvisionato
Tallis Chbr Ch, ECO, M. Viotti (r1992)
(6/93) (ERAT) ① [2] **4509-91701-2**

Adina K. Battle
Nemorino L. Pavarotti
Belcore J. Pons
Dulcamara E. Dara
Giannetta K. Uecker
NY Met Op Chor, NY Met Op Orch, James Levine, B. Large (pp1991)
(7/93) (DG) ◖ [2] **072 432-1GH2**
(DG) ▭ **072 432-3GH**

Adina R. Carteri
Nemorino L. Alva
Belcore R. Panerai
Dulcamara G. Taddei
Giannetta A. Vercelli
La Scala Chor, La Scala Orch, T. Serafin (r c1958)
(5/94) (CFP) ① [2] **CD-CFPD4733**
(5/94) (CFP) ▭ **TC-CFPD4733**

Adina H. Gueden
Nemorino G. di Stefano
Belcore R. Capecchi
Dulcamara F. Corena
Giannetta L. Mandelli
MMF Chor, MMF Orch, F. Molinari-Pradelli (r1955)
(7/95) (DECC) ① [2] **443 542-2LF2**

1a-3, 6a-8b, 10a-11b, 13a-c, 17, 19, 21, 22. K. Battle, L. Pavarotti, L. Nucci, E. Dara, D. Upshaw, NY Met Op Chor, NY Met Op Orch, James Levine (DG) ① **435 880-2GH**
2. B. Gigli, orch, Rosario Bourdon (r1925)
(NIMB) ① **NI7817**
(NIMB) ▭ **NC7817**
2. B. Gigli, orch, Rosario Bourdon (r1925)
(CONI) ① **CDHD170**
2. F. Wunderlich, Bavarian St Orch, H. Müller-Kray (Ger) (EMI) ① [3] **CZS7 62993-2**
2. B. Gigli, orch (r1925) (IMP) ① **GLRS102**
2. A. Bonci, orch (r1913)
(PEAR) ① **GEMMCD9168**
2. B. Gigli, orch (r1925)
(5/90) (PEAR) ① **GEMMCD9367**
2. B. Gigli, orch, Rosario Bourdon (r1925)
(10/90) (RCA) ① **GD87811**
(10/90) (RCA) ▭ **GK87811**
2, 19. L. Pavarotti, Rome SO, N. Bonavolontà (pp1967) (10/95) (RCA) ① **09026 62541-2**
3, 6a, 18c, 20b R. Scotto, MMF Chor, MMF Orch, G. Gavazzeni (pp1967)
(MEMO) ① [2] **HR4291/2**
5a A. Scotti, anon (r1905)
(PEAR) ① **GEMMCD9937**
5a T. Gobbi, Philh, A. Erede (r1963)
(10/89) (EMI) ① **CDM7 63109-2**
5a A. Scotti, anon (r1905)
(4/94) (RCA) ① [6] **09026 61580-2(1)**
5a D. Hvorostovsky, Philh, I. Marin (r1992)
(9/94) (PHIL) ① **434 912-2PH**
(9/94) (PHIL) ▭ **434 912-4PH**
6a G. Aragall, E. Tumagian, Bratislava RSO, A. Rahbari (r1992) (12/94) (NAXO) ① **8 550684**
6a, 6b M. Freni, L. Pavarotti, Ater Orch, L. Magiera (pp)
(5/94) (DECC) ① [2] **443 018-2DF2**
6a, 20a, 20b A. Scarabelli, C. Merritt, Parma Teatro Regio Chor, Toscanini SO, H. Soudant
(NUOV) ① **6905**
6b L. Pavarotti, R. Grist, San Francisco Op Orch, G. Patanè (pp1969) (BUTT) ① **BMCD015**
(BUTT) ▭ **BMK015**
6b L. Pavarotti, M. Freni, Ater Orch, L. Magiera (pp1980) (BELA) ① **450 002-2**
(BELA) ▭ **450 002-4**
6b J. Sutherland, L. Pavarotti, ECO, R. Bonynge (1970) (DECC) ① **436 313-2DA**
(DECC) ▭ **436 313-4DA**

8a A. Didur, orch (r c1919)
(1/94) (CLUB) ① **CL99-089**
8a S. Baccaloni, orch (r1930)
(4/94) (EMI) ① [3] **CHS7 64864-2(1)**
8a F. Corradetti, anon, anon (r1907)
(12/94) (BONG) ① **GB1043-2**
8a, 8b F. Corena, MMF Chor, MMF Orch, F. Molinari-Pradelli (r1955)
(10/93) (DECC) ① **436 464-2DM**
8a, 8b, 9a-c G. Taddei, L. Pavarotti, Vienna St Op Chor, Vienna St Op Orch, N. Bareza (pp1984) (ACAN) ① **49 402**
8a, 8b, 9a-c, 18a-c S. Bruscantini, C. Merritt, A. Scarabelli, Parma Teatro Regio Chor, Toscanini SO, H. Soudant (pp1988)
(MEMO) ① [2] **HR4300/1**
9a, 18a-c L. Pavarotti, P. Pace, E. Dara, Bologna Teatro Comunale Orch, L. Magiera (pp1991) (DECC) ◖ **071 140-1DH**
(DECC) ▭ **071 140-3DH**
9b F. de Lucia, E. Badini, anon (r1907)
(1/95) (SYMP) ① **SYMCD1149**
10a-d K. Battle, P. Domingo, NY Met Op Orch, James Levine (pp1988)
(DG) ① **445 552-2GMA**
(DG) ▭ **445 552-4GMA**
10c P. Domingo, A. Panagulias, Miami SO, E. Kohn (pp1991) (IMP) ① **MCD43**
11b T. Schipa, orch (r1928)
(2/89) (PEAR) ① **GEMMCD9322**
11b T. Schipa, orch, Rosario Bourdon (r1928)
(10/90) (MSCM) ① [2] **MM30231**
(MSCM) ▭ [2] **MM40086**
11b T. Schipa, orch, Rosario Bourdon (r1928)
(4/94) (RCA) ① [6] **09026 61580-2(4)**
11b, 19. T. Schipa, orch, Anon (cond) (pp1928/9) (MEMO) ① [2] **HR4220/1**
15a, 15b T. Gobbi, N. Monti, Rome Op Orch, G. Santini (r1953)
(10/89) (EMI) ① **CDM7 63109-2**
15b E. Caruso, G. De Luca, orch, J. Pasternack (r1919) (PEAR) ① [3] **GEMMCDS9159(2)**
15b T. Hampson, J. Hadley, WNO Orch, C. Rizzi (r1992) (TELD) ① **4509-98824-2**
15b E. Caruso, G. De Luca, orch, J. Pasternack (r1919) (7/91) (RCA) ① [12] **GD60495(6)**
15b E. Caruso, G. De Luca, orch, J. Pasternack (r1919) (10/91) (PEAR) ① [3] **EVC4(2)**
15b J. Hadley, T. Hampson, WNO Orch, C. Rizzi (r1992) (11/93) (TELD) ① **9031-73283-2**
15b, 19. P. Domingo, I. Wixell, ROH Chor, ROHO, J. Pritchard (SONY) ① **SBK46548**
(SONY) ▭ **SBT46548**
18a, 18c V. Zeani, N. Rossi-Lemeni, Turin RAI Orch, F. Vernizzi (pp1958)
(BONG) ① **GB1060-2**
19. J. Björling, Stockholm Royal Op Orch, N. Grevillius (r1957) (RCA) ▭ **GK85277**
19. M. Lanza, Hollywood Bowl SO, E. Ormandy (pp1947) (IMP) ① **PWKS4230**
19. P. Domingo, Los Angeles PO, C.M. Giulini
(DG) ① [3] **427 708-2GX3**
19. P. Domingo, Los Angeles PO, C.M. Giulini
(DG) ▭ **419 091-4GW**
19. B. Gigli, orch (r1929) (CONI) ① **CDHD149**
(CONI) ▭ **MCHD149**
19. P. Domingo, LSO, N. Santi
(RCA) ① **GD84265**
19. M. Lanza, RCA Victor Orch, C. Callinicos (r1950) (RCA) ① **GD60049**
(RCA) ▭ **GK60049**
19. A. Dermota, Berlin St Op Orch, A. Rother (r1950s) (PREI) ① **90022**
19. T. Schipa, orch, C. Sabajno (r1931)
(EMI) ① **CDC7 54016-2**
19. B. Gigli, orch, Rosario Bourdon (r1929)
(NIMB) ① **NI7817**
(NIMB) ▭ **NC7817**
19. T. Schipa, La Scala Orch, C. Sabajno (r1929) (MMOI) ① **CDMOIR405**
(MMOI) ▭ **CMOIR405**
19. J. Carreras, Turin RAI Orch, C. Scimone
(PHIL) ① **432 692-2PH**
(PHIL) ▭ **432 692-4PH**
19. P. Domingo, LSO, N. Santi
(RCA) ① [2] **GD60866**
(RCA) ▭ [2] **GK60866**
19. G. di Stefano, MMF Orch, F. Molinari-Pradelli (r1955) (DECC) ① **433 065-2DWO**
(DECC) ▭ **433 065-4DWO**
19. J. Carreras, LPO, J. López-Cobos
(PHIL) ① **434 152-2PM**
19. Alfredo Kraus, Madrid SO, G.P. Sanzogno (pp1991) (IMP) ① [2] **DPCD998**

19. L. Canonici, Lyon Op Chor, Lyon Op Orch, P. Verrot (ERAT) Ⓓ **2292-45797-2**
(ERAT) ⊟ **2292-45797-4**
19. Alfredo Kraus, Madrid SO, G.P. Sanzogno (RNE) Ⓓ [2] **650004**
19. A. Cupido, Danish Rad Concert Orch, M. Elquist (DENO) Ⓓ **CO-79785**
19. P. Domingo, LSO, N. Santi (r1971) (RCA) Ⓓ **09026 61356-2**
(RCA) ⊟ **09026 61356-4**
19. E. Caruso, anon (r1904) (MCI) Ⓓ **MCCD086**
(MCI) ⊟ **MCTC086**
19. J. Schmidt, BPO, S. Meyrowitz (r1931) (RELI) Ⓓ **CR921036**
19. C. Bergonzi, Verona Arena Orch, A. Guadagno (pp1992) (MCI) Ⓓ **MCCD099**
19. G. di Stefano, MMF Orch, F. Molinari-Pradelli (r1955) (DECC) Ⓓ **440 403-2DM**
19. J. Carreras, LPO, J. López-Cobos (r1980) (BELA) Ⓓ **450 059-2**
(BELA) ⊟ **450 059-4**
19. P. Domingo, N. Santi, LSO (RCA) Ⓓ **09026 61440-2**
(RCA) ⊟ **09026 61440-4**
19. J. Schmidt, orch, F. Günther (r1934) (EMI) Ⓓ [2] **CHS7 64673-2**
19. J. Carreras, Turin RAI Orch, C. Scimone (r1984) (PHIL) Ⓓ **442 600-2PH**
(PHIL) ⊟ **442 600-4PH**
19. J. McCormack, orch (r1910) (ASV) Ⓓ **CDAJA5137**
(ASV) ⊟ **ZCAJA5137**
19. P. Domingo, J. Pritchard, J. Pritchard (SONY) Ⓓ **MDK47176**
(SONY) ⊟ **MDT47176**
19. P. Domingo, Los Angeles PO, C.M. Giulini (r1980) (DG) Ⓓ **445 525-2GMA**
(DG) ⊟ **445 525-4GMA**
19. D. Borgioli, orch, L. Molajoli (r1927) (PEAR) Ⓓ **GEMMCD9091**
19. J. Carreras, English Concert Chor, BBC Concert Orch, E. Ricci (pp1994) (TELD) ◖ **4509-96080-6**
(TELD) ▣ **4509-96080-3**
19. T. Beltrán, RPO, R. Stapleton (r1994) (SILV) Ⓓ **SILKD6005**
(SILV) ⊟ **SILKC6005**
19. A. Bonci, orch (r1912: 2 vers) (PEAR) Ⓓ **GEMMCD9168**
19. M. Lanza, orch, R. Sinatra (r1971) (RCA) Ⓓ **09026 62550-2**
19. B. Gigli, orch, J. Barbirolli (r1933) (PEAR) Ⓓ [2] **GEMMCDS9176**
19. L. Pavarotti, ECO, R. Bonynge (7/86) (DECC) Ⓓ [2] **417 011-2DH2**
19. P. Domingo, Los Angeles PO, C.M. Giulini (7/86) (DG) Ⓓ **415 366-2GH**
19. B. Gigli, orch, J. Barbirolli (r1933) (9/88) (EMI) Ⓓ **CDH7 61051-2**
19. J. Björling, Stockholm Royal Op Orch, N. Grevillius (r1945) (10/88) (EMI) Ⓓ **CDH7 61053-2**
19. Alfredo Kraus, Paris Op Orch, M. Veltri (pp1987) (12/88) (EMI) Ⓓ **CDC7 49067-2**
19. M. André, Toulouse Capitole Orch, M. Plasson (arr tpt) (1/89) (EMI) Ⓓ **CDC7 49219-2**
19. T. Schipa, La Scala Orch, C. Sabajno (r1931) (2/89) (PEAR) Ⓓ **GEMMCD9322**
19. E. Caruso, S. Cottone (r1902) (5/89) (EMI) Ⓓ **CDH7 61046-2**
19. H. Nash, orch (Eng: r1926) (8/89) (PEAR) Ⓓ **GEMMCD9319**
19. K. Walker, J. Drake (arr bn) (10/89) (REGE) Ⓓ **REGCD104**
(10/89) (REGE) ⊟ **REGC104**
19. E. Caruso, anon (r1904) (10/89) (NIMB) Ⓓ **NI7803**
(NIMB) ⊟ **NC7803**
19. T. Schipa, orch, Rosario Bourdon (r1925) (12/89) (RCA) Ⓓ **GD87969**
19. J. Patzak, Berlin St Op Orch (r1932) (3/90) (PEAR) Ⓓ **GEMMCD9383**
19. J. Schmidt, orch (r1934) (4/90) (EMI) Ⓓ **CDM7 69478-2**
19. T. Schipa, La Scala Orch, C. Sabajno (r1929) (4/90) (EMI) Ⓓ **CDH7 63200-2**
19. B. Gigli, orch, Rosario Bourdon (r1929) (5/90) (PEAR) Ⓓ **GEMMCD9367**
19. R. Giménez, Scottish CO, M. Veltri (5/90) (NIMB) Ⓓ **NI5224**
(5/90) (NIMB) ⊟ **NC5224**
19. L. Pavarotti, ECO, R. Bonynge (7/90) (DECC) Ⓓ [2] **425 681-2DM2**
(7/90) (DECC) ⊟ [2] **425 681-4DM2**
19. E. Caruso, anon (r1904) (7/90) (CLUB) Ⓓ **CL99-060**
19. D. Smirnov, orch (r1912) (7/90) (CLUB) Ⓓ **CL99-031**
19. T. Schipa, orch, Rosario Bourdon (r1925) (10/90) (MSCM) Ⓓ [2] **MM30231**
(MSCM) ⊟ [2] **MM40086**
19. G. Morino, Warmia Nat PO, B. Amaducci (10/90) (NUOV) Ⓓ **6851**
19. B. Gigli, orch, Rosario Bourdon (r1929) (10/90) (RCA) Ⓓ **GD87811**
(10/90) (RCA) ⊟ **GK87811**
19. E. Caruso, anon (r1904) (12/90) (PEAR) Ⓓ [3] **EVC1(1)**
19. E. Caruso, anon (r1903) (12/90) (PEAR) Ⓓ [3] **EVC1(1)**
19. E. Caruso, S. Cottone (r1902) (12/90) (PEAR) Ⓓ [3] **EVC1(1)**
19. D. Borgioli, orch (r1923) (12/90) (CLUB) Ⓓ **CL99-014**
19. E. Caruso, orch (r1911) (3/91) (PEAR) Ⓓ [3] **EVC2**
19. E. Caruso, orch (r1911) (7/91) (RCA) Ⓓ [12] **GD60495(4)**
19. E. Caruso, S. Cottone (r1902) (7/91) (RCA) Ⓓ [12] **GD60495(1)**
19. E. Caruso, anon (r1904) (7/91) (RCA) Ⓓ [12] **GD60495(1)**
19. E. Caruso, anon (r1903) (7/91) (RCA) Ⓓ [12] **GD60495(1)**
19. Ferruccio Tagliavini, RCA Victor Orch, A. Dorati (r1947) (4/92) (EMI) Ⓓ [7] **CHS7 69741-2(7)**
19. J. McCormack, orch (r1910) (10/92) (TEST) Ⓓ **SBT1005**
19. R. Vargas, ECO, M. Viotti (11/92) (CLAV) Ⓓ **CD50-9202**
19. J. McCormack, orch (r1910) (5/93) (MMOI) Ⓓ **CDMOIR418**
19. B. Gigli, orch, J. Barbirolli (r1933) (6/93) (MMOI) Ⓓ **CDMOIR417**
19. Ferruccio Tagliavini, EIAR Orch, U. Tansini (r1940) (3/94) (CENT) Ⓓ **CRC2164**
19. T. Schipa, La Scala Orch, C. Sabajno (r1929) (4/94) (EMI) Ⓓ [3] **CHS7 64864-2(1)**
19. R. Crooks, orch, W. Pelletier (r1938) (5/94) (CLAR) Ⓓ **CDGSE78-50-52**
19. L. Pavarotti, Ater Orch, L. Magiera (pp) (5/94) (DECC) Ⓓ [2] **443 018-2DF2**
19. A. Pertile, La Scala Orch, C. Sabajno (r1929) (10/94) (PREI) Ⓓ **89072**
19. B. Gigli, orch (r1929) (12/94) (MMOI) Ⓓ **CDMOIR425**
19. P. Bertin, A. Scholl, D. Visse, Camargue PO, Reinhardt Wagner (r1995: arr R Wagner) (8/95) (HARM) Ⓓ **HMC90 1552**
20b M. Callas, Paris Cons, N. Rescigno (6/86) (EMI) Ⓓ **CDC7 47283-2**

Emilia di Liverpool– opera: 2 acts (1824—Naples) (Lib. after Scatizzi)

Emilia Y. Kenny
Candida A. Mason
Luigia B. Mills
Don Romualdo S. Bruscantini
Claudio di Liverpool G. Dolton
Federico C. Merritt
Il Conte C. Thornton-Holmes
G. Mitchell Ch, Philh, D. Parry
(5/92) (OPRA) Ⓓ [3] **ORC008**
(6/88) (OPRA) ⊙ [4] **OR008**

Enrico di Borgogna– opera: 2 acts (1818—Venice) (Lib. Merelli)

Elisa! Elisa! Oh! me infelice!... Care aurette che spiegate D. Jones, Philh, D. Parry (10/90) (OPRA) Ⓓ [3] **ORCH103**

L' Eremitaggio di Liverpool– opera: 2 acts (1828—Naples) (Lib. G. Checcherini)

Claudio di Liverpool G. Dolton
Emilia Y. Kenny
Colonel Villars C. Merritt
Count Asdrubale S. Bruscantini
Bettina B. Mills
Candida A. Mason
Giacomo C. Thornton-Holmes
G. Mitchell Ch, Philh, D. Parry
(5/92) (OPRA) Ⓓ [3] **ORC008**
(6/88) (OPRA) ⊙ [4] **OR008**

Il Falegname di Livonia, o Pietro il grande, Czar delle Russie– opera: 2 acts (1819—Venice) (Lib. Bevilacqua-Aldovrandini)

Ah qual colpo, oh ciel, qual fremito R. Smythe, M. Hill Smith, K. John, S. Bickley, M. Moreno, J. Best, Philh, D. Parry (10/90) (OPRA) Ⓓ [3] **ORCH103**

Fausta– opera: 2 acts (1832—Naples) (Lib. Gilardoni & cpsr)

Fausta R. Kabaivanska
Emperor Constantine R. Bruson
Crispo G. Giacomini
Irella G. Dalle Molle
Massimiano L. Roni
Licinia A. Vespasiani
Albino T. Pane
Rome Op Chor, Rome Op Orch, D. Oren (pp1981)
(ITAL) Ⓓ [3] **LO7701/3**

La Favorita– opera: 4 acts (1840—Paris) (Lib. Royer & Väez)

EXCERPTS—ACT 1: 1. Bell'alba, foriera; 2. Quella preghiera non odi tu?; 3. Una vergine, un' angel di Dio; 4. Non sai tu; 5. Bei raggi lucenti; 6a. Messaggera gentile; 6b. Ah, mio bene!; 7a. Ah! Signora!; 7b. Sì, che un solo accento. ACT 2: 8a. Ma de' malvagi invan; 8b. Vieni, amor/Leonora! A' piedi tuoi; 8c. De' nemici tuoi; 9a. Quando le soglie paterne; 9b. In questo suol a lusingar; 9c. Ah, l'alto ardor che nutro; 10a. Ah, Sire!; 10b. Qual tumulto!; 11. Il nome del Pastor. ACT 3: 12. A lei son presso alfine!; 13. A tanto amor, Leonora; 14a. Fia dunque vero?; 14b. O mio Fernando; 15. Di già nella cappella. ACT 4: 16a. Fratelli! andiam; 16b. Splendon più belle; 17. Figlio diletto, ascolta!; 18a. Favorita del re!; 18b. Spirto gentil; 19a. Fernando! Dove mai lo troverò?; 19b. Pietoso al par del Nume; 20a. Addio! Fuggir mi lascia!; 20b. Vieni, ah vien!.

Leonora F. Cossotto
Fernando Alfredo Kraus
Alfonso S. Bruscantini
Baldassarre R. Raimondi
Ines M. Zotti
Don Gasparo A. Pedroni
NHK Italian Op Chor, NHK SO, O. de Fabritiis (pp1971)
(FOYE) Ⓓ [2] **2-CF2054**

Léonor G. Scalchi
Fernand L. Canonici
Alphonse R. Massis
Balthazar G. Surian
Inès M. Laurenza
Don Gaspar E. Gavazzi
Milan RAI Chor, Milan RAI SO, D. Renzetti (pp1991: Fr)
(FONI) Ⓓ [3] **RFCD2015**

Leonora F. Cossotto
Fernando L. Pavarotti
Alfonso G. Bacquier
Baldassarre N. Ghiaurov
Ines I. Cotrubas
Don Gasparo P. de Palma
Bologna Teatro Comunale Chor, Bologna Teatro Comunale Orch, R. Bonynge
(10/90) (DECC) Ⓓ [3] **430 038-2DM3**

Leonora A. Tabiadon
Fernando G. Morino
Alfonso P. Coni
Baldassarre A. Verducci
Ines A. Ruffini
Don Gasparo M. Farruggia
Slovak Phil Chor, Italian International Orch, F. Luisi (pp1989)
(10/91) (NUOV) Ⓓ [2] **6823/4**

Ballet Music Orch, R. Bonynge (VAI) ▣ **VAI69108**
3. T. Schipa, orch (r1927) (PEAR) Ⓓ **GEMMCD9364**
3. Alfredo Kraus, Milan RAI SO, A. Basile (pp1959) (MEMO) Ⓓ [2] **HR4233/4**
3. T. Schipa, orch, Anon (cond) (pp1928) (MEMO) Ⓓ [2] **HR4220/1**
3. J. Sempere, Verona Arena Orch, A. Guadagno (pp1992) (MCI) Ⓓ **MCCD099**
3. M. Fleta, orch (r1926) (PEAR) Ⓓ **GEMMCD9129**
3. L. Signoretti, anon (r1901) (12/89) (SYMP) Ⓓ **SYMCD1065**

3. M. Fleta, orch (r1927)
(2/90) (PREI) Ⓓ **89002**
3. A. Pertile, La Scala Orch, C. Sabajno (r1930)
(9/90) (PREI) Ⓓ **89007**
3. F. Marconi, orch (r1908)
(10/90) (SYMP) Ⓓ **SYMCD1069**
3. T. Schipa, orch, Rosario Bourdon (r1928)
(10/92) (TEST) Ⓓ **SBT1005**
3. A. Cortis, orch (r1925)
(3/94) (NIMB) Ⓓ **NI7850**
3. F. de Lucia, anon (r1904)
(1/95) (SYMP) Ⓓ **SYMCD1149**
3, 18a, 18b A. Cupido, Danish Rad Concert Orch, M. Elquist (DENO) Ⓓ **CO-79785**
3, 18a, 18b R. Giménez, Scottish CO, M. Veltri
(5/90) (NIMB) Ⓓ **NI5224**
(5/90) (NIMB) ▭ **NC5224**
3, 18b A. Bonci, orch (r1913)
(PEAR) Ⓓ **GEMMCD9168**
4b M. Horne, Monte Carlo PO, L. Foster (r1984: Fr) (ERAT) Ⓓ **4509-98501-2**
6b, 9a A. Tabiadon, G. Morino, P. Coni, Bratislava Phil Ch, Italian International Orch, F. Luisi (NUOV) Ⓓ **6905**
8a-c, 13. S. Bruscantini, F. Cossotto, A. Pedroni, Alfredo Kraus, NHK SO, O. de Fabritiis (pp1971)
(MEMO) Ⓓ [2] **HR4300/1**
8a, 8b G. Taddei, Naples San Carlo Op Orch, U. Rapalo (PREI) Ⓓ **90020**
8b M. Battistini, orch (r1921)
(PEAR) Ⓓ **GEMMCD9016**
8b G. De Luca, anon (r1902)
(PEAR) Ⓓ [3] **GEMMCDS9159(1)**
8b T. Ruffo, orch, C. Sabajno (r1912)
(11/90) (NIMB) Ⓓ **NI7810**
(NIMB) ▭ **NC7810**
8b J.B. Faure, anon (French: r c1900)
(9/91) (SYMP) Ⓓ **SYMCD1089**
8b A. Endrèze, orch, F. Ruhlmann (French: r c1932) (11/92) (MSCM) Ⓓ **MM30451**
8b G. De Luca, anon (r1902)
(8/93) (SYMP) Ⓓ **SYMCD1111**
8b M. Battistini, orch, C. Sabajno (r1906)
(4/94) (EMI) Ⓓ [3] **CHS7 64860-2(1)**
8b, 8c M. Battistini, orch, C. Sabajno (r1913)
(10/92) (NIMB) Ⓓ **NI7831**
(10/92) (NIMB) ▭ **NC7831**
8b, 8c, 13. R. Bruson, Berlin RSO, R. Paternostro (10/89) (CAPR) Ⓓ **10 247**
(10/89) (CAPR) ▭ **CC27 247**
8b, 13. G. De Luca, anon (r1907)
(PEAR) Ⓓ [3] **GEMMCDS9159(1)**
8b, 13. R. Stracciari, orch (r1925)
(PEAR) Ⓓ **GEMMCD9178**
8b, 13. D. Hvorostovsky, Philh, I. Marin (r1992)
(9/94) (PHIL) Ⓓ **434 912-2PH**
(9/94) (PHIL) ▭ **434 912-4PH**
9a P. Coni, S. Verrett, Bologna Teatro Comunale Orch, L. Magiera (pp1991)
(DECC) ◐ **071 140-1DH**
(DECC) ▣ **071 140-3DH**
9b, 9c P. Amato, M. Matzenauer, orch (r1912)
(PREI) Ⓓ **89064**
9c P. Amato, M. Matzenauer, orch (r1912)
(PEAR) Ⓓ **GEMMCD9104**
9c G. De Luca, E. Ceresoli, anon (r1902)
(PEAR) Ⓓ [3] **GEMMCDS9159(1)**
9c G. De Luca, E. Ceresoli, anon (r1902)
(8/93) (SYMP) Ⓓ **SYMCD1111**
12. F. Cossotto, Bologna Teatro Comunale Orch, R. Bonynge (DECC) Ⓓ **433 069-2DWO**
(DECC) ▭ **433 069-4DWO**
13. M. Battistini, orch (r1924)
(PEAR) Ⓓ **GEMMCD9016**
13. G. De Luca, orch (r1918)
(PEAR) Ⓓ [3] **GEMMCDS9160(1)**
13. A. Magini-Coletti, orch (r1908)
(PREI) Ⓓ **89995**
13. G. De Luca, orch (r1918)
(1/92) (PREI) Ⓓ **89036**
13. M. Battistini, orch (r1906)
(2/92) (PREI) Ⓓ **89045**
13. P. Silveri, LSO, W. Goehr (r1948)
(4/92) (EMI) Ⓓ [7] **CHS7 69741-2(7)**
13. M. Ancona, orch (r1907)
(7/92) (PEAR) Ⓓ [3] **GEMMCDS9923(2)**
13. M. Battistini, orch, C. Sabajno (r1906)
(10/92) (NIMB) Ⓓ **NI7831**
(10/92) (NIMB) ▭ **NC7831**
13. G. Bellantoni, orch (r1910)
(11/92) (MEMO) Ⓓ [2] **HR4408/9(2)**
13. M. Ancona, orch (r1907)
(7/93) (NIMB) Ⓓ [2] **NI7840/1**
13. G. Bellantoni, orch (r c1910)
(12/94) (BONG) Ⓓ **GB1043-2**

14a, 14b S. Verrett, RCA Italiana Op Orch, G. Prêtre (r1967) (RCA) Ⓓ **09026 61457-2**
14a, 14b E. Stignani, Rome Academy Orch, V. Bellezza (r1946)
(4/92) (EMI) Ⓓ [7] **CHS7 69741-2(7)**
14a, 14b S. Verrett, RCA Italiana Op Orch, G. Prêtre (r1967)
(4/94) (RCA) Ⓓ [6] **09026 61580-2(8)**
14b S. Pasqualini, Berlin RSO, R. Buckley
(SCHW) Ⓓ [2] **314052**
14b D. Graves, Rio de Janeiro Municipal Th Chor, Rio de Janeiro Municipal Th Orch, J. DeMain (pp1992) (SONY) ◐ **SLV48362**
(SONY) ▣ **SHV48362**
14b G. Simionato, MMF Orch, A. Erede (1955)
(DECC) Ⓓ **440 406-2DM**
14b E. Stignani, EIAR Orch, U. Tansini (r1937)
(1/91) (PREI) Ⓓ **89014**
14b S. Onegin, orch, Rosario Bourdon (r1929)
(2/91) (PREI) Ⓓ **89027**
14b R. Anday, Vienna St Op Orch, K. Alwin (r1929) (5/92) (PREI) Ⓓ **89046**
14b K. Branzell, orch (r1928)
(8/92) (PREI) Ⓓ **89039**
14b D. Soffel, Swedish CO, M. Liljefors (pp1988)
(4/93) (CPRI) Ⓓ **CAP21428**
14b F. Cossotto, Bologna Teatro Comunale Orch, R. Bonynge (r1974)
(10/93) (DECC) Ⓓ **436 462-2DM**
14b F. Litvinne, orch (r1907: Fr)
(12/94) (SYMP) Ⓓ **SYMCD1128**
14b, 19a, 19b I. Minghini-Cattaneo, L. Cecil, La Scala Orch, C. Sabajno (r1930)
(6/90) (PREI) Ⓓ **89008**
14b, 19b E. Burzio, orch (r1913)
(1/91) (CLUB) Ⓓ [2] **CL99-587/8**
16b E. Pinza, orch (r1924)
(2/89) (PEAR) Ⓓ **GEMMCD9306**
16b E. Pinza, NY Met Op Chor, NY Met Op Orch, G. Setti (r1930) (3/92) (PREI) Ⓓ **89050**
16b O. Luppi, orch (r1905)
(11/92) (MEMO) Ⓓ [2] **HR4408/9(1)**
18a Alfredo Kraus, Buenos Aires Colón Th Orch, B. Bartoletti (pp1967)
(MEMO) Ⓓ [2] **HR4233/4**
18a, 18b P. Domingo, Barcelona SO, G. Navarro
(11/92) (RCA) ▭ **09026 61204-4**
18a, 18b B.S. Rosenberg, Budapest Concert Orch, J. Acs (pp1990) (OLYM) Ⓓ **OCD370**
18a, 18b P. Domingo, Barcelona SO, G. Navarro
(RCA) ⓞⓞ **09026 61204-5**
18a, 18b L. Pavarotti, Bologna Teatro Comunale Orch, R. Bonynge
(7/86) (DECC) Ⓓ [2] **417 011-2DH2**
18a, 18b P. Dvorský, Bratislava RSO, Czech RSO, O. Lenárd (10/89) (OPUS) Ⓓ **9156 1824**
18a, 18b Alfredo Kraus, WNO Orch, C. Rizzi (r1994; sung in French)
(8/95) (PHIL) Ⓓ **442 785-2PH**
(8/95) (PHIL) ▭ **442 785-4PH**
18b B. Gigli, orch (r1921) (CONI) Ⓓ **CDHD170**
18b L. Pavarotti, Vienna Op Orch, E. Downes (r1968) (DECC) Ⓓ **433 065-2DWO**
(DECC) ▭ **433 065-4DWO**
18b L. Pavarotti, Vienna Op Orch, E. Downes (r1967) (DECC) Ⓓ **436 314-2DA**
(DECC) ▭ **436 314-4DA**
18b B. Gigli, orch (r1918)
(ASV) Ⓓ **CDAJA5137**
(ASV) ▭ **ZCAJA5137**
18b D. Borgioli, orch (r1922)
(PEAR) Ⓓ **GEMMCD9091**
18b P. Domingo, Barcelona SO, G. Navarro (r1992) (RCA) Ⓓ **09026 62550-2**
18b B. Gigli, orch (r1921)
(5/90) (NIMB) Ⓓ **NI7807**
(NIMB) ▭ **NC7807**
18b A. Pertile, La Scala Orch, G. Nastrucci (r1930) (9/90) (PREI) Ⓓ **89007**
18b B. Gigli, orch, J. Pasternack (r1921)
(10/90) (RCA) Ⓓ **GD87811**
(10/90) (RCA) ▭ **GK87811**
18b E. Caruso, orch (r1906)
(12/90) (PEAR) Ⓓ [3] **EVC1(2)**
18b D. Borgioli, orch (r1923)
(12/90) (CLUB) Ⓓ **CL99-014**
18b E. Caruso, orch (r1906)
(7/91) (RCA) Ⓓ [12] **GD60495(2)**
18b E. Caruso, orch (r1906)
(7/91) (MSCM) Ⓓ **MM30352**
18b A. Piccaver, orch (r1913)
(8/93) (PREI) Ⓓ **89060**
18b L. Pavarotti, Vienna Op Orch, E. Downes (r1968) (12/93) (DECC) Ⓓ **433 437-2DA**
(DECC) ▭ **433 437-4DA**

18b E. Caruso, orch (r1906)
(7/95) (NIMB) Ⓓ **NI7866**
20b A. Alvarez, M. Delna, anon (r1905)
(7/92) (PEAR) Ⓓ [3] **GEMMCDS9923(1)**
21. LSO, R. Bonynge (r1962)
(DECC) Ⓓ **444 108-2DA**

La **Fille du régiment, 'Daughter of the Regiment'– opéra-comique: 2 acts (1840—Paris) (Lib. Saint-Georges and Bayard)**

1. Overture. ACT 1. 2. L'ennemi s'avance (Armiamci in silenzio); 3. Pour une femme de mon nom (not in Italian version); 4a. Sacré nom (Corpo di mille diavoli); 4b. Au bruit de la guerre (Apparvi alla luce sula campo guerrier); 5. Quel bel jour (Oh! che bel giorno); 6. Allons, allons, march', march' (Avanti, avanti); 7. Chacun le sait (Ciascun lo dice); 8a. Dès que l'appel sonne (È l'ora dell'appello); 8b. Attention! en marche (not in Italian version); 9a. Ils l'ont emmené brutalement (L'hanno condotto); 9b. Depuis l'instant (Da quell'instante); 10. Ah! mille z'yeux! (Lo dico con il cuore); 11. Rataplan (Rataplan); 12. Ah! mes amis (Miei buoni amiche); 13. Pour mon âme (Qual destino); 14a. Je suis soldat (Suo padre me l'ha data); 14b. Il faut partir (Convien partir); 15. Ah! si vous nous quitter (Ah se voi mi lascia). ACT 2: 16. Le jour naissant dans le bocage (Sorge va il dì bosco in seno); 17a. C'en est donc fait (Deciso è dunque!); 17b. Par le rang et par l'opulance (Le ricchezze ed il rango); 17c. Pour ce contrat fatal (Per questo imen fatal); 17d. Qu'est-ce que c'est que t'entends (Oh trasporto); 17e. Salut à la France (Salvezza alla Francia); 18. Tonio! Marie! (Tonio! Maria!); 19. Tous les trois réunis (Stretti insiem tutte tre); 20. Entr'acte: Tyrolienne; 21. Pour me rapprocher de Marie (not in Italian version); 22a. Ah! c'est elle (Eccola: Madre mia); 22b. Au secours de notre fille (Per giovar a nostra figlia); 22c. Quand le destin (Quando il destino).

Marie	J. Sutherland
Tonio	L. Pavarotti
Sulpice	S. Malas
Marquise	M. Sinclair
Duchess	E. Coates
Hortensius	J. Bruyère
Corporal	E. Garrett
Peasant	Alan Jones II

ROH Chor, ROHO, R. Bonynge (r1968)
(11/86) (DECC) Ⓓ [2] **414 520-2DH2**
Eccomi finalmente, 9a, 9b, 12, 13. A. Scarabelli, W. Matteuzzi, G. Musinu, Bologna Teatro Comunale Chor, Bologna Teatro Comunale Orch, B. Campanella (Ital: pp1989)
(NUOV) Ⓓ **6892**
Excs J. Sutherland, Orch, Anon (cond), D. Bailey (11/92) (DECC) ◐ **071 135-1DH**
1. Black Dyke Mills Band, G. Brand (arr G Langford) (10/91) (CHAN) Ⓓ **CHAN6539**
(10/91) (CHAN) ▭ **MBTD6539**
1. Black Dyke Mills Band, D. Hurst (arr brass band: G Langford)
(9/93) (CHAN) Ⓓ **CHAN4514**
(9/93) (CHAN) ▭ **BBTD4514**
4b, Cet amant J. Sutherland, H. Begg, G. Yurisch, Sydney Eliz Orch, R. Bonynge
(DECC) ◐ **071 149-1DH**
(DECC) ▣ **071 149-3DH**
7, 14b; A viva forza l'han condotto via; Deciso è dunque L. Serra, W. Matteuzzi, Bologna Teatro Comunale Orch, B. Campanella (Ital) (NUOV) Ⓓ **6820**
7, 17b T. dal Monte, La Scala Orch, La Scala Chor, G. Santini (r1928)
(2/90) (PREI) Ⓓ **89001**
7, 9b, 16, 17a M. Freni, L. Pavarotti, A. di Stasio, W. Ganzarolli, La Scala Chor, La Scala Orch, N. Sanzogno (Ital: pp1969)
(MEMO) Ⓓ [2] **HR4277/8**
9a, 9b L. Serra, W. Matteuzzi, Bologna Teatro Comunale Chor, Bologna Teatro Comunale Orch, B. Campanella (Ital) (NUOV) Ⓓ **6905**
9b J. Sutherland, L. Pavarotti, ROHO, R. Bonynge (r1967) (DECC) Ⓓ **436 313-2DA**
(DECC) ▭ **436 313-4DA**
9b J. Anderson, Alfredo Kraus, Paris Op Orch, M. Veltri (pp1987)
(12/88) (EMI) Ⓓ **CDC7 49067-2**
9b F. Hempel, H. Jadlowker, orch (Ger: r1900s)
(12/91) (CLUB) Ⓓ **CL99-042**
12. E. Ferretti, G. Saks, Ernst-Senff Chbr Chor, Berlin RSO, R. Buckley
(SCHW) Ⓓ [2] **314052**
12. Alfredo Kraus, Seville SO, L.A. Garcia-Navarro (pp1991) (RCA) Ⓓ **RD61191**

12. Alfredo Kraus, Seville SO, L.A. Garcia-Navarro (pp1991) (RCA) OO **09026 61191-5**
12. F. de la Mora, WNO Orch, C. Mackerras (r1994-5) (TELA) Ⓓ **CD80411**
12. L. Pavarotti, E. Garrett, ROH Chor, ROHO, R. Bonynge (7/86) (DECC) Ⓓ [2] **417 011-2DH2**
12. Alfredo Kraus, J-N. Bèguelin, Paris Op Chor, Paris Op Orch, B. Campanella (pp1986) (10/89) (EMI) Ⓓ **CDM7 63104-2**
12. R. Giménez, Scottish Phil Sngrs, Scottish CO, M. Veltri (5/90) (NIMB) Ⓓ **NI5224** (5/90) (NIMB) ▭ **NC5224**
12, 13. L. Pavarotti, E. Garrett, ROH Chor, ROHO, R. Bonynge (r1967) (12/93) (DECC) Ⓓ **433 437-2DA** (DECC) ▭ **433 437-4DA**
12, 13. Alfredo Kraus, WNO Orch, C. Rizzi (r1994) (8/95) (PHIL) Ⓓ **442 785-2PH** (8/95) (PHIL) ▭ **442 785-4PH**
12, 13. L. Pavarotti, G. Morresi, La Scala Chor, La Scala Orch, N. Sanzogno (pp1969) (10/95) (RCA) Ⓓ **09026 62541-2**
13. B.S. Rosenberg, Budapest Concert Orch, J. Acs (pp1990) (OLYM) Ⓓ **OCD370**
14b M. Callas, N. Rescigno, Paris Cons (6/86) (EMI) Ⓓ **CDC7 47283-2**
14b T. dal Monte, Orch, J. Pasternack (r1926) (2/90) (PREI) Ⓓ **89001**
14b T. dal Monte, orch, J. Pasternack (Ital: r1926) (2/92) (MMOI) Ⓓ **CDMOIR408**
14b M. Freni, Ater Orch, L. Magiera (pp: Ital) (5/94) (DECC) Ⓓ [2] **443 018-2DF2**
17a, 17b M. Horne, ROHO, H. Lewis (Ital) (DECC) Ⓓ **421 891-2DA**
17b T. dal Monte, chor, La Scala Orch, G. Santini (r1928: Ital) (4/94) (EMI) Ⓓ [3] **CHS7 64864-2(1)**
17c-e J. Sutherland, ROH Chor, ROHO, R. Bonynge (DECC) Ⓓ **417 780-2DM**
17e R. Doria, orch (r1954) (MSCM) Ⓓ **MM30221** (MSCM) ▭ **MM040079**
20. E. Berger, Berlin St Op Orch, L. Blech (r1935: arr sop: Ger) (PREI) Ⓓ **89092**
21. G. Morino, Warmia Nat PO, B. Amaducci (10/90) (NUOV) Ⓓ **6851**

Gabriella di Vergy– opera: 3 acts (1869—Naples) (Lib. A L Tottola, after Du Belloy)

Gabriella L. Andrew
Fayel C. du Plessis
Raoul de Coucy M. Arthur
Philip II J. Tomlinson
Almeide J. Davies
Armando J. Winfield
G. Mitchell Ch, RPO, A. Francis (r1978) (9/94) (OPRA) Ⓓ [2] **ORC003**

Gabriella di Vergy– opera: 2 acts (1826) (Lib. A L Tottola, after Du Belloy)

EXCERPTS: 1a. Respiro alfin; 1b. A te sola; 1c. Ah, she fra palpiti; 2a. Minacciosa perchè me sgridi; 2b. Un padre severo; 2c. Che abisso d'orror!; 3a. Ah fermate!; 3b. Perchè non chiusi al dì.

1a-c D. Jones, RPO, A. Francis (r1978) (9/94) (OPRA) Ⓓ [2] **ORC003**
2a-c E. Harrhy, D. Jones, RPO, A. Francis (r1978) (9/94) (OPRA) Ⓓ [2] **ORC003**
3a, 3b E. Harrhy, RPO, A. Francis (r1978) (9/94) (OPRA) Ⓓ [2] **ORC003**

Gemma di Vergy– opera seria: 2 acts (1834—Milan) (Lib. E. Bidera, after Dumas)

Eccomi sola alfine M. Caballé, NY Op Orch, E. Queler (pp1976) (SONY) Ⓓ **SMK48155** (SONY) ▭ **SMT48155**
Eccomi sola alfine M. Caballé, NY Op Orch, E. Queler (pp1976) (SONY) ● **SM48155**
Lascia, Guido...Una voce al cor...Egli riede M. Caballé, Ambrosian Op Chor, LSO, C.F. Cillario (11/92) (RCA) Ⓓ [2] **GD60941**
Qui pagnale!...Ah! nel cuor; Ecco il pegno...Questa soave immagine R. Bruson, Berlin RSO, R. Paternostro (10/89) (CAPR) Ⓓ **10 247** (10/89) (CAPR) ▭ **CC27 247**

Gianni di Parigi– opera: 2 acts (1839—Milan) (Lib. F. Romani, after Saint-Just)

Principessa di Navarra L. Serra
Steward A. Romero
Gianni di Parigi G. Morino
Oliviero E. Zilio
Pedrigo E. Fissore
Lorezza S. Manga
Milan RAI Chor, Milan RAI SO, C.F. Cillario (pp1988) (10/91) (NUOV) Ⓓ [2] **6752/3**

Ah, quanto e qual diletto; Ho simulato assai L. Serra, Milan RAI SO, C.F. Cillario (NUOV) Ⓓ **6820**
Mira o bella il trovatore M. Elkins, Philh, J. Judd (r1979) (9/94) (OPRA) Ⓓ **ORC004**

Imelda de' Lambertazzi– opera seria: 2 acts (1830—Naples) (Lib. L. A. Tottola)

Imelda F. Sovilla
Lamberto D. d'Auria
Lambertazzi F. Tenzi
Geremei A. Martin
Ubaldo G. Sarti
Lugano Rad & TV Ch, Lugano Rad & TV Orch, M. Andreae (pp1989) (NUOV) Ⓓ [2] **6778/9**

Imelda lasciarti ... Deh, cedi F. Sovilla, A. Martin, Lugano Rad & TV Ch, Lugano Rad & TV Orch, M. Andreae (NUOV) Ⓓ **6905**
Vincesti alfin...Amarti e nel martoro M. Elkins, Philh, J. Judd (r1979) (9/94) (OPRA) Ⓓ **ORC004**

Linda di Chamounix– opera: 3 acts (1842—Vienna) (Lib. Rossi, after D'Ennery and Lemoine)

ACT 1: 1. Overture; 2. Ambo nati in questa valle; 3a. Ah! tardai troppo; 3b. O luce di quest' anima; 4a. Cari luoghi ov'io passai; 4b. Per sua madre andò una figlia; 5a. Linda! Linda!; 5b. Da quel dì che t'incontrai. ACT 2: 6a. Già scorsero tre mesi; 6b. Al bel destin; 7. Se tanto in ira agli uomini; 8. Un buon servo del Visconte; 9a. Linda!...A che pensate?; 9b. A consolarmi affrettati.

Linda M. Rinaldi
Carlo Alfredo Kraus
Marquis de Boisfleury E. Dara
Antonio R. Bruson
Pierotto E. Zilio
Prefect C. Cava
Maddelena M.G. Allegri
Intendant A. Ceroni
La Scala Chor, La Scala Orch, G. Gavazzeni (pp1972) (FOYE) Ⓓ [2] **2-CF2045**

Linda E. Gruberová
Carlo D. Bernardini
Marquis de Boisfleury A. Melander
Antonio E. Kim
Pierotto M. Groop
Prefect S. Palatchi
Maddalena U. Precht
Intendant K. Hedlund
Mikaeli Chbr Ch, Swedish RSO, F. Haider (r1993) (9/94) (NIGH) Ⓓ [3] **NC070561-2**

Linda A. Stella
Carlo C. Valletti
Marquis de Boisfleury R. Capecchi
Antonio G. Taddei
Pierotto F. Barbieri
Prefect G. Modesti
Maddalena R. Corsi
Intendant P. de Palma
Naples San Carlo Op Chor, Naples San Carlo Op Orch, T. Serafin (r1956) (9/94) (PHIL) Ⓓ [2] **442 093-2PM2**

1. Philh, T. Serafin (r1961) (EMI) Ⓓ [2] **CES5 68541-2**
2. G. De Luca, anon (r1907) (PEAR) Ⓓ [3] **GEMMCDS9159(2)**
2. M. Battistini, orch, C. Sabajno (r1912) (10/92) (NIMB) Ⓓ **NI7831** (10/92) (NIMB) ▭ **NC7831**
3a, 3b A. Moffo, Munich RO, K. Eichhorn (EURO) Ⓓ **GD69113**
3a, 3b R. Streich, Berlin Deutsche Op Orch, R. Peters (DG) Ⓓ [2] **435 748-2GDO2**
3a, 3b J. Sutherland, Paris Cons, N. Santi (r1959) (DECC) Ⓓ **440 404-2DM**
3a, 3b K. Battle, LPO, B. Campanella (r1991) (DG) OO **435 866-5CH**
3a, 3b L. Aliberti, Munich RO, L. Gardelli (11/86) (ORFE) Ⓓ **C119841A**
3a, 3b A. Galli-Curci, orch (r1922) (2/89) (PEAR) Ⓓ **GEMMCD9308**
3a, 3b K. Battle, LPO, B. Campanella (r1991) (12/93) (DG) Ⓓ **435 866-2GH**
3b M. Foley, Orch (r1949-53) (ODE) Ⓓ **CDODE1062**
3b T. dal Monte, La Scala Orch, C. Sabajno (r1929) (2/90) (PREI) Ⓓ **89001**
3b A. Galli-Curci, orch, J. Pasternack (r1922) (5/90) (NIMB) Ⓓ **NI7806** (NIMB) ▭ **NC7806**
3b L. Tetrazzini, orch, P. Pitt (r1910) (9/92) (EMI) Ⓓ [3] **CHS7 63802-2(1)**
3b L. Tetrazzini, orch (r1911) (9/92) (EMI) Ⓓ [3] **CHS7 63802-2(1)**
3b L. Tetrazzini, orch (r1914) (9/92) (PEAR) Ⓓ **GEMMCD9225**
3b L. Tetrazzini, orch, P. Pitt (r1910) (9/92) (PEAR) Ⓓ **GEMMCD9222**
3b L. Tetrazzini, orch (r1911) (9/92) (PEAR) Ⓓ **GEMMCD9222**
3b L. Orgonášová, Bratislava RSO, W. Humburg (2/93) (NAXO) Ⓓ **8 550605**
3b A. Galli-Curci, orch, J. Pasternack (r1922) (8/94) (ROMO) Ⓓ [2] **81004-2**
4b J. Kowalski, Berlin RSO, H. Fricke (CAPR) ● **80 416**
4b J. Kowalski, Berlin RSO, H. Fricke (CAPR) OO **70 416**
4b E. Stignani, EIAR Orch, U. Tansini (r1937) (1/91) (PREI) Ⓓ **89014**
4b J. Kowalski, Berlin RSO, H. Fricke (10/92) (CAPR) Ⓓ **10 416**
4b E. Bruno, anon (r1902) (4/94) (EMI) Ⓓ [3] **CHS7 64860-2(2)**
5a, 7. R. Vargas, ECO, M. Viotti (11/92) (CLAV) Ⓓ **CD50-9202**
7. A. Cupido, Danish Rad Concert Orch, M. Elquist (DENO) Ⓓ **CO-79785**

Lucia di Lammermoor, '(The) Bride of Lammermoor'– opera: 3 acts (1835—Naples) (Lib. Cammarano, after Scott)

ACT 1: 1a. Percorrete le spiagge vicine; 1b. Tu sei turbato; 1c. Cruda, funesta smania; 1d. La pietade in suo favore; 2a. Ancor non giunse?; 2b. Regnava nel silenzio; 2c. Quando rapito in estasi; 3a. Egli s'avanza; 3b. Lucia perdona; 3c. Sulla tomba; 3d. Ah! Verrano a te; ACT 2: 4. Lucia fra poco a te verrà; 5a. Appressati, Lucia; 5b. Il pallor funesto; 5c. Soffriva nel pianto; 5d. Se tradirmi; 6. Ebben?...Di tua speranza; 7a. Per te d'immenso giubilo; 7b. Per poco fra le tenebre; 7c. Dov'è Lucia?; 8. Chi mi frena (Sextet); 9. T'allontana, sciagurato. ACT 3: 10. Orrida è questa notte (Wolf's Crag Scene); 11. D'immenso giubilo; 12. Dalle stanze; 13a. Il dolce suono; 13b. Ardon gl'incensi; 13c. Alfin son tua; 13d. Spargi d'amaro pianto (Mad Scene); 14. Si tragga altrove; 15a. Tombe degl'avi miei; 15b. Fra poco a me ricovero; 15c. Giusto ciel, rispondete; 15d. Tu che a Dio. ALTERNATIVE ARIA FOR EXCERPT 2: 16a. Ancor non giunse?; 16b. Perchè non ho del vento.

Lucia J. Sutherland
Edgardo R. Greager
Enrico M. Donnelly
Raimondo C. Grant
Alisa P. Price
Arturo S. Baigildin
Normanno R. Donald
Australian Op Chor, Sydney Eliz Orch, R. Bonynge, J. Copley (MCEG) ▣ **VVD779**

Lucia D. Mazzola
Edgardo G. Morino
Enrico S. Carroli
Raimondo M. Rinaudo
Alisa E. Ruta
Arturo S. Paolillo
Normanno M. Ferrara
Naples San Carlo Op Chor, Naples San Carlo Op Orch, M. de Bernart (pp1989) (NUOV) Ⓓ [3] **6794/6**

Lucia R. Scotto
Edgardo G. Raimondi
Enrico G. Guelfi
Raimondo A. Ferrin
Alisa F. Raffanelli
Arturo B. Prior
Normanno P. de Palma
La Scala Chor, La Scala Orch, C. Abbado (pp1967) (MEMO) Ⓓ [2] **HR4287/8**

Lucia C. Deutekom
Edgardo L. Pavarotti
Enrico D. Trimarchi
Raimondo S. Pagliuca
Arturo B. Sebastian
Normanno M. Ferrara
Naples San Carlo Op Chor, Naples San Carlo Op Orch, C. Franci (pp1970) (BUTT) Ⓓ [2] **BMCD003** (BUTT) ▭ [2] **BMK003**

Lucia L. Pons
Edgardo F. Jagel
Enrico J. Brownlee
Raimondo E. Pinza
Alisa T. Votipka
NY Met Op Chor, NY Met Op Orch, G. Papi (pp1937)
(FORT) Ⓓ [2] **FT1511/2**
Lucia J. Sutherland
Edgardo L. Pavarotti
Enrico S. Milnes
Raimondo N. Ghiaurov
Alisa H. Tourangeau
Arturo R. Davies
Normanno P.F. Poli
ROH Chor, ROHO, R. Bonynge
(11/85) (DECC) Ⓓ [3] **410 193-2DH3**
Lucia M. Callas
Edgardo Ferruccio Tagliavini
Enrico P. Cappuccilli
Raimondo B. Ladysz
Alisa M. Elkins
Arturo L. del Ferro
Normanno R. Casellato
Philh Chor, Philh, T. Serafin
(1/87) (EMI) Ⓓ [2] **CDS7 47440-8**
Lucia A. Moffo
Edgardo C. Bergonzi
Enrico M. Sereni
Raimondo E. Flagello
Alisa C. Vozza
Arturo P. Duval
Normanno V. Pandano
RCA Italiana Op Chor, RCA Italiana Op Orch, G. Prêtre (r1966)
(9/88) (RCA) Ⓓ [2] **GD86504**
Lucia M. Callas
Edgardo G. di Stefano
Enrico T. Gobbi
Raimondo R. Arié
Alisa A.M. Canali
Arturo V. Natali
Normanno G. Sarri
MMF Chor, MMF Orch, T. Serafin (r1953)
(10/89) (EMI) Ⓓ [2] **CMS7 69980-2**
Lucia J. Sutherland
Edgardo R. Cioni
Enrico R. Merrill
Raimondo C. Siepi
Alisa A.R. Satre
Arturo K. Macdonald
Normanno R. Pelizzoni
Santa Cecilia Academy Chor, Santa Cecilia Academy Orch, J. Pritchard
(12/89) (DECC) Ⓓ [2] **411 622-2DM2**
Lucia M. Caballé
Edgardo J. Carreras
Enrico V. Sardinero
Raimondo S. Ramey
Alisa A. Murray
Arturo C.H. Ahnsjö
Normanno V. Bello
Ambrosian Op Chor, New Philh, J. López-Cobos
(1/91) (PHIL) Ⓓ [2] **426 563-2PM2**
Lucia M. Callas
Edgardo G. di Stefano
Enrico R. Panerai
Raimondo N. Zaccaria
Alisa L. Villa
Arturo G. Zampieri
Normanno Mario Carlin
La Scala Chor, Berlin RIAS Orch, H. von Karajan (pp1955)
(2/91) (EMI) Ⓓ [2] **CMS7 63631-2**
Lucia E. Gruberová
Edgardo N. Shicoff
Enrico A. Agache
Raimondo A. Miles
Alisa D. Montague
Arturo B. Lombardo
Normanno F. Piccoli
Ambrosian Sngrs, LSO, R. Bonynge
(11/92) (TELD) Ⓓ [2] **9031-72306-2**
Lucia E. Gruberová
Edgardo Alfredo Kraus
Enrico R. Bruson
Raimondo R. Lloyd
Alisa K. Kuhlmann
Arturo B. Bottone
Normanno B. Lazzaretti
Ambrosian Op Chor, RPO, N. Rescigno (r1983)
(3/93) (EMI) Ⓓ [2] **CMS7 64622-2**
Lucia J. Sutherland
Edgardo R. Greager
Enrico M. Donnelly
Raimondo C. Grant
Alisa P. Price
Arturo S. Baigildin
Normanno R. Donald
Australian Op Chor, Sydney Eliz Orch, R. Bonynge, J. Copley
(4/93) (PION) ◐ [2] **PLMCC00641**
Lucia C. Studer
Edgardo P. Domingo
Enrico J. Pons
Raimondo S. Ramey
Alisa J. Larmore
Arturo F. de la Mora
Normanno A. Laciura
Ambrosian Op Chor, LSO, I. Marin (r1990)
(4/93) (DG) Ⓓ [2] **435 309-2GH2**

Excs R. Scotto, L. Pavarotti, P. Cappuccilli, G. Manganotti, A. Ferrin, A. di Stasio, F. Ricciardi, Turin RAI Chor, Turin RAI Orch, F. Molinari-Pradelli (pp1967) (BUTT) Ⓓ **BMCD017**
(BUTT) ⊟ **BMK017**
Excs J. Sutherland, Orch, Anon (cond), D. Bailey (11/92) (DECC) ◐ **071 135-1DH**
1a, 1c, 2b, 2c, 3c, 3d, 5c, 8, 11, 12, 13a-d, 15b, 15d A. Agache, E. Gruberová, N. Shicoff, B. Lombardo, A. Miles, D. Montague, F. Piccoli, Ambrosian Sngrs, LSO, R. Bonynge
(TELD) Ⓓ **4509-93692-2**
1c R. Stracciari, orch (r1925)
(2/90) (PREI) Ⓓ **89003**
1c D. Hvorostovsky, Philh, I. Marin (r1992)
(9/94) (PHIL) Ⓓ **434 912-2PH**
(9/94) (PHIL) ⊟ **434 912-4PH**
1c, 1d, 2b, 2c, 3c, 3d, 5c, 8, 12, 13b-d, 15a, 15d J. Sutherland, L. Pavarotti, S. Milnes, N. Ghiaurov, H. Tourangeau, R. Davies, P.F. Poli, ROH Chor, ROHO, R. Bonynge
(DECC) Ⓓ **421 885-2DA**
(DECC) ⊟ **421 885-4DA**
1c, 2b, 2c, 3b, 3c, 5c, 5d, 8, 12, 13a-d, 15a, 15b M. Callas, Ferruccio Tagliavini, P. Cappuccilli, B. Ladysz, L. del Ferro, M. Elkins, R. Casellato, Philh Chor, Philh, T. Serafin (r1959)
(EMI) Ⓓ **CDM7 63934-2**
2a-c, 13a-d R. Scotto, La Scala Chor, La Scala Orch, C. Abbado (pp1967)
(MEMO) Ⓓ [2] **HR4291/2**
2a-c, 13a-d M. Callas, Berlin RSO, H. von Karajan (pp1954) (MEMO) Ⓓ **HR4293/4**
2a-c, 13a-d J. Sutherland, N. Sautereau, Paris Op Chor, Paris Cons, N. Santi (r1959)
(DECC) Ⓓ **440 404-2DM**
2a, 2b E. Gruberová, V. Walterová, Czech PO, F. Haider (SUPR) Ⓓ **11 0345-2**
2b L. Tetrazzini, orch (r1909)
(10/90) (NIMB) Ⓓ **NI7808**
(10/90) (NIMB) ⊟ **NC7808**
2b T. dal Monte, orch (r1926)
(7/92) (PEAR) Ⓓ [3] **GEMMCDS9925(2)**
2b T. Dal Monte, orch, J. Pasternack (r1926)
(4/94) (RCA) Ⓓ [6] **09026 61580-2(3)**
2b, 2c L. Aliberti, Munich RO, L. Gardelli
(11/86) (ORFE) Ⓓ **C119841A**
2b, 2c M. Callas, M. Elkins, Philh, T. Serafin
(2/90) (EMI) Ⓓ **CDM7 63182-2**
2b, 2c L. Tetrazzini, orch, P. Pitt (r1909)
(9/92) (EMI) Ⓓ [3] **CHS7 63802-2(1)**
2b, 2c L. Tetrazzini, orch, P. Pitt (r1909)
(9/92) (PEAR) Ⓓ **GEMMCD9221**
2b, 2c, 3b, 3d V. Zeani, Alfredo Kraus, Piacenza SO, A. Zedda (pp1964) (BONG) Ⓓ **GB1060-2**
2b, 13a-d R. Streich, Berlin RSO, K. Gaebel
(DG) Ⓓ [2] **435 748-2GDO2**
2b, 13c, 13d T. dal Monte, Orch, J. Pasternack (r1926) (2/90) (PREI) Ⓓ **89001**
2c F. Toresella, anon (r1900)
(12/89) (SYMP) Ⓓ **SYMCD1065**
2c, 13b G. Pareto, orch (r1907)
(PEAR) Ⓓ **GEMMCD9117**
3a-d D. Mazzola, G. Morino, Naples San Carlo Op Chor, Naples San Carlo Op Orch, M. de Bernart (NUOV) Ⓓ **6905**
3b-d Alfredo Kraus, Paris Op Orch, M. Veltri (pp1987) (12/88) (EMI) Ⓓ **CDC7 49067-2**
3b-d, 8. L. Pavarotti, J. Anderson, S. Verrett, G. Sabbatini, P. Cappuccilli, G. Furlanetto, Bologna Teatro Comunale Orch, L. Magiera (pp1991)
(DECC) ◐ **071 140-1DH**
(DECC) ⊡ **071 140-3DH**
3b, 3c M. Callas, G. di Stefano, La Scala Chor, Berlin RIAS Orch, H. von Karajan (pp1955)
(MEMO) Ⓓ **HR4372/3**
3c M. Caballé, J. Carreras, New Philh, J. López-Cobos (PHIL) Ⓓ **434 986-2PM**
3c F. Hempel, H. Jadlowker, orch (Ger: r1900s)
(12/91) (CLUB) Ⓓ **CL99-042**
3c G. Zenatello, M. Barrientos, anon (r1906)
(5/94) (PEAR) Ⓓ [4] **GEMMCDS9073(1)**
3c G. Zenatello, M. Barrientos, anon (r1906)
(5/94) (SYMP) Ⓓ **SYMCD1168**
3c, 3d J. Sutherland, L. Pavarotti, ROHO, R. Bonynge (r1971) (DECC) Ⓓ **436 315-2DA**
(DECC) ⊟ **436 315-4DA**
3c, 3d J. Sutherland, L. Pavarotti, ROHO, R. Bonynge (r1971) (DECC) Ⓓ **436 313-2DA**
(DECC) ⊟ **436 313-4DA**
3c, 3d L. Pavarotti, N. Gustafson, Bologna Teatro Comunale Orch, L. Magiera (pp1994)
(DECC) Ⓓ **444 460-2DH**
(DECC) ⊟ **444 460-4DH**
3c, 3d M. Talley, B. Gigli, Vitaphone Orch, H. Heller (r1927)
(5/90) (PEAR) Ⓓ **GEMMCD9367**
3c, 3d A. Pertile, A. Rozsa, La Scala Orch, C. Sabajno, G. Nastrucci (r1930)
(9/90) (PREI) Ⓓ **89007**
3d T. Schipa, A. Galli-Curci, orch (r1924)
(PEAR) Ⓓ **GEMMCD9364**
3d A. Galli-Curci, T. Schipa, orch, Rosario Bourdon (r1928) (12/89) (RCA) Ⓓ **GD87969**
3d A. Galli-Curci, T. Schipa, orch, Rosario Bourdon (r1924) (5/90) (NIMB) Ⓓ **NI7806**
(NIMB) ⊟ **NC7806**
3d T. Schipa, A. Galli-Curci, orch, Rosario Bourdon (r1924)
(10/90) (MSCM) Ⓓ [2] **MM30231**
(MSCM) ⊟ [2] **MM40086**
3d A. Galli-Curci, T. Schipa, orch (r1924)
(3/94) (CONI) Ⓓ **CDHD201**
(3/94) (CONI) ⊟ **MCHD201**
3d A. Galli-Curci, T. Schipa, orch, Rosario Bourdon (r1924)
(8/94) (ROMO) Ⓓ [2] **81004-2**
3d, 8. L. Pavarotti, R. Scotto, G. Manganotti, A. Ferrin, A. di Stasio, F. Ricciardi, Turin RAI Chor, Turin RAI Orch, F. Molinari-Pradelli (pp1967)
(BUTT) Ⓓ **BMCD015**
(BUTT) ⊟ **BMK015**
7a K. Collins, ROH Chor, ROHO, L. Gardelli
(EMI) Ⓓ **CDM7 64356-2**
7a Ambrosian Op Chor, RPO, N. Rescigno (r1983) (EMI) Ⓓ [2] **CZS5 68559-2**
7a, 11. ROH Chor, ROHO, B. Haitink
(12/89) (EMI) Ⓓ **CDC7 49849-2**
8. E. Steber, B. Sullivan, J. Hines, R. Rounseville, R. Stevens, T.L. Thomas, Orch, Anon (cond) (bp1953) (VAI) ⊡ **VAI69112**
8. J. Sutherland, H. Tourangeau, L. Pavarotti, R. Davies, S. Milnes, N. Ghiaurov, ROH Chor, ROHO, R. Bonynge
(DECC) Ⓓ **433 064-2DWO**
8. M. Sembrich, G. Severina, E. Caruso, F. Daddi, A. Scotti, M. Journet, orch, W.B. Rogers (r1908) (NIMB) Ⓓ **NI7834**
(NIMB) ⊟ **NC7834**
8. J. Sutherland, H. Tourangeau, L. Pavarotti, R. Davies, S. Milnes, N. Ghiaurov, ROH Chor, ROHO, R. Bonynge (r1971)
(DECC) Ⓓ **436 300-2DX**
(DECC) ⊟ **436 300-4DX**
8. A. Galli-Curci, M. Egener, E. Caruso, A. Bada, G. De Luca, M. Journet, orch, J. Pasternack (r1917: 2 vers)
(PEAR) Ⓓ [3] **GEMMCDS9159(2)**
8. A. Galli-Curci, L. Homer, B. Gigli, A. Bada, G. De Luca, E. Pinza, orch (r1927)
(PEAR) Ⓓ [3] **GEMMCDS9160(2)**
8. A. Galli-Curci, L. Homer, B. Gigli, A. Bada, G. De Luca, E. Pinza, NY Met Op Orch, G. Setti (r1927) (9/88) (EMI) Ⓓ **CDH7 61051-2**
8. A. Galli-Curci, L. Homer, B. Gigli, A. Bada, G. De Luca, E. Pinza, NY Met Op Orch, G. Setti (r1927) (5/90) (PEAR) Ⓓ **GEMMCD9367**
8. M. Sembrich, G. Severina, E. Caruso, F. Daddi, A. Scotti, M. Journet, orch, W.B. Rogers (r1908) (12/90) (PEAR) Ⓓ [3] **EVC1(2)**
8. L. Tetrazzini, J. Jacoby, E. Caruso, A. Bada, P. Amato, M. Journet, orch, W.B. Rogers (r1912)
(7/91) (RCA) Ⓓ [12] **GD60495(4)**
8. A. Galli-Curci, M. Egener, E. Caruso, A. Bada, G. De Luca, M. Journet, orch, J. Pasternack (2 vers: r1917) (7/91) (RCA) Ⓓ [12] **GD60495(6)**
8. M. Sembrich, G. Severina, E. Caruso, F. Daddi, A. Scotti, M. Journet, orch, W.B. Rogers (r1908) (7/91) (RCA) Ⓓ [12] **GD60495(2)**
8. A. Galli-Curci, M. Egener, E. Caruso, A. Bada, G. De Luca, M. Journet, orch (r1917)
(7/91) (MSCM) Ⓓ **MM30352**
8. L. Tetrazzini, J. Jacoby, E. Caruso, A. Bada, P. Amato, M. Journet, orch, W.B. Rogers (r1912)
(10/91) (PEAR) Ⓓ [3] **EVC3(1)**

8. A. Galli-Curci, M. Egener, E. Caruso, A. Bada, G. De Luca, M. Journet, orch, J. Pasternack (2 vers: r1917) (10/91) (PEAR) ① [3] **EVC4(1)**
8. L. Tetrazzini, J. Jacoby, E. Caruso, A. Bada, P. Amato, M. Journet, orch (r1912) (9/92) (PEAR) ① **GEMMCD9224**
8. A. Galli-Curci, M. Egener, E. Caruso, A. Bada, G. De Luca, M. Journet, orch, J. Pasternack (r1917: two vers) (3/94) (ROMO) ① [2] **81003-2**
8. M. Rappold, M. Matzenauer, G. Zenatello, A. Middleton, T. Chalmers, E. Baroni, orch (r1916) (5/94) (PEAR) ① [4] **GEMMCDS9074(2)**
8. A. Galli-Curci, L. Homer, B. Gigli, A. Bada, G. De Luca, E. Pinza, NY Met Op Orch, G. Setti (r1927) (8/94) (NIMB) ① **NI7852**
8, 15c, 15d A. Galli-Curci, L. Homer, B. Gigli, A. Bada, G. De Luca, E. Pinza, NY Met Op Chor, NY Met Op Orch, G. Setti (r1927) (CONI) ① **CDHD227** (CONI) ▭ **MCHD227**
10. J. Hadley, T. Hampson, WNO Orch, C. Rizzi (r1992) (11/93) (TELD) ① **9031-73283-2**
10. J. Lotrič, I. Morozov, Slovak RSO, J. Wildner (r1994) (2/95) (NAXO) ① **8 553030**
12. M. Pertusi, Bulgarian Nat Chor, Sofia PO, E. Tabakov (r1994) (CAPR) ① **10 704**
12. E. Pinza, Chor, orch, C. Sabajno (r1923) (2/89) (PEAR) ① **GEMMCD9306**
12. M. Journet, orch (r1916) (7/92) (PEAR) ① [3] **GEMMCDS9924(2)**
12. E. Pinza, chor, orch, C. Sabajno (r1923) (4/94) (EMI) ① [3] **CHS7 64864-2(1)**
13a M. Korjus, Berlin St Op Orch, B. Seidler-Winkler (r1936) (DANT) ① **LYS001**
13a M. Korjus, Berlin St Op Orch, B. Seidler-Winkler (r1936) (10/93) (PREI) ① **89054**
13a A. Galli-Curci, orch, J. Pasternack (r1917) (3/94) (ROMO) ① [2] **81003-2**
13a A. Galli-Curci, orch (r1917) (8/94) (NIMB) ① **NI7852**
13a-d J. Sutherland, C. Siepi, R. Merrill, R. Pelizzoni, Santa Cecilia Academy Chor, Santa Cecilia Academy Orch, J. Pritchard (DECC) ① **417 780-2DM**
13a-d L. Pons, Orch, Rosario Bourdon (r1930) (MSCM) ① **MM30446**
13a-d E. Gruberová, A. Agache, A. Miles, Ambrosian Sngrs, LSO, R. Bonynge (TELD) ① **4509-93691-2**
13a-d E. Gruberová, Munich RO, G. Kuhn (r c1980) (EMIN) ① **CD-EMX2234**
13a-d M. Callas, G. Sarri, R. Arié, MMF Chor, MMF Orch, T. Serafin (r1953) (2/90) (EMI) ① [4] **CMS7 63244-2**
13a-d L. Orgonášová, Bratislava RSO, W. Humburg (2/93) (NAXO) ① **8 550605**
13a-d J. Sutherland, Paris Op Chor, Paris Cons, N. Santi (r1959) (10/93) (DECC) ① **436 461-2DM**
13a-d S. Jo, Monte Carlo PO, P. Olmi (r1994) (6/95) (ERAT) ① **4509-97239-2**
13a-d, 14. M. Callas, Philh, T. Serafin (EMIN) ① **CD-EMX9519** (EMIN) ▭ **TC-EMX2099**
13a, 13b Dilbèr, Estonia Op Orch, E. Klas (9/92) (ONDI) ① **ODE768-2**
13a, 13b, 13c, 13d M. Devia, Svizzera Italiana Orch, M. Rota (pp1992) (10/94) (BONG) ① **GB2513-2**
13b M. Ivogün, orch (r1917) (PREI) ① **89094**
13b N. Melba, J. Lemmoné, orch, W.B. Rogers (r1910) (3/89) (LARR) ① **CDLRH221**
13b L. Tetrazzini, orch (r1911) (10/90) (NIMB) ① **NI7808** (10/90) (NIMB) ▭ **NC7808**
13b M. Ivogün, orch (r1917) (8/92) (NIMB) ① **NI7832** (8/92) (NIMB) ▭ **NC7832**
13b L. Tetrazzini, orch, P. Pitt (r1907) (9/92) (EMI) ① [3] **CHS7 63802-2(1)**
13b L. Tetrazzini, orch, P. Pitt (r1907) (9/92) (PEAR) ① **GEMMCD9221**
13b L. Tetrazzini, orch (r1911) (9/92) (PEAR) ① **GEMMCD9223**
13b N. Melba, orch (r1910) (7/93) (NIMB) ① [2] **NI7840/1**
13b F. Hempel, orch (r1910: Ger) (3/94) (NIMB) ① **NI7849**
13b A. Galli-Curci, orch (r1917) (3/94) (CONI) ① **CDHD201** (3/94) (CONI) ▭ **MCHD201**
13b N. Melba, orch, W.B. Rogers (r1910) (5/95) (ROMO) ① [3] **81011-2(2)**
13b-d J. Sutherland, M. Donnelly, C. Grant, Sydney Eliz Orch, R. Bonynge (DECC) ● **071 149-1DH** (DECC) ▣ **071 149-3DH**
13b-d M. Mesplé, Paris Op Orch, G-F. Masini (r1974) (EMI) ① [2] **CZS7 67813-2**
13b-d L. Pons, orch, Rosario Bourdon (r1930) (4/92) (MSOU) ① **DFCDI-111**
13b-d M. Sembrich, orch, D. Lyons (r1906) (4/94) (RCA) ① [6] **09026 61580-2(1)**
13b, 13d L. Pons, orch, Rosario Bourdon (r1930) (RCA) ① **09026 61411-2**
13b, 15d R. Peters, Mario Carlin, G. Tozzi, Rome Op Chor, Rome Op Orch, E. Leinsdorf (r1957) (RCA) ① **09026 62689-2**
13c M. Michailova, anon (r1905: Russ) (PEAR) ① [3] **GEMMCDS9111(1)**
13c N. Melba, orch, W.B. Rogers (r1907) (5/95) (ROMO) ① [3] **81011-2(1)**
13d J. Sutherland, Paris Cons, N. Santi (r1959) (DECC) ① **436 300-2DX** (DECC) ▭ **436 300-4DX**
13d M. Callas, Philh Chor, Philh, T. Serafin (r1959) (EMI) ① **CDC5 55016-2**
13d L. Pagliughi, La Scala Orch, C. Sabajno (r1928) (PEAR) ① [2] **GEMMCDS9180**
13d A. Galli-Curci, orch, Rosario Bourdon (r1922) (5/90) (NIMB) ① **NI7806** (NIMB) ▭ **NC7806**
13d L. Tetrazzini, anon (r c1904) (9/92) (PEAR) ① **GEMMCD9225**
13d N. Melba, anon (r1904) (11/92) (MEMO) ① [2] **HR4408/9(1)**
13d A. Galli-Curci, orch (r1922) (3/94) (CONI) ① **CDHD201** (3/94) (CONI) ▭ **MCHD201**
13d A. Galli-Curci, orch (r1922) (8/94) (NIMB) ① **NI7852**
13d A. Galli-Curci, orch, J. Pasternack (r1922) (8/94) (ROMO) ① [2] **81004-2**
15a B. Gigli, NY Met Op Orch, G. Setti (r1927) (CONI) ① **CDHD170**
15a-d B. Gigli, NY Met Op Orch, G. Setti (r1927) (NIMB) ① **NI7817** (NIMB) ▭ **NC7817**
15a-d R. Giménez, F. Carroll, Scottish Phil Sngrs, Scottish CO, M. Veltri (5/90) (NIMB) ① **NI5224** (5/90) (NIMB) ▭ **NC5224**
15a-d B. Gigli, E. Pinza, NY Met Op Chor, NY Met Op Orch, G. Setti (r1927) (10/90) (RCA) ① **GD87811** (10/90) (RCA) ▭ **GK87811**
15a-d A. Pertile, La Scala Orch, C. Sabajno (r1929) (10/94) (PREI) ① **89072**
15a, 15b P. Domingo, Los Angeles PO, C.M. Giulini (DG) ▭ **419 091-4GW**
15a, 15b A. Cupido, Danish Rad Concert Orch, M. Elquist (DENO) ① **CO-79785**
15a, 15b P. Domingo, Los Angeles PO, C.M. Giulini (r1980) (DG) ① **445 525-2GMA** (DG) ▭ **445 525-4GMA**
15a, 15b P. Domingo, NY Met Op Orch, James Levine (pp1988) (DG) ① **445 552-2GMA** (DG) ▭ **445 552-4GMA**
15a, 15b R. Alagna, LPO, R. Armstrong (EMI) ① **CDC5 55540-2** (EMI) ▭ **EL5 55540-4**
15a, 15b Alfredo Kraus, RPO, N. Rescigno (10/89) (EMI) ① **CDM7 63104-2**
15a, 15b B. Gigli, NY Met Op Orch, G. Setti (r1927) (5/90) (PEAR) ① **GEMMCD9367**
15a, 15b L. Pavarotti, RPO, K.H. Adler (pp1982) (8/91) (DECC) ① **430 716-2DM** (8/91) (DECC) ▭ **430 716-4DM**
15a, 15b R. Vargas, ECO, M. Viotti (11/92) (CLAV) ① **CD50-9202**
15a, 15b J. Hislop, orch, J. Harrison (r1923) (1/93) (PEAR) ① **GEMMCD9956**
15a, 15b J. Peerce, Rome Op Orch, E. Leinsdorf (r1957) (4/94) (RCA) ① [6] **09026 61580-2(5)**
15a, 15b L. Pavarotti, chor, Turin SO, F. Molinari-Pradelli (pp1967) (10/95) (RCA) ① **09026 68014-2**
15a, 15b, 15d F. Marconi, orch (r1908) (10/90) (SYMP) ① **SYMCD1069**
15b P. Domingo, Miami SO, E. Kohn (pp1991) (IMP) ① **MCD43**
15b R. Greager, Australian Op & Ballet Orch, R. Bonynge (pp1986) (KIWI) ① **CDSLD-82**
15b L. Pavarotti, Toscanini SO, E. Buckley (SONY) ① **MDK47176** (SONY) ▭ **MDT47176**
15b G. Zenatello, anon (r c1912) (5/94) (PEAR) ① [4] **GEMMCDS9074(1)**
15b L. Pavarotti, NYPO, L. Magiera (pp1993) (2/95) (DECC) ① **444 450-2DH** (2/95) (DECC) ▭ **444 450-4DH**
15b A. Giorgini, orch (r c1913) (4/95) (RECO) ① **TRC3**
15c, 15d B. Gigli, E. Pinza, NY Met Op Chor, NY Met Op Orch, G. Setti (r1927) (IMP) ① **GLRS102**
15c, 15d B. Gigli, NY Met Op Orch, G. Setti (r1927) (5/90) (PEAR) ① **GEMMCD9367**
15d J. Carreras, S. Ramey, Ambrosian Op Chor, New Philh, J. López-Cobos (PHIL) ① **432 692-2PH** (PHIL) ▭ **432 692-4PH**
15d C. Valletti, Orch, A. Basile (pp1955) (MEMO) ① [2] **HR4191/2**
15d T. Schipa, orch, Anon (cond) (pp1913) (MEMO) ① [2] **HR4220/1**
15d J. Carreras, New Philh, J. López-Cobos (PHIL) ① **434 152-2PM**
15d J. Carreras, New Philh, J. López-Cobos (PHIL) ① **442 602-2PM** (PHIL) ▭ **442 602-4PM**
15d T. Schipa, orch, C. Sabajno (r1913) (4/90) (EMI) ① **CDH7 63200-2**
15d J. Palet, anon (r1905) (11/92) (MEMO) ① [2] **HR4408/9(2)**
16a, 16b L. Korsoff, orch (Fr: r1913) (8/92) (IRCC) ① **IRCC-CD802**

Lucrezia Borgia– opera seria: prologue, 2 acts (1833—Milan) (Lib. F. Romani, after V. Hugo)

EXCERPTS: PROLOGUE: 1. Prelude; 2. Nella fatal di Rimini; 3. Tranquillo ei posa; 4. Com'è bello!; 5. Ciel! - Che vegg'io?; 6. Di pescatore ignobile; 7. Gente appressa; 8. Maffio Orsini, signora, son io. ACT 1: 9. Nel veneto corteggio lo ravvisasti?; 10. Vieni: la mia vendetta; 11. Addio, Gennaro; 12. Qui che fai?; 13. Non far motto, parti, sgombra; 14. Tutto eseguisti?; 15. Così turbata?; 16. Soli noi siamo; 17. E sì avverso a Gennaro che vi fè; 18. Oh! a te bada, a te stesso pon mente; 19. Trafitto tosto ei sia; 20. Della Duchessa ai prieghi; 21. Guai se ti sfugge un moto; 22. Infelice! il veleno bevesti. ACT 2: 23. Partir degg'io:lo vuol Lucrezia; 24. T'amo qual dama un angelo; 25. Rischiarata è la finestra; 26. Sei tu? - Son io; 27. Minacciata è la mia vita; 28. Va, se vuoi: tentar m'è caro; 29. Stolti! ei corre alla Negroni!; 30. Viva il Madera!; 31. Il segreto per esser felici (Brindisi); 32. La gioia de' profani è un fumo passaggier; 33. Tu pur qui? non sei fuggito?; 34. M'odi, ah m'odi; 35. Madre se ognor lontano; 36. Era desso il figlio mio.

Lucrezia	J. Sutherland
Gennaro	G. Aragall
Alfonso	I. Wixell
Orsini	M. Horne
Liverotto	G. Clark
Vitellozzo	P. de Palma
Gazella	L. Visser
Petrucci	J. Bröcheler
Rustighello	G. Ewer
Gubetta	R. Van Allan
Astolfo	N. Zaccaria
Servant	D. Wilson-Johnson
Cupbearer	P. Taylor

London Op Chor, National PO, R. Bonynge (3/90) (DECC) ① [2] **421 497-2DM2**

Lucrezia	M. Caballé
Gennaro	Alfredo Kraus
Alfonso	E. Flagello
Orsini	S. Verrett
Liveretto	F. Ricciardi
Vitellozzo	F. Iacopucci
Gazella	F. Romano
Petrucci	F. Mazzoli
Rustighello	G. Baratti
Gubetta	V.M. Brunetti
Astolfo	R. El Hage
Servant	C. Sforza
Cupbearer	F. Ruta
Off-stage voice	A. Mineo

RCA Italiana Op Chor, RCA Italiana Op Orch, J. Perlea (r1966) (9/90) (RCA) ① [2] **GD86642**

Excs J. Sutherland, Orch, Anon (cond), D. Bailey (11/92) (DECC) ● **071 135-1DH**
3. M. Horne, LSO, R. Bonynge (DECC) ① **421 891-2DA**
3, 4. M. Caballé, Philh, N. Rescigno (11/92) (RCA) ▭ [2] **RK61044**
3, 4. M. Caballé, La Scala Orch, E. Gracis (pp1970) (MEMO) ① [2] **HR4279/80**

3, 4. M. Callas, N. Rescigno, Paris Cons (6/86) (EMI) ⓒ **CDC7 47283-2**
3, 4. M. Callas, Philh, A. Tonini (2/93) (EMI) ⓒ **CDC7 54437-2**
4. K. Ricciarelli, Svizzera Italiana Orch, B. Amaducci (r1979) (ERMI) ⓒ **ERM151**
4. L. Aliberti, Munich RO, L. Gardelli (11/86) (ORFE) ⓒ **C119841A**
4, 34. G. Arangi-Lombardi, La Scala Orch, L. Molajoli (r1933) (10/90) (PREI) ⓒ **89013**
4, 36. J. Sutherland, G. Ewer, R. Allman, Sydney Eliz Orch, R. Bonynge (DECC) **071 149-1DH** (DECC) **071 149-3DH**
6. F. Marconi, C. Sabajno (r1907) (10/90) (SYMP) ⓒ **SYMCD1069**
6. F. Marconi, anon (r1907) (7/93) (NIMB) ⓒ [2] **NI7840/1**
10. F. Chaliapin, orch (r1912) (PREI) ⓒ **89030**
10. R. Raimondi, Madrid SO, G.P. Sanzogno (RNE) ⓒ [2] **650004**
10. G. Rossi, orch (r1906) (5/91) (SYMP) ⓒ **SYMCD1077**
10. F. Navarini, anon (r1907) (7/92) (PEAR) ⓒ [3] **GEMMCDS9923(1)**
10. J. Van Dam, Loire PO, M. Soustrot (r1992) (8/93) (FORL) ⓒ **UCD16681**
10, 16. K. Ricciarelli, R. Raimondi, Madrid SO, G.P. Sanzogno (pp1991) (IMP) ⓒ [2] **DPCD998**
16. K. Ricciarelli, R. Raimondi, Madrid SO, G.P. Sanzogno (RNE) ⓒ [2] **650004**
23, 24. Alfredo Kraus, WNO Orch, C. Rizzi (r1994) (8/95) (PHIL) ⓒ **442 785-2PH** (8/95) (PHIL) **442 785-4PH**
31. M. Brandt, anon (r1905: Ger) (SYMP) ⓒ **SYMCD1085**
31. E. Schumann-Heink, orch (r1909) (10/89) (NIMB) ⓒ **NI7801** (NIMB) **NC7801**
31. G. Fabbri, S. Cottone (r1903) (12/89) (SYMP) ⓒ **SYMCD1065**
31. E. Schumann-Heink, orch (Ger: r1906) (2/91) (NIMB) ⓒ **NI7811** (2/91) (NIMB) **NC7811**
31. S. Onegin, orch, Rosario Bourdon (r1928) (2/91) (PREI) ⓒ **89027**
34. E. Teodorini, anon (r1903: two versions) (5/91) (SYMP) ⓒ **SYMCD1077**
34. I. de Frate, orch (r1908) (11/92) (MEMO) ⓒ [2] **HR4408/9(1)**
34. E. Teodorini, anon (r1903) (4/94) (EMI) ⓒ [3] **CHS7 64860-2(1)**
35. F. Marconi, B. Mililotti, C. Sabajno (r1907) (10/90) (SYMP) ⓒ **SYMCD1069**

Maria di Rohan– opera seria: 3 acts (1843—Venice) (Lib. S. Cammarano)
EXCERPTS: 1. Overture. ACT 1: 2. Ed è cor; 3a. Non seguite la caccia; 3b. Quando il cor da lei piaggato; 4a. Conte! Agitata siete!; 4b. Cupa fatal mestizia; 5a. Cavalieri! Che veggio!; 5b. Per non istare in ozio; 6. Gemea in tetro carcare; 7. Sparve il nembo minaccioso. ACT 2: 8a. Nel fragor della festa; 8b. Alma soave e cara; 8c. Dorme un sonno affanoso!; 9. Son leggero è ver d'amore; 10a. T'aspettai finora; 10b. Ah! no, tinganni; 11a. Che mai potrà commuoverti?; 11b. A morir incominicai. ACT 3: 12a. Ah, così santo affetto; 12b. Voler d'iniquiasorte; 13. Avvi un Dio che in sua clemenza; 14a. Son cifre di Riccardo; 14b. Bella e di sol vestita; 14c. Voce fatal di morte; 15. So per prova il tuo bel core; 16. Vivo non t'è concesso.
Maria M. Nicolesco
Giuseppe G. Morino
Enrico P. Coni
Armando di Gondì F. Franci
Visconte di Suze V. Alaimo
De Fiesque G. Colafelice
Slovak Phil Chor, Italian International Op Orch, M. de Bernart (pp1988) (10/91) (NUOV) ⓒ [2] **6732/3**
8a, 8b A. Cupido, Danish Rad Concert Orch, M. Elquist (DENO) ⓒ **CO-79785**

Maria di Rudenz– opera seria: 3 acts (1838—Venice) (Lib. Cammarano)
Maria di Rudenz K. Ricciarelli
Matilde S. Baleani
Corrado L. Nucci
Enrico A. Cupido
Rambaldo G. Surian
Chancellor S. Eupani
Venice La Fenice Chor, Venice La Fenice Orch, E. Inbal (pp1981) (ITAL) ⓒ [2] **LO7706/7**

Maria Padilla– opera: 3 acts (1841—Milan) (Lib. G. Rossi, after Ancelot)
Maria L. McDonall
Inès D. Jones
Don Ruiz G. Clark
Don Pedro C. du Plessis
Ramiro R. Earle
Don Luigi I. Caley
Don Alfonso R. Kennedy
Francisca J. Davies
G. Mitchell Ch, LSO, A. Francis (2/93) (OPRA) ⓒ [3] **ORC006**

Maria Stuarda– opera: 3 acts (1835—Milan) (Lib. G. Bardari, after Schiller)
EXCERPTS: 1. Prelude. ACT 1: 1a. Qui si sttende; 2a. Sì, vuol di Francia il Rege; 2b. Ah, quando all'aura; 2c. In tal giorno di contento; 3. Fra noi perchè non veggio Leicester; 4a. Questa imago, questo foglio; 4b. Ah! rimiro il bel sembiante; 5a. Sei tu confuso?; 5b. Era d'amor l'immagine. ACT 2: 6a. Allenta il più, Regina; 6b. O nube che lieve per l'aria; 7a. Ah! non m'inganna la gioia!; 7b. Da tutti abbandonata; 8. Qual loco è questo?; 9. È sempre la stessa; 10a. Deh! l'accogli; 10b. Morta al mondo, e morta al trono; 11. Va preparati, furente. ACT 3: 12a. E pensi? e tardi?; 12b. Quella vita a me funesta; 13a. Regina!—A lei s'affretta il supplizio; 13b. Deh! per pietà sospendi; 13c. D'una sorella, o barbara; 14. La perfida insultarmi anche volea; 15a. Oh mio buon Talbot!; 15b. Delle mie colpe lo squadillo fantasma; 15c. Quando di luce rosea; 15d. Un'altra colpa a piangere; 16. Vedeste?—Vedemmo. Oh truce apparato!; 17a. Anna!—Qui più sommessi favallate; 17b. Deh! vi rivedo alfin; 17c. Deh! Tu di un umile preghiera; 18a. Oh colpo!... 18b. D'un cor che muore reca il perdono; 18c. Giunge il Conte; 18d. Ah! se un giorno.
Maria Stuarda J. Baker
Elisabetta R. Plowright
Leicester D. Rendall
Talbot J. Tomlinson
Cecil A. Opie
Anna A. Bostock
ENO Chor, ENO Orch, C. Mackerras, J. Copley (CAST) **CVI2038**
Maria Stuarda M. Caballé
Elisabetta M.V. Menendez
Leicester J. Carreras
Talbot M. Mazzieri
Cecil E. Serra
Anna R. Bezinian
Paris ORTF Lyric Chor, Paris ORTF Lyric Orch, N. Santi (pp1972) (FOYE) ⓒ [2] **2-CF2093**
Maria Stuarda E. Gruberová
Elisabetta A. Baltsa
Leicester F. Araiza
Talbot F.E. d'Artegna
Cecil S. Alaimo
Anna I. Vermillion
Bavarian Rad Chor, Munich RO, G. Patanè (r1989) (4/90) (PHIL) ⓒ [2] **426 233-2PH2**
Maria Stuarda J. Sutherland
Elisabetta H. Tourangeau
Leicester L. Pavarotti
Talbot R. Soyer
Cecil J. Morris
Anna M. Elkins
Bologna Teatro Comunale Chor, Bologna Teatro Comunale Orch, R. Bonynge (9/90) (DECC) ⓒ [2] **425 410-2DM2**
Excs J. Baker (CAST) **CVI2030**
7b J. Sutherland, L. Pavarotti, Bologna Teatro Comunale Orch, R. Bonynge (r1974/5) (DECC) ⓒ **436 313-2DA** (DECC) **436 313-4DA**
17a, 17b E. Gruberová, J. Marková, Smetana Th Chor, Czech PO, F. Haider (SUPR) ⓒ **11 0345-2**
18a-d M. Caballé, Ambrosian Op Chor, Philh, N. Rescigno (11/92) (RCA) [2] **RK61044**
18b-d L. Gencer, MMF Orch, F. Molinari-Pradelli (pp1967) (MEMO) ⓒ [2] **HR4239/40**

Les **Martyrs– opera: 4 acts (1840—Paris) (reworking of 'Poliuto'. Lib. Scribe)**
Pauline L. Gencer
Polyeucte O. Garaventa
Félix F. Furlanetto
Sévère R. Bruson
Callisthène F. Signor
Néarque O. di Credico
A Christian M. Guggia
Venice La Fenice Chor, Venice La Fenice Orch, G. Gelmetti (10/94) (ITAL) ⓒ [3] **LO7716/8**

Ne m'oubliez pas– opera: 3 acts (incomplete) (1842) (Lib. J H V de Saint-Georges)
Henriette M. Elkins
André A. Oliver
Franz C. du Plessis
G. Mitchell Ch, Philh, J. Judd (r1979) (9/94) (OPRA) ⓒ **ORC004**

Le **Nozze in villa– dramma buffo: 2 acts (1820—Mantua) (Lib. B. Merelli)**
In lei vegg'io l'oggetto D. Montague, P. Nilon, J. Viera, Philh, D. Parry (8/95) (OPRA) ⓒ [3] **ORCH104**

Il **Paria– melo-dramma: 2 acts (1829—Naples) (Lib. D Gilardoni)**
Notte, ch'eterna a me parevi...Qui pel figlio una madre gridava J. Rawnsley, G. Mitchell Ch, Philh, D. Parry (8/95) (OPRA) ⓒ [3] **ORCH104**

Parisina d'Este– opera: 3 acts (1833—Florence) (Lib. F. Romani, after Byron)
No, più salir non ponno...Ciel sei tu che in tal momento...Ugo è spento M. Caballé, M. Elkins, T. McDonnell, Ambrosian Op Chor, LSO, C.F. Cillario (11/92) (RCA) ⓒ [2] **GD60941**

I **pazzi per progetto– opera farsa: 1 act (1824—Naples) (Lib D. Gilardoni)**
Darlemont L. Monreale
Norina S. Rigacci
Blinval G. Polidori
Cristina A. Cicogna
Venanzio V. M. Brunetti
Eustachio E. Fissore
Frank G. Sarti
Toscanini SO, B. Rigacci (pp1988) (7/95) (BONG) ⓒ **GB2070-2**

Poliuto– opera seria: 3 acts (1848—Naples) (Lib. Cammarano, after Corneille)
Poliuto N. Martinucci
Paolina E. Connell
Severo R. Bruson
Callistene F. Federici
Nearco A. dell'Innocenti
Felice B. Lazzaretti
A Christian G. Mazzini
Rome Op Chor, Rome Op Chor, J. Latham-König (pp1988) (10/89) (NUOV) ⓒ [2] **6776/7**
Decio, signor del mondo...No, l'acciar non fu spietato; Donna...il più lieto dei viventi E. Bastianini, M. Callas, La Scala Chor, La Scala Orch, A. Votto (pp1960) (MEMO) ⓒ [2] **HR4400/1**
Di tua beltade immagine D. Hvorostovsky, Philh, I. Marin (r1992) (9/94) (PHIL) ⓒ **434 912-2PH** (9/94) (PHIL) **434 912-4PH**
D'un alma troppo fervida; Sfolgoró divino raggio; Donna - malvagio! F. Corelli, La Scala Orch, A. Votto (pp1960) (MEMO) ⓒ [2] **HR4204/5**
Fu macchiato l'onor mio C. Merritt, Munich RSO, J. Fiore (r1993) (9/94) (PHIL) ⓒ **434 102-2PH**
Sfolgorò divino raggio J. Carreras, Vienna SO, O. Caetani (SONY) ⓒ **SMK48155** (SONY) **SMT48155**
Sfolgorò divino raggio J. Carreras, Vienna SO, O. Caetani ( ) (SONY) **SM48155**

Roberto Devereux, ossia Il conte di Essex– opera: 3 acts (1837—Naples) (Lib. Cammarano, after Ancelot)
EXCERPTS—; 1. Overture. ACT 1: 2. All' afflitto è dolce il pianto; 3a. Duchessa, alle fervide preci; 3b. L'amor suo mi fè' beata; 4a. Ieri, taceva il giorno; 4b. Forse in quel co sensible; 4c. Qui ribelle; 5a. Tutto è silenzio; 5b. Dacchè tornasti, ahi misera!; 5c. E quando fuggirai? ACT 2: 8. Un perfido, un vile, un mentitore tu sei; 9a. Non venni mai sì vento; 9b. Su lui non piombi il fulmine; 11. Sì scellerata! Non sol che un nume vindice. ACT 3: 15a. Ed ancor la tremenda porta; 15b. Come un spirito angelico; 15c. Odo un suon per l'aria cieca; 15d. Bagnato il sen di lagrime; 18a. E sara in questi orribili momenti; 18b. Vivi

ingrato; 18c. Qual sangue versato al cielo.
Roberto D. Bernardini
Elisabetta E. Gruberová
Sara D. Ziegler
Nottingham E. Kim
Cecil B. Boutet
Raleigh M. Kazbek
Page F. Richert
Rhine Op Chor, Strasbourg PO, F. Haider (r1994)
(5/95) (NIGH) Ⓓ [2] **NC070563-2**
1. South-West German RSO, K. Arp (r1994)
(PIER) Ⓓ **PV730050**
2. M. Elkins, Philh, J. Judd (r1979)
(9/94) (OPRA) Ⓓ **ORC004**
3a, 3b E. Gruberová, J. Marková, L.M. Vodička, P. Horáček, Smetana Th Chor, Czech PO, F. Haider (SUPR) Ⓓ **11 0345-2**
4a, 4b, 9a, 9b, 11. L. Gencer, A.M. Rota, P. Cappuccilli, Naples San Carlo Op Chor, Naples San Carlo Op Orch, M. Rossi (pp1964)
(MEMO) Ⓓ [2] **HR4273/4**
15a-d A. Cupido, Danish Rad Chbr Ch, Danish Rad Concert Orch, M. Elquist
(DENO) Ⓓ **CO-79785**
18a, 18b M. Caballé, Chor, Orch, C.F. Cillario
(11/92) (RCA) ▭ [2] **RK61044**

Torquato Tasso– opera: 3 acts (1833—Rome) (Lib. J. Ferretti)
Fatal, Goffredo!...Trono e corona M. Caballé, LSO, C.F. Cillario
(11/92) (RCA) Ⓓ [2] **GD60941**

Ugo, Conte di Parigi– opera: 2 acts (1832—Milan) (Lib. F. Romani)
Ugo M. Arthur
Luigi V D. Jones
Emma E. Harrhy
Bianca J. Price
Adelia Y. Kenny
Folco di Angiò C. du Plessis
G. Mitchell Ch, New Philh, A. Francis
(12/90) (OPRA) Ⓓ [3] **ORC001**

La **Zingara– opera: 2 acts (1822—Naples) (Lib. A. L. Tottola)**
A te nell'appressarmi B. Ford, I. Platt, J. Rawnsley (8/95) (OPRA) Ⓓ [3] **ORCH104**
Fra l'erbe cosparse E. Orel, anon (Russ: r c1902) (7/93) (SYMP) Ⓓ **SYMCD1105**
Fra l'erbe cosparse M. Korjus, Berlin St Op Orch, B. Seidler-Winkler (Ger: r1936)
(10/93) (PREI) Ⓓ **89054**

DOSTAL, Nico *(1891–1981)* Austria

Clivia– operetta: 3 acts (1933—Berlin) (Lib. C Amberg)
EXCERPTS: 1a. Warum trieb das Schicksal; 1b. Ich bin verliebt.
1a, 1b R. Holm, W. Krenn, Vienna Volksoper Orch, A. Paulik (r1970)
(LOND) Ⓓ **436 898-2DM**
1b E. Harwood, BBC SO, V. Tausky (pp1976)
(BBCR) Ⓓ **BBCRD9103**

Die **Ungarische Hochzeit– operetta: prologue, 3 acts (1939—Stuttgart) (Lib. H Hermecke, after K Mikszáth)**
EXCERPTS: 1. Heimat, deine Lieder; 2. Märchentraum der Liebe; 3a. Am alten Brunnen; 3b. Spiel das Lied von Glück und Treu; 4. Hungarian March.
3a, 3b R. Holm, W. Krenn, Vienna Volksoper Orch, A. Paulik (r1970)
(LOND) Ⓓ **436 898-2DM**
3b L. Popp, ASMF, N. Marriner
(6/88) (EMI) Ⓓ **CDC7 49700-2**

DUBOIS, Théodore (François Clement) *(1837–1924)* France

Aben-Hamet– opera: prologue & 4 acts (1884—Paris) (Lib. L. Detroyat, after Chateaubriand)
Reine! toi qu'Hamet salue M. Imbert, orch (r1900s) (8/92) (IRCC) Ⓓ **IRCC-CD802**

DUKAS, Paul (Abraham) *(1865–1935)* France

Ariane et Barbe-bleue– opera: 3 acts, Paris (1907) (Wds. Maeterlinck)
Prelude, Act 3. FRNO, J. Martinon
(1/90) (EMI) Ⓓ **CDM7 63160-2**

DUNI, Egidio (Romualdo) *(1708–1775)* Italy

Demofoonte– opera seria (1737—London) (Lib. after Metastasio)
Misero pargoletto A. Christofellis, Seicentonovecento Ens, F. Colusso (r1993/4)
(EMI) Ⓓ **CDC5 55250-2**
Prudente mi chiedi A. Christofellis, Inst Ens (r1987/8) (EMI) Ⓓ **CDC5 55259-2**

DURÓN, Sebastián *(1660–1716)* Spain

Salir el Amor del Mundo– zarzuela (1696—Madrid) (Lib Cañizares)
EXCERPTS: 1. Sosieguen, descansen.
1. Romanesca (r1991-2)
(11/94) (GLOS) Ⓓ **GCD920201**

DUSAPIN, Pascal *(b 1955)* France

Medeamaterial– opera (1992—Brussels) (Wds. Heiner Müller)
1. Jason mein Erstes; 2. Herrin ich; 3. Weib was für eine Stimme; 4. Zwei Söhne gab; 5. Bist du mein Mann; 6. Und meinen Bruder; 7. Das kleid der Liebe; 8. Jetzt tritt der Bräutigam; 9. Aus meinen Händchen; 10. Ist att sein küssen.
Medea H. Leidland
Chor, Collegium Vocale, Chapelle Royale Orch, P. Herreweghe (r1992)
(6/93) (HARM) Ⓓ **HMC90 5215**

Romeo and Juliet– opera: 9 numbers (1989—Montpellier) (Wds. O. Cadiot)
1. Prologue; 2. Le début; 3. Le matin; 4. Avant; 5. La révolution; 6. Après; 7. Le soir; 8. La fin; 9. Epilogue.
Juliette 1 F. Kubler
Romeo 1 N. Isherwood
Juliette 2 C. Gerstenhaber
Romeo 2 J. Combey
Bill O. Cadiot
Bill P. Sausy
France Groupe Vocal, Rhin-Mulhouse SO, L. Pfaff
(ACCO) Ⓓ **20116-2**

DUVERNOY, Victor Alphonse *(1842–1907)* France

Hellé– opera: 4 acts (1896—Paris) (Lib. C. DuLocle & C. Nuitter)
Voici le soir, la nuit s'avance R. Caron, anon (r1904) (8/92) (IRCC) Ⓓ **IRCC-CD802**
Voici le soir, la nuit s'avance R. Caron, anon (r1904) (12/94) (SYMP) Ⓓ **SYMCD1172**

DVOŘÁK, Antonín *(1841–1904)* Bohemia

B–Numbers from Burghauser's chronological catalogue of Dvořák's complete works

Armida– opera: 4 acts, B206 (Op. 115) (1904—Prague) (Lib. J. Vrchlický)
At dawn, as I merrily pursued a slender gazelle L. Popp, Munich RO, S. Soltesz (r1987)
(4/89) (EMI) Ⓓ **CDC7 49319-2**
Overture Košice St PO, R. Stankovsky
(MARC) Ⓓ **8 223272**
Overture Prague SO, M. Konvalinka (r1982)
(PRAG) Ⓓ **PR254 045**

Dimitrij– opera: 4 acts, B127 (Op. 64), rev as B186 (1882—Prague) (Lib. M. Cervinková-Riegrová)
Dimitri Ivanovich L.M. Vodička
Marfa Ivanovna D. Drobková
Marina Mnishkova M. Hajóssyová
Xenia Borisnova L. Aghova
Pyotr Fyodorovich Basmanov P. Mikuláš
Prince Shuisky I. Kusnjer
Iov L. Vele
Czech Phil Chor, Prague Rad Chor, Czech PO, G. Albrecht
(3/93) (SUPR) Ⓓ [3] **11 1259-2**
From the wild storm of life L.M. Vodička, Czech PO, G. Albrecht (r1989)
(KOCH) Ⓓ **34036-2**
(KOCH) ▭ **24036-4**
Overture Košice St PO, R. Stankovsky
(MARC) Ⓓ **8 223272**

The **Jacobin– opera: 3 acts, B159 (Op. 84): rev as B200 (1889—Prague) (Lib. M Červinková-Riegrová)**
Bohuš V. Zítek
Jiří V. Přibyl
Terinka D. Šounová-Brouková
Count Vilém K. Průša
Adolf R. Tuček
Julie M. Machotková
Filip K. Berman
Benda B. Blachut
Lotinka I. Mixová
Kantiléna Children's Chor, Kühn Chor, Brno St PO, J. Pinkas (r1977)
(12/94) (SUPR) Ⓓ [2] **11 2190-2**
Excs V. Zítek, V. Přibyl, D. Šounová-Brouková, K. Průša, R. Tuček, M. Machotková, K. Berman, B. Blachut, I. Mixová, Kantiléna Children's Chor, Kühn Chor, Brno St PO, J. Pinkas (r1977)
(SUPR) Ⓓ **11 2250-2**
Overture Košice St PO, R. Stankovsky
(MARC) Ⓓ **8 223272**

Kate and the Devil– opera: 3 acts, B201 (Op. 112) (1899—Prague) (Lib. A. Wenig)
Kate A. Barová
Devil Marbuel R. Novák
Shepherd Jirka M. Ježil
Kate's mother D. Suryová
Lucifer J. Horáček
Devil the Gate-keeper J. Hladík
Devil the Guard A. Šťáva
Princess B. Šulcová
Chamber maid N. Romanová
Marshall P. Kamas
Musician O. Polášek
Brno Janáček Op Chor, Brno Janáček Op Orch, J. Pinkas (r1979)
(9/94) (SUPR) Ⓓ [2] **11 1800-2**
Overture Košice St PO, R. Stankovsky
(MARC) Ⓓ **8 223272**
Overture Czech PO, V. Neumann
(9/90) (ORFE) Ⓓ **C180891A**
Overture, Act 3. Czech PO, V. Neumann
(SUPR) Ⓓ **11 1287-2**
Prelude to Act 2. Brno Janáček Op Orch, J. Pinkas (r1979) (KOCH) Ⓓ **34036-2**
(KOCH) ▭ **24036-4**

King and Charcoal Burner– opera: 3 acts, B21, rev as B42 and B151 (1929—Prague) (comp. 1871. Lib. B J Lobeský)
Overture Košice St PO, R. Stankovsky
(MARC) Ⓓ **8 223272**

Rusalka– opera: 3 acts, B203 (Op. 114) (1901—Prague) (Lib. Kvapil)
EXCERPTS: 1. Overture. ACT 1: 2. Ho, ho, ho!; 3. Watersprite, my father dear; 4. He comes here frequently; 5. O, moon high up in the deep, deep sky (O silver moon); 6. Your ancient wisdom knows everything; 7. Abracadabra; 8. Here she appeared; 9. The hunt is over, return home at once; 10. I know you're but magic that will pass. ACT 2: 11. Well them, well then; 12. A week now do you dwell with me; 13. Festival music: Ballet (Polonaise); 14. No one this world can give you; 16. Rusalka, daughter, I am here; 17. O, useless it is; 18. Strange fire in your eyes is burning. ACT 3: 19. Insensible water power (God of the lake); 20. Ah, ah! Already you have come back?; 21. Only human blood can cleanse you; 22. I'll rather suffer; 23. Uprooted and banished; 24. That you're afraid? Don't be silly; 25. Who is noisy?; 26. Hair, golden hair have I; 27. Where are you, my white doe?; 28. Do you still know me, lover?.
Rusalka E. Hannan
Watergnome R. Macann
Witch A. Howard
Prince J. Treleaven
Foreign Princess P. Cannan
Woodsprite I C. Pope
Woodsprite II E. Hulse
Woodsprite III L. McLeod
Turnspit F. Kimm
Hunter E. Byles
ENO Chor, ENO Orch, M. Elder, D. Pountney
(MCEG) ▭ **VVD392**

Rusalka G. Beňačková
Watergnome R. Novák
Witch V. Soukupová
Prince W. Ochman
Foreign Princess D. Drobková
Woodsprite I J. Jonášová
Woodsprite II D. Šounová-Brouková
Woodsprite III A. Barová
Turnspit J. Marková
Hunter R. Tuček
Prague Phil Chor, Czech PO, V. Neumann (r1982/3)
(SUPR) ① [3] **10 3641-2**
Rusalka M. Šubrtová
Watersprite E. Haken
Witch M. Ovčačíková
Prince I. Žídek
Foreign Princess A. Míková
Watersprite I J. Wysoczanská
Watersprite II E. Hlobilová
Watersprite III V. Krilová
Turnspit I. Mixová
Hunter V. Bednář
Prague Nat Th Chor, Prague Nat Th Orch, Z. Chalabala (r1961)
(SUPR) ① [2] **SU0013-2**
1. Czech PO, V. Neumann
(SUPR) ① **11 0624-2**
1. Košice St PO, R. Stankovsky
(MARC) ① **8 223272**
2, 5, 7, 9(pt), 10, 12-14, 19, 26, 28. G. Beňačková, R. Novák, V. Soukupová, W. Ochman, D. Drobková, J. Jonášová, D. Šounová-Brouková, A. Barová, Prague Phil Chor, Czech PO, V. Neumann (r1982/3)
(SUPR) ① **11 2252-2**
5. P. Lorengar, Santa Cecilia Academy Orch, G. Patanè (DECC) ① **425 853-2DWO**
(DECC) ▭ **425 853-4DWO**
5. J. Barstow, RPO, R. Stapleton
(RPO) ① **CDRPO7009**
(RPO) ▭ **ZCRPO7009**
5. P. Lorengar, Santa Cecilia Academy Orch, G. Patanè (r1966) (DECC) ① **433 065-2DWO**
(DECC) ▭ **433 065-4DWO**
5. R. Streich, Berlin RSO, K. Gaebel
(DG) ① [2] **435 748-2GDO2**
5. L. Popp, Munich RO, S. Soltesz
(CFP) ① **CD-CFP4606**
(CFP) ▭ **TC-CFP4606**
5. J. Barstow, RPO, R. Stapleton (r1991)
(RPO) ① [2] **CDRPD9006**
(RPO) ▭ [2] **ZCRPD9006**
5. G. Groves, J. Partridge (r1994)
(ASV) ① **CDWHL2088**
5. F. Von Stade, Boston SO, S. Ozawa (pp1993)
(SONY) ◐ **SLV53488**
(SONY) ▭ **SHV53488**
5. P. Lorengar, Santa Cecilia Academy Orch, G. Patanè (r1966) (DECC) ① **443 765-2DF2**
5. L. Price, New Philh, N. Santi (r1977)
(RCA) ① **09026 62596-2**
5. E. Destinn, orch, W.B. Rogers (r1915: Ger)
(PEAR) ① **GEMMCD9172**
5. N. Gustafson, Bologna Teatro Comunale Orch, L. Magiera (pp1994)
(DECC) ① **444 460-2DH**
(DECC) ▭ **444 460-4DH**
5. P. Lorengar, Santa Cecilia Academy Orch, G. Patanè (r1966) (DECC) ① **443 931-2DM**
5. Czech PO, V. Neumann
(5/89) (PHIL) ① **422 387-2PH**
5. L. Garrett, Philh, A. Greenwood (r1990-1)
(11/91) (SILV) ① **SONGCD903**
(11/91) (SILV) ▭ **SONGC903**
5. P. McCann, Black Dyke Mills Band, P. Parkes (r1984: arr P Parkes)
(11/92) (CHAN) ① **CHAN4501**
(11/92) (CHAN) ▭ **BBTD4501**
5. L. Price, New Philh, N. Santi (r1977)
(12/92) (RCA) ① [4] **09026 61236-2**
5. J. Hammond, Philh, V. Tausky (r1952)
(12/92) (TEST) ① **SBT1013**
5. J. Novotná, G. King (r1956)
(4/93) (SUPR) ① **11 1491-2**
5. Black Dyke Mills Band, J. Watson (r1992: arr Langford) (9/93) (POLY) ① **QPRL053D**
(9/93) (POLY) ▭ **CPRL053D**
5. E. Destinn, orch, W.B. Rogers (r1915: Ger)
(11/93) (ROMO) ① [2] **81002-2**
5. A. Roocroft, LPO, F. Welser-Möst
(10/94) (EMI) ① **CDC5 55090-2**
(10/94) (EMI) ▭ **EL5 55090-4**
5. E. Destinn, orch, W.B Rogers (r1915: Ger)
(12/94) (SUPR) ① [12] **11 2136-2(5)**
5. L. Popp, G. Parsons (pp1981)
(6/95) (ORFE) ① **C363941B**
5. S. Bullock, A. Bryn Parri (r1994)
(11/95) (SAIN) ① **SCDC2070**
5, 23. L. Popp, Munich RO, S. Soltesz (r1987)
(4/89) (EMI) ① **CDC7 49319-2**
7. E. Randová, Brno St PO, O. Lenárd (pp1992)
(SUPR) ① **11 1846-2**
7. V. Soukupová, Czech PO, V. Neumann (r1982-83) (KOCH) ① **34036-2**
(KOCH) ▭ **24036-4**
26. J. Novotná, A. Sándor (r1931)
(4/93) (SUPR) ① **11 1491-2**

Vanda– opera: 5 acts, B55 (Op. 25) (1876—Prague) (Lib. V. B. Šumavský, after J. Surzycki)
Overture BBC PO, S. Gunzenhauser (r1992)
(10/93) (NAXO) ① **8 550600**

ECCLES, John *(c1668–1735) England*

The **Judgment of Paris– masque (1701—London) (Wds. Congreve)**
EXCERPTS: 1. Symphony for Mercury (Trumpet Sonata); 2. Awake, awake, thy Spirits Raise.
1. Parley of Instr, R. Goodman, P. Holman
(11/88) (HYPE) ① **CDA66108**
2. E. Kirkby, English Tpt Virtuosi, A. Hoskins (tpt/dir), M. Hoskins (tpt/dir) (r1994)
(10/95) (MOSC) ① **070979**

EGK, Werner *(1901–1983) Germany*

Columbus– opera (1932, staged 1942—Frankfurt)
Excs P. Schoeffler, J. Witt, E. Réthy, F. Jelinek, F. Worff, F. Normann, E. Kunz, W. Franter, H. Gallos, Vienna St Op Chor, Vienna St Op Orch, L. Ludwig (pp1942) (SCHW) ① [2] **314712**

Peer Gynt– opera: 3 acts (1938—Berlin) (Lib. cpsr, after Ibsen)
Peer Gynt R. Hermann
Solveig N. Sharp
Aase C. Wulkopf
Ingrid J. Perry
Mads H. Hopfner
Old Man H. Hopf
The Redhead K. Lövaas
Vogt; Merchant I H. Weber
Schmied; Merchant II P. Hansen
The President; Merchant III P. Lika
Unknown Man W. Wild
Lord of the Trolls F. Lenz
Bavarian Rad Chor, Munich RO, H. Wallberg (r1981)
(10/89) (ORFE) ① [2] **C005822H**

Die **Verlobung in San Domingo– opera: 2 acts (1963—Munich) (Lib. cpsr, after H von Kleist)**
Jeanne E. Lear
Babekan M. Bence
Hoango H.G. Nöcker
Nanky H. Nasseri
Christoph von Ried F. Wunderlich
Gottfried von Ried M. Yahia
Herr Schwarz Richard Holm
Herr Weiss K.C. Kohn
Bavarian St Orch, W. Egk (pp1963)
(9/94) (ORFE) ① [2] **C343932I**

EINEM, Gottfried von *(b 1918) Austria*

Dantons Tod– opera: 2 parts (1947—Salzburg) (Lib. cpsr and B. Blacher, after G. Büchner)
Georg Danton T. Adam
Camille Desmoulins W. Hollweg
Hérault de Séchelles W. Gahmlich
Robespierre H. Hiestermann
Lucile K. Laki
Saint Just H. Berger-Tuna
Herrmann K. Rydl
Simon F. Wyzner
Young Man C. Doig
Executioner I K. Terkal
Executioner II A. Muff
Julie I. Mayr
Lady G. Sima
Simon's Wife M. Lipovšek
Austrian Rad Chor, Austrian RSO, L. Zagrosek (pp1983)
(1/90) (ORFE) ① [2] **C102842H**

Der **Prozess, '(The) Trial'– opera: 2 acts, Op. 14 (1953—Salzburg) (Lib. Blacher & von Cramer, after Kafka)**
Josef K M. Lorenz
Deputy Director; Student P. Klein
Albert K E. Koréh
A lad E. Majkut
Frau Grubach P. Batic
Solicitor A. Poell
Titorelli L. Szemere
Supervisor; Passer-by; Prison Chaplain; Manufacturer L. Hofmann
Magistrate; Hit-man O. Czerwenka
Franz; Office Manager W. Berry
Willem; Bailiff A. Pernerstorfer
Fräulein Bürstner; Bailiff's Wife L. della Casa
A hunchbacked girl Luise Leitner
Vienna St Op Chor, VPO, K. Böhm (pp1953)
(ORFE) ① [2] **C393952I**

ELGAR, Sir Edward (William) *(1857–1934) England*

Crown of India– imperial masque, Op. 66 (1911-12—London) (Wds. H. Hamilton)
1a. Introduction; 1b. Dance of Nautch Girls; 2. Menuetto; 3. Warriors' Dance; 4. Intermezzo; 5. March of the Mogul Emperors.
Cpte SNO, A. Gibson (r1978)
(CHAN) ① **CHAN6523**
(CHAN) ▭ **MBTD6523**
Cpte LPO, D. Barenboim (r1973)
(SONY) ① **SBK48265**
Cpte SNO, A. Gibson
(6/87) (CHAN) ① **CHAN8429**
Cpte LPO, D. Barenboim
(9/91) (CBS) ① [2] **CD46465**
Cpte LSO, E. Elgar (r1930)
(2/93) (EMI) ① [3] **CDS7 54564-2**
5. BBC SO, L. Bernstein (r1982)
(11/84) (DG) ① **413 490-2GH**

The **Spanish Lady– opera (sketches only), Op. 89 (Lib. B. Jackson, from B. Jonson's 'The Devil is an Ass')**
Sketches ed P Young: 1955-56; 1. Country Dance: Allegretto e leggiero; 2. Burlesco: Allegro; 3. Adagio; 4. Sarabande: Maestoso; 5. Bourrée: Vivace. SONGS: 6. Modest and Fair; 7. Still to be Neat.
2. Bournemouth Sinfonietta, G. Hurst
(8/87) (CHAN) ① **CHAN8432**
2. Bournemouth Sinfonietta, G. Hurst (r1975)
(2/92) (CHAN) ① **CHAN6544**
2, 4, 5. English Stg Orch, W. Boughton (r1983)
(NIMB) ▭ **NC5008**

ENNA, Auguste (Emil) *(1859–1939) Denmark*

The **Match Girl– opera (1897—Copenhagen) (Lib. cpsr, after Andersen)**
Ov Odense SO, O. Schmidt
(1/87) (UNIC) ▭ **DKPC9036**

ERKEL, Ferenc *(1810–1893) Hungary*

Dózsa György– opera: 5 acts (1867—Budapest) (Lib. E. Szigligeti, after M. Jókai)
Rózsa's Death-Song I. Kassai (arr pf)
(MARC) ① **8 223318**

Hunyadi László– opera (1844—Budapest) (Lib. Egressy, after L. Tóth)
Ah rebéges L. Nordica, anon (r1907)
(7/93) (NIMB) ① [2] **NI7840/1**
Csárdás Budapest PO, J. Sándor
(LASE) ① **15 621**
(LASE) ▭ **79 621**

ESSYAD, Ahmed *(b 1940) Morocco*

Le **Collier des Ruses, '(The) Necklace of Guiles'– chamber opera (1977—Avignon) (Lib after El Hamadhani)**
Cpte C. Bonnet, F. Gonzalez, V. Reinbold, Ens, P. Nahon (r1994) (K617) ① [2] **K617051**

EYSLER, Edmund (1874–1949) Austria

Bruder Straubinger– operetta (3 acts) (1903—Vienna) (Lib. M. West and I. Schnitzer)
Küssen ist keine Sünd B. Weikl, Austrian RSO, K. Eichhorn (ORFE) Ⓓ **C077831A**
Küssen ist keine Sünd P. Morrison, Chandos Concert Orch, S. Barry (Eng) (2/90) (CHAN) Ⓓ **CHAN8759**
(2/90) (CHAN) ⊟ **LBTD023**

FACCIO, Franco (1840–1891) Italy

Amleto– opera: 4 acts (1865—Genoa) (Lib. A Boito)
Principe Amleto C. Owen, anon (r1950/60s) (6/94) (IRCC) Ⓓ **IRCC-CD808**

FALL, Leo (1873–1925) Austria

Der **Fidele Bauer– operetta (3 acts) (1907—Mannheim) (Lib. Leon)**
Kleinen Kindern und auch süssen kleinen Frauen...O frag' mich nicht, mein süsser Schatz F. Wunderlich, Graunke SO, C. Michalski (EMI) Ⓓ [3] **CZS7 62993-2**
O, frag' mich nicht P. Domingo, ECO, J. Rudel (2/87) (EMI) Ⓓ **CDC7 47398-2**

Die **Rose von Stambul– operetta (3 acts) (1916—Vienna) (Lib. Brammer and Grünwald)**
Ein Walzer muss es sein; Ihr stillen, süssen Frau'n; O Rose von Stambul F. Wunderlich, Graunke SO, C. Michalski (EMI) Ⓓ [3] **CZS7 62993-2**
Excs E. Köth, R. Schock, Günther Arndt Ch, Berlin SO, F. Fox (2/91) (EURO) Ⓓ **GD69023**
Ihr stillen, süssen Frau'n P. Domingo, Ambrosian Sngrs, ECO, J. Rudel (2/87) (EMI) Ⓓ **CDC7 47398-2**
Ihr stillen, süsser Frauen H.E. Groh, orch (r1932) (3/92) (PEAR) Ⓓ **GEMMCD9419**
Man sagt uns nach...O Rose von Stambul; Zwei Augen, die wollen mir nicht aus dem Sinn F. Wunderlich, Bavarian St Orch, H. Moltkau (EMI) Ⓓ [3] **CZS7 62993-2**
Waltz Vienna SO, R. Stolz (EURO) Ⓓ **258 667**

FALLA (Y MATHEU), Manuel de (1876–1946) Spain

El **Corregidor y la molinera– farsa mimica (2 scenes) (1917—Madrid)**
Teatre Iliure CO, J. Pons (r1994) (7/95) (HARM) Ⓓ **HMC90 1520**

El **Retablo de maese Pedro– puppet opera (1923—Paris) (Lib. cpsr, after Cervantes)**

El Trujamán	T. Tourné
Maese Pedro	P. Lavirgen
Don Quixote	R. Cesari

Madrid Concerts Orch, P. de Freitas Branco (GME) Ⓓ **GME221**

El Trujamán	S. Linay
Maese Pedro	Adrian Thompson
Don Quixote	M. Best

Matrix Ens, R. Ziegler (7/91) (ASV) Ⓓ **CDDCA758**

El Trujamán	J. Smith
Maese Pedro	A. Oliver
Don Quixote	P. Knapp

London Sinfonietta, S. Rattle (9/92) (DECC) Ⓓ [2] **433 908-2DM2**

El Trujamán	X. Cabero
Maese Pedro	J. Cabero
Don Quixote	J. Diaz

Opera Atelier, Montreal SO, C. Dutoit (6/93) (DECC) ◖ **071 145-1DH**
(6/93) (DECC) ▭ **071 145-3DH**
Sinfonia A. de Larrocha (r1992; trans pf) (9/94) (RCA) Ⓓ **09026 61389-2**

La **Vida breve– opera: 2 acts - 4 scenes (1913—Nice) (Lib. C. Fernández Shaw)**
1. Prelude, Act 1; 2. Danse espagnole No.1; 3. Danse espagnole No.2; 4. Vivan los que rien!; 5. Alli está! Riyendo.

Salud	A. Nafé
Paco	A. Ordóñez
Carmela	K. Notare
Grandmother	C. Keen
Uncle Sarvaor	M. Wadsworth
Voices	M. Cid
Manuel	W. McGraw
Singer	G. Moreno

M. May Fest Chor, Cincinnati SO, J. López-Cobos (TELA) Ⓓ **CD80317**

Salud	T. Berganza
Carmela; Street Vendor I & III	P.P. Iñigo
Grandmother; Street Vendor II	A. Nafé
Paco	J. Carreras
Uncle Salvador	J. Pons
Singer	M. Mairena
Manuel	R. Contreras
Voice in smithy; Voice in distance; voice of hawker	M. Cid

Ambrosian Op Chor, LSO, G. Navarro (10/92) (DG) Ⓓ **435 851-2GH**
1, 2. Mexico St SO, E. Bátiz (IMP) Ⓓ **PCD2028**
1, 2. Cincinnati SO, J. López-Cobos (11/87) (TELA) Ⓓ **CD80149**
1, 2. SRO, E. Ansermet (4/89) (DECC) Ⓓ **417 771-2DM**
1, 2. SRO, E. Ansermet (9/92) (DECC) Ⓓ [2] **433 908-2DM2**
2. D. Sitkovetsky, B. Canino (arr Kreisler) (ORFE) Ⓓ **C048831A**
2. M. Rost (trs gtr) (LASE) Ⓓ **15 602**
(LASE) ⊟ **79 602**
2. W. Feybli, D. Erni (arr Pujol:2 gtrs) (ORFE) Ⓓ **C189891A**
2. J. Christensen, M. Fukačová (arr gtr/vc) (KONT) Ⓓ **32044**
2. F. Kreisler, F. Rupp (arr Kreisler: r1938) (BIDD) Ⓓ **LAB040**
2. R. de Haan, E. Westerhof (arr 2 gtrs) (OTTA) Ⓓ **OTRC48710**
2. English Gtr Qt (r1992) (SAYD) Ⓓ **CD-SDL399**
(SAYD) ⊟ **CSDL399**
2. NYPO, L. Bernstein (SONY) Ⓓ **SFK47279**
2. Württemberg St Orch, G. Navarro (pp1991) (CAPR) Ⓓ **10 461**
2. J. Heifetz, E. Bay (r1935: arr vn/pf: Kreisler) (EMI) Ⓓ [2] **CHS7 64929-2**
2. R. Gauk (trans K. Fuji: gtr) (MARQ) Ⓓ **ERAD137**
2. Mexico City PO, E. Bátiz (ASV) Ⓓ **CDQS6121**
2. M. Gendron, P. Gallion (r1960; arr Gendron) (PHIL) Ⓓ [3] **438 960-2PM3**
2. R. Hill, P. Wiltschinsky (trans Hill/Wiltschinsky) (TELD) Ⓓ **4509-94523-2**
2. C. Ferras, J-C. Ambrosini (arr Kreisler) (BELA) Ⓓ **461 003-2**
(BELA) ⊟ **461 003-4**
2. Mexico City PO, F. Lozano (FORL) Ⓓ **FF047**
2. Philadelphia, L. Stokowski (r1928) (CALA) Ⓓ **CACD0501**
2. Moscow Virtuosi, V. Spivakov (r1994) (RCA) Ⓓ **09026 68185-2**
2. C-L. Lin, S. Rivers (arr. Kreisler) (7/85) (CBS) Ⓓ **CD39133**
2. LSO, G. Simon (10/86) (CHAN) Ⓓ **CHAN8457**
2. F. Kreisler, C. Lamson (r1928: arr Kreisler) (1/90) (PEAR) Ⓓ **GEMMCD9324**
2. J. Szigeti, N. Magaloff (r1932) (1/90) (BIDD) Ⓓ [2] **LAB007/8**
2. Mexico City PO, E. Bátiz (9/91) (ASV) Ⓓ **CDDCA735**
2. Y. Menuhin, A. Balsam (arr Kreisler: r1932) (9/91) (TEST) Ⓓ **SBT1003**
2. J. Thibaud, G. de Lausnay (r1929: arr vn/pf: Kreisler) (10/91) (MSCM) Ⓓ **MM30321**
2. Y. Menuhin, A. Balsam (arr Kreisler; r1932) (12/91) (BIDD) Ⓓ **LAB046**
2. Brodsky Qt (arr M. Thomas) (4/92) (TELD) Ⓓ **2292-46015-2**
2. R. Holmes, J. Walker (r1974: arr Kreisler) (5/92) (DECC) Ⓓ **433 220-2DWO**
(5/92) (DECC) ⊟ **433 220-4DWO**
2. Paris Cons, R. Frühbeck de Burgos (7/92) (EMI) Ⓓ [2] **CZS7 67474-2**
2. F. Kreisler, A. Sándor (arr Kreisler: r1926) (9/92) (BIDD) Ⓓ [2] **LAB049/50**
2. F. Kreisler, M. Raucheisen (arr Kreisler: r1926) (9/92) (BIDD) Ⓓ [2] **LAB049/50**
2. I. Haendel, A. Kotowska (arr Kreisler: r1942) (10/92) (PEAR) Ⓓ **GEMMCD9939**
2. T. Kropat, T. Krumeich (arr 2 gtrs) (7/93) (CHNN) Ⓓ **CG9103**
2. J. Bream, J. Williams (r1971; arr Pujol, rev Bream) (11/93) (RCA) Ⓓ **09026 61450-2**
(11/93) (RCA) ⊟ **09026 61450-4**
2. F. Kreisler, F. Rupp (r1938: arr Kreisler) (12/93) (EMI) Ⓓ **CDH7 64701-2**
2. F. Kreisler, C. Lamson (r1928: arr Kreisler) (12/93) (BIDD) Ⓓ **LAB080**
2. A. de Larrocha (r1992; trans pf) (9/94) (RCA) Ⓓ **09026 61389-2**
2. J. Heifetz, E. Bay (r1935) (11/94) (RCA) Ⓓ [65] **09026 61778-2(03)**
2. J. Thibaud, G. de Lausnay (r1929: arr Kreisler) (12/94) (APR) Ⓓ [2] **APR7028**
2. M. Kliegel, B. Glemser (r1993: arr vc/pf: G Pekkera) (1/95) (NAXO) Ⓓ **8 550785**
2. S. Nakarjakov, A. Markovich (r1994: arr tpt/pf) (6/95) (TELD) Ⓓ **4509-94554-2**
2, 3. Spanish Nat Orch, R. Frühbeck de Burgos (EMI) Ⓓ [2] **CMS7 64467-2**
2, 3. K. Labèque, M. Labèque (r1993; trans Samazeuilh: 2 pfs) (9/94) (PHIL) Ⓓ **438 938-2PH**
(9/94) (PHIL) ⊟ **438 938-4PH**
3. A. de Larrocha (r1950s: arr pf) (12/92) (EMI) Ⓓ **CDM7 64527-2**
4. V. de los Angeles, Spanish Nat Orch, R. Frühbeck de Burgos (EMI) Ⓓ **CDM7 64359-2**
4, 5. V. de los Angeles, Philh, S. Robinson (r1948) (4/92) (EMI) Ⓓ **CDH7 64028-2**

FAURÉ, Gabriel (Urbain) (1845–1924) France

Pénélope– drame lyrique: 3 acts (1913—Monte Carlo) (Lib. R. Fauchois)

Pénélope	J. Norman
Ulysse	A. Vanzo
Eurymaque	P. Huttenlocher
Eumée	J. Van Dam
Euryclée	J. Taillon
Alkandre	C. Alliot-Lugaz
Phylo	C. Barbaux
Lydie	D. Borst
Mélantho	M. Command
Cléone	N. Lerer
Ctésippe	P. Guigue
Léodès	G. Friedmann
Pisandre	F. Le Roux

J. Laforge Choral Ens, Monte Carlo PO, C. Dutoit (4/92) (ERAT) Ⓓ [2] **2292-45405-2**
Overture Loire PO, M. Soustrot (r1992) (6/94) (PIER) Ⓓ **PV792051**

Prométhée– tragédie lyrique: 3 acts (1900—Béziers) (Lib. J. Lorrain & A. F. Hérold)

Prométhée	F. Soulié
Pandore	E. Berger
Hermes	J. Castellat
Aenoe	R. Esso
Bia	V. Millot
Gaia	L. Vignon
Andros	Guy Fletcher
Héphaistos	O. Lallouette
Kratos	R. Velazquez

Ariège-Pyrénées Voc Ens, Equinoxe, Midi-Pyrénées Regional Orch, D. Dondeyne (r1992) (SCAL) Ⓓ **ARI155**

FÉNELON, Philippe (b 1952) France

Le **Chevalier Imaginaire– opera: prologue, 2 acts (1984-86) (Lib. cpsr, after Cervantes & Kafka)**

Sancho, Narrator, Black figure	L. Villanueva
Don Quixote	A. Tomicich
Niece	M. Armitstead
Housekeeper	M. Davies
Priest	P. Doghan
Barber	L. Masson

Paris InterContemporain Ens, P. Eötvös (pp1992) (11/95) (ERAT) Ⓓ **4509-96394-2**

FENNIMORE, Joseph (b 1940) USA

Eventide– opera: 1 act (1974) (Lib. cpsr)

Mahala	K. Williams
Plumy	H. Johnsson
Teeboy	P. Creech

Chelsea Chbr Ens, T. Rolek (ALBA) Ⓓ **TROY023-2**

FÉVRIER, Henry *(1875–1957)* *France*

Gismonda– opéra-comique: 4 acts (1919—Chicago) (Lib. H Cain & L Payen, after Sardou)

Toute blanche, les deux seins nus M. Namara, anon (r1930s) (8/92) (IRCC) ① **IRCC-CD802**

Monna Vanna– opera (1909—Paris) (Lib. after M. Maeterlinck)

Ce n'est pas un vieillard Vanni-Marcoux, orch, P. Coppola (r1924) (PEAR) ① **GEMMCD9912**

Ce n'est pas un vieillard Vanni-Marcoux, orch (r1924) (1/94) (CLUB) ① **CL99-101**

C'est étrange; Elle est à moi F. Ansseau, orch, P. Coppola (r1929) (1/91) (PREI) ① **89022**

C'est étrange que l'homme; Ah! j'aurais mieux aimé. F. Ansseau, orch, P. Coppola (r1929) (8/92) (IRCC) ① **IRCC-CD802**

FIBICH, Zdeněk (Antonín Václav) *(1850–1900)* *Bohemia*

The **Bride of Messina– opera: 3 acts, Op. 18 (1884—Prague) (Lib. O Hostinský, after Schiller)**

Donna Isabella L. Márová
Don Manuel V. Zítek
Don Cesar I. Žídek
Beatrice G. Beňačková
Diego K. Hanuš
Cayetan J. Horáček
Bohemund M. Švejda
Page N. Šormová

Prague Rad Chor, Prague Nat Th Chor, Prague Nat Th Orch, F. Jílek (r1975) (12/94) (SUPR) ① [2] **11 1492-2**

You are the elder I. Žídek, V. Zítek, J. Horáček, Prague Nat Th Chor, Prague Nat Th Orch, F. Jílek (r1975) (KOCH) ① **34036-2** (KOCH) ▭ **24036-4**

The **Fall of Arkona– opera: prologue (Helga) & 3 acts (Dargun), Opp. 55 and 60 (1900—Prague) (Lib. A Schulzová)**

Overture Prague SO, V. Válek (r1984) (SUPR) ① **11 1823-2**

Šárka– opera: 3 acts, Op. 51 (1897) (Lib. A. Schulzová)

Prince Přemsyl V. Zítek
Ctirad V. Přibyl
Vitoraz J. Klán
Šárka E. Děpoltová
Vlasta E. Randová
Libina J. Janská
Svatava B. Effenberková
Mlada J. Pavlová
Radka A. Barová
Hosta V. Bakalová
Častava D. Suryová

Brno Janáček Op Chor, Brno St PO, J. Štych (10/88) (SUPR) ① [3] **CO-1746/8**

FLOTOW, Friedrich (Adolf Ferdinand) von *(1812–1883)* *Germany*

Alessandro Stradella– opera: 3 acts (1844—Hamburg) (Lib. Riese)

Overture Berlin St Op Orch, A. von Zemlinsky (r1928) (SCHW) ① **310037**

Wie freundlich strahlt...Jungfrau Maria G. Ljungberg, orch, F. Günther (r1934) (EMI) ① [2] **CHS7 64673-2**

Wie freundlich strahlt W. Ludwig, Berlin City Op Orch, W. Ladwig (r1932) (7/95) (PREI) ① **89088**

Martha– opera: 4 acts (1847—Vienna) (Lib. Riese)

ACT 1: 1. Overture; 2. Darf mit nächtig; 3a. Teure Lady!; 3b. Von den edlen Kavalieren (Duet); 4a. Gnaden Tristan Mickleford; 4b. Schöne Lady (Trio); 5. Wohlgemut junges Blut; 6. Mädchen, brav und treu; 7. Wie das schnattert (Duet)...Ja! Seit früher Kindheit Tagen; 8a. Der Markt beginnt; 8b. Sieh nur (Quartet); 9. Hier! Da nehmt die Abstandssumme. ACT 2: 10. Nur näher, schöne Mädchen; 11a. Mädels, dort is eure Kammer; 11b. Was soll ich dazu sagen? (Quartet); 12a. Nancy! Julia!; 12b. Blickt sein Auge (Duet); 12c. Letzte Rose (Ballad); 12d. Martha - Herr!; 12e. Martha, nimme zum frommen Bunde (Duet); 13a. Warte nur!; 13b. Mitternacht! (Notturno); 14. Nancy! Lady! Was nun weiter? (Finale). ACT 3: 15a. Entr'acte; 15b. Lasst mich euch fragen (Porter Song); 16. Jägerin, schlau im Sinn; 17a. Blitz! Die wilde Jagd!; 17b. An dem Frechen; 18a. Darum pflück' ich; 18b. Ach so fromm (M'appari tutt'amor); 19a. Die Herrin rastet dort; 19b. Hier in den stillen Schattengründen; 20. Mag der Himmel (Quintet). ACT 4: 21a. Entr'acte; 21b. Zum treuen Freunde; 21c. Den Teuren zu versöhnen; 22. Der Lenz ist gekommen; 23a. Fasst Euch, Lady!; 23b. Ja! Was Nun? (Duet); 24. Hier die Buden (Finale). ADDITIONAL ITEM FOR ITALIAN VERSION—; 25a. Povero Lionello; 25b. Il mio Lionel.

Harriet L. Popp
Nancy D. Soffel
Lionel S. Jerusalem
Plunkett K. Ridderbusch
Tristram S. Nimsgern
Sherriff P. Lika

Bavarian Rad Chor, Munich RO, H. Wallberg (2/89) (EURO) ① [2] **352 878**

Harriet A. Rothenberger
Nancy B. Fassbaender
Lionel N. Gedda
Plunkett H. Prey
Tristram D. Weller
Sheriff H.G. Knoblich

Bavarian St Op Chor, Bavarian St Orch, R. Heger (5/89) (EMI) ① [2] **CMS7 69339-2**

Exc L. Homer, orch (r1906) (IRCC) ① **IRCC-CD810**

1. Vienna St Op Orch, L. Reichwein (r1938) (SCHW) ① [2] **311162**

7. F. Wunderlich, G. Frick, Berlin SO, B. Klobučar (EMI) ① [3] **CZS7 62993-2**

7. E. Caruso, M. Journet, orch, W.B. Rogers (r1910: Ital) (NIMB) ① **NI7834** (NIMB) ▭ **NC7834**

7. R. Tauber, B. Ziegler, orch (r1923) (PEAR) ① **GEMMCD9145**

7. E. Caruso, M. Journet, orch (Ital: r1910) (3/91) (PEAR) ① [3] **EVC2**

7. E. Caruso, M. Journet, orch, W.B. Rogers (r1910: Ital) (7/91) (RCA) ① [12] **GD60495(3)**

9. L. Pavarotti, National PO, O. de Fabritiis (Ital) (7/90) (DECC) ① [2] **425 681-2DM2** (7/90) (DECC) ▭ [2] **425 681-4DM2**

10, 11a, 11b, 13a F. Alda, J. Jacoby, E. Caruso, M. Journet, orch (Ital: r1912) (3/91) (PEAR) ① [3] **EVC2**

10, 11a, 11b, 13a F. Alda, J. Jacoby, E. Caruso, M. Journet, orch, W.B. Rogers (Ital: r1912) (7/91) (RCA) ① [12] **GD60495(4)**

12b, 12c F. Marconi, B. Mililotti, C. Sabajno (r1907: Ital) (10/90) (SYMP) ① **SYMCD1069**

12c W. Bennett, C. Benson (arr fl/pf) (BRAV) ① **BVA8634** (BRAV) ▭ **BVA8632**

12c L. Garrett, Philh, I. Bolton (Eng) (SILV) ① **SONGCD907** (SILV) ▭ **SONGC907**

12c J. Sutherland, LSO, R. Bonynge (Eng) (DECC) ① **425 048-2DX** (DECC) ▭ **425 048-4DX**

12c C. White, orch (r c1913: Eng) (IRCC) ① **IRCC-CD810**

12c E. Berger, Berlin St Op Orch, L. Blech (r1935) (PREI) ① **89092**

12c M. Favero, orch (r c1929: Ital) (VAI) ① **VAIA1071**

12c M. Favero, orch (r c1929: Ital) (BONG) ① **GB1078-2**

12c F. Saville, anon (r c1902) (10/92) (SYMP) ① **SYMCD1093**

12c L. Price, LSO, E. Downes (Eng) (12/92) (RCA) ① [4] **09026 61236-2**

12c E. Mason, orch (r1924) (8/93) (SYMP) ① **SYMCD1136**

12c A. Galli-Curci, orch, J. Pasternack (r1917: Eng) (3/94) (ROMO) ① [2] **81003-2**

12c A. Galli-Curci, orch, J. Pasternack (r1921: Eng) (8/94) (ROMO) ① [2] **81004-2**

12c E. Mason, orch, F. Black (r1924) (8/94) (ROMO) ① **81009-2**

12c E. Mason, orch, F. Black (r1925) (8/94) (ROMO) ① **81009-2**

12c E. Steber, orch, H. Barlow (bp1946) (11/95) (VAI) ① **VAIA1072**

12c, 18b H. Roswaenge, orch (r1935: Ger) (4/95) (PREI) ① [2] **89209**

13a F. Alda, J. Jacoby, E. Caruso, M. Journet, orch, W.B. Rogers (r1912: Ital) (NIMB) ① **NI7834** (NIMB) ▭ **NC7834**

15b T. Ruffo, orch, J. Pasternack (r1922) (PEAR) ① **GEMMCD9088**

15b M. Journet, orch (r1905: Ital) (PEAR) ① **GEMMCD9122**

15b L. Hofmann, orch, J. Prüwer (r1929) (PREI) ① **89102**

15b A. Kipnis, Berlin St Op Orch, C. Schmalstich (r1930) (12/90) (PREI) ① **89019**

15b P. Plançon, orch (Fr: r1907) (9/91) (PEAR) ① **GEMMCD9497**

15b E. de Reszke, anon (Ital: r1903) (7/92) (PEAR) ① [3] **GEMMCDS9923(1)**

15b T. Ruffo, orch (Ital: r1922) (2/93) (PREI) ① [3] **89303(2)**

15b E. de Reszke, anon (r1903: Ital) (7/93) (NIMB) ① [2] **NI7840/1**

15b A. Didur, orch (r c1918: Ital) (1/94) (CLUB) ① **CL99-089**

15b P. Plançon, orch (r1907: Ital) (12/94) (ROMO) ① [2] **82001-2**

16. D. Soffel, Swedish CO, M. Liljefors (pp1984) (4/93) (CPRI) ① **CAP21428**

18b P. Domingo, Bavarian St Orch, C. Kleiber (DG) ① [3] **427 708-2GX3**

18b J. Björling, Stockholm Royal Op Orch, N. Grevillius (Ital: r1957) (RCA) ▭ **GK85277**

18b L. Pavarotti, New Philh, R. Bonynge (Ital) (7/75) (DECC) ▭ **400 053-4DH**

18b B. Gigli, orch (Ital: r1929) (CONI) ① **CDHD149** (CONI) ▭ **MCHD149**

18b T. Schipa, orch, Anon (cond) (Ital:pp1925) (MEMO) ① [2] **HR4220/1**

18b P. Domingo, LSO, N. Santi (Ital) (RCA) ① [2] **GD60866** (RCA) ▭ [2] **GK60866**

18b P. Domingo, LSO, N. Santi (r1971; Ital) (RCA) ① **09026 61356-2** (RCA) ▭ **09026 61356-4**

18b J. Vickers, Rome Op Orch, T. Serafin (r1961: Ital) (VAI) ① **VAIA1016**

18b B. Gigli, orch (r1929: Ital) (IMP) ① **GLRS102**

18b J. Björling, orch, N. Grevillius (r1939: Ital) (PEAR) ① **GEMMCD9043**

18b J. Schmidt, orch, F. Günther (r1934) (EMI) ① [2] **CHS7 64673-2**

18b L. Pavarotti, New Philh, R. Bonynge (r1973: Ital) (DECC) ① **436 314-2DA** (DECC) ▭ **436 314-4DA**

18b P. Domingo, LSO, N. Santi (Ital) (RCA) ① **09026 61886-2** (RCA) ▭ **09026 61886-4**

18b M. del Monaco, Milan SO, T. Benintende-Neglia (r1952: Ital) (TEST) ① **SBT1039**

18b B. Gigli, orch (r1923: Ital) (ASV) ① **CDAJA5137** (ASV) ▭ **ZCAJA5137**

18b J. Björling, H. Ebert (pp1956: Ital) (BLUE) ① **ABCD057**

18b P. Seiffert, Munich RO, J. Kout (r1992-3) (RCA) ① **09026 61214-2**

18b R. Tauber, orch (r1930) (PEAR) ① **GEMMCD9145**

18b P. Anders, Berlin Deutsche Op Orch, J. Schüler (r1937) (TELD) ① **4509-95512-2**

18b Capitol SO, C. Dragon (r1958: arr Dragon) (EMI) ① **CDM5 65430-2**

18b A. Bonci, orch (r1912: Ital) (PEAR) ① **GEMMCD9168**

18b E. Caruso, orch, J. Pasternack (r1917: Ital) (RCA) ① **09026 62550-2**

18b A. Piccaver, Berlin St Op Orch, M. Gurlitt (r1929: Ital) (PREI) ① [2] **89217**

18b R. Alagna, LPO, R. Armstrong (Ital) (EMI) ① **CDC5 55540-2** (EMI) ▭ **EL5 55540-4**

18b P. Domingo, Los Angeles PO, C.M. Giulini (7/86) (DG) ① **415 366-2GH**

18b J. Björling, orch, N. Grevillius (r1939: Ital) (10/88) (EMI) ① **CDH7 61053-2**

18b T. Schipa, orch (Ital: r1927) (2/89) (PEAR) ① **GEMMCD9322**

18b J. Patzak, Berlin St Op Orch, A. Melichar (r1932) (3/90) (PEAR) ① **GEMMCD9383**

18b J. Schmidt, Berlin St Op Orch, C. Schmalstich (r1929) (4/90) (EMI) ① **CDM7 69478-2**

18b B. Gigli, orch, Rosario Bourdon (Ital: r1923) (5/90) (NIMB) ① **NI7807** (NIMB) ▭ **NC7807**

18b E. Caruso, orch (Ital: r1906)
(7/90) (CLUB) Ⓓ **CL99-060**
18b E. Caruso, orch (Ital: r1906)
(12/90) (PEAR) Ⓓ [3] **EVC1(2)**
18b E. Caruso, orch, J. Pasternack (Ital: r1917)
(7/91) (RCA) Ⓓ [12] **GD60495(6)**
18b E. Caruso, orch (r1906: Ital)
(7/91) (RCA) Ⓓ [12] **GD60495(2)**
18b E. Caruso, orch, J. Pasternack (Ital: r1917)
(10/91) (PEAR) Ⓓ [3] **EVC4(1)**
18b L. Pavarotti, James Levine, B. Large (Ital)
(2/92) (DECC) ◐ **071 119-1DH**
(2/92) (DECC) ▣ **071 119-3DH**
18b R. Tauber, orch (r1930)
(9/92) (MMOI) Ⓓ **CDMOIR409**
18b L. Sobinov, anon (r1904: Russ)
(6/93) (PEAR) Ⓓ [3] **GEMMCDS9997/9(2)**
18b B. Gigli, orch, Rosario Bourdon (Ital: r1929)
(6/93) (MMOI) Ⓓ **CDMOIR417**
18b P. Anders, Berlin St Op Orch, J. Schüler (bp1944) (8/93) (ACAN) Ⓓ **43 268**
18b J. Björling, orch, N. Grevillius (r1939: Ital)
(10/93) (NIMB) Ⓓ **NI7842**
18b E. Caruso, orch (r1917/32: Ital)
(5/94) (CLAR) Ⓓ **CDGSE78-50-52**
18b J. Björling, orch, N. Grevillius (r1939: Ital)
(9/94) (IMP) Ⓓ **GLRC103**
18b J. Björling, orch, N. Grevillius (r1939: Ital)
(9/94) (CONI) Ⓓ **CDHD214**
(9/94) (CONI) ▭ **MCHD214**
18b H. Roswaenge, orch (r1935)
(9/94) (NIMB) Ⓓ **NI7856**
18b A. Pertile, La Scala Orch, C. Sabajno (r1930: Ital) (10/94) (PREI) Ⓓ **89072**
18b E. Caruso, orch (r1906: Ital)
(7/95) (NIMB) Ⓓ **NI7866**
20. H. von Debička, E. Leisner, H. Roswaenge, R. Watzke, orch (r1928)
(2/92) (PREI) Ⓓ [2] **89201**
25a, 25b M. Battistini, orch, C. Sabajno (r1906)
(10/92) (NIMB) Ⓓ **NI7831**
(10/92) (NIMB) ▭ **NC7831**
25a, 25b M. Battistini, orch, C. Sabajno (r1906)
(10/92) (PEAR) Ⓓ **GEMMCD9936**
25b M. Battistini, orch (r1906: Ital)
(2/92) (PREI) Ⓓ **89045**

L' **Ombre– opera (3 acts) (1870—Paris) (Lib. Saint-Georges and de Leuven)**
Quand je monte cocotte; Midi, minuit L. Fugère, orch (r c1929)
(6/93) (SYMP) Ⓓ **SYMCD1125**

FLOYD, Carlisle *(b 1926) USA*

Susannah– music drama: 2 acts (1954—Tallahassee) (Lib. cpsr)

Susannah Polk	C. Studer
Sam Polk	J. Hadley
Olin Blitch	S. Ramey
Little Bat McLean	K. Chester
Elder McLean	M. Druiett
Elder Gleaton	S. Cole
Elder Hayes	S. Kale
Elder Ott	D. Pittsinger
Mrs McLean	A. Howells
Mrs Gleaton	D. Jones
Mrs Hayes	J. Glennon
Mrs Ott	E. Laurence

Lyon Op Chor, Lyon Op Orch, K. Nagano
(10/94) (VIRG) Ⓓ [2] **VCD5 45039-2**
Hear me, O Lord S. Ramey, NY Met Op Orch, J. Conlon (pp1991)
(6/93) (RCA) Ⓓ **09026 61509-2**

FOERSTER, Josef Bohuslav *(1859–1951) Bohemia*

Eva– opera (3 acts) (1899—Prague) (Lib. cpsr, after Pressová)

Eva	E. Děpoltová
Mánek	L.M. Vodička
Mešjanovka	A. Barová
Samko	J. Souček
Zuzka	L. Márová
Rubač	K. Petr

Prague Rad Chor, Prague RSO, F. Vajnar
(5/85) (SUPR) ⊙ [3] **1116 3311/3**

FORTNER, Wolfgang *(1907–1987) Germany*

Die **Bluthochzeit– opera: 2 acts (1957) (Lib. after Lorca)**
Interlude N German RSO, G. Wand (pp1985)
(1/92) (RCA) Ⓓ **RD60827**

FRANCHETTI, (Baron) Alberto *(1860–1942) Italy*

Cristoforo Colombo– opera: 3 acts and epilogue (1892—Genoa) (Lib. L. Illica)
EXCERPTS: 1. Aman lassù le stelle; 2. Dunque ho sognato?.

Cristoforo Colombo	R. Bruson
Don Roldano Ximenes	R. Scandiuzzi
Isabella; Iguamota	R. Ragatzu
Don Fernan Guevara	M. Berti
Anacoana	G. Pasino
Matheos	V. Ombuena
Yanika	A. Ulbrich
Bobadilla	E. Turco
Diaz	P. Lefebvre
Marguerite	F. Previati
Old Man	D. Jenis

Hungarian Rad Chor, Frankfurt RSO, M. Viotti (pp1991)
(7/92) (SCHW) Ⓓ [3] **310302**
1. T. Ruffo, orch (r1914)
(2/93) (PREI) Ⓓ [3] **89303(1)**
2. T. Ruffo, orch (r1921)
(2/93) (PREI) Ⓓ [3] **89303(2)**
3. E. Giraldoni, anon (r1902)
(6/90) (SYMP) Ⓓ **SYMCD1073**

La **figlia di Iorio– opera (1906—Milan) (Lib. after d'Annunzio)**
Che c'è egli? G. Zenatello, E. Giraldoni, anon (r1906) (4/94) (EMI) Ⓓ [3] **CHS7 64860-2(2)**
Che c'è egli?; Rinverdisca per noi G. Zenatello, E. Giraldoni, anon (r1906)
(5/94) (PEAR) Ⓓ [4] **GEMMCDS9073(1)**
Che c'è egli?; Rinverdisca per noi G. Zenatello, E. Giraldoni, anon (r1906)
(5/94) (SYMP) Ⓓ **SYMCD1168**

Germania– opera: prologue, 2 scenes and epilogue (1902—Milan) (Lib. Illica)
EXCERPTS: PROLOGUE: 1. Studenti udite.
ACT 1: 2. Non, non chiuder gli occhi vaghi.
Ferito prigionier G. De Luca, anon (r1907)
(PEAR) Ⓓ [3] **GEMMCDS9159(2)**
1. E. Caruso, orch (r1910)
(RCA) Ⓓ **09026 61243-2**
1. M. Gilion, orch (r c1909)
(BONG) Ⓓ **GB1076-2**
1, 2. E. Caruso, S. Cottone (r1902)
(5/89) (EMI) Ⓓ **CDH7 61046-2**
1, 2. E. Caruso, S. Cottone (r1902)
(12/90) (PEAR) Ⓓ [3] **EVC1(1)**
1, 2. E. Caruso, orch (r1910)
(3/91) (PEAR) Ⓓ [3] **EVC2**
1, 2. E. Caruso, orch (r1910)
(7/91) (RCA) Ⓓ [12] **GD60495(3)**
1, 2. E. Caruso, S. Cottone (r1902)
(7/91) (RCA) Ⓓ [12] **GD60495(1)**
1, 2. G. Zenatello, orch (r1910)
(5/94) (SYMP) Ⓓ **SYMCD1168**
1, 2. G. Zenatello, orch (r1910)
(5/94) (PEAR) Ⓓ [4] **GEMMCDS9073(2)**
2. E. Caruso, anon (r1903)
(12/90) (PEAR) Ⓓ [3] **EVC1(1)**
2. E. Caruso, anon (r1903)
(7/91) (RCA) Ⓓ [12] **GD60495(1)**
2. E. Caruso, S. Cottone (r1902)
(4/94) (EMI) Ⓓ [3] **CHS7 64860-2(2)**
3. A. Pinto, S. Cottone (r1902)
(4/94) (EMI) Ⓓ [3] **CHS7 64860-2(2)**
4. P. Amato, orch (r1913) (PREI) Ⓓ **89064**
4. M. Sammarco, anon (r1902)
(7/92) (PEAR) Ⓓ [3] **GEMMCDS9924(2)**
4. M. Sammarco, anon (r1902)
(4/94) (EMI) Ⓓ [3] **CHS7 64860-2(2)**
5. A. Pinto, anon (r1902)
(8/93) (SYMP) Ⓓ **SYMCD1111**

FRANCK, César (-Auguste-Jean-Guillaume-Hubert) *(1822–1890) Belgium/France*

Hulda– opera: 4 acts and epilogue (1894—Monte Carlo) (Lib. C. Grandmougin, after Bjørson)
Entr'acte pastorale; Chanson de l'hermine; Marche Royale; Ballet du Printemps D. Blumenthal, J. Bogart (r1991; arr pf duet/2 pfs)
(SCHW) Ⓓ **313772**

FREDERICK II, King of Prussia *(1712–1786) Germany*

known as Frederick the Great

Il **Ré pastore– serenata (1747—Berlin)**
Sulle più belle piante J. Kowalski, Berlin CO, M. Pommer (9/88) (CAPR) Ⓓ **10 113**
(9/88) (CAPR) ▭ **CC27 127**

FRIED, Grigori *(b 1915) Russia*

The **Diary of Anne Frank– opera-monodrama: 4 scenes (1972—Moscow) (Lib. cpsr based on Diary)**
Cpte E. Ben-Zvi, Bolshoi Th Orch, A. Chistiakov
(CDM) Ⓓ **LDC288 045**

FRIML, (Charles) Rudolf *(1879–1972) Czechoslovakia/USA*

The **Firefly– operetta (1912—New York) (Lib. Harbach)**
EXCERPTS: 1. The Donkey Serenade; 2. A Woman's Smile.
1. M. Lanza, orch, R. Sinatra (r1952)
(IMP) Ⓓ **PWKS4230**
1. M. Lanza, orch, R. Sinatra (r1952)
(RCA) Ⓓ **09026 61420-2**
(RCA) ▭ **09026 61420-4**
1. M. Lanza, J. Alexander Ch, orch, H. René (r1956) (RCA) Ⓓ **74321 18574-2**
(RCA) ▭ **74321 18574-4**
1. J. Hadley, American Th Orch, P. Gemignani (r1993; orch W. D. Brohn)
(RCA) Ⓓ **09026 62681-2**
2. C. Campbell, Orig Broadway Cast (r1913)
(5/94) (PEAR) Ⓓ [3] **GEMMCDS9053/5**

Rose Marie– operetta (1924—New York) (Lib. Hammerstein and Harbach)
EXCERPTS: 1. Indian Love Call; 2. Rose Marie.
1. J. Sutherland, Ambrosian Light Op Chor, New Philh, R. Bonynge (arr Gamley)
(DECC) Ⓓ **433 223-2DWO**
(DECC) ▭ **433 223-4DWO**
1. J. Sutherland, Ambrosian Light Op Chor, New Philh, R. Bonynge (arr Gamley)
(DECC) Ⓓ **425 048-2DX**
(DECC) ▭ **425 048-4DX**
1. F. Kreisler, C. Lamson (r1926: arr Kreisler)
(12/93) (BIDD) Ⓓ **LAB075**
1. V. Masterson, T. Allen, Philh, J.O. Edwards (r1990) (5/94) (TER) Ⓓ **CDVIR8317**
(5/94) (TER) ▭ **ZCVIR8317**
1. B. Hendricks, G. Quilico, Lyon Op Orch, L. Foster (r1993) (6/95) (EMI) Ⓓ **CDC5 55151-2**
2. A. Baugé, orch (r1930s: French)
(FORL) Ⓓ **UCD19022**
2. A. Baugé, orch, G. Andolfi (French)
(EMI) Ⓓ [2] **CZS5 68292-2**

The **Three Musketeers– operetta (1928—New York) (Lib. McGuire and others after A. Dumas)**
March of the Musketeers L. Warren (bp1953)
(VAI) ▣ **VAI69105**

The **Vagabond King– operetta (1925—New York) (Lib. Hooker & Post, after E M Royle)**
EXCERPTS: 1. Overture; 2. Some day; 3. The Vagabond King Waltz; 4. The Scotch Archer's Song; 5. Only a rose; 6. Love me tonight; 7. Drinking Song; 8. This same heart; 9. Song of the Vagabonds; 10. Tomorrow; 11. Nocturne; 12. Finale.
2, 5-7, 9-12. M. Lanza, J. Raskin, Chor, Orch, C. Callinicos (r1959) (RCA) Ⓓ **09026 68130-2**
5. J. Gimpel, M. Lanza, orch, C. Callinicos (r1959) (RCA) Ⓓ **RD86218**
5. M. Lanza, J. Alexander Ch, orch, H. René
(RCA) Ⓓ **GD60720**
(RCA) ▭ **GK60720**
5. R. Crooks, orch (r1930)
(PEAR) Ⓓ **GEMMCD9093**
5. J. Björling, Stockholm Royal Op Orch, N. Grevillius (r1937)
(12/94) (MMOI) Ⓓ **CDMOIR425**
9. J. Hadley, Harvard Glee Club, American Th Orch, P. Gemignani (r1993; orch W. D. Brohn)
(RCA) Ⓓ **09026 62681-2**

FUX, Johann Joseph *(1660–1741) Austria*

Dafne in Lauro– chamber opera (1714—Vienna) (Lib. Pariati)

Diana M. van der Sluis
Dafne L. Åkerlund
Apollo G. Lesne
Amore S. Piccollo
Mercurio M. Klietmann
Cappella Voc Ens, Clemencic Consort, R. Clemenčić (pp1990)
(NUOV) ① [2] **6930/1**

GANNE, (Gustave) Louis *(1862–1923) France*

Hans, le Jouer de Flûte– operetta: 3 acts (1906—Monte Carlo) (Lib. M. Vaucaire & G. Mitchell)

Hans M. Dens
Lisbeth N. Broissin
Yoris J. Peyron
Pippermann A. Balbon
Ketchen G. Parat
Guillaume R. Lenoty
Mme Pippermann M. Sansonnetti
Van Pott G. Rey
Tantendorff Génio
Loskitch P. Roi
Steinbeck M. Enot
Karteifle R. Liot
Marchande de plaisir J. Levasseur
Nightwatchman J. Mollien
Sergeant A. Caurat
Newspaper seller M. Rossignol
French Rad Chor, French Rad Lyric Orch, J. Gressier (bp1957)
(3/92) (MUSD) ① [2] **20151-2**

Les **Saltimbanques– opéra-comique (3 acts) (1899—Paris) (Lib. M. Ordonneau)**

C'est l'amour F. Révoil, orch, M. Cariven
(EMI) ① [2] **CZS5 68292-2**
C'est l'amour M. Hill Smith, P. Morrison, Chandos Sngrs, Chandos Concert Orch, S. Barry (Eng) (2/90) (CHAN) ① **CHAN8759**
(2/90) (CHAN) ▭ **LBTD023**
Excs J. Micheau, R. Massard, G. Moizan, R. Amade, M. Roux, chor, orch, P. Dervaux (bp1958) (3/92) (MUSD) ① [2] **20151-2**

GARCÍA, Manuel *(1775–1832) Spain*

Il **Califfo di Bagdad– opera (2 acts) (1813—Naples) (Lib. Tottola)**

Ogni piacere è grato M. Moreno, K. John, Philh, D. Parry (10/90) (OPRA) ① [3] **ORCH103**

GAY, John *(1685–1732) England*

The Beggar's Opera (1728—London) (Lib. cpsr: composed in association with Pepusch)

EXCERPTS: 1. Overture. ACT 1: 2. Through all the employments of life; 3. 'Tis woman that seduces all mankind; 4. If any wench Venus' girdle wear; 5. If love the virgin's heart invade; 6. A maiden is like the golden ore; 7. Virgins are like the fair flower in its lustre; 8. Our Polly is a sad slut!; 9. Can love be control'd by advice?; 10. O Polly, you might have toy'd and kissed; 11. I like a ship in storms was tossed; 12. A fox may steal your hens, sir; 13. Oh, ponder well!; 14. The turtle thus with plaintive crying; 15. Pretty Polly say; 16. My heart was so free; 17. When I laid on Greenland's coast; 18. O what pain it is to part!; 19. The miser thus a shilling sees. ACT 2: 20. Fill ev'ry glass, for wine inspires us; 21. Let us take the road; 22. If the heart of a man is deprest; 23. Youth's the season made for joys; 24. Before the barn door crowing; 25. The gamesters and lawyers are jugglers alike; 26. At the Tree I shall suffer with pleasure; 27. Man may escape from rope and gun; 28. Thus when a good huswife sees a rat; 29. How cruel are the traitors; 30. The first time at the looking-glass; 31. When you censure the age; 32. Is then his fate decreed, sir?; 33. You'll think e'er many ways ensure; 34. If you at an office solicit your due; 35. This when the swallow seeking prey; 36. How happy could I be with either; 37. I'm bubbled; 38. Cease your fuming; 39. Why how now, Madame Flirt?; 40. No power on earth can e'er divide; 41. I like the fox shall grieve. ACT 3: 42. When young at the bar; 43. My love is all madness and folly; 44. Thus gamesters united in friendship are found; 45. The modes of court so common are grown; 46. What gudgeons are we men!; 47. In the days of my youth; 48. I'm like a skiff on the ocean tossed; 49. When a wife's in her pout; 50. A curse attends that woman's love; 51. Among the men, coquets we find; 52. Come, sweet lass; 53. Hither, dear husband; 54. Which way shall I turn me?; 55. When my hero in court appears; 56. When he holds up his hand; 57. Ourselves, like the great; 58. The charge is prepar'd; 59. O cruel, cruel, cruel case!; 60. Of all the friends in time of grief; 61. Since I must swing; 62. But now again my spirits sink; 63. But valour the stronger grows; 64. If thus a man must die; 65. So I drink off this bumper; 66. But can I leave my pretty hussies; 67. Their eyes, their lips, their busses; 68. Since laws were made for ev'ry degree; 69. Would I might be hung'd; 70. Thus I stand like a Turk.

Polly C. Hall
Macheath R. Daltrey
Lucy R. Ashe
Lockit P. Bayliss
Peachum S. Johns
Mrs Peachum P. Routledge
Mrs Trapes G. Brown
Filch G. Tibbs
Matt A. Pedley
Jenny Diver I. Blair
Dolly Trull E. Sharling
Jemmy Twitcher K. Stott
Beggar B. Hoskins
Player G. Crowden
EBS, J.E. Gardiner, J. Miller
(PHIL) ◖ [2] **070 408-1PHE2**

Polly E. Morison
Polly Z. Walker
Macheath J. Cameron
Macheath J. Neville
Lucy M. Sinclair
Lucy R. Roberts
Lockit I. Wallace
Lockit E. Porter
Peachum O. Brannigan
Peachum P. Rogers
Mrs Peachum; Mrs Trapes C. Shacklock
Mrs Peachum; Mrs Trapes D. Heard
Filch A. Young
Filch R. Hardy
Jenny Diver A. Pollak
Jenny Diver J. Jacobs
Pro Arte Chor, PAO, M. Sargent (r1955: arr Austin/Pepusch)
(CFP) ① [2] **CD-CFPSD4778**

Polly K. Te Kanawa
Macheath J. Morris
Lucy J. Sutherland
Lockit S. Dean
Peachum A. Marks
Mrs Peachum A. Lansbury
Mrs Trapes R. Resnik
Filch A. Rolfe Johnson
Matt G. Clark
Jenny Diver A. Murray
Dolly Trull A. Wilkens
Jemmy Twitcher J. Gibbs
Beggar W. Mitchell
Player M. Hordern
London Voices, National PO, R. Bonynge (arr Bonynge/Gamley)
(5/91) (DECC) ① [2] **430 066-2DH2**

Polly B. Mills
Macheath Adrian Thompson
Lucy Anne Dawson
Lockit R. Jackson
Peachum C. Daniels
Mrs. Peachum Sarah Walker
Mrs Trapes Sarah Walker
Filch I. Honeyman
Matt R. Bryson
Jenny Diver C. Wyn-Rogers
Beggar B. Hoskins
Player I. Caddy
Broadside Band, J. Barlow
(1/92) (HYPE) ① [2] **CDA66591/2**

Polly A. Murray
Macheath P. Langridge
Lucy Y. Kenny
Lockit J. Rawnsley
Peachum R. Lloyd
Mrs Peachum A. Collins
Mrs Trapes N. Willis
Filch C. Gillett
Beggar D. Mulholland
Aldeburgh Fest Ch, Aldeburgh Fest Orch, S. Bedford (ed/arr Britten)
(9/93) (ARGO) ① [2] **436 850-2ZHO2**

Polly J. Waters
Macheath P. Gilmore
Lucy F. Cuka
Lockit J. Carter
Peachum J. Cossins
Mrs Peachum; Mrs Trapes H. Hazell
Filch P. Kenton
Matt D. Calder
Jenny Diver A. Richards
Beggar R. Durden
London Cast, N. Rhoden (r1968; ed Turner, orch Pearce-Higgins; without dialogue)
(10/94) (SONY) ① **SMK66171**

7, 38. K. Te Kanawa, National PO, R. Bonynge
(11/87) (DECC) ① **417 645-2DH**

10, 16, 17. C. Willis, A. Mildmay, Roy Henderson, M. Redgrave, orch, M. Mudie (r1940) (6/94) (EMI) ① **CDH5 65072-2**

45. Broadside Band (Tune: Lilliburlero)
(3/88) (AMON) ① **CD-SAR28**
(AMON) ▭ **CSAR28**

GAZTAMBIDE, Joaquín *(1822–1870) Spain*

Una **Vieja– zarzuela: 1 act (1860—Madrid) (Lib. D. F. Camprodon)**

Un español que vien A. Cortis, orch (r1925)
(3/94) (NIMB) ① **NI7850**

GAZZANIGA, Giuseppe *(1743–1818) Italy*

Don Giovanni Tenorio o sia Il convitato di pietra– opera: 1 act (1787—Venice) (Lib. Bertati)

Don Giovanni J. Aler
Donna Anna E. Steinsky
Donna Elvira P. Coburn
Donna Ximena M. Kinzel
Commendatore G. von Kannen
Duca Ottavio R. Swensen
Maturina J. Kaufman
Pasquariello J-L. Chaignaud
Biagio A. Scharinger
Lanterna A. Rosner
Bavarian Rad Chor, Munich RO, S. Soltesz
(4/91) (ORFE) ① [2] **C214902H**

Don Giovanni D. Johnson
Donna Anna E. Szmytka
Donna Elvira L. Serra
Donna Ximena E. Schmid
Commendatore J. Tilli
Duca Ottavio C. Allemano
Maturina E. Szmytka
Pasquariello F. Furlanetto
Biagio A. Scharinger
Lanterna H. Wildhaber
Stuttgart Chbr Ch, Tafelmusik, B. Weil (omits recits)
(1/92) (SONY) ① **SK46693**

GENERALI, Pietro *(1773–1832) Italy*

Adelina– opera (1 act), Lib. Rossi (1810—Venice)

Giusto cielo! correte, andate M. Hill Smith, P. Guy-Bromley, R. Smythe, Philh, D. Parry
(10/90) (OPRA) ① [3] **ORCH103**

GERMAN, Sir Edward *(1862–1936) England*

Merrie England– operetta: 2 acts (1902—London) (Lib. B. Hood)

EXCERPTS: 1. Overture. ACT 1: 2. Opening chorus; 3. Oh! where the deer do lie; 5. I do counsel that your playtime; 6. That every Jack should have a Jill; 7. Love is meant to make us glad; 8. She had a letter from her love; 9. When true love hath found a man; 10. When a man is a lover; 11. The Yeomen of England; 12a. Entrance of Queen Elizabeth...God save Elizabeth; 12b. O peaceful England; 13. King Neptune sat on his lonely throne; 14. Finale. ACT 2: 15. The month of May has come today; 16. In England, Merrie England; 17. The big brass band; 18. It is the merry month of May;

19a. The Queen of May is crowned today; 19b. Rustic dance; 20. Dan Cupid hath a garden (The English Rose); 21. Two merry men a-drinking; 22. Who shall say that love is cruel?; 23. When Cupid first this old world trod; 24. Oh! here's a to-do to die today; 25. Finale.

Queen Elizabeth M. Sinclair
Sir Walter Raleigh W. McAlpine
Earl of Essex P. Glossop
Bessie Throckmorton J. Bronhill
Jill-All-Alone P. Kern
Walter Wilkins H. Glynne

Rita Williams Sngrs, M. Collins Orch, M. Collins (r c1959)
(CFP) ⓓ [2] **CD-CFPSD4796**

11. P. Morrison, Ambrosian Sngrs, Chandos Concert Orch, S. Barry
(7/88) (CHAN) ⓓ **CHAN8561**
(7/88) (CHAN) ⊟ **LBTD019**

20. Webster Booth, orch, C. Greenwood (r1939)
(PEAR) ⓓ **GEMMCD9024**

20. R. Tauber, orch (r1938)
(2/92) (LYRC) ⓓ [2] **SRO830**

20. J. Johnston, Philh, J. Robertson (r1950)
(4/95) (TEST) ⓓ **SBT1058**

22. M. Hill Smith, Southern Fest Orch, R. White
(5/93) (CHAN) ⓓ **CHAN9110**
(5/93) (CHAN) ⊟ **LBTD031**

Tom Jones– comic opera: 3 acts (1907—Manchester) (Lib. Courtneidge, Thomson & Taylor, after Fielding)

EXCERPTS—ACT 1: 1. Dont' you find the weather charming?; 2. On a January night in Zummersetsheer; 3. West Country lad; 4. Today my spinet; 5. Wisdon says 'Festina lente'; 6. The Barley Mow; 7. Here's a paradox for lovers; 8. For Aye, My Love. ACT 2: 9. Hurry, Bustle!; 10. A Person of Parts; 11. Dream o'Day Jill; 12. Gurt Uncle Jan Tappit; 13. My Lady's coach has been attacked; 14. As all the Maises; 15. You have a pretty wit; 16. A soldier's scarlet coat; 17. Hey Dewy Down; 18. Where be my daughter?; 19. Love maketh a garden fair. ACT 3: 20a. Morris Dance; 20b. Gavotte; 20c. Jig; 21. The Green Ribbon; 22. If lov'es content; 23a. Which is my own truw self; 23b. For tonight (Waltz Song); 24. Wise Old Saws; 25. Hark! the merry marriage bells. ADDITIONAL ITEM: 26. We Redcoat Soldiers serve the King.

4, 5, 8, 9, 21, 23b, 26. New SO, M. Sargent (r1932: arr orch) (PEAR) ⓓ **GEMMCD9024**

23b J. Sutherland, New Philh, R. Bonynge
(DECC) ⓓ **433 223-2DWO**
(DECC) ⊟ **433 223-4DWO**

23b J. Sutherland, Ambrosian Light Op Chor, New Philh, R. Bonynge
(DECC) ⓓ **425 048-2DX**
(DECC) ⊟ **425 048-4DX**

23b Bratislava RSO, A. Leaper (r1991; arr Tomlinson) (6/93) (MARC) ⓓ **8 223419**

GERSHWIN, George
(1898–1937) USA

Blue Monday Blues– opera: 1 act (1925—New York) (Lib. De Sylva)

Vi A. Burton
Joe G. Hopkins
Tom; Sweet Pea W. Sharp
Sam A. Woodley
Mike J.J. Offenbach

Concordia, M. Alsop (r1992/3)
(1/94) (EMI) ⓓ **CDC7 54851-2**

Has anyone seen Joe? B. Hendricks, K. Labèque, M. Labèque (arr. Jeanneau)
(1/87) (PHIL) ⓓ **416 460-2PH**

Porgy and Bess– opera: 3 acts (1935—Boston) (Lib. Heyward and I. Gershwin)

EXCERPTS: ACT ONE: 1. Introduction...Jasbo Brown Blues; 2. Summertime; 3. A woman is a sometime thing; 4. Here come de honey man; 5. Don't you ever let a woman; 6. Oh, little stars; 7. Wake up an' hit it out; 8. Gone, gone, gone; 9. Overflow; 10. Um! A saucer-burial; 11. My man's gone now; 12. Headin' for the Promis' Lan'. ACT 2: 13. It takes a long pull; 14. I got plenty o' nuttin'; 15. I hates yo' struttin' style; 16. Buzzard Song; 17. Bess, you is my woman now; 18. Oh, I can't sit down; 19. I ain' got no shame; 20. It ain't necessarily so; 21. What you want wid Bess?; 22. Honey, dat's all de breakfast; 23. Oh, doctor Jesus; 24. Oh dey's so fresh an' fine; 25a. Now de time; 25b. Porgy, dat you there; 26. I loves you, Porgy; 27. Why you been out on that wharf; 28. Oh, Doctor Jesus; 29. Oh, de Lawd shake de Heavens; 30. Oh, dere's somebody; 31. A red-headed woman. ACT 3: 32. Clara, don't you be downhearted; 33. Interlude; 34a. Introduction; 34b. Wait for us at the corner, Al; 35. You've got to go, Porgy; 36. There's a boat dat's leavin'; 37a. Introduction; 37b. Good mornin', sistuh!; 38. Dem white folks; 39. Oh, Bess; 40. Bess is gone; 41. Oh Lawd, I'm on my way.

Porgy W. White
Bess C. Haymon
Clara H. Blackwell
Serena C. Clarey
Sportin' Life D. Evans
Maria M. Simpson
Crown Gregg Baker
Jake B. Hubbard
Mingo B. Coleman
Robbins J. Worthy
Jim Curtis Watson
Peter M. Wallace
Lily M. Brathwaite
Undertaker A. Paige
Frazier W. Johnson
Annie P. Ingram
Scipio L. Thompson
Nelson; Crab Man Colenton Freeman
Strawberry Woman C. Johnson
Detective A. Tilvern
Coroner B.J. Mitchell
Mr Archdale T. Maynard
Policeman R. Travis
Jasbo Brown W. Marshall

Glyndebourne Fest Chor, LPO, S. Rattle, T. Nunn (r1988)
(EMI) ◖ [2] **LDB49 1131-4**
(EMI) ▭ [2] **MVD49 1131-3**

Porgy W. White
Bess L. Mitchell
Clara B. Hendricks
Serena F. Quivar
Sportin' Life F. Clemmons
Maria; Strawberry Woman B. Conrad
Crown M. Boatwright
Jake Arthur Thompson
Mingo; Undertaker J.V. Pickens
Robbins; Crab Man S. Hagan
Peter; Nelson William Brown
Frazier; Jim C. Deane
Annie A. Ford
Lily I. Jones
Mr Archdale J. Buck
Detective R. Snook
Policeman R. Nealley
Coroner A. Leatherman
Scipio D. Zucca
Jasbo Brown J. Jones

Cleveland Orch Children's Chor, Cleveland Orch Chor, Cleveland Orch, L. Maazel
(2/86) (DECC) ⓓ [3] **414 559-2DH3**

Porgy D.R. Albert
Bess C. Dale
Clara B. Lane
Serena W. Shakesnider
Sportin' Life L. Marshall
Maria C. Brice
Crown Andrew Smith
Jake A.B. Smalls

Houston Grand Op Chor, Houston Grand Op Orch, J. DeMain
(9/86) (RCA) ⓓ [3] **RD82109**

Porgy W. White
Bess C. Haymon
Clara H. Blackwell
Serena C. Clarey
Sportin' Life D. Evans
Maria M. Simpson
Crown Gregg Baker
Jake B. Hubbard
Mingo B. Coleman
Robbins J. Worthy
Jim Curtis Watson
Peter M. Wallace
Lily M. Brathwaite
Undertaker A. Paige
Frazier W. Johnson
Annie P. Ingram
Scipio L. Thompson
Nelson; Crab Man Colenton Freeman
Strawberry Woman C. Johnson
Detective A. Tilvern
Coroner B.J. Mitchell
Mr Archdale T. Maynard
Policeman R. Travis
Jasbo Brown W. Marshall

Glyndebourne Fest Chor, LPO, S. Rattle (r1988)
(6/89) (EMI) ⓓ [3] **CDS7 49568-2**

orch, F. Chacksfield (r1973: arr R Shaw)
(DECC) ⓓ **443 389-2DWO**
(DECC) ⊟ **443 389-4DWO**

Excs Munich Brass (arr brass ens)
(ORFE) ⓓ **C247911A**

Excs Stuttgart RSO, N. Marriner (pp1985)
(CAPR) ⓓ **10 466**

Fantasy E. Wild (trans Wild)
(10/90) (CHES) ⓓ **Chesky CD32**

1. C. Barbaosa-Lima, S. Isbin (arr 2 gtrs)
(CCOR) ⓓ **CCD42012**
(CCOR) ⊟ **CC2012**

1, 2, 11, 14, 17, 20, 36, 41. HR-Brass, J. Whigham (r1991; arr Honetschläger)
(CAPR) ⓓ **10 429**

1, 2, 3, 8, 11, 14, 17, 20, 21, 26, 36, 39, 41. L. Price, B. Webb, B. Hall, M. Stewart, M. Burton, J.W. Bubbles, R. Henson, W. Warfield, M. Boatwright, Alonzo Jones, RCA Victor Chor, RCA Victor Orch, S. Henderson (r1963)
(RCA) ⓓ **74321 24218-2**

1, 2, 3, 9, 11, 12, 14, 17, 18, 20, 36, 41. R. Alexander, Gregg Baker, NY Choral Artists, NYPO, Z. Mehta (r1990)
(TELD) ⓓ **4509-97444-2**

1-3, 11, 12, 14-18, 20, 21, 31, 36, 38-41. W. White, C. Haymon, D. Evans, C. Clarey, H. Blackwell, B. Hubbard, M. Simpson, Gregg Baker, B. Coleman, J. Worthy, M. Wallace, M. Brathwaite, A. Paige, P. Ingram, W. Marshall, Glyndebourne Fest Chor, LPO, S. Rattle
(EMI) ⓓ **CDC7 54325-2**
(EMI) ⊟ **EL754325-4**

1-3, 8, 11, 12, 14, 17, 18, 20, 36, 41. D. Newman, A. Woodley, Oklahoma City Ambassadors Ch, Minería SO, H. de la Fuente, New Philh (IMP) ⓓ **PCD1057**

1-3, 8, 14, 17, 20, 21, 26, 36, 39, 41. L. Price, W. Warfield, J.W. Bubbles, R. Henson, B. Webb, M. Burton, Alonzo Jones, B. Hall, RCA Victor Chor, RCA Victor Orch, S. Henderson (r1963)
(4/89) (RCA) ⓓ **GD85234**
(4/89) (RCA) ⊟ **GK85234**

1-3, 8, 9, 11, 12, 14, 17, 18, 20, 21, 36, 39, 41. D.R. Albert, C. Dale, Andrew Smith, W. Shakesnider, B. Lane, C. Brice, A.B. Smalls, L. Marshall, Houston Grand Op. Chor, Houston Grand Op Orch, J. DeMain
(2/86) (RCA) ⓓ **RD84680**

2. K. Battle, W. Jones, H. Burton (pp1991)
(DG) ▭ **072 189-3GH**

2. E. Steber, Orch, Anon (cond) (bp1954)
(VAI) ▭ **VAI69112**

2. O. Harnoy, C. Wilson (arr vc/pf)
(RCA) ⓓ **RD60697**

2. Vanessa-Mae, New Belgian CO, N. Cleobury (r1991; arr Heifetz: vn & orch)
(TRIT) ⓓ **TCvan27102**
(TRIT) ⊟ **TCvan45-27102**

2. J. Anderson, S. Wynberg (trans cor ang/gtr: Anderson/Wynberg) (CHAN) ⓓ **CHAN6581**

2. L. Garrett, Philh, I. Bolton
(SILV) ⓓ **SONGCD907**
(SILV) ⊟ **SONGC907**

2. L. Price, orch (r1960)
(DECC) ⓓ **440 402-2DM**

2. X. Wei, Pam Nicholson
(ASV) ⓓ **CDQS6114**

2. ASMF Chbr Ens (r1993: arr M Latchem)
(CHAN) ⓓ **CHAN9216**

2. D. Newman, Minería SO, H. de la Fuente (r1993)
(IMP) ⓓ **PCDS26**
(IMP) ⊟ **PCDSC26**

2. K. Te Kanawa, NY Choral Artists, New Princess Th Orch, J. McGlinn (r1986)
(EMI) ⓓ **CDC5 55095-2**

2. R. Alexander, NYPO, Z. Mehta
(TELD) ⓓ **4509-96231-2**
(TELD) ⊟ **4509-96231-4**

2. K. Te Kanawa, NY Choral Artists, New Princess Th Orch, J. McGlinn
(10/87) (EMI) ⓓ **CDC7 47454-2**

2. C. Berberian, B. Canino
(7/89) (WERG) ⓓ **WER60054-50**

2. K. Battle, M. Garrett (pp1991)
(7/92) (DG) ⓓ **435 440-2GH**

2. Thurston Cl Qt (arr cl qt: Bland)
(10/93) (ASV) ⓓ **CDWHL2076**
(10/93) (ASV) ⊟ **ZCWHL2076**

2. LPO, RPO, Philh (r1994; arr Milone)
(9/95) (CALA) ◑ **CACD0105**

2, 11, 17(pt) M. McGovern, Jazz Ens
(SONY) Ⓘ **SK44995**
2, 14, 17, 20, 26. Budapest Stgs (arr anon)
(11/90) (LASE) Ⓘ **15 606**
(11/90) (LASE) ⊟ **79 606**
2, 17. Brodsky Qt (arr M. Thomas)
(4/92) (TELD) Ⓘ **2292-46015-2**
2, 17, 20. E. Rousseau, H. Graf (trans Rousseau: sax/pno) (DELO) Ⓘ **DE1007**
2, 17, 20. X. Wei, Pam Nicholson (arr Heifetz)
(9/90) (ASV) Ⓘ **CDDCA698**
2, 26. K. Battle, St Luke's Orch, A. Previn (r1992) (DG) Ⓘ **437 787-2GH**
2, 26. B. Hendricks, K. Labèque, M. Labèque (arr. Jeanneau) (1/87) (PHIL) Ⓘ **416 460-2PH**
2, 26, 36. M. Marshall, W. Marshall
(MEL) Ⓘ **MELCD022-2**
2, 3, 11, 14, 17, 20, 26, 36. G. Rabol (r1992; arr Rabol: pf) (O111) Ⓘ **OPS30-64**
2, 3, 11, 17, 20, 36. J. Heifetz, E. Bay (r1945)
(11/94) (RCA) Ⓘ [65] **09026 61778-2(19)**
2, 3, 11, 17, 20, 36. J. Heifetz, B. Smith (r1965)
(11/94) (RCA) Ⓘ [65] **09026 61778-2(40)**
2, 3, 20. S. Whang, K. Hashimoto (arr Heifetz: vn/pf) (INTU) Ⓘ **INT3113-2**
3, 14, 20, 36. E.B. Holmes, S. Katz
(SCHW) Ⓘ **312642**
11. Daniel Smith, J. Still, Caravaggio Ens (arr bn/pf; r1993) (ASV) Ⓘ **CDWHL2078**
(ASV) ⊟ **ZCWHL2078**
12. D. Woods, Collegiate Chorale, NY Met Op Orch, J. Conlon (pp1991)
(6/93) (RCA) Ⓘ **09026 61509-2**
12, 29. J. Kaye, W. Sharp, S. Blier
(7/91) (KOCH) Ⓘ **37028-2**
14. S. Ramey, London Studio SO, E. Stratta (r1993) (TELD) Ⓘ **4509-90865-2**
14, 17, 22, 27, 32, 37b, 41. J. Gibbons (r1992-3; trans Gibbons: pf) (ASV) Ⓘ [3] **CDWLS328**
14, 17, 22, 27, 32, 37b, 41. J. Gibbons (r1992-3; trans Gibbons: pf)
(3/95) (ASV) Ⓘ **CDWHL2082**
(3/95) (ASV) ⊟ **ZCWHL2082**
14, 39. L. Tibbett, Orch, A. Smallens (r1935)
(3/90) (RCA) Ⓘ **GD87808**
17. X. Wei, Pam Nicholson (arr vn/pf: Heifetz)
(ASV) Ⓘ **CDQS6126**
17. G. Groves, J. Watson, J. Partridge (r1994)
(ASV) Ⓘ **CDWHL2088**
17. L. Price, W. Warfield, RCA Victor SO, S. Henderson (RCA) Ⓘ **09026 62699-2**
(RCA) ⊟ **09026 62699-4**
17. J. Lloyd Webber, RPO, N. Cleobury (arr vc)
(3/87) (PHIL) Ⓘ **416 698-2PH**
17. E. Parkin (arr Parkin)
(10/89) (CLOU) Ⓘ **ACN6002**
17. I. Stern, Columbia SO, M. Katims (arr Harris)
(7/90) (SONY) Ⓘ **SK45816**
17. R. Stoltzman, LSO, E. Stern (r1993; arr Silverman) (12/93) (RCA) Ⓘ **09026 61790-2**
17. W. White, C. Haymon, LPO, S. Rattle (r1988)
(6/94) (EMI) Ⓘ **CDH5 65072-2**
17, 20. O. Harnoy, H. Bowkun (arr Heifetz)
(MSOU) Ⓘ **DFCDI-012**
20. J. Heifetz, B. Smith (r1970; arr Heifetz)
(7/95) (RCA) ▣ **09026 62706-3**
20. V. Spivakov, S. Bezrodny (arr Heifetz)
(RCA) Ⓘ **RD60861**
20. S. Chang, S. Rivers (trans Heifetz)
(1/93) (EMI) Ⓘ **CDC7 54352-2**
20. J. Heifetz, B. Smith (r1970)
(11/94) (RCA) Ⓘ [65] **09026 61778-2(35)**
20. A. A. Meyers, S. Rivers (r1993; trans Heifetz: vn/pf) (4/95) (RCA) Ⓘ **09026 62546-2**
20. ASMF, BBC SO, LPO, ENO Orch, G. Simon (r1995; arr va: J. Milone)
(9/95) (CALA) ◑ **CACD0106**

Porgy and Bess– concert suite from opera
A. Paratore, J. Paratore (arr Grainger)
(SCHW) Ⓘ **310115**
Hollywood Bowl SO, L. Slatkin
(EMIN) Ⓘ **CD-EMX2175**
M. Turkovic, Stuttgart CO, M. Sieghart
(ORFE) Ⓘ **C223911A**
Hamilton PO, B. Brott (CBC) Ⓘ **SMCD5111**
Philadelphia, E. Ormandy
(SONY) Ⓘ **SBK39454**
RLPO, Carl Davis (arr Russell Bennett)
(CFP) Ⓘ **CD-CFP4601**
(CFP) ⊟ **TC-CFP4601**
Kammerspiel (r1994; arr Bateman)
(TIMB) Ⓘ **DMHCD1**
Detroit SO, A. Dorati
(8/91) (DECC) Ⓘ **430 712-2DM**
Bournemouth SO, J. Farrer (r1993; arr Russell Bennett) (8/94) (IMP) Ⓘ **MCD75**

GIACOMELLI, Geminiano *(1692–1742) Italy*

Merope– opera (1734—Venice) (Wds. A Zeno)
Quel usignuolo A. Christofellis, Seicentonovecento Ens, F. Colusso (r1993/4)
(EMI) Ⓘ **CDC5 55250-2**

GIMÉNEZ (Y BELLIDO), Jerónimo *(1854–1923) Spain*

El **barbero de Sevilla– zarzuela (1901—Madrid) (Lib. Perrin & Palacios)**
Me llaman la primorosa I. Rey, ECO, E. Ricci (r1994) (2/95) (ERAT) Ⓘ **4509-95789-2**
(2/95) (ERAT) ⊟ **4509-95789-4**

La **Boda de Luis Alonso o La noche del encierro– zarzuela (1897—Madrid) (Lib. Burgos)**
EXCERPTS: 1. Intermezzo; 2. Malagueña; 3. Zapateado.
1. Austrian RSO, G. Navarro
(SONY) Ⓘ **MK39210**
1. Orch (EDL) Ⓘ **EDL2562-2**
(EDL) ⊙ **EDL2562-1** ⊟ **EDL2562-4**
1. Miami SO, E. Kohn (pp1991)
(IMP) Ⓘ **MCD43**
2, 3. P. Romero, Celedonio Romero, Celín Romero, Celino Romero (r1993; arr Moreno Torroba jr & P Romero)
(PHIL) Ⓘ **442 781-2PH**
(PHIL) ⊟ **442 781-4PH**

El **Mundo comedia es, o El baile de Luis Alonso– zarzuela (1896—Madrid) (Lib. Burgos)**
EXCERPTS: 1. Intermedio.
1. P. Romero, Celedonio Romero, Celín Romero, Celino Romero (r1993; arr P Romero)
(PHIL) Ⓘ **442 781-2PH**
(PHIL) ⊟ **442 781-4PH**

La **Tempranica– zarzuela (1900—Madrid) (Lib. J. Romea)**
Canción de la Tempranica P. Perez Inigo, Madrid SO, E. G. Asensio (pp1991)
(11/92) (IMP) Ⓘ **MCD45**
La tarántula é un bich mú malo V. de los Angeles, Spanish Nat Orch, R. Frühbeck de Burgos (r1967) (EMI) Ⓘ **CDM5 65579-2**

La **Torre del oro– zarzuela: 1 act (1902—Madrid) (Lib. Perrin & Palacios)**
Preludio Seville SO, E. Colomer (pp1991)
(RCA) Ⓘ **RD61191**
Preludio Seville SO, E. Colomer (pp1991)
(RCA) ꝏ **09026 61191-5**

GIORDANO, Umberto *(1867–1948) Italy*

Andrea Chénier– opera: 4 acts (1896—Milan) (Lib. Illica)
ACT 1: 1a. Questo azzurro sofà; 1b. Son sessant'anni; 2. T'odio, casa dorata!; 3. Per stasera pazienza!; 4. O Pastorelle; 5. Signor Chénier; 6a. Colpito qui m'avete; 6b. Un dì all'azzurro spazio (Improvviso); 7. Perdonatemi!. ACT 2: 8. Per l'ex inferno!; 9a. Credo a una possanza; 9b. Io non ho amato ancor; 10a. Ecco l'altare; 10b. Udite! Son sola!; 10c. Ora soave. ACT 3: 11. Dumouriez traditore; 12. Prendi! è un ricordo; 13a. Nemico della Patria?; 13b. Un dì m'era di gioia; 14. Sta bene! Ove trovarti se; 15a. Come sa amare!; 15b. La mamma morta; 16. E l'angelo si accosta; 17a. Gravier de Vergennes; 17b. Si, fui soldato; 18. Udiamo i testimoni!; ACT 4: 19a. Cittadino, men duol; 19b. Come un bel dì di maggio; 20. Viene a costei concesso; 21a. Benedico il destino!; 21b. Vicino a te s'acqueta; 21c. La nostra morte.
Andrea Chénier P. Domingo
Maddalena A. Tomowa-Sintow
Carlo Gerard G. Zancanaro
Incredibile J. Dobson
Countess P. Johnson
Bersi C. Buchan
Roucher J. Summers
ROH Chor, ROHO, J. Rudel, M. Hampe
(CAST) ▣ **CVI2058**
Andrea Chénier J. Carreras
Maddalena E. Marton
Carlo Gerard P. Cappuccil
La Scala Chor, La Scala Orch, R. Chailly, L. Puggelli
(CAST) ▣ **CVI200**
Andrea Chénier M. del Monac
Maddalena R. Tebald
Carlo Gerard E. Bastianin
Incredibile M. Carus
Countess M.T. Mandala
Bersi F. Cossott
Roucher S. Maionic
Fléville D. Mantovan
Fouquier-Tinville V. Polott
Schmidt; Dumas D. Casel
Abate A. Mercuria
Maestro di casa M. Cazzat
Madelon A. Guid
Mathieu F. Coren
Santa Cecilia Academy Chor, Santa Cecilia Academy Orch, G. Gavazzeni
(DECC) Ⓘ [2] **425 407-2DM**
Andrea Chénier F. Bonisol
Maddalena M. Gulegin
Carlo Gerard R. Bruso
Incredibile H. Zedni
Countess E. Dundekov
Bersi G. Pasin
Roucher; Dumas; Maestro di casa M. Pertus
Fléville H. Helm
Fouquier-Tinville; Schmidt C. Otel
Abate P. Lefebvr
Madelon G. Lino
Mathieu S. Rinaldi-Milian
Hungarian Rad Chor, Frankfurt RSO, M. Viotti
(CAPR) Ⓘ [2] **60 014-**
Andrea Chenier L. Pavarot
Maddalena M. Caball
Carlo Gerard L. Nucc
Incredibile P. de Palm
Countess A. Varna
Bersi K. Kuhlman
Roucher T. Kraus
Fléville H. Cuéno
Fouquier-Tinville; Maestro di casa N. Howle
Schmidt G. Morre
Dumas R. Hame
Abate F. Andreol
Madelon C. Ludwi
Mathieu G. Tade
WNO Chor, National PO, R. Chailly
(2/85) (DECC) Ⓘ [2] **410 117-2DH**
Andrea Chénier J. Carrera
Maddalena E. Marto
Carlo Gerard G. Zancanar
Incredibile T. Pan
Countess T. Takác
Bersi K. Takác
Roucher F. Federi
Fléville G. Vághel
Fouquier-Tinville T. Bát
Schmidt J. Tót
Dumas K. Sárkán
Abate I. Rozso
Maestro di casa J. Moldva
Madelon E. Farka
Mathieu J. Grego
Hungarian Rad & TV Chor, Hungarian St Orch, G. Patanè
(11/87) (CBS) Ⓘ [2] **CD4236**
Andrea Chénier P. Doming
Maddalena R. Scott
Carlo Gerard S. Milne
Incredibile M. Sénécha
Countess J. Kraf
Bersi M. Ewin
Roucher A. Mon
Fléville T. Sharp
Fouquier-Tinville S. Harlin
Schmidt I. Bushki
Dumas M. Kin
Abate P. de Palm
Maestro di casa N. Beava
Madelon G. Killebrew
Mathieu E. Dar
John Alldis Ch, National PO, James Levine (r1976)
(9/89) (RCA) Ⓘ [2] **GD8204**
Andrea Chenier F. Corel
Maddalena A. Stell
Carlo Gérard M. Seren
Incredibile; Abate P. De Palm
Countess L. Monet
Bersi S. Malag
Rouchier; Fouquier-Tinville G. Modest

Fléville D. Mantovani
Schmidt; Dumas; Maestro di Casa P. Pedani
Madelon A. di Stasio
Mathieu P. Montarsolo
Rome Op Chor, Rome Op Orch, G. Santini (r1963) (7/95) (EMI) Ⓓ [2] **CMS5 65287-2**
1b G. Taddei, Naples San Carlo Op Orch, U. Rapalo (PREI) Ⓓ **90020**
1b R. Stracciari, orch (r1925) (PEAR) Ⓓ **GEMMCD9178**
1b, 13a T. Ruffo, orch (r1920) (2/93) (PREI) Ⓓ [3] **89303(2)**
4. John Alldis Ch, National PO, James Levine (r1976) (RCA) Ⓓ **74321 24209-2**
4. ROH Chor, ROHO, B. Haitink (12/89) (EMI) Ⓓ **CDC7 49849-2**
6a, 6b M. del Monaco, Santa Cecilia Academy Orch, G. Gavazzeni (DECC) Ⓓ **433 069-2DWO**
(DECC) ⊟ **433 069-4DWO**
6a, 6b Deng, A. Juffinger (SCHW) Ⓓ **312642**
6a, 6b Deng, Württemberg PO, R. Paternostro (SINE) Ⓓ **39820222**
6a, 6b G. di Stefano, Santa Cecilia Academy Orch, F. Patanè (r1958) (DECC) Ⓓ **440 403-2DM**
6a, 6b M. del Monaco, Santa Cecilia Academy Orch, G. Gavazzeni (r1957) (DECC) Ⓓ **440 407-2DM**
6a, 6b G. di Stefano, Santa Cecilia Academy Orch, F. Patanè (r1958) (DECC) Ⓓ **443 379-2DM**
6a, 6b A. Pertile, orch (r1925) (4/94) (EMI) Ⓓ [3] **CHS7 64864-2(1)**
6a, 6b G. Zenatello, anon (r1905) (5/94) (SYMP) Ⓓ **SYMCD1168**
6a, 6b G. Zenatello, anon (r1905/6: 2 vers) (5/94) (PEAR) Ⓓ [4] **GEMMCDS9073(1)**
6a, 6b, 17b, 19b L. Pavarotti, National PO, R. Chailly (r1979) (DECC) Ⓓ **440 400-2DM**
6a, 6b, 17b G. Zenatello, orch (r1908) (5/94) (PEAR) Ⓓ [4] **GEMMCDS9073(1)**
6a, 6b, 17b G. Zenatello, orch (r1908) (5/94) (SYMP) Ⓓ **SYMCD1168**
6a, 6b, 19b, 21b F. Corelli, Vienna St. Op Orch, L. von Matačić (pp1960) (MEMO) Ⓓ [2] **HR4204/5**
6a, 6b, 19b J. Vickers, Rome Op Orch, T. Serafin (r1961) (VAI) Ⓓ **VAIA1016**
6a, 6b, 19b B. Heppner, Munich RO, R. Abbado (r1993/4) (11/95) (RCA) Ⓓ **09026 62504-2**
6b M. Lanza, Hollywood Bowl SO, E. Ormandy (pp1947) (IMP) Ⓓ **PWKS4230**
6b J. Carreras, MMF Orch, Rome Op Orch, Z. Mehta (pp1990) (DECC) ● **071 123-1DH**
(DECC) ⊡ **071 123-3DH**
6b B. Prevedi, ROHO, E. Downes (DECC) Ⓓ **433 623-2DSP**
(DECC) ⊟ **433 623-4DSP**
6b J. Carreras, MMF Orch, Rome Op Orch, Z. Mehta (pp1990) (DECC) OO **430 433-5DH**
6b E. Caruso, orch (r1907) (RCA) Ⓓ **09026 61243-2**
6b B. Prevedi, ROHO, E. Downes (r1964) (BELA) Ⓓ **450 005-2**
(BELA) ⊟ **450 005-4**
6b B. Prevedi, ROHO, E. Downes (r1964) (DECC) Ⓓ **436 314-2DA**
(DECC) ⊟ **436 314-4DA**
6b M. del Monaco, Milan SO, A. Quadri (r1948) (TEST) Ⓓ **SBT1039**
6b J. Carreras, Hungarian St Orch, G. Patanè (SONY) Ⓓ **MDK47176**
(SONY) ⊟ **MDT47176**
6b A. Pertile, La Scala Orch, C. Sabajno (r1927) (PEAR) Ⓓ **GEMMCD9129**
6b B. Gigli, orch (r1922) (NIMB) Ⓓ **NI7864**
6b G. Martinelli, orch, J. Pasternack (r1926) (10/89) (NIMB) Ⓓ **NI7804**
(NIMB) ⊟ **NC7804**
6b B. Gigli, La Scala Orch, U. Berrettoni (r1941) (5/90) (EMI) Ⓓ **CDH7 61052-2**
6b G. Zenatello, anon (r1903) (6/90) (SYMP) Ⓓ **SYMCD1073**
6b G. Lauri-Volpi, La Scala Orch, F. Ghione (r1934) (9/90) (PREI) Ⓓ **89012**
6b B. Gigli, orch, J. Pasternack (r1922) (10/90) (RCA) Ⓓ **GD87811**
(10/90) (RCA) ⊟ **GK87811**
6b J. Carreras, MMF Orch, Rome Op Orch, Z. Mehta (pp1990) (10/90) (DECC) Ⓓ **430 433-2DH**
(10/90) (DECC) ⊟ **430 433-4DH**
6b E. Caruso, orch (r1907) (12/90) (PEAR) Ⓓ [3] **EVC1(2)**
6b E. Caruso, orch (r1907) (7/91) (RCA) Ⓓ [12] **GD60495(2)**
6b G. Zenatello, orch (r c1916) (11/91) (CLUB) Ⓓ **CL99-025**
6b F. Tamagno, Anon (pf) (r1903-04) (2/92) (OPAL) Ⓓ **OPALCD9846**
6b B. Gigli, La Scala Orch, U. Berrettoni (r1941) (7/92) (PEAR) Ⓓ [3] **GEMMCDS9926(2)**
6b G. Lauri-Volpi, La Scala Orch, F. Ghione (r1934) (7/92) (PEAR) Ⓓ [3] **GEMMCDS9925(2)**
6b G. Martinelli, orch, J. Pasternack (r1926) (3/93) (PREI) Ⓓ **89062**
6b B. Gigli, orch, J. Pasternack (r1922) (6/93) (MMOI) Ⓓ **CDMOIR417**
6b G. Lauri-Volpi, La Scala Orch, F. Ghione (r1934) (7/93) (NIMB) Ⓓ **NI7845**
6b G. Zenatello, anon (r1903) (5/94) (PEAR) Ⓓ [4] **GEMMCDS9073(1)**
6b G. Zenatello, orch (r1916) (5/94) (PEAR) Ⓓ [4] **GEMMCDS9074(1)**
6b R. Zanelli, La Scala Orch, C. Sabajno (r1929) (9/94) (NIMB) Ⓓ **NI7856**
6b A. Pertile, La Scala Orch, C. Sabajno (r1927) (10/94) (PREI) Ⓓ **89072**
6b B. Gigli, La Scala Orch, O. de Fabritiis (r1941) (12/94) (MMOI) Ⓓ **CDMOIR425**
6b E. Caruso, orch (r1907) (7/95) (NIMB) Ⓓ **NI7866**
6b, 19b B. Gigli, orch (r1922) (5/90) (NIMB) Ⓓ **NI7807**
(NIMB) ⊟ **NC7807**
6b, 17b F. Merli, orch, L. Molajoli (r1928) (1/91) (PREI) Ⓓ **89026**
6b, 17b, 19b A. Paoli, orch (r1911) (PREI) Ⓓ **89998**
6b, 19b B. Gigli, orch, J. Pasternack (r1922) (CONI) Ⓓ **CDHD170**
6b, 19b P. Domingo, National PO, James Levine (RCA) Ⓓ [2] **GD60866**
(RCA) ⊟ [2] **GK60866**
9a G. Zenatello, orch (r1910) (5/94) (PEAR) Ⓓ [4] **GEMMCDS9073(2)**
9a G. Zenatello, orch (r1909) (5/94) (SYMP) Ⓓ **SYMCD1168**
9b A. Cortis, La Scala Orch, C. Sabajno (r1930) (10/91) (PREI) Ⓓ **89043**
10a, 15b R. Tebaldi, Milan RAI Chor, Vienna St Op Orch, L. von Matačić (pp1960) (MEMO) Ⓓ [2] **HR4235/6**
10b, 21b, 21c M. Seinemeyer, T. Pattiera, orch, F. Weissmann (r1926: Ger) (PEAR) Ⓓ **GEMMCD9082**
13a H. Schlusnus, Berlin St Op Orch, M. Gurlitt (r1928) (PREI) Ⓓ [2] **89212**
13a T. Gobbi, Rome Op Orch, O. de Fabritiis (r1955) (10/89) (EMI) Ⓓ **CDM7 63109-2**
13a L. Tibbett, orch (pp1935) (3/91) (PEAR) Ⓓ [2] **GEMMCDS9452**
13a C. Galeffi, La Scala Orch, L. Molajoli (r1930) (2/92) (PREI) Ⓓ **89040**
13a T. Ruffo, orch (r1929) (2/93) (PREI) Ⓓ [3] **89303(2)**
13a G. Hüsch, Berlin St Op Orch, H.U. Müller (r1937: Ger) (3/94) (PREI) Ⓓ **89071**
13a C. Formichi, orch, H. Harty (r1927) (11/94) (PREI) Ⓓ **89055**
13a J.C. Thomas, Victor SO, F. Tours (r1939) (10/95) (NIMB) Ⓓ **NI7867**
13a, 13b T. Gobbi, Rome Op Orch, O. de Fabritiis (r1955) (4/92) (EMI) Ⓓ [7] **CHS7 69741-2(7)**
13a, 13b J. Van Dam, Loire PO, M. Soustrot (r1992) (8/93) (FORL) Ⓓ **UCD16681**
13a, 15b E. Bastianini, R. Tebaldi, Vienna St Op Chor, Vienna St Op Orch, L. von Matačić (pp1960) (MEMO) Ⓓ [2] **HR4400/1**
13b A. Granforte, La Scala Orch, C. Sabajno (r1927) (PREI) Ⓓ **89105**
13b M. Sammarco, orch (r1908) (7/92) (PEAR) Ⓓ [3] **GEMMCDS9924(1)**
13b E. Giraldoni, orch (r1909) (11/92) (MEMO) Ⓓ [2] **HR4408/9(2)**
13b M. Sammarco, orch (r1908) (4/94) (EMI) Ⓓ [3] **CHS7 64860-2(1)**
15b Lotte Lehmann, Berlin City Op Orch, F. Zweig (Ger: r1927) (PEAR) Ⓓ **GEMMCD9410**
15b M. Caballé, National PO, R. Chailly (r1984) (DECC) Ⓓ **436 472-2DM**
15b R. Tebaldi, Santa Cecilia Academy Orch, G. Gavazzeni (r1957) (DECC) Ⓓ **440 408-2DM**
15b M. Seinemeyer, orch, F. Weissmann (r1928) (PEAR) Ⓓ **GEMMCD9082**
15b M. Callas, Philh, T. Serafin (r1954) (EMI) Ⓓ **CDC5 55216-2**
(EMI) ⊟ **EL555216-4**
15b M. Caballé, National PO, R. Chailly (r1984) (DECC) Ⓓ **443 377-2DM**
15b L. Price, RCA Italiana Op Orch, F. Molinari-Pradelli (r1960s) (RCA) Ⓓ **09026 62596-2**
15b R. Kabaivanska, Bulgarian RSO, V. Stefanov (r1970s) (FORL) Ⓓ **UCD16742**
15b K. Te Kanawa, LSO, Myung-Whun Chung (r1989) (EMI) Ⓓ **CDM5 65578-2**
15b A. Tomowa-Sintow, Munich RO, P. Sommer (11/86) (ORFE) Ⓓ **C106841A**
15b M. Callas, Philh, T. Serafin (r1954) (11/86) (EMI) Ⓓ **CDC7 47282-2**
15b C. Muzio, orch (r1920) (5/90) (BOGR) Ⓓ [2] **BIM705-2**
15b M. Seinemeyer, Berlin St Op Orch, F. Weissmann (r1928) (11/90) (PREI) Ⓓ **89029**
15b G. Cigna, orch, L. Molajoli (r1931) (11/90) (LYRC) Ⓓ **SRO805**
15b K. Te Kanawa, LSO, Myung-Whun Chung (11/90) (EMI) Ⓓ **CDC7 54062-2**
15b C. Muzio, orch, L. Molajoli (r1935) (4/91) (NIMB) Ⓓ **NI7814**
(4/91) (NIMB) ⊟ **NC7814**
15b R. Tebaldi, Santa Cecilia Academy Orch, G. Gavazzeni (8/91) (DECC) Ⓓ [2] **430 481-2DX2**
15b M. Freni, Venice La Fenice Orch, R. Abbado (9/92) (DECC) Ⓓ **433 316-2DH**
15b J. Hammond, Philh, L. Collingwood (r1947) (12/92) (TEST) Ⓓ **SBT1013**
15b L. Price, RCA Italiana Op Orch, F. Molinari-Pradelli (12/92) (RCA) Ⓓ [4] **09026 61236-2**
15b R. Pampanini, orch, L. Molajoli (r1927) (8/93) (PREI) Ⓓ **89063**
15b E. Carelli, S. Cottone (r1904) (8/93) (SYMP) Ⓓ **SYMCD1111**
15b R. Raisa, orch (r1933) (1/94) (CLUB) Ⓓ **CL99-052**
15b C. Muzio, orch (r1920) (1/94) (ROMO) Ⓓ [2] **81005-2**
15b Z. Milanov, RCA SO, A. Basile (r1958) (4/94) (RCA) Ⓓ [6] **09026 61580-2(5)**
15b E. Rethberg, orch (r1925) (7/94) (PREI) Ⓓ **89051**
15b M. Reining, Vienna St Op Orch, R. Moralt (r1942: Ger) (9/94) (PREI) Ⓓ **89065**
15b E. Rethberg, orch (r1924) (2/95) (ROMO) Ⓓ [2] **81012-2**
15b(pt) Lotte Lehmann, Vienna St Op Orch, R. Heger (pp1933: Ger) (11/95) (SCHW) Ⓓ [2] **314622**
15b, 21b, 21c M. Caballé, L. Pavarotti, B. Giaiotti, National PO, R. Chailly (r1984) (DECC) Ⓓ **443 928-2DM**
17a, 17b, 21b J. Carreras, E. Marton, P. Cappuccilli, La Scala Chor, La Scala Orch, R. Chailly (CAST) ⊡ **CVI2067**
17b J. Carreras, La Scala Orch, R. Chailly (TELD) ● **9031-77676-6**
(TELD) ⊡ **9031-77676-3**
17b M. del Monaco, Milan SO, T. Benintende-Neglia (r1952) (TEST) Ⓓ **SBT1039**
17b B. Gigli, La Scala Orch, C. Sabajno (r1933) (PEAR) Ⓓ [2] **GEMMCDS9176**
17b B. Gigli, La Scala Orch, O. de Fabritiis (r1941) (9/88) (EMI) Ⓓ **CDH7 61051-2**
17b B. Gigli, La Scala Orch, C. Sabajno (r1933) (9/88) (EMI) Ⓓ **CDH7 61051-2**
17b G. Zenatello, orch, Rosario Bourdon (r1929) (11/91) (CLUB) Ⓓ **CL99-025**
17b G. Zenatello, orch, Rosario Bourdon (r1929) (11/91) (PREI) Ⓓ **89038**
17b G. Zenatello, orch (r1908) (7/92) (PEAR) Ⓓ [3] **GEMMCDS9924(1)**
17b B. Gigli, La Scala Orch, C. Sabajno (r1933) (4/94) (EMI) Ⓓ [3] **CHS7 64864-2(2)**
17b G. Zenatello, orch, B. Reibold (r1929) (5/94) (PEAR) Ⓓ [4] **GEMMCDS9074(2)**
19b J. Björling, Stockholm Royal Op Orch, N. Grevillius (r1957) (RCA) ⊟ **GK85277**
19b F. Corelli, Rome Op Orch, G. Santini (EMI) Ⓓ **CDC7 54016-2**
19b T. Schipa, orch, Anon (cond) (pp1938) (MEMO) Ⓓ [2] **HR4220/1**
19b A. Davies, RPO, R. Stapleton (RPO) Ⓓ **CDRPO7009**
(RPO) ⊟ **ZCRPO7009**
19b J. Carreras, Hungarian St Op Orch, G. Patanè (SONY) Ⓓ **SMK48155**
(SONY) ⊟ **SMT48155**
19b J. Björling, B. Bokstedt (BLUE) Ⓓ **ABCD042**
19b T. Harper, Bratislava RSO, M. Halász (NAXO) Ⓓ **8 550497**
19b E. Caruso, orch, J. Pasternack (r1916) (RCA) Ⓓ **09026 61243-2**

19b J. Carreras, Hungarian St Op Orch, G. Patanè ( ) (SONY) ● **SM48155**
19b A. Davies, RPO, R. Stapleton (r1991) (RPO) Ⓓ [2] **CDRPD9006**
(RPO) ▭ [2] **ZCRPD9006**
19b G. di Stefano, Zurich Tonhalle Orch, F. Patanè (r1958) (DECC) Ⓓ **440 403-2DM**
19b M. del Monaco, Santa Cecilia Academy Orch, G. Gavazzeni (r1957)
(DECC) Ⓓ **436 314-2DA**
(DECC) ▭ **436 314-4DA**
19b M. del Monaco, Milan SO, A. Quadri (r1952)
(TEST) Ⓓ **SBT1039**
19b B. Gigli, orch (r1922)
(ASV) Ⓓ **CDAJA5137**
(ASV) ▭ **ZCAJA5137**
19b J. Björling, H. Ebert (pp1950)
(BLUE) Ⓓ **ABCD057**
19b J. Björling, orch, N. Grevillius (r1943)
(PEAR) Ⓓ **GEMMCD9129**
19b C. Bergonzi, Santa Cecilia Academy Orch, G. Gavazzeni (r1957)
(DECC) Ⓓ **440 417-2DM**
19b G. di Stefano, Turin RAI Orch, O. de Fabritiis (bp1953) (FONI) Ⓓ **CDMR5003**
19b A. Piccaver, Berlin St Op Orch, J. Prüwer (r1930) (PREI) Ⓓ [2] **89217**
19b G. Martinelli, orch, Rosario Bourdon (r1927)
(10/89) (NIMB) Ⓓ **NI7804**
(NIMB) ▭ **NC7804**
19b F. Giraud, S. Cottone (r1904)
(6/90) (SYMP) Ⓓ **SYMCD1073**
19b E. Caruso, orch, J. Pasternack (r1916)
(7/91) (RCA) Ⓓ [12] **GD60495(5)**
19b E. Caruso, orch, J. Pasternack (r1916)
(10/91) (PEAR) Ⓓ [3] **EVC4(1)**
19b G. Martinelli, orch, Rosario Bourdon (r1927)
(3/93) (PREI) Ⓓ **89062**
19b J. Björling, orch, N. Grevillius (r1944)
(10/93) (EMI) Ⓓ **CDH7 64707-2**
19b A. Pertile, La Scala Orch, C. Sabajno (r1929) (10/94) (PREI) Ⓓ **89072**
19b E. Caruso, orch (r1916)
(7/95) (NIMB) Ⓓ **NI7866**
21b, 21c A. Stella, F. Corelli, P. Pedani, Rome Op Orch, G. Santini (CFP) Ⓓ **CD-CFP9013**
(CFP) ▭ **TC-CFP4498**
21b, 21c A. Pertile, M. Sheridan, La Scala Orch, C. Sabajno (r1928) (10/94) (PREI) Ⓓ **89072**

La **Cena delle Beffe**– opera (1924—Milan) (Lib. Benelli)

Ah, che tormento; Mi svesti A. Cortis, orch (r1927) (3/94) (NIMB) Ⓓ **NI7850**
Ed io non ne godevo...Sempre così. F. Alda, orch, Rosario Bourdon (r1925)
(4/94) (RCA) Ⓓ [6] **09026 61580-2(2)**

Fedora– opera: 3 acts (1898—Milan) (Lib. Colautti, after Sardou)

ACT 1: 1a. Ed ecco il suo ritratto; 1b. O grandi gli occhi lucenti; 2a. Continuate; 2b. Su questa santa croce. ACT 2: 3a. Signori, vi presento Lazinski; 3b. Io sono lo sbadiglio molesto; 4. La donna russa; 5. Amor ti vieta; 6. Appena giunta; 7. Intermezzo; 8a. Loris, Ipanoff, oggi lo Zar; 8b. Mia madre, la mia vecchia madre; 9. La fante mi svela; 10a. Ma chi m'accusa; 10b. Vedi, io piango; 11a. Lascia che pianga sola; 11b. Dove ten vai?. ACT 3: 12. Dice la capinera; 13. E voi più non tubate?; 14. Quel truce sgherro; 15. Son pronta; 16. La montanina mia; 17. Dio di giustizia; 18a. O bianca madre; 18b. Jariskin recò all'Imperatore; 18c. Morti per me; 19a. Se quella sciagurata; 19b. Forse con te; 19c. Se quell'infelice; 20. Tutto tramonta.

Fedora E. Marton
Loris J. Carreras
Siriex J. Martin
Olga V. Kincses
Grech J. Gregor
Désiré I. Rozsos
Cirillo K. Kováts
Dmitri J. Bokor
Lorek J. Németh
Baron Rouvel A. Fülöp
Boroff P. Kovács
Sergio I. Baski
Nicola; Michele S. Blazsó
Boleslao Lazinski I. Rohmann
Un piccolo Savoiardo T. Csányi
Hungarian Rad & TV Chor, Hungarian Radio & TV Orch, G. Patanè (r1986)
(SONY) Ⓓ [2] **M2K42181**
Fedora M. Olivero
Loris M. del Monaco
Siriex T. Gobbi
Grech S. Maionica
Olga L. Cappellino
Désiré R. Cassinelli
Cirillo P. Binder
Dimitri K. Te Kanawa
Lorek L. Monreale
Boroff V. Carbonari
Sergio A. Cesarini
Nicola L. Monreale
Michele A. Bokatti
Un piccolo Savoiardo S. Caspari
Boleslao Lazinski P. Rogers
Baron Rouvel P. de Palma
Monte Carlo Op Chor, Monte Carlo Nat Op Orch, L. Gardelli
(3/92) (DECC) Ⓓ [2] **433 033-2DM2**
1b G. Bellincioni, S. Cottone (r1903)
(6/90) (SYMP) Ⓓ **SYMCD1073**
1b, 17. M. Jeritza, orch (r1923)
(4/94) (PREI) Ⓓ **89079**
4. T. Gobbi, Philh, A. Erede (r1963)
(10/89) (EMI) Ⓓ **CDM7 63109-2**
4. T. Gobbi, Philh, A. Erede (r1963)
(4/94) (EMI) Ⓓ [3] **CHS7 64864-2(2)**
5. L. Pavarotti, National PO, O. de Fabritiis
(DECC) Ⓓ **430 470-2DH**
(DECC) ▭ **430 470-4DH**
5. B. Prevedi, ROHO, E. Downes
(DECC) Ⓓ **433 623-2DSP**
(DECC) ▭ **433 623-4DSP**
5. P. Domingo, Orch (EDL) Ⓓ **EDL2562-2**
(EDL) ⊙ **EDL2562-1** ▭ **EDL2562-4**
5. J. Björling, MMF Orch, A. Erede
(DECC) Ⓓ **433 064-2DWO**
5. J. Björling, MMF Orch, A. Erede (r1957)
(DECC) Ⓓ **436 300-2DX**
(DECC) ▭ **436 300-4DX**
5. E. Caruso, U. Giordano (r1902)
(MCI) Ⓓ **MCCD086**
(MCI) ▭ **MCTC086**
5. Deng, Württemberg PO, R. Paternostro
(SINE) Ⓓ **39820222**
5. M. del Monaco, New SO, A. Erede (r1956)
(DECC) Ⓓ **440 407-2DM**
5. L. Pavarotti, National PO, O. de Fabritiis (r1979) (DECC) Ⓓ **440 400-2DM**
5. B. Prevedi, ROHO, E. Downes (r1964)
(BELA) Ⓓ **450 005-2**
(BELA) ▭ **450 005-4**
5. J. Björling, MMF Orch, A. Erede (r1957)
(DECC) Ⓓ **436 314-2DA**
(DECC) ▭ **436 314-4DA**
5. P. Domingo, Berlin Deutsche Op Orch, N. Santi (ERAT) Ⓓ **4509-91715-2**
(ERAT) ▭ **4509-91715-4**
5. L. Pavarotti, Toscanini SO, E. Buckley
(SONY) Ⓓ **MDK47176**
(SONY) ▭ **MDT47176**
5. E. Scaramberg, orch (r1905: Fr)
(SYMP) Ⓓ **SYMCD1173**
5. G. Martinelli, orch (r1926)
(PEAR) Ⓓ **GEMMCD9129**
5. T. Beltrán, RPO, R. Stapleton (r1994)
(SILV) Ⓓ **SILKD6005**
(SILV) ▭ **SILKC6005**
5. A. Bonci, orch (r1912)
(PEAR) Ⓓ **GEMMCD9168**
5. A. Piccaver, Berlin St Op Orch, J. Prüwer (r1930: Ger) (PREI) Ⓓ [2] **89217**
5. F. de Lucia, anon (r1902)
(BONG) Ⓓ [2] **GB1064/5-2**
5. F. de la Mora, WNO Orch, C. Mackerras (r1994-5) (TELA) Ⓓ **CD80411**
5. J. Björling, orch, N. Grevillius (r1944)
(10/88) (EMI) Ⓓ **CDH7 61053-2**
5. E. Caruso, U. Giordano (r1902)
(5/89) (EMI) Ⓓ **CDH7 61046-2**
5. G. Martinelli, orch, J. Pasternack (r1926)
(10/89) (NIMB) Ⓓ **NI7804**
(NIMB) ▭ **NC7804**
5. B. Gigli, orch, U. Berrettoni (r1940)
(5/90) (EMI) Ⓓ **CDH7 61052-2**
5. L. Pavarotti, National PO, O. de Fabritiis
(7/90) (DECC) Ⓓ [2] **425 681-2DM2**
(7/90) (DECC) ▭ [2] **425 681-4DM2**
5. E. Caruso, U. Giordano (r1902)
(12/90) (PEAR) Ⓓ [3] **EVC1(1)**
5. D. Borgioli, orch (r c1923)
(12/90) (CLUB) Ⓓ **CL99-014**
5. E. Caruso, U. Giordano (r1902)
(7/91) (RCA) Ⓓ [12] **GD60495(1)**
5. M. del Monaco, New SO, A. Erede (r1956)
(10/93) (DECC) Ⓓ **436 463-2DM**
(10/93) (DECC) ▭ **436 463-4DM**
5. G. Anselmi, anon (r1907)
(7/95) (SYMP) Ⓓ **SYMCD1170**
5. J. Björling, MMF Orch, A. Erede (r1959)
(10/95) (DECC) Ⓓ **443 930-2DM**
5. A. Davies, A. Bryn Parri (r1994)
(11/95) (SAIN) Ⓓ **SCDC2085**
5, 8b G. Martinelli, orch, J. Pasternack (r1926)
(3/93) (PREI) Ⓓ **89062**
5, 8b A. Giorgini, anon (r1904)
(4/95) (RECO) Ⓓ **TRC3**
7. Gothenburg SO, N. Järvi
(DG) Ⓓ **439 152-2GMA**
(DG) ▭ **439 152-4GMA**
7. RPO, A. Licata (r1994) (TRIN) Ⓓ **TRP044**
7. BPO, H. von Karajan
(10/87) (DG) Ⓓ [3] **419 257-2GH3**
7. Gothenburg SO, N. Järvi
(6/90) (DG) Ⓓ **429 494-2GDC**
(6/90) (DG) ▭ **429 494-4GDC**
10b E. Garbin, G. Russ, orch (r1908)
(7/92) (PEAR) Ⓓ [3] **GEMMCDS9924(2)**
10b F. de Lucia, anon (r1904)
(1/95) (SYMP) Ⓓ **SYMCD1149**
20. E. Carelli, E. Ventura, anon (r1904)
(11/92) (MEMO) Ⓓ [2] **HR4408/9(2)**
20. E. Carelli, E. Ventura, S. Cottone (r1904)
(8/93) (SYMP) Ⓓ **SYMCD1111**

Madame Sans-Gêne– opera: 3 acts (1915—New York)

Che me ne faccio del vostro castello C. Muzio, orch (r1922)
(5/90) (BOGR) Ⓓ [2] **BIM705-2**
Che me ne faccio del vostro castello C. Muzio, orch (r1922)
(1/94) (ROMO) Ⓓ [2] **81005-2**
Che me ne faccio del vostro castello C. Muzio, orch (r1917)
(1/95) (ROMO) Ⓓ [2] **81010-2**

Marcella– opera: 3 acts (1907—Milan) (Lib. L. Stecchetti, after H. Cain, J. Adonis)

Dolce notte misteriosa T. Schipa, orch, Anon (cond) (pp1938) (MEMO) Ⓓ [2] **HR4220/1**
No, non pensarci più. E. Perea, orch (r1910)
(11/92) (MEMO) Ⓓ [2] **HR4408/9(2)**

Siberia– opera: 3 acts (1927—Milan) (Lib. Illica)

E qui con te G. Zenatello, R. Storchio, R. Delle Ponti (r1903)
(5/94) (PEAR) Ⓓ [4] **GEMMCDS9073(1)**
Gleby!...Alfin, è così qua...Quest' orgoglio G. De Luca, R. Storchio, R. delle Ponti (r1903)
(PEAR) Ⓓ [3] **GEMMCDS9159(1)**
Gléby!...Quest'orgoglio R. Storchio, G. De Luca, R. Delle Ponti (r1903)
(4/94) (EMI) Ⓓ [3] **CHS7 64860-2(2)**
La connobbi G. De Luca, R. delle Ponti (r1903)
(PEAR) Ⓓ [3] **GEMMCDS9159(1)**
No! se un pensier...Nel suo amor R. Storchio, R. Delle Ponti (r1903)
(4/94) (EMI) Ⓓ [3] **CHS7 64860-2(2)**
O bella mia G. De Luca, G. Pini-Corsi, O. Gennari, V. Pozzi-Camolla, R. delle Ponti (r1903) (PEAR) Ⓓ [3] **GEMMCDS9159(1)**
Orride steppe G. Zenatello, R. Delle Ponti (r1903) (4/94) (EMI) Ⓓ [3] **CHS7 64860-2(2)**
Orride steppe; No, mio onore...T'incontrai per via G. Zenatello, R. Delle Ponti (r1903)
(5/94) (PEAR) Ⓓ [4] **GEMMCDS9073(1)**
T'incontrai per via G. Zenatello, orch (r1911)
(5/94) (PEAR) Ⓓ [4] **GEMMCDS9073(2)**

GLASS, Philip *(b 1937) USA*

Akhnaten– opera: 3 acts (1984—Stuttgart) (Lib. cpsr)

EXCERPTS: ACT 1: 1. Year 1 of Akhnaten's Reign—Thebes; 2. Prelude—Refrain and Three Verses; 3. Scene 1: Funeral of Amenhotep III; 4. Scene 2: The Coronation of Akhnaten; 5. Scene 3: The Window of Appearances. ACT 2: 6. Years 5 to 15—Thebes and Akhnaten; 7. Scene 1: The Temple; 8. Scene 2: Akhnaten and Nefertiti; 9. Scene 3: The City. Dance; 10. Scene 4: Hymn. ACT 3: 11. Year 17 and the Present—Akhnaten; 12. Scene 1: The Family; 13. Scene 2: Attack and Fall; 14. Scene 3: The Ruins; 15. Scene 4: Epilogue.

Akhnaten P. Esswood
Nefertiti M. Vargas
Queen Tye M. Liebermann
Horemhab T. Hannula
Amon High Priest H. Holzapfel
Aye C. Hauptmann
Scribe D. Warrilow
Stuttgart Op Chor, Stuttgart Op Orch, D.R. Davies
(2/88) (CBS) Ⓓ [2] **CD42457**

1c, 2d P. Esswood, Stuttgart St Orch, Stuttgart State Chor (1/94) (SONY) ① **SK64133**
(1/94) (SONY) ⊟ **ST64133**

Belle et la Bête– opera: 19 sections (1994—Sicily) (Lib. cpsr, after J Cocteau)

La Belle J. Felty
La Bête; Avenant; Ardent; Officiel G. Purnhagen
Le Père; L'Usurier J. Kuether
Félicie A. M. Martinez
Adélaïde H. Neill
Ludovic Z. Zhou
Philip Glass Ens, M. Riesman (r1994)
(NONE) ① [2] **7559-79347-2**

Einstein on the Beach– opera (4 acts) (1975—Paris) (Lib. Wilson)

Cpte L. Childs, S. Johnson, P. Mann, S. Sutton, P. Zukofsky, Philip Glass Ens, M. Riesman (9/86) (CBS) ① [4] **CD38875**
Cpte L. Childs, G. Dolbashian, J. McGruder, S. Sutton, G. Fulkerson, chor, Philip Glass Ens, M. Riesman (r1993) (1/94) (NONE) ① [3] **7559-79323-2**
Bed J. Gibson (r1992; arr sax) (6/93) (PNT) ① **434 873-2PTH**
Bed J. Pendarvis (1/94) (SONY) ① **SK64133**
(1/94) (SONY) ⊟ **ST64133**
Suite G. Fulkerson (r1981) (NEW) ① **80313-2**

Hydrogen Jukebox– theatrical piece (1990—Philadelphia) (Lib. A. Ginsberg)

EXCERPTS: 1. from Iron Horse; 2. Jaweh and Allah Battle; 3. from Iron Horse; 4. To P. O. 5. from Crossing Nation; 6. From Wichita Vortex Sutra; 7. from Howl Part II; 8. from Cabin in the Rockies; 9. from Nagasaki Days; 10. Aunt Rose; 11. from The Green Automobile; 12. from N. S. A. Dope Calypso; 13. from Nagasaki Days; 14. Ayers Rock/Uluru Song; 15. Father Death Blues.
Cpte M. Goldray, C. Wincene, A. Sterman, F. Cassara, J. Pugliese, R. Peck, E. Futral, M.A. Eaton, M.A. Hart, R. Fracker, G. Purnhagen, N. Watson, A. Ginsberg, P. Glass, M. Goldray (r1992-3) (1/94) (NONE) ① **7559-79286-2**

Satyagraha– opera: 3 acts (1980—Rotterdam)

EXCERPTS: 1. ACT 1: Tolstoy—; 1a. Scene 1: The Kuru Field of Justice; 1b. Scene 2: Tolstoy Farm (1910); 1c. Scene 3: The Vow (1906); 2. ACT 2: Tagore—; 2a. Scene 1: Confrontation and Rescue (1896); 2b. Scene 2: Indian Opinion; 2c. Scene 3: Protest. ACT 3: 3. King—Newcastle March (1913).
Ghandi D. Perry
Miss Schlesen C. Cummings
Kasturbai; Mrs Alexander R. Liss
Kallenbach; Prince Arjuna R. McFarland
Parsi Rustomji; Lord Krishna S. Reeve
Mrs Naidoo S. Woods
NYC Op Chor, NYC Op Orch, C. Keene (9/86) (CBS) ① [3] **CD39672**
Act III Conclusion D. Joyce (r1993; arr Riesman: org) (1/94) (CATA) ① **09026 61825-2**
1a, 2c D. Perry, NYC Op Orch, NYC Op Chor (1/94) (SONY) ① **SK64133**
(1/94) (SONY) ⊟ **ST64133**

GLIÈRE, Reinhold
(1875–1956) Ukraine/USSR

Gyul'sara– music drama (1937—Moscow)

EXCERPTS: 1. Overture.
1. St Petersburg State SO, A. Anichanov (r1994) (MARC) ① **8 223675**

Shakh-Senem– opera (1926—Baku) (work rev 1934)

EXCERPTS: 1. Overture.
1. St Petersburg State SO, A. Anichanov (r1994) (MARC) ① **8 223675**

GLINKA, Mikhail Ivanovich
(1804–1857) Russia

Life for the Tsar– opera: 4 acts (1836—St Petersburg) (Lib. G. Rosen)

Ivan Susanin E. Nesterenko
Antonida M. Mescheriakova
Sobinin A. Lomonosov
Vanya E. Zaremba
Polish Commander B. Bezhko
Bolshoi Th Chor, Bolshoi SO, A. Lazarev, N. Kuznetsov (r1992)
(TELD) ● **4509-92051-6**
(6/94) (TELD) ⊟ **4509-92051-3**
Ivan Susanin B. Martinovich
Antonida A. Pendachanska
Sobinin C. Merritt
Vanya S. Toczyska
Polish Commander S. Georgiev
Messenger M. Popov
Russian Commander K. Videv
Sofia National Op Chor, Sofia Fest Orch, E. Tchakarov (9/91) (SONY) ① [3] **S3K46487**
Antonida's Romance N. Davrath, Vienna St Op Orch, V. Golschmann (r1960s) (VANG) ① [2] **08.9081.72**
Antonida's romance J. M. Leonard, V. L. Becker (arr sax/pf: J M Leonard) (ASV) ① **CDWHL2085**
Ballet Music Philh, E. Kurtz (r1961) (9/93) (EMI) ① [2] **CZS7 67729-2**
Brothers, follow me H. Roswaenge, Berlin St Op Orch, B. Seidler-Winkler (r1940: Ger) (PREI) ① [2] **89211**
Brothers, follow me H. Roswaenge, Berlin St Op Orch, B. Seidler-Winkler (r1940: Ger) (5/90) (PREI) ① **89018**
Do not weep, little orphan D. Zakharova, anon (r1912) (PEAR) ① [3] **GEMMCDS9111(2)**
Final chorus Bulgarian Nat Ch, Sofia PO, R. Raichev (FORL) ① **FF060**
Finale Bolshoi Th Chor, Bolshoi Th Orch, A. Chistiakov (CDM) ① **LDC288 022**
I do not grieve for that E. Bronskaya, orch (r1913) (3/95) (NIMB) ① **NI7865**
I look over the bare field M. Michailova, orch (r1906) (PEAR) ① [3] **GEMMCDS9111(2)**
Introduction; Polonaise; Final Chorus Bolshoi Th Chor, Bolshoi SO, A. Lazarev (r1993) (5/94) (ERAT) ① **4509-91723-2**
It is not for that that I grieve M. Kuznetsova, orch (r1904) (6/93) (PEAR) ① [3] **GEMMCDS9004/6(1)**
It is not for that that I grieve A. Nezhdanova, anon (r1907) (6/93) (PEAR) ① [3] **GEMMCDS9007/9(1)**
It is not for that I grieve E. Orel, anon (r c1902) (7/93) (SYMP) ① **SYMCD1105**
My dawn will come F. Chaliapin, anon (r1902) (7/93) (SYMP) ① **SYMCD1105**
My poor horse fell in the field E. Kurmangaliev, Moscow Maly SO, V. Ponkin (MEZH) ① **MK417047**
My poor horse fell in the field E. Zbrueva, anon (r1903) (6/93) (PEAR) ① [3] **GEMMCDS9004/6(2)**
My poor horse fell...Open up!; Light the fires!...Saddle your horses E. Zbrueva, chor, orch (r1913) (6/93) (PEAR) ① [3] **GEMMCDS9004/6(2)**
Our hearts rejoice...O God, love our Tsar M. Michailova, A. Makarova, N. Bolshakov, L. Sibiriakov, anon (r1905) (PEAR) ① [3] **GEMMCDS9111(2)**
Overture Bolshoi Th Orch, A. Chistiakov (r1992) (CDM) ① **LDC288 053**
The rose that blooms M. Michailova, G. Nikitina, A. Labinsky, L. Sibiriakov, orch (r1909) (PEAR) ① [3] **GEMMCDS9111(2)**
The rose that blooms L. Sibiriakov, M. Michailova, G. Nikitina, A. Labinsky, orch (r1908) (6/93) (PEAR) ① [3] **GEMMCDS9007/9(2)**
They guess the truth P. Gluboky, Soviet Cinema Orch, E. Khachaturian (r1990) (CDM) ① [2] **LDC288 005/6**
(CDM) ⊟ **KC488 005**
They guess the truth F. Chaliapin, anon (r1914) (6/88) (EMI) ① **CDH7 61009-2**
They guess the truth N. Rossi-Lemeni, Philh, T. Benintende-Neglia (r1952) (4/92) (EMI) ① [7] **CHS7 69741-2(7)**
They guess the truth M. Reizen, Bolshoi Th Orch, V. Nebolsin (r1955) (12/92) (PREI) ① **89059**
They guess the truth L. Sibiriakov, orch (r1908) (6/93) (PEAR) ① [3] **GEMMCDS9001/3(2)**
They guess the truth D. Bukhtoyarov, anon (r1902) (6/93) (PEAR) ① [3] **GEMMCDS9001/3(1)**
Vanya's Air A. Milcheva, Bulgarian RSO, V. Stefanov (r1970s) (FORL) ① **UCD16743**
What about a wedding? L. Sibiriakov, chor, orch (r1910) (6/93) (PEAR) ① [3] **GEMMCDS9007/9(2)**

Ruslan and Lyudmila– opera: 5 acts (1842—St. Petersburg) (Lib. V F Shirkov, after S Pushkin)

EXCERPTS: 1. Overture. ACT 1: 2. There is a desert country (The Bard's song); 3. Soon I must leave thee (Lyudmila's cavatina). ACT 2: 5. Introduction (entr'acte); 8. The happy day is gone (Farlaf's rondo); 9. O say, ye fields! (Ruslan's aria). ACT 3: 11. The evening shadows (Persian song); 12. O my Ratmir! (Gorislava's romance and cavatina); 13. The wondrous dream of love (Ratmir's aria); 14. Dances. ACT 4: 19. Chernomor's march; 20. Oriental dances.
Ah, thou my fate A. Nezhdanova, anon, anon (r1907) (6/93) (PEAR) ① [3] **GEMMCDS9007/9(1)**
Scene of the Finn and Ruslan G. Nelepp, I. Petrov, USSR RSO, K. Kondrashin (r c1950) (PREI) ① **89081**
1. Czech PO, K. Ančerl (SUPR) ⊟ **11 0640-4**
1. USSR RSO, V. Fedoseyev (CLTS) ⊟ **CML2004**
1. Philh, W. Boughton (NIMB) ① **NI5120**
(NIMB) ⊟ **NC5120**
1. USSR RSO, V. Fedoseyev (OLYM) ① **OCD121**
1. New PO, J. Sándor (LASE) ① **15 514**
(LASE) ⊟ **79 514**
1. LSO, Y. Ahronovitch (IMP) ① **PCDS8**
(IMP) ⊟ **PCDSC8**
1. LSO, M. Shostakovich, H. Chappell (PION) ● **PLMCB00551**
1. NYPO, L. Bernstein (r1963) (SONY) ① **SMK47607**
1. Philh, W. Boughton (NIMB) ① **NI5387**
(NIMB) ⊟ **NC5387**
1. LSO, G. Solti (r1966) (BELA) ① **450 017-2**
(BELA) ⊟ **450 017-4**
1. LSO, Y. Ahronovitch (r1985) (IMP) ① **PCDS25**
(IMP) ⊟ **PCDSC25**
1. New England Conservatory Youth PO, B. Zander (r1993) (CPI) ① **CPI329402**
1. Russian Federation St SO, E. Svetlanov (r1992) (CANY) ① **EC3657-2**
1. Polish Chmbr PO, W. Rajski (INTE) ① **INT830 899**
1. LSO, Y. Ahronovitch (IMP) ① **PCD804**
1. Rhineland-Pfalz State PO, K. Redel (r1979) (FORL) ① **FF058**
1. Philh, C. Silvestri (r1959) (EMI) ① [2] **CZS5 68550-2**
1. RPO, Y. Simonov (r1994) (TRIN) ① **TRP030**
1. Baltimore SO, D. Zinman (r1989) (TELA) ① **CD80378**
1. CBO, G. Weldon (r1946) (EMI) ① [2] **CHS5 65590-2**
1. St. Louis SO, L. Slatkin (12/83) (TELA) ① **CD80072**
1. LPO, C. Mackerras (11/87) (CFP) ① **CD-CFP9000**
1. Moscow PO, L. Leighton Smith (2/88) (SHEF) ① **CD25**
(2/88) (SHEF) ⊙ **TLP25** ⊟ **CAS25**
1. Chicago SO, F. Reiner (1/90) (RCA) ① **GD60176**
1. Berlin SO, C.P. Flor (pp1988) (4/90) (RCA) ① **RD60119**
1. Leningrad PO, E. Mravinsky (pp) (6/92) (ERAT) ① [11] **2292-45763-2**
1. Leningrad PO, E. Mravinsky (pp) (6/92) (ERAT) ① **2292-45757-2**
1. LSO, A. Coates (r1928) (12/92) (KOCH) ① **37700-2**
1. Malmö SO, J. DePreist (1/93) (BIS) ① **BIS-CD570**
1. Queen's Hall Orch, Henry Wood (r1937) (1/94) (BEUL) ① **1PD3**
1. Kirov Th Orch, V. Gergiev (r1993) (4/94) (PHIL) ① **442 011-2PH**
(4/94) (PHIL) ⊟ **442 011-4PH**
1. Chicago SO, F. Reiner (r1959) (8/94) (RCA) ① **09026 61958-2**
1. Philh, C. Silvestri (r1959) (11/94) (EMI) ① [2] **CZS5 68229-2**
1. Russian Nat Orch, M. Pletnev (12/94) (DG) ① **439 892-2GH**
(DG) ⊟ **439 892-4GH**
2. D. Smirnov, orch (r1913) (PEAR) ① **GEMMCD9106**
2. D. Smirnov, orch (r1913) (6/93) (PEAR) ① [3] **GEMMCDS9004/6(1)**

2. A. Bogdanovich, anon (r1903)
(6/93) (PEAR) Ⓓ [3] **GEMMCDS9007/9(1)**
3. E. Orel, anon (r c1902)
(7/93) (SYMP) Ⓓ **SYMCD1105**
3, 8, 9. A. Safiulin, Soviet Cinema Orch, E. Khachaturian (r1990)
(CDM) Ⓓ [2] **LDC288 005/6**
(CDM) ⊟ **KC488 005**
8. F. Chaliapin, LSO, M. Steinmann (r1931)
(CONI) Ⓓ **CDHD226**
(CONI) ⊟ **MCHD226**
8. F. Chaliapin, LSO, M. Steinmann (r1931)
(6/88) (EMI) Ⓓ **CDH7 61009-2**
8. F. Chaliapin, LSO, M. Steinmann (r1931)
(12/89) (PEAR) Ⓓ **GEMMCD9314**
8. M. Reizen, Bolshoi Th Orch, A. Melik-Pashayev (r1948) (12/92) (PREI) Ⓓ **89059**
8. V. Kastorsky, orch (r1908)
(6/93) (PEAR) Ⓓ [3] **GEMMCDS9001/3(1)**
9. F. Chaliapin, orch, I.P. Arkadiev (r1908)
(PREI) Ⓓ **89030**
9. A. Pirogov, Bolshoi Th Orch, A. Melik-Pashayev (r c1950) (PREI) Ⓓ **89078**
9. F. Chaliapin, orch (r1908)
(6/88) (EMI) Ⓓ **CDH7 61009-2**
9. M. Reizen, Bolshoi Th Orch, S. Samosud (r1948) (12/92) (PREI) Ⓓ **89059**
9. P. Orlov, anon (r1902)
(6/93) (PEAR) Ⓓ [3] **GEMMCDS9001/3(1)**
11. E. Zimbalist, E. Bay (r1925: arr Zimbalist)
(7/93) (APR) Ⓓ [2] **APR7016**
12. M. Kuznetsova, orch (r1904)
(6/93) (PEAR) Ⓓ [3] **GEMMCDS9004/6(1)**
12. M. Kuznetsova, anon (r1905)
(7/93) (SYMP) Ⓓ **SYMCD1105**
13. E. Kurmangaliev, Moscow Maly SO, V. Ponkin (MEZH) Ⓓ **MK417047**
13, And blazing heat, She is my life E. Zbrueva, orch (r1907)
(6/93) (PEAR) Ⓓ [3] **GEMMCDS9004/6(2)**

GLUCK, Christoph Willibald (Ritter von) *(1714–1787)* *Bohemia*

Alceste– opera: 3 acts (1776—Paris) (Lib. Calzabigi)

EXCERPTS—; 1. Overture. ACT 1: 2. Grands Dieux, du destin qui m'accable; 3a. Où suis-je? O malheureuse Alceste!; 3b. Non, ce n'est point un sacrifice; 4. Tes destins sont remplis; 5. Divinités du Styx. ACT 2: 6a. O moment délicieux!; 6b. Bannis la crainte et les alarmes; 7a. Ciel!...Tu pleurs? Je tremble!; 7b. Je n'ai jamais chéri la vie; 8a. Tu m'aimes, je t'adore; 8b. Barbare! Non, sans toi, je ne puis vivre; 9a. Grands Dieux! Pour mon époux j'implore; 9b. Ah, malgré moi, mon faible coeur. ACT 3: 10. Nous ne pouvons trop trop répandre des larmes; 11. Après de longs travaux; 12a. Grands Dieux, soutenez mon courage!; 12b. Ah, divinités implacables; 13. Reçois, Dieu bienfaisant; 14. O mes amis!...O mes enfants!.

Alceste J. Norman
Admète N. Gedda
High Priest T. Krause
Evandre R. Gambill
Herald P. Lika
Hercule S. Nimsgern
Apollo B. Weikl
Oracle R. Bracht
Thanatos K. Rydl
Bavarian Rad Chor, BRSO, S. Baudo (r1982)
(6/87) (ORFE) Ⓓ [3] **C027823F**
Excs J. Norman, N. Gedda, S. Nimsgern, T. Krause, R. Gambill, Bavarian Rad Chor, BRSO, S. Baudo (r1982) (ORFE) Ⓓ **C027901A**
Gavotte I. Friedman (r1928: arr pf: Brahms)
(PEAR) Ⓓ [4] **IF2000(1)**
Gavotte J. Hofmann (r1916: arr pf: Brahms)
(VAI) Ⓓ [2] **VAIA1036**
Gavotte J. Hofmann (r1923: arr pf: Brahms)
(VAI) Ⓓ **VAIA1047**
Gavotte E. Petri (pp1959: arr pf: Brahms)
(3/94) (MUSI) Ⓓ [4] **MACD-772**
1. BPO, W. Furtwängler (r1942)
(TELD) Ⓓ **9031-76435-2**
1. Concertgebouw, W. Mengelberg (r1935)
(7/90) (SYMP) Ⓓ **SYMCD1078**
1. Concertgebouw, W. Mengelberg (arr Mottl: r1935) (1/91) (KOCH) Ⓓ **37011-2**
5. S. Balguérie, orch, A. Wolff (r1932)
(MSCM) Ⓓ **MM30221**
(MSCM) ⊟ **MM040079**
5. M. Callas, FRNO, G. Prêtre (r1961)
(EMI) Ⓓ **CDC5 55016-2**
5. M. Anderson, FNO, J. Horenstein (pp1956)
(MUSI) Ⓓ [2] **MACD-784**
5. M. Horne, SRO, H. Lewis (r1965)
(DECC) Ⓓ **440 415-2DM**
5. L. Price, LSO, E. Downes (r1960s-70)
(RCA) Ⓓ **09026 62596-2**
5. H. Wildbrunn, orch (r1924: Ger)
(PREI) Ⓓ **89097**
5. G. Bumbry, Stuttgart RSO, S. Soltesz
(11/86) (ORFE) Ⓓ **C081841A**
5. M. Callas, FRNO, G. Prêtre
(2/88) (EMI) Ⓓ **CDC7 49059-2**
5. M. Callas, FRNO, G. Prêtre
(2/90) (EMIN) Ⓓ **CD-EMX2123**
(2/88) (EMIN) ⊟ **TC-EMX2123**
5. E. Stignani, EIAR Orch, U. Tansini (Ital: r1941)
(1/91) (PREI) Ⓓ **89014**
5. L. Price, LSO, E. Downes
(12/92) (RCA) Ⓓ [4] **09026 61236-2**
5. M. Klose, Berlin St Op Orch, B. Seidler-Winkler (r1938: Ger) (7/95) (PREI) Ⓓ **89082**
6b G. Thill, Orch, E. Bigot (r1930)
(1/89) (EMI) Ⓓ **CDM7 69548-2**
6b G. Thill, orch, E. Bigot (r1930)
(8/95) (FORL) Ⓓ **UCD16727**
9b R. Bampton, Victor SO, W. Pelletier (r1941)
(4/92) (EMI) Ⓓ [7] **CHS7 69741-2(1)**
9b R. Bampton, RCA SO, W. Pelletier (r1941)
(4/94) (RCA) Ⓓ [6] **09026 61580-2(4)**

Armide– opera: 5 acts (1777—Paris) (Lib. P. Quinnault)

Ah! si la liberté. F. Leider, orch, J. Barbirolli (r1928) (2/90) (PREI) Ⓓ **89004**
Ah! si la liberté. F. Leider, orch, J. Barbirolli (r1928)
(7/92) (PEAR) Ⓓ [3] **GEMMCDS9926(1)**
Musette J. Woods (arr. J. Woods)
(IMP) Ⓓ **PCD1086**

Le Cinesi– opera-serenade: 1 act (1754—Vienna) (Wds. Metastasio)

Sivene I. Poulenard
Lisinga A.S. von Otter
Tangia G. Banditelli
Silango G. de Mey
SCB, R. Jacobs
(DHM) Ⓓ **GD77174**
Sivene K. Erickson
Lisinga A. Milcheva
Tangia M. Schiml
Silango T. Moser
Munich RO, L. Gardelli (r1983)
(1/90) (ORFE) Ⓓ **C178891A**

La Corona– opera: 1 act (composed 1765 - not performed) (Wds. Metastasio)

Atalanta A. Słowakiewicz
Meleagro H. Górzyńska
Climene L. Juranek
Asteria B. Nowicka
Bavarian Rad Chor, Warsaw Chbr Op Orch, T. Bugaj (r1983)
(3/88) (ORFE) Ⓓ [2] **C135872H**

La Danza– opera: 1 act (1755—Vienna) (Wds. Metastasio)

Nice E. Ignatowicz
Tirsi K. Myrlak
Warsaw Chbr Op Orch, T. Bugaj (r1983)
(3/88) (ORFE) Ⓓ [2] **C135872H**

Echo et Narcisse– drame lyrique: prologue and 3 acts (1770—Paris) (Lib. L. T. von Tschudi)

Echo S. Boulin
Narcisse K. Streit
Amour D. Massell
Cynire P. Galliard
Egle G. Hoffstedt
Aglae C. Högman
Thanaïs H. Krogen
Sylphie E.M. Tersson
Hamburg St Op Chor, Concerto Cologne, R. Jacobs (pp1987)
(11/88) (HARM) ⊟ [2] **HMC40 5210/2**

Iphigénie en Aulide– tragedy: 3 acts (1774—Paris) (Lib. du Roullet, after Racine)

Iphigénie L. Dawson
Agamemnon J. Van Dam
Clytemnestra A. S. von Otter
Achilles J. Aler
Patroclus B. Delétré
Calchas G. Cachemaille
Arcas R. Schirrer
Diana G. Laurens
1st Greek Lady; Slave A. Monoyios
2nd Greek Lady I. Eschenbrenner
Monteverdi Ch, Lyon Op Orch, J. E. Gardiner (r1987)
(ERAT) Ⓓ [6] **4509-99607-2**
Iphigénie L. Dawson
Agamemnon J. Van Dam
Clytemnestra A.S. von Otter
Achilles J. Aler
Patroclus B. Delétré
Calchas G. Cachemaille
Arcas R. Schirrer
Diana G. Laurens
1st Greek Lady; Slave A. Monoyios
2nd Greek Lady I. Eschenbrenner
Monteverdi Ch, Lyon Op Orch, J.E. Gardiner
(6/90) (ERAT) Ⓓ [2] **2292-45003-2**
Agammemnon's recit & aria B. Christoff, Bulgarian RSO, E. Gracis (r1979)
(FORL) Ⓓ **UCD16651**
Air et Danse;Tambourin;Gavotte;Chaconne NY Nat SO, W. Damrosch (r1929)
(SCHW) Ⓓ [2] **311162**
Diane impitoyable B. Christoff, Philh, A. Fistoulari (r1951: Ital) (EMI) Ⓓ **CDH5 65500-2**
Excs P. Schoeffler, H. Braun, H. Konetzni, S. Svanholm, S. Roth, H. Schweiger, Vienna St Op Chor, Vienna St Op Orch, L. Ludwig (pp1942: Ger) (SCHW) Ⓓ [2] **314692**
Gavotte H. Samuel (arr Brahms: r1928)
(KOCH) Ⓓ [2] **37137-2**
Gavotte M. Levitzki (arr Brahms: r1927)
(6/92) (APR) Ⓓ [2] **APR7020**
Gavotte I. Biret (r1993: trans pf: Brahms)
(5/95) (NAXO) Ⓓ **8 550958**
L'ai-je bien entendu...En croirai-je mes yeux? C. Ludwig, J. King, VPO, K. Böhm (pp1962: Ger)
(ORFE) Ⓓ **C365941A**
Overture Czech PO, B. Liška
(SUPR) ⊟ **11 0640-4**
Overture German Fest Orch, A. Scholz
(CAVA) Ⓓ **CAVCD017**
Overture R. Greiss, G. Bach (arr vn/gtr: Porro)
(FSM) Ⓓ **FCD91114**
Overture BPO, R. Strauss (r1928)
(KOCH) Ⓓ **37119-2**
Overture NBC SO, A. Toscanini (bp1952)
(RCA) Ⓓ **GD60280**
Overture Philh, O. Klemperer
(8/92) (EMI) Ⓓ **CDM7 64143-2**

Iphigénie en Tauride– opera: 4 acts (1779—Paris) (Lib. Guillard and Du Roullet)

EXCERPTS: ACT 1: 1. Grands Dieux! soyez-nous secourables; 2a. Iphigénie, ô ciel!; 2b. Ô songe affreux!; 3a. Ô race de Pélops; 3b. Ô toi qui prolongeas mes jours; 3c. Quand verrons-nous tarir nos pleurs?; 4. Ballet; 5. Il nous fallait du sang. ACT 2: 6a. Quel silence effrayant!; 6b. Dieux qui me poursuivez; 7a. Quel langage accablant; 7b. Unis dès la plus tendre enfance; 8a. Dieux! la malheur en tous lieux suit mes pas; 8b. De noirs pressentiments; 9a. Les Dieux apaisent leur courroux; 9b. Dieux! étouffez en moi; 10a. Et vous, à vos Dieux tutélaires; 10b. Il nous fallait du sang; 11. Etrangers malheureux; 12a. Dieux protecteurs; 12b. Le calme rentre dans mon coeur; 13. Vengeons et la nature et les Dieux; 14. Je vois toute l'horreur; 15a. Patrie infortunée; 15b. Ô malheureuse Iphigénie!; 15c. Honorez avec moi ce héros; 15d. Contemplez ces tristes apprêts; 15e. Ô mon frère. ACT 3: 16a. Je cède à vos désirs; 16b. D'une image, hélas! trop chérie; 17. Voici ces captifs malheureux; 18a. Ô joie inattendue!; 18b. Je pourrais du tyran tromper la barbarie; 19a. Ô moment trop heureux!; 19b. Et tu prétends encore que tu m'aimes; 19c. Quoi! je ne vaincrai pas; 19d. Ah! mon ami, j'implore ta pitié!; 19e. Pylade!...Ah! mon ami, j'implore ta pitié!; 20a. Malgré toi, je saurai t'arracher au trépas!; 20b. Quoi? toujours à mes voeux; 21a. Puisque le ciel à vos jours s'intéresse; 21b. Divinité des grandes âmes; 22a. Non, cet affreux devoir; 22b. Je t'implore et je tremble; 23a. Ô Diane, sois-nous propice; 23b. La force m'abandonne; 23c. Chaste fille de Latone; 23d. Quel moment! Dieux puissants; 24. Tremblez! tremblez!; 25. De tes forfaits la trame est découverte; 26. Qu'oses-tu proposer, barbare?; 27. C'est à toi de mourir!; 28. Arrêtez! écoutez mes decrets éternels; 29a. Ta soeur! qu'ai-je entendu?; 29b. Dans cet objet touchant; 29c. Les Dieux, longtemps en courroux.

Iphigénie R. Crespin
Pylade G. Chauvet
Oreste R. Massard
Diana M. Benegas

Thoas V. de Narké
Buenos Aires Colón Th Chor, Buenos Aires Colón Th Orch, G. Sébastian (pp1964: mono, on L then R channels)
(CHNT) Ⓓ **LDC278 769**
Iphigénie D. Montague
Pylade J. Aler
Oreste T. Allen
1st Priestess N. Argenta
2nd Priestess S. Boulton
Diana C. Alliot-Lugaz
Thoas R. Massis
Monteverdi Ch, Lyon Op Orch, J.E. Gardiner (r1985)
(6/86) (PHIL) Ⓓ [2] **416 148-2PH2**
Iphigénie P. Lorengar
Pylade F. Bonisolli
Oreste W. Groenroos
1st Priestess A.J. Smith
2nd Priestess S. Klare
Diana A. Nowski
Thoas D. Fischer-Dieskau
Bavarian Rad Chor, BRSO, L. Gardelli (r1982)
(12/87) (ORFE) Ⓓ [2] **C052832H**
Iphigenie C. Vaness
Pylade G. Winbergh
Oreste T. Allen
1st Priestess A. Zoroberto
2nd Priestess M. Remor
Diana S. Brunet
Thoas G. Surian
Scythian A. Veccia
Minister of the Sanctuary E. Turco
Greek woman S. Krasteva
La Scala Chor, La Scala Orch, R. Muti (pp1992)
(10/93) (SONY) Ⓓ [2] **S2K52492**
3b R. Crespin, SRO, A. Lombard (r1970/1)
(DECC) Ⓓ **440 416-2DM**
3b K. Te Kanawa, ROHO, J. Tate (r1988)
(EMI) Ⓓ **CDM5 65578-2**
3b K. Te Kanawa, ROHO, J. Tate
(2/90) (EMI) Ⓓ **CDC7 49863-2**
7b, 19a, 19b F. Wunderlich, H. Prey, BRSO, R. Kubelík (Ger: bp)
(DG) Ⓓ [5] **435 145-2GX5(1)**
8b V. Maurel, anon (r1903)
(10/92) (SYMP) Ⓓ **SYMCD1101**
15b M. Callas, Paris Cons, G. Prêtre
(2/88) (EMI) Ⓓ **CDC7 49059-2**
15b M. Callas, Paris Cons, G. Prêtre
(2/90) (EMI) Ⓓ [4] **CMS7 63244-2**

Orfeo ed Euridice– opera: 3 acts (1762—Vienna) (Lib. Calzabigi. Italian version of Orphée et Eurydice)

EXCERPTS: ACT 1: 1a. Overture; 1b. Introduction...Ah! se intorno; 2. Amici, quel lamento; 3. Pantomime; 4. Ah! se intorno; 5. Restar vogl'io; 6. Ritornello; 7. Chiamo il mio ben; 8. Euridice, Euridice; 9. Cerco il mio ben; 10. Euridice! Euridice!; 11. Piango il mio ben; 12. O Numi, barbari Numi; 13. Se il dolce suon; 14. Ciel! rivederla potrò!; 15. Gli sguardi trattieni; 16. Che disse!; 17. Addio, addio. ACT 2: 18. Danza in E flat; 19. Chi mai dell'Erebo; 20. Ballo in C minor; 21. Chi mai dell'Erebo; 22. Deh! placetevi; 23. Misero giovine!; 24. Mille pene; 25. Ah! quale incognito affetto; 26. Men tiranno; 27. Ah! quale incognito affetto; 28. Dance of the Furies; 29. Ballet in F; 30. Ballet in D minor (Dance of the Blessed Spirits): (flute solo); 31. Ballet in C; 32. Questo asilo; 33. Che puro ciel!; 34. Vieni ai regni; 35. Dance of hero; 36. Oh voi, ombre felici; 37. Torna, o bella. ACT 3: 38. Vieni! segui i miei passi; 39. Vieni appaga il tuo consorte; 40. Qual vita; 41. Che fiero momento; 42. Ecco novel tormento; 43. Che farò senza Euridice; 44. Ah! finisca e per sempre; 45. Trionfi Amore; 46. Grazioso; 47. Gavotte; 48. Ballet; 49. Minuet; 50. Divo Amore; 51. Ballet in A; 52. Ballet in D; 53. Ciaccona in D.

Orfeo J. Kowalski
Euridice G. Webster
Amor J. Budd
ROH Chor, ROHO, Hartmut Haenchen, H. Kupfer
(MCEG) ▣ **VVD986**
Orfeo J. Baker
Euridice E. Speiser
Amor E. Gale
Glyndebourne Fest Chor, LPO, R. Leppard, P. Hall (r1982)
(CAST) ▣ **CVI2035**
Orfeo G. Simionato
Euridice S. Jurinac
Amor G. Sciutti
Vienna St Op Chor, VPO, H. von Karajan (pp1959)
(MEMO) Ⓓ [2] **HR4382/3**
Orfeo J. Kowalski
Euridice G. Webster
Amor J. Budd
ROH Chor, ROHO, Hartmut Haenchen, H. Kupfer
(PION) ◐ **PLMCB00621**
Orfeo G. Bumbry
Euridice A. Rothenberger
Amor R-M. Pütz
Leipzig Rad Chor, Leipzig Gewandhaus, V. Neumann (r1966)
(BERL) Ⓓ [2] **0090 332BC**
Orfeo D. Fischer-Dieskau
Euridice E. Söderström
Amor R-M. Pütz
Cologne Rad Chor, Cappella Coloniensis, F. Leitner (pp1964)
(ORFE) Ⓓ [2] **C391952I**
Orfeo M. Horne
Euridice P. Lorengar
Amor H. Donath
ROH Chor, ROHO, G. Solti
(8/89) (DECC) Ⓓ [2] **417 410-2DM2**
Orfeo R. Jacobs
Euridice M. Kweksilber
Amor M. Falewicz
Ghent Collegium Vocale, Petite Bande, S. Kuijken (Ed. Andriessen & S. Kuijken)
(1/90) (ACCE) Ⓓ [2] **ACC48223/4D**
Orfeo J. Kowalski
Euridice D. Schellenberger
Amor C. Fliegner
Berlin Rad Chor, CPE Bach Orch, Hans Haenchen
(1/90) (CAPR) Ⓓ [2] **60 008-2**
Orfeo S. Verrett
Euridice A. Moffo
Amor J. Raskin
Rome Polyphonic Chor, Virtuosi di Roma, R. Fasano
(1/91) (RCA) Ⓓ [2] **GD87896**
Orfeo A. Baltsa
Euridice M. Marshall
Amor E. Gruberová
Ambrosian Op Chor, Philh, R. Muti
(3/91) (EMI) Ⓓ [2] **CMS7 63637-2**
Orfeo M. Chance
Euridice N. Argenta
Amor S. Beckerbauer
Stuttgart Chbr Ch, Tafelmusik, F. Bernius
(8/92) (SONY) Ⓓ [2] **SX2K48040**
Orfeo M. Forrester
Euridice T. Stich-Randall
Amor H. Steffek
Vienna Academy Ch, Vienna St Op Orch, C. Mackerras
(12/92) (VANG) Ⓓ [2] **08.4040.72**
Orfeo J. Baker
Euridice E. Speiser
Amor E. Gale
Glyndebourne Fest Chor, LPO, R. Leppard
(5/93) (ERAT) Ⓓ [2] **2292-45864-2**
Orfeo G. Simionato
Euridice S. Jurinac
Amor G. Sciutti
Vienna St Op Chor, VPO, H. von Karajan (pp1959)
(11/93) (DG) Ⓓ [2] **439 101-2GX2**
Orfeo D.L. Ragin
Euridice S. McNair
Amore C. Sieden
Monteverdi Ch, EBS, J.E. Gardiner (r1991)
(2/94) (PHIL) Ⓓ [2] **434 093-2PH2**
Orfeo J. Bowman
Euridice L. Dawson
Amor C. McFadden
Namur Chbr Ch, Grande Ecurie, J-C. Malgoire (pp1994)
(1/95) (ASTR) Ⓓ [2] **E8538**
Orfeo D. Fischer-Dieskau
Euridice M. Stader
Amor R. Streich
Berlin RIAS Chbr Ch, Berlin Motet Ch, Berlin RSO, F. Fricsay (r1956: Ger)
(2/95) (DG) Ⓓ [2] **439 711-2GX2**
Act 2. N. Merriman, B. Gibson, R. Shaw Chorale, NBC SO, A. Toscanini (bp1952)
(RCA) Ⓓ **GD60280**
Dance of the furies; 30. Orpheus CO (r1992)
(DG) OO **437 782-5GH**
Dance of the furies; 30. Orpheus CO (r1992)
(DG) Ⓓ **437 782-2GH**
Excs J. Baker (CAST) ▣ **CVI2030**
1. Munich Bach Orch, K. Richter
(DG) Ⓓ [2] **447 364-2GDB2**
1a, 1b, 7, 20-23, 30, 33, 39, 40-45. S. McNair, D. L. Ragin, C. Sieden, Monteverdi Ch, EBS, J. E. Gardiner (r1991) (PHIL) Ⓓ **442 383-2PH**
4, 8, 11, 15, 16, 19, 22, 23, 33, 34, 38, 39, 41, 43-45. K. Ferrier, A. Ayars, Z. Vlachopoulos, Glyndebourne Fest Chor, Southern PO, F. Stiedry (r1947) (6/92) (DECC) Ⓓ **433 468-2DM**
7-11, 43. E. Kurmangaliev, Moscow Maly SO, V. Ponkin (MEZH) Ⓓ **MK417047**
7, 22, 33, 43. K. Ferrier, Netherlands Op Chor, Netherlands Op Orch, C. Bruck (r1951)
(6/88) (EMI) Ⓓ **CDH7 61003-2**
7, 9, 11, 22, 33, 43. G. Simionato, VPO, H. von Karajan (pp1959) (MEMO) Ⓓ [2] **HR4386/7**
10, 43. E. Leisner, orch (r1913: Ger)
(PREI) Ⓓ [2] **89210**
11, 43. M. Klose, Berlin St Op Orch, B. Seidler-Winkler (r1938: Ger) (7/95) (PREI) Ⓓ **89082**
16, 17. J. Baker, LPO, R. Leppard (pp1982)
(10/95) (BBCR) Ⓓ [2] **DMCD98**
16, 17, 31, 33, 43. C. Watkinson, Amsterdam Bach Sols, J.W. de Vriend
(3/89) (ETCE) Ⓓ **KTC1064**
28. AAM, C. Hogwood (r1980)
(L'OI) Ⓓ [2] **443 267-2OX2**
28, 30. S. Preston, AAM, C. Hogwood
(12/83) (L'OI) Ⓓ **410 553-2OH**
28, 30. I. Biret (trans Kempff)
(5/93) (MARC) Ⓓ **8 223452**
28, 30. Calgary PO, M. Bernardi (r1992)
(12/94) (CBC) Ⓓ **SMCD5125**
29-31, 35. Luxembourg Rad & TV SO, L. de Froment (FORL) Ⓓ **FF046**
30. ASMF, N. Marriner, D. Heather
(6/87) (EMI) ▣ **MVP99 1042 2**
30. E. Feuermann, T. van der Pas (arr vc/pf: r1934) (PEAR) Ⓓ **GEMMCD9442**
30. F. Kreisler, G. Falkenstein (r1912: arr Kreisler) (BIDD) Ⓓ **LAB019**
30. BPO, H. von Karajan (DG) Ⓓ **413 309-2GH**
(DG) ▭ **413 309-4GH**
30. G. von Bahr, Stockholm Chbr Ens
(BIS) Ⓓ **BIS-CD100**
30. Adelaide SO, J. Serebrier
(MCI) Ⓓ **OQ0011**
30. E. Wild (trans Sgambati: pp1981)
(AUDI) Ⓓ [2] **CD72008**
30. Budapest PO, A. Kórodi (LASE) Ⓓ **15 513**
(LASE) ▭ **79 513**
30. H. Rucker, Dresden PO, H. Kegel
(LASE) Ⓓ **15 625**
(LASE) ▭ **79 625**
30. London Fest Orch, R. Pople
(HYPE) Ⓓ **CDH88030**
(HYPE) ▭ **KH88030**
30. ECO, J. Judd (NOVA) Ⓓ **150 044-2**
30. RLPO, C. Groves (CFP) Ⓓ **CD-CFP4515**
(CFP) ▭ **TC-CFP4515**
30. F Liszt CO, J. Rolla (vn/dir)
(TELD) Ⓓ **9031-74789-2**
30 (pt) B. Hoff, R. Levin (arr vn/pf: Kreisler)
(VICT) Ⓓ **VCD19037**
30. L. Jones, K. Sturrock (vn/pf)
(SAIN) Ⓓ **SCD4058**
30. J. Baker, P. Sykes (arr fl/org)
(CENT) Ⓓ **CRC2084**
30. ASMF, N. Marriner
(EMI) Ⓓ [2] **CZS7 67425-2**
30. J. Galway, National PO, C. Gerhardt (arr Gerhardt) (RCA) Ⓓ **GD60924**
30. NBC SO, A. Toscanini (r1946)
(RCA) Ⓓ **GD60280**
30. M. Maisky, P. Gililov (arr vc/pf)
(DG) OO **431 544-5GH**
30. A. Goldstone (r1993; arr Sgambati)
(AMPH) Ⓓ **PHICD123**
(AMPH) ▭ **PHI123**
30. G. Novaes (r1950s; arr Sgambati: pf)
(VOX) Ⓓ [2] **CDX2 5501**
30. C. Conway, D. Watkins (arr fl/hp)
(MERI) Ⓓ **CDE84241**
30. W. Kempff (r1975: arr pf: Kempff)
(DG) Ⓓ **439 108-2GGA**
30. E. Moguilevsky (r1992)
(PAVA) Ⓓ **ADW7277**
30. S. Rachmaninov (r1925: arr pf: Sgambati)
(DECC) Ⓓ **440 066-2DM**
30. G. Neveu, B. Seidler-Winkler (r1938: arr vn/pf: Kreisler) (PEAR) Ⓓ **GEMMCD9125**
30. ASMF, N. Marriner (r1977)
(CFP) Ⓓ **CD-CFP4660**
(CFP) ▭ **TC-CFP4660**

30. S. Accardo, L. Manzini (r1993; arr Kreisler) (FONE) ⦶ **94F04**
30. A. Markov, D. Cogan (r1993: arr vn/pf) (ERAT) ⦶ **4509-98481-2**
30. H. Szeryng, C. Reiner (r1963; arr Kreisler) (MERC) ⦶ **434 351-2MM**
30. ECO, R. Leppard (r1980) (SONY) ⦶ **SMK66940**
30. P-L. Graf, Zurich Camerata, R. Tschupp (11/87) (JECK) ⦶ **JD506-2**
30. RLPO, C. Groves (1/89) (EMIL) ⦶ **CDZ114**
(EMIL) ▭ **LZ114**
30. M. Hambourg (r1929: arr pf: Sgambati) (4/89) (OPAL) ⦶ **OPALCD9839**
30. ASMF, N. Marriner (11/89) (CFP) ⦶ **CD-CFP4557**
(11/89) (CFP) ▭ **TC-CFP4557**
30. NYPSO, A. Toscanini (r1929) (3/90) (PEAR) ⦶ [3] **GEMMCDS9373**
30. X. Wei, Pam Nicholson (arr vn/pf) (9/90) (ASV) ⦶ **CDDCA698**
30. J. Kubelík, anon (arr Wilhelmj: r1912) (6/91) (BIDD) ⦶ [2] **LAB033/4**
30. M. Maisky, P. Gililov (arr vc/pf) (7/91) (DG) ⦶ **431 544-2GH**
30. G. Neveu, B. Seidler-Winkler (r1938) (10/92) (TEST) ⦶ **SBT1010**
30. NYPSO, A. Toscanini (r1929) (11/92) (RCA) ⦶ **GD60318**
30. M. Levitzki (arr Sgambati: r1923) (1/93) (APR) ⦶ [2] **APR7014**
30. S. Rachmaninov (r1925; arr Sgambati: pf) (3/93) (RCA) ⦶ [10] **09026 61265-2(1)**
30. Midori, R. McDonald (r1992; arr vn/pf Kreisler) (6/93) (SONY) ⦶ **SK52568**
(6/93) (SONY) ▭ **ST52568**
30. Barthold Kuijken, Tafelmusik, J. Lamon (r1991) (7/93) (SONY) ⦶ **SK48045**
30. N. Milstein, G. Moore (r1932: arr Kreisler) (7/93) (APR) ⦶ [2] **APR7016**
30. B. Huberman, P. Frenkel (r1923: arr Wilhelmj) (3/94) (BIDD) ⦶ [2] **LAB077/8**
30. E. Petri (pp1959: arr pf: Sgambati) (3/94) (MUSI) ⦶ [4] **MACD-772**
30. N. Milstein, L. Pommers (r1956: arr Kreisler) (5/94) (EMI) ⦶ [6] **ZDMF7 64830-2**
30. W. Kempff (r1975: arr pf: Kempff) (11/94) (DG) ⦶ [2] **439 672-2GX2**
30. J. Heifetz, E. Bay (r1945) (11/94) (RCA) ⦶ [65] **09026 61778-2(19)**
30. J. Bálint, N. Mercz (r1992: arr fl/hp: Mercz) (12/94) (NAXO) ⦶ **8 550741**
30. I. Perlman, S. Sanders (r1985: arr Kreisler) (6/95) (EMI) ⦶ [20] **CZS4 83177-2(2)**
30. E. Petri (r1936: arr pf: Sgambati) (8/95) (APR) ⦶ [2] **APR7027**
30, 49. R. Aitken, E. Goodman (r c1981: arr fl/hp) (IMP) ⦶ **PCD1091**
33. T. Berganza, ROHO, A. Gibson (DECC) ⦶ **433 067-2DWO**
(DECC) ▭ **433 067-4DWO**
33. T. Berganza, ROHO, A. Gibson (r1960) (DECC) ⦶ **443 378-2DM**
33, 43. J. Baker, LPO, R. Leppard (CAST) ▣ **CVI2071**
43. Alfredo Kraus, J. Tordesillas (NIMB) ⦶ **NI5102**
43. L. Pavarotti, Philh, P. Gamba (arr A Faris) (DECC) ⦶ **417 796-2DM**
43. T. Schipa, orch, Anon (cond) (pp1932) (MEMO) ⦶ [2] **HR4220/1**
43. T. Berganza, ROHO, A. Gibson (r1960) (DECC) ⦶ **433 065-2DWO**
(DECC) ▭ **433 065-4DWO**
43. J. Baker, Glyndebourne Fest Chor, LPO, R. Leppard (ERAT) ⦶ **2292-45797-2**
(ERAT) ▭ **2292-45797-4**
43. E. Himy (arr Sgambati: pf) (BNL) ⦶ **BNL112822**
43. F. von Stade, Utah SO, J. Silverstein (pp1991) (DECC) ⦶ **436 284-2DH**
43. J. Baker, Glyndebourne Fest Orch, R. Leppard (TELD) ● **9031-77676-6**
(TELD) ▣ **9031-77676-3**
43. T. Schipa, La Scala Orch, C. Sabajno (r1932) (NIMB) ⦶ **NI7870**
43. R. Stevens, Rome Op Orch, P. Monteux (r1957) (RCA) ⦶ **09026 62689-2**
43. B. Fassbaender, Stuttgart RSO, H. Graf (11/86) (ORFE) ⦶ **C096841A**
43. T. Schipa, orch, C. Sabajno (r1932) (4/90) (EMI) ⦶ **CDH7 63200-2**
43. M. Lipovšek, Munich RO, G. Patanè (6/90) (ORFE) ⦶ **C179891A**
43. E. Stignani, EIAR Orch, A. la Rosa Parodi (r1940) (1/91) (PREI) ⦶ **89014**
43. S. Onegin, orch, Rosario Bourdon (r1928) (2/91) (PREI) ⦶ **89027**
43. K. Ferrier, LSO, M. Sargent (Eng: r1946) (6/91) (DECC) ⦶ **430 096-2DWO**
(6/91) (DECC) ▭ **430 096-4DWO**
43. L. Pavarotti, Philh, P. Gamba (arr A Faris) (12/91) (DECC) ⦶ **433 710-2DH**
(12/91) (DECC) ▭ **433 710-4DH**
43. K. Ferrier, LSO, M. Sargent (r1946: Eng) (6/92) (DECC) ⦶ **433 470-2DM**
(6/92) (DECC) ▭ **433 470-4DM**
43. L. Kirkby-Lunn, orch, P. Pitt (r1915) (7/92) (PEAR) ⦶ [3] **GEMMCDS9924(1)**
43. C. Butt, orch, Henry Wood (r c1916) (7/92) (PEAR) ⦶ [3] **GEMMCDS9925(1)**
43. K. Branzell, orch (Ger: r1927) (8/92) (PREI) ⦶ **89039**
43. K. Flagstad, Philh, W. Braithwaite (r1948) (7/93) (TEST) ⦶ **SBT1018**
43. K. Thorborg, Berlin St Op Orch, F. Weissmann (r1933: Ger) (4/95) (PREI) ⦶ **89084**
49. Munich Pro Arte Orch, K. Redel (FORL) ⦶ **FF051**

Orphée et Eurydice– opera: 3 acts (1774—Paris) (Lib. R de Calzabigi, trans P-L Moline)

EXCERPTS: 1a. Overture. ACT 1: 1b. Ah! dans ce bois tranquille; 2. Vos plaintes, vos regrets; 3. Pantomime; 4. Ah! dans ce bois lugubre et sombre; 5. Éloignez-vous!; 6. Ritournelle in C minor; 7a. Eurydice! Eurydice! Ombre chère; 7b. Object de mon amour; 7c. Eurydice, Eurydice, de ce doux nom; 7d. Accablé de regrets; 7e. Plein de troubles; 8. Divinités de l'Achéron; 9. L'Amour vient au secours; 10. Si les doux accords; 11. Dieux! Je la reverrais!; 12. Soumis au silence; 13. Qu'entends-je? Qu'a-t-il dit?; 14. Amours, viens rendre à mon âme. ACT 2: 15. Danse des Furies; 16. Prélude; 17. Quel est l'audacieux; 18. Air de Furie in D minor; 19. Quel est l'audacieux; 20. Laissez-vous toucher; 21. Qui t'amène; 22. Ah1 la flamme qui me dévore; 23. Par quels puissants accords; 24. La tendresse qui me presse; 25. Quels chants doux; 26. Air de Furies in D minor; 27. Ballet des Ombres heureuses; 28. Cet asile aimable et tranquille; 29. Ritournelle in F; 30. Quel nouveau ciel pour ces lieux; 31. Viens dans ce séjour paisible; 32. Ballet (Lent); 33. Ô vous, ombres que j'implore; 34. Près du tendre objet qu'on aime. ACT 3: 35. Viens, viens, Eurydice, suis-moi; 36. Viens, suis un époux; 37. Mais d'où vient qu'il persiste; 38a. Fortune ennemie; 38b. Je goûtais les charmes; 38c. Fortune ennemie (reprise); 39. Quelle épreuve cruelle!; 40. J'ai perdu mon Eurydice; 41. Ah! puisse ma douleur; 42. Arrête, Orphée!; 43. Tendre amour!; 44. Le dieu de Paphos et de Gnide; 45. Ballet.

Orphée A.S. von Otter
Eurydice B. Hendricks
Amour B. Fournier
Monteverdi Ch, Lyon Op Orch, J.E. Gardiner (r1989) (2/90) (EMI) ⦶ [2] **CDS7 49834-2**
Abridged A. Raveau, G. Féraldy, J. Delille, Vlassof Chor, Vlassof Orch, H. Tomasi (r1935) (2/92) (MSCM) ⦶ **MM30325**
Orphée L. Simoneau
Eurydice S. Danco
Amour P. Alarie
R. Blanchard Voc Ens, Lamoureux Orch, H. Rosbaud (r1956) (5/93) (PHIL) ⦶ [2] **434 784-2PM2**
Abridged A. Raveau, G. Féraldy, J. Delille, Vlassof Chor, Paris SO, H. Tomasi (r1935) (PEAR) ⦶ **GEMMCD9169**
14. S. Verrett, RCA Italiana Op Orch, G. Prêtre (r1967) (RCA) ⦶ **09026 61457-2**
15. K. Ott, C. Keller (12/90) (CPO) ⦶ **CPO999 044-2**
27. I. Perlman, S. Sanders (arr. Kreisler) (EMI) ⦶ **CDC7 47467-2**
36. M. Mesplé, N. Gedda, Paris Op Orch, P. Dervaux (r1974) (EMI) ⦶ [2] **CZS7 67813-2**
40. J. Kowalski, Berlin RSO, H. Fricke (CAPR) ◘ **80 416**
40. J. Kowalski, Berlin RSO, H. Fricke (CAPR) OO **70 416**
40. M. Callas, FRNO, G. Prêtre (r1961) (EMI) ⦶ **CDC5 55016-2**
40. L. Simoneau, Lamoureux Orch, H. Rosbaud (PHIL) ⦶ **442 602-2PM**
(PHIL) ▭ **442 602-4PM**
40. A. Raveau, Paris SO, H. Tomasi (r1935) (PEAR) ⦶ **GEMMCD9169**
40. M. Callas, FRNO, G. Prêtre (2/88) (EMI) ⦶ **CDC7 49059-2**
40. M. Callas, FRNO, G. Prêtre (2/90) (EMI) ⦶ **CDM7 63182-2**
40. R. Anday, orch (Ger: r1924) (5/92) (PREI) ⦶ **8904**
40. J. Kowalski, Berlin RSO, H. Fricke (10/92) (CAPR) ⦶ **10 41**

Paride ed Elena– opera: 5 acts (1770—Vienna) (Lib. Calzibigi)

EXCERPTS: 1. Overture. ACT ONE: 2a. Non sdegnare, o bella Venere; 2b. O del mio dolce ardor; 2c. Dall'aurea sua stella; 2d. Spiaggate amate; 3a. Stranier, la mia Regina; 3b. Ma, chie sei?; 4a. Felice te, che possessor sarai; 4b. Nell'idea ch'ei volge in mente; 4c. Ballo. ACT TWO: 5. Si presenti, mi vegga di Priamo il figlio; 6a. Regina! Oh Dei!; 6b. Forse più d'una beltà; 7a. Tutto qui mi sorprende; 7b. Le belle immagini d'un dolce amore. ACT THREE: 8a. Prence, la tuo presenza il popolo di Sparta; 8b. Negli strali, nell'arco possente; 8c. non più! L'eroe trojano, illustri atleti; 8d. Lodi al Nume nell'arco possente; 8e. Per te, Signor; 8f. Quegli occhi belli; 8g. Ah ferma!...Ah senti!; 8h. Mi fugge spietata; 8i. Maestoso. ACT FOUR: 9. Temerario! E non basta; 10a. Vengo, o Regina; 10b. Ah, lo veggo, ad ingannarmi; 11a. Si, spietata, s'accende; 11b. Di te scordarmi, e vivere!; 12. Lo temei: non mi sento. ACT FIVE: 13a. Elena a me s'asconde!; 13b. Donzelle semplici, no, non credete; 13c. Consolati, o Regina!; 14. Opportuno giungesti, Elena t'ama!; 15. T'inganni, il tu destino; 16a. Che udii?; 16b. Sempre a te sarò fedele!; 17a. Vieni al mar tranquilla è l'onda; 17b. Presto fugge la beltà.

Paride R. Alexande
Elena C. McFadder
Amore D. Frey
Pallade K. Ganninge
Stagione Voc Ens, Stagione, M. Schneider (pp1991) (6/93) (CAPR) ⦶ [2] **60 027-2**
Chaconne Stuttgart CO, K. Münchinger (DECC) ⦶ **433 631-2DSP**
(DECC) ▭ **433 631-4DSP**
2b Alfredo Kraus, J. Tordesillas (NIMB) ⦶ **NI5102**
2b B. Gigli, La Scala Orch, D. Olivieri (r1935) (NIMB) ⦶ **NI7817**
(NIMB) ▭ **NC7817**
2b R. Bruson, C. Sheppard (pp1980) (CHAN) ⦶ **CHAN6551**
2b M. Elman, J. Seiger (arr Ries: vn/pf) (VANG) ⦶ **08.8029.71**
2b J. Carreras, ECO, V. Sutej (r1992; arr Agostinelli) (PHIL) OO **434 926-5PH**
2b M. Battistini, orch (r1923) (PEAR) ⦶ **GEMMCD9016**
2b C. de Rothschild, D. Watkins (r1994) (NATI) ⦶ **NTCD006**
2b J. Carreras, ECO, V. Sutej (r1992; arr Agostinelli) (6/93) (PHIL) ⦶ **434 926-2PH**
2b T. Berganza, ROHO, A. Gibson (r1960) (10/93) (DECC) ⦶ **436 462-2DM**
2b R. Tebaldi, R. Bonynge (r1972) (9/94) (DECC) ⦶ **436 202-2DM**
2b K. Vayne, orch (bp1958-9) (6/95) (PREI) ⦶ **89996**
2b M. Klose, Berlin St Op Orch, B. Seidler-Winkler (r1938) (7/95) (PREI) ⦶ **89082**
2d C. Muzio, orch (r1923) (5/90) (BOGR) ⦶ [2] **BIM705-2**
2d C. Muzio, anon (r1923) (1/94) (ROMO) ⦶ [2] **81005-2**

La Rencontre imprévue– opera: 3 acts (1764—Vienna) (Lib. L. H. Dancourt)

Rezia L. Dawson
Balkis C. Le Coz
Dardané C. Dubosc
Amine S. Marin-Degor
Ali G. de Mey
Osmin J-L. Viala
Sultan G. Flechter
Vertigo J-P. Lafont
Calender G. Cachemaille
Chef de Caravane F. Dudziak
Lyon Op Orch, J. E. Gardiner (r1990) (ERAT) ⦶ [6] **4509-99607-2**
Rezia L. Dawson
Balkis C. Le Coz
Dardané C. Dubosc
Amine S. Marin-Degor
Ali G. de Mey
Osmin J-L. Viala

Sultan G. Flechter
Vertigo J-P. Lafont
Calender G. Cachemaille
Chef de Caravane F. Dudziak
Lyon Op Orch, J.E. Gardiner
(10/91) (ERAT) Ⓓ [2] **2292-45516-2**
Rezia J. Kaufman
Balkis I. Vermillion
Dardané A. Stumphius
Amine A-M. Rodde
Ali R. Gambill
Osmin C.H. Ahnsjö
Sultan U. Ress
Vertigo M. Walker
Calender J-H. Rootering
Chef de Caravane P. Orecchia
Munich RO, L. Hager
(12/92) (ORFE) Ⓓ [2] **C242912H**
C'est un torrent E. Schwarzkopf, M. Raucheisen (Ger: bp1944)
(6/87) (ACAN) Ⓓ **43 801**
C'est un torrent E. Schwarzkopf, G. Moore (Ger: r1954) (12/90) (EMI) Ⓓ **CDM7 63654-2**
C'est un torrent L. Fugère, anon (r1929)
(6/93) (SYMP) Ⓓ **SYMCD1125**
C'est un torrent L. Fugère, anon (r1928)
(7/93) (NIMB) Ⓓ [2] **NI7840/1**
Un ruisselet bien clair G. Farrar, orch (r1912: Ger) (IRCC) Ⓓ **IRCC-CD805**

La **Semiramide riconosciuta– opera: 3 acts (1748—Vienna) (Wds. Metastasio)**
Vieni che poi sereno P. Frijsh, C. Dougherty (1940)
(4/95) (PEAR) Ⓓ [2] **GEMMCDS9095(1)**

Telemaco, or L'isola di Circe– dramma per musica: 2 acts (1765—Vienna) (Lib. Coltellini, after Capece)
Ah!, non turbi; Ahimè! Che miro! ... Perchè t'involi J. Kowalski, Berlin RSO, H. Fricke
(CAPR) ◙ **80 416**
Ah!, non turbi; Ahimè! Che miro! ... Perchè t'involi J. Kowalski, Berlin RSO, H. Fricke
(CAPR) ⚬⚬ **70 416**
Ah!, non turbi; Ahimè! Che miro! ... Perchè t'involi J. Kowalski, Berlin RSO, H. Fricke
(10/92) (CAPR) Ⓓ **10 416**

GODARD , Benjamin (Louis Paul) *(1849–1895) France*

Danté et Béatrice– opera: 4 acts (1890) (Lib. E Blau)
Nous allons partir E. Clément, G. Farrar, orch, Rosario Bourdon (r1913)
(8/95) (ROMO) Ⓓ **82002-2**

Jocelyn– opera: 4 acts, Op. 109 (1888—Brussels) (Lib. Capoul and Silvestre)
EXCERPTS: 1. Oh! ne t'éveille pas encor (Berceuse).
1. Lotte Lehmann, Berlin St Op Orch, F. Zweig (r1927) (PEAR) Ⓓ **GEMMCD9409**
1. J. McCormack, F. Kreisler, V. O'Brien (r1914)
(BIDD) Ⓓ **LAB022**
1. K. McKellar, Orch, P. Knight
(DECC) Ⓓ **425 849-2DWO**
(DECC) ▭ **425 849-4DWO**
1. Fairey Band, K. Dennison (arr brass band: G Langford) (CHAN) Ⓓ **CHAN6530**
1. S. Walkley, Sun Life Band, B. Hurdley (arr E. Ball) (GRAS) Ⓓ **GRCD41**
1. P. Casals, N. Mednikoff (r1926: arr vc/pf)
(MSCM) Ⓓ **MM30428**
1. R. Streich, Berlin RSO, K. Gaebel
(DG) Ⓓ [2] **435 748-2GDO2**
1. T. Rossi, orch, M. Cariven (r1936)
(FORL) Ⓓ **UCD19053**
1. R. Crooks, orch (r1933)
(CLAR) Ⓓ **CDGSE78-50-58**
1. Stuttgart RSO, N. Marriner (r1987)
(CFP) Ⓓ **CD-CFP4661**
(CFP) ▭ **TC-CFP4661**
1. J. McCormack, F. Kreisler, V. O'Brien (r1914: Eng) (9/89) (PEAR) Ⓓ **GEMMCD9315**
1. P. Casals, N. Mednikoff (arr vc/pf: r1926)
(10/91) (BIDD) Ⓓ **LAB017**
1. P. Domingo, I. Perlman, NY Studio Orch, J. Tunick (r1990) (3/92) (EMI) Ⓓ **CDC7 54266-2**
1. B. Crosby, J. Heifetz, orch, V. Young (r1946)
(11/94) (RCA) Ⓓ [65] **09026 61778-2(19)**
1. V. Capoul, anon (r1905)
(12/94) (SYMP) Ⓓ **SYMCD1172**
1. P. Gallois, London Fest Orch, R. Pople (r1993: arr fl: F.Pierre)
(5/95) (DG) Ⓓ **445 822-2GH**

1. E. Clément, orch (r1911)
(8/95) (ROMO) Ⓓ **82002-2**
1. E. Clément, orch (r1911)
(8/95) (PEAR) Ⓓ **GEMMCD9161**

La **Vivandière– opéra-comique: 3 acts (1895—Paris) (Lib. Cain. Orch cpted Vidal)**
(ACT 1); 4. Viens avec nous, petit.
Viens avec nous S. Michel, Paris Opéra-Comique Orch, L. Fourestier (r1951)
(4/92) (EMI) Ⓓ [7] **CHS7 69741-2(3)**
4. M. Horne, Monte Carlo PO, L. Foster (r1984)
(ERAT) Ⓓ **4509-98501-2**

GOETZ, Hermann (Gustav) *(1840–1876) Germany*

Widerspenstigen Zähmung– opera: 4 acts (1874—Mannheim) (Lib. J. V. Widmann, after Shakespeare)
Es schweige die Klage Lotte Lehmann, orch (r1919) (6/92) (PREI) Ⓓ [3] **89302**
Overture G. Schneider, Hanover Rad PO, W.A. Albert (r1991) (CPO) Ⓓ **CPO999 076-2**

GOLDMARK , Károly *(1830–1915) Austro-Hungary*

Das **Heimchen am Herd– opera: 3 acts (1896—Vienna) (Lib. A M Willner, after Dickens)**
EXCERPTS: 1. Ein Geheimnis wundersüss; 2. Ach, das ist herrlich.
1, 2. M. Jeritza, orch (r1914)
(4/94) (PREI) Ⓓ **89079**

Die **Königin von Saba– opera: 4 acts, Op. 27 (1879—Vienna) (Lib. Mosenthal)**
EXCERPTS—ACT 1: 1. Dein Freund ist dein (Sulamith & Chorus); 2a. Am Fuss des Libanon (Assad); 2b. Da plätschert eine Silberquelle; 3. March; 4. Ballet Music. ACT 2: 5. Aus dem Jubels Festgepränge (Queen); 6. Magische Töne (Assad); 7. Blick empor zu jenen Räumen! (Solomon). ACT 3: 8. Ballet Music; 9a. Die Stunde, die ihn mir geraubt (Sulamith); 9b. Doch eh! ich in des Todes Tal (Sulamith). ACT 4: 10a. Komm, Tod, geendet sind die Qualen (Assad); 10b. Du Ew'ger, der mein Aug' gelichtet (Assad).
2b L. Slezak, orch (r1905)
(2/91) (PREI) Ⓓ **89020**
2b, 6. K. Erb, orch (r1914) (PREI) Ⓓ **89095**
6. E. Caruso, orch, W.B. Rogers (r1909: Ital)
(MCI) Ⓓ **MCCD086**
(MCI) ▭ **MCTC086**
6. P. Seiffert, Munich RO, J. Kout (r1992-3)
(RCA) Ⓓ **09026 61214-2**
6. E. Caruso, orch (r1909: Ital)
(10/89) (NIMB) Ⓓ **NI7803**
(NIMB) ▭ **NC7803**
6. E. Caruso, orch (Ital: r1909)
(3/91) (PEAR) Ⓓ [3] **EVC2**
6. E. Caruso, orch, W.B. Rogers (r1909: Ital)
(7/91) (RCA) Ⓓ [12] **GD60495(3)**
6. L. Slezak, orch (r1909)
(9/94) (NIMB) Ⓓ **NI7856**
10b L. Slezak, orch (r1908)
(2/91) (PREI) Ⓓ **89020**

GOLDSCHMIDT, Berthold *(b 1903) Germany/England*

Beatrice Cenci– opera: 3 acts (1988—London) (Lib. M Esslin, after P B Shelley)
Cenci S. Estes
Lucretia D. Jones
Beatrice R. Alexander
Bernardo F. Kimm
Cardinal Camillo P. Rose
Orsino E. Wottrich
Marzio S. Lorenz
Olimpio R. Beyer
Colonna S. Stoll
Judge J. D. de Haan
Tenor Solo I. Bostridge
Berlin Rad Chor, Berlin Deutsches SO, L. Zagrosek (r1994)
(7/95) (SONY) Ⓓ [2] **S2K66836**

Der **gewaltige Hahnrei– Musikalische Tragikomodie: 3 acts, Op. 14 (1932—Mannheim) (Lib. after F. Crommelynck)**
Stella R. Alexander
Bruno R. Wörle
Petrus M. Kraus
Ochsenhirt C. Otelli
Mémé H. Lawrence
Estrugo M. Petzold
Young Man E. Wottrich
Cornelie M. Posselt
Florence C. Berggold
Gendarm F-J. Kapellmann
Berlin Rad Chor, Berlin Deutsches SO, L. Zagrosek (r1992)
(3/94) (DECC) Ⓓ [2] **440 850-2DHO2**

GOMES, (Antonio) Carlos *(1836–1896) Brazil*

Il **Guarany– opera: 4 acts (1870—Milan) (Lib. Scalvini and d'Ormeville)**
EXCERPTS: 1. Prelude. ACT 1: 2. Ave Maria; 3. Gentile di cuore; 4. Sento una forza indomita. ACT 2: 5. Vanto io pur superba cuna; 6. Sena tetto, senza cuna. ACT 3: 7. Regina della tribù; 8. Perchè di mesti.
Il torvo sguardo A. Amadi, orch (r1910s)
(6/94) (IRCC) Ⓓ **IRCC-CD808**
3. B. Sayão, orch (r c1930)
(6/94) (IRCC) Ⓓ **IRCC-CD808**
4. F. Marconi, B. Mililotti, C. Sabajno (r1907)
(10/90) (SYMP) Ⓓ **SYMCD1069**
4. G. Zenatello, E. Mazzoleni, orch (r1911)
(5/94) (SYMP) Ⓓ **SYMCD1168**
4. G. Zenatello, E. Mazzoleni, orch (r1911)
(5/94) (PEAR) Ⓓ [4] **GEMMCDS9074(1)**
4. E. Mazzoleni, G. Zenatello, orch (r c1910)
(6/94) (IRCC) Ⓓ **IRCC-CD808**
5. B. Gigli, orch, E. Sivieri (r1951)
(10/90) (RCA) Ⓓ **GD87811**
(10/90) (RCA) ▭ **GK87811**
6. F. Merli, B. Scacciati, orch, L. Molajoli (r1929)
(PREI) Ⓓ **89091**
6. E. Destinn, E. Caruso, orch, W.B. Rogers (r1914) (7/91) (RCA) Ⓓ [12] **GD60495(5)**
6. E. Caruso, E. Destinn, orch, W.B. Rogers (r1914) (10/91) (PEAR) Ⓓ [3] **EVC3(1)**
6. M. Battistini, orch (r1924)
(7/93) (NIMB) Ⓓ [2] **NI7840/1**
6. E. Destinn, E. Caruso, orch (r1914)
(11/93) (ROMO) Ⓓ [2] **81002-2**
6. P. Amato, orch (r1912)
(6/94) (IRCC) Ⓓ **IRCC-CD808**
6. E. Destinn, E. Caruso, orch, W.B Rogers (r1914) (12/94) (SUPR) Ⓓ [12] **11 2136-2(5)**
8. G. Zenatello, M. Pereira, anon (r c1912)
(5/94) (PEAR) Ⓓ [4] **GEMMCDS9074(1)**

Salvator Rosa– opera: 4 acts (1874—Genoa) (Lib. Ghislanzoni)
EXCERPTS: 1. Mia piccirella; 2. Di sposa, di padre; 3. È quanto.
1. C. Muzio, orch (r1920)
(5/90) (BOGR) Ⓓ [2] **BIM705-2**
1. E. Caruso, orch, J. Pasternack (r1919)
(7/91) (RCA) Ⓓ [12] **GD60495(6)**
1. E. Caruso, orch, J. Pasternack (r1919)
(10/91) (PEAR) Ⓓ [3] **EVC4(2)**
1. C. Muzio, orch (r1920)
(1/94) (ROMO) Ⓓ [2] **81005-2**
2. C. Siepi, Santa Cecilia Academy Orch, A. Erede (r1954) (DECC) Ⓓ **440 418-2DM**
2. M. Pertusi, Sofia PO, E. Tabakov (r1994)
(CAPR) Ⓓ **10 704**
2. A. Didur, orch (r c1918)
(1/94) (CLUB) Ⓓ **CL99-089**

Lo **Schiavo– opera: 4 acts (1889—Rio de Janeiro) (Lib. R. Paravicini, after Taunay)**
EXCERPTS: 1. Prelude; 2a. L'importuna insistenza; 2b. Quando nascesti tu; 3. Sogni d'amore; 4. Ciel di Parahyba.
1. Rio de Janeiro Municipal Th Orch, J. DeMain (pp1992) (SONY) ◖ **SLV48362**
(SONY) ▭▭ **SHV48362**
2a, 2b E. Caruso, orch (r1911)
(10/89) (NIMB) Ⓓ **NI7803**
(NIMB) ▭ **NC7803**
2a, 2b B. Gigli, orch, E. Sivieri (r1951)
(10/90) (RCA) Ⓓ **GD87811**
(10/90) (RCA) ▭ **GK87811**
2a, 2b E. Caruso, orch (r1911)
(3/91) (PEAR) Ⓓ [3] **EVC2**
2a, 2b E. Caruso, orch (r1911)
(7/91) (RCA) Ⓓ [12] **GD60495(4)**
2a, 2b E. Caruso, orch (r1911)
(7/91) (MSCM) Ⓓ **MM30352**
2a, 2b E. Caruso, orch (r1911)
(12/93) (NIMB) Ⓓ **NI7851**
2b G. Lauri-Volpi, orch, Rosario Bourdon (r1928)
(9/90) (PREI) Ⓓ **89012**

2b G. Lauri-Volpi, orch, Rosario Bourdon (r1929) (7/93) (NIMB) Ⓓ **NI7845**
3. A. Orda, Polish RSO, K. Missona (bp1977) (SYMP) Ⓓ **SYMCD1117**

GOSSEC , François-Joseph *(1734–1829) Belgium/France*

Le **Camp du Grand pré– opera (1793)**
Tambourin M. Elman, P. Kahn (arr Burmester: r1911) (BIDD) Ⓓ **LAB035**

Rosine, ou L'épouse abandonnée– opera: 3 acts (1786—Paris) (Lib. N. Gersin)
Gavotte
M. Larrieu, S. Mildonian (DENO) Ⓓ **C37-7301**
M. Elman, P. Kahn (arr Elman: r1910) (BIDD) Ⓓ **LAB035**
K-W. Chung, P. Moll (arr Meyer) (9/87) (DECC) Ⓓ **417 289-2DH**
A. Busch, B. Seidler-Winkler (arr Burmester: r1921) (6/93) (SYMP) Ⓓ **SYMCD1109**

GÖTZE, Walter Wilhelm *(1883–1961) Germany*

Der **Page des Königs– operetta (Lib. Rheinberg)**
Was wär mein Lied J. Schmidt, orch, F. Weissmann (r1933) (EMI) Ⓓ [2] **CHS7 64673-2**

GOUNOD , Charles (François) *(1818–1893) France*

Cinq Mars– opéra dialogué: 4 acts (1877—Paris) (Lib. Poirson and Gallet, after de Vigny)
Nuit resplenissante C. Tirard, orch (r1930) (MSCM) Ⓓ **MM30221**
(MSCM) ▭ **MM040079**
Nuit resplendissante F. Pollet, Montpellier PO, C. Diederich (r1989) (ERAT) Ⓓ **4509-98502-2**
Nuit silencieuse R. Doria, J. Boguet (12/91) (MSCM) Ⓓ **MM30373**

Faust– opéra: 5 acts (1859—Paris) (Lib. Barbier and Carré)
EXCERPTS: ACT 1: 1. Introduction; 2a. Rien! En vain j'interroge; 2b. Salut! ô mon dernier matin; 3a. Mais ce Dieu; 3b. Me voici! D'où vient ta surprise?; 4a. A moi les plaisirs; 4b. O merveille!; ACT 2: 5. Vin ou bière (Kermesse Scene); 6a. O sainte médaille; 6b. Avant de quitter; 7. Le veau d'or; 8. A votre santé! (Sword Scene); 9a. Nous nous retrouverons; 9b. Ainsi que la brise légère; 9c. Ne permettrez-vous pas; 9d. Valse. ACT 3: 10. Faites-lui mes aveux; 11a. Quel trouble inconnu; 11b. Salut! demeure chaste et pure; 12a. Je voudrais bien savoir; 12b. Il était un roi de Thulé; 13a. O Dieu! que de bijoux!; 13b. Ah! je ris (Jewel Song); 14a. Seigneur Dieu, que vois-je!; 14b. Prenez mon bras; 15a. Il était temps!; 15b. Il se fait tard!; 15c. O nuit d'amour; 15d. Il m'aime!. ACT 4: 16. Elles ne sont plus là!; 17. Si le bonheur (When all was young); 18a. Déposons les armes (Soldiers' Chorus); 18b. Gloire immortelle; 19a. Qu'attendez-vous encore?; 19b. Vous qui faites l'endormie (Serenade); 20. Que voulez-vous, messieurs? (Duel Scene); 21a. Par ici! (Death of Valentine); 21b. Écoute-moi bien; 22. Seigneur, daignez permettre (Church Scene). ACT 5: 23. Walpurgis Night; 24a. Mon coeur est pénétré d'épouvante!; 24b. Attends! Voici la rue; 25a. Alerte! alerte!; 25b. Anges purs; 26. BALLET MUSIC; 26a. Les nubiennes; 26b. Adagio; 26c. Danse antique; 26d. Variations de Cléopâtre; 26e. Les troyens; 26f. Variations du miroir; 26g. Danse de Phryné.

Faust P. Domingo
Marguérite M. Freni
Méphistophélès N. Ghiaurov
Valentin T. Allen
Siebel M. Command
Marthe J. Taillon
Wagner M. Vento
Paris Op Chor, Paris Op Orch, G. Prêtre (4/87) (EMI) Ⓓ [3] **CDS7 47493-8**

Faust F. Araiza
Marguérite K. Te Kanawa
Méphistophélès E. Nesterenko
Valentin A. Schmidt
Siebel P. Coburn
Marthe M. Lipovšek
Wagner G. Cachemaille
Bavarian Rad Chor, BRSO, Colin Davis (5/87) (PHIL) Ⓓ [3] **420 164-2PH3**

Faust N. Gedda
Marguérite V. de los Angeles
Méphistophélès B. Christoff
Valentin E. Blanc
Siebel L. Berton
Marthe R. Gorr
Wagner V. Autran
Paris Op Chor, Paris Op Orch, A. Cluytens (r1958) (7/89) (EMI) Ⓓ [3] **CMS7 69983-2**

Faust F. Corelli
Marguérite J. Sutherland
Méphistophélès N. Ghiaurov
Valentin R. Massard
Siebel M. Elkins
Marthe M. Sinclair
Wagner R. Myers
Ambrosian Op Chor, LSO, R. Bonynge (r1966) (12/91) (DECC) Ⓓ [3] **421 240-2DM3**

Faust R. Leech
Marguérite C. Studer
Méphistophélès J. Van Dam
Valentin T. Hampson
Siebel M. Mahé
Marthe N. Denize
Wagner M. Barrard
French Army Chor, Toulouse Capitole Chor, Toulouse Capitole Orch, M. Plasson (12/91) (EMI) Ⓓ [3] **CDS7 54228-2**

Faust G. Aragall
Marguérite M. Caballé
Méphistophélès P. Plishka
Valentin P. Huttenlocher
Siebel A. Terzian
Marthe J. Taillon
Wagner J. Brun
Rhine Op Chor, Strasbourg PO, A. Lombard (4/92) (ERAT) Ⓓ [3] **2292-45685-2**

Faust C. Vezzani
Marguérite M. Berthon
Méphistophélès M. Journet
Valentin L. Musy
Siebel M. Coiffier
Marthe J. Montfort
Wagner M. Cozette
chor, orch, H. Busser (r1930) (9/93) (PEAR) Ⓓ [2] **GEMMCDS9987**

Faust H. Nash
Marguérite M. Licette
Méphistophélès R. Easton
Valentin H. Williams
Siebel D. Vane
Marthe M. Brunskill
Wagner R. Carr
BBC Ch, SO, T. Beecham, C. Raybould (r1929/30: Eng) (5/94) (DUTT) Ⓓ [2] **2CDAX2001**

Faust J. Hadley
Marguérite C. Gasdia
Méphistophélès S. Ramey
Valentin A. Agache
Siébel S. Mentzer
Marthe B. Fassbaender
Wagner P. Fourcade
WNO Chor, WNO Orch, C. Rizzi (r1993) (7/94) (TELD) Ⓓ [3] **4509-90872-2**

Faust K. Jörn
Marguérite E. Destinn
Méphistophélès P. Knüpfer
Valentin D. Zádor
Siebel M. Götze
Marthe I. von Scheele-Müller
Wagner A. Neudahm
Berlin Court Op Chor, orch, B. Seidler-Winkler (r1908: Ger) (12/94) (SUPR) Ⓓ [12] **11 2136-2(3)**

Faust N. Gedda
Marguérite V. de los Angeles
Méphistophélès B. Christoff
Valentin J. Borthayre
Siebel M. Angelici
Marthe S. Michel
Wagner R. Jeantet
Paris Op Chor, Paris Op Orch, A. Cluytens (r1953) (9/95) (EMI) Ⓓ [3] **CMS5 65256-2**

Excs R. Leech, J. Van Dam, C. Studer, T. Hampson, Toulouse Capitole Chor, Toulouse Capitole Orch, M. Plasson (EMI) Ⓓ **CDC7 54358-2**
Excs N. Gedda, V.de los Angeles, R. Gorr, L. Berton, B. Christoff, E. Blanc, V. Autran, Paris Op Chor, Paris Op Orch, A. Cluytens (r1958) (EMIN) Ⓓ **CD-EMX2215**
Excs A. Siloti (arr pf: r1930s) (8/93) (PEAR) Ⓓ **GEMMCD9993**
Excs H. Roswaenge, J. Berglund, L. Helletsgruber, A. Sved, Vienna St Op Orch, J. Krips (pp1936: Ger/Swed) (11/95) (SCHW) Ⓓ [2] **314622**
Waltz Cölln Salon Orch (arr Weninger) (EURO) Ⓓ **GD69296**
Waltz BRSO, F. Fricsay (BELA) Ⓓ **450 139-2**
(BELA) ▭ **450 139-4**
2a, 2b, 3a, 3b, 4a, 4b, 24a, 24b, 25a, 25b H. Nash, M. Licette, R. Easton, BBC Chor, SO, T. Beecham (r1929/30; sung in English) (9/91) (PEAR) Ⓓ **GEMMCD9473**
3a, 3b M. Journet, F. Ansseau, orch, P. Coppola (r1929) (PREI) Ⓓ **89021**
3a, 3b F. Ansseau, M. Journet, Paris Op Orch, P. Coppola (r1929) (MSCM) Ⓓ **MM30377**
3b, 19b A. Pirogov, I. Kozlovsky, Bolshoi Th Orch, V. Nebolsin (r c1950: Russ) (PREI) Ⓓ **89078**
3, 7, 19, 24, 25. M. Journet, M. Berthon, C. Vezzani, SO, H. Busser (r1930) (1/94) (CLUB) Ⓓ **CL99-034**
4b E. Caruso, M. Journet, orch (r1910) (3/91) (PEAR) Ⓓ [3] **EVC2**
4b E. Caruso, M. Journet, orch, W.B. Rogers (r1910) (10/94) (NIMB) Ⓓ **NI7859**
4b, 14a, 14b, 15b, 15c, 20, 24a, 24b, 25a E. Caruso, M. Journet, G. Farrar, G. Lejeune-Gilibert, orch, W.B. Rogers (r1910) (RCA) Ⓓ **09026 61244-2**
4b, 14, 15b, 15c, 20, 24, 25a G. Farrar, G. Lejeune-Gilibert, E. Caruso, A. Scotti, M. Journet, orch, W.B. Rogers (r1910) (7/91) (RCA) Ⓓ [12] **GD60495(3)**
5, 6a, 6b, 7, 9a-c, 11a, 11b, 12a, 12b, 13a, 13b, 15b-d, 22, 25a, 25b P. Domingo, M. Freni, N. Ghiaurov, T. Allen, M. Command, M. Vento, Paris Op. Chor, Paris Op. Orch, G. Prêtre (r1978) (EMI) Ⓓ **CDM7 63090-2**
6a, 6b M. Battistini, orch (r1911: Ital) (PEAR) Ⓓ **GEMMCD9016**
6a, 6b A. Granforte, La Scala Orch, C. Sabajno (r1927: Ital) (PREI) Ⓓ **89105**
6a, 6b L. Tibbett, Orch, N. Shilkret (r1934) (3/90) (RCA) Ⓓ **GD87808**
6a, 6b L. Tibbett, orch, N. Shilkret (r1934) (3/91) (PEAR) Ⓓ [2] **GEMMCDS9452**
6a, 6b M. Battistini, orch, C. Sabajno (Ital: r1911) (7/92) (PEAR) Ⓓ [3] **GEMMCDS9924(1)**
6a, 6b L. Warren, RCA SO, W. Pelletier (r1941) (4/94) (RCA) Ⓓ [6] **09026 61580-2(5)**
6b L. Warren, Orch, H. Barlow (bp1953) (VAI) ▣ **VAI69105**
6b H. Prey, Berlin SO, H-M. Rabenstein (Ger) (EURO) Ⓓ **GD69019**
6b A. Scotti, orch (r1909: Ital) (PEAR) Ⓓ **GEMMCD9937**
6b G. Laperrière, Three Rivers SO, G. Bellemare (r1992) (CBC) Ⓓ **SMCD5127**
6b T. Ruffo, orch, W.B. Rogers (r1915) (PEAR) Ⓓ **GEMMCD9088**
6b H. Schlusnus, Berlin St Op Orch, L. Blech (r1935: Ger) (PREI) Ⓓ [2] **89212**
6b G. De Luca, orch (r1919: Ital) (PEAR) Ⓓ [3] **GEMMCDS9160(1)**
6b G. De Luca, orch (r1929: Ital) (PEAR) Ⓓ [3] **GEMMCDS9160(2)**
6b G. De Luca, orch (r1919: Ital) (PREI) Ⓓ **89995**
6b R. Stracciari, orch, G. Polacco (r1917: Ital) (PEAR) Ⓓ **GEMMCD9178**
6b D. Fischer-Dieskau, Berlin RSO, G. Patanè (r1973: Ger) (EMI) Ⓓ [2] **CMS5 65621-2**
6b G. De Luca, orch (Ital: r1919) (1/92) (PREI) Ⓓ **89036**
6b C. Galeffi, La Scala Orch, L. Molajoli (r1926: Ital) (2/92) (PREI) Ⓓ **89040**
6b G. De Luca, anon (Ital: r1907) (7/92) (PEAR) Ⓓ [3] **GEMMCDS9925(1)**
6b A. Endrèze, orch, F. Ruhlmann (r c1932) (11/92) (MSCM) Ⓓ **MM30451**
6b T. Ruffo, orch (Ital: r1922) (2/93) (PREI) Ⓓ [3] **89303(2)**
6b A. Scotti, anon (Ital: r1902) (3/93) (SYMP) Ⓓ **SYMCD1100**
6b P. Lisitsian, Bolshoi Th Orch, V. Nebolsin (r1947: Russ) (8/93) (PREI) Ⓓ **89061**
6b G. Hüsch, Berlin St Op Orch, H.U. Müller (r1937: Ger) (3/94) (PREI) Ⓓ **89071**

6b G. De Luca, NY Met Op Orch, G. Setti (r1929: Ital) (10/94) (PREI) Ⓓ **89073**
6b, 11b, 13b, 24a Jenny Williams, T. Burns (r1992;Eng (A Faust Travesty) (RCA) Ⓓ **GD61175**
6b, 19b, 22(pt) T. Ruffo, orch (Ital: r1915) (2/93) (PREI) Ⓓ [3] **89303(1)**
6b, 21b H. Hermann Nissen, Berlin SO, F. Zweig (r1929: Ger) (PREI) Ⓓ **89090**
6b, 25a J. Björling, A. Sved, A. Kipnis, E. Réthy, Vienna St Op Orch, J. Krips (pp1937: Ger/Swed) (12/94) (SCHW) Ⓓ [2] **314542**
7. M. Journet, orch, H. Busser (r1930) (PREI) Ⓓ **89021**
7. M. McEachern, orch (Eng: r1923) (PEAR) Ⓓ **GEMMCD9455**
7. N. Ghiaurov, London Sym Chor, LSO, E. Downes (DECC) Ⓓ **433 069-2DWO** (DECC) ⊟ **433 069-4DWO**
7. P. Plançon, chor, orch (r1906) (PEAR) Ⓓ **GEMMCD9122**
7. E. Pinza, NY Met Op Chor, NY Met Op Orch, G. Setti (r1929) (2/89) (PEAR) Ⓓ **GEMMCD9306**
7. T. Pasero, orch (Ital: r1927) (6/90) (PREI) Ⓓ **89010**
7. P. Plançon, orch (r1906) (9/91) (PEAR) Ⓓ **GEMMCD9497**
7. E. Pinza, NY Met Op Chor, NY Met Op Orch, G. Setti (r1929) (3/92) (PREI) Ⓓ **89050**
7. A. Didur, anon (r1900: Ital) (6/93) (PEAR) Ⓓ [3] **GEMMCDS9997/9(2)**
7. L. Sibiriakov, orch (r1908: Russ) (6/93) (PEAR) Ⓓ [3] **GEMMCDS9001/3(2)**
7. E. Pinza, NY Met Op Chor, NY Met Op Orch, G. Setti (r1929) (9/93) (RCA) Ⓓ **09026 61245-2**
7. P. Plançon, anon (r1904/5: 2 vers) (12/94) (ROMO) Ⓓ [2] **82001-2**
7. P. Plançon, orch (r1906) (12/94) (ROMO) Ⓓ [2] **82001-2**
7, 11b C. Kullman, E. Pinza, Vienna St Op Chor, Vienna St Op Orch, K. Alwin (pp1935: Fr/Ger) (7/94) (SCHW) Ⓓ [2] **314512**
7, 15a, 19. N. Ghiaurov, G. Raimondi, La Scala Chor, La Scala Orch, G. Prêtre (pp1967) (MEMO) Ⓓ [2] **HR4223/4**
7, 15a, 19b M. Reizen, Bolshoi Th Orch, V. Nebolsin (r1950: Russ) (2/95) (PREI) Ⓓ **89080**
7, 19b F. Chaliapin, orch (Russian: r1907) (PREI) Ⓓ **89030**
7, 19b J. von Manowarda, orch (r1922: Ger) (PREI) Ⓓ **89069**
7, 19b F. Chaliapin, M. Cozette, Paris Op Chor, Paris Op Orch, H. Busser (r1930) (CONI) Ⓓ **CDHD226** (CONI) ⊟ **MCHD226**
7, 19b E. List, Berlin St Op Orch, F. Weissmann (r1930: Ger) (PREI) Ⓓ **89083**
7, 19b L. Hofmann, Berlin St Op Orch, F.A. Schmidt (r1932: Ger) (PREI) Ⓓ **89102**
7, 19b N. Ghiuselev, N. Ghiaurov, Bulgarian RSO, I. Marinov, R. Raichev (r1970s) (FORL) Ⓓ **UCD16741**
7, 19b A. Kipnis, Berlin St Op Orch, C. Schmalstich (Ger: r1930) (12/90) (PREI) Ⓓ **89019**
7, 19b A. Kipnis, orch (r1927) (10/91) (PEAR) Ⓓ **GEMMCD9451**
7, 19b M. Journet, orch (r1906) (10/94) (NIMB) Ⓓ **NI7859**
8. P. Amato, M. Journet, NY Met Op Chor, orch (r1912) (PEAR) Ⓓ **GEMMCD9104**
9a-d F. Chaliapin, M. Cozette, Paris Op Chor, Paris Op Orch, H. Büsser (r1930) (12/89) (PEAR) Ⓓ **GEMMCD9314**
9d, 26. Rotterdam PO, D. Zinman (r1980) (PHIL) Ⓓ [2] **438 763-2PM2**
9d, 26. BPO, H. von Karajan (r1971) (10/94) (DG) Ⓓ [2] **437 404-2GX2**
10. M. Command, Paris Op Orch, G. Prêtre (CFP) Ⓓ **CD-CFP4582** (CFP) ⊟ **TC-CFP4582**
10. C. Supervia, orch, G. Cloëz (r1931) (9/90) (CLUB) Ⓓ **CL99-074**
10, 17. K. Branzell, orch (r1928) (8/92) (PREI) Ⓓ **89039**
11. J. Björling, Hilversum RO, F. Weissmann (pp1939) (8/88) (BLUE) Ⓓ **ABCD006**
11. G. Thill, Orch, E. Bigot (r1930) (1/89) (EMI) Ⓓ **CDM7 69548-2**
11. B. Gigli, orch, E. Goossens (Ital: r1931) (10/92) (TEST) Ⓓ **SBT1005**
11a, 11b G. di Stefano, Zurich Tonhalle Orch, F. Patanè (DECC) Ⓓ **433 623-2DSP** (DECC) ⊟ **433 623-4DSP**
11a, 11b P. Domingo, New Philh, N. Santi (RCA) Ⓓ [2] **GD60866** (RCA) ⊟ [2] **GK60866**
11a, 11b J. Carreras, ROHO, J. Delacôte (EMI) Ⓓ **CDC7 54524-2**
11a, 11b P. Domingo, Paris Op Orch, G. Prêtre (EMI) Ⓓ **CDM7 64359-2**
11a, 11b P. Domingo, LSO, N. Santi (r1972) (RCA) Ⓓ **09026 61356-2** (RCA) ⊟ **09026 61356-4**
11a, 11b G. di Stefano, Zurich Tonhalle Orch, F. Patanè (r1958) (DECC) Ⓓ **440 403-2DM**
11a, 11b F. Corelli, LSO, R. Bonynge (r1966) (DECC) Ⓓ **443 379-2DM**
11a, 11b B. Gigli, orch, E. Goossens (r1931: Ital) (PEAR) Ⓓ [2] **GEMMCDS9176**
11a, 11b L. Pavarotti, Vienna Volksoper Orch, L. Magiera (7/86) (DECC) Ⓓ [2] **417 011-2DH2**
11a, 11b B. Gigli, orch, E. Goossens (Ital: r1931) (9/88) (EMI) Ⓓ **CDH7 61051-2**
11a, 11b Alfredo Kraus, Paris Op Orch, M. Veltri (pp1987) (12/88) (EMI) Ⓓ **CDC7 49067-2**
11a, 11b P. Domingo, Paris Op Orch, G. Prêtre (r1978) (6/94) (EMI) Ⓓ **CDC5 55017-2**
11a, 11b Alfredo Kraus, WNO Orch, C. Rizzi (r1994) (8/95) (PHIL) Ⓓ **442 785-2PH** (8/95) (PHIL) ⊟ **442 785-4PH**
11a, 11b, 15b P. Dvorský, M. Hajóssyová, S. Kopčák, Bratislava RSO, Czech RSO, O. Lenárd (10/89) (OPUS) Ⓓ **9156 1824**
11b L. Pavarotti, Vienna Volksoper Orch, L. Magiera (7/75) (DECC) ⊟ **400 053-4DH**
11b J. Björling, orch, H. Barlow (bp1950) (VAI) ▣ **VAI69101**
11b B. Gigli, orch, E. Goossens (r1931: Ital) (NIMB) Ⓓ **NI7817** (NIMB) ⊟ **NC7817**
11b H. Nash, orch, C. Raybould (Eng: r1930) (MMOI) Ⓓ **CDMOIR405** (MMOI) ⊟ **CMOIR405**
11b B.S. Rosenberg, Budapest Concert Orch, J. Acs (pp1990) (OLYM) Ⓓ **OCD370**
11b T. Schipa, orch, Anon (cond) (Ital: pp1913) (MEMO) Ⓓ [2] **HR4220/1**
11b E. Caruso, orch (r1906) (RCA) Ⓓ **09026 61244-2**
11b B. Gigli, orch, E. Goossens (r1931: Ital) (IMP) Ⓓ **GLRS102**
11b G. Di Stefano, Zurich Tonhalle Orch, F. Patanè (r1959) (BELA) Ⓓ **450 005-2** (BELA) ⊟ **450 005-4**
11b J. Björling, orch, N. Grevillius (r1939) (PEAR) Ⓓ **GEMMCD9043**
11b B. Gigli, orch, E. Goossens (r1931: Ital) (CONI) Ⓓ **CDHD227** (CONI) ⊟ **MCHD227**
11b H. Roswaenge, Berlin St Op Orch, B. Seidler-Winkler (r1939: Ger) (PREI) Ⓓ [2] **89211**
11b W. Widdop, orch, L. Collingwood (r1930: Eng) (PEAR) Ⓓ **GEMMCD9112**
11b D. Borgioli, orch (r c1924: Ital) (PEAR) Ⓓ **GEMMCD9091**
11b K. Erb, orch (r1914: Ger) (PREI) Ⓓ **89095**
11b T. Beltrán, RPO, R. Stapleton (r1994) (SILV) Ⓓ **SILKD6005** (SILV) ⊟ **SILKC6005**
11b A. Bonci, orch (r1913: Ital) (PEAR) Ⓓ **GEMMCD9168**
11b F. de Lucia, anon (r1906: Ital: 2 vers) (BONG) Ⓓ [2] **GB1064/5-2**
11b C. Kullman, orch, O. Dobrindt (r1932: Eng) (MMOI) Ⓓ **CDMOIR429**
11b F. de la Mora, WNO Orch, C. Mackerras (r1994-5) (TELA) Ⓓ **CD80411**
11b J. Björling, orch, N. Grevillius (r1939) (10/88) (EMI) Ⓓ **CDH7 61053-2**
11b H. Nash, orch (Eng: r1926) (8/89) (PEAR) Ⓓ **GEMMCD9319**
11b B. Gigli, orch (Ital: r1921) (5/90) (NIMB) Ⓓ **NI7807** (NIMB) ⊟ **NC7807**
11b G. Zenatello, anon (Ital: r1903) (6/90) (SYMP) Ⓓ **SYMCD1073**
11b G. Lauri-Volpi, orch, Rosario Bourdon (r1930) (9/90) (PREI) Ⓓ **89012**
11b G. Morino, Warmia Nat PO, B. Amaducci (10/90) (NUOV) Ⓓ **6851**
11b B. Gigli, orch, J. Pasternack (r1921) (10/90) (RCA) Ⓓ **GD87811** (10/90) (RCA) ⊟ **GK87811**
11b E. Caruso, orch (r1906) (12/90) (PEAR) Ⓓ [3] **EVC1(2)**
11b E. Caruso, orch (r1906) (7/91) (RCA) Ⓓ [12] **GD60495(2)**
11b A. Cortis, La Scala Orch, C. Sabajno (Ital: r1930) (10/91) (PREI) Ⓓ **89043**
11b H. Roswaenge, orch (r1928: Ger) (2/92) (PREI) Ⓓ [2] **89201**
11b P. Dvorský, Bratislava RSO, O. Lenárd (5/92) (NAXO) Ⓓ **8 550343**
11b J. Hislop, orch, E. Goossens (pp1928) (7/92) (PEAR) Ⓓ [3] **GEMMCDS9926(1)**
11b J. Björling, orch, N. Grevillius (r1939) (9/92) (MMOI) Ⓓ **CDMOIR409**
11b W. Widdop, Orch, L. Collingwood (Eng: r1930) (11/92) (CLAR) Ⓓ **CDGSE78-50-46**
11b J. Hislop, orch, G.W. Byng (r1926) (1/93) (PEAR) Ⓓ **GEMMCD9956**
11b L. Sobinov, D.G. Kornilov (r1904: Russ) (6/93) (PEAR) Ⓓ [3] **GEMMCDS9997/9(2)**
11b A. Labinsky, anon (Russ: r1905) (7/93) (SYMP) Ⓓ **SYMCD1105**
11b G. Lauri-Volpi, orch, Rosario Bourdon (r1930) (7/93) (NIMB) Ⓓ **NI7845**
11b J. Björling, orch, N. Grevillius (r1939) (10/93) (NIMB) Ⓓ **NI7842**
11b C. Kullman, orch (Eng: r1932) (11/93) (PREI) Ⓓ **89057**
11b A. Cortis, La Scala Orch, C. Sabajno (r1930: Ital) (3/94) (NIMB) Ⓓ **NI7850**
11b G. Zenatello, orch (r1908: Ital) (5/94) (SYMP) Ⓓ **SYMCD1168**
11b G. Zenatello, orch (r1908: Ital) (5/94) (PEAR) Ⓓ [4] **GEMMCDS9073(2)**
11b G. Zenatello, anon (r1903: Ital) (5/94) (PEAR) Ⓓ [4] **GEMMCDS9073(1)**
11b G. Zenatello, orch (r1916: Ital) (5/94) (PEAR) Ⓓ [4] **GEMMCDS9074(2)**
11b J. Björling, orch, N. Grevillius (r1939) (9/94) (IMP) Ⓓ **GLRS103**
11b J. Björling, orch, N. Grevillius (r1939) (9/94) (CONI) Ⓓ **CDHD214** (9/94) (CONI) ⊟ **MCHD214**
11b E. Caruso, orch (r1906) (10/94) (NIMB) Ⓓ **NI7859**
11b F. de Lucia, anon (r1906: Ital) (1/95) (SYMP) Ⓓ **SYMCD1149**
11b J. Johnston, ROHO, L. Collingwood (r1947: Eng) (4/95) (TEST) Ⓓ **SBT1058**
11b H. Nash, Liverpool PO, M. Sargent (r1944: Eng) (11/95) (PEAR) Ⓓ **GEMMCD9175**
11b, 13a, 13b, 18a G. Aragall, M. Caballé, Rhine Op Chor, Strasbourg PO, A. Lombard (ERAT) Ⓓ **2292-45797-2** (ERAT) ⊟ **2292-45797-4**
11, 15b P. Domingo, M. Freni, Paris Op Orch, G. Prêtre (EMI) Ⓓ **CDM7 63103-2**
12a, 12b(pt) G. Farrar, anon (bp1935) (IRCC) Ⓓ **IRCC-CD805**
12a, 12b G. Farrar, orch (r1910) (10/94) (NIMB) Ⓓ **NI7859**
12a, 12b, 13a, 13b M. Callas, Paris Cons, G. Prêtre (EMI) Ⓓ **CDC7 49005-2**
12a, 12b, 13a, 13b C. Studer, Toulouse Capitole Orch, M. Plasson (r1991) (EMI) Ⓓ **CDC5 55350-2**
12a, 12b, 13a A. Pendachanska, Sofia SO, M. Angelov (r1994) (CAPR) Ⓓ **10 706**
12b M. Caballé, Rhine Op Chor, Strasbourg PO, A. Lombard (ERAT) Ⓓ **4509-91715-2** (ERAT) ⊟ **4509-91715-4**
12b C. Supervia, orch, G. Cloëz (r1931) (3/93) (NIMB) Ⓓ [2] **NI7836/7**
12b, 13a, 13b M. Caballé, Strasbourg PO, A. Lombard (r1977) (ERAT) Ⓓ **4509-98499-2**
12b, 13a, 13b G. Cigna, orch, L. Molajoli (r1930: Ital) (11/90) (LYRC) Ⓓ **SRO805**
12b, 13a, 13b M. Caballé, New Philh, R. Giovaninetti (r1970) (5/93) (DG) Ⓓ **431 103-2GB**
12b, 13a, 13b R. Pampanini, orch, A. Albergoni (Ital: r1927) (8/93) (PREI) Ⓓ **89063**
12b, 13b E. Eames, orch (r1906) (11/93) (ROMO) Ⓓ [2] **81001-2**
12b, 13b E. Destinn, Odeon Orch, A. Pilz (r1908: Ger) (12/94) (SUPR) Ⓓ [12] **11 2136-2(2)**
12b, 13b E. Rethberg, Victor SO, Rosario Bourdon (r1929) (10/95) (ROMO) Ⓓ [2] **81014-2**
12b, 15d, 25a Lotte Lehmann, R. Hutt, M. Bohnen, orch (Ger: r1916) (6/92) (PREI) Ⓓ [3] **89302**
12b, 16. M. Freni, La Scala Chor, La Scala Orch, G. Prêtre (pp1967) (MEMO) Ⓓ [2] **HR4277/8**
13. J. Sutherland, ROHO, F. Molinari-Pradelli (DECC) Ⓓ **417 780-2DM**
13. J. Sutherland, ROHO, F. Molinari-Pradelli (DECC) Ⓓ **433 066-2DWO** (DECC) ⊟ **433 066-4DWO**

13. V. de los Angeles, Philh, W. Susskind (r1949) (8/90) (EMI) ⏀ **CDH7 63495-2**

13a K. Te Kanawa, LSO, J. Mauceri (12/90) (DECC) ▣ **084 474-3**

13a, 13b N. Melba, orch, W.B. Rogers (r1910) (3/89) (LARR) ⏀ **CDLRH221**

13a, 13b J. Sutherland, ROHO, F. Molinari-Pradelli (1/90) (DECC) ⏀ [2] **425 493-2DM2**

13a, 13b G. Cigna, orch, L. Molajoli (Ital: r1930) (11/90) (PREI) ⏀ **89016**

13b A. Moffo, Orch, G. Osser (bp1963) (VAI) ▣ **VAI69114**

13b J. Sutherland, ROHO, F. Molinari-Pradelli (DECC) ⏀ **433 624-2DSP**

13b E. Ap Robert, A. Bryn Parri (SAIN) ⏀ **SCDC2002** (SAIN) ⊟ **C2002**

13b G. Farrar, orch (r1905: Ger) (IRCC) ⏀ **IRCC-CD805**

13b R. Carteri, Milan RAI SO, O. de Fabritiis (bp1956: Ital) (FONI) ⏀ **CDMR5014**

13b N. Melba, Rosario Bourdon, W. B. Rogers (r1910) (RCA) ⏀ **74321 24284-2** (RCA) ⊟ **74321 24284-4**

13b V. de los Angeles, Paris Op Orch, A. Cluytens (r1958) (EMI) ⏀ **CDM5 65579-2**

13b A. Patti, L. Ronald (r1905) (4/90) (PEAR) ⏀ **GEMMCD9312**

13b M. Cebotari, VPO, F. Prohaska (r1949) (12/90) (PREI) ⏀ **90034**

13b L. Garrett, Philh, A. Greenwood (r1990-1) (11/91) (SILV) ⏀ **SONGCD903** (11/91) (SILV) ⊟ **SONGC903**

13b L. Tetrazzini, orch (Ital: r1914) (9/92) (EMI) ⏀ [3] **CHS7 63802-2(2)**

13b L. Tetrazzini, orch (Ital: r1914) (9/92) (PEAR) ⏀ **GEMMCD9223**

13b S. Adams, anon (r1902) (3/93) (SYMP) ⏀ **SYMCD1100**

13b A. Nezhdanova, U. Masetti (r1906: Russ) (6/93) (PEAR) ⏀ [3] **GEMMCDS9007/9(1)**

13b E. Orel, anon (Russ: r c1902) (7/93) (SYMP) ⏀ **SYMCD1105**

13b E. Mason, orch (r1924) (8/93) (SYMP) ⏀ **SYMCD1136**

13b N. Melba, orch, W.B. Rogers (r1910) (9/93) (RCA) ⏀ **09026 61412-2**

13b E. Eames, anon (r1905) (11/93) (ROMO) ⏀ [2] **81001-2**

13b E. Destinn, orch, A. Pilz (r1908: Ger) (5/94) (SUPR) ⏀ **11 1337-2**

13b E. Mason, orch, F. Black (r1924) (8/94) (ROMO) ⏀ **81009-2**

13b E. Mason, orch, F. Black (r1925: 2 vers) (8/94) (ROMO) ⏀ **81009-2**

13b G. Farrar, orch (r1913) (10/94) (NIMB) ⏀ **NI7859**

13b E. Eames, anon (r1905) (1/95) (NIMB) ⏀ **NI7860**

13b N. Melba, orch, W.B. Rogers (r1907) (5/95) (ROMO) ⏀ [3] **81011-2(1)**

13b N. Melba, orch, W.B. Rogers (r1910) (5/95) (ROMO) ⏀ [3] **81011-2(2)**

13b, 16(pt) K. Te Kanawa, BRSO, Colin Davis (PHIL) ⏀ **434 725-2PM** (PHIL) ⊟ **434 725-4PM**

14a, 14b, 15a-d G. Farrar, G. Gilibert, E. Caruso, M. Journet, orch (r1910) (3/91) (PEAR) ⏀ [3] **EVC2**

15a F. Chaliapin, Moscow Imperial Op Orch, M.I. Semenov (Russian: r1910) (PREI) ⏀ **89030**

15a E. Pinza, NY Met Op Orch, W. Pelletier (bp1940) (7/91) (MMOI) ⏀ **CDMOIR404** (MMOI) ⊟ **CMOIR404**

15a A. Kipnis, orch (Ger: r c1916) (10/91) (PEAR) ⏀ **GEMMCD9451**

15a F. Chaliapin, orch, E. Goossens (pp1928) (7/92) (PEAR) ⏀ [3] **GEMMCDS9926(1)**

15a M. Journet, orch (r1910) (10/94) (NIMB) ⏀ **NI7859**

15a, 19b L. Sibiriakov, orch (r1909: Russ) (6/93) (PEAR) ⏀ [3] **GEMMCDS9001/3(2)**

15b D. Borgioli, M. Zamboni, orch, L. Molajoli (r1927: Ital) (PEAR) ⏀ **GEMMCD9091**

15b A. Piccaver, M. Angerer, Berlin St Op Orch, M. Gurlitt (r1929: Ger) (PREI) ⏀ [2] **89217**

15b C. Ferrani, G. Apostolu, anon (Ital: r1902) (5/91) (SYMP) ⏀ **SYMCD1077**

15b G. Bréjean-Silver, E. Scaramberg, anon (r1905) (12/93) (SYMP) ⏀ **SYMCD1113**

15b G. Zenatello, A. Nielsen, orch (r c1913) (5/94) (SYMP) ⏀ **SYMCD1168**

15b G. Zenatello, A. Verlet, orch (r1916) (5/94) (PEAR) ⏀ [4] **GEMMCDS9074(2)**

15b F. de Lucia, C. Boninsegna, anon (r1904: Ital) (1/95) (SYMP) ⏀ **SYMCD1149**

15b, 15c G. Zenatello, A. Nielsen, orch (r1911) (5/94) (PEAR) ⏀ [4] **GEMMCDS9074(1)**

15b, 15c G. Farrar, E. Caruso, orch (r1910) (10/94) (NIMB) ⏀ **NI7859**

15d H. Spani, La Scala Orch, C. Sabajno (Ital: r1928) (9/90) (CLUB) ⏀ [2] **CL99-509/10**

15d H. Spani, La Scala Orch, C. Sabajno (Ital: r1928) (12/92) (PREI) ⏀ **89037**

16. Z. Dolukhanova, USSR Rad Orch, O. Bron (r1950s) (PREI) ⏀ **89066**

17. E. Zbrueva, anon (r1903: Russ) (6/93) (PEAR) ⏀ [3] **GEMMCDS9004/6(2)**

18a Fairey Band, K. Dennison (arr Langford) (CHAN) ⏀ **CHAN6530**

18a R. Massard, M. Elkins, M. Sinclair, LSO, R. Bonynge (DECC) ⏀ **433 064-2DWO**

18a ROH Chor, RPO, R. Stapleton (r1990) (RPO) ⏀ [2] **CDRPD9006** (RPO) ⊟ [2] **ZCRPD9006**

18a M. Elkins, M. Sinclair, R. Massard, Ambrosian Op Chor, LSO, R. Bonynge (r1966) (DECC) ⏀ **433 443-2DA** (DECC) ⊟ **433 443-4DA**

18a LSO, LSC, R. Hickox (r1988) (IMP) ⏀ **PCDS22** (IMP) ⊟ **PCDSC22**

18a Orphei Drängar Ch, Swedish RSO, E. Ericson, L. Segerstam (pp1978) (7/88) (BIS) ⏀ **BIS-CD383**

18a ROH Chor, RPO, R. Stapleton (10/90) (IMP) ⏀ **MCD15** (10/90) (IMP) ⊟ **MCC15**

18a, 18b R. Shaw Chorale, RCA Victor Orch, Robert Shaw (RCA) ⏀ **GD60205**

18b LSC, LSO, R. Hickox (IMP) ⏀ **PCDS4** (IMP) ⊟ **PCDSC4**

18b LSC, LSO, R. Hickox (IMP) ⏀ **PCDS10** (IMP) ⊟ **PCDSC10**

18b Paris Op Chor, Paris Op Orch, G. Prêtre (r1978) (CFP) ⏀ **CD-CFP4602** (CFP) ⊟ **TC-CFP4602**

18b A. Silja, E. Waechter, Bayreuth Fest Chor, Bayreuth Fest Orch, W. Pitz (r1963) (BELA) ⏀ **450 052-2** (BELA) ⊟ **450 052-4**

18b Ambrosian Op Chor, LSO, R. Bonynge (r1965) (DECC) ⏀ **440 947-2DH** (DECC) ⊟ **440 947-4DH**

18b LSC, LSO, R. Hickox (r1988) (IMP) ⏀ [3] **TCD1070**

18b LSC, LSO, R. Hickox (r1987/8) (IMP) ⏀ [3] **TCD1073**

18b Capitol SO, C. Dragon (r1958: arr Dragon) (EMI) ⏀ **CDM5 65430-2**

18b LSC, LSO, R. Hickox (4/89) (IMP) ⏀ **PCD908**

19b M. Journet, orch, Rosario Bourdon (r1925) (PREI) ⏀ **89021**

19b N. Ghiaurov, LSO, E. Downes (DECC) ⏀ **433 067-2DWO** (DECC) ⊟ **433 067-4DWO**

19b R. Raimondi, Orch, Anon Cond (pp1991) (MCI) ⏀ **MCCD090** (MCI) ⊟ **MCTC090**

19b M. Pertusi, Sofia PO, E. Tabakov (r1994) (CAPR) ⏀ **10 704**

19b T. Pasero, orch, L. Molajoli (Ital: r1927) (6/90) (PREI) ⏀ **89010**

19b E. Pinza, orch, H. Barlow (bp1944) (7/91) (MMOI) ⏀ **CDMOIR404** (MMOI) ⊟ **CMOIR404**

19b L. Melchissédec, anon (r1903) (9/91) (SYMP) ⏀ **SYMCD1089**

19b P. Plançon, anon (r1902) (9/91) (PEAR) ⏀ **GEMMCD9497**

19b N. de Angelis, orch, L. Molajoli (Ital: r1927) (7/92) (PREI) ⏀ **89042**

19b P. Plançon, anon (r1904) (7/92) (PEAR) ⏀ [3] **GEMMCDS9923(1)**

19b P. Gailhard, anon (r1905) (7/92) (PEAR) ⏀ [3] **GEMMCDS9923(1)**

19b V. Arimondi, anon (Ital: r1904) (7/92) (PEAR) ⏀ [3] **GEMMCDS9924(1)**

19b A. Didur, S. Cottone (r1903: Ital) (6/93) (PEAR) ⏀ [3] **GEMMCDS9997/9(2)**

19b A. Didur, orch (r c1919) (1/94) (CLUB) ⏀ **CL99-089**

19b P. Plançon, orch (r1906) (12/94) (ROMO) ⏀ [2] **82001-2**

19b P. Plançon, anon (r1904) (12/94) (ROMO) ⏀ [2] **82001-2**

19b P. Gailhard, anon (r1905: 2 vers: Fr/Ital) (12/94) (SYMP) ⏀ **SYMCD1172**

19b P. Plançon, orch (r1906) (1/95) (NIMB) ⏀ **NI7860**

19b T. Pasero, orch, A. Sabino (r1943: Ital) (4/95) (PREI) ⏀ **89074**

20. E. Caruso, A. Scotti, M. Journet, orch (r1910) (3/91) (PEAR) ⏀ [3] **EVC2**

20. E. Caruso, A. Scotti, M. Journet, orch, W.B. Rogers (r1910) (10/94) (NIMB) ⏀ **NI7859**

21a M. Battistini, E. Barbieri, orch (r1913: Ital) (PEAR) ⏀ **GEMMCD9016**

21a E. Badini, A. de Revers, L. Mellerio, orch (r1909: Ital) (12/94) (BONG) ⏀ **GB1043-2**

21b A. Scotti, chor, orch (r1911) (7/92) (PEAR) ⏀ [3] **GEMMCDS9923(2)**

21b A. Scotti, orch (r1911) (10/94) (NIMB) ⏀ **NI7859**

22. F. Chaliapin, M. Michailova, Moscow Imperial Op Orch, M.I. Semenov (Russian: r1910) (PREI) ⏀ **89030**

22. E. List, M. Seinemeyer, Berlin St Op Orch, F. Weissmann (r1929: Ger) (PREI) ⏀ **89083**

22. L. Sibiriakov, E. Katulskaya, orch, G.I. Wahrlich (r1913: Russ) (PEAR) ⏀ [3] **GEMMCDS9111(1)**

22. F. Austral, F. Chaliapin, orch, A. Coates (r1925) (PEAR) ⏀ **GEMMCD9146**

22(pt) G. Rossi, anon (Ital: r1903) (5/91) (SYMP) ⏀ **SYMCD1077**

22. N. de Angelis, G. Cigna, orch, L. Molajoli (Ital: r1929) (7/92) (PREI) ⏀ **89042**

22. F. Litvinne, anon (r1903) (10/92) (SYMP) ⏀ **SYMCD1101**

24a, 24b G. Farrar, E. Caruso, orch, W.B. Rogers (r1910) (10/94) (NIMB) ⏀ **NI7859**

24a, 24b, 25a H. Roswaenge, M. Teschemacher, W. Strienz, Berlin St Op Orch, B. Seidler-Winkler (r1938: Ger) (PREI) ⏀ [2] **89211**

24a, 24b, 25a, 25b G. Farrar, E. Caruso, M. Journet, orch (r1910) (3/91) (PEAR) ⏀ [3] **EVC2**

25. E. Steber, B. Sullivan, J. Hines, Orch, Anon (cond) (bp1953) (VAI) ▣ **VAI69112**

25a K. Ricciarelli, Alfredo Kraus, R. Raimondi, Madrid SO, G.P. Sanzogno (pp1991) (IMP) ⏀ [2] **DPCD998**

25a K. Ricciarelli, Alfredo Kraus, R. Raimondi, Madrid SO, G.P. Sanzogno (RNE) ⏀ [2] **650004**

25a E. Eames, C. Dalmores, P. Plançon, orch (r1907) (11/93) (ROMO) ⏀ [2] **81001-2**

25a G. Farrar, E. Caruso, M. Journet, orch, W.B. Rogers (r1910) (10/94) (NIMB) ⏀ **NI7859**

25a P. Plançon, E. Eames, C. Dalmores, orch (r1907) (12/94) (ROMO) ⏀ [2] **82001-2**

25a, 25b A. Besançon, Suisse Romande Brass Ens. (arr Brass) (CASC) ⏀ **VEL1015**

25a, 25b J. Sutherland, F. Corelli, N. Ghiaurov, Ambrosian Op Chor, R. Bonynge, R. Bonynge (DECC) ⏀ **433 064-2DWO**

25a, 25b N. Ghiaurov, J. Sutherland, F. Corelli, Ambrosian Op Chor, R. Bonynge (r1966) (DECC) ⏀ **433 440-2DA** (DECC) ⊟ **433 440-4DA**

25a, 25b G. Cigna, P. Civil, T. Pasero, orch, L. Molajoli (Ital: r c1930) (6/90) (PREI) ⏀ **89010**

25a, 25b G. Cigna, P. Civil, T. Pasero, orch, L. Molajoli (Ital: r1930) (11/90) (PREI) ⏀ **89016**

26. Bratislava RSO, O. Lenárd (NAXO) ⏀ **8 550081**

26. Adelaide SO, J. Serebrier (MCI) ⏀ **OQ0008**

26. Paris Cons, R. Leibowitz (CHES) ⏀ **Chesky CD57**

26. Eastman Wind Ens, F. Fennell (r1959. arr Winterbottom) (MERC) ⏀ **434 322-2MM**

26. Bolshoi Th Orch, G. Zhemchuzhin (PILZ) ⏀ [6] **441002-2**

26. Montreal SO, C. Dutoit (DECC) ⏀ **436 475-2DM**

26. Slovak PO, K. Redel (r1990) (PIER) ⏀ **PV730023**

26. Luxembourg Rad & TV SO, L. de Froment (r1992) (FORL) ⏀ **FF044**

26. F. Corelli, N. Ghiaurov, LSO, R. Bonynge (r1966) (DECC) ⏀ **444 108-2DA**

26. Budapest PO, J. Sándor (5/90) (LASE) ⏀ **15 616** (LASE) ⊟ **79 616**

26. Montreal SO, C. Dutoit (8/91) (DECC) ⏀ **430 718-2DM**

26. RPO, T. Beecham (r1957) (9/92) (EMI) ⏀ **CDM7 63401-2**

26. NYPO, L. Bernstein (r1967) (9/93) (SONY) ⏀ **SMK47600**

26. San Francisco SO, P. Monteux (r1947) (9/94) (RCA) ⏀ [15] **09026 61893-2**

26. RPO, T. Beecham (r1958; rehearsal & perf)
(4/95) (TELD) ⬖ **4509-95038-6**
(4/95) (TELD) ▣ **4509-95038-3**
26a-g Luxembourg Rad & TV SO, L. de Froment
(FORL) Ⓓ **FF028**
26a, 26b LPO, T. Beecham (bp1939)
(11/91) (SYMP) Ⓓ [2] **SYMCD1096/7**
26a, 26b LPO, T. Beecham (bp1939)
(5/94) (DUTT) Ⓓ [2] **2CDAX2001**

Le **Médecin malgré lui– opéra-comique: 3 acts (1858—Paris) (Lib. J Barbier & M Carré, after Molière)**
Qu'ils sont doux L. Fugère, anon (r1929)
(6/93) (SYMP) Ⓓ **SYMCD1125**

Mireille– opéra dialogué: 5 acts (1864—Paris) (Lib. Carré after Mistral)
ACT 1: 1. Overture; 2. Chantez, chantez, Magnanarelles; 3a. Adieu, bonne Taven!; 3b. Vincenette a votre âge. ACT 2: 4. La Farandole; 5a. Puisque Vincent le veut; 5b. La brise est douce (Chanson de Magali); 6. Voici la saison; 7a. Trahir Vincent; 7b. Mon coeur ne peut changer!; 8. Si les filles d'Arles. ACT 3: 9. Ils s'éloignent!. ACT 4: 10. Le jour se lève; 11. Heureux petit berger; 12. Voici la vaste plaine. ACT 5: 13a. Mon coeur est plein d'un noir souci!; 13b. Anges du paradis; 14. Ah! la voici! c'est elle!;. ADDITIONAL ARIA: 15. O légère hirondelle (Waltz Song).
Mireille J. Vivalda
Vincent N. Gedda
Taven C. Gayraud
Ourrias M. Dens
Vincenette M. Ignal
Ramon A. Vessières
Clémence C. Jacquin
Ambroise M. Cortis
Shepherd R. Tropin
Aix-en-Provence Fest Chor, Paris Cons, A. Cluytens (r1954)
(12/92) (EMI) Ⓓ [2] **CMS7 64382-2**
3b M. Mesplé, N. Gedda, Paris Op Orch, P. Dervaux (r1974) (EMI) Ⓓ [2] **CZS7 67813-2**
5b A. Garulli, E. Bendazzi-Garulli, anon (r1902)
(5/91) (SYMP) Ⓓ **SYMCD1077**
10-12. R. Doria, Paris Sols Orch, J. Etcheverry
(SYMP) Ⓓ **SYMCD1103**
11, 15. P. Alarie, Lamoureux Orch, P. Dervaux (r1953) (11/94) (PHIL) Ⓓ [2] **438 953-2PM2**
15. L. Pons, Orch, G. Cloëz (r1929)
(MSCM) Ⓓ **MM30446**
15. E. Gruberová, Tokyo PO, F. Haider (pp1993)
(NIGH) Ⓓ **NC090560-2**
15. L. Tetrazzini, orch, P. Pitt (Ital: r1909)
(9/92) (EMI) Ⓓ [3] **CHS7 63802-2(1)**
15. L. Tetrazzini, orch, P. Pitt (Ital: r1909)
(9/92) (PEAR) Ⓓ **GEMMCD9222**
15. A. Nezhdanova, anon (r1908)
(6/93) (PEAR) Ⓓ [3] **GEMMCDS9007/9(2)**
15. M. Korjus, Berlin St Op Orch, B. Seidler-Winkler (Ger: r1935) (10/93) (PREI) Ⓓ **89054**
15. F. Hempel, orch (r1912: Ital)
(3/94) (NIMB) Ⓓ **NI7849**
15. E. Katulskaya, orch (r1913: Russ)
(3/95) (NIMB) Ⓓ **NI7865**

Philémon et Baucis– opéra (1860—Paris) (Lib. Barbier and Carré)
Philémon A. Misciano
Baucis R. Scotto
Jove R. Panerai
Vulcane P. Montarsolo
Bacchante J. Torriani
Milan RAI Chor, Milan RAI SO, N. Sanzogno (Ital: pp1961)
(FOYE) Ⓓ [2] **2-CF2016**
Philémon J-C. Orliac
Baucis A-M. Rodde
Jupiter P. Néquecaur
Vulcan F. Giband
French Rad Lyric Orch, H. Gallois (bp1975)
(11/93) (MUSD) Ⓓ **20234-2**
Au bruit des lourds marteaux S. Gehrman, N. Walker (NIMB) Ⓓ **NI5214**
Au bruit des lourds marteaux P. Plançon, anon (r1902) (9/91) (PEAR) Ⓓ **GEMMCD9497**
Au bruit des lourds marteaux P. Plançon, anon (r1905)
(7/92) (PEAR) Ⓓ [3] **GEMMCDS9923(1)**
Au bruit des lourds marteaux P. Plançon, anon (r1902) (3/93) (SYMP) Ⓓ **SYMCD1100**
Au bruit des lourds marteaux M. Journet, orch (r1910) (10/94) (NIMB) Ⓓ **NI7859**
Au bruit des lourds marteaux P. Plançon, anon (r1905) (12/94) (ROMO) Ⓓ [2] **82001-2**

O riante nature A. Galli-Curci, orch (r1930)
(PEAR) Ⓓ **GEMMCD9450**
O riante nature A. Galli-Curci, orch (r1930)
(8/94) (NIMB) Ⓓ **NI7852**
Que les songes sont heureux G. Souzay, New SO, P. Bonneau (r1956)
(DECC) Ⓓ **440 419-2DM**
Rêverie R. Doria, J. Boguet
(12/91) (MSCM) Ⓓ **MM30373**

Polyeucte– opéra: 5 acts (1864—Paris) (Wds. Barbier and Carré, after Corneille)
Source délicieuse R. Alagna, LPO, R. Armstrong (EMI) Ⓓ **CDC5 55540-2**
(EMI) ⊟ **EL5 55540-4**
Source délicieuse L. Escalais, anon (r1906)
(8/92) (IRCC) Ⓓ **IRCC-CD802**
Source délicieuse L. Escalais, anon (r1906)
(12/94) (SYMP) Ⓓ **SYMCD1128**

La **Reine de Saba– opéra: 4 acts (1862—Paris) (Lib. Barbier & Carré, after Nerval)**
Ballet Music LSO, R. Bonynge (r1971)
(DECC) Ⓓ **444 108-2DA**
Faiblesse de la race humaine!...Inspirez-moi, race divine E. Caruso, orch, W.B. Rogers (r1916) (7/91) (RCA) Ⓓ [12] **GD60495(5)**
Faiblesse de la race humaine!...Inspirez-moi, race divine E. Caruso, orch, W.B. Rogers (r1916) (10/91) (PEAR) Ⓓ [3] **EVC3(2)**
Inspirez-moi, race divine E. Scaramberg, anon (r1905) (SYMP) Ⓓ **SYMCD1173**
Inspirez-moi, race divine W. Widdop, orch, M. Sargent (r1929: Eng)
(PEAR) Ⓓ **GEMMCD9112**
Inspirez-moi, race divine W. Widdop, orch, M. Sargent (r1929: Eng)
(5/94) (CLAR) Ⓓ **CDGSE78-50-52**
Inspirez-moi, race divine E. Caruso, orch (r1916) (7/95) (NIMB) Ⓓ **NI7866**
Plus grand dans son obscurité. F. Pollet, Montpellier PO, C. Diederich (r1989)
(ERAT) Ⓓ **4509-98502-2**
Plus grand dans son obscurité. M. Rappold, orch (Eng: r1920s)
(8/92) (IRCC) Ⓓ **IRCC-CD802**
Reine du matin R. Doria, J. Boguet
(12/91) (MSCM) Ⓓ **MM30373**

Roméo et Juliette, 'Romeo and Juliet'– opéra: 5 acts (1867—Paris) (Lib. Barbier and Carré, after Shakespeare)
EXCERPTS. ACT 1: 1. L'heure s'envoie; 2. Écoutez! écoutez!; 3. Allons! jeunes gens!; 4a. Enfin la place est libre; 4b. Mab, la reine des mensonges; 4c. Eh bien! que l'avertissment; 5. Je veux vivre (Waltz); 6a. Le nom de cette belle enfant?; 6b. Ange adorable; 7a. Quelqu'un!; 7b. Le voici. ACT 2: 8a. O nuit! sous tes ailes; 8b. L'amour, l'amour; 8c. Ah! lève-toi, soleil; 9. Hélas! moi, le haïr!; 10a. O nuit divine; 10b. Ah! ne fuis pas encore. ACT 3: 11. Mon père! Dieu vous garde!; 12. Dieu qui fit l'homme; 13a. Depius hier je cherche en vain mon maître!; 13b. Que faites-tu, blance tourterelle; 14. Ah! voici nos gens!; 15. Eh quoi? toujours du sang?. ACT 4: 16a. Va! Je t'ai pardonné; 16b. Nuit d'hymenée!; 16c. Non, ce n'est pas le jour; 17a. Quoi! ma fille; 17b. Que l'hymne nuptiale; 18a. Mon père! tout m'accable; 18b. Buvez donc ce breuvage; 19. Dieu! quel frisson court dans mes veines!; 20. Cortège nuptial; 21. Ma fille, cède aux voeux (Finale). ACT 5: 22. Le sommeil de Juliette; 23. Salut! tombeau sombre.
Roméo R. Alagna
Juliette L. Vaduva
Frère Laurent R. Lloyd
Mercutio F. Le Roux
Stéphano A. M. Panzarella
Capulet P. Sidhom
Gertrud Sarah Walker
Tybalt P. C. Clarke
ROH Chor, ROHO, C. Mackerras, B. Large (pp1993)
(10/95) (PION) ▣ **CVI1771**
Roméo F. Corelli
Juliette M. Freni
Frère Laurent X. Depraz
Mercutio H. Gui
Stephano E. Lublin
Capulet C. Calès
Gertrude M. Vilma
Tybalt R. Cardona
Paris Y. Bisson
Gregorio C. Grigoriou
Benvolio M. Auzeville
Duo P. Thau
Paris Op Chor, Paris Op Orch, A. Lombard (r1968)
(EMI) Ⓓ [2] **CMS5 65290-2**
Roméo Alfredo Kraus
Juliette C. Malfitano
Frère Laurent J. Van Dam
Mercutio G. Quilico
Stephano A. Murray
Capulet G. Bacquier
Gertrude J. Taillon
Tybalt C. Burles
Paris K. Ollmann
Gregorio J-M. Frémeau
Midi-Pyrenees Regional Ch, Toulouse Capitole Chor, Toulouse Capitole Orch, M. Plasson
(3/87) (EMI) Ⓓ **CDS7 47365-8**
Roméo R. Jobin
Juliette J. Micheau
Gertrude O. Ricquier
Friar Lawrence H. Rehfuss
Capulet C. Cambon
Tybalt L. Rialland
Mercutio P. Mollet
Prince; Gregorio A. Philippe
Stephano C. Collart
Paris C. Roquetty
Paris Op Chor, Paris Op Orch, A. Erede (r1953)
(6/95) (DECC) Ⓓ [2] **443 539-2LF2**
March SO, T. Beecham (r1917)
(11/91) (SYMP) Ⓓ [2] **SYMCD1096/7**
3. L. Melchissédec, anon (r1907)
(9/91) (SYMP) Ⓓ **SYMCD1089**
3. P. Plançon, anon (r1904)
(9/91) (PEAR) Ⓓ **GEMMCD9497**
3. P. Plançon, anon (r1904)
(7/92) (PEAR) Ⓓ [3] **GEMMCDS9923(2)**
3. P. Plançon, anon (r1902)
(3/93) (SYMP) Ⓓ **SYMCD1100**
3. P. Plançon, anon (r1904)
(12/94) (ROMO) Ⓓ [2] **82001-2**
3. P. Plançon, anon (r1904)
(1/95) (NIMB) Ⓓ **NI7860**
4b G. Souzay, New SO, P. Bonneau (r1956)
(DECC) Ⓓ **440 419-2DM**
5. L. Bori, orch (r1922)
(PEAR) Ⓓ **GEMMCD9458**
5. A. Moffo, Munich RO, K. Eichhorn
(EURO) Ⓓ **GD69113**
5. M. Callas, FRNO, G. Prêtre
(EMI) Ⓓ **CDC7 54702-2**
(EMI) ⊟ **EL754702-4**
5. M. Mesplé, Paris Op Orch, J-P. Marty (r1968)
(EMI) Ⓓ [2] **CZS7 67813-2**
5. G. Farrar, orch (r1906)
(IRCC) Ⓓ **IRCC-CD805**
5. J. Harjanne, J. Lagerspetz (r1992)
(FINL) Ⓓ **4509-95583-2**
5. E. Gruberová, Munich RO, G. Kuhn (r c1980)
(EMIN) Ⓓ **CD-EMX2234**
5. A. Pendachanska, Sofia SO, M. Angelov (r1994) (CAPR) Ⓓ **10 706**
5. G. Farrar, orch (r1911) (NIMB) Ⓓ **NI7872**
5. L. Bori, Victor Orch, Rosario Bourdon (r1922)
(ROMO) Ⓓ [2] **81016-2**
5. M. Callas, FRNO, G. Prêtre
(2/88) (EMI) Ⓓ **CDC7 49059-2**
5. E. Norena, orch (r1928)
(10/89) (NIMB) Ⓓ **NI7802**
(NIMB) ⊟ **NC7802**
5. J. Sutherland, ROHO, F. Molinari-Pradelli
(1/90) (DECC) Ⓓ [2] **425 493-2DM2**
5. M. Callas, FRNO, G. Prêtre
(2/90) (EMI) Ⓓ **CDM7 63182-2**
5. A. Galli-Curci, orch, J. Pasternack (r1917)
(5/90) (NIMB) Ⓓ **NI7806**
(NIMB) ⊟ **NC7806**
5. R. Pinkert, anon (r1906)
(7/92) (PEAR) Ⓓ [3] **GEMMCDS9923(1)**
5. L. Tetrazzini, orch, P. Pitt (Ital: r1908)
(9/92) (EMI) Ⓓ [3] **CHS7 63802-2(1)**
5. L. Tetrazzini, anon (r c1904)
(9/92) (PEAR) Ⓓ **GEMMCD9225**
5. L. Tetrazzini, orch, P. Pitt (Ital: r1908)
(9/92) (PEAR) Ⓓ **GEMMCD9221**
5(pt) R. Pinkert, anon (r1906)
(11/92) (MEMO) Ⓓ [2] **HR4408/9(1)**
5. S. Adams, anon (r1902)
(3/93) (SYMP) Ⓓ **SYMCD1100**
5. M. Caballé, New Philh, R. Giovaninetti (r1970)
(5/93) (DG) Ⓓ **431 103-2GB**
5. A. Nezhdanova, U. Masetti (r1906: Russ)
(6/93) (PEAR) Ⓓ [3] **GEMMCDS9007/9(1)**
5. E. Eames, anon (r1905)
(11/93) (ROMO) Ⓓ [2] **81001-2**

5. E. Eames, orch (r1906)
(11/93) (ROMO) Ⓓ [2] **81001-2**
5. A. Galli-Curci, orch, J. Pasternack (r1917)
(3/94) (ROMO) Ⓓ [2] **81003-2**
5. M. Devia, Svizzera Italiana Orch, M. Rota (pp1992) (10/94) (BONG) Ⓓ **GB2513-2**
5. P. Alarie, Lamoureux Orch, P. Dervaux (r1953) (11/94) (PHIL) Ⓓ [2] **438 953-2PM2**
5. E. Eames, orch (r1906)
(1/95) (NIMB) Ⓓ **NI7860**
5. L. Garrett, RPO, P. Robinson (r1994)
(4/95) (SILV) Ⓓ **SILKD6004**
(4/95) (SILV) ▭ **SILKC6004**
5. I. Galante, Latvian Nat SO, A. Vilumanis (r1994) (11/95) (CAMP) Ⓓ **RRCD1335**
(11/95) (CAMP) ▭ **RRMC8035**
6a, 6b, 8b, 8c, 10b, 16a, 16b, 23. H. Schymberg, J. Björling, Stockholm Royal Op Orch, N. Grevillius (Swedish; pp1940)
(3/92) (BLUE) Ⓓ **ABCD013**
6b M. Mesplé, N. Gedda, Paris Op Orch, P. Dervaux (r1974) (EMI) Ⓓ [2] **CZS7 67813-2**
6b G. Farrar, E. Clément, orch (r1913)
(NIMB) Ⓓ **NI7872**
6b F. Marconi, B. Mililotti, C. Sabajno (r1907: Ital) (10/90) (SYMP) Ⓓ **SYMCD1069**
6b L. Bori, B. Gigli, orch, Rosario Bourdon (r1923) (10/90) (RCA) Ⓓ **GD87811**
(10/90) (RCA) ▭ **GK87811**
6b E. Scaramberg, G. Bréjean-Silver, anon (r1905)
(7/92) (PEAR) Ⓓ [3] **GEMMCDS9923(2)**
6b J. Björling, A-L. Björling, Stockholm Concert Soc Orch, N. Grevillius (r1949)
(8/92) (BLUE) Ⓓ **ABCD016**
6b E. Clément, G. Farrar, orch, Rosario Bourdon (r1913) (8/95) (ROMO) Ⓓ **82002-2**
6b E. Clément, G. Farrar, orch, Rosario Bourdon (r1913) (8/95) (PEAR) Ⓓ **GEMMCD9161**
6b, 10b L. Bori, B. Gigli, orch (r1923)
(PEAR) Ⓓ **GEMMCD9458**
6b, 10b L. Bori, B. Gigli, Victor Orch, Rosario Bourdon (r1923) (ROMO) Ⓓ [2] **81016-2**
8b, 8c Alfredo Kraus, Toulouse Capitole Orch, M. Plasson (EMI) Ⓓ **CDC7 54016-2**
8b, 8c P. Domingo, New Philh, N. Santi
(RCA) Ⓓ [2] **GD60866**
(RCA) ▭ [2] **GK60866**
8b, 8c J. Carreras, ROHO, J. Delacôte
(EMI) Ⓓ **CDC7 54524-2**
8b, 8c G. Thill, Orch, P. Gaubert (r1927)
(1/89) (EMI) Ⓓ **CDM7 69548-2**
8b, 8c Alfredo Kraus, Toulouse Capitole Orch, M. Plasson (10/89) (EMI) Ⓓ **CDM7 63104-2**
8b, 10b L. Bori, B. Gigli, orch, Rosario Bourdon (r1923) (CONI) Ⓓ **CDHD170**
8c G. Thill, orch, P. Gaubert (r c1925)
(PEAR) Ⓓ **GEMMCD9947**
8c A. Cupido, Verona Arena Orch, A. Guadagno (pp1992) (MCI) Ⓓ **MCCD099**
8c J. Björling, orch, N. Grevillius (r1930: Swed)
(PEAR) Ⓓ **GEMMCD9043**
8c P. Domingo, New Philh, N. Santi
(RCA) Ⓓ **09026 61886-2**
(RCA) ▭ **09026 61886-4**
8c E. Scaramberg, anon (r1905)
(SYMP) Ⓓ **SYMCD1173**
8c P. Franz, orch (r1912) (PREI) Ⓓ **89099**
8c F. de la Mora, WNO Orch, C. Mackerras (r1994-5) (TELA) Ⓓ **CD80411**
8c G. Morino, Warmia Nat PO, B. Amaducci
(10/90) (NUOV) Ⓓ **6851**
8c L. Slezak, orch (Ger: r1907)
(2/91) (PREI) Ⓓ **89020**
8c J. Björling, Stockholm Royal Op Orch, N. Grevillius (r1946)
(4/92) (EMI) Ⓓ [7] **CHS7 69741-2(5)**
8c J. Björling, orch, N. Grevillius (r1945)
(8/92) (BLUE) Ⓓ **ABCD016**
8c I. Alchevsky, anon (r1900s)
(7/93) (SYMP) Ⓓ **SYMCD1105**
8c A. Piccaver, orch (r1912: Ger)
(8/93) (PREI) Ⓓ **89060**
8c J. Björling, Stockholm Royal Op Orch, N. Grevillius (r1945)
(10/93) (EMI) Ⓓ **CDH7 64707-2**
8c E. Clément, anon (r1905)
(8/95) (ROMO) Ⓓ **82002-2**
8c G. Thill, orch, P. Gaubert (r1927)
(8/95) (FORL) Ⓓ **UCD16727**
8c A. Davies, A. Bryn Parri (r1994)
(11/95) (SAIN) Ⓓ **SCDC2085**
8c, 22. F. Ansseau, orch (r1926)
(1/91) (PREI) Ⓓ **89022**
10a, 16b F. Hempel, H. Jadlowker, orch (Ger: r1900s) (12/91) (CLUB) Ⓓ **CL99-042**
10b B. Gigli, L. Bori, orch (r1923)
(ASV) Ⓓ **CDAJA5137**
(ASV) ▭ **ZCAJA5137**
13a, 13b G. Swarthout, RCA SO, W. Pelletier (r1942) (4/94) (RCA) Ⓓ [6] **09026 61580-2(4)**
16a-c K. Battle, P. Domingo, NY Met Op Orch, James Levine (pp1988)
(DG) Ⓓ **445 552-2GMA**
(DG) ▭ **445 552-4GMA**
16a-c P. Domingo, R. Scotto, National PO, K. H. Adler (r 1970s) (SONY) Ⓓ **SMK39030**
16a, 16b B. Frittoli, V. Ombuena, Berlin RSO, J. Märkl (r1991) (SCHW) Ⓓ [2] **312682**
22. RPO, T. Beecham (r1959)
(EMI) Ⓓ **CDM7 63412-2**
23. P. Cornubert, anon (r1905)
(SYMP) Ⓓ **SYMCD1173**
23. P. Franz, orch (r1911) (PREI) Ⓓ **89099**
23. R. Alagna, LPO, R. Armstrong
(EMI) Ⓓ **CDC5 55540-2**
(EMI) ▭ **EL5 55540-4**
23. G. Thill, G. Féraldy, Orch, J. Szyfer (r1929)
(1/89) (EMI) Ⓓ **CDM7 69548-2**

Sapho– opéra: 3 acts (1851—Paris) (Lib. Augier)
EXCERPTS: 1a. Introduction and March; 1b. O Jupiter; 2a. Tu ne suis pas la multitude; 2b. Puis-je oublier; 3. Violà Sapho; 4a. Quel entretien si doux; 4b. Quand de choisir elle me presse; 5a. Salut Alcée; 5b. Les entrailles des victimes; 5c. Les Dieux d'un oeil clément; 6. O Liberté, déesse austère; 7a. Meure le tyrannie; 7b. Sapho! Sapho! Sapho!; 8. Héros sur la tour solitaire; 9. Fille d'Apollon. ACT 2: 10a. Gloire à Bachus; 10b. Assez chante! Phaon, fais sortit; 11. Oui, jourons tous; 12a. Reste là! Pythéas; 12b. Comprends-moi bien, ma bonne Phèdre; 13. Ma vie en se séjour; 14. Glycère ici! Que cherche-t-elle; 15a. Je viens sauver ta tête; 15b. O Douleur qui m'oppresse. ACT 3: 15c. Prelude; 16a. J'arrive le premier; 16b. O jours heureux; 17a. Adieu Patrie; 17b. La mer et la vaisseau; 17c. Sois béni; 17d. Adieu, adieu Patrie; 18. Broutez le thym; 19a. Où suis-je; 19b. O ma lyre immortelle.

Sapho	M. Command
Glycère	S. Coste
Phaon	C. Papis
Alcée	E. Faury
Pythéas	L. Sarrazin
Cygénire, High Priest	P. Georges
Goat-herd	S. Martinez

Saint-Etienne Lyric Chor, Saint-Etienne Nouvel Orch, P. Fournillier (r1992)
(7/94) (SCHW) Ⓓ [2] **313112**
8, 19b M. Horne, Monte Carlo PO, L. Foster (r1984) (ERAT) Ⓓ **4509-98501-2**
19a, 19b M. Horne, SRO, H. Lewis (1965)
(DECC) Ⓓ **440 415-2DM**
19a, 19b S. Verrett, RCA Italiana Op Orch, G. Prêtre (r1967) (RCA) Ⓓ **09026 61457-2**
19b R. Crespin, SRO, A. Lombard (r1970/1)
(DECC) Ⓓ **440 416-2DM**
19b G. Bumbry, Stuttgart RSO, S. Soltesz
(11/86) (ORFE) Ⓓ **C081841A**
19b F. Litvinne, anon (r1903)
(10/92) (SYMP) Ⓓ **SYMCD1101**

Le **Tribut de Zamora– opéra: 4 acts (1881—Paris) (Lib. d'Ennery & Brésil)**
Garde la couronne des reines Z. de Lussan, anon (r1906) (8/92) (IRCC) Ⓓ **IRCC-CD802**
Waltz LSO, R. Bonynge (r1971)
(DECC) Ⓓ **444 111-2DA**

GRABU, Louis *(fl 1665–1694) France/England*

Albion and Albanius– opera (1685—London) (Lib. J Dryden)
EXCERPTS: 1. Concert of Venus.
1. Parley of Instr, P. Holman (r1993)
(6/94) (HYPE) Ⓓ **CDA66667**

GRAENER, Paul *(1872–1944) Germany*

Friedemann Bach– opera: 3 acts, Op. 90 (1931—Schwerin) (Lib. R Lothar, after A E Brachvogel)
Preis dir und Dank; Kein Hälmlein wächst auf Erden W. Ludwig, Berlin City Op Orch, W. Ladwig (r1932) (7/95) (PREI) Ⓓ **89088**

GRANADOS (Y CAMPIÑA), Enrique *(1867–1916) Spain*

Goyescas– opera: 1 act (1916—New York) (Lib. F. Periquet y Zuaznabar)
EXCERPTS: 1. Intermezzo; 2. La maja y el ruiseñor (Lover and the nightingale); 3. Elegia eterna.
1. N. Zumbro (trans cpsr: pf)
(CONC) Ⓓ **CACD9004**
(CONC) ▭ **FED4-TC-9004**
1. I. Presti, A. Lagoya (trans Lagoya)
(PHIL) Ⓓ **422 979-2PCC**
1. J. Christensen, M. Fukačová (arr gtr/vc)
(KONT) Ⓓ **32044**
1. P. Casals, N. Mednikoff (arr Cassado: r1927)
(MSCM) Ⓓ **MM30428**
1. P. Romero, Celín Romero (arr gtr)
(PHIL) Ⓓ **434 727-2PM**
(PHIL) ▭ **434 727-4PM**
1. NYPO, A. Kostelanetz
(SONY) Ⓓ **SFK47279**
1. Madrid SO, E.F. Arbós (r1928)
(VAI) Ⓓ **VAIA1046**
1. Mexico City PO, E. Bátiz
(ASV) Ⓓ **CDQS6121**
1. I. Presti, A. Lagoya (arr gtr duet)
(BELA) Ⓓ **450 146-2**
(BELA) ▭ **450 146-4**
1. A. Lamasse, D. Hovora (trans. G. Cassado)
(FORL) Ⓓ **FF038**
1. J. Katrama, M. Rahkonen (r1981: arr db/pf)
(FINL) Ⓓ **4509-95605-2**
1. J. Bream, J. Williams (r1971: arr Pujol)
(RCA) Ⓓ **74321 25821-2**
(RCA) ▭ **74321 25821-4**
1. New Philh, R. Frühbeck de Burgos
(10/89) (DECC) Ⓓ **417 786-2DM**
1. LSO, R. Frühbeck de Burgos
(11/89) (IMP) Ⓓ **PCD924**
(11/89) (IMP) ▭ **CIMPC924**
1. Mexico City PO, E. Bátiz
(9/91) (ASV) Ⓓ **CDDCA735**
1. P. Casals, N. Mednikoff (arr Cassadó: r1927)
(10/91) (BIDD) Ⓓ **LAB017**
1. M. Hanskov, T. Lønskov (arr db/pf)
(3/92) (DANA) Ⓓ **DACOCD378**
1. M. Kliegel, R. Havenith (arr vc/pf)
(9/92) (MARC) Ⓓ **8 223403**
1. T. Kropat, T. Krumeich (arr gtr duet)
(7/93) (CHNN) Ⓓ **CG9103**
1. J. Bream, J. Williams (r1971; arr Pujol)
(11/93) (RCA) Ⓓ **09026 61450-2**
(11/93) (RCA) ▭ **09026 61450-4**
1, 3. C. Heurtefeux, R. Flachot (r1989; arr Heurtefeux: gtr/vc) (MAND) Ⓓ **MAN4806**
2. V. de los Angeles, Philh, A. Fistoulari (r1950)
(4/92) (EMI) Ⓓ **CDH7 64028-2**
2. M. Caballé, M. Burgueras (pp1994)
(1/95) (RCA) Ⓓ **09026 62547-2**

GRANIER, Jean *(19th Cent)*

Pierre l'ermite– opera
Scène pour ténor L. Escalais, anon (r1906)
(12/93) (SYMP) Ⓓ **SYMCD1126**

GRAUN, Carl Heinrich *(1703/4–1759) Germany*

Artaserse– opera (1743—Berlin) (Lib. Metastasio)
Sulle sponde del torbido lete J. Kowalski, Berlin CO, M. Pommer
(9/88) (CAPR) Ⓓ **10 113**
(9/88) (CAPR) ▭ **CC27 127**

Cleopatra e Cesare– opera (1742—Berlin) (Lib. Botarelli, after Corneille)
Cortese il cielo non può donare J. Kowalski, Berlin CO, M. Pommer
(9/88) (CAPR) Ⓓ **10 113**
(9/88) (CAPR) ▭ **CC27 127**

Montezuma– opera (1775—Berlin) (Lib. Frederick II, trans Tagliazucchi)
Non han calma J. Sutherland, LPO, R. Bonynge (r1966; ed Bonynge) (DECC) Ⓓ **421 881-2DA**

Rodelinda– opera (1741—Berlin) (Lib. Botarelli, after Salvi)
Pompe vane di morte...Se a questa vita J. Kowalski, Berlin CO, M. Pommer
(9/88) (CAPR) Ⓓ **10 113**
(9/88) (CAPR) ▭ **CC27 127**

GRECHANINOV, Alexandr Tikhonovich *(1864–1956) Russia/USA*

Dobrinya Nikitich– opera, Op. 22 (1903—Moscow) (Lib. cpsr)
Flowers were blooming in the fields L. Sobinov, anon (r1901) (6/93) (PEAR) ① [3] **GEMMCDS9997/9(1)**
Flowers were blooming in the fields D. Smirnov, orch, P. Pitt (r1921) (6/93) (PEAR) ① [3] **GEMMCDS9004/6(2)**
Zabava's aria A. Nezhdanova, U. Masetti (r1906) (6/93) (PEAR) ① [3] **GEMMCDS9007/9(1)**

GRÉTRY, André-Ernest-Modeste *(1741–1813) Belgium*

La **Caravane di Caire– opéra-ballet: 3 acts (1783—Fontainebleu) (Lib. E. Morelde Chédeville)**
1. Pas de trois; 2. Marche du Pacha.

Le Pacha	J. Bastin
Tamorin	G. Ragon
Florestan	P. Huttenlocher
Saint-Phar	G. de Mey
Husca	V. Le Texier
Zélime	I. Poulenard
Almaide	G. de Reyghere
Esclave italienne	C. Napoli
Esclave française	M-N. De Callataÿ
Esclave allemande, Coryphée	E. Crommen
Coryphée	M-P. Fayt
Osmin	J. Dur
Furville	C. Massoz

Namur Chbr Ch, Ricercar Acad, M. Minkowski (RICE) ① [2] **RIC100084/5**
1, 2. Ricercar Consort (RICE) ① [3] **RIC93001**

Céphale et Procis– opera: 3 acts (1773—Paris) (Lib. Marmontel, after Ovid)
Gavotte M. Elman, P. Kahn (arr Franko: r1911) (BIDD) ① **LAB035**

Les **Fausses apparences ou L'amant jaloux– opéra-comique: 3 acts (1778—Paris) (Lib. d'Hèle, after S. Centlivre)**
EXCERPTS: 1. Je romps la chaîne qui m'engage.
Sérénade L. Campagnola, orch (r1913) (MSCM) ① **MM30377**
1. S. Jo, ECO, R. Bonynge (r1993) (9/94) (DECC) ① **440 679-2DH**

Le **Jugement de Midas– opéra-comique: 3 acts (1778—Paris) (Lib. T. d'Hèle)**
Excs M. van der Sluis, F. Vanhecke, S. Gari, J. Elwes, J. Bastin, M. Verschaeve, Paris Chapelle Royale Chor, Petite Bande, G. Leonhardt (r1980) (RICE) ① **RIC063033**

le **Magnifique– opéra-comique (3 acts) (1773—Paris) (Lib. J. M. Sedaine, after La Fontaine)**
Overture Munich RO, K. Redel (PIER) ① **PV786104**

Richard Coeur-de-Lion– opéra-comique: 3 acts (1784—Paris) (Lib. Sedaine)
O Richard, o mon roi G. Soulacroix, anon (r1904) (9/91) (SYMP) ① **SYMCD1089**

Zémire et Azor– opéra-comique: 4 acts (1771—Fontainebleau) (Lib. Marmontel)
Ballet music RPO, T. Beecham (r1956) (9/92) (EMI) ① **CDM7 63401-2**
La fauvette et ses petits L. Pons, H. Bove, Renaissance Qt (r1940) (MSCM) ① **MM30446**
Pantomime and Finale Richard Hickox Orch, R. Hickox (DECC) ① **425 848-2DWO** (DECC) ⊡ **425 848-4DWO**

GRIEG, Edvard (Hagerup) *(1843–1907) Norway*

CW denotes work without Op. number

Olav Trygvason– operatic fragment (1873) (first three scenes only)
T. Carlsen, V. Hanssen, A. Hansli, Oslo Phil Chor, LSO, P. Dreier (UNIC) ① **UKCD2056** (UNIC) ⊡ **UKC364**
R. Stene, A. Gjevang, H. Hagegård, Gothenburg Sym Chor, Gothenburg SO, N. Järvi (r1992) (DG) ① [6] **437 842-2GH6**
R. Stene, A. Gjevang, H. Hagegård, Gothenburg Sym Chor, Gothenburg SO, N. Järvi (r1992) (6/93) (DG) ① **437 523-2GH**
S. Kringelborn, R. Stene, P. Vollestad, Trondheim Sym Chor, Trondheim SO, O.K. Ruud (r1993) (4/95) (VIRG) ① **VC5 45051-2**

GRUENBERG, Louis *(1884–1964) USA*

The **Emperor Jones– opera: 2 acts, Op. 36 (1931) (Lib. cpsr and K. de Jaffa, after O'Neill)**
Standin' in the need of prayer L. Tibbett, NY Met Op Orch, W. Pelletier (r1934) (3/90) (RCA) ① **GD87808**
Standin' in the need of prayer L. Tibbett, orch (pp1934) (3/91) (PEAR) ① [2] **GEMMCDS9452**

GUERRERO (Y TORRES), Jacinto *(1895–1951) Spain*

Los **Gavilanes– zarzuela (1923—Madrid) (Lib. J R Martín)**
Marcha de la Amistad G. Sanchez, T. Verdera, P. Perez Inigo, P. Domingo, Madrid SO, E. G. Asensio (pp1991) (11/92) (IMP) ① **MCD45**
Mi aldea!; Flor roja P. Domingo, Madrid SO, M. Moreno-Buendia (r1987) (1/89) (EMI) ① **CDC7 49148-2**

El **Huésped del Sevillano– zarzuela (Madrid) (Lib. E. Reoyo and J. I. Luca de Tena)**
Canto a la espada P. Domingo, Barcelona SO, G. Navarro (ACAN) ① **49 390**
Canto a la espada P. Domingo, Madrid SO, E. G. Asensio (pp1991) (11/92) (IMP) ① **MCD45**
Canto a la espada J. Carreras, ECO, E. Ricci (r1994) (2/95) (ERAT) ① **4509-95789-2** (2/95) (ERAT) ⊡ **4509-95789-4**
Mujer de los negros ojos P. Domingo, Madrid SO, M. Moreno-Buendia (r1987) (1/89) (EMI) ① **CDC7 49148-2**

La **Rosa del azafrán– zarzuela (1930) (Lib. F Romero & G Fernández-Shaw)**
Cuando siembro voy cantando P. Domingo, Madrid Zarzuela Chor, Madrid SO, M. Moreno-Buendia (r1987) (1/89) (EMI) ① **CDC7 49148-2**

GURLITT, Manfred *(1890–1972) Germnay*

Wozzeck– opera: 18 scenes & epilogue, Op. 16 (1926—Bremen) (Lib. after G Büchner)
EXCERPTS: SCENE 1: 1. Langsam, Wozzeck, langsam. SCENE 2: 2. Du, der Platz ist verflucht! SCENE 3A: 3. He Bub! Sasa! Rarara! Da kommen sie! SCENE 3B: 4. Mädel, was fängst du jetzt an? SCENE 3C: 5. Wer da? Bist du's Franz? Komm herein! SCENE 4: 6. Marie! Geh einmal vor dich hin. SCENE 5A: 7. Wie die Steine glänzen! SCENE 5B: 8. Unter dein en Fingern glänzts ja. SCENE 6: 9. Wohin so elig, geehrtester Herr Sargnagel? SCENE 7: 10. Guten Tag, Franz. SCENE 8: 11. Frau Wirtin hat eine brave Magd. SCENE 9: 12. Ein Jäger aus dem Pfalz ritt einst durch einen Grünen Wald. SCENE 10: 13. Immerzu! Still! Musik! SCENE 11: 14. Andres! Ich kann nicht schlafen! SCENE 12: 15. Ich bin ein Mann! Ich hab' ein Weibsbild. SCENE 13: 16. Und ist kein Betrug in seinem Munde erfunden worden. SCENE 14: 17. Das Pistölchen ist zu teuer. SCENE 15A: 18. Wie heute schön die Sonne scheint. SCENE 15B: 19. Es war einmal ein arm Kind. SCENE 16: 20. Das Kamisölchen, Andres, gehört mit zur Montur. SCENE 17: 21. Dort links gehts in die Stadt. SCENE 17: 22. Das Messer! Wo ist das Messer! Wo ist das Messer! EPILOGUE: 23. Lament for Wozzeck.

Wozzeck	R. Hermann
Marie	C. Lindsley
Captain	A. Scharinger
Drum-major	J. Gottschick
Doctor	R. Wörle
Andres	E. Wottrich
First Girl	C. Berggold
Jew	R. Ginzel
Solo Soprano	R. Schudel
Old Woman; Solo Contralto	G. Schreckenbach

Berlin RIAS Chbr Ch, Berlin Rad Children's Ch, Berlin Deutsches SO, G. Albrecht (r1993) (11/95) (CAPR) ① **60 052**

HÁBA, Alois *(1893–1973) Czechoslovakia*

The **Mother– quarter-tone opera (1927-29) (Lib. cpsr)**

Maruša, the mother	V. Urbanová
Křen	O. Spisar
Francka	M. Lemariová
Nanka	M. Sandtnerová
Maruša	J. Polívková
Francek	L. Havlák
Vincek	M. Borský
Maruša's Father	V. Jedenáctík
Sister-in-law	E. Zikmundová
Brother-in-law	P. Kočí
Priest	J. Janoušek

Prague Nat Th Chor, Prague Nat Th Orch, J. Jirouš (r1964) (1/94) (SUPR) ① [2] **10 8258-2**
Rock-a-bye baby my Tonecek V. Urbanová, Prague Nat Th Orch, J. Jirouš (r1964) (KOCH) ① **34036-2** (KOCH) ⊡ **24036-4**

The **new land– opera: 3 acts, Op. 47 (1934-36) (Lib. F Gladkov & F Pujman)**
EXCERPTS: 1. Overture.
1. Film SO, Š. Koníček (r1985) (SUPR) ① [3] **11 1865-2**

HAEFFNER, Johann Christian Friedrich *(1759–1833) Germany/Sweden*

Electra– tragic opera: 3 acts (1787—Stockholm) (Lib Guillard, after Sophocles)

Electra	H. Martinpelto
Orest	P. Mattei
Klytemnestra	H. Hinz
Aegisth	M. Samuelson
Pilad	K. Hedlund
Arcas	S. Tysklind
High Priest	A. Häggstam
Ismene	C. Högman
One of the Crowd	L. Wedin
A General	S-E. Alexandersson

Stockholm Rad Chor, Drottningholm Baroque Ens, T. Schuback (r1992) (7/94) (CPRI) ① [2] **CAP22030**

HAGEMAN, Richard *(1882–1966) The Netherlands/USA*

Caponsacchi– opera (1932—Freiburg)
I know you better...This very vivid morn H. Jepson, RCA SO, A. Smallens (r1936) (4/94) (RCA) ① [6] **09026 61580-2(4)**

HAHN, Reynaldo *(1875–1947) Venezuela/France*

Ciboulette– operetta (1923—Paris) (Lib. De Flers and De Croisset)
EXCERPTS: ACT 1: 1. Nous sommes six hussards; 2. Est-ce monsieur Thiers?; 3. Bien des jeunes gens; 4. Toi! Vous!; 5. Après cette nuit d'orgie; 6. Nous sommes les bons maraîchers; 7a. La voilà! La voilà!; 7b. C'est le printemps qui m'a surprise; 8a. Y a des femm's qui font la folie; 8b. Moi m'appelle Ciboulette; 9. Oh! mon Dieu!; 10. Les parents, quand on est bébé; 11. Mettons nos tabliers coquets. ACT 2: 12a. Prelude; 12b. C'est le doux silence des champs; 13. Nous avons fait un beau voyage; 14. Y a des arbes...C'est sa banlieue; 15. C'est nous; 16. Ah! si vous étiez Nicolas; 17. Qu'il est doux de fair campagne; 18. Moi j'aime (Mélodrame); 19. C'est tout ce qui me reste d'elle; 20. Nous somm's les bons villageois. ACT 3: 21. Ah! Monsieur Métra!; 22. J'ai vingt-huit ans; 23. Mon amour, daigne me permettre; 24. C'est le moment inévitable de la chanson.

1, 3, 4, 7a, 8a, 8b, 10, 11, 13-17, 22-24. A. Grandjean, W. Clément, M. Hamel, F. Ogéas, J-C. Benoit, P. Carton, Paris Champs-Élysées Chor, Paris Champs-Élysées Orch, P. Bonneau (r1955) (EMI) ① [2] **CZS5 68286-2**
7b, 14. R. Crespin, SRO, A. Lombard (r1970/1) (DECC) ① **440 416-2DM**
13. B. Hendricks, G. Quilico, Lyon Op Orch, L. Foster (r1993) (6/95) (EMI) ① **CDC5 55151-2**

HALÉVY, (Jacques-François)Fromental(-Elie) *(1799–1862) France*

Charles VI– opera: 5 acts (1843—Paris) (Lib. C and G. Delavigne)
Avec la douce chansonnette J. Noté, anon (r1903) (9/91) (SYMP) ① **SYMCD1089**

La **Juive– opera: 5 acts (1835—Paris) (Lib. Scribe)**
ACT 1: 1. Overture; 2. Introduction; 3. Si la rigueur. ACT 2: 4. O Dieu, Dieu de nos pères (Passover Music); 5. Dieu! que ma voix tremblante; 6. Il va venir; 7. Lorsqu'à toi. ACT 3: 8. Mon doux seigneur et maître (Boléro); 9. Vous qui du Dieu vivant. ACT 4: 10. Ah, que ma voix plaintive; 11a. Va prononcer ma mort; 11b. Rachel, quand du Seigneur. ACT 5: 12. Dieu m'éclaire; 13. Il est temps! (Finale).

Eleázar J. Carreras
Rachel J. Varady
Princess Eudoxie J. Anderson
Cardinal de Brogni F. Furlanetto
Prince Léopold D. Gonzalez
Ruggiero R. Massis
Albert R. Schirrer

Ambrosian Op Chor, Philh, A. de Almeida (11/89) (PHIL) ① [3] **420 190-2PH3**
Ah, j'implore en tremblant L. Slezak, W. Hesch, orch (Ger: r1908) (2/91) (PREI) ① **89020**
Ah, j'implore en tremblant A. Didur, T. Leliwa, orch (r c1911: Ital) (1/94) (CLUB) ① **CL99-089**
Pour lui, pour moi, mon père J. Korolewicz-Wayda, anon (r1900s: Pol) (6/93) (PEAR) ① [3] **GEMMCDS9004/6(1)**
3. C. Siepi, Santa Cecilia Academy Orch, A. Erede (r1954) (DECC) ① **440 418-2DM**
3. E. Pinza, orch, C. Sabajno (Ital: r1923) (2/89) (PEAR) ① **GEMMCD9306**
3. E. Pinza, NY Met Op Orch, F. Cleva (r1946: Ital) (4/90) (CBS) ① **CD45693**
3. I. Andrésen, orch (Ger: r1929) (10/90) (PREI) ① **89028**
3. A. Kipnis, Berlin Charlottenburg Op Orch, J. Heidenreich (r1923) (10/91) (PEAR) ① **GEMMCD9451**
3. L. Sibiriakov, anon (r1906: Russ) (6/93) (PEAR) ① [3] **GEMMCDS9001/3(2)**
3, 9. E. Pinza, orch, Rosario Bourdon (r1927) (3/92) (PREI) ① **89050**
4. F. Völker, chor, Berlin Staatskapelle, A. Melichar (r1933: Ger) (8/94) (PREI) ① **89070**
5. R. Verdière, orch (r1930) (MSCM) ① **MM30377**
5. L. Slezak, orch (Ger: r1907) (2/91) (PREI) ① **89020**
6. R. Ponselle, orch (r1924) (PEAR) ① [2] **GEMMCDS9964**
6. F. Pollet, Montpellier PO, C. Diederich (r1989) (ERAT) ① **4509-98502-2**
6. Lotte Lehmann, orch (Ger: r1921) (6/92) (PREI) ① [3] **89302**
6. R. Ponselle, orch, R. Romani (r1924) (10/93) (NIMB) ① **NI7846**
6. E. Destinn, orch (r1911: Ger) (12/94) (SUPR) ① [12] **11 2136-2(4)**
9. E. Pinza, orch (Ital: r1924) (2/89) (PEAR) ① **GEMMCD9306**
9. N. de Angelis, orch, L. Molajoli (Ital: r1928) (7/92) (PREI) ① **89042**
9. F. Navarini, anon (Ital: r1906) (11/92) (MEMO) ① [2] **HR4408/9(1)**
9. A. Didur, S. Cottone (r1903: Ital) (6/93) (PEAR) ① [3] **GEMMCDS9997/9(2)**
9. L. Sibiriakov, orch (r1908: Russ) (6/93) (PEAR) ① [3] **GEMMCDS9001/3(2)**
9. F. Navarini, anon (r1907: Ital) (4/94) (EMI) ① [3] **CHS7 64860-2(1)**
11a, 11b L. Slezak, Berlin St Op Orch, M. Gurlitt (r1928: Ger) (PREI) ① [2] **89203**
11a, 11b, 12. L. Escalais, anon (2 vers, Fr/Ital: r1905/6) (12/93) (SYMP) ① **SYMCD1126**
11b M. Lorenz, Berlin St Op Orch, C. Schmalstich (Ger: r1928) (PREI) ① **89053**
11b J. Carreras, ROHO, J. Delacôte (EMI) ① **CDC7 54524-2**
11b E. Caruso, orch, J. Pasternack (r1920) (RCA) ① **09026 61244-2**
11b P. Domingo, RPO, E. Downes (r1968) (RCA) ① **09026 61356-2** (RCA) ▭ **09026 61356-4**
11b J. Schmidt, BPO, S. Meyrowitz (r1931: Ger) (RELI) ① **CR921036**
11b M. Gilion, orch (r c1909: Ital) (BONG) ① **GB1076-2**
11b P. Domingo, Los Angeles PO, C.M. Giulini (r1980) (DG) ① **445 525-2GMA** (DG) ▭ **445 525-4GMA**
11b E. Caruso, orch, J. Pasternack (r1920) (10/89) (NIMB) ① **NI7803** (NIMB) ▭ **NC7803**
11b F. Völker, Berlin St Op Orch, A. Melichar (r1933: Ger) (2/90) (PREI) ① **89005**
11b B. Gigli, ROHO, R. Zamboni (r1946) (5/90) (EMI) ① **CDH7 61052-2**
11b E. Caruso, orch, J. Pasternack (r1920) (7/91) (RCA) ① [12] **GD60495(6)**
11b E. Caruso, orch, J. Pasternack (r1920) (10/91) (PEAR) ① [3] **EVC4(2)**
11b A. Davidov, anon (r1901: Russ) (6/93) (PEAR) ① [3] **GEMMCDS9007/9(1)**
11b E. Caruso, orch, J. Pasternack (r1920) (4/94) (RCA) ① [6] **09026 61580-2(1)**
11b G. Thill, orch, E. Bigot (r1931) (8/95) (FORL) ① **UCD16727**
12. L. Escalais, anon (r1905: Ital) (4/94) (EMI) ① [3] **CHS7 64860-2(1)**

Le **Val d'Andorre– opéra-comique: 3 acts (1848—Paris) (Lib. J H Vernoy de Saint-Georges)**
Chanson du chevrier L. Fugère, orch (r1930) (6/93) (SYMP) ① **SYMCD1125**

HANDEL, George Frideric *(1685–1759) Germany/England*

HWV—Numbers used in B. Baselt (comp), Versichnis der Werke G.F. Händels (1979)

Admeto, re di Tessaglia– opera: 3 acts, HWV22 (1727—London) (Lib. cpsr)
1. Overture; 2. Introduction; 3. Admeto's Aria: 3a. Orride larve; 3b. Chiudetevi, miei lumi; 4. Se l'arco avessi (Trazimede's Aria); 5. Cangio d'aspetto; 6. Sinfonia.
1, 2, 3a, 3b, 6. A. Köhler, Halle Op House Handel Fest Orch, H. Arman (r1994) (6/95) (CAPR) ① **10 547**
3, 4. E. Kurmangaliev, Moscow Maly SO, V. Ponkin (r1991) (MEZH) ① **MK417047**
5. K. Ferrier, P. Spurr (bp1949; Eng) (6/92) (DECC) ① **433 473-2DM**
6. AAM, C. Hogwood (PHIL) ◖ **070 155-1PH** (PHIL) ▣ **070 155-3PH**
6. AAM, C. Hogwood (8/94) (PHIL) ① **434 992-2PH** (8/94) (PHIL) ▭ **434 992-4PH**

Agrippina– opera: 3 acts (1709—Venice) (Lib. Grimani)
EXCERPTS: 1. Sinfonia. ACT 1: 2. Nerone amato figlio; 3. Con saggio tuo consiglio; 4. Per così grand'impresa; 5. La mia sorte fortunata; 6. Or che Pallante è vinto; 7a. Volo pronto; 7b. Quanto fa; 8. L'alma mia; 9a. Qual piacer; 9b. Amici al sen; 11. Alle tue piante; 12a. Tù ben degno; 12b. L'ultima del gioir; 13. Lusinghiera; 14. Vaghe perle; 15. Otton, Claudio, Nerone; 16. E' un foco quel d'amore; 17. Mà qui Agrippina viene; 18a. Hò un non sò; 18b. Cieli, quai strani; 19a. Fà quanto vuoi; 19b. Non veggo alcun; 20a. Pur ritorno; 21a. Vieni, o cara; 21b. Che mai farò; 22. E quando mai?; 23. Pur al fin; 24a. Non hò cor; 24b. Se Ottone m'inganno; 25. Se giunge un dispetto. ACT 2: 26. Dunque noi siam traditi?; 27a. Coronato il crin; 27b. Roma, piu ch'il trionfo; 28. Ecco il superbo!; 29a. Di timpani, e trombe; 29b. Bella Brittania; 30. Cade il Mondo; 31. Signor, quanto il mio core; 32a. Nulla sperar da me; 32b. Tuo ben è'l Trono; 33a. Sotto il lauro; 33b. Scherzo son; 34. Otton, Otton, qual portentoso; 35. Voi, che udite; 37a. Bella pur nel mio diletto; 37b. Il tormento d'Ottone; 38. Vaghe fonti; 39. Mà qui che veggo!; 40a. Ti vo' giusta; 40b. Da quali ordite; 41. Ingannata una sol; 43a. Col peso del tuo amor; 43b. Qual bramato; 44. Quando invita; 45a. Pensieri; 45b. Quel ch'oprai; 46. Se ben nemica; 47. Col raggio placido; 48. Di giunger non dispero; 49a. Spererò; 49b. Per dar la pace; 50a. Vagheggiar de tuoi; 50b. Vorrei della bellezza; 51a. Basta, che sol tù chieda; 51b. Favorevol; 52. Ogni vento. ACT 3: 53. Il caro Otton; 54a. Tacerò; 54b. Attendo qui Nerone; 55. Anelante ti reco; 57. Amico Ciel; 58. Io di Roma il Giove sono; 59. Pur al fin se n'andò; 60. Pur ch'io ti stringa; 61a. Piega pur del mio cor; 61b. Bel piacere; 62. Contantò osò Poppea?; 63. Come nube; 64. Evvi donna più empia?; 65. Adorato mio sposo; 66. Se vuol pace; 67. Ecco la mia rivale; 68. D'Ottone e di Poppea; 69. V'accendano le Tede; 70. Lieto il Tebro increspi l'onda.

Agrippina S. Bradshaw
Nero W. Hill
Poppea L. Saffer
Claudius N. Isherwood
Otho D. Minter
Pallas M. Dean
Narcissus R. Popken
Lesbo B. Szilágyi
Juno G. Banditelli

Capella Savaria, N. McGegan (3/93) (HARM) ① [3] **HMU90 7063/5**
1. ASMF, K. Sillito (r1993) (8/94) (CAPR) ① **10 420**
45a, 52. L. Hunt, Philh Baroque Orch, N. McGegan (3/93) (HARM) ① **HMU90 7056**
52. L. Hunt, Philh Baroque Orch, N. McGegan (r1991) (HARM) ① **HMU90 7149**
61b M. Horne, Solisti Veneti, C. Scimone (ERAT) ① **2292-45186-2**
61b K. te Kanawa, AAM, C. Hogwood (PHIL) ◖ **070 155-1PH** (PHIL) ▣ **070 155-3PH**
61b K. te Kanawa, AAM, C. Hogwood (8/94) (PHIL) ① **434 992-2PH** (8/94) (PHIL) ▭ **434 992-4PH**

Alcina– opera: 3 acts, HWV34 (1735—London) (Lib. after Ariosto)
EXCERPTS: 1. Overture. ACT 1: 2a. Oh Dei! quivi non scorgo; 2b. O s'apre al riso; 3a. Questo è il cielo; 3b. Ballet; 3c. Ecco l'infido; 3d. Di', cor mio, quanto t'amai; 4a. Generosi guerrier; 4b. Chi m'insegna il caro padre?; 5a. Mi ravvisi, Ruggier, dimmi; 5b. Di te mi rido; 6. Qua dunque ne veniste; 7. È gelosia; 8. Io dunque; 9a. La cerco in vano; 9b. Semplicetto!; 10. Ah, infedele; 11a. Regina: il tuo soggiorno; 11b. Sì; son quella!; 12. Se nemico mi fossi; 13a. Bradamante favella?; 13b. La bocca vaga; 14. A quai strani perigli; 15a. Tornami a vagheggiar; 15b. Gavotte - Sarabande - Menuet - Gavotte. ACT 2: 16a. Musette—Menuet; 16b. Col celarvi; 16c. Qual portento; 16d. Pensa a chi geme; 17a. Qual odio ingiusto; 17b. Vorrei vendicarmi; 18a. Chi scopre al mio pensiero; 18b. Mi lusinga il dolce affetto; 19. S'acquieti il rio; 20. Ama, sospira; 21a. Non scorgo nel tuo viso; 21b. Mio bel tesoro; 22a. Reina: io cerco in vano; 22b. Tra speme e timore; 23a. Reina, sei tradita; 23b. Ah! mio cor! schernito sei!; 24. Or, che dici; 25. È un folle; 26. Ed è ver che mi narri?; 27. Verdi prati, selve amene; 28a. Ah! Ruggiero crudel; 28b. Ombre pallide; 29. Ballet (Dream Music). ACT 3: 30. Sinfonia; 31a. Voglio amar; 31b. Credete al mio dolore; 31c. M'inganna, me n'avveggo; 31d. Un momento di contento; 32a. Molestissimo incontro!; 32b. Ma quando tornerai; 33a. Tutta d'armate squadre; 33b. Sta nell'Ircana; 34a. Vanne tu seco ancora; 34b. All'alma fedel; 35a. Niuna forza lo arresta; 35b. Mi restano le lagrime; 36a. Sin per le vie del sole; 36b. Già vicino è il momento; 36c. Barbara! Io ben lo so; 37a. Le lusinghe; 37b. Non è amor; 38. Prendi e vivi; 39a. Dall'orror di notte cieca; 39b. Ballet; 39c. Dopo tante amare pene.

Alcina J. Sutherland
Ruggiero T. Berganza
Bradamante M. Sinclair
Oronte L. Alva
Morgana G. Sciutti
Oberto M. Freni
Melisso E. Flagello

LSO, R. Bonynge (DECC) ① [3] **433 723-2DMO3**

Alcina A. Auger
Ruggiero D. Jones
Bradamante K. Kuhlmann
Morgana E. Harrhy
Oberto P. Kwella
Oronte M. Davies
Melisso J. Tomlinson

Op Stage Chor, City of London Baroque Sinfonia, R. Hickox (r1985) (11/88) (EMI) ① [3] **CDS7 49771-2**

Excs J. Sutherland, Orch, Anon (cond), D. Bailey (11/92) (DECC) ◐ **071 135-1DH**
1. ASMF, N. Marriner (2/92) (DECC) ① **430 261-2DM**
(2/92) (DECC) ▭ **430 261-4DM**
1. ASMF, K. Sillito (r1993) (8/94) (CAPR) ① **10 420**
1, 16a, 29. ECO, C. Mackerras (r1994) (NOVA) ① **150 108-2**
1, 28a, 28b, 29. K. te Kanawa, AAM, C. Hogwood (PHIL) ◐ **070 155-1PH**
(PHIL) ▣ **070 155-3PH**
1, 28a, 28b, 29. K. te Kanawa, AAM, C. Hogwood (8/94) (PHIL) ① **434 992-2PH**
(8/94) (PHIL) ▭ **434 992-4PH**
1, 29. NYPSO, W. Mengelberg (r1929: arr Göhler) (PEAR) ① **GEMMCD9474**
1, 29. NYPSO, W. Mengelberg (r1929) (7/90) (ARHI) ⊙ [2] **AD105/6**
15. K. Battle, ASMF, N. Marriner (7/90) (EMI) ① **CDC7 49179-2**
15a J. Sutherland, Sydney Eliz Orch, R. Bonynge (MCEG) ▣ **VVD780**
15a K. Battle, ASMF, N. Marriner (r1988) (EMI) ① **CDC5 55095-2**
15a, 28b J. Sutherland, Philomusica of London, A. Lewis (r1959) (DECC) ① [2] **436 227-2DM2**
15a, 31b E. Kirkby, AAM, C. Hogwood (r1991) (7/93) (L'OI) ① **436 132-2OH**
15b Halle Op House Handel Fest Orch, H. Arman (r1994) (6/95) (CAPR) ① **10 547**
18b, 27, 33b A. Murray, OAE, C. Mackerras (r1994) (8/95) (FORL) ① **UCD16738**
27. J. Kowalski, CPE Bach Orch, Hartmut Haenchen (CAPR) **OO 70 213**
27. J. Kowalski, CPE Bach Orch, Hartmut Haenchen (CAPR) ◎ **80 213**
27. J. Kowalski, CPE Bach Orch, Hartmut Haenchen (3/88) (CAPR) ① **10 213**
(3/88) (CAPR) ▭ **CC27 213**
27. J. Bowman, King's Consort, R. King (12/91) (HYPE) ① **CDA66483**
(12/91) (HYPE) ▭ **KA66483**

Alessandro– opera: 3 acts (1726—London) (Lib. Rolli)

EXCERPTS: 1. Overture; 2a. ACT 1: E tanto ancor s'indugia; 2b. Sinfonia; 3a. Grazie all'eterno Giove; 3b. Fra la stragi; 4. Che vidi!; 5a. Ecco Tassile; 5b. Quanto dolce amor saria; 5c. Ne'trofei d'Alessandro; 5d. Lusinghe più care; 5e. Sventurato ch'io sono!; 6a. Fra le guerre; 6b. Apprestasti, oh Cleone; 7a. Dalla vittoria; 7b. No, più soffrir; 8a. Vilipese bellezze; 8b. Men fedele; 8c. Si, lusingando; 8d. Un lusinghiero; 9a. Tu, che Rossane adori; 9b. Pregi son; 9c. Sempre sel suo valor; 9d. A sprone, a fren leggiero; 14a. Sinfonia; 14b. Al magnanimo; 14c. Primo motor; 14d. Figlio del Re; 14e. Placa l'alma; 14f. Fra gli uomini; 14g. Da un breve riposo. ACT 2: 15a. Solitudini amate; 15b. Aure, fonti; 16a. Eccola in preda al sonno; 16b. Vano amore; 17a. Tiranna passion; 17b. Sempre fido e disprezzato; 17c. Pur troppo veggio; 17d. Che tiranna d'Amor; 18a. Qui aspetto l'inconstante; 18b. Alla sua gabbia; 19a. Vincitor generoso; 19b. Risolvo abbandonar; 19c. Finto sereno; 19d. La cervetta nei lacci avvolta; 20. Dopo il sublime onor; 21. Oh Dei!; 22a. Sire, il popol già vento; 22b. Il cor mio; 22c. Svanisci, oh reo; 22d. Dica il falso. ACT 3: 23a. Sfortunato è il mio valore; 23b. L'adulador s'appressa; 24a. Rendetti, o muori; 24b. Saro qual vento; 25a. La resa liberta; 25b. Si, m'e caro imitar; 25c. Sento un'inferno; 25d. Brilla nell'alma; 26a. Qual tormento crudel; 26b. L'amor, che per te sento; 27a. E qual fisso pensier; 27b. Pupille amati; 27c. Numi eterni; 27d. Tempesta e calma; 28a. D'uom fiero nel soglio; 28b. Chi osera traditore; 28c. Prove sono di grandezza; 29a. Spegni o supremo; 29b. Si festeggi il bel giorno; 29c. In generoso onor.

Alessandro	R. Jacobs
Rossane	S. Boulin
Lisaura	I. Poulenard
Tassile	J. Nirouët
Clito	S. Varcoe
Leonato	G. de Mey
Cleone	R. Bollen

Petite Bande, S. Kuijken (2/91) (DHM) ① [3] **GD77110**

26b L. Saffer, Philh Baroque Orch, N. McGegan (12/91) (HARM) ① **HMU90 7036**

Almira– opera: 3 acts (1705—Hamburg) (Lib. F. C Feustking, after G Pamcieri)

Rigaudon Queen's Hall Orch, Henry Wood (r1937) (1/94) (BEUL) ① **1PD3**

Amadigi di Gaula– opera: 3 acts (1715—London) (Lib. Haym)

EXCERPTS: 1. Overture. ACT 1: 2a. Or che di negro ammanto; 2b. Pugnero contro del fato; 3a. Oh notte! oh cara notte; 3b. Notte amica dei riposi; 3c. Che miro; 4a. Et tu cerchi fuggir?; 4b. Non sa temere; 5a. Il crudel m'abbandona; 5b. Ah! spietato!; 6a. Risveglian queste fiamme; 6b. Vado, corro al mio tesoro; 7a. Deh! ferma, oh Dio!; 7b. Agitato il cor mi sento; 7c. Sinfonia; 8a. Cieli, che fia?; 8b. Gioie, venite in sen; 8c. In questo istante; 8d. E si dolce il mio contento; 8e. Andiamo ora, mio ben; 8f. Oh caro mio tesor; 9a. Cieli! Numi!; 9b. Io godo, scherzo, e rido; 10a. Ferma, deh!; 11a. Io ramingo men vado; 11b. Sussurrate, onde vezzose; 11c. Numi! che veggio?; 12. Svenne Amadigi; 13a. Cieli! che sara mai?; 13b. S'estinto e l'idol mio; 13c. Ma, qual scampo; 13d. T'amai, quant'il mio cor; 13e. Che mai creduto havria; 13f. Ti pentirai, crudel!; 14a. Dunquel colei; 14b. Crudel, tu non farai; 15a. D'un sventurato amante; 15b. Pena tiranna; 16a. Arresta, oh Prence!; 16b. Se tu brami di godere; 17. Ma, se questo no basta; 18a. Amadigi, mio bene!; 18b. Tu mia speranza; 18c. Ma qui il rival!; 19a. Cieli! Numi! soccorso; 19b. Afannami, torementami; 20a. Mi dreide l'amante; 20b. Destero dall'empia Dite. ACT 3: 21a. Dove mi guida; 21b. Dolve vita del mio petto; 22a. Sento, ne so che sia; 22b. Vanne lungi dal mio petto; 23a. Se t'offese Oriana; 23b. Cangia al fine; 24. Han'penetrato; 25a. Cieli! ingiusti, e inclementi; 25b. Addio, crudo Amadigi!; 25c. Che orrore!; 25d. Sinfonia; 26a. Son finiti i tormenti; 26b. Sento la gioia; 26c. Godete omai felici; 26d. Godete, oh cori amanti; 27. Ballo.

Amadigi	N. Stutzmann
Oriana	J. Smith
Melissa	E. Harrhy
Dardano	B. Fink
Orgando	P. Bertin

Musiciens du Louvre, M. Minkowski (9/91) (ERAT) ① [2] **2292-45490-2**
5b R. White, City of London Baroque Sinfonia, I. Bolton (12/91) (VIRG) ① **VJ7 59644-2**
(12/91) (VIRG) ▭ **VJ7 59644-4**
15b King's Consort, R. King (HYPE) ① **KING 1**
15b J. Bowman, King's Consort, R. King (12/91) (HYPE) ① **CDA66483**
(12/91) (HYPE) ▭ **KA66483**
20b H. Field, Philh, S. Wright (NIMB) ① **NI5123**

Arianna in Creta– opera (1734—London) (Lib. cpsr)

Mirami altero in volto L. Hunt, Philh Baroque Orch, N. McGegan (r1991) (HARM) ① **HMU90 7149**
Mirami; Qual leon L. Hunt, Philh Baroque Orch, N. McGegan (3/93) (HARM) ① **HMU90 7056**
Quel crudele di me Z. Dolukhanova, Moscow CO, R. Barshai (r1950s) (PREI) ① **89066**

Ariodante– opera: 3 acts (1735—London) (Lib. adapted from Salvi)

EXCERPTS: 1. Overture. ACT ONE: 2a. Vezzi, lusinghe, e brio; 2b. Ami dunque, o signora?; 3a. Ginevra?; 3b. Orrida agli occhi miei; 4a. Orgogliosa beltade!; 4b. Apri le luci, e mira; 5a. Mie speranze, che fate?; 5b. Coperta la frode; 6a. Qui d'amor; 6b. T'amerò dunque sempre; 6c. Prendi da questa mano; 7a. Non vi turbate; 7b. Volate, amori; 8a. Vanne pronto, Odoardo; 8b. Voli colla sua tromba; 9a. Oh! felice mio core!; 9b. Con l'ali di costanza; 10a. Conosco il merto tuo; 10b. Spero per voi; 11a. Dalinda, in occidente; 11b. Del mio sol vezzosi rai; 12a. Ah! che quest'alma amante; 12b. Il primo ardor; 13a. Pare, ovunque m'aggiri; 13b. E qual propizia stella; 13c. Sinfonai pastorale (Il ballo); 13d. Se rinasce nel mio cor; 13e. Si godete al vostro amor; 13f. Ballet. ACT TWO: 14a. Preludio (Notte con lume di luna); 14b. Di Dalinda l'amore; 15a. Tu preparati a morire; 15b. Ginevra?; 15c. Tu vivi, e punito; 16a. E vivo ancora?; 16b. Scherza infida in grembo al drudo; 17a. Lo stral ferì nel segno; 17b. Se tanto piace al cor; 18a. Felice fu il mio inganno; 18b. Se l'inganno sortisce felice; 19a. Andiam, fidi, al consiglio; 19b. Invida sorte avara; 20a. Mi palpita il core; 20b. Sta' lieta, o principessa!; 21a. Mio Re!; 21b. Il tuo sangue; 22. Quante sventure un giorno sol ne porta!; 23a. A me impudica?; 23b. Il mio crudel martoro; 23c. Ballet; 23d. Che vidi? Oh Dei! ACT THREE: 24a. Numi! Lasciarmi vivere; 24b. Perfidi! io son tradita!; 24c. Cieca notte, infidi sguardi; 25a. Ingrato Polinesso!; 25b. Neghittosi, or voi che fate?; 26a. Sire, deh, non negare; 26b. Dover, giustizia, amor; 27. Or venga a me la figlia; 28a. Io ti bacio; 28b. Figlia, da dubbia sorte; 28c. Al sen ti stringo; 29a. Così mi lascia il padre?; 29b. Si, morrò, ma l'onor mio; 30. Arrida il cielo alla giustizia; 31. Dopo notte, atra e funesta; 32a. Dalinda! ecco risorge; 32b. Dite spera, e son contento; 33a. Da dubbia infausta sorte; 33b. Manca, oh Dei!; 34a. Fuglia! innocente figlia!; 34b. Bramo aver mille vite... 35a. Ognuno acclami bella virtute; 35b. Ballet; 35c. Sa trionfar ognor.

Ariodante	J. Baker
Ginevra	E. Mathis
Dalinda	N. Burrowes
Polinesso	J. Bowman
Lurcanio	D. Rendall
King of Scotland	S. Ramey
Odoardo	A. Oliver

London Voices, ECO, R. Leppard (r1978) (12/94) (PHIL) ① [3] **442 096-2PM3**
1. Grande Ecurie, J-C. Malgoire (r1985) (SONY) ① **SBK48285**
1. ASMF, N. Marriner (2/92) (DECC) ① **430 261-2DM**
(2/92) (DECC) ▭ **430 261-4DM**
1. ASMF, K. Sillito (r1993) (8/94) (CAPR) ① **10 420**
9a, 9b, 16a, 16b, 31. J. Baker, ECO, R. Leppard (PHIL) ① **426 450-2PBQ**
13c AAM, C. Hogwood (PHIL) ◐ **070 155-1PH**
(PHIL) ▣ **070 155-3PH**
13c ECO, C. Mackerras (r1994) (NOVA) ① **150 108-2**
13c AAM, C. Hogwood (8/94) (PHIL) ① **434 992-2PH**
(8/94) (PHIL) ▭ **434 992-4PH**
16a, 16b, 31. A. Christofellis, Seicentonovecento Ens, F. Colusso (r1993/4) (EMI) ① **CDC5 55250-2**
16b J. Bowman, King's Consort, R. King (12/91) (HYPE) ① **CDA66483**
(12/91) (HYPE) ▭ **KA66483**
16b, 31. A. Murray, OAE, C. Mackerras (r1994) (8/95) (FORL) ① **UCD16738**
25b E. Kirkby, AAM, C. Hogwood (r1991) (7/93) (L'OI) ① **436 132-2OH**
31. J. Baird, Brewer CO, R. Palmer (NEWP) ① **NPD85568**
31. J. Larmore, Lausanne CO, J. López-Cobos (r1994) (TELD) ① **4509-96800-2**
31. C. Watkinson, Amsterdam Bach Sols, J.W. de Vriend (3/89) (ETCE) ① **KTC1064**

Atalanta– opera: 3 acts (1736—London) (Lib. adapted from Valeriano)

EXCERPTS: 1. Overture. ACT 1: 2. Care selve, ombre beate; 3. Sempre ti lagni; 4a. Ecco Aminta!; 4b. Lascia ch'io parta solo; 5a. Ch'io rimanga con te?; 5b. S'è tuo piacer; 6a. Perchè sospesa; 6b. Impara, ingrata; 7a. Ah! Che purtroppo adoro; 7b. Come alla tortorella langue; 8a. Al varco, oh pastori!; 8b. Oh Tirsi, e tu; 9a. Cerchi in vano la morte; 9b. Sinfonia; 9c. Trattenetelo, og fidi; 9d. Riportai gloriosa palma; 10a. Ah! che tu sei la fera; 10b. Non sarà poco. ACT 2: 11. Oggi rimbombano di feste; 12a. Sei pur sola una volta; 12b. Lassa! ch'io t'ho perduta; 13. Amarilli?; 14a. Ah! ch'io ancora; 14b. Sì, sì, mel raccorderò; 15a. Il mio caro pastore; 15b. Soffri in pace il tuo dolore; 16a. E non moro d'affanno?; 16b. Di ad Irene, tiranna; 17a. Ma giunge il caro mio; 17b. M'allontano, sdegnose pupille; 18a. Poveri affetti miei!; 18b. Se nasce un rivoletto. ACT 3: 19. Sinfonia; 20a. E dalla man di Tirsi; 20b. Bench'io non sappia ancor; 21a. Sono Irene?; 21b. Diedi il core ad altra Ninfa; 22a. Ohimè! che pene!; 22b. Ben'io sento l'ingrata; 23. Oh! del crudo mio bene; 24a. Io vo morir; 24b. Custodite, o dolci sogni; 24c. Io vo morir; 25a. Re Meleagro; 25b. Oh, forza del destin!; 25c. Caro!/Cara!; 25d. Sinfonia; 26a. Del supremo Tonante; 26b. Sol prova contenti; 26c. Dalla stirpe degli Eroi; 26d. Con voce giuliva; 26e. Gridiam tutti!; 26f. Sonifonia; 26g. Viva la face, viva l'amor; 26h. Gavotta; 26i. Con voce giuliva.

March Menuhin FO, Y. Menuhin (r c1968) (EMI) ① [2] **CES5 68523-2**
2. J. Baker, ECO, R. Leppard (PHIL) ① **426 450-2PBQ**

2. L. Pavarotti, Bologna Teatro Comunale Orch, R. Bonynge (arr Gamley) (DECC) Ⓓ **425 037-2DM**
2. A. Auger, Mostly Mozart Orch, G. Schwarz (11/86) (DELO) Ⓓ **DE3026**
2. E. Norena, orch, J. Messner (r1938) (3/91) (PREI) Ⓓ **89041**
2. F. Quartararo, RCA Victor Orch, J-P. Morel (r1947) (4/92) (EMI) Ⓓ [7] **CHS7 69741-2(1)**
2. L. Price, RCA Italiana Op Orch, F. Molinari-Pradelli (12/92) (RCA) Ⓓ [4] **09026 61236-2**
2. J. McCormack, E. Schneider (r1924: Eng) (5/93) (MMOI) Ⓓ **CDMOIR418**
7b K. Ferrier, P. Spurr (bp1949: Eng) (6/92) (DECC) Ⓓ **433 473-2DM**
16b N. Gedda, E. Werba (pp1961) (EMI) Ⓓ **CDH5 65352-2**

Berenice– opera: 3 acts, HWV38 (1737—London)
EXCERPTS: 1. Overture; 1a. Minuet.
Scottish CO, J. Laredo (IMP) Ⓓ **PCD2001**
Chi t'intende S.S. Frank, S.L. Bloom, B. Karp, P. Sykes (CENT) Ⓓ **CRC2084**
Si, tra i ceppi A. Orda, Polish RSO, H. Debich (bp1967) (SYMP) Ⓓ **SYMCD1117**
1. Scottish CO, J. Laredo (vn/dir) (IMP) Ⓓ **PCD802**
1. Stuttgart CO, K. Münchinger (DECC) Ⓓ **417 781-2DM**
1. AAM, C. Hogwood (hpd/dir) (r1978) (L'OI) Ⓓ **443 201-2OM**
1. ASMF, N. Marriner (r1964) (DECC) Ⓓ [2] **444 543-2DF2**
1. AAM, C. Hogwood (12/83) (L'OI) Ⓓ **410 553-2OH**
1. Y. Menuhin (vn/dir), C. Ferras (1/89) (EMIL) Ⓓ **CDZ114**
(EMIL) ⊟ **LZ114**
1. ASMF, K. Sillito (r1993) (8/94) (CAPR) Ⓓ **10 420**
1a ASMF, N. Marriner, D. Heather (6/87) (EMI) ▣ **MVP99 1042 2**
1a F. Jackson (r1990; arr W.T. Best: org) (AMPH) ⊟ **PHI120**
1a ASMF, N. Marriner (CFP) Ⓓ **CD-CFP4616**
1a C. Dearnley (arr org: Dearnley) (IMP) Ⓓ **ORCD11009**
(IMP) ⊟ **ORZC11009**
1a ASMF, N. Marriner (r1964) (DECC) Ⓓ **444 388-2DWO**
(DECC) ⊟ **444 388-4DWO**
1a ECO, R. Leppard (r1980) (SONY) Ⓓ **SMK66940**
1a ASMF, N. Marriner (10/91) (DECC) Ⓓ **430 500-2DWO**
(10/91) (DECC) ⊟ **430 500-4DWO**

Ezio– opera: 3 acts (1732—London) (Lib adapted from Metastasio)
Perchè tanto tormento? Se un bell'ardire; Follè colui; Nasce al bosco; Che indegno! Già risonar D. Thomas, Philh Baroque Orch, N. McGegan (8/90) (HARM) Ⓓ **HMU90 7016**
Tergi l'ingiuste lagrime P. Domingo, National PO, E. Kohn (11/90) (EMI) Ⓓ **CDC7 54053-2**

Flavio, Rè di Longobardi– opera: 3 acts (1723—London) (Lib. Haym)
Flavio J. Gall
Guido D.L. Ragin
Emilia L. Lootens
Teodata B. Fink
Vitige C. Högman
Ugone G. Fagotto
Lotario U. Messthaler
Ens 415, R. Jacobs (r1989) (7/90) (HARM) Ⓓ [2] **HMC90 1312/3**
(7/90) (HARM) ⊟ [2] **HMC40 1312/3**
Amor, nel mio penar D. Minter, Philh Baroque Orch, N. McGegan (4/88) (HARM) Ⓓ **HMC90 5183**
Amor nel mio penar; Rompo i lacci A. Köhler, Halle Op House Handel Fest Orch, H. Arman (r1994) (6/95) (CAPR) Ⓓ **10 547**
Chi mai l'intende ... Amante stravagante L. Saffer, Philh Baroque Orch, N. McGegan (12/91) (HARM) Ⓓ **HMU90 7036**
Chi può mirare Z. Dolukhanova, Moscow CO, R. Barshai (r1950s) (PREI) Ⓓ **89066**
Overture ECCO, E. Aadland (12/91) (ASV) Ⓓ **CDDCA766**
Rompo i lacci D.L. Ragin, Ens 415, R. Jacobs (HARM) Ⓓ **HMP390 804**

Floridante– opera: 3 acts (1721—London) (Lib. Rolli, after Silvani)
Floridante D. Minter
Timante M. Zádori
Oronte I. Gáti
Coralbo J. Moldvay
Elmira A. Markert
Rossane K. Farkas
Capella Savaria, N. McGegan (pp1990) (1/93) (HUNG) Ⓓ [3] **HCD31304/6**
Alma mia L. Pons, Renaissance Qnt (r1940) (RCA) Ⓓ **09026 61411-2**
Alma mia R. Crooks, F. Schauwecker (r1941) (PEAR) Ⓓ **GEMMCD9093**
Alma mia E. Pinza, F. Kitzinger (r1940) (9/93) (RCA) Ⓓ **09026 61245-2**
Bramo te sola; Se dolce m'era gia N. Stutzmann, Hanover Band, R. Goodman (3/93) (RCA) Ⓓ **09026 61205-2**
Excs N. Argenta, I. Attrot, C. Robbin, L. Maguire, M. Braun, Tafelmusik, A. Curtis (hpd/dir) (1/93) (CBC) Ⓓ **SMCD5110**

Giulio Cesare, 'Julius Caesar'– opera: 3 acts, HWV17 (1724—London) (Lib. Haym)
EXCERPTS: 1a. Overture. ACT 1: 1b. Viva, il nosto Alcide; 2. Presto omai l'Egizia terra; 3. Empio, dirò, tu sei; 4. Priva son d'ogni conforto; 5. Svegliatevi nel core; 6. Non disperar, chi sa?; 7. L'empio sleale, indegno; 8. Alma del gran Pompeo; 9. Non è si vago e bello; 10. Tutto può donna vezzosa; 11. Nel tu seno; 12. Cara speme, questo core; 13. Tu la mia stella sei; 14. Va tacito e nascosto; 15. Tu sei il cor di questo core; 16. Son nata a lagrimar. ACT 2: 17. V'adoro, pupille; 18. Se in fiorito ameno prato; 19. Deh piangete, oh mesti lumi; 20. Se a me non sei crudele; 21. Sì spietata, il tuo rigore; 22. Cessa omai di sospirare!; 23. L'angue offeso mai riposa; 24. Venere bella, per un istante; 25. Al lampo dell'armi; 26. Che sento? oh Dio!; 27. Se pietà di me non senti; 28. Belle dea di questo core; 29. L'aure che spira. ACT 3: 30. Dal fulgor di questa spada; 31a. Sinfonia; 31b. Domerò la tua fierezza; 32. Piangerò, la sorte mia; 33. Dall' ondoso periglio; 34. Quel torrente, che cade dal monte; 35. La giustizia; 36. Voi, che mie fide ancelle; 37. Da tempeste il legno infranto; 38. Non ha più che temere; 39a. Sinfonia and March; 39b. Caro! Più amabile beltà; 40. Ritorni omai.
Giulio Cesare J. Baker
Cleopatra V. Masterson
Cornelia Sarah Walker
Sextus D. Jones
Ptolemy J. Bowman
Achillas J. Tomlinson
Curio J. Kitchiner
Nirenus T.E. Williams
ENO Chor, ENO Orch, C. Mackerras, J. Copley (Eng) (MCEG) ▣ **VVD383**
Giulio Cesare N. Treigle
Cleopatra B. Sills
Cornelia M. Forrester
Sextus B. Wolff
Ptolemy S. Malas
Achillas D. Cossa
Curio W. Beck
Nirenus M. Devlin
NY Met Op Chor, NY Met Op Orch, J. Rudel (RCA) Ⓓ **GD86182**
Giulio Cesare M. Dupuy
Cleopatra P. Orciani
Cornelia R. Pierotti
Sextus J. Ligi
Ptolemy S. Anselmi
Achillas P. Spagnoli
Curio G. De Matteis
Nirenus S. Mingardo
Bassano Pro Arte Orch, M. Panni (NUOV) Ⓓ [3] **6863/5**
Giulio Cesare J. Baker
Cleopatra V. Masterson
Cornelia Sarah Walker
Sextus D. Jones
Ptolemy J. Bowman
Achilles J. Tomlinson
Curio C. Booth-Jones
Nirenus D. James
ENO Chor, ENO Orch, C. Mackerras (Eng: ed. Mackerras) (5/89) (EMI) Ⓓ [3] **CMS7 69760-2**
Giulio Cesare J. Larmore
Cleopatra B. Schlick
Cornelia B. Fink
Sextus M. Rørholm
Ptolemy D.L. Ragin
Achillas F. Zanasi
Curio O. Lallouette
Nirenus D. Visse
Cologne Concerto, R. Jacobs (Appendix; Qui perde un momento - 1725 vers) (4/92) (HARM) Ⓓ [4] **HMC90 1385/7**
(HARM) ⊟ **HMC40 1385/7**
Guilio Cesare J. Gall
Cleopatra S. Larson
Cornelia M. Westbrook-Geha
Sextus L. Hunt
Ptolemy D. Minter
Achillas J. Maddalena
Curio H. Hildebrand
Nirenus C. Cobb
Staatskapelle Dresden, C. Smith, P. Sellars (8/93) (DECC) ◐ [5] **071 408-1DH3**
(8/93) (DECC) ▣ [2] **071 408-3DH2**
Giulio Cesare W. Berry
Cleopatra L. Popp
Cornelia C. Ludwig
Sextus F. Wunderlich
Ptolemy K.C. Kohn
Achillas H.G. Nöcker
Curio H.B. Ernst
Nirenus M. Proebstl
Stuttgart Rad Chor, Munich PO, F. Leitner (bp1965: Ger) (3/95) (ORFE) Ⓓ [3] **C351943D**
Giulio Cesare J. Baker
Cleopatra V. Masterson
Cornelia Sarah Walker
Sextus D. Jones
Ptolemy J. Bowman
Achillas J. Tomlinson
Curio J. Kitchiner
Nirenus T.E. Williams
Pothinus B. Casey
ENO Chor, ENO Orch, C. MacKerras (6/95) (PION) ◐ [2] **PLMCD00771**
1b, 4, 5, 7, 8, 10, 14, 15, 22, 25-29, 32, 39a J. Larmore, B. Fink, M. Rørholm, B. Schlick, D.L. Ragin, F. Zanasi, Cologne Concerto, R. Jacobs (r1991) (HARM) Ⓓ **HMC90 1458**
4, 13, 17, 21, 24, 27, 29, 32, 37. J. Sutherland, M. Elkins, M. Horne, M. Sinclair, R. Conrad, New SO, R. Bonynge (DECC) Ⓓ [3] **433 723-2DMO3**
4, 19. E. Leisner, orch (r1926: Ger) (PREI) Ⓓ [2] **89210**
5. P. Domingo, National PO, E. Kohn (11/90) (EMI) Ⓓ **CDC7 54053-2**
5. P. Domingo, National PO, E. Kohn (r1989) (6/94) (EMI) Ⓓ **CDC5 55017-2**
5, 12, 23, 29, 35. L. Hunt, Philh Baroque Orch, N. McGegan (3/93) (HARM) Ⓓ **HMU90 7056**
5, 16, 23. F. Wunderlich, C. Ludwig, Munich PO, F. Leitner (Ger: bp) (DG) Ⓓ [5] **435 145-2GX5(1)**
6, 13, 17, 31a, 32. K. te Kanawa, AAM, C. Hogwood (PHIL) ◐ **070 155-1PH**
(PHIL) ▣ **070 155-3PH**
6, 13, 17, 31a, 32. K. te Kanawa, AAM, C. Hogwood (8/94) (PHIL) Ⓓ **434 992-2PH**
(8/94) (PHIL) ⊟ **434 992-4PH**
9. B. Fassbaender, Stuttgart RSO, H. Graf (11/86) (ORFE) Ⓓ **C096841A**
9, 14. D. Minter, Philh Baroque Orch, N. McGegan (4/88) (HARM) Ⓓ **HMC90 5183**
13, 39b I. Seefried, D. Fischer-Dieskau, Berlin RSO, K. Böhm (r1960) (9/93) (DG) Ⓓ [2] **437 677-2GDO2**
14. D. Minter, Philh Baroque Orch, N. McGegan (HARM) Ⓓ **HMP390 804**
14. J. Kowalski, CPE Bach Orch, Hartmut Haenchen (CAPR) ◙ **80 213**
14. J. Kowalski, CPE Bach Orch, Hartmut Haenchen (CAPR) ◘◘ **70 213**
14. J. Kowalski, CPE Bach Orch, Hartmut Haenchen (3/88) (CAPR) Ⓓ **10 213**
(3/88) (CAPR) ⊟ **CC27 213**
14. A. Köhler, Halle Op House Handel Fest Orch, H. Arman (r1994) (6/95) (CAPR) Ⓓ **10 547**
14, 18. N. Stutzmann, Hanover Band, R. Goodman (3/93) (RCA) Ⓓ **09026 61205-2**
14, 18, 32, 33. A. Murray, OAE, C. Mackerras (r1994) (8/95) (FORL) Ⓓ **UCD16738**
14, 25. J. Bowman, King's Consort, R. King (12/91) (HYPE) Ⓓ **CDA66483**
(12/91) (HYPE) ⊟ **KA66483**
17. C. Ludwig, Berlin SO, H. Stein (Ger) (9/92) (EMI) Ⓓ [4] **CMS7 64074-2(2)**
26, 27, 32, 37. L. Saffer, Philh Baroque Orch, N. McGegan (12/91) (HARM) Ⓓ **HMU90 7036**
27, 37. R. Alexander, VCM, N. Harnoncourt (r c1988) (TELD) Ⓓ **4509-98645-2**

31a ECO, C. Mackerras (r1994)
(NOVA) ① **150 108-2**
32. K. Battle, W. Jones, H. Burton (pp1991)
(DG) ▭ **072 189-3GH**
32. K. Te Kanawa, Chelsea Op Group Orch, W. Southgate (pp1990) (KIWI) ① **CDSLD-82**
32. A. Auger, Mostly Mozart Orch, G. Schwarz
(11/86) (DELO) ① **DE3026**
32. L. Popp, ECO, G. Fischer (r1967)
(10/88) (EMI) ① **CDM7 69546-2**
32. K. Battle, ASMF, N. Marriner
(7/90) (EMI) ① **CDC7 49179-2**
32. A.S. von Otter, Drottningholm Baroque Ens, A. Öhrwall (10/91) (PROP) ① **PRCD9008**
(10/91) (PROP) ⊙ **PROP9911**
32. K. Battle, M. Garrett (pp1991)
(7/92) (DG) ① **435 440-2GH**
32. M. Forrester, Vienna St Op Orch, R. Zeller
(12/92) (CBC) ① **PSCD2002**
32. A. Roocroft, LPO, F. Welser-Möst
(10/94) (EMI) ① **CDC5 55090-2**
(10/94) (EMI) ▭ **EL5 55090-4**
40. A. Schoenberg Ch, VCM, N. Harnoncourt, L. Popp, P. Esswood (TELD) ① **4509-95498-2**

Giustino– opera: 3 acts (1737—London) (Wds. after N. Beregani)

EXCERPTS: 1. Overture. ACT ONE: 1a. Tema il nemico; 1b. Viva Augusto eterno impero; 1c. Ah! mio Sovrano Augusto; 2a. Vitaliano, il di cui Nome; 2b. Un vostro sguardo; 3a. Arianna, che pensi?; 3b. Da tuoi begl'occhi impara; 4a. Può ben nascer tra li Boschi; 4b. Ah! perché non poss'io; 4c. Bel ristoro de'mortali; 5a. Corri, vola, a'tuoi Trofei; 5b. Chi mi chiama alla gloria?; 5c. Se parla nel mio cor; 6a. Cieli! Numi soccorso!; 6b. Sinfonia; 6c. Oh! eterni Numi!; 6d. Nacque al Bosco, nacque al Prato; 7a. Amanzio!; 7b. È Virtute insin la frode; 8a. Leggo nel tuo sembiante; 8b. Allor, ch'io forte avrò; 9a. Sia fausta ognor la sorte; 9b. Non si vanti un'alma audace; 10a. All'armi, o Guerrieri; 10b. Signor, ti arrise il Fato; 11. Vanne sì, superba và; 12a. Dunque si poco temi; 12b. Mio dolce amato Sposo. ACT TWO: 13. Sinfonia; 14. A Dispetto dell'Onde; 15a. Questa è la cruda Spiaggia; 15b. Ritrosa belezza; 16a. Numi! che'l Ciel reggete; 16b. Sinfonia; 16c. Respiro: e'tutto deggio; 17a. Mio bel tesoro!; 17b. Ma quale orrido Mostro; 18. Per Voi soave e bella; 19. Troppo fosti, o mio core; 20a. Ah! quai crudeli pene; 20b. Sventurata Navicella; 21a. Verdi Lauri; 21b. Vieni, barbaro, altero; 21c. Sull'Altar di questo Nume; 22a. Già il valor di Giustino; 22b. Quel Torrente che s'innalza. ACT THREE: 23. Sinfonia; 24a. Amici, tutto devo; 24b. Il piacer della vendetta; 24c. Signor', a'tuoi Trionfi; 24d. O fiero e rio sospetto; 25a. Generoso Giustino, oh! quanto ammiro; 25b. Zeffiretto, che scorre nel prato; 26a. E fia ver, che infedele; 26b. Di Re sdegnato l'ira tremenda; 27a. Qual'infernal veleno; 27b. Il mio cor già piu non sà; 28a. Giustino, anima mia!; 28b. Augelletti garruletti; 29a. Riusci il bel disegno; 29b. Dall'occaso in oriente; 30. Fortuna, m'hai tradito!; 31a. Prima che splenda in oriente il sole; 31b. Trattien l'acciar; 31c. Qual voce ascolto; 31d. Sollevar'il mondo oppresso; 32. Or che cinto ho il crin d'alloro; 33a. Qual marzial fragor?; 33b. Olà? Renditi a me!; 33c. Ti rendo questo cor; 33d. Signor, se vile intercessor non sono; 33e. In braccio a te la calma.

Giustino M. Chance
Arianna D. Röschmann
Anastasio D. Kotoski
Fortuna J. Gondek
Polidarte D. Ely
Leocasta J. Lane
Vitaliano M. Padmore
Amanzio D. Minter
Halle Cantamus Chbr Ch, Freiburg Baroque Orch, N. McGegan (r1994)
(HARM) ① [3] **HMU90 7130/2**
Adagio AAM, C. Hogwood
(PHIL) ● **070 155-1PH**
(PHIL) ▭ **070 155-3PH**
Adagio AAM, C. Hogwood
(8/94) (PHIL) ① **434 992-2PH**
(8/94) (PHIL) ▭ **434 992-4PH**
5b, 5c J. Kowalski, CPE Bach Orch, Hartmut Haenchen (CAPR) ● **80 213**
5b, 5c J. Kowalski, CPE Bach Orch, Hartmut Haenchen (CAPR) ○○ **70 213**
5b, 5c J. Kowalski, CPE Bach Orch, Hartmut Haenchen (3/88) (CAPR) ① **10 213**
(3/88) (CAPR) ▭ **CC27 213**

5c, 25b J. Bowman, King's Consort, R. King
(12/91) (HYPE) ① **CDA66483**
(12/91) (HYPE) ▭ **KA66483**

Imeneo– opera: 3 acts (1740—London) (Lib. adapted from Stampiglia)

Imeneo J. Ostendorf
Rosmene J. Baird
Tirinto D. Fortunato
Clomiri B. Hoch
Argenio J. Opalach
Brewer Chbr Chor, Brewer CO, R. Palmer
(8/93) (VOX) ① [2] **115451-2**

Muzio Scevola (Act 3)– opera: 3 acts (1721—London) (Lib Rolli. Act 1, Amadei; Act 2, Bononcini)

EXCERPTS: 1. Overture. ACT 3: 2a. Doppo l'arrivi degl'illustri; 2b. Lungo pensar e dubitar; 3a. Eccessi di virtu; 3b. Soave affetti miei; 4a. Pensoso a passo lento; 4b. Pupille sdegnose!; 4c. Io altro regno; 4d. Dimmi, crudele Amore; 4e. Chi mai più giusto sdegno; 4f. Volate più dei venti; 5a. Mio cor, pria ti ricorda; 5b. Il confine della vita; 6a. Patria della bellezza; 6b. Non ti fidar; 7b. Come, se ti vedro; 7c. Oh come passi al coer; 7d. Con lui volate; 8a. Gia m'udiste; 8b. Spera che tra le care; 9a. Ahi che pur troppo; 9b. Ah, dolce nome; 10a. Lasciate d'inseguir; 10b. Vivo senza alma; 11a. Piene di lor contento; 11b. Ma come amar e come mai fidar; 11c. Dono d'alta fortuna; 11d. Romani, udite!; 11e. Unica erede; 12. Si sara più dolce amore.

Porsenna J. Ostendorf
Muzio D. Fortunato
Clelia J. Baird
Orazio E. Mills
Irene J. Lane
Fidalma A. Matthews
Tarquinio F. Urrey
Brewer CO, R. Palmer
(3/93) (NEWP) ① [2] **NPD85540**
1. Brewer CO, R. Palmer
(NEWP) ① **NPD85568**
2b J. Baird, Brewer CO, R. Palmer
(NEWP) ① **NPD85568**
4c, 4d L. Hunt, Philh Baroque Orch, N. McGegan (3/93) (HARM) ① **HMU90 7056**

Orlando– opera: 3 acts, HWV31 (1733—London) (Lib. adapted from Capece, after L. Arioso)

EXCERPTS: 1. Overture. ACT 1: 2. Giergliofici eterni; 3a. Stimulato dalla gloria; 3b. Purgalo ormai da effeminati sensi; 3c. Sinfonia; 3d. Lascia Amor; 4a. Imagini funeste; 4b. Non fu già men forte Alcide; 5a. Quanto diletto avea; 5b. Io non so; 5c. Itene pur tremendo; 5d. Ho un certu rossore; 6a. M'hai vinto al fin; 6b. Ritornava al suo bel viso; 6c. Spera, mio ben; 6d. Chi possessore; 7a. Ecco Dorinda; 7b. Se il cor mai ti dirà; 8a. Povera me!; 8b. O care parolette; 9a. Noti a me sono; 9b. Se fedel vuoi; 10a. T'ubbirdirò, crudele; 10b. Fammi combattere; 11. Angelica,deh lascia; 12a. O Angelica, o Medoro; 12b. Consolati o bella. ACT 2: 13. Quando spieghi i tuoi tormenti; 14a. Perchè, gentil Dorinda; 14b. Se mi rivolgo al prato; 15a. E' questa la mercede; 15b. Cielo! Se tu il consenti; 16a. A qual rischio vi espone; 16b. Tra caligini profonde; 17a. Da queste amiche piante; 17b. Verdi allori sempre unito; 18a. Dopo tanti perigli; 18b. Non potrà dirmi ingrata; 19a. Dove, dove giudate, Furi; 19b. Verdi piante; 20a. Tutto a poter partire; 20b. Ah perfida, qui sei!; 21. Ohime! Che miro!; 22. Amor, caro amore; 23a. Ah Stigie larve!; 23b. Già latra Cerbero; 23c. Ma la Furia; 23d. Vaghe pupille, non piangete. ACT 3: 24. Sinfonia; 25a. Di Dorinda alle mura; 25b. Vorrei poterti amar; 26. Più obbligata gli sono; 27a. Pur ti trovo, o mio bene; 27b. Unisca amor in noi; 27c. Già lo stringo, gia l'abbraccio; 28a. Di Dorinda all'albergo; 28b. Così giusta è questa speme; 29a. S'è corrisposto un core; 29b. Amor è qual vento; 30a. Impari ognum da Orlando; 30b. O voi del mio poter; 30c. Sorge infausta una procella; 31. Dorinda, e perchè piangi?; 32a. Più non fuggir petrai; 32b. Finchè prendi ancora il sangue; 32c. Vieni—Vanne precipitando; 32d. Già per la man d'Orlando; 32e. Già l'ebro mio ciglio; 33b. Tu che del gran tonante; 33c. Sinfonia; 33d. Ah! non che fate signor?; 33e. Dormo ancora, o son desto?; 33f. Per fa mia diletta; 34a. Che vedo, oh dei!; 34b. Vinse incanti; 34c. Trionfa oggi'l mio cor.

Orlando J. Bowman
Angelica A. Auger
Medoro C. Robbin
Dorinda E. Kirkby
Zoroastro D. Thomas
AAM, C. Hogwood
(8/91) (L'OI) ① [3] **430 845-2OH3**
3d, 30a-c D. Thomas, Philh Baroque Orch, N. McGegan (8/90) (HARM) ① **HMU90 7016**
10a, 10b, 15a, 15b, 23a-d, 32d, 32e D. Minter, Philh Baroque Orch, N. McGegan
(4/88) (HARM) ① **HMC90 5183**
10b M. Horne, Solisti Veneti, C. Scimone
(ERAT) ① **2292-45186-2**
10b, 15b A. Köhler, Halle Op House Handel Fest Orch, H. Arman (r1994)
(6/95) (CAPR) ① **10 547**
10b, 23a-c N. Stutzmann, Hanover Band, R. Goodman (3/93) (RCA) ① **09026 61205-2**
23a A. Deller, Handel Fest Orch, A. Lewis (r1960) (1/95) (VANG) ① **08.5069.71**
30c D. Thomas, Philh Baroque Orch, N. McGegan (HARM) ① **HMP390 804**

Ottone– opera: 3 acts (1723—London) (Lib. N. Haym)

EXCERPTS: 1. Overture. ACT 1: 2. Pur che regni; 3a. Chi più lento è di me?; 3b. La speranza è giunta in porto; 4a. Vien di Romano inclita figlia; 4b. Bel labbro formato; 5a. È tale Otton?; 5b. Falsa immagine; 6. Concerto; 7a. Te, che assalir le nostre navi osati; 7b. Del minacciar del vento; 8a. Tutto a più leite cure; 8b. Ritorna, o dolce amore; 9a. Anch'io sperai; 9b. Diresti poi così?; 10a. Tu la madre d'Otton; 10b. Pensa ad amare; 11a. Adelaide, di cui con tanta lode; 11b. Indietro, indietro; 12a. Giunge Otton?; 12b. Affanni del pensier; 13. Sinfonia; 14a. Cedi il ferro, o la vita; 14b. Tu puoi straziarmi; 15a. È di più mio rival?; 15b. Dell'onda ai fiero moti. ACT 2: 16. Sinfonia; 17a. Per berve spazio a me colui; 17b. Lascia, nel suo viso; 18a. (Ah! che più non resisto); 18b. Ah! tu non sai; 19a. Ah, Matilda, Matilda; 19b. Vieni, o figlio; 20. Spera sì; 21a. (Quegli, è certo il mio sposo); 21b. All'orror d'un duolo eterno; 22a. O illustre Teofane; 22b. Alla fama; 23a. Con gelosi sospetti; 23b. Dopo l'orrore; 24a. O grati orrori; 24b. S'io dir potessi; 25a. Dal gran sasso; 25b. Le profonde vie dell'onde; 26a. (Ode gente); 26b. Deh! non dir; 27. Già d'ogni interno; 28a. Odo il suono; 28b. Notte cara. ACT 3: 29. Dove sei; 30a. Già t'invola; 30b. Trema, tiranno; 31a. Io son tradito; 31b. Tanti affanni; 32. Sinfonia; 33a. Empi, al vostro attentato; 33b. D'innalzar i flutti; 34. Perchè in vita tornai?; 35a. Si, mi traete alme; 35b. Benchè mi sia crudele; 36a. Deh! ti trattiene; 36b. No, non temere, o bella; 37a. Pur cangiasti alla fin; 37b. Gode l'alma consolata; 38a. Uno de'servi miei; 38b. Nel suo sangue; 39. Matilda, arresta il piede; 40a. Frena, crudel; 40b. A'teneri affetti; 41a. Ma qual caso; 41b. Faccia ritorno l'antica pace.

Ottone D. Minter
Teofane L. Saffer
Emireno M. Dean
Gismonda J. Gondek
Adelberto R. Popken
Matilda P. Spence
Freiburg Baroque Orch, N. McGegan
(3/93) (HARM) ① [3] **HMU90 7073/5**
Ottone J. Bowman
Teofane C. McFadden
Emireno M. George
Gismonda J. Smith
Adelberto D. Visse
Matilda C. Denley
King's Consort, R. King (r1993)
(7/93) (HYPE) ① [3] **CDA66751/3**
Vinto è d'amor L. Popp, ECO, G. Fischer (r1967) (10/88) (EMI) ① **CDM7 69546-2**
3b M. Forrester, Vienna St Op Orch, R. Zeller
(12/92) (CBC) ① **PSCD2002**
3b, 19b K. Ferrier, G. Moore (r1945: Eng)
(6/88) (EMI) ① **CDH7 61003-2**
5a, 5b, 12a, 12b L. Saffer, Philh Baroque Orch, N. McGegan (12/91) (HARM) ① **HMU90 7036**
5b J. Baird, Brewer CO, R. Palmer
(NEWP) ① **NPD85568**
19b L. Hunt, Philh Baroque Orch, N. McGegan (r1991) (HARM) ① **HMU90 7149**
19b L. Hunt, Philh Baroque Orch, N. McGegan
(3/93) (HARM) ① **HMU90 7056**
31b J. Bowman, King's Consort, R. King
(12/91) (HYPE) ① **CDA66483**
(12/91) (HYPE) ▭ **KA66483**

Partenope– opera: 3 acts (1730—London) (Lib. adapted from Stampiglia)

EXCERPTS: 1. Overture. ACT 1: 2a. Tu

dell'eccelse mura; 2b. Viva, viva, Partenope viva; 2c. Miei fidi arride il cielo; 3. Arsace—Armindo; 4a. Regina, in folte schiere; 4b. L'amor ed il destin; 4c. O Eurimene; 5a. Cavalier, se gli Dei; 5b. Se non ti sai spiegar; 5c. Armindo ardisci e prova; 5d. Voglio dire al mio tesoro; 6a. Ah! ch'un volto fatal; 6b. Un altra volta ancor; 6c. Rosmira, oh! Dio!; 6d. Sento amor con novi dardi; 7a. Stan pronit i miei guerrieri; 7b. T'appresta forse amore; 8. Signora—Armindo; 9. E di che reo son io?; 10a. E se giunge Eurimene?; 10b. Sei mia gioia; 10c. I novelli amor tuoi; 10d. Dimmi pietoso ciel; 11a. Ecco Emilio; 11b. Anch'io pugnar saprò; 12a. Arsace, tu sarai; 12b. Io ti levo l'impero dell'armi; 13a. Lascai deh!; 13b. E' figlio il mio timore; 14a. Prence, di te mi lagno; 14b. Io seguo sol fiero. ACT 2: 15a. Sinfonia; 15b. Forti mie schiere; 15c. Marcia; 15d. Ma le nemiche squadre; 15e. Con valorosa mano—Battaglia I; 15f. Soccorso—Battaglia II; 15g. Renditi, o pure estinto; 15h. Vi circondi la gloria; 16a. Contro un pudico amor; 16b. Barbaro fato si; 17a. Care mura in sei bel giorno; 17b. Emilio!—Alta Regina; 17c. Voglio amare infin ch'io moro; 18a. Ti bramo amico; 18b. E vuoi con dure tempre; 19a. Non più darsi in un petto; 19b. Furie son dell'alma mia; 20a. A prò di chi t'offese; 20b. Poterti dir vorrei; 21a. Regina—Arminda, ancora; 21b. Non chiedo o luci vaghe; 21c. Più d'ogn'altro; 21d. Qual farfalletta; 22. Quanto godo Eurimene; 23a. Rosmira mia; 23b. Furibondo spira il vento. ACT 3: 24a. Sinfonia; 24b. Regina ti compiace; 24c. Non è incauto mio consiglio; 25a. Partenope, Eurimene; 25b. Arscae, oh Dio!; 25c. Chi m'apre i lumi; 25d. Spera e godi o mio tesoro; 26a. Prencipe ardir; 26b. La speme ti consoli; 27a. Rosmira, dove ti guida; 27b. Ch'io parta; 27c. Oh Dio!; 27d. Quel volto mi piace; 28a. Ormonte, ti destino giudice; 28b. Nobil core, che ben ama; 29a. Non chiedo, o miei tromenti!; 29b. Ma quai note di mesti lamenti; 30. Cieli che miro; 31a. Ma Partenope vien; 31b. Un cor infedele si deve punir; 31c. Passo di duolo in duolo; 31d. Fatto è Amor un Dio d'inferno; 32a. Di bel desire avvampo; 32b. La gloria in nobil alma; 33a. Sinfonia; 33b. Regina, in queste arene; 33c. Si scherza sì; 33d. Arminda sia mio sposo; 33e. D'Imeneo le belle.

Partenope K. Laki
Arsace R. Jacobs
Armindo J.Y. Skinner
Ormonte S. Varcoe
Rosmira H. Müller-Molinari
Emilio M. Hill

Petite Bande, S. Kuijken
(2/91) (DHM) ① [3] **GD77109**
10b R. Crooks, F. Schauwecker (r1941)
(PEAR) ① **GEMMCD9093**
23b M. Horne, Solisti Veneti, C. Scimone
(ERAT) ① **2292-45186-2**
23b N. Stutzmann, Hanover Band, R. Goodman
(3/93) (RCA) ① **09026 61205-2**

Il Pastor Fido– opera: 3 acts (1712 rev 1734) (Lib. Rossi)

EXCERPTS: 1. Overture. ACT 1: 2. Ah! infelice mia patria!; 3. D'amor a fier contrasti; 4. Lontan del mio tesoro; 5. Frode, sol a te rivolta; 6. Finchè un Zeffiro soave; 7. Quanto mai felici siete; 8. Non vo' mai seguitar; 9. Ballets: 9a. March; 9b. Pour les Chasseurs; 9c. Hunters' dance; 10. Oh! quanto bella gloria. ACT 2: 11. Caro amor; 13. Ho un non sò che nel cor; 14. Torni pure un bel splendore; 15. Finte labbra; 16. Sol nel mezzo risona del core; 17. Se in ombre nascosto; 18. Sì, rivedrò; 19. Scherza in mar la navicella; 20a. Accorrete, voi pastori; 21. Ballets: 21a. Shepherds' dance; 21b. Musette; 21c. Menuets I and II. ACT 3: 22. Sinfonia; 23. Oh! quanto bella gloria; 24. Sento nel sen; 25. Secondaste al fine; 26a. Oh! Mirtillo, Mirtillo; 26b. Ah! non son io che parlo; 27a. Sciogliete quelle mani; 27b. Per te, mio dolce bene; 27c. Si unisce al tuo martir; 28a. Dell'empia frode il velo; 28b. Caro/Cara; 28c. Sciolga dunque al ballo; 29. Ballets: 29a. General dance; 29b. Gavotte; 29c. Ballet; 29d. Chorus and General Dance: Replicati al ballo.

9a-c, 21a-c, 29a-c Cologne Stravaganza
(12/92) (DENO) ① **CO-79250**

Poro, re dell'Indie– opera: 3 acts (1731—London) (Lib after Metastasio)

Poro G. Banditelli
Cleofide R. Bertini
Erissena B. Fink
Gandarte G. Lesne
Alessandro Il Grande S. Naglia
Timagene R. Abbondanza

Europa Galante, F. Biondi (r1994)
(11/94) (O111) ① [3] **OPS30-113/5**

Radamisto– opera: 3 acts, HWV12a (1720—London) (Lib. Haym)

EXCERPTS: 1. Overture. ACT ONE: 2. Sommi Dei; 3a. Reina, infausto avviso; 3b. Deh! fuggi un traditore; 4a. Seguirem dunque la crudele impresa; 4b. L'ingrato non amar; 5a. Ecco l'infido sposo; 5b. Tu vuoi ch'io parta; 6a. Il crudel odio tuo; 6b. Con la strage; 7a. Ove seguirmi vuoi; 7b. Cara sposa, amato bene; 8a. Ver le nemiche mura; 8b. Son contenta di morire; 9a. Seguila, o figlio!; 9b. Perfido, di a quell'empio tiranno; 10a. Fraarte, omai quel ferro; 10b. Son lievi le catene; 11a. Coraggio, amici!; 11b. Sinfonia (Battle Symphony); 12a. Già vint'è il nemico; 12b. Segni di crudeltà; 13a. Pur troppo è vero; 13b. Dopo l'orride procelle. ACT TWO: 14a. Sposo, vien meno il piè; 14b. Quando mai, spietata sorte; 15a. Oh crudo ciel!; 15b. Vuol ch'io serva; 16a. Prencipe generoso; 16b. Ombra cara di mia sposa; 17a. Mitiga il grave affanno; 17b. lascia pur amica spene; 18a. Oh senza esempio dispietata sorte!; 18b. Già che morir non posso; 19a. Signor...E che mi rechi?; 19b. Si che ti renderai; 20a. Nulla già di speranza; 20b. Fatemi, o cieli, almen; 21a. Questo vago giardin; 21b. La sorte, il ciel, amor; 22a. Adorato german, quanto più lieta; 22b. Vanne, sorella ingrata; 23a. Trà il german, trà lo sposo; 23b. Che farà quest'alma mia; 24. Troppo sofferse; 25a. Due seggi, olà!; 25b. Empio, perverso cor!; 26a. Ascolta, Ismen; 26b. Se teco vive il cor. ACT THREE: 27a. Stanco di più soffrir; 27b. S'adopri il braccio armato; 28. So ben che nel mio amore; 28a. So ben che nel mio maore; 28b. So ch'è vana la speranza; 29a. Non temo, idolo mio; 29b. Dolce bene di quest'alma; 30a. O della Tracia, o dell'Armenia; 30b. Vieni, d'empietà mostro; 30c. Vile! se mi dai vita; 31a. Mio Rè, mio Tiridate, ascolta; 31b. Barbaro! partirò; 32a. Farasmane la segua; 32b. Alzo al volo; 33a. Di Radamisto il capo?; 33b. Deggio dunque, oh Dio; 34a. Oh Dio! parte Zenobia; 34b. Qual nave smarrita; 35a. In questo tempio; 35b. O cedere o perir; 36a. Arrestatevi, o fidi!; 36b. non ho più affanni; 37a. Festeggi omai la reggia; 37b. Un dì più felice.

Radamisto R. Popken
Zenobia J. Gondek
Polissena L. Saffer
Tigrane D. Hanchard
Fraarte M. Frimmer
Tiridate M. Dean
Farasmane N. Cavallier

Freiburg Baroque Orch, N. McGegan (hpd/dir) (r1993: 1720 ver)
(6/94) (HARM) ① [3] **HMU90 7111/3**
Passacaille; Giga Halle Op House Handel Fest Orch, H. Arman (r1994)
(6/95) (CAPR) ① **10 547**
1. Sydney Eliz Orch, R. Bonynge
(MCEG) ▭ **VVD780**
1. A. Noble (r1995; arr hpd)
(HERA) ① **HAVPCD181**
(HERA) ⊟ **HAVPC181**
16b N. Stutzmann, Hanover Band, R. Goodman
(3/93) (RCA) ① **09026 61205-2**
16b, 34b L. Hunt, Philh Baroque Orch, N. McGegan (3/93) (HARM) ① **HMU90 7056**
34b L. Hunt, Philh Baroque Orch, N. McGegan (r1991) (HARM) ① **HMU90 7149**

Riccardo Primo, Rè di Inghilterra– opera: 3 acts (1727—London) (Lib. Rolli after F. Briani)

Il volo così fido L. Saffer, Philh Baroque Orch, N. McGegan (12/91) (HARM) ① **HMU90 7036**
Nube che il sole adombra; Agitato da fiere tempeste D. Minter, Philh Baroque Orch, N. McGegan (4/88) (HARM) ① **HMC90 5183**

Rinaldo– opera: 3 acts, HWV7a (1711—London) (Lib. Rossi)

EXCERPTS. 1. Overture. ACT 1: 2a. Della nostre fatiche; 2b. Sovra balze scoscesce; 3a. Signor, già dal tuo senno; 3b. Rinaldo, amato sposo; 3c. Combatti da forte; 4a. Questi saggi consigli; 4b. Ogni indugio; 5a. Signor, che delle stelle; 5b. Sulla ruota di fortuna; 6a. Sibillar gli'angui d'Aletto; 6b. Goffredo, se t'arrise; 6c. No, no, che quest'alma; 7a. Infra dubbii di Marte; 7b. Vieni, o cara; 8. Furie terribili!; 9b. Molto voglio, molto spero; 10. Augelletti; 11a. Al suon di quel bel labbro; 11b. Scherzando sul tuo volto; 12a. Al valor del mio brando; 12b. Sinfonia; 12c. Cara sposa; 13a. Ch'insolito stupore; 13b. Tale stupor m'occupa; 13c. Cor'ingrato; 14. Un mio giusto; 15a. Di speranza un bel raggio; 15b. Venti, turbini, prestate. ACT 2: 16. Siam prossimi al porto; 17. A qual sasso; 18a. Per raccòr d'Almirena; 18b. Il vostro maggio; 19a. Qual incognita forza; 19b. Il Tricerbo umilato; 20a. Signor strano ardimento!; 20b. Mio cor, che mi sai dir?; 21a. Armida dispietata!; 21b. Lascia ch'io pianga; 21c. Basta, che sol tu chieda; 22. Cingetemi d'alloro; 23a. Perfida, un cor illustre; 24a. Crudel, tù ch'involasti; 24b. Sfinge un penoso horrore; 25a. Dunque i lacci d'un volto; 25b. Ah! crudel; 26. Riprendiam d'Almirena; 27a. Adorata Almirena; 27b. Anima mia, ti rasserena; 27c. Vo'far guerra, e vincer voglio. ACT 3: 28. Sinfonia; 29. Tu, a cui concesso; 30a. La causa che vi spinge; 30b. Andante, o forti; 31. Mori svenata!; 32a. Nella guardata soglia; 32b. Vinto il furor d'inferno; 32c. Sorge nel petto; 33a. Al trionfo s'affretti; 34. Chiuso frà quelle mura; 34b. È un incendio frà due venti; 35. Per fomentar lo sdegno; 36a. Sinfonia; 36b. Al trionfo del nostre furore; 37a. Di quei strani accidenti; 37b. Bel piacere; 38a. Signor, l'hoste nemica; 38b. De Sion nell'alta sede; 39a. Sinfonia; 39b. Se cio t'è in grado, oprence; 39c. Or la tromba in suon festante; 40. Miei fidi; 41a. Maganimi campioni; 41b. Battaglia; 42. Ecco, il superbo; 43. Vinto è sol della virtù.

Rinaldo M. Horne
Almirena C. Gasdia
Goffredo E. Palacio
Armida C. Weidinger
Argante N. de Carolis
Christian Magician C. Colombara
Siren I C. Calvi
Siren C. Tosetta

Venice La Fenice Orch, J. Fisher (pp1989)
(4/90) (NUOV) ① [2] **6813/4**
1. ECO, C. Mackerras (r1994)
(NOVA) ① **150 108-2**
1. ECCO, E. Aadland
(12/91) (ASV) ① **CDDCA766**
1, 21b K. te Kanawa, AAM, C. Hogwood
(PHIL) ◉ **070 155-1PH**
(PHIL) ▭ **070 155-3PH**
1, 21b K. te Kanawa, AAM, C. Hogwood
(8/94) (PHIL) ① **434 992-2PH**
(8/94) (PHIL) ⊟ **434 992-4PH**
4b, 12c, 13c, 15b, 39c M. Horne, Venice La Fenice Orch, J. Fisher (pp1989)
(MEMO) ① [2] **HR4392/3**
12c J. Larmore, Lausanne CO, J. López-Cobos (r1994) (TELD) ① **4509-96800-2**
12c D. Fischer-Dieskau, J-P. Rampal, R. Veyron-Lacroix, J. Neilz (r1971)
(EMI) ① [2] **CMS5 65621-2**
12c C. Watkinson, Amsterdam Bach Sols, J.W. de Vriend (3/89) (ETCE) ① **KTC1064**
12c N. Stutzmann, Hanover Band, R. Goodman
(3/93) (RCA) ① **09026 61205-2**
12c, 13c J. Kowalski, Berlin RSO, H. Fricke
(CAPR) ◘ **80 416**
12c, 13c J. Kowalski, Berlin RSO, H. Fricke
(CAPR) **OO** **70 416**
12c, 13c J. Kowalski, Berlin RSO, H. Fricke
(10/92) (CAPR) ① **10 416**
12c, 13c, 15b, 21b, 39c M. Horne, Solisti Veneti, C. Scimone (ERAT) ① **2292-45186-2**
12c, 15b, 39c, 41a J. Bowman, King's Consort, R. King (12/91) (HYPE) ① **CDA66483**
(12/91) (HYPE) ⊟ **KA66483**
15b A. Köhler, Halle Op House Handel Fest Orch, H. Arman (r1994)
(6/95) (CAPR) ① **10 547**
21a-c J. Norman, G. Parsons (pp1987)
(8/88) (PHIL) ① **422 048-2PH**
21a-c J. Norman, G. Parsons (pp1987)
(6/89) (PHIL) ① **422 235-2PH**
21a, 21b G. De Luca, orch (r1918)
(PEAR) ① [3] **GEMMCDS9160(1)**
21b B. Streisand, Columbia SO, C. Ogerman (arr Ogerman) (SONY) ◘ **SM33452**
21b B. Streisand, Columbia SO, C. Ogerman (arr Ogerman) (SONY) ① **SK33452**
21b M. Horne, Solisti Veneti, C. Scimone
(ERAT) ① **2292-45797-2**
(ERAT) ⊟ **2292-45797-4**
21b Vienna Boys' Ch, U.C. Harrer
(PHIL) ① **434 726-2PM**
(PHIL) ⊟ **434 726-4PH**

21b L. Garrett, Philh, I. Bolton
(SILV) Ⓓ **SONGCD907**
(SILV) ⊟ **SONGC907**
21b J. Carreras, ECO, V. Sutej (r1992; arr Agostinelli) (PHIL) OO **434 926-5PH**
21b J. Baird, Brewer CO, R. Palmer
(NEWP) Ⓓ **NPD85568**
21b A. Auger, Mostly Mozart Orch, G. Schwarz
(11/86) (DELO) Ⓓ **DE3026**
21b C. Muzio, orch (r1922)
(5/90) (BOGR) Ⓓ [2] **BIM705-2**
21b E. Schumann-Heink, orch (r1909)
(2/91) (NIMB) Ⓓ **NI7811**
(2/91) (NIMB) ⊟ **NC7811**
21b Vienna Boys' Ch, U.C. Harrer
(12/91) (PHIL) Ⓓ **426 307-2PH**
21b R. White, City of London Baroque Sinfonia, I. Bolton (12/91) (VIRG) Ⓓ **VJ7 59644-2**
(12/91) (VIRG) ⊟ **VJ7 59644-4**
21b J. Carreras, ECO, V. Sutej (r1992; arr Agostinelli) (6/93) (PHIL) Ⓓ **434 926-2PH**
21b C. Muzio, orch (r1922)
(1/94) (ROMO) Ⓓ [2] **81005-2**
39c J. Kowalski, CPE Bach Orch, Hartmut Haenchen (CAPR) ◙ **80 213**
39c J. Kowalski, CPE Bach Orch, Hartmut Haenchen (CAPR) OO **70 213**
39c J. Kowalski, CPE Bach Orch, Hartmut Haenchen (3/88) (CAPR) Ⓓ **10 213**
(3/88) (CAPR) ⊟ **CC27 213**
39c, 41b H. Field, J. Wallace, Philh, S. Wright
(NIMB) Ⓓ **NI5123**
41b ECO, R. Bonynge (r1967;ed R. Bonynge)
(DECC) Ⓓ [2] **444 543-2DF2**

Rodelinda– opera: 3 acts, HWV19 (1725—London) (Lib. Haym, after A. Salvi)

EXCERPTS: 1a. Overture; 1b. Menuet. ACT 1: 2a. Hò perduto il caro sposo; 2b. Regina!; 2c. L'empio rigor del fato; 3. Duca, vedesti mai; 4a. E tanto da che sei Rè; 4b. Io già t'amai, ritrosa; 5a. E tu dice d'amarmi?; 5b. Lo farò, dirò spietato; 6a. Eduige, t'inganni; 6b. Di Cupido impiego i vanni; 7a. Pompe vane di morte!; 7b. Dove sei, amato bene!; 7c. Mà giunge Unulfo; 8. Ombre, piante; 9a. Baci inutili, e vani; 9b. Morrai sì, l'empia; 10a. E ben, Duca, poss'io; 10b. Se per te giungo a godere; 11a. Unulfo, oh Dio!; 11b. Sono i colpi della sorte; 12a. Sì, l'infida consorte; 12b. Confusa si miri. ACT 2: 13. Già perdesti, oh signora; 14a. Rodelinda, si mesta ritorni; 14b. De'miei scherni; 15a. Rodelinda, è pur ver?; 15b. Spietati, io vi giurai; 16a. Unulfo, Garibaldo; 16b. Prigioniera hò l'alma; 16c. Massime così indegne; 16d. Tirannia gli diede il regno; 16e. Sì, sì fellon, t'intendo; 16f. Frà tempeste funeste; 17a. Con rauco mormorio; 17b. Ah, nò; che non m'inganna; 17c. Scacciata dal suo nido; 18a. Vive il mio sposo?; 18b. Ritorna, oh caro e dolce; 19a. Ah! sì, ecco lo sposo; 19b. Tuo drudo è mio rivale; 19c. Non ti bastò, consorte; 19d. Io t'abbraccio. ACT 3: 20a. Del german nel periglio; 20b. Un geffiro spirò; 20c. Con opra giusta; 20d. Quanto più fiera tempesta; 21a. O falso è Bertarido; 21b. Trà sospetti, affetti; 22a. Che di voi fù più infedele; 22b. Mà non che sò dal remoto; 23a. Non temere, Signore!; 23b. Se'l mio duol; 24a. Fatto inferno è il mio; 24b. Pastorello d'un povero; 25. Che miro? amica sorte; 26a. Tu morrai, traditor!; 26b. Vivi tiranno!; 26c. Dunque sei Bertarido?; 27a. Ecco ti innanzi il reo; 27b. Mio caro bene!; 27c. Sposa, figlio sorella; 27d. Dopo la notte oscura.

Rodelinda	B. Schlick
Eduige	C. Schubert
Bertarido	D. Cordier
Unulfo	K. Wessel
Grimoaldo	C. Prégardien
Garibaldo	G. Schwarz

Stagione, M. Schneider (pp1990)
(1/93) (DHM) Ⓓ [3] **RD77192**
1. J. Gray, R. Pearl (r1994; arr. Gray/Pearl)
(DORI) Ⓓ **DOR90209**
2a, 8. L. Popp, ECO, G. Fischer (r1967)
(10/88) (EMI) Ⓓ **CDM7 69546-2**
7a, 7b J. Baker, ECO, R. Leppard
(PHIL) Ⓓ **426 450-2PBQ**
7a, 7b C. Watkinson, Amsterdam Bach Sols, J.W. de Vriend (3/89) (ETCE) Ⓓ **KTC1064**
7a, 7b A. Köhler, Halle Op House Handel Fest Orch, H. Arman (r1994)
(6/95) (CAPR) Ⓓ **10 547**
7a, 7b, 17a M. Forrester, Vienna RSO, B. Priestman (12/92) (CBC) Ⓓ **PSCD2002**
7b M. Horne, Vienna Cantata Orch, H. Lewis (r1967) (DECC) Ⓓ **433 065-2DWO**
(DECC) ⊟ **433 065-4DWO**
7b I. Baillie, CBO, B. Cameron (r1941: Eng)
(PEAR) Ⓓ **GEMMCD9934**
7b E. Leisner, orch (r1926: Ger)
(PREI) Ⓓ [2] **89210**
7b B. Greevy, ASMF, R. Leppard (r1965)
(DECC) Ⓓ [2] **444 543-2DF2**
7b K. Ferrier, LSO, M. Sargent (1946: Eng)
(6/91) (DECC) Ⓓ **430 096-2DWO**
(6/91) (DECC) ⊟ **430 096-4DWO**
7b M. Horne, Vienna Cantata Orch, H. Lewis
(10/91) (DECC) Ⓓ **430 500-2DWO**
(10/91) (DECC) ⊟ **430 500-4DWO**
7b K. Ferrier, LSO, M. Sargent (r1946: Eng)
(6/92) (DECC) Ⓓ **433 470-2DM**
(6/92) (DECC) ⊟ **433 470-4DM**
7b I. Baillie, CBO, B. Cameron (r1941: Eng)
(7/95) (DUTT) Ⓓ **CDLX7013**
7b, 26b M. Horne, Vienna Cantata Orch, H. Lewis (r1967) (DECC) Ⓓ **440 415-2DM**
8, 15b L. Saffer, Philh Baroque Orch, N. McGegan (12/91) (HARM) Ⓓ **HMU90 7036**
26b J. Kowalski, CPE Bach Orch, Hartmut Haenchen (CAPR) ◙ **80 213**
26b J. Kowalski, CPE Bach Orch, Hartmut Haenchen (CAPR) OO **70 213**
26b M. Horne, Vienna Cantata Orch, H. Lewis (r1967) (DECC) Ⓓ [2] **444 543-2DF2**
26b J. Kowalski, CPE Bach Orch, Hartmut Haenchen (3/88) (CAPR) Ⓓ **10 213**
(3/88) (CAPR) ⊟ **CC27 213**
26b D. Minter, Philh Baroque Orch, N. McGegan
(4/88) (HARM) Ⓓ **HMC90 5183**

Rodrigo– opera: 3 acts (1707—Florence) (Lib. Haym)

Overture ASMF, K. Sillito (r1993)
(8/94) (CAPR) Ⓓ **10 420**
Sailors' Dance Queen's Hall Orch, Henry Wood (r1937) (1/94) (BEUL) Ⓓ **1PD3**

Scipione– opera: 3 acts, HWV20 (1726—London) (Lib. Rolli)

EXCERPTS: 1. Overture. ACT ONE: 2a. March; 2b. Abbiam vinto; 2c. A Tiberio; 2d. Scaccia, Oh Bella; 2e. Oh Lucejo!; 2f. Un caro amante; 3a. Quando vengo; 3b. Lamentandomi corro; 4. Oh quante grazie Amore; 5a. Libera chi non é; 5b. Indegna é; 6a. No, non si teme; 6b. Oh! Sventurati; 6c. Dolci aurette; 7a. Dimmi, carra; 7b. Ah! T'ascondi; 8. Vanne!; 9a. Giunsi a tempo; 9b. Figlia di reo timor. ACT TWO: 10a. Overture; 10b. Mercè del Vincitor; 10c. Braccio si valoroso; 11a. Tutta raccolta ancor; 11b. Di libertade il dono; 11c. Pensa, Oh Bella; 12a. Ecco, Oh Prence; 12b. Parto, fuggo; 12c. Seguilo, O Duce!; 12d. Com'onda incalza; 13a. Importuno tu sei; 13b. Temo che lusinghiero; 13c. Lusingarlo mi giova; 13d. Voglio contenta allor; 14. Qui torno e qui; 15. Oh Bella!; 16. Tanto s'ardisce ancora; 17a. Numi, lo difendete!; 17b. Cedo a Roma; 17c. Signor, del tuo fisso; 17d. Scoglio d'immota fronte. ACT THREE: 18a. Sinfonia & Recit: Miseri affetti miei!; 18b. Se mormora; 18c. Più resister non posso; 18d. Ah! Scipione; 19. Già cessata; 20a. Sinfonia; 20b. All'invito; 21a. Oh dolce Figlia!; 21b. Gioia si, speri si; 22a. Tu, d'indibile Figlia; 22b. Del debellar la Gloria; 23a. Dove, Oh Prencipe amator?; 23b. Bella notte; 23c. Squarciasi'l fosco; 23d. Come al nazio boschetto; 24a. Dopo il nemico oppresso; 24b. Venga Lucejo; 24c. Si fuggano i tormenti; 24d. Marte riposi; 24e. Finale: Faranno gioia intera.

Scipione	D. L. Ragin
Berenice	S. Piau
Lucejo	D. Lamprecht
Ernando	O. Lallouette
Armira	V. Tabery
Lelio	G. Flechter

Talens Lyriques, C. Rousset (r1993)
(6/94) (FNAC) Ⓓ [3] **592245**
2a ECO, C. Mackerras (r1994)
(NOVA) Ⓓ **150 108-2**
11a O. Natzke, H. Robinson Cleaver (r1939; Eng) (4/92) (EMI) Ⓓ [7] **CHS7 69741-2(2)**
17d L. Saffer, Philh Baroque Orch, N. McGegan
(12/91) (HARM) Ⓓ **HMU90 7036**
23d L. Czidra, Z. Pertis (r1992; arr rec)
(NAXO) Ⓓ **8 550700**

Serse, 'Xerxes'– opera: 3 acts (1738—London) (Lib. adapted from Minato as rev Stampiglia, 1694)

EXCERPTS: ACT 1: 1a. Fronde tenere; 1b. Ombra mai fu (Largo); 2. Se cangio Spoglia; 3. Soggetti al mio volere; 4. Non so se sia speme; 5. Se l'Idol mio Rapir mi vuoi; 6. Un cenno leggiadretto. ACT 2: 7. Speranze mie fermate; 8. Dirà che amor; 9. Quella che tutta fe; 10. Gran pena é gelosia!. ACT 3: 11. No, se tu mi sprezzi; 12. Del Ciel d'amore; 13. Caro voi siete. 14. Più che penso alle fiamme del core; 15. Se bramate d'amar, chi vi sdegna; 16. Crude furie degl'orrido abissi.

Io le dirò che l'amo A. Christofellis, Seicentonovecento Ens, F. Colusso (r1993/4)
(EMI) Ⓓ **CDC5 55250-2**
Overture J. Bowman, King's Consort, R. King
(12/91) (HYPE) Ⓓ **CDA66483**
(12/91) (HYPE) ⊟ **KA66483**
Va godendo vezzoso e bello G. Anselmi, Bettinelli (r1910)
(7/95) (SYMP) Ⓓ **SYMCD1170**
1. M. André, J. Parker-Smith (arr Defaye tpt/org)
(EMI) Ⓓ **CDM7 69062-2**
1. E. Caruso, orch, J. Pasternack (r1920)
(12/90) (NIMB) Ⓓ **NI7809**
(12/90) (NIMB) ⊟ **NC7809**
1. E. Caruso, orch, J. Pasternack (r1920)
(7/91) (RCA) Ⓓ [12] **GD60495(6)**
1. E. Caruso, orch, J. Pasternack (r1920)
(10/91) (PEAR) Ⓓ [3] **EVC4(2)**
1. K. Battle, M. Garrett (pp1991)
(7/92) (DG) Ⓓ **435 440-2GH**
1a, 1b M. Larrieu, S. Mildonian
(DENO) Ⓓ **C37-7301**
1a, 1b Alfredo Kraus, J. Tordesillas
(NIMB) Ⓓ **NI5102**
1a, 1b J. Baker, ECO, R. Leppard
(PHIL) Ⓓ **426 450-2PBQ**
1a, 1b J. Kowalski, CPE Bach Orch, Hartmut Haenchen (CAPR) ◙ **80 213**
1a, 1b J. Kowalski, CPE Bach Orch, Hartmut Haenchen (CAPR) OO **70 213**
1a, 1b E. Caruso, orch (r1920)
(ASV) Ⓓ **CDAJA5137**
(ASV) ⊟ **ZCAJA5137**
1a, 1b T. Schipa, orch (r1926)
(NIMB) Ⓓ **NI7870**
1a, 1b B. Gigli, orch, J. Barbirolli (r1933)
(PEAR) Ⓓ [2] **GEMMCDS9176**
1a, 1b J. Kowalski, CPE Bach Orch, Hartmut Haenchen (3/88) (CAPR) Ⓓ **10 213**
(3/88) (CAPR) ⊟ **CC27 213**
1a, 1b J. Björling, Bergen SO, C. Garaguly (pp1954) (8/88) (BLUE) Ⓓ **ABCD006**
1a, 1b J. Bowman, King's Consort, R. King
(8/88) (IMP) Ⓓ **PCD894**
1a, 1b B. Gigli, orch, J. Barbirolli (r1933)
(9/88) (EMI) Ⓓ **CDH7 61051-2**
1a, 1b T. Schipa, orch (r1927)
(2/89) (PEAR) Ⓓ **GEMMCD9322**
1a, 1b C. Watkinson, Amsterdam Bach Sols, J.W. de Vriend (3/89) (ETCE) Ⓓ **KTC1064**
1a, 1b M. Lipovšek, Munich RO, G. Patanè
(6/90) (ORFE) Ⓓ **C179891A**
1a, 1b R. White, City of London Baroque Sinfonia, I. Bolton
(12/91) (VIRG) Ⓓ **VJ7 59644-2**
(12/91) (VIRG) ⊟ **VJ7 59644-4**
1a, 1b K. Ferrier, LSO, M. Sargent (r1949)
(6/92) (DECC) Ⓓ **433 470-2DM**
(6/92) (DECC) ⊟ **433 470-4DM**
1a, 1b, 14-16. F. Wunderlich, BRSO, R. Kubelík (Ger: bp) (DG) Ⓓ [5] **435 145-2GX5(1)**
1a, 1b, 15; Per rendermi beato parto M. Forrester, Vienna RSO, B. Priestman
(12/92) (CBC) Ⓓ **PSCD2002**
1a, 1b, 15, 16. A. Murray, OAE, C. Mackerras (r1994) (8/95) (FORL) Ⓓ **UCD16738**
1b Cölln Salon Orch (arr. Anon)
(EMI) Ⓓ **CDC7 49819-2**
1b K. Battle, W. Jones, H. Burton (pp1991)
(DG) ▣ **072 189-3GH**
1b Adelaide SO, J. Serebrier (MCI) Ⓓ **OQ0011**
1b F. Wunderlich, Berlin SO, G. Becker
(EURO) Ⓓ **GD69018**
(EURO) ⊟ **GK69018**
1b LSO, G. Szell (DECC) Ⓓ **425 851-2DWO**
(DECC) ⊟ **425 851-4DWO**
1b T. Burke, orch (r1929)
(PEAR) Ⓓ **GEMMCD9411**
1b G. Zamfir, D. Bish (arr panpipes/org)
(PHIL) Ⓓ **426 057-2PH**
(PHIL) ⊟ **426 057-4PH**
1b F. Wunderlich, Bavarian St Orch, H. Müller-Kray (EMI) Ⓓ [3] **CZS7 62993-2**
1b T. Schipa, orch, Anon (cond) (pp1926)
(MEMO) Ⓓ [2] **HR4220/1**
1b M. Horne, Solisti Veneti, C. Scimone
(ERAT) Ⓓ **2292-45186-2**

1b F Liszt CO, J. Rolla (vn/dir) (TELD) ① **9031-74789-2**
1b ASMF, N. Marriner (EMI) ① [2] **CZS7 67425-2**
1b M. Horne, Solisti Veneti, C. Scimone (ERAT) ① **2292-45797-2** (ERAT) ⊟ **2292-45797-4**
1b Boston Pops, A. Fiedler (r1959) (RCA) ① **09026 61207-2** (RCA) ⊟ **09026 61207-4**
1b G. Zamfir, D. Bish (arr panpipes/org) (PHIL) **OO** **426 057-5PH**
1b R. Oostwoud, S. Harrison (SCHW) ① **312642**
1b G. Revell (arr org) (APPL) ① **APC003**
1b C. Curley (r1989;arr Curley: org) (ARGO) ① **436 260-2ZH**
1b F. Wunderlich, Bavarian St Op Orch, H. Müller-Kray (CFP) ① **CD-CFP4616**
1b J. Carreras, ECO, V. Sutej (r1992; arr Agostinelli) (PHIL) **OO** **434 926-5PH**
1b R. Wolfgang, Orpheus CO (DG) ① **439 147-2GMA** (DG) ⊟ **439 147-4GMA**
1b S. Cleobury (arr Cleobury) (BELA) ① **450 013-2** (BELA) ⊟ **450 013-4**
1b LSO, G. Szell (r1971; arr Reinhard) (BELA) ① **450 001-2** (BELA) ⊟ **450 001-4**
1b J. Bowman, King's Consort, R. King (IMP) ① **ORCD11010** (IMP) ⊟ **ORZC11010**
1b B. Gigli, orch, J. Barbirolli (r1933) (CONI) ① **CDHD227** (CONI) ⊟ **MCHD227**
1b M. Gendron, P. Gallion (r1960; arr Gendron) (PHIL) ① [3] **438 960-2PM3**
1b M. André, J. Parker-Smith (arr. Defaye tpt/org) (EMIL) ① **CDZ112** (EMIL) ⊟ **LZ112**
1b Munich Pro Arte Orch, K. Redel (FORL) ① **FF051**
1b P. Casals, orch (r1915: arr vc/orch) (SONY) ① **SMK66573**
1b E. Leisner, orch (r1913: Ger) (PREI) ① [2] **89210**
1b Guildhall Str Ens, R. Salter (vn/dir) (r1992) (RCA) ① **74321 25819-2** (RCA) ⊟ **74321 25819-4**
1b C. Kullman, orch, O. Dobrindt (r1932) (MMOI) ① **CDMOIR429**
1b J. Larmore, Lausanne CO, J. López-Cobos (r1994) (TELD) ① **4509-96800-2**
1b ECO, C. Mackerras (r1994) (NOVA) ① **150 108-2**
1b LSO, G. Szell (r1961) (DECC) ① [2] **444 543-2DF2**
1b R. Kilbey Stgs, R. Kilbey (arr. orch: Byfield) (1/89) (EMIL) ① **CDZ114** (EMIL) ⊟ **LZ114**
1b Solisti Italiani (10/89) (DENO) ① **CO-73335**
1b T. Schipa, orch, Rosario Bourdon (r1926) (12/89) (RCA) ① **GD87969**
1b K. Ferrier, LSO, M. Sargent (r1949) (6/91) (DECC) ① **430 096-2DWO** (6/91) (DECC) ⊟ **430 096-4DWO**
1b E. Pinza, orch, H. Barlow (bp1944) (7/91) (MMOI) ① **CDMOIR404** (MMOI) ⊟ **CMOIR404**
1b P. Domingo, I. Perlman, NY Studio Orch, J. Tunick (r1990) (3/92) (EMI) ① **CDC7 54266-2**
1b E. Albani, anon (r1904) (10/92) (SYMP) ① **SYMCD1093**
1b T. Schipa, orch, Rosario Bourdon (r1926) (1/93) (MMOI) ① **CDMOIR411** (1/93) (MMOI) ⊟ **CMOIR411**
1b J. Carreras, ECO, V. Sutej (r1992; arr Agostinelli) (6/93) (PHIL) ① **434 926-2PH**
1b K. Flagstad, Philh, W. Braithwaite (r1948) (7/93) (TEST) ① **SBT1018**
1b F. Kreisler, C. Lamson (r1924: arr Kreisler) (9/93) (BIDD) ① [2] **LAB068/9**
1b Guildhall Str Ens, R. Salter (vn/dir) (r1992) (2/94) (RCA) ① **09026 61275-2**
1b E. Rethberg, orch (r1928) (2/95) (ROMO) ① [2] **81012-2**
6. L. Popp, ECO, G. Fischer (r1967) (10/88) (EMI) ① **CDM7 69546-2**
16. G. Sabbatini, A. Juffinger (SCHW) ① **314073**

Siroe, Rè di Persia– opera: 3 acts (1728—London) (Lib. Haym, after Metastasio)

Siroe	D. Fortunato
Emira	J. Baird
King Cosroe	J. Ostendorf
Laodice	A. Matthews
Medarse	S. Rickards
Arasse	F. Urrey

Brewer CO, R. Palmer (5/92) (NEWP) ① [3] **NCD60125**
Gigue Brewer CO, R. Palmer (NEWP) ① **NPD85568**
La mia speranza J. Baird, Brewer CO, R. Palmer (NEWP) ① **NPD85568**

Sosarme– opera: 3 acts (1732—London) (Lib. after Metastasio)

EXCERPTS: 1. Overture. ACT ONE: 2a. Di mio padre al furore; 2b. Voi, miei fidi compagni; 2c. Alla stragge, alla morte, alla vittoria!; 3a. Madre e Regina!; 3b. Rendi'l sereno il ciglio; 4a. Giusti Numi; 4b. Forte inciampo al suo furore; 5a. Melo, mio prence; 5b. Fra l'ombre e gl'orrori; 5c. Come più dell'usato; 5d. Sì, minaccia e vinta; 6a. Non più contese!; 6b. Il mio valore ch'albergo in petto; 6c. Così dunque sospiran; 6d. La turba adulatrice; 7a. Amici, troppo oscuro; 7b. Alla stragge, alla morte (reprise); 7c. Mà chi ritorna in vita; 7d. Oh Diva Hecate; 7e. Dite pace. ACT TWO: 8a. Padre, germano, e sposo; 8b. E ben dall'alta torre; 8c. Se m'ascolti; 9a. Mio Rè, l'ultimo sforzo; 9b. Se discordia ci disciolse; 10a. E così tu disprezzi; 10b. Sò ch'il Ciel ben spesso gode; 10c. Quanto più Melo ha sdegno; 10d. Sento il cor che lieto gode; 11a. Grazie al Cielo; 11b. Per le porte del tormento; 11c. Signor, tuo regio sangue; 11d. Alle sfere della gloria; 11e. Viva! viva e regni fortunato; 12a. Son tuo congiunto; 12b. Vado al campo; 12c. Mio sposo, ahi qual orror; 12d. In mille dolci modi; 12e. Parmi ch'un dolce; 12f. Vola l'augello. ACT THREE: 13. Sinfonia; 14a. Mi siegue la Regina; 14b. S'io cadrò per tuo consiglio; 15a. Melo, dov'è il tuo zelo?; 15b. Cuor di madre e cuor di moglia; 15c. A deluder le frodi; 15d. Sincero affetto; 16a. Per la segreta porta; 16b. Altomaro, si renda libera lo steccato!; 16c. Tiene Giove; 16d. Signor, qui giunge Argone; 16e. Tu caro, caro sei; 16f. Fugga da questo; 16g. Dopo l'ire si funeste.

Sosarme	D. Fortunato
King Haliate	J. Aler
Elmira	J. Baird
Melo	D. Minter
Varo	N. Watson
Erenice	J. Lane
Argone	R. Pellerin

Taghkanic Chorale, Amor Artis Orch, J. Somary (r1993) (12/94) (NEWP) ① [2] **NPD85575**
3b E. Rethberg, orch (r1928) (2/95) (ROMO) ① [2] **81012-2**
5a, 5b, 10c, 10d, 16b, 16c D. Thomas, Philh Baroque Orch, N. McGegan (8/90) (HARM) ① **HMU90 7016**

Tamerlano– opera: 3 acts (1724—London) (Lib. Haym)

Tamerlano	D.L. Ragin
Bajazet	N. Robson
Asteria	N. Argenta
Andronico	M. Chance
Irene	J. Findlay
Leone	R. Schirrer

EBS, J.E. Gardiner (pp1985) (ERAT) ① [3] **2292-45408-2**
Serav Asteria ... Se non mi vuol amar L. Saffer, Philh Baroque Orch, N. McGegan (12/91) (HARM) ① **HMU90 7036**

Teseo– opera: 5 acts (1713—London) (Lib. Haym, after Quinault)

EXCERPTS: 1. Overture. ACT 1: 2. Sia qual'vuole il mio fato; 3a. Clizia, son'gli Ateniesi; 3b. E pur' bello, in' nobil core; 4a. Ora svelaci Arcane; 4b. Deh' serbatè ò giusti Dei!; 5a. Parte Agilea; 5b. Ti credo, si ben' mio; 5c. Commanda dunque ò bella; 5d. Ah! cruda gelosia!; 5e. Dunque all'affetto mio; 5f. Addio! mio caro mio; 6a. Serenatevi, oh luci belle!; 6b. Or'ch'affermito o il soglio; 6c. Ricordati, oh bella; 6d. Ah, che sol'er Teseo; 6e. M'adora l'idol mio. ACT 2: 7a. Dolce riposo, ed innocente pace!; 7b. L'infelice Medea; 7c. Quell'amor, ch'è nato à forza; 8a. Delle armi nostre; 8b. Si ti lascio; 9. Sire, tutto è periglio; 10a. Ogn'un acclami il nostro Alcide!; 10b. Amici, à bastanza nostrate il vostro affretto; 11a. Teseo, dove ten'vai!; 11b. Quanto che à mè siam' care; 11c. Ai vostri amori; 11d. Non so più che bramar; 12a. Ira, sdegno, e furore; 12b. O stringerò nel' sen. ACT 3: 13a. Risplendete, amiche stelle; 13b. Perdona, omai perdona; 13c. Più non cerca liberta; 14a. Quivi sarà frà poco; 14b. Vieni, torna, idolo mio; 14c. Teseo qui giunge; 15a. Pur ti riveggio al'fine; 15b. S'armi il fato, s'armi amore!; 16. Egeo di qui venir m'impose; 17a. Tu ben'sai Principessa; 17b. Numi, chi ci soccorre!; 17c. Deh'dammi aita Arcane; 17d. Ombre, sortite dall' eterna notte!; 17e. O ciel, che mai sara!; 17f. Sibillando, ululando, fulminate, la rival. ACT 4: 18a. Sire, come imponesti; 18b. Voglio stragi; 18c. Amor per Agilea; 18d. Benchè tuoni e l'etra auvampi; 19a. Cruda, ed'ancor'non vuoi; 19b. E che mai veggio oh Dio!; 20b. E ancor su'gli occhi miei; 20c. Dal cupo baratro; 20d. S'arma contro di me tutto l'inferno?; 21a. Chi ritorna alla mia mente; 21b. Mira qual'cura prendo!; 22a. Agilea più non m'ama; 22b. Qual' tigre o qual' megera t'impresse; 22c. Tu piangi! e à me, l'ascondi!; 22d. Amarti si vorrei; 23a. Troppo un rè che t'adora; 23b. Chi di non più beato?; 24. Cara/caro, ti dono in pegno il cor. ACT 5: 25a. Dunque per vendicarmi; 25b. Morirò, ma vendicata; 25c. Scopria, mà non veduta; 26a. Questo vaso he miri; 26b. Non è da Rè quel cor; 26c. Ma del Popolo l'odio; 27a. Giuro per questo acciaro; 27b. Che miro oh Ciel!; 28a. Ah! perfida Medea!; 28b. Tegno in pugno; 28c. Signore in questo giorno; 28d. Unito à un puro affetto; 29. Essenti del mio sdegno; 30a. Socorretici o Numi!; 30b. Il ciel gia si compiace; 30c. Goda ogn'alma in si bel giorno.

Teseo	E. James
Agilea	J. Gooding
Medea	D. Jones
Egeo	D.L. Ragin
Clizia	C. Napoli
Arcane	J. Gall
Sacerdote di Minerva	F. Bazola-Minori

Musiciens du Louvre, M. Minkowski (3/93) (ERAT) ① [2] **2292-45806-2**

Tolomeo, Rè di Egitto– opera: 3 acts (1728—London) (Lib. Haym)

EXCERPTS: 1. Overture; 2. Non lo dirò col labbro ('Silent worship'); 3a. Che più si tarda si trada omai; 3b. Stille amare; 4. Piangi pur.
1. G. Gifford (trans hpd) (5/90) (LIBR) ① **LRCD156** (5/90) (LIBR) ⊟ **LRS156**
2. M. Ashton, Concert Royal (England) (r1991) (GEOR) ⊟ **GR002**
2. K. McKellar, ROHO, A. Boult (Eng) (DECC) ① **425 851-2DWO** (DECC) ⊟ **425 851-4DWO**
2. T. Allen, J. Constable (Eng) (4/92) (GAMU) ① **GAMD506**
3a, 3b D. Minter, Philh Baroque Orch, N. McGegan (4/88) (HARM) ① **HMC90 5183**
4. D. Thomas, Philh Baroque Orch, N. McGegan (8/90) (HARM) ① **HMU90 7016**

HANSON , Howard *(1896–1981) USA*

Merry Mount– opera: 3 acts, Op. 31 (1933—New York) (Lib. R. L. Stokes, after Hawthorne)

Suite Seattle SO, G. Schwarz (7/92) (DELO) ① **DE3105**
'Tis an earth defiled L. Tibbett, NY Met Op Orch, W. Pelletier (r1934) (3/90) (RCA) ① **GD87808**

HARTMANN , Johan Peter Emilius *(1805–1900) Denmark*

Little Christine– opera (1 act), Op. 44 (1846—Copenhagen) (Wds. H. C. Anderson)

Now, my young swain L. Melchior, A. Neumann, Orch (r1913) (8/88) (DANA) ① [2] **DACOCD311/2**
Sverkel's Romance L. Melchior, Orch (Danish: r c1920) (8/88) (DANA) ① [2] **DACOCD311/2**

The **Raven– opera (1832—Copenhagen)**

Ov Odense SO, O. Schmidt (1/87) (UNIC) ⊟ **DKPC9036**

HARTMANN , Karl Amadeus *(1905–1963) Germany*

Simplicius Simplicissimus—three scenes from his youth– chamber opera (1948—Munich)

Simplicius Simplicissimus	H. Donath

Einsiedel E. Büchner
Gouverneur K. König
Landsknecht B. Brinkmann
Hauptmann R. Scholze
Bauer H. Berger-Tuna
W. Euba
Munich Concert Ch, BRSO, H. Fricke (r1985)
(11/95) (WERG) Ⓓ [2] **WER6259-2**

HASSE, Johann (Adolph)
(1699–1783) Germany

Artaserse– opera: 3 acts (1730—Venice) (Lib. Lalli, after Metastasio)
Palido il sole J. Kowalski, Berlin RSO, H. Fricke
(CAPR) ꝏ **70 416**
Palido il sole J. Kowalski, Berlin RSO, H. Fricke
(CAPR) ● **80 416**
Palido il sole J. Kowalski, Berlin RSO, H. Fricke
(10/92) (CAPR) Ⓓ **10 416**
Pallido il sole A. Christofellis, Seicentonovecento Ens, F. Colusso (r1993/4)
(EMI) Ⓓ **CDC5 55250-2**
Per questo dolce amplesso A. Christofellis, Inst Ens (r1987/8) (EMI) Ⓓ **CDC5 55259-2**

La **Clemenza di Tito– opera (3 acts) (1735—Dresden) (Lib. Metastasio)**
Tardi s'avvedde d'un tradimento J. Kowalski, Berlin CO, M. Pommer
(9/88) (CAPR) Ⓓ **10 113**
(9/88) (CAPR) ▭ **CC27 127**

Cleofide (Alessandro nell'Indie)– opera (3 acts) (1731—Leipzig) (Wds. Boccardi, after Metastasio)
Cleofide E. Kirkby
Erissena A. Mellon
Poro D.L. Ragin
Alessandro D. Visse
Gandarte R. Wong
Timagene D. Cordier
Cappella Coloniensis, W. Christie
(2/88) (CAPR) Ⓓ [4] **10 193/6**

Lucio Papirio– opera (3 acts) (1742—Dresden) (Lib. Zeno)
All'onor mio rifletti J. Kowalski, Berlin CO, M. Pommer (9/88) (CAPR) Ⓓ **10 113**
(9/88) (CAPR) ▭ **CC27 127**

Piramo e Tisbe– intermezzo tragico (2 acts) (1768—Vienna) (Lib. M. Coltellini)
Piramo B. Schlick
Tisbe A. Monoyios
Father W. Jochens
Stagione, M. Schneider (r1993)
(CAPR) Ⓓ [2] **60 043-2**
Piramo B. Schlick
Tisbe S. Gari
Father M. Lecocq
Capella Clementina, H. Müller-Brühl (r1984)
(4/94) (SCHW) Ⓓ [2] **310882**

HAYDN, Franz Joseph
(1732–1809) Austria

Hob—Numbers from Hoboken's Thematic Catalogue of Haydn's works (1957-71)

Acide e Galatea– festa teatrale: 1 act, HobXXVIII/1 (1763—Einsentadt) (Lib. Migliavacca)
EXCERPTS: 1. Overture (pub 1959).
Tergi i vezzosi rai D. Fischer-Dieskau, Vienna Mozart Orch, R. Peters (r1969)
(DECC) Ⓓ **440 409-2DM**
Tergi i vezzosi rai M. Devlin, Lausanne CO, A. Dorati (r1980)
(6/93) (PHIL) Ⓓ [3] **432 416-2PH3**
1. Sinfonia, D. Vermeulen (r1994)
(DINT) Ⓓ **DICD920289**

Ah crudel! poiché lo brami– Insertion soprano aria for 'La vendemmia' by Gazza, Hob XXXc/5 (1780)
T. Berganza, Scottish CO, R. Leppard (r1982)
(ERAT) Ⓓ **4509-98498-2**

L' **Anima del filosofo, ossia Orfeo ed Euridice– dramma per music: 4 acts (1791) (Lib. Badini: probably unfinished)**
Orfeo R. Swensen
Euridice H. Donath
Genio S. Greenberg
Creonte T. Quasthoff
Pluto P. Hansen
Baccante A. Suzuki
Bavarian Rad Chor, Munich RO, L. Hager (r1992)
(9/95) (ORFE) Ⓓ [2] **C262932H**

Armida– opera: 3 acts, HobXXVIII/12 (1783—Eszterháza) (Lib. cpsr)
1. Sinfonia; 2. March; 3. Parti Rinaldo; 4. Se pietade avete; 5. Caro sarò fedele; 6. Barbaro! E ardici ancor; 7. Odio, furor, dispetto; 8. Ah, non ferir.
Armida J. Norman
Rinaldo C.H. Ahnsjö
Zelmira N. Burrowes
Idreno S. Ramey
Ubaldo R. Leggate
Clotarco A. Rolfe Johnson
Lausanne CO, A. Dorati (r1978)
(6/93) (PHIL) Ⓓ [2] **432 438-2PH2**
1. Orpheus CO (r1992)
(12/93) (DG) Ⓓ **437 783-2GH**

La **Canterina– intermezzo in musica: 2 acts, HobXXVIII/2 (1766—Bratislava) (Lib. from Piccinni's 'L'Origille')**
EXCERPTS: 1. Che visino delicato; 2a. Che mai deggio?; 2b. Io sposarl'empio tiranno?; 3. Che dici?; 4. Scellerata! mancatrice!; 5. Oh, rovinate noi!; 6. Signor mio; 7. Che mai vuol dir tal cosa?; 8. Non v'è chi m'aiuta; 9. Misera! Dove andrà?; 10. O stelle! Aiuto!; 11. Apri pur, mia dea terrestre.
Gasparina B. Harris
Don Pelagio J. Garrison
Apollonia D. Fortunato
Don Ettore J. Guyer
Palmer CO, R. Palmer (r1994)
(NEWP) Ⓓ **NPD85595**

La **Circe, ossia L'isola incantata– pasticcio (1789) (attrib Haydn)**
EXCERPTS: 1. Terzetto: Lavatevi presto.
1. C.H. Ahnsjö, A. Baldin, M. Devlin, Lausanne CO, A. Dorati (r1980)
(6/93) (PHIL) Ⓓ [3] **432 416-2PH3**

La **Fedeltà premiata– opera: 3 acts, HobXXVIII/10 (1780—Eszterháza) (Lib. after Lorenzi)**
Sinfonia
Overture Versailles Camerata, A. du Closel
(2/89) (FORL) Ⓓ **UCD16567**
Per te m'accese amore; Vanne...fuggi...traditore!; Barbaro conte...Dell' amor mio fedele F. von Stade, Lausanne CO, A. Dorati
(PHIL) Ⓓ **420 084-2PH**
RPO, S. Sanderling (r1994) (TRIN) Ⓓ **TRP021**

Il meglio mio carratere– Insertion soprano aria for 'L'impresario in Angust, HobXXIVb/17 (1790)
T. Berganza, Scottish CO, R. Leppard (r1982)
(ERAT) Ⓓ **4509-98498-2**

L' **Incontro improvviso– opera: 3 acts, HobXXVIII/6 (1775—Eszterháza) (Lib. Friebert)**
Overture
Ali C.H. Ahnsjö
Rezia L. Zoghby
Balkis M. Marshall
Dardane D. Jones
Osmin D. Trimarchi
Calandro B. Luxon
Sultan; Dervish J. Prescott
Official; Dervish J. Hooper
Dervish N. Scarpinati
Lausanne CO, A. Dorati (r1979)
(6/93) (PHIL) Ⓓ [3] **432 416-2PH3**

L' **Infedeltà delusa– opera: 2 acts, HobXXVIII/5 (1773—Eszterháza) (Lib. Coltellini)**
1. Overture; 2. Intermezzo.
Vespina N. Argenta
Sandrina L. Lootens
Nencio M. Schäfer
Filippo C. Prégardien
Nanni S. Varcoe
Petite Bande, S. Kuijken (r1987-8)
(DHM) Ⓓ [2] **05472 77316-2**

La **Moglie quando è buona– insertion soprano aria for 'Giannina e Bernadone', HobXXIVb/18 (1790)**
T. Berganza, Scottish CO, R. Leppard (r1982)
(ERAT) Ⓓ **4509-98498-2**

Il **Mondo della luna– opera: 3 acts, HobXXVIII/7 (1777—Eszterháza) (Lib. Goldoni)**
1. Overture; (ACT 2); 12. Sinfonia; 13. Ballet music; 14. Ballet music; 17. March; 23. Ballet music.
Una donna come me F. von Stade, Lausanne CO, A. Dorati (PHIL) Ⓓ **420 084-2PH**
1. COE, C. Abbado (pp1993)
(10/95) (DG) Ⓓ **439 932-2GH**

Orlando Paladino– opera: 3 acts, HobXXVIII/11 (1782—Eszterháza) (Lib. Badini and Porta)
Sinfonia
Angelica A. Auger
Eurilla E. Ameling
Alcina G. Killebrew
Orlando G. Shirley
Medoro C.H. Ahnsjö
Rodomonte B. Luxon
Pasquale D. Trimarchi
Caronte M. Mazzieri
Licone G. Carelli
Lausanne CO, A. Dorati (r1976)
(6/93) (PHIL) Ⓓ [3] **432 434-2PH3**

Lo **Speziale– opera: 3 acts, HobXXVIII/3 (1768—Esterháza) (Lib. Goldoni)**
Overture Versailles Camerata, A. du Closel
(2/89) (FORL) Ⓓ **UCD16567**

La **Vera costanza– opera: 3 acts, HobXXVIII/8 (1779—Eszterháza) (Lib. Puttini)**
1. Sinfonia; 2. Con un tenero sospiro; 3a. Misera, chi m'aiuta; 3b. Dove fuggo; 4a. Eccomi giuta al colmo; 4b. Care spiagge; 5. Caro figlio, partiamo; 6. Rosina vezzosina.
1. Versailles Camerata, A. du Closel
(2/89) (FORL) Ⓓ **UCD16567**
1. Austro-Hungarian Haydn Orch, A. Fischer (r1991) (1/94) (NIMB) Ⓓ **NI5341**

HAYDN, (Johann) Michael
(1737–1806) Austria

P—Nos. from Perger (1907); MH—Nos. from Sherman/Thomas (1993)

Andromeda e Perseo– opera seria: 2 acts, MH438 (P25) (1787—Salzburg)
EXCERPTS: 1. Sinfonia in C.
1. Oradea PO, R. Rîmbu (r1994)
(OLYM) Ⓓ **OCD485**

HEISE, Peter (Arnold)
(1830–1879) Denmark

Drot og Marsk, 'King and Marshall'– opera: 4 acts (1878—Copenhagen) (Lib. C. Richardt)
King Erik P. Elming
Stig Andersen B. Norup
Ingeborg E. Johansson
Rane Johnsen K. Westi
Count Jakob C. Christiansen
Jens Grand A. Haugland
Arved Bengtsen O. Hedegaard
Aase I. Nielsen
Herald R. Johansen
Danish Nat Rad Ch, Danish Nat RSO, M. Schønwandt (r1992)
(6/93) (CHAN) Ⓓ [3] **CHAN9143/5**

HENZE, Hans Werner *(b 1926)*
Germany

Die **Bassariden– opera: 1 act (1956-66—Salzburg) (Lib. W H Auden & C Kallman, after Euripides)**
Dionysus; Voice K. Riegel
Pentheus A. Schmidt
Cadmus M. Burt
Tiresias R. Tear
Captain W. Murray
Agave K. Armstrong
Autonoe C. Lindsley

Beroe O. Wenkel
Berlin Rad Chbr Ch, South German Rad Chor, Berlin RSO, G. Albrecht
(10/91) (SCHW) Ⓓ [2] **314006**

Boulevard Solitude– opera: 7 scenes (1952—Hanover) (Lib. W. Jokisch, after G. Weil)
Manon Lescaut E. Vassilieva
Armand des Grieux J. Pruett
Lescaut C-J. Falkman
Francis J-M. Salzmann
Lilaque père B. Brewer
Lilaque fils D. Ottevaere
Children's Chor, Lausanne Op Chor, Rencontres Musicales Orch, I. Anguelov (pp1987)
(12/92) (CASC) Ⓓ [2] **VEL1006**

The **English Cat– opera (1983—Stuttgart) (Lib. E. Bond)**
Lord Puff R. Berkeley-Steele
Arnold M. Coles
Jones A. Watt
Tom I. Platt
Peter J. Pike
Minette L. Kennedy
Babette G. Nilsson
Louise D. Bennett
Miss Crisp C. Court
Mrs Gomfit J. Bremar
Lady Toodle R. Hallawell
Mr. Plunkett G. Davenport
Parnassus Orch, M. Stenz
(12/92) (WERG) Ⓓ [2] **WER6204-2**

Der **junge Lord– opera: 2 acts (1965—Berlin) (Lib. I Bachmann, after W Hauff)**
Sir Edgar's Secretary B. McDaniel
Lord Barrat L. Driscoll
Begonia V. Little
Bürgermeister M. Röhrl
Magistrate Hasentreffer I. Sardi
Comptroller Scharf E. Krukowski
Professor von Mucker H. Krebs
Baroness Grünwiesel P. Johnson
Frau von Hufnagel R. Hesse
Frau Hasentreffer L. Otto
Luise E. Mathis
Ida B. Jasper
Chambermaid M. Türke
Wilhelm D. Grobe
Amintore G. Treptow
Lamplighter F. Hoppe
Schöneberg Boys' Ch, Berlin Deutsche Op Chor, Berlin Deutsche Op Orch, C. von Dohnányi (r1960s)
(9/94) (DG) Ⓓ [2] **445 248-2GC2**

HERBERT, Victor August *(1859–1924) USA*

Angel Face– operetta (1919—Chicago) (Book & Lyrics H B Smith & R B Smith)
EXCERPTS: 1. I Might Be Your 'Once-in-a-While'.
1. J. Hadley, American Th Orch, P. Gemignani (r1993; orch W. D. Brohn)
(RCA) Ⓓ **09026 62681-2**

Babes in Toyland– operetta (1903—Chicago) (Lib. MacDonough)
EXCERPTS: 1. March of the Toys; 2. Toyland; 3. Floretta; 4. The moon will help you out; 5. Jane; 6. Eccentric Dance; 7. Never mind, Bo-Peep; 8. Children's Theme; 9. Before and After; 10. I can't do the sum.
1. Boston Pops, A. Fiedler (RCA) Ⓓ **GD60700**
1. Boston Pops, J. T. Williams (r1992)
(SONY) Ⓓ **SK48232**
(SONY) ⊟ **ST48232**
1. St Louis SO, L. Slatkin
(6/89) (RCA) Ⓓ **RD87716**
1. Boston Pops, A. Fiedler (r1958)
(1/94) (RCA) Ⓓ **09026 61249-2**
1, 10. Pittsburgh SO, L. Maazel (r1991: arr H Sanford) (SONY) Ⓓ **SK52491**
1-9. Eastman-Dryden Orch, D. Hunsberger (arr O. Langley) (ARAB) Ⓓ **Z6547**
10. Cincinnati Uni Sngrs, Cincinnati Uni Th Orch, E. Rivers (r1978) (4/94) (NEW) Ⓓ **80221-2**

Eileen– operetta (1917—Cleveland) (Lib. Blossom. Orig. title Hearts of Erin)
EXCERPTS: 1. The Irish Have a Great Night Tonight; 2. Thine Alone; 3. Ireland, My Sireland; 4. Free Trade and a Misty Moon.
1. Pittsburgh SO, L. Maazel (r1991: arr H Sanford) (SONY) Ⓓ **SK52491**
1, 3, 4. G. Evans, V. Stiles, S. Welsh, Orig Broadway Cast, V. Herbert (r1917)
(5/94) (PEAR) Ⓓ [3] **GEMMCDS9059/61**
2. J. Peerce, Orch, H. Barlow (bp1950)
(VAI) ▣ **VAI69117**

The **Enchantress– operetta (1911—Washington) (Lib. F de Gresac & H B Smith)**
I want to be a Prima Donna L. Garrett, Philh, I. Bolton (SILV) Ⓓ **SONGCD907**
(SILV) ⊟ **SONGC907**

The **Fortune Teller– operetta (1898—Toronto) (Lib. H. B. Smith)**
EXCERPTS: 1. Gypsy Love Song; 2. Romany Life; 3. Opening Chorus of Schoolgirls; 4. Always Do as People Say You Should; 5. 2nd Act Finale: Chorus of Trumpets and Drums.
1. Pittsburgh SO, L. Maazel (r1991: arr H Sanford) (SONY) Ⓓ **SK52491**
1. J. Hadley, American Th Orch, P. Gemignani (r1993; orch W. D. Brohn)
(RCA) Ⓓ **09026 62681-2**
1. C. Kullman, orch, W. Goehr (r1938)
(MMOI) Ⓓ **CDMOIR429**
1. E. Cowles, Broadway Cast (r1906)
(5/94) (PEAR) Ⓓ [3] **GEMMCDS9050/2(1)**
2. M. Hill Smith, Chandos Sngrs, Chandos Concert Orch, S. Barry
(2/90) (CHAN) Ⓓ **CHAN8759**
(2/90) (CHAN) ⊟ **LBTD023**
3-5. A. Nielsen, Broadway Cast (r1898)
(5/94) (PEAR) Ⓓ [3] **GEMMCDS9050/2(1)**

It happened in Nordland– operetta (1904—Harrisburg, PA) (Lib. McDonough)
EXCERPTS: 1. Absinthe Frappé.
1. Pittsburgh SO, L. Maazel (r1991: arr H Sanford) (SONY) Ⓓ **SK52491**

Mademoiselle Modiste– operetta: 2 acts (1905—Trenton, New Jersey) (Lib. H. Blossom)
EXCERPTS: 1. Kiss me again.
1. R. Ponselle, orch (r1920)
(PEAR) Ⓓ [2] **GEMMCDS9964**
1. Pittsburgh SO, L. Maazel (r1991: arr H Sanford) (SONY) Ⓓ **SK52491**
1. R. Ponselle, orch, R. Romani (r1920)
(10/93) (NIMB) Ⓓ **NI7846**
1. R. Ponselle, orch, R. Romani (r1920)
(12/93) (NIMB) Ⓓ **NI7851**
1. A. Galli-Curci, orch, Rosario Bourdon (r1923)
(8/94) (ROMO) Ⓓ [2] **81004-2**

Natoma– opera: 3 acts (1911—Philadelphia) (Lib. J D Redding)
I list the trill C. White, orch (r c1913)
(IRCC) Ⓓ **IRCC-CD810**

Naughty Marietta– operetta (1910—New York) (Lib. Young)
EXCERPTS: 1. Tramp! Tramp! Tramp; 2. Ah! sweet mystery of life (Song of the fountain); 3. It can never, never can be love; 4. If I were anybody else but me; 5. 'Neath a Southern moon; 6. Zing, Zing (Italian Street Song); 7. Turna like dat-a, Pierrette (Dance of the marionettes); 8. You may a marionette; 9. New Orleans, jeunesse Dorée; 10. The loves of New Orleans; 11. The sweet by-and-by; 12. Live for today; 13. It's pretty soft for Simon; 14. I'm falling in with some one.
I'm falling in love with someone R. Crooks, orch (r1929)
(9/93) (CLAR) Ⓓ **CDGSE78-50-50**
1. P. Morrison, Chandos Concert Orch, S. Barry
(6/85) (CHAN) Ⓓ **CHAN8362**
(6/85) (CHAN) ⊟ **LBTD013**
2. M. Lanza, orch, R. Sinatra
(RCA) Ⓓ **GD60720**
(RCA) ⊟ **GK60720**
2. R. Crooks, orch (r1928)
(PEAR) Ⓓ **GEMMCD9093**
2. J. Peerce, Philh, A. Fistoulari (r1950)
(4/92) (EMI) Ⓓ [7] **CHS7 69741-2(2)**
2, 6. B. Hendricks, Ambrosian Sngrs, Philh, L. Foster (r1992) (8/93) (EMI) Ⓓ **CDC7 54626-2**
6. L.I. Marsh, orch (r1911)
(IRCC) Ⓓ **IRCC-CD810**
6, 10. E. Steber, orch, H. Barlow (bp1949)
(VAI) ▣ **VAI69102**
6, 14. Pittsburgh SO, L. Maazel (r1991: arr H Sanford) (SONY) Ⓓ **SK52491**
13. M. Lanza, C. Callinicos (pp1958)
(RCA) Ⓓ **09026 61884-2**
(RCA) ⊟ **09026 61884-4**
14. J. Hadley, American Th Orch, P. Gemignani (r1993; orch W. D. Brohn)
(RCA) Ⓓ **09026 62681-2**
14. C. Kullman, orch, F. Hartley (r1938)
(MMOI) Ⓓ **CDMOIR429**

The **Only Girl– operetta (1914) (Lib. H. Blossom, arr. G. Trinkhaus)**
EXCERPTS—; 1. When you're away.
1. T. Ringholz, Eastman-Dryden Orch, D. Hunsberger (arr G. Trinkhaus)
(ARAB) Ⓓ **Z6547**
1. Pittsburgh SO, L. Maazel (r1991: arr H Sanford) (SONY) Ⓓ **SK52491**
1. J. Hadley, American Th Orch, P. Gemignani (r1993; orch W. D. Brohn)
(RCA) Ⓓ **09026 62681-2**

Orange Blossoms– operetta (1922)
A kiss in the dark E. Steber, orch, H. Barlow (bp1951) (VAI) ▣ **VAI69102**
A kiss in the dark C. Muzio, orch (r1924)
(5/90) (BOGR) Ⓓ [2] **BIM705-2**
A kiss in the dark F. Kreisler, C. Lamson (r1924: arr Kreisler)
(9/93) (BIDD) Ⓓ [2] **LAB068/9**
A kiss in the dark C. Muzio, orch (r1924)
(1/94) (ROMO) Ⓓ [2] **81005-2**
A kiss in the dark A. Galli-Curci, orch, Rosario Bourdon (r1923)
(8/94) (ROMO) Ⓓ [2] **81004-2**

The **Princess Pat– operetta (1915—Atlantic City) (Lib. Blossom)**
EXCERPTS: 1. Neapolitan Love Song; 2. Love is the Best of All.
1. R. Tucker, Orch, H. Barlow (bp1957)
(VAI) ▣ **VAI69109**
1. J. Björling, orch, H. Barlow (bp1950)
(VAI) ▣ **VAI69101**
1. J. Björling, Orch, H. Barlow (bp1950)
(VAI) ▣ **VAI69111**
1. J. Hadley, American Th Orch, P. Gemignani (r1993; orch W. D. Brohn)
(RCA) Ⓓ **09026 62681-2**
2. E. Painter, Orig Broadway Cast (r1915)
(5/94) (PEAR) Ⓓ [3] **GEMMCDS9056/8**

The **Red Mill– operetta (1906—Buffalo) (Lib. Blossom)**
EXCERPTS—; 1. For every day is Ladies' Day for me; 2. In the isle of our dreams; 3. Whistle it; 4. Dance I want you to marry me; 5. You can never tell about a woman; 6. The Legend of the Mill; 7. Because you're you; 8. The streets of New York.
1. R. Merrill, Orch, H. Barlow (bp1957)
(VAI) ▣ **VAI69116**
1-6. Eastman-Dryden Orch, D. Hunsberger (arr O. Langley) (ARAB) Ⓓ **Z6547**
1, 8. J. Hadley, Harvard Glee Club, American Th Orch, P. Gemignani (r1993; orch W. D. Brohn)
(RCA) Ⓓ **09026 62681-2**
7. Pittsburgh SO, L. Maazel (r1991: arr H Sanford) (SONY) Ⓓ **SK52491**

The **Serenade– operetta (1897—New York) (Lyrics H B Smith)**
EXCERPTS: 1. Don Jose of Sevilla; 2. Dreaming, Dreaming.
1, 2. H. C. Barnabee, J. B. Davis, H. Fredricks, G. Frothingham, W. H. MacDonald, Broadway Cast (r1898)
(5/94) (PEAR) Ⓓ [3] **GEMMCDS9050/2(1)**

Sweethearts– operetta (1913—Baltimore) (Lib. H.B. & R.B. Smith, De Gresac)
EXCERPTS—; 1. On Parade; 2. Every lover must meet his fate; 3. Sweethearts; 4. In the convent they never taught me that; 5. The fame of love; 6. Mother Goose; 7. Angelus; 8. Pretty as a picture; 9. The cricket on the hearth; 10. Jeanette's wooden shoes.
1-10. Eastman-Dryden Orch, D. Hunsberger (arr H. Sanford) (ARAB) Ⓓ **Z6547**
2. E. Steber, orch, H. Barlow (bp1952)
(VAI) ▣ **VAI69102**
3, 7, 9. C. McDonald, Orig Broadway Cast (r1913)
(5/94) (PEAR) Ⓓ [3] **GEMMCDS9056/8**

HÉROLD, (Louis Joseph) Ferdinand *(1791–1833)* France

Le **Pré aux Clercs– opera: 3 acts (1832—Paris) (Lib. Planard, after Mérimée)**
EXCERPTS: 1. Jours de mon enfance; 2. Souvenir de jeune age.

Jours de mon enfance; Souvenirs de jeune age R. Doria, Paris Sols Orch, J. Etcheverry
(SYMP) Ⓓ **SYMCD1103**
Jours de mon enfance S. Jo, ECO, R. Bonynge (r1993) (9/94) (DECC) Ⓓ **440 679-2DH**

Zampa– opera: 3 acts (1831—Paris) (Lib. Mélesville)
Overture Philh, W. Boughton
(NIMB) Ⓓ **NI5120**
(NIMB) ▣ **NC5120**
Overture Sydney Eliz Orch, R. Bonynge
(MCEG) ◙ **VVD780**
Overture NBC SO, A. Toscanini (r1952)
(RCA) Ⓓ **GD60310**
Overture Bournemouth Municipal Orch, D. Godfrey (r1928) (BEUL) Ⓓ **1PD4**
Overture Munich RO, K. Redel
(PIER) Ⓓ **PV786104**
Pourquoi tremblez-vous? M. Battistini, orch (r1906: Ital) (2/92) (PREI) Ⓓ **89045**
Pourquoi tremblez-vous? M. Battistini, orch, C. Sabajno (Ital: r1906) (10/92) (NIMB) Ⓓ **NI7831**
(10/92) (NIMB) ▣ **NC7831**
Pourquoi tremblez-vous? M. Battistini, orch, C. Sabajno (Ital: r1906)
(10/92) (PEAR) Ⓓ **GEMMCD9936**

HERRMANN , Bernard *(1911–1975) USA*

Wuthering Heights– opera: 4 acts (1982—Portland, Oregon) (Lib. L. Fletcher, after Brontë)
Catherine Earnshaw M. Beaton
Heathcliffe D. Bell
Hindley Earnshaw J. Kitchiner
Isabella Linton P. Bowden
Edgar Linton J. Ward
Nelly Linton E. Bainbridge
Joseph M. Rippon
Mr Lockwood D. Kelly
Hareton Earnshaw M. Snashall
Elizabethan Sngrs, PAO, B. Herrmann (r1966)
(8/93) (UNIC) Ⓓ [3] **UKCD2050/2**

HEUBERGER, Richard (Franz Joseph) *(1850–1914) Austria*

Der **Opernball, 'Opera Ball'– opera (1898—Vienna)**
EXCERPTS: 1. Overture; 2. Im chambre separée.
Midnight bells G. Farrar, orch (r1927: Eng)
(IRCC) Ⓓ **IRCC-CD805**
Midnight Bells X. Wei, Pam Nicholson (arr Kreisler) (9/90) (ASV) Ⓓ **CDDCA698**
Waltz Vienna SO, R. Stolz (EURO) Ⓓ **258 667**
1. BPO, E. Kleiber (r1932) (BIDD) Ⓓ **WHL002**
1. VPO, W. Boskovsky (r1968)
(LOND) Ⓓ **436 785-2LM**
1. BPO, E. Kleiber (r1933)
(TELD) Ⓓ **4509-95513-2**
1. BPO, E. Kleiber (r1932)
(5/94) (ARCI) Ⓓ **ARC102**
2. London Salon Ens (arr salon orch)
(MERI) Ⓓ **CDE84264**
2. J. Kolomyjec, M. DuBois, Kitchener-Waterloo SO, R. Armenian (CBC) Ⓓ **SMCD5126**
2. E. Schwarzkopf, Philh, O. Ackermann (r1957)
(EMI) Ⓓ **CDM5 65577-2**
2. E. Schumann, orch, W. Goehr (r1938)
(ROMO) Ⓓ **81019-2**
2. E. Schwarzkopf, Philh, O. Ackermann
(1/86) (EMI) Ⓓ **CDC7 47284-2**
2. R. Tauber, Odeon Künstlerorchester, F. Weissmann (r1931)
(12/89) (EMI) Ⓓ **CDH7 69787-2**
2. Raphaele Concert Orch, P. Walden (arr Waldenmaier) (5/91) (MOZA) Ⓓ **MECD1002**
2. H.E. Groh, orch (r1936)
(3/92) (PEAR) Ⓓ **GEMMCD9419**
2. F. Kreisler, C. Lamson (r1923: arr Kreisler)
(9/93) (BIDD) Ⓓ [2] **LAB068/9**
2. F. Kreisler, M. Raucheisen (r1930: arr Kreisler) (12/93) (EMI) Ⓓ **CDH7 64701-2**
2. J. Migenes, Vienna Volksoper Orch, L. Schifrin (r1993)
(1/94) (ERAT) Ⓓ **4509-92875-2**
(1/94) (ERAT) ▣ **4509-92875-4**
2. B. Hendricks, G. Quilico, Lyon Op Orch, L. Foster (r1993) (6/95) (EMI) Ⓓ **CDC5 55151-2**

HIDALGO, Juan *(1612/16–1685) Spain*

Celos aun del aire matan– opera: 3 acts (1660—Madrid) (Lib. Calderón)
EXCERPTS: 1. Noble en Tinacria naciste (jácara); 2. A to dos miro (recit).
1, 2. Newberry Consort, M. Springfels
(7/92) (HARM) Ⓓ **HMU90 7022**

La **Estatua de Prometeo– zarzuela (1672—Madrid) (Lib. Calderón)**
1. Tonante Dios!.
1. Romanesca (r1991-2)
(11/94) (GLOS) Ⓓ **GCD920201**

Los celos hacen estrellas– zarzuela (1672—Madrid) (performed for the birthday of Queen Mariana)
EXCERPTS: 1. De los ceños del diciembre; 2. Como ha de saber Belilla?; 3. De los luces que en el mar; 4. La noche tenebrosa; 5. Trompi cábalas amor; 6. Trom picávalas amor; 7. Peynándose estaba un olmo.
1-5. Newberry Consort, M. Springfels
(7/92) (HARM) Ⓓ **HMU90 7022**
3, 7. Romanesca (r1991-2)
(11/94) (GLOS) Ⓓ **GCD920201**

El **templo de Palas– zarzuela (1675—Madrid) (Lib Avellaneda)**
EXCERPTS: 1. Ay que si, ay que no.
1. Newberry Consort, M. Springfels
(7/92) (HARM) Ⓓ **HMU90 7022**
1. Romanesca (r1991-2)
(11/94) (GLOS) Ⓓ **GCD920201**

HINDEMITH, Paul *(1895–1963) Germany*

Cardillac– opera: 3 acts, Op. 39 (1926) (Lib. F. Lion, after Hoffmann)
Cardillac S. Nimsgern
Cardillac's daughter V. Schweizer
Officer R. Schunk
Gold Merchant H. Stamm
Cavalier J. Protschka
Lady G. Schnaut
Chief of Military Police A. Schmidt
Berlin Rad Chbr Ch, Berlin RSO, G. Albrecht
(7/89) (WERG) Ⓓ [2] **WER60148/9-50**
Cardillac D. Fischer-Dieskau
Cardillac's daughter L. Kirschstein
Officer D. Grobe
Gold Merchant K.C. Kohn
Cavalier E. Katz
Lady E. Söderström
Chief of Military Police W. Nett
Cologne Rad Chor, Cologne RSO, J. Keilberth (1926 vers)
(12/91) (DG) Ⓓ [2] **431 741-2GC2**

Mathis der Maler– opera: 7 scenes (1938—Zurich) (Lib. cpsr)
Mathis R. Hermann
Albrecht J. Protschka
Lorenz von Pommersfelden V. von Halem
Capito H. Winkler
Riedinger H. Stamm
Schwalb H. Kruse
Truchsess von Waldburg U. Hielscher
Sylvester von Schaumberg U. Ress
Ursula S. Hass
Regina G. Rossmanith
Countess Helfenstein M. Schmiege
N German Rad Chor, Cologne Rad Chor, Cologne RSO, G. Albrecht (r1990)
(9/94) (WERG) Ⓓ [3] **WER6255-2**
Mathis D. Fischer-Dieskau
Albrecht J. King
Lorenz von Pommersfelden G. Feldhoff
Capito M. Schmidt
Riedinger P. Meven
Schwalb W. Cochran
Truchsess von Waldburg A. Malta
Sylvester von Schaumberg D. Grobe
Ursula R. Wagemann
Regina U. Koszut
Countess Helfenstein T. Schmidt
Bavarian Rad Chor, BRSO, R. Kubelík (r1977)
(7/95) (EMI) Ⓓ [3] **CDS5 55237-2**
Auf denn zum letzten Stück des Weges D. Fischer-Dieskau, BRSO, R. Kubelík (r1977)
(EMI) Ⓓ [2] **CMS5 65621-2**
Excs D. Fischer-Dieskau, P. Lorengar, D. Grobe, Berlin RSO, L. Ludwig
(12/91) (DG) Ⓓ [2] **431 741-2GC2**

Mörder, Hoffnung der Frauen– opera: 1 act, Op. 12 (1919) (Lib. O. Kokoschka)
Man F. Grundheber
Woman G. Schnaut
Soldier I W. Gahmlich
Soldier II V. von Halem
Soldier III B-O. Magnusson
Maiden I L. Peacock
Maiden II G. Schreckenbach
Maiden III B. Haldas
Berlin RIAS Chbr Ch, Berlin RSO, G. Albrecht
(2/89) (WERG) Ⓓ **WER60132-50**

Neues vom Tage– opera: 3 parts (1929—Berlin) (Lib. M. Schiffer)
EXCERPTS: 1a. Overture; 1b. Overture (concert version: 1930).
Laura E. Werres
Eduard C. Nicolai
Herr Hermann R. Pries
Herr M H. Hiestermann
Frau M M. Borst
Hotel manager O.G. de Gracia
Registrar A. Sandner
1st Manager; Head waiter C. Antunes
2nd Manager W. Geuer
3rd Manager T. Donecker
4th Manager; Tourist guide C. Scheeben
5th Manager D. Gillessen
6th Manager H. Feckler
Chamber maid S. Bitter
Cologne Pro Musica, Cologne RSO, J. Latham-König
(WERG) Ⓓ [2] **WER6192-2**
1b Cologne RSO, O. Maga
(THOR) Ⓓ **CTH2044**
1b Melbourne SO, W.A. Albert (r1991)
(CPO) Ⓓ **CPO999 007-2**
1b Bamberg SO, K.A. Rickenbacher (r1989)
(VIRG) Ⓓ **CUV5 61201-2**
1b BBC PO, Y. P. Tortelier
(10/92) (CHAN) Ⓓ **CHAN9060**

Das **Nusch-Nuschi– play for Burmese marionettes: 1 act, Op. 20 (1920) (Lib. F. Blei)**
Mung Tha Bya; Bettler; Herald I; Writer II H. Stamm
Ragweng M. Schumacher
Field-Marshall Kyce-Waing; Master of Ceremonies V. von Halem
Henker J. Becker
Susulu D. Knutson
Tum Tum W. Gahmlich
Kamadewa; Writer I P. Maus
Herald II A. Ramirez
Bangsa; Maiden I V. Schweizer
Osasa C. Lindsley
Twaise; Maiden II G. Schreckenbach
Ratasata; Maiden III G. Sieber
Bajadere I G. Resick
Bajadere II G. Pohl
Training monkey I W. Marschall
Training monkey II M. Kleber
Berlin RSO, G. Albrecht
(7/89) (WERG) Ⓓ **WER60146-50**

Sancta Susanna– opera: 1 act, Op. 21 (1921) (Lib. Stramm)
Susanna H. Donath
Klementia G. Schnaut
Old Nun G. Schreckenbach
Berlin RIAS Chbr Ch, Berlin RSO, G. Albrecht (r1984)
(2/89) (WERG) Ⓓ **WER60106-50**

HOLBROOKE, Joseph *(1878–1958) England*

Bronwen– opera, Op. 75 (1929—Huddersfield) (Lib. H. de Walden)
EXCERPTS: 1. Overture. ACT 1: 2. Bran's answer; 3. The Bard's song. ACT 2: 4. Cradle song. ACT 3: 5. Taliessin's song; 6. Funeral march.
1. Bratislava RSO, A. Leaper (r1992)
(11/93) (MARC) Ⓓ **8 223446**
1-6. D. Vane, J. Coates, SO, C. Powell (r1929)
(4/93) (SYMP) Ⓓ **SYMCD1130**

The **Children of Don– drama, Op. 56 (1911—London) (Lib H. de Walden)**
EXCERPTS: 1. Overture; 2. Noden's song.
1. Ukraine National SO, A. Penny (r1994)
(MARC) Ⓓ **8 223721**

1. orch, A. Hammond (r1937)
(4/93) (SYMP) Ⓓ **SYMCD1130**
2. N. Walker, orch, C. Raybould (r1937)
(4/93) (SYMP) Ⓓ **SYMCD1130**

Dylan– drama, Op. 53 (1914—London) (Lib. H. de Walden)
EXCERPTS: 1. Overture; 2. The Sea King's song; 3. Prelude.
1. orch, C. Raybould (r1937)
(4/93) (SYMP) Ⓓ **SYMCD1130**
2. N. Walker, orch, J. Holbrooke (r1937)
(4/93) (SYMP) Ⓓ **SYMCD1130**
3. Ukraine National SO, A. Penny (r1994)
(MARC) Ⓓ **8 223721**

The **Enchanter– opera, Op. 70 (1915)**
EXCERPTS: 2. Dance.
2. J. Holbrooke (trans pf: cpsr: r1930)
(4/93) (SYMP) Ⓓ **SYMCD1130**

HOLDRIDGE, Lee *(b 1944) USA*

Lazarus and His Beloved– concert suite from opera (1974)
LSO, L. Holdridge (r1980) (BAY) Ⓓ **BCD-1025**
LSO, L. Holdridge (r1980) (KLVI) Ⓓ **CTD88104**

HOLLAND, Jan David *(1746–1827) Germany/Poland*

Agatha, or The Host's Arrival– opera: 3 acts (1784—Nieświez) (Lib. M. Radziwiłł)
1. Overture.
1. Warsaw CO, M. Sewen (OLYM) Ⓓ **OCD382**

HOLLIGER, Heinz *(b 1939) Switzerland*

Der **magische Tänzer– 1963-65 (Lib. N Sachs)**
Marina E. Gilhofer
David H. Riediker
Neighbour D. Dorow
Magic dancer P. Langridge
Stuttgart Schola Cantorum, Basle Th Ch, Basle SO, H. Zender (r1970)
(10/94) (DG) Ⓓ **445 251-2GC**

HOLST, Gustav(us Theodore von) *(1874–1934) England*

H—numbers used in I. Holst Thematic Catalogue (1972)

At the Boar's Head– opera: 1 act, Op. 156 (Op. 42) (1925—Manchester) (Lib. after Shakespeare's 'Henry IV')
Prince Hal P. Langridge
Falstaff J. Tomlinson
Mistress Quickly E. Ross
Doll Tearsheet F. Palmer
Pistol D. Wilson-Johnson
Peto P. Hall
Bardolph R. Suart
Poins M. George
Liverpool Phil Ch, RLPO, D. Atherton (r1981)
(EMI) Ⓓ **CDM5 65127-2**

The **Perfect Fool– opera: 1 act, H150 (Op. 39) (1923—London) (Wds. cpsr, after Shakespeare)**
EXCERPTS: 1. Ballet Music.
1. Philh, W. Boughton (NIMB) Ⓓ **NI5117**
(NIMB) ▭ **NC5117**
1. LPO, A. Boult (DECC) Ⓓ **433 620-2DSP**
1. Philh, W. Boughton (r1988)
(NIMB) Ⓓ [4] **NI5450/3**
1. RLPO, C. Mackerras (r1988)
(VIRG) Ⓓ **CUV5 61257-2**
1. LPO, A. Boult (r1961)
(DECC) Ⓓ [2] **444 549-2DF2**
1. Black Dyke Mills Band, P. Parkes (arr brass band: Parkes) (9/93) (CHAN) Ⓓ **CHAN4507**
(9/93) (CHAN) ▭ **BBTD4507**
1. LPO, A. Boult (r1961)
(4/94) (DECC) Ⓓ **440 318-2DWO**
(4/94) (DECC) ▭ **440 318-4DWO**
1. ECO, Y. Menuhin (r1993)
(12/94) (EMIN) Ⓓ **CD-EMX2227**
(12/94) (EMIN) ▭ **TC-EMX2227**

1. LPO, M. Sargent (r1946)
(7/95) (BEUL) Ⓓ **1PD13**

Sāvitri– opera di camera: 1 act, H96 (Op. 25) (1916—London) (Lib. cpsr)
Sāvitri F. Palmer
Satyavān P. Langridge
Death S. Varcoe
Richard Hickox Sngrs, CLS, R. Hickox (r1983)
(2/88) (HYPE) Ⓓ **CDA66099**

Sita– opera: 3 acts, H89 (Op. 23) (1900-06) (Lib. cpsr)
EXCERPTS: ACT 3: 1. Interlude; 2. Closing scene.
1. L. McAslan, A. Baillie, LPO, LSO, D. Atherton (ed C Matthews) (6/93) (LYRI) Ⓓ **SRCD209**

The **Wandering Scholar– chamber orchestra: 1 act, H176 (Op. 50) (1934—Liverpool) (Lib. C Bax, after H Waddell)**
Louis M. Rippon
Alison N. Burrowes
Father Philippe M. Langdon
Pierre R. Tear
ECO, S. Bedford (r1974)
(EMI) Ⓓ **CDM5 65127-2**

HONEGGER, Arthur *(1892–1955) France/Switzerland*

H—Numbers from Halbreich's chronological catalogue

Les **aventures du roi Pausole– operetta: 3 acts (1930—Paris) (Lib. A. Willemetz, after Louÿs)**
Overture; Ballet Odeon Grand Orch, A. Honegger (r1930) (4/94) (MUSI) Ⓓ **MACD-767**

HÖPKEN, Arvid Niclas von *(1710–1778) Sweden*

Catone in Utica– opera (1753) (Lib. Metastasio)
EXCERPTS—; 1. Sinfonia in D.
1. Swedish Nat Museum CO, C. Génetay
(MSVE) Ⓓ **MSCD412**

HOSCHNA, Karl *(1877–1911) USA*

Madame Sherry– operetta (1910—New York) (Lib. Hauerbach)
Ev'ry little movement L. Tetrazzini, T. Amici (Fr: r1922)
(9/92) (EMI) Ⓓ [3] **CHS7 63802-2(2)**
Je ne sais comment L. Tetrazzini, orch (r1922)
(9/92) (PEAR) Ⓓ **GEMMCD9225**

HUBAY, Jenö *(1858–1937) Hungary*

The **Cremona lutenist– opera: 2 acts, Op. 40 (1894—Budapest) (Lib. F. Coppée & H. Beauclair)**
Intermezzo J. Hubay, O. Herz (r1928)
(12/91) (BIDD) Ⓓ **LAB045**

HUMPERDINCK, Engelbert *(1854–1921) Germany*

Dornröschen– opera: 3 acts (1902—Frankfurt am Main) (Lib. E. Ebeling & B. Filhès, after Perrault)
EXCERPTS—; 1. Introduction; 2. Ballade; 3. Irrfahrten; 4. Das Dornenschloss; 5. Festklänge.
1-5. Bratislava RSO, M. Fischer-Dieskau
(MARC) Ⓓ **8 223369**
1-5. Bamberg SO, K.A. Rickenbacher (r1990)
(11/94) (VIRG) Ⓓ **CUV5 61128-2**

Hänsel und Gretel– opera: 3 acts (1893—Weimar) (Lib. Wette)
EXCERPTS: ACT 1: 1. Prelude; 2a. Suse, liebe, Suse; 2b. Brüderchen, komm, tanz' mit mir (Dance Duet); 3. Hallo! Himmel, die Mutter; 4a. Rallalala, rallalala; 4b. Ach, wir armen, armen Leute. ACT 2: 5. Hexenritt (Witch's Ride); 6. Ein Männlein steht im Walde; 7a. Der kleine Sandmann bin ich; 7b. Abends will ich schlafen gehn (Evening Hymn); 8. Dream Pantomime. ACT 3: 9. Prelude; 10a. Der kleine Taumann heiss ich; 10b. Wo bin ich? Wach ich? Ist es ein Traum?; 11. Bleib' stehn! Bleib' stehn!; 12. Knusper, knusper Knäuschen; 13. Erlöst, befreit!; 14a. Vater! Mutter!; 14b. Kinder schaut das Wunder an.
Hänsel A. Moffo
Gretel H. Donath
Father D. Fischer-Dieskau
Mother C. Berthold
Sandman A. Auger
Dew Fairy L. Popp
Witch C. Ludwig
Tolz Boys' Ch, Munich RSO, K. Eichhorn (r1971)
(EURO) Ⓓ [2] **GD69294**
Hänsel A. Moffo
Gretel H. Donath
Father D. Fischer-Dieskau
Mother C. Berthold
Sandman A. Auger
Dew Fairy L. Popp
Witch C. Ludwig
Tolz Boys' Ch, Munich RO, K. Eichhorn (r1971)
(RCA) Ⓓ [2] **74321 25281-2**
Hänsel M-L. Schilp
Gretel E. Berger
Mother E. Waldenau
Father H. Heinz Nissen
Sandman H. Erdmann
Dew Fairy G. Walker
Witch M. Arndt-Ober
Berlin Deutsche Op Chor, Berlin RSO, A. Rother (bp1944)
(PREI) Ⓓ [2] **90209**
Hänsel I. Seefried
Gretel A. Rothenberger
Mother G. Hoffman
Father W. Berry
Sandman; Dew Fairy L. Maikl
Witch E. Höngen
Vienna Boys' Ch, VPO, A. Cluytens (r1963)
(EMI) Ⓓ [2] **CMS5 65661-2**
Hänsel E. Grümmer
Gretel E. Schwarzkopf
Mother M. von Ilosvay
Father J. Metternich
Sandman; Dew Fairy A. Felbermayer
Witch E. Schürhoff
Loughton High School for Girls Ch, Bancroft's School Chor, Philh, H. von Karajan (r1953)
(4/88) (EMI) Ⓓ [2] **CMS7 69293-2**
Hänsel F. von Stade
Gretel I. Cotrubas
Mother C. Ludwig
Father S. Nimsgern
Sandman K. Te Kanawa
Dew Fairy R. Welting
Witch E. Söderström
Cologne Op Children's Ch, Cologne Gürzenich Orch, J. Pritchard
(11/88) (CBS) Ⓓ [2] **CD79217**
Hänsel A.S. von Otter
Gretel B. Bonney
Mother H. Schwarz
Father A. Schmidt
Sandman B. Hendricks
Dew Fairy E. Lind
Witch M. Lipovšek
Tolz Boys' Ch, BRSO, J. Tate
(11/90) (EMI) Ⓓ [2] **CDS7 54022-2**
Hänsel A. Murray
Gretel E. Gruberová
Mother G. Jones
Father F. Grundheber
Sandman B. Bonney
Dew Fairy C. Oelze
Witch C. Ludwig
Staatskapelle Dresden, Colin Davis (r1992)
(10/93) (PHIL) Ⓓ [2] **438 013-2PH2**
Hänsel J. Larmore
Gretel R. Ziesak
Mother H. Behrens
Father B. Weikl
Sandman R. Joshua
Dew Fairy C. Schäfer
Witch H. Schwarz
Tolz Boys' Ch, BRSO, D. Runnicles (r1994)
(1/95) (TELD) Ⓓ [2] **4509-94549-2**
Excs Cölln Salon Orch (arr. Artok)
(EMI) Ⓓ **CDC7 49819-2**
1. NYPSO, W. Mengelberg (r1930)
(PEAR) Ⓓ **GEMMCD9474**
1. T. Murray (arr org: Lemare)
(PRIO) Ⓓ **PRCD338**
1. NBC SO, A. Toscanini (r1952)
(RCA) Ⓓ **GD60310**
1. BPO, H. von Karajan
(EMI) Ⓓ **CDM7 64629-2**

1. LSO, A. Coates (r1926) (4/93) (KOCH) ① [2] 37704-2
1. Bamberg SO, K.A. Rickenbacher (r1990) (11/94) (VIRG) ① CUV5 61128-2
1. BBC SO, A. Boult (r1932) (2/95) (BEUL) ① 1PD12
1, 2a, 2b, 4a, 6, 7a, 7b, 8, 10a, 10b, 11-13, 14b F. Grundheber, G. Jones, A. Murray, E. Gruberová, C. Ludwig, B. Bonney, C. Oelze, Dresden St Op Chor, Staatskapelle Dresden, Colin Davis (r1992) (PHIL) ① 442 435-2PH
2a, 2b E. Schwarzkopf, I. Seefried, Philh, J. Krips (r1947) (3/89) (EMI) ① CDH7 69793-2
2a, 2b C. Supervia, I.M. Ferraris, orch, A. Albergoni (r1928: Ital) (9/90) (CLUB) ① CL99-074
2a, 2b C. Supervia, I.M. Ferraris, orch, A. Albergoni (Ital: r1928) (9/90) (PREI) ① 89023
2a, 2b, 3, 6, 7a, 7b, 8, 10b, 11-13. A.S. von Otter, B. Bonney, M. Lipovšek, H. Schwarz, A. Schmidt, B. Hendricks, Tolz Boys' Ch, BRSO, J. Tate (EMI) ① CDC7 54327-2
2b Manchester Children's Ch, Hallé, H. Harty (r1929: Eng) (BEUL) ① 1PD4
2b C. Supervia, I.M. Ferraris, orch, A. Albergoni (r1928: Ital) (4/94) (EMI) ① [3] CHS7 64864-2(1)
4a G. Hüsch, Berlin St Op Orch, H.U. Müller (r1937) (10/93) (NIMB) ① NI7848
4a G. Hüsch, Berlin St Op Orch, H.U. Müller (r1936) (3/94) (PREI) ① 89071
7a K. Te Kanawa, Cologne Gürzenich Orch, J. Pritchard (CBS) ① CD39208
7a, 7b G. Groves, J. Watson, J. Partridge (r1994) (ASV) ① CDWHL2088
7b Vienna Boys' Ch, U. Harrer, H. Deutsch (KOCH) ① 321 214
7b S. Van Dyck, T. Huffman, A. Piccolo (NEWP) ① NPD85514
7b K. Battle, F. von Stade, St Luke's Orch, A. Previn (pp1991) (SONY) SLV48361 (SONY) SHV48361
7b Luboff Ch, New SO, L. Stokowski (r1962; arr Luboff & Stott) (RCA) ① 09026 61867-2
7b L. Popp, B. Fassbaender, VPO, G. Solti (r1978) (DECC) ① 443 335-2LRX (DECC) 443 335-4LRX
7b Hollywood Bowl SO, C. Dragon (r1958) (CFP) ① CD-CFP4660 (CFP) TC-CFP4660
7b K. Battle, F. von Stade, Orch, A. Previn (pp1991) (12/92) (SONY) ① SK48235 (12/92) (SONY) ST48235
7b Fine Arts Brass Ens, M. Shepherd, P. Spicer (r1992; arr Roberts) (12/93) (BIRM) ① BBCCD2
8. RCA Victor Orch, F. Reiner (r1950) (8/94) (RCA) ① 09026 61792-2
10b E. Schwarzkopf, E. Grümmer, Philh, H. von Karajan (r1953) (12/90) (EMI) ① CDM7 63657-2

Die **Königskinder– melodrama: 3 acts (1897—Munich) (Lib. E. Rosmer)**
EXCERPTS—; 1. Hellafest, Kinderreigen; 2. Introduction, Act 3.

King's Son	A. Dallapozza
Goose-Girl	H. Donath
Minstrel	H. Prey
Witch	H. Schwarz
Woodcutter	K. Ridderbusch
Broom-maker	G. Unger
Broom-maker's Daughter	B. Lindner
Landlord	G. Wewel
Landlord's Daughter	H. Ankersen
Tailor	F. Lenz
Stable Maid	O. Wenkel
Leader of the Councillors	T. Nicolai

Tolz Boys' Ch, Bavarian Rad Chor, Munich RO, H. Wallberg (8/89) (EMI) ① [3] CMS7 69936-2
Verdorben, gestorben G. Hüsch, Berlin St Op Orch, H.U. Müller (r1936) (3/94) (PREI) ① 89071
Verdorben! Gestorben! T. Hampson, Pestalozzi Children's Ch, Munich RO, F. Luisi (r1994) (9/95) (EMI) ① CDC5 55233-2
Weisst noch das grosse Nest; Lieber Spielmann G. Farrar, orch (r1912) (IRCC) ① IRCC-CD805
1, 2. Bamberg SO, K.A. Rickenbacher (r1990) (11/94) (VIRG) ① CUV5 61128-2

Die **Marketenderin– comic opera: 2 acts (1914—Cologne) (Lib. R. Misch)**
EXCERPTS: 1. Prelude.
1. Bratislava RSO, M. Fischer-Dieskau (MARC) ① 8 223369

ISOUARD, Nicolas *(1775–1818) France*

Joconde– opera: 3 acts (1814—Paris) (Lib. Etienne)
Dans un délire extrême M-N. Bouvet, anon (r1903) (9/91) (SYMP) ① SYMCD1089

IVANOV, Mikhail Mikhaylovich *(1849–1927) Russia*

Zabava Putyatishna– opera
Solovej Budomirovich's serenade L. Sobinov, anon (r1901) (6/93) (PEAR) ① [3] GEMMCDS9997/9(1)

JACOBI, Victor *(1883–1921) Hungary*

Sybil– operetta (1914—Budapest) (Lib. Bródy and Martos)
The Colonel of the Crimson Hussars M. Hill Smith, Ambrosian Sngrs, Chandos Concert Orch, S. Barry (7/88) (CHAN) ① CHAN8561 (7/88) (CHAN) LBTD019

JAMES, Joseph *(20th Cent) UK?*

The **Scarlet Letter– opera (Based on the Romance by Nathanial Hawthorne)**
1. The Prison Door; 2. The Interview; 3. Pearl; 4. The Governor's Hall; 5. The Elf-Child and the Minister; 6. The Leech and his patient; 7. The Meteor; 8. A Forest Walk; 9. A flood of sunshine; 10. Chorus - Adorn thyself with me!; 11. Conclusion - Be true!.
1-11. V. Tierney, D.M. Anderson, Philh, A. Greenwood (10/92) (NOVL) Novelbond1

JANÁČEK, Leoš *(1854–1928) Moravia*

The **Cunning Little Vixen– opera: 3 acts (1924—Brno) (Lib. cpsr, after R. Těsnohlídek)**

Vixen	L. Popp
Fox	E. Randová
Dog	L. Márová
Cock	G. Jahn
Hen; Woodpecker; Innkeeper's Wife	I. Mixová
Badger; Parson	R. Novák
Owl; Forester's Wife	E. Zikmundová
Forester	D. Jedlička
Schoolmaster	V. Krejčík
Innkeeper	B. Blachut
Harašta	V. Zítek

Bratislava Children's Ch, Vienna St Op Chor, VPO, C. MacKerras (11/86) (DECC) ① [2] 417 129-2DH2

Vixen	L. Watson
Fox	D. Montague
Dog	K. Shelby
Cock	M. King
Hen	G. Groves
Badger; Parson	G. Howell
Owl; Forester's Wife	G. Knight
Woodpecker	P. Purcell
Forester	T. Allen
Schoolmaster	R. Tear
Innkeeper	J. Dobson
Innkeeper's Wife	E. Bainbridge
Harašta	N. Folwell

ROH Chor, ROHO, S. Rattle (Eng) (3/92) (EMI) ① [2] CDS7 54212-2

Vixen	M. Hajóssyová
Fox	G. Beňačková
Dog	I. Mixová
Cock; Jay	L. Domanínská
Hen	B. Effenberková
Badger; Parson	K. Průša
Owl; Forester's Wife	H. Buldrová
Woodpecker	M. Mrázová
Foreseter	R. Novák
Schollmaster; Gnat	M. Frydlewicz
Innkeeper	K. Hanuš
Innkeeper's Wife	D. Tikalová
Harašta	J. Souček

Kühn Children's Chor, Czech Phil Chor, Czech PO, V. Neumann (r1979/80) (4/93) (SUPR) ① [2] 10 3471-2
My name is Goldskin M. Hajóssyová, G. Beňačková, Czech PO, V. Neumann (r1979-80) (KOCH) ① 34036-2 (KOCH) 24036-4
Suite Czech PO, F. Jílek (11/85) (SUPR) ① C37-7303
Suite Czech PO, J. Bělohlávek (11/92) (CHAN) ① CHAN9080
Suite Czech PO, V. Talich (r1954; arr Talich) (1/94) (SUPR) ① 11 1905-2

Cunning Little Vixen– concert suite from opera
Prague SO, P. Altrichter (r1992) (SUPR) ① 11 1810-2
Leningrad PO, G. Rozhdestvensky (r1976) (RCA) ① 74321 29251-2
VPO, C. MacKerras (arr. Talich) (11/86) (DECC) ① [2] 417 129-2DH2

The **Excursions of Mr Brouček to the Moon and to the 15th Century– opera: 4 acts (1920—Prague) (Lib. V Dyk & F S Procházka)**

Brouček	L. Fehenberger
Mazal, Azurean, Peter	F. Wunderlich
Sexton, Lunigrove, Domšík	K. Böhme
Málinka, Etherea, Kunka	W. Lipp
Würfl, Wonderglitter, Councillor	K. Engen
Apprentice-waiter, Child-prodigy, Student	A. Fahberg
Housewife, Kedruta	L. Benningsen
Poet, Miroslav	P. Kuen
Cloudy, Voice, Vacek	K. Ostertag

Bavarian St Orch, Bavarian St Op Chor, J. Keilberth (pp1959) (2/95) (ORFE) ① [2] C354942I

Brouček	V. Přibyl
Mazal, Azurean, Peter	M. Švejda
Sexton, Lunigrove, Domšík	Bohumil Maršík
Málinka, Etherea, Kunka	J. Jonášová
Würfl, Wonderglitter, Councillor	R. Novák
Apprentice-waiter, Child-prodigy, Student	J. Marková
Housewife, Kedruta	L. Márová
Rainbowglory, Voice, Vojta	V. Krejčík
Cloudy, Voice, Vacek	J. Souček
Poet, Miroslav	J. Olejníček
Apparition	R. Tuček
1st Taborite	K. Hanuš

Czech Phil Chor, Czech PO, F. Jílek (r1980) (2/95) (SUPR) ① [2] 11 2153-2
Postlude to Part 1. M. Kopp, A. Barová, J. Janská, V. Doležal, Y. Tannenbergerova, M. Ungrová, Brno St PO, L. Svárovský (r1994) (3/95) (SUPR) ① 11 1878-2

Fate (Osud)– opera: 3 acts, Brno Radio (1934) (Lib. F. Bartošová and cpsr)

Živný	V. Přibyl
Mila Valková	M. Hajóssyová
Mila's Mother	J. Palivcová
Dr Suda	V. Krejčík
Student	J. Holešovský
First Lady	J. Pokorná
Second Lady	J. Krátká
Old Slovak Woman	D. Suryová
Major's wife	Z. Kareninová
Lhotský	R. Novák
Konečný	F. Caban
Hrázda	J. Olejníček
Miss Stuhlá	M. Steinerová
Miss Pacovská	M. Polášková
Verva	J. Souček
First Guest	A. Jurečka
Second Guest	J. Doubek
Waiter	B. Kurfürst
Kosinská	A. Barová
Součková	J. Janská
Fanča	J. Hladíková
Doubek	J. Škrobánek
Young Doubek	M. Jílková

Brno Janáček Op Chor, Brno Janáček Op Orch, F. Jílek (r1975-76) (SUPR) ① SU0045-2

Mila Valková	H. Field
Živný	P. Langridge
Mila's mother	K. Harries
Poet; Student; Hrazda	P. Bronder
Dr. Suda	S. Kale
First lady; Kosinská	C. Teare
Second Lady	E. Gaskell
Old Slovak woman	D. Hood
Major's wife	Mary Davies
Councillor's wife	G. Keeble

Lhotský; Verva B. Mora
Konrčný M. Holland
Miss Stuhlá C. Bell
Miss Pacovská R. Moseley-Morgan
First guest; First young gentleman G. Rhys-Davies
Second guest; Second young gentleman P. Lloyd-Evans
Walter R. Mason
Engineer T. German
Young widow F. Manning
Fanča C. Edwards
Young Doubek S. Linay
Součková Y. Jones
Doubek M. Preston-Roberts
WNO Chor, WNO Orch, C. Mackerras (Eng)
(9/90) (EMI) Ⓓ **CDC7 49993-2**
Suite Czech PO, F. Jílek
(11/85) (SUPR) Ⓓ **C37-7303**

From the House of the Dead– opera: 3 acts, Brno (1930) (Lib. cpsr, after F. Dostoyevsky)
Goryanchikov N. Ghiaurov
Alyeya E. Szmytka
Luka B. McCauley
Tall Prisoner B. Nikolov
Short Prisoner R. Novák
Commandant H. Peeters
Old Prisoner J. Veverka
Skuratov P. Langridge
Chekunov P. Kamas
Don Juan R. Haan
Wench C. Young
Kedril A. Oliver
Shapkin H. Zednik
Shishkov M. Pederson
Cherevin M. Kopp
Voice A. Rost
Vienna St Op Chor, VPO, C. Abbado, K.M. Grüber (pp)
(10/95) (DG) ▣ **072 139-3GH**
Goryanchikov D. Jedlička
Alyeya J. Janská
Luka J. Zahradníček
Tall Prisoner V. Krejčík
Short Prisoner R. Novák
Commandant A. Švorc
Old Prisoner B. Blachut
Skuratov I. Žídek
Chekunov; Don Juan J. Souček
Wench E. Zikmundová
Kedril; Shapkin Z. Soušek
Shishkov V. Zítek
Cherevin; Voice Z. Švehla
Vienna St Op Chor, VPO, C. Mackerras
(10/91) (DECC) Ⓓ [2] **430 375-2DH2**
Goryanchikov R. Novák
Alyeya M. Jirglová
Luka V. Přibyl
Tall Prisoner J. Stříška
Short Prisoner K. Berman
Commandant J. Horáček
Old Prisoner B. Blachut
Skuratov I. Žídek
Chekunov J. Jindrák
Don Juan K. Průša
Wench A. Míková
Kedril; Shapkin M. Karpíšek
Shishkov J. Souček
Cherevin V. Kočí
Voice M. Švejda
Czech Phil Chor, Czech PO, V. Neumann (r1979)
(9/94) (SUPR) Ⓓ [2] **10 2941-2**
Prelude Philh, L. Pešek
(6/92) (VIRG) Ⓓ **VC7 59076-2**
Suite Czech PO, F. Jílek
(11/85) (SUPR) Ⓓ **C37-7303**
Wretched creature! I. Žídek, B. Blachut, J. Horáček, K. Berman, Czech Phil Chor, Czech PO, V. Neumann (r1979) (KOCH) Ⓓ **34036-2**
(KOCH) ▭ **24036-4**

Jenufa– opera: 3 acts (1904—Brno) (Lib. cpsr, after G. Preissová)
Jenufa R. Alexander
Laca P. Langridge
Kostelnička A. Silja
Števa M. Baker
Karolka A. Hagley
Grandmother Buryja M. Davies
Stárek R. Poulton
Mayor G. Sandison
Mayor's Wife L. Ormiston
Pastuchyňa H. Cannell
Tetka D. Cowley
Barena S. Pring
Jano L. Davies
Glyndebourne Fest Chor, LPO, A. Davis, N. Lehnhoff (r1989)
(MCEG) ▣ **VVD928**
Jenufa G. Beňačková
Laca W. Ochman
Kostelnička Leonie Rysanek
Števa P. Kazaras
Karolka K. Cowdrick
Grandmother Buryja B. Schramm
Stárek K. Shaw
Mayor F. Barr
Mayor's Wife N.L. Hartliep
Pastuchyňa; Tetka M. Partamian
Barena A. Rubstein
Jano K. Johnson
NY Schola Cantorum, NY Op Orch, E. Queler (pp1988)
(BIS) Ⓓ [2] **BIS-CD449/50**
Jenufa L. Domanínská
Laca V. Přibyl
Kostelnička N. Kniplová
Števa I. Žídek
Karolka M. Boháčová
Grandmother Buryja M. Mrázová
Stárek J. Jindrák
Mayor Z. Kroupa
Mayor's Wife J. Procházková
Shepherdess E. Hlobilová
Barena B. Effenberková
Tetka A. Rousková
Prague Nat Th Chor, Prague Nat Th Orch, B. Gregor (r1969)
(EMI) Ⓓ [2] **CMS5 65476-2**
Jenufa E. Söderström
Laca W. Ochman
Kostelnička E. Randová
Števa P. Dvorský
Karolka L. Popp
Grandmother Buryja M. Mrázová
Stárek V. Zítek
Mayor D. Jedlička
Mayor's Wife I. Mixová
Pastuchyňa; Tetka V. Soukupová
Barena J. Pokorná
Jano J. Jonášová
Vienna St Op Chor, VPO, C. MacKerras (r1982)
(12/85) (DECC) Ⓓ [2] **414 483-2DH2**
Jenufa G. Beňačková
Laca V. Přibyl
Kostelnička N. Kniplová
Števa V. Krejčík
Karolka J. Pokorná
Grandmother Buryja A. Barová
Miller K. Berman
Mayor V. Halíř
Mayor's Wife K. Belanová
Shepherdess D. Suryová
Barena C. Strádalová
Jano J. Janská
Brno Janáček Op Chor, Brno Janáček Op Orch, F. Jílek (r1977/8)
(4/93) (SUPR) Ⓓ [2] **10 2751-2**
And that's how we would go...Ah, he was so strong J. Pavlová, Y. Tannenbergerova, Brno St PO, L. Svárovský (r1994)
(3/95) (SUPR) Ⓓ **11 1878-2**
Steva, I know it was joy G. Beňačková, A. Barová, V. Krejčík, Brno Janáček Op Orch, F. Jílek (r1977-78) (KOCH) Ⓓ **34036-2**
(KOCH) ▭ **24036-4**
This is my mother's room L. Popp, Munich RO, S. Soltesz (r1987)
(4/89) (EMI) Ⓓ **CDC7 49319-2**

Káťa Kabanová– opera: 3 acts (1921—Prague) (Wds. cpsr, aster A.N. Ostrovosky)
Káťa Kabanová N. Gustafson
Boris B. McCauley
Kabanicha F. Palmer
Dikoj D. Adams
Tichon R. Davies
Kudrjáš J. Graham-Hall
Varvara L. Winter
Kuligin R. Poulton
Gláša C. Bunning
Fekluša L. Ormiston
Glyndebourne Fest Chor, LPO, A. Davis, N. Lehnhoff (r1988)
(MCEG) ▣ **VVD929**
Káťa Kabanová E. Söderström
Boris P. Dvorský
Kabanicha N. Kniplová
Dikoj D. Jedlička
Tichon V. Krejčík
Kudrjáš Z. Švehla
Varvara L. Márová
Kuligin J. Souček
Glaša J. Pavlová
Fekluša G. Jahn
Vienna St Op Chor, VPO, C. Mackerras
(10/89) (DECC) Ⓓ [2] **421 852-2DH2**
Káťa Kabanová D. Tikalová
Boris B. Blachut
Kabanicha L. Komancová
Dikoj Z. Kroupa
Tichon B. Vích
Kudrjáš V. Kočí
Varvara I. Mixová
Kuligin R. Jedlička
Glaša E. Hlobilová
Fekluša M. Lemariová
Prague Nat Th Chor, Prague Nat Th Orch, J. Krombholc (r1959)
(11/93) (SUPR) Ⓓ [2] **10 8016-2**
Guess what occurred to me! D. Tikalová, I. Mixová, Prague Nat Th Orch, J. Krombholc (r1959) (KOCH) Ⓓ **34036-2**
(KOCH) ▭ **24036-4**

The Living Corpse– opera fragment (1916) (Lib. cpsr, after Tolstoy)
Y. Tannenbergerova, J. Janská, J. Jiskrová, Brno St PO, L. Svárovský (r1994)
(3/95) (SUPR) Ⓓ **11 1878-2**

The Makropulos Affair– opera: 3 acts (1926—Prague) (Wds. cpsr, after K. Čapek)
Emilia Marty S. Sundine
Albert Gregor G. Clark
Vítek R. Margison
Kristina K. Brett
Jaroslav Prus C. Opthof
Janek B. Boutet
Kolenatý R. Orth
Stage Technician S. Horst
Hauk-Šendorf G. Rideout
Chambermaid G. Prata
Canadian Op Chor, Canadian Op Orch, R. Klobučar, L. Mansouri (pp1989)
(PICK) ▣ **RPT2032**
Emilia Marty E. Söderström
Albert Gregor P. Dvorský
Vítek V. Krejčík
Kristina A. Czaková
Jaroslav Prus V. Zítek
Janek Z. Švehla
Kolenatý D. Jedlička
Stage Technician J. Joran
Cleaning Woman I. Mixová
Hauk-Šendorf B. Blachut
Chambermaid B. Vítková
Vienna St Op Chor, VPO, C. Mackerras (r1978)
(10/91) (DECC) Ⓓ [2] **430 372-2DH2**
Emilia Marty L. Prylová
Albert Gregor I. Žídek
Vítek R. Vonásek
Kristina H. Tattermuschová
Jaroslav Prus P. Kočí
Janek V. Kočí
Kolenatý K. Berman
Stage Technician J. Joran
Cleaning Woman J. Procházková
Hauk-Šendorf M. Karpíšek
Chambermaid M. Musilová
Prague Nat Th Chor, Prague Nat Th Orch, B. Gregor (r1965/6)
(5/95) (SUPR) Ⓓ [2] **10 8351-2**

Šárka– opera: 3 acts (1925—Brno) (Lib. J. Zeyer (work written 1887-88, rev 1918-19 & 1924-25)
Šárka A. Nováková
Ctirad A. Jurečka
Přemsyl F. Kunc
Lumír J. Válka
Brno Rad Chor, Brno RSO, B. Bakala (r1953)
(6/94) (MULT) Ⓓ **310154-2**

JESSEL, Leon *(1871–1942)* *Germany*

Schwarzwaldmädel– operetta (3 acts) (1917—Berlin) (Lib. A. Neidhart)
Excs M. Schramm, A. Herrfurth, L. Schädle, U. Schirrmacher, R. Schock, K-E. Mercker, F. Ollendorff, W. Reichert, Berlin RIAS Chbr Ch, Berlin SO, W. Schmidt-Boelcke
(2/91) (EURO) Ⓓ **GD69027**

JOMMELLI, Nicolò *(1714–1774) Italy*

Armida abbandonata– opera: 3 acts (1770—Naples) (Lib. Saverio de' Rogati, after Tasso)

Armida E. Malas-Godlewska
Rinaldo C. Brua
Tancredi G. Ragon
Erminia V. Gens
Rambaldo L. Polverelli
Ubaldo P. Petibon
Dano C. Perrin
Talens Lyriques, C. Rousset (r1994)
(4/95) (FNAC) Ⓓ [3] **592326**

Didone abbandonata– opera: 3 acts (1747—Rome) (Lib. Metastasio)

Son regina, e sono amante M. Dragoni, Munich RSO, G. Kuhn (r1991) (ORFE) Ⓓ **C261921A**

Pelope– opera: 3 acts (1755—Stuttgart) (Lib. Verazi)

EXCERPTS: 1. Fra speme e timore.
1. R. Sonnenschmidt, Sephira Ens (r1989)
(BAYE) Ⓓ **BR100083**

JOPLIN, Scott *(1868–1917) USA*

Treemonisha– opera: 3 acts (1915—New York) (Lib. cpsr)

Treemonisha C. Balthrop
Monisha B. Allen
Remus C. Rayam
Ned W. White
Zodzetrick B. Harney
Lucy C. Johnson
Andy K. Hicks
Luddud D. Duckens
Cephus D. Ransom
Simon R. Bazemore
Parson Alltalk E. Pierson
Houston Grand Op Chor, Houston Grand Op Orch, G. Schuller
(8/92) (DG) Ⓓ [2] **435 709-2GX2**

KABALEVSKY, Dmitry Borisovich *(1904–1987) USSR*

Colas Breugnon– opera: 3 acts, Op. 24 (1938—Leningrad) (Lib. Bragin, after Rolland)

EXCERPTS: 1. Overture.
Colas Breugnon L. Boldin
Selina N. Isakova
Jacqueline V. Kayevchenko
Gifflard E. Masimenko
Chamaille G. Dudarev
Robinet N. Gutorovich
Duke d'Asnois A. Mishchevski
Mademoiselle de Termes A. Shitkova
Herald L. Yeliseev
Parishioner I M. Syromyatnikov
Parishioner II V. Zamberg
Moscow Stanislavsky Th Chor, Moscow Stanislavsky Th Orch, G. Zhemchuzhin (r1973)
(5/93) (OLYM) Ⓓ [2] **OCD291**
1. BBC SO, A. Davis (pp1994)
(TELD) ▭ **4509-97869-3**
1. NBC SO, A. Toscanini (r1946)
(RCA) Ⓓ **GD60310**
1. Phil Pops Orch, C. Gerhardt (r1967)
(CHES) Ⓓ **Chesky CD108**
1. NBC SO, A. Toscanini (bp1943)
(1/90) (DELL) Ⓓ **CDDA9020**
1. Chicago SO, F. Reiner (r1959)
(8/94) (RCA) Ⓓ **09026 61958-2**
1. Russian Nat Orch, M. Pletnev
(12/94) (DG) Ⓓ **439 892-2GH**
(DG) ⊟ **439 892-4GH**

KÁLMÁN, Imre (Emmerich) *(1882–1953) Hungary/USA*

Die **Bajadere– operetta: 3 acts (1921—Vienna) (Lib. J. Brammer and A. Grünwald)**

O Bajadere Innsbruck Salon Qnt (r1991; arr qnt)
(SCHW) Ⓓ **310212**

Die **Csárdásfürstin, '(The) Gypsy Princess'– operetta: 3 acts (1915—Vienna) (Lib. Stein & Jenbach)**

EXCERPTS—; 1. Introduction. ACT 1: 2. Heia, heia, in den Bergen ist mein Heimatland; 3a. Alle sind wir Sünder; 3b. Die Mädis von Chantant; 4a. Sylva, ich will nur dich; 4b. Ja, Mädchen gibt es wunderfeine; 5a. Aus ist's mit der Liebe; 5b. Ganz ohne Weiber geht die Chose nicht; 6. O jag' dem Glück nicht nach; 7a. Ich, Edwin Ronald; 7b. Jetzt, gerade jetzt!; 7c. Heissa, so verliebt zu sein. ACT 2: 8. Entr'acte; 9. Erstrahlen die Lichter (Tanzwalzer); 10a. Ich warte auf das grosse wunder; 10b. Machen wir's den Schwalben nach; 11. Jubel; 12a. Liebchen, mich reisst es; 12b. Dance with dialogue; 12c. Weisst du es noch?; 13a. Mädel, guck; 13b. Das ist die Liebe; 14a. Tanzen möcht' ich; 14b. Tausend kleine Engel singen; 15a. Verzeih', Papa; 15b. Lieben sich zwei Menschenkinder. ACT 3: 16a. Intermezzo; 16b. Nimm, Zigeuner, deine Geige; 16c. Jaj, Mamán, Bruderherz, ich kauf' mir die Welt; 17. Mädel, guck ... Das list die Liebe (reprise); 18. Tausend kleine Engel singen (finale).
Excs Lotte Rysanek, E. Liebesberg, R. Christ, H. Prikopa, Vienna Volksoper Chor, Vienna Volksoper Orch, F. Bauer-Theussl
(KOCH) Ⓓ **399 226**
2. M. Hill Smith, Philh, J.O. Edwards (r1989-91; Eng) (10/91) (TER) Ⓓ **CDVIR8314**
(10/91) (TER) ⊟ **ZCVIR8314**
2, 3a, 3b, 4a, 4b, 5a, 5b, 6, 10a, 10b, 13a, 13b, 14a, 14b, 16b A. Rothenberger, N. Gedda, O. Miljakovic, W. Brokmeier, W. Anheisser, Bavarian St Op Chor, Graunke SO, W. Mattes
(EMI) Ⓓ [2] **CMS7 64309-2**
5b, 9, 12b, 14a Innsbruck Salon Qnt (r1991; arr qnt) (SCHW) Ⓓ **310212**
6. P. Lorengar, Vienna Op Orch, W. Weller (r1970) (LOND) Ⓓ **436 898-2DM**
10a, 10b, 14a, 14b J. Kolomyjec, M. DuBois, Kitchener-Waterloo SO, R. Armenian
(CBC) Ⓓ **SMCD5126**
12c P. Domingo, I. Perlman, NY Studio Orch, J. Tunick (r1990) (3/92) (EMI) Ⓓ **CDC7 54266-2**
14a E.C. Lund, Vienna Op Ball Orch, U. Theimer
(VICT) Ⓓ **VCD19008**
14a, 14b M. Hill Smith, P. Morrison, Chandos Concert Orch, S. Barry (Eng)
(6/85) (CHAN) Ⓓ **CHAN8362**
(6/85) (CHAN) ⊟ **LBTD013**

Die **Faschingsfee– operetta (1917—Vienna) (Lib. Willner & Oesterreicher)**

Liebe Himmelvater; Liebe, ich sehn' mich Innsbruck Salon Qnt (r1991; arr qnt)
(SCHW) Ⓓ **310212**
Lieber Himmelvater M. Hill Smith, Chandos Concert Orch, S. Barry
(10/91) (CHAN) Ⓓ **CHAN8978**

Gräfin Mariza, 'Countess Maritza'– operetta: 3 acts (1924—Vienna) (Lib. Brammer and Grünwald)

EXCERPTS—; 1. Overture. ACT 1: 2. Glück ist ein schöner Traum; 4a. Wenn es Abend wird; 4b. Grüss mir die süssen (Grüss mir mein Wien); 5a. Höre ich Zigeunergeigen; 5b. Wo wohnt die Liebe; 6a. Sonnenschein, hüll' dich ein; 6b. O schöne Kinderzeit; 7a. Ich bitte, nicht lachen; 7b. Komm mit nach Varasdin; 8a. Zigeunermusik; 8b. Auch war einst feiner Csárdáskavalier; 8c. Komm, Zigány; 8d. Ei bravo, Herr Verwalter; 8e. Bitte sehr, das ist noch gar nix, nein!; 8f. Geigen schallen, Lichter blitzen; 8g. Eh' ein kurzer Mond ins Land mag entfliehen; 8h. Komm, Zigány. ACT 2: 9. Schwesterlein, Schwesterlein; 10a. Wenn ich abends schlafen geh'; 10b. Ich möchte trämen vor dir, mein Pickikám!; 11. Genung, genug, ich will mit Geschäften; 12a. Herrgott, was ist denn heut' los; 12b. Einmal möcht' ich wieder tanzen; 13a. Junger Mann ein Mädchen liebt; 13b. Behüt' dich Gott, komm gut nach Haus; 14a. Geigen schallen, Lichter blitzen; 14b. Ja!, Heut' um Zehn sind wir in Tabarin; 15a. Mein lieber Schatz; 15b. Sag' ja, mein Lieb, sag' ja; 16a. Hei, Mariza, hei; 16b. Hab' mich einmal toll verliebt; 16c. Eh' ein Kurzer Mond ins Land mag entfliehen. ACT 3: 17. Zigeunermusik; 18a. Ungarmädel, Haut wie Rosen; 18b. Braunes Mädel von der Puszta; 18c. Fein könnt' auf der Welt es sein; 18d. Wer hat euch erdacht, ihr süssen Frau'n; 19. Komm mit nach Varasdin; 20a. Ich trag' mit starker Hand; 20b. Sag' ja, die Stunde des Glücks ist da.
Excs M. Hill Smith, R. Remedios, L. Barber, T. Davies, L. Livingstone, J. Moyle, New Sadlers Wells Op Chor, New Sadlers Wells Op Orch, B. Wordsworth (r1983; Eng)
(TER) Ⓓ **CDTEO1007**
(TER) ⊟ **ZCTEO1007**
Excs M. Hill Smith, R. Remedios, L. Barber, L. Livingstone, T. Davies, J. Moyle, New Sadler's Wells Op Chor, New Sadler's Wells Op Orch, B. Wordsworth (Eng: trans Douglas)
(TER) Ⓓ **CDTER1051**
(1/84) (TER) ⊟ **ZCTER1051**
1, 2, 10a, 10b, 14a, 15a, 15b, 18a-d, 19. A. Rothenberger, E. Moser, N. Gedda, O. Miljakovic, W. Brokmeier, K. Böhme, Graunke SO, W. Mattes (EMI) Ⓓ [2] **CMS7 64309-2**
4a, 4b R. Tauber, Odeon Künstlerorchester, F. Weissmann (r1932)
(12/89) (EMI) Ⓓ **CDH7 69787-2**
4a, 4b, 8b, 8c F. Wunderlich, Bavarian St Orch, H. Moltkau (EMI) Ⓓ [3] **CZS7 62993-2**
4a, 4b, 8b, 9. R. Karczykowski, Polish Nat RSO, R. Bibl (POLS) Ⓓ **PNCD087**
4a, 4b, 8b, 8c P. Domingo, Ambrosian Sngrs, ECO, J. Rudel (EMI) Ⓓ [2] **CMS7 64309-2**
4b B. Weikl, Austrian RSO, K. Eichhorn
(ORFE) Ⓓ **C077831A**
4b R. Tauber, Vienna Th an der Wien Orch, A. Paulik (r1924) (12/92) (NIMB) Ⓓ **NI7833**
(12/92) (NIMB) ⊟ **NC7833**
4b, 16c, 19. Innsbruck Salon Qnt (r1991; arr qnt)
(SCHW) Ⓓ **310212**
4, 8b, 8c P. Domingo, Ambrosian Sngrs, ECO, J. Rudel (2/87) (EMI) Ⓓ **CDC7 47398-2**
5a J. Migenes, Vienna Volksoper Orch, L. Schifrin (r1993)
(1/94) (ERAT) Ⓓ **4509-92875-2**
(1/94) (ERAT) ⊟ **4509-92875-4**
8b, 8c J. Kolomyjec, Kitchener-Waterloo SO, R. Armenian (CBC) Ⓓ **SMCD5126**
15b M. Hill Smith, New Sadler's Wells Op Orch, B. Wordsworth (r1989-91; Eng)
(10/91) (TER) Ⓓ **CDVIR8314**
(10/91) (TER) ⊟ **ZCVIR8314**

Ein **Herbstmanöver– operetta (1909—Vienna)**

Küsslied Innsbruck Salon Qnt (r1991; arr qnt)
(SCHW) Ⓓ **310212**

Die **Herzogin von Chicago– operetta (1928—Vienna) (Lib. Brammer & Grünwald)**

Abschied; Ein kleiner Slowfox Innsbruck Salon Qnt (r1991; arr qnt) (SCHW) Ⓓ **310212**
Ein kleiner Slowfix mit Mary M. Hill Smith, Chandos Concert Orch, S. Barry
(10/91) (CHAN) Ⓓ **CHAN8978**

Hollandweibchen– operetta (1920—Vienna) (Lib. Stein & Jenbach)

Ein Glaserl Wein; Ach, wer weiss mir Innsbruck Salon Qnt (r1991; arr qnt)
(SCHW) Ⓓ **310212**
O du holde Zeit M. Hill Smith, Chandos Concert Orch, S. Barry (10/91) (CHAN) Ⓓ **CHAN8978**

Kaiserin Josephine– operetta (1936—Zurich) (Lib. Knepler & Herczeg)

Liebe singt ihr Zauberlied; Mein Traum, mein Traum; Du bist die Frau; Nur ein Gedanke immerzu O. Miljakovic, A. Dallapozza, Graunke SO, C. Wildmann (EMI) Ⓓ [2] **CMS7 64309-2**
Mein Traum; Schöne Marquise M. Hill Smith, Chandos Concert Orch, S. Barry
(10/91) (CHAN) Ⓓ **CHAN8978**

Das **Veilchen vom Montmartre– operetta (1930—Vienna) (Lib. Brammer & Grünwald)**

Das Veilchen vom Montmartre M. Hill Smith, Chandos Concert Orch, S. Barry
(10/91) (CHAN) Ⓓ **CHAN8978**
Heut, nacht hab' ich geträumt von dir N. Gedda, Graunke SO, W. Mattes
(EMI) Ⓓ [2] **CMS7 64309-2**

Der **Zigeunerprimas, 'Sari'– operetta (1912—Vienna) (Lib. F. Grünbaum and J. Wilhelm)**

Alter Rácz Innsbruck Salon Qnt (r1991; arr qnt)
(SCHW) Ⓓ **310212**

Mein alter Stradivari B. Kusche, Graunke SO, W. Mattes (EMI) Ⓓ [2] **CMS7 64309-2**

Die **Zirkusprinzessin, 'Circus Princess'– operetta: 3 acts (1926—Vienna) (Lib. Brammer & Grünwald)**

EXCERPTS—ACT 1: 1. Bravo, bravo, Herr Direktor!; 2a. Was in der Welt geschieht; 2b. Ja, ist denn die Liebe wirklich gar so schön; 3a. Wenn ein einsames Wienerkind; 3b. Wo ist der Himmel so blau wie in Wien; 4. Es is noch Zeit!; 5a. Weider hinaus ins strahlende Licht; 5b. Zwei Märchenaugen; 6a. Wenn ich in den Zirkus gehe; 6b. Die kleine Mäderln im Trikot; 7a. Manchal treibt das Schicksal; 7b. Wer wind denn gleich weinen, mein Kind; 8. Hoheit hat uns eingelanden heute zum Souper!; 9a. Heissa, die Nacht erwacht; 9b. Juppla, Josefinchen. ACT 2: 10. Freut euch des Lebens; 11a. Der Husar; 11b. Mädel, gib acht!, Schleis dein Fenster; 12a. Wollen sie mir nicht gestehen; 12b. Mein Darling!, muss so sein wie Du!; 13a. Wieder blüht die Primel; 13b. Leise, leise, komm mit mir auf die Wesse; 14a. Süsseste von allen Frauen; 14b. Ich und Du - Du und ich!; 15a. Iwan Peter Petrowitsch; 15b. Mein heissgeliebter, süssen Iwan; 16. Ein Hochzeitsfest, welche Pracht! (finale). ACT 3: 17a. Nimmt man Abschied von dieser Stadt; 17b. Wo ist der Himmel so blau in Wien!; 18. Glaubst Du denn, ich werd' mich kränken; 18b. Wenn Du mich sitzen lässt; 19. Der alte Herrgott, der weiss war et tut; 20. Mein darling muss lieb sein wie du.

2a M. Hill Smith, Chandos Concert Orch, S. Barry (10/91) (CHAN) Ⓓ **CHAN8978**
5a, 5b F. Wunderlich, Bavarian St Orch, H. Moltkau (EMI) Ⓓ [2] **CMS7 64309-2**
5b R. Schock, orch, W. Schüchter (r1956) (EMI) Ⓓ **CDM7 69475-2**
5b F. Wunderlich, Berlin SO, A. Melichar (EURO) Ⓓ **GD69018** (EURO) ⊟ **GK69018**
5b Innsbruck Salon Qnt (r1991; arr qnt) (SCHW) Ⓓ **310212**
5b R. Holm, W. Krenn, Vienna Volksoper Orch, A. Paulik (r1970) (LOND) Ⓓ **436 898-2DM**
5b R. Tauber, Berlin Künstlertheater Orch, E. Hauke (r1927) (12/89) (EMI) Ⓓ **CDH7 69787-2**
5b R. Tauber, Berlin Künstlertheater Orch, E. Hauke (r1927) (12/92) (NIMB) Ⓓ **NI7833** (12/92) (NIMB) ⊟ **NC7833**

KALOMIRIS, Manolis *(1883–1962) Greece*

The Mother's Ring– opera: 3 acts (1917 rev 1939—Athens)

Yannakis	Z. Terzakis
Erofili	M. Koromantzou
Mother; Old Woman	J. Sfekas-Karvelas
Sotiris	A. Kouloumbis
Kyriakos	F. Voutsinos
Dame Destiny	T. Genova
Maid	C. Athanassova
Nymph	D. Valkova

Bulgarian Nat Chor, Sofia PO, Y. Daras (8/85) (ATHE) ⊙ [3] **04/6/83**

KARETNIKOV, Nikolai *(1930–1994) USSR*

Till Eulenspiegel– opera: 2 acts (1983) (Lib. cpsr & Lounguin, after C de Coster)

Tyl	B. Kudriavtsev
Nele	E. Mazo
Lamme	A. Martynov
Katline, etc	L. Mkrtchian
Prince, etc	A. Pruzhansky
Klaas, etc	A. Mochalov
Joost, etc	P. Gluboky

Chor, Soviet Cinema Orch, E. Khachaturian, V. Polianski (r1988) (7/92) (CDM) Ⓓ [2] **LDC288 029/30**

KASPAROV, Yuri *(b 1955) Armenia*

Nevermore– opera-monodrama: baritone and chamber ensemble (1992) (Wds. E. A. Poe: 'The Ravens')

EXCERPTS: 1. Overture.

1. Moscow Contemp Music Ens, A. Vinogradov (r1992) (9/93) (CDM) Ⓓ **LDC288 060**

KATTNIGG, Rudolf *(1895–1955) Austria*

Bel Ami– operetta (1948)

EXCERPTS: 1. Bel ami, schöner Mai.

1. R. Holm, W. Krenn, Vienna Volksoper Orch, A. Paulik (r1970) (LOND) Ⓓ **436 898-2DM**

Mädels vom Rhein– operetta (1938—Bremen)

EXCERPTS: 1. Ich weiss mir ein Mädel.

1. R. Holm, W. Krenn, Vienna Volksoper Orch, A. Paulik (r1970) (LOND) Ⓓ **436 898-2DM**

KEISER, Reinhard *(1674–1739) Germany*

Croesus– opera: 3 acts (1710, rev 1730—?Hamburg) (Lib. Postel)

Croesus	M. Klietmann
Cyrus	S. Mizugushi
Elmira	P. Grigorova
Atis	M. van der Sluis
Orsanes	A. Martin
Eliates	M. Tucker
Clerida/Trigesta	L. Åkerlund
Solon/Elcius	J. Benet
Halimacus	U. Targler
Nerillus	P. Mildenhall

Cappella Voc Ens, Clemencic Consort, R. Clemenčić (rev.version; pp1990) (NUOV) Ⓓ [2] **6934/5**

Masagniello furioso, oder Die Neapolitanische Fischer-Empörung– opera: 3 acts (1706—Hamburg) (Lib. B. Feind)

Masagniello	M. Schopper
Mariane	B. Schlick
Aloysia	D. Röschmann
Duca d'Arcos	D. Cordier
Don Velsaco	W. Jochens
Don Antonio	H. van der Kamp
Don Pedro	H. Meens
Perrone	J. Dreyer
Bassian	W. Mikus

Bremen Voc Ens, Fiori Musicali, T. Albert (pp1989) (11/93) (CPO) Ⓓ [2] **CPO999 110-2**

KIENZL, Wilhelm *(1857–1941) Austria*

Der **Evangelimann– musical play: 2 acts, Op. 45 (1894—Berlin) (Lib. cpsr, after Meissner)**

EXCERPTS: ACT 2: 13. O schöne Jugendtage; 16a. Selig sind, die Verfolgung leiden; 16b. Lasset die Kleinen zu mir kommen!.

13. R. Anday, orch (r1926) (5/92) (PREI) Ⓓ **89046**
13. K. Branzell, orch (r1928) (8/92) (PREI) Ⓓ **89039**
16a P. Anders, Berlin Deutsche Op Chor, Berlin Deutsche Op Orch, W. Lutze (r1938) (TELD) Ⓓ **4509-95512-2**
16a P. Anders, South-West German RSO, O. Ackermann (bp1952) (8/93) (ACAN) Ⓓ **43 268**
16a, 16b F. Wunderlich, Munich St Wolfgang Children's Ch, Bavarian St Orch, H. Müller-Kray (EMI) Ⓓ [3] **CZS7 62993-2**
16a, 16b M. Höffgen, N. Gedda, Munich St. Wolfgang Children's Ch, Bavarian St Orch, R. Heger (CFP) Ⓓ **CD-CFP4616**
16a, 16b J. Schmidt, orch, F. Günther (r1933) (EMI) Ⓓ [2] **CHS7 64673-2**
16a, 16b R. Tauber, orch (r1919) (12/92) (NIMB) Ⓓ **NI7830** (12/92) (NIMB) ⊟ **NC7830**
16a, 16b W. Ludwig, Berlin St Op Orch, G. Steeger (r1940) (7/95) (PREI) Ⓓ **89088**

Der **Kuhreigen– opera: 3 acts, Op. 85 (1911—Vienna) (Lib. R Batka, after R H Bartsch)**

Lug, Dursel, lug ... Zu Strassburg auf der Schanz F. Wunderlich, Stuttgart Rad Chor, Stuttgart RSO, A. Rischner (bp1959) (10/89) (ACAN) Ⓓ **43 267**
Zu Strassburg auf der Schanz W. Ludwig, Berlin St Op Orch, G. Steeger (r1940) (7/95) (PREI) Ⓓ **89088**

KLEMPERER, Otto *(1885–1973) Germany*

Das **Ziel– opera (1915 rev 1970)**

1. Merry Waltz.

1. New Philh, L. Stokowski (pp1974) (3/95) (BBCR) Ⓓ **BBCRD9107**

KLISCHNEGG, Felix

Die **Kätzchen– operetta (Lib. Niedt)**

Unter dem Lindenbaum E. Sack, Berlin Staatskapelle (r1937) (DANT) Ⓓ **LYS2**

KNAIFEL, Aleksandr *(b 1943) USSR*

The **Canterville Ghost– opera: 3 acts (1974—Leningrad) (Lib. T. Kramarova, after O. Wilde)**

EXCERPTS—; 1. The Ghost Monologue One; 2. Virginia (scene without a singer); 3. The Ghost Monologue Two; 4. The Ghost (passacaglia for organ); 5. The Ghost and Virginia.

1-5. S. Suleymanov, T. Monogarova, A. Levental, Moscow Forum Th Orch, M. Yurovsky (CDM) Ⓓ **LDC288 009** (CDM) ⊟ **KC488 009**

KNUSSEN, (Stuart) Oliver *(b 1952) England*

Higglety Pigglety Pop!– fantasy opera: 1 act (1985—Glyndebourne) (Lib. M Sendak)

Jennie	C. Buchan
Potted plant; Baby; Mother Goose	D. Rees
Pig-in-Sandwich Board; Ash Tree	A. Gallacher
Cat-Milkman; Ash Tree	N. Jenkins
Baby's Mother	R. Hardy
Lion	S. Richardson

London Sinfonietta, O. Knussen, F. Corsaro (r1985) (CAST) ▣ **CVI2048**

Where the Wild Things are– fantasy opera: 1 act (1984—London) (Lib. M Sendak)

Max	R. Hardy
Mama; Tzippy	M. King
Moishe; Goat	H. Hetherington
Bruno	S. Richardson
Emile	S. Rhys-Williams
Bernard	A. Gallacher

London Sinfonietta, O. Knussen (r1984) (6/85) (UNIC) ⊟ **DKPC9044**

Max	K. Beardsley
Mama; Tzippy	M. King
Moishe; Goat	H. Hetherington
Bruno	J. Munro
Emile	S. Rhys-Williams
Bernard	A. Gallacher

London Sinfonietta, O. Knussen, F. Corsaro (r1984) (CAST) ▣ **CVI2048**

KODÁLY, Zoltán *(1882–1967) Hungary*

Háry János– Singspiel: 5 scenes, Op. 15 (1926—Budapest) (Lib. Paulini and Harsáyni)

Cpte E. Komlóssy, L. Palócz, G. Melis, Z. Bende, O. Szönyi, Margit László, P. Ustinov, Edinburgh Fest Chor, Wandsworth Sch Boys' Ch, LSO, I. Kertész (r1968) (10/95) (DECC) Ⓓ [2] **443 488-2DF2**
3. Hungarian St SO, A. Fischer (r1990) (NIMB) Ⓓ **NI7010**

Háry János– concert suite from opera, Op. 15 (1927)

1. Prelude; 2. Viennese Musical Clock; 3. Song; 4. Battle and Defeat of Napoleon; 5. Intermezzo; 6. Entrance of the Emperor and his court.

Minneapolis SO, A. Dorati (MERC) Ⓓ **432 005-2MM**
Chicago SO, N. Järvi (pp1990) (CHAN) Ⓓ **CHAN8877**
Hungarian St Orch, A. Fischer (NIMB) Ⓓ **NI5284** (NIMB) ⊟ **NC5284**
Philh Hungarica, A. Dorati (DECC) Ⓓ **425 034-2DM**
Cleveland Orch, G. Szell (r1969) (SONY) Ⓓ **SBK48162**

Helsinki PO, J. Fürst (r1993)
(KONT) ① [2] **32153/4**
Budapest RSO, L. Stokowski (r1967)
(MUSI) ① **MACD-771**
Philh Hungarica, A. Dorati (r1973)
(DECC) ① [2] **443 006-2DF2**
LSO, I. Kertész (r1964) (BELA) ① **461 012-2**
(BELA) ▭ **461 012-4**
Concertgebouw, W. Mengelberg (pp1940)
(ARHI) ① **ADCD115**
LSO, R. Frühbeck de Burgos
(7/90) (NIMB) ① **NI5194**
NBC SO, A. Toscanini (bp1947)
(1/91) (RCA) ① **GD60279**
L. Kaptain, Chicago SO, G. Solti (pp1993)
(1/95) (DECC) ① **443 444-2DH**
3. Hungarian Nat PO, T. Ferenc
(IMP) ① **PCDS24**
(IMP) ▭ **PCDSC24**
5. J. Szigeti, A. Foldes (r1941: arr vn/pf: Szigeti)
(7/94) (BIDD) ① [2] **LAB070/1**

The **Transylvanian Spinning-Room, 'Székely fono'– music for lyrical play: Act 1 (1932—Budapest) (Wds. trad folk texts)**
Under the mountains of Csitári J. Simándy, I. Tokody, orch, Anon (cond) (pp1991/2)
(VAI) ① **VAIA1009**

KOKKONEN, Joonas *(b 1921) Finland*

The **Last Temptations– opera: 2 acts (1975—Helsinki)**
Interludes Lahti SO, O. Vänskä
(8/92) (BIS) ① **BIS-CD498**

KORNGOLD, Erich Wolfgang *(1897–1957) Austro-Hungary/USA*

Die **Kathrin– opera: 3 acts, Op. 28 (1939—Stockholm) (Lib. E. Decsey)**
Ich bin ein Liedersänger G. Janowitz, R. Christ, Austrian St Rad Orch, W. Loibner (bp)
(5/92) (CAMB) ① **CD-1032**
Letter scene I. Steingruber, Austrian St Rad Orch, G. Kassowitz (bp)
(5/92) (CAMB) ① **CD-1032**
Malignac's aria A. Poell, Austrian St Rad Orch, J. Strobl (bp) (5/92) (CAMB) ① **CD-1032**
Soldaten Marsch und Gebet I. Steingruber, Austrian St Rad Orch, G. Kassowitz (bp)
(5/92) (CAMB) ① **CD-1032**
Szene in Nachtlokal R. Schwaiger, A. Dermota, Austrian St Rad Orch, G. Kassowitz (bp)
(5/92) (CAMB) ① **CD-1032**
The prayer; The letter song P.J. Baker, G. Calusdian (ENTR) ① **ESCD6502**
Wanderlied A. Dermota, Austrian St Rad Orch, E. Korngold (bp1949)
(5/92) (CAMB) ① **CD-1032**

Der **Ring des Polykrates– opera: 1 act, Op. 7 (1916—Munich) (Lib. after H. Tewles)**
Tagesbuch der Laura G. Janowitz, Austrian St Rad Orch, W. Loibner (bp)
(5/92) (CAMB) ① **CD-1032**
The diary song P.J. Baker, G. Calusdian
(ENTR) ① **ESCD6502**

The **Silent Serenade– operetta, Op. 46 (1946) (Lib. cpsr and H. Reisfeld)**
Song of Bliss; With you P.J. Baker, G. Calusdian (ENTR) ① **ESCD6502**

Die **Tote Stadt– opera: 3 acts, Op. 12 (1920—Hamburg and Cologne) (Lib. Schott, after Rodenbach)**
EXCERPTS - ACT 1: 6a. Nun, zu der alten Laute; 6b. Glück, das mir verblieb (Mariettalied). ACT 2: 8. Prelude; 12. Mein Sehnen, mein Wähnen (Pierrotlied). ACT 3: 14. Prelude; 16. Und der Erste, der Lieb mich gelehrt (Marietta); 18. O Freund, ich werde sie nicht wiedersehen.

Paul	R. Kollo
Marietta	C. Neblett
Frank	B. Luxon
Brigitta	R. Wageman
Fritz	H. Prey
Juliette	G. Fuchs
Lucienne	P. Clark
Gaston, Victorin	A. de Ridder
Count Albert	W. Brokmeier

Tolz Boys' Ch, Bavarian Rad Chor, Munich RO, E. Leinsdorf (r1975)
(11/89) (RCA) ① [2] **GD87767**
6b P.J. Baker, G. Calusdian
(ENTR) ① **ESCD6502**
6b J. Schmidt, orch, O. Dobrindt (r1933)
(EMI) ① [2] **CHS7 64673-2**
6b M. Jeritza, orch, J. Pasternack (r1922)
(NIMB) ① **NI7864**
6b L. Price, New Philh, N. Santi (r1977)
(RCA) ① **09026 62596-2**
6b P. Lorengar, Vienna St Op Orch, W. Weller (r1970) (DECC) ① **443 931-2DM**
6b J. Schmidt, orch (r1933)
(4/90) (EMI) ① **CDM7 69478-2**
6b J. Hammond, Philh, W. Susskind (r1953)
(4/92) (EMI) ① [7] **CHS7 69741-2(1)**
6b I. Steingruber, A. Dermota, Austrian St Rad Orch, E. Korngold (bp1949)
(5/92) (CAMB) ① **CD-1032**
6b L. Price, New Philh, N. Santi (r1977)
(12/92) (RCA) ① [4] **09026 61236-2**
6b M. Németh, orch (r1930s)
(1/94) (CLUB) ① **CL99-007**
6b M. Jeritza, orch, J. Pasternack, F. Lapitino (r1922) (4/94) (RCA) ① [6] **09026 61580-2(3)**
6b M. Jeritza, orch (r1927)
(4/94) (PREI) ① **89079**
6b, 18. R. Tauber, Lotte Lehmann, orch, G. Szell (r1924) (3/92) (EMI) ① **CDH7 64029-2**
6b, 18. R. Tauber, Lotte Lehmann, orch, G. Szell (r1924) (12/92) (NIMB) ① **NI7830**
(12/92) (NIMB) ▭ **NC7830**
12. T. Indermühle, Salonisti (arr Artok)
(EURO) ① **GD69298**
12. R. Schwaiger, A. Poell, Austrian St Rad Orch, E. Korngold (bp1949)
(5/92) (CAMB) ① **CD-1032**
12. F. Kreisler, C. Lamson (r1924: arr Kreisler)
(9/93) (BIDD) ① [2] **LAB068/9**
12. T. Hampson, Munich RO, F. Luisi (r1994)
(9/95) (EMI) ① **CDC5 55233-2**
16. Lotte Lehmann, Berlin St Op Orch, G. Szell (r1924) (6/92) (PREI) ① [3] **89302**
18. R. Tauber, orch, G. Szell (r1924)
(10/92) (TEST) ① **SBT1005**

Violanta– opera: 1 act, Op. 8 (1916—Munich) (Lib. H. Müller)

Violanta	E. Marton
Alfonso	S. Jerusalem
Simone Troval	W. Berry
Giovanni Bracca	H. Laubenthal
Bice	G. Stoklassa
Barbara	R. Hesse
Matteo	M. Schmidt
First Soldier	H. Weber
Second Soldier	P. Hansen
First Maid	K. Hautermann
Second Maid	R. Freyer

Bavarian Rad Chor, Munich RO, M. Janowski
(9/89) (CBS) ① **CD79229**
Prelude; Carnival Austrian RSO, M. Schönherr (r1949) (3/93) (CAMB) ① **CD-1066**
Wie schön seid ihr H. Hillebrecht, H. Hoppe, Austrian St Rad Orch, J. Strobl (bp)
(5/92) (CAMB) ① **CD-1032**

Das **Wunder der Heliane– opera: 3 acts, Op. 20 (1927—Hamburg) (Lib. Muller, after H. Kaltneker)**

Heliane	A. Tomowa-Sintow
Ruler	H. Welker
Stranger	J.D. de Haan
Messenger	R. Runkel
Porter	R. Pape
Blind Judge	N. Gedda
Young Man	M. Petzold

Berlin Rad Chor, Berlin RSO, J. Mauceri (r1992)
(4/93) (DECC) ① [3] **436 636-2DH3**
Ich ging zu ihm I. Steingruber, Austrian St Rad Orch, J. Strobl (bp) (5/92) (CAMB) ① **CD-1032**

KORTEKANGAS, Olli *(b 1955) Finland*

Grand Hotel– opera: 1 act (1985) (Lib. A. Melleri)
E-L. Saarinen, S. Tiilikainen, K. Laurikainen, Avanti CO, Finnish Chbr Ch, Tapiola Chbr Ch, O. Pohjola, E-O. Söderström
(ONDI) ① **ODE749-2**

KOVAŘOVIC, Karel *(1862–1920) Czechoslovakia*

The **Dogs' Heads– opera: 3 acts (1898—Prague) (Lib. Šípek, after A Jirásek)**
Belle cruelle E. Destinn, orch, B. Seidler-Winkler (r1908)
(12/94) (SUPR) ① [12] **11 2136-2(1)**
Zelení hájové. J. Novotná, orch (r1926)
(4/93) (SUPR) ① **11 1491-2**

Nazarene– opera (unfinished)
Slovácká Pisen E. Destinn, orch, W.B. Rogers (r1915) (11/93) (ROMO) ① [2] **81002-2**
Slovácká píseň. E. Destinn, orch, W.B Rogers (r1915) (12/94) (SUPR) ① [12] **11 2136-2(5)**

KRÁSA, Hans *(1899–1944) Czechoslovakia*

Brundibár, '(The) Bumble Bee'– children's opera: 2 acts (1938) (Lib. K. Hoffmeister)

Brundibár	P. Krištofová
Little Joe	V. Ondračka
Annette	G. Přibilová
Ice cream man	T. Staněk
Baker	M. Alexandridis
Milkman	K. Tichá
Policeman	D. Horáčková
Sparrow	J. Kratěnová
Cat	B. Drofová
Dog	J. Flegl

Disman Rad Children's Ch, Disman Rad Children's Orch, J. Karas (r1992)
(8/93) (CHNN) ① **CCS5193**
Bambini di Praga, Prague FISYO, M. Klemens (bp1990) (8/92) (ROMA) ① [2] **RR1941**

KREISLER, Fritz *(1875–1962) Austria/USA*

Apple Blossoms– operetta (1919)
I'm in love; Letter song H. Kreisler, F. Kreisler (r1921: arr. Kreisler)
(7/90) (BIDD) ① [2] **LAB009/10**
Star of love G. Farrar, orch, J. Pasternack (r1920) (BIDD) ① **LAB022**
Who can tell? F. Kreisler, orch, J. Pasternack (r1920) (BIDD) ① **LAB021**

Sissy– operetta (1923) (later filmed as 'The King Steps Out', 1936)
EXCERPTS: 1. Ich glaub' das Glück (Caprice viennois).
1. E. Schumann, orch, L. Collingwood (r1935)
(ROMO) ① **81019-2**

KRENEK, Ernst *(1900–1991) Austria/USA*

Jonny spielt auf– opera: 2 acts, Op. 45 (1927—Leipzig) (Lib. cpsr)

Jonny	K. St. Hill
Max	H. Kruse
Anita	A. Marc
Daniello	M. Kraus
Yvonne	M. Posselt
Manager	D. Scholz
Bahnangestellter;Erster Polizist	M. Petzold
Zweiter Polizist	M. Weichert
Dritter Polizist	E. Noack

Leipzig Op Chor, Chinchilla, Leipzig Gewandhaus, L. Zagrosek (r1991)
(4/93) (DECC) ① [2] **436 631-2DH2**
Jetzt ist die Geige mein; Leb wohl, mein Schatz L. Hofmann, Berlin City Op Orch, M. Gurlitt (r1927) (PREI) ① **89102**

Der **Sprüng den Schatten– opera: 3 acts (1924—Frankfurt) (Lib. cpsr)**

Kuno	T. Brüning
Leonore	L. Kemeny
Blandine	S. Maclean
Odette	D. Amos
Dr. Berg	J. Pflieger
Marcus	U. Neuweiler
Laurenz Goldhaar	J. Dürmüller

Bielefeld City Th Chor, Bielefeld PO, D. de Villiers (pp1989)
(CPO) ① [2] **CPO999 082-2**

KREUTZER, Conradin (1780–1849) Germany

Das **Nachtlager in (von) Granada– romantic opera (2 acts) (1834—Vienna) (Lib. von Braun, after Kind)**

1. Overture. ACT ONE: 2. Da mir alles nun entrissen; 3a. Wie traurig und wie schön; 3b. Trauernd trieb ich meine Herde; 4. Ach, könnt ich mit ihm gehn!; 5a. Nun, Gott, sei Dank; 5b. Ein Schütz bin ich; 6. Welch feurig Aug!; 7. Hinweg!; 8a. Vom Berg ziehn wir hernieder; 8b. Zeigt dem Gast dass er wilkommen; 8c. Nun, liebes Mädchen; 8d. Wer klagt am Gitterfenster; 8e. Schon die Abendglocken klangen. ACT TWO: 9a. Wem mag das Ross wohl angehören; 9b. Nur froh vertraut der Hunde Laut; 10. Nun saget, lieber Herr; 11. Die Nacht ist schön; 12a. Leise wehet, leise wallet; 12b. Wacht auf, o Herr; 12c. Nicht ohne Grund scheint ihr Verdacht!; 12d. Ist alles still?; 13a. Ha, Bube!; 13b. Was soll des Hornes Ruf bedeuten?; 14a. Doch nun zu dir, du Holde; 14b. Trenne nicht das Band der Liebe.

Huntsman H. Prey
Gabriele R. Klepper
Gomez M. Pabst
Vasco W.M. Friedrich
Pedro C. Hauptmann
Ambrosio M. Blasius

Cologne Rad Chor, Cologne RSO, H. Froschauer (r1992) (1/94) (CAPR) ① [2] **60 029**

11. H. Prey, Berlin Deutsche Op Orch, H. Hollreiser (EURO) ① **GD69019**

11. T. Hampson, Munich RO, F. Luisi (r1994) (9/95) (EMI) ① **CDC5 55233-2**

14a, 14b F. Wunderlich, E. Köth, H. Prey, Munich RO, K. Eichhorn (bp) (DG) ① [5] **435 145-2GX5(1)**

Der **Verschwender– Zaubermärchen (3 acts) (1834—Vienna) (Lib. Raimund)**

Da streiten sich die Leut' herum B. Weikl, Austrian RSO, K. Eichhorn (ORFE) ① **C077831A**

KUHLAU, (Daniel) Friedrich (Rudolph) (1786–1832) Germany/Denmark

Lulu– opera: 2 acts, Op. 65 (1824—Copenhagen) (Lib. C F Güntelberg)

EXCERPTS: 1. Overture.

Lulu R. Saarman
Sidi A. Frellesvig
Vela T. Kiberg
Dilfeng U. Cold
Barca E. Harbo
Shepherd K. von Binzer
Water Elf H. Jakobsen
Black Elf B. Øland
Witch I H. Rummel
Witch II B. Friboe
Witch III H. Ørvad
Periferihme L. Lind

Danish Rad Chor, Danish RSO, M. Schønwandt (KONT) ① [3] **32009/11**

1. Odense SO, E. Serov (5/93) (UNIC) ① **DKPCD9132**

The **robber's castle (Røverborgen)– Singspiel (1814—Copenhagen) (Wds. A. Oehlenschlaeger)**

EXCERPTS: 1. Overture.

1. Odense SO, E. Serov (5/93) (UNIC) ① **DKPCD9132**

KÜNNEKE, Eduard (1885–1953) Germany

Die **Grosse Sünderin– operetta: 3 acts (1935—Berlin) (Lib. Stoll and Roemmer)**

EXCERPTS: 1. Histörchen, Geschichten; 2. Das Lied vom Leben des Schrenk; 3. Immerzu singt dein Herz meinem Herzen zu; 4. Das Lied vom indischen Märchen.

1, 4. H. Roswaenge, Berlin St Op Orch, B. Seidler-Winkler (r1935) (4/95) (PREI) ① [2] **89209**

2, 3. H. Roswaenge, T. Lemnitz, Berlin St Op Orch, E. Künneke (r1935) (4/95) (PREI) ① [2] **89209**

Die **Vetter aus Dingsda– operetta: 3 acts (1921—Berlin) (Lib Haller & Rideamus)**

EXCERPTS: ACT 1: 1a. Noch ein Gläschen Bordeaux?; 1b. Onkel und Tante, ja das sind Verwandte; 2. Strahlender Mond, der am Himmelszelt thront; 3. O werter, verehrter, von Liebe Betörter...Überleg's Dir's; 4a. Hallo, hallo, hier rief's doch irgendwo; 4b. Ich hab' mich verlaufen; 4c. Sag' an, wer bist Du Holde, sag' an; 4d. Ich bin nur ein armer Wandergesell. ACT 2: 5a. Ganz unverhofft kommt oft das Glück; 5b. Wenn Du glaubst, dass ich weiss, wer das ist; 5d. Der Roderich, der Roderich; 6a. Weisst Du noch, wie wir als Kinder gespiel?; 6b. Kindchen, Du musst nicht so schrecklich viel denken; 7a. Ich hab' an sie nur stets gedacht; 7b. Mann, o Mann; 8. Sieben Jahre lebt' ich in Batavia; 9a. Nicht wahr, hier ist's wie im Zauberreich; 9b. Und im Märchen, da wurden die beiden ein Paar; 9c. Ich bin nur ein armer Wandergesell; 10. Ach Heil'ger Nikolaus. ACT 3: 11a. Ganz unverhofft kommt oft das Glück; 11b. Dort ist er, dort steht er, der Lump, der Verräter; 11c. Er ist's, er ist's, der Augustin!.

Ich bin nur ein armer Wandergesell R. Schock, orch, W. Schüchter (r1953) (EMI) ① **CDM7 69475-2**

1a, 1b, 2, 3, 4a-d, 5a-d, 6a, 6b, 7a, 7b, 8, 9a-c, 10, 11a-c R. Holm, U. Schirrmacher, E. Krukowski, B. Mira, K-E. Mercker, R. Schock, C. Nicolai, Berlin SO, W. Schmidt-Boelcke (2/91) (EURO) ① **GD69025**

4d R. Karczykowski, Polish Nat RSO, R. Bibl (POLS) ① **PNCD087**

4d P. Anders, Berlin Deutsche Op Orch, N. Schultze (r1936) (MMOI) ① **CDMOIR419**
(MMOI) ▭ **CMOIR419**

4d R. Holm, W. Krenn, Vienna Volksoper Orch, A. Paulik (r1970) (LOND) ① **436 898-2DM**

4d C. Kullman, orch, O. Dobrindt (r1933: Eng) (MMOI) ① **CDMOIR429**

LALO, Edouard(-Victoire-Antoine) (1823–1892) France

Le **Roi d'Ys– opera: 3 acts (1888—Paris) (Lib. E. Blau)**

EXCERPTS: 1. Overture; 2. Noël!; 3. Margared, ô ma soeur!; 4. Vainement j'ai parlé; 5. Désireux d'accomplir. ACT 2: 6. De tous côtes j'aperçois; 7. Hélas, pourrais-je en mes alarmes; 8. Tais-toi, Margared!; 9. Victoire!; 10. Perdu! ACT 3: 11. Vous qui venez ici; 12a. Puisqu'on ne peut fléchir; 12b. Vainement, ma bien-aimée! (Aubade); 13. Voici l'heure; 14. Salut á l'époux; 15. Ces rumeurs, ces cris d'alarm; 16. Ô Puissance infinie!.

1. Luxembourg Rad & TV SO, L. de Froment (r1992) (FORL) ① **FF044**

1. RPO, Y. Butt (10/90) (ASV) ① **CDDCA709**

1. San Francisco SO, P. Monteux (r1942) (9/94) (RCA) ① [15] **09026 61893-2**

1. Luxembourg Rad & TV SO, L. de Froment (r1992) (11/94) (FORL) ① **FF045**

3. N. Vallin, M. Sibille, orch (r c1930) (PEAR) ① **GEMMCD9948**

6. S. Juyol, Paris Op Orch, L. Fourestier (r1947) (4/92) (EMI) ① [7] **CHS7 69741-2(3)**

12a, 12b J. Carreras, ROHO, J. Delacôte (EMI) ① **CDC7 54524-2**

12a, 12b T. Rossi, chor, orch, M. Cariven (r1937) (FORL) ① **UCD19053**

12a, 12b B. Gigli, orch (r1922) (5/90) (NIMB) ① **NI7807**
(NIMB) ▭ **NC7807**

12a, 12b B. Gigli, ROHO, R. Zamboni (r1946) (5/90) (EMI) ① **CDH7 61052-2**

12a, 12b B. Gigli, orch, J. Pasternack (r1922) (10/90) (RCA) ① **GD87811**
(10/90) (RCA) ▭ **GK87811**

12a, 12b N. Melba, orch, W.B. Rogers (r1910) (5/95) (ROMO) ① [3] **81011-2(2)**

12a, 12b Alfredo Kraus, WNO Orch, C. Rizzi (r1994) (8/95) (PHIL) ① **442 785-2PH**
(8/95) (PHIL) ▭ **442 785-4PH**

12b G. Morino, Warmia Nat PO, B. Amaducci (10/90) (NUOV) ① **6851**

12b J. Szigeti, A. Farkas (arr Szigeti: r1941) (5/93) (SONY) ① **MPK52569**

12b N. Melba, orch, W.B. Rogers (r1910) (9/93) (RCA) ① **09026 61412-2**

12b J. Szigeti, A. Foldes (r1941: arr vn/pf: Szigeti) (7/94) (BIDD) ① [2] **LAB070/1**

12b E. Clément, orch (r1911) (8/95) (ROMO) ① **82002-2**

12b E. Clément, orch (r1911) (8/95) (PEAR) ① **GEMMCD9161**

14(pt) M. Mesplé, N. Gedda, Paris Op Orch, P. Dervaux (r1974) (EMI) ① [2] **CZS7 67813-2**

LAMPE, John Frederick (c1703–1751) England

Britannia– opera (1732—London) (Lib. Lediard)

EXCERPTS: 1. Welcome Mars.

1. E. Kirkby, AAM, C. Hogwood (r1991) (7/93) (L'OI) ① **436 132-2OH**

Dione– opera (1733—London) (Lib. Gay and others)

EXCERPTS: 1. Pretty warblers.

1. E. Kirkby, AAM, C. Hogwood (r1991) (7/93) (L'OI) ① **436 132-2OH**

Pyramus and Thisbe– mock opera: 1 act (1745—London) (Lib. ?cspr, after Shakespeare)

EXCERPTS: 1. Overture; 2. The wretched sighs and groans (Wall air); 3. And thou, O wall; 4. O wicked wall; 5. Fly, swift good Time; 6. Not Shafulus (Whispering duetto); 7. I go without delay; 8. Ladies don't fright you; 9. The man in the moon I am, sir; 10. Where is my love, my Pyre dear; 11. Sweet moon, I thank thee; 12. Approach, ye furies fell; 13. Now I am dead; 14. These lily lips; 15. Dance; 16. Thus folding, beholding; 17. Now e'er you remove.

Pyramus M. Padmore
Thisbe S. Bisatt
Wall; Master M. Sanderson
Moon; Prompter A. Treharne
Lion; Prologue A. Knight
Mr Semibrief P. Milne
First Gentleman A. McMahon
Second Gentleman J. Edwards
P. Hyde
C. Baldy

Opera Restor'd, P. Holman (r1994) (HYPE) ① **CDA66759**

LANDI, Stefano (1586 or 1587–1639) Italy

La **Mort d'Orfeo– tragicommedia pastorale: 5 acts (1619—?Rome)**

1. Calliope's Aria (Act IV).

Cpte J. Elwes, J. Koslowsky, D. Cordier, M. Chance, M. Kroese, W. Jochens, N. van der Meel, H. van der Kamp, L. Deroo, Currende Voc Ens, Tragicomedia, S. Stubbs (10/88) (ACCE) ① [2] **ACC8746/7D**

Instrumental suite Tragicomedia (EMI) ① **CDC7 54312-2**

1. Ricercar Consort (RICE) ① [3] **RIC93001**

LANDOWSKI, Marcel (b 1915) France

Le **Fou– lyric drama in five tableaux (1956—Nancy)**

C. Carlson, J. Van Dam, P. Huttenlocher, R. Corazza, Rhine Op Chor, Strasbourg PO, A. Lombard (r1980) (ERAT) ① [9] **4509-96971-2**

LANGGAARD, Rued (1893–1952) Denmark

BVN Nos. from Bendt Viinholdt Nielsen Catalogue, 1991

Antikrist– opera (1916-36) (Lib cpsr, after Book of Revelation)

EXCERPTS: 1. Prelude.

1. Rubinstein PO, I. Stupel (12/94) (DANA) ① **DACOCD410**

LAPARRA, Raoul (1876–1943) France

La **Habanera– opera: 3 acts (1908)**

Et c'est á moi que l'on dit 'Chante'; Le sort m'a designé. Vanni-Marcoux, orch, P. Coppola (r1931) (PEAR) ① **GEMMCD9912**

Et c'est à moi que l'on dit 'Chante!'; Le sort m'a designé. Vanni-Marcoux, orch (r1931)
(1/94) (CLUB) ① **CL99-101**

Illustre Fregona– zarzuela
Mélancolique tombe le soir J. Björling, orch, N. Grevillius (r1933: Swed) (NIMB) ① **NI7835**
Mélancolique tombe le soir J. Björling, orch, N. Grevillius (r1933: Swed)
(PEAR) ① **GEMMCD9043**

LAVALLÉE, Calixa *(1842–1891) Canada*

The **Indian Question– opera (1891)**
EXCERPTS: 1. Marche Indienne.
1. Hannaford St Silver Band, S. Chenette (r1991)
(CBC) ① **SMCD5103**

The **Widow– comic opera (1881—Boston) (Lib. F H Nelson)**
EXCERPTS: 2. Oh! Trust my love; 23. Smiling hope.
2, 23. J. Kolomyjec, M. DuBois, Kitchener-Waterloo SO, R. Armenian
(CBC) ① **SMCD5126**

LECOCQ, (Alexandre) Charles *(1832–1918) France*

Le **Coeur et la main– operetta (1883—Paris) (Lib. Nuitter and Beaumont)**
Boléro F. Révoil, orch, M. Cariven
(EMI) ① [2] **CZS5 68292-2**
Bonsoir Perez le Capitaine J. Sutherland, SRO, R. Bonynge (r1969)
(DECC) ① **436 316-2DA**
(DECC) ▭ **436 316-4DA**

La **Fille de Madame Angot– operetta: 3 acts (1872—Brussels) (Lib. Clairville, Koning and Siraudin)**
EXCERPTS: 1. Introduction. ACT 1: 2. Marchande de marée; 3. Certainment, j'aimais Clairette; 4. Jadis les rois. ACT 2: 5. Elle est tellement innocente; 6. Voyons monsieur, raisonnons politique; 7. Quand on conspire, quand sans frayeur; 8a. Ah! je te trouve; 8b. Tournes, tournez. ACT 3: 9. Vous aviez fait de la dépense; 10. De la mère Angot; 11. Ah! c'est donc toi, Madame Barras.
Certainement, j'aimais Clairette A. Baugé, orch, G. Andolfi (r1935)
(EMI) ① [2] **CZS5 68292-2**
Voyons, Monsieur, raisonnons politique N. Vallin, A. Baugé, orch, G. Andolfi (r1936)
(EMI) ① [2] **CZS5 68292-2**
6. N. Vallin, A. Baugé, orch (r1930s)
(FORL) ① **UCD19022**

Le **Jour et la Nuit– operetta: 3 acts (1881—Paris) (Lib. E. Letterier & A. Vanloo)**

Manola	L. Berton
Beatrix	L. Dachary
Sanchette	F. Betti
Anita	C. Manfredini
Pepita	M. Siderer
Catana	G. Aurel
Prince Calabazas	H. Bedex
Don Braseiro	G. Rey
Miguel	M. Hamel
Don Degomez	G. Moryn
Crastoval	P. Roi

French Rad Lyric Orch, R. Ellis (with dialogue: bp)
(3/92) (MUSD) ① [2] **20136-2**

Le **petit duc– operetta: 3 acts (Paris) (Lib. Meilhac & Halévy)**
Excs N. Renaux, L. Berton, W. Clément, R. Hérent, F. Betti, Raymond St Paul Chor, Lamoureux Concerts Orch, J. Gressier (r1953)
(EMI) ① [2] **CZS5 68295-2**
Rondeau de la paysanne F. Révoil, orch, M. Cariven (r1935) (EMI) ① [2] **CZS5 68292-2**

LEFLEM, Paul *(1881–1984) France*

La **Magicienne de la Mer– concert interludes from opera (1947)**
1. Dahut's Call; 2. Ys drowned, is reborn in dream.
Britanny Orch, C. Schnitzler (pp1993)
(TIMP) ① **1C1021**

LEGRENZI, Giovanni *(1626–1690) Italy*

Eteocle e Polinice– opera (1675—Venice)
Che fiero costume E. Pinza, F. Kitzinger (r1940) (9/93) (RCA) ① **09026 61245-2**

LEHÁR, Franz *(1870–1948) Hungary/Austria*

Die **Blaue Mazur, '(The) Blue Mazurka'– operetta: 2 acts (1920—Vienna) (Lib. L. Stein & B. Jenbach)**
Ich bin zum ersten Mal verliebt Berlin Ens
(5/91) (ORFE) ① **C126901A**

Eva (Das Fabriksmädel)– operetta: 3 acts (1911—Vienna) (Lib. Willner, Bodanzky and E. Spero)
EXCERPTS: 1. Overture. ACT 1: 2. Heissa, jucheia, jetzt gibt's was zu seh'n; 3a. Im heimlichen Dämmer der silbernen Ampel; 3b. Wär' es auch nichts als ein Augenblick; 4. Bestimmung—Fatum—das ist alles!; 5. Glück und Glas, kingeling; 6a. Nur keine Angst—hier kann uns nichts passieren; 6b. Pipsi, holdes Pipsi; 7a. Um zwölf in der Nacht; 7b. Die Geister von Montmartre; 8. Halt! Ein Augenblick, ihr Leute (finale). ACT 2: 9. Retten Sie mich, Dagobert, die Herren sind zu keck!; 10a. Hat man das erste Stiefelpaar vetreten in Paris; 10b. O du Pariser Pflaster; 11a. Rechts das Männchen meiner Wahl; 11b. Geschieden muss sein, so heisst es im Lied; 12. Erschrecken Sie nicht—ich bin's!; 13a. Nur das eine Wort—sprich es aus!; 13b. Schwül aus tiefen Kelchen lockt dich ein Duft; 14. Octave, gesteh' dir's ein—du bist verliebt!; 15a. Ziehe hin zu deinem Vater; 15b. Sei nicht bös—nicht nervös; 16a. Mädel! Mein süsses Aschenbrödel du; 16b. Wär' es auch nichts als ein Augenblick; 17. Silentium! Silentium! Ich bringe einen Toast! (finale). ACT 3: 18a. Wenn die Pariserin spazieren fährt; 18b. Manches diskret man zeigt; 19a. Gib acht, gib acht, mein schönes Kind; 19b. Herrgott, lass mir doch meinen Leichtsinn nur; 20. Pipse, holdes Pipsi (reprise); 21. Ein Mädel wie Sie, so nett und so fein (finale).
1, 3a, 3b M. Reining, VPO, F. Lehár (r1942)
(1/94) (PREI) ① **90150**
1, 3a, 3b M. Reining, VPO, F. Lehár (r1942)
(1/94) (EMI) ① **CDC7 54838-2**
3a, 3b Lotte Lehmann, Berlin St Op Orch, H. Weigert (r1928) (PEAR) ① **GEMMCD9410**
3a, 3b M. Reining, VPO, F. Lehár (r1942)
(4/92) (EMI) ① [7] **CHS7 69741-2(4)**
3a, 3b M. Reining, VPO, F. Lehár (r1942)
(9/94) (PREI) ① **89065**
3b B. Weikl, Austrian RSO, K. Eichhorn
(ORFE) ① **C077831A**
3b P. Lorengar, Vienna Op Orch, W. Weller (r1970) (LOND) ① **436 897-2DM**
3b M. Hill Smith, Chandos Concert Orch, S. Barry (10/91) (CHAN) ① **CHAN8978**

Frasquita– operetta: 3 acts (1922—Vienna) (Lib. A M Willner & H Reichert, after P Louys)
EXCERPTS: 1. Overture. ACT 1; 2a. Neun gegen acht—das nenn ich Glück; 2b. Gib mit dem Fächer ein Zeichen mir; 3. Weit war uns're Wand'rung heut; 4. Wer hat das gesagt?; 5a. Wie wird sie wohl sein?; 5b. Sag mir, sag' mir; 6a. Einem Kavalier, der so wie dieser; 6b. Wenn ganz sacht über Nacht; 7. Fragst mich, was Liebe ist?; 8. Meine Mutter hat eine Gans; 9a. Tanzen, das ist jetzt die grosse Mode; 9b. Darum Mädel suchst du einem Mann; 10. Ich hab' meine Jugend im Sonnenlicht (finale); 11a. Wenn eine Rose ich schenke; 11b. Du siehst auf jedem kleinen Blatt. ACT 2: 12a. Schwärmerisch sprach Don Rodrigo; 12b. Geh' mit mir in die Alhambra; 13a. Wüsst' ich, wer morgen mein Liebster ist; 13b. Wüsst' ich wer morgen mein Liebster ist; 14a. So weit sind wir noch lange nicht; 14b. Weisst du nicht was ein Herz voller Sehnsucht begehrt?; 15a. Amelie, die gute Tante gab den Rat mir immer; 15b. Ich gäb' was drum; 16a. Schatz, ich bitt' dich, komm heut' Nacht; 16b. Hab' ein blaues Himmelbett; 17a. Kinder, heute fühl' ich mich wie zwanzig Jahr; 17b. Jung ist jeder, der jung sich noch fühlt; 18. Sehr viel verlangen Sie, mein Freund! (finale); 18a. War in einem Städtchen einst ein armes Mädchen; 19. Lasst den Tage seine Sonne. ACT 3: 20. Durch die schwarze Maske; 21a. Oh, glaub' mir, mein Freund; 21b. Wo du weilst, was du immer tust; 22. Kinder! Kinder! Heut' ist Karneval!; 23a. Wenn zwei sich immer küssen; 23b. Da küss mich immerzu; 24. Träumen möcht' ich für mich hin (finale).
Passion Rose...Rest with the dew of the morning G. Farrar, orch (r1927: Eng)
(IRCC) ① **IRCC-CD805**
7. M. Hill Smith, Chandos Concert Orch, S. Barry
(10/91) (CHAN) ① **CHAN8978**
14b J. Migenes, Vienna Volksoper Orch, L. Schifrin (r1993)
(1/94) (ERAT) ① **4509-92875-2**
(1/94) (ERAT) ▭ **4509-92875-4**
16b S. Burrows, National PO, R. Stapleton (Eng)
(DECC) ① **433 223-2DWO**
(DECC) ▭ **433 223-4DWO**
16b F. Kreisler, C. Lamson (r1926: arr Kreisler)
(IMP) ① **GLRS106**
16b T. Folgar, orch (r1932)
(PEAR) ① [2] **GEMMCDS9180**
16b F. Kreisler, C. Lamson (arr Kreisler: vn/pf: r1926) (1/90) (PEAR) ① **GEMMCD9324**
16b F. Kreisler, C. Lamson (r1926: arr Kreisler)
(12/93) (BIDD) ① **LAB075**
16b R. Tauber, Berlin Künstlertheater Orch, E. Hauke (r1927) (12/94) (MMOI) ① **CDMOIR425**
16b I. Perlman, S. Sanders (arr vn/pf: Kreisler)
(6/95) (EMI) ① [20] **CZS4 83177-2(2)**

Der **Fürst der Berge– operetta: 2 acts (1934—Berlin)**
Lange Jahre; Schweig, zogendes Herz R. Tauber, orch (r1932)
(3/89) (PEAR) ① **GEMMCD9310**

Giuditta– opera: 5 acts (1934—Vienna) (Lib. Knepler and Löhner)
ACT 1: 1a. Prelude; 1b. O mia cara Donna Emilia; 1c. Du lieber, alter Knabe; 2a. Unser Schiff geht Schlag acht Uhr; 2b. So, mein Kleines Vögelchen; 3a. Alle Tag' nichts, als Müh und Plag; 3b. Also hier ist die Osteria; 4a. Freund, das Leben ist lebenswert!; 4b. O Signora, o Signora!; 5a. Ah!...Wohin, wohin will es mich treiben; 5b. In einem Meer von Liebe; 5c. He Wirt, zahlen!; 5d. Schönste der Frau'n; 5e. 'Giuditta' hat ergesagt; 6a. Mein kleiner Vogel; 6b. Weit über's Meer; 6c. Giuditta! Giuditta!; 6d. Herr Kapitän, der Weg ist weit; 6e. Pierrino, ich habe mein Kätzchen vergessen!; 6f. Da, schau, Sebastiano!. ACT 2: 7a. Das ist das Haus, in dem Giuditta; 7b. Zwei, die sich lieben, vergessen die Welt; 7c. Schönste der Frau'n, dann soll das Glück; 8. Schön, wie die blaue Sommernacht; 9. Anita! Anita!. ACT 3: 10. Unsre Heimat ist die Wüste; 11a. Welch tiefes Rätsel ist die Liebe; 11b. Du bist meine Sonne; 12a. Giuditta! Was machst du hier!; 12b. Octavio, es ist Zeit!; 12c. Und das soll Liebe sein?; 12d. In die Stirne fällt die Locke; 12e. Mein Herz ruft Tag und Nacht mir zu; 12f. Entr'acte. ACT 4: 13a. In einem Meer von Liebe; 13b. Bravo!, Hoch, Giuditta; 14a. Ich bin nicht schön, dass weiss ich; 14b. Ja, die Liebe ist so wie ein Schaukelbrett; 14c. Wen sucht du kenn, Kleiner?; 15a. Ich hab'ich mich so gehr gesehnt; 15b. Schaut der Mond; 15c. Herr Direktor!; 16a. Ich weiss es selber nicht; 16b. Meine Lippen, sie küssen so heiss; 16c. Giuditta... 16d. Wollen der Herr hier Platz; 17a. So wie um den Sonnenball; 17b. Wo ist Giuditta?; 17c. Prelude. ACT 5: 18a. 'Schönste der Frau'n' begann das Lied; 18b. Ist alles in Ordnung?; 18c. Unser Lied!; 19. Octavio! Octavio! Du?; 20. Finale: Ich danke Ihnen.

Giuditta	E. Moser
Octavio	N. Gedda
Manuele Biffi	K. Hirte
Antonio	L. Baumann
Lord Barrymore	J. Jung
The Duke	T. Wiedenhofer
Duke's Adjutant	J. von Pawels
Martini	G. Wewel
Anita	B. Lindner
Pierrino	M. Finke
Sebastiano	F. Lenz

Munich Concert Chor, Munich RO, W. Boskovsky (r1983/4: with dialogue)
(2/95) (EMI) ① [2] **CMS5 65378-2**
Excs T. Indermühle, Salonisti (arr Hruby)
(EURO) ① **GD69298**
Serenade F. Kreisler, C. Lamson (arr Kreisler: r1926) (1/90) (PEAR) ① **GEMMCD9324**
Serenade F. Kreisler, C. Lamson (r1926: arr Kreisler) (12/93) (BIDD) ① **LAB075**
1. VJSO, W. Boskovsky
(8/84) (EMI) ① **CDC7 47020-2**

1a-c, 2a, 2b, 3a, 4a, 4b, 5a-e, 7a, 7b, 8, 11a, 12a-e, 13a, 13b, 14a, 15b, 16a, 16b, 18a, 19. H. Gueden, E. Loose, W. Kmentt, M. Dickie, E. Majkut, K. Equiluz, K. Dönch, H. Duhan, W. Berry, H. Pröglhöf, Vienna St Op Chor, Vienna St Op Orch, R. Moralt (r1957)
(6/95) (LOND) Ⓓ **436 900-2LA**

4a F. Wunderlich, Berlin SO, A. Melichar
(EURO) Ⓓ **GD69018**
(EURO) ⊟ **GK69018**

4a F. Wunderlich, Bavarian St Orch, H. Moltkau
(EMI) Ⓓ [3] **CZS7 62993-2**

4a R. Karczykowski, Polish Nat RSO, R. Bibl
(POLS) Ⓓ **PNCD087**

4a F. Wunderlich, Berlin SO, A. Melichar (r1960s) (RCA) Ⓓ **09026 62550-2**

4a F. Araiza, Munich RSO, R. Weikert
(3/93) (RCA) Ⓓ **09026 61163-2**

4a, 5d, 8, 11b, 16b, 17a J. Novotná, R. Tauber, VPO, F. Lehár (r1934)
(3/89) (PEAR) Ⓓ **GEMMCD9310**

4a, 8, 11b, 18a R. Tauber, J. Novotná, VPO, F. Lehár (r1934) (1/94) (PREI) Ⓓ **90150**

4a, 8, 11b, 16b, 17a, 18a J. Novotná, R. Tauber, VPO, F. Lehár (r1934)
(1/94) (EMI) Ⓓ **CDC7 54838-2**

4a, 11b H. Roswaenge, Berlin Volksoper Orch, B. Seidler-Winkler (r1943)
(PREI) Ⓓ [2] **89211**

5b M. Hill Smith, Chandos Concert Orch, S. Barry (10/91) (CHAN) Ⓓ **CHAN8978**

5b, 16b L. Popp, Ambrosian Op. Chor, ASMF, N. Marriner (6/88) (EMI) Ⓓ **CDC7 49700-2**

11b G. Thill, orch, G. Bret (r1935: Fr)
(MMOI) Ⓓ **CDMOIR419**
(MMOI) ⊟ **CMOIR419**

11b W. Kmentt, Vienna St Op Orch, R. Moralt (r1957) (DECC) Ⓓ **436 316-2DA**
(DECC) ⊟ **436 316-4DA**

11b R. Tauber, VPO, F. Lehár (r1934)
(7/89) (EMI) Ⓓ **CDM7 69476-2**

11b R. Tauber, Vienna St Op Orch, F. Lehár (pp1935) (7/94) (SCHW) Ⓓ [2] **314512**

16b E.C. Lund, Vienna Op Ball Orch, U. Theimer
(VICT) Ⓓ **VCD19008**

16b H. Gueden, Vienna St Op Orch, W. Loibner (r1951) (PREI) Ⓓ **90227**

16b M. Hill Smith, Chandos Concert Orch, S. Barry (Eng) (6/85) (CHAN) Ⓓ **CHAN8362**
(6/85) (CHAN) ⊟ **LBTD013**

16b E. Schwarzkopf, Philh, O. Ackermann
(1/86) (EMI) Ⓓ **CDC7 47284-2**

16b B. Hendricks, Philh, L. Foster (r1992)
(8/93) (EMI) Ⓓ **CDC7 54626-2**

16b E. Réthy, VPO, F. Lehár (r1940)
(1/94) (PREI) Ⓓ **90150**

16b J. Novotná, Vienna St Op Orch, F. Lehár (pp1934) (7/94) (SCHW) Ⓓ [2] **314512**

16b L. Garrett, RPO, P. Robinson (r1994; Eng)
(4/95) (SILV) Ⓓ **SILKD6004**
(4/95) (SILV) ⊟ **SILKC6004**

Der **Graf von Luxemburg, '(The) Count of Luxembourg'– operetta: 3 acts (1909—Vienna) (Lib. Willner & Bodanzky)**

ACT 1: 1. Karneval, ja, du allerschönste Zeit (Introduction); 2. Mein Anherr war der Luxemburg; 3. Ein Stübchen so klein; 4a. Pierre, der schreibt an kleine Fleurette; 4b. Denn doppelt schmekt's dem Bübchen; 5. So liri, liri, lari; 6. Ich bin verliebt; 7. Ein Scheck auf die englische Bank!; 8a. Heut' noch werd' ich Ehefrau; 8b. Unbekannt deshalb nich minder intressant; 9a. Frau Gräfin, Sie erlauben wohl!; 9b. Sie geht links, er geht rechts; 9c. Bist du's, lachendes Glück; 9d. Sah nur die kleine Hand; 9e. Leichsinn ist die Parole. ACT 2: 10a. Hoch, evöe, Angèle Didier; 10b. Ich danke, meine Herrn und meine Damen; 11a. Sind Sie von Sinnen, Herr Baron?; 11b. Lieber Freund, man greift nicht nach von Sternen; 12a. Schau'n Sie freundlichst mich an; 12b. Mädel klein, Mädel fein; 13. Ach seh'n Sie doch, er ist ganz blass; 14. Der Handshuch, wie pikant; 15. Es duftet nach Trèfle incarnat; 16. Ein Löwe war ich im Salon (Polkatänzer); 17. Kam ein Falter leicht geflattert; 18a. Bin jener Graf von Luxemburg; 18b. Adieuu, Angèle. ACT 3: 19. Introduction; 20. Alles mit Ruhe geniessen; 21. Mädel klein, Mädel fein; 22a. Packt die Liebe einem Alten; 22b. Liebe, ach, du Sonnenschein; 23. Es duftet nach Trèfle incarnat; 24. Wir bummeln durch's Leben (finale).

Count René N. Gedda
Prince Basil K. Böhme
Countess Stasa G. Litz
Armand Brissard; Pawel von Pawlowitsch W. Brokmeier
Angèle Didier L. Popp
Juliette Vermont R. Holm
Sergei Metschikoff H.G. Grimm
Pélégrin W. Anheisser
Manager of the Grand Hotel H. Günther

Bavarian St Op Chor, Graunke SO, W. Mattes (r1968)
(EMI) Ⓓ [2] **CMS5 65375-2**

Excs M. Hill Smith, N. Jenkins, V. Tierney, H. Nicoll, L. Richard, New Sadler's Wells Op. Chor, New Sadler's Wells Op. Orch, B. Wordsworth (Eng) (TER) Ⓓ **CDTER1050**
(1/84) (TER) ⊟ **ZCTER1050**

Excs M. Hill Smith, N. Jenkins, V. Tierney, H. Nicoll, L. Richard, New Sadler's Wells Op Chor, New Sadler's Wells Op Orch, B. Wordsworth (Eng) (TER) Ⓓ **CDTEO1004**
(TER) ⊟ **ZCTEO1004**

1, 3, 4b, 9a, 9c, 11b, 12a, 16, 19, 22b H. Brauner, R. Holm, E. Liebesberg, D. Hermann, R. Christ, H. Prikopa, Vienna Volksoper Chor, Vienna Volksoper Orch, F. Bauer-Theussl
(KOCH) Ⓓ **399 223**

2. B. Weikl, Austrian RSO, K. Eichhorn
(ORFE) Ⓓ **C077831A**

7, 8a, 8b, 9a, 9b, 9c, 23, 24. H. Gueden, W. Kmentt, Vienna Volksoper Chor, Vienna Volksoper Orch, M. Schönherr (r1965)
(6/95) (LOND) Ⓓ **436 896-2LA**

8a, 10a E. Schwarzkopf, chor, Philh, O. Ackermann (1/86) (EMI) Ⓓ **CDC7 47284-2**

11b G. Alpar, H.E. Groh, orch, O. Dobrindt (r1932) (MMOI) Ⓓ **CDMOIR419**
(MMOI) ⊟ **CMOIR419**

11b R. Holm, W. Krenn, Vienna Volksoper Orch, A. Paulik (r1970) (DECC) Ⓓ **436 316-2DA**
(DECC) ⊟ **436 316-4DA**

11b R. Holm, W. Krenn, Vienna Volksoper Orch, A. Paulik (r1970) (LOND) Ⓓ **436 897-2DM**

12a N. Vallin, A. Baugé, orch, G. Andolfi (r1934: French) (EMI) Ⓓ [2] **CZS5 68292-2**

18b M. Hill Smith, New Sadler's Wells Op Chor, New Sadler's Wells Op Orch, B. Wordsworth (r1989-91; Eng) (10/91) (TER) Ⓓ **CDVIR8314**
(10/91) (TER) ⊟ **ZCVIR8314**

Das **Land des Lächelns, 'Land of Smiles'– operetta: 3 acts (1929—Berlin) (Lib. L Herzer & F Löhner)**

EXCERPTS: 1a. Overture. ACT 1: 1b. Hoch soll sie leben; 1c. Ich danke fur die Huldigung; 1d. Heut! meine Herr'n was win Tag; 1e. Flirten, bisschen flirten; 1f. Gern, gern, wär'ich verliebt; 2. Es ist nicht das erstemal; 3a. Ich trete ins Zimmer, von Sehnsucht durchbebt; 3b. Immer nur lächeln und immer vergnügt; 3c. Ich kann es nicht sagen, ich sage es nie; 4a. Ach, trinken Sie vielleicht; 4b. Bei einem Tee en deux; 5. Von Apfelblüten einem Kranz; 6a. Wir sind allein; 6b. Ein Lied, es verfolget mich Tag und Nacht; 6c. Es wird schon so sein. ACT 2: 7a. Prelude; 7b. Dschinthien wuomen ju chon ma goa can; 7c. In Namen unseres Wen Sway Jeh; 8a. Dich sehe ich und nur dich sehe ich!; 8b. Wer hat die Liebe uns ins Herz; 9. Im Salon zur blau'n Pagode; 10a. Als Gott die Welt erschuf; 10b. Meine Liebe, deine Liebe; 11. Dein ist mein ganzes Herz! (You are my heart's delight); 12a. Alles vorbei!; 12b. Ich möcht' einmal die Heimat seh'n; 13a. Mit welchem Recht?!; 13b. Du hast mich vor allen gedemütigt; 13c. Ihr Götter, sagt, was ist mir gescheh'n? ACT 3: 14a. Liebe besiegt; 14b. Märchen von Glück; 15a. Wenn die Chyrsanthemen blüh'n; 15b. Du bist so zart; 15c. Wie rasch verwelkte doch das kleine Blümchen Glück!; 16a. Dieselbe Sonne, die über Europa scheint; 16b. Liebes Schwesterlein.

Lisa E. Schwarzkopf
Gustl E. Kunz
Sou-Chong N. Gedda
Mi E. Loose
Tschang O. Kraus

BBC Chor, Philh, O. Ackermann (r1953)
(11/88) (EMI) Ⓓ [2] **CHS7 69523-2**

Lisa A. Rothenberger
Gustl H. Friedauer
Sou-Chong N. Gedda
Mi R. Holm
Tschang J. Moeller

Bavarian Rad Chor, Graunke SO, W. Mattes (r1967: with dialogue)
(2/95) (EMI) Ⓓ [2] **CMS5 65372-2**

Excs M. Dens, C. Devos, L. Noguera, L. Berton, C. Collart, Raymond St Paul Chor, Orch, M. Cariven (r1956: Fr)
(EMI) Ⓓ [2] **CZS7 67872-**

1a, 1b M. Hill Smith, Chandos Concert Orch, S. Barry (Eng) (2/90) (CHAN) Ⓓ **CHAN875**
(2/90) (CHAN) ⊟ **LBTD02**

1a, 1b, 3a, 4b, 5, 6a-c, 7a-c, 8a, 8b, 9, 10a, 10b, 11, 12a, 12b, 15a-c, 16a, 16b M. Schramm, F. Gruber, R. Schock, L. Schmidt, Günther Arndt Ch, Berlin SO, R. Stolz
(4/88) (EURO) Ⓓ **258 37**

1a, 2, 3a, 4b, 5, 6b, 8b, 9, 11, 14a, 15c, 16a, 16b G. di Stefano, D. Koller, V. Goodall, H. Holecek, Vienna Volksoper Orch, H. Lambrecht (r1967) (PREI) Ⓓ **9314**

3b, 4b, 5, 11. R. Tauber, V. Schwarz, Berlin Staatskapelle, F. Lehár (r1929)
(12/89) (EMI) Ⓓ **CDH7 69787-**

3b, 4b, 5, 6b, 8a, 8b, 11. R. Tauber, V. Schwarz, Berlin St Op Orch, F. Lehár (r1929)
(3/89) (PEAR) Ⓓ **GEMMCD931**

3b, 4b, 5, 8b, 11, 12a, 12b, 13c V. Schwarz, R. Tauber, Berlin Staatskapelle, F. Lehár (r1929)
(1/94) (EMI) Ⓓ **CDC7 54838-**

3b, 5, 8b, 15b I. Eisinger, J. Schmidt, Berlin City Op Orch, S. Meyrowitz (r1929)
(RELI) Ⓓ **CR92103**

4a, 4b B. Hendricks, G. Quilico, Lyon Op Orch, L. Foster (r1993)
(6/95) (EMI) Ⓓ **CDC5 55151-**

4a, 4b, 8, 11. R. Holm, W. Krenn, Vienna Volksoper Orch, A. Paulik (r1970)
(LOND) Ⓓ **436 897-2D**

4a, 4b, 11, 12b J. Kolomyjec, M. DuBois, Kitchener-Waterloo SO, R. Armenian
(CBC) Ⓓ **SMCD512**

5. F. Wunderlich, Graunke SO, C. Michalski
(EMI) Ⓓ [3] **CZS7 62993-**

5. R. Tauber, Berlin Staatskapelle, F. Lehár (r1929) (12/92) (NIMB) Ⓓ **NI783**
(12/92) (NIMB) ⊟ **NC783**

5. A. Davies, S. Bullock, A. Bryn Parri (r1994; sung in English) (11/95) (SAIN) Ⓓ **SCDC208**

8a, 8b M. Hill Smith, Chandos Concert Orch, S. Barry (10/91) (CHAN) Ⓓ **CHAN897**

11. P. Domingo, MMF Orch, Rome Op Orch, Z. Mehta (pp1990) (DECC) ◖ **071 123-1D**
(DECC) ▣ **071 123-3D**

11. P. Domingo, LSO, K-H. Loges (arr Loges)
(DG) Ⓓ [3] **427 708-2GX**

11. P. Domingo, LSO, K-H. Loges
(DG) ⊟ **419 091-4GW**

11. M. Feinstein, A. Guzelimian (Eng)
(5/90) (EMI) ⊟ **EG749768-**

11. R. Merrill, Orch, H. Barlow (bp1957)
(VAI) ▣ **VAI6911**

11. P. Domingo, LSO, K-H. Loges (arr. Loges)
(DG) Ⓓ **413 451-2G**

11. R. Schock, orch, W. Schüchter (r1957)
(EMI) Ⓓ **CDM7 69475-**

11. J. Carreras, ECO, R. Benzi
(PHIL) Ⓓ **416 973-2P**
(PHIL) ⊟ **416 973-4P**

11. R. Karczykowski, Polish Nat RSO, R. Bibl
(POLS) Ⓓ **PNCD08**

11. S. Burrows, National PO, R. Stapleton (Eng)
(DECC) Ⓓ **433 223-2DW**
(DECC) ⊟ **433 223-4DW**

11. J. Locke, orch, R. Martin (Eng)
(EMI) Ⓓ **CDP7 98844-**
(EMI) ⊙ **GO203**

11. M. Lanza, orch, R. Sinatra (Eng: bp1952)
(RCA) Ⓓ [3] **GD60889(1**

11. J. Carreras, ECO, R. Benzi
(PHIL) Ⓓ **434 152-2P**

11. P. Domingo, MMF Orch, Rome Op Orch, Z. Mehta (pp1990) (DECC) ⓄⓄ **430 433-5D**

11. R. Tauber, orch (r1935: Eng)
(MMOI) Ⓓ **CDMOIR41**
(MMOI) ⊟ **CMOIR41**

11. R. Tauber, orch (r1935)
(ASV) Ⓓ **CDAJA511**
(ASV) ⊟ **ZCAJA511**

11. P. Domingo, LSO, K-H. Loges (arr Loges)
(BELA) Ⓓ **450 036-**
(BELA) ⊟ **450 036-**

11. J. Björling, Inst Ens (r1960: Ger/Swed)
(DECC) Ⓓ **436 316-2D**
(DECC) ⊟ **436 316-4D**

11. J. Carreras, ECO, R. Benzi
(PHIL) Ⓓ **442 602-2P**
(PHIL) ⊟ **442 602-4P**

11. R. Tauber, orch (r1935: Eng)
(PEAR) Ⓓ **GEMMCD912**

11. J. Björling, orch (r1959)
(DECC) ⦶ **443 379-2DM**
11. F. Araiza, Munich RO, R. Weikert (r1992)
(RCA) ⦶ **09026 62550-2**
11. P. Domingo, ECO, J. Rudel
(2/87) (EMI) ⦶ **CDC7 47398-2**
11. J. Lloyd Webber, RPO, N. Cleobury (arr vc/orch) (3/87) (PHIL) ⦶ **416 698-2PH**
11. R. Tauber, Berlin St Op Orch, F. Lehár (r1929) (7/89) (EMI) ⦶ **CDM7 69476-2**
11. P. Domingo, MMF Orch, Rome Op Orch, Z. Mehta (pp1990)
(10/90) (DECC) ⦶ **430 433-2DH**
(10/90) (DECC) ⊟ **430 433-4DH**
11. F. Araiza, Munich RSO, R. Weikert
(3/93) (RCA) ⦶ **09026 61163-2**
11. J. Björling, orch, N. Grevillius (r1932: Swed)
(12/94) (MMOI) ⦶ **CDMOIR425**
11. O. Bjarnason, W. Jones (pp1994)
(1/95) (RCA) ⦶ **09026 62547-2**
11. J. Björling, Inst Ens (r1959)
(10/95) (DECC) ⦶ **443 930-2DM**
12b L. Popp, ASMF, N. Marriner
(6/88) (EMI) ⦶ **CDC7 49700-2**

Die **Lustige Witwe, '(The) Merry Widow'– operetta: 3 acts (1905—Vienna) (Lib. Léon & Stein)**

EXCERPTS—ACT 1: 1a. Verehrteste Damen und Herren (Introduction); 1b. Ballroom music; 2. So kommen Sie!...Ich bin eine anständ'ge Frau (Valencienne, Camille); 3a. Bitte, meine Herr'n (Entrance song: Hanna, ensemble); 3b. Ballroom music; 4. O Vaterland...Da geh' ich zu Maxim (Entrance song: Danilo); 5. Ja was? ein trautes Zimmerlein (Zauber der Häuslichkeit (Val, Cam); 6. Damenwahl!...O kommet doch, o kommt, Ihr Ballsiren). ACT 2: 7a. Ich bin, hier jetzt zu verweilen (Introduction and Dance); 7b. Es lebt eine Vilja, ein Waldmägdelein (Vilja-Lied: Hanna, chorus); 8. Heia, Mädel, aufgeschaut...Dummer, dummer Reitersmann (Hanna, Danilo); 9. Wie die Weiber man behandelt? (March-septet); 10. Play-scene and Dance duet (Hanna, Danilo); 11. Mein Freund, Vernunft!...Wie eine Rosenknospe (Valencienne, Camille); 12. Ha! Ha! Wir fragen...Es waren zwei Königskinder (Finale). ACT 3: 13a. Entr'acte (Vilja-song); 13b. Maxim's music; 13c. Dance scene (Cake-walk); 14a. Ja, wir sind es, die Grisetten (Valencienne, Grisettes); 14b. Da geh' ich zu Maxim (Reminiscence: Danilo, Grisettes); 15. Lippen schweigen (Hanna, Danilo); 16. Ja, das Stadium der Weiber ist schwerz (Finale). ADDITIONAL NUMBERS: 17. Overture (composed 1940); 18. Butterflies (Grisettes: London, 1907); 19. I was born, by cruel fate (Njegus: London, 1907).

Hanna J. Sutherland
Baron Zeta G. Wilcock
Valencienne A-M. McDonald
Danilo R. Stevens
Camille A. Austin
Cascade N. Kirkby
Brioche C. Dawes
Bogdanovich D. Brennan
Sylviane C. Clack
Kromov J. Germain
Olga I. Cassimatis
Pritschsch D. Soloman
Praskovia R. Raisbeck
Njegus G. Ewer
Australian Op Chor, Sydney Eliz PO, R. Bonynge, V. Lumsden
(MCEG) ▣ **VVD828**
Cpte Canada Nat Ballet, Canada Nat Ballet Orch, E. Florio, N. Campbell (arr Lanchberry)
(PION) ◐ **PLMCB00271**
Hanna Glawari F. Lott
Danilo T. Hampson
Mirko Zeta R. Poulton
Camille J. Aler
Valencienne E. Szmytka
Raoul R. Schasching
Cascada K. Azesberger
Glyndebourne Fest Chor, LPO, F. Welser-Möst (pp1993: omits dialogue)
(EMI) ⦶ **CDC5 55141-2**
Hanna Glawari E. Schwarzkopf
Danilo E. Waechter
Mirko Zeta J. Knapp
Camille N. Gedda
Valencienne H. Steffek
Raoul H. Strohbauer
Cascada K. Equiluz
Njegus F. Böheim
Philh Chor, Philh, L. von Matačić (omits 5,13c)
(4/86) (EMI) ⦶ [2] **CDS7 47178-8**
Hanna Glawari E. Schwarzkopf
Danilo E. Kunz
Mirko Zeta A. Niessner
Camille N. Gedda
Valencienne E. Loose
Raoul J. Schmidinger
Cascada O. Kraus
BBC Chor, Philh, O. Ackermann (omits 5,10,13a,13b,13c,14b: r1953)
(11/88) (EMI) ⦶ **CDH7 69520-2**
Hanna Glawari E. Harwood
Danilo R. Kollo
Mirko Zeta Z. Kélémen
Camille W. Hollweg
Valencienne T. Stratas
Raoul W. Krenn
Cascada D. Grobe
Berlin Deutsche Op Chor, BPO, H. von Karajan
(8/92) (DG) ⦶ [2] **435 712-2GX2**
Hanna Glawari F. Lott
Danilo T. Hampson
Mirko Zeta R. Poulton
Camille J. Aler
Valencienne E. Szmytka
Raoul R. Schasching
Cascada K. Azesberger
Njegus D. Bogarde
Glyndebourne Fest Chor, LPO, F. Welser-Möst (pp1993: Eng narr)
(9/94) (EMI) ⦶ [2] **CDS5 55152-2**
Hanna C. Studer
Danilo B. Skovhus
Zeta B. Terfel
Camille R. Trost
Valencienne B. Bonney
Raoul U. Peper
Cascada K-M. Fredriksson
Njegus H. Zednik
Bogdanowitsch R. Savage
Sylviane L. Alcantara
Kromow P. Salmon
C. Backes
Pritschitsch J. Clarkson
Praškowia A. Kazimierczuk
Wiener Tschuschenkapelle, VPO, J. E. Gardiner (r1994: with dialogue)
(2/95) (DG) ⦶ **439 911-2GH**
(2/95) (DG) ⊟ **439 911-4GH**
Ballet version Canada Nat Ballet (arr Lanchberry) (MCEG) ▣ **VVD390**
Excs J. Vivalda, M. Dens, M. Linval, R. Amade, P. Germain, J. Pruvost, J-C. Benoit, R. Duclos Ch, Paris Cons, F. Pourcel (r1960: Fr)
(EMI) ⦶ [2] **CZS7 67872-2**
Gar oft hab' ich gehört A. Moffo, H. Galatis Orch, H. Galatis (arr Galatis)
(EURO) ⦶ **GD69113**
1a, 1b, 2, 3a, 3b, 4, 6, 7a, 7b, 8, 9, 14a, 14b, 15, 16. E. Harrhy, H. Kucharek, J. Moyle, A. Oke, G. Winslade, P. Parfitt, M. Curtis, New Sadler's Wells Op Chor, New Sadler's Wells Op Orch, B. Wordsworth (Eng) (TER) ⦶ **CDTEO1003**
(TER) ⊟ **ZCTEO1003**
1a, 1b, 2, 3a, 4, 6, 7b, 8-10, 14a, 15, 16. E. Harwood, T. Stratas, R. Kollo, W. Hollweg, Z. Kélémen, D. Grobe, W. Krenn, Berlin Deutsche Op Chor, BPO, H. von Karajan (r1972)
(3/86) (DG) ⦶ **415 524-2GH**
1a, 2, 3a, 4, 5, 6, 7a, 7b, 8, 11, 12, 14a, 15. J. Bronhill, D. Dowling, H. Glynne, M. Lowe, T. Round, W. McAlpine, J. Kentish, R. Herincx, J. Larsen, William Booth, Sadler's Wells Op Chor, Sadler's Wells Op Orch, W. Reid (Eng: r1957)
(CFP) ⦶ **CD-CFP4485**
(CFP) ⊟ **TC-CFP4485**
1a, 2, 3a, 4, 6-9, 11, 12, 14a, 15. A. Rothenberger, E. Köth, N. Gedda, R. Ilosfalvy, Bavarian Rad Chor, Graunke SO, W. Mattes
(EMI) ⦶ **CDM7 69090-2**
1a, 2, 3a, 4, 6, 7a, 8, 9, 11, 12, 14a, 15, 16. S. Németh, M. Tiboldi, M. Vásári, G. Leblanc, L. Kokas, L. Csere, L. Hadics, Budapest Operetta Chor, Budapest Operetta Orch, L. Makláry
(LASE) ⦶ **14 212**
1a, 2, 3a, 4-6, 7a, 7b, 8-12, 13a, 13b, 14a, 15, 16. H. Gueden, E. Loose, P. Grunden, W. Kmentt, P. Klein, K. Equiluz, K. Dönch, H. Duhan, M. Rus, L. Pantscheff, Vienna St Op Chor, Vienna St Op Orch, R. Stolz (r1958)
(6/95) (LOND) ⦶ **436 899-2LA**
1-4, 6-9, 11-16. E. Harrhy, H. Kucharek, J. Moyle, A. Oke, G. Winslade, P. Parfitt, M. Curtis, New Sadler's Wells Op. Chor, New Sadler's Wells Op. Orch, B. Wordsworth (Eng)
(12/86) (TER) ⦶ **CDTER1111**
(12/86) (TER) ⊟ **ZCTER1111**
3a, 15. J. Sutherland, R. Stevens, Sydney Eliz PO, R. Bonynge (DECC) ◐ **071 149-1DH**
(DECC) ▣ **071 149-3DH**
3b National SO, J.O. Edwards
(TER) ⦶ **CDVIR8315**
4. R. Schock, Berlin FFB Orch, W. Schmidt-Boelcke (EMI) ⦶ **CDM7 69475-2**
4. R. Karczykowski, Polish Nat RSO, R. Bibl
(POLS) ⦶ **PNCD087**
4, 7b, 15. N. Gedda, T. Gedda, Stockholm Palm Court Orch, L. Almgren (pp1987)
(BLUE) ⦶ **ABCD014**
6(pt) R. Tauber, orch, D. Bela (French: r c1933)
(3/89) (PEAR) ⦶ **GEMMCD9310**
7a, 7b J. Sutherland, Ambrosian Light Op Chor, New Philh, R. Bonynge
(DECC) ⦶ **417 780-2DM**
7a, 7b J. Sutherland, Ambrosian Light Op Chor, New Philh, R. Bonynge (Eng)
(DECC) ⦶ **433 223-2DWO**
(DECC) ⊟ **433 223-4DWO**
7a, 7b J. Sutherland, Ambrosian Light Op Chor, New Philh, R. Bonynge (r1966)
(DECC) ⦶ **436 316-2DA**
(DECC) ⊟ **436 316-4DA**
7a, 7b E. Schwarzkopf, Philh Chor, Philh, L. von Matačić (r1962) (EMI) ⦶ **CDC5 55095-2**
7a, 7b L. Popp, Ambrosian Op. Chor, ASMF, N. Marriner (6/88) (EMI) ⦶ **CDC7 49700-2**
7a, 7b M. Hill Smith, Ambrosian Sngrs, Chandos Concert Orch, S. Barry (Eng)
(7/88) (CHAN) ⦶ **CHAN8561**
(7/88) (CHAN) ⊟ **LBTD019**
7b E. Bettendorf, orch (r1929)
(MMOI) ⦶ **CDMOIR419**
(MMOI) ⊟ **CMOIR419**
7b R. Scotto, Eslovaca Philharmonica Orch, K. Leitner (r1992) (IMP) ⦶ **PCDS21**
(IMP) ⊟ **PCDSC21**
7b J. Lloyd Webber, ECO, N. Cleobury (arr C Palmer) (3/85) (PHIL) ⦶ **412 231-2PH**
7b R. Tauber, Orch (r1932)
(12/89) (EMI) ⦶ **CDH7 69787-2**
7b E. Schwarzkopf, Philh, O. Ackermann (r1953)
(12/90) (EMI) ⦶ **CDM7 63657-2**
7b B. Hendricks, Philh, L. Foster (r1992)
(8/93) (EMI) ⦶ **CDC7 54626-2**
7b J. Migenes, Vienna Volksoper Orch, L. Schifrin (r1993)
(1/94) (ERAT) ⦶ **4509-92875-2**
(1/94) (ERAT) ⊟ **4509-92875-4**
7b H. Donath, K. Donath (pp1994)
(1/95) (RCA) ⦶ **09026 62547-2**
7b L. Popp, G. Parsons (pp1981)
(6/95) (ORFE) ⦶ **C363941B**
7b, 15. V. Zeani, A. Lazzari, Rome RAI Orch, B. Maderna (pp1968) (BONG) ⦶ **GB1060-2**
11. A. Rautawaara, P. Anders, Berlin Deutsche Op Orch, P. Hühn (r1937)
(MMOI) ⦶ **CDMOIR419**
(MMOI) ⊟ **CMOIR419**
11. N. Vallin, A. Baugé, orch (r1930s: French)
(FORL) ⦶ **UCD19022**
14b P. Domingo, ECO, J. Rudel
(2/87) (EMI) ⦶ **CDC7 47398-2**
14b, 15. M. Hill Smith, P. Morrison, Chandos Concert Orch, S. Barry (Eng)
(6/85) (CHAN) ⦶ **CHAN8362**
(6/85) (CHAN) ⊟ **LBTD013**
15. E.C. Lund, Vienna Op Ball Orch, U. Theimer
(VICT) ⦶ **VCD19008**
15. J. Sutherland, W. Krenn, National PO, R. Bonynge (Eng) (DECC) ⦶ **433 223-2DWO**
(DECC) ⊟ **433 223-4DWO**
15. R. Tauber, orch, E. Korngold (r1931)
(MMOI) ⦶ **CDMOIR419**
(MMOI) ⊟ **CMOIR419**
15. R. Holm, W. Krenn, Vienna Volksoper Orch, A. Paulik (r1970) (DECC) ⦶ **436 316-2DA**
(DECC) ⊟ **436 316-4DA**
15. R. Holm, W. Krenn, Vienna Volksoper Orch, A. Paulik (r1970) (LOND) ⦶ **436 897-2DM**
15. K. Battle, P. Domingo, NY Met Op Orch, James Levine (pp1988: Eng)
(DG) ⦶ **445 552-2GMA**
(DG) ⊟ **445 552-4GMA**
15. N. Vallin, A. Baugé, orch, G. Andolfi (r1934: French) (EMI) ⦶ [2] **CZS5 68292-2**
15. R. Tauber, Orch, E. Korngold (r1931)
(12/89) (EMI) ⦶ **CDH7 69787-2**
15. R. Tauber, Odeon Künstlerorchester, E. Korngold (r1932) (12/92) (NIMB) ⦶ **NI7833**
(12/92) (NIMB) ⊟ **NC7833**
15. B. Hendricks, G. Quilico, Lyon Op Orch, L. Foster (r1993) (6/95) (EMI) ⦶ **CDC5 55151-2**

17. VPO, F. Lehár (r1940)
(1/94) (EMI) ⓘ **CDC7 54838-2**

Paganini– operetta: 3 acts (1925—Berlin) (Lib. Knepler and Jenbach)
ACT 1: 1. Violin solo; 2. Mein lieber Freund; 3. Schönes Italien; 4. So jung noch; 5. Feuersglut Lodert; 6. Niemals habe ich mich interessiert; 7. Die Fürstin Anna Elisa. ACT 2: 8. Wenn keine Liebe wär'; 9. Gern hab' ich die Frau'n geküsst; 10. Deinen süssen Rosenmund; 11. Launisch sind alle Frau'n; 12a. Sag' mir, wieviel süsse; 12b. Niemand liebt dich so wie; 13a. Ich kann es nicht fassen; 13b. Liebe du Himmel auf Erden; 14. Was ist's, das unsern Sinn erregt?. ACT 3: 15. Neapolitanisches Lied und Tanz; 16. Schnapslied; 17. Melodram und Reminiszenz; 18. Jetzt beginnt ein neues Leben; 19. Wo meine Wiege stand; 20. Du bist geflohen.

Excs E. Liebesberg, E. Mechera, R. Christ, K. Equiluz, Vienna Volksoper Chor, Vienna Volksoper Orch, F. Bauer-Theussl
(KOCH) ⓘ **399 226**

Excs A. Forli, M. Dens, N. Sautereau, G. Godin, Paris Cons, F. Pourcel (r1962: Fr)
(EMI) ⓘ [2] **CZS7 67872-2**

3, 9. R. Tauber, Berlin St Op Orch, H. Weigert (r1925) (12/92) (NIMB) ⓘ **NI7833**
(12/92) (NIMB) ▭ **NC7833**

9. R. Karczykowski, Polish Nat RSO, R. Bibl
(POLS) ⓘ **PNCD087**

9. S. Burrows, National PO, R. Stapleton (Eng)
(DECC) ⓘ **433 223-2DWO**
(DECC) ▭ **433 223-4DWO**

9. R. Tauber, orch (r1927)
(MMOI) ⓘ **CDMOIR419**
(MMOI) ▭ **CMOIR419**

9. A. Baugé, orch (r1930s: French)
(FORL) ⓘ **UCD19022**

9. P. Baillie, NZ SO, C. Roller (r1982)
(KIWI) ⓘ **CDSLD-82**

9. R. Tauber, Berlin St Op Orch, H. Weigert (r1925) (NIMB) ⓘ **NI7864**

9. A. Baugé, orch, G. Andolfi (r1935: French)
(EMI) ⓘ [2] **CZS5 68292-2**

9. P. Domingo, ECO, J. Rudel
(2/87) (EMI) ⓘ **CDC7 47398-2**

9. M. Hill Smith, Chandos Concert Orch, S. Barry (Eng) (7/88) (CHAN) ⓘ **CHAN8561**
(7/88) (CHAN) ▭ **LBTD019**

9. R. Tauber, Berlin Künstlertheater Orch, E. Hauke (r1927) (12/89) (EMI) ⓘ **CDH7 69787-2**

9, 12a, 12b, 13a, 13b R. Holm, W. Krenn, Vienna Volksoper Orch, A. Paulik (r1970)
(LOND) ⓘ **436 897-2DM**

9, 12b, 13b N. Gedda, T. Gedda, Stockholm Palm Court Orch, L. Almgren (pp1987)
(BLUE) ⓘ **ABCD014**

13b J. Sutherland, Ambrosian Light Op Chor, New Philh, R. Bonynge (Eng)
(DECC) ⓘ **433 223-2DWO**
(DECC) ▭ **433 223-4DWO**

13b M. Reining, Berlin Deutsche Op Orch, W. Lutze (r1939) (9/92) (PREI) ⓘ **90083**

13b E. Réthy, VPO, F. Lehár (r1940)
(1/94) (PREI) ⓘ **90150**

13b E. Réthy, VPO, F. Lehár (r1940)
(1/94) (EMI) ⓘ **CDC7 54838-2**

13b J. Migenes, Vienna Volksoper Orch, L. Schifrin (r1993)
(1/94) (ERAT) ⓘ **4509-92875-2**
(1/94) (ERAT) ▭ **4509-92875-4**

13b, 15. M. Hill Smith, Chandos Concert Orch, S. Barry (10/91) (CHAN) ⓘ **CHAN8978**

Der **Rastelbinder– operetta: 2 acts (1902—Vienna) (Lib. Léon)**
Wenn zwei sich lieben R. Tauber, C. Vanconti, orch (r1928) (3/89) (PEAR) ⓘ **GEMMCD9310**

Schön ist die Welt, 'Beautiful World'– operetta: 3 acts (1930—Berlin) (Lib. F. Löhrer and L. Herzer)
EXCERPTS: 1. Overture. ACT 1: 2. Nichts zu seh'n, gar nichts zu seh'n; 3a. Wie süss muss die Liebe sein; 3b. Sag', armes Herzchen, sag; 4. Herzogin Marie; 5. Nur ein Viertelstündchen; 6a. Bruder Leichtsinn, so werd'ich genannt; 6b. Schön ist die Welt; 7a. Ein Ausflug mit Ihnen; 7b. Frei und jung dabei; 8a. Tropfenglut hat ihr Blut; 8b. Rio de Janeiro; 9. Ja, was ist mit mir? (finale). ACT 2: 10. Jetzt mit der rechten Hand; 11. Es steht vom Lieben so oft geschrieben; 12. Liebste, glaub' an mich; 13. Was ist geschehen? Eine Lawine! (finale). ACT 3: 14. Herr Direcktor, bitte sehr!; 15. Ja, die Liebe ist brutal; 16a. Dort in der kleinen Tanzbar; 16b. In der kleinen Bar; 17. Ich bin verliebt; 18a. Heimlich wie in der Nacht die Diebe; 18b. Schön sind lachende Frau'n; 19. Liebste, glaub' an mich (finale).

3b, 17. J. Migenes, Vienna Volksoper Orch, L. Schifrin (r1993)
(1/94) (ERAT) ⓘ **4509-92875-2**
(1/94) (ERAT) ▭ **4509-92875-4**

6b F. Wunderlich, Berlin SO, A. Melichar
(EURO) ⓘ **GD69018**
(EURO) ▭ **GK69018**

6b W. Krenn, Vienna Volksoper Orch, A. Paulik (r1970) (DECC) ⓘ **436 316-2DA**
(DECC) ▭ **436 316-4DA**

6b, 7a, 7b, 17. R. Holm, W. Krenn, Vienna Volksoper Orch, A. Paulik (r1970)
(LOND) ⓘ **436 897-2DM**

6b, 7b, 9 (pt), 11, 17, 19. R. Schock, S. Geszty, Berlin SO, W. Schmidt-Boelcke
(2/91) (EURO) ⓘ **GD69021**

17. M. Hill Smith, Chandos Concert Orch, S. Barry (10/91) (CHAN) ⓘ **CHAN8978**

17. E. Réthy, Vienna SO, F. Lehár (r1942)
(1/94) (PREI) ⓘ **90150**

17. E. Réthy, Vienna SO, F. Lehár (r1942)
(1/94) (EMI) ⓘ **CDC7 54838-2**

Wo die Lerche singt, 'Where the Lark sings'– operetta (1918—Vienna) (Lib. Willner & Reichert, after F. Martos)
Durch die weiten singt M. Hill Smith, Chandos Concert Orch, S. Barry
(10/91) (CHAN) ⓘ **CHAN8978**

Der **Zarewitsch, '(The) Czarevich'– operetta: 3 acts (1927—Berlin) (Wds. B. Jenbach & H. Reichart)**
EXCERPTS: ACT 1: 1. Es steht ein Soldat am Wolgastrand; 2. Hell erklingt ein liebliches frohed Heimatlied (Melodram); 3a. War' ein echter Schwerenöter; 3b. Wo die Lerche singt; 4. Schaukle, Liebchen, schaulke; 5. Einer wird kommen; 6. Allein! Wieder allein (Wolgalied); 7a. Win Weib! Du ein Weib?; 7b. Geh' trinke deinen Tee; 7c. Trinkt man auf du und du. ACT 2: 8. Herz, warum schlägst du so bang?; 9. Ich Name war Amalie von Bretzenheim; 10. Hab' nur dich allein; 11. Heute hab' ich (Napolitana); 12. O Komm, es hat der Frühling ach nur einen Mai; 13. Heute Abend komm' ich zu dir; 14. Das Leben ruft; 15a. Liebe mich, küsse mich; 15b. Setz' dich her! Denke du bist ein Märchenprinz!; 15c. Ich bin verliebt; 15d. Berauscht har mich der heimatliche Tanz! (Finale). ACT 3: 16. Intermezzo; 17. Kosende Wellen; 18. Warum hat jeder Frühling, ach, nur einen Mai?; 20. Ich ben bereit! zu jeder Zeit!; 21a. Für den grossen Zar; 21b. Wir wollen dir dienen; 22. Warum hat jeder Frühling, ach, nur einen Mai? (reprise).

1, 2, 5, 7c, 10, 17. H. Gueden, W. Kmentt, Vienna Volksoper Chor, Vienna Volksoper Orch, M. Schönherr (r1965)
(6/95) (LOND) ⓘ **436 896-2LA**

1, 3, 4, 5, 6c, 7, 9, 10, 14, 15. G. di Stefano, D. Koller, D. Hanak, H. Holecek, Orig Volga Cossacks Chor, Vienna Operetta Chor, Vienna Operetta Orch, Balalaika Sols, E-G. Scherzer
(SCHW) ⓘ **312732**

1, 4-6, 7c, 8, 13, 14, 16, 21b R. Schock, P. von Felinau, R. Holm, K-E. Mercker, H. Wisniewska, K. Lang, Berlin Deutsche Op Chor, Berlin SO, R. Stolz (EURO) ⓘ **258 357**

4. J. Migenes, Vienna Volksoper Orch, L. Schifrin (r1993)
(1/94) (ERAT) ⓘ **4509-92875-2**
(1/94) (ERAT) ▭ **4509-92875-4**

5. A. Moffo, H. Galatis Orch, H. Galatis (arr Galatis) (EURO) ⓘ **GD69113**

5. E. Schwarzkopf, Philh, O. Ackermann
(1/86) (EMI) ⓘ **CDC7 47284-2**

5. M. Reining, Berlin Deutsche Op Orch, W. Lutze (r1939) (9/92) (PREI) ⓘ **90083**

5. E. Réthy, Vienna SO, F. Lehár (r1942)
(1/94) (PREI) ⓘ **90150**

5. E. Réthy, Vienna SO, F. Lehár (r1942)
(1/94) (EMI) ⓘ **CDC7 54838-2**

5, 17. M. Hill Smith, Chandos Concert Orch, S. Barry (10/91) (CHAN) ⓘ **CHAN8978**

6. F. Wunderlich, Berlin SO, A. Melichar
(EURO) ⓘ **GD69018**
(EURO) ▭ **GK69018**

6. F. Araiza, Munich RSO, R. Weikert
(3/93) (RCA) ⓘ **09026 61163-2**

6, 13. R. Schock, E. Köth, orch, W. Schüchter (r1957) (EMI) ⓘ **CDM7 69475-2**

6, 17. R. Holm, W. Krenn, Vienna Volksoper Orch, A. Paulik (r1970)
(LOND) ⓘ **436 897-2DM**

10, 17. F. Wunderlich, M. Muszely, Graunke SO, C. Michalski (EMI) ⓘ [3] **CZS7 62993-2**

Ziguenerliebe, 'Gipsy Love'– operetta: 3 acts (1910—Vienna) (Lib. Willner and Bodanzky)
EXCERPTS–; 1. Introduction. ACT 1: 2. Heissa, heissa!; 3. So sprach noch niemals ein Mann zu mir!; 4. Es liegt in blauen Fernen; 5. So treaska! Liebe Gäste!; 6. Trägst den Zweig in deinen Händchen rosig zart; 7. Will die Männer ich berücken; 8. Zuerst such man Gelegenheit; 9a. Da habt Ihr nun den Mond in voller Pracht; 9b. Lass' uns nach dem Garten ziehen; 9c. Glück hat als Gast - nie lange Rast!. ACT 2: 10. Kutyalácos, der Spektakel; 11. Ich bin ein Zigeunerkind; 12. Endlich, Józsi, bist di hier!; 13. Welche von uns allen, würde Dir gefallen; 14a. War einst ein Mädel; 14b. Gib mir dort vom Himmelszelt; 15a. Ich weiss ein Rezept; 15b. Nur die Liebe macht uns jung; 16. Liebes Männchen, folge mir; 17. Ha, ha, das find'ich köstlich; 18a. Lass Dich bezaubernm ach, durch mein Fleh'n; 18b. Zorika, Zorika, kehre zrück; 19. Vorwärts, Mädeln, rührt die Hände; 20. Ich bin ein Zigeunerkind. ACT 3: 21. Gib mir das Zweiglein; 22. Lieber Onkel, hör mich nur an; 23. Hör' ich Cymbalklänge; 24. Ich bin ein Zigeunerkind (reprise); 25. Zorika, Zorika, nun bist du mein. LATER INTERPOLATIONS: 26. Wer nennt nicht die Liebe sein einziges Glück.

1. H.H. Bollman, Berlin SO, F. Lehár (r c1926)
(3/89) (PEAR) ⓘ **GEMMCD9310**

4. R. Tauber, V. Schwarz, orch (r1928)
(3/89) (PEAR) ⓘ **GEMMCD9310**

14b M. Hill Smith, Chandos Concert Orch, S. Barry (10/91) (CHAN) ⓘ **CHAN8978**

20. J. Schmidt, orch, F. Günther (r1936)
(EMI) ⓘ [2] **CHS7 64673-2**

20. J. Schmidt, orch (r1936)
(4/90) (EMI) ⓘ **CDM7 69478-2**

23. P. Lorengar, Vienna Op Orch, W. Weller (r1970) (LOND) ⓘ **436 897-2DM**

23. R. Tauber, Berlin Künstlertheater Orch, E. Hauke (r1927) (12/89) (EMI) ⓘ **CDH7 69787-2**

23. M. Hill Smith, Philh, J.O. Edwards (r1989-91; Eng) (10/91) (TER) ⓘ **CDVIR8314**
(10/91) (TER) ▭ **ZCVIR8314**

23. R. Tauber, Berlin Künstlertheater Orch, E. Hauke (r1927) (12/92) (NIMB) ⓘ **NI7833**
(12/92) (NIMB) ▭ **NC7833**

23. E. Réthy, Vienna SO, F. Lehár (r1942)
(1/94) (PREI) ⓘ **90150**

23. E. Réthy, Vienna SO, F. Lehár (r1942)
(1/94) (EMI) ⓘ **CDC7 54838-2**

LEKEU, Guillaume (Jean Joseph Nicholas) *(1870–1894)* *Belgium*

Barberine– opera (1889) (Lib. A. de Musset. Work incomplete)
EXCERPTS: 1. Prelude, Act 2; 2. various fragments only.

1. Liège PO, P. Bartholomée
(RICE) ⓘ **RIS084067**

Les **Burgraves– drama lyrique (1887) (Wds. V. Hugo)**
EXCERPTS: 1. Symphonic Introduction: Part 1 (1889); 2. Symphonic Introduction: Part 2 (1889).
Liège PO, P. Bartholomée
(10/92) (RICE) ⓘ **RIS099083**

LEO, Leonardo *(1694–1744)* *Italy*

Catone in Utica– opera (1729—Venice) (Lib. Metastasio)
Sarebbe un bel diletto A. Christofellis, Inst Ens (r1987/8) (EMI) ⓘ **CDC5 55259-2**

LEONCAVALLO, Ruggiero *(1858–1919) Italy*

La **Bohème, 'Bohemian Life'– opera: 4 acts (1897—Venice) (Lib. cpsr)**
EXCERPTS: ACT 1: 1. No, signor mio, così non può durare; 2. Bella dama; 3a. Musette svaria sulla bocca viva; 3b. Se insieme lo cercassimo; 4. Platonico è l'amante; 5. Mimì Pinson la biondinetta; 6. Vita mia!...O Musette; 7. Senti Marcello! ACT 2: 8. Auf! ce n'è ancora?; 9. Io non ho che una povera stanzetta; 10. L'immenso tesoro; 11a. Ed ora vengano; 11b. Qualcun... 12. Dei vent'anni fra l'ebbrezza (Inno della Bohème);

13. Domando la parola; 14. Da quel suon soavemente; 15. Brav! Bravissima!; 16. Alza l'occhio celeste; 17. Ma quando smettete? ACT 3: 18. E che! Ti pur sei vedo?; 19. Addio!...È destin! Debbo andarmene...Coraggio!; 20. Tu qui! Perchè? Che vuoi?; 21. Sei proprio tu che hai scritto ciò?; 22. Va via, fantasma del passato!; 23a. Musette! o gioia della mia dimora; 23b. Testa adorata. ACT 4: 24. Scuoti, o vento, fra i sibili; 25. Brrr! Che freddo!; 26. Mimì, Buona sera!...V'incomodo; 27. Mimì Pinson la biondinetta; 28. No, morir non voglio.

Mimì L. Mazzaria
Rodolfo J. Summers
Marcello M. Malagnini
Musette M. Senn
Schaunard B. Praticò
Colline; Paolo P. Spagnoli
Barbemuche S. Pagliuca
Durand; Gaudenzio R. Emili
Eufemia C. de Mola
Turin Fenice Chor, Turin Fenice Orch, J. Latham-König (r1990)
(NUOV) Ⓓ [3] **6917/9**

Mimì L. Popp
Rodolfo B. Weikl
Marcello F. Bonisolli
Musette A. Milcheva
Schaunard A. Titus
Colline R. Grumbach
Barbemuche A. Malta
Durand N. Orth
Eufemia S. Lis
Paolo J.W. Wilsing
Gaudenzio F. Lenz
Bavarian Rad Chor, Munich RO, H. Wallberg (r1981)
(8/88) (ORFE) Ⓓ [2] **C023822H**

5. R. Storchio, orch (r1910)
(11/92) (MEMO) Ⓓ [2] **HR4408/9(1)**
9. G. Zenatello, orch (r1911)
(5/94) (PEAR) Ⓓ [4] **GEMMCDS9073(2)**
9, 23b E. Caruso, orch (r1911)
(RCA) Ⓓ **09026 61243-2**
9, 23b E. Caruso, orch (r1911)
(3/91) (PEAR) Ⓓ [3] **EVC2**
9, 23b E. Caruso, orch (r1911)
(7/91) (RCA) Ⓓ [12] **GD60495(4)**
9, 23b E. Caruso, orch (r1911)
(7/95) (NIMB) Ⓓ **NI7866**
23a, 23b B. Heppner, Munich RO, R. Abbado (r1993/4) (11/95) (RCA) Ⓓ **09026 62504-2**
23b B.S. Rosenberg, Budapest Concert Orch, J. Acs (pp1990) (OLYM) Ⓓ **OCD370**
23b P. Domingo, LSO, N. Santi (r1971)
(RCA) Ⓓ **09026 61356-2**
(RCA) ⊟ **09026 61356-4**
23b M. del Monaco, Milan SO, A. Quadri (r1951)
(TEST) Ⓓ **SBT1039**
23b J. Carreras, RPO, R. Benzi (r1979)
(PHIL) Ⓓ **442 600-2PH**
(PHIL) ⊟ **442 600-4PH**
23b E. Caruso, orch (r1911)
(5/89) (PEAR) Ⓓ **GEMMCD9309**

Chatterton– opera: 4 acts (1896—Rome) (Lib. cpsr, after A de Vigny)
1. T. Ruffo, orch, C. Sabajno (r1908)
(PEAR) Ⓓ **GEMMCD9088**

I Medici
Ascolta il canto mio G. Kaschmann, S. Cottone (r1903) (12/89) (SYMP) Ⓓ **SYMCD1065**
Ascolta il canto mio G. Kaschmann, S. Cottone (r1903) (4/94) (EMI) Ⓓ [3] **CHS7 64860-2(1)**

Pagliacci, '(The) Clowns'– opera: prologue and 2 acts (1892—Milan) (Lib. Cpsr)
1. Si può? (Prologue); ACT 1: 2. Son qua!; 3. Un grande spettacolo; 4. Un tal gioco; 5a. I zampognari!; 5b. Din, don (Bell Chorus); 6a. Qual fiamma avea nel guardo!; 6b. Oh! Che volo d'augelli; 6c. Stridono lassù; 7a. Sei là!; 7b. So ben che difforme; 8a. Silvio! A quest'ora; 8b. Decidi il mio destin; 8c. E allor perchè; 9a. Recitar!; 9b. Vesti la giubba; 10. Intermezzo. ACT 2: 11. Presto, affrettiamoci; 12a. Pagliaccio, mio marito; 12b. O Colombina (Serenade); 12c. È dessa!; 13a. Versa il filtro; 13b. No, Pagliaccio non son; 14a. Ebben, se mi giudichi; 14b. No, per mia madre!.

Canio G. Masini
Nedda O. Fineschi
Tonio; Silvio T. Gobbi
Beppe G. Sinimberghi
Rome Op Chor, Rome Op Orch, G. Morelli, M. Costa (r1946)
(7/90) (IMP) 📼 **SL1058**

Canio P. Domingo
Nedda T. Stratas
Tonio J. Pons
Silvio A. Rinaldi
Beppe F. Andreolli
La Scala Orch, La Scala Chor, G. Prêtre, F. Zeffirelli
(PHIL) ● **070 104-1PHI**
(7/90) (PHIL) 📼 **070 104-3PH**

Canio P. Domingo
Nedda M. Caballé
Tonio S. Milnes
Silvio B. McDaniel
Beppe L. Goeke
John Alldis Ch, LSO, N. Santi
(RCA) Ⓓ [2] **GD60865**

Canio B. Gigli
Nedda I. Pacetti
Tonio M. Basiola I
Silvio L. Paci
Beppe G. Nessi
La Scala Chor, La Scala Orch, F. Ghione (r1934)
(NIMB) Ⓓ [2] **NI7843/4**

Canio R. Tucker
Nedda M. Sighele
Tonio K. Nurmela
Silvio W. Alberti
Beppe E. Lorenzi
MMF Chor, MMF Orch, R. Muti (pp1971)
(MEMO) Ⓓ **HR4576**

Canio M. del Monaco
Nedda R. Noli
Tonio A. Poli
Silvio O. Borgonova
Beppe P. de Palma
Naples San Carlo Op Chor, Naples San Carlo Op Orch, V. Bellezza (pp1957)
(LYRC) Ⓓ **LCD181**

Canio V. Atlantov
Nedda L. Popp
Tonio B. Weikl
Silvio W. Brendel
Beppe A. Ionita
Tolz Boys' Ch, Bavarian Rad Chor, Munich RO, L. Gardelli (r1983)
(RCA) Ⓓ [2] **74321 25282-2**

Canio A. Valente
Nedda A. Saraceni
Tonio A. Granforte
Silvio L. Basi
Beppe N. Palai
La Scala Chor, La Scala Orch, C. Sabajno (r1929/30)
(VAI) Ⓓ [2] **VAIA1082**

Canio P. Domingo
Nedda T. Stratas
Tonio J. Pons
Silvio A. Rinaldi
Beppe F. Andreolli
La Scala Chor, La Scala Orch, G. Prêtre
(2/86) (PHIL) Ⓓ **411 484-2PH**

Canio G. di Stefano
Nedda M. Callas
Tonio T. Gobbi
Silvio R. Panerai
Beppe N. Monti
La Scala Chor, La Scala Orch, T. Serafin (r1954)
(10/87) (EMI) Ⓓ [3] **CDS7 47981-8**

Canio C. Bergonzi
Nedda J. Carlyle
Tonio G. Taddei
Silvio R. Panerai
Beppe U. Benelli
La Scala Chor, La Scala Orch, H. von Karajan
(10/87) (DG) Ⓓ [3] **419 257-2GH3**

Canio L. Pavarotti
Nedda M. Freni
Tonio I. Wixell
Silvio L. Saccomani
Beppe V. Bello
London Voices, National PO, G. Patanè
(1/89) (DECC) Ⓓ [2] **414 590-2DH2**

Canio J. Björling
Nedda V. de los Angeles
Tonio L. Warren
Silvio R. Merrill
Beppe P. Franke
Columbus Boychoir, R. Shaw Chorale, RCA Victor Orch, R. Cellini (r1953)
(12/89) (EMI) Ⓓ **CDC7 49503-2**

Canio J. Carreras
Nedda R. Scotto
Tonio K. Nurmela
Silvio T. Allen
Beppe U. Benelli
Ambrosian Op Chor, Philh, R. Muti (r1979)
(3/91) (EMI) Ⓓ [2] **CMS7 63650-2**

Canio F. Corelli
Nedda L. Amara
Tonio T. Gobbi
Silvio M. Zanasi
Beppe M. Spina
La Scala Chor, La Scala Orch, L. von Matačić (r1960)
(3/92) (EMI) Ⓓ [2] **CMS7 63967-2**

Canio N. Martinucci
Nedda M. Gauci
Tonio E. Tumagian
Silvio B. Skovhus
Beppe M. Dvorský
Slovak Phil Chor, Bratislava RSO, A. Rahbari
(4/93) (NAXO) Ⓓ **8 660021**

Canio L. Pavarotti
Nedda D. Dessì
Tonio J. Pons
Silvio P. Coni
Beppe E. Gavazzi
Westminster Symphonic Ch, Philadelphia Boys' Ch, Philadelphia, R. Muti (pp1992)
(4/93) (PHIL) Ⓓ **434 131-2PH**

Canio L. Pavarotti
Nedda D. Dessì
Tonio J. Pons
Silvio P. Coni
Beppe E. Gavazzi
Westminster Symphonic Ch, Philadelphia Boys' Ch, Philadelphia, R. Muti (pp1992)
(4/93) (PHIL) OO **434 131-5PH**

Excs J. Björling, M. Bokor, F. Ginrod, Vienna St Op Chor, Vienna St Op Orch, K. Alwin (pp1937: Ger/Swed) (12/94) (SCHW) Ⓓ [2] **314542**
Excs T. Mazaroff, G. Monthy, A. Michalsky, Vienna St Op Chor, Vienna St Op Orch, W. Loibner (pp1938)
(12/94) (SCHW) Ⓓ [2] **314542**
1. R. Merrill, Orch, H. Barlow (bp1955)
(VAI) 📼 **VAI69116**
1. I. Wixell, National PO, G. Patanè
(DECC) Ⓓ **433 066-2DWO**
(DECC) ⊟ **433 066-4DWO**
1. A. Orda, Polish RSO, S. Rachoń (bp1964)
(SYMP) Ⓓ **SYMCD1117**
1. E.B. Holmes, S. Harrison
(SCHW) Ⓓ **312642**
1. P. Amato, orch, W.B. Rogers (r1911)
(PEAR) Ⓓ **GEMMCD9104**
1. H. Hotter, Berlin Deutsche Op Orch, A. Rother (r1942: Ger) (PREI) Ⓓ **90200**
1. T. Ruffo, orch, C. Sabajno (r1912)
(PEAR) Ⓓ **GEMMCD9088**
1. T. Ruffo, orch, C. Sabajno (r1912)
(NIMB) Ⓓ **NI7864**
1. S. Milnes, Minería SO, H. de la Fuente (r1981)
(IMP) Ⓓ **PCD1109**
1. R. Tauber, orch (r1931: Ger)
(PEAR) Ⓓ **GEMMCD9145**
1. R. Merrill, New SO, E. Downes (r1963)
(DECC) Ⓓ **443 380-2DM**
1. H. Schlusnus, Berlin St Op Orch, L. Blech (r1935: Ger) (PREI) Ⓓ [2] **89212**
1. H. Hotter, Vienna St Op Orch, A. Paulik (pp1943: Ger) (SCHW) Ⓓ [2] **314722**
1. A. Granforte, La Scala Orch, C. Sabajno (r1927) (PREI) Ⓓ **89105**
1. G. Bechi, Santa Cecilia Academy Orch, V. Bellezza (r1946) (2/90) (PREI) Ⓓ **89009**
1. R. Stracciari, orch (r1925)
(2/90) (PREI) Ⓓ **89003**
1. L. Tibbett, Orch, Rosario Bourdon (r1926)
(3/90) (RCA) Ⓓ **GD87808**
1. J. Hynninen, Estonian SO, E. Klas
(4/90) (ONDI) Ⓓ **ODE731-2**
1. H. Schlusnus, Berlin St Op Orch, L. Blech (Ger: r1935) (9/90) (PREI) Ⓓ **89006**
1. T. Ruffo, orch, C. Sabajno (r1912)
(11/90) (NIMB) Ⓓ **NI7810**
(NIMB) ⊟ **NC7810**
1. C. Tagliabue, Turin EIAR Orch, U. Tansini (r1939) (11/90) (PREI) Ⓓ **89015**
1. L. Tibbett, orch, Rosario Bourdon (r1926)
(3/91) (PEAR) Ⓓ [2] **GEMMCDS9452**
1. C. Galeffi, La Scala Orch, L. Molajoli (r1930)
(2/92) (PREI) Ⓓ **89040**
1. L. Warren, RCA Orch, R. Cellini (r1953)
(4/92) (EMI) Ⓓ [7] **CHS7 69741-2(2)**
1. D. Noble, Sadlers Wells Op Orch, W. Braithwaite (Eng: r1939)
(7/92) (PEAR) Ⓓ [3] **GEMMCDS9925(1)**
1. M. Ancona, C. Sabajno (r1904)
(7/92) (PEAR) Ⓓ [3] **GEMMCDS9923(1)**

1. M. Battistini, orch, C. Sabajno (r1911)
(10/92) (PEAR) Ⓓ **GEMMCD9936**
1. P. Lisitsian, Bolshoi Th Orch, S. Samosud (r1955: Russ) (8/93) (PREI) Ⓓ **89061**
1. L. Warren, orch, W. Pelletier (r1940)
(8/93) (VAI) Ⓓ **VAIA1017**
1. T. Gobbi, RPO, A. Erede (r1948)
(8/93) (TEST) Ⓓ **SBT1019**
1. J. Van Dam, Loire PO, M. Soustrot (r1992)
(8/93) (FORL) Ⓓ **UCD16681**
1. E. Tumagian, Bratislava RSO, A. Rahbari (r1992) (12/94) (NAXO) Ⓓ **8 550684**
1, 13b H. Roswaenge, Berlin St Op Orch, B. Seidler-Winkler (r1940: Ger)
(PREI) Ⓓ [2] **89211**
1, 4, 5a, 5b, 6c, 8c, 9a, 9b, 13a, 13b, 14b P. Domingo, T. Stratas, J. Pons, A. Rinaldi, F. Andreolli, La Scala Chor, La Scala Orch, G. Prêtre (r1983) (PHIL) Ⓓ **442 482-2PH**
1, 4, 5b, 6c, 7a, 9a, 9b, 13b L. Pavarotti, M. Freni, L. Saccomani, I. Wixell, V. Bello, Finchley Children's Music Group, London Op Chor, National PO, G. Patanè
(DECC) Ⓓ **421 870-2DA**
(DECC) ▭ **421 870-4DA**
1, 6a, 8c, 9a, 9b, 13b J. Carreras, R. Scotto, K. Nurmela, T. Allen, U. Benelli, Southend Boys' Ch, Ambrosian Op Chor, Philh, R. Muti
(EMI) Ⓓ **CDM7 63933-2**
(EMI) ▭ **EG763933-4**
1, 7b T. Gobbi, Milan RAI SO, A. Simonetto (pp1954) (MEMO) Ⓓ [2] **HR4376/7**
2, 5b Ambrosian Op Chor, LSO, N. Santi (r1971)
(RCA) Ⓓ **74321 24209-2**
4. G. Zenatello, orch, Rosario Bourdon (r1929)
(11/91) (CLUB) Ⓓ **CL99-025**
4. G. Zenatello, orch, Rosario Bourdon (r1929)
(11/91) (PREI) Ⓓ **89038**
4. F. de Lucia, orch (r1917)
(7/92) (PEAR) Ⓓ [3] **GEMMCDS9923(2)**
4. G. Zenatello, anon (r1907)
(5/94) (SYMP) Ⓓ **SYMCD1158**
4. G. Zenatello, anon (r1907)
(5/94) (PEAR) Ⓓ [4] **GEMMCDS9073(1)**
4. G. Zenatello, orch, Rosario Bourdon (r1929)
(5/94) (PEAR) Ⓓ [4] **GEMMCDS9074(2)**
4, 13b G. Zenatello, orch (r1909)
(5/94) (SYMP) Ⓓ **SYMCD1158**
4, 13b G. Zenatello, orch (r1909)
(5/94) (PEAR) Ⓓ [4] **GEMMCDS9073(2)**
4, 9a, 9b J. Björling, R. Moberg, Stockholm Royal Op Orch, L. Gardelli (Swedish; pp1954)
(3/92) (BLUE) Ⓓ **ABCD028**
4, 9b H. Roswaenge, Berlin St Op Orch, B. Seidler-Winkler (r1939: Ger)
(PREI) Ⓓ [2] **89211**
4, 9b L. Pavarotti, Philadelphia, R. Muti
(PHIL) Ⓓ **442 602-2PM**
(PHIL) ▭ **442 602-4PM**
5a, 5b J. McCracken, Santa Cecilia Academy Chor, Santa Cecilia Academy Orch, L. Gardelli (r1967) (DECC) Ⓓ **433 443-2DA**
(DECC) ▭ **433 443-4DA**
5b Fiesole School of Music Female Chor, MMF Chor, MMF Orch, M. Arena (ACAN) Ⓓ **43 540**
5b J. McCracken, Ragazza del Colosseo Chor, Santa Cecilia Academy Chor, Santa Cecilia Academy Orch, L. Gardelli
(DECC) Ⓓ **433 066-2DWO**
(DECC) ▭ **433 066-4DWO**
5b Bayreuth Fest Chor, Bayreuth Fest Orch, W. Sawallisch (r1976) (BELA) Ⓓ **450 052-2**
(BELA) ▭ **450 052-4**
5b Ambrosian Op Chor, Philh, R. Muti (r1979)
(EMI) Ⓓ [2] **CZS5 68559-2**
5b, 9b L. Pavarotti, Philh Chor, Philh, L. Magiera
(DECC) OO **436 320-5DH**
5b, 9b L. Pavarotti, Philh Chor, Philh, L. Magiera
(11/91) (DECC) ◐ **071 150-1DH**
(11/91) (DECC) ▣ **071 150-3DH**
6a R. Ponselle, orch (r1924)
(PEAR) Ⓓ [2] **GEMMCDS9964**
6a A. Moffo, Munich RO, K. Eichhorn
(EURO) Ⓓ **GD69113**
6a I. Cotrubas, Czech SO, A. Krieger (pp1991)
(IMP) Ⓓ **MCD42**
6a J. Wiener-Chenisheva, Bulgarian Nat Op Orch, I. Marinov (r1970s)
(FORL) Ⓓ **UCD16742**
6a L. Bori, Victor Orch, W.B. Rogers (r1914)
(ROMO) Ⓓ [2] **81016-2**
6a C. Muzio, orch (r1917)
(1/95) (ROMO) Ⓓ [2] **81010-2**
6a I. Galante, Latvian Nat SO, A. Vilumanis (r1994) (11/95) (CAMP) Ⓓ **RRCD1335**
(11/95) (CAMP) ▭ **RRMC8035**
6a-c A. Moffo, Orch, A. Fiedler (bp1963)
(VAI) ▣ **VAI69114**
6a-c M. Freni, National PO, G. Patanè (r1977)
(DECC) Ⓓ **440 412-2DM**
6a-c M. Callas, La Scala Orch, T. Serafin (r1954)
(EMI) Ⓓ **CDC5 55216-2**
(EMI) ▭ **EL555216-4**
6a-c V. de los Angeles, RCA Victor Orch, R. Cellini (r1953) (EMI) Ⓓ **CDM5 65579-2**
6a-c K. Te Kanawa, LSO, Myung-Whun Chung (r1989) (EMI) Ⓓ **CDM5 65578-2**
6a-c K. Te Kanawa, LSO, Myung-Whun Chung
(11/90) (EMI) Ⓓ **CDC7 54062-2**
6a-c L. Price, Philh, H. Lewis (r1979)
(12/92) (RCA) Ⓓ [4] **09026 61236-2**
6a-c A. Gluck, orch (r1911)
(4/94) (RCA) Ⓓ [6] **09026 61580-2(2)**
6a, 6b, 8a C. Muzio, M. Laurenti, orch (r1921)
(5/90) (BOGR) Ⓓ [2] **BIM705-2**
6a, 8a C. Muzio, M. Laurenti, orch (r1921)
(1/94) (ROMO) Ⓓ [2] **81005-2**
6a, 8a, 8b X. Belmas, W. Domgraf-Fassbaender, orch, A. Kitschin (r1929)
(10/92) (PREI) Ⓓ **89047**
6c C. White, orch (r c1913)
(IRCC) Ⓓ **IRCC-CD810**
6c C. Muzio, orch (r1917)
(PEAR) Ⓓ **GEMMCD9143**
6c M. Favero, orch (r c1929)
(VAI) Ⓓ **VAIA1071**
6c M. Favero, orch (r c1929)
(BONG) Ⓓ **GB1078-2**
6c E. Destinn, orch (r1912)
(5/94) (SUPR) Ⓓ **11 1337-2**
6c E. Destinn, orch (r1912: 2 vers)
(12/94) (SUPR) Ⓓ [12] **11 2136-2(5)**
6c E. Destinn, orch, B. Seidler-Winkler (r1908: Ger) (12/94) (SUPR) Ⓓ [12] **11 2136-2(2)**
6c, 9b, 13b(pt) A. Piccaver, G. Monthy, E. Schumann, Vienna St Op Chor, Vienna St Op Orch, K. Alwin (pp1937: Ger)
(6/95) (SCHW) Ⓓ [2] **314632**
7a J. Herrmann, M. Düren, orch (r1943: Ger)
(PREI) Ⓓ **89076**
7a, 7b A. Granforte, A. Saraceni, La Scala Orch, C. Sabajno (r1929) (12/91) (PREI) Ⓓ **89048**
7b M. Basiola I, La Scala Orch, F. Ghione (r1934) (PREI) Ⓓ **89995**
8a-c H. Spani, A. Granforte, La Scala Orch, C. Sabajno (r1927)
(9/90) (CLUB) Ⓓ [2] **CL99-509/10**
8b H. Spani, A. Granforte, La Scala Orch, C. Sabajno (r1927) (12/92) (PREI) Ⓓ **89037**
8b E. Steber, G. Cehanovsky, L. Warren, orch, W. Pelletier (r1940) (11/95) (VAI) Ⓓ **VAIA1072**
9a, 9b L. Pavarotti, Vienna Volksoper Orch, L. Magiera (7/75) (DECC) ▭ **400 053-4DH**
9a, 9b M. Lanza, orch, C. Callinicos (r1950)
(RCA) Ⓓ **RD86218**
9a, 9b J. Carreras, Barcelona SO, G. Navarro
(11/92) (RCA) ▭ **09026 61204-4**
9a, 9b B. Gigli, orch (r1924)
(CONI) Ⓓ **CDHD149**
(CONI) ▭ **MCHD149**
9a, 9b P. Domingo, LSO, N. Santi
(RCA) Ⓓ **GD84265**
9a, 9b J. Carreras, Philh, R. Muti
(EMI) Ⓓ **CDM7 63111-2**
9a, 9b M. Lanza, RCA Victor Orch, C. Callinicos (r1950) (RCA) Ⓓ **GD60049**
(RCA) ▭ **GK60049**
9a, 9b E. Caruso, S. Cottone (r1902)
(EMI) Ⓓ **CDC7 54016-2**
9a, 9b T. Burke, orch (Eng: r1932)
(PEAR) Ⓓ **GEMMCD9411**
9a, 9b M. Lanza, Rome Op Orch, C. Callinicos (r1957) (RCA) Ⓓ **GD60516**
9a, 9b M. del Monaco, Santa Cecilia Academy Orch, F. Molinari-Pradelli
(DECC) Ⓓ **433 068-2DWO**
(DECC) ▭ **433 068-4DWO**
9a, 9b L. Slezak, Berlin St Op Orch, M. Gurlitt (r1928: Ger) (PREI) Ⓓ [2] **89203**
9a, 9b M. Lanza, RCA Victor Orch, C. Callinicos (r1950) (RCA) Ⓓ [3] **GD60889(2)**
9a, 9b H. Roswaenge, Philh Hungarica, Z. Rozsnyai (pp1959) (PREI) Ⓓ **90103**
9a, 9b M. Lorenz, Berlin St Op Orch, C. Schmalstich (Ger: r1929) (PREI) Ⓓ **89053**
9a, 9b J. Carreras, Philh, R. Muti
(EMI) Ⓓ **CDM7 64359-2**
9a, 9b J. Carreras, Philh, R. Muti
(EMI) Ⓓ **CDC7 54524-2**
9a, 9b T. Harper, Bratislava RSO, M. Halász
(NAXO) Ⓓ **8 550497**
9a, 9b E. Caruso, orch (r1907)
(RCA) Ⓓ **09026 61243-2**
9a, 9b P. Domingo, LSO, N. Santi (r1971)
(RCA) Ⓓ **09026 61356-2**
(RCA) ▭ **09026 61356-4**
9a, 9b J. Carreras, Barcelona SO, G. Navarro
(RCA) OO **09026 61204-5**
9a, 9b E. Barham, RPO, R. Stapleton (r1990)
(RPO) Ⓓ [2] **CDRPD9006**
(RPO) ▭ [2] **ZCRPD9006**
9a, 9b E. Caruso, orch (r1907)
(MCI) Ⓓ **MCCD086**
(MCI) ▭ **MCTC086**
9a, 9b Deng, Württemberg PO, R. Paternostro
(SINE) Ⓓ **39820222**
9a, 9b E. Caruso, SO (r1907/30)
(ASV) Ⓓ **CDAJA5112**
(ASV) ▭ **ZCAJA5112**
9a, 9b M. del Monaco, Santa Cecilia Academy Orch, F. Molinari-Pradelli (r1959)
(DECC) Ⓓ **440 407-2DM**
9a, 9b M. del Monaco, Philomusica of London, A. Dorati (BELA) Ⓓ **450 015-2**
(BELA) ▭ **450 015-4**
9a, 9b L. Pavarotti, National PO, G. Patanè (r1977) (DECC) Ⓓ **440 947-2DH**
(DECC) ▭ **440 947-4DH**
9a, 9b P. Domingo, LSO, N. Santi
(RCA) Ⓓ **09026 61440-2**
(RCA) ▭ **09026 61440-4**
9a, 9b J. Schmidt, orch, O. Dobrindt (r1933: Ger)
(EMI) Ⓓ [2] **CHS7 64673-2**
9a, 9b M. Lanza, orch, C. Callinicos (r1950)
(RCA) Ⓓ **74321 18574-2**
(RCA) ▭ **74321 18574-4**
9a, 9b J. McCracken, Vienna Op Orch, D. Bernet (r1965) (DECC) Ⓓ **436 314-2DA**
(DECC) ▭ **436 314-4DA**
9a, 9b M. del Monaco, Milan SO, A. Quadri (r1951) (TEST) Ⓓ **SBT1039**
9a, 9b L. Pavarotti, Toscanini SO, E. Buckley
(SONY) Ⓓ **MDK47176**
(SONY) ▭ **MDT47176**
9a, 9b E. Caruso, orch (r1907)
(ASV) Ⓓ **CDAJA5137**
(ASV) ▭ **ZCAJA5137**
9a, 9b F. Corelli, La Scala Orch, L. von Matačić
(EMIL) Ⓓ **CDZ103**
(EMIL) ▭ **LZ103**
9a, 9b P. Domingo, LSO, N. Santi
(RCA) Ⓓ **74321 25817-2**
(RCA) ▭ **74321 25817-4**
9a, 9b A. Bonci, orch (r1913)
(PEAR) Ⓓ **GEMMCD9168**
9a, 9b A. Piccaver, Berlin St Op Orch, M. Gurlitt (r1929) (PREI) Ⓓ [2] **89217**
9a, 9b L. Pavarotti, National PO, G. Patanè
(7/86) (DECC) Ⓓ [2] **417 011-2DH2**
9a, 9b L. Melchior, LSO, J. Barbirolli (r1930; Ger) (8/88) (DANA) Ⓓ [2] **DACOCD315/6**
9a, 9b J. Björling, orch, N. Grevillius (r1944)
(10/88) (EMI) Ⓓ **CDH7 61053-2**
9a, 9b E. Caruso, S. Cottone (r1902)
(5/89) (EMI) Ⓓ **CDH7 61046-2**
9a, 9b G. Martinelli, orch, Rosario Bourdon (r1927) (10/89) (NIMB) Ⓓ **NI7804**
(NIMB) ▭ **NC7804**
9a, 9b E. Caruso, orch (r1907)
(10/89) (NIMB) Ⓓ **NI7803**
(NIMB) ▭ **NC7803**
9a, 9b M. Fleta, orch (r1927)
(2/90) (PREI) Ⓓ **89002**
9a, 9b J. Schmidt, orch (r1933; Ger)
(4/90) (EMI) Ⓓ **CDM7 69478-2**
9a, 9b L. Pavarotti, National PO, O. de Fabritiis
(7/90) (DECC) Ⓓ [2] **425 681-2DM2**
(7/90) (DECC) ▭ [2] **425 681-4DM2**
9a, 9b E. Caruso, anon (r1904)
(12/90) (PEAR) Ⓓ [3] **EVC1(1)**
9a, 9b E. Caruso, orch (r1907)
(12/90) (PEAR) Ⓓ [3] **EVC1(2)**
9a, 9b E. Caruso, S. Cottone (r1902)
(12/90) (PEAR) Ⓓ [3] **EVC1(1)**
9a, 9b E. Caruso, S. Cottone (r1902)
(7/91) (RCA) Ⓓ [12] **GD60495(1)**
9a, 9b E. Caruso, anon (r1904)
(7/91) (RCA) Ⓓ [12] **GD60495(1)**
9a, 9b E. Caruso, orch (r1907)
(7/91) (RCA) Ⓓ [12] **GD60495(2)**
9a, 9b E. Caruso, orch, W.B. Rogers (r1907)
(10/92) (TEST) Ⓓ **SBT1005**
9a, 9b M. del Monaco, Santa Cecilia Academy Orch, F. Molinari-Pradelli (r1959)
(10/93) (DECC) Ⓓ **436 463-2DM**
(10/93) (DECC) ▭ **436 463-4DM**

9a, 9b J. Vickers, Rome Op Orch, T. Serafin (r1961) (4/94) (RCA) Ⓓ [6] **09026 61580-2(7)**
9a, 9b G. Zenatello, anon (r1905/6: 2 vers) (5/94) (PEAR) Ⓓ [4] **GEMMCDS9073(1)**
9a, 9b G. Zenatello, orch (r1908) (5/94) (PEAR) Ⓓ [4] **GEMMCDS9073(2)**
9a, 9b G. Zenatello, orch (r1916) (5/94) (PEAR) Ⓓ [4] **GEMMCDS9074(2)**
9a, 9b G. Zenatello, orch (r1912) (5/94) (PEAR) Ⓓ [4] **GEMMCDS9074(1)**
9a, 9b A. Pertile, La Scala Orch, C. Sabajno (r1927) (10/94) (PREI) Ⓓ **89072**
9a, 9b A. Giorgini, orch (r c1913) (4/95) (RECO) Ⓓ **TRC3**
9a, 9b G. Thill, orch, E. Bigot (r c1928: Fr) (8/95) (FORL) Ⓓ **UCD16727**
9a, 9b, 12a B. Gigli, I. Pacetti, La Scala Orch, F. Ghione (r1934) (CONI) Ⓓ **CDHD227** (CONI) ▭ **MCHD227**
9a, 9b, 13b J. Vickers, Rome Op Orch, T. Serafin (r1961) (VAI) Ⓓ **VAIA1016**
9a, 9b, 13b F. Ansseau, orch, P. Coppola (r1927) (1/91) (PREI) Ⓓ **89022**
9b R. Tucker, Orch, H. Barlow (bp1959) (VAI) ▣ **VAI69109**
9b J. Björling, orch, H. Barlow (bp1951) (VAI) ▣ **VAI69101**
9b J. Peerce, Orch, H. Barlow (bp1950) (VAI) ▣ **VAI69117**
9b M. Wittrisch, Berlin St Op Orch, K. Bendix (Ger: r1931) (PREI) Ⓓ **89024**
9b J. Carreras, LSO, J. López-Cobos (PHIL) Ⓓ **432 692-2PH** (PHIL) ▭ **432 692-4PH**
9b J. Carreras, Philh, R. Muti (EMI) Ⓓ [2] **CDEMTVD59** (EMI) ⊙ [2] **EMTVD59**
9b L. Pavarotti, Orch (EDL) Ⓓ **EDL2562-2** (EDL) ⊙ **EDL2562-1** ▭ **EDL2562-4**
9b P. Domingo, LSO, N. Santi (RCA) Ⓓ [2] **GD60866** (RCA) ▭ [2] **GK60866**
9b J. Carreras, LSO, J. López-Cobos (PHIL) Ⓓ **434 152-2PM**
9b J. Björling, orch, N. Grevillius (r1933: Swed) (NIMB) Ⓓ **NI7835**
9b P. Domingo, Berlin Deutsche Op Chor, N. Santi (ERAT) Ⓓ **2292-45797-2** (ERAT) ▭ **2292-45797-4**
9b J. Oakman, Czech PO, J. Bigg (with instr track for singing) (IMP) Ⓓ [2] **DPCD1015** (IMP) ▭ **CIMPCD1015**
9b J. Carreras, London Studio SO, M. Viotti (r1993) (TELD) Ⓓ **4509-92369-2** (TELD) ▭ **4509-92369-4**
9b J. Carreras, LSO, J. López-Cobos (r1979) (BELA) Ⓓ **450 059-2** (BELA) ▭ **450 059-4**
9b J. Oakman, Czech SO, J. Bigg (r1992) (IMP) Ⓓ **PCDS23** (IMP) ▭ **PCDSC23**
9b J. Oakman, Czech SO, J. Bigg (IMP) Ⓓ [3] **TCD1070**
9b L. Melchior, LSO, J. Barbirolli (r1930: Ger) (PREI) Ⓓ **89086**
9b J. Carreras, RPO, R. Benzi (r1979) (PHIL) Ⓓ **442 600-2PH** (PHIL) ▭ **442 600-4PH**
9b P. Domingo, Los Angeles PO, Z. Mehta (pp1994) (TELD) **OO** **4509-96200-5**
9b P. Domingo, Los Angeles PO, Z. Mehta (pp1994) (TELD) ◘ **4509-96200-8**
9b Capitol SO, C. Dragon (r1958: arr Dragon) (EMI) Ⓓ **CDM5 65430-2**
9b E. Caruso, orch (r1907) (5/89) (PEAR) Ⓓ **GEMMCD9309**
9b R. Tauber, orch, W. Goehr (Eng: r1936) (7/89) (EMI) Ⓓ **CDM7 69476-2**
9b F. Völker, Berlin St Op Orch, H. Weigert (r1930: Ger) (2/90) (PREI) Ⓓ **89005**
9b B. Gigli, orch (r1922) (5/90) (NIMB) Ⓓ **NI7807** (NIMB) ▭ **NC7807**
9b E. Barham, RPO, R. Stapleton (10/90) (IMP) Ⓓ **MCD15** (10/90) (IMP) ▭ **MCC15**
9b A. Garulli, anon (r1902) (5/91) (SYMP) Ⓓ **SYMCD1077**
9b G. Zenatello, orch (r c1917) (11/91) (CLUB) Ⓓ **CL99-025**
9b G. Lugo, orch, F. Weiss (Fr: r1933) (2/92) (PREI) Ⓓ **89034**
9b H.E. Groh, orch (Ger: r1933) (3/92) (PEAR) Ⓓ **GEMMCD9419**
9b G. Martinelli, orch, Rosario Bourdon (r1927) (3/93) (PREI) Ⓓ **89062**
9b D. Yuzhin, anon (r1902: Russ) (6/93) (PEAR) Ⓓ [3] **GEMMCDS9001/3(1)**
9b G. Lauri-Volpi, orch (r1923) (7/93) (NIMB) Ⓓ **NI7845**
9b E. Caruso, orch (r1907/32) (5/94) (CLAR) Ⓓ **CDGSE78-50-52**
9b G. Zenatello, orch (r1908) (5/94) (SYMP) Ⓓ **SYMCD1158**
9b G. Zenatello, anon (r1906) (5/94) (SYMP) Ⓓ **SYMCD1158**
9b P. Domingo, Los Angeles PO, Z. Mehta (pp1994) (12/94) (TELD) Ⓓ **4509-96200-2** (12/94) (TELD) ⊙ **4509-96200-1** ▭ **4509-96200-4**
9b B. Gigli, La Scala Orch, F. Ghione (r1934) (12/94) (MMOI) Ⓓ **CDMOIR425**
9b J. Johnston, orch, M. Mudie (r1948: Eng) (4/95) (TEST) Ⓓ **SBT1058**
9b(pt) H. Roswaenge, Vienna St Op Orch (pp1930s) (11/95) (SCHW) Ⓓ [2] **314622**
9b, 12b G. Anselmi, anon (r1907) (7/95) (SYMP) Ⓓ **SYMCD1170**
9b, 13b H. Roswaenge, Berlin St Op Orch, B. Seidler-Winkler (r1939: Ger) (5/90) (PREI) Ⓓ **89018**
9b, 13b F. Merli, orch, L. Molajoli (r1929) (1/91) (PREI) Ⓓ **89026**
10. BPO, H. von Karajan, H. Burton (r1985) (SONY) ◐ **SLV46402** (SONY) ▣ **SHV46402**
10. Brno St PO, O. Lenárd (pp1992) (SUPR) Ⓓ **11 1846-2**
10. Philh, I. Westrip (r1993) (IMP) Ⓓ **PCD1075**
10. RPO, A. Licata (r1994) (TRIN) Ⓓ **TRP044**
10. Gothenburg SO, N. Järvi (6/90) (DG) Ⓓ **429 494-2GDC** (6/90) (DG) ▭ **429 494-4GDC**
12a, 12b B. Gigli, I. Pacetti, La Scala Orch, F. Ghione (r1934) (PEAR) Ⓓ [2] **GEMMCDS9176**
12b I. Kozlovsky, USSR SO, Anon (cond) (r1930-50) (MYTO) Ⓓ **1MCD921.55**
12b J. Björling, H. Ebert (pp1950) (BLUE) Ⓓ **ABCD057**
12b T. Schipa, orch (r1926) (2/89) (PEAR) Ⓓ **GEMMCD9322**
12b H. Nash, M. Licette, BNOC Orch, E. Goossens (Eng: r1927) (8/89) (PEAR) Ⓓ **GEMMCD9319**
12b T. Schipa, orch, Rosario Bourdon (r1926) (12/89) (RCA) Ⓓ **GD87969**
12b I. Pacetti, B. Gigli, La Scala Orch, F. Ghione (r1934) (5/90) (EMI) Ⓓ **CDH7 61052-2**
12b T. Schipa, orch, Rosario Bourdon (r1925) (10/90) (MSCM) Ⓓ [2] **MM30231** (MSCM) ▭ [2] **MM40086**
12b G. Zenatello, orch (r1911) (5/94) (SYMP) Ⓓ **SYMCD1158**
12b G. Zenatello, orch (r1911) (5/94) (PEAR) Ⓓ [4] **GEMMCDS9073(2)**
13b A. Paoli, orch (r1907) (PREI) Ⓓ **89998**
13b E. Caruso, orch (r1910) (RCA) Ⓓ **09026 61243-2**
13b M. del Monaco, Milan SO, A. Quadri (r1951) (TEST) Ⓓ **SBT1039**
13b B. Gigli, orch, J. Barbirolli (r1933) (PEAR) Ⓓ [2] **GEMMCDS9176**
13b B. Gigli, orch, J. Barbirolli (r1933) (9/88) (EMI) Ⓓ **CDH7 61051-2**
13b E. Caruso, orch (r1910) (5/89) (PEAR) Ⓓ **GEMMCD9309**
13b E. Caruso, orch (r1910) (10/89) (NIMB) Ⓓ **NI7801** (NIMB) ▭ **NC7801**
13b E. Caruso, orch (r1910) (10/89) (NIMB) Ⓓ **NI7803** (NIMB) ▭ **NC7803**
13b G. Anthony, G. Martinelli, chor, orch, G. Setti (r1927) (10/89) (NIMB) Ⓓ **NI7804** (NIMB) ▭ **NC7804**
13b E. Caruso, orch (r1910) (3/91) (PEAR) Ⓓ [3] **EVC2**
13b E. Caruso, orch (r1910) (7/91) (RCA) Ⓓ [12] **GD60495(3)**
13b G. Martinelli, G. Anthony, NY Met Op Chor, NY Met Op Orch, G. Setti (r1927) (3/93) (PREI) Ⓓ **89062**
13b F. Völker, Berlin Staatskapelle, J. Schüler (r1937: Ger) (8/94) (PREI) Ⓓ **89070**
13b B. Gigli, LSO, J. Barbirolli (r1933) (9/94) (NIMB) Ⓓ **NI7856**
13b, 14b F. Völker, W. Achsel, E. Schipper, K. Hammes, Vienna St Op Chor, Vienna St Op Orch, K. Alwin (pp1934: Ger) (9/95) (SCHW) Ⓓ [2] **314662**

Der **Roland von Berlin– opera: 4 acts (1904—Berlin) (Lib. cpsr, after W Alexis)**
Fahr wohl! Trautgesell! G. Farrar, anon (r1904) (IRCC) Ⓓ **IRCC-CD805**
Hennig darf ein Patrizierkind; Fahr wohl, Trautgesell E. Destinn, R. Leoncavallo (r1905) (12/94) (SUPR) Ⓓ [12] **11 2136-2(1)**
Ratenow's Prayer F.M. Bonini, anon (r1905) (12/94) (BONG) Ⓓ **GB1043-2**

Zazà– opera: 4 acts (1900—Milan) (Lib. cpsr, after P. Berton & C. Simon)
EXCERPTS: ACT 1: 1. A voi, su presto; 2. Salute a tutti; 3. Lo sai tu che vuol dire; 4. Augusto, buona sera; 5. Ah, ah, là, là; 6. Signor, entrate. ACT 2: 7. È deciso, tu parti; 8. Or lasciami andare!; 9. Ecco gli stivaletti; 10. Toh, o che quadretto; 11. Buona Zazà del mio buon tempo; 12. Hai ragione. ACT 3: 13. O mio piccolo tavolo; 14. Eccomi pronta; 15a. Mama usciva di casa; 15b. Dir che ci sono al mondo. ACT 4: 16. Dunque nessuna nuova; 17. Zazà, piccola zingara; 18. Che non vorresti farlo; 19. Tu non m'amavi più; 20. Ed ora io mi domando.
È un riso gentil G. Martinelli, orch, Rosario Bourdon (r1927) (3/93) (PREI) Ⓓ **89062**
È un riso gentil G. Martinelli, orch (r1922) (9/94) (NIMB) Ⓓ **NI7856**
Non so capir G. Farrar, G. De Luca, orch (r1920) (PEAR) Ⓓ [3] **GEMMCDS9160(1)**
11. G. De Luca, anon (r1907) (PEAR) Ⓓ [3] **GEMMCDS9159(2)**
11, 17. R. Stracciari, orch (r1925) (PEAR) Ⓓ **GEMMCD9178**
11, 17. T. Gobbi, La Scala Orch, U. Berrettoni (r1942) (10/89) (EMI) Ⓓ **CDM7 63109-2**
11, 17. T. Ruffo, orch (r1912) (11/90) (NIMB) Ⓓ **NI7810** (NIMB) ▭ **NC7810**
11, 17. A. Granforte, La Scala Orch, C. Sabajno (r1929) (12/91) (PREI) Ⓓ **89048**
11, 17. T. Ruffo, orch (r1912) (2/93) (PREI) Ⓓ [3] **89303(1)**
15a, 15b I. Tokody, orch, Anon (cond) (pp1991/2) (VAI) Ⓓ **VAIA1009**
15a, 15b C. Muzio, Anon (pf) (r1921) (5/90) (BOGR) Ⓓ [2] **BIM705-2**
15a, 15b C. Muzio, orch (r1921) (1/94) (ROMO) Ⓓ [2] **81005-2**
17. R. Stracciari, orch (r1925) (MSCM) Ⓓ [2] **MM30276**
17. G. De Luca, anon (r1905) (PEAR) Ⓓ [3] **GEMMCDS9159(1)**
17. A. Granforte, La Scala Orch, C. Sabajno (r1929) (PREI) Ⓓ **89995**
17. P. Lisitsian, Bolshoi Th Orch, V. Piradov (r1948: Russ) (8/93) (PREI) Ⓓ **89061**
17. R. Zanelli, orch (r1919) (10/95) (NIMB) Ⓓ **NI7867**

LEONI, Franco *(1864–1949)* *Italy*

L' **Oracolo– opera: 1 act (1905—London)**
Mio figlio A. Didur, orch (r c1919) (1/94) (CLUB) Ⓓ **CL99-089**

LEROUX , Xavier *(1863–1919)* *France*

La **Reine Fiammette– opéra-comique: 4 acts (1903—Paris) (Lib. C. Mendès)**
Tu sais...Je ne suis plus reine M. Carré, X. Leroux (r1904) (8/92) (IRCC) Ⓓ **IRCC-CD802**

LEVY , Marvin David *(b 1932)* *USA*

Mourning Becomes Electra– opera (3 acts) (1967—New York) (Lib. after O'Neill)
Too weak to kill the man I hate S. Milnes, NY Met Op Orch, J. Conlon (pp1991) (6/93) (RCA) Ⓓ **09026 61509-2**
Too weak to kill S. Milnes, New Philh, A. Guadagno (r1968) (4/94) (RCA) Ⓓ [6] **09026 61580-2(8)**

LIDHOLM, Ingvar (Natanael) *(b 1921) Sweden*

A **Dream Play– opera: prelude and 2 acts (1992—Stockholm) (Lib. cspr, after J. Strindberg)**

Daughter H. Martinpelto
Officer H. Hagegård
Stage-Door Keeper I. Tobiasson
Advocate S. Wahlund
Poet C. Appelgren
Bill-Poster; Dean of Theology L. Kullenbo
Schoolmaster; Dean of Law A. Helleland
Glazier; Blind man A. Bergström
Chancellor S. Sandlund
Dean of Philosophy H. Westberg
Policeman; Dean of Medecine R. Cederlöf
Victoria; She N. Stemme
He C. Unander-Scharin
Stockholm Royal Ch, Stockholm Royal Orch, K. Ingebretsen (r1992/3)
(9/93) (CPRI) ⓘ [2] **CAP22029**

LIGETI, Gyorgy (Sandor) *(b 1923) Hungary/Austria*

Le **Grand Macabre– opera: 2 acts (1978—Stockholm) (Lib. Meschke & cpsr, after Ghelderode)**

Chief of Secret Police, Gepopo E. Davies
Venus E. Davies
Amanda P. Walmsley-Clark
Amando O. Fredricks
Prince Go-Go K. Smith
Mescalina C. Puhlmann-Richter
Piet the Pot P. Haage
Nekrotzar D. Weller
Astradamors U. Krekow
Ruffiak J. Leutgeb
Schobiak E. Salzer
Schabernack L. Modos
White Minister H. Prikopa
Black Minister E.L. Strachwitz
Gumpoldskirchner Spatzen, Austrian Rad Chor, A. Schoenberg Ch, Austrian RSO, E. Howarth
(12/91) (WERG) ⓘ [2] **WER6170-2**
Scènes et Interludes I. Nielsen, O. Fredricks, P. Haage, D. Weller, French Rad New PO, G. Amy
(ADES) ⓘ [4] **14122-2**

LINCKE, (Carl Emile) Paul *(1866–1946) Germany*

Frau Luna– operetta-revue: 1 act (1899—Berlin) (Lib. Bolten-Baeckers)

Castles in the Air R. Crooks, orch (r1933: Eng)
(9/93) (CLAR) ⓘ **CDGSE78-50-50**
Schlösser, die im Monde liegen L. Popp, ASMF, N. Marriner
(6/88) (EMI) ⓘ **CDC7 49700-2**

Im Reiche des Indra– operetta (1 act) (1899—Berlin) (Lib. Bolten-Baeckers)

Es war einmal B. Weikl, Austrian RSO, K. Eichhorn (ORFE) ⓘ **C077831A**
Es war einmal R. Tauber, orch (r1929)
(7/89) (EMI) ⓘ **CDM7 69476-2**

Lysistrata– operetta

Glühwürmchen-Idyll E. Sack, Berlin Staatskapelle (r1937) (DANT) ⓘ **LYS2**

LLOYD, George *(b 1913) England*

Iernin– opera: 3 acts (1934—Penzance) (Lib. W. Lloyd)

M. Hill Smith, G. Pogson, H. Herford, M. Rivers, J. Robarts, J. White, S. Jackson, C. Powell, BBC Sngrs, BBC Concert Orch, G. Lloyd (r1985)
(9/94) (ALBA) ⓘ [3] **TROY121/3**

John Socman– opera: 3 acts (1951—Bristol) (Lib. W. Lloyd)

EXCERPTS: 1. Overture. ACT 1; 2. Scene 1; 3. Scene 2; 4. Scene 3. ACT 2: 5. Scene 1; 6. Scene 2; 7. ACT 3.
1. BBC PO, G. Lloyd (r1988)
(8/89) (ALBA) ⓘ **TROY015-2**
(ALBA) ▭ **TROY015-4**
2, 3, 5, 7. D. Wilson-Johnson, T. Booth, J. Watson, D. Montague, J. Winfield, M. George, M. Rivers, P. Sheffield, S. Adler, London Voices, Trinity Boy's Ch, Philh, G. Lloyd (r1994)
(1/95) (ALBA) ⓘ **TROY131-2**

LOCKE, Matthew *(1621/2–1677) England*

Cupid and Death– masque (1659—London) (Lib. J. Shirley. Collab. with C. Gibbons)

EXCERPTS: 1. The Lovers' Grove.
1. A. Rooley (r1990; arr Rooley)
(MOSC) ⓘ **070971**

LORTZING, (Gustav) Albert *(1801–1851) Germany*

Die **Beiden Schützen– operetta: 3 acts (1837—Leipzig) (Lib. after G. Cords)**

Da, wo schöne Mädchen wohnen H. Prey, Berlin Deutsche Op Orch, H. Hollreiser
(EURO) ⓘ **GD69019**

Hans Sachs– operetta: 3 acts (1840—Leipzig) (Lib. after L. F. Deinhardstein)

Wo bist du, Sachs? H. Prey, Berlin Deutsche Op Orch, H. Hollreiser (EURO) ⓘ **GD69019**

Undine– opera: 4 acts (1845—Magdeburg) (Lib. after de la Motte-Fouqué)

EXCERPTS: 1. Overture; 2. Da lieg, du altes Mordgewehr; 3. Ach, welche Freude, welche Wonne; 4. Ich ritt zum grossen Waffenspiele; 5. Zürchtig Bräutlein, darfst erscheinen; 6. Uns beiden ist die Hauptstadt wohlbekannt!; 7. Ihr seid nun vereint; 8. Viel schöne Gaben; 9. Doch halt, wo ist der Mann. ACT 2: 10. Introduction; 11. Was seh' ich! Ihr seid glücklich wieder da?; 12. So wisse, dass in allen Elementen; 13. Für Euch, o Fürstin, eine frohe Kunde; 14. Was ergreift mit bangem Schrecken; 15. Seid zweifach mir willkommen; 16. Vernehmet, Ritter und Vasallen; 17. Es wohnt' am Seegestade; 18. Was ich sagte, bleibet wahr!. ACT 3: 19. Auf ihr Zecher; 20. Vater, Mutter, Schwestern, Brüder; 21. Ich lasse dich nicht, nein, nein; 22. Was seh' ich?; 23. Nun ist's vollbracht!; 24. O kehr zurück!—Schwanengesang, Schwanenklang. ACT 4: 25. Introduction; 26. Hinweg! Hinweg! Dein dräuend Angesicht; 27. Ich war in meinen Jungen Jahren; 28. Hört nur, wie es unten Kocht und braust; 29. Ha! es schlägst Mitternacht.

Undine M. Krause
Hugo J. Protschka
Bertalda C. Hampe
Kühleborn J. Janssen
Tobias K. Häger
Marthe I. Most
Veit H. Kruse
Hans A. Schmidt
Heilmann G. Wewel
Messenger D. Schortemeier
Cologne Rad Chor, Cologne RSO, K. Eichhorn
(3/91) (CAPR) ⓘ [2] **60 017-2**
12. Lotte Lehmann, orch (r1919)
(6/92) (PREI) ⓘ [3] **89302**
20. F. Wunderlich, Berlin SO, A. Rother
(EURO) ⓘ **GD69018**
(EURO) ▭ **GK69018**
20. P. Anders, Berlin Deutsche Op Orch, J. Schüler (r1937) (TELD) ⓘ **4509-95512-2**
20. R. Tauber, orch (r1928)
(7/89) (PEAR) ⓘ **GEMMCD9327**
20. F. Wunderlich, Stuttgart RSO, A. Rischner (bp1957) (10/89) (ACAN) ⓘ **43 267**
20. R. Schock, Berlin Deutsche Op Orch, W. Schüchter (r1952)
(4/92) (EMI) ⓘ [7] **CHS7 69741-2(4)**
20. R. Tauber, Berlin Schauspielhaus Orch, E. Hauke (r1928) (12/92) (NIMB) ⓘ **NI7830**
(12/92) (NIMB) ▭ **NC7830**
20. P. Anders, Berlin RSO, A. Rother (bp1943)
(8/93) (ACAN) ⓘ **43 268**
20. R. Tauber, orch (r1928)
(12/94) (MMOI) ⓘ **CDMOIR425**
23. G. Hüsch, Berlin St Op Orch, H.U. Müller (r1935) (3/94) (PREI) ⓘ **89071**
23, 24. D. Fischer-Dieskau, R. Streich, Berlin Deutsche Op Chor, Berlin SO, W. Schüchter (r1953) (EMI) ⓘ [2] **CMS5 65621-2**
27(pt) L. Hofmann, A. Peters, orch, J. Prüwer (r1929) (PREI) ⓘ **89102**

Der **Waffenschmied– opera: 3 acts (1846—Vienna) (Lib. after von Ziegler)**

Auch ich war ein Jüngling K. Moll, Munich RO, K. Eichhorn (r1981) (ORFE) ⓘ **C009821A**
Auch ich war ein Jüngling E. List, orch, O. Dobrindt (r1929) (PREI) ⓘ **89083**
Auch ich war ein Jüngling L. Hofmann, orch, J. Prüwer (r1929) (PREI) ⓘ **89102**
Auch ich war ein Jüngling E. Kunz, Philh, O. Ackermann (r1953) (9/95) (TEST) ⓘ **SBT1059**
Er schläft M. Teschemacher, Berlin City Op Orch, H.U. Müller (r1934)
(11/92) (PREI) ⓘ **89049**
Festmarsch Innsbruck Postmusik, F. Pedarnig
(KOCH) ⓘ **322 559**
Man wird ja einmal nur geboren F. Wunderlich, Munich RO, H. Moltkau (bp)
(DG) ⓘ [5] **435 145-2GX5(1)**
Man wird ja einmal nur geboren; War einst ein junger Springinsfeld F. Wunderlich, Stuttgart Rad Chor, Stuttgart RSO, A. Rischner (bp1957) (10/89) (ACAN) ⓘ **43 267**
Man wird ja einmal nur geboren F. Wunderlich, Munich RO, H. Moltkau
(5/93) (DG) ⓘ **431 110-2GB**

Der **Wildschütz– opera: 3 acts (1842—Leipzig) (Wds. cpsr)**

Count Eberbach G. Hornik
Countess Eberbach D. Soffel
Baron Kronthal P. Schreier
Baroness Kronthal E. Mathis
Nanette G. von Ottenthal
Baculus H. Sotin
Gretchen G. Resick
Pancratius R. Süss
Guest B. Riedel
Berlin Rad Children's Ch, Berlin Rad Chor, Berlin Staatskapelle, B. Klee (r1980/2)
(BERL) ⓘ [2] **0011 432BC**
Auf des Lebens raschen Wogen; Ihr Weib?...Mein teures Weib! I. Seefried, E. Haefliger, Bamberg SO, C. Stepp (r1965)
(9/93) (DG) ⓘ [2] **437 677-2GDO2**
Auf des Lebens raschen Wagen F. Hempel, orch (r c1914/5) (3/94) (NIMB) ⓘ **NI7849**
Bleiben soll ich...Aus dem Parke erklingen die lieblichen Töne F. Wunderlich, A. Rothenberger, G. Litz, Bavarian St Orch, R. Heger (EMI) ⓘ [3] **CZS7 62993-2**
Fünftausend Taler G. Hann, Berlin RSO, H. Steinkopf (bp1943)
(MYTO) ⓘ [2] **2MCD943103**
Fünftausend Taler A. Kipnis, Berlin St Op Orch, E. Orthmann (r1931) (12/90) (PREI) ⓘ **89019**
Fünftausend Taler E. Kunz, Philh, O. Ackermann (r1953) (9/95) (TEST) ⓘ **SBT1059**
Ihr Weib?...Mein teures Weib! F. Wunderlich, A. Rothenberger, Bavarian St Orch, R. Heger
(EMI) ⓘ [3] **CZS7 62993-2**
Wie freundlich strahlt D. Fischer-Dieskau, BPO, W. Schüchter (r1955)
(EMI) ⓘ [2] **CMS5 65621-2**
Wie freundlich strahlt...Heiterkeit und Fröhlichkeit T. Hampson, Munich RO, F. Luisi (r1994) (9/95) (EMI) ⓘ **CDC5 55233-2**
Wie freundlich strahlt G. Hüsch, Berlin St Op Orch, F. Weissmann (r1928)
(10/95) (NIMB) ⓘ **NI7867**

Zar und Zimmermann– comic opera: 3 acts (1837—Leipzig) (Lib after C. C. Römers)

Peter the Great G. Hann
Peter Ivanov H. Buchta
Marie M. Gripekoven
General Lefort B. Müller
Van Bett W. Strienz
Widow Browe E. Mayer
Lord Syndham H. Hölzlin
Marquis de Chateauneuf H. Schmid-Berikoven
Stuttgart Rad Chor, Stuttgart RO, B. Zimmermann (bp1936)
(MYTO) ⓘ [2] **2MCD943103**
Den hohen Herrscher würdig zu empfangen K. Moll, Munich RO, K. Eichhorn (r1981)
(ORFE) ⓘ **C009821A**
Lebe wohl, mein flandrisch Mädchen F. Wunderlich, I. Hallstein, Bavarian Rad Chor, Bamberg SO, H. Gierster
(DG) ⓘ [5] **435 145-2GX5(1)**
Lebe wohl, mein flandrisch Mädchen P. Anders, Berlin Deutsche Op Orch, J. Schüler (r1937) (TELD) ⓘ **4509-95512-2**
Lebe wohl, mein flandrisch Mädchen F. Wunderlich, I. Hallstein, Bavarian Rad Chor, Bamberg SO, H. Gierster
(5/93) (DG) ⓘ **431 110-2GB**
O sancta justitia!; Den hohen Herrscher; Heil sei dem Tag G. Hann, chor, Berlin RSO, H. Steinkopf (bp1943)
(MYTO) ⓘ [2] **2MCD943103**

O Sancta Justitia E. Kunz, Philh, O. Ackermann (r1953) (9/95) (TEST) ① **SBT1059**
Sonnst spielt ich L. Hofmann, Berlin Staatskapelle (r1928) (PREI) ① **89102**
Sonst spielt ich H. Schlusnus, Berlin St Op Orch, J. Schüler (r1937) (PREI) ① [2] **89212**
Sonst spielt ich D. Fischer-Dieskau, BPO, W. Schüchter (r1955) (EMI) ① [2] **CMS5 65621-2**
Sonst spielt ich H. Schlusnus, Berlin St Op Orch, J. Schüler (r1937) (9/90) (PREI) ① **89006**
Sonst spielt ich G. Hüsch, Berlin St Op Orch, H.U. Müller (r1937) (3/94) (PREI) ① **89071**
Verraten H. Prey, Berlin Deutsche Op Orch, H. Hollreiser (EURO) ① **GD69019**
Verraten!...Die Macht des Szepters B. Weikl, Munich RO, H. Wallberg (3/89) (ACAN) ① **43 266**
Verraten!...Die Macht des Zeptes T. Hampson, Munich RO, F. Luisi (r1994) (9/95) (EMI) ① **CDC5 55233-2**

LOTTI, Antonio *(c1667–1740) Italy*

Arminio– pasticcio (1714)
EXCERPTS: 1. Pur dicesti.
1. A. Patti, L. Ronald (r1905) (4/90) (PEAR) ① **GEMMCD9312**
1. H. Jadlowker, anon (r1927) (12/91) (CLUB) ① **CL99-042**
1. L. Tetrazzini, P. Pitt (r1910) (9/92) (EMI) ① [3] **CHS7 63802-2(2)**
1. C. Bartoli, G. Fischer (12/92) (DECC) ① **436 267-2DH** (12/92) (DECC) ▭ **436 267-4DH**
1. J. Baker, ASMF, N. Marriner (1/93) (PHIL) ① **434 173-2PM**

LUDERS , Gustav (Carl) *(1865–1913) Germany/USA*

The **Prince of Pilsen– operetta (1903—New York)**
EXCERPTS: 1. The Heidelberg Stein Song.
Excs R. Tucker, Orch, H. Barlow (bp1957) (VAI) ▭ **VAI69109**
1. Cincinnati Uni Sngrs, Cincinnati Uni Th Orch, E. Rivers (r1978) (4/94) (NEW) ① **80221-2**

LULLY, Jean-Baptiste *(1632–1687) Italy/France*

Alceste (ou le triomphe d'Alcide)– tragédie lyrique: prologue and 5 acts (1674—Paris) (Lib. Quinault)
Alceste C. Alliot-Lugaz
Alcide J-P. Lafont
Admète H. Crook
Céphise; La Gloire S. Marin-Degor
Lychas G. Ragon
Straton J-F. Gardeil
Lycomède; Pluton F. Loup
Caron G. Reinhart
Phérès M. Dens
Prosperine; Femme affligée; Nymphe de la Marne V. Gens
Thétis; Nymphe de la Mer C. Le Coz
Nymphe de la Seine M. Ruggeri
Eole; Cléante; Homme désolé O. Lallouette
Alecton; Apollon D. Nasrawi
Grande Ecurie, Sagittarius Ens, Compagnie Barocco, J-C. Malgoire (pp1992) (4/93) (ASTR) ① [3] **E8527**

Amadis– opera (prologue and 5 acts) (1686—Versailles) (Lib. Quinault)
Bois épais E. Caruso, orch, J. Pasternack (r1920) (7/91) (RCA) ① [12] **GD60495(6)**
Bois épais E. Caruso, orch, J. Pasternack (r1920) (10/91) (PEAR) ① [3] **EVC4(2)**

Armide– opera: prologue, 5 acts (1686—Paris) (Lib. Quinault)
G. Laurens, H. Crook, V. Gens, N. Rime, B. Delétré, G. Ragon, J. Hancock, L. Coadou, Collegium Vocale, Chapelle Royale Ch, Chapelle Royale Orch, P. Herreweghe (r1992) (8/93) (HARM) ① [2] **HMC90 1456/7**
Les Sourdines; Passacaille O. Baumont (trans J-H. d'Anglebert) (REM) ① **REM310990**

Atys– opera (prologue and 5 acts) (1675—Saint-Germain) (Lib. Quinault)
Le Temps, Phobétor, Sangar B. Delétré
Flore M. Zanetti
Zephir, Morphée, Trio J-P. Fouchécourt
Zephir, Le sommeil G. Ragon
Melpomene A. Steyer
Iris, Sangaride A. Mellon
Atys G. de Mey
Idas J. Bona
Doris F. Semellaz
Cybèle G. Laurens
Mélisse N. Rime
Célénus J-F. Gardeil
Phantase M. Laplénie
Un song funeste S. Maciejewski
Trio I. Desrochers V. Gens
Arts Florissants Chor, Arts Florissants Orch, W. Christie (7/87) (HARM) ① [3] **HMC90 1257/9** (HARM) ▭ [3] **HMC40 1257/9**
Act 3, Scene 4; Act 5, Final Scene G. Laurens, J-P. Fouchécourt, G. Ragon, M. Laplénie, B. Delétré, Arts Florissants Chor, Arts Florissants Orch, W. Christie (r1987) (HARM) ① **HMP390 805**
Excs B. Delétré, J-P. Fouchécourt, G. Ragon, A. Mellon, G. de Mey, J. Bona, F. Semellaz, G. Laurens, N. Rime, J-F. Gardeil, M. Laplénie, I. Desrochers, V. Gens, Arts Florissants Chor, Arts Florissants Orch, W. Christie (HARM) ① **HMC90 1249**

Cadmus et Hermione– opera (1673—Paris)
London Ob Band, M-A. Petit, P. Goodwin (r1994) (4/95) (HARM) ① **HMU90 7122**

Phaëton– opera (prologue, 5 acts) (1683—Versailles) (Lib. Quinault)
Phaëton H. Crook
Clymène R. Yakar
Théone J. Smith
Libye V. Gens
Epaphus G. Thervel
Triton; Le Soleil; La Déesse de la terre J-P. Fouchécourt
Mérops P. Huttenlocher
Saturne; Protée L. Naouri
Astrée; Une Heure du jour V. Pochon
L'Automne; Jupiter J. Varnier
Une Bergère; Une Heure du jour F. Couderc
Sagittarius Ens, Musiciens du Louvre, M. Minkowski (r1993) (8/94) (ERAT) ① [2] **4509-91737-2**

LUNA (Y CARNÉ) , Pablo *(1879–1942) Spain*

El **Niño judío– zarzuela (1918—Madrid)**
EXCERPTS—; 1. De España vengo; 2. Danza India; 3. Soy un rayito de luna.
1. M. Caballé, Barcelona SO, E.M. Marco (11/92) (RCA) ▭ [2] **RK61044**
1. P. Lorengar, Austrian RSO, G. Navarro (SONY) ① **MK39210**
1. V. de los Angeles, Sinfonia of London, R. Frühbeck de Burgos (orch Gamley) (10/88) (EMI) ① **CDM7 69502-2**

L' **Pícara molinera– zarzuela (1928—Madrid)**
Paxarin, tu que vuelas P. Domingo, Barcelona SO, G. Navarro (ACAN) ① **49 390**

Sangre de Reyes– zarzuela (1926—Pavón)
Adiós para siempre J. Carreras, ECO, E. Ricci (r1994) (2/95) (ERAT) ① **4509-95789-2** (2/95) (ERAT) ▭ **4509-95789-4**

LUTYENS, (Agnes) Elisabeth *(1906–1983) England*

Isis and Osiris– lyric drama: 8vv and small orchestra, Op. 74 (1970)
Lament of Isis on the death of Osiris J. Manning (r1992) (10/93) (NMC) ① **NMCD011**

MACCUNN, Hamish *(1868–1916) Scotland*

Jeanie Deans– opera (4 acts) (1894—Edinburgh) (Lib. Bennett after Scott)
Effie's Cradle Song
O would that I could see again P. MacMahon, L. Glover (LINN) ① [2] **CKD008** (LINN) ⦿ **CKH008** ▭ **CKC008**

MACHOVER , Tod *(b 1953) USA*

Valis– opera (two parts) (1987—Paris)
Cpte P. Mason, J. Felty, T. Edwards, T. Bogdan, M. King, D. Runswick, A. Azéma, D. Ciampolini, E. Stephenson, T. Machover (BRID) ① **BCD9007**

MACKEBEN , Theo *(1897–1953) Germany*

Der **Goldene Käfig– operetta (1943)**
EXCERPTS: 1. Walzer der Freude.
1. Cologne RSO, E. Smola (r1994) (CAPR) ① **10 705**

MACKENZIE, Sir Alexander (Campbell) *(1847–1935) Scotland*

The **Cricket on the Hearth– opera: 3 acts, Op. 62 (1901; staged 1914—London) (Lib. J Sturgis, after Dickens)**
EXCERPTS: 1. Overture.
1. BBC Scottish SO, M. Brabbins (r1994) (5/95) (HYPE) ① **CDA66764**

MACMILLAN, James *(b 1959) Scotland*

Búsqueda– music-theatre piece (1988) (Texts trans. D G Markus)
Cpte J. Stevenson, Ruth Anderson, C. Spink, A. Bentley, Scottish CO, J. MacMillan (r1993) (4/95) (CATA) ① **09026 62669-2** (4/95) (CATA) ▭ **09026 62669-4**

Visitatio Sepulchri– sacred opera: 3 scenes (1993—Glasgow) (Text 13th-Century Latin Easter play)
Cpte O. Blackburn, C. Bunning, T. Dives, R. O. Forbes, A. Oke, S. Richardson, R. Bryson, Scottish CO, I. Bolton (r1993) (4/95) (CATA) ① **09026 62669-2** (4/95) (CATA) ▭ **09026 62669-4**

MADERNA, Bruno *(1920–1973) Italy*

Hyperion– opera (1960-69) (Lib. after Hölderlin)
Cpte P. Walmsley-Clark, B. Ganz, J. Zoon, Jeunes Sols Voc Ens, Asko Ens, P. Eötvös (pp1992) (9/93) (MONT) ① [2] **782014**
P. Walmsley-Clark, B. Ganz, J. Zoon, Jeunes Sols Voc Ens, ASKO Ens, P. Eötvös (pp1992) (AUVI) ① [2] **MO782014**

Satyricon– opera: 1 act (1973—Scheveningen) (Lib. Maderna & Strasfogel, after Petronius)
Trimalcione W. Neill
Fortunata D. Brown
Habinna P. Sperry
Eumolpo M. Kraak
Scintilla P. Holden
Niceros T. Haenen
Criside A. Haenen
Quartilla E. Lioni
Hilversum RO, Milan RAI Chor, Milan RAI SO, B. Maderna (r1973) (STDV) ① **STR10061**
Trimalchio; Habinnas P. Sperry
Niceros; Eumolpus A. Tomicich
Criside L. Oliveri
Fortunata M. Vargas
Divertimento Ens, S. Gorli (r1991) (9/93) (SALA) ① **SCD9101**

MADETOJA , Leevi *(1897–1947) Finland*

Juha– opera: 6 tableaux, Op. 74 (1935—Helsinki) (Lib. cpsr & Ackté, after Aho)
Juha J. Hynninen
Marja M. Lokka
Shemeikka E. Erkkilä
Mother-in-Law A. Välkki
Kaisa M. Haverinen
Vicar T. Valtasaari
Anja M. Wirkkala
Maiden I M. Metsomäki

Maiden II K. Haartti
Man I K. Airinen
Man II K. Olli
Finnish Rad Youth Ch, Finnish RSO, J. Jalas (r1977)
(11/92) (ONDI) Ⓓ [2] **ODE714-2**

The **Ostrobothnians– concert suite from opera, Op. 52 (1922)**
Iceland SO, P. Sakari
(8/92) (CHAN) Ⓓ **CHAN9036**
Finnish RSO, J-P. Saraste (r1993)
(4/95) (FINL) Ⓓ **4509-96867-2**

MAILLART, Aimé *(1817–1871) France*

Les **Dragons de Villars– opera (1856—Paris) (Lib. J. P. Lockroy and Cormon)**
Ne parle pas, Rose, je t'en supplie F. Wunderlich, Munich RO, H. Moltkau (Ger: bp)
(DG) Ⓓ [5] **435 145-2GX5(1)**
Overture Berlin St Op Orch, A. von Zemlinsky (r1928) (SCHW) Ⓓ **310037**

MALIPIERO, Gian Francesco *(1882–1973) Italy*

Il **Finto Arlecchino– opera (1925) (Lib. cpsr)**
Symphonic fragments Veneto PO, P. Maag (r1991) (9/93) (MARC) Ⓓ **8 223397**

MANCINI, Francesco *(1672–1737) Italy*

Gl'Amanti Generosi– opera (1705—Naples)
Sinfonia C. Steele-Perkins, Parley of Instr
(1/89) (HYPE) Ⓓ **CDA66255**

MANFROCE, Nicola Antonio *(?–1813) Italy*

Ecuba– opera: 3 acts (1812—Naples) (Lib. Schmidt, after Milcent)
Sì tenero amatore M. Bovino, H. Nichol, Y. Kenny, P. Nilon, Philh, D. Parry
(10/90) (OPRA) Ⓓ [3] **ORCH103**

MARAIS, Marin *(1656–1728) France*

Alcyone– tragédie lyrique: prologue and 5 acts (1706) (Lib. A. Houdar de la Motte)
Alcyone J. Smith
Ceix G. Ragon
Pelée P. Huttenlocher
Pan; Phorbas V. le Texier
Ismène, Matelotte I S. Boulin
Tmole, Grand Prêtre, Neptune B. Delétré
Apollon, Le Sommeil J-P. Fouchécourt
Prêtesse, Matelotte II V. Gens
Musiciens du Louvre, M. Minkowski
(4/92) (ERAT) Ⓓ [3] **2292-45522-2**
Suites Concert des Nations, J. Savall (r1993)
(2/95) (ASTR) Ⓓ **E8525**

MARCHETTI, Filippo *(1831–1902) Italy*

Ruy Blas– dramma lirico: 4 acts (1869—Milan) (Lib. D'Ormeville after Hugo)
Ah, tu mi fuggivi...O dolce voluttà. C. Boninsegna, L. Colazza, orch (r1907)
(6/94) (IRCC) Ⓓ **IRCC-CD808**
Ai miei rivali A. Orda, Polish RSO, S. Rachoń (bp1964) (SYMP) Ⓓ **SYMCD1117**
Ai miei rivali T. Parvis, orch (r1910)
(11/92) (MEMO) Ⓓ [2] **HR4408/9(2)**
Ai miei rivali T. Parvis, orch (r c1910)
(12/94) (BONG) Ⓓ **GB1043-2**
Dal suo labbro benchè muto L. del Lungo, E. Caronna, orch (r1910s)
(6/94) (IRCC) Ⓓ **IRCC-CD808**
Ed ei non viene ancor F. Marconi, orch (r1908)
(10/90) (SYMP) Ⓓ **SYMCD1069**
Grazie Signor...Io che tentai F. Merli, B. Scacciati, orch, L. Molajoli (r1929)
(PREI) Ⓓ **89091**
Io scacciato...Ai miei rivali E. Bucalo, anon (r1904) (6/94) (IRCC) Ⓓ **IRCC-CD808**
O dolce volutta G. Zenatello, E. Mazzoleni, orch (r1911) (12/93) (SYMP) Ⓓ **SYMCD1148**
O madre mia dal intimo; Larva adorata T. Desana, orch (r1910s)
(6/94) (IRCC) Ⓓ **IRCC-CD808**
Per me...O dolce volutta G. Zenatello, E. Mazzoleni, orch (r1911)
(5/94) (PEAR) Ⓓ [4] **GEMMCDS9073(2)**

MARSCHNER, Heinrich (August) *(1795–1861) Germany*

Der **Bäbu– comic opera: 3 acts, Op. 98 (1838—Hanover) (Lib. W A Wohlbrück)**
EXCERPTS: 1. Overture.
1. Košice St PO, A. Walter (r1994)
(9/95) (MARC) Ⓓ **8 223342**

Des **Falkners Braut– comic opera: 3 acts (1832—Dresden)**
EXCERPTS: 1. Overture.
1. Košice St PO, A. Walter (r1993)
(9/95) (MARC) Ⓓ **8 223342**

Hans Heiling– romantic opera: prologue and 3 acts (1833—Berlin) (Lib. E. Devrient)
EXCERPTS: PROLOGUE: 1a. Rastlos geschafft; 1b. Genug, beendet euer emsig Treiben; 2. Overture. ACT 1: 3. O bleib' bei mir!; 4. Ha, welche Zeichen!; 5. An jenem Tag; 6. Wohlan, wohlan!; 7. Juchheisa!; 8. Ein sprödes allerliebstes Kind; 9. Wie hüpft mir vor Freude das Herz. ACT 2: 10. Einst war so tiefer Friede; 11. Aus der Klüfte; 12. Wohl durch den grünen Wald; 13. Ha dieses Wort; 14. Des Nachts wohl auf der Haide; 15. Ihr hört es! ACT 3: 16a. O Mutter, hätt ich dir geglaubt; 16b. Herauf, ihr Geister aus Höhl'; 17. Peasants' Wedding March; 18. Es wollte vor Zeiten; 19. Segne Allmächtiger; 20. Nun bist du mein; 21. So wollen wir auf kurze Zeit.
Hans Heiling T. Mohr
Queen of the Earth Spirits M. Hajóssyová
Anna E. Seniglová
Gertrude M. Eklöf
Konrad K. Markus
Stephan L. Neshyba
Slovak Phil Chor, Slovak PO, E. Körner (omits dialogue)
(11/91) (MARC) Ⓓ [2] **8 223306/7**
5. J. Herrmann, Berlin St Op Orch, B. Seidler-Winkler (r1942) (PREI) Ⓓ **89076**
5. H. Hotter, Berlin Deutsche Op Orch, A. Rother (bp1943) (PREI) Ⓓ **90200**
5. H. Schlusnus, Berlin St Op Orch, L. Blech (r1935) (PREI) Ⓓ [2] **89212**
5. H. Hermann Nissen, Berlin SO, F. Zweig (r1929) (PREI) Ⓓ **89090**
5. B. Weikl, Munich RO, H. Wallberg
(3/89) (ACAN) Ⓓ **43 266**
5. H. Schlusnus, Berlin St Op Orch, L. Blech (r1935) (9/90) (PREI) Ⓓ **89006**
5. T. Hampson, Munich RO, F. Luisi (r1994)
(9/95) (EMI) Ⓓ **CDC5 55233-2**
5. H. Schlusnus, orch (r1917)
(10/95) (NIMB) Ⓓ **NI7867**

Kaiser Adolph von Nassau– romantic opera: 4 acts, Op. 130 (1845—Dresden) (Lib. H Rau)
EXCERPTS: 1. Overture.
1. Košice St PO, A. Walter (r1993)
(9/95) (MARC) Ⓓ **8 223342**

Lukretia– opera: 2 acts, Op. 67 (1827—Danzing) (Lib. A Eckschlager)
EXCERPTS: 1. Overture.
1. Košice St PO, A. Walter (r1993)
(9/95) (MARC) Ⓓ **8 223342**

Der **Templer und die Jüdin– romantic opera: 3 acts, Op. 60 (1829—Leipzig) (Lib. W A Wohlbrück)**
EXCERPTS: 1. Overture.
1. Košice St PO, A. Walter (r1994)
(9/95) (MARC) Ⓓ **8 223342**

Der **Vampyr– romantic opera (1828—Leipzig) (Lib. W. A. Wohlbrück, after C. Nodier)**
Ha, noch einen ganzen Tag...Ha, welche Lust B. Weikl, Munich RO, H. Wallberg
(3/89) (ACAN) Ⓓ **43 266**
Ha! Noch einen ganzen Tag T. Hampson, Munich RO, F. Luisi (r1994)
(9/95) (EMI) Ⓓ **CDC5 55233-2**

MARTIN, Frank *(1890–1974) Switzerland*

Le **Mystère de la Nativité– oratorio/spectacle (1957-59) (Wds. after A. Greban)**
E. Ameling, A. Heynis, L. Devos, H. Cuénod, E. Tappy, P. Mollet, D. Olsen, A. Vessières, C. Clavensy, Jeunes de l'Eglise Ch, Geneva Motet Ch, SRO, E. Ansermet (pp1959)
(11/92) (CASC) Ⓓ [2] **VEL2006**

Der **Sturm– opera (3 acts) (1956—Vienna) (Lib. after Shakespeare)**
EXCERPTS; 1. Overture; 2. Mein Ariel: Hast du der Luft nur ist; 3. Hin sind meine Zauberei'n.
1-3. D. Fischer-Dieskau, SRO, E. Ansermet (pp1961) (11/92) (CASC) Ⓓ **VEL2001**

MARTIN Y GUERRERO *(19th Cent) Spain*

Gavilanes– zarzuela
Flor rota T. Folgar, orch (r1929)
(PEAR) Ⓓ [2] **GEMMCDS9180**

MARTINŮ, Bohuslav (Jan) *(1890–1959) Bohemia*

Alexandre bis– opera: 1 act (1937: fp—1964—Mannheim) (Lib. A. Wurmser)
Armande C. Collart
Alexandre A. Doniat
Orscar G. Friedmann
Portrait M. Vigneron
Philomene B. Kal
French Rad Lyric Orch, J. Doussard (pp1969)
(CHNT) Ⓓ **LDC278 994**
Armande D. Šounová-Brouková
Alexandre R. Tuček
Oscar V. Krejčík
Portrait R. Novák
Philomene A. Barová
Brno Janáček Op Orch, F. Jílek (r1982)
(SUPR) Ⓓ [2] **11 2140-2**

Ariane– opera: 1 act (1961—Gelsenkirchen/Brno) (Lib. cpsr, after Neveux)
Ariadne C. Lindsley
Theseus N. Phillips
Burun V. Doležal
Minotaur R. Novák
Guard M. Kopp
Old Man L. Vele
Czech PO, V. Neumann
(12/92) (SUPR) Ⓓ **10 4395-2**
Sinfonia 3. Czech PO, V. Neumann (r1986)
(KOCH) Ⓓ **34036-2**
(KOCH) ▭ **24036-4**

Comedy on the Bridge– radio opera: 1 act (1935) (Lib. cpsr, after Klicpera)
Popelka N. Sautereau
Jean B. Demigny
Eva J. Berbié
Bedron J. Mars
Instituteur J. Giraudeau
Sentinelle Ennemie J. Peyron
Sentinelle Amie G. Friedmann
Officier L. Lovano
French Rad Lyric Orch, M. Rosenthal (pp1963)
(CHNT) Ⓓ **LDC278 994**
Popelka J. Krátká
Jean R. Tuček
Eva A. Barová
Bedron R. Novák
Instituteur V. Krejčík
Sentinelle Ennemie J. Hladík
Sentinelle Amie J. Dufek
Officier B. Kurfürst
Brno Janáček Op Orch, F. Jílek (r1973)
(SUPR) Ⓓ [2] **11 2140-2**
Popelka J. Krátká
Sykoš R. Tuček
Bedroň R. Novák
Eve A. Barová
Schoolmaster V. Krejčík
Friendly sentry J. Hladík
Enemy sentry J. Dufek

Friendly officer B. Kurfürst
Brno Janáček Chbr Op Orch, F. Jílek
(5/85) (SUPR) ⊙ 1116 3314G

The Greek Passion– opera (4 acts) (1961—Zurich) (Lib. cpsr, afer Kazantzakis)
Manolios J. Mitchinson
Katerina H. Field
Grigoris J. Tomlinson
Kostandis P. Joll
Fotis G. Moses
Yannakos A. Davies
Lenio R. Cullis
Nikolios; Old woman C. Savory
Panait; Andonis J. Lawton
Michelis J. Harris
Old man; Patriarcheas D. Gwynne
Despinio J. Jonášová
Ladas M. Geliot
Kühn Children's Chor, Czech Phil Chor, Brno St PO, C. Mackerras
(3/91) (SUPR) ⓘ [2] 10 3611-2
Manolios, when shall we get married? R. Cullis, H. Field, J. Mitchinson, A. Davies, J. Tomlinson, Czech Phil Chor, Brno St PO, C. Mackerras (r1981) (KOCH) ⓘ 34036-2
(KOCH) ⊟ 24036-4

Julietta– opera: 3 acts (1938—Prague) (Lib. cpsr, after Neveux)
Julietta A. Esposito
Michel J. Giraudeau
Official, Policeman, Young Sailor, Worker J. Peyron
Man at Window, Old Man, Blind Man, Souvenir Seller B. Demigny
Man in Helmet, Old Sailor P. Germain
Old Arab, Grandfather Youth, Beggar L. Lovano
Bird Seller, Man, Old Woman, Hunter S. Michel
Small Arab, Man, Fortune-Teller B. Kal
Fish Seller, Man, Small Old Woman I. Kolassi
Chorale Madrigal, French Rad Lyric Orch, C. Bruck (r1962)
(CHNT) ⓘ [2] LDC278 995/6
Julietta M. Tauberová
Michel I. Žídek
Police Officer; Postman; Forest Warden A. Zlesák
Man with the Helmet Z. Otava
Man in the Window V. Bednář
Small Arab I. Mixová
Old Arab V. Jedenáctík
Bird-Seller J. Procházková
Fishmonger L. Hanzalíková
Old Man Youth J. Horáček
Grandfather K. Kalaš
Grandmother M. Čadikovičová
Old Lady S. Jelínková
Fortune-Teller V. Soukupová
Souvenir Seller J. Jindrák
Old Sailor J. Veverka
Young Sailor Z. Švehla
Errand-Boy M. Lemariová
Beggar K. Berman
Convict D. Jedlička
Engine Driver J. Stříška
Night Watchman B. Lalák
Prague Nat Th Chor, Prague Nat Th Orch, J. Krombholc (r1964)
(6/93) (SUPR) ⓘ [3] 10 8176-2
Good evening, ladies and gentlemen M. Čadikovičová, K. Kalaš, J. Horáček, Prague Nat Th Orch, J. Krombholc (r1964)
(KOCH) ⓘ 34036-2
(KOCH) ⊟ 24036-4

The Miracles of Mary– opera: prologue and 3 parts (1935—Brno) (Lib. cpsr, after H. Ghéon)
Archangel Gabriel; Sister Marta A. Barová
Mariken J. Marková
The Devil V. Zítek
Blacksmith D. Jedlička
Sister Paskalina E. Děpoltová
Maria; Maiden A. Kratochvílová
Foolish virgin; Mother of God M. Mrázová
Dealer in Oils I J. Jindrák
Dealer in Oils II Bohumil Maršík
Mascaron V. Kocián
God the Son I. Kusnjer
Drunkard J. Vavruška
Blacksmith's daughter; Girl B. Vítková
Inn-keeper K. Průša
Prague Children's Ch, Prague Rad Chor, Prague SO, J. Bělohlávek (r1982/3)
(1/94) (SUPR) ⓘ [2] 11 1802-2
Mariken dances with the Devil J. Marková, Prague Rad Chor, Prague SO, J. Bělohlávek (1982-83) (KOCH) ⓘ 34036-2
(KOCH) ⊟ 24036-4

MASCAGNI, Pietro (1863–1945) Italy

L' amico Fritz– opera: 3 acts (1891—Rome) (Lib. Dasparo)
EXCERPTS; 1. Preludio. ACT 1: 2. Son pochi fiori; 3. Laceri, miseri, tanti bambini. ACT 2: 4a. Suzel, buon dì (Cherry Duet); 4b. Tutto tace; 5. Intermezzo. ACT 3: 6. O pallida, che un giorno mi guardasti; 7a. Ed anchè Beppe amò; 7b. O Amore, o bella luce; 8. Non mi resta che il pianto.
Suzel S. Pacetti
Fritz Kobus P. Ballo
Beppe P. Romanò
David A. Ariostini
Federico C. Bosi
Hanezò F. Militano
Caterina A. Rossi
Cooperativa Artisti Associati Chor, Tuscan Accademia Strumentale Orch, A. Pinzauti (pp1991)
(FONE) ⓘ [2] 93F10
Suzel M. Freni
Fritz Kobus L. Pavarotti
Beppe L. Didier Gambardella
David V. Sardinero
Hanezò B. di Bella
Federico L. Pontiggia
Caterina M. Major
ROH Chor, ROHO, G. Gavazzeni
(8/87) (EMI) ⓘ [3] CDS7 47905-8
2. M. Favero, La Scala Orch, G. Antonicelli (r1936) (VAI) ⓘ VAIA1071
2. M. Favero, La Scala Orch, G. Antonicelli (r1936) (BONG) ⓘ GB1078-2
2. C. Muzio, orch (r1923)
(5/90) (BOGR) ⓘ [2] BIM705-2
2. C. Muzio, anon (r1923)
(1/94) (ROMO) ⓘ [2] 81005-2
2. M. Favero, La Scala Orch, G. Antonicelli (r1936) (4/94) (EMI) ⓘ [3] CHS7 64864-2(2)
2, 8. L. Bori, Victor Orch, N. Shilkret (r1923)
(ROMO) ⓘ [2] 81016-2
3. E. Stignani, EIAR Orch, U. Tansini (r1941)
(1/91) (PREI) ⓘ 89014
4a T. Schipa, M. Favero, orch, Anon (cond) (pp1937) (MEMO) ⓘ [2] HR4220/1
4a, 4b M. Favero, T. Schipa, La Scala Orch, G. Antonicelli (r1937) (VAI) ⓘ VAIA1071
4a, 4b M. Favero, T. Schipa, La Scala Orch, G. Antonicelli (r1937) (10/89) (NIMB) ⓘ NI7801
(NIMB) ⊟ NC7801
4a, 4b M. Favero, T. Schipa, La Scala Orch, G. Antonicelli (r1937)
(4/90) (EMI) ⓘ CDH7 63200-2
4a, 4b R. Pampanini, D. Borgioli, orch, L. Molajoli (r1930) (8/93) (PREI) ⓘ 89063
4a, 4b M. Freni, L. Pavarotti, Ater Orch, L. Magiera (pp)
(5/94) (DECC) ⓘ [2] 443 018-2DF2
4a, 4b, 7a, 7b Ferruccio Tagliavini, M. Olivero, EIAR Orch, U. Tansini (r1940)
(3/94) (CENT) ⓘ CRC2164
4a, 7b D. Borgioli, R. Pampanini, orch, L. Molajoli (r1930) (PEAR) ⓘ GEMMCD9091
4a, 7b D. Borgioli, R. Pampanini, orch (r1928)
(12/90) (CLUB) ⓘ CL99-014
4b L. Bori, M. Fleta, Victor Orch, Rosario Bourdon (r1924) (ROMO) ⓘ [2] 81016-2
4b M. Fleta, L. Bori, orch (r1924)
(2/90) (PREI) ⓘ 89002
4b L. Bori, M. Fleta, C. Linton, orch, Rosario Bourdon (r1924)
(4/94) (RCA) ⓘ [6] 09026 61580-2(2)
5. Monte Carlo PO, L. Foster
(ERAT) ⓘ 2292-45860-2
5. BPO, H. von Karajan
(EMI) ⓘ CDM7 64629-2
5. BPO, H. von Karajan
(10/87) (DG) ⓘ [3] 419 257-2GH3
5. Gothenburg SO, N. Järvi
(6/90) (DG) ⓘ 429 494-2GDC
(6/90) (DG) ⊟ 429 494-4GDC
7a J. Carreras, LSO, J. López-Cobos
(PHIL) ⓘ 434 152-2PM
7a F. de Lucia, orch (r1917)
(BONG) ⓘ [2] GB1064/5-2
7a, 7b L. Pavarotti, ROHO, G. Gavazzeni (r1968) (CFP) ⓘ CD-CFP4602
(CFP) ⊟ TC-CFP4602
7a, 7b M. del Monaco, Milan SO, T. Benintende-Neglia (r1952) (TEST) ⓘ SBT1039
7a, 7b B. Gigli, orch, R. Zamboni (r1948)
(5/90) (EMI) ⓘ CDH7 61052-2
8. M. Favero, orch (r c1929)
(VAI) ⓘ VAIA1071
8. M. Favero, orch (r c1929)
(BONG) ⓘ GB1078-2

Cavalleria Rusticana– opera: 1 act (1890—Rome) (Lib. Targioni-Tozzetti and Menasci)
1. Prelude; 2. O Lola (Siciliana); 3. Gli aranci olezzano; 4. Dite, mamma Lucia; 5a. Il cavallo scalpita; 5b. Beato voi; 6a. Regina coeli; 6b. Inneggiamo, il Signor (Easter Hymn); 7. Voi lo sapete; 8. Tu qui, Santuzza?; 9. Fior di giaggiolo; 10. No, no, Turiddu, rimani; 11. Oh! Il Signore vi manda; 12. Comare Santa; 13. Intermezzo; 14. A casa, a casa; 15a. Viva il vino (Brindisi); 15b. A voi tutti salute!; 16. Mamma, quel vino è generoso.
Santuzza R. Scotto
Turiddu P. Domingo
Alfio P. Elvira
Lola I. Jones
Mamma Lucia J. Kraft
Ambrosian Op. Chor, National PO, James Levine
(RCA) ⓘ RD83091
Santuzza E. Obraztsova
Turiddu P. Domingo
Alfio R. Bruson
Lola A. Goll
Mamma Lucia F. Barbieri
La Scala Chor, La Scala Orch, G. Prêtre, F. Zeffirelli
(PHIL) 070 103-1PH
(PHIL) 070 103-3PH
Santuzza R. Tebaldi
Turiddu J. Björling
Alfio E. Bastianini
Lola L. Dani
Mamma Lucia R. Corsi
MMF Chor, MMF Orch, A. Erede
(DECC) ⓘ 425 985-2DM
Santuzza L.B. Rasa
Turiddu B. Gigli
Alfio G. Bechi
Lola M. Marcucci
Mamma Lucia G. Simionato
La Scala Chor, La Scala Orch, P. Mascagni (r1940)
(NIMB) ⓘ [2] NI7843/4
Santuzza G. Simionato
Turridu M. del Monaco
Alfio C. MacNeil
Lola A.R. Satre
Mamma Lucia A. di Stasio
Santa Cecilia Academy Chor, Santa Cecilia Academy Orch, T. Serafin (r1961)
(BELA) ⓘ 450 016-2
(BELA) ⊟ 450 016-4
Santuzza M. Arroyo
Turiddu F. Bonisolli
Alfio B. Weikl
Lola L. Budai
Mamma Lucia J. Falk
Bavarian Rad Chor, Munich RO, L. Gardelli (r1981)
(RCA) ⓘ [2] 74321 25282-2
Santuzza D. Sanzio
Turiddu G. Breviario
Alfio P. Biasini
Lola M. Pantaleoni
Mamma Lucia O. de Franco
La Scala Chor, La Scala Orch, C. Sabajno (r1929/30)
(VAI) ⓘ [2] VAIA1082
Santuzza E. Obraztsova
Turiddu P. Domingo
Alfio R. Bruson
Lola A. Gall
Mamma Lucia F. Barbieri
La Scala Chor, La Scala Orch, G. Prêtre
(2/86) (PHIL) ⓘ 416 137-2PH
Santuzza M. Callas
Turiddu G. di Stefano
Alfio R. Panerai
Lola A.M. Canali

Mamma Lucia E. Ticozzi
La Scala Chor, La Scala Orch, T. Serafin (r1953) (10/87) (EMI) Ⓓ [3] **CDS7 47981-8**

Santuzza F. Cossotto
Turiddu C. Bergonzi
Alfio G. Guelfi
Lola A. Martino
Mamma Lucia M.G. Allegri
La Scala Chor, La Scala Orch, H. von Karajan (10/87) (DG) Ⓓ [3] **419 257-2GH3**

Santuzza Z. Milanov
Turiddu J. Björling
Alfio R. Merrill
Lola C. Smith
Mamma Lucia M. Roggero
R. Shaw Chorale, RCA Orch, R. Cellini (r1953) (8/88) (RCA) Ⓓ **GD86510**

Santuzza J. Varady
Turiddu L. Pavarotti
Alfio P. Cappuccilli
Lola C. Gonzales
Mamma Lucia I. Bormida
London Voices, National PO, G. Gavazzeni (1/89) (DECC) Ⓓ [2] **414 590-2DH2**

Santuzza M. Caballé
Turiddu J. Carreras
Alfio M. Manuguerra
Lola J. Hamari
Mamma Lucia A. Varnay
Southend Boys' Ch, Ambrosian Op Chor, Philh, R. Muti (r1979) (3/91) (EMI) Ⓓ [2] **CMS7 63650-2**

Santuzza J. Norman
Turiddu G. Giacomini
Alfio D. Hvorostovsky
Lola M. Senn
Mamma Lucia R. Laghezza
Paris Orch Chor, Paris Orch, S. Bychkov (12/91) (PHIL) Ⓓ **432 105-2PH** (12/91) (PHIL) ▭ **432 105-4PH**

Santuzza V. de los Angeles
Turiddu F. Corelli
Alfio M. Sereni
Lola A. Lazzarini
Mamma Lucia C. Vozza
Rome Op Chor, Rome Op Orch, G. Santini (r1962) (3/92) (EMI) Ⓓ [2] **CMS7 63967-2**

Santuzza S. Evstatieva
Turiddu G. Aragall
Alfio E. Tumagian
Lola A. di Mauro
Mamma Lucia A. Michalková
Slovak Phil Chor, Bratislava RSO, A. Rahbari (r1992) (3/93) (NAXO) Ⓓ **8 660022**

Excs G. Cernay, G. Micheletti, A. Endrèze, A. Hena, M. Arty, chor, orch, G. Cloëz (French: r c1932) (11/92) (MSCM) Ⓓ **MM30451**

Excs M. Jeritza, H. Roswaenge, E. Schipper, B. Paalen, M. Bokor, Vienna St Op Chor, Vienna St Op Orch, H. Reichenberger (pp1933: Ger) (11/95) (SCHW) Ⓓ [2] **314622**

1. La Scala Orch, H. von Karajan (DG) Ⓓ [2] **447 364-2GDB2**

1, 15a, 16. J. Carreras, J. Hamari, A. Varnay, Ambrosian Op Chor, Philh, R. Muti (EMI) Ⓓ **CDC7 54524-2**

1, 2. E. Caruso, BNOC Orch, A. Buesst (r1910/32) (5/94) (CLAR) Ⓓ **CDGSE78-50-52**

1, 2, 15b A. di Mauro, G. Aragall, E. Tumagian, Bratislava RSO, A. Rahbari (r1992) (12/94) (NAXO) Ⓓ **8 550684**

1, 2, 5a, 6a, 6b, 7, 10, 13, 15a, 16. M. Caballé, J. Carreras, M. Manuguerra, J. Hamari, A. Varnay, Ambrosian Op Chor, Philh, R. Muti (EMI) Ⓓ **CDM7 63933-2** (EMI) ▭ **EG763933-4**

1, 2, 5a, 6a, 6b, 7, 10, 11, 13, 15a, 16. P. Domingo, E. Obraztsova, R. Bruson, A. Gall, F. Barbieri, La Scala Chor, La Scala Orch, G. Prêtre (r1983) (PHIL) Ⓓ **442 482-2PH**

2. J. Björling, RCA Orch, R. Cellini (r1953) (RCA) ▭ **GK85277**

2. J. Björling, orch, N. Grevillius (r1934: Swed) (NIMB) Ⓓ **NI7835**

2. E. Caruso, F. Lapitino (r1910) (RCA) Ⓓ **09026 61243-2**

2. M. del Monaco, Milan SO, A. Quadri (r1952) (TEST) Ⓓ **SBT1039**

2. E. Scaramberg, anon (r1905: Fr) (SYMP) Ⓓ **SYMCD1173**

2. A. Piccaver, anon (r1929) (PREI) Ⓓ [2] **89217**

2. F. de Lucia, anon (r1902) (BONG) Ⓓ [2] **GB1064/5-2**

2. E. Caruso, S. Cottone (r1902) (5/89) (EMI) Ⓓ **CDH7 61046-2**

2. G. Martinelli, F. Lapitino, orch, J. Pasternack (r1915) (10/89) (NIMB) Ⓓ **NI7804** (NIMB) ▭ **NC7804**

2. T. Schipa, orch, C. Sabajno (r1913) (4/90) (EMI) Ⓓ **CDH7 63200-2**

2. B. Gigli, Anon (hp), P. Mascagni (r1940) (5/90) (EMI) Ⓓ **CDH7 61052-2**

2. E. Caruso, anon (r1904) (12/90) (PEAR) Ⓓ [3] **EVC1(1)**

2. E. Caruso, S. Cottone (r1902) (12/90) (PEAR) Ⓓ [3] **EVC1(1)**

2. E. Caruso, anon (r1903) (12/90) (PEAR) Ⓓ [3] **EVC1(1)**

2. E. Caruso, orch (r1910) (3/91) (PEAR) Ⓓ [3] **EVC2**

2. E. Caruso, anon (r1903) (7/91) (RCA) Ⓓ [12] **GD60495(1)**

2. E. Caruso, S. Cottone (r1902) (7/91) (RCA) Ⓓ [12] **GD60495(1)**

2. E. Caruso, F. Lapitino (r1910) (7/91) (RCA) Ⓓ [12] **GD60495(3)**

2. E. Caruso, anon (r1904) (7/91) (RCA) Ⓓ [12] **GD60495(1)**

2. A. Cortis, La Scala Orch, C. Sabajno (r1929) (10/91) (PREI) Ⓓ **89043**

2. H. Roswaenge, orch (r1928: Ger) (2/92) (PREI) Ⓓ [2] **89201**

2. G. Lugo, orch, F. Weiss (Fr: r1933) (2/92) (PREI) Ⓓ **89034**

2. F. de Lucia, orch (r1920) (7/92) (PEAR) Ⓓ [3] **GEMMCDS9923(1)**

2. E. Caruso, anon (r1904) (7/92) (PEAR) Ⓓ [3] **GEMMCDS9923(2)**

2. J. Björling, Stockholm Royal Op Orch, N. Grevillius (r1948) (8/92) (BLUE) Ⓓ **ABCD016**

2. F. Valero, anon (r1903) (11/92) (MEMO) Ⓓ [2] **HR4408/9(1)**

2. G. Martinelli, orch, Rosario Bourdon (r1927) (3/93) (PREI) Ⓓ **89062**

2. A. Davidov, anon (r1901: Russ) (6/93) (PEAR) Ⓓ [3] **GEMMCDS9007/9(1)**

2. J. Björling, Stockholm Royal Op Orch, N. Grevillius (r1948) (10/93) (EMI) Ⓓ **CDH7 64707-2**

2. A. Cortis, La Scala Orch, C. Sabajno (r1929) (3/94) (NIMB) Ⓓ **NI7850**

2. G. Anselmi, anon (r1907) (4/94) (EMI) Ⓓ [3] **CHS7 64860-2(2)**

2. G. Zenatello, orch (r1912) (5/94) (PEAR) Ⓓ [4] **GEMMCDS9074(1)**

2. A. Pertile, orch (r1923) (9/94) (NIMB) Ⓓ **NI7856**

2. F. de Lucia, anon (r1903) (1/95) (SYMP) Ⓓ **SYMCD1149**

2. G. Anselmi, anon (r1907) (7/95) (SYMP) Ⓓ **SYMCD1170**

2. E. Clément, anon (r c1911: Fr) (8/95) (PEAR) Ⓓ **GEMMCD9161**

2, 14, 15a, 16. H. Nash, M. Parry, J. Griffiths, BNOC Chor, BNOC Orch, A. Buesst (r1928: Eng) (11/95) (PEAR) Ⓓ **GEMMCD9175**

2, 15a T. Schipa, orch, Anon (cond) (pp1913) (MEMO) Ⓓ [2] **HR4220/1**

2, 15a F. Valero, anon (r1903) (6/90) (SYMP) Ⓓ **SYMCD1073**

2, 15a, 16. J. Carreras, A. Varnay, Ambrosian Op Chor, Philh, R. Muti (EMI) Ⓓ **CDM7 63111-2**

2, 16. J. Schmidt, BPO, S. Meyrowitz (r1929: Ger) (RELI) Ⓓ **CR921036**

2, 5b, 6a, 6b, 7, 10, 13, 15a, 16. J. Varady, L. Pavarotti, I. Bormida, P. Cappuccilli, C. Gonzales, London Op Chor, National PO, G. Gavazzeni (DECC) Ⓓ **421 870-2DA** (DECC) ▭ **421 870-4DA**

3. Fiesole School of Music Female Chor, MMF Chor, MMF Orch, M. Arena (ACAN) Ⓓ **43 540**

3. R. Shaw Chorale, RCA Victor Orch, R. Cellini (RCA) Ⓓ **GD60205**

3. Ambrosian Op Chor, National PO, James Levine (r1979) (RCA) Ⓓ **74321 24209-2**

3, 6a Ambrosian Op Chor, Philh, R. Muti (r1979) (EMI) Ⓓ [2] **CZS5 68559-2**

5b, 6a Santa Cecilia Academy Chor, Santa Cecilia Academy Orch, T. Serafin (r1960s) (BELA) Ⓓ **450 117-2** (BELA) ▭ **450 117-4**

6. P. Tinsley, ROH Chor, ROHO, L. Gardelli (EMI) Ⓓ **CDM7 64356-2**

6a C. Brewer, Atlanta Sym Chor, Atlanta Sym Chbr Chor, Atlanta SO, Robert Shaw (r1993) (TELA) Ⓓ **ECHOCD2**

6a, 6b J. Varady, London Op Chor, National PO, G. Gavazzeni (r1976) (DECC) Ⓓ **433 065-2DW** (DECC) ▭ **433 065-4DW**

6a, 6b H. Field, ROH Chor, ROHO, B. Haitink (12/89) (EMI) Ⓓ **CDC7 49849-**

6a, 6b, 7. J. Barstow, ROH Chor, RPO, R. Stapleton (r1991) (RPO) Ⓓ [2] **CDRPD900** (RPO) ▭ [2] **ZCRPD900**

6b J. Barstow, ROH Chor, RPO, R. Stapleton (IMP) Ⓓ [3] **TCD107**

6b P. Tinsley, ROH Chor, ROHO, L. Gardelli (EMIL) Ⓓ **CDZ10** (EMIL) ▭ **LZ10**

6, 7. J. Barstow, ROH Chor, RPO, R. Stapleton (RPO) Ⓓ **CDRPO700** (RPO) ▭ **ZCRPO700**

7. R. Ponselle, orch (r1919) (PEAR) Ⓓ [2] **GEMMCDS996**

7. R. Tebaldi, New Philh, O. de Fabritiis (DECC) Ⓓ **433 069-2DW** (DECC) ▭ **433 069-4DW**

7. M. Callas, E. Ticozzi, La Scala Chor, La Scala Orch, T. Serafin (r1953) (EMI) Ⓓ **CDC7 54702-** (EMI) ▭ **EL754702-**

7. E. Suliotis, A. di Stasio, Rome Orch, S. Varviso (r1967) (DECC) Ⓓ **440 405-2D**

7. E. Randová, Brno St PO, O. Lenárd (pp1992) (SUPR) Ⓓ **11 1846-**

7. F. Litvinne, anon (r1905) (SYMP) Ⓓ **SYMCD117**

7. C. Boninsegna, orch (r1907) (PEAR) Ⓓ **GEMMCD913**

7. H. Wildbrunn, orch (r1919: Ger) (PREI) Ⓓ **8909**

7. M. Nikolova, Bulgarian RSO, V. Stefanov (r1970s) (FORL) Ⓓ **UCD1674**

7. V. de los Angeles, C. Vozza, Rome Op Orch, G. Santini (r1962) (EMI) Ⓓ **CDM5 65579-**

7. M. Caballé, A. Varnay, Philh, R. Muti (r1979) (EMI) Ⓓ **CDM5 65575-**

7. E. Turner, orch, T. Beecham (r1928) (9/89) (EMI) Ⓓ **CDH7 69791-**

7. G. Bellincioni, S. Cottone (r1903) (6/90) (SYMP) Ⓓ **SYMCD107**

7. V. de los Angeles, Rome Op Orch, G. Morelli (r1954) (8/90) (EMI) Ⓓ **CDH7 63495-**

7. G. Arangi-Lombardi, La Scala Orch, L. Molajoli (r1930) (10/90) (PREI) Ⓓ **8901**

7. E. Burzio, orch (r c1906) (1/91) (CLUB) Ⓓ [2] **CL99-587/**

7. C. Muzio, orch, L. Molajoli (r1934) (4/91) (NIMB) Ⓓ **NI781** (4/91) (NIMB) ▭ **NC781**

7. J. Gadski, orch (r1908) (7/91) (CLUB) Ⓓ **CL99-10**

7. R. Tebaldi, New Philh, O. de Fabritiis (8/91) (DECC) Ⓓ [2] **430 481-2DX**

7. G. Bellincioni, S. Cottone (r1903) (7/92) (PEAR) Ⓓ [3] **GEMMCDS9923(1**

7. E. Calvé, orch (r1907) (7/92) (PEAR) Ⓓ [3] **GEMMCDS9923(1**

7. M. Freni, Venice La Fenice Orch, R. Abbado (9/92) (DECC) Ⓓ **433 316-2D**

7. X. Belmas, orch, A. Kitschin (r1928) (10/92) (PREI) Ⓓ **8904**

7. G. Bellincioni, anon (r1903) (11/92) (MEMO) Ⓓ [2] **HR4408/9(2**

7. L. Price, E. Bainbridge, New Philh, N. Santi (r1977) (12/92) (RCA) Ⓓ [4] **09026 61236-**

7. E. Calvé, anon (r1902) (3/93) (SYMP) Ⓓ **SYMCD110**

7. A. Pinto, anon (r1902) (8/93) (SYMP) Ⓓ **SYMCD111**

7. E. Carelli, S. Cottone (r1904) (8/93) (SYMP) Ⓓ **SYMCD111**

7. R. Ponselle, orch, R. Romani (r1919) (10/93) (NIMB) Ⓓ **NI784**

7. E. Eames, orch (r1906: two vers) (11/93) (ROMO) Ⓓ [2] **81001-**

7. R. Raisa, orch (r1933) (1/94) (CLUB) Ⓓ **CL99-05**

7. M. Jeritza, orch (r1923) (4/94) (PREI) Ⓓ **8907**

7. E. Destinn, orch (r1911) (5/94) (SUPR) Ⓓ **11 1337-**

7. F. Litvinne, anon (r1905) (12/94) (SYMP) Ⓓ **SYMCD112**

7. E. Destinn, orch, F. Kark (r1908: Ger) (12/94) (SUPR) Ⓓ [12] **11 2136-2(2**

7. E. Destinn, orch, B. Seidler-Winkler (r1908: Ger) (12/94) (SUPR) Ⓓ [12] **11 2136-2(2**

7. E. Destinn, orch, B. Seidler-Winkler (r1908: Ger) (12/94) (SUPR) Ⓓ [12] **11 2136-2(1**

7. E. Destinn, orch (r1912) (12/94) (SUPR) Ⓓ [12] **11 2136-2(4)**
7. C. Muzio, orch (r1918) (1/95) (ROMO) Ⓓ [2] **81010-2**
7. E. Rethberg, Berlin SO, F. Weissmann (r1933) (10/95) (ROMO) Ⓓ [2] **81014-2**
7, 10, 13. K. Ricciarelli, J. Carreras, Orch, Anon Cond (pp1991) (MCI) Ⓓ **MCCD090** (MCI) ▭ **MCTC090**
7, 11. E. Destinn, D. Gilly, orch (r1911) (12/94) (SUPR) Ⓓ [12] **11 2136-2(4)**
7, 8. M. Callas, A.M. Canali, E. Ticozzi, G. di Stefano, La Scala Chor, La Scala Orch, T. Serafin (r1953) (2/90) (EMI) Ⓓ [4] **CMS7 63244-2**
8. J. Carreras, I. Tokody, orch, Anon (cond) (pp1991/2) (VAI) Ⓓ **VAIA1009**
8. H. Spani, P. Masini, orch (r1925) (9/90) (CLUB) Ⓓ [2] **CL99-509/10**
8. B. Gigli, D. Giannini, La Scala Orch, C. Sabajno (r1932) (6/93) (MMOI) Ⓓ **CDMOIR417**
8(pt) G. Zenatello, E. Mazzoleni, orch (r c1911) (5/94) (SYMP) Ⓓ **SYMCD1158**
8. G. Zenatello, M. Gay, orch (r1911) (5/94) (PEAR) Ⓓ [4] **GEMMCDS9074(1)**
8. J. Johnston, A. Shuard, Philh, M. Mudie (r1951: Eng) (4/95) (TEST) Ⓓ **SBT1058**
8, 10. B. Gigli, D. Giannini, La Scala Orch, C. Sabajno (r1932) (PEAR) Ⓓ [2] **GEMMCDS9176**
8, 10. E. Burzio, G. Acerbi, orch (r1915) (1/91) (CLUB) Ⓓ [2] **CL99-587/8**
8(pt), 10. G. Zenatello, E. Mazzoleni, orch (r1911) (5/94) (PEAR) Ⓓ [4] **GEMMCDS9074(1)**
8, 12, 15a, 16. J. Björling, A. Nordmo-Løvberg, B. Björling, M. Sehlmark, G. Svedenbrant, Stockholm Royal Op Chor, Stockholm Royal Op Orch, K. Bendix (pp1954) (3/92) (BLUE) Ⓓ **ABCD028**
8, 15a, 16. J. Björling, R. Tebaldi, L. Dani, R. Corsi, MMF Chor, MMF Orch, A. Erede (r1959) (10/95) (DECC) Ⓓ **443 930-2DM**
8, 9. A. Baltsa, J. Carreras, LSO, P. Domingo (r1990-91) (SONY) Ⓓ **SK53968**
10. M. Caballé, J. Carreras, Philh, R. Muti (EMI) Ⓓ **CDM7 64359-2**
10. D. Giannini, B. Gigli, La Scala Orch, C. Sabajno (r1932) (5/90) (EMI) Ⓓ **CDH7 61052-2**
10. H. Roswaenge, M. Jeritza, Vienna St Op Orch, H. Reichenberger (pp1933: Ger) (6/94) (SCHW) Ⓓ **314502**
11. X. Belmas, W. Domgraf-Fassbaender, orch, A. Kitschin (r1929) (10/92) (PREI) Ⓓ **89047**
11(pt), 12. R. Raisa, G. Rimini, orch (r1929) (1/94) (CLUB) Ⓓ **CL99-052**
13. Philh, R. Muti (EMI) Ⓓ **CDM7 69596-2**
13. J. McCormack, F. Kreisler, V. O'Brien (r1914) (BIDD) Ⓓ **LAB022**
13. German Fest Orch, A. Scholz (CAVA) Ⓓ **CAVCD018**
13. National PO, G. Gavazzeni (DECC) Ⓓ **425 848-2DWO** (DECC) ▭ **425 848-4DWO**
13. RPO, M. Reed (pp1989) (RPO) Ⓓ [2] **CDRPD9001** (RPO) ▭ [2] **ZCRPD9001**
13. T. Indermühle, Salonisti (EURO) Ⓓ **GD69298**
13. National PO, G. Gavazzeni (DECC) Ⓓ **433 822-2DH** (DECC) ▭ **433 822-4DH**
13. Santa Cecilia Academy Orch, T. Serafin (r1960) (DECC) Ⓓ **433 065-2DWO** (DECC) ▭ **433 065-4DWO**
13. La Scala Orch, G. Prêtre (DECC) ◖ **071 142-1DH** (DECC) ▣ **071 142-3DH**
13. Philh, L. Magiera (DECC) OO **436 320-5DH**
13. Gothenburg SO, N. Järvi (DG) Ⓓ **439 152-2GMA** (DG) ▭ **439 152-4GMA**
13. RPO, M. Reed (IMP) Ⓓ **PCDS23** (IMP) ▭ **PCDSC23**
13. National SO, G. Gavazzeni (r1977) (DECC) Ⓓ [2] **443 585-2DF2** (DECC) ▭ [2] **433 585-4DWO2**
13. Philh, I. Westrip (r1993) (IMP) Ⓓ **PCD1075**
13. BBC Concert Orch, E. Ricci (pp1994) (TELD) ◖ **4509-96080-6** (TELD) ▣ **4509-96080-3**
13. Hallé, M. Handford (r1981) (CFP) Ⓓ **CD-CFP4658** (CFP) ▭ **TC-CFP4658**
13. V. Fox (r1962: arr org) (EMI) Ⓓ **CDM5 65426-2**
13. La Scala Orch, A. Guarnieri (r1927) (BONG) Ⓓ **GB1039-2**
13. RPO, A. Licata (r1994) (TRIN) Ⓓ **TRP044**
13. Gothenburg SO, N. Järvi (6/90) (DG) Ⓓ **429 494-2GDC** (6/90) (DG) ▭ **429 494-4GDC**
13. Philh, L. Magiera (11/91) (DECC) ◖ **071 150-1DH** (11/91) (DECC) ▣ **071 150-3DH**
13. SO, T. Beecham (r c1912) (11/91) (SYMP) Ⓓ [2] **SYMCD1096/7**
13. LPO, RPO, Philh (r1994; arr Milone) (9/95) (CALA) ◑ **CACD0105**
15a B. Gigli, NY Met Op Chor, NY Met Op Orch, G. Setti (r1929) (CONI) Ⓓ **CDHD149** (CONI) ▭ **MCHD149**
15a P. Domingo, G. Psaros, John Alldis Ch, New Philh, N. Santi (RCA) Ⓓ **GD84265**
15a M. Wittrisch, Berlin St Op Orch, L. Blech (Ger: r1935) (PREI) Ⓓ **89024**
15a P. Domingo, G. Psaros, John Alldis Ch, New Philh, N. Santi (RCA) Ⓓ [2] **GD60866** (RCA) ▭ [2] **GK60866**
15a E. Caruso, anon (r1905) (RCA) Ⓓ **09026 61243-2**
15a P. Domingo, G. Psaros, John Alldis Ch, LSO, N. Santi (r1972) (RCA) Ⓓ **09026 61356-2** (RCA) ▭ **09026 61356-4**
15a B. Gigli, orch (r1928) (IMP) Ⓓ **GLRS102**
15a A. Piccaver, Berlin St Op Orch, M. Gurlitt (r1928) (PREI) Ⓓ [2] **89217**
15a D. Smirnov, orch (r1913) (7/90) (CLUB) Ⓓ **CL99-031**
15a E. Caruso, anon (r1905) (12/90) (PEAR) Ⓓ [3] **EVC1(1)**
15a E. Caruso, anon (r1905) (7/91) (RCA) Ⓓ [12] **GD60495(1)**
15a F. Valero, anon (r1903) (7/92) (PEAR) Ⓓ [3] **GEMMCDS9923(2)**
15a F. Valero, anon (r1903) (4/94) (EMI) Ⓓ [3] **CHS7 64860-2(1)**
15a G. Zenatello, orch (r1911) (5/94) (PEAR) Ⓓ [4] **GEMMCDS9074(1)**
15a E. Caruso, anon (r1905) (7/95) (NIMB) Ⓓ **NI7866**
15a, 15b(pt) A. Piccaver, E. Schipper, Vienna St Op Chor, Vienna St Op Orch, K. Alwin (pp1937: Ger) (6/95) (SCHW) Ⓓ [2] **314632**
15a, 16. F. Corelli, orch, W. Pelletier (bp1963) (VAI) ▣ **VAI69100**
15a, 16. F. Merli, orch, L. Molajoli (r1926) (1/91) (PREI) Ⓓ **89026**
15a, 16. G. Lauri-Volpi, orch (r1923) (7/93) (NIMB) Ⓓ **NI7845**
16. M. Wittrisch, Berlin St Op Orch, K. Bendix (Ger: r1931) (PREI) Ⓓ **89024**
16. B. Prevedi, ROHO, E. Downes (DECC) Ⓓ **433 623-2DSP** (DECC) ▭ **433 623-4DSP**
16. M. Lanza, RCA Victor Orch, C. Callinicos (r1950) (RCA) Ⓓ [3] **GD60889(2)**
16. H. Roswaenge, Philh Hungarica, Z. Rozsnyai (pp1959) (PREI) Ⓓ **90103**
16. E. Caruso, orch (r1913) (RCA) Ⓓ **09026 61243-2**
16. E. Caruso, orch (r1913) (MCI) Ⓓ **MCCD086** (MCI) ▭ **MCTC086**
16. A. Solovianenko, Verona Arena Orch, A. Guadagno (pp1992) (MCI) Ⓓ **MCCD099**
16. M. Lanza, orch, C. Callinicos (r1952) (RCA) Ⓓ **09026 61420-2** (RCA) ▭ **09026 61420-4**
16. B. Prevedi, ROHO, E. Downes (r1964) (BELA) Ⓓ **450 005-2** (BELA) ▭ **450 005-4**
16. M. Gilion, orch (r c1909) (BONG) Ⓓ **GB1076-2**
16. B. Gigli, La Scala Orch, C. Sabajno (r1933) (CONI) Ⓓ **CDHD227** (CONI) ▭ **MCHD227**
16. M. del Monaco, Milan SO, T. Benintende-Neglia (r1952) (TEST) Ⓓ **SBT1039**
16. P. Domingo, E. Obraztsova, F. Barbieri, La Scala Chor, La Scala Orch, G. Prêtre (PHIL) Ⓓ **442 602-2PM** (PHIL) ▭ **442 602-4PM**
16. E. Caruso, orch (r1913) (ASV) Ⓓ **CDAJA5137** (ASV) ▭ **ZCAJA5137**
16. J. Björling, H. Ebert (pp1951) (BLUE) Ⓓ **ABCD057**
16. E. Caruso, orch (r1913) (PEAR) Ⓓ **GEMMCD9129**
16. A. Piccaver, Berlin St Op Orch, M. Gurlitt (r1929) (PREI) Ⓓ [2] **89217**
16. B. Gigli, La Scala Orch, C. Sabajno (r1933) (PEAR) Ⓓ [2] **GEMMCDS9176**
16. B. Gigli, La Scala Orch, C. Sabajno (r1933) (9/88) (EMI) Ⓓ **CDH7 61051-2**
16. P. Dvorský, M. Nitranová, Bratislava RSO, Czech RSO, O. Lenárd (10/89) (OPUS) Ⓓ **9156 1824**
16. G. Martinelli, orch, J. Pasternack (r1927) (10/89) (NIMB) Ⓓ **NI7804** (NIMB) ▭ **NC7804**
16. J. Varady, I. Bormida, L. Pavarotti, London Op Chor, National PO, G. Gavazzeni (7/90) (DECC) Ⓓ [2] **425 681-2DM2** (7/90) (DECC) ▭ [2] **425 681-4DM2**
16. E. Caruso, orch (r1913) (7/91) (RCA) Ⓓ [12] **GD60495(4)**
16. E. Caruso, orch (r1913) (7/91) (MSCM) Ⓓ **MM30352**
16. E. Caruso, orch (r1913) (10/91) (PEAR) Ⓓ [3] **EVC3(1)**
16. J. Björling, orch, N. Grevillius (r1944) (8/92) (BLUE) Ⓓ **ABCD016**
16. J. Hislop, orch, J. Barbirolli (r1928) (1/93) (PEAR) Ⓓ **GEMMCD9956**
16. G. Martinelli, orch, Rosario Bourdon (r1927) (3/93) (PREI) Ⓓ **89062**
16. J. Björling, orch, N. Grevillius (r1944) (10/93) (EMI) Ⓓ **CDH7 64707-2**
16. A. Piccaver, orch, M. Gurlitt (r c1929) (12/93) (NIMB) Ⓓ **NI7851**
16. G. Zenatello, orch (r1908) (5/94) (SYMP) Ⓓ **SYMCD1158**
16. G. Zenatello, orch (r1908) (5/94) (PEAR) Ⓓ [4] **GEMMCDS9073(2)**
16. J. Johnston, O. Price, orch, M. Mudie (r1948: Eng) (4/95) (TEST) Ⓓ **SBT1058**

Guglielmo Ratcliff– opera: four parts (1895—Milan) (Lib. H. Heine, trans A. Maffei)

EXCERPTS: 1a. Introduction. PART 1: 1b. Ucciso ho la mia cara; 2a. Sposo e sposa voi siete; 2b. È sempre il vecchio andazzo; 3. Sia lode al mio saio scozzese; 4. Apro, piccina; 5. Io n'ho stupore; 6. Vecchia volpe è quest'uomo. PART 2: 7. Willie, sai recitarmi; 8. Che intendere voleste; 9. Il Dugla viene?; 10. Quando fanciullo ancora; 11. Ti scendo ora alfin nel pensier. PART 3: 12. Oh, come il vento fischia; 13. Non m'è nuova la voce; 14. Intermezzo; 15. Non altro che delirio. PART 4: 16. Ah! Ah! Ah! Ah!; 17. O buon Dio, quale angoscia; 18. D'indole dolce e manusueta; 19. O Sancta vergine; 20. I tuoi sembianti son più belli; 21. T'arresta, e non fuggirmi.

2. C. Galeffi, La Scala Orch, L. Molajoli (r1928) (2/92) (PREI) Ⓓ **89040**
2. G. Pacini, anon (r1904) (4/94) (EMI) Ⓓ [3] **CHS7 64860-2(1)**

Iris– opera: 3 acts (1898—Rome) (Lib. Illica)

EXCERPTS - ACT 1: 1. La notte—I primi albori; 2. I fiori; 3. L'aurora: Son lo la vita! (Hymn to the Sun); 4. Ho fatto un triste sogno; 5. È lei! È lei!; 6. Voglio posare; 7. Al rio! Al rio!; 8. In pure stille; 9. Giù per la vita; 10. Io son Danjuro; 11. Misera! Ognor qui sola!; 12. Apri la tua finestra!; 13. È questa poesia; 14. La bellezza; La morte; Il vampiro; 15. Grazie, mousmè!; 16. Vieni! Dammi il braccio! ACT 2: 17. (Una guècha, susurrando); 18. Là che ci fate; 19. Donne, vampiri; 20. Ognora sogni; 21. Io pingo; 22. A un cenno mio; 23. Un dì (ero piccina); 24. Or dammi il braccio; 25. Da un'ora; 26. Annotta!; 27. Oh, maraviglia; 28. Datemi il passo! ACT 3: 29. Introduzione; 30. La notte—Ad ora bruna; 31. Perchè? Perchè?; 32. Ancora il triste sogno; 33. Un grand'occhio mi guarda!.

Iris	M. Olivero
Osaka	S. Puma
Kyoto	S. Meletti
Blind Man	G. Neri
Geisha	A. Oliva
Ragpicker	S. De Tommaso
Pedlar	Mario Carlin

Turin RAI Chor, Turin RAI Orch, A. Questa (pp1956) (FONI) Ⓓ [2] **CDAR2023**

3. Rio de Janeiro Municipal Th Chor, Rio de Janeiro Municipal Th Orch, J. DeMain (pp1992) (SONY) ◖ **SLV48362** (SONY) ▣ **SHV48362**

8, 23. L. Bori, Victor Orch, W.B. Rogers (r1915)
(ROMO) Ⓓ [2] **81016-2**
12. B. Gigli, orch (r1921) (CONI) Ⓓ **CDHD170**
12. L. Pavarotti, National PO, O. de Fabritiis (r1979) (DECC) Ⓓ **440 400-2DM**
12. P. Domingo, Munich RO, G. Patanè
(SONY) Ⓓ **MDK47176**
(SONY) ▭ **MDT47176**
12. G. di Stefano, Turin RAI Orch, O. de Fabritiis (bp1953) (FONI) Ⓓ **CDMR5003**
12. F. de Lucia, orch (r1920)
(BONG) Ⓓ [2] **GB1064/5-2**
12. E. Caruso, S. Cottone (r1902)
(5/89) (EMI) Ⓓ **CDH7 61046-2**
12. G. Martinelli, F. Lapitino, orch, J. Pasternack (r1917) (10/89) (NIMB) Ⓓ **NI7804**
(NIMB) ▭ **NC7804**
12. B. Gigli, orch (r1921)
(5/90) (NIMB) Ⓓ **NI7807**
(NIMB) ▭ **NC7807**
12. E. Caruso, S. Cottone (r1902)
(12/90) (PEAR) Ⓓ [3] **EVC1(1)**
12. E. Caruso, S. Cottone (r1902)
(7/91) (RCA) Ⓓ [12] **GD60495(1)**
12. A. Cortis, La Scala Orch, C. Sabajno (r1929)
(10/91) (PREI) Ⓓ **89043**
12. A. Cortis, La Scala Orch, C. Sabajno (r1929)
(3/94) (NIMB) Ⓓ **NI7850**
12. F. De Lucia, anon (r1920)
(4/94) (EMI) Ⓓ [3] **CHS7 64860-2(1)**
12. G. Anselmi, anon (r1907)
(7/95) (SYMP) Ⓓ **SYMCD1170**
21. M. Farneti, orch (r1931)
(11/92) (MEMO) Ⓓ [2] **HR4408/9(1)**
23. M. Freni, Venice La Fenice Orch, R. Abbado
(9/92) (DECC) Ⓓ **433 316-2DH**
23. R. Pampanini, EIAR Orch, U. Tansini (r1940)
(8/93) (PREI) Ⓓ **89063**
23. E. Carelli, S. Cottone (r1904)
(8/93) (SYMP) Ⓓ **SYMCD1111**

Isabeau– opera: 3 acts (1911—Buenos Aires) (Lib. Illica, after Lady Godiva legend)
EXCERPTS. ACT 1: 1. L'ecchio à cieco; 2. Il sogno à Dio; 3. Non colombelle. ACT 2: 4. Or solo ritorno; 5. E passera la viva creatura. ACT 3: 6. Fu vile l'editto; 7. I tuoi occhi.
E passerà la viva creatura B. De Muro, orch (r1912) (4/94) (EMI) Ⓓ [3] **CHS7 64860-2(2)**

Lodoletta– opera: 3 acts (1917—Rome) (Lib. Forzano)
EXCERPTS. ACT 1: 1. Coro delle olandesine. ACT 2: 2. Che corsa. ACT 3: 3a. Se Franz dicesse il vero; 3b. Ah! ritrolva; 4a. Ah! il suo name; 4b. Flammen, perdonami.
Lodoletta M. Spacagna
Mad woman A. Ulbrich
Maud Z. Bazsinka
La Vanard J. Sánta
Flammen P. Kelen
Giannotto K. Szilágyi
Franz M. Kálmándi
Antonio L. Polgár
Tenor voice A. Laczó
Postman J. Mukk
Hungarian St Op Children's Chor, Hungarian Rad & TV Chor, Hungarian St Orch, C. Rosekrans
(6/91) (HUNG) Ⓓ [2] **HCD31307/8**
3a, 3b B. Gigli, D. Giannini, U. Berrettoni (r1941)
(5/90) (EMI) Ⓓ **CDH7 61052-2**
4a, 4b M. Freni, Venice La Fenice Orch, R. Abbado (9/92) (DECC) Ⓓ **433 316-2DH**
4b M. Favero, orch, A. Sabino (r1941)
(VAI) Ⓓ **VAIA1071**
4b M. Favero, orch, A. Sabino (r1941)
(BONG) Ⓓ **GB1078-2**

Nerone– opera: 3 acts (1935—Milan) (Lib. Targioni-Tozzetti, after Cossa)
Perchè dovrei tremare? R. Scotto, I. Davis (pp1983) (10/86) (ETCE) Ⓓ **KTC2002**
(ETCE) ▭ **XTC2002**
Vergini Muse...Quando al soave anelito P. Domingo, National PO, E. Kohn
(11/90) (EMI) Ⓓ **CDC7 54053-2**
Vergini Muse...Quando al soave anelito P. Domingo, National PO, E. Kohn (r1989)
(6/94) (EMI) Ⓓ **CDC5 55017-2**

Il **Piccolo Marat– opera: 3 acts (1921—Rome) (Lib. Forzano & Targiono-Tozzetti)**
Piccolo Marat U. Borsò
L'Orco, Presidente del Comitato N. Rossi-Lemeni
Mariella V. Zeani
La Principessa C. Betner
Soldier R. Rota
Carpenter A. Poli
Il Tigre M. Frosini
Spy R. Spagli
Thief A. Frati
Captain E. Vessari
Voci interne C.M. Sperti
Livorno Teatro La Gran Guardia Chor, Livorno Teatro La Gran Guardia Orch, O. de Fabritiis (pp1961)
(FONE) Ⓓ [2] **88F17-37**
Piccolo Marat D. Galvez-Vallejo
L'Orco, Presidente del Comitato F. Vassar
Mariella S. Neves
La Principessa C. Pfeiler
Soldier; Captain S. Cowan
Spy H. Claessens
Thief M. Dirks
La Tigre L. Visser
Carpenter D. Henry
Netherlands Rad Chor, Netherlands RSO, K. Bakels (r1992)
(BONG) Ⓓ [2] **GB2168/9-2**

I **Rantzau– opera: 4 acts (1892—Florence) (Lib. Targioni-Tozzetti and Tenasci)**
(ACT 4) Giorgio si batte
Gianni Rantzau B. Anderson
Giacomo Rantzau G. Boldrini
Fiorenzo D. Colaianni
Giorgio O. Garaventa
Lebel C. Bosi
Luisa R. Lantieri
Giulia F. Bertoli
Livorno Cel-Teatro Chor, Livorno Cel-Teatro Orch, B. Rigacci (pp1992)
(FONE) Ⓓ [2] **93F13**

Zanetto– opera: 1 act (1896—Pesaro) (Lib. Targioni-Tozzetti and Tenasci, after Coppée)
Senti bambino R. Scotto, I. Davis (pp1983)
(10/86) (ETCE) Ⓓ **KTC2002**
(ETCE) ▭ **XTC2002**

MASCHERONI, Edoardo *(1859–1941) Italy*

Lorenza– opera (1901—Rome) (Lib. I. Illica)
Susanna al bagno E. Carelli, M. Sammarco, E. Mascheroni (r1904)
(8/93) (SYMP) Ⓓ **SYMCD1111**

MASSÉ, Victor *(1822–1884) France*

Les **Noces de Jeannette– opéra-comique: 1 act (1853—Paris) (Lib. J. Barbier & M. Carré)**
Jeanette R. Doria
Jean L. Huberty
Pasdeloup Ass Orch, J. Allain (r1955)
(ACCO) Ⓓ **20119-2**
Air du rossignol P. Gallois, London Fest Orch, R. Pople (r1993: arr fl: F.Pierre)
(5/95) (DG) Ⓓ **445 822-2GH**
Halte-là! s'il vous plaît N. Vallin, A. Baugé, orch, G. Andolfi (r1934)
(EMI) Ⓓ [2] **CZS5 68292-2**

Paul et Virginie– opera: 3 acts (1876—Paris) (Lib. Barbier and Carré)
L'oiseau s'envole J. Lassalle, anon (r1902)
(9/91) (SYMP) Ⓓ **SYMCD1089**

La **Reine Topaze– opéra-comique: 3 acts (1856—Paris) (Lib. J P Lockroy & L Battu)**
EXCERPTS: 1. Ninette est jeune et belle, 'Carnaval de Venise'.
1. S. Jo, ECO, R. Bonynge (r1993)
(9/94) (DECC) Ⓓ **440 679-2DH**

Les **Saisons– opera: 3 acts (1855—Paris) (Lib. J Barbier & M Carré)**
Chanson de blé. L. Fugère, orch (r1928)
(6/93) (SYMP) Ⓓ **SYMCD1125**

MASSENET, Jules (Emile Frédéric) *(1842–1912) France*

Amadis– opera: 4 acts (1922—Monte Carlo) (Lib. Claretia)
Amadis H. Perraguin
Floriane D. Streiff
Galaor D. Henry
King Raimbert A. Garcin
Fairy N. Chabrier
Huntsman P. Descombe
Hauts-de-Seine Maîtrise, Paris Op Chor, Paris Op Orch, P. Fournillier
(6/89) (FORL) Ⓓ [2] **UCD16578/**

Ariane– opera: 5 acts (1906—Paris) (Lib. C Mendes)
EXCERPTS: 1. Andante et Menuet des Graces; 2. Ce Sarrasin disait (Air des roses); 3. Lamento d'Ariane.
3. National PO, R. Bonynge (r1975)
(DECC) Ⓓ **444 108-2D**
4, 5. L. Muratore, orch (r1910s)
(8/92) (IRCC) Ⓓ **IRCC-CD80**

Cendrillon– concert suite from opera
1. Marche des princesses; 2. Les filles de noblesse; 3. Menuet de Cendrillon.
Hong Kong PO, K. Jean
(1/92) (MARC) Ⓓ **8 22335**

Cendrillon, 'Cinderella'– opera: 4 acts (1899—Paris) (Lib. Cain. after Perrault)
Cendrillon F. von Stad
Prince Charming N. Gedd
Madame de la Haltière J. Berbi
Pandolfe J. Basti
Fairy R. Weltin
Noémie T. Cah
Dorothée E. Bainbridg
King; Voice of the Herald C. Melor
Dean of the Faculty P. Croo
Master of Ceremonies C. du Plessi
Prime Minister J. Nobl
Ambrosian Op Chor, Philh, J. Rudel
(9/89) (CBS) Ⓓ [2] **CD7932**
Valse RPO, T. Beecham (r1957)
(9/92) (EMI) Ⓓ **CDM7 63401-**

Chérubin– opera: 3 acts (1903—Monte Carlo) (Lib. F. de Croisset & H. Cain)
Chérubin F. von Stad
Jacoppo S. Rame
L'Ensoleillad J. Anderso
Nina D. Upshav
Count J-M. Ivalc
Countess H. Garet
Baron M. Trempor
Baroness B. Balley
Duke M. Sénécha
Ricardo C.H. Ahnsj
Innkeeper A. Arapia
Officer R. Scholz
Bavarian St Op Chor, Munich RSO, P. Steinberg
(12/92) (RCA) Ⓓ [2] **09026 60593-**
Air de Nina J. Sutherland, Ambrosian Light Op Chor, New Philh, R. Bonynge (arr Gamley)
(DECC) Ⓓ **425 048-2D**
(DECC) ▭ **425 048-4D**
Lorsque vous n'aurez rien à faire D. Upshaw, Munich RSO, P. Steinberg
(RCA) Ⓓ **09026 61886-**
(RCA) ▭ **09026 61886-**
Viva amour E. Eames, anon (r1908)
(11/93) (ROMO) Ⓓ [2] **81001-**

Le **Cid– opera: 4 acts (1885—Paris) (Lib. d'Ennery, Blau and Gallet)**
EXCERPTS. ACT 1: 1. O noble lame étincelante. ACT 2: BALLET MUSIC: 2a. Castillane; 2b. Andalouse; 2c. Aragonaise; 2d. Aubade; 2e. Catalane; 2f. Madrilène; 2g. Navarraise. ACT 3: 3a. De cet affreux combat; 3b. Pleurez, mes yeux; 4a. Ah! tout est bien fini; 4b. O souverain, ô juge, ô père. ACT 4: 5. Il a fait noblement.
Don Arias C. Ingran
Don Alonzo T. Hodge
Count de Gormas A. Voketaiti
Chimène G. Bumbr
Infanta E. Bergquis
King J. Gardne
Rodrigue P. Doming
Don Diegue P. Plishk
Moorish Envoy P. Lightfoo
St Jacques J. Adam
Byrne Camp Chorale, NY Op Orch, E. Queler (pp1976)
(2/90) (CBS) Ⓓ [2] **CD7930**
1. G. Thill, orch, E. Bigot (r1933)
(8/95) (FORL) Ⓓ **UCD1672**
1, 4a, 4b A. Paoli, orch (r1909; Ital)
(PREI) Ⓓ **8999**
1, 4a, 4b G. Thill, Orch, E. Bigot (r1933)
(1/89) (EMI) Ⓓ **CDM7 69548-**
2a-g CBSO, L. Frémaux (r1971)
(EMI) Ⓓ **CDM5 65150-**

2a-g National PO, R. Bonynge (r1975) (DECC) ⓘ **444 110-2DA**
2a-g National PO, R. Bonynge (1/90) (DECC) ⓘ [2] **425 475-2DM2**
2a, 2f Orch, Anon Cond (pp1991) (MCI) ⓘ **MCCD090** (MCI) ▭ **MCTC090**
2c-g RPO, B. Tovey (RPO) ⓘ **CDRPO7010** (RPO) ▭ **ZCRPO7010**
3a, 3b M. Callas, FRNO, G. Prêtre (2/88) (EMI) ⓘ **CDC7 49059-2**
3a, 3b K. Te Kanawa, ROHO, J. Tate (2/90) (EMI) ⓘ **CDC7 49863-2**
3b M. Caballé, Philh, J. Collado (11/92) (RCA) ▭ [2] **RK61044**
3b A. Schläger, anon (r1904: Ger) (SYMP) ⓘ **SYMCD1085**
3b M. Caballé, Seville SO, P. Domingo (pp1991) (RCA) ⓘ **RD61191**
3b M. Caballé, Seville SO, P. Domingo (pp1991) (RCA) **ОО 09026 61191-5**
3b F. Pollet, Montpellier PO, C. Diederich (r1989) (ERAT) ⓘ **4509-98502-2**
3b G. Bumbry, Stuttgart RSO, S. Soltesz (11/86) (ORFE) ⓘ **C081841A**
3b M. Callas, FRNO, G. Prêtre (2/90) (EMI) ⓘ **CDM7 63182-2**
3b F. Litvinne, anon (r1903) (10/92) (SYMP) ⓘ **SYMCD1101**
3b M. Jeritza, orch (r1925) (4/94) (PREI) ⓘ **89079**
3b F. Litvinne, orch (r1907) (12/94) (SYMP) ⓘ **SYMCD1128**
3b D. Visse, Camargue PO, Reinhardt Wagner (r1995: arr R Wagner) (8/95) (HARM) ⓘ **HMC90 1552**
4a, 4b P. Domingo, Barcelona SO, G. Navarro (11/92) (RCA) ▭ **09026 61204-4**
4a, 4b E. Caruso, orch, W.B. Rogers (r1916) (RCA) ⓘ **09026 61244-2**
4a, 4b P. Domingo, LSO, N. Santi (r1971) (RCA) ⓘ **09026 61356-2** (RCA) ▭ **09026 61356-4**
4a, 4b P. Domingo, Barcelona SO, G. Navarro (RCA) **ОО 09026 61204-5**
4a, 4b J. Schmidt, orch, O. Dobrindt (r1932: Ger) (EMI) ⓘ [2] **CHS7 64673-2**
4a, 4b J. Schmidt, orch (r1932; Ger) (4/90) (EMI) ⓘ **CDM7 69478-2**
4a, 4b E. Caruso, orch, W.B. Rogers (r1916) (7/91) (RCA) ⓘ [12] **GD60495(5)**
4a, 4b E. Caruso, orch, W.B. Rogers (r1916) (10/91) (PEAR) ⓘ [3] **EVC3(2)**
4a, 4b L. Escalais, anon (r1906) (12/93) (SYMP) ⓘ **SYMCD1126**
4a, 4b B. Heppner, Munich RO, R. Abbado (r1993/4) (11/95) (RCA) ⓘ **09026 62504-2**
4b B.S. Rosenberg, Budapest Concert Orch, J. Acs (pp1990) (OLYM) ⓘ **OCD370**
4b P. Domingo, NY Op Orch, E. Queler (SONY) ⓘ **MDK47176** (SONY) ▭ **MDT47176**
4b J. Carreras, Los Angeles PO, Z. Mehta (pp1994) (TELD) ⓘ **4509-96200-8**
4b J. Carreras, Los Angeles PO, Z. Mehta (pp1994) (TELD) **ОО 4509-96200-5**
4b J. Carreras, Los Angeles PO, Z. Mehta (pp1994) (12/94) (TELD) ⓘ **4509-96200-2**

(12/94) (TELD) ⊙ **4509-96200-1** ▭ **4509-96200-4**

Cléopâtre– opera: 4 acts (1914—Monte Carlo) (Lib. L. Payen)

Cléopâtre	K. Harries
Marc-Antoine	D. Henry
Spakos	J-L. Maurette
Octavie	D. Streiff
Charmion	M. Olmeda
Ennius	M. Hacquard
Amnhès, Sévérus	C. Massoz
Slave	P. Georges

Massenet Fest Chor, Saint-Etienne Nouvel Orch, P. Fournillier (pp1990) (10/92) (SCHW) ⓘ [2] **310322**
A-t-il dit vrai?...Solitaire sur ma terrasse Vanni-Marcoux, orch (r1931) (1/94) (CLUB) ⓘ **CL99-101**
exc Vanni-Marcoux, orch, P. Coppola (r1931) (PEAR) ⓘ **GEMMCD9912**

Don César de Bazan– comic opera (1872—Paris) (Lib. D'Ennery, Dumanoir and Chantepie)
EXCERPTS: 2. A Séville, belles Señoras (Sevillana); 3. Entr'acte (Act 3).
1. N. Melba, orch, W.B. Rogers (r1910) (9/93) (RCA) ⓘ **09026 61412-2**
1. A. Galli-Curci, orch, Rosario Bourdon (r1923) (8/94) (ROMO) ⓘ [2] **81004-2**
2. A. Galli-Curci, orch (r1923) (10/89) (NIMB) ⓘ **NI7802** (NIMB) ▭ **NC7802**
2. S. Jo, ECO, R. Bonynge (r1993) (9/94) (DECC) ⓘ **440 679-2DH**
2. N. Melba, orch, W.B. Rogers (r1910) (5/95) (ROMO) ⓘ [3] **81011-2(2)**
2, 3. LSO, R. Bonynge (r1971) (DECC) ⓘ **444 111-2DA**

Don Quichotte– comédie héroïque: 5 acts (1910—Monte Carlo) (Lib. Cain, after J. Le Lorrain)

Don Quichotte	B. Christoff
Sancho Pança	C. Badioli
Dulcinée	T. Berganza
Pedro	O. Rovero
Garcias	P. Malgarini
Rodriguez	A. Nobile
Juan	T. Frascati
Bandit Chief	C. Bagno

Milan RAI Chor, Milan RAI SO, A. Simonetto (pp1957: Ital) (FONI) ⓘ [2] **CDAR2025**

Don Quichotte	N. Ghiaurov
Sancho Pança	G. Bacquier
Dulcinée	R. Crespin
Pedro	M. Command
Garcias	A. Dutertre
Rodriguez	P. Garazzi
Juan	J-M. Frémeau
Bandit Chief	J. Loreau

Suisse Romande Rad Chor, SRO, K. Kord (r1978) (4/92) (DECC) ⓘ [2] **430 636-2DM2**

Don Quichotte	J. Van Dam
Sancho Pança	A. Fondary
Dulcinée	T. Berganza
Pedro	I. Vernet
Garcias	M-A. Todorovitch
Rodriguez	C. Papis
Juan	N. Rivenq
Bandit Chief	J-C. Barbier

Toulouse Capitole Chor, Toulouse Capitole Orch, M. Plasson (r1992) (12/93) (EMI) ⓘ [2] **CDS7 54767-2**
Death scene F. Chaliapin, O. Kline, orch, Rosario Bourdon (r1927) (NIMB) ⓘ **NI7864**
Death Scene F. Chaliapin, orch, E. Goossens (r1927) (12/89) (PEAR) ⓘ **GEMMCD9314**
Écoute, mon ami...prends cette île Vanni-Marcoux, O. Ricquier, M. Cozette, orch, P. Coppola (r1934) (PEAR) ⓘ **GEMMCD9912**
Écoute, mon ami ... prends cette île Vanni-Marcoux, O. Ricquier, M. Cozette, orch (r1934) (1/94) (CLUB) ⓘ **CL99-101**
Interlude; Mort de Don Quichotte R. Raimondi, Paris Op Orch, E. Tchakarov (r1981) (ERAT) ⓘ **4509-98503-2**
Interludes Monte Carlo Op Orch, J.E. Gardiner (2/93) (ERAT) ⓘ **2292-45859-2**
Quand apparaissent les étoiles Vanni-Marcoux, orch (r1924) (1/94) (CLUB) ⓘ **CL99-101**

Esclarmonde– opera: 4 acts (1889—Paris) (Lib. Gallet and L. de Gramont)

Esclarmonde	D. Mazzola
Roland	J. Sempere
Parséis	H. Perraguin
Enéas	G. Gabelle
Bishop of Blois	C. Treguier
King Cléomer; Emperor Phorcas	J-P. Courtis

Massenet Fest Chor, Budapest Liszt SO, P. Fournillier (pp1992) (SCHW) ⓘ [3] **312692**

Esclarmonde	J. Sutherland
Roland	G. Aragall
Parséis	H. Tourangeau
Enéas	R. Davies
Bishop of Blois	L. Quilico
King Cléomer	R. Lloyd
Saracen Envoy	I. Caley
Byzantine Herald	G. Clark
Emperor Phorcas	C. Grant

Finchley Children's Music Group, John Alldis Ch, National PO, R. Bonynge (8/90) (DECC) ⓘ [3] **425 651-2DM3**

Esclarmonde– concert suite from opera
1. Evocation; 2. L'île magique; 3. Hymenée; 4. Dans la forêt: Pastorale: Chasse.
Hong Kong PO, K. Jean (1/92) (MARC) ⓘ **8 223354**

Grisélidis– conte lyrique: 3 acts (1901—Paris) (Lib. A. Silvestre and E. Morand)

Grisélidis	M. Command
Fiamina	C. Larcher
Bertrade	B. Desnoues
Le Diable	J-P. Courtis
Alain	J-L. Viala
Le Marquis	D. Henry
Le Prieur	C. Treguier
Gondebaud	M. Sieyes

Lyon Nat Ch, Lyon Op Chor, Budapest F. Liszt SO, P. Fournillier (r1992) (12/94) (SCHW) ⓘ [2] **312702**
Voir Griseldis; Je suis l'oiseau M. Villabella, orch (r1928) (MSCM) ⓘ **MM30377**

Hérodiade– opera: 4 acts (1881—Brussels) (Lib. Millet, Grémont & Zamadini, after Flaubert)
EXCERPTS; 1. Prelude. ACT 1: 2a. Ah! Salomé! dans ce palais; 2b. Il est doux, il est bon; 3a. Venge-moi d'une suprême offense!; 3b. Hérod! Ne me refuse pas; 4. Calmez donc vos fureurs. ACT 2: 5a. Ce breuvage pourrait me donner un tel rêve!; 5b. Vision fugutive. ACT 3: 6a. Dors, ô cité perverse; 6b. Astres étincelants; 6c. Ah! Phanuel!; 6d. L'horizon devient menaçant; 7a. Je souffre!; 7b. Charme des jours passés; 8a. C'en est fait!; 8b. Demande au prisonnier; 8c. Que m'oses-tu dire? ACT 4: 9a. Ne pouvant réprimer les élans de la foi; 9b. Adieu donc, vains objets; 10. Quand nos jours s'éteindront; 11. Ballet music.
2a, 2b K. Te Kanawa, ROHO, J. Tate (2/90) (EMI) ⓘ **CDC7 49863-2**
2b M. Caballé, Barcelona SO, G. Navarro (11/92) (RCA) ▭ **09026 61204-4**
2b E. Calvé, orch (r1908) (MSCM) ⓘ **MM30221** (MSCM) ▭ **MM040079**
2b N. Vallin, orch, G. Cloëz (r c1927-32) (PEAR) ⓘ **GEMMCD9948**
2b M. Caballé, Barcelona SO, G. Navarro (RCA) **ОО 09026 61204-5**
2b A. Pendachanska, Sofia SO, M. Angelov (r1994) (CAPR) ⓘ **10 706**
2b K. Te Kanawa, ROHO, J. Tate (r1988) (EMI) ⓘ **CDM5 65578-2**
2b C. Muzio, orch (r1922: Ital.) (5/90) (BOGR) ⓘ [2] **BIM705-2**
2b E. Calvé, orch (r1908) (7/92) (PEAR) ⓘ [3] **GEMMCDS9924(1)**
2b M. Garden, orch (r1911) (8/93) (SYMP) ⓘ **SYMCD1136**
2b C. Muzio, orch (r1922: Ital) (1/94) (ROMO) ⓘ [2] **81005-2**
2b M. Jeritza, orch (r1926) (4/94) (PREI) ⓘ **89079**
2b A. Adini, anon (r1905) (12/94) (SYMP) ⓘ **SYMCD1172**
2b E. Steber, orch, H. Barlow (bp1949) (11/95) (VAI) ⓘ **VAIA1072**
2b, 3b, Jean je le revois, 5b, 6b, 7b, Salomé laisse-moi t'aimer, 9a, 10, 11. D. Scharley, M. Le Bris, G. Chauvet, R. Massard, A. Legros, Paris ORTF Lyric Orch, J. Etcheverry (r1961) (MUSD) ⓘ **20427-2**
3a M. Horne, Monte Carlo PO, L. Foster (r1984) (ERAT) ⓘ **4509-98501-2**
5a, 5b A. Orda, Polish RSO, S. Rachoń (bp1964) (SYMP) ⓘ **SYMCD1117**
5a, 5b G. Laperrière, Three Rivers SO, G. Bellemare (r1992) (CBC) ⓘ **SMCD5127**
5a, 5b G. De Luca, orch (r1919) (PEAR) ⓘ [3] **GEMMCDS9160(1)**
5b M. Battistini, orch (r1912: Ital) (PEAR) ⓘ **GEMMCD9016**
5b G. De Luca, anon (r1907: Ital) (PEAR) ⓘ [3] **GEMMCDS9159(1)**
5b G. Taddei, orch (r1951: Ital) (PREI) ⓘ **89995**
5b E. Giraldoni, anon (r1902) (6/90) (SYMP) ⓘ **SYMCD1073**
5b L. Tibbett, orch (pp1935) (3/91) (PEAR) ⓘ [2] **GEMMCDS9452**
5b G. De Luca, orch (r1919) (1/92) (PREI) ⓘ **89036**
5b R. Merrill, RCA Orch, J-P. Morel (r1946) (4/92) (EMI) ⓘ [7] **CHS7 69741-2(2)**
5b M. Renaud, orch (r1906) (7/93) (NIMB) ⓘ [2] **NI7840/1**
5b G. Bellantoni, orch (r c1910: Ital) (12/94) (BONG) ⓘ **GB1043-2**

8b A. Endrèze, orch, H. Defosse (r c1931) (11/92) (MSCM) Ⓓ **MM30451**
9a P. Franz, orch (r1929) (PREI) Ⓓ **89099**
9a G. Lugo, orch, E. Cohen (r1935) (2/92) (PREI) Ⓓ **89034**
9a G. Thill, orch, F. Heurteur (r1927) (8/95) (FORL) Ⓓ **UCD16727**
9a, 9b G. Thill, orch, F. Heurteur (r c1925) (PEAR) Ⓓ **GEMMCD9947**
9a, 9b R. Maison, SO, P. Coppola (r1934) (MSCM) Ⓓ **MM30377**
9a, 9b B. Heppner, Munich RO, R. Abbado (r1993/4) (11/95) (RCA) Ⓓ **09026 62504-2**
9b L. Escalais, anon (r1906) (12/94) (SYMP) Ⓓ **SYMCD1128**
9b, 10. F. Tamagno, Anon (pf) (r1903-04) (2/92) (OPAL) Ⓓ **OPALCD9846**
10. F. Tamagno, anon (r1903) (7/93) (NIMB) Ⓓ [2] **NI7840/1**
11. NZ SO, J-Y. Ossonce (r1994) (9/95) (NAXO) Ⓓ **8 553124**

Le **Jongleur de Notre Dame– opera: 3 acts (1902—Monte Carlo) (Lib. Lena)**
EXCERPTS: 1. Overture. ACT 1: 2. Pour Notre-Dame des cieux; 3. Attention! avancez; 4. Pardonnez-moi, Sainte Vierge Marie; 5. C'est le Prieur! Fuyons!; 6. Il pleure; 7a. Dame des cieux; 7b. Liberté!; 8. Pour la Vierge d'abord; 10. Prelude. ACT 2: 11. Ave coeleste lilium; 12. Mes frères, c'est très bien; 13. Mes frères, je connaise ma triste indignité; 14. Jongleur, piteux métier; 15. Seul, je n'offre rien à Marie; 16. La Vierge entend fort bien; 17. La sauge et en effet précieuse en cuisine; 18. Prelude. ACT 3: 19. Un regard, le dernier; 20. Personne...Allons, courage!; 21. Mais ce vacarme...Belle Doètte; 22. Et maintenant voulez-vous des tours; 23. Arrière tous; 24. C'est le Prieur!; 25. Spectacle radieux!.
Jean A. Vanzo
Boniface R. Massard
Prior J. Bastin
Poet-monk J. Dupouy
Painter-monk C. Meloni
Sculptor-monk P. Thau
Musician-monk Y. Bisson
ORTF Chor, French Rad Maîtrise, ORTF PO, P. Dervaux (bp1973) (CHNT) Ⓓ [2] **LDC278 911/2**
7b C. Friant, orch (r1927) (MSCM) Ⓓ **MM30377**
7b M. Garden, orch (r1911) (8/93) (SYMP) Ⓓ **SYMCD1136**
8, 17. L. Fugère, orch (r1928) (6/93) (SYMP) Ⓓ **SYMCD1125**
16(pt) M. Journet, orch, Rosario Bourdon (r1926) (PREI) Ⓓ **89021**
16. G. Souzay, New SO, P. Bonneau (r1956) (DECC) Ⓓ **440 419-2DM**
16. G. Soulacroix, anon (r1902) (9/91) (SYMP) Ⓓ **SYMCD1089**
16. M. Journet, orch (r1908) (10/94) (NIMB) Ⓓ **NI7859**
16(pt) C. Formichi, orch, H. Harty (r1924) (11/94) (PREI) Ⓓ **89055**
17. Vanni-Marcoux, orch, P. Coppola (r1930) (PEAR) Ⓓ **GEMMCD9912**
17. L. Fugère, orch (r1928) (10/95) (NIMB) Ⓓ **NI7867**

Le **Mage– opera: 5 acts (1891—Paris) (Lib. J. Richepin)**
Ah! parais, ostre de mon ciel L. Escalais, anon (r1905) (12/93) (SYMP) Ⓓ **SYMCD1126**

Manon– opera: 5 acts (1884—Paris) (Lib. Meilhac and Gille)
ACT 1: 1. Prelude; 2a. Holà! Hé! Monsieur l'Hôtelier?; 2b. Hors d'oeuvre de choix; 3a. C'est très bien le diner!; 3b. Entendez-vous la cloche; 3c. C'est bon!; 4. Les voilà! les voilà!; 5a. Voyez cette jeune fille!; 5b. Je suis encore tout étourdie; 6a. Partez! On sonne!; 6b. Revenez, Guillot, revenez!; 7a. Il vous parlait, Manon?; 7b. Regardez-moi; 7c. Ne bronchez pas; 8a. Restons ici; 8b. Voyons, Manon!; 9a. J'ai marqué l'heure du départ; 9b. Et je sais votre nom; 9c. Non! Je ne veux pas croire; 10a. Par aventure; 10b. Nous vivrons à Paris; 11. Ce sont elles. ACT 2: 12a. Introduction; 12b. J'écris à mon père; 12c. On l'appelle Manon; 12d. Tu le veux?; 13a. Enfin, les amoureux; 13b. Venir ici sous un déguisement?; 14a. Allons! Il le faut pour lui-même; 14b. Adieu, notre petite table; 15a. C'est vrai; 15b. Instant charmant; 15c. En ferment les yeux; 15d. C'est un rêve. ACT 3: 16a. Entr'acte; 16b. Voyez mules à fleurettes!; 17a. A quoi bon l'économie; 17b. O Rosalinde; 18. Voici les élégantes!; 19a. Suis-je gentille ainsi?; 19b. Je marche sur tous les chemins; 19c. Obéissons quand leur voix appelle (Gavotte); 20a. Voici les élégantes!; 20b. Elle est charmante; 21a. L'Opéra! voici l'Opéra!; 21b. Ballet; 22. Quelle éloquence!; 23a. Les grands mots que voilà!; 23b. Épouse quelque brave fille; 24a. Je suis seul!; 24b. Ah! fuyez, douce image; 25a. Toi! Vous!; 25b. N'est-ce plus ma main. ACT 4: 26a. Le jouer sans prudence; 26b. J'enfourche aussi Pégase. ACT 5: 27a. Manon! Pauvre Manon!; 27b. Capitaine, ô gué; 28. Ah! Des Grieux!; Alternative Aria: 29. Oui, dans les bois... Fabliau (to replace Gavotte).
Manon M. Freni
Des Grieux L. Pavarotti
Lescaut W. Ganzarolli
Comte des Grieux A. Zerbini
de Brétigny G. Morresi
Guillot F. Ricciardi
La Scala Chor, La Scala Orch, P. Maag (Ital: pp1969) (BUTT) Ⓓ [2] **BMCD004**
(BUTT) ▣ [2] **BMK004**
Manon I. Cotrubas
Des Grieux Alfredo Kraus
Lescaut G. Quilico
Comte des Grieux J. Van Dam
De Bretigny J-M. Frémeau
Guillot C. Burles
Poussette G. Raphanel
Javotte C. Alliot-Lugaz
Rosette M. Mahé
Innkeeper J. Loreau
Toulouse Capitole Chor, Toulouse Capitole Orch, M. Plasson (11/88) (EMI) Ⓓ [3] **CDS7 49610-2**
Manon G. Féraldy
Des Grieux J. Rogatchewsky
Lescaut G. Villier
Comte des Grieux L. Guénot
De Brétigny A. Gaudin
De Brétigny J. Vieuille
Guillot E. de Creus
Poussette A. Vavon
Javotte Mlle Rambert
Javotte Mlle Ravery
Rosette A. Bernadet
Rosette M. Fenoyer
Innkeeper P. Payen
Servant M. Julliot
Paris Opéra-Comique Chor, Paris Opéra-Comique Orch, E. Cohen (r1928/9) (11/90) (EPM) Ⓓ [2] **150 012**
Minuet SO, T. Beecham (r1916) (11/91) (SYMP) Ⓓ [2] **SYMCD1096/7**
5b R. Kabaivanska, Bulgarian RSO, V. Stefanov (r1970s) (FORL) Ⓓ **UCD16741**
5b, 14b, 25a, 25b M. Freni, L. Pavarotti, La Scala Chor, La Scala Orch, P. Maag (pp1969; Ital) (MEMO) Ⓓ [2] **HR4277/8**
5b, 19a M. Mesplé, Paris Op Orch, J-P. Marty (r1968) (EMI) Ⓓ [2] **CZS7 67813-2**
8a, 19c F. Saville, anon (Ger: r c1902) (10/92) (SYMP) Ⓓ **SYMCD1093**
8b, 19b H. Schymberg, Stockholm Royal Orch, N. Grevillius (r1943: Swed) (ALTN) Ⓓ **CDAN3**
9a-c L. Pavarotti, M. Freni, La Scala Orch, P. Maag (pp1969; Ital) (BUTT) Ⓓ **BMCD015**
(BUTT) ▣ **BMK015**
9a-c M. Mesplé, N. Gedda, Paris Op Orch, P. Dervaux (r1974) (EMI) Ⓓ [2] **CZS7 67813-2**
12b, 12c G. Farrar, E. Caruso, orch (r1912) (10/94) (NIMB) Ⓓ **NI7859**
12c E. Caruso, G. Farrar, orch, W.B. Rogers (r1912) (RCA) Ⓓ **09026 61244-2**
12c G. Farrar, E. Caruso, orch, W.B. Rogers (r1912) (7/91) (RCA) Ⓓ [12] **GD60495(4)**
12c G. Farrar, E. Caruso, orch, W.B. Rogers (r1912) (10/91) (PEAR) Ⓓ [3] **EVC3(1)**
12c H. von Debička, H. Roswaenge, orch (r1929: Ger) (2/92) (PREI) Ⓓ [2] **89201**
14a, 14b L. Price, RCA Italiana Op Orch, F. Molinari-Pradelli (r1960s) (RCA) Ⓓ **09026 62596-2**
14a, 14b G. Farrar, orch (r1908) (NIMB) Ⓓ **NI7872**
14a, 14b V. de los Angeles, Paris Opéra-Comique Orch, P. Monteux (r1955) (EMI) Ⓓ **CDM5 65579-2**
14a, 14b M. Freni, La Scala Orch, A. Votto (10/89) (EMI) Ⓓ **CDM7 63110-2**
14a, 14b M. Callas, Paris Cons, G. Prêtre (2/90) (EMIN) Ⓓ **CD-EMX2123**
(2/88) (EMIN) ▣ **TC-EMX2123**
14a, 14b V. de los Angeles, Philh, W. Susskind (r1949) (8/90) (EMI) Ⓓ **CDH7 63495-2**
14a, 14b H. Spani, La Scala Orch, C. Sabajno (r1929; Ital) (9/90) (CLUB) Ⓓ [2] **CL99-509/10**
14a, 14b Lotte Lehmann, Berlin St Op Orch, K. Besl (r1924; Ger) (6/92) (PREI) Ⓓ [3] **89302**
14a, 14b L. Price, RCA Italiana Op Orch, F. Molinari-Pradelli (12/92) (RCA) Ⓓ [4] **09026 61236-2**
14a, 14b L. Garrett, RPO, P. Robinson (r1994) (4/95) (SILV) Ⓓ **SILKD6004**
(4/95) (SILV) ▣ **SILKC6004**
14a, 14b, 19c R. Streich, Berlin Deutsche Op Chor, Berlin Deutsche Op Orch, R. Peters (DG) Ⓓ [2] **435 748-2GDO2**
14a, 14b, 19a-c M. Callas, Paris Cons, G. Prêtre (2/88) (EMI) Ⓓ **CDC7 49059-2**
14a, 14b, 19b, 19c K. Te Kanawa, ROHO, J. Tate (2/90) (EMI) Ⓓ **CDC7 49863-2**
14b M. Callas, Paris Cons, G. Prêtre (r1963) (EMI) Ⓓ **CDC5 55216-2**
(EMI) ▣ **EL555216-4**
14b G. Farrar, orch (r1908) (PEAR) Ⓓ **GEMMCD9130**
14b R. Tebaldi, Rome RAI Orch, A. Basile (bp1961: Ital) (FONI) Ⓓ **CDMR5023**
14b L. Bori, Victor Orch, Rosario Bourdon (r1923) (ROMO) Ⓓ [2] **81016-2**
14b E. Bendazzi-Garulli, anon (Ital: r1902) (5/91) (SYMP) Ⓓ **SYMCD1077**
14b H. Spani, La Scala Orch, C. Sabajno (Ital: r1929) (12/92) (PREI) Ⓓ **89037**
14b E. Carelli, S. Cottone (Ital: r1904) (8/93) (SYMP) Ⓓ **SYMCD1111**
15a-d F. Wunderlich, Bavarian St Orch, H. Müller-Kray (Ger) (EMI) Ⓓ [3] **CZS7 62993-2**
15b D. Smirnov, orch (r1921: Ital) (PEAR) Ⓓ **GEMMCD9106**
15b, 15c B. Gigli, orch, J. Barbirolli (r1931: Ital) (NIMB) Ⓓ **NI7817**
(NIMB) ▣ **NC7817**
15b, 15c G. di Stefano, Zurich Tonhalle Orch, F. Patanè (r1958) (DECC) Ⓓ **440 403-2DM**
15b, 15c J. Björling, orch, N. Grevillius (r1938) (PEAR) Ⓓ **GEMMCD9043**
15b, 15c B. Gigli, orch, J. Barbirolli (r1931: Ital) (CONI) Ⓓ **CDHD227**
(CONI) ▣ **MCHD227**
15b, 15c G. di Stefano, Zurich Tonhalle Orch, G. Patanè (r1958) (DECC) Ⓓ **436 314-2DA**
(DECC) ▣ **436 314-4DA**
15b, 15c H. Roswaenge, Berlin St Op Orch, B. Seidler-Winkler (r1939: Ger) (PREI) Ⓓ [2] **89211**
15b, 15c B. Gigli, orch, J. Barbirolli (r1931: Ital) (PEAR) Ⓓ [2] **GEMMCDS9176**
15b, 15c B. Gigli, orch, J. Barbirolli (Ital: r1931) (9/88) (EMI) Ⓓ **CDH7 61051-2**
15b, 15c G. Morino, Warmia Nat PO, B. Amaducci (10/90) (NUOV) Ⓓ **6851**
15b, 15c J. Björling, orch, N. Grevillius (r1938) (10/93) (EMI) Ⓓ **CDH7 64707-2**
15b, 15c J. Björling, orch, N. Grevillius (r1938) (9/94) (CONI) Ⓓ **CDHD214**
(9/94) (CONI) ▣ **MCHD214**
15b, 15c, 24a, 24b A. Bonci, orch (r1913: Ital) (PEAR) Ⓓ **GEMMCD9168**
15b, 24b M. Freni, L. Pavarotti, La Scala Orch, P. Maag (pp1969) (10/95) (RCA) Ⓓ **09026 62541-2**
15c T. Burke, orch (Ital: r1920/1) (PEAR) Ⓓ **GEMMCD9411**
15c J. Björling, orch, N. Grevillius (r1938: Ital) (NIMB) Ⓓ **NI7835**
15c T. Rossi, orch, M. Cariven (r1937) (FORL) Ⓓ **UCD19053**
15c J. McCormack, orch (r1913: Ital) (ASV) Ⓓ **CDAJA5137**
(ASV) ▣ **ZCAJA5137**
15c A. Piccaver, Berlin St Op Orch, J. Prüwer (r1928: Ger) (PREI) Ⓓ [2] **89217**
15c F. de Lucia, orch (r1917: Ital) (BONG) Ⓓ [2] **GB1064/5-2**
15c J. Björling, Hilversum RO, F. Weissmann (pp1939) (8/88) (BLUE) Ⓓ **ABCD006**
15c E. Caruso, S. Cottone (Ital: r1902) (5/89) (EMI) Ⓓ **CDH7 61046-2**
15c E. Caruso, anon (r1904: Ital) (10/89) (NIMB) Ⓓ **NI7803**
(NIMB) ▣ **NC7803**
15c T. Schipa, orch, Rosario Bourdon (Ital: r1926) (12/89) (RCA) Ⓓ **GD87969**
15c J. Patzak, orch (Ger: r1929) (3/90) (PEAR) Ⓓ **GEMMCD9383**

15c D. Smirnov, orch (Ital: r1921)
(7/90) (CLUB) Ⓓ **CL99-031**
15c E. Caruso, anon (Ital: r1904)
(12/90) (PEAR) Ⓓ [3] **EVC1(1)**
15c E. Caruso, S. Cottone (Ital: r1902)
(12/90) (PEAR) Ⓓ [3] **EVC1(1)**
15c E. Caruso, S. Cottone (Ital: r1902)
(7/91) (RCA) Ⓓ [12] **GD60495(1)**
15c E. Caruso, anon (Ital: r1904)
(7/91) (RCA) Ⓓ [12] **GD60495(1)**
15c H. Nash, orch (Eng: r1932)
(9/91) (PEAR) Ⓓ **GEMMCD9473**
15c L. Sobinov, orch (r1910: Russ)
(6/93) (PEAR) Ⓓ [3] **GEMMCDS9997/9(2)**
15c F. de Lucia, anon (r1907: Ital)
(7/93) (NIMB) Ⓓ [2] **NI7840/1**
15c Ferruccio Tagliavini, EIAR Orch, U. Tansini (r1943: Ital) (3/94) (CENT) Ⓓ **CRC2164**
15c R. Crooks, orch, N. Shilkret (r1933)
(5/94) (CLAR) Ⓓ **CDGSE78-50-52**
15c J. Björling, orch, N. Grevillius (r1938: Ital)
(9/94) (IMP) Ⓓ **GLRS103**
15c E. Clément, F. La Forge (r1911)
(9/94) (NIMB) Ⓓ **NI7856**
15c G. Anselmi, anon (r1907: Ital)
(7/95) (SYMP) Ⓓ **SYMCD1170**
15c E. Clément, F. La Forge (r1911)
(8/95) (ROMO) Ⓓ **82002-2**
15c E. Clément, F. la Forge (r1911)
(8/95) (PEAR) Ⓓ **GEMMCD9161**
15c, 24a, 24b Alfredo Kraus, Toulouse Capitole Orch, M. Plasson
(10/89) (EMI) Ⓓ **CDM7 63104-2**
15c, 24b E. Clément, anon (r1905)
(8/95) (ROMO) Ⓓ **82002-2**
19a-c N. Vallin, orch, F. Ruhlmann (r1932)
(2/92) (MMOI) Ⓓ **CDMOIR408**
19b, 19c K. Te Kanawa, ROHO, J. Tate (r1988)
(EMI) Ⓓ **CDM5 65578-2**
19c B. Sayão, Orch, H. Barlow (bp1951)
(VAI) ▣ **VAI69103**
19c L. Garrett, Philh, I. Bolton
(SILV) Ⓓ **SONGCD907**
(SILV) ⊟ **SONGC907**
19c C. Muzio, orch (r1918)
(PEAR) Ⓓ **GEMMCD9143**
19c P. Lorengar, Santa Cecilia Academy Orch, G. Patanè (r1966) (DECC) Ⓓ **443 931-2DM**
19c A. Galli-Curci, orch (r1923)
(2/89) (PEAR) Ⓓ **GEMMCD9308**
19c A. Galli-Curci, orch (r1923)
(10/89) (NIMB) Ⓓ **NI7802**
(NIMB) ⊟ **NC7802**
19c Lotte Lehmann, orch (Ger: r1917)
(6/92) (PREI) Ⓓ [3] **89302**
19c L. Schöne, Berlin St Op Orch, L. Blech (r c1929: Ger) (1/94) (CLUB) Ⓓ **CL99-020**
19c R. Crooks, RCA SO, W. Pelletier (r1938)
(4/94) (RCA) Ⓓ [6] **09026 61580-2(4)**
19c A. Galli-Curci, orch, Rosario Bourdon (r1923) (8/94) (ROMO) Ⓓ [2] **81004-2**
19c C. Muzio, orch (r1918)
(1/95) (ROMO) Ⓓ [2] **81010-2**
24a, 24b G. di Stefano, LSO, A. Erede (r1947; Ital) (EMI) Ⓓ **CDM7 63105-2**
24a, 24b N. Gedda, FRNO, G. Prêtre
(EMI) Ⓓ **CDC7 54016-2**
24a, 24b T. Schipa, orch, Anon (cond) (pp1913; Ital) (MEMO) Ⓓ [2] **HR4220/1**
24a, 24b P. Domingo, LSO, N. Santi (r1971)
(RCA) Ⓓ **09026 61356-2**
(RCA) ⊟ **09026 61356-4**
24a, 24b E. Caruso, orch, W.B. Rogers (r1911)
(RCA) Ⓓ **09026 61244-2**
24a, 24b J. Schmidt, Berlin City Op Orch, F. Weissmann (r1932: Ger)
(EMI) Ⓓ [2] **CHS7 64673-2**
24a, 24b E. Scaramberg, anon (r1905)
(SYMP) Ⓓ **SYMCD1173**
24a, 24b E. Scaramberg, orch (r1905)
(SYMP) Ⓓ **SYMCD1173**
24a, 24b A. Piccaver, Berlin St Op Orch, J. Prüwer (r1930: Ger) (PREI) Ⓓ [2] **89217**
24a, 24b J. Björling, Stockholm Royal Op Orch, N. Grevillius (r1945)
(10/88) (EMI) Ⓓ **CDH7 61053-2**
24a, 24b E. Caruso, orch (r1911)
(10/89) (NIMB) Ⓓ **NI7803**
(NIMB) ⊟ **NC7803**
24a, 24b T. Schipa, La Scala Orch, F. Ghione (r1934; Ital) (4/90) (EMI) Ⓓ **CDH7 63200-2**
24a, 24b B. Gigli, ROHO, R. Zamboni (r1946; Ital) (5/90) (EMI) Ⓓ **CDH7 61052-2**
24a, 24b E. Caruso, orch (r1911)
(3/91) (PEAR) Ⓓ [3] **EVC2**
24a, 24b E. Caruso, orch, W.B. Rogers (r1911)
(7/91) (RCA) Ⓓ [12] **GD60495(4)**
24b T. Schipa, orch (Ital: r1934)
(PEAR) Ⓓ **GEMMCD9364**
24b C. Valletti, Orch, A. Basile (pp1955)
(MEMO) Ⓓ [2] **HR4191/2**
24b P. Cornubert, anon (r1905)
(SYMP) Ⓓ **SYMCD1173**
24b J. Patzak, orch, M. Gurlitt (Ger: r1929)
(3/90) (PEAR) Ⓓ **GEMMCD9383**
24b D. Smirnov, orch (r1910)
(7/90) (CLUB) Ⓓ **CL99-031**
24b D. Smirnov, orch (Ital: r c1928)
(7/90) (CLUB) Ⓓ **CL99-031**
24b A. Cortis, La Scala Orch, C. Sabajno (Ital: r1929) (10/91) (PREI) Ⓓ **89043**
24b G. Lugo, orch, E. Cohen (r1935)
(2/92) (PREI) Ⓓ **89034**
24b A. Cortis, La Scala Orch, C. Sabajno (r1929: Ital) (3/94) (NIMB) Ⓓ **NI7850**
24b G. Thill, orch, E. Bigot (r c1936)
(9/94) (NIMB) Ⓓ **NI7856**
24b H. Roswaenge, BPO, F.A. Schmidt (r1933: Ger) (4/95) (PREI) Ⓓ [2] **89209**
25a F. Heldy, F. Ansseau, orch, P. Coppola (r1927)
(7/92) (PEAR) Ⓓ [3] **GEMMCDS9926(1)**
25a, 25b P. Domingo, R. Scotto, National PO, K. H. Adler (r1970s) (SONY) Ⓓ **SMK39030**
29. G. Féraldy, orch (r1928)
(11/90) (EPM) Ⓓ [2] **150 012**

Marie-Magdeleine– drame sacré: 3 acts (Paris—1873) (Lib. Gallet)
Oh! bien-aimé. G. Martinelli, orch (r1931)
(MSCM) Ⓓ **MM30221**
(MSCM) ⊟ **MM040079**

La **Navarraise– opera: 2 acts (1894—London) (Lib. Claretie and Cain)**
EXCERPTS: 1. Overture; 2. ACT 1: L'ssaut a coûté cher; 3. Vierge très bonne, Marie; 4. Je ne pensais qu'à toi; 5. Araqui! mon père; 6. Deux mille duros!; 7. Êtes-vous de la compagnie; 8. Général! Qu'est-ce encore?; 9. Grénelons les maisons; 10. Ô bien-aimée, pourquoi n'es-tu pas la?; 11. Anita! La Navarraise?; 12. A moi, á moi; 13. Interlude. ACT 2: 14. Alerte! On attaque!; 15. Le bonheur! Araquil; 16. Blessé, mourant, j'espère; 17. Mon fils! Père!; 18. Nocturne.

Araquil	A. Vanzo
Anita	G. Moizan
Garrido	J. Mars
Remiglio	L. Lovano
Ramon	J. Peyron
Bustamente	M. Vigneron

French Rad Lyric Chor, French Rad Lyric Orch, J-C. Hartemann (bp1963)
(CHNT) Ⓓ [2] **LDC278 911/2**
Nocturne LSO, R. Bonynge (r1972)
(LOND) Ⓓ **440 081-2LRX**
18. LSO, R. Bonynge (r1971)
(DECC) Ⓓ **444 111-2DA**

Panurge– operetta: 3 acts (1913—Paris) (Lib. M. Boukay & G. Spitzmüller, after Rabelais)
Touraine est un pays Vanni-Marcoux, P. Coppola (r1930) (PEAR) Ⓓ **GEMMCD9912**
Touraine est un pays Vanni-Marcoux, anon (r1931) (1/94) (CLUB) Ⓓ **CL99-101**

Le **Roi de Lahore– opéra: 5 acts (1877—Paris) (Lib. Gallet)**
EXCERPTS: ACT 3: 1. Adagio and Waltz. ACT 4: 2. Promesse de mon avenir (O casto fior). ACT 5: 3. Entr'acte.

Alim	L. Lima
Sitâ	J. Sutherland
Scindia	S. Milnes
Indra	N. Ghiaurov
Timour	J. Morris
Kaled	H. Tourangeau

London Voices, National PO, R. Bonynge
(2/93) (DECC) Ⓓ [2] **433 851-2DMO2**
Promesse de mon avenir G. De Luca, anon (r1907: Ital)
(PEAR) Ⓓ [3] **GEMMCDS9159(1)**
Promesse de mon avenir G. De Luca, anon (r1902: Ital)
(PEAR) Ⓓ [3] **GEMMCDS9159(1)**
1. LSO, R. Bonynge (r1971)
(DECC) Ⓓ **444 108-2DA**
2. A. Orda, Polish RSO, S. Rachoń (bp1964: Ital)
(SYMP) Ⓓ **SYMCD1117**
2. A. Scotti, anon (r1905: Ital)
(PEAR) Ⓓ **GEMMCD9937**
2. R. Stracciari, orch (r1925: Ital)
(2/90) (PREI) Ⓓ **89003**
2. J. Lassalle, anon (r1902)
(9/91) (SYMP) Ⓓ **SYMCD1089**
2. J. Lassalle, anon (r1902)
(7/92) (PEAR) Ⓓ [3] **GEMMCDS9923(1)**
2. A. Cotogni, anon (Ital: r1908)
(11/92) (MEMO) Ⓓ [2] **HR4408/9(1)**
2. A. Endrèze, orch, H. Defosse (r c1931)
(11/92) (MSCM) Ⓓ **MM30451**
2. T. Ruffo, orch (Ital: r1920)
(2/93) (PREI) Ⓓ [3] **89303(2)**
2. G. De Luca, anon (Ital: r1902)
(8/93) (SYMP) Ⓓ **SYMCD1111**
2. G. Pacini, anon (r1904: Ital)
(4/94) (EMI) Ⓓ [3] **CHS7 64860-2(1)**
2. M. Renaud, orch (r1906)
(10/95) (NIMB) Ⓓ **NI7867**

Roma– opera: 5 acts (1912—Monte Carlo) (Lib. H. Cain, after A. Parodi)
Le soleil se couchait L. Dupré, orch (r1912)
(8/92) (IRCC) Ⓓ **IRCC-CD802**
Soir admirable L. Beyle, orch (r1912)
(8/92) (IRCC) Ⓓ **IRCC-CD802**

Sapho– pièce lyrique (1897—Monte Carlo) (Lib. Cain and Bernède)
Ah! qu'il est loin mon pays G. Thill, orch, E. Bigot (r1930) (8/95) (FORL) Ⓓ **UCD16727**
Pendant un an je fus ta femme F. Pollet, Montpellier PO, C. Diederich (r1989)
(ERAT) Ⓓ **4509-98502-2**

Thaïs– comédie lyrique: 3 acts (1894—Paris) (Lib. Gallet, after France)
EXCERPTS. ACT 1: 1a. Hélas! enfant encore; 1b. Toi qui mis la pitié; 2a. Va mendiant!; 2b. Voilà donc la terrible cité. ACT 2: 3a. Ah! je suis seule; 3b. Dis-moi que je suis belle; 4a. Étranger, te voila; 4b. Ah! pitié; 5. Méditation; 6. L'amour est une vertu rare. ACT 3: 7a. L'ardent soleil; 7b. O messager de Dieu; 7c. Baigne d'eau; 8. Que te fait si sévère; 9. Te souvient-il.

Thaïs	B. Sills
Athanaël	S. Milnes
Nicias	N. Gedda
Palémon	R. Van Allan
Crobyle	A-M. Connors
Myrtale	A. Murray
Albine	P. Kern
La Charmeuse	N. Burrowes
Servant	B. Etheridge

John Alldis Ch, New Philh, L. Maazel (r1976)
(EMI) Ⓓ [2] **CMS5 65479-2**
La paix soit avec vous; Honte! horreur! ténèbres éternelles M. Journet, orch, P. Coppola (r1928) (PREI) Ⓓ **89021**
1a, 1b, 2a, 2b M. Journet, M. Cozette, SO, P. Coppola (r1928) (1/94) (CLUB) Ⓓ **CL99-034**
1a, 2b T. Ruffo, orch, W.B. Rogers (r1914: Ital)
(PEAR) Ⓓ **GEMMCD9088**
1a, 2b T. Ruffo, orch (Ital: r1914)
(2/93) (PREI) Ⓓ [3] **89303(1)**
1a, 2b C. Formichi, orch, H. Harty (r1924)
(11/94) (PREI) Ⓓ **89055**
2b M. Journet, M. Cozette, orch, P. Coppola (r1928) (PREI) Ⓓ **89021**
2b C. Whitehill, orch (r1913)
(IRCC) Ⓓ **IRCC-CD810**
2b T. Ruffo, orch, W.B. Rogers (Ital: r1914)
(11/90) (NIMB) Ⓓ **NI7810**
(NIMB) ⊟ **NC7810**
3a, 3b L. Price, LSO, E. Downes
(12/92) (RCA) Ⓓ [4] **09026 61236-2**
3a, 3b J. Hammond, Philh, S. Robinson (r1951)
(12/92) (TEST) Ⓓ **SBT1013**
3b R. Doria, Paris Sols Orch, J. Etcheverry
(SYMP) Ⓓ **SYMCD1103**
3b L. Monteyrol, Budapest SO, A. Déry (r1992)
(AUVI) Ⓓ **V4682**
3b, 6. M. Jeritza, orch (r1926)
(4/94) (PREI) Ⓓ **89079**
5. BBC SO, A. Davis (pp1994)
(TELD) ▣ **4509-97869-3**
5. F. Kreisler, G. Falkenstein (r1910: arr Marsick)
(BIDD) Ⓓ **LAB019**
5. Hallé, M. Handford (CFP) Ⓓ **CD-CFP4543**
5. Budapest PO, A. Kórodi (LASE) Ⓓ **15 513**
(LASE) ⊟ **79 513**
5. Budapest PO, A. Kórodi (LASE) Ⓓ **15 625**
(LASE) ⊟ **79 625**
5. N. Kennedy, National PO, R. Bonynge
(DECC) Ⓓ **425 849-2DWO**
(DECC) ⊟ **425 849-4DWO**
5. RLPO, C. Groves (CFP) Ⓓ **CD-CFP4515**
(CFP) ⊟ **TC-CFP4515**
5. T. Nishizaki, J. Jandó (arr. Marsick)
(NAXO) Ⓓ **8 550306**

5. Cölln Salon Orch (arr Hötter) (EURO) Ⓓ **GD69295**
5. S-O. Svarfvar, Örebro CO, G.W. Nilson (arr Nilson) (BLUE) Ⓓ **ABCD038**
5. M. Rabin, Hollywood Bowl SO, F. Slatkin (r1959) (EMI) Ⓓ [6] **CMS7 64123-2**
5. P. Graffin, RPO, Y. Menuhin (ETCE) Ⓓ **KTC1125**
5. J. Georgiadis, RPO, E. Bátiz (RPO) Ⓓ **CDRPO5006** (RPO) ▭ **ZCRPO5006**
5. L. Nashman, J. Arpin (fl/pf) (PRO) Ⓓ **CDD585**
5. M. Elman, J. Seiger (arr vn/pf) (VANG) Ⓓ **08.8029.71**
5. J. Bell, RPO, A. Litton (DECC) **OO** **433 519-5DH**
5. A. Smith, Orch, Anon Cond (pp1991) (MCI) Ⓓ **MCCD090** (MCI) ▭ **MCTC090**
5. K. Smith, P. Rhodes (arr Madden) (ASV) Ⓓ **CDWHL2072** (ASV) ▭ **ZCWHL2072**
5. A. Smith, Orch, Anon Cond (pp1991) (MCI) Ⓓ **MCCD090** (MCI) ▭ **MCTC090**
5. A-S. Mutter, BPO, H. von Karajan (EMI) Ⓓ **CDM7 64629-2**
5. RPO, E. Bátiz (IMP) Ⓓ **PCDS013** (IMP) ▭ **PCDSC013**
5. RPO, E. Bátiz (IMP) Ⓓ **PCDS012** (IMP) ▭ **PCDSC012**
5. R. Marchesi, R. Guglielmo (r1992;trans vn & pf) (MDIT) Ⓓ **MED92102**
5. J-L. Garcia, ECO, P. Tortelier (r1987) (VIRG) Ⓓ **VJ5 61109-2**
5. A-S. Mutter, VPO, James Levine (r1992) (DG) **OO** **437 544-5GH**
5. M. Hasson, I. Brown (r1992) (IMP) Ⓓ **PCDS22** (IMP) ▭ **PCDSC22**
5. M. Beier, M. Eriksson (r1986) (DANA) Ⓓ **DACOCD306**
5. N. Kennedy, National SO, R. Bonynge (r1983) (DECC) Ⓓ [2] **443 585-2DF2** (DECC) ▭ [2] **433 585-4DWO2**
5. M. Schwalbé, BPO, H. von Karajan (BELA) Ⓓ **450 137-2** (BELA) ▭ **450 137-4**
5. D. Nolan, Philh, I. Westrip (r1993) (IMP) Ⓓ **PCD1075**
5. F. Kreisler, C. Lamson (r1928: arr Marsick) (IMP) Ⓓ **GLRS106**
5. M. Langdon-Davies, M. Tanner (r1993: arr Weston) (COLN) Ⓓ **VAN201**
5. C. Ferras, J-C. Ambrosini (arr vn/pf; Marsick) (BELA) Ⓓ **461 003-2** (BELA) ▭ **461 003-4**
5. Y.P. Tortelier (vn/dir), Renaissance Sngrs, Ulster Orch (r1989: arr Bradbury) (CHAN) Ⓓ **CHAN6608**
5. Hallé, M. Handford (r1979) (CFP) Ⓓ **CD-CFP4661** (CFP) ▭ **TC-CFP4661**
5. BPO, H. Von Karajan (r1967) (DG) Ⓓ **445 282-2GH** (DG) ▭ **445 282-4GH**
5. A. Markov, D. Cogan (r1993: arr vn/pf) (ERAT) Ⓓ **4509-98481-2**
5. J. Katrama, M. Rahkonen (r1993; arr db/pf: J. Katrama) (FINL) Ⓓ **4509-97894-2**
5. V. Fox (r1960: arr org) (EMI) Ⓓ **CDM5 65426-2**
5. I. Perlman, Abbey Road Ens, L. Foster (r1995) (EMI) Ⓓ **CDC5 55475-2**
5. A. Dumay, Monte Carlo PO, A. Dumay (6/87) (EMI) Ⓓ **CDC7 47544-2**
5. BPO, H. von Karajan (10/87) (DG) Ⓓ [3] **419 257-2GH3**
5. J-L. Garcia, ECO, P. Tortelier (7/88) (VIRG) Ⓓ **VC7 59668-2**
5. F. Kreisler, C. Lamson (arr Marsick: vn/pf; r1928) (1/90) (PEAR) Ⓓ **GEMMCD9324**
5. Gothenburg SO, N. Järvi (6/90) (DG) Ⓓ **429 494-2GDC** (6/90) (DG) ▭ **429 494-4GDC**
5. LPO, T. Beecham (bp1939) (11/91) (SYMP) Ⓓ [2] **SYMCD1096/7**
5. N. Kennedy, National PO, R. Bonynge (1/92) (DECC) Ⓓ **433 604-2DSP**
5. J. Bell, RPO, A. Litton (1/92) (DECC) Ⓓ **433 519-2DH**
5. N. Kennedy, National PO, R. Bonynge (r1983) (5/92) (DECC) Ⓓ **433 220-2DWO** (5/92) (DECC) ▭ **433 220-4DWO**
5. J. Hassid, G. Moore (arr Marsick: r1940) (10/92) (PEAR) Ⓓ **GEMMCD9939**
5. J. Hassid, G. Moore (arr Marsick: r1940) (10/92) (TEST) Ⓓ **SBT1010**
5. Chee-Yun, A. Eguchi (trans Marsick: vn, pf) (12/93) (DENO) Ⓓ **CO-75118**
5. F. Kreisler, C. Lamson (r1928: arr Marsick: two vers) (12/93) (BIDD) Ⓓ **LAB080**
5. A-S. Mutter, VPO, James Levine (r1992) (12/93) (DG) Ⓓ **437 544-2GH** (12/93) (DG) ▭ **437 544-4GH**
5. A.A. Meyers, Philh, A. Litton (r1993) (2/94) (RCA) Ⓓ **09026 61700-2**
5. N. Milstein, L. Pommers (r1956: arr Marsick) (5/94) (EMI) Ⓓ [6] **ZDMF7 64830-2**
5. J. Bálint, N. Mercz (r1992: arr fl/hp: Mercz) (12/94) (NAXO) Ⓓ **8 550741**
5. BBC SO, A. Davis (r1994) (2/95) (TELD) Ⓓ **4509-97868-2** (2/95) (TELD) ▭ **4509-97868-4**
5. P. Gallois, London Fest Orch, R. Pople (r1993: arr fl: Prezman) (5/95) (DG) Ⓓ **445 822-2GH**
6. M. Garden, orch (r c1913) (8/93) (SYMP) Ⓓ **SYMCD1136**
7c M. Battistini, A. Janni, orch (r1911: Ital) (PEAR) Ⓓ **GEMMCD9016**
7c C. Formichi, G. Holst, orch (r1927) (11/94) (PREI) Ⓓ **89055**
7c E. Katulskaya, L. Sibiriakov, orch (r1913: Russ) (3/95) (NIMB) Ⓓ **NI7865**
9. G. Farrar, orch (r1918) (NIMB) Ⓓ **NI7872**

Werther– opera: 4 acts (1892—Vienna) (Lib. Blau, Milliet and Hartmann)

ACT 1: 1. Prelude; 2. Assez! Assez!; 3a. Je ne sais si je veille; 3b. O nature, pleine de grâce; 4. Jésus vient de naître!; 5. O spectacle idéal d'amour; 6. Sophie! Albert!; 7a. Elle m'aime; 7b. Interlude (Clair de lune); 7c. Il faut nous séparer; 7d. Si vous l'aviez connue!. ACT 2: 8a. Prelude; 8b. Vivat Bacchus!; 9. Trois mois!; 10a. Un autre est son époux!; 10b. J'aurais sur ma poitrine; 11a. Au bonheur; 11b. Je vous sais un coeur loyal et fort; 12a. Frère, voyez le beau bouquet!; 12b. Du gai soleil, plein de flamme; 12c. Va porter ton bouquet; 13a. Ah! qu'il est loin ce jour; 13b. N'est-il donc pas d'autre femme; 14. Lorsque l'enfant revient d'un voyage. ACT 3: 15a. Werther! Qui m'aurait dit la place; 15b. Des cris joyeux; 16. Bonjour, grande soeur!; 17. Ah! le rire est béni; 18a. Va! Laisse couler; 18b. Les larmes qu'on ne pleure pas; 19. Ah! mon courage m'abandonne; 20. Oui, c'est moi!; 21a. Traduire; 21b. Pourquoi me réveiller?; 22. N'achevez pas!; 23. Werther est de retour. ACT 4: 24a. Prelude (Le nuit de Noël); 24b. Werther!...Rien!...Dieu! Ah! du sang!; 25. Noël! Noël!; 26. Là-bas, au fond du cimetière. 27. Finale.

Werther A. Lance
Charlotte R. Gorr
Albert G. Bacquier
Sophie M. Mesplé
Magistrate J. Giovannetti
Schmidt R. Andreozzi
Johann J. Mars

FNR Maîtrise, FRNO, J. Etcheverry (ADES) Ⓓ [2] **14083-2**

Werther Ferruccio Tagliavini
Charlotte G. Simionato
Albert G. Orlandini
Sophie D. Gatta
Magistrate S. Bruscantini
Schmidt V. Pandano
Johann E. Campi
Käthchen I. Ligabue

La Scala Chor, La Scala Orch, F. Capuana (pp1951: Ital) (BONG) Ⓓ [2] **GB1101/2-2**

Werther J. Carreras
Charlotte F. von Stade
Albert T. Allen
Sophie I. Buchanan
Magistrate R. Lloyd
Schmidt P. Crook
Johann M. King
Kätchen L. Humphries
Brühlmann D. Bell

ROHO, Colin Davis (r1980) (2/87) (PHIL) Ⓓ [2] **416 654-2PH2**

Werther Alfredo Kraus
Charlotte T. Troyanos
Albert M. Manuguerra
Sophie C. Barbaux
Magistrate J. Bastin
Schmidt P. Langridge
Johann J-P. Lafont
Käthchen L. Richardson
Brühlmann M. Lewis

Covent Garden Sngrs, LPO, M. PLasson (4/89) (EMI) Ⓓ [2] **CMS7 69573-2**

Werther G. Thill
Charlotte N. Vallin
Albert M. Roque
Sophie G. Féraldy
Magistrate A. Narçon
Schmidt H. Niel
Johann L. Guénot

Cantoria Children's Ch, Paris Opéra-Comique Chor, Paris Opéra-Comique Orch, E. Cohen (r1931) (3/90) (EMI) Ⓓ [2] **CHS7 63195-2**

Werther N. Gedda
Charlotte V. de los Angeles
Albert R. Soyer
Sophie M. Mesplé
Magistrate J-C. Benoit
Schmidt A. Mallabrera
Johann C. Grigoriou

French Rad Maîtrise, Paris Orch, G. Prêtre (5/92) (EMI) Ⓓ [2] **CMS7 63973-2**

3a G. Thill, Orch, F. Heurteur (r1927) (1/89) (EMI) Ⓓ **CDM7 69548-2**
3a, 3b T. Schipa, orch, M. Cordone (r1942; Ital) (4/90) (EMI) Ⓓ **CDH7 63200-2**
3a, 3b G. Thill, orch, F. Heurteur (r1927) (10/92) (TEST) Ⓓ **SBT1005**
3a, 3b P. Domingo, Cologne RSO, R. Chailly (r1979) (6/94) (BELA) Ⓓ **450 121-2** (6/94) (BELA) ▭ **450 121-4**
3a, 3b, 21a, 21b Alfredo Kraus, LPO, M. Plasson (10/89) (EMI) Ⓓ **CDM7 63104-2**
3a, 7b, 10a, 14, 15a, 18a, 18b, 19, 21a, 21b T. Troyanos, Alfredo Kraus, C. Barbaux, M. Manuguerra, L. Richardson, M. Lewis, LPO, M. Plasson (EMI) Ⓓ **CDM7 63936-2**
3b G. Thill, orch (r c1925) (PEAR) Ⓓ **GEMMCD9947**
3b T. Schipa, orch, M. Cordone (r1942: Ital) (9/94) (NIMB) Ⓓ **NI7856**
3b, 10b F. Ansseau, orch (r1927) (1/91) (PREI) Ⓓ **89022**
3b, 21b C. Valletti, Orch, A. Basile (pp1955) (MEMO) Ⓓ [2] **HR4191/2**
3b, 21b A. Piccaver, orch (r1914: Ger) (8/93) (PREI) Ⓓ **89060**
7b-d A. Baltsa, J. Carreras, LSO, P. Domingo (r1990-91) (SONY) Ⓓ **SK53968**
10a A. Giorgini, orch (r1908: Ital) (4/95) (RECO) Ⓓ **TRC3**
10a, 10b E. Scaramberg, orch (r1905) (SYMP) Ⓓ **SYMCD1173**
10a, 10b E. Scaramberg, anon (r1905) (SYMP) Ⓓ **SYMCD1173**
10a, 10b G. Thill, Orch, M. Frigara (r1927) (1/89) (EMI) Ⓓ **CDM7 69548-2**
10a, 10b R. Jobin, Paris Opéra-Comique Orch, A. Cluytens (r1948) (4/92) (EMI) Ⓓ [7] **CHS7 69741-2(3)**
10b G. Micheletti, orch (r1929) (MSCM) Ⓓ **MM30377**
14. N. Shicoff, Toulouse Capitole Orch, M. Plasson (EMI) Ⓓ **CDC7 54016-2**
14. J. Rogatchewsky, orch (1927) (MSCM) Ⓓ **MM30377**
15a A. Milcheva, Bulgarian RSO, V. Stefanov (r1970s) (FORL) Ⓓ **UCD16741**
15a G. Simionato, Milan SO, A. Quadri (Ital: r1951) (4/92) (EMI) Ⓓ [7] **CHS7 69741-2(7)**
15a, 15b M. Callas, Paris Cons, G. Prêtre (EMI) Ⓓ **CDC7 49005-2**
15a, 15b M. Callas, Paris Cons, G. Prêtre (EMI) Ⓓ **CDC7 49502-2**
15a, 15b S. Verrett, RCA Italiana Op Orch, G. Prêtre (r1967) (RCA) Ⓓ **09026 61457-2**
15a, 15b M. Lipovšek, Munich RO, G. Patanè (6/90) (ORFE) Ⓓ **C179891A**
18a J. M. Leonard, V. L. Becker (arr sax/pf: J M Leonard) (ASV) Ⓓ **CDWHL2085**
18a, 18b G. Simionato, Santa Cecilia Academy Orch, F. Previtali (r1956) (DECC) Ⓓ **440 406-2DM**
18a, 18b S. Verrett, RCA Italiana Op Orch, G. Prêtre (r1967) (RCA) Ⓓ **74321 24284-2** (RCA) ▭ **74321 24284-4**
18a, 18b B. Fassbaender, Stuttgart RSO, H. Graf (11/00) (ORFE) Ⓓ **C096841A**
18b Z. Dolukhanova, USSR Rad Orch, O. Bron (r1950s) (PREI) Ⓓ **89066**
21a, 21b T. Schipa, orch (r1925) (2/89) (PEAR) Ⓓ **GEMMCD9322**

21a, 21b T. Schipa, La Scala Orch, F. Ghione (r1934; Ital) (4/90) (EMI) ① **CDH7 63200-2**
21b T. Schipa, orch (Ital: r1934) (PEAR) ① **GEMMCD9364**
21b F. Corelli, Milan RAI SO, M. Rossi (Ital; pp1955) (MEMO) ① [2] **HR4204/5**
21b Alfredo Kraus, Milan RAI SO, A. Basile (Ital; pp1959) (MEMO) ① [2] **HR4233/4**
21b T. Schipa, orch, Anon (cond) (pp1925) (MEMO) ① [2] **HR4220/1**
21b T. Schipa, orch, Anon (cond) (Ital: pp1934) (MEMO) ① [2] **HR4220/1**
21b G. di Stefano, Zurich Tonhalle Orch, F. Patanè (DECC) ① **433 623-2DSP** (DECC) ⊟ **433 623-4DSP**
21b L. Pavarotti, National PO, O. de Fabritiis (DECC) ① **430 470-2DH** (DECC) ⊟ **430 470-4DH**
21b G. di Stefano, Zurich Tonhalle Orch, F. Patanè (DECC) ① **433 066-2DWO** (DECC) ⊟ **433 066-4DWO**
21b J. Carreras, Orch, Anon Cond (pp1991) (MCI) ① **MCCD090** (MCI) ⊟ **MCTC090**
21b L. Pavarotti, Philh, L. Magiera (DECC) **OO** **436 320-5DH**
21b L. Pavarotti, National PO, O. de Fabritiis (r1979) (DECC) ① **436 472-2DM**
21b P. Ballo, Verona Arena Orch, A. Guadagno (pp1992) (MCI) ① **MCCD099**
21b G. di Stefano, Zurich Tonhalle Orch, F. Patanè (r1958) (DECC) ① **440 403-2DM**
21b L. Pavarotti, National PO, O. de Fabritiis (r1979) (DECC) ① **440 400-2DM**
21b J. Carreras, ROHO, Colin Davis (r1980) (BELA) ① **450 059-2** (BELA) ⊟ **450 059-4**
21b L. Pavarotti, Ater Orch, L. Magiera (pp1980) (BELA) ① **450 002-2** (BELA) ⊟ **450 002-4**
21b G. Di Stefano, Zurich Tonhalle Orch, F. Patanè (BELA) ① **450 005-2** (BELA) ⊟ **450 005-4**
21b G. di Stefano, Zurich Tonhalle Orch, G. Patanè (r1958) (DECC) ① **436 314-2DA** (DECC) ⊟ **436 314-4DA**
21b M. del Monaco, Milan SO, A. Quadri (r1952: Ital) (TEST) ① **SBT1039**
21b P. Cornubert, anon (r1905) (SYMP) ① **SYMCD1173**
21b N. Gedda, E. Werba (pp1961) (EMI) ① **CDH5 65352-2**
21b L. Pavarotti, Los Angeles PO, Z. Mehta (pp1994) (TELD) ◘ **4509-96200-8**
21b L. Pavarotti, Los Angeles PO, Z. Mehta (pp1994) (TELD) **OO** **4509-96200-5**
21b G. Prandelli, Rome RAI Orch, A. Basile (bp1961: Ital) (FONI) ① **CDMR5023**
21b A. Piccaver, Berlin St Op Orch, J. Prüwer (r1930: Ger) (PREI) ① [2] **89217**
21b F. de Lucia, anon (r1902: Ital) (BONG) ① [2] **GB1064/5-2**
21b R. Alagna, LPO, R. Armstrong (EMI) ① **CDC5 55540-2** (EMI) ⊟ **EL5 55540-4**
21b F. de la Mora, WNO Orch, C. Mackerras (r1994-5) (TELA) ① **CD80411**
21b P. Dvorský, Bratislava RSO, Czech RSO, O. Lenárd (10/89) (OPUS) ① **9156 1824**
21b T. Schipa, orch, Rosario Bourdon (r1925) (12/89) (RCA) ① **GD87969**
21b J. Patzak, orch (Ger: r1937) (3/90) (PEAR) ① **GEMMCD9383**
21b B. Gigli, ROHO, R. Zamboni (Ital: r1946) (5/90) (EMI) ① **CDH7 61052-2**
21b L. Pavarotti, National PO, O. de Fabritiis (7/90) (DECC) ① [2] **425 681-2DM2** (7/90) (DECC) ⊟ [2] **425 681-4DM2**
21b A. Cortis, La Scala Orch, C. Sabajno (Ital: r1929) (10/91) (PREI) ① **89043**
21b L. Pavarotti, Philh, L. Magiera (11/91) (DECC) ◖ **071 150-1DH** (11/91) (DECC) ▣ **071 150-3DH**
21b L. Pavarotti, James Levine, B. Large (2/92) (DECC) ◖ **071 119-1DH** (2/92) (DECC) ▣ **071 119-3DH**
21b G. Lugo, orch, F. Weiss (r1933) (2/92) (PREI) ① **89034**
21b G. Prandelli, Milan SO, A. Quadri (Ital: r1949) (4/92) (EMI) ① [7] **CHS7 69741-2(7)**
21b P. Dvorský, Bratislava RSO, O. Lenárd (5/92) (NAXO) ① **8 550343**
21b M. Battistini, orch, C. Sabajno (Ital: r1911) (10/92) (NIMB) ① **NI7831** (10/92) (NIMB) ⊟ **NC7831**
21b M. Battistini, orch, C. Sabajno (Ital: r1911) (10/92) (PEAR) ① **GEMMCD9936**
21b J. Hislop, orch, G.W. Byng (r1926) (1/93) (PEAR) ① **GEMMCD9956**
21b L. Sobinov, orch (r1910: Russ) (6/93) (PEAR) ① [3] **GEMMCDS9997/9(2)**
21b G. Lauri-Volpi, orch (r1922: Ital) (7/93) (NIMB) ① **NI7845**
21b G. di Stefano, Zurich Tonhalle Orch, F. Patanè (r1958) (10/93) (DECC) ① **436 463-2DM** (10/93) (DECC) ⊟ **436 463-4DM**
21b A. Cortis, La Scala Orch, C. Sabajno (r1929: Ital) (3/94) (NIMB) ① **NI7850**
21b T. Schipa, La Scala Orch, F. Ghione (r1934: Ital) (4/94) (EMI) ① [3] **CHS7 64864-2(2)**
21b L. Pavarotti, Ater Orch, L. Magiera (pp) (5/94) (DECC) ① [2] **443 018-2DF2**
21b E. Van Dyck, anon (r1905) (12/94) (SYMP) ① **SYMCD1172**
21b L. Pavarotti, Los Angeles PO, Z. Mehta (pp1994) (12/94) (TELD) ① **4509-96200-2**
(12/94) (TELD) ⊙ **4509-96200-1** ⊟ **4509-96200-4**
21b F. de Lucia, anon (r1903: Ital) (1/95) (SYMP) ① **SYMCD1149**
21b L. Pavarotti, NYPO, L. Magiera (pp1993) (2/95) (DECC) ① **444 450-2DH** (2/95) (DECC) ⊟ **444 450-4DH**
21b G. Anselmi, anon (r1907: Ital) (7/95) (SYMP) ① **SYMCD1170**
21b E. Clément, orch (r1911) (8/95) (ROMO) ① **82002-2**
21b E. Clément, orch (r1911) (8/95) (PEAR) ① **GEMMCD9161**

MAXWELL DAVIES , Sir Peter *(b 1934) England*

The **Lighthouse– opera: prologue, 1 act (1980—Edinburgh) (Lib. cpsr)**
Sandy, Officer 1 N. Mackie
Blazes, Officer 2 C. Keyte
Arthur, Officer 3, Voice of the Cards I. Comboy
BBC PO, P. Maxwell Davies (pp1994) (1/95) (COLL) ① **Coll1415-2**
Excs N. Mackie, C. Keyte, I. Comboy, BBC PO, P. Maxwell Davies (pp1994) (COLL) ① **Coll1444-2**

The **Martyrdom of St Magnus– chamber opera: 9 scenes (1977—Orkney) (Lib. cpsr, after George Mackay Brown)**
Blind Mary; Ingerth; Mary O'Connell T. Dives
Earl Magnus C. Gillett
Norse Herald; King of Norway; Keeper; Lifolf P. Thomson
Welsh Herald; Tempter R. Morris
Bishop of Orkney; Earl Hakon K. Thomas
Scottish Chbr Op Ens, M. Rafferty (3/91) (UNIC) ① **DKPCD9100**

Miss Donnithorne's Maggot– music theatre work: mezzo and ensemble (1974) (Lib. R. Stow)
M. Thomas, Fires of London, P. Maxwell Davies (3/88) (UNIC) ① **DKPCD9052** (UNIC) ⊟ **DKPC9052**

Resurrection– opera: prologue & one act (1987—Darmstadt) (Wds. cpsr)
Elder Sister; Phoebus Apollo; Antichrist D. Jones
Mam; Zeus or Hera C. Robson
Headmaster; Surgeon 1; White Abbot; Bishop M. Hill
Vicar; Pluto; Hot Gospeller N. Jenkins
Dad; Surgeon 2; The Rev'd Minister; Policeman H. Herford
Younger Brother; Surgeon 3; Sir Croesus Wright; Judge G. Finley
Surgeon 4; Comrade Serbsky; Trade-Union Leader J. Best
BBC PO, P. Maxwell Davies (r1994) (8/95) (COLL) ① [2] **Coll7034-2**

The **Two Fiddlers– children's opera: 2 acts (1978—Kirkwall) (Lib. cpsr, after G. Mackay Brown)**
Dances Scottish CO, P. Maxwell Davies (12/88) (UNIC) ① **DKPCD9070**

MAYER, William (Robert) *(b 1925) USA*

A **Death in the Family– opera (1982) (Lib. cpsr, after J Agee)**
Butterfly Aria; How far we all come away from ourselves J. Christin, G. Mercer, J. McKeel, New Calliope Sngrs, P. Schubert (ALBA) ① **TROY068-2**

One Christmas Long Ago– opera (1962) (Lib. cpsr)
Alleluia Florilegium Chbr Ch, New Calliope Sngrs, J. Rice (ALBA) ① **TROY068-2**

MAYR , (Johannes) Simon *(1763–1845) Germany*

also known as Giovanni Simone Mayr

Adelasia ed Aleramo– opera: 2 acts (1807—Rome) (Lib. Morelli, after Rossi)
Storm; Dove salvarmi?....Oh Dio!; Ah! ch'io fra voi N. Christie, S. Dugdale, E. Harrhy, Philh, D. Parry (OPRA) ⊙ **ORH102**

Alfredo il Grande– opera: 2 acts (1818—Rome) (Lib. Morelli, after Rossi)
Ov'è la bella vergine D. Montague, M. Moreno, K. John, R. Smythe, Philh, D. Parry (OPRA) ⊙ **ORH102**
Ov'2 la bella vergine? D. Montague, K. John, M. Moreno, R. Smythe, Philh, D. Parry (10/90) (OPRA) ① [3] **ORCH103**

Cora– opera: 2 acts (1815—Naples) (Lib. Salfa-Benco)
Sempre uniti insiem saremo Y. Kenny, P. Doghan, K. John, R. Leggate, R. Smythe, Philh, D. Parry (OPRA) ⊙ **ORH102**
Sempre uniti insiem saremo Y. Kenny, P. Doghan, K. John, R. Leggate, R. Smythe, Philh, D. Parry (10/90) (OPRA) ① [3] **ORCH103**

Elena (e Costantino)– opera: 2 acts (1814—Naples) (Lib. Tottola)
Ah! se mirar potessi R. Smythe, Philh, D. Parry (OPRA) ⊙ **ORH102**
Ah! se mirar potessi R. Smythe, Philh, D. Parry (10/90) (OPRA) ① [3] **ORCH103**

Fedra– opera: 2 acts (1820—Milan) (Lib. Romanelli)
Se fiero, Ippolito P. Walker, Philh, D. Parry (OPRA) ⊙ **ORH102**
Se fiero, Ippolito P. Walker, Philh, D. Parry (8/95) (OPRA) ① [3] **ORCH104**

La **Finte Rivali– opera: 2 acts (1803—Milan) (Lib. Romanelli)**
Il pesciolin guizzando D. Montague, P. Doghan, Philh, D. Parry (OPRA) ⊙ **ORH102**

Ginevra di Scozia– opera: 2 acts (1801—Trieste) (Lib. Rossi)
Per pietà, deh! M. Hill Smith, D. Jones, Philh, D. Parry (OPRA) ⊙ **ORH102**

Medea in Corinto– opera: 2 acts (1813—Naples) (Lib. Romani)
Medea J. Eaglen
Creusa Y. Kenny
Giasone B. Ford
Egeo R. Giménez
Creonte A. Miles
Ismene A. Mason
Tideo P. Nilon
Evandro N. Archer
G. Mitchell Ch, Philh, D. Parry (r1993) (11/94) (OPRA) ① [3] **ORC011**
Amiche cingete; Caro albergo Y. Kenny, G. Mitchell Ch, S. Drake, Philh, D. Parry (10/90) (OPRA) ① [3] **ORCH103**

La **Rosa bianca e la rosa rossa– opera: 2 acts (1813—Genoa) (Lib. Romani)**
Dov'è la destra? infida! Y. Kenny, P. Walker, P. Doghan, Philh, D. Parry (OPRA) ⊙ **ORH102**
Dov'è la destra? infida! Y. Kenny, P. Walker, P. Doghan, Philh, D. Parry (10/90) (OPRA) ① [3] **ORCH103**

MÉHUL, Nicholas Etienne *(1763–1817) France*

La **chasse de jeune Henri– opera: 2 acts (1797—Paris) (Lib. J P Bouilly)**
EXCERPTS: 1. Overture.
1. Horreaux-Trehard Duo (arr 2 gtrs) (CALL) ① **CAL9218**

1. Munich RO, K. Redel (PIER) Ⓓ **PV786104**
1. Lisbon Gulbenkian Orch, M. Swierczewski (7/89) (NIMB) Ⓓ [2] **NI5184/5**

Joseph– opera (2 acts) (1807—Paris) (Lib. Marsollier)
Champs paternels R. Tauber, orch, H. Geehl (Ger: r1945) (3/92) (EMI) Ⓓ **CDH7 64029-2**
Vainement, Pharaon...Champs paternals G. Thill, orch (r1927) (MSCM) Ⓓ **MM30377**
Vainement Pharaon G. Thill, orch, E. Bigot (r1930) (8/95) (FORL) Ⓓ **UCD16727**

Le **Trésor supposé– opera (1 act) (1802—Paris) (Lib. F-B. Hofmann)**
Overture Lisbon Gulbenkian Orch, M. Swierczewski (7/89) (NIMB) Ⓓ [2] **NI5184/5**

MENDELSSOHN (-BARTHOLDY) , (Jakob Ludwig) Felix *(1809–1847) Germany*

Die **beiden Pädagogen– singspiel: 1 act (?1821—Berlin) (Lib. J L Caspar, after E Scribe)**
Probatum est, dies ruf' ich mir D. Fischer-Dieskau, Munich RO, H. Wallberg (r1978) (EMI) Ⓓ [2] **CMS5 65621-2**

Der **Heimkehr aus der Fremde, 'Son and Stranger'– Liederspiel: 1 act (1829—Berlin) (Lib. K Klingemann)**
EXCERPTS: 1. Overture; 2. Ich bin ein veilgereister Mann (I'm a roamer bold).
1. Nuremberg SO, K. Seibel (COLO) Ⓓ **COL34 9007**
1. M. McEachern, orch (Eng: r1934) (PEAR) Ⓓ **GEMMCD9455**
1. Philh, F. D'Avalos (IMP) Ⓓ **MCD88**
1. Berne SO, P. Maag (IMP) Ⓓ **PCD2003**
1. Berne SO, P. Maag (6/86) (IMP) Ⓓ **PCD824**
2. P. Dawson, orch (r c1912) (PEAR) Ⓓ **GEMMCD9122**
2. D. Fischer-Dieskau, Munich RO, H. Wallberg (r1977) (EMI) Ⓓ [2] **CMS5 65621-2**

Die **Hochzeit des Camacho– opera: 2 acts, Op. 10 (1827—Berlin) (Lib. K. Klingemann, after Cervantes: dialogue lost)**
Quiteria R. Schudel
Lucinda C. Swanson
Basilio C. Bieber
Vivaldo W. Mok
Camacho V. Horn
Carrasco R. Lukas
Sancho Panza J. Becker
Don Quixote W. Murray
Alkalde F. Molsberger
Berlin RIAS Chbr Ch, BRSO, B. Klee (9/91) (SCHW) Ⓓ [2] **314042**
Quiteria R. Hofman
Lucinda A. Ulbrich
Basilio S. Weir
Vivaldo H. Rhys-Evans
Camacho N. van der Meel
Carrasco W. Wild
Sancho Panza U. Malmberg
Don Quixote U. Cold
Aachen Youth Ch, Modus Novus Ch, Anima Eterna, J. van Immerseel (r1992) (12/93) (CHNN) Ⓓ [2] **CCS5593**
Overture Nuremberg SO, K. Seibel (COLO) Ⓓ **COL34 9007**
Overture Philh, F. d'Avalos (r1993) (IMP) Ⓓ **MCD81**
Overture Bamberg SO, C.P. Flor (1/89) (RCA) Ⓓ **RD87905**

MENOTTI, Gian Carlo *(b 1911) Italy/USA*

Amahl and the Night Visitors– opera: 1 act (1951—NBC (New York) (Lib. cpsr)
Amahl J. Rainbird
Mother L. Haywood
King Kaspar J. Dobson
King Melchior D. Maxwell
King Balthazar Curtis Watson
Page C. Painter
ROH Chor, ROHO, D. Syrus (7/88) (TER) Ⓓ **CDTER1124**
(7/88) (TER) ▭ **ZCTER1124**
Introduction; March; Shepherd's Dance NZ SO, A. Schenck (r1989) (9/90) (KOCH) Ⓓ **37005-2**

Amelia al ballo– opera: 1 act (1937—Philadelphia) (Lib. cpsr)
Overture NY Met Op Orch, J. Conlon (pp1991) (6/93) (RCA) Ⓓ **09026 61509-2**
While I waste these precious hours L. Price, New Philh, N. Santi (r1977) (12/92) (RCA) Ⓓ [4] **09026 61236-2**

The **Boy who grew too fast– children's opera (1982—Wilmington) (Lib. cpsr)**
Poponel G. Godfrey
Miss Hope J. Howarth
Mrs Skrosvodmonit M. Morelle
Dr Shrinck P. Crook
Mad Dog E. Garrett
Miss Proctor E. Bainbridge
Small Poponel D. Wallder
Lizzie Spender A. Machell
Ricky T. Duffy
Policeman A. Plant
ROHO, D. Syrus (r1986) (TER) Ⓓ **CDTER1125**
(TER) ▭ **ZCTER1125**

The **Consul– opera: 3 acts (1950—Philadelphia) (Lib. cpsr)**
I shall find you shells N. Pelle, Montreal I Musici, Y. Turovsky (r1993: orch P Jaffe) (CHAN) Ⓓ **CHAN9304**
My child is dead! I. Borkh, Berlin St Op Orch, A. Rother (Ger: r1951) (4/92) (EMI) Ⓓ [7] **CHS7 69741-2(4)**

The **Telephone– opera: opera buffa (1946—New York) (Lib. cpsr)**
Lucy C. Farley
Ben R. Smythe
Scottish CO, J. Serebrier, M. Newman (5/93) (DECC) ◖ **071 143-1DH**
(5/93) (DECC) ▬ **071 143-3DH**

MERCADANTE , (Giuseppe) Saverio (Raffaele) *(1795–1870) Italy*

Amleto– melodramma tragico: 2 acts (1822—Milan) (Lib. F Romani)
Qui fu commesso, o populi S. McCulloch, T. Goble, D. Montague, I. Thompson, A. Thorburn, G. Mitchell Ch, Philh, D. Parry (8/95) (OPRA) Ⓓ [3] **ORCH104**

Andronico– melodramma tragico: 2 acts (1821—Venice) (Lib. D Tindario)
EXCERPTS; 1. Nel seggio placido.
1. G. Groves, J. Watson, J. Partridge (r1994) (ASV) Ⓓ **CDWHL2088**

L' **Apoteosi d'Ercole– opera: 2 acts (1819—Naples) (Lib. Schmidt)**
Ambo unite!...Come palpiti cor mio! G. Dolton, E. Harrhy, D. Jones, P. Nilon, Philh, D. Parry (10/90) (OPRA) Ⓓ [3] **ORCH103**

Il **Bravo– melodramma: 3 acts (1839—Milan) (Lib. G. Rossi)**
Il Bravo D. di Domenico
Teodora A. Tabiadon
Violetta J. Perry
Pisani S. Bertocchi
Foscari S. Antonucci
Capellio L. de Lisi
Marco A. Riva
Luigi G. de Matteis
Michelina M.C. Zanni
Bratislava Phil Ch, Italian International Orch, B. Aprea (NUOV) Ⓓ [3] **6971/3**

Elena da Feltre– dramma tragico: 3 acts (1838—Naples) (Lib. Cammarano)
EXCERPTS: 1. Overture.
1. Moldava SO, S. Frontalini (BONG) Ⓓ **GB2144-2**

Gabriella di Vergy– dramma tragico: 2 acts (1828—Lisbon) (Lib. A L Tottola, adapted A Profumo)
Ah che dici!...Quant'immagini crudeli C. Daniels, J. Rhys-Davies, P. Nilon, I. Sharpe, K. M. Daymond, J. Viera, Philh, D. Parry (8/95) (OPRA) Ⓓ [3] **ORCH104**

Il **Giuramento– opera: 3 acts (1837—Milan) (Lib. Rossi)**
Elaisa G. de Liso
Viscardo G. Morino
Bianca M. Olmeda
Manfredo M. Barrard
Isaura E. Procuronoff
Brunoro P. Aubert
Nantes Op Chor, Loire PO, G. Carella (pp1993) (NUOV) Ⓓ [2] **7179/80**
La dea di tutti...Bella adorata; Compiuta è omai...Fu celeste J. Carreras, RPO, R. Benzi (PHIL) Ⓓ **434 152-2PM**

Nitocri– melodramma serio: 2 acts (1824—Turin) (Lib. Poisasco, after Zeno)
EXCERPTS: 1. Overture.
Numi, che intesi mai?...Se m'abbandoni D. Jones, Philh, D. Parry (8/95) (OPRA) Ⓓ [3] **ORCH104**
1. Moldava SO, S. Frontalini (BONG) Ⓓ **GB2144-2**

I **Normanni a Parigi– tragedia lirica: 4 acts (1832—Turin) (Lib. Romani)**
EXCERPTS: 1. Overture.
1. Moldava SO, S. Frontalini (BONG) Ⓓ **GB2144-2**

Orazi e Curiazi– tregedia lirica: 3 acts (1846—Naples) (Lib. Cammarano)
Camilla N. Miricioiu
Orazio A. Michaels-Moore
Curiazio M. Jerome
Vecchio Orazio A. Miles
Sabina J. Rhys-Davies
Gran Sacerdote P. Nilon
G. Mitchell Ch, Philh, D. Parry (r1993) (OPRA) Ⓓ [3] **ORC12**

Il **Reggente– dramma lirico: 3 acts (1843—Turin) (Lib. Cammarano, after Scribe)**
EXCERPTS: 1. Overture.
1. Moldava SO, S. Frontalini (BONG) Ⓓ **GB2144-2**

La **Schiava saracena, ovvero Il campo di Gerosolima– melodramma tragico: 4 acts (1848—Milan) (Lib F M Piave)**
EXCERPTS: 1. Overture.
1. Moldava SO, S. Frontalini (BONG) Ⓓ **GB2144-2**

Gli **Sciti– dramma per musica: 2 acts (1823—Naples) (Lib. Tottola)**
EXCERPTS: 1. Overture.
1. Moldava SO, S. Frontalini (BONG) Ⓓ **GB2144-2**

La **Testa di bronzo– melodramma eroi-comico: 2 acts (1827—Laranjeiras) (Lib. F Romani)**
Overture Philh, D. Parry (8/95) (OPRA) Ⓓ [3] **ORCH104**

MESSAGER , André (Charles Prosper) *(1853–1929) France*

L' **amour masqué– operetta (1923—Paris) (Lib. Guitry)**
EXCERPTS: 1. Overture; 2. Veuillez accepter cette rose; 3. Vingt ans, vingt ans; 4. J'ai deux amants; 5. Valentine a perdu la tête; 6. Kartoum bella; 7. Toute l'histoire en quatre mots; 8. Voulez-vous voir un homme extremement heureux; 9. Viens, s'il est vrai que tu m'attends; 10. J'aime pas les bonnes; 11. Chant birman; 12. Le Koutchiska, c'est le ragout; 13. Il était pour moi; 14. Ah! quelle nuit; 15. Excellente combinaison; 16. C'était vous.
4. R. Crespin, Vienna Volksoper Orch, A. Lombard (r1970/1) (DECC) Ⓓ **440 416-2DM**
4. B. Hendricks, Philh, L. Foster (r1992) (8/93) (EMI) Ⓓ **CDC7 54626-2**

La **Basoche– opéra-comique (1890—Pris) (Lib. A. Carré)**
EXCERPTS: 1. Prelude. ACT 1: 2. C'est aujord'hui que la Basoche; 3. En attendant l'heure de la bataille; 4. Quand tu connaitras Colette; 5. Midi, c'est l'heure; 6. Bonjour, ami!; 7. Dans ce grand Paris; 8. Trop lourd est le poids du veuvage; 9. Vive le roi; 10. Quoi, se dire un simple mortel! ACT 2: 11. Voici le guet qui passe; 12. Il était une fois; 13. Ah, Colette, c'est toi!; 14. A table aupres de moi; 15. Eh! que ne parliez-vous?; 16. Il faut agir adroitment. ACT 3: 17. Jour de liesse et de réjouissance; 18. El l'honneur de hyménée; 19. Elle m'aime; 20. A ton amour simple et sincère; 21. Arrêtez, s'il s'agit d'être pendu!.
Colette N. Sautereau
Clément Marot C. Maurane

Marie d'Angleterre I. Jaumillot
Le Duc de Longueville L. Noguera
Roland L. Lovano
L'Éveillé A. Doniat
Louis XII J. Scellier
Guillot Génio
Jeune Fille I G. Parat
Jeune Fille II A. Martineau
Le Chancelier J. Villisech
L'Écuyer P. Saugey
French Rad Lyric Chor, French Rad Lyric Orch, T. Aubin (bp1960)
(4/94) (MUSD) ① [2] **202572**
Elle m'aime; Trop lourd est le poids L. Fugère, orch (r1928) (6/93) (SYMP) ① **SYMCD1125**
Excs L. Berton, N. Broissin, H. Legay, M. Dens, Colonne Concerts Orch, J. Pernoo (r1961)
(EMI) ① [2] **CZS5 68295-2**
Quand tu connaîtras Collette G. Soulacroix, anon (r1900) (9/91) (SYMP) ① **SYMCD1089**

Coups de Roulis– operetta: 3 acts (1928—Paris) (Lib. A. Willemetz, after M. Larrouy)
Béatrice L. Dachary
Sola Myrrhis C. Collart
Puy Pradal G. Rey
Gerville D. Tirmont
Kermao A. Doniat
Pinson J. Pruvost
Saint-Mesmin P. Saugey
Bellory M. Fauchey
Muriac R. Lenoty
Haubourdin C. Daguerressar
Blangy Génio
Subervielle J. Hoffmann
ORTF Lyric Chorale, ORTF Lyric Orch, M. Cariven (bp1963)
(11/93) (MUSD) ① [2] **20238-2**

Fortunio– operetta: 5 acts (1907—Paris) (Lib. de Caillavet and de Flers)
Fortunio T. Dran
Jacqueline C. Alliot-Lugaz
Clavaroche G. Cachemaille
Landry F. Dudziak
Maître André M. Trempont
Maître Subtil P. Rocca
Guillaume R. Schirrer
D'Azincourt M. Fockenoy
De Verbois N. Rivenq
Madelon B. Desnoues
Gertrude S. Stewart
Lyon Op Chor, Lyon Op Orch, J.E. Gardiner (r1987)
(ERAT) ① [2] **2292-45983-2**
Excs L. Berton, M. Sénéchal, M. Dens, J-C. Benoit, G. Godin, P. Germain, Colonne Concerts Orch, J. Pernoo (r1961)
(EMI) ① [2] **CZS5 68295-2**
J'aimais ma vieille maison grise G. Thill, orch, P. Chagnon (r1932)
(8/95) (FORL) ① **UCD16727**
La maison grise N. Vallin, P. Darck (r c1933-8)
(PEAR) ① **GEMMCD9948**

Madame Chrysanthème– operetta: 4 acts (1893—Paris) (Lib. G Hartmann & A Alexandre, after P Loti)
EXCERPTS: 1. Le jour sous le soleil béni.
1. B. Hendricks, Philh, L. Foster (r1992)
(8/93) (EMI) ① **CDC7 54626-2**
1. S. Jo, ECO, R. Bonynge (r1993)
(9/94) (DECC) ① **440 679-2DH**

Monsieur Beaucaire– opérette romantique: prologue and 3 acts (1919—London) (Eng lib. Lonsdale, trans Rivoire & Veber)
EXCERPTS: 1. Introduction. ACT 1: 2a. Au jardin où les fleurs; 2b. O rose; 3. Pour faire une prisonnière; 4a. Souhaitons la bienvenue; 4b. Vous me reprochez ma froideur; 5. Qui donc vient là-bas vers nous; 6. Vous me demander une rose. ACT 2: 7. A femme jolie; 8a. Le jour diminue; 8b. Ah! rossignol; 9. Quoi! si doux. ACT 3: 10. Je connais une belle; 11. Quand vous series fée; 12. Oh! mer écumante.
Monsieur Beaucaire W. Clément
Lady Mary Carlisle L. Dachary
Lady Lucy N. Broissin
Molyneux R. Lenoty
Winterset L. Lovano
Nash H. Bedex
Bantinson J. Pruvost
Townbrake G. Foix
Rakell M. Enot
Captain Badger A. Balbon
Mirepoix G. Moryn
French Rad Lyric Chor, French Rad Lyric Orch, J. Gressier (bp1958)
(11/93) (MUSD) ① [2] **20241-2**
La rose rouge A. Baugé, orch, G. Andolfi (r1935) (EMI) ① [2] **CZS5 68292-2**
2a, 2b N. Vallin, A. Baugé, orch
(FORL) ① **UCD19022**
9. M. Hill Smith, Chandos Sngrs, Chandos Concert Orch, S. Barry (Eng)
(2/90) (CHAN) ① **CHAN8759**
(2/90) (CHAN) ▭ **LBTD023**
10. M. Hill Smith, P. Morrison, Chandos Concert Orch, S. Barry (Eng)
(7/88) (CHAN) ① **CHAN8561**
(7/88) (CHAN) ▭ **LBTD019**

Passionêment– operetta: 3 acts (1926—Paris) (Lib. M. Hennequin & A. Willemetz)
Ketty L. Dachary
Hélène C. Harbell
Julia C. Collart
Perceval A. Doniat
Stevenson D. Tirmont
Captain Harris G. Friedmann
Le Barrios Hieronimus
John R. Lenoty
ORTF Lyric Orch, J-P. Kreder (bp1964)
(3/92) (MUSD) ① [2] **20135-2**

La **Petite fonctionnaire– operetta (1921—Paris) (Lib. X. Roux, after A. Capus)**
Je regrette mon Prassigny F. Révoil, orch, M. Cariven (r1935) (EMI) ① [2] **CZS5 68292-2**

Les **P'tites Michu– operetta: 3 acts (1897—Paris) (Lib. A. Vanloo & G. Duval)**
Excs C. Collart, C. Harbell, C. Maurane, C. Devos, French Rad Lyric Orch, R. Ellis (bp1958)
(3/92) (MUSD) ① [2] **20135-2**

Véronique– opéra-comique: 3 acts (1898—Paris) (Lib. Vanloo and Duval)
EXCERPTS: 1. Overture. ACT 1: 2. La bel état que celui de fleuriste; 3. Ah! la charmante promenade; 4. Vrai Dieu, mes bons amis!; 5. Petite dinde; 6. Les voitures sont à la porte. ACT 2: 7. De-ci, de là; 8. Duo de l'escarpolette; 9. Lisette avait peur du loup; 10. Une grisette mignonne; 11. Adieu, je pars. ACT 3: 12. Chut, chut; 13. Voyons, ma tante; 14. Ma foi! pour venir de province; 15. Eh bien! par ordre procédons; 16. Par une faveur insigne; 17. Voyons, par ordre procédons (final duet).
5. M. Hill Smith, P. Morrison, Chandos Concert Orch, S. Barry (Eng)
(6/85) (CHAN) ① **CHAN8362**
(6/85) (CHAN) ▭ **LBTD013**
5; C'est Estelle et Véronique F. Révoil, orch, E. Beruilly (r1935) (EMI) ① [2] **CZS5 68292-2**
6. E. Eames, E. de Gogorza, orch (r1911: Eng)
(11/93) (ROMO) ① [2] **81001-2**
7, 8. S. Laydeker, A. Baugé, orch, G. Andolfi (r1935) (EMI) ① [2] **CZS5 68292-2**
7, 8. B. Hendricks, G. Quilico, Lyon Op Orch, L. Foster (r1993) (6/95) (EMI) ① **CDC5 55151-2**

MESSIAEN , Olivier
(1908–1992) France

Saint François d'Assisi– opera (Paris)
L'Ange C. Eda-Pierre
Saint François J. Van Dam
Le Lépreux K. Riegel
Frère Léon M. Philippe
Frère Massée G. Gautier
Frère Elie M. Sénéchal
Frère Bernard J-P. Courtis
Paris Op Chor, Paris Op Orch, S. Ozawa (pp)
(12/88) (CYBE) ① [4] **CY833/6**
Frères oiseaux, en tous temps et lieux D. Fischer-Dieskau, Austrian RSO, L. Zagrosek (pp1985) (ORFE) ① **C335931A**

MEYERBEER, Giacomo
(1791–1864) Germany

L' **Africaine, '(The) African Maid'– opera: 5 acts (1865—Paris) (Lib. Scribe and Fétis)**
ACT 1: 1. Overture; 2. Adieu, mon doux rivage. ACT 2: 3. Sur mes genoux; 4. Fille des rois; 5. Combien tu m'es chère. ACT 3: 6. Holà! Matelots; 7. Adamastor, roi des vagues. ACT 4: 8. Prelude; 9a. Pays merveilleux; 9b. O Paradis; 9c. Conduisez-moi; 10. L'avoir tant adorée (Averla tanto amata). ACT 5: 11. Erreur fatal.
Sélika S. Verrett
Vasco da Gama P. Domingo
Inès R.A. Swenson
Nélusko J. Diaz
Don Pedro M. Devlin
Don Diego P. Skinner
Grand Inquisitor J. Rouleau
Don Alvar K. Anderson
Anna P. Spence
High Priest of Brahma M. Delavan
San Francisco Op Chor, San Francisco Op Orch, M. Arena, B. Large
(MCEG) ▭ **VVD673**
Selika J. Norman
Vasco da Gama V. Luchetti
Nelusko G. Guelfi
Inez M. Sighele
Don Pedro A. Ferrin
Don Diego G. Casarini
Don Alvaro D. Formichini
Anna G. Matteini
Grand Inquisitor G. del Vivo
High Priest M. Rinaudo
MMF Chor, MMF Orch, R. Muti (Ital: pp1971)
(MEMO) ① [3] **HR4213/5**
Selika S. Verrett
Vasco da Gama P. Domingo
Nelusko J. Diaz
Inez R.A. Swenson
Don Pedro M. Devlin
Don Diego P. Skinner
Anna P. Spence
Grand Inquisitor J. Rouleau
High Priest M. Delavan
San Francisco Op Chor, San Francisco Op Ballet, San Francisco Op Orch, M. Arena, B. Large
(3/93) (PION) ◐ [2] **PLMCD00601**
Excs J. Schwarz, orch (Ger: r1916)
(PREI) ① **89033**
1, 2, 4. M. Lanza, orch, C. Callinicos (r1951: Ital)
(RCA) ① **09026 61420-2**
(RCA) ▭ **09026 61420-4**
2. E. Rethberg, orch (r1920: Ger)
(7/94) (PREI) ① **89051**
2. E. Rethberg, Berlin SO, F. Weissmann (r1933: Ger) (10/95) (ROMO) ① [2] **81014-2**
3. R. Ponselle, orch (r1923: Ital)
(PEAR) ① [2] **GEMMCDS9964**
3. R. Ponselle, orch, Rosario Bourdon (Ital: r1925) (1/90) (RCA) ① **GD87810**
3. C. Muzio, orch (r1922)
(5/90) (BOGR) ① [2] **BIM705-2**
3. E. Burzio, orch (Ital: r1913)
(1/91) (CLUB) ① [2] **CL99-587/8**
3. L. Price, RCA Italiana Op Orch, F. Molinari-Pradelli (12/92) (RCA) ① [4] **09026 61236-2**
3. R. Raisa, orch (r1917: Ital)
(1/94) (CLUB) ① **CL99-052**
3. C. Muzio, orch (r1922: Ital)
(1/94) (ROMO) ① [2] **81005-2**
3. R. Ponselle, orch, Rosario Bourdon (r1925: 2 vers: Ital) (11/94) (ROMO) ① [2] **81006-2**
3. F. Litvinne, anon (r1905)
(12/94) (SYMP) ① **SYMCD1128**
3. F. Litvinne, orch (r1907)
(12/94) (SYMP) ① **SYMCD1128**
3. E. Destinn, orch, F. Kark (r1908: Ger)
(12/94) (SUPR) ① [12] **11 2136-2(2)**
4. H. Hermann Nissen, Berlin SO, F. Zweig (r1929: Ger) (PREI) ① **89090**
4. H. Schlusnus, orch (r1921: Ger)
(PREI) ① **89110**
4. L. Melchissédec, orch (r1907)
(9/91) (SYMP) ① **SYMCD1089**
6. T. Ruffo, orch, W.B. Rogers (Ital: r1915)
(11/90) (NIMB) ① **NI7810**
(NIMB) ▭ **NC7810**
6. T. Ruffo, orch (Ital: r1915)
(2/93) (PREI) ① [3] **89303(1)**
6. P. Gailhard (r1904)
(12/94) (SYMP) ① **SYMCD1172**
6, 11. G. Campanari, anon (r1903; Ital)
(4/94) (RCA) ① [6] **09026 61580-2(1)**
6, 7. P. Amato, chor, orch (r1910: Ital)
(PEAR) ① **GEMMCD9104**
7. R. Stracciari, orch (Ital: r1925)
(MSCM) ① [2] **MM30276**
7. P. Amato, chor, orch (r1914: Ital)
(PREI) ① **89064**
7. R. Stracciari, orch (r1925: Ital)
(2/90) (PREI) ① **89003**
7. T. Ruffo, orch (Ital: r1929)
(2/93) (PREI) ① [3] **89303(2)**
7. T. Ruffo, orch (Ital: r1920)
(2/93) (PREI) ① [3] **89303(1)**

9a-c P. Domingo, Los Angeles PO, C.M. Giulini (DG) ⊟ **419 091-4GW**

9a-c L. Pavarotti, National PO, O. de Fabritiis (Ital) (DECC) Ⓓ **430 470-2DH** (DECC) ⊟ **430 470-4DH**

9a-c C. Bergonzi, Santa Cecilia Academy Orch, G. Gavazzeni (Ital) (DECC) Ⓓ **433 068-2DWO** (DECC) ⊟ **433 068-4DWO**

9a-c B. Gigli, orch (r1928: Ital) (IMP) Ⓓ **GLRS102**

9a-c C. Bergonzi, Santa Cecilia Academy Orch, G. Gavazzeni (1957: Ital) (DECC) Ⓓ **436 314-2DA** (DECC) ⊟ **436 314-4DA**

9a-c J. Björling, Hilversum RO, F. Weissmann (pp1939; Ital) (8/88) (BLUE) Ⓓ **ABCD006**

9a-c J. Björling, orch, N. Grevillius (r1937: Ital) (10/88) (EMI) Ⓓ **CDH7 61053-2**

9a-c P. Domingo, ROHO, J. Barker (pp1988) (9/89) (EMI) Ⓓ **CDC7 49811-2**

9a-c F. Völker, Berlin St Op Orch, J. Prüwer (r1928: Ger) (2/90) (PREI) Ⓓ **89005**

9a-c J. Schmidt, Berlin St Op Orch, C. Schmalstich (r1929; Ger) (4/90) (EMI) Ⓓ **CDM7 69478-2**

9a-c E. Caruso, orch (r1907; Ital) (12/90) (PEAR) Ⓓ [3] **EVC1(2)**

9a-c E. Caruso, orch (r1907: Ital) (7/91) (RCA) Ⓓ [12] **GD60495(2)**

9a-c B. Gigli, orch, Rosario Bourdon (r1923; Ital) (4/94) (RCA) Ⓓ [6] **09026 61580-2(3)**

9a-c H. Roswaenge, BPO, F.A. Schmidt (r1933: Ger) (4/95) (PREI) Ⓓ [2] **89209**

9a, 9b P. Domingo, MMF Orch, Rome Op Orch, Z. Mehta (pp1990) (DECC) ◐ **071 123-1DH** (DECC) ▣ **071 123-3DH**

9a, 9b B. Gigli, orch (Ital) (CONI) Ⓓ **CDHD149** (CONI) ⊟ **MCHD149**

9a, 9b C. Bergonzi, Santa Cecilia Academy Orch, G. Gavazzeni (Ital) (DECC) Ⓓ **433 623-2DSP** (DECC) ⊟ **433 623-4DSP**

9a, 9b M. Lorenz, Berlin St Op Orch, C. Schmalstich (Ger: r1929) (PREI) Ⓓ **89053**

9a, 9b P. Domingo, MMF Orch, Rome Op Orch, Z. Mehta (pp1990) (DECC) ΟΟ **430 433-5DH**

9a, 9b P. Domingo, LSO, N. Santi (r1971; Ital) (RCA) Ⓓ **09026 61356-2** (RCA) ⊟ **09026 61356-4**

9a, 9b C. Bergonzi, Verona Arena Orch, A. Guadagno (pp1992) (MCI) Ⓓ **MCCD099**

9a, 9b M. del Monaco, New SO, A. Erede (r1956: Ital) (DECC) Ⓓ **440 407-2DM**

9a, 9b L. Pavarotti, National PO, O. de Fabritiis (r1979: Ital) (DECC) Ⓓ **440 400-2DM**

9a, 9b J. Björling, Stockholm Royal Op Orch, N. Grevillius (r1937: Ital) (PEAR) Ⓓ **GEMMCD9043**

9a, 9b L. Melchior, LSO, J. Barbirolli (r1930: Ger) (PREI) Ⓓ **89086**

9a, 9b P. Cornubert, anon (r1905) (SYMP) Ⓓ **SYMCD1173**

9a, 9b J. Björling, H. Ebert (pp1950: Ital) (BLUE) Ⓓ **ABCD057**

9a, 9b C. Bergonzi, Santa Cecilia Academy Orch, G. Gavazzeni (r1957: Ital) (DECC) Ⓓ **440 417-2DM**

9a, 9b P. Domingo, Los Angeles PO, C.M. Giulini (r1980) (DG) Ⓓ **445 525-2GMA** (DG) ⊟ **445 525-4GMA**

9a, 9b A. Piccaver, Berlin St Op Orch, M. Gurlitt (r1928: Ital) (PREI) Ⓓ [2] **89217**

9a, 9b L. Melchior, LSO, J. Barbirolli (Ger: r1930) (8/88) (DANA) Ⓓ [2] **DACOCD315/6**

9a, 9b B. Gigli, orch, Rosario Bourdon (Ital: r1928) (9/88) (PEAR) Ⓓ **GEMMCD9316**

9a, 9b E. Caruso, orch (r1907: Ital) (10/89) (NIMB) Ⓓ **NI7803** (NIMB) ⊟ **NC7803**

9a, 9b P. Domingo, MMF Orch, Rome Op Orch, Z. Mehta (pp1990) (10/90) (DECC) Ⓓ **430 433-2DH** (10/90) (DECC) ⊟ **430 433-4DH**

9a, 9b C. Bergonzi, Santa Cecilia Academy Orch, G. Gavazzeni (r1957: Ital) (10/93) (DECC) Ⓓ **436 463-2DM** (10/93) (DECC) ⊟ **436 463-4DM**

9a, 9b L. Pavarotti, Ater Orch, L. Magiera (pp: Ital) (5/94) (DECC) Ⓓ [2] **443 018-2DF2**

9a, 9b P. Domingo, ROHO, J. Barker (pp1988) (6/94) (EMI) Ⓓ **CDC5 55017-2**

9a, 9b B. Heppner, Munich RO, R. Abbado (r1993/4) (11/95) (RCA) Ⓓ **09026 62504-2**

9b G. Lauri-Volpi, La Scala Orch, F. Ghione (Ital: r1934) (MMOI) Ⓓ **CDMOIR405** (MMOI) ⊟ **CMOIR405**

9b B.S. Rosenberg, Budapest Concert Orch, J. Acs (pp1990) (OLYM) Ⓓ **OCD370**

9b P. Domingo, Miami SO, E. Kohn (pp1991) (IMP) Ⓓ **MCD43**

9b J. Björling, orch, N. Grevillius (r1937: Ital) (NIMB) Ⓓ **NI7835**

9b L. Pavarotti, Philh, L. Magiera (Ital) (DECC) ΟΟ **436 320-5DH**

9b P. Domingo, Rio de Janeiro Municipal Th Orch, J. DeMain (pp1992) (SONY) ◐ **SLV48362** (SONY) ▣ **SHV48362**

9b L. Pavarotti, Ater Orch, L. Magiera (pp1980) (BELA) Ⓓ **450 002-2** (BELA) ⊟ **450 002-4**

9b C. Bergonzi, Santa Cecilia Academy Orch, G. Gavazzeni (BELA) Ⓓ **450 005-2** (BELA) ⊟ **450 005-4**

9b M. Gilion, orch (r c1909: Ital) (BONG) Ⓓ **GB1076-2**

9b J. Schmidt, orch, O. Dobrindt (r1933: Ger) (EMI) Ⓓ [2] **CHS7 64673-2**

9b M. del Monaco, Milan SO, A. Quadri (r1948: Ital) (TEST) Ⓓ **SBT1039**

9b B. Gigli, orch (r1923: Ital) (ASV) Ⓓ **CDAJA5137** (ASV) ⊟ **ZCAJA5137**

9b P. Domingo, MMF Orch, Rome Op Orch, Z. Mehta (pp1990) (DECC) Ⓓ **440 410-2DM**

9b G. Prandelli, Rome RAI Orch, A. Basile (bp1961: Ital) (FONI) Ⓓ **CDMR5023**

9b A. Bonci, orch (r1913: Ital) (PEAR) Ⓓ **GEMMCD9168**

9b F. de Lucia, orch (r1917: Ital) (BONG) Ⓓ [2] **GB1064/5-2**

9b L. Melchior, orch (Ger: r1926) (8/88) (DANA) Ⓓ [2] **DACOCD313/4**

9b E. Caruso, orch (r1907) (5/89) (PEAR) Ⓓ **GEMMCD9309**

9b H. Nash, orch (Eng: r1926) (8/89) (PEAR) Ⓓ **GEMMCD9319**

9b M. Fleta, orch (r1927: Ital) (2/90) (PREI) Ⓓ **89002**

9b B. Gigli, orch, Rosario Bourdon (Ital: r1923) (5/90) (NIMB) Ⓓ **NI7807** (NIMB) ⊟ **NC7807**

9b L. Pavarotti, National PO, O. de Fabritiis (Ital) (7/90) (DECC) Ⓓ [2] **425 681-2DM2** (7/90) (DECC) ⊟ [2] **425 681-4DM2**

9b G. Lauri-Volpi, La Scala Orch, F. Ghione (Ital: r1934) (9/90) (PREI) Ⓓ **89012**

9b F. Marconi, S. Cottone (r1903: Ital) (10/90) (SYMP) Ⓓ **SYMCD1069**

9b F. Marconi, orch (r1908: Ital) (10/90) (SYMP) Ⓓ **SYMCD1069**

9b F. Ansseau, orch (r1923) (1/91) (PREI) Ⓓ **89022**

9b F. Merli, orch, L. Molajoli (Ital: r1926) (1/91) (PREI) Ⓓ **89026**

9b A. Cortis, La Scala Orch, C. Sabajno (Ital: r1930) (10/91) (PREI) Ⓓ **89043**

9b L. Pavarotti, Philh, L. Magiera (Ital) (11/91) (DECC) ◐ **071 150-1DH** (11/91) (DECC) ▣ **071 150-3DH**

9b J. Björling, orch, N. Grevillius (r1937: Ital) (9/92) (MMOI) Ⓓ **CDMOIR409**

9b F. Viñas, anon (Ital: r1905) (11/92) (MEMO) Ⓓ [2] **HR4408/9(1)**

9b B. Gigli, orch, Rosario Bourdon (Ital: r1928) (6/93) (MMOI) Ⓓ **CDMOIR417**

9b A. Davidov, anon (r1901: Russ) (6/93) (PEAR) Ⓓ [3] **GEMMCDS9007/9(1)**

9b G. Lauri-Volpi, La Scala Orch, F. Ghione (r1934: Ital) (7/93) (NIMB) Ⓓ **NI7845**

9b L. Escalais, anon (r1905) (12/93) (SYMP) Ⓓ **SYMCD1126**

9b J. Björling, orch, N. Grevillius (r1937: Ital) (9/94) (IMP) Ⓓ **GLRS103**

9b J. Björling, orch, N. Grevillius (r1937: Ital) (9/94) (CONI) Ⓓ **CDHD214** (9/94) (CONI) ⊟ **MCHD214**

9b A. Giorgini, anon (r1904: Ital) (4/95) (RECO) Ⓓ **TRC3**

9c E. Caruso, orch, J. Pasternack (Ital: r1920) (7/91) (RCA) Ⓓ [12] **GD60495(6)**

9c E. Caruso, orch, J. Pasternack (Ital: r1920) (10/91) (PEAR) Ⓓ [3] **EVC4(2)**

9c E. Caruso, orch (r1920: Ital) (7/95) (NIMB) Ⓓ **NI7866**

10. H. Schlusnus, orch (r1922: Ger) (PREI) Ⓓ **89110**

Il Crociato in Egitto– opera: 2 acts (1824—Venice) (Lib. G. Rossi)

Aladino	I. Platt
Adriano	B. Ford
Armando	D. Montague
Palmide	Y. Kenny
Felicia	D. Jones
Alma	L. Kitchen
Osmino	U. Benelli

G. Mitchell Ch, RPO, D. Parry (9/92) (OPRA) Ⓓ [4] **ORC010**

O solinghi recessi!...D'una madre disperata Y. Kenny, I. Platt, L. Kitchen, U. Benelli, G. Mitchell Ch, RPO, D. Parry (r1990) (OPRA) Ⓓ **ORR201**

Popoli dell'Egitto Alfredo Kraus, WNO Chor, WNO Orch, C. Rizzi (r1994) (8/95) (PHIL) Ⓓ **442 785-2PH** (8/95) (PHIL) ⊟ **442 785-4PH**

Dinorah, '(Le) pardon de Ploërmel'– opera: 3 acts (1859—Paris) (Lib. Barbier and Carré)

EXCERPTS: 1. Overture. ACT 1: 2. Le jour radieux; 3. Bellah! ma chèvre chérie!; 4. Dors petite; 5. Je suis chez moi!; 6. Dieu nous donne è chacun; 7. Qui va là?; 8. Sonne, sonne, gai sonneur?; 9. Holà! hé! vieil Alain!; 10. O puissante magie!; 11. Me voici!; 13. Un trésor!; 14. Ce tintement que l'on entend. ACT 2: 15. Qu'il est bon; 16. Dites-moi, dites vite; 17. Me voici! me voici!; 18. Ombre légère (Shadow Song); 19. Arrive!; 20. Ah! que j'ai froid!; 21. Grand Dieu! Quelqu'un!; 22. Quand l'heure sonnera; 23. Tu frémis? Que m'importe; 24. Taisez-vous!; 25. De l'oiseau dans le bocage. ACT 3: 26. En chasse, piqueurs adroits!; 27. Les blés sont sons è faucher; 28. Sous les génèvriers; 29. Bonjour, faucher!; 30. La force m'abandonne; 31. Ah! mon remaords te venge; 32. Grand Dieu! son teint s'anime; 33. Vois!...regarde ces lieux!; 34. Sainte Marie!.

Dinorah	D. Cook
Hoël	C. du Plessis
Corentin	A. Oliver
Goatherd	D. Jones
Goatgirl	M. Hill Smith
Huntsman	R. Earle
Reaper	I. Caley

G. Mitchell Ch, Philh, J. Judd (r1979) (4/94) (OPRA) Ⓓ [3] **ORC005**

Dors, petite A. Galli-Curci, orch, Rosario Bourdon (r1924: Ital) (8/94) (ROMO) Ⓓ [2] **81004-2**

En chasse P. Plançon, anon (r1905) (12/94) (ROMO) Ⓓ [2] **82001-2**

1. NBC SO, A. Toscanini (bp1938) (6/90) (DELL) Ⓓ **CDDA9021**

2, 3. G. Huguet, orch (r1906: Ital) (9/92) (IRCC) Ⓓ **IRCC-CD800**

3, 31. A. Galli-Curci, orch, Rosario Bourdon, Folkmann (r1924: Ital) (4/94) (RCA) Ⓓ [6] **09026 61580-2(3)**

18. R. Doria, Pasdeloup Ass Orch, J. Allain (SYMP) Ⓓ **SYMCD1103**

18. L. Pons, Orch, A. Kostelanetz (r1940) (MSCM) Ⓓ **MM30446**

18. M. Callas, Milan RAI SO, A. Simonetto (r1954: Ital) (SUIT) Ⓓ **CDS1-5001**

18. R. Streich, Berlin RSO, K. Gaebel (Ital) (DG) Ⓓ [2] **435 748-2GDO2**

18. M. Korjus, Berlin St Op Orch, F. Schönbaumsfeld (r1934) (DANT) Ⓓ **LYS001**

18. L. Pons, orch, A. Kostelanetz (r1940) (RCA) Ⓓ **09026 61411-2**

18. E. Gruberová, Tokyo PO, F. Haider (pp1993) (NIGH) Ⓓ **NC090560-2**

18. M. Callas, Philh, T. Serafin (r1954: Ital) (EMI) Ⓓ **CDC5 55216-2** (EMI) ⊟ **EL555216-4**

18. M. Callas, Philh, T. Serafin (Ital: r1954) (11/86) (EMI) Ⓓ **CDC7 47282-2**

18. A. Galli-Curci, orch, J. Pasternack (r1917: Ital) (5/90) (NIMB) Ⓓ **NI7806** (NIMB) ⊟ **NC7806**

18. L. Pons, Columbia SO, P. Cimara (r1942) (7/90) (CBS) Ⓓ **CD45694**

18. Dilbèr, Estonia Op Orch, E. Klas (9/92) (ONDI) Ⓓ **ODE768-2**

18. F. Hempel, orch (r1918: Ital) (9/92) (IRCC) Ⓓ **IRCC-CD800**

18. L. Tetrazzini, orch, P. Pitt (r1907) (9/92) (EMI) Ⓓ [3] **CHS7 63802-2(1)**

18. L. Tetrazzini, orch, P. Pitt (r1907: Ital) (9/92) (PEAR) Ⓓ **GEMMCD9221**

18. L. Tetrazzini, orch (r1913: Ital) (9/92) (PEAR) Ⓓ **GEMMCD9224**

18. M. Korjus, Berlin St Op Orch, F. Schönbaumsfeld (r1934: Ger) (10/93) (PREI) Ⓓ **89054**

18. M. Barrientos, anon (r1904: Ital) (12/93) (SYMP) Ⓓ **SYMCD1113**

18. A. Galli-Curci, orch, J. Pasternack (r1917: Ital) (3/94) (ROMO) ① [2] **81003-2**
18. S. Jo, Monte Carlo PO, P. Olmi (r1994) (6/95) (ERAT) ① **4509-97239-2**
22. J. Hadley, T. Hampson, WNO Orch, C. Rizzi (r1992) (11/93) (TELD) ① **9031-73283-2**
26. L. Fugère, orch (r1928) (9/92) (IRCC) ① **IRCC-CD800**
26. L. Fugère, orch (r1930) (6/93) (SYMP) ① **SYMCD1125**
26. P. Plançon, anon (r1905) (1/95) (NIMB) ① **NI7860**
31. P. Amato, orch (r1914: Ital) (PREI) ① **89064**
31. G. De Luca, anon (r1902: Ital) (PEAR) ① [3] **GEMMCDS9159(1)**
31. G. De Luca, anon (r1907: Ital) (PEAR) ① [3] **GEMMCDS9159(1)**
31. G. De Luca, orch (r1924: Ital) (PEAR) ① [3] **GEMMCDS9160(2)**
31. R. Stracciari, orch (r1925: Ital) (PEAR) ① **GEMMCD9178**
31. R. Stracciari, orch (r1925: Ital) (2/90) (PREI) ① **89003**
31. G. De Luca, orch (r1924: Ital) (1/92) (PREI) ① **89036**
31. M. Ancona, orch (r1908: Ital) (9/92) (IRCC) ① **IRCC-CD800**
31. T. Ruffo, orch (r1914: Ital) (2/93) (PREI) ① [3] **89303(1)**

Emma– opera: 2 acts (1819—Venice) (Lib. Rossi)
Di gioja, di pace B. Mills, D. Montague, P. Nilon, H. Nichol, G. Dolton, M. Bovino, Philh, D. Parry (10/90) (OPRA) ① [3] **ORCH103**

L' **Esule di Granata– melodramma serio: 2 acts (1822—Milan) (Lib. F Romani)**
Sì, mel credi P. Spence, A. Miles, G. Mitchell Ch, Philh, D. Parry (8/95) (OPRA) ① [3] **ORCH104**

L' **Etoile du nord– opera: 3 acts (1854—Paris) (Lib. Scribe)**
La, la, la L. Tetrazzini, orch (Ital: r1913) (9/92) (EMI) ① [3] **CHS7 63802-2(2)**
La, la, la L. Tetrazzini, orch (Ital: r1913) (9/92) (PEAR) ① **GEMMCD9223**
O jours heureux P. Plançon, orch (r1908) (9/91) (PEAR) ① **GEMMCD9497**
O jours heureux P. Plançon, orch (r1908) (12/94) (ROMO) ① [2] **82001-2**
O jours heureux P. Plançon, orch (r1908) (1/95) (NIMB) ① **NI7860**
Veille sur eux A. Galli-Curci, orch (r1922) (2/89) (PEAR) ① **GEMMCD9308**
Veille sur eux A. Galli-Curci, orch, J. Pasternack (r1922) (8/94) (ROMO) ① [2] **81004-2**

Les **Huguenots– opera: 5 acts (1836—Paris) (Lib. Scribe and Deschamps)**
ACT 1: 1. Overture; 2. Des beaux jours; 3a. De ces lieux enchanteurs; 3b. Sous le beau ciel de Touraine; 4. Bonheur de la table; 5a. Non loin des vieilles tours; 5b. Ah! quel spectacle; 5c. Plus blanche que la blanche hermine; 6a. Quelle étrange figure; 6b. Seigneur, rempart et seul; 7. Eh! mais-plus je le vois; 8. Piff paff, piff paff; 9. Au maitre de ces lieux; 10. L'aventure est singulière; 11. Honneur au conquérant; 12a. Nobles seigneurs; 12b. Une dame noble et sage; 13a. Trop de mérite aussi; 13b. Vous savez si je suis un ami; 13c. Les plaisirs, les honneurs. ACT 2: 14. Entracte; 15a. O beau pays de la Touraine; 15b. Belle forêt; 15c. Sombre chimère; 15d. A cet mot seul s'anime; 16. Jeunes beautés; 17. Non, non, non, vous n'avez jamais; 18a. Le voici, du silence; 18b. Pareille loyauté; 19a. Beauté divine; 19b. Preux doit vivre; 19c. Si j'étais coquette; 19d. A vous et ma vie et mon ame; 20. Allons! toujours le page; 21. Par l'honneur, par le nom; 22a. Et maintenant je dois offrir; 22b. O transport. ACT 3: 23. Entracte; 24. C'est le jour de dimanche; 25a. Rataplan; 25b. Prenant son sabre de batailles; 26. Vierge Marie; 27. Profanes, impies; 28a. Gypsy Round; 28b. Gypsy Dance; 29. Pour remplir un voeu solennel; 30. Rentrez, habitants de Paris; 31a. O terreur! Je tressaille; 31b. Dans la nuit; 31c. Ah! l'ingrat; 31d. Ah! tu ne peux; 32. Un danger le menace; 33. En mon bon droit j'ai confiance; 34. Nous voila! félons, arrière; 35a. Ma fille; 35b. Au banquet. ACT 4: 36. Entracte; 37a. Je suis seule; 37b. Parmi les pleurs; 38. Juste ciel! est-ce lui; 39a. Des troubles renaissants; 39b. Qu'en ce riche quartier; 40. Gloire au grand Dieu vengeur; 41a. O ciel! Où courez vous; 41b. Tu l'as dit. ACT 5: 42. Entracte and Ball; 43a. Aux armes!; 43b. A la lueur de leurs torches; 44. C'est toi; 45. Dieu Seigneur, rempart et seul soutien; 46. Savez-vous qu'en joignant vos mains; 47. Abjurez, huguenots!; 48. Ah! voyez, le ciel s'ouvre; 49. Par le fer et par l'incendie.

Marguerite	J. Sutherland
Valentine	M. Arroyo
Urbain	H. Tourangeau
Comte de St Bris	G. Bacquier
Comte de Nevers	D. Cossa
Cossé	J. Ward
Méru	J. Gibbs
Thoré; Nightwatchman	J. Noble
Tavannes; Bois-Rosé; Monk I	J. Wakefield
De Retz	G. Thomas
Raoul de Nangis	A. Vrenios
Marcel	N. Ghiuselev
Maurevert; Monk III	C. Grant
Léonard	J. Coster
Maid of Honour I	K. Te Kanawa
Maid of Honour II	J. Clément
Gipsy I	A. Auger
Gipsy II	M. Lehane
Monk II	A. Opie

Ambrosian Op Chor, New PO, R. Bonynge (r1969) (DECC) ① [4] **430 549-2DM4**

Marguerite	J. Sutherland
Valentine	A. Thane
Urbain	S. Johnston
Comte de St Bris	J. Wegner
Comte de Nevers	J. Pringle
Cossé	L. Gaffney
Méru	D. Lemke
Thoré	K. Henderson
Tavannes	D. Collins-White
De Retz	N. Kirkby
Raoul de Nangis	A. Austin
Marcel	C. Grant
Bois-Rosé	S. Baigildin
Léonard	K. Harms
Nightwatchman	N. Wilkie
Maid of Honour I	J. Cole
Maid of Honour II	K.E. Brown
Gipsy I	M. McKay
Gipsy II	J. Bermingham
Monk I	D. Hibbard
Monk II	S. Bennett
Monk III	G. Scott

Australian Op Dance Ens, Australian Op Chor, Australian Op & Ballet Orch, R. Bonynge, V. Lumsden (PION) [2] **PLMCD00181**
Dieu le veut J-F. Delmas, chor, orch (r1907) (9/92) (IRCC) ① **IRCC-CD800**
Excs J. Sutherland, Orch, Anon (cond), D. Bailey (11/92) (DECC) **071 135-1DH**
3b E. Caruso, anon (r1903) (5/89) (EMI) ① **CDH7 61046-2**
3b E. Caruso, anon (Ital: r1903) (12/90) (PEAR) ① [3] **EVC1(1)**
3b E. Caruso, anon (Ital: r1903) (7/91) (RCA) ① [12] **GD60495(1)**
3b, 5b, 5c P. Cornubert, anon (r1905) (SYMP) ① **SYMCD1173**
5a F. Corelli, La Scala Orch, G. Gavazzeni (Ital; pp1962) (MEMO) ① [2] **HR4204/5**
5a-c G. Morino, Warmia Nat PO, B. Amaducci (Ital) (10/90) (NUOV) ① **6851**
5b, 5c E. Caruso, anon (r1905: Ital) (MCI) ① **MCCD086**
(MCI) **MCTC086**
5b, 5c E. Caruso, anon (Ital: r1905) (12/90) (PEAR) ① [3] **EVC1(1)**
5b, 5c E. Caruso, orch, W.B. Rogers (r1909: Ital) (7/91) (RCA) ① [12] **GD60495(3)**
5b, 5c E. Caruso, anon (Ital: r1905) (7/91) (RCA) ① [12] **GD60495(1)**
5b, 5c G. Zenatello, orch (r1910: Ital) (5/94) (PEAR) ① [4] **GEMMCDS9073(2)**
5c A. Paoli, orch (Ital: r1911) (PREI) ① **89998**
5c M. Gilion, orch (r c1909: Ital) (BONG) ① **GB1076-2**
5c D. Smirnov, orch (r1913: Russ) (PEAR) ① **GEMMCD9106**
5c P. Franz, orch (r1912) (PREI) ① **89099**
5c L. Slezak, orch (Ger: r1907) (2/91) (PREI) ① **89020**
5c E. Caruso, orch (Ital: r1909) (3/91) (PEAR) ① [3] **EVC2**
5c I. Ershov, anon (r1903: Russ) (6/93) (PEAR) ① [3] **GEMMCDS9997/9(1)**
5c D. Yuzhin, anon (r1902: Russ) (6/93) (PEAR) ① [3] **GEMMCDS9001/3(1)**
5c A. Labinsky, anon (Russ: r1905) (7/93) (SYMP) ① **SYMCD1105**
5c G. Lauri-Volpi, orch, Rosario Bourdon (r1929: Ital) (7/93) (NIMB) ① **NI7845**
5c G. Zenatello, orch (r1910: Ital) (5/94) (SYMP) ① **SYMCD1168**
5c H. Roswaenge, Berlin St Op Orch, F.A. Schmidt (r1932: Ger) (4/95) (PREI) ① [2] **89209**
5c E. Caruso, orch (r1909: Ital) (7/95) (NIMB) ① **NI7866**
5c G. Thill, orch, E. Bigot (r1931) (8/95) (FORL) ① **UCD16727**
6b I. Andrésen, orch (Ger: r1929) (10/90) (PREI) ① **89028**
6b A. Kipnis, Berlin Charlottenburg Op Orch, J. Heidenreich (Ger: r1923) (10/91) (PEAR) ① **GEMMCD9451**
6b L. Sibiriakov, orch (r1908: Russ) (6/93) (PEAR) ① [3] **GEMMCDS9001/3(2)**
6b, 8. C. Siepi, Santa Cecilia Academy Orch, A. Erede (r1954) (DECC) ① **440 418-2DM**
8. A. Pirogov, Bolshoi Th Orch, S. Samosud (r c1950: Russ) (PREI) ① **89078**
8. J. Mardones, orch (r1910) (PEAR) ① **GEMMCD9122**
8. T. Pasero, orch, L. Molajoli (Ital: r1928) (6/90) (PREI) ① **89010**
8. L. Sibiriakov, orch (Russ: r1909) (7/92) (PEAR) ① [3] **GEMMCDS9925(1)**
8. P. Plançon, anon (r1902) (3/93) (SYMP) ① **SYMCD1100**
8. A. Didur, S. Cottone (r1903: Ital) (6/93) (PEAR) ① [3] **GEMMCDS9997/9(2)**
8. A. Didur, anon (r1900: Ital) (6/93) (PEAR) ① [3] **GEMMCDS9997/9(2)**
8. A. Didur, anon (r1906: Ital) (1/94) (CLUB) ① **CL99-089**
12a E. Gruberová, Munich RO, G. Kuhn (r c1980) (EMIN) ① **CD-EMX2234**
12a D. Soffel, Swedish CO, M. Liljefors (pp1984) (4/93) (CPRI) ① **CAP21428**
12a, 12b H. Kashiwagi, S. Harrison (SCHW) ① **312642**
12a, 12b Z. Dolukhanova, USSR Rad Orch, O. Bron (r1950s) (PREI) ① **89066**
12a, 12b S. Onegin, orch, Rosario Bourdon (r1928) (2/91) (PREI) ① **89027**
12b M. Ivogün, orch (r1917: Ger) (PREI) ① **89094**
12b Z. Dolukhanova, Moscow PO, G. Stolarov (pp1954: Russ) (RUSS) ① **RDCD15023**
12b M. Ivogün, orch (r1917: Ger) (8/92) (NIMB) ① **NI7832**
(8/92) (NIMB) **NC7832**
12b X. Belmas, orch, A. Kitschin (Ital: r1928) (10/92) (PREI) ① **89047**
15a J. Sutherland, Orch, R. Bonynge (Ital) (VAI) **VAI69108**
15a E. Norena, orch (r1930) (3/91) (PREI) ① **89041**
15a S. Kurz, orch (Ger: r1906) (7/92) (PEAR) ① [3] **GEMMCDS9924(1)**
15a E. Norena, orch (r1930) (9/92) (IRCC) ① **IRCC-CD800**
15a L. Tetrazzini, orch (Ital: r1912) (9/92) (EMI) ① [3] **CHS7 63802-2(2)**
15a L. Tetrazzini, orch (Ital: r1912) (9/92) (PEAR) ① **GEMMCD9223**
15a M. Caballé, New Philh, R. Giovaninetti (r1970) (5/93) (DG) ① **431 103-2GB**
15a A. Nezhdanova, orch (r1908: Russ) (6/93) (PEAR) ① [3] **GEMMCDS9007/9(2)**
15a F. Hempel, orch (r1911) (3/94) (NIMB) ① **NI7849**
15a-d J. Sutherland, ROHO, F. Molinari-Pradelli (1/90) (DECC) ① [2] **425 493-2DM2**
15a, 15d R. Doria, Pasdeloup Ass Orch, J. Allain (SYMP) ① **SYMCD1103**
15d O. Boronat, orch (r1908: Ital) (3/95) (NIMB) ① **NI7865**
17. M. Horne, Sydney Eliz Orch, R. Bonynge (MCEG) **VVD780**
17. A. Parsi-Pettinella, anon (Ital: r1906) (9/92) (IRCC) ① **IRCC-CD800**
18b F. Hempel, H. Jadlowker, orch (Ger: r1900s) (12/91) (CLUB) ① **CL99-042**
19a L. Landouzy, A. Affre, orch (r1907) (9/92) (IRCC) ① **IRCC-CD800**
19a-d M. Mesplé, N. Gedda, Paris Op Orch, P. Dervaux (r1974) (EMI) ① [2] **CZS7 67813-2**
19c J. Sutherland, A. Austin, Australian Op & Ballet Orch, R. Bonynge (DECC) **071 149-1DH**
(DECC) **071 149-3DH**
31b J. Nivette, A. Talexis, orch (r c1908) (7/92) (PEAR) ① [3] **GEMMCDS9924(2)**

31b M. Lafargue, A. Gresse, orch (r1912)
(9/92) (IRCC) Ⓓ **IRCC-CD800**
31b, 41a G. Simionato, N. Ghiaurov, F. Corelli, La Scala Chor, La Scala Orch, G. Gavazzeni (Ital: pp1962) (MEMO) Ⓓ [2] **HR4386/7**
31d L. Sibiriakov, E. Bronskaya, orch (r1914: Russ) (PEAR) Ⓓ [3] **GEMMCDS9111(1)**
32. L. Sibiriakov, orch (r1909: Russ)
(PEAR) Ⓓ [3] **GEMMCDS9111(1)**
33. L. Escalais, A. Algos, F. Corradetti, O. Luppi, A. Magini-Coletti, G. Masotti, G. Sala, anon (Ital: r1905) (12/93) (SYMP) Ⓓ **SYMCD1126**
39a F. Schorr, chor, orch (Ger: r1922)
(PREI) Ⓓ **89052**
39a J-F. Delmas, orch (r1904)
(12/94) (SYMP) Ⓓ **SYMCD1172**
40. M. Journet, chor, orch (r1912)
(7/92) (PEAR) Ⓓ [3] **GEMMCDS9923(2)**
41a M. Wittrisch, M. Teschemacher, Berlin St Op Orch, E. Orthmann (Ger: r1932)
(PREI) Ⓓ **89024**
41a(pt) E. Destinn, K. Jörn, orch, B. Seidler-Winkler (r1908: Ger)
(12/94) (SUPR) Ⓓ [12] **11 2136-2(2)**
41a, 41b L. Slezak, E. Bland, orch (Ger: r1906)
(2/91) (PREI) Ⓓ **89020**
41a, 41b E. Destinn, K. Jörn, orch, B. Seidler-Winkler (r1908: Ger)
(12/94) (SUPR) Ⓓ [12] **11 2136-2(2)**

Margherita d'Anjou– melodramma semiserio: 2 acts (1820—Milan) (Lib. F Romani)
Quel parlar! Quell'aria incerta G. Dolton, R. Smythe, A. Miles, Philh, D. Parry
(8/95) (OPRA) Ⓓ [3] **ORCH104**

Le **Prophète– opera: 5 acts (1849—Paris) (Lib. Scribe)**
EXCERPTS: ACT ONE: 1. Prélude, 'La brise est muette'; 2. Mon couer est muette; 3. Fidès, ma bonne mère; 4. Ad nos salutarem undam; 5. Ainsi ces beaux châteaux?; 6. O roi des cieux; 7. Le Comte d'Oberthal; 8. Un jour, dans les flots; 9. Eh quoi! tant de candeur. ACT TWO: 10. Valsons toujours; 11. Ami, quel nuage; 12. Pour Berthe moi je soupire; 13. Ils partent, grâce au ciel; 14. Ah! mon fils, sois béni!; 15. O fureur! le ciel; 16. Gémissant sous le joug; 17. Ne sais-tu pas qu'en France; 18. Et la couronne. ACT THREE: 19. Entracte, 'Du sang!'; 20. Aussi nombreux que les étoiles; 21. Voici la fin du jour; 22. Voici les fermières; 23. Ballet; 24. Livrez-vous au repos, frères; 25. Sous votre bannière; 26. Pour prendre Munster; 27. Mais pourquoi dans l'ombre; 28. Qu'on le mène au supplice; 29. Par toi Munster nous fut promis; 30. Qui vous a sans mon ordre; 31. Éternel, Dieu sauveur; 32. Grand prophète; 33. Roi du ciel et des anges. ACT FOUR: 34. Entracte, 'Courbons notre tête'; 35. Donnez, donnez pour une pauvre âme; 36. C'est l'heure!...On nous attend; 37. Un pauvre pèlerin; 38a. Dernier espoir; 38b. Non, plus d'espoir; 39. Un matin je trouvai; 40. Coronation March; 41. Domine, salvum fac regem nostrum; 42. Le voilà, le Roi Prophète; 43. Qui je suis?; 44. Arrêtez!...Il prend ma defense!; 45. Tu cherissais ce fils. ACT FIVE: 46. Entracte, 'Ainsi vous l'attestez?'; 47. O prêtres de Baal; 48. O toi qui m'abandonnes; 49. Comme un éclair; 50. Ma mère!; 51a. Eh bien! si le remords; 51b. À la voix de ta mère; 52. Voici le souterrain; 53. Loin de la ville; 54. O spectre, ô spectre épouvantable!; 55. Hourra! gloire!; 56. Versez! que tout respire.

Fidès	M. Horne
Jean de Leyden	N. Gedda
Berthe	M. Rinaldi
Comte d'Oberthal	A. Giacomotti
Zacharie	R. Amis el Hage
Jonas	F. Peter
Mathisen	B. Carmeli

Turin RAI Chor, Turin RAI Orch, H. Lewis (pp1970)
(FOYE) Ⓓ [3] **3-CF2035**

Fidès	M. Horne
Jean de Leyden	J. McCracken
Berthe	R. Scotto
Comte d'Oberthal	J. Bastin
Zacharie	J. Hines
Jonas	J. Dupouy
Mathisen	C. du Plessis

Ambrosian Op Chor, Haberdashers' Aske's Sch Ch, RPO, H. Lewis
(10/89) (CBS) Ⓓ [3] **CD79400**
12. M. Gilion, orch (r c1909: Ital)
(BONG) Ⓓ **GB1076-2**
12. H. Winkelmann, anon (r1904; Ger)
(7/91) (SYMP) Ⓓ **SYMCD1081**
12. F. Tamagno, Anon (pf) (r1903-04)
(2/92) (OPAL) Ⓓ **OPALCD9846**
12. F. Viñas, anon (r1906; Ital)
(9/92) (IRCC) Ⓓ **IRCC-CD800**
12. D. Yuzhin, anon (r1902: Russ)
(6/93) (PEAR) Ⓓ [3] **GEMMCDS9001/3(1)**
12. F. Viñas, anon (r1906: Ital)
(7/93) (NIMB) Ⓓ [2] **NI7840/1**
12, 33. L. Slezak, orch (r1908; Ger)
(2/91) (PREI) Ⓓ **89020**
12, 56. I. Ershov, anon (r1903: Russ)
(6/93) (PEAR) Ⓓ [3] **GEMMCDS9997/9(1)**
14. M. Brandt, anon (r1905: Ger)
(SYMP) Ⓓ **SYMCD1085**
14. G. Fabbri, S. Cottone (r1903; Ital)
(12/89) (SYMP) Ⓓ **SYMCD1065**
14. E. Schumann-Heink, orch (r1909)
(2/91) (NIMB) Ⓓ **NI7811**
(2/91) (NIMB) ⊟ **NC7811**
14. S. Onegin, orch, Rosario Bourdon (r1928)
(2/91) (PREI) Ⓓ **89027**
14. K. Branzell, orch (r1927; Ger)
(8/92) (PREI) Ⓓ **89039**
14. S. Cahier, orch (r1928)
(9/92) (IRCC) Ⓓ **IRCC-CD800**
14, 35, 47. M. Horne, N. Gedda, Turin RAI Chor, Turin RAI Orch, H. Lewis (pp1970)
(MEMO) Ⓓ [2] **HR4392/3**
33. A. Paoli, orch (r1907; Ital) (PREI) Ⓓ **89998**
33. F. Tamagno, anon (r1903; Ital)
(7/92) (PEAR) Ⓓ [3] **GEMMCDS9923(2)**
33. L. Escalais, anon (r1905)
(12/93) (SYMP) Ⓓ **SYMCD1126**
35. K. Branzell, orch (r1928)
(8/92) (PREI) Ⓓ **89039**
37. M. Kurt, M. Matzenauer, orch (r1907; Ger)
(9/92) (IRCC) Ⓓ **IRCC-CD800**
38b M. Kurt, O. Metzger, orch (r1907; Ger)
(9/92) (IRCC) Ⓓ **IRCC-CD800**
40. NYPSO, W. Mengelberg (r1929)
(PEAR) Ⓓ **GEMMCD9474**
40. Berlin RSO, C. Richter (LASE) Ⓓ **15 510**
(LASE) ⊟ **79 510**
40. Philadelphia, E. Ormandy
(RCA) Ⓓ **09026 61211-2**
40. LSO, R. Bonynge (r1971)
(BELA) Ⓓ **461 004-2**
(BELA) ⊟ **461 004-4**
40. D. Hill (arr. Best) (IMP) Ⓓ **PCD2002**
40. LSO, C. Mackerras (r1961)
(MERC) Ⓓ **434 352-2MM**
40. D. Hill (trans Best) (9/86) (IMP) Ⓓ **PCD823**
40. St Louis SO, L. Slatkin
(6/89) (RCA) Ⓓ **RD87716**
40. Massed Brass Bands, J. H. Iles (r1935)
(11/93) (BEUL) Ⓓ **1PD2**
47. E. Schumann-Heink, orch (r1907)
(2/91) (NIMB) Ⓓ **NI7811**
(2/91) (NIMB) ⊟ **NC7811**
47. S. Onegin, orch, Rosario Bourdon (r1929)
(2/91) (PREI) Ⓓ **89027**
47. E. Schumann-Heink, orch (r1907)
(4/94) (RCA) Ⓓ [6] **09026 61580-2(1)**
48. L. Homer, anon (r1904)
(9/92) (IRCC) Ⓓ **IRCC-CD800**

Robert le Diable– opera: 5 acts (1831—Paris) (Lib. Scribe and Delavigne)
Ah! l'honnête homme! E. Clément, M. Journet, orch (r1913) (9/92) (IRCC) Ⓓ **IRCC-CD800**
De ma patrie A. Paoli, anon (Ital: r1909)
(PREI) Ⓓ **89998**
Du rendez-vous E. Clément, M. Journet, orch, Rosario Bourdon (r1912)
(8/95) (ROMO) Ⓓ **82002-2**
Du rendez-vous...Le bonheur E. Clément, M. Journet, orch, Rosario Bourdon (r1912)
(8/95) (PEAR) Ⓓ **GEMMCD9161**
Evocation G. Gravina, anon (Ital: r1902)
(12/89) (SYMP) Ⓓ **SYMCD1065**
Nonnes, qui reposez C. Siepi, Santa Cecilia Academy Orch, A. Erede (r1954)
(DECC) Ⓓ **440 418-2DM**
Nonnes, qui reposez E. Pinza, orch, Rosario Bourdon (Ital: r1927)
(2/89) (PEAR) Ⓓ **GEMMCD9306**
Nonnes, qui reposez E. Pinza, orch, Rosario Bourdon (Ital: r1927) (3/92) (PREI) Ⓓ **89050**
Nonnes, qui reposez N. de Angelis, orch, L. Molajoli (Ital: r1928) (7/92) (PREI) Ⓓ **89042**
Nonnes, qui reposez N. de Angelis, orch (Ital: r1927) (9/92) (IRCC) Ⓓ **IRCC-CD800**
Nonnes qui reposez A. Didur, anon (r1900: Ital)
(6/93) (PEAR) Ⓓ [3] **GEMMCDS9997/9(2)**
Nonnes qui reposez A. Didur, S. Cottone (r1903: Ital)
(6/93) (PEAR) Ⓓ [3] **GEMMCDS9997/9(2)**
Nonnes, qui reposez D. Bukhtoyarov, anon (r1901: Russ)
(6/93) (PEAR) Ⓓ [3] **GEMMCDS9001/3(1)**
Nonnes, qui reposez L. Sibiriakov, orch (r1908: Russ)
(6/93) (PEAR) Ⓓ [3] **GEMMCDS9001/3(2)**
Nonnes, qui reposez A. Didur, orch (r1907: Ital)
(1/94) (CLUB) Ⓓ **CL99-089**
Nonnes qui reposez P. Plançon, orch (r1908)
(12/94) (ROMO) Ⓓ [2] **82001-2**
Nonnes, qui reposez P. Plançon, orch (r1908)
(1/95) (NIMB) Ⓓ **NI7860**
Robert, toi que j'aime C. White, orch (r c1913: Ital) (IRCC) Ⓓ **IRCC-CD810**
Robert, toi que j'aime F. Hempel, orch (r1913)
(3/94) (NIMB) Ⓓ **NI7849**
Sicilienne L. Escalais, anon (r1905)
(12/93) (SYMP) Ⓓ **SYMCD1126**
Va! dit elle, va; Quand je quittai la Normandie E. Destinn, orch, F. Kark (r1908: Ger)
(12/94) (SUPR) Ⓓ [12] **11 2136-2(2)**
Va, dit-elle, va, mon enfant B.A. de Montalant, orch (r1908) (9/92) (IRCC) Ⓓ **IRCC-CD800**
Valse infernal M. Journet, chor, orch (r1912)
(9/92) (IRCC) Ⓓ **IRCC-CD800**
Voici donc les débris F. Chaliapin, orch (Ital: r1912) (PREI) Ⓓ **89030**

Romilda– opera: 2 acts (1817—Padua) (Lib. Rossi)
Che barbaro tormento B. Mills, A. Mason, C. Merritt, Philh, D. Parry
(10/90) (OPRA) Ⓓ [3] **ORCH103**

Semiramide riconosciuta– opera: 2 acts (1819—Turin) (Lib. Rossi, after Metastasio)
Il piacer, la gioja scenda Y. Kenny, G. Mitchell Ch, Philh, D. Parry
(10/90) (OPRA) Ⓓ [3] **ORCH103**

MILHAUD, Darius *(1892–1974)* *France*

L' **Abandon d'Ariane– opéra-minute: 5 scenes, Op. 98 (1927) (Lib. H. Hoppenot)**
M. Masquelin, C. Norrick, C. Calès, G. Garino, B-J. Mura, G. Mauclerc, C. Lara, F. Raynal, J. Laforge Choral Ens, Ars Nova Ens, A. Siranossian (r1982) (ARIO) Ⓓ **ARN68195**
Capella Cracoviensis, K.A. Rickenbacher
(5/93) (SCHW) Ⓓ **311392**
J. Bathori, J. Planel, G. Petit, M. Brega, Pro Musica Ens, D. Milhaud (r1929)
(9/93) (EPM) Ⓓ [3] **150 122**

Christophe Colomb– opera: 2 parts, Op. 102 (1930—Berlin) (Lib. P. Claudel)

Christopher Columbus I	R. Massard
Queen Isabella	J. Micheau
Christopher Columbus II	X. Depraz
Messenger	X. Depraz
Narrator	J. Marchat
Prosecutor	J. Davy
Spoken voice of Columbus	J. Davy
King of Spain	L. Lovano
Ship's Captain	L. Lovano
Sailors' spokesman	L. Lovano
Cook	J. Giraudeau
Major-domo	J. Giraudeau
	J. Peyron
	P. Germain
	J. Chalude

French Rad Chor, French Rad Lyric Orch, M. Rosenthal (pp1956)
(5/88) (MONT) Ⓓ [2] **TCE8750**

La **Déliverance de Thésée– opéra-minute: 6 scenes, Op. 99 (1927) (Wds. H. Hoppenot)**
M. Masquelin, C. Norrick, C. Calès, G. Garino, B-J. Mura, G. Mauclerc, C. Lara, F. Raynal, J. Laforge Choral Ens, Ars Nova Ens, A. Siranossian (r1982) (ARIO) Ⓓ **ARN68195**
Capella Cracoviensis, K.A. Rickenbacher
(5/93) (SCHW) Ⓓ **311392**
J. Bathori, J. Planel, G. Petit, A. Valencin, J. Hazart, Pro Musica Ens, D. Milhaud (r1929)
(9/93) (EPM) Ⓓ [3] **150 122**

L' **Enlèvement d'Europe– opéra-minute: 8 scenes, Op. 94 (1927)**
M. Masquelin, C. Norrick, C. Calès, G. Garino, B-J. Mura, G. Mauclerc, C. Lara, F. Raynal, J. Laforge Choral Ens, Ars Nova Ens, A. Siranossian (r1982) (ARIO) Ⓓ **ARN68195**
Capella Cracoviensis, K.A. Rickenbacher
(5/93) (SCHW) Ⓓ **311392**

J. Bathori, J. Planel, G. Petit, J. Hazart, Pro Musica Ens, D. Milhaud (r1929)
(9/93) (EPM) Ⓓ [3] **150 122**

Les **Malheurs d'Orphée– opera: 3 acts, Op. 85 (1926—Brussels) (Lib. A. Lunel)**

Orphée J. Cussac
Eurydice J. Brumaire
Le Maréchal, Le Sanglier S. Verzoub
Le Charron B. Demigny
Le Vannier, L'Ours A. Vessières
Le Renard, La Souer Jumelle C. Collart
Le Loup, La Souer Ainée C. Neumann
La Souer Cadette J. Collard
Paris Op Orch, D. Milhaud
(ADES) Ⓓ **13284-2**

Orphée M. Walker
Eurydice A. Steiger
Le Maréchal, Le Sanglier P. Harrhy
Le Charron P. Donnelly
Le Vannier, L'Ours M. Best
Le Renard, La Soeur Jumelle Gaynor Morgan
La Loup, La Soeur Ainée P. Bardon
La Soeur Cadette S. Bickley
Matrix Ens, R. Ziegler
(7/91) (ASV) Ⓓ **CDDCA758**

Le **Pauvre Matelot– opera: 3 acts, Op. 92 (1927—Paris) (Lib. J. Cocteau)**

The Wife J. Brumaire
The Sailor J. Giraudeau
His Father-in-law X. Depraz
His Friend A. Vessières
Paris Op Orch, D. Milhaud
(ADES) Ⓓ **13284-2**

MILLÖCKER, Carl *(1842–1899) Austria*

Der **Arme Jonathan– operetta (3 acts) (1890—Vienna) (Lib. Wittmann and Bauer)**

Ach, wir armen Primadonnen! L. Schöne, orch (r1925) (12/92) (NIMB) Ⓓ **NI7833**
(12/92) (NIMB) ▣ **NC7833**
The Doleful Prima Donna M. Hill Smith, Chandos Concert Orch, S. Barry
(7/88) (CHAN) Ⓓ **CHAN8561**
(7/88) (CHAN) ▣ **LBTD019**

Der **Bettlestudent, '(The) Beggar Student'– operetta: 3 acts, Vienna (1882) (Lib. Zell and Genée)**

ACT 1: 1. Ach unsre Lieben sperrte man ein; 2a. Und da soll man noch galant sein; 2b. Ach ich hab' sie ja nur auf die Schulter geküsst; 3. Die Welt hat das genialste Streben; 4. Juchheissa, hurra! Die Messe beginnt; 5. Einkäufe machen sollten wir eigentlich; 6. Ich knüpfte manche zarte Bande; 7. Bei solchem Feste (finale). ACT 2: 8. Einem Mann hat sie (hab' ich) gefunden; 9. Durch diesen Kuss sei unser Bund geweiht!; 10a. Soll ich reden, darf ich schweigen?; 10b. Ich setz' sen Fall; 11. Glückliche Braut! Dir strahlet hell das Leben; 12. Mit Geld und guten Worten; 13. Ach, ich hab' sie ja nur auf die Schulter geküsst. ACT 3: 14. Lumpen, Bagage, Bettelstudent; 15. Der Fürst soll nur ein Bettler sein; 16. Ich hab' kein Geld, bin vogelfrei; 17a. Still, man, kommt!...Dort steht der Patron; 17b. Die halbe Stunde ist vorbei; 17c. Jetzt lach' ich jeglicher Gefahr; 18. Befreit das Land! Geknüpft das Band!.

Palmatica G. Litz
Laura R. Streich
Bronislawa R. Holm
Ollendorf H. Prey
Jan G. Unger
Symon Rymanowicz N. Gedda
Enterich K.H. Bennert
Bavarian Rad Chor, Graunke SO, F. Allers (r1967/73: with dialogue)
(2/95) (EMI) Ⓓ [2] **CMS5 65387-2**
Nur das Eine bitt'ich dich Raphaele Concert Orch, P. Walden (arr Waldenmaier)
(5/91) (MOZA) Ⓓ **MECD1002**
6. R. Karczykowski, Polish Nat RSO, R. Bibl
(POLS) Ⓓ **PNCD087**
6. F. Völker, orch (r1934)
(3/90) (PEAR) Ⓓ **GEMMCD9383**
9. F. Wunderlich, L. Schmidt, Berlin SO, W. Schmidt-Boelcke (EMI) Ⓓ [3] **CZS7 62993-2**
10a, 10b R. Holm, W. Krenn, Vienna Volksoper Orch, A. Paulik (r1970)
(LOND) Ⓓ **436 898-2DM**
16. R. Schock, orch, W. Schüchter (r1955)
(EMI) Ⓓ **CDM7 69475-2**
16. J. Björling, B. Bokstedt
(BLUE) Ⓓ **ABCD042**
16. M. Wittrisch, orch (r1929)
(MMOI) Ⓓ **CDMOIR419**
(MMOI) ▣ **CMOIR419**
16. J. Björling, H. Ebert (pp1956: Swed)
(BLUE) Ⓓ **ABCD057**
16. J. Björling, orch, N. Grevillius (r1938: Swed)
(8/92) (BLUE) Ⓓ **ABCD016**
16. J. Björling, orch, N. Grevillius (r1938: Swed)
(9/92) (MMOI) Ⓓ **CDMOIR409**
16. J. Björling, orch, N. Grevillius (r1938: Swed)
(10/93) (NIMB) Ⓓ **NI7842**
16. J. Björling, orch, N. Grevillius (r1938: Swed)
(12/93) (NIMB) Ⓓ **NI7851**
16. J. Björling, orch, N. Grevillius (r1938: Swed)
(9/94) (IMP) Ⓓ **GLRS103**
16. J. Björling, orch, N. Grevillius (r1938: Swed)
(9/94) (CONI) Ⓓ **CDHD214**
(9/94) (CONI) ▣ **MCHD214**

Die **Dubarry– operetta (1931) (pastiche made by Theo Mackeben)**

EXCERPTS: 1a. Introduction; 1b. Immer nahen, immer nähen; 2. Heut' hab ich Glück; 3. Aber wenn es Feierabend. SCENE 2: 4. Seht, wie sich alles schön; 5. Heut' hab ich Glück; 6. Stets verliebt; 7a. Der Frühling zieht ins Land; 7b. Es lockt die Nacht; 8. Stets verliebt (chorus). SCENE 3: 9. Wie schön ist alles!; 10. Liebe, kleine Jeanne. SCENE 4: 11. Blicken dich zwei Augen an. SCENE 5: 12. Der Geige Klange lockt zur Nacht von Paris; 13. In dunkler Nacht zog mich Gesang; 14a. Ja, es ist ein alter Vorgang; 14b. Wenn verliebte bummeln gehr; 15a. Ich habe Liebe schon genossen; 15b. Ich schenk mein' Herz nur einem Mann; 16. Arme kleine Jeanne. SCENE 7: 17. Ob man gefällt oder nicht gefällt; 18a. Ügerglück macht die Liebe; 18b. Ich denk zûruck an jene Zeit; 19. Der uns führen soll ins grosse Glück!. SCENE 8: 20. Ich habe Liebe schon genossen (reprise); 21. Ich schenk mein' Herz (reprise). SCENE 9: 22. In Park von Trianon; 23a. Was ich im Leben beginne; 23b. Ja, so ist die, die Dubarry; 24a. Die Uniform freut mich enorm; 24b. Ich nehem' die Trommel an; 25. Mein Weg führt immer mich zu Dir zurück.

1a, 1b, 8, 9, 17, 18b, 23a, 23b E. Köth, H. Wilhelm, Günther Arndt Ch, Berlin SO, F. Fox
(2/91) (EURO) Ⓓ **GD69023**
9. H. Nash, orch (r1932: Eng)
(9/91) (PEAR) Ⓓ **GEMMCD9473**
15b G. Moore, orch, N. Shilkret (r1932: Eng)
(PEAR) Ⓓ **GEMMCD9130**
15b L. Popp, ASMF, N. Marriner
(6/88) (EMI) Ⓓ **CDC7 49700-2**
15b Raphaele Concert Orch, P. Walden (arr Waldenmaier) (5/91) (MOZA) Ⓓ **MECD1002**
15b, 23a, 23b E. Schwarzkopf, chor, Philh, O. Ackermann (1/86) (EMI) Ⓓ **CDC7 47284-2**
23b J. Sutherland, Ambrosian Light Op Chor, New Philh, R. Bonynge (Eng)
(DECC) Ⓓ **433 223-2DWO**
(DECC) ▣ **433 223-4DWO**
23b E. Sack, Berlin Staatskapelle (r1939)
(DANT) Ⓓ **LYS2**
23b E. Harwood, BBC SO, V. Tausky (pp1976)
(BBCR) Ⓓ **BBCRD9103**
24b G. Alpar, orch, T. Mackeben (r1932: Eng/Ger) (MMOI) Ⓓ **CDMOIR419**
(MMOI) ▣ **CMOIR419**

Gasparone– operetta: 3 acts (1884—Vienna) (Lib. F. Zell and R. Genée)

Carlotta A. Rothenberger
Baboleno Nasoni G. Wewel
Sindulfo W. Brokmeier
The stranger H. Prey
Luigi G.W. Dieberitz
Benozzo M. Finke
Sora G. Fuchs
Bavarian St Op Chor, Munich RO, H. Wallberg (r1981: with dialogue)
(2/95) (EMI) Ⓓ [2] **CMS5 65363-2**
Canzonetta J. Patzak, orch, M. Gurlitt (r1929)
(3/90) (PEAR) Ⓓ **GEMMCD9383**
Dunkelrote Rosen B. Weikl, Austrian RSO, K. Eichhorn (ORFE) Ⓓ **C077831A**
Er soll dein Herr sein Raphaele Concert Orch, E. Rondell (arr Waldenmaier)
(5/91) (MOZA) Ⓓ **MECD1002**
Wie freu'ich mich, Sie hier zu seh'n...Hüten Sie sich B. Hendricks, G. Quilico, Lyon Op Orch, L. Foster (r1993)
(6/95) (EMI) Ⓓ **CDC5 55151-2**

Das **Verwunschene Schloss– operetta: 3 acts (1878—Vienna) (Lib. Berla)**

Polonaise Raphaele Concert Orch, E. Rondell (arr Waldenmaier)
(5/91) (MOZA) Ⓓ **MECD1002**

MONDONVILLE, Jean-Joseph Cassanéa de *(1711–1772) France*

Titon et aurore– heroic pastorale: prologue and 3 acts (1753—Paris) (Lib. La Marre & Voiserion)

Titon J-P. Fouchécourt
L'Aurore C. Napoli
Prométhée; Eole P. Huttenlocher
Palès J. Smith
Amour; Nymphe A. Monoyios
F. Herr Voc Ens, Musiciens du Louvre, M. Minkowski (pp1991)
(10/92) (ERAT) Ⓓ [2] **2292-45715-2**

MONIUSZKO, Stanisław *(1819–1872) Poland*

The **Countess– opera: 4 acts (1859—Warsaw) (Lib. W. Wolski)**

Overture Katowice RSO, J. Krenz (r1952)
(8/93) (OLYM) Ⓓ **OCD386**
Overture Bydgoszcz PSO, R. Satanowski (r1991) (8/93) (CPO) Ⓓ **CPO999 113-2**

Halka– opera: 2 acts rev 4 acts (1848 rev 1858—Vilnius; Warsaw) (Lib. Wolski)

With the morning sun
Halka B. Zagórzanka
Jontek W. Ochman
Stolnik J. Ostapiuk
Zofia R. Racewicz
Janusz A. Hiolski
Dziemba M. Woiciechowski
Wielki Th Chor, Wielki Th Orch, R. Satanowski (pp1986)
(CPO) Ⓓ [2] **CPO999 032-2**
Heavenly Father Warsaw Cath Ch, A. Filaber
(POLS) Ⓓ **PNCD132**
Janusz's aria N. Shevelev, anon (r1901)
(6/93) (PEAR) Ⓓ [3] **GEMMCDS9007/9(2)**
Jontek's Scene and Dumka G. Nelepp, G. Korotkov, USSR RSO, K. Kondrashin (r c1950: Russ) (PREI) Ⓓ **89081**
Like the shrub in the whirlwind J. Korolewicz-Wayda, orch, O.I. Arkadiev (r1908)
(6/93) (PEAR) Ⓓ [3] **GEMMCDS9004/6(1)**
Like the wind in the hills A. Labinsky, orch (r1908) (3/95) (NIMB) Ⓓ **NI7865**
Overture Bydgoszcz PSO, R. Satanowski (r1991) (8/93) (CPO) Ⓓ **CPO999 113-2**
Overture; Mazurka Warsaw Nat PO, W. Rowicki (r1964) (8/93) (OLYM) Ⓓ **OCD386**
Polonaise A. Didur, anon (r1901)
(6/93) (PEAR) Ⓓ [3] **GEMMCDS9997/9(2)**
The wind whistles I. Kozlovsky, USSR SO, Anon (cond) (r1930-50)
(MYTO) Ⓓ **1MCD921.55**
The wind whistles L. Sobinov, anon (r1901)
(6/93) (PEAR) Ⓓ [3] **GEMMCDS9997/9(1)**
The wind whistles D. Yuzhin, anon (r1902)
(6/93) (PEAR) Ⓓ [3] **GEMMCDS9001/3(1)**

The **Haunted Manor– opera (4 acts) (1865—Warsaw) (Lib. Checiński)**

When I looked into her eyes A. Didur, anon (r1900)
(6/93) (PEAR) Ⓓ [3] **GEMMCDS9997/9(2)**

Jawnuta– operetta (1852 rev 1860—Warsaw) (Lib. F D Kniaźnin: rev of 'The Gypsies')

Overture Bydgoszcz PSO, R. Satanowski (r1991) (8/93) (CPO) Ⓓ **CPO999 113-2**

Paria– opera: prologue and 3 acts (1869—Warsaw) (Lib. Checiński)

Paria...Oh Paria
Overture Bydgoszcz PSO, R. Satanowski (r1991) (8/93) (CPO) Ⓓ **CPO999 113-2**
Overture Katowice RSO, G. Fitelberg (r1952)
(8/93) (OLYM) Ⓓ **OCD386**

The **Raftsman– opera: 1 act (1858—Warsaw) (Lib. W. Boguslawski)**

Overture Warsaw Nat PO, W. Rowicki (r1964)
(8/93) (OLYM) Ⓓ **OCD386**

Overture Bydgoszcz PSO, R. Satanowski (r1991) (8/93) (CPO) Ⓓ **CPO999 113-2**

Rokiczana– opera: 3 acts (1858-59)
1. Ballad of Florian the Grey.
A. Didur, anon (r1901) (6/93) (PEAR) Ⓓ [3] **GEMMCDS9997/9(2)**

Verbum nobile– opera: 1 act (1860—Warsaw) (Lib. J. Checiński)
Overture Bydgoszcz PSO, R. Satanowski (r1991) (8/93) (CPO) Ⓓ **CPO999 113-2**
Overture Katowice RSO, G. Fitelberg (r1952) (8/93) (OLYM) Ⓓ **OCD386**
Pan Marcin's aria A. Orda, Polish RSO, H. Debich (bp1965) (SYMP) Ⓓ **SYMCD1117**
Serwacy's Polonaise A. Didur, anon (r1901) (6/93) (PEAR) Ⓓ [3] **GEMMCDS9997/9(2)**

MONK, Meredith *(b 1943) USA*

Atlas– opera: 3 parts (1991)
Cpte C. Arávalo, T. Bogdan, J. Brenner, S-Z. Chen, A. Easter, R. Een, D. Emerson, E. Eyre, K. Geissinger, C. Gonzalez, D. Hanchard, W. Hill, S. Kalm, M. Monk, R. Osborne, W. Pauley, R. Wong, Orch, W. Hankin (r1992) (10/93) (ECM) Ⓓ [2] **437 773-2**

Education of the Girlchild– opera: 6 solo vv, electric org & pf (1972-73)
EXCERPTS: 1. The tale.
1. A. de Mare (KOCH) Ⓓ **37104-2**

Facing North– chamber opera: vv, pf & pitch pipe (1990—?New York)
M. Monk, R. Een (r1992) (ECM) Ⓓ **437 439-2**

Specimen Days– opera: 14 solo vv, 2pfs & 2 electric orgs (1981)
EXCERPTS: 1. Travel song.
1. A. de Mare (KOCH) Ⓓ **37104-2**

Vessel– opera epic (1971—New York)
M. Monk (r1992) (ECM) Ⓓ **437 439-2**

MONSIGNY, Pierre-Alexandre *(1729–1817) France*

Aline, reine de Golconde– opera: 3 acts (Paris) (Lib. M-J. Sedaine)
Rigaudon M. Elman, P. Kahn (arr Franko: r1911) (BIDD) Ⓓ **LAB035**
Rigaudon Y. Menuhin, H. Giesen (arr Franko: r1930) (4/91) (BIDD) Ⓓ **LAB032**

MONTÉCLAIR, Michel Pignolet de *(1667–1737) France*

Jephté– tragédie lyrique: prologue and 5 acts (1732—Paris) (Lib. S-J. Pellegrin)
Jephté J. Bona
Iphise S. Daneman
Almaise; Vénus C. Brua
Phinée; Apollon N. Rivenq
Ammon M. Padmore
Abdon B. Loonen
Abner J-C. Saragosse
Polhymnie; Israelite S. Pitour
Terpsichore S. Colas
Maspha Woman; Shepherdess; Truth M. Saint-Palais
Maspha Man F. Bazola-Minori
Hebrew P. Foucher
Elise A. Pichard
Arts Florissants Chor, Arts Florissants Orch, W. Christie (1/93) (HARM) Ⓓ [2] **HMC90 1424/5**

MONTEVERDI, Claudio (Giovanni Antonio) *(1567–1643) Italy*

L' Arianna– opera (1608—Mantua) (Lib. Rinuccini)
Lasciatemi morire a 1
Lasciatemi morire M. Lanza, C. Callinicos (pp1958) (RCA) Ⓓ **09026 61884-2**
(RCA) ⊟ **09026 61884-4**
Lasciatemi morire H. Sheppard, S. Le Sage, M. Worthley, P. Todd, A. Deller (alto/dir), M. Bevan, Deller Consort (4/94) (VANG) Ⓓ **08.2030.71**
N. Anfuso, J. Gray (AUVI) Ⓓ **AV6833**
Concerto Vocale (HARM) Ⓓ **HMC90 1129**
(HARM) ⊟ **HMC40 1129**
E. Pinza, F. Kitzinger (r1940) (9/93) (RCA) Ⓓ **09026 61245-2**

L' Incoronazione di Poppea, '(The) Coronation of Poppea'– opera (1642—Venice) (Lib. Busenello)
Poppea M. Ewing
Nerone D. Bailey
Ottavia C. Clarey
Ottone D. Duesing
Seneca R. Lloyd
Virtù H. Walker
Fortune P. Kern
Drusilla E. Gale
Arnalta A-M. Owens
Lucano K. Lewis
Lictor R. Bryson
Pallas J. Miller
Love L. Kitchen
Valetto P. Evangelides
Damigella L. Garrett
Glyndebourne Fest Chor, LPO, R. Leppard, P. Hall (r1984) (CAST) ▣ **CVI2040**
Poppea R. Yakar
Nerone E. Tappy
Ottavia T. Schmidt
Ottone P. Esswood
Seneca M. Salminen
Virtue H. Gardow
Fortune R. Lenhart
Drusilla J. Perry
Nurse M. Minetto
Arnalta A. Oliver
Lucano P. Huttenlocher
Love K. Brettschneider
Valletto P. Keller
Damigella S. Calabro
Zurich Op Monteverdi Ens, N. Harnoncourt, J-P. Ponnelle (DECC) ◐ [2] **071 406-1DH2**
(DECC) ▣ **071 406-3DH**
Poppea H. Donath
Nerone E. Söderström
Ottavia C. Berberian
Ottone P. Esswood
Seneca G. Luccardi
Virtue; Drusilla R. Hansmann
Fortune; Pallas; Darmigella J. Gartner
Nurse M. Minetto
Arnalta C. Gaifa
Lucano P. Langridge
Lictor; Mercury E. Fissore
Love Anon (treb)
Valletto Margaret Baker
VCM, N. Harnoncourt (r1973-74) (TELD) Ⓓ [4] **2292-42547-2**
Poppea D. Borst
Nerone G. Laurens
Ottavia J. Larmore
Ottone A. Köhler
Seneca M. Schopper
Drusilla L. Lootens
Virtue M.C. Kiehr
Fortune H.M. Ørbaek
Arnalta C. Homberger
Lucano G. de Mey
Lictor A. Lebeda
Venus; Pallas Athene R. Jakobi
Love M. Bovet
Mercury G. Türk
Valletto C. Högman
Concerto Vocale, R. Jacobs (4/91) (HARM) Ⓓ [3] **HMC90 1330/2**
(4/91) (HARM) ⊟ [3] **HMC40 1330/2**
N. Stanchiev, B. Christoff, Bulgarian RSO, E. Gracis (Seneca's aria) (FORL) Ⓓ **UCD16651**
A Dio Rome; Disprezzata Regina F. Von Stade, Scottish CO, R. Leppard (r1984) (ERAT) Ⓓ **4509-98504-2**
Adagiati Poppea; Pur ti miro M. van der Sluis, A. Köhler, Lautten Compagney (r1993) (CAPR) Ⓓ **10 470**
Adagiati Poppea; Eri già tutta mia R. Jacobs, K. Junghänel (r1985) (5/87) (HARM) Ⓓ **HMA190 1183**
Coronation M. Ewing, D. Bailey, LPO, R. Leppard (CAST) ▣ **CVI2071**
Disprezzata Regina G. Laurens, L. Pianca (r1991) (TELD) Ⓓ **4509-91181-2**
Excs Concerto Vocale, R. Jacobs (r1990) (HARM) Ⓓ **HMP390 806**
Oblivion soave E. Pinza, F. Kitzinger (r1940) (9/93) (RCA) Ⓓ **09026 61245-2**
Pur ti miro M. László, Richard Lewis, RPO, J. Pritchard (r1963) (6/94) (EMI) Ⓓ **CDH5 65072-2**
Pur ti muro, pur ti godo Concerto Vocale (HARM) Ⓓ **HMC90 1129**
(HARM) ⊟ **HMC40 1129**
Sinfonia Lautten Compagney (r1993) (CAPR) Ⓓ **10 470**

L' Orfeo– favola in musica (1607—Mantua) (Lib. Striggio)
Orfeo P. Huttenlocher
Euridice D. Turban
Music; Hope T. Schmidt
Messenger; Prosperina G. Linos
Nymph S. Calabro
Charon H. Franzen
Pluto W. Gröschel
Apollo R. Hermann
Shepherd I P. Keller
Shepherd II; Spirit I F. Araiza
Shepherd III; Spirit II R. Hartmann
Shepherd IV C. Boesch
Zurich Op Monteverdi Ens, N. Harnoncourt, J-P. Ponnelle (DECC) ◐ **071 103-1DH**
(DECC) ▣ **071 103-3DH**
Orfeo G. Quilico
Euridice; Hope; Echo A. Michael
Messenger C. Watkinson
Nymph S. Whittingham
Pluto; Charon F. Voutsinos
Apollo E. Tappy
Music C. Alliot-Lugaz
Prosperina D. Borst
Shepherd I; Spirit I F. Le Roux
Shepherd II; Spirit II G. de Mey
Shepherd III H. Ledroit
Chapelle Royale Ch, Lyon Op Orch, M. Corboz (r1985) (ERAT) Ⓓ [2] **4509-96958-2**
Orfeo E. Tappy
Euridice M. Schwartz
Music W. Staempfli
Messenger L. Sarti
Nymph Y. Perrin
Hope M. Conrad
Charon; Spirit II F. Loup
Prosperine J. Bise
Pluto J. Staempfli
Shepherd I; Apollo T. Altmeyer
Shepherd II V. Girod
Shepherd III; Spirit III P. Huttenlocher
Spirit I O. Dufour
Lausanne Voc Ens, Lausanne Instr Ens, M. Corboz (r1968) (ERAT) Ⓓ [2] **4509-98531-2**
Orfeo L. Dale
Euridice; Music E. Ben-Nun
Messenger J. Larmore
Hope A. Scholl
Charon P. Gérimon
Prosperina B. Fink
Pluto H. Peeters
Apollo N. Rivenq
Concerto Vocale, R. Jacobs (r1995) (HARM) Ⓓ [2] **HMC90 1553/4**
Orfeo L. Kozma
Euridice; Music R. Hansmann
Hope; Messenger C. Berberian
Prosperina; Nymph E. Katanosaka
Caronte N. Simkowsky
Plutone J. Villisech
Apollo; Shepherd IV; Spirit III M. van Egmond
Shepherd I G. Theuring
Shepherd II; Spirit I N. Rogers
Shepherd III; Spirit II K. Equiluz
VCM, N. Harnoncourt (7/85) (TELD) Ⓓ [2] **2292-42494-2**
Orfeo A. Rolfe Johnson
Euridice J. Baird
Music L. Dawson
Messenger A.S. von Otter
Nymph N. Argenta
Hope M. Nichols
Charon; Spirit III J. Tomlinson
Prosperina D. Montague
Plutone W. White
Echo; Shepherd I M. Tucker
Apollo; Shepherd II N. Robson
Shepherd III M. Chance
Shepherd IV S. Birchall
Spirit I H. Milner
Spirit II N. Robertson
Monteverdi Ch, EBS, His Majesties Sagbutts and Cornetts, J.E. Gardiner (12/87) (ARCH) Ⓓ [2] **419 250-2AH2**
Orfeo J.M. Ainsley
Euridice J. Gooding

Music; Messenger; Prosperina C. Bott
Nymph T. Bonner
Hope; Shepherd II C. Robson
Shepherd I; Spirit I; Echo; Apollo A. King
Shepherd III; Spirit II R. Evans
Plutone; Shepherd IV M. George
Caronte; Spirit III S. Grant
New London Consort, P. Pickett (r1991)
(2/93) (L'OI) ① [2] **433 545-2OH2**
Orfeo N. Rogers
Euridice P. Kwella
Music E. Kirkby
Proserpina J. Smith
Nymph H. Afonso
Hope C. Denley
Messenger G. Laurens
Apollo; Shepherd I M. Bolognesi
Shepherd II R. Covey-Crump
Shepherd III J. Potter
Shepherd IV; Pluto S. Varcoe
Charon D. Thomas
Spirit T. Edwards
Spirit G. Shaw
Chiaroscuro, London Cornett and Sackbutt Ens, T. Caudle, London Baroque, C. Medlam (r1983)
(4/94) (EMI) ① [2] **CMS7 64947-2**
Lasciate i monti; Vioeni Imeneo; Ecco pur ch'a voi ritorno; Moresca A. Rolfe Johnson, L. Dale, A. Woodrow, Monteverdi Ch, EBS, J.E. Gardiner (r1982) (ERAT) ① **2292-45984-2**
Lasciate i monti; Vieni Imeneo; Ecco pur ch'a voi ritorno; Moresca A. Rolfe Johnson, L. Dale, A. Woodrow, Monteverdi Ch, EBS, J. E. Gardiner (r1982) (ERAT) ① [5] **4509-99713-2**
Toccata J. Wallace, Philh, C. Warren-Green (trans Wallace) (NIMB) ① **NI5017**

Il **Ritorno d'Ulisse in Patria– opera: prologue and 3 acts (1641—Venice) (Lib. G. Badoaro)**
Ulisse; Humana fragilità S.O. Eliasson
Giove L. Anderko
Nettuno N. Simkowsky
Minerva; Amore R. Hansmann
Giunone; Servant; Fortuna M. Baker-Genovesi
Penelope N. Lerer
Telemaco K. Hansen
Antino; Tempo W. Wyatt
Pisandro K. Equiluz
Anfinomo P. Esswood
Eurimaco N. Rogers
Eumete M. van Egmond
Iro M. Dickie
Ericlea A-M. Mühle
Junge Kantorei, VCM, N. Harnoncourt (r1971)
(TELD) ① [3] **2292-42496-2**
Di misera Regina (Lamento di Penelope) E. Tubb, Consort of Musicke, A. Rooley
(4/88) (IMP) ① **PCD881**

MOORE, Douglas S(tuart) *(1893–1969) USA*

Carry Nation– opera: 2 acts (1966—Lawrence) (Lib. W N Jayme)
Carry Nation B. Wolff
Father A. Voketaitis
Mother E. Faull
Charles J. Patrick
Caretaker J. Bittner
Preacher E. Pierson
NYC Op Chor, NYC Op Orch, S. Krachmalnick
(7/90) (BAY) ① [2] **BCD-1012/3**

MORAN, John *(20th Cent) USA*

The **Manson Family– opera: 3 acts (1990—New York) (Lib. cpsr)**
Catherine Share R. Sortomme
Jack Lord, as The Prosecutor I. Pop
Lynette Fromme T. Roche
Susan D. Atkins P. Snell
Charles Manson J. Moran
Courtroom Host C. Lane
The Judge B. McGrath
Voice of Defense R. Greenawalt
Ens
(PNT) ① **432 967-2PTH**

MORAN, Robert *(b 1937) USA*

Desert of Roses– opera (1982)
EXCERPTS: 1. Movement 1; 2. I can go? I can go to my father?; 3. Movement 3; 4. Look into my eyes; 5. Movement 5.
1-5. J. West, Piano Circus Band, C. Smith
(8/92) (ARGO) ① **436 128-2ZH**

The **Dracula Diary– opera: one act (1994—Houston) (Lib. James Skofield)**
EXCERPTS: 1. Prologue: The Confessional; 2. The Convent; 3. The Singing Lesson; 4. The Nightmare; 5. The Rehearsal; 6. The Doctor/The Dressing Room; 7. The Gypsy; 8. The Dracula Diary; 9. The Murder; 10. The Party; 11. The Confessional.
Angela; Nemesis L. Knoop
Impresario J. Maddalena
Monk; The Tenor; Menippus R. Very
Confessor; Singing Master; Doctor; Apparition J. S. Sikon
Mother Superior; Courtier; Maid; Zorina; Party Guest J. Grove
Couriter; Party Guest M. Chioldi
Houston Op Studio, W. Holmquist (r1994)
(CATA) ① **09026 62638-2**

MORENO TORROBA, Federico *(1891–1982) Spain*

La **Chulapona– zarzuela (1934—Madrid)**
Noche madrileña P. Domingo, ROHO, J. Barker (pp1988) (9/89) (EMI) ① **CDC7 49811-2**
Tienes razón, amigo P. Domingo, Barcelona SO, G. Navarro (ACAN) ① **49 390**

Luisa Fernanda– zarzuela (1932—Madrid)
EXCERPTS: 1. De este apacible rincón; 2. Caballero del alto plumero; 3. Bien venidos, los vareadores.
Luisa Fernanda T. Tourné
Carolina E. Alsina
Vidal R. Cesari
Javier P. Lavirgen
Rosita J. Bermejo
Mariana A. Fernandez
Nogales P. Tamayo
Anibal J.R. Henche
Bizco A. Curros
Padre Lucas S. Videras
Don Florito V. Larrea
Captain R. Campos
Hispavox Lyric Chor, Madrid Concerts Orch, F. Moreno Torroba
(10/92) (HISP) ① **CDZ7 67329-2**
Coro de Vareadores P. Domingo, chor, Madrid SO, E. G. Asensio (pp1991)
(11/92) (IMP) ① **MCD45**
Los vareadores P. Domingo, Miami SO, E. Kohn (pp1991) (IMP) ① **MCD43**
1. P. Domingo, Barcelona SO, G. Navarro
(ACAN) ① **49 390**
1, 2. P. Domingo, Austrian RSO, G. Navarro
(SONY) ① **MK39210**
3. P. Domingo, Madrid Zarzuela Chor, Madrid SO, M. Moreno-Buendia (r1987)
(1/89) (EMI) ① **CDC7 49148-2**

Maravilla– zarzuela (1941) (Lib A Quintero & J M Arozamena)
Amor, vida de mi vida P. Domingo, Madrid SO, M. Moreno-Buendia (EMI) ① **CDM7 64359-2**
Amor, vida de mi Vida P. Domingo, Los Angeles PO, Z. Mehta (pp1994)
(TELD) OO **4509-96200-5**
Amor, vida de mi Vida P. Domingo, Los Angeles PO, Z. Mehta (pp1994)
(TELD) ◘ **4509-96200-8**
Amor, vida de mi vida P. Domingo, Madrid SO, M. Moreno-Buendia (r1987)
(1/89) (EMI) ① **CDC7 49148-2**
Amor, vida de mi Vida P. Domingo, Los Angeles PO, Z. Mehta (pp1994)
(12/94) (TELD) ① **4509-96200-2**

(12/94) (TELD) ⊙ **4509-96200-1** ▭ **4509-96200-4**

MOREY

Le **Vallière– opera**
Ja, du allein J. Schmidt, orch, F. Weissmann (r1933: Ger) (EMI) ① [2] **CHS7 64673-2**

MORLACCHI, Francesco *(1784–1841) Italy*

Il **Nuovo barbiere di Siviglia– opera (4 acts) (1816—Dresden) (Lib. Petrosellini)**
Giusto cielo!... Buona sera M. Hill Smith, K. John, P. Guy-Bromley, J. Best, R. Smythe, Philh, D. Parry (10/90) (OPRA) ① [3] **ORCH103**

MOSCA, Luigi *(1775–1824) Italy*

Le **Bestie in uomini– opera (2 acts) (1812—Milan) (Lib. Anelli)**
Mentre guardo, oh Dio! me stessa D. Montague, G. Mitchell Ch, Philh, D. Parry
(10/90) (OPRA) ① [3] **ORCH103**

MOURET, Jean-Joseph *(1682–1738) France*

Les **amours de Ragonde ou La soirée de village– comédie lyrique: 3 acts (1714 rev 1742—Sceaux) (Lib. Mericault-Destouches)**
Ragonde M. Verschaeve
Colin J-P. Fouchécourt
Colette S. Marin-Degor
Lucas J-L. Bindi
Mathurine N. Rime
Thibault G. Ragon
Blaise J-L. Serre
Musiciens du Louvre, M. Minkowski
(12/92) (ERAT) ① **2292-45823-2**

MOZART, Wolfgang Amadeus *(1756–1791) Austria*

K–Numbers used in L. von Koechel's W.A. Mozarts Werke

Apollo et Hyacinthus– Latin intermezzo, K38 (1767—Salzburg) (Wds. ?P. F. Widl)
EXCERPTS: 1. Overture. ACT ONE: 2. Amice! iam parata sunt omnia; 3. Numen o Latonium!; 4a. Heu me! perimus!; 4b. Saepe terrent Numina; 5a. Ah nate! vera loqueris; 5b. Iam pastor Apollo. ACT TWO: 6a. Amare numquid filia; 6b. Laetari, iocari; 7a. Rex! de salute filii est actum; 7b. En! duos conspicis; 8a. Heu! Numen! ecce!; 8b. Discede crudelis!. ACT THREE: 9a. Non est - Quis ergo; 9b. Ut navis in aequore luxuriante; 10a. Quocumque me converto; 10b. Natus cadit; 11a. Rex! me redire cogit; 11b. Tandem post turbida fulmina.
Apollo C. Günther
Hyacinthus S. Pratschske
Oebalus M. Schäfer
Melia C. Fliegner
Zephyrus P. Cieslewicz
Nice Baroque Ens, G. Schmidt-Gaden
(11/91) (PAVA) ① [2] **ADW7236/7**
Apollo C. Wulkopf
Hyacinthus E. Mathis
Oebalus A. Rolfe Johnson
Melia A. Auger
Zephyrus H. Schwarz
Salzburg Chbr Ch, Salzburg Mozarteum Orch, L. Hager (r1981)
(11/91) (PHIL) ① [2] **422 526-2PME2**
1. Prague CO, O. Vlček (r1989)
(SUPR) ① [2] **11 1166-2**

Ascanio in Alba– festa teatrale: 2 acts, K111 (1771—Milan) (Lib. G. Parini)
EXCERPTS: 1a. Overture. PART ONE: 1b. Andante grazioso; 2. Di te più amabile; 3a. Geni, Grazie, ed Amori; 3b. L'ombra de' rami tuoi; 4a. Ma la Ninfa gentil; 4b. Di te più amabile; 5a. Perché tacer degg'io?; 5b. Cara, lontano ancora; 6. Venga, de' sommi Eroi; 7a. Ma qual canto risona?; 7b. Venga, de' sommi Eroi; 8a. Ma tu, chi sei, che ignoto qui t'aggiri fra noi?; 8b. Se il labbro più non dice; 9a. Quanto soavi al core de la tua stirpe; 9b. Hai di Diana il core; 10a. Oh, generosa Diva; 10b. Venga, de' sommi Eroi; 11a. Di propria man la Dea a voi la donerà; 11b. Venga, de' sommi Eroi; 12a. Oh mia gloria, oh mia cura; 12b. Per la gioia in questo seno; 13a. Misera! Che farò?; 13b. Si, ma d'un altro amore; 14a. Ah no, Silvia t'inganni; 14b. Come è felice stato; 15a. Silvia, mira, che il sole omai s'avanza; 15b. Venga, de' sommi Eroi; 16a. Cielo! Che vidi mai?; 16b. Ah di sì nobil alma; 17a. Un'altra prova a te mirar conviene; 17b. Al chiaror di que' bei rai; 18. Di te più amabile, né

Dea maggiore. PART TWO: 19a. Star lontana non so; 19b. Spiega il desìo; 20. Già l'ore sen volano; 21a. Cerco di loco in loco; 21b. Silvia, ove sei?; 21c. Dal tuo gentil sembiante; 22a. Ahimè! Che veggio mai?; 22b. Al mio ben mi veggio avanti; 23a. Ferma, aspetta, ove vai?; 23b. Infelici affetti miei; 24a. Anima grande; 24b. Che strano evento; 25a. Ahi la crudel; 25b. Torna mio bene, ascolta; 26. Venga, de' sommi Eroi; 27a. Che strana meraviglia; 27b. Sento, che il cor mi dice; 28a. Si, Padre, alfin mi taccia; 28b. Scendi, celeste Venere; 29a. Ma, s'allontani almen; 29b. No, non possiamo vivere; 30a. Ecco ingombran l'altare; 30b. Scendi, celeste Venere; 31a. Invoca, o figlia; 31b. Ah caro sposo, oh Dio!; 32a. Eccovi al fin di vostre pene; 32b. Che bel piacer io sento; 33a. Ah chi nodi più forti; 33b. Alma Dea, tutto il mondo governa.

Ascanio G. Jahn
Silvia E. Gabry
Aceste W. Krenn
Venere S. Mangelsdorff
Fauno R. van Vrooman
Salzburg Fest Chbr Ch, Salzburg Mozarteum Orch, L. Hager (pp1967)
(FOYE) ① [2] **2-CF2032**

Ascanio M. Chance
Silvia J. Feldman
Aceste H. Milner
Venere L. Windsor
Fauno R. Mannion
Paris Sorbonne Uni Ch, Concerto Armonico, J. Grimbert (r1990)
(NAXO) ① [2] **8 660040/1**

Ascanio A. Baltsa
Silvia E. Mathis
Aceste P. Schreier
Venere L. Sukis
Fauno A. Auger
Salzburg Chbr Ch, Salzburg Mozarteum Orch, L. Hager (r1976)
(1/92) (PHIL) ① [3] **422 530-2PME3**

1a Staatskapelle Dresden, H. Vonk
(CAPR) ① **10 070**
(CAPR) ⊟ **CC27 086**
1a Prague CO, O. Vlček (r1989)
(SUPR) ① [2] **11 1166-2**
1a Staatskapelle Dresden, H. Vonk
(10/91) (CAPR) ① [3] **10 809**
5a, 5b, 16b J. Kowalski, Berlin RSO, H. Fricke
(CAPR) ◘ **80 416**
5a, 5b, 16b J. Kowalski, Berlin RSO, H. Fricke
(CAPR) **OO 70 416**
5a, 5b, 16b J. Kowalski, Berlin RSO, H. Fricke
(10/92) (CAPR) ① **10 416**
5b A. Raunig, Vienna Amadeus Ens, W. Kobera
(DIVE) ① **DIV31013**

Bastien und Bastienne– Singspiel: 1 act, K50/K46b (1768—Vienna) (Lib. F. W. Weiskern & J. A. Sachtner)

EXCERPTS: 1. Overture; 2. Mein liebster Freund hat mich verlassen; 3. Ich geh jetzt auf die Weide; 4. Entry of Colas; 5. Befraget mich ein zartes Kind; 6. Wenn mein Bastien einst im Scherze; 7. Würd ich auch, wie manche Buhlerinnen; 8. Auf den Rat, den ich gegeben; 9. Grossen Dank dir abzustatten; 10. Geh! du sagst mir eine Fabel; 11. Diggi, daggi; 12. Meiner Liebsten schöne Wangen; 13. Er war mir sonst treu und ergeben; 14. Geh hin! - Ich will mich in die Stadt begeben; 15. Dein Trotz vermehrt sich durch mein Leiden?; 16. Geh! Herz von Flandern!; 17. Kinder! Kinder.

Bastien V. Cole
Bastienne E. Gruberová
Colas L. Polgár
F. Liszt CO, R. Leppard (r1989)
(1/91) (SONY) ① **SK45855**

Bastien G. Nigl
Bastienne D. Orieschnig
Colas D. Busch
Vienna SO, U.C. Harrer (r1986)
(5/92) (PHIL) ① **422 527-2PME**

1. ECO, L. Hager (r1989)
(NOVA) ① **150 041-2**
1. Prague CO, O. Vlček (r1988)
(SUPR) ① [2] **11 1166-2**

La **Clemenza di Tito– opera seria: 2 acts, K621 (1791—Prague) (Lib. C. Mazzolà)**

EXCERPTS: 1. Overture. ACT ONE: 2. Come ti piace, imponi; 3. Deh se piacer; 4. Deh prendi un dolce amplesso; 5. Marcia; 6. Serbate, o Dei custodi; 7. Del più sublime soglio; 8. Ah perdona al primo affetto; 9. Ah, se fosse; 10. Parto, parto; 11. Vengo... aspettate... 12a. Oh Dei, che smania è questa; 12b. Deh conservate, oh Dei! (Finale). ACT TWO: 13. Torna di Tito a lato; 14. Se al volto mai ti senti; 15. Ah grazie si rendano; 16. Tardi s'avvede; 17. Tu fosti tradito; 18. Quello di Tito è il volto; 19. Deh per questo istante; 20. Se all'impero; 21. S'altro che lagrime; 22a. Ecco il punto, oh Vitellia; 22b. Non più di fiori; 23. Che del ciel; 24a. Ma che giorno è mai questo?; 24b. Tu, è ver, m'assolvi Augusto (Finale).

Cpte P. Bernold, BWV Trio (r1993; arr fl qt)
(SCHW) ① **315762**

Tito P. Schreier
Vitellia J. Varady
Sesto T. Berganza
Annio M. Schiml
Servilia E. Mathis
Publio T. Adam
Leipzig Rad Chor, Staatskapelle Dresden, K. Böhm (r1979)
(12/90) (DG) ① [2] **429 878-2GX2**

Tito A. Rolfe Johnson
Vitellia J. Varady
Sesto A.S. von Otter
Annio C. Robbin
Servilia S. McNair
Publio C. Hauptmann
Monteverdi Ch, EBS, J.E. Gardiner (pp1991)
(12/91) (ARCH) ① [2] **431 806-2AH2**

Tito S. Burrows
Vitellia J. Baker
Sesto Y. Minton
Annio F. von Stade
Servilia L. Popp
Publio R. Lloyd
ROH Chor, ROHO, Colin Davis (r1976)
(4/92) (PHIL) ① [2] **422 544-2PME2**

Tito P. Langridge
Vitellia L. Popp
Sesto A. Murray
Annio D. Ziegler
Servilia R. Ziesak
Publio L. Polgár
Zurich Op Hse Chor, Zurich Op Orch, N. Harnoncourt (r1993)
(5/94) (TELD) ① [2] **4509-90857-2**

Tito U. Heilmann
Vitellia D. Jones
Sesto C. Bartoli
Annio D. Montague
Servillia B. Bonney
Publio G. Cachemaille
AAM Chor, AAM, C. Hogwood (r1993)
(3/95) (L'OI) ① [2] **444 131-2OHO2**

Tito G. Winbergh
Vitellia C. Vaness
Sesto D. Ziegler
Annio M. Senn
Servilia C. Barbaux
Publio L. Polgár
Vienna St Op Chor, VPO, R. Muti (pp1988)
(10/95) (EMI) ① [2] **CDS5 55489-2**

1. Staatskapelle Dresden, H. Vonk
(CAPR) ① **10 070**
(CAPR) ⊟ **CC27 086**
1. ECO, L. Hager (r1989)
(NOVA) ① **150 041-2**
1. New Philh, O. Klemperer
(EMI) ① **CDM7 63619-2**
1. BPO, J. Horenstein (r1929)
(KOCH) ① **37054-2**
1. Zurich Tonhalle Orch, J. Krips
(ADES) ① **13225-2**
1. LPO, B. Haitink (PHIL) ① **432 512-2PSL**
1. Prague CO, O. Vlček (r1988)
(SUPR) ① [2] **11 1166-2**
1. ASMF, N. Marriner
(EMI) **OO DCC7 47014-5**
1. Sinfonia Varsovia, E. Krivine (r1990)
(DENO) ① **CO-75372**
1. ASMF, N. Marriner (EMI) ◘ **MDC7 47014-8**
1. Concertgebouw, Zurich Op Orch, Zurich Op Hse Mozart Orch, VCM, N. Harnoncourt
(TELD) ① **4509-95523-2**
1. Basle SO, M. Atzmon (r1973/4)
(RCA) ① **74321 29237-2**
1. ASMF, N. Marriner
(4/84) (EMI) ① **CDC7 47014-2**
1. Staatskapelle Dresden, H. Vonk
(10/91) (CAPR) ① [3] **10 809**
1. Tafelmusik, B. Weil
(5/92) (SONY) ① **SK46695**
1, 10. A. Ulbrich, Berlin RSO, J. Märkl (r1991)
(SCHW) ① [2] **312682**
1, 21. K. Te Kanawa, WNO Orch, C. Mackerras
(10/91) (EMI) ◖ **LDA9 91242-1**
(10/91) (EMI) ▣ **MVC9 91242-3**
1-3, 5, 8-10. Amadeus Ens, J. Rudel (arr Triebensee: Woodwind Octet and Bass)
(MUSM) ① [5] **67118-2**
1-3, 7, 8. Budapest Wind Ens, K. Berkes (arr Triebensee) (QUIN) ⊟ **QUI40 3008**
1-5, 7-11, 12b Consortium Classicum, D. Klöcker (arr various: wind ens) (BAYE) ① **BR100073**
5. Banda Classica, C. Siegmann (arr Triebensee) (SCHW) ① **310110**
6, 15. Zurich Op Hse Chor, Zurich Op Orch, N. Harnoncourt (r1993) (TELD) ① **4509-97505-2**
7, 9, 20. J. Dickie, Capella Istropolitana, J. Wildner (12/91) (NAXO) ① **8 550383**
9. G. Sabbatini, NHK Chbr Sols, R. Paternostro (pp1990) (CAPR) ① [3] **10 810**
9. G. Sabbatini, NHK Chbr Sols, R. Paternostro (pp1990) (10/91) (CAPR) ① **10 348**
9. P. Domingo, Munich RO, E. Kohn
(3/92) (EMI) ① **CDC7 54329-2**
9. L. Simoneau, Vienna SO, B. Paumgartner (r1954) (11/94) (PHIL) ① [2] **438 953-2PM2**
10. I. Siebert, D. Klöcker, South-West German RSO, K. Donath (SCHW) ① **314018**
10. L. Marshall, LSO, E. Pedrazzoli
(CBC) ① **PSCD2001**
10. A. Raunig, Vienna Amadeus Ens, W. Kobera
(DIVE) ① **DIV31013**
10. M. Horne, ROHO, H. Lewis (r1964)
(DECC) ① **440 415-2DM**
10. J. Baker, Scottish CO, R. Leppard (r1984)
(ERAT) ① **4509-98497-2**
10. C. Bartoli, L. Schatzberger, AAM, C. Hogwood (r1991-2) (DECC) ① **448 300-2DH**
(DECC) ⊟ **448 300-4DH**
10. B. Fassbaender, Stuttgart RSO, H. Graf
(11/86) (ORFE) ① **C096841A**
10. M. Lipovšek, Munich RO, G. Patanè
(6/90) (ORFE) ① **C179891A**
10. D. Soffel, Swedish CO, M. Liljefors (pp1988)
(4/93) (CPRI) ① **CAP21428**
10. T. Berganza, Vienna St Op Orch, I. Kertész (r1966/7) (4/93) (DECC) ① **421 899-2DA**
10. T. Berganza, LSO, J. Pritchard (r1962)
(4/93) (DECC) ① **421 899-2DA**
10. E. Ritchie, V. Soames, J. Purvis (r1992; arr Bergmann) (3/94) (CLRI) ① **CC0006**
10. M. Price, ECO, J. Lockhart (r1973)
(5/95) (RCA) ① [2] **09026 61635-2**
10, 19. J. Larmore, Lausanne CO, J. López-Cobos (r1994) (TELD) ① **4509-96800-2**
10, 19, 22b C. Bartoli, Vienna CO, G. Fischer
(12/91) (DECC) ① **430 513-2DH**
(DECC) ⊟ **430 513-4DH**
10, 20, 22b L. Popp, A. Murray, P. Langridge, Zurich Op Orch, N. Harnoncourt (r1993)
(TELD) ① **4509-97507-2**
10, 22a, 22b F. von Stade, Rotterdam PO, E. de Waart (PHIL) ① **420 084-2PH**
14. K. Te Kanawa, LSO, Colin Davis
(3/84) (PHIL) ① **411 148-2PH**
19. C. Bartoli, G. Fischer (pp1991)
(11/92) (DECC) ◖ **071 141-1DH**
(11/92) (DECC) ▣ **071 141-3DH**
20. R. Giménez, ROHO, B. Wordsworth
(NIMB) ① **NI5300**
20. E. Haefliger, ECO, J.E. Dähler
(CLAV) ① **CD50-8305**
20. P. Seiffert, Munich RO, J. Kout (r1992-3)
(RCA) ① **09026 61214-2**
20. J. Protschka, Munich RO, K. Eichhorn
(3/89) (CAPR) ① **10 109**
20. R. Blake, LSO, N. McGegan
(3/89) (ARAB) ① **Z6598**
(3/89) (ARAB) ⊟ **ABQC6598**
20. L. Simoneau, Paris Champs-Élysées Orch, A. Jouve (r1955)
(3/91) (EMI) ① [2] **CHS7 63715-2**
22b L. Popp, Munich RO, L. Slatkin (r1983)
(8/84) (EMI) ① **CDC7 47019-2**
22b C. Studer, ASMF, N. Marriner
(9/94) (PHIL) ① **442 410-2PM**

Così fan tutte– opera buffa: 2 acts, K588 (1790—Vienna) (Lib. L. da Ponte)

EXCERPTS: 1. Overture. ACT 1: 2. La mia Dorabella; 3a. Fuor la spada!; 3b. È la fede; 4a. Scioccherie di poeti!; 4b. Una bella serenata; 5. Ah guarda, sorella; 6. Vorrei dir; 7. Sento, o Dio; 8. Al fato dan legge; 9. Bella vita militar!; 10. Di scrivermi; 11. Soave sia il vento; 12. Smanie implacabili; 13. In uomini; 14. Alla bella Despinetta; 15a. Temerari! Sortite fuori di questo loco!; 15b. Come scoglio; 16. Non siate ritrosi; 17. Rivolgete a lui lo sguardo (alternative aria for

No. 16); 18. E voi ridete?; 19. Un' aura amorosa; 20. Ah, che tutta in momento; 21. Dove son? Che loco è questo?. ACT 2: 22a. Andate là; 22b. Una donna a quindici anni; 23a. Sorella, cosa dici?; 23b. Prenderò quel brunettino; 24. Secondate, aurette amiche; 25. La mano a me date; 26. Il core vi dono; 27a. Barbara! Perchè fuggi?; 27b. Ah, lo veggio; 28a. Ei parte...senti; 28b. Per pietà, ben mio; 29. Donne mie, la fate a tanti; 30a. In qual fiero contrasto; 30b. Tradito, schernito dal perfido cor; 31. È Amore un ladroncello; 32. Fra gli amplessi; 33. Tutti accusan le donne; 34. Richiamati, da regio contrordine; 35. Fortunato l'uom che prende (Finale).

Fiordiligi H. Döse
Dorabella S. Lindenstrand
Despina D. Perriers
Ferrando A. Austin
Guglielmo T. Allen
Don Alfonso F. Petri
Glyndebourne Fest Chor, LPO, J. Pritchard, A. Slack (pp1975)
(IMP) ▣ **SL2002**

Fiordiligi D. Dessì
Dorabella D. Ziegler
Despina A. Scarabelli
Ferrando J. Kundlák
Gugliemo A. Corbelli
Don Alfonso C. Desderi
La Scala Chor, La Scala Orch, R. Muti, M. Hampe
(5/90) (CAST) ▣ **CVI2062**

Fiordiligi A.C. Biel
Dorabella M. Höglind
Despina U. Severin
Ferrando L. Tibell
Guglielmo M. Lindén
Don Alfonso E. Florimo
Drottningholm Court Th Chor, Drottningholm Court Th Orch, A. Östman, T. Olofsson
(MCEG) ▣ **VVD475**

Fiordiligi R. El Hefni
Dorabella A. El Sharqawi
Despina A. Radi
Ferrando H. Kami
Guglielmo R. Zaidan
Don Alfonso R. Al Wakeel
Silesian Chbr Music Chor, Polish Nat RO, Y. El Sisi (r1988: Arabic)
(OIA) ① [3] **SADEK1001**

Fiordiligi A.C. Biel
Dorabella M. Höglind
Despina U. Severin
Ferrando L. Tibell
Guglielmo M. Lindén
Don Alfonso E. Florimo
Drottningholm Court Th Chor, Drottningholm Court Th Orch, A. Östman, W. Decker
(PHIL) ◐ [2] **070 416-1PHE2**

Fiordiligi K. Te Kanawa
Dorabella F. von Stade
Despina T. Stratas
Ferrando D. Rendall
Guglielmo P. Huttenlocher
Don Alfonso J. Bastin
Rhine Op Chor, Strasbourg PO, A. Lombard (r1977)
(ERAT) ① [3] **2292-45683-2**

Fiordiligi L. della Casa
Dorabella C. Ludwig
Despina E. Loose
Ferrando A. Dermota
Guglielmo E. Kunz
Don Alfonso P. Schoeffler
Vienna St Op Chor, VPO, K. Böhm (r1955)
(DECC) ① [2] **417 185-2DMO2**

Fiordiligi G. Janowitz
Dorabella B. Fassbaender
Despina R. Grist
Ferrando P. Schreier
Guglielmo H. Prey
Don Alfonso D. Fischer-Dieskau
Vienna St Op Chor, VPO, K. Böhm (pp1972)
(FOYE) ① [2] **2-CF2066**

Fiordiligi M. Caballé
Dorabella J. Baker
Despina I. Cotrubas
Ferrando N. Gedda
Guglielmo W. Ganzarolli
Don Alfonso R. Van Allan
ROH Chor, ROHO, Colin Davis
(4/87) (PHIL) ① [3] **416 633-2PH3**

Fiordiligi C. Vaness
Dorabella D. Ziegler
Despina L. Watson
Ferrando J. Aler
Guglielmo D. Duesing
Don Alfonso C. Desderi
Glyndebourne Fest Chor, LPO, B. Haitink (r1986)
(7/87) (EMI) ① [3] **CDS7 47727-8**

Fiordiligi L. Price
Dorabella T. Troyanos
Despina J. Raskin
Ferrando G. Shirley
Guglielmo S. Milnes
Don Alfonso E. Flagello
Ambrosian Op Chor, New Philh, E. Leinsdorf (r1967)
(9/88) (RCA) ① [3] **GD86677**

Fiordiligi E. Schwarzkopf
Dorabella C. Ludwig
Despina H. Steffek
Ferrando Alfredo Kraus
Guglielmo G. Taddei
Don Alfonso W. Berry
Philh Chor, Philh, K. Böhm (r1962)
(11/88) (EMI) ① [3] **CMS7 69330-2**

Fiordiligi E. Schwarzkopf
Dorabella N. Merriman
Despina L. Otto
Ferrando L. Simoneau
Guglielmo R. Panerai
Don Alfonso S. Bruscantini
Chor, Philh, H. von Karajan (r1954)
(12/88) (EMI) ① [3] **CHS7 69635-2**

Fiordiligi L. Cuberli
Dorabella C. Bartoli
Despina J. Rodgers
Ferrando K. Streit
Guglielmo F. Furlanetto
Don Alfonso J. Tomlinson
Berlin RIAS Chbr Ch, BPO, D. Barenboim (r1989)
(10/90) (ERAT) ① [3] **2292-45475-2**

Fiordiligi K. Mattila
Dorabella A.S. von Otter
Despina E. Szmytka
Ferrando F. Araiza
Guglielmo T. Allen
Don Alfonso J. Van Dam
Ambrosian Op Chor, ASMF, N. Marriner (r1988-9)
(11/90) (PHIL) ① [3] **422 381-2PH3**

Fiordiligi G. Janowitz
Dorabella B. Fassbaender
Despina R. Grist
Ferrando P. Schreier
Guglielmo H. Prey
Don Alfonso R. Panerai
Vienna St Op Chor, VPO, K. Böhm (pp1974)
(12/90) (DG) ① [2] **429 874-2GX2**

Fiordiligi J. Borowska
Dorabella R. Yachmi-Caucig
Despina P. Coles
Ferrando J. Dickie
Guglielmo A. Martin
Don Alfonso P. Mikuláš
Slovak Phil Chor, Capella Istropolitana, J. Wildner (r1990)
(3/91) (NAXO) ① [3] **8 660008/10**

Fiordiligi I. Souez
Dorabella L. Helletsgruber
Despina I. Eisinger
Ferrando H. Nash
Guglielmo W. Domgraf-Fassbaender
Don Alfonso J. Brownlee
Glyndebourne Fest Chor, Glyndebourne Fest Orch, F. Busch (r1935)
(3/91) (PEAR) ① [3] **GEMMCDS9406**

Fiordiligi I. Souez
Dorabella L. Helletsgruber
Despina I. Eisinger
Ferrando H. Nash
Guglielmo W. Domgraf-Fassbaender
Don Alfonso J. Brownlee
Glyndebourne Fest Chor, Glyndebourne Fest Orch, F. Busch (r1935)
(9/91) (EMI) ① [2] **CHS7 63864-2**

Fiordiligi M. Price
Dorabella Y. Minton
Despina L. Popp
Ferrando L. Alva
Guglielmo G. Evans
Don Alfonso H. Sotin
John Alldis Ch, New Philh, O. Klemperer
(9/91) (EMI) ① [3] **CMS7 63845-2**

Fiordiligi C. Margiono
Dorabella D. Ziegler
Despina A. Steiger
Ferrando D. van der Walt
Guglielmo G. Cachemaille
Don Alfonso T. Hampson
Netherlands Op Chor, Concertgebouw, N. Harnoncourt (r1991)
(11/91) (TELD) ① [3] **9031-71381-2**

Fiordiligi M. Caballé
Dorabella J. Baker
Despina I. Cotrubas
Ferrando N. Gedda
Guglielmo W. Ganzarolli
Don Alfonso R. Van Allan
ROH Chor, ROHO, Colin Davis (r1974)
(1/92) (PHIL) ① [3] **422 542-2PME3**
(PHIL) ⊟ **422 542-4PX2**

Fiordiligi A.C. Antonacci
Dorabella M. Bacelli
Despina L. Cherici
Ferrando R. Decker
Guglielmo A. Dohmen
Don Alfonso S. Bruscantini
Marchigiano V. Bellini Lyric Chor, Marchigiano PO, G. Kuhn (pp1990)
(10/92) (ORFE) ① [3] **C243913F**

Fiordiligi S. Isokoski
Dorabella M. Groop
Despina N. Argenta
Ferrando M. Schäfer
Guglielmo P. Vollestad
H. Claessens
Petite Bande Chor, Petite Bande, S. Kuijken (pp1992)
(2/94) (ACCE) ① [3] **ACC9296/8D**

Fiordiligi A. Roocroft
Dorabella R. Mannion
Despina E. James
Ferrando R. Trost
Guglielmo R. Gilfry
Don Alfonso C. Nicolai
Monteverdi Ch, EBS, J. E. Gardiner, P. Mumford (pp1992)
(2/94) (ARCH) ◐ [2] **072 436-1AH2**
(2/94) (ARCH) ▣ [2] **072 436-3AH2**

Fiordiligi A. Roocroft
Dorabella R. Mannion
Despina E. James
Ferrando R. Trost
Guglielmo R. Gilfry
Don Alfonso C. Feller
Monteverdi Ch, EBS, J. E. Gardiner (pp1992)
(2/94) (ARCH) ① [3] **437 829-2AH3**

Fiordiligi F. Lott
Dorabella M. McLaughlin
Despina N. Focile
Ferrando J. Hadley
Guglielmo A. Corbelli
Don Alfonso G. Cachemaille
Edinburgh Fest Chor, Scottish CO, C. Mackerras (r1993)
(4/94) (TELA) ① [3] **CD80360**

Fiordiligi T. Stich-Randall
Dorabella I. Malaniuk
Despina G. Sciutti
Ferrando W. Kmentt
Guglielmo W. Berry
Don Alfonso D. Ernster
Vienna St Op Chor, Vienna SO, R. Moralt (r1956)
(10/94) (PHIL) ① [3] **438 678-2PM3**

Fiordiligi I. Seefried
Dorabella D. Hermann
Despina L. Otto
Ferrando A. Dermota
Guglielmo E. Kunz
Don Alfonso P. Schoeffler
Vienna St Op Chor, VPO, K. Böhm (pp1954)
(2/95) (ORFE) ① [2] **C357942I**

1. BPO, D. Barenboim (pp1989)
(SONY) ▣ **SHV498602**

1. Staatskapelle Dresden, H. Vonk
(CAPR) ① **10 070**
(CAPR) ⊟ **CC27 086**

1. Berlin Charlottenburg Op Orch, A. von Zemlinsky (r1928) (SCHW) ① **310037**

1. Staatskapelle Dresden, H. Vonk
(LASE) ① **15 622**
(LASE) ⊟ **79 622**

1. ECO, L. Hager (r1989)
(NOVA) ① **150 041-2**

1. New Philh, O. Klemperer
(EMI) ① **CDM7 63619-2**

1. Zurich Tonhalle Orch, J. Krips
(ADES) ① **13225-2**

1. London Fest Orch, K. Redel
(INTR) ① **409 015-2**

1. LPO, B. Haitink (PHIL) ① **432 512-2PSL**

1. Prague CO, O. Vlček (r1988) (SUPR) Ⓓ [2] **11 1166-2**
1. ASMF, N. Marriner (EMI) ⓄⓄ **DCC7 47014-5**
1. Paris RSO, L. Bertrand (ROSE) Ⓓ **3229**
1. Sinfonia Varsovia, E. Krivine (r1990) (DENO) Ⓓ **CO-75372**
1. ASMF, N. Marriner (EMI) ◉ **MDC7 47014-8**
1. Glyndebourne Fest Orch, F. Busch (r1935) (EMI) Ⓓ [2] **CHS5 65058-2**
1. Concertgebouw, Zurich Op Orch, Zurich Op Hse Mozart Orch, VCM, N. Harnoncourt (TELD) Ⓓ **4509-95523-2**
1. RPO, Colin Davis (r c1961) (EMI) Ⓓ [2] **CES5 68533-2**
1. Basle SO, M. Atzmon (r1973/4) (RCA) Ⓓ **74321 29237-2**
1. ASMF, N. Marriner (4/84) (EMI) Ⓓ **CDC7 47014-2**
1. Staatskapelle Dresden, H. Vonk (10/91) (CAPR) Ⓓ [3] **10 809**
1. Tafelmusik, B. Weil (5/92) (SONY) Ⓓ **SK46695**
1. LSO, J. Krips (r1951) (7/95) (DECC) Ⓓ [2] **443 530-2LF2**
1, 11-13, 15b, 19, 22b, 23b, 26, 28a, 28b, 29, 30b, 31, 33-35. L. Cuberli, C. Bartoli, J. Rodgers, K. Streit, F. Furlanetto, J. Tomlinson, Berlin RIAS Chbr Ch, BPO, D. Barenboim (r1989) (ERAT) Ⓓ **4509-94821-2**
1, 16, 29. J. Van Dam, Paris Orch Ens, J-P. Wallez (pp) (5/88) (NOVA) Ⓓ **150 014-2**
1, 2, 3a, 3b, 4a, 4b, 5, 9, 11-14, 15b, 16, 18, 19, 21(pt), 23a, 23b, 26, 29, 32, 33, 35. G. Janowitz, B. Fassbaender, R. Grist, P. Schreier, H. Prey, R. Panerai, Vienna St Op Chor, VPO, K. Böhm (pp1974) (BELA) Ⓓ **450 114-2**
(BELA) ▭ **450 114-4**
1, 2, 3a, 3b, 4a, 4b, 11-14, 15b, 16, 18, 19 22b, 23a, 23b, 25, 28a, 28b, 29, 32, 33, 35. A. Roocroft, R. Mannion, E. James, R. Trost, R. Gilfry, C. Nicolai, EBS, J. E. Gardiner (pp1992) (ARCH) Ⓓ **437 994-2AH**
1, 2, 3b, 4b, 11-14, 15b, 16, 18, 19, 22b, 23b, 25, 26, 28a, 28b, 29, 32, 33, 35. E. Schwarzkopf, N. Merriman, L. Otto, L. Simoneau, R. Panerai, S. Bruscantini, Philh, H. von Karajan (r1954) (EMIN) Ⓓ **CD-EMX2211**
(EMIN) ▭ **TC-EMX2211**
1, 2, 4b, 5, 6, 11-14, 15b, 16, 18, 19, 22b, 23b, 25, 28b, 29, 32-35. C. Margiono, D. Ziegler, G. Cachemaille, D. van der Walt, A. Steiger, T. Hampson, Netherlands Op Chor, Concertgebouw, N. Harnoncourt (TELD) Ⓓ **9031-76455-2**
1, 2, 5-7, 9-13, 15b, 16, 18, 19, 22b, 25, 26, 27b, 28b, 29, 30b, 31-33. F. Lott, M. McLaughlin, N. Focile, J. Hadley, A. Corbelli, G. Cachemaille, Edinburgh Fest Chor, Scottish CO, C. Mackerras (r1993) (TELA) Ⓓ **CD80399**
1, 3b, 5, 9, 19, 23b-25. M. Bourgue Wind Ens (trans J. Wendt) (PIER) Ⓓ **PV787033**
1, 3b, 5, 9, 19, 22b, 23b, 26, 31, 35. Amadeus Ens, J. Rudel (arr Wendt: Woodwinds and Bass) (MUSM) Ⓓ [5] **67118-2**
1, 3b, 5, 9, 19, 23b, 24, 35. M. Bourgue Wind Ens (trans Wendt) (PIER) Ⓓ **PV730005**
1, 4b, 5, 11, 14, 19, 23b, 24, 28b, 31, 33(pt) Linos Ens (r1992; arr Tarkmann) (CAPR) Ⓓ **10 494**
2, 3a, 3b, 4a, 4b P. Schreier, H. Prey, D. Fischer-Dieskau, VPO, K. Böhm (pp1972) (ORFE) Ⓓ **C335931A**
2, 3a, 3b, 4a, 4b, 5, 7, 10, 11, 15b, 23b, 26, 28a, 28b, 32. S. Jurinac, B. Thebom, Richard Lewis, E. Kunz, M. Borriello, Glyndebourne Fest Orch, F. Busch (r1950: inc rehearsals for 23b,28b,32) (6/94) (TEST) Ⓓ **SBT1040**
4b H. Nash, W. Domgraf-Fassbaender, J. Brownlee, Glyndebourne Fest Orch, F. Busch (r1935) (6/94) (EMI) Ⓓ **CDH5 65072-2**
5. G. Janowitz, B. Fassbaender, VPO, K. Böhm (pp1972) (ORFE) Ⓓ **C394301B**
5, 11. K. Te Kanawa, F. von Stade, J. Bastin, Strasbourg PO, A. Lombard (ERAT) Ⓓ **2292-45797-2**
(ERAT) ▭ **2292-45797-4**
5, 15b, 28a, 28b S. Jurinac, B. Thebom, Glyndebourne Fest Orch, F. Busch (r1950) (1/90) (EMI) Ⓓ **CDH7 63199-2**
5, 23b, 25, 26, 32. A. Martin, D. Robin, Capella Istropolitana, J. Wildner (12/91) (NAXO) Ⓓ **8 550435**
7. I. Seefried, C. Ludwig, A. Dermota, E. Kunz, P. Schoeffler, VPO, K. Böhm (pp1956) (ORFE) Ⓓ **C394201B**
9. Netherlands Op Chor, Concertgebouw, N. Harnoncourt (r1991) (TELD) Ⓓ **4509-97505-2**
11. L. Popp, B. Fassbaender, T. Krause, Vienna Haydn Orch, I. Kertész (DECC) Ⓓ **433 066-2DWO**
(DECC) ▭ **433 066-4DWO**
11. Classic Buskers (arr Copley) (SEAV) Ⓓ **CD007365**
11. M. Marshall, A. Baltsa, J. Van Dam, VPO, R. Muti (CFP) Ⓓ **CD-CFP4612**
(CFP) ▭ **TC-CFP4612**
11. L. Popp, B. Fassbaender, T. Krause, Vienna Haydn Orch, I. Kertész (r1971) (DECC) Ⓓ **433 440-2DA**
(DECC) ▭ **433 440-4DA**
11. L. Popp, B. Fassbaender, T. Krause, Vienna Haydn Orch, I. Kertész (r1971) (DECC) Ⓓ **440 947-2DH**
(DECC) ▭ **440 947-4DH**
11. T. Hampson, C. Margiono, D. Ziegler, Concertgebouw, N. Harnoncourt (r1991) (TELD) Ⓓ **4509-98824-2**
11. L. Popp, B. Fassbaender, T. Krause, Vienna Op Orch, I. Kertész (6/91) (DECC) Ⓓ **430 498-2DWO**
(6/91) (DECC) ▭ **430 498-4DWO**
11. C. Vaness, D. Ziegler, C. Desderi, LPO, B. Haitink (r1986) (6/94) (EMI) Ⓓ **CDH5 65072-2**
11, 19. Swingle Sngrs (arr Rathbone) (VIRG) Ⓓ **VC7 59617-2**
11, 19. M. Marshall, A. Baltsa, J. Van Dam, F. Araiza, VPO, R. Muti (7/91) (EMIL) Ⓓ **CDZ7 67015-2**
12. J. Larmore, Lausanne CO, J. López-Cobos (r1994) (TELD) Ⓓ **4509-96800-2**
12. M. Lipovšek, Munich RO, G. Patanè (6/90) (ORFE) Ⓓ **C179891A**
12. T. Berganza, LPO, G. Solti (r1973) (4/93) (DECC) Ⓓ **421 899-2DA**
12, 31. F. Von Stade, Strasbourg PO, A. Lombard (r c1978) (ERAT) Ⓓ **4509-98504-2**
13. M. McLaughlin, VPO, James Levine (DG) ▭ **439 153-4GMA**
13. K. Battle, VPO, R. Muti (pp1982) (EMI) Ⓓ **CDC5 55095-2**
13. L. Bori, Victor Orch, Rosario Bourdon (r1922) (ROMO) Ⓓ [2] **81016-2**
13. C. Bartoli, G. Fischer (pp1991) (11/92) (DECC) ● **071 141-1DH**
(11/92) (DECC) ▣ **071 141-3DH**
13, 15a, b C. Bartoli, Vienna CO, G. Fischer (r1993) (DECC) Ⓓ **448 300-2DH**
(DECC) ▭ **448 300-4DH**
13, 15a, 15b, 28a, 28b C. Bartoli, Vienna CO, G. Fischer (r1993) (11/94) (DECC) Ⓓ **443 452-2DH**
(11/94) (DECC) ▭ **443 452-4DH**
13, 22b A. Noni, Philh, W. Susskind (r1950) (6/94) (TEST) Ⓓ **SBT1040**
15a, 15b C. Taha, Berlin RSO, J. Märkl (r1991) (SCHW) Ⓓ [2] **312682**
15a, 15b A. Winska, Warsaw PO, W. Michniewski (r1990) (PAVA) Ⓓ **ADW7289**
15a, 15b C. Studer, ASMF, N. Marriner (9/94) (PHIL) Ⓓ **442 410-2PM**
15a, 15b A. Roocroft, LPO, F. Welser-Möst (10/94) (EMI) Ⓓ **CDC5 55090-2**
(10/94) (EMI) ▭ **EL5 55090-4**
15a, 15b, 28a, 28b, 31. T. Berganza, LSO, J. Pritchard (r1962) (4/93) (DECC) Ⓓ **421 899-2DA**
15a, 15b, 28a, 28b I. Seefried, Vienna SO, F. Leitner (r1953) (9/93) (DG) Ⓓ [2] **437 677-2GDO2**
15b E. Schwarzkopf, Philh, K. Böhm (EMIN) Ⓓ **CD-EMX9519**
(EMIN) ▭ **TC-EMX2099**
15b A. Tomowa-Sintow, Bulgarian RSO, V. Stefanov (CAPR) Ⓓ [3] **10 810**
15b K. Te Kanawa, Rhine Op Chor, Strasbourg PO, A. Lombard (ERAT) Ⓓ **4509-91715-2**
(ERAT) ▭ **4509-91715-4**
15b H. Schymberg, Stockholm Royal Orch, N. Grevillius (r1946) (ALTN) Ⓓ **CDAN3**
15b E. Schwarzkopf, Philh, K. Böhm (r1962) (EMI) Ⓓ **CDM5 65577-2**
15b A. Rothenberger, VPO, S. Ozawa (pp1969) (ORFE) Ⓓ **C394301B**
15b L. Popp, Munich RO, L. Slatkin (r1983) (8/84) (EMI) Ⓓ **CDC7 47019-2**
15b C. Vaness, LPO, B. Haitink (7/91) (EMIL) Ⓓ **CDZ7 67015-2**
15b K. Te Kanawa, Strasbourg PO, A. Lombard (r1972) (4/94) (RCA) Ⓓ [6] **09026 61580-2(8)**
16, 17, 29. H. Prey, Salzburg Mozarteum Orch, B. Weil (5/88) (DENO) Ⓓ **CO-1741**
17, 29. N. De Carolis, Venice and Padua CO, B. Giuranna (CLAV) Ⓓ **CD50-9120**
17, 29. F. Furlanetto, Vienna SO, I. Marin (3/92) (SONY) Ⓓ **SK47192**
19. A. Dermota, Berlin St Op Orch, A. Rother (Ger: r1950s) (PREI) Ⓓ **90022**
19. G. Sabbatini, NHK Chbr Sols, R. Paternostro (pp1990) (CAPR) Ⓓ [3] **10 810**
19. H. Buff-Giessen, anon (r1906: Ger) (SYMP) Ⓓ **SYMCD1085**
19. S. Milnes, orch (EURO) Ⓓ **VD69256**
19. P. Schreier, orch (EURO) Ⓓ **VD69256**
19. H. Roswaenge, Philh Hungarica, Z. Rozsnyai (pp1959) (PREI) Ⓓ **90103**
19. Alfredo Kraus, Philh, K. Böhm (EMI) Ⓓ **CDM7 64359-2**
19. J. Aler, LPO, B. Haitink (CFP) Ⓓ **CD-CFP4606**
(CFP) ▭ **TC-CFP4606**
19. E. Haefliger, ECO, J.E. Dähler (CLAV) Ⓓ **CD50-8305**
19. D. van der Walt, Concertgebouw, N. Harnoncourt (r1991) (TELD) Ⓓ **4509-97507-2**
19. R. Blake, LSO, N. McGegan (3/89) (ARAB) Ⓓ **Z6598**
(3/89) (ARAB) ▭ **ABQC6598**
19. Alfredo Kraus, Philh, K. Böhm (10/89) (EMI) Ⓓ **CDM7 63104-2**
19. H. Roswaenge, Berlin St Op Orch, F. Weissmann (Ger: r1928) (5/90) (PEAR) Ⓓ **GEMMCD9394**
19. G. Sabbatini, NHK Chbr Sols, R. Paternostro (pp1990) (10/91) (CAPR) Ⓓ **10 348**
19. H. Roswaenge, orch (r1928: Ger) (2/92) (PREI) Ⓓ [2] **89201**
19. L. Pavarotti, James Levine, B. Large (2/92) (DECC) ● **071 119-1DH**
(2/92) (DECC) ▣ **071 119-3DH**
19. P. Domingo, Munich RO, E. Kohn (r1991) (6/94) (EMI) Ⓓ **CDC5 55017-2**
19. L. Simoneau, Vienna SO, B. Paumgartner (r1954) (11/94) (PHIL) Ⓓ [2] **438 953-2PM2**
19. H. Nash, Glyndebourne Fest Orch, F. Busch (r1935) (2/95) (DUTT) Ⓓ **CDLX7012**
19. W. Ludwig, Berlin St Op Orch, B. Seidler-Winkler (r1936: Ger) (7/95) (PREI) Ⓓ **89088**
19, 27b, 30a, 30b J. Dickie, Capella Istropolitana, J. Wildner (12/91) (NAXO) Ⓓ **8 550383**
19, 29. J. Patzak, K. Kronenberg, Bavarian St Op Orch, C. Krauss (pp1941: Ger) (SCHW) Ⓓ [2] **314712**
19, 30a, 30b R. Giménez, ROHO, B. Wordsworth (NIMB) Ⓓ **NI5300**
19, 30a, 30b J. Protschka, Munich RO, K. Eichhorn (3/89) (CAPR) Ⓓ **10 109**
19, 30a, 30b P. Domingo, Munich RO, E. Kohn (3/92) (EMI) Ⓓ **CDC7 54329-2**
21. M. Marshall, A. Baltsa, K. Battle, F. Araiza, J. Morris, J. Van Dam, VPO, R. Muti (pp1982) (ORFE) Ⓓ **C394301B**
22b L. Schöne, Berlin St Op Orch, F. Zweig (r c1928: Ger) (1/94) (CLUB) Ⓓ **CL99-020**
23a, 23b E. Schwarzkopf, C. Ludwig, VPO, K. Böhm (pp1958) (ORFE) Ⓓ **C394201B**
23a, 23b I. Seefried, N. Merriman, BPO, E. Jochum (r1962) (9/93) (DG) Ⓓ [2] **437 677-2GDO2**
23a, 23b, 26. C. Ludwig, I. Seefried, R. Panerai, VPO, K. Böhm (pp1959) (ORFE) Ⓓ **C365941A**
23b J. Zoon, H. de Vries, London Studio SO (arr Vrijens) (PHIL) Ⓓ **438 940-2PH**
23b, 24, 30b, 31. Budapest Wind Ens, K. Berkes (arr Wendt) (QUIN) ▭ **QUI40 3008**
26. E. Kunz, B. Thebom, Glyndebourne Fest Orch, F. Busch (r1950) (6/94) (EMI) Ⓓ **CDH5 65072-2**
28a, 28b A. Roocroft, ASMF, N. Marriner (EMI) Ⓓ **CDC5 55396-2**
(EMI) ▭ **EL5 55396-4**
28a, 28b K. Te Kanawa, LSO, Colin Davis (3/84) (PHIL) Ⓓ **411 148-2PH**
28a, 28b A. Tomowa-Sintow, Munich RO, P. Sommer (11/86) (ORFE) Ⓓ **C106841A**
28b E. Steber, Columbia SO, B. Walter (r1953) (SONY) Ⓓ [3] **SM3K47211**
28b E. Schwarzkopf, Philh, H. von Karajan (r1954) (12/90) (EMI) Ⓓ **CDM7 63657-2**
29. G. Laperrière, Three Rivers SO, G. Bellemare (r1992) (CBC) Ⓓ **SMCD5127**
29. G. Taddei, Philh, K. Böhm (7/91) (EMIL) Ⓓ **CDZ7 67015-2**
29. M. Rothmüller, Philh, J. Robertson (r1950) (4/92) (EMI) Ⓓ [7] **CHS7 69741-2(4)**
29. G. Hüsch, Berlin St Op Orch, H.U. Müller (r1939: Ger) (3/94) (PREI) Ⓓ **89071**

30b G. Morino, Warmia Nat PO, B. Amaducci
(10/90) (NUOV) Ⓓ **6851**
31. C. Bartoli, Vienna CO, G. Fischer
(12/91) (DECC) Ⓓ **430 513-2DH**
(DECC) ▭ **430 513-4DH**
32. I. Souez, H. Nash, Glyndebourne Fest Orch, F. Busch (r1935) (MMOI) Ⓓ **CDMOIR406**
(MMOI) ▭ **CMOIR406**
32. P. Domingo, C. Vaness, Munich RO, E. Kohn
(3/92) (EMI) Ⓓ **CDC7 54329-2**
32. I. Souez, H. Nash, orch, C. Raybould (r1934)
(2/95) (DUTT) Ⓓ **CDLX7012**

Don Giovanni– dramma giocoso: 2 acts, K527 (1787—Prague) (Lib. L. da Ponte)

EXCERPTS: 1a. Overture. ACT ONE: 1b. Notte e giorno; 2a. Ma qual mai s'offre; 2b. Fuggi, crudele; 3. Ah, chi mi dice; 4. Madamina il catalogo; 5. Giovinette, che fate all' amore; 6. Ho capito; 7. Là ci darem la mano; 8. Ah, fuggi il traditor; 9. Non ti fidar; 10a. Don Ottavio, son morta; 10b. Or sai chi l'onore; 10c. Dalla sua pace; 11. Finch' han dal vino; 12. Batti, batti; 13. Presto, presto; 13a. Minuet. ACT TWO: 14. Eh via, buffone; 15. Ah, taci in giusto core; 16. Deh! vieni alla finestra; 17a. Metà di voi; 17b. Se un uom e una ragazza; 18. Vedrai, carino; 19. Sola sola; 20. Ah pietà; 21. Il mio tesoro; 22. Per queste tue manine; 23a. In quali eccessi; 23b. Mi tradì quell' alma ingrata; 24. O statua gentilissima; 25a. Crudele! Ah no mio bene; 25b. Non mi dir; 26. Gia la mensa è preparata; 27. Ah, dovè il perfido?.

Don Giovanni B. Luxon
Donna Anna H. Branisteanu
Donna Elvira R. Yakar
Zerlina E. Gale
Don Ottavio L. Goeke
Leporello S. Dean
Masetto J. Rawnsley
Commendatore P. Thau
Glyndebourne Fest Chor, LPO, B. Haitink, P. Hall (pp1977)
(IMP) ▣ **SL2001**

Don Giovanni H. Hagegård
Donna Anna H. Döse
Donna Elvira B. Nordin
Zerlina A. Soldh
Don Ottavio G. Winbergh
Leporello E. Saedén
Masetto T. Wallström
Commendatore B. Rundgren
Drottningholm Baroque Ens, Drottningholm Court Th Chor, A. Östman, G. Järvefelt
(5/90) (MCEG) ▣ **VVD342**

Don Giovanni R. Raimondi
Donna Anna E. Moser
Donna Elvira K. Te Kanawa
Zerlina T. Berganza
Don Ottavio K. Riegel
Leporello J. Van Dam
Massetto M. King
Commendatore J. Macurdy
Paris Op Chor, Paris Op Orch, L. Maazel
(2/92) (ARTI) ▣ **ART014**

Don Giovanni C. Siepi
Donna Anna E. Grümmer
Donna Elvira L. della Casa
Zerlina E. Berger
Don Ottavio A. Dermota
Leporello O. Edelmann
Masetto W. Berry
Commendatore D. Ernster
Vienna St Op Chor, VPO, W. Furtwängler, H. Graf (r/pp1954)
(7/95) (DG) ▣ **072 440-3GH**

Don Giovanni T. Allen
Donna Anna E. Gruberová
Donna Elvira A. Murray
Zerlina S. Mentzer
Don Ottavio F. Araiza
Leporello C. Desderi
Masetto N. de Carolis
Commendatore S. Kopčák
La Scala Chor, La Scala Orch, R. Muti, G. Strehler
(5/90) (CAST) ▣ **CVI2061**

Don Giovanni E. Pinza
Donna Anna R. Bampton
Donna Elvira J. Novotná
Zerlina B. Sayão
Don Ottavio C. Kullman
Leporello A. Kipnis
Masetto M. Harrell
Commendatore N. Cordon
NY Met Op Chor, NY Met Op Orch, B. Walter (pp1942)
(MEMO) Ⓓ [3] **HR4225/7**

Don Giovanni N. Ghiaurov
Donna Anna G. Janowitz
Donna Elvira T. Zylis-Gara
Zerlina M. Freni
Don Ottavio Alfredo Kraus
Leporello G. Evans
Masetto R. Panerai
Commendatore V. von Halem
Vienna St Op Chor, VPO, H. von Karajan (pp1969)
(MEMO) Ⓓ [3] **HR4362/4**

Don Giovanni A. Dohmen
Donna Anna M. Pick-Hieronimi
Donna Elvira S. Isokoski
Zerlina B. Balleys
Don Ottavio S. MacAllister
Leporello P. Spagnoli
Masetto; Commendatore A. Kohn
Ludwigshafen Th Chor, Vienna Academy Orch, M. Haselböck (pp1991)
(NOVA) Ⓓ [3] **150 084-2**

Don Giovanni E. Perry
Donna Anna D. Labelle
Donna Elvira L. Hunt
Zerlina A.L. Zhu
Don Ottavio Carroll Freeman
Leporello H. Perry
Masetto E. James
Commendatore J. Patterson
A. Schoenberg Ch, VPO, C. Smith, P. Sellars
(DECC) ◖ [2] **071 411-1DH2**

Don Giovanni A. Campo
Donna Anna T. Stich-Randall
Donna Elvira S. Danco
Zerlina A. Moffo
Don Ottavio N. Gedda
Leporello M. Cortis
Masetto A. Vessières
Commendatore R. Arié
Aix-en-Provence Fest Chor, Paris Cons, H. Rosbaud (r1956)
(EMI) Ⓓ [3] **CMS7 64372-2**

Don Giovanni R. Al Wakeel
Donna Anna N. Allouba
Donna Elvira N. Erian
Zerlina T.S. El Din
Don Ottavio S. Bedair
Leporello R. Zaidan
Masetto; Commendatore C. Rathl
Silesian Chbr Music Chor, Polish Nat RO, Y. El Sisi (r1989: Arabic)
(OIA) Ⓓ [3] **SADEK1003**

Don Giovanni A. Titus
Donna Anna J. Varady
Donna Elvira A. Auger
Zerlina E. Mathis
Don Ottavio T. Moser
Leporello R. Panerai
Masetto R. Scholze
Commendatore J-H. Rootering
Bavarian Rad Chor, BRSO, R. Kubelík (r1985)
(RCA) Ⓓ [3] **74321 25284-2**

Don Giovanni T. Allen
Donna Anna C. Vaness
Donna Elvira M. Ewing
Zerlina E. Gale
Don Ottavio K. Lewis
Leporello R. Van Allan
Masetto J. Rawnsley
Commendatore D. Kavrakos
Glyndebourne Fest Chor, LPO, B. Haitink
(12/84) (EMI) Ⓓ [3] **CDS7 47037-8**

Don Giovanni S. Ramey
Donna Anna A. Tomowa-Sintow
Donna Elvira A. Baltsa
Zerlina K. Battle
Don Ottavio G. Winbergh
Leporello F. Furlanello
Masetto A. Malta
Commendatore P. Burchuladze
Berlin Deutsche Op Chor, BPO, H. von Karajan (r1985)
(10/86) (DG) Ⓓ [3] **419 179-2GH3**

Don Giovanni R. Raimondi
Donna Anna E. Moser
Donna Elvira K. Te Kanawa
Zerlina T. Berganza
Don Ottavio K. Riegel
Leporello J. Van Dam
Masetto M. King
Commendatore J. Macurdy
Paris Op Chor, Paris Op Orch, L. Maazel (r1979)
(11/87) (SONY) Ⓓ [3] **M3K35192**

Don Giovanni E. Waechter
Donna Anna J. Sutherland
Donna Elvira E. Schwarzkopf
Zerlina G. Sciutti
Don Ottavio L. Alva
Leporello G. Taddei
Masetto P. Cappuccilli
Commendatore G. Frick
Philh Chor, Philh, C.M. Giulini (r1959)
(12/87) (EMI) Ⓓ [3] **CDS7 47260-8**

Don Giovanni J. Brownlee
Donna Anna I. Souez
Donna Elvira L. Helletsgruber
Zerlina A. Mildmay
Don Ottavio K. von Pataky
Leporello S. Baccaloni
Masetto Roy Henderson
Commendatore D. Franklin
Glyndebourne Fest Chor, Glyndebourne Fest Orch, F. Busch (r1936)
(3/89) (EMI) Ⓓ [3] **CHS7 61030-2**

Don Giovanni C. Siepi
Donna Anna S. Danco
Donna Elvira L. della Casa
Zerlina H. Gueden
Don Ottavio A. Dermota
Leporello F. Corena
Masetto W. Berry
Commendatore K. Böhme
Vienna St Op Chor, VPO, J. Krips (r1955)
(9/89) (DECC) Ⓓ [3] **411 626-2DM3**

Don Giovanni T. Hampson
Donna Anna E. Gruberová
Donna Elvira R. Alexander
Zerlina B. Bonney
Don Ottavio H-P. Blochwitz
Leporello L. Polgár
Masetto A. Scharinger
Commendatore R. Holl
Netherlands Op Chor, Concertgebouw, N. Harnoncourt (r1988)
(3/90) (TELD) Ⓓ [3] **2292-44184-2**

Don Giovanni D. Fischer-Dieskau
Donna Anna B. Nilsson
Donna Elvira M. Arroyo
Zerlina R. Grist
Don Ottavio P. Schreier
Leporello E. Flagello
Masetto A. Mariotti
Commendatore M. Talvela
Czech Sngrs Chor, Prague Nat Th Orch, K. Böhm (r1967)
(12/90) (DG) Ⓓ [3] **429 870-2GX3**

Don Giovanni H. Hagegård
Donna Anna A. Auger
Donna Elvira D. Jones
Zerlina B. Bonney
Don Ottavio N. van der Meel
Leporello G. Cachemaille
Masetto B. Terfel
Commendatore K. Sigmundsson
Drottningholm Court Th Orch, Drottningholm Court Th Orch, A. Östman (r1989)
(12/90) (L'OI) Ⓓ [3] **425 943-2OH3**

Don Giovanni J. Brownlee
Donna Anna I. Souez
Donna Elvira L. Helletsgruber
Zerlina A. Mildmay
Don Ottavio K. von Pataky
Leporello S. Baccaloni
Masetto Roy Henderson
Commendatore D. Franklin
Glyndebourne Fest Chor, Glyndebourne Fest Orch, F. Busch (r1936)
(3/91) (PEAR) Ⓓ [3] **GEMMCDS9369**

Don Giovanni B. Weikl
Donna Anna M. Price
Donna Elvira S. Sass
Zerlina L. Popp
Don Ottavio S. Burrows
Leporello G. Bacquier
Masetto A. Sramek
Commendatore K. Moll
London Op Chor, LPO, G. Solti
(3/91) (DECC) Ⓓ [3] **425 169-2DM3**

Don Giovanni C. Siepi
Donna Anna E. Grümmer
Donna Elvira E. Schwarzkopf
Zerlina E. Berger
Don Ottavio A. Dermota
Leporello O. Edelmann
Masetto W. Berry

Commendatore D. Ernster
Vienna St Op Chor, VPO, W. Furtwängler (pp1954)
(7/91) (EMI) ① [3] **CHS7 63860-2**
Don Giovanni W. Shimell
Donna Anna C. Studer
Donna Elvira C. Vaness
Zerlina S. Mentzer
Don Ottavio F. Lopardo
Leporello S. Ramey
Masetto N. de Carolis
Commendatore J-H. Rootering
Vienna St Op Concert Ch, VPO, R. Muti
(7/91) (EMI) ① [3] **CDS7 54255-2**
Don Giovanni N. Ghiaurov
Donna Anna C. Watson
Donna Elvira C. Ludwig
Zerlina M. Freni
Don Ottavio N. Gedda
Leporello W. Berry
Masetto P. Montarsolo
Commendatore F. Crass
New Philh Chor, New Philh, O. Klemperer (r1966)
(9/91) (EMI) ① [3] **CMS7 63841-2**
Don Giovanni I. Wixell
Donna Anna M. Arroyo
Donna Elvira K. Te Kanawa
Zerlina M. Freni
Don Ottavio S. Burrows
Leporello W. Ganzarolli
Masetto R. Van Allan
Commendatore L. Roni
ROH Chor, ROHO, Colin Davis (r1973)
(1/92) (PHIL) ① [3] **422 541-2PME3**
(PHIL) ▭ **422 541-4PX2**
Don Giovanni T. Allen
Donna Anna S. Sweet
Donna Elvira K. Mattila
Zerlina M. McLaughlin
Don Ottavio F. Araiza
Leporello S. Alaimo
Masetto C. Otelli
Commendatore R. Lloyd
Ambrosian Op Chor, ASMF, N. Marriner (r1990)
(1/92) (PHIL) ① [3] **432 129-2PH3**
Don Giovanni F. Furlanetto
Donna Anna L. Cuberli
Donna Elvira W. Meier
Zerlina J. Rodgers
Don Ottavio U. Heilmann
Leporello J. Tomlinson
Masetto M. Pertusi
Commendatore M. Salminen
Berlin RIAS Chbr Ch, BPO, D. Barenboim
(3/92) (ERAT) ① [3] **2292-45588-2**
Don Giovanni A. Dohmen
Donna Anna F. Pedaci
Donna Elvira I. Galgani
Zerlina B. Lucarini
Don Ottavio M. Berti
Leporello E. Turco
Masetto A. Cauli
Commendatore A. Silvestrelli
Marchigiano V. Bellini Lyric Chor, Marchigiano PO, G. Kuhn (pp1991)
(5/92) (SCHW) ① [3] **314088**
Don Giovanni R. Bruson
Donna Anna S. Ghazarian
Donna Elvira G. Ottenthal
Zerlina P. Pace
Don Ottavio G. Sabbatini
Leporello N. Ghiuselev
Masetto S. Rinaldi-Miliani
Commendatore F. de Grandis
Cologne Rad Chor, Cologne RSO, N. Järvi (r1990)
(5/92) (CHAN) ① [3] **CHAN8920/2**
Don Giovanni S. Ramey
Donna Anna A. Tomowa-Sintow
Donna Elvira J. Varady
Zerlina K. Battle
Don Ottavio G. Winbergh
Leporello F. Furlanetto
Masetto A. Malta
Commendatore P. Burchuladze
Vienna St Op Chor, VPO, H. von Karajan, U. Märkle (pp1987)
(4/93) (SONY) ● [2] **SLV46383**
(4/93) (SONY) ▣ **SHV46383**
Don Giovanni D. Fischer-Dieskau
Donna Anna S. Jurinac
Donna Elvira M. Stader
Zerlina I. Seefried
Don Ottavio E. Haefliger
Leporello K.C. Kohn
Masetto I. Sardi
Commendatore W. Kreppel
Berlin RIAS Chbr Ch, Berlin RSO, F. Fricsay (r1958)
(5/93) (DG) ① [3] **437 341-2GDO3**
Don Giovanni H. Hagegård
Donna Anna H. Döse
Donna Elvira B. Nordin
Zerlina A. Soldh
Don Ottavio G. Winbergh
Leporello E. Saedén
Masetto T. Wallström
Commendatore B. Rundgren
Drottningholm Court Th Chor, Drottningholm Court Th Orch, A. Östman, G. Järvefelt (r1987)
(9/93) (PHIL) ● **070 419-1PHE2**
Don Giovanni A. Schmidt
Donna Anna A. Halgrimson
Donna Elvira L. Dawson
Zerlina N. Argenta
Don Ottavio J.M. Ainsley
Leporello G. Yurisch
Masetto G. Finley
Commendatore A. Miles
London Schütz Ch, LCP, R. Norrington (r1992)
(10/93) (EMI) ① [3] **CDS7 54859-2**
Don Giovanni G. London
Donna Anna H. Zadek
Donna Elvira S. Jurinac
Zerlina G. Sciutti
Don Ottavio L. Simoneau
Leporello W. Berry
Masetto E. Waechter
Commendatore L. Weber
Vienna Chbr Ch, Vienna SO, R. Moralt (r1955)
(10/94) (PHIL) ① [3] **438 674-2PM3**
Don Giovanni C. Siepi
Donna Anna E. Grümmer
Donna Elvira L. della Casa
Zerlina R. Streich
Don Ottavio L. Simoneau
Leporello F. Corena
Masetto W. Berry
Commendatore G. Frick
Vienna St. Op. Chor, VPO, D. Mitropoulos (pp1956)
(11/94) (SONY) ① [3] **SM3K64263**
Don Giovanni R. Gilfry
Donna Anna L. Orgonášová
Donna Elvira C. Margiono
Zerlina E. James
Don Ottavio C. Prégardien
Leporello I. D'Arcangelo
Masetto J. Clarkson
Commendatore A. Silvestrelli
Monteverdi Ch, EBS, J. E. Gardiner (pp1994)
(8/95) (ARCH) ① [3] **445 870-2AH3**
L. Price, P. de Palma, orch
(EURO) ① **VD69256**
1a Staatskapelle Dresden, H. Vonk
(CAPR) ① **10 070**
(CAPR) ▭ **CC27 086**
1a Berlin St Op Orch, A. von Zemlinsky (r1928)
(SCHW) ① **310037**
1a Staatskapelle Dresden, H. Vonk
(LASE) ① **15 622**
(LASE) ▭ **79 622**
1a ECO, L. Hager (r1989)
(NOVA) ① **150 041-2**
1a New Philh, O. Klemperer
(EMI) ① **CDM7 63619-2**
1a Chicago SO, F. Reiner (RCA) ① **VD60484**
(RCA) ▭ **VK60484**
1a Staatskapelle Dresden, H. Vonk
(CAPR) ① [3] **10 810**
1a Horreaux-Trehard Duo (arr 2 gtrs)
(CALL) ① **CAL9218**
1a Zurich Tonhalle Orch, J. Krips
(ADES) ① **13225-2**
1a LPO, B. Haitink (PHIL) ① **432 512-2PSL**
1a Prague CO, O. Vlček (r1988)
(SUPR) ① [2] **11 1166-2**
1a Czech PO, K. Ančerl (pp1966)
(PRAG) ① **PR254 005**
1a RPO, Colin Davis (CFP) ① **CD-CFP4612**
(CFP) ▭ **TC-CFP4612**
1a ASMF, N. Marriner (concert ending Mozart)
(EMI) ◎ **DCC7 47014-5**
1a Sinfonia Varsovia, E. Krivine (r1990)
(DENO) ① **CO-75372**
1a ASMF, N. Marriner (concert ending Mozart)
(EMI) ✪ **MDC7 47014-8**
1a LPO, T. Beecham (r1939/40)
(PEAR) ① **GEMMCD9081**
1a Prague Virtuosi, O. Vlček (r1992)
(DINT) ① **DICD920201**
1a ROHO, Colin Davis (r1973)
(BELA) ① **461 001-2**
(BELA) ▭ **461 001-4**
1a Concertgebouw, Zurich Op Orch, Zurich Op Hse Mozart Orch, VCM, N. Harnoncourt
(TELD) ① **4509-95523-2**
1a RPO, Colin Davis (r c1961)
(EMI) ① [2] **CES5 68533-2**
1a Basle SO, M. Atzmon (r1973/4)
(RCA) ① **74321 29237-2**
1a ASMF, N. Marriner (concert ending Mozart)
(4/84) (EMI) ① **CDC7 47014-2**
1a Staatskapelle Dresden, H. Vonk
(10/91) (CAPR) ① [3] **10 809**
1a National PO, L. Stokowski
(4/92) (EMI) ① **CDM7 64140-2**
1a Tafelmusik, B. Weil
(5/92) (SONY) ① **SK46695**
1a LPO, T. Beecham (r1939/40)
(10/94) (DUTT) ① **CDLX7009**
1a LSO, J. Krips (r1951)
(7/95) (DECC) ① [2] **443 530-2LF2**
1a, 1b, 2a, 2b, 4, 7, 10a, 10b, 11, 12, 14, 16, 18, 21, 23a, 23b, 27. S. Milnes, J. Macurdy, A. Tomowa-Sintow, P. Schreier, T. Zylis-Gara, W. Berry, D. Duesing, E. Mathis, Vienna St Op Chor, VPO, K. Böhm (r1977)
(DG) ① **445 463-2GMH**
1a, 1b, 3, 4, 5, 7, 9, 10c, 11, 12, 13a, 14, 16, 18, 25b, 26. Amadeus Ens, J. Rudel (arr Triebensee: Wind Octet and Bass)
(MUSM) ① [5] **67118-2**
1a, 1b, 3-5, 7, 11, 13, 14, 16. M. Bourgue Wind Ens (trans J. Triebensee) (PIER) ① **PV787033**
1a, 1b, 3-5, 7, 10a-c, 11, 12, 14-16, 18, 19, 21, 23a, 23b, 25b T. Allen, S. Sweet, K. Mattila, M. McLaughlin, F. Araiza, S. Alaimo, C. Otelli, R. Lloyd, ASMF, N. Marriner (r1990)
(PHIL) ① **438 494-2PH**
1a, 1b, 3-5, 7, 11, 13, 14, 16. M. Bourgue Wind Ens (trans Triebensee) (PIER) ① **PV730005**
1a, 1b, 3-5, 7, 9, 10c, 11-16, 17a, 18, 22, 23b, 25b, 26. Athena Ens (r1980; trans wind band: Triebensee) (4/94) (CHAN) ① **CHAN6597**
1a, 1b, 3-7, 9, 10c, 11-16, 17a, 18, 22, 23b, 25b, 26. Mozart Wind Ens (arr. wind ens)
(ORFE) ① **C063841A**
1a, 1b, 4, 5, 7, 9, 10b, 10c, 11, 12, 16, 18, 21, 23b, 24, 25b, 27. F. Furlanetto, M. Salminen, L. Cuberli, U. Heilmann, W. Meier, J. Tomlinson, M.Pertusi, J. Rodgers, Berlin RIAS Chbr Ch, Berlin CO, D. Barenboim (r1991)
(ERAT) ① **4509-94823-2**
1a, 1b, 4, 5, 7, 10c, 11, 13, 16, 18, 23b, 25b Netherlands Wind Ens (arr 8 wind instr: Triebensee)
(12/91) (PHIL) ① [3] **422 545-2PME3**
1a, 4, 7, 10a-c, 11, 12, 13(pt), 15, 16, 21, 23a, 25b, 26(pt) E. Waechter, J. Sutherland, E. Schwarzkopf, L. Alva, G. Sciutti, G. Taddei, P. Cappuccilli, Philh Chor, Philh, C.M. Giulini (r1959) (10/89) (EMI) ▭ **EG763078-4**
1a, 4, 7, 10a-c, 11, 12, 13(pt), 15, 16, 18, 21, 23a, 23b, 25b, 26(pt) W. Shimell, S. Ramey, C. Studer, C. Vaness, F. Lopardo, S. Mentzer, N. de Carolis, VPO, R. Muti
(EMI) ① **CDC7 54323-2**
1a, 25a, 25b C. Studer, BPO, C. Abbado (pp1991) (SONY) ● **SLV46405**
(SONY) ▣ **SHV46405**
1b S. Baccaloni, Glyndebourne Fest Orch, F. Busch (r1936) (PEAR) ① **GEMMCD9122**
1b, 3-5, 10c, 11-16, 17a, 18, 23b, 25b, 27. Linos Ens (arr Wind Band; r1991) (CAPR) ① **10 492**
1b, 4, 5, 7, 11, 16. Budapest Wind Ens, K. Berkes (arr Triebensee)
(QUIN) ▭ **QUI40 3008**
2a, 2b F. Wunderlich, E. Grümmer, Berlin SO, H. Zanotelli (Ger) (EMI) ① [3] **CZS7 62993-2**
2a, 2b P. Domingo, C. Vaness, Munich RO, E. Kohn (3/92) (EMI) ① **CDC7 54329-2**
2a, 10a-c, 21, 23a, 26. C. Valletti, VPO, H. von Karajan (pp1960) (MEMO) ① [2] **HR4191/2**
2a, 10a, 10b, 25a, 25b L. Price, C. Valletti, Vienna St Op Chor, VPO, H. von Karajan (pp1960) (MEMO) ① [2] **HR4396/7**
3, 8, 23a, 23b L. Price, VPO, E. Leinsdorf (r1960) (DECC) ① **440 402-2DM**
4. K. Moll, Munich RO, K. Eichhorn (r1981: Ger)
(ORFE) ① **C009821A**
4. R. Bruson, NHK Chbr Sols, R. Paternostro (pp1990) (CAPR) ① [3] **10 810**
4. E. Pinza, NY Met Op Orch, B. Walter (r1946)
(SONY) ① [3] **SM3K47211**

4. S. Page, Czech PO, J. Bigg (with instr track for singing) (IMP) Ⓓ [2] **DPCD1015**
(IMP) ▭ **CIMPCD1015**
4. D. Maxwell, English Northern Philh, P. Daniel (r1992) (EMI) Ⓓ **CDC7 54785-2**
4. S. Page, Czech PO, J. Bigg (r1992) (IMP) Ⓓ **PCD1043**
4. G. Evans, SRO, B. Balkwill (r1966) (DECC) Ⓓ **443 380-2DM**
4. B. Christoff, Philh, W. Schüchter (r1952) (EMI) Ⓓ **CDH5 65500-2**
4. R. Mayr, orch (r1922: Ger) (ORFE) Ⓓ **C394101B**
4. F. Chaliapin, orch, J. Barbirolli (r1928) (12/89) (PEAR) Ⓓ **GEMMCD9314**
4. E. Pinza, NY Met Op Orch, B. Walter (r1946) (4/90) (CBS) Ⓓ **CD45693**
4. A. Kipnis, Berlin St Op Orch, C. Schmalstich (Ger: r1930) (12/90) (PREI) Ⓓ **89019**
4. R. Bruson, NHK Chbr Sols, R. Paternostro (pp1990) (10/91) (CAPR) Ⓓ **10 348**
4. O. Natzke, orch (r1940s) (12/92) (ODE) Ⓓ **CDODE1365**
4. L. Fugère, orch (French: r1929) (6/93) (SYMP) Ⓓ **SYMCD1125**
4. T. Pasero, La Scala Orch, A. Sabino (r1941) (4/95) (PREI) Ⓓ **89074**
4. E. Kunz, VPO, O. Ackermann (r1949) (9/95) (TEST) Ⓓ **SBT1059**
4, 11. G. Bacquier, Collegium Academicum Orch, R. Dunand (GALL) Ⓓ **CD-816**
4, 11, 16. N. De Carolis, Venice and Padua CO, B. Giuranna (CLAV) Ⓓ **CD50-9120**
4, 11, 16. J. Van Dam, Paris Orch Ens, J-P. Wallez (pp) (5/88) (NOVA) Ⓓ **150 014-2**
4, 20, 24. S. Bruscantini, N. Ghiaurov, D. Petkov, Rome RAI Chor, Rome RAI Orch, C.M. Giulini (pp1970) (MEMO) Ⓓ [2] **HR4300/1**
4, 6, 11, 16, 17a, 17b H. Prey, Salzburg Mozarteum Orch, B. Weil (5/88) (DENO) Ⓓ **CO-1741**
4, 6, 11, 16, 17a F. Furlanetto, Vienna SO, I. Marin (3/92) (SONY) Ⓓ **SK47192**
4, 7, 10b, 10c, 11, 12, 13, 16, 18, 21, 23a, 23b, 25b, 27. G. Harman, R. Brünner, R. Knoll, Salzburg Mozarteum Chor, Salzburg Mozarteum Orch, K. Prestel (r1969) (5/94) (BELA) Ⓓ **450 080-2**
(5/94) (BELA) ▭ **450 080-4**
4, 7, 16, 18. A. Martin, D. Robin, Vienna Mozart Orch, K. Leitner (12/91) (NAXO) Ⓓ **8 550435**
7. G. Sciutti, E. Waechter, Philh, C.M. Giulini (CFP) Ⓓ **CD-CFP9013**
(CFP) ▭ **TC-CFP4498**
7. S. Ghazarian, R. Bruson, NHK Chbr Sols, R. Paternostro (pp1990) (CAPR) Ⓓ [3] **10 810**
7. N. Ghiaurov, M. Freni, VPO, H. von Karajan (pp1969) (MEMO) Ⓓ [2] **HR4223/4**
7. P. Munsel, E. Pinza, orch, A. Goodman (bp1946) (MMOI) Ⓓ **CDMOIR406**
(MMOI) ▭ **CMOIR406**
7. L. Popp, T. Krause, Vienna Haydn Orch, I. Kertész (DECC) Ⓓ **433 067-2DWO**
(DECC) ▭ **433 067-4DWO**
7. A. Scotti, G. Farrar, orch (r1909) (PEAR) Ⓓ **GEMMCD9937**
7. G. Furlanetto, P. Pace, Bologna Teatro Comunale Orch, L. Magiera (pp1991) (DECC) ◐ **071 140-1DH**
(DECC) ▣ **071 140-3DH**
7. H. Donath, R. Soyer, ECO, D. Barenboim (r1968) (CFP) Ⓓ **CD-CFP4602**
(CFP) ▭ **TC-CFP4602**
7. L. Popp, T. Krause, Vienna Haydn Orch, I. Kertész (r1971) (DECC) Ⓓ **440 947-2DH**
(DECC) ▭ **440 947-4DH**
7. J. Zoon, H. de Vries, London Studio SO (arr Vrijens) (PHIL) Ⓓ **438 940-2PH**
7. G. Groves, J. Watson, J. Partridge (r1994) (ASV) Ⓓ **CDWHL2088**
7. E. Mathis, A. Titus, BRSO, R. Kubelík (RCA) Ⓓ **09026 62699-2**
(RCA) ▭ **09026 62699-4**
7. M. Battistini, E. Corsi, orch (r1907) (PEAR) Ⓓ **GEMMCD9016**
7. K. Battle, P. Domingo, NY Met Op Orch, James Levine (pp1988) (DG) Ⓓ **445 552-2GMA**
(DG) ▭ **445 552-4GMA**
7. H. Schlusnus, E. Berger, Berlin St Op Orch, C. Krauss (r1936: Ger) (PREI) Ⓓ [2] **89212**
7. R. Stracciari, A. Rettore, orch (r1928) (PEAR) Ⓓ **GEMMCD9178**
7. M. Freni, N. Ghiaurov, VPO, H. von Karajan (pp1968) (ORFE) Ⓓ **C394301B**
7. R. Soyer, H. Donath, ECO, D. Barenboim (7/91) (EMIL) Ⓓ **CDZ7 67015-2**
7. S. Ghazarian, R. Bruson, NHK Chbr Sols, R. Paternostro (pp1990) (10/91) (CAPR) Ⓓ **10 348**
7. E. Berger, H. Schlusnus, Berlin St Op Orch, C. Krauss (Ger: r1936) (12/91) (PREI) Ⓓ **89035**
7. M. Battistini, E. Corsi, orch (r1906) (2/92) (PREI) Ⓓ **89045**
7. Lotte Lehmann, H. Schlusnus, orch (Ger: r1920) (6/92) (PREI) Ⓓ [3] **89302**
7. M. Battistini, E. Corsi, orch, C. Sabajno (r1906) (7/92) (PEAR) Ⓓ [3] **GEMMCDS9924(1)**
7. E. Eames, E. de Gogorza, orch (r1906/7: two vers) (11/93) (ROMO) Ⓓ [2] **81001-2**
7. T. Allen, E. Gale, LPO, B. Haitink (r1984) (6/94) (EMI) Ⓓ **CDH5 65072-2**
7. E. Eames, E. de Gogorza, orch (r1906) (1/95) (NIMB) Ⓓ **NI7860**
7. E. Kunz, I. Seefried, VPO, H. von Karajan (r1947) (9/95) (TEST) Ⓓ **SBT1059**
7, 11, 16, 26. T. Gobbi, Vienna St Op Chor, Vienna St Op Orch, W. Furtwängler (pp1950) (MEMO) Ⓓ [2] **HR4376/7**
7, 12, 18. M. Freni, N. Ghiaurov, VPO, H. von Karajan (pp1969) (MEMO) Ⓓ [2] **HR4277/8**
7, 8, 10b, 11. M. Bokor, L. Helletsgruber, E. Rethberg, E. Pinza, VPO, B. Walter (pp1937) (ORFE) Ⓓ **C394101B**
8. K. Te Kanawa, WNO Orch, C. Mackerras (10/91) (EMI) ◐ **LDA9 91242-1**
(10/91) (EMI) ▣ **MVC9 91242-3**
8, 23a, 23b K. Te Kanawa, Paris Op Orch, L. Maazel (CBS) Ⓓ **CD39208**
8, 23b K. Te Kanawa, Paris Op Orch, L. Maazel (SONY) Ⓓ **SBK46548**
(SONY) ▭ **SBT46548**
10a-c, 25a, 25b M. Major, P. Hornblow, NZ SO, J. Matheson (KIWI) Ⓓ **CDTRL075**
10a, 10b F. Leider, orch, J. Barbirolli (r1928) (MMOI) Ⓓ **CDMOIR406**
(MMOI) ▭ **CMOIR406**
10a, 10b K. Te Kanawa, ECO, J. Tate (PHIL) Ⓓ **434 725-2PM**
(PHIL) ▭ **434 725-4PM**
10a, 10b L. Price, P. de Palma, RCA Italiana Op Orch, F. Molinari-Pradelli (12/92) (RCA) Ⓓ [4] **09026 61236-2**
10a, 10b L. Price, P. de Palma, RCA Italiana Op Orch, F. Molinari-Pradelli (6/93) (RCA) Ⓓ **09026 61357-2**
10a, 10b, 25b K. Te Kanawa, ECO, J. Tate (10/88) (PHIL) Ⓓ **420 950-2PH**
10b C. Bartha, Swedish RSO, Vladimir Ashkenazy (TELD) ◐ **9031-76372-6**
(TELD) ▣ **9031-76372-3**
10b A. Tomowa-Sintow, BPO, H. von Karajan (DG) ▭ **439 153-4GMA**
10b H. Wildbrunn, orch (r1924: Ger) (PREI) Ⓓ **89097**
10b C. Studer, VPO, R. Muti (r1990) (EMI) Ⓓ **CDC5 55350-2**
10b F. Leider, orch, J. Barbirolli (r1928) (2/90) (PREI) Ⓓ **89004**
10b F. Leider, orch (r1925: Ger) (5/91) (PREI) Ⓓ [3] **89301**
10b Lilli Lehmann, anon (r1906) (7/92) (PEAR) Ⓓ [3] **GEMMCDS9923(2)**
10b, 16, 18. E. Gruberová, B. Bonney, T. Hampson, Concertgebouw, N. Harnoncourt (r1988) (TELD) Ⓓ **4509-97507-2**
10b, 23a, 23b, 25a, 25b M. Callas, Paris Cons, N. Rescigno (EMI) Ⓓ **CDC7 49005-2**
10b, 25a, 25b E. Gruberová, Concertgebouw, N. Harnoncourt (TELD) Ⓓ **4509-93691-2**
10b, 25a, 25b M. Cebotari, VPO, H. von Karajan (r1947) (12/90) (PREI) Ⓓ **90034**
10c J. Patzak, Berlin St Op Orch, L. Blech (Ger: r1935) (MMOI) Ⓓ **CDMOIR406**
(MMOI) ▭ **CMOIR406**
10c L. Simoneau, Vienna SO, R. Moralt (PHIL) Ⓓ **442 602-2PM**
(PHIL) ▭ **442 602-4PM**
10c A. Dermota, VPO, R. Moralt (pp1944: Ger) (PREI) Ⓓ **90249**
10c R. Tauber, orch (Ger: r1922) (7/89) (PEAR) Ⓓ **GEMMCD9327**
10c R. Tauber, orch (Ger: r1922) (7/89) (EMI) Ⓓ **CDM7 69476-2**
10c R. Tauber, orch (Ger: r1922) (3/92) (EMI) Ⓓ **CDH7 64029-2**
10c W. Midgley, ROHO, R. Goodall (r1951) (4/92) (EMI) Ⓓ [7] **CHS7 69741-2(2)**
10c H. Nash, orch (r1929) (7/92) (PEAR) Ⓓ [3] **GEMMCDS9926(1)**
10c R. Tauber, orch (Ger: r1922) (12/92) (NIMB) Ⓓ **NI7830**
(12/92) (NIMB) ▭ **NC7830**
10c A. Bonci, anon (r1905) (12/93) (SYMP) Ⓓ **SYMCD1113**
10c W. Ludwig, orch, H. von Benda (r1934: Ger) (7/95) (PREI) Ⓓ **89088**
10c, 12. E. Mathis, P. Schreier, VPO, K. Böhm (pp1977) (ORFE) Ⓓ **C394301B**
10c, 21. T. Schipa, orch (r1927) (PEAR) Ⓓ **GEMMCD9364**
10c, 21. J. Protschka, Munich RO, K. Eichhorn (CAPR) Ⓓ [3] **10 810**
10c, 21. Alfredo Kraus, VPO, H. von Karajan (pp1968) (MEMO) Ⓓ [2] **HR4233/4**
10c, 21. T. Schipa, orch, Anon (cond) (pp1927) (MEMO) Ⓓ [2] **HR4220/1**
10c, 21. R. Giménez, ROHO, B. Wordsworth (NIMB) Ⓓ **NI5300**
10c, 21. E. Haefliger, ECO, J.E. Dähler (CLAV) Ⓓ **CD50-8305**
10c, 21. R. Tauber, orch, W. Goehr (r1939) (PEAR) Ⓓ **GEMMCD9145**
10c, 21. J. Protschka, Munich RO, K. Eichhorn (3/89) (CAPR) Ⓓ **10 109**
10c, 21. R. Blake, LSO, N. McGegan (3/89) (ARAB) Ⓓ **Z6598**
(3/89) (ARAB) ▭ **ABQC6598**
10c, 21. H. Nash, orch (r1929) (8/89) (PEAR) Ⓓ **GEMMCD9319**
10c, 21. T. Schipa, orch, Rosario Bourdon (r1927) (12/89) (RCA) Ⓓ **GD87969**
10c, 21. J. Dickie, Capella Istropolitana, J. Wildner (12/91) (NAXO) Ⓓ **8 550383**
10c, 21. H. Roswaenge, orch (r1928: Ger) (2/92) (PREI) Ⓓ [2] **89201**
10c, 21. P. Domingo, Munich RO, E. Kohn (3/92) (EMI) Ⓓ **CDC7 54329-2**
10c, 21. P. Domingo, Munich RO, E. Kohn (r1991) (6/94) (EMI) Ⓓ **CDC5 55017-2**
10c, 21. L. Simoneau, Vienna SO, B. Paumgartner (r1954) (11/94) (PHIL) Ⓓ [2] **438 953-2PM2**
10c, 21. H. Nash, orch, C. Raybould (r1929) (2/95) (DUTT) Ⓓ **CDLX7012**
11. A. Titus, orch (EURO) Ⓓ **VD69256**
11. B. Weikl, LPO, G. Solti (DECC) Ⓓ **433 822-2DH**
(DECC) ▭ **433 822-4DH**
11. T. Krause, Vienna Haydn Orch, I. Kertész (DECC) Ⓓ **433 068-2DWO**
(DECC) ▭ **433 068-4DWO**
11. A. Scotti, anon (r1904) (PEAR) Ⓓ **GEMMCD9937**
11. P. Domingo, VPO, James Levine (DG) ◐ **072 187-1GH**
(DG) ▣ **072 187-3GH**
11. A. Scholz, Berlin RSO, J. Märkl (r1991) (SCHW) Ⓓ [2] **312682**
11. R. Raimondi, Paris Op Orch, E. Tchakarov (r1981) (ERAT) Ⓓ **4509-98503-2**
11. P. Domingo, VPO, James Levine (11/89) (DG) ◐ **072 110-1GH**
11. E. Pinza, orch, Rosario Bourdon (r1930) (7/91) (MMOI) Ⓓ **CDMOIR404**
(MMOI) ▭ **CMOIR404**
11. F. d'Andrade, orch (r1907) (7/92) (PEAR) Ⓓ [3] **GEMMCDS9923(1)**
11. A. Scotti, anon (r1904) (7/92) (PEAR) Ⓓ [3] **GEMMCDS9923(2)**
11. T. Ruffo, orch (r1914) (2/93) (PREI) Ⓓ [3] **89303(1)**
11. M. Battistini, anon (r1902) (7/93) (NIMB) Ⓓ [2] **NI7840/1**
11. E. Pinza, orch, Rosario Bourdon (r1930) (9/93) (RCA) Ⓓ **09026 61245-2**
11, 16. N. Ghiaurov, VPO, H. von Karajan (pp1969) (MEMO) Ⓓ [2] **HR4223/4**
11, 16. G. Laperrière, Three Rivers SO, G. Bellemare (r1992) (CBC) Ⓓ **SMCD5127**
11, 16. T. Hampson, Concertgebouw, N. Harnoncourt (ERAT) Ⓓ **4509-91715-2**
(ERAT) ▭ **4509-91715-4**
11, 16. C. Siepi, VPO, J. Krips (r1955) (DECC) Ⓓ **440 418-2DM**
11, 16. E. Pinza, Cibelli, orch, Rosario Bourdon (r1930) (2/89) (PEAR) Ⓓ **GEMMCD9306**
11, 16. J. Hynninen, Estonian SO, E. Klas (4/90) (ONDI) Ⓓ **ODE731-2**
11, 16. E. Pinza, orch, Rosario Bourdon (r1930) (3/92) (PREI) Ⓓ **89050**
11, 16. M. Battistini, anon (r1902) (10/92) (PEAR) Ⓓ **GEMMCD9936**
11, 16. A. Scotti, anon (r1902) (3/93) (SYMP) Ⓓ **SYMCD1100**

11, 21. A. Dermota, C. Siepi, VPO, W. Furtwängler (pp1953) (ORFE) Ⓓ **C394201B**
11, 23b T. Allen, M. Ewing, LPO, B. Haitink (7/91) (EMIL) Ⓓ **CDZ7 67015-2**
12. K. Battle, BPO, H. von Karajan (DG) ▭ **439 153-4GMA**
12. E. Schumann, orch, G.W. Byng (r1926) (MMOI) Ⓓ **CDMOIR406** (MMOI) ▭ **CMOIR406**
12. A. Patti, L. Ronald (r1905) (PEAR) Ⓓ **GEMMCD9130**
12. C. Bartoli, Vienna CO, G. Fischer (r1993) (DECC) Ⓓ **448 300-2DH** (DECC) ▭ **448 300-4DH**
12. A. Patti, L. Ronald (r1905) (4/90) (PEAR) Ⓓ **GEMMCD9312**
12. L. Tetrazzini, orch, P. Pitt (r1907) (9/92) (EMI) Ⓓ [3] **CHS7 63802-2(1)**
12. L. Tetrazzini, orch (r1911) (9/92) (EMI) Ⓓ [3] **CHS7 63802-2(1)**
12. L. Tetrazzini, orch (r1911) (9/92) (PEAR) Ⓓ **GEMMCD9222**
12. L. Tetrazzini, orch, P. Pitt (r1907) (9/92) (PEAR) Ⓓ **GEMMCD9221**
12. A. Patti, L. Ronald (r1905) (7/93) (NIMB) Ⓓ [2] **NI7840/1**
12. G. Farrar, orch (r1908) (10/94) (NIMB) Ⓓ **NI7857**
12. E. Rethberg, Victor SO, Rosario Bourdon (r1930) (10/95) (ROMO) Ⓓ [2] **81014-2**
12, 18. E. Schumann, orch (r1920) (PEAR) Ⓓ **GEMMCD9445**
12, 18. L. Bori, orch (r1937) (PEAR) Ⓓ **GEMMCD9458**
12, 18. E. Schumann, orch, G.W. Byng (r1926) (ROMO) Ⓓ **81019-2**
12, 18. E. Schumann, orch, G.W. Byng (r1926) (6/91) (PREI) Ⓓ **89031**
12, 18, 25a, 25b E. Schwarzkopf, Philh, J. Pritchard (r1952) (EMI) Ⓓ **CDH7 63708-2**
12, 23a, 23b C. Bartoli, Vienna CO, G. Fischer (r1993) (11/94) (DECC) Ⓓ **443 452-2DH** (11/94) (DECC) ▭ **443 452-4DH**
13a Philadelphia, E. Ormandy (SONY) Ⓓ **SBK39436**
13a W. Schulz, H. Schellenberger (arr fl/ob) (DG) Ⓓ **439 150-2GMA** (DG) ▭ **439 150-4GMA**
13a W. Landowska, orch, N. Shilkret (r1926) (BIDD) Ⓓ **LHW016**
14, 15. E. Schwarzkopf, E. Waechter, W. Berry, VPO, H. von Karajan (pp1960) (ORFE) Ⓓ **C394201B**
16. J. van Dam, RTBF SO, R. Zollman (r1990) (PRES) Ⓓ **PCOM1109**
16. Swingle Sngrs (arr Parry) (VIRG) Ⓓ **VC7 59617-2**
16. E. Pinza, orch, Rosario Bourdon (r1930) (MMOI) Ⓓ **CDMOIR406** (MMOI) ▭ **CMOIR406**
16. G. Bacquier, ECO, R. Bonynge (DECC) Ⓓ **433 068-2DWO** (DECC) ▭ **433 068-4DWO**
16. F. Schorr, orch (Ger: r1922) (PREI) Ⓓ **89052**
16. A. Scotti, anon (r1903) (PEAR) Ⓓ **GEMMCD9937**
16. W. Backhaus (r1923: arr Backhaus: pf roll) (COND) Ⓓ **690.07.013**
16. T. Ruffo, orch, W.B. Rogers (r1912) (PEAR) Ⓓ **GEMMCD9088**
16. T. Allen, LPO, B. Haitink (EMIL) Ⓓ **CDZ100** (EMIL) ▭ **LZ100**
16. G. Bacquier, ECO, R. Bonynge (r1968) (DECC) Ⓓ [2] **443 762-2DF2**
16. H. Schlusnus, Berlin St Op Orch, L. Blech (r1935: Ger) (PREI) Ⓓ [2] **89212**
16. G. De Luca, anon (r1902) (PEAR) Ⓓ [3] **GEMMCDS9159(1)**
16. G. De Luca, anon (r1907) (PEAR) Ⓓ [3] **GEMMCDS9159(1)**
16. H. Schlusnus, orch (r1925: Ger) (PREI) Ⓓ **89110**
16. H. Duhan, orch (r1922: Ger) (ORFE) Ⓓ **C394101B**
16. L. Howard (trans Busoni) (12/86) (HYPE) Ⓓ **CDA66090**
16. E. Petri (r1938: arr Busoni) (4/90) (PEAR) Ⓓ **GEMMCD9347**
16. E. Pinza, NY Met Op Orch, F. Cleva (r1947) (4/90) (CBS) Ⓓ **CD45693**
16. J. Lassalle, anon (French: r1902) (9/91) (SYMP) Ⓓ **SYMCD1089**
16. V. Maurel, anon (r1904) (7/92) (PEAR) Ⓓ [3] **GEMMCDS9923(1)**
16. G. De Luca, anon (r1907) (7/92) (PEAR) Ⓓ [3] **GEMMCDS9925(1)**
16. M. Renaud, orch (r1908) (7/92) (PEAR) Ⓓ [3] **GEMMCDS9923(2)**
16. E. Pinza, NY Met Op Orch, B. Walter (pp1942) (7/92) (PEAR) Ⓓ [3] **GEMMCDS9926(2)**
16. T. Ruffo, orch (r1920) (2/93) (PREI) Ⓓ [3] **89303(1)**
16. T. Ruffo, orch (r1912) (2/93) (PREI) Ⓓ [3] **89303(1)**
16. V. Maurel, anon (r1907) (7/93) (NIMB) Ⓓ [2] **NI7840/1**
16. G. De Luca, anon (r1902) (8/93) (SYMP) Ⓓ **SYMCD1111**
16. T. Gobbi, La Scala Orch, U. Berrettoni (r1942) (8/93) (TEST) Ⓓ **SBT1019**
16. Vanni-Marcoux, orch (r1927: French) (1/94) (CLUB) Ⓓ **CL99-101**
16. E. Pinza, Cibelli, orch, Rosario Bourdon (r1930) (4/94) (RCA) Ⓓ [6] **09026 61580-2(3)**
16. V. Maurel, anon (r1905) (12/94) (SYMP) Ⓓ **SYMCD1128**
16. P. Schoeffler, National SO, C. Krauss (r1947) (1/95) (PREI) Ⓓ **90190**
16. E. Petri (r1938: arr Busoni) (8/95) (APR) Ⓓ [2] **APR7027**
16, 26(pt) T. Hampson, L. Polgár, R. Holl, Netherlands Op Chor, Concertgebouw, N. Harnoncourt (r1988) (TELD) Ⓓ **4509-98824-2**
16, 26(pt) T. Hampson, L. Polgár, R. Holl, Netherlands Op Chor, Concertgebouw, N. Harnoncourt (r1988) (TELD) Ⓓ **4509-98824-2**
18. F. von Stade, Rotterdam PO, E. de Waart (PHIL) Ⓓ **420 084-2PH**
18. M. Favero, orch (r1941) (VAI) Ⓓ **VAIA1071**
18. M. Favero, orch (r1941) (BONG) Ⓓ **GB1078-2**
18. L. Bori, Victor Orch, J. Pasternack (r1921) (ROMO) Ⓓ [2] **81016-2**
18. E. Schumann, orch (r1917: Ger) (ORFE) Ⓓ **C394101B**
18. B. Bonney, Concertgebouw, N. Harnoncourt (r1989) (TELD) Ⓓ **0630-11470-2**
18. C. Bartoli, Vienna CO, G. Fischer (12/91) (DECC) Ⓓ **430 513-2DH** (DECC) ▭ **430 513-4DH**
18. I. Seefried, D. Fischer-Dieskau, I. Sardi, Berlin RSO, F. Fricsay (r1958) (9/93) (DG) Ⓓ [2] **437 677-2GDO2**
21. F. Wunderlich, Berlin SO, H. Stein (Ger) (EMI) Ⓓ [3] **CZS7 62993-2**
21. P. Domingo, orch (EURO) Ⓓ **VD69256**
21. R. Tauber, orch, W. Goehr (r1939) (MMOI) Ⓓ **CDMOIR406** (MMOI) ▭ **CMOIR406**
21. P. Domingo, RPO, E. Downes (RCA) Ⓓ [2] **GD60866** (RCA) ▭ [2] **GK60866**
21. K. Lewis, LPO, B. Haitink (r1984) (KIWI) Ⓓ **CDSLD-82**
21. J. McCormack, orch (r1916) (ASV) Ⓓ **CDAJA5137** (ASV) ▭ **ZCAJA5137**
21. D. Lloyd, Sadler's Wells Orch (r1940: Eng) (SAIN) Ⓓ **SCDC2076** (SAIN) ▭ **C2076**
21. R. Tauber, orch, W. Goehr (r1939) (NIMB) Ⓓ **NI7864**
21. P. Seiffert, Munich RO, J. Kout (r1992-3) (RCA) Ⓓ **09026 61214-2**
21. R. Tauber, orch, W. Goehr (r1939) (ORFE) Ⓓ **C394101B**
21. J. McCormack, orch, W.B. Rogers (r1916) (10/89) (NIMB) Ⓓ **NI7801** (NIMB) ▭ **NC7801**
21. H. Roswaenge, Berlin St Op Orch, F. Weissmann (Ger: r1928) (5/90) (PEAR) Ⓓ **GEMMCD9394**
21. N. Gedda, New Philh, O. Klemperer (7/91) (EMIL) Ⓓ **CDZ7 67015-2**
21. R. Tauber, orch, W. Goehr (r1939) (3/92) (EMI) Ⓓ **CDH7 64029-2**
21. H. Meyer-Welfing, VPO, R. Moralt (Ger: r1946) (4/92) (EMI) Ⓓ [7] **CHS7 69741-2(4)**
21. J. McCormack, orch (r1916) (7/92) (PEAR) Ⓓ [3] **GEMMCDS9924(2)**
21. J. McCormack, orch, W.B. Rogers (r1916) (5/93) (MMOI) Ⓓ **CDMOIR418**
21. R. Crooks, orch, W. Pelletier (r1937) (5/94) (CLAR) Ⓓ **CDGSE78-50-52**
21. R. Tauber, orch, W. Goehr (r1939) (9/94) (NIMB) Ⓓ **NI7856**
23a, 23b E. Schwarzkopf, Philh, C.M. Giulini (r1959) (EMI) Ⓓ **CDM5 65577-2**
23a, 23b C. Studer, ASMF, N. Marriner (9/94) (PHIL) Ⓓ **442 410-2P**
23a, 23b H. Konetzni, Vienna SO, H. Swarowsky (r1950) (1/95) (PREI) Ⓓ **9007**
23a, 23b, 25a, 25b E. Steber, Columbia SO, B. Walter (r1953) (SONY) Ⓓ [3] **SM3K4721**
23a, 23b, 25a, 25b L. Popp, Munich RO, L. Slatkin (r1983) (8/84) (EMI) Ⓓ **CDC7 47019-**
23a, 23b, 25a, 25b M. Price, ECO, J. Lockhart (r1973) (5/95) (RCA) Ⓓ [2] **09026 61635-**
23b S. Ghazarian, NHK Chbr Sols, R. Paternostro (pp1990) (CAPR) Ⓓ [3] **10 81**
23b M. Callas, Paris Cons, N. Rescigno (EMI) Ⓓ **CDC7 54702-** (EMI) ▭ **EL754702-**
23b A. Roocroft, ASMF, N. Marriner (EMI) Ⓓ **CDC5 55396-** (EMI) ▭ **EL5 55396-**
23b E. Schwarzkopf, VPO, W. Furtwängler (pp1954) (12/90) (EMI) Ⓓ **CDM7 63657-**
23b S. Ghazarian, NHK Chbr Sols, R. Paternostro (pp1990) (10/91) (CAPR) Ⓓ **10 34**
24. R. Stilwell, W. White, J. Tomlinson, ASMF, N. Marriner (LOND) Ⓓ [2] **825 126-**
24. M. Sammarco, O. Luppi, anon (r1905) (7/92) (PEAR) Ⓓ [3] **GEMMCDS9924(2**
25a M. Dragoni, Munich RSO, G. Kuhn (r1991) (ORFE) Ⓓ **C261921**
25a, 25b J. Sutherland, Philh, C.M. Giulini (EMIN) Ⓓ **CD-EMX951** (EMIN) ▭ **TC-EMX209**
25a, 25b J. Varady, orch (EURO) Ⓓ **VD6925**
25a, 25b L. Marshall, LSO, E. Pedrazzoli (CBC) Ⓓ **PSCD200**
25a, 25b J. Sutherland, Philh, C.M. Giulini (r1959) (EMI) Ⓓ **CDC5 55095-**
25a, 25b E. Urbanová, Prague SO, J. Bělohlávek (r1993) (SUPR) Ⓓ **11 1851-**
25a, 25b L. Price, LSO, E. Downes (12/92) (RCA) Ⓓ [4] **09026 61236-**
25a, 25b L. Price, LSO, E. Downes (6/93) (RCA) Ⓓ **09026 61357-**
25b J. Sutherland, Philh, C.M. Giulini (r1959) (CFP) Ⓓ **CD-CFP460** (CFP) ▭ **TC-CFP460**
25b A. Auger, Drottningholm Court Th Orch, A. Östman (r1989) (DECC) Ⓓ **440 414-2D**
25b M. Callas, MMF Orch, T. Serafin (r1953) (2/93) (EMI) Ⓓ **CDC7 54437-**
26. N. Ghiaurov, T. Zylis-Gara, G. Evans, V. von Halem, VPO, H. von Karajan (pp1969) (MEMO) Ⓓ [2] **HR4223**
26(pt) R. Ragatzu, O. Romanko, M. Bacelli, R. Wörle, M. Biscotti, G. Saks, Berlin RSO, R. Buckley (SCHW) Ⓓ [2] **31405**
27. L. Helletsgruber, A. Mildmay, K. von Pataky, Roy Henderson, I. Souez, S. Baccaloni, Glyndebourne Fest Orch, F. Busch (r1936) (6/94) (EMI) Ⓓ **CDH5 65072-**

Die **Entführung aus dem Serail, '(The) Abduction from the hareem'– singspiel: 3 acts, K384 (1782—Vienna) (Lib. C F Bretzn & J G Stephanie jr)**

EXCERPTS: 1. Overture. ACT 1: 2. Hier soll ich dich denn sehen; 3. Wer ein Liebchen hat gefunden; 4. Solche hergelaufne Laffen; 5. Konstanze...O wie ängstlich; 6. Singt dem grossen Bassa Lieder; 7. Ach ich liebte; 8. Konstanze! dich wiederzusehen...O wie ängstlich; 9. Durch Zärtlichkeit; 10. Ich gehe, doch rate ich dir; 11a. Welcher Kummer; 11b. Traurigkeit; 12. Martern aller Arten; 13. Welche Wonne, welche Lust; 14. Frisch zum Kampfe!; 15. Vivat Bacchus!; 16. Wenn der Freude Tränen fliessen; 17. Ach, Belmonte! ach mein Leben! (Quartet). ACT 3: 18. Ich baue ganz auf deine Stärke; 19. In Mohrenland gefangen war; 20. Ha, wie will ich triumphieren; 21a. Welch ein Geschick!; 21b. Ha, du solltest für mich sterben; 22. Nie werd' ich deine Huld verkennen (Vaudeville); 23. Chorus of Janissaries.

Constanze A. Winsk
Blonde E. Hellstror
Belmonte R. Cro
Pedrillo B-O. Morga
Osmin T. Szul
Bassa Selim E. Schaffe
Drottningholm Court Th Chor, Drottningholm Court Th Orch, A. Östman, H. Clemen (MCEG) ▣ **VVD8**

Constanze V. Masterso
Blonde L. Watso
Belmonte R. Davie
Pedrillo J. Hobac
Osmin W. Whi

Bassa Selim J. Bissmeier
Glyndebourne Fest Chor, LPO, G. Kuhn, P. Wood (r1980) (IMP) ⊟ **SLL7016**

Constanze E. Gruberová
Blonde R. Grist
Belmonte F. Araiza
Pedrillo N. Orth
Osmin M. Talvela
Bassa Selim T. Holtzmann
Bavarian St Op Chor, Bavarian St Orch, K. Böhm, A. Everding
(DG) ◐ **072 408-1GH**
(DG) ⊟ **072 408-3GH**

Constanze A. Rothenberger
Blonde R. Grist
Belmonte F. Wunderlich
Pedrillo G. Unger
Osmin F. Corena
Bassa Selim M. Heltau
Vienna St Op Chor, VPO, Z. Mehta (pp1965: with dialogue) (ORFE) Ⓓ [2] **C392952I**

Constanze E. Gruberová
Blonde K. Battle
Belmonte G. Winbergh
Pedrillo H. Zednik
Osmin M. Talvela
Bassa Selim W. Quadflieg
Vienna St Op Concert Ch, VPO, G. Solti (r1985: with dialogue) (4/87) (DECC) Ⓓ [2] **417 402-2DH2**

Constanze Y. Kenny
Blonde L. Watson
Belmonte P. Schreier
Pedrillo W. Gamlich
Osmin M. Salminen
Bassa Selim W. Reichmann
Zurich Op. Hse Chor, Zurich Op Hse Mozart Orch, N. Harnoncourt (with dialogue) (5/88) (TELD) Ⓓ [3] **2292-42643-2**

Constanze A. Rothenberger
Blonde L. Popp
Belmonte N. Gedda
Pedrillo G. Unger
Osmin G. Frick
Bassa Selim L. Rudolf
Vienna St Op Chor, VPO, J. Krips (with dialogue) (12/89) (EMI) Ⓓ [2] **CMS7 63263-2**

Constanze A. Auger
Blonde R. Grist
Belmonte P. Schreier
Pedrillo H. Neukirch
Osmin K. Moll
Bassa Selim O. Mellies
Leipzig Rad Chor, Staatskapelle Dresden, K. Böhm (with dialogue) (12/90) (DG) Ⓓ [2] **429 868-2GX2**

Constanze L. Marshall
Blonde I. Hollweg
Belmonte L. Simoneau
Pedrillo G. Unger
Osmin G. Frick
Bassa Selim H. Laubenthal
Beecham Choral Soc, RPO, T. Beecham (with dialogue) (3/91) (EMI) Ⓓ [2] **CHS7 63715-2**

Constanze C. Eda-Pierre
Blonde N. Burrowes
Belmonte S. Burrows
Pedrillo R. Tear
Osmin R. Lloyd
Bassa Selim C. Jürgens
John Alldis Ch, ASMF, Colin Davis (r1978: with dialogue) (4/92) (PHIL) Ⓓ [2] **422 538-2PME2**

Constanze C. Studer
Blonde E. Szmytka
Belmonte K. Streit
Pedrillo R. Gambill
Osmin G. Missenhardt
Bassa Selim M. Heltau
Vienna St Op Chor, Vienna SO, B. Weil (5/92) (SONY) Ⓓ [2] **S2K48053**

Constanze L. Orgonášová
Blonde C. Sieden
Belmonte S. Olsen
Pedrillo U. Peper
Osmin C. Hauptmann
Bassa Selim H-P. Minetti
Monteverdi Ch, EBS, J.E. Gardiner (r1991: with dialogue) (12/92) (ARCH) Ⓓ [2] **435 857-2AH2**

Constanze M. Stader
Blonde R. Streich
Belmonte E. Haefliger
Pedrillo M. Vantin
Osmin J. Greindl
Bassa Selim W. Franck
Berlin RIAS Chbr Ch, Berlin RIAS Orch, F. Fricsay (r1954: with dialogue) (7/95) (DG) Ⓓ [2] **445 412-2GDO2**

Constanze E. Köth
Blonde L. Schädle
Belmonte F. Wunderlich
Pedrillo F. Lenz
Osmin K. Böhme
Bassa Selim R. Boysen
Bavarian St Op Chor, BRSO, E. Jochum (with dialogue) (7/95) (DG) Ⓓ [2] **439 708-2GX2**

Constanze W. Lipp
Blonde E. Loose
Belmonte W. Ludwig
Pedrillo P. Klein
Osmin E. Koréh
Bassa Selim H. Woester
Vienna St Op Chor, VPO, J. Krips (r1950: omits dialogue) (7/95) (DECC) Ⓓ [2] **443 530-2LF2**

Constanze E. Gruberová
Blonde G. Ebel
Belmonte F. Araiza
Pedrillo N. Orth
Osmin R. Bracht
Bassa Selim H. Leipnitz
Bavarian Rad Chor, Munich RO, H. Wallberg (r1978) (10/95) (RCA) Ⓓ [2] **74321 25283-2**

(r1954: Ital) (FONI) Ⓓ **CDO104**

1. Staatskapelle Dresden, H. Vonk (CAPR) Ⓓ **10 070**
(CAPR) ⊟ **CC27 086**
1. Berlin Charlottenburg Op Orch, A. von Zemlinsky (r1928) (SCHW) Ⓓ **310037**
1. Philh, O. Klemperer (EMI) Ⓓ **CDM7 63619-2**
1. Zurich Tonhalle Orch, J. Krips (ADES) Ⓓ **13225-2**
1. LPO, B. Haitink (PHIL) Ⓓ **432 512-2PSL**
1. Prague CO, O. Vlček (r1988) (SUPR) Ⓓ [2] **11 1166-2**
1. Tafelmusik, B. Weil (arr Blombert) (SONY) Ⓓ **SK52498**
1. ASMF, N. Marriner (concert ending André) (EMI) ÕÕ **DCC7 47014-5**
1. Sinfonia Varsovia, E. Krivine (r1990) (DENO) Ⓓ **CO-75372**
1. ASMF, N. Marriner (concert ending André) (EMI) Õ **MDC7 47014-8**
1. NY Harmonie Ens, S. Richman (r1992: arr J Triebensee) (MUSI) Ⓓ **MACD-797**
1. Concertgebouw, Zurich Op Orch, Zurich Op Hse Mozart Orch, VCM, N. Harnoncourt (TELD) Ⓓ **4509-95523-2**
1. H. Roswaenge, orch (r1934) (PEAR) Ⓓ **GEMMCD9129**
1. RPO, Colin Davis (r c1961) (EMI) Ⓓ [2] **CES5 68533-2**
1. Bavarian St Op Orch, E. Jochum (DG) Ⓓ [2] **447 364-2GDB2**
1. Basle SO, M. Atzmon (r1973/4) (RCA) Ⓓ **74321 29237-2**
1. ASMF, N. Marriner (concert ending André) (4/84) (EMI) Ⓓ **CDC7 47014-2**
1. Staatskapelle Dresden, H. Vonk (10/91) (CAPR) Ⓓ [3] **10 809**
1. BPO, W. Furtwängler (r1933) (4/92) (KOCH) Ⓓ [2] **37059-2**
1. Tafelmusik, B. Weil (5/92) (SONY) Ⓓ **SK46695**
1, 2, 9, 10, 13, 15, 16, 20. Linos Ens (arr Wind Band;r1992) (CAPR) Ⓓ **10 493**
1, 2, 9, 10, 13, 15, 16, 20. Amadeus Ens, J. Rudel (arr Wendt: Woodwinds and Bass) (MUSM) Ⓓ [5] **67118-2**
1, 2, 9, 10, 13, 15, 16, 20. Netherlands Wind Ens (arr 8 wind instr: Wendt?) (12/91) (PHIL) Ⓓ [3] **422 545-2PME3**
1-3, 5, 10, 12, 14, 15, 17-20, 21a, 23. C. Studer, E. Szmytka, K. Streit, R. Gambill, G. Missenhardt, Vienna St Op Concert Ch, Vienna SO, B. Weil (r1991) (SONY) Ⓓ **SMK53500**
2. H. Roswaenge, Berlin St Op Orch, B. Seidler-Winkler (r1937) (4/95) (PREI) Ⓓ [2] **89209**
2, 16. F. Wunderlich, Bavarian St Op Orch, E. Jochum (DG) Ⓓ [5] **435 145-2GX5(1)**
2, 16. F. Wunderlich, Bavarian St Orch, E. Jochum (5/93) (DG) Ⓓ **431 110-2GB**
2, 16. P. Anders, Berlin Staatskapelle, R. Heger (bp1945) (8/93) (ACAN) Ⓓ **43 268**
2, 5, 16. A. Dermota, Berlin St Op Orch, A. Rother (r1950s) (PREI) Ⓓ **90022**
2, 5, 16, 18, 19. J. Dickie, Capella Istropolitana, J. Wildner (12/91) (NAXO) Ⓓ **8 550383**
2, 5, 19. P. Anders, Berlin Deutsche Op Orch, H. Schmidt-Isserstedt (r1935) (TELD) Ⓓ **4509-95512-2**
3. A. Kipnis, Berlin St Op Orch, E. Orthmann (r1931) (BEUL) Ⓓ **2PD4**
3. N. Mangin, LPO, J. Pritchard (r1972) (KIWI) Ⓓ **CDSLD-82**
3. A. Kipnis, Berlin St Op Orch, E. Orthmann (r1931) (12/90) (PREI) Ⓓ **89019**
3, 4, 20. M. Salminen, Lahti SO, E. Klas (8/92) (BIS) Ⓓ **BIS-CD520**
4. H. Alsen, VPO, R. Moralt (pp1944) (PREI) Ⓓ **90249**
4, 20. K. Moll, Munich RO, K. Eichhorn (r1981) (ORFE) Ⓓ **C009821A**
5. F. Wunderlich, Berlin SO, B. Klobučar (EMI) Ⓓ [3] **CZS7 62993-2**
5. F. Araiza, orch (EURO) Ⓓ **VD69256**
5. R. Tauber, orch (r1938) (PEAR) Ⓓ **GEMMCD9145**
5. F. Wunderlich, VPO, I. Kertész (pp1961) (ORFE) Ⓓ **C394301B**
5. H.E. Groh, orch (r1936) (3/92) (PEAR) Ⓓ **GEMMCD9419**
5. W. Ludwig, Berlin St Op Orch, B. Seidler-Winkler (r1936) (7/95) (PREI) Ⓓ **89088**
5, 14. P. Domingo, Munich RO, E. Kohn (3/92) (EMI) Ⓓ **CDC7 54329-2**
5, 16, 18. J. Protschka, Munich RO, K. Eichhorn (3/89) (CAPR) Ⓓ **10 109**
6. Ambrosian Op. Chor, ASMF, N. Marriner (LOND) Ⓓ [2] **825 126-2**
6. Berlin RIAS Chbr Ch, Berlin RSO, H.M. Schneidt (CAPR) Ⓓ [3] **10 810**
6, 23. Zurich Op Hse Chor, Zurich Op Hse Mozart Orch, N. Harnoncourt (r1985) (TELD) Ⓓ **4509-97505-2**
7. L. Pons, Orch, A. Kostelanetz (French: r1940) (MSCM) Ⓓ **MM30446**
7. M. Perras, Berlin St Op Orch, B. Seidler-Winkler (r1930s) (10/93) (NIMB) Ⓓ **NI7848**
7. M. Price, LPO, J. Pritchard (r1972) (6/94) (EMI) Ⓓ **CDH5 65072-2**
7, 11a, 11b, 12. L. Marshall, LSO, RPO, Anthony Bernard, T. Beecham, E. Pedrazzoli (CBC) Ⓓ **PSCD2001**
7, 11a, 11b, 12. A. Winska, Warsaw PO, W. Michniewski (r1990) (PAVA) Ⓓ **ADW7289**
7, 12. M. Németh, orch (r c1930) (1/94) (CLUB) Ⓓ **CL99-007**
7, 13. L. Pons, orch, B. Walter (r1942) (SONY) Ⓓ [3] **SM3K47211**
9. L. Pons, orch (r1929: Fr) (MSCM) Ⓓ **MM30221**
(MSCM) ⊟ **MM040079**
9. A. Martin, D. Robin, Vienna Mozart Orch, K. Leitner (12/91) (NAXO) Ⓓ **8 550435**
9. T. Dahl, Calgary PO, M. Bernardi (r1992) (12/94) (CBC) Ⓓ **SMCD5125**
9, 10, 15, 20. Budapest Wind Ens, K. Berkes (arr Wendt) (QUIN) ⊟ **QUI40 3008**
9, 13. R. Streich, Berlin RIAS Orch, F. Fricsay (r1950s) (DG) Ⓓ **431 875-2GDO**
11a, 11b E. Schwarzkopf, VPO, J. Krips (r1946) (EMI) Ⓓ **CDH7 63708-2**
11a, 11b M. Perras, VPO, K. Alwin (r1929) (ORFE) Ⓓ **C394101B**
11a, 11b L. Popp, Munich RO, L. Slatkin (r1983) (8/84) (EMI) Ⓓ **CDC7 47019-2**
11a, 11b, 12. M. Major, NZ SO, J. Matheson (KIWI) Ⓓ **CDTRL075**
11a, 11b, 12. K. Te Kanawa, ECO, J. Tate (10/88) (PHIL) Ⓓ **420 950-2PH**
11b E. Steber, Columbia SO, B. Walter (r1953) (SONY) Ⓓ [3] **SM3K47211**
12. E. Schwarzkopf, VPO, H. von Karajan (r1946) (EMI) Ⓓ **CDH7 63708-2**
12. E. Gruberová, orch (EURO) Ⓓ **VD69256**
12. M. Callas, Milan RAI SO, A. Simonetto (r1954) (SUIT) Ⓓ **CDS1-5001**
12. K. Te Kanawa, ECO, J. Tate (PHIL) Ⓓ **434 725-2PM**
(PHIL) ⊟ **434 725-4PM**
12. M. Korjus, Berlin St Op Orch, F. Schönbaumsfeld (r1934) (DANT) Ⓓ **LYS001**
12. M. Dragoni, Munich RSO, G. Kuhn (r1991) (ORFE) Ⓓ **C261921A**
12. M. Ivogün, orch (r1919) (PREI) Ⓓ **89094**
12. Y. Kenny, Zurich Op Hse Mozart Orch, N. Harnoncourt (r1985) (TELD) Ⓓ **4509-97507-2**

12. M. André, Toulouse Capitole Orch, M. Plasson (arr tpt) (1/89) (EMI) Ⓓ **CDC7 49219-2**
12. J. Sutherland, ROHO, F. Molinari-Pradelli (1/90) (DECC) Ⓓ [2] **425 493-2DM2**
12. M. Ivogün, orch (r1919) (7/92) (PEAR) Ⓓ [3] **GEMMCDS9926(1)**
12. M. Callas, Rome RAI Orch, A. Simonetto (Ital: pp1954) (2/93) (EMI) Ⓓ **CDC7 54437-2**
12. M. Ivogün, orch (r c1925) (1/94) (CLUB) Ⓓ **CL99-020**
12. C. Studer, ASMF, N. Marriner (9/94) (PHIL) Ⓓ **442 410-2PM**
12. M. Price, ECO, J. Lockhart (r1973) (5/95) (RCA) Ⓓ [2] **09026 61635-2**
12, 17. L. Aikin, V. Esposito, V. Ombuena, J. Sacher, Berlin RSO, J. Märkl (r1991) (SCHW) Ⓓ [2] **312682**
12, 20. A. Rothenberger, G. Frick, VPO, J. Krips (7/91) (EMIL) Ⓓ **CDZ7 67015-2**
13. K. Battle, VPO, G. Solti (r1984/5) (DECC) Ⓓ **443 377-2DM**
13. I. Hollweg, RPO, T. Beecham (7/91) (EMIL) Ⓓ **CDZ7 67015-2**
16. W. Ludwig, orch, H. von Benda (r1934) (7/95) (PREI) Ⓓ **89088**
16, 18. J. Protschka, Munich RO, K. Eichhorn (CAPR) Ⓓ [3] **10 810**
18. E. Haefliger, ECO, J.E. Dähler (CLAV) Ⓓ **CD50-8305**
18. R. Blake, LSO, N. McGegan (3/89) (ARAB) Ⓓ **Z6598** (3/89) (ARAB) ⊟ **ABQC6598**
18. L. Simoneau, Paris Champs-Élysées Orch, A. Jouve (r1955) (3/91) (EMI) Ⓓ [2] **CHS7 63715-2**
20. E. Pinza, NY Met Op Orch, B. Walter (r1946) (SONY) Ⓓ [3] **SM3K47211**
20. G. Frick, VPO, J. Krips (CFP) Ⓓ **CD-CFP4612** (CFP) ⊟ **TC-CFP4612**
20. E. Pinza, NY Met Op Orch, B. Walter (r1946: Ital) (4/90) (CBS) Ⓓ **CD45693**
21a M. Ivogün, K. Erb, orch (r1917) (PREI) Ⓓ **89094**
21a, 21b E. Köth, R. Schock, VPO, G. Szell (pp1956) (ORFE) Ⓓ **C394201B**
21a, 21b P. Anders, E. Berger, Berlin Staatskapelle, K. Schmidt (bp1946) (8/93) (ACAN) Ⓓ **43 268**
26. ASMF, N. Marriner (LOND) Ⓓ **827 267-2**

La **finta giardiniera– opera buffa: 3 acts, K196 (1775—Munich) (Lib. G. Petrosellini)**

EXCERPTS: 1. Overture. ACT 1: 2. Che lieto giorno, che contentezza; 3. Se l'augellin sen fugge; 4. Dentro il mio petto; 5. Noi donne poverine, tapine sfortunate; 6. A forza di martelli; 7. Che beltà, che leggiadria; 8. Si promette facilmente dagl'amanti; 9. Da scirocco a tramontana; 10a. Un marito! Oh Dio, vorrei; 10b. Un marito! Oh Dio! vorrei (alternative version); 11. Appena mi vedon chi cade chi sviene; 12. Geme la tortorella; 13. Numi! che incanto è questo. ACT 2: 14. Vorrei punirti, indegno; 15. Con un vezzo all'italiana; 16. Care pupille, pupille belle; 17. Una voce sento al core; 18. Una damina, una nipote?; 19. Dolce d'amor compagna; 20a. Ah non partir m'ascolta; 20b. Già di vento freddo; 21. Chi vuol godere il mondo; 22. Crudel, oh! Dio, fermate; 23. Ah dal pianto, dal singhiozzo; 24. Fra quest'ombre e quest'oscuro; 25. Mirate, che contrasto fa il sole; 26. Mio padronne, io dir volevo; 27. Và pure ad altri in braccio; 28a. Dove mai son!; 28b. Tu me lasci? o fiero istante; 29. Viva pur la giardiniera!.

Sandrina B-M. Aruhn
Podestà S. Kale
Belfiore R. Croft
Arminda E. Pilat
Ramiro A. Skoglund
Serpetta A.C. Biel
Nardo P. Salomaa

Drottningholm Court Th Chor, Drottningholm Court Th Orch, A. Östman, G. Järvefelt (MCEG) ▣ **VVD616**

Sandrina B-M. Aruhn
Podestà S. Kale
Belfiore R. Croft
Arminda E. Pilat
Ramiro A. Skoglund
Serpetta A.C. Biel
Nardo P. Salomaa

Drottningholm Court Th Chor, Drottningholm Court Th Orch, A. Östman, G. Järvefelt (PHIL) ◐ [2] **070 418-1PHE2**

Sandrina J. Conwell
Podestà E. di Cesare
Belfiore T. Moser
Arminda L. Sukis
Ramiro B. Fassbaender
Serpetta J-R. Ihloff
Nardo B. McDaniel

Salzburg Mozarteum Orch, L. Hager (r1980) (5/92) (PHIL) Ⓓ [3] **422 533-2PME3**

Sandrina H. Donath
Podestà G. Unger
Belfiore W. Hollweg
Arminda J. Norman
Ramiro T. Troyanos
Serpetta I. Cotrubas
Nardo H. Prey

N German Rad Chor, N German RSO, H. Schmidt-Isserstedt (r1972: Ger) (5/92) (PHIL) Ⓓ [3] **422 534-2PME3**

Sandrina E. Gruberová
Podestà T. Moser
Belfiore U. Heilmann
Arminda C. Margiono
Ramiro M. Bacelli
Serpetta D. Upshaw
Nardo A. Scharinger

VCM, N. Harnoncourt (pp1991) (3/93) (TELD) Ⓓ [3] **9031-72309-2**

1. Staatskapelle Dresden, H. Vonk (CAPR) Ⓓ **10 070** (CAPR) ⊟ **CC27 086**
1. English Sinfonia, C. Groves (IMP) Ⓓ [4] **BOXD9**
1. Zurich Tonhalle Orch, J. Krips (ADES) Ⓓ **13225-2**
1. Prague CO, O. Vlček (r1988) (SUPR) Ⓓ [2] **11 1166-2**
1. Concertgebouw, Zurich Op Orch, Zurich Op Hse Mozart Orch, VCM, N. Harnoncourt (TELD) Ⓓ **4509-95523-2**
1. RPO, Colin Davis (r c1961) (EMI) Ⓓ [2] **CES5 68533-2**
1. English Sinfonia, C. Groves (11/90) (IMP) Ⓓ **PCD939** (11/90) (IMP) ⊟ **CIMPC939**
1. Staatskapelle Dresden, H. Vonk (10/91) (CAPR) Ⓓ [3] **10 809**
5. I. Baillie, CBO, B. Cameron (r1941: Eng) (PEAR) Ⓓ **GEMMCD9934**
5. I. Baillie, CBO, B. Cameron (r1941: Eng) (7/95) (DUTT) Ⓓ **CDLX7013**
6, 15. H. Prey, Salzburg Mozarteum Orch, B. Weil (Ger) (5/88) (DENO) Ⓓ **CO-1741**
7. P. Domingo, Munich RO, E. Kohn (3/92) (EMI) Ⓓ **CDC7 54329-2**
20. R. Giménez, ROHO, B. Wordsworth (NIMB) Ⓓ **NI5300**
20a J. Protschka, Munich RO, K. Eichhorn (Ger) (CAPR) Ⓓ [3] **10 810**
20a J. Protschka, Munich RO, K. Eichhorn (Ger) (3/89) (CAPR) Ⓓ **10 109**
22. K. Te Kanawa, LSO, Colin Davis (3/84) (PHIL) Ⓓ **411 148-2PH**
27. J. Larmore, Lausanne CO, J. López-Cobos (r1994) (TELD) Ⓓ **4509-96800-2**

La **finta semplice– opera buffa: 3 acts, K51/K46a (1769—Salzburg) (Lib. M. Coltellini, after C. Goldini)**

EXCERPTS: 1. Overture, ACT ONE: 2. Bella cosa è far l'amore!; 3a. Ritiriamoci, amici!; 3b. Troppa briga a prender moglie; 4a. L'un de' patroni è alzato; 4b. Marito io vorrei; 5a. Oh, starem male insieme; 5b. Non c'è al mondo altro che donne; 6a. Con chi l'ha Don Cassandro?; 6b. Guarda la donna in viso; 7a. Eh! ben ben, ci vedremo; 7b. Colla bocca, e non col core; 8a. Sicché m'avete inteso?; 8b. Oh, la prendo da vero; 8c. Cosa ha mai la donna indosso; 9a. Grand'uomo che son io; 9b. Ella vuole ed io torrei; 10a. Eh ben, sorella mia?; 10b. Senti l'eco, ove t'aggiri; 11a. Ninetta - Che volete?; 11b. Chi mi vuol bene; 12a. Adesso è fatto tutto; 12b. Dove avete la creanza? ACT TWO: 13a. Sono i padroni miei; 13b. Un marito, donne care; 14a. Eh, quando sia mia sposa; 14b. Con certe persone vuol esser bastone; 15a. Non mi marito più; 15b. Se a maritarmi arrivo; 16a. Quando avrò moglie anch'io; 16b. Amoretti, che ascosi qui siete; 17a. Vado subitamente; 17b. Ubriaco non son io; 18a. Egli è venuto; 18b. Sposa cara, sposa bella; 19a. Mia signora Madama; 19b. Me ne vo' prender spasso; 19c. Ehi...dormite, signore?; 19d. Ho sentito a dir da tutte; 20a. Di voi cercavo appunto; 20b. Cospetton, cospettonaccio!; 21a. Dove andate, signore?; 21b. Siam quasi in porto adesso; 21c. Vieni a tempo, Simone; 21d. In voi, belle, è leggiadria; 22. T'ho detto, buffone. ACT THREE: 23. Vieni, vieni, oh mia Ninetta; 24a. Io non ho gran paura; 24b. Sono in amore, voglio marito; 25. Che scompiglio, che flagello; 26a. Che smorfie, che paura!; 26b. Nelle guerre d'amore; 27a. E così, Baronessa?; 27b. Eh ben, quando facciamo queste nozze, signora?; 27c. Se le pupille io giro.

Rosina H. Donath
Polidoro A. Rolfe Johnson
Giacinta T. Berganza
Cassandro R. Holl
Ninetta J-R. Ihloff
Fracasso T. Moser
Simone R. Lloyd

Salzburg Mozarteum Orch, L. Hager (r1983) (8/89) (ORFE) Ⓓ [3] **C085843F**

Rosina B. Hendricks
Don Cassandro S. Lorenz
Don Polidoro D. Johnson
Giacanta A. Murray
Ninetta E. Lind
Fracasso H-P. Blochwitz
Simone A. Schmidt

CPE Bach Orch, P. Schreier (r1988) (11/91) (PHIL) Ⓓ [2] **422 528-2PME2**

1. ECO, L. Hager (r1989) (NOVA) Ⓓ **150 041-2**
1. Prague CO, O. Vlček (r1989) (SUPR) Ⓓ [2] **11 1166-2**
1. Basle SO, M. Atzmon (r1973/4) (RCA) Ⓓ **74321 29237-2**
6b H-P. Blochwitz, Dresden PO, J-P. Weigle (PHIL) Ⓓ [8] **422 523-2PME8(2)**
9b N. De Carolis, Venice and Padua CO, B. Giuranna (CLAV) Ⓓ **CD50-9120**
11. D. Upshaw, VCM, N. Harnoncourt (ERAT) Ⓓ **4509-91715-2** (ERAT) ⊟ **4509-91715-4**
24b E. Szmytka, ASMF, Colin Davis (PHIL) Ⓓ [8] **422 523-2PME8(2)**
25. J. Larmore, Lausanne CO, J. López-Cobos (r1994) (TELD) Ⓓ **4509-96800-2**

Idomeneo, Rè di Creta, 'Idomeneo, King of Crete'– opera seria: 3 acts, K366 (1781—Munich) (Lib. G Varesco)

EXCERPTS - MUNICH VERSION: 1. Overture. ACT 1: 2a. Quando avran; 2b. Padre, germani, addio!; 3. Non ho colpa, e mi codanni; 4. Godiam la pace, trionfi Amore; 5a. Estinto è Idomeneo?; 5b. Tutte nel cor vi sento; 6. Pietà, Numi, pietà!; 7. Vedrommi intorno; 8a. Spietatissimi Dei!; 8b. Il padre adorato ritrovo; 9a. March in D; 9b. Ballet in G; 10. Nettuno s'onori! ACT 2: 11a. Tutto m'è noto; 11b. Se il tuo duol; 12. Se il padre perdei; 13a. Qual mi conturba i sensi equivoca favella; 13b. Fuor del mar; 14a. Chi mai del mio provò piacer più dolce; 14b. Idol mio, se ritroso; 15. March in C; 16. Placidò il mar; 17. Pria di partir, O Dio!; 18. Qual nuovo terrore!; 19. Corriamo, fuggiamo quel mostro spietato. ACT 3: 20a. Solitudini amiche; 20b. Zeffiretti lusinghieri; 21. S'io non moro a questi accenti; 22. Andrò ramingo e solo (quartet); 23. Se solà ne' fati è scritto; 24a. Volgi intorno lo sguardo; 24b. O, o voto tremendo; 25. March in F; 26. Accogli, o rè del mar; 27a. Padre, mio caro padre!; 27b. No, la morte io non pavento; 28a. Ma che più tradi? Idomeneo cessi esser rè; 28b. Ha vinto amore; 29a. O ciel pietoso!; 29b. Oh smania! oh furie!; 30. Popoli! A Voi l'ultima legge; 31. Torna la pace al core; 32. Scenda Amor, scende Imeneo. VARIANT ARIAS: 50. Spiegarti non poss'io, K489 (21); 51. Non più. Tutto ascoltai, K490 (11a); 52. Non temer, amato bene, K490 (11b); 53. D'Oreste, d'Aiace (29b); 54. Torna la pace (31); 55. Gavotte; 56. Ballet Music, K367.

Idomeneo S. Kale
Idamante D. Kuebler
Ilia A.C. Biel
Elettra A. Soldh
Arbace J-E. Jacobsson
High Priest L. Tibell
Oracle O. Sköld

Drottningholm Court Th Chor, Drottningholm Court Th Orch, A. Östman, M. Hampe (MCEG) ▣ **VVD946**

Idomeneo P. Langridge
Idamante J. Hadley
Ilia Y. Kenny
Elettra C. Vaness
Arbace T. Hemsley
High Priest A. Roden

Oracle R. Kennedy
Glyndebourne Fest Chor, LPO, B. Haitink, T. Nunn (r1983)
(CAST) ▭ CVI2019
Idomeneo Richard Lewis
Idamante L. Goeke
Ilia B. Betley-Sieradzka
Elettra J. Barstow
Arbace A. Oliver
High Priest J. Fryatt
Oracle D. Wicks
Glyndebourne Fest Chor, LPO, J. Pritchard, J. Cox (pp1974)
(IMP) ▭ SL2003
Idomeneo N. Gedda
Idamante A. Dallapozza
Ilia A. Rothenberger
Elettra E. Moser
Arbace P. Schreier
High Priest E. Büchner
Oracle T. Adam
Leipzig Rad Chor, Staatskapelle Dresden, H. Schmidt-Isserstedt
(EMI) ⓘ [3] **CMS7 63990-2**
Idomeneo Richard Lewis
Idamante L. Pavarotti
Ilia G. Janowitz
Elettra E. Tarrès
Arbace N. Taylor
High Priest D. Hughes
Oracle D. Wicks
Glyndebourne Fest Chor, LPO, J. Pritchard (pp1964)
(BUTT) ⓘ [2] **BMCD010**
(BUTT) ▭ [2] **BMK010**
Idomeneo W. Hollweg
Idamante T. Schmidt
Ilia R. Yakar
Elettra F. Palmer
Arbace K. Equiluz
High Priest R. Tear
Oracle S. Estes
Zurich Op Hse Chor, Zurich Op Hse Mozart Orch, N. Harnoncourt
(3/86) (TELD) ⓘ [3] **2292-42600-2**
Idomeneo L. Pavarotti
Idamante A. Baltsa
Ilia L. Popp
Elettra E. Gruberová
Arbace L. Nucci
High Priest Timothy Jenkins
Oracle N. Storozhev
Vienna St Op Concert Ch, VPO, J. Pritchard
(4/88) (DECC) ⓘ [3] **411 805-2DH3**
Idomeneo W. Ochman
Idamante P. Schreier
Ilia E. Mathis
Elettra J. Varady
Arbace H. Winkler
High Priest E. Büchner
Oracle S. Vogel
Leipzig Rad Chor, Staatskapelle Dresden, K. Böhm (r1977)
(12/90) (DG) ⓘ [3] **429 864-2GX3**
Idomeneo A. Rolfe Johnson
Idamante A.S. von Otter
Ilia S. McNair
Elettra H. Martinpelto
Arbace N. Robson
High Priest G. Winslade
Oracle C. Hauptmann
Monteverdi Ch, EBS, J.E. Gardiner (pp1990)
(6/91) (ARCH) ⓘ [3] **431 674-2AH3**
Idomeneo F. Araiza
Idamante S. Mentzer
Ilia B. Hendricks
Elettra R. Alexander
Arbace U. Heilmann
High Priest W. Hollweg
Oracle H. Peeters
Bavarian Rad Chor, BRSO, Colin Davis (r1991)
(12/91) (PHIL) ⓘ [3] **422 537-2PME3**
Idomeneo W. Kmentt
Idamante E. Haefliger
Ilia P. Lorengar
Elettra E. Grümmer
Arbace R. Capecchi
High Priest E. Waechter
Oracle G. Littasy
Vienna St Op Chor, VPO, F. Fricsay (pp1961: Paumgartner vers)
(9/95) (DG) ⓘ [3] **447 662-2GX3**
1. Staatskapelle Dresden, H. Vonk
(CAPR) ⓘ **10 070**
(CAPR) ▭ **CC27 086**
1. ECO, L. Hager (r1989)
(NOVA) ⓘ **150 041-2**
1. Zurich Tonhalle Orch, J. Krips
(ADES) ⓘ **13225-2**
1. LPO, B. Haitink (PHIL) ⓘ **432 512-2PSL**
1. Prague CO, O. Vlček (r1988)
(SUPR) ⓘ [2] **11 1166-2**
1. ASMF, N. Marriner
(EMI) ⓘⓘ **DCC7 47014-5**
1. Sinfonia Varsovia, E. Krivine (r1990)
(DENO) ⓘ **CO-75372**
1. ASMF, N. Marriner (EMI) ⓘ **MDC7 47014-8**
1. Concertgebouw, Zurich Op Orch, Zurich Op Hse Mozart Orch, VCM, N. Harnoncourt
(TELD) ⓘ **4509-95523-2**
1. RPO, Colin Davis (r c1961)
(EMI) ⓘ [2] **CES5 68533-2**
1. Basle SO, M. Atzmon (r1973/4)
(RCA) ⓘ **74321 29237-2**
1. ASMF, N. Marriner
(4/84) (EMI) ⓘ **CDC7 47014-2**
1. Staatskapelle Dresden, H. Vonk
(10/91) (CAPR) ⓘ [3] **10 809**
1. Tafelmusik, B. Weil
(5/92) (SONY) ⓘ **SK46695**
1, 12, 29a, 29b, 30-32. J. Sabel, E. Réthy, E. Böttcher, A. Konetzni, E. Kunz, M. Rus, H. Alsen, Vienna St Op Chor, Vienna St Op Orch, R. Strauss (pp1941: Ger: arr R Strauss)
(11/94) (SCHW) ⓘ [2] **314532**
2a, 2b B. Hendricks, L. Pearson, ECO, J. Tate
(6/85) (EMI) ⓘ **CDC7 47122-2**
2a, 2b, 12, 20b S. Jurinac, Glyndebourne Fest Orch, F. Busch (r1951)
(1/90) (EMI) ⓘ **CDH7 63199-2**
3. A. Baltsa, VPO, J. Pritchard (r1983)
(10/93) (DECC) ⓘ **436 462-2DM**
5a, 5b J. Varady, VPO, K. Böhm (pp1976)
(ORFE) ⓘ **C394301B**
5b R. Hunter, Tasmanian SO, D. Franks (r1989)
(10/95) (ABCC) ⓘ **8 7000 10**
7. Richard Lewis, Glyndebourne Fest Orch, F. Busch (r1951) (6/94) (EMI) ⓘ **CDH5 65072-2**
7, 31. J. Protschka, Munich RO, K. Eichhorn
(3/89) (CAPR) ⓘ **10 109**
7, 8a, 8b G. Sabbatini, NHK Chbr Sols, R. Paternostro (pp1990)
(10/91) (CAPR) ⓘ **10 348**
7, 8b G. Sabbatini, NHK Chbr Sols, R. Paternostro (pp1990) (CAPR) ⓘ [3] **10 810**
8b A. Raunig, Vienna Amadeus Ens, W. Kobera
(DIVE) ⓘ **DIV31013**
9a, 15, 25. Salzburg Mozarteum Orch, H. Graf
(11/89) (CAPR) ⓘ **10 253**
(11/89) (CAPR) ▭ **CC27 253**
9a, 15, 25. Salzburg Mozarteum Orch, H. Graf
(10/91) (CAPR) ⓘ [3] **10 809**
10. Zurich Op Hse Chor, Zurich Op Hse Mozart Orch, N. Harnoncourt (r1980)
(TELD) ⓘ **4509-97505-2**
12. K. Te Kanawa, LSO, Colin Davis
(PHIL) ⓘ **434 725-2PM**
(PHIL) ▭ **434 725-4PM**
12. A. Roocroft, ASMF, N. Marriner
(EMI) ⓘ **CDC5 55396-2**
(EMI) ▭ **EL5 55396-4**
12. K. Te Kanawa, LSO, Colin Davis
(3/84) (PHIL) ⓘ **411 148-2PH**
12. L. Price, New Philh, P.H. Adler
(6/93) (RCA) ⓘ **09026 61357-2**
12, 52. H. Gueden, VPO, C. Krauss (r1951)
(PREI) ⓘ **90227**
13a, 13b L. Simoneau, Vienna SO, B. Paumgartner (r1954)
(11/94) (PHIL) ⓘ [2] **438 953-2PM2**
13b W. Hollweg, Zurich Op Hse Mozart Orch, N. Harnoncourt (r1980) (TELD) ⓘ **4509-97507-2**
13b R. Blake, LSO, N. McGegan
(3/89) (ARAB) ⓘ **Z6598**
(3/89) (ARAB) ▭ **ABQC6598**
13b P. Domingo, Munich RO, E. Kohn
(3/92) (EMI) ⓘ **CDC7 54329-2**
14a, 14b M. Price, ECO, J. Lockhart (r1973)
(5/95) (RCA) ⓘ [2] **09026 61635-2**
20a, 20b L. Popp, Munich RO, L. Slatkin (r1983)
(8/84) (EMI) ⓘ **CDC7 47019-2**
20a, 20b A. Roocroft, LPO, F. Welser-Möst
(10/94) (EMI) ⓘ **CDC5 55090-2**
(10/94) (EMI) ▭ **EL5 55090-4**
20b E. Schwarzkopf, Philh, J. Pritchard (r1952)
(EMI) ⓘ **CDH7 63708-2**
20b V. de los Angeles, London Musicum Collegium, P. Casals (pp1959)
(MUSI) ⓘ [4] **MACD-689**
22. P. Langridge, Y. Kenny, J. Hadley, C. Vaness, LPO, B. Haitink (CAST) ▭ **CVI2071**
27b, 29b, 50-55. W. Hollweg, T. Schmidt, F. Araiza, R. Yakar, F. Palmer, Zurich Op Hse Mozart Orch, N. Harnoncourt (r1980)
(TELD) ⓘ **4509-95983-2**
29b, 29c L. Price, Philh, H. Lewis (r1979)
(12/92) (RCA) ⓘ [4] **09026 61236-2**
29b, 53. L. Price, New Philh, N. Santi
(6/93) (RCA) ⓘ **09026 61357-2**
29b, 53. C. Studer, ASMF, N. Marriner
(9/94) (PHIL) ⓘ **442 410-2PM**
31. J. Protschka, Munich RO, K. Eichhorn
(CAPR) ⓘ [3] **10 810**
31. E. Haefliger, ECO, J.E. Dähler
(CLAV) ⓘ **CD50-8305**
31. L. Simoneau, Paris Champs-Élysées Orch, A. Jouve (r1955)
(3/91) (EMI) ⓘ [2] **CHS7 63715-2**
50. H. Donath, P. Schreier, VPO, K. Böhm (pp1973) (ORFE) ⓘ **C394301B**
50. S. Jurinac, L. Simoneau, Glyndebourne Fest Orch, J. Pritchard (r1956)
(6/94) (EMI) ⓘ **CDH5 65072-2**
52. L. Popp, orch (EURO) ⓘ **VD69256**
52. P. Schreier (ten/dir), Staatskapelle Dresden
(PHIL) ⓘ [8] **422 523-2PME8(2)**
52. K. Te Kanawa, Vienna CO, G. Fischer (r1980) (DECC) ⓘ **440 401-2DM**
52. M. Marshall, Salzburg Mozarteum Orch, R. Weikert (pp1983) (ORFE) ⓘ **C394501B**
52. B. Hendricks, J-L. Garcia, ECO, J. Tate
(6/85) (EMI) ⓘ **CDC7 47122-2**
52. K. Battle, D. Harris, B. Griffiths, RPO, A. Previn (12/86) (EMI) ⓘ **CDC7 47355-2**
52. B. Hendricks, S. Mentzer, A. Röhn, BRSO, Colin Davis
(12/91) (PHIL) ⓘ [3] **422 545-2PME3**
52. I. Seefried, Vienna SO, F. Leitner (r1952)
(9/93) (DG) ⓘ [2] **437 677-2GDO2**
52. L. Simoneau, Vienna SO, B. Paumgartner (r1954) (11/94) (PHIL) ⓘ [2] **438 953-2PM2**
53. S. Sass, Hungarian St Op Orch, E. Lukács
(CAPR) ⓘ [3] **10 810**
55. M. Elman, P. Kahn (arr Auer: r1910)
(BIDD) ⓘ **LAB035**
56. NHK Chbr Sols, R. Paternostro (pp1990)
(CAPR) ⓘ [3] **10 810**
56. Netherlands CO, D. Zinman
(PHIL) ⓘ [2] **422 525-2PME2**
56. Prague CO, B. Novotný (r1990)
(SUPR) ⓘ [2] **11 1166-2**
56. NHK Chbr Sols, R. Paternostro (pp1990)
(10/91) (CAPR) ⓘ **10 348**

Lucio Silla– opera seria: 3 acts, K135 (1772—Milan) (Lib. G. de Gamerra)
EXCERPTS: 1. Overture. ACT 1: 2. Vieni ov'amour t'invita; 3a. Dunque sperar; 3b. Il tenero momento; 4. Se lusinghiera speme; 5. Dalla sponda tenebrosa; 6a. Mi piace? E il cor di Silla; 6b. Il desio di vendetta; 7a. Morte fatal; 7b. Fuor di queste urne; 8a. Se l'empio Silla; 8b. D'Eliso in sen m'attendi. ACT 2: 9. Guerrier, che d'un acciaro; 10a. Ah corri, vola, Cecilio a che t'arresti; 10b. Quest'improvviso tremito; 11. Se il labbro tumido; 12a. Vanne t'affretta; 12b. Ah se il crudel periglio; 13a. Ah sì, scuotasi omai; 13b. Nel fortunato istante; 14. D'ogni pietà mi spoglio perfida; 15a. Chi sa che non sia questa; 15b. Ah se morir mi chiama; 16. Quando sugl'arsi campi; 17a. In un istante; 17b. Parto m'affretto; 18. Se gloria in crin ti cinse; 19. Quell'orgoglioso sdegno. ACT 3: 20. Strider sento la procella; 21. De' più superbi il core; 22. Pupille amate non lagrimate; 23a. Sposo, mia vita. Ah dove. Dove vai?; 23b. Fra i pensier più funesti; 24. Il gran Silla che a Roma in seno.
Lucio Silla P. Schreier
Giunia E. Gruberová
Cecilio C. Bartoli
Lucio Cinna Y. Kenny
Celia D. Upshaw
A. Schoenberg Ch, VCM, N. Harnoncourt (pp1989)
(3/91) (TELD) ⓘ [2] **2292-44928-2**
Lucio Silla A. Holte Johnson
Giunia L. Cuberli
Cecilio A. Murray
Lucio Cinna B-M. Aruhn
Celia C. Barbaux
Aufidio A. Van Baasbank
Brussels Théâtre de la Monnaie Chor, Brussels Théâtre de la Monnaie Orch, S. Cambreling (pp1985)
(2/92) (RICE) ⓘ [3] **RIS090072/4**
Lucio Silla P. Schreier
Giunia A. Auger
Cecilio J. Varady

Lucio Cinna E. Mathis
Celia H. Donath
Aufidio W. Krenn
Salzburg Rad Chor, Salzburg Mozarteum Chor, Salzburg Mozarteum Orch, L. Hager (r1975)
(2/92) (PHIL) ① [3] **422 532-2PME3**
1. Staatskapelle Dresden, H. Vonk
(CAPR) ① **10 070**
(CAPR) ⊟ **CC27 086**
1. ECO, L. Hager (r1989)
(NOVA) ① **150 041-2**
1. LPO, B. Haitink (PHIL) ① **432 512-2PSL**
1. Concertgebouw, N. Harnoncourt
(TELD) ① **9031-74785-2**
1. Prague CO, O. Vlček (r1989)
(SUPR) ① [2] **11 1166-2**
1. ASMF, N. Marriner
(EMI) OO **DCC7 47014-5**
1. ASMF, N. Marriner (EMI) ◙ **MDC7 47014-8**
1. Concertgebouw, Zurich Op Orch, Zurich Op Hse Mozart Orch, VCM, N. Harnoncourt
(TELD) ① **4509-95523-2**
1. Basle SO, M. Atzmon (r1973/4)
(RCA) ① **74321 29237-2**
1. ASMF, N. Marriner
(4/84) (EMI) ① **CDC7 47014-2**
1. Staatskapelle Dresden, H. Vonk
(10/91) (CAPR) ① [3] **10 809**
3b C. Bartoli, VCM, N. Harnoncourt (pp1989)
(TELD) ① **4509-97507-2**
5. E. Gruberová, VCM, N. Harnoncourt
(TELD) ① **4509-93691-2**
7b, 18, 24. A. Schoenberg Ch, VCM, N. Harnoncourt (pp1989)
(TELD) ① **4509-97505-2**
12a, 12b E. Gruberová, Munich RO, L. Gardelli
(11/86) (ORFE) ① **C101841A**
15a, 15b I. Vermillion, Munich RSO, J-P. Weigle
(PHIL) ① [8] **422 523-2PME8(2)**
22. K. Te Kanawa, LSO, Colin Davis
(3/84) (PHIL) ① **411 148-2PH**
23b B. Hendricks, ECO, J. Tate
(6/85) (EMI) ① **CDC7 47122-2**

Mitridate, rè di Ponto– opera seria: 3 acts, K87 (1770—Milan) (Lib. V. A. Cigna-Santi)
EXCERPTS: 1. Overture. ACT 1: 2. Al destin, che la minaccia; 3a. Qual tumulto; 3b. Soffre il mio cor con pace; 4. L'odio nel cor frenate; 5. Nel sen mi palpita dolente il core; 6. Parto: nel gran cimento; 7. Venga pur, minacci; 8. March; 9. Se di lauri il crine adorno; 10. In faccia all'oggetto che'marde; 11a. Respira alfin, respira; 11b. Quel ribelle e quell'ingrato. ACT 2: 12. Va, va, l'error mio palesa; 13. Tu, che fedel mi sei; 14a. Non più Regina; 14b. Lungi da te, mio bene, se vuoi ch'io porti il piede; 15a. Grazie ai numi parti; 15b. Nel grave tormento; 16. So, quanto a te dispiace; 17. Son reo, l'error confesso e degno del tuo sdegno; 18. Già di pietà mi spoglio; 19a. Io sposa di quel mostro; 19b. Se viver non degg'io. ACT 3: 20. Tu sai per chi m'accese; 21. Vado incontro al fato estremo; 22. Se il rigor d'ingrata sorte; 23a. Ah ben ne fui presaga!; 23b. Pallid'ombre, che scorgete; 24. Se di regnar sei vago; 25a. Vadasi, oh ciel; 25b. Già dagli occhi il velo è tolto; 26. Non si ceda al Campidoglio.
Mitridate S. Kolk
Aspasia M. Zara
Sifare E. Gabry
Farnace B. Fassbaender
Ismene I. Cotrubas
Marzio P. Baillie
Arbate R. Didusch
Salzburg Mozarteum Orch, L. Hager (pp1970)
(MEMO) ① [2] **HR4156/7**
Mitridate W. Hollweg
Aspasia A. Auger
Sifare E. Gruberová
Farnace A. Baltsa
Ismene I. Cotrubas
Marzio D. Kuebler
Arbate C. Weidinger
Salzburg Mozarteum Orch, L. Hager (r1977)
(2/92) (PHIL) ① [3] **422 529-2PME3**
Mitridate G. Winbergh
Aspasia Y. Kenny
Sifare A. Murray
Farnace A. Gjevang
Ismene J. Rodgers
Marzio P. Straka
Arbate M. Roncato
VCM, N. Harnoncourt, J-P. Ponnelle
(11/92) (DECC) ◖ [2] **071 407-1DH2**
(11/92) (DECC) ▣ **071 407-3DH**
Mitridate B. Ford
Aspasia L. Orgonášová
Sifare A. Murray
Farnace J. Kowalski
Ismene L. Watson
Marzio J. Lavender
Arbate J. Fugelle
ROHO, P. Daniel
(7/95) (PION) ◖ **PLMCC00941**
1. ECO, L. Hager (r1989)
(NOVA) ① **150 041-2**
1. Prague CO, O. Vlček (r1989)
(SUPR) ① [2] **11 1166-2**
1. Basle SO, M. Atzmon (r1973/4)
(RCA) ① **74321 29237-2**
2, 10, 14a, 14b, 19a, 19b, 21. E. Wiens, E. Szmytka, G. Gudbjörnsson, ASMF, N. Marriner
(PHIL) ① [8] **422 523-2PME8(2)**
7, 12. J. Kowalski, CPE Bach Orch, Hartmut Haenchen (CAPR) ① [3] **10 810**
7, 12, 17, 25b J. Kowalski, CPE Bach Orch, Hartmut Haenchen (CAPR) ◙ **80 213**
7, 12, 17, 25b J. Kowalski, CPE Bach Orch, Hartmut Haenchen (CAPR) OO **70 213**
7, 12, 17, 25b J. Kowalski, CPE Bach Orch, Hartmut Haenchen (3/88) (CAPR) ① **10 213**
(3/88) (CAPR) ⊟ **CC27 213**
9, 21. R. Blake, LSO, N. McGegan
(3/89) (ARAB) ① **Z6598**
(3/89) (ARAB) ⊟ **ABQC6598**
11b J. Protschka, Munich RO, K. Eichhorn
(CAPR) ① [3] **10 810**
11b J. Protschka, Munich RO, K. Eichhorn
(3/89) (CAPR) ① **10 109**
14b K. Te Kanawa, ECO, J. Tate
(10/88) (PHIL) ① **420 950-2PH**
14b F. Lott, LMP, J. Glover
(2/90) (ASV) ① **CDDCA683**
25b J. Larmore, Lausanne CO, J. López-Cobos (r1994) (TELD) ① **4509-96800-2**

Le **Nozze di Figaro, '(The) Marriage of Figaro'– opera buffa: 4 acts, K492 (1786—Vienna) (Lib. L. da Ponte, after Beaumarchais)**
EXCERPTS: 1. Overture. ACT 1: 2. Cinque dieci; 3a. Cosa stai misurando; 3b. Se a caso madama; 4a. Bravo, signor padrone!; 4b. Se vuol ballare; 5. La vendetta; 6. Via, resti servita; 7. Non so più cosa son; 8. Cosa sento!; 9. Giovani liete; 10. Non più andrai. ACT 2: 11. Porgi, amor; 12. Voi che sapete; 13a. Bravo! che bella voce; 13b. Venite inginocchiatevi; 14. Quante buffonerie!; 15a. Che novità!; 15b. Susanna, or via, sortite; 16a. Dunque voi non aprite?; 16b. Aprite, presto, aprite; 17a. Tutto è come il lasciai; 17b. Esci, ormai, garzon malnato; 18. Dunque?...o ciel (Finale). ACT 3: 19. Crudel! perchè finora; 20a. 'Hai già vinta la causa!'; 20b. Vedrò mentr'io sospiro; 21. Riconosci in quest'amplesso; 22a. E Susanna non vien!; 22b. Dove sono; 23a. Cosa mi narri?; 23b. Sull'aria; 24. Ricevete o padroncina; 25. Ecco la marcia (Wedding March). ACT 4: 26. L'ho perduta; 27. Il capro e la capretta; 28. In quegli anni; 29a. Tutto è disposto; 29b. Aprite un po' quegl'occhi; 30a. Giunse alfin il momento; 30b. Deh vieni, non tardar; 31. Pian pianino; 32. Pace, pace, mio dolce tesoro!; 33. Contessa, perdono.
VARIANTS: V1. Signora mia garbata, K492g (Act 1: Marcellina); V2. Un moto di gioia, K579 (Act 2: Susanna); V3. Aprite, presto, aprite (Act 2: Susanna and Cherubino); V4. Ah no, lasciarti in pace, K577d (high version: Act 3: Almaviva); V5. Dove sono (second part: Act 3: Countess: 1789 version); V6. Al desio di chi t'adora, K577a (Act 4: Susanna).
Figaro H. Prey
Susanna M. Freni
Count Almaviva D. Fischer-Dieskau
Countess Almaviva K. Te Kanawa
Cherubino M. Ewing
Marcellina H. Begg
Bartolo P. Montarsolo
Don Basilio J. van Kesteren
Don Curzio W. Caron
Antonio H. Kraemmer
Barbarina J. Perry
VPO, K. Böhm, J-P. Ponnelle
(DG) ◖ [2] **072 403-1GH2**
(DG) ▣ **072 403-3GH**
Figaro K. Skram
Susanna I. Cotrubas
Count Almaviva B. Luxon
Countess Almaviva K. Te Kanawa
Cherubino F. von Stade
Marcellina N. Condò
Bartolo M. Rintzler
Don Basilio J. Fryatt
Don Curzio B. Dickerson
Antonio T. Lawlor
Barbarina E. Gale
Glyndebourne Fest Chor, LPO, J. Pritchard, P. Hall (r1973)
(IMP) ▣ **SLL7013**
Figaro W. Domgraf-Fassbaender
Susanna A. Mildmay
Count Almaviva Roy Henderson
Countess Almaviva A. Rautawaara
Cherubino L. Helletsgruber
Marcellina C. Willis
Bartolo N. Allin
Bartolo I. Tajo
Don Basilio H. Nash
Don Curzio M. Jones
Antonio F. Dunlop
Barbarina W. Radford
Glyndebourne Fest Chor, Glyndebourne Fest Orch, F. Busch (omits recits: r1934/5)
(PEAR) ① [2] **GEMMCDS9375**
Figaro E. Kunz
Susanna I. Seefried
Count Almaviva G. London
Countess Almaviva E. Schwarzkopf
Cherubino S. Jurinac
Marcellina E. Höngen
Bartolo M. Rus
Don Basilio; Don Curzio E. Majkut
Antonio W. Felden
Barbarina R. Schwaiger
Vienna St Op Chor, VPO, H. von Karajan (r1950: omits recits)
(EMI) ① [2] **CMS7 69639-2**
Figaro S. Sylvan
Susanna J. Ommerlé
Count Almaviva J. Maddalena
Countess Almaviva J. West
Cherubino S. Larson
Marcellina S.E. Kuzma
Bartolo D. Evitts
Don Basilio F. Kelley
Don Curzio W. Cotton
Antonio H. Hildebrand
Barbarina L. Torgove
A. Schoenberg Ch, Vienna SO, C. Smith, P. Sellars
(DECC) ◖ [2] **071 412-1DH2**
(DECC) ▣ **071 412-3DH**
Figaro R. Panerai
Susanna R. Streich
Count Almaviva H. Rehfuss
Countess Almaviva T. Stich-Randall
Cherubino P. Lorengar
Marcellina C. Gayraud
Bartolo M. Cortis
Don Basilio H. Cuénod
Don Curzio G. Friedmann
Antonio A. Vessières
Barbarina M. Ignal
Aix-en-Provence Fest Chor, Paris Cons, H. Rosbaud (pp1955)
(EMI) ① [2] **CMS7 64376-2**
Figaro R. Zaidan
Susanna; Barbarina N. Allouba
Count Almaviva R. Al Wakeel
Countess Almaviva N. Erian
Cherubino A. Radi
Marcellina A. El Sharqawi
Bartolo; Antonio C. Rathl
Don Basilio; Don Curzio S. Bedair
Silesian Chbr Music Chor, Polish Nat RO, Y. El Sisi (r1988: Arabic)
(OIA) ① [3] **SADEK1002**
Figaro M. Samuelson
Susanna G. Resick
Count Almaviva P-A. Wahlgren
Countess Almaviva S. Lindenstrand
Cherubino A. C. Biel
Marcellina K. Mang-Habashi
Bartolo E. Saedén
Don Basilio T. Lilleqvist
Don Curzio B. Leinmark
Antonio K-R. Lindgren
Barbarina B. Larsson
Drottningholm Court Th Chor, Drottningholm Court Th Orch, A. Östman, G. Järvefelt, T. Olofsson (r1981)
(PHIL) ◖ **070 421-1PHG2**
Figaro E. Kunz
Susanna I. Beilke
Count Almaviva H. Hotter
Countess Almaviva H. Braun
Cherubino G. Sommerschuh
Marcellina R. Fischer

Bartolo G. Neidlinger
Don Basilio J. Witt
Don Curzio W. Wernigk
Antonio F. Normann
Barbarina L. Timm
/ienna St Op Chor, VPO, C. Krauss (pp1942: Ger)
(PREI) Ⓓ [3] **90203**
Figaro S. Ramey
Susanna L. Popp
Count Almaviva T. Allen
Countess Almaviva K. Te Kanawa
Cherubino F. von Stade
Marcellina J. Berbié
Bartolo K. Moll
Don Basilio R. Tear
Don Curzio P. Langridge
Antonio G. Tadeo
Barbarina Y. Kenny
ondon Op Chor, LPO, G. Solti
(4/84) (DECC) Ⓓ [3] **410 150-2DH3**
Figaro J. Van Dam
Susanna B. Hendricks
Count Almaviva R. Raimondi
Countess Almaviva L. Popp
Cherubino A. Baltsa
Marcellina F. Palmer
Bartolo R. Lloyd
Don Basilio A. Baldin
Don Curzio N. Jenkins
Antonio D. Maxwell
Barbarina C. Pope
mbrosian Op Chor, ASMF, N. Marriner (r1985)
(7/86) (PHIL) Ⓓ [3] **416 370-2PH3**
Figaro J. Van Dam
Susanna I. Cotrubas
Count Almaviva T. Krause
Countess Almaviva A. Tomowa-Sintow
Cherubino F. von Stade
Marcellina J. Berbié
Bartolo J. Bastin
Don Basilio H. Zednik
Don Curzio K. Equiluz
Antonio Z. Kélémen
Barbarina C. Barbaux
ienna St Op Chor, VPO, H. von Karajan
(7/88) (DECC) Ⓓ [3] **421 125-2DH3**
Figaro C. Desderi
Susanna G. Rolandi
Count Almaviva R. Stilwell
Countess Almaviva F. Lott
Cherubino F. Esham
Marcellina A. Mason
Bartolo A. Korn
Don Basilio U. Benelli
Don Curzio A. Oliver
Antonio F. Davià
Barbarina Anne Dawson
yndebourne Fest Chor, LPO, B. Haitink
(7/88) (EMI) Ⓓ [3] **CDS7 49753-2**
Figaro P. Salomaa
Susanna B. Bonney
Count Almaviva H. Hagegård
Countess Almaviva A. Auger
Cherubino A. Nafé
Marcellina D. Jones
Bartolo C. Feller
Don Basilio E. Gimenez
Don Curzio F. Egerton
Antonio E. Florimo
Barbarina N. Argenta
ottningholm Court Th Chor, Drottningholm Court Th Orch, A. Östman (also contains alternative arias)
(12/88) (L'OI) Ⓓ [3] **421 333-2OH3**
Figaro G. Taddei
Susanna A. Moffo
Count Almaviva E. Waechter
Countess Almaviva E. Schwarzkopf
Cherubino F. Cossotto
Marcellina D. Gatta
Bartolo I. Vinco
Don Basilio; Don Curzio R. Ercolani
Antonio P. Cappuccilli
Barbarina E. Fusco
ilh Chor, Philh, C.M. Giulini (r1959)
(1/90) (EMI) Ⓓ [2] **CMS7 63266-2**
Figaro C. Siepi
Susanna H. Gueden
Count Almaviva A. Poell
Countess Almaviva L. della Casa
Cherubino S. Danco
Marcellina H. Rössl-Majdan
Bartolo F. Corena
Don Basilio M. Dickie

Don Curzio H. Meyer-Welfing
Antonio H. Pröglhöf
Barbarina A. Felbermayer
Vienna St Op Chor, VPO, E. Kleiber (r1955)
(2/90) (DECC) Ⓓ [3] **417 315-2DM3**
Figaro P. Schoeffler
Susanna M. Cebotari
Count Almaviva M. Ahlersmeyer
Countess Almaviva M. Teschemacher
Cherubino A. Kolniak
Marcellina E. Waldenau
Bartolo K. Böhme
Don Basilio K. Wessely
Don Curzio H. Buchta
Antonio H.H. Fiedler
Barbarina H. Franck
Stuttgart Rad Chor, Stuttgart RO, K. Böhm (Ger: bp1938)
(11/90) (PREI) Ⓓ [2] **90035**
Figaro H. Prey
Susanna E. Mathis
Count Almaviva D. Fischer-Dieskau
Countess Almaviva G. Janowitz
Cherubino T. Troyanos
Marcellina P. Johnson
Bartolo P. Lagger
Don Basilio E. Wohlfahrt
Don Curzio M. Vantin
Antonio K. Hirte
Barbarina B. Vogel
Berlin Deutsche Op Chor, Berlin Deutsche Op Orch, K. Böhm
(12/90) (DG) Ⓓ [3] **429 869-2GX3**
Figaro G. Evans
Susanna J. Blegen
Count Almaviva D. Fischer-Dieskau
Countess Almaviva H. Harper
Cherubino T. Berganza
Marcellina B. Finnilä
Bartolo W. McCue
Don Basilio J. Fryatt
Don Curzio J. Robertson
Antonio M. Donnelly
Barbarina E. Gale
John Alldis Ch, ECO, D. Barenboim
(5/91) (EMI) Ⓓ [3] **CMS7 63646-2**
Figaro J. Tomlinson
Susanna J. Rodgers
Count Almaviva A. Schmidt
Countess Almaviva L. Cuberli
Cherubino C. Bartoli
Marcellina P. Pancella
Bartolo G. von Kannen
Don Basilio G. Clark
Don Curzio R. Brunner
Antonio P. Rose
Barbarina H. Leidland
Berlin RIAS Chbr Ch, BPO, D. Barenboim
(5/91) (ERAT) Ⓓ [3] **2292-45501-2**
Figaro G. Evans
Susanna R. Grist
Count Almaviva G. Bacquier
Countess Almaviva E. Söderström
Cherubino T. Berganza
Marcellina A. Burmeister
Bartolo M. Langdon
Don Basilio W. Hollweg
Don Curzio W. Brokmeier
Antonio C. Grant
Barbarina M. Price
John Alldis Ch, New Philh, O. Klemperer
(9/91) (EMI) Ⓓ [3] **CMS7 63849-2**
Figaro S. Bruscantini
Susanna G. Sciutti
Count Almaviva F. Calabrese
Countess Almaviva S. Jurinac
Cherubino R. Stevens
Marcellina M. Sinclair
Bartolo I. Wallace
Don Basilio H. Cuénod
Don Curzio D. McCoshan
Antonio G. Griffiths
Barbarina J. Sinclair
Glyndebourne Fest Chor, Glyndebourne Fest Orch, V. Gui (r1955)
(9/91) (CFP) Ⓓ [2] **CD-CFPD4724**
(9/91) (CFP) ⊟ [2] **TC-CFPD4724**
Figaro A. Titus
Susanna H. Donath
Count Almaviva F. Furlanetto
Countess Almaviva J. Varady
Cherubino M. Schmiege
Marcellina C. Kallisch
Bartolo S. Nimsgern
Don Basilio H. Zednik
Don Curzio C.H. Ahnsjö

Antonio G. Auer
Barbarina I. Kertesi
Bavarian Rad Chor, BRSO, Colin Davis
(9/91) (RCA) Ⓓ [3] **RD60440**
Figaro F. Furlanetto
Susanna D. Upshaw
Count Almaviva T. Hampson
Countess Almaviva K. Te Kanawa
Cherubino A.S. von Otter
Marcellina T. Troyanos
Bartolo P. Plishka
Don Basilio A. Laciura
Don Curzio M. Forrest
Antonio R. Capecchi
Barbarina H. Grant-Murphy
NY Met Op Chor, NY Met Op Orch, James Levine
(9/91) (DG) Ⓓ [3] **431 619-2GH3**
Figaro W. Ganzarolli
Susanna M. Freni
Count Almaviva I. Wixell
Countess Almaviva J. Norman
Cherubino Y. Minton
Marcellina M. Casula
Bartolo C. Grant
Don Basilio R. Tear
Don Curzio D. Lennox
Antonio P. Hudson
Barbarina L. Watson
BBC Chor, BBC SO, Colin Davis (r1971)
(1/92) (PHIL) Ⓓ [3] **422 540-2PME3**
Figaro L. Gallo
Susanna M. McLaughlin
Count Almaviva R. Raimondi
Countess Almaviva C. Studer
Cherubino G. Sima
Marcellina M. Lilowa
Bartolo R. Mazzola
Don Basilio H. Zednik
Don Curzio F. Kasemann
Antonio I. Gáti
Barbarina Y. Tannenbergerova
Vienna St Op Chor, Vienna St Op Orch, C. Abbado, J. Miller
(2/94) (SONY) ◖ [2] **S2LV46406**
(2/94) (SONY) ▭ **SHV46406**
Figaro M. Pertusi
Susanna M. McLaughlin
Count Almaviva L. Gallo
Countess Almaviva K. Mattila
Cherubino M. Bacelli
Marcellina N. Curiel
Bartolo A. Nosotti
Basilio U. Benelli
Don Curzio G. Sica
Antonio G. Tadeo
MMF Chor, MMF Orch, Z. Mehta (r1992)
(6/94) (SONY) Ⓓ [3] **S3K53286**
Figaro B. Terfel
Susanna A. Hagley
Count Almaviva R. Gilfry
Countess Almaviva H. Martinpelto
Cherubino P. H. Stephen
Marcellina S. McCulloch
Bartolo C. Feller
Don Basilio; Don Curzio F. Egerton
Antonio J. Clarkson
Barbarina C. Backes
Monteverdi Ch, EBS, J. E. Gardiner (pp1993)
(8/94) (ARCH) Ⓓ [3] **439 871-2AH3**
Figaro R. Capecchi
Susanna I. Seefried
Count Almaviva D. Fischer-Dieskau
Countess Almaviva M. Stader
Cherubino H. Töpper
Marcellina L. Benningsen
Bartolo I. Sardi
Don Basilio P. Kuen
Don Curzio F. Lenz
Antonio G. Wieter
Barbarina R. Schwaiger
Berlin RIAS Chbr Ch, Berlin RSO, F. Fricsay (r1960)
(10/94) (DG) Ⓓ [3] **437 671-2GDO3**
Figaro W. Berry
Susanna R. Streich
Count Almaviva P. Schoeffler
Countess Almaviva S. Jurinac
Cherubino C. Ludwig
Marcellina I. Malaniuk
Bartolo O. Czerwenka
Don Basilio E. Majkut
Don Curzio M. Dickie
Antonio K. Dönch

Barbarina R. Schwaiger
Vienna St Op Chor, Vienna SO, K. Böhm (r1956)
(10/94) (PHIL) ⦶ [3] **438 670-2PM3**
Figaro A. Scharinger
Susanna B. Bonney
Count Almaviva T. Hampson
Countess Almaviva C. Margiono
Cherubino P. Lang
Marcellina A. Murray
Bartolo K. Moll
Don Basilio P. Langridge
Don Curzio C. Späth
Antonio K. Langan
Barbarina I. Rey
Netherlands Op Chor, Concertgebouw, N. Harnoncourt (r1993)
(10/94) (TELD) ⦶ [3] **4509-90861-2**
Figaro B. Terfel
Susanna A. Hagley
Count Almaviva R. Gilfry
Countess Almaviva H. Martinpelto
Cherubino P.H. Stephen
Marcellina S. McCulloch
Bartolo C. Feller
Don Basilio; Don Curzio F. Egerton
Antonio J. Clarkson
Barbarina C. Backes
Monteverdi Ch, EBS, J.E. Gardiner, J-L. Thamin (r1993)
(3/95) (ARCH) ◐ [2] **072 439-1AH2**
(3/95) (ARCH) ▣ **072 439-3AH**
Figaro A. Miles
Susanna N. Focile
Count Almaviva A. Corbelli
Countess Almaviva C. Vaness
Cherubino S. Mentzer
Marcellina S. Murphy
Bartolo; Antonio A. Antoniozzi
Don Basilio; Don Curzio R. Davies
Barbarina R. Evans
Scottish Chbr Chor, Scottish CO, C. Mackerras (r1994; with appendices)
(8/95) (TELA) ⦶ [3] **CD80388**
Figaro L. Gallo
Susanna S. McNair
Count Almaviva B. Skovhus
Countess Almaviva C. Studer
Cherubino C. Bartoli
Marcellina A. C. Antonacci
Bartolo I. d'Arcangelo
Don Basilio C. Allemano
Don Curzio P. Jelosits
Antonio I. Gáti
Barbarina A. Rost
Vienna St Op Chor, VPO, C. Abbado (r1994)
(10/95) (DG) ⦶ [3] **445 903-2GH3**
Excs M. Ahlersmeyer, M. Reining, M. Cebotari, M. Rohs, Vienna St Op Orch, K. Böhm (pp1941: Ger) (3/95) (SCHW) ⦶ [2] **314602**
V2, V6. J. Baker, Scottish CO, R. Leppard (r1984) (ERAT) ⦶ **4509-98497-2**
1. ASMF, N. Marriner (WIEN) ▣ **WNR2037**
1. BBC SO, Colin Davis (PHIL) ▭ **422 269-4PMI**
1. Staatskapelle Dresden, H. Vonk (CAPR) ⦶ **10 070**
(CAPR) ▭ **CC27 086**
1. Cleveland Orch, G. Szell (IMP) ⦶ [2] **DUET 15CD**
1. ECO, L. Hager (r1989) (NOVA) ⦶ **150 041-2**
1. LPO, G. Solti (DECC) ⦶ **425 851-2DWO**
(DECC) ▭ **425 851-4DWO**
1. Leningrad PO, E. Mravinsky (pp1965) (OLYM) ⦶ [6] **OCD5002**
1. New Philh, O. Klemperer (EMI) ⦶ **CDM7 63619-2**
1. Staatskapelle Dresden, H. Vonk (CAPR) ⦶ [3] **10 810**
1. English Sinfonia, C. Groves (IMP) ⦶ [4] **BOXD9**
1. BPO, J. Horenstein (r1929) (KOCH) ⦶ **37054-2**
1. LPO, G. Solti (DECC) ⦶ **433 323-2DH**
(DECC) ▭ **433 323-4DH**
1. Zurich Tonhalle Orch, J. Krips (ADES) ⦶ **13225-2**
1. LPO, B. Haitink (PHIL) ⦶ **432 512-2PSL**
1. RPO, E. Bátiz (ASV) ⦶ **CDQS6065**
(ASV) ▭ **ZCQS6065**
1. Paris Cons, R. Leibowitz (r1960) (CHES) ⦶ **Chesky CD61**
1. English Sinfonia, C. Groves (IMP) ⦶ **PCDS11**

1. Munich Brass (arr brass ens) (ORFE) ⦶ **C247911A**
1. BPO, W. Furtwängler (r1933) (SYMP) ⦶ **SYMCD1043**
1. Prague CO, O. Vlček (r1988) (SUPR) ⦶ [2] **11 1166-2**
1. NBC SO, A. Toscanini (bp1947) (RCA) ⦶ **GD60286**
1. RPO, E. Bátiz (ASV) ⦶ **CDQS6076**
(ASV) ▭ **ZCQS6076**
1. Cleveland Orch, G. Szell (SONY) ⦶ **SBK39436**
1. English Sinfonia, C. Groves (IMP) ⦶ [3] **TCD1014**
1. Manchester Camerata, C. Rizzi (MANC) ⦶ **MCL20**
1. LPO, Anon (cond) (WORD) ⦶ **FCD7404**
1. ASMF, N. Marriner (EMI) OO **DCC7 47014-5**
1. Sinfonia Varsovia, E. Krivine (r1990) (DENO) ⦶ **CO-75372**
1. ASMF, N. Marriner (EMI) ⬤ **MDC7 47014-8**
1. NY Met Op Orch, James Levine (DG) ⦶ **439 150-2GMA**
(DG) ▭ **439 150-4GMA**
1. English Sinfonia, C. Groves (IMP) ⦶ [3] **TCD1070**
1. RPO, J. Glover (r1993) (TRIN) ⦶ **TRP004**
(TRIN) ▭ **MCTRP004**
1. LPO, T. Beecham (r1937) (PEAR) ⦶ **GEMMCD9094**
1. Polish Chmbr PO, W. Rajski (INTE) ⦶ **INT830 899**
1. Concertgebouw, Zurich Op Orch, Zurich Op Hse Mozart Orch, VCM, N. Harnoncourt (TELD) ⦶ **4509-95523-2**
1. Vienna Haydn Orch, I. Kertész (r1971) (DECC) ⦶ [2] **443 762-2DF2**
1. RPO, Colin Davis (r c1961) (EMI) ⦶ [2] **CES5 68533-2**
1. Leningrad PO, E. Mravinsky (pp1965) (MELO) ⦶ [10] **74321 25189-2**
1. Leningrad PO, E. Mravinsky (pp1965) (MELO) ⦶ **74321 25191-2**
1. Berlin Deutsche Op Orch, K. Böhm (DG) ⦶ [2] **447 364-2GDB2**
1. St Paul CO, B. McFerrin (r1995) (SONY) ⦶ **SK64600**
1. Basle SO, M. Atzmon (r1973/4) (RCA) ⦶ **74321 29237-2**
1. ASMF, N. Marriner (4/84) (EMI) ⦶ **CDC7 47014-2**
1. RPO, E. Bátiz (11/89) (ASV) ⦶ **CDQS6033**
(11/89) (ASV) ▭ **ZCQS6033**
1. BPO (11/89) (RCA) ⦶ **RD60032**
1. English Sinfonia, C. Groves (11/90) (IMP) ⦶ **PCD939**
(11/90) (IMP) ▭ **CIMPC939**
1. Staatskapelle Dresden, H. Vonk (10/91) (CAPR) ⦶ [3] **10 809**
1. BPO, W. Furtwängler (r1933) (4/92) (KOCH) ⦶ [2] **37059-2**
1. Tafelmusik, B. Weil (5/92) (SONY) ⦶ **SK46695**
1. NYPO, L. Bernstein (r1968) (9/93) (SONY) ⦶ **SMK47601**
1. LPO, T. Beecham (r1937) (10/94) (DUTT) ⦶ **CDLX7009**
1. LSO, J. Krips (r1951) (7/95) (DECC) ⦶ [2] **443 530-2LF2**
1, 11, 22b K. Te Kanawa, WNO Orch, C. Mackerras (10/91) (EMI) ◐ **LDA9 91242-1**
(10/91) (EMI) ▣ **MVC9 91242-3**
1, 20a, 20b J. Van Dam, Paris Orch Ens, J-P. Wallez (pp) (5/88) (NOVA) ⦶ **150 014-2**
1, 22a, 22b K. Te Kanawa, LSO, J. Mauceri (12/90) (DECC) ▣ **084 474-3**
1, 22b K. Te Kanawa, LPO, G. Solti (6/91) (DECC) ⦶ **430 498-2DWO**
(6/91) (DECC) ▭ **430 498-4DWO**
1, 2, 3b, 4b, 10-12, 13b, 19, 21, 22b, 23b, 25, 30b, 33(pt) Consortium Classicum, D. Klöcker (arr various: wind ens) (BAYE) ⦶ **BR100073**
1, 2, 3b, 4b, 10-12, 13b, 19, 22b, 23b, 25, 30b, 33. Linos Ens (arr Wind Band; r1991) (CAPR) ⦶ **10 493**
1, 2, 3b, 4b, 10, 11, 12, 13b, 19, 21, 22b, 23b, 25, 30b, 31. Amadeus Ens, J. Rudel (arr Wendt: Woodwinds and Bass) (MUSM) ⦶ [5] **67118-2**
1, 2, 4b, 7, 10, 12, 19, 20a, 20b, 23b, 24, 26, 29a, 29b, 30a, 30b, 32. M. Freni, J. Norman, Y. Minton, L. Watson, W. Ganzarolli, I. Wixell, BBC Sym Chor, BBC SO, Colin Davis (BELA) ⦶ **450 047-2**
(BELA) ▭ **450 047-4**

1, 2, 9, 10, 19(pt), 33. A. Jerger, M. Reining, P. Schoeffler, M. Perras, D. With, O. Levko-Antosch, K. Ettl, W. Wernigk, H. Gallos, V. Madin, D. Komarek, Vienna St Op Chor, Vienna St Op Orch, W. Loibner (pp1938: Ger) (6/95) (SCHW) ⦶ [2] **314632**
1, 3b, 4b, 5, 7, 10-12, 13b, 20b, 22a, 22b, 23b, 26, 29b, 30a, 30b, 32(pt), 33. D. Fischer-Dieskau, G. Janowitz, E. Mathis, H. Prey, T. Troyanos, P. Lagger, B. Vogel, Berlin Deutsche Op Chor, Berlin Deutsche Op Orch, K. Böhm (DG) ⦶ **423 115-2GH**
1, 3b, 4b, 5, 7, 9-12, 18(pt), 20a, 20b, 21, 22a, 22b, 29a, 29b, 30a, 30b, 32(pt), 33. T. Hampson, K. Te Kanawa, D. Upshaw, F. Furlanetto, A.S. von Otter, P. Plishka, T. Troyanos, NY Met Op Chor, NY Met Op Orch, James Levine (DG) ⦶ **435 488-2GH**
1, 3b, 4b, 5, 7, 10-12, 13b, 20b, 22a, 22b, 23b, 26, 29b, 30a, 30b, 32(pt), 33. D. Fischer-Dieskau, G. Janowitz, E. Mathis, H. Prey, T. Troyanos, P. Lagger, B. Vogel, Berlin Deutsche Op Chor, Berlin Deutsche Op Orch, K. Böhm (r1968) (DG) ⦶ **439 449-2GCL**
(DG) ▭ **439 449-4GCL**
1, 3b, 4b, 5, 7, 9-12, 13b, 18, 19, 20a, 22a, 22b, 23a, 23b, 26, 29b, 30a, 30b, 33. B. Terfel, A. Hagley, R. Gilfry, H. Martinpelto, P. H. Stephen, S. McCulloch, C. Feller, F. Egerton, J. Clarkson, C. Backes, Monteverdi Ch, EBS, J. E. Gardiner (pp1993) (ARCH) ⦶ **445 874-2AH**
1, 4b, 5, 7, 10-12, 13b, 20a, 20b, 21, 22a, 22b, 23a, 23b, 29a, 29b, 30a, 30b, 32, 33. K. Te Kanawa, L. Popp, F. von Stade, S. Ramey, T. Allen, K. Moll, LPO, G. Solti (DECC) ⦶ **417 395-2DH**
1, 4b, 5, 7, 10-12, 13b, 20a, 21, 22a, 22b, 23b, 25, 29b, 30a, 30b, 33. R. Raimondi, L. Popp, B. Hendricks, J. Van Dam, A. Baltsa, F. Palmer, A. Baldin, N. Jenkins, R. Lloyd, D. Maxwell, C. Pope, Ambrosian Op Chor, ASMF, N. Marriner (PHIL) ⦶ **416 870-2PH**
1, 4b, 5, 7, 10-12, 13b, 20a, 20b, 21, 22a, 22b, 23a, 23b, 29a, 29b, 30a, 30b, 32, 33. K. Te Kanawa, L. Popp, F. von Stade, S. Ramey, T. Allen, K. Moll, LPO, G. Solti ( ) (DECC) OO **417 395-5DH**
1, 4b, 5, 7, 10-12, 13b, 20a, 20b, 21, 22a, 22b, 23b, 29b, 30b, 32. J. Van Dam, I. Cotrubas, T. Krause, A. Tomowa-Sintow, F. von Stade, J. Berbié, J. Bastin, H. Zednik, K. Equiluz, Z. Kélémen, C. Barbaux, Vienna St Op Chor, VPO, H. von Karajan (r1978) (DECC) ⦶ **436 311-2DA**
1, 4b, 5, 7, 10-12, 13b, 18(pt), 20a, 20b, 21, 22a, 22b, 29a, 29b, 30a, 30b, 31-33. P. Salomaa, B. Bonney, H. Hagegård, A. Auger, A. Nafé, D. Jones, C. Feller, E. Gimenez, F. Egerton, E. Florimo, N. Argenta, Drottningholm Court Th Chor, Drottningholm Court Th Orch, A. Östman (r1987) (L'OI) ⦶ **443 191-2OM**
1, 4b, 7, 9-12, 13b, 16b, 17a, 18(pt), 20b, 21, 22b, 23b, 26, 28, 29b, 31. J. Tomlinson, J. Rodgers, A. Schmidt, L. Cuberli, C. Bartoli, P. Pancella, G. von Kannen, G. Clark, R. Brunner, P. Rose, H. Leidland, Berlin RIAS Chbr Ch, BPO, D. Barenboim (r1990) (ERAT) ⦶ **4509-94822-2**
1, 8. SO, T. Beecham (r c1912/6) (11/91) (SYMP) ⦶ [2] **SYMCD1096/7**
2. G. Rolandi, C. Desderi, LPO, B. Haitink (r1987) (6/94) (EMI) ⦶ **CDH5 65072-2**
3b, 7, 8, 10-12, 15b, 16b, 17b(pt), 19(pt), 19, 20b, 22a, 22b, 23b, 29b, 30a, 30b, 31, 32. T. Allen, K. Battle, J. Hynninen, M. Price, A. Murray, K. Rydl, M. Nicolesco, A. Ramirez, E. Gavazzi, P. Pace, F. De Grandis, Vienna St Op Concert Ch, VPO, R. Muti (EMI) ⦶ **CDC7 54321-2**
4a, 4b G. De Luca, orch (r1917) (PEAR) ⦶ [3] **GEMMCDS9160(1**
4a, 4b, 5, 10, 20a, 20b, 29a, 29b F. Furlanetto, Vienna SO, I. Marin (3/92) (SONY) ⦶ **SK47192**
4a, 4b, 10. C. Siepi, VPO, E. Kleiber (r1955) (DECC) ⦶ **440 418-2DM**
4b R. Mayr, orch (r1922: Ger) (ORFE) ⦶ **C394101B**
4b G. De Luca, orch (r1917) (1/92) (PREI) ⦶ **89036**
4b P. Schoeffler, National SO, C. Krauss (r1947) (1/95) (PREI) ⦶ **9019**
4b, 29b E. Pinza, NY Met Op Orch, B. Walter (r1946) (SONY) ⦶ [3] **SM3K4721**

4b, 5, 10, 20a, 20b, 29a, 29b G. London, Columbia SO, B. Walter (r1953) (SONY) Ⓓ [3] **SM3K47211**
4b, 7, 10-12, 18, 19, 20a, 22a, 22b, 23b, 29a, 29b, 30a, 30b, 33. G. Taddei, A. Moffo, E. Waechter, E. Schwarzkopf, F. Cossotto, I. Vinco, D. Gatta, R. Ercolani, E. Fusco, P. Cappuccilli, Philh, C.M. Giulini (EMI) Ⓓ **CDM7 63409-2**
4b, 10, 12, 23b Budapest Wind Ens, K. Berkes (arr Wendt) (QUIN) ⊟ **QUI40 3008**
4b, 10, 16b, 20a N. De Carolis, Venice and Padua CO, B. Giuranna (CLAV) Ⓓ **CD50-9120**
4b, 10, 20a, 20b, 22b H. Prey, Salzburg Mozarteum Orch, B. Weil (5/88) (DENO) Ⓓ **CO-1741**
4b, 29a, 29b G. De Luca, anon (r1907) (PEAR) Ⓓ [3] **GEMMCDS9159(2)**
4b, 29b E. Pinza, NY Met Op Orch, B. Walter (r1946) (4/90) (CBS) Ⓓ **CD45693**
5. A. Kipnis, E. Ruziczka, Berlin St Op Orch, E. Orthmann (Ger: r1931) (12/90) (PREI) Ⓓ **89019**
5. A. Kipnis, E. Ruziczka, Berlin St Op Orch, E. Orthmann (Ger: r1931) (10/91) (PEAR) Ⓓ **GEMMCD9451**
7. C. Bartoli, Berlin RSO, R. Paternostro (CAPR) Ⓓ [3] **10 810**
7. L. Helletsgruber, Glyndebourne Fest Orch, F. Busch (r1935) (MMOI) Ⓓ **CDMOIR406** (MMOI) ⊟ **CMOIR406**
7. C. Supervia, orch, A. Albergoni (r1928) (NIMB) Ⓓ **NI7864**
7. A. Galli-Curci, orch (r1917) (PEAR) Ⓓ **GEMMCD9130**
7. G. Farrar, orch (r1927) (IRCC) Ⓓ **IRCC-CD805**
7. E. Steber, RCA Victor Orch, E. Leinsdorf (r1947) (RCA) Ⓓ **74321 24284-2** (RCA) ⊟ **74321 24284-4**
7. Z. Dolukhanova, Moscow PO, G. Stolarov (pp1954: Russ) (RUSS) Ⓓ **RDCD15023**
7. A. Galli-Curci, orch (r1917) (2/89) (PEAR) Ⓓ **GEMMCD9308**
7. P. McCann, Black Dyke Mills Band, P. Parkes (r1984: arr P Parkes) (11/92) (CHAN) Ⓓ **CHAN4501** (11/92) (CHAN) ⊟ **BBTD4501**
7. A. Galli-Curci, orch, J. Pasternack (r1917) (3/94) (ROMO) Ⓓ [2] **81003-2**
7, 11, 12, 22b, 30a, 30b E. Schwarzkopf, Philh, J. Pritchard (r1952) (EMI) Ⓓ **CDH7 63708-2**
7, 12. E. Schumann, orch (r1920) (PEAR) Ⓓ **GEMMCD9445**
7, 12. T. Berganza, ECO, D. Barenboim (EMI) Ⓓ **CDM7 64359-2**
7, 12. F. von Stade, Rotterdam PO, E. de Waart (PHIL) Ⓓ **420 084-2PH**
7, 12. C. Supervia, orch, A. Albergoni (r1928) (9/90) (CLUB) Ⓓ **CL99-074**
7, 12. C. Supervia, orch, A. Albergoni (r1928) (9/90) (PREI) Ⓓ **89023**
7, 12. T. Berganza, LSO, J. Pritchard (r1962) (4/93) (DECC) Ⓓ **421 899-2DA**
7, 12, 13b, 30b E. Schumann, orch, G.W. Byng (r1926) (6/91) (PREI) Ⓓ **89031**
7, 12, 30a, 30b C. Bartoli, Vienna CO, G. Fischer (12/91) (DECC) Ⓓ **430 513-2DH** (DECC) ⊟ **430 513-4DH**
7, 13b, 30b E. Schumann, orch, L. Collingwood (r1927) (ROMO) Ⓓ **81019-2**
7, 19, 22a, 22b, 30a, 30b H. Gueden, I. Seefried, E. Schwarzkopf, P. Schoeffler, VPO, W. Furtwängler (pp1953: Ger) (ORFE) Ⓓ **C394201B**
9, 24. Netherlands Op Chor, Concertgebouw, N. Harnoncourt (r1993) (TELD) Ⓓ **4509-97505-2**
9, 25. Berlin St Op Chor, Berlin Staatskapelle, O. Suitner (CAPR) Ⓓ [3] **10 810**
10. T. Allen, Scottish CO, R. Armstrong (EMIL) Ⓓ **CDZ104** (EMIL) ⊟ **LZ104**
10. M. Pertusi, Berlin RSO, R. Paternostro (CAPR) Ⓓ [3] **10 810**
10. B. Terfel, ASMF, N. Marriner (PHIL) Ⓓ [8] **422 523-2PME8(2)**
10. J. Diaz, ECO, E. Stratta (ASV) Ⓓ **CDQS6065** (ASV) ⊟ **ZCQS6065**
10. T. Krause, Vienna Haydn Orch, I. Kertész (DECC) Ⓓ **433 066-2DWO** (DECC) ⊟ **433 066-4DWO**
10. S. Ramey, LPO, G. Solti (r1981) (DECC) Ⓓ **440 947-2DH** (DECC) ⊟ **440 947-4DH**
10. C. Desderi, LPO, B. Haitink (7/91) (EMIL) Ⓓ **CDZ7 67015-2**
10. E. Pinza, orch, B. Reibold (r1939) (7/91) (MMOI) Ⓓ **CDMOIR404** (MMOI) ⊟ **CMOIR404**
10. C. Santley, anon (r1903) (10/92) (SYMP) Ⓓ **SYMCD1093**
10. T. Gobbi, Philh, J. Robertson (r1950) (8/93) (TEST) Ⓓ **SBT1019**
10. S. Ramey, LPO, G. Solti (r1981) (10/93) (DECC) Ⓓ **436 464-2DM**
10. P. Schoeffler, Vienna St Op Orch, W. Loibner (pp1938: Ger) (6/94) (SCHW) Ⓓ **314502**
10. E. Kunz, VPO, H. von Karajan (r1947) (9/95) (TEST) Ⓓ **SBT1059**
10a C. Desderi, LPO, B. Haitink (CFP) Ⓓ **CD-CFP4612** (CFP) ⊟ **TC-CFP4612**
10, 11, 12. C. Margiono, P. Lang, A. Scharinger, Concertgebouw, N. Harnoncourt (r1993) (TELD) Ⓓ **4509-97507-2**
10, 12. J. Novotná, E. Pinza, VPO, B. Walter (pp1937) (ORFE) Ⓓ **C394101B**
10, 19, 30b A. Martin, D. Robin, Vienna Mozart Orch, K. Leitner (12/91) (NAXO) Ⓓ **8 550435**
10, 20a, 20b R. Bruson, NHK Chbr Sols, R. Paternostro (pp1990) (10/91) (CAPR) Ⓓ **10 348**
11. K. Te Kanawa, NY Met Op Orch, James Levine (DG) ⊟ **439 153-4GMA**
11. M. Callas, Paris Cons, N. Rescigno (EMI) Ⓓ **CDC7 49005-2**
11. Lotte Lehmann, Berlin St Op Orch, M. Gurlitt (Ger: r1927) (MMOI) Ⓓ **CDMOIR406** (MMOI) ⊟ **CMOIR406**
11. L. Pons, orch, B. Walter (r1942) (SONY) Ⓓ [3] **SM3K47211**
11. J. Rodgers, English Northern Philh, P. Daniel (r1992) (EMI) Ⓓ **CDC7 54785-2**
11. J. Varady, BRSO, Colin Davis (RCA) Ⓓ **09026 61886-2** (RCA) ⊟ **09026 61886-4**
11. F. Austral, orch (r1927: Eng) (PEAR) Ⓓ **GEMMCD9146**
11. E. Schwarzkopf, Philh, C.M. Giulini (r1959) (EMI) Ⓓ **CDM5 65577-2**
11. V. de los Angeles, Philh, W. Susskind (r1949) (8/90) (EMI) Ⓓ **CDH7 63495-2**
11. E. Schwarzkopf, VPO, H. von Karajan (r1950) (12/90) (EMI) Ⓓ **CDM7 63657-2**
11. F. Leider, orch (r1925: Ger) (5/91) (PREI) Ⓓ [3] **89301**
11. J. Gadski, orch (r1910) (7/91) (CLUB) Ⓓ **CL99-109**
11. M. Price, VPO, R. Muti (7/91) (EMIL) Ⓓ **CDZ7 67015-2**
11. Lotte Lehmann, orch (Ger: r1917) (7/92) (PEAR) Ⓓ [3] **GEMMCDS9925(2)**
11. Lilli Lehmann, orch (r1907: Ger) (7/93) (NIMB) Ⓓ [2] **NI7840/1**
11. E. Rethberg, orch (r1921: Ger) (7/94) (PREI) Ⓓ **89051**
11. E. Destinn, orch, F. Kark (r1906: Ger) (12/94) (SUPR) Ⓓ [12] **11 2136-2(1)**
11. R. Hunter, Tasmanian SO, D. Franks (r1989) (10/95) (ABCC) Ⓓ **8 7000 10**
11. E. Rethberg, Berlin SO, F. Weissmann (r1930: Ger) (10/95) (ROMO) Ⓓ [2] **81014-2**
11, 12, 13b S. Jurinac, E. Lear, G. Sciutti, VPO, H. Wallberg (pp1962) (ORFE) Ⓓ **C394301B**
11, 12, 30a, 30b L. Popp, Munich RO, L. Slatkin (r1983) (8/84) (EMI) Ⓓ **CDC7 47019-2**
11, 22a, 22b K. Te Kanawa, LPO, G. Solti (r1981) (DECC) Ⓓ **440 401-2DM**
11, 22a, 22b A. Auger, Drottningholm Court Th Orch, A. Östman (r1987) (DECC) Ⓓ **440 414-2DM**
11, 22a, 22b M. Reining, VPO, J. Krips (r1950; Ger) (9/92) (PREI) Ⓓ **90083**
11, 22a, 22b, 30a, 30b M. Reining, Prussian St Orch, H.U. Müller (r1942: Ger) (9/94) (PREI) Ⓓ **89065**
11, 22a, 22b C. Studer, ASMF, N. Marriner (9/94) (PHIL) Ⓓ **442 410-2PM**
11, 22b E. Steber, orch, H. Barlow (bp1951-52) (VAI) ▣ **VAI69102**
11, 22b S. Ghazarian, NHK Chbr Sols, R. Paternostro (pp1990) (CAPR) Ⓓ [3] **10 810**
11, 22b T. Lemnitz, BPO, B. Seidler-Winkler (r1938) (10/90) (PREI) Ⓓ **89025**
11, 22b F. Leider, orch (r1921: Ger) (5/91) (PREI) Ⓓ [3] **89301**
11, 22b S. Ghazarian, NHK Chbr Sols, R. Paternostro (pp1990) (10/91) (CAPR) Ⓓ **10 348**
11, 30a, 30b L. Price, New Philh, P.H. Adler (6/93) (RCA) Ⓓ **09026 61357-2**
11, 30b Lotte Lehmann, orch (Ger: r1917) (6/92) (PREI) Ⓓ [3] **89302**
12. Preston's Pocket (trans fl) (AMON) Ⓓ **CD-SAR11** (5/84) (AMON) ⊟ **CSAR11**
12. T. Indermühle, Salonisti (arr Salabert) (EURO) Ⓓ **GD69298**
12. F. von Stade, LPO, G. Solti (DECC) Ⓓ **433 822-2DH** (DECC) ⊟ **433 822-4DH**
12. B. Fassbaender, Vienna Haydn Orch, I. Kertész (DECC) Ⓓ **433 064-2DWO**
12. I. Baillie, orch (Eng: r1927) (PEAR) Ⓓ **GEMMCD9934**
12. Z. Mehta, VPO, K. Böhm (DECC) ◖ **071 142-1DH** (DECC) ▣ **071 142-3DH**
12. T. Berganza, LSO, J. Pritchard (r1962) (DECC) Ⓓ **436 300-2DX** (DECC) ⊟ **436 300-4DX**
12. H. Kashiwagi, S. Harrison (SCHW) Ⓓ **312642**
12. L. Kitchen, English Northern Philh, P. Daniel (r1992) (EMI) Ⓓ **CDC7 54785-2**
12. F. von Stade, LPO, G. Solti (r1981) (DECC) Ⓓ **436 472-2DM**
12. W. Schulz, H. Schellenberger (arr fl/ob) (DG) Ⓓ **439 150-2GMA** (DG) ⊟ **439 150-4GMA**
12. C. Bartoli, Berlin RIAS Chor, BPO, D. Barenboim (ERAT) Ⓓ **4509-91715-2** (ERAT) ⊟ **4509-91715-4**
12. C. Ludwig, VPO, K. Böhm (pp1957) (ORFE) Ⓓ **C365941A**
12. E. Schumann, orch (r1926) (NIMB) Ⓓ **NI7864**
12. N. Melba, orch (r1910) (PEAR) Ⓓ **GEMMCD9130**
12. T. Berganza, LSO, J. Pritchard (r1962) (DECC) Ⓓ [2] **443 762-2DF2**
12. E. Schumann, orch, G.W. Byng (r1926) (ROMO) Ⓓ **81019-2**
12. J. Larmore, Lausanne CO, J. López-Cobos (r1994) (TELD) Ⓓ **4509-96800-2**
12. N. Melba, orch, W.B. Rogers (r1910) (3/89) (LARR) Ⓓ **CDLRH221**
12. A. Patti, L. Ronald (r1905) (4/90) (PEAR) Ⓓ **GEMMCD9312**
12. L. Garrett, Philh, A. Greenwood (r1990-1) (11/91) (SILV) Ⓓ **SONGCD903** (11/91) (SILV) ⊟ **SONGC903**
12. Lotte Lehmann, orch (Ger: r1921) (6/92) (PREI) Ⓓ [3] **89302**
12. L. Tetrazzini, orch, P. Pitt (r1907) (9/92) (EMI) Ⓓ [3] **CHS7 63802-2(1)**
12. L. Tetrazzini, orch, P. Pitt (r1907) (9/92) (PEAR) Ⓓ **GEMMCD9221**
12. C. Bartoli, G. Fischer (pp1991) (11/92) (DECC) ◖ **071 141-1DH** (11/92) (DECC) ▣ **071 141-3DH**
12. A. Patti, L. Ronald (r1905) (7/93) (NIMB) Ⓓ [2] **NI7840/1**
12. F. von Stade, LPO, G. Solti (r1981) (10/93) (DECC) Ⓓ **436 462-2DM**
12. G. Farrar, orch (r1908) (10/94) (NIMB) Ⓓ **NI7857**
12. N. Melba, orch, W.B. Rogers (r1910) (5/95) (ROMO) Ⓓ [3] **81011-2(2)**
12. N. Melba, orch, W.B. Rogers (r1907) (5/95) (ROMO) Ⓓ [3] **81011-2(1)**
12, 22a, 22b, 30a, 30b M. Price, ECO, J. Lockhart (r1973) (5/95) (RCA) Ⓓ [2] **09026 61635-2**
12, 30a, b C. Bartoli, Vienna CO, G. Fischer (r1989) (DECC) Ⓓ **448 300-2DH** (DECC) ⊟ **448 300-4DH**
12, 30b H. Gueden, VPO, C. Krauss (r1951) (PREI) Ⓓ **90227**
12, 30b F. Cossotto, A. Moffo, Philh, C.M. Giulini (7/91) (EMIL) Ⓓ **CDZ7 67015-2**
13b D. Upshaw, NY Met Op Orch, James Levine (DG) ⊟ **439 153-4GMA**
13b H. Gueden, VPO, A. Erede (r1952) (PREI) Ⓓ **90227**
13b E. Schumann, orch (r1927) (7/92) (PEAR) Ⓓ [3] **GEMMCDS9925(2)**
17b E. Schwarzkopf, I. Seefried, E. Kunz, D. Fischer-Dieskau, VPO, K. Böhm (pp1958) (ORFE) Ⓓ **C335931A**
19. A. Scotti, G. Farrar, orch (r1909) (PEAR) Ⓓ **GEMMCD9937**
19. M. Gerhart, H. Duhan, orch (r1924: Ger) (ORFE) Ⓓ **C394101B**
19. Lotte Lehmann, H. Schlusnus, orch (Ger: r1920) (6/92) (PREI) Ⓓ [3] **89302**

19. E. Eames, E. de Gogorza, orch (r1909) (11/93) (ROMO) Ⓓ [2] **81001-2**

19. E. Eames, E. de Gogorza, orch (r1909) (1/95) (NIMB) Ⓓ **NI7860**

19, 20a, 20b I. Seefried, D. Fischer-Dieskau, VPO, K. Böhm (pp1960) (ORFE) Ⓓ **C335931A**

19, 20a, 20b T. Hampson, B. Bonney, Concertgebouw, N. Harnoncourt (r1993) (TELD) Ⓓ **4509-98824-2**

20a, 20b R. Bruson, NHK Chbr Sols, R. Paternostro (pp1990) (CAPR) Ⓓ [3] **10 810**

20a, 20b G. Saks, Berlin RSO, R. Buckley (SCHW) Ⓓ [2] **314052**

20a, 20b D. Fischer-Dieskau, Vienna Mozart Orch, R. Peters (r1969: alternative ver) (DECC) Ⓓ **440 409-2DM**

20a, 20b G. Laperrière, Three Rivers SO, G. Bellemare (r1992) (CBC) Ⓓ **SMCD5127**

20a, 20b D. Fischer-Dieskau, VPO, K. Böhm (pp1957) (ORFE) Ⓓ **C394201B**

20a, 20b J. Hynninen, Estonian SO, E. Klas (4/90) (ONDI) Ⓓ **ODE731-2**

20a, 20b G. Hüsch, Berlin St Op Orch, H.U. Müller (r1939: Ger) (3/94) (PREI) Ⓓ **89071**

20a, 20b, 29a, 29b G. Bacquier, Collegium Academicum Orch, R. Dunand (GALL) Ⓓ **CD-816**

20b T. Hampson, Concertgebouw, N. Harnoncourt (r c1989-94) (TELD) Ⓓ **4509-97463-2**

20b T. Pasero, orch, A. Sabino (r1943) (4/95) (PREI) Ⓓ **89074**

20b, 31(pt), 32, 33. H. Braun, I. Beilke, G. Sommerschuh, R. Fischer, J. Witt, E. Kunz, G. Neidlinger, H. Hotter, VPO, C. Krauss (pp1942) (ORFE) Ⓓ **C394101B**

21. M. Sinclair, S. Bruscantini, I. Wallace, D. McCoshan, F. Calabrese, G. Sciutti, Glyndebourne Fest Orch, V. Gui (r1955) (6/94) (EMI) Ⓓ **CDH5 65072-2**

22a, 22b R. Ragatzu, Berlin RSO, R. Buckley (SCHW) Ⓓ [2] **314052**

22a, 22b E. Steber, Columbia SO, B. Walter (r1953) (SONY) Ⓓ [3] **SM3K47211**

22a, 22b K. Te Kanawa, LPO, G. Solti (DECC) Ⓓ **433 068-2DWO** (DECC) ▭ **433 068-4DWO**

22a, 22b K. Te Kanawa, LPO, G. Solti (r1981) (DECC) Ⓓ **440 947-2DH** (DECC) ▭ **440 947-4DH**

22a, 22b P. Lorengar, Vienna St Op Orch, W. Weller (r1970) (DECC) Ⓓ **443 931-2DM**

22a, 22b M. Cebotari, Philh, J. Krips (r1947) (ORFE) Ⓓ **C394101B**

22a, 22b B. Hendricks, ECO, J. Tate (6/85) (EMI) Ⓓ **CDC7 47122-2**

22a, 22b M. Freni, Rome Op Orch, F. Ferraris (10/89) (EMI) Ⓓ **CDM7 63110-2**

22a, 22b M. Cebotari, Philh, J. Krips (r1947) (12/90) (PREI) Ⓓ **90034**

22a, 22b L. Price, RCA Italiana Op Orch, F. Molinari-Pradelli (12/92) (RCA) Ⓓ [4] **09026 61236-2**

22a, 22b L. Price, RCA Italiana Op Orch, F. Molinari-Pradelli (6/93) (RCA) Ⓓ **09026 61357-2**

22a, 22b K. Te Kanawa, LPO, G. Solti (r1981) (10/93) (DECC) Ⓓ **436 461-2DM**

22a, 22b, 30a, V6. C. Bartoli, Vienna CO, G. Fischer (r1993) (11/94) (DECC) Ⓓ **443 452-2DH** (11/94) (DECC) ▭ **443 452-4DH**

22b J. Varady, BRSO, Colin Davis (RCA) Ⓓ **09026 61440-2** (RCA) ▭ **09026 61440-4**

22b E. Bettendorf, orch (r c1922: Ger) (PEAR) Ⓓ **GEMMCD9130**

22b K. Te Kanawa, LPO, G. Solti (11/87) (DECC) Ⓓ **417 645-2DH**

22b E. Destinn, orch, B. Seidler-Winkler (r1908: Ger) (5/94) (SUPR) Ⓓ **11 1337-2**

22b E. Destinn, orch, F. Kark (r1908: Ger) (12/94) (SUPR) Ⓓ [12] **11 2136-2(2)**

22b E. Destinn, orch, B. Seidler-Winkler (r1908: Ger) (12/94) (SUPR) Ⓓ [12] **11 2136-2(2)**

22b S. Bullock, A. Bryn Parri (r1994) (11/95) (SAIN) Ⓓ **SCDC2070**

22b, 23b M. Teschemacher, I. Beilke, Berlin St Op Orch, B. Seidler-Winkler (Ger: r1939) (11/92) (PREI) Ⓓ **89049**

23b R. Ragatzu, C. Gonzales, Berlin RSO, R. Buckley (SCHW) Ⓓ [2] **314052**

23b E. Berger, V. Ursuleac, Berlin St Op Orch, C. Krauss (Ger: r1936) (12/91) (PREI) Ⓓ **89035**

23b E. Eames, M. Sembrich, orch (r1908) (11/93) (ROMO) Ⓓ [2] **81001-2**

23b E. Eames, M. Sembrich, orch (r1908) (1/95) (NIMB) Ⓓ **NI7860**

23b, 24. A. Mildmay, A. Rautawaara, Glyndebourne Fest Chor, Glyndebourne Fest Orch, F. Busch (r1934) (6/94) (EMI) Ⓓ **CDH5 65072-2**

25. Salzburg Mozarteum Orch, H. Graf (11/89) (CAPR) Ⓓ **10 253** (11/89) (CAPR) ▭ **CC27 253**

25. Salzburg Mozarteum Orch, H. Graf (10/91) (CAPR) Ⓓ [3] **10 809**

25, 33. F. Lott, S. Ramey, R. Stilwell, I. Buchanan, W. White, A. Howells, D. Rees, P. Payne, A. Oliver, R. Leggate, J. Tomlinson, ASMF, N. Marriner (LOND) Ⓓ [2] **825 126-2**

26. L. Monteyrol, Budapest SO, A. Déry (r1992) (AUVI) Ⓓ **V4682**

28. R. Wörle, Berlin RSO, R. Buckley (SCHW) Ⓓ [2] **314052**

28. P. Domingo, Munich RO, E. Kohn (3/92) (EMI) Ⓓ **CDC7 54329-2**

29a, 29b G. Taddei, Vienna St Op Orch, K. Böhm (pp1981) (ACAN) Ⓓ **49 402**

29a, 29b W. Berry, VPO, K. Böhm (pp1966) (ORFE) Ⓓ **C394301B**

29b W. Domgraf-Fassbaender, Glyndebourne Fest Orch, F. Busch (r1935) (MMOI) Ⓓ **CDMOIR406** (MMOI) ▭ **CMOIR406**

29b T. Gobbi, Philh, J. Robertson (r1950) (10/89) (EMI) Ⓓ **CDM7 63109-2**

29b A. Kipnis, orch (Ger: r c1916) (10/91) (PEAR) Ⓓ **GEMMCD9451**

30a, 30b L. Price, orch (EURO) Ⓓ **VD69256**

30a, 30b R. Streich, Berlin RSO, K. Gaebel (DG) Ⓓ [2] **435 748-2GDO2**

30a, 30b G. Pareto, orch, P. Pitt (r1920) (PEAR) Ⓓ **GEMMCD9117**

30a, 30b M. Price, ECO, J. Lockhart (r1973) (RCA) Ⓓ **74321 24284-2** (RCA) ▭ **74321 24284-4**

30a, 30b E. Schwarzkopf, Philh, J. Pritchard (r1952) (EMI) Ⓓ **CDM5 65577-2**

30a, 30b B. Bonney, Concertgebouw, N. Harnoncourt (r1994) (TELD) Ⓓ **0630-11470-2**

30a, 30b E. Gruberová, F. Liszt CO, R. Leppard (r1989) (1/91) (SONY) Ⓓ **SK45855**

30a, 30b I. Seefried, Berlin RSO, F. Fricsay (r1960) (9/93) (DG) Ⓓ [2] **437 677-2GDO2**

30a, 30b B. Sayão, RCA SO, W. Pelletier (r1940) (4/94) (RCA) Ⓓ [6] **09026 61580-2(4)**

30b E. Schumann, orch (r1923) (PEAR) Ⓓ **GEMMCD9445**

30b T. dal Monte, orch (r1924) (MMOI) Ⓓ **CDMOIR406** (MMOI) ▭ **CMOIR406**

30b I. Cotrubas, New Philh, J. Pritchard (SONY) Ⓓ **SBK46548** (SONY) ▭ **SBT46548**

30b H. Schymberg, Stockholm Royal Orch, N. Grevillius (r1946) (ALTN) Ⓓ **CDAN3**

30b M. Sembrich, orch (r1906) (PEAR) Ⓓ **GEMMCD9130**

30b E. Schumann, orch, G.W. Byng (r1926) (ORFE) Ⓓ **C394101B**

30b L. Bori, Victor Orch, J. Pasternack (r1921) (ROMO) Ⓓ [2] **81016-2**

30b A. Pandolfini, S. Cottone (r1903) (6/90) (SYMP) Ⓓ **SYMCD1073**

30b E. Schumann, orch, G.W. Byng (r1926) (2/92) (MMOI) Ⓓ **CDMOIR408**

30b F. Hempel, orch (r1911) (3/94) (NIMB) Ⓓ **NI7849**

30b E. Rethberg, orch (r1927) (2/95) (ROMO) Ⓓ [2] **81012-2**

30b I. Baillie, orch (r1927) (7/95) (DUTT) Ⓓ **CDLX7013**

32. D. Lojarro, G. Ottenthal, S. Jo, C. Bartoli, G. Pasino, G. Sabbatini, M. Knapp, M. Chingari, C. Otelli, M. Pertusi, Berlin RSO, R. Paternostro (CAPR) Ⓓ [3] **10 810**

33. H. Hotter, H. Braun, I. Beilke, E. Kunz, G. Sommerschuh, G. Neidlinger, J. Witt, F. Normann, L. Timm, W. Wernigk, R. Fischer, Vienna St Op Chor, Vienna St Op Orch, C. Krauss (pp1942: Ger) (SCHW) Ⓓ [2] **314722**

L' **oca del Cairo, '(The) Cairo Goose'– opera buffa: 2 acts, K422 (1783) (Lib. Varesco: incomplete)**

Pippo H. Bekaert
Celidora R. Van der Paal
Biondello B. Loonen
Calandrino I. Micu
Lavina L. Schoon
Chicchibio R. Bischoff
Auretta G. Anthoni

Transparant Chbr Op Orch, H. Rotman (r1991; reconstr Rotman) (CPO) Ⓓ **CPO999 104-2**

Pippo D. Fischer-Dieskau
Celidora E. Wiens
Biondello P. Schreier
Calandrino D. Johnson
Lavina P. Coburn
Chicchibio A. Scharinger
Auretta I. Nielsen

CPE Bach Orch, P. Schreier (r1990) (5/92) (PHIL) Ⓓ **422 539-2PME**

Il **rè pastore, '(The) Shepherd king'– serenata: 2 acts, K208 (1775—Salzburg) (Lib P. Metastasio)**

EXCERPTS—; 1. Overture. ACT 1: 2. Intendo, amico rio; 3. Alla selva, al prato, al fonte; 4a. Ditelo voi pastori; 4b. Aer tranquillo e dì sereni; 5. Si spande al sole in faccia; 6. Per me rispondete; 7. Di tante sue procelle; 8a. Che! m'affretti; 8b. Vanne a regnar, ben mio. ACT 2: 9. Barbaro, oh Dio, mi vedi; 10. Se vincendo vi rendo felici; 11. L'amerò, sarò costante; 12. Se tu di me fai dono; 13. Sol può dir, come si trova; 14. Voi che fausti ognor donate; 15. Viva! l'invito duce!.

1. Prague CO, O. Vlček (r1988) (SUPR) Ⓓ [2] **11 1166-2**

4b R. Streich, Salzburg Mozarteum Camerata Academica, B. Paumgartner (DG) Ⓓ **431 875-2GDO**

4b, 11. E. Kirkby, AAM, C. Hogwood (4/91) (L'OI) Ⓓ **425 835-2OH**

5, 10. R. Giménez, ROHO, B. Wordsworth (NIMB) Ⓓ **NI5300**

11. L. Pons, orch, B. Walter (r1942) (SONY) Ⓓ [3] **SM3K47211**

11. I. Seefried, W. Schneiderhan, Czech PO, K. Ančerl (pp1966) (PRAG) Ⓓ **PR254 005**

11. V. Girard, Prague Virtuosi, O. Vlček (r1991) (DINT) Ⓓ **DICD920204**

11. E. Schumann, orch, G.W. Byng (r1926) (ROMO) Ⓓ **81019-2**

11. H. Gueden, Camerata Academica, B. Paumgartner (pp1963) (ORFE) Ⓓ **C394401B**

11. H. Gueden, VPO, A. Erede (r1952) (PREI) Ⓓ **90227**

11. K. Te Kanawa, LSO, Colin Davis (3/84) (PHIL) Ⓓ **411 148-2PH**

11. L. Popp, Munich RO, L. Slatkin (r1983) (8/84) (EMI) Ⓓ **CDC7 47019-2**

11. K. Battle, B. Griffiths, RPO, A. Previn (12/86) (EMI) Ⓓ **CDC7 47355-2**

11. E. Schumann, orch, G.W. Byng (r1926) (6/91) (PREI) Ⓓ **89031**

11. L. Price, New Philh, P.H. Adler (6/93) (RCA) Ⓓ **09026 61357-2**

11. N. Melba, J. Kubelík, G. Lapierre (r1913) (9/93) (RCA) Ⓓ **09026 61412-2**

11. I. Seefried, Vienna SO, F. Leitner (r1952) (9/93) (DG) Ⓓ [2] **437 677-2GDO2**

11. M. Ivogün, orch (r c1924) (1/94) (CLUB) Ⓓ **CL99-020**

11. M. Price, ECO, J. Lockhart (r1973) (5/95) (RCA) Ⓓ [2] **09026 61635-2**

11. N. Melba, J. Kubelík, G. Lapierre (r1913) (5/95) (ROMO) Ⓓ [3] **81011-2(2)**

11. E. Rethberg, Victor SO, Rosario Bourdon (r1930) (10/95) (ROMO) Ⓓ [2] **81014-2**

Der **Schauspieldirektor, '(The) Impresario'– Singspiel: 1 act, K486 (1786—Vienna) (Lib. G. Stephanie jr)**

EXCERPTS: 1. Overture; 2. Da schlägt die Abschiedsstunde; 3. Bester Jüngling! mit Entzükken; 4. Ich bin die erste Sängerin; 5. Jeder Künstler strebt nach Ehre.

Mme Herz R. Grist
Mlle Silberklang A. Auger
Vogelsang P. Schreier
Buff K. Moll

Staatskapelle Dresden, K. Böhm (omits dialogue) (12/90) (DG) Ⓓ [3] **429 877-2GX3**

Mme Herz R. Welting
Mlle Silberklang I. Cotrubas
Vogelsang A. Rolfe Johnson
Buff C. Grant

LSO, Colin Davis (r1975: omits dialogue) (4/92) (PHIL) Ⓓ [2] **422 536-2PME2**

Mme Herz M. Nador
Mlle Silberklang K. Laki
Vogelsang T. Hampson

Buff H. van der Kamp
oncertgebouw, N. Harnoncourt (r1986)
(3/95) (TELD) ① **4509-95979-2**

1. Staatskapelle Dresden, H. Vonk
(CAPR) ① **10 070**
(CAPR) ▭ **CC27 086**

1. ECO, L. Hager (r1989)
(NOVA) ① **150 041-2**

1. Zurich Tonhalle Orch, J. Krips
(ADES) ① **13225-2**

1. LPO, B. Haitink (PHIL) ① **432 512-2PSL**

1. Prague CO, O. Vlček (r1988)
(SUPR) ① [2] **11 1166-2**

1. ASMF, N. Marriner
(EMI) **OO DCC7 47014-5**

1. Sinfonia Varsovia, E. Krivine (r1990)
(DENO) ① **CO-75372**

1. ASMF, N. Marriner (EMI) **O MDC7 47014-8**

1. Concertgebouw, Zurich Op Orch, Zurich Op Hse Mozart Orch, VCM, N. Harnoncourt
(TELD) ① **4509-95523-2**

1. RPO, Colin Davis (r c1961)
(EMI) ① [2] **CES5 68533-2**

1. G. Bacquier, Collegium Academicum Orch, R. Dunand (GALL) ① **CD-816**

1. Basle SO, M. Atzmon (r1973/4)
(RCA) ① **74321 29237-2**

1. ASMF, N. Marriner
(4/84) (EMI) ① **CDC7 47014-2**

1. Staatskapelle Dresden, H. Vonk
(10/91) (CAPR) ① [3] **10 809**

1. Tafelmusik, B. Weil
(5/92) (SONY) ① **SK46695**

1. LSO, J. Krips (r1951)
(7/95) (DECC) ① [2] **443 530-2LF2**

3. E. Steber, Columbia SO, B. Walter (r1953)
(SONY) ① [3] **SM3K47211**

3. K. Te Kanawa, VPO, J. Pritchard (r1990)
(DECC) ① **440 401-2DM**

---

sogno di Scipione, 'Scipio's dream'– azione teatrale: 1 act, K126 (1772—Salzburg) (Lib. P. Metastasio)

Scipio P. Schreier
Costanza L. Popp
Fortuna E. Gruberová
Publio C.H. Ahnsjö
Emilio T. Moser
Licenza E. Mathis

alzburg Chbr Ch, Salzburg Mozarteum Orch, L. Hager (r1979)
(1/92) (PHIL) ① [2] **422 531-2PME2**

Overture Prague CO, O. Vlček (r1989)
(SUPR) ① [2] **11 1166-2**

Sposo deluso, '(The) Deluded Spouse'– opera buffa: 2 acts, K430/K424a (?1784) (Lib. ?L. da Ponte: unfinished)

1. Overture; 2. Trio; 3. Quartet.

Eugenia L. Schoon
Bettina R. Van der Paal
Pulcherio I. Micu
Don Asdrubale B. Loonen
Bocconio H. Bekaert

ansparant Chbr Op Orch, H. Rotman (r1991; reconstr Rotman)
(CPO) ① **CPO999 104-2**

Eugenia F. Palmer
Bettina I. Cotrubas
Pulcherio R. Tear
Don Asdrubale A. Rolfe Johnson
Bocconio C. Grant

O, Colin Davis (r1975)
(5/92) (PHIL) ① **422 539-2PME**

1. Basle SO, M. Atzmon (r1973/4)
(RCA) ① **74321 29237-2**

---

amos, König in Ägypten, 'Thamos, King of Egypt'– play with music: 5 acts, K345 (1774—Salzburg) (Wds. T P von Gebler)

EXCERPTS—; 1. Schon weichet dir, Sonne (chorus); 2. Intermezzo No. 1; 3. Intermezzo No. 2; 4. Intermezzo No. 3; 5. Intermezzo No. 4; 6. Gottheit, Gottheit, über alle mätchting (chorus); 7. Intermezzo No. 5; 8. Ihr (Wie) Kinder des Straubes, erzittert und behet (chorus); 9. Final Music for Act 5.

Cpte K. Eichstaedt, G. Pohl, E. Büchner, H.C. Polster, T. Adam, Berlin Rad Chor, Berlin Staatskapelle, B. Klee
(PHIL) ① [2] **422 525-2PME2**

Cpte A. Miles, Monteverdi Ch, EBS, J.E. Gardiner (r1991)
(2/94) (ARCH) ① **437 556-2AH**

Cpte T. Thomaschke, J. Perry, A-M. Mühle, M. van Altena, H. van der Kamp, Collegium Vocale, Netherlands Chbr Ch, Concertgebouw, N. Harnoncourt (r1980)
(3/95) (TELD) ① **4509-95979-2**

1, 6. Collegium Vocale, Netherlands Chbr Ch, Concertgebouw, N. Harnoncourt (r1980)
(TELD) ① **4509-97505-2**

3. RPO, T. Beecham (r1957)
(EMI) ① **CDM7 63412-2**

3-5, 7, 9. Sinfonia Varsovia, E. Krivine (r1990)
(DENO) ① **CO-75372**

Zaïde– Singspiel: 2 acts, K344/336b (1779-80—Salzburg) (Lib. J. A. Schachtner)

EXCERPTS: ACT ONE: 2. Unerforschliche Fügung; 3. Ruhe sanft, mein holdes Leben; 4. Rase Schicksal, wüte immer; 5. Meine Seele hüpft vor Freuden; 6. Herr und Freund!; 7. Nur mutig, mein Herz; 8. O selige Wonne! ACT TWO: 9a. Zaide entflohen!; 9b. Der stolze Löw'; 10. Wer hungrig bei der Tafel sitzt; 11. Ich bin so bös' als gut; 12. Trostlos schluchzet Philomele; 13. Tiger! wetze nur die Klauen; 14. Ihr Mächtigen seht ungerührt; 15. Freundin! stille deine Tränen.

Zaïde J. Blegen
Gomatz W. Hollweg
Allazim W. Schöne
Sultan Soliman T. Moser
Osmin R. Holl
Principal singer W. Bellon

Salzburg Mozarteum Orch, L. Hager (with dialogue)
(5/91) (ORFE) ① [2] **C055832I**

Zaïde E. Mathis
Gomatz P. Schreier
Allazim I. Wixell
Sultan Soliman W. Hollweg
Osmin R. Süss
Principal singer A. Ude

Berlin Staatskapelle, B. Klee (r1973: with dialogue)
(4/92) (PHIL) ① [2] **422 536-2PME2**

3. F. Lott, ASMF, N. Marriner (Eng)
(LOND) ① [2] **825 126-2**

3. E. Johnson, J. Drake (arr Johnson)
(ASV) ① **CDDCA800**
(ASV) ▭ **ZCDCA800**

3. L. Popp, Vienna Haydn Orch, I. Kertész (r1971) (DECC) ① **443 377-2DM**

3. K. Te Kanawa, LSO, Colin Davis
(3/84) (PHIL) ① **411 148-2PH**

3. F. Wunderlich, Stuttgart RSO, A. Rischner (bp1956) (10/89) (ACAN) ① **43 267**

3. F. Lott, LMP, J. Glover
(2/90) (ASV) ① **CDDCA683**

3. I. Seefried, LMP, H. Blech (r1953)
(4/94) (TEST) ① **SBT1026**

3. T. Dahl, Calgary PO, M. Bernardi (r1992)
(12/94) (CBC) ① **SMCD5125**

3, 12. E. Kirkby, AAM, C. Hogwood
(4/91) (L'OI) ① **425 835-2OH**

Die **Zauberflöte, '(The) Magic Flute'– singspiel: 2 acts, K620 (1791—Vienna) (Lib. E. Schikaneder)**

EXCERPTS: 1a. Overture. ACT 1: 1b. Zu Hilfe; 2. Der Vogelfänger bin ich ja; 3. Dies Bildnis ist bezaubernd schön; 4a. O zitt're nicht; 4b. Zum leiden; 5. H'm H'm H'm; 6. Du feines Täubchen; 7. Bei Männern; 8a. Zum Ziele führt dich; 8b. Wie stark ist nicht dein Zauberton; 9a. Schnelle Füsse; 9b. Das klinget so herrlich—könnte jeder brave Mann; 9c. Es lebe Sarastro. ACT 2: 10a. March; 10b. O, Isis und Osiris (aria); 11. Bewahret euch vor Weibertücken; 12. Wie? Wie? Wie?; 13. Alles fühlt der Liebe Freuden; 14. Der Hölle Rache; 15. In diesen heil'gen Hallen; 16. Seid uns zum zweitenmal willkommen; 17. Ach, ich fühl's; 18. O, Isis und Osiris (chorus); 19. Soll ich dich, Teurer, nicht mehr sehen?; 20. Ein Mädchen oder Weibchen; 21. Bald prangt; 22. Der, welcher wandert; 23. Papagena Weibchen; 24. Pa-Pa-Pa-Papagena; 25. Nur stille. 26. Die Strahlen der Sonne.

Pamina A.C. Biel
Queen of Night B.L. Frandsen
Tamino S. Dahlberg
Papageno M. Samuelson
Sarastro L. Polgár
Speaker P. Salomaa
Monostatos M. Khyle
Papagena B. Larsson
First Lady A. Soldh
Second Lady L. Sallay
Third Lady I. Blom
First Boy E. Berg
Second Boy A-C. Larsson
Third Boy A. Tomson
First Armed Man T. Annmo
Second Armed Man O. Sköld
First Priest T. Lilleqvist

Drottningholm Court Th Chor, Drottningholm Court Th Orch, A. Östman, T. Olofsson
(7/90) (MCEG) ■■ **VVD663**

Pamina M. Price
Queen of Night L. Serra
Tamino P. Schreier
Papageno M. Melbye
Sarastro K. Moll
Speaker; Second Priest T. Adam
Monostatos R. Tear
Papagena M. Venuti
First Lady M. McLaughlin
Second Lady A. Murray
Second Lady H. Schwarz
First Boy F. Höher
Second Boy M. Diedrich
Third Boy F. Klos
First Armed Man R. Goldberg
Second Armed Man H. Reeh
First Priest A. Ude

Leipzig Rad Chor, Staatskapelle Dresden, Colin Davis (with dialogue)
(PHIL) ■■ **070 429-3**

Pamina F. Lott
Queen of Night M. Sandoz
Tamino L. Goeke
Papageno B. Luxon
Sarastro T. Thomaschke
Speaker W. White
Monostatos J. Fryatt
Papagena E. Conquet
First Lady T. Cahill
Second Lady P. Parker
Third Lady F. Kimm
First Boy K. Flowers
Second Boy L. John
Third Boy E. Stokes
First Armed Man N. McKinnon
Second Armed Man; Second Priest J. Rath
First Priest R. Berkeley-Steele

Glyndebourne Fest Chor, LPO, B. Haitink, J. Cox (r1978)
(IMP) ■■ **SLL7015**

Pamina H. Gueden
Queen of Night W. Lipp
Tamino L. Simoneau
Papageno W. Berry
Sarastro K. Böhme
Speaker P. Schoeffler
Monostatos A. Jaresch
Papagena E. Loose
First Lady J. Hellwig
Second Lady C. Ludwig
Third Lady H. Rössl-Majdan
First Boy D. Siebert
Second Boy R. Boesch
Third Boy E. Boerner
First Armed Man J. Gostic
Second Armed Man L. Pantscheff
First Priest E. Majkut
Second Priest H. Pröglhöf

Vienna St Op Chor, VPO, K. Böhm (omits dialogue)
(DECC) ① [2] **414 362-2DM2**

Pamina T. Lemnitz
Queen of the Night E. Berger
Tamino H. Roswaenge
Papageno G. Hüsch
Sarastro W. Strienz
Speaker; Second Armed Man W. Grossmann
Monostatos; First Armed Man H. Tessmer
Pagagena; First Boy I. Beilke
First Lady H. Scheppan
Second Lady E. Marherr-Wagner
Third Lady; Third Boy R. Berglund
Second Boy C. Spletter
Priest E. Fabbry

Favres Solisten Vereinigung, BPO, T. Beecham (r1937/8: omits dialogue)
(NIMB) ① [2] **NI7827/8**

Pamina A.C. Biel
Queen of Night B.L. Frandsen
Tamino S. Dahlberg
Papageno M. Samuelson
Sarastro L. Polgár
Speaker P. Salomaa
Monostatos M. Khyle
Papagena B. Larsson
First Lady A. Soldh
Second Lady L. Sallay

Third Lady I. Blom
First Boy E. Berg
Second Boy A-C. Larsson
Third Boy A. Tomson
First Armed Man T. Annmo
Second Armed Man O. Sköld
First Priest T. Lilleqvist

Drottningholm Court Th Chor, Drottningholm Court Th Orch, A. Östman, G. Järvefelt, T. Olofsson
(PHIL) ◖ [2] **070 422-1PHG2**

Pamina I. Seefried
Queen of Night W. Lipp
Tamino A. Dermota
Papageno E. Kunz
Sarastro J. Greindl
Speaker P. Schoeffler
Monostatos P. Klein
Papagena E. Oravez
First Lady C. Goltz
Second Lady M. Kenney
Third Lady S. Wagner
First Boy H. Steffek
Second Boy Luise Leitner
Third Boy F. Meusburger
First Armed Man H. Beirer
Second Armed Man F. Bierbach
First Priest F. Liewehr
Second Priest F. Höbling

Vienna St Op Chor, VPO, W. Furtwängler (pp1951)
(EMI) ⓘ [3] **CHS5 65356-2**

Pamina G. Janowitz
Queen of Night L. Popp
Tamino N. Gedda
Papageno W. Berry
Sarastro G. Frick
Speaker; Second Armed Man; Second Priest F. Crass
Monostatos; First Priest G. Unger
Papagena R-M. Pütz
First Lady E. Schwarzkopf
Second Lady C. Ludwig
Third Lady M. Höffgen
First Boy A. Giebel
Second Boy A. Reynolds
Third Boy J. Veasey
First Armed Man K. Liebl

Philh Chor, Philh, O. Klemperer (r1964: omits dialogue)
(EMI) ⓘ [2] **CDS5 55173-2**

Pamina T. Eipperle
Queen of Night L. Piltti
Tamino W. Ludwig
Papageno K. Schmitt-Walter
Sarastro J. von Manowarda
Speaker; Second Priest G. Hann
Monostatos H. Buchta
Papagena L. Preisig
First Lady M. Martensen
Second Lady E. Pfeil
Third Lady Y. Hochreiter

Regensburg Cath Ch, E. Kristjansson, A. Welitsch, M. Osswald, Stuttgart Rad Chor, Stuttgart RO, J. Keilberth (bp1937: with dialogue)
(PREI) ⓘ [2] **90254**

Pamina E. Mathis
Queen of Night K. Ott
Tamino F. Araiza
Papageno G. Hornik
Sarastro J. Van Dam
Speaker C. Nicolai
Monostatos H. Kruse
Papagena J. Perry
First Lady A. Tomowa-Sintow
Second Lady A. Baltsa
Third Lady H. Schwarz
First Boy W. Bünten
Second Boy C. Schulz
Third Boy T. Pfülb
First Armed Man V. Horn
Second Armed Man V. von Halem
First Priest H. Hopfner
Second Priest L. Valenta

Berlin Deutsche Op Chor, BPO, H. von Karajan (r1980: with dialogue)
(1/85) (DG) ⓘ [3] **410 967-2GH3**

Pamina L. Popp
Queen of Night E. Gruberová
Tamino S. Jerusalem
Papageno W. Brendel
Sarastro R. Bracht
Speaker N. Bailey
Monostatos H. Zednik
Papagena B. Lindner
First Lady M. Richardson
Second Lady D. Soffel
Third Lady O. Wenkel
First Armed Man P. Hofmann
Second Armed Man A. Haugland
First Priest W. Kmentt
Second Priest E. Kunz
Third Priest A. von Mattoni

Tolz Boys' Ch, Bavarian Rad Chor, BRSO, B. Haitink (with dialogue)
(3/88) (EMI) ⓘ [3] **CDS7 47951-8**

Sarastro K. Moll
Queen of the Night E. Moser
Pamina A. Rothenberger
Tamino P. Schreier
Papageno W. Berry
Papagena O. Miljakovic
Speaker T. Adam
Monostatos W. Brokmeier
First Priest W. Badorek
Second Priest G. Wewel
First Armed Man W. Badorek
Second Armed Man G. Wewel
First Lady L. Kirschstein
Second Lady I. Gramatzki
Third Lady B. Fassbaender
First Boy W. Gampert
Second Boy P. Hinterreiter
Third Boy A. Stein

Bavarian St Op Chor, Bavarian St Op Orch, W. Sawallisch (with dialogue)
(3/88) (EMI) ⓘ [2] **CDS7 47827-8**

Pamina I. Seefried
Queen of Night W. Lipp
Tamino A. Dermota
Papageno E. Kunz
Sarastro L. Weber
Speaker G. London
Monostatoes P. Klein
Papagena E. Loose
First Lady S. Jurinac
Second Lady F. Riegler
Third Lady E. Schürhoff
First Boy H. Steinmassl
Second Boy E. Dörpinghans
Third Boy A. Stückl
First Armed Man; First Priest E. Majkut
Second Armed Man L. Pantscheff
Second Priest H. Pröglhöf

Vienna Singverein, VPO, H. von Karajan (r1950: omits dialogue)
(1/89) (EMI) ⓘ [2] **CHS7 69631-2**

Pamina B. Bonney
Queen of Night E. Gruberová
Tamino H-P. Blochwitz
Papageno A. Scharinger
Sarastro M. Salminen
Speaker T. Hampson
Monostatos P. Keller
Papagena E. Schmid
First Lady P. Coburn
Second Lady D. Ziegler
Third Lady M. Lipovšek
First Boy S. Gienger
Second Boy M. Baur
Third Boy A. Fischer
First Armed Man T. Moser
Second Armed Man A. Suhonen
First Priest A. Maly
Second Priest W. Kmentt

Vienna Singverein, G. Jesserer, Zurich Op Hse Chor, Zurich Op Orch, N. Harnoncourt (r1987; with narration)
(7/89) (TELD) ⓘ [2] **2292-42716-2**

Pamina I. Cotrubas
Queen of Night Z. Donat
Tamino E. Tappy
Papageno C. Boesch
Sarastro M. Talvela
Speaker J. Van Dam
Monostatos H. Hiestermann
Papagena E. Kales
First Lady R. Yakar
Second Lady T. Schmidt
Third Lady I. Mayr
First Boy M. Huber
Second Boy T. Paulsen
Third Boy C. Baumgartner
First Armed Man K. Terkal
Second Armed Man H. Von Bömches
First Priest P. Weber
Second Priest H. Nitsche

Vienna St Op Chor, VPO, James Levine (with dialogue)
(10/89) (RCA) ⓘ [3] **GD84586**

Pamina T. Lemnitz
Queen of Night E. Berge
Tamino H. Roswaeng
Papageno G. Husc
Sarastro W. Strien
Speaker; Second Armed Man W. Grossman
Monostatos; First Armed Man H. Tessme
Papagena; First Boy I. Beilk
First Lady H. Scheppa
Second Lady E. Marherr-Wagne
Third Lady; Third Boy R. Berglun
Second Boy C. Splette
Priest E. Fabbr

Favres Solisten Vereinigung, BPO, T. Beecham (r1937/8; omits dialogue)
(3/90) (EMI) ⓘ [2] **CHS7 61034-**

Pamina T. Lemnit
Queen of Night E. Berge
Tamino H. Roswaeng
Papageno G. Husc
Sarastro W. Strien
Speaker; Second Armed Man W. Grossman
Monostatos; First Armed Man H. Tessme
Papagena; First Boy I. Beilk
First Lady H. Scheppa
Second Lady E. Marherr-Wagne
Third Lady; Third Boy R. Berglun
Second Boy C. Splette
Priest E. Fabbr

Favres Solisten Vereinigung, BPO, T. Beecham (r1937/8: omits dialogue)
(3/90) (PEAR) ⓘ [2] **GEMMCDS937**

Pamina K. Te Kanaw
Queen of Night C. Stude
Tamino F. Araiz
Papageno O. Bä
Sarastro S. Rame
Monostatos A. Baldi
Papagena E. Lin
First Lady Y. Kenn
Second Lady I. Vermillio
Third Lady A. Collin
First Boy C. Fliegne
Second Boy M. Bau
Third Boy C. Günthe
First Armed Man E. Barhan
Second Armed Man H. Peeter
First Priest E. Barhan
Second Priest H. Peeter

Ambrosian Op Chor, ASMF, N. Marriner (with dialogue)
(11/90) (PHIL) ⓘ [2] **426 276-2PH**
(11/90) (PHIL) ▭ [2] **426 276-4PH**

Pamina E. Lea
Queen of Night R. Peter
Tamino F. Wunderlich
Papageno D. Fischer-Dieska
Sarastro F. Cras
Speaker H. Hotte
Monostatos F. Len
Papagena L. Ott
First Lady H. Hillebrech
Second Lady C. Ahlir
Third Lady S. Wagne
First Boy R. Schwaige
Second Boy A. Fahber
Third Boy R. Kosti
First Armed Man J. King
Second Armed Man M. Talvela

Berlin RIAS Chbr Ch, BPO, K. Böhm (with dialogue)
(12/90) (DG) ⓘ [3] **429 877-2GX**

Pamina L. Popp
Queen of Night E. Gruberov
Tamino F. Araiz
Papageno W. Brende
Sarastro K. Mo
Speaker J-H. Rooterin
Monostatos N. Ort
Papagena G. Siebe
First Lady P. Cobur
Second Lady D. Evangelato
Third Lady C. Wulkop
First Boy C. Rossdeutsche
Second Boy C. Immle
Third Boy S. Bandemeh
First Armed Man H. Winkle
Second Armed Man K. Helm
First Priest K. Böhme
Second Priest F. Klarweir
Third Priest G. Aue
Fourth Priest D. Thaw

Bavarian St Op Chor, Bavarian St Op Orch, W. Sawallisch, P. Windgassen
(9/91) (PHIL) ◖ [2] **070 405-1PHG2**
(7/90) (PHIL) ▭▭ **070 405-3PH**

Pamina R. Ziesak

Queen of Night S. Jo
Tamino U. Heilmann
Papageno M. Kraus
Sarastro K. Moll
Speaker A. Schmidt
Monostatos H. Zednik
Papagena Lotte Leitner
First Lady A. Pieczonka
Second Lady A. Kuettenbaum
Third Lady J. van Nes
First Boy M.E. Cencic
Second Boy M. Rausch
Third Boy M. Leitner
First Armed Man W. Schmidt
Second Armed Man H. Franzen
First Priest C. Bieber
Second Priest H.J. Porcher

Vienna Boys' Ch, Vienna St Op Concert Ch, VPO, G. Solti (with dialogue)
(10/91) (DECC) Ⓓ [2] **433 210-2DH2**

Pamina D. Upshaw
Queen of Night B. Hoch
Tamino A. Rolfe Johnson
Papageno A. Schmidt
Sarastro C. Hauptmann
Speaker O. Bär
Monostatos G. de Mey
Papagena C. Pierard
First Lady N. Argenta
Second Lady E. James
Third Lady C. Denley
First Boy T. Bonner
Second Boy E. Tubb
Third Boy C. Trevor
First Armed Man; Second Priest R. Müller
Second Armed Man R. Wistreich
First Priest W. Riedelbauch
Third Priest S. Birchall

London Schütz Ch, LCP, R. Norrington (with dialogue)
(11/91) (EMI) Ⓓ [2] **CDS7 54287-2**

Pamina B. Hendricks
Queen of Night J. Anderson
Tamino J. Hadley
Papageno T. Allen
Sarastro R. Lloyd
Speaker; Second Priest G. Hornik
Monostatos H. Wildhaber
Papgena U. Steinsky
First Lady P.M. Schnitzer
Second Lady G. Sima
Third Lady J. Bernheimer
First Boy D. Ison
Second Boy N. Watts
Third Boy J. Dawson
First Armed Man; First Priest P. Svensson
Second Armed Man A. Miles

Scottish Chbr Chor, Scottish CO, C. Mackerras (r1991: with dialogue)
(12/91) (TELA) Ⓓ [2] **CD80302**

Pamina M. Price
Queen of Night L. Serra
Tamino P. Schreier
Papageno M. Melbye
Sarastro K. Moll
Speaker; Second Priest T. Adam
Monostatos R. Tear
Papagena M. Venuti
First Lady M. McLaughlin
Second Lady A. Murray
Third Lady H. Schwarz
First Boy F. Höher
Second Boy M. Diedrich
Third Boy F. Klos
First Armed Man R. Goldberg
Second Armed Man H. Reeh
First Priest A. Ude

Leipzig Rad Chor, Staatskapelle Dresden, Colin Davis (r1984: with dialogue)
(4/92) (PHIL) Ⓓ [3] **422 543-2PME3**

Pamina K. Battle
Queen of Night L. Serra
Tamino F. Araiza
Papageno M. Hemm
Sarastro K. Moll
Speaker A. Schmidt
Monostatos H. Zednik
Papagena B. Kilduff
First Lady J. Gondek
Second Lady M. Lerner
Third Lady J. Christin
First Boy T. Huffman
Second Boy B. Schott
Third Boy P-C. Brevig
First Armed Man M. Baker
Second Armed Man M. Devlin
First Priest J. Courtney
Second Priest B. Fitch

NY Met Op Chor, NY Met Op Orch, James Levine, G. Mostart, B. Large
(4/93) (DG) ◐ **072 424-1GH2**
(4/93) (DG) ▣ **072 424-3GH**

Pamina M. Stader
Queen of Night R. Streich
Tamino E. Haefliger
Papageno D. Fischer-Dieskau
Sarastro J. Greindl
Speaker; Second Armed Man K. Borg
Monostatos M. Vantin
Papagena L. Otto
First Lady M. Schech
Second Lady L. Losch
Third Lady M. Klose
First Boy M. Guilleaume
Second Boy M. Reith
Third Boy D. Eustrati
First Armed Man; Priest H. Vandenburg

Berlin RIAS Chbr Ch, Berlin RIAS Orch, F. Fricsay (with dialogue: r1954)
(5/93) (DG) Ⓓ [2] **435 741-2GDO2**

Pamina B. Bonney
Queen of Night S. Jo
Tamino K. Streit
Papageno G. Cachemaille
Sarastro K. Sigmundsson
Speaker H. Hagegård
Monostatos M. Petzold
Papagena L. Watson
First Lady R. Ziesak
Second Lady P. Hansen
Third Lady I. Vermillion
First Boy D. Naseband
Second Boy K. Suzuki
Third Boy S. Schnorr
First Armed Man R. Wörle
Second Armed Man P. Salomaa
First Priest H. Lippert
Second Priest O. Widmer

Drottningholm Court Th Chor, Drottningholm Court Th Orch, A. Östman (r1992: with dialogue)
(2/94) (L'OI) Ⓓ [2] **440 085-2OHO2**

Pamina E. Norberg-Schulz
Queen of Night H. Kwon
Tamino H. Lippert
Papageno G. Tichy
Sarastro K. Rydl
Speaker R. Holzer
Monostatos W. Gahmlich
Papagena Lotte Leitner
First Lady J. Faulkner
Second Lady W. Winsauer
Third Lady A. Gonda
First Boy R. Pap
Second Boy M. Richter
Third Boy M. Uray
First Armed Man; Second Priest P. Jelosits
Second Armed man; First Priest P. Köves

Hungarian Fest Chor, Budapest Failoni Orch, M. Halász (r1993: with dialogue)
(7/94) (NAXO) Ⓓ [2] **8 660030/1**

Excs D. Upshaw, A. Schmidt, B. Hoch, A. Rolfe Johnson, LCP, R. Norrington
(EMI) Ⓓ **CDC7 54492-2**

1. BPO, K. Böhm (DG) Ⓓ [2] **447 364-2GDB2**
1a ASMF, N. Marriner (LOND) Ⓓ **827 267-2**
1a NYPSO, W. Mengelberg (r1930) (PEAR) Ⓓ **GEMMCD9474**
1a Czech PO, K. Ančerl (SUPR) ⊟ **11 0640-4**
1a Staatskapelle Dresden, H. Vonk (CAPR) Ⓓ **10 070**
(CAPR) ⊟ **CC27 086**
1a Bavarian St Orch, W. Sawallisch (ORFE) Ⓓ **C161871A**
1a Columbia SO, B. Walter (IMP) Ⓓ [2] **DUET 15CD**
1a Budapest PO, J. Sándor (LASE) Ⓓ **15 622**
(LASE) ⊟ **79 622**
1a Nice PO, K. Redel (FORL) Ⓓ **UCD16584**
1a ECO, L. Hager (r1989) (NOVA) Ⓓ **150 041-2**
1a Philh, O. Klemperer (EMI) Ⓓ **CDM7 63619-2**
1a A. Paratore, J. Paratore (arr Busoni) (SCHW) Ⓓ **310115**
1a Staatskapelle Dresden, H. Vonk (CAPR) Ⓓ [3] **10 810**
1a Swingle Sngrs (arr Parry) (VIRG) Ⓓ **VC7 59617-2**
1a Zurich Tonhalle Orch, J. Krips (ADES) Ⓓ **13225-2**
1a LPO, C. Rainer (INTR) Ⓓ **409 005-2**
1a LPO, B. Haitink (PHIL) Ⓓ **432 512-2PSL**
1a Berlin St Op Orch, R. Strauss (r1928) (KOCH) Ⓓ **37119-2**
1a Prague CO, O. Vlček (r1988) (SUPR) Ⓓ [2] **11 1166-2**
1a Tafelmusik, B. Weil (SONY) Ⓓ **SK52498**
1a NBC SO, A. Toscanini (bp1949) (RCA) Ⓓ **GD60310**
1a LPO, Anon (cond) (WORD) Ⓓ **FCD7404**
1a ASMF, N. Marriner (EMI) **OO DCC7 47014-5**
1a Sinfonia Varsovia, E. Krivine (r1990) (DENO) Ⓓ **CO-75372**
1a Czech PO, V. Talich (pp1954) (MULT) Ⓓ **310151-2**
1a ASMF, N. Marriner (EMI) ◘ **MDC7 47014-8**
1a Czech PO, K. Ančerl (r1960) (SUPR) Ⓓ **11 1935-2**
1a BBC SO, Colin Davis (r1971) (BELA) Ⓓ **461 001-2**
(BELA) ⊟ **461 001-4**
1a Concertgebouw, Zurich Op Orch, Zurich Op Hse Mozart Orch, VCM, N. Harnoncourt (TELD) Ⓓ **4509-95523-2**
1a RPO, Colin Davis (r c1961) (EMI) Ⓓ [2] **CES5 68533-2**
1a RPO, J. Lockhart (r1994) (TRIN) Ⓓ **TRP038**
1a Basle SO, M. Atzmon (r1973/4) (RCA) Ⓓ **74321 29237-2**
1a ASMF, N. Marriner (4/84) (EMI) Ⓓ **CDC7 47014-2**
1a Hungarian CO, V. Tátrai (5/90) (LASE) Ⓓ **15 511**
(5/90) (LASE) ⊟ **79 511**
1a Staatskapelle Dresden, H. Vonk (10/91) (CAPR) Ⓓ [3] **10 809**
1a Tafelmusik, B. Weil (5/92) (SONY) Ⓓ **SK46695**
1a BBC SO, A. Toscanini (r1938) (5/94) (BIDD) Ⓓ [2] **WHL008/9**
1a BPO, T. Beecham (r1937/8) (10/94) (DUTT) Ⓓ **CDLX7009**
1a LSO, J. Krips (r1951) (7/95) (DECC) Ⓓ [2] **443 530-2LF2**
1a, 1b, 2, 3, 4a, 4b, 7, 10b, 13-18, 20, 24, 26. E. Lear, R. Peters, F. Wunderlich, D. Fischer-Dieskau, F. Crass, F. Lenz, L. Otto, H. Hillebrecht, C. Ahlin, S. Wagner, A. Fahberg, R. Schwaiger, R. Kostia, Berlin RIAS Chbr Ch, BPO, K. Böhm (8/90) (DG) ⊟ **429 825-4GMM**
1a, 1b, 2, 3, 4a, 4b, 7, 10b, 13-18, 20, 24, 26. F. Crass, F. Wunderlich, R. Peters, E. Lear, H. Hillebrecht, C. Ahlin, S. Wagner, D. Fischer-Dieskau, L. Otto, F. Lenz, R. Schwaiger, A. Fahberg, R. Kostia, Berlin RIAS Chor, BPO, K. Böhm (DG) Ⓓ **419 424-2GB**
1a, 1b, 2, 3, 4a, 4b, 5, 7, 8a, 8b, 9a-c, 10b, 11-21. B. Hendricks, J. Hadley, T. Allen, R. Lloyd, J. Anderson, U. Steinsky, G. Hornik, P. Svensson, H. Wildhaber, P.M. Schnitzer, G. Sima, J. Bernheimer, D. Ison, N. Watts, J. Dawson, A. Miles, Scottish Chbr Chor, Scottish CO, C. Mackerras (r1991) (TELA) Ⓓ **CD80345**
1a, 1b, 2, 3, 4a, 4b, 5, 7, 8b, 9a, 10b, 13-15, 17, 20, 24, 25. K. Te Kanawa, C. Studer, F. Araiza, O. Bär, S. Ramey, A. Baldin, E. Lind, Y. Kenny, I. Vermillion, A. Collins, Ambrosian Op Chor, ASMF, N. Marriner (r1989) (PHIL) Ⓓ **438 495-2PH**
1a, 1b, 2, 3, 4a, 7, 10b, 13-18, 20, 24, 26. F. Crass, R. Peters, E. Lear, F. Wunderlich, D. Fischer-Dieskau, L. Otto, F. Lenz, Berlin RIAS Chbr Ch, BPO, K. Böhm (r1964) (DG) Ⓓ **445 464-2GMH**
1a, 1b, 2, 3, 4a, 4b, 7, 9a, 10b, 14, 15, 17, 18, 23, 26. R. Bracht, S. Jerusalem, N. Bailey, W. Kmentt, E. Kunz, A. von Mattoni, E. Gruberová, L. Popp, M. Richardson, D. Soffel, O. Wenkel, W. Brendel, B. Lindner, H. Zednik, P. Hofmann, A. Haugland, Bavarian Rad Chor, BRSO, B. Haitink (2/84) (EMI) Ⓓ **CDC7 47008-2**
1a, 1b, 2, 3, 4a, 4b, 7, 10b, 14-18, 20, 24, 26. E. Mathis, F. Araiza, K. Ott, J. Van Dam, G. Hornik, J. Perry, H. Kruse, A. Tomowa-Sintow, A. Baltsa, H. Schwarz, Berlin Deutsche Op Chor, BPO, H. von Karajan (r1980) (1/86) (DG) Ⓓ **415 287-2GH**
1a, 1b, 2, 3, 5-7, 8a, 8b, 9a, 9b, 10b, 12, 13, 16, 19, 20, 24. Munich Wind Ens (arr. Heidenreich) (ORFE) Ⓓ **C092841A**
1a, 1b(pt), 2, 3, 6, 8b, 9c(pt), 13, 14, 18-20, 22. Linos Ens (r1991; arr Heidenreich & Tarkmann) (CAPR) Ⓓ **10 494**

1a, 2, 3, 4a, 4b, 5, 7, 9a-c, 10b, 14, 15, 17, 20, 24, 25. N. Gedda, G. Janowitz, W. Berry, R-M. Pütz, G. Frick, L. Popp, G. Unger, E. Schwarzkopf, C. Ludwig, M. Höffgen, A. Giebel, A. Reynolds, J. Veasey, Philh Chor, Philh, O. Klemperer (r1964) (EMI) Ⓓ **CDM7 63451-2**
1a, 2, 3, 5, 7, 9b, 13, 18, 20, 24. Amadeus Ens, J. Rudel (arr Heidenreich: Woodwinds and Bass) (MUSM) Ⓓ [5] **67118-2**
1a, 2, 5, 6, 8b, 9b, 24. M. Bourgue Wind Ens (trans J. Heidenreich) (PIER) Ⓓ **PV787033**
1a, 2, 5, 6, 8b, 9b, 24. M. Bourgue Wind Ens (trans Heidenreich) (PIER) Ⓓ **PV730005**
1a, 2-5, 7, 8b, 9a, 10b, 12-15, 17, 19, 20, 24-26. I. Seefried, W. Lipp, A. Dermota, E. Kunz, L. Weber, G. London, S. Jurinac, F. Riegler, E. Schürhoff, E. Loose, P. Klein, Vienna Singverein, VPO, H. Von Karajan (r1950) (EMIN) Ⓓ **CD-EMX2220** (EMIN) ▭ **TC-EMX2220**
2. T. Allen, Scottish CO, R. Armstrong (EMIL) Ⓓ **CDZ105**
2. G. Hüsch, BPO, T. Beecham (r1937) (MMOI) Ⓓ **CDMOIR406** (MMOI) ▭ **CMOIR406**
2. T. Krause, Vienna Haydn Orch, I. Kertész (DECC) Ⓓ **433 068-2DWO** (DECC) ▭ **433 068-4DWO**
2. W. Berry, Bavarian St Op Orch, W. Sawallisch (r1972) (CFP) Ⓓ **CD-CFP4602** (CFP) ▭ **TC-CFP4602**
2. M. Kraus, VPO, G. Solti (r1990) (DECC) Ⓓ **440 947-2DH** (DECC) ▭ **440 947-4DH**
2. W. Schulz, H. Schellenberger (arr fl/ob) (DG) Ⓓ **439 150-2GMA** (DG) ▭ **439 150-4GMA**
2. E. Kunz, VPO, W. Furtwängler (pp1951) (ORFE) Ⓓ **C394201B**
2. E. Kunz, VPO, R. Moralt (r1947) (4/92) (EMI) Ⓓ [7] **CHS7 69741-2(4)**
2, 14, 20, 24. A. Martin, D. Robin, Vienna Mozart Orch, K. Leitner (12/91) (NAXO) Ⓓ **8 550435**
2, 15. J. Van Dam, Paris Orch Ens, J-P. Wallez (pp) (5/88) (NOVA) Ⓓ **150 014-2**
2, 15, 20. F. Furlanetto, Vienna SO, I. Marin (3/92) (SONY) Ⓓ **SK47192**
2, 20. H. Prey, Bratislava PO, K. Wöss (pp) (CAPR) Ⓓ [3] **10 810**
2, 20. L. Fugère, orch (French: r1929) (6/93) (SYMP) Ⓓ **SYMCD1125**
2, 20. E. Kunz, VPO, R. Moralt (r1947) (9/95) (TEST) Ⓓ **SBT1059**
2, 20, 24. H. Prey, Salzburg Mozarteum Orch, B. Weil (5/88) (DENO) Ⓓ **CO-1741**
2, 24. W. Berry, Bavarian St Op Orch, W. Sawallisch (7/91) (EMIL) Ⓓ **CDZ7 67015-2**
2, 3, 4a, 4b, 5, 7, 8b, 9a, 10b, 13-15, 17, 18, 20, 23-25. L. Serra, M. Price, K. Moll, P. Schreier, M. Melbye, Leipzig Rad Chor, Staatskapelle Dresden, Colin Davis (PHIL) ▭ **432 618-4PM**
2, 3, 4a, 4b, 7, 8b, 9a-c, 10b, 13-15, 17, 20, 22, 24, 25. R. Ziesak, S. Jo, U. Heilmann, M. Kraus, K. Moll, H. Zednik, Lotte Leitner, A. Pieczonka, A. Kuettenbaum, J. van Nes, W. Schmidt, H. Franzen, Vienna Boys' Ch, Vienna St Op Concert Ch, VPO, G. Solti (DECC) Ⓓ **433 667-2DH**
2, 3, 4a, 4b, 7, 8b, 9a-c, 10b, 13-15, 17, 20, 22, 24, 25. R. Ziesak, S. Jo, U. Heilmann, M. Kraus, K. Moll, H. Zednik, Lotte Leitner, A. Pieczonka, A. Kuettenbaum, J. van Nes, W. Schmidt, H. Franzen, Vienna Boys' Ch, Vienna St Op Concert Ch, VPO, G. Solti ( ) (DECC) **OO** **433 667-5DH**
2, 3, 4a, 4b, 7, 8b, 9a-c, 10b, 13-15, 17, 20, 22(pt), 24, 25. S. Burrows, P. Lorengar, C. Deutekom, M. Talvela, H. Prey, G. Stolze, R. Holm, H. van Bork, Y. Minton, H. Plümacher, Vienna St Op Chor, VPO, G. Solti (r1969) (DECC) Ⓓ **433 441-2DA** (DECC) ▭ **433 441-4DA**
2, 5, 8b, 9b, 24. Budapest Wind Ens, K. Berkes (arr Heidenreich) (QUIN) ▭ **QUI40 3008**
3. F. Wunderlich, Hamburg St Op Orch, A. Rother (EURO) Ⓓ **GD69018** (EURO) ▭ **GK69018**
3. J. Protschka, Munich RO, K. Eichhorn (CAPR) Ⓓ [3] **10 810**
3. Y. Kawahara, R. Hoffmann (arr. Kawahara) (LARG) Ⓓ **Largo 5105**
3. F. Wunderlich, orch (EURO) Ⓓ **VD69256**
3. P. Anders, Berlin St Op Orch, H. Schmidt-Isserstedt (r1937) (MMOI) Ⓓ **CDMOIR406** (MMOI) ▭ **CMOIR406**
3. R. Giménez, ROHO, B. Wordsworth (NIMB) Ⓓ **NI5300**
3. F. Wunderlich, BPO, K. Böhm (DG) Ⓓ [5] **435 145-2GX5(1)**
3. J. Björling, H. Ebert (BLUE) Ⓓ **ABCD042**
3. J. Schmidt, BPO, S. Meyrowitz (r1931) (RELI) Ⓓ **CR921036**
3. E. Haefliger, ECO, J.E. Dähler (CLAV) Ⓓ **CD50-8305**
3. E. Tappy, VPO, James Levine (RCA) Ⓓ **09026 61886-2** (RCA) ▭ **09026 61886-4**
3. H. Roswaenge, BPO, T. Beecham (r1937) (PREI) Ⓓ [2] **89211**
3. D. Lloyd, Sadler's Wells Orch (r1940: Eng) (SAIN) Ⓓ **SCDC2076** (SAIN) ▭ **C2076**
3. R. Tauber, orch (r1938) (PEAR) Ⓓ **GEMMCD9145**
3. P. Anders, Berlin Deutsche Op Orch, H. Schmidt-Isserstedt (r1935) (TELD) Ⓓ **4509-95512-2**
3. T. Beltrán, RPO, R. Stapleton (r1994) (SILV) Ⓓ **SILKD6005** (SILV) ▭ **SILKC6005**
3. F. Wunderlich, Hamburg St Op Orch, A. Rother (r1960s) (RCA) Ⓓ **09026 62550-2**
3. J. Protschka, Munich RO, K. Eichhorn (3/89) (CAPR) Ⓓ **10 109**
3. R. Tauber, orch (r1922) (7/89) (PEAR) Ⓓ **GEMMCD9327**
3. F. Wunderlich, Stuttgart RSO, C. Schuricht (bp1959) (10/89) (ACAN) Ⓓ **43 267**
3. R. Tauber, Vienna St Op Orch, K. Alwin (r1938) (10/89) (NIMB) Ⓓ **NI7801** (NIMB) ▭ **NC7801**
3. L. Simoneau, Paris Champs-Élysées Orch, A. Jouve (r1955) (3/91) (EMI) Ⓓ [2] **CHS7 63715-2**
3. M. Marshall, A. Baltsa, B. Haitink (7/91) (EMIL) Ⓓ **CDZ7 67015-2**
3. H.E. Groh, orch (r1936) (3/92) (PEAR) Ⓓ **GEMMCD9419**
3. P. Domingo, Munich RO, E. Kohn (3/92) (EMI) Ⓓ **CDC7 54329-2**
3. R. Tauber, orch (r1922) (3/92) (EMI) Ⓓ **CDH7 64029-2**
3. W. Ludwig, VPO, O. Ackermann (r1949) (4/92) (EMI) Ⓓ [7] **CHS7 69741-2(4)**
3. R. Tauber, Vienna St Op Orch, K. Alwin (r1938) (7/92) (PEAR) Ⓓ [3] **GEMMCDS9926(2)**
3. R. Tauber, orch (r1922) (12/92) (NIMB) Ⓓ **NI7830** (12/92) (NIMB) ▭ **NC7830**
3. F. Wunderlich, BPO, K. Böhm (5/93) (DG) Ⓓ **431 110-2GB**
3. P. Anders, Berlin Deutsche Op Orch, A. Grüber (bp1944) (8/93) (ACAN) Ⓓ **43 268**
3, 14. E. Gruberová, H-P. Blochwitz, Zurich Op Orch, N. Harnoncourt (r1987) (TELD) Ⓓ **4509-97507-2**
3, 17. E. Grümmer, A. Dermota, VPO, G. Solti (pp1956) (ORFE) Ⓓ **C394201B**
3, 6, 10b, 26. N. Hadden, C. Mackintosh, J. Schlapp, S. Comberti (arr Ehrenfried) (10/91) (CRD) Ⓓ **CRD3468** (10/91) (CRD) ▭ **CRDC4168**
3, 7, 15. J. Novotná, H. Roswaenge, W. Domgraf-Fassbaender, A. Kipnis, VPO, A. Toscanini (pp1937) (ORFE) Ⓓ **C394101B**
3, 8b H. Nash, orch (Eng: r1927) (8/89) (PEAR) Ⓓ **GEMMCD9319**
3, 8b J. Dickie, Capella Istropolitana, J. Wildner (12/91) (NAXO) Ⓓ **8 550383**
3, 8b F. Völker, Berlin Staatskapelle, F.A. Schmidt (r1937) (8/94) (PREI) Ⓓ **89070**
4a, 4b J. Sutherland, New SO, R. Bonynge (r1963) (DECC) Ⓓ **421 881-2DA**
4a, 4b H. Schymberg, Stockholm Royal Orch, N. Grevillius (r1943) (ALTN) Ⓓ **CDAN3**
4a, 4b E. Berger, BPO, B. Seidler-Winkler (r1938) (PREI) Ⓓ **89092**
4a, 4b, 7, 19. E. Gruberová, I. Cotrubas, E. Tappy, C. Boesch, M. Talvela, VPO, James Levine (pp1980) (ORFE) Ⓓ **C394301B**
4a, 4b, 14. R. Streich, Berlin RIAS Orch, F. Fricsay (r1954) (DG) Ⓓ **431 875-2GDO**
4a, 4b, 14. A. Winska, Warsaw PO, W. Michniewski (r1990) (PAVA) Ⓓ **ADW7289**
4a, 4b, 14. M. Ivogün, orch (r1916) (PREI) Ⓓ **89094**
4a, 14. M. Ivogün, orch (r 1916 or 1925) (1/94) (CLUB) Ⓓ **CL99-020**
4a, 14, 17. C. Studer, ASMF, N. Marriner (9/94) (PHIL) Ⓓ **442 410-2PM**
4b F. Hempel, orch (r1911: Ital) (3/94) (NIMB) Ⓓ **NI784**
4b, 17, 18, 26. E. Berger, M. Reining, J. von Manowarda, Vienna St Op Chor, Vienna St Op Orch, H. Knappertsbusch (pp1941) (SCHW) Ⓓ [2] **31467**
5, 16. Winchester Quiristers, R. Bottone, Julian Smith (MERI) Ⓓ **CDE8416** (MERI) ▭ **KE7716**
7. T. Lemnitz, G. Hüsch, BPO, T. Beecham (r1937) (MMOI) Ⓓ **CDMOIR40** (MMOI) ▭ **CMOIR40**
7. H. Schlusnus, S. Kurz, orch (r1923) (PREI) Ⓓ **8911**
7. Lotte Lehmann, H. Schlusnus, orch (r1920) (6/92) (PREI) Ⓓ [3] **8930**
7. E. Eames, E. de Gogorza, orch (r1906: Ital) (11/93) (ROMO) Ⓓ [2] **81001-**
7. E. Eames, E. de Gogorza, orch (r1906: Ital) (1/95) (NIMB) Ⓓ **NI786**
7, 20. F. Schorr, E. Bettendorf, orch (r1922) (PREI) Ⓓ **8905**
7, 20. F. Schorr, E. Bettendorf, orch (r1921) (9/91) (PEAR) Ⓓ **GEMMCD939**
7, 8b, 9a L. della Casa, L. Simoneau, W. Berry, K. Dönch, VPO, G. Szell (pp1959) (ORFE) Ⓓ **C394201B**
8b A. Dermota, Berlin St Op Orch, A. Rother (r1950s) (PREI) Ⓓ **9002**
8b H. Nash, orch (Eng: r1927) (MMOI) Ⓓ **CDMOIR40** (MMOI) ▭ **CMOIR40**
8b K. Erb, orch (r1911) (PREI) Ⓓ **8909**
8b W. Ludwig, Berlin St Op Orch, B. Seidler-Winkler (r1936) (7/95) (PREI) Ⓓ **8908**
9a-c S. Vihavainen, J. Silvasti, J. Falck, J. Rhyänen, Savonlinna Op Fest Chor, Savonlinna Op Fest Orch, U. Söderblom (BIS) Ⓓ [2] **BIS-CD373/**
10a Locke Brass Consort, J. Stobart (arr Stobart) (9/92) (CRD) Ⓓ **CRD340** (3/83) (CRD) ▭ **CRDC410**
10b A. Kipnis, Berlin St Op Orch, C. Schmalstich (r1930) (MMOI) Ⓓ **CDMOIR40** (MMOI) ▭ **CMOIR40**
10b E. List, Berlin St Op Orch, F. Weissmann (r1930) (PREI) Ⓓ **8908**
10b P. Knüpfer, orch (r1907) (PEAR) Ⓓ **GEMMCD912**
10b Vienna St Op Chor, VPO, K. Böhm (r1950s) (BELA) Ⓓ **450 117-** (BELA) ▭ **450 117-**
10b E. Pinza, orch, Rosario Bourdon (r1927) (2/89) (PEAR) Ⓓ **GEMMCD930**
10b E. Pinza, NY Met Op Chor, NY Met Op Orch, B. Walter (Eng: bp1942) (7/91) (MMOI) Ⓓ **CDMOIR40** (MMOI) ▭ **CMOIR40**
10b G. Frick, Berlin Deutsche Op Chor, Berlin SO, W. Schüchter (r1954) (4/92) (EMI) Ⓓ [7] **CHS7 69741-2(4**
10b N. Allin, orch (Eng: r c1920) (7/92) (PEAR) Ⓓ [3] **GEMMCDS9925(1**
10b O. Natzke, orch, H. Geehl (r1938) (12/92) (ODE) Ⓓ **CDODE136**
10b E. Pinza, NY Met Op Chor, NY Met Op Orch, G. Setti (r1928) (9/93) (RCA) Ⓓ **09026 61245-**
10b M. Talvela, Vienna St Op Chor, VPO, G. Solti (r1969) (10/93) (DECC) Ⓓ **436 464-2D**
10b M. Talvela, VPO, James Levine (r1980) (4/94) (RCA) Ⓓ [6] **09026 61580-2(8**
10b, 14. S. Clark, A. Romm (tbn/pf) (EBS) Ⓓ **EBS602**
10b, 15. L. Hofmann, orch, J. Prüwer (r1929) (PREI) Ⓓ **8910**
10b, 15. I. Andrésen, chor, Berlin St Op Orch, F. Zweig (r1928) (10/90) (PREI) Ⓓ **8902**
10b, 15. A. Kipnis, chor, Berlin St Op Orch, C. Schmalstich (r1930) (12/90) (PREI) Ⓓ **8901**
10b, 15. P. Plançon, anon (Ital: r1905) (9/91) (PEAR) Ⓓ **GEMMCD949**
10b, 15. M. Salminen, Lahti SO, E. Klas (8/92) (BIS) Ⓓ **BIS-CD52**
10b, 15. P. Plançon, anon (r1905: Ital) (12/94) (ROMO) Ⓓ [2] **82001-**
10b, 15. K. Borg, Munich PO, A. Rother (r1953) (12/94) (FINL) Ⓓ [3] **4509-95606-**
10b, 15. P. Schoeffler, LSO, K. Rankl (r1946) (1/95) (PREI) Ⓓ **9019**
10b, 15. P. Plançon, anon (r1905: Ital) (1/95) (NIMB) Ⓓ **NI786**
10b, 18. M. Salminen, Zurich Op Hse Chor, Zurich Op Orch, N. Harnoncourt (r1987) (TELD) Ⓓ **4509-97505-**

14. K. Ott, BPO, H. von Karajan
(DG) ▭ **439 153-4GMA**
14. L. Kennedy, ASMF, N. Marriner
(LOND) Ⓓ **827 267-2**
14. S. Jo, Berlin RSO, R. Paternostro (pp)
(CAPR) Ⓓ [3] **10 810**
14. E. Köth, orch (EURO) Ⓓ **VD69256**
14. L. Pons, orch, B. Walter (r1942)
(SONY) Ⓓ [3] **SM3K47211**
14. B. Hoch, Hong Kong PO, K. Schermerhorn
(IMP) Ⓓ **PCDS4**
(IMP) ▭ **PCDSC4**
14. B. Hoch, Hong Kong PO, K. Schermerhorn
(IMP) Ⓓ **PCDS6**
(IMP) ▭ **PCDSC6**
14. F. Foster-Jenkins, C. McMoon (r c1944)
(RCA) Ⓓ **GD61175**
14. V. Loukjanetz, P. Lerebours
(AUVI) Ⓓ **V4662**
14. S. Jo, Suisse Romande Chbr Ch, Lausanne Pro Arte Ch, Paris Orch Ens, A. Jordan
(ERAT) Ⓓ **2292-45797-2**
(ERAT) ▭ **2292-45797-4**
14. M. Foley, Orch (r1949-53)
(ODE) Ⓓ **CDODE1062**
14. M. Korjus, Berlin RSO, J. Müller (r1934)
(DANT) Ⓓ **LYS001**
14. E. Gruberová, BRSO, B. Haitink
(CFP) Ⓓ **CD-CFP4612**
(CFP) ▭ **TC-CFP4612**
14. B. Hoch, Hong Kong PO, K. Schermerhorn
(IMP) Ⓓ [3] **TCD1070**
14. E. Gruberová, Zurich Op Orch, N. Harnoncourt (TELD) Ⓓ **4509-93691-2**
14. J. Harjanne, J. Lagerspetz (r1992; arr picc tpt/pf: Lagerspetz/Harjanne)
(FINL) Ⓓ **4509-95583-2**
14. E. Berger, BPO, T. Beecham (r1937)
(PREI) Ⓓ **89092**
14. S. Jo, VPO, G. Solti (r1990)
(DECC) Ⓓ **443 377-2DM**
14. W. Lipp, VPO, W. Furtwängler (pp1949)
(ORFE) Ⓓ **C394201B**
14. B. Hoch, Hong Kong PO, K. Schermerhorn
(11/86) (IMP) Ⓓ **PCD827**
14. F. Hempel, orch (r1911)
(10/89) (NIMB) Ⓓ **NI7802**
(NIMB) ▭ **NC7802**
14. L. Popp, Philh, O. Klemperer
(7/91) (EMIL) Ⓓ **CDZ7 67015-2**
14. E. Köth, Berlin St Op Orch, A. Rother (r1954)
(4/92) (EMI) Ⓓ [7] **CHS7 69741-2(4)**
14. L. Tetrazzini, orch, P. Pitt (Ital: r1908)
(9/92) (EMI) Ⓓ [3] **CHS7 63802-2(2)**
14. L. Tetrazzini, orch (Ital: r1920)
(9/92) (PEAR) Ⓓ **GEMMCD9225**
14. M. Korjus, Berlin RO, J. Müller (r1934)
(10/93) (PREI) Ⓓ **89054**
14. F. Hempel, orch (r1911)
(3/94) (NIMB) Ⓓ **NI7849**
14. A. Nezhdanova, orch (r1912: Russ)
(3/95) (NIMB) Ⓓ **NI7865**
14. S. Jo, Paris Orch Ens, A. Jordan (r1994)
(6/95) (ERAT) Ⓓ **4509-97239-2**
14, 17. M. André, Toulouse Capitole Orch, M. Plasson (arr tpt)
(1/89) (EMI) Ⓓ **CDC7 49219-2**
15. M. Talvela, orch (EURO) Ⓓ **VD69256**
15. E. Pinza, NY Met Op Orch, B. Walter (r1946)
(SONY) Ⓓ [3] **SM3K47211**
15. P. Kang, S. Katz (SCHW) Ⓓ **312642**
15. O. Natzke, ROHO, K. Rankl (r1947: Eng)
(KIWI) Ⓓ **CDSLD-82**
15. W. Strienz, BPO, T. Beecham (r1937)
(PEAR) Ⓓ **GEMMCD9122**
15. E. Pinza, NY Met Op Orch, B. Walter (r1946: Ital) (4/90) (CBS) Ⓓ **CD45693**
15. A. Kipnis, orch (r1929)
(10/91) (PEAR) Ⓓ **GEMMCD9451**
15. I. Andrésen, orch, F. Zweig (r1928)
(7/92) (PEAR) Ⓓ [3] **GEMMCDS9926(2)**
15. O. Natzke, orch, W. Braithwaite (Eng: r1940)
(12/92) (ODE) Ⓓ **CDODE1365**
15. A. Kipnis, Berlin St Op Orch, E. Orthmann (r1930) (12/93) (NIMB) Ⓓ **NI7851**
15. T. Pasero, orch, A. Sabino (r1943: Ital)
(4/95) (PREI) Ⓓ **89074**
15-26. I. Seefried, E. Loose, E. Rutgers, H. Konetzni, E. Höngen, E. Nikolaidi, A. Dermota, P. Klein, J. Witt, E. Kunz, P. Schoeffler, H. Alsen, Vienna St Op Chor, VPO, K. Böhm (pp1944: with dialogue) (PREI) Ⓓ **90249**
17. K. Te Kanawa, LSO, J. Mauceri
(12/90) (DECC) ▣ **084 474-3**
17. E. Mathis, BPO, H. von Karajan
(DG) ▭ **439 153-4GMA**
17. E. Schumann, orch (r1923)
(PEAR) Ⓓ **GEMMCD9445**
17. E. Schwarzkopf, Philh, W. Braithwaite (Eng: r1948) (EMI) Ⓓ **CDH7 63708-2**
17. I. Cotrubas, orch (EURO) Ⓓ **VD69256**
17. L. Schöne, Berlin St Op Orch, F. Zweig (r1928) (MMOI) Ⓓ **CDMOIR406**
(MMOI) ▭ **CMOIR406**
17. E. Steber, Columbia SO, B. Walter (r1953)
(SONY) Ⓓ [3] **SM3K47211**
17. K. Te Kanawa, LSO, Colin Davis
(PHIL) Ⓓ **434 725-2PM**
(PHIL) ▭ **434 725-4PM**
17. I. Cotrubas, VPO, James Levine
(RCA) Ⓓ **09026 61440-2**
(RCA) ▭ **09026 61440-4**
17. B. Hendricks, ECO, J. Tate (r1984)
(EMI) Ⓓ **CDC5 55095-2**
17. B. Hendricks, Scottish CO, C. Mackerras (r1991) (TELA) Ⓓ **CD80407**
17. E. Destinn, orch, B. Seidler-Winkler (r1908)
(PEAR) Ⓓ **GEMMCD9172**
17. D. Maynor, Boston SO, S. Koussevitzky (r1939) (PEAR) Ⓓ **GEMMCD9179**
17. H. Gueden, VPO, A. Erede (r1952)
(PREI) Ⓓ **90227**
17. B. Bonney, Zurich Op Orch, N. Harnoncourt (r1987) (TELD) Ⓓ **0630-11470-2**
17. K. Te Kanawa, LSO, Colin Davis
(3/84) (PHIL) Ⓓ **411 148-2PH**
17. B. Hendricks, ECO, J. Tate
(6/85) (EMI) Ⓓ **CDC7 47122-2**
17. T. Lemnitz, BPO, T. Beecham (r1937)
(10/90) (PREI) Ⓓ **89025**
17. E. Norena, orch, P. Coppola (French: r1932)
(3/91) (PREI) Ⓓ **89041**
17. J. Gadski, orch (Ital: r1910)
(7/91) (CLUB) Ⓓ **CL99-109**
17. K. Te Kanawa, WNO Orch, C. Mackerras
(10/91) (EMI) ◐ **LDA9 91242-1**
(10/91) (EMI) ▣ **MVC9 91242-3**
17. T. Lemnitz, BPO, T. Beecham (r1937)
(2/92) (MMOI) Ⓓ **CDMOIR408**
17. D. Maynor, Boston SO, S. Koussevitzky (r1939) (4/92) (EMI) Ⓓ [7] **CHS7 69741-2(1)**
17. M. Licette, orch, P. Pitt (Eng: r1916)
(7/92) (PEAR) Ⓓ [3] **GEMMCDS9925(1)**
17. L. Price, New Philh, P.H. Adler
(6/93) (RCA) Ⓓ **09026 61357-2**
17. E. Destinn, orch, W.B. Rogers (r1915)
(11/93) (ROMO) Ⓓ [2] **81002-2**
17. L. Schöne, Berlin St Op Orch, L. Blech (r c1929) (1/94) (CLUB) Ⓓ **CL99-020**
17. E. Destinn, orch, W.B. Rogers (r1915)
(5/94) (SUPR) Ⓓ **11 1337-2**
17. M. Reining, Vienna St Op Orch, H. Knappertsbusch (pp1941)
(6/94) (SCHW) Ⓓ **314502**
17. E. Rethberg, orch (r1921)
(7/94) (PREI) Ⓓ **89051**
17. E. Destinn, orch, W.B Rogers (r1915)
(12/94) (SUPR) Ⓓ [12] **11 2136-2(5)**
17. E. Destinn, orch, B. Seidler-Winkler (r1908)
(12/94) (SUPR) Ⓓ [12] **11 2136-2(2)**
17. E. Destinn, Odeon Orch, A. Pilz (r1908)
(12/94) (SUPR) Ⓓ [12] **11 2136-2(2)**
17. E. Rethberg, orch (r1927)
(2/95) (ROMO) Ⓓ [2] **81012-2**
17. I. Galante, Latvian Nat SO, A. Vilumanis (r1994) (11/95) (CAMP) Ⓓ **RRCD1335**
(11/95) (CAMP) ▭ **RRMC8035**
18. ROH Chor, RPO, R. Stapleton
(RPO) Ⓓ **CDRPO7009**
(RPO) ▭ **ZCRPO7009**
18. Berlin Deutsche Op Chor, Berlin Deutsche Op Orch, G. Sinopoli (DG) **OO 415 283-5GH**
18. ROH Chor, RPO, R. Stapleton (r1991)
(RPO) Ⓓ [2] **CDRPD9006**
(RPO) ▭ [2] **ZCRPD9006**
18. ROH Chor, RPO, R. Stapleton
(IMP) Ⓓ [3] **TCD1070**
18. Berlin Deutsche Op Chor, Berlin Deutsche Op Orch, G. Sinopoli
(10/85) (DG) Ⓓ **415 283-2GH**
18, 26. Bulgarian Svetoslav Obretenov Ch, Sofia PO, G. Robev (CAPR) Ⓓ [3] **10 810**
19. P. Anders, T. Eipperle, G. Hann, Berlin RSO, A. Rother (bp1944) (8/93) (ACAN) Ⓓ **43 268**
22. C. Ingelse (arr organ) (LIND) Ⓓ **LBCD23**
24. G. Groves, J. Watson, J. Partridge (r1994)
(ASV) Ⓓ **CDWHL2088**
26. Timişoara Banatul Phil Chor, Timişoara Banatul PO, N. Boboc (ELCT) Ⓓ **ELCD109**

MUGNONE, Leopoldo *(1858–1941) Italy*

Vita brettone– opera: 3 acts (1905—Naples) (Lib. E. Golisciani)
Vivea nel tempo antico A. Didur, orch (r1906)
(1/94) (CLUB) Ⓓ **CL99-089**

MUSSORGSKY, Modest Petrovich *(1839–1881) Russia*

Boris Godunov– opera: prologue and 4 acts (1874—St Petersburg) (Lib. cpsr)
PROLOGUE: 1a. To whom are you abandoning us; 1b. Mityukha, what are we bawling about?; 1c. True Believers; 1d. The Angel of the Lord spake to the world; 2a. Like to the red sun; 2b. I am sick at heart (Coronation Scene). ACT 1: 3a. Yet one last tale; 3b. You have been writing; 4a. I caught a dove-coloured drake; 4b. For the building of a church; 4c. Once in the town of Kazan; 4d. How he rides...Hostess, where does this road lead?; 4e. Why, from here, for instance; 5. Who are you? Eh?. ACT 2: 6a. Where are you, my bridegroom?; 6b. Once a gnat was sawing wood; 6c. A tale of this and that; 7a. And you, my son, what are you busy with?; 7b. I have attained the highest power; 7c. Our poll parrot was sitting with the nannies; 7d. Your Majesty, I make obeisance; 7e. Ugh, it's oppressive (Clock Scene). ACT 3: 8a. On the banks of the azure Vistula; 8b. Enough! The beauteous lady is grateful; 8c. Marina's bored; 8d. Oh, it's you, father; 9a. At midnight in the garden; 9b. Tsarevich!...At my heels again; 9c. I don't believe in your passion (Polonaise and Chorus); 9d. The crafty Jesuit squeezed me hard; 9e. Oh tsarevich, I implore. ACT 4: 10a. Is the mass over, then?; 10b. Trrrr Tin hat; 10c. The moon is going; 10d. What is he crying for?; 10e. Gush forth, bitter tears; 11a. Well, let's put it to the vote; 11b. Your pardon, my lords; 11c. One day at the hour of vespers (Pimen's monologue); 11d. Farewell, my son, I am dying; 12a. Bring him down here; 12b. No falcon flies across the skies; 12c. The sun and moon have gone dark; 12d. Unleashed, raging our might has been; 12e. Oh Lord, save the king; 12f. Hail to thee, tsarevich; 12g. Gush forth, bitter tears.

Boris E. Nesterenko
Grigory V. Piavko
Marina T. Sinyavskaya
Bolshoi Th Chor, Bolshoi Th Orch, A. Lazarev, I. Morozova
(CAST) ▣ **CVI2041**

Boris N. Ghiaurov
Grigory L. Spiess
Marina G. Vishnevskaya
Pimen M. Talvela
Varlaam A. Diakov
Shuisky A. Maslennikov
Missail M. Paunov
Rangoni Z. Kélémen
Feodor O. Miljakovic
Xenia N. Dobrianova
Nurse B. Cvejic
Hostess M. Lilowa
Simpleton A. Maslennikov
Shchelkalov S. Markov
Lavitsky S.R. Frese
Chernikovsky P. Karolidis
Vienna Boys' Ch, Sofia Rad Chor, Vienna St Op Chor, VPO, H. von Karajan (arr Rimsky-Korsakov/Ippolitov-Ivanov)
(11/88) (DECC) Ⓓ [3] **411 862-2DH3**

Abridged A. Haugland, S.F. Andersen, H. Zednik, E. Harbo, A. Møller, S. Lillesøe, M. Myhus, G. Paevatalu, DR Rad Ch, DR RSO, D. Kitaienko (bp1986)
(6/90) (KONT) Ⓓ [2] **32036/7**

Boris R. Raimondi
Grigory V. Polozov
Marina; Hostess G. Vishnevskaya
Pimen P. Plishka
Varlaam R. Tesarowicz
Shuisky K. Riegel
Missail M. Raitzin
Rangoni N. Storozhev
Feodor M.A. Fish
Xenia C. Dubosc
Nurse M. Zakai
Simpleton N. Gedda

Shchelkalov L. Miller
Chevy Chase Sch Ch, Washington Oratorio Soc, Washington Chor Arts Soc, Washington NSO, M. Rostropovich
(6/90) (ERAT) Ⓓ [3] **2292-45418-2**
Boris N. Ghiaurov
Grigory M. Svetlev
Marina S. Mineva
Pimen N. Ghiuselev
Varlaam D. Petkov
Shuisky J. Franck
Missail Angel Petkov
Rangoni B. Martinovich
Feodor R. Troeva-Mircheva
Xenia L. Hadjieva
Nurse S. Popangelova
Hostess P. Dilova
Simpleton M. Popov
Bodra Smyana Children's Ch, Sofia National Op Chor, Sofia Fest Orch, E. Tchakarov (1872 vers)
(4/92) (SONY) Ⓓ [3] **S3K45763**
Boris R. Lloyd
Grigory A. Steblianko
Marina O. Borodina
Pimen A. Morozov
Varlaam V. Ognovenko
Shuisky Y. Boitsov
Missail I. Yan
Rangoni S. Leiferkus
Feodor L. Dyadkova
Xenia O. Kondina
Nurse E. Perlasova
Hostess L. Filatova
Simpleton V. Solodovnikov
Shchelakov M. Kit
Nikitich Y. Fedotov
Mityukha G. Karasyov
Kirov Th Chor, Kirov Th Orch, V. Gergiev, A. Tarkovsky (r1990)
(4/94) (DECC) ◖ [2] **071 409-1DH2**
(4/94) (DECC) ▣ [2] **071 409-3DH2**
Boris M. Talvela
Grigory N. Gedda
Marina B. Kinasz
Pimen L. Mróz
Varlaam A. Haugland
Shuisky B. Paprocki
Missail K. Pustelak
Rangoni; Shchelkalov A. Hiolski
Feodor W. Baniewicz
Xenia H. Lukomska
Nurse B. Brun-Barańska
Hostess S. Toczyska
Simpleton P. Raptis
Mityukha W. Zalewski
Krushchov J. Góralski
Cracow Boys' Ch, Polish Rad Chor, Cracow RSO, J. Semkow (r1976)
(5/94) (EMI) Ⓓ [3] **CDS7 54377-2**
Boris A. Kocherga
Grigory S. Larin
Marina M. Lipovšek
Pimen S. Ramey
Varlaam G. Nikolsky
Shuisky P. Langridge
Missail H. Wildhaber
Rangoni S. Leiferkus
Feodor L. Nichiteanu
Xenia V. Valente
Nurse Y. Gorokhovskaya
Hostess E. Zaremba
Simpleton; Boyar A. Fedin
Shchelkalov A. Shagidullin
Nikitich; Chernikovsky; Police Officer M. Krutikov
Mityukha; Krushchov; Lavitsky W. Drabowicz
Slovak Phil Chor, Berlin Rad Chor, Tolz Boys' Ch, BPO, C. Abbado (r1993: orig ver)
(5/94) (SONY) Ⓓ [3] **S3K58977**
Boris; Pimen; Varlaam B. Christoff
Grigory N. Gedda
Marina; Feodor E. Zareska
Shuisky; Missail; Krushchov A. Bielecki
Rangoni; Shchelkalov K. Borg
Xenia L. Lebedeva
Nurse; Hostess L. Romanova
Simpleton W. Pasternak
Lavitsky R. Bonte
Chernikovsky E. Bousquet
Paris Russian Chor, FRNO, I. Dobroven (r1952: arr Rimsky-Korsakov)
(12/94) (EMI) Ⓓ [3] **CHS5 65192-2**

Excs A. Kipnis, I. Petina, A. De Paolis, N. Moscona, NY Met Op Chor, NY Met Op Orch, G. Szell (pp1943) (MUSI) Ⓓ **MACD-867**
Forest scene Bolshoi Th Chor, Bolshoi SO, A. Lazarev (r1993)
(5/94) (ERAT) Ⓓ **4509-91723-2**
Symphonic Synthesis Philadelphia, L. Stokowski (r1936: arr Stokowski)
(11/94) (DUTT) Ⓓ **CDAX8009**
1a-d, 2a, 2b M. Talvela, U. Viitanen, J. Falck, H. Kilpeläinen, A. Alamikkotervo, Savonlinna Op Fest Chor, Savonlinna Op Fest Orch, K. Haatanen (BIS) Ⓓ [2] **BIS-CD373/4**
2a, 2b J. Rouleau, J. Lanigan, ROH Chor, ROHO, E. Downes (r1970s)
(BELA) Ⓓ **450 117-2**
(BELA) ⊟ **450 117-4**
2a, 2b, 4c, 4d, 7b, 7d, 7e, 11d A. Kipnis, A. Leskaya, I. Tamarin, Victor Chorale, Victor SO, N. Berezowski (r1945/6)
(9/92) (RCA) Ⓓ **GD60522**
2a, 2b, 7b, 11d N. Ghiaurov, chor, VPO, H. von Karajan (pp1966) (MEMO) Ⓓ [2] **HR4223/4**
2b N. Ghiaurov, A. Maslennikov, Vienna St Op Chor, VPO, H. von Karajan (r1970)
(DECC) Ⓓ **433 443-2DA**
(DECC) ⊟ **433 443-4DA**
2b N. Ghiaurov, Bulgarian Nat Ch, Sofia PO, E. Tchakarov (FORL) Ⓓ **FF060**
2b F. Chaliapin, Paris Russian Op Chor, Paris Russian Op Orch, M. Steinmann, chor, orch, E. Goossens (r1926/31)
(6/88) (EMI) Ⓓ **CDH7 61009-2**
2b Vanni-Marcoux, orch (r1934: French)
(1/94) (CLUB) Ⓓ **CL99-101**
2b Kirov Th Chor, Kirov Th Orch, V. Gergiev (r1993; arr Shostakovich; includes bonus sampler CD) (7/95) (PHIL) Ⓓ **442 775-2PH**
(7/95) (PHIL) ⊟ **442 775-4PH**
3a F. Chaliapin, orch, G.W. Byng (r1922)
(12/89) (PEAR) Ⓓ **GEMMCD9314**
3a B. Christoff, Philh, N. Malko (r1949)
(6/93) (EMI) Ⓓ **CDH7 64252-2**
3a, 3b D. Smirnov, K.E. Kaidanov, orch (r1924)
(6/93) (PEAR) Ⓓ [3] **GEMMCDS9004/6(2)**
3b D. Smirnov, K.E. Kaidanov, orch (r1924)
(PEAR) Ⓓ **GEMMCD9106**
4c A. Pirogov, Bolshoi Th Orch, A. Melik-Pashayev (r c1950) (PREI) Ⓓ **89078**
4c S. Preobrazhensky, anon (r1903)
(PEAR) Ⓓ [3] **GEMMCDS9111(2)**
4c F. Chaliapin, orch, Rosario Bourdon (r1927)
(PEAR) Ⓓ **GEMMCD9122**
4c F. Chaliapin, orch, Rosario Bourdon (1927)
(12/89) (PEAR) Ⓓ **GEMMCD9314**
4c B. Christoff, Philh, H. von Karajan (r1949)
(6/93) (EMI) Ⓓ **CDH7 64252-2**
4c L. Sibiriakov, orch (r1910)
(6/93) (PEAR) Ⓓ [3] **GEMMCDS9007/9(2)**
4c, 11b, 11c P. Gluboky, Soviet Cinema Orch, E. Khachaturian (r1990)
(CDM) Ⓓ [2] **LDC288 005/6**
(CDM) ⊟ **KC488 005**
7b A. Safiulin, Soviet Cinema Orch, E. Khachaturian (r1990)
(CDM) Ⓓ [2] **LDC288 005/6**
(CDM) ⊟ **KC488 005**
7b A. Pirogov, Bolshoi Th Orch, N. Golovanov (r c1950) (PREI) Ⓓ **89078**
7b E. Pinza, NY Met Op Chor, NY Met Op Orch, E. Cooper (r1944: Ital)
(4/90) (CBS) Ⓓ **CD45693**
7b E. Pinza, NY Met Op Orch, E. Panizza (Ital: bp1939) (7/91) (MMOI) Ⓓ **CDMOIR404**
(MMOI) ⊟ **CMOIR404**
7b G. London, V. Pleasants (r1950)
(4/92) (EMI) Ⓓ [7] **CHS7 69741-2(2)**
7b T. Pasero, orch (Ital: r1944)
(4/92) (EMI) Ⓓ [7] **CHS7 69741-2(7)**
7b F. Chaliapin, orch, V. Bellezza (pp1928)
(7/92) (PEAR) Ⓓ [3] **GEMMCDS9926(1)**
7b M. Reizen, Bolshoi Th Orch, N. Golovanov (r1948) (12/92) (PREI) Ⓓ **89059**
7b T. Pasero, SO, D. Marzollo (r1944: Ital)
(4/95) (PREI) Ⓓ **89074**
7b, 7e F. Chaliapin, LSO, M. Steinmann (r1931)
(CONI) Ⓓ **CDHD226**
(CONI) ⊟ **MCHD226**
7b, 7e F. Chaliapin, LSO, M. Steinmann (r1931)
(6/88) (EMI) Ⓓ **CDH7 61009-2**
7b, 7e F. Chaliapin, LSO, M. Steinmann (r1931)
(12/89) (PEAR) Ⓓ **GEMMCD9314**
7b, 7e, 11d A. Kipnis, NYPO, F. Reiner (pp1944: arr Shostakovich) (MUSI) Ⓓ **MACD-867**
7b, 7e, 11d Vanni-Marcoux, orch (r1927: French) (1/94) (CLUB) Ⓓ **CL99-101**

7b, 11c, 11d K. Borg, Berlin RSO, H. Stein (r1963) (12/94) (FINL) Ⓓ [3] **4509-95606-2**
7b, 11d N. Ghiaurov, Sofia PO, E. Tchakarov (r1970s) (FORL) Ⓓ **UCD16743**
7b, 11d B. Christoff, ROH Chor, Philh, I. Dobroven (r1949)
(6/93) (EMI) Ⓓ **CDH7 64252-2**
7e A. Kipnis, RCA SO, N. Berezowski (r1945)
(4/94) (RCA) Ⓓ [6] **09026 61580-2(5)**
9d(pt), 9e H. Roswaenge, F. Beckmann, Berlin St Op Orch, B. Seidler-Winkler (r1940: Ger)
(PREI) Ⓓ [2] **89211**
9e E. Lear, D. Uzunov, Sofia National Op Chor, Paris Cons, A. Cluytens
(CFP) Ⓓ **CD-CFP9013**
(CFP) ⊟ **TC-CFP4498**
9e D. Smirnov, M. Davydova, orch (r1923)
(PEAR) Ⓓ **GEMMCD9106**
9e(pt) P. Althouse, M. Ober, orch (r1915: Ital)
(IRCC) Ⓓ **IRCC-CD810**
11d Vanni-Marcoux, orch, P. Coppola (r1927: French) (PEAR) Ⓓ **GEMMCD9912**
11d F. Chaliapin, M. Carosio, ROH Chor, orch, V. Bellezza (pp1928) (CONI) Ⓓ **CDHD226**
(CONI) ⊟ **MCHD226**
11d R. Raimondi, Paris Op Orch, E. Tchakarov (r1981) (ERAT) Ⓓ **4509-98503-2**
11d F. Chaliapin, ROH Chor, ROHO, V. Bellezza (pp1928) (6/88) (EMI) Ⓓ **CDH7 61009-2**
11d F. Chaliapin, orch, L. Collingwood (r1927)
(12/89) (PEAR) Ⓓ **GEMMCD9314**
11d E. Pinza, Twentieth Cent Fox Chor, Twentieth Cent Fox SO, Alfred Newman (r1952)
(9/93) (RCA) Ⓓ **09026 61245-2**
11d O. Miljakovic, N. Ghiaurov, Vienna St Op Chor, Sofia Rad Chor, VPO, H. von Karajan (r1970) (10/93) (DECC) Ⓓ **436 464-2DM**
11d M. Reizen, B. Zlatogorova, Bolshoi Th Orch, N. Golovanov (r1948) (2/95) (PREI) Ⓓ **89080**
12a-d Bolshoi Th Chor, Bolshoi Th Orch, A. Chistiakov (CDM) Ⓓ **LDC288 022**
19a, 19b P. Althouse, M. Ober, orch, W.B. Rogers (r1915; Ital)
(4/94) (RCA) Ⓓ [6] **09026 61580-2(2)**

The **Fair at Sorochintsï, 'Sorochinskaya yarmarka'– opera (1913—Moscow) (Lib. afte Gogol opera finished Lyadov)**

Gopak Plovdiv PO, R. Raychev
(LASE) Ⓓ **15 621**
(LASE) ⊟ **79 621**
Gopak Andreas Trio (arr pf trio: Drucker)
(DIVO) Ⓓ **CDX29104-2**
Gopak J. Starker, G. Moore (r1958: arr vc/pf: Stutschewsky) (EMI) Ⓓ [6] **CZS5 68485-2**
Gopak Philh, C. Mackerras (r1956)
(EMI) Ⓓ [2] **CZS5 68550-2**
Gopak LSO, A. Coates (r1945)
(BEUL) Ⓓ **2PD11**
Gopak S. Rachmaninov (r1925; arr Rachmaninov: pf) (5/90) (RCA) Ⓓ **GD87766**
Gopak H. Shelley (r1991: arr pf: Rachmaninov)
(3/92) (HYPE) Ⓓ **CDA66486**
Gopak LSO, A. Coates (r1929)
(12/92) (KOCH) Ⓓ **37700-2**
Gopak S. Rachmaninov (r1925; arr Rachmaninov: pf)
(3/93) (RCA) Ⓓ [10] **09026 61265-2(2)**
Gopak Philh, G. Simon (r1992: orch Liadov)
(11/93) (CALA) Ⓓ **CACD1012**
(11/93) (CALA) ⊟ **CAMC1012**
Gopak H. Shelley (r1991: arr pf: Rachmaninov)
(3/94) (HYPE) Ⓓ [8] **CDS44041/8**
Gopak N. Milstein, orch, R. Irving (r1962: arr Jones) (5/94) (EMI) Ⓓ [6] **ZDMF7 64830-2**
Gopak J. Szigeti, A. Foldes (r1941: arr vn/pf: Dushkin) (7/94) (BIDD) Ⓓ [2] **LAB070/1**
Why, my sad heart D. Smirnov, orch (r1924: Fr)
(PEAR) Ⓓ **GEMMCD9106**
Why, my sad heart G. Vinogradov, Bolshoi Th Orch, S. Samosud (r c1948)
(4/92) (EMI) Ⓓ [7] **CHS7 69741-2(6)**
Why, my sad heart D. Smirnov, orch (r1924: Fr)
(6/93) (PEAR) Ⓓ [3] **GEMMCDS9004/6(2)**

Khovanshchina– opera: 5 acts (1872-80—St Petersburg) (Lib. cpsr)

1. Prelude (Dawn over the Moscow River). ACT 2: 14b. Mysterious forces (Marfa's divination). ACT 3: 21a. I walked all through the meadows (Marfa's aria); 24. The lair of the Streltsy is sunk in sleep (Shaklovity's aria). ACT 4: 34. Dance of the Persian Slave Girls; 36. Prelude (Scene 2). ACT 5: 41. Here on this spot (Dosifei's aria). ADDITIONAL ITEMS: 46. Intermezzo; 47. Golitsyn's journey.

Ivan Khovansky S. Elenkov

Andrey Khovansky Z. Gadjev
Golitsin L. Bodurov
Shaklovity S. Popov
Dosifey N. Ghiuselev
Marfa S. Mineva
Scribe Angel Petkov
Emma S. Marinova
Varsonofiev E. Ugrinov
Kuzka R. Doikov
Streshniev N. Vasilev
Strelets I D. Stanchev
Strelets II P. Bakardjiev
Strelets III W. Vrachovski
Sofia National Op Chor, Sofia National Op Orch, R. Raichev
(GEGA) Ⓓ [3] **GD113/5**

Ivan Khovansky M. Petri
Andrey Khovansky A. Berdini
Golitsin M. Picchi
Shaklovity G. Malaspina
Dosifey B. Christoff
Marfa I. Companeez
Scribe H. Handt
Emma J. Mancini
Varsonofiev; Strelets II D. Lopatto
Kuzka A. Mineo
Strelets I G. Canello
Rome RAI Chor, Rome RAI Orch, A. Rodzinski (pp1958: Ital)
(DATU) Ⓓ [2] **DAT12320**

Ivan Khovansky B. Minzhilkiev
Andrey Khovansky Y. Marusin
Golitsin; Scribe K. Pluzhnikov
Shaklovity V. Trofimov
Dosifey N. Okhotnikov
Marfa O. Borodina
Susanna E. Tselovalnik
Emma T. Kravtsova
Pastor V. Lebed
Varsonofiev M. Chernozhukov
Kuzka N. Gassiev
Streshniev V. Gerelo
Strelets I Y. Fedotov
Strelets II A. Khramtsov
Kirov Ballet, Kirov Th Chor, Kirov Th Orch, V. Gergiev, B. Large (r1992)
(PHIL) ◐ [2] **070 433-1PHG2**
(PHIL) ▣ **070 433-3PH2**

Ivan Khovansky N. Ghiaurov
Andrey Khovansky Z. Gadjev
Golitsin K. Kaludov
Shaklovity S. Popov
Dosifey N. Ghiuselev
Marfa A. Milcheva
Susanna M.P. Popova
Scribe Angel Petkov
Emma M. Dimchewska
Pastor; Strelets II D. Stanchev
Varsonofiev; Strelets I S. Georgiev
Kuzka R. Doikov
Streshniev A. Selimski
Sofia National Op Chor, Sofia National Op Orch, E. Tchakarov
(10/90) (SONY) Ⓓ [3] **S3K45831**

Ivan Khovansky A. Haugland
Andrey Khovansky V. Atlantov
Golitsin V. Popov
Shaklovity A. Kocherga
Dosifey P. Burchuladze
Marfa M. Lipovšek
Susanna B. Poschner-Klebel
Scribe H. Zednik
Emma J. Borowska
Kuzka W. Gahmlich
Vienna Boys' Ch, Slovak Phil Chor, Vienna St Op Chor, Vienna St Op Orch, C. Abbado (pp1989)
(11/90) (DG) Ⓓ [3] **429 758-2GH3**

Ivan Khovansky B. Minzhilkiev
Andrey Khovansky V. Galusin
Golitsin A. Steblianko
Shaklovity V. Alexeev
Dosifey N. Okhotnikov
Marfa O. Borodina
Susanna E. Tselovalnik
Scribe K. Pluzhnikov
Emma J. Prokina
Kuzka N. Gassiev
Streshniev V. Gerelo
Leningrad Kirov Th Chor, Leningrad Kirov Th Orch, V. Gergiev
(6/92) (PHIL) Ⓓ [3] **432 147-2PH3**

Ivan Khovansky N. Ghiaurov
Andrey Khovansky V. Atlantov
Golitsin Y. Marusin
Shaklovity A. Kocherga
Dosifey P. Burchuladze
Marfa L. Shemchuk
Susanna B. Poschner-Klebel
Scribe H. Zednik
Emma J. Borowska
Kuzka W. Gahmlich
Streshniev T. Breese
Slovak Phil Chor, Vienna Boys' Ch, Vienna St Op Chor, Vienna St Op Orch, C. Abbado, A. Kirchner
(4/93) (PION) ◐ **PLMCC00631**

Act 3, scenes 6 & 8. Bolshoi Th Chor, Bolshoi Th Orch, A. Chistiakov (CDM) Ⓓ **LDC288 022**
Dance of the Persian Slaves Philh, H. von Karajan (r1960) (EMI) Ⓓ [2] **CZS5 68550-2**
Excs Rotterdam PO, J. Conlon
(8/91) (ERAT) Ⓓ **2292-45596-2**
1. Leningrad PO, E. Mravinsky (pp1965)
(OLYM) Ⓓ [6] **OCD5002**
1. NYPO, L. Bernstein (r1963)
(SONY) Ⓓ **SMK47607**
1. LSO, G. Solti (r1966) (BELA) Ⓓ **450 017-2**
(BELA) ▭ **450 017-4**
1. Phil Pops Orch, C. Gerhardt (r1964)
(CHES) Ⓓ **Chesky CD108**
1. Russian Federation St SO, E. Svetlanov (r1992) (CANY) Ⓓ **EC3657-2**
1. Sydney SO, J. Serebrier
(IMG) Ⓓ **IMGCD1611**
1. Rhineland-Pfalz State PO, K. Redel (r1979)
(FORL) Ⓓ **FF058**
1. Leningrad PO, E. Mravinsky (r1982)
(RUSS) Ⓓ [2] **RDCD10905**
1. Moscow PO, L. Leighton Smith
(2/88) (SHEF) Ⓓ **CD25**
(2/88) (SHEF) ⊙ **TLP25** ▭ **CAS25**
1. Oslo PO, M. Jansons
(1/90) (EMI) Ⓓ **CDC7 49797-2**
1. RPO, Vladimir Ashkenazy (pp1989)
(5/90) (RPO) Ⓓ **CDRPO7014**
(5/90) (RPO) ▭ **ZCRPO7014**
1. RPO, Y. Temirkanov (arr Rimsky-Korsakov)
(3/92) (RCA) Ⓓ **RD60195**
1. Atlanta SO, Y. Levi
(4/92) (TELA) Ⓓ **CD80296**
1. Leningrad PO, E. Mravinsky (pp1981)
(6/92) (ERAT) Ⓓ **2292-45757-2**
1. Leningrad PO, E. Mravinsky (pp1981)
(6/92) (ERAT) Ⓓ [11] **2292-45763-2**
1. Russian Nat Orch, M. Pletnev
(12/94) (DG) Ⓓ **439 892-2GH**
(DG) ▭ **439 892-4GH**
1, 34. Bolshoi Th Orch, A. Chistiakov (r1992)
(CDM) Ⓓ **LDC288 053**
1, 34, 47. Rotterdam PO, J. Conlon (r1989)
(12/93) (ERAT) Ⓓ **4509-92870-2**
1, 47. LSO, C. Abbado (r1980)
(6/93) (RCA) Ⓓ **09026 61354-2**
1, 47. Philh, G. Simon (r1992; orch Rimsky-Korsakov/Stokowski)
(11/93) (CALA) Ⓓ **CACD1012**
(11/93) (CALA) ▭ **CAMC1012**
14b Z. Dolukhanova, Moscow PO, G. Stolarov (pp1954) (RUSS) Ⓓ **RDCD15023**
14b Z. Dolukhanova, orch (r1950s)
(4/92) (EMI) Ⓓ [7] **CHS7 69741-2(6)**
14b, 21a Z. Dolukhanova, USSR Rad Orch, A. Gauk (r1950s) (PREI) Ⓓ **89066**
21a A. Milcheva, Bulgarian RSO, V. Stefanov (r1970s) (FORL) Ⓓ **UCD16743**
24. A. Safiulin, Soviet Cinema Orch, E. Khachaturian (r1990)
(CDM) Ⓓ [2] **LDC288 005/6**
(CDM) ▭ **KC488 005**
24. A. Pirogov, Bolshoi Th Orch (r c1950)
(PREI) Ⓓ **89078**
34. Plovdiv PO, R. Raychev (LASE) Ⓓ **15 621**
(LASE) ▭ **79 621**
34. Slovak PO, K. Redel (r1990)
(PIER) Ⓓ **PV730023**
34, 46. Budapest PO, J. Sándor
(LASE) Ⓓ **14 012**
(LASE) ▭ **78 012**
36. Philadelphia, L. Stokowski (r1927: arr Stokowski) (11/94) (DUTT) Ⓓ **CDAX8009**
41. M. Reizen, Bolshoi Th Orch, V. Nebolsin (r1953) (12/92) (PREI) Ⓓ **89059**
41. B. Christoff, Philh, I. Dobroven (r1950)
(6/93) (EMI) Ⓓ **CDH7 64252-2**
41. K. Borg, Berlin RSO, H. Stein (r1963)
(12/94) (FINL) Ⓓ [3] **4509-95606-2**
46. Gothenburg SO, N. Järvi
(6/90) (DG) Ⓓ **429 494-2GDC**
(6/90) (DG) ▭ **429 494-4GDC**

The Marriage– comic opera: 1 act (1909—St. Petersburg) (Lib. Gogol: opera unfinished)
Podkolesin V. Khrulev
Kochkarev A. Podbolotov
Fiokla Ivanovna L. Kolmakova
Stepan V. Ribasenko
USSR Ministry of Culture SO, G. Rozhdestvensky (r1982: orch Rozhdestvensky)
(9/93) (OLYM) Ⓓ **OCD145**

Oedipus in Athens– opera (projected) (1858-60) (Lib. cpsr, after Ozerov)
Chorus of people in the temple LSC, LSO, C. Abbado (r1980)
(6/93) (RCA) Ⓓ **09026 61354-2**
Chorus of people in the temple Prague Phil Chor, BPO, C. Abbado (pp1993)
(2/95) (DG) Ⓓ **445 238-2GH**
(2/95) (DG) ▭ **445 238-4GH**

Salammbô– opera (incomplete) (1863-66) (Lib. cpsr, after Flaubert)
Balearic Song B. Christoff, A. Labinsky (r c1956) (8/89) (EMI) Ⓓ [3] **CHS7 63025-2**
Balearic Song A. Haugland, P. Rosenbaum (r1994) (4/95) (CHAN) Ⓓ [3] **CHAN9336/8**
Chorus of priestesses LSC, LSO, C. Abbado (r1980) (6/93) (RCA) Ⓓ **09026 61354-2**
Chorus of priestesses Prague Phil Chor, BPO, C. Abbado (pp1993)
(2/95) (DG) Ⓓ **445 238-2GH**
(2/95) (DG) ▭ **445 238-4GH**

MYSLIVEČEK, Josef
(1737–1781) Bohemia

II **Bellerofonte– opera: 3 acts (1767—Naples)**
Bellerofonte C. Lindsley
Argene G. May
Ariobate D. Ahlstedt
Atamante R. Giménez
Briseide K. Laki
Diomede S. Margita
Czech Phil Chor, Prague CO, Z. Peskó
(3/92) (SUPR) Ⓓ [3] **11 0006-2**
Sinfonia Prague CO, Z. Peskó (r1987)
(KOCH) Ⓓ **34036-2**
(KOCH) ▭ **24036-4**

NÁPRAVNÍK, Eduard
(1839–1916) Moravia

Dubrovsky– opera (4 acts), Op. 58 (1895—St Petersburg) (Lib. M. I. Tchaikovsky, after Pushkin)
Give me oblivion N. Gedda, E. Werba (pp1961)
(EMI) Ⓓ **CDH5 65352-2**
Give me oblivion I. Kozlovsky, Bolshoi Th Orch, A. Orlov (r1939)
(4/92) (EMI) Ⓓ [7] **CHS7 69741-2(6)**
Give me oblivion A. Labinsky, anon (r1901)
(6/93) (PEAR) Ⓓ [3] **GEMMCDS9001/3(1)**
Give me oblivion D. Smirnov, orch (r1912)
(6/93) (PEAR) Ⓓ [3] **GEMMCDS9004/6(1)**
Give me oblivion A. Davidov, anon (r1902)
(6/93) (PEAR) Ⓓ [3] **GEMMCDS9007/9(1)**
Ne jamais la voir ni l'entendre M. Mei-Figner, N. Figner, anon (r1901: Fr)
(6/93) (PEAR) Ⓓ [3] **GEMMCDS9997/9(1)**

Harold– opera: 5 acts, Op. 45 (1886—St. Petersburg) (Lib. P P Weinberg, after E von Wildenbruch)
Berceuse d'Harold F. Litvinne, A. Cortot (r1902)
(10/92) (SYMP) Ⓓ **SYMCD1101**
Hush thee, dear one, slumber well M. Michailova, anon (r1905)
(PEAR) Ⓓ [3] **GEMMCDS9111(1)**
Hush thee, dear one, slumber well M. Mei-Figner, anon (r1901)
(6/93) (PEAR) Ⓓ [3] **GEMMCDS9997/9(1)**
Hush thee, dear one, slumber well A. Nezhdanova, anon, anon (r1907)
(6/93) (PEAR) Ⓓ [3] **GEMMCDS9007/9(1)**

NAUMANN, Johann Gottlieb
(1741–1801) Germany

Amphion– prologue and opera-ballet: 1 act (1778—Stockholm) (Lib. G.G. Adlerbeth, after A.L. Thomas)
EXCERPTS: 1. Overture.

1. Stockholm Nat Museum CO, C. Génetay (MSVE) ⓓ **MSCD407**

NEDBAL, Oskar *(1874–1930)* *Bohemia*

Polenblut– operetta (1913—Vienna)
Mazurka Czech PO, V. Neumann (SUPR) ⓓ **11 1287-2**
Mazurka Czech PO, V. Neumann (9/90) (ORFE) ⓓ **C180891A**

NESSLER, Viktor E(rnst) *(1841–1890) Alsace*

Der **Trompeter von Säckingen– opera (1884) (Lib. R. Bunge, after V. von Scheffel)**
Behüt' dich Gott H. Prey, Berlin Deutsche Op Orch, H. Hollreiser (EURO) ⓓ **GD69019**
Behüt' dich Gott R. Tauber, Berlin Schauspielhaus Orch, E. Hauke (r1928) (PEAR) ⓓ **GEMMCD9145**
Behüt' dich Gott H. Schlusnus, Berlin St Op Orch, L. Blech (r1935) (PREI) ⓓ [2] **89212**
Behüt' dich Gott! L. Melchior, Orch (Danish: r1913) (8/88) (DANA) ⓓ [2] **DACOCD311/2**
Behüt' dich Gott H.E. Groh, orch (r1938) (3/92) (PEAR) ⓓ **GEMMCD9419**
Behüt' dich Gott R. Tauber, Berlin Schauspielhaus Orch, E. Hauke (r1928) (12/92) (NIMB) ⓓ **NI7833**
(12/92) (NIMB) ⊟ **NC7833**

NICOLAI, (Carl) Otto (Ehrenfried) *(1810–1849)* *Germany*

Die **Lustigen Weiber von Windsor, '(The) Merry Wives of Windsor'– opera: 3 acts (1849—Berlin) (Lib. Mosenthal, after Shakespeare)**
EXCERPTS: 1. Overture. ACT 1: 2. Nein, das ist wirklich doch zu keck!; 3. So geht indes hinein - Eure Tochter!; 4. Nun eilt herbei; 5a. So hab' ich dich errungen; 5b. Herein! Kommt all herein!. ACT 2: 6. Als Büblein klein; 7a. Gott grüss Euch, Sir!; 7b. In einem Waschkorb?; 8a. Dies ist die Stunde; 8b. Horch, die Lerche singt im Hain!; 8c. Fenton! - Mein Mädchen; 8d. Bestürmen denn die läst'gen Freier; 9. So! Jetzt hätt' ich ihn gefangen!; 10. Wer kloft? - Mach auf, Herr Fluth!. ACT 3: 11. Vom Jäger Herne die Mär ist alt; 12. Wohl dehn, gefasst ist der Entschluss!; 13. O süsser Mond!; 14. Die Glocke schlug schon Mitternacht; 15a. Ihr Elfen, weiss und rot und grau; 15b. Die Menschheit schläft; 16. Mücken, Wespen, Fliegenchor; 17a. Er gesteht noch immer nicht!; 17b. Fasst ihn, Geister, nach der Reih'; 18. So hat denn der Schwank der fröhlichen Nacht.

Mistress Ford R-M. Pütz
Mistress Page G. Litz
Ann Page E. Mathis
Sir John Falstaff G. Frick
Ford E. Gutstein
Page K. Engen
Fenton F. Wunderlich
Slender F. Lenz
Dr Caius C. Hoppe
Bavarian St Op Chor, Bavarian St Orch, R. Heger (r1963) (7/89) (EMI) ⓓ [2] **CMS7 69348-2**
Excs L. Hofmann, A. Jerger, K. Bollhammer, E. Majkut, Vienna St Op Chor, Vienna St Op Orch, F. Weingartner (pp1935) (3/95) (SCHW) ⓓ [2] **314602**
1. VPO, C. Kleiber, B. Large (pp1992) (PHIL) ▭ **070 152-3PH**
1. Philh, L. Siegel (LASE) ⓓ **15 514**
(LASE) ⊟ **79 514**
1. Philh, A. Scholz (r1980) (ROSE) ⓓ **3229**
1. VPO, W. Boskovsky (r1968) (LOND) ⓓ **436 785-2LM**
1. VPO, C. Kleiber (pp1992) (SONY) ⓓ [3] **SX3K53385**
1. LSO, C. Mackerras (r1961) (MERC) ⓓ **434 352-2MM**
1. LPO, T. Beecham (r1936) (7/93) (DUTT) ⓓ **CDLX7001**
1. Black Dyke Mills Band, D. Hurst (arr brass band: G Langford) (9/93) (CHAN) ⓓ **CHAN4514**
(9/93) (CHAN) ⊟ **BBTD4514**
1. NYPO, L. Bernstein (r1967) (9/93) (SONY) ⓓ **SMK47601**
2. E. Berger, C. Müller, Berlin City Op Orch, W.F. Reuss (r1933) (12/91) (PREI) ⓓ **89035**
4. R. Streich, Berlin RSO, K. Gaebel (DG) ⓓ [2] **435 748-2GDO2**
4. M. Ivogün, orch (r1919) (PREI) ⓓ **89094**
4. M. Cebotari, VPO, F. Prohaska (r1949) (12/90) (PREI) ⓓ **90034**
4. Lotte Lehmann, orch (r1919) (6/92) (PREI) ⓓ [3] **89302**
4. M. Ivogün, orch (r1917) (8/92) (NIMB) ⓓ **NI7832**
(8/92) (NIMB) ⊟ **NC7832**
4. L. Schöne, Berlin St Op Orch, E. Orthmann (r c1930) (1/94) (CLUB) ⓓ **CL99-020**
6. E. List, orch, O. Dobrindt (r1928) (PREI) ⓓ **89083**
6. L. Hofmann, Berlin Staatskapelle (r1928) (PREI) ⓓ **89102**
6. A. Kipnis, Berlin St Op Orch, E. Orthmann (r1931) (12/90) (PREI) ⓓ **89019**
7b D. Fischer-Dieskau, G. Frick, BPO, W. Schüchter (r1955) (EMI) ⓓ [2] **CMS5 65621-2**
7b G. Hüsch, E. Fuchs, Berlin City Op Orch, A. von Zemlinsky (r1932) (3/94) (PREI) ⓓ **89071**
8b P. Seiffert, Munich RO, J. Kout (r1992-3) (RCA) ⓓ **09026 61214-2**
8b K. Erb, orch (r1911) (PREI) ⓓ **89095**
8b P. Anders, Berlin Deutsche Op Orch, J. Schüler (r1937) (TELD) ⓓ **4509-95512-2**
8b J. Patzak, orch (r1936) (3/90) (PEAR) ⓓ **GEMMCD9383**
8b H.E. Groh, orch (r1933) (3/92) (PEAR) ⓓ **GEMMCD9419**
8b P. Anders, Berlin St Op Orch, J. Schüler (bp1942) (8/93) (ACAN) ⓓ **43 268**
8b W. Ludwig, Berlin St Op Orch, B. Seidler-Winkler (r1936) (7/95) (PREI) ⓓ **89088**
8c F. Wunderlich, E. Mathis, Bavarian St Orch, R. Heger (EMI) ⓓ [3] **CZS7 62993-2**

NICOLINI, Giuseppe *(1762–1842) Italy*

I **Baccanali di Roma– opera: 2 acts (1801—Milan) (Lib. L Romanelli)**
Parmi sentir nell'anima Y. Kenny, Philh, D. Parry (r1982) (OPRA) ⓓ **ORR201**

NIELSEN, Carl (August) *(1865–1931) Denmark*

FS—Numbers used in D. Fog and D. Schousboe, Carl Nielsen (1965)

Maskarade– opera, FS39 (1906—Copenhagen) (Lib. V. Andersen, after Holberg)
EXCERPTS -; 1. Prelude, Act 1; 2. Prelude, Act 2; 3. Dance of the Cockerels.

Jeronimus H. Byrding
Magdelone I. Steffensen
Leander T. Thygesen
Henrik E. Nørby
Arv M. Jacobsen
Leonard P. Wiedemann
Leonore R. Guldbaek
Pernille E.M. Edlers
Night Watchman; Master of the Masquerade G. Leicht
Tutor N.J. Bondo
Danish Rad Chor, Danish RSO, L. Grøndahl (bp1954) (DANA) ⓓ [3] **DACOCD357/9**

Jeronimus I. Hansen
Magdelone G. Plesner
Leander T. Landy
Henrik M. Schmidt Johansen
Arv C. Sørensen
Leonard G. Bastian
Leonora E. Brodersen
Pernille T. Hyldgaard
Night Watchman J. Klint
Tutor O.V. Hansen
Master of the Masquerade A. Haugland
Danish Rad Chor, Danish RSO, J. Frandsen (12/88) (UNIC) ⓓ [2] **DKPCD9073/4**
E.H. Thaysen, L.T. Bertelsen, Odense SO, E. Serov (11/95) (KONT) ⓓ **32203**
Overture; Magdelone's Dance Scene; Prelude, Act 2; Dance of the Cockerels Danish St RSO, T. Jensen (r1954) (DUTT) ⓓ **CDLXT2505**
1. Gothenburg SO, Myung-Whun Chung (8/86) (BIS) ⓓ **BIS-CD321**
1. BBC SO, A. Davis (4/91) (VIRG) ⓓ **VC7 59618-2**
1, 2. Philadelphia, E. Ormandy (1/91) (SONY) ⓓ [4] **S4K45989**
4. J. Klint, R. Bevan (12/90) (PAUL) ⓓ **PACD56**

Saul and David– opera: 4 acts, FS25 (1902—Copenhagen) (Lib. E. Christiansen)

Saul F. Andersson
David O. Svendsen
Mikal R. Guldbaek
Jonathan N. Møller
Witch of Endor I. Frey
Samuel O. Wolstad
Abner M. Wedel
Danish Rad Chor, Danish RSO, T. Jensen (bp1960) (DANA) ⓓ [3] **DACOCD357/9**

Saul A. Haugland
David P. Lindroos
Mikal T. Kiberg
Jonathan K. Westi
Witch of Endor A. Gjevang
Samuel C. Christiansen
Abner J. Klint
Danish Nat Rad Chor, Danish Nat RSO, N. Järvi (3/91) (CHAN) ⓓ [2] **CHAN8911/2**
(3/91) (CHAN) ⊟ [2] **DBTD2026**
Preludes to Acts II, III & IV Odense SO, E. Serov (r1992) (KONT) ⓓ **32157**
2. Swedish RSO, E-P. Salonen (r1992) (4/94) (SONY) ⓓ **SK53276**

Snefrid– melodram, FS17 (1893—Copenhagen) (Wds. H Drachmann)
Odense SO, E. Serov (r1993) (11/94) (KONT) ⓓ **32178**

NONO, Luigi *(1924–1990)* *Italy*

Intolleranza 1960– scenic action: 2 acts (1961—Venice) (Wds. from various texts)

An Emigrant D. Rampy
His Companion U. Koszut
A Woman K. Harries
An Algerian J. van der Schaaf
A Tortured Prisoner W. Probst
Policeman I J. Dieken
Policeman II C. Hoening
Policeman III C. Otto
Policeman IV H. Wenning
Stuttgart Op Chor, Stuttgart Op Orch, B. Kontarsky (pp1993) (10/95) (TELD) ⓓ **4509-97304-2**

Prometeo: Tragedia dell'ascolto– opera (1984—Venice) (Lib. Cacciari)
I. Ade-Jesemann
M. Bair-Ivenz
P. Hall
Freiburg Sols Ch, Modern Ens, I. Metzmacher (pp1993) (EMI) ⓓ [2] **CDS5 55209-2**

Promoteo– vocal suite from opera (1992)
1. 3 voci, 'Ascolta! Cogli quest'anima (wds. after W Benjamin); 2. Isola seconda, 'Doch uns ist gegeben' (wds. Hölderlin).
1, 2. I. Ade-Jesemann, M. Bair-Ivenz, S. Otto, P. Hall, U. Krumbiegel, M. Schadock, M. Hasel, M. Preis, C. Gössling, Freiburg Sols Ch, BPO, C. Abbado (pp1992) (1/95) (SONY) ⓓ **SK53978**

NØRGÅRD, Per *(b 1932)* *Denmark*

The **Divine Circus (Det guddommelige Tivoli)– opera (1983—Jutland)**
EXCERPTS: PROLOGUE: 1. A Kill (wds. T. Hughes); Silversweet Sound (wds. Shakespeare).
1. H. Stavad, P. Westenholz, M. Zeuthen (DANI) ⓓ **DCD8143**

Gilgamesh– opera in six days and seven nights (1973—Århus) (Lib. cpsr)

Gilgamesh B. Haugan
Enkido H. Lannerbäck
Aruru B-M. Aruhn
Huwawa J. Hviid
Siduri R. Eckhoff
Ishtar M. Baekkelund
Utnapishtim B. Eriksson
Utnapishtims mage S. Grippe
Ishara A. Bartler

Priest R. Leanderson
chor, Swedish RSO, T. Vetö
(1/93) (MARC) Ⓓ [2] **DCCD9001**

Siddhartha: Play for the Expected One– opera ballet: 3 acts (1983—Stockholm) (Lib. O Sarvig)

Siddharta Gotama S. F. Andersen
Suddhodana A. Haugland
Prajapati E. Guillaume
Asita E. Harbo
First Counsellor K. Janken
Second Counsellor C. Christiansen
Messenger P. Elming
Yasodhara T. Kiberg
Kamala A. Frellesvig
Gandarva M. Nyhus
G. Mortensen
Danish Nat Rad Ch, Danish Nat Rad Childrens' Ch, Danish Nat RSO, J. Latham-König (r1984)
(DACA) Ⓓ [2] **8 224031/2**

NOUGUÈS, Jean *(1875–1932)* *France*

L' **Aigle– opera: 3 acts (1912—Rouen) (Lib. H. Cain & L. Payen)**
Ah! mes fidèles H. Albers, orch (r c1911)
(8/92) (IRCC) Ⓓ **IRCC-CD802**

Quo vadis?– opera
Amici, l'ora attesa e questa; Errar sull'ampio M. Battistini, orch, C. Sabajno (Ital: r1912)
(10/92) (PEAR) Ⓓ **GEMMCD9936**
Errar sull'ampio mar M. Battistini, orch, C. Sabajno (Ital: r1912) (10/92) (NIMB) Ⓓ **NI7831**
(10/92) (NIMB) ▭ **NC7831**

OFFENBACH, Jacques *(1819–1880)* *Germany/France*

Barbe-Bleue– operetta: 3 acts (1866—Paris) (Lib. Meilhac and Halévy)
Faut-il y aller ou faut-il pas y aller? J. Rhodes, Bordeaux Aquitaine Orch, R. Benzi (r1970s)
(EMI) Ⓓ [2] **CZS5 68113-2**
Or depuis la rose nouvelle...Tous les deux, amoureux B. Hendricks, G. Quilico, Lyon Op Orch, L. Foster (r1993)
(6/95) (EMI) Ⓓ **CDC5 55151-2**
Overture CBSO, L. Frémaux
(KLVI) Ⓓ **KCD11040**
Overture BPO, H. von Karajan (German version) (3/83) (DG) Ⓓ **400 044-2GH**
Overture Vienna SO, B. Weil (r1992: arr F Hoffmann) (1/94) (SONY) Ⓓ **SK53288**

La **Belle Hélène, 'Beautiful Helen'– operetta: 3 acts (1864—Paris) (Lib. Meilhac and Halévy)**
1a. Overture (prep. E. Haensch). ACT 1: 1b. Vers tes autels, Jupin (chorus); 1c. C'est le devoir des jeunes filles (Chorus of girls); 2a. Amours divins! (Helen); 2b. Entrez, vite, Grande Reine! (Calchas, Helen); 3a. Au cabaret du labyrinthe (Oreste, Calchas, chorus); 3b. Tzing la la (Oreste, chorus); 4. Quoi?...Là-bas dans l'azur (melodrame); 5. Homme de 20 anns (melodrame); 6. Au mont Ida (Paris); 7a. Voici les rois de la Grèce (chorus); 7b. Ces rois remplis de vaillance (Kings); 7c. Nous commençons (ensemble); 7d. Fanfare! (Helen, chorus); 8. Gloire (finale). ACT 2: 9. Entr'acte; 10. Ô Reine, en ce jour (Helen, Bacchus, chorus); 11. On me nomme Hélène la Blonde (Hélène); 12. Le voici le Roi des Rois (March of the goose); 13. Vous le voyez (Gambling Scene); 14. En couronnes, tressons les roses (Helen, Paris, chorus); 15. C'est le ciel qui m'envoie (Helen, Paris); 16. A moi! Rois de la Grèce (finale: ensemble). ACT 3: 17. Entr'acte; 18a. Dansons, buvons (Oreste, chorus); 18b. Vénus au fond de notre âme (Oreste, chorus); 18c. Oh mais alors ce n'était pas un rêve (melodrame); 19. Là vrai, je ne suis pas coupable (Hélène); 20. Lorsque le Grèce (Menelaus, Calchas, Agamemnon); 21a. La galère de Cythère (chorus); 21b. Et tout d'abord, ô vile multitude (Paris, chorus); 22. Elle vient, c'est elle (finale: ensemble).

Hélène J. Norman
Paris J. Aler
Ménélas C. Burles
Agamennon G. Bacquier
Calchas J-P. Lafont
Oreste C. Alliot-Lugaz
Achille J. Loreau
Ajax I R. Trentin
Ajax II G. Desroches
Bacchis N. Carreras
Slave A. Levallier
Toulouse Capitole Chor, Toulouse Capitole Orch, M. Plasson
(9/86) (EMI) Ⓓ [2] **CDS7 47157-8**
1a Czech PO, V. Neumann
(SUPR) Ⓓ **11 0724-2**
1a Košice St PO, A. Walter
(NAXO) Ⓓ **8 550468**
1a CBSO, L. Frémaux (KLVI) Ⓓ **KCD11040**
1a BPO, H. von Karajan
(3/83) (DG) Ⓓ **400 044-2GH**
1a Berlin St Op Orch, O. Klemperer (r1929)
(2/89) (SYMP) Ⓓ **SYMCD1042**
1a Detroit SO, P. Paray (r1959)
(11/93) (MERC) Ⓓ **434 332-2MM**
1a Boston Pops, A. Fiedler (r1956)
(1/94) (RCA) Ⓓ **09026 61429-2**
1a Vienna SO, B. Weil (r1992: arr F Lehner)
(1/94) (SONY) Ⓓ **SK53288**
1a, 15. Raphaele Concert Orch, P. Walden (arr Waldenmaier) (5/91) (MOZA) Ⓓ **MECD1002**
1c, 6, 7a, 7b, 8, 11, 15, 18b, 20, 21b, 22. C. Devos, Duvaleix, M. Roux, B. Demigny, G. Rey, A. Doniat, W. Clément, D. Dassy, L. Berton, Raymond St Paul Chor, Lamoureux Orch, J. Gressier (r1950s)
(5/93) (EMI) Ⓓ [2] **CZS7 67515-2**
2a, 6, 7b, 20. D. Millet, C. Burles, M. Hamel, P. Guigue, J-C. Benoit, B. Sinclair, L. Masson, R. Duclos Ch, Lamoureux Orch, J-P. Marty
(EMI) Ⓓ [2] **CZS5 68113-2**
2a, 15, 19. J. Norman, J. Aler, Toulouse Capitole Orch, M. Plasson (r1984)
(EMI) Ⓓ **CDM5 65576-2**
6. H. Nash, orch (Eng: r1932)
(9/91) (PEAR) Ⓓ **GEMMCD9473**
6. J. Björling, orch, N. Grevillius (r1938: Swed)
(8/92) (BLUE) Ⓓ **ABCD016**
6. J. Björling, orch, N. Grevillius (r1938: Swed)
(10/93) (NIMB) Ⓓ **NI7842**
6. J. Björling, orch, N. Grevillius (r1938: Swed)
(10/93) (EMI) Ⓓ **CDH7 64707-2**
6. J. Björling, orch, N. Grevillius (r1938: Swed)
(9/94) (IMP) Ⓓ **GLRS103**
6. J. Björling, orch, N. Grevillius (r1938: Swed)
(12/94) (MMOI) Ⓓ **CDMOIR425**
11. J. Norman, Toulouse Capitole Orch, M. Plasson (EMI) Ⓓ **CDM7 69256-2**
11. J. Norman, Toulouse Capitole Orch, M. Plasson (r1984) (EMI) Ⓓ **CDC5 55095-2**
11. R. Crespin, SRO, A. Lombard (r1970/1)
(DECC) Ⓓ **440 416-2DM**
11, 21b J. Norman, J. Aler, Toulouse Capitole Chor, Toulouse Capitole Orch, M. Plasson (r1984) (EMI) Ⓓ [2] **CZS5 68113-2**

Les **Brigands– operetta: 3 acts (1869—Paris) (Lib. Meilhac and Halévy)**

Falsacappa T. Raffalli
Fiorella G. Raphanel
Fragoletto C. Alliot-Lugaz
Piétro M. Trempont
Carmagnola C. Jean
Domino F. Dudziak
Barbavano P-Y. Le Maigat
Princess of Granada V. Millot
Adolphe de Valladolid M. Fockenoy
Comte de Gloria-Cassis J-L. Viala
Duke of Mantua T. Dran
Baron de Campotasso F. le Roux
Antonio B. Pisani
Captain of the Carabinieri R. Schirrer
Pipo J. Loreau
Lyon Op Chor, Lyon Op Orch, J.E. Gardiner (r1988)
(2/90) (EMI) Ⓓ [2] **CDS7 49830-2**

Falsacappa M. Trempont
Fiorella V. Chevalier
Fragoletto C. Alliot-Lugaz
Piétro R. Cassinelli
Carmagnola G. Fletcher
Domino J-L. Meunier
Barbavano A. Garcin
Princess of Granada M. Barscha
Adolphe de Valladolid A. Normand
Comte de Gloria-Cassis J-L. Viala
Duke of Mantua J-L. Maurette
Baron de Campotasso G. Gautier
Antonio B. Pisani
Captain of the Carabinieri R. Schirrer
Pipo J. Loreau
Lyon Op Chor, Lyon Op Orch, C. Gibault, L. Erlo, A. Maratrat
(6/93) (PION) ◐ [3] **PLMCC00701**
Excs G. Raphanel, C. Alliot-Lugaz, T. Raffalli, M. Trempont, J-L. Viala, Lyon Op Chor, Lyon Op Orch, J.E. Gardiner (r c1989)
(EMI) Ⓓ [2] **CZS5 68113-2**

La **Chanson de Fortunio– operetta: 1 act (1861—Paris) (Lib. Crémieux and Halévy)**

Fortunio L. Lovano
Mme Fortunio L. Dachary
Valentin M. Hamel
Friquet R. Amade
Babet F. Betti
Guillaume A. Doniat
Landry R. Destain
Sylvain J. Pruvost
Saturnin P. Saugey
ORTF Lyric Orch, J-C. Hartemann (bp1963)
(3/92) (MUSD) Ⓓ [2] **20138-2**

Christopher Columbus– opera pastiche (1976—Belfast) (Lib. D White: music arr P Schmid)

Christopher Columbus M. Arthur
Beatriz J. Roberts
Rosa Columbus J. Peters
Fleurette Columbus L. Gray
Gretel Columbus M. Hill Smith
Luis de Torres C. du Plessis
Chief of Police A. Opie
Queen Isabella Anna Dawson
King Ferdinand A. Bregonzi
Tourist C. Harré
Waiter J. Duxbury
Princess Minnehaha Columbua; Esperanza R. Ashe
Carmelita C. Kite
Manuela K. Smales
Valencia A. Dixey
G. Mitchell Ch, LMP, A. Francis (r1977: Eng)
(4/93) (OPRA) Ⓓ [2] **ORC002**

Les **Contes d'Hoffmann, '(The) Tales of Hoffmann'– opera: prologue, 3 acts, epilogue (1881—Paris) (Lib. Barbier. Score completed Guiraud)**
PROLOGUE: 1. Prelude; 2. Glou! glou! glou!; 3a. Le conseilleur Lindorf, morbleu!; 3b. Dans les rôles d'amoureux langoureux; 4. Deux heures devant moi; 5. Drig, drig, drig; 6. Il était une fois à la cour d'Eisenach (Legend of Kleinsach); 7. Peuh! cette bière est détestable. ACT 1: 8. Entr'acte; 9. Là! dors en paix; 10a. Allons! courage et confiance; 10b. C'est elle!; 10c. Ah! vivre deux!; 11a. C'est moi, Coppélius (Je me nomme Coppélius); 11b. J'ai des veux; 12. Non aucun hôte vraiment; 13. Les oiseaux dans la charmille (Doll's Song); 14a. Le souper vous attend; 14b. Ils se sont éloignés enfin!; 15. Voici les valseurs (Waltz). ACT 2: 16. Belle nuit, ô nuit d'amour (Barcarolle); 17a. Et moi, ce n'est pa là; 17b. Que d'un brûlant désir; 18a. Scintille diamant!; 18b. Cher ange!; 19a. Malheureux!; 19b. O Dieu! de quelle ivresse; 20. Hélas! mon coeur s'égare encore!; 21. Ecoutez, messieurs!. ACT 3; 22. Elle a fui, la tourterelle; 23. Jour et nuit; 24a. C'est une chanson d'amour; 24b. J'ai le bonheur dans l'âme; 25. Qu'as-tu donc?; 26. Pour conjurer le danger; 27a. Ne chanteras plus?; 27b. Écoute! Antonia! Dieu, ma mère; 28. Mon enfant! ma fille! Antonia! (Finale). 29. Entr'acte. EPILOGUE: 30. Voilà quelle fut l'histoire; 31. Vidons les tonneaux; 32a. Et moi?; 32b. O Dieu! de quelle ivresse; 33. Non, ivre mort. 34. Barcarolle (orchestral version).

Hoffmann P. Domingo
Olympia L. Serra
Giulietta A. Baltsa
Antonia I. Cotrubas
Nicklausse; Muse C. Powell
Lindorf R. Lloyd
Coppélius G. Evans
Dapertutto S. Nimsgern
Dr Miracle N. Ghiuselev
Spalanzani R. Tear
Schlémil P. Gelling
Crespel G. Howell
Voice of Antonia's mother P. Cannan
Andrès; Cochenille P. Crook
Pitichinaccio F. Egerton
Frantz B. Dickerson
Luther E. Garrett
Nathaniel R. Leggate
Hermann J. Rawnsley

Stella D. Bergsma
ROH Chor, ROHO, G. Prêtre, J. Schlesinger
(CAST) ▣ **CVI2045**
Hoffmann P. Domingo
Olympia; Giulietta; Antonia; Stella J. Sutherland
Nicklausse; Muse H. Tourangeau
Lindorf; Coppélius; Dapertutto; Dr Miracle G. Bacquier
Spalanzani J. Charon
Schlémil A. Neury
Crespel P. Plishka
Voice of Antonia's mother M. Lilowa
Andrès; Cochenille; Pitichinaccio; Frantz H. Cuénod
Luther R. Jacques
Suisse Romande Rad Ch, SRO, R. Bonynge (with dialogue)
(11/86) (DECC) Ⓓ [2] **417 363-2DH2**
Hoffmann N. Shicoff
Olympia L. Serra
Giulietta J. Norman
Antonia R. Plowright
Stella D. Bryant
Nicklausse A. Murray
Lindorf; Coppélius; Dapertutto; Dr Miracle J. van Dam
Spalanzani A. Oliver
Schlémil D. Duesing
Crespel K. Rydl
Voice of Antonia's mother J. Taillon
Andrès; Cochenille; Pitichinaccio; Frantz R. Tear
Muse A. Murray
Luther K. Rydl
Brussels Nat Op Chor, Brussels Nat Op Orch, S. Cambreling (r1988)
(12/88) (EMI) Ⓓ [3] **CDS7 49641-2**
Hoffmann N. Gedda
Olympia G. d'Angelo
Giulietta E. Schwarzkopf
Antonia V. de los Angeles
Nicklausse J-C. Benoit
Lindorf N. Ghiuselev
Coppélius; Dr Miracle G. London
Dapertutto E. Blanc
Spalanzani M. Sénéchal
Schlemil; Luther J-P. Laffage
Crespel R. Geay
Mother's Voice C. Gayraud
J. Collard
R. Duclos Ch, Paris Cons, A. Cluytens (r1964/5)
(12/89) (EMI) Ⓓ [2] **CMS7 63222-2**
Hoffmann P. Domingo
Olympia; Antonia; Giulietta E. Gruberová
Nicklausse; Muse C. Eder
Lindorf A. Schmidt
Coppélius G. Bacquier
Dapertutto J. Diaz
Dr Miracle J. Morris
Spalanzani G. Friedmann
Schlémil R. Van Allan
Crespel H. Stamm
Voice of Antonia's mother C. Ludwig
Andrès R. Gambill
Cochenille; Pitichinaccio P. Crook
Frantz M. Sénéchal
Luther K. Rydl
Nathanaël R. Leggate
Hermann U. Malmberg
French Rad Chor, FNO, S. Ozawa (r1986)
(3/90) (DG) Ⓓ [2] **427 682-2GH2**
Hoffmann F. Araiza
Olympia E. Lind
Giulietta C. Studer
Antonia J. Norman
Nicklausse; Muse A.S. von Otter
Lindorf; Coppélius; Dapertutto; Dr Miracle S. Ramey
Spalanzani R. Cassinelli
Schlémil J-L. Chaignaud
Crespel B. Martinovich
Voice of Antonia's mother F. Palmer
Andrès; Cochenille; Pitichinaccio; Frantz G. Gautier
Luther R. Tomaszewski
Nathaniel; Wolfram P. Menzel
Hermann; Wilhelm J. Hartfiel
Leipzig Rad Chor, Staatskapelle Dresden, J. Tate (with dialogue)
(11/92) (PHIL) Ⓓ [3] **422 374-2PH3**
Hoffmann D. Galvez-Vallejo
Olympia N. Dessay
Giulietta I. Vernet
Antonia B. Hendricks
Nicklausse B. Balleys
Lindof; Coppelius; Dr Miracle; Dapertutto J. Van Dam
Spalanzan; Crespel; Schlemil G. Bacquier
Voice of Antonia's mother H. Jossoud
Frantz J. Verzier
Stella L. Malidor
Lyon Op Chor, Lyon Op Orch, K. Nagano
(6/95) (PION) ◖ **PLMCB00931**
Hoffmann R. Jobin
Olympia R. Doria
Giulietta V. Bovy
Antonia G. Boué
Nicklausse F. Revoil
Muse R. Faure
Lindorf L. Musy
Coppélius A. Pernet
Dapertutto C. Soix
Dr Miracle R. Bourdin
Spalanzani R. Lapelletrie
Schlémil C. Cambon
Crespel A. Philippe
Voice of Antonia's mother S. Borghese
Andrès; Cochenille; Pitichinaccio; Frantz Bourvil
Luther A. Vessières
Nathanael R. Amade
Hermann C. Maurane
Stella H. Delahaye
Paris Opéra-Comique Chor, Paris Opéra-Comique Orch, A. Cluytens (r1948)
(9/95) (EMI) Ⓓ [2] **CMS5 65260-2**
Excs P. Domingo (CAST) ▣ **CVI2021**
Excs P. Domingo, J. Sutherland, G. Bacquier, H. Cuénod, H. Tourangeau, Suisse Romande Rad Ch, Lausanne Pro Arte Ch, Du Brassus Ch, SRO, R. Bonynge (DECC) Ⓓ **421 866-2DA**
Excs P. Domingo, E. Gruberová, C. Eder, G. Bacquier, J. Diaz, J. Morris, French Rad Chor, FNO, S. Ozawa (DG) Ⓓ **429 788-2GH**
Excs N. Shicoff, A. Murray, L. Serra, R. Plowright, J. Norman, J. Van Dam, R. Tear, J. Taillon, M. Vanaud, D. Duesing, T. Dran, Brussels Nat Op Chor, Brussels Nat Op Orch, S. Cambreling (EMI) Ⓓ **CDC7 54322-2**
Excs F. Araiza, E. Lind, C. Studer, J. Norman, A.S. von Otter, S. Ramey, R. Cassinelli, F. Palmer, G. Gautier, R. Tomaszewski, P. Menzel, Leipzig Rad Chor, Staatskapelle Dresden, J. Tate (r1987-89) (PHIL) Ⓓ **438 502-2PH**
Excs J. Norman, A. Murray, N. Shicoff, D. Duesing, Brussels Théâtre de la Monnaie Chor, Brussels Théâtre de la Monnaie Orch, S. Cambreling (r1988) (EMI) Ⓓ **CDM5 65576-2**
Excs J. Sutherland, Orch, Anon (cond), D. Bailey (11/92) (DECC) ◖ **071 135-1DH**
1. Detroit SO, P. Paray (r1959)
(11/93) (MERC) Ⓓ **434 332-2MM**
1, 3b, 6, 10a, 11a, 13, 16, 18a, 19a, 20, 22, 23, 27a A. Lance, S. Sarroca, R. Massard, J. Giovannetti, S. Michel, R. Andreozzi, Y. Bisson, M. Mesplé, A. Guiot, G. Bacquier, G. Serkoyan, J. Giraudeau, R. Soyer, F. Arrauzau, orch, J. Etcheverry (ADES) Ⓓ **13208-2**
6. P. Domingo, SRO, R. Bonynge
(DG) Ⓓ [3] **427 708-2GX3**
6. R. Tauber, chor, SO (Ger: r1928)
(MMOI) Ⓓ **CDMOIR405**
(MMOI) ⊟ **CMOIR405**
6. P. Domingo, P. di Proenza, Lausanne Pro Arte Ch, SRO, R. Bonynge (r1971)
(DECC) Ⓓ **436 300-2DX**
(DECC) ⊟ **436 300-4DX**
6. P. Domingo, ROHO, G. Prêtre
(TELD) ◖ **9031-77676-6**
(TELD) ▣ **9031-77676-3**
6. P. Domingo, SRO, R. Bonynge
(7/86) (DG) Ⓓ **415 366-2GH**
6. G. Lauri-Volpi, NY Met Op Chor, NY Met Op Orch, G. Setti (r1929) (9/90) (PREI) Ⓓ **89012**
6. G. Lauri-Volpi, NY Met Op Chor, NY Met Op Orch, G. Setti (r1929) (7/93) (NIMB) Ⓓ **NI7845**
6. P. Domingo, Suisse Romande Rad Chor, Lausanne Pro Arte Ch, SRO, R. Bonynge (r1972) (10/93) (DECC) Ⓓ **436 463-2DM**
(10/93) (DECC) ⊟ **436 463-4DM**
6. Alfredo Kraus, P. Gyton, WNO Chor, WNO Orch, C. Rizzi (r1994)
(8/95) (PHIL) Ⓓ **442 785-2PH**
(8/95) (PHIL) ⊟ **442 785-4PH**
6, 10a-c, 19b P. Domingo, P. di Proenza, Suisse Romande Rad Chor, Pro Arte Ch, Brassus Chorale, SRO, R. Bonynge (r1972)
(DECC) Ⓓ **440 410-2DM**
6, 19b R. Tauber, orch (Ger: r1928)
(7/89) (PEAR) Ⓓ **GEMMCD9327**
6, 19b R. Tauber, chor, Berlin Staatskapelle, E. Hauke (Ger: r1928)
(3/92) (EMI) Ⓓ **CDH7 64029-2**
6, 19b R. Tauber, chor, Berlin Staatskapelle, E. Hauke (Ger: r1928) (12/92) (NIMB) Ⓓ **NI7830**
(12/92) (NIMB) ⊟ **NC7830**
6, 32b M. Wittrisch, Berlin St Op Orch, E. Orthmann (Ger: r1932) (PREI) Ⓓ **89024**
6, 32b J. Patzak, Berlin St Op Orch, H. Weigert (Ger: r1930) (3/90) (PEAR) Ⓓ **GEMMCD9383**
8. Boston Pops, A. Fiedler (r1956)
(1/94) (RCA) Ⓓ **09026 61429-2**
8, 16, 19a, 29. LPO, T. Beecham (r1936)
(7/94) (PEAR) Ⓓ **GEMMCD9065**
8, 19a, 29, 34. LPO, T. Beecham (r1936)
(6/94) (DUTT) Ⓓ **CDLX7003**
11a G. Souzay, New SO, P. Bonneau (r1956)
(DECC) Ⓓ **440 419-2DM**
11a A. Didur, orch (r c1916)
(1/94) (CLUB) Ⓓ **CL99-089**
13. E. Gruberová, French Rad Chor, FNO, S. Ozawa (DG) ⊟ **439 153-4GMA**
13. R. Streich, Berlin RIAS Chbr Ch, Berlin RSO, R. Kraus (DG) Ⓓ [2] **435 748-2GDO2**
13. M. Mesplé, Paris Op Orch, J-P. Marty (r1968) (EMI) Ⓓ [2] **CZS7 67813-2**
13. M. Robin, Paris Op Orch, P. Dervaux
(EMI) Ⓓ [2] **CZS5 68113-2**
13. M. André, Toulouse Capitole Chor, Toulouse Capitole Orch, M. Plasson (arr tpt)
(1/89) (EMI) Ⓓ **CDC7 49219-2**
13. L. Pons, orch, G. Cloëz (r1929)
(4/92) (MSOU) Ⓓ **DFCDI-111**
13. F. Saville, anon (Ger: r c1902)
(10/92) (SYMP) Ⓓ **SYMCD1093**
13. M. Korjus, Berlin St Op Orch, F. Schönbaumsfeld (Ger: r1934)
(10/93) (PREI) Ⓓ **89054**
13. F. Hempel, orch (r1913)
(3/94) (NIMB) Ⓓ **NI7849**
13. P. Alarie, Lamoureux Orch, P. Dervaux (r1953) (11/94) (PHIL) Ⓓ [2] **438 953-2PM2**
13. I. Baillie, orch, S. Robinson (r1930: Eng)
(7/95) (DUTT) Ⓓ **CDLX7013**
13, 16. L. Serra, A. Baltsa, C. Powell, P. Domingo, R. Tear, ROHO, G. Prêtre
(CAST) ▣ **CVI2065**
13, 16. J. Sutherland, M. Horne, Sydney Eliz Orch, R. Bonynge (MCEG) ▣ **VVD780**
13, 34. T. Dahl, Calgary PO, M. Bernardi (r1992)
(12/94) (CBC) Ⓓ **SMCD5125**
16. J. Carreras, Barcelona SO, G. Navarro
(11/92) (RCA) ⊟ **09026 61204-4**
16. J. McCormack, F. Kreisler, E. Schneider (r1916) (BIDD) Ⓓ **LAB022**
16. R. Ponselle, C. Ponselle, orch (r1919)
(PEAR) Ⓓ [2] **GEMMCDS9964**
16. J. Sutherland, H. Tourangeau, Suisse Romande Rad Chor, Lausanne Pro Arte Ch, SRO, R. Bonynge (DECC) Ⓓ **433 822-2DH**
(DECC) ⊟ **433 822-4DH**
16. J. Sutherland, H. Tourangeau, Suisse Romande Rad Ch, Lausanne Pro Arte Ch, SRO, R. Bonynge (DECC) Ⓓ **433 067-2DWO**
(DECC) ⊟ **433 067-4DWO**
16. G. Saba (arr Moszkowski) (IMP) Ⓓ **PCDS6**
(IMP) ⊟ **PCDSC6**
16. I. Cotrubas, E. Obraztsova, Czech SO, A. Krieger (pp1991) (IMP) Ⓓ **MCD42**
16. I. Baillie, N. Walker, orch (r1927: Eng)
(PEAR) Ⓓ **GEMMCD9934**
16. K. Ricciarelli, L.V. Terrani, Madrid SO, G.P. Sanzogno (pp1991) (IMP) Ⓓ [2] **DPCD998**
16. A. Scotti, G. Farrar, orch (r1912)
(PEAR) Ⓓ **GEMMCD9937**
16. K. Ricciarelli, L.V. Terrani, Madrid SO, G.P. Sanzogno (RNE) Ⓓ [2] **650004**
16. J. Carreras, Barcelona SO, G. Navarro
(RCA) ○○ **09026 61204-5**
16. K. Smith, P. Rhodes (arr Rhodes)
(ASV) Ⓓ **CDWHL2072**
(ASV) ⊟ **ZCWHL2072**
16. S. McCulloch, A-M. Owens, Czech PO, J. Bigg (with instr track for singing)
(IMP) Ⓓ [2] **DPCD1015**
(IMP) ⊟ **CIMPCD1015**
16. E. Schwarzkopf, J. Collard, R. Duclos Ch, Paris Cons, A. Cluytens (r1964)
(CFP) Ⓓ **CD-CFP4602**
(CFP) ⊟ **TC-CFP4602**
16. S. McCulloch, A-M. Owens, Czech PO, J. Bigg (r1992) (IMP) Ⓓ **PCD1043**
16. J. Sutherland, H. Tourangeau, Suisse Romande Rad Ch, Lausanne Pro Arte Ch, SRO, R. Bonynge (r1971) (DECC) Ⓓ **433 440-2DA**
(DECC) ⊟ **433 440-4DA**

16. S. McCulloch, A-M. Owens, Czech SO, J. Bigg (IMP) Ⓓ [3] **TCD1070**
16. J. Sutherland, H. Tourangeau, Suisse Romande Rad Ch, Lausanne Pro Arte Ch, SRO, R. Bonynge (r1971) (DECC) Ⓓ **436 315-2DA** (DECC) ▭ **436 315-4DA**
16. G. Groves, J. Watson, J. Partridge (r1994) (ASV) Ⓓ **CDWHL2088**
16. Dresden St Op Orch, S. Varviso (BELA) Ⓓ **450 126-2** (BELA) ▭ **450 126-4**
16. A. Gluck, L. Homer, orch (r c1913) (PEAR) Ⓓ **GEMMCD9130**
16. J. Sutherland, H. Tourangeau, Suisse Romande Rad Chor, Lausanne Pro Arte Ch, SRO, R. Bonynge (r1971) (DECC) Ⓓ **443 335-2LRX** (DECC) ▭ **443 335-4LRX**
16. M. Caballé, S. Verrett, New Philh, A. Guadagno (RCA) Ⓓ **09026 62699-2** (RCA) ▭ **09026 62699-4**
16. London Choral Soc, RPO, A. Inglis (r1994) (RPO) Ⓓ **CDRPO7025** (RPO) ▭ **ZCRPO7025**
16. M. Caballé, S. Verrett, New Philh, A. Guadagno (RCA) Ⓓ **74321 25817-2** (RCA) ▭ **74321 25817-4**
16. L. Hofmann, M. Salvatini, Berlin Staatskapelle, M. Gurlitt (r1927: Ger) (PREI) Ⓓ **89102**
16. G. Farrar, A. Scotti, orch (r1909) (NIMB) Ⓓ **NI7872**
16. G. Saba (trs. Moszkowski) (10/87) (IMP) Ⓓ **PCD858**
16. J. McCormack, F. Kreisler, E. Schneider (Eng: r1916) (9/89) (PEAR) Ⓓ **GEMMCD9315**
16. L. Garrett, Philh, A. Greenwood (r1990-1) (11/91) (SILV) Ⓓ **SONGCD903** (11/91) (SILV) ▭ **SONGC903**
16. P. Domingo, I. Perlman, NY Studio Orch, J. Tunick (r1990: arr ten/vn) (3/92) (EMI) Ⓓ **CDC7 54266-2**
16. M. Caballé, S. Verrett, New Philh, A. Guadagno (5/92) (RCA) Ⓓ **GD60818**
16. C. Muzio, K. Howard, orch (r1918) (1/95) (ROMO) Ⓓ [2] **81010-2**
16, 24a E. Schwarzkopf, J. Collard, V. de los Angeles, N. Gedda, R. Duclos Ch, Paris Cons, A. Cluytens (r1964/5) (EMI) Ⓓ [2] **CZS5 68113-2**
17a, 17b, 19b C. Kullman, Berlin St Op Orch, O. Dobrindt (Ger: r1931) (11/93) (PREI) Ⓓ **89057**
18a H. Prey, Berlin Deutsche Op Orch, H-M. Rabenstein (Ger) (EURO) Ⓓ **GD69019**
18a J. Schwarz, orch (Ger: r1916) (PREI) Ⓓ **89033**
18a A. Ivanov, Bolshoi Th Orch, A. Melik-Pashayev (r1940s: Russ) (PREI) Ⓓ **89067**
18a H. Schlusnus, Berlin St Op Orch, L. Blech (r1935: Ger) (PREI) Ⓓ [2] **89212**
18a H. Schlusnus, orch (r1925: Ger) (PREI) Ⓓ **89110**
18a H. Hasslo, orch, N. Grevillius (r1941: Swed) (4/92) (EMI) Ⓓ [7] **CHS7 69741-2(5)**
19b M. Wittrisch, Berlin St Op Orch, E. Orthmann (Ger: r1932) (MMOI) Ⓓ **CDMOIR405** (MMOI) ▭ **CMOIR405**
19b A. Piccaver, orch (r1920: Ger) (8/93) (PREI) Ⓓ **89060**
19b R. Tauber, orch (r1928: Ger) (12/94) (MMOI) Ⓓ **CDMOIR425**
22. Lotte Lehmann, Berlin St Op Orch, F. Weissmann (Ger: r1933) (PEAR) Ⓓ **GEMMCD9410**
22. L. Bori, Victor Orch, W.B. Rogers (r1915) (ROMO) Ⓓ [2] **81016-2**
22. K. Te Kanawa, ROHO, J. Tate (2/90) (EMI) Ⓓ **CDC7 49863-2**
22. C. Muzio, orch (r1924) (5/90) (BOGR) Ⓓ [2] **BIM705-2**
22. Lotte Lehmann, orch (Ger: r1921) (6/92) (PREI) Ⓓ [3] **89302**
22. J. Hammond, Philh, V. Tausky (r1952) (12/92) (TEST) Ⓓ **SBT1013**
22. C. Muzio, orch (r1924) (1/94) (ROMO) Ⓓ [2] **81005-2**
22. J. Novotná, RCA SO, F. Weissmann (r1945) (4/94) (RCA) Ⓓ [6] **09026 61580-2(5)**
23. Bourvil, A. Philippe, Paris Opéra-Comique Orch, A. Cluytens (r1948) (EMI) Ⓓ [2] **CZS5 68113-2**
24a, 24b H. Roswaenge, H. von Debička, Berlin St Op Orch, H. Weigert (r1931: Ger) (4/95) (PREI) Ⓓ [2] **89209**
24b H.E. Groh, E. Bettendorf, orch (Ger: r1931) (3/92) (PEAR) Ⓓ **GEMMCD9419**
34. Budapest PO, J. Sándor (LASE) Ⓓ **15 621** (LASE) ▭ **79 621**
34. SRO, R. Bonynge (r1972) (DECC) ▭ **433 870-4DWO**
34. Vienna Ravel Orch, J-P. Rouchon (DIVE) Ⓓ **DIV31011**
34. Cölln Salon Orch (arr Weninger) (EURO) Ⓓ **GD69296**
34. Paris Cons, R. Leibowitz (r1960) (CHES) Ⓓ **Chesky CD61**
34. Gothenburg SO, N. Järvi (DG) Ⓓ **439 152-2GMA** (DG) ▭ **439 152-4GMA**
34. Philh, I. Westrip (r1993) (IMP) Ⓓ **PCD1075**
34. Stuttgart RSO, N. Marriner (EMIL) Ⓓ **CDZ102** (EMIL) ▭ **LZ102**
34. BPO, H. von Karajan (arr M Rosenthal) (3/83) (DG) Ⓓ **400 044-2GH**
34. Gothenburg SO, N. Järvi (6/90) (DG) Ⓓ **429 494-2GDC** (6/90) (DG) ▭ **429 494-4GDC**
34. BPO, H. von Karajan (arr M Rosenthal) (8/91) (DG) Ⓓ **431 160-2GR**
34. Black Dyke Mills Band, G. Brand (arr G Langford) (10/91) (CHAN) Ⓓ **CHAN6539** (10/91) (CHAN) ▭ **MBTD6539**

La **Fille du tambour-major– operetta: 3 acts (1879—Paris) (Lib. Chivot and Duru)**
Overture Loire PO, M. Soustrot (PIER) Ⓓ **PV730022**
Overture Vienna SO, B. Weil (r1992) (1/94) (SONY) Ⓓ **SK53288**
Que m'importe un titre éclatant L. Chatel, R. Duclos Ch, Paris Cons, F. Nuvolone (EMI) Ⓓ [2] **CZS5 68113-2**

Geneviève de Brabant– operetta: 2 acts (1859—Paris) (Lib. Jaime and Tréfeu)
Duo des Gendarmes M. McEachern, chor, orch (Eng: r1933) (PEAR) Ⓓ **GEMMCD9455**
Galop Cincinnati Pops, E. Kunzel (11/92) (TELA) Ⓓ **CD80294** (11/92) (TELA) ▭ **CS30294**
Galop Boston Pops, A. Fiedler (r1956) (1/94) (RCA) Ⓓ **09026 61429-2**

Der **Goldschmied von Toledo– operetta: 3 acts (pastiche of Offenbach works: 1919)**
EXCERPTS: 1. Lieblichste alle Frauen.
1. J. Patzak, Berlin St Op Chor, Berlin St Op Orch, J. Prüwer (r1931) (3/90) (PEAR) Ⓓ **GEMMCD9383**

La **Grande-Duchesse de Gérolstein– operetta: 3 acts (1867—Paris) (Lib. Meilhac and Halévy)**
EXCERPTS: 1. Overture. ACT 1: 2. Tournons et valsons?; 3a. O mon Fritz; 3b. Allez, jeunes filles; 4. Pif, Paf, Pouf; 5. Me voici! me voici!; 6. Portez armes; 7a. Vous aimez le danger; 7b. Ah! Que j'aime les militaires; 8. Ah! c'est un fameux régiment; 9. Pour epouser une princesse (Chronique de la Gazette de Hollande); 9a. Ils vont tous partir; 9b. Voici le sabre de mon père. ACT 2: 10a. Enfin la guerre est terminée; 10b. Je t'ai sur mon coeur; 10c. Ah! lettre adorée; 11. Après le victoire; 12. En très bon ordre; 13a. Oui, Général; 13b. Dites-lui qu'on l'a remarqué distigué; 14a. Ne devinez-vous pas; 14b. Max était soldat de fortune; 15. Logeons-la donc. ACT 3: 16. Ce qu'on a fait; 17. Sortez, sortez; 18a. Nous amenons la jeune femme; 18b. Bonne nuit, monsieur; 19a. On peut être aimable; 19b. Ouvrez, ouvres; 19c. À cheval, à cheval; 19d. Notre auguste maîtresse; 20. Au repas comme à la Bataille; 21. Il était un de mes aïeux (Légende du Verre); 22. Voici revenir; 23. Enfin j'ai repris la panache.
1. CBSO, L. Frémaux (KLVI) Ⓓ **KCD11040**
1. BPO, H. von Karajan (arr F Hoffmann) (3/83) (DG) Ⓓ **400 044-2GH**
1. Boston Pops, A. Fiedler (r1956) (1/94) (RCA) Ⓓ **09026 61429-2**
1. Vienna SO, B. Weil (r1992: arr F Hoffmann) (1/94) (SONY) Ⓓ **SK53288**
7a, 7b J. Rhodes, Bordeaux Aquitaine Orch, R. Benzi (r1970s) (EMI) Ⓓ [2] **CZS5 68113-2**
7b SRO, Vienna Volksoper Orch, A. Lombard (r1970) (DECC) Ⓓ **436 316-2DA** (DECC) ▭ **436 316-4DA**
7b M. Horne, Monte Carlo PO, L. Foster (r1984) (ERAT) Ⓓ **4509-98501-2**
7b (pt), 7b R. Crespin, SRO, A. Lombard (r1970/1) (DECC) Ⓓ **440 416-2DM**
9b, 19c J-C. Benoit, E. Lublin, Paris Cons, J-P. Marty (EMI) Ⓓ [2] **CZS5 68113-2**
13b Y. Printemps, H. Büsser (r1929) (EMI) Ⓓ [2] **CZS5 68113-2**

M. Choufleuri restera chèz lui– operetta: 1 act (1861—Paris) (Lib. various)

Choufleuri	J-P. Lafont
Ernestine	M. Mesplé
Babylas	C. Burles
Petermann	M. Trempont
Balandard	M. Hamel
Mme Balandard	E. Greger

J. Laforge Choral Ens, Monte Carlo PO, M. Rosenthal (10/89) (EMI) Ⓓ [2] **CDS7 49361-2**
Pedro possède une guitare M. Mesplé, C. Burles, Monte Carlo PO, M. Rosenthal (r1982) (EMI) Ⓓ [2] **CZS5 68113-2**

Madame Favart– operetta: 3 acts (1878—Paris) (Lib. H Chivot & A Duru)
La ronde des vignes; Menuet et rondeau de la Vieille F. Révoil, orch, E. Beruilly (EMI) Ⓓ [2] **CZS5 68292-2**

Madame l'archiduc– operetta: 3 acts (1874—Paris) (Lib. Meilhac, Halévy & Millaud)

Marietta	L. Dachary
Countess	J. Levasseur
Giacometta	R. Bredy
Ernest	D. Tirmont
Giletti	P. Miguel
Fortunato	R. Amade
Count	G. Rey
Riccardo	A. Doniat
Pontefiascone	R. Lenoty
Bonaventura	J. Pruvost
Piano-Dolce	M. Martin
Frangipiano	M. Fauchey
Bonnardo	M. Vigneron

ORTF Lyric Chorale, ORTF Lyric Orch, J-C. Hartemann (bp1963) (3/92) (MUSD) Ⓓ [2] **20138-2**

Le **Mari à la porte– operetta: 1 act (1859—Paris) (Lib. A Delacour & L Morand)**
EXCERPTS: 1. J'entends, ma belle, 'Valse tyrolienne'.
1. S. Jo, ECO, R. Bonynge (r1993) (9/94) (DECC) Ⓓ **440 679-2DH**

Mesdames de la Halle– operetta: 1 act (1853—Paris) (Lib. A. Lapointe)

Madame Poiretapée	M. Hamel
Madame Beurrefondu	J-P. Lafont
Madama Madou	M. Trempont
La Marchande de Plaisir	M. Pouradier-Duteil
Marchande de Legumes	O. Dumaine
La Marchande d'Habits	M. Quillevéré
Raflafla	C. Burles
La Commissaire	J-M. Frémeau
Coute-au-pot	L. Pezzino
Ciboulette	M. Mesplé

J. Laforge Choral Ens, Monte Carlo PO, M. Rosenthal (10/89) (EMI) Ⓓ [2] **CDS7 49361-2**
Au beau jour; Quel bruit...Je suis la petite fruitière C. Burles, M. Mesplé, Monte Carlo PO, M. Rosenthal (r1982) (EMI) Ⓓ [2] **CZS5 68113-2**

Monsieur et Madame Denis– operetta: 1 act (1862—Paris) (Lib. M. Laurencin & M. Delaporte)
EXCERPTS: 1. Overture.
1. Vienna SO, B. Weil (r1992) (1/94) (SONY) Ⓓ **SK53288**

Orphée aux enfers, 'Orpheus in the Underworld'– operetta: 2 (later 4) acts (1858 rev 1874—Paris) (Lib. H Crémieux & L Halévy)
EXCERPTS: 1. Overture; 1a. Can-can. ACT 1: 3. La femme dont le coeur; 4. Ah! c'est ainsi!; 5. Ballet pastoral; 6a. Moi, je suis Aristée; 6b. Voici le tendre Aristée; 6c. Mélodrame; 7a. La mort m'apparaît; 7b. Violà une plume (Mélodrame); 8. Libre! ô bonheur. ACT 2: 9. Entr'acte and Chorus of Sleep; 10. Je suis Vénus!; 11. Tzing, tzing, tzing; 12. Par Saturne!; 13a. Eh hop! Eh hop!; 13b. Entry of Pluto; 14. Comme il me regarde!; 15. Aux armes, dieux et demi-dieux!; 16. Pour séduire Alcmène... 17. Il approche! Il s'avance...Le violà, oui, c'est bien lui!; 18. Entr'acte. ACT 3: 19. Ah! quelle triste destinée; 20a. Quand j'étais roi de Béotie; 20b. Ah! tenez, Madame (Mélodrame); 21. Ah! mon bras! (Mélodrame); 22. Nez au vent, oeil au guet; 23.

Allons, mes fins limiers; 24. Le beau bourdon que voilà; 25. Il m'a semblé sur mon épaule; 26a. Si j'étais roi de Béotie; 26b. Galop. ACT 4: 27. Vive le vin! Vive Pluton!; 28. J'ai vu le Dieu Bacchus; 29. Maintenant, je veux, moi qui (Menuet et Galop infernal); 30. Elle est assez bonne! (Mélodrame); 31. Ne regarde pas en arrière! (finale).

Orpheus	M. Sénéchal
Eurydice	M. Mesplé
Aristeus-Pluto	C. Burles
Jupiter	M. Trempont
Juno	D. Castaing
Public Opinion	J. Rhodes
John Styx	B. Brewer
Venus	M. Command
Cupid	J. Berbié
Diane	M. Péna
Mars	J-P. Lafont
Mercury	A. Mallabrera
Lictor	H. Brambilla
Minos	J-C. Bonnafous
Eache	R. Trentin
Rhadamante	H. Amiel

Petits Chanteurs à la Croix Potencée, Toulouse Capitole Chor, Toulouse Capitole Orch, M. Plasson (r1978)
(1/89) (EMI) Ⓓ [2] **CDS7 49647-2**

Orpheus	D. Fieldsend
Euridice	M. Hegarty
Aristeus/Pluto	B. Patterson
Jupiter	R. Suart
Juno	F. McCafferty
Public Opinion	J. Pert
John Styx	Gareth Jones
Venus	S. Wyn Gibson
Cupid	R. Arthars
Diana	J. Pullen
Mars	C. Donohue
Mercury	D. Cavendish
Minerva	P. Baxter
Morpheus	R. Woodall

D'Oyly Carte Op Chor, D'Oyly Carte Op Orch, J.O. Edwards (r1994: Eng)
(2/95) (SONY) Ⓓ [2] **SM2K66616**

Excs B. Bottone, S. Burgess, S. Kale, L. Watson, ENO Chor, ENO Orch, M. Elder (r1987; Eng) (TER) Ⓓ **CDTEO1008**
(TER) ▭ **ZCTEO1008**

Excs R. Angas, S. Squires, B. Bottone, C. Pope, E. Robinson, F. Kimm, S. Masterton-Smith, I. Morris, S. Burgess, S. Kale, L. Watson, E. Belcourt, E. Byles, G. Adams, ENO Chor, ENO Orch, M. Elder (r1987; Eng)
(TER) Ⓓ **CDTER1134**
(TER) ▭ **ZCTER1134**

Excs A. Doniat, M. Roux, C. Devos, C. Collart, A. Grandjean, H. Prudon, D. Dassy, F. Betti, L. Berton, Raymond St Paul Chor, Lamoureux Orch, J. Gressier (r1950s)
(5/93) (EMI) Ⓓ [2] **CZS7 67515-2**

1. SRO, E. Ansermet
(DECC) Ⓓ **425 848-2DWO**
(DECC) ▭ **425 848-4DWO**

1. Vienna Ravel Orch, J-P. Rouchon
(DIVE) Ⓓ **DIV31011**

1. Czech PO, V. Neumann
(SUPR) Ⓓ **11 0724-2**

1 (finale) RPO, M. Reed
(RPO) Ⓓ [2] **CDRPD9001**
(RPO) ▭ [2] **ZCRPD9001**

1. Cölln Salon Orch (arr Weninger)
(EURO) Ⓓ **GD69295**

1. Košice St PO, A. Walter
(NAXO) Ⓓ **8 550468**

1. Paris Cons, R. Leibowitz
(CHES) Ⓓ **Chesky CD57**

1 (finale) Classic Buskers, Chuckerbutty Ocarina Qt (arr Murray) (SEAV) Ⓓ **CD007366**

1(pt) Classic Buskers (arr Copley)
(SEAV) Ⓓ **CD007365**

1. Philadelphia, E. Ormandy
(RCA) Ⓓ **09026 61211-2**

1. CBSO, L. Frémaux (KLVI) Ⓓ **KCD11040**

1. National PO, C. Gerhardt (r1971)
(CHES) Ⓓ **Chesky CD108**

1. LSO, C. Mackerras (r1961)
(MERC) Ⓓ **434 352-2MM**

1. BPO, H. von Karajan
(3/83) (DG) Ⓓ **400 044-2GH**

1. Raphaele Concert Orch, P. Walden (arr Waldenmaier) (5/91) (MOZA) Ⓓ **MECD1002**

1. BPO, H. von Karajan
(8/91) (DG) Ⓓ **431 160-2GR**

1. NYPO, L. Bernstein
(11/92) (SONY) Ⓓ **SMK47532**

1. Detroit SO, P. Paray (r1959)
(11/93) (MERC) Ⓓ **434 332-2MM**

1. Boston Pops, A. Fiedler (r1956)
(1/94) (RCA) Ⓓ **09026 61429-2**

1. Vienna SO, B. Weil (r1992: arr Binder/Busch)
(1/94) (SONY) Ⓓ **SK53288**

1a RPO, M. Reed (r1990) (IMP) Ⓓ **PCDS22**
(IMP) ▭ **PCDSC22**

1a Empire Brass (r1992; arr. R. Smedvig)
(1/94) (TELA) Ⓓ **CD80305**
(1/94) (TELA) ▭ **CS30305**

1, 5. Philh, A. de Almeida
(PHIL) Ⓓ **442 403-2PM**

4, 6a, 11, 16, 25, 29. M. Mesplé, M. Sénéchal, C. Burles, M. Péna, J. Berbié, M. Command, M. Trempont, Toulouse Capitole Chor, Toulouse Capitole Orch, M. Plasson (r1978)
(EMI) Ⓓ [2] **CZS5 68113-2**

29 (pt) Cologne RSO, P. Steinberg
(LASE) Ⓓ **15 504**
(LASE) ▭ **79 504**

La **Périchole– operetta: 2 (later 3) acts (1868 rev 1874—Paris) (Lib. Meilhac and Halévy)**

EXCERPTS: 1a. Overture. ACT 1: 1b. Du vice-roi c'est aujourd'hui la fête; 1c. Promptes à servir la pratique; 1d. Ah! Qu'on y fait gaîment glouglou; 2. C'est lui, c'est notre vice-roi!; 3. Dis-moi, Piquillo? (Marche indienne); 4. Le conquérant dir à la jeune indienne; 5. Vous a-t-on dit souvent (Seguidille); 6. Levez-vous et prenez vos rangs; 7. O mon cher amant, je te jure; 8a. Ah! mon Dieu! (melodrame); 8b. Holà! hé!...holà! de là-bas; 8c. Et prenez les bras de vos clercs!; 8d. Ah! quel diner je viens de faire!; 8e. C'est un ange, messieurs!; 8f. Ah! les autres; 8g. Pourrais-je vous prier; 8h. Mon Dieu!...que de cérémonie; 8i. Et maintenant, séparez-les. ACT 2: 9. Entr'acte; 10. Cher seigneur, revenez à vous; 11. On vante partout son sourire; 12. Quel marché sa bassesse; 13a. Et là, maintentant que que nous sommes seuls; 13b. Est-ce bientôt cette présentation?; 13c. Son Altesse à l'heure ordinaire; 14a. Nous allons donc voir un mari; 14b. Que veulent dire ces colères; 14c. C'est vrai, j'ai tort de m'emporter; 14d. Sautez dessus!; 14e. Conduisez-le, bons courtisans. ACT 3: 15. Les maris courbaient le tête (Boléro); 16. On me proposait d;être infâme; 17a. Qui va là?; 17b. Dans ces couloirs obscurs; 17c. Tu n'es pas beau, tu n'es pas riche; 17d. Je t'adore, brigand, j'ai honte à l'avour; 18. Je suis le joli geôlier; 19. Roi pas plus haut qu' une botte!; 20a. Tais-toi!; 20b. Elle m'adore; 21a. En avant! en avant soldat!; 21b. Pauvres gens, où sont-ils?; 22. Écoutez, peup d'Amérique; 23. Tous deux, au temps de peine et de misère.

La Périchole	T. Berganza
Piquillo	J. Carreras
Don Andres de Ribeira	G. Bacquier
Don Pedro de Hinoyosa	M. Sénéchal
Le Comte de Panatelas	M. Trempont
Guadelena; Manuelita	P. Delange
Berginella	M. Command
Mastrilla	S. Nigoghossian
First Lawyer	H. Brambilla
Second Lawyer	H. Amiel

Toulouse Capitole Chor, Toulouse Capitole Orch, M. Plasson (r1981)
(3/87) (EMI) Ⓓ [2] **CDS7 47362-8**

Périchole	R. Crespin
Piquillo	A. Vanzo
Don Andrès	J. Bastin
Miguel de Panatellas	G. Friedmann
Don Pedro	J. Trigeau
Notary 1	A. Besançon
Notary 2	P. Guigue
Guadalena; Manuelita	R. Roberts
Berginella; Ninetta	E. Saurova
Mastrilla; Frasquinella	G. Baudoz
Bramdilla	I. Meister

Rhine Op Chor, Strasbourg PO, A. Lombard
(5/92) (ERAT) Ⓓ [2] **2292-45686-2**

Excs J. Sutherland, Orch, Anon (cond), D. Bailey (11/92) (DECC) ◖ **071 135-1DH**

Medley Boston Pops, A. Fiedler (r1956)
(1/94) (RCA) Ⓓ **09026 61429-2**

Overture Loire PO, M. Soustrot
(PIER) Ⓓ **PV730022**

1, 2(pt), 14b G. Bacquier, T. Berganza, Toulouse Capitole Chor, Toulouse Capitole Orch, M. Plasson (r1981)
(EMI) Ⓓ [2] **CZS5 68113-2**

4, 5, 13a, 16. J. Carreras, T. Berganza, Toulouse Capitole Orch, M. Plasson
(EMI) Ⓓ **CDM7 63111-2**

4, 8d T. Berganza, J. Carreras, Toulouse Capitole Orch, M. Plasson
(EMI) Ⓓ **CDM7 64359-2**

4, 8d, 14e S. Lafaye, R. Amade, L. Noguera, R. Duclos Ch, Lamoureux Orch, I. Markevitch (r c1960) (EMI) Ⓓ [2] **CZS5 68113-2**

7. R. Crespin, SRO, A. Lombard (r1970)
(DECC) Ⓓ **436 316-2DA**
(DECC) ▭ **436 316-4DA**

7, 8d, 17c, 17d R. Crespin, SRO, A. Lombard (r1970/1) (DECC) Ⓓ **440 416-2DM**

8d C. Novikova, orch (Russ: r1940s)
(4/92) (EMI) Ⓓ [7] **CHS7 69741-2(6)**

8d D. Visse, Camargue PO, Reinhardt Wagner (r1995: arr R Wagner)
(8/95) (HARM) Ⓓ **HMC90 1552**

16. J. Carreras, Toulouse Capitole Orch, M. Plasson (EMI) Ⓓ **CDC7 54524-2**

17c M. Teyte, orch (r1932)
(2/92) (MMOI) Ⓓ **CDMOIR408**

17c L. Price, LSO, E. Downes
(12/92) (RCA) Ⓓ [4] **09026 61236-2**

Pomme d'api– operetta: 1 act (1873—Paris) (Lib. Halévy and W. Busnach)

Rabastene	J-P. Lafont
Gustave	L. Pezzino
Catherine	M. Mesplé

Monte Carlo PO, M. Rosenthal
(10/89) (EMI) Ⓓ [2] **CDS7 49361-2**

Va donc chercher le gril M. Mesplé, J-P. Lafont, L. Pezzino, Monte Carlo PO, M. Rosenthal (r1982) (EMI) Ⓓ [2] **CZS5 68113-2**

Robinson Crusoé– operetta (1867—Paris) (Lib. Cormon and Crémieux)

Robinson Crusoe	J. Brecknock
Edwige	Y. Kenny
Sir William Crusoe	R. Kennedy
Lady Deborah Crusoe	E. Hartle
Suzanne	M. Hill Smith
Toby	A. Oliver
Man Friday	S. Browne
Jim Cocks	A. Opie
Will Atkins	W. Parfitt

G. Mitchell Ch, RPO, A. Francis (r1980: Eng)
(8/94) (OPRA) Ⓓ [3] **ORC007**

Vert-vert– operetta: 3 acts (1869—Paris) (Lib. Meilhac and Nuitter)

Overture BPO, H. von Karajan
(3/83) (DG) Ⓓ **400 044-2GH**

Overture Vienna SO, B. Weil (r1992: arr F Hoffmann) (1/94) (SONY) Ⓓ **SK53288**

La **Vie parisienne– operetta: 5 (later 4) acts (1866—Paris) (Lib. Meilhac and Halévy)**

Overture

Autrefois plus d'un amant B. Hendricks, Philh, L. Foster (r1992)
(8/93) (EMI) Ⓓ **CDC7 54626-2**

Excs J-C. Benoit, R. Crespin, L. Masson, M. Mesplé, M. Sénéchal, C. Château, E. Lublin, Toulouse Capitole Chor, Toulouse Capitole Orch, M. Plasson (r c1976)
(EMI) Ⓓ [2] **CZS5 68113-2**

Excs M. Roux, M. Hamel, W. Clément, L. Dachary, N. Renaux, L. Berton, D. Dassy, Raymond St Paul Chor, Lamoureux Orch, J. Gressier (r1950s)
(5/93) (EMI) Ⓓ [2] **CZS7 67515-2**

Overture CBSO, L. Frémaux
(KLVI) Ⓓ **KCD11040**

Overture Loire PO, M. Soustrot
(PIER) Ⓓ **PV730022**

Overture Vienna SO, B. Weil (r1992: arr B Wolff) (1/94) (SONY) Ⓓ **SK53288**

Le **Voyage dans la lune– fairy opera: 4 acts (1875—Paris) (Lib. Leyerrier, Vanloo and A. Mortier)**

Monde charmant B. Hendricks, Philh, L. Foster (r1992) (8/93) (EMI) Ⓓ **CDC7 54626-2**

Overture Loire PO, M. Soustrot
(PIER) Ⓓ **PV730022**

Overture; Ballet des flocons de neige Philh, A. de Almeida (PHIL) Ⓓ **442 403-2PM**

ORFF, Carl *(1895–1982)* *Germany*

Antigonae– Trauerspiel: 1 act (1949—Salzburg) (Wds. Sophoceles, after Hölderlin)

Antigonae	C. Goltz
Ismene	I. Barth
Kreon	H. Uhde
Guard	P. Kuen
Hämon	K. Ostertag

Tiresias E. Haefliger
Messenger K. Böhme
Eurydice M. Schech
Chorus leader B. Kusche
Bavarian St Op Chor, Bavarian St Orch, G. Solti (pp1951)
(ORFE) Ⓓ [2] **C407952I**
Antigonae I. Borkh
Ismene C. Hellmann
Kreon C. Alexander
Guard G. Stolze
Hämon F. Uhl
Tiresias E. Haefliger
Messenger K. Borg
Eurydike H. Plümacher
Chorus leader K. Engen
Bavarian Rad Chor, BRSO, F. Leitner (r1961)
(8/93) (DG) Ⓓ [3] **437 721-2GC3**

Die **Kluge– opera: 1 act (1943—Frankfurt)**
King T. Stewart
Peasant G. Frick
Peasant's daughter L. Popp
Jailor R. Kogel
Man with Donkey M. Schmidt
Man with Mule C. Nicolai
Vagabond I F. Gruber
Vagabond II H. Friedrich
Vagabond III K. Böhme
Munich RO, K. Eichhorn (r1970)
(RCA) Ⓓ [5] **74321 24790-2**
King T. Stewart
Peasant G. Frick
Peasant's daughter L. Popp
Jailer R. Kogel
Man with Donkey M. Schmidt
Man with Mule C. Nicolai
Vagabond I F. Gruber
Vagabond II H. Friedrich
Vagabond III K. Böhme
Munich RO, K. Eichhorn
(3/91) (EURO) Ⓓ [2] **GD69069**
King M. Cordes
Peasant G. Frick
Peasant's daughter E. Schwarzkopf
Jailer G. Wieter
Man with Donkey R. Christ
Man with Mule B. Kusche
Vagabond I P. Kuen
Vagabond II H. Prey
Vagabond III G. Neidlinger
Philh, W. Sawallisch
(3/91) (EMI) Ⓓ [2] **CMS7 63712-2**
Als die Treue ward geboren Mainz Wind Ens, K.R. Schöll (arr Wanek)
(WERG) Ⓓ **WER6174-2**

Der **Mond– opera: 1 act (1939—Munich) (Lib. cpsr, after Brothers Grimm)**
Narrator J. van Kesteren
Young Man I H. Friedrich
Young Man II R. Kogel
Young Man III F. Gruber
Young Man IV B. Kusche
Peasant R. Grumbach
Mayor H. Buchta
Old Man F. Crass
R. Kiermeyer Children's Ch, Bavarian Rad Chor, Munich RO, K. Eichhorn (r1970)
(RCA) Ⓓ [5] **74321 24790-2**
Narrator J. van Kesteren
Young Man I H. Friedrich
Young Man II R. Kogel
Young Man III F. Gruber
Young Man IV B. Kusche
Peasant R. Grumbach
Petrus F. Crass
Mayor H. Buchta
R. Kiermeyer Children's Ch, Bavarian Rad Chor, Munich RO, K. Eichhorn
(3/91) (EURO) Ⓓ [2] **GD69069**
Narrator R. Christ
Young Man I K. Schmitt-Walter
Young Man II H. Graml
Young Man III P. Kuen
Young Man IV P. Lagger
Peasant A. Peter
Petrus H. Hotter
Childrens' Chor, Philh, W. Sawallisch
(3/91) (EMI) Ⓓ [2] **CMS7 63712-2**
Three Dances Mainz Wind Ens, K.R. Schöll (arr Wanek) (WERG) Ⓓ **WER6174-2**

Orpheus– opera: 3 acts (1925 rev 1931 and 1940—Mannheim) (after Monteverdi)
Orpheus H. Prey
Euridike L. Popp
Die Botin R. Wageman
Der Wächter der Toten K. Ridderbusch
Sprecher C. Orff
Bavarian Rad Chor, Munich RSO, K. Eichhorn
(ACAN) Ⓓ [7] **44 2085-2**
Orpheus H. Prey
Euridike L. Popp
Die Botin R. Wageman
Der Wächter der Toten K. Ridderbusch
Sprecher C. Orff
Bavarian Rad Chor, Munich RSO, K. Eichhorn
(ACAN) Ⓓ **44 2089-2**

Prometheus– opera: 1 act (1966—Stuttgart) (Lib after Aeschylus)
Prometheus R. Hermann
Kratos J. Greindl
Hephaistos H. Cramer
Okeanos K. Engen
Chorführerin I E. Moser
Chorführerin II S. van Sante
Io C. Lorand
Hermes F. Uhl
W German Rad Chor, Cologne RSO, F. Leitner
(ACAN) Ⓓ [2] **44 2099-2**
Prometheus R. Hermann
Kratos J. Greindl
Hephaistos H. Cramer
Okeanos K. Engen
Chorführerin I E. Moser
Chorführerin II S. van Sante
Io C. Lorand
Hermes F. Uhl
W German Rad Chor, Cologne RSO, F. Leitner
(ACAN) Ⓓ [7] **44 2085-2**

Tanz der Spröden– opera: 1 act (1925 rev 1940—Karlsruhe) (after Monteverdi)
Amor L. Popp
Venus R. Wageman
Pluto K. Ridderbusch
Eine Spröde H. Schwarz
Bavarian Rad Chor, Munich RSO, K. Eichhorn
(ACAN) Ⓓ **44 2090-2**
Amor L. Popp
Venus R. Wageman
Pluto K. Ridderbusch
Eine Spröde H. Schwarz
Bavarian Rad Chor, Munich RSO, K. Eichhorn
(ACAN) Ⓓ [7] **44 2085-2**

PACINI, Giovanni *(1796–1867) Italy*

Adelaide e Comingio– opera: 2 acts (1817—Milan) (Lib. Rossi)
Overture Philh, D. Parry
(10/90) (OPRA) Ⓓ [3] **ORCH103**

Annetta e Lucindo– opera: 1 act (1813—Milan) (Lib. Marconi)
Fra l'orror di notte oscura E. Harrhy, P. Nilon, J. Cashmore, G. Dolton, Philh, D. Parry
(10/90) (OPRA) Ⓓ [3] **ORCH103**

Saffo– opera: 3 acts (1840—Naples) (Lib. S. Cammarano)
L'ama ognor E. Burzio, orch (r1913)
(1/91) (CLUB) Ⓓ [2] **CL99-587/8**

PADEREWSKI, Ignacy Jan *(1860–1941) Poland*

Manru– opera: 3 acts, Op. 20 (1901—Dresden) (Lib. A Nossig, after J I Kraszewski)
Come al sol cocente G. Anselmi, anon (r1907: Ital) (7/95) (SYMP) Ⓓ **SYMCD1170**

PAER, Ferdinando *(1771–1839) Italy*

Le **Maître de chapelle– opéra-comique: 2 acts (1821—Paris) (Lib. S. Gay)**
Ah quel plaisir L. Fugère, orch (r1930)
(6/93) (SYMP) Ⓓ **SYMCD1125**
Air G. Soulacroix, anon (r1904)
(9/91) (SYMP) Ⓓ **SYMCD1089**

Sargino, ossia L'allievo dell'amore– dramma eroicomico: 2 acts (1803—Dresden) (Lib. Foppa)
Una voca al cor mi parla E. Ritchie, V. Soames, J. Purvis (r1992; arr Waxman/Voxman)
(3/94) (CLRI) Ⓓ **CC0006**

PAISIELLO, Giovanni *(1740–1816) Italy*

L' **Amor contrastato, 'La Molinara'– opera: 3 acts (1789—Naples) (Lib. G. Palomba)**
EXCERPTS: 1. Nel cor più non mi sento.
1. M. Caballé, M. Zanetti
(FORL) Ⓓ **UCD10902**
1. J. Sutherland, Philomusica of London, Granville Jones (r1959)
(DECC) Ⓓ [2] **436 227-2DM2**
1. E. Pinza, orch, D. Voorhees (bp1950)
(7/91) (MMOI) Ⓓ **CDMOIR404**
(MMOI) ▭ **CMOIR404**
1. C. Bartoli, G. Fischer
(12/92) (DECC) Ⓓ **436 267-2DH**
(12/92) (DECC) ▭ **436 267-4DH**
1. J. Baker, ASMF, N. Marriner
(1/93) (PHIL) Ⓓ **434 173-2PM**
1. E. Pinza, F. Kitzinger (r1940)
(9/93) (RCA) Ⓓ **09026 61245-2**

Il **Barbiere di Siviglia, '(The) Barber of Seville'– dramma giocoso: 4 parts (1782—St Petersburg) (Lib. G Petrosellini)**
Overture Haydn Philh, E. Rojatti
(NUOV) Ⓓ **6726**

Don Chisciotte della Mancia– opera: 3 acts (1769—Naples) (Lib. G.B. Lorenzi)
Don Chischiotte P. Barbacini
Sancio Pancia R. Franceschetto
Countess M.A. Peters
Duchess E. Zilio
Don Calafrone M. Bolognesi
Don Platone B. Praticò
Carmosina B. Lucarini
Cardolella F. Arnone
Ricciardetta Ann Rossi
Rome Op Orch, P.G. Morandi (pp1990)
(4/92) (NUOV) Ⓓ [2] **6994/5**

Nina, o sia La pazza per amore– commedia in prosa e versi: 1 act (1789—Naples) (Lib. G. Carpani, after B. J. Mersollier)
EXCERPTS: 1. Overture; 2. Il mio ben quando verrà.
Nina M. Bolgan
Lindoro D. Bernardini
Count F. Musinu
Susanna F. Pediconi
Giorgio G. Surian
Shepherd C. Bosi
Peasant Girl B. Cegile
Catania Teatro Massimo Bellini Chor, Catania Teatro Massimo Bellini Orch, R. Bonynge (pp1989)
(9/91) (NUOV) Ⓓ [2] **6872/3**
Overture Haydn Philh, E. Rojatti
(NUOV) Ⓓ **6726**
2. C. Bartoli, G. Fischer
(12/92) (DECC) Ⓓ **436 267-2DH**
(12/92) (DECC) ▭ **436 267-4DH**

La **Serva Padrona– intermezzo: 2 acts (1781—Tsarskoye Selo) (Lib. G.A. Federico)**
Serpina A.V. Banks
Uberto G.L. Ricci
Milan CO, P. Vaglieri
(2/93) (NUOV) Ⓓ **7043**

Il **Zingari in fiera– commedia per musica: 2 acts (1789—Naples) (Lib. Palomba)**
EXCERPTS: 1. Overture; 2. Chi vuol la zingarella.
1. Haydn Philh, E. Rojatti (NUOV) Ⓓ **6726**
2. V. de los Angeles, G. Parsons (pp1990)
(12/91) (COLL) Ⓓ **Coll1247-2**
2. C. Bartoli, G. Fischer (r1990-1)
(12/92) (DECC) Ⓓ **436 267-2DH**
(12/92) (DECC) ▭ **436 267-4DH**

PALADILHE, Emil *(1844–1926) France*

Patrie!– opera: 5 acts (1886—Paris) (Lib. Sardou and Gallet)
Pauvre martyr obscur T. Ruffo, orch, J. Pasternack (r1920) (PEAR) Ⓓ **GEMMCD9088**
Pauvre martyr obscur T. Ruffo, orch (r1920)
(2/93) (PREI) Ⓓ [3] **89303(1)**
Pauvre martyr obscur J-F. Delmas, orch (r1904) (12/94) (SYMP) Ⓓ **SYMCD1172**

Suzanne– opéra-comique: 3 acts (1878—Paris) (Lib. Lockroy & E Cormon)
Comme un petit oiseau T. Schipa, orch, Mr Prince (r1924) (12/89) (RCA) Ⓓ **GD87969**

PALLAVICINO, Carlo *(1630–1688) Italy*

Il **Diocletiano– opera (1674—Venice)**
Sinfonia C. Steele-Perkins, Parley of Instr
(1/89) (HYPE) ① **CDA66255**

PATZELT, Joannes *(d 1748) Slovakia*

Castor et Pollux—Musica pro comoedia generali– opera-cantata (c1743) (Lib. P. Matzer)
Pollux K. Zajíčková-Vyskočilová
Castor J. Saparová
Jupiter, Charitas P. Oswald
Mors P. Mikuláš
Genius Justi V. Stracenská
Genius Justiniana, Echo M. Beňačková
Musica aeterna, P. Baxa
(OPUS) ① **9352 1719**

PAVESI, Stefano *(1779–1850) Italy*

Aginta, o la Virtu Premiata– opera: 2 acts (1814—Milan) (Lib. Fiorini)
Come Paride alle Grazie M. Hill Smith, A. Bolton, G. Dolton, Philh, D. Parry
(10/90) (OPRA) ① [3] **ORCH103**

PENDERECKI, Krzysztof *(b 1933) Poland*

Paradise Lost– sacra rappresentazione: 2 acts (1978—Chicago) (Lib. C Fry, after J Milton)
Polish Nat RO, A. Wit (Adagietto)
(6/90) (POLS) ① **PNCD020**

PENDLETON, Edmund J. *(1899–1987) USA*

The **Miracle of the Nativity– lyric drama: one act (1975) (Wds cpsr, arr from the Scriptures)**
Mary S. Bullock
Joseph S. Imbodem
Angel Gabriel D. Robinson
Caesar's Envoy J. Chaminé
M. Piquemal Voc Ens, Ile de France CO, J-W. Audoli
(CAMP) ① **RRCD1325**

PENELLA, Manuel *(1880–1939) Spain*

Don Gil de Alcalá– opera: 3 acts (1932—Barcelona) (Lib. cpsr)
Pavana G. Pérez-Quer, D. Kassner (arr Pérez-Quer) (PRES) ① **PCOM1120**

El **Gato Montés– opera: 3 acts (1916—Madrid) (Lib. cpsr)**
Juanillo J. Pons
Rafael Ruiz P. Domingo
Soleá V. Villarroel
Gypsy T. Berganza
Padre Antón C. Chausson
Frasquita M. Perelstein
Loliya A. Barrio
Hormigón C. Alvarez
Caireles P. Farrés
Pezuño M.L. Galindo
Recalcao; Alguacilillo C. Bergasa
Pastorcillo Angeles Blancas
Vendedor R. Muñiz
Madrid Zarzuela Chor, Madrid SO, M. Roa
(9/92) (DG) ① [2] **435 776-2GH2**
Exc P. Domingo, A. Panagulias, Miami SO, E. Kohn (pp1991) (IMP) ① **MCD43**
Me llambas, Rafaeliyo? P. Domingo, V. Alonso, VPO, James Levine (DG) ◖ **072 187-1GH**
(DG) ▣ **072 187-3GH**
Me llambas, Rafaeliyo? P. Domingo, V. Alonso, VPO, James Levine
(11/89) (DG) ◖ **072 110-1GH**
Si Torero quiero sé. J. Carreras, I. Rey, ECO, E. Ricci (r1994)
(2/95) (ERAT) ① **4509-95789-2**
(2/95) (ERAT) ⊟ **4509-95789-4**

PERGOLESI, Giovanni Battista *(1710–1736) Italy*

Adriano in Siria– opera seria: 3 acts (1734—Naples) (Lib. Metastasio)
Oh cari sdegni...Lieto così tal volta A. Christofellis, Seicentonovecento Ens, F. Colusso (r1993/4) (EMI) ① **CDC5 55250-2**
Sinfonia Santa Cecilia Orch da Camera, A. Vlad
(EURM) ① **350262**

Il **Flaminio– commedia musicale: 3 acts (1735—Naples) (Wds. Federico)**
Sinfonia Santa Cecilia Orch da Camera, A. Vlad
(EURM) ① **350262**

Lo **Frate 'nnamorato– commedia musicale: 3 acts (1732—Naples) (Lib. G. G. Federico)**
Nena A. Felle
Ascanio N. Focile
Marcaniello A. Corbelli
Don Pietro B. de Simone
Nina B. Manca di Nissa
Cardella N. Curiel
Vannella E. Norberg-Schulz
Luggrezia L. d'Intino
Carlo E. di Cesare
La Scala Orch, R. Muti (pp1989)
(7/91) (EMI) ① [3] **CDS7 54240-2**
D'ogni pena (Siciliana) B. Hoff, R. Levin (arr ob/pf) (VICT) ① **VCD19037**
Ogni pena più spietata J. Baker, ASMF, N. Marriner (1/93) (PHIL) ① **434 173-2PM**
Sinfonia Santa Cecilia Orch da Camera, A. Vlad
(EURM) ① **350262**

L' **Olimpiade– opera seria: 3 acts (1735—Rome) (Lib. Metastasio)**
Overture New Philh, R. Leppard (r1967)
(2/94) (PHIL) ① [10] **438 921-2PB10**
Sinfonia Santa Cecilia Orch da Camera, A. Vlad
(EURM) ① **350262**

Prigionier superbo– opera seria: 3 acts (1733—Naples)
Sinfonia Santa Cecilia Orch da Camera, A. Vlad
(EURM) ① **350262**

Salustia– opera seria: 3 acts (1732—Naples) (Lib. ?Morelli, after Zeno: Severo)
Sinfonia Santa Cecilia Orch da Camera, A. Vlad
(EURM) ① **350262**

La **Serva Padrona– intermezzo: 2 acts (1733—Naples) (Lib. G A Federico)**
M. Bonifaccio, S. Nimsgern, Collegium Aureum, F. Maier (vn/dir) (9/92) (DHM) ① **RD77184**
Stizzoso, mio stizzoso V. de los Angeles, G. Parsons (pp1990)
(12/91) (COLL) ① **Coll1247-2**

PERI, Jacopo *(1561–1633) Italy*

Euridice– opera: 5 scenes (1600—Florence) (Lib. cpsr: collab with G Caccini)
EXCERPTS: 1. Per quel vago boschetto (Aria di Dafne).
1. J. Feldman, N. North (LINN) ① **CKD005**
(LINN) ⊙ **CKH005**

PETERSON-BERGER, Wilhelm *(1867–1942) Sweden*

Arnljot– opera (1910—Stockholm) (Lib. cpsr)
Arnljot's greeting to Jämtland I. Wixell, Stockholm PO, J. Arnell (MSVE) ① **MSCD617**

Ran– music drama (1903—Stockholm) (Lib. cpsr)
Dancing Game Uppsala Univ Chmbr Ch, S. Parkman (MSVE) ① **MSCD612**

PETIT, Pierre *?France*

La **Maréchale sans gêne– operetta**
Le jour où je dirai 'je l'aime'; Margot avait deux amoureux F. Révoil, orch, R. Blareau
(EMI) ① [2] **CZS5 68292-2**

PETRELLA, Errico *(1813–1877) Italy*

La **Contessa d'Amalfi– opera: 4 acts (1864—Turin) (Lib. G Peruzzini)**
Fra i rami fulgida A. Santini, orch (r1908)
(6/94) (IRCC) ① **IRCC-CD808**

Jone, o L'ultimo giorno di Pompeo– opera: 4 acts (1858—Milan) (Lib. Peruzzini, after Bulwer-Lytton)
Della corona egizia; Sinistro è il ciel F. Corradetti, anon (r1907)
(12/94) (BONG) ① **GB1043-2**
O Jone, di quest'anima M. Gilion, orch (r c1909) (BONG) ① **GB1076-2**
O Jone di quest'anima A. Scampini, orch (r1908) (6/94) (IRCC) ① **IRCC-CD808**

PFITZNER, Hans (Erich) *(1869–1949) Germany*

Der **arme Heinrich– music drama: 3 acts (1895—Mainz) (Lib. J Graun & cpser, after H von Aue)**
Auf grüne Wipfel lacht nun wonnig der Lenz D. Fischer-Dieskau, BRSO, W. Sawallisch (r1979) (EMI) ① [2] **CMS5 65621-2**

Das **Christ-Elflein– opera: 1 act, Op. 20 (1906—Munich) (Lib. I von Stach & cpsr: work rev 1917)**
Overture Bratislava RSO, H. Beissel
(7/89) (MARC) ① **8 223162**
Overture Berlin St Op Orch, H. Pfitzner (r1927)
(5/95) (EMI) ① **CDC5 55225-2**

Das **Herz– music drama: 3 acts, Op. 39 (1931—Berlin & Munich) (Lib. H Mahner-Mons)**
Athanasias A. Wenhold
Asmodi; Councillor Modiger V. Horn
Helge von Laudenheim R. Cunningham
Gwendolin B. Johanning
Duchess K. Quandt
Prince Tancred R. Dressler
Young knight; Assistant physician II L. Chioreanu
Court Lady I I. Melle
Court Lady II R. Atanasova
Servant I L. Hübel
Servant II I. Christoph
Assistant Physician II N. Barowski
Thüringian Landestheater Chor, Thüringian SO, R. Reuter (r1993)
(11/94) (MARC) ① [2] **8 223627/8**
Love theme Bratislava RSO, H. Beissel
(7/89) (MARC) ① **8 223162**

Palestrina– opera: 3 acts (1917—Munich) (Lib. cpsr)
Palestrina N. Gedda
Pope Pius IV; Christoph Madruscht K. Ridderbusch
Morone B. Weikl
Novagerio H. Steinbach
Borromeo D. Fischer-Dieskau
Cardinal of Lorraine V. von Halem
Abdisu J. van Kesteren
Anton Brus P. Meven
Count Luna H. Prey
Bishop of Budoja F. Lenz
Theophilus Adalbert Kraus
Avosmediano F. Mazura
Ighino H. Donath
Silla B. Fassbaender
Severolus G. Nienstedt
Lukrezia R. Freyer
Tolz Boys' Ch, Bavarian Rad Chor, BRSO, R. Kubelík (r1970s)
(7/89) (DG) ① [3] **427 417-2GC3**
Excs J. Witt, H. Hotter, E. Schürhoff, E. Boettcher, E. Rutgers, M. Schober, A. Dermota, H. Gallos, W. Wernigk, F. Worff, A. Poell, S. Roth, E. Kunz, Alfred Vogel, H. Alsen, Vienna St Op Orch, R. Moralt (pp1942)
(SCHW) ① [2] **314712**
Excs J. Witt, A. Jerger, M. Bokor, E. Réthy, E. Szánthó, H. Alsen, K. Ettl, F. Destal, G. Maikl, W. Wernigk, D. Komarek, A. Gregorig, Vienna St Op Chor, Vienna St Op Orch, B. Walter (pp1937)
(2/95) (SCHW) ① [2] **314572**
Preludes to Acts 1-3. BRSO, W. Sawallisch
(ORFE) ① **C168881A**

Preludes to Acts 1-3. Berlin St Op Orch, H. Pfitzner (r1931) (5/95) (EMI) ① **CDC5 55225-2**

Die **Rose vom Liebesgarten– opera: prologue, 2 acts & epilogue (1901—Elberfeld) (Lib. J Grun)**
Miracle of the Blossoms; Funeral March
BRSO, W. Sawallisch (ORFE) ① **C168881A**

PHILIDOR, André Danican *(c1647–1730) France*

Le **Mariage de la Grosse Cathos, 'Fat Kate's Wedding'– opéra-ballet (1688—Versailles)**
London Ob Band, M-A. Petit, P. Goodwin (r1994) (4/95) (HARM) ① **HMU90 7122**

PHILLIPS, Montague F(awcett) *(1885–1969) England*

The **Rebel Maid– romantic light opera (1921—London) (Lib. G. Dodson and A. M. Thomson)**
Sail my ships M. Hill Smith, Southern Fest Orch, R. White (5/93) (CHAN) ① **CHAN9110**
(5/93) (CHAN) ▭ **LBTD031**

PICCINNI, (Vito) Niccolò (Marcello Antonio Giacomo) *(1728–1800) Italy*

La **Cecchina, '(La) Buona figliuola'– commedia: 3 acts (1760—Rome) (Lib. Goldoni)**
EXCERPTS: 1. Sinfonia. ACT 1: 2. Che piacer, che bel diletto; 3a. Cara Cecchina mia; 3b. Quel che d'amore; 3c. Eh, Mengotto; 3d. Ogni amatore; 3e. Ah, Cecchina, al mio foco; 3f. Non comoda all'amante; 4a. Poverina, tutto il dì; 4b. Poc'anzi le parlai; 4c. E'pur bella la Cecchina; 5a. E' tantovero; 5b. Sono una giovane; 6a. Amo e' ver, la Marchesa; 6b. Della sposa il bel sembiante; 7a. Si, signora; 7b. Che superbia maledetta; 8. Una povera ragazza; 9a. No, non gli riuscira; 9b. Furie di donna irata; 10. Vo cercando, e non ritrovo (Finale). ACT 2: 11. Dov'è Cecchina; 12a. Ah, povero Mangotto; 12b. Ah, Cecchina...il tuo Mengotto; 12c. O nix tu donne piu pensar; 12d. Star trompette, star tampurri; 13a. Ah! che distante e troppo; 13b. Cara, s'è ver ch'io v'ami; 14. Per il buco della chiave; 15a. Che risolvo, che fo?; 15b. So che fedel m'adora; 16a. Via di qua; 16b. Alla larga, signore; 17. Vederete una figliola; 18a. Almen fra queste piante; 18b. Vieni, il mio seno; 19. Padre mio, dove sei tu?; 20. Si, signora, di lassù (Finale). ACT 3: 21. Si, signori, vi dico; 22a. La vostra man per mio; 22b. Chi più di me contento; 23a. Ah, tu mi poni in core; 23b. Sento che il cor mi dice; 24a. Fol feder, fol parlar; 24b. Ah, comme tutte je consolar; 25a. Baronessa, mio bene; 25b. La Baronessa amabile; 26a. So che no'l meriti; 26b. Son tenera di pasta; 27a. Mi spiaceria pur tanto; 27b. Vedi la bianca; 28. Porgetemi la destra (Finale).

Cecchina	M.A. Peters
Conchiglia	G. Morino
Tagliaferro	B. Praticò
Armidoro	A. Ruffini
Lucinda	G. Morigi
Mengotto	P. Spagnoli
Paoluccia	S. Mingardo
Sandrina	M.C. Zanni

PAO, B. Campanella (pp1990) (MEMO) ① **DR3101/3**
9b J. Sutherland, New SO, R. Bonynge (r1963) (DECC) ① **421 881-2DA**
9b J. Sutherland, Philomusica of London, Granville Jones (r1959) (DECC) ① [2] **436 227-2DM2**

Le **faux Lord– opéra-comique: 1 acts (1783—Paris) (Lib. G. M. Piccinni)**
EXCERPTS: 1. O notte, o dea del mistro.
1. R. Bruson, C. Sheppard (pp1980) (CHAN) ① **CHAN6551**
1. J. Baker, ASMF, N. Marriner (1/93) (PHIL) ① **434 173-2PM**

La **Pescatrice, ovvero L'erede riconosciuta– intermezzo: 2 acts (1766—Rome) (Lib. after ?Goldini)**
EXCERPTS: 1. Sinfonia. ACT 1: 2. Aiuto, buona gente; 3a. Gran meraviglia al certo; 3b. Non sentite che a Levante; 4a. Ah, se il mar si placasse; 4b. Se mai qualcun venisse; 5a. Io non credea che gli uomini; 5b. Pescatrici semplicette; 5c. Male, questa canzon non fa per me; 5d. Se sapeste, o donzellette; 5e. Oibò, non so che farmene; 5f. Un amante rispettoso; 5g. State lì fin ch'io non torno; 6a. Dunque obbedir convien; 6b. Chi vuol veder la statua; 7. Si prendessero gioco; 8a. Ah, vigliacco!; 8b. Se d'una figlia amabile; 9a. Non conosce chi è Silvia; 9b. Colla mia Silvia; 10. Care amiche e compagne; 11. V'era al tempo delle fate. ACT 2: 12. Ecco qui la vera crede; 13a. Olà, così si tratta coi cavalieri; 13b. Signor Conte, mi dispiace; 14a. Sia maledetto il foglio; 14b. Quanti giovani vi sono; 15a. Quanto da quel che fui; 15b. Già sono un'ombra pallida; 16. No. Recate pur via questi vani ornamenti; 17a. Marchesina mia bella; 17b. Se m'abbandoni, morirò di dolor; 17c. Povera bambinella; 18a. M'ha commosso; 18b. Quando è l'alba la mattina; 19a. Insomma, hanno le donne; 19b. Silvia bella...ah l'ho perduta!; 19c. Silvia bella, ah l'ho perduta!; 20a. Ah, che dite Dorilla!; 20b. Dimmi pria se in mezzo al petto; 21. Che pazzo core è il mio; 22. Invidiosa non son io.

Silvia	M. Pennicchi
Dorilla	M.L. Garbato
Count	M. Comencini
Licone	G. Gatti

Sassari SO, C. Rizzi (BONG) ① [2] **GB2073/4-2**

PIERNÉ, (Henri Constant) Gabriel *(1863–1937) France*

Fragonard– operetta: 3 acts & 4 tableaux (1934—Paris) (Lib. A Rivoire & R Coolus)
Ah si tu savais; Ah! ça, mais, qu'est-ce qui me prend F. Révoil, orch, M. Cariven (r1935) (EMI) ① [2] **CZS5 68292-2**

Ramuntcho– musique de scène pour le drame de Pierre Loti (1908)
Paris Op Orch, J-B. Mari (EMI) ① **CDM7 64278-2**
Overture Paris Cons, J-B. Mari (r1961) (MAND) ① **MAN4805**
Stes Nos 1 and 2. Lorraine PO, J. Houtmann (8/88) (BIS) ① **BIS-CD381**

PIETRI, Giuseppe *(1886–1946) Italy*

Maristella– opera (1934—Naples) (Lib. M Salvini, after S Di Giacomo)
Io conosco un giardino B. Gigli, orch, U. Berrettoni (r1940) (9/88) (EMI) ① **CDH7 61051-2**
Uno strano senso arcano; Oh! la mia casa R. Pampanini, orch, L. Molajoli (r1934) (8/93) (PREI) ① **89063**

PLANQUETTE, (Jean) Robert *(1848–1903) France*

Les **cloches de Corneville– operetta: 3 acts (1877—Paris) (Lib. Clairville and Gabet)**
EXCERPTS: 1. Overture. ACT 1: 2. Nous avons hélas; 3. J'ai fait trois fois le tour du monde. ACT 2: 4. Mesdames, messieurs, voici le cortège; 5. Ne parlez pas de mon courage; 6. Non, vous le voyez, mes aïeux étaient restés; 7. Gloire au valeureux Grenicheux. ACT 3: 8. La pomme est un fruit...Viv'le cidr' de Normandie; 9. Ah! Monsiegneur à peine je respire; 10. Pour ce trésor que tu nous abandonnes; 11. Je régardais en l'air.
C'est la salle de mes ancêtres; J'ai fait trois fois le tour du monde A. Baugé, orch, G. Andolfi (r1935) (EMI) ① [2] **CZS5 68292-2**
3. A. Baugé, orch (r1930s) (FORL) ① **UCD19022**

Rip van Winkle– operetta: 3 acts (1882—London) (Lib. H. B. Farnie)

Rip	C. Daguerressar
Nelly	L. Dachary
Ichabod	J. Pruvost
Kate	F. Betti
Derrick	L. Lovano
Nick	R. Lenoty
Jacques	J. Peyron
Jacinthe	C. Collart
Lowna	J. Pierre
Jacques, child	P. Oriadey
Captain Hudson	J. Giovannetti

French Rad Lyric Chor, French Rad Lyric Orch, M. Cariven (with dialogue: bp1961) (3/92) (MUSD) ① **20160-2**
C'est un rien A. Baugé, orch (r1930s) (FORL) ① **UCD19022**

POISE, (Jean Alexandre) Ferdinand *(1828–1892) France*

Joli Gilles– opéra-comique: 2 acts (1884—Paris) (Lib. Monselet, after S d'Allainval)
Voici le matin la grive a chanté. A. Ghasne, orch (r1906) (9/91) (SYMP) ① **SYMCD1089**

POISSL, Johann Nepomuk *(1783–1865) Germany*

Athalia– opera: 3 acts (1814) (Lib. Wohlbrück, after Racine)
Ihr weintet meinem Schmerz I. Siebert, D. Klöcker, South-West German RSO, K. Donath (SCHW) ① **314018**

PONCHIELLI, Amilcare *(1834–1886) Italy*

Il **Figliuol prodigo– melodrama: 4 acts (1880—Milan) (Lib. Zanardini)**
Raccogli e calma A. Orda, Polish RSO, K. Missona (bp1977) (SYMP) ① **SYMCD1117**

La **Gioconda– opera: 4 acts (1876—Milan) (Lib. T Gorrio (A Boito)**
ACT 1: 1. Prelude; 2. Feste! Pane!; 3. Figlia, che reggi; 4a. La vidi stamane; 4b. Assassini!; 5a. Voce di donna; 5b. A te questo rosario; 6a. Enzo Grimaldo, Principe di Santafior; 6b. Oh grido di quest'anima; 7. Oh monumento!; 8. Angele Dei. ACT 2: 9a. Ho! He!; 9b. Pescator, affonda l'esca; 10. Cielo e mar!; 11a. Deh! non turbare; 11b. Deh! non tremar; 11c. Laggiù nelle nebbie remote; 12. Stella del marinar!; 13a. E un anatema!; 13b. L'amo come il fulgor del creato!; 14a. Laura, Laura! ove sei?; 14b. Vedi là, nel canal morto. ACT 3: 15a. Si! morir ella de'!; 15b. Là turbini e farnetichi; 15c. Bella così, madonna; 16. Benvenuti, messeri!; 17. Dance of the hours; 18a. D'un vampiro fatal; 18b. Già ti veggo. ACT 4: 19a. Suicidio!; 19b. Ecco il velen; 20a. Gioconda!...Enzo!; 20b. Oh furibonda; 20c. Oh gioia!; 21a. Ecco la barca; 21b. Quest'ultimo bacio; 22. Ora posso morir; 23a. Così mantieni il patto?; 23b. Ebbrezza! delirio!.

La Gioconda	E. Marton
Enzo	P. Domingo
Barnaba	M. Manuguerra
La Cieca	M. Lilowa
Alvise	K. Rydl
Laura	L. Shemchuk
Zuàne	A. Sramek
Isèpo	J. Pita
Pilot	G. Simic
Singer	A. Burgstaller

Vienna St Op Chor, Vienna St Op Orch, A. Fischer, H. Käch (MCEG) ▭ **VVD726**

La Gioconda	R. Tebaldi
Enzo	C. Bergonzi
Barnaba	R. Merrill
La Cieca	O. Dominguez
Alvise	N. Ghiuselev
Laura	M. Horne
Zuàne; Pilot	S. Maionica
Isèpo	P. De Palma

Santa Cecilia Academy Chor, Santa Cecilia Academy Orch, L. Gardelli (DECC) ① [3] **430 042-2DM3**

La Gioconda	Z. Milanov
Enzo	G. Martinelli
Barnaba	C. Morelli
La Cieca	A. Kaskas
Alvise	N. Moscona
Laura	B. Castagna
Zuàne	W. Engelman
Isèpo	G. Paltrinieri

NY Met Op Chor, NY Met Op Orch, E. Panizza (pp1939) (SYMP) ① [2] **SYMCD1176/7**

La Gioconda	M. Caballé
Enzo	L. Pavarotti
Barnaba	S. Milnes
La Cieca	A. Hodgson

Alvise N. Ghiaurov
Laura A. Baltsa
Zuàne J. Del Carlo
Isèpo R. Romani
Pilot N. Jenkins
Singer S. Varcoe
London Op Chor, Finchley Children's Music Group, National PO, B. Bartoletti
(7/85) (DECC) ① [3] **414 349-2DH3**

La Gioconda M. Callas
Enzo P.M. Ferraro
Barnaba P. Cappuccilli
La Cieca I. Companeez
Alvise I. Vinco
Laura F. Cossotto
Zuàne L. Monreale
Isèpo R. Ercolani
Pilot; Singer C. Forti
La Scala Chor, La Scala Orch, A. Votto (r1959)
(2/88) (EMI) ① [3] **CDS7 49518-2**

La Gioconda A. Cerquetti
Enzo M. del Monaco
Barnaba E. Bastianini
La Cieca F. Sacchi
Alvise C. Siepi
Laura G. Simionato
Zuàne G. Giorgetti
Isèpo A. Cesarini
MMF Chor, MMF Orch, G. Gavazzeni (r1957)
(9/93) (DECC) ① [2] **433 770-2DMO2**

3, 5a, 11c, 13b I. Minghini-Cattaneo, D. de Martis, L. Cecil, A. Granforte, La Scala Orch, C. Sabajno (r1930) (6/90) (PREI) ① **89008**

4b G. Lauri-Volpi, NY Met Op Chor, NY Met Op Orch, G. Setti (r1929) (9/90) (PREI) ① **89012**

5a K. Branzell, orch (r1927) (8/92) (PREI) ① **89039**

5a L. Homer, orch (r1912) (4/94) (RCA) ① [6] **09026 61580-2(1)**

5a E. Petri, chor, orch (r1908) (4/94) (EMI) ① [3] **CHS7 64860-2(2)**

6a B. Gigli, G. De Luca, orch, Rosario Bourdon (r1927) (CONI) ① **CDHD170**

6a B. Gigli, G. De Luca, orch (r1927) (PEAR) ① [3] **GEMMCDS9160(2)**

6a B. Gigli, G. De Luca, orch, Rosario Bourdon (r1927) (PEAR) ① [3] **GEMMCDS9159(2)**

6a P. Domingo, S. Milnes, LSO, A. Guadagno (r1970) (RCA) ① **09026 62595-2**

6a B. Gigli, orch, Rosario Bourdon (r1929) (5/90) (PEAR) ① **GEMMCD9367**

6a B. Gigli, T. Ruffo, orch, Rosario Bourdon (r1926) (10/90) (RCA) ① **GD87811**
(10/90) (RCA) ▭ **GK87811**

6a B. Gigli, T. Ruffo, orch, Rosario Bourdon (r1926) (11/90) (NIMB) ① **NI7810**
(NIMB) ▭ **NC7810**

6a T. Ruffo, B. Gigli, orch (r1926) (2/93) (PREI) ① [3] **89303(2)**

6a G. De Luca, B. Gigli, orch, Rosario Bourdon (r1927) (10/94) (PREI) ① **89073**

6a G. Aragall, E. Tumagian, Bratislava RSO, A. Rahbari (r1992) (12/94) (NAXO) ① **8 550684**

6a, 6b C. Bergonzi, D. Fischer-Dieskau, BRSO, J. López-Cobos (ORFE) ① **C028821A**

6a, 6b F. de Lucia, B. Franci, orch (r1920) (BONG) ① [2] **GB1064/5-2**

6a, 6b B. Gigli, G. De Luca, orch, Rosario Bourdon (r1927) (9/88) (PEAR) ① **GEMMCD9316**

6a, 6b G. Zenatello, P. Amato, anon (r1907) (12/93) (SYMP) ① **SYMCD1148**

6a, 6b P. Amato, R. Grassi, orch (r1909) (4/94) (EMI) ① [3] **CHS7 64860-2(2)**

6a, 6b G. Zenatello, P. Amato, anon (r1907) (5/94) (PEAR) ① [4] **GEMMCDS9073(1)**

7. E. Suliotis, Rome Orch, S. Varviso (r1967) (DECC) ① **440 405-2DM**

7. G. De Luca, anon (r1907) (PEAR) ① [3] **GEMMCDS9159(2)**

7. A. Granforte, orch, G.W. Byng (r1925) (PREI) ① **89105**

7. R. Stracciari, orch (r1925) (2/90) (PREI) ① **89003**

7. T. Ruffo, orch, C. Sabajno (r1912) (11/90) (NIMB) ① **NI7810**
(NIMB) ▭ **NC7810**

7. G. De Luca, anon (r1907) (7/92) (PEAR) ① [3] **GEMMCDS9924(2)**

8(pt) G. Arangi-Lombardi, G. Zinetti, La Scala Orch, L. Molajoli (r1929) (10/90) (PREI) ① **89013**

9b P. Amato, NY Met Op Chor, orch, W.B. Rogers (r1911) (PEAR) ① **GEMMCD9104**

9b G. De Luca, NY Met Op Chor, NY Met Op Orch (r1928) (PEAR) ① [3] **GEMMCDS9160(2)**

9b T. Ruffo, orch, C. Sabajno (r1912) (11/90) (NIMB) ① **NI7810**
(NIMB) ▭ **NC7810**

9b G. De Luca, NY Met Op Chor, NY Met Op Orch, G. Setti (r1928) (10/94) (PREI) ① **89073**

10. G. Aragall, Barcelona SO, G. Navarro (11/92) (RCA) ▭ **09026 61204-4**

10. M. Lanza, RCA Victor Orch, C. Callinicos (r1950) (RCA) ① **GD60049**
(RCA) ▭ **GK60049**

10. B. Gigli, orch, C. Sabajno (r1918) (EMI) ① **CDC7 54016-2**

10. B. Gigli, orch, Rosario Bourdon (r1929) (NIMB) ① **NI7817**
(NIMB) ▭ **NC7817**

10. B. Gigli, orch, Rosario Bourdon (r1929) (CONI) ① **CDHD170**

10. T. Schipa, orch, Anon (cond) (pp1913) (MEMO) ① [2] **HR4220/1**

10. J. Björling, MMF Orch, A. Erede (DECC) ① **433 066-2DWO**
(DECC) ▭ **433 066-4DWO**

10. J. Carreras, LSO, J. López-Cobos (PHIL) ① **434 152-2PM**

10. J. Björling, orch, N. Grevillius (r1937) (NIMB) ① **NI7835**

10. T. Harper, Bratislava RSO, M. Halász (NAXO) ① **8 550497**

10. G. Aragall, Barcelona SO, G. Navarro (RCA) ꝏ **09026 61204-5**

10. E. Caruso, orch (r1910) (RCA) ① **09026 61243-2**

10. J. Vickers, Rome Op Orch, T. Serafin (r1961) (VAI) ① **VAIA1016**

10. B. Gigli, orch (r1929) (IMP) ① **GLRS102**

10. Deng, Württemberg PO, R. Paternostro (SINE) ① **39820222**

10. G. di Stefano, Santa Cecilia Academy Orch, F. Previtali (r1958) (DECC) ① **440 403-2DM**

10. M. del Monaco, MMF Orch, G. Gavazzeni (r1957) (DECC) ① **440 407-2DM**

10. J. Björling, Stockholm Royal Op Orch, N. Grevillius (r1937) (PEAR) ① **GEMMCD9043**

10. L. Pavarotti, Ater Orch, L. Magiera (pp1980) (BELA) ① **450 002-2**
(BELA) ▭ **450 002-4**

10. P. Domingo, Berlin Deutsche Op Orch, N. Santi (ERAT) ① **4509-91715-2**
(ERAT) ▭ **4509-91715-4**

10. J. Björling, B. Bokstedt (pp1957) (BLUE) ① **ABCD057**

10. C. Bergonzi, Santa Cecilia Academy Orch, L. Gardelli (r1967) (DECC) ① **440 417-2DM**

10. B. Gigli, orch, Rosario Bourdon (r1929) (PEAR) ① **GEMMCD9129**

10. A. Bonci, orch (r1913) (PEAR) ① **GEMMCD9168**

10. A. Piccaver, Berlin St Op Orch, J. Prüwer (r1928) (PREI) ① [2] **89217**

10. F. de Lucia, orch (r1917) (BONG) ① [2] **GB1064/5-2**

10. F. de la Mora, WNO Orch, C. Mackerras (r1994-5) (TELA) ① **CD80411**

10. L. Pavarotti, New Philh, L. Magiera (7/86) (DECC) ① [2] **417 011-2DH2**

10. M. André, Toulouse Capitole Orch, M. Plasson (arr tpt) (1/89) (EMI) ① **CDC7 49219-2**

10. E. Caruso, S. Cottone (r1902) (5/89) (EMI) ① **CDH7 61046-2**

10. T. Schipa, orch, C. Sabajno (r1913) (4/90) (EMI) ① **CDH7 63200-2**

10. B. Gigli, T. Ruffo, orch, Rosario Bourdon (r1926) (5/90) (PEAR) ① **GEMMCD9367**

10. B. Gigli, orch, C. Sabajno (r1918) (5/90) (NIMB) ① **NI7807**
(NIMB) ▭ **NC7807**

10. F. Marconi, S. Cottone (r1903) (6/90) (SYMP) ① **SYMCD1073**

10. L. Pavarotti, New Philh, L. Magiera (7/90) (DECC) ① [2] **425 681-2DM2**
(7/90) (DECC) ▭ [2] **425 681-4DM2**

10. A. Pertile, La Scala Orch, C. Sabajno (r1928) (9/90) (PREI) ① **89007**

10. B. Gigli, orch, Rosario Bourdon (r1929) (10/90) (RCA) ① **GD87811**
(10/90) (RCA) ▭ **GK87811**

10. E. Caruso, S. Cottone (r1902) (12/90) (PEAR) ① [3] **EVC1(1)**

10. E. Caruso, anon (r1905) (12/90) (PEAR) ① [3] **EVC1(1)**

10. F. Merli, orch, L. Molajoli (r1928) (1/91) (PREI) ① **89026**

10. E. Caruso, orch (r1910) (3/91) (PEAR) ① [3] **EVC2**

10. E. Caruso, anon (r1905) (7/91) (RCA) ① [12] **GD60495(1)**

10. E. Caruso, orch (r1910) (7/91) (RCA) ① [12] **GD60495(3)**

10. E. Caruso, S. Cottone (r1902) (7/91) (RCA) ① [12] **GD60495(1)**

10. R. Tucker, NY Met Op Orch, E. Cooper (r1947) (4/92) (EMI) ① [7] **CHS7 69741-2(2)**

10. F. Marconi, S. Cottone (r1903) (7/92) (PEAR) ① [3] **GEMMCDS9923(1)**

10. B. Gigli, orch (r1929) (9/92) (MMOI) ① **CDMOIR409**

10. J. Björling, orch, N. Grevillius (r1937) (10/92) (TEST) ① **SBT1005**

10. D. Yuzhin, anon (r1902: Russ) (6/93) (PEAR) ① [3] **GEMMCDS9001/3(1)**

10. J. Björling, MMF Orch, A. Erede (r1957) (10/93) (DECC) ① **436 463-2DM**
(10/93) (DECC) ▭ **436 463-4DM**

10. J. Björling, Stockholm Royal Op Orch, N. Grevillius (r1937) (10/93) (EMI) ① **CDH7 64707-2**

10. A. Bonci, anon (r1905) (12/93) (SYMP) ① **SYMCD1113**

10. J. Björling, orch, N. Grevillius (r1937) (12/93) (NIMB) ① **NI7851**

10. G. Zenatello, orch (r1908) (12/93) (SYMP) ① **SYMCD1148**

10. F. Marconi, S. Cottone (r1903) (4/94) (EMI) ① [3] **CHS7 64860-2(1)**

10. G. Zenatello, orch (r1908) (5/94) (PEAR) ① [4] **GEMMCDS9073(1)**

10. G. Zenatello, anon (r1907) (5/94) (PEAR) ① [4] **GEMMCDS9073(1)**

10. G. Zenatello, orch (r1911) (5/94) (PEAR) ① [4] **GEMMCDS9074(1)**

10. L. Pavarotti, Ater Orch, L. Magiera (pp) (5/94) (DECC) ① [2] **443 018-2DF2**

10. J. Björling, orch, N. Grevillius (r1937) (9/94) (CONI) ① **CDHD214**
(9/94) (CONI) ▭ **MCHD214**

10. D. Yuzhin, orch (r1908: Russ) (3/95) (NIMB) ① **NI7865**

10. J. Björling, MMF Orch, A. Erede (r1959) (10/95) (DECC) ① **443 930-2DM**

11c R. Tebaldi, F. Corelli, R. Cambiata, SRO, A. Guadagno (r1972) (10/93) (DECC) ① **436 301-2DA**

12. A. Baltsa, National PO, B. Bartoletti (r1980) (DECC) ① **443 378-2DM**

13a, 13b M. Caballé, A. Baltsa, L. Pavarotti, S. Milnes, National PO, B. Bartoletti (12/91) (DECC) ① **430 724-2DM**

13a, 13b M. Caballé, S. Verrett, New Philh, A. Guadagno (5/92) (RCA) ① **GD60818**

13a, 13, 19a A. Cerquetti, G. Simionato, M. del Monaco, E. Bastianini, MMF Chor, MMF Orch, G. Gavazzeni (r1957) (DECC) ① **440 411-2DM**

13a, 19a, 21a, 21b M. Caballé, A. Baltsa, L. Pavarotti, S. Milnes, London Op Chor, National PO, B. Bartoletti (r1980) (DECC) ① **443 928-2DM**

13b G. Cigna, C. Elmo, EIAR Orch, U. Tansini (r1941) (11/90) (PREI) ① **89016**

13b E. Destinn, L. Kirkby-Lunn, orch, P. Pitt (r1911) (12/94) (SUPR) ① [12] **11 2136-2(4)**

14a, 14b, 20a G. Zenatello, E. Mazzoleni, orch (r c1910) (12/93) (SYMP) ① **SYMCD1148**

14a, 20a G. Zenatello, E. Mazzoleni, orch (r1911) (5/94) (PEAR) ① [4] **GEMMCDS9074(1)**

15a T. Pasero, orch, L. Molajoli (r1928) (6/90) (PREI) ① **89010**

15a, 15b C. Siepi, Santa Cecilia Academy Orch, G. Gavazzeni (r1957) (DECC) ① **440 418-2DM**

15b G. Gravina, anon (r1902) (12/89) (SYMP) ① **SYMCD1065**

17. Budapest PO, A. Kórodi (LASE) ① **15 621**
(LASE) ▭ **79 621**

17. Bratislava RSO, O. Lenárd (NAXO) ① **8 550081**

17. ASMF, N. Marriner (EMIL) ① **CDZ104**
(EMIL) ▭ **LZ104**

17. Budapest PO, A. Kórodi (LASE) ① **15 504**
(LASE) ▭ **79 504**

17. Budapest PO, A. Kórodi (LASE) ① **15 513**
(LASE) ▭ **79 513**

17. Sinfonia of London, R. Irving (EMI) ① [2] **CDEMTVD59**
(EMI) ⊙ [2] **EMTVD59**

17. Munich Brass (arr brass ens) (ORFE) ① **C247911A**

17. Sinfonia of London, R. Irving (CFP) Ⓓ **CD-CFP4606** (CFP) ▭ **TC-CFP4606**
17. National PO, B. Bartoletti (DECC) Ⓓ **436 475-2DM**
17. Philh, I. Westrip (r1993) (IMP) Ⓓ **PCD1075**
17. Slovak PO, K. Redel (r1990) (PIER) Ⓓ **PV730023**
17. National PO, B. Bartoletti (DECC) Ⓓ **443 331-2LRX** (DECC) ▭ **443 331-4LRX**
17. Staatskapelle Dresden, S. Varviso (r1983) (PHIL) Ⓓ [2] **442 550-2PM2**
17. RPO, Y. Simonov (r1994) (TRIN) Ⓓ **TRP030**
17. Gothenburg SO, N. Järvi (6/90) (DG) Ⓓ **429 494-2GDC** (6/90) (DG) ▭ **429 494-4GDC**
17. NBC SO, A. Toscanini (r1952) (1/91) (RCA) Ⓓ **GD60308**
17. NYPO, L. Bernstein (r1967) (9/93) (SONY) Ⓓ **SMK47600**
18b E. Turner, E. Rubadi, F. Ciniselli, L. Paci, B. Carmassi, La Scala Chor, orch, L. Molajoli (r1926) (9/89) (EMI) Ⓓ **CDH7 69791-2**
18b E. Mazzoleni, G. Armanini, R. Stracciari, N. de Angelis, orch (r1910) (12/93) (SYMP) Ⓓ **SYMCD1113**
19a R. Ponselle, orch (r1923) (PEAR) Ⓓ [2] **GEMMCDS9964**
19a E. Suliotis, Rome Orch, S. Varviso (DECC) Ⓓ **433 624-2DSP**
19a E. Suliotis, Rome Orch, S. Varviso (DECC) Ⓓ **433 068-2DWO** (DECC) ▭ **433 068-4DWO**
19a M. Callas, Turin RAI Orch, A. Votto (r1953) (SUIT) Ⓓ **CDS1-5001**
19a M. Callas, La Scala Orch, A. Votto (EMI) Ⓓ **CDC7 54702-2** (EMI) ▭ **EL754702-4**
19a M. Jeritza, orch (r1923) (PEAR) Ⓓ **GEMMCD9130**
19a C. Muzio, orch (r1917) (PEAR) Ⓓ **GEMMCD9143**
19a M. Callas, Turin RAI Orch, A. Votto (r1952) (FONI) Ⓓ **CDO104**
19a H. Wildbrunn, orch (r1922) (PREI) Ⓓ **89097**
19a E. Destinn, orch, W.B. Rogers (r1914) (PEAR) Ⓓ **GEMMCD9172**
19a G. Dimitrova, Bulgarian RSO, R. Raichev (r1970s) (FORL) Ⓓ **UCD16742**
19a E. Turner, orch, L. Molajoli (r1926) (9/89) (EMI) Ⓓ **CDH7 69791-2**
19a R. Ponselle, orch, Rosario Bourdon (r1925) (10/89) (NIMB) Ⓓ **NI7805** (NIMB) ▭ **NC7805**
19a R. Ponselle, orch, Rosario Bourdon (r1925) (1/90) (RCA) Ⓓ **GD87810**
19a M. Callas, La Scala Orch, A. Votto (2/90) (EMI) Ⓓ **CDM7 63182-2**
19a M. Callas, C. Forti, La Scala Chor, La Scala Orch, A. Votto (r1959) (2/90) (EMI) Ⓓ [4] **CMS7 63244-2**
19a G. Cigna, orch, L. Molajoli (r1931) (11/90) (LYRC) Ⓓ **SRO805**
19a R. Tebaldi, New Philh, O. de Fabritiis (8/91) (DECC) Ⓓ [2] **430 481-2DX2**
19a R. Ponselle, orch (r1925) (7/92) (PEAR) Ⓓ [3] **GEMMCDS9926(1)**
19a A. Pinto, anon (r1902) (8/93) (SYMP) Ⓓ **SYMCD1111**
19a M. Caballé, R. Tebaldi, B. Bartoletti (r1980) (10/93) (DECC) Ⓓ **436 461-2DM**
19a E. Destinn, orch (r1914) (11/93) (ROMO) Ⓓ [2] **81002-2**
19a R. Raisa, orch (r1933) (1/94) (CLUB) Ⓓ **CL99-052**
19a R. Raisa, orch (r1923) (1/94) (CLUB) Ⓓ **CL99-052**
19a M. Jeritza, orch (r1923) (4/94) (PREI) Ⓓ **89079**
19a G. Cigna, orch, L. Molajoli (r1932) (4/94) (EMI) Ⓓ [3] **CHS7 64864-2(2)**
19a G. Cobelli, orch (r1925) (4/94) (EMI) Ⓓ [3] **CHS7 64864-2(1)**
19a E. Destinn, orch, W.B. Rogers (r1914) (5/94) (SUPR) Ⓓ **11 1337-2**
19a R. Ponselle, orch, Rosario Bourdon (r1925: 2 vers) (11/94) (ROMO) Ⓓ [2] **81006-2**
19a E. Destinn, orch, W.B Rogers (r1914) (12/94) (SUPR) Ⓓ [12] **11 2136-2(5)**
19a E. Destinn, orch (r1911) (12/94) (SUPR) Ⓓ [12] **11 2136-2(4)**
19a C. Muzio, orch (r1917) (1/95) (ROMO) Ⓓ [2] **81010-2**
19a R. Hunter, Tasmanian SO, D. Franks (r1989) (10/95) (ABCC) Ⓓ **8 7000 10**
19a, 19b G. Bumbry, Stuttgart RSO, S. Soltesz (11/86) (ORFE) Ⓓ **C081841A**
21a E. Teodorini, anon (r1903) (5/91) (SYMP) Ⓓ **SYMCD1077**
21b E. Burzio, orch (r1913) (1/91) (CLUB) Ⓓ [2] **CL99-587/8**
23a G. De Luca, E. Burzio, anon (r1907) (PEAR) Ⓓ [3] **GEMMCDS9159(2)**
23a G. Arangi-Lombardi, E. Molinari, La Scala Orch, L. Molajoli (r1929) (10/90) (PREI) Ⓓ **89013**
23a E. Burzio, G. De Luca, orch (r c1906) (1/91) (CLUB) Ⓓ [2] **CL99-587/8**
23a G. De Luca, E. Burzio, anon (r1907) (4/94) (EMI) Ⓓ [3] **CHS7 64860-2(2)**
23b M. Battistini, J. de Witt, orch (r1921) (PEAR) Ⓓ **GEMMCD9016**

Lina– opera (1877—Milan) (Lib. C D'Ormeville: revision of 'La savoiarda')
La madre mia M. Carosio, orch (r1946) (6/94) (IRCC) Ⓓ **IRCC-CD808**

I **Lituani– opera: prologue & 3 acts (1874—Milan) (Lib. S Ghislanzoni)**

Walter	O. Garaventa
Aldona	Y. Hayashi
Arnoldo	A. Cassis
Albano	C. De Bortoli
Vitoldo	A. Riva
A Minstrel	S. Ghione

Turin RAI Chor, Turin RAI Orch, G. Gavazzeni (bp1979) (ITAL) Ⓓ [2] **LO7708/9**
O rimembranze gioje A. Orda, Polish RSO, S. Rachoń (bp1964) (SYMP) Ⓓ **SYMCD1117**
Sinfonia Minsk PO, S. Frontalini (r1990) (1/94) (BONG) Ⓓ **GB2115-2**

I **promessi sposi– melodramma: 4 parts (1856—Cremona) (Lib. after Manzoni)**
Al tuo trono E. Vannuccini, orch (r1910s) (6/94) (IRCC) Ⓓ **IRCC-CD808**
Sinfonia Minsk PO, S. Frontalini (r1990) (1/94) (BONG) Ⓓ **GB2115-2**

PORRINO, Ennio *(1910–1959)* Italy

Gli **orazi– opera: 1 act (1941—Milan) (Lib. C Guastalla)**
Io per l'antico diritto T. Pasero, SO, D. Marzollo (r1944) (4/95) (PREI) Ⓓ **89074**

PORTUGAL, Marco Antônio (da Fonseca) *(1762–1830)* Portugal

La **Morte di Semiramide– opera: 3 acts (1801 rev 1806—Lisbon) (Lib. G. Caravita)**
Sconsigliata che fo!...Son Regina Y. Kenny, Philh, D. Parry (r1982) (OPRA) Ⓓ **ORR201**

POULENC, Francis (Jean Marcel) *(1899–1963)* France

Les **Dialogues des Carmélites– opera: 3 acts (1957—Milan) (Lib. cpsr, after G Bernanos)**

Blanche de La Force	D. Duval
Madame Lidoine	R. Crespin
Madame de Croissy	D. Scharley
Soeur Constance	L. Berton
Mère Marie	R. Gorr
Marquis de La Force	X. Depraz
Chevalier de La Force	P. Finel
Mère Jeanne	J. Fourrier
Soeur Mathilde	G. Desmoutiers
L'Aumônier	L. Rialland
Le Geôlier	R. Bianco
L'Officier	J. Mars
Commissaire 1	R. Romagnoni
Commissaire 2	C. Paul
Thierry	M. Forel
Javelinot	M. Conti

Paris Op Chor, Paris Op Orch, P. Dervaux (7/88) (EMI) Ⓓ [2] **CDS7 49331-2**

Blanche de la Force	C. Dubosc
Madame Lidoine	R. Yakar
Madame de Croissy	R. Gorr
Soeur Constance	B. Fournier
Mère Marie	M. Dupuy
Marquis de la Force	J. Van Dam
Chevalier de la Force	J-L. Viala
L'aumônier	M. Sénéchal
Le geôlier	F. le Roux

Lyon Op Chor, Lyon Op Orch, K. Nagano (9/92) (VIRG) Ⓓ [2] **VCD7 59227-2**
Excs J. Sutherland, Orch, Anon (cond), D. Bailey (11/92) (DECC) ◖ **071 135-1DH**
Mes filles, voilà s'achève J. Sutherland, P. Price, Sydney Eliz Orch, R. Bonynge (DECC) ◖ **071 149-1DH** (DECC) ▭ **071 149-3DH**
Mes filles, violà s'schève L. Price, LSO, E. Downes (12/92) (RCA) Ⓓ [4] **09026 61236-2**

Les **Mamelles de Tirésias– opéra bouffe: prologue & 2 acts (1947—Paris) (Lib. Apollinaire)**

Thérèse; Fortune-teller	D. Duval
Marchande de journaux; Grosse Dame	M. Legouhy
Husband	J. Giraudeau
Policeman	E. Rousseau
Director	R. Jeantet
Presto	J. Thirache
Lacouf	F. Leprin
Journalist	S. Rallier
Son	J. Hivert
Monsieur barbu	G. Jullia

Paris Opéra-Comique Chor, Paris Opéra-Comique Orch, A. Cluytens (r1953) (EMI) Ⓓ **CDM5 65565-2**

La **Voix humaine– tragédie lyrique: 1 act (1959—Paris) (Lib. Cocteau)**
La Femme C. Farley
Scottish CO, J. Serebrier, M. Newman (5/93) (DECC) ◖ **071 143-1DH** (5/93) (DECC) ▭ **071 143-3DH**
La Femme D. Duval
Paris Opéra-Comique Orch, G. Prêtre (r1959) (10/94) (EMI) Ⓓ **CDM5 65156-2**

PREDIERI, Luca Antonio *(1688–1767)* Italy

Zenobia– opera (1740—Vienna) (Lib. Metastasio)
Pace una volta H. Field, Philh, S. Wright (NIMB) Ⓓ **NI5123**
Pace una volta K. Battle, W. Marsalis, St Luke's Orch, J. Nelson (8/92) (SONY) Ⓓ **SK46672** (8/92) (SONY) ▭ **ST46672**

PROBST, Dominique *(b 1954)* France

Maximilien Kolbe– opera: 3 parts (1981-88) (Lib. E Ionesco)

Maximilien Kolbe	A. Snarski
Father of a family	V. Sanso
Camp Commander	P. Gérimon
Pouchovski	P. Danais

Childrens' Ch, Male Chor, Inst Ens, O. Holt (pp1989) (CYBE) Ⓓ **CY879**

PROKOFIEV, Sergey (Sergeyevich) *(1891–1953)* Russia/USSR

The **Fiery Angel– opera: 5 acts, Op. 37 (1954—Paris) (Lib. V. Bryusov)**

Renata	N. Secunde
Ruprecht	S. Lorenz
Agrippa; Mephistopheles	H. Zednik
Faust	P. Salomaa
Inquisitor	K. Moll
Jacob Glock; Doctor	G. Zachrisson
Mathias; Servant	B. Terfel
Landlady	R. Lang
Fortune-teller; Mother Superior	R. Engert-Ely
Innkeeper	C.G. Holmgren

Ohlin Voc Ens, Gothenburg Pro Musica Chbr Ch, Gothenburg SO, N. Järvi (7/91) (DG) Ⓓ [2] **431 669-2GH2**

The **Love for Three Oranges– opera: prologue & 4 acts, Op. 33 (1919—Chicago)**
SUITE—; 1. Les ridicules; 2. Scène infernale; 3. Marche; 4. Scherzo; 5. Le Prince et la Princesse; 6. La fruite.

King of Clubs	W. White
Prince	R. Davies
Princess Clarissa	N. Condò
Leandro	J. Pringle
Truffaldino	U. Benelli

Pantaloon P-C. Runge
Farfarello D. Hammond-Stroud
Tchelio R. Van Allan
Fata Morgana N. Morpurgo
Linetta Y. Lea
Nicoletta S. Moore
Ninetta C. Alliot-Lugaz
Cook; Herald R. Bryson
Smeraldina F. Kimm
Master of Ceremonies H. Hetherington
Glyndebourne Fest Chor, LPO, B. Haitink, F. Corsaro (r1982)
(CAST) ▣ **CVI2050**
King of Clubs G. Bacquier
Prince J-L. Viala
Princess Clarissa H. Perraguin
Leandro V. Le Texier
Truffaldino G. Gautier
Pantaloon; Farfarello; Master of Ceremonies D. Henry
Tchelio G. Reinhart
Fata Morgana M. Lagrange
Linetta C. Caroli
Nicoletta B. Fournier
Ninetta C. Dubosc
Cook J. Bastin
Smeraldina B. Uria-Monzon
Lyon Op Chor, Lyon Op Orch, K. Nagano, L. Erlo (Fr)
(12/90) (MCEG) ▣ **VVD805**
King of Clubs G. Bacquier
Prince J-L. Viala
Princess Clarissa H. Perraguin
Leandro V. Le Texier
Truffaldino G. Gautier
Pantaloon; Farfarello; Master of Ceremonies D. Henry
Tchelio G. Reinhart
Fata Morgana M. Lagrange
Linetta C. Caroli
Nicoletta B. Fournier
Ninetta C. Dubosc
Cook J. Bastin
Smeraldina B. Uria-Monzon
Lyon Op Chor, Lyon Op Orch, K. Nagano (Fr)
(12/89) (VIRG) Ⓓ [2] **VCD7 59566-2**
(12/89) (VIRG) ⊟ [2] **VCD7 59566-4**
1-3, 5. Moscow RSO, V. Fedoseyev (r1993)
(CANY) Ⓓ **EC3687-2**
1-4. Pittsburgh SO, W. Steinberg (r1957)
(EMI) Ⓓ **CDM5 65424-2**
3. J. Heifetz, B. Smith (r1970; arr Heifetz)
(7/95) (RCA) ▣ **09026 62706-3**
3. D. Briggs (r1990s: arr org)
(MAYH) Ⓓ **KMCD1007**
(MAYH) ⊟ **KMK1007**
3. Bekova Sisters (r1994; arr pf trio: Bekova)
(CHAN) Ⓓ **CHAN9364**
3. Moscow Virtuosi, V. Spivakov (r1994)
(RCA) Ⓓ **09026 68185-2**
3. Empire Brass (r1992; arr. E. Smedvig)
(1/94) (TELA) Ⓓ **CD80305**
(1/94) (TELA) ⊟ **CS30305**

The **Love for Three Oranges– concert suite from opera**
EXCERPTS: 1. Les ridicules; 2. Scène infernale; 3. March; 4. Scherzo; 5. Le Prince et la Princesse; 6. La fruite.
RPO, O. Danon (CHES) Ⓓ **Chesky CD56**
Minneapolis SO, A. Dorati
(MERC) Ⓓ **432 753-2MM**
Montreal SO, C. Dutoit (r1992)
(DECC) ⓞⓞ **440 331-5DH**
LPO, E. Bátiz (r1982) (IMG) Ⓓ **IMGCD1603**
LSO, N. Marriner (r1980)
(PHIL) Ⓓ [2] **442 278-2PM2**
Armenian PO, L. Tjeknavorian
(ASV) Ⓓ **CDDCA886**
(ASV) ⊟ **ZCDCA886**
SNO, N. Järvi (9/89) (CHAN) Ⓓ **CHAN8729**
(9/89) (CHAN) ⊟ **ABTD1369**
LSO, N. Marriner
(11/90) (PHIL) Ⓓ **426 640-2PSL**
Montreal SO, C. Dutoit (r1992)
(1/94) (DECC) Ⓓ **440 331-2DH**
Philadelphia, E. Ormandy (r1963)
(7/94) (SONY) Ⓓ **SBK53261**
(SONY) ⊟ **SBT53261**
1-5. Philh, N. Malko (CFP) Ⓓ **CD-CFP4523**
1-5. LPO, W. Weller
(1/92) (DECC) Ⓓ **433 612-2DSP**
3. Budapest PO, J. Sándor (LASE) Ⓓ **15 621**
(LASE) ⊟ **79 621**
3. SNO, N. Järvi (CHAN) Ⓓ **CHAN6511**
(CHAN) ⊟ **MBTD6511**

3. A. Shirinsky, N. Rozova (r1991; arr vn/pf)
(MEZH) Ⓓ **MK417030**
3. M. Rabin, L. Pommers (r1959: arr Heifetz)
(EMI) Ⓓ [6] **CMS7 64123-2**
3. I. Perlman, J.G. Guggenheim (arr Heifetz; pp1990) (EMI) ◐ **LDB9 91243-1**
(EMI) ▣ **MVD9 91243-3**
3. Philadelphia, E. Ormandy (r1963)
(SONY) Ⓓ **SBK39446**
3. Bavarian St Orch, W. Sawallisch
(EMI) Ⓓ [2] **CZS7 67546-2**
3. NYPO, L. Bernstein (r1971)
(SONY) Ⓓ **SMK47607**
3. Los Angeles PO, M. Tilson Thomas
(SONY) Ⓓ **SK53549**
3. E. Fodor, D. Saunders (r1992: trans Heifetz)
(NEWP) Ⓓ **NPD85551**
3. LSO, Y. Ahronovitch (IMP) Ⓓ **PCD804**
3. R. Pöntinen (arr pf)
(11/85) (BIS) Ⓓ **BIS-CD300**
3. A. Rubinstein (arr.Rubinstein)
(10/87) (RCA) Ⓓ **RD85666**
3. St Louis SO, L. Slatkin
(6/89) (RCA) Ⓓ **RD87716**
3. X. Wei, Pam Nicholson (arr Heifetz)
(9/90) (ASV) Ⓓ **CDDCA698**
3. I. Perlman, J.G. Guggenheim (pp1990)
(2/91) (EMI) Ⓓ **CDC7 54108-2**
3. S. Chang, S. Rivers (arr Heifetz)
(1/93) (EMI) Ⓓ **CDC7 54352-2**
3. Midori, R. McDonald (r1992; arr vn/pf Heifetz)
(6/93) (SONY) Ⓓ **SK52568**
(6/93) (SONY) ⊟ **ST52568**
3. A. Rubinstein (r1961; arr pf)
(8/94) (RCA) Ⓓ **09026 61863-2**
3. J. Heifetz, E. Bay (r1945)
(11/94) (RCA) Ⓓ [65] **09026 61778-2(19)**
3. J. Heifetz, B. Smith (r1970)
(11/94) (RCA) Ⓓ [65] **09026 61778-2(40)**
3-5. Košice St PO, A. Mogrelia
(9/91) (NAXO) Ⓓ **8 550381**
4, 5. V. Feltsman, LSO, M. Tilson Thomas (r1981) (SONY) Ⓓ **SMK64243**

Semyon Kotko– opera: 5 acts, Op. 81 (1940—Moscow) (Lib. V Katayev & cpsr)
EXCERPTS: 1. Overture.
1. Russian Nat Orch, M. Pletnev
(12/94) (DG) Ⓓ **439 892-2GH**
(DG) ⊟ **439 892-4GH**

War and Peace– opera: 5 acts & epigraph, Op. 91 (1944—Moscow) (Lib. cpsr, after Tolstoy)
EXCERPTS: 1. Overture; 2. Scene 1: The radiance of the sky (Svetlaje vesenneje neba); 3. Scene 2: 3a. Ballet Music; 3b. Chorus! let the chorus begin! (Hor! Pust' nachinajet hor!); 4. Scene 3: The young prince's fiancée (Nevesta maladova kn'az'a); 5. Scene 4: The charming, delightful Natasha! (Maja prelesnaja); 6. Scene 5: At ten o'clock in the evening (Vecheram v des'at'); 7. Scene 6: Oh, my dear Miss Natasha (Oj, baryshn'a); 8. Scene 7: Picture the scene, Countess (Padumajte, grafin'a); 9. Epigraph (chorus): The forces of two and ten European nations; 10. Scene 8: Come on, lads! (Pashla rib'ata!); 11. Scene 9: The wine is uncorked (Vino atkuporena); 12. Scene 10: And so, gentlemen (Itak, gospoda); 13. Scene 11: Moscow's deserted! (Maskva pusta!); 14. Scene 12: It's stretching higher and further (T'anesta); 15. Scene 13: We've burnt our bridges (Karabli sazheny).
Prince Bolkonsky L. Miller
Natasha G. Vishnevskaya
Sonya Katherine Ciesinski
Maria M. Paunova
Count Rostov D. Petkov
Pierre Bezoukhov W. Ochman
Helena S. Toczyska
Anatol Kuragin N. Gedda
Dolokhov V. de Kanel
Denissov M. Smith
Marshal Kutuzov N. Ghiuselev
Napoleon E. Tumagian
French Rad Chor, FNO, M. Rostropovich (r1986)
(4/92) (ERAT) Ⓓ [4] **2292-45331-2**
Prince Bolkonsky A. Gergalov
Natasha Y. Prokina
Sonya S. Volkova
Maria L. Kanunnikova
Count Rostov S. Alexashkin
Pierre Bezhoukhov G. Gregorian
Helena O. Borodina
Anatol Kuragin Y. Marusin
Dolokhov A. Morozov
Denissov M. Kit
Marshal Kutuzov N. Okhotnikov
V. Gerelo
Kirov Th Chor, Kirov Th Orch, V. Gergiev (r1991)
(6/93) (PHIL) Ⓓ [3] **434 097-2PH3**
Excs A. Gergalov, Y. Prokina, S. Alexashkin, G. Grigorian, Y. Marusin, I. Bogacheva, S. Volkova, N. Okhotnikov, V. Gerelo, Kirov Th Chor, Kirov Th Orch, V. Gergiev (r1991)
(PHIL) Ⓓ **442 437-2PH**
What right have they? L. Popp, Munich RO, S. Soltesz (r1987) (4/89) (EMI) Ⓓ **CDC7 49319-2**
3. ASMF, BBC SO, LPO, ENO Orch, G. Simon (r1995; arr va: J. Milone)
(9/95) (CALA) ◑ **CACD0106**

War and Peace– concert suite from the opera (arr. C Palmer)
EXCERPTS: 1. The Ball: 1a. Fanfare and Polonaise; 1b. Waltz; 1c. Mazurka; 2. Intermezzo—May Night; 3. Finale: 3a. Snowstorm; 3b. Battle; 3c. Victory.
Philh, N. Järvi (r1991)
(3/93) (CHAN) Ⓓ **CHAN9096**
1b Bekova Sisters (r1994; arr pf trio: Bekova)
(CHAN) Ⓓ **CHAN9364**

PUCCINI, Giacomo (Antonia Domenico Michele Secondo Maria) *(1858–1924) Italy*

La **Bohème, 'Bohemian Life'– opera: 4 acts (1896—Turin) (Lib. Illica and Giacosa)**
EXCERPTS: ACT 1: 1a. Questo Mar Rosso; 1b. Nei cieli bigi; 1c. Pensier profondo! Giusto color!; 1d. Legna! Sigari! Bordo!; 1e. Si può? Chi è là? Benoit!; 1f. Io resto per terminar l'articolo; 1g. Non sono in vena. Chi è là!; 1h. Si sente meglio? Sì. Qui cè tanto freddo; 2. Che gelida manina; 3. Sì. Mi chiamano Mimì; 4. O soave fanciulla. ACT 2: 5. Aranci, datteri!; 6a. Chi guardi?; 6b. Eccoci qui!; 7a. Come un facchino; 7b. Quando me'n vo' soletta (Musetta's Waltz). ACT 3: 8. Ohè, là, le guardie; 9. Mimì?!...Speravo di trovarvi; 10a. Marcello...Finalmente; 10b. Mimì è una civetta; 11. Donde lieta uscì (Mimì's Farewell); 12. Addio dolce svegliare. ACT 4: 13a. In un coupè?; 13b. O Mimì, tu più non torni; 14. Che ora sia?; 15. Musetta!...C'è Mimì; 16. Vecchia zimarra (Coat song); 17a. Sono andati?; 17b. Tornò al nido; 17c. Oh Dio! Mimì!.
Mimì I. Cotrubas
Rodolfo N. Shicoff
Musetta M. Zschau
Marcello T. Allen
Schaunard J. Rawnsley
Colline G. Howell
Benoit B. Donlan
Alcindoro J. Gibbs
ROH Chor, ROHO, L. Gardelli, J. Copley
(CAST) ▣ **CVI2014**
Mimì M. Freni
Rodolfo L. Pavarotti
Musetta S. Pacetti
Marcello G. Quilico
Schaunard S. Dickson
Colline N. Ghiaurov
Alcindoro; Benoit I. Tajo
San Francisco Op Chor, San Francisco Op Orch, T. Severini, F. Zambello
(MCEG) ▣ **VVD603**
Mimì A. Moffo
Rodolfo R. Tucker
Musetta M. Costa
Marcello R. Merrill
Schaunard P. Maero
Colline G. Tozzi
Benoit F. Corena
Alcindoro G. Onesti
Parpignol; Sergeant A. Zagonara
Customs Officer F. Tosin
Rome Op Chor, Rome Op Orch, E. Leinsdorf
(RCA) Ⓓ [2] **GD83969**
Mimì R. Scotto
Rodolfo Alfredo Kraus
Musetta C. Neblett
Marcello S. Milnes
Schaunard M. Manuguerra
Colline P. Plishka
Benoit I. Tajo
Alcindoro R. Capecchi
Parpignol P. Crook
Sergeant M. Lewis

Customs Officer J. Noble
Trinity Boys' Ch, Ambrosian Op Chor, National PO, James Levine
(CFP) Ⓓ [2] **CD-CFPD4708**
(CFP) ▭ [2] **TC-CFPD4708**
Mimì M. Freni
Rodolfo L. Pavarotti
Musetta M. Oran
Marcello G. Taddei
Schaunard N. Carta
Colline R. Arié
Madrid Zarzuela Chor, Madrid Zarzuela Orch, N. Sanzogno (pp1970)
(BUTT) Ⓓ [2] **BMCD007**
(BUTT) ▭ [2] **BMK007**
Mimì R. Tebaldi
Rodolfo G. Prandelli
Musetta H. Gueden
Marcello G. Inghilleri
Schaunard F. Corena
Colline R. Arié
Benoit; Alcindoro M. Luise
Sergeant I. Santafe
Santa Cecilia Academy Chor, Santa Cecilia Academy Orch, A. Erede (r1951)
(LOND) Ⓓ [2] **440 233-2LF2**
Mimì M. Freni
Rodolfo L. Pavarotti
Musetta E. Harwood
Marcello R. Panerai
Schaunard G. Maffeo
Colline N. Ghiaurov
Benoit; Alcindoro M. Sénéchal
Parpignol G. Pietsch
Sergeant H-D. Appelt
Customs Officer H-D. Pohl
Schöneberg Boys' Ch, Berlin Deutsche Op Chor, BPO, H. von Karajan (r1972)
(DECC) Ⓓ [11] **443 204-2DH11(2)**
Mimì A. Stella
Rodolfo G. Poggi
Musetta B. Rizzoli
Marcello R. Capecchi
Schaunard G. Mazzini
Colline G. Modesti
Benoit M. Luise
Alcindoro G. Onesti
Parpignol P. de Palma
Customs Officer G. Gaudioso
Customs Officer A. Terrosi
Naples San Carlo Op Chor, Naples San Carlo Op Orch, F. Molinari-Pradelli (r1957)
(PHIL) Ⓓ [2] **442 106-2PM2**
Mimì M. Caballé
Rodolfo P. Domingo
Musetta J. Blegen
Marcello S. Milnes
Schaunard V. Sardinero
Colline R. Raimondi
Benoit N. Mangin
Alcindoro N. Castel
Parpignol A. Byers
Sergeant F. Whiteley
Customs Officer W. Mason
Wandsworth Sch Boys' Ch, John Alldis Ch, LPO, G. Solti
(9/86) (RCA) Ⓓ [2] **RD80371**
Mimì K. Ricciarelli
Rodolfo J. Carreras
Musetta A. Putnam
Marcello I. Wixell
Schaunard H. Hagegård
Colline R. Lloyd
Benoit G. de Angelis
Alcindoro W. Elvin
Parpignol F. Egerton
Sergeant R. Hazell
Customs Officer D. Whelan
ROH Chor, ROHO, Colin Davis (r1979)
(5/87) (PHIL) Ⓓ [2] **416 492-2PH2**
(PHIL) ▭ **416 492-4PX2**
Mimì V. de los Angeles
Rodolfo J. Björling
Musetta L. Amara
Marcello R. Merrill
Schaunard J. Reardon
Colline G. Tozzi
Benoit; Alcindoro F. Corena
Parpignol W. Nahr
Sergeant G. del Monte
Customs Officer T. Powell
Columbus Boychoir, RCA Victor Chor, RCA Victor SO, T. Beecham (r1956)
(6/87) (EMI) Ⓓ [2] **CDS7 47235-8**
Mimì M. Freni
Rodolfo L. Pavarotti
Musetta E. Harwood
Marcello R. Panerai
Schaunard G. Maffeo
Colline N. Ghiaurov
Benoit M. Sénéchal
Alcindoro M. Sénéchal
Parpignol G. Pietsch
Sergeant H-D. Appelt
Customs Officer H-D. Pohl
Schöneberg Boys' Ch, Berlin Deutsche Op Chor, BPO, H. von Karajan (r1972)
(11/87) (DECC) Ⓓ [2] **421 049-2DH2**
Mimì M. Callas
Rodolfo G. di Stefano
Musetta A. Moffo
Marcello R. Panerai
Schaunard M. Spatafora
Colline N. Zaccaria
Benoit; Alcindoro C. Badioli
Parpignol F. Ricciardi
Sergeant C. Forti
Customs Officer E. Coda
La Scala Chor, La Scala Orch, A. Votto (r1956)
(11/87) (EMI) Ⓓ [2] **CDS7 47475-8**
Mimì B. Hendricks
Rodolfo J. Carreras
Musetta A.M. Blasi
Marcello G. Quilico
Schaunard R. Cowan
Colline F.E. d'Artegna
Benoit; Alcindoro F. Davià
Parpignol M. Sénéchal
FRN Chor, FNR Maîtrise, FNO, J. Conlon
(5/88) (ERAT) Ⓓ [2] **2292-45311-2**
Mimì A. Réaux
Rodolfo J. Hadley
Musetta B. Daniels
Marcello T. Hampson
Schaunard J. Busterud
Colline P. Plishka
Benoit J. McKee
Alcindoro G. Beni
Parpignol D. Bernardini
Sergeant P. Kreider
Children's Ch, Santa Cecilia Academy Chor, Santa Cecilia Academy Orch, L. Bernstein (pp1987)
(8/88) (DG) Ⓓ [2] **423 601-2GH2**
Mimi M. Freni
Rodolfo G. Raimondi
Musetta A. Martino
Marcello R. Panerai
Schaunard G. Maffeo
Colline I. Vinco
Benoit C. Badioli
La Scala Chor, La Scala Orch, H. von Karajan, F. Zeffirelli
(10/88) (DG) ◐ [2] **072 105-1GH2**
(DG) ▣ **072 105-3GH**
Mimì R. Tebaldi
Rodolfo C. Bergonzi
Musetta G. d'Angelo
Marcello E. Bastianini
Schaunard R. Cesari
Colline C. Siepi
Benoit; Alcindoro F. Corena
Parpignol P. de Palma
Sergeant A. d'Orazi
Santa Cecilia Academy Chor, Santa Cecilia Academy Orch, T. Serafin
(2/90) (DECC) Ⓓ [2] **425 534-2DM2**
Mimì V. Kincses
Rodolfo P. Dvorský
Musetta S. Haljáková
Marcello I. Konsulov
Schaunard B. Póka
Colline D. Niemirowicz
Benoit S. Benňačka
Alcindoro S. Janči
Parpignol V. Schrenkel
Bratislava Children's Ch, Bratislava Nat Op Chor, Bratislava RSO, O. Lenárd
(5/90) (OPUS) Ⓓ [2] **9156 0931/2**
Mimì L. Orgonášová
Rodolfo J. Welch
Musetta C. Gonzales
Marcello F. Previati
Schaunard B. Senator
Colline I. Urbas
Benoit R. Novák
Alcindoro J. Sulzenko
Parpignol L. Hallon
Sergeant S. Benacka
Bratislava Children's Ch, Slovak Phil Chor, Bratislava RSO, W. Humburg
(4/91) (NAXO) Ⓓ [2] **8 660003/4**
Mimì L. Albanese
Rodolfo J. Peerce
Musetta A. McKnight
Marcello F. Valentino
Schaunard G. Cehanovsky
Colline N. Moscona
Benoit; Alcindoro S. Baccaloni
Chor, NBC SO, A. Toscanini (bp1946)
(9/91) (RCA) Ⓓ [2] **GD60288**
Mimì M. Freni
Rodolfo N. Gedda
Musetta M. Adani
Marcello M. Sereni
Schaunard M. Basiola II
Colline F. Mazzoli
Benoit C. Badioli
Alcindoro P. Montarsolo
Parpignol V. Pandano
Sergeant M. Rinaudo
Rome Op Chor, Rome Op Orch, T. Schippers (r1962/3)
(4/92) (EMI) Ⓓ [2] **CMS7 69657-2**
Mimì M. Freni
Rodolfo L. Pavarotti
Musetta S. Pacetti
Marcello G. Quilico
Schaunard S. Dickson
Colline N. Ghiaurov
Benoit; Alcindoro I. Tajo
Pargignol D. Harper
Sergeant M. Coles
San Francisco Op Chor, San Francisco Op Orch, T. Severini, B. Large
(5/93) (PION) ◐ **PLMCB00281**
Mimì M. Gauci
Rodolfo G. Aragall
Musetta M. Krause
Marcello V. Sardinero
Schaunard C. Bergasa
Colline, Sergeant M. Rosca
Benoit, Alcindoro J. Joris
Parpignol F. De Moor
Customs Official W. Brans
Brussels BRT Phil Chor, Brussels BRT PO, A. Rahbari (r1993)
(1/94) (DINT) Ⓓ [2] **DICD920107/8**
Mimì K. Ricciarelli
Rodolfo J. Carreras
Musetta A. Putnam
Marcello I. Wixell
Schaunard H. Hagegård
Colline R. Lloyd
Benoit G. de Angelis
Alcindoro W. Elvin
Parpignol F. Egerton
Sergeant R. Hazell
Customs Officer D. Whelan
ROH Chor, ROHO, Colin Davis (r1979)
(10/94) (PHIL) Ⓓ [2] **442 260-2PM2**
Mimì L. Albanese
Rodolfo B. Gigli
Musetta T. Menotti
Marcello A. Poli
Schaunard A. Baracchi
Colline D. Baronti
Benoit; Alcindoro C. Scattola
Parpignol N. Palai
La Scala Chor, La Scala Orch, U. Berrettoni (r1938)
(3/95) (NIMB) Ⓓ [2] **NI7862/3**
Mimì R. Torri
Rodolfo A. Giorgini
Musetta T. Vitulli
Marcello E. Badini
Schaunard A. Baracchi
Colline L. Manfrini
Benoit; Alcindoro S. Baccaloni
Parpignol G. Nessi
La Scala Chor, La Scala Orch, C. Sabajno (r1928)
(3/95) (VAI) Ⓓ [2] **VAIA1078**
Mimì K. Te Kanawa
Rodolfo R. Leech
Musetta N. Gustafson
Marcello A. Titus
Colline R. Scandiuzzi
Beniot C. Chausson
Alcindoro A. Ewing
Parpignol B. Banks
Sergeant L. Fyson
Ambrosian Sngrs, St Clement Danes Sch Ch, LSO, K. Nagano (r1994)
(11/95) (ERAT) Ⓓ [2] **0630-10699-2**
Mimì K. Ricciarelli
Rodolfo F. Araiza
Musetta L. Broglia

Marcello S. Antonucci
Schaunard A. Noli
Colline P. Burchuladze
Benoit A. Mariotti
Alcindoro C. Giombi
Parpignol A. Casertano
Sergeant A. Piccinni
Limberg Cath Children's Ch, Verona Arena Chor, Verona Arena Orch, A. Guadagno (r1995) (11/95) (SCHW) ⦶ [2] **315922**
Act 4. D. Labbette, H. Nash, S. Andreva, J. Brownlee, R. Alva, R. Easton, LPO, T. Beecham (r1935) (9/91) (PEAR) ⦶ **GEMMCD9473**
Act 4. D. Labbette, S. Andreva, H. Nash, J. Brownlee, R. Alva, R. Easton, LPO, T. Beecham (r1935) (2/95) (DUTT) ⦶ **CDLX7012**
Excs C. Steele-Perkins, L. Pearson (r1989: arr Pearson) (LDR) ⦶ **LDRCD1006** (LDR) ⊟ **LDRZC1006**
Excs Munich Brass (arr brass ens) (ORFE) ⦶ **C247911A**
Excs M. Freni, L. Pavarotti, R. Talarico, S. Bruscantini, G. Maffeo, N. Ghiuselev, Rome RAI Chor, Rome RAI Orch, T. Schippers (pp1969) (BUTT) ⦶ **BMCD016** (BUTT) ⊟ **BMK016**
Fantasia Cölln Salon Orch (arr Gauwin) (EURO) ⦶ **GD69295**
1a-h, 2-5, 7b, 10b, 12, 13b, 16, 17a-c A. Moffo, R. Tucker, M. Costa, R. Merrill, G. Tozzi, P. Maero, Rome Op Chor, Rome Op Orch, E. Leinsdorf (RCA) ⦶ **GD60189** (RCA) ⊟ **GK60189**
1a, 1b, 2-4. H. Schymberg, J. Björling, S. Herdenberg, C. Richter, L. Björker, Stockholm Royal Op Orch, N. Grevillius (Swedish; pp1940) (3/92) (BLUE) ⦶ **ABCD013**
1a, 3, 4, 5, 7a, 7b, 11, 12, 13b, 17a-c R. Scotto, J. Meneguzzer, G. Poggi, E. Guagni, T. Gobbi, G. Giorgetti, V. Carbonari, G. Modesti, MMF Chor, MMF Orch, A. Votto (r1961) (BELA) ⦶ **450 134-2** (BELA) ⊟ **450 134-4**
1b G. Zenatello, M. Sammarco, orch (r1909) (7/92) (PEAR) ⦶ [3] **GEMMCDS9924(1)**
1b, 13b G. Zenatello, M. Sammarco, orch (r1909) (5/94) (SYMP) ⦶ **SYMCD1158**
1b, 13b G. Zenatello, M. Sammarco, orch (r1909) (5/94) (PEAR) ⦶ [4] **GEMMCDS9073(2)**
1g, 1h, 2. H. Roswaenge, M. Cebotari, Berlin RSO, H. Steinkopf (bp1941: Ger) (PREI) ⦶ [2] **89211**
1g, 2-4, 7b, 11, 12, 13a, 13b, 16, 17a-c M. Freni, L. Pavarotti, R. Panerai, E. Harwood, N. Ghiaurov, G. Maffeo, M. Sénéchal, Berlin Deutsche Op Chor, BPO, H. von Karajan (DECC) ⦶ **421 245-2DH** (DECC) ⊟ **421 245-4DH**
1, 17a I. Cotrubas, N. Shicoff, T. Allen, M. Zschau, J. Rawnsley, G. Howell, ROHO, L. Gardelli (CAST) ▣ **CVI2070**
2. G. Thill, orch (r1931: Fr) (PEAR) ⦶ **GEMMCD9947**
2. L. Pavarotti, BPO, H. von Karajan (7/75) (DECC) ⊟ **400 053-4DH**
2. P. Domingo, LPO, G. Solti (RCA) ⦶ **GD84265**
2. L. Pavarotti, BPO, H. von Karajan (DECC) ⦶ **425 850-2DWO** (DECC) ⊟ **425 850-4DWO**
2. J. Björling, orch, N. Grevillius (r1937) (EMI) ⦶ **CDC7 54016-2**
2. T. Burke, orch (r1920/1) (PEAR) ⦶ **GEMMCD9411**
2. M. Wittrisch, Berlin St Op Orch, E. Orthmann (Ger: r1932) (PREI) ⦶ **89024**
2. B. Gigli, orch, E. Goossens (r1931) (NIMB) ⦶ **NI7817** (NIMB) ⊟ **NC7817**
2. J. Carreras, ROHO, Colin Davis (PHIL) ⦶ **432 692-2PH** (PHIL) ⊟ **432 692-4PH**
2. M. Lanza, RCA Victor Orch, C. Callinicos (r1949) (RCA) ⦶ **GD60516**
2. B.S. Rosenberg, Budapest Concert Orch, J. Acs (pp1990) (OLYM) ⦶ **OCD370**
2. T. Schipa, orch, Anon (cond) (pp1913) (MEMO) ⦶ [2] **HR4220/1**
2. C. Bergonzi, Santa Cecilia Academy Orch, T. Serafin (DECC) ⦶ **433 636-2DSP** (DECC) ⊟ **433 636-4DSP**
2. L. Pavarotti, Orch (EDL) ⦶ **EDL2562-2** (EDL) ⊙ **EDL2562-1** ⊟ **EDL2562-4**
2. L. Pavarotti, BPO, H. von Karajan (DECC) ⦶ **433 822-2DH** (DECC) ⊟ **433 822-4DH**
2. P. Domingo, LPO, G. Solti (RCA) ⦶ [2] **GD60866** (RCA) ⊟ [2] **GK60866**
2. L. Pavarotti, BPO, H. von Karajan (DECC) ⦶ **433 066-2DWO** (DECC) ⊟ **433 066-4DWO**
2. J. Carreras, ROHO, Colin Davis (PHIL) ⦶ **434 152-2PM**
2. M. Fleta, orch (r1927) (MMOI) ⦶ **CDMOIR412**
2. G. Raimondi, La Scala Orch, H. von Karajan (DECC) ◖ **071 142-1DH** (DECC) ▣ **071 142-3DH**
2. J. Björling, orch, N. Grevillius (r1936) (NIMB) ⦶ **NI7835**
2. L. Pavarotti, BPO, H. von Karajan (r1972) (DECC) ⦶ **436 300-2DX** (DECC) ⊟ **436 300-4DX**
2. T. Harper, Bratislava RSO, M. Halász (NAXO) ⦶ **8 550497**
2. P. Domingo, LPO, G. Solti (r1973) (RCA) ⦶ **09026 61356-2** (RCA) ⊟ **09026 61356-4**
2. E. Caruso, orch (r1906) (RCA) ⦶ **09026 61243-2**
2. E. Caruso, orch (r1906) (MCI) ⦶ **MCCD086** (MCI) ⊟ **MCTC086**
2. S. Fisichella, Verona Arena Orch, A. Guadagno (pp1992) (MCI) ⦶ **MCCD099**
2. B. Gigli, orch, E. Goossens (r1931) (IMP) ⦶ **GLRS102**
2. Deng, Württemberg PO, R. Paternostro (SINE) ⦶ **39820222**
2. J. Carreras, ROHO, Colin Davis (r1979) (BELA) ⦶ **450 059-2** (BELA) ⊟ **450 059-4**
2. J. Björling, orch, N. Grevillius (r1937) (PEAR) ⦶ **GEMMCD9043**
2. B. Gigli, orch, E. Goossens (r1931) (CONI) ⦶ **CDHD227** (CONI) ⊟ **MCHD227**
2. R. Tucker, Rome Op Orch, E. Leinsdorf (RCA) ⦶ **09026 61886-2** (RCA) ⊟ **09026 61886-4**
2. J. Carreras, ROHO, Colin Davis (r1976) (PHIL) ⦶ **442 600-2PH** (PHIL) ⊟ **442 600-4PH**
2. F. Araiza, ECO, A. Zedda (PHIL) ⦶ **442 602-2PM** (PHIL) ⊟ **442 602-4PM**
2. L. Pavarotti, Toscanini SO, E. Buckley (SONY) ⦶ **MDK47176** (SONY) ⊟ **MDT47176**
2. J. McCormack, orch (r1910) (ASV) ⦶ **CDAJA5137** (ASV) ⊟ **ZCAJA5137**
2. J. Björling, H. Ebert (pp1956) (BLUE) ⦶ **ABCD057**
2. J. Hammond, D. Lloyd, CBO, L. Heward (r1941: Eng) (SAIN) ⦶ **SCDC2076** (SAIN) ⊟ **C2076**
2. C. Bergonzi, Santa Cecilia Academy Orch, L. Gardelli (r1958) (DECC) ⦶ **440 417-2DM**
2. T. Beltrán, RPO, R. Stapleton (r1994) (SILV) ⦶ **SILKD6005** (SILV) ⊟ **SILKC6005**
2. A. Bonci, orch (r1912) (PEAR) ⦶ **GEMMCD9168**
2. A. Piccaver, Berlin St Op Orch, M. Gurlitt (r1929) (PREI) ⦶ [2] **89217**
2. J. Björling, RCA Orch, R. Cellini (r1951) (RCA) ⦶ **09026 62550-2**
2. B. Gigli, orch, E. Goossens (r1931) (PEAR) ⦶ [2] **GEMMCDS9176**
2. F. de Lucia, orch (r1917) (BONG) ⦶ [2] **GB1064/5-2**
2. J. Björling, orch, N. Grevillius (r1936) (CONI) ⦶ **CDHD235**
2. R. Alagna, LPO, R. Armstrong (EMI) ⦶ **CDC5 55540-2** (EMI) ⊟ **EL5 55540-4**
2. R. Tucker, Rome Op Orch, E. Leinsdorf (r1961) (RCA) ⦶ **09026 62689-2**
2. F. de la Mora, WNO Orch, C. Mackerras (r1994-5) (TELA) ⦶ **CD80411**
2. L. Pavarotti, BPO, H. von Karajan (7/86) (DECC) ⦶ [2] **417 011-2DH2**
2. J. Björling, Hilversum RO, F. Weissmann (pp1939) (8/88) (BLUE) ⦶ **ABCD006**
2. B. Gigli, orch, E. Goossens (r1931) (9/88) (EMI) ⦶ **CDH7 61051-2**
2. J. Björling, orch, N. Grevillius (r1936) (10/88) (EMI) ⦶ **CDH7 61053-2**
2. C. Bergonzi, Santa Cecilia Academy Orch, T. Serafin (1/89) (DECC) ⦶ **417 686-2DC**
2. M. André, Toulouse Capitole Orch, M. Plasson (arr tpt) (1/89) (EMI) ⦶ **CDC7 49219-2**
2. E. Caruso, orch (r1906) (5/89) (PEAR) ⦶ **GEMMCD9309**
2. Alfredo Kraus, National PO, James Levine (10/89) (EMI) ⦶ **CDM7 63104-2**
2. B. Gigli, orch, E. Goossens (r1931) (10/89) (NIMB) ⦶ **NI7801** (NIMB) ⊟ **NC7801**
2. M. Fleta, orch (r1927) (2/90) (PREI) ⦶ **89002**
2. J. Patzak, Berlin St Op Orch (Ger: r1931) (3/90) (PEAR) ⦶ **GEMMCD9383**
2. T. Schipa, orch, C. Sabajno (r1913) (4/90) (EMI) ⦶ **CDH7 63200-2**
2. L. Pavarotti, BPO, H. von Karajan (7/90) (DECC) ⦶ [2] **425 681-2DM2** (7/90) (DECC) ⊟ [2] **425 681-4DM2**
2. D. Smirnov, orch (r1913) (7/90) (CLUB) ⦶ **CL99-031**
2. N. Gedda, ROHO, G. Patanè (8/90) (CFP) ⦶ **CD-CFP4569** (8/90) (CFP) ⊟ **TC-CFP4569**
2. E. Caruso, orch (r1906) (12/90) (PEAR) ⦶ [3] **EVC1(2)**
2. E. Caruso, orch (r1906) (7/91) (RCA) ⦶ [12] **GD60495(2)**
2. A. Cortis, La Scala Orch, C. Sabajno (r1930) (10/91) (PREI) ⦶ **89043**
2. H. Roswaenge, orch (r1927: Ger) (2/92) (PREI) ⦶ [2] **89201**
2. G. Lugo, orch, A. Wolff (Fr: r1932) (2/92) (PREI) ⦶ **89034**
2. G. Lugo, orch (r1939) (2/92) (PREI) ⦶ **89034**
2. A. Bonci, anon (r1905) (7/92) (PEAR) ⦶ [3] **GEMMCDS9923(2)**
2. J. Hislop, orch (r1922) (7/92) (PEAR) ⦶ [3] **GEMMCDS9925(1)**
2. D. Borgioli, orch (r c1924) (7/92) (PEAR) ⦶ [3] **GEMMCDS9926(1)**
2. G. Anselmi, anon (r1909) (7/92) (PEAR) ⦶ [3] **GEMMCDS9924(2)**
2. R. Tauber, orch, K. Besl (Ger: r1924) (12/92) (NIMB) ⦶ **NI7830** (12/92) (NIMB) ⊟ **NC7830**
2. J. Hislop, orch, J. Barbirolli (r1928) (1/93) (PEAR) ⦶ **GEMMCD9956**
2. G. Martinelli, orch, J. Pasternack (r1926) (3/93) (PREI) ⦶ **89062**
2. B. Gigli, orch, E. Goossens (r1931) (6/93) (MMOI) ⦶ **CDMOIR417**
2. G. Lauri-Volpi, orch (r1923) (7/93) (NIMB) ⦶ **NI7845**
2. A. Piccaver, orch (r1914) (8/93) (PREI) ⦶ **89060**
2. L. Pavarotti, BPO, H. von Karajan (r1972) (10/93) (DECC) ⦶ **436 463-2DM** (10/93) (DECC) ⊟ **436 463-4DM**
2. L. Pavarotti, BPO, H. von Karajan (r1972) (12/93) (DECC) ⦶ **433 437-2DA** (DECC) ⊟ **433 437-4DA**
2. A. Cortis, La Scala Orch, C. Sabajno (r1930) (3/94) (NIMB) ⦶ **NI7850**
2. Ferruccio Tagliavini, EIAR Orch, U. Tansini (r1940) (3/94) (CENT) ⦶ **CRC2164**
2. G. di Stefano, RCA SO, R. Cellini (r1951) (4/94) (RCA) ⦶ [6] **09026 61580-2(6)**
2. E. Caruso, orch (r1906) (4/94) (EMI) ⦶ [3] **CHS7 64860-2(1)**
2. G. Lugo, orch (r1939) (4/94) (EMI) ⦶ [3] **CHS7 64864-2(2)**
2. E. Caruso, orch, C. Nicholls (r1906/92) (5/94) (CLAR) ⦶ **CDGSE78-50-52**
2. G. Zenatello, orch (r1908) (5/94) (SYMP) ⦶ **SYMCD1158**
2. G. Zenatello, orch (r1908) (5/94) (PEAR) ⦶ [4] **GEMMCDS9073(1)**
2. G. Zenatello, anon (r c1912) (5/94) (PEAR) ⦶ [4] **GEMMCDS9074(1)**
2. J. Björling, orch, N. Grevillius (r1936) (9/94) (IMP) ⦶ **GLRS103**
2. A. Pertile, La Scala Orch, G. Nastrucci (r1930) (10/94) (PREI) ⦶ **89072**
2. J. Björling, orch, N. Grevillius (r1936) (12/94) (MMOI) ⦶ **CDMOIR425**
2(pt) A. Giorgini, orch (r1924) (4/95) (RECO) ⦶ **TRC3**
2. J. Johnston, ROHO, L. Collingwood (r1947: Eng) (4/95) (TEST) ⦶ **SBT1058**
2. E. Caruso, orch (r1906) (7/95) (NIMB) ⦶ **NI7866**
2. L. Pavarotti, Rome SO, N. Bonavolontà (pp1967) (10/95) (RCA) ⦶ **09026 62541-2**

2. H. Nash, orch, J. Batten (r1932: Eng) (11/95) (PEAR) Ⓓ **GEMMCD9175**
2, 10a, 13a, 13b I. Kozlovsky, E. Shumskaya, I. Burlak, USSR SO, Anon (cond) (r1930-50) (MYTO) Ⓓ **1MCD921.55**
2, 10b J. Schmidt, Berlin SO, O. Dobrindt (r1932: Ger) (EMI) Ⓓ [2] **CHS7 64673-2**
2, 13a, 13b L. Pavarotti, G. Sabbatini, P. Cappuccilli, Bologna Teatro Comunale Orch, L. Magiera (pp1991) (DECC) ◐ **071 140-1DH** (DECC) ◘ **071 140-3DH**
2, 3, 4, 7b, 13a, b R. Tebaldi, G. d'Angelo, C. Bergonzi, R. Cesari, E. Bastianini, C. Siepi, F. Corena, Santa Cecilia Academy Orch, T. Serafin (r1959) (DECC) Ⓓ [2] **444 555-2DF2**
2, 3, 7b M. Freni, E. Harwood, L. Pavarotti, M. Sénéchal, R. Panerai, BPO, H. von Karajan (r1972) (DECC) Ⓓ **436 317-2DA** (DECC) ▣ **436 317-4DA**
2, 3, 7b, 12. N. Shicoff, I. Cotrubas, M. Zschau, T. Allen, ROHO, L. Gardelli (CAST) ◘ **CASH5051**
2-4. J. Barstow, A. Davies, RPO, R. Stapleton (RPO) Ⓓ **CDRPO7009** (RPO) ▣ **ZCRPO7009**
2-4. J. Carreras, B. Hendricks, French Rad Chor, FNO, J. Conlon (ERAT) Ⓓ **2292-45797-2** (ERAT) ▣ **2292-45797-4**
2-4. M. Freni, L. Pavarotti, BPO, H. von Karajan (DECC) Ⓓ **421 896-2DA**
2-4. J. Barstow, A. Davies, RPO, R. Stapleton (r1991) (RPO) Ⓓ [2] **CDRPD9006** (RPO) ▣ [2] **ZCRPD9006**
2-4. Anne Dawson, D.M. Anderson, K. Latham, S. Dowson, B. Budd, English Northern Philh, P. Daniel (r1992) (EMI) Ⓓ **CDC7 54785-2**
2-4. B. Frittoli, V. Ombuena, A. Scholz, A. Anisimov, Berlin RSO, J. Märkl (r1991) (SCHW) Ⓓ [2] **312682**
2-4. Hollywood Bowl SO, Alfred Newman (r1959: arr orch) (EMI) Ⓓ **CDM5 65430-2**
2-4. M. Callas, G. di Stefano, M. Spatafora, N. Zaccaria, R. Panerai, La Scala Orch, A. Votto (10/88) (EMI) Ⓓ **CDM7 69543-2**
2-4. M. Freni, L. Pavarotti, R. Panerai, G. Maffeo, N. Ghiaurov, BPO, H. von Karajan (r1972) (12/93) (DECC) Ⓓ **433 439-2DA** (DECC) ▣ **433 439-4DA**
2, 4, 12, 13b P. Dvorský, V. Kincses, S. Halјáková, I. Konsulov, Bratislava RSO, Czech RSO, O. Lenárd (10/89) (OPUS) Ⓓ **9156 1824**
2, 4, 17a-c F.I. d'Amico, P. Dvorský, Berlin RSO, R. Paternostro (ACAN) Ⓓ **43 123**
2-4, 6a, 6b, 7b, 9, 10a, 11, 12, 16, 17a-c N. Gedda, M. Freni, M. Sereni, M. Adami, M. Basiola II, F. Mazzoli, P. Montarsolo, Rome Op Chor, Rome Op Orch, T. Schippers (EMI) Ⓓ **CDM7 63932-2**
2-4, 7a, 7b, 11, 12, 16, 17a-c R. Tebaldi, C. Bergonzi, G. d'Angelo, E. Bastianini, R. Cesari, C. Siepi, F. Corena, P. de Palma, A. d'Orazi, Santa Cecilia Academy Chor, Santa Cecilia Academy Orch, T. Serafin (r1959) (DECC) Ⓓ **436 312-2DA** (DECC) ▣ **436 312-4DA**
2-4, 7b M. Freni, E. Harwood, L. Pavarotti, M. Sénéchal, G. Maffeo, R. Panerai, N. Ghiaurov, BPO, H. von Karajan (DECC) Ⓓ **433 865-2DWO** (DECC) ▣ **433 865-4DWO**
2, 4, 7b B. Daniels, A. Réaux, J. Hadley, T. Hampson, J. Busterud, G. Beni, P. Plishka, Santa Cecilia Academy Orch, L. Bernstein (DG) Ⓓ **439 151-2GMA** (DG) ▣ **439 151-4GMA**
2-4, 7b, 9, 17a Cincinnati Pops, E. Kunzel (inst arr Beck, Bernstein, Kunzel) (TELA) Ⓓ **CD80260**
2, 7b S. McCulloch, J. Oakman, Czech PO, J. Bigg (with instr track for singing) (IMP) Ⓓ [2] **DPCD1015** (IMP) ▣ **CIMPCD1015**
2, 7b S. McCulloch, J. Oakman, Czech PO, J. Bigg (r1992) (IMP) Ⓓ **PCD1043**
3. Lotte Lehmann, Berlin St Op Orch, F. Weissmann (Ger: 1929) (PEAR) Ⓓ **GEMMCD9409**
3. R. Ponselle, orch (r1923) (PEAR) Ⓓ [2] **GEMMCDS9964**
3. M. Freni, Rome Op Orch, T. Schippers (EMIN) Ⓓ **CD-EMX9519** (EMIN) ▣ **TC-EMX2099**
3. L. Bori, orch (r1928) (PEAR) Ⓓ **GEMMCD9458**
3. I. Cotrubas, New Philh, J. Pritchard (SONY) Ⓓ **SBK46548** (SONY) ▣ **SBT46548**
3. M. Callas, BBC SO, M. Sargent (pp1959) (MEMO) Ⓓ **HR4293/4**
3. M. Chiara, Vienna Volksoper Orch, N. Santi (DECC) Ⓓ **433 624-2DSP**
3. M. Chiara, Vienna Volksoper Orch, N. Santi (DECC) Ⓓ **433 636-2DSP** (DECC) ▣ **433 636-4DSP**
3. M. Freni, L. Pavarotti, BPO, H. von Karajan (DECC) Ⓓ **433 064-2DWO**
3. I. Cotrubas, Czech SO, A. Krieger (pp1991) (IMP) Ⓓ **MCD42**
3. R. Pampanini, La Scala Orch, L. Molajoli (r1927) (MMOI) Ⓓ **CDMOIR412**
3. S. Murphy, WNO Orch, J. Smith (COLL) Ⓓ **Coll3025-2**
3. M. Callas, Philh, T. Serafin (r1954) (EMI) Ⓓ **CDC7 54702-2** (EMI) ▣ **EL754702-4**
3. L. Garrett, Philh, I. Bolton (SILV) Ⓓ **SONGCD907** (SILV) ▣ **SONGC907**
3. R. Tebaldi, C. Bergonzi, Santa Cecilia Academy Orch, T. Serafin (r1958) (DECC) Ⓓ **440 408-2DM**
3. M. Freni, Philh, G. Sinopoli (DG) Ⓓ **439 151-2GMA** (DG) ▣ **439 151-4GMA**
3. M. Caballé, LPO, G. Solti (RCA) Ⓓ **09026 61440-2** (RCA) ▣ **09026 61440-4**
3. M. Ivogün, orch (r1919: Ger) (PREI) Ⓓ **89094**
3. G. Bréjean-Silver, anon (r1905: Fr) (SYMP) Ⓓ **SYMCD1173**
3. H. Schymberg, Stockholm Royal Orch, N. Grevillius (r1946) (ALTN) Ⓓ **CDAN3**
3. C. Muzio, orch (r1921) (PEAR) Ⓓ **GEMMCD9143**
3. M. Favero, orch (r1937) (VAI) Ⓓ **VAIA1071**
3. M. Caballé, LPO, G. Solti (r1976) (RCA) Ⓓ **74321 25817-2** (RCA) ▣ **74321 25817-4**
3. L. Albanese, RCA Victor Orch, J-P. Morel (r1949) (RCA) Ⓓ **74321 24284-2** (RCA) ▣ **74321 24284-4**
3. P. Lorengar, Santa Cecilia Academy Orch, G. Patanè (r1966) (DECC) Ⓓ **443 931-2DM**
3. C. Muzio, orch, L. Molajoli (r1935) (CONI) Ⓓ **CDHD235**
3. M. Favero, orch (r1937) (BONG) Ⓓ **GB1078-2**
3. V. de los Angeles, RCA Victor Orch, T. Beecham (r1956) (EMI) Ⓓ **CDM5 65579-2**
3. L. Bori, Victor Orch, Rosario Bourdon (r1922) (ROMO) Ⓓ [2] **81016-2**
3. M. Freni, Hamburg PO, L. Magiera (11/88) (ACAN) Ⓓ **49 384**
3. M. Chiara, Vienna Volksoper Orch, N. Santi (1/89) (DECC) Ⓓ **417 686-2DC**
3. C. Muzio, orch (r1921) (5/90) (BOGR) Ⓓ [2] **BIM705-2**
3. R. Scotto, National PO, James Levine (8/90) (CFP) Ⓓ **CD-CFP4569** (8/90) (CFP) ▣ **TC-CFP4569**
3. G. Arangi-Lombardi, La Scala Orch, L. Molajoli (r1932) (10/90) (PREI) Ⓓ **89013**
3. M. Seinemeyer, Berlin St Op Orch, F. Weissmann (Ger: r1926) (11/90) (PREI) Ⓓ **89029**
3. C. Muzio, orch (r1911) (4/91) (NIMB) Ⓓ **NI7814** (4/91) (NIMB) ▣ **NC7814**
3. R. Tebaldi, C. Bergonzi, Santa Cecilia Academy Orch, T. Serafin (8/91) (DECC) Ⓓ [2] **430 481-2DX2**
3. Lotte Lehmann, orch (Ger: r1917) (6/92) (PREI) Ⓓ [3] **89302**
3. J. Cross, orch (Eng: r1935) (7/92) (PEAR) Ⓓ [3] **GEMMCDS9926(2)**
3. M. Kousnietzoff, orch (r1917) (7/92) (PEAR) Ⓓ [3] **GEMMCDS9924(2)**
3. C. Muzio, orch (r1911) (7/92) (PEAR) Ⓓ [3] **GEMMCDS9925(1)**
3. M. Gauci, Belgian Rad & TV Orch, A. Rahbari (11/92) (NAXO) Ⓓ **8 550606**
3. R. Pampanini, orch, L. Molajoli (r1928) (8/93) (PREI) Ⓓ **89063**
3. M. Freni, L. Pavarotti, BPO, H. von Karajan (r1972) (10/93) (DECC) Ⓓ **436 461-2DM**
3. C. Muzio, orch (r1911) (1/94) (ROMO) Ⓓ [2] **81005-2**
3. C. Muzio, orch (r1921) (1/94) (ROMO) Ⓓ [2] **81005-2**
3. M. Caballé, LPO, G. Solti (r1973) (4/94) (RCA) Ⓓ [6] **09026 61580-2(8)**
3. E. Rethberg, orch (r1925) (7/94) (PREI) Ⓓ **89051**
3. M. Reining, Vienna St Op Orch, R. Moralt (r1942: Ger) (9/94) (PREI) Ⓓ **89065**
3. C. Muzio, orch (r1917) (1/95) (ROMO) Ⓓ [2] **81010-2**
3. E. Rethberg, orch (r1924) (2/95) (ROMO) Ⓓ [2] **81012-2**
3. E. Steber, orch, H. Barlow (bp1949) (11/95) (VAI) Ⓓ **VAIA1072**
3, 11. E. Marton, Munich RO, G. Patanè (SONY) Ⓓ **SK48094** (SONY) ▣ **ST48094**
3, 11. M. Freni, BPO, H. von Karajan (r1972) (DECC) Ⓓ **440 412-2DM**
3, 11. M. Caballé, LSO, C. Mackerras (10/87) (EMI) Ⓓ **CDC7 47841-2**
3, 11. M. Callas, Philh, T. Serafin (r1954) (12/87) (EMI) Ⓓ **CDC7 47966-2**
3, 11. V. de los Angeles, Rome Op Orch, G. Morelli (r1954) (8/90) (EMI) Ⓓ **CDH7 63495-2**
3, 11. C. Muzio, orch, L. Molajoli (r1935) (4/91) (NIMB) Ⓓ **NI7814** (4/91) (NIMB) ▣ **NC7814**
3, 11. C. Ferrani, anon (r1902) (5/91) (SYMP) Ⓓ **SYMCD1077**
3, 11. X. Belmas, orch, A. Kitschin (r1927) (10/92) (PREI) Ⓓ **89047**
3, 11. G. Farrar, orch (r1912) (10/94) (NIMB) Ⓓ **NI7857**
3, 11. J. Varady, Berlin RSO, M. Viotti (r1993) (5/95) (ORFE) Ⓓ **C323941A**
3, 11. N. Melba, orch, W.B. Rogers (r1907) (5/95) (ROMO) Ⓓ [3] **81011-2(1)**
3, 11. N. Melba, orch, W.B. Rogers (r1910) (5/95) (ROMO) Ⓓ [3] **81011-2(1)**
3, 12. I. Galante, Latvian Nat SO, A. Vilumanis (r1994) (11/95) (CAMP) Ⓓ **RRCD1335** (11/95) (CAMP) ▣ **RRMC8035**
3, 17a-c M. Freni, G. Raimondi, La Scala Chor, La Scala Orch, H. von Karajan (pp1963) (MEMO) Ⓓ [2] **HR4277/8**
3, 4. R. Tebaldi, R. Tucker, Rome RAI Orch, A. Paoletti (pp1954) (MEMO) Ⓓ [2] **HR4235/6**
3, 4. R. Tebaldi, C. Bergonzi, R. Cesari, C. Siepi, E. Bastianini, Santa Cecilia Academy Orch, T. Serafin (r1959) (BELA) Ⓓ **450 007-2** (BELA) ▣ **450 007-4**
3, 4. M. Freni, L. Pavarotti, G. Maffeo, R. Panerai, N. Ghiaurov, BPO, H. von Karajan (r1972) (DECC) Ⓓ **440 947-2DH** (DECC) ▣ **440 947-4DH**
3, 4. L. Bori, J. McCormack, Victor Orch, W.B. Rogers (r1914) (ROMO) Ⓓ [2] **81016-2**
3, 4. M. Cebotari, M. Wittrisch, Berlin St Op Orch, F. Zweig (Ger: r c1933) (12/90) (PREI) Ⓓ **90034**
3, 7b E. Berger, Berlin City Op Orch, H. Schmidt-Isserstedt (r1940: Ger) (PREI) Ⓓ **89092**
4. M. Freni, N. Gedda, M. Sereni, Rome Op Orch, T. Schippers (CFP) Ⓓ **CD-CFP9013** (CFP) ▣ **TC-CFP4498**
4. J. Björling, A-L. Björling, orch, H. Barlow (bp1950) (VAI) ◘ **VAI69101**
4. F. Yeend, M. Lanza, Hollywood Bowl SO, E. Ormandy (pp1947) (IMP) Ⓓ **PWKS4230**
4. F. Wunderlich, A. Rothenberger, Berlin SO, B. Klobučar (Ger) (EMI) Ⓓ [3] **CZS7 62993-2**
4. R. Tebaldi, G. di Stefano, Rome RAI Orch (bp1954) (MEMO) Ⓓ **HR4372/3**
4. M. Freni, L. Pavarotti, BPO, H. von Karajan (DECC) Ⓓ **430 470-2DH** (DECC) ▣ **430 470-4DH**
4. M. Favero, A. Ziliani, orch (r1934) (MMOI) Ⓓ **CDMOIR412**
4. E. Caruso, N. Melba, orch, W.B. Rogers (r1907) (RCA) Ⓓ **09026 61243-2**
4. M. Freni, N. Gedda, M. Sereni, Rome Op Orch, T. Schippers (r1963) (CFP) Ⓓ **CD-CFP4602** (CFP) ▣ **TC-CFP4602**
4. E. Caruso, G. Farrar, orch, W.B. Rogers (r1912) (MCI) Ⓓ **MCCD086** (MCI) ▣ **MCTC086**
4. L. Pavarotti, NYC Op Orch, R. Bonynge (r1981: pp) (DECC) Ⓓ **436 472-2DM**
4. R. Tebaldi, C. Bergonzi, Santa Cecilia Academy Orch, T. Serafin (r1959) (BELA) Ⓓ **450 006-2** (BELA) ▣ **450 006-4**
4. M. Seinemeyer, T. Pattiera, orch, F. Weissmann (r1926: Ger) (PEAR) Ⓓ **GEMMCD9082**

4. H. Schymberg, J. Björling, Swedish RSO, T. Mann (bp1945) (ALTN) ① **CDAN3**
4. M. Callas, G. di Stefano, La Scala Orch, A. Votto (r1956) (EMI) ① **CDC5 55216-2** (EMI) ▭ **EL555216-4**
4. M. Freni, L. Pavarotti, Bologna Teatro Comunale Orch, L. Magiera (RCA) ① **09026 62699-2** (RCA) ▭ **09026 62699-4**
4. M. Favero, A. Ziliani, La Scala Orch, F. Ghione (r1935) (VAI) ① **VAIA1071**
4. B. Gigli, M. Caniglia, orch, W. Goehr (r1937) (PEAR) ① [2] **GEMMCDS9176**
4. M. Caniglia, B. Gigli, orch, W. Goehr (r1937) (CONI) ① **CDHD235**
4. M. Favero, A. Ziliani, La Scala Orch, F. Ghione (r1935) (BONG) ① **GB1078-2**
4. B. Gigli, M. Caniglia, orch, W. Goehr (r1937) (9/88) (EMI) ① **CDH7 61051-2**
4. J. Björling, A-L. Björling, orch, N. Grevillius (r1941) (10/88) (EMI) ① **CDH7 61053-2**
4. M. Freni, F. Bonisolli, Hamburg PO, L. Magiera (11/88) (ACAN) ① **49 384**
4. N. Melba, E. Caruso, orch, W.B. Rogers (r1907) (3/89) (LARR) ① **CDLRH221**
4. E. Caruso, N. Melba, orch (r1907) (5/89) (PEAR) ① **GEMMCD9309**
4. E. Caruso, G. Farrar, orch, W.B. Rogers (r1912) (7/90) (CLUB) ① **CL99-060**
4. M. Seinemeyer, T. Pattiera, Berlin St Op Orch, F. Weissmann (Ger: r1926) (11/90) (PREI) ① **89029**
4. N. Melba, E. Caruso, orch, W.B. Rogers (r1907) (12/90) (PEAR) ① [3] **EVC1(2)**
4. G. Farrar, E. Caruso, orch, W.B. Rogers (r1912) (7/91) (RCA) ① [12] **GD60495(4)**
4. N. Melba, E. Caruso, orch, W.B. Rogers (r1907) (7/91) (RCA) ① [12] **GD60495(2)**
4. G. Farrar, E. Caruso, orch, W.B. Rogers (r1912) (10/91) (PEAR) ① [3] **EVC3(1)**
4. F. Hempel, H. Jadlowker, orch (Ger: r1900s) (12/91) (CLUB) ① **CL99-042**
4. N. Melba, E. Caruso, orch (r1907) (7/92) (PEAR) ① [3] **GEMMCDS9924(1)**
4. J. Björling, H. Schymberg, orch, N. Grevillius (r1941) (10/93) (NIMB) ① **NI7842**
4. J. Björling, A-L. Björling, Stockholm Concert Soc Orch, N. Grevillius (r1949) (10/93) (EMI) ① **CDH7 64707-2**
4. M. Cebotari, M. Wittrisch, Berlin St Op Orch, F. Zweig (r1932: Ger) (10/93) (NIMB) ① **NI7848**
4. G. Zenatello, A. Verlet, orch (r1916) (5/94) (PEAR) ① [4] **GEMMCDS9074(2)**
4. G. Farrar, E. Caruso, orch (r1912) (10/94) (NIMB) ① **NI7857**
4. N. Melba, E. Caruso, orch, W.B. Rogers (r1907) (5/95) (ROMO) ① [3] **81011-2(1)**
4. E. Caruso, N. Melba, orch (r1907) (7/95) (NIMB) ① **NI7866**
4. M. Freni, L. Pavarotti, Modena Teatro Comunale Orch, L. Magiera (pp1967) (10/95) (RCA) ① **09026 62541-2**
4. A. Davies, S. Bullock, A. Bryn Parri (r1994) (11/95) (SAIN) ① **SCDC2085**
4, 12, 13a, 13b L. Pavarotti, M. Freni, S. Bruscantini, R. Talarico, Rome RAI Orch, T. Schippers (pp1969) (BUTT) ① **BMCD015** (BUTT) ▭ **BMK015**
4, 17a A. Piccaver, M. Angerer, Berlin St Op Orch, M. Gurlitt (r1929) (PREI) ① [2] **89217**
4, 17a H. von Debička, H. Roswaenge, orch (r1929: Ger) (2/92) (PREI) ① [2] **89201**
4, 17a-c H. von Debička, H. Roswaenge, Berlin St Op Orch, M. Gurlitt (Ger: r1929) (5/90) (PEAR) ① **GEMMCD9394**
5, 6a, 6b, 7a, 7b I. Cotrubas, T. Allen, G. Howell, J. Rawnsley, ROHO, L. Gardelli (TELD) ● **9031-77676-6** (TELD) ▣ **9031-77676-3**
6b, 17a G. Zenatello, L. Cannetti, orch (r1911) (5/94) (SYMP) ① **SYMCD1158**
6b, 17a, 17b G. Zenatello, L. Cannetti, orch (r1911) (5/94) (PEAR) ① [4] **GEMMCDS9073(2)**
7b I. Cotrubas, M. Zschau, N. Shicoff, T. Allen, J. Rawnsley, G. Howell, ROHO, L. Gardelli (CAST) ▣ **CVI2065**
7b A. Moffo, Orch, H. Barlow (bp1958) (VAI) ▣ **VAI69114**
7b K. Te Kanawa, LPO, J. Pritchard (SONY) ① **SBK46548** (SONY) ▭ **SBT46548**
7b V. Zeani, Santa Cecilia Academy Orch, F. Patanè (DECC) ① **433 636-2DSP** (DECC) ▭ **433 636-4DSP**
7b E. Harwood, M. Freni, R. Panerai, M. Sénéchal, BPO, H. von Karajan (DECC) ① **433 068-2DWO** (DECC) ▭ **433 068-4DWO**
7b L. Schöne, Berlin St Op Orch, L. Blech (r1929) (MMOI) ① **CDMOIR412**
7b K. Te Kanawa, LPO, J. Pritchard (SONY) ① **SK48094** (SONY) ▭ **ST48094**
7b S. McCulloch, Czech SO, J. Bigg (IMP) ① [3] **TCD1070**
7b L. Bori, orch (r1927) (PEAR) ① **GEMMCD9130**
7b C. Muzio, orch (r1918) (PEAR) ① **GEMMCD9143**
7b Capitol SO, C. Dragon (r1958: arr Dragon) (EMI) ① **CDM5 65430-2**
7b L. Bori, orch, Rosario Bourdon (r1927) (CONI) ① **CDHD235**
7b L. Bori, Victor Orch, N. Shilkret (r1923) (ROMO) ① [2] **81016-2**
7b K. Te Kanawa, LPO, J. Pritchard (5/85) (CBS) ① **MK37298** (CBS) ▭ **40-37298**
7b V. Zeani, Santa Cecilia Academy Orch, F. Patanè (1/89) (DECC) ① **417 686-2DC**
7b C. Supervia, orch, G. Cloëz (r1931: Fr) (9/90) (CLUB) ① **CL99-074**
7b L. Garrett, Philh, A. Greenwood (r1990-1) (11/91) (SILV) ① **SONGCD903** (11/91) (SILV) ▭ **SONGC903**
7b E. Berger, Berlin St Op Orch, A. Melichar (Ger: r1934) (12/91) (PREI) ① **89035**
7b R. Tebaldi, New Philh, R. Bonynge (r1969) (10/93) (DECC) ① **436 301-2DA**
7b E. Destinn, orch (r1912: 2 vers) (12/94) (SUPR) ① [12] **11 2136-2(5)**
7b C. Muzio, orch (r1918) (1/95) (ROMO) ① [2] **81010-2**
7b, 11. M. Adani, M. Freni, Rome Op Orch, T. Schippers (EMI) ① **CDM7 69596-2**
9. L. Albanese, A. Poli, La Scala Orch, U. Berrettoni (r1938) (4/94) (EMI) ① [3] **CHS7 64864-2(2)**
9. G. Farrar, A. Scotti, orch (r1909) (10/94) (NIMB) ① **NI7857**
9(pt), 11. N. Melba, J. Brownlee, orch, V. Bellezza (pp1926) (7/92) (PEAR) ① [3] **GEMMCDS9925(2)**
10b J. Schmidt, Berlin SO, F. Weissmann (Ger: r1932) (4/90) (EMI) ① **CDM7 69478-2**
10b A. Cortis, orch (r1925) (3/94) (NIMB) ① **NI7850**
11. J. Sutherland, Orch, R. Bonynge (VAI) ▣ **VAI69108**
11. R. Tebaldi, orch (bp1959) (VAI) ▣ **VAI69100**
11. C. Muzio, orch, L. Molajoli (r1935) (MMOI) ① **CDMOIR412**
11. I. Tokody, orch, Anon (cond) (pp1991/2) (VAI) ① **VAIA1009**
11. M. Callas, Philh, T. Serafin (r1954) (EMI) ① **CDC5 55016-2**
11. M. Favero, orch (r c1929) (VAI) ① **VAIA1071**
11. C. Muzio, orch, L. Molajoli (r1935) (CONI) ① **CDHD235**
11. M. Caballé, LSO, C. Mackerras (r1970) (EMI) ① **CDM5 65575-2**
11. A. Gheorghiu, ROHO, E. Downes (r1995) (ROH) ① **75605 55013-2** (ROH) ▭ **75605 55013-4**
11. L. Bori, Victor Orch, N. Shilkret (r1925) (ROMO) ① [2] **81016-2**
11. N. Melba, orch, W.B. Rogers (r1910) (10/89) (NIMB) ① **NI7802** (NIMB) ▭ **NC7802**
11. H. Spani, La Scala Orch, C. Sabajno (r1927) (9/90) (CLUB) ① [2] **CL99-509/10**
11. D. Labbette, LPO, T. Beecham (r1936) (9/91) (PEAR) ① **GEMMCD9473**
11. S. Scuderi, LSO, A. Erede (r1948) (4/92) (EMI) ① [7] **CHS7 69741-2(7)**
11. G. Moore, orch (r c1934) (7/92) (PEAR) ① [3] **GEMMCDS9926(2)**
11. H. Spani, La Scala Orch, C. Sabajno (r1927) (12/92) (PREI) ① **89037**
11. J. Hammond, Hallé, L. Heward (r1941: Eng) (12/92) (TEST) ① **SBT1013**
11. I. Bohuss, anon (r1902: Pol) (6/93) (PEAR) ① [3] **GEMMCDS9004/6(1)**
11. E. Carelli, S. Cottone (r1904) (8/93) (SYMP) ① **SYMCD1111**
11. N. Melba, orch, W.B. Rogers (r1910) (9/93) (RCA) ① **09026 61412-2**
11. E. Carelli, anon (r1905) (4/94) (EMI) ① [3] **CHS7 64860-2(1)**
11. N. Melba, orch, W.B. Rogers (r1909) (5/95) (ROMO) ① [3] **81011-2(1)**
11, 17a M. Favero, orch (r c1929) (BONG) ① **GB1078-2**
12. L. Bori, orch (r1925) (PEAR) ① **GEMMCD9458**
12. G. Farrar, G. Ciaparelli-Viafora, E. Caruso, A. Scotti, orch, W.B. Rogers (r1908) (NIMB) ① **NI7834** (NIMB) ▭ **NC7834**
12. E. Caruso, G. Farrar, G. Ciaparelli-Viafora, A. Scotti, orch, W.B. Rogers (r1908) (RCA) ① **09026 61243-2**
12(pt) M. Ivogün, K. Erb, orch (r1917: Ger) (PREI) ① **89094**
12. G. Farrar, G. Ciaparelli-Viafora, E. Caruso, A. Scotti, orch, W.B. Rogers (r1908) (12/90) (PEAR) ① [3] **EVC1(2)**
12. G. Farrar, G. Ciaparelli-Viafora, E. Caruso, A. Scotti, orch, W.B. Rogers (r1908) (7/91) (RCA) ① [12] **GD60495(2)**
12. F. Hüni-Mihacsek, T. de Garmo, H. Roswaenge, T. Scheidl, orch (r1928: Ger) (2/92) (PREI) ① [2] **89201**
12. M. Camporelli, A. Stehle, E. Garbin, M. Sammarco, anon (r1905) (12/93) (SYMP) ① **SYMCD1113**
12. P. Tassinari, M. Huder, Ferruccio Tagliavini, E. Mascherini, EIAR Orch, U. Tansini (r1943) (3/94) (CENT) ① **CRC2164**
12. G. Farrar, E. Caruso, A. Scotti, G. Ciaparelli-Viafora, orch (r1908) (10/94) (NIMB) ① **NI7857**
13a, 13b B. Gigli, G. De Luca, orch (r1927) (CONI) ① **CDHD149** (CONI) ▭ **MCHD149**
13a, 13b C. Bergonzi, D. Fischer-Dieskau, BRSO, J. López-Cobos (ORFE) ① **C028821A**
13a, 13b F. Wunderlich, M. Cordes, Berlin SO, B. Klobučar (Ger) (EMI) ① [3] **CZS7 62993-2**
13a, 13b F. Wunderlich, H. Prey, Munich RO, K. Eichhorn (Ger: bp) (DG) ① [5] **435 145-2GX5(1)**
13a, 13b B. Gigli, G. De Luca, orch, Rosario Bourdon (r1927) (MMOI) ① **CDMOIR412**
13a, 13b L. Pavarotti, R. Panerai, BPO, H. von Karajan (DECC) ① **421 896-2DA**
13a, 13b B. Gigli, G. De Luca, orch (r1927) (IMP) ① **GLRS102**
13a, 13b P. Domingo, S. Milnes, LSO, A. Guadagno (RCA) ① **09026 62699-2** (RCA) ▭ **09026 62699-4**
13a, 13b B. Gigli, G. De Luca, orch (r1927) (PEAR) ① [3] **GEMMCDS9160(2)**
13a, 13b J. Hislop, A. Granforte, orch, G. W. Byng (r1926) (CONI) ① **CDHD235**
13a, 13b P. Domingo, S. Milnes, LSO, A. Guadagno (r1970) (RCA) ① **09026 62595-2**
13a, 13b D. Fischer-Dieskau, R. Schock, Berlin SO, W. Schüchter (r1954: Ger) (EMI) ① [2] **CMS5 65621-2**
13a, 13b B. Gigli, G. De Luca, orch, Rosario Bourdon (r1927) (9/88) (PEAR) ① **GEMMCD9316**
13a, 13b J. Björling, R. Merrill, RCA Victor SO, R. Cellini (2/89) (RCA) ① **GD87799** (RCA) ▭ **GK87799**
13a, 13b P. Domingo, T. Allen, ROHO, J. Barker (pp1988) (9/89) (EMI) ① **CDC7 49811-2**
13a, 13b J. Hislop, A. Granforte, orch, G.W. Byng (r1926) (1/93) (PEAR) ① **GEMMCD9956**
13b E. Caruso, A. Scotti, orch (r1907) (RCA) ① **09026 61243-2**
13b H. Roswaenge, G. Hüsch, Berlin St Op Orch, B. Seidler-Winkler (r1937: Ger) (PREI) ① [2] **89211**
13b J. Carreras, G. Quilico, French Rad Chor, FNO, J. Conlon (ERAT) ① **4509-91715-2** (ERAT) ▭ **4509-91715-4**
13b T. Hampson, J. Hadley, WNO Orch, C. Rizzi (r1992) (TELD) ① **4509-98824-2**
13b T. Hampson, J. Hadley, WNO Orch, C. Rizzi (r c1989-94) (TELD) ① **4509-97463-2**
13b H. Schlusnus, R. Hutt, orch (r1921: Ger) (PREI) ① **89110**
13b E. Caruso, A. Scotti, orch (r1907) (5/89) (PEAR) ① **GEMMCD9309**
13b H. Nash, D. Noble, orch (Eng: r1930) (8/89) (PEAR) ① **GEMMCD9319**
13b H. Roswaenge, G. Hüsch, Berlin St Op Orch, B. Seidler-Winkler (Ger: r1937) (5/90) (PEAR) ① **GEMMCD9394**
13b E. Caruso, A. Scotti, orch (r1907) (12/90) (PEAR) ① [3] **EVC1(2)**

13b D. Borgioli, G. Vanelli, orch (r1927)
(12/90) (CLUB) Ⓓ **CL99-014**
13b E. Caruso, A. Scotti, orch (r1907)
(7/91) (RCA) Ⓓ [12] **GD60495(2)**
13b T. Ruffo, B. Gigli, orch (r1926)
(2/93) (PREI) Ⓓ [3] **89303(2)**
13b F. Wunderlich, H. Prey, Munich RO, K. Eichhorn (Ger) (5/93) (DG) Ⓓ **431 110-2GB**
13b J. Hadley, T. Hampson, WNO Orch, C. Rizzi (r1992) (11/93) (TELD) Ⓓ **9031-73283-2**
13b G. De Luca, B. Gigli, orch, Rosario Bourdon (r1927) (10/94) (PREI) Ⓓ **89073**
16. Vanni-Marcoux, orch, P. Coppola (r1927)
(PEAR) Ⓓ **GEMMCD9122**
16. E. Pinza, orch, Rosario Bourdon (r1927)
(CONI) Ⓓ **CDHD235**
16. E. Pinza, NY Met Op Orch, F. Cleva (r1946)
(4/90) (CBS) Ⓓ **CD45693**
16. E. Caruso, orch, W.B. Rogers (r1916)
(7/90) (CLUB) Ⓓ **CL99-060**
16. E. Caruso, orch, W.B. Rogers (r1916)
(7/91) (RCA) Ⓓ [12] **GD60495(5)**
16. E. Pinza, orch, Rosario Bourdon (r1927)
(7/91) (MMOI) Ⓓ **CDMOIR404**
(MMOI) ⊟ **CMOIR404**
16. E. Caruso, orch (r1916)
(7/91) (MSCM) Ⓓ **MM30352**
16. E. Caruso, orch, W.B. Rogers (r1916)
(10/91) (PEAR) Ⓓ [3] **EVC3(2)**
16. E. Pinza, orch, Rosario Bourdon (r1927)
(3/92) (PREI) Ⓓ **89050**
16. M. Journet, orch (r1912)
(7/92) (PEAR) Ⓓ [3] **GEMMCDS9923(2)**
16. M. Salminen, Lahti SO, E. Klas
(8/92) (BIS) Ⓓ **BIS-CD520**
16. J. Van Dam, Loire PO, M. Soustrot (r1992)
(8/93) (FORL) Ⓓ **UCD16681**
16. E. Pinza, orch, Rosario Bourdon (r1927)
(9/93) (RCA) Ⓓ **09026 61245-2**
16. M. Journet, orch (r1912)
(4/94) (RCA) Ⓓ [6] **09026 61580-2(1)**
16. O. Luppi, orch, E. Vitale (r1909)
(4/94) (EMI) Ⓓ [3] **CHS7 64860-2(2)**
16. E. Caruso, orch (r1916)
(7/95) (NIMB) Ⓓ **NI7866**
17a T. Schipa, L. Bori, orch (r1925)
(PEAR) Ⓓ **GEMMCD9364**
17a-c L. Bori, T. Schipa, orch (r1925)
(PEAR) Ⓓ **GEMMCD9458**
17a-c L. Bori, T. Schipa, orch, Rosario Bourdon (r1925) (CONI) Ⓓ **CDHD235**
17a-c D. Labbette, H. Nash, S. Andreva, J. Brownlee, R. Alva, R. Easton, orch, T. Beecham (r1935) (7/92) (PEAR) Ⓓ [3] **GEMMCDS9926(2)**
17a, 17c L. Bori, T. Schipa, Victor Orch, Rosario Bourdon (r1925) (ROMO) Ⓓ [2] **81016-2**

Edgar– opera: 4 acts (1889—Milan) (Lib. Fontana, after de Musset)
EXCERPTS: 1. Prelude. ACT 1: 2. Qual voce lontano; 3. O fior del giorno; 4. Già il mandorlo; 5. Ah! Ah! Ah! Tu qui?; 6. Ove fosti stanotte?; 7. Questo amor, vergogna mia; 8. Tu il cuor mi strazi; 9. Che fu?; 10. T'arresta!; 11. Or dunque, addio! ACT 2: 12. Splendida notte, notte gioconda; 13. Orgia, chimera dall'occhio vitreo; 14. Edgar...Edgar... 15. Urrà! Uno squillo marzial!; 16. Prelude. ACT 3: 17. Requiem aeternam!; 18. Addio, addio, mio dolce amor!; 19. Del prode Edgar; 20. V'è alcun fra voi; 21. D'ogni dolor; 22. Voglio passar!; 23. Bella Signora; 24. All'armi! All'armi!; 25. È ver!.

Fidelia	R. Scotto
Edgar	C. Bergonzi
Tigrana	G. Killebrew
Frank	V. Sardinero
Gualtiero	M. Munkittrick

NY Schola Cantorum, NY City Op Children's Chor, NY Op Orch, E. Queler (pp1977)
(10/89) (CBS) Ⓓ [2] **CD79213**
1, 16. Berlin RSO, R. Chailly (r1982)
(DECC) Ⓓ **444 154-2DM**
18. N. Rautio, ROHO, E. Downes (r1995)
(ROH) Ⓓ **75605 55013-2**
(ROH) ⊟ **75605 55013-4**
21. R. Scotto, I. Davis (pp1983)
(10/86) (ETCE) Ⓓ **KTC2002**
(ETCE) ⊟ **XTC2002**

La Fanciulla del West, '(The) Girl of the Golden West'– opera: 3 acts, Lib. Civinni and Zangarini (1910—New York)
ACT 1: 1. Che faranno i vecchi miei; 2. Jim, perchè piangi?; 3a. Dove eravamo?; 3b. Lavami e sarò bianco; 4a. Ti voglio bene, Minnie; 4b. Minnie, dalla mia casa; 5. Laggiù nel Soledad; 6a. Mister Johnson siete rimasto; 6b. Non so, non so. ACT 2: 7. Oh, se sapeste; 8a. Sì! Tanto!; 8b. Perchè questa parola?; 9a. Una parola sola!; 9b. Sono Ramerrez; 9c. Or son sei mesi; 10. Che c'è di nuovo, Jack?; 11. Siete pronto?. ACT 3: 12. Ch'ella mi creda libero; 13a. Ah!...Ah!; 13b. Non vi fu mai chi disse.

Minnie	C. Neblett
Dick Johnson	P. Domingo
Jack Rance	S. Carroli
Nick	F. Egerton
Ashby	R. Lloyd
Jake Wallace	G. Howell
Billy Jackrabbit	P. Hudson
Wowkle	A. Wilkens
Sonora	J. Summers
Trin	J. Dobson
Sid	M. Rivers
Bello	T. McDonnell
Harry	P. Crook
Joe	R. Leggate
Happy	W. Elvin
Jim Larkens	M. King
José Castro	E. Garrett
Postillion	H. Owen

ROH Chor, ROHO, N. Santi, P. Faggioni
(CAST) ▣ **CVI2020**

Minnie	C. Neblett
Dick Johnson	P. Domingo
Jack Rance	S. Milnes
Nick	F. Egerton
Ashby	R. Lloyd
Jake Wallace	G. Howell
Billy Jackrabbit	P. Hudson
Wowkle	A. Wilkens
Sonora	J. Summers
Trin	J. Dobson
Sid	M. Rivers
Bello	T. McDonnell
Harry	P. Crook
Joe	R. Leggate
Happy	W. Elvin
Jim Larkens	M. King
José Castro	E. Garrett
Postillion	H. Owen

ROH Chor, ROHO, Z. Mehta
(11/87) (DG) Ⓓ [2] **419 640-2GH2**

Minnie	B. Nilsson
Dick Johnson	J. Gibin
Jack Rance	A. Mongelli
Nick	R. Ercolani
Ashby	A. Cassinelli
Jake Wallace	N. Zaccaria
Billy Jackrabbit; José Castro	C. Forti
Wowkle	G. Carturan
Sonora	E. Sordello
Trin	F. Andreolli
Sid	G. Costariol
Bello	D. Mantovani
Harry	D. Formichini
Joe	A. Costantino
Happy	L. Monreale
Jim Larkens	G. Morresi
Postillion	A. Mercuriali

La Scala Chor, La Scala Orch, L. von Matačić
(4/92) (EMI) Ⓓ [2] **CMS7 63970-2**

Minnie	M. Zampieri
Dick Johnson	P. Domingo
Jack Rance	J. Pons
Nick	S. Bertocchi
Ashby	L. Roni
Jake Wallace	M. Chingari
Billy Jackrabbit	A. Bramante
Wowkle	N. Verri
Sonora	A. Salvadori
Trin	E. Gavazzi
Sid	G. Savoiardo
Bello	O. Mori
Harry	F. Memeo
Joe	A. Bottion
Happy	E. Panariello
Jim Larkens	P. Spagnoli
José Castro	C. Giombi
Postillion	U. Scalavino

La Scala Chor, La Scala Orch, L. Maazel (pp1991)
(6/92) (SONY) Ⓓ [2] **S2K47189**

Minnie	E. Marton
Dick Johnson	D. O'Neill
Jack Vance	A. Fondary
Nick	W. Planté
Ashby	J-H. Rootering
Jake Wallace	B. Montgomery
Billy Jackrabbit	F. Hawlata
José Castro	H. Berger-Tuna
Wowkle	C. Wulkopf
Sonora	J-M. Ivaldi
Trin	R. Swensen
Sid	D. Serraiocco
Bello	M. Cooke
Harry	J. Vacik
Joe	H. Weber
Happy	L. Baumann
Larkens	R. Scholze
Postillion	R. Kandblinder

Bavarian Rad Chor, Munich RSO, L. Slatkin
(11/92) (RCA) Ⓓ [2] **09026 60597-2**

Minnie	G. Jones
Dick Johnson	C. Murgu
Jack Rance	C. Otelli
Nick	V. Ombuena
Ashby	F. E. D'Artegna
Jake Wallace	M. Pertusi
Billy Jackrabbit	E. Turco
Wowkle	G. Pasino
Sonora	G. de Angelis
Trin	P. Lefebvre
Sid	O. Mori
Bello	M. Taghadossi
Harry	C. Bosi
Joe	F. Montagud
Happy	A. Stragapede
Jim Larkens	D. Serraiocco
Postillion	F. Memeo

Hungarian Rad Chor, Frankfurt RSO, M. Viotti (r1992)
(1/94) (SINE) Ⓓ [2] **39820212**

Minnie	B. Daniels
Dick Johnson	P. Domingo
Jack Rance	S. Milnes
Nick	A. Laciura
Ashby	J. Robbins
Jake Wallace	Y. Yannissis
Billy Jackrabbit	H.J. Tian
Wowkle	S. Kelly
Sonora	K. Josephson
Trin	C. Anthony
Sid	J. Courtney
Bello	R. Vernon
Harry	B. Fitch
Joe	M. Forest
Happy	K. Short
Jim Larkens	D. Croft
José Castro	V. Hartman
Pony Express rider	Michael Best

NY Met Op Chor, NY Met Op Orch, L. Slatkin, G. del Monaco, B. Large (r1992)
(4/94) (DG) ◐ [2] **072 433-1GH2**
(4/94) (DG) ▣ **072 433-3GH**
Excs P. Domingo, C. Neblett, ROHO, N. Santi
(CAST) ▣ **CVI2070**
Excs P. Domingo (CAST) ▣ **CVI2021**
1, 3a, 4b, 5, 6a, 7, 10, 12, 13b C. Neblett, P. Domingo, S. Milnes, F. Egerton, J. Summers, J. Dobson, M. Rivers, T. McDonnell, P. Crook, R. Leggate, W. Elvin, M. King, A. Wilkens, G. Howell, ROH Chor, ROHO, Z. Mehta (r1977)
(DG) Ⓓ **445 465-2GMH**
4a, 10. T. Gobbi, La Scala Orch, A. Votto (pp1956) (MEMO) Ⓓ [2] **HR4376/7**
4b S. Milnes, LPO, S. Varviso (r1973)
(DECC) Ⓓ **436 317-2DA**
(DECC) ⊟ **436 317-4DA**
4b T. Gobbi, Rome Op Orch, O. de Fabritiis (r1955) (10/89) (EMI) Ⓓ **CDM7 63109-2**
4b T. Gobbi, La Scala Orch, U. Berrettoni (r1942) (8/93) (TEST) Ⓓ **SBT1019**
5. R. Tebaldi, Santa Cecilia Academy Orch, F. Capuana (r1958) (DECC) Ⓓ **440 408-2DM**
5. G. Cigna, orch, L. Molajoli (r1932)
(11/90) (PREI) Ⓓ **89016**
5. G. Cigna, orch, L. Molajoli (r1932)
(11/90) (LYRC) Ⓓ **SRO805**
5. E. Burzio, orch (r1913)
(1/91) (CLUB) Ⓓ [2] **CL99-587/8**
5. T. Poli-Randaccio, orch (r1922)
(4/94) (EMI) Ⓓ [3] **CHS7 64860-2(2)**
8a(pt), 8b P. Domingo, C. Neblett, A. Wilkens, ROHO, Z. Mehta (r1977)
(6/94) (BELA) Ⓓ **450 121-2**
(6/94) (BELA) ⊟ **450 121-4**
9a-c, 12. G. di Stefano, La Scala Orch, A. Votto (r1955) (EMI) Ⓓ **CDM7 63105-2**
9b, 12. G. Zenatello, orch (r1911)
(5/94) (SYMP) Ⓓ **SYMCD1158**
9c G. Martinelli, anon (r1962)
(11/92) (MEMO) Ⓓ [2] **HR4408/9(2)**
9c G. Zenatello, orch (r1911)
(5/94) (PEAR) Ⓓ [4] **GEMMCDS9074(1)**
9c, 12. J. Schmidt, Berlin City Op Orch, F. Weissmann (Ger: r1933)
(EMI) Ⓓ [2] **CHS7 64673-2**

10. R. Tebaldi, F. Corelli, Rome RAI Orch, A. Basile (pp1961) (MEMO) Ⓓ [2] **HR4235/6**
10. E. Johnson, orch, J. Pasternack (r1919) (4/94) (RCA) Ⓓ [6] **09026 61580-2(3)**
12. P. Domingo, ROHO, N. Santi (CAST) ▣ **CASH5051**
12. P. Domingo, ROHO, Z. Mehta (DG) ⊟ **419 091-4GW**
12. P. Domingo, Orch (EDL) Ⓓ **EDL2562-2** (EDL) ⊙ **EDL2562-1** ⊟ **EDL2562-4**
12. L. Pavarotti, National PO, O. de Fabritiis (DECC) Ⓓ **430 470-2DH** (DECC) ⊟ **430 470-4DH**
12. B. Prevedi, ROHO, E. Downes (DECC) Ⓓ **433 623-2DSP** (DECC) ⊟ **433 623-4DSP**
12. J. Björling, MMF Orch, A. Erede (DECC) Ⓓ **433 636-2DSP** (DECC) ⊟ **433 636-4DSP**
12. J. Björling, MMF Orch, A. Erede (DECC) Ⓓ **433 069-2DWO** (DECC) ⊟ **433 069-4DWO**
12. H. Roswaenge, Philh Hungarica, Z. Rozsnyai (pp1959) (PREI) Ⓓ **90103**
12. J. Björling, orch, N. Grevillius (r1937) (MMOI) Ⓓ **CDMOIR412**
12. J. Björling, orch, N. Grevillius (r1935: Swed) (NIMB) Ⓓ **NI7835**
12. T. Harper, Bratislava RSO, M. Halász (NAXO) Ⓓ **8 550497**
12. P. Domingo, LSO, N. Santi (r1971) (RCA) Ⓓ **09026 61356-2** (RCA) ⊟ **09026 61356-4**
12. B. Prevedi, ROHO, E. Downes (DECC) Ⓓ **433 865-2DWO** (DECC) ⊟ **433 865-4DWO**
12. V. Scuderi, Verona Arena Orch, A. Guadagno (pp1992) (MCI) Ⓓ **MCCD099**
12. L. Pavarotti, National PO, R. Chailly (r1979) (DECC) Ⓓ **440 400-2DM**
12. M. del Monaco, Santa Cecilia Academy Orch, F. Capuana (r1958) (DECC) Ⓓ **440 407-2DM**
12. B. Prevedi, ROHO, E. Downes (r1964) (BELA) Ⓓ **450 005-2** (BELA) ⊟ **450 005-4**
12. B. Prevedi, ROHO, E. Downes (r1964) (BELA) Ⓓ **450 007-2** (BELA) ⊟ **450 007-4**
12. J. Björling, Stockholm Royal Op Orch, N. Grevillius (r1937) (PEAR) Ⓓ **GEMMCD9043**
12. L. Pavarotti, National PO, O. de Fabritiis (r1979) (DECC) Ⓓ **436 317-2DA** (DECC) ⊟ **436 317-4DA**
12. A. Bonci, orch (r1913?) (PEAR) Ⓓ **GEMMCD9168**
12. A. Piccaver, Berlin St Op Orch, M. Gurlitt (r1928) (PREI) Ⓓ [2] **89217**
12. A. Valente, La Scala Orch, G. Nastrucci (r1928) (CONI) Ⓓ **CDHD235**
12. J. Botha, ROHO, E. Downes (r1995) (ROH) Ⓓ **75605 55013-2** (ROH) ⊟ **75605 55013-4**
12. J. Björling, MMF Orch, A. Erede (r1959) (DECC) Ⓓ [2] **444 555-2DF2**
12. J. Björling, orch, N. Grevillius (r1937) (10/88) (EMI) Ⓓ **CDH7 61053-2**
12. J. Björling, MMF Orch, A. Erede (1/89) (DECC) Ⓓ **417 686-2DC**
12. P. Domingo, ROHO, J. Barker (pp1988) (9/89) (EMI) Ⓓ **CDC7 49811-2**
12. J. Patzak, Berlin St Op Orch (Ger: r1931) (3/90) (PEAR) Ⓓ **GEMMCD9383**
12. J. Schmidt, Berlin St Op Orch, F. Weissmann (Ger: r1933) (4/90) (EMI) Ⓓ **CDM7 69478-2**
12. L. Pavarotti, National PO, O. de Fabritiis (7/90) (DECC) Ⓓ [2] **425 681-2DM2** (7/90) (DECC) ⊟ [2] **425 681-4DM2**
12. G. Campora, Rome Op Orch, G. Santini (8/90) (CFP) Ⓓ **CD-CFP4569** (8/90) (CFP) ⊟ **TC-CFP4569**
12. I. Calleja, orch (Eng: r1914) (11/92) (MEMO) Ⓓ [2] **HR4408/9(2)**
12. P. Domingo, ROHO, Z. Mehta (5/93) (DG) Ⓓ **431 104-2GB**
12. G. Lauri-Volpi, SO, M. Cordone (r1942) (7/93) (NIMB) Ⓓ **NI7845**
12. A. Piccaver, orch (r1914: Ger) (8/93) (PREI) Ⓓ **89060**
12. J. Björling, orch, N. Grevillius (r1937) (10/93) (NIMB) Ⓓ **NI7842**
12. G. Zenatello, orch (r1911) (5/94) (PEAR) Ⓓ [4] **GEMMCDS9073(2)**
12. P. Domingo, ROHO, J. Barker (pp1988) (6/94) (EMI) Ⓓ **CDC5 55017-2**
12. J. Björling, orch, N. Grevillius (r1937) (9/94) (IMP) Ⓓ **GLRS103**
12. J. Björling, orch, N. Grevillius (r1937) (9/94) (CONI) Ⓓ **CDHD214** (9/94) (CONI) ⊟ **MCHD214**
12. T. Ralf, Saxon St Orch, K. Böhm (r1941: Ger) (10/94) (PREI) Ⓓ **89077**
12(pt) A. Giorgini, orch (r1924) (4/95) (RECO) Ⓓ **TRC3**
12. A. Piccaver, Vienna St Op Orch, H. Duhan (pp1937: Ger) (6/95) (SCHW) Ⓓ [2] **314632**
12. J. Björling, MMF Orch, A. Erede (r1959) (10/95) (DECC) Ⓓ **443 930-2DM**
12. B. Heppner, Munich RO, R. Abbado (r1993/4) (11/95) (RCA) Ⓓ **09026 62504-2**

Gianni Schicchi– opera: 1 act (1918—New York) (Lib. Adami)
1. Firenze è come un albero fiorito; 2. O mio babbino caro; 3. Lauretta mia.

Gianni Schicchi J. Pons
Lauretta C. Gasdia
Rinuccio Y. Marusin
La Scala Chor, La Scala Orch, G. Gavazzeni, S. Bussotti (CAST) ▣ **CVI2057**

Gianni Schicchi G. Taddei
Lauretta G. Rapisardi
Rinuccio G. Savio
Zita A. Dubbini
Gherardo G. del Signore
Nella R. Ferrari
Betto di Signa P.L. Latinucci
Simone F. Corena
Marco A. Albertini
La Ciesca L. Avogadro
Spinelloccio; Notary F. Calabrese
Turin RAI Orch, A. Simonetto (bp1949) (PREI) Ⓓ **90074**

Gianni Schicchi R. Capecchi
Lauretta B. Rizzoli
Rinuccio A. Lazzari
Zita V. Palombini
Gherardo P. de Palma
Nella O. Rovero
Gherardino N. Tarallo
Betto di Signa P. Clabassi
Simone G. Modesti
Marco A. La Porta
La Ciesca M. Minetto
Spinelloccio F. Mazzoli
Pinellino G. Onesti
Guccio G. Gaudioso
Naples San Carlo Op Chor, Naples San Carlo Op Orch, F. Molinari-Pradelli (r1956) (PHIL) Ⓓ [2] **442 106-2PM2**

Gianni Schicchi T. Gobbi
Lauretta I. Cotrubas
Rinuccio P. Domingo
Zita A. di Stasio
Gherardo F. Andreolli
Nella S. Fortunato
Gherardino A. Domingo
Betto di Signa A. Mariotti
Simone G. Luccardi
Marco C. del Bosco
La Ciesca S. Malagù
LSO, L. Maazel (11/88) (CBS) Ⓓ [3] **CD79312**

Gianni Schicchi R. Panerai
Lauretta H. Donath
Rinuccio P. Seiffert
Zita W. Baniewicz
Gherardo T. Pane
Nella V. Errante
Gherardino C. Kunz
Betto di Signa G. Auer
Simone F. Federici
Marco R. Riener
La Ciesca M. Georg
Bavarian Rad Chor, Munich RO, G. Patanè (4/90) (EURO) Ⓓ [3] **GD69043**

Gianni Schicci F. Corena
Lauretta R. Tebaldi
Rinuccio A. Lazzari
Zita L. Danieli
Gherardo R. Ercolani
Nella D. Carral
Gherardino A. di Ninno
Betto di Signa G. Foiani
Simone P. Washington
Marco S. Maionica
La Ciesca M.T. Pace
MMF Chor, MMF Orch, L. Gardelli (2/91) (DECC) Ⓓ [3] **411 665-2DM3**

Gianni Schicchi T. Gobbi
Lauretta V. de los Angeles
Rinuccio C. del Monte
Zita A.M. Canal
Gherardo A. Zagonara
Nella L. Marimpietr
Gherardino C. Cornold
Betto di Signa S. Melett
Simone P. Montarsolo
Marco F. Valentin
La Ciesca G. Raymond
Rome Op Orch, G. Santini (r1958) (6/93) (EMI) Ⓓ [3] **CMS7 64165-2**

Gianni Schicchi E. Tumagian
Lauretta M. Gauc
Rinuccio Y. Ramiro
Zita M. Perelstein
Gherardo F. Careccia
Nella D. Verdoodt
Gherardino O. Van De Voorde
Betto di Signa F. Van Eetveldt
Simone; Guccio M. Rosca
Marco; Pinellino M. Meersman
La Ciesca R. Fabry
Spinelloccio J. Joris
Brussels BRT PO, A. Rahbari (r1993) (7/94) (DINT) Ⓓ **DICD920119**

Gianni Schicchi L. Nucci
Lauretta M. Freni
Rinuccio R. Alagna
Zita E. Podles
Gherardo R. Cassinelli
Nella B. Frittoli
Gherardino B. Guerrini
Betto G. Giorgetti
Simone E. Fissore
Marco O. Mori
La Ciesca N. Curiel
Spinelloccio C. Cue
Notary A. Mariotti
Pinellio D. Jenis
Guccio D. Serraiocco
MMF Chor, MMF Orch, B. Bartoletti (r1991) (8/94) (DECC) Ⓓ [3] **436 261-2DHO3**

Gianni Schicchi R. Panerai
Lauretta H. Donath
Rinuccio P. Seiffert
Zita W. Baniewicz
Gherardo T. Pane
Nella V. Errante
Gherardino C. Kunz
Betto di Signa G. Auer
Simone F. Federici
Marco R. Riener
La Ciesca M. Georg
Bavarian Rad Chor, Munich RO, G. Patanè (r1987) (6/95) (RCA) Ⓓ **74321 25285-2**

Avete torto! G. di Stefano, La Scala Orch, A. Votto (r1955) (EMI) Ⓓ **CDM7 63105-2**
Excs A. Jerger, E. Réthy, D. With, E. Godin, W. Wernigk, M. Schober, O. Drapal, N. Zec, V. Madin, F. Worff, W. Achsel, K. Ettl, F. Skokan, F. Schramm, Vienna St Op Orch, W. Loibner (pp1938: Ger) (3/95) (SCHW) Ⓓ [2] **314602**
1. P. Domingo, LSO, L. Maazel (SONY) Ⓓ **MDK47176** (SONY) ⊟ **MDT47176**
1, 2. C. del Monte, V. de los Angeles, Rome Op Orch, G. Santini (EMI) Ⓓ **CDM7 69596-2**
2. K. Battle, W. Jones, H. Burton (pp1991) (DG) ▣ **072 189-3GH**
2. M. Caballé, Philh, J. Collado (11/92) (RCA) ⊟ [2] **RK61044**
2. B. Sayão, Orch, H. Barlow (bp1951) (VAI) ▣ **VAI69103**
2. J. Björling, orch, H. Barlow (bp1950) (VAI) ▣ **VAI69101**
2. K. Te Kanawa, LPO, J. Pritchard (CBS) Ⓓ **CD39208**
2. M. Caballé, LSO, C. Mackerras (EMIL) Ⓓ **CDZ105**
2. Cincinnati Pops, E. Kunzel (inst arr Beck, Bernstein, Kunzel) (TELA) Ⓓ **CD80260**
2. K. Te Kanawa, LPO, J. Pritchard (SONY) Ⓓ **SBK46548** (SONY) ⊟ **SBT46548**
2. R. Tebaldi, MMF Orch, L. Gardelli (DECC) Ⓓ **433 624-2DSP**
2. F. Weathers, Vienna Op Orch, A. Quadri (DECC) Ⓓ **433 636-2DSP** (DECC) ⊟ **433 636-4DSP**
2. R. Tebaldi, MMF Orch, L. Gardelli (DECC) Ⓓ **433 822-2DH** (DECC) ⊟ **433 822-4DH**
2. R. Tebaldi, MMF Orch, L. Gardelli (r1962) (DECC) Ⓓ **433 065-2DWO** (DECC) ⊟ **433 065-4DWO**

2. A. Panagulias, Miami SO, E. Kohn (pp1991) (IMP) ① **MCD43**
2. R. Scotto, Czech SO, A. Krieger (pp1991) (IMP) ① **MCD42**
2. K. Ricciarelli, Madrid SO, G.P. Sanzogno (pp1991) (IMP) ① [2] **DPCD998**
2. M. Caballé, LSO, C. Mackerras (EMI) ① **CDM7 64359-2**
2. S. Murphy, WNO Orch, J. Smith (COLL) ① **Coll3025-2**
2. J. Hammond, Hallé, L. Heward (Eng: r1941) (MMOI) ① **CDMOIR412**
2. K. Ricciarelli, Madrid SO, G.P. Sanzogno (RNE) ① [2] **650004**
2. K. Te Kanawa, LPO, J. Pritchard (SONY) ① **SK48094** (SONY) ▭ **ST48094**
2. R. Streich, Berlin Deutsche Op Orch, R. Peters (DG) ① [2] **435 748-2GDO2**
2. I. Tokody, orch, Anon (cond) (pp1991/2) (VAI) ① **VAIA1009**
2. B. Glenn, S. Katz (SCHW) ① **312642**
2. M. Callas, Philh, T. Serafin (r1954) (EMI) ① **CDC7 54702-2** (EMI) ▭ **EL754702-4**
2. L. Mitchell, National PO, K.H. Adler (DECC) ① **433 865-2DWO** (DECC) ▭ **433 865-4DWO**
2. S. McCulloch, Czech PO, J. Bigg (with instr track for singing) (IMP) ① [2] **DPCD1015** (IMP) ▭ **CIMPCD1015**
2. K. Ricciarelli, Orch, Anon Cond (pp1991) (MCI) ① **MCCD090** (MCI) ▭ **MCTC090**
2. M. Caballé, LSO, C. Mackerras (CFP) ① **CD-CFP4606** (CFP) ▭ **TC-CFP4606**
2. V. Masterson, RPO, R. Stapleton (r1990) (RPO) ① [2] **CDRPD9006** (RPO) ▭ [2] **ZCRPD9006**
2. J. Rodgers, English Northern Philh, P. Daniel (r1992) (EMI) ① **CDC7 54785-2**
2. S. McCulloch, Czech PO, J. Bigg (r1992) (IMP) ① **PCD1043**
2. R. Tebaldi, MMF Orch, L. Gardelli (r1961) (DECC) ① **440 408-2DM**
2. L. Mitchell, National PO, K.H. Adler (r1980) (BELA) ① **450 007-2** (BELA) ▭ **450 007-4**
2. M. Freni, Venice La Fenice Orch, R. Abbado (DG) ① **439 151-2GMA** (DG) ▭ **439 151-4GMA**
2. R. Tebaldi, MMF Orch, L. Gardelli (r1962) (DECC) ① **433 440-2DA** (DECC) ▭ **433 440-4DA**
2. F. Weathers, Vienna Op Orch, A. Quadri (BELA) ① **450 015-2** (BELA) ▭ **450 015-4**
2. F. Alda, orch (r1919) (KIWI) ① **CDSLD-82**
2. H. Donath, Munich RSO, G. Patanè (RCA) ① **09026 61440-2** (RCA) ▭ **09026 61440-4**
2. S. McCulloch, Czech SO, J. Bigg (IMP) ① [3] **TCD1070**
2. J. M. Leonard, V. L. Becker (arr sax/pf: J M Leonard) (ASV) ① **CDWHL2085**
2. R. Tebaldi, MMF Orch, L. Gardelli (r1962) (DECC) ① **436 317-2DA** (DECC) ▭ **436 317-4DA**
2. M. Caballé, LSO, C. Mackerras (r1970) (EMI) ① **CDC5 55095-2**
2. Cincinnati Pops, E. Kunzel (arr Bernstein, Kunzel & Beck) (TELA) ① **CD80401**
2. C. Muzio, orch (r1918) (PEAR) ① **GEMMCD9143**
2. R. Tebaldi, Rome RAI Orch, A. Basile (bp1961) (FONI) ① **CDMR5023**
2. H. Donath, Munich RO, G. Patanè (RCA) ① **74321 25817-2** (RCA) ▭ **74321 25817-4**
2. L. Price, New Philh, E. Downes (r1971) (RCA) ① **74321 24284-2** (RCA) ▭ **74321 24284-4**
2. J. Hammond, Hallé, L. Heward (r1941: Eng) (CONI) ① **CDHD235**
2. P. Lorengar, Santa Cecilia Academy Orch, G. Patanè (r1966) (DECC) ① **443 931-2DM**
2. V. de los Angeles, Rome Op Orch, G. Santini (r1958) (EMI) ① **CDM5 65579-2**
2. A. Gheorghiu, ROHO, E. Downes (r1995) (ROH) ① **75605 55013-2** (ROH) ▭ **75605 55013-4**
2. H. Gueden, Santa Cecilia Academy Orch, A. Erede (r1954) (PREI) ① **90227**
2. R. Tebaldi, MMF Orch, L. Gardelli (r1962) (DECC) ① [2] **444 555-2DF2**
2. K. Te Kanawa, LPO, J. Pritchard (5/85) (CBS) ① **MK37298** (CBS) ▭ **40-37298**
2. M. Caballé, LSO, C. Mackerras (10/87) (EMI) ① **CDC7 47841-2**
2. M. Callas, Philh, T. Serafin (r1954) (12/87) (EMI) ① **CDC7 47966-2**
2. M. Freni, Hamburg PO, L. Magiera (11/88) (ACAN) ① **49 384**
2. F. Weathers, Vienna Op. Orch, A. Quadri (1/89) (DECC) ① **417 686-2DC**
2. M. Freni, Orch, L. Magiera (10/89) (EMI) ① **CDM7 63110-2**
2. A. Stella, LSO, A. Erede (8/90) (CFP) ① **CD-CFP4569** (8/90) (CFP) ▭ **TC-CFP4569**
2. V. Masterson, RPO, R. Stapleton (10/90) (IMP) ① **MCD15** (10/90) (IMP) ▭ **MCC15**
2. R. Tebaldi, MMF Orch, L. Gardelli (8/91) (DECC) ① [2] **430 481-2DX2**
2. L. Garrett, Philh, A. Greenwood (r1990-1) (11/91) (SILV) ① **SONGCD903** (11/91) (SILV) ▭ **SONGC903**
2. M. Freni, Venice La Fenice Orch, R. Abbado (9/92) (DECC) ① **433 316-2DH**
2. P. McCann, Black Dyke Mills Band, P. Parkes (r1984: arr G Langford) (11/92) (CHAN) ① **CHAN4501** (11/92) (CHAN) ▭ **BBTD4501**
2. M. Gauci, Belgian Rad & TV Orch, A. Rahbari (11/92) (NAXO) ① **8 550606**
2. J. Hammond, Hallé, L. Heward (r1941: Eng) (12/92) (TEST) ① **SBT1013**
2. L. Price, LSO, E. Downes (12/92) (RCA) ① [4] **09026 61236-2**
2. L. Orgonášová, Bratislava RSO, W. Humburg (2/93) (NAXO) ① **8 550605**
2. A. Roocroft, LPO, F. Welser-Möst (10/94) (EMI) ① **CDC5 55090-2** (10/94) (EMI) ▭ **EL5 55090-4**
2. C. Muzio, orch (r1918) (1/95) (ROMO) ① [2] **81010-2**
2. J. Varady, Berlin RSO, M. Viotti (r1993) (5/95) (ORFE) ① **C323941A**
2. L. Popp, G. Parsons (pp1981) (6/95) (ORFE) ① **C363941B**
2. E. Steber, orch, H. Barlow (bp1949) (11/95) (VAI) ① **VAIA1072**
2. I. Galante, Latvian Nat SO, A. Vilumanis (r1994) (11/95) (CAMP) ① **RRCD1335** (11/95) (CAMP) ▭ **RRMC8035**
3. M. Freni, F. Bonisolli, Hamburg PO, L. Magiera (11/88) (ACAN) ① **49 384**

Madama Butterfly– opera: 2 acts (1904—Milan) (Lib. Giacosa and Illica)

EXCERPTS: ACT 1: 1a. E soffitto; 1b. Questa è la cameriera; 2. Dovunque al mondo; 3a. Ed è bella la sposa?; 3b. Amore o grillo; 4a. Ah! ah! quanto cielo!; 4b. Ancora un passo; 5a. Gran ventura; 5b. L'Imperial Commissario; 6. Vieni, amor mio!; 7a. Ieri son salita tutta sola; 7b. Ed eccoci in famiglia; 8a. Viene la sera; 8b. Bimba, dagli occhi; 8c. Vogliatemi bene; 8d. Un po' di vero c'è. ACT 2: 9. E Izaghi e Izanami; 10. Un bel dì vedremo; 11a. C'è. Entrate; 11b. Ora a noi; 11c. Ebbene, che fareste; 11d. E questo?; 12. Che tua madre; 13a. Il cannone del porto!; 13b. Scuoti quella fronda; 13c. Tutti i fior; 13d. Or vienmi ad adornar; 14. Humming Chorus; 15. Intermezzo; 16. Già il sole!; 17a. Povera Butterfly; 17b. Ve lo dissi?; 17c. Io so che alle sue pene; 18a. Non ve l'avevo detto?; 18b. Addio, fiorito asil; 18c. Glielo dirai?; 19a. Che vuol da me; 19b. Come una mosca prigioniera; 20a. Con onor muore; 20b. Tu? tu? piccolo iddio.

Madama Butterfly Y. Hayashi
Pinkerton P. Dvorský
Sharpless G. Zancanaro
Suzuki H-N. Kim
Goro E. Gavazzi
Kate Pinkerton A.C. Antonacci
The Bonze S. Fontana
La Scala Chor, La Scala Orch, L. Maazel, K. Asari (5/90) (MCEG) ▭ **VVD341**

Madama Butterfly M. Freni
Pinkerton P. Domingo
Sharpless R. Kerns
Suzuki C. Ludwig
Goro M. Sénéchal
Prince Yamadori G. Stendoro
Kate Pinkerton E. Schary
The Bonze M. Rintzler
Vienna St Op Chor, VPO, H. von Karajan, J-P. Ponnelle (5/90) (DECC) ▭ **071 404-3DH**

Madama Butterfly R. Kabaivanska
Pinkerton N. Antinori
Sharpless L. Saccomani
Suzuki E. Jankovic
Goro M. Ferrara
Prince Yamadori G. Zecchillo
Kate Pinkerton M. Zotti
The Bonze G. Brunelli
Verona Arena Chor, Verona Arena Orch, M. Arena, G. Chazalettes (CAST) ▭ **CVI2007**

Madama Butterfly Y. Hayashi
Pinkerton P. Dvorský
Sharpless G. Zancanaro
Suzuki H-N. Kim
Goro E. Gavazzi
Prince Yamadori A. Testa
Kate Pinkerton A.C. Antonacci
The Bonze S. Fontana
Imperial Commissioner C. Giombi
La Scala Chor, La Scala Orch, L. Maazel, D. Bailey (PION) ● **PLMCC00261**

Madama Butterfly R. Tebaldi
Pinkerton G. Campora
Sharpless G. Inghilleri
Suzuki N. Rankin
Goro P. de Palma
Prince Yamadori M. Luise
Kate Pinkerton G. Diozzi
The Bonze F. Corena
Imperial Commissioner M. Calvino
Registrar L. Pizzeri
Santa Cecilia Academy Chor, Santa Cecilia Academy Orch, A. Erede (r1951) (LOND) ① [2] **440 230-2LF2**

Madama Butterfly R. Scotto
Pinkerton P. Domingo
Sharpless I. Wixell
Suzuki G. Knight
Goro F. Andreolli
Prince Yamadori J. Summers
Kate Pinkerton A. Murray
The Bonze M. King
Imperial Commissioner C. Keyte
Registrar A. Byers
Ambrosian Op Chor, Philh, L. Maazel (6/87) (SONY) ① [2] **M2K35181**

Madama Butterfly M. Freni
Pinkerton L. Pavarotti
Sharpless R. Kerns
Suzuki C. Ludwig
Goro M. Sénéchal
Prince Yamadori G. Stendoro
Kate Pinkerton E. Schary
The Bonze M. Rintzler
Imperial Commissioner H. Helm
Registrar S.R. Frese
Vienna St Op Chor, VPO, H. von Karajan (r1974) (6/87) (DECC) ① [3] **417 577-2DH3**

Madama Butterfly M. Callas
Pinkerton N. Gedda
Sharpless M. Borriello
Suzuki L. Danieli
Goro R. Ercolani
Prince Yamadori Mario Carlin
Kate Pinkerton L. Villa
The Bonze P. Clabassi
Imperial Commissioner E. Campi
La Scala Chor, La Scala Orch, H. von Karajan (r1955) (10/87) (EMI) ① [2] **CDS7 47959-8**

Madama Butterfly L. Price
Pinkerton R. Tucker
Sharpless P. Maero
Suzuki R. Elias
Goro P. de Palma
Prince Yamadori R. Kerns
Kate Pinkerton A. di Stasio
The Bonze V. Carbonari
Imperial Commissioner A. la Porta
Registrar M. Rinaudo
RCA Italiana Op Chor, RCA Italiana Op Orch, E. Leinsdorf (3/88) (RCA) ① [2] **RD86160**

Madama Butterfly A. Moffo
Pinkerton C. Valletti
Sharpless R. Cesari
Suzuki R. Elias
Goro Mario Carlin
Prince Yamadori N. Catalani

Kate Pinkerton M.T. Pace
The Bonze F. Corena
Imperial Commissioner L. Monreale
Rome Op Chor, Rome Op Orch, E. Leinsdorf (r1957)
(9/88) (RCA) ⓘ [2] **GD84145**
Madama Butterfly M. Freni
Pinkerton J. Carreras
Sharpless J. Pons
Suzuki T. Berganza
Goro A. Laciura
Prince Yamadori M. Curtis
Kate Pinkerton M. Rørholm
The Bonze K. Rydl
Yakuside P. Salomaa
Imperial Commissioner; Registrar H. Komatsu
Ambrosian Op Chor, Philh, G. Sinopoli (r1987)
(12/88) (DG) ⓘ [3] **423 567-2GH3**
Madama Butterfly R. Scotto
Pinkerton C. Bergonzi
Sharpless R. Panerai
Suzuki A. di Stasio
Goro P. de Palma
Prince Yamadori G. Morresi
Kate Pinkerton S. Padoan
The Bonze P. Montarsolo
Imperial Commissioner M. Rinaudo
Rome Op Chor, Rome Op Orch, J. Barbirolli (r1966)
(5/89) (EMI) ⓘ [2] **CMS7 69654-2**
Madama Butterfly R. Tebaldi
Pinkerton C. Bergonzi
Sharpless E. Sordello
Suzuki F. Cossotto
Goro A. Mercuriali
Prince Yamadori M. Cazzato
Kate Pinkerton L. Nerozzi
The Bonze P. Washington
Yakuside; Registrar O. Nanni
Imperial Commissioner V. Carbonari
Santa Cecilia Academy Chor, Santa Cecilia Academy Orch, T. Serafin
(3/90) (DECC) ⓘ [2] **425 531-2DM2**
Madama Butterfly V. de los Angeles
Pinkerton J. Björling
Sharpless M. Sereni
Suzuki M. Pirazzini
Goro P. de Palma
Prince Yamadori A. la Porta
Kate Pinkerton S. Bertona
The Bonze P. Montarsolo
Yakuzide B. Giaiotti
Imperial Commissioner A. Sacchetti
Registrar P. Caroli
Rome Op. Chor, Rome Op. Orch, G. Santini
(3/91) (EMI) ⓘ [2] **CMS7 63634-2**
(8/85) (EMI) ⊟ [2] **TC-CFPD4446**
Madama Butterfly M. Gauci
Pinkerton Y. Ramiro
Sharpless G. Tichy
Suzuki N. Boschková
Goro J. Abel
Prince Yamadori R. Szücs
Kate Pinkerton A. Michalková
The Bonze J. Špaček
Imperial Commissioner; Registrar V. Kubovčik
Slovak Phil Chor, Bratislava RSO, A. Rahbari
(5/92) (NAXO) ⓘ [2] **8 660015/6**

2. I. Kozlovsky, P. Selivanov, USSR SO, Anon (cond) (r1930-50) (MYTO) ⓘ **1MCD921.55**

2, 3b J. Hislop, W. Parnis, D. Gilly, orch, J. Harrison (r1923)
(1/93) (PEAR) ⓘ **GEMMCD9956**

2, 8a-c, 10, 13a, 13b, 18a, 18b, 20a, 20b R. Tebaldi, F. Cossotto, C. Bergonzi, E. Sordello, Santa Cecilia Academy Chor, Santa Cecilia Academy Orch, T. Serafin
(DECC) ⓘ **421 873-2DA**
(DECC) ⊟ **421 873-4DA**

2, 8a-d, 10, 13a-d, 14, 17c, 18a-c, 20a, 20b M. Freni, L. Pavarotti, C. Ludwig, R. Kerns, M. Sénéchal, Vienna St Op Chor, VPO, H. von Karajan (DECC) ⓘ **421 247-2DH**
(DECC) ⊟ **421 247-4DH**

2, 8a-d, 10, 13a, 13b, 17c, 18b, 20a, 20b M. Collier, A. Robson, C. Craig, G. Griffiths, Sadler's Wells Op Orch, B. Balkwill (r1959-60: Eng) (CFP) ⓘ **CD-CFP4600**
(CFP) ⊟ **TC-CFP4600**

3b J. Hislop, D. Gilly, orch (r1923)
(7/92) (PEAR) ⓘ [3] **GEMMCDS9925(1)**

3b, 4a, 4b, 10. M. Freni, J. Carreras, J. Pons, A. Laciura, Ambrosian Op Chor, Philh, G. Sinopoli
(DG) ⓘ **439 151-2GMA**
(DG) ⊟ **439 151-4GMA**

3b, 8a-d, 13b, 20a, 20b R. Scotto, G. Knight, P. Domingo, Ambrosian Op Chor, Philh, L. Maazel
(SONY) ⓘ **SK48094**
(SONY) ⊟ **ST48094**

3b, 18a E. Caruso, A. Scotti, orch (r1910)
(NIMB) ⓘ **NI7834**
(NIMB) ⊟ **NC7834**

3b, 18a E. Caruso, A. Scotti, orch (r1910)
(3/91) (PEAR) ⓘ [3] **EVC2**

3b, 18a E. Caruso, A. Scotti, orch (r1910)
(10/94) (NIMB) ⓘ **NI7857**

3b, 18a, 18b E. Caruso, A. Scotti, orch (r1910)
(RCA) ⓘ **09026 61243-2**

3b, 18a, 18b E. Caruso, A. Scotti, orch (r1910)
(7/91) (RCA) ⓘ [12] **GD60495(3)**

3b, 18b W. Ludwig, G. Hüsch, Berlin St Op Orch, F. Zaun (r1934: Ger)
(7/95) (PREI) ⓘ **89088**

4a, 4b, 8b, 10, 11d, 12, 13b, 14, 18a-c, 19a, 19b, 20a, 20b R. Scotto, C. Bergonzi, A. di Stasio, R. Panerai, S. Padoan, Rome Op Chor, Rome Op Orch, J. Barbirolli (r1966)
(EMI) ⓘ **CDM7 63411-2**

4a, 10. Lotte Lehmann, orch (Ger: r1917)
(6/92) (PREI) ⓘ [3] **89302**

4b Lotte Lehmann, chor, Berlin St Op Orch, M. Gurlitt (Ger: r1932) (PEAR) ⓘ **GEMMCD9409**

4b M. Seinemeyer, Berlin St Op Chor, Berlin St Op Orch, F. Weissmann (r1928)
(MMOI) ⓘ **CDMOIR412**

4b C. Muzio, orch (r1917)
(PEAR) ⓘ **GEMMCD9143**

4b M. Favero, orch (r c1929)
(VAI) ⓘ **VAIA1071**

4b M. Favero, orch (r c1929)
(BONG) ⓘ **GB1078-2**

4b E. Mason, orch (r1924)
(8/93) (SYMP) ⓘ **SYMCD1136**

4b E. Mason, orch, F. Black (r1924)
(8/94) (ROMO) ⓘ **81009-2**

4b C. Muzio, orch (r1917)
(1/95) (ROMO) ⓘ [2] **81010-2**

4b, 7a, 10, 12, 20a G. Farrar, orch (r1909)
(10/94) (NIMB) ⓘ **NI7857**

4b, 8c, 10, 14, 15. Cincinnati Pops, E. Kunzel (inst arr Beck, Bernstein, Kunzel)
(TELA) ⓘ **CD80260**

4b, 10. E. Mason, orch, F. Black (r1925)
(8/94) (ROMO) ⓘ **81009-2**

6, 7a, 7b, 8a-d R. Tebaldi, G. di Stefano, Rome RAI Orch (pp1950) (MEMO) ⓘ **HR4372/3**

8. Hollywood Bowl SO, Alfred Newman (r1959: arr orch) (EMI) ⓘ **CDM5 65430-2**

8a H. Roswaenge, M. Cebotari, Berlin RSO, A. Rother (Ger: bp1940s) (PREI) ⓘ **90096**

8a G. Nelepp, V. Barsova, Bolshoi Th Orch, V. Nebolsin (r c1950: Russ) (PREI) ⓘ **89081**

8a-d F. Wunderlich, P. Lorengar, S. Wagner, Berlin SO, B. Klobučar (Ger)
(EMI) ⓘ [3] **CZS7 62993-2**

8a-d M. Freni, L. Pavarotti, G. Aragall, H. von Karajan (DECC) ⓘ **421 896-2DA**

8a-d K. Ricciarelli, P. Domingo, Santa Cecilia Academy Orch, G. Gavazzeni (r1972)
(RCA) ⓘ **09026 62595-2**

8a-d R. Tauber, E. Rethberg, orch (Ger: r1922)
(3/92) (EMI) ⓘ **CDH7 64029-2**

8a-d R. Pampanini, F. Ciniselli, orch, E. Panizza (r1928) (8/93) (PREI) ⓘ **89063**

8a-d M. Freni, C. Ludwig, L. Pavarotti, VPO, H. von Karajan (r1974)
(12/93) (DECC) ⓘ **433 439-2DA**
(DECC) ⊟ **433 439-4DA**

8a-d E. Rethberg, R. Tauber, orch (r1922: Ger)
(7/94) (PREI) ⓘ **89051**

8a-d, 18b F.I. d'Amico, P. Dvorský, Berlin RSO, R. Paternostro (ACAN) ⓘ **43 123**

8a, 10, 13b, 14, 20a, b R. Tebaldi, F. Cossotto, C. Bergonzi, Santa Cecilia Academy Chor, Santa Cecilia Academy Orch, T. Serafin (r1958)
(DECC) ⓘ [2] **444 555-2DF2**

8b R. Tebaldi, C. Bergonzi, Santa Cecilia Academy Orch, T. Serafin (r1958)
(BELA) ⓘ **450 006-2**
(BELA) ⊟ **450 006-4**

8b M. Favero, A. Ziliani, orch, G. Antonicelli (r1936) (VAI) ⓘ **VAIA1071**

8b M. Favero, A. Ziliani, orch, G. Antonicelli (r1936) (BONG) ⓘ **GB1078-2**

8b P. Domingo, R. Scotto, Philh, L. Maazel (r1970s) (SONY) ⓘ **SMK39030**

8b M. Freni, F. Bonisolli, Hamburg PO, L. Magiera (11/88) (ACAN) ⓘ **49 384**

8b H. von Debička, H. Roswaenge, orch (r1929: Ger) (2/92) (PREI) ⓘ [2] **89201**

8b M. Sheridan, A. Pertile, La Scala Orch, C. Sabajno (r1927)
(7/92) (PEAR) ⓘ [3] **GEMMCDS9925(2)**

8b-d V. de los Angeles, J. Björling, Rome Op Orch, G. Santini (CFP) ⓘ **CD-CFP9013**
(CFP) ⊟ **TC-CFP4498**

8b-d L. Price, E. Bainbridge, P. Domingo, LSO, N. Santi (r1974) (RCA) ⓘ **09026 61634-2**

8b-d M. Sheridan, A. Pertile, La Scala Orch, C. Sabajno (r1927) (CONI) ⓘ **CDHD235**

8b-d M. Callas, N. Gedda, La Scala Chor, La Scala Orch, H. von Karajan (r1955)
(2/90) (EMI) ⓘ [4] **CMS7 63244-2**

8b-d H. von Debička, H. Roswaenge, Berlin St Op Orch, M. Gurlitt (Ger: r1929)
(5/90) (PEAR) ⓘ **GEMMCD9394**

8b-d, 10, 18b R. Scotto, P. Domingo, Philh, L. Maazel (SONY) ⓘ **SBK46548**
(SONY) ⊟ **SBT46548**

8b, 10. S. Bullock, A. Davies, A. Bryn Parri (r1994) (11/95) (SAIN) ⓘ **SCDC2070**

8c R. Kabaivanska, N. Antinori, Verona Arena Orch, M. Arena (CAST) ▣ **CVI2070**

8c M. Callas, N. Gedda, La Scala Orch, H. von Karajan (r1955) (EMI) ⓘ **CDC5 55216-2**
(EMI) ⊟ **EL555216-4**

8c V. de los Angeles, J. Björling, Rome Op Orch, G. Santini (r1959) (EMI) ⓘ **CDM5 65579-2**

8c R. Tauber, V. Schwarz, orch (Ger: r1930)
(7/89) (EMI) ⓘ **CDM7 69476-2**

8c G. Zenatello, L. Cannetti, orch (r1911)
(5/94) (SYMP) ⓘ **SYMCD1158**

8c J. Johnston, J. Gartside, ROHO, L. Collingwood (r1947: Eng)
(4/95) (TEST) ⓘ **SBT1058**

8c, 8d F. Yeend, M. Lanza, Hollywood Bowl SO, E. Ormandy (pp1947) (IMP) ⓘ **PWKS4230**

8c, 8d R. Tebaldi, C. Bergonzi, Santa Cecilia Academy Orch, T. Serafin
(DECC) ⓘ **433 064-2DWO**

8c, 8d G. Zenatello, L. Cannetti, orch (r1911)
(5/94) (PEAR) ⓘ [4] **GEMMCDS9073(2)**

8c, 8d, 10, 13b, 13c R. Tebaldi, F. Cossotto, C. Bergonzi, Santa Cecilia Academy Chor, Santa Cecilia Academy Orch, T. Serafin
(DECC) ⓘ **433 865-2DWO**
(DECC) ⊟ **433 865-4DWO**

8c, 10, 14. R. Tebaldi, C. Bergonzi, Santa Cecilia Academy Chor, Santa Cecilia Academy Orch, T. Serafin (r1958) (BELA) ⓘ **450 007-2**
(BELA) ⊟ **450 007-4**

8d E. Caruso, G. Farrar, orch, W.B. Rogers (r1908) (RCA) ⓘ **09026 61243-2**

8d E. Caruso, G. Farrar, orch, W.B. Rogers (r1908) (MCI) ⓘ **MCCD086**
(MCI) ⊟ **MCTC086**

8d G. Farrar, E. Caruso, orch, W.B. Rogers (r1908) (12/90) (PEAR) ⓘ [3] **EVC1(2)**

8d G. Farrar, E. Caruso, orch, W.B. Rogers (r1908) (7/91) (RCA) ⓘ [12] **GD60495(2)**

8d G. Farrar, E. Caruso, orch (r1908)
(10/94) (NIMB) ⓘ **NI7857**

10. Lotte Lehmann, Berlin St Op Orch, F. Weissmann (Ger: r1930)
(PEAR) ⓘ **GEMMCD9409**

10. R. Kabaivanska, Verona Arena Orch, M. Arena (CAST) ▣ **CASH5051**

10. R. Tebaldi, orch (bp1959)
(VAI) ▣ **VAI69100**

10. B. Sayão, Orch, H. Barlow (bp1952)
(VAI) ▣ **VAI69103**

10. A. Moffo, Orch, H. Barlow (bp1958)
(VAI) ▣ **VAI69114**

10. E. Steber, Orch, Anon (cond) (bp1954)
(VAI) ▣ **VAI69112**

10. R. Ponselle, orch (r1919)
(PEAR) ⓘ [2] **GEMMCDS9964**

10. M. Callas, La Scala Orch, H. von Karajan (r1955) (EMI) ⓘ **CDC7 49502-2**

10. R. Scotto, Rome Op Orch, J. Barbirolli
(EMIN) ⓘ **CD-EMX9519**
(EMIN) ⊟ **TC-EMX2099**

10. M. Caballé, LSO, C. Mackerras
(EMIL) ⓘ **CDZ104**
(EMIL) ⊟ **LZ104**

10. R. Tebaldi, Santa Cecilia Academy Orch, T. Serafin (DECC) ⓘ **425 847-2DWO**
(DECC) ⊟ **425 847-4DWO**

10. R. Tebaldi, Rome RAI Orch, A. Paoletti (pp1954) (MEMO) ⓘ [2] **HR4235/6**

10. M. Caballé, Madrid Zarzuela Orch, G. Rivoli (pp1968) (MEMO) ⓘ [2] **HR4279/80**

10. M. Freni, VPO, H. von Karajan
(DECC) Ⓓ **433 822-2DH**
(DECC) ▭ **433 822-4DH**

10. A. Moffo, Munich RO, K. Eichhorn
(EURO) Ⓓ **GD69113**

10. F. Weathers, Vienna Op Orch, A. Quadri
(DECC) Ⓓ **433 636-2DSP**
(DECC) ▭ **433 636-4DSP**

10. R. Crespin, ROHO, E. Downes
(DECC) Ⓓ **433 624-2DSP**

10. M. Freni, VPO, H. von Karajan
(DECC) Ⓓ **433 069-2DWO**
(DECC) ▭ **433 069-4DWO**

10. M. Freni, VPO, H. von Karajan
(DECC) ◐ **071 142-1DH**
(DECC) ▣ **071 142-3DH**

10. M. Caballé, LSO, C. Mackerras
(EMI) Ⓓ **CDM7 64359-2**

10. Lotte Lehmann, Berlin St Op Orch, F. Weissmann (Ger: r1932)
(MMOI) Ⓓ **CDMOIR412**

10. S. Murphy, WNO Orch, J. Smith
(COLL) Ⓓ **Coll3025-2**

10. K. Te Kanawa, LPO, J. Pritchard
(SONY) Ⓓ **SK48094**
(SONY) ▭ **ST48094**

10. R. Tebaldi, Santa Cecilia Academy Orch, T. Serafin (r1958) (DECC) Ⓓ **436 300-2DX**
(DECC) ▭ **436 300-4DX**

10. M. Callas, Philh, T. Serafin (r1954)
(EMI) Ⓓ **CDC7 54702-2**
(EMI) ▭ **EL754702-4**

10. S. McCulloch, Czech PO, J. Bigg (with instr track for singing) (IMP) Ⓓ [2] **DPCD1015**
(IMP) ▭ **CIMPCD1015**

10. G. Moore, Concertgebouw, W. Mengelberg (pp1936) (ARHI) Ⓓ **ADCD109**

10. M. Dragoni, Munich RSO, G. Kuhn (r1991)
(ORFE) Ⓓ **C261921A**

10. M. Caballé, LSO, C. Mackerras
(CFP) Ⓓ **CD-CFP4608**
(CFP) ▭ **TC-CFP4608**

10. V. Masterson, RPO, R. Stapleton (r1990)
(RPO) Ⓓ [2] **CDRPD9006**
(RPO) ▭ [2] **ZCRPD9006**

10. J. Cairns, English Northern Philh, P. Daniel (r1992) (EMI) Ⓓ **CDC7 54785-2**

10. S. McCulloch, Czech PO, J. Bigg (r1992)
(IMP) Ⓓ **PCD1043**

10. R. Tebaldi, Santa Cecilia Academy Orch, T. Serafin (r1958) (DECC) Ⓓ **440 408-2DM**

10. R. Crespin, ROHO, E. Downes (r1963)
(DECC) Ⓓ **433 440-2DA**
(DECC) ▭ **433 440-4DA**

10. L. Price, RCA Italiana Op Orch, E. Leinsdorf
(RCA) Ⓓ **09026 61440-2**
(RCA) ▭ **09026 61440-4**

10. S. McCulloch, Czech SO, J. Bigg (r1992)
(IMP) Ⓓ **PCDS23**
(IMP) ▭ **PCDSC23**

10. R. Buckman, orch, E. Goossens (r1924: Eng)
(KIWI) Ⓓ **CDSLD-82**

10. M. Freni, VPO, H. von Karajan (r1974)
(DECC) Ⓓ **436 317-2DA**
(DECC) ▭ **436 317-4DA**

10. A. Moffo, Rome Op Orch, E. Leinsdorf
(RCA) Ⓓ **09026 61886-2**
(RCA) ▭ **09026 61886-4**

10. V. de los Angeles, Rome Op Orch, G. Santini (r1959) (EMI) Ⓓ **CDC5 55095-2**

10. H. Schymberg, Stockholm Royal Orch, N. Grevillius (r1946) (ALTN) Ⓓ **CDAN3**

10. M. Carosio, Turin RAI Orch, O. de Fabritiis (bp1953) (FONI) Ⓓ **CDMR5003**

10. Capitol SO, C. Dragon (r1958: arr Dragon)
(EMI) Ⓓ **CDM5 65430-2**

10. E. Destinn, orch, B. Seidler-Winkler (r1908)
(PEAR) Ⓓ **GEMMCD9172**

10. K. Ricciarelli, Svizzera Italiana Orch, B. Amaducci (r1979) (ERMI) Ⓓ **ERM151**

10. A. Tomowa-Sintow, Bulgarian Nat Op Orch, I. Marinov (r1970s) (FORL) Ⓓ **UCD16742**

10. L. Albanese, RCA Victor Orch, F. Weissmann (r1945) (RCA) Ⓓ **74321 24284-2**
(RCA) ▭ **74321 24284-4**

10. P. Lorengar, Santa Cecilia Academy Orch, G. Patanè (r1966) (DECC) Ⓓ **443 931-2DM**

10. M. Farneti, orch, L. Molajoli (r1931)
(CONI) Ⓓ **CDHD235**

10. M. Caballé, LSO, C. Mackerras (r1970)
(EMI) Ⓓ **CDM5 65575-2**

10. A. Gheorghiu, ROHO, E. Downes (r1995)
(ROH) Ⓓ **75605 55013-2**
(ROH) ▭ **75605 55013-4**

10. A. Moffo, Rome Op Orch, E. Leinsdorf (r1957) (RCA) Ⓓ **09026 62689-2**

10. J. Hammond, CBO, L. Heward (r1941: Eng)
(EMI) Ⓓ [2] **CHS5 65590-2**

10. K. Te Kanawa, LPO, J. Pritchard
(5/85) (CBS) Ⓓ **MK37298**
(CBS) ▭ **40-37298**

10. M. Freni, Hamburg PO, L. Magiera
(11/88) (ACAN) Ⓓ **49 384**

10. F. Weathers, Vienna Op. Orch, A. Quadri
(1/89) (DECC) Ⓓ **417 686-2DC**

10. E. Turner, orch, J. Batten (r1933: Eng)
(9/89) (EMI) Ⓓ **CDH7 69791-2**

10. R. Ponselle, orch, R. Romani (r1919)
(10/89) (NIMB) Ⓓ **NI7802**
(NIMB) ▭ **NC7802**

10. M. Freni, Orch, L. Magiera
(8/90) (CFP) Ⓓ **CD-CFP4569**
(8/90) (CFP) ▭ **TC-CFP4569**

10. H. Spani, orch (r1925)
(9/90) (CLUB) Ⓓ [2] **CL99-509/10**

10. V. Masterson, RPO, R. Stapleton
(10/90) (IMP) Ⓓ **MCD15**
(10/90) (IMP) ▭ **MCC15**

10. R. Tebaldi, Santa Cecilia Academy Orch, T. Serafin (8/91) (DECC) Ⓓ [2] **430 481-2DX2**

10. E. Berger, Berlin St Op Orch, L. Blech (Ger: r1934) (12/91) (PREI) Ⓓ **89035**

10. M. Seinemeyer, Berlin St Op Orch, F. Weissmann (r1928)
(2/92) (MMOI) Ⓓ **CDMOIR408**

10. G. dalla Rizza, orch (r1925)
(7/92) (PEAR) Ⓓ [3] **GEMMCDS9925(1)**

10. P. McCann, Black Dyke Mills Band, P. Parkes (r1984: arr G Langford)
(11/92) (CHAN) Ⓓ **CHAN4501**
(11/92) (CHAN) ▭ **BBTD4501**

10. J. Hammond, CBO, L. Heward (r1941: Eng)
(12/92) (TEST) Ⓓ **SBT1013**

10. D. Giannini, Berlin St Op Orch, C. Schmalstich (r1928) (4/93) (PREI) Ⓓ **89044**

10. N. Ermolenko-Yuzhina, orch (r1911: Russ)
(6/93) (PEAR) Ⓓ [3] **GEMMCDS9001/3(2)**

10. R. Pampanini, orch, A. Albergoni (r1927)
(8/93) (PREI) Ⓓ **89063**

10. E. Mason, orch (r1925)
(8/93) (SYMP) Ⓓ **SYMCD1136**

10. R. Crespin, ROHO, E. Downes (r1963)
(10/93) (DECC) Ⓓ **436 461-2DM**

10. R. Ponselle, orch, R. Romani (r1919)
(10/93) (NIMB) Ⓓ **NI7846**

10. E. Destinn, orch (r1914)
(11/93) (ROMO) Ⓓ [2] **81002-2**

10. R. Pampanini, orch, L. Molajoli (r1927)
(4/94) (EMI) Ⓓ [3] **CHS7 64864-2(1)**

10. E. Destinn, orch (r1911)
(5/94) (SUPR) Ⓓ **11 1337-2**

10. E. Rethberg, orch (r1925)
(7/94) (PREI) Ⓓ **89051**

10. A. Galli-Curci, orch, Rosario Bourdon (r1922)
(8/94) (ROMO) Ⓓ [2] **81004-2**

10. E. Destinn, orch, B. Seidler-Winkler (r1908: Ger) (12/94) (SUPR) Ⓓ [12] **11 2136-2(1)**

10. E. Destinn, orch, P. Pitt (r1911)
(12/94) (SUPR) Ⓓ [12] **11 2136-2(4)**

10. E. Destinn, orch (r1914)
(12/94) (SUPR) Ⓓ [12] **11 2136-2(5)**

10. E. Destinn, orch (r1911)
(12/94) (SUPR) Ⓓ [12] **11 2136-2(4)**

10. C. Muzio, orch (r1918)
(1/95) (ROMO) Ⓓ [2] **81010-2**

10. E. Rethberg, orch (r1924)
(2/95) (ROMO) Ⓓ [2] **81012-2**

10. L. Garrett, RPO, P. Robinson (r1994)
(4/95) (SILV) Ⓓ **SILKD6004**
(4/95) (SILV) ▭ **SILKC6004**

10. R. Hunter, Tasmanian SO, D. Franks (r1989)
(10/95) (ABCC) Ⓓ **8 7000 10**

10. E. Rethberg, Berlin SO, F. Weissmann (r1930: Ger) (10/95) (ROMO) Ⓓ [2] **81014-2**

10b L. Price, RCA Italiana Op Orch, E. Leinsdorf
(RCA) Ⓓ **74321 25817-2**
(RCA) ▭ **74321 25817-4**

10, 12. E. Destinn, orch, B. Seidler-Winkler (r1908)
(7/92) (PEAR) Ⓓ [3] **GEMMCDS9924(1)**

10, 12, 20b E. Destinn, Odeon Orch, A. Pilz (r1908) (12/94) (SUPR) Ⓓ [12] **11 2136-2(2)**

10, 12, 20b J. Varady, Berlin RSO, M. Viotti (r1993) (5/95) (ORFE) Ⓓ **C323941A**

10, 13b, 13c H. Konetzni, M-L. Schilp, Berlin St Op Orch, H. Schmidt-Isserstedt (r1937: Ger)
(1/95) (PREI) Ⓓ **90078**

10, 19b, 20a, 20b M. Freni, C. Ludwig, L. Pavarotti, Bologna Teatro Comunale Orch, H. von Karajan (r1974) (DECC) Ⓓ **440 412-2DM**

10, 20a R. Scotto, Rome Op Orch, J. Barbirolli
(EMI) Ⓓ **CDM7 69596-2**

10, 20a M. Callas, Philh, T. Serafin (r1954)
(12/87) (EMI) Ⓓ **CDC7 47966-2**

10, 20a M. Cebotari, VPO, F. Prohaska (r1948)
(12/90) (PREI) Ⓓ **90034**

10, 20a, 20b E. Destinn, orch, B. Seidler-Winkler (r1908) (12/94) (SUPR) Ⓓ [12] **11 2136-2(2)**

10, 20b M. Caballé, LSO, C. Mackerras
(10/87) (EMI) Ⓓ **CDC7 47841-2**

10, 20b M. Freni, Orch, L. Magiera
(10/89) (EMI) Ⓓ **CDM7 63110-2**

11b G. Farrar, A. Scotti, orch (r1909)
(10/94) (NIMB) Ⓓ **NI7857**

12. M. Reining, Vienna St Op Orch, R. Moralt (r1942: Ger) (9/94) (PREI) Ⓓ **89065**

13a M. Freni, T. Berganza, Philh, G. Sinopoli
(DG) ▭ **439 153-4GMA**

13a-d M. Seinemeyer, H. Jung, Berlin St Op Orch, F. Weissmann (Ger: r1929)
(11/90) (PREI) Ⓓ **89029**

13a-d M. Caballé, S. Verrett, New Philh, A. Guadagno (5/92) (RCA) Ⓓ **GD60818**

13b M. Freni, C. Ludwig, VPO, H. von Karajan (r1974) (DECC) Ⓓ **436 315-2DA**
(DECC) ▭ **436 315-4DA**

13b L. Price, M. Horne, NY Met Op Orch, James Levine (RCA) Ⓓ **09026 62699-2**
(RCA) ▭ **09026 62699-4**

13c R. Scotto, A. di Stasio, Rome Op Orch, J. Barbirolli (CFP) Ⓓ **CD-CFP4582**
(CFP) ▭ **TC-CFP4582**

13c G. Farrar, J. Jacoby, orch (r1909)
(10/94) (NIMB) Ⓓ **NI7857**

14. Fiesole School of Music Female Chor, MMF Chor, MMF Orch, M. Arena (ACAN) Ⓓ **43 540**

14. Rome Op Chor, Rome Op Orch, E. Leinsdorf
(RCA) Ⓓ **GD60205**

14. Vienna St Op Orch, VPO, H. von Karajan
(DECC) Ⓓ **433 067-2DWO**
(DECC) ▭ **433 067-4DWO**

14. ROH Chor, ROHO, L. Gardelli
(EMI) Ⓓ **CDM7 64356-2**

14. Mormon Tabernacle Ch, Utah SO, J. Silverstein (pp1991) (DECC) Ⓓ **436 284-2DH**

14. Vienna St Op Chor, VPO, H. von Karajan (r1974) (DECC) Ⓓ **440 947-2DH**
(DECC) ▭ **440 947-4DH**

14. Vienna St Op Chor, VPO, H. von Karajan (r1974) (DECC) Ⓓ **433 443-2DA**
(DECC) ▭ **433 443-4DA**

14. Santa Cecilia Academy Chor, Santa Cecilia Academy Orch, C. Franci (r1950s)
(BELA) Ⓓ **450 117-2**
(BELA) ▭ **450 117-4**

14. Rome Op Chor, Rome Op Orch, J. Barbirolli (r1966) (CFP) Ⓓ **CD-CFP4661**
(CFP) ▭ **TC-CFP4661**

14. Mormon Tabernacle Ch, Utah SO, J. Silverstein (pp1991) (LOND) Ⓓ **443 381-2LM**

14. RCA Italiana Op Chor, RCA Italiana Op Orch, E. Leinsdorf (r1963)
(RCA) Ⓓ **74321 24209-2**

14. ROH Chor, ROHO, L. Gardelli (r1971)
(EMI) Ⓓ [2] **CZS5 68559-2**

14. ROH Chor, ROHO, L. Gardelli
(8/90) (CFP) Ⓓ **CD-CFP4569**
(8/90) (CFP) ▭ **TC-CFP4569**

18a, 18b G. Lauri-Volpi, L. Borgonovo, La Scala Orch, F. Ghione (r1934)
(MMOI) Ⓓ **CDMOIR412**

18a, 18b G. Lauri-Volpi, L. Borgonovo, La Scala Orch, F. Ghione (r1934) (CONI) Ⓓ **CDHD235**

18b F. Wunderlich, H. Prey, Berlin SO, B. Klobučar (Ger) (EMI) Ⓓ [3] **CZS7 62993-2**

18b Deng, Württemberg PO, R. Paternostro
(SINE) Ⓓ **39820222**

18b M. del Monaco, New SO, A. Erede (r1956)
(DECC) Ⓓ **440 407-2DM**

18b P. Domingo, I. Wixell, Philh, L. Maazel
(SONY) Ⓓ **MDK47176**
(SONY) ▭ **MDT47176**

18b A. Piccaver, T. Scheidl, Berlin St Op Orch, M. Gurlitt (r1928) (PREI) Ⓓ [2] **89217**

18b R. Tauber, orch (Ger: r1925)
(7/89) (PEAR) Ⓓ **GEMMCD9327**

18b P. Dvorský, Bratislava RSO, Czech RSO, O. Lenárd (10/89) (OPUS) Ⓓ **9156 1824**

18b G. Lauri-Volpi, L. Borgonovo, La Scala Orch, F. Ghione (r1934)
(9/90) (PREI) Ⓓ **89012**

18b P. Dvorský, Bratislava RSO, O. Lenárd
(5/92) (NAXO) Ⓓ **8 550343**

18b R. Tauber, orch, H. Weigert (Ger: r1925)
(12/92) (NIMB) Ⓓ **NI7830**
(12/92) (NIMB) ▭ **NC7830**

18b G. Lauri-Volpi, L. Borgonovo, La Scala Orch, F. Ghione (r1934) (7/93) (NIMB) Ⓓ **NI7845**
18b G. Masini, orch (r1929) (4/94) (EMI) Ⓓ [3] **CHS7 64864-2(2)**
18b H. Roswaenge, BPO, E. Orthmann (r1933: Ger) (4/95) (PREI) Ⓓ [2] **89209**
18b A. Davies, A. Bryn Parri (r1994) (11/95) (SAIN) Ⓓ **SCDC2085**
19b, 20. M. Freni, C. Ludwig, L. Pavarotti, VPO, H. von Karajan (r1974) (DECC) Ⓓ **443 377-2DM**
20a L. Albanese, RCA SO, V. Trucco (r1949) (4/94) (RCA) Ⓓ [6] **09026 61580-2(5)**
20a, 20b I. Tokody, orch, Anon (cond) (pp1991/2) (VAI) Ⓓ **VAIA1009**
20b H. Spani, orch, Berlin St Op Orch (r1929) (MMOI) Ⓓ **CDMOIR412**
20b H. Spani, orch, C. Sabajno (r1929) (9/90) (CLUB) Ⓓ [2] **CL99-509/10**
20b H. Spani, La Scala Orch, C. Sabajno (r1929) (12/92) (PREI) Ⓓ **89037**

Manon Lescaut– opera: 4 acts (1893—Turin) (Lib. Various)

ACT 1: 1. Ave, sera gentile; 2a. No, non ancora; 2b. Tra voi, belle; 3a. Cortese damigella; 3b. Manon Lescaut mi chiamo; 4. Donna non vidi mai; 5. La sua ventura; 6. Vedete? Io son fedele. ACT 2: 7a. Dispettosetto questo riccio!; 7b. Buon giorno; 8. In quelle trine morbide; 9. Sulla vetta (Madrigal); 10. L'ora, o Tirsi; 11a. Tu, tu, amore? Tu?; 11b. O tentatrice!; 12. Ah! Manon, mi tradisce; 13. Intermezzo. ACT 3: 14. Ansia, eterna, crudel; 15a. Ah! non v'avvicinate!; 15b. No!...No!...pazzo son. ACT 4: 16. Prelude; 17a. Tutta su me ti posa; 17b. Manon... 18. Sola, perduta, abbandonata; 19. Nulla rinvenni.

Manon Lescaut M. Olivero
Des Grieux P. Domingo
Lescaut G. Fioravanti
Geronte A. Mariotti
Edmondo E. Lorenzi
Singer R. Pallini
Innkeeper F. Federici
Dancing Master F. Ricciardi
Sergeant G. Casarini
Lamplighter O. Begali
Captain C. del Bosco
Verona Arena Chor, Verona Arena Orch, N. Santi (pp1970) (FOYE) Ⓓ [2] **2-CF2033**

Manon Lescaut K. Te Kanawa
Des Grieux P. Domingo
Lescaut T. Allen
Geronte F. Robinson
Edmondo R. Leggate
Singer A. Cooper
Innkeeper G. Macpherson
Dancing Master J. Fryatt
Lamplighter M. Curtis
Captain R. Earle
ROH Chor, ROHO, G. Sinopoli, G. Friedrich (CAST) ▣ **CVI2028**

Manon Lescaut M. Caballé
Des Grieux P. Domingo
Lescaut V. Sardinero
Geronte N. Mangin
Edmondo R. Tear
Singer D. Wallis
Innkeeper R. Van Allan
Dancing Master B. Dickerson
Sergeant R. Lloyd
Lamplighter I. Partridge
Captain G. Howell
Ambrosian Op Chor, New Philh, B. Bartoletti (r1971) (EMI) Ⓓ [2] **CMS7 64852-2**

Manon Lescaut M. Freni
Des Grieux L. Pavarotti
Lescaut D. Croft
Geronte G. Taddei
Edmondo R. Vargas
Singer C. Bartoli
Innkeeper; Captain F. Davià
Dancing Master A. Laciura
Lamplighter P. Groves
Sergeant J. Courtney
NY Met Op Chor, NY Met Op Orch, James Levine (r1992) (DECC) Ⓓ [11] **443 204-2DH11(5)**

Manon Lescaut M. Freni
Des Grieux P. Domingo
Lescaut R. Bruson
Geronte K. Rydl
Edmondo R. Gambill
Singer B. Fassbaender
Innkeeper G. Macpherson
Dancing Master J. Fryatt
Sergeant H. Thomas
Lamplighter M. Curtis
Captain J. Tomlinson
ROH Chor., Philh, G. Sinopoli (3/85) (DG) Ⓓ [2] **413 893-2GH2**

Manon Lescaut M. Callas
Des Grieux G. di Stefano
Lescaut G. Fioravanti
Geronte F. Calabrese
Edmondo D. Formichini
Singer F. Cossotto
Innkeeper C. Forti
Dancing Master V. Tatone
Sergeant G. Morresi
Lamplighter F. Ricciardi
Captain F. Ventriglia
La Scala Chor, La Scala Orch, T. Serafin (r1957) (9/86) (EMI) Ⓓ [2] **CDS7 47393-8**

Manon Lescaut K. Te Kanawa
Des Grieux J. Carreras
Lescaut P. Coni
Geronte I. Tajo
Edmondo W. Matteuzzi
Singer M. Zimmermann
Innkeeper L. Freschi
Dancing Master P. de Palma
Sergeant G. Tadeo
Lamplighter C. Gaifa
Captain N. de Carolis
Bologna Teatro Comunale Chor, Bologna Teatro Comunale Orch, R. Chailly (r1987) (9/88) (DECC) Ⓓ [2] **421 426-2DH2**

Manon Lescaut R. Tebaldi
Des Grieux M. del Monaco
Lescaut M. Borriello
Geronte F. Corena
Edmondo P. de Palma
Singer L. Ribacchi
Innkeeper; Sergeant A. Sacchetti
Dancing Master A. Zagonara
Lamplighter A. Mercuriali
Captain D. Caselli
Santa Cecilia Academy Chor, Santa Cecilia Academy Orch, F. Molinari-Pradelli (8/91) (DECC) Ⓓ [2] **430 253-2DM2**

Manon Lescaut L. Albanese
Des Grieux J. Björling
Lescaut R. Merrill
Geronte; Sergeant F. Calabrese
Edmondo; Dancing Master; Lamplighter Mario Carlin
Singer A.M. Rota
Innkeeper; Captain E. Campi
Rome Op Chor, Rome Op Orch, J. Perlea (r1954) (10/91) (RCA) Ⓓ [2] **GD60573**

Manon Lescaut M. Gauci
Des Grieux K. Kaludov
Lescaut V. Sardinero
Geronte M. Rosca
Edmondo D. George
Singer L. Van Deyck
Innkeeper; Sergeant; Captain H. Lauwers
Dancing Master; Lamplighter L. Van Gijsegem
J. Gregoor Ch, Brussels BRT Phil Chor, Brussels BRT PO, A. Rahbari (12/92) (NAXO) Ⓓ [2] **8 660019/20**

Manon Lescaut N. Rautio
Des Grieux P. Dvorský
Lescaut G. Quilico
Geronte L. Roni
Edmondo M. Berti
Singer C. N. Bandera
Innkeeper A. Bramante
Dancing Master M. Bolognesi
Sergeant S. Sammaritano
Lamplighter E. Cossutta
Captain E. Panariello
La Scala Chor, La Scala Orch, L. Maazel (r1992) (7/93) (SONY) Ⓓ [2] **S2K48474**

Manon Lescaut M. Freni
Des Grieux L. Pavarotti
Lescaut D. Croft
Geronte G. Taddei
Edmondo R. Vargas
Singer C. Bartoli
Innkeeper; Captain F. Davià
Dancing Master A. Laciura
Lamplighter P. Groves
Sergeant J. Courtney
NY Met Op Chor, NY Met Op Orch, James Levine (r1992) (11/93) (DECC) Ⓓ [2] **440 200-2DHO2**

Excs P. Domingo (CAST) ▣ **CVI2021**
1, 2b, 3a, 4, 6, 8, 11a, 14, 15b, 17a, 17b, 18. M. Freni, R. Bruson, P. Domingo, K. Rydl, R. Gambill, G. MacPherson, M. Curtis, J. Tomlinson, ROH Chor, Philh, G. Sinopoli (r1983-4) (DG) Ⓓ **445 466-2GMH**
2a, 2b, 4, 15a, 15b L. Pavarotti, N. Howlett, National PO, O. de Fabritiis (r1979) (DECC) Ⓓ **440 400-2DM**
2b J. Björling, MMF Orch, A. Erede (r1959) (10/95) (DECC) Ⓓ **443 930-2DM**
2b, 4. L. Pavarotti, Philh, L. Magiera (DECC) OO **436 320-5DH**
2b, 4. A. Pertile, La Scala Orch, C. Sabajno (r1929) (9/90) (PREI) Ⓓ **89007**
2b, 4. L. Pavarotti, Philh, L. Magiera (11/91) (DECC) ◐ **071 150-1DH**
(11/91) (DECC) ▣ **071 150-3DH**
2b, 4. J. Carreras, W. Matteuzzi, Bologna Teatro Comunale Orch, R. Chailly (r1987) (10/93) (DECC) Ⓓ **436 463-2DM**
(10/93) (DECC) ▭ **436 463-4DM**
2b, 6, 12, 15a, 17a, 18. H. Schymberg, J. Björling, H. Hasslo, B. Lundborg, Stockholm Royal Op Chor, Stockholm Royal Op Orch, N. Grevillius (pp1959) (3/92) (BLUE) Ⓓ **ABCD028**
3a, 3b, 4. P. Domingo, M. Freni, R. Bruson, Philh, G. Sinopoli (r1983/4) (DG) Ⓓ **445 525-2GMA**
(DG) ▭ **445 525-4GMA**
4. J. Björling, Rome Op. Orch, J. Perlea (r1954) (RCA) ▭ **GK85277**
4. B. Gigli, orch (r1926) (CONI) Ⓓ **CDHD149**
(CONI) ▭ **MCHD149**
4. B. Gigli, orch, J. Pasternack (r1926) (NIMB) Ⓓ **NI7817**
(NIMB) ▭ **NC7817**
4. B. Gigli, orch, J. Pasternack (r1926) (MMOI) Ⓓ **CDMOIR405**
(MMOI) ▭ **CMOIR405**
4. J. Carreras, LSO, J. López-Cobos (PHIL) Ⓓ **432 692-2PH**
(PHIL) ▭ **432 692-4PH**
4. J. Carreras, Bologna Teatro Comunale Orch, R. Chailly (DECC) Ⓓ **433 822-2DH**
(DECC) ▭ **433 822-4DH**
4. L. Pavarotti, National PO, O. de Fabritiis (DECC) Ⓓ **430 470-2DH**
(DECC) ▭ **430 470-4DH**
4. C. Bergonzi, Santa Cecilia Academy Orch, G. Gavazzeni (DECC) Ⓓ **433 636-2DSP**
(DECC) ▭ **433 636-4DSP**
4. C. Bergonzi, Santa Cecilia Academy Orch, G. Gavazzeni (DECC) Ⓓ **433 069-2DWO**
(DECC) ▭ **433 069-4DWO**
4. C. Bergonzi, Santa Cecilia Academy Orch, G. Gavazzeni (r1957) (DECC) Ⓓ **436 300-2DX**
(DECC) ▭ **436 300-4DX**
4. T. Harper, Bratislava RSO, M. Halász (NAXO) Ⓓ **8 550497**
4. E. Caruso, orch (r1913) (RCA) Ⓓ **09026 61243-2**
4. P. Domingo, New Philh, B. Bartoletti (r1971) (CFP) Ⓓ **CD-CFP4602**
(CFP) ▭ **TC-CFP4602**
4. E. Caruso, orch (r1913) (MCI) Ⓓ **MCCD086**
(MCI) ▭ **MCTC086**
4. J. Carreras, National PO, R. Chailly (r1987) (DECC) Ⓓ **436 472-2DM**
4. B. Gigli, orch (r1926) (IMP) Ⓓ **GLRS102**
4. Deng, Württemberg PO, R. Paternostro (SINE) Ⓓ **39820222**
4. P. Domingo, Philh, G. Sinopoli (DG) Ⓓ **439 151-2GMA**
(DG) ▭ **439 151-4GMA**
4. M. del Monaco, Milan SO, A. Quadri (r1951) (TEST) Ⓓ **SBT1039**
4. C. Bergonzi, Santa Cecilia Academy Orch, G. Gavazzeni (r1957) (DECC) Ⓓ **440 417-2DM**
4. A. Bonci, orch (r1913) (PEAR) Ⓓ **GEMMCD9168**
4. B. Gigli, orch, J. Pasternack (r1926) (CONI) Ⓓ **CDHD235**
4. J. Botha, ROHO, E. Downes (r1995) (ROH) Ⓓ **75605 55013-2**
(ROH) ▭ **75605 55013-4**
4. B. Gigli, orch, J. Pasternack (r1926) (9/88) (PEAR) Ⓓ **GEMMCD9316**
4. C. Bergonzi, Santa Cecilia Academy Orch, G. Gavazzeni (1/89) (DECC) Ⓓ **417 686-2DC**

4. E. Caruso, orch (r1913) (10/89) (NIMB) Ⓓ **NI7803** (NIMB) ▭ **NC7803**
4. L. Pavarotti, National PO, O. de Fabritiis (7/90) (DECC) Ⓓ [2] **425 681-2DM2** (7/90) (DECC) ▭ [2] **425 681-4DM2**
4. D. Smirnov, orch (r1913) (7/90) (CLUB) Ⓓ **CL99-031**
4. C. Craig, Orch, M. Collins (8/90) (CFP) Ⓓ **CD-CFP4569** (8/90) (CFP) ▭ **TC-CFP4569**
4. E. Caruso, orch (r1913) (7/91) (RCA) Ⓓ [12] **GD60495(4)**
4. E. Caruso, orch (r1913) (10/91) (PEAR) Ⓓ [3] **EVC3(1)**
4. E. Caruso, orch (r1913) (7/92) (PEAR) Ⓓ [3] **GEMMCDS9924(1)**
4. G. Martinelli, orch (r1914) (7/92) (PEAR) Ⓓ [3] **GEMMCDS9925(1)**
4. J. Björling, Stockholm Royal Op Orch, N. Grevillius (r1948) (8/92) (BLUE) Ⓓ **ABCD016**
4. J. Björling, Stockholm Royal Op Orch, N. Grevillius (r1948) (10/93) (EMI) Ⓓ **CDH7 64707-2**
4. A. Ziliani, La Scala Orch, F. Ghione (r1935) (4/94) (EMI) Ⓓ [3] **CHS7 64864-2(2)**
4. G. Zenatello, anon (r1903) (5/94) (PEAR) Ⓓ [4] **GEMMCDS9073(1)**
4. G. Zenatello, anon (r c1912) (5/94) (PEAR) Ⓓ [4] **GEMMCDS9074(1)**
4. B. Gigli, orch, J. Pasternack (r1926) (12/94) (MMOI) Ⓓ **CDMOIR425**
4. B. Heppner, Munich RO, R. Abbado (r1993/4) (11/95) (RCA) Ⓓ **09026 62504-2**
4, 12. P. Domingo, New Philh, B. Bartoletti (EMI) Ⓓ **CDM7 63103-2**
4, 12. A. Piccaver, orch (r1920) (8/93) (PREI) Ⓓ **89060**
4, 12. G. Zenatello, orch (r1909) (5/94) (SYMP) Ⓓ **SYMCD1158**
4, 12. G. Zenatello, orch (r1909) (5/94) (PEAR) Ⓓ [4] **GEMMCDS9073(2)**
4, 12. P. Domingo, M. Caballé, New Philh, B. Bartoletti (r1972) (6/94) (EMI) Ⓓ **CDC5 55017-2**
4, 13. P. Dvorský, Bratislava RSO, O. Lenárd (5/92) (NAXO) Ⓓ **8 550343**
4, 15a G. Zenatello, anon (r1907) (5/94) (SYMP) Ⓓ **SYMCD1158**
4, 15a G. Zenatello, anon (r1907) (5/94) (PEAR) Ⓓ [4] **GEMMCDS9073(1)**
4, 15a, 15b P. Dvorský, I. Gáti, Budapest Op Orch, A. Mihály (ACAN) Ⓓ **43 123**
4, 8, 11a K. Te Kanawa, J. Carreras, Bologna Teatro Comunale Orch, R. Chailly (r1987) (DECC) Ⓓ [2] **444 555-2DF2**
8. R. Ponselle, orch (r1921) (PEAR) Ⓓ [2] **GEMMCDS9964**
8. R. Ponselle, orch (r1923) (PEAR) Ⓓ [2] **GEMMCDS9964**
8. Cincinnati Pops, E. Kunzel (inst arr Beck, Bernstein, Kunzel) (TELA) Ⓓ **CD80260**
8. S. Murphy, WNO Orch, J. Smith (COLL) Ⓓ **Coll3025-2**
8. M. Chiara, Vienna Volksoper Orch, N. Santi (DECC) Ⓓ **433 865-2DWO** (DECC) ▭ **433 865-4DWO**
8. K. Te Kanawa, Bologna Teatro Comunale Orch, R. Chailly (r1987) (DECC) Ⓓ **436 472-2DM**
8. R. Tebaldi, Santa Cecilia Academy Orch, F. Molinari-Pradelli (r1954) (DECC) Ⓓ **440 408-2DM**
8. M. Chiara, Vienna Volksoper Orch, N. Santi (r1972) (BELA) Ⓓ **450 007-2** (BELA) ▭ **450 007-4**
8. M. Callas, Philh, T. Serafin (r1954) (EMI) Ⓓ **CDC5 55016-2**
8. M. Chiara, Vienna Volksoper Orch, Z. Mehta, N. Santi (r1971) (DECC) Ⓓ **436 317-2DA** (DECC) ▭ **436 317-4DA**
8. C. Muzio, orch (r1917) (PEAR) Ⓓ **GEMMCD9143**
8. M. Favero, orch (r1937) (VAI) Ⓓ **VAIA1071**
8. M. Favero, orch (r1937) (BONG) Ⓓ **GB1078-2**
8. M. Caballé, New Philh, B. Bartoletti (r1971) (EMI) Ⓓ **CDM5 65575-2**
8. K. Te Kanawa, LPO, J. Pritchard (5/85) (CBS) Ⓓ **MK37298** (CBS) ▭ **40-37298**
8. A. Tomowa-Sintow, Munich RO, P. Sommer (11/86) (ORFE) Ⓓ **C106841A**
8. M. Freni, Hamburg PO, L. Magiera (11/88) (ACAN) Ⓓ **49 384**
8. M. Freni, Orch, L. Magiera (10/89) (EMI) Ⓓ **CDM7 63110-2**
8. H. Spani, La Scala Orch, C. Sabajno (r1927) (9/90) (CLUB) Ⓓ [2] **CL99-509/10**
8. H. Spani, orch (r1925) (9/90) (CLUB) Ⓓ [2] **CL99-509/10**
8. M. Seinemeyer, Berlin St Op Orch, F. Weissmann (r1927) (11/90) (PREI) Ⓓ **89029**
8. C. Ferrani, anon (r1902) (5/91) (SYMP) Ⓓ **SYMCD1077**
8. R. Tebaldi, SRO, A. Erede (r1949) (4/92) (EMI) Ⓓ [7] **CHS7 69741-2(7)**
8. Lotte Lehmann, Berlin St Op Orch, K. Besl (Ger: r1924) (6/92) (PREI) Ⓓ [3] **89302**
8. R. Pampanini, orch (r1927) (7/92) (PEAR) Ⓓ [3] **GEMMCDS9926(1)**
8. L. Cavalieri, orch (r1910) (11/92) (MEMO) Ⓓ [2] **HR4408/9(2)**
8. C. Ferrani, anon (r1903) (11/92) (MEMO) Ⓓ [2] **HR4408/9(1)**
8. H. Spani, La Scala Orch, C. Sabajno (r1927) (12/92) (PREI) Ⓓ **89037**
8. J. Hammond, Philh, L. Collingwood (r1947) (12/92) (TEST) Ⓓ **SBT1013**
8. D. Giannini, Berlin St Op Orch, C. Schmalstich (r1928) (4/93) (PREI) Ⓓ **89044**
8. R. Pampanini, orch, L. Molajoli (r1927) (8/93) (PREI) Ⓓ **89063**
8. R. Ponselle, orch, R. Romani (r1923) (10/93) (NIMB) Ⓓ **NI7846**
8. D. Kirsten, RCA SO, J-P. Morel (r1947) (4/94) (RCA) Ⓓ [6] **09026 61580-2(6)**
8. M. Reining, Vienna St Op Orch, R. Moralt (r1942: Ger) (9/94) (PREI) Ⓓ **89065**
8. A. Roocroft, LPO, F. Welser-Möst (10/94) (EMI) Ⓓ **CDC5 55090-2** (10/94) (EMI) ▭ **EL5 55090-4**
8. C. Muzio, orch (r1917) (1/95) (ROMO) Ⓓ [2] **81010-2**
8, 18. M. Freni, Philh, G. Sinopoli (DG) ▭ **439 153-4GMA**
8, 18. M. Caballé, LSO, C. Mackerras (10/87) (EMI) Ⓓ **CDC7 47841-2**
8, 18. M. Callas, Philh, T. Serafin (r1954) (12/87) (EMI) Ⓓ **CDC7 47966-2**
8, 18. M. Gauci, Belgian Rad & TV Orch, A. Rahbari (11/92) (NAXO) Ⓓ **8 550606**
8, 18. J. Varady, Berlin RSO, M. Viotti (r1993) (5/95) (ORFE) Ⓓ **C323941A**
10, 17a, 17b, 18. K. Te Kanawa, P. Domingo, ROHO, G. Sinopoli (CAST) ▣ **CASH5051**
11a M. Caballé, P. Domingo, New Philh, B. Bartoletti (EMI) Ⓓ **CDM7 64359-2**
11a M. Callas, G. di Stefano, La Scala Orch, T. Serafin (r1957) (EMI) Ⓓ **CDC5 55216-2** (EMI) ▭ **EL555216-4**
11a M. Freni, F. Bonisolli, Hamburg PO, L. Magiera (11/88) (ACAN) Ⓓ **49 384**
11a J. Björling, L. Albanese, Rome Op Orch, J. Perlea (2/89) (RCA) Ⓓ **GD87799** (RCA) ▭ **GK87799**
11a M. Caballé, B. Marti, LSO (8/90) (CFP) Ⓓ **CD-CFP4569** (8/90) (CFP) ▭ **TC-CFP4569**
11a, 11b K. Te Kanawa, J. Carreras, Bologna Teatro Comunale Orch, R. Chailly (DECC) Ⓓ **421 896-2DA**
11a, 11b L. Price, P. Domingo, LSO, N. Santi (r1974) (RCA) Ⓓ **09026 61634-2**
11a, 11b M. Callas, G. di Stefano, La Scala Orch, T. Serafin (10/88) (EMI) Ⓓ **CDM7 69543-2**
11a, 11b K. Te Kanawa, J. Carreras, Bologna Teatro Comunale Orch, R. Chailly (12/91) (DECC) Ⓓ **430 724-2DM**
11a, 11b M. Caballé, P. Domingo, NY Met Op Orch, James Levine (pp) (5/93) (DG) Ⓓ **431 103-2GB**
11a, 11b P. Domingo, M. Caballé, NY Met Op Orch, James Levine (5/93) (DG) Ⓓ **431 104-2GB**
11a, 11b R. Tebaldi, F. Corelli, SRO, A. Guadagno (r1972) (10/93) (DECC) Ⓓ **436 301-2DA**
11a, 11b R. Tebaldi, F. Corelli, SRO, A. Guadagno (r1972) (12/93) (DECC) Ⓓ **433 439-2DA** (DECC) ▭ **433 439-4DA**
11a, 11b A. Pertile, M. Sheridan, La Scala Orch, C. Sabajno (r1928) (10/94) (PREI) Ⓓ **89072**
11a, 14. P. Domingo, K. Te Kanawa, T. Allen, M. Curtis, ROHO, G. Sinopoli (CAST) ▣ **CVI2070**
11c J. Carreras, RPO, R. Benzi (r1979) (PHIL) Ⓓ **442 600-2PH** (PHIL) ▭ **442 600-4PH**
12. P. Dvorský, Verona Arena Orch, A. Guadagno (pp1992) (MCI) Ⓓ **MCCD099**
12. B. Gigli, La Scala Orch, U. Berrettoni (r1941) (CONI) Ⓓ **CDHD227** (CONI) ▭ **MCHD227**
12. A. Pertile, La Scala Orch, C. Sabajno (r1930) (9/90) (PREI) Ⓓ **89007**
12. G. Zenatello, orch, Rosario Bourdon (r1929) (11/91) (CLUB) Ⓓ **CL99-025**
12. G. Zenatello, orch, Rosario Bourdon (r1929) (11/91) (PREI) Ⓓ **89038**
12. G. Zenatello, orch (r1909) (7/92) (PEAR) Ⓓ [3] **GEMMCDS9924(1)**
12. P. Schiavazzi, orch (r1910) (11/92) (MEMO) Ⓓ [2] **HR4408/9(2)**
12. G. Zenatello, orch, Rosario Bourdon (r1929) (5/94) (PEAR) Ⓓ [4] **GEMMCDS9074(2)**
12. A. Pertile, La Scala Orch, C. Sabajno (r1930) (10/94) (PREI) Ⓓ **89072**
13. Orch (EDL) Ⓓ **EDL2562-2** (EDL) ⊙ **EDL2562-1** ▭ **EDL2562-4**
13. Paris Cons, R. Leibowitz (r1960) (CHES) Ⓓ **Chesky CD61**
13. Miami SO, E. Kohn (pp1991) (IMP) Ⓓ **MCD43**
13. BPO, H. von Karajan (EMI) Ⓓ **CDM7 64629-2**
13. BPO, H. von Karajan, H. Burton (r1985) (SONY) ◐ **SLV46402** (SONY) ▣ **SHV46402**
13. Philh, I. Westrip (r1993) (IMP) Ⓓ **PCD1075**
13. Berlin RSO, R. Chailly (r1982) (DECC) Ⓓ **444 154-2DM**
13. RPO, A. Licata (r1994) (TRIN) Ⓓ **TRP044**
13. BPO, H. von Karajan (10/87) (DG) Ⓓ [3] **419 257-2GH3**
13. Gothenburg SO, N. Järvi (6/90) (DG) Ⓓ **429 494-2GDC** (6/90) (DG) ▭ **429 494-4GDC**
15a B. Gigli, G. Noto, orch, U. Berrettoni (r1940) (CONI) Ⓓ **CDHD227** (CONI) ▭ **MCHD227**
15a E. Garbin, S. Cottone (r1902) (4/94) (EMI) Ⓓ [3] **CHS7 64860-2(1)**
15a A. Pertile, A. Granforte, La Scala Orch, C. Sabajno (r1927) (10/94) (PREI) Ⓓ **89072**
15a, 15b K. Te Kanawa, P. Domingo, ROHO, G. Sinopoli (CAST) ▣ **CVI2065**
15a, 15b A. Pertile, A. Granforte, La Scala Orch, C. Sabajno (r1927) (CONI) Ⓓ **CDHD235**
15a, 15b G. Lauri-Volpi, L. Borgonovo, La Scala Orch, F. Ghione (r1934) (9/90) (PREI) Ⓓ **89012**
15a, 15b G. Lauri-Volpi, L. Borgonovo, La Scala Orch, F. Ghione (r1934) (7/93) (NIMB) Ⓓ **NI7845**
15a, 15b J. Björling, E. Campi, Rome Op Orch, Rome Op Chor, J. Perlea (r1954) (4/94) (RCA) Ⓓ [6] **09026 61580-2(5)**
18. M. Caballé, New Philh, B. Bartoletti (EMI) Ⓓ **CDM7 69596-2**
18. R. Tebaldi, R. Tucker, Rome RAI Orch, A. Paoletti (pp1954) (MEMO) Ⓓ [2] **HR4235/6**
18. R. Scotto, LSO, G. Gavazzeni (SONY) Ⓓ **SK48094** (SONY) ▭ **ST48094**
18. R. Scotto, LSO, G. Gavazzeni (SONY) Ⓓ **SK53549**
18. R. Tebaldi, Rome RAI Orch, A. Basile (bp1961) (FONI) Ⓓ **CDMR5023**
18. N. Rautio, ROHO, E. Downes (r1995) (ROH) Ⓓ **75605 55013-2** (ROH) ▭ **75605 55013-4**
18. A. Stella, LSO, A. Erede (8/90) (CFP) Ⓓ **CD-CFP4569** (8/90) (CFP) ▭ **TC-CFP4569**
18. R. Pampanini, EIAR Orch, U. Tansini (r1940) (8/93) (PREI) Ⓓ **89063**

La **Rondine, '(The) Swallow'– opera: 3 acts (1917—Monte Carlo) (Lib. Adami)**

EXCERPTS: ACT ONE: 1. Ah! no! no!; 2. Chi il bel sogno di Doretta; 3. Dolcessa! Ebbrezza!; 4. La Doretta della mia fantasia; 5. Denaro! Nient'altro che denaro!; 6. Ore dolci e divine; 7. E poi? Basta. È finito; 8. O mio giovine amico; 9. Forse, come la rondine. ACT TWO: 10. Fiori freschi!; 11. Chi è? Mai vista!; 12. Scusatemi, scusate; 13. Che caldo! Che sete!; 14. Perchè mai cercate di saper; 15. Zitti! Non disturbiamoli!; 16. Bevo al tuo fresco sorriso; 17. Rambaldo! Ah, M'aiutate!; 18. Nella trepida luce d'un mattin. ACT THREE: 19. Senti? Anche il mare respira sommesso; 20. E siam fuggiti qui per nasconderlo!; 21. Dimmi che vuoi seguirmi; 22. Che più dirgli? Che fare?; 23. È qui? Non so!; 24. Ma come voi?; 25. Amore mio! Mia madre!.

Magda K. Te Kanawa
Ruggero P. Domingo
Lisetta M. Nicolesco
Prunier D. Rendall
Rambaldo L. Nucci
Yvette L. Watson
Bianca G. Knight
Suzy L. Finnie
Solo Soprano E. Gale
Majordomo O. Broome
Georgette M. Midgley
Gabriella M. Thomas
Lolette U. Connors
Rabonnier B. Ogston
Gobin V. Midgley
Périchaud L. Benson
Crébillon D. Beavan
Young Man A. Byers
Solo Tenor W. Evans
Ambrosian Op. Chor, LSO, L. Maazel (r1981)
(10/85) (CBS) ⓓ [2] **CD37852**
Magda A. Moffo
Ruggero D. Barioni
Lisette G. Sciutti
Prunier P. de Palma
Rambaldo M. Sereni
Yvette S. Brigham-Dimiziani
Bianca V. de Notaristefani
Suzy F. Mattiucci
Perichaud M. Basiola II
Gobin F. Iacopucci
Crebillon R. El Hage
RCA Italiana Op Chor, RCA Italiana Op Orch, F. Molinari-Pradelli (r1966)
(9/90) (RCA) ⓓ [2] **GD60459**
1. K. Te Kanawa, Philh, L. Maazel
(SONY) ⓓ **SK48094**
(SONY) ▭ **ST48094**
1. M. Caballé, LSO, C. Mackerras (r1970)
(EMI) ⓓ **CDM5 65575-2**
1. R. Tebaldi, New PO, O. de Fabritiis (r1964)
(DECC) ⓓ [2] **444 555-2DF2**
2. K. Te Kanawa, LSO, J. Mauceri
(12/90) (DECC) ▭ **084 474-3**
2. N. Miricioiu, D. Harper (pp1985)
(ETCE) ▭ **XTC1041**
2. M. Caballé, LSO, C. Mackerras
(EMI) ⓓ **CDM7 69596-2**
2. R. Tebaldi, New Philh, O. de Fabritiis
(DECC) ⓓ **433 069-2DWO**
(DECC) ▭ **433 069-4DWO**
2. L. Mitchell, National PO, K.H. Adler
(DECC) ⓓ **433 865-2DWO**
(DECC) ▭ **433 865-4DWO**
2. L. Garrett, Philh, I. Bolton
(SILV) ⓓ **SONGCD907**
(SILV) ▭ **SONGC907**
2. L. Mitchell, National PO, K.H. Adler (r1980)
(BELA) ⓓ **450 007-2**
(BELA) ▭ **450 007-4**
2. R. Tebaldi, New Philh, O. de Fabritiis (r1964)
(DECC) ⓓ **436 317-2DA**
(DECC) ▭ **436 317-4DA**
2. P. Lorengar, Santa Cecilia Academy Orch, G. Patanè (r1966) (DECC) ⓓ **443 931-2DM**
2. A. Gheorghiu, ROHO, E. Downes (r1995)
(ROH) ⓓ **75605 55013-2**
(ROH) ▭ **75605 55013-4**
2. K. Te Kanawa, LPO, J. Pritchard
(5/85) (CBS) ⓓ **MK37298**
(CBS) ▭ **40-37298**
2. M. Caballé, LSO, C. Mackerras (r1970)
(10/87) (EMI) ⓓ **CDC7 47841-2**
2. M. Freni, Orch, L. Magiera
(10/89) (EMI) ⓓ **CDM7 63110-2**
2. N. Miricioiu, D. Harper (pp1985)
(5/90) (ETCE) ⓓ **KTC1041**
2. R. Tebaldi, New Philh, O. de Fabritiis
(8/91) (DECC) ⓓ [2] **430 481-2DX2**
2. D. Kirsten, RCA Victor Orch, J-P. Morel (r1949) (4/92) (EMI) ⓓ [7] **CHS7 69741-2(1)**
2. L. Orgonášová, Bratislava RSO, W. Humburg
(2/93) (NAXO) ⓓ **8 550605**
2. A. Roocroft, LPO, F. Welser-Möst
(10/94) (EMI) ⓓ **CDC5 55090-2**
(10/94) (EMI) ▭ **EL5 55090-4**
2. J. Varady, Berlin RSO, M. Viotti (r1993)
(5/95) (ORFE) ⓓ **C323941A**
2. I. Galante, Latvian Nat SO, A. Vilumanis (r1994) (11/95) (CAMP) ⓓ **RRCD1335**
(11/95) (CAMP) ▭ **RRMC8035**
25. P. Domingo, K. Te Kanawa, LSO, L. Maazel (r1970s) (SONY) ⓓ **SMK39030**

Suor Angelica, 'Sister Angelica'– opera: 1 act (1918—New York) (Wds. Forzano)
EXCERPTS. 1. Tutto ho offerto; 2. Intermezzo; 3. Senza mamma, O bimbo; 4. Amici fiori che nel.
Suor Angelica R. Plowright
Princess D. Vejzovic
La Scala Chor, La Scala Orch, G. Gavazzeni, S. Bussotti
(CAST) ▭ **CVI2057**
Suor Angelica R. Scotto
Princess M. Horne
Abbess P. Payne
Sister Monitor G. Knight
Mistress of the Novices A. Howard
Suor Genovieffa I. Cotrubas
Suor Osmina D. Cryer
Suor Dolcina M. Cable
Infirmary Sister E. Bainbridge
Almoner Sister I S. Minty
Almoner Sister II G. Jennings
Lay Sister I U. Connors
Lay Sister II A. Gunson
Novice D. Jones
Desborough School Ch, Ambrosian Op Chor, New Philh, L. Maazel
(11/88) (CBS) ⓓ [3] **CD79312**
Suor Angelica L. Popp
Princess M. Lipovšek
Abbess M. Schiml
Sister Monitor D. Jennings
Mistress of the Novices B. Calm
Suor Genovieffa; Suor Osmina M.G. Ferroni
Suor Dolcina M. Georg
Infirmary Sister V. Errante
Almoner Sister I; Novice E. van Lier
Almoner Sister II K. Hautermann
Lay Sister I M. Schmitt
Lay Sister II A. Schiller
Bavarian Rad Chor, Munich RO, G. Patanè
(4/90) (EURO) ⓓ [3] **GD69043**
Suor Angelica R. Tebaldi
Princess G. Simionato
Abbess; Lay Sister II L. Danieli
Sister Monitor M.T. Pace
Mistress of the Novices; Infirmary Sister A. di Stasio
Suor Genovieffa; Almoner Sister II; Novice D. Carral
Suor Osmina; Almoner Sister I J. Valtriani
Suor Dolcina; Lay Sister I G. Tavolaccini
MMF Chor, MMF Orch, L. Gardelli
(2/91) (DECC) ⓓ [3] **411 665-2DM3**
Suor Angelica V. de los Angeles
Princess F. Barbieri
Abbess; Mistress of the novices M. Doro
Sister Monitor C. Vozza
Suor Genovieffa; Almoner Sister I L. Marimpietri
Suor Osmina; Almoner Sister II; Novice S. Chissari
Suor Dolcina A. Marcangeli
Infirmary Sister T. Cantarini
Lay Sister I S. Bertona
Lay Sister II M. Huder
Rome Op Chor, Rome Op Orch, T. Serafin (r1957)
(6/93) (EMI) ⓓ [3] **CMS7 64165-2**
Suor Angelica M. Gauci
Princess L. Van Deyck
Abbess; Infirmary Sister M. Karadjian
Sister Monitor R. Fabry
Mistress of the Novices; Almoner Sister II D. Grossberger
Suor Genovieffa B. Degelin
Suor Osmina; Almoner Sister I D. Verdoodt
Suor Dolcina; A Novice M. Vliegen
J. Greggoor Chor, Brussels BRT PO, A. Rahbari (r1993)
(7/94) (DINT) ⓓ **DICD920120**
Suor Angelica M. Freni
Princess E. Suliotis
Abbess G. Scalchi
Sister Monitor E. Podles
Mistress of the Novices N. Curiel
Suor Genovieffa B. Frittoli
Suor Osmina; Almoner Sister II V. Esposito
Suor Dolcina O. Romanko
Infirmary Sister; Lay Sister I D. Beronesi
Almoner Sister I; Novice L. Cherici
Lay Sister II S. Macculi
Prato Voci Bianche Chor, MMF Chor, MMF Orch, B. Bartoletti (r1991)
(8/94) (DECC) ⓓ [3] **436 261-2DHO3**
2. BPO, H. von Karajan
(EMI) ⓓ **CDM7 64629-2**
2. Philh, I. Westrip (r1993) (IMP) ⓓ **PCD1075**
2. RPO, A. Licata (r1994) (TRIN) ⓓ **TRP044**
2. BPO, H. von Karajan
(10/87) (DG) ⓓ [3] **419 257-2GH3**
2. Gothenburg SO, N. Järvi
(6/90) (DG) ⓓ **429 494-2GDC**
(6/90) (DG) ▭ **429 494-4GDC**
3. M. Major, NZ SO, J. Matheson
(KIWI) ⓓ **CDTRL075**
3. A. Moffo, Munich RO, K. Eichhorn
(EURO) ⓓ **GD69113**
3. R. Scotto, New Philh, L. Maazel
(SONY) ⓓ **SK48094**
(SONY) ▭ **ST48094**
3. V. Zeani, Santa Cecilia Academy Orch, F. Patanè (DECC) ⓓ **433 865-2DWO**
(DECC) ▭ **433 865-4DWO**
3. R. Tebaldi, MMF Orch, L. Gardelli (r1961)
(DECC) ⓓ **440 408-2DM**
3. F. Weathers, Vienna Op Orch, A. Quadri (r1967) (BELA) ⓓ **450 007-2**
(BELA) ▭ **450 007-4**
3. M. Chiara, Vienna Volksoper Orch, N. Santi (r1971) (DECC) ⓓ **436 317-2DA**
(DECC) ▭ **436 317-4DA**
3. C. Muzio, orch (r1918)
(PEAR) ⓓ **GEMMCD9143**
3. L. Price, RCA Italiana Op Orch, F. Molinari-Pradelli (r1960s) (RCA) ⓓ **09026 62596-2**
3. K. Te Kanawa, LSO, Myung-Whun Chung (r1989) (EMI) ⓓ **CDM5 65578-2**
3. V. de los Angeles, Rome Op Orch, T. Serafin (r1957) (EMI) ⓓ **CDM5 65579-2**
3. N. Rautio, ROHO, E. Downes (r1995)
(ROH) ⓓ **75605 55013-2**
(ROH) ▭ **75605 55013-4**
3. M. Chiara, Vienna Op Orch, N. Santi (r1971)
(DECC) ⓓ [2] **444 555-2DF2**
3. M. Callas, Philh, T. Serafin (r1954)
(12/87) (EMI) ⓓ **CDC7 47966-2**
3. M. Freni, Rome Op Orch, F. Ferraris
(10/89) (EMI) ⓓ **CDM7 63110-2**
3. F. Cavalli, RPO, A. Fistoulari
(8/90) (CFP) ⓓ **CD-CFP4569**
(8/90) (CFP) ▭ **TC-CFP4569**
3. K. Te Kanawa, LSO, Myung-Whun Chung
(11/90) (EMI) ⓓ **CDC7 54062-2**
3. R. Tebaldi, MMF Orch, L. Gardelli
(8/91) (DECC) ⓓ [2] **430 481-2DX2**
3. M. Gauci, Belgian Rad & TV Orch, A. Rahbari
(11/92) (NAXO) ⓓ **8 550606**
3. L. Price, RCA Italiana Op Orch, F. Molinari-Pradelli (12/92) (RCA) ⓓ [4] **09026 61236-2**
3. A. Oltrabella, orch, G. Antonicelli (r1936)
(4/94) (EMI) ⓓ [3] **CHS7 64864-2(2)**
3. C. Muzio, orch (r1918)
(1/95) (ROMO) ⓓ [2] **81010-2**
3. J. Varady, Berlin RSO, M. Viotti (r1993)
(5/95) (ORFE) ⓓ **C323941A**
3, 4. Lotte Lehmann, orch (Ger: r1920)
(6/92) (PREI) ⓓ [3] **89302**

Il Tabarro, '(The) Cloak'– opera: 1 act (1918—New York) (Lib. Adami)
EXCERPTS. 1. Hai ben ragione; 2a. È ben altro il mio sogno!; 2b. Ma chi lascia il sobborgo; 2c. O Luigi!; 2d. Folle di gelosia!; 3. Perchè non m'ami più; 4a. Scorri, fiume eterno (original version of Michelè's aria); 4b. Nulla! Silenzio! (replacement version of Michelè's aria).
Michele P. Cappuccilli
Giorgetta S. Sass
Luigi N. Martinucci
La Scala Chor, La Scala Orch, G. Gavazzeni, S. Bussotti
(CAST) ▭ **CVI2057**
Michele S. Milnes
Giorgetta L. Price
Luigi P. Domingo
Tinca P. de Palma
Talpa R. El Hage
Frugola O. Dominguez
John Alldis Ch, New Philh, E. Leinsdorf
(RCA) ⓓ [2] **GD60865**
Michele I. Wixell
Giorgetta R. Scotto
Luigi P. Domingo
Tinca M. Sénéchal
Talpa D. Wicks
Frugola G. Knight
Ambrosian Op Chor, New Philh, L. Maazel
(11/88) (CBS) ⓓ [3] **CD79312**
Michele S. Nimsgern
Giorgetta I. Tokody
Luigi G. Lambert
Tinca T. Pane
Talpa G. Auer

Frugola W. Baniewicz
Bavarian Rad Chor, Munich RO, G. Patanè
(4/90) (EURO) ① [3] **GD69043**
Michele R. Merrill
Giorgetta R. Tebaldi
Luigi M. del Monaco
Tinca R. Ercolani
Talpa S. Maionica
Frugola L. Danieli
MMF Chor, MMF Orch, L. Gardelli
(2/91) (DECC) ① [3] **411 665-2DM3**
Michele T. Gobbi
Giorgetta M. Mas
Luigi G. Prandelli
Tinca P. de Palma
Talpa P. Clabassi
Frugola M. Pirazzini
Rome Op Chor, Rome Op Orch, V. Bellezza (r1955)
(6/93) (EMI) ① [3] **CMS7 64165-2**
Michele J. Pons
Giorgetta M. Freni
Luigi G. Giacomini
Tinca P. de Palma
Talpa F. de Grandis
Frugola G. Scalchi
Song-pedlar R. Cassinelli
Amante I B. Frittoli
Amante II R. Emili
MMF Chor, MMF Orch, B. Bartoletti (r1991)
(8/94) (DECC) ① [3] **436 261-2DHO3**
Michele E. Tumagian
Giorgetta M. Slatinaru
Luigi N. Martinucci
Tinca A. Leonel
Talpa M. Rosca
Frugola L. van Deyck
. Gregoor Ch, Brussels BRT Phil Chor, Brussels BRT PO, A. Rahbari (r1994)
(4/95) (DINT) ① **DICD920209**
1. D. Smirnov, orch (r1921)
(PEAR) ① **GEMMCD9106**
1. D. Smirnov, orch (r1921)
(7/90) (CLUB) ① **CL99-031**
2c S. Sass, N. Martinucci, P. Cappuccilli, La Scala Orch, G. Gavazzeni
(CAST) ▬ **CVI2070**
4a L. Tibbett, orch (pp1935)
(3/91) (PEAR) ① [2] **GEMMCDS9452**
4b A. Michaels-Moore, ROHO, E. Downes (r1995)
(ROH) ① **75605 55013-2**
(ROH) ▭ **75605 55013-4**

Tosca– opera: 3 acts (1900—Rome) (Lib. Illica and Giacosa)

ACT 1: 1a. Ah! Finalmente!; 1b. E sempre lava!; 1c. Sante ampolle!; 2. Recondita armonia; 3a. Mario!; 3b. Perchè chiuso?; 3c. Ora stammi a sentir; 3d. Non la sospiri; 3e. Or lasciami al lavoro; 3f. Ah, quegli occhi!; 4. È buona la mia Tosca; 5. Sommo giubilo; 6a. Un tal baccano in chiesa!; 6b. Fu grave sbaglio; 7a. Or tutto è chiaro; 7b. Tosca divina; 7c. O che v'offende; 8. Tre sbirri (Te Deum). ACT 2: 9a. Tosca è un buon falco; 9b. Ella verrà; 10a. Sale, ascende...A te quest'inno (Cantata); 10b. Mario, tu qui?; 11a. La povera mia cena; 11b. Già, mi dicon venal; 11c. Se la giurata; 12. Vissi d'arte; 13a. Sei troppo bella; 13b. Tosca. finalmente mia!. ACT 3: 14. Prelude; 15a. Io de' sospiri; 15b. Mario Cavaradossi?; 16. E lucevan le stelle; 17a. Franchigia a Floria Tosca; 17b. O dolci mani; 17c. Senti, l'ora è vicina; 18a. Amaro sol per te; 18b. Trionfal...Di nova speme; 19a. Son pronto; 19b. Com'è lunga l'attesa!.

Tosca E. Marton
Cavaradossi G. Aragall
Scarpia I. Wixell
Verona Arena Chor, Verona Arena Orch, D. Oren, S. Bussotti
(CAST) ▬ **CVI2006**
Tosca R. Tebaldi
Cavaradossi E. Tobin
Scarpia G. London
Angelotti G. Grefe
Spoletta H. Buchta
Sacristan H. Cramer
Sciarrone S. Fischer-Sandt
Gaoler W. Baur
Shepherd Boy C. Hellmann
Stuttgart Op Chor, Stuttgart Op Orch, F. Patanè (pp1961)
(VAI) ▬ **VAI69216**
Tosca R. Tebaldi
Cavaradossi G. Campora
Scarpia E. Mascherini
Angelotti D. Caselli
Spoletta P. de Palma
Sacristan F. Corena
Sciaronne; Gaoler A. Sacchetti
Shepherd Boy G. F. Volante
Santa Cecilia Academy Chor, Santa Cecilia Academy Orch, A. Erede (r1951)
(LOND) ① [2] **440 236-2LF2**
Tosca M. Freni
Cavaradossi L. Pavarotti
Scarpia S. Milnes
Angelotti R. Van Allan
Spoletta M. Sénéchal
Sacristan I. Tajo
Sciarrone P. Hudson
Gaoler J. Tomlinson
Shepherd Boy W. Baratti
Wandsworth Sch Boys' Ch, London Op Chor, National PO, N. Rescigno (r1978)
(DECC) ① [11] **443 204-2DH11(1)**
Tosca K. Ricciarelli
Cavaradossi J. Carreras
Scarpia R. Raimondi
Angelotti G. Hornik
Spoletta H. Zednik
Sacristan F. Corena
Sciarrone; Gaoler V. von Halem
Shepherd Boy W. Bünten
Berlin Deutsche Op Chor, BPO, H. von Karajan
(3/85) (DG) ① [2] **413 815-2GH2**
Tosca M. Callas
Cavaradossi G. di Stefano
Scarpia T. Gobbi
Angelotti F. Calabrese
Spoletta A. Mercuriali
Sacristan M. Luise
Sciarrone; Gaoler D. Caselli
Shepherd Boy A. Cordova
La Scala Chor, La Scala Orch, V. de Sabata (r1953)
(9/85) (EMI) ① [2] **CDS7 47175-8**
Tosca M. Caballé
Cavaradossi J. Carreras
Scarpia I. Wixell
Angelotti S. Ramey
Spoletta P. de Palma
Sacristan D. Trimarchi
Sciarrone; Gaoler W. Elvin
Shepherd Boy A. Murray
ROH Chor, ROHO, Colin Davis
(4/86) (PHIL) ① [2] **412 885-2PH2**
(PHIL) ▭ [2] **412 885-4PX2**
Tosca K. Te Kanawa
Cavaradossi G. Aragall
Scarpia L. Nucci
Angelotti M. King
Spoletta P. de Palma
Sacristan S. Malas
Sciarrone P. Hudson
Gaoler N. Folwell
Shepherd Boy I. Martinez
ROH Children's Chor, WNO Chor, National PO, G. Solti
(11/86) (DECC) ① [2] **414 597-2DH2**
Tosca L. Price
Cavaradossi P. Domingo
Scarpia S. Milnes
Angelotti C. Grant
Spoletta F. Egerton
Sacristan P. Plishka
Sciarrone J. Gibbs
Gaoler M. Rippon
Shepherd Boy D. Pearl
Wandsworth Sch Boys' Ch, John Alldis Ch, New Philh, Z. Mehta
(11/86) (RCA) ① [2] **RD80105**
Tosca R. Kabaivanska
Cavaradossi P. Domingo
Scarpia S. Milnes
Angelotti G. Luccardi
Spoletta M. Ferrara
Sacristan A. Mariotti
Sciarrone B. Grella
Gaoler D. Medici
Shepherd P. Domingo jnr
Ambrosian Sngrs, New Philh, B. Bartoletti, G. de Bosio
(10/88) (DECC) ◖ [2] **071 402-1DH2**
(DECC) ▬ **071 402-3DH**
Tosca Z. Milanov
Cavaradossi J. Björling
Scarpia L. Warren
Angelotti L. Monreale
Spoletta Mario Carlin
Sacristan F. Corena
Sciarrone N. Catalani
Gaoler V. Preziosa
Shephard Boy G. Bianchini
Rome Op Chor, Rome Op Orch, E. Leinsdorf
(1/89) (RCA) ① [2] **GD84514**
Tosca R. Scotto
Cavaradossi P. Domingo
Scarpia R. Bruson
Angelotti J. Cheek
Spoletta A. Velis
Sacristan R. Capecchi
Sciarrone P. Hudson
Gaoler I. Perlman
Shepherd Boy D. Martinez
Ambrosian Op Chor, St Clement Danes Sch Ch, Philh, James Levine (r1980)
(1/89) (EMI) ① [2] **CDS7 49364-2**
Tosca M. Freni
Cavaradossi L. Pavarotti
Scarpia S. Milnes
Angelotti R. Van Allan
Spoletta M. Sénéchal
Sacristan I. Tajo
Sciarrone P. Hudson
Gaoler J. Tomlinson
Shepherd Boy W. Baratti
Wandsworth Sch Boys' Ch, London Op Chor, National PO, N. Rescigno
(1/89) (DECC) ① [2] **414 036-2DH2**
Tosca L. Price
Cavaradossi G. di Stefano
Scarpia G. Taddei
Angelotti C. Cava
Spoletta P. de Palma
Sacristan F. Corena
Sciarrone L. Monreale
Gaoler A. Mariotti
Shepherd Boy H. Weiss
Vienna St Op Chor, VPO, H. von Karajan
(1/89) (DECC) ① [2] **421 670-2DM2**
Tosca M. Callas
Cavaradossi C. Bergonzi
Scarpia T. Gobbi
Angelotti; Gaoler L. Monreale
Spoletta R. Ercolani
Sacristan G. Tadeo
Sciarrone U. Trama
Shepherd Boy D. Sellar
Paris Op Chor, Paris Cons, G. Prêtre (r1964)
(8/89) (EMI) ① [2] **CMS7 69974-2**
Tosca E. Marton
Cavaradossi J. Carreras
Scarpia J. Pons
Angelotti I. Gáti
Spoletta F. Gerdesits
Sacristan I. Tajo
Sciarrone J. Németh
Gaoler J. Gregor
Shepherd Boy B. Héja
Hungarian Rad & TV Chor, Hungarian St Orch, M. Tilson Thomas
(10/90) (SONY) ① [2] **S2K45847**
Tosca R. Tebaldi
Cavaradossi M. del Monaco
Scarpia G. London
Angelotti S. Maionica
Spoletta P. de Palma
Sacristan F. Corena
Sciarrone; Gaoler G. Morese
Shepherd boy E. Palerini
Santa Cecilia Academy Chor, Santa Cecilia Academy Orch, F. Molinari-Pradelli
(8/91) (DECC) ① [2] **411 871-2DM2**
Tosca N. Miricioiu
Cavaradossi G. Lamberti
Scarpia S. Carroli
Angelotti A. Piccinni
Spoletta M. Dvorský
Sacristan J. Špaček
Sciarrone J. Durco
Gaoler S. Benacka
Slovak Phil Chor, Bratislava RSO, A. Rahbari
(10/91) (NAXO) ① [2] **8 660001/2**
Tosca H. Behrens
Cavaradossi P. Domingo
Scarpia C. MacNeil
Angelotti J. Courtney
Spoletta A. Laciura
Sacristan I. Tajo
Sciarrone R. Christopher
Gaoler R. Vernon
Shepherd Boy M. Fogerty
NY Met Op Chor, NY Met Op Orch, G. Sinopoli, F. Zeffirelli
(7/92) (DG) ◖ [2] **072 426-1GH2**
(7/92) (DG) ▬ **072 426-3GH**
Tosca M. Freni
Cavaradossi P. Domingo

Scarpia S. Ramey
Angelotti B. Terfel
Spoletta A. Laciura
Sacristan A. Veccia
Sciarrone R. Lukas
Gaoler B. Secombe
Shepherd Boy L. Tiernan
ROH Chor, Philh, G. Sinopoli (r1990)
(7/92) (DG) Ⓓ [2] **431 775-2GH2**
Tosca M. Caballé
Cavaradossi J. Carreras
Scarpia I. Wixell
Angelotti S. Ramey
Spoletta P. de Palma
Sacristan D. Trimarchi
Sciarrone; Gaoler W. Elvin
Shepherd Boy A. Murray
ROH Chor, ROHO, Colin Davis (r1976)
(8/93) (PHIL) Ⓓ [2] **438 359-2PM2**
Tosca C. Vaness
Cavaradossi G. Giacomini
Scarpia G. Zancanaro
Angelotti D. Serraiocco
Spoletta P. de Palma
Sacristan A. Mariotti
Sciarrone O. Mori
Gaoler C. Austin
Shepherd boy J. Smith
Philadelphia Boys' Ch, Westminster Symphonic Ch, Philadelphia, R. Muti (pp1991/2)
(9/93) (PHIL) Ⓓ [2] **434 595-2PH2**
Tosca C. Malfitano
Cavaradossi P. Domingo
Scarpia R. Raimondi
Angelotti G. Prestia
Spoletta M. Buffoli
Sacristan G. Gatti
Sciarrone S. Sammaritano
Gaoler F. Federici
Shepherd Boy S. Scatarzi
Rome RAI Chor, Rome RAI Orch, Z. Mehta (r1992)
(10/93) (TELD) ◐ [2] **4509-90212-6**
(10/93) (TELD) ▣ **4509-92698-3**
Tosca R. Kabaivanska
Cavaradossi L. Pavarotti
Scarpia I. Wixell
Angelotti F. Federici
Spoletta M. Bolognesi
Sacristan A. Mariotti
Sciarrone U. Carosi
Gaoler G. Zecchillo
Shpeherd Boy V. Gricolo
Rome Op Chor, Rome Op Orch, D. Oren (pp1990)
(12/93) (RCA) Ⓓ [2] **09026 61806-2**
Tosca B. Nilsson
Cavaradossi F. Corelli
Scarpia D. Fischer-Dieskau
Angelotti S. Maionica
Spoletta P. de Palma
Sacristan A. Mariotti
Sciarrone D. Mantovani
Gaoler L. Arbace
Shepherd Boy P. Veronelli
Santa Cecilia Academy Chor, Santa Cecilia Academy Orch, L. Maazel (r1966)
(4/94) (DECC) Ⓓ [2] **440 051-2DMO2**
Tosca C. Melis
Cavaradossi P. Pauli
Scarpia A. Granforte
Angelotti; Sciarrone G. Azzimonti
Spoletta N. Palai
Sacristan A. Gelli
Shepherd Boy G. Bottini
La Scala Chor, La Scala Orch, C. Sabajno (r1929)
(4/95) (VAI) Ⓓ [2] **VAIA1076**

Act 2. M. Callas, T. Gobbi, A. Lance, L. Rialland, J-P. Hurteau, Paris Op Orch, G. Sébastian (pp1958) (11/91) (EMI) ◐ **LDB9 91258-1**
(11/91) (EMI) ▣ **MVC9 91258-3**
Act 2. M. Callas, R. Cioni, T. Gobbi, R. Bowman, D. Wicks, ROH Chor, ROHO, C.F. Cillario, F. Zeffirelli (pp1964)
(3/95) (EMI) ◐ **LDB4 91283-1**
(3/95) (EMI) ▣ **MVD4 91283-3**
Act 3. H. Roswaenge, G. Behm, M. Abendroth, W. Stoll, H. Braun, Berlin St Op Orch, H. Löwlein (pp1957) (PREI) Ⓓ **90103**
Excs P. Domingo (CAST) ▣ **CVI2021**
Excs M. Freni, P. Domingo, S. Ramey, B. Terfel, A. Laciura, A. Veccia, R. Lukas, L. Tiernan, B. Secombe, Philh, G. Sinopoli (r1990)
(DG) Ⓓ **437 547-2GH**
Excs N. Vallin, E. di Mazzei, A. Endrèze, Paris Opéra-Comique Chor, Paris Opéra-Comique Orch, G. Cloëz (French: r1932)
(4/92) (MSCM) Ⓓ **MM30376**
1a, 1b, 2, 3a, 3d, 8, 10b(pt), 12, 16, 17, 19b Z. Milanov, J. Björling, L. Warren, Rome Op Chor, Rome Op Orch, E. Leinsdorf
(RCA) Ⓓ **GD60192**
(RCA) ▭ **GK60192**
1a, 2, 3a, 3f, 8, 10a, 10b, 12, 16, 17a, 17b, 18a, 19b K. Ricciarelli, J. Carreras, R. Raimondi, G. Hornik, H. Zednik, F. Corena, V. von Halem, Berlin Deutsche Op Chor, BPO, H. von Karajan
(DG) Ⓓ **423 113-2GH**
1a, 2, 3a, 3f, 8, 10b(pt), 12, 13b, 15b, 16, 17b, 18a(pt), 19b K. Ricciarelli, J. Carreras, R. Raimondi, G. Hornik, H. Zednik, F. Corena, V. von Halem, Schöneberg Boys' Ch, Berlin Deutsche Op Chor, BPO, H. von Karajan (r1979)
(DG) Ⓓ **439 461-2GCL**
(DG) ▭ **439 461-4GCL**
1c, 2, 3a-f, 8, 9a, 12, 13b, 15a, 15b, 16, 17c, 19b M. Freni, L. Pavarotti, S. Milnes, R. Van Allan, M. Sénéchal, I. Tajo, P. Hudson, J. Tomlinson, W. Baratti, Wandsworth Sch Boys' Ch, London Op Chor, National PO, N. Rescigno
(DECC) Ⓓ **421 888-2DA**
(DECC) ▭ **421 888-4DA**
1c, 2, 3a-f, 8, 10b, 12, 13a, b, 16, 17a-c, 18a, b, 19a, b C. Vaness, G. Giacomini, P. de Palma, G. Zancanaro, C. Austin, O. Mori, A. Mariotti, Philadelphia Boys' Ch, Westminster Symphonic Ch, Philadelphia, R. Muti (pp1991/2)
(PHIL) Ⓓ **442 438-2PH**
1c, 2, 3a-f, 8, 12, 16. M. Freni, L. Pavarotti, M. Sénéchal, S. Milnes, I. Tajo, London Op Chor, Wandsworth Sch Boys Ch, National PO, N. Rescigno (r1978)
(DECC) Ⓓ [2] **444 555-2DF2**
1c, 3a, 3d, 3f, 8, 10a, 10b, 11b, 11c, 12, 15a, 15b, 16, 17a-c, 18a, 18b, 19b E. Marton, J. Carreras, J. Pons, F. Gerdesits, I. Tajo, J. Németh, J. Gregor, B. Héja, Hungarian Rad & TV Chor, Hungarian St Orch, M. Tilson Thomas (r1988) (SONY) Ⓓ **SMK53550**
2. B. Gigli, orch (r1926) (CONI) Ⓓ **CDHD149**
(CONI) ▭ **MCHD149**
2. P. Dvorský, Berlin RSO, R. Paternostro
(ACAN) Ⓓ **43 123**
2. T. Burke, orch (r1920)
(PEAR) Ⓓ **GEMMCD9411**
2. J. Björling, orch, N. Grevillius (r1936)
(MMOI) Ⓓ **CDMOIR405**
(MMOI) ▭ **CMOIR405**
2. F. Corelli, NY Met Op Orch, K.H. Adler (pp1962) (MEMO) Ⓓ [2] **HR4204/5**
2. L. Pavarotti, National PO, N. Rescigno
(DECC) Ⓓ **430 470-2DH**
(DECC) ▭ **430 470-4DH**
2. P. Domingo, P. Plishka, New Philh, Z. Mehta
(RCA) Ⓓ [2] **GD60866**
(RCA) ▭ [2] **GK60866**
2. B. Gigli, G. Tomei, Rome Op Orch, O. de Fabritiis (r1938) (MMOI) Ⓓ **CDMOIR412**
2. B. Prevedi, ROHO, E. Downes
(DECC) Ⓓ **433 865-2DWO**
(DECC) ▭ **433 865-4DWO**
2. J. Vickers, Rome Op Orch, T. Serafin (r1961)
(VAI) Ⓓ **VAIA1016**
2. F. Corelli, A. Mariotti, Santa Cecilia Academy Orch, L. Maazel (r1966)
(DECC) Ⓓ **433 440-2DA**
(DECC) ▭ **433 440-4DA**
2. J. Björling, orch, N. Grevillius (r1936)
(PEAR) Ⓓ **GEMMCD9043**
2. L. Pavarotti, Rome Op Orch, D. Oren
(RCA) Ⓓ **09026 61886-2**
(RCA) ▭ **09026 61886-4**
2. R. Crooks, Berlin St Op Orch, C. Schmalstich (r1927: Ger) (PEAR) Ⓓ **GEMMCD9093**
2. J. Carreras, D. Trimarchi, ROHO, Colin Davis (r1976) (PHIL) Ⓓ **442 600-2PH**
(PHIL) ▭ **442 600-4PH**
2. B. Gigli, orch (r1921) (ASV) Ⓓ **CDAJA5137**
(ASV) ▭ **ZCAJA5137**
2. F. de Lucia, orch (r1917)
(BONG) Ⓓ [2] **GB1064/5-2**
2. J. Hislop, orch, J. Barbirolli (r1929)
(CONI) Ⓓ **CDHD235**
2. B. Gigli, orch, J. Pasternack (r1926)
(9/88) (PEAR) Ⓓ **GEMMCD9316**
2. E. Caruso, orch (r1909)
(5/89) (PEAR) Ⓓ **GEMMCD9309**
2. P. Dvorský, Bratislava RSO, Czech RSO, O. Lenárd (10/89) (OPUS) Ⓓ **9156 1824**
2. B. Gigli, G. Tomei, Rome Op Orch, O. de Fabritiis (r1938) (5/90) (EMI) Ⓓ **CDH7 61052-2**
2. C. Craig, Orch, M. Collins
(8/90) (CFP) Ⓓ **CD-CFP4569**
(8/90) (CFP) ▭ **TC-CFP4569**
2. P. Domingo, National PO, E. Kohn
(11/90) (EMI) Ⓓ **CDC7 54053-2**
2. L. Pavarotti, James Levine, B. Large
(2/92) (DECC) ◐ **071 119-1DH**
(2/92) (DECC) ▣ **071 119-3DH**
2. G. Anselmi, anon (r1907)
(7/92) (PEAR) Ⓓ [3] **GEMMCDS9924(1)**
2. R. Tauber, orch (r1932: Ger)
(9/92) (MMOI) Ⓓ **CDMOIR409**
2. R. Tauber, orch (Ger: r1922)
(12/92) (NIMB) Ⓓ **NI7830**
(12/92) (NIMB) ▭ **NC7830**
2. G. Lauri-Volpi, orch (r1922)
(7/93) (NIMB) Ⓓ **NI7845**
2. A. Piccaver, orch (r1914: Ger)
(8/93) (PREI) Ⓓ **89060**
2. J. Björling, orch, N. Grevillius (r1936)
(10/93) (NIMB) Ⓓ **NI7842**
2. R. Crooks, Berlin St Op Orch, C. Schmalstich (r1929: Ger)
(5/94) (CLAR) Ⓓ **CDGSE78-50-52**
2. G. Zenatello, orch (r1908)
(5/94) (SYMP) Ⓓ **SYMCD1158**
2. G. Zenatello, orch (r1908)
(5/94) (PEAR) Ⓓ [4] **GEMMCDS9073(2)**
2. P. Domingo, National PO, E. Kohn (r1989)
(6/94) (EMI) Ⓓ **CDC5 55017-2**
2. J. Björling, orch, N. Grevillius (r1936)
(9/94) (IMP) Ⓓ **GLRS103**
2. J. Björling, orch, N. Grevillius (r1936)
(9/94) (CONI) Ⓓ **CDHD214**
(9/94) (CONI) ▭ **MCHD214**
2. F. de Lucia, anon (r1903)
(1/95) (SYMP) Ⓓ **SYMCD1149**
2. A. Giorgini, anon (r1904)
(4/95) (RECO) Ⓓ **TRC3**
2. E. Caruso, orch (r1909)
(7/95) (NIMB) Ⓓ **NI7866**
2, 12, 16. B. Nilsson, F. Corelli, A. Mariotti, L. Maazel (r1966) (DECC) Ⓓ **436 317-2DA**
(DECC) ▭ **436 317-4DA**
2, 16. P. Domingo, L. Pavarotti, MMF Orch, Rome Op Orch, Z. Mehta (pp1990)
(DECC) ◐ **071 123-1DH**
(DECC) ▣ **071 123-3DH**
2, 16. M. Lanza, RCA Victor Orch, C. Callinicos (r1950) (RCA) Ⓓ **GD60049**
(RCA) ▭ **GK60049**
2, 16. A. Dermota, Berlin St Op Orch, A. Rother (r1950s) (PREI) Ⓓ **90022**
2, 16. T. Schipa, orch, Anon (cond) (pp1913)
(MEMO) Ⓓ [2] **HR4220/1**
2, 16. G. di Stefano, Santa Cecilia Academy Orch, F. Patanè (DECC) Ⓓ **433 636-2DSP**
(DECC) ▭ **433 636-4DSP**
2, 16. G. di Stefano, Santa Cecilia Academy Orch, F. Patanè (DECC) Ⓓ **433 623-2DSP**
(DECC) ▭ **433 623-4DSP**
2, 16. F. Corelli, A. Mariotti, Santa Cecilia Academy Orch, L. Maazel (r1966)
(DECC) Ⓓ **433 065-2DWO**
(DECC) ▭ **433 065-4DWO**
2, 16. J. Björling, orch, N. Grevillius (r1933: Swed) (NIMB) Ⓓ **NI7835**
2, 16. P. Domingo, L. Pavarotti, MMF Orch, Rome Op Orch, Z. Mehta (pp1990)
(DECC) ѺѺ **430 433-5DH**
2, 16. T. Harper, Bratislava RSO, M. Halász
(NAXO) Ⓓ **8 550497**
2, 16. E. Caruso, orch, W.B. Rogers (r1909)
(RCA) Ⓓ **09026 61243-2**
2, 16. E. Barham, RPO, R. Stapleton (r1990)
(RPO) Ⓓ [2] **CDRPD9006**
(RPO) ▭ [2] **ZCRPD9006**
2, 16. J. Schmidt, BPO, S. Meyrowitz (r1929: Ger) (RELI) Ⓓ **CR921036**
2, 16. L. Pavarotti, Philh, L. Magiera
(DECC) ѺѺ **436 320-5DH**
2, 16. Deng, Württemberg PO, R. Paternostro
(SINE) Ⓓ **39820222**
2, 16. M. del Monaco, F. Corena, Santa Cecilia Academy Orch, F. Molinari-Pradelli (r1959)
(DECC) Ⓓ **440 407-2DM**
2, 16. G. di Stefano, Zurich Tonhalle Orch, F. Patanè (r1958) (DECC) Ⓓ **440 403-2DM**
2, 16. G. Di Stefano, Santa Cecilia Academy Orch, F. Patanè (r1959) (BELA) Ⓓ **450 005-2**
(BELA) ▭ **450 005-4**
2, 16. J. Schmidt, Berlin City Op Orch, F. Weissmann (r1933)
(EMI) Ⓓ [2] **CHS7 64673-2**

12. R. Kabaivanska, New PO, B. Bartoletti (DECC) ● **071 142-1DH**
(DECC) ▣ **071 142-3DH**

12. K. Ricciarelli, Madrid SO, G.P. Sanzogno (RNE) Ⓓ [2] **650004**

12. E. Marton, Hungarian St Orch, M. Tilson Thomas (SONY) Ⓓ **SK48094**
(SONY) ▭ **ST48094**

12. M. Freni, National PO, N. Rescigno (r1978) (DECC) Ⓓ **436 300-2DX**
(DECC) ▭ **436 300-4DX**

12. M. Callas, Paris Cons, G. Prêtre (EMI) Ⓓ **CDC7 54702-2**
(EMI) ▭ **EL754702-4**

12. J. Sutherland, New Philh, R. Bonynge (DECC) Ⓓ **433 865-2DWO**
(DECC) ▭ **433 865-4DWO**

12. M. Callas, Paris Cons, G. Prêtre (r1965) (CFP) Ⓓ **CD-CFP4602**
(CFP) ▭ **TC-CFP4602**

12. M. Dragoni, Munich RSO, G. Kuhn (r1991) (ORFE) Ⓓ **C261921A**

12. J. Barstow, RPO, R. Stapleton (r1991) (RPO) Ⓓ [2] **CDRPD9006**
(RPO) ▭ [2] **ZCRPD9006**

12. L. Price, VPO, H. von Karajan (r1962) (DECC) Ⓓ **440 402-2DM**

12. R. Tebaldi, Santa Cecilia Academy Orch, F. Molinari-Pradelli (r1959) (DECC) Ⓓ **440 408-2DM**

12. J. Sutherland, New Philh, R. Bonynge (r1973) (BELA) Ⓓ **450 007-2**
(BELA) ▭ **450 007-4**

12. E. Urbanová, Prague SO, J. Bělohlávek (r1993) (SUPR) Ⓓ **11 1851-2**

12. M. Freni, National PO, N. Rescigno (r1978) (DECC) Ⓓ **440 412-2DM**

12. A. Cerquetti, MMF Orch, G. Gavazzeni (r1956) (DECC) Ⓓ **440 411-2DM**

12. C. Muzio, orch (r1917) (PEAR) Ⓓ **GEMMCD9143**

12. H. Wildbrunn, orch (r1919) (PREI) Ⓓ **89097**

12. K. Ricciarelli, Svizzera Italiana Orch, B. Amaducci (r1979) (ERMI) Ⓓ **ERM151**

12. L. Price, New Philh, E. Downes (r1971) (RCA) Ⓓ **74321 24284-2**
(RCA) ▭ **74321 24284-4**

12. H. Spani, La Scala Orch, C. Sabajno (r1929) (CONI) Ⓓ **CDHD235**

12. M. Caballé, LSO, C. Mackerras (r1970) (EMI) Ⓓ **CDM5 65575-2**

12. Z. Milanov, Rome Op Orch, E. Leinsdorf (r1957) (RCA) Ⓓ **09026 62689-2**

12. K. Te Kanawa, LPO, J. Pritchard (5/85) (CBS) Ⓓ **MK37298**
(CBS) ▭ **40-37298**

12. R. Scotto, I. Davis (pp1983) (10/86) (ETCE) Ⓓ **KTC2002**
(ETCE) ▭ **XTC2002**

12. M. Caballé, LSO, C. Mackerras (10/87) (EMI) Ⓓ **CDC7 47841-2**

12. K. Te Kanawa, National PO, G. Solti (11/87) (DECC) Ⓓ **417 645-2DH**

12. A. Cerquetti, MMF Orch, G. Gavazzeni (1/89) (DECC) Ⓓ **417 686-2DC**

12. E. Turner, orch, J. Batten (r1933: Eng) (9/89) (EMI) Ⓓ **CDH7 69791-2**

12. M. Freni, Orch, L. Magiera (10/89) (EMI) Ⓓ **CDM7 63110-2**

12. M. Callas, Paris Cons, G. Prêtre (2/90) (EMI) Ⓓ **CDM7 63182-2**

12. M. Callas, Paris Cons, G. Prêtre (2/90) (EMIN) Ⓓ **CD-EMX2123**
(2/88) (EMIN) ▭ **TC-EMX2123**

12. N. Miricioiu, D. Harper (pp1985) (5/90) (ETCE) Ⓓ **KTC1041**

12. A. Stella, LSO, A. Erede (8/90) (CFP) Ⓓ **CD-CFP4569**
(8/90) (CFP) ▭ **TC-CFP4569**

12. H. Spani, orch, C. Sabajno (r1929) (9/90) (CLUB) Ⓓ [2] **CL99-509/10**

12. H. Spani, orch (r1925) (9/90) (CLUB) Ⓓ [2] **CL99-509/10**

12. G. Arangi-Lombardi, La Scala Orch, L. Molajoli (r1932) (10/90) (PREI) Ⓓ **89013**

12. C. Muzio, orch, L. Molajoli (r1935) (4/91) (NIMB) Ⓓ **NI7814**
(4/91) (NIMB) ▭ **NC7814**

12. F. Leider, orch (r1921: Ger) (5/91) (PREI) Ⓓ [3] **89301**

12. R. Tebaldi, Santa Cecilia Academy Orch, F. Molinari-Pradelli (8/91) (DECC) Ⓓ [2] **430 481-2DX2**

12. G. Brouwenstijn, Hilversum RO, P. Van Kempen (r1951) (4/92) (EMI) Ⓓ [7] **CHS7 69741-2(4)**

12. Lotte Lehmann, Berlin St Op Orch, K. Besl (Ger: r1924) (6/92) (PREI) Ⓓ [3] **89302**

12. A. Marc, NZ SO, H. Wallberg (6/92) (DELO) Ⓓ **DE3108**
(6/92) (DELO) ▭ **CS3108**

12. E. Destinn, orch, P. Pitt (r1911) (7/92) (PEAR) Ⓓ [3] **GEMMCDS9924(2)**

12. C. Melis, orch (r c1910) (7/92) (PEAR) Ⓓ [3] **GEMMCDS9926(1)**

12. M. Jeritza, orch, Rosario Bourdon (r1928) (7/92) (PEAR) Ⓓ [3] **GEMMCDS9925(2)**

12. M. Gauci, Belgian Rad & TV Orch, A. Rahbari (11/92) (NAXO) Ⓓ **8 550606**

12. H. Spani, La Scala Orch, C. Sabajno (r1929) (12/92) (PREI) Ⓓ **89037**

12. J. Hammond, Hallé, L. Heward (r1941: Eng) (12/92) (TEST) Ⓓ **SBT1013**

12. M. Mei-Figner, anon (r1901) (6/93) (PEAR) Ⓓ [3] **GEMMCDS9997/9(1)**

12. J. Korolewicz-Wayda, anon (r1904) (6/93) (PEAR) Ⓓ [3] **GEMMCDS9004/6(1)**

12. A. Pinto, anon (two versions: r1902) (8/93) (SYMP) Ⓓ **SYMCD1111**

12. E. Carelli, S. Cottone (r1904) (8/93) (SYMP) Ⓓ **SYMCD1111**

12. R. Ponselle, orch, R. Romani (r1919) (10/93) (NIMB) Ⓓ **NI7846**

12. E. Eames, orch (r1908) (11/93) (ROMO) Ⓓ [2] **81001-2**

12. E. Eames, anon (r1905) (11/93) (ROMO) Ⓓ [2] **81001-2**

12. E. Destinn, orch (r1914) (11/93) (ROMO) Ⓓ [2] **81002-2**

12. R. Ponselle, orch, R. Romani (r1919) (12/93) (NIMB) Ⓓ **NI7851**

12. R. Raisa, orch (r1933) (1/94) (CLUB) Ⓓ **CL99-052**

12. M. Németh, orch (1/94) (CLUB) Ⓓ **CL99-007**

12. M. Jeritza, orch (r1914) (4/94) (PREI) Ⓓ **89079**

12. E. Eames, orch (r1908) (4/94) (RCA) Ⓓ [6] **09026 61580-2(1)**

12. E. Destinn, orch (r1911) (5/94) (SUPR) Ⓓ **11 1337-2**

12. M. Freni, Ater Orch, L. Magiera (pp) (5/94) (DECC) Ⓓ [2] **443 018-2DF2**

12. E. Rethberg, orch (r1925) (7/94) (PREI) Ⓓ **89051**

12. G. Farrar, orch (r1913) (10/94) (NIMB) Ⓓ **NI7857**

12. E. Destinn, orch (r1912) (12/94) (SUPR) Ⓓ [12] **11 2136-2(4)**

12. E. Destinn, orch (r1914) (12/94) (SUPR) Ⓓ [12] **11 2136-2(5)**

12. E. Destinn, orch (r1911) (12/94) (SUPR) Ⓓ [12] **11 2136-2(4)**

12. E. Destinn, orch, B. Seidler-Winkler (r1909) (12/94) (SUPR) Ⓓ [12] **11 2136-2(2)**

12. E. Destinn, orch, P. Pitt (r1911) (12/94) (SUPR) Ⓓ [12] **11 2136-2(4)**

12. H. Konetzni, Berlin St Op Orch, H. Schmidt-Isserstedt (r1937: Ger) (1/95) (PREI) Ⓓ **90078**

12. C. Muzio, orch (r1917) (1/95) (ROMO) Ⓓ [2] **81010-2**

12. E. Rethberg, orch (r1924) (2/95) (ROMO) Ⓓ [2] **81012-2**

12. J. Varady, Berlin RSO, M. Viotti (r1993) (5/95) (ORFE) Ⓓ **C323941A**

12. N. Melba, orch, W.B. Rogers (r1907) (5/95) (ROMO) Ⓓ [3] **81011-2(1)**

12. N. Melba, orch, W.B. Rogers (r1910) (5/95) (ROMO) Ⓓ [3] **81011-2(2)**

12. K. Vayne, orch (bp1958-9) (6/95) (PREI) Ⓓ **89996**

12. R. Hunter, Tasmanian SO, D. Franks (r1989) (10/95) (ABCC) Ⓓ **8 7000 10**

14. D. Sellar, RPO, C. Gerhardt (r1964) (CHES) Ⓓ **Chesky CD108**

15b, 16, 17a-c, 18a, 18b, 19a, 19b H. Roswaenge, H. Ranczak, H. Wrana, Berlin RSO, H. Steinkopf (Ger: bp1940s) (PREI) Ⓓ **90096**

16. P. Domingo, ECO, R. Armstrong (9/92) (ABMU) ▣ **95542**

16. M. Lanza, Hollywood Bowl SO, E. Ormandy (pp1947) (IMP) Ⓓ **PWKS4230**

16. L. Pavarotti, RPO, L. Magiera (7/75) (DECC) ▭ **400 053-4DH**

16. P. Domingo, New Philh, Z. Mehta (RCA) Ⓓ **GD84265**

16. P. Dvorský, Budapest Op Orch, A. Mihály (ACAN) Ⓓ **43 123**

16. G. di Stefano, orch, A. Erede (r1947) (EMI) Ⓓ **CDM7 63105-2**

16. C. Bergonzi, Paris Cons, G. Prêtre (EMI) Ⓓ **CDC7 54016-2**

16. T. Burke, orch (r1927) (PEAR) Ⓓ **GEMMCD9411**

16. B. Gigli, La Scala Orch, F. Ghione (r1934) (NIMB) Ⓓ **NI7817**
(NIMB) ▭ **NC7817**

16. J. Carreras, ROHO, Colin Davis (PHIL) Ⓓ **432 692-2PH**
(PHIL) ▭ **432 692-4PH**

16. F. Wunderlich, South-West German RSO, E. Smola (Ger: bp) (DG) Ⓓ [5] **435 145-2GX5(1)**

16. P. Domingo, New Philh, Z. Mehta (RCA) Ⓓ [2] **GD60866**
(RCA) ▭ [2] **GK60866**

16. J. Carreras, Hungarian St Op Orch, M. Tilson Thomas (SONY) Ⓓ **SMK48155**
(SONY) ▭ **SMT48155**

16. J. Carreras, ROHO, Colin Davis (PHIL) Ⓓ **434 152-2PM**

16. G. Aragall, Seville SO, E. Garcia-Asensio (pp1991) (RCA) Ⓓ **RD61191**

16. P. Domingo, Miami SO, E. Kohn (pp1991) (IMP) Ⓓ **MCD43**

16. G. Lauri-Volpi, orch, Rosario Bourdon (r1928) (MMOI) Ⓓ **CDMOIR412**

16. P. Domingo, Philh, James Levine (EMI) Ⓓ **CDM7 64359-2**

16. F. Corelli, Santa Cecilia Academy Orch, L. Maazel (r1966) (DECC) Ⓓ **436 300-2DX**
(DECC) ▭ **436 300-4DX**

16. G. Aragall, Seville SO, E. Garcia-Asensio (pp1991) (RCA) ◘◘ **09026 61191-5**

16. J. McCracken, Santa Cecilia Academy Orch, National PO (DECC) Ⓓ **433 865-2DWO**
(DECC) ▭ **433 865-4DWO**

16. J. Carreras, Hungarian St Op Orch, M. Tilson Thomas ( ) (SONY) ◘ **SM48155**

16. G. Aragall, National PO, G. Solti (r1984) (DECC) Ⓓ **436 472-2DM**

16. P. Domingo, Rio de Janeiro Municipal Th Orch, J. DeMain (pp1992) (SONY) ● **SLV48362**
(SONY) ▣ **SHV48362**

16. G. Tieppo, Verona Arena Orch, A. Guadagno (pp1992) (MCI) Ⓓ **MCCD099**

16. J. Carreras, London Studio SO, M. Viotti (r1993) (TELD) Ⓓ **4509-92369-2**
(TELD) ▭ **4509-92369-4**

16. J. Carreras, ROHO, Colin Davis (r1976) (BELA) Ⓓ **450 059-2**
(BELA) ▭ **450 059-4**

16. J. Björling, Stockholm Royal Op Orch, N. Grevillius (r1937) (PEAR) Ⓓ **GEMMCD9043**

16. P. Domingo, MMF Orch, Rome Op Orch, Z. Mehta (pp1990) (DECC) Ⓓ **440 947-2DH**
(DECC) ▭ **440 947-4DH**

16. J. McCracken, Santa Cecilia Academy Orch, L. Gardelli (r1969) (BELA) Ⓓ **450 007-2**
(BELA) ▭ **450 007-4**

16. B. Gigli, La Scala Orch, F. Ghione (r1934) (CONI) Ⓓ **CDHD227**
(CONI) ▭ **MCHD227**

16. J. Zoon, H. de Vries, London Studio SO (arr Vrijens) (PHIL) Ⓓ **438 940-2PH**

16. E. Barham, RPO, R. Stapleton (IMP) Ⓓ [3] **TCD1070**

16. M. Lanza, orch, C. Callinicos (r1950) (RCA) Ⓓ **74321 18574-2**
(RCA) ▭ **74321 18574-4**

16. L. Pavarotti, Rome Op Orch, D. Oren (RCA) Ⓓ **09026 61886-2**
(RCA) ▭ **09026 61886-4**

16. J. Carreras, ROHO, Colin Davis (r1976) (PHIL) Ⓓ **442 600-2PH**
(PHIL) ▭ **442 600-4PH**

16. J. Carreras, Hungarian St Orch, M. Tilson Thomas (SONY) Ⓓ **MDK47176**
(SONY) ▭ **MDT47176**

16. P. Domingo, Philh, James Levine (EMIL) Ⓓ **CDZ102**
(EMIL) ▭ **LZ102**

16. M. Lanza, C. Callinicos (pp1958) (RCA) Ⓓ **09026 61884-2**
(RCA) ▭ **09026 61884-4**

16. G. Prandelli, Rome RAI Orch, A. Basile (bp1961) (FONI) Ⓓ **CDMR5023**

16. F. Ansseau, orch, P. Coppola (r1927) (CONI) Ⓓ **CDHD235**

16. B. Gigli, La Scala Orch, F. Ghione (r1934) (PEAR) Ⓓ [2] **GEMMCDS9176**

16. F. de Lucia, orch (r1920) (BONG) Ⓓ [2] **GB1064/5-2**

16. J. Botha, ROHO, E. Downes (r1995)
(ROH) ⊙ **75605 55013-2**
(ROH) ▭ **75605 55013-4**
16. B. Gigli, La Scala Orch, F. Ghione (r1934)
(9/88) (EMI) ⊙ **CDH7 61051-2**
16. E. Caruso, S. Cottone (r1902)
(5/89) (EMI) ⊙ **CDH7 61046-2**
16. E. Caruso, anon (r1902)
(5/89) (PEAR) ⊙ **GEMMCD9309**
16. E. Caruso, orch (r1904)
(10/89) (NIMB) ⊙ **NI7803**
(NIMB) ▭ **NC7803**
16. M. Fleta, orch (r1924)
(2/90) (PREI) ⊙ **89002**
16. J. Schmidt, Berlin St Op Orch, F. Weissmann (r1933) (4/90) (EMI) ⊙ **CDM7 69478-2**
16. L. Pavarotti, National PO, N. Rescigno
(7/90) (DECC) ⊙ [2] **425 681-2DM2**
(7/90) (DECC) ▭ [2] **425 681-4DM2**
16. D. Smirnov, orch (r1909)
(7/90) (CLUB) ⊙ **CL99-031**
16. F. Corelli, Orch, F. Ferraris
(8/90) (CFP) ⊙ **CD-CFP4569**
(8/90) (CFP) ▭ **TC-CFP4569**
16. G. Lauri-Volpi, orch, Rosario Bourdon (r1928) (9/90) (PREI) ⊙ **89012**
16. E. Caruso, anon (r1903)
(12/90) (PEAR) ⊙ [3] **EVC1(1)**
16. E. Caruso, S. Cottone (r1902)
(12/90) (PEAR) ⊙ [3] **EVC1(1)**
16. E. Caruso, anon (r1903)
(12/90) (PEAR) ⊙ [3] **EVC1(1)**
16. E. Caruso, anon (r1903)
(7/91) (RCA) ⊙ [12] **GD60495(1)**
16. E. Caruso, anon (r1903)
(7/91) (RCA) ⊙ [12] **GD60495(1)**
16. E. Caruso, S. Cottone (r1902)
(7/91) (RCA) ⊙ [12] **GD60495(1)**
16. B. Gigli, La Scala Orch, F. Ghione (r1934)
(9/92) (MMOI) ⊙ **CDMOIR409**
16. B. Gigli, La Scala Orch, F. Ghione (r1934)
(10/92) (TEST) ⊙ **SBT1005**
16. R. Tauber, orch, K. Besl (Ger: r1923)
(12/92) (NIMB) ⊙ **NI7830**
(12/92) (NIMB) ▭ **NC7830**
16. G. Martinelli, orch, J. Pasternack (r1926)
(3/93) (PREI) ⊙ **89062**
16. F. Wunderlich, South-West German RSO, E. Smola (Ger) (5/93) (DG) ⊙ **431 110-2GB**
16. J. Björling, orch, N. Grevillius (r1937)
(10/93) (NIMB) ⊙ **NI7842**
16. G. Zenatello, orch (r1911)
(5/94) (PEAR) ⊙ [4] **GEMMCDS9074(1)**
16. G. Zenatello, anon (r c1912)
(5/94) (PEAR) ⊙ [4] **GEMMCDS9074(1)**
16. P. Domingo, Philh, James Levine (r1980)
(6/94) (EMI) ⊙ **CDC5 55017-2**
16. J. Björling, orch, N. Grevillius (r1937)
(9/94) (IMP) ⊙ **GLRS103**
16. J. Björling, orch, N. Grevillius (r1937)
(9/94) (CONI) ⊙ **CDHD214**
(9/94) (CONI) ▭ **MCHD214**
16(pt) A. Giorgini, orch (r1924)
(4/95) (RECO) ⊙ **TRC3**
16, 17a-c, 18a, 18b, 19a, 19b M. Callas, G. di Stefano, A. Mercuriali, La Scala Chor, La Scala Orch, V. de Sabata
(10/88) (EMI) ⊙ **CDM7 69543-2**
16, 17b G. Zenatello, M. Gay, orch, Rosario Bourdon (r1929) (11/91) (CLUB) ⊙ **CL99-025**
16, 17b G. Zenatello, M. Gay, orch, Rosario Bourdon (r1929) (11/91) (PREI) ⊙ **89038**
16, 17b G. Zenatello, orch, Rosario Bourdon (r1929)
(5/94) (PEAR) ⊙ [4] **GEMMCDS9074(2)**
17b B. Gigli, orch, J. Pasternack (r1921)
(5/90) (NIMB) ⊙ **NI7807**
(NIMB) ▭ **NC7807**
17b B. Gigli, orch, J. Pasternack (r1922)
(10/90) (RCA) ⊙ **GD87811**
(10/90) (RCA) ▭ **GK87811**
17b G. Lugo, orch, F. Weiss (Fr: r1933)
(2/92) (PREI) ⊙ **89034**
17b Ferruccio Tagliavini, EIAR Orch, U. Tansini (r1942) (3/94) (CENT) ⊙ **CRC2164**
17b, 18a G. Zenatello, E. Mazzoleni, orch (r1911)
(5/94) (PEAR) ⊙ [4] **GEMMCDS9074(1)**
17b, 18a, 18b M. Callas, C. Bergonzi, Paris Cons, Philh (CFP) ⊙ **CD-CFP9013**
(CFP) ▭ **TC-CFP4498**
18a E. Marton, G. Aragall, Verona Arena Orch, D. Oren (CAST) ▣ **CVI2070**
18a M. Fleta, F. Austral, orch (r1923)
(2/90) (PREI) ⊙ **89002**
18a, 18b G. Ljungberg, J. Schmidt, Berlin St. Op. Orch, L. Blech (r1929: Ger)
(EMI) ⊙ [2] **CHS7 64673-2**

Turandot– opera: 3 acts (1926—Milan) (cpted Alfano: Lib. Adami and Simoni)

ACT 1: 1. Popolo di Pekino!; 2. Gira la cote!; 3. Perchè tarda la luna?; 4. O giovinetto!; 5. Principessa! Pietà!; 6. Fermo! che fai?; 7. Non indugiare!; 8. Signore, ascolta!; 9. Non piangere, Liù!; 10. Ah! per l'ultima volta!. ACT 2. 11a. Olà, Pang! Olà, Pong!; 11b. O China; 11c. Ho una casa; 11d. Vi ricordate il principe regal; 11e. Addio, amore; 12a. Gravi, enormi; 12b. Un giuramento; 12c. Popolo di Pekino!; 13a. In questa Reggia; 13b. O Principe, che a lunghe carovane; 14. Straniero, ascolta!; 15. Tre enigmi. ACT 3: 16. Così comanda Turandot; 17. Nessun dorma!; 18. Tu che guardi le stelle; 19. Principessa divina!; 20. Tanto amore; 21. Tu, che di gel sei cinta; 22. Liù!; 23. Principessa di morte!; 24a. Del primo pianto; 24b. Diecimila anni al nostro Imperatore!.

Turandot G. Dimitrova
Calaf N. Martinucci
Liù C. Gasdia
Ping G. Polidori
Pang P.F. Poli
Pong A. Bevacqua
Timur I. Vinco
Emperor G. Corradi
Mandarin O. Mori
Verona Arena Chor, Verona Arena Orch, M. Arena, G. Montaldo
(CAST) ▣ **CVI2004**

Turandot E. Marton
Calaf P. Domingo
Liù L. Mitchell
Ping B. Schexnayder
Pang A. Glassman
Pong A. Laciura
Timur P. Plishka
Emperor H. Cuénod
Mandarin Arthur Thompson
NY Met Op Ballet, NY Met Op Chor, NY Met Op Orch, James Levine, F. Zeffirelli
(DG) ◐ [2] **072 410-1GH2**
(DG) ▣ **072 410-3GH**

Turandot B. Nilsson
Calaf F. Corelli
Liù R. Scotto
Ping G. Mazzini
Pang F. Ricciardi
Pong P. de Palma
Timur B. Giaiotti
Emperor A. Mercuriali
Mandarin G. Morresi
Rome Op Chor, Rome Op Orch, F. Molinari-Pradelli (r1965)
(EMI) ⊙ [2] **CMS7 69327-2**

Turandot J. Sutherland
Calaf L. Pavarotti
Liù M. Caballé
Ping T. Krause
Pang P.F. Poli
Pong P. de Palma
Emperor N. Ghiaurov
Emperor P. Pears
Mandarin S. Markov
Wandsworth Sch Boys' Ch, John Alldis Ch, LPO, Z. Mehta (r1972)
(DECC) ⊙ [11] **443 204-2DH11(3)**

Turandot G. Cigna
Calaf F. Merli
Liù M. Olivero
Ping A. Poli
Pang G. del Signore
Pong A. Zagonara
Timur L. Neroni
Emperor A. Giannotti
Mandarin G. Bravura
Turin EIAR Chor, Turin EIAR Orch, F. Ghione (r1937)
(FONI) ⊙ [2] **CDO28**

Turandot K. Ricciarelli
Calaf P. Domingo
Liù B. Hendricks
Ping G. Hornik
Pang H. Zednik
Pong F. Araiza
Timur R. Raimondi
Emperor P. de Palma
Mandarin S. Nimsgern
Vienna St Op Chor, Vienna Boys' Ch, VPO, H. von Karajan
(6/84) (DG) ⊙ [2] **423 855-2GH2**

Turandot J. Sutherland
Calaf L. Pavarotti
Liù M. Caballé
Ping T. Krause
Pang P.F. Poli
Pong P. de Palma
Timur N. Ghiaurov
Emperor P. Pears
Mandarin S. Markov
Wandsworth Sch Boys' Ch, John Alldis Ch, LPO, Z. Mehta (r1971)
(5/85) (DECC) ⊙ [2] **414 274-2DH2**

Turandot E. Marton
Calaf J. Carreras
Liù K. Ricciarelli
Ping R. Kerns
Pang H. Wildhaber
Pong H. Zednik
Timur J.P. Bogart
Emperor W. Kmentt
Mandarin K. Rydl
Vienna Boys' Ch, Vienna St Op Chor, Vienna St Op Orch, L. Maazel (pp1983)
(10/85) (CBS) ⊙ [2] **CD39160**

Turandot B. Nilsson
Calaf J. Björling
Liù R. Tebaldi
Ping M. Sereni
Pang P. de Palma
Pong T. Frascati
Timur G. Tozzi
Emperor A. de Paolis
Mandarin L. Monreale
Prince of Persia A. Zagonara
Rome Op Chor, Rome Op Orch, E. Leinsdorf
(9/87) (RCA) ⊙ [2] **RD85932**

Turandot M. Callas
Calaf E. Fernandi
Liù E. Schwarzkopf
Ping M. Borriello
Pang R. Ercolani
Pong P. de Palma
Timur N. Zaccaria
Emperor G. Nessi
Mandarin G. Mauri
La Scala Chor, La Scala Orch, T. Serafin (r1957)
(11/87) (EMI) ⊙ [2] **CDS7 47971-8**

Turandot G. Dimitrova
Calaf N. Martinucci
Liù C. Gasdia
Ping G. Ceccarini
Pang T. Pane
Pong P. de Palma
Timur R. Scandiuzzi
Emperor A. Casertano
Mandarin A. Giacomotti
Genoa Teatro Comunale Chor, Genoa Teatro Comunale Orch, D. Oren (pp1989)
(11/89) (NUOV) ⊙ [2] **6786/7**

Turandot I. Borkh
Calaf M. del Monaco
Liù R. Tebaldi
Ping F. Corena
Pang Mario Carlin
Pong R. Ercolani
Timur N. Zaccaria
Emperor G. Fanelli
Mandarin E. Giordano
Santa Cecilia Academy Chor, Santa Cecilia Academy Orch, A. Erede (r1955)
(8/93) (DECC) ⊙ [2] **433 761-2DMO2**

Turandot E. Marton
Calaf B. Heppner
Liù M. Price
Ping B. de Simone
Pang R. Swensen
Pong U. Ress
Timur J-H. Rootering
Emperor C.H. Ahnsjö
Mandarin O. Mori
Augsburg Cath Boys' Ch, Bavarian Rad Chor, Munich RO, R. Abbado (r1992)
(12/93) (RCA) ⊙ [2] **09026 60898-2**

Turandot M. Caballé
Calaf J. Carreras
Liù M. Freni
Ping V. Sardinero
Pang R. Corazza
Pong R. Cassinelli
Timur P. Plishka
Emperor M. Sénéchal
Mandarin E. Tumagian
Strasbourg Cath Maîtrise, Rhine Op Chor, Strasbourg PO, A. Lombard (r1977)
(12/94) (EMI) ⊙ [2] **CMS5 65293-2**

Excs J. Kiepura, M. Németh, Vienna St Op Chor, Vienna St Op Orch, H. Reichenberger (pp1934: Ger) (3/95) (SCHW) Ⓓ [2] **314602**
Fantasia T. Indermühle, Salonisti (arr Nastrucci) (EURO) Ⓓ **GD69298**
1-3, 8-10, 11a, 11c, 13a, 13b, 14(pt), 17, 19(pt), 21, 23, 24a, 24b E. Marton, W. Kmentt, J.P. Bogart, J. Carreras, K. Ricciarelli, R. Kerns, H. Wildhaber, H. Zednik, K. Rydl, Vienna Boys' Ch, Vienna St Op Chor, Vienna St Op Orch, L. Maazel (pp1983) (CBS) Ⓓ **CD42168**
1-3, 8-10, 11c, 13a, 13b, 14, 15, 17, 20-22, 24a, 24b G. Dimitrova, N. Martinucci, C. Gasdia, R. Scandiuzzi, Genoa Teatro Comunale Chor, Genoa Teatro Comunale Orch, D. Oren (NUOV) Ⓓ **6871**
2. ROH Chor, ROHO, L. Gardelli (EMI) Ⓓ **CDM7 64356-2**
2, 3. Strasbourg Cath Maîtrise, Rhine Op Chor, Strasbourg PO, A. Lombard (r1977) (EMI) Ⓓ [2] **CZS5 68559-2**
2, 3, 4. Augsburg Cath Boys' Ch, Munich Rad Chor, Munich RO, R. Abbado (r1992) (RCA) Ⓓ **74321 24209-2**
2, 3, 8-10, 11a, 13a, 15, 17, 20, 21, 24a, 24b K. Ricciarelli, P. de Palma, R. Raimondi, P. Domingo, B. Hendricks, G. Hornik, H. Zednik, F. Araiza, Vienna St Op Chor, Vienna Boys' Ch, VPO, H. von Karajan (r1981) (DG) Ⓓ **410 645-2GH**
2, 3, 9, 10, 11a, 11c, 13a, 15 (pt), 17, 18 (pt), 20, 21, 24a, 24b J. Sutherland, L. Pavarotti, M. Caballé, T. Krause, P.F. Poli, P. de Palma, N. Ghiaurov, P. Pears, John Alldis Ch, Wandsworth Sch Boys' Ch, LPO, Z. Mehta (r1972) (DECC) Ⓓ **433 438-2DA** (DECC) ⊟ **433 438-4DA**
3. Fiesole School of Music Female Chor, MMF Chor, MMF Orch, M. Arena (ACAN) Ⓓ **43 540**
3, 4, 8, 9, 13a, 14, 17, 21, 24b M. Caballé, J. Carreras, M. Freni, P. Plishka, V. Sardinero, R. Corazza, R. Cassinelli, M. Sénéchal, Rhine Op Chor, Strasbourg PO, A. Lombard (EMI) Ⓓ **CDM7 63410-2**
8. B. Hendricks, BPO, H. von Karajan (DG) ⊟ **439 153-4GMA**
8. M. Chiara, Vienna Volksoper Orch, N. Santi (DECC) Ⓓ **433 067-2DWO** (DECC) ⊟ **433 067-4DWO**
8. R. Streich, Berlin Deutsche Op Orch, R. Peters (DG) Ⓓ [2] **435 748-2GDO2**
8. M. Caballé, LPO, Z. Mehta (r1973) (DECC) Ⓓ **436 300-2DX** (DECC) ⊟ **436 300-4DX**
8. M. Caballé, LPO, Z. Mehta (r1972) (DECC) Ⓓ **440 947-2DH** (DECC) ⊟ **440 947-4DH**
8. R. Tebaldi, M. del Monaco, N. Zaccaria, F. Corena, Mario Carlin, R. Ercolani, Santa Cecilia Academy Chor, Santa Cecilia Academy Orch, A. Erede (r1959) (BELA) Ⓓ **450 007-2** (BELA) ⊟ **450 007-4**
8. M. Price, Munich RSO, R. Abbado (RCA) Ⓓ **09026 61886-2** (RCA) ⊟ **09026 61886-4**
8. M. Callas, Philh, T. Serafin (r1954) (EMI) Ⓓ **CDC5 55216-2** (EMI) ⊟ **EL555216-4**
8. M. Favero, La Scala Orch, G. Antonicelli (r1936) (VAI) Ⓓ **VAIA1071**
8. M. Favero, La Scala Orch, G. Antonicelli (r1936) (BONG) Ⓓ **GB1078-2**
8. M. Caballé, LSO, C. Mackerras (r1970) (EMI) Ⓓ **CDM5 65575-2**
8. M. Freni, Rome Op Orch, F. Ferraris (10/89) (EMI) Ⓓ **CDM7 63110-2**
8. E. Schwarzkopf, La Scala Orch, T. Serafin (r1957) (12/90) (EMI) Ⓓ **CDM7 63657-2**
8. L. Schöne, Berlin St Op Orch, F. Zweig (r1928) (2/92) (MMOI) Ⓓ **CDMOIR408**
8. L. Schöne, Berlin St Op Orch, F. Zweig (r1928) (7/92) (PEAR) Ⓓ [3] **GEMMCDS9926(1)**
8. L. Schöne, Berlin St Op Orch, F. Zweig (r1928) (10/93) (NIMB) Ⓓ **NI7848**
8. M. Zamboni, orch (r1926) (4/94) (EMI) Ⓓ [3] **CHS7 64864-2(1)**
8. E. Steber, orch (bp1946: Eng) (11/95) (VAI) Ⓓ **VAIA1072**
8-10, 13a, 13b J. Sutherland, M. Caballé, M. Chiara, P. F. Poli, P. de Palma, T. Krause, N. Ghiaurov, John Alldis Ch, LPO, Z. Mehta (r1972) (DECC) Ⓓ **436 317-2DA** (DECC) ⊟ **436 317-4DA**
8, 13a, 13b, 17. R. Tebaldi, B. Nilsson, J. Björling, Rome Op Chor, Rome Op Orch, NY Met Op Orch (r1959) (RCA) Ⓓ **09026 62689-2**
8, 13a, 21. M. Callas, Philh, T. Serafin (r1954) (12/87) (EMI) Ⓓ **CDC7 47966-2**
8, 13a, 21. J. Varady, Berlin RSO, M. Viotti (r1993) (5/95) (ORFE) Ⓓ **C323941A**
8, 21. M. Caballé, John Alldis Ch, LPO, Z. Mehta (r1972) (DECC) Ⓓ **443 928-2DM**
8, 21. H. Gueden, Santa Cecilia Academy Orch, A. Erede (r1954) (PREI) Ⓓ **90227**
8, 21. M. Caballé, LSO, C. Mackerras (10/87) (EMI) Ⓓ **CDC7 47841-2**
8, 21. M. Freni, Hamburg PO, L. Magiera (11/88) (ACAN) Ⓓ **49 384**
8, 21. K. Te Kanawa, LSO, Myung-Whun Chung (11/90) (EMI) Ⓓ **CDC7 54062-2**
8, 21. M. Gauci, Belgian Rad & TV Orch, A. Rahbari (11/92) (NAXO) Ⓓ **8 550606**
8, 21. L. Orgonášová, Bratislava RSO, W. Humburg (2/93) (NAXO) Ⓓ **8 550605**
8, 21. R. Pampanini, orch, L. Molajoli (r1927) (8/93) (PREI) Ⓓ **89063**
8, 21. L. Schöne, Berlin St Op Orch, F. Zweig (r1928) (1/94) (CLUB) Ⓓ **CL99-020**
8, 9. J. Björling, R. Tebaldi, G. Tozzi, M. Sereni, P. de Palma, T. Frascati, Rome Op Orch, Rome Op Chor, E. Leinsdorf (2/89) (RCA) Ⓓ **GD87799** (RCA) ⊟ **GK87799**
8, 9, 10, 13a, 17. J. Sutherland, M. Caballé, L. Pavarotti, P.F. Poli, P. de Palma, T. Krause, N. Ghiaurov, John Alldis Ch, LPO, Z. Mehta (r1972) (DECC) Ⓓ [2] **444 555-2DF2**
8, 9, 17. A. Gheorghiu, J. Botha, F. Egerton, R. Leggate, A. Michaels-Moore, M. Druiett, ROH Chor, ROHO, E. Downes (r1995) (ROH) Ⓓ **75605 55013-2** (ROH) ⊟ **75605 55013-4**
8, 9, 21. L. Price, N. Zaccaria, G. di Stefano, Vienna St Op Chor, Vienna St Op Orch, F. Molinari-Pradelli (pp1961) (MEMO) Ⓓ [2] **HR4396/7**
9. F. Corelli, orch, W. Pelletier (bp1963) (VAI) ▣ **VAI69100**
9. P. Domingo, New Philh, N. Santi (RCA) Ⓓ [2] **GD60866** (RCA) ⊟ [2] **GK60866**
9. A. Valente, orch, M. di Veroli (r1927) (MMOI) Ⓓ **CDMOIR412**
9. B. Prevedi, ROHO, E. Downes (DECC) Ⓓ **433 865-2DWO** (DECC) ⊟ **433 865-4DWO**
9. J. Carreras, Vienna St Op Orch, L. Maazel (SONY) Ⓓ **MDK47176** (SONY) ⊟ **MDT47176**
9. A. Piccaver, Berlin St Op Orch, M. Gurlitt (r1928) (PREI) Ⓓ [2] **89217**
9. R. Tauber, orch, G. Szell (Ger: r1926) (12/92) (NIMB) Ⓓ **NI7830** (12/92) (NIMB) ⊟ **NC7830**
9. G. di Stefano, MMF Orch, F. Patanè (r1958) (10/93) (DECC) Ⓓ **436 463-2DM** (10/93) (DECC) ⊟ **436 463-4DM**
9, 10. P. Domingo, L. Mitchell, P. Plishka, B. Schexnayder, A. Glassman, A. Laciura, NY Met Op Ballet, NY Met Op Chor, NY Met Op Orch, James Levine (DECC) ◐ **071 142-1DH** (DECC) ▣ **071 142-3DH**
9, 10, 17. M. Caballé, L. Pavarotti, N. Ghiaurov, T. Krause, John Alldis Ch, LPO, Z. Mehta (DECC) Ⓓ **433 822-2DH** (DECC) ⊟ **433 822-4DH**
9, 17. J. Björling, R. Tebaldi, G. Tozzi, Rome Op. Orch, E. Leinsdorf (RCA) ⊟ **GK85277**
9, 17. G. di Stefano, La Scala Orch, A. Votto (r1955) (EMI) Ⓓ **CDM7 63105-2**
9, 17. J. Carreras, M. Freni, Rhine Op Chor, Strasbourg PO, A. Lombard (EMI) Ⓓ **CDM7 63111-2**
9, 17. G. di Stefano, La Scala Orch, A. Votto (pp1958) (MEMO) Ⓓ **HR4372/3**
9, 17. B. Prevedi, ROHO, E. Downes (DECC) Ⓓ **433 623-2DSP** (DECC) ⊟ **433 623-4DSP**
9, 17. H. Roswaenge, Berlin RSO, H. Steinkopf (Ger: bp1940s) (PREI) Ⓓ **90096**
9, 17. J. Carreras, M. Freni, P. Plishka, Rhine Op Chor, Strasbourg PO, A. Lombard (EMI) Ⓓ **CDC7 54524-2**
9, 17. G. di Stefano, Zurich Tonhalle Orch, F. Patanè (r1958) (DECC) Ⓓ **440 403-2DM**
9, 17. B. Prevedi, ROHO, E. Downes (r1964) (BELA) Ⓓ **450 005-2** (BELA) ⊟ **450 005-4**
9, 17. J. Schmidt, orch, W. Goehr (r1934) (EMI) Ⓓ [2] **CHS7 64673-2**
9, 17. R. Tauber, orch (r1926: Ger) (PEAR) Ⓓ **GEMMCD9145**
9, 17. A. Cortis, La Scala Orch, C. Sabajno (r1929) (10/91) (PREI) Ⓓ **89043**
9, 17. R. Tauber, Berlin St Op Orch, G. Szell (Ger: r1926) (3/92) (EMI) Ⓓ **CDH7 64029-2**
9, 17. C. Kullman, Berlin St Op Orch, C. Schmalstich (Ger: r1932) (11/93) (PREI) Ⓓ **89057**
9, 17. H. Roswaenge, Berlin St Op Orch (r1935: Ger) (4/95) (PREI) Ⓓ [2] **89209**
9, 17, 23. F. Corelli, La Scala Orch, G. Gavazzeni (pp1964) (MEMO) Ⓓ [2] **HR4204/5**
9, 23. N. Martinucci, C. Gasdia, I. Vinco, G. Dimitrova, Verona Arena Chor, Verona Arena Orch, M. Arena (CAST) ▣ **CVI2068**
11a A. Baracchi, E. Venturini, G. Nessi, orch (r1927) (4/94) (EMI) Ⓓ [3] **CHS7 64864-2(1)**
12a Locke Brass Consort, J. Stobart (arr Stobart) (9/92) (CRD) Ⓓ **CRD3402** (3/83) (CRD) ⊟ **CRDC4102**
13a S. Murphy, WNO Orch, J. Smith (COLL) Ⓓ **Coll3025-2**
13a M. Callas, Philh, T. Serafin (r1954) (EMI) Ⓓ **CDC7 54702-2** (EMI) ⊟ **EL754702-4**
13a M. Caballé, J. Carreras, Rhine Op Chor, Strasbourg PO, A. Lombard (r1977) (EMI) Ⓓ **CDM5 65575-2**
13a E. Turner, orch, S. Robinson (r1928) (9/89) (EMI) Ⓓ **CDH7 69791-2**
13a A. Shuard, ROHO, E. Downes (8/90) (CFP) Ⓓ **CD-CFP4569** (8/90) (CFP) ⊟ **TC-CFP4569**
13a G. Cigna, F. Merli, Turin EIAR Orch, F. Ghione (r1938) (11/90) (LYRC) Ⓓ **SRO805**
13a A. Marc, NZ SO, H. Wallberg (6/92) (DELO) Ⓓ **DE3108** (6/92) (DELO) ⊟ **CS3108**
13a M. Németh, orch (Ger: r c1928) (7/92) (PEAR) Ⓓ [3] **GEMMCDS9926(2)**
13a, 13b M. Callas, La Scala Chor, La Scala Orch, H. von Karajan (r1957) (EMI) Ⓓ **CDC7 49502-2**
13a, 13b R. Tebaldi, New Philh, O. de Fabritiis (DECC) Ⓓ **433 636-2DSP** (DECC) ⊟ **433 636-4DSP**
13a, 13b E. Turner, orch, L. Molajoli (r1928) (MMOI) Ⓓ **CDMOIR412**
13a, 13b E. Marton, J. Carreras, Vienna St Op Chor, Vienna St Op Orch, L. Maazel (SONY) Ⓓ **SK48094** (SONY) ⊟ **ST48094**
13a, 13b E. Turner, orch, S. Robinson (1928) (CONI) Ⓓ **CDHD235**
13a, 13b R. Tebaldi, New Philh, O. de Fabritiis (1/89) (DECC) Ⓓ **417 686-2DC**
13a, 13b E. Turner, orch, S. Robinson (r1928) (10/89) (NIMB) Ⓓ **NI7801** (NIMB) ⊟ **NC7801**
13a, 13b R. Tebaldi, New Philh, O. de Fabritiis (8/91) (DECC) Ⓓ [2] **430 481-2DX2**
13a, 13b L. Price, D. Barioni, Ambrosian Op Chor, New Philh, N. Santi (r1977) (12/92) (RCA) Ⓓ [4] **09026 61236-2**
13a, 13b B. Nilsson, J. Björling, Rome Op Orch, E. Leinsdorf (r1959) (4/94) (RCA) Ⓓ [6] **09026 61580-2(7)**
13a, 13b, 23, 24a, 24b B. Nilsson, F. Corelli, La Scala Chor, La Scala Orch, G. Gavazzeni (pp1964) (MEMO) Ⓓ [2] **HR4275/6**
13a, 17. P. Domingo, K. Ricciarelli, Vienna St Op Chor, VPO, H. von Karajan (DG) Ⓓ **439 151-2GMA** (DG) ⊟ **439 151-4GMA**
13a, 17, 24b G. Dimitrova, N. Martinucci, Verona Arena Chor, Verona Arena Orch, M. Arena (CAST) ▣ **CASH5051**
15, 17. M. Németh, T. Mazaroff, Vienna St Op Chor, Vienna St Op Orch, R. Moralt (pp1941: Ger) (12/94) (SCHW) Ⓓ [2] **314542**
16. B. Prevedi, ROHO, E. Downes (DECC) Ⓓ **433 636-2DSP** (DECC) ⊟ **433 636-4DSP**
17. J. Carreras, Rhine Op Chor, Strasbourg PO, A. Lombard (EMI) Ⓓ **CDM7 69596-2**
17. L. Pavarotti, John Alldis Ch, LPO, Z. Mehta (7/75) (DECC) ⊟ **400 053-4DH**
17. J. Carreras, P. Domingo, L. Pavarotti, MMF Orch, Rome Op Orch, Z. Mehta (pp1990) (DECC) ◐ **071 123-1DH** (DECC) ▣ **071 123-3DH**

17. L. Pavarotti, MMF Orch, Rome Op Orch, Z. Mehta (pp1990) (DECC) ◐ **071 123-1DH** (DECC) ▣ **071 123-3DH**
17. P. Domingo, VPO, H. von Karajan (DG) ① [3] **427 708-2GX3**
17. P. Dvorský, Berlin RSO, R. Paternostro (ACAN) ① **43 123**
17. F. Corelli, Rome Op Orch, F. Molinari-Pradelli (CFP) ① **CD-CFP4277**
17. J. Carreras, Rhine Op Chor, Strasbourg PO, A. Lombard (EMI) ① **CDC7 54016-2**
17. T. Burke, orch (r1927) (PEAR) ① **GEMMCD9411**
17. J. Carreras, LSO, J. López-Cobos (PHIL) ① **432 692-2PH** (PHIL) ▭ **432 692-4PH**
17. Cincinnati Pops, E. Kunzel (inst arr Beck, Bernstein, Kunzel) (TELA) ① **CD80260**
17. L. Pavarotti, RPO, K.H. Adler (DECC) ① **430 470-2DH** (DECC) ▭ **430 470-4DH**
17. L. Pavarotti, Orch (EDL) ① **EDL2562-2** (EDL) ⊙ **EDL2562-1** ▭ **EDL2562-4**
17. J. Carreras, Vienna St Op Orch, L. Maazel (pp1983) (SONY) ① **SMK48155** (SONY) ▭ **SMT48155**
17. L. Pavarotti, John Alldis Ch, LPO, Z. Mehta (DECC) ① **433 064-2DWO**
17. J. Carreras, LSO, J. López-Cobos (PHIL) ① **434 152-2PM**
17. L. Pavarotti, MMF Orch, Rome Op Orch, Z. Mehta (DECC) ◐ **071 142-1DH** (DECC) ▣ **071 142-3DH**
17. A. Cortis, orch (r1929) (MMOI) ① **CDMOIR412**
17. J. Carreras, Rhine Op Chor, Strasbourg PO, A. Lombard (EMI) ① **CDM7 64359-2**
17. P. Domingo, Berlin Deutsche Op Chor, N. Santi (ERAT) ① **2292-45797-2** (ERAT) ▭ **2292-45797-4**
17. J. Carreras, P. Domingo, L. Pavarotti, MMF Orch, Rome Op Orch, Z. Mehta (pp1990) (DECC) ꝏ **430 433-5DH**
17. L. Pavarotti, MMF Orch, Rome Op Orch, Z. Mehta (pp1990) (DECC) ꝏ **430 433-5DH**
17. T. Harper, Bratislava RSO, M. Halász (NAXO) ① **8 550497**
17. Deng, A. Juffinger (SCHW) ① **312642**
17. G. di Stefano, Santa Cecilia Academy Orch, F. Patanè (DECC) ① **433 865-2DWO** (DECC) ▭ **433 865-4DWO**
17. J. Oakman, Prague Phil Chor, Czech PO, J. Bigg (with instr track for singing) (IMP) ① [2] **DPCD1015** (IMP) ▭ **CIMPCD1015**
17. J. Carreras, Vienna St Op Orch, L. Maazel (pp1983) (SONY) ◙ **SM48155**
17. N. Gedda, ROHO, G. Patanè (r1967) (CFP) ① **CD-CFP4602** (CFP) ▭ **TC-CFP4602**
17. N. Gedda, ROHO, G. Patanè (CFP) ① **CD-CFP4613** (CFP) ▭ **TC-CFP4613**
17. E. Barham, ROH Chor, RPO, R. Stapleton (r1990) (RPO) ① [2] **CDRPD9006** (RPO) ▭ [2] **ZCRPD9006**
17. L. Pavarotti, Philh, L. Magiera (DECC) ꝏ **436 320-5DH**
17. E. Barham, Op North Chor, English Northern Philh, P. Daniel (r1992) (EMI) ① **CDC7 54785-2**
17. M. Malagnini, Verona Arena Orch, A. Guadagno (pp1992) (MCI) ① **MCCD099**
17. J. Oakman, Prague Phil Chor, Czech PO, J. Bigg (r1992) (IMP) ① **PCD1043**
17. Deng, Württemberg PO, R. Paternostro (SINE) ① **39820222**
17. M. del Monaco, Santa Cecilia Academy Chor, Santa Cecilia Academy Orch, A. Erede (r1955) (DECC) ① **440 407-2DM**
17. L. Pavarotti, Verona Arena Orch, A. Gatto (pp1980) (BELA) ① **450 002-2** (BELA) ▭ **450 002-4**
17. G. di Stefano, Santa Cecilia Academy Orch, F. Patanè (r1959) (BELA) ① **450 007-2** (BELA) ▭ **450 007-4**
17. J. Carreras, LSO, J. López-Cobos (r1979) (BELA) ① **450 059-2** (BELA) ▭ **450 059-4**
17. B. Heppner, Munich RSO, R. Abbado (RCA) ① **09026 61440-2** (RCA) ▭ **09026 61440-4**
17. J. Oakman, Prague Phil Chor, Czech SO, J. Bigg (IMP) ① [3] **TCD1070**
17. G. Groves, J. Watson, J. Partridge (r1994: arr W Belshaw) (ASV) ① **CDWHL2088**

17. M. del Monaco, Milan SO, A. Quadri (r1948) (TEST) ① **SBT1039**
17. J. Carreras, RPO, R. Benzi (r1979) (PHIL) ① **442 600-2PH** (PHIL) ▭ **442 600-4PH**
17. L. Pavarotti, Toscanini SO, E. Buckley (SONY) ① **MDK47176** (SONY) ▭ **MDT47176**
17. J. Björling, H. Ebert (pp1951) (BLUE) ① **ABCD057**
17. L. Pavarotti, Los Angeles PO, Z. Mehta (pp1994) (TELD) ꝏ **4509-96200-5**
17. L. Pavarotti, Los Angeles PO, Z. Mehta (pp1994) (TELD) ◙ **4509-96200-8**
17. P. Domingo, Vienna St Op Chor, VPO, H. von Karajan (r1981) (DG) ① **445 525-2GMA** (DG) ▭ **445 525-4GMA**
17. R. Leech, Cincinnati Pops, E. Kunzel (TELA) ① **CD80401**
17. B. Heppner, Munich RO, H. Lewis (RCA) ① **74321 25817-2** (RCA) ▭ **74321 25817-4**
17. B. Heppner, Munich RO, R. Abbado (r1992) (RCA) ① **09026 62550-2**
17. A. Piccaver, Berlin St Op Orch, J. Prüwer (r1930) (PREI) ① [2] **89217**
17. A. Cortis, La Scala Orch, C. Sabajno (r1929) (CONI) ① **CDHD235**
17. L. Pavarotti, LPO, Z. Mehta (7/86) (DECC) ① [2] **417 011-2DH2**
17. P. Domingo, VPO, H. von Karajan (7/86) (DG) ① **415 366-2GH**
17. J. Björling, orch, N. Grevillius (r1944) (10/88) (EMI) ① **CDH7 61053-2**
17. B. Prevedi, ROHO, E. Downes (1/89) (DECC) ① **417 686-2DC**
17. J. Schmidt, orch, W. Goehr (r1934) (4/90) (EMI) ① **CDM7 69478-2**
17. B. Gigli, chor, Philh, S. Robinson (r1949) (5/90) (EMI) ① **CDH7 61052-2**
17. L. Pavarotti, John Alldis Ch, LPO, Z. Mehta (7/90) (DECC) ① [2] **425 681-2DM2** (7/90) (DECC) ▭ [2] **425 681-4DM2**
17. N. Gedda, ROHO, G. Patanè (8/90) (CFP) ① **CD-CFP4569** (8/90) (CFP) ▭ **TC-CFP4569**
17. L. Pavarotti, MMF Orch, Rome Op Orch, Z. Mehta (pp1990) (10/90) (DECC) ① **430 433-2DH** (10/90) (DECC) ▭ **430 433-4DH**
17. J. Carreras, P. Domingo, L. Pavarotti, MMF Orch, Rome Op Orch, Z. Mehta (pp1990) (10/90) (DECC) ① **430 433-2DH** (10/90) (DECC) ▭ **430 433-4DH**
17. E. Barham, RPO, R. Stapleton (10/90) (IMP) ① **MCD15** (10/90) (IMP) ▭ **MCC15**
17. L. Pavarotti, RPO, K.H. Adler (pp1982) (8/91) (DECC) ① **430 716-2DM** (8/91) (DECC) ▭ **430 716-4DM**
17. L. Pavarotti, Philh, L. Magiera (11/91) (DECC) ◐ **071 150-1DH** (11/91) (DECC) ▣ **071 150-3DH**
17. L. Pavarotti, James Levine, B. Large (2/92) (DECC) ◐ **071 119-1DH** (2/92) (DECC) ▣ **071 119-3DH**
17. P. Dvorský, Bratislava RSO, O. Lenárd (5/92) (NAXO) ① **8 550343**
17. A. Cortis, La Scala Orch, C. Sabajno (r1929) (7/92) (PEAR) ① [3] **GEMMCDS9926(2)**
17. Britannia Building Soc Band, H. Snell (r1990; arr Snell: cornet) (8/92) (DOYE) ① **DOYCD004** (DOYE) ▭ **DOYMC004**
17. R. Tauber, orch (r1926: Ger) (9/92) (MMOI) ① **CDMOIR409**
17. P. McCann, Black Dyke Mills Band, P. Parkes (r1984: arr P Parkes) (11/92) (CHAN) ① **CHAN4501** (11/92) (CHAN) ▭ **BBTD4501**
17. G. Lauri-Volpi, SO, M. Cordone (r1942) (7/93) (NIMB) ① **NI7845**
17. A. Cortis, La Scala Orch, C. Sabajno (r1929) (3/94) (NIMB) ① **NI7850**
17. G. Lauri-Volpi, orch, M. Cordone (r1942) (4/94) (EMI) ① [3] **CHS7 64864-2(2)**
17. L. Pavarotti, Verona Arena Orch (pp) (5/94) (DECC) ① [2] **443 018-2DF2**
17. J. Björling, orch, N. Grevillius (r1944) (9/94) (NIMB) ① **NI7856**
17. L. Pavarotti, Los Angeles PO, Z. Mehta (pp1994) (12/94) (TELD) ① **4509-96200-2** (12/94) (TELD) ⊙ **4509-96200-1** ▭ **4509-96200-4**

17. L. Pavarotti, NYPO, L. Magiera (pp1993) (2/95) (DECC) ① **444 450-2DH** (2/95) (DECC) ▭ **444 450-4DH**
17. L. Pavarotti, Grudgionz Fest Chor, Grudgionz Fest Orch, G-F. Masini (pp1964) (10/95) (RCA) ① **09026 68014-2**
17. B. Heppner, Bavarian Rad Chor, Munich RO, R. Abbado (r1993/4) (11/95) (RCA) ① **09026 62504-2**
20, 21. E. Norena, orch, P. Coppola (r1932) (3/91) (PREI) ① **89041**
21. M. Freni, Philh, G. Sinopoli (DG) ▭ **439 153-4GMA**
21. F. Weathers, Vienna Op Orch, A. Quadri (DECC) ① **433 069-2DWO** (DECC) ▭ **433 069-4DWO**
21. E. Marton, Munich RO, G. Patanè (SONY) ① **SK48094** (SONY) ▭ **ST48094**
21. V. Zeani, Santa Cecilia Academy Orch, F. Patanè (DECC) ① **433 865-2DWO** (DECC) ▭ **433 865-4DWO**
21. R. Tebaldi, Santa Cecilia Academy Orch, A. Erede (r1955) (DECC) ① **440 408-2DM**
21. M. Favero, orch (r c1929) (VAI) ① **VAIA1071**
21. P. Lorengar, Santa Cecilia Academy Orch, G. Patanè (r1966) (DECC) ① **443 931-2DM**
21. M. Favero, orch (r c1929) (BONG) ① **GB1078-2**
21. A. Tomowa-Sintow, Munich RO, P. Sommer (11/86) (ORFE) ① **C106841A**
21. M. Freni, Rome Op Orch, F. Ferraris (8/90) (CFP) ① **CD-CFP4569** (8/90) (CFP) ▭ **TC-CFP4569**
21. E. Arizmendi, orch, J.E. Martini (r c1953) (4/92) (EMI) ① [7] **CHS7 69741-2(7)**
21. K. Ricciarelli, Verona Arena Orch, B. Martinotti (pp) (5/94) (DECC) ① [2] **443 018-2DF2**
23. J. Sutherland, L. Pavarotti, LPO, Z. Mehta (DECC) ① **421 896-2DA**
23, 24a, 24b L. Kelm, J.F. West, chor, orch, C. Keene (pp1985: original Alfano completion) (10/93) (LYRC) ① [2] **SRO839**
24a Lotte Lehmann, Berlin City Op Orch, F. Zweig (Ger: r1927) (PEAR) ① **GEMMCD9409**
24b E. Marton, Bavarian Rad Chor, Munich RO, R. Abbado (r1990s) (RCA) ① **09026 62674-2**

Le **Villi– opera: 2 acts (1884—Milan) (Lib. Fontana)**

EXCERPTS. ACT 1: 1. Prelude; 2. Evviva! Evviva!; 3. Se come voi piccina io fossi; 4. Non esser, Anna mia; 5. Presto! Presto in vaggio. ACT 2: 6. L'Abbandono; 7. La Tregenda; 8. No, possibil non è; 9a. Ecco la casa; 9b. Torna ai felice; 10. Roberto!.

Guglielmo	L. Nucci
Anna	R. Scotto
Roberto	P. Domingo
Narrator	T. Gobbi

Ambrosian Op Chor, National PO, L. Maazel (5/88) (CBS) ① **CD76890**
1. P. Dvorský, Bratislava RSO, O. Lenárd (5/92) (NAXO) ① **8 550343**
1, 7. Berlin RSO, R. Chailly (r1982) (DECC) ① **444 154-2DM**
3. R. Scotto, Czech SO, A. Krieger (pp1991) (IMP) ① **MCD42**
3. K. Te Kanawa, LPO, J. Pritchard (SONY) ① **SK48094** (SONY) ▭ **ST48094**
3. N. Rautio, ROHO, E. Downes (r1995) (ROH) ① **75605 55013-2** (ROH) ▭ **75605 55013-4**
3. K. Te Kanawa, LPO, J. Pritchard (5/85) (CBS) ① **MK37298** (CBS) ▭ **40-37298**
3. M. Caballé, LSO, C. Mackerras (10/87) (EMI) ① **CDC7 47841-2**
3. M. Gauci, Belgian Rad & TV Orch, A. Rahbari (11/92) (NAXO) ① **8 550606**
9b B.S. Rosenberg, Budapest Concert Orch, J. Acs (pp1990) (OLYM) ① **OCD370**

PUCITTA (PUCCITTA), Vincenzo *(1778–1861) Italy*

La **Vestale– opera: 2 acts (1810—London)**
Viva di Roma...Guidò Marte i nostri passi P. Nilon, G. Mitchell Ch, Philh, D. Parry (10/90) (OPRA) ① [3] **ORCH103**

PURCELL, Daniel
(c1660–1717) England

The **Pilgrim– secular masque (1700—London) (Wds. Dryden)**
EXCERPTS: 1. With horns and with hounds.
1. E. Kirkby, English Tpt Virtuosi, A. Hoskins (tpt/dir), M. Hoskins (tpt/dir) (r1994) (10/95) (MOSC) ① **070979**

PURCELL, Henry II
(1659–1695) England

Z–Numbers from F.F. Zimmerman's Analytic Catalogue, 1963

Dido and Aeneas– opera: 3 acts, Z626 (1689—London) (Lib. N. Tate)
EXCERPTS: 1. Overture. ACT 1 SCENE 1: 2. Shake the cloud; 3. Ah! Belinda; 4. Grief increases by concealing; 5. When monarchs unite; 6. When sould so much virtue spring; 7. Fear no danger to ensue. ACT 1 SCENE 2: 8. See, your royal guest apperas; 9. Cupid only throws the dart; 10. If not for mine; 11. Pursue thy conquest, Love; 12. A Dance Gittars Chacony; 13. To the hills and the vales; 14. The Triumphing Dance. ACT 2 SCENE 1: 15. Wayward sisters; 16. Harm's our delight; 17. The Queen of Carthage; 18. Ho, ho, ho; 19. Ruin'd ere the set of sun?; 20. But ere we this perform; 21. In our deep vaulted cell; 22. Echo Dance of the Furies. ACT 2 SCENE 2: 23. Ritornelle; 24. Thanks to these lonesome vales; 26. Oft she visits this loved mountain; 27. Behold, upon my bend spear; 28. Haste, haste to town; 29. Stay, Prince, and hear; 30. Jove's commands shall be obey'd; 31. Then since our charms have sped; 32. The Groves' Dance. ACT 3 SCENE 1; 33. Come away, fellow sailors; 34. The Sailors' Dance; 35. See, see the flags; 36. Our next motion; 37. Destruction's our delight; 38. The Witches' Dance (Jack of the Lanthorn Dance). ACT 3 SCENE 2: 39. Your counsel all is urg'd in vain; 40. But Death, alas!; 41. Great minds against themselves conspire; 42. Thy hand, Belinda; 43. When I am laid in earth; 44. With drooping wings ye Cupids come.

Dido K. Flagstad
Aeneas T. Hemsley
Belinda; Second Lady; Attendant Spirit E. Schwarzkopf
Sorceress A. Mandikian
First Lady E. McNab
First Witch S. Rex
Second Witch A. Pollak
Sailor D. Lloyd
Mermaid Sngrs, Mermaid Orch, Geraint Jones (r1952)
(EMI) ① **CDH7 61006-2**

Dido A. Murray
Aeneas A. Scharinger
Belinda R. Yakar
Sorceress T. Schmidt
Second Lady; First Witch E. von Magnus
Second Witch H. Gardow
Spirit P. Esswood
Sailor J. Köstlinger
A. Schoenberg Ch, VCM, N. Harnoncourt (r1983)
(TELD) ① **4509-93686-2**

Dido C. Bott
Aeneas J. M. Ainsley
Belinda E. Kirkby
Sorceress D. Thomas
First Witch E. Priday
Second Witch S. Stowe
Second Woman J. Baird
First Sailor D. Lochmann
Spirit M. Chance
AAM Chor, AAM, C. Hogwood (r1992)
(L'OI) **ꝏ 436 992-5OHO**

Dido V. de los Angeles
Aeneas P. Glossop
Belinda H. Harper
Sorceress P. Johnson
Second Woman E. Robson
Sailor R. Tear
Ambrosian Sngrs, ECO, J. Barbirolli (r1965)
(EMI) ① **CDM5 65664-2**

Dido M. Ewing
Aeneas K.M. Daymond
Belinda R. Evans
Sorceress S. Burgess
First Witch M. Plazas
Second Witch P.H. Stephen
Second Woman P. Rozario
Sailor J. MacDougall
Spirit J. Bowman
Collegium Musicum 90 Chor, Collegium Musicum 90, R. Hickox
(CHAN) ① **CHAN0586**

Dido J. Norman
Aeneas T. Allen
Belinda M. McLaughlin
Sorceress P. Kern
Second Woman E. Gale
First Witch H. Walker
Second Witch D. Jones
Spirit D.L. Ragin
Sailor P. Power
Chor, ECO, R. Leppard (ed Dent?)
(7/86) (PHIL) ① **416 299-2PH**

Dido G. Laurens
Aeneas P. Cantor
Belinda J. Feldman
Sorceress D. Visse
First Witch; Woman A. Mellon
Second Witch B. Borden
Spirit E. Lestrigant
Sailor M. Laplénie
Arts Florissants Voc Ens, Arts Florissants Instr Ens, W. Christie
(7/86) (HARM) ① **HMC90 5173**
(7/86) (HARM) ▭ **HMC40 5173**

Dido J. Baker
Aeneas R. Herincx
Belinda P. Clark
Sorceress M. Sinclair
Second Woman E. Poulter
First Witch R. James
Second Witch C. Wilson
Spirit D. Dorow
Sailor J. Mitchinson
St Anthony Sngrs, ECO, A. Lewis (ed Laurie/Dart)
(12/90) (DECC) ① **425 720-2DM**

Dido E. Kirkby
Aeneas D. Thomas
Belinda J. Nelson
Sorceress J. Noorman
Second Woman J. Rees
First Witch E. Van Evera
Second Witch; Sailor R. Bevan
Spirit T. Bonner
Taverner Ch, Taverner Plyrs, A. Parrott
(11/91) (CHAN) ① **CHAN0521**

Dido T. Troyanos
Aeneas R. Stilwell
Belinda F. Palmer
Sorceress P. Kern
Second Woman E. Gale
First Witch; Spirit A. Hodgson
Second Witch L. Maxwell
Sailor P. Langridge
ECO Chor, ECO, R. Leppard
(11/91) (ERAT) ① **2292-45263-2**

Dido D. Jones
Aeneas P. Harvey
Belinda D. Deam
Sorceress S. Bickley
First Witch N. Jenkin
Second Witch M. Marshall
Second Woman; Spirit C. Ashton
Sailor A. Murgatroyd
St James's Sngrs, St James's Baroque Plyrs, I. Bolton (r1989)
(9/93) (TELD) ① **4509-91191-2**

Dido C. Watkinson
Aeneas G. Mosley
Belinda R. Holton
Sorceress T. Shaw
Second Woman E. Priday
First Witch D. Deam
Second Witch S. Beesley
Sailor P. Tindall
Spirit J. Kenny
Monteverdi Ch, EBS, J. E Gardiner (r1990)
(3/94) (PHIL) ① **432 114-2PH**

Dido M. Thomas
Aeneas M. Bevan
Belinda; First Witch; First Woman H. Sheppard
Sorceress H. Watts
Second Witch; Second Woman E. Dales
Spirit; Sailor R. Tear
Oriana Concert Ch, Oriana Concert Orch, H. Lester, A. Deller (r1960s)
(4/94) (VANG) ① **08.2032.71**

Dido C. Bott
Aeneas J. M. Ainsley
Belinda E. Kirkby
Sorceress D. Thomas
First Witch E. Priday
Second Witch S. Stowe
Second Woman J. Baird
First Sailor D. Lochmann
Spirit M. Chance
AAM Chor, AAM, C. Hogwood (r1992)
(7/94) (L'OI) ① **436 992-2OHO**

Dido L. Hunt
Aeneas M. Dean
Belinda L. Saffer
Sorceress E. Rabiner
Second Woman D. Deam
First Witch; Spirit C. Brandes
Second Witch R. Rainero
Sailor P. Elliott
Cambridge Clare College Ch, Philh Baroque Orch (r1993)
(4/95) (HARM) ① **HMU90 7110**

Dido V. Gens
Aeneas N. Berg
Belinda S. Marin-Degor
Sorceress C. Brua
Second Woman; First Witch S. Daneman
Second Witch G. Mechaly
Spirit; Sailor J-P. Fouchécourt
Arts Florissants Voc Ens, Arts Florissants Instr Ens, W. Christie (r1994)
(6/95) (ERAT) ① **4509-98477-2**

Dido G. Laurens
Aeneas P. Cantor
Belinda J. Feldman
Sorceress D. Visse
First Witch; Woman A. Mellon
Second Witch B. Borden
Spirit E. Lestrigant
Sailor M. Laplénie
Arts Florissants Voc Ens, Arts Florissants Instr Ens, W. Christie (r1985)
(7/95) (HARM) ① [6] **HMX290 1528/33(1)**

Dido T. Troyanos
Aeneas B. McDaniel
Belinda S. Armstrong
Sorceress P. Johnson
Second Woman; First Witch Margaret Baker
Second Witch M. Lensky
Spirit P. Esswood
Sailor N. Rogers
Hamburg Monteverdi Ch, Hamburg NDR CO, C. Mackerras (r1967)
(7/95) (ARCH) ① **447 148-2AP**

Excs Freiburg Baroque Orch, T. Hengelbrock (arr Hengelbrock) (3/92) (DHM) ① **RD77231**
Suite ECO, J-L. Garcia (vn/dir) (r1977) (SONY) ① **SMK58936**
1. Taverner Plyrs, A. Parrott (7/83) (CHAN) ① **CHAN8301**
(CHAN) ▭ **CBTD1008**
1-3, 5, 20, 40-44. V. de los Angeles, H. Harper, P. Johnson, Ambrosian Sngrs, ECO, J. Barbirolli (r1965) (EMI) ① **CDM5 65341-2**
1, 3-5, 8-11, 15-20, 27, 28, 42, 43. T. Troyanos, S. Armstrong, B. McDaniel, P. Johnson, Margaret Baker, M. Lensky, Hamburg Monteverdi Ch, Hamburg NDR CO, C. Mackerras (r1967) (DG) ① **439 474-2GCL**
(DG) ▭ **439 474-4GCL**
1, 43. C. Watkinson, Amsterdam Bach Sols, J.W. de Vriend (3/89) (ETCE) ① **KTC1064**
2. J. Feldman, N. North, S. Cunningham (1/93) (ARCA) ① **A02**
33. J. Woods (arr. J. Woods) (IMP) ① **PCD1086**
40-44. A. Deller, St Anthony Sngrs, ECO, A. Lewis (r1961) (DECC) ① **443 393-2DWO**
(DECC) ▭ **443 393-4DWO**
42, 43. E. Kirkby, AAM Chor, AAM, C. Hogwood (hpd/dir) (r1992) (L'OI) ① **444 620-2OH**
42, 43. L. Price, RCA Italiana Op Orch, F. Molinari-Pradelli (r1960s) (RCA) ① **09026 62596-2**
42, 43. L. Price, RCA Italiana Op Orch, F. Molinari-Pradelli (12/92) (RCA) ① [4] **09026 61236-2**
42, 43. K. Flagstad, Philh, W. Braithwaite (r1948) (7/93) (TEST) ① **SBT1018**
42-44. J. Baker, St Anthony Sngrs, ECO, A. Lewis (r1961) (10/93) (DECC) ① **436 462-2DM**
43. J. Norman, I. Gage (pp1971) (MEMO) ① **HR4271**
43. V. de los Angeles, ECO, J. Barbirolli (EMIL) ① **CDZ7 67253-2**
43. G. Laurens, Arts Florissants Orch, W. Christie (r1985) (HARM) ① **HMP390 807**

43. King's Consort, R. King (treb/dir), G. Fisher (r1988) (IMP) ① **PCDS19** (IMP) ⊟ **PCDSC19**
43. G. Fisher, King's Consort, R. King (HYPE) ① **KING2**
43. M. Caballé, RCA Italiana Op Orch, F. Molinari-Pradelli (RCA) ① **74321 25817-2** (RCA) ⊟ **74321 25817-4**
43. G. Fisher, King's Consort, R. King (8/88) (IMP) ① **PCD894**
43. K. Flagstad, Philh, W. Braithwaite (r1948) (4/92) (EMI) ① [7] **CHS7 69741-2(5)**
43. BBC SO, L. Stokowski (r1954) (4/95) (TELD) **4509-95038-6** (4/95) (TELD) **4509-95038-3**

The History of **Dioclesian, or The Prophetess– semi-opera: 5 acts, Z627 (1691—London) (Lib. T Betterton. Work rev 1694)**

EXCERPTS: 1. First Musick; 2. Second Musick; 3. Overture. ACT 1: 4. First Act Tune (Hornpipe). ACT 2: 5a. Great Diocles the Boar has kill'd (song: bass); 5b. Sing Iôs! (chorus); 6. Charon the peaceful Shade invites (song: soprano); 7. Symphony (trumpets and violins); 8. Let all mankind the pleasure share (duet: soprano, bass); 9a. Let the soldiers rejoice, 'Martial song' (tenor); 9b. Rejoice with a general voice (2 tenors, bass); 9c. Retornello I (trumpets and oboes); 9d. To Mars let 'em raise...Rejoice with a general voice (TTB); 9e. Retornello II (trumpets and oboes); 10a. A Symphony of Flutes; 10b. Since the toils and the hazards (song: alto); 10c. Let the priests (SATB); 10d. All sing (chorus); 11. Dance of Furies; 12. Second Act Tune. ACT 3: 13a. Two in one upon a Ground; 13b. Chaconne for Flutes; 14. The Chair Dance; 15a. Prelude for Oboes; 15b. What I shall do? (song: tenor); 16. Third Act Tune. ACT 4: 17. Butterfly Dance; 18. Tune for Trumpets; 19. Sound Fame, thy brazen trumpet sound (song: tenor); 20. Let all rehearse (chorus); 21. Fourth Act Tune. APPENDICES: 22. Country Dance in the Fifth Act; 23. Since from my dear Astrea's sight (song: soprano); 24. When first I saw (song: tenor); 25. MASQUE: 26. Call the nymphs (Cupid, chorus); 27. Come, come away (duet); 28. Behold, O mighty'st of Gods (chorus); 29. Paspe (The first entry of heros on the stage); 30. Oh, the sweet delights of love! (duet); 31. Let mortals fight (Fawn, chorus); 32a. Make room...(2 Bacchanals, Bacchus: the second entry); 32b. Dance of Bacchanals; 33. Still I'm wishing (Follower of Cupid); 34. Canaries; 35. Tell me why (Shepherd, Shepherdess: The third entry); 36. Dance; 37a. All our days...(A Pleasure, Chorus: the fourth entry); 37b. Let us dance; 37c. Dance; 38. Triumph, victorious Love (Trio, chorus: the last entry).

Cpte N. Argenta, A. Monoyios, P. Agnew, R. Edgar-Wilson, S. Gadd, S. Birchall, L. Wallington, B. Bannatyne-Scott, English Concert Ch, English Concert, T. Pinnock (r1994) (ARCH) ① [2] **447 071-2AH2**
Cpte C. Pierard, J. Bowman, J. M. Ainsley, M. Padmore, M. George, Collegium Musicum 90 Chor, Collegium Musicum 90, R. Hickox (r1994) (7/95) (CHAN) ① **CHAN0568**
1-24. L. Dawson, G. Fisher, R. Covey-Crump, P. Elliott, M. George, S. Varcoe, Monteverdi Ch, EBS, J.E. Gardiner (r1987) (7/95) (ERAT) ① [2] **4509-96556-2**
1-24. L. Dawson, G. Fisher, R. Covey-Crump, P. Elliott, M. George, S. Varcoe, Monteverdi Ch, EBS, J.E.Gardiner (r1987) (7/95) (ERAT) ① [8] **4509-96371-2**
3. P. Esswood, J. Sonnleitner, C. Medlam (12/89) (HYPE) ① **CDA66070**
3. N. Argenta, N. North, R. Boothby, P. Nicholson (r1992) (6/94) (VIRG) ① **VC7 59324-2**
9a Deller Consort, A. Deller (alto/dir) (r1969) (HARM) ① **HMA190 214**
9a M. Chance, Freiburg Baroque Orch, G. von der Goltz (r1993) (10/94) (DHM) ① **05472 77295-2**
15b A. Deller, W. Bergmann (r1950s) (9/93) (VANG) ① [2] **08.2003.72**
15b, 23. J. Bowman, King's Consort, R. King (7/89) (HYPE) ① **CDA66288**
19. E. Kirkby, English Tpt Virtuosi, A. Hoskins (tpt/dir), M. Hoskins (tpt/dir) (r1994) (10/95) (MOSC) ① **070979**
23. A. Deller, W. Kuijken, W. Christie, R. Skeaping (r1979) (HARM) ① **HMC90 249** (HARM) ⊟ **HMC40 249**
23. A. Dalton, F. Borstlap, A. Uittenbosch (ETCE) ① **KTC1013**
23. A. Deller, H. Lester (bp1977) (INA) ① **262004**
23. R. Jacobs, W. Kuijken, K. Junghänel (8/85) (ACCE) ① **ACC57802D**
23. J. Feldman, N. North, S. Cunningham (1/93) (ARCA) ① **A02**
23. A. Mellon, W. Kuijken, C. Rousset (r1992) (9/93) (ASTR) ① **E8757**
23. A. Deller, W. Kuijken, W. Christie, R. Skeaping (r1979) (7/95) (HARM) ① [6] **HMX290 1528/33(2)**
25. C. Pierard, J. Bowman, J. M. Ainsley, I. Bostridge, M. George, M. Brook, N. Berg, Collegium Musicum 90, R. Hickox (r1993) (11/94) (CHAN) ① **CHAN0558**
35. E. Kirkby, D. Thomas, A. Rooley (6/88) (HYPE) ① **CDA66056**
37c S. Sanford, B. Wissick, R. Erickson (r1991) (10/95) (ALBA) ① **TROY127-2**

Don Quixote: The Musical– music by Purcell & others (1995) (Book & revised lyrics Don Taylor)

EXCERPTS: ACT ONE: 1. Fanfare (J Eccles); 2. Overture (Anon); 3. Knighting music (Anon); 4. Sing all ye muses; 5. Knighting music (Anon); 6. Funeral entrance music (J Eccles); 7. Young Chrysostom (J Eccles); 8. The dirge (J Eccles); 9. The Barber's song (Anon); 10. When the world first knew creation; 11. Let the dreadful engines; 12. 'Twas early one morning (J Eccles); 13. With this sacred charming wand; 14. Pastoral Suite (J Lenton). ACT TWO: 15a. Slow pastoral (J Lenton); 15b. Artful Shepherds (J Stanley); 16. If you will love me (Anon); 17. Ye nymphs and sylvan gods (J Eccles); 18. Damon, let a friend (Colonel Pack); 19. Riding through the whistling air; 20. Hornpipe (T Tollet); 21. Lads and lasses; 22. Masque overture (Mr Orme); 23. Vertumnus Flora (R Courtville); 24. Here is Hymen (R Courtville); 25. Cease, Hymne, cease (R Courtville); 26. Happy mortals (B Compton); 27. Come tell what befell (Anon); 28. The old wife (Anon); 29. Theresa was as sweet (Anon); 30. Marcella's distraught narrative; 31. I burn, I burn (J Eccles); 32. You can never trust a Frenchman (Anon); 33. Genius of England; 34. From rosy bowers; 35a. Puppet overture(T Tollet); 35b. Sweetheart, my passion (Anon); 36. Now sleep my knight; 37. While thus we bow.

Don Quixote P. Scofield
Sancho Panza R. Hudd
Altisdora E. Kirkby
Marcella E. Tubb
Cardenio D. Thomas

Consort of Musicke, City Waites, Purcell Simfony, A. Rooley (r1995) (10/95) (MOSC) ① [2] **070973**

The **Fairy Queen– semi-opera: 5 acts, Z629 (1692—London) (Lib. ?E. Settle, after Shakespeare)**

EXCERPTS: 1. First Musick: 1a. Prelude; 1b. Hornpipe; 2. Second Musick: 2a. Air; 2b. Rondeau; 2c. Overture. ACT 1: 3. Come let us leave the town; 4. Fill up the bowl (Scene of the Drunken Poet); 5. First Act Tune: Jig. ACT 2: 6a. Prelude; 6b. Come all ye songsters of the sky; 7a. May the God of Wit inspire; 7b. Echo (trumpet); 8. Now join your warbling voices all; 9a. Sing while we trip it; 9b. Dance of the Fairies; 10. See, even Night herself is here; 11. I am come to lock all fast; 12. One charming night; 13. Hush, no more; 14. Dance of the followers of Night; 15. Second Act Tune: Air. ACT 3: 16. If love's a sweet passion; 17. Symphony while the swans come forward; 18. Dance of the Fairies; 19. Dance of the Green Men; 20. Ye gentle spirits of the air; 21. Now the maids and the men (Coridon and Mopsa Dialogue); 22. Dance of the Haymakers; 23. When I have often heard; 24. A thousand ways; 25. Third Act Tune: Hornpipe. ACT 4: 26. Symphony; 27. Now the night is chased away; 28. Let the fifes and the clarions; 29. Entry of Phoebus; 30. When a cruel long winter; 31. Hail! Great parent of us all; 32. Thus ever grateful Spring; 33. Here's the Summer; 34. See my many coloured fields; 35. Next Winter comes slowly; 36. Hail! Great parent (reprise); 37. Fourth Act Tune: Air. ACT 5: 38. Prelude; 39. Thrice happy lovers (Epithalamium); 40. O let me weep (The Plaint); 41. Entry Dance; 42. Symphony; 43. Thus the gloomy world; 44. Thus happy and free; 45. Yes, Xansi; 46. Monkeys' Dance; 47. Hark! now all things; 48. Hark! the echoing air; 49. Sure the dull God of Marriage; 50. Prelude; 51a. See, I obey; 51b. Turn then thine eyes; 51c. My torch indeed; 52. They shall be as happy as they're fair (Trio); 53. Chaconne: Dance of the Chinese Man and Woman; 54. They shall be as happy (chorus).

Cpte Deller Consort, Stour Music Fest Chor, Stour Music Fest CO, A. Deller (alto/dir) (HARM) ① [2] **HMP390 257/8**
Cpte B. Bonney, E. von Magnus, S. McNair, M. Chance, L. Dale, R. Hall, A. Michaels-Moore, A. Schoenberg Ch, VCM, N. Harnoncourt (r1994) (TELD) ① [2] **4509-97684-2**
Cpte E. Harrhy, J. Smith, J. Nelson, T. Penrose, A. Stafford, W. Evans, M. Hill, S. Varcoe, D. Thomas, Monteverdi Ch, EBS, J.E. Gardiner (8/87) (ARCH) ① [2] **419 221-2AH2**
Cpte N. Argenta, L. Dawson, I. Desrochers, W. van Gent, V. Gens, S. Piau, N. Rime, C. Daniels, J-P. Fouchécourt, M. le Brocq, C. le Paludier, B. Loonen, F. Piolino, T. Randle, F. Bazola-Minori, J. Corréas, G. Banks-Martin, B. Delétré, T. Lander, R. Taylor, Arts Florissants Chor, Arts Florissants Orch, W. Christie (r1989) (1/90) (HARM) ① [2] **HMC90 1308/9** (1/90) (HARM) ⊟ [2] **HMC40 1308/9**
Cpte G. Fisher, L. Anderson, A. Murray, M. Chance, J.M. Ainsley, I. Partridge, R. Suart, M. George, The Sixteen, The Sixteen Orch, H. Christophers (4/92) (COLL) ① [2] **Coll7013-2**
Cpte J. Vyvyan, M. Wells, N. Burrowes, A. Hodgson, J. Bowman, C. Brett, P. Pears, I. Partridge, O. Brannigan, J. Shirley-Quirk, Ambrosian Op Chor, ECO, B. Britten (r1970: ed/arr Britten, I Holst, Ledger & Pears) (5/92) (DECC) ① [2] **433 163-2DM2**
Cpte Scholars Baroque Ens (r1992) (7/94) (NAXO) ① [2] **8 550660/1**
Cpte L. Hunt, C. Pierard, S. Bickley, H. Crook, M. Padmore, D. Wilson-Johnson, R. Wistreich, London Schütz Ch, LCP, R. Norrington (r1993) (2/95) (EMI) ① [2] **CDS5 55234-2**
ECO, B. Britten (r1968) (DECC) ① **443 393-2DWO** (DECC) ⊟ **443 393-4DWO**
C. Bott, Jeffrey Thomas, M. Schopper, Amsterdam Baroque Ch, Amsterdam Baroque Orch, T. Koopman (r1994) (6/95) (ERAT) ① [2] **4509-98507-2**
Excs C. Bonell (arr Bonell) (ASV) ① **CDQS6038** (ASV) ⊟ **ZCQS6038**
Excs Freiburg Baroque Orch, T. Hengelbrock (arr Hengelbrock) (3/92) (DHM) ① **RD77231**
Excs M. André, H. Bilgram (tpt/org) (1/93) (EMI) ① **CDC7 54330-2**
Suite Folger Consort (DELO) ① **DE1003**
Suite English Gtr Qt (arr Gallery) (11/91) (SAYD) ① **CD-SDL386** (11/91) (SAYD) ⊟ **CSDL386**
Suites 1 and 2. Arion Ens, A. Lascae (PART) ① **Part1118-2**
1b, 2b, 2c, 6a, 7b, 46, 53. Oxford City Orch, M. Papadopoulos (r1994) (IMP) ① **PCD1104**
1, 2, 5, 6a, 10, 18, 22, 26, 29, 42. J. Carlyle, Bath Fest Orch, Y. Menuhin (r1965) (EMI) ① **CDM5 65341-2**
1-4. E. Kirkby, C. Hogwood, A. Rooley, R. Campbell, C. Mackintosh (9/86) (L'OI) ① **417 123-2OH**
1, 5. J. Bowman, King's Consort, R. King (7/89) (HYPE) ① **CDA66288**
1, 7a, 7b, 8, 9a, 9b, 21. N. Argenta, J-P. Fouchécourt, B. Delétré, Arts Florissants Chor, Arts Florissants Orch, W. Christie (r1989) (HARM) ① **HMP390 807**
2b Brandenburg Consort, R. Goodman (r1992) (HYPE) ① **CDA66600**
2, 3, 8. D. Minter, P. O'Dette, M. Springfels (1/93) (HARM) ① **HMU90 7035**
2-4. J. Feldman, N. North, S. Cunningham (1/93) (ARCA) ① **A02**
2, 4, 13, 21, 40, 46, 48. E. Harrhy, J. Nelson, E. Priday, J. Smith, T. Penrose, S. Varcoe, D. Thomas, Monteverdi Ch, EBS, J.E. Gardiner (r1981) (DG) ① **439 474-2GCL** (DG) ⊟ **439 474-4GCL**
2, 48. H. Crook, Capriccio Stravagante, S. Sempé (hpd/dir) (9/92) (DHM) ① **RD77252**
5. Deller Consort, A. Deller (alto/dir) (r1969) (HARM) ① **HMA190 214**
6a, 6b K. Battle, James Levine (pp1984) (DG) ① **445 524-2GMA**
8. K. Ferrier, P. Spurr (bp1949) (6/92) (DECC) ① **433 473-2DM**

10, 16, 32, 47. C. Bott, Purcell Qt (r1994) (CHAN) ⦶ **CHAN0571**

16, 20, 48. S. Sanford, B. Wissick, R. Erickson (r1991) (10/95) (ALBA) ⦶ **TROY127-2**

16, 48. G. Simpson, B. Mason (AMON) ⦶ **CD-SAR50**

26. ECO, B. Britten (r1970) (DECC) ⦶ **443 393-2DWO** (DECC) ▭ **443 393-4DWO**

29-36. Taverner Ch, Taverner Plyrs, A. Parrott (r1994) (VIRG) ⦶ **VC5 45116-2**

39. A. Deller, W. Bergmann (r1950) (EMI) ⦶ **CDH5 65501-2**

39. A. Deller, G. Malcolm (r1950s) (9/93) (VANG) ⦶ [2] **08.2003.72**

39. A. Mellon, W. Kuijken, C. Rousset (r1992) (9/93) (ASTR) ⦶ **E8757**

39. M. Hill, A. Ball (r1994; arr Tippett & Bergmann) (4/95) (HYPE) ⦶ **CDA66749**

39, 40. A. Deller, W. Kuijken, W. Christie, R. Skeaping (r1979) (7/95) (HARM) ⦶ [6] **HMX290 1528/33(2)**

40. A. Deller, W. Kuijken, W. Christie, R. Skeaping (r1979) (HARM) ⦶ **HMC90 249** (HARM) ▭ **HMC40 249**

40. P. Memelsdorff, A. Staier (r1994; arr Memelsdorff & Staier) (DHM) ⦶ **05472 77318-2**

40. E. Kirkby, C. Mackintosh, R. Campbell, A. Rooley (r1982) (L'OI) ⦶ **444 620-2OH**

40. Suzie Le Blanc, Tragicomedia (r1994) (7/95) (TELD) ⦶ **4509-95068-2**

40, 48. S. McNair, C. Steele-Perkins, S. Standage, AAM, C. Hogwood (r1994) (9/95) (PHIL) ⦶ **446 081-2PH**

45. J. Griffett, Early Instr Chbr Ens, M. Venhoda (CAMP) ⦶ **RRCD1323**

47. A. Deller, T. Weil, B. Lam, stg orch (r1953) (EMI) ⦶ **CDH5 65501-2**

48. N. Argenta, N. North, R. Boothby, P. Nicholson (r1992) (6/94) (VIRG) ⦶ **VC7 59324-2**

48. F. Lott, G. Johnson (r1995; arr Britten) (11/95) (HYPE) ⦶ [2] **CDA67061/2**

The **Indian Queen– semi-opera (final masque by D. Purcell), Z630 (1695—London) (Lib. J. Dryden and R. Howard)**

EXCERPTS: 1. First Music; 2. Second Music; 3. Overture; 4. Trumpet Tune. PROLOGUE: 5. Wake, Quivera; 6. Why should men quarrel; 7. By ancient prophecies; 8. Trumpet tune (reprise). ACT 2: 9. Symphony; 10. I come to sing great Zempoalla's Story; 11. What flattering noise is this; 12. Scorn'd envy, here's nothing; 13. I fly from the place; 14. Begone, curst fiends of hell; 15. I come to sing. ACT 3: 16. Air; 17. Minuet; 18. Ye twice ten thousand deities; 19. Symphony; 20. Seek not to know; 21. Trumpet Overture; 22. Ah, how happy are we; 23. We the Spirits of the Air; 24. I attempt from love's sickness; 25. Third Act Tune. ACT 4: 26. They tell us that your mighty powers; 27. Fourth Act Tune. ACT 5: 28. While thus we bow.

Cpte S. Varcoe, J. Smith, M. Hill, J. Elwes, R. Hardy, G. Fisher, A. Stafford, D. Thomas, D. Harris, Monteverdi Ch, EBS, J.E. Gardiner (ERAT) ⦶ **2292-45556-2**

Cpte M. Bevan, H. Sheppard, M. Deller, P. Elliott, A. Deller, Deller Ch, King's Musick, A. Deller (omits final masque) (8/87) (HARM) ⦶ **HMC90 243** (HARM) ▭ **HMA43 243**

Cpte R. Hardy, M. Hill, J. Elwes, A. Stafford, D. Thomas, S. Varcoe, G. Fisher, D. Harris, J. Smith, Monteverdi Ch, EBS, J.E. Gardiner (r1979) (7/95) (ERAT) ⦶ **4509-96551-2**

Cpte S. Varcoe, J. Smith, M. Hill, J. Elwes, R. Hardy, G. Fisher, A. Stafford, D. Thomas, D. Harris, Monteverdi Ch, EBS, J.E.Gardiner (r1979) (7/95) (ERAT) ⦶ [8] **4509-96371-2**

Cpte T. Bonner, C. Bott, R. Covey-Crump, P. Harvey, Purcell Simfony Voices, Purcell Simfony (r1994) (9/95) (LINN) ⦶ **CKD035**

Let us wander K. Ferrier, I. Baillie, G. Moore (r1945) (6/88) (EMI) ⦶ **CDH7 61003-2**

Let us wander E. Söderström, K. Meyer, J. Eyron (r1974) (9/93) (BIS) ⦶ **BIS-CD017**

Let us wander V. de los Angeles, D. Fischer-Dieskau, G. Moore (r1960: arr Moffat) (4/94) (EMI) ⦶ [4] **CMS5 65061-2(2)**

1-3, 5, 9, 10, 17-22, 24, 26, 28. C. Keyte, A. Cantelo, Wilfred Brown, I. Partridge, R. Tear, St Anthony Sngrs, ECO, C. Mackerras (r1965) (5/92) (DECC) ⦶ [2] **433 166-2DM2**

1-4. B. Tracey (trans hpd) (DHM) ⦶ **GD77233**

1, 4, 9, 19, 24, 27, 28. J. Carlyle, Bath Fest Orch, Y. Menuhin (r1965) (EMI) ⦶ **CDM5 65341-2**

3. G. Reiche Consort (AMBI) ⦶ **amb97865**

5, 18. Deller Consort, A. Deller (alto/dir) (r1969) (HARM) ⦶ **HMA190 214**

8, 9. Taverner Plyrs, A. Parrott (12/88) (EMI) ⦶ **CDM7 69853-2**

19. Parley of Instr Baroque Orch (r1994) (10/95) (HYPE) ⦶ [3] **CDA67001/3**

19, 21. Taverner Plyrs, A. Parrott (r1987) (VIRG) ⦶ **VC5 45116-2**

21. M. Murphy, Consort of London, R. Haydon Clark (COLL) ⦶ **Coll3008-2**

22. T. Penrose, J. Griffett, Early Instr Chbr Ens, M. Venhoda (CAMP) ⦶ **RRCD1323**

24. A. Deller, W. Kuijken, W. Christie, R. Skeaping (r1979) (HARM) ⦶ **HMC90 249** (HARM) ▭ **HMC40 249**

24. A. Dalton, F. Borstlap, A. Uittenbosch (ETCE) ⦶ **KTC1013**

24. A. Murray, G. Johnson (r1991) (7/92) (EMI) ⦶ **CDC7 54411-2**

24. J. Feldman, N. North, S. Cunningham (1/93) (ARCA) ⦶ **A02**

24. D. Minter, M. Meyerson (1/93) (HARM) ⦶ **HMU90 7035**

24. A. Deller, W. Bergmann (r1950s) (9/93) (VANG) ⦶ [2] **08.2003.72**

24. N. Argenta, P. Nicholson (r1992) (6/94) (VIRG) ⦶ **VC7 59324-2**

24. A. Deller, W. Kuijken, W. Christie, R. Skeaping (r1979) (7/95) (HARM) ⦶ [6] **HMX290 1528/33(2)**

24. S. McNair, AAM, C. Hogwood (r1994) (9/95) (PHIL) ⦶ **446 081-2PH**

24. S. Sanford, B. Wissick, R. Erickson (r1991) (10/95) (ALBA) ⦶ **TROY127-2**

24. S. Gritton, G. Johnson (r1995; arr Britten) (11/95) (HYPE) ⦶ [2] **CDA67061/2**

King Arthur– semi-opera, Z628 (1691—London) (Lib. J. Dryden)

EXCERPTS: 1. First Music; 2. Second Music; 3. Overture. ACT 1: 4. SACRIFICE SCENE: 4a. Woden, first to thee; 4b. The White Horse neigh'd aloud; 4c. The Lot is cast; 4d. Brave souls; 5. Come if you care; 6. First Act Tune: Come if you date. ACT 2: 7a. Hither this way; 7b. Let not a Moon-born Elf; 7c. Hither this way (chorus); 7d. Come follow me; 8a. How blest are the Shepherds; 8b. Shepherd, shepherd, leave Decoying; 8c. Come shepherds; 8d. Hornpipe; 9. Second Act Tune: Air. ACT 3: 10. FROST SCENE: 10a. What ho; 10b. What Power art thou; 10c. Thou Doting Fool; 10d. Great love; 10e. No part of my Dominion; 10f. Prelude; 10g. See, see, we assemble; 10h. 'Tis I that have warm'd ye; 10i. Sound a Parley; 11. Third Act Tune: Hornpipe. ACT 4: 12. Two daughters; 13a. Passacaglia; 13b. How happy the Lover; 13c. For love ev'ry creature; 14. Fourth Act Tune: Air. ACT 5: 15. Trumpet Tune; 16. Ye blust'ring Brethren; 17. Symphony; 18. Round the coast; 19. For folded flocks; 20. Your Hay it is Mow'd (Harvest Home); 21. Fairest isle; 22. You say,Tis love; 23. Warlike Consort; 24a. Saint George, the patron of our isle; 24b. Our natives not alone appear.

Cpte H. Sheppard, J. Knibbs, R. Hardy, A. Deller, M. Deller, P. Elliott, L. Nixon, M. Bevan, N. Beavan, Deller Ch, King's Musick, A. Deller (HARM) ⦶ [2] **HMC90 252/3** (HARM) ▭ [2] **HMC40 252/3**

Cpte E. Morison, H. Harper, M. Thomas, J. Whitworth, D. Galliver, Wilfred Brown, J. Cameron, H. Alan, T. Anthony, St Anthony Sngrs, Philomusica of London, A. Lewis (r1958) (5/92) (DECC) ⦶ [2] **433 166-2DM2**

Cpte N. Argenta, J. Gooding, L. Perillo, J. MacDougall, M. Tucker, B. Bannatyne-Scott, G. Finley, English Concert Ch, English Concert, T. Pinnock (9/92) (ARCH) ⦶ [2] **435 490-2AH2**

Cpte V. Gens, C. McFadden, S. Piau, S. Waters, M. Padmore, I. Paton, J. Best, P. Salomaa, F. Bazola-Minori, Arts Florissants Chor, Arts Florissants Orch, W. Christie (6/95) (ERAT) ⦶ [2] **4509-98535-2**

Cpte J. Smith, G. Fisher, E. Priday, G. Ross, A. Stafford, P. Elliott, S. Varcoe, Monteverdi Ch, EBS, J.E. Gardiner (r1983) (7/95) (ERAT) ⦶ [2] **4509-96552-2**

Cpte J. Smith, G. Fisher, E. Priday, G. Ross, A. Stafford, P. Elliott, S. Varcoe, Monteverdi Ch, EBS, J.E.Gardiner (r1983) (7/95) (ERAT) ⦶ [8] **4509-96371-2**

Excs Deller Consort, King's Musick, A. Deller (r1978) (HARM) ⦶ **HMA190 200** (HARM) ▭ **HMA43 200**

Excs J. Smith, G. Fisher, E. Priday, A. Stafford, P. Elliott, S. Varcoe, Monteverdi Ch, EBS, J.E. Gardiner (ERAT) ⦶ **2292-45919-2**

Excs Freiburg Baroque Orch, T. Hengelbrock (arr Hengelbrock) (3/92) (DHM) ⦶ **RD77231**

Excs H. Sheppard, J. Knibbs, R. Hardy, A. Deller, M. Deller, P. Elliott, L. Nixon, M. Bevan, N. Beavan, Deller Ch, King's Musick, A. Deller (r1978) (7/95) (HARM) ⦶ [6] **HMX290 1528/33(2)**

2, 9, 13a, 15, 17, 21. J. Carlyle, Bath Fest Orch, Y. Menuhin (r1965) (EMI) ⦶ **CDM5 65341-2**

8a, 8b, 21. F. Lott, S. Gritton, Sarah Walker, J. M. Ainsley, G. Johnson (r1995; arr Britten) (11/95) (HYPE) ⦶ [2] **CDA67061/2**

8b K. Ferrier, I. Baillie, G. Moore (r1945) (6/88) (EMI) ⦶ **CDH7 61003-2**

10. R. Hardy, M. Bevan, Deller Consort, King's Musick, A. Deller (r1978) (HARM) ⦶ **HMP390 807**

10b T. Anthony, Philomusica of London, A. Lewis (r1958) (DECC) ⦶ **443 393-2DWO** (DECC) ▭ **443 393-4DWO**

12. E. Söderström, K. Meyer, J. Eyron (r1974) (9/93) (BIS) ⦶ **BIS-CD017**

13a, 14, 15, 17. Bath Fest Orch, Y. Menuhin (r1965) (EMI) ⦶ [2] **CZS7 67425-2**

13c, 22. E. Kirkby, D. Thomas, A. Rooley (6/88) (HYPE) ⦶ **CDA66056**

15. C. Dearnley (r1977: trans org) (GUIL) ⦶ **GMCD7102**

20. L. Skeaping, J. Potter, Broadside Band, J. Barlow (r1992; arr J. Barlow) (6/93) (SAYD) ⦶ **CD-SDL400** (6/93) (SAYD) ▭ **CSDL400**

21. A. Deller, W. Kuijken, W. Christie, R. Skeaping (r1979) (HARM) ⦶ **HMC90 249** (HARM) ▭ **HMC40 249**

21. A. Dalton, F. Borstlap, A. Uittenbosch (ETCE) ⦶ **KTC1013**

21. P. Huttenlocher, J.E. Dähler (CLAV) ⦶ **CD50-0705**

21. A. Deller, W. Kuijken, W. Christie (r1979) (HARM) ⦶ **HMP390 807**

21. J. Bowman, King's Consort, R. King (HYPE) ⦶ **KING2**

21. H. Harper, Philomusica of London, A. Lewis (r1958) (DECC) ⦶ **443 393-2DWO** (DECC) ▭ **443 393-4DWO**

21. C. Bott, P. Chateauneuf (r1994) (L'OI) ⦶ **444 620-2OH**

21. J. Bowman, King's Consort, R. King (7/89) (HYPE) ⦶ **CDA66288**

21. P. Esswood, J. Sonnleitner, C. Medlam (12/89) (HYPE) ⦶ **CDA66070**

21. F. Lott, G. Johnson (r1991) (7/92) (EMI) ⦶ **CDC7 54411-2**

21. J. Feldman, N. North, S. Cunningham (1/93) (ARCA) ⦶ **A02**

21. A. Deller, W. Bergmann (r1950s) (9/93) (VANG) ⦶ [2] **08.2003.72**

21. A. Mellon, W. Kuijken, C. Rousset (r1992) (9/93) (ASTR) ⦶ **E8757**

21. N. Argenta, N. North (r1992) (6/94) (VIRG) ⦶ **VC7 59324-2**

21. A. Deller, W. Kuijken, W. Christie, R. Skeaping (r1979) (7/95) (HARM) ⦶ [6] **HMX290 1528/33(2)**

21. S. McNair, AAM, C. Hogwood (r1994) (9/95) (PHIL) ⦶ **446 081-2PH**

The **Tempest– semi-opera, Z631 (c1695) (Lib. Shadwell)**

1. Dear pretty youth; 2. Full fathom five; 3. Come unto these yellow sands; 4. Dry those eyes (attrib).

Cpte D. Thomas, R. Earle, C. Hall, R. Hardy, J. Smith, S. Varcoe, J. Elwes, Monteverdi Ch, Monteverdi Orch, J.E. Gardiner (r1979) (7/95) (ERAT) ⦶ **4509-96555-2**

Cpte J. Smith, R. Hardy, C. Hall, J. Elwes, S. Varcoe, D. Thomas, R. Earle, Monteverdi Ch, EBS, J.E.Gardiner (r1979) (7/95) (ERAT) ⦶ [8] **4509-96371-2**

1. E. Kirkby, C. Hogwood, A. Rooley, R. Campbell, C. Mackintosh (9/86) (L'OI) ⦶ **417 123-2OH**

1. J. Feldman, N. North, S. Cunningham (1/93) (ARCA) ⦶ **A02**

1. N. Argenta, N. North, R. Boothby (r1992) (6/94) (VIRG) ⦶ **VC7 59324-2**

1. S. Sanford, B. Wissick, R. Erickson (r1991) (10/95) (ALBA) ⦶ **TROY127-2**

2. St Peter ad Vincula Ch, Hurwitz Chbr Ens, A. Davis, J.T. Williams (CHAN) ⓘ **CHAN6560**
(CHAN) ▭ **MBTD6560**
2, 3. Folger Consort (DELO) ⓘ **DE1003**
4. C. Brandes, Arcadian Academy, N. McGegan (hpd/dir) (r1994) (HARM) ⓘ **HMU90 7167**
5. H. Alan, Philomusica of London, A. Lewis (r1958) (DECC) ⓘ **443 393-2DWO**
(DECC) ▭ **443 393-4DWO**

RABAUD, Henri *(1873–1949) France*

Mârouf, savetier du Caire– opera: 5 acts (1914—Paris) (Lib. L Népoty)
A travers le désert R. Alagna, LPO, R. Armstrong (EMI) ⓘ **CDC5 55540-2**
(EMI) ▭ **EL5 55540-4**
Dances Loire PO, P. Dervaux (3/92) (EMI) ⓘ **CDM7 63951-2**
Dances Rhineland-Pfalz State PO, L. Segerstam (r1990) (1/95) (MARC) ⓘ **8 223503**

RACHMANINOV, Sergey (Vasil'yevich) *(1873–1943) Russia/USA*

Aleko– opera: 1 act (1893—Moscow) (Lib. Nemirovich-Danchenko, after Pushkin)
EXCERPTS—; 1. Intermezzo; 2. Gipsy chorus; 3. Old Gipsy's story; 4. Scena and chorus; 5. Gipsy Girls' dance; 6. Men's dance; 7. Chorus; 8. Duet; 9. Zemfira's song; 10. Aleko's cavatina; 11. Intermezzo; 12. Young Gipsy's song; 13. Duet and finale.
Aleko V. Matorin
Zemfira N. Erassova
Old Gipsy V. Pochapsky
Young Gipsy V. Taraschenko
Old Gipsy Woman G. Borisova
Russian St Ch, Orch, A. Chistiakov (r1993) (10/94) (CDM) ⓘ **LDC288 079**
Excs P. Kurchumov, D. Petkov, N. Ghiuselev, Bulgarian RSO, Plovdiv PO, V. Stefanov, R. Raichev (r1970s) (FORL) ⓘ **UCD16743**
1. BPO, L. Maazel (9/92) (DG) ⓘ **435 594-2GGA**
1. St Petersburg PO, Y. Temirkanov (r1992) (4/95) (RCA) ⓘ **09026 62710-2**
1, 5. Philh, N. Järvi (CHAN) ⓘ **CHAN9081**
1, 5. LSO, A. Previn (r1976) (10/93) (EMI) ⓘ [3] **CMS7 64530-2**
3, 10. M. Reizen, Bolshoi Th Orch, V. Nebolsin (r1955) (12/92) (PREI) ⓘ **89059**
10. A. Ivanov, Bolshoi Th Orch (r1940s) (PREI) ⓘ **89067**
10. A. Pirogov, Bolshoi Th Orch, N. Golovanov (r c1950) (PREI) ⓘ **89078**
10. E. Nesterenko, E. Shenderovich (r1993) (RUSS) ⓘ **RDCD11372**
10. F. Chaliapin, orch, L. Collingwood (r1929) (6/88) (EMI) ⓘ **CDH7 61009-2**
10. D. Hvorostovsky, Kirov Th Orch, V. Gergiev (r1993) (5/94) (PHIL) ⓘ **438 872-2PH**
(5/94) (PHIL) ▭ **438 872-4PH**
12. N. Gedda, E. Werba (pp1961) (EMI) ⓘ **CDH5 65352-2**

Francesca da Rimini– opera: prologue, 2 scenes & epilogue, Op. 25 (1906—Moscow) (Lib. M Tchaikovsky, after Dante)
Cpte M. Lapina, V. Taraschenko, V. Matorin, N. Rechetniak, N. Vasiliev, Russian St Ch, Bolshoi Th Orch, A. Chistiakov (r1992) (CDM) ⓘ **LDC288 081**
Lanceotto's aria A. Pirogov, Bolshoi Th Orch, S. Samosud (r c1950) (PREI) ⓘ **89078**

The **miserly knight– opera: 3 scenes, Op. 24 (1906—Moscow) (Lib. Pushkin)**
The Baron M. Krutikov
Albert V. Kudriashov
The Jew A. Arkhipov
The Duke V. Verestnikov
The Servant P. Gluboky
Bolshoi Th Orch, A. Chistiakov (r1993) (10/94) (CDM) ⓘ **LDC288 080**

Monna Vanna– opera: act 1 in piano score; act 2 sketch only (1907) (Lib. Slonov, after Maeterlinck)
Act 1. S. Milnes, S. McCoy, B. Walker, N. Karousatos, J. Thorsteinsson, Icelandic Op Chor, Iceland SO, I. Buketoff (orch Buketoff) (3/92) (CHAN) ⓘ **CHAN8987**

RAFF, (Joseph) Joachim *(1822–1882) Switzerland/Germany*

Dame Kobold– comic opera: 3 acts, Op. 154 (1870—Weimar) (Lib. P Reber, after Calderón)
EXCERPTS: 1. Overture.
1. Košice St PO, U. Schneider (r1994) (MARC) ⓘ **8 223638**

RAMEAU, Jean-Philippe *(1683–1764) France*

Abaris (Les Boréades)– tragédie lyrique: 5 acts (Lib. anon, attrib Cahusac)
Orchestral Suite Eighteenth Century Orch, F. Brüggen (11/87) (PHIL) ⓘ **420 240-2PH**

Castor et Pollux– tragédie en musique: prologue & 5 acts (1737 rev 1754—Paris) (Lib. Bernard)
EXCERPTS: 1. Ouverture. PROLOGUE: 2. Vénus, ô Vénus; 3. Symphonie; 4. Je vous revois, belle Déesse; 5a. Gavottes; 5b. Renais, plus brillante; 6a. Premier Menuet & Tambourin; 6b. Naissez, dons de Flore; 7a. Deuxième Menuet & Tambourin; 7b. D'un spectacle nouveau. ACT ONE: 8. Que tout gémisse; 9. Où courez-vous?; 10. Tristes apprêts, pâles flambeaux; 11a. Symphonie guerrière; 11b. D'où partent ces cris nouveaux?; 11c. Eclatez, fières trompettes (Premier Air des Athlètes); 12. Deuxième et Troisième Airs des Athlètes; 13. Je Remets à vos pieds. ACT TWO: 14. Nature, Amour, qui partagez mon coeur; 15. Le souverain des Dieux; 16. Ma voix, puissant maître du monde; 17. Connaissez notre puissance; 18. Qu'Hébé de fleurs; 19. Voici des Dieux. ACT THREE: 20. Rassemblez-vous, peuples; 21. Son char a reculé; 22. Sortez d'esclavage; 23. Brisons tous nos fers; 24. Tout cède à ce héros vainqueur. ACT FOUR: 25. Séjour de l'éternelle paix; 26. Qu'il soit heureux comme nous; 27. Ici se lève l'aurore; 28a. Gavotte; 28b. Sur les Ombres fugitives; 29a. Passepieds; 29b. Autant d'amours que de fleurs; 30. Fuyez, Ombres légères; 31. Rassurez-vous, habitants fortunés; 32. Mais, qui s'offre à mes yeux; 33. Revenez sur les rivages sombres. ACT FIVE: 34. Castor revoit le jour; 35. Le Ciel est donc touché; 36. Vivez, heureux époux; 37. Peuples, éloignez-vous; 38. Eh quoi! tous ces objets; 39. Qu'ai-je entendu!; 40. Les Destins sont contents; 41. Mon frère...ô Ciel!; 42. Palais de ma grandeur; 43. Tant de vertus doivent prétendre; 44. Entrée des Astres. Gigue; 45a. Ariette; 45b. Brillez, Astres nouveaux; 46a. Chaconne; 46b. Que les Cieux.
Castor; Amour Z. Vandersteene
Pollux G. Souzay
Minerve; Télaïre J. Scovotti
Venus; Maid I; Ombre heureuse; Planète M. Schéle
Mars; Athlete II R. Leanderson
Phébé N. Lerer
Jupiter J. Villisech
Maid II H. Reiter
High Priest; Athlete I S-E. Alexandersson
Stockholm Chbr Ch, VCM, N. Harnoncourt (r1972) (TELD) ⓘ [3] **2292-42510-2**
Castor H. Crook
Pollux J. Corréas
Télaïre A. Mellon
Phébé V. Gens
Mars; Jupiter R. Schirrer
Vénus; A Happy Spirit; A Planet S. Piau
Love; High Priest M. Padmore
Minerve C. Brua
Follower of Hebe; A Celestial Pleasure S. Daneman
Athlete I A. Brand
Athlete II J-C. Sarragosse
Arts Florissants Chor, Arts Florissants Orch, W. Christie (r1992) (7/93) (HARM) ⓘ [3] **HMC90 1435/7**
Castor P. Jeffes
Pollux P. Huttenlocher
Télaïre J. Smith
Phébé C. Buchan
Jupiter L. Wallington
Mercure; Athlete I B. Parsons
Cléone; Suivante d'Hébé J. Rees
Ombre G. Fisher
Spartiate J. Hancorn
Grand Prêtre H. Herford
English Bach Fest Chor, English Bach Fest Baroque Orch, C. Farncombe (r1982) (5/95) (ERAT) ⓘ [2] **4509-95311-2**
Suite Musicholiers, A. Einhorn (arr F-A. Gevaert) (ARIO) ⓘ **ARN68067**
Suite Eighteenth Century Orch, F. Brüggen (4/91) (PHIL) ⓘ **426 714-2PH**
1, 2, 8, 10, 11a-c, 19, 22, 23, 25-27, 33, 44, 45a, 45b, 46a, 46b H. Crook, J. Corréas, A. Mellon, V. Gens, S. Piau, M. Padmore, C. Brua, S. Daneman, A. Brand, J-C. Sarragosse, Arts Florissants Chor, Arts Florissants Orch, W. Christie (r1992) (HARM) ⓘ **HMC90 1501**

Dardanus– tragédie en musique: prologue & 5 acts (1739 rev 1744—Paris) (Lib. Le Clerc de la Bruyère)
1. Ouverture; 2. Entrée pour les Guerriers; 3. Bruit de guerre; 4. Premier Air: Grave; 5. Deuxième Air: Vivement; 6. Tambourins; 7. Les songes; 8. Chaconne.
Vénus C. Eda-Pierre
Iphise F. von Stade
Dardanus G. Gautier
Anténor M. Devlin
Teucer R. Soyer
Isménor J. Van Dam
Phrygienne V. Dietschy
Songe H. Garetti
Songe A. Dutertre
Songe M. Marandon
Songe J-P. Courtis
Paris Op Chor, Paris Op Orch, R. Leppard (r1980) (5/95) (ERAT) ⓘ [2] **4509-95312-2**
Antenor's aria N. Stanchiev, Bulgarian RSO, E. Gracis (r1979) (FORL) ⓘ **UCD16651**
Antenor's Aria B. Christoff, Bulgarian RSO, E. Gracis (r1970s) (FORL) ⓘ **UCD16741**
Menuet tendre en rondeau Brandenburg Consort, R. Goodman (r1992) (HYPE) ⓘ **CDA66600**
Riguadon G. Cziffra (r1980-81; arr pf) (3/95) (EMI) ⓘ **CDM5 65253-2**
Riguadon G. Cziffra (r1969; arr pf) (3/95) (EMI) ⓘ **CDM5 65255-2**
Suite Collegium Aureum, R. Peters (r1964) (8/93) (DHM) ⓘ **05472 77269-2**
Suites 1 & 2. Musicholiers, A. Einhorn (arr V. d'Indy) (ARIO) ⓘ **ARN68067**
1, 4, 6. A. Besançon, Suisse Romande Brass Ens. (arr Brass) (CASC) ⓘ **VEL1015**
1-8. Eighteenth Century Orch, F. Brüggen (11/87) (PHIL) ⓘ **420 240-2PH**

Les **Fêtes d'Hébé– opéra-ballet: prologue & 3 entrées (1739—Paris)**
Le Tambourin B. Hoff, R. Levin (arr ob/pf) (VICT) ⓘ **VCD19037**
Musette et Tambourin ECO, R. Leppard (EMI) ⓘ [2] **CZS7 67425-2**
Tambourin F. Kreisler, M. Eisner (r1917: arr Kreisler) (BIDD) ⓘ **LAB019**
Tambourin F. Kreisler, G. Falkenstein (r1910: arr Kreisler) (BIDD) ⓘ **LAB019**
Tambourin J. Thibaud, H. Craxton (arr Kreisler: r1922) (BIDD) ⓘ **LAB014**
Tambourin Queen's Hall Orch, Henry Wood (r1923) (1/94) (BEUL) ⓘ **1PD3**

Hippolyte et Aricie– tragédie en musique: prologue & 5 acts (1733—Paris) (Lib. Pellegrin)
Hippolyte J-P. Fouchécourt
Aricie V. Gens
Phèdre B. Fink
Thésée R. Smythe
Diane T. Feighan
Cupid; Shepherdess; Female Sailor A. Massis
Pluton; Neptune; Jupiter L. Naouri
Oenone F. Katz
Mercure; Arcas J-L. Georgel
Tisiphone L. Coadou
Fate I J-L. Meunier
Fate II J-F. Loiseleur des Longchamps
Fate III J. Varnier
High Priestess M. Simon
Follower of Cupid S. van Dyck
Priestess K. Okada
Huntress M. Hall
Sagittarius Ens, Musiciens du Louvre, M. Minkowski (pp1994) (9/95) (ARCH) ⓘ [3] **445 853-2AH3**

Nightingale Song E. Schwarzkopf, G. Scheck, M. Raucheisen (Ger: bp1944)
(6/87) (ACAN) Ⓓ **43 801**
Suite Petite Bande, S. Kuijken (r1978)
(7/90) (DHM) Ⓓ **GD77009**

Les **Indes galantes– opéra-ballet: prologue & 4 entrées (1735-1761—Paris) (Lib. Fuzelier)**
Hébé; Zima C. McFadden
Bellone; Ali J. Corréas
L'Amour; Phanie I. Poulenard
Osman; Adario N. Rivenq
Emilie M. Ruggeri
Valère; Damon H. Crook
Huascar; Don Alvar B. Delétré
Tacmas J-P. Fouchécourt
Zaïre S. Piau
Fatime N. Rime
Arts Florissants Chor, Arts Florissants Orch, W. Christie
(2/92) (HARM) Ⓓ [3] **HMC90 1367/9**
(2/92) (HARM) ⊟ [3] **HMC40 1367/9**
Orchestral Suite Luxembourg Rad & TV SO, L. de Froment (FORL) Ⓓ **FF042**
Rondeau Brandenburg Consort, R. Goodman (r1992) (HYPE) Ⓓ **CDA66600**
Soleil, on a detruit G. Souzay, New SO, P. Bonneau (r1956) (DECC) Ⓓ **440 419-2DM**
Suite Collegium Aureum, G. Leonhardt (r1967)
(8/93) (DHM) Ⓓ **05472 77269-2**
Suites 1 & 2. Musicholiers, A. Einhorn (arr P. Dukas) (ARIO) Ⓓ **ARN68067**

Naïs– pastorale-héroïque: 3 acts (1749—Paris) (Lib. Cahusac)
1. Overture; 2. Entrée majesteuse; 3. Sarabande; 4. Gavotte Vive; 5. Riguadons; 6. Entrée des Lutteures; 7. Chaconne; 8. Air de Triomphe; 9. Menuets; 10. Tambourins; 11. Musette; 12. Sarabande; 13. Gavottes; 14. Pas de deux; 15. Air gai; 16. Tambourins; 17. Menuets; 18. Contredanse général.
Naïs L. Russell
Neptune I Caley
Jupiter; Telenus I. Caddy
Pluton J. Tomlinson
Tiresie R. Jackson
Asterion B. Parsons
Palemon A. Ransome
Flore; 2ème Bergère A. Mackay
1re Bergère J. Smith
English Bach Fest Chor, English Bach Fest Orch, N. McGegan (r1980)
(11/95) (ERAT) Ⓓ [2] **4509-98532-2**
1-18. Philh Baroque Orch, N. McGegan (r1994)
(7/95) (HARM) Ⓓ **HMU90 7121**

Platée– comédie-lyrique: prologue & 3 acts (1745—Versailles) (Lib. J Autreau & A J Le Valois d'Orville)
Platée G. Ragon
La folie; Thalie J. Smith
Thespis; Mercure G. de Mey
Jupiter; A satyr V. le Texier
Junon G. Laurens
Cithéron; Momus B. Delétré
L'amour; Clarine V. Gens
Momus M. Verschaeve
F. Herr Voc Ens, Musiciens du Louvre, M. Minkowski (r1988)
(9/90) (ERAT) Ⓓ [2] **2292-45028-2**
Suite Musicholiers, A. Einhorn (arr G. Marty)
(ARIO) Ⓓ **ARN68067**

Le **temple de la gloire– opéra-ballet: 5 acts (1745—Versailles) (Lib. Voltaire)**
1. Overture; 2. Air tendre pour les Muses; 3. Musette en Rondeau; 4. Gavotte en Musette; 5. Air; 6. Gigue un peu gaie; 7. Air de Triomphe; 8. Gigue vive; 9. Passacaille; 10. Entrée des Bergers et Bergères; 11. Loure Grave pour une Entrée Brillante; 12. Air Gai; 13. Entrée de la Jeunesse; 14. Suite de la Passacaille; 15. Air très gai.
Airs gay; Ramages Concert Spirituel Orch, H. Niquet (r1992) (10/93) (FNAC) Ⓓ **592196**
1-15. Philh Baroque Orch, N. McGegan (r1994)
(7/95) (HARM) Ⓓ **HMU90 7121**

Zoroastre– tragédie en musique: prologue & 5 acts (1749 rev 1756—Paris) (Lib. Cahusac)
Zoroastre J. Elwes
Amélite G. de Reyghere
Erinice M. van der Sluis
Céphie A. Mellon
Abramane G. Reinhart
Oromasés; Voice from the Underworld J. Bona
Zopire M. Verschaeve
Narbanor F. Fauché
God of Revenge P. Cantor
Ghent Collegium Vocale, Petite Bande, S. Kuijken
(6/91) (DHM) Ⓓ [3] **GD77144**

RAPCHAK, Lawrence *(20th cent) USA*

The **Lifework of Juan Diaz– opera: 1 act (1990—Chicago) (Lib. R Bradbury, adapted Ratner)**
Juan Diaz R. Hovencamp
Maria Diaz C. Loverde
Alejandro R. Alderson
Ricardo D. Rowader
Jorge J. Whitmer
Ramona; Child voice 2 A. Armato
Josefina; Child voice 1 J. Lind
Chicago Chbr Op Orch, L. Rapchak (r1990)
(ALBA) Ⓓ **TROY091-2**

RAUTAVAARA, Einojuhani *(b 1928) Finland*

Vincent– opera: 3 acts (1990—Helsinki) (Lib. cpsr)
Vincent J. Hynninen
Theo M. Heinikari
Paul M. Putkonen
Maria Hoornik E-L. Saarinen
Gaby S. Rautavaara
Finnish Nat Op Chor, Finnish Nat Op Orch, F. Manchurov
(ONDI) Ⓓ **ODE750-2**

RAVEL, (Joseph) Maurice *(1875–1937) France*

L' **Enfant et les sortilèges, 'Bewitched Child'– opera: 2 parts (1925—Monte Carlo) (Lib. Colette)**
Child S.D. Wyner
Mother; Chinese Cup; Dragonfly; Little Owl J. Taillon
Armchair; Tree J. Bastin
Sofa; Bat; Squirrel J. Berbié
Grandfather Clock; Black Cat P. Huttenlocher
Teapot; Old Man; Frog P. Langridge
Fire; Princess; Nightingale A. Auger
Shepherd; White Cat L. Finnie
Shepherdess L. Richardson
Ambrosian Sngrs, LSO, A. Previn (r1981)
(EMIN) Ⓓ **CD-EMX2241**
Child F. Wend
Mother; Chinese Cup; Dragonfly M-L. de Montmollin
Sofa; She-cat; Bat G. Touraine
Fire; Nightingale A. Migliette
Princess; Squirrel S. Danco
Owl; Shepherd J. Bise
Shepherdess G. Bobillier
Armchairl; Tree L. Lovano
Clock; Tom-cat P. Mollet
Teapot; Old Man; Frog H. Cuénod
Geneva Motet Ch, SRO, E. Ansermet (r1954)
(6/93) (DECC) Ⓓ [2] **433 400-2DM2**
Child M. Mahé
Mother; Chinese Cup; Dragonfly A. Chedel
Fire; Princess; Nightingale E. Vidal
She-cat; Squirrel; Shepherd M. Damonte
Shepherdess; Owl; Sofa; Bat M. Lagrange
Armchair; Tree V. le Texier
Clock; Tom-cat M. Barrard
Teapot; Old Man; Frog L. Pezzino
Bordeaux Th Chor, Bordeaux Aquitaine Orch, A. Lombard (r1992)
(9/93) (AUVI) Ⓓ **V4670**
Child N. Sautereau
Mother; Chinese Cup; Dragonfly D. Scharley
Sofa; Squirrel; Shepherd S. Michel
Fire; Nightingale O. Turba-Rabier
Bat; Owl; Shepherdess C. Verneuil
Armchair; Tree A. Vessières
Clock; Tom-cat Y. le Marc'Hadour
Teapot; Frog J. Peyron
Princess M. Angelici
She-cat M. Legouhy
Old Man M. Prigent
French Rad Maîtrise, FRN Chor, FRNO, E. Bour (r1947)
(2/95) (TEST) Ⓓ **SBT1044**
Child C. Alliot-Lugaz
Sofa; Bat; Owl; Princess C. Dubosc
Shepherdess; Fire; Nightingale M-F. Lefort
Squirrel; Dragonfly; She-cat O. Beaupré
Mother; Chinese cup; Shepherd C. Carlson
Teapot; Old Man; Frog G. Gautier
Clock; Tom-cat D. Henry
Armchair; Tree L. Sarrazin
Montreal SO, C. Dutoit (r1992)
(10/95) (DECC) Ⓓ **440 333-2DH**
Five o'clock Foxtrot N. Petrov (pp)
(OLYM) Ⓓ **OCD273**
Five o'clock Foxtrot Philh, G. Simon (arr. Palmer) (11/91) (CALA) Ⓓ **CACD1005**
(11/91) (CALA) ⊟ **CAMC1005**

L' **Heure espagnole– opera: 1 act (1911—Paris) (Lib. Franc-Nohain)**
Concepcion J. Berbié
Gonzalve M. Sénéchal
Torquemada J. Giraudeau
Ramiro G. Bacquier
Don Inigo Gomez J. Van Dam
FRNO, L. Maazel (r1965)
(3/89) (DG) Ⓓ **423 719-2GH**
Concepcion S. Danco
Gonzalve P. Derenne
Torquemada M. Hamel
Ramiro H. Rehfuss
Don Inigo Gomez A. Vessières
SRO, E. Ansermet (r1953)
(6/93) (DECC) Ⓓ [2] **433 400-2DM2**
Concepcion J. Krieger
Gonsalve L. Arnoult
Torquemada R. Gilles
Ramiro J. Aubert
Don Inigo Gomez H. Dufranne
SO, G. Truc (r1929)
(9/95) (VAI) Ⓓ **VAIA1073**
Concepción D. Duval
Gonsalve J. Giraudeau
Torquemada R. Hérent
Ramiro J. Vieuille
Don Inigo Gómez C. Clavensy
Paris Opéra-Comique Orch, A. Cluytens (r1953)
(9/95) (EMI) Ⓓ **CDM5 65269-2**
Excs Salonisti (arr Mouton)
(EURO) Ⓓ **GD69299**

RAYMOND, Fred *(1900–1954) Germany*

Maske in Blau– operetta (1937—Berlin) (Lib. H. Hentschke & G. Schwann)
Excs M. Schramm, M. Rökk, R. Schock, K-E. Mercker, Berlin Deutsche Op Chor, Berlin SO, W. Schmidt-Boelcke
(2/91) (EURO) Ⓓ **GD69029**

REBIKOV, Vladimir Ivanovich *(1866–1920) Russia*

The **Christmas Tree– children's opera: 1 act (1903—Moscow)**
EXCERPTS: 1. Valse.
1. Bekova Sisters (r1994; arr pf trio: Bekova)
(CHAN) Ⓓ **CHAN9364**

REFICE, Licinio *(1885–1954) Italy*

Cecilia– opera (1922—Rome) (Lib. E Mucci)
Grazie sorelle R. Tebaldi, Santa Cecilia Academy Orch, A. Erede
(8/91) (DECC) Ⓓ [2] **430 481-2DX2**

REINHARDT, Heinrich *(1865–1922) Austria*

The **Spring Maid– operetta (1910) (Lyrics Harry B. Smith)**
EXCERPTS: 1. The Three Trees; 2. Two Little Love Bees; 3. Day Dreams, Visions of Bliss.
1-3. C. McDonald, T. McNaughton, Orig Broadway Cast (r1911)
(5/94) (PEAR) Ⓓ [3] **GEMMCDS9053/5**

RESPIGHI, Ottorino *(1879–1936) Italy*

Belfagor– opera: prologue, 2 acts & epilogue (1923—Milan) (Lib. C. Guastalla)
Belfagor L. Miller
Candida S. Sass
Baldo G. Lamberti

Mirocleto L. Polgár
Olympia K. Takács
Fidelia M. Kalmár
Maddalena M. Zempléni
Old Man P.L. Bárány
Boy Z. Komarniczky
Menica M. Lukin
Don Biagio J. Tóth
Hungarian Rad & TV Chor, Hungarian St Orch, L. Gardelli
(1/90) (HUNG) Ⓓ [2] **HCD12850/1**

Semirama– opera: 3 acts (1910—Bologna) (Lib. A Cerè)
Semirama E. Marton
Susania V. Kincses
Merodach L. Bartolini
Falasar L. Miller
Ormus L. Polgár
Satibara T. Clementis
Hungarian Rad & TV Chor, Hungarian St Orch, L. Gardelli (r1990)
(7/93) (HUNG) Ⓓ [2] **HCD31197/8**

REYER, (Louis-Etienne-)Ernest *(1823–1909) France*

Sigurd– opera: 4 acts (1884—Brussels) (Lib. du Locle and Blau)
EXCERPTS: 1. Overture. ACT 1: 2. Brodons des étendards; 3. Ma mère, un songe malgré moi; 4. Fille des rois, que te sert d'être belle?; 5. Les destins n'ont pas de secrets; 6. Quand on court depuis le matin; 7. J'aime à voir assis; 8. Il est une île sombre; 9. Prince du Rhin, nous partons; 10. Prince du Rhin, au pays de mon père; 11. O file de Sigemon. ACT 2: 12. Dieux terribles qui vous plaisez; 13. Et toi, Freia, déesse de l'amour; 14. O Brunehild, ô vierge armée; 15. Et bien, puisqu'ici-bas; 16. Lequel de nous va tenter l'aventure?; 17. Lequel de vous, guerriers; 18a. Le bruit des chants s'éteint; 18b. Espirits gardiens; 19. Mais non! Point de triste présage; 20. Je suis vainqueur!; 21. Salut, splendeur du jour!; 22. O Gunther mon ami. ACT 3: 23. À la voix des esprits de l'air; 24. Oui, Sigurd est vainqueur!; 25. La violà donc, la déesse; 26. Je suis Gunther, Roi des Burgondes; 27. Les premiers feux du matin; 28. Au nom du roi Gunther, peuple; 29. Roi Gunther, digne fils; 30. Frappons les airs joyeux. ACT 4: 31. Emplissons nos urnes; 32. O palais radieux; 33. Jeune reine, ma soeur; 34. Compagnons, parmi les sentiers; 35. La nuit sera belle; 36. Un souvenir poignant; 37. Sigurd, les dieux dans leur clémence; 38. La nuit sera belle; 39. De nos pères suivant l'usage; 40. O prodige!...Oubliez les maux.
10. E. Scaramberg, orch (r1906)
(MSCM) Ⓓ **MM30377**
10. E. Scaramberg, anon (r1905)
(SYMP) Ⓓ **SYMCD1173**
10. M. Renaud, anon (r1903)
(9/91) (SYMP) Ⓓ **SYMCD1089**
13. M. Renaud, anon (r1903)
(8/92) (IRCC) Ⓓ **IRCC-CD802**
18a P. Franz, orch (r1929) (PREI) Ⓓ **89099**
18a, 18b P. Cornubert, anon (r1905)
(SYMP) Ⓓ **SYMCD1173**
18b, 36. P. Franz, orch (r1912)
(PREI) Ⓓ **89099**
21. F. Pollet, Montpellier PO, C. Diederich (r1989) (ERAT) Ⓓ **4509-98502-2**
21. G. Lubin, orch, H. Defosse (r1929)
(5/91) (CLUB) Ⓓ **CL99-022**
21, 32. M. Lawrence, Pasdeloup Orch, P. Coppola (r1934) (5/90) (PREI) Ⓓ **89011**
37. R. Caron, anon (r1904)
(8/92) (IRCC) Ⓓ **IRCC-CD802**
37(pt) A. Talexis, L. Escalais, anon (r1905)
(8/92) (IRCC) Ⓓ **IRCC-CD802**
37 (pt) L. Escalais, A. Talexis, anon (r1906)
(12/93) (SYMP) Ⓓ **SYMCD1126**
37. R. Caron, anon (r1904)
(12/94) (SYMP) Ⓓ **SYMCD1172**

REZNIČEK , E(mil) N(ikolaus) von *(1860–1945) Austria*

Donna Diana– opera: 3 acts (1894—Prague) (Lib. cpsr)
Overture
Overture VPO, W. Boskovsky (r1968)
(LOND) Ⓓ **436 785-2LM**
Overture VPO, C. Abbado (pp1988)
(7/88) (DG) Ⓓ **423 662-2GH**
Overture NYPO, L. Bernstein (r1967)
(9/93) (SONY) Ⓓ **SMK47601**
Overture BPO, E. Kleiber (r1932)
(5/94) (ARCI) Ⓓ **ARC102**

RICCI, Federico *(1809–1877) Italy*

Crispino e la comare– melodramma fantastico-giocoso: 4 acts (1850—Venice) (Lib. F Piave: comp with L Ricci)
Io non sono J. Sutherland, LSO, R. Bonynge
(DECC) Ⓓ **425 048-2DX**
(DECC) ▣ **425 048-4DX**
Io non sono L. Tetrazzini, orch (r1913)
(9/92) (EMI) Ⓓ [3] **CHS7 63802-2(2)**
Io non sono L. Tetrazzini, orch (r1913)
(9/92) (PEAR) Ⓓ **GEMMCD9223**

RICCI, Luigi *(1805–1859) Italy*

Il diavolo condannato nel mondo a prender moglie– azione comica spettacolosa: 3 acts (1827—Naples) (Lib. A L Tottola)
Io ti ho dato il sangue mio P. Nilon, J. Rawnsley, J. Viera, A. Thorburn, Philh, D. Parry
(8/95) (OPRA) Ⓓ [3] **ORCH104**

RIHM , Wolfgang *(b 1952) Germany*

Die **Eroberung von Mexico– music drama (1992—Hamburg) (Lib. Artaud & Paz)**
Cortez R. Salter
Montezuma R. Behle
Soprano C. Fugiss
Alto S. Otto
Shouting Man P. Kollek
Speaker H. J. Frey
Speaker G. Becker
Hamburg St Op Chor, Hamburg PO, I. Metzmacher (pp1992)
(CPO) Ⓓ [2] **CPO999 185-2**

RIMSKY-KORSAKOV, Nikolay Andreyevich *(1844–1908) Russia*

Christmas Eve– opera: 4 acts (1895—St Petersburg) (Lib. cpsr, after Gogol)
1. Christmas night; 2. Ballet of the stars; 3. Witches' sabbath and ride on the Devil's back; 4. Polonaise; 5. Vakula and the slippers.
Koliadka Bolshoi Th Chor, Bolshoi SO, A. Lazarev (r1993)
(5/94) (ERAT) Ⓓ **4509-91723-2**
1. Armenian PO, L. Tjeknavorian
(ASV) Ⓓ **CDQS6106**
(ASV) ▣ **ZCQS6106**
1. Armenian PO, L. Tjeknavorian
(ASV) Ⓓ **CDQS6116**
1-5. SNO, N. Järvi
(CHAN) Ⓓ [3] **CHAN8327/9**
(12/84) (CHAN) ▣ [3] **DBTD3004**
1-5. Armenian PO, L. Tjeknavorian
(9/92) (ASV) Ⓓ **CDDCA772**
(9/92) (ASV) ▣ **ZCDCA772**
1-5. SRO, E. Ansermet (r1958)
(9/95) (DECC) Ⓓ [2] **443 464-2DF2**
4. Philadelphia, E. Ormandy
(IMP) Ⓓ [2] **DUET 4CD**

The **Golden Cockerel– concert suite from opera (prep. Glazunov & M. Steinberg)**
1. Introduction and Dodon's sleep; 2. King Dodon on the battlefield; 3. Queen of Shemakha's Dance; King Dodon's Dance; 4. Wedding Feast, Death of King Dodon and Finale.
1, 2, 4. Prague SO, V. Smetáček (r1959)
(SUPR) Ⓓ **11 1107-2**
1-4. USSR Academy SO, E. Svetlanov
(CLTS) ▣ **CML2020**
1-4. SNO, N. Järvi
(CHAN) Ⓓ [3] **CHAN8327/9**
(12/84) (CHAN) ▣ [3] **DBTD3004**
1-4. Philadelphia, E. Ormandy
(IMP) Ⓓ [2] **DUET 4CD**
1-4. LSO, A. Dorati (MERC) Ⓓ **434 308-2MM**
1-4. Boston Pops, A. Fiedler (r1956)
(RCA) Ⓓ **09026 61497-2**
1-4. Philh, E. Kurtz (r1961)
(EMI) Ⓓ [2] **CZS5 68098-2**
1-4. Pittsburgh SO, W. Steinberg (r1957)
(EMI) Ⓓ **CDM5 65424-2**
1, 4 (pt) Bratislava RSO, O. Lenárd
(10/90) (NAXO) Ⓓ **8 550098**
1-4. Armenian PO, L. Tjeknavorian
(9/92) (ASV) Ⓓ **CDDCA772**
(9/92) (ASV) ▣ **ZCDCA772**
1-4. Bratislava RSO, D. Johanos
(9/92) (NAXO) Ⓓ **8 550486**
1-4. Philh, E. Kurtz (r1961)
(9/93) (EMI) Ⓓ [2] **CZS7 67729-2**
1-4. Bolshoi SO, A. Lazarev (r1992)
(8/94) (ERAT) Ⓓ **4509-94808-2**
4. FNO, P. Monteux (pp1958)
(MONT) Ⓓ [2] **TCE8740**

The **Golden Cockerel, '(Le) Coq d'Or'– opera: 3 acts (1909—Moscow) (Lib. Bel'sky, sfter Pushkin)**
EXCERPTS: 1. Overture. ACT 2: 2. Hymn to the Sun. ACT 3: 3. Wedding March.
1, 3. LSO, A. Coates (r1945) (BEUL) Ⓓ **2PD11**
2. J. Thibaud, H. Craxton (r1927: trans vn/pf: Kreisler) (BIDD) Ⓓ **LAB024**
2. J. Thibaud, H. Craxton (r1922: trans vn/pf: Kreisler) (BIDD) Ⓓ **LAB014**
2. F. Kreisler, F. Rupp (r1938: trans vn/pf: Kreisler) (BIDD) Ⓓ **LAB040**
2. R. Doria, Paris Sols Orch, J-C. Hartemann (French) (SYMP) Ⓓ **SYMCD1103**
2. L. Pons, Orch, A. Kostelanetz (r1940: French)
(MSCM) Ⓓ **MM30446**
2. R. Streich, Berlin RSO, K. Gaebel
(DG) Ⓓ [2] **435 748-2GDO2**
2. M. Korjus, Berlin St Op Orch, B. Seidler-Winkler (r1936: Ger) (DANT) Ⓓ **LYS001**
2. L. Pons, orch, A. Kostelanetz (r1940)
(RCA) Ⓓ **09026 61411-2**
2. A. Rubinstein (r1925: pf roll)
(COND) Ⓓ **690.07.007**
2. F. Kreisler, F. Rupp (r1938: arr Kreisker)
(IMP) Ⓓ **GLRS106**
2. Rhineland-Pfalz State PO, K. Redel (r1979)
(FORL) Ⓓ **FF058**
2. S. Accardo, L. Manzini (r1993; arr Kreisler)
(FONE) Ⓓ **94F04**
2. P. Fournier, L. Crowson (r1969: arr vc/pf: Kreisler) (DG) Ⓓ [2] **447 349-2GDB2**
2. L. Pons, orch, A. Kostelanetz (r1940: French)
(4/92) (MSOU) Ⓓ **DFCDI-111**
2. L. Kaufman, P. Ulanowsky (r1950s: trans vn/pf: Kreisler) (8/92) (CAMB) Ⓓ **CD-1063**
2. A. Nezhdanova, orch (r1910)
(6/93) (PEAR) Ⓓ [3] **GEMMCDS9007/9(2)**
2. F. Kreisler, C. Lamson (r1921: trans vn/pf: Kreisler) (9/93) (BIDD) Ⓓ [2] **LAB068/9**
2. M. Korjus, Berlin St Op Orch, B. Seidler-Winkler (r1936: Ger) (10/93) (PREI) Ⓓ **89054**
2. A. Galli-Curci, orch (r1921)
(3/94) (CONI) Ⓓ **CDHD201**
(3/94) (CONI) ▣ **MCHD201**
2. L. Pons, RCA SO, A. Kostelanetz (r1940: Fr)
(4/94) (RCA) Ⓓ [6] **09026 61580-2(4)**
2. A. Galli-Curci, orch (r1921)
(8/94) (NIMB) Ⓓ **NI7852**
2. A. Galli-Curci, orch, J. Pasternack (r1921)
(8/94) (ROMO) Ⓓ [2] **81004-2**
2. J. Heifetz, E. Bay (r1945)
(11/94) (RCA) Ⓓ [65] **09026 61778-2(19)**
3. Philadelphia, E. Ormandy
(RCA) Ⓓ **09026 61209-2**
(RCA) ▣ **09026 61209-4**

Kaschey the Deathless– autumnal parable: 1 act (1902—Moscow) (Lib. cpsr, after E M Petrovsky)
EXCERPTS: 1. Kashcheyevna's Aria; 2. Prince Ivan Karalevich's Aria: In this, night's darkest hour.
Kashchey A. Arkhipov
Princess I. Jourina
Kashcheyevna N. Terentieva
Ivan Korolevitch V. Verestnikov
Storm Knight V. Matorin
Yurlov Russian Ch, Bolshoi Th Orch, A. Chistiakov
(CDM) Ⓓ **LDC288 046**
1. Z. Dolukhanova, USSR Rad Orch, A. Kovalyov (r1950s) (PREI) Ⓓ **89066**
1. Z. Dolukhanova, Moscow PO, G. Stolarov (pp1954) (RUSS) Ⓓ **RDCD15023**

2. D. Hvorostovsky, Kirov Th Orch, V. Gergiev (r1993) (5/94) (PHIL) Ⓓ **438 872-2PH**
(5/94) (PHIL) ▭ **438 872-4PH**

Legend of the Invisible City of Kitezh and the Maiden Fevroniya– opera: 4 acts (1907—St Petersburg) (Lib. Bel'sky, after various)

1. Prelude: A Hymn to Nature; 2. Wedding Procession; 3. Tartar invasion and Battle of Kershenets; 4. Death of Fevroniya and Apotheosis of the Invisible City.

Prague SO, V. Smetáček (r1967) (PRAG) Ⓓ **PR250 035**

O vain illusion of glory and grandeur B. Christoff, Philh, W. Schüchter (r1952) (6/93) (EMI) Ⓓ **CDH7 64252-2**

The disaster is approaching Bolshoi Th Chor, Bolshoi SO, A. Lazarev (r1993) (5/94) (ERAT) Ⓓ **4509-91723-2**

1, 3. Bolshoi Th Orch, A. Chistiakov (r1992) (CDM) Ⓓ **LDC288 053**

1-4. SNO, N. Järvi (CHAN) Ⓓ [3] **CHAN8327/9**
(12/84) (CHAN) ▭ [3] **DBTD3004**

1-4. Prague SO, V. Smetáček (r1958) (SUPR) Ⓓ **11 1107-2**

1-4. Odense SO, E. Serov (KONT) Ⓓ **32117**

May Night– opera: 3 acts (1880—St. Petersburg) (Lib. cpsr, after Gogol)

1. Overture.

How relieved I am I. Damaev, E. Katulskaya, orch (r1913) (PEAR) Ⓓ [3] **GEMMCDS9111(2)**

Serenade S. Krasovsky, orch (r c1940) (PEAR) Ⓓ **GEMMCD9122**

Sleep, my beauty I. Damaev, orch (r1910) (PEAR) Ⓓ [3] **GEMMCDS9111(2)**

Sleep, my beauty L. Sobinov, anon (r1901) (6/93) (PEAR) Ⓓ [3] **GEMMCDS9997/9(1)**

Sleep, my beauty D. Yuzhin, anon (r1902) (6/93) (PEAR) Ⓓ [3] **GEMMCDS9001/3(1)**

Sleep, my beauty L. Sobinov, orch (r1910) (9/94) (NIMB) Ⓓ **NI7856**

The sun descends D. Smirnov, orch (r1912) (PEAR) Ⓓ **GEMMCD9106**

1. SNO, N. Järvi (CHAN) Ⓓ [3] **CHAN8327/9**
(12/84) (CHAN) ▭ [3] **DBTD3004**

1. Mexico City PO, E. Bátiz (ASV) Ⓓ **CDQS6089**
(ASV) ▭ **ZCQS6089**

1. Philh, C. Silvestri (r1959) (EMI) Ⓓ [2] **CZS5 68098-2**

1. LSO, A. Coates (r1929) (12/92) (KOCH) Ⓓ **37700-2**

1. SRO, E. Ansermet (6/94) (BELA) Ⓓ **450 132-2**
(BELA) ▭ **450 132-4**

1. Bolshoi SO, A. Lazarev (r1992) (8/94) (ERAT) Ⓓ **4509-94808-2**

1. Philh, C. Silvestri (r1959) (11/94) (EMI) Ⓓ [2] **CZS5 68229-2**

1. SRO, E. Ansermet (r1959) (9/95) (DECC) Ⓓ [2] **443 464-2DF2**

Mlada– opera-ballet (1872) (collab with Borodin, Cui, Mussorgsky & Minkus)

1. Introduction; 2. Redowa; 3. A Bohemian Dance; 4. Lithuanian Dance; 5. Indian Dance; 6. Procession of the Nobles.

Princess Mlada	N. Ananiashvili
Prince Yaromir	O. Kulko
Princess Voislava	M. Gavrilova
Prince Mstivoy	G. Nikolsky
Morena	G. Borisova
Priest	M. Maslov
Lumir	L. Nam
Lada	O. Velichko
Man from Novgorod	V. Kudriashov
Man from Novgorod's Wife	T. Pechuria
Mayor	Y. Statnik
Soul of Yaromir	K. Nikitin
Witch	Y. Malkhassiants

Bolshoi Ballet, Bolshoi Th Chor, Bolshoi SO, A. Lazarev, B. Pokrovsky (r1992) (TELD) ◐ **4509-92052-6**
(8/94) (TELD) ▣ **4509-92052-3**

Sacrificial Chorus Bolshoi Th Chor, Bolshoi Th Orch, A. Chistiakov (CDM) Ⓓ **LDC288 022**

Suite Philh, E. Svetlanov (9/92) (COLL) Ⓓ **Coll1348-2**

1, 2, 4-6. Bratislava RSO, D. Johanos (9/92) (NAXO) Ⓓ **8 550486**

1-5. SNO, N. Järvi (CHAN) Ⓓ [3] **CHAN8327/9**
(12/84) (CHAN) ▭ [3] **DBTD3004**

2, 4, 5. SNO, N. Järvi (CHAN) Ⓓ **CHAN6598**

6. Budapest PO, J. Sándor (LASE) Ⓓ **15 621**
(LASE) ▭ **79 621**

6. SNO, N. Järvi (CHAN) Ⓓ **CHAN6511**
(CHAN) ▭ **MBTD6511**

6. Boston Pops, A. Fiedler (RCA) Ⓓ **GD60700**

6. Bolshoi Th Orch, A. Chistiakov (r1992) (CDM) Ⓓ **LDC288 053**

6. Cincinnati Pops, E. Kunzel (9/86) (TELA) Ⓓ **CD80115**

6. LSO, A. Coates (r1930) (12/92) (KOCH) Ⓓ **37700-2**

6. Bolshoi Th Chor, Bolshoi SO, A. Lazarev (r1993) (5/94) (ERAT) Ⓓ **4509-91723-2**

6. Russian St SO, E. Svetlanov (r1993) (10/95) (RCA) Ⓓ **09026 62684-2**

Mozart and Salieri– opera: 1 act, Op. 48 (1898—Moscow) (Lib. Pushkin)

Mozart	A. Fedin
Salieri	E. Nesterenko

Bolshoi Th Orch, M. Ermler (r1986) (9/93) (OLYM) Ⓓ **OCD145**

Mozart	V. Bogachev
Salieri	N. Storozhev

Montreal I Musici, Y. Turovsky (r1992) (9/93) (CHAN) Ⓓ **CHAN9149**

Sadko– opera: 7 scenes (1898—Moscow) (Lib. cpsr and Bel'sky)

EXCERPTS -; 1. Greetings, ye merchants of Novgorod; 2. O you dark forests (Sadko's aria); 3. O fearful crags (Song of the Viking Guest); 4. Song of the Indian Guest; 5. Song of the Venetian Guest; 6. Farewell, my friends (Sadko's aria); 7. Sleep went along the river (Berceuse); 8. Songs of the Venetian Merchant: 8a. The paragon of cities; 8b. Beautiful city!.

Sadko	G. Nelepp
Volkhova	E. Shumskaya
Okean-More	S. Krasovsky
Lyubava Buslayevna	V. Davydova
Nezhata	E. Antonova
Viking Guest	M. Reizen
Hindu Guest	I. Kozlovsky
Venetian Guest	P. Lisitsian
Duda	S. Koltypin
Sopel	A. Peregudov
Apparition	I. Bogdanov
Foma Nazar'ich	T. Tshernakov
Luca Zinov'ich	S. Nikolau

Bolshoi Th Chor, Bolshoi Th Orch, N. Golovanov (r c1951-2) (ARLE) Ⓓ [3] **ARL23/5**

Sadko	V. Galusin
Volkhova	V. Tsidipova
Okean-More	S. Alexashkin
Lyubava Buslayevna	M. Tarassova
Nezhata	L. Dyadkova
Viking	B. Minzhilkiev
Hindu	G. Grigorian
Venetian	A. Gergalov
Duda	V. Ognovenko
Sopel	N. Gassiev
Apparition	N. Putilin
Foma Nazarich	Y. Boitsov
Luka Zinovich	G. Bezebenkov

Kirov Th Chor, Kirov Th Orch, V. Gergiev (pp1993) (1/95) (PHIL) Ⓓ [3] **442 138-2PH3**

Sadko	V. Galusin
Volkhova	V. Tsidipova
Okean-More	S. Alexashkin
Lyubava Buslayevna	M. Tarassova
Nezhata	L. Dyadkova
Viking	B. Minzhilkiev
Indian	G. Grigorian
Venetian	A. Gergalov
Duda	V. Ognovenko
Sopel	N. Gassiev
Apparition	N. Putilin
Foma Nazarich	Y. Boitsov
Luka Zinovich	G. Bezebenkov

Kirov Ballet, Kirov Th Chor, Kirov Th Orch, V. Gergiev, B. Large (pp1993) (7/95) (PHIL) ◐ [2] **070 439-1PHG2**
(7/95) (PHIL) ▣ **070 439-3PH**

Chorus Bulgarian Nat Ch, Sofia PO, R. Raichev (FORL) Ⓓ **FF060**

Excs G. Morskoi, anon (r1901) (ARLE) Ⓓ [3] **ARL23/5**

Excs G. Morskoi, anon (r1901) (6/93) (PEAR) Ⓓ [3] **GEMMCDS9001/3(1)**

Lubava's aria; Sadko & Lubava duet N. Obukhova, N. Ozerov, Bolshoi Th Orch, L. Steinberg (r1937) (ARLE) Ⓓ [3] **ARL23/5**

Praise to the King of the Sea D. Smirnov, Berlin St Op Orch, F. Weissmann (r1929) (ARLE) Ⓓ [3] **ARL23/5**

Sadko & Volkhova duet E. Vitting, E. Katulskaya, orch (r1913) (ARLE) Ⓓ [3] **ARL23/5**

Sadko & Volkhova duet V. Damaev, S. Druzhiakina, orch (r1911) (ARLE) Ⓓ [3] **ARL23/5**

Sadko's orders in Novgorod V. Petrov, Bolshoi Th Orch, A. Lazarev (r c1970) (ARLE) Ⓓ [3] **ARL23/5**

Your tresses shine like honey-hued dew E. Katulskaya, E. Vitting, orch (r1912) (PEAR) Ⓓ [3] **GEMMCDS9111(2)**

3. A. Safiulin, Soviet Cinema Orch, E. Khachaturian (r1990) (CDM) Ⓓ [2] **LDC288 005/6**
(CDM) ▭ **KC488 005**

3. A. Pirogov, Bolshoi Th Orch (r c1950) (PREI) Ⓓ **89078**

3. S. Preobrazhensky, anon (r1903) (PEAR) Ⓓ [3] **GEMMCDS9111(2)**

3. M. Reizen, orch (r1942) (PEAR) Ⓓ **GEMMCD9122**

3. N. Ghiaurov, VPO, E. Downes (r1962) (DECC) Ⓓ **443 380-2DM**

3. F. Chaliapin, D. Pokhitonov (r1913) (ARLE) Ⓓ [3] **ARL23/5**

3. M. Mikhailov, Bolshoi Th Orch, S. Samosud (r1942) (ARLE) Ⓓ [3] **ARL23/5**

3. F. Chaliapin, orch, A. Coates (r1927) (6/88) (EMI) Ⓓ **CDH7 61009-2**

3. A. Kipnis, Victor SO, N. Berezowski (r1945) (9/92) (RCA) Ⓓ **GD60522**

3. M. Reizen, Bolshoi Th Orch, N. Golovanov (r1952) (12/92) (PREI) Ⓓ **89059**

3. L. Sibiriakov, anon (r1905) (6/93) (PEAR) Ⓓ [3] **GEMMCDS9001/3(2)**

3. B. Christoff, Philh, I. Dobroven (r1950) (6/93) (EMI) Ⓓ **CDH7 64252-2**

4. R. Ponselle, orch (r1920) (PEAR) Ⓓ [2] **GEMMCDS9964**

4. F. Kreisler, orch, J. Pasternack (r1919: arr Kreisler) (BIDD) Ⓓ **LAB021**

4. G. Thill, orch (r1934: Fr) (PEAR) Ⓓ **GEMMCD9947**

4. LSO, Y.P. Tortelier (arr Lotter) (CIRR) Ⓓ **CICD1001**

4. B. Gigli, orch, N. Shilkret (r1932) (NIMB) Ⓓ **NI7817**
(NIMB) ▭ **NC7817**

4. F. Kreisler, F. Rupp (arr Kreisler: r1938) (BIDD) Ⓓ **LAB040**

4. Armenian PO, L. Tjeknavorian (ASV) Ⓓ **CDDCA771**
(ASV) ▭ **ZCDCA771**

4. J. Björling, orch, N. Grevillius (r1936: Swed) (NIMB) Ⓓ **NI7835**

4. K. Smith, P. Rhodes (arr Smith/Rhodes) (ASV) Ⓓ **CDWHL2072**
(ASV) ▭ **ZCWHL2072**

4. M. Korjus, Berlin St Op Orch, B. Seidler-Winkler (r1936: Ger) (DANT) Ⓓ **LYS001**

4. M. Lanza, orch, R. Sinatra (r1953) (RCA) Ⓓ **74321 18574-2**
(RCA) ▭ **74321 18574-4**

4. D. Smirnov, orch (r1921) (PEAR) Ⓓ **GEMMCD9106**

4. Luxembourg Rad & TV SO, L. de Froment (r1979) (FORL) Ⓓ **FF029**

4. C. Ferras, J-C. Ambrosini (BELA) Ⓓ **461 003-2**
(BELA) ▭ **461 003-4**

4. I. Kozlovsky, orch (r1941) (PEAR) Ⓓ **GEMMCD9129**

4. S. Accardo, L. Manzini (r1993; arr Kreisler) (FONE) Ⓓ **94F04**

4. D. Smirnov, orch (r1912) (ARLE) Ⓓ [3] **ARL23/5**

4. Capitol SO, C. Dragon (r1958: arr Dragon) (EMI) Ⓓ **CDM5 65430-2**

4. S. Lemeshev, All-Union Rad Orch, A. Orlov (r1945) (ARLE) Ⓓ [3] **ARL23/5**

4. J. Lloyd Webber, RPO, N. Cleobury (arr vc) (3/87) (PHIL) Ⓓ **416 698-2PH**

4. A. Galli-Curci, orch (r1922) (2/89) (PEAR) Ⓓ **GEMMCD9308**

4. B. Gigli, orch, N. Shilkret (French: r1932) (5/90) (PEAR) Ⓓ **GEMMCD9367**

4. E. Feuermann, G. Moore (arr vc/pf: r1939) (10/91) (PEAR) Ⓓ **GEMMCD9443**

4. L. Pons, orch, A. Kostelanetz (Fr: r1941) (4/92) (MSOU) Ⓓ **DFCDI-111**

4. I. Alchevsky, anon (r1900s) (7/93) (SYMP) Ⓓ **SYMCD1105**

4. M. Korjus, Berlin St Op Orch, B. Seidler-Winkler (Ger: r1936) (10/93) (PREI) Ⓓ **89054**
4. R. Ponselle, orch, R. Romani (r1920) (10/93) (NIMB) Ⓓ **NI7846**
4. F. Kreisler, F. Rupp (r1938: arr Kreisler) (12/93) (EMI) Ⓓ **CDH7 64701-2**
4. A. Galli-Curci, orch (r1922) (8/94) (NIMB) Ⓓ **NI7852**
4. A. Galli-Curci, orch, J. Pasternack (r1922) (8/94) (ROMO) Ⓓ [2] **81004-2**
4. J. Bálint, N. Mercz (r1992: arr fl/hp: Mercz) (12/94) (NAXO) Ⓓ **8 550741**
5. A. Orda, Polish RSO, S. Rachoń (bp1964) (SYMP) Ⓓ **SYMCD1117**
5. D. Gamrekeli, Bolshoi Th Orch, V. Nebolsin (r1946) (ARLE) Ⓓ [3] **ARL23/5**
5. I. Gryzunov, orch, B. Seidler-Winkler (r1910) (ARLE) Ⓓ [3] **ARL23/5**
5. P. Lisitsian, Bolshoi Th Orch, N. Golovanov (r c1953) (4/92) (EMI) Ⓓ [7] **CHS7 69741-2(6)**
5. P. Lisitsian, Bolshoi Th Orch, N. Golovanov (r1952) (8/93) (PREI) Ⓓ **89061**
6. V. Damaev, anon (r1905) (ARLE) Ⓓ [3] **ARL23/5**
6. G. Pozemkovsky, orch, A. Labinsky (r1931) (ARLE) Ⓓ [3] **ARL23/5**
7. R. Streich, Berlin Deutsche Op Orch, R. Peters (DG) Ⓓ [2] **435 748-2GDO2**
7. Z. Dolukhanova, USSR Rad Orch, A. Kovalyov (r1950s) (PREI) Ⓓ **89066**
7. N. Davrath, Vienna St Op Orch, V. Golschmann (r1960s) (VANG) Ⓓ [2] **08.9081.72**
7. N. Zabela-Vrubel, anon (r1912) (ARLE) Ⓓ [3] **ARL23/5**
7. N. Koshetz, orch, B. Reibold (r1928) (ARLE) Ⓓ [3] **ARL23/5**
7. A. Nezhdanova, U. Mazetti (r1907) (ARLE) Ⓓ [3] **ARL23/5**
7. E. Stepanova, Bolshoi Th Orch, L. Steinberg (r1937) (ARLE) Ⓓ [3] **ARL23/5**
7. G. Vishnevskaya, LPO, M. Rostropovich (r1976) (EMI) Ⓓ [3] **CMS5 65716-2**
7. N. Koshetz, orch (r1928) (10/89) (NIMB) Ⓓ **NI7802** (NIMB) ⊟ **NC7802**
7. N. Zabela-Vrubel, anon (r1912) (6/93) (PEAR) Ⓓ [3] **GEMMCDS9004/6(1)**
7. A. Nezhdanova, anon (r1907) (6/93) (PEAR) Ⓓ [3] **GEMMCDS9007/9(1)**
7. L. Garrett, RPO, P. Robinson (r1994) (4/95) (SILV) Ⓓ **SILKD6004** (4/95) (SILV) ⊟ **SILKC6004**
8a, 8b D. Hvorostovsky, Kirov Th Orch, V. Gergiev (r1993) (5/94) (PHIL) Ⓓ **438 872-2PH** (5/94) (PHIL) ⊟ **438 872-4PH**

Snow Maiden (second version)– opera: 4 acts (1898—St. Petersburg) (Lib. cpsr, after Ostrovsky)

1. Introduction; 2. Danse des oiseaux; 3. Cortège; 4. Danse des bouffons.

Carnival Procession; Chorus of Blind Psalterists; Song of the Grain Bolshoi Th Chor, Bolshoi SO, A. Lazarev (r1993) (5/94) (ERAT) Ⓓ **4509-91723-2**
Clouds plotted with thunder E. Zbrueva, anon (r1903) (6/93) (PEAR) Ⓓ [3] **GEMMCDS9004/6(2)**
Going berrying N. Davrath, Vienna St Op Orch, V. Golschmann (r1960s) (VANG) Ⓓ [2] **08.9081.72**
Going berrying X. Belmas, orch, A. Kitschin (r1929) (10/92) (PREI) Ⓓ **89047**
How painful here; But what ails me? L. Lipkowska, orch (r1912) (6/93) (PEAR) Ⓓ [3] **GEMMCDS9004/6(1)**
How painful E. Orel, anon (r c1902) (7/93) (SYMP) Ⓓ **SYMCD1105**
How painful L. Lipkowska, orch (r1912) (3/95) (NIMB) Ⓓ **NI7865**
I know all the songs L. Bori, orch (French: r1922) (PEAR) Ⓓ **GEMMCD9458**
I know all the songs L. Bori, Victor Orch, Rosario Bourdon (r1922: Fr) (ROMO) Ⓓ [2] **81016-2**
Joyous day departs L. Sobinov, orch (r1911) (6/93) (PEAR) Ⓓ [3] **GEMMCDS9997/9(2)**
Lel's 3rd Song E. Kurmangaliev, Moscow Maly SO, V. Ponkin (MEZH) Ⓓ **MK417047**
Mighty nature, full of wonder L. Sobinov, anon (r1901) (6/93) (PEAR) Ⓓ [3] **GEMMCDS9997/9(1)**
Mizgir's Aria: Under the warm blue sea D. Hvorostovsky, Kirov Th Orch, V. Gergiev (r1993) (5/94) (PHIL) Ⓓ **438 872-2PH** (5/94) (PHIL) ⊟ **438 872-4PH**
So full of wonder I. Zhadan, Bolshoi Th Orch, A. Orlov (r1937) (4/92) (EMI) Ⓓ [7] **CHS7 69741-2(6)**
So full of wonder D. Smirnov, orch, J. Harrison (r1924) (6/93) (PEAR) Ⓓ [3] **GEMMCDS9004/6(2)**
With friends to gather berries A. Nezhdanova, orch (r1908) (6/93) (PEAR) Ⓓ [3] **GEMMCDS9007/9(2)**
1-4. SNO, N. Järvi (CHAN) Ⓓ [3] **CHAN8327/9** (12/84) (CHAN) ⊟ [3] **DBTD3004**
1-4. Odense SO, E. Serov (KONT) Ⓓ **32117**
1-4. Philh, E. Kurtz (r1963) (EMI) Ⓓ [2] **CZS5 68098-2**
1-4. Bratislava RSO, D. Johanos (9/92) (NAXO) Ⓓ **8 550486**
1-4. Philh, E. Kurtz (r1963) (9/93) (EMI) Ⓓ [2] **CZS7 67729-2**
1-4. Geneva Motet Ch, SRO, E. Ansermet (r1957) (9/95) (DECC) Ⓓ [2] **443 464-2DF2**
4. Budapest PO, J. Sándor (LASE) Ⓓ **15 621** (LASE) ⊟ **79 621**
4. Philadelphia, E. Ormandy (IMP) Ⓓ [2] **DUET 4CD**
4. SNO, N. Järvi (CHAN) Ⓓ **CHAN6598**
4. National SO, A. Coates (r1945) (BEUL) Ⓓ **2PD11**
4. Cincinnati Pops, E. Kunzel (9/86) (TELA) Ⓓ **CD80115**
4. LSO, A. Coates (r1932) (12/92) (KOCH) Ⓓ **37700-2**
4. NYPO, L. Bernstein (r1967) (9/93) (SONY) Ⓓ **SMK47600**

The **Tale of Tsar Saltan– opera: prologue & 4 acts (1900—Moscow) (Lib. Bel'sky, after Pushkin)**

1. Tsar's farewell and departure; 2. Tsarina in a barrel at sea; 3. Flight of the bumble-bee; 4. The three wonders; 5. March.

Tsar Saltan	I. Petrov
Militrissa	E. Smolenskaya
Court Weaver	L. Nikitina
Royal Cook	E. Shumilova
Barbarikha	E. Verbitskaya
Guidon	V. Ivanovsky
Swan Princess	G. Oleinichenko
Old Man	P. Chekin
Messenger	A. Ivanov

Bolshoi Th Chor, Bolshoi Th Orch, V. Nebolsin (CHNT) Ⓓ [2] **LDC278 1037/8**
Chorus Bulgarian Nat Ch, Sofia PO, R. Raichev (FORL) Ⓓ **FF060**
Tsar Saltan's aria A. Pirogov, Bolshoi Th Orch, A. Melik-Pashayev (r c1950) (PREI) Ⓓ **89078**
1, 2, 4. Odense SO, E. Serov (KONT) Ⓓ **32117**
1, 2, 4. Philh, P. Kletzki (r1958) (EMI) Ⓓ [2] **CZS5 68098-2**
1, 2, 4. Philh, P. Kletzki (r1958) (9/93) (EMI) Ⓓ [2] **CZS7 67726-2**
1, 2, 4. Chicago SO, D. Barenboim (r1993) (12/93) (ERAT) Ⓓ **4509-91717-2**
1, 2, 4. Philh, E. Bátiz (r1992) (6/94) (NAXO) Ⓓ **8 550726**
1, 2, 4. SRO, E. Ansermet (r1959) (9/95) (DECC) Ⓓ [2] **443 464-2DF2**
1-4. SNO, N. Järvi (CHAN) Ⓓ [3] **CHAN8327/9** (12/84) (CHAN) ⊟ [3] **DBTD3004**
1-4. Armenian PO, L. Tjeknavorian (9/92) (ASV) Ⓓ **CDDCA772** (9/92) (ASV) ⊟ **ZCDCA772**
3. Paris Cons, A. Cluytens (r1959) (EMI) Ⓓ **CDM7 69110-2**
3. C. Lindberg, R. Pöntinen (r1983) (BIS) Ⓓ **BIS-CD258**
3. E. Wild (trans Rachmaninov: pp1981) (AUDI) Ⓓ [2] **CD72008**
3. Budapest PO, A. Kórodi (LASE) Ⓓ **15 504** (LASE) ⊟ **79 504**
3. E. Glennie, National PO, B. Wordsworth (arr Palmer) (RCA) Ⓓ **RD60242** (RCA) ⊟ **RK60242**
3. SNO, N. Järvi (CHAN) Ⓓ **CHAN6511** (CHAN) ⊟ **MBTD6511**
3. B. Ringeissen (pf) (ADES) Ⓓ [2] **14166-2**
3. O. Harnoy, C. Wilson (arr Harnoy) (RCA) Ⓓ **RD60697**
3. ASMF, N. Marriner (EMI) Ⓓ [2] **CDEMTVD59** (EMI) ⊙ [2] **EMTVD59**
3. Örebro CO, G.W. Nilson (arr Nilson) (BLUE) Ⓓ **ABCD038**
3. M. Rabin, Hollywood Bowl SO, F. Slatkin (r1959: arr Heifetz) (EMI) Ⓓ [6] **CMS7 64123-2**
3. Canadian Brass (r1990; arr Cable) (PHIL) Ⓓ **432 571-2PH**
3. J. Galway, National PO, C. Gerhardt (arr Gerhardt) (RCA) Ⓓ **GD60924**
3. E. Johnson, J. Drake (arr Johnson/Drake) (ASV) Ⓓ **CDDCA800** (ASV) ⊟ **ZCDCA800**
3. K. Smith, P. Rhodes (arr Smith/Rhodes) (ASV) Ⓓ **CDWHL2072** (ASV) ⊟ **ZCWHL2072**
3. ASMF, N. Marriner (CFP) Ⓓ **CD-CFP4613** (CFP) ⊟ **TC-CFP4613**
3. W. Marsalis, Eastman Wind Ens, D. Hunsberger (arr D Hunsberger) (SONY) **O** **SM42137**
3. Canadian Brass (r1990; arr Cable) (PHIL) **OO** **432 571-5PH**
3. M. Gendron, P. Gallion (r1960) (PHIL) Ⓓ [3] **438 960-2PM3**
3. Philh, C. Mackerras (r1956) (EMI) Ⓓ [2] **CZS5 68098-2**
3. S. Nakarjakov, A. Markovich (TELD) Ⓓ **4509-96231-2** (TELD) ⊟ **4509-96231-4**
3. ASMF, N. Marriner (EMIL) Ⓓ **CDZ103** (EMIL) ⊟ **LZ103**
3. Luxembourg Rad & TV SO, L. de Froment (r1979) (FORL) Ⓓ **FF029**
3. A. Lamasse, D. Hovora (arr. J. Strimer) (FORL) Ⓓ **FF038**
3. P. Casals, Blas-Net (r1929: arr vc/pf) (PEAR) Ⓓ **GEMMCD9128**
3. L. Sirota (r c1938: arr Strimer) (PEAR) Ⓓ **GEMMCD9156**
3. D. Briggs (r1990s: arr org) (MAYH) Ⓓ **KMCD1007** (MAYH) ⊟ **KMK1007**
3. P. Fournier, L. Crowson (r1969: arr vc/pf: Strimer) (DG) Ⓓ [2] **447 349-2GDB2**
3. F. Höricke (r1993; arr Rachmaninov) (MDG) Ⓓ **MDG611 0547-2**
3. Boston Pops, A. Fiedler (r1958) (RCA) Ⓓ **09026 68132-2**
3. J. O'Conor (r1995: arr Rachmaninov) (TELA) Ⓓ **CD80391**
3. J. Lloyd Webber, ECO, N. Cleobury (arr C Palmer) (3/85) (PHIL) Ⓓ **412 231-2PH**
3. W. Marsalis, Eastman Wind Ens, D. Hunsberger (arr D Hunsberger) (9/87) (SONY) Ⓓ **MK42137**
3. K. Walker, J. Drake (arr bn Waterhouse) (10/89) (REGE) Ⓓ **REGCD104** (10/89) (REGE) ⊟ **REGC104**
3. J. Szigeti, N. Magaloff (arr Hartmann: r1933) (1/90) (BIDD) Ⓓ [2] **LAB007/8**
3. V. Horowitz (arr Rachmaninov: r1932) (3/90) (EMI) Ⓓ [3] **CHS7 63538-2**
3. S. Rachmaninov (r1929; arr Rachmaninov: pf) (5/90) (RCA) Ⓓ **GD87766**
3. S. Rachmaninov (arr Rachmaninov: pf roll) (6/90) (DECC) Ⓓ **425 964-2DM**
3. I. Stern, Columbia SO, M. Katims (arr Harris) (7/90) (SONY) Ⓓ **SK45816**
3. Y. Menuhin, A. Balsam (arr Hartmann: r1932) (9/91) (TEST) Ⓓ **SBT1003**
3. J. Heifetz, E. Bay (arr Heifetz; r1932) (12/91) (APR) Ⓓ [2] **APR7015**
3. Y. Menuhin, A. Balsam (arr Hartmann; r1932) (12/91) (BIDD) Ⓓ **LAB046**
3. H. Shelley (r1991: arr pf: Rachamninov) (3/92) (HYPE) Ⓓ **CDA66486**
3. S. Rachmaninov (r1929; arr Rachmaninov: pf) (3/93) (RCA) Ⓓ [10] **09026 61265-2(2)**
3. S. Nakarjakov, A. Markovich (arr tpt/pf) (5/93) (TELD) Ⓓ **9031-77705-2**
3. N. Milstein, G. Moore (r1932: arr Hartmann) (7/93) (APR) Ⓓ [2] **APR7016**
3. W. Lang, M. Murphy, J. Shepherd, P. McCann, Black Dyke Mills Band, P. Parkes (pp1987: arr Woodfield) (11/93) (CHAN) Ⓓ **CHAN4513** (CHAN) ⊟ **BBTD4513**
3. Chee-Yun, A. Eguchi (trans Heifetz) (12/93) (DENO) Ⓓ **CO-75118**
3. J. Weber (r1992: arr pf: Rachmaninov) (12/93) (IMP) Ⓓ **PCD1051**
3. H. Shelley (r1991: arr pf: Rachmaninov) (3/94) (HYPE) Ⓓ [8] **CDS44041/8**
3. N. Milstein, L. Pommers (r1956: arr Hartmann) (5/94) (EMI) Ⓓ [6] **ZDMF7 64830-2**
3. J. Heifetz, E. Bay (r1946) (11/94) (RCA) Ⓓ [65] **09026 61778-2(06)**

3. J. Heifetz, A. Sándor (r1934)
(11/94) (RCA) Ⓓ [65] **09026 61778-2(02)**
3. Philh, D.V. Yu (r1993)
(1/95) (IMP) Ⓓ **MCD82**
3. SRO, E. Ansermet (r1958)
(9/95) (DECC) Ⓓ [2] **443 464-2DF2**
3. A. Janigro, D. Lipatti (r1947: arr vc/pf)
(10/95) (ARCI) Ⓓ [2] **ARC112/3**
3. G. Malcolm (r1962; arr Malcolm)
(11/95) (DECC) Ⓓ **444 390-2DWO**
(11/95) (DECC) ⊟ **444 390-4DWO**
3, 5. LSO, A. Previn (RCA) Ⓓ **VD60487**
4. Bolshoi Th Orch, A. Chistiakov (r1992)
(CDM) Ⓓ **LDC288 053**
4. Russian St SO, E. Svetlanov (r1993)
(10/95) (RCA) Ⓓ **09026 62684-2**
5. J. Fletcher, PJBE (CLAV) Ⓓ **CD50-8503**
5. RPO, A. Previn (r1984)
(5/85) (TELA) Ⓓ **CD80107**

The **Tsar's Bride– opera: 4 acts (1899—Moscow) (Lib. I F Tyumrnrv, after May)**
EXCERPTS: 1. Overture.

Sobakin	E. Nesterenko
Marfa	G. Vishnevskaya
Griaznoy	V. Valaitis
Skuratov	B. Morozov
Likov	V. Atlantov
Liubasha	I. Arkhipova
Bomelius	A. Sokolov
Saburova	E. Andreeva
Duniasha	G. Borisova
Petrovna	V. Borisenko
Coachman	V. Malchenko
Servant	N. Lebedeva
Boy	K. Baskov

Bolshoi Th Chor, Bolshoi Th Orch, F. Mansorov (r1973)
(CHNT) Ⓓ [2] **LDC278 1035/6**

Sobakin	P. Gluboky
Marfa	E. Kudriavchenko
Griaznoy	V. Verestnikov
Skuratov	N. Nizinenko
Likov	A. Mishenkin
Liubasha	N. Terentieva
Bomelius	V. Kudriashov
Saburova	I. Udalova
Duniasha	E. Okolycheva
Petrovna	T. Pechuria
Coachman	V. Pashinsky
Servant	N. Larionova
Boy	Y. Markelov

Sveshnikov Russian Academy Ch, Bolshoi Th Orch, A. Chistiakov (r1992)
(8/93) (CDM) Ⓓ [2] **LDC288 056/7**
All the livelong day L. Lipkowska, orch (r1912)
(6/93) (PEAR) Ⓓ [3] **GEMMCDS9004/6(1)**
Gryaznoi's aria A. Ivanov, Bolshoi Th Orch, K. Kondrashin (r1940s) (PREI) Ⓓ **89067**
Gryaznoy's Aria: Still the beauty haunts my mind D. Hvorostovsky, Kirov Th Orch, V. Gergiev (r1993) (5/94) (PHIL) Ⓓ **438 872-2PH**
(5/94) (PHIL) ⊟ **438 872-4PH**
Haste thee, mother mine Y. Menuhin, H. Giesen (arr Franko: r1930)
(4/91) (BIDD) Ⓓ **LAB032**
Haste thee, mother mine Y. Menuhin, H. Giesen (arr Franko: r1930)
(9/91) (TEST) Ⓓ **SBT1003**
Hop-Picker's Chorus Bolshoi Th Chor, Bolshoi Th Orch, A. Chistiakov (CDM) Ⓓ **LDC288 022**
Hop-Picker's Chorus Bolshoi Th Chor, Bolshoi SO, A. Lazarev (r1993)
(5/94) (ERAT) Ⓓ **4509-91723-2**
In Novgorod M. Korjus, Berlin St Op Orch, B. Seidler-Winkler (r1936; Ger)
(DANT) Ⓓ **LYS001**
In Novgorod M. Korjus, Berlin St Op Orch, B. Seidler-Winkler (Ger: r1936)
(10/93) (PREI) Ⓓ **89054**
Ivan Sergeivich, come into the garden M. Seinemeyer, Berlin St Op Orch, F. Weissmann (Ger: r1927) (11/90) (PREI) Ⓓ **89029**
Look there, above your head A. Nezhdanova, orch (r1912)
(6/93) (PEAR) Ⓓ [3] **GEMMCDS9007/9(2)**
Marfa's Scene & Aria; Lyubasha's Aria G. Vishnevskaya, LPO, M. Rostropovich (r1976)
(EMI) Ⓓ [3] **CMS5 65716-2**
Overture Bolshoi SO, A. Lazarev (r1992)
(8/94) (ERAT) Ⓓ **4509-94808-2**
Overture Russian Nat Orch, M. Pletnev
(12/94) (DG) Ⓓ **439 892-2GH**
(DG) ⊟ **439 892-4GH**
She lay asleep L. Sibiriakov, anon (r1905)
(6/93) (PEAR) Ⓓ [3] **GEMMCDS9001/3(2)**
Sobakin's aria A. Pirogov, Bolshoi Th Orch (r c1950) (PREI) Ⓓ **89078**
The threatening cloud has passed away G. Morskoi, anon (r1901)
(6/93) (PEAR) Ⓓ [3] **GEMMCDS9001/3(1)**
1. Russian St SO, E. Svetlanov (r1993)
(10/95) (RCA) Ⓓ **09026 62684-2**

ROLAND , Marc *(b 1894)* *Germany*

Ferien vom Ich– operetta
Unter dem Sternenzelt F. Wunderlich, Berlin SO, G. Becker (EURO) Ⓓ **GD69018**
(EURO) ⊟ **GK69018**

ROMANO , Enrico *(1877–?)* *Italy*

Zulma– opera
Da tanto tempo; O si ricordiamo E. Burzio, orch (r1913) (1/91) (CLUB) Ⓓ [2] **CL99-587/8**

ROMBERG, Sigmund *(1887–1951) Hungary/USA*

Maytime– operetta (1917) (Lib. R. J. Young)
EXCERPTS: 1. Will You Remember?.
1. L. Warren, E. Steber, Orch, H. Barlow (bp1949) (VAI) ▣ **VAI69110**
1. M. Lanza, J. Alexander Ch, orch, H. René (r1956) (RCA) Ⓓ [3] **GD60889(1)**
1. J. C. Thomas, Orig Broadway Cast (r1922)
(5/94) (PEAR) Ⓓ [3] **GEMMCDS9059/61**

The **New Moon– operetta: 2 acts (1928—New York) (Lyrics O. Hammerstein, F. Mandel & L. Schwarz)**
EXCERPTS: 1. Overture. ACT 1: 2. Dainty wisp of thistledown; 3. Marianne; 4. The girl on the prow; 5. An interrupted love song; 6. Tavern song; 7. Softly, as in a morning sunrise; 8. Stout-hearted men; 9. One kiss; 10. The trial; 11. Wanting you. ACT 2: 12. Funny little sailor men; 13. Lover, come back to me; 14. Love is quite a simple thing; 15a. Marriage number; 15b. Try her out at dances; 16a. Never for you; 16b. Lover, come back to me (reprise); 17a. One kiss (reprise); 17b. Wanting you (reprise).
3, 7, 8. J. Hadley, Harvard Glee Club, American Th Orch, P. Gemignani (r1993; orch W. D. Brohn) (RCA) Ⓓ **09026 62681-2**
7. M. Lanza, orch, R. Sinatra (r1951)
(IMP) Ⓓ **PWKS4230**
7. M. Lanza, C. Callinicos (pp1958)
(RCA) Ⓓ [3] **GD60889(2)**
7. M. Lanza, C. Callinicos (pp1958)
(RCA) Ⓓ **09026 61884-2**
(RCA) ⊟ **09026 61884-4**
9, 13. B. Hendricks, Ambrosian Sngrs, Philh, L. Foster, G. Quilico (r1992)
(8/93) (EMI) Ⓓ **CDC7 54626-2**
11. M. Lanza, orch, R. Sinatra (bp)
(RCA) Ⓓ **GD60720**
(RCA) ⊟ **GK60720**
11. B. Hendricks, G. Quilico, Lyon Op Orch, L. Foster (r1993) (6/95) (EMI) Ⓓ **CDC5 55151-2**

Nina Rosa– operetta (1930—New York) (Wds. Harbach & I. Caesar)
EXCERPTS: 1. March of Nina Rosa; 2. How unfaithful are women.
1, 2. A. Baugé, orch (r1930s: French)
(FORL) Ⓓ **UCD19022**
1, 2. A. Baugé, orch, G. Andolfi (French)
(EMI) Ⓓ [2] **CZS5 68292-2**

The **Student Prince– operetta (1924) (Lib. Donnelly)**
EXCERPTS. 1. Overture. ACT 1: 2. Prologue - By our bearing so sedate; 3. Golden days; 4. Garlands bright; 5. To the Inn we're marching (Entrance of Students and Kathie); 6. Drinking Song; 7. I'm coming at your call; 8. A student has a happy lot; 9. Come boys, let's all be gay, boys; 10. Entrance of the Prince and Engel; 11. Heidelberg, beloved vision; 12. In Heidelberg fair; 13. Gaudeamus igitur; 14. Drinking Song (reprise); 15. Golden days (reprise); 16. Deep in my heart, dear; 17. Come sir, will you join our noble Saxon corps; 18. To our native land of freedom; 19. Come answer to our call; 20. Drinking song (reprise); 21. Serenade; 22. Carnival of Springtime; 23. Come boys, let's all be gay, boys. ACT 2: 24. Introduction; 25. Farmer Jacob lay a-snoring; 26. Student life; 27. Thoughts will come to me of days; 28. We're off to Paris, city of joy; 29. Deep in my heart, dear (reprise). ACT 3: 30. Opening; 31. Ballet; 32. Waltz; 33. Just we two; 34. The flag that flies above; 35. Gavotte; 36. Never more will come again those days of youth; 37. Serenade Intermezzo. ACT 4: 38. Let us sing a song; 39. To the Inn we're marching (reprise); 40. The flag that flies above us (reprise); 41. Serenade (reprise); 42. Come boys, let's all be gay, boys (reprise); 43. Scene; 44. Deep in my heart, dear (reprise).

Prince Karl Franz	D. Rendall
Kathie	M. Hill Smith
Dr Engel	N. Bailey
Princess Margaret	D. Montague
Ruder	J. Howard
Gretchen	R. Ashe
Von Asterberg	N. Jenkins
Lucas	D. Maxwell
Detlef	B. Bottone
Lutz	Leon Greene
Tarnitz	S. Page
Hubert	A. Mutis
Fritz	N. Colicos
Lackey I	S. Green
Lackey II	B. Rankin
Lackey III	R. Hart
Lackey IV	R. Lock
Serving Wench	M. Friedman

Ambrosian Chor, Philh, J.O. Edwards
(3/91) (TER) Ⓓ [2] **CDTER2 1172**
(3/91) (TER) ⊟ [2] **ZCTED 1172**
J. Locke, E. Broadbent, orch, N. Paramor
(EMI) Ⓓ **CDP7 98844-2**
(EMI) ⊙ **GO2034**
Excs R. Tucker, Orch, H. Barlow (bp1957)
(VAI) ▣ **VAI69109**
1, 3, 6, 13, 16, 21. E. Doubleday, M. Lanza, chor, orch, C. Callinicos (r1953)
(RCA) Ⓓ **GD60048**
(RCA) ⊟ **GK60048**
1, 3, 9, 12, 13, 15, 16, 20, 21, 27, 29, 33, 37, 43, 44. C. Jeffreys, E. Geisen, D. Hönig, Hamburg St Op Chor, Hamburg St Op Orch, S. Gyártó
(BAYE) Ⓓ **BR150004**
2, 3, 5-7, 9, 13, 16, 21-23, 26-29, 33, 36, 37, 44. D. Rendall, M. Hill Smith, N. Bailey, D. Montague, J. Howard, R. Ashe, N. Jenkins, D. Maxwell, B. Bottone, S. Page, Ambrosian Chor, Philh, J.O. Edwards (r1989)
(TER) Ⓓ **CDTEO1005**
(TER) ⊟ **ZCTEO1005**
2, 6, 16, 21. E. Doubleday, M. Lanza, J. Alexander Ch, RCA Victor Orch, C. Callinicos (r1953) (RCA) Ⓓ [3] **GD60889(1)**
3. J. Hadley, M. Lanza, American Th Orch, P. Gemignani (r1993; orch W. D. Brohn; Lanza's vocal r1952) (RCA) Ⓓ **09026 62681-2**
3, 6, 21. M. Lanza, chor, orch, C. Callinicos (r1952) (RCA) Ⓓ **74321 18574-2**
(RCA) ⊟ **74321 18574-4**
6, 21. J. Hadley, Harvard Glee Club, American Th Orch, P. Gemignani (r1993; orch W. D. Brohn) (RCA) Ⓓ **09026 62681-2**
16. M. Hill Smith, Philh, J.O. Edwards (r1989-91)
(10/91) (TER) Ⓓ **CDVIR8314**
(10/91) (TER) ⊟ **ZCVIR8314**
16. F. Kreisler, C. Lamson (r1926: arr Kreisler)
(12/93) (BIDD) Ⓓ **LAB075**
16. B. Hendricks, G. Quilico, Lyon Op Orch, L. Foster (r1993) (6/95) (EMI) Ⓓ **CDC5 55151-2**
16, 21. M. Lanza, orch, R. Sinatra (r1952)
(RCA) Ⓓ **09026 61420-2**
(RCA) ⊟ **09026 61420-4**
21. M. Lanza, orch, C. Callinicos
(RCA) Ⓓ **GD60720**
(RCA) ⊟ **GK60720**
21. J. Sutherland, Ambrosian Light Op Chor, New Philh, R. Bonynge (arr Gamley)
(DECC) Ⓓ **433 223-2DWO**
(DECC) ⊟ **433 223-4DWO**
21. J. Carreras, Ambrosian Sngrs, London Studio SO, M. Viotti (r1993; arr Packh/Palmer)
(TELD) Ⓓ **4509-92369-2**
(TELD) ⊟ **4509-92369-4**
21. R. Crooks, chor, orch (r1930)
(PEAR) Ⓓ **GEMMCD9093**
21. J. Carreras, English Concert Chor, BBC Concert Orch, E. Ricci (pp1994)
(TELD) ◖ **4509-96080-6**
(TELD) ▣ **4509-96080-3**
21. B. Bowman, Cincinnati Wind Sym, E. Corporon (r1994: arr D Godfrey)
(KLVI) Ⓓ **KCD11060**
21. P. Domingo, I. Perlman, NY Studio Orch, J. Tunick (r1990) (3/92) (EMI) Ⓓ **CDC7 54266-2**

29. S. Burrows, National PO, R. Stapleton (arr P Hope) (DECC) ① **433 223-2DWO**
(DECC) ▭ **433 223-4DWO**
32. Philh, J.O. Edwards (TER) ① **CDVIR8315**

ROPARTZ, Joseph Guy (Marie) *(1864–1955) France*

La **Miracle de Saint Nicolas– legend: 2 parts—16 scenes: sols, chorus & orch (1905) (Wds. R d'Avril)**
C. Papis, D. Henry, V. le Texier, I. Brissot, E. LeBrun, C. Lajarrige, Ile de France Regional Ch, Nancy SO, M. Piquemal (r1994)
(MARC) ① **8 223774**

ROREM, Ned *(b 1923) USA*

A **Childhood Miracle– opera: 1 act (1956—Philadelphia) (Lib. E Stein)**
Violet D. Dunn
Peony M. Couture
Mother M. Tsingopoulos
Father P. Castaldi
Emma M. Cidoni
Snowman P. Greene
Magic Circle CO, R. Evans Harrell (r c1994)
(10/95) (NEWP) ① **NPD85594**

Miss Julie– opera: 2 acts (1965—New York) (Lib. K. Elmslie after Strindberg)
Miss Julie T. Fried
John P. Torre
Christine H. Sarris
Mr Niels D. Blackburn
Young Boy M. Mulligan
Young Girl Laurelyn Watson
Bass Soloist J. Ernster
MSM Op Chor, MSM Op Orch, D. Gilbert (pp1994)
(NEWP) ① [2] **NPD85605**

Three Sisters Who Are Not Sisters– opera: 1 act (1971—Philadelphia) (Lib. G Stein)
Jenny A. Matthews
Samuel F. Urrey
Helen C. Flamm
Ellen M. Tsingopoulos
Sylvester M. Singer
J. van Buskirk
Magic Circle CO, R. Evans Harrell (r c1994)
(10/95) (NEWP) ① **NPD85594**

ROSSI, Luigi *(c1597–1653) Italy*

Orfeo– opera: prologue & 3 acts (1647—Paris) (Lib. F. Buti)
Orfeo A. Mellon
Euridice M. Zanetti
Nutrice; Bacco D. Favat
Aristeo S. Piau
Satiro N. Isherwood
Amore C. Pelon
Venere; Vittoria N. Rime
Vecchia; Giove J-P. Fouchécourt
Endimione J. Corréas
Giunone M. Boyer
Gelosia C. Eloir
Augura; Plutone B. Delétré
Apollo; Mercurio B. Thivel
Caronte; Momo J-M. Salzmann
Proserpina D. Michel-Dansac
Himeneo B. Malleret
Arts Florissants Voc Ens, Arts Florissants Instr Ens, W. Christie
(3/92) (HARM) ▭ [3] **HMU40 1358/60**

Il **palazzo incantato, overo La guerriera amante– opera (1642—Rome)**
Corrente Tragicomedia (r1992)
(10/93) (TELD) ① **4509-90799-2**

ROSSINI, Gioachino (Antonio) *(1792–1868) Italy*

Adelaide di Borgogna– dramma: 2 acts (1817—Rome) (Lib. G. Schmidt)
EXCERPTS: 1. Soffia la tua ventura; 2. Salve, Italia, un di regnante.
Adelaide M. Devia
Ottone M. Dupuy
Berengario A. Caforio
Adalberto A. Bertolo
Eurice E. Tandura
Iroldo M. Farruggia
Ernesto G. Fallisi
New Cambridge Chor, M. Franca Fest Orch, A. Zedda (pp1984)
(4/95) (FONI) ① [2] **CDC64**
1, 2. D. Jones, Richard Hickox Sngrs, CLS, R. Hickox (2/91) (CHAN) ① **CHAN8865**
(2/91) (CHAN) ▭ **ABTD1480**

Armida– dramma: 3 acts (1817—Naples) (Lib. G. Schmidt, after Tasso)
EXCERPTS: 1. Overture. ACT 1: 2. Lieto, ridente oltre usato; 3. Ah, no! Sia questo di tregua il giorno; 4. Arditi, all'ire farem ritorno; 5. Germano, a te richiede; 6a. Signor, tanto il tuo nome ovunque suona; 6b. Sventurata! or che mi resta; 7. Or che farò? Ceder dovrò?; 8. German, se togli al campo; 9. Cedei guerrieri, è ver; 10a. Oh sorte infida! Come! a Dudon costui succede?; 10b. Non soffrirò l'offesa; 10c. Ah! tutti v'unite; 11. Grata quest'alma costante; 12a. Ecco il guerriero, il duce; 12b. Se pari agli accenti; 13. Che terribile momento!; 14. Sappia il duce il caso orrendo; 15. Vieni, o duce, punisci l'errore; 16. M'invita la sorte. ACT 2: 17. Alla voce d'Armida possente; 18a. Sovr'umano potere; 18b. Di ferro e fiamme cinti; 19. Dove son io!; 20a. Mio ben, questa che premi; 20b. No; d'Amor la reggia è questa; 21. Ballet; 22. D'Amore al dolce impero. ACT 3: 23. Come l'aurette placide; 24. Rimira: a noi sen viene; 25. Fuggite infernei mostri; 26. Soavi catene; 27. Resta, mio ben; 28. Lo splendor di que' rai; 29. In quale aspetto imbelle; 30. Se al mio crudel tormento; 31a. Dove son io!; 31b. È ver gode quest'anima.
Armida C. Deutekom
Goffredo; Carlo O. Garaventa
Ubaldo; Gernando E. Gimenez
Rinaldo P. Bottazzo
Eustazio B. Trotta
Idraote A. Maddalena
Astarotte G. Antonini
Venice La Fenice Chor, Venice La Fenice Orch, C. Franci (pp1970)
(MEMO) ① [2] **HR4152/3**
Armida C. Deutekom
Goffredo; Carlo O. Garaventa
Ubaldo; Gernando E. Gimenez
Rinaldo P. Bottazzo
Eustazio B. Trotta
Idraote A. Maddalena
Astarotte G. Antonini
Venice La Fenice Chor, Venice La Fenice Orch, C. Franci (pp1970)
(FOYE) ① [2] **2-CF2030**
Armida C. Gasdia
Goffredo; Carlo W. Matteuzzi
Ubaldo; Gernando B. Ford
Rinaldo C. Merritt
Eustazio C.H. Workman
Idraote; Astarotte F. Furlanetto
Ambrosian Op Chor, Solisti Veneti, C. Scimone
(12/91) (EURM) ① [2] **350211**
Armida R. Fleming
Goffredo D. Kaasch
Rinaldo G. Kunde
Idraote I. d'Arcangelo
Gernando J. Francis
Eustazio C. Bosi
Ubaldo I. Zennaro
Carlo B. Fowler
Astarotte S. Zadvorny
Bologna Teatro Comunale Chor, Bologna Teatro Comunale Orch, D. Gatti (pp1993)
(3/95) (SONY) ① [3] **S3K58968**
1. ASMF, N. Marriner (r1979)
(10/92) (PHIL) ① [3] **434 016-2PM3**
22. M. Callas, Rome RAI Orch, A. Simonetto (pp1954) (MEMO) ① **HR4293/4**
22. M. Callas, Milan RAI SO, A. Simonetto (r1954) (SUIT) ① **CDS1-5001**
22. M. Caballé, C. Vozza, RCA Italiana Op Orch, C.F. Cillario (11/92) (RCA) ① [2] **GD60941**
22. M. Callas, Rome RAI Orch, A. Simonetto (pp1954) (2/93) (EMI) ① **CDC7 54437-2**
28. R. Blake, P. Jeffes, P. Bronder, LSO, M. Valdes (12/89) (ARAB) ① **Z6612**
(12/89) (ARAB) ▭ **ABQC6612**
28. M. Callas, Rome RAI Orch, A. Simonetto (pp1954)
(4/92) (EMI) ① [7] **CHS7 69741-2(7)**

Il **Barbiere di Siviglia, '(The) Barber of Seville'– commedia: 2 acts (1816—Rome) (Lib. C. Sterbini, after Beaumarchais)**
EXCERPTS: 1. Overture. ACT 1: 2a. Piano, pianissimo; 2b. Ecco, ridente in cielo; 3. Mille grazie; 4. Largo al factotum; 5. Se il mio nome; 6a. Oh cielo; 6b. All'idea di quel metallo; 6c. Numero quindici; 7a. Una voce poco fa; 7b. Io son docile; 8. La calunnia; 9. Dunque io son?; 10. A un dottor della mia sorte; 11. Ehi, di casa!; 12. Fredda ed immobile. ACT 2: 13. Pace e gioia; 14. Contro un cor (Lesson Scene); 15. Don Basilio!...Cosa veggo!; 16. Buona sera, mio signore; 17. Il vecchiotto cerca moglie; 18. Storm Music; 19a. Ah! qual colpo; 19b. Zitti, zitti; 20. Cessa di più resistere; 21. Di si felice. REPLACEMENT ARIAS: 22a. Ma forse, ahimè Lindoro; 22b. L'innocenza di Lindoro (No. 7); 23. La mia pace, la mia calma (No. 14).
Figaro H. Prey
Rosina T. Berganza
Almaviva L. Alva
Doctor Bartolo E. Dara
Don Basilio P. Montarsolo
Berta S. Malagù
Fiorello R. Cesari
Officer L. Roni
La Scala Chor, La Scala Orch, C. Abbado, J-P. Ponnelle
(DG) ◖ [2] **072 404-1GH2**
(DG) ▭ **072 404-3GH**
Figaro J. Rawnsley
Rosina M. Ewing
Almaviva M-R. Cosotti
Doctor Bartolo C. Desderi
Don Basilio F. Furlanetto
Berta C. McCord
Fiorello R. Dean
Glyndebourne Fest Chor, LPO, S. Cambreling, J. Cox (r1981)
(CAST) ▭ **CVI2016**
Figaro R. Stracciari
Rosina M. Capsir
Almaviva D. Borgioli
Doctor Bartolo S. Baccaloni
Don Basilio V. Bettoni
Berta C. Ferrani
Fiorello A. Bordonali
La Scala Chor, La Scala Orch, L. Molajoli (r1929)
(MSCM) ① [2] **MM30276**
Figaro L. Nucci
Rosina K. Battle
Almaviva R. Blake
Doctor Bartolo E. Dara
Don Basilio F. Furlanetto
Berta L. di Franco
Fiorello D. Hamilton
NY Met Op Chor, NY Met Op Orch, R. Weikert
(DG) ▭ **072 414-3GH**
Figaro E. Bastianini
Rosina G. Simionato
Almaviva A. Misciano
Doctor Bartolo F. Corena
Don Basilio C. Siepi
Berta R. Cavallari
Fiorello A. La Porta
Official G. Zampieri
MMF Chor, MMF Orch, A. Erede (r1956)
(DECC) ① [2] **443 536-2LF2**
Figaro A. Opie
Rosina D. Jones
Almaviva B. Ford
Doctor Bartolo A. Shore
Don Basilio P. Rose
Berta J. Rhys-Davies
Fiorillo P. Snipp
Officer C. Ross
ENO Chor, ENO Orch, G. Bellini (Eng)
(CHAN) ① [2] **CHAN7023/4**
Figaro T. Allen
Rosina A. Baltsa
Almaviva F. Araiza
Doctor Bartolo D. Trimarchi
Don Basilio R. Lloyd
Berta S. Burgess
Fiorello M. Best
Ambrosian Op Chor, ASMF, N. Marriner (r1982)
(4/84) (PHIL) ① [2] **446 448-2PH2**
Figaro H. Prey
Rosina T. Berganza
Almaviva L. Alva
Doctor Bartolo E. Dara
Don Basilio P. Montarsolo
Berta S. Malagù
Fiorello R. Cesari
Ambrosian Op Chor, LSO, C. Abbado (r1971)
(10/86) (DG) ① [2] **415 695-2GH2**
Figaro T. Gobbi
Rosina M. Callas

Almaviva L. Alva
Doctor Bartolo F. Ollendorff
Don Basilio N. Zaccaria
Berta G. Carturan
Fiorello Mario Carlin
chor, Philh, A. Galliera
(6/87) (EMI) ① [2] **CDS7 47634-8**

Figaro R. Merrill
Rosina R. Peters
Almaviva C. Valletti
Doctor Bartolo F. Corena
Don Basilio G. Tozzi
Berta M. Roggero
Fiorello C. Marsh
NY Met Op Chor, NY Met Op Orch, E. Leinsdorf
(9/88) (RCA) ① [3] **GD86505**

Figaro L. Nucci
Rosina M. Horne
Almaviva P. Barbacini
Doctor Bartolo E. Dara
Don Basilio S. Ramey
Berta R. Pierotti
Fiorello S. Alaimo
La Scala Chor, La Scala Orch, R. Chailly (r1982)
(9/88) (SONY) ① [3] **S3K37862**

Figaro L. Nucci
Rosina C. Bartoli
Almaviva W. Matteuzzi
Doctor Bartolo E. Fissore
Don Basilio P. Burchuladze
Berta G. Banditelli
Fiorello M. Pertusi
Bologna Teatro Comunale Chor, Bologna Teatro Comunale Orch, G. Patanè
(9/89) (DECC) ① [3] **425 520-2DH3**

Figaro M. Ausensi
Rosina T. Berganza
Almaviva U. Benelli
Doctor Bartolo F. Corena
Don Basilio N. Ghiaurov
Berta S. Malagù
Fiorello D. Mantovani
Naples Scarlatti Chor, Naples Scarlatti Orch, S. Varviso
(5/92) (DECC) ① [2] **417 164-2DM2**

Figaro S. Bruscantini
Rosina V. de los Angeles
Almaviva L. Alva
Doctor Bartolo I. Wallace
Don Basilio C. Cava
Berta L. Sarti
Fiorello D. Robertson
Glyndebourne Fest Chor, RPO, V. Gui (r1962)
(5/92) (EMI) ① [2] **CMS7 64162-2**
(9/87) (EMI) ▭ [2] **TC-CFPD4704**

Figaro P. Domingo
Rosina K. Battle
Almaviva F. Lopardo
Doctor Bartolo L. Gallo
Don Basilio R. Raimondi
Berta G. Sima
Fiorello C. Chausson
Venice La Fenice Chor, COE, C. Abbado
(12/92) (DG) ① [2] **435 763-2GH2**

Figaro H. Hagegård
Rosina J. Larmore
Almaviva R. Giménez
Doctor Bartolo A. Corbelli
Don Basilio S. Ramey
Berta B. Frittoli
Fiorello U. Malmberg
Geneva Grand Th Chor, Lausanne CO, J. López-Cobos (r1992)
(11/93) (TELD) ① [2] **9031-74885-2**

Figaro T. Hampson
Rosina S. Mentzer
Almaviva J. Hadley
Doctor Bartolo B. Praticò
Don Basilio S. Ramey
Berta A. Felle
Fiorello J. Fardilha
Chor, Tuscan Orch, G. Gelmetti (r1992)
(11/93) (EMI) ① [3] **CDS7 54863-2**

Figaro R. Servile
Rosina S. Ganassi
Almaviva R. Vargas
Doctor Bartolo A. Romero
Don Basilio F. de Grandis
Berta I. Kertesi
Fiorello K. Sárkány
Hungarian Rad Chor, Failoni CO, W. Humburg (r1992)
(3/94) (NAXO) ① [3] **8 660027/9**

Excs Munich Rococo Sols (arr Trautner) (9/90) (SCHW) ① **310061**
Excs F. de Lucia, F. Novelli, M. Resemba, G. Schottler, S. Valentino, A. di Tommaso, N. Sabatano, Naples San Carlo Op Chor, Naples San Carlo Op Orch, S. Sassano (r1918) (9/91) (LYRC) ① **SRO819**
Excs J. Sutherland, Orch, Anon (cond), D. Bailey (11/92) (DECC) ◖ **071 135-1DH**
Manca un foglio A. Pini-Corsi, orch (r1912) (7/92) (PEAR) ① [3] **GEMMCDS9923(1)**
1. Plovdiv PO, R. Raychev (HARM) ▭ **HMC40 466**
1. Scottish CO, J.Laredo (NIMB) ① **NI5078**
1. Zagreb PO, M. Halász (NAXO) ① **8 550236**
1. C. Lindberg, R. Pöntinen (arr Lindberg/Pöntinen) (BIS) ① **BIS-CD328**
1 (bars 1-34) Stockholm PO, A. Toscanini (pp1933) (BIS) ① [8] **BIS-CD421/4(2)**
1. Budapest PO, J. Sándor (LASE) ① **15 622** (LASE) ▭ **79 622**
1. RPO, M. Reed (RPO) ① [2] **CDRPD9001** (RPO) ▭ [2] **ZCRPD9001**
1(pt) Philh, R. Muti (EMI) ① [2] **CDEMTVD59** (EMI) ⊙ [2] **EMTVD59**
1. Classic Buskers (arr Copley) (SEAV) ① **CD007365**
1. Philh, C.M. Giulini (EMI) ① [2] **CZS7 67440-2**
1. BPO, W. Furtwängler (r1935) (SYMP) ① **SYMCD1043**
1. RPO, E. Bátiz (RPO) ① **CDRPO5006** (RPO) ▭ **ZCRPO5006**
1. Tedesco Duo (arr Giuliani/Hölzer: 2 gtrs) (SCHW) ① **310402**
1. LSO, P. Gamba (DECC) ① **433 606-2DSP**
1. Philh, C.M. Giulini (CFP) ① **CD-CFP4606** (CFP) ▭ **TC-CFP4606**
1. Plovdiv PO, R. Raychev (HARM) ① **HMP390 466**
1. LCP, R. Norrington (EMI) **ꝏ** **DCC7 54091-5**
1. RPO, M. Reed (r1990) (RPO) ① **CDRPO5010**
1. NYPO, L. Bernstein (r1963) (SONY) ① **SMK47606**
1. LCP, R. Norrington (EMI) ◙ **MDC7 54091-8**
1. Mexico St SO, E. Bátiz (ASV) ① **CDDCA857** (ASV) ▭ **ZCDCA857**
1. BPO, H. von Karajan (r1971) (DG) ① **439 415-2GCL**
1. COE, J. Judd (r1985) (IMP) ① **PCDS23** (IMP) ▭ **PCDSC23**
1. COE, J. Judd (IMP) ① [3] **TCD1070**
1. Ricercar Acad, M. Ponseele (r1993; arr Sedlak: Wind Ens) (RICE) ① **RIC126114**
1. NY Harmonie Ens, S. Richman (r1992: arr W Sedlak) (MUSI) ① **MACD-797**
1. Luxembourg Rad & TV SO, P. Cao (FORL) ① **FF027**
1. Minneapolis SO, A. Dorati (r1957) (MERC) ① **434 345-2MM**
1. ROHO, C. Rizzi (r1990) (CONI) ① **75605 55004-2**
1. VPO, M. Sargent (EMI) ① [2] **CES5 68541-2**
1. BPO, H. von Karajan (DG) ① [2] **447 364-2GDB2**
1. ASMF, N. Marriner (r1974) (PHIL) ① **446 196-2PM**
1. Hanover Band, R. Goodman (r1994) (RCA) ① **09026 68139-2**
1. COE, J. Judd (8/85) (IMP) ① **PCD805**
1. Philh, C.M. Giulini (12/87) (EMI) ① **CDM7 69042-2**
1. LSO, C. Abbado (5/88) (DG) ① **419 869-2GGA**
1. ASMF, N. Marriner (2/89) (EMI) ① **CDC7 49155-2**
1. Philh, H. von Karajan (11/89) (EMI) ① **CDM7 63113-2**
1. NYPSO, A. Toscanini (r1929) (3/90) (PEAR) ① [3] **GEMMCDS9373**
1. BPO, H. von Karajan (5/90) (DG) ① **429 164-2GR**
1. Chicago SO, F. Reiner (9/90) (RCA) ① **GD60387**
1. Plovdiv PO, R. Raychev (10/90) (LASE) ① **15 506** (10/90) (LASE) ▭ **79 506**
1. LCP, R. Norrington (4/91) (EMI) ① **CDC7 54091-2**
1. COE, C. Abbado (5/91) (DG) ① **431 653-2GH** (5/91) (DG) ▭ **431 653-4GH**

1. SO, T. Beecham (r1916) (11/91) (SYMP) ① [2] **SYMCD1096/7**
1. BPO, W. Furtwängler (r1935) (4/92) (KOCH) ① [2] **37059-2**
1. ASMF, N. Marriner (r1974) (10/92) (PHIL) ① [3] **434 016-2PM3**
1. NBC SO, A. Toscanini (r1945) (11/92) (RCA) ① **GD60289**
1. NYPSO, A. Toscanini (r1929) (11/92) (RCA) ① **GD60318**
1. I. Seefried, M. Forrester, E. Haefliger, D. Fischer-Dieskau, Berlin St Hedwig's Cath Ch, BPO, F. Fricsay, H. Krebs, T. Varga, Berlin RIAS Chbr Ch, Berlin RIAS Orch, H. Geusser, W. Fugmann, M. Weber, G. Herzog, Berlin RSO, VPO, E. Grümmer, G. Pitzinger, H. Hotter, Y. Menuhin (r1954) (11/94) (DG) ① [11] **445 400-2GDO10**
1. Berlin RIAS Orch, F. Fricsay (r1954) (11/94) (DG) ① **445 406-2GDO**
1. Atlanta SO, Y. Levi (r1993) (11/94) (TELA) ① **CD80334**
1. National PO, R. Chailly (r1984) (9/95) (DECC) ① [2] **443 850-2DF2**
1, 18. Rome Op Orch, T. Serafin (r1960s) (BELA) ① **450 106-2** (BELA) ▭ **450 106-4**
1, 2b, 4, 5, 6b, 7a, 8-10, 14, 17, 18, 19a, 20, 21. R. Giménez, A. Corbelli, J. Larmore, H. Hagegård, S. Ramey, B. Frittoli, Geneva Grand Th Chor, Lausanne CO, J. López-Cobos (r1992) (TELD) ① **4509-93693-2**
1, 2b, 4, 6b, 7a, 8, 9, 15, 19a, 21. M. Callas, L. Alva, T. Gobbi, F. Ollendorff, N. Zaccaria, G. Carturan, chor, Philh, A. Galliera (r1957) (EMI) ① **CDM7 63076-2**
1, 2b, 4, 7a, 8, 10, 13-15, 19a, 21. L. Alva, E. Dara, T. Berganza, H. Prey, P. Montarsolo, S. Malagù, Ambrosian Op Chor, LSO, C. Abbado (r1971) (DG) ① **423 584-2GH**
1, 2b, 4, 7a, 8-10, 12, 14, 16, 19a, 21. R. Merrill, R. Peters, C. Valletti, G. Tozzi, F. Corena, M. Roggero, NY Met Op Chor, NY Met Op Orch, E. Leinsdorf (RCA) ① **GD60188** (RCA) ▭ **GK60188**
1, 2b, 4, 7a, 8-10, 13-15, 17, 18, 19a, 21. K. Battle, P. Domingo, F. Lopardo, L. Gallo, R. Raimondi, COE, C. Abbado (r1992) (DG) ① **437 841-2GH**
1, 4, 7a, 7, 8-10, 12b, 13, 14, 17, 18, 19a, 20, 21. M. Horne, R. Pierotti, P. Barbacini, L. Nucci, E. Dara, S. Ramey, S. Sammaritano, La Scala Chor, La Scala Orch, R. Chailly (r1982) (SONY) ① **SMK53501**
1, 7a M. Callas, Paris Op Orch, G. Sébastian (pp1958) (11/91) (EMI) ◖ **LDB9 91258-1** (11/91) (EMI) ▣ **MVC9 91258-3**
2b M. Wittrisch, Berlin St Op Orch, C. Schmalstich (Ger: r1931) (PREI) ① **89024**
2b H. Buff-Giessen, anon (r1906: Ger) (SYMP) ① **SYMCD1085**
2b C. Valletti, Orch, A. Basile (pp1955) (MEMO) ① [2] **HR4191/2**
2b G. di Stefano, Mexico Palacio Chor, Mexico Palacio Orch, R. Cellini (pp1949) (MEMO) ① **HR4372/3**
2b Combattimento (MERI) ① **CDE84196** (MERI) ▭ **KE77196**
2b T. Beltrán, RPO, R. Stapleton (r1994) (SILV) ① **SILKD6005** (SILV) ▭ **SILKC6005**
2b T. Schipa, orch, Rosario Bourdon (r1926) (12/89) (RCA) ① **GD87969**
2b D. Borgioli, orch (r1927) (12/90) (CLUB) ① **CL99-014**
2b Ferruccio Tagliavini, EIAR Orch, U. Tansini (r1942) (3/94) (CENT) ① **CRC2164**
2b C. Valletti, NY Met Op Orch, E. Leinsdorf (r1958) (4/94) (RCA) ① [6] **09026 61580-2(6)**
2b E. Clément, anon (r1905: Fr) (8/95) (ROMO) ① **82002-2**
2b, 5. D. Borgioli, orch (r c1921) (PEAR) ① **GEMMCD9091**
2b, 5. R. Giménez, D. Goodall, Scottish CO, M. Veltri (8/88) (NIMB) ① **NI5106** (NIMB) ▭ **NC5106**
2b, 5. T. Schipa, orch (r1926) (2/89) (PEAR) ① **GEMMCD9322**
2b, 5. H. Nash, orch (Eng: r1929) (8/89) (PEAR) ① **GEMMCD9319**
2b, 5. F. de Lucia, anon (r1908) (7/92) (PEAR) ① [3] **GEMMCDS9923(2)**
2b, 5. R. Vargas, ECO, M. Viotti (11/92) (CLAV) ① **CD50-9202**
2b, 5. F. de Lucia, anon (r1908) (1/95) (SYMP) ① **SYMCD1149**

7a, 7b C. Bartoli, Bologna Teatro Comunale Orch, G. Patanè (r1989)
(DECC) Ⓓ **440 947-2DH**
(DECC) ⊟ **440 947-4DH**
7a, 7b M. Mesplé, Paris Op Orch, G-F. Masini (r1974) (EMI) Ⓓ [2] **CZS7 67813-2**
7a, 7b M. Callas, Philh, A. Galliera (r1957)
(EMI) Ⓓ **CDC5 55095-2**
7a, 7b E. Gruberová, Munich RO, G. Kuhn (r c1980) (EMIN) Ⓓ **CD-EMX2234**
7a, 7b A. Galli-Curci, orch, J. Pasternack (r1917)
(RCA) Ⓓ **74321 24284-2**
(RCA) ⊟ **74321 24284-4**
7a, 7b V. de los Angeles, RPO, V. Gui (r1962)
(EMI) Ⓓ **CDM5 65579-2**
7a, 7b M. Callas, Philh, T. Serafin (r1954)
(11/86) (EMI) Ⓓ **CDC7 47282-2**
7a, 7b M. Callas, Philh, A. Galliera
(2/90) (EMIN) Ⓓ **CD-EMX2123**
(2/88) (EMIN) ⊟ **TC-EMX2123**
7a, 7b M. Callas, Philh, T. Serafin (r1954)
(2/90) (EMI) Ⓓ [4] **CMS7 63244-2**
7a, 7b A. Galli-Curci, orch, J. Pasternack (r1917)
(5/90) (NIMB) Ⓓ **NI7806**
(NIMB) ⊟ **NC7806**
7a, 7b L. Pons, orch, A. Kostelanetz (r1947)
(7/90) (CBS) Ⓓ **CD45694**
7a, 7b C. Supervia, orch, A. Albergoni (r1927)
(9/90) (PREI) Ⓓ **89023**
7a, 7b D. Jones, CLS, R. Hickox
(2/91) (CHAN) Ⓓ **CHAN8865**
(2/91) (CHAN) ⊟ **ABTD1480**
7a, 7b E. Berger, Berlin St Op Orch, F. Zweig (r1932; Ger) (12/91) (PREI) Ⓓ **89035**
7a, 7b C. Supervia, orch, A. Albergoni (r1927)
(3/93) (NIMB) Ⓓ [2] **NI7836/7**
7a, 7b L. Lipkowska, orch (r1912: Russ)
(6/93) (PEAR) Ⓓ [3] **GEMMCDS9004/6(1)**
7a, 7b P. McCann, Black Dyke Mills Band, P. Parkes (arr Parkes)
(7/93) (CHAN) Ⓓ **CHAN4505**
(CHAN) ⊟ **BBTD4505**
7a, 7b C. Bartoli, Bologna Teatro Comunale Orch, G. Patanè (r1988)
(10/93) (DECC) Ⓓ **436 462-2DM**
7a, 7b M. Ivogün, orch (r1925)
(1/94) (CLUB) Ⓓ **CL99-020**
7a, 7b F. Hempel, orch (r1910: Ger)
(3/94) (NIMB) Ⓓ **NI7849**
7a, 7b E. De Hidalgo, orch (r1908)
(4/94) (EMI) Ⓓ [3] **CHS7 64864-2(1)**
7a, 7b S. Jo, Monte Carlo PO, P. Olmi (r1994)
(6/95) (ERAT) Ⓓ **4509-97239-2**
7a, 7b, 14. L. Serra, R. Blake, Turin Teatro Regio Orch, B. Campanella (NUOV) Ⓓ **6820**
7b I. Abendroth, anon (r1902: Ger)
(SYMP) Ⓓ **SYMCD1085**
7b M. Ivogün, orch (r1916: Ger)
(PREI) Ⓓ **89094**
8. M. Journet, orch, Rosario Bourdon (r1925)
(PREI) Ⓓ **89021**
8. F. Chaliapin, La Scala Orch, C. Sabajno (r1912) (PREI) Ⓓ **89030**
8. S. Ramey, Munich RO, J. Delacôte
(EMI) Ⓓ [2] **CZS7 67440-2**
8. R. Raimondi, Madrid SO, G.P. Sanzogno (pp1991) (IMP) Ⓓ [2] **DPCD998**
8. R. Raimondi, Madrid SO, G.P. Sanzogno
(RNE) Ⓓ [2] **650004**
8. F. Chaliapin, orch, E. Goossens (r1926)
(CONI) Ⓓ **CDHD226**
(CONI) ⊟ **MCHD226**
8. F. Chaliapin, orch, E. Goossens (r1926)
(PEAR) Ⓓ **GEMMCD9122**
8. R. Raimondi, LSO, James Levine
(10/88) (EMI) Ⓓ **CDM7 69549-2**
8. F. Chaliapin, orch, E. Goossens (r1926)
(12/89) (PEAR) Ⓓ **GEMMCD9314**
8. E. Pinza, NY Met Op Orch, F. Cleva (r1946)
(4/90) (CBS) Ⓓ **CD45693**
8. T. Pasero, orch, L. Molajoli (r1927)
(6/90) (PREI) Ⓓ **89010**
8. A. Kipnis, Berlin St Op Orch, E. Orthmann (Ger: r1931) (12/90) (PREI) Ⓓ **89019**
8. N. de Angelis, orch, L. Molajoli (r1927)
(7/92) (PREI) Ⓓ **89042**
8. M. Salminen, Lahti SO, E. Klas
(8/92) (BIS) Ⓓ **BIS-CD520**
8. V. Bettoni, La Scala Orch, L. Molajoli (r1929)
(11/92) (MEMO) Ⓓ [2] **HR4408/9(2)**
8. A. Didur, orch (r1908)
(12/92) (TEST) Ⓓ **SBT1008**
8. O. Natzke, orch, H. Geehl (r1938)
(12/92) (ODE) Ⓓ **CDODE1365**
8. L. Sibiriakov, anon (r1906: Russ)
(6/93) (PEAR) Ⓓ [3] **GEMMCDS9001/3(2)**
8. J. Van Dam, Loire PO, M. Soustrot (r1992)
(8/93) (FORL) Ⓓ **UCD16681**
8. E. Pinza, RCA Victor Orch, E. Leinsdorf (r1951) (9/93) (RCA) Ⓓ **09026 61245-2**
8. F. Navarini, anon (r1907)
(4/94) (EMI) Ⓓ [3] **CHS7 64860-2(1)**
8. K. Borg, Munich PO, A. Rother (r1955)
(12/94) (FINL) Ⓓ [3] **4509-95606-2**
8. M. Reizen, Bolshoi Th Orch, S. Samosud (r1951) (2/95) (PREI) Ⓓ **89080**
8. T. Pasero, Rome Teatro Reale Orch, L. Ricci (r1943) (4/95) (PREI) Ⓓ **89074**
9. M. Callas, T. Gobbi, Philh, A. Galliera
(CFP) Ⓓ **CD-CFP9013**
(CFP) ⊟ **TC-CFP4498**
9. M. Callas, T. Gobbi, Philh, A. Galliera (r1957)
(CFP) Ⓓ **CD-CFP4602**
(CFP) ⊟ **TC-CFP4602**
9. M. Callas, T. Gobbi, Philh, A. Galliera (r1957)
(EMI) Ⓓ **CDC5 55216-2**
(EMI) ⊟ **EL555216-4**
9. L. Pons, G. De Luca, orch (r1940)
(PEAR) Ⓓ [3] **GEMMCDS9160(2)**
9. M. Barrientos, R. Stracciari, orch (r1919)
(PEAR) Ⓓ **GEMMCD9178**
9. L. Pons, G. De Luca, orch, W. Pelletier (r1940) (4/92) (MSOU) Ⓓ **DFCDI-111**
9. M. Barrientos, R. Stracciari, orch (r1919)
(12/92) (TEST) Ⓓ **SBT1008**
14. L. Pons, G. De Luca, Orch, W. Pelletier (r1940) (MSCM) Ⓓ **MM30446**
14. C. Supervia, G. Manuritta, orch, A. Albergoni (r1928) (9/90) (PREI) Ⓓ **89023**
14. C. Supervia, G. Manuritta, orch, A. Albergoni (r1928) (3/93) (NIMB) Ⓓ [2] **NI7836/7**
18. Budapest PO, A. Kórodi (LASE) Ⓓ **15 504**
(LASE) ⊟ **79 504**
18. Helsinki PO, S. Comissiona
(PRO) Ⓓ **CDS580**
19a F. de Lucia, J. Huguet, A. Pini-Corsi, anon (r1906) (BONG) Ⓓ [2] **GB1064/5-2**
19a G. Huguet, F. de Lucia, A. Pini-Corsi, anon (r1906) (12/92) (TEST) Ⓓ **SBT1008**
19a J. Huguet, F. de Lucia, A. Pini-Corsi, anon (r1906) (7/93) (NIMB) Ⓓ [2] **NI7840/1**
19a V. de los Angeles, L. Alva, S. Bruscantini, RPO, V. Gui (r1962)
(6/94) (EMI) Ⓓ **CDH5 65072-2**
19a F. de Lucia, A. Pini-Corsi, M. Galvany, anon (r1906) (1/95) (SYMP) Ⓓ **SYMCD1149**
20. R. Blake, Ambrosian Sngrs, LSO, J. McCarthy (4/88) (ARAB) Ⓓ **Z6582**
(4/88) (ARAB) ⊟ **ABQC6582**

Bianca e Falliero (or Il consiglio dei tre)– melodramma: 2 acts (1819—Rome) (Lib. F. Romani, after A. van Arnhault)

Bianca	K. Ricciarelli
Falliero	M. Horne
Contareno	C. Merritt
Capellio	G. Surian
Costanza	P. Orciani
Priuli	A. Riva
Pisani	E. Gavazzi
Officer; Usher	D. D'Auria

Prague Phil Chor, London Sinf Op Orch, D. Renzetti (pp1986)
(9/94) (FONI) Ⓓ [3] **RFCD2008**
Cielo il mio labbro ispira M. Fortuna, M. Horne, C. Merritt, H. Runey, NY Concert Chorale, St Luke's Orch, R. Norrington (pp1992)
(6/93) (EMI) ◖ **LDB491007-1**
(6/93) (EMI) ▣ **MVD491007-3**
Della rosa il bel vermiglio K. Ricciarelli, Lyon Op Chor, Lyon Op Orch, G. Ferro (r1989)
(11/94) (VIRG) Ⓓ **CUV5 61139-2**
Overture ASMF, N. Marriner (r1979)
(10/92) (PHIL) Ⓓ [3] **434 016-2PM3**
Tu non sai qual colpo atroce D. Jones, CLS, R. Hickox (2/91) (CHAN) Ⓓ **CHAN8865**
(2/91) (CHAN) ⊟ **ABTD1480**

La cambiale di matrimonio– farsa comica: 1 act (1810—Venice) (Lib. G. Rossi)

EXCERPTS: 1. Overture; 2. Non c'è il vecchio sussurrone; 3. Chi mai trova il dritto, il fondo; 4. Ecco un lettera per voi, signore; 5a. Ma, signore, questa lettera; 5b. Isacchetto!; 5c. Signor et caetera et caetera; 5d. Povera Miss Fanny!; 6. Tornami a dir che m'ami; 7a. Sì cara mia, speriam; 7b. Avete voi veduto; 8. Presto, presto; 9. Grazie ... grazie ... 10. Sicchè, dunque, istruitemi; 11a. Servo! proprio in Europa; 11b. Volea dirlo ... sicchè dunque saprete; 12. Darei per si'bel fondo; 13. Quell'amabile visino; 14a. Non si farà; 14b. Anch'io son giovine; 15. Eccolo appunto; 16. Ipotecato! - Diavolo! - Madama; 17. Dite presto, dove sta questa gran difficoltà; 18. Venite, sono andati; 19a. Bravi! Bravi!; 19b. Ragazzi miei; 20a. Come tacer; 20b. Vorrei spiegarvi; 21. Eppur lo cred'anch'io che il far del bene; 22a. Metti là tutto, e parti; 22b. Porterò così il cappello; 23. Qual'ira, oh ciel; 24. Vi prego un momento, signore.

1. Plovdiv PO, R. Raychev
(HARM) ⊟ **HMC40 466**
1. Haydn Philh, E. Rojatti (NUOV) Ⓓ **6726**
1. Plovdiv PO, R. Raychev
(HARM) Ⓓ **HMP390 466**
1. RPO, T. Beecham (r1958/9)
(EMI) Ⓓ [2] **CES5 68541-2**
1. ASMF, N. Marriner
(2/89) (EMI) Ⓓ **CDC7 49155-2**
1. Plovdiv PO, R. Raychev
(10/90) (LASE) Ⓓ **15 520**
(10/90) (LASE) ⊟ **79 520**
1. ASMF, N. Marriner (r1974)
(10/92) (PHIL) Ⓓ [3] **434 016-2PM3**
1. National PO, R. Chailly (r1984)
(9/95) (DECC) Ⓓ [2] **443 850-2DF2**
20b J. Sutherland, Sydney Eliz Orch, R. Bonynge (MCEG) ▣ **VVD780**

La Cenerentola, or La bontà in trionfo, 'Cinderella'– dramma giocoso: 2 acts (1817—Rome) (Lib. G. Ferretti)

EXCERPTS: 1. Overture. ACT 1: 2a. No, no, no; 2b. Una volta c'era un re; 2c. Un tantin di carità; 2d. O figlie amabili; 2e. Cenerentola, vien qua; 3. Miei rampolli femminini; 4a. Tutto è deserto; 4b. Un soave non so che; 5a. Non so che dir; 5b. Scegli la sposa, affrettati; 5c. Come un'ape ne' giorni d'aprile; 6. Signor, una parola; 7. Là del ciel nell'arcano profondo; 8. Zitto, zitto, piano, piano; 8a. Conciossiacosacche; 8b. Noi Don Magnifico; 8c. Zitto, zitto, piano, piano; 8d. Signor...Altezza, è in tavolo. ACT 2: 9a. Mi par che quei birbanti; 9b. Sia qualunque delle figlie; 10a. Ah! questa bella incognita; 10b. E allor... 10c. Sì, ritrovarla io giuro; 11a. Ma dunque io son un ex; 11b. Un segreto d'importanza; 12a. Ma ve l'avevo detto; 12b. Temporale; 13a. Son qui; 13b. Siete voi?; 14a. Della Fortuna; 14b. Nacqui all'affanno, al pianto; 14c. Non più mesta accanto al fuoco.

Angelina	K. Kuhlmann
Don Ramiro	L. Dale
Dandini	A. Rinaldi
Don Magnifico	C. Desderi
Clorinda	M. Taddei
Tisbe	L. Zannini
Alidoro	R. Kennedy

Glyndebourne Fest Chor, LPO, D. Renzetti, J. Cox (r1983)
(CAST) ▣ **CVI2053**

Angelina	A. Murray
Don Ramiro	F. Araiza
Dandini	G. Quilico
Don Magnifico	W. Berry
Clorinda	A. Denning
Tisbe	D. Evangelatos
Alidoro	W. Schöne

Vienna St Op Chor, VPO, R. Chailly, M. Hampe
(7/90) (MCEG) ▣ **VVD665**

Angelina	F. von Stade
Don Ramiro	F. Araiza
Dandini	C. Desderi
Don Magnifico	P. Montarsolo
Clorinda	M. Guglielmi
Tisbe	L. Zannini
Alidoro	P. Plishka

La Scala Chor, La Scala Orch, C. Abbado, J-P. Ponnelle
(DG) ▣ **072 402-3GH**

Angelina	T. Berganza
Don Ramiro	L. Alva
Dandini	R. Capecchi
Don Magnifico	P. Montarsolo
Clorinda	M. Guglielmi
Tisbe	L. Zannini
Alidoro	U. Trama

Scottish Op Chor, LSO, C. Abbado (r1971)
(DG) Ⓓ [2] **423 861-2GH2**

Angelina	A. Baltsa
Don Ramiro	F. Araiza
Dandini	S. Alaimo
Don Magnifico	R. Raimondi
Clorinda	C. Malone
Tisbe	F. Palmer
Alidoro	J. del Carlo

Ambrosian Op Chor, ASMF, N. Marriner (r1987)
(11/88) (PHIL) Ⓓ [3] **420 468-2PH3**

Angelina	L.V. Terrani

Don Ramiro F. Araiza
Dandini D. Trimarchi
Don Magnifico E. Dara
Clorinda E. Ravaglia
Tisbe M. Schmiege
Alidoro A. Corbelli
W German Rad Chor, Cappella Coloniensis, G. Ferro
(6/91) (SONY) ① [2] **S2K46433**
Angelina M. de Gabarain
Don Ramiro J. Oncina
Dandini S. Bruscantini
Don Magnifico I. Wallace
Clorinda A. Noni
Tisbe F. Cadoni
Alidoro H. Alan
Glyndebourne Fest Chor, Glyndebourne Fest Orch, V. Gui, B. Balkwill (r1953/4)
(5/92) (EMI) ① [2] **CMS7 64183-2**
Angelina A. Murray
Don Ramiro F. Araiza
Dandini G. Quilico
Don Magnifico W. Berry
Clorinda A. Denning
Tisbe D. Evangelatos
Alidoro W. Schöne
Vienna St Op Chor, VPO, R. Chailly, M. Hampe, C. Viller (pp1988)
(3/93) (PION) ⏾ [2] **PLMCD00151**
Angelina C. Bartoli
Don Ramiro W. Matteuzzi
Dandini A. Corbelli
Don Magnifico E. Dara
Clorinda F. Costa
Tisbe G. Banditelli
Alidoro M. Pertusi
Bologna Teatro Comunale Chor, Bologna Teatro Comunale Orch, R. Chailly (r1992)
(11/93) (DECC) ① [2] **436 902-2DHO2**
Angelina J. Larmore
Ramiro R. Giménez
Dandini G. Quilico
Don Magnifico A. Corbelli
Clorinda A. Scarabelli
Tisbe L. Polverelli
Alidoro A. Miles
ROH Chor, ROHO, C. Rizzi (r1994)
(4/95) (TELD) ① [2] **4509-94553-2**
1. Plovdiv PO, R. Raychev
(HARM) ▭ **HMC40 466**
1. Zagreb PO, M. Halász (NAXO) ① **8 550236**
1. Scottish CO, J.Laredo (NIMB) ① **NI5078**
1. Philh, C.M. Giulini
(EMI) ① [2] **CZS7 67440-2**
1. Plovdiv PO, R. Raychev
(HARM) ① **HMP390 466**
1. Lamoureux Concerts Orch, R. Benzi (r1964)
(BELA) ① **461 001-2**
(BELA) ▭ **461 001-4**
1. Minneapolis SO, A. Dorati (r1957)
(MERC) ① **434 345-2MM**
1. ROHO, C. Rizzi (r1990)
(CONI) ① **75605 55004-2**
1. Philh, T. Serafin (r1961)
(EMI) ① [2] **CES5 68541-2**
1. ASMF, N. Marriner (r1976)
(PHIL) ① **446 196-2PM**
1. Philh, C.M. Giulini
(12/87) (EMI) ① **CDM7 69042-2**
1. LSO, C. Abbado
(5/88) (DG) ① **419 869-2GGA**
1. ASMF, N. Marriner
(2/89) (EMI) ① **CDC7 49155-2**
1. Chicago SO, F. Reiner
(9/90) (RCA) ① **GD60387**
1. Plovdiv PO, R. Raychev
(10/90) (LASE) ① **15 520**
(10/90) (LASE) ▭ **79 520**
1. COE, C. Abbado
(5/91) (DG) ① **431 653-2GH**
(5/91) (DG) ▭ **431 653-4GH**
1. ASMF, N. Marriner (r1976)
(10/92) (PHIL) ① [3] **434 016-2PM3**
1. NBC SO, A. Toscanini (r1945)
(11/92) (RCA) ① **GD60289**
1. Black Dyke Mills Band, P. Parkes (arr Parkes)
(7/93) (CHAN) ① **CHAN4505**
(CHAN) ▭ **BBTD4505**
1, 2d, 2e, 3, 5b, 8c, 9a, 9b, 10b, 12a, 13a, 14b, 14c L. V. Terrani, E. Ravaglia, M. Schmiege, F. Araiza, D. Trimarchi, E. Dara, A. Corbelli, W German Rad Chor, Cappella Coloniensis, G. Ferro (r1988) (SONY) ① **SMK53502**
2b, 2c, 4a, 4b, 5b, 5c, 8d, 9b, 10, 14a, 14c C. Bartoli, W. Matteuzzi, A. Corbelli, E. Dara, F. Costa, G. Banditelli, M. Pertusi, Bologna Teatro Comunale Chor, Bologna Teatro Comunale Orch, R. Chailly (r1992)
(DECC) ① **444 183-2DH**
3. G. Taddei, Vienna St Op Orch, R. Abbado (pp1981) (ACAN) ① **49 402**
3. A. Rossi, orch (r1905)
(12/92) (TEST) ① **SBT1008**
4b, 8c K. Kuhlmann, L. Dale, Glyndebourne Fest Chor, LPO, D. Renzetti (CAST) ▣ **CVI2071**
5c, 7. S. Ramey, WNO Chor, WNO Orch, G. Ferro (TELD) ① **9031-73242-2**
6. J. Oncina, M. de Gabarain, I. Wallace, S. Bruscantini, Glyndebourne Fest Orch, V. Gui (r1953) (6/94) (EMI) ① **CDH5 65072-2**
9a, 9b K. Kuhlmann, L. Dale, M. Taddei, L. Zannini, C. Desderi, R. Kennedy, A. Rinaldi, A. Howells, D. Renzetti (TELD) ⏾ **9031-77676-6**
(TELD) ▣ **9031-77676-3**
10b(pt), 10c R. Giménez, Scottish Phil Sngrs, Scottish CO, M. Veltri (8/88) (NIMB) ① **NI5106**
(NIMB) ▭ **NC5106**
14a-c F. von Stade, J. Opalach, C. Estep, M. Fortuna, M. Lerner, H. Runey, NY Concert Chorale, St Luke's Orch, R. Norrington (pp1992)
(12/94) (EMI) ① **CDC7 54643-2**
14b G. Simionato, Milan RAI SO, N. Sanzogno (pp1956) (MEMO) ① [2] **HR4386/7**
14b C. Supervia, orch, A. Albergoni (r1927)
(7/92) (PEAR) ① [3] **GEMMCDS9926(2)**
14b M. Fortuna, M. Lerner, F. von Stade, C. Estep, J. Opalach, H. Runey, NY Concert Chorale, St Luke's Orch, R. Norrington (pp1992)
(6/93) (EMI) ⏾ **LDB491007-1**
(6/93) (EMI) ▣ **MVD491007-3**
14b, c C. Bartoli, Bologna Teatro Comunale Chor, Bologna Teatro Comunale Orch, R. Chailly (r1992) (DECC) ① **448 300-2DH**
(DECC) ▭ **448 300-4DH**
14b, 14c M. Callas, Philh, A. Tonini (r1961/2)
(EMI) ① **CDC7 49428-2**
14b, 14c M. Callas, Paris Cons, N. Rescigno
(EMI) ① **CDC7 49005-2**
14b, 14c M. Callas, FRNO, G. Prêtre (pp1963)
(MEMO) ① **HR4293/4**
14b, 14c C. Bartoli, A. Schoenberg Ch, Vienna Volksoper Orch, G. Patanè
(DECC) ① **436 133-2DWO**
14b, 14c M. Callas, Paris Cons, N. Rescigno
(EMI) ① [2] **CZS7 67440-2**
14b, 14c L. Garrett, Philh, I. Bolton
(SILV) ① **SONGCD907**
(SILV) ▭ **SONGC907**
14b, 14c M. Horne, ROHO, H. Lewis
(DECC) ① **421 891-2DA**
14b, 14c F. von Stade, Rotterdam PO, E. de Waart (PHIL) ① **420 084-2PH**
14b, 14c G. Simionato, Santa Cecilia Academy Orch, F. Ghione (r1954)
(DECC) ① **440 406-2DM**
14b, 14c C. Bartoli, Vienna Volksoper Orch, G. Patanè (9/89) (DECC) ① **425 430-2DH**
(9/89) (DECC) ▭ **425 430-4DH**
14b, 14c V. de los Angeles, Rome Op Orch, G. Morelli (r1954) (8/90) (EMI) ① **CDH7 63495-2**
14b, 14c C. Supervia, orch, A. Albergoni (r1927)
(9/90) (PREI) ① **89023**
14b, 14c D. Jones, C. Smith, K. Steffan, H. Nicholl, G. Finley, S. Birchall, Richard Hickox Sngrs, CLS, R. Hickox
(2/91) (CHAN) ① **CHAN8865**
(2/91) (CHAN) ▭ **ABTD1480**
14b, 14c C. Supervia, orch, A. Albergoni (r1927)
(12/92) (TEST) ① **SBT1008**
14b, 14c C. Supervia, orch, A. Albergoni (r1927)
(3/93) (NIMB) ① [2] **NI7836/7**
14b, 14c M. Horne, ROHO, H. Lewis (r1964)
(10/93) (DECC) ① **436 462-2DM**

Le **Comte Ory– opéra/opéra comique: 2 acts (1828—Paris) (Lib. E. Scribe & C.G. Delestre-Poirson)**

EXCERPTS: 1. Overture. ACT 1: 2. Jouvencelles, venez vite; 3. Que les destins prospères; 4. Moi, je réclame; 5. De grâce, encore un mot; 6. Je ne puis plus longtemps; 7. Veiller sans cesse; 8. Vous, notre appui; 9. Cette aventure fort singulière; 10. Cet ermite, ma belle enfant; 11. Une dame de haut parage; 12. Isolier dans ces lieux; 13. En proie à la tristesse; 14. Vous avez entendu sa touchante prière; 15a. Ô bon ermite; 15b. C'est bien, je suis content; 16. Ciel! - Ô terreur, ô peine extrême; 17. Cet écrit, noble châtelaine; 18. Venez amis, retirons-nous. ACT 2: 19a. Dans ce séjour calme et tranquille; 19b. Noble châtelaine; 19c. Quand tomberont sur lui; 20. Ah! quel respect, Madame; 21. Ce téméraire; 22. Voici vos compagnes fidèles; 23. Ah! la bonne folie!; 24. Eh! mais, quelle triste observance; 25. Dans ce lieu solitaire; 26. Buvons, buvons; 27. Elle revient ... silence!; 28. A la faveur de cette nuit obscure; 29. J'entends d'ici le bruit des armes; 30. Ecoutez ces chants de victoire.

Comte Ory J. Aler
Adèle S. Jo
Gouverneur G. Cachemaille
Isolier D. Montague
Raimbaud G. Quilico
Ragonde R. Pierotti
Alice M. Castets
Nobleman I F. Dudziak
Nobleman II N. Rivenq
Lyon Op Chor, Lyon Op Orch, J.E. Gardiner
(10/89) (PHIL) ① [2] **422 406-2PH2**
Comte Ory J. Oncina
Adèle S. Barabas
Gouverneur I. Wallace
Isolier C. Canne-Meijer
Raimbaud M. Roux
Ragonde M. Sinclair
Alice J. Sinclair
Nobleman D. Troy
Glyndebourne Fest Chor, Glyndebourne Fest Orch, V. Gui (r1956)
(5/92) (EMI) ① [2] **CMS7 64180-2**
3. R. Blake, LSO, J. McCarthy
(4/88) (ARAB) ① **Z6582**
(4/88) (ARAB) ▭ **ABQC6582**
13, 20. R. Doria, M. Sénéchal, A. Migliette, chor, orch, P. Stoll (pp) (SYMP) ① **SYMCD1103**
15a C. Canne-Meijer, J. Oncina, S. Barabas, Glyndebourne Fest Chor, Glyndebourne Fest Orch, V. Gui (r1956)
(6/94) (EMI) ① **CDH5 65072-2**

Demetrio e Polibio– dramma serio: 2 acts (1812—Rome) (Lib. V. Viganò-Mombelli)

EXCERPTS: 1. Overture.
1. ASMF, N. Marriner (r1979)
(10/92) (PHIL) ① [3] **434 016-2PM3**

La **Donna del lago, '(The) Lady of the Lake'– melodramma: 2 acts (1819—Naples) (Lib. A.L. Tottola, after Sir Walter Scott)**

EXCERPTS: 1. Overture. ACT 1: 2. O, mattutini albori; 3. Qual suon!; 4. Uberto! Ah! Dove t'ascondi?; 5. Sei già nel tetto mio; 6. D'Inibaca Donzella; 7. Sei già sposa?; 8. Quali accenti!... 9. Ma son sorpreso... 10. Mura felici; 11. Elena! o tu, che chiamo!; 12. O quante lacrime; 13. Figlia! È così; 14. Taci, lo voglio; 15. E nel fatal conflitto; 16. Vivere io non potrò; 17. Qual rapido torrente; 18. Eccomi a voi; 19. Ma dov'è colei; 20. Se a'miei voti; 21. Alfin mi è dato; 22. Vieni, o stella; 23. Quanto a quest'alma; 24. La mia spada; 25. Quest'amplesso; 26. Crudele sospetto... 27. Sul colle a Morve; 28. Già un raggio; 29. Su...amici!. ACT 2: 30. O fiamma soave; 31. Va, non temer; 32. Alla ragion deh rieda; 33. Numi, se a'miei sospiri... 34. Vincesti!...Addio!... 35. Qual pena in me; 36. Parla...che sei?; 37. Io son la misera; 38. Quante sciagure; 39. Ah! Si pera; 40. Douglas! Douglas! Ti salva!; 41. Che sento!; 42. Attendi: Il Re fra poco; 43. Che sento! Qual soave armonia!; 44. Stelle! Sembra egli stesso!; 45. Eccolo! Amica sorte; 46. Impogna il Re: 47. Ah! Che vedo!; 48. Tanti affetti; 49. Fra il padre.

Elena K. Ricciarelli
Malcolm L.V. Terrani
Uberto/Giacomo D. Gonzalez
Rodrigo di Dhu D. Raffanti
Douglas d'Angus S. Ramey
Albina C. Valdenassi
Serano O. di Credico
Bertram A. d'Uva
Prague Philharmonic Ch, COE, M. Pollini (r1983)
(8/88) (SONY) ① [3] **S2K39311**
2, 48. M. Caballé, Turin RAI Orch, P. Bellugi (pp1970) (MEMO) ① [2] **HR4279/80**
10. M. Horne, Sydney Eliz Orch, R. Bonynge
(MCEG) ▣ **VVD780**
10. M. Horne, NYC Op Orch, R. Bonynge (r1981: pp) (DECC) ① **436 472-2DM**
10. M. Horne, NYC Op Orch, R. Bonynge (pp1981) (DECC) ① **440 415-2DM**
10. M. Horne, St Luke's Orch, R. Norrington (pp1992) (6/93) (EMI) ⏾ **LDB491007-1**
(6/93) (EMI) ▣ **MVD491007-3**

10. M. Horne, St Luke's Orch, R. Norrington (pp1992) (12/94) (EMI) Ⓓ **CDC7 54643-2**
10, 11. C. Bartoli, Vienna Volksoper Orch, G. Patanè (9/89) (DECC) Ⓓ **425 430-2DH**
(9/89) (DECC) ▭ **425 430-4DH**
10-12. D. Jones, CLS, R. Hickox
(2/91) (CHAN) Ⓓ **CHAN8865**
(2/91) (CHAN) ▭ **ABTD1480**
10, 48. M. Horne, Ambrosian Op Chor, RPO, H. Lewis (DECC) Ⓓ **421 306-2DA**
18. R. Vargas, ECO, M. Viotti
(11/92) (CLAV) Ⓓ **CD50-9202**
30. R. Blake, LSO, J. McCarthy
(4/88) (ARAB) Ⓓ **Z6582**
(4/88) (ARAB) ▭ **ABQC6582**
48. M. Horne, orch (pp)
(MEMO) Ⓓ [2] **HR4392/3**
48. C. Bartoli, Venice La Fenice Chor, Venice La Fenice Orch, I. Martin
(DECC) **OO 436 075-5DH**
48. M. Horne, Ambrosian Op Chor, RPO, H. Lewis (r1972) (DECC) Ⓓ **443 378-2DM**
48. C. Bartoli, Venice La Fenice Chor, Venice La Fenice Orch, I. Martin
(2/92) (DECC) Ⓓ **436 075-2DH**
48. C. Bartoli, G. Fischer (pp1991)
(11/92) (DECC) ● **071 141-1DH**
(11/92) (DECC) ▣ **071 141-3DH**
48. M. Caballé, RCA Italiana Op Chor, RCA Italiana Op Orch, C.F. Cillario
(11/92) (RCA) Ⓓ [2] **GD60941**
48. D. Soffel, Swedish CO, M. Liljefors (pp1988)
(4/93) (CPRI) Ⓓ **CAP21428**

Eduardo e Cristina– dramma: 2 acts (1819—Venice) (Lib. G. Schmidt, after Pavesi)

EXCERPTS: 1. Overture.

1. ASMF, N. Marriner (r1979)
(10/92) (PHIL) Ⓓ [3] **434 016-2PM3**

Elisabetta, Regina d'Inghilterra– dramma: 2 acts (1815—Naples) (Lib. G. Schmidt, after Federici)

EXCERPTS: 1. Overture. ACT 1: 2. Più lieta, più bella; 3. Nel giubilo comun, signore; 4a. Esulta, Elisa, omai; 4b. Qant'è grato all'alma mia; 4c. Questo cor ben lo comprende; 5a. Grandi del regno; 5b. Vieni, o prode; 6. Alta Regina; 7. Incauta, che festi!; 8a. Sconsigliata!; 8b. Sento un'interna voce; 9. Che intesi!; 10b. Perché mai, destin crudele; 10c. Misera! A quale stato; 11. Guglielmo, ascolta; 12a. Che penso; 12b. Se mi serbasti il soglio; 12c. Qual colpo inaspettato; 12d. Duce, il tal guisa. ACT 2: 13a. Dov'è Matilde?; 13b. Pensa che sol per poco; 13c. Non bastan quelle lagrime; 14a. Misero me!...La sposa; 14b. L'avverso mio destino; 14c. Ah! Fra poco, in faccia a morte; 15. Chiede Norfolk a te l'accesso; 16. Qui soffermiamo il piè; 17a. Che intesi!...Oh annunzio!; 17b. Deh! Troncate i ceppi suoi; 18a. Della cieca fortuna; 18b. Sposa amata; 19a. E l'adorata sposa; 19b. Deh! scusa i trasporti; 20a. Tu regina!...deh! come; 20b. Fellon, la pena avrai; 20c. Bell'alme generose; 20d. Leicester!.

Elisabetta	M. Caballé
Leicester	J. Carreras
Matilde	V. Masterson
Enrico	R. Creffield
Norfolk	U. Benelli
Guglielmo	N. Jenkins

Ambrosian Sngrs, LSO, G-F. Masini
(12/92) (PHIL) Ⓓ [2] **432 453-2PM2**
4b K. Ricciarelli, Lyon Op Chor, Lyon Op Orch, G. Ferro (r1989)
(11/94) (VIRG) Ⓓ **CUV5 61139-2**
4b, 20b C. Bartoli, Venice La Fenice Chor, Venice La Fenice Orch, I. Martin
(DECC) **OO 436 075-5DH**
4b, 20b C. Bartoli, Venice La Fenice Chor, Venice La Fenice Orch, I. Martin
(2/92) (DECC) Ⓓ **436 075-2DH**
8b M. Major, NZ SO, P. Gamba
(KIWI) Ⓓ **CDTRL075**
14a M. Caballé, J. Carreras, V. Masterson, LSO, G-F. Masini (PHIL) Ⓓ **434 986-2PM**
17a R. Blake, LSO, J. McCarthy
(4/88) (ARAB) Ⓓ **Z6582**
(4/88) (ARAB) ▭ **ABQC6582**
18a C. Merritt, Munich RSO, J. Fiore (r1993)
(9/94) (PHIL) Ⓓ **434 102-2PH**

Ermione– azione tragica: 2 acts (1819—Naples) (Lib. A.L. Tottola, after Racine)

EXCERPTS: 1. Overture. ACT 1: 1a. Mi guarda, e impallidisce!; 2. Troja! qual fosti un di!; 3. Mia delizia! un solo istante; 4. All'ombra del tuo sposo; 5. Dall'Oriente l'astro del giorno; 6a. A tante cure, o amiche; 6b. Non proseguir; 7. Sul lido di Agamennone; 8. Venga il Greco Orator; 9a. Reggia abborrita; 9b. Che sorda al mesto pianto; 9c. Ah! come nascondere; 9d. Che fai di te; 10. March; 11a. Mi guarda e impallidisce; 11b. Balena in man del figlio; 12a. Deh serena i mesti rai; 12b. Non pavento: quest'alma; 12c. Periglioso e il restar; 13a. E Pirro ancor; 13b. Amarti?; 14. Alfin l'Eroe da forte; 15. Sperar poss'io; 16. A me Astianatte. ACT 2: 17a. Liete novelle; 17b. Ombra del caro sposo; 17c. Vieni a giurar; 18a. Sia compiuto il mio fato; 18b. Essa corre al trionfo; 18c. Di, che vedesti piangere; 19a. Il voglia il Ciel; 19b. Amata, l'amai; 20a. Ma che ascolto?; 20b. Un'empia mel rapi; 21. Il tuo dolor ei affretta; 22a. Ah! qual sovrasta a Pirro; 22b. A cosi triste immagine; 23a. Che feci? dove son?; 23b. Parmi, che ad ogn'istante; 25. Ah! ti rinvenni!.

Ermione	C. Gasdia
Andromaca	M. Zimmermann
Pirro	E. Palacio
Oreste	C. Merritt
Pilade	W. Matteuzzi
Fenicio	S. Alaimo
Attalo	M. Bolognesi
Cleonte; Cefisa	E. Tandura

Prague Phil Chor, Monte Carlo PO, C. Scimone
(ERAT) Ⓓ [2] **2292-45790-2**
1. ASMF, N. Marriner (r1979)
(10/92) (PHIL) Ⓓ [3] **434 016-2PM3**
9a-c R. Blake, P. Jeffes, LSO, M. Valdes
(12/89) (ARAB) Ⓓ **Z6612**
(12/89) (ARAB) ▭ **ABQC6612**
11b C. Merritt, Munich RSO, J. Fiore (r1993)
(9/94) (PHIL) Ⓓ **434 102-2PH**

La **Gazza ladra, '(The) Thieving Magpie'– melodramma: 2 acts (1817—Milan) (Lib. G. Gheradini, after d'Aubigny & Caigniez)**

EXCERPTS: 1. Overture. ACT 1: 2. Oh che giorno fortunato; 3. Marmotte, che fate; 4. Egli viene, o mia Lucia; 5. Là, seduto l'amato Giannetto; 6. Oh cospetto! Undici ore già passate; 7. Di piacer mi balza il cor; 8. Tutto sorridere; 9. Alfin sei giunta; 10. Stringhe e ferri; 11. Oh, senti il vecchio Isacco; 12a. Ma qual suono; 12b. Bravo, bravo! Ben tornato; 13. Vieni fra queste braccia; 14. Bravo, bravo. Ma quel piacer; 15. Tocchiamo, beviamo; 16a. Oh madre, ancor no mi diceste; 16b. Idol mio!; 17. Ieri, sul tramontar del sole; 18. Come frenare il pianto; 19. Per questo amplesso; 20. Io tremo, pavento; 21. Il mio piano è preparato; 22. Sì, sì, Ninetta; 23a. Un altro, un altro; 23b. Questo piego presante; 23c. Ah! Padre udiste?; 24. M'affretto di mandarvi; 25. Respiro ... Mia cara!; 26. Siamo soli: Amor seconda; 27. Non so quel che farei!; 28a. Stringhe e ferri da calzette; 28b. Ecco la gabbia; 28c. Andiam tosto; 28d. Eccovi, o miei signori; 28e. E sopra sotto; 29. In casa di Messere; 30. Iasacco chiamaste; 31. Mi sento opprimere; 32. In prigione costei. ACT 2: 32b. Ahimè; 33a. In quell'orrendo; 33c. Oh troppe grazie!; 34. Forse un dì conoscerete; 35. Oh mio signor partite; 36. Ah destino crudel; 37a. Sì per voi, pupille amate; 37b. Chi m'aiuta?; 38. Udrai la sentenza; 39. Podestà, Poedstà!; 40. Deh pensa domani; 41. Infelice Ninetta; 42. Chi è? Fernando!; 43. Eterni Dei, che sento!; 44. Ah lungi, il timore!; 45a. Ora mi par che il core; 45b. A questo seno; 45c. Saprò correggerre; 46. A pieni voti; 47. Tremate, o popoli; 48. Infelice donzella; 49. Aspettate sopendete; 50. Ah no! Fermate!; 51. Sino il pianto è negato; 52a. Che razza di villaggio; 52b. Ora che nel castagno; 53. Infelice, sventurata; 54. Deh tu reggi in tal momento; 55. Giorgio, Giorgio?; 56. Che scampanare è questo?; 57. Figlia mia!; 58. Ecco cessato il vento.

Ninetta	K. Ricciarelli
Giannetto	W. Matteuzzi
Gottardo	S. Ramey
Pippo	B. Manca di Nissa
Lucia	L. d'Intino
Fernando Villabella	F. Furlanetto
Fabrizio Vingradito	R. Coviello
Isacco	O. di Credico
Antonio	P. Lefebre
Giorgio	F. Musinu
Ernesto	M. Lippi

Prague Phil Chor, Turin RSO, G. Gelmetti (pp1989)
(10/90) (SONY) Ⓓ [3] **S3K45850**

1. Plovdiv PO, R. Raychev
(HARM) ▭ **HMC40 466**
1. Zagreb PO, M. Halász (NAXO) Ⓓ **8 550236**
1. Berlin St Op Orch, A. von Zemlinsky (r1929)
(SCHW) Ⓓ **310037**
1. National PO, R. Chailly
(DECC) Ⓓ **425 852-2DWO**
(DECC) ▭ **425 852-4DWO**
1. VPO, C. Abbado (pp1991)
(DG) ● **072 175-1GH**
(DG) ▣ **072 175-3GH**
1. National PO, R. Chailly
(DECC) Ⓓ **436 133-2DWO**
1. Philh, R. Muti (EMI) Ⓓ [2] **CZS7 67440-2**
1. RPO, E. Bátiz (ASV) Ⓓ **CDQS6076**
(ASV) ▭ **ZCQS6076**
1. National PO, R. Chailly
(DECC) **OO 400 049-5DH**
1. LSO, P. Gamba (DECC) Ⓓ **433 606-2DSP**
1. Plovdiv PO, R. Raychev
(HARM) Ⓓ **HMP390 466**
1. LCP, R. Norrington
(EMI) **OO DCC7 54091-5**
1. NYPO, L. Bernstein (r1960)
(SONY) Ⓓ **SMK47606**
1. LCP, R. Norrington (EMI) **◘ MDC7 54091-8**
1. BPO, H. von Karajan (r1971)
(DG) Ⓓ **439 415-2GCL**
1. Rome Op Orch, T. Serafin (r1960s)
(BELA) Ⓓ **450 106-2**
(BELA) ▭ **450 106-4**
1. LPO, T. Beecham (r1934)
(PEAR) Ⓓ **GEMMCD9084**
1. Lamoureux Concerts Orch, R. Benzi (r1964)
(BELA) Ⓓ **461 001-2**
(BELA) ▭ **461 001-4**
1. Minería SO, H. de la Fuente (r1987)
(IMP) Ⓓ **PCD1109**
1. Minneapolis SO, A. Dorati (r1957)
(MERC) Ⓓ **434 345-2MM**
1. ROHO, C. Rizzi (r1990)
(CONI) Ⓓ **75605 55004-2**
1. RPO, T. Beecham (r1958)
(EMI) Ⓓ [2] **CES5 68541-2**
1. La Scala Orch, A. Guarnieri (r1927)
(BONG) Ⓓ **GB1039-2**
1. BPO, H. von Karajan
(DG) Ⓓ [2] **447 364-2GDB2**
1. ASMF, N. Marriner (r1976)
(PHIL) Ⓓ **446 196-2PM**
1. Hanover Band, R. Goodman (r1994)
(RCA) Ⓓ **09026 68139-2**
1. Philh, C.M. Giulini
(12/87) (EMI) Ⓓ **CDM7 69042-2**
1. LSO, C. Abbado
(5/88) (DG) Ⓓ **419 869-2GGA**
1. ASMF, N. Marriner
(2/89) (EMI) Ⓓ **CDC7 49155-2**
1. Philh, H. von Karajan
(11/89) (EMI) Ⓓ **CDM7 63113-2**
1. BPO, H. von Karajan
(5/90) (DG) Ⓓ **429 164-2GR**
1. Chicago SO, F. Reiner
(9/90) (RCA) Ⓓ **GD60387**
1. Plovdiv PO, R. Raychev
(10/90) (LASE) Ⓓ **15 506**
(10/90) (LASE) ▭ **79 506**
1. LCP, R. Norrington
(4/91) (EMI) Ⓓ **CDC7 54091-2**
1. COE, C. Abbado
(5/91) (DG) Ⓓ **431 653-2GH**
(5/91) (DG) ▭ **431 653-4GH**
1. BPO, W. Furtwängler (r1930)
(4/92) (KOCH) Ⓓ [2] **37059-2**
1. ASMF, N. Marriner (r1976)
(10/92) (PHIL) Ⓓ [3] **434 016-2PM3**
1. NBC SO, A. Toscanini (r1945)
(11/92) (RCA) Ⓓ **GD60289**
1. St Luke's Orch, R. Norrington (pp1992)
(6/93) (EMI) ● **LDB491007-1**
(6/93) (EMI) ▣ **MVD491007-3**
1. LPO, T. Beecham (r1934)
(7/93) (DUTT) Ⓓ **CDLX7001**
1. Philh, G. Cantelli (r1952)
(11/94) (TEST) Ⓓ **SBT1034**
1. Berlin RIAS Orch, F. Fricsay (r1953)
(11/94) (DG) Ⓓ **445 406-2GDO**
1. Atlanta SO, Y. Levi (r1993)
(11/94) (TELA) Ⓓ **CD80334**

26, 27. M. Freni, National PO, R. Chailly (r1979: Ital) (DECC) ① **440 412-2DM**
26, 27. F. Pollet, Montpellier PO, C. Diederich (r1989) (ERAT) ① **4509-98502-2**
26, 27. R. Tebaldi, Santa Cecilia Academy Orch, A. Erede (Ital) (8/91) (DECC) ① [2] **430 481-2DX2**
26, 27. K. Ricciarelli, Lyon Op Chor, Lyon Op Orch, G. Ferro (r1989) (11/94) (VIRG) ① **CUV5 61139-2**
27. C. Muzio, orch (r1918: Ital) (PEAR) ① **GEMMCD9143**
27. R. Tebaldi, Milan RAI SO, N. Sanzogno (bp1953: Ital) (FONI) ① **CDMR5023**
27. M. Caballé, RPO, L. Gardelli (r1972) (EMI) ① **CDM5 65575-2**
27. G. Martinelli, orch, N. Shilkret (Ital: r1923) (10/89) (NIMB) ① **NI7804** (NIMB) ▭ **NC7804**
27. E. Norena, orch, H. Defosse (r1930) (3/91) (PREI) ① **89041**
27. L. Pagliughi, orch (Ital: r c1938) (12/92) (TEST) ① **SBT1008**
34. G. Martinelli, G. De Luca, J. Mardones, orch, N. Shilkret (r1923: Ital) (PEAR) ① [3] **GEMMCDS9159(2)**
34, 56, 57. G. De Luca, G. Martinelli, J. Mardones, orch (r1923) (PEAR) ① [3] **GEMMCDS9160(1)**
35. G. Martinelli, G. De Luca, J. Mardones, orch (Ital: r1923) (12/92) (TEST) ① **SBT1008**
35. L. Escalais, O. Luppi, A. Magini-Coletti, anon (Ital: r1905) (12/93) (SYMP) ① **SYMCD1126**
35. L. Escalais, anon (r1905) (12/93) (SYMP) ① **SYMCD1126**
37. H. Spani, La Scala Orch, C. Sabajno (r1931: Ital) (4/94) (EMI) ① [3] **CHS7 64864-2(2)**
49a, 49b, 50, 56, 57, 61, 62-64, 72. G. Zancanaro, C. Studer, C. Merritt, G. Surian, A. Felle, L. d'Intino, La Scala Chor, La Scala Orch, R. Muti, G. Bertola (CAST) ▬ **CVI2064**
57. J. Schwarz, orch (Ger: r1916) (PREI) ① **89033**
57. A. Ivanov, Bolshoi Th Orch, S. Samosud (r1940s: Russ) (PREI) ① **89067**
57. A. Sved, orch, D. Olivieri (r1940: Ital) (PREI) ① **89096**
57. G. De Luca, anon (r1907: Ital) (PEAR) ① [3] **GEMMCDS9159(2)**
57. B. Franci, orch (r1929: Ital) (PREI) ① **89995**
57. T. Gobbi, Philh, A. Erede (r1963: Ital) (10/89) (EMI) ① **CDM7 63109-2**
57. G. De Luca, orch (Ital: r1923) (1/92) (PREI) ① **89036**
57. A. Endrèze, orch, F. Ruhlmann (r c1932) (11/92) (MSCM) ① **MM30451**
57. A. Sved, orch (Ital: r1940) (12/92) (TEST) ① **SBT1008**
57. J. Van Dam, Loire PO, M. Soustrot (r1992; Ital) (8/93) (FORL) ① **UCD16681**
57. D. Hvorostovsky, Philh, I. Marin (r1992) (9/94) (PHIL) ① **434 912-2PH** (9/94) (PHIL) ▭ **434 912-4PH**
61, 62. J. Carreras, LPO, J. López-Cobos (PHIL) ① **434 152-2PM**
61, 62. M. Gilion, anon (r1906: Ital) (BONG) ① **GB1076-2**
61, 62. R. Alagna, LPO, R. Armstrong (EMI) ① **CDC5 55540-2** (EMI) ▭ **EL5 55540-4**
61, 62. C. Merritt, NY Concert Chorale, St Luke's Orch, R. Norrington (pp1992) (12/94) (EMI) ① **CDC7 54643-2**
61-64. L. Pavarotti, Vienna Op Chor, Vienna Op Orch, N. Rescigno (r1969: Ital) (DECC) ① **443 379-2DM**
61-64. L. Pavarotti, Vienna Op Chor, Vienna Op Orch, N. Rescigno (r1969: Ital) (12/93) (DECC) ① **433 437-2DA** (DECC) ▭ **433 437-4DA**
62. G. Thill, orch, E. Bigot (r1931) (EMI) ① **CDC7 54016-2**
62. B.S. Rosenberg, Budapest Concert Orch, J. Acs (Ital; pp1990) (OLYM) ① **OCD370**
62. G. Thill, Orch, E. Bigot (r1931) (1/89) (EMI) ① **CDM7 69548-2**
62. F. Signorini, orch (Ital: r1908) (11/92) (MEMO) ① [2] **HR4408/9(1)**
62. A. d'Arkor, orch (r1930) (12/92) (TEST) ① **SBT1008**
62. C. Merritt, NY Concert Chorale, St Luke's Orch, R. Norrington (pp1992) (6/93) (EMI) ◐ **LDB491007-1** (6/93) (EMI) ▬ **MVD491007-3**
62. G. Thill, orch, E. Bigot (r1931) (8/95) (FORL) ① **UCD16727**
62, 64. F. Tamagno, Anon (pf) (r1903-04) (2/92) (OPAL) ① **OPALCD9846**
64. F. Tamagno, anon (Ital: r1903) (12/92) (TEST) ① **SBT1008**

L' **Inganno felice– farsa: 1 act (1812—Venice) (Lib. G. Foppa after Paisiello)**

EXCERPTS: 1. Overture; 2a. Cosa dite! ma cosa dite!; 2b. Ebben, che ascendi; 3a. Qual tenero diletto; 3b. Né posson due lustri; 4. Ebben, che tenta; 5. Chi mi chiama?; 6a. Prima d'andar; 6b. Una voce m'ha colpito; 7. Egli restò indeciso; 8. Ciel protettor; 9a. Oh, Cielo; 9b. Quel sembiante, quello sguardo; 10. Oh, l'impressione è fatta; 11a. Quale inchiesta!; 11b. Tu mi conosci, e sai che; 12a. Mel pagherà tua vita!; 12b. Va taluno mormorando; 13. È deciso!; 14a. Al nuovo dì col mio fedele; 14b. Al più dolce e caro oggetto; 15. Son fuor di me!; 16. Oarmi tutto disposto; 17. Finale: Tacita notte amica, deh.

Batone N. de Carolis
Isabella A. Felle
Bertrando I. Zennaro
Tarabotto F. Previati
Ormondo D. Serraiocco
ECO, M. Viotti (r1992) (5/93) (CLAV) ① **CD50-9211**

Isabella E. Cundari
Bertrando F. Jacopucci
Batone P. Montarsolo
Tarabotto G. Tadeo
Ormondo Sergio Pezzetti
Naples RAI Orch, C. Franci (5/93) (NOTE) ① [2] **PGP21001**

1. Polish CO, J. Maksymiuk (EMI) ① [2] **CES5 68541-2**
1. ASMF, N. Marriner (r1974) (10/92) (PHIL) ① [3] **434 016-2PM3**

L' **Italiana in Algeri, '(The) Italian Girl in Algiers'– dramma giocoso: 2 acts (1816—Rome) (Lib. A. Anelli)**

EXCERPTS: 1. Overture. ACT 1: 2. Serenate il mesto ciglio; 3. Il mio schiavo italian; 4. Languir per una bella; 5a. Ah, quando fia; 5b. Se inclinassi a prender moglie; 6a. Quanta roba!; 6b. Cruda sorte!; 7. Misericordia; 8a. Ah! Isabella; 8b. Ai capricci della sorte; 9a. E ricusar potresti; 9b. Ascoltami, italiano; 9c. Dunque degg'io lasciarvi?; 10. Già d'insolito; 11a. Viva, viva; 11b. O! Che muso; 12a. Vo' star con mia; 12b. Pria di dividerci. ACT 2: 13a. Uno stupido; 13b. Amiche, andate a dir all'italiana; 13c. Qual disdetta; 14. Ah, come il cor di giubilo; 15a. Viva il grande Kaimakan; 15b. Ho un gran peso; 16a. Dunque a momenti; 16b. Per lui che adoro; 17a. Io non resisto più; 17b. Ti presento; 18a. Con tutta la sua boria; 18b. La femmine d'Italia; 19. E tu speri di togliere Isabella; 20. Orsù, la tua nipote; 21a. Pappataci; 21b. Voi mi deste; 22. E può la tua padrone; 23a. Tutti i nostri Italiani; 23b. Pronti abbiamo; 23c. Amici, in ogni evento; 23d. Pensa alla patria; 23e. Qual piacer!; 24a. Che bel cor; 24b. Dei Pappataci; 25a. Non sei tu che il grado eletto; 25b. Son l'aure seconde; 25c. Mio Signore. ADDITIONAL ARIA: 26. Concedi, concedi, amor pietoso.

Isabella T. Berganza
Lindoro L. Alva
Taddeo R. Panerai
Mustafà F. Corena
Elvira G. Tavolaccini
Zulma M.T. Pace
Haly P. Montarsolo
MMF Chor, MMF Orch, S. Varviso (7/89) (DECC) ① [2] **417 828-2DM2**

Isabella A. Baltsa
Lindoro F. Lopardo
Taddeo E. Dara
Mustafà R. Raimondi
Elvira P. Pace
Zulma A. Gonda
Haly A. Corbelli
Vienna St Op Chor, VPO, C. Abbado (r1987) (10/89) (DG) ① [2] **427 331-2GH2**

Isabella G. Simionato
Lindoro C. Valletti
Taddeo M. Cortis
Mustafà M. Petri
Elvira G. Sciutti
Zulma M. Masini
Haly E. Campi
La Scala Chor, La Scala Orch, C.M. Giulini (r1954) (11/91) (EMI) ① [2] **CHS7 64041-2**

Isabella M. Horne
Lindoro E. Palacio
Taddeo D. Trimarchi
Mustafà S. Ramey
Elvira K. Battle
Zulma C. Foti
Haly N. Zaccaria
Prague Phil Chor, Solisti Veneti, C. Scimone (1/92) (ERAT) ① [2] **2292-45404-2**

1. Plovdiv PO, R. Raychev (HARM) ▭ **HMC40 466**
1. Scottish CO, J.Laredo (NIMB) ① **NI5078**
1. Zagreb PO, M. Halász (NAXO) ① **8 550236**
1. National PO, R. Chailly (DECC) ∞ **400 049-5DH**
1. Plovdiv PO, R. Raychev (HARM) ① **HMP390 466**
1. LCP, R. Norrington (EMI) ∞ **DCC7 54091-5**
1. NYPO, L. Bernstein (r1960) (SONY) ① **SMK47606**
1. LCP, R. Norrington (EMI) ◉ **MDC7 54091-8**
1. BPO, H. von Karajan (r1971) (DG) ① **439 415-2GCL**
1. Mexico St SO, E. Bátiz (ASV) ① **CDDCA857** (ASV) ▭ **ZCDCA857**
1. Ricercar Acad, M. Ponseele (r1993; arr Legrand: Wind Ens) (RICE) ① **RIC126114**
1. Polish Chmbr PO, W. Rajski (INTE) ① **INT830 899**
1. Minneapolis SO, A. Dorati (r1957) (MERC) ① **434 345-2MM**
1. ROHO, C. Rizzi (r1990) (CONI) ① **75605 55004-2**
1. NY Met Op Orch, James Levine (pp1988) (DG) ① **445 552-2GMA** (DG) ▭ **445 552-4GMA**
1. Philh, A. Galliera (r1959) (EMI) ① [2] **CES5 68541-2**
1. ASMF, N. Marriner (r1974) (PHIL) ① **446 196-2PM**
1. Hanover Band, R. Goodman (r1994) (RCA) ① **09026 68139-2**
1. Philh, C.M. Giulini (12/87) (EMI) ① **CDM7 69042-2**
1. LSO, C. Abbado (5/88) (DG) ① **419 869-2GGA**
1. Philh, H. von Karajan (11/89) (EMI) ① **CDM7 63113-2**
1. NYPSO, A. Toscanini (r1936) (3/90) (PEAR) ① [3] **GEMMCDS9373**
1. BPO, H. von Karajan (5/90) (DG) ① **429 164-2GR**
1. Plovdiv PO, R. Raychev (10/90) (LASE) ① **15 506** (10/90) (LASE) ▭ **79 506**
1. LCP, R. Norrington (4/91) (EMI) ① **CDC7 54091-2**
1. COE, C. Abbado (5/91) (DG) ① **431 653-2GH** (5/91) (DG) ▭ **431 653-4GH**
1. ASMF, N. Marriner (r1974) (10/92) (PHIL) ① [3] **434 016-2PM3**
1. NBC SO, A. Toscanini (pp1950) (11/92) (RCA) ① **GD60289**
1. NYPO, A. Toscanini (r1936) (11/92) (RCA) ① **GD60318**
1. Black Dyke Mills Band, P. Parkes (arr brass band: P Parkes) (9/93) (CHAN) ① **CHAN4514** (9/93) (CHAN) ▭ **BBTD4514**
1. Atlanta SO, Y. Levi (r1993) (11/94) (TELA) ① **CD80334**
1. National PO, R. Chailly (r1981) (9/95) (DECC) ① [2] **443 850-2DF2**
1, 4, 5b, 6b, 8b, 10, 11b, 12b(pt), 13a, 14, 15a, 15b, 16b, 16b, 17b, 18b, 21b, 25. L. V. Terrani, J. M. Bima, L. Rizzi, F. Araiza, A. Corbelli, E. Dara, W. Ganzarolli, W German Rad Chor, Cappella Coloniensis, G. Ferro (r1979) (SONY) ① **SMK53504**
4. C. Valletti, Orch, A. Basile (pp1955) (MEMO) ① [2] **HR4191/2**
4. W. Matteuzzi, Teatro La Fenice Chor, Teatro La Fenice Orch, V. Parisi (pp1989) (NUOV) ① **6892**
4. R. Blake, LSO, J. McCarthy (4/88) (ARAB) ① **Z6582** (4/88) (ARAB) ▭ **ABQC6582**
4. R. Vargas, ECO, M. Viotti (11/92) (CLAV) ① **CD50-9202**

4, 26. R. Giménez, Scottish CO, M. Veltri (8/88) (NIMB) ① **NI5106** (NIMB) ⊟ **NC5106**

6a, 6b D. Jones, Richard Hickox Sngrs, CLS, R. Hickox (2/91) (CHAN) ① **CHAN8865** (2/91) (CHAN) ⊟ **ABTD1480**

6b T. Berganza, Barcelona SO, G. Navarro (11/92) (RCA) ⊟ **09026 61204-4**

6b T. Berganza, Barcelona SO, G. Navarro (RCA) OO **09026 61204-5**

6b M. Horne, ROHO, H. Lewis (DECC) ① **421 891-2DA**

6b M. Horne, Prague Phil Chor, Solisti Veneti, C. Scimone (ERAT) ① **4509-91715-2** (ERAT) ⊟ **4509-91715-4**

6b C. Bartoli, A. Schoenberg Ch, Vienna Volksoper Orch, G. Patanè (r1988) (DECC) ① **443 378-2DM**

6b D. Soffel, Swedish CO, M. Liljefors (pp1984) (4/93) (CPRI) ① **CAP21428**

6b M. Horne, Solisti Veneti, C. Scimone (r1980) (4/94) (RCA) ① [6] **09026 61580-2(8)**

6b, 16b, 23c, 23d M. Horne, Turin RAI Chor, Turin RAI Orch, C. Franci (pp1968) (MEMO) ① [2] **HR4392/3**

6b, 23b-d C. Bartoli, A. Schoenberg Ch, Vienna Volksoper Orch, G. Patanè (9/89) (DECC) ① **425 430-2DH** (9/89) (DECC) ⊟ **425 430-4DH**

8b C. Supervia, C. Scattola, orch, A. Albergoni (r1927) (3/93) (NIMB) ① [2] **NI7836/7**

10. M. Pertusi, Sofia PO, E. Tabakov (r1994) (CAPR) ① **10 704**

11b A. Baltsa, R. Raimondi, Orch, Anon Cond (pp1991) (MCI) ① **MCCD090** (MCI) ⊟ **MCTC090**

12a, 15b S. Bruscantini, T. Berganza, M. Petri, V. Meucci, Milan RAI Chor, Milan RAI SO, N. Sanzogno (pp1957) (MEMO) ① [2] **HR4300/1**

12b C. Gonzales, M. Bacelli, S. Pasqualini, E. Ferretti, G. Saks, Berlin RSO, R. Buckley (SCHW) ① [2] **314052**

18b S. Ramey, WNO Orch, G. Ferro (TELD) ① **9031-73242-2**

21a R. Blake, T. Hampson, J. Opalach, St Luke's Orch, R. Norrington (pp1992) (6/93) (EMI) ◐ **LDB491007-1** (6/93) (EMI) ▣ **MVD491007-3**

23b-d M. Horne, Geneva Op Chor, SRO, H. Lewis (DECC) ① **421 891-2DA**

23b-d M. Horne, Geneva Op Chor, SRO, H. Lewis (r1965) (DECC) ① **440 415-2DM**

23c, 23d G. Simionato, Milan RAI SO, N. Sanzogno (pp1956) (MEMO) ① [2] **HR4386/7**

23d G. Fabbri, S. Cottone (r1903) (12/89) (SYMP) ① **SYMCD1065**

Maometto Secondo– dramma: 2 acts (1820—Naples) (Lib. C. della Valle)

EXCERPTS: 1. Overture. ACT 1: 2. Al tou cenno, Erisso; 3. Risponda a te primiero; 4. Sì, giuriam!; 5. Ah! che invan su questo ciglio; 6. Petoso ciel; 7a. No, tacer non deggio; 7b. Ohimè, qual fulmine; 7c. Dal cor l'iniquo affetto; 7d. Misere! ... or dove, ahimè; 8a. Giusto Cielo, in tal periglio; 8b. Ahi padre!; 9. Figlia, mi lascia; 10. Mira, signor, quel pianto; 11. Dal ferro, dal foco; 12. Sorgete, sorgete; 13. Del mondo al vincitor; 14a. Compiuta ancor del tutto; 14b. Signor, di liete nuove; 14c. Appressatevi, o prodi; 15. Giusto Ciel, che strazio è questo!; 16. Guardie, olà, costor si traggano; 17. Rendemi il padre, o barbaro; 18. Ah! perchè fra le spade nemiche. ACT 2: 19. È follia sul fior degli anni; 20. Tacete. - Ahimè!; 21. Anna, tu piangi?; 22. Gli estremi sensi ascolta; 23. Ma qual tumulto ascolto?; 24a. Ah che più tardi ancor?; 24b. All'invito generoso; 24c. Dell'araba tromba; 25. Sieguimi, o Calbo; 26. Tenera sposa; 27. Non temer: d'un basso affetto; 28. Del periglio al fiero aspetto; 29. Oh, come al cor soavi; 30. In questi estremi istanti; 31a. Alfin compita è la metà; 31b. Nume, cui'l sole è trono; 32. Sventurata! fuggir sol ti resta; 33. Quella morte che s'avanza; 34. Sì, ferite: il chieggo, il merto; 35. Già fra le tombe?.

Anna	J. Anderson
Calbo	M. Zimmermann
Erisso	E. Palacio
Maometto	S. Ramey
Condulmiero; Selimo	L. Dale

Ambrosian Op. Chor, Philh, C. Scimone (9/85) (PHIL) ① [3] **412 148-2PH3**

1. ASMF, N. Marriner (r1979) (10/92) (PHIL) ① [3] **434 016-2PM3**

5, 8a C. Bartoli, Venice La Fenice Chor, Venice La Fenice Orch, I. Martin (DECC) OO **436 075-5DH**

5, 8a C. Bartoli, Venice La Fenice Chor, Venice La Fenice Orch, I. Martin (2/92) (DECC) ① **436 075-2DH**

8a C. Bartoli, Venice La Fenice Orch, I. Marin (r1991) (DECC) ① **448 300-2DH** (DECC) ⊟ **448 300-4DH**

27. D. Soffel, Swedish CO, M. Liljefors (pp1984) (4/93) (CPRI) ① **CAP21428**

Matilde di Shabran (or Bellezza e cuor di ferro)– melodramma giocoso: 2 acts (1821—Rome) (Lib. G. Ferretti)

EXCERPTS: 1. Overture.

Overture Plovdiv PO, R. Raychev (10/90) (LASE) ① **15 520** (10/90) (LASE) ⊟ **79 520**

1. Ricercar Acad, M. Ponseele (r1993; arr Sedlak: Wind Ens) (RICE) ① **RIC126114**

Mosè– opera: 3 acts (1827—Rome) (Italian version of Moïse et Pharaon')

Mosè	N. Rossi-Lemeni
Elisero	A. Lazzari
Faraone	G. Taddei
Aménofi	M. Filippeschi
Aufide	P. de Palma
Osiride	P. Clabassi
Maria	L. Danieli
Anaide	C. Mancini
Sinaide	B. Rizzoli
Mysterious voice	F. Mazzoli

Naples San Carlo Op Chor, Naples San Carlo Op Orch, T. Serafin (r1956) (3/95) (PHIL) ① [2] **442 100-2PM2**

Mosè in Egitto– azione tragico-sacra: 3 acts (1818—Naples) (Lib. A.L. Tottola, after Ringhieri)

EXCERPTS: 1. Introduction. ACT 1: 2. Mano ultrice d'un Dio; 3. Eterno! immenso!; 4a. Celeste man placata!; 4b. Egizi! Faraone!; 4c. Voci di giubilo; 5. E avete, avverse stelle; 6a. Ah! se puoi così lasciarmi; 6b. Non è ver che stringa il cielo; 6c. Ah! quel suon già d'Israele; 7. Ah! dov'è Faraone?; 8a. Cade dal ciglio in velo; 8b. Ove m'ascondo?; 9. All'etra, al ciel; 10. Tutto mi ride intorno; 11a. Che narri?...Il ver; 11b. All'idea di tanto eccesso; 11c. Padre...Signor... ACT 2: 12. Ecco in tua mano, Aronne; 13a. Parlar, spiegar non posso; 13b. (Non merta più consiglio); 14. Gentil Regina, oh quanto; 15a. La pace mia smarrita; 15b. Deh, ti consola e spera; 16. Nuove sciagure, o mio german!; 17a. Dove mi guidi?; 17b. Quale assalto, qual cimento!; 17c. Ah mira!...Oh ciel!; 17d. Involto in fiamma rea; 17e. Mi manca la voce; 17f. Fiera guerra mi sento nel seno; 18. Che potrai dir?; 19. Tu di ceppi m'aggravi; 20. O Nume Osiri; 21. Se a mitigar tue cure; 22. Sì, popoli d'Egitto; 23a. Porgi la destra amata; 23b. E ancor resisti?; 23c. Tormenti, affanni e smanie; 24. Eccone in salvo, o figli; 25a. Dal tuo stellato soglio; 25b. Ma qual fragor!; 25c. Son fuggiti! Oh cieli, che miro!.

Mosè	R. Raimondi
Elcia	J. Anderson
Amaltea	Z. Gal
Amenosi	S. Browne
Aronne	S. Fisichella
Osiride	E. Palacio
Mambre	K. Lewis
Faraone	S. Nimsgern

Ambrosian Op Chor, Philh, C. Scimone (1819 vers) (12/92) (PHIL) ① [2] **420 109-2PM2**

Prayer Ambrosian Op. Chor, Philh, C. Scimone (12/85) (PHIL) ① [2] **412 548-2PH2**

3. N. Ghiaurov, Rome RAI Chor, Rome RAI Orch, W. Sawallisch (pp1968) (MEMO) ① [2] **HR4223/4**

3. N. De Angelis, orch (r1929) (4/94) (EMI) ① [3] **CHS7 64864-2(1)**

3, 25a E. Cheni, I. Mannarini, E. Venturini, N. de Angelis, orch, L. Molajoli (r1929) (7/92) (PREI) ① **89042**

25a N. Ghiaurov, T. Zylis-Gara, G. Lane, G. Corradi, Rome RAI Chor, Rome RAI Orch, W. Sawallisch (pp1968) (MEMO) ① [2] **HR4223/4**

25a P. Tinsley, E. Shelley, D. Hughes, R. Lloyd, ROH Chor, ROHO, L. Gardelli (EMI) ① **CDM7 64356-2**

25a P. Tinsley, E. Shelley, D. Hughes, R. Lloyd, ROH Chor, ROHO, L. Gardelli (r1971) (EMI) ① [2] **CZS5 68559-2**

25a E. Pinza, A.M. Turchetti, chor, orch (r1923) (12/92) (TEST) ① **SBT1008**

L' Occasione fa il ladro– burletta: 1 act (1812—Venice) (Lib. L. Prividali)

EXCERPTS: 1. Overture; 2. Frema in cielo il nembo irato; 3a. Il tuo rigore insano; 3b. Grato conforto è l'incontrar per viaggio; 4a. Paghiamo il conto; 4b. Che sorte, che accidente; 5. Non lo permetto; 6a. Vicino è il momento; 6b. Sposarsi ad un; 7. Eccomi al gran cimento; 8a. Alma coraggio!; 8b. Quel gentil, quel vago oggetto; 9. Se non m'inganna il core; 10. Dov'è questo aposo?; 11. Non so più cosa far; 12a. Qual strano caso è il mio!; 12b. D'ogni più sacro impegno; 13a. Per conoscer l'inganno; 13b. Voi la sposa!; 14a. Qui non c'è scampo; 14b. Il mio padrone è un uomo; 15. Voi qui appunto io cercava; 16a. Qual chiasso è questo?; 16b. Ma se incerti voi siete; 16c. Fermatevi; 17a. Il suo trascorso alfine; 17b. Quello, ch'io fui, ritorno; 18. On quanto son grate; 19. Finale: Miei signore, allegramente.

Berenice	S. Patterson
Don Parmenione	N. de Carolis
Conte Alberto	R. Gambill
Ernestina	M. Bacelli
Martino	A. Corbelli
Don Eusebio	S. Kale

Stuttgart RSO, G. Gelmetti (r1992) (TELD) ◐ **4509-92170-6** (TELD) ▣ **4509-92170-3**

Berenice	M. Bayo
Don Parmenione	N. de Carolis
Count Alberto	I. Zennaro
Ernestina	F. Provvisionato
Martino	F. Previati
Don Eusebio	F. Massa

ECO, M. Viotti (r1992) (5/93) (CLAV) ① [2] **CD50-9208/9**

12b R. Giménez, Scottish CO, M. Veltri (8/88) (NIMB) ① **NI5106** (NIMB) ⊟ **NC5106**

12b R. Vargas, ECO, M. Viotti (11/92) (CLAV) ① **CD50-9202**

Otello (or Il moro di Venezia)– dramma: 3 acts (1816—Naples) (Lib. F. Berio di Salsa, after Shakespeare)

EXCERPTS: 1. Overture. ACT 1: 2. Viva Otello, via il prode; 3a. Vincemno, prodi; 3b. Ah! sì, per voi già sento; 4a. Rodrigo! Elmiro!; 4b. No, no temer, serena; 5a. Inutile è quel pianto; 5b. Ah! ch'io pavento; 6a. Ma che miro?; 6b. Giunto è Rodrigo, il fortunato istante; 6c. Padre, permetti; 6d. Dove son? Che mai veggio; 6f. L'infida, ahimè che miro?; 6g. Padre!...Non v'è perdono. ACT 2: 7a. Lasciami; 7b. Che ascolto? ahimè, che dici?; 8a. M'abbandò, disparve; 8b. Che feci?; 9a. E a tanto giunger puote; 9b. Ahimè! fermate, udite; 10a. Desdemona! che veggo!; 10b. Qual nuova a me recate? ACT 3: 11a. Ah! Dagli affani oppressa; 11b. Assia a piè d'un salice; 11c. Che dissi!; 11d. Deh calma, o ciel, nel sonno; 12a. Eccomi giunto inosservato, e solo; 12b. Che miro! ahimè!; 12c. Non arrestare il colpo; 12d. Per me la tua colpa. ADDITIONAL ITEM FOR 1844 PARIS REVIVAL: 13. Ballet.

Otello	J. Carreras
Desdemona	F. von Stade
Iago	G. Pastine
Rodrigo	S. Fisichella
Emilia	N. Condò
Elmiro	S. Ramey
Lucio	K. Lewis
Doge; Gondoliere	A. Leoz

Ambrosian Op Chor, Philh, J. López-Cobos (12/92) (PHIL) ① [2] **432 456-2PM2**

1. ASMF, N. Marriner (r1979) (10/92) (PHIL) ① [3] **434 016-2PM3**

1. National PO, R. Chailly (r1984) (9/95) (DECC) ① [2] **443 850-2DF2**

2. M. Horne, SRO, H. Lewis (DECC) ① **421 306-2DA**

2. F. von Stade, Rotterdam PO, E. de Waart (PHIL) ① **420 084-2PH**

2. C. Bartoli, Vienna Volksoper Orch, G. Patanè (9/89) (DECC) ① **425 430-2DH** (9/89) (DECC) ⊟ **425 430-4DH**

3b C. Merritt, Munich RSO, J. Fiore (r1993) (9/94) (PHIL) ① **434 102-2PH**

7b R. Blake, LSO, M. Valdes (12/89) (ARAB) ① **Z6612** (12/89) (ARAB) ⊟ **ABQC6612**

11a-d M. Caballé, C. Vozza, RCA Italiana Op Chor, RCA Italiana Op Orch, G. Prêtre (r1967)
(RCA) Ⓓ **74321 24284-2**
(RCA) ▭ **74321 24284-4**
11a-d M. Caballé, C. Vozza, RCA Italiana Op Orch, C.F. Cillario
(11/92) (RCA) Ⓓ [2] **GD60941**
11b M. Horne, orch (pp1971)
(MEMO) Ⓓ [2] **HR4392/3**
11b D. Jones, C. Smith, CLS, R. Hickox
(2/91) (CHAN) Ⓓ **CHAN8865**
(2/91) (CHAN) ▭ **ABTD1480**
11b-d K. Ricciarelli, Lyon Op Chor, Lyon Op Orch, G. Ferro (r1989)
(11/94) (VIRG) Ⓓ **CUV5 61139-2**
12c, 12d J. Carreras, F. von Stade, Philh, J. López-Cobos (r1978) (PHIL) Ⓓ **442 600-2PH**
(PHIL) ▭ **442 600-4PH**

La **pietra del paragone– melodramma giocoso: 2 acts (1812—Milan) (Lib. L. Romanelli)**

Giocondo P. Barbacini
Clarice H. Müller-Molinari
Aspasia A. Trovarelli
Fulvia M.C. Nocentini
Asdrubale R. Scaltriti
Macrobio V. di Matteo
Pacuvio P. Rumetz
Fabrizio A. Svab
Modena Teatro Comunale Chor, Camerata Musicale Orch, C. Desderi (pp1992)
(5/93) (NUOV) Ⓓ [2] **7132/3**
Oh, come il fosco ...Quell'alme pupille R. Giménez, Scottish CO, M. Veltri
(8/88) (NIMB) Ⓓ **NI5106**
(NIMB) ▭ **NC5106**
Se l'Italie contrade...Se per voi lo care io torno C. Bartoli, A. Schoenberg Ch, Vienna Volksoper Orch, G. Patanè
(9/89) (DECC) Ⓓ **425 430-2DH**
(9/89) (DECC) ▭ **425 430-4DH**

Ricciardo e Zoriade– dramma: 2 acts (1818—Naples) (Lib. F. Berio di Salsa)
Contro cento, e cento prodi D. Montague, P. Doghan, P. Nilon, G. Dolton, G. Mitchell Ch, Philh, D. Parry
(10/90) (OPRA) Ⓓ [3] **ORCH103**
Overture Ambrosian Sngrs, ASMF, N. Marriner (r1979) (10/92) (PHIL) Ⓓ [3] **434 016-2PM3**
S'ella m'è ognor fedele R. Blake, P. Jeffes, LSO, M. Valdes (12/89) (ARAB) Ⓓ **Z6612**
(12/89) (ARAB) ▭ **ABQC6612**

La **Scala di seta, '(The) Silken Ladder'– farsa comica: 1 act (1812—Venice) (Lib G Foppa, after Gaveaux)**
EXCERPTS: 1. Overture; 2. Va' sciocco, non seccarmi; 3. Siamo sicuri. Uscite!; 4. Egli è sceso... 5a. Signor padron; 5b. Io so ch'hai buon core; 6. Oh senza ceremonia... 7a. E che? tu ti mariti?; 7b. Va lesto; 7c. Vedrò qual sommo incanto; 8a. Io non so conquistare un cor di donna?; 8b. Sì che unito a cara sposa; 9. Va' là presto; 10a. Or andiam dal tutor... 10b. Sento talor nell'anima; 11. Bellissima! il cassetto è proprio nuovo!; 12. E ognum mi dice sciocco!; 13a. Sollecitiam perchè Blansac; 13b. Ma se mai; 13c. Il mio ben sospiro e chiamo; 14a. Brava! vada, si serva...; 15. Come? come?; 16. Buono! non c'è persona; 17. Dorme ognuno in queste soglie; 18. Finale: Finir conviene la scena.

Germano A. Corbelli
Giulia L. Serra
Dorvil D. Kuebler
Blansac A. Rinaldi
Lucilla J. Bunnell
Dormont D. Griffith
Stuttgart RSO, G. Gelmetti, M. Hampe
(TELD) ◖ **9031-73828-6**
(TELD) ▬ **9031-73828-3**
Germano R. Coviello
Giulia L. Serra
Dorvil W. Matteuzzi
Blansac N. de Carolis
Lucilla C. Bartoli
Dormont O. di Credico
Bologna Teatro Comunale Orch, G. Ferro (pp1988)
(FONI) Ⓓ [2] **RFCD2003**
1. Zagreb PO, M. Halász (NAXO) Ⓓ **8 550236**
1. Plovdiv PO, R. Raychev
(HARM) ▭ **HMC40 466**
1. Scottish CO, J.Laredo (NIMB) Ⓓ **NI5078**
1. Haydn Philh, E. Rojatti (NUOV) Ⓓ **6726**
1. National PO, R. Chailly
(DECC) Ⓓ **436 133-2DWO**
1. Philh, R. Muti (EMI) Ⓓ [2] **CZS7 67440-2**
1. National PO, R. Chailly
(DECC) ◘◘ **400 049-5DH**
1. LSO, P. Gamba (DECC) Ⓓ **433 606-2DSP**
1. Polish CO, J. Maksymiuk
(CFP) Ⓓ **CD-CFP4608**
(CFP) ▭ **TC-CFP4608**
1. Plovdiv PO, R. Raychev
(HARM) Ⓓ **HMP390 466**
1. LCP, R. Norrington
(EMI) ◘◘ **DCC7 54091-5**
1. NYPO, L. Bernstein (r1963)
(SONY) Ⓓ **SMK47606**
1. LCP, R. Norrington (EMI) ◙ **MDC7 54091-8**
1. Mexico St SO, E. Bátiz
(ASV) Ⓓ **CDDCA857**
(ASV) ▭ **ZCDCA857**
1. BPO, H. von Karajan (r1971)
(DG) Ⓓ **439 415-2GCL**
1. Rome Op Orch, T. Serafin (r1960s)
(BELA) Ⓓ **450 106-2**
(BELA) ▭ **450 106-4**
1. LPO, T. Beecham (r1933)
(PEAR) Ⓓ **GEMMCD9084**
1. Polish Chmbr PO, W. Rajski
(INTE) Ⓓ **INT830 899**
1. Minneapolis SO, A. Dorati (r1957)
(MERC) Ⓓ **434 345-2MM**
1. ROHO, C. Rizzi (r1990)
(CONI) Ⓓ **75605 55004-2**
1. Philh, A. Galliera (r1959)
(EMI) Ⓓ [2] **CES5 68541-2**
1. ASMF, N. Marriner (r1974)
(PHIL) Ⓓ **446 196-2PM**
1. Hanover Band, R. Goodman (r1994)
(RCA) Ⓓ **09026 68139-2**
1. Philh, C.M. Giulini
(12/87) (EMI) Ⓓ **CDM7 69042-2**
1. ASMF, N. Marriner
(2/89) (EMI) Ⓓ **CDC7 49155-2**
1. Philh, H. von Karajan
(11/89) (EMI) Ⓓ **CDM7 63113-2**
1. BPO, H. von Karajan
(5/90) (DG) Ⓓ **429 164-2GR**
1. Chicago SO, F. Reiner
(9/90) (RCA) Ⓓ **GD60387**
1. Plovdiv PO, R. Raychev
(10/90) (LASE) Ⓓ **15 506**
(10/90) (LASE) ▭ **79 506**
1. LCP, R. Norrington
(4/91) (EMI) Ⓓ **CDC7 54091-2**
1. COE, C. Abbado
(5/91) (DG) Ⓓ **431 653-2GH**
(5/91) (DG) ▭ **431 653-4GH**
1. ASMF, N. Marriner (r1974)
(10/92) (PHIL) Ⓓ [3] **434 016-2PM3**
1. Black Dyke Mills Band, P. Parkes (arr Parkes)
(7/93) (CHAN) Ⓓ **CHAN4505**
(CHAN) ▭ **BBTD4505**
1. LPO, T. Beecham (r1933)
(7/93) (DUTT) Ⓓ **CDLX7001**
1. BBC SO, A. Toscanini (r1938)
(5/94) (BIDD) Ⓓ [2] **WHL008/9**
1. LPO, T. Beecham (r1933)
(10/94) (DUTT) Ⓓ **CDLX7009**
1. Atlanta SO, Y. Levi (r1993)
(11/94) (TELA) Ⓓ **CD80334**
1. National PO, R. Chailly (r1981)
(9/95) (DECC) Ⓓ [2] **443 850-2DF2**

Semiramide– melodramma tragico: 2 acts (1823—Venice) (Lib. G. Rossi, after Voltaire)
EXCERPTS: 1. Overture. ACT 1: 2. Sì...gran Nume...t'intesi; 3. Suoni festevoli; 4. Là dal Gange a te primiero; 5. Di plausi qual clamor; 6. Di tanti regi e populi; 7. Ah! già il sacro foco è spento; 8. Eccomi alfine in Babilonia; 9. Ah! quel giorno ognor rammento; 10. Io t'attendeva, Arsace; 11. Bella imago; 12. Serena i vaghi rai; 13a. Bel raggio lusinghier; 13b. Dolce pensiero; 13c. Mitrane! E che rechi?; 14. Serbami ognor sì fido; 15. Alle più calde immagini; 16. March; 17. Ergi omai la fronte altera; 18. I vostri voti omai; 19. L'alto eroe; 20. Qual mesto gemito; 21. D'un semidio che adoro; 22. Ah! Sconvolta nell'ordine eterno. ACT 2: 23. Assur, i cenni miei; 24. Se la vita; 25. Quekka, ricordati; 26. La forza primiera; 27. Ebben, compiasi omai; 28. In sì barbara sciagura; 29. Su, ti scuoti; 30. No: non ti lascio; 31. Ebben...a tei; ferisci; 32. Giorno d'orrore!; 33. Madre—addio; 34. La speranza più soave; 35. Sì, sperar voglio contento; 36. Il di già cade; 37. Deh! ti ferma; 38. Que' numi furenti; 39. Qual densa notte!; 40. Al mio pregar t'arrendi; 41. Dei! qual sospiro!; 42. Ninia, ferisci!.

Semiramide I. Tamar
Arsace G. Scalchi
Assur M. Pertusi
Idreno G. Kunde
Azema M. Valenti
Oroe I. d'Arcangelo
Ghost of Nino S. Zadvorny
Mitrane L. Petroni
Prague Phil Chor, Bologna Teatro Comunale Orch, A. Zedda (pp1992)
(FONI) Ⓓ [3] **RFCD2018**
Semiramide J. Sutherland
Arsace M. Horne
Assur J. Rouleau
Idreno J. Serge
Azema P. Clark
Oroe S. Malas
Ghost of Nino M. Langdon
Mitrane L. Fyson
Ambrosian Op Chor, LSO, R. Bonynge
(2/90) (DECC) Ⓓ [3] **425 481-2DM3**
Semiramide C. Studer
Arsace J. Larmore
Assur S. Ramey
Idreno F. Lopardo
Azema J. Faulkner
Oroe J-H. Rootering
Ghost of Nino R. Tesarowicz
Mitrane O. Arévalo
Ambrosian Op Chor, LSO, I. Marin
(2/94) (DG) Ⓓ [3] **437 797-2GH3**
Excs J. Sutherland, Orch, Anon (cond), D. Bailey (11/92) (DECC) ◖ **071 135-1DH**
Fantasie E. Wild (arr Thalberg: pp1981)
(AUDI) Ⓓ [2] **CD72008**
1. Zagreb PO, M. Halász (NAXO) Ⓓ **8 550236**
1. Plovdiv PO, R. Raychev
(HARM) ▭ **HMC40 466**
1. Scottish CO, J.Laredo (NIMB) Ⓓ **NI5078**
1. Horreaux-Trehard Duo (arr 2 gtrs)
(CALL) Ⓓ **CAL9218**
1. Philh, R. Muti (EMI) Ⓓ [2] **CZS7 67440-2**
1. LSO, P. Gamba (DECC) Ⓓ **433 606-2DSP**
1. Plovdiv PO, R. Raychev
(HARM) Ⓓ **HMP390 466**
1. LCP, R. Norrington
(EMI) ◘◘ **DCC7 54091-5**
1. E. Segre (r1992; arr gtr: Giuliani)
(CLAV) Ⓓ **CD50-9303**
1. NYPO, L. Bernstein (r1960)
(SONY) Ⓓ **SMK47606**
1. LCP, R. Norrington (EMI) ◙ **MDC7 54091-8**
1. Mexico St SO, E. Bátiz
(ASV) Ⓓ **CDDCA857**
(ASV) ▭ **ZCDCA857**
1. BPO, H. von Karajan (r1971)
(DG) Ⓓ **439 415-2GCL**
1. Rome Op Orch, T. Serafin (r1960s)
(BELA) Ⓓ **450 106-2**
(BELA) ▭ **450 106-4**
1. Ricercar Acad, M. Ponseele (r1993; arr Sedlak: Wind Ens) (RICE) Ⓓ **RIC126114**
1. NY Harmonie Ens, S. Richman (r1992: arr W Sedlak) (MUSI) Ⓓ **MACD-797**
1. LPO, T. Beecham (r1939)
(PEAR) Ⓓ **GEMMCD9084**
1. ASMF, N. Marriner (r1976)
(PHIL) Ⓓ **446 196-2PM**
1. South-West German RSO, K. Arp (r1994)
(PIER) Ⓓ **PV73005(**
1. Hanover Band, R. Goodman (r1994)
(RCA) Ⓓ **09026 68139-2**
1. Philh, C.M. Giulini
(12/87) (EMI) Ⓓ **CDM7 69042-2**
1. ASMF, N. Marriner
(2/89) (EMI) Ⓓ **CDC7 49155-2**
1. Philh, H. von Karajan
(11/89) (EMI) Ⓓ **CDM7 63113-2**
1. NYPSO, A. Toscanini (r1936)
(3/90) (PEAR) Ⓓ [3] **GEMMCDS9373**
1. Plovdiv PO, R. Raychev
(10/90) (LASE) Ⓓ **15 506**
(10/90) (LASE) ▭ **79 506**
1. LCP, R. Norrington
(4/91) (EMI) Ⓓ **CDC7 54091-2**
1. COE, C. Abbado
(5/91) (DG) Ⓓ **431 653-2GH**
(5/91) (DG) ▭ **431 653-4GH**
1. ASMF, N. Marriner (r1976)
(10/92) (PHIL) Ⓓ [3] **434 016-2PM3**
1. NBC SO, A. Toscanini (r1951)
(11/92) (RCA) Ⓓ **GD60289**
1. NYPO, A. Toscanini (r1936)
(11/92) (RCA) Ⓓ **GD60318**
1. BBC SO, A. Toscanini (pp1935)
(4/93) (TEST) Ⓓ **SBT1015**

1. LPO, T. Beecham (r1939) (7/93) (DUTT) Ⓓ **CDLX7001**
1. Berlin RIAS Orch, F. Fricsay (r1951) (11/94) (DG) Ⓓ **445 406-2GDO**
1. I. Seefried, M. Forrester, E. Haefliger, D. Fischer-Dieskau, Berlin St Hedwig's Cath Ch, BPO, F. Fricsay, H. Krebs, T. Varga, Berlin RIAS Chbr Ch, Berlin RIAS Orch, H. Geusser, W. Fugmann, M. Weber, G. Herzog, Berlin RSO, VPO, E. Grümmer, G. Pitzinger, H. Hotter, Y. Menuhin (r1951) (11/94) (DG) Ⓓ [11] **445 400-2GDO10**
1. Atlanta SO, Y. Levi (r1993) (11/94) (TELA) Ⓓ **CD80334**
1. National PO, R. Chailly (r1984) (9/95) (DECC) Ⓓ [2] **443 850-2DF2**
3. L.V. Terrani, Madrid SO, G.P. Sanzogno (pp1991) (IMP) Ⓓ [2] **DPCD998**
5. J. Sutherland, M. Horne, LSO, R. Bonynge (DECC) Ⓓ **436 133-2DWO**
8. L.V. Terrani, Madrid SO, G.P. Sanzogno (RNE) Ⓓ [2] **650004**
9. M. Horne, ROHO, H. Lewis (DECC) Ⓓ **421 891-2DA**
9. Z. Dolukhanova, USSR Rad Orch, A. Kovalyov (1950s: Russ) (PREI) Ⓓ **89066**
9. Z. Dolukhanova, Moscow PO, G. Stolarov (pp1954) (RUSS) Ⓓ **RDCD15023**
9. G. Fabbri, S. Cottone (r1903) (12/89) (SYMP) Ⓓ **SYMCD1065**
9. E. Stignani, EIAR Orch, A. la Rosa Parodi (r1940) (1/91) (PREI) Ⓓ **89014**
12, 13a, 13b K. Ricciarelli, Lyon Op Chor, Lyon Op Orch, G. Ferro (r1989) (11/94) (VIRG) Ⓓ **CUV5 61139-2**
13a I. Abendroth, anon (r1902: Ger) (SYMP) Ⓓ **SYMCD1085**
13a M. Dragoni, Munich RSO, G. Kuhn (r1991) (ORFE) Ⓓ **C261921A**
13a A. Pendachanska, Sofia SO, M. Angelov (r1994) (CAPR) Ⓓ **10 706**
13a C. Bartoli, Venice La Fenice Orch, I. Marin (r1991) (DECC) Ⓓ **448 300-2DH**
(DECC) ▭ **448 300-4DH**
13a M. André, Toulouse Capitole Orch, M. Plasson (arr tpt) (1/89) (EMI) Ⓓ **CDC7 49219-2**
13a L. Tetrazzini, orch, P. Pitt (r1910) (9/92) (EMI) Ⓓ [3] **CHS7 63802-2(1)**
13a L. Tetrazzini, orch, P. Pitt (r1910) (9/92) (PEAR) Ⓓ **GEMMCD9222**
13a C. Boninsegna, orch (r1910) (12/92) (TEST) Ⓓ **SBT1008**
13a A. Galli-Curci, orch (r1924) (3/94) (CONI) Ⓓ **CDHD201**
(3/94) (CONI) ▭ **MCHD201**
13a A. Galli-Curci, orch, Rosario Bourdon (r1924) (8/94) (ROMO) Ⓓ [2] **81004-2**
13a-c J. Sutherland, ROHO, F. Molinari-Pradelli (1/90) (DECC) Ⓓ [2] **425 493-2DM2**
13a, 13b J. Sutherland, Orch, R. Bonynge (VAI) ▣ **VAI69108**
13a, 13b M. Callas, Philh, A. Tonini (r1960) (EMI) Ⓓ **CDC7 49428-2**
13a, 13b M. Callas, Paris Cons, N. Rescigno (EMI) Ⓓ **CDC7 49005-2**
13a, 13b A. Galli-Curci, orch (r1924) (PEAR) Ⓓ **GEMMCD9450**
13a, 13b M. Callas, FRNO, G. Prêtre (pp1963) (MEMO) Ⓓ **HR4293/4**
13a, 13b J. Anderson, Paris Op Orch, M. Veltri (EMI) Ⓓ [2] **CZS7 67440-2**
13a, 13b M. Horne, Geneva Op Chor, SRO, H. Lewis (DECC) Ⓓ **421 891-2DA**
13a, 13b C. Bartoli, Venice La Fenice Chor, Venice La Fenice Orch, I. Martin (DECC) OO **436 075-5DH**
13a, 13b E. Gruberová, Munich RO, G. Kuhn (r c1980) (EMIN) Ⓓ **CD-EMX2234**
13a, 13b J. Anderson, Paris Op Orch, M. Veltri (pp1987) (12/88) (EMI) Ⓓ **CDC7 49067-2**
13a, 13b C. Bartoli, Venice La Fenice Chor, Venice La Fenice Orch, I. Martin (2/92) (DECC) Ⓓ **436 075-2DH**
13a, 14, 15, 30-33. J. Sutherland, M. Horne, L. Fyson, LSO, R. Bonynge (r1965) (10/93) (DECC) Ⓓ **436 303-2DA**
13b E. Stignani, orch (r c1938) (12/92) (TEST) Ⓓ **SBT1008**
14. J. Sutherland, M. Horne, Sydney Eliz Orch, R. Bonynge (MCEG) ▣ **VVD780**
14. G. Sakharova, Z. Dolukhanova, USSR Rad Orch, A. Kovalyov (1950s: Russ) (PREI) Ⓓ **89066**
14, 15. J. Sutherland, M. Horne, LSO, R. Bonynge (r1963) (DECC) Ⓓ **421 881-2DA**
14, 15. M. Caballé, S. Verrett, New Philh, A. Guadagno (5/92) (RCA) Ⓓ **GD60818**
15. J. Sutherland, M. Horne, Sydney Eliz Orch, R. Bonynge (DECC) ◐ **071 149-1DH**
(DECC) ▣ **071 149-3DH**
34. R. Blake, Ambrosian Sngrs, LSO, M. Valdes (12/89) (ARAB) Ⓓ **Z6612**
(12/89) (ARAB) ▭ **ABQC6612**
36-38. S. Ramey, WNO Chor, WNO Orch, G. Ferro (TELD) Ⓓ **9031-73242-2**
37. T. Pasero, EIAR Orch, U. Tansini (r1940) (4/95) (PREI) Ⓓ **89074**

Le **Siège de Corinthe, 'Assedio di Corinto'– tragédie lyrique: 3 acts (1826—Paris) (Lib. L. Balocchi)**

EXCERPTS: 1. Overture. ACT 1: 2. Ta noble voix seigneur; 3. Ta fille m'est promise; 4. La ville coupable; 5. Qu'à ma voix la victoire s'arrête; 6. Nous avons triomphé. ACT 2: 7. L'hymen lui donne une couronne; 8. Que vais-je devenir; 9. Rassure-toi mon pouvoir t'environne; 10. Air de danse; 11. Divin prophète entends nos voeux; 12. Il est mon frère; 13. Corinthe nous défie. ACT 3: 14. Avançons, oui ces murs; 15. Oh toi qui tout révère; 16. Grand Dieu faut-il qu'un peuple qui t'adore; 17. Céleste providence; 18. Je viens de parcourir; 19. Répondons à ce cri de victoire; 20a. L'heure fatale approche; 20b. Juste ciel! ah, ta clémence est ma seule espérance; 21. Mais quels accens se font entendre.

Pamira B. Sills
Neocle S. Verrett
Maometto J. Diaz
Cleomene H. Theyard
Jero G. Howell
Omar R. Lloyd
Ismene D. Wallis
Adrasto G. Scano
Ambrosian Op Chor, LSO, T. Schippers (r1974: Ital) (4/93) (EMI) Ⓓ [3] **CMS7 64335-2**
Pamyra L. Serra
Mahomet II M. Lippi
Néocles M. Comencini
Cléomène D. Raffanti
Hiéros A. Gaforio
Adastre V. Martino
Omar F. Facini
Ismène F. Provvisionato
Prague Phil Chor, Genoa Carlo Felice Th Chor, Genoa Carlo Felice Th Orch, P. Olmi (pp1992) (5/93) (NUOV) Ⓓ [3] **7140/2**
1. Mexico St SO, E. Bátiz (ASV) Ⓓ **CDDCA857**
(ASV) ▭ **ZCDCA857**
1. Hanover Band, R. Goodman (r1994) (RCA) Ⓓ **09026 68139-2**
1. LSO, C. Abbado (5/88) (DG) Ⓓ **419 869-2GGA**
1. Plovdiv PO, R. Raychev (10/90) (LASE) Ⓓ **15 506**
(10/90) (LASE) ▭ **79 506**
1. ASMF, N. Marriner (r1976) (10/92) (PHIL) Ⓓ [3] **434 016-2PM3**
1. NBC SO, A. Toscanini (r1945) (11/92) (RCA) Ⓓ **GD60289**
1. Santa Cecilia Academy Orch, G. Cantelli (r1949) (7/93) (TEST) Ⓓ **SBT1017**
1. National PO, R. Chailly (r1984) (9/95) (DECC) Ⓓ [2] **443 850-2DF2**
5. S. Ramey, NY Concert Chorale, St Luke's Orch, R. Norrington (pp1992) (6/93) (EMI) ◐ **LDB491007-1**
(6/93) (EMI) ▣ **MVD491007-3**
5. S. Ramey, NY Concert Chorale, St Luke's Orch, R. Norrington (pp1992) (12/94) (EMI) Ⓓ **CDC7 54643-2**
11. Ambrosian Op Chor, LSO, T. Schippers (r1974: Ital) (EMI) Ⓓ [2] **CZS5 68559-2**
14. M. Horne, P. de Palma, La Scala Orch, T. Schippers (Ital: pp1969) (MEMO) Ⓓ [2] **HR4392/3**
14. D. Soffel, Swedish CO, M. Liljefors (pp1984; Ital) (4/93) (CPRI) Ⓓ **CAP21428**
14, 20a, 20b M. Horne, Ambrosian Op Chor, RPO, H. Lewis (Ital) (DECC) Ⓓ **421 306-2DA**
20a, 20b M. Caballé, RCA Italiana Op Chor, RCA Italiana Op Orch, C.F. Cillario (Ital) (11/92) (RCA) ▭ [2] **RK61044**
20a, 20b M. Caballé, RCA Italiana Op Chor, RCA Italiana Op Orch, C.F. Cillario (Ital) (11/92) (RCA) Ⓓ [2] **GD60941**
20a, 20b K. Ricciarelli, Lyon Op Chor, Lyon Op Orch, G. Ferro (r1989) (11/94) (VIRG) Ⓓ **CUV5 61139-2**

Sigismondo– opera: 2 acts (1814—Venice) (Lib. G Foppa)

Sigismondo S. Ganassi
Aldimira R. Ragatzu
Ladislao B. Lazzaretti
Aangilda N. Zanini
Ulderico; Zenovito G. Prestia
Radoski F. Pina
Trevigiano Autunno Chor, Rovigo Venezze Cons Orch, R. Bonynge (pp1992) (BONG) Ⓓ [2] **GB2131/2-2**

Il **Signor Bruschino (or Il figlio per azzardo)– farsa giocosa: 1 act (1813—Venice) (Lib. G. Foppa, after Chazet & Maurice Ourry)**

EXCERPTS: 1. Overture; 2a. Deh! tu m'assisti amore; 2b. Marianna! ... Voi signore?; 2c. Quanto è dolce a un'alma amante; 3. A voi lieto ritorno; 4. Ah se il colpo arrivo a fare; 5. A noi su, trasformiamoci; 6. Nel teatro del gran mondo; 7a. Ho trovato a Sofia un buon partito; 7b. Lasciatemi... che violenza!; 8. Per un figlio già pentito; 9a. Impaziente son io; 9b. Sì, tentiamo; 10. Ah donate il caro sposo; 11. Qui convien finirla; 12. Ho la testa, o è andata via?; 13. Va tutto ben; 14. È bel nodo, che due cori; 15. Ebben, ragion, dovere; 16. È tornato Filiberto.

Gaudenzio E. Dara
Bruschino padre A. Rinaldi
Sofia M. Devia
Florville D. Gonzalez
Filiberto A. Antoniozzi
Marianna N. Curiel
Bruschino figlio E. Favano
Commissario M. Farruggia
Turin RAI Orch, D. Renzetti (pp1988) (FONI) Ⓓ [2] **RFCD2002**
Gaudenzio B. Praticò
Bruschino padre N. de Carolis
Sofia P. Orciani
Florville L. Canonici
Filiberto P. Spagnoli
Marianna K. Lytting
Bruschino figlio; Commissario F. Massa
Turin PO, M. Viotti (r1988) (10/89) (CLAV) Ⓓ [2] **CD50-8904/5**
Gaudenzio A. Corbelli
Bruschino padre A. Rinaldi
Sofia A. Felle
Florville D. Kuebler
Filberto C. Feller
Marianna J. Hall
Bruschino figlio V. Gobbi
Commisario O. di Credico
Stuttgart RSO, G. Gelmetti, M. Hampe (11/91) (TELD) ◐ **9031-71482-6**
(11/91) (TELD) ▣ **9031-71482-3**
Gaudenzio J. Mahler
Bruschino padre J. Wolański
Sofia A. Słowakiewicz
Florville K. Myrlak
Filiberto D. Niemirowicz
Marianna H. Górzyńska
Bruschino figlio K. Moleda
Commissario B. Jaszkowski
Warsaw Chbr Op Orch, J. Kaspszyk (5/93) (PAVA) Ⓓ **ADW7158**
Gaudenzio S. Ramey
Bruschino padre C. Desderi
Sofia K. Battle
Florville F. Lopardo
Filiberto M. Pertusi
Marianna J. Larmore
Bruschino figlio; Commissario O. Arévalo
ECO, I. Marin (r1991) (12/93) (DG) Ⓓ **435 865-2GH**
1. Scottish CO, J.Laredo (NIMB) Ⓓ **NI5078**
1. Zagreb PO, M. Halász (NAXO) Ⓓ **8 550236**
1. National PO, R. Chailly (DECC) OO **400 049-5DH**
1. LCP, R. Norrington (EMI) OO **DCC7 54091-5**
1. LCP, R. Norrington (EMI) ◉ **MDC7 54091-8**
1. Mexico St SO, E. Bátiz (ASV) Ⓓ **CDDCA857**
(ASV) ▭ **ZCDCA857**
1. Minneapolis SO, A. Dorati (r1957) (MERC) Ⓓ **434 345-2MM**
1. RPO, Colin Davis (EMI) Ⓓ [2] **CES5 68541-2**
1. ASMF, N. Marriner (r1974) (PHIL) Ⓓ **446 196-2PM**

1. Philh, C.M. Giulini
(12/87) (EMI) Ⓓ **CDM7 69042-2**
1. LSO, C. Abbado
(5/88) (DG) Ⓓ **419 869-2GGA**
1. Chicago SO, F. Reiner
(9/90) (RCA) Ⓓ **GD60387**
1. LCP, R. Norrington
(4/91) (EMI) Ⓓ **CDC7 54091-2**
1. ASMF, N. Marriner (r1974)
(10/92) (PHIL) Ⓓ [3] **434 016-2PM3**
1. NBC SO, A. Toscanini (r1945)
(11/92) (RCA) Ⓓ **GD60289**
1. I. Seefried, M. Forrester, E. Haefliger, D. Fischer-Dieskau, Berlin St Hedwig's Cath Ch, BPO, F. Fricsay, H. Krebs, T. Varga, Berlin RIAS Chbr Ch, Berlin RIAS Orch, H. Geusser, W. Fugmann, M. Weber, G. Herzog, Berlin RSO, VPO, E. Grümmer, G. Pitzinger, H. Hotter, Y. Menuhin (r1951)
(11/94) (DG) Ⓓ [11] **445 400-2GDO10**
1. Berlin RIAS Orch, F. Fricsay (r1951)
(11/94) (DG) Ⓓ **445 406-2GDO**
1. National PO, R. Chailly (r1981)
(9/95) (DECC) Ⓓ [2] **443 850-2DF2**
2a-c R. Giménez, Scottish CO, M. Veltri
(8/88) (NIMB) Ⓓ **NI5106**
(NIMB) ▭ **NC5106**
10. D. Jones, CLS, R. Hickox
(2/91) (CHAN) Ⓓ **CHAN8865**
(2/91) (CHAN) ▭ **ABTD1480**

Tancredi– melodramma eroico: 2 acts (1813—Venice) (Lib. G. Rossi, after Voltaire)

EXCERPTS: 1. Overture. ACT 1: 2. Pace, onore, fede amore; 3. Se amistà verace; 4a. Più dolci e placide; 4b. Come dolce all'alma mia; 5. Amenaide sventurata!; 6a. Oh patria!; 6b. Di tanti palpiti; 7. E voi nella gran piazza; 8a. Andante, al gran tempi'; 8b. Pensa, pensa che sei mia figlia; 9a. Che feci! incauta!; 9b. L'aura che intorno spiri; 10. Amori scendete; 11. Alla gloria, al trionfo; 11e. Si, la patria si difenda; 12. Amici, Cavalieri; 13a. E morte infame; 13b. Ciel! che feci!; 13c. Ah! se giusto, o ciel. ACT 2: 14. Vedesti? L'indegna!; 15a. Io padre più non sono; 15b. Oh Dio! Crudel!; 15c. Ah! segnar invano; 16a. Trionfa, esulta; 16b. Tu che i miseri; 17a. Di mia vita infelice; 17b. No, che il morir non è; 18. Di già l'ora; 19. Fermate!; 20a. M'abbraccia, Argirio; 20b. Ah! se de'mali; 20c. Ecco le trome; 21. Ov'è? ... dov'è?; 22a. Gran Dio! Deh! tu proteggi; 22b. Giusto Dio; 23. Plaudite, o popoli; 24a. T'arresta; 24b. Lasciami: non t'ascolto; 24c. Ah! come mai quell'anima; 24d. Dunque? ... Addio; 25. Infelice Tancredi!; 26a. S'avverassero pure; 26b. Torni alfin; 27a. Dove son io?; 27b. Ah! che scordar; 27c. Regna il terror; 28a. Ecco, amici; 28b. Perchè turbar; 28c. Traitrice; 29. Quanti tormenti; 30a. Gran Dio!; 30b. Muore il prode; 30c. Oh Dio ... lasciarti; 30d. Amenaide ... serbami. REPLACEMENT ARIAS: 31a. A sospirato lido!; 31b. Dolci d'amor parole; 31c. Voce, che tenera; 32a. Qual suon? che miro?; 32b. Solamir d'Amenaide; 32c. Va, palese è troppo omai; 32d. E' questa la fede; 32e. Si, la patria si difenda.

Tancredi M. Horne
Amenaide L. Cuberli
Argirio E. Palacio
Orbazzano N. Zaccaria
Isaura B. Manca di Nissa
Roggiero P. Schuman
Venice La Fenice Chor, Venice La Fenice Orch, R. Weikert (pp1983)
(8/88) (SONY) Ⓓ [3] **S3K39073**
Tancredi P. Price
Amenaide H. Francis
Argirio K. Lewis
Orbazzano T. McDonnell
Isaura E. Stokes
Roggiero P. Jeffes
London Voices, Centre d'Action Musicale de l'Ouest Orch, J. Perras (pp1976)
(5/94) (ARIO) Ⓓ [3] **ARN368200**
Tancredi E. Podles
Amenaide S. Jo
Argirio S. Olsen
Orbazzano P. Spagnoli
Isaura A. M. di Micco
Roggiero L. Lendi
L. Baert
F. Coryn
E. Demeyere
Capella Brugensis, Collegium Instr Brugense, A. Zedda (r1994)
(11/95) (NAXO) Ⓓ [2] **8 660037/8**
1. Scottish CO, J.Laredo (NIMB) Ⓓ **NI5078**
1. BBC Wireless Military Band, B.W. O'Donnell (r1930) (BEUL) Ⓓ **2PD4**
1. Ricercar Acad, M. Ponseele (r1993; arr Legrand: Wind Ens) (RICE) Ⓓ **RIC126114**
1. ROHO, C. Rizzi (r1990)
(CONI) Ⓓ **75605 55004-2**
1. Plovdiv PO, R. Raychev
(10/90) (LASE) Ⓓ **15 506**
(10/90) (LASE) ▭ **79 506**
1. ASMF, N. Marriner (r1974)
(10/92) (PHIL) Ⓓ [3] **434 016-2PM3**
1. Black Dyke Mills Band, T. Walmsley (arr Rimmer) (7/93) (CHAN) Ⓓ **CHAN4505**
(CHAN) ▭ **BBTD4505**
1. Berlin RIAS Orch, F. Fricsay (r1952)
(11/94) (DG) Ⓓ **445 406-2GDO**
1. I. Seefried, M. Forrester, E. Haefliger, D. Fischer-Dieskau, Berlin St Hedwig's Cath Ch, BPO, F. Fricsay, H. Krebs, T. Varga, Berlin RIAS Chbr Ch, Berlin RIAS Orch, H. Geusser, W. Fugmann, M. Weber, G. Herzog, Berlin RSO, VPO, E. Grümmer, G. Pitzinger, H. Hotter, Y. Menuhin (r1952)
(11/94) (DG) Ⓓ [11] **445 400-2GDO10**
1. Atlanta SO, Y. Levi (r1993)
(11/94) (TELA) Ⓓ **CD80334**
1. National PO, R. Chailly (r1984)
(9/95) (DECC) Ⓓ [2] **443 850-2DF2**
4a, 4b K. Ricciarelli, Lyon Op Chor, Lyon Op Orch, G. Ferro (r1989)
(11/94) (VIRG) Ⓓ **CUV5 61139-2**
6a, 6b M. Horne, SRO, H. Lewis
(DECC) Ⓓ **421 306-2DA**
6a, 6b G. Simionato, Milan RAI SO, N. Sanzogno (pp1956) (MEMO) Ⓓ [2] **HR4386/7**
6a, 6b C. Bartoli, Vienna Volksoper Orch, G. Patanè (9/89) (DECC) Ⓓ **425 430-2DH**
(9/89) (DECC) ▭ **425 430-4DH**
6a, 6b M. Caballé, RCA Italiana Op Orch, C.F. Cillario (11/92) (RCA) Ⓓ [2] **GD60941**
6a, 6b, 27a, 27b J. Kowalski, Berlin RSO, H. Fricke (CAPR) **OO 70 416**
6a, 6b, 27a, 27b J. Kowalski, Berlin RSO, H. Fricke (CAPR) **O 80 416**
6a, 6b, 27a, 27b J. Kowalski, Berlin RSO, H. Fricke (10/92) (CAPR) Ⓓ **10 416**
6b M. Horne, SRO, H. Lewis
(DECC) Ⓓ **436 133-2DWO**
6b T. Berganza, Seville SO, E. Garcia-Asensio (pp1991) (RCA) Ⓓ **RD61191**
6b M. Horne, SRO, H. Lewis (r1965)
(DECC) Ⓓ **436 300-2DX**
(DECC) ▭ **436 300-4DX**
6b T. Berganza, Seville SO, E. Garcia-Asensio (pp1991) (RCA) **OO 09026 61191-5**
6b Combattimento (MERI) Ⓓ **CDE84196**
(MERI) ▭ **KE77196**
6b D. Soffel, Swedish CO, M. Liljefors (pp1984)
(4/93) (CPRI) Ⓓ **CAP21428**
15b, 15c R. Giménez, Scottish Phil Sngrs, Scottish CO, M. Veltri (8/88) (NIMB) Ⓓ **NI5106**
(NIMB) ▭ **NC5106**
22a, 22b K. Battle, Ambrosian Op Chor, LPO, B. Campanella (r1991) (DG) **OO 435 866-5CH**
22a, 22b K. Battle, Ambrosian Op Chor, LPO, B. Campanella (r1991)
(12/93) (DG) Ⓓ **435 866-2GH**

Torvaldo e Dorliska– dramma semiserio: 2 acts (1815—Rome) (Lib. C. Sterbini)

EXCERPTS: 1. Overture. ACT ONE: 2. È un bel dir che tutto al mondo; 3. Dunque invano; 4. Il padrone? Ben tornato eccellenza!; 5. Ormondo, la mia gente; 6. Dove son? chi m'aita; 7. Oh, giusto Ciel; 8. Ah! per pietà; 9. Ella... oh Ciel!; 10. Dove corri, sconsigliata?; 11. Ella più non mi fugge; 12a. Tutto è silenzio; 12b. Fra un istante; 13. Finché niun qui m'osserva; 14. Ah qual raggio di speranza; 15. A Dorliska tu n'andrai; 16. Dunqu... Andiamo; 17. Delle nostre notturne bagattelle; 18. Sopra quell'albero; 19. Oh! via, Signora mia; 20. Immota, stolida; 21. Ella manca. ACT TWO: 22. Bravi, bravi; quà venite; 23. Oh, Giorgio; 24. Dille, che solo a lei; 25. No, pentirsi non giova; 26. Ferma, costante, immobile; 27. Ah!... morir pel caro sposo; 28. Insensata!... e non vede; 29. Una voce lusinghiera; 30. Ah non posso!; 31. Dunque tu vuoi ch'io parta?; 32. Quest'ultimo addio; 33. Alme ree! tremate! invano; 34. Vieni; 35. Cedi... 36. Grazie al destin pietoso.

Torvaldo E. Palacio
Dorliska F. Pediconi
Duke of Ordow S. Antonucci
Giorgio M. Buda
Carlotta N. Ciliento
Ormondo A. Maran
Cantemus, Lugano Rad & TV Ch, Lugano Rad & TV Orch, M. de Bernart (pp1992)
(11/94) (AKAD) Ⓓ [2] **2CDAK12**
1. ASMF, N. Marriner (r1979)
(10/92) (PHIL) Ⓓ [3] **434 016-2PM3**
1. National PO, R. Chailly (r1984)
(9/95) (DECC) Ⓓ [2] **443 850-2DF2**
12a, 12b C. Merritt, Philh, D. Parry
(10/90) (OPRA) Ⓓ [3] **ORCH103**

Il Turco in Italia– dramma buffo: 2 acts (1814—Milan) (Lib. F. Romani)

EXCERPTS: 1. Overture (Sinfonia). ACT 1: 2a. Nostra patria è il mondo intero; 2b. Ho da far un dramma buffo; 3a. Ah! se di questi zingari l'arrivo; 3b. Vado in traccia d'una Zingara; 3c. Ah! mia moglie; 4a. Brava! Intesi ogni cosa; 4b. Non si dà follia maggiore; 4c. Voga, voga; 4e. Bella Italia, alfin ti miro; 4f. Serva...Servo; 4g. Della Zingara amante; 4h. Un vago sembiante; 4i. Amici...Soccorretemi; 5. Un marito scimunito!; 6a. Olà: tosto il caffè; 6b. Siete dei Turchi; 6c. Io stupisco, mi sorprende; 6d. Come! Sì grave torto; 7a. Sono arrivato tardi; 7b. Per piacere alla signora; 7c. Non mia vita, mio tesoro; 8a. Ho quasi del mio dramma; 8b. Gran maraviglie; 8c. Per la fuga è tutto lesto; 8d. Perchè mai se son tradito; 8e. Evviva d'amore; 8f. Chi servir non brama amor; 8g. Qui mia moglie ha da venire; 8h. Ah! che il cor non m'ingannava; 8i. Vada via: si guardi bene; 8j. Quando il vento. ACT 2: 9a. Via...cosa serve?; 9b. D'un bell'uso in Turchia; 9c. Se Fiorilla di vender bramate; 9d. Ed invece di pagarla; 10a. Credeva che questa scena; 10b. Non v'è piacer perfetto; 11a. Che Turca impertinente!; 11b. Credete alla femmine; 11c. In Italia certamente; 12a. Sentite!; 12b. Intesi: ah! tutto intesi; 12c. Oh! che fatica! che cervello duro!; 12d. Zaida infelice!; 12e. Ah! sarebbe troppo dolce; 13. Amor la danza mova; 14a. Eccomi qui; 14b. Oh! quardate che accidente; 14c. Dunque seguitemi; 14d. Questo vecchio maledetto; 15a. Benedetta la festa; 15b. I vostri cenci vi mando; 15c. Squallida veste; 15d. Caro padre, madre amata; 16a. Che dramma!; 16b. Son la vite campo appassita; 16c. Rida a voi sereno il Cielo.

Selim N. Rossi-Lemen
Fiorilla M. Callas
Geronio F. Calabrese
Narciso N. Gedda
Zaida J. Gardino
Albazar P. de Palma
Prosdocimo M. Stabile
La Scala Chor, La Scala Orch, G. Gavazzeni (r1954)
(12/87) (EMI) Ⓓ [2] **CDS7 49344-2**
Selim S. Ramey
Fiorilla M. Caballé
Geronio E. Dara
Narciso E. Palacio
Zaida J. Berbié
Albazar P. Barbacini
Prosdocimo L. Nucci
Ambrosian Op Chor, National PO, R. Chailly (r1981)
(9/89) (SONY) Ⓓ [2] **S2K37859**
Selim S. Alaimo
Fiorilla S. Jo
Geronio E. Fissore
Narciso R. Giménez
Zaida S. Mentzer
Albazar P. Bronder
Prosdocimo A. Corbelli
Ambrosian Op Chor, ASMF, N. Marriner
(12/92) (PHIL) Ⓓ [2] **434 128-2PH2**
1. National PO, R. Chailly
(DECC) **OO 400 049-5DH**
1. Mexico St SO, E. Bátiz
(ASV) Ⓓ **CDDCA857**
(ASV) ▭ **ZCDCA857**
1. ASMF, N. Marriner (r1974)
(PHIL) Ⓓ **446 196-2PM**
1. ASMF, N. Marriner (r1974)
(10/92) (PHIL) Ⓓ [3] **434 016-2PM3**
1. National PO, R. Chailly (r1981)
(9/95) (DECC) Ⓓ [2] **443 850-2DF2**
1, 3b, 4b, 4c, 4e, 7b, 8b, 8d, 8e, 8h, 9b, 10a, 10b, 12c, 12e, 14b, 15c, 16b, 16c M. Caballé, J. Berbié, E. Palacio, P. Barbacini, E. Dara, L. Nucci, S. Ramey, Ambrosian Op Chor, National PO, R. Chailly (r1981) (SONY) Ⓓ **SMK53505**
4b M. Caballé, National PO, R. Chailly
(SONY) Ⓓ **SMK48155**
(SONY) ▭ **SMT48155**

4b M. Caballé, National PO, R. Chailly ( ) (SONY) ◘ **SM48155**
4e, 8c, 11b S. Bruscantini, G. Sciutti, R. Mattioli, Milan RAI Chor, Milan RAI SO, N. Sanzogno (pp1958) (MEMO) Ⓓ [2] **HR4300/1**
11a-c M. Callas, F. Calabrese, La Scala Orch, G. Gavazzeni (r1954) (2/90) (EMI) Ⓓ [4] **CMS7 63244-2**
12b R. Blake, LSO, J. McCarthy (4/88) (ARAB) Ⓓ **Z6582**
(4/88) (ARAB) ▭ **ABQC6582**

Ugo re d'Italia– opera ("lost' opera for London, 1825)
Vieni, o cara B. Ford, P. Nilon, Philh, D. Parry (8/95) (OPRA) Ⓓ [3] **ORCH104**

Il viaggio a Reims (or L'albergo del giglio d'oro)– dramma giocoso: 1 act (1825—Paris) (Lib. L. Balocchi)
EXCERPTS: 1. Overture. 2a. Presto, presto, su coraggio; 2b. Benché grazie al mio talento; 3. Di vaghi raggi adorno; 4a. Partire io pur vorrei; 4b. Amabil Contessina; 4c. Che accede; 5a. Ahimè! sta in gran pericolo; 5b. Partir, oh ciel! desio; 5c. Che miro! ah! qual sorpresa; 5d. Eh! senti, mastro Antonio; 6a. Sì, di matti una gran gabbia; 6b. La mia quota a voi consegno; 6c. Donna ingrata; 6d. Naturale è l'impazienza; 7. Non pavento alcun periglio; 8. Arpa gentil; 9. Zitti. Non canta più; 10a. Ah! perchè la conobbi?; 10b. Invan strappar dal core; 11. Milord, una parola; 12a. Sola ritrovo alfin la bella Dea; 12b. Nel suo divin sembiante; 12c. Bravo il signor Ganimede!; 13a. Medaglie incomparabili; 13b. Vedeste il Cavaliere?; 14a. Ah! A tal colpo inaspettato; 14b. Signor, ecco una lettera; 14c. Son qua, cosa comanda?; 15a. Di che son reo?; 15b. D'alma celeste, oh Dio; 15c. Madama qui mi manda; 16a. Or che regna; 16b. Ai prodi guerrieri; 16c. Onore, gloria ed alto omaggio; 16d. Omaggio all'Augusto Duce; 16e. Dell'aurea pianta; 16f. Madre el nuovo Enrico; 16g. Più vivace e più fecondo; 17a. Corinna, or tacca a voi; 17b. All'ombra amena; 18. Viva il diletto augusto Regnator.

Corinna	C. Gasdia
Madama Cortese	K. Ricciarelli
Contessa di Folleville	L. Cuberli
Marchesa Melibea	L.V. Terrani
Cavalier Belfiore	E. Gimenez
Conte di Libenskof	F. Araiza
Lord Sidney	S. Ramey
Don Profondo	R. Raimondi
Barone di Trombonok	E. Dara
Don Prudenzio	G. Surian
Don Alvaro	L. Nucci

Prague Phil Chor, COE, C. Abbado (pp1984) (1/86) (DG) Ⓓ [2] **415 498-2GH2**

Corinna	S. McNair
Madama Cortese	C. Studer
Contessa di Folleville	L. Serra
Marchesa Melibea	L.V. Terrani
Cavalier Belfiore	R. Giménez
Conte di Libenskof	W. Matteuzzi
Lord Sidney	S. Ramey
Don Profondo	R. Raimondi
Barone di Trombonok	E. Dara
Don Prudenzio	G. Surian
Don Alvaro	L. Gallo

Berlin Rad Chor, BPO, C. Abbado (pp1992) (12/93) (SONY) Ⓓ [2] **S2K53336**
1. National PO, R. Chailly (DECC) ОО **400 049-5DH**
1. VPO, M. Sargent (EMI) Ⓓ [2] **CES5 68541-2**
1. Plovdiv PO, R. Raychev (10/90) (LASE) Ⓓ **15 520**
(10/90) (LASE) ▭ **79 520**
1. ASMF, N. Marriner (r1976) (10/92) (PHIL) Ⓓ [3] **434 016-2PM3**
1. National PO, R. Chailly (r1981) (9/95) (DECC) Ⓓ [2] **443 850-2DF2**
5b K. Battle, Ambrosian Op Chor, LPO, B. Campanella (r1991) (DG) ОО **435 866-5CH**
5b K. Battle, Ambrosian Op Chor, LPO, B. Campanella (r1991) (12/93) (DG) Ⓓ **435 866-2GH**
10a, 10b S. Ramey, WNO Orch, G. Ferro (TELD) Ⓓ **9031-73242-2**
14a M. Fortuna, D. Voigt, M. Horne, K. Kuhlmann, M. Lerner, F. von Stade, R. Blake, C. Estep, C. Merritt, T. Hampson, J. Opalach, H. Runey, G. Hogan, S. Ramey, NY Concert Chorale, St Luke's Orch, R. Norrington (pp1992) (6/93) (EMI) ◖ **LDB491007-1**
(6/93) (EMI) ▣ **MVD491007-3**
14a, 14b M. Fortuna, D. Voigt, M. Horne, K. Kuhlmann, M. Lerner, F. von Stade, R. Blake, C. Estep, C. Merritt, T. Hampson, J. Opalach, H. Runey, G. Hogan, S. Ramey, St Luke's Orch, R. Norrington (pp1992) (12/94) (EMI) Ⓓ **CDC7 54643-2**
14b C. Gonzales, R. Ragatzu, O. Romanko, M. Bacelli, S. Pasqualini, E. Ferretti, R. Wörle, M. Biscotti, G. Saks, A. Silvestrelli, Ernst-Senff Chbr Chor, Berlin RSO, R. Buckley (SCHW) Ⓓ [2] **314052**
15b J. Zoon, H. de Vries, London Studio SO (arr Vrijens) (PHIL) Ⓓ **438 940-2PH**

Zelmira– dramma: 2 acts (1822—Naples) (Lib. A.L. Tottola, after Dormont de Belloy)
EXCERPTS: 1. Overture. ACT 1: 2. Oh, sciagura!; 3. Che vidi amici!; 4. Della tenda real; 5. Non fuggirmi ... 6. Ah! gia trascorse il dì; 7. Ma m'illude il desio?; 8. S'intessano agli allori; 9a. Terra amica; 9b. Godi, o Signor; 10. O cielo! Egli è fra suoi; 11. Dimmi ... al tuo padre; 12. T'intendo, istabil Diva; 13. Mentre qual fiera ingorda; 14. Di luce sfavillante; 15a. Emma fedel; 15b. Perche mi guardi; 16. Si sparga di fiori; 17. Si figli miei; 18. Il figlio mio; 19. La sorpresa ... lo stupore; 20. Alla strage ognor ti guida. ACT 2: 21a. Gran cose, o Re!; 21b. Pian, piano inoltrisi; 22. Ciel, pietoso, ciel clemente; 23a. A che difendi; 23b. In estasi di gioja; 24. Chi sciolse i lacci miei; 25. Ne lacci miei cadesti; 26. Di Azor le ceneri; 27. Perigliosi; 28. Riedi al soglio; 29. Fa piu grato. ADDITIONAL ARIA: 30. Da te spero.

Zelmira	C. Gasdia
Emma	B. Fink
Ilo	W. Matteuzzi
Antenore	C. Merritt
Polidoro	J. Garcia
Leucippo	B. Senator
Eacide	V. Midgley
High Priest	L. Fyson

Ambrosian Sngrs, Solisti Veneti, C. Scimone (6/90) (ERAT) Ⓓ [2] **2292-45419-2**
Prchè mi guardi, e piangi? E. Harrhy, D. Jones, Philh, D. Parry (8/95) (OPRA) Ⓓ [3] **ORCH104**
8, 9a R. Blake, Ambrosian Sngrs, LSO, M. Valdes (12/89) (ARAB) Ⓓ **Z6612**
(12/89) (ARAB) ▭ **ABQC6612**
9a R. Blake, NY Concert Chorale, St Luke's Orch, R. Norrington (pp1992) (6/93) (EMI) ◖ **LDB491007-1**
(6/93) (EMI) ▣ **MVD491007-3**
9a R. Blake, NY Concert Chorale, St Luke's Orch, R. Norrington (pp1992) (12/94) (EMI) Ⓓ **CDC7 54643-2**
15b D. Voigt, K. Kuhlmann, St Luke's Orch, R. Norrington (pp1992) (6/93) (EMI) ◖ **LDB491007-1**
(6/93) (EMI) ▣ **MVD491007-3**
28. C. Bartoli, Venice La Fenice Chor, Venice La Fenice Orch, I. Martin (DECC) ОО **436 075-5DH**
28. C. Bartoli, Venice La Fenice Chor, Venice La Fenice Orch, I. Martin (2/92) (DECC) Ⓓ **436 075-2DH**

ROUSSEL, Albert (Charles Paul Marie) *(1869–1937) France*

Padmâvatî– opera-ballet: 2 acts (1923—Paris) (Lib. L. Laloy)

Padmâvatî	M. Horne
Ratan-Sen	N. Gedda
Alaouddin	J. Van Dam
Nakamti	J. Berbié
Brahmmin	C. Burles
Gora	M. Vento
Badal	L. Dale

Orféon Donostiarra, Toulouse Capitole Orch, M. Plasson (9/88) (EMI) Ⓓ [2] **CDS7 47891-8**

RUBINSTEIN , Anton (Grigor'yevich) *(1829–1894) Russia*

The Demon– opera: 3 acts (1875—St Petersburg) (Lib. Viskovatov)
EXCERPTS; 1. Overture. ACT 1: 2. Accursed world!; 3. Thou wilt be the world's queen; 4. On desire's soft, fleeting wing. ACT 2: 5. Lezginka (Caucasian Dance); 6. Ballet Music; 7. Do not weep, my child (Demon's aria); 8. On the airy ocean. ACT 3: 9. Calm and clear is the night; 10. I am he whom you called; 11. I swear by the eternal truth.
Night chorus Bolshoi Th Chor, Bolshoi Th Orch, A. Chistiakov (CDM) Ⓓ **LDC288 022**
Sinodal's aria A. Labinsky, anon (r1905) (7/93) (SYMP) Ⓓ **SYMCD1105**
Soaring like a falcon L. Sobinov, orch (r1910) (3/95) (NIMB) Ⓓ **NI7865**
2. A. Ivanov, Bolshoi Th Orch, S. Samosud (r1940s) (PREI) Ⓓ **89067**
2. L. Sibiriakov, orch (r1912) (6/93) (PEAR) Ⓓ [3] **GEMMCDS9007/9(2)**
4. A. Bogdanovich, anon (r1903) (6/93) (PEAR) Ⓓ [3] **GEMMCDS9007/9(1)**
7. F. Chaliapin, orch (r1911) (PREI) Ⓓ **89030**
7. M. Battistini, anon (r1903: Ital) (PEAR) Ⓓ **GEMMCD9016**
7. F. Chaliapin, orch (r1911) (6/88) (EMI) Ⓓ **CDH7 61009-2**
7. E. Giraldoni, anon (r1902) (6/90) (SYMP) Ⓓ **SYMCD1073**
7. M. Reizen, Bolshoi Th Orch, V. Nebolsin (r1955) (12/92) (PREI) Ⓓ **89059**
7. T. Ruffo, orch (r1922) (2/93) (PREI) Ⓓ [3] **89303(2)**
7, 10. I. Tartakov, anon (r1901) (6/93) (PEAR) Ⓓ [3] **GEMMCDS9997/9(1)**
7, 8. N. Shevelev, anon (r1901) (6/93) (PEAR) Ⓓ [3] **GEMMCDS9007/9(2)**
7, 8, 10. A. Safiulin, Soviet Cinema Orch, E. Khachaturian (r1990) (CDM) Ⓓ [2] **LDC288 005/6**
(CDM) ▭ **KC488 005**
7, 8, 10. D. Hvorostovsky, Kirov Th Orch, V. Gergiev (r1993) (5/94) (PHIL) Ⓓ **438 872-2PH**
(5/94) (PHIL) ▭ **438 872-4PH**
8. F. Chaliapin, M. Kovalenko, orch (r1911) (PREI) Ⓓ **89030**
8. A. Ivanov, Bolshoi Th Orch, K. Kondrashin (r1940s) (PREI) Ⓓ **89067**
8. P. Orlov, anon (r1902) (6/93) (PEAR) Ⓓ [3] **GEMMCDS9001/3(1)**

Dmitry Donskoy– opera: 3 acts (1852—St. Petersburg) (Lib. V A Sollogub & V R Zotov, after Ozerov)
EXCERPTS -; 1. Overture.
1. Bucharest George Enescu PO, H. Andreescu (MARC) Ⓓ **8 223320**

Feramors– opera: 3 acts (1863—Dresden) (Lib. J. Rodenberg, after T. Moore)
Moscow St SO, I. Golovshin (r1993) (10/94) (RUSS) Ⓓ **RDCD11356**

Kalashnikov the Merchant– opera: 3 acts (1880—St Petersburg) (Lib. N. Kulikov, after Lermontov)
Merchant's aria N. Shevelev, anon (r1901) (6/93) (PEAR) Ⓓ [3] **GEMMCDS9007/9(2)**

Nero– opera: 4 acts (1879—Hamburg) (Lib. Barbier)
EXCERPTS: 1. Vindex's Epithalamium: I sing to you, Hymen divine!.
Epithalamium A. Ivanov, Bolshoi Th Orch (r1940s) (PREI) Ⓓ **89067**
Imen! Imen! P. Lisitsian, Bolshoi Th Orch, A. Melik-Pashayev (r1957) (8/93) (PREI) Ⓓ **89061**
Invan, invan F. Marconi, anon (r1907: Ital) (10/90) (SYMP) Ⓓ **SYMCD1069**
Invan, invan F. Marconi, S. Cottone (r1903: Ital) (10/90) (SYMP) Ⓓ **SYMCD1069**
Oh, light of the day E. Caruso, orch, J. Pasternack (2 vers: French: r1917) (7/91) (RCA) Ⓓ [12] **GD60495(6)**
Oh, light of the day E. Caruso, orch, J. Pasternack (2 vers: French: r1917) (10/91) (PEAR) Ⓓ [3] **EVC4(1)**
Oh, light of the day E. Caruso, orch (r1917: Fr) (7/95) (NIMB) Ⓓ **NI7866**
Zulima's Bacchic song E. Zbrueva, chor, orch (r1911) (6/93) (PEAR) Ⓓ [3] **GEMMCDS9004/6(2)**
1. D. Hvorostovsky, Kirov Th Orch, V. Gergiev (r1993) (5/94) (PHIL) Ⓓ **438 872-2PH**
(5/94) (PHIL) ▭ **438 872-4PH**

RUGGI, Francesco Jnr *(1826–1901) Italy*

I due Ciabattini– opera (1860—Naples) (Lib. A Spadetta)
Arsenico! Veleno! G. De Luca, F. Corradetti, anon (r1907) (PEAR) Ⓓ [3] **GEMMCDS9159(2)**

Arsenico! Veleno! G. De Luca, F. Corradetti, anon (r1907) (6/94) (IRCC) ① **IRCC-CD808**

SACCHINI, Antonio *(1730–1786) Italy*

La **contadina in Corte– opera buffa: 2 acts (1765—Rome) (Lib. N Tassi)**

Sandrina C. Forte
Tancia S. Rigacci
Ruggiero E. Palacio
Berto G. Gatti
Sassari SO, G. Catalucci (pp1991)
(1/95) (BONG) ① [2] **GB2145/6-2**

SACRATI, Francesco *(1605–1650) Italy*

Proserpina rapita– opera (1644—Venice)
E dove t'aggiri V. de los Angeles, G. Moore (r1960) (4/94) (EMI) ① [4] **CMS5 65061-2(2)**

SAINT-SAËNS, (Charles) Camille *(1835–1921) France*

Ascanio– opéra: 5 acts (1890—Paris) (Lib. Gallet, after P Meierice)
EXCERPTS: 1. Enfants, je ne vous en veux; 2. Airs de ballet: 2a. Adagio et Variation; 2g. Valse-finale.
1. J. Lassalle, anon (r1902)
(9/91) (SYMP) ① **SYMCD1089**
2. W. Bennett, ECO, S. Bedford
(10/89) (ASV) ① **CDDCA652**
2. S. Milan, CLS, R. Hickox
(10/90) (CHAN) ① **CHAN8840**
2. K. Jones, C. Edwards (r1993; arr fl/pf)
(10/94) (CONI) ① [2] **CDCF905**
2a J. Galway, National PO, C. Gerhardt
(RCA) ① **GD60924**
2a R. Aitken, E. Westenholz (r1980)
(BIS) ① **BIS-CD166**
2g LPO, G. Simon (r1993)
(CALA) ① **CACD1015**
(CALA) ⊟ **CAMC1015**

Les **Barbares– opera: 3 acts (1901—Paris) (Lib. V. Sardou & P. B. Gheusi)**
N'oublions pas les sacrifices C. Rousselière, anon (r1903) (8/92) (IRCC) ① **IRCC-CD802**

Etienne Marcel– opera: 4 acts (1879—Lyon) (Lib. L. Gallet)
O beaux rêves évanouis J. Hammond, Philh, W. Susskind (r1953)
(12/92) (TEST) ① **SBT1013**

Henry VIII– opéra: 4 acts (1883—Paris) (Lib. L Détroyat & A Silvestre)
EXCERPTS: ACT 1: 4. Qui donc commande, quand il aime. ACT 2: 4b. Qui donc commande, quand il aime. ACT 2: 14. Chère Anne; 18. Ballet-divertissement: 18a. Introduction—Entré des Clans; 18b. Idylle écossaise; 18c. La fête du houblon; 18d. Danse de la gitane; 18e. Scherzetto; 18f. Gigue et Finale; 22a. O souvenirs cruel!.

Henry VIII P. Rouillon
Catherine d'Aragon M. Command
Anne Boleyn L. Vignon
Don Gomez de Feria A. Gabriel
Duc de Norfolk P. Bohée
Comte de Surrey A. Laiter
Cardinal Campeggio G. Serkoyan
Cranmer J-M. Loisel
Rouen Théâtre des Arts Chor, French Lyrique Orch, A. Guingal (pp1991)
(4/93) (CHNT) ① [3] **LDC278 1083/5**
18. NY Nat SO, W. Damrosch (r1929)
(SCHW) ① [2] **311162**
18d LSO, R. Bonynge (r1971)
(DECC) ① **444 108-2DA**
22a F. Pollet, Montpellier PO, C. Diederich (r1989) (ERAT) ① **4509-98502-2**

La **princesse jaune– opéra-comique: 1 act, Op. 30 (18971—Paris) (Lib. L. Gallet)**
EXCERPTS: 1. Overture.
1. LPO, G. Simon (r1993)
(CALA) ① **CACD1016**
(CALA) ⊟ **CAMC1016**

Samson et Dalila– opera: 3 acts (1877—Weimar) (Lib. F. Lemaire)
ACT 1: 1. Dieu d'Israël!; 2. Arrêtez, ô mes frères; 3. Qui donc élève ici la voix?; 4. Que vois-je!; 5. Maudite à jamais; 6. Hymne de joie; 7. Je viens célébrer la victoire; 8. Danse des prêtresses de Dagon; 9. Printemps qui commence. ACT 2: 10. Prelude; 11a. Samson, recherchant; 11b. Amour! viens aider ma faiblesse!; 12a. J'ai gravi la montagne; 12b. La victoire facile; 13a. En ces lieux, malgré moi; 13b. Mon coeur s'ouvre à ta voix. ACT3: 14. Vois ma misère; 15. L'aube qui blanchit; 16. Bacchanale; 17. Gloire à Dagon.

Samson J. Vickers
Dalila S. Verrett
Priest J. Summers
Abimelech J. Tomlinson
Old Hebrew G. Howell
Messenger J. Dobson
First Philistine M. Davies
Second Philistine M. Best
ROH Chor, ROHO, Colin Davis, E. Moshinsky
(CAST) ▣ **CVI2026**

Samson P. Domingo
Dalila S. Verrett
Priest W. Brendel
Abimelech A. Voketaitis
Old Hebrew K. Langan
Messenger R. Tate
San Francisco Op Chor, San Francisco Op Orch, J. Rudel, N. Joel
(MCEG) ▣ **VVD393**

Samson J. Vickers
Dalila R. Gorr
Priest E. Blanc
Abimelech A. Diakov
Old Hebrew A. Diakov
Messenger R. Corazza
First Philistine J. Potier
Second Philistine J-P. Hurteau
R. Duclos Ch, Paris Op Orch, G. Prêtre
(7/88) (EMI) ① [2] **CDS7 47895-8**

Samson J. Carreras
Dalila A. Baltsa
Priest J. Summers
Abimelech S. Estes
Old Hebrew P. Burchuladze
Messenger R. Swensen
Philistine I D.G. Smith
Philistine II U. Malmberg
Bavarian Rad Chor, BRSO, Colin Davis (r1989)
(1/91) (PHIL) ① [2] **426 243-2PH2**

Samson P. Domingo
Dalila E. Obraztsova
Priest R. Bruson
Abimelech P. Thau
Old Hebrew R. Lloyd
Messenger G. Friedmann
Philistine I C. Zaharia
Philistine II M. Huber
Paris Orch Chor, Paris Orch, D. Barenboim
(11/91) (DG) ① [2] **413 297-2GX2**

Samson P. Domingo
Dalila W. Meier
Priest A. Fondary
Abimelech J-P. Courtis
Old Hebrew S. Ramey
Messenger C. Papis
Philistine I D. Galvez-Vallejo
Philistine II F. Harismendy
Paris Opéra-Bastille Chor, Paris Opéra-Bastille Orch, Myung-Whun Chung
(2/93) (EMI) ① [2] **CDS7 54470-2**

Samson J. Luccioni
Dalila H. Bouvier
Priest P. Cabanel
Abimelech C. Cambon
Paris Op Chor, Paris Op Orch, L. Fourestier (r1946)
(9/95) (EMI) ① [2] **CMS5 65263-2**

Dalila's Aria A. Milcheva, Bulgarian RSO, V. Stefanov (r1970s) (FORL) ① **UCD16741**
Excs R. Anday, R. Maison, Vienna St Op Orch, H. Reichenberger (pp1933)
(12/94) (SCHW) ① [2] **314542**
Grande fantasie LPO, G. Simon (r1993: orch arr A Luigini) (CALA) ① **CACD1016**
(CALA) ⊟ **CAMC1016**
1, 2, 5, 9, 11a, 13a, 13b, 14, 16, 17. A. Baltsa, J. Carreras, J. Summers, S. Estes, P. Burchuladze, R. Swensen, D.G. Smith, U. Malmberg, Bavarian Rad Chor, BRSO, Colin Davis (r1989)
(PHIL) ① **438 504-2PH**
2. P. Franz, orch (r1911) (PREI) ① **89099**
2. F. Tamagno, Anon (pf) (r1903-04)
(2/92) (OPAL) ① **OPALCD9846**
2. L. Escalais, anon (r1905)
(12/93) (SYMP) ① **SYMCD1126**
2. G. Zenatello, orch (r1908: Ital)
(5/94) (PEAR) ① [4] **GEMMCDS9073(1)**
2. G. Zenatello, orch (r1908: Ital)
(5/94) (SYMP) ① **SYMCD1168**
2, 13b M. Gilion, N. Frascani, orch (r c1909: Ital)
(BONG) ① **GB1076-2**
2, 3(pt) A. Paoli, orch (Ital: r1907)
(PREI) ① **89998**
2, 5, 9, 11a, 11b, 13b, 14, 16, 17. J. Vickers, R. Gorr, E. Blanc, R. Corazza, J. Potier, J-P. Hurteau, R. Duclos Ch, Paris Op Orch, G. Prêtre
(EMI) ① **CDM7 63935-2**
3(pt) A. Paoli, chor, orch (r1907: Ital)
(4/94) (EMI) ① [3] **CHS7 64860-2(2)**
5. C. Formichi, orch, H. Harty (r1924)
(11/94) (PREI) ① **89055**
7. E. Caruso, L. Homer, M. Journet, orch, J. Pasternack (r1919) (RCA) ① **09026 61244-2**
7. L. Homer, E. Caruso, M. Journet, orch, J. Pasternack (r1919)
(7/91) (RCA) ① [12] **GD60495(6)**
7. L. Homer, E. Caruso, M. Journet, orch, J. Pasternack (r1919)
(10/91) (PEAR) ① [3] **EVC4(2)**
8, 16. RPO, T. Beecham (r1958/9)
(EMI) ① **CDM7 63412-2**
9. G. Simionato, Santa Cecilia Academy Orch, F. Previtali (r1956) (DECC) ① **440 406-2DM**
9. M. Callas, FRNO, G. Prêtre (r1961)
(EMI) ① **CDC5 55016-2**
9. C. Supervia, orch, G. Cloëz (r1931)
(NIMB) ① **NI7864**
9. B. Fassbaender, Stuttgart RSO, H. Graf
(11/86) (ORFE) ① **C096841A**
9. M. Callas, FRNO, G. Prêtre
(2/90) (EMIN) ① **CD-EMX2123**
(2/88) (EMIN) ⊟ **TC-EMX2123**
9. C. Supervia, orch, A. Albergoni (r1927: Ital)
(9/90) (CLUB) ① **CL99-074**
9. C. Supervia, orch, A. Albergoni (Ital: r1927)
(9/90) (PREI) ① **89023**
9. R. Anday, Berlin St Op Orch, J. Prüwer (r1928) (5/92) (PREI) ① **89046**
9. E. Thornton, orch (Eng: r1908)
(7/92) (PEAR) ① [3] **GEMMCDS9925(1)**
9. L. Kirkby-Lunn, orch, P. Pitt (r1915)
(7/92) (PEAR) ① [3] **GEMMCDS9924(2)**
9. K. Branzell, orch (r1928)
(8/92) (PREI) ① **89039**
9. C. Supervia, orch, G. Cloëz (r1931)
(3/93) (NIMB) ① [2] **NI7836/7**
9. A. Parsi-Pettinella, anon (Ital: r1904)
(12/93) (SYMP) ① **SYMCD1113**
9. A. Parsi-Pettinella, orch (r1907: Ital)
(4/94) (EMI) ① [3] **CHS7 64860-2(1)**
9, 11a, 11b, 13b M. Callas, FRNO, G. Prêtre
(2/88) (EMI) ① **CDC7 49059-2**
9, 11a, 11b, 13. M. Lipovšek, Munich RO, G. Patanè (6/90) (ORFE) ① **C179891A**
9, 11b E. Stignani, EIAR Orch, U. Tansini (Ital: r1937) (1/91) (PREI) ① **89014**
9, 13b E. Leisner, orch (r1921: Ger)
(PREI) ① [2] **89210**
9, 13b S. Onegin, Berlin St Op Orch, L. Blech (Ger: r1929) (2/91) (PREI) ① **89027**
11a, 11b Z. Dolukhanova, Moscow PO, G. Stolarov (pp1954: Russ)
(RUSS) ① **RDCD15023**
11b M. Anderson, orch, L. Collingwood (r1930: Eng) (ASV) ① **CDAJA5112**
(ASV) ⊟ **ZCAJA5112**
11b H. Bouvier, Paris Op Orch, L. Fourestier (r1946) (4/92) (EMI) ① [7] **CHS7 69741-2(3)**
11b, 13b R. Anday, Vienna St Op Orch, K. Alwin (Ger: r1931) (5/92) (PREI) ① **89046**
11b, 13b K. Branzell, orch (Ger: r1927)
(8/92) (PREI) ① **89039**
13b M. Caballé, Philh, J. Collado
(11/92) (RCA) ⊟ [2] **RK61044**
13b M. Horne, Sydney Eliz Orch, R. Bonynge
(MCEG) ▣ **VVD780**
13b M. Horne, Vienna Op Orch, H. Lewis (r1967)
(DECC) ① **425 854-2DWO**
(DECC) ⊟ **425 854-4DWO**
13b M. Horne, Vienna Op Orch, H. Lewis
(DECC) ① **433 067-2DWO**
(DECC) ⊟ **433 067-4DWO**
13b E. Obraztsova, Czech SO, A. Krieger (pp1991) (IMP) ① **MCD42**
13b M. Callas, FRNO, G. Prêtre
(EMI) ① **CDC7 54702-2**
(EMI) ⊟ **EL754702-4**
13b A-M. Owens, Czech PO, J. Bigg (with instr track for singing) (IMP) ① [2] **DPCD1015**
(IMP) ⊟ **CIMPCD1015**
13b A-M. Owens, Czech PO, J. Bigg (r1992)
(IMP) ① **PCD1043**

13b D. Graves, Rio de Janeiro Municipal Th Orch, J. DeMain (pp1992) (SONY) **SLV48362** (SONY) **SHV48362**
13b M. Ilgenfritz (r1917: arr Ilgenfritz: pf roll) (COND) ⓘ **690.07.004**
13b M. Horne, Vienna Op Orch, H. Lewis (r1967) (DECC) ⓘ **433 440-2DA** (DECC) **433 440-4DA**
13b A-M. Owens, Czech SO, J. Bigg (IMP) ⓘ [3] **TCD1070**
13b G. Groves, J. Watson, J. Partridge (r1994: arr W Belshaw) (ASV) ⓘ **CDWHL2088**
13b M. Horne, Monte Carlo PO, L. Foster (ERAT) ⓘ **4509-91715-2** (ERAT) **4509-91715-4**
13b M. Callas, FRNO, G. Prêtre (EMIL) ⓘ **CDZ100** (EMIL) **LZ100**
13b M. Horne, Vienna Op Orch, H. Lewis (r1967) (DECC) ⓘ **443 334-2LRX** (DECC) **443 334-4LRX**
13b M. Horne, Vienna Op Orch, H. Lewis, ROHO (1967) (DECC) ⓘ **440 415-2DM**
13b S. Verrett, RCA Italiana Op Orch, G. Prêtre (r1967) (RCA) ⓘ **09026 61457-2**
13b Capitol SO, C. Dragon (r1957: arr Dragon) (EMI) ⓘ **CDM5 65430-2**
13b M. Horne, Monte Carlo PO, L. Foster (r1984) (ERAT) ⓘ **4509-98501-2**
13b M. Horne, Vienna Op Orch, H. Lewis (r1967) (DECC) ⓘ [2] **444 552-2DF2**
13b M. Anderson, orch, L. Collingwood (Eng: r1930) (10/89) (NIMB) ⓘ **NI7801** (NIMB) **NC7801**
13b M. Callas, FRNO, G. Prêtre (2/90) (EMI) ⓘ **CDM7 63182-2**
13b I. Minghini-Cattaneo, orch, J. Barbirolli (Ital: r1929) (6/90) (PREI) ⓘ **89008**
13b B. Thebom, LSO, W. Braithwaite (r1950) (4/92) (EMI) ⓘ [7] **CHS7 69741-2(1)**
13b F. Litvinne, anon (r1903) (10/92) (SYMP) ⓘ **SYMCD1101**
13b F. Litvinne, A. Cortot (r1902) (10/92) (SYMP) ⓘ **SYMCD1101**
13b Grimethorpe Colliery Band, E. Howarth (arr Langford) (12/92) (DOYE) ⓘ **DOYCD013** (12/92) (DOYE) **DOYMC013**
13b R. Resnik, ROHO, E. Downes (r1961) (10/93) (DECC) ⓘ **436 462-2DM**
13b F. Litvinne, orch (r1907) (12/94) (SYMP) ⓘ **SYMCD1128**
13b E. Destinn, orch (r1911: Ger) (12/94) (SUPR) ⓘ [12] **11 2136-2(4)**
13b K. Thorborg, Berlin St Op Orch, F. Weissmann (r1933: Ger) (4/95) (PREI) ⓘ **89084**
13b M. Klose, Berlin St Op Orch, F.A. Schmidt (r1932: Ger) (7/95) (PREI) ⓘ **89082**
13b P. Bertin, Camargue PO, Reinhardt Wagner (r1995: arr R Wagner) (8/95) (HARM) ⓘ **HMC90 1552**
14. E. Caruso, NY Met Op Chor, orch, J. Pasternack (r1916) (RCA) ⓘ **09026 61244-2**
14. G. Thill, Orch, P. Gaubert (r1936) (1/89) (EMI) ⓘ **CDM7 69548-2**
14. E. Caruso, NY Met Op Chor, orch, J. Pasternack (r1916) (7/91) (RCA) ⓘ [12] **GD60495(5)**
14. E. Caruso, NY Met Op Chor, orch, J. Pasternack (r1916) (10/91) (PEAR) ⓘ [3] **EVC4(1)**
14. P. Franz, chor, orch (r1919) (7/92) (PEAR) ⓘ [3] **GEMMCDS9925(1)**
14. G. Thill, chor, orch, P. Gaubert (r1936) (7/92) (PEAR) ⓘ [3] **GEMMCDS9926(1)**
16. Philadelphia, E. Ormandy (IMP) ⓘ [2] **DUET 10CD**
16. Philadelphia, E. Ormandy (r1964) (SONY) ⓘ **SBK47655**
16. Classic Buskers (arr Copley) (SEAV) ⓘ **CD007365**
16. Montreal SO, C. Dutoit (DECC) ⓘ **436 475-2DM**
16. Montreal SO, C. Dutoit (r1987) (DECC) ⓘ [2] **444 552-2DF2**
16. Cincinnati Pops, E. Kunzel (9/86) (TELA) ⓘ **CD80115**
16. Paris Orch, D. Barenboim (4/87) (DG) ⓘ **415 847-2GGA**
16. Paris Op Orch, G. Prêtre (6/88) (EMI) ⓘ **CDM7 69112-2**
16. Montreal SO, C. Dutoit (6/89) (DECC) ⓘ **421 527-2DH**
16. H. Fagius, Stockholm PO, J. DePreist (r1992) (7/93) (BIS) ⓘ **BIS-CD555**
16. NYPO, L. Bernstein (r1967) (9/93) (SONY) ⓘ **SMK47600**
16. Empire Brass (r1992; arr. R. Smedvig) (1/94) (TELA) ⓘ **CD80305** (1/94) (TELA) **CS30305**
16. Philadelphia, L. Stokowski (r1927) (8/95) (BIDD) ⓘ **WHL012**

SALIERI, Antonio *(1750–1825) Italy/Austria*

L' **Angiolina, ossia Il Matrimonio per sussurro– opera buffa: 2 acts (1800—Vienna) (Lib. C.P. Defranceschi)**
Overture Bratislava RSO, M. Dittrich (r1992) (1/94) (MARC) ⓘ **8 223381**

Annibale in Capua– dramma per musica (1801) (Lib. Sografi)
A fulminas m'invita A. Raunig, Vienna Amadeus Ens, W. Kobera (DIVE) ⓘ **DIV31013**

Armida– opera seria: 3 acts (1771) (Lib. Coltellini)
Lungi da te A. Raunig, Vienna Amadeus Ens, W. Kobera (DIVE) ⓘ **DIV31013**
Overture Bratislava RSO, M. Dittrich (r1992) (1/94) (MARC) ⓘ **8 223381**

Axur, Re d'Ormus– opera: 4 acts (1788—Vienna) (Lib. Da Ponte)
Cpte A. Martin, C. Rayam, E. Mei, E. Nova, A. Vespasiani, M. Valentini, M. Porcelli, M. Cecchetti, S. Turchetta, G.B. Palmieri, Guido d'Arezzo Ch, Russian PO, R. Clemencic (hpd/dir) (12/90) (NUOV) ⓘ [3] **6852/4**
Finale Ambrosian Op Chor, ASMF, N. Marriner (LOND) ⓘ **827 267-2**
Overture Bratislava RSO, M. Dittrich (r1991) (1/94) (MARC) ⓘ **8 223381**
Perdermi? A. Raunig, Vienna Amadeus Ens, W. Kobera (DIVE) ⓘ **DIV31013**

Cesare in Farmacusa– opera eroico-comica: 2 acts (1800—Vienna) (Lib. C.P. Defranceschi)
Overture Bratislava RSO, M. Dittrich (r1991) (1/94) (MARC) ⓘ **8 223381**

Les **Danaides– opera: 5 acts (1784—Paris) (Lib. Du Roullet and Tschudi)**
Overture Bratislava RSO, M. Dittrich (r1991) (1/94) (MARC) ⓘ **8 223381**

Don Chisciotte alle nozze di Gamace– divertimento teatrale: 1 act (1770—Vienna) (Lib. G. Boccherini)
Overture Bratislava RSO, M. Dittrich (r1992) (1/94) (MARC) ⓘ **8 223381**

Eraclito e Democrito– opera filosofico-buffa: 2 acts (1795—Vienna) (Lib. Gamerra)
Overture Bratislava RSO, M. Dittrich (r1991) (1/94) (MARC) ⓘ **8 223381**

La **grotta di Trofonio– opera: 2 acts (1785—Vienna) (Lib. G.B. Casti)**
Overture Bratislava RSO, M. Dittrich (r1991) (1/94) (MARC) ⓘ **8 223381**

La **Locandiera– opera: 3 acts (1773—Vienna) (Lib. D. Poggi, after Goldoni)**

Mirandolina	A. Ruffini
Marquis	G. Sarti
Count	O. di Credico
Fabrizio	P. Guarnera
Cavalier	L. Petroni
Lena	P. Leolini

Toscanini SO, F. Luisi (pp1989) (NUOV) ⓘ [2] **6888/9**

Il **moro– opera buffa: 2 acts (1796—Vienna) (Lib. Gamerra)**
Overture Bratislava RSO, M. Dittrich (r1991) (1/94) (MARC) ⓘ **8 223381**

Prima la musica e poi le parole– divertimento teatrale: 1 act (1786—Vienna) (Lib. Casti)

Music Director	G. Polidori
Poet	G. Gatti
Eleonora	M. Casula
Tonina	K. Gamberucci

Boemia del Nord Phil CO, D. Sanfilippo (pp1968) (BONG) ⓘ **GB2063/4-2**

Il **ricco d'un giorno– opera buffa: 3 acts (1784—Vienna) (Lib. Da Ponte)**
Overture Bratislava RSO, M. Dittrich (r1991) (1/94) (MARC) ⓘ **8 223381**

La **Scuola de' gelosi– opera buffa: 2 acts (1778—Venice) (Lib. C Mazzolà)**
EXCERPTS: 1. Sinfonia in D, 'La Veneziana'.
1. Budapest Stgs, K. Botvay (r1994) (CAPR) ⓘ **10 530**

La **secchia rapita– opera buffa: 3 acts (1772—Vienna) (Lib. G. Boccherini)**
Overture Bratislava RSO, M. Dittrich (r1991) (1/94) (MARC) ⓘ **8 223381**

Il **talismano– opera buffa: 3 acts (1788—Vienna) (Lib. Da Ponte)**
Overture Bratislava RSO, M. Dittrich (r1991) (1/94) (MARC) ⓘ **8 223381**

SALLINEN , Aulis *(b 1935) Finland*

Kullervo– opera: 2 acts (1988—Los Angeles) (Lib. cpsr)

Kullervo	J. Hynninen
Mother	E-L. Saarinen
Kalervo	M. Salminen
Kimmo	J. Silvasti
Sister	S. Vihavainen
Smith's Wife	A-L. Jakobson
Hunter	P. Mäkelä
Unto	J. Kotilainen
Unto's Wife	P. Etelävuori
Tiera	M. Putkonen
First Man	M. Heinikari
Second Man	E. Ruuttunen
Blind Singer	V-M. Loiri

Finnish Nat Op Chor, Finnish Nat Op Orch, U. Söderblom (8/92) (ONDI) ⓘ [3] **ODE780-2**

SALMHOFER, Franz *(1900–1975) Austria*

Iwan Tarassenko– opera: prologue & 1 act (1938—Vienna)
Excs A. Konetzni, T. Mazaroff, A. Jerger, G. Monthy, K. Ettl, K. Kolowratnik, R. Tomek, F. Szkokan, J. Sawka, Vienna St Op Chor, Vienna St Op Orch, W. Loibner (pp1938) (6/95) (SCHW) ⓘ [2] **314632**

SAMARA , Spiro *(1861–1917) Greece*

Mademoiselle de belle Isle– opera (1905—Genoa)
Oui, je l'aime A. Paoli, anon (Ital: r1907) (PREI) ⓘ **89998**

SAMUEL-ROUSSEAU, Marcel *(1882–1955) France*

Tarass Boulba– opera: 5 acts (1919—Paris)
Non, je n'ai pas sommeil M. Kuznetsova, orch (r1920) (6/93) (PEAR) ⓘ [3] **GEMMCDS9004/6(1)**

SARTI, Giuseppe *(1729–1802) Italy*

Armida e Rinaldo– opera: 2 acts (1786—St Petersburg) (Lib. M. Coltellini)
Lungi dal caro bene E. Pinza, F. Kitzinger (r1940) (9/93) (RCA) ⓘ **09026 61245-2**

SATIE, Erik (Alfred Leslie) *(1866–1925) France*

Geneviève de Brabant– miniature marionette opera (1899 orch 1925-26) (Wds. C de Latour: orch R Desormière)
M. Mesplé, J-C. Benoit, P. Bertin, Paris Op Chor, Paris Orch, P. Dervaux (EMI) ⓘ [2] **CZS7 62877-2**

SAXTON, Robert *(b 1953) England*

Caritas– opera: 2 acts (1991—Wakefield) (Lib. A. Wesker)
Christine E. Davies
Bishop of Norwich J. Best
Robert Lonle C. Ventris
Agnes L. Hibberd
William R. Bryson
Richard Lonle; Travelling Priest D. Gwynne
Mathew P. Wilson
Bailiff G. Bell
Villager B. Budd
Tax Collector B. Cookson
Matilde L. Ormiston
English Northern Philh, D. Masson (pp1991) (7/92) (COLL) ⦶ **Coll1350-2**

SCARLATTI, (Pietro) Alessandro (Gaspare) *(1660–1725) Italy*

Clearco in Negroponte– dramma per musica: 3 acts (1686—Naples) (Lib. A Arcoleo)
Vengo a stringerti Alfredo Kraus, J. Tordesillas (NIMB) ⦶ **NI5102**

La **Donna ancora è fedele– dramma per musica: 3 acts (1698—Naples) (Lib. after Contini)**
EXCERPTS: 1. Son tutta duolo; 2. Se Florindo è fedele.
1. T. Schipa, orch, D. Olivieri (r1939) (NIMB) ⦶ **NI7870**
1. T. Schipa, orch, D. Olivieri (r1939) (4/90) (EMI) ⦶ **CDH7 63200-2**
1, 2. C. Bartoli, G. Fischer (12/92) (DECC) ⦶ **436 267-2DH**
(12/92) (DECC) ⊟ **436 267-4DH**
2. H. Spani, orch, G. Nastrucci (r1929) (9/90) (CLUB) ⦶ [2] **CL99-509/10**

Il **Flavio– dramma per musica: 3 acts (1688—Naples) (Lib. after M Noris)**
Che vuole innamorarsi E. Pinza, F. Kitzinger (r1940) (9/93) (RCA) ⦶ **09026 61245-2**
Chi vuole innamorarsi Alfredo Kraus, J. Tordesillas (NIMB) ⦶ **NI5102**

La **Griselda– dramma per musica: 3 acts (1721—Rome) (Lib. ?F M Rusponi, after A Zeno)**
EXCERPTS: 1. In voler ciò che tu brami; 2. Nell'aspro mio dolor; 3. Mi rivedi, o selva ombrosa; 4. Figlio! Tiranno!; 5. Finirá, barbara sorte.
No, non sospira l'amor; Vago sei, volto amoroso; Peno...Ho in seno due fiammelle S. Bruscantini, Naples Scarlatti Chor, Naples Scarlatti Orch, N. Sanzogno (pp1970) (MEMO) ⦶ [2] **HR4300/1**
1-5. M. Freni, Naples Scarlatti Chor, Naples Scarlatti Orch, N. Sanzogno (pp1970) (MEMO) ⦶ [2] **HR4277/8**

L' **Honestà negli amore– dramma per musica: 3 acts (1680—Rome) (Lib. F Parnasso)**
EXCERPTS: 1. Già il sole dal Gange.
1. M. Lanza, C. Callinicos (pp1958) (RCA) ⦶ **09026 61884-2**
(RCA) ⊟ **09026 61884-4**
1. C. Bartoli, G. Fischer (12/92) (DECC) ⦶ **436 267-2DH**
(12/92) (DECC) ⊟ **436 267-4DH**
1. J. Baker, ASMF, N. Marriner (1/93) (PHIL) ⦶ **434 173-2PM**

Lesbina e Adolfo– intermezzo (1700—Naples) (Lib. A Zeno)
Lesbina D. Uccello
Adolfo G. Gatti
Boemia del Nord Phil CO, D. Sanfilippo (pp1968) (BONG) ⦶ **GB2063/4-2**

Il **Pirro e Demetrio– dramma per musica: 3 acts (1694—Naples) (Lib. Morselli)**
Le violette Alfredo Kraus, J. Tordesillas (NIMB) ⦶ **NI5102**
Le violette M. Bayo, U. Duetschler (CLAV) ⦶ **CD50-9023**
Le violette S.S. Frank, P. Sykes (CENT) ⦶ **CRC2084**
Le violette T. Schipa, orch, D. Olivieri (r1939) (NIMB) ⦶ **NI7870**
Le Violette V. de los Angeles, G. Parsons (pp1990) (12/91) (COLL) ⦶ **Coll1247-2**
Le violette V. de los Angeles, G. Moore (r1960) (4/94) (EMI) ⦶ [4] **CMS5 65061-2(2)**
Rugiadose, odorose T. Schipa, orch, D. Olivieri (r1939) (4/90) (EMI) ⦶ **CDH7 63200-2**

Il **Pompeo– dramma per musica: 3 acts (1683—Rome) (Lib. N Minato)**
EXCERPTS: 1. O cessate di piagarmi; 2. Toglietemi la vita ancor; 3. Già il sole dal Gange.
1. C. Bartoli, G. Fischer (12/92) (DECC) ⦶ **436 267-2DH**
(12/92) (DECC) ⊟ **436 267-4DH**
1. R. Tebaldi, R. Bonynge (r1972) (9/94) (DECC) ⦶ **436 202-2DM**
1, 2. Alfredo Kraus, J. Tordesillas (NIMB) ⦶ **NI5102**
1-3. J. Carreras, ECO, V. Sutej (r1992; arr Agostinelli) (PHIL) OO **434 926-5PH**
1-3. J. Carreras, ECO, V. Sutej (r1992; arr Agostinelli) (6/93) (PHIL) ⦶ **434 926-2PH**
3. M. Bayo, U. Duetschler (CLAV) ⦶ **CD50-9023**
3. L. Pavarotti, Bologna Teatro Comunale Orch, R. Bonynge (DECC) ⦶ **425 037-2DM**

Il **Prigioniero fortunato– dramma per musica: 3 acts (1698—Naples) (Lib. Paglia)**
Sinfonia J. Wallace, Philh, S. Wright (NIMB) ⦶ **NI5123**

SCHILLINGS, Max von *(1868–1933) Germany*

Moloch– opera (1906—Dresden) (Lib. E. Gerhäuser)
Harvest festival Košice St PO, A. Walter (4/92) (MARC) ⦶ **8 223324**

Mona Lisa– opera: 2 acts, Op. 31 (1915—Vienna) (Lib. B Dovsky)
Mona Lisa; Wife B. Bilandzija
Francesco del Giocondo; Stranger K. Wallprecht
Giovanni de Salviati; Lay brother A. Bonnema
Pietro Tumoni M. Gasztecki
Arrigo Oldofredi K. Russ
Alessio Beneventi; Sisto U. Köberle
Sandro da Luzzano J. Sabrowski
Masolino Pedruzzi B. Gebhardt
Mona Ginevra E. Reimer
Dianora A. Lawrence
Piccarda G. Kosbahn
Kiel Op Chor, Kiel PO, K. Seibel (r1994) (8/95) (CPO) ⦶ [2] **CPO999 303-2**

SCHMALSTICH, Clemens *(1880–1960) Germany*

Peterchens Mondfahrt– opera
Reigen Cölln Salon Orch (arr. Schulz) (EMI) ⦶ **CDC7 49819-2**

SCHMIDT, Franz *(1874–1939) Austria*

Notre Dame– opera: 2 acts (1902-04) (Lib. cpsr after Hugo)
Intermezzo
Esmeralda G. Jones
Phoebus J. King
Gringoire H. Laubenthal
Archdeacon H. Welker
Quasimodo K. Moll
An Officer H. Helm
Old Falourdel K. Borris
Berlin St Hedwig's Cath Ch, Berlin RIAS Chbr Ch, Berlin RSO, C. Perick (5/89) (CAPR) ⦶ [2] **10 248/9**
Excs A. Jerger, H. Alsen, K. Friedrich, J. Witt, E. Schulz, G. Monthy, Vienna St Op Chor, Vienna St Op Orch, R. Moralt (pp1943) (2/95) (SCHW) ⦶ [2] **314572**
Intermezzo Monte Carlo PO, L. Foster (ERAT) ⦶ **2292-45860-2**
Intermezzo BPO, H. von Karajan (EMI) ⦶ **CDM7 64629-2**
Intermezzo BPO, H. von Karajan (10/87) (DG) ⦶ [3] **419 257-2GH3**
Intermezzo Gothenburg SO, N. Järvi (6/90) (DG) ⦶ **429 494-2GDC**
(6/90) (DG) ⊟ **429 494-4GDC**
Intermezzo Vienna St Op Orch, W. Loibner (pp1938) (6/94) (SCHW) ⦶ **314502**
Intermezzo Vienna St Op Orch, W. Loibner (pp1938) (6/95) (SCHW) ⦶ [2] **314632**

SCHOECK, Othmar *(1886–1957) Switzerland*

Massimilla Doni– opera: 4 acts (6 scenes), Op. 50 (1937—Dresden) (Lib. Rüger, after Balzac)
Massimilla Doni E. Mathis
Emilio Memmi J. Protschka
Duke Cattaneo H. Winkler
Capraja H. Stamm
Prince Vendramin R. Hermann
Genovese D. van der Walt
Tinti C. Lindsley
Page; Maid; Shepherd; Fruiterer A. Küttenbaum
Director; News-vendor U. Ress
Cologne Rad Chor, Cologne RSO, G. Albrecht (bp1986) (11/89) (SCHW) ⦶ [2] **314025**

Penthesilea– opera: 1 act (1925—Dresden) (Lib. cpsr, after Kleist)
1. Suite (arr. Delfs).
Penthesilea H. Dernesch
Prothoe J. Marsh
Meroe M. Gessendorf
High Priestess M. Lipovšek
Priestess G. Sima
Achilles T. Adam
Diomede H. Hiestermann
Herold P. Weber
Austrian Rad Chor, Austrian RSO, G. Albrecht (pp1982) (3/95) (ORFE) ⦶ **C364941B**
1. Swiss YSO, A. Delfs (2/93) (CLAV) ⦶ **CD50-9201**

Venus– opera: 3 acts, Op. 32 (1922—Zurich) (Lib. A. Rüeger, after Merimée)
Baron de Zarandelle F. Lang
Simone L. Popp
Horace J. O'Neal
Madame de Lauriens H. Fassbender
Raimond B. Skovhus
Lucile Z. Alföldi
Heidelberg Chbr Ch, Basle Boys' Ch, Swiss Workshop PO, M. Venzago (r1991) (10/94) (MGB) ⦶ [2] **CD6112**

SCHOENBERG, Arnold (Franz Walther) *(1874–1951) Austria/USA*

Erwartung– monodrama: 1 act, Op. 17 (1909—Prague) (Lib. M. Pappenheim)
Cpte J. Norman, NY Met Op Orch, James Levine (r1989) (PHIL) OO **426 261-5PH**
Cpte A. Silja, VPO, C. von Dohnányi (2/89) (DECC) ⦶ [2] **417 348-2DH2**
Cpte J. Norman, NY Met Op Orch, James Levine (r1989) (9/93) (PHIL) ⦶ **426 261-2PH**
Cpte J. Martin, BBC SO, P. Boulez (r1977) (12/93) (SONY) ⦶ **SMK48466**
Cpte P. Bryn-Julson, CBSO, S. Rattle (r1993) (4/95) (EMI) ⦶ **CDC5 55212-2**

Die **glückliche Hande– drama with music: 1 act, Op. 18 (1924—Vienna) (Wds. cpsr)**
S. Nimsgern, BBC Sngrs, BBC SO, P. Boulez (r1981) (12/93) (SONY) ⦶ **SMK48464**

Moses und Aron– opera: 3 acts (1930-32: fp 1951) (Lib. cpsr)
Moses W. Haseleu
Aron R. Goldberg
Priest L. Mróz
Young Girl R. Krahmer
Invalid Woman G. Pohl
Young Man; Naked Youth A. Ude
Another Man H. C. Polster
Ephraimite K-H. Stryczek
Leipzig Rad Chor, Dresden Cath Boys' Ch, Leipzig RSO, H. Kegel (r1976) (BERL) ⦶ [2] **0011162BC**
Moses F. Mazura
Aron P. Langridge
Priest A. Haugland
Young Girl B. Bonney
Invalid Woman M. Zaka
Young Man; Youth D. Harper
Naked Youth T. Dymit
A Man; Ephraimite H. Wittges
Another Man; An Elder K. Link
Naked Woman I J. Braham

Naked Woman II B. Pearson
Naked Woman III C. Anderson
Naked Woman IV K. Zajac
First Elder R. Cohn
Second Elder P. Grizzell
Solo voice in the orchestra I S. Schweikert
Solo voice in the orchestra II E. Gottlieb
Solo voice in the orchestra III K. Brunssen
Solo voice in the orchestra IV Roald Henderson
Solo voice in the orchestra V B. Nystrom
Solo voice in the orchestra VI W. Kirkwood
ɜlen Ellyn Children's Chor, Chicago Sym Chor, Chicago SO, G. Solti (r1984)
(1/85) (DECC) Ⓓ [2] **414 264-2DH2**
Moses G. Reich
Aron R. Cassilly
Priest R. Angas
Young Girl; Naked Woman II F. Palmer
Invalid Woman G. Knight
Young Man; Youth J. Winfield
Ephramite R. Hermann
An Elder J. Noble
Naked Man I; Solo voice in the orchestra I J. Manning
Naked Woman III; Solo voice in the orchestra III G. Knight
Naked Woman IV; Solo voice in the orchestra IV H. Watts
Solo voice in the orchestra V P. Langridge
Solo voice in the orchestra V M. Rippon
Solo voice in the orchestra VI D. Wicks
BC Sngrs, Orpheus Boys' Ch, BBC SO, P. Boulez (r1974)
(12/93) (SONY) Ⓓ [2] **SM2K48456**
Moses G. Reich
Aron L. Devos
Priest W. Mann
Young Girl E. Csapó
Invalid Woman E. Obrowsky
Young Man; Naked Youth R. Lucas
Another Man R. Salter
Ephraimite L. Illavský
ienna Boys' Ch, Austrian Rad Chor, Austrian RSO, M. Gielen (r1974)
(4/94) (PHIL) Ⓓ [2] **438 667-2PM2**
Dance of the Golden Calf (Act II Scene III) Hamburg RO, Hamburg Rad Ch, H. Rosbaud (r1954) (STDV) Ⓓ **STR10022**

SCHREKER , Franz
(1878–1934) Austria

er **Ferne Klang– opera: 3 acts (1912—Frankfurt) (Lib. cpsr)**
Grete Graumann E. Grigorescu
Fritz T. Harper
Dr Vigelius A. Haller
Ham actor H. Fiehl
Old Graumann R. Bunse
Old Graumann's wife E. Pilarl
Landlord P. Friess
Count W. Hahn
Baron P.N. Kante
Chevalier R. Leisenheimer
Rudolf W. Pickersgill
agen Op Chor, Hagen PO, M. Halász (r1989)
(8/90) (MARC) Ⓓ [2] **8 223270/1**
Grete Graumann G. Schnaut
Fritz T. Moser
Dr Viglius S. Nimsgern
Ham actor H. Helm
Old Graumann V. von Halem
Old Graumann's wife B. Scherler
Landlord J.W. Prein
Count R. Hermann
Baron G. Saks
Chevalier R. Wörle
Rudolf C. Otelli
Old woman J. Juon
erlin RIAS Chbr Ch, Berlin Rad Chor, Berlin RSO, G. Albrecht
(12/91) (CAPR) Ⓓ [2] **60 024-2**
In einem Lande ein bleicher König T. Hampson, Munich RO, F. Luisi (r1994)
(9/95) (EMI) Ⓓ **CDC5 55233-2**

ie **Gezeichneten– opera: 3 acts (1918—Frankfurt) (Lib. cpsr)**
Herzog Antoniotto Adorno C. van Tassel
Count Andrae Vitelozzo Tamare S. Cowan
Lodovico Nardi, Podestà W. Oosterkamp
Carlotta Nardi M. Schmiege
Alviano Salvago W. Cochran
G. Usodimare H. Meens
Menaldo Negroni F. Lang
Michelotto Cibo E.D. Smid
Gonsalvo Fieschi M. Dirks
Julian Pinelli E. Godding
Capitaneo di Giustizia C. van Tassel
Ginevra Scotti E. Bollongino
Dutch Rad Phil Chor, Dutch Rad PO, E. de Waart (pp1990)
(12/91) (MARC) Ⓓ [3] **8 223328/30**
Duke Adorno; Capitaneo di Giustizia A. Muff
Count Vitelozzo Tamare M. Pederson
Lodovico Nardi L. Polgár
Calotta Nardi E. Connell
Alviano Salvago H. Kruse
Guidobald Usodimare R. Wörle
Menaldo Negroni E. Wottrich
Michelotto Cibo O. Widmer
Gonsalvo Fieschi M. Görne
Julian Pinelli K. Sigmundsson
Paolo Calvi P. Salomaa
Ginevra Scotti M. Posselt
Martuccia C. Berggold
Pietro M. Petzold
Youth H. Lippert
Friend; Servant; Third Citizen; Third Young Man R. Beyer
Girl M. Rüping
Giant Citizen J. Becker
Father G. Schwarz
Mother K. Borris
Small boy I. Nguyen-Huu
Maidservant R. Schudel
First Senator R. Ginzel
Second Senator J. Gottschick
Third Senator F. Molsberger
First Citizen P. Menzel
Second Citizen M. Köhler
First Young Man J. Metzger
Second Young Man H. Czerny
Berlin Rad Chor, Berlin Deutsches SO, L. Zagrosek (r1993/4)
(6/95) (DECC) Ⓓ [3] **444 442-2DHO3**

Irrelohe– opera: 3 acts (1924—Cologne) (Lib. cpsr)
Count Heinrich M. Pabst
Eva L. DeVol
Forester; Anselmus G. Simic
Lola E. Randová
Peter M. Pederson
Christobald H. Zednik
Parson; Strahlbusch N. Belamaric
Miller; Ratzekahl S. Holecek
Fünkchen; A Lackey H. Wildhaber
Vienna Singverein, Vienna SO, P. Gülke (pp1989)
(SONY) Ⓓ [2] **S2K66850**

Der **Schatzgräber– opera: prologue, 4 acts & epilogue (1920—Frankfurt) (Lib. cpsr)**
Elis J. Protschka
Els G. Schnaut
King H. Stamm
Fool P. Haage
Bailiff H. Helm
Albi H. Kruse
Innkeeper C. Schultz
Chancellor; Scribe P. Galliard
Count; Herald U. Malmberg
Young Nobleman F.F. Nentwig
Schoolmaster U. Krekow
Mayor D. Weller
Hamburg St Op Chor, Hamburg St Op Orch, G. Albrecht (pp1989)
(5/90) (CAPR) Ⓓ [2] **60 010-2**

SCHUBERT , Franz (Peter)
(1797–1828) Austria

Alfonso und Estrella– opera: 3 acts, D732 (1854—Weimar) (Lib. F. von Schober)
Overture Tuscany Rad & TV Orch, D. Renzetti
(EURM) Ⓓ **350213**

Claudine von Villa Bella– Singspiel: 3 acts, D239 (1913—Vienna) (Lib. Goethe. Only Overture and Act 1 complete)
1. Overture; 2. Das hast du wohl bereitet; 3. Fröhlicher, seliger, herrlicher Tag; 4. Hin und wieder fliegen die Pfeile; 5. Alle Freuden, alle Gaben; 6. Es erhebt sich eine Stimme; 7. Liebe schwärmt auf allen Wegen; 8. Mit Mädeln sich vertragen; 9. Deinem Willen nachzugeben; 10. Liebliches Kind, kannst du mir sagen; 11. Mich umfängt ein banger Schauer.
4. E. Schumann, G. Moore (r1949)
(4/92) (EMI) Ⓓ [7] **CHS7 69741-2(4)**
4, 7. A. Auger, G. Johnson (r1989)
(1/91) (HYPE) Ⓓ **CDJ33009**
(1/91) (HYPE) ▭ **KJ33009**
7. A. Auger, D. Baldwin (r1988)
(DELO) Ⓓ **DE3029**
7. M. Musacchio, M. Dedieu-Vidal
(REM) Ⓓ **REM311151**
7. B. Van den Bosch, Concertgebouw, W. Mengelberg (pp1940) (ARHI) Ⓓ **ADCD109**
7. K. Battle, James Levine
(12/88) (DG) Ⓓ **419 237-2GH**
7. E. Wiens, R. Jansen
(5/93) (CBC) Ⓓ **MVCD1053**
7. R. Streich, E. Werba (r1959)
(10/94) (DG) Ⓓ [2] **437 680-2GDO2**
7. P. Frijsh, D. Bucktrout (r1932)
(4/95) (PEAR) Ⓓ [2] **GEMMCDS9095(2)**

Fierrabras– opera: 3 acts, D796 (1897—Karlsruhe) (Lib. J Kupelwieser)
Fierrabras J. Protschka
Emma K. Mattila
Charlemagne R. Holl
Roland T. Hampson
Eginhard R. Gambill
Boland L. Polgár
Florinda C. Studer
Maragond B. Balleys
Brutamente H. Welker
A. Schoenberg Ch, COE, C. Abbado (pp1988: omits dialogue)
(10/90) (DG) Ⓓ [2] **427 341-2GH2**
Beschlossen ist's, ich löse seine Ketten! F. Wunderlich, Stuttgart Rad Chor, Berne St Orch, H. Müller-Kray (bp1959)
(10/89) (ACAN) Ⓓ **43 267**
Overture Tuscany Rad & TV Orch, D. Renzetti
(EURM) Ⓓ **350213**
Overture VPO, I. Kertész
(4/92) (DECC) Ⓓ [4] **430 773-2DC4**

Die **Freunde von Salamanka– Singspiel: 2 acts, D326 (1928—Halle) (Lib. J. Mayrhofer)**
Overture Tuscany Rad & TV Orch, D. Renzetti
(EURM) Ⓓ **350213**

Des **Teufels Lustschloss– opera: 3 acts, D84 (1879—Vienna) (Lib. von Kotzebue: two versions (1813-1815)**
Overture VPO, I. Kertész
(4/92) (DECC) Ⓓ [4] **430 773-2DC4**
Overture L. Rose, NYPO, L. Bernstein (r1967)
(9/93) (SONY) Ⓓ **SMK47609**

Die **Verschworenen (Der häusliche Krieg)– Singspiel: 1 act, D787 (1861—Vienna) (Lib. F. Castelli, after Aristophanes)**
EXCERPTS: 1. Overture; 3. Ich schleiche bang und still.
1. English Sinfonia, C. Groves
(5/92) (IMP) Ⓓ **PCD967**
3. D. Aalbers, F. van den Brink, S. Hoogland
(PART) Ⓓ **Part1132-2**
3. I. Siebert, D. Klöcker, South-West German RSO, K. Donath (SCHW) Ⓓ **314018**
3. A. Auger, T. King, G. Johnson (r1989: ed Spiegel) (1/91) (HYPE) Ⓓ **CDJ33009**
(1/91) (HYPE) ▭ **KJ33009**
3. E. Wiens, J. Valdepeñas, R. Jansen
(5/93) (CBC) Ⓓ **MVCD1053**

Der **Vierjährige Posten– Singspiel: 1 act, D190 (1896—Dresden) (Lib. T. Körner)**
EXCERPTS: 5. Gott! höre meine Stimme.
5. A. Auger, G. Johnson (r1989)
(1/91) (HYPE) Ⓓ **CDJ33009**
(1/91) (HYPE) ▭ **KJ33009**

Die **Zwillingsbrüder– Singspiel: 1 act, D647 (1820—Vienna) (Lib. G von Hofmann)**
Mag es stürmen, donnern, blitzen; Liebe teure Muttererde D. Fischer-Dieskau, Bavarian St Op Orch, W. Sawallisch (r1975)
(EMI) Ⓓ [2] **CMS5 65621-2**
Overture Tuscany Rad & TV Orch, D. Renzetti
(EURM) Ⓓ **350213**
Overture English Sinfonia, C. Groves
(IMP) Ⓓ **PCDS11**
Overture English Sinfonia, C. Groves
(3/93) (IMP) Ⓓ **PCD968**
(3/93) (IMP) ▭ **CIMPC968**

SCHULHOFF, Ervín
(1894–1942) Bohemia

Plameny, 'Flammen'– opera: 2 acts (1927-8—Prague) (Lib. K J Beneš)
1. Festliches Vorspiel (Ouvertüre).
Don Juan K. Westi

Donna Anna; Nun; Woman; Marguerite J. Eaglen
Death I. Vermillion
Commendatore J.W. Prein
Harlequin G. Wolf
Shadow C. Lindsley
Shadow C. Höhn
Shadow R. Schudel
Shadow E. Dressen
Shadow C. Berggold
Shadow K. Borris
Berlin RIAS Chbr Ch, Berlin Deutsches SO, J. Mauceri (r1993/4)
(DECC) ① [2] **444 630-2DHO2**
1. Brno St PO, I. Yinon (r1994)
(8/95) (SCHW) ① **314372**

SCHULTZE, Norbert *(b 1911)* *Germany*

Schwarzer Peter– opera for young and old people: 6 scenes (1936—Hamburg) (Lib. W. Lieck)
King Hans T. Altmeyer
King Klaus H.G. Knoblich
Minstrel B. McDaniel
Astrologer G. Vespermann
Captain; Narrator O. Höpfner
Roderick H. Kruse
Erica G. van Jüten
Queen Margaret M. Mödl
Broom-maker F. Müller-Heuser
First Midwife B. Mira
Second Midwife C. Genest
Old Shepherd W. Schneider
Innkeeper J. Schoenenberg
Tailor K-R. Liecke
Shoemaker A. Goerke
Blacksmith Heiner Kruse
Baker J. Meinertzhagen
Cook E. Hallhuber
Siegland Cantata Ch, Cologne Children's Ch, Cologne RSO, N. Schultze
(SCHW) ① [2] **314061**

SCHUMAN, William (Howard) *(1910–1992) USA*

The **Mighty Casey– baseball opera: 3 scenes (1953—Hartford) (Lib. J Gury, after E L Thayer)**
Casey S. Robinson
Watchman F. Pomponi
Merry C. Thorpe
Thatcher D. Corman
Snedeker R. Cusick
Charlie D. Dreyer
Umpire Buttenheiser C. Conde
Manager A. Parks
Concessionaire J. Russell
Male Fan K. Chester
Female Fan S. Rosenbaum
Juilliard Op Center, Juilliard Orch, G. Schwarz (pp1990)
(9/94) (DELO) ① **DE1030**

A **Question of Taste– opera: 1 act (1989—New York) (Lib. J D McClatchy, after R Dahl)**
Louise A. Norton
Mrs Hudson E. Grohowski
Tom T. P. Groves
Mrs Schofield E. Bishop
Mr Schofield D. Corman
Phillisto Pratte S. Wilde
Sarah C. Scimone
Juilliard Op Center, Juilliard Orch, G. Schwarz (pp1990)
(9/94) (DELO) ① **DE1030**

SCHUMANN, Robert (Alexander) *(1810–1856)* *Germany*

Genoveva– opera: 4 acts, Op. 81 (1850—Leipzig) (Lib. Reinick, after Tieck and Hebbel)
1. Overture.
Genoveva J. Faulkner
Golo K. Lewis
Hidulfus; Caspar H. Stamm
Siegfried A. Titus
Margaretha R. Behle
Drago C. Schultz
Balthasar J. Tilli
Hamburg St Op Chor, Hamburg PO, G. Albrecht (pp1992)
(1/94) (ORFE) ① [2] **C289932H**
1. Boston SO, C. Munch (r1951)
(RCA) ① **GD60682**
1. Polish Nat RSO, J. Wildner (r1992)
(NAXO) ① **8 550608**
1. LSO, N. Järvi (r1986)
(CHAN) ① **CHAN6548**
1. BPO, R. Kubelík (DG) ① [2] **437 395-2GX2**
1. LSO, N. Järvi (12/88) (CHAN) ① **CHAN8595**
(12/88) (CHAN) ▭ **ABTD1290**
1. NYPO, L. Bernstein (r1963)
(9/93) (SONY) ① **SMK47609**
1. Concertgebouw, B. Haitink (r1984)
(7/94) (PHIL) ① [2] **442 079-2PB2**

SEROV, Alexander Nikolayevich *(1820–1871)* *Russia*

Judith– opera: 5 acts (1863—St Peterburg) (Lib. cpsr, after Bible)
Judith I. Udulova
Avra E. Zaremba
Holofernes M. Krutikov
Bagoas N. Vassiliev
Ozias A. Babikin
Achior V. Kudriashov
Asfaneses S. Suleymanov
Eliachim P. Gluboky
Charmis M. Mikhailov
1st Odalisque I. Zhurina
2nd Odalisque M. Shutova
Hindu singer L. Kuznetsov
Russian Academic Chbr Chor, Male Chbr Ch, Bolshoi Th Orch, A. Chistiakov
(CDM) ① [2] **LDC288 035/6**
Cease your grumbling L. Sibiriakov, orch (r1913) (PEAR) ① [3] **GEMMCDS9111(1)**
Cease your grumbling L. Sibiriakov, orch (r1913) (3/95) (NIMB) ① **NI7865**
Holofernes war song V. Sharonov, anon (r1901)
(6/93) (PEAR) ① [3] **GEMMCDS9001/3(1)**
I shall don my robe of byssus N. Ermolenko-Yuzhina, orch (r1909)
(6/93) (PEAR) ① [3] **GEMMCDS9001/3(2)**

The **Power of Evil– opera: 5 acts (1871—St Petersburg) (cpted Soloy'nov and Serova)**
Merry Shrovetide F. Chaliapin, Paris Russian Op Chor, Balalaika Orch, O. Tchernoyarov (r1931) (12/89) (PEAR) ① **GEMMCD9314**

SERRANO (SIMÉON), José *(1873–1941) Spain*

La **Alegría del batallón– zarzuela (1907—Madrid) (Lib. Arniches and Quintana)**
A una gitana preciosa C. Supervia, orch, P. Godes (r1932) (3/93) (NIMB) ① [2] **NI7836/7**
Canción del soldado A. Cortis, orch (r1925)
(3/94) (NIMB) ① **NI7850**

Alma da Dios– zarzuela (1 act) (1907—Madrid) (Lib. Arniches and Alvarez)
Canción Húngara P. Lavirgen, Seville SO, E. Colomer (pp1991) (RCA) ① **RD61191**
Canción Húngara P. Lavirgen, Seville SO, E. Colomer (pp1991) (RCA) **ОО 09026 61191-5**
Canción Húngara T. Schipa, orch (r1926)
(NIMB) ① **NI7870**
Canción Húngara T. Folgar, chor, orch (r1929)
(PEAR) ① [2] **GEMMCDS9180**
Exc J. Carreras, Orch (EDL) ① **EDL2562-2**
(EDL) ⊙ **EDL2562-1** ▭ **EDL2562-4**

La **Canción del Olvidó– zarzuela: 1 act (1916—Valencia) (Lib. F. Romero & G. Fernández Shaw)**
Canción de Marinela M. Caballé, Barcelona SO, E.M. Marco
(11/92) (RCA) ▭ [2] **RK61044**
Junto al puente de la peña P. Domingo, Madrid SO, M. Moreno-Buendia (r1987)
(1/89) (EMI) ① **CDC7 49148-2**

Los **Claveles– zarzuela: 1 act (1929—Madrid) (Lib. L. Fernández de Svilla & A. C. Carreño)**
Romance de Rosa G. Sanchez, Madrid SO, E. G. Asensio (pp1991) (11/92) (IMP) ① **MCD45**

La **Dolorosa– zarzuela: 2 acts (1930—Madrid) (Lib. Lorente)**
La roca fría del Calvario
Relato de Rafael J. Carreras, ECO, E. Ricci (r1994) (2/95) (ERAT) ① **4509-95789-**
(2/95) (ERAT) ▭ **4509-95789-**
P. Domingo, Austrian RSO, G. Navarro
(SONY) ① **MK3921**

Los de Aragón– zarzuela: 1 act (1927—Madrid) (Lib. Lorente)
Cuantas veces solo P. Domingo, Barcelona SO, G. Navarro (ACAN) ① **49 39**

El **Mal de Amores– zarzuela (Lib. S. & J. Alvarez Quintero)**
Canción de la gitanita C. Supervia, orch, P. Godes (r1932) (3/93) (NIMB) ① [2] **NI7836/**

El **Trust de los Tenorios– zarzuela**
EXCERPTS: 1. Te quiero, morena; 2. Jota.
Española J. Schmidt, orch (r1930)
(4/90) (EMI) ① **CDM7 69478-**
1. P. Domingo, Barcelona SO, G. Navarro
(ACAN) ① **49 39**
1. P. Domingo, Austrian RSO, G. Navarro
(SONY) ① **MK3921**
1. J. Schmidt, orch, C. Schmalstich (r1930)
(EMI) ① [2] **CHS7 64673-**
1. J. Carreras, ECO, E. Ricci (r1994)
(2/95) (ERAT) ① **4509-95789-**
(2/95) (ERAT) ▭ **4509-95789-**
2. P. Domingo, Rio de Janeiro Municipal Th Orch, J. DeMain (pp1992)
(SONY) ◖ **SLV4836**
(SONY) ▭ **SHV4836**

SHAW, Thomas *(c1760/5–c1830) England*

The **Stranger– pasticcio (1798—London)**
EXCERPTS: 1. I have a silent sorrow here (G. Cavendish arr Shaw).
1. P. Wright, J. Gillaspie (r1989)
(PEAR) ① **SHECD961**

SHIELD, William *(1748–1829)* *England*

Robin Hood– comic opera: 3 acts (1784—London) (Lib. MacNally)
EXCERPTS: 1. Her hair is like a golden clue.
1. P. Wright, J. Gillaspie (r1989)
(PEAR) ① **SHECD961**

Rosina– afterpiece: 2 acts (1782—London) (Lib. Mrs Brooke)
EXCERPTS: 1. Overture; 2. Light as thistledown; 3. When William at eve; 4. Whilst with village maids.
2, 3. J. Sutherland, New SO, R. Bonynge (r1963)
(DECC) ① **421 881-2D**
2-4. J. Sutherland, Philomusica of London, Granville Jones (r1959)
(DECC) ① [2] **436 227-2DM**

SHOSTAKOVICH, Dmitry (Dmitriyevich) *(1906–1975)* *USSR*

The **Gamblers, 'Igroki'– opera: 3 acts (1941—Wuppertal) (Lib. N Gogol: cpted K Meyer 1980-81)**
Ikharyov V. Bogache
Gavryushka A. Babiki
Uteshityelny S. Suleymano
Shvokhnyev A. Naumenk
Krugel A. Arkhipo
Alexey N. Nizinenk
Mikhayl Glov M. Krutiko
Alexander Glov V. Verestniko
Zamukhrishkin A. Maslenniko
NW German PO, M. Yurovsky (r1993)
(6/95) (CAPR) ① [2] **60 062-**

Katerina Izmaylova– opera: 4 acts, Op. 114 (1963—Moscow) (Lib. Preys, after Leskov)
Suite SNO, N. Järvi
(7/88) (CHAN) ① **CHAN858**
(7/88) (CHAN) ▭ **ABTD127**
Suite SNO, N. Järvi (r1988)
(5/95) (CHAN) ① [2] **CHAN7000/**

Lady Macbeth of the Mtsensk district– opera: 4 acts, Op. 29 (1934—Leningrad) (Lib. cpsr & Preys, after Leskov)
Katerina Izmailova G. Vishnevskay
Sergei N. Gedd
Boris Izmailov D. Petko
Zinovi Izmailov W. Kren
Shabby Peasant R. Tea

Aksinya T. Valjakka
Teacher M. Hill
Priest L. Mróz
Sergeant A. Haugland
Sonyetka B. Finnilä
Old Convict A. Malta
Millhand; Officer L. Fyson
Porter S. Emmerson
Steward J. Noble
Coachman; Foreman I C. Appleton
Foreman II A. Byers
Foreman III J. Lewington
Policeman O. Broome
Drunken Guest E. Fleet
Sentry D. Beavan
Woman Convict L. Richardson
Ambrosian Op Chor, LPO, M. Rostropovich (r1978)
(5/90) (EMI) ① [2] **CDS7 49955-2**
Katerina Izmailova M. Ewing
Sergei S. Larin
Boris Izmailov A. Haugland
Zinovi Izmailov P. Langridge
Shabby Peasant H. Zednik
Aksinya Kristine Ciesinski
Teacher I. Levinsky
Priest R. Tesarowicz
Police Sergeant A. Kocherga
Sonyetka E. Zaremba
Old Convict K. Moll
Millhand G. Gritziuk
Officer C. Alvarez
Porter G. Petitot
Steward J-P. Mazaloubaud
Coachman A. Woodrow
Foreman I J-C. Costa
Foreman II J. Savignol
Foreman III J. Ochagavia
Policeman P. Duminy
Drunken Guest M. Agnetti
Sentry J. Tilli
Woman Convict M.J. Wray
Paris Opéra-Bastille Chor, Paris Opéra-Bastille Orch, Myung-Whun Chung (r1992)
(12/93) (DG) ① [2] **437 511-2GH2**
Entr'acte Sym of the Air, L. Stokowski (r1958-9)
(EMI) ① [2] **ZDMB5 65427-2**
Passacaglia A. Fiseisky (org)
(ETCE) ① [2] **KTC2019**
Passacaglia C. Herrick (arr cpsr: org)
(10/92) (HYPE) ① **CDA66605**
Passacaglia K. John
(11/92) (PRIO) ① **PRCD370**

The Nose– concert suite from opera, Op. 15a (1927-28)
L. Löbl, J. Jindrák, B. Avksentiev, Czech PO, G. Rozhdestvensky (pp1973)
(PRAG) ① **PR250 003**

SIBELIUS , Jean (Julius Christian) *(1865–1957) Finland*

The Maiden in the Tower– opera: 1 act (8 scenes) (1896) (Lib. Hertzberg)
The Maiden M.A. Häggander
The Lover E. Hagegård
The Bailiff J. Hynninen
The Chatelaine T. Kruse
Gothenburg Concert Hall Ch, Gothenburg SO, N. Järvi
(3/85) (BIS) ① **BIS-CD250**

SIMON, Anton *(1850–1916) France/Russia*

Song of love triumphant– opera, Op. 46 (1897—Moscow) (Lib. N. Vilde, after Turgenev)
O pure creature N. Shevelev, anon (r1901)
(6/93) (PEAR) ① [3] **GEMMCDS9007/9(2)**

SKROUP , František Jan *(1801–1862) Bohemia*

Dratenik/Tinker's Wedding– opera (1835 rev 1849) (Lib. Chmelenský)
Tamo čemu vylne I. Siebert, D. Klöcker, South-West German RSO, K. Donath
(SCHW) ① **314018**

SMETANA, Bedřich *(1824–1884) Bohemia*

B nos. from Bartoš (1973); T nos. from Teige (1893)

The Bartered Bride– opera: 3 acts (1866—Prague) (Lib. Sabine)
EXCERPTS -; 1. Overture. ACT 1: 2. Let us rejoice; 3. Should I ever happen to learn; 4. While a mother's love; 5. Faithful love cannot be marred; 6. As I'm saying my dear fellow; 7. Things like these can't be fixed; 8. He is timid; 9a. You don't even suspect the hitch; 9b. And where everybody fails; 9c. Polka. ACT 2: 10. Beer's no doubt a gift; 11. Furiant; 12. My...my...mother dear; 13. I know of a maiden fair; 14. Every man maintains his wife is best; 15. I know a girl; 16a. How could they believe; 16b. Come inside, people!; 16c. Is it really true?; 16d. Quite a bargain. ACT 3: 17. I can't get it off my mind; 18. March of the Comedians; 19. Dance of the Comedians (Skočná); 20a. We will make a graceful little bear of you; 20b. What? He does not want her?; 20c. Well then, she's Mařenka; 21. Think it over, Mařenka; 22a. Oh, what a grief!; 22b. That dream of love; 23. Are you really so stubborn?; 24. Calm down, dear; 25a. Now I shall call in your parents; 25b. What have you decided, Mařenka?; 25c. Oh, he's a cunning man all right!; 25d. Ha ha ha ha.
Mařenka T. Stratas
Jeník R. Kollo
Vašek H. Zednik
Kečal W. Berry
Krušina J.W. Wilsing
Háta G. Wewezow
Micha A. Malta
Ludmilla M. Bence
Esmeralda J. Perry
Circus-master K. Dönch
Indian T. Nicolai
Bavarian Rad Chor, Munich RSO, J. Krombholc (r1975; Ger)
(EURO) ① [2] **352 887**
Mařenka G. Beňačková
Jeník P. Dvorský
Vašek M. Kopp
Kečal R. Novák
Krušina J. Jindrák
Háta M. Mrázová
Micha J. Horáček
Ludmila M. Veselá
Esmeralda J. Jonášová
Circus-master A. Hampel
Indian K. Hanuš
Czech Phil Chor, Czech PO, Z. Košler (r1980/1)
(10/91) (SUPR) ① [3] **10 3511-2**
Mařenka H. Konetzni
Jeník R. Tauber
Vašek H. Tessmer
Kečal F. Krenn
Krušina M. Rothmüller
Háta M. Jarred
Micha A. Matters
Ludmila S. Kalter
Esmerelda S. Andreva
Circus-master G. Hinze
Indian G. Clifford
ROH Chor, LPO, T. Beecham (pp1939; Ger)
(2/92) (LYRC) ① [2] **SRO830**
Mařenka L. Červinková
Jeník B. Blachut
Vašek R. Vonásek
Kečal K. Kalaš
Krušina L. Mráz
Háta V. Krilová
Micha J. Heriban
Ludmila J. Palivcová
Esmeralda J. Pechová
Circus-master B. Vich
Indian J. Soumar
Prague Rad Chor, Prague RSO, K. Ančerl (r1947)
(9/94) (MULT) ① [2] **310185-2**
Excs A. Dermota, E. Réthy, E. Kaufmann, O. Levko-Antosch, G. Monthy, E. Nikolaidi, A. Pernerstorfer, Vienna St Op Chor, Vienna St Op Orch, R. Moralt (pp1942: Ger)
(2/95) (SCHW) ① [2] **314572**
1. Czech PO, V. Neumann
(SUPR) ① **11 0624-2**
1. J. Sándor, Budapest SO (LASE) ① **15 514**
(LASE) ▭ **79 514**
1. NBC SO, A. Toscanini (bp1946)
(RCA) ① **GD60310**
1. Brno St PO, Y. Menuhin (r1992)
(SUPR) ① **11 1837-2**
1. Frankfurt RSO, E. Inbal
(TELD) ① **4509-94530-2**
1. Polish Chmbr PO, W. Rajski
(INTE) ① **INT830 899**
1. Solti Orchestral Project, G. Solti (pp1994)
(DECC) ① **444 458-2DH**
1. Czech PO, K. Ančerl (pp1963)
(ORFE) ① **C395951B**
1. Black Dyke Mills Band, J. Watson (r1992: arr Broadbent) (9/93) (POLY) ① **QPRL053D**
(9/93) (POLY) ▭ **CPRL053D**
1. NYPO, L. Bernstein (r1963)
(9/93) (SONY) ① **SMK47601**
1. RCA Victor SO, L. Stokowski (r1960)
(3/94) (RCA) ① **09026 61503-2**
1. LSO, B. Walter (r1938)
(8/94) (DUTT) ① **CDLX7008**
1. NBC SO, B. Walter (pp1940)
(2/95) (PEAR) ① **GEMMCD9131**
1. Chicago SO, F. Reiner (r1955)
(8/95) (RCA) ① **09026 62587-2**
1. LPO, H. Harty (r1933)
(9/95) (DUTT) ① **CDLX7016**
1, 2, , 11, 18 (pt), 19. LSO, G. Simon
(8/86) (CHAN) ① **CHAN8412**
(8/86) (CHAN) ▭ **ABTD1149**
1, 9c, 11. Philh, W. Boughton
(NIMB) ① **NI5120**
(NIMB) ▭ **NC5120**
1, 9c, 11. Prague Nat Th Chor, Prague Nat Th Orch, Z. Chalabala (SUPR) ① **11 1115-2**
1, 9c, 11. Israel PO, I. Kertész (r1962)
(DECC) ① [2] **443 015-2DF2**
1, 9c, 11, 19. Prague SO, J. Bělohlávek
(SUPR) ① **11 0377-2**
1, 9c, 11, 19. Luxembourg RSO, L. Hager (r1983) (FORL) ① **FF049**
1, 9c, 11, 19. VPO, James Levine (r1986)
(8/89) (DG) ① **427 340-2GH**
1, 9c, 11, 19. RLPO, L. Pešek (r1990)
(11/94) (VIRG) ① **VC7 59285-2**
3. E. Destinn, anon (r1905: Ger)
(PEAR) ① **GEMMCD9172**
3. E. Destinn, anon (r1905)
(12/94) (SUPR) ① [12] **11 2136-2(1)**
3, 22a-c L. Popp, Munich RO, S. Soltesz (r1987)
(4/89) (EMI) ① **CDC7 49319-2**
5. G. Beňačková, P. Dvorský, Czech PO, Z. Košler (r1980-81) (KOCH) ① **34036-2**
(KOCH) ▭ **24036-4**
5. E. Rethberg, R. Tauber, orch (r1921: Ger)
(7/94) (PREI) ① **89051**
5, 16a R. Tauber, E. Rethberg, orch (Ger: r1919)
(3/92) (EMI) ① **CDH7 64029-2**
5, 23. E. Destinn, O. Mařák, orch, B. Seidler-Winkler (r1909)
(12/94) (SUPR) ① [12] **11 2136-2(2)**
9c RPO, E. Bátiz (RPO) ① **CDRPO5006**
(RPO) ▭ **ZCRPO5006**
9c, 11. RTL SO, L. Hager (LASE) ① **15 504**
(LASE) ▭ **79 504**
9c, 11, 19. BPO, H. von Karajan (r1971)
(DG) ① **439 451-2GCL**
9c, 11, 19. Cleveland Orch, G. Szell
(6/93) (SONY) ① **SBK48279**
(6/93) (SONY) ▭ **SBT48279**
11, 19. Czech PO, V. Neumann
(SUPR) ① **11 1287-2**
11, 19. Czech PO, V. Neumann
(9/90) (ORFE) ① **C180891A**
14, 15. F. Wunderlich, G. Frick, Bamberg SO, R. Kempe (Ger) (EMI) ① [3] **CZS7 62993-2**
14, 15. P. Anders, W. Schirp, Berlin Deutsche Op Orch, H. Schmidt-Isserstedt (r1940: Ger)
(TELD) ① **4509-95512-2**
15. J. Schmidt, M. Bohnen, BPO, S. Meyrowitz (r1929: Ger) (RELI) ① **CR921036**
15. C. Kullman, E. Fuchs, Berlin City Op Orch, A. von Zemlinsky (Ger: r1931)
(11/93) (PREI) ① **89057**
16a R. Tauber, orch (Ger: r1919)
(7/89) (EMI) ① **CDM7 69476-2**
16a J. Patzak, orch, M. Gurlitt (Ger: r1929)
(3/90) (PEAR) ① **GEMMCD9383**
16a R. Tauber, orch (Ger: r1919)
(12/92) (NIMB) ① **NI7830**
(12/92) (NIMB) ▭ **NC7830**
16a, 23. G. Nelepp, E. Shumilova, USSR RSO, K. Kondrashin (r c1950: Russ)
(PREI) ① **89081**
18. L. Warren (bp1953) (VAI) ▭ **VAI69105**

19. Sun Life Band, R. Newsome (arr R. Newsome) (GRAS) ① **GRCD41**
19. LSO, C. Mackerras (r1961) (MERC) ① **434 352-2MM**
22a-c E. Schwarzkopf, Philh, Helmut Schmidt (Ger) (10/88) (EMI) ① **CDM7 69501-2**
22a-c S. Jurinac, Philh, W. Braithwaite (r1950; Ger) (1/90) (EMI) ① **CDH7 63199-2**
22a-c S. Danco, SRO, I. Karr (bp1953) (1/93) (CASC) ① **VEL2010**
22a-c J. Novotná, orch, A. Wallenstein (bp1942) (4/93) (SUPR) ① **11 1491-2**
22a, 22b E. Schwarzkopf, Philh, H. Schmidt (r1956: Ger) (EMI) ① **CDM5 65577-2**
22a, 22b E. Destinn, orch, B. Seidler-Winkler (r1908) (12/94) (SUPR) ① [12] **11 2136-2(2)**
22a, 22b H. Konetzni, VPO, H. von Karajan (r1947: Ger) (1/95) (PREI) ① **90078**
22b E. Destinn, orch, B. Seidler-Winkler (r1908) (5/94) (SUPR) ① **11 1337-2**
23. F. Wunderlich, P. Lorengar, Bamberg SO, R. Kempe (Ger) (EMI) ① [3] **CZS7 62993-2**

The **Brandenburgers in Bohemia– opera: 3 acts (1866—Prague) (Lib. K Sabina)**

Volfram Olbramovič K. Kalaš
Oldřich Rokycanský J. Joran
Junoš I. Žídek
Jan Tausendmark Z. Otava
Varneman A. Votava
Jíra B. Vich
Ludiše M. Šubrtová
Vlčenka M. Fidlerová
Děčena V. Soukupová
Old villager E. Haken
Town crier J. Jindrák
Prague Nat Th Chor, Prague Nat Th Orch, J.H. Tichý (r1963) (5/94) (SUPR) ① [2] **11 1804-2**

The night is quiet I. Žídek, B. Vich, Prague Nat Th Chor, Prague Nat Th Orch, J.H. Tichý (r1963) (KOCH) ① **34036-2** (KOCH) ▭ **24036-4**

Dalibor– opera: 3 acts, B133 (1868—Prague) (Lib. J. Wenzig, trans E. Špindler)

EXCERPTS: 1. Overture. ACT 1: 2. Oh no! From the prison's pit; 3. You know by now; 4a. Oh hear of what I must complain; 4b. The sun did set; 5a. I won't deny it; 5b. When Ždeněk mine; 6. Oh, didst thou hear it, friend; 7. What storm here in my bosom. ACT 2: 8. Oh yes, the gayest is this our world; 9. My dearest, my yearning; 10. Oh, how saddening is a jailer's life; 11. Oh, goodness! Now so quickly came to me; 12a. It was he again; 12b. Oh, Ždeněk, just one fleeting; 13. You're asking who I can!; 14. Oh, unspeakable charm of love. ACT 3: 15. It will be near to forty years; 16a. At this late hour; 16b. Beautiful aim that any king; 17a. It's the third night; 17b. Oh, God! I'll be free again!; 18. Let so it be!.

Dalibor V. Přibyl
Vladislav J. Jindrák
Milada N. Kniplová
Budivoj A. Švorc
Beneš J. Horáček
Vítek Z. Švehla
Jitka H. Svobodová-Janků
Judge D. Jedlička
Prague Nat Th Chor, Prague Nat Th Orch, J. Krombholc (r1967) (SUPR) ① [2] **11 2185-2**

Dalibor L.M. Vodička
Vladislav I. Kusnjer
Milada E. Urbanová
Budivoj V. Kříž
Beneš J. Kalendocsky
Vítek M. Kopp
Jitka J. Marková
Judge Bohuslav Maršík
Prague Nat Th Chor, Prague Nat Th Orch, Z. Košler (r1995) (SUPR) ① [2] **SU0077-2**

Ah, whose is the spell B. Blachut, Prague Op Orch, J. Charvát (r1947) (4/92) (EMI) ① [7] **CHS7 69741-2(6)**
Excs A. Jerger, H. Konetzni, T. Mazaroff, Vienna St Op Chor, Vienna St Op Orch, L. Ludwig (pp1942: Ger) (SCHW) ① [2] **314692**
How confused I feel! L. Popp, Munich RO, S. Soltesz (r1987) (4/89) (EMI) ① **CDC7 49319-2**
O Zdeněk; Ah, whose is the spell F. Völker, Berlin Staatskapelle, G. Steeger (r1940: Ger) (8/94) (PREI) ① **89070**
6. H. Winkelmann, anon (r1904: Ger) (7/91) (SYMP) ① **SYMCD1081**
11. E. Destinn, orch, B. Seidler-Winkler (r1909: Ger) (PEAR) ① **GEMMCD9172**
11. E. Destinn, orch, B. Seidler-Winkler (r1908) (5/94) (SUPR) ① **11 1337-2**
11. E. Destinn, orch, B. Seidler-Winkler (r1908) (12/94) (SUPR) ① [12] **11 2136-2(1)**
11. E. Destinn, orch, B. Seidler-Winkler (r1909: Ger) (12/94) (SUPR) ① [12] **11 2136-2(2)**
18(pt) H. Konetzni, W. Franter, E. Réthy, Vienna St Op Chor, Vienna St Op Orch, L. Ludwig (pp1942: Ger) (SCHW) ① [2] **314692**

The **Devil's Wall– comic-romantic opera: 3 acts, T129 (1882—Prague) (Lib. E Krásnohorská)**

EXCERPTS: 1. Overture. ACT 1: 2. A horse without a rider; 3a. No-one? Happy me; 3b. The morn's greetings!; 4a. I bid you welcome, my maiden!; 4b. Thus to rest in your arms; 5. Ha, ha, ha, my dearest one; 6a. Welcome home ... Our commander; 6b. O, my lord!; 6c. O, woe is me!; 7a. A swift messenger is approaching; 7b. Only one lovely woman's beauty touched me. ACT 2: 8a. Who will offer shelter to the weary?; 8b. Where can I flee before so sweet an image?; 8c. Sleep, my innocent one; 9. It is hard to get accustomed to!; 10. Do something, Father; 11a. Jarek! My dear friend!; 11b. Like an orphaned bird; 12. Welcome to this castle; 13. O, what a whirl!; 14. What is your grave news? ACT 3: 15. There's the monastery; 16. Where are you taking me?; 17. My eyes have seen it!; 18. I am a good shepherd of sheep; 19. Come, quietly and stealthily; 20. Ah! Run for safety!; 21. I know why that Záviš; 22. Save yourselves!; 23. To pray alone.

Vok Vítkovic V. Bednář
Záviš Vítkovic I. Mixová
Jarek I. Žídek
Hedvika M. Šubrtová
Michálek A. Votava
Katuška L. Domanínská
Beneš K. Berman
Rarach L. Mráz
Prague Nat Th Chor, Prague Nat Th Orch, Z. Chalabala (r1960) (11/95) (SUPR) ① [2] **11 2201-2**

The **Kiss– opera: 2 acts (1876—Prague) (Lib E. Krásnohorská after K. Světlá)**

EXCERPTS: 1. Overture. ACT 1: 2a. Today with his friends he has drowned his sorrow; 2b. We are united; 3a. Let us drink now to their health; 3b. Never, never, in my despair; 3c. Here you are, my guiltless child; 3d. Till the wedding I shall wait; 3e. I only want to kiss your cheek; 4. What I've now foreseen has now arrived; 5. How could he ever forget our love; 6a. I'm, my dear girl, old by now; 6b. Cradle song; 7. Play musicians, play a jump dance. ACT 2: 8. Let's go; 9. If I knew how to redeem my guilt; 10. Just go and pray; 11. O, why ever did I believe follishly; 12. Well did he show to me; 13. The Lark's song: Herald, skylark, herald, a new day; 14. O yes, I forgive you, young man.

Paloucký E. Haken
Vendulka E. Děpoltová
Lukáš L.M Vodička
Tomĕs V. Zítek
Martinka L. Márová
Matovš K. Hanuš
Barče B. Effenberková
Guard Z. Jankovský
Brno Janáček Op Chor, Brno Janáček Op Orch, F. Vajnar (r1980) (9/95) (SUPR) ① [2] **11 2180-2**

Cradle song E. Destinn, orch, B. Seidler-Winkler (r1908) (PEAR) ① **GEMMCD9172**
1. Czech PO, V. Neumann (SUPR) ① **11 0624-2**
6b E. Schumann, orch, W. Goehr (r1936: Ger) (PEAR) ① **GEMMCD9445**
6b E. Schumann, orch (r1937: Ger) (BEUL) ① **2PD4**
6b S. Jurinac, Philh, W. Braithwaite (Ger: r1950) (1/90) (EMI) ① **CDH7 63199-2**
6b J. Novotná, RCA Victor Orch, F. Weissmann (r1945) (4/93) (SUPR) ① **11 1491-2**
6b E. Destinn, orch, J. Pasternack (r1921) (11/93) (ROMO) ① [2] **81002-2**
6b E. Destinn, orch, J. Pasternack (r1921) (12/94) (SUPR) ① [12] **11 2136-2(5)**
6b E. Destinn, orch, B. Seidler-Winkler (r1908) (12/94) (SUPR) ① [12] **11 2136-2(2)**
13. J. Novotná, orch (r1926) (4/93) (SUPR) ① **11 1491-2**

Libuše– opera: 3 acts (1881—Prague) (Lib. J Wenzig, trans Spindler)

EXCERPTS: 1. Prelude; 2. Eternal gods, you that dwell above the clouds; 3. You elders, nobles. ACT 2: 4. My father; 5. When in the sweet yearning of love; 6. Without rest onwards and out in the fields; 7. The sun is blazing; 8. O, ye lime trees; 9. Ah, look into his face; 10. Peace be with you. ACT 3: 11. Introduction; 12. Welcome!; 13. Hail, Stronghold of Vyšehrad!; 14. O gods almighty.

Libuše E. Urbanová
Přemysl V. Kříž
Chrudoš L. Vele
Štáhlav J. Markvart
Lutobor M. Podskalský
Radovan P. Červinka
Krasava H. Kaupová
Radmila M. Volková
Prague Nat Th Chor, Prague Nat Th Orch, O. Dohnányi (pp1995) (SUPR) ① [2] **SU0200-2**

Libuse G. Beňačková
Přemysl V. Zítek
Chrudoš A. Švorc
Štáhlav L.M. Vodička
Lubtor K. Průša
Radovan R. Tuček
Krasava E. Děpoltová
Radmila V. Soukupová
Prague Nat Th Chor, Prague Nat Th Orch, Z. Košler (pp1983) (4/94) (SUPR) ① [3] **11 1276-2**

Fanfares Prague Nat Th Orch, Z. Košler (r1982) (SUPR) ① **11 2118-2**
1. Prague SO, J. Bělohlávek (SUPR) ① **11 0377-2**
1. Prague RSO, V. Talich (r1953) (MULT) ① **310151-2**
2. L. Dvořáková, Prague RSO, V. Talich (r1953) (MULT) ① **310151-2**
14. G. Beňačková, Prague Nat Th Chor, Prague Nat Th Orch, Z. Košler (pp1983) (KOCH) ① **34036-2** (KOCH) ▭ **24036-4**

The **Two Widows– opera: 2 acts (1874: rev vers 1878—Prague) (Lib. E. Züngel, after P J F Mallefille)**

Karolina J. Jonášová
Anežka M. Machotková
Ladislav M. Švejda
Mumlal D. Jedlička
Toník A. Hampel
Lidunka D. Šounová-Brouková
Prague Rad Chor, Prague RSO, J. Krombholc (bp1974) (6/93) (PRAG) ① [2] **PR250 022/3**

Karolina N. Šormová
Anežka M. Machotková
Ladislav J. Zahradníček
Mumlal J. Horáček
Toník Z. Švehla
Lidunka D. Šounová-Brouková
Prague Nat Th Chor, Prague Nat Th Orch, F. Jílek (r1975) (10/94) (SUPR) ① [2] **11 2122-2**

SMYTH, Dame Ethel (Mary) *(1858–1944) England*

The **Boatswain's Mate– opera: 2 acts (1916—London) (Lib. cpsr, after W W Jacobs)**

EXCERPTS: 1. Overture. ACT 1: 2. When rocked on the billows; 3. The Keeper; 4. A friend and I were on the piece; 5a. Contrariness—Suppose you mean to do a given thing; 5b. What if I were young again. ACT 2: 6. Oh! dear, if I had known; 7. The first thing to do is to get rid of the body; 8. When the sun is setting.

5a, 5b E. Harrhy, Plymouth Music Series Orch, P. Brunelle (8/91) (VIRG) ① **VC7 59022-2**

The **Wreckers– opera: 3 acts (1906—Leipzig) (Lib. cpsr)**

EXCERPTS: 1. Overture.

Pascoe P. Sidhom
Lawrence D. Wilson-Johnson
Harvey; A Man B. Bannatyne-Scott
Tallan A. Roden
Jack A. Sand
Mark J. Lavender
Thirza A-M. Owens

Avis J. Howarth
Huddersfield Choral Soc, BBC PO, O. de la Martinez (pp1994)
(11/94) (CONI) ① [2] **CDCF250/1**
1. SNO, A. Gibson (r1968)
(CFP) ① **CD-CFP4635**

SORIANO, Perez *(?19th Cent) Spain*

El **Guitarrico– zarzuela**
El guitarrico T. Ruffo, orch (r1914)
(2/93) (PREI) ① [3] **89303(1)**
Jota de Perico J. Carreras, ECO, E. Ricci (r1994) (2/95) (ERAT) ① **4509-95789-2**
(2/95) (ERAT) ▭ **4509-95789-4**
Serenata P. Domingo, Barcelona SO, G. Navarro (ACAN) ① **49 390**

SOROZÁBAL, Pablo *(1897–1988) Spain*

Del manojo de rosas– zarzuela: 2 acts (1934)
EXCERPTS: 1. Madrilena bonita.
1. P. Domingo, Miami SO, E. Kohn (pp1991)
(IMP) ① **MCD43**
1. P. Domingo, Madrid SO, M. Moreno-Buendia (r1987) (1/89) (EMI) ① **CDC7 49148-2**

Katiuska– zarzuela: 2 acts (1931)
Katiuska P. Lorengar
Prince Sergio Alfredo Kraus
Pedro Stakoff R. Cesari
Bruno Brunovich M. Gas
Olga E. Serrano
Tatiana S.P. Carpio
Miska A.M. Fernandez
Boni F. Maroto
Amadeo Pich J. Marin
Madrid Coros Cantores, Madrid Concerts Orch, P. Sorozábal
(10/92) (HISP) ① **CDZ7 67330-2**

La **Tabernera del puerto– zarzuela: 3 acts (1940—Madrid) (Lib. Fernandez & Romero)**
EXCERPTS -; 1. No puede ser.
1. P. Domingo, MMF Orch, Rome Op Orch, Z. Mehta (pp1990) (DECC) ◐ **071 123-1DH**
(DECC) ▭▭ **071 123-3DH**
1. J. Carreras, Seville SO, E. Garcia-Asensio (pp1991) (RCA) ① **RD61191**
1. P. Domingo, MMF Orch, Rome Op Orch, Z. Mehta (pp1990) (DECC) **OO 430 433-5DH**
1. J. Carreras, Seville SO, E. Garcia-Asensio (pp1991) (RCA) **OO 09026 61191-5**
1. P. Domingo, Rio de Janeiro Municipal Th Orch, J. DeMain (pp1992)
(SONY) ◐ **SLV48362**
(SONY) ▭▭ **SHV48362**
1. P. Domingo, Madrid SO, M. Moreno-Buendia (r1987) (1/89) (EMI) ① **CDC7 49148-2**
1. P. Domingo, MMF Orch, Rome Op Orch, Z. Mehta (pp1990)
(10/90) (DECC) ① **430 433-2DH**
(10/90) (DECC) ▭ **430 433-4DH**
1. P. Domingo, Madrid SO, E. G. Asensio (pp1991) (11/92) (IMP) ① **MCD45**
1. J. Carreras, ECO, E. Ricci (r1994)
(2/95) (ERAT) ① **4509-95789-2**
(2/95) (ERAT) ▭ **4509-95789-4**

SOUTULLO , Reveriano *(1884–1932) Spain*

La **Del Soto Parral– zarzuela: 2 acts (1927) (comp with J V Carbonell. Lib Carreño & Ardavín)**
Ya mis horas felices P. Domingo, Madrid SO, M. Moreno-Buendia (r1987)
(1/89) (EMI) ① **CDC7 49148-2**

La **Leyenda de Beso– operetta: 2 acts (Cpsd with Juan Vert)**
Amor mi raza sabe conquistar
Hecho de un rayo de luna P. Domingo, Barcelona SO, G. Navarro (ACAN) ① **49 390**
P. Lorengar, P. Domingo, Austrian RSO, G. Navarro (SONY) ① **MK39210**

Ultimo romantico– operetta: 2 acts (Cpsd with Juan Vert)**
Bella enamorada P. Domingo, Barcelona SO, G. Navarro (ACAN) ① **49 390**
Bella enamorada P. Domingo, Madrid SO, E. G. Asensio (pp1991) (11/92) (IMP) ① **MCD45**

Noche de amor P. Domingo, ROHO, J. Barker (pp1988) (9/89) (EMI) ① **CDC7 49811-2**

SPOHR, Louis *(1784–1859) Germany*

Der **Alchymist– opera: 3 acts (1830—Kassel) (Lib. K. Pfeiffer, after Irving)**
EXCERPTS: 1. Overture.
1. Berlin RSO, C. Fröhlich (r1991)
(CPO) ① **CPO999 093-2**

Der **Berggeist– opera: 3 acts, Op. 73 (1825—Kassel) (Lib. G. Döring)**
EXCERPTS: 1. Overture.
1. Berlin RSO, C. Fröhlich (r1991)
(CPO) ① **CPO999 093-2**

Faust– opera: 2 (later 3) acts (1816—Prague) (Lib. J K Bernhard)
Faust M. Vier
Mephistopheles E. von Jordis
Kunigunde D. Jennings
Gulf I. Bric
Kaylinger M. Eichwalder
Wohlhaldt D. Walker
Wagner U. Neuweiler
Moor H. Kegler
Count Hugo W. Pugh
Röschen C. Taha
Franz D. Abbott
Sycorax M. Kowollik
Bielefeld Op Chor, Bielefeld PO, G. Moull (pp1993)
(8/94) (CPO) ① [2] **CPO999 247-2**
Faust B. Skovhus
Mephistopheles F. Hawlata
Kunigunde H. Martinpelto
Gulf; Kaylinger A. Reiter
Wohlhaldt R. Orrego
Wagner U. Wand
Count Hugo R. Swensen
Röschen B. Wohlfarth
Franz C. Späth
Sycorax M. Borst
Stuttgart Rad Chor, Kaiserslautern Rad Orch, K. Arp (r1993)
(12/94) (CAPR) ① [2] **60 049-2**
Der Hölle selbst will ich...Liebe ist die zarte Blüte T. Hampson, Munich RO, F. Luisi (r1994)
(9/95) (EMI) ① **CDC5 55233-2**
Ich bin allein, des Abends Nähe I. Siebert, D. Klöcker, South-West German RSO, K. Donath
(SCHW) ① **314018**
Ich bin allein E. Ritchie, V. Soames, J. Purvis (r1992) (3/94) (CLRI) ① **CC0006**
Overture Budapest SO, A. Walter
(MARC) ① **8 223122**

Jessonda– opera: 3 acts, Op. 63 (1823—Kassel) (Lib. Gehe)
Overture
Jessonda J. Varady
Amazili R. Behle
Dandau K. Moll
Nadori T. Moser
Tristan d'Acunha D. Fischer-Dieskau
Pedro Lopes P. Haage
Indian Officer P. Galliard
A Bayadère C. Meyer-Esche
Hamburg St Op Chor, Hamburg PO, G. Albrecht
(11/91) (ORFE) ① [2] **C240912H**
Overture Budapest SO, A. Walter
(MARC) ① **8 223122**
Overture Berlin RSO, C. Fröhlich (r1991)
(CPO) ① **CPO999 093-2**

Pietro von Abano– romantic opera: 2 acts, Op. 76 (1827—Kassel) (Lib. K. Pfeiffer, after Treck)
EXCERPTS: 1. Overture.
1. Berlin RSO, C. Fröhlich (r1991)
(CPO) ① **CPO999 093-2**

SPONTINI , Gaspare (Luigi Pacifico) *(1774–1851) Italy*

Agnes von Hohenstaufen– opera: 2 (later 3) acts (1827 rev 1829 aand 1837—Berlin) (Lib. E Raupach rev Lichtenstein)
EXCERPTS: 1. O re dei cieli.
O Re dei Cieli A. Cerquetti, Milan RAI SO, A. Basile (bp1956) (FONI) ① **CDMR5014**
Quando Zefiro; Solo tu M. Caballé, Rome RAI Chor, Rome RAI Orch, R. Muti (pp1970)
(MEMO) ① [2] **HR4279/80**
1. A. Cerquetti, MMF Orch, G. Gavazzeni (r1956) (DECC) ① **440 411-2DM**

Fernand Cortez (La conquète du Mexique)– tragic opera: 3 acts (1809—Paris) (Lib. Jouy, J. A. d'Esmenard)
1. Overture.
1. Horreaux-Trehard Duo (arr 2 gtrs)
(CALL) ① **CAL9218**

Olimpie– tragédie lyrique: 3 acts (1821—Berlin) (Lib. Dieulafoy and Briffaut)
Olympia J. Varady
Statira S. Toczyska
Cassandre Ferruccio Tagliavini
Antigonè D. Fischer-Dieskau
L'Hiérophante G. Fortune
Hermas J. Becker
Berlin RIAS Chbr Ch, Berlin Deutsche Op Chor, Berlin RSO, G. Albrecht (Ital: rev 1826)
(11/87) (ORFE) ① [3] **C137862H**

La **Vestale– tragédie lyrique: 3 acts (1807—Paris) (Lib. V J E de Jouy)**
EXCERPTS: 1. Overture. ACT 1: 1b. Périsse la vestale impié; 2a. Près de ce temple auguste, à Vesta consacre?; 2b. Dans le sein d'un ami fidèle; 3a. Eh bien! partage donc mon crime ma fureur; 3b. Quand l'amitié seconde mon courage; 4. Fille du ciel, éternelle Vesta; 5a. Prêtresse dans ce jour, Rome victorieuse; 5b. L'amour est un mostre; 5c. Au nom de tous les Dieux; 6a. Ô d'un pouvoir funeste, invincible ascendant!; 6b. Licinius, je vais donc te revoir; 7. De lauriers couvrons les chemins. ACT 2: 8. Feu créateur, âme du monde; 9a. Du plus auguste ministre; 9b. Toi que j'implore avec effroi (Tu che invoco con orrore); 10a. Impitoyables dieux! (O Nume, tutelar degli infelici); 10b. L'arret et prononcé, ma carrière est remplie; 11a. Julia...Je l'entends; 11b. Les dieux prendront pitié du sort qui nous accable; 11c. Vénus doit à l'amour son appui protecteur; 12. Quel trouble! Quels transports!; 13a. Suis moi!—Quelqu' in vient; 13b. Ah! si je te suis chère; 14a. Il vivra!...D'un oeil ferme; 14b. Vengeancede leurs projects criminels; 14c. Sa bouche a prononcé l'arrêt. ACT 3: 15a. Qu'ai je vu! quels apprêts! quel spectacle d'horreur!; 15b. Non, non, je vis encore; 16a. Cinna, que fait l'armée?; 16b. Ce n'est plus le temps d'écouter; 17a. Mais avant de tenter un combat inégal; 17b. C'est à toi de trembler!; 18a. Différons, croyez-moi, l'instant du sacrifice; 18b. Périsse la vestale impié; 19a. Adieu, mes tendres soeurs; 20a. Sur l'autel profané de la chaste déesse; 20b. Vesta nous t'implorons pour le vierge coupable; 21a. Les dieux ont prononcé son juste châtiment; 21b. Toi, que je laisse sur la terre (Caro ogetto, il di cui nome); 22a. Arrêtez, ministres de la mort!; 22b. Ô terreur! ô disgrace!.
Julia K. Huffstodt
Licinius A. M. Moore
Cinna J. P. Raftery
Chief Vestal D. Graves
Pontiff D. Kavrakos
Haruspex A. Bramante
Consul S. Sammaritano
La Scala Chor, La Scala Orch, R. Muti (pp1993)
(SONY) ① [3] **S3K66357**
Julia R. Plowright
Licinius F. Araiza
Cinna P. Lefebre
Chief Vestal G. Pasino
Pontiff A. Cauli
Haruspex F. de Grandis
Bavarian Rad Chor, Munich RSO, G. Kuhn (r1991)
(7/93) (ORFE) ① [2] **C256922H**
Overture La Scala Orch, A. Guarnieri (r1927)
(BONG) ① **GB1039-2**
1. La Scala Orch, A. Guarnieri (r1928)
(4/94) (EMI) ① [3] **CHS7 64864-2(1)**
9b M. Callas, Milan RAI SO, A. Simonetto (r1956) (FONI) ① **CDO104**
9b M. Callas, La Scala Orch, T. Serafin (r1955: Ital) (2/90) (EMI) ① [4] **CMS7 63244-2**
9b R. Ponselle, orch, Rosario Bourdon (r1926: Ital) (2/92) (MMOI) ① **CDMOIR408**
9b E. Mazzoleni, orch (r1909/11: Ital)
(4/94) (EMI) ① [3] **CHS7 64860-2(2)**
9b K. Vayne, orch (r1950s)
(6/95) (PREI) ① **89996**
9b, 10a R. Ponselle, orch, Rosario Bourdon (r1926: Ital) (10/89) (NIMB) ① **NI7805**
(NIMB) ▭ **NC7805**

9b, 10a (2 vers) R. Ponselle, orch, Rosario Bourdon (r1926: Ital) (11/94) (ROMO) ⓓ [2] **81007-2**
9b, 10a, 21b M. Callas, La Scala Orch, T. Serafin (r1955: Ital) (11/86) (EMI) ⓓ **CDC7 47282-2**
10a M. Callas, La Scala Orch, T. Serafin (r1955: Ital) (EMI) ⓓ **CDC5 55216-2** (EMI) ⊟ **EL555216-4**
10a R. Ponselle, orch, Rosario Bourdon (r1926: Ital) (1/90) (RCA) ⓓ **GD87810**
15a, 15b P. Domingo, National PO, E. Kohn (Ital) (11/90) (EMI) ⓓ **CDC7 54053-2**

STANFORD, Sir Charles Villiers *(1852–1924) Ireland/England*

Shamus O'Brien– comic opera: 2 acts, Op. 61 (1896—London) (Lib. G H Jessop, after J S Le Fanu)
EXCERPTS: 1. Ochone! When I Used to Be Young; 2. Where is the Man?; 3. The Song of the Banshee.
1. J. O'Mara, anon (r1901) (10/92) (SYMP) ⓓ **SYMCD1093**
1. J. O'Mara (r1901) (5/94) (PEAR) ⓓ [3] **GEMMCDS9050/2(1)**

STEFFANI, Agostino *(1654–1728) Italy*

Henrico Leone– opera: 3 acts (1689—Hanover) (Lib. O. Mauro)
Henrico R. Popken
Metilda M. Frimmer
Almaro D. Diwiak
Idalba S. Szameit
Errea N. Yoko
Ircano, Demone G. Faulstich
Eurillo C. Guber
Capella A. Steffani, L. Rovatkay (CALI) ⓓ **CAL50855**

STOLZ, Robert *(1880–1975) Austria*

Der **Favorit– operetta: 2 acts (1916—Berlin) (Lib. F Grünbaum & W Sterk)**
Du sollst der Kaiser meiner Seele sein A. Moffo, H. Galatis Orch, H. Galatis (arr Galatis) (EURO) ⓓ **GD69113**
Du sollst der Kaiser I. Eisinger, Berlin City Op Orch, S. Meyrowitz (r1931) (RELI) ⓓ **CR921036**
Du sollst der Kaiser meiner Seele sein L. Popp, ASMF, N. Marriner (6/88) (EMI) ⓓ **CDC7 49700-2**
Du sollst der Kaiser meiner Seele sein B. Hendricks, Philh, L. Foster, H. Bean (r1992) (8/93) (EMI) ⓓ **CDC7 54626-2**
Du sollst der Kaiser meiner Seele sein J. Migenes, Vienna Volksoper Orch, L. Schifrin (r1993) (1/94) (ERAT) ⓓ **4509-92875-2** (1/94) (ERAT) ⊟ **4509-92875-4**

Frühjahrsparade– operetta: 2 acts (1964—Vienna) (Lib. Marischka and H. Wiener)
Wien wird schön erst bei Nacht L. Popp, ASMF, N. Marriner (6/88) (EMI) ⓓ **CDC7 49700-2**

Venus im Seide– operetta: 3 acts (1932—Zurich) (Lib. Grünwald and L. Herzer)
Spiel auf deiner Geige J. Migenes, Vienna Volksoper Orch, L. Schifrin (r1993) (1/94) (ERAT) ⓓ **4509-92875-2** (1/94) (ERAT) ⊟ **4509-92875-4**

Zwei Herzen in Dreivierteltakt– operetta (1948—Vienna) (Wds. W. Reisch and F. Schulz)
Zwei Herzen in Dreivierteltakt M. Feinstein, A. Guzelimian (Eng) (5/90) (EMI) ⊟ **EG749768-2**

STRADELLA, Alessandro *(1644–1682) Italy*

Il **Moro per amore– opera per musica: 3 acts (1681—Genoa) (Lib. F Orsini, Duca di Bracciano)**
Rodrigo R. Ristori
Eurinda R. Invernizzi
Lucinda S. Piccollo
Lindora M. Lazzara
Feraspe; Floridoro V. Matacchini
Fiorino M. G. Liguori
Filandro M. Beasley
A. Stradella Consort, E. Velardi (r1992) (BONG) ⓓ [3] **GB2153/5-2**

STRAUS, Oscar *(1870–1954) Austria*

Didi– operetta (1906)
EXCERPTS: 1. Overture; 2. Waltz.
Waltz V. Kincses, Budapest Strauss SO, A. Walter (MARC) ⓓ **8 223596**

Drei Walzer– operetta: 3 acts (1935—Zurich) (Lib. P. Knepler & A. Robinson)
EXCERPTS: 1. Overture. SCENE 1: 2. Mehr im Takt, meine Damen; 3a. Aber gehn S'- sein S' net so grantig; 3b. Wein ist ein Liebeslied; 4a. Sie gestatten, aber hattenwir nicht längst die Ehre schon; 4b. Was der Gärtner für, die Rosen; 5. Gerne suchen wir Talent (finaletto). SCENE 2: 6. Hast du was g'hört?; 7. So ein Eklat war noch nicht da (finale). SCENE 3: 8a. Du bist der Tag, du bist die Welt; 8b. Wien ist ein Liebeslied; 9. Radetzky March.
Excs: French R. Crespin, Vienna Volksoper Orch, A. Lombard (r1970/1) (DECC) ⓓ **440 416-2DM**
3b A. Auger, D. Baldwin (1988: French) (DELO) ⓓ **DE3029**
8b J. Micheau, Raymond St Paul Chor, SO, P. Bonneau (r1950s: Fr) (EMI) ⓓ [2] **CZS7 67875-2**

Der **Letzte Walzer– operetta: 3 acts (1920—Berlin) (Lib. J. Brammer & A. Grünwald)**
EXCERPTS: 1. Overture. ACT 1: 2. Es lebe der Herr General!; 3. Bei Lied und Wein; 4. Rosen, die wir nicht erreichten; 5. Mama, Mama! Wir wollen einen Mann!; 6. O kommt, o kommt und tanzt mit mir; 7. Das ist der letzte Walzer; 8. Graf Sarrasow, Sie geh'n zu weit (finale). ACT 2: 9. Hört ihr die liebliche, zwingende; 10. Dann weiss der Jüngling, dass es Zeit; 11. Tanze, vera Lisaweta; 12. Du hast zwei Grübchen; 13. Hast du es nicht erraten?; 14. Der Klang des Guslizither (finale) ACT 3: 15. Wir sind die Balletteusen; 16. Bei Lied und Wein (reprise); 17. O du pikantes, kleines O-la-la; 18. Du lieber letzer Walzer (finale).
Das ist der letzte Walzer M. Schramm, R. Schock, Berlin SO, R. Stolz (2/91) (EURO) ⓓ **GD69022**

Rund um die Liebe– operetta: 3 acts (1914—Vienna) (Lib. R. Bodanzky & F. Thelen)
EXCERPTS: 1. Overture; 2. Es gibt Dinge, die muss man vergessen.
1. Budapest Strauss SO, A. Walter (r1993) (MARC) ⓓ **8 223596**
1, 2. R. Schock, Berlin SO, R. Stolz (2/91) (EURO) ⓓ **GD69022**

Der **Tapfere Soldat– operetta: 3 acts (1908—Vienna) (Lib. Bernauer and Jacobson. Eng: The Chocolate Sol)**
EXCERPTS: 1. Overture. ACT 1: 2. Wir marschieren durch die Nacht; 3. Mein Held!; 4. Wie schön ist dieses Männerbild; 5. Komm', Komm! Held meiner Träume; 6. In meinen Leben sah ich nie einen Helden; 7. Ach, du kleiner Praliné-Soldat; 8a. Es ist ein Schicksal, schwer zu tragen; 8b. Weil's Leben süss und herlich ist; 9. Suchet alle Mann, der Serbe nict entwischen Kann!; 10a. Drei Frauensassen am Feuerherd; 10b. Tiralala! (finale). ACT 2: 11. Ein Hoch ein Hoch der Heldenschar!; 12a. Ich bin gewöhnt stets nur zu siegen; 12b. Mein Mädchenherz, das schlägt; 13. Ich habe die Feinde gesschlagen auf's Haupt; 14a. Ein Jeder hat es schon erhahren; 14b. Wenn man so dürfte, wie man wollte; 15. Ach, es ist doch ein schönes Vergnügen; 16. Es war einmal ein Fräulein; 17. Leute, Leute, kommt herbei; 18. Ich was der Helder deiner Träume. ACT 3: 19. Mein lieber Herr von Bumerli; 20. Pardon! Ich steig' ja nur auf den Balcon!; 21a. Du magst dein Köpfchen noch so heftig schütteln; 21b. Freundchen, Freundchen nur nicht toben; 22a. Wenn ein Mann ein Mädchen; 22b. Lieber Schwiegerpapa, liebe Schweigermama; 23. Ich geb' Dir morgens einem Kuss.
Held meiner Träume E. Steber, Orch, Anon (cond) (bp1951) (VAI) ▭ **VAI69112**
Held meiner Träume E. Steber, Orch, H. Barlow (bp1949) (VAI) ▭ **VAI69110**
Held meiner Träume J. Sutherland, New Philh, R. Bonynge (Eng) (DECC) ⓓ **433 223-2DWO** (DECC) ⊟ **433 223-4DWO**
Held meiner Träume M. Hill Smith, Chandos Concert Orch, S. Barry (Eng) (6/85) (CHAN) ⓓ **CHAN8362** (6/85) (CHAN) ⊟ **LBTD013**
Komm, Held meiner Träume M. Schramm, Berlin SO, R. Stolz (2/91) (EURO) ⓓ **GD69022**
Komm'! Held meiner Träume R. Tauber, P. Kahn (pp or bp) (2/92) (LYRC) ⓓ [2] **SRO830**
Komm, Held meiner Träume J. Migenes, Vienna Volksoper Orch, L. Schifrin (r1993) (1/94) (ERAT) ⓓ **4509-92875-2** (1/94) (ERAT) ⊟ **4509-92875-4**
Komm, komm, Held meiner Träume;Bulgaren March V. Kincses, Budapest Strauss SO, A. Walter (MARC) ⓓ **8 223596**

Ein **Walzertraum, '(A) Waltz Dream'– operetta: 3 acts (1907—Vienna) (Lib. Dörmann and Jacobson)**
EXCERPTS: 1. Overture. ACT 1: 2. Wir sind so aufgererf; 3. Ein Mädchen, das so lieb und brav; 4. O Jubel sondergleichen; 5a. Ich hab' mit Freuden angelhört; 5b. Alles was kock und fesch; 6a. Vorüber ist die Feier; 6b. Ich hab' einen Mann; 7a. Ah, was vernehm'ich!; 7b. Und die arm Dynastie; 8a. Da draussen im duftigen Garten; 8b. Leise, ganz leise klingt's durch den Raum; 9. Meiner lieber Freund, du lässt mich lang allein!. ACT 2: 10. G'stelle Mädl'n, resch und fesch; 11a. Kom'her, du mein reizendes Mäderl!; 11b. O du liebeer, o du g'scheiter; 12a. Das Geheimnis sollst du verraten; 12b. Temperamant! Temperament!; 13a. Lehn'dine Wang an meine Wang; 13b. Piccolo! Piccolo! Tsin-tsin-tsin; 14a. Wenn zwei Menschen sich anschau'n; 14b. Du bist der Traum, den oft ich geträumt; 15. Ich es möglich (finale). ACT 3: 16. Es geht von Mund zu Mond; 17. Ja, was ist denn nur los mit dir, Niki!; 18. Mann muss manches im Leben vergessen; 19. Mächt's auf die Tür'n, machtes auf die Fenster; 20. Einmal noch beben, eh'es vorbei.
Entrance March;Waltz;G'stellte Mäd'ln Budapest Strauss SO, A. Walter (r1993) (MARC) ⓓ **8 223596**
1, 2, 5a, 5b, 6a, 7a, 8a, 8b, 10, 11a, 12b, 13b, 14b, 20. H. Brauner, R. Holm, E. Liebesberg, D. Hermann, R. Christ, H. Prikopa, Vienna Volksoper Chor, Vienna Volksoper Orch, F. Bauer-Theussl (r1960) (KOCH) ⓓ **399 223**
6a, 6b, 8a, 8b, 10, 11a, 13b, 20. R. Schock, W. Lipp, L. Schmidt, F. Gruber, M. Schramm, Günther Arndt Ch, Berlin SO, R. Stolz (2/91) (EURO) ⓓ **GD69022**
8a, 8b R. Schock, M. Schmidt, orch, W. Schüchter (r1958) (EMI) ⓓ **CDM7 69475-2**
8a, 8b R. Tauber, Orch, F. Schönbaumsfeld (r1932) (12/89) (EMI) ⓓ **CDH7 69787-2**
8a, 8b M. Hill Smith, P. Morrison, Chandos Concert Orch, S. Barry (Eng) (2/90) (CHAN) ⓓ **CHAN8759** (2/90) (CHAN) ⊟ **LBTD023**
8b B. Weikl, Austrian RSO, K. Eichhorn (ORFE) ⓓ **C077831A**
8b Vienna SO, R. Stolz (EURO) ⓓ **258 667**
8b A. Baugé, orch (r1930s: French) (FORL) ⓓ **UCD19022**
8b P. Domingo, ECO, J. Rudel (2/87) (EMI) ⓓ **CDC7 47398-2**
8b R. Crooks, orch (r1933: Eng) (9/93) (CLAR) ⓓ **CDGSE78-50-50**

STRAUSS, Johann (Baptist) II *(1825–1899) Austria*

Blindekuh– operetta: 3 acts (1878—Vienna) (Lib. R. Kneisel)
Overture VJSO, W. Boskovsky (1/90) (EMI) ⓓ [2] **CZS7 62751-2**

Cagliostro in Wien– opera: 3 acts (1875—Vienna) (Lib. Lib. Zell and Genée)
Overture VJSO, J. Francek (LASE) ⓓ **15 619** (LASE) ⊟ **79 619**
Overture Vienna SO Strauss Ens, J. Wildner (r1992; arr Totzauer) (ORFE) ⓓ **C291931A**
Overture VPO, W. Boskovsky (r1967) (LOND) ⓓ **436 785-2LM**

Zigeunerkind, wie glänzt dein Haar L. Schöne, orch (r1925) (12/92) (NIMB) ⓘ **NI7833**
(12/92) (NIMB) ▭ **NC7833**

Der **Carneval in Rom, '(The) Carnival in Rome'– operetta: 3 acts (1873—Vienna) (Lib. Braun and Lindau)**
Overture VPO, W. Boskovsky (r1973)
(LOND) ⓘ **436 785-2LM**

Die **Fledermaus, '(The) Bat'– operetta: 3 acts (1874—Vienna) (Lib. Haffner and Genée, after Meilhac and Halevy)**
EXCERPTS: 1. Overture. ACT 1: 2. Täubchen, das entflattert ist; 3. Du darfst heut' nicht; 4. Nein, mit solchen Advokaten; 5. Komm' mit mir zum Souper; 6. So muss allein ich bleiben; 7. Trinke, Liebchen, trinke schnell; 8. Mein Herr, was dächten Sie; 9. Nein, nein, ich zweifle gar nicht mehr. ACT 2: 10a. Ein Souper heut uns winkt; 10b. Chacun à son goût!; 11a. Ach, meine Herr'n und Damen; 11b. Mein Herr Marquis; 12. Dieser Anstand, so manierlich; 13. Klänge der Heimat (Czardas); 14a. In Feuerstrom der Reben; 14b. Brüderlein und Schwesterlein; 15. Ballet; 16. Genug damit, genug!; ACT 3: 17. Spiel' ich die Unschuld; 18. Ich stehe voll Zagen; 19. O Fledermaus.

Rosalinde K. Te Kanawa
Adele H. Heichele
Eisenstein H. Prey
Alfred D. O'Neill
Doctor Falke B. Luxon
Orlovsky D. Soffel
Frosch J. Meinrad
ROH Chor, ROHO, P. Domingo, L. Lindtberg
(CAST) ▣ **CVI2023**

Rosalinde J. Sutherland
Adèle M. Brynnel
Orlofsky H. Begg
Alfred A. Austin
Falke M. Lewis
Blind G. Wilcock
Ida A-M. McDonald
Eisenstein R. Gard
Frank G. Yurisch
Frosch G. Ewer
Australian Op Chor, Sydney Eliz Orch, R. Bonynge, A. Besch
(MCEG) ▣ **VVD781**

Rosalinde N. Gustafson
Adele J. Howarth
Eisenstein L. Otey
Alfred B. Bottone
Doctor Falke A. Michaels-Moore
Orlovsky J. Kowalski
Frank E. Garrett
Blind J. Dobson
Ida G. Groves
Frosch J. Sessions
Guest 1 J. Sutherland
Guest 2 L. Pavarotti
Guest 3 M. Horne
ROH Chor, ROHO, R. Bonynge, H. Burton (pp1989; Eng)
(MCEG) ▣ **VVD952**

Cpte A. Schlemm, R. Streich, P. Anders, H. Krebs, H. Brauer, A. Müller, H. Wocke, E. Heyer, S. Menz, F. Hoppe, Berlin RIAS Chbr Ch, Berlin RIAS Orch, F. Fricsay (r1949)
(DG) ⓘ [2] **447 370-2GDB2**

Rosalinde R. Arthars
Adele A. Grummet
Eisenstein D. Fieldsend
Alfred K. Mahsoori
Falke G. Sandison
Orlovsky D. Hawksley
Frank L. Black
Blind H. Ludlow
Ida W. Schoemann
Frosch P. Barnhill
D'Oyly Carte Op Chor, D'Oyly Carte Op Orch, J. O. Edwards (r1995: Eng)
(SONY) ⓘ [2] **S2K64573**

Rosalinde G. Scheyrer
Adele W. Lipp
Eisenstein K. Terkal
Alfred A. Dermota
Doctor Falke E. Waechter
Orlovsky C. Ludwig
Frank W. Berry
Blind E. Majkut
Ida L. Martini
Frosch E. Kunz
Philh Chor, Philh, O. Ackermann (r1959: with dialogue)
(CFP) ⓘ [2] **CD-CFPSD4793**

Rosalinde L. Popp
Adele E. Lind
Eisenstein P. Seiffert
Alfred P. Domingo
Doctor Falke W. Brendel
Orlovsky A. Baltsa
Frank K. Rydl
Blind H. Zednik
Ida U. Steinsky
Frosch H. Lohner
Bavarian Rad Chor, Munich RO, P. Domingo (with dialogue)
(5/87) (EMI) ⓘ [2] **CDS7 47480-8**

Rosalinde H. Gueden
Adele E. Köth
Eisenstein W. Kmentt
Alfred G. Zampieri
Doctor Falke W. Berry
Orlovsky R. Resnik
Frank E. Waechter
Blind P. Klein
Ida H. Schubert
Frosch E. Kunz
Guest 1 R. Tebaldi
Guest 2 F. Corena
Guest 3 B. Nilsson
Guest 4 M. del Monaco
Guest 5 T. Berganza
Guest 6 J. Sutherland
Guest 7 J. Björling
Guest 8 L. Price
Guest 9 G. Simionato
Guest 10 E. Bastianini
Guest 11 L. Welitsch
Vienna St Op Chor, VPO, H. von Karajan (with dialogue & Act 2 Gala)
(12/87) (DECC) ⓘ [2] **421 046-2DH2**

Rosalinde P. Coburn
Adele J. Perry
Eisenstein E. Waechter
Alfred J. Hopferwieser
Doctor Falke W. Brendel
Orlovsky B. Fassbaender
Frank B. Kusche
Blind F. Gruber
Ida I. Steinbeisser
Frosch F. Muxeneder
Ivan I. Ungar
Bavarian St Op Ballet, Bavarian St Op Chor, Bavarian St Op Orch, C. Kleiber, O. Schenk
(9/91) (DG) ◐ **072 400-1GH2**
(DG) ▣ **072 400-3GH**

Rosalinde K. Te Kanawa
Adele E. Gruberová
Eisenstein W. Brendel
Alfred R. Leech
Doctor Falke O. Bär
Orlovsky B. Fassbaender
Frank T. Krause
Blind A. Wendler
Ida K. Göttling
Frosch O. Schenk
Vienna St Op Chor, VPO, A. Previn (r1990: with dialogue)
(9/91) (PHIL) ⓘ [2] **432 157-2PH2**

Rosalinde N. Gustafson
Adele J. Howarth
Eisenstein L. Otey
Alfred B. Bottone
Doctor Falke A. Michaels-Moore
Orlovsky J. Kowalski
Frank E. Garrett
Blind J. Dobson
Ida G. Groves
Frosch J. Sessions
Guest 1 J. Sutherland
Guest 2 L. Pavarotti
Guest 3 M. Horne
ROH Chor, ROHO, R. Bonynge, H. Burton (pp1989; Eng)
(9/93) (PION) ◐ **PLMCD00721**

Rosalinde G. Fontana
Adele B. Karwautz
Eisenstein J. Dickie
Alfred J. Hopferwieser
Doctor Falke A. Martin
Orlovsky R. Yachmi-Caucig
Frank A. Werner
Blind E. Wessner
Frosch H. Krämmer
Ida A. Calix
Ivan A.E. Hollander
Bratislava City Chor, Bratislava RSO, J. Wildner (r1991)
(1/94) (NAXO) ⓘ [2] **8 660017/8**

Act 2. H. Prey, B. Daniels, G. Hornik, A.S. von Otter, B. Kilduff, G. Millo, A. Dobriansky, J. Anderson, K. Battle, F. Furlanetto, T. Hampson, A. Millo, S. Milnes, S. Ramey, F. von Stade, NY Met Op Chor, NY Met Op Orch, James Levine
(DG) ◐ [2] **072 428-1GH2**
(DG) ▣ **072 428-3GH**
Excs P. Domingo (CAST) ▣ **CVI2021**
Excs A. Paratore, J. Paratore (arr Luboschutz)
(SCHW) ⓘ **310115**
Excs J. Sutherland, Orch, Anon (cond), D. Bailey (11/92) (DECC) ◐ **071 135-1DH**
Fledermäuschen Kings Sngrs (arr D. Runswick)
(EMI) ⓘ **CDC7 54057-2**
1. Philh, W. Boughton (NIMB) ⓘ **NI5120**
(NIMB) ▭ **NC5120**
1. Paris Cons, B. Walter (r1938)
(PEAR) ⓘ **GEMMCD9945**
1. VPO, C. Kleiber, B. Large (pp1989)
(DG) ▣ **072 146-3GH**
1. VPO, W. Boskovsky
(DECC) ⓘ **417 747-2DM**
1. VJSO, J. Francek (LASE) ⓘ **15 619**
(LASE) ▭ **79 619**
1. VPO, L. Maazel (pp1980)
(DG) ⓘ [2] **429 562-2GX2**
1. Mazovian PO, P. Kantschieder
(SCHW) ⓘ **311155**
1. Czech PO, V. Neumann
(SUPR) ⓘ **11 0724-2**
1. Vienna SO, W. Sawallisch (pp1967)
(ORFE) ⓘ **C236901A**
1. Munich RO, P. Domingo
(EMI) ⓘ [2] **CDEMTVD59**
(EMI) ⊙ [2] **EMTVD59**
1. Košice St PO, A. Walter
(NAXO) ⓘ **8 550468**
1. VPO, H. von Karajan (pp1987)
(SONY) ◐ **SLV45985**
1. Polish Nat RSO, R. Bibl
(POLS) ⓘ **PNCD087**
1. NYPO, B. Walter (r1956) (CBS) ⓘ **CD47682**
1. Vienna St Op Orch, J. Horenstein
(CHES) ⓘ **Chesky CD70**
1. VPO, C. Krauss (r1929) (PREI) ⓘ **90139**
1. Minnesota Orch, Anon (cond)
(WORD) ⓘ **FCD7409**
1. Chicago SO, D. Barenboim (r1992)
(ERAT) ⓘ **2292-45998-2**
1. LPO, F. Welser-Möst
(EMI) ⓞⓞ **DCC7 54089-5**
1. Philh, A. Scholz (r1980) (ROSE) ⓘ **3229**
1. BPO, E. Kleiber (r1933) (BIDD) ⓘ **WHL002**
1. VPO, W. Boskovsky (r1968)
(LOND) ⓘ **436 781-2LM**
1. LPO, F. Welser-Möst
(EMI) ◘ **MDC7 54089-8**
1. LSO, J. Georgiadis (IMP) ⓘ **ORCD11015**
(IMP) ▭ **ORZC11015**
1. LSO, J. Georgiadis (IMP) ⓘ [3] **TCD1070**
1. VPO, C. Kleiber (pp1989)
(SONY) ⓘ [3] **SX3K53385**
1. VPO, L. Maazel (pp1980)
(DG) ⓘ **439 439-2GCL**
1. Luxembourg Rad & TV SO, P. Cao
(FORL) ⓘ **FF046**
1. BPO, E. Kleiber (r1933)
(TELD) ⓘ **4509-95513-2**
1. VPO, R. Kempe
(EMI) ⓘ [2] **CES5 68535-2**
1. Bavarian St Orch, C. Kleiber
(DG) ⓘ [2] **447 364-2GDB2**
1. VPO, C. Abbado (pp1988)
(7/88) (DG) ⓘ **423 662-2GH**
1. LSO, J. Georgiadis (4/89) (IMP) ⓘ **PCD902**
1. VPO, C. Kleiber (pp1989)
(2/91) (SONY) ⓘ **SK45938**
1. Hallé, B. Tovey
(2/91) (CFP) ⓘ **CD-CFP4577**
1. Black Dyke Mills Band, G. Brand (arr Winter)
(10/91) (CHAN) ⓘ **CHAN6539**
(10/91) (CHAN) ▭ **MBTD6539**
1(pt) SO, T. Beecham (r1910)
(11/91) (SYMP) ⓘ [2] **SYMCD1096/7**
1. Berlin RSO, F. Fricsay
(12/91) (DG) ⓘ [2] **413 432-2GW2**
(DG) ▭ **413 432-4GW2**
1. LPO, F. Welser-Möst
(12/91) (EMI) ⓘ **CDC7 54089-2**
1. LPO, Carl Davis
(12/91) (VIRG) ⓘ **VJ7 59654-2**
(12/91) (VIRG) ▭ **VJ7 59654-4**
1. VPO, L. Maazel
(2/92) (DG) ⓘ [2] **435 335-2GWP2**
1. BPO, W. Furtwängler (r1937)
(4/92) (KOCH) ⓘ [2] **37073-2**

1. Philh, O. Klemperer (9/92) (EMI) Ⓓ **CDM7 64144-2**
1. Vienna Ens (arr M Bjelik) (9/92) (SONY) Ⓓ **SK47187**
1. VPO, C. Krauss (r1929) (11/92) (PREI) Ⓓ **90112**
1. Concertgebouw, N. Harnoncourt (12/92) (TELD) Ⓓ **9031-74786-2**
1. NYPO, L. Bernstein (r1970) (9/93) (SONY) Ⓓ **SMK47601**
1. Columbia SO, B. Walter (r1956) (8/95) (SONY) Ⓓ **SMK64467**
1, 10b, 11b, 14b B. Fassbaender, N. Gedda, R. Holm, A. Rothenberger, W. Berry, D. Fischer-Dieskau, Vienna St Op Chor, Vienna SO, W. Boskovsky (CFP) Ⓓ **CD-CFP4499** (CFP) ▭ **TC-CFP4499**
1, 15. VPO, H. von Karajan (r1960) (DECC) Ⓓ [9] **448 042-2DC9**
1-19. G. Fontana, J. Hopferwieser, J. Dickie, B. Karwautz, R. Yachmi-Caucig, A. Martin, A. Werner, E. Wessner, A. Calix, Bratislava City Chor, Bratislava RSO, J. Wildner (r1991) (NAXO) Ⓓ **8 553171**
1, 2, 6-8, 10a, 11b, 12, 13, 14a, 14b, 17, 19. R. Schock, W. Lipp, W. Berry, E. Steiner, C. Curzi, C. Nicolai, R. Holm, I. Dressel, Vienna St Op Chor, Vienna SO, R. Stolz (EURO) Ⓓ **258 369**
1-4, 6, 7, 10a, 10b, 11a, 11b, 12, 13, 14a, 16, 17, 19. W. Hollweg, E. Gruberová, C. Boesch, M. Lipovšek, J. Protschka, A. Scharinger, W. Kmentt, B. Bonney, E. von Magnus, Netherlands Op Chor, Concertgebouw, N. Harnoncourt (r1987) (7/93) (TELD) Ⓓ **4509-91974-2**
1, 6-8, 11a, 11b, 12, 13, 14a, 14b, 16, 17, 19. K. Te Kanawa, E. Gruberová, W. Brendel, R. Leech, O. Bär, B. Fassbaender, T. Krause, K. Göttling, A. Previn, Vienna St Op Chor, VPO (r1990) (PHIL) Ⓓ **438 503-2PH**
2, 4-7, 10a, 10b, 11a, 11b, 12, 13, 14a, 14b, 16-19. G. Janowitz, R. Holm, S. Lukan, W. Kmentt, W. Windgassen, E. Waechter, H. Holecek, E. Kunz, E. Kuchar, Vienna St Op Chor, VPO, K. Böhm (r1971) (DECC) Ⓓ **421 898-2DM**
2, 5-8, 11b, 12, 13, 14a, 14b, 16, 17, 19. J. Brumaire, L. Berton, P. Fleta, R. Corazza, J-C. Benoit, J. Pruvost, M. Roux, A. Forli, R. Duclos Ch, Société des Concerts du Conservatoire Orch, F. Pourcel (r1965) (EMI) Ⓓ [2] **CZS7 67869-2**
5. J. Hadley, T. Hampson, WNO Orch, C. Rizzi (r1992) (11/93) (TELD) Ⓓ **9031-73283-2**
5. H. Nash, D. Noble, orch, C. Raybould (r1930: Eng) (2/95) (DUTT) Ⓓ **CDLX7012**
5. H. Nash, D. Noble, orch, C. Raybould (r1930: Eng) (11/95) (PEAR) Ⓓ **GEMMCD9175**
6, 13. J. Sutherland, R. Gard, M. Brynnel, Sydney Eliz Orch, R. Bonynge (DECC) ◐ **071 149-1DH** (DECC) ▣ **071 149-3DH**
8. A. Moffo, H. Galatis Orch, H. Galatis (arr Galatis) (EURO) Ⓓ **GD69113**
8. L. Garrett, Philh, I. Bolton (Eng) (SILV) Ⓓ **SONGCD907** (SILV) ▭ **SONGC907**
8. L. Schöne, Berlin St Op Orch, L. Blech (r1928) (MMOI) Ⓓ **CDMOIR419** (MMOI) ▭ **CMOIR419**
8. Lotte Lehmann, orch, F. Weissmann (r1931) (7/92) (PEAR) Ⓓ [3] **GEMMCDS9926(2)**
8, 13. Lotte Lehmann, Berlin St Op Orch, F. Weissmann (r1931) (PEAR) Ⓓ **GEMMCD9409**
11b K. Battle, W. Jones, H. Burton (pp1991) (DG) ▣ **072 189-3GH**
11b E. Schumann, orch, K. Alwin (r1927) (PEAR) Ⓓ **GEMMCD9445**
11b F. Foster-Jenkins, C. McMoon (r c1944;Eng) (RCA) Ⓓ **GD61175**
11b E. Schumann, orch, K. Alwin (r1927) (MMOI) Ⓓ **CDMOIR419** (MMOI) ▭ **CMOIR419**
11b H. Gueden, Vienna St Op Orch, R. Stolz (r1961) (DECC) Ⓓ **436 316-2DA** (DECC) ▭ **436 316-4DA**
11b G. Janowitz, VPO, K. Böhm (r1971) (DECC) Ⓓ **436 316-2DA** (DECC) ▭ **436 316-4DA**
11b E. Schumann, orch, K. Alwin (r1927) (ROMO) Ⓓ **81019-2**
11b K. Battle, M. Garrett (pp1991) (7/92) (DG) Ⓓ **435 440-2GH**
11b E. Schumann, orch, K. Alwin (r1927) (7/92) (PEAR) Ⓓ [3] **GEMMCDS9926(2)**
11b T. Dahl, Calgary PO, M. Bernardi (r1992) (12/94) (CBC) Ⓓ **SMCD5125**
11b, 13. J. Migenes, Vienna Volksoper Orch, L. Schifrin (r1993) (1/94) (ERAT) Ⓓ **4509-92875-2** (1/94) (ERAT) ▭ **4509-92875-4**
11b, 17. R. Streich, Berlin RIAS Chbr Ch, Berlin RSO, K. Gaebel (DG) Ⓓ [2] **435 748-2GDO2**
11b, 17. E. Sack, Berlin Staatskapelle (r1938) (DANT) Ⓓ **LYS2**
11b, 17. E. Berger, Berlin St Op Orch, W. Schütze (r1934) (12/91) (PREI) Ⓓ **89035**
12. R. Tauber, V. Schwarz, orch (r1928) (7/89) (PEAR) Ⓓ **GEMMCD9327**
12. R. Tauber, V. Schwarz, orch (r1928) (7/89) (EMI) Ⓓ **CDM7 69476-2**
12. R. Tauber, V. Schwarz, Berlin Staatskapelle, F. Weissmann (r1928) (12/89) (EMI) Ⓓ **CDH7 69787-2**
13. E. Steber, Orch, Anon (cond) (bp1953) (VAI) ▣ **VAI69112**
13. T. Gedda, Stockholm Palm Court Orch, L. Almgren (pp1987) (BLUE) Ⓓ **ABCD014**
13. I. Cotrubas, Czech SO, A. Krieger (pp1991) (IMP) Ⓓ **MCD42**
13. K. Te Kanawa, VPO, A. Previn (PHIL) Ⓓ **434 725-2PM** (PHIL) ▭ **434 725-4PM**
13. E. Rethberg, orch, Rosario Bourdon (r1931) (MMOI) Ⓓ **CDMOIR419** (MMOI) ▭ **CMOIR419**
13. C. Studer, ROHO, J. Barker (pp1988) (EMI) Ⓓ **CDC5 55095-2**
13. E. Gruberová, Concertgebouw, N. Harnoncourt (TELD) Ⓓ **4509-93691-2**
13. L.I. Marsh, orch (r1912: Eng) (IRCC) Ⓓ **IRCC-CD810**
13. E. Schwarzkopf, Philh, H. von Karajan (r1955) (EMI) Ⓓ **CDM5 65577-2**
13. C. Studer, ROHO, J. Barker (pp1988) (9/89) (EMI) Ⓓ **CDC7 49811-2**
13. E. Schwarzkopf, Philh, H. von Karajan (r1955) (12/90) (EMI) Ⓓ **CDM7 63657-2**
13. M. Ivogün, Berlin St Op Orch, L. Blech (r1932) (8/92) (NIMB) Ⓓ **NI7832** (8/92) (NIMB) ▭ **NC7832**
13. M. Reining, Berlin Deutsche Op Orch, W. Lutze (r1939) (9/92) (PREI) Ⓓ **90083**
13. L. Price, New Philh, N. Santi (r1977) (12/92) (RCA) Ⓓ [4] **09026 61236-2**
13. B. Hendricks, Philh, L. Foster (r1992) (8/93) (EMI) Ⓓ **CDC7 54626-2**
13. M. Ivogün, orch (r1932) (1/94) (CLUB) Ⓓ **CL99-020**
13. E. Rethberg, Victor SO, Rosario Bourdon (r1931) (10/95) (ROMO) Ⓓ [2] **81014-2**
13, 17. K. Te Kanawa, J. Meinrad, ROHO, P. Domingo (TELD) ◐ **9031-77676-6** (TELD) ▣ **9031-77676-3**
14b R. Shaw Chorale, RCA Victor Orch, Robert Shaw (RCA) Ⓓ **GD60205**
16. Lotte Lehmann, R. Tauber, K. Branzell, W. Staegemann, Berlin St Op Chor, Berlin St Op Orch, F. Weissmann (r1928) (PEAR) Ⓓ **GEMMCD9409**
16. R. Tauber, Lotte Lehmann, K. Branzell, G. Merrem-Nikisch, W. Staegemann, Chor, Berlin Staatskapelle, F. Weissmann (r1928) (12/89) (EMI) Ⓓ **CDH7 69787-2**
17. E. Schumann, Vienna St Op Orch, K. Alwin (r1929) (ROMO) Ⓓ **81019-2**
17. B. Bonney, E. von Magnus, C. Boesch, Concertgebouw, N. Harnoncourt (r1988) (TELD) Ⓓ **0630-11470-2**
17. L. Schöne, orch (r1924) (12/92) (NIMB) Ⓓ **NI7833** (12/92) (NIMB) ▭ **NC7833**
19. Grimethorpe Colliery Band, E. Howarth (arr Winter) (12/92) (DOYE) Ⓓ **DOYCD013** (12/92) (DOYE) ▭ **DOYMC013**

Indigo und die vierzig Räuber, 'Indigo and the 40 Thieves'– operetta: 3 acts (1871—Vienna) (Lib. M Steiner)

EXCERPTS: 1. Overture. ACT 1: 2. Intermezzo; 3. Sternelied; 4. Lasst frei nun erschallen; 5. Launisches Glück (interpolated song by J Bürger, after Strauss); 6. Musik der Nacht; 7. Bacchanale.

1. VPO, W. Boskovsky (r1970) (LOND) Ⓓ **436 785-2LM**
1. VPO, L. Maazel (pp1983) (DG) Ⓓ **439 439-2GCL**
1. VPO, R. Muti (pp1993) (3/93) (PHIL) Ⓓ **438 493-2PH** (3/93) (PHIL) ▭ **438 493-4PH**
5. J. Schmidt, Berlin Staatskapelle, F. Weissmann (r1932) (4/90) (EMI) Ⓓ **CDM7 69478-2**
5. C. Kullman, orch, E. Hauke (r1932) (11/93) (PREI) Ⓓ **89057**
6. Kings Sngrs, M. Barrueco (arr B. Chilcott) (EMI) Ⓓ **CDC7 54057-2**
7. L. Schöne, orch (r1925) (12/92) (NIMB) Ⓓ **NI7833** (12/92) (NIMB) ▭ **NC7833**

Der **Lustige Krieg, '(The) Merry War'– operetta: 3 acts (1882—Hamburg) (Lib. Zell and Genée)**

Nur für Natur J. Patzak, orch, M. Gurlitt (r1929) (3/90) (PEAR) Ⓓ **GEMMCD9383**
Nur für Natur E. Kunz, VPO, O. Ackermann (r1951) (9/95) (TEST) Ⓓ **SBT1059**
Was ist an einem Kuss gelegen? L. Schöne, orch (r1925) (12/92) (NIMB) Ⓓ **NI7833** (12/92) (NIMB) ▭ **NC7833**

Eine **Nacht in Venedig, '(A) Night in Venice'– operetta: 3 acts (1883—Vienna) (Lib. Zell & Genée)**

EXCERPTS (1923 version by Korngold): 1. Overture. ACT 1: 2. Wenn vom Lido sacht; 3. Ihr Venetianer hört ... Drum sei fröhlich, sei selig, Venetia; 4. 'S ist wahr, ich bin nicht ... Wenn du dich kränkst; 5. Seht, oh seht! ... Frutti di mare!; 6. Evviva, Caramello! ... Willkommen, liebe Freunde!; 7. Annina! Caramello! ... Pellegrina rondinella; 8. Alle maskiert, alle maskiert; 9. Sei mir gegrüsst, du holdes Venetia!; 10. Hier ward es still ... der Mond hat schere Klag' erhoben; 11. Hast du mir ein Kostüm gebracht; 12. Komm' in die Gondel, mein Liebchen; 13. Messere Delacqua!; 14. Schnell zur Serenade!; 15. Kaum dass mein Liebchen die schaukelnde entführt. ACT 2: 16. Wo bleibt nur Caramello? ... Venedigs Frauen herzuführen; 17a. Was mir der Zufall gab; 17b. Treu sein, das liegt mir nicht; 18. Hör' mich. Annina, komm in die Gondel; 19. Sie sagten meinem Liebesfleh'n; 20. Solch' ein Wirtshaus lob' ich mir ... Marietta, come va?; 21. Ninana, Ninana, hier will ich singen; 22. Lasset die Andern tanzen da, tra la la!; 23. Jetzt ist Zeit ... Horch! von San Marco der Glocken Geläut. ACT 3: 24. Karneval ruft Euch zum Ball; 25. Die Tauben von San Marco; 26. Ach, wie herrlich zu schau'n; 27. Tacke, tacke, tacke ... Aber wenn man erst gekostet hat; 28. Wie sichs gebührt, hat es gespürt.

Annina	E. Réthy
Duke	K. Friedrich
Ciboletta	R. Boesch
Caramello	K. Preger
Delacqua	A. Jerger
Pappacoda	H. Mayer-Gänsbacher
Barbara	M. Schober

Bregenz Fest Chor, Vienna SO, A. Paulik (r1951: orig ver: omits dialogue) (SCHW) Ⓓ **312722**

Annina	E. Schwarzkopf
Duke	N. Gedda
Ciboletta	E. Loose
Caramello	E. Kunz
Delacqua	K. Dönch
Pappacoda	P. Klein
Agricola	H. Ludwig
Barbara	H. Ludwig

Chor, Philh, O. Ackermann (r1954) (11/88) (EMI) Ⓓ **CDH7 69530-2**

1. VJSO, J. Francek (arr Korngold) (LASE) Ⓓ **15 619** (LASE) ▭ **79 619**
1. Košice St PO, A. Walter (NAXO) Ⓓ **8 550468**
1. VJSO, W. Boskovsky (CFP) Ⓓ **CD-CFP4607** (CFP) ▭ **TC-CFP4607**
1. VJSO, W. Boskovsky (1/90) (EMI) Ⓓ [2] **CZS7 62751-2**
1. Raphaele Concert Orch, P. Walden (arr Waldenmaier) (5/91) (MOZA) Ⓓ **MECD1002**
1, 9, 17a, 17b, 19. J. Kolomyjec, M. DuBois, Kitchener-Waterloo SO, R. Armenian (CBC) Ⓓ **SMCD5126**
6, 7. F. Wunderlich, L. Otto, Günther Arndt Ch, Berlin SO, F. Walter (EMI) Ⓓ [3] **CZS7 62993-2**
9. R. Schock, Berlin FFB Orch, W. Schmidt-Boelcke (EMI) Ⓓ **CDM7 69475-2**
9. N. Gedda, Stockholm Palm Court Orch, L. Almgren (pp1987) (BLUE) Ⓓ **ABCD014**
9, 12, 26. R. Karczykowski, Polish Nat RSO, R. Bibl (POLS) Ⓓ **PNCD087**
12. R. Schock, orch, W. Schüchter (r1952) (EMI) Ⓓ **CDM7 69475-2**

12. F. Wunderlich, R. Schock, Berlin SO, F. Walter (EMI) ① [3] **CZS7 62993-2**
12. P. Anders, Berlin St Op Orch, P. Hühn (r1936) (MMOI) ① **CDMOIR419** (MMOI) ⊟ **CMOIR419**
12. W. Krenn, Vienna Volksoper Orch, A. Paulik (r1970) (DECC) ① **436 316-2DA** (DECC) ⊟ **436 316-4DA**
12. P. Domingo, ECO, J. Rudel (2/87) (EMI) ① **CDC7 47398-2**
12. J. Patzak, Berlin St Op Orch, H. Weigert (r1930) (3/90) (PEAR) ① **GEMMCD9383**
12. H.E. Groh, orch, O. Dobrindt (r1931) (3/92) (PEAR) ① **GEMMCD9419**
12. C. Kullman, orch, E. Hauke (r1932) (11/93) (PREI) ① **89057**
12, 16. F. Wunderlich, Berlin RIAS Chor, Berlin SO, A. Melichar (EURO) ① **GD69018** (EURO) ⊟ **GK69018**
12, 26. E. Kunz, Vienna Volksoper Orch, A. Paulik (r1949) (9/95) (TEST) ① **SBT1059**
17b M. Wittrisch, Berlin St Op Orch, C. Schmalstich (r1930) (MMOI) ① **CDMOIR419** (MMOI) ⊟ **CMOIR419**
17b E. Kunz, VPO, O. Ackermann (r1951) (9/95) (TEST) ① **SBT1059**
17b, 26. R. Holm, W. Krenn, Vienna Volksoper Orch, A. Paulik (r1970) (LOND) ① **436 898-2DM**
25. Kings Sngrs (Eng: arr B Chilcott) (EMI) ① **CDC7 54057-2**
26. B. Weikl, Austrian RSO, K. Eichhorn (ORFE) ① **C077831A**
26. F. Wunderlich, Munich RO, W. Schmidt-Boelcke (EURO) ① **GD69018** (EURO) ⊟ **GK69018**
26. F. Wunderlich, Berlin SO, F. Walter (EMI) ① [3] **CZS7 62993-2**
26. J. Patzak, Berlin St Op Orch, A. Melichar (r1934) (MMOI) ① **CDMOIR419** (MMOI) ⊟ **CMOIR419**

Prinz Methusalem– operetta: 3 acts (1877—Vienna) (Lib. C. Treumann, after Delacour & Wildér)
Overture VPO, W. Boskovsky (r1968) (LOND) ① **436 785-2LM**
Overture Vienna Strauss Festival Orch, P. Guth (pp1993; arr. Schönherr) (DINT) ① **DICD920149**

Ritter Pásmán– comic opera: 3 acts (1892—Vienna) (Lib. L. Dóczi, after J. Arany)
EXCERPTS—ACT 3: 1. Ballet music.
1. VPO, W. Boskovsky (r1967) (LOND) ① **436 781-2LM**

Simplizius– operetta: 3 acts (1887—Vienna) (Lib. Léon)
Wenn nicht die Hoffnung wär J. Schmidt, orch, F. Günther (r1935) (EMI) ① [2] **CHS7 64673-2**

Das **Spitzentuch der Königin, '(The) Queen's Lace Handkerchief'– operetta (1880—Vienna) (Lib. Bohrmann-Riegen and Genée)**
Overture VPO, W. Boskovsky (r1967) (LOND) ① **436 785-2LM**

Die **Tänzerin Fanny Elssler, '(The) Dancer Fanny Elssler'– operetta (1934—Berlin) (arr. O. Stalla)**
Draussen in Sievering blüht schon der Flieder B. Weikl, Austrian RSO, K. Eichhorn (ORFE) ① **C077831A**
Draussen in Sievering F. Wunderlich, Vienna Volksoper Orch, Spilar Schrammeln, R. Stolz (DG) ① [5] **435 145-2GX5(2)**
Draussen in Sievering E. Sack, Berlin Staatskapelle (r1935: arr Weninger) (DANT) ① **LYS2**
Draussen in Sievering L. Popp, ASMF, N. Marriner (6/88) (EMI) ① **CDC7 49700-2**

Ein **Tausend und eine Nacht, '(A) Thousand and One Nights'– operetta (1906—Vienna) (rev E Reiterer from 'Indigo')**
1. Intermezzo.
1. Vienna Op Ball Orch, U. Theimer (8/92) (DENO) ① **CO-77949**
2. J. Schmidt, Berlin Staatskapelle, F. Weissmann (r1932) (EMI) ① [2] **CHS7 64673-2**

Waldmeister– operetta (1895—Berlin) (Lib. Davis)
EXCERPTS: 1. Overture.
1. VPO, L. Maazel (DG) ① [2] **429 562-2GX2**
1. VPO, C. Abbado (pp1991) (DG) ◖ **072 175-1GH** (DG) ▣ **072 175-3GH**
1. VPO, W. Boskovsky (r1969) (LOND) ① **436 785-2LM**
1. VPO, C. Abbado (pp1991) (4/91) (DG) ① **431 628-2GH**
1. VPO, W. Boskovsky (r1957) (2/92) (DG) ① [2] **435 335-2GWP2**

Wiener Blut, 'Vienna Blood'– operetta: 3 acts (1899—Vienna) (Lib. Léon and Stein. Music arr. and adpted Mül)
Das eine kann ich nicht verzeih'n...Wiener Blut B. Hendricks, G. Quilico, Lyon Op Orch, L. Foster (r1993) (6/95) (EMI) ① **CDC5 55151-2**
Excs B. Kusche, R. Schock, H. Gueden, F. Liewehr, M. Schramm, E. Kunz, W. Lipp, F. Gruber, Vienna St Op Chor, Vienna SO, R. Stolz (4/88) (EURO) ① **258 370**
Grüss dich Gott, du liebes Nesterl J. Migenes, Vienna Volksoper Orch, L. Schifrin (r1993) (1/94) (ERAT) ① **4509-92875-2** (1/94) (ERAT) ⊟ **4509-92875-4**
Ich war ein echtes Wiener Blut N. Gedda, T. Gedda, Stockholm Palm Court Orch, L. Almgren (pp1987) (BLUE) ① **ABCD014**
Overture VJSO, J. Francek (arr Korngold) (LASE) ① **15 619** (LASE) ⊟ **79 619**
Wiener Blut H. Gueden, Vienna Operetta Chor, Vienna St Op Orch, R. Stolz (r1961) (DECC) ① **436 316-2DA** (DECC) ⊟ **436 316-4DA**

Der **Zigeunerbaron, '(The) Gipsy Baron'– operetta: 3 acts (1885—Vienna) (Lib. Schnitzer, after Jókai)**
1a. Overture. ACT 1: 1b. Das wär' kein rechter Schifferknecht; 2. Als flotter Geist; 3a. So träuschte mich die Ahnung nicht!; 3b. Ja, das Schreiben und das Lesen; 4. Just sind es vierundzwanzig Jahre; 5a. Dem Freier naht die Braut; 5b. Ein Falter schwirrt ums Licht; 6. So elend und so treu; 7a. Arsena! Arsena; 7b. Ha, was hör' ich da für Klänge; 7c. Nun zu des bösen Nachbarn Haus (finale). ACT 2: 8a. Entr'acte; 8b. Mein Aug' bewachte; 9a. Ein Greis ist mir im Traum erschienen; 9b. Ha, seht, es winkt; 10. Auf, auf, vorbei ist die Nacht; 11. Wer uns getraut; 12. Her die Hand, es muss ja sein; 13. Nach Wien! ACT 3: 14a. Entr'acte; 15. Ein Mädchen hat es gar nicht gut; 16. Von des Tajos Strand; 17. Hurrah, die Schlacht mitgebracht (Entrance March); 18. Heiraten, Vivat!.

Sáffi	P. Coburn
Barinkay	H. Lippert
Homonay	W. Holzmair
Zsupán	R. Schasching
Arsena	C. Oelze
Czipra	J. Hamari
Mirabella	E. von Magnus
Carnero	J. Flimm
Pali	R. Florianschütz
Ottokar	H-J. Lazar

A. Schoenberg Ch, Vienna SO, N. Harnoncourt (pp1994) (6/95) (TELD) ① [2] **4509-94555-2**
Entrance March Berlin Phil Wind Qnt, H. von Karajan (r1973: arr Villinger) (5/94) (DG) ① **439 346-2GX2**
Waltz Royal Prom Orch, Anon (cond) (WORD) ① **FCD7411**
1. VPO, C. Kleiber, B. Large (pp1992) (PHIL) ▣ **070 152-3PH**
1. VPO, H. von Karajan (pp1968) (DG) ① **439 104-2GDO**
1. Columbia SO, B. Walter (r1956) (8/95) (SONY) ① **SMK64467**
1a Mazovian PO, P. Kantschieder (SCHW) ① **311155**
1a Košice St PO, A. Walter (NAXO) ① **8 550468**
1a VPO, H. von Karajan (pp1987) (SONY) ◖ **SLV45985**
1a NYPO, B. Walter (r1956) (CBS) ① **CD47682**
1a Vienna St Op Orch, J. Horenstein (CHES) ① **Chesky CD70**
1a BPO, H. von Karajan (EMI) ① **CDM7 64629-2**
1a LPO, F. Welser-Möst (EMI) OO **DCC7 54089-5**
1a BPO, E. Kleiber (r1933) (BIDD) ① **WHL002**
1a LPO, F. Welser-Möst (EMI) ◘ **MDC7 54089-8**
1a BPO, E. Kleiber (r1933) (TELD) ① **4509-95513-2**
1a VPO, H. von Karajan (r1960) (DECC) ① [9] **448 042-2DC9**
1a Hallé, B. Tovey (2/91) (CFP) ① **CD-CFP4577**
1a BPO, H. von Karajan (12/91) (DG) ① [2] **413 432-2GW2** (DG) ⊟ **413 432-4GW2**
1a LPO, F. Welser-Möst (12/91) (EMI) ① **CDC7 54089-2**
1a Concertgebouw, N. Harnoncourt (12/92) (TELD) ① **9031-74786-2**
1a BPO, E. Kleiber (r1933) (5/94) (ARCI) ① **ARC102**
1a, 1b BPO, H. von Karajan, U. Märkle (r1983) (SONY) ◖ **SLV46401** (SONY) ▣ **SHV46401**
1a, 1b VPO, C. Kleiber (pp1992) (SONY) ① [3] **SX3K53385**
1a, 1b, 2, 3b, 6, 8b, 9b, 10-12, 16-18. J-C. Benoit, J. Micheau, J. Danjou, C. Gayraud, G. Chauvet, M. Lecocq, R. Duclos Ch, Pasdeloup Ass Orch, A. Lombard (r1962-3) (EMI) ① [2] **CZS7 67869-2**
1a, 1b, 17. VPO, W. Boskovsky (r1965) (LOND) ① **436 781-2LM**
1a, 2. R. Karczykowski, Polish Nat RSO, R. Bibl (POLS) ① **PNCD087**
1a, 17. VJSO, J. Francek (LASE) ① **15 619** (LASE) ⊟ **79 619**
2. R. Schock, orch, W. Schüchter (r1953) (EMI) ① **CDM7 69475-2**
2. F. Wunderlich, R. Lamy Sngrs, Munich RO, W. Schmidt-Boelcke (EURO) ① **GD69018** (EURO) ⊟ **GK69018**
2. M. Wittrisch, orch (r1928) (MMOI) ① **CDMOIR419** (MMOI) ⊟ **CMOIR419**
2. J. Schmidt, Berlin St. Op. Orch, F. Weissmann (r1932) (EMI) ① [2] **CHS7 64673-2**
2. R. Tauber, orch (r1929) (PEAR) ① **GEMMCD9145**
2. R. Tauber, Berlin Staatskapelle, E. Hauke (r1929) (12/89) (EMI) ① **CDH7 69787-2**
2. J. Schmidt, Berlin Staatskapelle, F. Weissmann (r1932) (4/90) (EMI) ① **CDM7 69478-2**
2. H.E. Groh, orch (r1938) (3/92) (PEAR) ① **GEMMCD9419**
2. R. Tauber, Vienna Th Orch, A. Paulik (r1924) (10/92) (TEST) ① **SBT1005**
2, 11. C. Kullman, E. Berger, Berlin St Op Orch, C. Schmalstich (r1932) (11/93) (PREI) ① **89057**
3b E. Kunz, Vienna Volksoper Orch, A. Paulik (r1949) (9/95) (TEST) ① **SBT1059**
6. P. Lorengar, Vienna Volksoper Orch, W. Weller (r1970) (DECC) ① **436 316-2DA** (DECC) ⊟ **436 316-4DA**
6. P. Lorengar, Vienna Op Orch, W. Weller (r1970) (LOND) ① **436 898-2DM**
6. M. Cebotari, VPO, H. von Karajan (r1948) (12/90) (PREI) ① **90034**
6. E. Rethberg, orch (r1921) (7/94) (PREI) ① **89051**
6. E. Rethberg, Berlin SO, F. Weissmann (r1930) (10/95) (ROMO) ① [2] **81014-2**
7a-c, 18. Lotte Lehmann, R. Tauber, K. Branzell, W. Staegemann, H. Lange, Berlin St Op Chor, Berlin St Op Orch, F. Weissmann (r1928) (PEAR) ① **GEMMCD9409**
11. H. Schymberg, J. Björling, orch, N. Grevillius (r1938: Swed) (MMOI) ① **CDMOIR419** (MMOI) ⊟ **CMOIR419**
11. R. Holm, W. Krenn, Vienna Volksoper Orch, A. Paulik (r1970) (LOND) ① **436 898-2DM**
11. R. Tauber, C. Vanconti, orch (r1928) (PEAR) ① **GEMMCD9145**
11. R. Tauber, C. Vantoni, Berlin Staatskapelle, E. Hauke (r1928) (12/89) (EMI) ① **CDH7 69787-2**
11. J. Björling, H. Schymberg, orch, N. Grevillius (r1938: Swed) (8/92) (BLUE) ① **ABCD016**
11. J. Björling, H. Schymberg, orch, N. Grevillius (r1938: Swed) (10/93) (NIMB) ① **NI7842**
11. J. Björling, H. Schymberg, orch, N. Grevillius (r1938: Swed) (9/94) (IMP) ① **GLRS103**
11. B. Hendricks, G. Quilico, Lyon Op Orch, L. Foster (r1993) (6/95) (EMI) ① **CDC5 55151-2**
12. B. Weikl, Austrian RSO, K. Eichhorn (ORFE) ① **C077831A**
17. Vienna Strauss Festival Orch, P. Guth (pp1993; arr. Schönherr) (DINT) ① **DICD920149**

17. VPO, L. Maazel (pp1981)
(DG) Ⓓ **439 439-2GCL**
17. VPO, Z. Mehta (pp1990)
(4/90) (SONY) Ⓓ **SK45808**
17. Raphaele Concert Orch, P. Walden (arr Waldenmaier) (5/91) (MOZA) Ⓓ **MECD1002**
17. Vienna Op Ball Orch, U. Theimer
(8/92) (DENO) Ⓓ **CO-77949**
17. VPO, C. Krauss (r1929)
(11/92) (PREI) Ⓓ **90112**

STRAUSS, Richard (Georg) *(1864–1949) Germany*

AV nos from catalogue by E.H. Mueller von Asow

Die **Aegyptische Helena– opera: 2 acts, Op. 75 (1928—Dresden) (Lib. H von Hofmannsthal)**

EXCERPTS: ACT ONE: 1. Das Mahl ist gerichtet; 2. Ist es wirklich Helena?; 3. Wo bin ich?; 4. Bei jener Nacht, der keuschen einzig einen; 5. Ihr grünen Augen im weissen Gesicht; 6. Du bist durchnässt; 7. Ai!...Im weissen Gewand; 8. Zerspalten das Herz!; 9a. Helen's awakening; 9b. O Engel!; 10. Das Nötigste nur in eine Truhe. ACT TWO: 11. Zweite Brautnacht!; 12. Wo ist das Haus?; 13. Aus flirrender Stille was naht heran?; 14. Ich werde neben dir reiten!; 15. So schön bedient; 16. Aithra! Liebe Herrliche!; 17. O dreifache Törin!; 18. Mein Geliebter! Menelas!; 18a. Funeral march; 18b. Mein Geliebter! Menelas!; 19. Unter geschlossenem Lid; 20. Helena, oder wie ich sonst dich nenne; 21. Bei jener Nacht, der keuschen einzig einen; 22. Ewig erwählt von diesem Blick!; 23. Wie du aufs neue die Nacht durchglänzest.

Helena G. Jones
Menelaus M. Kastu
Hermione; First Elf D. Bryant
Aithra B. Hendricks
Altair W. White
Da-ud C. Rayam
First Servant B. Lane
Second Servant G. Kirkland
Second Elf P. Dell
Third Elf M. Cimarella
Fourth Elf K. Grimshaw
K. Jewell Chorale, Detroit SO, A. Dorati (r1979)
(1/92) (DECC) Ⓓ [2] **430 381-2DM2**
4, 11. R. Pauly, Berlin St Op Orch, F. Busch (r1928) (3/90) (PEAR) Ⓓ [2] **GEMMCDS9365**
4(pt), 5, 9b(pt), 11, 13(pt), 20. V. Ursuleac, F. Völker, M. Bokor, H. Roswaenge, A. Jerger, Vienna St Op Chor, Vienna St Op Orch, C. Krauss (pp1933)
(11/94) (SCHW) Ⓓ [2] **314552**
9a, 18a Berlin St Op Orch, F. Busch (r1928)
(3/90) (PEAR) Ⓓ [2] **GEMMCDS9365**
11. L. Price, Boston SO, E. Leinsdorf
(8/90) (RCA) Ⓓ **GD60398**

Arabella– opera: 3 acts, Op. 79 (1933—Dresden) (Lib. H von Hofmannsthal)

ACT 1: 1a. Ich danke, Fräulein; 1b. Aber der Richtige; 1c. Mandryka! Der reiche Kerl!; 2a. Mein Elemer!; 2b. Nach dem Matteo. ACT 2: 3a. Sie wollen mich heiraten; 3b. So wie Sie sind; 4. Und jetzt sag' ich adieu. ACT 3: 5. Das war sehr gut.

Arabella A. Putnam
Zdenka G. Rolandi
Mandryka J. Bröcheler
Waldner A. Korn
Adelaide R. Sarfaty
Fiakermilli G. Bradley
Matteo K. Lewis
Elemer G. Winslade
Dominik J. Munro
Lamoral G. Moses
Fortune-teller E. Hartle
Welko J. Hall
Glyndebourne Fest Chor, LPO, B. Haitink, J. Cox (r1984)
(CAST) ▣ **CVI2036**
Arabella G. Janowitz
Zdenka S. Ghazarian
Mandryka B. Weikl
Waldner H. Kraemmer
Adelaide M. Lilowa
Fiakermilli E. Gruberová
Matteo R. Kollo
Elemer G. Fransson
Dominik H. Helm
Lamoral K. Rydl
Fortune Teller M. Mödl
VPO, G. Solti, O. Schenk
(DECC) ◖ [2] **071 405-1DH2**
(DECC) ▣ **071 405-3DH**
Arabella L. della Casa
Zdenka H. Gueden
Mandryka G. London
Waldner O. Edelmann
Adelaide I. Malaniuk
Matteo A. Dermota
Elemer W. Kmentt
Dominik E. Waechter
Lamoral H. Pröglhöf
Fiakermilli M. Coertse
Vienna St Op Chor, VPO, G. Solti (r1957)
(5/92) (DECC) Ⓓ [2] **430 387-2DM2**
Arabella L. della Casa
Zdenka A. Rothenberger
Mandryka D. Fischer-Dieskau
Waldner K.C. Kohn
Adelaide I. Malaniuk
Fiakermilli E.M. Rogner
Matteo G. Paskuda
Elemer F. Uhl
Dominik C. Hoppe
Lamoral H. Günter
Fortune-teller C. Reich
Welko W. Matthes
Bavarian St Op Chor, Bavarian St Orch, J. Keilberth (pp1963)
(8/93) (DG) Ⓓ [3] **437 700-2GX3**
Arabella M. Reining
Zdenka L. della Casa
Mandryka H. Hotter
Waldner G. Hann
Adelaide R. Anday
Fiakermilli H. Handl
Matteo H. Taubmann
Elemer J. Patzak
Dominik J. Witt
Lamoral A. Poell
Fortune-teller R. Michaelis
Welko F. Szkokan
Vienna St Op Chor, VPO, K. Böhm (pp1947)
(11/94) (DG) Ⓓ [3] **445 342-2GX3**
Excs V. Ursuleac, M. Bokor, A. Jerger, A. Kern, G. Rünger, R. Mayr, Vienna St Op Chor, Vienna St Op Orch, C. Krauss (pp1933)
(10/95) (SCHW) Ⓓ [2] **314652**
1a-c, 2a, 2b, 3a, 3b, 5. E. Schwarzkopf, J. Metternich, A. Felbermayer, Philh, L. von Matačić (r1954) (4/88) (EMI) Ⓓ **CDH7 61001-2**
1b, 2a, 2b Lotte Lehmann, K. Heidersbach, Berlin St Op Orch, R. Jäger (r1933)
(MSCM) Ⓓ [2] **MM30285**
(MSCM) ▭ [2] **MM40107**
1b, 3a, 5. P. Coburn, R. Klepper, B. Skovhus, Munich RSO, M. Honeck (pp1992)
(CAPR) Ⓓ **10 481**
1b, 5. L. della Casa, H. Gueden, A. Poell, VPO, R. Moralt (r1953)
(4/90) (DECC) Ⓓ **425 959-2DM**
1b, 5. M. Teschemacher, I. Beilke, Berlin St Op Orch, B. Seidler-Winkler (r1939)
(11/92) (PREI) Ⓓ **89049**
1c, 3a L. della Casa, D. Fischer-Dieskau, O. Edelmann, VPO, J. Keilberth (pp1958)
(ORFE) Ⓓ **C335931A**
1(pt), 2. Lotte Lehmann, K. Heidersbach, Berlin St Op Orch, R. Jäger (r1933)
(PEAR) Ⓓ **GEMMCD9410**
3a L. della Casa, P. Schoeffler, VPO, H. Hollreiser (r1954)
(4/90) (DECC) Ⓓ **425 959-2DM**
5. E. Schwarzkopf, J. Metternich, Philh, L. von Matačić (r1954) (EMI) Ⓓ **CDM5 65577-2**
5. Leonie Rysanek, Philh, W. Schüchter (r1952)
(4/92) (EMI) Ⓓ [7] **CHS7 69741-2(4)**
5. Leonie Rysanek, Philh, W. Schüchter (r1952)
(2/95) (EMI) Ⓓ **CDH5 65201-2**

Ariadne auf Naxos– opera: prologue and 1 act, Op. 60 (1916—Vienna) (Lib. H von Hofmannsthal)

PROLOGUE: 1. Introduction; 2. Mein Herr Haushofmeister!; 3. Du allmächtiger Gott!; 4. 'Die ungetreue Zerbinetta'; 5. Ein Augenblick ist wenig; 6. Sein wir wieder gut. OPERA: 7. Overture; 8. Schläft sie?; 9. Wo war ich? Tot?; 10. Lieben, Hassen, Hoffen, Zagen; 11. Es gibt ein Reich; 12. Die Dame gibt mit trübem Sinn; 13. Grossmächtige Prinzessin; 14. Hübsch gepredigt!; 15. Ein schönes Wunder!; 16. Circe, kannst du mich hören?; 17. Das waren Zauberworte!.

Ariadne G. Janowitz
Composer T. Schmidt
Zerbinetta E. Gruberová
Bacchus R. Kollo
Music Master W. Berry
Harlequin B. McDaniel
Truffaldino M. Jungwirth
Brighella; Dancing Master H. Zednik
Scaramuchio K. Equiluz
Naiad H. de Groote
Dryad A. Gall
Echo O. Miljakovic
Major-Domo E. Kunz
Footman A. Sramek
Officer P. Weber
Wig-Maker G. Tichy
VPO, K. Böhm, F. Sanjust
(11/94) (DG) ▣ **072 442-3GH**
Ariadne J. Norman
Composer T. Troyanos
Zerbinetta K. Battle
Bacchus J. King
Music Master F.F. Nentwig
Harlequin S. Dickson
Truffaldino A. Korn
Brighella A. Laciura
Scaramuchio A. Glassman
Naiad B. Bonney
Dryad G. Bean
Echo D. Upshaw
Dancing Master J. Franck
Major-Domo N. Castel
NY Met Op Orch, James Levine, B. Large
(10/91) (DG) ▣ **072 411-3GH**
Ariadne E. Schwarzkopf
Composer I. Seefried
Zerbinetta R. Streich
Bacchus R. Schock
Music Master K. Dönch
Harlequin H. Prey
Truffaldino F. Ollendorff
Brighella H. Krebs
Scaramuchio G. Unger
Naiad L. Otto
Dryad G. Hoffman
Echo A. Felbermayer
Dancing Master H. Cuénod
Major-Domo A. Neugebauer
Philh, H. von Karajan (r1954)
(EMI) Ⓓ [2] **CDS5 55176-2**
Ariadne Leonie Rysanek
Composer S. Jurinac
Zerbinetta R. Peters
Bacchus J. Peerce
Music Master; Harlequin W. Berry
Truffaldino G. Adam
Brighella; Dancing Master M. Dickie
Scaramuchio; Officer K. Equiluz
Naiad M. Coertse
Dryad H. Rössl-Majdan
Echo L. Maikl
Major-domo K. Preger
Footman L. Pantscheff
Wig-maker H. Pröglhöf
VPO, E. Leinsdorf (r1959)
(DECC) Ⓓ [2] **443 675-2DMO2**
Ariadne M. Reining
Composer I. Seefried
Zerbinetta A. Noni
Bacchus M. Lorenz
Music Master P. Schoeffler
Harlequin E. Kunz
Truffaldino M. Rus
Brighella P. Klein
Scaramuchio R. Sallaba
Naiad E. Loose
Dryad M. Frutschnigg
Echo E. Rutgers
Dancing Master J. Witt
Major-Domo A. Muzzarelli
Footman H. Schweiger
Officer F. Jelinek
Wig-Maker H. Baier
Vienna St Op Orch, K. Böhm (pp1944)
(SCHW) Ⓓ [2] **314732**
Ariadne A. Tomowa-Sintow
Composer A. Baltsa
Zerbinetta K. Battle
Bacchus G. Lakes
Music Master H. Prey
Harlequin U. Malmberg
Truffaldino K. Rydl
Brighella H. Sojer
Scaramuchio J. Protschka
Naiad B. Bonney
Dryad H. Müller-Molinari
Echo D. Upshaw
Dancing Master H. Zednik

Major-Domo	O. Schenk

VPO, James Levine
(5/87) (DG) ① [2] **419 225-2GH2**

Ariadne	J. Norman
Composer	J. Varady
Zerbinetta	E. Gruberová
Bacchus	P. Frey
Music Master	D. Fischer-Dieskau
Harlequin	O. Bär
Truffaldino	G. Wolf
Brighella	A. Conrad
Scaramuchio	M. Finke
Naiad	E. Lind
Dryad	M. Rørholm
Echo	J. Kaufman
Dancing Master	M. Finke
Major-Domo	R. Asmus

Leipzig Gewandhaus, K. Masur (r1988)
(11/88) (PHIL) ① [2] **422 084-2PH2**

Ariadne	L. Price
Composer	T. Troyanos
Zerbinetta	E. Gruberová
Bacchus	R. Kollo
Music Master	W. Berry
Harlequin	B. McDaniel
Truffaldino	M. Jungwirth
Brighella	G. Unger
Scaramuchio	K. Equiluz
Naiad	D. Cook
Dryad	E. Hartle
Echo	N. Burrowes
Dancing Master	H. Zednik
Major-Domo	E. Kunz
Footman	A. Sramek
Officer	P. Weber
Wig-Maker	G. Tichy

LPO, G. Solti (r1977-78)
(5/92) (DECC) ① [2] **430 384-2DM2**

Ariadne	G. Janowitz
Composer	T. Zylis-Gara
Zerbinetta	S. Geszty
Bacchus	J. King
Music Master	T. Adam
Harlequin	H. Prey
Truffaldino	S. Vogel
Brighella	H.J. Rotzsch
Scaramuchio; Dancing Master	P. Schreier
Naiad	E. Wüstmann
Dryad	A. Burmeister
Echo	A. Stolte
Major-Domo	E-A. Winds

Staatskapelle Dresden, R. Kempe (r1968)
(11/92) (EMI) ① [2] **CMS7 64159-2**

Ariadne	M. Reining
Composer	I. Seefried
Zerbinetta	A. Noni
Bacchus	M. Lorenz
Music Master	P. Schoeffler
Harlequin	E. Kunz
Truffaldino	M. Rus
Brighella	P. Klein
Scaramuchio	R. Sallaba
Naiad	E. Loose
Dryad	M. Frutschnigg
Echo	E. Rutgers
Dancing Master	J. Witt
Major-Domo	A. Muzzarelli
Footman	H. Schweiger
Officer	F. Jelinek
Wig-Maker	H. Baier

Vienna St Op Orch, K. Böhm (pp1944)
(11/94) (PREI) ① [2] **90217**

Ariadne	L. della Casa
Composer	I. Seefried
Zerbinetta	H. Gueden
Bacchus	R. Schock
Music Master	P. Schoeffler
Harlequin	A. Poell
Truffaldino	O. Czerwenka
Brighella	M. Dickie
Scaramuccio	A. Jaresch
Naiad	R. Streich
Dryad	H. Rössl-Majdan
Echo	L. Otto
Dancing Master	P. Klein
Major-Domo	A. Neugebauer

VPO, K. Böhm (pp1954)
(11/94) (DG) ① [2] **445 332-2GX2**

Excs L. Della Casa, L. Otto, N. Puttar, L. Kirschstein, R. Schock, BPO, A. Erede (r1959) (11/94) (TEST) ① **SBT1036**

Excs A. Konetzni, S. Svanholm, A. Kern, E. Schulz, A. Jerger, A. Pichler, A. Muzzarelli, F. Jelinek, H. Baier, D. Komarek, E. Nikolaidi, E. Rutgers, A. Poell, W. Wernigk, Alfred Vogel, R. Sallaba, Vienna St Op Orch, R. Moralt (pp1941) (10/95) (SCHW) ① [2] **314652**

6. C. Ludwig, P. Schoeffler, VPO, K. Böhm (pp1955) (ORFE) ① **C365941A**

7, 10. Northern Sinfonia, R. Hickox (r1994: orch) (CHAN) ① **CHAN9354**

9(pt), 11. C. Ludwig, U. Schirrmacher, A. Bernard, Y. Nagano, Berlin Deutsche Op Orch, H. Hollreiser (r1963-4) (TESS) ① **049-2**

11. Lotte Lehmann, Berlin St Op Orch, H. Weigert (r1928) (PEAR) ① **GEMMCD9410**

11. M. Crider, Munich RSO, M. Honeck (pp1992) (CAPR) ① **10 481**

11. L. Price, LPO, G. Solti (r1960) (DECC) ① **440 402-2DM**

11. C. Ludwig, VPO, K. Böhm (pp1964) (ORFE) ① **C365941A**

11. E. Schwarzkopf, Philh, H. von Karajan (r1954) (EMI) ① **CDM5 65577-2**

11. A. Tomowa-Sintow, Munich RO, P. Sommer (11/86) (ORFE) ① **C106841A**

11. L. della Casa, VPO, H. Hollreiser (r1954) (4/90) (DECC) ① **425 959-2DM**

11. L. Price, LSO, F. Cleva (8/90) (RCA) ① **GD60398**

11. M. Cebotari, VPO, H. von Karajan (r1948) (12/90) (PREI) ① **90034**

11. E. Schwarzkopf, Philh, H. von Karajan (r1954) (12/90) (EMI) ① **CDM7 63657-2**

11. F. Leider, orch (r1925) (5/91) (PREI) ① [3] **89301**

11. Lotte Lehmann, Berlin St Op Orch, F. Weissmann (r1928) (7/92) (PEAR) ① [3] **GEMMCDS9925(2)**

13. E. Berger, Berlin RO, C. Krauss (bp1935) (PREI) ① **89092**

13. E. Gruberová, Munich RO, L. Gardelli (11/86) (ORFE) ① **C101841A**

13. M. Ivogün, Berlin St Op Orch, L. Blech (r1932) (7/92) (PEAR) ① [3] **GEMMCDS9925(2)**

13. Dilbèr, Estonia Op Orch, E. Klas (9/92) (ONDI) ① **ODE768-2**

13. T. Dahl, Calgary PO, M. Bernardi (r1992) (12/94) (CBC) ① **SMCD5125**

13(pt) S. Jo, Monte Carlo PO, P. Olmi (r1994) (6/95) (ERAT) ① **4509-97239-2**

15. N. Sylvest, T. Lønskov (arr vc/pf: Heldburg) (CANZ) ① **CAN33009**

Capriccio– conversation piece for music: 1 act, Op. 85 (1942—Munich) (Lib. C Krauss)

EXCERPTS; 1. Prelude (string sextet); 2. Kein andres (Flamand); 3. Interlude (moonlight music); 4a. Wo ist mein Bruder?; 4b. Morgen mittag um elf!; 4c. Kein andres (Countess).

Countess	E. Schwarzkopf
Count	E. Waechter
Flamand	N. Gedda
Olivier	D. Fischer-Dieskau
La Roche	H. Hotter
Clairon	C. Ludwig
Taupe	R. Christ
Italian Soprano	A. Moffo
Italian Tenor	D. Troy
Majordomo	K. Schmitt-Walter

Philh, W. Sawallisch (r1957/8)
(11/87) (EMI) ① [2] **CDS7 49014-8**

Countess	G. Janowitz
Count	D. Fischer-Dieskau
Flamand	P. Schreier
Olivier	H. Prey
La Roche	K. Ridderbusch
Clairon	T. Troyanos
Taupe	D. Thaw
Italian Soprano	A. Auger
Italian Tenor	A. de Ridder
Majordomo	K.C. Kohn

BRSO, K. Böhm (r1971)
(11/94) (DG) ① [2] **445 347-2GX2**

Countess	K. te Kanawa
Count	H. Hagegård
Flamand	D. Kuebler
Olivier	S. Keenlyside
La Roche	V. Braun
Clairon	T. Troyanos
Taupe	M. Sénéchal
Major Domo	D. Travis

San Francisco Op Orch, D. Runnicles (r1993)
(6/95) (DECC) [2] **071 426-1DH2**
(6/95) (DECC) **071 426-3DH**

Excs V. Ursuleac, F. Klarwein, H. Hotter, K. Kronenberg, G. Hann, G. Wieter, Bavarian St Op Orch, C. Krauss (pp1942) (MYTO) ① **1MCD943104**

Excs P. Schoeffler, M. Cebotari, A. Jerger, A. Dermota, E. Kunz, M. Rohs, W. Wenkoff, A. Noni, T. Neralič, Vienna St Op Orch, K. Böhm (pp1944) (SCHW) ① [2] **314712**

1. Medici Qt (NIMB) ① **NI5076**

1. Uppsala Chbr Sols (BLUE) ① **ABCD011**

1. Stuttgart RSO, N. Marriner (9/92) (CAPR) ① **10 369**

1. Rotterdam PO, J. Tate (4/93) (EMI) ① **CDC7 54581-2**

1. ASMF Chbr Ens (r1992) (5/93) (CHAN) ① **CHAN9131**

1. Vienna Stg Sextet (r1993) (2/95) (EMI) ① **CDC5 55108-2**

1. Raphael Ens (r1993) (3/95) (HYPE) ① **CDA66704**

1, 3. VPO, A. Previn (r1992) (11/93) (DG) ① **437 790-2GH**

1, 3, 4b, 4c F. Lott, SNO, N. Järvi (2/90) (CHAN) ① **CHAN8758**

2. M. Crider, Munich RSO, M. Honeck (pp1992) (CAPR) ① **10 481**

2. A. Dermota, VPO, K. Böhm (r1950) (4/92) (EMI) ① [7] **CHS7 69741-2(4)**

3. B. Tuckwell, RPO, Vladimir Ashkenazy (9/92) (DECC) ① **430 370-2DH**

3, 4a-c L. della Casa, F. Bierbach, VPO, H. Hollreiser (r1954) (4/90) (DECC) ① **425 959-2DM**

4a, 4b E. Schwarzkopf, K. Schmitt-Walter, Philh, W. Sawallisch (r1957) (12/90) (EMI) ① **CDM7 63657-2**

4b, 4c C. Farley, RTBF New SO, J. Serebrier (CHAN) ① **CHAN8364**

4b, 4c E. Schwarzkopf, Philh, O. Ackermann (r1953) (4/88) (EMI) ① **CDH7 61001-2**

4b, 4c G. Janowitz, BRSO, K. Böhm (r1971) (4/95) (DG) ① **439 467-2GCL**
(4/95) (DG) **439 467-4GCL**

Daphne– opera: 1 act, Op. 82 (1938—Munich) (Lib. J Gregor)

EXCERPTS: 1a. Introduction; 1b. Kleontes! Adrast! Wo bleibst du?; 2a. Leb wohl, du Tag; 2b. O bleib, geliebter Tag; 3a. Leukippos, du!; 3b. Ja, ich selbst, ich war der Baum!; 4. Daphne! Mutter! Wir warten dein!; 5a. Ei, so fliegt sie vorbei; 5b. Höre uns, Brüder; 6a. Seid ihr um mich, ihr Hirten alle?; 6b. Wisset, ich sah ihn, Phoibos Apollon!; 7. Ich grüsse dich, weiser, erfahrener Fischer; 8a. Was führt dich her im niedern Gewande; 8b. Was seh ich? Was schreitet dort?; 9a. Wie bist du gewaltig, fremder Hirte; 9b. Was können an Weite menschliche Augen forschend ermessen; 10. Dieser Kuss, dies Umarmen, du nanntest dich: Bruder; 11. Allüberall blüht Dionysos; 12. O selge Dämonen; 13. Trinke, du Tochter; 14a. Furchtbare Schmach dem Gotte!; 14b. Was sagt der da?; 14c. Ein Zeichen wollt ihr?; 15a. Zu dir nun, Knabe; 15b. Ja, ich bekenne; 16. Wahrheit? Jeden heiligen Morgen; 17a. Was blendet so?; 17b. Daphne...Gespielen... 17c. Unheilvolle Daphne; 18a. Was erblicke ich? Himmlische Schönheit; 18b. Götter! Brüder im hohen Olympos!; 19. Ich komme...Ich komme, grünende Brüder.

Daphne	L. Popp
Apollo	R. Goldberg
Peneios	K. Moll
Leukippos	P. Schreier
Gaea	O. Wenkel
Shepherd I	L. Baumann
Shepherd II	A. Senger
Shepherd III	W. Vater
Shepherd IV	M. Hölle
Maiden I	D. Wirtz
Maiden II	U-M. Flake

Bavarian Rad Chor, BRSO, B. Haitink
(1/89) (EMI) ① [2] **CDS7 49309-2**

Daphne	H. Gueden
Apollo	J. King
Peneios	P. Schoeffler
Leukippos	F. Wunderlich
Gaea	V. Little
Shepherd I	H. Braun
Shepherd II	K. Equiluz
Shepherd III	H. Pröglhöf
Maiden I	R. Streich
Maiden II	E. Mechera

Vienna St Op Chor, Vienna SO, K. Böhm (pp1964)
(11/94) (DG) ① [2] **445 322-2GX2**

Daphne M. Reining
Apollo K. Friedrich
Peneios H. Alsen
Leukippos A. Dermota
Gaea M. Frutschnigg
Shepherd I G. Monthy
Shepherd II R. Sallaba
Shepherd III H. Schweiger
Shepherd IV H. Baier
Maiden I E. Loose
Maiden II M. Schober
Vienna St Op Chor, VPO, K. Böhm (pp1944)
(11/95) (PREI) ① [2] **90237**

Excs M. Reining, A. Dermota, A. Rauch, Vienna St Op Chor, Vienna St Op Orch, R. Moralt (pp1942) (11/94) (SCHW) ① [2] **314552**

2b, 18b, 19(pt) M. Teschemacher, T. Ralf, Dresden St Op Orch, K. Böhm (r1938) (11/95) (PREI) ① [2] **90237**

2c, 19b M. Teschemacher, Saxon St Orch, K. Böhm (r1938) (11/92) (PREI) ① **89049**

18a M. Cebotari, Berlin RSO, A. Rother (bp1943) (8/95) (PREI) ① **90222**

18a B. Heppner, Toronto SO, A. Davis (r1994) (11/95) (CBC) ① **SMCD5142**

18b T. Ralf, Saxon St Orch, K. Böhm (r1938) (10/94) (PREI) ① **89077**

19a C. Farley, RTBF New SO, J. Serebrier (CHAN) ① **CHAN8364**

19a A. Tomowa-Sintow, Munich RO, P. Sommer (11/86) (ORFE) ① **C106841A**

Elektra– opera: 1 act, Op. 58 (1909—Dresden) (Lib. H von Hofmannsthal)

EXCERPTS: 1. Wo bleibt Elektra?; 2. Allein! Weh, ganz allein; 3. Elektra!; 4. Ich kann nicht sitzen und ins Dunkel starren; 5. Es geht ein Lärm los; 6. Was willst du? Seht doch, dort!; 7. Die Götter! bist doch selber eine Göttin; 8. Ich will nichts hören!; 9. Ich habe keine guten Nächte; 10. Wenn das rechte Blutopfer; 11. Was bluten muss?; 12. Was sagen sie ihr denn?; 13. Orest! Orest ist tot!; 14. Platz da! Wer lungert so vor einer Tür?; 15. Nun muss es hier von uns geschehn; 16. Du! Du! denn du bist stark!; 17. Nun denn, allein!; 18. Was willst du, fremder Mensch?; 19. Elektra! Elektra; 20. Orest! (Recognition Scene); 21. Du wirst es tun? Allein?; 22. Seid ihr von Sinnen; 23. Ich habe ihm das Beil nicht geben können!; 24. Es muss etwas geschehen sein; 25. He! Lichter! Lichter!; 26. Elektra! Schwester!; 27. Ob ich nich höre?; 28. Hörst du denn nicht, sie tragen ihn; 29. Schweig, und tanze.

Elektra I. Borkh
Klytemnestra J. Madeira
Chrysothemis L. della Casa
Aegisthus M. Lorenz
Orestes K. Böhme
Tutor A. Pernerstorfer
Confidante A. Felbermayer
Trainbearer K. Loraine
Young Servant E. Majkut
Old Servant G. Littasy
Overseer A. Gerber-Candy
Maidservant I K. Meyer
Maidservant II S. Draksler
Maidservant III S. Wagner
Maidservant IV M. Horne
Maidservant V L. Otto
Vienna St Op Chor, VPO, D. Mitropoulos (pp1957)
(MEMO) ① [2] **HR4380/1**

Elektra B. Nilsson
Klytemnestra R. Resnik
Chrysothemis M. Collier
Aegisthus G. Stolze
Orestes T. Krause
Tutor T. Franc
Confidante M. Sjöstedt
Trainbearer M. Lilowa
Young Servant G. Unger
Old Servant L. Heppe
Overseer P. Tinsley
Maidservant I H. Watts
Maidservant II M. Lehane
Maidservant III Y. Minton
Maidservant IV J. Cook
Maidservant V F. Weathers
VPO, G. Solti (r1966/7)
(12/86) (DECC) ① [2] **417 345-2DH2**

Elektra Leonie Rysanek
Klytemnestra A. Varnay
Chrysothemis C. Ligendza
Aegisthus H. Beirer
Orestes D. Fischer-Dieskau
Tutor J. Greindl
Confidante C. Reppel
Trainbearer O. Varla
Young Servant C. Doig
Old Servant K. Böhme
Overseer C. Lorand
Maidservant I K. Borris
Maidservant II A. Gall
Maidservant III R. Yachmi-Caucig
Maidservant IV M. Nikolova
Maidservant V M. Vance
Vienna St Op Chor, VPO, K. Böhm, G. Friedrich
(11/88) (DECC) ◖ [2] **071 400-1DH2**
(DECC) ▭ **071 400-3DH**

Elektra H. Behrens
Klytemnestra C. Ludwig
Chrysothemis N. Secunde
Aegisthus R. Ulfung
Orestes J. Hynninen
Tutor; Old Servant B. Matthews
Confidante; Maidservant IV E. Rawlins
Trainbearer D. Labelle
Young Servant B. Cresswell
Overseer M. Napier
Maidservant I J. Khara
Maidservant II W. Hillhouse
Maidservant III D. Kesling
Maidservant V C. Haymon
Tanglewood Fest Chor, Boston SO, S. Ozawa (pp1988)
(4/89) (PHIL) ① [2] **422 574-2PH2**

Elektra E. Marton
Klytemnestra M. Lipovšek
Chrysothemis C. Studer
Aegisthus H. Winkler
Orestes B. Weikl
Tutor K. Moll
Confidante V. Wheeler
Trainbearer D. Giepel
Young Servant U. Ress
Old Servant A. Kuhn
Overseer C. Anhorn
Maidservant I D. Evangelatos
Maidservant II S. Close
Maidservant III B. Calm
Maidservant IV J. Faulkner
Maidservant V C.M. Petrig
Bavarian Rad Chor, BRSO, W. Sawallisch (r1990)
(12/90) (EMI) ① [2] **CDS7 54067-2**

Elektra E. Marton
Klytemnestra B. Fassbaender
Chrysothemis C. Studer
Aegisthus J. King
Orestes F. Grundheber
Tutor G. Simic
Confidante W. Winsauer
Trainbearer N. Sasaki
Young Servant W. Gahmlich
Old Servant C. Otelli
Overseer G. Lechner
Maidservant I M. Lilowa
Maidservant II G. Sima
Maidservant III M. Hintermeier
Maidservant IV B. Poschner-Klebel
Maidservant V J. Borowska
Vienna St Op Chor, Vienna St Op Orch, C. Abbado, B. Large
(4/93) (PION) ◖ **PLMCB00221**

Elektra E. Schlüter
Klytemnestra G. Hammer
Chrysothemis A. Kupper
Aegisthus P. Markwort
Orestes R. Hager
Tutor G. Neidlinger
Confidante E. Schwier
Trainbearer K. Lange
Young Servant F. Göllnitz
Old Servant H. Siegel
Overseer C. Autenrieth
Maidservant I M. von Ilosvay
Maidservant II H. Gura
Maidservant III M. Wulf
Maidservant IV L. Bischof
Maidservant V S. Mirtsch
Hamburg St Op Chor, Hamburg PO, E. Jochum (pp1944)
(7/93) (ACAN) ① [2] **ACAN44 2128-2**

Elektra I. Borkh
Klytemnestra J. Madeira
Chrysothemis M. Schech
Aegisthus F. Uhl
Orestes D. Fischer-Dieskau
Tutor F. Teschler
Confidante R. Reinecke
Trainbearer H. Ambros
Young Servant G. Unger
Old Servant S. Vogel
Overseer I. Steingruber
Maidservant I C. Ahlin
Maidservant II M. Sjöstedt
Maidservant III S. Wagner
Maidservant IV J. Hellwig
Maidservant V G. Schreyer
Dresden St Op Chor, Staatskapelle Dresden, K. Böhm (r1960)
(11/94) (DG) ① [2] **445 329-2GX2**

Excs G. Rünger, H. Konetzni, Vienna St Op Chor, Vienna St Op Orch, H. Knappertsbusch (pp1941) (9/95) (SCHW) ① [2] **314662**

Paraphrase G. Gould (trans Gould; bp1966) (SONY) ◖ [6] **S6LV48400**
(SONY) ▭ [12] **S12HV48400(2)**

Paraphrase G. Gould (bp1966) (SONY) ◖ **SLV48433**
(SONY) ▭ **SHV48433**

2. B. Nilsson, VPO, G. Solti (r1966/7) (10/93) (DECC) ① **436 461-2DM**

2, 20. R. Pauly, E. Schipper, Vienna St Op Orch, H. Knappertsbusch (pp1936) (SCHW) ① [2] **314672**

2, 6, 26. I. Borkh, P. Schoeffler, F. Yeend, Chicago Lyric Op Chor, Chicago SO, F. Reiner (r1956) (5/93) (RCA) ① **GD60874**

4. C. Studer, E. Marton, BRSO, W. Sawallisch (r1990) (EMI) ① **CDC5 55350-2**

18-21. C. Ludwig, W. Berry, Berlin Deutsche Op Orch, H. Hollreiser (r1963-4) (TESS) ① **049-2**

Feuersnot– opera: 1 act, Op. 50 (1901—Dresden) (Lib. E von Wolzogen)

Feuersnot! Minnegebot! J. Varady, B. Weikl, Munich RO, H. Fricke (3/89) (ACAN) ① **43 266**

Feuersnot! Minnegebot! M. Cebotari, K. Schmitt-Walter, Berlin RSO, A. Rother (bp1943) (8/95) (PREI) ① **90222**

Love scene Toronto SO, A. Davis (r1994) (11/95) (CBC) ① **SMCD5142**

Die **Frau ohne Schatten– opera: 3 acts, Op. 65 (1919—Vienna) (Lib. H von Hofmannsthal)**

EXCERPTS: ACT ONE: 1. Licht überm See; 2. Amme! Wachst du?; 3. Ist mein Liebster dahin; 4. Wie soll ich denn nicht weinen?; 5. Amme, um alles, wo find' ich den Schatten?; 6. Flight down to Earth; 7. Dieb! Da nimm!; 8. Sie aus dem Hause; 9. Dritthalb Jahr bin ich dein Weib; 10. Was wollt ihr hier?; 11. Ach, Herrin, süsse Herrin!; 12. Hat es dich blutige Tränen gekostet; 13. Mutter, Mutter, lass uns nach Hause!; 14. Trag' ich die Ware selber zu Markt; 15. Sie haben es mir gesagt. ACT TWO: 16. Komm bald wieder nach Haus, mein Gebieter; 17. Was ist nun deine Rede, du Prinzessin; 18. Orchestral Interlude; 19. Falke, Falke, du wiedergefundener; 20. Stille...O weh, Falke, o weh!; 21. Es gibt derer, die haben immer Zeit; 22. Schlange, was hab' ich mit dir zu schaffen; 23. Ein Handwerk verstehst du sicher nicht; 24. Wer da?; 25. Sieh - Amme - sieh; 26. Zum Lebenswasser!; 27. Wehe, mein Mann!; 28. Es dunkelt, dass ich nicht sehe zur Arbeit; 29. Es gibt derer; 30. Das Weib ist irre; 31. Barak, ich hab' es nicht getan!. ACT THREE: 32. Schweigt doch, ihr Stimmen!; 33. Mir anvertraut; 34. Auf, geh nach oben, Mann; 35. Sie kommen!; 36. Fort mit uns; 37. Aus unsern Taten steigt ein Gericht!; 38. Was Menschen bedfürfen?; 39. Keikobad! Deine Dienerin; 40. Weh uns Armen!; 41. Vater, bist du's?; 42. Goldenen Trank; 43. Ach! Weh mir! Mein Liebster starr!; 44. Wenn das Herz aus Kristall... 45. Sind das die Cherubim; 46. Engel sind's, die von sich sagen!; 47. Trifft mich sein Lieben nicht; 48. Nun will ich jubeln; 49. Vater, dir drohet nichts.

Empress J. Varady
Emperor P. Domingo
Dyer's Wife H. Behrens
Barak the Dyer J. Van Dam
Nurse R. Runkel
Spirit-Messenger A. Dohmen
Voice of the Falcon S. Jo
Apparition of a Young Man R. Gambill
Voice from above E. Ardam
Guardian of the Threshold E. Lind
One-eyed Brother G. Hornik
One-armed Brother H. Franzen
Hunchback Brother W. Gahmlich
Vienna Boys' Ch, Vienna St Op Chor, VPO, G. Solti
(5/92) (DECC) ① [3] **436 243-2DH3**

Empress C. Studer

Emperor T. Moser
Dyer's Wife E. Marton
Barak the Dyer R. Hale
Nurse M. Lipovšek
Spirit-Messenger B. Terfel
Voice of the Falcon A. Rost
Apparition of a Young Man H. Lippert
Guardian of the Temple E. Norberg-Schulz
Voice from Above E. Ardam
One-eyed Brother M. Hemm
One-armed Brother H. Franzen
Hunchback Brother W. Gahmlich
Vienna St Op Chor, Salzburg Children's Ch, VPO, G. Solti, G. Friedrich (pp1992)
(4/94) (DECC) [2] **071 425-1DH2**
(4/94) (DECC) [2] **071 425-3DH2**
Empress Leonie Rysanek
Emperor J. King
Dyer's Wife B. Nilsson
Barak the Dyer W. Berry
Nurse R. Hesse
Spirit-Messenger P. Wimberger
Voice of the Falcon; Guardian of the Temple Lotte Rysanek
Apparition of a Young Man E. Aichberger
Voice from Above G. Jahn
One-eyed Brother H. Helm
One-armed Brother L. Alvary
Hunchback Brother M. Dickie
Vienna St Op Chor, Vienna St Op Orch, K. Böhm (pp1977)
(11/94) (DG) ① [3] **445 325-2GX3**
Excs F. Völker, V. Ursuleac, G. Rünger, Vienna St Op Chor, Vienna St Op Orch, C. Krauss (pp1933) (9/95) (SCHW) ① [2] **314662**
Symphonic fantasy Rotterdam PO, J. Tate (4/93) (EMI) ① **CDC7 54581-2**
1, 2(pt), 3, 12(pt), 13, 15, 18, 27, 31, 33, 34, 35(pt), 36(pt), 37, 41, 42(pt), 48. R. Kollo, C. Studer, A. Muff, U. Vinzing, H. Schwarz, BRSO, W. Sawallisch (r1987) (EMI) ① **CDC7 54494-2**
2(pt), 3, 8(pt), 9, 11, 12(pt), 15(pt), 19, 25, 31-33, 36(pt), 37, 41, 44, 47, 48. T. Ralf, H. Konetzni, E. Höngen, H. Alsen, E. Loose, W. Wenkoff, E. Boettcher, M. Frutschnigg, J. Herrmann, E. Schulz, G. Monthy, M. Rus, W. Wernigk, A. Poell, T. Neralič, R. Neumann, Vienna St Op Chor, Vienna St Op Orch, K. Böhm (pp1943) (11/94) (SCHW) ① [2] **314552**
19. T. Ralf, Saxon St Orch, K. Böhm (bp1943) (10/94) (PREI) ① **89077**
19, 20. P. Domingo, VPO, G. Solti (r1991) (DECC) ① **440 410-2DM**
19, 20. B. Heppner, Toronto SO, A. Davis (r1994) (11/95) (CBC) ① **SMCD5142**
25, 41. E. Steber, S. Svanholm, O. Wiener, C. Goltz, I. Steingruber, Orch, K. Böhm (bp1953) (VAI) ① **VAIA1012**
32, 33. C. Ludwig, W. Berry, VPO, K. Böhm (pp1974) (ORFE) ① **C365941A**
32-34. C. Ludwig, W. Berry, S. Wagner, Berlin Deutsche Op Orch, H. Hollreiser (r1963-4) (TESS) ① **049-2**
35. L. Price, New Philh, E. Leinsdorf (8/90) (RCA) ① **GD60398**
41. C. Studer, C. Sieden, U. Vinzing, A. Muff, Bavarian Rad Chor, BRSO, W. Sawallisch (r1987) (EMI) ① **CDC5 55350-2**
41. H. Konetzni, Vienna St Op Orch, K. Böhm (pp1943) (6/94) (SCHW) ① **314502**

Friedenstag– opera: 3 acts, Op. 81 (1938—Munich) (Lib. J Gregor)
Commandant R. Roloff
Maria A. Marc
Sergeant W. Wilderman
Rifleman G. Shirley
Corporal M. Wittges
Musketeer P. van Derick
Bugler P. Schmidt
A Piedmontese R. Broitman
Officer; Front-Line Officer S. Lusmann
Holsteiner T. Cook
Burgomaster R. Cassilly
Prelate J. Wood
Woman of the People K. Williams
NY Gay Men's Chor, Collegiate Chorale, Collegiate Orch, R. Bass (pp1989)
(1/92) (KOCH) ① **37111-2**
Commandant H. Hotter
Maria V. Ursuleac
Sergeant H. Alsen
Rifleman J. Witt
Corporal H. Wiedemann
Musketeer C. Bissuti
Bugler N. Zec
A Piedmontese A. Dermota
Officer H. Gallos
Front-Line Officer G. Monthy
Holsteiner K. Kamann
Burgomaster W. Franter
Prelate V. Madin
Woman of the People M. Bugarinovic
Vienna St Op Chor, Vienna St Op Orch, C. Krauss (pp1939)
(10/95) (SCHW) ① [2] **314652**

Guntram– opera: 3 acts, Op. 25 (1884, rev 1940—Weimar) (Lib. cpsr)
EXCERPTS: 1. Overture. ACT 1: 2. Hier, ihr Guten, rastet, erholt euch; 3. Ein glückliches Loos?; 4. Endlich, endlich entflohn dem Schwarm; 5. Freihild!...Was hör ich?; 6. Freihild, mein Kind, mein süsses Kind!; 7. Verdammtes Volk, hab ich euch gefasst? ACT 2: 8. Prelude; 9. Heil dem Herrscher, dessen Seele; 10. Freihild! Noch scheinst du traurig; 11. Was soll der Sang?; 12. Kreig, Kreig, Kreig, mein Herzog; 13. So verfalle das Reich in Schutt and Staub; 14. Fass'ich sie bang. ACT 3: 15. Prelude; 16. Ex lux perpetua; 17. Guntram! Guntram! was ist dir?; 18. Gegrüsst Guntram, grosser Sünder; 19a. Heil dir, Geliebter; 19b. Ewig einsam; 19c. Wenn du einst die Gauen; 20. Freihild, leb' wohl.
Prelude Rotterdam PO, J. Tate (4/93) (EMI) ① **CDC7 54581-2**
14. L. Price, New Philh, E. Leinsdorf (8/90) (RCA) ① **GD60398**
19b, 19c B. Heppner, Toronto SO, A. Davis (r1994) (11/95) (CBC) ① **SMCD5142**

Intermezzo– opera: 2 acts, Op. 72 (1924—Dresden) (Lib. cpsr)
EXCERPTS: ACT 1: 1. Anna! Anna! Wo bleibt denn nur die dumme Gans?; 2. Haben Sie alles für den Herrn?; 3. Interlude I; 4. Nun wollen wir frisieren!; 5. Ach! Frau Huss! Ja, Grüss Gott!; 6. Interlude II; 7a. Bahn frei!; 7b. Doch, aber Sie waren zu schnell!; 8a. Interlude III (Waltz); 8b. Ich kann nicht mehr; 9. Interlude IV; 10. Wissen Sie, mein Mann, der immer an der Arbeit sitzt; 11. Interlude V; 12. Es ist wirlich ein sehr netter; 13. Ha, ha, ha, ha. Der Hauptmann Sturtz hat seinen Abschied; 14a. Ein hübscher Mensch!; 14b. Interlude VI; 15a. Frau Notar! Können Sie mir meinen Koffer heraufschicken?; 15b. Interlude VII; 16. Tausend Mark will er haben!; 17a. Interlude VII; 17b. Mein lieber, lieber Bubi! ACT 2: 18. Ach, Sie kennen sie nicht, Herr Justizrat!; 19a. Verfluchte Chose! Frau Christine wird toben!; 19b. Postlude I; 20. Guten Tag, Herr Notar; 21. Interlude IX; 22. Postlude II; 23. Introduction (Scene 4); 24. Ah! Anna! Ich hätte den Baron doch nicht dahin schicken sollen; 25. Interlude X; 26. Er kommt! Herrgott, wie ich mich freue!; 27. Da bin ich, gnäd'ge Frau; 28. Er ist sicher kein Gauner.
Christine F. Lott
Little Franzl R. Ashford
Robert Storch J. Pringle
Anna E. Gale
Baron Lummer I. Caley
Notary R. Bryson
Notary's Wife R. Woodland
Conductor G. Winslade
Commercial Councillor I. Caddy
Legal Councillor B. Donlan
Singer A. Gallacher
Fanny Y. Howard
Marie D. Brook
Therese M. Jagusz
Resi C. Pierard
Glyndebourne Fest Chor, LPO, G. Kuhn, J. Cox (r1983: Eng)
(CAST) **CVI2024**
Christine L. Popp
Little Franzl P. Brammer
Robert Storch D. Fischer-Dieskau
Anna G. Fuchs
Baron Lummer A. Dallapozza
Notary K. Hirte
Notary's Wife G. Greindl-Rosner
Conductor M. Finke
Commercial Councillor R. Grumbach
Legal Councillor J.W. Wilsing
Singer K. Moll
Fanny E. Woska
Marie E. Rüggeberg
Therese E. Rüggeberg
Resi K. Hautermann
BRSO, W. Sawallisch (r1980)
(1/89) (EMI) ① [2] **CDS7 49337-2**

Intermezzo– symphonic interludes from the opera (arr cpsr from Interludes in opera)
EXCERPTS: 1. Reisefieber und Walzerszene; 2. Träumerei am Kamin; 3. Am Spieltisch; 4. Fröhlicher Beschluss.
1-4. Seattle SO, G. Schwarz (9/90) (DELO) ① **DE3052**
1-4. Rotterdam PO, J. Tate (4/93) (EMI) ① **CDC7 54581-2**
1-4. VPO, A. Previn (r1992) (11/93) (DG) ① **437 790-2GH**
2. Tokyo PO, F. Haider (pp1993) (NIGH) ① **NC090560-2**
3, 4. Toronto SO, A. Davis (r1994) (11/95) (CBC) ① **SMCD5142**

Die **Liebe der Danae– opera: 3 acts, Op. 83 (1952—Salzburg) (Lib. J Gregor, after H von Hofmannsthal)**
EXCERPTS: 10. Symphonic Fragment (arr from Act 3: C. Krauss: 1952).
10. Toronto SO, A. Davis (r1985) (SONY) ① **SMK66938**
10. Slovak PO, Z. Košler (2/91) (NAXO) ① **8 550342**
11, 12. B. Heppner, Toronto SO, A. Davis (r1994) (11/95) (CBC) ① **SMCD5142**

Der **Rosenkavalier– opera: 3 acts, Op. 59 (1911—Dresden) (Lib. H von Hofmannsthal)**
EXCERPTS: 1. Prelude. ACT 1: 2. Wie du warst! Wie du bist; 3. Der Feldmarschall sitzt im krowatischen Wald; 4. Selbstverständlich empfängt mich Ihro Gnaden; 5. Macht das einen lahmen Esel aus mir?; 6a. I komm' glei; 6b. Drei arme adelige Waisen; 7. Di rigori armato; 8. Mein lieber Hippolyte; 9. Da geht er hin; 10. Ach, du bist wieder da!; 11. Die Zeit, die ist ein sonderbar Ding. ACT 2: 12. Ein ernster Tag, ein grosser Tag!; 13. In dieser feierlichen Stunde der Prüfung; 14. Mir ist die Ehre (Presentation of the Rose); 15. Ich kenn' Ihn schon recht wohl; 16. Jetzt aber kommt mein Herr Zukünftiger; 17. Hab' nichts dawider; 18. Mit Ihren Augen voll Tränen; 19. Herr Baron von Lerchenau!; 20a. Da lieg' ich!; 20b. Herr Kavalier! (Letter Scene); 20c. Baron Ochs' Waltz. ACT 3: 21. Prelude; 22. Hab'n Euer Gnaden; 23. Nein, nein! I trink' kein Wein; 24. Wie die Stund' hingeht; 25. Halt! Keiner rührt sich!; 26. Ihre hochfürstliche Gnaden; 27. Ist halt vorbei; 28. Mein Gott, es war nicht mehr; 29. Heut oder morgen oder den übernächsten Tag; 30. Marie Theres'...Hab' mir's gelobt (Trio); 31. Ist ein Traum (Finale). 32. ORCHESTRAL SUITE: 32a. Prelude, Act 1; 32b. Presentation of the Rose, Act 2; 32c. Baron Ochs's Waltz, Act 2; 32d. Ist ein Traum, Act 3; 32e. Waltz Reprise; 33. WALTZ SEQUENCES, Act 2 and 3.
Die Feldmarschallin K. Te Kanawa
Octavian A. Baltsa
Baron Ochs A. Haugland
Sophie B. Bonney
Faninal J. Summers
Italian Tenor Y. Ramiro
Annina C. Buchan
Valzacchi R. Tear
Milliner S. Maisey
Notary J. Gibbs
Police Commissioner R. Earle
Marschallin's Major-domo K. Begley
Faninal's Major-domo J. Dobson
Landlord P. Crook
ROH Chor, ROHO, G. Solti, J. Schlesinger
(CAST) **CVI2017**
Die Feldmarschallin A. Tomowa-Sintow
Octavian A. Baltsa
Baron Ochs K. Moll
Sophie J. Perry
Faninal G. Hornik
Italian Tenor V. Cole
Annina H. Müller-Molinari
Valzacchi H. Zednik
Leitmetzerin W. Lipp
Milliner G. Sima
Notary C. Feller
Police commissioner V. von Halem
Marschallin's Major-domo K. Equiluz
Faninal's Major-domo F. Kasemann
Landlord K. Terkal
Orphan I B. Poschner-Klebel
Orphan II W. Winsauer
Orphan III M. Hintermeier
Animal Seller H. Nitsche

Footman I A. Tomaschek
Footman II J. Reinprecht
Footman III W. Scheider
Footman IV G. Panzenböck
Waiter I I. Koblitz
Waiter II W. Holzherr
Waiter III W. Zeh
Waiter IV H. Lichtenberger
Porter J. Reautschnigg

Vienna St Op Concert Ch, VPO, H. von Karajan (r1982-4)
(9/84) (DG) ① [3] **423 850-2GH3**

Die Feldmarschallin R. Crespin
Octavian Y. Minton
Baron Ochs M. Jungwirth
Sophie H. Donath
Faninal O. Wiener
Italian Tenor L. Pavarotti
Annina A. Howells
Valzacchi M. Dickie
Leitmetzerin E. Loose
Milliner R. Schwaiger
Notary A. Jerger
Police Commissioner H. Lackner
Marschallin's Majordomo H. Prikopa
Faninal's Majordomo K. Equiluz
Landlord A. Dermota
Orphan I A. Auger
Orphan II R. Yachmi-Caucig
Orphan III I. Mayr
Animal seller K. Terkal
Footman I H. Pipal
Footman II A. Tomaschek
Footman III A. Maly
Footman IV L. Heppe
Waiter I A. Tomaschek
Waiter II F. Setzer
Waiter III F. Strack
Waiter IV N. Simkowsky
Porter J. Reautschnigg

Vienna St Op Chor, VPO, G. Solti
(3/87) (DECC) ① [3] **417 493-2DH3**

Die Feldmarschallin; Orphan I E. Schwarzkopf
Octavian; Orphan II C. Ludwig
Baron Ochs O. Edelmann
Sophie T. Stich-Randall
Faninal; Footman III; Waiter III E. Waechter
Italian Tenor N. Gedda
Annina; Orphan III K. Meyer
Valzacchi; Animal Seller P. Kuen
Leitmetzerin L. Welitsch
Milliner A. Felbermayer
Notary; Footman IV H. Pröglhöf
Police Commissioner; Waiter IV F. Bierbach
Marschallin's Majordomo; Footman II; Waiter II E. Majkut
Faninal's Majordomo; Footman I; Waiter I G. Unger
Landlord K. Friedrich

Loughton High School for Girls' Ch, Bancroft School Boys' Ch, Philh Chor, Philh, H. von Karajan
(1/88) (EMI) ① [3] **CDS7 49354-2**

Die Feldmarschallin C. Ludwig
Octavian G. Jones
Baron Ochs W. Berry
Sophie L. Popp
Faninal E. Gutstein
Italian Tenor P. Domingo
Annina M. Lilowa
Valzacchi M. Dickie
Leitmetzerin E. Loose
Milliner L. Dutoit
Notary L. Pantscheff
Police Commissioner H. Lackner
Marschallin's Majordomo H. Pröglhöf
Faninal's Majordomo E. Aichberger
Landlord K. Terkal
Orphan I E. Mühlberger
Orphan II H. Saidula
Orphan III J. Herndl
Animal seller M. Guggia
Footman I F. Setzer
Footman II R. Resch
Footman III K. Bernhard
Footman IV L. Hoppe
Waiter I H. Gneuer
Waiter II F. Riedl
Waiter III A. Maly
Waiter IV K. Neugebauer
Porter M. Heigl

Vienna St Op Chor, VPO, L. Bernstein
(9/88) (CBS) ① [3] **CD42564**

Abridged Lotte Lehmann, M. Olczewska, R. Mayr, E. Schumann, V. Madin, B. Paalen, H. Gallos, A. Michalsky, K. Ettl, Vienna St Op Chor, VPO, R. Heger (r1933)
(3/90) (PEAR) ① [2] **GEMMCDS9365**

Die Feldmarschallin M. Reining
Octavian S. Jurinac
Baron Ochs L. Weber
Sophie H. Gueden
Faninal A. Poell
Italian Tenor A. Dermota
Annina H. Rössl-Majdan
Valzacchi P. Klein
Leitmetzerin J. Hellwig
Milliner B. Seidl
Notary F. Bierbach
Police Commissioner W. Berry
Marschallin's Majordomo H. Pröglhöf
Faninal's Majordomo A. Jaresch
Landlord; Animal seller E. Majkut
Orphan I W. Loibner
Orphan II E. Hochstätter
Orphan III M. Trupp
Footman I A. Buchbauer
Footman II L. Fleck
Footman III F. Maier
Footman IV O. Vajda
Waiter I W. Daucha
Waiter II R. Stumper
Waiter III F. Erbner
Waiter IV F. Settmacher

Vienna St Op Chor, VPO, E. Kleiber (r1954)
(5/90) (DECC) ① [3] **425 950-2DM3**

Die Feldmarschallin G. Jones
Octavian B. Fassbaender
Baron Ochs M. Jungwirth
Sophie L. Popp
Faninal B. Kusche
Italian Tenor F. Araiza
Annina G. Wewezow
Valzacchi D. Thaw
Leitmetzerin A. Waas
Milliner S. Sonnenschein
Notary H. Wilbrink
Police Commissioner A. Peter
Marschallin's Majordomo G. Paskuda
Faninal's Majordomo F. Lenz
Landlord N. Orth
Animal Seller O. Kobayashi

Bavarian St Op Chor, Bavarian St Op Orch, C. Kleiber, O. Schenk (r1979)
(9/91) (DG) ◖ **072 405-1GH2**
(DG) ▭ **072 405-3GH**

Die Feldmarschallin K. Te Kanawa
Octavian A.S. von Otter
Baron Ochs K. Rydl
Sophie B. Hendricks
Faninal F. Grundheber
Italian Tenor R. Leech
Annina C. Powell
Valzacchi G. Clark
Leitmetzerin J. Faulkner
Milliner S. Brohm
Notary A. Sramek
Police Commissioner B. Schwanbeck
Marschallin's Majordomo F. Gruber
Faninal's Majordomo M. Kraus
Landlord H. Zednik
Orphan I B. Bonitz
Orphan II M. Harnisch
Orphan III H. Liebmann
Animal Seller A. Ude
Footman I J. Schroeter
Footman II B. Beyer
Footman III R. Zakowsky
Footman IV W. Czerny
Waiter I C. Bodenstein
Waiter II J. Urban
Waiter III R. Steffek
Waiter IV H-J. Staude
Porter W. Eggars

Dresden Kreuzchor Children's Voices, Dresden St Op Chor, Staatskapelle Dresden, B. Haitink
(9/91) (EMI) ① [3] **CDS7 54259-2**

Abridged Lotte Lehmann, M. Olczewska, R. Mayr, E. Schumann, V. Madin, B. Paalen, H. Gallos, A. Michalsky, K. Ettl, W. Wernigk, Vienna St Op Chor, VPO, R. Heger (r1933)
(4/93) (EMI) ① [2] **CHS7 64487-2**

Die Feldermarschallin A. Tomowa-Sintow
Octavian A. Baltsa
Baron Ochs K. Moll
Sophie J. Perry
Faninal G. Hornik
Italian Tenor V. Cole
Annina H. Müller-Molinari
Valzacchi H. Zednik
Leitmetzerin W. Lipp
Milliner G. Sima
Notary A. Sramek
Police commissioner K. Rydl
Marschallin's Major-domo J. van Kesteren
Faninal's Major-domo F. Kasemann
Landlord K. Terkal
Orphan I G. Ottenthal
Orphan II G. de Gyldenfeldt
Orphan III C. Slania
Animal Seller H. Nitsche
Footman I A. Tomaschek
Footman II J. Reinprecht
Footman III W. Scheider
Footman IV G. Panzenböck
Waiter I I. Koblitz
Waiter II W. Holzherr
Waiter III W. Zeh
Waiter IV H. Lichtenberger
Porter M. Heigl

Vienna St Op Concert Ch, VPO, H. von Karajan, H. von Karajan (r1984)
(6/94) (SONY) ◖ [2] **S2LV48313**
(6/94) (SONY) ▭ [2] **S2HV48313**

Die Feldmarschallin C. Ludwig
Octavian T. Troyanos
Baron Ochs T. Adam
Sophie E. Mathis
Faninal O. Wiener
Italian Tenor A. de Ridder
Annina C. Ahlin
Valzacchi G. Unger
Leitmetzerin K. Lövaas
Notary L. Pantscheff
Police Commissioner K. Hirte
Marschallin's Majordomo A. Pfeifle
Faninal's Majordomo S.R. Frese
Landlord R. Licha

Vienna St Op Chor, VPO, K. Böhm (pp1969)
(11/94) (DG) ① [3] **445 338-2GX3**

Die Feldmarschallin E. Lear
Octavian F. von Stade
Baron Ochs J. Bastin
Sophie R. Welting
Faninal D. Hammond-Stroud
Italian Tenor J. Carreras
Annina S. van Sante
Valzacchi J. Atherton
Leitmetzerin N. Morpurgo
Milliner R. van Haarlem
Notary; Police Commissioner H. Smit
Marschallin's Majordomo W. Goedhardt
Faninal's Majordomo; Animal Seller M. Coppens
Landlord A. van Limpt
Orphan I A. Bello
Orphan II M. Dieleman
Orphan III T. van der Putten
Footman I; Waiter I F. Fiselier
Footman II; Waiter II P. Bindels
Footman III; Waiter III A. Kooijmans
Footman IV; Waiter IV W. Huisman
Porter R. Vedder

Netherlands Op Chor, Rotterdam PO, E. de Waart (r1976)
(12/94) (PHIL) ① [3] **442 086-2PM3**

Die Feldmarschallin F. Lott
Octavian A.S. von Otter
Baron Ochs K. Moll
Sophie B. Bonney
Faninal G. Hornik
Italian Tenor K. Ikaia-Purdy
Annina A. Gonda
Valzacchi H. Zednik
Leitmetzerin O. Miljakovic
Milliner Lotte Leitner
Notary W. Bankl
Police Commissioner P. Wimberger
Marschallin's Majordomo W. Kmentt
Faninal's Majordomo F. Kasemann
Landlord P. Jelosits

Vienna St Op Chor, Vienna St Op Orch, C. Kleiber, O. Schenk (r1994)
(4/95) (DG) ◖ [2] **070 443-1GH2**
(4/95) (DG) ▭ [2] **072 443-3GH2**

Excs Lotte Lehmann, E. Hadrabová, V. Madin, E. Schumann, A. Michalsky, R. Tomek, B. Sterneck, B. Paalen, W. Wernigk, Vienna St Op Chor, Vienna St Op Orch, H. Knappertsbusch (pp1936) (11/95) (SCHW) ① [2] **314622**

1, 2, 7, 9, 11, 14, 15, 20a-c, 23, 30, 31. K. Te Kanawa, A.S. von Otter, B. Hendricks, K. Rydl, F. Grundheber, C. Powell, R. Leech, A. Sramek, Dresden St Op Chor, Staatskapelle Dresden, B. Haitink (r1990) (EMI) ① **CDC7 54493-2**

1-3, 7, 9, 14, 20a-c, 23, 24, 30, 31. A. Tomowa-Sintow, K. Moll, A. Baltsa, G. Hornik, J. Perry, H. Müller-Molinari, V. Cole, Vienna St Op Chor, VPO, H. von Karajan (r1982-4)
(8/85) (DG) Ⓓ **415 284-2GH**

2, 14, 23, 30, 31. I. Seefried, M. Schech, R. Streich, D. Fischer-Dieskau, K. Böhme, I. Steingruber, Dresden St Op Chor, Staatskapelle Dresden, K. Böhm (r1958)
(9/93) (DG) Ⓓ [2] **437 677-2GDO2**

2, 27. B. Sterneck, A. Konetzni, E. Schumann, E. Flesch, B. Paalen, H. Gallos, G. Maikl, Vienna St Op Orch, H. Knappertsbusch (pp1936)
(SCHW) Ⓓ [2] **314672**

2, 4, 5, 6a, 6b, 7, 8, 9(pt), 18, 31. V. Ursuleac, R. Mayr, E. Hadrabová, M. Gerhart, H. Gallos, B. Paalen, K. von Pataky, Vienna St Op Orch, C. Krauss (pp1933)
(7/94) (SCHW) Ⓓ [2] **314512**

7. H. Roswaenge, Philh Hungarica, Z. Rozsnyai (pp1959) (PREI) Ⓓ **90103**

7. H. Roswaenge, Berlin St Op Orch, B. Seidler-Winkler (r1938) (PREI) Ⓓ [2] **89211**

7. J. Carreras, Rotterdam PO, E. de Waart (r1976) (PHIL) Ⓓ **442 600-2PH**
(PHIL) ▭ **442 600-4PH**

7. P. Domingo, VPO, L. Bernstein
(SONY) Ⓓ **MDK47176**
(SONY) ▭ **MDT47176**

7. P. Seiffert, Munich RO, J. Kout (r1992-3)
(RCA) Ⓓ **09026 61214-2**

7. T. Beltrán, RPO, R. Stapleton (r1994)
(SILV) Ⓓ **SILKD6005**
(SILV) ▭ **SILKC6005**

7. L. Pavarotti, VPO, G. Solti
(7/86) (DECC) Ⓓ [2] **417 011-2DH2**

7. H. Roswaenge, Berlin St Op Orch, B. Seidler-Winkler (r1938) (5/90) (PREI) Ⓓ **89018**

7. R. Tauber, orch (r1920)
(12/92) (NIMB) Ⓓ **NI7830**
(12/92) (NIMB) ▭ **NC7830**

7. C. Kullman, Berlin City Op Orch, F. Zweig (r1932) (11/93) (PREI) Ⓓ **89057**

7. L. Pavarotti, VPO, G. Solti (r1968)
(12/93) (DECC) Ⓓ **433 437-2DA**
(DECC) ▭ **433 437-4DA**

7. Alfredo Kraus, WNO Orch, C. Rizzi (r1994)
(8/95) (PHIL) Ⓓ **442 785-2PH**
(8/95) (PHIL) ▭ **442 785-4PH**

7. B. Heppner, Toronto SO, A. Davis (r1994)
(11/95) (CBC) Ⓓ **SMCD5142**

7, 31. L. Aikin, C. Taha, A. Ulbrich, V. Ombuena, Berlin RSO, J. Märkl (r1991)
(SCHW) Ⓓ [2] **312682**

9. E. Schwarzkopf, Philh, H. von Karajan (r1956)
(EMI) Ⓓ **CDM5 65577-2**

9. L. Price, New Philh, E. Leinsdorf
(8/90) (RCA) Ⓓ **GD60398**

9(pt) Lotte Lehmann, Berlin St Op Orch, H. Weigert (r1925) (6/92) (PREI) Ⓓ [3] **89302**

9(pt) M. Siems, orch (r1911)
(7/92) (PEAR) Ⓓ [3] **GEMMCDS9925(1)**

9(pt) V. Ursuleac, Vienna St Op Orch, C. Krauss (pp1933) (6/94) (SCHW) Ⓓ **314502**

9(pt) H. Konetzni, VPO, H. von Karajan (r1947)
(1/95) (PREI) Ⓓ **90078**

9-11. C. Ludwig, T. Troyanos, VPO, K. Böhm (pp1969) (ORFE) Ⓓ **C365941A**

9, 11(pt) K. Te Kanawa, Staatskapelle Dresden, B. Haitink (r1990) (EMI) Ⓓ **CDM5 65578-2**

9, 11(pt) M. Reining, Zurich Tonhalle Orch, H. Knappertsbusch (r1949)
(9/92) (PREI) Ⓓ **90083**

9-11, 14, 15, 20b, 20c, 23, 30, 31. E. Schwarzkopf, O. Edelmann, C. Ludwig, T. Stich-Randall, E. Waechter, K. Meyer, Philh Chor, Philh, H. von Karajan (r1956)
(EMI) Ⓓ **CDM7 63452-2**

9, 11, 30. Leonie Rysanek, E. Grümmer, E. Köth, BPO, W. Schüchter (r1955)
(2/95) (EMI) Ⓓ **CDH5 65201-2**

11. Lotte Lehmann, Berlin St Op Orch, M. Gurlitt (r1927) (PEAR) Ⓓ **GEMMCD9410**

11(pt) E. Schwarzkopf, Philh, H. von Karajan (r1956) (12/90) (EMI) Ⓓ **CDM7 63657-2**

11(pt), 13(pt), 14. H. Konetzni, E. Schumann, M. Bokor, A. Michalsky, Vienna St Op Chor, Vienna St Op Orch, H. Knappertsbusch (pp1937)
(SCHW) Ⓓ [2] **314672**

14. E. Schwarzkopf, I. Seefried, VPO, H. von Karajan (3/89) (EMI) Ⓓ **CDH7 69793-2**

14, 20a, 20b, 30. P. Coburn, R. Klepper, M. Borst, F. Hawlata, Bavarian Rad Chor, Munich RSO, M. Honeck (pp1992) (CAPR) Ⓓ **10 481**

14, 31. C. Supervia, I.M. Ferraris, orch, A. Albergoni (r1928: Ital)
(9/90) (CLUB) Ⓓ **CL99-074**

14, 31. C. Supervia, I.M. Ferraris, orch, A. Albergoni (Ital: r1928) (9/90) (PREI) Ⓓ **89023**

20a E. List, E. Schürhoff, Lower Austria Orch, W. Loibner (r1951) (PREI) Ⓓ **89083**

20a-c R. Mayr, A. Andrassy, orch, B. Walter (r1929)
(7/92) (PEAR) Ⓓ [3] **GEMMCDS9925(2)**

20a(pt), 20b R. Mayr, B. Paalen, Vienna St Op Chor, VPO, R. Heger (r1933)
(PEAR) Ⓓ **GEMMCD9122**

20a, 20b C. Ludwig, W. Berry, Berlin Deutsche Op Chor, Berlin Deutsche Op Orch, H. Hollreiser (r1963-4) (TESS) Ⓓ **049-2**

20b A. Kipnis, E. Ruziczka, Berlin St Op Orch, E. Orthmann (r1931) (12/90) (PREI) Ⓓ **89019**

20b E. Ruziczka, A. Kipnis, Berlin St Op Orch, E. Orthmann (r1931) (10/93) (NIMB) Ⓓ **NI7848**

20c Hollywood Bowl SO, J. Mauceri (r1993)
(6/94) (PHIL) Ⓓ **438 685-2PH**
(6/94) (PHIL) ▭ **438 685-4PH**

30. A. Tomowa-Sintow, A. Baltsa, J. Perry, VPO, H. von Karajan (DG) ▭ **439 153-4GMA**

30. K. Te Kanawa, B. Bonney, A. Howells, ROHO, G. Solti (CAST) ▣ **CVI2065**

30. K. Te Kanawa, A. Howells, B. Bonney, ROHO, G. Solti (TELD) ◐ **9031-77676-6**
(TELD) ▣ **9031-77676-3**

30. M. Cebotari, P. Buchner, T. Lemnitz, Berlin RSO, A. Rother (bp1943)
(8/95) (PREI) Ⓓ **90222**

30, 31. E. Schwarzkopf, C. Ludwig, T. Stich-Randall, E. Waechter, Philh, H. von Karajan (r1956) (CFP) Ⓓ **CD-CFP4656**
(CFP) ▭ **TC-CFP4656**

30, 31. R. Fleming, K. Battle, F. von Stade, A. Schmidt, BPO, C. Abbado (pp1992)
(7/93) (SONY) Ⓓ **SK52565**

31. E. Berger, T. Lemnitz, Berlin St Op Orch, C. Krauss (r1936) (12/91) (PREI) Ⓓ **89035**

31. E. Berger, T. Lemnitz, Berlin St Op Orch, C. Krauss (r1936) (10/93) (NIMB) Ⓓ **NI7848**

31. R. Stevens, E. Berger, RCA SO, F. Reiner (r1951) (4/94) (RCA) Ⓓ [6] **09026 61580-2(5)**

31. E. Hadrabová, M. Gerhard, Vienna St Op Orch, C. Krauss (pp1933)
(6/94) (SCHW) Ⓓ **314502**

32. RCA SO, C. Gerhardt (arr Gerhardt)
(CHES) Ⓓ **Chesky CD35**

32. Quebec Cons Orch, F-P. Decker
(REM) Ⓓ **REM311120**

32. Minneapolis SO, A. Dorati (r1955: arr Dorati)
(MERC) Ⓓ **434 348-2MM**

32. Cincinnati SO, J. López-Cobos (r1994)
(TELA) Ⓓ **CD80371**

32. SNO, N. Järvi
(2/90) (CHAN) Ⓓ **CHAN8758**

32. BBC Welsh SO, T. Otaka
(9/90) (NIMB) Ⓓ **NI5235**

32. Stuttgart RSO, N. Marriner
(9/92) (CAPR) Ⓓ **10 369**

32. VPO, A. Previn (r1992)
(11/93) (DG) Ⓓ **437 790-2GH**

32. Hallé, J. Barbirolli (pp1969)
(10/95) (BBCR) Ⓓ [2] **DMCD98**

32a-e BRSO, L. Maazel (r1995)
(10/95) (RCA) Ⓓ **09026 68225-2**

32e Bavarian St Orch, R. Strauss (r1941)
(8/95) (PREI) Ⓓ [2] **90205**

33(Act III) BPO, K. Böhm (BELA) Ⓓ **450 139-2**
(BELA) ▭ **450 139-4**

33. BPO, E. Kleiber (arr Singer)
(BIDD) Ⓓ **WHL002**

33. Concertgebouw, E. Jochum (r1960)
(PHIL) Ⓓ [2] **442 281-2PM2**

33. Staatskapelle Dresden, R. Kempe (r1973: arr Kempe) (EMI) Ⓓ [2] **CZS5 68110-2**

33. SNO, N. Järvi
(12/90) (CHAN) Ⓓ **CHAN8834**
(12/90) (CHAN) ▭ **ABTD1457**

33. Slovak PO, Z. Košler
(2/91) (NAXO) Ⓓ **8 550342**

33. SO, T. Beecham (r1916)
(11/91) (SYMP) Ⓓ [2] **SYMCD1096/7**

33. Seattle SO, G. Schwarz
(10/92) (DELO) Ⓓ **DE3109**

33. Chicago SO, F. Reiner (r1957)
(12/92) (RCA) Ⓓ **09026 60930-2**

33. Staatskapelle Dresden, R. Kempe (r1973: arr Kempe) (12/92) (EMI) Ⓓ [3] **CMS7 64346-2**

Der **Rosenkavalier– music for the film version, Av112 (1925)**

Tivoli Augmented Orch, R. Strauss (r1926)
(1/93) (KOCH) Ⓓ **37132-2**

Tivoli Augmented Orch, R. Strauss (r1926)
(4/93) (EMI) Ⓓ **CDC7 54610-2**

Hong Kong PO, K. Schermerhorn
(MARC) Ⓓ **8 220323**

Salome– opera: 1 act, Op. 54 (1905—Dresden) (Lib. O Wilde, trans H Lachmann)

1. Dance of the Seven Veils; 2. Ach, du wolltest mich nicht deinen Mund küssen lassen.

Salome	M. Ewing
Jokanaan	M. Devlin
Herod	K. Riegel
Herodias	G. Knight
Narraboth	R. Leggate

ROHO, E. Downes, P. Hall
(10/93) (CGP) ▣ **CVI1720**

Salome	T. Stratas
Jokanaan	B. Weikl
Herod	H. Beirer
Herodias	A. Varnay
Narraboth	W. Ochman
Page	H. Schwarz

VPO, K. Böhm
(DG) ◐ **072 109-1GH**
(DG) ▣ **072 109-3GH**

Salome	B. Nilsson
Jokanaan	E. Waechter
Herod	G. Stolze
Herodias	G. Hoffman
Narraboth	W. Kmentt
Page	J. Veasey
Nazarene I	T. Krause
Narazene II	N. Douglas
Soldier I	Z. Koznowski
Soldier II	H. Holecek
Cappadocian	T. Kirschbichler
Slave	L. Maikl

VPO, G. Solti
(7/85) (DECC) Ⓓ [2] **414 414-2DH2**

Salome	M. Caballé
Jokanaan	S. Milnes
Herod	Richard Lewis
Herodias	R. Resnik
Narraboth	J. King
Page	J. Hamari
Nazarene I	M. Rippon
Nazarene II	G. Griffiths
Soldier I	N. Howlett
Soldier II	D. Kelly
Cappadocian	D. Wicks
Slave	E. Bainbridge

LSO, E. Leinsdorf (r1968)
(9/90) (RCA) Ⓓ [2] **GD86644**

Salome	C. Studer
Jokanaan	B. Terfel
Herod	H. Hiestermann
Herodias	Leonie Rysanek
Narraboth	C. Bieber
Page	M. Rørholm
Nazarene I	F. Molsberger
Nazarene II	R. Lukas
Soldier I	W. Murray
Soldier II	B. Rundgren
Cappadocian	K. Lang

Berlin Deutsche Op Orch, G. Sinopoli
(9/91) (DG) Ⓓ [2] **431 810-2GH2**

Salome	C. Malfitano
Jokanaan	S. Estes
Herod	H. Hiestermann
Herodias	Leonie Rysanek
Narraboth	C. Bieber
Page	C. Capasso
Nazarene I	F. Molsberger
Nazarene II	R. Lukas
Soldier I	W. Murray
Soldier II	B. Rundgren
Cappadocian	K. Lang
Slave	A.E. Willis

Berlin Deutsche Op Orch, G. Sinopoli, P. Weigl, B. Large
(7/92) (TELD) ◐ **9031-73827-6**
(7/92) (TELD) ▣ **9031-73827-3**

Salome	M. Ewing
Jokanaan	M. Devlin
Herod	K. Riegel
Herodias	G. Knight
Narraboth	R. Leggate

ROHO, E. Downes, P. Hall
(9/93) (PION) ◐ **PLMCB00791**

Salome	W. Wegner
Jokanaan	J. Metternich
Herod	L. Szemere
Herodias	G. von Milinkovic
Narraboth	W. Kmentt
Page	D. Hermann
Nazarene I; Cappadocian	O. Czerwenka

Nazarene II W. Berry
Soldier I Adolf Vogel
Soldier II H. Pröglhöf
Slave D. Frass
Vienna SO, R. Moralt (r1952)
(5/94) (PHIL) ① [2] **438 664-2PM2**
Salome I. Borkh
Jokanaan H. Hotter
Herod M. Lorenz
Herodias I. Barth
Narraboth L. Fehenberger
Page K. Sabo
Nazarene I M. Proebstl
Nazarene II A. Peter
Soldier I A. Keil
Soldier II F. Friedrich
Cappadocian C. Hoppe
Slave G. Ebeling
Bavarian St Orch, J. Keilberth (pp1951)
(9/94) (ORFE) ① [2] **C342932I**
Salome J. Norman
Jokanaan J. Morris
Herod W. Raffeiner
Herodias K. Witt
Narraboth R. Leech
Page A. Markert
Nazarene I F. Schiller
Nazarene II H. Peeters
Soldier I J. Commichau
Soldier II R. Tomaszewski
Cappadocian M. Henneberg
Staatskapelle Dresden, S. Ozawa (r1990)
(10/94) (PHIL) ① [2] **432 153-2PH2**
Salome G. Jones
Jokanaan D. Fischer-Dieskau
Herod R. Cassilly
Herodias M. Dunn
Narraboth W. Ochman
Page U. Boese
Nazarene I H. Sotin
Nazarene II H. Wilhelm
Soldier I K. Moll
Soldier II C. Schultz
Cappadocian F. Grundheber
Slave W. Hartmann
Hamburg St Op Orch, K. Böhm (pp1970)
(11/94) (DG) ① [2] **445 319-2GX2**
Salome C. Malfitano
Jokanaan B. Terfel
Herod K. Riegel
Herodias H. Schwarz
Narraboth K. Begley
Page R. Stene
Nazarene I P. Rose
Nazarene II M. Gantner
Soldier I F. Olsen
Soldier II G. Paucker
Cappadocian W. Zeh
Slave R. Braga
VPO, C. von Dohnányi (r1994)
(4/95) (DECC) ① [2] **444 178-2DHO2**
Cincinnati SO, J. López-Cobos (r1994)
(TELA) ① **CD80371**
Excs J. Witt, E. Schürhoff, E. Schulz, P. Schoeffler, A. Dermota, D. With, H. Alsen, H. Schweiger, C. Bissuti, K. Ettl, Vienna St Op Orch, R. Strauss (pp1942)
(11/94) (SCHW) ① [2] **314532**
Excs H. Hotter, E. Schulz, A. Dermota, J. Sattler, M. Bugarinovic, Vienna St Op Orch, R. Strauss (pp1942)
(11/94) (SCHW) ① [2] **314532**
Excs M. Jeritza, G. Graarud, B. Paalen, E. Schipper, G. Maikl, J. von Manowarda, Wolken, Vienna St Op Orch, H. Reichenberger (pp1933)
(11/95) (SCHW) ① [2] **314622**
Jokanaan, ich bin verliebt J. Gadski, orch (r1908) (7/91) (CLUB) ① **CL99-109**
Jokanaan, ich bin verliebt E. Destinn, orch, B. Seidler-Winkler (r1907)
(5/94) (SUPR) ① **11 1337-2**
Jokanaan, ich bin verliebt E. Destinn, orch, B. Seidler-Winkler (r1907)
(12/94) (SUPR) ① [12] **11 2136-2(1)**
1. RPO, A. Dorati (CHES) ① **Chesky CD36**
1. Philadelphia, E. Ormandy (r1962)
(SONY) ① **SBK53511**
(SONY) ▭ **SBT53511**
1. Staatskapelle Dresden, R. Kempe (r1970)
(EMI) ① [2] **CZS5 68110-2**
1. German Nat Youth Orch, C. Prick (r1992)
(ARSM) ① **AMP5014-2**
1. Philadelphia, L. Stokowski (r1937)
(CALA) ① **CACD0502**
1. BPO, H. von Karajan (r1972/3)
(DG) ① **447 441-2GOR**

1. VPO, H. von Karajan (r1960)
(DECC) ① [9] **448 042-2DC9**
1. BPO, H. von Karajan (r1972)
(4/88) (DG) ① **415 853-2GGA**
1. SNO, N. Järvi (2/90) (CHAN) ① **CHAN8758**
1. Philh, O. Klemperer
(5/90) (EMI) ① **CDM7 63350-2**
1. Seattle SO, G. Schwarz
(9/90) (DELO) ① **DE3052**
1. Berlin St Op Orch, O. Klemperer (r1928)
(11/91) (KOCH) ① **37053-2**
1. Berlin RSO, H.M. Schneidt
(5/92) (CAPR) ① **10 380**
1. NBC SO, A. Toscanini (bp1939)
(11/92) (RCA) ① **GD60296**
1. Staatskapelle Dresden, R. Kempe (r1970)
(12/92) (EMI) ① [3] **CMS7 64346-2**
1. Chicago SO, F. Reiner (r1954)
(5/93) (RCA) ① **GD60874**
1. VPO, C. Krauss (r1941)
(5/93) (KOCH) ① **37129-2**
1. VPO, A. Previn (r1992)
(11/93) (DG) ① **437 790-2GH**
1. NYPO, L. Bernstein (r1968)
(9/94) (SONY) ① **SMK47625**
1. NY Stadium SO, L. Stokowski (r c1958)
(4/95) (EVER) ① **EVC9004**
1, 2. L. Price, Boston SO, E. Leinsdorf
(8/90) (RCA) ① **GD60398**
2. M. Lawrence, Pasdeloup Orch, P. Coppola (French: r1934) (5/90) (PREI) ① **89011**
2. I. Borkh, Chicago SO, F. Reiner (r1955)
(5/93) (RCA) ① **GD60874**
2. M. Caballé, FNO, L. Bernstein
(5/93) (DG) ① **431 103-2GB**
2. M. Cebotari, Berlin RSO, A. Rother (bp1943)
(8/95) (PREI) ① **90222**

Salomé– opera: 1 act (1907—Paris) (Lib. O Wilde)
Salomé K. Huffstodt
Iokanann J. Van Dam
Hérod J. Dupouy
Hérodias H. Jossoud
Narraboth J-L. Viala
Page H. Perraguin
Nazaréen I J. Bastin
Nazaréen II A. Gabriel
Soldat I V. le Texier
Soldat II F. Dumont
Cappadocien Y. Bisson
Esclave C. Goldsack
Lyon Op Orch, K. Nagano
(1/92) (VIRG) ① [2] **VCD7 59054-2**

Die **Schweigsame Frau, '(The) Silent Woman'– opera: 3 acts, Op. 80 (1935—Dresden) (Lib. S Zweig, after B Johnson)**
EXCERPTS: 1. Potpourri (Overture). ACT 1: 2. Ei, die Ehre, die Ehre!; 3. Ruhe? Warum soll ich Ruhe halten?; 4. Ha! Eine schweigsame Frau? Ein Meer ohne Salz?; 5. Es wird Abend, der Ofen friert kalt; 6a. Ah! Mein Stock!; 6b. Henry?; 7a. Kleiner humoristischer Marsch; 7b. Das deine Truppen? Deine Soldaten?; 8. Ruhe! Ruhe in meinem Haus!; 9. Oh Gott, war das ein saurer Empfang!; 10. Da unten im Keller stehn allerhand Kisten; 11. Nicht am mich, an mich, Geliebter, denke; 12. Sehr rechtschaffen gedacht, junger Herr; 13a. Nun, meine Schätzchen, hätte nicht eine von euch Lust; 13b. Ich würde lachen; 13c. Ich würde singen!; 14. Hah!..Was ist?...Mir fällt etwas ein!; 15a. Seid ihr bereit?; 15b. Ja, das wollen wir probieren. ACT 2: 16. Den Paraderock mit den vergoldeten Schnüren!; 17. Euer Gnaden gehorsamster Diener!; 18. Nur das Eine lasst Euch bitten; 19. Wohl tut ihr, das Haupt zu neigen; 20. Ui je, i hab an Angst!; 21. Dieses ist ein junges Fräulein; 22. Gestattet, dass ich Euch noch dieses edle Fräulein präsentiere!; 23. Sie ist die Rechte!; 24. So stumm, mein Kind, und noch immer so scheu?; 25. Ei, ei, wie rasch das Arcanum wirkt!; 26. Anhiero gestatte ich mir, hochverehrliche Herren; 27. Ich dank Euch, ehrwürdiger, und Euch, hochgelehrter Herr; 28a. Potz Deubel, so hat die alte Hur diesmal doch; 28b. Vorwärts, brave Kameramden; 28c. Heda Nachbarn, heda Leute; 28d. Ist es möglich, Sir Morosus?; 29. Nehmt's nicht so streng als es erscheint; 30. Du bist so still und scheinst bedrückt!; 31. Ruhe! hab ich dir gesagt!!!; 32. Was geht hier vor? Sind die Türken im Haus?; 33. Siehst du, Ohm, das ist die richtige Art; 34. Aminta! Aminta! Du süssester Engel. ACT 3: 35. Introduction; 36. Hier die Spiegel, die Konsolen; 37. 'L'incoronazione di Poppea' - Sento un certo non so che; 38. Dolce amor!; 39. Seine illustre Lordschaft, der Chef-Justice, werden in wenigen Minuten; 40. Mit Reverenz! Vieledle Dame!; 41. Gnädigster Herr...zwei Karossen sind angefahren; 42a. Meinen submissesten Respekt; 42b. Es haben der hochgeborene Lord Morosus und die hochgeborene Lady Morosus; 43. Könnt ihr bezungen, dass Lady Morusus Umgang; 44. Hohes Gericht, ich habe einen weiteren Zeugen bereit; 45. Willst du wirklich mich nicht kennen?; 46a. Endlich bin ich ihrer ledig!; 46b. Ich opponiere!; 47. Teurer Ohm! Nicht länger kann ich Eure Not und Sorge schaun; 48. Wie? Was? Kameraden... 49. Die Ihr feindlich aufgenommen; 50. Wie schön ist doch die
Sir Morosus H. Hotter
Housekeeper G. von Milinkovic
Barber H. Prey
Henry Morosus F. Wunderlich
Aminta H. Gueden
Isotta P. Alarie
Carlotta H. Plümacher
Morbio J. Knapp
Vanuzzi K. Dönch
Farfallo A. Pernerstorfer
Vienna St Op Chor, VPO, K. Böhm (pp1959)
(11/94) (DG) ① [2] **445 335-2GX2**
1. Rotterdam PO, J. Tate
(4/93) (EMI) ① **CDC7 54581-2**
1. Toronto SO, A. Davis (r1994)
(11/95) (CBC) ① **SMCD5142**
40. M. Salminen, Lahti SO, E. Klas
(8/92) (BIS) ① **BIS-CD520**

STRAVINSKY, Igor (Fyodorovich) *(1882–1971)* *Russia/France/USA*

Mavra– opera buffa: 1 act (1922—Paris) (Lib. Kochno, after Pushkin)
Cpte S. Belinck, M. Simmons, P. Rideout, S. Kolk, CBC SO, I. Stravinsky
(7/91) (SONY) ① [22] **SM22K46290(3)**
Chanson russe C. Ferras, J-C. Ambrosini (Stravinsky/Dushkin) (BELA) ① **461 003-2**
(BELA) ▭ **461 003-4**
Maiden's Song Z. Dolukhanova, N. Svetlanova (r1968) (RUSS) ① **RDCD11341**
Parasha's aria J. Manning, Robert Russell Bennett (r1977) (10/91) (CHAN) ① **CHAN6535**
(10/91) (CHAN) ▭ **MBTD6535**
Parasha's Song L. Mordkovitch, M. Gusak-Grin (trans cpsr) (3/87) (CHAN) ① **CHAN8500**
(3/87) (CHAN) ▭ **ABTD1210**
Song of Parasha P. Bryn-Julson, Paris InterContemporain Ens, P. Boulez
(2/92) (DG) ① **431 751-2GC**

The **Nightingale– musical fairy tale: 3 acts (1914—Paris) (Lib. cpsr and S. Mitusov, after H. Andersen)**
Nightingale J. Micheau
Fisherman J. Giraudeau
Cook G. Moizan
Chamberlain M. Roux
Emperor L. Lovano
Bonze B. Cottret
Death C. Gayraud
French Rad and TV Chor, FNO, A. Cluytens (pp1955)
(MONT) ① [2] **TCE8760**
Nightingale P. Bryn-Julson
Fisherman I. Caley
Cook F. Palmer
Chamberlain J. Tomlinson
Emperor N. Howlett
Bonze M. George
Death E. Laurence
BBC Sngrs, BBC SO, P. Boulez (r1990)
(ERAT) ① [3] **4509-98955-2**
Nightingale R. Grist
Fisherman L. Driscoll
Cook M. Picassi
Chamberlain K. Smith
Emperor D. Gramm
Bonze H. Beattie
Death E. Bonazzi
Washington Op Soc Chor, Washington Op Soc Orch, I. Stravinsky
(7/91) (SONY) ① [22] **SM22K46290(4)**
Nightingale P. Bryn-Julson
Fisherman I. Caley
Cook F. Palmer
Chamberlain J. Tomlinson
Emperor N. Howlett

Bonze M. George
Death E. Laurence
BBC Sngrs, BBC SO, P. Boulez
(7/92) (ERAT) Ⓓ **2292-45627-2**

Oedipus rex– opera-oratorio: 2 acts (1927 rev 1948—Paris) (Text J Cocteau)
Oedipus L. Simoneau
Jocasta E. Zareska
Creon B. Cottret
Tiresias G. Serkoyan
Shepherd M. Hamel
Messenger G. Abdoun
Narrator J. Cocteau
French Rad and TV Chor, FNO, I. Stravinsky (pp1952)
(MONT) Ⓓ [2] **TCE8760**
Oedipus T. Moser
Jocasta J. Norman
Creon; Messenger S. Nimsgern
Tiresias R. Bracht
Shepherd A. Ionita
Narrator M. Piccoli
Bavarian Rad Male Chor, BRSO, Colin Davis
(ORFE) Ⓓ **C071831A**
Cpre NY Choral Artists, St Luke's Orch, R. Craft
(MUSM) Ⓓ [2] **67078-2**
Oedipus G. Shirley
Jocasta S. Verrett
Creon D. Gramm
Tiresias Chester Watson
Shepherd L. Driscoll
Messenger J. Reardon
Narrator J. Westbrook
Washington Op Soc Chor, Washington Op Soc Orch, I. Stravinsky
(7/91) (SONY) Ⓓ [22] **SM22K46290(3)**

Perséphone– melodrama: 3 scenes (1934—Paris) (Text Gide)
Cpte V. Zorina, M. Molese, Ithaca Coll Concert Ch, Texas Boys' Ch, Columbia SO, I. Stravinsky
(7/91) (SONY) Ⓓ [22] **SM22K46290(3)**
Cpte A. Rolfe Johnson, A. Fournet, Tiffin Boys' Ch, LP Ch, LPO, K. Nagano
(6/92) (VIRG) Ⓓ [2] **VCK7 59077-2**
Exc V. Zorina, orch, I. Stravinsky
(12/93) (ARHI) Ⓓ **ADCD110**

The **Rake's Progress– opera: 3 acts (1951—Venice) (Lib. W H Auden & C Kallman)**
Tom Rakewell L. Goeke
Anne F. Lott
Nick Shadow S. Ramey
Baba the Turk R. Elias
Sellem J. Fryatt
Mother Goose N. Willis
Truelove R. Van Allan
Keeper T. Lawlor
Glyndebourne Fest Chor, LPO, B. Haitink, J. Cox (r1977)
(IMP) ▣ **SL2008**
Tom Rakewell A. Young
Anne J. Raskin
Nick Shadow J. Reardon
Baba the Turk R. Sarfaty
Sellem K. Miller
Mother Goose J. Manning
Truelove D. Garrard
Keeper P. Tracey
Sadler's Wells Op Chor, RPO, I. Stravinsky (r1964)
(SONY) Ⓓ [2] **SM2K46299**
Tom Rakewell P. Langridge
Anne C. Pope
Nick Shadow S. Ramey
Baba the Turk Sarah Walker
Sellem J. Dobson
Mother Goose A. Varnay
Truelove S. Dean
Keeper M. Best
London Sinfonietta Chor, London Sinfonietta, R. Chailly
(2/85) (DECC) Ⓓ [2] **411 644-2DH2**
Tom Rakewell A. Young
Anne J. Raskin
Nick Shadow J. Reardon
Baba the Turk R. Sarfaty
Sellem K. Miller
Mother Goose J. Manning
Truelove D. Garrard
Keeper P. Tracey
Sadler's Wells Op Chor, RPO, I. Stravinsky
(7/91) (SONY) Ⓓ [22] **SM22K46290(4)**
Tom Rakewell J. Garrison
Anne J. West
Nick Shadow J. Cheek
Baba the Turk W. White
Sellem M. Lowery
Mother Goose S. Love
Truelove A. Woodley
Keeper J. Johnson
Gregg Smith Sngrs, St Luke's Orch, R. Craft (r1993)
(3/95) (MUSM) Ⓓ [2] **67131-2**

Renard– burlesque in song and dance (1922—Paris)
Cpte T. Baker, D. Martin, D. Evitts, W. Pauley, St Luke's Orch, R. Craft (r1991-93)
(9/94) (MUSM) Ⓓ **67110-2**
G. Shirley, L. Driscoll, W. Murphy, D. Gramm, T. Koves, Columbia Chbr Ens, I. Stravinsky
(7/91) (SONY) Ⓓ [22] **SM22K46290(4)**
H. Hetherington, P. Harrhy, P. Donnelly, N. Cavallier, Matrix Ens, R. Ziegler
(7/91) (ASV) Ⓓ **CDDCA758**
J. Aler, N. Robson, J. Tomlinson, D. Wilson-Johnson, London Sinfonietta, E-P. Salonen
(1/92) (SONY) Ⓓ **SK45965**
G. Shirley, L. Driscoll, W. Murphy, D. Gramm, T. Koves, Columbia Chbr Ens, I. Stravinsky
(8/92) (SONY) Ⓓ [3] **SM3K46291**

SUCHOŇ, Eugen *(1908–1993)* *Slovakia*

The **Whirlpool (Krútňava)– opera: 6 scenes (1949) (Lib. cpsr & S. Hoza, after M. Urban)**
Ondrej Zimon P. Dvorský
Katrena G. Beňačková
Stelina O. Malachovský
Zimon V. Kubovčik
Zimonka A. Michalková
Zalcika J. Sedlarova
Skolnica O. Hanakova
Marka E. Antoličová
Zuzka L. Barikova
Shepherd Boy J. Valásková
Krupa J. Kundlák
Hrin J. Martvon
Olen P. Mikuláš
Master of Wedding Cermony S. Benňačka
Mistress of Wedding Ceremony A. Kubankova
Bridesman L. Ludha
Woman; Cook A. Martvonova
Gendarme J. Valentik
Slovak Phil Chor, Bratislava RSO, O. Lenárd
(11/90) (CAMP) Ⓓ [2] **RR2CD1311/2**
(11/90) (CAMP) ▭ [2] **WL2M411/2**

SUDER, Joseph *(1892 – 1980)* *Germany*

Kleider machen Leute– opera (cpted 1934: première 1964) (Lib. cpsr, after Keller)
Ladislaus Strapinski K. König
Burgomaster von Goldach Morris Morgan
Annette P. Coburn
Melchior W. Probst
Innkeeper W. Plate
Vreneli S. Klare
Policeman J-H. Rootering
Postman K. Geber
Coachman B. Nachbaur
Youth B. Lindner
Attendant D. Pauli
Bavarian Rad Chor, Bamberg SO, U. Mund
(5/92) (ORFE) Ⓓ [2] **C124862H**

SULLIVAN, Sir Arthur (Seymour) *(1842–1900)* *England*

Cox and Box (or The Long-lost Brothers)– operetta: 1 act (1866—London) (Wds. F. C. Burnand, after J. M. Morton)
Cox A. Styler
Box J. Riordan
Bouncer D. Adams
New SO, I. Godfrey (with dialogue)
(LOND) Ⓓ [2] **417 355-2LM2**
Overture PAO, M. Sargent
(CFP) Ⓓ **CD-CFP4529**
Overture PAO, M. Sargent
(EMI) Ⓓ [2] **CMS7 64409-2**

The **Gondoliers (or The King of Barataria)– comic operetta: 2 acts (1889—London) (Lib. W. S. Gilbert)**
EXCERPTS: 1. Overture. ACT 1: 2a. List and learn; 2b. Good morrow, pretty maids; 2c. For the merriest fellow; 2d. Buon giorno, signorine; 2e. We're called gondolieri; 2f. And now to choose our brides; 2g. Thank you gallant gondolieri; 3. From the sunny Spanish shore; 4. In enterprise of martial kind; 5. O rapture; 6. There was a time; 7. I stole the prince; 8. But, bless my heart consider my position; 9. Try we lifelong; 10a. Bridegroom and bride; 10b. When a merry maiden marries; 11a. Kind sir you cannot have the heart; 11b. Then one of us. ACT 2: 12. Of happiness the very pith; 13. Rising early in the morning; 14. Take a pair of sparkling eyes; 15. Here we are; 16a. Dance a cachucha; 16b. Dance; 17. There lived a King; 18. In a contemplative fashion; 19. With ducal pomp; 20. On the day; 21a. To help unhappy commoners; 21b. Small titles and orders; 22. I am a courtier grave and serious; 23. Here is a case unprecedented; 24a. Now let the loyal lieges; 24b. The Royal Prince; 24c. This statement we receive; 24d. Once more gondolieri.
Marco Palmieri T. Round
Giuseppe Palmieri A. Styler
Gianetta M. Sansom
Tessa J. Wright
Duke of Plaza-Toro J. Reed
Duchess of Plaza-Toro G. Knight
Casilda J. Toye
Luiz J. Skitch
Don Alhambra K. Sandford
Inez J. Roach
Antonio; Annibale M. Wakeham
Francesco J. Riordan
Giorgio G. Cook
Fiametta D. Bradshaw
Vittoria C. Jones
Giulia D. Gill
D'Oyly Carte Op Chor, New SO, I. Godfrey (with dialogue)
(DECC) ▭ [2] **417 254-4DY2**
Marco Palmieri D. Oldham
Giuseppe Palmieri George Baker
Gianetta W. Lawson
Tessa A. Davies
Duke of Plaza-Toro H. Lytton
Duchess of Plaza-Toro B. Lewis
Casilda M. Bennett
Luiz A. Hosking
Don Alhambra L. Sheffield
Inez G. Gowrie
Antonio R. Walker
Francisco H. Aitken
Giorgio R. Stear
Fiametta S. Gordon
Vittoria B. Elburn
Guilia D. Hemingway
D'Oyly Carte Op Chor, orch, H. Norris (omits dialogue: r1927)
(PEAR) Ⓓ [2] **GEMMCDS9961**
Marco Palmieri Richard Lewis
Giuseppe Palmieri J. Cameron
Gianetta E. Morison
Tessa M. Thomas
Duke of Plaza-Toro G. Evans
Duchess of Plaza-Toro M. Sinclair
Casilda E. Graham
Luiz; Francesco A. Young
Don Alhambra O. Brannigan
Inez; Giulia H. Watts
Antonio; Giorgio J. Milligan
Fiametta S. Hitchens
Vittoria L. Renton
Glyndebourne Fest Chor, PAO, M. Sargent (omits dialogue)
(EMI) Ⓓ [2] **CMS7 64394-2**
Abridged George Baker, William Booth, S. Granville, D. Oldham, L. Rands, L. Hubbard, S. Robertson, D'Oyly Carte Op Chor, SO, M. Sargent (r1931) (7/89) (ARAB) Ⓓ [2] **Z8095-2**
Marco Palmieri T. Round
Giuseppe Palmieri A. Styler
Gianetta M. Sansom
Tessa J. Wright
Duke of Plaza-Toro J. Reed
Duchess of Plaza-Toro G. Knight
Casilda J. Toye
Luiz J. Skitch
Don Alhambra K. Sandford
Inez J. Roach
Antonio; Annibale M. Wakeham
Francesco J. Riordan
Giorgio G. Cook
Fiametta D. Bradshaw
Vittoria C. Jones

Giulia D. Gill
D'Oyly Carte Op Chor, New SO, I. Godfrey (with dialogue)
(1/90) (DECC) Ⓓ [2] **425 177-2LM2**
Marco Palmieri D. Fieldsend
Giuseppe Palmieri A. Oke
Gianetta L.E. Ross
Tessa R. Hanley
Duke of Plaza-Toro R. Suart
Duchess of Plaza-Toro J. Pert
Casilda E. Woollett
Luiz P. Creasey
Don Alhambra J. Rath
Inez C. Kelly
Antonio T. Morgan
Francesco D. Cavendish
Giorgio T. Barrett
Annibale G. Vaughan
Fiametta Y. Patrick
Vittoria P. Baxter
Giulia E. Elliott
D'Oyly Carte Op Chor, D'Oyly Carte Op Orch, J. Pryce-Jones (r1991)
(5/92) (TER) Ⓓ [2] **CDTER2 1187**
(5/92) (TER) ▭ **ZCTED 1187**
1. PAO, M. Sargent (CFP) Ⓓ **CD-CFP4529**
1. Scottish CO, A. Faris (NIMB) Ⓓ **NI5066**
(NIMB) ▭ **NC5066**
1. ASMF, N. Marriner (r1992)
(PHIL) **OO 434 916-5PH**
1. New Sadler's Wells Op Orch, S. Phipps (r1977) (5/93) (TER) Ⓓ **CDVIR8316**
(5/93) (TER) ▭ **ZCVIR8316**
1. ASMF, N. Marriner (r1992)
(6/93) (PHIL) Ⓓ **434 916-2PH**
2a Glyndebourne Fest Chor, PAO, M. Sargent
(CFP) Ⓓ **CD-CFP4582**
(CFP) ▭ **TC-CFP4582**
2e, 4, 14, 16a J. Toye, G. Knight, T. Round, A. Styler, J. Reed, J. Skitch, D'Oyly Carte Op Chor, New SO, I. Godfrey
(6/91) (DECC) Ⓓ **430 095-2DWO**
(6/91) (DECC) ▭ **430 095-4DWO**
3, 4, 14, 20, 21b, 24d M. Studholme, J. Allister, E. Bohan, I. Wallace, English Chorale, London Concert Orch, M. Dods (IMP) Ⓓ **PWK1157**
3, 6, 11b, 21a J. Reed, C. Palmer, J. Goss, P. Potter, A. Guthrie, R. Mason, P. Wales, T. Lawlor, RPO, J. Walker (r1960s)
(BELA) Ⓓ **461 006-2**
(BELA) ▭ **461 006-4**
3, 7, 11b J. Wright, J. Toye, M. Sansom, G. Knight, T. Round, J. Skitch, J. Reed, K. Sandford, A. Styler, New SO, I. Godfrey
(2/93) (DECC) Ⓓ **433 868-2DWO**
(2/93) (DECC) ▭ **433 868-4DWO**
10b, 14, 18, 24d A. Davies, W. Lawson, D. Oldham, George Baker, D'Oyly Carte Op Chor, SO, H. Norris (r1927) (MMOI) Ⓓ **CDMOIR413**
11a V. Essex, orch (r1923)
(SYMP) Ⓓ **SYMCD1123**
13, 15. King's Sngrs (r1993; arr Gritton)
(5/94) (RCA) Ⓓ **09026 61885-2**
(5/94) (RCA) ▭ **09026 61885-4**
14. Fairey Band, K. Dennison (arr Langford)
(CHAN) Ⓓ **CHAN6530**
14. J. Coates, anon (r1906)
(SYMP) Ⓓ **SYMCD1123**
14. H. Nash, orch (r1926)
(8/89) (PEAR) Ⓓ **GEMMCD9319**
14, 16a, 22. Richard Lewis, G. Evans, M. Sinclair, E. Graham, J. Cameron, Glyndebourne Fest Chor, PAO, M. Sargent
(CFP) Ⓓ **CD-CFP4238**
(CFP) ▭ **TC-CFP40238**
16a, 16b T. Round, D'Oyly Carte Op Chor, D'Oyly Carte Op Orch, New SO, I. Godfrey
(DECC) Ⓓ **425 850-2DWO**
(DECC) ▭ **425 850-4DWO**
18, 24d T. Dahl, M. Forrester, T. Chiles, R. Suart, D. Grant, D. Morphy, Winnipeg Sngrs, Winnipeg G & S Soc, Winnipeg SO, B. Tovey (r1994) (6/95) (CBC) Ⓓ **SMCD5139**
20. C. Herwin, orch (r1923)
(SYMP) Ⓓ **SYMCD1123**

The **Grand Duke (or The Statutory Duel)– operetta: 2 acts (1896—London) (Lib. W. S. Gilbert)**
EXCERPTS: 1. Overture. ACT 1: 2a. Won't it be a pretty wedding; 2b. Pretty Lisa, fair and tasty; 3. By the mystic regulation; 4. Were I a king in very truth; 5. How would I play this part; 6a. My goodness me; 6b. Ten minutes since, I met a chap; 7. About a century since; 8. Strange the views some people hold; 9. Now take a card; 10a. The good Grand Duke; 10b. A pattern to professors; 11. As o'er our penny roll we sing; 12. When you find your a broken down critter; 13. Come hither all you people. ACT 2: 14. As before you we defile; 15a. Your loyalty our Ducal heartstrings touches; 15b. At the outset I may mention; 16a. Yes Ludwig and his Julia are mated; 16b. Take care of him; 17. Now Julia come consider it; 18a. Your Highness there's a party; 18b. With fury indescribable I burn; 19. Now away to the wedding we go; 20a. So ends my dream; 20b. Broken ev'ry promise; 21. If the light of love's lingering ember; 22. Come, bumpers; 23. Why, who is this approaching; 24. The Prince of Monte Carlo; 25. His Highness we know not; 26. We're rigged out in magnificent way; 27. Dance; 28. Take my advice; 29a. Away to the wedding; 29b. Well you're a pretty king of fellow; 30. Happy couples lightly treading.
Grand Duke Rudolph J. Reed
Ernest Dummkopf M. Reid
Ludwig K. Sandford
Dr Tannhäuser M. Rayner
Prince of Monte Carlo J. Ayldon
Ben Hashbaz J. Ellison
Herald J. Conroy-Ward
Princess of Monte Carlo B. Lilley
Baroness von Krakenfeldt L. Holland
Julia Jellicoe J. Goss
Lisa J. Metcalfe
Elsa; Second Girl P. Leonard
Gretchen; First Girl A. Eggleston
Bertha; Third Girl B. Lloyd-Jones
Olga G. Prendergast
D'Oyly Carte Op Chor, RPO, R. Nash (r1976)
(LOND) Ⓓ [2] **436 813-2LM2**

HMS Pinafore (or The Lass that Loved a Sailor)– comic operetta: 2 acts (1878—London) (Lib. W. S. Gilbert)
EXCERPTS: 1. Overture. ACT 1: 2. We sail the ocean blue; 3a. Hail, men-o'-war's men; 3b. I'm called little Buttercup; 4a. But, tell me; 4b. The Nightingale; 4c. A maiden fair to see; 5a. My gallant crew; 5b. I am the Captain of the Pinafore; 6a. Sir you are sad; 6b. Sorry her lot who loves too well; 7. Over the bright blue sea; 8a. Sir Joseph's barge is seen; 8b. Gaily tripping, lightly skipping; 9. I am the monarch of the sea; 10. When I was a lad I served a term; 11. A British tar is a soaring soul; 12. Refrain, audacious tar; 13a. Can I survive this overbearing; 13b. Oh joy, oh rapture unforseen; 13c. Let's give three cheers for a sailor's bride; 14a. Entr'acte. ACT 2: 14b. Fair moon, to thee I sing; 15. Things are seldom what they seem; 16. The hours creep on apace; 17. Never mind the why and wherefore; 18. Kind Captain, i've important information; 19a. Carefully on tiptoe stealing; 19b. He is an Englishman; 19c. Did you hear him?; 20. Farewell my own; 21. A many years ago; 22. Oh joy, oh rapture unforseen.
Sir Joseph Porter H. Lytton
Little Buttercup B. Lewis
Josephine E. Griffin
Captain Corcoran George Baker
Ralph Rackstraw C. Goulding
Dick Deadeye D. Fancourt
Hebe N. Briercliffe
Bill Bobstay S. Granville
Bob Becket S. Robertson
D'Oyly Carte Op Chor, Orch, M. Sargent (r1930: omits dialogue)
(PRO) Ⓓ **CDD598**
Sir Joseph Porter George Baker
Captain Corcoran; Bob Beckett J. Cameron
Ralph Rackstraw Richard Lewis
Josephine E. Morison
Dick Deadeye O. Brannigan
Bill Bobstay J. Milligan
Hebe M. Thomas
Little Buttercup M. Sinclair
Glyndebourne Fest Chor, PAO, M. Sargent (omits dialogue)
(EMI) Ⓓ [2] **CMS7 64397-2**
Sir Joseph Porter H. Lytton
Captain Corcoran George Baker
Ralph Rackstraw C. Goulding
Josephine E. Griffin
Dick Deadeye D. Fancourt
Bill Bobstay S. Granville
Hebe N. Briercliffe
Little Buttercup B. Lewis
Bob Becket S. Robertson
D'Oyly Carte Op Chor, SO, M. Sargent (r1930: omits dialogue)
(HAPY) Ⓓ [2] **CDHD253/4**
(HAPY) ▭ [2] **MCHD253/4**
Sir Joseph Porter N. Grace
Captain Corcoran G. Sandison
Ralph Rackstraw C. Gillett
Josephine E. Ritchie
Dick Deadeye T. Lawlor
Bill Bobstay P. Parfitt
Bob Becket P. Thomson
Hebe J. Roebuck
Little Buttercup L. Ormiston
New Sadler's Wells Op Chor, New Sadler's Wells Op Orch, S. Phipps (ed Russell Hume)
(5/88) (TER) Ⓓ [2] **CDTER2 1150**
(5/88) (TER) ▭ [2] **ZCTED 1150**
Sir Joseph Porter J. Reed
Captain Corcoran J. Skitch
Ralph Rackstraw T. Round
Josephine J. Hindmarsh
Dick Deadeye D. Adams
Bill Bobstay G. Cook
Bob Becket E. Wilson Hyde
Hebe J. Wright
Little Buttercup G. Knight
D'Oyly Carte Op Chor, New SO, I. Godfrey (with dialogue)
(1/90) (DECC) Ⓓ [2] **414 283-2LM2**
(12/84) (DECC) ▭ [2] **414 283-4DY2**
Sir Joseph Porter R. Suart
Little Buttercup F. Palmer
Josephine R. Evans
Captain Corcoran T. Allen
Ralph Rackstraw M. Schade
Dick Deadeye D. Adams
Hebe V. Seymour
Bill Bobstay R. Van Allan
Bob Becket J. King
Bob Becket P. Lloyd-Evans
WNO Chor, WNO Orch, C. Mackerras (r1994: omits dialogue)
(1/95) (TELA) Ⓓ **CD80374**
Excs J. Reed, J. Skitch, T. Round, D. Adams, G. Cook, E. Wilson Hyde, J. Hindmarsh, J. Wright, G. Knight, D'Oyly Carte Op. Chor, New SO, I. Godfrey (DECC) Ⓓ **436 145-2DSP**
(DECC) ▭ **436 145-4DSP**
1. PAO, M. Sargent (CFP) Ⓓ **CD-CFP4529**
1. Scottish CO, A. Faris (NIMB) Ⓓ **NI5066**
(NIMB) ▭ **NC5066**
1. ASMF, N. Marriner (r1992)
(PHIL) **OO 434 916-5PH**
1. New Sadler's Wells Op Orch, S. Phipps (r1977) (5/93) (TER) Ⓓ **CDVIR8316**
(5/93) (TER) ▭ **ZCVIR8316**
1. ASMF, N. Marriner (r1992)
(6/93) (PHIL) Ⓓ **434 916-2PH**
2, 3a, 3b, 4a-c, 5a, 5b, 6a, 6b, 9-11, 14b, 17, 20-22. N. Grace, L. Ormiston, E. Ritchie, G. Sandison, C. Gillett, T. Lawlor, J. Roebuck, P. Parfitt, P. Thomson, New Sadler's Wells Op Chor, New Sadler's Wells Op Orch, S. Phipps
(KOCH) Ⓓ **34029-2**
(KOCH) ▭ **24029-4**
2, 3b, 5b, 10, 17, 19b B. Lewis, George Baker, H. Lytton, E. Griffin, S. Granville, D'Oyly Carte Op Chor, SO, M. Sargent (r1930)
(MMOI) Ⓓ **CDMOIR413**
2, 3b, 5b, 22. Richard Lewis, E. Morison, M. Thomas, M. Sinclair, J. Cameron, O. Brannigan, Glyndebourne Fest Chor, PAO, M. Sargent
(CFP) Ⓓ **CD-CFP4238**
(CFP) ▭ **TC-CFP40238**
2, 5a, 5b, 13b J. Hindmarsh, J. Wright, G. Knight, T. Round, J. Skitch, D'Oyly Carte Op Chor, New SO, I. Godfrey
(2/93) (DECC) Ⓓ **433 868-2DWO**
(2/93) (DECC) ▭ **433 868-4DWO**
3a, 3b, 10, 17. M. Studholme, J. Allister, E. Bohan, I. Wallace, English Chorale, London Concert Orch, M. Dods (IMP) Ⓓ **PWK1157**
3b Classic Buskers, Chuckerbutty Ocarina Qt (arr Copley) (SEAV) Ⓓ **CD007366**
3b, 9, 10, 17. J. Reed, J. Skitch, J. Wright, G. Knight, J. Hindmarsh, D'Oyly Carte Op Chor, New SO, I. Godfrey
(6/91) (DECC) Ⓓ **430 095-2DWO**
(6/91) (DECC) ▭ **430 095-4DWO**
9, 10, 17, 22. E. Morison, George Baker, J. Cameron, Glyndebourne Fest Chor, PAO, M. Sargent (CFP) Ⓓ **CD-CFP4609**
(CFP) ▭ **TC-CFP4609**
11. King's Sngrs (r1993; arr Gritton)
(5/94) (RCA) Ⓓ **09026 61885-2**
(5/94) (RCA) ▭ **09026 61885-4**

16, 17. T. Dahl, M. Forrester, T. Chiles, R. Suart, D. Grant, D. Morphy, Winnipeg Sngrs, Winnipeg G & S Soc, Winnipeg SO, B. Tovey (r1994)
(6/95) (CBC) ① **SMCD5139**

Iolanthe (or The Peer and the Peri)– comic operetta: 2 acts (1882—London) (Lib. W. S. Gilbert)

EXCERPTS: 1. Overture. ACT 1: 2. Tripping hither tripping thither; 3. Iolanthe; 4. Good morrow, good mother; 5. Fare thee well attractive stranger; 6a. Good morrow, good lover; 6b. None shall part us; 7. Loudly let the trumpet bray (March of the Peers); 8a. Entrance of Lord Chancellor; 8b. The law is the true embodiment; 9a. My well-loved Lord and Guardian; 9b. Of all the young ladies; 10. Nay tempt me not; 11. Spurn not the nobly born; 12. My Lords it may not be; 13. When I went to the Bar as a very young man; 14a. When darkly looms the day; 14b. In babyhood; 14c. For riches and rank I do not long. ACT 2: 15. When all night long a chap remains; 16. Strephon's a Member of Parliament; 17. When Britain really ruled the waves; 18. In vain to us you plead; 19. Oh foolish fay; 20. Tho' p'r'aps I may incur your blame; 21a. Love, unrequited; 21b. When you're lying awake with a dismal headache; 22. If you go in, you're sure to win; 23. If we're weak enough to tarry; 24a. My Lord, a suppliant at your feet; 24b. He loves if in the bygone years; 25. It may not be; 26. Soon as we may.

Iolanthe M. Thomas
Strephon J. Cameron
Queen of the Fairies M. Sinclair
Phyllis E. Morison
Lord Chancellor George Baker
Earl of Mountararat I. Wallace
Earl Tolloller A. Young
Private Willis O. Brannigan
Celia A. Cantelo
Leila H. Harper

Glyndebourne Fest Chor, PAO, M. Sargent (r1958: omits dialogue)
(EMI) ① [2] **CMS7 64400-2**

Iolanthe Y. Newman
Strephon A. Styler
Queen of the Fairies G. Knight
Phyllis M. Sansom
Lord Chancellor J. Reed
Earl of Mountararat D. Adams
Earl Tolloller T. Round
Private Willis K. Sandford
Celia J. Toye
Leila P. Wales
Fleta D. Bradshaw

D'Oyly Carte Op Chor, Grenadier Guards Band, New SO, I. Godfrey (with dialogue)
(1/90) (DECC) ① [2] **414 145-2LM2**
(DECC) ▭ [2] **414 145-4DY2**

Iolanthe R. Hanley
Strephon Philip Blake Jones
Queen of the Fairies J. Pert
Phyllis E. Woollett
Lord Chancellor R. Suart
Earl of Mountararat L. Richard
Earl Tolloller P. Creasey
Private Willis J. Rath
Celia Y. Patrick
Leila M. Mitchell
Fleta L. Owen

D'Oyly Carte Op Chor, D'Oyly Carte Op Orch, J. Pryce-Jones (omits dialogue)
(5/92) (TER) ① [2] **CDTER2 1188**
(5/92) (TER) ▭ [2] **ZCTED 1188**

1. PAO, M. Sargent (CFP) ① **CD-CFP4529**

1. Scottish CO, A. Faris (NIMB) ① **NI5066**
(NIMB) ▭ **NC5066**

1. ASMF, N. Marriner (r1992)
(PHIL) ⊙⊙ **434 916-5PH**

1. D'Oyly Carte Op Orch, J. Pryce-Jones (r1991)
(5/93) (TER) ① **CDVIR8316**
(5/93) (TER) ▭ **ZCVIR8316**

1. ASMF, N. Marriner (r1992)
(6/93) (PHIL) ① **434 916-2PH**

1. Kneller Hall Band, F. Renton (r1992: arr N Richardson) (9/93) (BAND) ① **BNA5067**
(9/93) (BAND) ▭ **BND61075**

1, 19, 21a T. Dahl, M. Forrester, T. Chiles, R. Suart, D. Grant, D. Morphy, Winnipeg Sngrs, Winnipeg G & S Soc, Winnipeg SO, B. Tovey (r1994) (6/95) (CBC) ① **SMCD5139**

1, 6b, 7, 10, 11, 13, 14c, 15-17, 19, 21a, 21b, 22, 23, 24a, 24b, 25, 26. E. Shilling, D. Dowling, S. Bevan, Leon Greene, E. Harwood, J. Moyle, H. Begg, P. Kern, E. Robson, C. Morey, Sadlers Wells Op Chor, Sadlers Wells Op Orch, A. Faris (r c1961) (4/94) (CFP) ① [2] **CD-CFPD4730**
(4/93) (CFP) ▭ [2] **TC-CFPD4730**

2, 4, 6b, 7, 13, 14a-c, 15, 23, 24a, 26. R. Stuart, L. Richard, P. Creasey, J. Rath, Philip Blake Jones, J. Pert, R. Hanley, Y. Patrick, M. Mitchell, L. Owen, E. Woollett, D'Oyly Carte Op Chor, D'Oyly Carte Op Orch, J. Pryce-Jones
(KOCH) ① **34028-2**
(KOCH) ▭ **24028-4**

6b H. Lytton, L. Henri, anon (r1902)
(SYMP) ① **SYMCD1123**

6b, 13, 20, 21a, 21b, 22. J. Reed, A. Guthrie, R. Mason, T. Lawlor, J. Ayldon, K. Sandford, RPO, J. Walker (r1960s) (BELA) ① **461 006-2**
(BELA) ▭ **461 006-4**

7. Kneller Hall Band, F. Renton (r1992: arr F Renton) (9/93) (BAND) ① **BNA5067**
(9/93) (BAND) ▭ **BND61075**

7, 22. T. Round, J. Reed, D. Adams, D'Oyly Carte Op Chor, New SO, I. Godfrey
(6/91) (DECC) ① **430 095-2DWO**
(6/91) (DECC) ▭ **430 095-4DWO**

7, 23, 26. E. Morison, M. Thomas, M. Sinclair, George Baker, I. Wallace, A. Young, J. Cameron, Glyndebourne Fest Chor, PAO, M. Sargent (CFP) ① **CD-CFP4238**
(CFP) ▭ **TC-CFP40238**

15. H. Dearth, orch (r1906)
(SYMP) ① **SYMCD1123**

15. D. Adams, New SO, I. Godfrey
(2/93) (DECC) ① **433 868-2DWO**
(2/93) (DECC) ▭ **433 868-4DWO**

17. J. Carreras, Sadler's Wells Op Chor, Sadler's Wells Op Orch, A. Faris (r1962)
(KIWI) ① **CDSLD-82**

17, 22. D. Fancourt, D. Oldham, George Baker, D'Oyly Carte Op Chor, SO, M. Sargent (r1929)
(MMOI) ① **CDMOIR413**

17, 22, 23. E. Morison, A. Young, George Baker, J. Cameron, I. Wallace, Glyndebourne Fest Chor, PAO, M. Sargent (CFP) ① **CD-CFP4609**
(CFP) ▭ **TC-CFP4609**

Ivanhoe– opera: 3 acts (1891—London) (Lib. J. Sturgis, after W. Scott)

Ho! Jolly Jenkin D. Bispham, orch (r1909)
(SYMP) ① **SYMCD1123**

Lord of our chosen race E. Evans, orch (r1916)
(SYMP) ① **SYMCD1123**

Woo thou thy snowflake P. Dawson, orch (r1922) (SYMP) ① **SYMCD1123**

The **Mikado (or The Town of Titipu)– comic operetta: 2 acts (1885—London) (Lib. W. S. Gilbert)**

EXCERPTS: 1. Overture. ACT 1: 2. If you want to know who we are; 3a. Gentleman, I pray you tell me; 3b. A wandering minstrel I; 4. Our great Mikado; 5. Young men despair; 6a. And have I journey'd for a month; 6b. Behold the Lord High Executioner; 6c. Taken from the county jail; 7. As some day it may happen; 8. Comes a train of little ladies; 9. Three little maids; 10. So please you, sir; 11. Were you not to Ko-Ko plighted?; 12. I am so proud; 13a. With aspect stern; 13b. Your revels cease; 13c. The hour of gladness. ACT 2: 14. Braid the raven hair; 15. The sun, whose rays are all ablaze; 16. Brightly dawns our wedding day; 17. Here's a how-de-do!; 18. Miya sama, miya sama; 19. From every kind of man; 20. A more humane Mikado; 21. The criminal cried; 22. See how the Fates; 23. The flowers that bloom in the spring; 24a. Alone, and yet alive; 24b. Hearts do not break!; 25. On a tree by a river a little tom-tit (Tit Willow); 26. There is beauty in the bellow of the blast; 27. For he's gone and married Yum-Yum.

The Mikado D. Adams
Nanki-Poo T. Round
Ko-Ko P. Pratt
Pooh-Bah K. Sandford
Pish-Tush A. Styler
Yum-Yum J. Hindmarsh
Pitti-Sing B. Dixon
Peep-Bo J. Toye
Katisha A. Drummond-Grant
Go-To O. Grundy

D'Oyly Carte Op Chor, New SO, I. Godfrey (omits dialogue)
(7/85) (DECC) ▭ [2] **414 341-4DY2**

The Mikado O. Brannigan
Nanki-Poo Richard Lewis
Ko-Ko G. Evans
Pooh-Bah I. Wallace
Pish-Tush J. Cameron
Yum-Yum E. Morison
Pitti-Sing M. Thomas
Peep-Bo J. Sinclair
Katisha M. Sinclair

Glyndebourne Fest Chor, PAO, M. Sargent (omits dialogue)
(EMI) ① [2] **CMS7 64403-2**

Mikado D. Fancourt
Nanki-Poo D. Oldham
Ko-Ko M. Green
Pooh-Bah S. Granville
Pish-Tush L. Rands
Yum-Yum B. Bennett
Pitti-Sing M. Eyre
Peep-Bo E. Nickell-Lean
Katisha Jo Curtis

D'Oyly Carte Op Chor, SO, M. Sargent (r1936: omits dialogue)
(HAPY) ① [2] **CDHD253/4**
(HAPY) ▭ [2] **MCHD253/4**

The Mikado J. Ayldon
Nanki-Poo C. Wright
Ko-Ko J. Reed
Pooh-Bah K. Sandford
Pish-Tush M. Rayner
Yum-Yum V. Masterson
Pitti-Sing P.A. Jones
Peep-Bo P. Wales
Katisha L. Holland
Go-To J. Broad

D'Oyly Carte Op Chor, RPO, R. Nash (omits dialogue)
(1/90) (LOND) ① [2] **425 190-2LM2**

The Mikado M. Ducarel
Nanki-Poo B. Bottone
Ko-Ko E. Roberts
Pooh-Bah M. Rivers
Pish-Tush Gareth Jones
Yum-Yum D. Rees
Pitti Sing T. Ker
Peep-Bo Y. Patrick
Katisha S. Gorton

D'Oyly Carte Op Chor, D'Oyly Carte Op Orch, J. Pryce-Jones (omits dialogue)
(9/90) (TER) ① [2] **CDTER2 1178**
(9/90) (TER) ▭ [2] **ZCTED 1178**

The Mikado D. Adams
Nanki-Poo A. Rolfe Johnson
Ko-Ko R. Suart
Pooh-Bah R. Van Allan
Pish-Tush N. Folwell
Yum-Yum M. McLaughlin
Pitti-Sing A. Howells
Peep-Bo J. Watson
Katisha F. Palmer

WNO Chor, WNO Orch, C. Mackerras (omits dialogue)
(5/92) (TELA) ① **CD80284**
(5/92) (TELA) ▭ **CS30284**

The Mikado J. Holmes
Nanki-Poo J. Wakefield
Ko-Ko C. Revill
Pooh-Bah D. Dowling
Pish-Tush J.H. Nash
Yum-Yum M. Studholme
Pitti-Sing P. Kern
Peep-Bo D. Nash
Katisha J. Allister

Sadlers Wells Op Chor, Sadlers Wells Op Orch, A. Faris (r1962: omits dialogue)
(4/94) (CFP) ① [2] **CD-CFPD4730**
(4/93) (CFP) ▭ [2] **TC-CFPD4730**

Quadrille London Salon Ens
(MERI) ① **CDE84264**

1. PAO, M. Sargent (CFP) ① **CD-CFP4529**

1. ASMF, N. Marriner (r1992)
(PHIL) ⊙⊙ **434 916-5PH**

1. NYPO, J. Stransky (r1919)
(4/92) (PEAR) ① [3] **GEMMCDS9922**

1. D'Oyly Carte Op Orch, J. Pryce-Jones (r1990)
(5/93) (TER) ① **CDVIR8316**
(5/93) (TER) ▭ **ZCVIR8316**

1. ASMF, N. Marriner (r1992)
(6/93) (PHIL) ① **434 916-2PH**

1, 2, 3a, 3b, 4, 6b, 7, 9, 10, 13a-c(pt), 14, 15, 18-21, 23, 25-27. J. Ayldon, C. Wright, J. Reed, K. Sandford, M. Rayner, J. Broad, V. Masterson, P.A. Jones, P. Wales, L. Holland, D'Oyly Carte Op Chor, RPO, R. Nash
(1/92) (DECC) ① **433 618-2DSP**
(1/92) (DECC) ▭ **433 618-4DSP**

2, 3a, 3b, 7, 9, 10, 11, 14, 15, 17, 20, 23, 24a, 25, 26. L. Garrett, S. Bullock, F. Palmer, J. Rigby, B. Bottone, E. Idle, M. Richardson, R. Angas, R. Van Allan, ENO Chor, ENO Orch, Peter Robinson (r c1986) (KOCH) Ⓓ **34027-2**
(KOCH) ⊟ **24027-4**

2, 3b, 4, 5, 6b, 7-11, 13(part), 14, 15, 17, 20, 23, 24a, 25, 26. R. Angas, B. Bottone, E. Idle, R. Van Allan, M. Richardson, L. Garrett, J. Rigby, S. Bullock, F. Palmer, ENO Chor, ENO Orch, Peter Robinson (3/87) (TER) Ⓓ **CDTER1121**
(3/87) (TER) ⊟ **ZCTER1121**

2, 3b, 9, 17, 23, 25. D. Oldham, R. Flynn, B. Bennett, M. Eyre, E. Nickell-Lean, M. Green, S. Granville, D'Oyly Carte Op Chor, SO, I. Godfrey (r1936) (MMOI) Ⓓ **CDMOIR413**

2, 3b, 15, 27. Richard Lewis, E. Morison, M. Thomas, G. Evans, Glyndebourne Fest Chor, PAO, M. Sargent (CFP) Ⓓ **CD-CFP4238**
(CFP) ⊟ **TC-CFP40238**

3b, 6b, 9, 20. E. Morison, J. Sinclair, M. Thomas, Richard Lewis, G. Evans, O. Brannigan, Glyndebourne Fest Chor, PAO, M. Sargent (CFP) Ⓓ **CD-CFP4609**
(CFP) ⊟ **TC-CFP4609**

3b, 7, 15, 17, 25-27. M. Studholme, J. Allister, E. Bohan, I. Wallace, English Chorale, London Concert Orch, M. Dods (IMP) Ⓓ **PWK1157**

3b, 7, 9, 23, 25. J. Reed, P. Potter, P. Wales, K. Sandford, P.A. Jones, V. Masterson, D'Oyly Carte Op Chor, RPO, M. Sargent (r1960s) (BELA) Ⓓ **461 006-2**
(BELA) ⊟ **461 006-4**

3b, 7, 9, 23, 25. V. Masterson, P.A. Jones, P. Wales, C. Wright, J. Reed, D'Oyly Carte Op Chor, RPO, R. Nash (6/91) (DECC) Ⓓ **430 095-2DWO**
(6/91) (DECC) ⊟ **430 095-4DWO**

3b, 15-17, 20, 25. King's Sngrs (r1993; arr Gritton, Chilcott & Runswick) (5/94) (RCA) Ⓓ **09026 61885-2**
(5/94) (RCA) ⊟ **09026 61885-4**

6b, 26, 27. P.A. Jones, V. Masterson, P. Wales, L. Holland, C. Wright, J. Reed, K. Sandford, M. Rayner, D'Oyly Carte Op Chor, New SO, R. Nash (2/93) (DECC) Ⓓ **433 868-2DWO**
(2/93) (DECC) ⊟ **433 868-4DWO**

7, 9, 23, 24a, 25, 26, 27. T. Dahl, M. Forrester, T. Chiles, R. Suart, D. Grant, D. Morphy, Winnipeg Sngrs, Winnipeg G & S Soc, Winnipeg SO, B. Tovey (r1994) (6/95) (CBC) Ⓓ **SMCD5139**

9. Kneller Hall Band, F. Renton (r1992: arr P Stredwick) (9/93) (BAND) Ⓓ **BNA5067**
(9/93) (BAND) ⊟ **BND61075**

15. M. McLaughlin, WNO Chor, WNO Orch, C. Mackerras (r1991) (TELA) Ⓓ **CD80407**

15. B. Hendricks, Philh, L. Foster (r1992) (8/93) (EMI) Ⓓ **CDC7 54626-2**

15. L. Garrett, RPO, P. Robinson (r1994) (4/95) (SILV) Ⓓ **SILKD6004**
(4/95) (SILV) ⊟ **SILKC6004**

20. H. Williams, orch (r1923) (SYMP) Ⓓ **SYMCD1123**

23. Richard Lewis, G. Evans, PAO, M. Sargent (CFP) Ⓓ **CD-CFP4582**
(CFP) ⊟ **TC-CFP4582**

25. Classic Buskers, Chuckerbutty Ocarina Qt (arr Copley) (SEAV) Ⓓ **CD007366**

Patience (or Bunthorne's Bride)– operetta: 2 acts (1881—London) (Lib. W. S. Gilbert)

EXCERPTS: 1. Overture. ACT 1: 2. Twenty lovesick maidens; 3a. Still brooding on their mad infatuation; 3b. I cannot tell what this love may be; 4a. The Soldiers of our Queen; 4b. If you want a receipt; 5. In a doleful train; 6. When I first put this uniform on; 7a. Am I alone and unobserved?; 7b. If you're anxious for to shine; 8. Long years ago, fourteen maybe; 9. Prithee pretty maiden; 10a. Let the merry cymbals sound; 10b. True love must single-hearted be. ACT 2: 11. On such eyes as maidens cherish; 12a. Sad is that woman's lot; 12b. Silvered is the raven hair; 13. Turn, oh turn in this direction; 14. A magnet hung in a hardware shop; 15. Love is a plaintive song; 16. So go to him and say to him; 17. It's clear that medieval art alone retains its zest; 18. If Saphir I choose to marry; 19. When I go out of door; 20. I'm a Waterloo House young man; 21. After much debate internal.

Patience E. Morison
Bunthorne George Baker
Grosvenor J. Cameron
Lady Angela M. Thomas
Lady Ella H. Harper
Lady Saphir E. Harwood
Lady Jane M. Sinclair
Colonel Calverley J. Shaw
Major Murgatroyd T. Anthony
Duke of Dunstable A. Young

Glyndebourne Fest Chor, PAO, M. Sargent (r1961: omits dialogue) (EMI) Ⓓ [2] **CMS7 64406-2**

Patience W. Lawson
Bunthorne George Baker
Grosvenor L. Rands
Lady Angela N. Briercliffe
Lady Ella R. Mackay
Lady Saphir M. Eyre
Lady Jane B. Lewis
Colonel Calverley D. Fancourt
Major Murgatroyd M. Green
Duke of Dunstable D. Oldham

D'Oyly Carte Op Chor, SO, M. Sargent (r1930: omits dialogue) (7/89) (ARAB) Ⓓ [2] **Z8095-2**

Patience M. Sansom
Bunthorne J. Reed
Grosvenor K. Sandford
Lady Angela Y. Newman
Lady Ella J. Toye
Lady Saphir B. Lloyd-Jones
Lady Jane G. Knight
Colonel Calverley D. Adams
Major Murgatroyd J. Cartier
Duke of Dunstable P. Potter

D'Oyly Carte Op Chor, New SO, I. Godfrey (with dialogue) (1/90) (LOND) Ⓓ [2] **425 193-2LM2**

1. PAO, M. Sargent (CFP) Ⓓ **CD-CFP4529**

1. Scottish CO, A. Faris (NIMB) Ⓓ **NI5066**
(NIMB) ⊟ **NC5066**

1. ASMF, N. Marriner (r1992) (PHIL) **OO** **434 916-5PH**

1. D'Oyly Carte Op Orch, J.O. Edwards (r1992) (5/93) (TER) Ⓓ **CDVIR8316**
(5/93) (TER) ⊟ **ZCVIR8316**

1. ASMF, N. Marriner (r1992) (6/93) (PHIL) Ⓓ **434 916-2PH**

6, 14, 16. M. Sinclair, George Baker, J. Shaw, Glyndebourne Fest Chor, PAO, M. Sargent (CFP) Ⓓ **CD-CFP4609**
(CFP) ⊟ **TC-CFP4609**

7a, 7b, 16. G. Knight, J. Reed, New SO, I. Godfrey (2/93) (DECC) Ⓓ **433 868-2DWO**
(2/93) (DECC) ⊟ **433 868-4DWO**

The **Pirates of Penzance (or The Slave of Duty)– operetta: 2 acts (1879—Paignton) (Lib. W. S. Gilbert)**

EXCERPTS: 1. Overture. ACT 1: 2. Pour, o pour the pirate sherry; 3. When Frederic was a little lad; 4. Oh better far to live and die; 5a. O false one; 5b. You told me you were fair; 5c. What shall I do; 6. Climbing over rocky mountains; 7a. Stop ladies pray; 7b. Oh is there not one maiden breast?; 8. Poor wandering one; 9. What ought we to do?; 10. How beautifully blue the sky; 11. Stay, we must not lose our senses; 12a. Hold, monsters; 12b. Here's a first-class opportunity; 13. I am the very model of a modern Major-General; 14. Oh, men of dark and dismal fate. ACT 2: 15. Oh dry the glistening tear; 16a. Now Frederic, let your escort; 16b. When the foeman bares his steel; 17. Now the Pirates' lair; 18. When you had left our pirate fold; 19. Away, away; 20. All is prepared; 21a. Stay, Fredric; 21b. Ah, leave me not; 22a. Now I'll be brave; 22b. When a felon's not engaged; 23. A rollicking band; 24. With cat-like tread; 25a. Hush hush not a word; 25b. Sighing softly; 25c. Now what is this; 25d. We triumph now; 25e. Poor wandering ones.

Pirate King D. Adams
Frederic P. Potter
Major-General Stanley J. Reed
Mabel V. Masterson
Samuel G. Cook
Police Sergeant O. Brannigan
Ruth C. Palmer
Kate P. Wales
Edith J. Allister
Isobel S. Maisey

D'Oyly Carte Op Chor, RPO, I. Godfrey (with dialogue) (12/84) (DECC) ⊟ [2] **414 286-4DY2**

Major-General Stanley George Baker
Pirate King P. Dawson
Samuel S. Robertson
Frederic D. Oldham
Police Sergeant L. Sheffield
Mabel E. Griffin
Edith N. Briercliffe
Kate N. Walker
Ruth D. Gill

D'Oyly Carte Op Chor, SO, M. Sargent (r1929: omits dialogue) (PRO) Ⓓ **CDD597**

Pirate King J. Milligan
Frederic Richard Lewis
Major-General Stanley George Baker
Mabel E. Morison
Samuel J. Cameron
Police Sergeant O. Brannigan
Ruth M. Sinclair
Kate M. Thomas
Edith H. Harper

Glyndebourne Fest Chor, PAO, M. Sargent (omits dialogue) (EMI) Ⓓ [2] **CMS7 64409-2**

Pirate-King P. Dawson
Frederic D. Oldham
Major-General Stanley George Baker
Mabel E. Griffin
Samuel S. Robertson
Police Sergeant L. Sheffield
Ruth D. Gill
Kate N. Walker
Edith N. Briercliffe

D'Oyly Carte Op Chor, SO, M. Sargent (r1929: omits dialogue) (11/87) (ARAB) Ⓓ [2] **Z8068-2**

Pirate King D. Adams
Frederic P. Potter
Major-General Stanley J. Reed
Mabel V. Masterson
Samuel G. Cook
Police Sergeant O. Brannigan
Ruth C. Palmer
Kate P. Wales
Edith J. Allister
Isobel S. Maisey

D'Oyly Carte Op Chor, RPO, I. Godfrey (with dialogue) (1/90) (LOND) Ⓓ [2] **425 196-2LM2**

Pirate King M. Rivers
Frederic P. Creasey
Major-General Stanley E. Roberts
Mabel M. Hill Smith
Samuel Gareth Jones
Police Sergeant S. Masterton-Smith
Ruth S. Gorton
Kate P. Birchall
Edith P. Cameron

D'Oyly Carte Op Chor, D'Oyly Carte Op Orch, J. Pryce-Jones (omits dialogue) (9/90) (TER) Ⓓ [2] **CDTER2 1177**
(9/90) (TER) ⊟ [2] **ZCTED 1177**

Pirate King D. Adams
Frederic J.M. Ainsley
Major-General Stanley R. Suart
Mabel R. Evans
Samuel N. Folwell
Police Sergeant R. van Allan
Ruth G. Knight
Kate J. Williams
Edith J. Gossage

WNO Chor, WNO Orch, C. Mackerras (omits dialogue) (11/93) (TELA) Ⓓ **CD80353**
(11/93) (TELA) ⊟ **CS30353**

B. Hendricks, Ambrosian Sngrs, Philh, L. Foster (r1992) (8/93) (EMI) Ⓓ **CDC7 54626-2**

1. PAO, M. Sargent (CFP) Ⓓ **CD-CFP4529**

1. Scottish CO, A. Faris (NIMB) Ⓓ **NI5066**
(NIMB) ⊟ **NC5066**

1. ASMF, N. Marriner (r1992) (PHIL) **OO** **434 916-5PH**

1. D'Oyly Carte Op Orch, J. Pryce-Jones (r1990) (5/93) (TER) Ⓓ **CDVIR8316**
(5/93) (TER) ⊟ **ZCVIR8316**

1. ASMF, N. Marriner (r1992) (6/93) (PHIL) Ⓓ **434 916-2PH**

1-4, 6, 7b, 8, 10, 11, 13, 15, 16b, 21a, 21b, 22b, 24, 25a, 25b D. Adams, P. Potter, J. Reed, V. Masterson, G. Cook, C. Palmer, P. Wales, J. Allister, S. Maisey, D'Oyly Carte Op Chor, RPO, I. Godfrey (DECC) Ⓓ **436 148-2DSP**
(DECC) ⊟ **436 148-4DSP**

2, 3, 6, 7b, 8, 13, 14, 15, 16b, 22b, 24, 25c-e M. Rivers, Gareth Jones, P. Creasey, E. Roberts, S. Masterton-Smith, P. Birchall, P. Cameron, J. Arthur, S. Gorton, D'Oyly Carte Op Chor, D'Oyly Carte Op Orch, J. Pryce-Jones (KOCH) Ⓓ **34026-2**
(KOCH) ⊟ **24026-4**

4. R. Temple, anon (r1903) (SYMP) Ⓓ **SYMCD1123**

4, 21b, 24. King's Sngrs (r1993; arr Chilcott)
(5/94) (RCA) ⦶ **09026 61885-2**
(5/94) (RCA) ▭ **09026 61885-4**

4, 8, 13, 22b, 24. E. Morison, J. Milligan, George Baker, J. Cameron, O. Brannigan, Glyndebourne Fest Chor, PAO, M. Sargent
(CFP) ⦶ **CD-CFP4609**
(CFP) ▭ **TC-CFP4609**

7a, 7b, 8, 13, 20, 21a T. Dahl, M. Forrester, T. Chiles, R. Suart, D. Grant, D. Morphy, Winnipeg Sngrs, Winnipeg G & S Soc, Winnipeg SO, B. Tovey (r1994) (6/95) (CBC) ⦶ **SMCD5139**

7b, 8, 13, 22b Richard Lewis, E. Morison, George Baker, O. Brannigan, Glyndebourne Fest Chor, PAO, M. Sargent (CFP) ⦶ **CD-CFP4238**
(CFP) ▭ **TC-CFP40238**

7b, 8, 13, 22b, 24. D. Oldham, E. Griffin, George Baker, L. Sheffield, D'Oyly Carte Op Chor, SO, M. Sargent (r1929) (MMOI) ⦶ **CDMOIR413**

8. I. Jay, inst ens (r1904)
(SYMP) ⦶ **SYMCD1123**

8, 13, 16b, 22b V. Masterson, J. Allister, J. Reed, O. Brannigan, D'Oyly Carte Op Chor, RPO, I. Godfrey
(6/91) (DECC) ⦶ **430 095-2DWO**
(6/91) (DECC) ▭ **430 095-4DWO**

8, 21a, 21b, 22b M. Studholme, E. Bohan, I. Wallace, English Chorale, London Concert Orch, M. Dods (IMP) ⦶ **PWK1157**

24, 25e V. Masterson, P. Wales, C. Palmer, J. Allister, P. Potter, G. Cook, D'Oyly Carte Op Chor, RPO, I. Godfrey
(2/93) (DECC) ⦶ **433 868-2DWO**
(2/93) (DECC) ▭ **433 868-4DWO**

Princess Ida (or Castle Adamant)– operetta: 3 acts (1884—London) (Lib. W. S. Gilbert)

EXCERPTS: 1. Overture. ACT 1: 2. Search throughout the panorama; 3. Now hearken to my strict command; 4a. Today we meet; 4b. Ida was a twelvemonth old; 5. From the distant panorama; 6. We are warriors three; 7. If you give me your attention; 8a. Perhaps, if you address the lady; 8b. Expressive glances; 8c. For a month to dwell. ACT 2: 9. Towards the empyrean heights; 10. Mighty maiden; 11a. Minerva; 11b. Oh goddess wise; 11c. And thus to empyrean height; 12. Come, mighty Must; 13. Gently, gently; 14. I am a maiden, cold and steely; 15. The world is but a broken toy; 16. A lady fair, of lineage high; 17. The woman of the wisest wit; 18. Now would'nt you like to rule; 19. Merrily ring the luncheon bell; 20. Would you like to know the kind of maid; 21a. Oh joy, our chief is saved; 21b. Whom thou hast chained must wear his chain. ACT 3: 22. Death to the invader; 23. When'er I spoke sarcastic joke; 24. I built upon a rock; 25. When anger spreads his wing; 26. This helmet, I suppose; 27. This is our duty plain; 28. With joy abiding.

King Hildeband	K. Sandford
Hilarion	P. Potter
Cyril	D. Palmer
Florian	J. Skitch
King Gama	J. Reed
Arac	D. Adams
Guron	A. Raffell
Scynthius	G. Cook
Princess Ida	E. Harwood
Lady Blanche	C. Palmer
Lady Psyche	A. Hood
Melissa	V. Masterson

D'Oyly Carte Op Chor, RPO, M. Sargent (r1965)
(LOND) ⦶ [2] **436 810-2LM2**

1. PAO, M. Sargent (CFP) ⦶ **CD-CFP4529**

1. Scottish CO, A. Faris (NIMB) ⦶ **NI5066**
(NIMB) ▭ **NC5066**

1. PAO, M. Sargent
(EMI) ⦶ [2] **CMS7 64409-2**

1. D'Oyly Carte Op Orch, J.O. Edwards (r1992)
(5/93) (TER) ⦶ **CDVIR8316**
(5/93) (TER) ▭ **ZCVIR8316**

7, 24, 26. E. Harwood, J. Reed, A. Raffell, G. Cook, D'Oyly Carte Op Chor, M. Sargent
(2/93) (DECC) ⦶ **433 868-2DWO**
(2/93) (DECC) ▭ **433 868-4DWO**

15. London Concert Artists, J. Partridge
(ASV) ⦶ **CDWHL2070**
(ASV) ▭ **ZCWHL2070**

The **Rose of Persia (or The Story-teller and the Slave)– operetta: 2 acts (1899—London) (Lib. B. Hood)**

Drinking song W. Glynne, anon (r1920)
(SYMP) ⦶ **SYMCD1123**

Small street Arab C.H. Workman, orch (r1912)
(SYMP) ⦶ **SYMCD1123**

Ruddigore (or The Witch's Curse)– operetta: 2 acts (1887—London) (Lib. W. S. Gilbert)

EXCERPTS: 1. Overture (Geoffrey Toye version: 1921). ACT 1: 2. Fair is Rose; 3. Sir Rupert Murgatroyd; 4. If somebody there chanced to be; 5. I know a youth; 6a. From the briny sea; 6b. I shipped, d'ye see; 7a. Hornpipe; 7b. My boy, you may take it from me; 8. The battle's roar is over; 9. If well his suit has sped; 10. In sailing o'er life's ocean wide; 11a. Cheerily carols the lark; 11b. To a garden full of posies; 12. Welcome gentry for your entry; 13. O why am I moody and sad?; 14. You understand?; 15a. Hail the bride of seventeen summers; 15b. When the buds are blossoming; 15c. Hold, bride and bridegroom; 15d. As pure and blameless peasant; 15e. Within this breast; 15f. Farewell; 15g. Dance. ACT 2: 16. I once was as meek; 17. Happily coupled; 18. In bygone days; 19. Painted emblems of a race; 20. When the night wind howls (The Ghosts' High-Noon); 21. He yields! He answers to your call!; 22a. Away, Remorse!; 22b. Ye well-to-do squires; 23. I once was a very abandon'd person; 24. My eyes are fully open; 25. There grew a little flower; 26. On, happy the lily ADDITIONAL ITEM: 27. Overture (original Hamilton Clarke version: 1887).

Rose Maybud	M. Hill Smith
Sir Ruthven Murgatroyd	G. Sandison
Dame Hannah	J. Davies
Zorah	A. Hann
Mad Margaret	L. Ormiston
Old Adam	J. Ayldon
Richard Dauntless	D. Hillman
Sir Despard Murgatroyd	H. Innocent
Sir Roderick Murgatroyd	T. Lawlor

New Sadler's Wells Op Chor, New Sadler's Wells Op Orch, S. Phipps (recording contains extra numbers from original 1887 score)
(TER) ⦶ [2] **CDTER2 1128**
(9/87) (TER) ▭ **ZCTED 1128**

Rose Maybud	E. Morison
Sir Ruthven Murgatroyd	George Baker
Dame Hannah	M. Sinclair
Zorah	E. Harwood
Mad Margaret	P. Bowden
Old Adam	H. Blackburn
Richard Dauntless	Richard Lewis
Sir Despard Murgatroyd	O. Brannigan
Sir Roderick Murgatroyd	J. Rouleau

Glyndebourne Fest Chor, PAO, M. Sargent (omits dialogue)
(EMI) ⦶ [2] **CMS7 64412-2**

Rose Maybud	J. Hindmarsh
Sir Ruthven Murgatroyd	J. Reed
Dame Hannah	G. Knight
Zorah	M. Sansom
Mad Margaret	J. Allister
Old Adam	S. Riley
Richard Dauntless	T. Round
Sir Despard Murgatroyd	K. Sandford
Sir Roderick Murgatroyd	D. Adams

D'Oyly Carte Op Chor, ROHO, I. Godfrey (omits dialogue)
(LOND) ⦶ [2] **417 355-2LM2**

1. PAO, M. Sargent (CFP) ⦶ **CD-CFP4529**

1. Scottish CO, A. Faris (NIMB) ⦶ **NI5066**
(NIMB) ▭ **NC5066**

1, 27. New Sadler's Wells Op Orch, S. Phipps (r1987) (5/93) (TER) ⦶ **CDVIR8316**
(5/93) (TER) ▭ **ZCVIR8316**

5, 7b, 8, 10, 25. J. Reed, C. Palmer, J. Goss, P. Potter, J. Ayldon, RPO, J. Walker (r1960s)
(BELA) ⦶ **461 006-2**
(BELA) ▭ **461 006-4**

11b P. Bowden, PAO, M. Sargent
(CFP) ⦶ **CD-CFP4582**
(CFP) ▭ **TC-CFP4582**

13. J. Reed, RPO, I. Godfrey
(2/93) (DECC) ⦶ **433 868-2DWO**
(2/93) (DECC) ▭ **433 868-4DWO**

20. King's Sngrs (r1993; arr Runswick)
(5/94) (RCA) ⦶ **09026 61885-2**
(5/94) (RCA) ▭ **09026 61885-4**

The **Sapphire Necklace– opera: 4 acts (1860s) (Lib. H. Chorley)**

EXCERPTS: 1. Overture (recons R. Spencer).

1. RTE Concert Orch, A. Penny (r1992)
(6/93) (MARC) ⦶ **8 223461**

The **Sorcerer– operetta: 2 acts (1877—London) (Lib. W. S. Gilbert)**

EXCERPTS: 1. Overture. ACT 1: 2. Ring forth ye bells; 3a. Constance, my daughter; 3b. When he is here; 4a. The air is charged; 4b. Time was when Love and I; 5. Sir Marmaduke; 6. With heart and voice; 7a. My kindly friends; 7b. Oh happy young heart; 8. My child; 9. With heart and with voice; 10. Welcome joy; 11. All is prepared; 12. Love feeds on many kinds of food; 13. My name is John Wellington Wells; 14a. Sprites of earth and air; 14b. Let us fly; 15a. Now to the banquet; 15b. Eat, drink and be gay. ACT 2: 16. 'Tis twelve; 17. Dear friends, take pity; 18. Thou hast the power; 19. I rejoice that it's decided; 20. Alexis doubt me not; 21. Hate me!; 22. Oh, my voice is sad and low; 23. Oh, joyous boon!; 24. Prepare for sad surprises; 25. Or he or I must die.

Sir Marmaduke Pointdextre	D. Adams
Alexis	D. Palmer
Dr Daly	A. Styler
Notary	S. Riley
John Wellington Wells	J. Reed
Lady Sangazure	C. Palmer
Aline	V. Masterson
Mrs Partlet	J. Allister
Constance	A. Hood

D'Oyly Carte Op Chor, RPO, I. Godfrey (r1966: omits dialogue)
(LOND) ⦶ [2] **436 807-2LM2**

Abridged D. Fancourt, D. Oldham, L. Rands, S. Robertson, George Baker, D. Gill, M. Dickson, A. Bethell, A. Moxon, D'Oyly Carte Op Chor, SO, I. Godfrey (r1933)
(11/87) (ARAB) ⦶ [2] **Z8068-2**

1. PAO, M. Sargent (CFP) ⦶ **CD-CFP4529**

1. Scottish CO, A. Faris (NIMB) ⦶ **NI5066**
(NIMB) ▭ **NC5066**

1. PAO, M. Sargent
(EMI) ⦶ [2] **CMS7 64409-2**

13. W. Passmore, orch (r1911)
(SYMP) ⦶ **SYMCD1123**

13. J. Reed, RPO, I. Godfrey
(2/93) (DECC) ⦶ **433 868-2DWO**
(2/93) (DECC) ▭ **433 868-4DWO**

Thespis (or The Gods Grown Old)– operatic extraganza: 2 acts (1871—London) (Lib. W S Gilbert: fragments recons 1990)

EXCERPTS—ACT 2: 1. Ballet Music; 1a. Introduction; 1b. Pas de Châles; 1c. Valse; 1d. St George and the Dragon; 2. Galop.

1c D'Oyly Carte Op Orch, J. Pryce-Jones
(TER) ⦶ **CDVIR8315**

1, 2. D'Oyly Carte Op Orch, J. Pryce-Jones
(5/92) (TER) ⦶ [2] **CDTER2 1188**
(5/92) (TER) ▭ [2] **ZCTED 1188**

1, 2. RTE Concert Orch, A. Penny (r1992)
(6/93) (MARC) ⦶ **8 223460**

Trial by Jury– operetta: 1 act (1866—London) (Lib. W. S. Gilbert)

EXCERPTS: 1. Hark the hour; 2a. Is this the Court; 2b. When first my old, old love I knew; 3. All hail, great Judge; 4. When I, good friends was called to the Bar; 5. Swear thou the Jury; 6. Comes the broken flower; 7. Oh, never since I joined the human race; 8. May it please you my lud; 9. That she is reeling; 10. Oh gentlemen listen; 11. That seems a reasonable proposition; 12. A nice dilemma we have here; 13. I love him, I love him, with fervour unceasing; 14. Oh joy unbounded.

Plaintiff	W. Lawson
Defendant	D. Oldham
Judge	L. Sheffield
Counsel	A. Hosking
Usher	George Baker

D'Oyly Carte Op Chor, orch, H. Norris (r1927)
(PEAR) ⦶ [2] **GEMMCDS9961**

Plaintiff	E. Morison
Defendant	Richard Lewis
Judge	George Baker
Counsel	J. Cameron
Usher	O. Brannigan
Foreman	B. Turgeon

Glyndebourne Fest Chor, PAO, M. Sargent
(EMI) ⦶ [2] **CMS7 64397-2**

Plaintiff	A. Hood
Defendant	T. Round
Judge	J. Reed
Counsel	K. Sandford
Usher	D. Adams
Foreman	A. Raffell

ROHO, I. Godfrey
(1/90) (DECC) ⦶ [2] **417 358-2LM2**
(DECC) ▭ [2] **417 358-4DY2**

4. L. Sheffield, D'Oyly Carte Op Chor, SO, H. Norris (r1927) (MMOI) ⦶ **CDMOIR413**

14. T. Dahl, M. Forrester, T. Chiles, R. Suart, D. Grant, D. Morphy, Winnipeg Sngrs, Winnipeg G & S Soc, Winnipeg SO, B. Tovey (r1994)
(6/95) (CBC) ① **SMCD5139**

Utopia Limited (or The Flowers of Progress)– operetta: 2 acts (1893—London) (Wds. W. S. Gilbert)
EXCERPTS: ACT 1: 1. In lazy languor; 2a. O make way for the Wise Men; 2b. In every mental lore; 3. Let all your doubts take wing; 4a. Quaff the nectar; 4b. A King of autocratic power; 4c. Although of native maids the cream; 4d. Bold faced ranger; 5. First you're born; 6. Subjected to your heavenly gaze; 7. Oh maiden rich; 8. Ah gallant soldier; 9. It's understood I think; 10. Oh admirable art; 11a. Although your royal summons; 11b. What these may be; 11c. I'm Captain Corcoran KCB; 11d. Some seven men form an Association. ACT 2; 12a. Oh, Zara; 12b. A tenor all singers above; 13. Words of love too lordly spoken; 14. Society has quite forsaken; 15. Entrance of Court; 16. Drawing Room Music; 17a. This ceremonial our wish displays; 17b. Eagle high; 18. With fury deep; 19. If you think that when banded in unity; 20. With wily brain; 21. A wonderful joy; 22. Then I may sing and play?; 23a. Oh would some demon power; 23b. When a maid is fifteen years; 24a. Ah, Lady Sophy; 24b. Oh rapture unrestrained; 24c. Tarantella; 25. Upon our sea-girt land; 26. There's a little group of isles.

King Paramount K. Sandford
Scaphio J. Reed
Phantis J. Ayldon
Tarara J. Ellison
Calynx M. Buchan
Lord Dramaleigh J. Conroy-Ward
Captain FitzBattleaxe M. Reid
Captain Corcoran J. Broad
Mr Goldbury M. Rayner
Sir Bailey Barre C. Wright
Mr Blushington D. Porter
Princess Zara P. Field
Princess Nekaya J. Goss
Princess Kalyba J. Merri
Lady Sophy L. Holland
Phylla R. Griffiths
D'Oyly Carte Op Chor, RPO, R. Nash (r1975)
(LOND) ① [2] **436 816-2LM2**

The **Yeomen of the Guard (or The Merryman and his Maid)– operetta: 2 acts (1888—London) (Lib. W. S. Gilbert)**
EXCERPTS: 1. Overture. ACT 1: 2. When maiden loves, she sits and sighs; 3. Tower Warders, Under orders; 4. When our gallant Norman foes; 5. Alas! I waver to and fro; 6. Is life a boon?; 7. Here's a man of jollity; 8. I have a song to sing, O!; 9. Here's a man, maiden; 10a. I've jibe and joke and quip and crank; 10b. I've wisdom from the East; 11a. 'Tis done! I am a bride!; 11b. Though tear and long-drawn sigh; 12. Were I thy bride. Finale: 13a. Oh, Sergeant Meryll, is it true; 13b. Didst thou not, oh Leonard Meryll; 13c. To thy fraternal care; 13d. The prisoner comes to meet his doom. ACT 2: 14a. Night has spread her pall once more; 14b. Warders are ye?; 15. Oh! a private buffoon; 16. Herupon we're both agreed; 17. Free from his fetters grim; 18. Strange adventure; 19. Hark! what was that, sir?; 20. A man who would woo a fair maid; 21. When a wooer goes a-wooing; 22. Rapture, rapture; 23. Comes the pretty young bride. ADDITIONAL EXCERPTS: 24. When jealous torments rack my soul (Act 1); 25. A laughing boy (Act 1); 26. Is life a boon? (original version).

Sir Richard Cholmondeley D. Dowling
Colonel Fairfax Richard Lewis
Sergeant Meryll J. Carol Case
Leonard; First Yeoman A. Young
Jack Point G. Evans
Shadbolt O. Brannigan
Elsie E. Morison
Phoebe M. Thomas
Dame Carruthers M. Sinclair
Kate D. Hume
Second Yeoman J. Carol Case
Glyndebourne Fest Chor, PAO, M. Sargent (omits dialogue)
(EMI) ① [2] **CMS7 64415-2**

Sir Richard Cholmondeley A. Raffell
Colonel Fairfax P. Potter
Sergeant Meryll D. Adams
Leonard D. Palmer
Jack Point J. Reed
Shadbolt K. Sandford
Elsie E. Harwood
Phoebe A. Hood
Dame Carruthers G. Knight
Kate M. Eales
First Yeoman D. Palmer
Second Yeoman T. Lawlor
D'Oyly Carte Op Chor, RPO, M. Sargent (omits dialogue)
(1/90) (DECC) ① [2] **417 358-2LM2**
(DECC) ▬ [2] **417 358-4DY2**

Sir Richard Cholmondeley D. Maxwell
Colonel Fayrfax D. Fieldsend
Sergeant Meryll T. Sharpe
Leonard J. Jenson
Jack Point F. Gray
Shadbolt G. Montaine
Elsie L.E. Ross
Phoebe J. Roebuck
Dame Carruthers J. Pert
Kate C. Lesley-Green
D'Oyly Carte Op Chor, D'Oyly Carte Op Orch, J.O. Edwards (r1991: omits dialogue)
(5/93) (TER) ① [2] **CDTER2 1195**
(5/93) (TER) ▬ **ZCTED 1195**

Sir Richard Cholmondley R. Lloyd
Colonel Fairfax K. Streit
Sergeant Meryll S. Dean
Leonard; First Yeoman N. Mackie
Jack Point T. Allen
Shadbolt B. Terfel
Elsie S. McNair
Phoebe J. Rigby
Dame Carruthers A. Collins
Kate J. Howarth
Second Yeoman A. Michaels-Moore
ASMF Chor, ASMF, N. Marriner (r1992: with dialogue)
(11/93) (PHIL) ① [2] **438 138-2PH2**

1. PAO, M. Sargent (CFP) ① **CD-CFP4529**
1. Scottish CO, A. Faris (NIMB) ① **NI5066**
(NIMB) ▬ **NC5066**
1. Besses o' the Barn Band, R. Newsome (arr M Sargent) (CHAN) ① [2] **CHAN6571/2**
1. ASMF, N. Marriner (r1992)
(PHIL) **ΌΌ 434 916-5PH**
1. D'Oyly Carte Op Orch, J. Pryce-Jones (r1991)
(5/93) (TER) ① **CDVIR8316**
(5/93) (TER) ▬ **ZCVIR8316**
1. ASMF, N. Marriner (r1992)
(6/93) (PHIL) ① **434 916-2PH**
1. Kneller Hall Band, F. Renton (r1992: arr W J Duthoit) (9/93) (BAND) ① **BNA5067**
(9/93) (BAND) ▬ **BND61075**
1. Besses o' the Barn Band, Black Dyke Mills Band, Yorkshire Imperial Band, H. Mortimer (pp1987: arr brass band: Sargent)
(11/93) (CHAN) ① **CHAN4513**
(CHAN) ▬ **BBTD4513**
1. Black Dyke Mills Band, R. Newsome (r1977; arr brass band: M. Sargent)
(1/94) (CHAN) ① **CHAN4528**
(1/94) (CHAN) ▬ **BBTD4528**
1, 2, 4, 6-9, 10a, 11a, 12, 14a, 15, 16, 18-21. S. McNair, J. Howarth, J. Rigby, A. Collins, K. Streit, T. Allen, B. Terfel, R. Lloyd, S. Dean, ASMF Chor, ASMF, N. Marriner (r1992)
(PHIL) ① **442 436-2PH**
2, 3. A. Hood, T. Lawlor, ROHO, I. Godfrey
(2/93) (DECC) ① **433 868-2DWO**
(2/93) (DECC) ▬ **433 868-4DWO**
2, 8. E. Morison, M. Thomas, G. Evans, PAO, M. Sargent (CFP) ① **CD-CFP4238**
(CFP) ▬ **TC-CFP40238**
2, 8. E. Morison, M. Thomas, G. Evans, PAO, M. Sargent (CFP) ① **CD-CFP4609**
(CFP) ▬ **TC-CFP4609**
4, 7. E. Harwood, G. Knight, J. Reed, D'Oyly Carte Op Chor, RPO, M. Sargent
(6/91) (DECC) ① **430 095-2DWO**
(6/91) (DECC) ▬ **430 095-4DWO**
6, 12. D. Oldham, N. Briercliffe, SO, M. Sargent (r1929) (MMOI) ① **CDMOIR413**
8. Classic Buskers, Chuckerbutty Ocarina Qt (arr Copley) (SEAV) ① **CD007366**
8. T. Dahl, M. Forrester, T. Chiles, R. Suart, D. Grant, D. Morphy, Winnipeg Sngrs, Winnipeg G & S Soc, Winnipeg SO, B. Tovey (r1994)
(6/95) (CBC) ① **SMCD5139**
10a, 16, 20, 21. J. Reed, P. Potter, A. Guthrie, K. Sandford, P.A. Jones, RPO, J. Walker (r1960s)
(BELA) ① **461 006-2**
(BELA) ▬ **461 006-4**
12. E. Jones-Hudson, orch (r1907)
(SYMP) ① **SYMCD1123**
24, 25, 26. D. Maxwell, D. Fieldsend, T. Sharpe, J. Jenson, F. Gray, G. Montaine, L.E. Ross, J. Roebuck, J. Pert, C. Lesley-Green, D'Oyly Carte Op Chor, D'Oyly Carte Op Orch, J.O. Edwards (r1991: omits dialogue)
(5/93) (TER) ① [2] **CDTER2 1195**
(5/93) (TER) ▬ **ZCTED 1195**

The **Zoo– operetta: 1 act (1875—London) (Lib B. Rowe)**

Aesculapius Carboy M. Reid
Thomas Brown K. Sandford
Mr Grinder J. Ayldon
Laetitia J. Goss
Eliza Smith J. Metcalfe
Narrator G. Shovelton
D'Oyly Carte Op Chor, RPO, R. Nash (r1977)
(LOND) ① [2] **436 807-2LM2**

SUPPÉ, Franz (von)
(1819–1895) Austria

Afrikareise– operetta: 3 acts (1883—Vienna) (Lib. M. Wert, Genée & O F Berg)
EXCERPTS: 1. Overture; 2. Titania Waltz.
2. Košice St PO, A. Walter (r1994)
(MARC) ① **8 223683**

Banditenstreiche, 'The Jolly Robbers'– comic operetta: 1 act (1867—Vienna) (Lib. R Boutonnier)
1. Overture.
1. German Fest Orch, A. Scholz
(CAVA) ① **CAVCD017**
1. RPO, G. Kuhn (EURO) ① **RD69037**
1. Košice St PO, A. Walter (r1993)
(MARC) ① **8 223647**
1. LSO, C. Mackerras (r1961)
(MERC) ① **434 352-2MM**
1. Montreal SO, C. Dutoit
(2/86) (DECC) ① **414 408-2DH**
1. Hungarian St Op Orch, J. Sandor
(11/90) (LASE) ① **15 611**
(11/90) (LASE) ▬ **79 611**
1. BPO, H. von Karajan
(8/92) (DG) ① [2] **435 712-2GX2**

Boccaccio– operetta: 3 acts (1879—Vienna) (Lib. Zell & Genée, after Boccaccio)
EXCERPTS: 1. Overture; 2. Florenz hat schöne Frauen; 3. Hab'ich nur deine Liebe; 4. Mia bella fiorentina; 5. Menuet and Tarantella.
Excs R. Holm, U. Schirrmacher, A. Oelke, R. Glawitsch, R. Schock, E. Marlo, P. Manuel, E. Krukowski, Günther Arndt Ch, Berlin SO, F. Fox
(EURO) ① **258 376**
1. Detroit SO, P. Paray
(MERC) ① **434 309-2MM**
1. Košice St PO, A. Walter (r1994)
(MARC) ① **8 223683**
1. Košice St PO, A. Walter (r1993)
(6/95) (MARC) ① **8 223648**
2, 3. Raphaele Concert Orch, P. Walden (arr Waldenmaier) (5/91) (MOZA) ① **MECD1002**
3. R. Streich, Berlin RSO, K. Gaebel
(DG) ① [2] **435 748-2GDO2**
3. E. Schwarzkopf, Philh, O. Ackermann
(1/86) (EMI) ① **CDC7 47284-2**
3. L. Popp, ASMF, N. Marriner
(6/88) (EMI) ① **CDC7 49700-2**
3. J. Patzak, Berlin St Op Orch (r1934)
(3/90) (PEAR) ① **GEMMCD9383**
3. M. Reining, Berlin Deutsche Op Orch, W. Lutze (r1939) (9/92) (PREI) ① **90083**
3. E. Rethberg, Victor SO, Rosario Bourdon (r1931) (10/95) (ROMO) ① [2] **81014-2**
3, 4. R. Holm, W. Krenn, Vienna Volksoper Orch, A. Paulik (r1970) (LOND) ① **436 898-2DM**
5. Košice St PO, A. Walter (r1993)
(MARC) ① **8 223647**

(unidentified) Carnaval
EXCERPTS: 1. Overture.
1. Košice St PO, A. Walter (r1993)
(MARC) ① **8 223647**

Dichter und Bauer, 'Poet and Peasant'– comedy with songs: 3 acts (1846—Vienna) (Lib. F Kaiser)
1. Overture.
1. Philh, W. Boughton (NIMB) ① **NI5120**
(NIMB) ▬ **NC5120**
1. German Fest Orch, A. Scholz
(CAVA) ① **CAVCD017**
1. RPO, G. Kuhn (EURO) ① **RD69037**
1. VPO, G. Solti (DECC) ① **425 853-2DWO**
(DECC) ▬ **425 853-4DWO**
1. Czech PO, V. Neumann
(SUPR) ① **11 0724-2**

1. New SO, A. Gibson (CHES) Ⓓ **Chesky CD62**
1. Detroit SO, P. Paray (MERC) Ⓓ **434 309-2MM**
1. Minnesota Orch, Anon (cond) (WORD) Ⓓ **FCD7409**
1. Paris RSO, L. Bertrand (ROSE) Ⓓ **3229**
1. NYPO, L. Bernstein (r1963) (SONY) Ⓓ **SMK47606**
1. Košice St PO, A. Walter (r1993) (MARC) Ⓓ **8 223647**
1. Montreal SO, C. Dutoit (2/86) (DECC) Ⓓ **414 408-2DH**
1. ASMF, N. Marriner (10/90) (EMI) Ⓓ **CDC7 54056-2**
1. Hungarian St Op Orch, J. Sandor (11/90) (LASE) Ⓓ **15 611**; (11/90) (LASE) ⊟ **79 611**
1. NBC SO, A. Toscanini (bp1943) (1/91) (RCA) Ⓓ **GD60308**
1. BPO, H. von Karajan (8/92) (DG) Ⓓ [2] **435 712-2GX2**
1. T. Trotter (r1992: trans org: E. Evans) (4/94) (DECC) Ⓓ **436 656-2DH**

Donna Juanita– operetta: 3 acts (1880—Vienna) (Lib. R Genée & F Zell)
EXCERPTS: 1. Overture; 2. March.
1. Košice St PO, A. Walter (r1993) (6/95) (MARC) Ⓓ **8 223648**
2. Košice St PO, A. Walter (r1993) (MARC) Ⓓ **8 223647**

Fatinitza– operetta: 3 acts (1876—Vienna) (Lib. R Genée & F Zell)
1. Overture; 2. March.
1. Košice St PO, A. Walter (r1994) (MARC) Ⓓ **8 223683**
1. Montreal SO, C. Dutoit (2/86) (DECC) Ⓓ **414 408-2DH**
1. Hungarian St Op Orch, J. Sandor (11/90) (LASE) Ⓓ **15 611**; (11/90) (LASE) ⊟ **79 611**
2. Vienna SO, R. Stolz (EURO) Ⓓ **258 665**
2. Košice St PO, A. Walter (r1993) (6/95) (MARC) Ⓓ **8 223648**

Die **Flotten Burschen– operetta: 1 act (1863—Vienna) (Lib. J Braun)**
1. Overture.
1. Hungarian St Op Orch, J. Sandor (11/90) (LASE) Ⓓ **15 611**; (11/90) (LASE) ⊟ **79 611**

Franz Schubert– operetta: 1 act (1864—Vienna) (Wds. H Max)
EXCERPTS: 1. Overture.
1. Košice St PO, A. Walter (r1994) (MARC) Ⓓ **8 223683**

Die **Frau Meisterin, 'The Lady Mistress'– magical operetta: 3 acts (1868—Vienna) (Lib. C Costa)**
EXCERPTS: 1. Overture.
1. Košice St PO, A. Walter (r1993) (MARC) Ⓓ **8 223647**
1. ASMF, N. Marriner (10/90) (EMI) Ⓓ **CDC7 54056-2**

Die **Heimkehr von der Hochzeit, 'Homecoming from the Wedding'– opera: 3 acts (1853—Vienna) (Lib. Feldman)**
EXCERPTS: 1. Overture.
1. Košice St PO, A. Walter (r1994) (MARC) Ⓓ **8 223683**

Die **Irrfahrt um's Glück (Die Jagd nach dem Glück), 'Fortune's Labyrinth'– operetta: 3 acts (1880—Vienna) (Lib. R Genée & F Zell)**
EXCERPTS: 1. Overture.
1. Košice St PO, A. Walter (r1993) (MARC) Ⓓ **8 223647**
1. ASMF, N. Marriner (10/90) (EMI) Ⓓ **CDC7 54056-2**

Isabella– comic operetta: 1 act (1869—Vienna) (Lib. J Wely)
EXCERPTS: 1. Overture.
1. Košice St PO, A. Walter (r1993) (6/95) (MARC) Ⓓ **8 223648**

Der **Krämer und sein Kommis– farce with songs: 2 acts (1844—Vienna) (Wds. F Kaiser)**
EXCERPTS: 1. Overture.
1. Košice St PO, A. Walter (r1993) (6/95) (MARC) Ⓓ **8 223648**

Leichte Kavallerie, 'Light Cavalry'– comic operetta: 2 acts (1866—Vienna) (Lib. C Costa)
1. Overture.
1. German Fest Orch, A. Scholz (CAVA) Ⓓ **CAVCD017**
1. H. Britton (arr Britton) (ASV) Ⓓ **CDQS6028**; (ASV) ⊟ **ZCQS6028**
1. RPO, G. Kuhn (EURO) Ⓓ **RD69037**
1. Czech PO, V. Neumann (SUPR) Ⓓ **11 0724-2**
1. RPO, M. Reed (RPO) Ⓓ [2] **CDRPD9001**; (RPO) ⊟ [2] **ZCRPD9001**
1. Košice St PO, A. Walter (NAXO) Ⓓ **8 550468**
1. Detroit SO, P. Paray (MERC) Ⓓ **434 309-2MM**
1. RPO, M. Reed (IMP) Ⓓ [3] **TCD1014**
1. BBC PO, E. Downes (IMP) Ⓓ **PCD1023**
1. RPO, M. Reed (IMP) Ⓓ **PCDS018**; (IMP) ⊟ **PCDSC018**
1. Paris RSO, L. Bertrand (ROSE) Ⓓ **3229**
1. NYPO, L. Bernstein (r1967) (SONY) Ⓓ **SMK47606**
1. RPO, M. Reed (r1990) (RPO) Ⓓ **CDRPO5010**
1. BBC PO, E. Downes (r1992) (IMP) Ⓓ **PCDS21**; (IMP) ⊟ **PCDSC21**
1. Košice St PO, A. Walter (r1994) (MARC) Ⓓ **8 223683**
1. BBC PO, E. Downes (r1990) (IMP) Ⓓ **PCD2045**
1. Montreal SO, C. Dutoit (2/86) (DECC) Ⓓ **414 408-2DH**
1. ASMF, N. Marriner (10/90) (EMI) Ⓓ **CDC7 54056-2**
1. Hungarian St Op Orch, J. Sandor (11/90) (LASE) Ⓓ **15 611**; (11/90) (LASE) ⊟ **79 611**
1. BPO, H. von Karajan (8/92) (DG) Ⓓ [2] **435 712-2GX2**
1. Black Dyke Mills Band, P. Parkes (arr brass band: G Langford) (9/93) (CHAN) Ⓓ **CHAN4514**; (9/93) (CHAN) ⊟ **BBTD4514**

Das **Modell– operetta: 3 acts (1895—Vienna) (Lib. V Léon & L Held)**
EXCERPTS: 1. Overture.
1. Košice St PO, A. Walter (r1993) (6/95) (MARC) Ⓓ **8 223648**

Ein **Morgen, ein Mittag, ein Abend in Wien, 'Morning, Noon and Night in Vienna'– local play with songs: 2 acts (1844—Vienna) (Wds. F X Told)**
1. Overture.
1. RPO, G. Kuhn (EURO) Ⓓ **RD69037**
1. Cölln Salon Orch (EURO) Ⓓ **GD69297**
1. Košice St PO, A. Walter (NAXO) Ⓓ **8 550468**
1. Detroit SO, P. Paray (MERC) Ⓓ **434 309-2MM**
1. LPO, T. Beecham (r1939) (PEAR) Ⓓ **GEMMCD9094**
1. Montreal SO, C. Dutoit (2/86) (DECC) Ⓓ **414 408-2DH**
1. ASMF, N. Marriner (10/90) (EMI) Ⓓ **CDC7 54056-2**
1. Hungarian St Op Orch, J. Sandor (11/90) (LASE) Ⓓ **15 611**; (11/90) (LASE) ⊟ **79 611**
1. BPO, H. von Karajan (8/92) (DG) Ⓓ [2] **435 712-2GX2**
1. LPO, T. Beecham (r1939) (7/93) (DUTT) Ⓓ **CDLX7001**

Paragraph drei– opera: 3 acts (1858—Vienna)
EXCERPTS: 1. Overture.
1. Košice St PO, A. Walter (r1990) (6/95) (MARC) Ⓓ **8 223648**

Pique Dame, 'Queen of Spades'– comic opera: 2 acts (1864—Vienna) (Lib. T Treumann. Rev from 'Die Kartenschlägerin')
1. Overture.
1. RPO, G. Kuhn (EURO) Ⓓ **RD69037**
1. Detroit SO, P. Paray (MERC) Ⓓ **434 309-2MM**
1. Košice St PO, A. Walter (r1993) (MARC) Ⓓ **8 223647**
1. Montreal SO, C. Dutoit (2/86) (DECC) Ⓓ **414 408-2DH**
1. ASMF, N. Marriner (10/90) (EMI) Ⓓ **CDC7 54056-2**
1. Hungarian St Op Orch, J. Sandor (11/90) (LASE) Ⓓ **15 611**; (11/90) (LASE) ⊟ **79 611**
1. Raphaele Concert Orch, P. Walden (arr Waldenmaier) (5/91) (MOZA) Ⓓ **MECD1002**
1. BPO, H. von Karajan (8/92) (DG) Ⓓ [2] **435 712-2GX2**

Die **schöne Galathee, 'Beautiful Galatea'– operetta: 1 act (1865—Berlin) (Lib. P Henrion)**
1. Overture.
Excs A. Moffo, R. Kollo, R. Wagemann, F. Gruber, Bavarian Rad Chor, Munich RO, K. Eichhorn (Ger) (EURO) Ⓓ **258 376**
Trinklied; Was sagst du? Ich lausche L. Schöne, orch (r1925) (12/92) (NIMB) Ⓓ **NI7833**; (12/92) (NIMB) ⊟ **NC7833**
1. German Fest Orch, A. Scholz (CAVA) Ⓓ **CAVCD017**
1. RPO, G. Kuhn (EURO) Ⓓ **RD69037**
1. Vienna St Op Orch, L. Reichwein (r1938) (SCHW) Ⓓ [2] **311162**
1. Košice St PO, A. Walter (NAXO) Ⓓ **8 550468**
1. Detroit SO, P. Paray (MERC) Ⓓ **434 309-2MM**
1. Paris RSO, L. Bertrand (ROSE) Ⓓ **3229**
1. VPO, W. Boskovsky (r1972) (LOND) Ⓓ **436 785-2LM**
1. Staatskapelle Dresden, O. Suitner (r1975) (BELA) Ⓓ **461 001-2**; (BELA) ⊟ **461 001-4**
1. Montreal SO, C. Dutoit (2/86) (DECC) Ⓓ **414 408-2DH**
1. Hungarian St Op Orch, J. Sandor (11/90) (LASE) Ⓓ **15 611**; (11/90) (LASE) ⊟ **79 611**
1. BPO, H. von Karajan (8/92) (DG) Ⓓ [2] **435 712-2GX2**
1. NYPO, L. Bernstein (11/92) (SONY) Ⓓ **SMK47532**
1. Black Dyke Mills Band, D. Hurst (arr brass band: G Langford) (9/93) (CHAN) Ⓓ **CHAN4514**; (9/93) (CHAN) ⊟ **BBTD4514**
1. Košice St PO, A. Walter (r1993) (6/95) (MARC) Ⓓ **8 223648**

Tantalusqualen, 'The Torments of Tantalus'– comic opera: 1 act (1868—Vienna) (Lib. cpsr, after L Angely)
1. Overture.
1. ASMF, N. Marriner (10/90) (EMI) Ⓓ **CDC7 54056-2**
1. Košice St PO, A. Walter (r1993) (6/95) (MARC) Ⓓ **8 223648**

Tricoche und Cacolet– humoresque: 3 acts (1873—Vienna) (Lib. H Meilhac & LHalévy)
EXCERPTS: 1. Overture.
1. Košice St PO, A. Walter (r1994) (MARC) Ⓓ **8 223683**

Des **Wanderers Ziel, 'The Goal of the Wanderer'– Festspiel: 1 act (1845—Vienna) (Lib. K Meisl)**
EXCERPTS: 1. Overture.
1. Košice St PO, A. Walter (r1993) (MARC) Ⓓ **8 223647**

SZYMANOWSKI, Karol (Maciej) *(1882–1937) Poland*

King Roger– opera: 3 acts, Op. 46 (1926—Warsaw) (Lib. cpsr and J. Iwaszkiewicz)

Roger II	F. Skulski
Roxana	B. Zagórzanka
Edrisi	Z. Nikodem
Shepherd	S. Kowalski
Archbishop	J. Ostapiuk
Deaconess	R. Racewicz

Warsaw Wiekl Th Chor, Warsaw Wiekl Th Orch, R. Satanowski (SCHW) Ⓓ [2] **314014**

Roger II	A. Hiolski
Roxana	B. Zagórzanka
Edrisi	H. Grychnik
Shepherd	W. Ochman
Archbishop	L. Mróz
Deaconess	A. Malewicz-Madey

Cracow Phil Boys' Chor, Katowice St Phil Chor, Katowice St Phil Orch, K. Stryja (r1990) (MARC) Ⓓ [2] **8 223339/40**

Roxana's song J. Heifetz, E. Bay (r1935: arr vn/pf: Kochanski) (EMI) Ⓓ [2] **CHS7 64929-2**
Roxana's Song K. Danczowska, K. Zimerman (arr vn/pf) (8/91) (DG) Ⓓ **431 469-2GGA**
Roxana's song H. Temianka, J. Graudan (arr Kochanski: r1937) (2/93) (BIDD) Ⓓ [2] **LAB059/60**

Roxana's Song J. Heifetz (r1935)
(11/94) (RCA) Ⓓ [65] **09026 61778-2(03)**

TAUBER, Richard
(1891–1948) Austria/England

Old Chelsea– musical romance: 2 acts (1943—London) (Lib. Tysh and Ellis)

My heart and I J. Locke, orch, G. Scott-Wood (r1947) (EMI) Ⓓ **CDP7 98844-2**
(EMI) ⊙ **GO2034**

My heart and I P. Morrison, Chandos Concert Orch, S. Barry (6/85) (CHAN) Ⓓ **CHAN8362**
(6/85) (CHAN) ▭ **LBTD013**

My heart and I R. Tauber, orch (r1943)
(2/92) (LYRC) Ⓓ [2] **SRO830**

TAYLOR, (Joseph) Deems
(1885–1966) USA

The **King's Henchman– opera: 3 acts, Op. 19 (1927—New York) (Lib. Millay)**

Nay, Maccus, lay him down L. Tibbett, NY Met Op Orch, NY Met Op Chor, G. Setti (r1928)
(4/94) (RCA) Ⓓ [6] **09026 61580-2(3)**

Oh, Caesar, great wert thou!; Nay, Maccus, lay him down L. Tibbett, NY Met Op Chor, NY Met Op Orch, G. Setti (r1928)
(3/91) (PEAR) Ⓓ [2] **GEMMCDS9452**

TCHAIKOVSKY, Pyotr Il'yich
(1840–1893) Russia

The **Enchantress– opera: 4 acts (1887—St. Petersburg) (Lib. I Shpazhinsky)**

Ah, the image of that enchantress N. Shevelev, anon (r1901)
(6/93) (PEAR) Ⓓ [3] **GEMMCDS9007/9(2)**

Business, official duties D. Hvorostovsky, Rotterdam PO, V. Gergiev
(7/90) (PHIL) Ⓓ **426 740-2PH**

Looking down from Nizhni N. Ermolenko-Yuzhina, orch (r1910)
(6/93) (PEAR) Ⓓ [3] **GEMMCDS9001/3(2)**

Love duet H. Roswaenge, T. Lemnitz, Berlin St Op Orch, E. Baltzer (r1941: Ger)
(PREI) Ⓓ [2] **89211**

Polya's Arias from Acts 1 & 4. C. Farley, Sicilian SO, J. Serebrier (r1992)
(IMP) Ⓓ **MCD64**

The Prince's aria P. Lisitsian, Bolshoi Th Orch, A. Melik-Pashayev (r1960)
(8/93) (PREI) Ⓓ **89061**

Yuri's arioso G. Nelepp, Bolshoi Th Orch, S. Samosud (r c1950) (PREI) Ⓓ **89081**

Eugene Onegin– opera: 3 acts (1879—Moscow) (Lib. Pushkin)

EXCERPTS: 1. Introduction. ACT 1: 2. Have you not heard (Slikhali i vi za roschei glas nochnai); 3. My swift little feet ache (Bolyat moyi skori nozhenki); 4. One day across the bridge (Uzh kak po mostu, mostochku); 5. How I love to dream (Kak ya lyublyu pod zvuki pesen etikh); 6. 'One day across the bridge' ('Uzk kak po mostu, mostochki'); 7. Well, my frolicsome one (Nu ti, moya vostrushka); 8. Mesdames, I've taken the liberty (Mesdames! Ya na sebya vzyal smyelost); 9. Tell, which is Tatyana? (Skazhi, kororaya Tatyana?); 10. How happy, how happy I am! (Kak shchastliv, kak shchastilv ya!); 11. I love you (Ya lyublyu vas); 12. Ah, there you are! (A, vot i vi!); 13. Well, I've let my tongue run on! (Nu, zaboltalas ya!); 14. Let me perish, but first let me summon (Puskai pogibnu ya, no pryezde); 15. Ah, night is past (Akh, noch minula); 16. Pretty maidens, dear companions (Dyevitsi-krasavsti); 17. He's here! He's here! Yevgeni! (Zdyes on, zdyes on, Yevgeni!); 18. You wrote to me (Kogda bi zhizn domashnim krugom). ACT 2: 19. Waltz; 20. Well, what a surprise (Vot tak syurpriz!); 21. Have I deserved such riducule from you (Uzhel ya zasluzhil ot vas); 22. Please do not interrupt me (A cette fête convié); 23. Ladies and gentlemen (Messieurs, mesdames, mesta zanyat izvolte); 24a. Aren't you dancing, Lenski? (Ti ne tantsuyesh, Lenski?); 24b. Mazurka; 25. In your house! (V vashem dome!); 26. What's this? (Nu, shto zhe?); 27. Faint echo of my youth (Kuda, kuda, kuda vi udalilis—Lenski's aria); 28. Ah, here they are! (A, vot oni!). ACT 3: 29. Polonaise; 30. I'm bored here too (I zdyes mnye skuchno!); 31. Princess Greminia! Look! (Knyaginya Gremina! Smotrite!); 32. Everyone knows love on earth (Lyubvi vsye vozrasti pokorni—Gremin's aria); 33. So come, I'll present (Itak, poidyom, tebya predstavlyu ya); 34. Can this really be the same Tatyana? (Uzhel ta samaya Tatyana); 35. O, how distressed I am! (O! Kak mnye tyazhelo!); 36. Onegin! I was younger then (Onegin! Ya togda molozhe).

Eugene Onegin W. Brendel
Tatyana M. Freni
Lensky P. Dvorský
Olga Sandra Walker
Prince Gremin N. Ghiaurov
Larina J. Craft
Filipyevna G. Bean
Triquet J. Fryatt
Chicago City Ballet, Chicago Lyric Op Chor, Chicago Lyric Op Orch, B. Bartoletti, P.L. Samaritani
(CAST) ▣ **CVI2037**

Eugene Onegin B. Weikl
Tatyana T. Kubiak
Lensky S. Burrows
Olga J. Hamari
Prince Gremin N. Ghiaurov
Larina A. Reynolds
Filipyevna E. Hartle
Triquet M. Sénéchal
Zaretsky R. Van Allan
Captain W. Mason
John Alldis Ch, ROHO, G. Solti
(8/87) (DECC) Ⓓ [2] **417 413-2DH2**

Eugene Onegin Y. Mazurok
Tatyana T. Milashkina
Lensky V. Atlantov
Olga T. Sinyavskaya
Prince Gremin E. Nesterenko
Larina T. Tugarinova
Filipyevna L. Avdeyeva
Triquet L. Kuznetsov
Zaretsky V. Yaroslavtsev
Captain A. Yapridze
Bolshoi Th. Chor, Bolshoi Th. Orch, M. Ermler
(12/87) (OLYM) Ⓓ [2] **OCD115**

Eugene Onegin T. Allen
Tatiana M. Freni
Lensky N. Shicoff
Olga A.S. von Otter
Prince Gremin P. Burchuladze
Larina R. Lang
Filipievna R. Engert-Ely
Triquet M. Sénéchal
Captain J. Hartfiel
Leipzig Rad Chor, Staatskapelle Dresden, James Levine (r1987)
(3/89) (DG) Ⓓ [2] **423 959-2GH2**

Eugene Onegin Y. Mazurok
Tatyana A. Tomowa-Sintow
Lensky N. Gedda
Olga R. Troeva-Mircheva
Prince Gremin N. Ghiuselev
Larina S. Popangelova
Filipyevna M. Lilowa
Triquet M. Lecocq
Captain S. Georgiev
Zaretzky D. Stanchev
Sofia National Op Chor, Sofia Fest Orch, E. Tchakarov
(3/91) (SONY) Ⓓ [2] **S2K45539**

Eugene Onegin B. Weikl
Tatyana T. Kubiak
Lensky S. Burrows
Olga J. Hamari
Prince Gremin N. Ghiaurov
Larina A. Reynolds
Filipyevna E. Hartle
Triquet M. Sénéchal
Zaretsky R. Van Allan
Captain W. Mason
John Alldis Ch, ROHO, G. Solti, P. Weigl
(2/92) (DECC) ● **071 124-1DH**
(2/92) (DECC) ▣ **071 124-3DH**

Eugene Onegin D. Hvorostovsky
Tatyana N. Focile
Lensky N. Shicoff
Olga O. Borodina
Prince Gremin A. Anisimov
Larina Sarah Walker
Filipievna I. Arkhipova
Triquet F. Egerton
Captain H. Hennequin
Zaretsky S. Zadvorny
St Petersburg Chbr Ch, Paris Orch, S. Bychkov (r1990)
(12/93) (PHIL) Ⓓ [2] **438 235-2PH2**

Eugene Onegin P. Nortsov
Tatyana G. Zhukovskaya
Lensky S. Lemeshev
Olga B. Zlatogorova
Prince Gremin A. Pirogov
Larina M. Butienina
Filipyevna K. Antarova
Triquet I. Kovalenko
Zaretzky A. Yakhontov
Captain Y. Manchavin
Bolshoi Th Chor, Bolshoi Th Orch, V. Nebolsin (r1936)
(1/94) (DANT) Ⓓ [2] **LYS10/1**

Eugene Onegin T. Hampson
Tatyana K. Te Kanawa
Lensky N. Rosenshein
Olga P. Bardon
Prince Gremin J. Connell
Larina L. Finnie
Filipyevna E. Bainbridge
Triquet N. Gedda
Zaretsky; Captain R. Van Allan
WNO Chor, WNO Orch, C. Mackerras (r1992: Eng)
(4/94) (EMI) Ⓓ [2] **CDS5 55004-2**

Eugene Onegin E. Belov
Tatiana G. Vishnevskaya
Lensky S. Lemeshev
Olga L. Avdeyeva
Prince Gremin I. Petrov
Larina V. Petrova
Filipievna E. Verbitskaya
Triquet A. Sokolov
Zaretzky I. Mikhailov
Captain G. Pankov
Bolshoi Th Chor, Bolshoi Th Orch, B. Khaikin (r1955)
(12/94) (MELO) Ⓓ [2] **74321 17090-2**

Ballet version Canada Nat Ballet (arr/orch Stolze) (MCEG) ▣ **VVD343**

Excs Y. Mazurok, T. Milashkina, V. Atlantov, Bolshoi Th Chor, Bolshoi Th Orch, M. Ermler
(CLTS) ▭ **CML2037**

1. Staatskapelle Dresden, James Levine
(DG) Ⓓ [2] **447 364-2GDB2**

1, 11, 14, 27-29, 32, 35, 36. M. Freni, A.S. von Otter, T. Allen, N. Shicoff, P. Burchuladze, J. Hartfiel, Leipzig Rad Chor, Staatskapelle Dresden, James Levine (r1987)
(DG) Ⓓ [10] **431 601-2GCE10**

1, 14, 18, 19, 29, 34, 36. L. Shernikh, A. Nenadovsky, Moscow RSO, V. Fedoseyev, R. Greenberg (PION) ● **PLMCB00501**

1, 2, 10, 11, 14, 17, 18, 20, 27-29, 32, 35, 36. Sarah Walker, N. Focile, O. Borodina, I. Arkhipova, D. Hvorostovsky, N. Shicoff, A. Anisimov, St Petersburg Chbr Ch, Paris Orch, S. Bychkov (r1992) (PHIL) Ⓓ **442 384-2PH**

1, 2, 10, 11, 14, 17-19, 26-28, 32, 35, 36. T. Allen, M. Freni, N. Shicoff, A.S. von Otter, P. Burchuladze, R. Lang, R. Engert-Ely, J. Hartfiel, Leipzig Rad Chor, Staatskapelle Dresden, James Levine (r1987) (DG) Ⓓ **445 467-2GMH**

2. M. Michailova, E. Zbrueva, orch (r1910)
(PEAR) Ⓓ [3] **GEMMCDS9111(2)**

3, 11. Bolshoi Th Chor, Bolshoi Th Orch, A. Chistiakov (CDM) Ⓓ **LDC288 022**

6, 16. Bulgarian Nat Ch, Sofia PO, R. Raichev
(FORL) Ⓓ **FF060**

9. A. Pendachanska, Sofia SO, M. Angelov (r1994) (CAPR) Ⓓ **10 706**

9. K. Te Kanawa, WNO Orch, C. Mackerras (r1992) (EMI) Ⓓ **CDM5 65578-2**

11. L. Sobinov, orch (r1910)
(PEAR) Ⓓ **GEMMCD9129**

11. D. Smirnov, orch (r1913)
(6/93) (PEAR) Ⓓ [3] **GEMMCDS9004/6(1)**

11. L. Sobinov, orch (r1911)
(6/94) (MMOI) Ⓓ **CDMOIR422**

11, 27 (two vers) L. Sobinov, anon (r1901)
(6/93) (PEAR) Ⓓ [3] **GEMMCDS9997/9(1)**

11, 27. A. Labinsky, orch, B. Seidler-Winkler (r1905)
(6/93) (PEAR) Ⓓ [3] **GEMMCDS9001/3(1)**

14. H. Field, M. Silver, Swedish RSO, Vladimir Ashkenazy (TELD) ● **9031-76372-6**
(TELD) ▣ **9031-76372-3**

14. N. Davrath, Vienna St Op Orch, V. Golschmann (r1960s)
(VANG) Ⓓ [2] **08.9081.72**

14. C. Farley, Melbourne SO, J. Serebrier
(IMP) Ⓓ **PCD1055**

14. C. Farley, Melbourne SO, J. Serebrier
(IMP) Ⓓ [3] **TCD1070**

14 (pt) M. Michailova, E. Zbrueva, orch (r1911)
(PEAR) Ⓓ [3] **GEMMCDS9111(2)**

14. M. Michailova, orch (r1906/7)
(PEAR) Ⓓ [3] **GEMMCDS9111(2)**

14. Brno St PO, J. Serebrier (r1994)
(IMG) Ⓓ **IMGCD1617**

14. E. Schwarzkopf, LSO, A. Galliera (Ger) (10/88) (EMI) ⓓ **CDM7 69501-2**
14. L. Popp, Munich RO, S. Soltesz (r1987) (4/89) (EMI) ⓓ **CDC7 49319-2**
14 (pt) C. Muzio, orch (r1920: Ital) (5/90) (BOGR) ⓓ [2] **BIM705-2**
14. E. Hannan, LPO, S. Edwards (1/92) (EMIN) ⓓ **CD-EMX2187**
14(pt) Lotte Lehmann, orch (Ger: r1917) (6/92) (PREI) ⓓ [3] **89302**
14. J. Hammond, RLPO, C. Lambert (r1943: Eng) (12/92) (TEST) ⓓ **SBT1013**
14(pt) C. Muzio, orch (r1920: Ital) (1/94) (ROMO) ⓓ [2] **81005-2**
14 (pt) Lotte Lehmann, orch (r c1917) (6/94) (MMOI) ⓓ **CDMOIR422**
14, 25. C. Farley, Melbourne SO, J. Serebrier (r1980) (IMP) ⓓ **MCD64**
18. A. Ivanov, E. Kruglikova, Bolshoi Th Orch, A. Orlov (r1948) (PREI) ⓓ **89067**
18. H. Schlusnus, Berlin St Op Orch, L. Blech (r1934: Ger) (PREI) ⓓ [2] **89212**
18. H. Schlusnus, orch (r1925: Ger) (PREI) ⓓ **89110**
18. J. Hynninen, Estonian SO, E. Klas (4/90) (ONDI) ⓓ **ODE731-2**
18. H. Schlusnus, Berlin St Op Orch, L. Blech (Ger: r1934) (9/90) (PREI) ⓓ **89006**
18. M. Battistini, anon (r1902: Ital) (10/92) (NIMB) ⓓ **NI7831** (10/92) (NIMB) ⊟ **NC7831**
18 (pt) N. Shevelev, anon (r1901) (6/93) (PEAR) ⓓ [3] **GEMMCDS9007/9(2)**
18. P. Lisitsian, Bolshoi Th Orch, A. Melik-Pashayev (r1960) (8/93) (PREI) ⓓ **89061**
18. E. Giraldoni, anon (r1906: Ital) (4/94) (EMI) ⓓ [3] **CHS7 64860-2(1)**
18, 34. D. Hvorostovsky, Rotterdam PO, V. Gergiev (7/90) (PHIL) ⓓ **426 740-2PH**
18, 35. M. Karakash, E. Popova, orch (r1913) (PEAR) ⓓ [3] **GEMMCDS9111(2)**
19. RPO, T. Beecham (CFP) ⓓ **CD-CFP4277**
19. Staatskapelle Dresden, H. Vonk (LASE) ⓓ **15 610** (LASE) ⊟ **79 610**
19. RPO, T. Beecham (r1959) (EMI) ⓓ **CDM7 63412-2**
19. BRSO, F. Fricsay (BELA) ⓓ **450 139-2** (BELA) ⊟ **450 139-4**
19. Houston SO, S. Comissiona (PRO) ⓓ **CDS584**
19. RPO, T. Beecham (r1959) (EMI) ⓓ **CDC7 54778-2**
19. RPO, T. Beecham (r1959) (EMI) ⓓ [5] **CZS7 67700-2**
19. D. Popovich, D. Startz, Belgrade Nat Op Chor, Belgrade Nat Op Orch, O. Danon (r1970s) (BELA) ⓓ **450 117-2** (BELA) ⊟ **450 117-4**
19. Slovak PO, K. Redel (r1990) (PIER) ⓓ **PV730023**
19. NYPO, K. Masur (pp1994) (TELD) ⓓ **4509-94571-2**
19, 29. Staatskapelle Dresden, H. Vonk (LASE) ⓓ **15 504** (LASE) ⊟ **79 504**
19, 29. Philadelphia, E. Ormandy (SONY) ⓓ **SBK47657**
19, 29. Minneapolis SO, A. Dorati (MERC) ⓓ **434 305-2MM**
19, 29. Bolshoi SO, A. Lazarev (ERAT) ⓓ **2292-45964-2**
19, 29. S. Burrows, B. Weikl, John Alldis Ch, ROHO, G. Solti (r1974) (DECC) ⓓ **436 406-2DWO** (DECC) ⊟ **436 406-4DWO**
19, 29. RPO, Y. Simonov (r1994) (TRIN) ⓓ **TRP015** (TRIN) ⊟ **MCTRP015**
19, 29. BPO, H. von Karajan (12/86) (DG) ⓓ **419 176-2GH**
19, 29. BPO, H. von Karajan (r1966) (4/88) (DG) ⓓ **415 855-2GGA**
19, 29. Kirov Th Orch, V. Gergiev (r1993; includes bonus sampler CD) (7/95) (PHIL) ⓓ **442 775-2PH** (7/95) (PHIL) ⊟ **442 775-4PH**
19, 29, 31b ROHO, Colin Davis (11/84) (PHIL) ⓓ **411 448-2PH**
25. D. Smirnov, orch (r1912) (6/93) (PEAR) ⓓ [3] **GEMMCDS9004/6(1)**
25. D. Smirnov, orch (r1912) (6/94) (MMOI) ⓓ **CDMOIR422**
26. A. Milcheva, Plovdiv PO, E. Tchakarov (r1970s) (FORL) ⓓ **UCD16743**
27. J. Björling, Stockholm Royal Op Orch, N. Grevillius (r1957: Swed) (RCA) ⊟ **GK85277**
27. A. Dermota, Berlin St Op Orch, A. Rother (r1950s: Ger) (PREI) ⓓ **90022**
27. B.S. Rosenberg, Budapest Concert Orch, J. Acs (pp1990) (OLYM) ⓓ **OCD370**
27. F. Wunderlich, Bavarian St Op Orch, O. Gerdes (Ger) (DG) ⓓ [5] **435 145-2GX5(1)**
27. P. Domingo, RPO, E. Downes (RCA) ⓓ [2] **GD60866** (RCA) ⊟ [2] **GK60866**
27. O. Harnoy, LPO, C. Mackerras (arr vc/orch: J Harnoy) (RCA) ꝏ **09026 60758-5**
27. J. Schmidt, orch, F. Weissmann (r1932: Ger) (EMI) ⓓ [2] **CHS7 64673-2**
27. D. Smirnov, orch (r1921) (PEAR) ⓓ **GEMMCD9106**
27. H. Roswaenge, Berlin St Op Orch, B. Seidler-Winkler (r1940: Ger) (PREI) ⓓ [2] **89211**
27. W. Widdop, orch, L. Collingwood (r1926: Eng) (PEAR) ⓓ **GEMMCD9112**
27. D. Smirnov, orch (r1921) (PEAR) ⓓ **GEMMCD9129**
27. R. Tauber, orch (r1923: Ger) (PEAR) ⓓ **GEMMCD9145**
27. G. Martinelli, orch, J. Pasternack (r1921: Ital) (10/89) (NIMB) ⓓ **NI7804** (NIMB) ⊟ **NC7804**
27. J. Patzak, orch, M. Gurlitt (Ger: r1929) (3/90) (PEAR) ⓓ **GEMMCD9383**
27. F. Marconi, S. Cottone (r1903: Ital) (10/90) (SYMP) ⓓ **SYMCD1069**
27. E. Caruso, orch, J. Pasternack (r1916: French) (7/91) (RCA) ⓓ [12] **GD60495(5)**
27. E. Caruso, orch, J. Pasternack (French: r1916) (10/91) (PEAR) ⓓ [3] **EVC4(1)**
27. R. Tauber, orch, K. Besl (r1923: Ger) (3/92) (EMI) ⓓ **CDH7 64029-2**
27. O. Harnoy, LPO, C. Mackerras (arr vc/orch: J Harnoy) (10/92) (RCA) ⓓ **RD60758**
27. R. Tauber, orch, K. Besl (r1923: Ger) (12/92) (NIMB) ⓓ **NI7830** (12/92) (NIMB) ⊟ **NC7830**
27. F. Wunderlich, Bavarian St Op Orch, O. Gerdes (Ger) (5/93) (DG) ⓓ **431 110-2GB**
27. D. Yuzhin, anon (r1902) (6/93) (PEAR) ⓓ [3] **GEMMCDS9001/3(1)**
27. D. Smirnov, orch (r1909) (6/93) (PEAR) ⓓ [3] **GEMMCDS9004/6(1)**
27. A. Bogdanovich, anon (r1903) (6/93) (PEAR) ⓓ [3] **GEMMCDS9007/9(1)**
27. I. Alchevsky, anon (r1900s) (7/93) (SYMP) ⓓ **SYMCD1105**
27. A. Piccaver, orch (r1920: Ger) (8/93) (PREI) ⓓ **89060**
27. C. Kullman, orch (r1935: Ger) (11/93) (PREI) ⓓ **89057**
27. F. Wunderlich, Bavarian St Orch, M. von Zallinger (r1962: Ger) (12/93) (NIMB) ⓓ **NI7851**
27. G. Martinelli, orch, J. Pasternack (r1921; Ital) (4/94) (RCA) ⓓ [6] **09026 61580-2(2)**
27. P. Domingo, Philh, R. Behr (r1993) (4/94) (EMI) ⓓ **CDC5 55018-2**
27. C. Kullman, Vienna St Op Orch, H. Reichenberger (pp1934: Ger) (7/94) (SCHW) ⓓ [2] **314512**
27. D. Smirnov, orch (r1909) (9/94) (NIMB) ⓓ **NI7856**
27. E. Caruso, orch (r1916: French) (7/95) (NIMB) ⓓ **NI7866**
28b (pt) F. Wunderlich, H. Prey, Bavarian St Orch, M. von Zallinger (Ger) (EMI) ⓓ [3] **CZS7 62993-2**
29. Philadelphia, E. Ormandy (IMP) ⓓ [2] **DUET 8CD**
29. Leningrad PO, Y. Temirkanov (pp1990) (RCA) ⓓ **RD60739**
29. Leningrad PO, Y. Temirkanov (pp1990) (RCA) ꝏ **09026 60739-5**
29. Bournemouth SO, A. Litton (r1988) (VIRG) ⓓ [3] **VMT7 59699-2**
29. NYPO, L. Bernstein (r1971) (SONY) ⓓ **SMK47636**
29. Kirov Th Orch, V. Gergiev (PHIL) ◖ **070 166-1PH** (PHIL) ▣ **070 166-3PH**
29. Bolshoi SO, A. Lazarev (ERAT) ⓓ **4509-96529-2** (ERAT) ⊟ **4509-96529-4**
29. Baltimore SO, D. Zinman (r1990) (TELA) ⓓ **CD80378**
29. Boston Pops, A. Fiedler (r1959) (RCA) ⓓ **09026 68132-2**
29. Cleveland Orch, C. von Dohnányi (r1986) (10/87) (TELA) ⓓ **CD80130**
29. J. Patzak, Berlin St Op Orch, Wolfgang Martin (r1936: Ger) (6/94) (MMOI) ⓓ **CDMOIR422**
32. P. Gluboky, Soviet Cinema Orch, E. Khachaturian (r1990) (CDM) ⓓ [2] **LDC288 005/6** (CDM) ⊟ **KC488 005**
32. N. Ghiaurov, ROHO, G. Solti (DECC) ⓓ **433 064-2DWO**
32. I. Te Wiata, BBC SO, M. Sargent (pp1961: Eng) (KIWI) ⓓ **CDSLD-82**
32. A. Kipnis, orch (r1921) (PEAR) ⓓ **GEMMCD9122**
32. M. Salminen, Lahti SO, E. Klas (8/92) (BIS) ⓓ **BIS-CD520**
32. A. Kipnis, Victor SO, N. Berezowski (r1945) (9/92) (RCA) ⓓ **GD60522**
32. M. Reizen, Bolshoi Th Orch, A. Melik-Pashayev (r1948) (12/92) (PREI) ⓓ **89059**
32. L. Sibiriakov, orch (r1906) (6/93) (PEAR) ⓓ [3] **GEMMCDS9001/3(2)**
32. D. Bukhtoyarov, anon (r1901) (6/93) (PEAR) ⓓ [3] **GEMMCDS9001/3(1)**
32. B. Christoff, Philh, W. Schüchter (r1952) (6/93) (EMI) ⓓ **CDH7 64252-2**
32. K. Borg, Berlin RSO, H. Stein (r1963) (12/94) (FINL) ⓓ [3] **4509-95606-2**
32. V. Kastorsky, orch (r1908) (3/95) (NIMB) ⓓ **NI7865**
34. F. Wunderlich, Berlin SO, H. Stein (Ger) (EMI) ⓓ [3] **CZS7 62993-2**
34. G. Baklanoff, orch (r1918) (6/94) (MMOI) ⓓ **CDMOIR422**

Iolanta– opera: 1 act (1892—St Petersburg) (Lib. M. Tchaikovsky)

Iolanta	G. Vishnevskaya
Vaudémont	N. Gedda
Robert	W. Groenroos
King René	D. Petkov
Ibn Hakia	T. Krause
Martha	V. Cortez
Alméric	J. Anderson
Brigitte	T. Gedda
Laura	C. Gaetano
Bertrand	F. Dumont

France Groupe Vocal, Paris Orch, M. Rostropovich (pp1984) (5/86) (ERAT) ⓓ [2] **2292-45973-2**
Duke Robert's aria M. Maksakov, orch (r c1908) (6/94) (MMOI) ⓓ **CDMOIR422**
Iolanta's arioso C. Farley, Melbourne SO, J. Serebrier (r1980) (IMP) ⓓ **MCD64**
Iolanta's arioso L. Lipkowska, anon (r1912) (6/94) (MMOI) ⓓ **CDMOIR422**
O God, if I have sinned A. Safiulin, Soviet Cinema Orch, E. Khachaturian (r1990) (CDM) ⓓ [2] **LDC288 005/6** (CDM) ⊟ **KC488 005**
O God, if I have sinned L. Sibiriakov, anon (r1906) (6/93) (PEAR) ⓓ [3] **GEMMCDS9001/3(2)**
Who can compare with my Mathilde? D. Hvorostovsky, Rotterdam PO, V. Gergiev (7/90) (PHIL) ⓓ **426 740-2PH**
Who can compare? V. Kastorsky, orch (r c1910) (6/94) (MMOI) ⓓ **CDMOIR422**

The Maid of Orleans– opera: 4 acts (1881—St Petersburg) (Lib. cpsr)

EXCERPTS. ACT 1: 1a. Oui, Dieu le veut!; 1b. Adieu, fôrets (Joan's aria).

Joan of Arc	N. Rautio
King Charles VII	O. Kulko
Agnès Sorel	M. Gavrilova
Dunois	M. Krutikov
Lionel	V. Redkin
Archbishop	G. Nikolsky
Raymond	A. Mishenkin
Bertrand	M. Mikhailov
Soldier	A. Babikin
Angel	Z. Smolyaninova

Bolshoi Th Chor, Bolshoi SO, A. Lazarev, B. Pokrovsky (r1993) (TELD) ◖ **4509-94191-6**
Joan's Arias from Acts 2 & 4. C. Farley, Sicilian SO, J. Serebrier (r1992) (IMP) ⓓ **MCD64**
1. C. Farley, Melbourne SO, J. Serebrier (r1980) (IMP) ⓓ **MCD64**
1. O. Ouroussov, Henry Wood (Eng: r1908) (10/92) (SYMP) ⓓ **SYMCD1093**
1b J. Norman, Leningrad PO, Y. Temirkanov (pp1990) (RCA) ⓓ **RD60739**

1b J. Norman, Leningrad PO, Y. Temirkanov (pp1990) (RCA) OO **09026 60739-5**
1b Z. Dolukhanova, Moscow PO, G. Stolarov (pp1954) (RUSS) Ⓓ **RDCD15023**
1b B. Fassbaender, Stuttgart RSO, H. Graf (11/86) (ORFE) Ⓓ **C096841A**
1b S. Jurinac, Philh, L. Collingwood (Ger: r1950) (1/90) (EMI) Ⓓ **CDH7 63199-2**
1b M. Jeritza, orch (r1926: Fr) (4/94) (PREI) Ⓓ **89079**
1b M. Jeritza, orch (r1927: Fr) (6/94) (MMOI) Ⓓ **CDMOIR422**

Mazeppa– opera: 3 acts (1884—Moscow) (Lib. cpsr & V Burenin, after Pushkin)
EXCERPTS: 1. Introduction. ACT ONE: 2a. I weave my fragrant garland; 2b. Greetings Maria, greetings, my beauty; 3a. You love the songs, dear companions; 3b. Maria...Oh! You frightened me!; 4. Well, Vasily, you honour me; 5. There is no bridge here; 6. Hopak (Cossack Dance); 7. That's fine, I like that; 8a. Mazeppa, I'm distressed by what you say; 8b. You crazy old man, tell me; 8c. The shameless, disgraceful old man, how could he?; 8d. Father! O Hetman! Cease your quarrelling; 9. As the storm brings clouds over the sky; 10a. Abandon your grief, Kochubey; 10b. But it is time we gave warning of the hetman's intrigues; 10c. Send me, send me to the Tsar!. ACT TWO: 11a. So this is the reward for my information; 11b. It's you, cruel man; 11c. No, you are not mistaken; 12a. How still is the Ukrainian night; 12b. Well?; 13. O Maria, Maria; 14a. My dearest love; 14b. My dear, you are unjust!; 14c. Would I, at my age; 14d. O my dearest, you will be Tsar of our homeland; 15a. How the stars twinkle in the sky; 15b. You alone can assuage their fury; 16. Will it be soon?; 17a. Hey-ho, fiddle-de-dee; 17b. My friend, Let us offer up for the last time. ACT THREE: 18. The Battle of Poltava; 19a. In bloody battle, on the field of honour; 19b. Here days passed by in happy succession; 20a. I hear in the distance the clatter of horses hooves; 20b. You destroyer of sacred innocence; 21a. Unhappy man!; 21b. Oh hush, hush, hush, my dear; 21c. Let's run away, I hear a noise; 22a. The old man's gone, how my heart beats; 22b. Sleep my baby, my pretty.

Mazeppa S. Leiferkus
Maria G. Gorchakova
Kochubey A. Kocherga
Liubov L. Dyadkova
Andrei S. Larin
Orlik M. Pederson
Iskra R. Margison
Drunken Cossack H. Zednik
Stockholm Royal Op Chor, Gothenburg SO, N. Järvi (r1993) (11/94) (DG) Ⓓ [3] **439 906-2GH3**

6. Dallas SO, E. Mata (PRO) Ⓓ **CDS539**
6. Dallas SO, Anon (cond) (WORD) Ⓓ **FCD7406**
6. Hallé, H. Harty (r1932) (BEUL) Ⓓ **1PD4**
6. LSO, C. Mackerras (r1961) (MERC) Ⓓ **434 352-2MM**
6. Cincinnati SO, E. Kunzel (12/83) (TELA) Ⓓ **CD80041**
6. Leipzig Gewandhaus, K. Masur (r1991) (5/93) (TELD) Ⓓ **9031-76456-2**
6, 18. LSO, G. Simon (7/84) (CHAN) Ⓓ [2] **CHAN8310/1**
6, 18. LSO, G. Simon (r1981) (7/94) (CHAN) Ⓓ **CHAN9190**
11c A. Ivanov, Bolshoi Th Orch, S. Samosud (r1947) (PREI) Ⓓ **89067**
11c A. Ivanov, orch (r1947) (4/92) (EMI) Ⓓ [7] **CHS7 69741-2(6)**
13. A. Orda, Polish RSO, S. Rachoń (bp1964) (SYMP) Ⓓ **SYMCD1117**
13. D. Hvorostovsky, Rotterdam PO, V. Gergiev (7/90) (PHIL) Ⓓ **426 740-2PH**
13. P. Lisitsian, Bolshoi Th Orch, A. Melik-Pashayev (r1960) (8/93) (PREI) Ⓓ **89061**
15a, 22b C. Farley, Sicilian SO, J. Serebrier (r1992) (IMP) Ⓓ **MCD64**
18. Bolshoi Th Orch, A. Chistiakov (r1992) (CDM) Ⓓ **LDC288 053**
22b N. Milstein, G. Pludermacher (pp1986: arr vn/pf) (5/95) (TELD) Ⓓ **4509-95998-2**

Oprichnik, '(The) Guardsman'– opera: 4 acts (1874—St Petersburg) (Lib. cpsr)
Danses
I swear before God N. Figner, anon (r1901) (6/93) (PEAR) Ⓓ [3] **GEMMCDS9997/9(1)**
Little nightingale M. Michailova, orch (r1906) (PEAR) Ⓓ [3] **GEMMCDS9111(2)**
Little nightingale N. Ermolenko-Yuzhina, orch (r1911) (6/93) (PEAR) Ⓓ [3] **GEMMCDS9001/3(2)**
Natalia's Arias from Acts 1 & 3. C. Farley, Sicilian SO, J. Serebrier (r1992) (IMP) Ⓓ **MCD64**
Overture National SO, A. Fistoulari (r1944) (5/95) (DUTT) Ⓓ **CDK1200**
ROHO, Colin Davis (11/84) (PHIL) Ⓓ **411 448-2PH**

The **Queen of Spades, 'Pique Dame'– opera: 3 acts (1890—St. Petersburg) (Lib. cpsr and M. Tchaikovsky)**
EXCERPTS: 1. Introduction. ACT 1: 2. Shine, sun, bright!; 3a. How did the play end yesterday; 3b. I do not know her name; 3c. If this is the case, we must get to work!; 4a. At last heaven has sent us a sunny day!; 4b. But are you sure that she's not noticed you?; 4c. Happy day, I bless you; 4d. Tell us, whom are you marrying?; 5. I feel afraid! There again he is; 6a. What an old witch, that Countess; 6b. Once at Versailles; 7. Se non è vero; 8. 'Tis evening...the cloudy spaces darken; 9a. Fascinating!and delightful!; 9b. Yes, that's it...'My darling friends'; 9c. Come on, bright-eyed Mashenka; 10. What a noise you are making; 11a. It is time now to break up your party; 11b. You need not shut the door, leave it open; 11c. What am I crying for, what is it?; 11d. Stay, I beg of you!; 11e. Forgive me, loveliest of creatures; 11f. Liza! Open the door; 11g. ...he who, impelled by burning passion. ACT 2: 12a. Entr'acte; 12b. In joy and merriment; 13a. The host asks his worthy guests; 13b. I love you beyond all measure; 14. After the performance wait for me in the hall; 15a. In the deep shadows; 15b. Dance of the Shepherds and Shepherdesses; 15c. My tender friend, my darling shepherd; 15d. How sweet you are my beauty!; 16a. 'He who is impelled by burning passion...'; 16b. The Empress! Her Majesty!; 17a. Yes, everything is just as she said; 17b. And how our noble benefactress enjoys herself; 17c. Enough of your flatteries!; 17d. Je crains de lui parles la nuit; 18a. Don't be frightened!; 18b. What is all that noise? ACT 3: 19a. Entr'acte; 19b. I do not believe you intended the Countess's death; 20a. It is terrifying!; 20b. I have come to you against my will; 21a. It is close on midnight already; 21b. Ah! I am weary with sorrow; 22a. Ah, what if midnight chimes answer; 22b. Yes, I have come, my darling; 23a. Drink and make merry!; 23b. Make your bids!; 24a. If darling girls could fly like birds; 24b. When the weather was wet; 25a. And now, gentlemen, to business; 25b. What is our life? A game!; 25c. No more play!; 25d. Prince! Prince! forgive me!; 25e. Lord, pardon him!.

Herman Y. Marusin
Lisa N. Gustafson
Countess F. Palmer
Tomsky S. Leiferkus
Yeletsky D. Kharitonov
Pauline M-A. Todorovitch
Chekalinsky G. Matheson-Bruce
Surin A. Slater
Chaplitsky R. Burt
Major-domo G. Pogson
Narumov C. Thornton-Holmes
Governess E. Hartle
Masha R. Tovey
Glyndebourne Fest Chor, LPO, A. Davis, G. Vick (r1992) (PION) ◐ **PLMCC00841**

Herman W. Ochman
Lisa S. Evstatieva
Countess P. Dilova
Count Tomsky I. Konsulov
Prince Yeletsky Y. Mazurok
Chekalinsky Angel Petkov
Surin P. Petrov
Chaplitsky; Major-Domo M. Popov
Narumov S. Georgiev
Polina S. Toczyska
Governess W. Katsarova
Masha R. Bareva
Prilepa E. Stoyanova
Gouslarche Boys' Ch, Svetoslav Obretenov Nat Chor, Sofia Fest Orch, E. Tchakarov (12/90) (SONY) Ⓓ [3] **S3K45720**

Herman V. Atlantov
Lisa M. Freni
Countess M. Forrester
Count Tomsky S. Leiferkus
Prince Yeletsky D. Hvorostovsky
Pauline Katherine Ciesinsk
Chekalinsky E. Gavazz
Surin J. Rodescu
Chaplitsky D. Petersen
Major-domo R. Clemen
Narumov J. Chamine
Governess J. Taylo
Masha D. Labelle
American Boychoir, Tanglewood Fest Chor, Boston SO, S. Ozawa (11/92) (RCA) Ⓓ [3] **09026 60992-2**

Herman G. Grigorian
Lisa M. Guleginа
Countess I. Arkhipova
Count Tomsky N. Putilin
Prince Yeletsky V. Chernov
Pauline O. Borodina
Chekalinsky V. Solodovnikov
Surin S. Alexashkin
Chapiltsky E. Boitsov
Major domo N. Gassiev
Narumov G. Bezebenkov
Governess L. Filatova
Masha T. Filimonova
Kirov Th Chor, Kirov Th Orch, V. Gergiev (r1992) (10/93) (PHIL) Ⓓ [3] **438 141-2PH3**

Herman G. Grigorian
Lisa M. Guleginа
Countess L. Filatova
Count Tomsky S. Leiferkus
Prince Yeletsky A. Gergalov
Pauline O. Borodina
Chekalinsky V. Solodovnikov
Surin S. Alexashkin
Chaplitsky E. Boitsov
Major-domo N. Gassiev
Narumov G. Bezebenkov
Governess E. Perlasova
Masha T. Filimonova
Kirov Th Chor, Kirov Th Orch, V. Gergiev, Y. Temirkanov (6/94) (PHIL) ◐ [2] **070 434-1PH2**
(6/94) (PHIL) ▣ **070 434-3PH**

Herman V. Atlantov
Lisa T. Milashkina
Countess V. Levko
Count Tomsky V. Valaitis
Prince Yeletsky A. Fedoseyev
Pauline G. Borisova
Chekalinsky A. Sokolov
Surin V. Yaroslavtsev
Chaplitsky V. Vlasov
Major-domo K. Baskov
Narumov Y. Dementiev
Governess N. Grigorieva
Masha N. Lebedeva
Bolshoi Th Chor, Bolshoi Th Orch, M. Ermler (r1974) (10/94) (MELO) Ⓓ [3] **74321 17091-2**

Herman N. Khanayev
Lisa X. Derzhinskaya
Countess F. Petrova
Count Tomsky A. Baturin
Prince Yeletsky P. Selivanov
Pauline N. Obukhova
Chekalinsky S. Ostroumov
Surin Y. Manchavin
Chaplitsky M. Novoyenin
Narumov K. Terekin
Governess L. Stavrovskaya
Macha N. Chubienko
Bolshoi Th Chor, Bolshoi Th Orch, S. Samosud (r1937) (8/95) (DANT) Ⓓ [3] **LYS013/5**

Excs N. Khanayev, A. Baturin, P. Nortsov, K. Terekin, B. Zlatogorova, X. Derzhinskaya, S. Ostroumov, Y. Manchavin, M. Novoyenin, M. Maksakova, V. Barsova, V. Politkovsky, Bolshoi Th Chor, Bolshoi Th Orch, S. Samosud (r1942) (8/95) (DANT) Ⓓ [3] **LYS013/5**
Suite C. Lindberg, R. Pöntinen (arr Lindberg) (BIS) Ⓓ **BIS-CD47**
1, 3b, 6b, 8, 9b, 11c-e, 13b, 17a-d, 21b, 22a, b, 24a, b, 25b-d M. Gulegina, T. Filimonova, I. Arkhipova, O. Borodina, G. Grigorian, V. Solodovnikov, E. Boitsov, N. Putilin, V. Chernov, S. Alexashkin, G. Bezebenkov, Kirov Th Chor, Kirov Th Orch, V. Gergiev (r1992) (PHIL) Ⓓ **442 439-2PH**
3b, 11e, 25b G. Nelepp, Bolshoi Th Orch, V. Nebolsin (r c1950) (PREI) Ⓓ **8908**
3b, 25b G. Nelepp, Bolshoi Th Chor, Bolshoi Th Orch, S. Samosud (r1940s) (8/95) (DANT) Ⓓ [3] **LYS013/5**

6b A. Didur, anon (r1906)
(4/94) (EMI) Ⓓ [3] **CHS7 64860-2(2)**
6b, 24a A. Didur, anon (r1906: Pol)
(1/94) (CLUB) Ⓓ **CL99-089**
7(pt) E. Vitting, orch (r1913)
(3/95) (NIMB) Ⓓ **NI7865**
8. J. Zoon, H. de Vries, London Studio SO (arr Vrijens) (PHIL) Ⓓ **438 940-2PH**
8, 15c M. Michailova, K. Tugarinova, anon (r1905) (PEAR) Ⓓ [3] **GEMMCDS9111(1)**
8, 15c, 21a E. Destinn, M. Duchêne, orch, W.B Rogers (r1915: Ger/Fr)
(12/94) (SUPR) Ⓓ [12] **11 2136-2(5)**
8, 21a E. Destinn, M. Duchêne, orch, W.B. Rogers (r1915: Ger)
(11/93) (ROMO) Ⓓ [2] **81002-2**
9a, 23a Bulgarian Nat Ch, Sofia PO, R. Raichev
(FORL) Ⓓ **FF060**
9b A. Panina, anon (r1907)
(6/93) (PEAR) Ⓓ [3] **GEMMCDS9001/3(2)**
9b E. Zbrueva, anon (r1907)
(6/93) (PEAR) Ⓓ [3] **GEMMCDS9004/6(2)**
9b E. Destinn, M. Duchêne, orch, W.B. Rogers (r1915: Fr) (11/93) (ROMO) Ⓓ [2] **81002-2**
11b, 25b J. Rogatchewsky, orch (r1928: Fr)
(6/94) (MMOI) Ⓓ **CDMOIR422**
11c, 21a C. Farley, Melbourne SO, J. Serebrier (r1980) (IMP) Ⓓ **MCD64**
11d, 11e, 11g F. Wunderlich, M. Muszely, Bavarian St Orch, M. von Zallinger (Ger)
(EMI) Ⓓ [3] **CZS7 62993-2**
11e N. Figner, anon (r1901)
(6/93) (PEAR) Ⓓ [3] **GEMMCDS9997/9(1)**
11e A. Davidov, anon (r1902)
(6/93) (PEAR) Ⓓ [3] **GEMMCDS9007/9(1)**
11e, 25b D. Smirnov, orch, J. Harrison (r1923)
(PEAR) Ⓓ **GEMMCD9106**
11e, 25b D. Smirnov, orch, J. Harrison (r1923)
(6/93) (PEAR) Ⓓ [3] **GEMMCDS9004/6(2)**
13b H. Choi, Moscow PO, D. Kitaienko (pp1990)
(TELD) ▣ **9031-72674-3**
13b D. Hvorostovsky, Boston SO, S. Ozawa
(RCA) Ⓓ **09026 61440-2**
(RCA) ▭ **09026 61440-4**
13b M. Karakash, orch (r1913)
(PEAR) Ⓓ [3] **GEMMCDS9111(2)**
13b H. Schlusnus, Berlin St Op Orch, A. Melichar (r1932: Ger) (PREI) Ⓓ [2] **89212**
13b J. Hynninen, Estonian SO, E. Klas
(4/90) (ONDI) Ⓓ **ODE731-2**
13b D. Hvorostovsky, Rotterdam PO, V. Gergiev
(7/90) (PHIL) Ⓓ **426 740-2PH**
13b H. Schlusnus, Berlin St Op Orch, A. Melichar (r1932: Ger) (9/90) (PREI) Ⓓ **89006**
13b N. Shevelev, anon (r1901)
(6/93) (PEAR) Ⓓ [3] **GEMMCDS9007/9(2)**
13b P. Lisitsian, Bolshoi Th Orch, A. Melik-Pashayev (r1952) (8/93) (PREI) Ⓓ **89061**
13b H. Schlusnus, Berlin St Op Orch, A. Melichar (r1932: Ger)
(6/94) (MMOI) Ⓓ **CDMOIR422**
13b M. Karakash, orch (r1913)
(3/95) (NIMB) Ⓓ **NI7865**
15c M. Michailova, K. Tugarinova, anon (r c1905) (6/94) (MMOI) Ⓓ **CDMOIR422**
15c M. Kovalenko, E. Zbrueva, orch (r1910)
(3/95) (NIMB) Ⓓ **NI7865**
17d A. Panina, orch (r1907)
(6/93) (PEAR) Ⓓ [3] **GEMMCDS9001/3(2)**
21a D. Voigt, Moscow PO, D. Kitaienko (pp1990)
(TELD) ▣ **9031-72674-3**
21a N. Davrath, Vienna St Op Orch, V. Golschmann (r1960s)
(VANG) Ⓓ [2] **08.9081.72**
21a E. Destinn, orch, W.B. Rogers (r1915: Ger)
(PEAR) Ⓓ **GEMMCD9172**
21a L. Popp, Munich RO, S. Soltesz (r1987)
(4/89) (EMI) Ⓓ **CDC7 49319-2**
21a S. Jurinac, Philh, L. Collingwood (Ger: r1950) (1/90) (EMI) Ⓓ **CDH7 63199-2**
21a S. Jurinac, Philh, L. Collingwood (r1950: Ger) (4/92) (EMI) Ⓓ [7] **CHS7 69741-2(4)**
21a X. Belmas, orch, A. Kitschin (r1927)
(10/92) (PREI) Ⓓ **89047**
21a M. Mei-Figner, anon (r1901)
(6/93) (PEAR) Ⓓ [3] **GEMMCDS9997/9(1)**
21a E. Destinn, orch, W.B. Rogers (r1915: Ger)
(4/94) (RCA) Ⓓ [6] **09026 61580-2(2)**
21a E. Destinn, orch, B. Seidler-Winkler (r1909: Ger) (5/94) (SUPR) Ⓓ **11 1337-2**
21a X. Belmas, orch, A. Kitschin (r1927)
(6/94) (MMOI) Ⓓ **CDMOIR422**
21a E. Destinn, orch, B. Seidler-Winkler (r1909: Ger) (12/94) (SUPR) Ⓓ [12] **11 2136-2(2)**
21a K. Vayne, orch (bp1958-9)
(6/95) (PREI) Ⓓ **89996**

24a M. Maksakov, anon (r1901)
(PEAR) Ⓓ [3] **GEMMCDS9111(2)**
24a G. De Luca, anon (r1907: Ital)
(PEAR) Ⓓ [3] **GEMMCDS9159(1)**
24a V. Kastorsky, chor, orch (r1906)
(6/93) (PEAR) Ⓓ [3] **GEMMCDS9001/3(1)**
24a A. Didur, anon (r1906: Ital)
(6/94) (MMOI) Ⓓ **CDMOIR422**
25b A. Davidov, anon (r1901)
(6/93) (PEAR) Ⓓ [3] **GEMMCDS9007/9(1)**

TELEMANN, Georg Philipp *(1681–1767) Germany*

TWV—Nos from M. Ruhnke, Telemann—Werkverzeichnis

Don Quichotte auf der Hochzeit des Comacho– comic opera/serenata (1761) (Lib. D. Schiebeler)

Don Quichotte	R. Nolte
Sancho Pansa	M. Schopper
Pedrillo	S. Stapf
Grisostomo	M. Bach
Quiteria	H. Hallaschka
Comacho	A. Köhler
Basilio	K-H. Brandt

Bremen Voc Ens, Stagione, M. Schneider (pp1993)
(9/94) (CPO) Ⓓ **CPO999 210-2**

Flavius Bertaridus– opera: 3 acts (1729—Hamburg) (Lib. Wend)
Lieto suono di trombe guerriere J. Kowalski, Berlin CO, M. Pommer
(9/88) (CAPR) Ⓓ **10 113**
(9/88) (CAPR) ▭ **CC27 127**

Pimpinone– intermezzo: 2 acts (1728—Hamburg) (Lib. J.P. Praetorius, after P. Pariati)

Pimpinone	J. Ostendorf
Vespetta	J. Baird

St Luke's Baroque Orch, R. Palmer
(1/92) (NEWP) Ⓓ **NCD60117**

Pimpinone	M. Schopper
Vespetta	M. Bach

Stagione, M. Schneider (r1992)
(4/94) (DHM) Ⓓ **05472 77284-2**

TERRASSE, Claude (Antoine) *(1867–1923) France*

La **Fiancée du Scaphandrier– operetta: 1 act (1902—?Paris) (Lib. Franc-Nohain)**

Baroness	L. Dachary
Elisa	C. Jacquin
Julot	G. Friedmann
Bézard	J. Tharande
Alexis	M. Hamel

ORTF Lyric Orch, J. Doussard (with dialogue: bp)
(3/92) (MUSD) Ⓓ [2] **20179-2**

Les **Travaux d'Hercule– operetta: 3 acts (1901—Paris) (Lib. R. de Flers & G. A. de Caillavet)**

Hercule	G. Rey
Omphale	L. Dachary
Augias	D. Tirmont
Erichtona	C. Harbell
Palémon	R. Lenoty
Orphée	B. Alvi
Lysius	L. Lovano
Amphiteus	M. Fauchey
Hannon	Lestelly
Xanthias	C. Daguerressar
Chrysis	M. Siderer
Myrtion; Naïs	H. Hennetier
Mousarion; Philine	G. Parat

French Rad Lyric Chor, French Rad Lyric Orch, M. Cariven (with dialogue: bp)
(3/92) (MUSD) Ⓓ [2] **20179-2**

THOMAS, (Charles Louis) Ambroise *(1811–1896) France*

Le **Caïd– opera: 2 acts (1849—Paris) (Lib. Sauvage)**
Enfant chéri...Le tambour-major E. Pinza, orch, Rosario Bourdon (r1927)
(PEAR) Ⓓ **GEMMCD9122**
Enfant chéri...Le tambour-major E. Pinza, orch, Rosario Bourdon (r1927)
(2/89) (PEAR) Ⓓ **GEMMCD9306**
Enfant chéri...Le tambour-major E. Pinza, orch, Rosario Bourdon (r1927)
(7/91) (MMOI) Ⓓ **CDMOIR404**
(MMOI) ▭ **CMOIR404**
Enfant chérie...Le tambour-major P. Plançon, orch (r1907) (9/91) (PEAR) Ⓓ **GEMMCD9497**
Enfant chérie...Le tambour-major P. Plançon, anon (r1903) (9/91) (PEAR) Ⓓ **GEMMCD9497**
Enfant chérie...Le tambour-major P. Plançon, anon (r1902) (3/93) (SYMP) Ⓓ **SYMCD1100**
Enfant chéri...Le Tambour-Major P. Plançon, orch (r1907) (1/95) (NIMB) Ⓓ **NI7860**
Enfin chéri...Le tambour-major P. Plançon, orch (r1906/7: 2 vers)
(12/94) (ROMO) Ⓓ [2] **82001-2**
Enfin chéri...Le tambour-major P. Plançon, anon (r1903) (12/94) (ROMO) Ⓓ [2] **82001-2**
Le tambour-major tout galonné d'or E. Pinza, orch, Rosario Bourdon (r1927)
(3/92) (PREI) Ⓓ **89050**
Le tambour-major tout galonné d'or E. Pinza, orch, Rosario Bourdon (r1927)
(9/93) (RCA) Ⓓ **09026 61245-2**

Françoise de Rimini– opera: 5 acts (1882—Paris) (Lib. J. Barbier & Carré, after Dante)
Ballet Suite English Concert Orch, R. Bonynge
(11/90) (DECC) Ⓓ [2] **421 818-2DH2**

Hamlet– opera: 5 acts (1869—Paris) (Lib. Carré, after Shakespeare)
EXCERPTS: ACT 1: 1. Prelude; 2a. Vains regrets!; 2b. Doute de la lumière; 3. Spectre infernal!. ACT 2: 4a. Se main depuis hier n'a pas touché ma main!; 4b. Adieu, dit-il; 5. Dans son regard; 6. O vin, dissipe la tristesse (Brindisi). ACT 3: 7. Etre ou ne pas être!; 8. Je t'implore, ô mon frère!. ACT 4: 9a. Entr'acte; 9b. Ballet; 10a. A vos jeux (Mad Scene); 10b. Des larmes de la nuit; 10c. Partagez-vous mes fleurs!; 10d. Pâle et blonde. ACT 5: 11. Comme une pâle fleur.

Hamlet	S. Milnes
Ophélie	J. Sutherland
Laërte	G. Winbergh
Gertrude	B. Conrad
Claudius	J. Morris
Ghost	J. Tomlinson
Marcellus	K. Lewis
Polonius	A.H. Morgan
Horatio	P. Gelling
First Gravedigger	P. Garazzi
Second Gravedigger	J. Rouleau

WNO Chor, WNO Orch, R. Bonynge
(5/93) (DECC) Ⓓ [3] **433 857-2DMO3**

Hamlet	T. Hampson
Ophélie	J. Anderson
Laërte	G. Kunde
Gertrude	D. Graves
Claudius	S. Ramey
Ghost	J-P. Courtis
Marcellus	G. Garino
Polonius	M. Trempont
Horatio	F. Le Roux
First Gravedigger	T. Félix
Second Gravedigger	J-P. Furlan

Ambrosian Op Chor, LPO, A. de Almeida (r1993)
(1/94) (EMI) Ⓓ [3] **CDS7 54820-2**
Exc R. Blanchart, anon (Ital: r1901)
(11/92) (MEMO) Ⓓ [2] **HR4408/9(1)**
2a, 2b M. Journet, F. Heldy, SO (r1930)
(1/94) (CLUB) Ⓓ **CL99-034**
2a, 11. A. Ivanov, I. Maslennikova, Bolshoi Th Orch, S. Samosud (r1940s: Russ)
(PREI) Ⓓ **89067**
4a, 4b E. Norena, orch, P. Coppola (r1932)
(3/91) (PREI) Ⓓ **89041**
6. R. Merrill, Orch, H. Barlow (bp1956)
(VAI) ▣ **VAI69116**
6. G. Laperrière, Three Rivers SO, G. Bellemare (r1992) (CBC) Ⓓ **SMCD5127**
6. T. Ruffo, orch, C. Sabajno (r1907: Ital)
(PEAR) Ⓓ **GEMMCD9088**
6. H. Schlusnus, Berlin St Op Orch, J. Heidenreich (r1927: Ger) (PREI) Ⓓ [2] **89212**
6. T. Ruffo, orch (r1907: Ital) (PREI) Ⓓ **89995**
6. G. Kaschmann, S. Cottone (Ital: r1903)
(12/89) (SYMP) Ⓓ **SYMCD1065**
6. T. Ruffo, orch, C. Sabajno (Ital: r1907)
(11/90) (NIMB) Ⓓ **NI7810**
(NIMB) ▭ **NC7810**
6. M. Battistini, La Scala Chor, orch, C. Sabajno (Ital: r1911) (10/92) (NIMB) Ⓓ **NI7831**
(10/92) (NIMB) ▭ **NC7831**
6. T. Ruffo, orch (Ital: r1920)
(2/93) (PREI) Ⓓ [3] **89303(1)**

6. E. Badini, orch (r1909: Ital) (12/94) (BONG) Ⓓ **GB1043-2**
6, 11. M. Battistini, orch (r1911: Ital) (PEAR) Ⓓ **GEMMCD9016**
6, 11. M. Battistini, orch (r1911: Ital) (2/92) (PREI) Ⓓ **89045**
7. Vanni-Marcoux, orch, P. Coppola (r1931) (PEAR) Ⓓ **GEMMCD9912**
7. Vanni-Marcoux, orch (r1931) (1/94) (CLUB) Ⓓ **CL99-101**
9b National PO, R. Bonynge (r1982) (DECC) Ⓓ **444 110-2DA**
10a A. Galli-Curci, orch (r1925) (PEAR) Ⓓ **GEMMCD9450**
10a J. Sutherland, ROHO, F. Molinari-Pradelli (1/90) (DECC) Ⓓ [2] **425 493-2DM2**
10a N. Melba, orch, L. Ronald (r1904) (7/92) (PEAR) Ⓓ [3] **GEMMCDS9923(1)**
10a L. Tetrazzini, orch (Ital: r1911) (9/92) (EMI) Ⓓ [3] **CHS7 63802-2(1)**
10a L. Tetrazzini, orch (Ital: r1911) (9/92) (PEAR) Ⓓ **GEMMCD9222**
10a A. Galli-Curci, orch (r1925: Ital) (8/94) (NIMB) Ⓓ **NI7852**
10a-c L. Aikin, Berlin RSO, J. Märkl (r1991) (SCHW) Ⓓ [2] **312682**
10a-c M. Mesplé, Paris Op Orch, J-P. Marty (r1968) (EMI) Ⓓ [2] **CZS7 67813-2**
10a-c E. Gruberová, Munich RO, G. Kuhn (r c1980) (EMIN) Ⓓ **CD-EMX2234**
10a-d M. Callas, Philh Chor, Philh, N. Rescigno (6/86) (EMI) Ⓓ **CDC7 47283-2**
10a-d N. Melba, orch (r1907) (4/94) (RCA) Ⓓ [6] **09026 61580-2(1)**
10a, 10d N. Melba, orch, W.B. Rogers (r1907) (9/93) (RCA) Ⓓ **09026 61412-2**
10a, 10d N. Melba, orch, W.B. Rogers (r1907) (5/95) (ROMO) Ⓓ [3] **81011-2(1)**
10b E. Norena, orch, H. Defosse (r1930) (3/91) (PREI) Ⓓ **89041**
10b N. Melba, orch, W.B. Rogers (r1910) (5/95) (ROMO) Ⓓ [3] **81011-2(2)**
10b, 10d N. Melba, orch (r1910) (7/93) (NIMB) Ⓓ [2] **NI7840/1**
10d E. Bronskaya, orch (r1913: Russ) (3/95) (NIMB) Ⓓ **NI7865**
11. G. De Luca, anon (r1902: Ital) (PEAR) Ⓓ [3] **GEMMCDS9159(1)**
11. G. De Luca, anon (r1907: Ital) (PEAR) Ⓓ [3] **GEMMCDS9159(2)**
11. R. Stracciari, orch (r1925: Ital) (PEAR) Ⓓ **GEMMCD9178**
11. M. Renaud, orch (r1908) (7/92) (PEAR) Ⓓ [3] **GEMMCDS9923(2)**
11. G. De Luca, anon (Ital: r1902) (8/93) (SYMP) Ⓓ **SYMCD1111**

Mignon– opera: 3 acts (1866—Paris) (Lib. Carré and Barbier)

EXCERPTS: 1. Overture. ACT 1: 2. Fugitif et tremblant; 3a. Laërte, amis; 3b. O filles de Bohême; 4a. Oui, je veux par le monde; 4b. Si l'amour sur la route; 5. Connais-tu le pays?; 6. Légères hirondelles (Swallow Duet); 7. Me voici, tu m'as rachetée. ACT 2: 8. Entr'acte; 9. Plus de soucis, Mignon (Trio); 10a. Me voilà seule hélas!; 10b. Je connais un pauvre enfant (Styrienne); 11a. C'est moi; 11b. Me voici dans son boudoir (Gavotte); 12. Adieu, Mignon! Courage!; 13a. Elle est là; 13b. Elle est aimée!; 14. As-tu souffert?; 15a. Oui, pour ce soir; 15b. Je suis Titania (Polonaise). ACT 3: 15c. Ah! Au soufflé léger du vent (Barcarolle); 16. De son coeur, j'ai calmé (Berceuse); 17a. Etrange regard!; 17b. Elle ne croyait pas; 17c. Ah! que ton âme enfin; 18. O Vierge Marie. ALTERNATIVE OPENING TO ACT 2: 19. A merveille!; ALTERNATIVE FINALE TO ACT 3: 20. Dansons, dansons, amis!.

Excs J. Sutherland, Orch, Anon (cond), D. Bailey (11/92) (DECC) ◖ **071 135-1DH**
La tua bell'alma; 12. F. de Lucia, anon (r1905: Ital) (BONG) Ⓓ [2] **GB1064/5-2**
Où suis-je?...Oui, crois au bonheur F. Wunderlich, P. Lorengar, Berlin SO, B. Klobučar (Ger) (EMI) Ⓓ [3] **CZS7 62993-2**
1. Cölln Salon Orch (arr Mouton) (EURO) Ⓓ **GD69296**
1. NBC SO, A. Toscanini (r1942) (RCA) Ⓓ **GD60310**
1. RPO, Y. Simonov (r1994) (TRIN) Ⓓ **TRP030**
1. LSO, C. Mackerras (r1961) (MERC) Ⓓ **434 352-2MM**
1. NBC SO, A. Toscanini (r1952) (11/92) (RCA) Ⓓ **GD60322**
1. Detroit SO, P. Paray (r1960) (8/93) (MERC) Ⓓ **434 321-2MM**
1. NYPO, L. Bernstein (r1963) (9/93) (SONY) Ⓓ **SMK47601**
4a H. Roswaenge, orch (r1935: Ger) (4/95) (PREI) Ⓓ [2] **89209**
5. T. Berganza, Barcelona SO, G. Navarro (11/92) (RCA) ▭ **09026 61204-4**
5. G. Farrar, F. Kreisler, orch, W.B. Rogers (r1915) (BIDD) Ⓓ **LAB022**
5. T. Berganza, Barcelona SO, G. Navarro (RCA) **OO 09026 61204-5**
5. G. Simionato, Santa Cecilia Academy Orch, F. Previtali (r1956) (DECC) Ⓓ **440 406-2DM**
5. E. Destinn, orch (r c1913: Ger) (PEAR) Ⓓ **GEMMCD9130**
5. C. Muzio, orch (r1917: Ital) (PEAR) Ⓓ **GEMMCD9143**
5. E. Destinn, anon (r1905: Ger) (PEAR) Ⓓ **GEMMCD9172**
5. G. Farrar, orch, W.B. Rogers (r1915) (NIMB) Ⓓ **NI7872**
5. A. Patti, A. Barili (r1906) (4/90) (PEAR) Ⓓ **GEMMCD9312**
5. K. Branzell, orch (r1928) (8/92) (PREI) Ⓓ **89039**
5. C. Supervia, orch, G. Cloëz (r1931) (3/93) (NIMB) Ⓓ [2] **NI7836/7**
5. E. Destinn, orch (r1914: Ger) (11/93) (ROMO) Ⓓ [2] **81002-2**
5. E. Destinn, orch (r1914: Ger) (5/94) (SUPR) Ⓓ **11 1337-2**
5. E. Destinn, orch (r1914: Ger) (12/94) (SUPR) Ⓓ [12] **11 2136-2(5)**
5. E. Destinn, anon (r1904: Ger) (12/94) (SUPR) Ⓓ [12] **11 2136-2(1)**
5. C. Muzio, orch (r1917: Ital) (1/95) (ROMO) Ⓓ [2] **81010-2**
5, 10b X. Belmas, orch, A. Kitschin (r1928) (10/92) (PREI) Ⓓ **89047**
5, 10b E. Destinn, anon (r1905: Ger) (12/94) (SUPR) Ⓓ [12] **11 2136-2(1)**
5, 10b E. Destinn, orch, B. Seidler-Winkler (r1908: Ger) (12/94) (SUPR) Ⓓ [12] **11 2136-2(1)**
5, 10b, 13b E. Destinn, orch (r1911: Ger) (12/94) (SUPR) Ⓓ [12] **11 2136-2(4)**
5, 11b L. Bori, orch (r1928) (PEAR) Ⓓ **GEMMCD9458**
5, 13a Lotte Lehmann, orch (Ger: r1917) (6/92) (PREI) Ⓓ [3] **89302**
5, 18. E. Destinn, orch, F. Kark (r1905: Ger) (PEAR) Ⓓ **GEMMCD9172**
5(pt), 18. E. Destinn, orch, F. Kark (r1906: Ger) (12/94) (SUPR) Ⓓ [12] **11 2136-2(1)**
5, 6. C. Supervia, V. Bettoni, orch, A. Albergoni (r1929: Ital) (9/90) (CLUB) Ⓓ **CL99-074**
6. Lotte Lehmann, H. Schlusnus, orch (Ger: r1920) (6/92) (PREI) Ⓓ [3] **89302**
6. G. Farrar, M. Journet, orch (r1910) (10/94) (NIMB) Ⓓ **NI7859**
6, 14, 16. G. Zinetti, T. Pasero, orch, L. Molajoli (Ital: r1928) (6/90) (PREI) Ⓓ **89010**
7. T. Schipa, orch, Anon (cond) (Ital: pp1924) (MEMO) Ⓓ [2] **HR4220/1**
8. Philadelphia, L. Stokowski (r1930s) (8/95) (BIDD) Ⓓ **WHL011**
10b G. Farrar, orch (r1908) (NIMB) Ⓓ **NI7872**
10b E. Stignani, EIAR Orch, U. Tansini (Ital: r1937) (1/91) (PREI) Ⓓ **89014**
10b, 13a I. Seefried, Lamoureux Orch, J. Fournet (r1963: Ger) (9/93) (DG) Ⓓ [2] **437 677-2GDO2**
12. F. Wunderlich, Berlin SO, B. Klobučar (Ger) (EMI) Ⓓ [3] **CZS7 62993-2**
12. H. Buff-Giessen, anon (r1906: Ger) (SYMP) Ⓓ **SYMCD1085**
12. G. Walter, anon (r1904: Ger) (SYMP) Ⓓ **SYMCD1085**
12. T. Schipa, orch (Ital: r1924) (2/89) (PEAR) Ⓓ **GEMMCD9322**
12. J. Patzak, orch (Ger: r1935) (3/90) (PEAR) Ⓓ **GEMMCD9383**
12. H.E. Groh, orch, F. Weissmann (Ger: r1931) (3/92) (PEAR) Ⓓ **GEMMCD9419**
12. G. di Stefano, La Scala Orch, E. Tieri (Ital: r1947) (4/92) (EMI) Ⓓ [7] **CHS7 69741-2(7)**
12. Ferruccio Tagliavini, EIAR Orch, U. Tansini (r1943: Ital) (3/94) (CENT) Ⓓ **CRC2164**
12. J. Patzak, orch (r c1934: Ger) (9/94) (NIMB) Ⓓ **NI7856**
12. W. Ludwig, Berlin City Op Orch, W. Ladwig (r1932: Ger) (7/95) (PREI) Ⓓ **89088**
12, 17b G. di Stefano, orch, A. Erede (Ital: r1947) (EMI) Ⓓ **CDM7 63105-2**
12, 17b K. Erb, orch (r1912: Ger) (PREI) Ⓓ **89095**
12, 17b B. Gigli, orch, Rosario Bourdon (Ital: r1928) (9/88) (PEAR) Ⓓ **GEMMCD931**
12, 17b D. Borgioli, orch (Ital: r c1923) (12/90) (CLUB) Ⓓ **CL99-01**
12, 17b R. Tauber, orch, K. Besl (Ger: r1923) (3/92) (EMI) Ⓓ **CDH7 64029-**
12, 17b A. Piccaver, orch (r1914: Ger) (8/93) (PREI) Ⓓ **8906**
13a, 13b N. Vallin, orch (r1928) (MSCM) Ⓓ **MM3022** (MSCM) ▭ **MM04007**
15a-c E. Gruberová, Munich RO, L. Gardelli (11/86) (ORFE) Ⓓ **C101841**
15a-c M. Callas, FRNO, G. Prêtre (2/90) (EMI) Ⓓ **CDM7 63182-**
15a-c P. Munsel, RCA SO, S. Levin (r1945) (4/94) (RCA) Ⓓ [6] **09026 61580-2(6**
15a, 15b M. Mesplé, Paris Op Orch, J-P. Marty (r1968) (EMI) Ⓓ [2] **CZS7 67813-**
15b I. Abendroth, anon (r1902: Ger) (SYMP) Ⓓ **SYMCD108**
15b L. Pons, Orch, A. Kostelanetz (r1940) (MSCM) Ⓓ **MM3044**
15b M. Callas, FRNO, G. Prêtre (r1961) (EMI) Ⓓ **CDC5 55016-**
15b M. Licette, orch, P. Pitt (r1915) (PEAR) Ⓓ **GEMMCD913**
15b M. Callas, FRNO, G. Prêtre (2/88) (EMI) Ⓓ **CDC7 49059-**
15b L. Tetrazzini, orch (r1911) (10/89) (NIMB) Ⓓ **NI780** (NIMB) ▭ **NC780**
15b T. dal Monte, La Scala Orch, C. Sabajno (r1929: Ital) (2/90) (PREI) Ⓓ **8900**
15b A. Galli-Curci, orch, J. Pasternack (Ital: r1919) (5/90) (NIMB) Ⓓ **NI780** (NIMB) ▭ **NC780**
15b L. Pons, Columbia SO, A. Kostelanetz (r1949) (7/90) (CBS) Ⓓ **CD4569**
15b L. Tetrazzini, orch (Ital: r1911) (10/90) (NIMB) Ⓓ **NI780** (10/90) (NIMB) ▭ **NC780**
15b L. Tetrazzini, orch, P. Pitt (Ital: r1908) (9/92) (EMI) Ⓓ [3] **CHS7 63802-2(**
15b L. Tetrazzini, orch (Ital: r1911) (9/92) (EMI) Ⓓ [3] **CHS7 63802-2(1**
15b L. Tetrazzini, orch, P. Pitt (Ital: r1907) (9/92) (EMI) Ⓓ [3] **CHS7 63802-2(1**
15b L. Tetrazzini, orch (Ital: r1911) (9/92) (PEAR) Ⓓ **GEMMCD922**
15b L. Tetrazzini, orch (Ital: r1911) (9/92) (PEAR) Ⓓ **GEMMCD922**
15b L. Tetrazzini, orch, P. Pitt (Ital: r1907) (9/92) (PEAR) Ⓓ **GEMMCD922**
15b A. Galli-Curci, orch, J. Pasternack (r1919: Ital) (3/94) (ROMO) Ⓓ [2] **81003-**
15b P. Alarie, Lamoureux Orch, P. Dervaux (r1953) (11/94) (PHIL) Ⓓ [2] **438 953-2PM**
15b E. Steber, orch, E. Goossens (bp1942) (11/95) (VAI) Ⓓ **VAIA107**
15c R. Shaw Chorale, RCA Victor Orch, Robert Shaw (RCA) Ⓓ **GD6020**
16. P. Plançon, orch (r1908) (9/91) (PEAR) Ⓓ **GEMMCD949**
16. E. Pinza, orch, Rosario Bourdon (r1927) (3/92) (PREI) Ⓓ **8905**
16. A. Didur, orch (r c1918) (1/94) (CLUB) Ⓓ **CL99-08**
16. G. Hüsch, Berlin St Op Orch, H.U. Müller (r1937: Ger) (3/94) (PREI) Ⓓ **8907**
16. P. Plançon, orch (r1908: Ital) (12/94) (ROMO) Ⓓ [2] **82001-**
17b T. Schipa, orch (Ital: r1924) (PEAR) Ⓓ **GEMMCD936**
17b B. Gigli, orch, Rosario Bourdon (r1928: Ital) (NIMB) Ⓓ **NI781** (NIMB) ▭ **NC781**
17b G. di Stefano, La Scala Orch, E. Tieri (Ital: pp1947) (MEMO) Ⓓ **HR4372/**
17b A. Bogdanovich, anon (r1905: Russ) (PEAR) Ⓓ [3] **GEMMCDS9111(**
17b J. Björling, B. Bokstedt (pp1957: Swed) (BLUE) Ⓓ **ABCD0**
17b G. Prandelli, Rome RAI Orch, A. Basile (bp1961: Ital) (FONI) Ⓓ **CDMR502**
17b H. Nash, orch (Eng: r1926) (8/89) (PEAR) Ⓓ **GEMMCD931**
17b L. Sobinov, orch (r1911: Russ) (6/93) (PEAR) Ⓓ [3] **GEMMCDS9997/9(**
17b A. Bonci, anon (Ital: r1905) (12/93) (SYMP) Ⓓ **SYMCD111**
17b T. Schipa, orch (r1924: Ital) (12/93) (NIMB) Ⓓ **NI785**
17b L. David, anon (r1905) (12/94) (SYMP) Ⓓ **SYMCD117**

17b G. Anselmi, anon (r1907: Ital)
(7/95) (SYMP) ① **SYMCD1170**
17c A. Bonci, orch (r1913: Ital)
(PEAR) ① **GEMMCD9168**

Raymond– opera: 3 acts (1851—Paris) (Lib. Rosier and de Leuven)
Overture Montreal SO, C. Dutoit
(6/89) (DECC) ① **421 527-2DH**
Overture Detroit SO, P. Paray (r1960)
(8/93) (MERC) ① **434 321-2MM**

Le Songe d'une nuit d'été– opera: 3 acts (1850—Paris) (Lib. J B Rosier & A de Leuven)
EXCERPTS: 1. Malgré l'éclat qui m'environne.
1. S. Jo, ECO, R. Bonynge (r1993)
(9/94) (DECC) ① **440 679-2DH**

THOMAS, Arthur Goring *(1850–1892) England*

Esmeralda– opera: 4 acts (1883 rev 1890—London) (Lib. Marzials & Randegger, after V Hugo)
EXCERPTS: 1a. All is yet tranquil; 1b. What would I do for my Queen; 2. O vision entrancing.
2. T. Burke, Anon (pf) (1927)
(PEAR) ① **GEMMCD9411**
2. W. Widdop, orch, M. Sargent (r1930)
(PEAR) ① **GEMMCD9112**

THOMSON, Virgil *(1896–1989) USA*

Lord Byron– opera: 3 acts (1972—New York) (Lib. J. Larson)
EXCERPTS: ACT ONE: 1. Byron is dead; 2a. Ay me that dreerie death; 2b. Spenser, Thomson, Milton, Chaucer; 2c. We shall all do our duty; 2d. Byron is dead; 2e. Interlude; 2f. I've no great cause. ACT TWO: 3a. It truly reminds me of him; 3b. Remember, the poet we knew; 4a. Alas! the love of woman!; 4b. Mi-lord, we should not pay such attention; 4c. Byron! Byron!; 4d. They have started the waltz lesson; 4e. No! I have no desire to spin round and round; 4f. She referred to my foot; 4g. A wanderer from the British world of fashion; 4h. You are very bitter; 4i. You are too late; 4j. Ah! Ah!; 5a. Prelude; 5b. God bless you, my love (Lady Caroline's Aria); 5c. God! I am more degenerate; 5d. Ask not for valour; 5e. Seductive waltz!; 5f. My sister waltzes; 5g. Sweet lady; 6a. Prelude; 6b. Should auld acquaintance; 6c. I take him from this day; 6d. I should hate to be a cuckold; 6e. Let us retire; 6f. Should auld acquaintance. ACT THREE: 7a. How we two; 7b. My baby Byron!; 7c. Dear, your house is so charming; 7d. Kisses, give your baby kisses; 7e. Your being here; 7f. You walk in beauty; 7g. I did not retire; 7h. I'd sooner burn in hell; 7i. As once I wept; 7j. 'Tis my nature; 7k. Fare thee well; 8a. Eventful volume!; 8b. Please! What are you burning?; 8c. Saviour, breathe an ev'ning blessing; 8d. Interlude; 8e. They weigh a life; 8f. Ah, he has outsoared the shadow; 8g. From mighty wrongs.

Lord Byron M. Lord
Thomas Moore R. Zeller
Lady Byron D. Fortunato
John Hobhouse R. Johnson
Mrs Leigh J. Ommerlé
John Murray G. Mercer
Contessa Guiccioli A. Csengery
Count Gamba T. Woodman
John Ireland S. Owen
Lady Melbourne L. Jonason
Lady Charlotte; Lady Caroline D. Vanderlinde
Lady Jane M. Dry
Monadnock Fest Chor, Monadnock Fest Orch, J. Bolle (pp1991)
(5/93) (KOCH) ① [2] **37124-2**
4a, 4g, 5g, 7h, 7k M. Hill, Budapest SO, J. Bolle
(4/90) (ALBA) ① **TROY017-2**

The Mother of us all– opera: 2 acts (1947—New York) (Lib. G. Stein)
Susan B Anthony M. Dunn
Jo the Loiterer J. Atherton
Daniel Webster P. Booth
Anne B. Godfrey
John Adams W. Lewis
Indiana Elliott L. Maxwell
Constance Fletcher H. Vanni
Thaddeus Stevens D. Perry
Angel More A. Putnam
Chris the Citizen J. McKee
Virgil T G. Ives
Santa Fé Op Chor, Santa Fé Op Orch, R. Leppard (r1976)
(7/90) (NEW) ① [2] **NW288/9-2**

THUILLE, Ludwig *(1861–1907) Austria*

Lobetanz– opera: 3 acts, Op. 10 (1898—Karlsruhe) (Lib. O. J. Bierbaum)
An allen Zweigen J. Gadski, orch (r1914)
(7/91) (CLUB) ① **CL99-109**

TIPPETT, Sir Michael (Kemp) *(b 1905) England*

The Ice Break– opera: 3 acts (1977—London) (Lib. cpsr)
Nadia H. Harper
Lev D. Wilson-Johnson
Yuri S. Sylvan
Gayle C. Page
Hannah C. Clarey
Olympian T. Randle
Luke B. Bottone
Lieutenant D. Maxwell
Astron C. Robson
Astron Sarah Walker
London Sinfonietta Chor, London Sinfonietta, D. Atherton
(2/92) (VIRG) ① **VC7 59048-2**

King Priam– opera: 3 acts (1962—Coventry) (Lib. cpsr)
Priam R. Macann
Hecuba J. Price
Hector O. Ebrahim
Andromache Sarah Walker
Paris H. Haskin
Helen A. Mason
Achilles N. Jenkins
Patroclus J. Hancorn
Nurse E. Hartle
Old Man R. Suart
Young Guard M. Curtis
Hermes C. Gillett
Kent Op Chor, Kent Op Orch, R. Norrington, N. Hynter
(MCEG) ▭ **VVD664**

The Knot Garden– opera: 3 acts (1970—London) (Lib. cpsr)
Faber R. Herincx
Thea Y. Minton
Flora J. Gomez
Denise J. Barstow
Mel T. Carey
Dov R. Tear
Mangus T. Hemsley
ROHO, Colin Davis (r1973)
(9/95) (PHIL) ① [2] **446 331-2PH2**

The Midsummer Marriage– opera: 3 acts (1955—London) (Lib. cpsr)
1. Ritual Dances; 2. Sosostris's Dances.
Mark A. Remedios
Jenifer J. Carlyle
King Fisher R. Herincx
Bella E. Harwood
Jack S. Burrows
Sosostris H. Watts
He-Ancient S. Dean
She-Ancient E. Bainbridge
Half-Tipsy Man D. Whelan
Dancing Man A. Daniels
ROH Chor, ROHO, Colin Davis (r1970)
(LYRI) ① [2] **SRCD2217**
1, 2. R. Cullis, M. Curtis, A. Hodgson, M. Best, Op. North Chor, English Northern Philh, M. Tippett
(4/90) (NIMB) ① **NI5217**

New Year– concert suite from opera (1990)
1. The Space Ship lands; 2. Prelude; 3. The Shaman Dance; 4. The Hunt for the Scapegoat; 5. Donny's Skarade; 6. Donny's Dream; 7. Dream Interlude; 8. Jo Ann's Dreamsong; 9. Love Scene for Jo Ann and Pelegrin; 10. Paradise Dance; 11. The Beating-Out of the Scapegoat; 12. Ringing in the New Year; 13. The Space Ship takes off again.
Bournemouth SO, R. Hickox (r1994)
(10/94) (CHAN) ① **CHAN9299**

TOMASI, Henri *(1901–1971) France*

Don Juan de Mañara– opera: 4 acts & 6 tableaux (1952—Paris) (Lib. after Milosz)
Miguel Mañara R. Jobin
Girolama M. Angelici
Don Fernand, Frère Jardinier A. Vessières
L'Ombre, L'Esprit du Ciel J. Brumaire
L'Esprit de la Terre B. Demigny
Johannes Melendez P. Cabanel
Don Jaime, Réligieux II J. Peyron
Deux Esprits H. Vermeil
French Rad Chor, FNO, H. Tomasi (r1952)
(10/92) (FORL) ① [2] **UCD16652/3**

TRAETTA, Tommaso (Michele Francesco Saverio) *(1727–1779) Italy*

Buovo d'Antona– comic opera: 3 acts (1758—Venice) (Lib. C. Goldoni)
Buovo d'Antona H. Crook
Maccabruno C. Trogu-Röhrich
Drusiana R. Balconi
Menichina D. del Monaco
Cecchina F. R. Ermolli
Capoccio G. Fagotto
Striglia G. Zambon
Teatro la Fenice Orch, A. Curtis (pp1993)
(4/94) (O111) ① [2] **OPS30-90/1**

TROJAHN, Manfred *(b 1949) Germany*

Enrico– dramatic comedy: nine scenes (1990—Munich) (Lib. C H Henneberg after L Pirandello)
Enrico R. Salter
Marchesa Matilda Spina T. Schmidt
Frida F. Lucey
Carlo di Nolli L. Magnusson
Barone Tito Belcredi H. G. Nöcker
Dottore J. Zinkler
Landolfo E. Lorenz
Bertoldo P. Umstadt
Arialdo T. Mohr
Ordulfo R. Trebes
Giovanni N. Hillebrand
Stuttgart RSO, D. R. Davies (pp1991)
(CPO) ① [2] **CPO999 160-2**

TUBIN, Eduard *(1905–1982) Estonia*

Barbara von Tisenhusen– opera: 3 acts (1968) (Lib. A. Kallas & J. Kross)
Barbara von Tisenhusen H. Raamat
Matthias Jeremias Friesner T. Sild
Anna von Tödwen M. Jõgeva
Johann von Tödwen U. Kreen
Franz Bonnius I. Kuusk
Jürgen V. Puura
Reinhold A. Kollo
Bartholomeus H. Miilberg
Reinhold von Tisenhusen M. Palm
Estonia Op Chor, Estonia Op Orch, P. Lilje
(4/93) (ONDI) ① [2] **ODE776-2**

TURNAGE, Mark-Anthony *(b 1960) England*

Greek– opera: 2 acts (1988—Munich) (Lib. S Berkoff, from stage play)
Eddy Q. Hayes
Dad; Cafe Manager; Chief of Police R. Suart
Wife; Doreen; Waitress 1; Sphinx 2 F. Kimm
Mum; Waitress 2; Sphinx 1 H. Charnock
Ens, R. Bernas (r1992)
(7/94) (ARGO) ① **440 368-2ZHO**
(7/94) (ARGO) ▭ **440 368-4ZHO**

ULLMANN, Viktor *(1898–1944) Austria/Hungary*

Der Kaiser von Atlantis, oder Die Tod-Verweigerung– opera: 1 act, Op. 49 (1943) (Lib. P Kien)
Kaiser Overall M. Kraus
Loudspeaker F. Mazura
Soldier M. Petzold
Bubikopf C. Oelze

Death W. Berry
Harlequin H. Lippert
Drummer-girl I. Vermillion
Leipzig Gewandhaus, L. Zagrosek (r1993)
(12/94) (DECC) ① **440 854-2DH**

USANDIZAGA, José Maria *(1887–1915) Spain*

Las **Golondrinas– zarzuela: 3 acts (1914—Madrid) (Lib. G Martinez Sierra. Rev as opera: fp 1929)**
Lisa J. Cubeiro
Cecilia I. Rivas
Puck V. Sardinero
Roberto R. Alonso
Madrid Coros Cantores, Spanish Lyric Orch, F. Moreno Torroba
(10/92) (HISP) ① **CDZ7 67453-2**

USIGLIO, Emilio *(1841–1910) Italy*

Le **Educande di Sorrento– opera: 3 acts (1868—Florence)**
Ma zitta, giunge alcun...Un bacio rendimi E. Petri, F. Corradetti, anon (r1906-7)
(6/94) (IRCC) ① **IRCC-CD808**

UTTINI, Francesco Antonio Baldassare *(1723–1795) Italy*

Aline, Queen of Golconda– opera: 3 acts (1776—Stockholm) (Lib. C B Zibet, after J M Sedaine)
EXCERPTS: 1. Overture; 2. Entr'acte.
1, 2. Stockholm Nat Museum CO, C. Génetay
(MSVE) ① **MSCD407**

Thetis and Peleus– opera: 5 acts (1773—Stockholm) (Lib J Wellander, after B Fontenelle)
EXCERPTS: 1. Ballet music.
1. Stockholm Nat Museum CO, C. Génetay
(MSVE) ① **MSCD407**

VACCAI, Nicola *(1790–1848) Italy*

Giulietta e Romeo– opera: 2 acts (1825—Milan) (Lib. F. Romani)
Ah! se tu dormi G. Fabbri, S. Cottone (r1903)
(12/89) (SYMP) ① **SYMCD1065**

VALVERDE, Joaquín *(1846–1910) Spain*

Nina Pancha– zarzuela
Habañera L. Bori, Victor Orch, W.B. Rogers (r1914) (ROMO) ① [2] **81016-2**

VAN GILSE, Jan *(1881–1944) Netherlands*

Thijl– dramtic legend (1940)
Funeral music Hague PO, E. Spanjaard (r1992)
(OLYM) ① **OCD507**
Funeral music Hague PO, E. Spanjaard
(OLYM) ① [8] **OCD5008**

VARIOUS, (composers)

for works involving a multiplicity of composers

The **Grand Vizier– operetta (1895—New York)**
EXCERPTS: 1. Who is Egen? (Tracy).
1. T. Q. Seabrooke, Broadway Cast (r1904)
(5/94) (PEAR) ① [3] **GEMMCDS9050/2(1)**

VARNEY, Louis *(1844–1908) France*

L' **amour mouillé– operetta: 3 acts (1887—Paris) (Lib. J Prével & A Liorat)**
Valse d'oiseau L. Bori, Victor Orch, N. Shilkret (r1924) (ROMO) ① [2] **81016-2**

VAUGHAN WILLIAMS, Ralph *(1872–1958) England*

Hugh the Drover– ballad opera: 2 acts (1924—London) (Lib. H Child)
EXCERPTS: ACT 1: 1. Buy, buy, buy! Who'll buy?; 2. Who'll buy my sweet primroses; 3. Cold blows the wind on Cotsall; 4. Ballads! Buy me ballads, pretty ballads!; 5. As I was a-walking on morning in spring; 6. Bless! What's this?; 7. Show me a richer man in all this town; 8. See, see here they come! Way for the morris men!; 9. They're gone!...My husabnd that's to be!; 10. Sweetheart, life must be full of care; 11. Alone I would be as the wind and as free; 12. Hey! She will obey; 13. Sweet little linnet that longs to be free; 14. Horse hoofs, thunder down the valley (Hugh's Song of the Road); 15. Mary, come back I say!; 16. In the night-time I have seen you riding (Love duet); 17. Mary! Mary!; 18. Who'll fight? A fight! Who's for a fight?; 19. Brave English lads, lovers of manly sport; 20. Down, down with John the Butcher!; 21. Alone and friendless, on this foreign ground I am to die; 22. Are you ready? Go!; 23. Hugh the Drover!; 24. Oh, the devil and Bonyparty. ACT 2: 25. Past four o'clock, and dawn is coming; 26. Gaily I go to die; 27. Hugh! My dear one!; 28. Rise up, my Mary; come away; 29. Dear sun, I crave a boon; 30. O I've been rambling all this night; 31. Here, queen uncrowned, in this most royal place; 32. The soldiers!; 33. Dropped from the ranks on a winter night; 34. Now you are mine!; 35. Halloo! Halloo, Mary and Hugh.
Hugh B. Bottone
Mary R. Evans
Constable R. Van Allan
John the Butcher A. Opie
Aunt Jane Sarah Walker
Turnkey N. Jenkins
Sergeant R. Poulton
Showman K. M. Daymond
Cheap-Jack H. Nicoll
Shellfish Seller A. Hutton
Primrose Seller J. Gooding
Ballad Seller W. Evans
Susan J. Saunders
Nancy A. Coote
William L. Atkinson
Robert P. Robinson
Fool J. Pearce
Innkeeper P. Im Thurn
New London Children's Ch, Corydon Sngrs, Corydon Orch, M. Best (r1994)
(10/94) (HYPE) ① [2] **CDA66901/2**
Hugh R. Tear
Mary S. Armstrong
Constable R. Lloyd
John the Butcher M. Rippon
Aunt Jane H. Watts
Turnkey J. Fryatt
Sergeant H. Newman
Showman T. Sharpe
Cheap-Jack L. Fyson
Shell-fish Seller O. Broome
Primrose Seller S. Burgess
Ballad Singer D. Johnston
Susan L. Richardson
Nancy S. Minty
William N. Jenkins
Robert B. Ogston
Innkeeper D. Read
Fool S. Davies
St Paul's Cath Ch, Ambrosian Op Chor, RPO, C. Groves (r1978)
(10/94) (EMI) ① [2] **CMS5 65224-2**
Abridged Mary Lewis, C. Willis, N. Walker, T. Davies, F. Collier, P. Dawson, W. Anderson, chor, orch, M. Sargent (r1920s)
(PEAR) ① **GEMMCD9468**
14. J. Johnston, Philh, J. Robertson (r1950)
(4/92) (EMI) ① [7] **CHS7 69741-2(2)**
14. J. Johnston, Philh, J. Robertson (r1950)
(4/95) (TEST) ① **SBT1058**
16. Mary Lewis, T. Davies, orch, M. Sargent (r1924) (7/95) (BEUL) ① **1PD13**

The **Pilgrim's Progress– morality: 4 acts (1951—London) (Lib. cpsr, after J. Bunyan)**
Pilgrim J. Noble
John Bunyan; Lord Hate-Good R. Herincx
Evangelist J. Carol Case
Pliable W. Evans
Obstinate; Judas Escariot; Pontius Pilate C. Keyte
Mistrust; Demas G. Shaw
Timorous; Usher B. Dickerson
Shining One 1 S. Armstrong
Shining One 2; Madam Wanton M. Hayward Segal
Shining One 3; Madam By-Ends G. Jennings
Interpreter; Superstition I. Partridge
Watchful J. Shirley-Quirk
Herald T. Sharpe
Appollyon R. Lloyd
Branchbearer; Malice N. Burrowes
Cupbearer; Pickthank A. Hodgson
Lord Lechery J. Ward
Simon Magus; Envy R. Angas
Worldly Glory J. Elwes
Madam Bubble D. Wallis
Woodcutter's Boy W. Eathorne
Mister By-Ends G. English
LP Ch, LPO, A. Boult (with rehearsal)
(EMI) ① [2] **CMS7 64212-2**
Pilgrim R. Whitehouse
John Bunyan W. Griffiths
Evangelist J. Neale
Pliable; Superstition G. Wili
Obstinate; Envy M. Wharfedale
Mistrust P. Westhead
Timorous; Mister By-Ends; Angel 3 S. Chaundy
Shining One 1 M. Murphy
Shining One 2 C. Bradshaw
Shining One 3 A. Kettlewell
Interpreter; Shepherd 1 J. Lloyd-Roberts
Watchful D. Moore
Herald M. Snell
Apollyon; Pontius Pilate H. Waddington
Heavenly Being 1 M. Pope
Heavenly Being 2 R. Peel
Lord Lechery; Celestial Messenger J. Marsden
Demas A. Morris
Judas Iscariot; Shepherd 2 D. Vaughan-Lewis
Simon Magus H. Matthews
Worldly Glory R. Simonetti
Madam Wanton A. Rasmussen
Madam Bubble S. Wallace
Usher A. Fraser
Lord Hate-Good G. Taylor
Malice K. Caun
Pickthank E. Pollard
Woodcutter's Boy T. Jackson
Madam By-Ends K. Wilkinson
Shepherd 3 S. Parr
Bird L. Rushton
Angel 1 E. Môn
Angel 2 A. Coote
RNCM Op Chor, RNCM Op Orch, I. Kennaway (pp1992)
(RNCM) ① [2] **RNCMPP1**

The **Poisoned Kiss– romantic extravaganza: 3 acts (1936—Cambridge) (Lib. E. Sharp, aft R. Garnett)**
Overture Bournemouth Sinfonietta, G. Hurst
(8/87) (CHAN) ① **CHAN8432**
Overture Bournemouth Sinfonietta, G. Hurst (r1975) (11/92) (CHAN) ① **CHAN6545**

Riders to the Sea– opera: 1 act (1937—London) (Lib. cpsr, after J.M. Synge)
Nora N. Burrowes
Cathleen M. Price
Maurya H. Watts
Bartley B. Luxon
Woman P. Stevens
Ambrosian Sngrs, London Orch Nova, M. Davies (r1970)
(4/94) (EMI) ① **CDM7 64730-2**
Nora I. Attrot
Cathleen L. Dawson
Maurya L. Finnie
Bartley K. M. Daymond
Woman P. H. Stephen
Northern Sinfonia, R. Hickox (r1995)
(11/95) (CHAN) ① **CHAN9392**

The **Shepherds of the Delectable Mountains– pastoral episode: 1 act (1921—London) (Lib. cpsr, after J Bunyan)**
L. Kitchen, J.M. Ainsley, Adrian Thompson, A. Opie, B. Terfel, J. Best, Corydon Sngrs, CLS, M. Best (8/92) (HYPE) ① **CDA66569**

VERACINI, Francesco Maria *(1690–1768) Italy*

Rosalinda– opera (1744—London) (Lib. Rolli)
Meco verrai L. Tetrazzini, orch (r1914)
(BEUL) ① **1PD4**
Meco verrai L. Tetrazzini, orch (r1913)
(10/90) (NIMB) ① **NI7808**
(10/90) (NIMB) ▭ **NC7808**
Meco verrai L. Tetrazzini, orch (r1914)
(9/92) (EMI) ① [3] **CHS7 63802-2(2)**

Meco verrai L. Tetrazzini, orch (r1913)
(9/92) (PEAR) Ⓓ **GEMMCD9224**
Meco verrai L. Tetrazzini, orch (r1914)
(9/92) (PEAR) Ⓓ **GEMMCD9223**

VERDI, Giuseppe (Fortunino Francesco) *(1813–1901) Italy*

Aida– opera: 4 acts (1871—Cairo) (Lib. A Ghislanzoni, after A Mariette)

EXCERPTS: 1. Prelude. ACT 1: 2. Sì, corre voce; 3a. Se quel guerrier; 3b. Celeste Aida; 4a. Quale insolita gioia; 4b. Vieni o diletta; 5a. Alta cagion v'aduna; 5b. Or di vulcano al tempio; 5c. Sul del Nilo; 6a. Ritorna vincitor; 6b. L'insana parola; 6c. I sacri nomi; 7a. Possente Possenta—Immenso Ftha; 7b. Dance of the Priestesses; 7c. Mortal diletto. ACT 2: 8a. Chi mai; 8b. Dance of the Moorish slaves; 9a. Fu la sortè dell' armi; 9b. Amore, amore; 10a. Gloria all' Egitto; 10b. March ('Grand March'); 10c. Ballabile; 10d. Vieni, o guerriero; 10e. Quest'assisa; 11. O Re, pei sacri Numi. ACT 3: 12a. O tu che sei d'Osiride; 12b. Vieni d'Iside; 12c. Qui Radames verrà; 12d. O patria mia; 13. Ciel mio padre; 14a. Pur' ti riveggo; 14b. Fuggiam gli ardor ... Là, tra foreste vergini; 14c. Tu! Amonasro!...Io son disonorato!. ACT 4: 15a. Introduction; 15b. L'abborita rivale; 15c. Già i sacerdoti; 15d. Misero appien mi festi; 16a. Ohimè morir mi sento; 16b. Spirto del nume; 17a. La fatale pietra; 17b. Morir si pura e bella; 18a. Immenso immenso; 18b. O terra addio.

Aida M. Chiara
Amneris F. Cossotto
Radamès N. Martinucci
Amonasro G. Scandola
Ramfis C. Zardo
King A. Zanazzo
Messenger G. Corradi
erona Arena Ballet, Verona Arena Chor, Verona Arena Orch, A. Guadagno, G. Sbragia
(CAST) ▣ **CVI2013**

Aida M. Chiara
Amneris G. Dimitrova
Radamès L. Pavarotti
Amonasro J. Pons
Ramphis N. Ghiaurov
King P. Burchuladze
Messenger E. Gavazzi
Priestess F. Garbi
a Scala Chor, La Scala Orch, L. Maazel, L. Ronconi
(MCEG) ▣ **VVD378**

Aida D. Giannini
Amneris I. Minghini-Cattaneo
Radamès A. Pertile
Amonasro G. Inghilleri
Ramfis L. Manfrini
King G. Masini
Messenger G. Nessi
a Scala Chor, La Scala Orch, C. Sabajno (r1928)
(PEAR) Ⓓ **GEMMCDS9402**

Aida H. Nelli
Amneris E. Gustavson
Radamès R. Tucker
Amonasro G. Valdengo
Ramfis N. Scott
King D. Harbour
Messenger V. Assandri
Priestess T. Stich-Randall
Shaw Chorale, NBC SO, A. Toscanini (bp1949)
(RCA) Ⓓ [3] **GD60300**

Aida A. Millo
Amneris D. Zajick
Radamès P. Domingo
Amonasaro S. Milnes
Ramfis P. Burchuladze
King D. Kavrakos
Messenger M. Baker
Priestess M.J. Wray
Met Op Ballet, NY Met Op Chor, NY Met Op Orch, James Levine, B. Large
(DG) ◐ [2] **072 416-1GH2**
(DG) ▣ **072 416-3GH**

Aida R. Tebaldi
Amneris E. Stignani
Radamès M. del Monaco
Amonasro A. Protti
Ramfis D. Caselli
King F. Corena
Messenger P. de Palma
Santa Cecilia Academy Chor, Santa Cecilia Academy Orch, A. Erede (r1952)
(LOND) Ⓓ [2] **440 239-2LF2**

Aida M. Curtis Verna
Amneris M. Pirazzini
Radamès F. Corelli
Amanasro G. Guelfi
Ramfis G. Neri
King A. Zerbini
Messenger A. Cesarini
Turin Rad Chor, Turin RSO, A. Questa (bp1956)
(FONI) Ⓓ [2] **CDO29**

Aida G. Arangi-Lombardi
Amneris M. Capuana
Radamès A. Lindi
Amonasro A. Borgioli
Ramfis T. Pasero
King S. Baccaloni
Messenger G. Nessi
La Scala Chor, Milan SO, L. Molajoli (r1928)
(VAI) Ⓓ [2] **VAIA1083**

Aida K. Ricciarelli
Amneris E. Obraztsova
Radamès P. Domingo
Amanasro L. Nucci
Ramfis N. Ghiaurov
King R. Raimondi
Messenger P. de Palma
Priestess L.V. Terrani
La Scala Chor, La Scala Orch, C. Abbado
(12/82) (DG) Ⓓ [3] **410 092-2GH3**

Aida M. Caballé
Amneris F. Cossotto
Radamès P. Domingo
Amonasro P. Cappuccilli
Ramfis N. Ghiaurov
King L. Roni
Messenger N. Martinucci
Priestess E. Casas
ROH Chor, New Philh, R. Muti (r1974)
(1/87) (EMI) Ⓓ [3] **CDS7 47271-8**

Aida L. Price
Amneris R. Gorr
Radamès J. Vickers
Amonasro R. Merrill
Ramfis G. Tozzi
King P. Clabassi
Messenger F. Ricciardi
Priestess M. Sighele
Rome Op Chor, Rome Op Orch, G. Solti (r1961)
(9/87) (DECC) Ⓓ [3] **417 416-2DH3**

Aida M. Callas
Amneris F. Barbieri
Radamès R. Tucker
Amonasro T. Gobbi
Ramfis G. Modesti
King N. Zaccaria
Messenger F. Ricciardi
Priestess E. Galassi
La Scala Chor, La Scala Orch, T. Serafin (r1955)
(11/87) (EMI) Ⓓ [3] **CDS7 49030-8**

Aida M. Freni
Amneris A. Baltsa
Radamès J. Carreras
Amonasro P. Cappuccilli
Ramfis R. Raimondi
King J. Van Dam
Messenger T. Moser
Priestess K. Ricciarelli
Vienna St Op Chor, VPO, H. von Karajan (r1979)
(4/88) (EMI) Ⓓ [3] **CMS7 69300-2**

Aida L. Price
Amneris G. Bumbry
Radamès P. Domingo
Amonasro S. Milnes
Ramfis R. Raimondi
King H. Sotin
Messenger B. Brewer
Priestess J. Mathis
John Alldis Ch, LSO, E. Leinsdorf (r1970)
(8/88) (RCA) Ⓓ [3] **RD86198**

Aida Z. Milanov
Amneris F. Barbieri
Radamès J. Björling
Amonasro L. Warren
Ramfis B. Christoff
King P. Clabassi
Messenger Mario Carlin
Priestess B. Rizzoli
Rome Op Chor, Rome Op Orch, J. Perlea (r1955)
(8/88) (RCA) Ⓓ [3] **GD86652**

Aida R. Tebaldi
Amneris G. Simionato
Radamès C. Bergonzi
Amonasro C. MacNeil
Ramfis A. Van Mill
King F. Corena
Messenger P. de Palma
Priestess E. Ratti
Vienna Singverein, VPO, H. von Karajan
(1/89) (DECC) Ⓓ [3] **414 087-2DM3**

Aida B. Nilsson
Amneris G. Bumbry
Radamès F. Corelli
Amonasro M. Sereni
Ramfis B. Giaiotti
King F. Mazzoli
Messenger P. de Palma
Priestess M. Fiorentini
Rome Op Chor, Rome Op Orch, Z. Mehta (r1966)
(1/90) (EMI) Ⓓ [2] **CMS7 63229-2**

Aida M. Chiara
Amneris G. Dimitrova
Radamès L. Pavarotti
Amonasro L. Nucci
Ramfis P. Burchuladze
King L. Roni
Messenger E. Gavazzi
Priestess M. Renée
La Scala Chor, La Scala Orch, L. Maazel
(5/90) (DECC) Ⓓ [3] **417 439-2DH3**

Aida M. Caniglia
Amneris E. Stignani
Radamès B. Gigli
Amonasro G. Bechi
Ramfis T. Pasero
King I. Tajo
Messenger A. Zagonara
Priestess M. Huder
Rome Op Chor, Rome Op Orch, T. Serafin (r1946)
(5/90) (EMI) Ⓓ [2] **CHS7 63331-2**

Aida H. Nelli
Amneris E. Gustavson
Radamès R. Tucker
Amonasro G. Valdengo
Ramfis N. Scott
King D. Harbour
Messenger V. Assandri
Priestess T. Stich-Randall
R. Shaw Chorale, NBC SO, A. Toscanini (bp1949)
(5/90) (RCA) Ⓓ [7] **GD60326**

Aida A. Millo
Amneris D. Zajick
Radamès P. Domingo
Amonasro J. Morris
Ramfis S. Ramey
King T. Cook
Messenger C. Anthony
Priestess H-K. Hong
NY Met Op Chor, NY Met Op Orch, James Levine
(5/91) (SONY) Ⓓ [3] **S3K45973**

Aida H. Nelli
Amneris E. Gustavson
Radames R. Tucker
Amonasro G. Valdengo
Ramfis N. Scott
King D. Harbour
Messenger V. Assandri
Priestess T. Stich-Randall
R. Shaw Chorale, NBC SO, A. Toscanini (bp1949)
(9/91) (RCA) ◐ [2] **780 346**
(5/90) (RCA) ▣ **790 346**

Aida M. Dragoni
Amneris B. Dever
Radamès K. Johannsson
Amonasro M. Rucker
Ramfis F.E. D'Artegna
King R. Ferrari
Messenger A. Marceno
Priestess M. Trini
RTE Phil Ch, RTE Chbr Ch, Culwick Choral Soc, Bray Choral Soc, Dublin County Ch, Dun Laoghaire Choral Soc, Cantabile Sngrs, Goethe Institut Ch, Musica Sacra Sngrs, Phoenix Sngrs, Irish Army Band, Ireland National SO, R. Saccani (r1994)
(10/95) (NAXO) Ⓓ [2] **8 660033/4**

Excs J. Björling, M. Németh, K. Thorborg, A. Sved, L. Hofmann, Vienna St Op Chor, Vienna St Op Orch, V. de Sabata (pp1936: Ger/Swed) (12/94) (SCHW) ⊙ [2] **314542**

Excs M. Németh, R. Anday, K. von Pataky, A. Sved, N. Zec, C. Bissuti, Vienna St Op Chor, Vienna St Op Orch, V. de Sabata (pp1936: Ger) (12/94) (SCHW) ⊙ [2] **314542**

Excs T. Mazaroff, M. Németh, K. Thorborg, A. Sved, H. Alsen, Vienna St Op Chor, Vienna St Op Orch, B. Walter (pp1937: Ger) (2/95) (SCHW) ⊙ [2] **314572**

Excs S. Svanholm, D. Ilitsch, H. Hotter, E. Nikolaidi, J. von Manowarda, M. Rus, Vienna St Op Chor, Vienna St Op Orch, V. Gui (pp1941: Ger) (4/95) (SCHW) ⊙ [2] **314582**

Excs B. Gigli, M. Németh, R. Anday, N. Zec, A. Sved, A. Kipnis, Vienna St Op Chor, Vienna St Op Orch, K. Alwin (pp1937: Ital/Ger) (6/95) (SCHW) ⊙ [2] **314632**

1. Sofia SO, V. Stefanov (LASE) ⊙ **15 519** (LASE) ▭ **79 519**

1. Forum PO, G. Bellini (EURM) ⊙ **350214**

1. RPO, E. Bátiz (RPO) ⊙ **CDRPO5006** (RPO) ▭ **ZCRPO5006**

1. Mexico St SO, E. Bátiz (r1990s) (ASV) ⊙ **CDDCA856** (ASV) ▭ **ZCDCA856**

1. Hungarian St Op Orch, P.G. Morandi (r1994) (NAXO) ⊙ **8 553018**

1. Philh, T. Serafin (r1959) (EMI) ⊙ [2] **CES5 68541-2**

1. BPO, H. von Karajan (DG) ⊙ [2] **447 364-2GDB2**

1. RPO, A. Licata (r1994) (TRIN) ⊙ **TRP044**

1. La Scala Orch, C. Abbado (6/87) (CBS) ⊙ **CD37228**

1. BPO, H. von Karajan (10/87) (DG) ⊙ **419 622-2GH**

1. BPO, H. von Karajan (5/90) (DG) ⊙ **429 164-2GR**

1. BPO, V. de Sabata (r1939) (11/92) (KOCH) ⊙ **37126-2**

1. Berlin RIAS Orch, F. Fricsay (r1953) (11/94) (DG) ⊙ **445 406-2GDO**

1. I. Seefried, M. Forrester, E. Haefliger, D. Fischer-Dieskau, Berlin St Hedwig's Cath Ch, BPO, F. Fricsay, H. Krebs, T. Varga, Berlin RIAS Chbr Ch, Berlin RIAS Orch, H. Geusser, W. Fugmann, M. Weber, G. Herzog, Berlin RSO, VPO, E. Grümmer, G. Pitzinger, H. Hotter, Y. Menuhin (r1953) (11/94) (DG) ⊙ [11] **445 400-2GDO10**

1. BPO, H. von Karajan (1/95) (DG) ⊙ **439 972-2GGA2**

1, 3a, 3b P. Dvorský, Bratislava RSO, O. Lenárd (5/92) (NAXO) ⊙ **8 550343**

1, 3a, 3b, 4b, 6a, 6c, 10a, 10e, 11, 12d, 13, 14a, 14b, 15c, 18a, 18b K. Ricciarelli, E. Obraztsova, P. Domingo, L. Nucci, N. Ghiaurov, R. Raimondi, La Scala Chor, La Scala Orch, C. Abbado (9/85) (DG) ⊙ **415 286-2GH**

1, 3a, 3b, 5a-c, 6a, 7c, 10a-c, 10e, 12c, 12d, 13, 17a, 18a, 18b K. Ricciarelli, P. Domingo, R. Raimondi, E. Obraztsova, L. Nucci, N. Ghiaurov, P. de Palma, La Scala Chor, La Scala Orch, C. Abbado (r1981) (DG) ⊙ **439 482-2GCL** (DG) ▭ **439 482-4GCL**

2, 3b, 5c, 6a, 6b, 10a, 10b, 10d Cincinnati Pops, E. Kunzel (r1994; arr & orch Kunzel & Beck) (TELA) ⊙ **CD80364** (TELA) ▭ **CS30364**

3a, 3b M. Lanza, RCA Victor Orch, C. Callinicos (r1949) (RCA) ⊙ **RD86218**

3a, 3b L. Pavarotti, Vienna Volksoper Orch, L. Magiera (7/75) (DECC) ▭ **400 053-4DH**

3a, 3b P. Domingo, La Scala Orch, C. Abbado (DG) ⊙ [3] **427 708-2GX3**

3a, 3b J. Björling, Rome Op. Orch, J. Perlea (r1955) (RCA) ▭ **GK85277**

3a, 3b P. Domingo, Los Angeles PO, C.M. Giulini (DG) ▭ **419 091-4GW**

3a, 3b P. Domingo, New Philh, R. Muti (EMI) ⊙ **CDC7 54016-2**

3a, 3b P. Domingo, New Philh, R. Muti (EMI) ⊙ **CDM7 63103-2**

3a, 3b P. Domingo, New Philh, R. Muti (CFP) ⊙ **CD-CFP4575** (CFP) ▭ **TC-CFP4575**

3a, 3b M. Lanza, RCA Victor Orch, C. Callinicos (r1949) (RCA) ⊙ **GD60516**

3a, 3b C. Bergonzi, Santa Cecilia Academy Orch, G. Gavazzeni (DECC) ⊙ **433 623-2DSP** (DECC) ▭ **433 623-4DSP**

3a, 3b L. Pavarotti, La Scala Orch, M. Freni (DECC) ⊙ **430 470-2DH** (DECC) ▭ **430 470-4DH**

3a, 3b C. Bergonzi, New Philh, N. Santi (PHIL) ⊙ [3] **432 486-2PM3**

3a, 3b P. Domingo, LSO, E. Leinsdorf (RCA) ⊙ [2] **GD60866** (RCA) ▭ [2] **GK60866**

3a, 3b L. Pavarotti, Vienna Volksoper Orch, L. Magiera (DECC) ⊙ **433 069-2DWO** (DECC) ▭ **433 069-4DWO**

3a, 3b J. Vickers, Rome Op Chor, G. Solti (r1961) (DECC) ⊙ **433 221-2DWO** (DECC) ▭ **433 221-4DWO**

3a, 3b M. Lanza, RCA Victor Orch, C. Callinicos (r1949) (RCA) ⊙ [3] **GD60889(2)**

3a, 3b M. Lorenz, Berlin St Op Orch, C. Schmalstich (r1928: Ger) (PREI) ⊙ **89053**

3a, 3b A. Paoli, orch (r1911) (PREI) ⊙ **89998**

3a, 3b H. Roswaenge, Berlin RSO, A. Rother (Ger: bp1940s) (PREI) ⊙ **90096**

3a, 3b J. Björling, orch, N. Grevillius (r1936) (NIMB) ⊙ **NI7835**

3a, 3b T. Harper, Bratislava RSO, M. Halász (NAXO) ⊙ **8 550497**

3a, 3b E. Caruso, orch, W.B. Rogers (r1911) (RCA) ⊙ **09026 61242-2**

3a, 3b P. Domingo, LSO, E. Leinsdorf (r1970) (RCA) ⊙ **09026 61356-2** (RCA) ▭ **09026 61356-4**

3a, 3b P. Domingo, New Philh, R. Muti (CFP) ⊙ **CD-CFP4608** (CFP) ▭ **TC-CFP4608**

3a, 3b E. Caruso, orch, W.B. Rogers (r1911) (MCI) ⊙ **MCCD086** (MCI) ▭ **MCTC086**

3a, 3b A. Davies, RPO, R. Stapleton (r1991) (RPO) ⊙ [2] **CDRPD9006** (RPO) ▭ [2] **ZCRPD9006**

3a, 3b A. Solovianenko, Verona Arena Orch, A. Guadagno (pp1992) (MCI) ⊙ **MCCD099**

3a, 3b Deng, Württemberg PO, R. Paternostro (SINE) ⊙ **39820222**

3a, 3b M. del Monaco, Santa Cecilia Academy Orch, A. Erede (r1952) (DECC) ⊙ **440 407-2DM**

3a, 3b C. Bergonzi, Santa Cecilia Academy Orch, G. Gavazzeni (r1958) (BELA) ⊙ **450 005-2** (BELA) ▭ **450 005-4**

3a, 3b L. Pavarotti, Vienna Volksoper Orch, L. Magiera (r1972) (DECC) ⊙ **433 440-2DA** (DECC) ▭ **433 440-4DA**

3a, 3b J. Vickers, Rome Op Orch, G. Solti (r1961) (DECC) ⊙ **433 442-2DA**

3a, 3b M. Lanza, RCA Victor SO, C. Callinicos (RCA) ⊙ **09026 61440-2** (RCA) ▭ **09026 61440-4**

3a, 3b C. Bergonzi, Santa Cecilia Academy Orch, G. Gavazzeni (BELA) ⊙ **450 133-2** (BELA) ▭ **450 133-4**

3a, 3b M. del Monaco, Milan SO, A. Quadri (r1951) (TEST) ⊙ **SBT1039**

3a, 3b H. Roswaenge, Berlin St Op Orch, B. Seidler-Winkler (r1940: Ger) (PREI) ⊙ [2] **89211**

3a, 3b C. Bergonzi, New Philh, N. Santi (PHIL) ⊙ **442 602-2PM** (PHIL) ▭ **442 602-4PM**

3a, 3b J. Carreras, VPO, H. von Karajan (r1979) (CFP) ⊙ **CD-CFP4656** (CFP) ▭ **TC-CFP4656**

3a, 3b J. Björling, H. Ebert (pp1956) (BLUE) ⊙ **ABCD057**

3a, 3b P. Domingo, Los Angeles PO, C.M. Giulini (r1980) (DG) ⊙ **445 525-2GMA** (DG) ▭ **445 525-4GMA**

3a, 3b C. Bergonzi, Santa Cecilia Academy Orch, G. Gavazzeni (r1957) (DECC) ⊙ **440 417-2DM**

3a, 3b M. Lanza, RCA Victor Orch, C. Callinicos (r1949) (RCA) ⊙ **74321 25817-2** (RCA) ▭ **74321 25817-4**

3a, 3b A. Piccaver, Berlin St Op Orch, J. Prüwer (r1930: Ger) (PREI) ⊙ [2] **89217**

3a, 3b J. Björling, Rome Op Chor, Rome Op Orch, J. Perlea (r1955) (RCA) ⊙ **09026 62550-2**

3a, 3b B. Gigli, orch, W. Goehr (r1937) (PEAR) ⊙ [2] **GEMMCDS9176**

3a, 3b L. Pavarotti, Vienna Volksoper Orch, L. Magiera (7/86) (DECC) ⊙ [2] **417 011-2DH2**

3a, 3b P. Domingo, La Scala Orch, C. Abbado (7/86) (DG) ⊙ **415 366-2GH**

3a, 3b B. Gigli, orch, W. Goehr (r1937) (9/88) (EMI) ⊙ **CDH7 61051-2**

3a, 3b J. Björling, orch, N. Grevillius (r1936) (10/88) (EMI) ⊙ **CDH7 61053-2**

3a, 3b G. Martinelli, orch, J. Pasternack (r1926) (10/89) (NIMB) ⊙ **NI7804** (NIMB) ▭ **NC7804**

3a, 3b E. Caruso, orch (r1911) (10/89) (NIMB) ⊙ **NI7803** (NIMB) ▭ **NC7803**

3a, 3b F. Völker, Berlin St Op Orch, H. Weigert (r1930: Ger) (2/90) (PREI) ⊙ **89005**

3a, 3b M. Fleta, orch (r1927) (2/90) (PREI) ⊙ **89002**

3a, 3b H. Roswaenge, Berlin St Op Orch, B. Seidler-Winkler (r1940: Ger) (5/90) (PREI) ⊙ **89018**

3a, 3b L. Pavarotti, Vienna Volksoper Orch, L. Magiera (7/90) (DECC) ⊙ [2] **425 681-2DM2** (7/90) (DECC) ▭ [2] **425 681-4DM2**

3a, 3b E. Caruso, orch (r1911) (3/91) (PEAR) ⊙ [3] **EVC2**

3a, 3b E. Caruso, orch, W.B. Rogers (r1911) (7/91) (RCA) ⊙ [12] **GD60495(4)**

3a, 3b E. Caruso, orch (r1911) (7/91) (MSCM) ⊙ **MM30352**

3a, 3b G. Martinelli, orch (r1926) (7/92) (PEAR) ⊙ [3] **GEMMCDS9925(1)**

3a, 3b G. Martinelli, orch, J. Pasternack (r1926) (3/93) (PREI) ⊙ **89062**

3a, 3b D. Yuzhin, anon (r1902: Russ) (6/93) (PEAR) ⊙ [3] **GEMMCDS9001/3(1)**

3a, 3b J. Vickers, Rome Op Orch, R. Chailly (r1961) (10/93) (DECC) ⊙ **436 463-2DM** (10/93) (DECC) ▭ **436 463-4DM**

3a, 3b C. Kullman, Berlin St Op Orch, E. Orthmann (Ger: r1931) (11/93) (PREI) ⊙ **89057**

3a, 3b R. Tucker, A. Toscanini, NBC SO (r1949) (4/94) (RCA) ⊙ [6] **09026 61580-2(6)**

3a, 3b P. Domingo, New Philh, R. Muti (r1974) (6/94) (EMI) ⊙ **CDC5 55017-2**

3a, 3b J. Björling, orch, N. Grevillius (r1936) (9/94) (IMP) ⊙ **GLRS103**

3a, 3b J. Björling, orch, N. Grevillius (r1936) (9/94) (CONI) ⊙ **CDHD214** (9/94) (CONI) ▭ **MCHD214**

3a, 3b J. Björling, orch, N. Grevillius (r1936) (12/94) (MMOI) ⊙ **CDMOIR425**

3a, 3b H. Roswaenge, BPO, E. Orthmann (r1933: Ger) (4/95) (PREI) ⊙ [2] **89209**

3a, 3b J. Johnston, Philh, M. Mudie (r1951) (4/95) (TEST) ⊙ **SBT1058**

3a, 3b B. Heppner, Munich RO, R. Abbado (r1993/4) (11/95) (RCA) ⊙ **09026 62504-2**

3a, 3b, 5b, 6a, 6b, 10a, 10b, 10d, 12c, 12d, 13, 14a, 14b, 15c, 16a, 16b, 17a, 17b, 18a, 18b L. Price, R. Gorr, J. Vickers, R. Merrill, G. Tozzi, P. Clabassi, F. Ricciardi, Rome Op Chor, Rome Op Orch, G. Solti (r1961) (DECC) ⊙ **433 444-2DA** (DECC) ▭ **433 444-4DA**

3a, 3b, 6a-c, 10a-d, 12c, 12d, 13, 14a, 14b, 15b-d, 17a, 17b, 18b A. Millo, D. Zajick, P. Domingo, J. Morris, S. Ramey, T. Cook, C. Anthony, NY Met Op Chor, NY Met Op Orch, James Levine (r1990) (SONY) ⊙ **SMK53506**

3a, 3b, 6a, 6b, 10a, 12d, 13, 15c, 17a, 18b R. Tebaldi, C. Bergonzi, G. Simionato, C. MacNeil, A. Van Mill, F. Corena, P. de Palma, Vienna Singverein, VPO, H. von Karajan (DECC) ⊙ **417 763-2DM**

3a, 3b, 6a, 6b, 10a, 10b, 10d, 12c, 12d, 13, 14a-c, 15c, 17a, 17b, 18b M. Chiara, G. Dimitrova, L. Pavarotti, L. Nucci, P. Burchuladze, L. Roni, E. Gavazzi, La Scala Chor, La Scala Orch, L. Maazel (r1985/6) (DECC) ⊙ **433 162-2DH**

3a, 3b, 6a, 6b, 10a, 10b, 10d, 12c, 12d, 13, 14a-c, 15c, 17a, 17b, 18b M. Chiara, G. Dimitrova, L. Pavarotti, L. Nucci, P. Burchuladze, L. Roni, E. Gavazzi, La Scala Chor, La Scala Orch, L. Maazel (r1985/6) (DECC) **ꝏ** **433 162-5DH**

3a, 3b, 6a, 10a, 10e, 12c, 12d, 13, 14a, 15c, 17b, 18a, 18b M. Caballé, P. Domingo, F. Cossotto, N. Ghiaurov, P. Cappuccilli, L. Roni, ROH Chor, New Philh, R. Muti (r1974) (EMI) ⊙ **CDM7 63450-2**

3a, 3b, 14a, 14b, 14c J. Carreras, M. Freni, A. Baltsa, P. Cappuccilli, R. Raimondi, VPO, H. von Karajan (EMI) ⊙ **CDC7 54524-2**

3a, 3b, 18b J. Carreras, M. Freni, A. Baltsa, Vienna St Op Chor, VPO, H. von Karajan (EMI) ⊙ **CDM7 63111-2**

3b R. Tucker, Orch, H. Barlow (bp1957) (VAI) ▣ **VAI6910**

3b P. Domingo, New Philh, R. Muti (EMIL) ⊙ **CDZ104** (EMIL) ▭ **LZ104**

3b P. Domingo, LSO, E. Leinsdorf (RCA) Ⓓ **GD84265**
3b T. Burke, orch (r1920/1) (PEAR) Ⓓ **GEMMCD9411**
3b A. Davies, RPO, R. Stapleton (RPO) Ⓓ **CDRPO7009** (RPO) ▭ **ZCRPO7009**
3b L. Muratore, orch (r1911; French) (MSCM) Ⓓ **MM30377**
3b P. Domingo, Berlin Deutsche Op Chor, N. Santi (ERAT) Ⓓ **2292-45797-2** (ERAT) ▭ **2292-45797-4**
3b A. Davies, RPO, R. Stapleton (IMP) Ⓓ [3] **TCD1070**
3b G. Nelepp, Bolshoi Th Orch, A. Melik-Pashayev (r c1950: Russ) (PREI) Ⓓ **89081**
3b J. Björling, Rome Op Orch, J. Perlea (RCA) Ⓓ **09026 61886-2** (RCA) ▭ **09026 61886-4**
3b R. Crooks, Berlin St Op Orch, C. Schmalstich (r1927: Ger) (PEAR) Ⓓ **GEMMCD9093**
3b E. Caruso, orch (r1908) (ASV) Ⓓ **CDAJA5137** (ASV) ▭ **ZCAJA5137**
3b P. Althouse, orch (r1914) (IRCC) Ⓓ **IRCC-CD810**
3b P. Franz, orch (r1911: Fr) (PREI) Ⓓ **89099**
3b F. de Lucia, orch (r1917) (BONG) Ⓓ [2] **GB1064/5-2**
3b E. Caruso, S. Cottone (r1902) (5/89) (EMI) Ⓓ **CDH7 61046-2**
3b E. Caruso, orch (r1908) (5/89) (PEAR) Ⓓ **GEMMCD9309**
3b E. Caruso, orch (r1906) (7/90) (CLUB) Ⓓ **CL99-060**
3b E. Caruso, S. Cottone (r1902) (7/90) (CLUB) Ⓓ **CL99-060**
3b E. Caruso, orch (r1906) (12/90) (PEAR) Ⓓ [3] **EVC1(2)**
3b E. Caruso, anon (r1904) (12/90) (PEAR) Ⓓ [3] **EVC1(1)**
3b E. Caruso, S. Cottone (2 vers: r1902) (12/90) (PEAR) Ⓓ [3] **EVC1(1)**
3b F. Merli, orch, L. Molajoli (r1928) (1/91) (PREI) Ⓓ **89026**
3b E. Caruso, orch (r1908) (3/91) (PEAR) Ⓓ [3] **EVC2**
3b E. Caruso, orch (r1906) (7/91) (RCA) Ⓓ [12] **GD60495(2)**
3b E. Caruso, S. Cottone (r1902: 2 vers) (7/91) (RCA) Ⓓ [12] **GD60495(1)**
3b E. Caruso, orch (r1908) (7/91) (RCA) Ⓓ [12] **GD60495(3)**
3b E. Caruso, anon (r1904) (7/91) (RCA) Ⓓ [12] **GD60495(1)**
3b F. Viñas, anon (r1905) (7/92) (PEAR) Ⓓ [3] **GEMMCDS9924(1)**
3b A. Davidov, anon (r1901: Russ) (6/93) (PEAR) Ⓓ [3] **GEMMCDS9007/9(1)**
3b L. Escalais, anon (r1906: Fr) (12/93) (SYMP) Ⓓ **SYMCD1126**
3b G. Zenatello, anon (r1906) (12/93) (SYMP) Ⓓ **SYMCD1138**
3b G. Zenatello, orch (r1909) (12/93) (SYMP) Ⓓ **SYMCD1148**
3b G. Zenatello, anon (r1906) (5/94) (PEAR) Ⓓ [4] **GEMMCDS9073(1)**
3b G. Zenatello, orch (r1909) (5/94) (PEAR) Ⓓ [4] **GEMMCDS9073(2)**
3b G. Zenatello, orch (r1912) (5/94) (PEAR) Ⓓ [4] **GEMMCDS9074(1)**
3b M. Lorenz, Vienna St Op Orch, L. Ludwig (pp1942: Ger) (6/94) (SCHW) Ⓓ **314502**
3b G. Martinelli, orch, J. Pasternack (r1926) (7/95) (MMOI) Ⓓ **CDMOIR428**
3b G. Thill, orch, E. Bigot (r1930: Fr) (8/95) (FORL) Ⓓ **UCD16727**
3b, 10a, 10e, 12a, 12c, 12d M. Chiara, N. Martinucci, F. Cossotto, G. Scandola, Verona Arena Chor, Verona Arena Orch, A. Guadagno (CAST) ▭ **CASH5052**
3b, 12d, 14a, 14b, 15c(pt), 17a, 18b M. Lorenz, D. Ilitsch, E. Nikolaidi, M. Ahlersmeyer, H. Aisen, Vienna St Op Chor, Vienna St Op Orch, L. Ludwig (pp1942: Ger) (1/95) (SCHW) Ⓓ [2] **314562**
4a, 4b, 5a, 5b, 5c, 8a, 9a, 15b-d, 16a, 16b C. Ludwig, L. Amara, R. Tucker, E. Flagello, E. Karlsrud, R. MacWherter, NY Met Op Chor, NY Met Op Orch, F. Cleva (pp1970) (MELD) Ⓓ [2] **MEL26516**
5c, 10a ROH Chor, New Philh, R. Muti (r1974) (EMI) Ⓓ [2] **CZS5 68559-2**
5a K. Ricciarelli, La Scala Orch, C. Abbado (DG) ▭ **439 153-4GMA**

6a M. Chiara, ROHO, N. Santi (BELA) Ⓓ **450 133-2** (BELA) ▭ **450 133-4**
6a E. Urbanová, Prague SO, J. Bělohlávek (r1993) (SUPR) Ⓓ **11 1851-2**
6a R. Tebaldi, Rome RAI Orch, A. Basile (bp1961) (FONI) Ⓓ **CDMR5023**
6a A. Tomowa-Sintow, Sofia PO, R. Raichev (r1970s) (FORL) Ⓓ **UCD16742**
6a T. Lemnitz, Berlin St Op Orch, F.A. Schmidt (Ger: r1937) (10/90) (PREI) Ⓓ **89025**
6a C. Muzio, orch (r1917) (1/95) (ROMO) Ⓓ [2] **81010-2**
6a R. Ponselle, orch, Rosario Bourdon (r1928) (7/95) (MMOI) Ⓓ **CDMOIR428**
6a R. Hunter, Tasmanian SO, D. Franks (r1989) (10/95) (ABCC) Ⓓ **8 7000 10**
6a, 6b R. Ponselle, orch (r1923) (PEAR) Ⓓ [2] **GEMMCDS9964**
6a, 6b A. Shuard, ROHO, E. Downes (CFP) Ⓓ **CD-CFP4575** (CFP) ▭ **TC-CFP4575**
6a, 6b L. Price, Rome Op Orch, G. Solti (DECC) Ⓓ **433 067-2DWO** (DECC) ▭ **433 067-4DWO**
6a, 6b R. Tebaldi, VPO, H. von Karajan (r1959) (DECC) Ⓓ **440 408-2DM**
6a, 6b V. Zeani, Naples San Carlo Op Orch, F. Previtali (pp1969) (BONG) Ⓓ **GB1060-2**
6a, 6b L. Price, Rome Op Orch, G. Solti (r1961) (DECC) Ⓓ **433 442-2DA**
6a, 6b M. Callas, Paris Cons, N. Rescigno (r1964) (EMI) Ⓓ **CDC5 55016-2**
6a, 6b R. Ponselle, orch, Rosario Bourdon (r1928) (RCA) Ⓓ **74321 24284-2** (RCA) ▭ **74321 24284-4**
6a, 6b M. Callas, Paris Cons, N. Rescigno (9/87) (EMI) Ⓓ **CDC7 47730-2**
6a, 6b E. Turner, orch, T. Beecham (r1928) (9/89) (EMI) Ⓓ **CDH7 69791-2**
6a, 6b E. Turner, orch, T. Beecham (r1928) (10/89) (NIMB) Ⓓ **NI7802** (NIMB) ▭ **NC7802**
6a, 6b R. Ponselle, orch, Rosario Bourdon (r1928) (1/90) (RCA) Ⓓ **GD87810**
6a, 6b M. Callas, Paris Cons, N. Rescigno (2/90) (EMI) Ⓓ **CDM7 63182-2**
6a, 6b G. Arangi-Lombardi, Milan SO, L. Molajoli (r1928) (10/90) (PREI) Ⓓ **89013**
6a, 6b M. Seinemeyer, Berlin St Op Orch, F. Weissmann (Ger: r1926) (11/90) (PREI) Ⓓ **89029**
6a, 6b F. Leider, orch (r1922: Ger) (5/91) (PREI) Ⓓ [3] **89301**
6a, 6b J. Gadski, orch (r1909) (7/91) (CLUB) Ⓓ **CL99-109**
6a, 6b R. Tebaldi, VPO, H. von Karajan (8/91) (DECC) Ⓓ [2] **430 481-2DX2**
6a, 6b L. Welitsch, Philh, J. Krips (r1947) (4/92) (EMI) Ⓓ [7] **CHS7 69741-2(4)**
6a, 6b G. Russ, anon (r1905) (7/92) (PEAR) Ⓓ [3] **GEMMCDS9923(2)**
6a, 6b R. Pampanini, EIAR Orch, U. Tansini (r1940) (8/93) (PREI) Ⓓ **89063**
6a, 6b R. Tebaldi, New Philh, R. Bonynge (r1969) (10/93) (DECC) Ⓓ **436 301-2DA**
6a, 6b R. Ponselle, orch, Rosario Bourdon (r1928) (10/93) (NIMB) Ⓓ **NI7846**
6a, 6b L. Price, ROHO, G. Solti (r1961) (10/93) (DECC) Ⓓ **436 461-2DM**
6a, 6b E. Turner, orch, T. Beecham (r1928) (12/93) (NIMB) Ⓓ **NI7851**
6a, 6b M. Freni, Ater Orch, L. Magiera (pp) (5/94) (DECC) Ⓓ [2] **443 018-2DF2**
6a, 6b, 12c, 12d G. Jones, ROHO, E. Downes (DECC) Ⓓ **433 624-2DSP**
6a, 6b, 12c, 12d L. Price, Rome Op Orch, G. Solti (r1961) (DECC) Ⓓ **440 402-2DM**
6a, 6b, 12c, 12d J. Barstow, ENO Orch, M. Elder (1/89) (TER) Ⓓ **CDVIR8307** (1/89) (TER) ▭ **ZCVIR8307**
6a, 6b, 12c, 12d A. Marc, NZ SO, H. Wallberg (6/92) (DELO) Ⓓ **DE3108** (6/92) (DELO) ▭ **CS3108**
6a, 6b, 12c, 12d D. Giannini, La Scala Orch, C. Sabajno (r1928) (4/93) (PREI) Ⓓ **89044**
6a, 6c E. Destinn, anon (r1905) (PEAR) Ⓓ **GEMMCD9172**
6a, 6c E. Destinn, anon (r1905: Ger) (12/94) (SUPR) Ⓓ [12] **11 2136-2(1)**
6a, 6c E. Destinn, orch, B. Seidler-Winkler (r1908: Ger) (12/94) (SUPR) Ⓓ [12] **11 2136-2(1)**
6a, 6c, 12d E. Destinn, orch (r1911: Ger) (12/94) (SUPR) Ⓓ [12] **11 2136-2(4)**

6a, 6c, 12d E. Destinn, orch (r1912) (12/94) (SUPR) Ⓓ [12] **11 2136-2(4)**
6a, 12d L. Price, Rome Op Orch, O. de Fabritiis (RCA) Ⓓ **RD87016**
6a, 12d R. Ponselle, orch, Rosario Bourdon (r1923: 2 vers of 6a) (11/94) (ROMO) Ⓓ [2] **81006-2**
6a(2 vers), 12d R. Ponselle, orch, Rosario Bourdon (r1926/8) (11/94) (ROMO) Ⓓ [2] **81007-2**
6a, 12d E. Rethberg, orch (r1927) (2/95) (ROMO) Ⓓ [2] **81012-2**
6a, 12d E. Rethberg, orch (r1924) (2/95) (ROMO) Ⓓ [2] **81012-2**
6a, 12d E. Rethberg, Berlin SO, F. Zweig (r1927) (10/95) (ROMO) Ⓓ [2] **81014-2**
6a, 12d, 18b R. Raisa, G. Crimi, orch (r1923) (1/94) (CLUB) Ⓓ **CL99-052**
6a, 13. X. Belmas, W. Domgraf-Fassbaender, orch, A. Kitschin (r1929) (10/92) (PREI) Ⓓ **89047**
6a, 13(pt), 14a(pt), 17a, 17b, 18a, 18b R. Bampton, L. Summers, A. Carron, L. Warren, chor, orch, W. Pelletier (r1940) (VAI) Ⓓ **VAIA1084**
6b, 6c L. Tetrazzini, orch (r1911) (9/92) (EMI) Ⓓ [3] **CHS7 63802-2(1)**
6b, 6c L. Tetrazzini, orch (r1911) (9/92) (PEAR) Ⓓ **GEMMCD9222**
6b, 9b(pt) E. Destinn, L. Kirkby-Lunn, orch, P. Pitt (r1911) (12/94) (SUPR) Ⓓ [12] **11 2136-2(4)**
6c C. Muzio, orch (r1917) (PEAR) Ⓓ **GEMMCD9143**
6c F. Litvinne, anon (r1905: Fr) (7/92) (PEAR) Ⓓ [3] **GEMMCDS9923(2)**
6c F. Litvinne, anon (r1905: Fr) (12/94) (SYMP) Ⓓ **SYMCD1128**
7c(pt) A. Paoli, A. de Segurola, orch (r1909) (PREI) Ⓓ **89998**
7c J. Carreras, R. Raimondi, Vienna St Op Chor, VPO, H. von Karajan (10/88) (EMI) Ⓓ **CDM7 69549-2**
7c E. Pinza, G. Martinelli, NY Met Op Chor, NY Met Op Orch, G. Setti (r1927/8) (2/89) (PEAR) Ⓓ **GEMMCD9306**
7c(pt) G. Martinelli, E. Pinza, NY Met Op Chor, NY Met Op Orch, G. Setti (r1927) (3/93) (PREI) Ⓓ **89062**
7c(pt) E. Garbin, O. Luppi, La Scala Chor, anon (r1905) (12/93) (SYMP) Ⓓ **SYMCD1113**
7c(pt) A. Didur, T. Leliwa, orch (r c1911) (1/94) (CLUB) Ⓓ **CL99-089**
7c(pt) G. Zenatello, J. Mardones, chor, orch (r1912) (5/94) (PEAR) Ⓓ [4] **GEMMCDS9074(1)**
8b, 10c NY Met Op Orch, James Levine (r1992) (6/94) (SONY) Ⓓ **SK52489**
9a, 9b R. Scotto, E. Obraztsova, Czech SO, A. Krieger (pp1991) (IMP) Ⓓ **MCD42**
9a, 9b G. Cigna, C. Elmo, Turin EIAR Orch, U. Tansini (r1941) (11/90) (LYRC) Ⓓ **SRO805**
9a, 9b M. Caballé, S. Verrett, Ambrosian Op Chor, New Philh, A. Guadagno (5/92) (RCA) Ⓓ **GD60818**
9a, 9b M. Klose, M. Perras, Berlin St Op Orch, B. Seidler-Winkler (r1937: Ger) (7/95) (PREI) Ⓓ **89082**
9b(pt) J. Gadski, L. Homer, orch (r1909) (7/92) (PEAR) Ⓓ [3] **GEMMCDS9923(2)**
10a ROH Chor, New Philh, R. Muti (EMI) Ⓓ **CDC7 47274-2**
10a John Alldis Ch, LSO, E. Leinsdorf (RCA) Ⓓ **GD60205**
10a ROH Chor, ROHO, L. Gardelli (EMI) Ⓓ **CDM7 64356-2**
10a Chicago Sym Chor, Chicago SO, G. Solti (DECC) OO **430 226-5DH**
10a Chor, Orch, Anon (cond) (BELA) Ⓓ **450 052-2** (BELA) ▭ **450 052-4**
10a E. Turner, E. Rubadi, F. Ciniselli, L. Paci, B. Carmassi, La Scala Chor, orch, L. Molajoli (r1926) (9/89) (EMI) Ⓓ **CDH7 69791-2**
10a ROH Chor, ROHO, B. Haitink (12/89) (EMI) Ⓓ **CDC7 49849-2**
10a Chicago Sym Chor, Chicago SO, G. Solti (4/91) (DECC) Ⓓ **430 226-2DH**
10a Slovak Phil Chor, Bratislava RSO, O. Dohnányi (4/91) (NAXO) Ⓓ **8 550241**
10a-c London Choral Soc, Scots Guards Band, Welsh Guards Band, RPO, M. Reed (pp1989: Eng) (RPO) Ⓓ [2] **CDRPD9001** (RPO) ▭ [2] **ZCRPD9001**

10a-c Rome Op Chor, Rome Op Orch, G. Solti (r1961) (DECC) ⓓ **433 221-2DWO** (DECC) ⊟ **433 221-4DWO**
10a-d R. Viljakainen, U. Sippola, P. Lindroos, W. Groenroos, M. Salminen, J. Tilli, Savonlinna Op Fest Chor, Savonlinna Op Fest Orch, L. Segerstam (BIS) ⓓ [2] **BIS-CD373/4**
10a-e NY Met Op Ballet, NY Met Op Chor, NY Met Op Orch, James Levine (DECC) ◐ **071 142-1DH** (DECC) ▣ **071 142-3DH**
10a-e Santa Cecilia Academy Chor, Santa Cecilia Academy Orch, C. Franci (r1964) (DECC) ⓓ **433 443-2DA** (DECC) ⊟ **433 443-4DA**
10a-e Santa Cecilia Academy Chor, Santa Cecilia Academy Orch, C. Franci (r1964) (DECC) ⓓ [2] **443 585-2DF2** (DECC) ⊟ [2] **433 585-4DWO2**
10a, 10b London Choral Soc, RPO, M. Reed (IMP) ⓓ [3] **TCD1070**
10a, 10b Locke Brass Consort, J. Stobart (arr Lake) (9/92) (CRD) ⓓ **CRD3402** (3/83) (CRD) ⊟ **CRDC4102**
10a, 10b, 10d, 10e Santa Cecilia Academy Chor, Santa Cecilia Academy Orch, C. Franci (DECC) ⓓ **425 849-2DWO** (DECC) ⊟ **425 849-4DWO**
10a, 10b, 10d La Scala Chor, La Scala Orch, L. Maazel (DECC) ⓓ **433 822-2DH** (DECC) ⊟ **433 822-4DH**
10a, 10b, 10d LSC, LSO, R. Hickox (r1987) (IMP) ⓓ **PCDS10** (IMP) ⊟ **PCDSC10**
10a, 10b, 10d LSC, LSO, R. Hickox (r1987) (IMP) ⓓ **PCDS15** (IMP) ⊟ **PCDSC15**
10a, 10b, 10d LSC, LSO, R. Hickox (r1987) (IMP) ⓓ [3] **TCD1073**
10a, 10b, 10d LSC, LSO, R. Hickox (r1987) (4/89) (IMP) ⓓ **PCD908**
10a, 10d Berlin Deutsche Op Chor, Berlin Deutsche Op Orch, G. Sinopoli (DG) **OO 415 283-5GH**
10a, 10d Berlin Deutsche Op Chor, Berlin Deutsche Op Orch, G. Sinopoli (10/85) (DG) ⓓ **415 283-2GH**
10a, 10d Atlanta Sym Chor, Atlanta SO, Robert Shaw (3/88) (TELA) ⓓ [2] **CD80152**
10b H. Britton (arr Britton) (ASV) ⓓ **CDQS6028** (ASV) ⊟ **ZCQS6028**
10b Boston Pops, A. Fiedler (RCA) ⓓ **GD60700**
10b VPO, H. Knappertsbusch (r1940) (PREI) ⓓ **90116**
10b ROHO, B. Haitink (EMI) ⓓ [2] **CZS7 67546-2**
10b A. Marsden-Thomas (r1992: arr org: Brown) (CRAM) ⓓ **CRACD 1**
10b St Louis SO, L. Slatkin (6/89) (RCA) ⓓ **RD87716**
10b NYPO, L. Bernstein (r1968) (9/93) (SONY) ⓓ **SMK47600**
10b Boston Pops, A. Fiedler (r1958) (1/94) (RCA) ⓓ **09026 61249-2**
10b, 10c Bologna Teatro Comunale Orch, R. Chailly (DECC) ⓓ **436 475-2DM**
10c National PO, C. Gerhardt (r1971) (CHES) ⓓ **Chesky CD108**
10c NYPO, L. Bernstein (r1968) (9/93) (SONY) ⓓ **SMK47600**
10d La Scala Chor, La Scala Orch, L. von Matačić (CFP) ⓓ **CD-CFP4575** (CFP) ⊟ **TC-CFP4575**
10d John Alldis Ch, LSO, E. Leinsdorf (r1971) (RCA) ⓓ **74321 24209-2**
10e(pt) M. Lanza, chor, Rome Op Orch, C. Callinicos (r1957) (RCA) ⓓ **GD60516**
10e E. Giraldoni, anon (r1902) (6/90) (SYMP) ⓓ **SYMCD1073**
10e C. Galeffi, La Scala Orch, L. Molajoli (r1926) (2/92) (PREI) ⓓ **89040**
10e B. Franci, orch (r1920) (7/92) (PEAR) ⓓ [3] **GEMMCDS9925(2)**
10e L. Montesanto, orch (r1912) (12/94) (BONG) ⓓ **GB1043-2**
10e, 13. E. Bastianini, L. Price, Vienna St Op Chor, VPO, L. von Matačić (pp1963) (MEMO) ⓓ [2] **HR4400/1**
10e, 13(pt) L. Warren, L. Alvary, R. Bampton, chor, A. Carron, L. Summers, N. Cordon, chor, orch, W. Pelletier (r1940) (8/93) (VAI) ⓓ **VAIA1017**

11(pt) A. Parsi-Pettinella, L. Pasini-Vitale, I. Calleja, A. Magini-Coletti, F. Corradetti, O. Luppi, orch (r1910) (12/93) (SYMP) ⓓ **SYMCD1113**
12a, 12b L. Manfrini, I. Minghini-Cattaneo, La Scala Chor, La Scala Orch, C. Sabajno (r1928) (7/94) (NIMB) ⓓ **NI7853**
12c, 12d M. Caballé, New Philh, R. Muti (EMIN) ⓓ **CD-EMX9519** (EMIN) ⊟ **TC-EMX2099**
12c, 12d A. Cerquetti, MMF Orch, G. Gavazzeni (DECC) ⓓ **433 069-2DWO** (DECC) ⊟ **433 069-4DWO**
12c, 12d A. Cerquetti, MMF Orch, G. Gavazzeni (r1956) (DECC) ⓓ **433 442-2DA**
12c, 12d M. Callas, La Scala Orch, T. Serafin (r1955) (EMI) ⓓ **CDC5 55216-2** (EMI) ⊟ **EL555216-4**
12c, 12d A. Cerquetti, MMF Orch, G. Gavazzeni (r1956) (DECC) ⓓ **440 411-2DM**
12c, 12d M. Caballé, New Philh, R. Muti (r1974) (EMI) ⓓ **CDM5 65575-2**
12c, 12d M. Caballé, New Philh, R. Muti (10/88) (EMI) ⓓ **CDM7 69500-2**
12c, 12d E. Turner, orch, S. Robinson (r1928) (9/89) (EMI) ⓓ **CDH7 69791-2**
12c, 12d R. Ponselle, orch, Rosario Bourdon (r1923) (10/89) (NIMB) ⓓ **NI7805** (NIMB) ⊟ **NC7805**
12c, 12d C. Boninsegna, orch, C. Sabajno (r1909) (7/92) (PEAR) ⓓ [3] **GEMMCDS9924(1)**
12c, 12d J. Hammond, Philh, G. Curiel (r1955) (12/92) (TEST) ⓓ **SBT1013**
12c, 12d C. Boninsegna, orch, C. Sabajno (r1909) (4/94) (EMI) ⓓ [3] **CHS7 64860-2(2)**
12c, 12d K. Ricciarelli, Parma Teatro Regio Orch, G. Patanè (pp1976) (5/94) (DECC) ⓓ [2] **443 018-2DF2**
12c, 12d E. Rethberg, Berlin St Op Orch, F. Zweig (r1927) (7/94) (NIMB) ⓓ **NI7853**
12c, 12d, 14a, 14b, 18. L. Price, G. Simionato, D. Usunow, Vienna St Op Chor, VPO, L. von Matačić (pp1963) (MEMO) ⓓ [2] **HR4396/7**
12c, 12d, 14a, 14b N. Ermolenko-Yuzhina, D. Yuzhin, orch (r1908: Russ) (6/93) (PEAR) ⓓ [3] **GEMMCDS9001/3(2)**
12c, 12d, 17a, 18b Leonie Rysanek, S. Wagner, R. Schock, Berlin Deutsche Op Chor, Berlin SO, W. Schüchter (r1955: Ger) (2/95) (EMI) ⓓ **CDH5 65201-2**
12d R. Ponselle, orch (r1918) (PEAR) ⓓ [2] **GEMMCDS9964**
12d E. Turner, orch (r1928) (PEAR) ⓓ **GEMMCD9130**
12d L.I. Marsh, orch (r1910s) (IRCC) ⓓ **IRCC-CD810**
12d C. Muzio, orch (r1918) (PEAR) ⓓ **GEMMCD9143**
12d A. Cerquetti, Milan RAI SO, A. Basile (bp1956) (FONI) ⓓ **CDMR5014**
12d E. Destinn, orch, B. Seidler-Winkler (r1908: Ger) (PEAR) ⓓ **GEMMCD9172**
12d R. Ponselle, orch, Rosario Bourdon (r1923) (1/90) (RCA) ⓓ **GD87810**
12d E. Burzio, orch (r c1907) (1/91) (CLUB) ⓓ [2] **CL99-587/8**
12d F. Leider, orch (r1921: Ger) (5/91) (PREI) ⓓ [3] **89301**
12d J. Gadski, orch (r1906) (7/91) (CLUB) ⓓ **CL99-109**
12d E. Rethberg, orch (r1924) (7/92) (PEAR) ⓓ [3] **GEMMCDS9925(2)**
12d E. Destinn, orch (r1912) (7/92) (PEAR) ⓓ [3] **GEMMCDS9924(1)**
12d E. Destinn, orch (r1914) (11/93) (ROMO) ⓓ [2] **81002-2**
12d M. Németh, orch (1/94) (CLUB) ⓓ **CL99-007**
12d G. Arangi-Lombardi, orch, L. Molajoli (r1928) (4/94) (EMI) ⓓ [3] **CHS7 64864-2(1)**
12d E. Destinn, orch (r1914) (5/94) (SUPR) ⓓ **11 1337-2**
12d E. Destinn, orch (r1914) (12/94) (SUPR) ⓓ [12] **11 2136-2(5)**
12d E. Destinn, orch, B. Seidler-Winkler (r1908: Ger) (12/94) (SUPR) ⓓ [12] **11 2136-2(2)**
12d C. Muzio, orch (r1918) (1/95) (ROMO) ⓓ [2] **81010-2**
12d R. Ponselle, orch, Rosario Bourdon (r1923) (7/95) (MMOI) ⓓ **CDMOIR428**
13. P. Amato, J. Gadski, orch (r1913) (PEAR) ⓓ **GEMMCD9104**
13. H. Hotter, H. Scheppan, Berlin Staatskapelle, A. Rother (bp1942: Ger) (PREI) ⓓ **90200**
13. A. Granforte, H. Monti, La Scala Orch, C. Sabajno (r1928) (PREI) ⓓ **89105**

13. C. Galeffi, L.B. Rasa, La Scala Orch, L. Molajoli (r1928) (2/92) (PREI) ⓓ **8904**
13. E. Rethberg, G. De Luca, orch, Rosario Bourdon (r1930) (7/94) (NIMB) ⓓ **NI785**
13. G. De Luca, E. Rethberg, orch, Rosario Bourdon (r1930) (10/94) (PREI) ⓓ **8907**
13, 14a-c E. Rethberg, G. Lauri-Volpi, G. De Luca, orch, Rosario Bourdon (r1929/30) (PEAR) ⓓ [3] **GEMMCDS9159(2**
13, 14a, 14b E. Rethberg, G. Lauri-Volpi, G. De Luca, Victor SO, Rosario Bourdon (r1930) (10/95) (ROMO) ⓓ [2] **81014-**
14a M. Seinemeyer, T. Pattiera, orch, F. Weissmann (r1928) (PEAR) ⓓ **GEMMCD908**
14a R. Ponselle, G. Martinelli, orch, Rosario Bourdon (r1924) (10/89) (NIMB) ⓓ **NI780** (NIMB) ⊟ **NC780**
14a F. Leider, C. Günther, orch (r1922: Ger) (5/91) (PREI) ⓓ [3] **8930**
14a R. Ponselle, G. Martinelli, orch, Rosario Bourdon (r1924) (7/95) (MMOI) ⓓ **CDMOIR42**
14a, 14b E. Gentner-Fischer, M. Lorenz, Berlin St Op Orch, C. Schmalstich (r1930: Ger) (PREI) ⓓ **8905**
14a, 14b E. Rethberg, G. Lauri-Volpi, orch (r1929) (7/92) (PEAR) ⓓ [3] **GEMMCDS9926(2**
14a, 14b M. Callas, F. Corelli, Paris Op Orch, G. Prêtre (2/93) (EMI) ⓓ **CDC7 54437-**
14a, 14b E. Rethberg, G. Lauri-Volpi, G. De Luca, orch, Rosario Bourdon (r1929/30) (7/94) (NIMB) ⓓ **NI785**
14a, 14b, 14c G. Lauri-Volpi, E. Rethberg, G. De Luca, orch, Rosario Bourdon (r1929/30) (9/90) (PREI) ⓓ **8901**
14a, 14b, 17a, 18b G. Zenatello, M. Rappold, orch (r1916/7) (11/91) (CLUB) ⓓ **CL99-02**
14a, 14b, 17a, 18b G. Zenatello, M. Rappold, chor, orch (r1916) (5/94) (PEAR) ⓓ [4] **GEMMCDS9074(2**
14a, 14b, 17a, 18b R. Ponselle, G. Martinelli, orch, Rosario Bourdon (r1924: 2 vers of 17a) (11/94) (ROMO) ⓓ [2] **81006-**
14a, 17a, 17b, 18a, 18b F. Hüni-Mihacsek, H. Roswaenge, orch (r1928: Ger) (2/92) (PREI) ⓓ [2] **8920**
14b L.I. Marsh, P. Althouse, orch (r1914) (IRCC) ⓓ **IRCC-CD81**
14b G. Zenatello, E. Mazzoleni, orch (r c1908) (12/93) (SYMP) ⓓ **SYMCD114**
14b G. Zenatello, E. Mazzoleni, orch (r1911) (5/94) (PEAR) ⓓ [4] **GEMMCDS9074(**
14b, 18b F. Merli, G. Arangi-Lombardi, orch, L. Molajoli (r1926) (1/91) (PREI) ⓓ **8902**
15. G. Bumbry, P. Domingo, LSO, E. Leinsdorf (r1970) (4/94) (RCA) ⓓ [6] **09026 61580-2(7**
15a-d R. Tebaldi, F. Corelli, SRO, A. Guadagno (r1972) (10/93) (DECC) ⓓ **436 301-2D**
15b E. Randová, P. Domingo, ROHO, J. Barker (pp1988) (9/89) (EMI) ⓓ **CDC7 49811-**
15b I. Minghini-Cattaneo, A. Pertile, La Scala Orch, C. Sabajno (r1928) (6/90) (PREI) ⓓ **8900**
15b-d, 16a, 16b G. Simionato, Vienna St Op Chor, VPO, L. von Matačić (pp1963) (MEMO) ⓓ [2] **HR4386/**
15c L. Melchior, M. Arndt-Ober, orch (Ger: r1923) (PREI) ⓓ **8903**
15c H. Roswaenge, F. Beckmann, Berlin St Op Orch, B. Seidler-Winkler (r1943: Ger) (PREI) ⓓ [2] **8921**
15c L. Melchior, M. Ober, orch (r1923: Ger) (8/88) (DANA) ⓓ [2] **DACOCD313/**
15c E. Leisner, H. Roswaenge, orch (r1929: Ger) (2/92) (PREI) ⓓ [2] **8920**
15c G. Zenatello, E. Bruno, orch (r1911) (12/93) (SYMP) ⓓ **SYMCD114**
15c, 15d E. Caruso, L. Homer, orch (r1910) (3/91) (PEAR) ⓓ [3] **EVC**
15c, 15d L. Homer, E. Caruso, orch (r1910) (7/91) (RCA) ⓓ [12] **GD60495(**
15c, 15d G. Zenatello, N. Frascani, anon (r1906) (12/93) (SYMP) ⓓ **SYMCD113**
15c, 15d G. Zenatello, E. Bruno, orch (r1911) (5/94) (PEAR) ⓓ [4] **GEMMCDS9073(2**
15c, 15d G. Zenatello, N. Frascani, anon (r1906) (5/94) (PEAR) ⓓ [4] **GEMMCDS9073(**
15c, 15d G. Zenatello, M. Gay, orch (r1911) (5/94) (PEAR) ⓓ [4] **GEMMCDS9074(**
15d G. Lauri-Volpi, G. Rünger, Vienna St Op Orch, H. Reichenberger (pp1934) (7/94) (SCHW) ⓓ [2] **31451**
16b(pt) I. Minghini-Cattaneo, La Scala Chor, La Scala Orch, C. Sabajno (r1928) (7/92) (PEAR) ⓓ [3] **GEMMCDS9926(**

17a E. Caruso, J. Gadski, orch, W.B. Rogers (r1909) (RCA) Ⓓ **09026 61242-2**
17a E. Caruso, J. Gadski, orch (r1909) (7/91) (MSCM) Ⓓ **MM30352**
17a R. Raisa, G. Crimi, orch (r1921) (1/94) (CLUB) Ⓓ **CL99-052**
17a, 17b F. Merli, orch, L. Molajoli (r1926) (1/91) (PREI) Ⓓ **89026**
17a, 17b, 18a, 18b L. Price, G. Bumbry, P. Domingo, John Alldis Ch, LSO, E. Leinsdorf (r1970) (RCA) Ⓓ **09026 61634-2**
17a, 17b, 18a, 18b J. Björling, Z. Milanov, Rome Op Orch, J. Perlea (2/89) (RCA) Ⓓ **GD87799** (RCA) ▭ **GK87799**
17a, 17b, 18a, 18b M. Fleta, F. Austral, E. Thornton, orch (r1923) (2/90) (PREI) Ⓓ **89002**
17a, 17b, 18a, 18b J. Gadski, E. Caruso, orch, W.B. Rogers (r1909) (7/91) (RCA) Ⓓ [12] **GD60495(3)**
17a, 17b, 18a, 18b R. Ponselle, G. Martinelli, E. Baker, chor, orch, Rosario Bourdon (r1926) (10/93) (NIMB) Ⓓ **NI7846**
17a, 17b, 18a, 18b R. Ponselle, E. Baker, G. Martinelli, orch, Rosario Bourdon (r1926) (7/95) (MMOI) Ⓓ **CDMOIR428**
17a, 18b J. Gadski, E. Caruso, orch (r1909) (NIMB) Ⓓ **NI7834** (NIMB) ▭ **NC7834**
17a, 18b E. Caruso, J. Gadski, orch (r1909) (3/91) (PEAR) Ⓓ [3] **EVC2**
17a, 18b R. Ponselle, G. Martinelli, E. Baker, chor, orch, Rosario Bourdon (r1926) (11/94) (ROMO) Ⓓ [2] **81007-2**
17b L. Slezak, S. Sedlmair, orch (r1904) (7/92) (PEAR) Ⓓ [3] **GEMMCDS9924(2)**
17b, 18. S. Sedlmair, L. Slezak, anon (r1904: Ger) (7/91) (SYMP) Ⓓ **SYMCD1081**
18b R. Ponselle, C. Hackett, orch (r1920) (PEAR) Ⓓ [2] **GEMMCDS9964**
18b F. Austral, M. Fleta, E. Thornton, chor, orch, C. Sabajno (r1923) (7/92) (PEAR) Ⓓ [3] **GEMMCDS9925(1)**
18b G. Zenatello, E. Mazzoleni, orch (r1911) (12/93) (SYMP) Ⓓ **SYMCD1148**
18b G. Zenatello, E. Mazzoleni, orch (r1911) (5/94) (PEAR) Ⓓ [4] **GEMMCDS9073(2)**
18b G. Zenatello, E. Destinn, chor, orch (r1912) (5/94) (PEAR) Ⓓ [4] **GEMMCDS9074(1)**
18b E. Destinn, G. Zenatello, chor, orch (r1912) (12/94) (SUPR) Ⓓ [12] **11 2136-2(5)**

[Al]zira– opera: prologue & 2 acts (1845—Naples) (Lib. S. Cammarano)

EXCERPTS: 1. Overture. PROLOGUE: 2. Muoia, muoia coverto d'insulti; 3a. Ah! Tu! Fia vero!; 3b. Ed a' nemici ancora; 3c. Una Inca...eccesso orribile!; 3d. Risorto fra le tenebre; 3e. Dio della guerra. ACT 1: 4. Giunse or, da lido ispano; 5a. Alta cagion qui v'assembrava; 5b. Eterna la memoria; 5c. Quanto un mortal puo chiedere; 6a. Riposa. Tutte, in suo dolor vegliante; 6b. Da Gusman, su fragil barca; 6c. Nell'astro più che fulgido; 7. Figlia! Padre!; 8a. Anima mia!; 8b. Risorge ne'tuoi lumi; 9a. Qual ardimento! Ola?; 9b. Teco sperai combattare; 9c. Nella polvem, genuflesso; 9d. Qual suon? Che avvenne?; 9e. Trema, trema...a ritorni fra l'armi. ACT 2: 10. Mesci, mesci, Vittoria! Vittoria!; 11a. Guerreri, al nuovi di, fra voi le opime; 11b. Il pianto, l'angoscia di lena mi priva; 12a. Di pira non più; 12b. Colma di gioia ho l'anima; 13. Amici! Propizio; 14a. Miserandi avanzi; 14b. Irne lunghi ancor dovrei; 14c. Non di codarde lagrime; 15. Tergi del pianto America; 16a. Prodi figli d'Iberia; 16b. E dolce la trombla che suo vittorio; 17a. La mano e questa che a te si deve; 17b. Altre virtudo, insam.

[A]lvaro J-H. Rootering
[G]usmano R. Bruson
[O]vando D. George
[Z]amoro F. Araiza
Ataliba D. Bonilla
[A]lzira I. Cotrubas
[Z]uma S. Lis
[O]tumbo A. Ionita

[Ba]varian Rad Chor, Munich RO, L. Gardelli ([r]1982) (ORFE) Ⓓ [2] **C057832A**
[1]. Hungarian St Op Orch, P.G. Morandi (r1994) (NAXO) Ⓓ **8 553018**
[1]. BPO, H. von Karajan (1/95) (DG) Ⓓ **439 972-2GGA2**
[6]a, 6b M. Caballé, RCA Italiana Op Chor, RCA Italiana Op Orch, A. Guadagno (11/92) (RCA) Ⓓ [2] **GD60941**

14a, 14b C. Bergonzi, Ambrosian Sngrs, New Philh, N. Santi (r1974) (PHIL) Ⓓ [3] **432 486-2PM3**

Aroldo– opera: 4 acts (1857—Rimini) (Lib. F. Piave)

EXCERPTS: 1. Overture. ACT 1: 2. Tocchiamo!; 3. Ciel, ch'io respiri!; 4. Salvami to, gran Dio; 5. Egli vieni; 6. Sotto il sol di Siria; 7. Ma lagrima ti grondano!; 8. Ebben, parlatemi; 9. Tosto ei disse!; 10. Dite che il fallo; 11. Ed io pure in faccia; 12. Or meco venite; 13. O Mina, tu mi sfuggi; 14. E'bello di guerra; 15. Eterna vivra in Kenth; 16. Vi fi in Palestina; 17. Oh, qual m'invade; 18. Chi ti salve. ACT 2: 19. Oh cielo! Ove son io?; 20. Ah, dagli scanni; 21. Mina!...Voi qui!; 22. Ah, dal sen di quella tomba; 23. Io resto; 24. Ah! Era vero?; 25. Dessa non è; 26. Non punirmi, o Signor. ACT 3: 27. Ei fugge!; 28. Mina, pensa che un angelo; 29. Oh, gioia inesprimibile; 30. L'istante s'avvicina!; 31. Opposto è il calle; 32. Non allo sposo; 33. Ah si, voliamo al tempio. ACT 4: 34. Cade il giorno; 35. Cantan felici!; 36. Angiol di Dio; 37. A lago (Burrasca); 38. Ah! più non reggo; 39. Ah, da me fuggi; 40. Allora che gli anni.

Mina M. Caballé
Aroldo G. Cecchele
Briano L. Lebherz
Egberto J. Pons
Godvino V. Manno
Enrico P. Rogers
Elena M. Busching

NY Oratorio Soc, Westchester Ch Soc, NY Op Orch, E. Queler (pp1979) (12/89) (CBS) Ⓓ [2] **CD79328**
1. Sofia SO, V. Stefanov (LASE) Ⓓ **15 519** (LASE) ▭ **79 519**
1. Mexico St SO, E. Bátiz (r1990s) (ASV) Ⓓ **CDDCA856** (ASV) ▭ **ZCDCA856**
1. Hungarian St Op Orch, P.G. Morandi (r1994) (NAXO) Ⓓ **8 553018**
1. BPO, H. von Karajan (1/95) (DG) Ⓓ **439 972-2GGA2**
3, 20. M. Caballé, NY Op Orch, E. Queler (pp1979) (SONY) Ⓓ **SMK48155** (SONY) ▭ **SMT48155**
3, 20. M. Caballé, NY Op Orch, E. Queler (pp1979) (SONY) ● **SM48155**
3, 4, 19. M. Callas, Paris Cons, N. Rescigno (9/87) (EMI) Ⓓ **CDC7 47943-2**
6. C. Bergonzi, New Philh, N. Santi (PHIL) Ⓓ [3] **432 486-2PM3**
19, 20. M. Caballé, L. Kozma, RCA Italiana Op Orch, A. Guadagno (11/92) (RCA) Ⓓ [2] **GD60941**

Attila– dramma lirico: prologue, 3 acts (1846—Venice) (Lib. Solera and Piave)

EXCERPTS: 1. Overture. PROLOGUE: 2. Urli, rapine; 3. Eroi, levatevi; 4a. Di vergini straniere; 4b. Santo di patria indefinito amor!; 5. Allor che i forti corrono; 6. Da te questo or m'è concesso; 7. Uldino, a me dinanzi l'inviato; 8. Attila!...Oh, il nobil messo!; 9. Trado per gli anni, e tremulo; 10. Vanitosi!; 11. Qual notte!; 12. L'alito del mattin...Preghiam!; 13. Quai voci!; 14. Ella in poter del barbaro!; 15. Cara patria. ACT 1: 16a. Liberamente or piangi; 16b. Oh! nel fuggente nuvolo; 17. Qual suon di passi!; 18a. Sì, quell'io son; 18b. Va! Racconta al sacrilego; 18c. Oh! t'inebria nell'amplesso; 19a. Uldino! Uldini!; 19b. Mentre gonfiarsi l'anima; 19c. Oltre a quel limite t'attendo; 20. Parla, imponi...Vieni. Le menti visita; 21. No!...non é sogno. ACT 2: 22a. Tregua è cogl'Unni; 22b. Dagli immortali vertici; 22c. Che vien?...Salute ad Ezio; 22d. È gettata la mie sorte; 23a. Del ciel l'immensa volta; 23b. Ezio, ben vieni!; 23c. Chi dona luce al cor?... 23d. Ah!...Lo spirto de'monti; 23e. L'orrenda procella; 23f. Si riaccendan le quercie; 23g. Oh, miei prodi!. ACT 3: 24. Qui del convengo è il loco; 25. Che non avrebbe il misero; 26. Che più s'indugia; 27. Cessa, seh, cessa; 28. Te sol, te sol quest'anima; 29. Non involarti, seguimi; 30a. Tu, rea donna; 30b. Nella tenda. ADDITIONAL ITEM: 31. Oh Dolore.

Attila E. Nesterenko
Odabella M. Chiara
Ezio S. Carroli
Foresto V. Luchetti

Verona Arena Chor, Verona Arena Orch, N. Santi, G. Montaldo (CAST) ▭▭ **CVI2055**

Attila R. Raimondi
Odabella C. Deutekom
Ezio S. Milnes
Foresto C. Bergonzi
Uldino R. Cassinelli
Leone J. Bastin

Finchley Children's Music Group, Ambrosian Sngrs, RPO, L. Gardelli (r1972) (3/90) (PHIL) Ⓓ [2] **426 115-2PM2**

Attila S. Ramey
Odabella C. Studer
Ezio G. Zancanaro
Foresto N. Shicoff
Uldino E. Gavazzi
Leone G. Surian

La Scala Chor, La Scala Orch, R. Muti (5/90) (EMI) Ⓓ [2] **CDS7 49952-2**
1. Hungarian St Op Orch, P.G. Morandi (r1994) (NAXO) Ⓓ **8 553018**
1. BPO, H. von Karajan (1/95) (DG) Ⓓ **439 972-2GGA2**
2. Santa Cecilia Academy Chor, Santa Cecilia Academy Orch, C. Franci (r1960s) (BELA) Ⓓ **450 117-2** (BELA) ▭ **450 117-4**
2, 23a, 23c La Scala Chor, La Scala Orch, R. Muti (EMI) Ⓓ **CDC7 54484-2**
4b, 4c J. Sutherland, LSO, R. Bonynge (r1963) (DECC) Ⓓ **440 404-2DM**
4b, 5. J. Sutherland, London Sym Chor, LSO, R. Bonynge (r1963) (DECC) Ⓓ **421 881-2DA**
6. C. Studer, S. Ramey, La Scala Chor, La Scala Orch, R. Muti (r1989) (EMI) Ⓓ **CDC5 55350-2**
7. E. Rethberg, B. Gigli, E. Pinza, orch, Rosario Bourdon (r1930) (CONI) Ⓓ **CDHD227** (CONI) ▭ **MCHD227**
9. M. Pertusi, C. Alvarez, Sofia PO, E. Tabakov (r1994) (CAPR) Ⓓ **10 704**
11, 12, 24, 25. C. Bergonzi, New Philh, N. Santi (PHIL) Ⓓ [3] **432 486-2PM3**
14, 15. P. Domingo, Ambrosian Op Chor, National PO, E. Kohn (11/90) (EMI) Ⓓ **CDC7 54053-2**
16a, 16b M. Callas, Paris Op Orch, N. Rescigno (r1969) (EMI) Ⓓ **CDC7 49428-2**
16a, 16b M. Callas, Paris Cons, N. Rescigno (9/87) (EMI) Ⓓ **CDC7 47943-2**
16a, 16b M. Caballé, RCA Italiana Op Orch, A. Guadagno (11/92) (RCA) Ⓓ [2] **GD60941**
19b J. Van Dam, Loire PO, M. Soustrot (r1992) (8/93) (FORL) Ⓓ **UCD16681**
22b I. Gorin, Victor SO, B. Reibold (r1941) (10/95) (NIMB) Ⓓ **NI7867**
28. E. Rethberg, B. Gigli, E. Pinza, orch, Rosario Bourdon (r1930) (10/90) (RCA) Ⓓ **GD87811** (10/90) (RCA) ▭ **GK87811**
28. E. Rethberg, B. Gigli, E. Pinza, Victor SO, Rosario Bourdon (r1930: 2 takes) (10/95) (ROMO) Ⓓ [2] **81014-2**
31. L. Pavarotti, La Scala Orch, C. Abbado (6/87) (CBS) Ⓓ **CD37228**

Un **ballo in maschera, '(A) masked ball'– opera: 3 acts (1859—Rome) (Lib. Somma)**

EXCERPTS: 1. Prelude; ACT 1: 2a. Posa in pace; 2b. Amici miei...soldati; 2c. La rivedrà nell'estasi; 3a. Conte...Oh ciel!; 3b. Alla vita che t'arride; 4a. Il primo giudice; 4b. Volta la terrea; 4c. Sia condonnata; 5a. Zitti...l'incanto non dèssi turbare; 5b. Re dell'abisso; 5c. Arrivo il primo!; 5d. È lui, è lui!; 6. Su, fatemi largo; 7a. Sentite, la mia Signora; 7b. Che v'agita cosi?; 7c. Della città all'occaso; 8a. Su, profetessa; 8b. Di' tu se fedele; 9. Chi voi siate; 10. È scherzo od è follia; 11a. Finisci il vaticinio; 11b. O figlio d'Inghilterra. ACT 2: 12a. Prelude; 12b. Ecco l'orrido campo; 12c. Ma dall'arido stelo divulsa; 13a. Teco io sto; 13b. M'ami. m'ami; 13c. Oh, qual soave brivido; 14a. Ahimè! S'appressa; 14b. Amico, gelosa; 14c. Odi tu come fremono cupi; 15a. Seguitemi; 15b. Ve', se di notte. ACT 3: 16a. A tal colpa; 16b. Morrò, ma prima in grazia; 17a. Alzati! là tuo figlio; 17b. Eri tu che macchiavi; 18a. Siam soli; 18b. Dunque l'onta; 19a. Il messaggio entri; 19b. Di che fulgor; 20a. Forse la soglia; 20b. Ma se m'è forza perderti; 21a. Fervono amori; 21b. Saper vorreste; 22a. Ah! perchè qui!; 22b. T'amo, si, t'amo; 23a. E tu ricevi il mio!; 23b. Ah! Morte, infamia; 23c. Ella è pura (Finale).

Amelia Leonie Rysanek
Riccardo C. Bergonzi
Renato R. Merrill
Oscar A. Rothenberger
Ulrica J. Madeira
Sam L. Vichey
Tom B. Giaiotti
Silvano C. Marsh
Judge A. Velis

Servant R. Nagy
NY Met Op Chor, NY Met Op Orch, N. Santi (pp1962)
(MEMO) ① [2] **HR4374/5**

Amelia M. Arroyo
Riccardo L. Pavarotti
Renato F. Bordoni
Oscar H. Donath
Ulrica I. Dalis
Sam R. Mundt
Tom P. Booth
Silvano A. Monk
Judge J. Pinedo
Servant D. Sullivan
San Francisco Op Chor, San Francisco Op Orch, C. Mackerras (pp1971)
(BUTT) ① [2] **BMCD022**
(BUTT) ▭ [2] **BMK022**

Amelia M. Price
Riccardo L. Pavarotti
Renato R. Bruson
Oscar K. Battle
Ulrica C. Ludwig
Sam R. Lloyd
Tom M. King
Silvano P. Weber
Judge A. Oliver
Servant P. Hall
London Op Chor, RCM Jnr Chor, National PO, G. Solti (r1982/3)
(9/85) (DECC) ① [2] **410 210-2DH2**

Amelia M. Callas
Riccardo G. di Stefano
Renato T. Gobbi
Oscar E. Ratti
Ulrica F. Barbieri
Sam S. Maionica
Tom N. Zaccaria
Silvano E. Giordano
Judge; Servant R. Ercolani
La Scala Chor, La Scala Orch, A. Votto (r1956)
(9/87) (EMI) ① [2] **CDS7 47498-8**

Amelia L. Price
Riccardo C. Bergonzi
Renato R. Merrill
Oscar R. Grist
Ulrica S. Verrett
Sam E. Flagello
Tom F. Mazzoli
Silvano M. Basiola II
Judge P. de Palma
Servant F. Iacopucci
RCA Italiana Op Chor, RCA Italiana Op Orch, E. Leinsdorf
(11/88) (RCA) ① [2] **GD86645**

Amelia M. Arroyo
Riccardo P. Domingo
Renato P. Cappuccilli
Oscar R. Grist
Ulrica F. Cossotto
Sam G. Howell
Tom R. Van Allan
Silvano G. Giorgetti
Judge K. Collins
Servant D. Barrett
Haberdashers' Aske's Sch Girls' Ch, ROH Chor, Medici Qt, New Philh, R. Muti
(11/88) (EMI) ① [2] **CMS7 69576-2**

Amelia J. Barstow
Riccardo P. Domingo
Renato L. Nucci
Oscar S. Jo
Ulrica F. Quivar
Sam K. Rydl
Tom G. Simic
Silvano J-L. Chaignaud
Judge W. Witte
Servant A. Tomaschek
Vienna St Op Chor, VPO, H. von Karajan (r1989)
(11/89) (DG) ① [2] **427 635-2GH2**

Amelia M. Caballé
Riccardo J. Carreras
Renato I. Wixell
Oscar S. Ghazarian
Ulrica P. Payne
Sam R. Lloyd
Tom G. Howell
Silvano J. Summers
Judge R. Leggate
Servant W. Elvin
ROH Chor, ROHO, Colin Davis
(1/91) (PHIL) ① [2] **426 560-2PM2**

Amelia H. Nelli
Riccardo J. Peerce
Renato R. Merrill
Oscar V. Haskins
Ulrica C. Turner
Sam N. Moscona
Tom N. Scott
Silvano G. Cehanovsky
Judge; Servant J.C. Rossi
R. Shaw Chorale, NBC SO, A. Toscanini (bp1954)
(7/91) (RCA) ① [2] **GD60301**

Amelia Z. Milanov
Riccardo J. Björling
Renato A. Sved
Oscar S. Andreva
Ulrica B. Castagna
Sam N. Cordon
Tom N. Moscona
Silvano A. Kent
Judge J. Carter
Servant L. Oliviero
NY Met Op Chor, NY Met Op Orch, E. Panizza (pp1940)
(2/94) (MYTO) ① [2] **2MCD90317**

Amelia R. Tebaldi
Riccardo L. Pavarotti
Renato S. Milnes
Oscar H. Donath
Ulrica R. Resnik
Sam L. Monreale
Tom N. Christov
Silvano J. van Dam
Judge P. F. Poli
Servant M. Alessandrini
Santa Cecilia Academy Chor, Santa Cecilia Academy Orch, B. Bartoletti (r1970)
(5/94) (DECC) ① [2] **440 042-2DMO2**

Excs M. Lorenz, M. Ahlersmeyer, H. Konetzni, E. Nikolaidi, A. Noni, S. Roth, M. Rus, F. Worff, Vienna St Op Chor, Vienna St Op Orch, K. Böhm (pp1942: Ger) (4/95) (SCHW) ① [2] **314582**

Excs P. Gallois, London Fest Orch, R. Pople (r1993: arr fl: Genin/Pierre)
(5/95) (DG) ① **445 822-2GH**

1. Hungarian St Op Orch, P.G. Morandi (r1994)
(NAXO) ① **8 553018**

1. RPO, A. Licata (r1994) (TRIN) ① **TRP044**

1. BPO, H. von Karajan
(10/87) (DG) ① **419 622-2GH**

1. BPO, H. von Karajan
(5/90) (DG) ① **429 164-2GR**

1. BPO, H. von Karajan
(1/95) (DG) ① **439 972-2GGA2**

1, 12a Mexico St SO, E. Bátiz (r1990s)
(ASV) ① **CDDCA856**
(ASV) ▭ **ZCDCA856**

2a Chicago Sym Chor, Chicago SO, G. Solti
(DECC) **OO** **430 226-5DH**

2a Chicago Sym Chor, Chicago SO, G. Solti
(4/91) (DECC) ① **430 226-2DH**

2b, 2c E. Caruso, F. Hempel, L. Rothier, A. de Segurola, NY Met Op Chor, orch, G. Scognamiglio (r1914) (RCA) ① **09026 61242-2**

2b, 2c, 10. F. Hempel, M. Duchêne, E. Caruso, L. Rothier, A. de Segurola, NY Met Op Chor, orch, G. Scognamiglio (r1914)
(7/91) (RCA) ① [12] **GD60495(5)**

2b, 2c, 10. F. Hempel, M. Duchêne, E. Caruso, A. de Segurola, L. Rothier, NY Met Op Chor, orch, G. Scognamiglio (r1914)
(10/91) (PEAR) ① [3] **EVC3(1)**

2c K. Battle, L. Pavarotti, R. Lloyd, M. King, London Op Chor, National PO, G. Solti
(7/90) (DECC) ① [2] **425 681-2DM2**
(7/90) (DECC) ▭ [2] **425 681-4DM2**

2c, 8a, 8b S. Stahlman, C. Bergonzi, F. Corena, L. Arbace, Santa Cecilia Academy Chor, G. Solti (r1961) (DECC) ① **440 417-2DM**

2c, 8b L. Slezak, orch (Ger: r1907)
(2/91) (PREI) ① **89020**

2c, 8b G. Zenatello, anon (r1905)
(12/93) (SYMP) ① **SYMCD1138**

2c, 8b G. Zenatello, chor, orch (r1908)
(12/93) (SYMP) ① **SYMCD1138**

2c, 8b G. Zenatello, chor, orch (r1908)
(5/94) (PEAR) ① [4] **GEMMCDS9073(2)**

2c, 8b G. Zenatello, chor, anon (r1905)
(5/94) (PEAR) ① [4] **GEMMCDS9073(1)**

2c, 10. F. Hempel, M. Duchêne, E. Caruso, L. Rothier, A. de Segurola, NY Met Op Chor, orch, G. Scognamiglio (r1914) (NIMB) ① **NI7834**
(NIMB) ▭ **NC7834**

3b H. Schlusnus, Berlin St Op Orch, H. Weigert (r1930: Ger) (PREI) ① [2] **89212**

3b T. Ruffo, orch (r1912)
(2/93) (PREI) ① [3] **89303(1)**

3b M. Ahlersmeyer, Vienna St Op Orch, K. Böhm (pp1942: Ger) (6/94) (SCHW) ① **314502**

3b, 17a, 17b B. Weikl, Munich RO, H. Wallberg
(ACAN) ① **43 327**

3b, 17a, 17b D. Fischer-Dieskau, BPO, A. Erede (r1959) (EMI) ① [2] **CMS5 65621-2**

3b, 17b J. Schwarz, orch (Ger: r1916)
(PREI) ① **89033**

3b, 17b A. Sved, Berlin St Op Orch, C. Krauss (r1936: Ger) (PREI) ① **89096**

3b, 17b G. De Luca, anon (r1907)
(PEAR) ① [3] **GEMMCDS9159(1)**

3b, 17b R. Stracciari, orch (r1917)
(PEAR) ① **GEMMCD9178**

3b, 17b M. Battistini, orch (r1906)
(2/92) (PREI) ① **89045**

3b, 17b M. Battistini, orch, C. Sabajno (r1906)
(10/92) (NIMB) ① **NI7831**
(10/92) (NIMB) ▭ **NC7831**

3b, 17b M. Battistini, orch, C. Sabajno (r1906)
(10/92) (PEAR) ① **GEMMCD9936**

3b, 17b P. Lisitsian, Bolshoi Th Orch, O. Bron (r1952: Russ) (8/93) (PREI) ① **8906**

4b F. Hempel, orch (r1916)
(3/94) (NIMB) ① **NI7849**

5a, 5b G. Simionato, C. Bergonzi, Santa Cecilia Academy Chor, Santa Cecilia Academy Orch, G. Solti (r1960/1) (DECC) ① **440 406-2DM**

5a, 5b S. Verrett, C. Bergonzi, RCA Italiana Op Chor, RCA Italiana Op Orch, E. Leinsdorf (r1966) (RCA) ① **09026 61457-2**

5b P. Payne, J. Carreras, ROH Chor, ROHO, Colin Davis (r1979) (KIWI) ① **CDSLD-82**

5b E. Randová, Brno St PO, O. Lenárd (pp1992)
(SUPR) ① **11 1846-2**

5b M. Anderson, NY Met Op Chor, NY Met Op Orch, D. Mitropoulos (r1955)
(RCA) ① **74321 24284-2**
(RCA) ▭ **74321 24284-4**

5b M. Anderson, NY Met Op Chor, NY Met Op Orch, D. Mitropoulos (r1955)
(1/90) (RCA) ① **GD87911**

5b I. Minghini-Cattaneo, La Scala Orch, C. Sabajno (r1930) (6/90) (PREI) ① **89008**

5b E. Stignani, EIAR Orch, A. la Rosa Parodi (r1940) (1/91) (PREI) ① **89014**

5b K. Branzell, orch (Ger: r1927)
(8/92) (PREI) ① **89039**

5b M. Anderson, NY Met Op Orch, D. Mitropoulos (r1955)
(4/94) (RCA) ① [6] **09026 61580-2(6)**

5b M. Klose, Berlin St Op Orch, B. Seidler-Winkler (r1936: Ger) (7/95) (PREI) ① **89082**

7b G. Zenatello, E. Burzio, E. Petri, anon (r1907)
(5/94) (PEAR) ① [4] **GEMMCDS9073(1)**

8a, 8b, 20a, 20b P. Domingo, R. Grist, ROH Chor, New Philh, R. Muti (r1975)
(6/94) (EMI) ① **CDC5 55017-2**

8a, 8b, 23c G. Zenatello, G. Marion, A. Boemi, Apollo Chor, orch, Rosario Bourdon (r1930)
(5/94) (PEAR) ① [4] **GEMMCDS9074(2)**

8b N. Gedda, ROHO, G. Patanè
(CFP) ① **CD-CFP4575**
(CFP) ▭ **TC-CFP4575**

8b P. Domingo, New Philh, N. Santi
(RCA) ① [2] **GD6086**
(RCA) ▭ [2] **GK6086**

8b E. Caruso, NY Met Op Chor, orch (r1911)
(RCA) ① **09026 61242-2**

8b C. Bergonzi, New Philh, N. Santi
(PHIL) ① **442 602-2PM**
(PHIL) ▭ **442 602-4PM**

8b J. Björling, B. Bokstedt (pp1957)
(BLUE) ① **ABCD057**

8b A. Bonci, orch (r1913)
(PEAR) ① **GEMMCD916**

8b J. Björling, orch, N. Grevillius (r1944)
(10/88) (EMI) ① **CDH7 61053-2**

8b E. Caruso, orch (r1911)
(5/89) (PEAR) ① **GEMMCD930**

8b E. Caruso, NY Met Op Chor, orch (r1911)
(10/89) (NIMB) ① **NI780**
(NIMB) ▭ **NC780**

8b J. Patzak, orch, M. Gurlitt (Ger: r1929)
(3/90) (PEAR) ① **GEMMCD938**

8b E. Caruso, NY Met Op Chor, orch (r1911)
(7/91) (RCA) ① [12] **GD60495(4)**

8b G. Zenatello, chor, orch (r1916)
(5/94) (PEAR) ① [4] **GEMMCDS9074(2)**

8b H. Roswaenge, Berlin St Op Orch, B. Seidler-Winkler (r1936: Ger)
(4/95) (PREI) ① [2] **8920**

8b J. Björling, MMF Orch, A. Erede (r1959)
(10/95) (DECC) ① **443 930-2DM**

8b, 20a, 20b P. Domingo, La Scala Orch, C. Abbado (DG) ① [3] **427 708-2GX3**

8b, 20a, 20b C. Bergonzi, Ambrosian Sngrs, New Philh, N. Santi (PHIL) Ⓓ [3] **432 486-2PM3**
8b, 20a, 20b T. Harper, Slovak Phil Chor, Bratislava RSO, M. Halász (NAXO) Ⓓ **8 550497**
8b, 20a, 20b P. Domingo, La Scala Orch, C. Abbado (7/86) (DG) Ⓓ **415 366-2GH**
8b, 20a, 20b E. Caruso, NY Met Op Chor, orch (r1911) (3/91) (PEAR) Ⓓ [3] **EVC2**
8b, 20b M. Gilion, orch (r c1909) (BONG) Ⓓ **GB1076-2**
8b, 23b, 23c G. Zenatello, G. Marion, A. Boemi, Apollo Chor, orch, Rosario Bourdon (r1930) (11/91) (CLUB) Ⓓ **CL99-025**
8b, 23b, 23c G. Zenatello, G. Marion, A. Boemi, Apollo Chor, orch, Rosario Bourdon (r1930) (11/91) (PREI) Ⓓ **89038**
12a Sofia SO, V. Stefanov (LASE) Ⓓ **15 519** (LASE) ⊟ **79 519**
12a-c R. Hunter, Tasmanian SO, D. Franks (r1989) (10/95) (ABCC) Ⓓ **8 7000 10**
12b L. Gencer, Bologna Teatro Comunale Orch, O. de Fabritiis (pp1961) (MEMO) Ⓓ [2] **HR4239/40**
12b, 12c E. Urbanová, Prague SO, J. Bělohlávek (r1993) (SUPR) Ⓓ **11 1851-2**
12b, 12c M. Seinemeyer, orch, F. Weissmann (r1929: Ger) (PEAR) Ⓓ **GEMMCD9082**
12b, 12c A. Tomowa-Sintow, Munich RO, P. Sommer (11/86) (ORFE) Ⓓ **C106841A**
12b, 12c M. Callas, Paris Cons, N. Rescigno (9/87) (EMI) Ⓓ **CDC7 47730-2**
12b, 12c M. Seinemeyer, Berlin St Op Orch, F. Weissmann (Ger: r1929) (11/90) (PREI) Ⓓ **89029**
12b, 12c, 16b J. Varady, Bavarian St Orch, D. Fischer-Dieskau (r1995) (ORFE) Ⓓ **C186951**
12b, 12c, 13. M. Callas, G. di Stefano, La Scala Chor, La Scala Orch, A. Votto (r1956) (2/90) (EMI) Ⓓ [4] **CMS7 63244-2**
12b, 12c, 16b R. Tebaldi, New Philh, O. de Fabritiis (8/91) (DECC) Ⓓ [2] **430 481-2DX2**
12b, 16b S. Murphy, WNO Orch, J. Smith (COLL) Ⓓ **Coll3025-2**
12c L. Price, RCA Italiana Op Orch, E. Leinsdorf (RCA) Ⓓ **RD87016**
12c C. Muzio, orch (r1918) (PEAR) Ⓓ **GEMMCD9143**
12c H. Spani, La Scala Orch, C. Sabajno (r1927) (9/90) (CLUB) Ⓓ [2] **CL99-509/10**
12c J. Gadski, orch (r1914) (7/91) (CLUB) Ⓓ **CL99-109**
12c C. Boninsegna, orch, C. Sabajno (r1905) (7/92) (PEAR) Ⓓ [3] **GEMMCDS9924(1)**
12c H. Spani, La Scala Orch, C. Sabajno (r1927) (12/92) (PREI) Ⓓ **89037**
12c C. Muzio, orch (r1918) (1/95) (ROMO) Ⓓ [2] **81010-2**
12c E. Rethberg, Victor SO, Rosario Bourdon (r1929) (10/95) (ROMO) Ⓓ [2] **81014-2**
12c, 16b H. Wildbrunn, orch (r1922: Ger) (PREI) Ⓓ **89097**
12c, 16b G. Arangi-Lombardi, La Scala Orch, L. Molajoli (r1933) (10/90) (PREI) Ⓓ **89013**
12c, 16b G. Cigna, orch, L. Molajoli (r1932) (11/90) (PREI) Ⓓ **89016**
12c, 16b G. Cigna, orch, L. Molajoli (r1932) (11/90) (LYRC) Ⓓ **SRO805**
12c, 16b M. Németh, orch (Ger) (1/94) (CLUB) Ⓓ **CL99-007**
13a H. Roswaenge, H. Scheppan, Berlin RSO, A. Rother (Ger: bp1940s) (PREI) Ⓓ **90096**
13a K. Ricciarelli, P. Domingo, Santa Cecilia Academy Orch, G. Gavazzeni (12/87) (RCA) Ⓓ **GD86534**
13a-c L. Price, P. Domingo, LSO, N. Santi (r1974) (RCA) Ⓓ **09026 61634-2**
13a, 13b M. Price, L. Pavarotti, National PO, G. Solti (12/91) (DECC) Ⓓ **430 724-2DM**
13a(pt), 13b G. Zenatello, E. Burzio, anon (r1906) (5/94) (PEAR) Ⓓ [4] **GEMMCDS9073(1)**
13a, 13b, 13c M. Callas, G. di Stefano, La Scala Orch, A. Votto (10/88) (EMI) Ⓓ **CDM7 69543-2**
13b, 13c G. Zenatello, E. Mazzoleni, orch (r1909) (5/94) (PEAR) Ⓓ [4] **GEMMCDS9073(2)**
13c G. Zenatello, E. Burzio, anon (r1906) (12/93) (SYMP) Ⓓ **SYMCD1138**
13c G. Zenatello, E. Mazzoleni, orch (r1909) (12/93) (SYMP) Ⓓ **SYMCD1138**
14a, 14b G. Russ, L. Longobardi, G. Pacini, anon (r1904) (12/93) (SYMP) Ⓓ **SYMCD1113**
15b F. Leider, H. Schlusnus, O. Helgers, M. Abendroth, orch (Ger: r1925) (5/91) (PREI) Ⓓ [3] **89301**
16b R. Tebaldi, New Philh, O. de Fabritiis (DECC) Ⓓ **433 067-2DWO** (DECC) ⊟ **433 067-4DWO**
16b R. Scotto, Czech SO, A. Krieger (pp1991) (IMP) Ⓓ **MCD42**
16b E. Suliotis, Rome Op Orch, O. de Fabritiis (r1966) (DECC) Ⓓ **440 405-2DM**
16b E. Suliotis, Rome Orch, S. Varviso (r1967) (DECC) Ⓓ **440 405-2DM**
16b R. Tebaldi, New Philh, O. de Fabritiis (r1964) (DECC) Ⓓ **433 442-2DA**
16b M. Callas, Paris Cons, N. Rescigno (9/87) (EMI) Ⓓ **CDC7 47943-2**
16b E. Burzio, orch (r1913) (1/91) (CLUB) Ⓓ [2] **CL99-587/8**
16b E. Destinn, orch, J. Pasternack (r1921) (11/93) (ROMO) Ⓓ [2] **81002-2**
16b K. Ricciarelli, Verona Arena Orch, B. Martinotti (pp) (5/94) (DECC) Ⓓ [2] **443 018-2DF2**
16b E. Destinn, orch, J. Pasternack (r1921) (12/94) (SUPR) Ⓓ [12] **11 2136-2(5)**
16b E. Rethberg, Victor SO, Rosario Bourdon (r1930) (10/95) (ROMO) Ⓓ [2] **81014-2**
16b, 16c M. Caballé, Rome RAI Orch, B. Bartoletti (pp1969) (MEMO) Ⓓ [2] **HR4279/80**
17. M. Biscotti, Berlin RSO, R. Buckley (SCHW) Ⓓ [2] **314052**
17. P. Amato, orch (r1914) (4/94) (RCA) Ⓓ [6] **09026 61580-2(2)**
17a P. Coni, Madrid SO, G.P. Sanzogno (RNE) Ⓓ [2] **650004**
17a, 17b J. Pons, Barcelona SO, G. Navarro (11/92) (RCA) ⊟ **09026 61204-4**
17a, 17b G. Taddei, Naples San Carlo Op Orch, U. Rapalo (PREI) Ⓓ **90020**
17a, 17b P. Coni, Madrid SO, G.P. Sanzogno (pp1991) (IMP) Ⓓ [2] **DPCD998**
17a, 17b J. Pons, Barcelona SO, G. Navarro (RCA) OO **09026 61204-5**
17a, 17b G. Laperrière, Three Rivers SO, G. Bellemare (r1991) (CBC) Ⓓ **SMCD5127**
17a, 17b T. Gobbi, LSO, W. Braithwaite (r1952) (10/89) (EMI) Ⓓ **CDM7 63109-2**
17a, 17b J. Hynninen, Estonian SO, E. Klas (4/90) (ONDI) Ⓓ **ODE731-2**
17a, 17b T. Ruffo, orch, W.B. Rogers (r1915) (11/90) (NIMB) Ⓓ **NI7810** (NIMB) ⊟ **NC7810**
17a, 17b G. Bechi, Rome Op Orch, T. Serafin (r1943) (4/94) (EMI) Ⓓ [3] **CHS7 64864-2(2)**
17b L. Warren, Orch, H. Barlow (bp1952) (VAI) ▣ **VAI69105**
17b A. Scotti, anon (r1905) (PEAR) Ⓓ **GEMMCD9937**
17b P. Amato, orch, W.B. Rogers (r1914) (PREI) Ⓓ **89064**
17b P. Amato, orch, W.B. Rogers (r1914) (PEAR) Ⓓ **GEMMCD9104**
17b H. Schlusnus, Berlin St Op Orch, L. Blech (r1935: Ger) (PREI) Ⓓ [2] **89212**
17b G. De Luca, anon (r1902) (PEAR) Ⓓ [3] **GEMMCDS9159(1)**
17b G. De Luca, orch (r1917) (PEAR) Ⓓ [3] **GEMMCDS9160(1)**
17b A. Granforte, orch, G.W. Byng (r1926) (PREI) Ⓓ **89105**
17b M. Ancona, orch (r1907) (PREI) Ⓓ **89995**
17b L. Tibbett, orch, Rosario Bourdon (r1929) (10/89) (NIMB) Ⓓ **NI7801** (NIMB) ⊟ **NC7801**
17b G. Bechi, La Scala Orch, U. Berrettoni (r1941) (2/90) (PREI) Ⓓ **89009**
17b L. Tibbett, Orch, Rosario Bourdon (r1930) (3/90) (RCA) Ⓓ **GD87808**
17b H. Schlusnus, Berlin St Op Orch, L. Blech (Ger: r1935) (9/90) (PREI) Ⓓ **89006**
17b C. Tagliabue, Turin EIAR Orch, U. Tansini (r1939) (11/90) (PREI) Ⓓ **89015**
17b L. Tibbett, orch, N. Shilkret (r1929) (3/91) (PEAR) Ⓓ [2] **GEMMCDS9452**
17b G. De Luca, orch (r1917) (1/92) (PREI) Ⓓ **89036**
17b C. Galeffi, La Scala Orch, L. Molajoli (r1926) (2/92) (PREI) Ⓓ **89040**
17b G. Danise, orch (r1921) (11/92) (MEMO) Ⓓ [2] **HR4408/9(2)**
17b T. Ruffo, orch (r1915) (2/93) (PREI) Ⓓ [3] **89303(1)**
17b G. De Luca, anon (r1902) (8/93) (SYMP) Ⓓ **SYMCD1111**
17b G. Hüsch, Berlin St Op Orch, H.U. Müller (r1937: Ger) (3/94) (PREI) Ⓓ **89071**
17b M. Ancona, orch (r1907) (10/95) (NIMB) Ⓓ **NI7867**
20a, 20b P. Domingo, New Philh, R. Muti (EMI) Ⓓ **CDM7 63103-2**
20a, 20b C. Bergonzi, Santa Cecilia Academy Orch, G. Gavazzeni (DECC) Ⓓ **433 623-2DSP** (DECC) ⊟ **433 623-4DSP**
20a, 20b H. Roswaenge, Berlin RSO, H. Steinkopf (bp1940s; Ger) (PREI) Ⓓ **90096**
20a, 20b J. Schmidt, BPO, S. Meyrowitz (r1931: Ger) (RELI) Ⓓ **CR921036**
20a, 20b Deng, Württemberg PO, R. Paternostro (SINE) Ⓓ **39820222**
20a, 20b M. del Monaco, New SO, A. Erede (r1958) (DECC) Ⓓ **440 407-2DM**
20a, 20b A. Erede, M. del Monaco, New SO (1958) (DECC) Ⓓ **436 314-2DA** (DECC) ⊟ **436 314-4DA**
20a, 20b J. Carreras, RPO, R. Benzi (r1976) (PHIL) Ⓓ **442 600-2PH** (PHIL) ⊟ **442 600-4PH**
20a, 20b C. Bergonzi, Santa Cecilia Academy Orch, G. Gavazzeni (r1957) (DECC) Ⓓ **440 417-2DM**
20a, 20b E. Caruso, orch (r1911) (10/89) (NIMB) Ⓓ **NI7803** (NIMB) ⊟ **NC7803**
20a, 20b E. Caruso, orch, W.B. Rogers (r1911) (7/91) (RCA) Ⓓ [12] **GD60495(4)**
20a, 20b E. Caruso, orch (r1911) (7/91) (MSCM) Ⓓ **MM30352**
20a, 20b P. Domingo, La Scala Orch, C. Abbado (6/94) (BELA) Ⓓ **450 121-2** (6/94) (BELA) ⊟ **450 121-4**
20b C. Bergonzi, Santa Cecilia Academy Orch, G. Gavazzeni (r1958) (BELA) Ⓓ **450 005-2** (BELA) ⊟ **450 005-4**
20b H. Roswaenge, Berlin St Op Orch (r1935: Ger) (4/95) (PREI) Ⓓ [2] **89209**
21b L. Tetrazzini, orch (r1911) (10/89) (NIMB) Ⓓ **NI7802** (NIMB) ⊟ **NC7802**
21b L. Tetrazzini, orch (r1911) (10/90) (NIMB) Ⓓ **NI7808** (10/90) (NIMB) ⊟ **NC7808**
21b S. Kurz, orch (r c1909) (7/92) (PEAR) Ⓓ [3] **GEMMCDS9924(1)**
21b L. Tetrazzini, orch, P. Pitt (r1909) (9/92) (EMI) Ⓓ [3] **CHS7 63802-2(1)**
21b L. Tetrazzini, orch, P. Pitt (r1909) (9/92) (PEAR) Ⓓ **GEMMCD9221**
21b L. Tetrazzini, orch (r1911) (9/92) (PEAR) Ⓓ **GEMMCD9223**
21b K. Battle, National PO, G. Solti (r1983) (10/93) (DECC) Ⓓ **436 461-2DM**
22a M. Caballé, J. Carreras, I. Wixell, S. Ghazarian, R. Lloyd, G. Howell, ROH Chor, ROHO, Colin Davis (PHIL) Ⓓ **434 986-2PM**

La **battaglia di Legnano, '(The) Battle of Legnano'– opera: 4 acts (1849—Rome) (Lib. S. Cammarano)**

EXCERPTS: 1. Overture. ACT 1: 2. Viva Italia!; 3a. O magnanima e prima; 3b. La pia materna mano; 4a. Viva Italia forte ed una; 4b. Spento tra la fiamme du Susa; 4c. Ah! m'abbraccia; 5. Giulive trombe!; 6. Plaude all'arrivo Milan dei forti; 7a. Voi lo diceste; 7b. Quante volte come un dono; 8. Che...signor!; 9. A frenarti, o cor; 10. Sposa... 11a. È ver? Sei d'altri; 11b. T'amai, t'amai qual angelo. ACT 2: 12a. Udiste?; 12b. Sì, tradi e invano; 13. Invia la baldanzosa Lombarda Lega; 14a. Ah! ben vi scorgo; 14b. Favellaste acerbi detti; 15. A che smarriti e pallidi?; 16. Le mie possenti squadre. ACT 3: 17a. Fra queste dense tenebre; 17b. Campioni della Morte; 18. Giuriam d'Italia; 19. Lida, Lida? Ove corri?; 20. Digli ch'è sangue italico; 21. Tu m'appellavi; 22. Se al nuovo di pugnando; 23. Rolando? M'ascolta; 24a. Regna la notte ancor; 24b. Ah! d'un consorte, o perfidi; 25. Vendetta d'un momento. ACT 4: 26. Deus meus, pone illos ut rotam; 27. Vittoria! Vittoria!; 28. Per la salvata Italia.

Lida	K. Ricciarelli
Arrigo	J. Carreras
Rolando	M. Manuguerra
Federico	N. Ghiuselev
Consul I	H. Lichtenberger
Consul II	D. Kavrakos
Marcovaldo	J. Summers
Podestà	F. Handlos
Imelda	A. Murray

Austrian Rad Chor, Austrian RSO, L. Gardelli (r1977) (11/89) (PHIL) Ⓓ [2] **422 435-2PM2**

1. Sofia SO, V. Stefanov (LASE) Ⓓ **15 519**
(LASE) ⊟ **79 519**
1. Hungarian St Op Orch, P.G. Morandi (r1994) (NAXO) Ⓓ **8 553089**
1. BPO, H. von Karajan (10/87) (DG) Ⓓ **419 622-2GH**
1. BPO, H. von Karajan (1/95) (DG) Ⓓ **439 972-2GGA2**
3a, 3b C. Bergonzi, New Philh, N. Santi (PHIL) Ⓓ [3] **432 486-2PM3**
3a, 3b, 11a, 11b F. Corelli, La Scala Orch, G. Gavazzeni (pp1961) (MEMO) Ⓓ [2] **HR4204/5**
3b J. Carreras, Vienna RSO, L. Gardelli (r1977) (PHIL) Ⓓ **442 600-2PH**
(PHIL) ⊟ **442 600-4PH**
11a J. Carreras, K. Ricciarelli, Vienna RSO, L. Gardelli (r1977) (PHIL) Ⓓ **442 600-2PH**
(PHIL) ⊟ **442 600-4PH**
18, 26. Slovak Phil Chor, Bratislava RSO, O. Dohnányi (4/91) (NAXO) Ⓓ **8 550241**

Il Corsaro– opera: 3 acts (1848—Trieste) (Lib. F Piave, after Byron)

EXCERPTS: 1. Prelude. ACT 1: 2. Come liberi volano i venti; 3a. Ah! sì, ben dite; 3b. Tutto parea sorridere; 3c. Della brezza col favore; 4. Si: de' corsari il fulmine; 5a. Egli non riede ancora!; 5b. Non so le tetre immagini; 6a. È pur tristo, o Medora; 6b. No, tu non sai comprendere; 6c. Tornerai, ma forse spenta. ACT 2: 7. Oh qual perenne gaudio t'aspetta; 8a. Nè sulla terra creatura alcuna; 8b. Vola talor dal carcere; 8c. Seide celebra con gioia e festa; 8d. Ah conforto è sol la speme; 9a. Sol grida di festa; 9b. O prodi miei, sorgete; 9c. Salve, Allah!; 10a. Giunge un Dervis; 10b. Di': que' ribaldi tremano; 11a. Resta ancora; 11b. Audace cotanto mostrarti pur sai?; 11c. Signor, trafitti giacciono. ACT 3: 12. Alfin questo corsaro è mio prigione!; 13a. Cento leggiarde vergini; 13b. Ma pria togliam dall'anima; 13c. S'avvicina il tuo momento; 14a. Eccola!...fingasi; 14b. Sia l'istante maledetto; 15. Eccomi progioniero!; 16. Ei dorme?; 17a. Seid la vuole; 17b. Non sai ti che sulla testa; 18. Sul capo mio discenda; 19. La terra, il ciel m'abborrino; 20a. Voi tacete; 20b. Per me felice; 20c. O mio Corrado, appressati.

Corrado J. Carreras
Medora J. Norman
Gulnara M. Caballé
Seid G-P. Mastromei
Selimo J. Noble
Giovanni C. Grant
Black Eunuch A. Oliver
Ambrosian Sngrs, New Philh, L. Gardelli (r1975) (3/90) (PHIL) Ⓓ [2] **426 118-2PM2**

1. Hungarian St Op Orch, P.G. Morandi (r1994) (NAXO) Ⓓ **8 553018**
1. BPO, H. von Karajan (10/87) (DG) Ⓓ **419 622-2GH**
1. BPO, H. von Karajan (1/95) (DG) Ⓓ **439 972-2GGA2**
5a, 5b K. Ricciarelli, Rome PO, G. Gavazzeni (12/87) (RCA) Ⓓ **GD86534**
5a, 5b M. Caballé, RCA Italiana Op Orch, A. Guadagno (11/92) (RCA) Ⓓ [2] **GD60941**
5a, 5b K. Ricciarelli, Parma Teatro Regio Orch, G. Patanè (pp1976) (5/94) (DECC) Ⓓ [2] **443 018-2DF2**
5a, 5b, 8a, 8b M. Callas, Paris Op Orch, N. Rescigno (9/87) (EMI) Ⓓ **CDC7 47943-2**
5b K. Ricciarelli, Svizzera Italiana Orch, B. Amaducci (r1979) (ERMI) Ⓓ **ERM151**
15. C. Bergonzi, New Philh, N. Santi (PHIL) Ⓓ [3] **432 486-2PM3**
16. M. Caballé, J. Carreras, New Philh, L. Gardelli (PHIL) Ⓓ **434 986-2PM**

Don Carlo– opera: 5 acts (1867 rev 1884—Paris) (Lib. Méry & du Locle. Italian version of Don Carlos)

EXCERPTS: ACT 1: 1. Su, cacciator; 2a. Fontainebleau! Foresta immensa; 2b. Io la vidi; 3a. Io suon del corno; 3b. Io sono uno stranier; 3c. Che mai fate voi?; 3d. Di qual amor; 4a. Al fedel ch'ora viene; 4b. L'ora fatale; 5. Inni di festa; 6. Il glorioso Re di Francia. ACT 2: 7. Carlo il sommo Imperatore; 8. Al chiostro di San Giusto; 9a. È lui! desso! l'Infante!; 9b. Qual pallor; 9c. Dio, che nell'alma infondere; 10. Sotto ai folti; 11. Nei giardin del bello; 12. La Regina!; 13. Che mai si fa nel suol francese; 14. Carlo ch'è sol il nostro amor; 15a. Io vengo a domandar; 15b. Perduta ben, mio sol tesor; 15c. Qual voce; 16a. Il Re!; 16b. Non pianger, mia compagna; 17a. Restate! Presso alla mia persona; 17b. O Signor, di Fiandre arrivo. ACT 3: 18a. A mezza-notte, ai giardin della Regina; 18b. Sei tu, sei tu; 19. Che disse mai?!; 20. Spuntato ecco il dì d'esultanza; 21. Nel posar sul mio capo la corona; 22. Sire, no, l'ora estrema. ACT 4: 23a. Ella giammai m'amò; 23b. Dormirò sol nel manto mio regal; 24a. Il Grande Inquisitor!...Son io dinanzi al Re?; 24b. Nell'ispano suol mai; 25a. Giustizia! o Sire; 25b. Ah! sii maledetto; 26. Pietà!; 27a. Ah! più non vedrò; 27b. O don fatale; 28a. Son io, mio Carlo; 28b. Convien qui dirci addio!; 28c. Per me giunto; 28d. O Carlo, ascolta; 28e. Io morrò; 29a. Mio Carlo, a te la spada; 29b. Ciel! suona a stormo!. ACT 5: 30. Tu che le vanità; 31a. È dessa!...Un detto, un sol; 31b. Vago sogno m'arrise; 31c. Ma lassù ci vedremo; 31d. Sì, per sempre! ADDITIONAL ARIAS: 32. Io l'ho perduta (for Italian 4-act version: Act 1 Scene 1).

Don Carlo L. Lima
Elisabetta I. Cotrubas
Eboli B. Baglioni
Rodrigo G. Zancanaro
Philip II R. Lloyd
Grand Inquisitor J. Rouleau
Monk M. Best
Voice from Heaven L. Biagioni
ROH Chor, ROHO, B. Haitink, L. Visconti (CAST) ▭ **CVI2033**

Don Carlo F. Corelli
Elisabetta M. Caballé
Eboli G. Bumbry
Rodrigo S. Milnes
Philip II C. Siepi
Grand Inquisitor J. Macurdy
Monk P. Plishka
Tebaldo F. von Stade
Conte di Lerma L. Goeke
Herald R. MacWherter
Voice from Heaven L. Amara
NY Met Op Chor, NY Met Op Orch, F. Molinari-Pradelli (4-act vers: pp1972) (FOYE) Ⓓ [2] **2-CF2092**

Don Carlo L. Pavarotti
Elisabetta D. Dessì
Eboli L. d'Intino
Rodrigo P. Coni
Philip II S. Ramey
Grand Inquisitor A. Anisimov
Monk A. Silvestrelli
Tebaldo M. Laurenza
Conte di Lerma O. Zanetti
Herald M. Bolognesi
Voice from Heaven N. Focile
La Scala Chor, La Scala Orch, R. Muti, F. Zeffirelli (pp1992: 4-act vers) (EMI) ◖ [2] **LDD4 91134-1**
(EMI) ▭ [2] **MVB4 91134-3**

Don Carlo P. Domingo
Elisabetta M. Caballé
Eboli S. Verrett
Rodrigo S. Milnes
Philip II R. Raimondi
Grand Inquisitor G. Foiani
Monk S. Estes
Tebaldo D. Wallis
Conte di Lerma R. Davies
Herald J. Noble
Voice from Heaven M-R. del Campo
Ambrosian Op Chor, ROHO, C.M. Giulini (7/87) (EMI) Ⓓ [3] **CDS7 47701-8**

Don Carlo J. Carreras
Elisabetta M. Freni
Eboli A. Baltsa
Rodrigo P. Cappuccilli
Philip II N. Ghiaurov
Grand Inquisitor R. Raimondi
Monk J. Van Dam
Tebaldo E. Gruberová
Conte di Lerma H. Nitsche
Herald C. Meletti
Voice from Heaven B. Hendricks
Berlin Deutsche Op Chor, BPO, H. von Karajan (r1978: 4-act vers) (4/88) (EMI) Ⓓ [3] **CMS7 69304-2**

Don Carlo F. Labò
Elisabetta A. Stella
Eboli F. Cossotto
Rodrigo E. Bastianini
Philip II B. Christoff
Grand Inquisitor I. Vinco
Monk A. Maddalena
Tebaldo A. Cattelani
Conte di Lerma F. Piva
Herald P. de Palma
Voice from Heaven G. Matteir
La Scala Chor, La Scala Orch, G. Santini (r1961) (9/91) (DG) Ⓓ [3] **437 730-2GX**

Don Carlo M. Sylveste
Elisabetta A. Mill
Eboli D. Zajic
Rodrigo V. Cherno
Philip II F. Furlanett
Grand Inquisitor S. Rame
Monk P. Plishk
Tebaldo J. Bunne
Conte di Lerma D. Cro
Herald J. H. Murra
Voice from Heaven K. Battl
NY Met Op Chor, NY Met Op Orch, James Levine (r1992) (4/93) (SONY) Ⓓ [3] **S3K5250**

Don Carlo M. Filippesch
Elisabetta A. Stell
Eboli E. Nicola
Rodrigo T. Gobb
Philip II B. Christof
Grand Inquisitor G. Ner
Monk P. Clabass
Tebaldo L. di Leli
Conte di Lerma; Herald P. Caro
Voice from Heaven O. Moscucc
Rome Op Chor, Rome Op Orch, G. Santini (r1954: 4-act ver) (4/93) (EMI) Ⓓ [3] **CMS7 64642-**

Don Carlo J. Carrera
Elisabetta F.I. D'Amic
Eboli A. Balts
Rodrigo P. Cappuccil
Philip II F. Furlanett
Grand Inquisitor M. Salmine
Monk F. de Grandi
Tebaldo; Voice from Heaven A. Bandel
Conte di Lerma H. Nitsch
Herald V. Horr
Bulgarian Nat Chor, Vienna St Op Chor, Salzburg Chbr Ch, BPO, H. von Karajan, U. Märkle (pp1986; 4-act vers) (8/93) (SONY) ◖ [3] **S2LV4831**
(8/93) (SONY) ▭ **S2HV4831**

Don Carlo L. Pavarott
Elisabetta D. Dess
Eboli L. d'Intin
Rodrigo P. Con
Philip II S. Rame
Grand Inquisitor A. Anisimov
Monk A. Silvestrel
Tebaldo M. Laurenz
Conte di Lerma O. Zanett
Herald M. Bolognes
Voice from Heaven N. Focil
La Scala Chor, La Scala Orch, R. Muti (pp1992: 4-act vers) (5/94) (EMI) Ⓓ [3] **CDS7 54867-**

Don Carlo E. Fernand
Elisabetta S. Jurina
Eboli G. Simionat
Rodrigo E. Bastianin
Philip II C. Siep
Grand Inquisitor M. Stefanon
Monk N. Zaccari
Tebaldo N. Balatsc
Conte di Lerma C. Schmid
Herald N. Foste
Voice from Heaven A. Rothenberge
Vienna St Op Chor, VPO, H. von Karajan (pp1958: 4-act ver) (9/95) (DG) Ⓓ [2] **447 655-2GX**

Excs T. Mazaroff, P. Pierotic, M. Reining, P. Tutsek, C. Bissuti, H. Alsen, Vienna St Op Chor, Vienna St Op Orch, B. Walter (pp1937: Ger/Bulg) (12/94) (SCHW) Ⓓ [2] **31454**
Excs F. Völker, A. Kipnis, N. Ardelli, A. Jerger, H. Konetzni, E. Nikolaidi, L. Helletsgruber, H. Alsen, Vienna St Op Chor, Vienna St Op Orch, B. Walter (pp1936/7: Ger) (3/95) (SCHW) Ⓓ [2] **31460**
Excs F. Völker, J. von Manowarda, E. Schipper, A. Jerger, V. Ursuleac, G. Rünger, Vienna St Op Orch, C. Krauss (pp1933: Ger) (9/95) (SCHW) Ⓓ [2] **31466**
1, 2a, 2b P. Domingo, Ambrosian Op Chor, ROHO, C.M. Giulini (r1970) (6/94) (EMI) Ⓓ **CDC5 55017-**
1(pt), 2a, 2b, 9a, 9b, 9c, 11, 15a, 15b, 20, 23a, 23b, 27a, 27b, 28a, 28c, 28d, 30. A. Millo, D. Zajick, J. Bunnell, M. Sylvester, J. H. Murray, V. Chernov, F. Furlanetto, P. Plishka, NY Met Op Chor, NY Met Op Orch, James Levine (r1992) (SONY) Ⓓ **SMK5350**

2a, 2b C. Bergonzi, New Philh, N. Santi (PHIL) Ⓓ [3] **432 486-2PM3**

2a, 2b C. Bergonzi, ROHO, G. Solti (r1965) (DECC) Ⓓ **440 417-2DM**

2a, 2b, 9c P. Domingo, S. Milnes, S. Estes, Ambrosian Op Chor, ROHO, C.M. Giulini (EMI) Ⓓ **CDM7 63103-2**

2a, 11, 15a, 23a, 25b, 27b, 28c, 28d, 30. P. Domingo, M. Caballé, S. Verrett, R. Raimondi, S. Milnes, G. Foiani, D. Wallis, Ambrosian Op Chor, ROHO, C.M. Giulini (EMI) Ⓓ **CDM7 63089-2**

2b J. Carreras, BPO, H. von Karajan (EMI) Ⓓ **CDC7 54524-2**

2b T. Harper, Bratislava RSO, M. Halász (NAXO) Ⓓ **8 550497**

2b M. Gilion, orch (r c1909) (BONG) Ⓓ **GB1076-2**

9a-c C. Bergonzi, D. Fischer-Dieskau, T. Franc, ROH Chor, ROHO, G. Solti (r1965) (DECC) Ⓓ **436 315-2DA** (DECC) ⊟ **436 315-4DA**

9a-c P. Domingo, S. Milnes, LSO, A. Guadagno (RCA) Ⓓ **09026 62699-2** (RCA) ⊟ **09026 62699-4**

9a-c D. Fischer-Dieskau, N. Gedda, Berlin RSO, G. Patanè (r1973: Ger) (EMI) Ⓓ [2] **CMS5 65621-2**

9a-c G. Aragall, E. Tumagian, Bratislava RSO, A. Rahbari (r1992) (12/94) (NAXO) Ⓓ **8 550684**

9a-c, 17a, 17b, 28a-c B. Prevedi, U. Carosi, P. Cappuccilli, N. Ghiaurov, Rome RAI Chor, Rome RAI Orch, T. Schippers (pp1969) (MEMO) Ⓓ [2] **HR4273/4**

9a, 17a, 17b, 28a T. Gobbi, Chicago Lyric Op Chor, Chicago Lyric Op Orch, A. Votto (pp1960) (MEMO) Ⓓ [2] **HR4376/7**

9b(pt), 9c J. Björling, R. Merrill, E. Markow, RCA Victor SO, R. Cellini (2/89) (RCA) Ⓓ **GD87799** (RCA) ⊟ **GK87799**

9c C. Bergonzi, D. Fischer-Dieskau, BRSO, J. López-Cobos (ORFE) Ⓓ **C028821A**

9c P. Domingo, S. Milnes, LSO, A. Guadagno (RCA) Ⓓ [2] **GD60866** (RCA) ⊟ [2] **GK60866**

9c E. Caruso, A. Scotti, orch, W.B. Rogers (r1912) (RCA) Ⓓ **09026 61242-2**

9c E. Caruso, A. Scotti, orch, W.B. Rogers (r1912) (7/91) (RCA) Ⓓ [12] **GD60495(4)**

9c E. Caruso, A. Scotti, orch, W.B. Rogers (r1912) (10/91) (PEAR) Ⓓ [3] **EVC3(1)**

9c T. Mazaroff, P. Pierotic, Vienna St Op Orch, B. Walter (pp1937: Ger) (6/94) (SCHW) Ⓓ **314502**

9c, 15b, 32. J. Carreras, P. Cappuccilli, M. Freni, Berlin Deutsche Op Chor, BPO, H. von Karajan (EMI) Ⓓ **CDM7 63111-2**

9c, 23a L. Lima, G. Zancanaro, R. Lloyd, ROHO, B. Haitink (CAST) ▣ **CVI2065**

9c, 28a, 28c, 28d G. De Luca, G. Martinelli, orch (r1921) (PEAR) Ⓓ [3] **GEMMCDS9160(1)**

11. A. Baltsa, E. Gruberová, Berlin Deutsche Op Chor, BPO, H. von Karajan (r1978) (CFP) Ⓓ **CD-CFP4656** (CFP) ⊟ **TC-CFP4656**

11, 12, 18a, 18b, 19, 20, 23a, 23b, 24a, 24b, 25a, 25b, 27b C. Ludwig, G. Jones, P. Domingo, K. Paskalis, N. Ghiaurov, H. Hotter, Leonie Rysanek, Vienna St Op Chor, Vienna St Op Orch, B. Klobučar (pp1967) (MELD) Ⓓ [2] **MEL26516**

14. G. Kaschmann, S. Cottone (r1903) (12/89) (SYMP) Ⓓ **SYMCD1065**

14. G. Kaschmann, S. Cottone (r1903) (4/94) (EMI) Ⓓ [3] **CHS7 64860-2(1)**

16b M. Caballé, S. Milnes, R. Raimondi, Ambrosian Op Chor, ROHO, C.M. Giulini (r1970) (EMI) Ⓓ **CDM5 65575-2**

16b K. Ricciarelli, Rome Polyphonic Chor, Rome PO, G. Gavazzeni (12/87) (RCA) Ⓓ **GD86534**

16b, 27b M. Callas, Paris Cons, N. Rescigno (9/87) (EMI) Ⓓ **CDC7 47943-2**

16b, 30. L. Gencer, Rome Op Orch, F. Previtali (pp1968) (MEMO) Ⓓ [2] **HR4239/40**

17. N. Ghiaurov, P. Cappuccilli, Rome RAI Orch, T. Schippers (pp1969) (MEMO) Ⓓ [2] **HR4223/4**

20. Chicago Sym Chor, Chicago SO, G. Solti (DECC) OO **430 226-5DH**

20. Chor, Orch, Anon (cond) (BELA) Ⓓ **450 052-2** (BELA) ⊟ **450 052-4**

20. Berlin Deutsche Op Chor, BPO, H. von Karajan (r1978) (EMI) Ⓓ [2] **CZS5 68559-2**

20. Atlanta Sym Chor, Atlanta SO, Robert Shaw (3/88) (TELA) Ⓓ [2] **CD80152**

20. Chicago Sym Chor, Chicago SO, G. Solti (4/91) (DECC) Ⓓ **430 226-2DH**

20. Slovak Phil Chor, Bratislava RSO, O. Dohnányi (4/91) (NAXO) Ⓓ **8 550241**

20, 21, 22. R. Viljakainen, P. Talola, P. Lindroos, J. Hynninen, P. Raanoja, M. Salminen, Savonlinna Op Fest Chor, Savonlinna Op Fest Orch, L. Segerstam (BIS) Ⓓ [2] **BIS-CD373/4**

23. R. Raimondi, Ambrosian Op Chor, ROHO, C.M. Giulini (10/88) (EMI) Ⓓ **CDM7 69549-2**

23a A. Anisimov, Berlin RSO, J. Märkl (r1991) (SCHW) Ⓓ [2] **312682**

23a M. Pertusi, Sofia PO, E. Tabakov (r1994) (CAPR) Ⓓ **10 704**

23a, 23b N. Ghiaurov, Rome RAI Orch, T. Schippers (pp1969) (MEMO) Ⓓ [2] **HR4223/4**

23a, 23b R. Lloyd, ROHO, B. Haitink (TELD) ● **9031-77676-6** (TELD) ▣ **9031-77676-3**

23a, 23b L. Sibiriakov, orch (r1910: Russ) (PEAR) Ⓓ [3] **GEMMCDS9111(1)**

23a, 23b C. Siepi, Santa Cecilia Academy Orch, A. Erede (r1954) (DECC) Ⓓ **440 418-2DM**

23a, 23b B. Christoff, Philh, H. von Karajan (r1949) (EMI) Ⓓ **CDH5 65500-2**

23a, 23b T. Pasero, orch, L. Molajoli (r1928) (6/90) (PREI) Ⓓ **89010**

23a, 23b A. Kipnis, Berlin St Op Orch, C. Schmalstich (Ger: r1930) (12/90) (PREI) Ⓓ **89019**

23a, 23b A. Kipnis, orch (Ger: r1922) (10/91) (PEAR) Ⓓ **GEMMCD9451**

23a, 23b N. de Angelis, orch, L. Molajoli (r1927) (7/92) (PREI) Ⓓ **89042**

23a, 23b M. Salminen, Lahti SO, E. Klas (8/92) (BIS) Ⓓ **BIS-CD520**

23a, 23b J. Van Dam, Loire PO, M. Soustrot (r1992) (8/93) (FORL) Ⓓ **UCD16681**

23a, 23b P. Burchuladze, English Concert Orch, E. Downes (r1984) (10/93) (DECC) Ⓓ **436 464-2DM**

23a, 23b T. Pasero, orch (r c1938) (4/94) (EMI) Ⓓ [3] **CHS7 64864-2(1)**

23a, 23b K. Borg, Bamberg SO, A. Rother (r1957) (12/94) (FINL) Ⓓ [3] **4509-95606-2**

23a, 23b M. Reizen, Bolshoi Th Orch, S. Samosud (r1951) (2/95) (PREI) Ⓓ **89080**

23b F. Chaliapin, orch (r1910) (PREI) Ⓓ **89030**

23b E. Pinza, orch (r1927) (PEAR) Ⓓ **GEMMCD9122**

23b E. Pinza, orch, Rosario Bourdon (r1927) (2/89) (PEAR) Ⓓ **GEMMCD9306**

23b E. Pinza, orch, Rosario Bourdon (r1927) (7/91) (MMOI) Ⓓ **CDMOIR404** (MMOI) ⊟ **CMOIR404**

23b E. Pinza, orch, Rosario Bourdon (r1927) (3/92) (PREI) Ⓓ **89050**

23b A. Didur, anon (r1900) (6/93) (PEAR) Ⓓ [3] **GEMMCDS9997/9(2)**

24. N. Ghiaurov, R. Raimondi, BPO, H. von Karajan (10/88) (EMI) Ⓓ **CDM7 69549-2**

24a, 24b N. Ghiaurov, D. Petkov, S. Artale, Rome RAI Orch, T. Schippers (pp1969) (MEMO) Ⓓ [2] **HR4223/4**

24a, 24b, 25a, 25b, 26, 27a, 27b H. Konetzni, E. Höngen, G. Oeggl, A. Pernerstorfer, A. Welitsch, Vienna St Op Orch, E. Baltzer (pp1950: Ger) (5/94) (PREI) Ⓓ [2] **90175**

27b E. Obraztsova, Philh, R. Stapleton (CFP) Ⓓ **CD-CFP4575** (CFP) ⊟ **TC-CFP4575**

27b G. Bumbry, ROHO, G. Solti (DECC) Ⓓ **433 067-2DWO** (DECC) ⊟ **433 067-4DWO**

27b M. Mödl, Berlin City Op Orch, H. Löwlein (Ger: r1951) (PREI) Ⓓ **90136**

27b Z. Dolukhanova, USSR Rad Orch, A. Kovalyov (r1950s) (PREI) Ⓓ **89066**

27b G. Simionato, Santa Cecilia Academy Orch, F. Ghione (r1954) (DECC) Ⓓ **440 406-2DM**

27b M. Callas, Paris Cons, N. Rescigno (r1964) (EMI) Ⓓ **CDC5 55016-2**

27b E. Leisner, orch (r1924) (PREI) Ⓓ [2] **89210**

27b E. Leisner, orch (r1922: Ger) (PREI) Ⓓ [2] **89210**

27b Z. Dolukhanova, Moscow PO, G. Stolarov (pp1954) (RUSS) Ⓓ **RDCD15023**

27b M. Lipovšek, Munich RO, G. Patanè (6/90) (ORFE) Ⓓ **C179891A**

27b E. Stignani, EIAR Orch, A. la Rosa Parodi (r1940) (1/91) (PREI) Ⓓ **89014**

27b S. Onegin, orch, Rosario Bourdon (r1929) (2/91) (PREI) Ⓓ **89027**

27b F. Leider, orch (Ger: r1926) (5/91) (PREI) Ⓓ [3] **89301**

27b M. Callas, Philh, A. Tonini (2/93) (EMI) Ⓓ **CDC7 54437-2**

27b G. Bumbry, ROHO, G. Solti (r1965) (10/93) (DECC) Ⓓ **436 462-2DM**

27b M. Klose, Berlin St Op Orch, B. Seidler-Winkler (r1936: Ger) (7/95) (PREI) Ⓓ **89082**

28a, 28b, 28c G. Laperrière, Three Rivers SO, G. Bellemare (r1991) (CBC) Ⓓ **SMCD5127**

28a, 28b, 28c, 28d D. Hvorostovsky, Rotterdam PO, V. Gergiev (7/90) (PHIL) Ⓓ **426 740-2PH**

28a, 28b, 28c, 28d R. Merrill, RCA SO, R. Cellini (r1950) (4/94) (RCA) Ⓓ [6] **09026 61580-2(6)**

28b, 28c T. Gobbi, La Scala Orch, U. Berrettoni (r1942) (8/93) (TEST) Ⓓ **SBT1019**

28c P. Coni, Madrid SO, G.P. Sanzogno (pp1991) (IMP) Ⓓ [2] **DPCD998**

28c A. Scotti, anon (r1905) (PEAR) Ⓓ **GEMMCD9937**

28c P. Coni, Madrid SO, G.P. Sanzogno (RNE) Ⓓ [2] **650004**

28c S. Milnes, F. Becerra, Minería SO, H. de la Fuente (r1981) (IMP) Ⓓ **PCD1109**

28c H. Schlusnus, orch (r1925) (PREI) Ⓓ **89110**

28c D. Fischer-Dieskau, BPO, A. Erede (r1959) (EMI) Ⓓ [2] **CMS5 65621-2**

28c E. Giraldoni, anon (r1902) (6/90) (SYMP) Ⓓ **SYMCD1073**

28c, 28d H. Schlusnus, Berlin St Op Orch, A. Rother (r1943: Ger) (PREI) Ⓓ [2] **89212**

28c, 28d G. De Luca, orch (r1921) (1/92) (PREI) Ⓓ **89036**

28c, 28d M. Battistini, orch, C. Sabajno (r1913) (10/92) (NIMB) Ⓓ **NI7831** (10/92) (NIMB) ⊟ **NC7831**

28c, 28e J. Hynninen, Estonian SO, E. Klas (4/90) (ONDI) Ⓓ **ODE731-2**

28d D. Fischer-Dieskau, ROHO, G. Solti (r1965) (DECC) Ⓓ **440 409-2DM**

28d M. Battistini, orch (r1924) (PEAR) Ⓓ **GEMMCD9016**

28d G. De Luca, orch (r1929) (PEAR) Ⓓ [3] **GEMMCDS9160(2)**

28d G. Bechi, Milan SO, A. Quadri (r1949) (4/92) (EMI) Ⓓ [7] **CHS7 69741-2(7)**

28d G. De Luca, orch, Rosario Bourdon (r1929) (10/94) (PREI) Ⓓ **89073**

28d, 28e G. Taddei, Naples San Carlo Op Orch, U. Rapalo (PREI) Ⓓ **90020**

28d, 28e B. Weikl, Munich RO, H. Wallberg (ACAN) Ⓓ **43 327**

28d, 28e T. Gobbi, La Scala Orch, U. Berrettoni (r1942) (10/89) (EMI) Ⓓ **CDM7 63109-2**

28e S. Milnes, Xalapa SO, H. de la Fuente (r1981) (IMP) Ⓓ **PCD1109**

28e G. Bechi, Milan SO, A. Quadri (r1949) (2/90) (PREI) Ⓓ **89009**

30. M. Callas, Concertgebouw, N. Rescigno (pp1959) (EMI) Ⓓ **CDC7 49428-2**

30. M. Callas, N German RSO, N. Rescigno (pp1959) (MEMO) Ⓓ **HR4293/4**

30. S. Murphy, WNO Orch, J. Smith (COLL) Ⓓ **Coll3025-2**

30. M. Dragoni, Munich RSO, G. Kuhn (r1991) (ORFE) Ⓓ **C261921A**

30. V. Zeani, Turin RAI Orch, P. Urbini (pp1969) (BONG) Ⓓ **GB1060-2**

30. E. Urbanová, Prague SO, J. Bělohlávek (r1993) (SUPR) Ⓓ **11 1851-2**

30. K. Te Kanawa, LPO, J. Pritchard (5/85) (CBS) Ⓓ **MK37298** (CBS) ⊟ **40-37298**

30. M. Callas, Philh, N. Rescigno (9/87) (EMI) Ⓓ **CDC7 47730-2**

30. M. Caballé, ROHO, C.M. Giulini (10/88) (EMI) Ⓓ **CDM7 69500-2**

30. J. Barstow, ENO Orch, M. Elder (1/89) (TER) Ⓓ **CDVIR8307** (1/89) (TER) ⊟ **ZCVIR8307**

30. M. Callas, Philh, N. Rescigno (2/90) (EMIN) Ⓓ **CD-EMX2123** (2/88) (EMIN) ⊟ **TC-EMX2123**

30. M. Seinemeyer, Berlin St Op Orch, F. Weissmann (r1927) (11/90) (PREI) Ⓓ **89029**

30. R. Tebaldi, New Philh, O. de Fabritiis (8/91) (DECC) Ⓓ [2] **430 481-2DX2**

30. M. Grandi, RPO, A. Erede (r1948) (4/92) (EMI) Ⓓ [7] **CHS7 69741-2(7)**

30. M. Teschemacher, Berlin St Op Orch, B. Seidler-Winkler (Ger: r1939) (11/92) (PREI) Ⓓ **89049**

30. M. Gauci, Belgian Rad & TV Orch, A. Rahbari (11/92) (NAXO) Ⓓ **8 550606**

30. J. Hammond, Philh, V. Tausky (r1952) (12/92) (TEST) Ⓓ **SBT1013**

30. M. Callas, ROHO, G. Prêtre (pp1962)
(3/95) (EMI) **LDB4 91283-1**
(3/95) (EMI) **MVD4 91283-3**
32. J. Vickers, Rome Op Orch, T. Serafin (r1961)
(VAI) ① **VAIA1016**

Don Carlos– opera: 5 acts (1867—Paris) (Lib. Méry & du Locle. French version of Don Carlo)

EXCERPTS: ACT 1: 1. Le cerf s'enfuit sous la ramure; 2a. Fontainebleau! Forêt immense; 2b. Je l'ai vue; 3a. Le bruit du cor; 3b. Je suis un étranger; 3c. Que faites-vous donc?; 3d. De quels transport; 4a. A celui qui vous vient; 4b. L'heure fatale est sonnée!; 5. O chants de fête; 6. Le trè-glorieux Roi de France. ACT 2: 7. Charles-Quint, l'auguste Empereur; 8. Au couvent de Saint-Just; 9a. Le voilà! C'est l'Infant!; 9b. Tu pâlis; 9c. Dieu, tu semas dans nos âmes; 10. Sous ces bois; 11. Au palais des fées; 12. La Reine!; 13. Que fait-on à la cour de France; 14. L'Infant Carlos; 15a. Je viens solliciter de la Reine; 15b. O bien perdu; 15c. Par quelle douce voix; 16a. Le Roi!; 16b. O ma chère compagne; 17a. Restez! Auprès de ma personne; 17b. O Roi! J'arrive de Flandre. ACT 3: 18a. Prélude; 18b. À minuit, aux jardins de la Reine; 18c. C'est vous!; 19. Que dit-il? Il est en délire; 20. Ce jour heureux; 21. En plačant sur mon front; 22. Sire, la dernière heure. ACT 4: 23a. Elle ne m'aime pas!; 23b. Je dormirai dans mon manteau royal; 24a. Le Grand Inquisiteur!...Suis-je devant le Roi?; 24b. Dans ce beau pays; 25a. Justice! Sire! J'ai foi; 25b. Maudit soit le soupčon infâme; 26. Pitié!; 27a. Ah! Je ne verrai plus la Reine!; 27b. O don fatal; 28a. C'est moi, Carlos!; 28b. Il faut nous dire adieu!; 28c. Oui, Carlos! C'est mon jour suprême; 28d. Carlos, écoute; 28e. Ah! Je meurs l'âme joyeuse; 29a. Mon fils, reprenez votre épée; 29b. Ciel! Le tocsin. ACT 5: 30. Toi qui sus le néant des grandeurs; 31a. C'est elle!...Un mot; 31b. J'avais fait un beau rêve!; 31c. Au revoir dans un monde; 31d. Oui, pour toujours!. ITEMS OMITTED PRIOR TO PREMIÈRE IN 1867: ACT 1: 32. L'hiver est long! (Prelude and Introduction); ACT 3: Scene 1: 33. Que de fleurs...Viens Eboli; (Introduction and Chorus); ACT 3: Scene 2: 34. Le Ballet de la Reine; ACT 4: Scene 1: 35. J'ai tout compris; ACT 4: Scene 2: 36. Mons fils, reprenez votre épée (Finale: part 1 - reconstructed); ACT 5; 37. Oui, pour toujours! (Finale).

Don Carlos P. Domingo
Elisabeth K. Ricciarelli
Eboli L.V. Terrani
Rodrigue L. Nucci
Philippe II R. Raimondi
Grand Inquisitor N. Ghiaurov
Monk N. Storozhev
Thibault A. Murray
Comte de Lerme T. Raffalli
Herald A. Savastano
Voice from Heaven A. Auger
La Scala Chor, La Scala Orch, C. Abbado (includes appendix)
(12/85) (DG) ① [4] **415 316-2GH4**

1, 2a, 7, 11, 15a, 20, 23a, 23b, 26, 27a, 27b, 28a-e, 31a-d R. Raimondi, P. Domingo, L. Nucci, N. Ghiaurov, N. Storozhev, K. Ricciarelli, L.V. Terrani, A. Murray, La Scala Chor, La Scala Orch, C. Abbado (r1983/4)
(DG) ① **415 981-2GH**
2a, 2b P. Domingo, La Scala Orch, C. Abbado (r1983-4) (DG) ① **445 525-2GMA**
(DG) **445 525-4GMA**
9a T. Hampson, J. Hadley, WNO Orch, C. Rizzi (r1992) (TELD) ① **4509-98824-2**
9a J. Hadley, T. Hampson, WNO Orch, C. Rizzi (r1992) (11/93) (TELD) ① **9031-73283-2**
9a, 9b F. Wunderlich, H. Prey, Munich RO, H. Stein (Ger: bp) (DG) ① [5] **435 145-2GX5(1)**
9a, 9b F. Wunderlich, H. Prey, Munich RO, H. Stein (Ger) (5/93) (DG) ① **431 110-2GB**
18a Hungarian St Op Orch, P.G. Morandi (r1994) (NAXO) ① **8 553089**
23a, 23b Vanni-Marcoux, orch, P. Coppola (r1931) (PEAR) ① **GEMMCD9912**
23b P. Plançon, orch (r1907)
(9/91) (PEAR) ① **GEMMCD9497**
23b P. Plançon, orch (r1907)
(7/93) (NIMB) ① [2] **NI7840/1**
23b P. Plançon, orch (r1907)
(12/94) (ROMO) ① [2] **82001-2**
28a, 28b, 28c S. Milnes, LPO, S. Varviso (r1972)
(DECC) ① **443 380-2DM**

30. F. Pollet, Montpellier PO, C. Diederich (r1989) (ERAT) ① **4509-98502-2**
30. K. Te Kanawa, ROHO, J. Tate
(2/90) (EMI) ① **CDC7 49863-2**
34. Monte Carlo Op Orch, A. de Almeida (r1973)
(PHIL) ① [2] **442 550-2PM2**
34. NY Met Op Orch, James Levine (r1992)
(6/94) (SONY) ① **SK52489**

I due Foscari, '(The) Two Foscaris'– opera: 3 acts (1844—Rome) (Lib. F Piave, after Byron)

EXCERPTS: 1. Prelude. ACT 1: 2. Silenzio; 3a. Qui ti rimani; 3b. Brezza del suol natio; 3c. Dal più remoto esilio; 3d. Odio solo, ed odio atroce; 4a. No...mi lasciate; 4b. Tu al cui sguardo onnipossente; 4c. Che mi rechi?; 5. Tacque il reo!; 6a. Eccomi solo alfine; 6b. O vecchio cor, che batti; 7a. L'illustre dama Foscari; 7b. Tu pur lo sai; 7c. Di sua innocenza dubiti? ACT 2: 8. Prelude; 9a. Notte! perpetua notte; 9b. Non maledirmi, o prode; 10a. Ah, sposo mio!; 10b. No, non morrai; 10c. Tutta è calma la laguna; 10d. Sperenza dolce ancora; 11a. Ah, padre!; 11b. Nel tuo paterno amplesso; 11c. Addio... 12. Ah sì, il tempo; 13. Che più si tarda?; 14a. O patrizi; 14b. Queste innocenti lagrime. ACT 3: 15a. Alla gioia!; 15b. Tace il vento; 16a. Donna infelice; 16b. All'infelice veglio; 17a. Egli ora parte; 17b. Più non vive!; 18a. Signor, chiedon parlarti; 18b. Questa dunque è l'inquia mercede; 18c. Che venga a me, se lice; 18d. Quel bronzo infernale.

Francesco Foscari R. Bruson
Jacopo Foscari A. Cupido
Lucrezia L. Roark-Strummer
Loredano L. Roni
Barbarigo R. Cazzaniga
Pisana M. Tagliasacchi
Officer A. Bottion
Servant A. Bramante
La Scala Chor, La Scala Orch, G. Gavazzeni, P. L. Pizzi
(CAST) **CVI2060**

Francesco Foscari G. Guelfi
Jacopo Foscari C. Bergonzi
Lucrezia M. Vitale
Loredano P. Lombardo
Barbarigo M. Bersieri
Pisana L. Pellegrino
Officer A. Bertocci
Servant G. Barbieri
Milan RAI Chor, Milan RAI SO, C.M. Giulini (pp1951)
(FONI) ① [2] **CDAR2022**

Francesco Foscari P. Cappuccilli
Jacopo Foscari J. Carreras
Lucrezia K. Ricciarelli
Loredano S. Ramey
Barbarigo V. Bello
Pisana E. Connell
Officer M. Antoniak
Servant F. Handlos
Austrian Rad Chor, Austrian RSO, L. Gardelli (r1976)
(12/89) (PHIL) ① [2] **422 426-2PM2**

1. Hungarian St Op Orch, P.G. Morandi (r1994)
(NAXO) ① **8 553089**
3a, 3c L. Pavarotti, A. Savastano, La Scala Orch, C. Abbado (6/87) (CBS) ① **CD37228**
4a, 4b M. Caballé, M. Sunara, RCA Italiana Op Orch, A. Guadagno
(11/92) (RCA) ① [2] **GD60941**
6b P. Amato, orch (r1913) (PREI) ① **89064**
6b P. Amato, orch (r1913)
(PEAR) ① **GEMMCD9104**
6b P. Amato, orch (r1913) (PREI) ① **89995**
6b P. Amato, orch (r1913)
(10/95) (NIMB) ① **NI7867**
9a, 9b C. Bergonzi, New Philh, N. Santi
(PHIL) ① [3] **432 486-2PM3**
18b E. Molinari, orch (r1928) (PREI) ① **89995**

Ernani– opera: 4 acts (1844—Venice) (Lib. F Piave)

EXCERPTS: ACT 1: 1. Prelude; 2. Evviva!; 3a. Mercè, dilette amici; 3b. Come rugiada al cespite; 3c. O tu che l'alma adora; 4a. Surta è la notte; 4b. Ernani! Ernani, involami; 4c. Tutto sprezzo che d'Ernani; 5a. Fa che a me venga; 5b. Qui mi trasse amor possente; 5c. Da quel dì che t'ho veduta; 6. Tu se', Ernani!; 7a. Che mai vegg'io!; 7b. Infelice! E tuo credevi; 7c. L'offeso onor, signori; 8. Vedi come il buon vegliardo. ACT 2: 9. Esultiamo; 10. Oro, Quant'oro; 11. Ah, morir; 12. No, vendetta più tremenda; 13a. Cugino, a che munito; 13b. Lo vedremo, veglio audace; 14. Vieni meco, sol di rose. 15. A te, scegli, seguimi!. ACT 3: 16a. Prelude; 16b. È questo il loco; 17a. Gran Dio!; 17b. Oh, de' verd'anni miei; 18a. Un patto!; 18b. Si ridesti; 19. O sommo Carlo. ACT 4: 20. Oh, come felici; 21a. Tutto ora tace intorno; 21b. Solingo, errante e misero.

Ernani P. Domingo
Elvira M. Freni
Don Carlo R. Bruson
De Silva N. Ghiaurov
La Scala Chor, La Scala Orch, R. Muti, L. Ronconi
(CAST) **CVI2047**

Ernani F. Corelli
Elvira L. Price
Don Carlos M. Sereni
De Silva C. Siepi
Giovanna C. Ordassy
Don Riccardo C. Anthony
Jago C. Russel
NY Met Op Chor, NY Met Op Orch, T. Schippers (pp1965)
(MEMO) ① [2] **HR4370/1**

Ernani P. Domingo
Elvira M. Freni
Don Carlos R. Bruson
De Silva N. Ghiaurov
Giovanna J. Michiel
Don Riccardo G. Manganotti
Jago A. Giacomotti
La Scala Chor, La Scala Orch, R. Muti (pp1982)
(1/84) (EMI) ① [3] **CDS7 47083-8**

Ernani C. Bergonzi
Elvira L. Price
Don Carlos M. Sereni
De Silva E. Flagello
Giovanna J. Hamari
Don Riccardo F. Iacopucci
Jago H. Mueller
RCA Italiana Op Chor, RCA Italiana Op Orch, T. Schippers (r1967)
(8/88) (RCA) ① [2] **GD86503**

D'Ernani i fidi...Odi il voto (Act 2) L. Pavarotti, G. Morresi, A. Giacomotti, La Scala Orch, C. Abbado (6/87) (CBS) ① **CD37228**
Excs P. Domingo (CAST) **CVI2021**
1. Hungarian St Op Orch, P.G. Morandi (r1994)
(NAXO) ① **8 553089**
1. BPO, H. von Karajan
(10/87) (DG) ① **419 622-2GH**
1. BPO, H. von Karajan
(1/95) (DG) ① **439 972-2GGA2**
2, 18a RCA Italiana Op Chor, RCA Italiana Op Orch, T. Schippers (r1967)
(RCA) ① **74321 24209-2**
2, 9. La Scala Chor, La Scala Orch, R. Muti (pp1982) (EMI) ① [2] **CZS5 68559-2**
3. P. Domingo, R. Wagner Chorale, Los Angeles PO, C.M. Giulini (DG) **419 091-4GW**
3a F. Corelli, NY Met Op Orch, T. Schippers (pp1965) (MEMO) ① [2] **HR4204/5**
3a-c P. Domingo, R. Wagner Chorale, Los Angeles PO, C.M. Giulini (r1980)
(DG) ① **445 525-2GMA**
(DG) **445 525-4GMA**
3a, 3b C. Bergonzi, New Philh, N. Santi
(PHIL) ① [3] **432 486-2PM3**
3a, 3b F. de Lucia, orch (r1917)
(BONG) ① [2] **GB1064/5-2**
3a, 3b G. Martinelli, orch, W.B. Rogers (r1915)
(10/89) (NIMB) ① **NI7804**
(NIMB) **NC7804**
3a, 3b G. Martinelli, orch, W.B. Rogers (r1915)
(7/95) (MMOI) ① **CDMOIR428**
3a, 3b, 3c M. del Monaco, New SO, A. Erede (r1958) (DECC) ① **440 407-2DM**
3b L. Slezak, orch (Ger: r1907)
(2/91) (PREI) ① **89020**
4a, 4b L. Price, RCA Italiana Op Orch, T. Schippers (RCA) ① **RD87016**
4a, 4b M. Callas, N German RSO, Athens Fest Orch (pp1962) (MEMO) ① **HR4293/4**
4a, 4b O. Romanko, Ernst-Senff Chbr Chor, Berlin RSO, R. Buckley
(SCHW) ① [2] **314052**
4a, 4b M. Caballé, Milan RAI Chor, Milan RAI SO, G. Gavazzeni (pp1969)
(MEMO) ① [2] **HR4279/80**
4a, 4b E. Gruberová, Smetana Th Chor, Czech PO, F. Haider (SUPR) ① **11 0345-2**
4a, 4b L. Price, NY Met Op Chor, NY Met Op Orch, T. Schippers (pp1965)
(MEMO) ① [2] **HR4396/7**

4a, 4b M. Korjus, Berlin St Op Orch, B. Seidler-Winkler (r1936; Ger) (DANT) ① **LYS001**
4a, 4b S. Dunn, Bologna Teatro Comunale Orch, R. Chailly (r1987) (DECC) ① **436 472-2DM**
4a, 4b J. Sutherland, Paris Cons, N. Santi (r1959) (DECC) ① **440 404-2DM**
4a, 4b M. Callas, Philh, N. Rescigno (r1958) (EMI) ① **CDC5 55016-2**
4a, 4b A. Cerquetti, MMF Orch, G. Gavazzeni (r1956) (DECC) ① **440 411-2DM**
4a, 4b A. Tomowa-Sintow, Munich RO, P. Sommer (11/86) (ORFE) ① **C106841A**
4a, 4b M. Callas, Philh, N. Rescigno (9/87) (EMI) ① **CDC7 47730-2**
4a, 4b R. Ponselle, orch, Rosario Bourdon (r1924) (10/89) (NIMB) ① **NI7805**
(NIMB) ⊟ **NC7805**
4a, 4b R. Ponselle, orch, Rosario Bourdon (r1928) (1/90) (RCA) ① **GD87810**
4a, 4b M. Callas, Philh, N. Rescigno (2/90) (EMI) ① **CDM7 63182-2**
4a, 4b V. de los Angeles, Rome Op Orch, G. Morelli (r1954) (8/90) (EMI) ① **CDH7 63495-2**
4a, 4b F. Hempel, orch (r1915) (3/94) (NIMB) ① **NI7849**
4a, 4b C. Muzio, orch (r1918) (1/95) (ROMO) ① [2] **81010-2**
4b M. Freni, La Scala Orch, R. Muti (CAST) ■■ **CASH5052**
4b E. Steber, Orch, Anon (cond) (bp1951) (VAI) ■■ **VAI69112**
4b R. Ponselle, orch (r1922) (PEAR) ① [2] **GEMMCDS9964**
4b S. Murphy, WNO Orch, J. Smith (COLL) ① **Coll3025-2**
4b M. Foley, Orch (r1949-53) (ODE) ① **CDODE1062**
4b A. Cerquetti, Milan RAI SO, A. Basile (bp1956) (FONI) ① **CDMR5014**
4b X. Belmas, orch, A. Kitschin (r1928) (10/92) (PREI) ① **89047**
4b M. Korjus, Berlin St Op Orch, B. Seidler-Winkler (Ger: r1936) (10/93) (PREI) ① **89054**
4b R. Raisa, orch (r1923) (1/94) (CLUB) ① **CL99-052**
4b R. Ponselle, orch, Rosario Bourdon (r1923/4: 2 vers) (11/94) (ROMO) ① [2] **81006-2**
4b R. Ponselle, orch, Rosario Bourdon (r1927/8 (2 vers) (11/94) (ROMO) ① [2] **81007-2**
4b K. Vayne, anon (r1949) (6/95) (PREI) ① **89996**
4b E. Steber, orch, W. Pelletier (bp1940) (11/95) (VAI) ① **VAIA1072**
4b, 4c R. Ponselle, orch, Rosario Bourdon (r1928) (7/95) (MMOI) ① **CDMOIR428**
5a-c, 16b, 17a, 17b E. Bastianini, M. del Monaco, A. Cerquetti, A. Cesarini, MMF Chor, MMF Orch, D. Mitropoulos (pp1957) (MEMO) ① [2] **HR4400/1**
5c G. Arangi-Lombardi, E. Molinari, La Scala Orch, L. Molajoli (r1929) (10/90) (PREI) ① **89013**
5c, 13b, 14, 19. M. Battistini, E. Corsi, A. Sillich, L. Colazza, orch (r1906) (2/92) (PREI) ① **89045**
7a-c B. Christoff, Philh, A. Fistoulari (r1951) (EMI) ① **CDH5 65500-2**
7a, 7b C. Siepi, Santa Cecilia Academy Orch, A. Erede (r1954) (DECC) ① **440 418-2DM**
7a, 7b E. Pinza, orch, Rosario Bourdon (r1929) (2/89) (PEAR) ① **GEMMCD9306**
7a, 7b E. Pinza, orch, Rosario Bourdon (r1929) (7/91) (MMOI) ① **CDMOIR404**
(MMOI) ⊟ **CMOIR404**
7a, 7b E. Pinza, orch, Rosario Bourdon (r1929) (9/93) (RCA) ① **09026 61245-2**
7b F. Chaliapin, orch (r1912) (PREI) ① **89030**
7b T. Pasero, orch, L. Molajoli (r1927) (6/90) (PREI) ① **89010**
7b E. Pinza, orch, Rosario Bourdon (r1929) (3/92) (PREI) ① **89050**
7b A. Didur, anon (r1900: Pol) (6/93) (PEAR) ① [3] **GEMMCDS9997/9(2)**
7b E. Pinza, orch, Rosario Bourdon (r1929) (12/93) (NIMB) ① **NI7851**
10, 11, 18b P. Domingo, M. Freni, R. Bruson, N. Ghiaurov, La Scala Chor, La Scala Orch, R. Muti (CAST) ■■ **CVI2067**
11. P. Domingo, M. Freni, La Scala Orch, R. Muti (TELD) ◐ **9031-77676-6**
(TELD) ■■ **9031-77676-3**
13b M. Sammarco, orch (r1911) (PREI) ① **89995**
13b, 17b T. Ruffo, orch (r1921) (2/93) (PREI) ① [3] **89303(2)**
14, 19. M. Battistini, E. Corsi, L. Colazza, A. Sillich, La Scala Chor, orch, C. Sabajno (r1906) (10/92) (NIMB) ① **NI7831**
(10/92) (NIMB) ⊟ **NC7831**
15. M. Wittrisch, W. Strienz, Berlin St Op Orch, L. Blech (Ger: r1935) (PREI) ① **89024**
17a, 17b R. Stracciari, orch (r1917) (PEAR) ① **GEMMCD9178**
17b G. De Luca, orch (r1916) (PEAR) ① [3] **GEMMCDS9160(1)**
17b G. De Luca, anon (r1907) (PEAR) ① [3] **GEMMCDS9159(1)**
17b G. Kaschmann, S. Cottone (r1903) (12/89) (SYMP) ① **SYMCD1065**
17b C. Tagliabue, La Scala Orch, U. Berrettoni (r1946) (11/90) (PREI) ① **89015**
17b G. Kaschmann, anon (r1903) (11/92) (MEMO) ① [2] **HR4408/9(1)**
17b M. Battistini, orch (r1906) (7/93) (NIMB) ① [2] **NI7840/1**
17b M. Battistini, orch, C. Sabajno (r1906) (4/94) (EMI) ① [3] **CHS7 64860-2(1)**
17b G. De Luca, orch (r1916) (10/95) (NIMB) ① **NI7867**
18a, 18b La Scala Chor, La Scala Orch, R. Muti (EMI) ① **CDC7 54484-2**
18b Forum Op Chor, Forum PO, G. Bellini (EURM) ① **350214**
18b Slovak Phil Chor, Bratislava RSO, O. Dohnányi (4/91) (NAXO) ① **8 550241**
19. G. Anthony, A. Tedesco, G. De Luca, NY Met Op Chor, NY Met Op Orch, G. Setti (r1928) (PEAR) ① [3] **GEMMCDS9160(2)**
19. C. Galeffi, La Scala Orch, L. Molajoli (r1926) (2/92) (PREI) ① **89040**
19. G. De Luca, G. Anthony, A. Tedesco, NY Met Op Chor, NY Met Op Orch, G. Setti (r1928) (10/94) (PREI) ① **89073**
21b L. Signoretti, anon (r1901) (12/89) (SYMP) ① **SYMCD1065**

Falstaff– opera: 3 acts (1893—Milan) (Lib. A Boito, after Shakespeare)

EXCERPTS: ACT 1: 1. Falstaff! Olà!; 2. So che se andiam,la notte; 3. Ma è tempo d'assottigliar l'ingegno; 4a. Ehi! paggio!; 4b. L'Onore! Ladri!; 5. Alice... Meg... Nannetta; 6a. Fulgida Alice! amor t'offro; 6b. Quell'otre! quel tino!; 6c. È un ribaldo, un furbo, un labro; 7. In due parole; 8a. Pst, pst, Nannetta; 8b. Labbro di foco!; 8c. Falstaff m'ha canzonata; 8d. Torno all'assalto; 9. Del tuo barbaro diagnostico. ACT 2: 10a. Siam pentiti e contriti; 10b. Reverenza!; 11a. Alice, è mia!; 11b. Va, vecchio John; 12. Signore, v'assista il cielo!; 13a. C'è Windsor una dama; 13b. V'ascolto; 14a. È sogno? o realtà; 14b. Eccomi qua. Son pronto; 15a. Presenteremo un bill; 15b. Giunta all'Albergo della Giarrettiera; 16a. Fra poco s'incomincia la commedia; 16b. A noi! Tu la parte farai che ti spetta; 17. Alfin t'ho colto; 18a. Quand'ero paggio; 18b. Voi mi celiate; 19a. Mia signora!; 19b. Vien qua; 19c. Al ladro; 20a. C'è. C'è; 20b. Facciamo le viste. ACT 3: 21a. Ehi! Taverniere!; 21b. Mondo ladro; 22a. Reverenza. La bella Alice; 22b. Quando il rintocco; 23. Sarai la Fata Regina delle Fate; 24a. Dal labbro il canto; 24b. Nossignore! Tu indossa; 25a. Una, due, tre, quattro; 25b. Odo un soave passo!; 26a. Ninfe! Elfi! Silfi!; 26b. Sul fil d'un soffio etesio; 27a. Alto là; 27b. Pizzica, pizzica; 28. Ogni sorta di gente dozzinale; 29a. Facciamo il paremtado; 29b. Tutto nel mondo è burla.

Falstaff G. Bacquier
Ford R. Stilwell
Alice K. Armstrong
Nannetta J-R. Ihloff
Fenton M-R. Cosotti
Mistress Quickly M. Szirmay
Meg Page S. Lindenstrand
Doctor Caius J. Lanigan
Bardolph P. Maus
Pistol U. Cold
Schöneberg Boys' Ch, Berlin Deutsche Op Chor, Vienna St Op Chor, VPO, G. Solti, G. Friedrich (r1979)
(9/93) (DECC) ■■ **071 403-3DH**

Falstaff D. Gramm
Ford B. Luxon
Alice K. Griffel
Nannetta E. Gale
Fenton M-R. Cosotti
Mistress Quickly N. Condò
Meg Page R. Penkova
Doctor Caius J. Fryatt
Bardolph B. Dickerson
Pistol U. Trama
Glyndebourne Fest Chor, LPO, J. Pritchard, J-P. Ponnelle (pp1976)
(IMP) ■■ **SLL7014**

Falstaff R. Bruson
Ford L. Nucci
Alice K. Ricciarelli
Nannetta B. Hendricks
Fenton D. Gonzalez
Mistress Quickly L.V. Terrani
Meg Page B. Boozer
Doctor Caius J. Dobson
Bardolph F. Egerton
Pistol W. Wilderman
ROH Chor, ROHO, C.M. Giulini, R. Eyre
(CAST) ■■ **CVI2001**

Falstaff G. Valdengo
Ford F. Guarrera
Alice H. Nelli
Nannetta T. Stich-Randall
Fenton A. Madasi
Mistress Quickly C. Elmo
Meg Page N. Merriman
Doctor Caius G. Carelli
Bardolph J.C. Rossi
Pistol N. Scott
R. Shaw Chorale, NBC SO, A. Toscanini (bp1950)
(RCA) ① [2] **GD60251**

Falstaff M. Stabile
Ford P. Silveri
Alice R. Tebaldi
Nannetta A. Noni
Fenton C. Valletti
Mistress Quickly C. Elmo
Meg Page A.M. Canali
Doctor Caius M. Caruso
Bardolph G. Nessi
Pistol S. Maionica
La Scala Chor, La Scala Orch, V. de Sabata (pp1951)
(MEMO) ① [2] **HR4500/1**

Falstaff G. Rimini
Ford E. Ghirardini
Alice P. Tassinari
Nannetta I.A. Tellini
Fenton R. d'Alessio
Mistress Quickly A. Buades
Meg Page R. Monticone
Doctor Caius E. Venturini
Bardolph G. Nessi
Pistol S. Baccaloni
La Scala Chor, Milan SO, L. Molajoli (r1932)
(VAI) ① [2] **VAIA1098**

Falstaff R. Bruson
Ford L. Nucci
Alice K. Ricciarelli
Nannetta B. Hendricks
Fenton D. Gonzalez
Mistress Quickly L.V. Terrani
Meg Page B. Boozer
Doctor Caius M. Sells
Bardolph F. Egerton
Pistol W. Wilderman
Los Angeles Master Chorale, Los Angeles PO, C.M. Giulini (pp1982)
(12/83) (DG) ① [2] **410 503-2GH2**

Falstaff T. Gobbi
Ford R. Panerai
Alice E. Schwarzkopf
Nannetta A. Moffo
Fenton L. Alva
Mistress Quickly F. Barbieri
Meg Page N. Merriman
Doctor Caius T. Spataro
Bardolph R. Ercolani
Pistol N. Zaccaria
Chor, Philh, H. von Karajan
(9/88) (EMI) ① [2] **CDS7 49668-2**

Falstaff G. Evans
Ford R. Merrill
Alice I. Ligabue
Nannetta M. Freni
Fenton Alfredo Kraus
Mistress Quickly G. Simionato
Meg Page R. Elias
Doctor Caius J. Lanigan
Bardolph P. de Palma
Pistol G. Foiani
RCA Italiana Op Chor, RCA Italiana Op Orch, G. Solti
(3/90) (DECC) ① [2] **417 168-2DM2**

Falstaff G. Valdengo
Ford F. Guarrera
Alice H. Nelli
Nannetta T. Stich-Randall

Fenton A. Madasi
Mistress Quickly C. Elmo
Meg Page N. Merriman
Doctor Caius G. Carelli
Bardolph J.C. Rossi
Pistol N. Scott

R. Shaw Chorale, NBC SO, A. Toscanini (bp1950)
(5/90) (RCA) Ⓓ [7] **GD60326**

Falstaff R. Panerai
Ford A. Titus
Alice S. Sweet
Nannetta J. Kaufmann
Fenton F. Lopardo
Mistress Quickly M. Horne
Meg Page S. Quittmeyer
Doctor Caius P. de Palma
Bardolph U. Ress
Pistol F.E. d'Artegna

Bavarian Rad Chor, BRSO, Colin Davis
(10/92) (RCA) Ⓓ [2] **09026 60705-2**

Falstaff G. Taddei
Ford R. Panerai
Alice R. Kabaivanska
Nannetta J. Perry
Mistress Quickly C. Ludwig
Meg Page T. Schmidt
Doctor Caius P. de Palma
Bardolph H. Zednik
Pistol F. Davià

Salzburg Ballet Sch, Vienna St Op Ballet, Vienna St Op Chor, VPO, H. von Karajan, H. von Karajan (r1982)
(9/93) (SONY) ◐ [2] **S2LV48422**
(9/93) (SONY) ▣ **SHV48422**

Falstaff J. Pons
Ford R. Frontali
Alice D. Dessì
Nannetta M. O'Flynn
Fenton R. Vargas
Mistress Quickly B. Manca di Nissa
Meg Page D. Ziegler
Doctor Caius E. Gavazzi
Bardolph P. Barbacini
Pistol L. Roni

La Scala Chor, La Scala Orch, R. Muti (pp1993)
(11/94) (SONY) Ⓓ [2] **S2K58961**

Falstaff P. Plishka
Ford B. Pola
Alice M. Freni
Nannetta B. Bonney
Fenton F. Lopardo
Mistress Quickly M. Horne
Meg Page S. Graham
Doctor Caius P. de Palma
Bardolph A. Laciura
Pistol J. Courtney

NY Met Op Chor, NY Met Op Orch, James Levine, F. Zeffirelli (r1992)
(10/95) (DG) ◐ [2] **072 434-1GH2**
(10/95) (DG) ▣ **072 434-3GH**

excs K. Ricciarelli, B. Hendricks, D. Gonzalez, R. Bruson, ROHO, C.M. Giulini
(CAST) ▣ **CVI2065**

Excs A. Jerger, G. Monthy, E. Réthy, D. Komarek, A. Dermota, G. Maikl, O. Levko-Antosch, E. Nikolaidi, W. Wernigk, N. Zec, Vienna St Op Chor, Vienna St Op Orch, W. Loibner (pp1939: Ger)
(3/95) (SCHW) Ⓓ [2] **314602**

Excs G. Hann, K. Kronenberg, E. Réthy, A. Kern, A. Dermota, J. Witt, M. Bugarinovic, E. Nikolaidi, W. Wernigk, M. Rus, Vienna St Op Chor, Vienna St Op Orch, C. Krauss (pp1941: Ger) (4/95) (SCHW) Ⓓ [2] **314582**

4a, 4b, 21b D. Fischer-Dieskau, BPO, A. Erede (r1959) (EMI) Ⓓ [2] **CMS5 65621-2**

4b T. Ruffo, orch, J. Pasternack (r1921)
(PEAR) Ⓓ **GEMMCD9088**

4b T. Gobbi, Philh, H. von Karajan (r1956)
(CFP) Ⓓ **CD-CFP4656**
(CFP) ⊟ **TC-CFP4656**

4b M. Stabile, orch (r1926) (PREI) Ⓓ **89995**

4b G. Bechi, Milan SO, A. Quadri (r1951)
(2/90) (PREI) Ⓓ **89009**

4b M. Stabile, orch (r1926)
(7/92) (PEAR) Ⓓ [3] **GEMMCDS9926(1)**

4b T. Ruffo, orch (r1921)
(2/93) (PREI) Ⓓ [3] **89303(2)**

4b T. Ruffo, orch (r1921)
(10/95) (NIMB) Ⓓ **NI7867**

4b, 10b, 12, 21a, 21b V. Palombini, G. Nessi, M. Stabile, A. Poli, L. Donaggio, La Scala Orch, A. Erede (r1942) (TELD) Ⓓ **9031-76437-2**

4b, 18a A. Scotti, orch (r1909)
(PEAR) Ⓓ **GEMMCD9937**

4b, 21a H. Hotter, Leipzig RSO, H. Weisbach (bp1939: Ger) (PREI) Ⓓ **90200**

9, 29b R. Bruson, B. Boozer, J. Dobson, F. Egerton, D. Gonzalez, B. Hendricks, L. Nucci, K. Ricciarelli, L.V. Terrani, W. Wilderman, ROH Chor, ROHO, C.M. Giulini
(CAST) ▣ **CASH5052**

12. M. Stabile, A. Poli, G. Nessi, L. Donaggio, La Scala Orch, A. Erede (r1942)
(4/94) (EMI) Ⓓ [3] **CHS7 64864-2(2)**

14a G. Laperrière, Three Rivers SO, G. Bellemare (r1991) (CBC) Ⓓ **SMCD5127**

14a L. Tibbett, Orch, Rosario Bourdon (r1926)
(3/90) (RCA) Ⓓ **GD87808**

14a L. Tibbett, orch (pp1935)
(3/91) (PEAR) Ⓓ [2] **GEMMCDS9452**

18a T. Gobbi, Philh, A. Erede (r1963)
(10/89) (EMI) Ⓓ **CDM7 63109-2**

18a T. Ruffo, orch, J. Pasternack (r1922)
(11/90) (NIMB) Ⓓ **NI7810**
(NIMB) ⊟ **NC7810**

18a V. Maurel, anon (r1907)
(7/92) (PEAR) Ⓓ [3] **GEMMCDS9923(1)**

18a A. Scotti, anon (r1903)
(7/92) (PEAR) Ⓓ [3] **GEMMCDS9925(1)**

18a D. Bispham, anon (r1902)
(10/92) (SYMP) Ⓓ **SYMCD1093**

18a V. Maurel, anon (r1907)
(11/92) (MEMO) Ⓓ [2] **HR4408/9(1)**

18a T. Ruffo, orch (r1922)
(2/93) (PREI) Ⓓ [3] **89303(2)**

18a A. Scotti, anon (r1902)
(3/93) (SYMP) Ⓓ **SYMCD1100**

18a V. Maurel, anon (r1907)
(7/93) (NIMB) Ⓓ [2] **NI7840/1**

18a V. Maurel, anon (r1907)
(4/94) (EMI) Ⓓ [3] **CHS7 64860-2(1)**

18a V. Maurel, anon (r1907)
(12/94) (SYMP) Ⓓ **SYMCD1128**

18a A. Magini-Coletti, E. Petri, orch (r1906)
(10/95) (NIMB) Ⓓ **NI7867**

24a C. Bergonzi, New Philh, N. Santi
(PHIL) Ⓓ [3] **432 486-2PM3**

24a K. Erb, orch (r1917: Ger) (PREI) Ⓓ **89095**

24a T. Schipa, orch (r1921)
(4/90) (EMI) Ⓓ **CDH7 63200-2**

24a Ferruccio Tagliavini, EIAR Orch, U. Tansini (r1940) (3/94) (CENT) Ⓓ **CRC2164**

26b R. Streich, Berlin Deutsche Op Chor, Berlin Deutsche Op Orch, R. Peters
(DG) Ⓓ [2] **435 748-2GDO2**

26b M. Freni, RCA Italiana Op Chor, RCA Italiana Op Orch, G. Solti (r1963)
(DECC) Ⓓ **440 412-2DM**

26b H. Gueden, Santa Cecilia Academy Orch, A. Erede (r1954) (PREI) Ⓓ **90227**

26b T. dal Monte, La Scala Orch, C. Sabajno (r1929) (2/90) (PREI) Ⓓ **89001**

26b K. Ricciarelli, Parma Teatro Regio Orch, G. Patanè (pp1976)
(5/94) (DECC) Ⓓ [2] **443 018-2DF2**

29b Cincinnati Pops, E. Kunzel (r1994; arr & orch Kunzel & Beck) (TELA) Ⓓ **CD80364**
(TELA) ⊟ **CS30364**

La **forza del destino, '(The) force of destiny'– opera: 4 acts (1862—St Petersburg) (Lib. F. Piave)**

EXCERPTS: 1. Overture. ACT 1: 2. Buona notte, mia figlia; 3a. Temea restasse; 3b. Me pellegrina ed orfana; 4a. Ah! per sempre; 4b. Seguirti fino agl'ultimi; 5a. È tardi; 5b. Vil seduttor!. ACT 2: 6a. Holà (Ballabile); 6b. La cena è pronto; 7a. Viva la guerra!; 7b. Al suon del tamburo; 8a. Padre Eterno Signor; 8b. Viva la buona compagnia; 9a. Poich'imberbe è l'incognito; 9b. Son Pereda, son ricco d'onore; 10. Sta bene (Finale); 11a. Son giunta!; 11b. Madre, pietosa Vergine; 12a. Chi siete?; 12b. Chi mi cerca?; 12c. Or siam soli... 12d. Infelice, delusa, reietta; 12e. Sull'alba il piede; 13a. Il santo nome; 13b. La Vergine degli angeli. ACT 3: 14a. Attenti al gioco; 14b. La vita è inferno; 14c. Oh, tu che in seno; 15a. Al tradimento; 15b. Amici in vita, in morte; 15c. All'armi!; 16a. Arde la mischia! (Battle Scene); 16b. Piano, qui posi; 16c. Solenne in quest'ora; 17a. Morir! Tremenda cosa!; 17b. Urna fatale; 17c. Ah! Egli è salvo; 18. Compagni, sostiamo; 19a. Nè gustare m'è dato; 19b. Sleale! Il segreto; 20a. Lorchè pifferi; 20b. Qua, vivandiere, un sorso; 20c. A buon mercato; 20d. Pane, pan per carità; 20e. Che vergogna!; 21a. Nella guerra, è la follia; 21b. Toh, toh! Poffare il mondo; 22a. Lasciatelo ch'ei vada; 22b. Rataplan. ACT 4: 23a. Fate la carità; 23b. Che? Siete all'osteria?; 24a. Auf! Pazienza; 24b. Del mondo i disinganni; 25a. Giunge qualcun; 25b. Siete il portiere?; 25c. Invano Alvaro; 25d. Le minaccie; 26. Pace, pace, mio Dio; 27a. Io muoio! Confessione!; 27b. Non imprecare, umiliata.

Leonora M. Freni
Don Alvaro P. Domingo
Don Carlo G. Zancanaro
Padre Guardiano P. Plishka
Preziosilla D. Zajick
Melitone S. Bruscantini
Marchese G. Surian
Trabuco E. Gavazzi
Curra F. Garbi
Mayor S. Sammaritano

La Scala Chor, La Scala Orch, R. Muti (r1986)
(5/87) (EMI) Ⓓ [3] **CDS7 47485-8**

Leonora R. Plowright
Don Alvaro J. Carreras
Don Carlo R. Bruson
Padre Guardiano P. Burchuladze
Preziosilla A. Baltsa
Melitone J. Pons
Marchese J. Tomlinson
Trabuco M. Curtis
Curra J. Rigby
Mayor R. Van Allan
Surgeon P. Salomaa

Ambrosian Op Chor, Philh, G. Sinopoli
(5/87) (DG) Ⓓ [3] **419 203-2GH3**

Leonora M. Callas
Don Alvaro R. Tucker
Don Carlo C. Tagliabue
Padre Guardiano N. Rossi-Lemeni
Preziosilla E. Nicolai
Melitone R. Capecchi
Marchese P. Clabassi
Trabuco G. del Signore
Curra R. Cavallari
Mayor; Surgeon D. Caselli

La Scala Chor, La Scala Orch, T. Serafin (r1954)
(10/87) (EMI) Ⓓ [3] **CDS7 47581-8**

Leonora L. Price
Don Alvaro P. Domingo
Don Carlo S. Milnes
Padre Guardiano B. Giaiotti
Preziosilla F. Cossotto
Melitone G. Bacquier
Marchese K. Moll
Trabuco M. Sénéchal
Curra G. Knight
Mayor M. King
Surgeon W. Elvin

John Alldis Ch, LSO, James Levine
(10/87) (RCA) Ⓓ [3] **RD81864**

Leonora L. Price
Don Alvaro R. Tucker
Don Carlo R. Merrill
Padre Guardiano G. Tozzi
Preziosilla S. Verrett
Melitone E. Flagello
Marchese G. Foiani
Trabuco P. de Palma
Curra C. Vozza
Mayor R. Bottcher
Surgeon M. Rinaudo

RCA Italiana Op Chor, RCA Italiana Op Orch, T. Schippers (r1964)
(12/88) (RCA) Ⓓ [3] **GD87971**

Leonora M. Arroyo
Don Alvaro C. Bergonzi
Don Alvaro P. Cappuccilli
Padre Guardiano R. Raimondi
Preziosilla B. Casoni
Melitone G. Evans
Marchese A. Zerbini
Trabuco F. Andreolli
Curra M. Cova
Mayor V. Carbonari
Surgeon D. Hammond-Stroud

Ambrosian Op Chor, RPO, L. Gardelli (r1969)
(6/93) (EMI) Ⓓ [3] **CMS7 64646-2**

Excs Grimethorpe Colliery Band, E. Howarth (arr Wright) (12/92) (DOYE) Ⓓ **DOYCD013**
(12/92) (DOYE) ⊟ **DOYMC013**

1. Czech PO, Z. Chalabala
(SUPR) ⊟ **11 0640-4**

1. Philh, C.M. Giulini (EMI) Ⓓ **CDM7 69596-2**

1. Philh, W. Boughton (NIMB) Ⓓ **NI5120**
(NIMB) ⊟ **NC5120**

1. LSO, J. Mauceri
(12/90) (DECC) ▣ **084 474-3**

1. BPO, H. von Karajan (r1978)
(DG) ▣ **072 196-3GH**

1. New Philh, R. Muti (EMI) Ⓓ **CDC7 47274-2**
1. Bavarian St Orch, W. Sawallisch (ORFE) Ⓓ **C161871A**
1. Sofia SO, V. Stefanov (LASE) Ⓓ **15 519** (LASE) ▣ **79 519**
1. Forum PO, G. Bellini (EURM) Ⓓ **350214**
1. NBC SO, A. Toscanini (r1945) (RCA) Ⓓ **GD60310**
1. Mexico St SO, E. Bátiz (r1990s) (ASV) Ⓓ **CDDCA856** (ASV) ▣ **ZCDCA856**
1. Brno St PO, O. Lenárd (pp1992) (SUPR) Ⓓ **11 1846-2**
1. New Philh, I. Markevitch (r1968) (BELA) Ⓓ **461 001-2** (BELA) ▣ **461 001-4**
1. Hungarian St Op Orch, P.G. Morandi (r1994) (NAXO) Ⓓ **8 553089**
1. LSO, A. Dorati (r1957) (MERC) Ⓓ **434 345-2MM**
1. NY Met Op Orch, James Levine (pp1988) (DG) Ⓓ **445 552-2GMA** (DG) ▣ **445 552-4GMA**
1. RPO, T. Serafin (r1959) (EMI) Ⓓ [2] **CES5 68541-2**
1. BPO, H. von Karajan (DG) Ⓓ [2] **447 364-2GDB2**
1. RPO, A. Licata (r1994) (TRIN) Ⓓ **TRP044**
1. South-West German RSO, K. Arp (r1994) (PIER) Ⓓ **PV730050**
1. BPO, H. von Karajan (10/87) (DG) Ⓓ **419 622-2GH**
1. BPO, H. von Karajan (5/90) (DG) Ⓓ **429 164-2GR**
1. Paris Op Orch, G. Sébastian (pp1958) (11/91) (EMI) ● **LDB9 91258-1** (11/91) (EMI) ▭ **MVC9 91258-3**
1. Black Dyke Mills Band, P. Parkes (arr brass band: F Wright) (9/93) (CHAN) Ⓓ **CHAN4514** (9/93) (CHAN) ▣ **BBTD4514**
1. I. Seefried, M. Forrester, E. Haefliger, D. Fischer-Dieskau, Berlin St Hedwig's Cath Ch, BPO, F. Fricsay, H. Krebs, T. Varga, Berlin RIAS Chbr Ch, Berlin RIAS Orch, H. Geusser, W. Fugmann, M. Weber, G. Herzog, Berlin RSO, VPO, E. Grümmer, G. Pitzinger, H. Hotter, Y. Menuhin (r1953) (11/94) (DG) Ⓓ [11] **445 400-2GDO10**
1. Berlin RIAS Orch, F. Fricsay (r1953) (11/94) (DG) Ⓓ **445 406-2GDO**
1. BPO, H. von Karajan (1/95) (DG) Ⓓ **439 972-2GGA2**
1. NBC SO, A. Toscanini (r1944) (4/95) (TELD) ● **4509-95038-6** (4/95) (TELD) ▭ **4509-95038-3**
1, 4a, 4b, 8a, 9b, 14b, 14c, 16c, 17b, 17c, 19a, 19b, 20a, 22b, 26, 27a, 27b R. Plowright, R. Bruson, J. Carreras, A. Baltsa, P. Burchuladze, J. Rigby, R. Van Allan, M. Curtis, P. Salomaa, Ambrosian Op Chor, Philh, G. Sinopoli (r1985) (DG) Ⓓ **423 148-2GH**
3b E. Burzio, orch (r1913) (1/91) (CLUB) Ⓓ [2] **CL99-587/8**
3b, 4a, 11a, 13b, 26. R. Tebaldi, G. di Stefano, Florence Teatro Comunale Orch, D. Mitropoulos (pp1953) (MEMO) Ⓓ [2] **HR4235/6**
3b, 9b, 11, 12c, 13b, 14b, 14c, 16c, 17b, 22b, 25d, 26, 27. M. Freni, P. Domingo, G. Zancanaro, D. Zajick, P. Plishka, S. Bruscantini, S. Sammaritano, La Scala Chor, La Scala Orch, R. Muti (EMI) Ⓓ **CDC7 54326-2**
3b, 11b G. Cigna, orch, L. Molajoli (r1930) (11/90) (PREI) Ⓓ **89016**
3b, 11b G. Cigna, orch, L. Molajoli (r1930) (11/90) (LYRC) Ⓓ **SRO805**
3b, 26. A. Marc, NZ SO, H. Wallberg (6/92) (DELO) Ⓓ **DE3108** (6/92) (DELO) ▣ **CS3108**
9b, 17a-c C. Tagliabue, Turin EIAR Orch, G. Marinuzzi (r1941) (11/90) (PREI) Ⓓ **89015**
9b, 17a, 17b H. Schlusnus, Berlin St Op Orch, J. Prüwer (r1928: Ger) (PREI) Ⓓ [2] **89212**
11a, 11b, 12a-e, 13a, 13b G. Cigna, G. Vaghi, E. Ghirardini, Rome RAI Chor, Rome RAI Orch, O. de Fabritiis (bp1938) (2/94) (LYRC) Ⓓ [2] **LCD173**
11a, 11b, 26. D. Giannini, orch, J. Barbirolli (r1928) (4/93) (PREI) Ⓓ **89044**
11b L. Price, RCA Italiana Op Chor, RCA Italiana Op Orch, T. Schippers (r1964) (RCA) Ⓓ **74321 24284-2** (RCA) ▣ **74321 24284-4**
11b E. Burzio, orch (r c1907) (1/91) (CLUB) Ⓓ [2] **CL99-587/8**
11b, 13b, 26. L. Price, RCA Italiana Op Orch, T. Schippers (RCA) Ⓓ **RD87016**
12c, 12d, 26. L. Gencer, La Scala Orch, A. Votto (pp1957) (MEMO) Ⓓ [2] **HR4239/40**
12d, 12e, 13b M. Arroyo, R. Raimondi, Ambrosian Op Chor, RPO, L. Gardelli (10/88) (EMI) Ⓓ **CDM7 69549-2**
13a B. Christoff, Rome Op Chor, Rome Op Orch, V. Gui (r1955) (EMI) Ⓓ **CDH5 65500-2**
13a I. Andrésen, chor, Berlin St Op Orch, F. Weissmann (Ger: r1927) (10/90) (PREI) Ⓓ **89028**
13a, 13b M. del Monaco, Santa Cecilia Academy Orch, F. Molinari-Pradelli (r1955) (DECC) Ⓓ **440 407-2DM**
13a, 22b R. Raimondi, B. Casoni, Ambrosian Op Chor, RPO, L. Gardelli (EMI) Ⓓ **CDM7 64356-2**
13a, 22b Ambrosian Op Chor, RPO, L. Gardelli (r1969) (EMI) Ⓓ [2] **CZS5 68559-2**
13b R. Ponselle, orch (r1918) (PEAR) Ⓓ [2] **GEMMCDS9964**
13b M. Foley, Orch (r1949-53) (ODE) Ⓓ **CDODE1062**
13b G. Groves, J. Watson, J. Partridge (r1994: arr W Belshaw) (ASV) Ⓓ **CDWHL2088**
13b R. Ponselle, E. Pinza, NY Met Op Chor, NY Met Op Orch, G. Setti (r1928) (10/89) (NIMB) Ⓓ **NI7805** (NIMB) ▣ **NC7805**
13b D. Giannini, La Scala Orch, C. Sabajno (r1928) (4/93) (PREI) Ⓓ **89044**
13b R. Ponselle, chor, orch, R. Romani (r1918) (10/93) (NIMB) Ⓓ **NI7846**
13b R. Ponselle, E. Pinza, NY Met Op Chor, orch, G. Setti (r1928) (11/94) (ROMO) Ⓓ [2] **81007-2**
13b E. Destinn, chor, orch (r1912) (12/94) (SUPR) Ⓓ [12] **11 2136-2(5)**
13b R. Ponselle, E. Pinza, NY Met Op Chor, NY Met Op Orch, G. Setti (r1928) (7/95) (MMOI) Ⓓ **CDMOIR428**
13b, 18, 21a, 22b M. Freni, D. Zajick, La Scala Chor, La Scala Orch, R. Muti (EMI) Ⓓ **CDC7 54484-2**
14b F. Merli, orch, L. Molajoli (r1926) (1/91) (PREI) Ⓓ **89026**
14b, 14c B. Gigli, La Scala Orch, U. Berrettoni (r1941) (5/90) (EMI) Ⓓ **CDH7 61052-2**
14b, 14c G. di Stefano, La Scala Orch, A. Votto (r1955) (EMI) Ⓓ **CDM7 63105-2**
14b, 14c B. Prevedi, ROHO, E. Downes (DECC) Ⓓ **433 623-2DSP** (DECC) ▣ **433 623-4DSP**
14b, 14c C. Bergonzi, New Philh, N. Santi (PHIL) Ⓓ [3] **432 486-2PM3**
14b, 14c P. Domingo, LSO, James Levine (RCA) Ⓓ [2] **GD60866** (RCA) ▣ [2] **GK60866**
14b, 14c H. Roswaenge, Philh Hungarica, Z. Rozsnyai (pp1959) (PREI) Ⓓ **90103**
14b, 14c M. Lorenz, Berlin St Op Orch, C. Schmalstich (Ger: r1929) (PREI) Ⓓ **89053**
14b, 14c P. Domingo, VPO, James Levine (DG) ● **072 187-1GH** (DG) ▭ **072 187-3GH**
14b, 14c E. Ivanov, Verona Arena Orch, A. Guadagno (pp1992) (MCI) Ⓓ **MCCD099**
14b, 14c M. Lanza, orch, C. Callinicos (r1952) (RCA) Ⓓ **09026 61420-2** (RCA) ▣ **09026 61420-4**
14b, 14c G. di Stefano, Santa Cecilia Academy Orch, F. Previtali (r1959) (DECC) Ⓓ **440 403-2DM**
14b, 14c J. McCracken, Vienna Op Orch, D. Bernet (r1965) (DECC) Ⓓ **436 314-2DA** (DECC) ▣ **436 314-4DA**
14b, 14c C. Bergonzi, Santa Cecilia Academy Orch, G. Gavazzeni (r1957) (DECC) Ⓓ **440 417-2DM**
14b, 14c C. Bergonzi, Santa Cecilia Academy Orch, G. Gavazzeni (r1957) (DECC) Ⓓ **443 379-2DM**
14b, 14c G. Martinelli, orch, Rosario Bourdon (r1927) (10/89) (NIMB) Ⓓ **NI7804** (NIMB) ▣ **NC7804**
14b, 14c P. Domingo, VPO, James Levine (11/89) (DG) ● **072 110-1GH**
14b, 14c B. Heppner, Munich RO, R. Abbado (r1993/4) (11/95) (RCA) Ⓓ **09026 62504-2**
14b, 14c, 16c, 25c, 25d G. di Stefano, A. Protti, La Scala Orch, A. Votto (pp1957) (MEMO) Ⓓ **HR4372/3**
14c E. Caruso, orch, W.B. Rogers (r1909) (RCA) Ⓓ **09026 61242-2**
14c B. Prevedi, ROHO, E. Downes (r1964) (BELA) Ⓓ **450 005-2** (BELA) ▣ **450 005-4**
14c G. di Stefano, Turin RAI Orch, O. de Fabritiis (bp1953) (FONI) Ⓓ **CDMR5003**
14c A. Piccaver, Berlin St Op Orch, J. Prüwer (r1928) (PREI) Ⓓ [2] **89217**
14c F. de Lucia, orch (r1917) (BONG) Ⓓ [2] **GB1064/5-2**
14c E. Caruso, orch (r1909) (5/89) (PEAR) Ⓓ **GEMMCD9309**
14c E. Caruso, orch (r1909) (10/89) (NIMB) Ⓓ **NI7803** (NIMB) ▣ **NC7803**
14c A. Pertile, La Scala Orch, C. Sabajno (r1928) (9/90) (PREI) Ⓓ **89007**
14c E. Caruso, orch (r1909) (3/91) (PEAR) Ⓓ [3] **EVC2**
14c E. Caruso, orch, W.B. Rogers (r1909) (7/91) (RCA) Ⓓ [12] **GD60495(3)**
14c E. Caruso, orch (r1909) (7/91) (MSCM) Ⓓ **MM30352**
14c G. Zenatello, orch (r1909) (12/93) (SYMP) Ⓓ **SYMCD1138**
14c G. Zenatello, orch (r1909) (5/94) (PEAR) Ⓓ [4] **GEMMCDS9073(2)**
14c P. Domingo, La Scala Orch, R. Muti (r1986) (6/94) (EMI) Ⓓ **CDC5 55017-2**
14c H. Roswaenge, Berlin St Op Orch (r1935: Ger) (4/95) (PREI) Ⓓ [2] **89209**
14c, 25c, 25d G. Martinelli, G. De Luca, orch, Rosario Bourdon (r1927) (3/93) (PREI) Ⓓ **89062**
16c B. Gigli, G. De Luca, orch (r1927) (CONI) Ⓓ **CDHD149** (CONI) ▣ **MCHD149**
16c C. Bergonzi, D. Fischer-Dieskau, BRSO, J. López-Cobos (ORFE) Ⓓ **C028821A**
16c B. Gigli, G. De Luca, orch, Rosario Bourdon (r1927) (NIMB) Ⓓ **NI7817** (NIMB) ▣ **NC7817**
16c M. del Monaco, E. Bastianini, Santa Cecilia Academy Orch, F. Molinari-Pradelli (DECC) Ⓓ **433 068-2DWO** (DECC) ▣ **433 068-4DWO**
16c P. Domingo, J. Pons, Seville SO, L.A. Garcia-Navarro (pp1991) (RCA) Ⓓ **RD61191**
16c E. Caruso, A. Scotti, orch (r1906) (NIMB) Ⓓ **NI7834** (NIMB) ▣ **NC7834**
16c P. Domingo, J. Pons, Seville SO, L.A. Garcia-Navarro (pp1991) (RCA) **OO** **09026 61191-5**
16c E. Caruso, A. Scotti, orch (r1906) (RCA) Ⓓ **09026 61242-2**
16c E. Caruso, A. Scotti, orch (r1906) (MCI) Ⓓ **MCCD086** (MCI) ▣ **MCTC086**
16c G. di Stefano, L. Warren, Santa Cecilia Academy Orch, F. Previtali (r1960) (BELA) Ⓓ **450 006-2** (BELA) ▣ **450 006-4**
16c M. Gilion, F.M. Bonini, anon (r1906) (BONG) Ⓓ **GB1076-2**
16c M. del Monaco, E. Bastianini, Santa Cecilia Academy Orch, F. Molinari-Pradelli (r1955) (DECC) Ⓓ **436 315-2DA** (DECC) ▣ **436 315-4DA**
16c H. Roswaenge, G. Hüsch, Berlin St Op Orch, B. Seidler-Winkler (r1937: Ger) (PREI) Ⓓ [2] **89211**
16c F. Merli, G. Vanelli, orch, L. Molajoli (r1929) (PREI) Ⓓ **89091**
16c P. Domingo, S. Milnes, LSO, A. Guadagno (RCA) Ⓓ **09026 62699-2** (RCA) ▣ **09026 62699-4**
16c B. Gigli, G. De Luca, orch (r1927) (PEAR) Ⓓ [3] **GEMMCDS9160(2)**
16c C. Hackett, R. Stracciari, orch (r1919) (PEAR) Ⓓ **GEMMCD9178**
16c H. Schlusnus, R. Hutt, orch (r1921: Ger) (PREI) Ⓓ **89110**
16c B. Gigli, T. Ruffo, orch, Rosario Bourdon (r1926) (PEAR) Ⓓ [2] **GEMMCDS9176**
16c J. Björling, R. Merrill, RCA Victor SO, R. Cellini (2/89) (RCA) Ⓓ **GD87799** (RCA) ▣ **GK87799**
16c R. Tauber, B. Ziegler, orch (Ger: r1922) (7/89) (PEAR) Ⓓ **GEMMCD9327**
16c H. Roswaenge, G. Hüsch, Berlin St Op Orch, B. Seidler-Winkler (Ger: r1937) (5/90) (PEAR) Ⓓ **GEMMCD9394**
16c F. Marconi, N. della Torre, orch (r1908) (10/90) (SYMP) Ⓓ **SYMCD1069**
16c E. Caruso, A. Scotti, orch (r1906) (12/90) (PEAR) Ⓓ [3] **EVC1(2)**
16c E. Caruso, A. Scotti, orch (r1906) (7/91) (RCA) Ⓓ [12] **GD60495(2)**

16c H.E. Groh, G. Hüsch, orch (r1932) (3/92) (PEAR) ⦶ **GEMMCD9419**
16c J. Hislop, A. Granforte, orch, G.W. Byng (r1926) (1/93) (PEAR) ⦶ **GEMMCD9956**
16c T. Ruffo, B. Gigli, orch (r1926) (2/93) (PREI) ⦶ [3] **89303(2)**
16c B. Gigli, G. De Luca, orch, Rosario Bourdon (r1927) (6/93) (MMOI) ⦶ **CDMOIR417**
16c C. Kullman, W. Grossmann, Berlin St Op Orch, E. Orthmann (Ger: r1931) (11/93) (PREI) ⦶ **89057**
16c E. Garbin, M. Sammarco, anon (r1905) (12/93) (SYMP) ⦶ **SYMCD1113**
16c G. De Luca, B. Gigli, orch, Rosario Bourdon (r1927) (10/94) (PREI) ⦶ **89073**
16c, 17a-c E. Bastianini, F. Corelli, NY Met Op Chor, NY Met Op Orch, N. Santi (pp1965) (MEMO) ⦶ [2] **HR4400/1**
16c, 25c P. Domingo, S. Milnes, LSO, A. Guadagno (r1970) (RCA) ⦶ **09026 62595-2**
16c, 25c G. Bechi, G. Lauri-Volpi, Rome Op Orch, R. Arduini (r1943) (2/90) (PREI) ⦶ **89009**
16c, 25c, 25d G. Lauri-Volpi, G. Bechi, Rome Op Orch, R. Arduini (r1943) (7/94) (NIMB) ⦶ **NI7853**
16c, 25c, 25d G. Aragall, E. Tumagian, Bratislava RSO, A. Rahbari (r1992) (12/94) (NAXO) ⦶ **8 550684**
17a, 17b B. Weikl, Munich RO, H. Wallberg (ACAN) ⦶ **43 327**
17a, 17b H. Schlusnus, Berlin St Op Orch, J. Schüler (r1937: Ger) (PREI) ⦶ [2] **89212**
17a, 17b E. Bastianini, E. Coda, Santa Cecilia Academy Orch, F. Molinari-Pradelli (r1955) (10/93) (DECC) ⦶ **436 464-2DM**
17b M. Battistini, orch (r1923) (PEAR) ⦶ **GEMMCD9016**
17b T. Gobbi, Philh, J. Robertson (r1950) (10/89) (EMI) ⦶ **CDM7 63109-2**
17b J. Hynninen, Estonian SO, E. Klas (4/90) (ONDI) ⦶ **ODE731-2**
17b T. Ruffo, orch (r1915) (2/93) (PREI) ⦶ [3] **89303(1)**
17b G. Viviani, orch (r c1924) (12/94) (BONG) ⦶ **GB1043-2**
17c M. Battistini, orch, C. Sabajno (r1921) (10/92) (PEAR) ⦶ **GEMMCD9936**
18. John Alldis Ch, LSO, James Levine (r1976) (RCA) ⦶ **74321 24209-2**
19. E. Caruso, G. De Luca, orch, J. Pasternack (r1918) (7/91) (RCA) ⦶ [12] **GD60495(6)**
19a, 19b G. De Luca, E. Caruso, orch (r1918) (PEAR) ⦶ [3] **GEMMCDS9160(1)**
19a, 19b E. Caruso, G. De Luca, orch, J. Pasternack (r1918) (10/91) (PEAR) ⦶ [3] **EVC4(1)**
19a, 25c J. Lotrič, I. Morozov, Slovak RSO, J. Wildner, Slovak Op Chor (r1994) (2/95) (NAXO) ⦶ **8 553030**
22b B. Casoni, Ambrosian Op Chor, L. Gardelli (CFP) ⦶ **CD-CFP4575**
(CFP) ⊟ **TC-CFP4575**
22b G. Simionato, Santa Cecilia Academy Chor, Santa Cecilia Academy Orch, F. Molinari-Pradelli (r1956) (DECC) ⦶ **440 406-2DM**
22b S. Verrett, RCA Italiana Op Chor, RCA Italiana Op Orch, T. Schippers (r1964) (RCA) ⦶ **09026 61457-2**
22b E. Stignani, EIAR Orch, G. Marinuzzi (r1941) (1/91) (PREI) ⦶ **89014**
22b Slovak Phil Chor, Bratislava RSO, O. Dohnányi (4/91) (NAXO) ⦶ **8 550241**
25c L. Pavarotti, P. Cappuccilli, Bologna Teatro Comunale Orch, L. Magiera (pp1991) (DECC) ◐ **071 140-1DH**
(DECC) ▣ **071 140-3DH**
25c F. Merli, G. Vanelli, orch, L. Molajoli (r1929) (1/91) (PREI) ⦶ **89026**
25c, 25d E. Caruso, P. Amato, orch (r1911) (NIMB) ⦶ **NI7834**
(NIMB) ⊟ **NC7834**
25c, 25d E. Caruso, P. Amato, orch (r1911) (PEAR) ⦶ **GEMMCD9104**
25c, 25d G. Martinelli, G. De Luca, orch (r1927) (PEAR) ⦶ [3] **GEMMCDS9160(2)**
25c, 25d G. Martinelli, G. De Luca, orch, Rosario Bourdon (r1928) (10/89) (NIMB) ⦶ **NI7804**
(NIMB) ⊟ **NC7804**
25c, 25d E. Caruso, P. Amato, orch (r1911) (3/91) (PEAR) ⦶ [3] **EVC2**
25c, 25d E. Caruso, P. Amato, orch (r1911) (7/91) (RCA) ⦶ [12] **GD60495(4)**
25d L. Montesanto, N. Fusati, orch (r c1918) (12/94) (BONG) ⦶ **GB1043-2**
25d F.M. Bonini, G.M. Patti, anon (r1906) (12/94) (BONG) ⦶ **GB1043-2**
26. R. Ponselle, orch (r1920) (PEAR) ⦶ [2] **GEMMCDS9964**
26. E. Steber, orch, H. Barlow (bp1952) (VAI) ▣ **VAI69102**
26. F. Cavalli, RPO, A. Fistoulari (CFP) ⦶ **CD-CFP4575**
(CFP) ⊟ **TC-CFP4575**
26. M. Callas, Athens Fest Orch, A. Votto (pp1957) (MEMO) ⦶ **HR4293/4**
26. G. Jones, Vienna Op Orch, A. Quadri (DECC) ⦶ **433 221-2DWO**
(DECC) ⊟ **433 221-4DWO**
26. S. Murphy, WNO Orch, J. Smith (COLL) ⦶ **Coll3025-2**
26. R. Tebaldi, Santa Cecilia Academy Orch, F. Molinari-Pradelli (r1955) (DECC) ⦶ **440 408-2DM**
26. E. Suliotis, Rome Orch, S. Varviso (r1967) (DECC) ⦶ **440 405-2DM**
26. V. Zeani, Turin RAI Orch, M. Rossi (pp1965) (BONG) ⦶ **GB1060-2**
26. L. Price, RCA Italiana Op Orch, T. Schippers (RCA) ⦶ **09026 61440-2**
(RCA) ⊟ **09026 61440-4**
26. M. Caballé, RPO, A. Guadagno (r1971) (EMI) ⦶ **CDC5 55095-2**
26. E. Urbanová, Prague SO, J. Bělohlávek (r1993) (SUPR) ⦶ **11 1851-2**
26. A. Cerquetti, MMF Orch, G. Gavazzeni (r1956) (DECC) ⦶ **440 411-2DM**
26. A. Cerquetti, Milan RAI SO, A. Basile (bp1956) (FONI) ⦶ **CDMR5014**
26. L. Price, New Philh, T. Schippers (RCA) ⦶ **74321 25817-2**
(RCA) ⊟ **74321 25817-4**
26. K. Ricciarelli, Svizzera Italiana Orch, B. Amaducci (r1979) (ERMI) ⦶ **ERM151**
26. A. Tomowa-Sintow, Sofia PO, R. Raichev (r1970s) (FORL) ⦶ **UCD16742**
26. J. Varady, Bavarian St Orch, D. Fischer-Dieskau (r1995) (ORFE) ⦶ **C186951**
26. G. Bumbry, Stuttgart RSO, S. Soltesz (11/86) (ORFE) ⦶ **C081841A**
26. M. Caballé, RPO, A. Guadagno (10/88) (EMI) ⦶ **CDM7 69500-2**
26. J. Barstow, ENO Orch, M. Elder (1/89) (TER) ⦶ **CDVIR8307**
(1/89) (TER) ⊟ **ZCVIR8307**
26. R. Ponselle, orch, Rosario Bourdon (r1928) (1/90) (RCA) ⦶ **GD87810**
26. C. Muzio, orch (r1922) (5/90) (BOGR) ⦶ [2] **BIM705-2**
26. K. Te Kanawa, LSO, Myung-Whun Chung (11/90) (EMI) ⦶ **CDC7 54062-2**
26. E. Burzio, orch (r c1908) (1/91) (CLUB) ⦶ [2] **CL99-587/8**
26. C. Muzio, orch, L. Molajoli (r1935) (4/91) (NIMB) ⦶ **NI7814**
(4/91) (NIMB) ⊟ **NC7814**
26. R. Tebaldi, Santa Cecilia Academy Orch, F. Molinari-Pradelli (8/91) (DECC) ⦶ [2] **430 481-2DX2**
26. R. Ponselle, orch, Rosario Bourdon (r1928) (7/92) (PEAR) ⦶ [3] **GEMMCDS9926(2)**
26. L. Tetrazzini, orch (r1914) (9/92) (EMI) ⦶ [3] **CHS7 63802-2(2)**
26. L. Tetrazzini, orch (r1914) (9/92) (PEAR) ⦶ **GEMMCD9225**
26. M. Gauci, Belgian Rad & TV Orch, A. Rahbari (11/92) (NAXO) ⦶ **8 550606**
26. C. Muzio, orch (r1922) (1/94) (ROMO) ⦶ [2] **81005-2**
26. R. Ponselle, orch, Rosario Bourdon (r1924) (4/94) (RCA) ⦶ [6] **09026 61580-2(3)**
26. K. Ricciarelli, Parma Teatro Regio Orch, G. Patanè (pp1976) (5/94) (DECC) ⦶ [2] **443 018-2DF2**
26. R. Ponselle, orch, Rosario Bourdon (r1923/4: 3 vers) (11/94) (ROMO) ⦶ [2] **81006-2**
26. R. Ponselle, orch, Rosario Bourdon (r1928 (2 vers) (11/94) (ROMO) ⦶ [2] **81007-2**
26. C. Muzio, orch (r1917) (1/95) (ROMO) ⦶ [2] **81010-2**
26. Leonie Rysanek, Berlin SO, W. Schüchter (r1955: Ger) (2/95) (EMI) ⦶ **CDH5 65201-2**
26. K. Vayne, orch (bp1959) (6/95) (PREI) ⦶ **89996**
26. R. Ponselle, orch, Rosario Bourdon (r1928) (7/95) (MMOI) ⦶ **CDMOIR428**
26. R. Hunter, Tasmanian SO, D. Franks (r1989) (10/95) (ABCC) ⦶ **8 7000 10**
27a R. Ponselle, G. Martinelli, E. Pinza, NY Met Op Chor, NY Met Op Orch, G. Setti (r1928) (10/89) (NIMB) ⦶ **NI7804**
(NIMB) ⊟ **NC7804**
27a, 27b R. Ponselle, G. Martinelli, E. Pinza, orch, Rosario Bourdon (r1928) (1/90) (RCA) ⦶ **GD87810**
27a, 27b R. Ponselle, G. Martinelli, E. Pinza, orch, Rosario Bourdon (r1928 (2 vers) (11/94) (ROMO) ⦶ [2] **81007-2**
27a, 27b R. Ponselle, G. Martinelli, E. Pinza, orch, Rosario Bourdon (r1928) (7/95) (MMOI) ⦶ **CDMOIR428**
27b B. Scacciati, F. Merli, T. Pasero, orch, L. Molajoli (r1929) (6/90) (PREI) ⦶ **89010**

Un **giorno di regno, '(A) king for a day'– opera: 2 acts (1840—Milan) (Lib. F Romani)**

EXCERPTS: 1. Overture. ACT 1: 2. Mai no rise un più bel dì; 3. Tesoriere garbatissimo; 4a. Sua Maestà, signori; 4b. Compagnoni di Parigi; 4c. Verrà pur troppo il giorno; 5a. Al doppio matrimonio; 5b. Sire tremante io vengo; 6a. Proverò che degno io sono; 6b. Infiammato da spirito guerriero; 7a. Ah, non m'hanno ingannata!; 7b. Grave a core innamorato; 8a. Sì festevola mattina; 8b. Non san quant'io nel petto; 8c. Non vo' quel vecchio, non son sì sciocca; 9. Ebben, Giuletta mia; 10a. Cara Giulia, alfin ti vedo; 10b. Madamine, il mio scudiere; 11. In te, cugina, io spero; 12. Bella speranza invero; 13. Quanto diceste mostra un gran talento; 14. Diletto genero, a voi ne vengo; 15a. Tesorier! io creder voglio; 15b. In qual punto il Re ci ha colto!; 16a. Olà spiegatemi tosto, o Barone; 16b. Affidate alla mente reale. ACT 2: 17a. Ma la nozze non si fanno?; 17b. Pietoso al lungo pianto; 17c. Deh, lasciate a un'alma amante; 18. Bene, scudiero, vi ritrovo in tempo; 19a. Un mio castello! cinque mila scudi!; 19b. Tutte l'armi si può prendere; 20. Ch'io non posso il ver comprendere?; 21. Nipote, un quest'istante; 22a. Perchè dunque non vien?; 22b. Sì, scordar saprò l'infido; 23a. Oh me felice appieno!; 23b. Ah! non sia, mio ben, fallace; 24a. Sì, caro conte!; 24b. A tal colpo preparata; 25a. Sire, venne in quest'istante; 25b. Eh! facciamo da buoni amici.

1. Hungarian St Op Orch, P.G. Morandi (r1994) (NAXO) ⦶ **8 553089**
1. RPO, K.H. Adler (pp1982) (8/91) (DECC) ⦶ **430 716-2DM**
(8/91) (DECC) ⊟ **430 716-4DM**
1. BPO, H. von Karajan (1/95) (DG) ⦶ **439 972-2GGA2**
7a, 7b M. Caballé, RCA Italiana Op Orch, A. Guadagno (11/92) (RCA) ⦶ [2] **GD60941**
17b C. Bergonzi, New Philh, N. Santi (PHIL) ⦶ [3] **432 486-2PM3**

Giovanna d'Arco, 'Joan of Arc'– dramma lirico: 4 acts (1845—Milan) (Lib. Solera, after Schiller)

EXCERPTS: 1. Overture; 2. Qual v'ha speme?; 3. Il Re!; 4. Sotto una quercia parvemi; 5. V'ha dunque un loco simile; 6. Pondo è letal, martiro; 7. Gelo, terrore m'invade!; 8. O, ben s'addice questo torbido; 9. Sempre all'alba ed alla sera; 10. Paventi, Carlo, tu forse?; 11. Tu sei bella; 12. Pronta sono!...Son guerriera... ACT 1: 13. Ai lari!...Alla patria!; 14. Questa rea che vi percuote; 15. Franco son io, ma in core; 16. So che per via di triboli; 17. Qui! qui...dove più s'apre libero il cielo; 18. O faticida foresta; 19. Ho risolto... 20. T'arretri e palpiti!; 21. Taci!...Le vie traboccano; 22. Vieni al tempio. ACT 2: 23. Dal cielo a noi chi viene; 24. Ecco il luogo....Speme al vecchio era una figlia... 25. Te, Dio, lodiam; 26. Compiuto è il rito!...Non fuggir, donzella!; 27. No! forme d'angelo...L'amaro calice sommessa io bevo; 28. Ti discopla!...Imbianca e tace!. ACT 3: 29. I Franchi!...Oh qual mi scuote rumor di guerra?; 30. A lui pensa!...Amai, ma un solo istante; 31. Tu che all'eletto Sàulo; 32. Or dal padre benedetta; 33. Ecco! Ella vola; 34. Di novel prodigo il ciel ne arrise; 35. Qual più fido amico; 36. Un suon funero; 37. Che mai fu?...S'apre il cielo.

Giovanna M. Caballé
Carlo VII P. Domingo
Giacomo S. Milnes
Delil K. Erwen
Talbot R. Lloyd
Ambrosian Op Chor, LSO, James Levine (11/89) (EMI) ⦶ [2] **CMS7 63226-2**

Giovanna S. Dunn
Carlo VII V. La Scola
Giacomo R. Bruson

Delil P. Lefebre
Talbot P. Spagnoli
Parma Teatro Regio Chor, Bologna Teatro Comunale Chor, Bologna Teatro Comunale Orch, R. Chailly, W. Herzog
(3/92) (TELD) ◐ [2] **9031-71478-6**
(3/92) (TELD) ▣ **9031-71478-3**
1. Hungarian St Op Orch, P.G. Morandi (r1994)
(NAXO) ① **8 553089**
1. RPO, A. Licata (r1994) (TRIN) ① **TRP044**
1. BPO, H. von Karajan
(1/95) (DG) ① **439 972-2GGA2**
3, 4. C. Bergonzi, New Philh, N. Santi
(PHIL) ① [3] **432 486-2PM3**
4, 5, 6. P. Domingo, Ambrosian Op Chor, LSO, James Levine (EMI) ① **CDM7 63103-2**
8, 12. R. Tebaldi, G. di Stefano, A. Simonetto (pp1951) (MEMO) ① [2] **HR4235/6**
8, 9. R. Tebaldi, New Philh, O. de Fabritiis
(8/91) (DECC) ① [2] **430 481-2DX2**
11, 23. Ambrosian Op Chor, LSO, James Levine (r1972) (EMI) ① [2] **CZS5 68559-2**
17, 18. K. Ricciarelli, Rome PO, G. Gavazzeni
(12/87) (RCA) ① **GD86534**
18. M. Caballé, LSO, James Levine (r1972)
(EMI) ① **CDM5 65575-2**

Io la vidi– scene: two tenors & orchestra (c1832-35) (Wds. Bassi)
L. Pavarotti, La Scala Orch, C. Abbado
(6/87) (CBS) ① **CD37228**

Jérusalem– opera: 4 acts (1847—Paris) (Lib. A. Royer and G. Vaëz)
Ave Maria K. Ricciarelli, Rome PO, G. Gavazzeni (12/87) (RCA) ① **GD86534**
Je veux encore entendre L. Escalais, anon (r1906) (12/93) (SYMP) ① **SYMCD1126**

I Lombardi alla prima crociata– opera: 4 acts (1843—Milan) (Lib. Solera)
EXCERPTS: 1. Prelude and Introduction. ACT 1: 2. Oh nobile esempio; 3. A te nell'ora infausta; 4. Sciagurata! hai tu creduto; 5. Tutta tremante ancor; 6a. Te, Vergin santa; 6b. Salve Maria!; 7. Vieni! Già posa Arvino. ACT 2: 8. É dunque vero!; 9a. Oh madre mia; 9b. La mia letizia infondere; 10. Come poteva un angelo; 11. È ancor silenzio; 12. Al tuo guerrier; 13. Sei tu l'uom della caverna?; 14. Stolto Allhà!; 15. La bella straniera; 16a. O madre dal cielo; 16b. Se vano è il pregare. ACT 3: 17. Gerusalem!; 18a. Dove sola m'inoltro; 18b. Teco io fuggo; 19a. Che vid'io mai?; 19b. Sì! del ciel che non punisce; 20a. Qui posa il fianco; 20b. Qual voluttà (Trio). ACT 4: 21. Componi, o cara vergine; 22. In cielo benedetto; 23a. Qual prodigio! (Polonaise); 23b. Non fu sogno; 24. O Signore, del tetto natio (Chorus); 25a. Al Siloè!; 25b. Quali voci!; 26. Guerra! guerra!; 27. Questa è mia tenda; 28. Te lodiamo (Finale).
Giselda G. Dimitrova
Oronte J. Carreras
Pagano S. Carroli
Arvino C. Bini
La Scala Chor, La Scala Orch, G. Gavazzeni, G. Lavia
(CAST) ▣ **CVI2027**
Giselda R. Scotto
Oronte L. Pavarotti
Pagano R. Raimondi
Arvino U. Grilli
Pirro M. Rinaudo
Acciano A. Colella
Sofia S. Mezzetti
Prior F. Iacopucci
Viclinda A. di Stasio
Rome Op Chor, Rome Op Orch, G. Gavazzeni (pp1969)
(MEMO) ① [2] **HR4337/8**
Giselda R. Scotto
Oronte L. Pavarotti
Pagano R. Raimondi
Arvino U. Grilli
Pirro M. Rinaudo
Acciano A. Colella
Sofia S. Mezzetti
Prior F. Iacopucci
Viclinda A. di Stasio
Rome Op Chor, Rome Op Orch, G. Gavazzeni (pp1969)
(BUTT) ① [2] **BMCD008**
(BUTT) ⊟ [2] **BMK008**
Giselda C. Deutekom
Oronte P. Domingo
Pagano R. Raimondi
Arvino J. lo Monaco
Pirro S. Dean
Acciano C. Grant
Sofia M. Aparici
Prior K. Erwen
Viclinda D. Malvisi
Ambrosian Sngrs, RPO, L. Gardelli (r1971)
(11/89) (PHIL) ① [2] **422 420-2PM2**
1, 20b R. Marchesi, R. Guglielmo (r1992;trans vn & pf) (MDIT) ① **MED92102**
6a M. Callas, Paris Cons, N. Rescigno
(2/93) (EMI) ① **CDC7 54437-2**
6a, 6b M. Callas, Paris Op Orch, N. Rescigno (r1969) (EMI) ① **CDC7 49428-2**
6a, 16a G. Arangi-Lombardi, La Scala Orch, L. Molajoli (r1933) (10/90) (PREI) ① **89013**
6a, 16b R. Scotto, Rome Op Orch, G. Gavazzeni (pp1969) (MEMO) ① [2] **HR4291/2**
9a, 9b S. Mazzetti, L. Pavarotti, Rome Op Orch, G. Gavazzeni (pp1969)
(10/95) (RCA) ① **09026 68014-2**
9b L. Pavarotti, Philh, L. Magiera
(DECC) OO **436 320-5DH**
9b L. Pavarotti, Parma Teatro Regio Orch, G. Patanè (pp1980) (BELA) ① **450 002-2**
(BELA) ⊟ **450 002-4**
9b L. Pavarotti, RPO, K.H. Adler (pp1982)
(8/91) (DECC) ① **430 716-2DM**
(8/91) (DECC) ⊟ **430 716-4DM**
9b L. Pavarotti, Philh, L. Magiera
(11/91) (DECC) ◐ **071 150-1DH**
(11/91) (DECC) ▣ **071 150-3DH**
9b L. Pavarotti, James Levine, B. Large
(2/92) (DECC) ◐ **071 119-1DH**
(2/92) (DECC) ▣ **071 119-3DH**
9b L. Escalais, anon (r1906)
(12/93) (SYMP) ① **SYMCD1126**
9b Ferruccio Tagliavini, EIAR Orch, U. Tansini (r1940) (3/94) (CENT) ① **CRC2164**
9b L. Pavarotti, Parma Teatro Regio Orch, G. Patanè (pp1976)
(5/94) (DECC) ① [2] **443 018-2DF2**
9b, Risorgimento J. Carreras, La Scala Chor, La Scala Orch, G. Gavazzeni
(CAST) ▣ **CASH5052**
9b, 10. C. Bergonzi, New Philh, N. Santi
(PHIL) ① [3] **432 486-2PM3**
10. P. Domingo, M. Aparici, RPO, L. Gardelli
(PHIL) ① **442 602-2PM**
(PHIL) ⊟ **442 602-4PM**
16. M. Callas, Paris Cons, N. Rescigno
(9/87) (EMI) ① **CDC7 47730-2**
16a C. Muzio, orch (r1922)
(1/94) (ROMO) ① [2] **81005-2**
16a, 16b C. Muzio, orch (r1922)
(5/90) (BOGR) ① [2] **BIM705-2**
16a, 16b L. Price, LSO, E. Downes
(12/92) (RCA) ① [4] **09026 61236-2**
16a, 20b G. Dimitrova, S. Carroli, J. Carreras, La Scala Chor, La Scala Orch, G. Gavazzeni
(CAST) ▣ **CVI2067**
17. BRS Chor, BRSO, Colin Davis (r1987)
(BELA) ① **450 052-2**
(BELA) ⊟ **450 052-4**
17. Monte Carlo Op Orch, A. de Almeida (r1973)
(PHIL) ① [2] **442 550-2PM2**
17, 24. Chicago Sym Chor, Chicago SO, G. Solti
(DECC) OO **430 226-5DH**
17, 24. La Scala Chor, La Scala Orch, R. Muti
(EMI) ① **CDC7 54484-2**
17, 24. Chicago Sym Chor, Chicago SO, G. Solti
(4/91) (DECC) ① **430 226-2DH**
20a, 20b F. Merli, B. Scacciati, N. de Angelis, orch, L. Molajoli (r1932) (PREI) ① **89091**
20a, 20b V. della Chiesa, J. Peerce, N. Moscona, NBC SO, A. Toscanini (bp1943)
(6/91) (RCA) ① **GD60276**
20b F. Alda, E. Caruso, M. Journet, orch, W.B. Rogers (r1912) (NIMB) ① **NI7834**
(NIMB) ⊟ **NC7834**
20b L. Pavarotti, R. Scotto, F. Iacopucci, Rome Op Orch, G. Gavazzeni (pp1969)
(BUTT) ① **BMCD015**
(BUTT) ⊟ **BMK015**
20b E. Caruso, F. Alda, M. Journet, orch, W.B. Rogers (r1912) (RCA) ① **09026 61242-2**
20b E. Rethberg, B. Gigli, E. Pinza, orch, Rosario Bourdon (r1930) (CONI) ① **CDHD227**
(CONI) ⊟ **MCHD227**
20b E. Rethberg, B. Gigli, E. Pinza, orch, Rosario Bourdon (r1930)
(5/90) (PEAR) ① **GEMMCD9367**
20b E. Rethberg, B. Gigli, E. Pinza, orch, Rosario Bourdon (r1930)
(10/90) (RCA) ① **GD87811**
(10/90) (RCA) ⊟ **GK87811**
20b F. Alda, E. Caruso, M. Journet, orch, W.B. Rogers (r1912)
(7/91) (RCA) ① [12] **GD60495(4)**
20b E. Caruso, M. Journet, F. Alda, orch, W.B. Rogers (r1912)
(10/91) (PEAR) ① [3] **EVC3(1)**
20b E. Rethberg, B. Gigli, E. Pinza, Victor SO, Rosario Bourdon (r1930: 2 takes)
(10/95) (ROMO) ① [2] **81014-2**
23a, 23b A. Moffo, Munich RO, K. Eichhorn
(EURO) ① **GD69113**
23a, 23b M. Caballé, RCA Italiana Op Orch, A. Guadagno (11/92) (RCA) ① [2] **GD60941**
24. Ambrosian Op. Chor, Philh, R. Muti
(EMI) ① **CDC7 47274-2**
24. Fiesole School of Music Female Chor, MMF Chor, MMF Orch, M. Arena (ACAN) ① **43 540**
24. Forum Op Chor, Forum PO, G. Bellini
(EURM) ① **350214**
24. Berlin Deutsche Op Chor, Berlin Deutsche Op Orch, G. Sinopoli (DG) OO **415 283-5GH**
24. Bayreuth Fest Chor, Bayreuth Fest Orch, W. Nelsson (r1986) (BELA) ① **450 052-2**
(BELA) ⊟ **450 052-4**
24. Berlin Deutsche Op Chor, Berlin Deutsche Op Orch, G. Sinopoli
(10/85) (DG) ① **415 283-2GH**

Luisa Miller– opera: 3 acts (1849—Naples) (Lib. S Cammarano)
EXCERPTS: 1. Overture. ACT 1: 2a. Ti desta, Luisa, regina de' cori; 2b. Non temer: più nobil spirto; 2c. Lo vidi, e'l primo palpito; 3a. T'amo d'amor ch'esprimere; 3b. Mia diletta!; 3c. Ferma ed ascolta!; 3d. Sacra la scelta è d'un consorte; 4. Ah! fu giusto il mio sospetto!; 5a. Che mai narrasti!; 5b. Il mio sangue; 5c. Padre...M'abbraccia; 6a. Quale un sorriso d'amica sorte; 6b. Dall'aule raggiante de vano splendor; 6c. Deh! La parola amara; 7a. Sciogliete i levrieri; 7b. Luisa, non temer; 7c. Fra' mortali ancora oppressa; 7d. Ad immagina tua creata. ACT 2: 8a. Ah! Luisa, Luisa, ove sei?; 8b. E segnare questa mano; 8c. Tu puniscimi, o Signore; 9a. Egli delira: sul mattin degli anni; 9b. L'alto retaggio; 9c. O meco incolume sarai; 9d. Vien la Duchessa!; 9e. Presentati alla Duchessa puoi, Luisa; 9f. Come celar la smanie; 10a. Il foglio dunque?; 10b. Oh! fede negar potessi; 10c. Quando le sere al placido; 11a. Di me chiedeste?; 11b. L'ara, o l'avello apprestami. ACT 3: 12a. Come in un giorno solo; 12b. La tombaè un letto; 13a. Ah! l'ultima preghiera; 13b. Ah, piangi! Il tuo dolore; 13c. Avean mio padre i barbari; 13d. Padre, ricevi l'estremo addio.
Luisa K. Ricciarelli
Rodolfo P. Domingo
Miller R. Bruson
Walter G. Howell
Federica E. Obraztsova
Wurm W. Ganzarolli
Laura A. Michael
Peasant L. de Corato
ROH Chor, ROHO, L. Maazel (r1979)
(5/88) (DG) ① [2] **423 144-2GH2**
Luisa A. Moffo
Rodolfo C. Bergonzi
Miller C. MacNeil
Walter G. Tozzi
Federica S. Verrett
Wurm E. Flagello
Laura G. Carturan
Peasant P. de Palma
RCA Italiana Op Chor, RCA Italiana Op Orch, F. Cleva (r1964)
(10/88) (RCA) ① [2] **GD86646**
Luisa M. Caballé
Rodolfo L. Pavarotti
Miller S. Milnes
Walter B. Giaiotti
Federica A. Reynolds
Wurm R. Van Allan
Laura A. Céline
Peasant F. Pavarotti
London Op Chor, National PO, P. Maag
(10/88) (DECC) ① [2] **417 420-2DH2**
Luisa A. Millo
Rodolfo P. Domingo
Miller V. Chernov
Walter J-H. Rootering
Federica F. Quivar
Wurm P. Plishka
Laura W. White
Peasant J. Bills
NY Met Op Chor, NY Met Op Orch, James Levine
(9/92) (SONY) ① [2] **S2K48073**

Luisa J. Anderson
Rodolfo T. Ichihara
Miller E. Tumagian
Walter P. Plishka
Frederica S. Anselmi
Wurm R. Tesarowicz
Laura B. Desnoues
Peasant M. Pastor
Montpellier Op Chor, Lyon Op Chor, Lyon Op Orch, M. Arena, C. Viller (r1988)
(9/93) (PION) ◐ **PLMCC00711**

1. Mexico St SO, E. Bátiz (r1990s)
(ASV) Ⓓ **CDDCA856**
(ASV) ⊟ **ZCDCA856**

1. Hungarian St Op Orch, P.G. Morandi (r1994)
(NAXO) Ⓓ **8 553018**

1. RPO, A. Licata (r1994) (TRIN) Ⓓ **TRP044**

1. BPO, H. von Karajan
(10/87) (DG) Ⓓ **419 622-2GH**

1. BPO, H. von Karajan
(1/95) (DG) Ⓓ **439 972-2GGA2**

1, 10c L. Pavarotti, Philh, L. Magiera
(DECC) ◎◎ **436 320-5DH**

1, 10c L. Pavarotti, Philh, L. Magiera
(11/91) (DECC) ◐ **071 150-1DH**
(11/91) (DECC) ▣ **071 150-3DH**

1, 2c, 5b, 6b, 7a-c, 8c, 10c, 11a, 11b, 12b, 13a-d A. Millo, P. Domingo, V. Chernov, J-H. Rootering, F. Quivar, P. Plishka, W. White, NY Met Op Chor, NY Met Op Orch, James Levine (r1991) (SONY) Ⓓ **SMK53508**

2a, 3a, 4, 5a, 5b, 8a, 9a, 9c, 9e, 9f, 10c Hagen Qt (r1994: arr stg qt: E Muzio)
(DG) Ⓓ **447 069-2GH**

3d D. Hvorostovsky, Rotterdam PO, V. Gergiev
(7/90) (PHIL) Ⓓ **426 740-2PH**

3d, 4. G. Taddei, M. Smith, Vienna St Op Orch, A. Erede (pp1974) (ACAN) Ⓓ **49 402**

5b T. Pasero, La Scala Orch, A. Sabino (r1942)
(4/95) (PREI) Ⓓ **89074**

8b, 8c, 12b, 13d M. Caballé, NY Met Op Chor, NY Met Op Orch, T. Schippers (pp1968)
(MEMO) Ⓓ [2] **HR4279/80**

8c, 8d E. Suliotis, Rome Op Orch, O. de Fabritiis (r1966) (DECC) Ⓓ **440 405-2DM**

8c, 13d M. Caballé, L. Pavarotti, S. Milnes, B. Giaiotti, London Op Chor, National PO, P. Maag (r1975) (DECC) Ⓓ **443 928-2DM**

10b, 10c P. Domingo, ROHO, L. Maazel
(DG) Ⓓ [3] **427 708-2GX3**

10b, 10c J. Peerce, NBC SO, A. Toscanini (bp1943) (RCA) Ⓓ [2] **GD60299**

10b, 10c J. Carreras, RPO, R. Benzi
(PHIL) Ⓓ **432 692-2PH**
(PHIL) ⊟ **432 692-4PH**

10b, 10c G. di Stefano, Palermo Teatro Massimo Orch, N. Sanzogno (pp1963)
(MEMO) Ⓓ **HR4372/3**

10b, 10c C. Bergonzi, Santa Cecilia Academy Orch, G. Gavazzeni (DECC) Ⓓ **433 623-2DSP**
(DECC) ⊟ **433 623-4DSP**

10b, 10c P. Domingo, RPO, E. Downes
(RCA) Ⓓ [2] **GD60866**
(RCA) ⊟ [2] **GK60866**

10b, 10c C. Bergonzi, New Philh, N. Santi
(PHIL) Ⓓ [3] **432 486-2PM3**

10b, 10c C. Bergonzi, Santa Cecilia Academy Orch, G. Gavazzeni
(DECC) Ⓓ **433 066-2DWO**
(DECC) ⊟ **433 066-4DWO**

10b, 10c C. Bergonzi, Santa Cecilia Academy Orch, G. Gavazzeni
(DECC) Ⓓ **433 221-2DWO**
(DECC) ⊟ **433 221-4DWO**

10b, 10c G. Pastine, Verona Arena Orch, A. Guadagno (pp1992) (MCI) Ⓓ **MCCD099**

10b, 10c Deng, Württemberg PO, R. Paternostro
(SINE) Ⓓ **39820222**

10b, 10c C. Bergonzi, Santa Cecilia Academy Orch, G. Gavazzeni (r1958)
(BELA) Ⓓ **450 005-2**
(BELA) ⊟ **450 005-4**

10b, 10c C. Bergonzi, Santa Cecilia Academy Orch, G. Gavazzeni (r1957)
(DECC) Ⓓ **433 442-2DA**

10b, 10c C. Bergonzi, Santa Cecilia Academy Orch, G. Gavazzeni (BELA) Ⓓ **450 133-2**
(BELA) ⊟ **450 133-4**

10b, 10c L. Pavarotti, Toscanini SO, E. Buckley
(SONY) Ⓓ **MDK47176**
(SONY) ⊟ **MDT47176**

10b, 10c C. Bergonzi, Santa Cecilia Academy Orch, G. Gavazzeni (r1957)
(DECC) Ⓓ **440 417-2DM**

10b, 10c P. Domingo, ROHO, L. Maazel
(7/86) (DG) Ⓓ **415 366-2GH**

10b, 10c J. Peerce, NBC SO, A. Toscanini (bp1943) (5/90) (RCA) Ⓓ [7] **GD60326**

10b, 10c L. Pavarotti, Vienna Op Orch, E. Downes (7/90) (DECC) Ⓓ [2] **425 681-2DM2**
(7/90) (DECC) ⊟ [2] **425 681-4DM2**

10b, 10c L. Pavarotti, RPO, K.H. Adler (pp1982)
(8/91) (DECC) Ⓓ **430 716-2DM**
(8/91) (DECC) ⊟ **430 716-4DM**

10b, 10c C. Bergonzi, Santa Cecilia Academy Orch, G. Gavazzeni (r1957)
(10/93) (DECC) Ⓓ **436 463-2DM**
(10/93) (DECC) ⊟ **436 463-4DM**

10b, 10c A. Bonci, anon (r1906)
(9/94) (NIMB) Ⓓ **NI7856**

10b, 10c L. Pavarotti, NYPO, L. Magiera (pp1993) (2/95) (DECC) Ⓓ **444 450-2DH**
(2/95) (DECC) ⊟ **444 450-4DH**

10b, 10c G. Anselmi, anon (r1907)
(7/95) (SYMP) Ⓓ **SYMCD1170**

10b, 10c L. Pavarotti, Rome SO, N. Bonavolontà (pp1967) (10/95) (RCA) Ⓓ **09026 68014-2**

10b, 10c B. Heppner, Munich RO, R. Abbado (r1993/4) (11/95) (RCA) Ⓓ **09026 62504-2**

10b, 10c, 13b P. Domingo, K. Ricciarelli, ROHO, L. Maazel (r1979) (6/94) (BELA) Ⓓ **450 121-2**
(6/94) (BELA) ⊟ **450 121-4**

10c P. Domingo, ECO, R. Armstrong
(9/92) (ABMU) ▣ **95542**

10c A. Pertile, La Scala Orch, C. Sabajno (r1927) (MMOI) Ⓓ **CDMOIR405**
(MMOI) ⊟ **CMOIR405**

10c T. Schipa, orch, Anon (cond) (pp1928)
(MEMO) Ⓓ [2] **HR4220/1**

10c P. Domingo, Orch (EDL) Ⓓ **EDL2562-2**
(EDL) ⊙ **EDL2562-1** ⊟ **EDL2562-4**

10c A. Bonci, orch (r1913)
(PEAR) Ⓓ **GEMMCD9168**

10c F. de Lucia, anon (r1908)
(BONG) Ⓓ [2] **GB1064/5-2**

10c L. Signoretti, anon (r1901)
(12/89) (SYMP) Ⓓ **SYMCD1065**

10c A. Pertile, La Scala Orch, C. Sabajno (r1927) (9/90) (PREI) Ⓓ **89007**

10c F. Giraud, anon (r1904)
(5/91) (SYMP) Ⓓ **SYMCD1077**

10c G. Lugo, orch (r1939)
(2/92) (PREI) Ⓓ **89034**

10c F. Giraud, anon (r1904)
(11/92) (MEMO) Ⓓ [2] **HR4408/9(1)**

10c G. Lauri-Volpi, Rome Op Orch, R. Arduini (r1943) (7/94) (NIMB) Ⓓ **NI7853**

10c F. de Lucia, anon (r1908)
(1/95) (SYMP) Ⓓ **SYMCD1149**

10c A. Giorgini, orch (r1905)
(4/95) (RECO) Ⓓ **TRC3**

Macbeth– opera: 4 acts (1847—Florence) (Lib. Piave and Maffei)

EXCERPTS: 1. Prelude. ACT 1: 2. Che faceste? dite su!; 3a. Giorno non vidi mai; 3b. Due vaticini compiuto or sono; 4. S'allontanarono!; 5a. Nel dì della vittoria; 5b. Vieni! t'affretta!; 5c. Ambizioso spirto; 5d. Or tutti sorgete; 6. Oh donna mia!; 7a. Sappia la sposa mia; 7b. Regna il sonno; 7c. Fatal mia donna!; 8a. Di destarlo per tempo; 8b. Schiudi, inferno, la bocca. ACT 2: 9a. Perchè mi sfuggi; 9b. La luce langue; 10. Chi osò mandarvi a noi?; 11a. Studia il passo; 11b. Come dal ciel precipita; 12a. Salve, o Re!; 12b. Si colmi il calice; 12c. Va', spirto d'abisso!. ACT 3: 13. Tre volte miagola; 14. Ballet Music; 15a. Finchè appelli; 15b. Fuggi, regal fantasima; 16. Ondine e Silfidi; 17a. Ove son io?; 17b. Ora di morte. ACT 4: 18. Patria oppressa!; 19a. O figli, o figli miei!; 19b. Ah, la paterna mano; 20. Dove siam? che bosco è quello?; 21a. Vegliammo invan due notti; 21b. Una macchia è qui tuttora; 22a. Perfidi! All'Anglo contro me v'unite!; 22b. Pietà, rispetto, amore; 23. Ella è morta!; 24. Vittoria! (Finale). SUPPLEMENTARY NUMBERS: ACT 2: 25. Trionfai!. ACT 3: 26. Vada in fiamme e in polve cada. ACT 4: 27. Mal per me che m'affidai (Death of Macbeth).

Macbeth R. Bruson
Lady Macbeth M. Zampieri
Banquo J. Morris
Macduff D. O'Neill
Malcolm D. Griffith
Berlin Deutsche Op Chor, Berlin Deutsche Op Orch, G. Sinopoli, B. Large
(MCEG) ▣ **VVD384**

Macbeth K. Paskalis
Lady Macbeth J. Barstow
Banquo J. Morris
Macduff K. Erwen
Malcolm I. Caley
Doctor B. Donlan
Servant I. Caddy
Assassin J. Tomlinson
Lady-in-waiting R. Woodland
Glyndebourne Fest Chor, LPO, J. Pritchard, M. Hadjimischev (r1972)
(IMP) ▣ **SLL7017**

Macbeth R. Bruson
Lady Macbeth G. Jones
Banquo R. Scandiuzzi
Macduff A. Cupido
Malcolm M. Tashiro
Doctor; Servant; Herald G. de Angelis
Lady-in-waiting T. Kohama
Fujiwara Op Chor, Tokyo PO, G. Kuhn (pp1992)
(SINE) Ⓓ [2] **39820242**

Macbeth R. Bruson
Lady Macbeth M. Zampieri
Banquo R. Lloyd
Macduff N. Shicoff
Malcolm C.H. Ahnsjö
Doctor P. Salomaa
Servant; Assassin M. Nikolič
Herald A. Schmidt
Lady-in-waiting L. Aliberti
Berlin Deutsche Op Chor, Berlin Deutsche Op Orch, G. Sinopoli (r1983)
(2/85) (PHIL) Ⓓ [3] **412 133-2PH3**

Macbeth P. Cappuccilli
Lady Macbeth S. Verrett
Banquo N. Ghiaurov
Macduff P. Domingo
Malcolm A. Savastano
Doctor C. Zardo
Servant G. Foiani
Herald S. Fontana
Assassin A. Mariotti
Lady-in-waiting S. Malagù
La Scala Chor, La Scala Orch, C. Abbado (r1976)
(9/86) (DG) Ⓓ [3] **415 688-2GH3**

Macbeth L. Warren
Lady Macbeth Leonie Rysanek
Banquo J. Hines
Macduff C. Bergonzi
Malcolm W. Olvis
Doctor G. Pechner
Servant H. Sternberg
Assassin O. Hawkins
Lady-in-waiting C. Ordassy
NY Met Op Chor, NY Met Op Orch, E. Leinsdorf (r1959)
(9/88) (RCA) Ⓓ [2] **GD84516**

Macbeth S. Milnes
Lady Macbeth F. Cossotto
Banquo R. Raimondi
Macduff J. Carreras
Malcolm G. Bernardi
Doctor C. del Bosco
Servant L. Fyson
Herald N. Taylor
Assassin J. Noble
Lady-in-waiting M. Borgato
Ambrosian Op Chor, New Philh, R. Muti (r1976)
(2/93) (EMI) Ⓓ [2] **CMS7 64339-2**

Macbeth L. Nucci
Lady Macbeth S. Verrett
Banquo S. Ramey
Macduff V. Luchetti
Malcolm A. Barasorda
Doctor S. Fontana
Servant G. Casarini
Herald G. Morresi
Assassin G. Sarti
Lady-in-waiting A.C. Antonacci
Bologna Teatro Comunale Chor, Bologna Teatro Comunale Orch, R. Chailly, C. D'Anna
(5/93) (DECC) ◐ [2] **071 422-1DH2**
(5/93) (DECC) ▣ **071 422-3DH**

Macbeth E. Mascherini
Lady Macbeth M. Callas
Banquo I. Tajo
Macduff G. Penno
Malcolm L. Della Pergola
Doctor D. Caselli
Servant A. Barbesi
Herald I. Vinco
Assassin M. Tommasini
Lady-in-Waiting A. Vercelli
La Scala Chor, La Scala Orch, V. de Sabata (pp1952)
(1/94) (EMI) Ⓓ [2] **CMS7 64944-2**

Macbeth M. Ahlersmeyer
Lady Macbeth E. Höngen
Banquo H. Alsen
Macduff J. Witt

Malcolm W. Franter
Doctor V. Madin
Assassin K. Ettl
Lady-in-Waiting E. Boettcher
Vienna St Op Chor, Vienna St Op Orch, K. Böhm (pp1943: Ger)
(5/94) (PREI) Ⓓ [2] 90175

Macbeth D. Fischer-Dieskau
Lady Macbeth E. Suliotis
Banquo N. Ghiaurov
Macduff L. Pavarotti
Malcolm R. Cassinelli
Doctor R. Myers
Servant J. Noble
Herald D. Reed
Assassin L. Fyson
Lady in waiting H. Lawrence
Ambrosian Op Chor, LPO, L. Gardelli (r1970)
(7/94) (DECC) Ⓓ [2] 440 048-2DMO2

1. Sofia SO, V. Stefanov (LASE) Ⓓ 15 519
(LASE) ⊟ 79 519
1. Hungarian St Op Orch, P.G. Morandi (r1994) (NAXO) Ⓓ 8 553089
1. BPO, H. von Karajan (10/87) (DG) Ⓓ 419 622-2GH
1. BPO, H. von Karajan (1/95) (DG) Ⓓ 439 972-2GGA2
2. LSC, LSO, R. Hickox (r1987/8) (IMP) Ⓓ [3] TCD1073
2. LSC, LSO, R. Hickox (4/89) (IMP) Ⓓ PCD908
3b M. Pertusi, C. Alvarez, Bulgarian Nat Chor, Sofia PO, E. Tabakov (r1994) (CAPR) Ⓓ 10 704
5a, 5b M. Callas, N German RSO, N. Rescigno (pp1959) (MEMO) Ⓓ HR4293/4
5a, 5b, 5c, 9b, 21b L. Gencer, Venice La Fenice Orch, G. Gavazzeni (pp1968) (MEMO) Ⓓ [2] HR4239/40
5a, 5b, 5c, 5d E. Suliotis, Rome Op Orch, O. de Fabritiis (r1966) (DECC) Ⓓ 440 405-2DM
5, 9b, 21b M. Callas, Philh, N. Rescigno (9/87) (EMI) Ⓓ CDC7 47730-2
7a-c, 22a, 22b G. Bumbry, D. Fischer-Dieskau, VPO, W. Sawallisch (pp1964) (ORFE) Ⓓ C335931A
9a, 9b R. Hunter, Tasmanian SO, D. Franks (r1989) (10/95) (ABCC) Ⓓ 8 7000 10
9b M. Callas, Philh, N. Rescigno (2/90) (EMIN) Ⓓ CD-EMX2123
(2/88) (EMIN) ⊟ TC-EMX2123
9b L. Price, New Philh, N. Santi (r1977) (12/92) (RCA) Ⓓ [4] 09026 61236-2
9b, 19a, 19b, 22b Leonie Rysanek, C. Bergonzi, L. Warren, NY Met Op Orch, E. Leinsdorf (r1959) (RCA) Ⓓ 09026 62689-2
9b, 21b M. Mödl, Berlin City Op Orch, H. Löwlein (Ger: r1951) (PREI) Ⓓ 90136
9b, 21b J. Barstow, S. Burgess, J. Connell, ENO Orch, M. Elder (1/89) (TER) Ⓓ CDVIR8307
(1/89) (TER) ⊟ ZCVIR8307
11. R. Raimondi, New Philh, R. Muti (10/88) (EMI) Ⓓ CDM7 69549-2
11. J. Hines, NY Met Op Orch, E. Leinsdorf (r1959) (4/94) (RCA) Ⓓ [6] 09026 61580-2(6)
11a, 11b S. Ramey, Bologna Teatro Comunale Orch, R. Chailly (r1986) (DECC) Ⓓ 443 380-2DM
11a, 11b B. Christoff, Bulgarian RSO, E. Gracis (r1979) (FORL) Ⓓ UCD16651
11a, 11b I. Andrésen, orch (Ger: r1929) (10/90) (PREI) Ⓓ 89028
11b M. Salminen, Lahti SO, E. Klas (8/92) (BIS) Ⓓ BIS-CD520
13, 18. Chicago Sym Chor, Chicago SO, G. Solti (DECC) OO 430 226-5DH
13, 18. Chicago Sym Chor, Chicago SO, G. Solti (4/91) (DECC) Ⓓ 430 226-2DH
14. New Philh, R. Muti (EMI) Ⓓ CDC7 47274-2
14. Slovak PO, K. Redel (r1990) (PIER) Ⓓ PV730023
14. LSO, A. de Almeida (r1972) (PHIL) Ⓓ [2] 442 550-2PM2
14. SNO, A. Gibson (9/85) (CHAN) Ⓓ CHAN8379
14. NY Met Op Orch, James Levine (r1992) (6/94) (SONY) Ⓓ SK52489
18. Ambrosian Op. Chor, New Philh, R. Muti (EMI) Ⓓ CDC7 47274-2
18. Fiesole School of Music Female Chor, MMF Chor, MMF Orch, M. Arena (ACAN) Ⓓ 43 540
18. Forum Op Chor, Forum PO, G. Bellini (EURM) Ⓓ 350214
18. ROH Chor, ROHO, L. Gardelli (EMI) Ⓓ CDM7 64356-2
18. Berlin Deutsche Op Chor, Berlin Deutsche Op Orch, G. Sinopoli (DG) OO 415 283-5GH
18. La Scala Chor, La Scala Orch, R. Muti (EMI) Ⓓ CDC7 54484-2
18. Chor, Orch, Anon (cond) (BELA) Ⓓ 450 052-2
(BELA) ⊟ 450 052-4
18. Ambrosian Op Chor, LPO, L. Gardelli (r1971) (DECC) Ⓓ 433 443-2DA
(DECC) ⊟ 433 443-4DA
18. NY Met Op Chor, NY Met Op Orch, E. Leinsdorf (r1959) (RCA) Ⓓ 74321 24209-2
18. Ambrosian Op Chor, New Philh, R. Muti (r1976) (EMI) Ⓓ [2] CZS5 68559-2
18. Berlin Deutsche Op Chor, Berlin Deutsche Op Orch, G. Sinopoli (10/85) (DG) Ⓓ 415 283-2GH
18. Atlanta Sym Chor, Atlanta SO, Robert Shaw (3/88) (TELA) Ⓓ [2] CD80152
18. Slovak Phil Chor, Bratislava RSO, O. Dohnányi (4/91) (NAXO) Ⓓ 8 550241
19. P. Domingo, La Scala Orch, C. Abbado (DG) ⊟ 419 091-4GW
19. J. Carreras, New Philh, R. Muti (EMI) Ⓓ CDC7 54524-2
19. P. Domingo, ROHO, J. Barker (pp1988) (9/89) (EMI) Ⓓ CDC7 49811-2
19a, 19b C. Bergonzi, New Philh, N. Santi (PHIL) Ⓓ [3] 432 486-2PM3
19a, 19b T. Harper, Bratislava RSO, M. Halász (NAXO) Ⓓ 8 550497
19a, 19b P. Dvorský, Verona Arena Orch, A. Guadagno (pp1992) (MCI) Ⓓ MCCD099
19a, 19b E. Caruso, orch (r1916) (7/91) (MSCM) Ⓓ MM30352
19a, 19b L. Pavarotti, RPO, K.H. Adler (pp1982) (8/91) (DECC) Ⓓ 430 716-2DM
(8/91) (DECC) ⊟ 430 716-4DM
19a, 19b E. Caruso, orch, W.B. Rogers (r1916) (10/91) (PEAR) Ⓓ [3] EVC3(2)
19a, 19b P. Domingo, La Scala Orch, C. Abbado (5/93) (DG) Ⓓ 431 104-2GB
19a, 19b P. Domingo, La Scala Orch, C. Abbado (r1976) (6/94) (BELA) Ⓓ 450 121-2
(6/94) (BELA) ⊟ 450 121-4
19b P. Domingo, Seville SO, E. Colomer (pp1991) (RCA) Ⓓ RD61191
19b P. Domingo, Seville SO, E. Colomer (pp1991) (RCA) OO 09026 61191-5
19b E. Caruso, orch, W.B. Rogers (r1916) (RCA) Ⓓ 09026 61242-2
19b L. Pavarotti, Parma Teatro Regio Orch, G. Patanè (pp1980) (BELA) Ⓓ 450 002-2
(BELA) ⊟ 450 002-4
19b E. Caruso, orch, W.B. Rogers (r1916) (7/91) (RCA) Ⓓ [12] GD60495(5)
19b L. Pavarotti, Parma Teatro Regio Orch, G. Patanè (pp1976) (5/94) (DECC) Ⓓ [2] 443 018-2DF2
19b E. Caruso, orch (r1916) (7/95) (NIMB) Ⓓ NI7866
21. M. Caballé, E. Bainbridge, T. Allen, RPO, A. Guadagno (10/88) (EMI) Ⓓ CDM7 69500-2
21. Leonie Rysanek, G. Pechner, C. Ordassy, NY Met Op Orch, E. Leinsdorf (r1959) (4/94) (RCA) Ⓓ [6] 09026 61580-2(7)
21a, 21b L. Price, C. Vozza, R. El Hage, RCA Italiana Op Orch, F. Molinari-Pradelli (12/92) (RCA) Ⓓ [4] 09026 61236-2
21b L. Price, RCA Italiana Op Orch, F. Molinari-Pradelli (RCA) Ⓓ RD87016
21b M. Caballé, E. Bainbridge, T. Allen, RPO, A. Guadagno (r1971) (EMI) Ⓓ CDM5 65575-2
21b M. Callas, Philh, N. Rescigno (2/90) (EMI) Ⓓ [4] CMS7 63244-2
22. B. Weikl, Munich RO, H. Wallberg (ACAN) Ⓓ 43 327
22. T. Gobbi, Rome Op Orch, O. de Fabritiis (r1955) (10/89) (EMI) Ⓓ CDM7 63109-2
22. D. Hvorostovsky, Rotterdam PO, V. Gergiev (7/90) (PHIL) Ⓓ 426 740-2PH
22. A. Sved, orch (r1940) (4/94) (EMI) Ⓓ [3] CHS7 64864-2(2)
22a, 22b J. Pons, Barcelona SO, G. Navarro (11/92) (RCA) ⊟ 09026 61204-4
22a, 22b J. Pons, Barcelona SO, G. Navarro (RCA) OO 09026 61204-5
22a, 22b D. Fischer-Dieskau, LPO, L. Gardelli (r1970) (DECC) Ⓓ 440 409-2DM
22a, 22b M. Battistini, C. Sabajno (r1912) (10/92) (NIMB) Ⓓ NI7831
(10/92) (NIMB) ⊟ NC7831
22b A. Sved, orch, D. Olivieri (r1940) (PREI) Ⓓ 89096
22b T. Gobbi, LSO, W. Braithwaite (r1952) (8/93) (TEST) Ⓓ SBT1019
199. C. Bergonzi, NY Met Op Orch, E. Leinsdorf (r1959) (4/94) (RCA) Ⓓ [6] 09026 61580-2(7)

Masnadieri– opera: 4 acts (1847—London) (Lib. Maffei, after Schiller)

EXCERPTS: 1. Prelude. ACT 1: 2a. Quando io leggo in Plutarco; 2b. O mio castel paterno; 3a. Ecco un foglio; 3b. Nell'argilla maledetta; 4a. Vecchio! spiccai da te; 4b. La sua lampada vitale; 5a. Trionfo, trionfo!; 5b. Tremate o miseri; 6a. Venerabile o padre; 6b. Lo sguardo avea degli angeli; 7a. Mio Carlo; 7b. Carlo! io muoio; 8a. Un messaggero; 8b. Sul capo mio colpevole. ACT 2: 9a. Dall'infame banchetto; 9b. Tu del mio Carlo; 9c. Ah, signora!; 9d. Carlo vive?; 10a. Perchè fuggisti; 10b. Io t'amo, Amalia; 10c. Tracotante!; 10d. Ti scosta, o malnato; 11a. Tutto quest'oggi; 11b. I cittadini correano alla festa; 12a. Come splendido; 12b. Di ladroni attorniato; 13. Capitano!. ACT 3: 14. Dio, ti ringrazio; 15a. Qual mare, qual terra; 15b. Qui nel bosco?; 15c. Lassù risplendere; 16. Le rube, gli stupri; 17a. Ben giunto, o Capitano!; 17b. Tutto è buio e silenzio; 17c. Un ignoto; 17d. Destatevi, o pietre!. ACT 4: 18. Tradimento!; 19. Pareami che sorto; 20a. M'hai chiamato; 20b. Precipita dal momte un foribondo; 21. Francesco! mio figlio!; 22. Come il bacio d'un padre; 23. Qui son essi!; 24. Caduto è il reprobo!.

Massimiliano R. Raimondi
Carlo C. Bergonzi
Francesco P. Cappuccilli
Amalia M. Caballé
Arminio J. Sandor
Moser M. Mazzieri
Rolla W. Elvin
Ambrosian Sngrs, New Philh, L. Gardelli (r1974)
(11/89) (PHIL) Ⓓ [2] 422 423-2PM2

Amalia J. Sutherland
Carlo F. Bonisolli
Francesco M. Manuguerra
Massimiliano S. Ramey
Arminio A. Davies
Moser S. Alaimo
Rolla J. Harris
WNO Chor, WNO Orch, R. Bonynge (r1982)
(7/93) (DECC) Ⓓ [2] 433 854-2DMO2

1. Hungarian St Op Orch, P.G. Morandi (r1994) (NAXO) Ⓓ 8 553089
1. BPO, H. von Karajan (10/87) (DG) Ⓓ 419 622-2GH
1. BPO, H. von Karajan (1/95) (DG) Ⓓ 439 972-2GGA2
2a, 2b, 12a, 12b C. Bergonzi, RPO, L. Gardelli (PHIL) Ⓓ [3] 432 486-2PM3
9a, 9b, 9c, 9d K. Ricciarelli, R. Truffelli, Rome PO, G. Gavazzeni (12/87) (RCA) Ⓓ GD86534
9c, 9d J. Sutherland, NYC Op Orch, R. Bonynge (r1981: pp) (DECC) Ⓓ 436 472-2DM
16. Chicago Sym Chor, Chicago SO, G. Solti (DECC) OO 430 226-5DH
16. Chicago Sym Chor, Chicago SO, G. Solti (4/91) (DECC) Ⓓ 430 226-2DH

Nabucco– opera: 4 acts (1842—Milan) (Lib. Solera)

EXCERPTS: 1. Overture. ACT 1: 2. Gli arredi festivi; 3a. Sperate, o figli!; 3b. D'Egitto là sui lidi; 3c. Come notte; 4a. Fenena! O mia diletta!; 4b. Io t'amava!; 5. Prode guerrier!; 6. Lo vedeste?; 7a. Viva Nabucco!; 7b. Che tenti?; 7c. Tremin gl'insani; 8a. O vinti, il capo; 8b. Mio furore. ACT 2: 9a. Ben io t'avenni; 9b. Anch'io dischiuso un giorno; 9c. Salgo già del trono; 10a. Vieni, o Levita!; 10b. Tu sul labbro; 11a. Che si vuol?; 11b. Il maledetto non ha fratelli; 12a. Deh, fratelli; 12b. S'appressan gl'istanti; 12c. S'oda or me!; 12d. Chi mi toglie il regio scettro?. ACT 3: 13. E l'Assiria una regina; 14. Eccelsa Donna; 15. Donna, chi sei?; 16. Oh, di qual'onta aggravisi; 17. Deh, perdona; 18. Va pensiero, sull'ali dorata; 19a. Oh, chi piange?; 19b. Del futuro nel buio discerno. ACT 4: 20. Son pur queste mie membra!; 21. Dio di Giuda!; 22. Cadran, cadranno i perfidi; 23a. Marcia funebra; 23b. Va! la palma del martirio; 23c. Oh, dischiuso; 24a. Viva Nabucco!; 24b. Oh! chi vegg'io?; 24c. Su me...morente.

Nabucco R. Bruson
Abigaille G. Dimitrova
Ismaele O. Garaventa
Fenena B. Baglioni
Zaccaria D. Petkov
High Priest F.E. d'Artegna
Abdallo A. Ceroni

Anna G. di Rocco
Verona Arena Chor, Verona Arena Orch, M. Arena, R. Giacchieri (CAST) ▣ **CVI2003**
Nabucco R. Bruson
Abigaille G. Dimitrova
Ismaele B. Beccaria
Fenena R. Pierotti
Zaccaria P. Burchuladze
La Scala Chor, La Scala Orch, R. Muti, R. de Simone (CAST) ▣ **CVI2029**
Nabucco P. Cappuccilli
Abigaille G. Dimitrova
Ismaele P. Domingo
Fenena L.V. Terrani
Zaccaria E. Nesterenko
High Priest K. Rydl
Abdallo V. Horn
Anna L. Popp
Berlin Deutsche Op Chor, Berlin Deutsche Op Orch, G. Sinopoli (5/84) (DG) Ⓓ [2] **410 512-2GH2**
Nabucco T. Gobbi
Abigaille E. Suliotis
Ismaele B. Prevedi
Fenena D. Carral
Zaccaria C. Cava
High Priest G. Foiani
Abdallo W. Kräutler
Anna A. d'Auria
Vienna St Op Chor, Vienna St Op Orch, L. Gardelli (1/87) (DECC) Ⓓ [2] **417 407-2DH2**

1. Sofia SO, V. Stefanov (LASE) Ⓓ **15 519** (LASE) ▭ **79 519**
1. Mexico St SO, E. Bátiz (r1990s) (ASV) Ⓓ **CDDCA856** (ASV) ▭ **ZCDCA856**
1. Hungarian St Op Orch, P.G. Morandi (r1994) (NAXO) Ⓓ **8 553089**
1. LSO, A. Dorati (r1957) (MERC) Ⓓ **434 345-2MM**
1. Philh, T. Serafin (r1959) (EMI) Ⓓ [2] **CES5 68541-2**
1. BPO, H. von Karajan (DG) Ⓓ [2] **447 364-2GDB2**
1. South-West German RSO, K. Arp (r1994) (PIER) Ⓓ **PV730050**
1. BPO, H. von Karajan (10/87) (DG) Ⓓ **419 622-2GH**
1. BPO, H. von Karajan (5/90) (DG) Ⓓ **429 164-2GR**
1. Berlin RIAS Orch, F. Fricsay (bp1952) (11/94) (DG) Ⓓ **445 406-2GDO**
1. I. Seefried, M. Forrester, E. Haefliger, D. Fischer-Dieskau, Berlin St Hedwig's Cath Ch, BPO, F. Fricsay, H. Krebs, T. Varga, Berlin RIAS Chbr Ch, Berlin RIAS Orch, H. Geusser, W. Fugmann, M. Weber, G. Herzog, Berlin RSO, VPO, E. Grümmer, G. Pitzinger, H. Hotter, Y. Menuhin (bp1952) (11/94) (DG) Ⓓ [11] **445 400-2GDO10**
1. BPO, H. von Karajan (1/95) (DG) Ⓓ **439 972-2GGA2**
1, 18. New Philh, R. Muti (EMI) Ⓓ **CDC7 47274-2**
1, 18. Forum Op Chor, Forum PO, G. Bellini (EURM) Ⓓ **350214**
1, 2, 3a, 6, 9b, 9c, 10a, 10b, 12c, 16, 18, 21, 23b M. Manuguerra, V. Luchetti, N. Ghiaurov, R. Scotto, E. Obraztsova, R. Lloyd, K. Collins, A. Edwards, Ambrosian Op Chor, Philh, R. Muti (r1977/8) (EMI) Ⓓ **CDM7 63092-2**
1, 2, 3c, 4a, 4b, 5, 9a-c, 11a, 11b, 12b-d, 17, 18, 21, 22, 24b, 24c P. Cappuccilli, P. Domingo, E. Nesterenko, G. Dimitrova, L.V. Terrani, K. Rydl, V. Horn, Berlin Deutsche Op Chor, Berlin Deutsche Op Orch, G. Sinopoli (DG) Ⓓ **413 321-2GH**
2. La Scala Chor, La Scala Orch, G. Prêtre (r1984) (BELA) Ⓓ **450 052-2** (BELA) ▭ **450 052-4**
2, 13, 18. Ambrosian Op Chor, Philh, R. Muti (r1977) (EMI) Ⓓ [2] **CZS5 68559-2**
2, 18. Fiesole School of Music Female Chor, MMF Chor, MMF Orch, M. Arena (ACAN) Ⓓ **43 540**
2, 18. Chicago Sym Chor, Chicago SO, G. Solti (DECC) ◎◎ **430 226-5DH**
2, 18. La Scala Chor, La Scala Orch, R. Muti (EMI) Ⓓ **CDC7 54484-2**
2, 18. LSC, LSO, R. Hickox (r1987/8) (IMP) Ⓓ [3] **TCD1073**
2, 18. LSC, LSO, R. Hickox (4/89) (IMP) Ⓓ **PCD908**
2, 18. Chicago Sym Chor, Chicago SO, G. Solti (4/91) (DECC) Ⓓ **430 226-2DH**
2, 18. Slovak Phil Chor, Bratislava RSO, O. Dohnányi (4/91) (NAXO) Ⓓ **8 550241**
2, 9a-c, 10a-d, 12b-d, 16, 18, 20, 21, 24a T. Gobbi, B. Prevedi, C. Cava, E. Suliotis, D. Carral, A. d'Auria, G. Foiani, W. Kräutler, Vienna St Op Chor, Vienna St Op Orch, L. Gardelli (DECC) Ⓓ **421 867-2DA** (DECC) ▭ **421 867-4DA**
3a B. Christoff, Rome Op Orch, V. Gui (r1955) (4/92) (EMI) Ⓓ [7] **CHS7 69741-2(6)**
3a, 3b M. McEachern, orch (r1925) (PEAR) Ⓓ **GEMMCD9455**
3a, 3b, 19a, 19b B. Christoff, Rome Op Chor, Rome Op Orch, V. Gui (r1955) (EMI) Ⓓ **CDH5 65500-2**
3a, 10b N. de Angelis, orch, L. Molajoli (r1928) (7/92) (PREI) Ⓓ **89042**
3, 10b, 19. N. Ghiaurov, La Scala Chor, La Scala Orch, G. Gavazzeni (pp1966) (MEMO) Ⓓ [2] **HR4223/4**
4b, 5, 18. G. Dimitrova, O. Garaventa, B. Baglioni, Verona Arena Chor, Verona Arena Orch, M. Arena (CAST) ▣ **CASH5052**
7b, 7c T. Ruffo, orch, W.B. Rogers (r1914) (11/90) (NIMB) Ⓓ **NI7810** (NIMB) ▭ **NC7810**
7c T. Ruffo, orch (r1914) (2/93) (PREI) Ⓓ [3] **89303(1)**
7c, 12b, 21. R. Bruson, P. Burchuladze, G. Dimitrova, La Scala Chor, La Scala Orch, R. Muti (CAST) ▣ **CVI2067**
9. M. Callas, Philh, N. Rescigno (9/87) (EMI) Ⓓ **CDC7 47730-2**
9a A. Tomowa-Sintow, Sofia PO, R. Raichev (r1970s) (FORL) Ⓓ **UCD16742**
9a, 9b M. Callas, FRNO, G. Prêtre (pp1963) (MEMO) Ⓓ **HR4293/4**
9a, 9b M. Callas, Turin RAI Orch, O. de Fabritiis (r1952) (SUIT) Ⓓ **CDS1-5001**
9a, 9b A. Cerquetti, MMF Orch, G. Gavazzeni (r1956) (DECC) Ⓓ **440 411-2DM**
9a, 9b J. Varady, Bavarian St Orch, D. Fischer-Dieskau (r1995) (ORFE) Ⓓ **C186951**
9a, 9b, 9c E. Suliotis, G. Foiani, Vienna St Op Concert Ch, Vienna Op Orch, L. Gardelli (r1965) (DECC) Ⓓ **440 405-2DM**
9c E. Suliotis, Vienna St Op Chor, Vienna Op Orch, L. Gardelli (r1965) (DECC) Ⓓ **436 300-2DX** (DECC) ▭ **436 300-4DX**
10a, 10b C. Siepi, Santa Cecilia Academy Orch, A. Erede (r1954) (DECC) Ⓓ **440 418-2DM**
10a, 10b J. Van Dam, Loire PO, M. Soustrot (r1992) (8/93) (FORL) Ⓓ **UCD16681**
10b T. Pasero, La Scala Orch, A. Sabino (r1942) (4/95) (PREI) Ⓓ **89074**
11a, 11b P. Domingo, Berlin Deutsche Op Chor, Berlin Deutsche Op Orch, G. Sinopoli (r1982) (DG) Ⓓ **445 525-2GMA** (DG) ▭ **445 525-4GMA**
12d, 21. R. Stracciari, orch (r1925) (MSCM) Ⓓ [2] **MM30276**
12d, 21. R. Stracciari, orch (r1925) (2/90) (PREI) Ⓓ **89003**
18. R. Shaw Chorale, RCA Victor Orch, Robert Shaw (RCA) Ⓓ **GD60205**
18. Vienna St Op Chor, Vienna Op Orch, L. Gardelli (DECC) Ⓓ **425 847-2DWO** (DECC) ▭ **425 847-4DWO**
18. Westminster Ch, NBC SO, A. Toscanini (bp1943) (RCA) Ⓓ [2] **GD60299**
18. La Scala Chor, La Scala Orch, L. von Matačić (CFP) Ⓓ **CD-CFP4575** (CFP) ▭ **TC-CFP4575**
18. London Choral Soc, RPO, M. Reed (Eng:pp1989) (RPO) Ⓓ [2] **CDRPD9001** (RPO) ▭ [2] **ZCRPD9001**
18. Ambrosian Op Chor, Philh, R. Muti (EMI) Ⓓ [2] **CDEMTVD59** (EMI) ⊙ [2] **EMTVD59**
18. H. Britton (org) (ASV) Ⓓ **CDWHL2064** (ASV) ▭ **ZCWHL2064**
18. Chicago Sym Chor, Chicago SO, G. Solti (DECC) Ⓓ **433 822-2DH** (DECC) ▭ **433 822-4DH**
18. Classic Buskers (arr Copley) (SEAV) Ⓓ **CD007365**
18. Vienna St Op Chor, Vienna Op Orch, L. Gardelli (r1965) (DECC) Ⓓ **433 065-2DWO** (DECC) ▭ **433 065-4DWO**
18. Ambrosian Sngrs, LSO, C. Abbado (DECC) Ⓓ **433 221-2DWO** (DECC) ▭ **433 221-4DWO**
18. Brighton Fest Chor, RPO, Carl Davis (RPO) Ⓓ **CDRPO7018** (RPO) ▭ **ZCRPO7018**
18. ROH Chor, ROHO, L. Gardelli (EMI) Ⓓ **CDM7 64356-2**
18. Vienna St Op Chor, Vienna Op Orch, L. Gardelli (r1965) (DECC) Ⓓ **436 300-2DX** (DECC) ▭ **436 300-4DX**
18. Berlin Deutsche Op Chor, Berlin Deutsche Op Orch, G. Sinopoli (DG) ◎◎ **415 283-5GH**
18. Rome Op Chor, Rome Op Orch, G. Santini (r c1958) (CFP) Ⓓ **CD-CFP4602** (CFP) ▭ **TC-CFP4602**
18. Ambrosian Op Chor, Philh, R. Muti (CFP) Ⓓ **CD-CFP4613** (CFP) ▭ **TC-CFP4613**
18. Ljubljana Rad Orch, Ljubljana Rad Chor, Anon (cond) (WORD) Ⓓ **FCD7410**
18. ROH Chor, RPO, R. Stapleton (r1990) (RPO) Ⓓ [2] **CDRPD9006** (RPO) ▭ [2] **ZCRPD9006**
18. Philh Chor, Philh, L. Magiera (DECC) ◎◎ **436 320-5DH**
18. Op North Chor, English Northern Philh, P. Daniel (r1992) (EMI) Ⓓ **CDC7 54785-2**
18. RPO, London Choral Soc, Scots Guards Band, Welsh Guards Band, M. Reed (pp1989; arr orch) (RPO) Ⓓ **CDRPO5009**
18. Dresden St Op Chor, Dresden St Op Orch, S. Varviso (r1985) (BELA) Ⓓ **450 052-2** (BELA) ▭ **450 052-4**
18. Vienna St Op Chor, Vienna Op Orch, N. Rescigno (r1965) (DECC) Ⓓ **433 440-2DA** (DECC) ▭ **433 440-4DA**
18. Vienna St Op Chor, VPO, L. Gardelli (r1965) (DECC) Ⓓ **433 443-2DA** (DECC) ▭ **433 443-4DA**
18. La Scala Chor, La Scala Orch, R. Muti (TELD) ◐ **9031-77676-6** (TELD) ▣ **9031-77676-3**
18. LSC, LSO, R. Hickox (r1988) (IMP) Ⓓ **PCDS23** (IMP) ▭ **PCDSC23**
18. LSC, LSO, R. Hickox (r1988) (IMP) Ⓓ [3] **TCD1070**
18. Santa Cecilia Academy Chor, Santa Cecilia Academy Orch, C. Franci (BELA) Ⓓ **450 133-2** (BELA) ▭ **450 133-4**
18. Vienna St Op Chor, Vienna Op Orch, L. Gardelli (r1965) (DECC) Ⓓ [2] **443 585-2DF2** (DECC) ▭ [2] **433 585-4DWO2**
18. Santa Cecilia Academy Orch, C. Rizzi, Santa Cecilia Academy Chor (TELD) Ⓓ **4509-96035-2** (TELD) ▭ **4509-96035-4**
18. Santa Cecilia Academy Chor, Santa Cecilia Academy Orch, C. Franci (r1960s) (BELA) Ⓓ **450 117-2** (BELA) ▭ **450 117-4**
18. ROH Chor, ROHO, L. Gardelli (EMIL) Ⓓ **CDZ101** (EMIL) ▭ **LZ101**
18. Mormon Tabernacle Ch, Utah SO, J. Rudel (r1989) (LOND) Ⓓ **443 381-2LM**
18. Cincinnati Pops, E. Kunzel (r1994; arr & orch Kunzel & Beck) (TELA) Ⓓ **CD80364** (TELA) ▭ **CS30364**
18. R. Shaw Chorale, orch, Robert Shaw (r1965) (RCA) Ⓓ **74321 24209-2**
18. Berlin Deutsche Op Chor, Berlin Deutsche Op Orch, G. Sinopoli (10/85) (DG) Ⓓ **415 283-2GH**
18. Atlanta Sym Chor, Atlanta SO, Robert Shaw (3/88) (TELA) Ⓓ [2] **CD80152**
18. ROH Chor, ROHO, B. Haitink (12/89) (EMI) Ⓓ **CDC7 49849-2**
18. Westminster Ch, NBC SO, A. Toscanini (bp1943) (5/90) (RCA) Ⓓ [7] **GD60326**
18. ROH Chor, RPO, R. Stapleton (10/90) (IMP) Ⓓ **MCD15** (10/90) (IMP) ▭ **MCC15**
18. Philh Chor, Philh, L. Magiera (11/91) (DECC) ◐ **071 150-1DH** (11/91) (DECC) ▣ **071 150-3DH**
18. La Scala Chor, La Scala Orch, V. Veneziani (r1928) (4/94) (EMI) Ⓓ [3] **CHS7 64864-2(2)**
20, 21, 22. T. Gobbi, W. Kräutler, Vienna St Op Concert Ch, Vienna Op Orch, L. Gardelli (r1965) (10/93) (DECC) Ⓓ **436 464-2DM**
21. C. Galeffi, orch (r1916) (PREI) Ⓓ **89995**
21. T. Gobbi, Rome Op Orch, O. de Fabritiis (r1955) (10/89) (EMI) Ⓓ **CDM7 63109-2**

21. C. Galeffi, orch (r1916)
(4/94) (EMI) Ⓓ [3] **CHS7 64860-2(2)**

Oberto, Conte di San Bonifaco– dramma: 2 acts (1839—Milan) (Lib. Soleva)

EXCERPTS: 1. Overture. ACT 1: 2a. Di vermiglia, amabil luce; 2b. Son fra voi! Già parmi udire il fremito; 3a. Ah, sgombro è il loco alfin; 3b. Sotto il paterno tetto; 3c. Oh, potesi nel mio core; 4. Oh patria terra, alfina io ti rivedo; 5a. Al cader della notte; 5b. Guardami! sul mio ciglio; 5c. Non ti basto il periglio; 5d. Del tuo favour soccorrimi; 5e. Un amplesso riceri, o pentita; 6. Findanzata avventurosa; 7a. Basta, basta, o fedeli!; 7b. Cuniza, ah parmi; 7c. Il pensier d'amore felice; 7d. Fra il timpre è la speme; 8. Alta cagione adunque; 9. A, perchè tanto in petto; 10a. Son io stresso! A te davanti; 10b. Su quella fronte impressa; 11a. A me gli amici! Mira!; 11b. A quell' aspetto un fremito. ACT 2: 12. Infelice! Nel core; 13a. Riccardo! E che gli resta?; 13b. Oh, chi torna l'ardente; 13c. Più che i vezzi e lo splendore; 14. Dov'è l'astro che nel cielo; 15a. Ei tarda ancor!; 15b. L'onor del tradimento; 15c. Ma tu, superbo giovane; 16. Eccolo! è desso! or son tranquillo; 17a. Ferma! Ah troppo in questa terra; 17b. La vergogna ed il dispetto; 17c. Ah Riccardo, se a misera amante; 18. Li vedeste; 19. Ciel, che feci!; 20. Dove son? il cerco invano!; 21a. Vieni, o misera, cresciuta; 21b. Sciagurata! a questa lido; 22. Una messaggio a questa volta?.

Cuniza R. Baldani
Leonora G. Dimitrova
Imelda A. Browner
Riccardo C. Bergonzi
Oberto R. Panerai
Bavarian Rad Chor, Munich RO, L. Gardelli
(6/87) (ORFE) Ⓓ [2] **C105842H**

1. Hungarian St Op Orch, P.G. Morandi (r1994)
(NAXO) Ⓓ **8 553018**

1. BPO, H. von Karajan
(1/95) (DG) Ⓓ **439 972-2GGA2**

19. C. Bergonzi, New Philh, N. Santi
(PHIL) Ⓓ [3] **432 486-2PM3**

Otello– opera: 4 acts (1887—Milan) (Lib. A Boito, after Shakespeare)

EXCERPTS: ACT 1: 1a. Una vela!; 1b. Esultate!; 2. Roderigo, ebben che pensi?; 3. Fuoco di gioia!; 4a. Roderigo, beviam!; 4b. Inaffia l'ugola! (Brindisi); 5a. Capitano, v'attende; 5b. Abbasso le spade!; 6a. Già nella notte densa (Love Duet); 6b. Venga la morte!. ACT 2: 7a. Non ti crucciar; 7b. Vanne! la tua meta; 7c. Credo in un Dio crudel; 8a. Ciò m'accora... 8b. Dove guardi; 9. D'un uom che geme; 10a. Desdemona rea!... 10b. Tu?! Indietro! fuggi!; 10c. Ora e per sempre; 11. Era la notte (Dream); 12a. Oh! mostruosa colpa!; 12b. Ah! mille vite; 12c. Si, pel ciel (Oath Duet). ACT 3: 13. La vedetta del porto; 14a. Dio ti giocondi; 14b. Esterrefatta fisso; 15. Dio! mi potevi (Monologue); 16a. Vieni; l'aula è deserta; 16b. Questa è una ragna; 17a. Quest'è il segnale; 17b. Come la ucciderò; 18a. Viva! Evviva!; 18b. Eccolo! È lui!; 18c. A terra!; 19. Ballabile. ACT 4: 20a. Era più calmo?; 20b. Mia madre aveva; 20c. Piangea cantando (Willow Song); 21. Ave Maria; 22. Chi è là? (Death of Desdemona); 23. Niun mi tema.

Otello V. Atlantov
Desdemona K. Te Kanawa
Iago P. Cappuccilli
Cassio A. Bevacqua
Roderigo A. Schiavon
Emilia F. Raffanelli
Lodovico G. Casarini
Montano O. Mori
Verona Arena Chor, Verona Arena Orch, Z. Peskó, G. De Bosio
(CAST) ▭ **CVI2025**

Otello J. Vickers
Desdemona M. Freni
Iago P. Glossop
Cassio A. Bottion
Roderigo M. Sénéchal
Emilia S. Malagù
Lodovico J. Van Dam
Montano M. Macchi
Berlin Deutsche Op Chor, BPO, H. von Karajan
(DG) ▭ **072 401-3GH**

Otello P. Domingo
Desdemona K. Te Kanawa
Iago S. Leiferkus
Cassio R. Leggate
Roderigo R. Remedios
Emilia C. Powell
Lodovico M. Beesley
Montano R. Earle
Herald C. Lackner
ROH Chor, ROHO, G. Solti, E. Moshinsky
(9/93) (CGP) ▭ **CVI1718**

Otello M. del Monaco
Desdemona G. Tucci
Iago T. Gobbi
Cassio M. Caruso
Roderigo G. De Julïis
Emilia A. di Stasio
Lodovico P. Clabassi
Montano T. Okamura
NHK Sym Chor, NHK SO, A. Erede (pp1959)
(MEMO) Ⓓ [2] **HR4406/7**

Otello P. Domingo
Desdemona K. Te Kanawa
Iago S. Leiferkus
Cassio R. Leggate
Roderigo R. Remedios
Emilia C. Powell
Lodovico M. Beesley
Montano R. Earle
Herald C. Lackner
ROH Chor, ROHO, G. Solti, E. Moshinsky (r1992)
(PION) ◖ **PLMCC00851**

Otello J. McCracken
Desdemona G. Jones
Iago D. Fischer-Dieskau
Cassio P. De Palma
Roderigo F. Andreolli
Emilia A. di Stasio
Lodovico A. Giacomotti
Montano L. Monreale
Herald G. Thomas
Upton Hse School Boys' Ch, Hammersmith School Girls' Ch, Ambrosian Op Chor, New Philh, J. Barbirolli (r1968)
(EMI) Ⓓ [2] **CMS5 65296-2**

Otello C. Craig
Desdemona R. Plowright
Iago N. Howlett
Cassio B. Bottone
Roderigo S. Kale
Emilia S. Squires
Lodovico S. Rea
Montano M. Rivers
Herald G. Traynor
ENO Chor, ENO Orch, M. Elder (pp1983: Eng)
(CFP) Ⓓ [2] **CD-CFPD4736**
(CFP) ▬ [2] **TC-CFPD4736**

Otello T. Ralf
Desdemona H. Konetzni
Iago P. Schoeffler
Cassio J. Witt
Roderigo P. Klein
Emilia E. Nikolaidi
Lodovico T. Neralič
Montano V. Madin
Herald R. Neumann
Vienna St Op Chor, Vienna St Op Orch, K. Böhm (pp1944: Ger)
(PREI) Ⓓ [2] **90230**

Otello R. Vinay
Desdemona D. Martinis
Iago P. Schoeffler
Cassio A. Dermota
Roderigo A. Jaresch
Emilia S. Wagner
Lodovico J. Greindl
Montano G. Monthy
Herald F. Bierbach
Vienna St Op Chor, VPO, W. Furtwängler (pp1951)
(EMI) Ⓓ [2] **CHS5 65751-2**

Otello J. Vickers
Desdemona R. Kabaivanska
Iago G-P. Mastromei
Cassio E. Valori
Roderigo V. Tavini
Emilia I. Casey
Lodovico J. Algorta
Montano P. de Vescovi
Herald H. Barbieri
Buenos Aires Colón Th Chor, Buenos Aires Colón Th Orch, B. Klobučar (pp)
(ATRI) Ⓓ [2] **ATR005/6CD**

Otello P. Domingo
Desdemona R. Scotto
Iago S. Milnes
Cassio F. Little
Roderigo P. Crook
Emilia J. Kraft
Lodovico P. Plishka
Montano; Herald M. King
Ambrosian Op Chor, National PO, James Levine (r1978)
(3/86) (RCA) Ⓓ [2] **GD82951**

Otello P. Domingo
Desdemona K. Ricciarelli
Iago J. Diaz
Cassio E. Di Cesare
Roderigo C. Zaharia
Emilia P. Malakova
Lodovico J. Macurdy
Montano E. Tumagian
Herald G. Pigliucci
La Scala Chor, La Scala Orch, L. Maazel (r1985)
(12/86) (EMI) Ⓓ [2] **CDS7 47450-8**

Otello M. del Monaco
Desdemona R. Tebaldi
Iago A. Protti
Cassio N. Romanato
Roderigo A. Cesarini
Emilia A.R. Satre
Lodovico F. Corena
Montano T. Krause
Herald L. Arbace
Vienna Children's Ch, Vienna St Op Chor, VPO, H. von Karajan (r1961)
(3/87) (DECC) Ⓓ [2] **411 618-2DH2**

Otello J. Vickers
Desdemona M. Freni
Iago P. Glossop
Cassio A. Bottion
Roderigo M. Sénéchal
Emilia S. Malagù
Lodovico J. Van Dam
Montano M. Macchi
Herald H. Helm
Berlin Deutsche Op Chor, BPO, H. von Karajan (r1973)
(4/88) (EMI) Ⓓ [2] **CMS7 69308-2**

Otello J. Vickers
Desdemona Leonie Rysanek
Iago T. Gobbi
Cassio F. Andreolli
Roderigo Mario Carlin
Emilia M. Pirazzini
Lodovico F. Mazzoli
Montano F. Calabrese
Herald R. Kerns
Rome Op Chor, Rome Op Orch, T. Serafin (r1960)
(11/88) (RCA) Ⓓ [2] **GD81969**

Otello G. Martinelli
Desdemona E. Rethberg
Iago L. Tibbett
Cassio N. Massue
Emilia T. Votipka
Lodovico N. Moscona
Montano G. Cehanovsky
NY Met Op Chor, NY Met Op Orch, E. Panizza (pp1938)
(9/91) (MUSI) Ⓓ [2] **MACD-645**

Otello L. Pavarotti
Desdemona K. Te Kanawa
Iago L. Nucci
Cassio A. Rolfe Johnson
Roderigo J. Keyes
Emilia E. Ardam
Lodovico D. Kavrakos
Montano A. Opie
Herald R. Cohn
NY Met Op Children's Ch, Chicago Sym Chor, Chicago SO, G. Solti (pp1991)
(11/91) (DECC) Ⓓ [2] **433 669-2DH2**

Otello R. Vinay
Desdemona H. Nelli
Iago G. Valdengo
Cassio V. Assandri
Roderigo L. Chabay
Emilia N. Merriman
Lodovico N. Moscona
Montano A. Newman
Chor, NBC SO, A. Toscanini (r1947)
(3/92) (RCA) Ⓓ [2] **GD60302**

Otello C. Murgu
Desdemona M. Gulegina
Iago R. Bruson
Cassio M. Saltarin
Roderigo H. Yoshida
Emilia G. Pasino
Lodovico M. Pertusi
Montano; Herald G. de Angelis
Tokyo Little Sngrs, Fujiwara Op Chor, Tokyo PO, G Kuhn (pp1991)
(6/92) (SCHW) Ⓓ [2] **314074**

Otello M. del Monaco

Desdemona R. Tebaldi
Iago A. Protti
Cassio P. de Palma
Roderigo A. Mercuriali
Emilia L. Ribacchi
Lodovico F. Corena
Montano P. L. Latinucci
Herald D. Caselli
Santa Cecilia Academy Chor, Santa Cecilia Academy Orch, A. Erede (r1954)
(5/94) (LOND) Ⓓ [2] **440 245-2LF2**

Otello C. Cossutta
Desdemona M. Price
Iago G. Bacquier
Cassio P. Dvorský
Roderigo K. Equiluz
Emilia J. Berbié
Lodovico K. Moll
Montano S. Dean
Herald H. Helm
Vienna Boys' Ch, Vienna St Op Chor, VPO, G. Solti (r1977)
(5/94) (DECC) Ⓓ [2] **440 045-2DMO2**

Otello P. Domingo
Desdemona C. Studer
Iago S. Leiferkus
Cassio R. Vargas
Roderigo M. Schade
Emilia D. Graves
Lodovico I. d'Arcangelo
Montano G. Prestia
Herald P. Duminy
Hauts-de-Seine Maîtrise, Paris Opéra-Bastille Chor, Paris Opéra-Bastille Orch, Myung-Whun Chung (r1993)
(12/94) (DG) Ⓓ [2] **439 805-2GH2**

Act 3. P. Domingo, M. Freni, J. Diaz, U. Heilmann, S. Kelly, P. Plishka, C. Anthony, D. Croft, NY Met Op Chor, NY Met Op Orch, James Levine (DG) ◐ [2] **072 428-1GH2**
(DG) ▣ **072 428-3GH**

Excs P. Domingo (CAST) ▣ **CVI2021**

1a M. del Monaco, T. Krause, A. Protti, A. Cesarini, Vienna St Op Chor, VPO, H. von Karajan (r1961) (DECC) Ⓓ **433 443-2DA**
(DECC) ▭ **433 443-4DA**

1a, 1b A. Paoli, V. de Goetzen, G. Sala, orch (r1911) (PREI) Ⓓ **89998**

1a, 1b, 3, 4a, 4b, 5a, 5b, 6a, 6b, 7b, 7c, 9, 10a-c, 11, 12a, 12c, 15, 20a-c, 21, 23. P. Domingo, C. Studer, S. Leiferkus, R. Vargas, M. Schade, D. Graves, I. d'Arcangelo, G. Prestia, P. Duminy, Hauts-de-Seine Maîtrise, Paris Opéra-Bastille Chor, Paris Opéra-Bastille Orch, Myung-Whun Chung (r1993) Ⓓ **445 867-2GH**

1a, 1b, 6a, 6b, 7b, 7c, 10a, 10b, 10c, 11, 12a, 12b, 12c, 15, 20a, 20b, 20c, 21, 23. K. Te Kanawa, E. Ardam, L. Pavarotti, A. Rolfe Johnson, L. Nucci, Chicago Sym Chor, Chicago SO, G. Solti (pp1991) (DECC) Ⓓ **440 843-2DH**

1a, 1b, 6a(pt), 6b, 12c G. Zenatello, A. Granforte, H. Spani, La Scala Chor, La Scala Orch, C. Sabajno (r1926)
(5/94) (PEAR) Ⓓ [4] **GEMMCDS9074(2)**

1a, 1b, 6b, 12b, 12c G. Zenatello, H. Spani, A. Granforte, La Scala Orch, C. Sabajno (r1926)
(11/91) (PREI) Ⓓ **89038**

1a, 1b, 12b, 12c G. Zenatello, A. Granforte, La Scala Orch, C. Sabajno (r1926)
(11/91) (CLUB) Ⓓ **CL99-025**

1a, 3, 14a, 14b, 15, 23. G. Cigna, A. Pertile, La Scala Chor, La Scala Orch, A. Erede (r1942)
(TELD) Ⓓ **9031-76437-2**

1b M. del Monaco, Milan SO, A. Quadri (r1951)
(EMI) Ⓓ **CDC7 54016-2**

1b M. del Monaco, Milan SO, A. Quadri (r1951)
(4/92) (EMI) Ⓓ [7] **CHS7 69741-2(7)**

1b F. Tamagno, anon (r1903)
(7/92) (PEAR) Ⓓ [3] **GEMMCDS9923(2)**

1b F. Tamagno, anon (r1903)
(11/92) (MEMO) Ⓓ [2] **HR4408/9(1)**

1b, 4b, 6a, 6b, 7b, 7c, 10b, 10c, 11, 12c, 15, 18c, 20b, 20c, 21, 23. P. Domingo, K. Ricciarelli, J. Diaz, E. di Cesare, C. Zaharia, J. Macurdy, E. Tumagian, P. Malakova, La Scala Chor, La Scala Orch, L. Maazel (EMI) Ⓓ **CDM7 69059-2**

1b, 6a, 6b, 10c, 12c, 15, 23. G. Lauri-Volpi, M. Caniglia, M. Basiola I, La Scala Orch, G. Marinuzzi (r1941) (7/94) (NIMB) Ⓓ **NI7853**

1b, 10c F. Tamagno, anon (r1903)
(4/94) (EMI) Ⓓ [3] **CHS7 64860-2(1)**

1b, 10c, 15. M. del Monaco, Milan SO, A. Quadri (r1951) (TEST) Ⓓ **SBT1039**

1b, 10c, 23. F. Tamagno, Anon (pf) (r1903-04)
(2/92) (OPAL) Ⓓ **OPALCD9846**

1b, 23. F. Tamagno, anon (r1903)
(9/94) (NIMB) Ⓓ **NI7856**

1, 6, 7, 11, 12, 15, 20, 21, 23. J. Vickers, M. Freni, P. Glossop, A. Bottion, M. Sénéchal, M. Machi, S. Malagù, Berlin Deutsche Op Chor, BPO, H. von Karajan (EMI) Ⓓ **CDM7 63454-2**

3. Santa Cecilia Academy Chor, Santa Cecilia Academy Orch, C. Franci
(DECC) Ⓓ **433 069-2DWO**
(DECC) ▭ **433 069-4DWO**

3. ROH Chor, ROHO, L. Gardelli
(EMI) Ⓓ **CDM7 64356-2**

3. Chicago Sym Chor, Chicago SO, G. Solti
(DECC) OO **430 226-5DH**

3. Santa Cecilia Academy Chor, Santa Cecilia Academy Orch, C. Franci (r1960s)
(BELA) Ⓓ **450 117-2**
(BELA) ▭ **450 117-4**

3. ROH Chor, ROHO, L. Gardelli (r c1972)
(EMI) Ⓓ [2] **CZS5 68559-2**

3. Ambrosian Op Chor, National PO, James Levine (r1977) (RCA) Ⓓ **74321 24209-2**

3. La Scala Chor, La Scala Orch, A. Guarnieri (r1927) (BONG) Ⓓ **GB1039-2**

3. Atlanta Sym Chor, Atlanta SO, Robert Shaw
(3/88) (TELA) Ⓓ [2] **CD80152**

3. ROH Chor, ROHO, B. Haitink
(12/89) (EMI) Ⓓ **CDC7 49849-2**

3. Chicago Sym Chor, Chicago SO, G. Solti
(4/91) (DECC) Ⓓ **430 226-2DH**

3. Slovak Phil Chor, Bratislava RSO, O. Dohnányi (4/91) (NAXO) Ⓓ **8 550241**

3. Vienna St Op Chor, Vienna St Op Orch, V. de Sabata (pp1935: Ger)
(7/94) (SCHW) Ⓓ [2] **314512**

4b A. Scotti, orch (r1907)
(PEAR) Ⓓ **GEMMCD9937**

4b P. Amato, A. Bada, NY Met Op Chor, NY Met Op Orch, G. Setti (r1911) (PREI) Ⓓ **89064**

4b J. Herrmann, W. Treffner, H. Tessmer, orch (r1943: Ger) (PREI) Ⓓ **89076**

4b P. Amato, A. Bada, NY Met Op Chor, orch, G. Setti (r1911) (PEAR) Ⓓ **GEMMCD9104**

4b H. Schlusnus, Berlin St Op Orch, M. Gurlitt (r1928: Ger) (PREI) Ⓓ [2] **89212**

4b A. Scotti, orch (r1907) (PREI) Ⓓ **89995**

4b A. Granforte, P. Girardi, N. Palai, La Scala Orch, C. Sabajno (r1931)
(12/91) (PREI) Ⓓ **89048**

4b G. Inghilleri, O. Dua, L. Cilla, chor, orch, J. Barbirolli (r1929)
(7/92) (PEAR) Ⓓ [3] **GEMMCDS9926(1)**

4b, 7c, 11. R. Stracciari, orch (r1925)
(2/90) (PREI) Ⓓ **89003**

6. C. Studer, P. Domingo, ROHO, J. Barker (pp1988) (9/89) (EMI) Ⓓ **CDC7 49811-2**

6. G. Lauri-Volpi, M. Caniglia, Rome Op Orch, D. Olivieri (r1941)
(4/94) (EMI) Ⓓ [3] **CHS7 64864-2(2)**

6a P. Domingo, K. Ricciarelli, Santa Cecilia Academy Orch, G. Gavazzeni
(RCA) Ⓓ [2] **GD60866**
(RCA) ▭ [2] **GK60866**

6a L. Pavarotti, K. Ricciarelli, Parma Teatro Regio Orch, G. Patanè (pp1980)
(BELA) Ⓓ **450 002-2**
(BELA) ▭ **450 002-4**

6a K. Te Kanawa, V. Atlantov, Verona Arena Orch, Z. Peskó (TELD) ◐ **9031-77676-6**
(TELD) ▣ **9031-77676-3**

6a L. Price, P. Domingo, New Philh, N. Santi
(RCA) Ⓓ **09026 62699-2**
(RCA) ▭ **09026 62699-4**

6a(pt) H. Spani, G. Zenatello, La Scala Orch, C. Sabajno (r1926)
(9/90) (CLUB) Ⓓ [2] **CL99-509/10**

6a, 6b M. Seinemeyer, T. Pattiera, orch, F. Weissmann (r1928) (PEAR) Ⓓ **GEMMCD9082**

6a, 6b M. Freni, J. Vickers, BPO, H. von Karajan (r1973) (CFP) Ⓓ **CD-CFP4656**
(CFP) ▭ **TC-CFP4656**

6a, 6b L. Price, P. Domingo, LSO, N. Santi (r1974) (RCA) Ⓓ **09026 61634-2**

6a, 6b M. Seinemeyer, T. Pattiera, Berlin St Op Orch, F. Weissmann (r1928)
(11/90) (PREI) Ⓓ **89029**

6a, 6b J. Sutherland, K. Te Kanawa, NYC Op Orch, R. Bonynge
(12/91) (DECC) Ⓓ **430 724-2DM**

6a, 6b G. Zenatello, E. Mazzoleni, orch (r c1910)
(12/93) (SYMP) Ⓓ **SYMCD1148**

6a, 6b G. Zenatello, L. Pasini-Vitale, orch (r1909) (12/93) (SYMP) Ⓓ **SYMCD1148**

6a, 6b M. Price, C. Cossutta, VPO, G. Solti (r1977) (12/93) (DECC) Ⓓ **433 439-2DA**
(DECC) ▭ **433 439-4DA**

6a, 6b G. Zenatello, L. Pasini-Vitale, orch (r1909)
(5/94) (PEAR) Ⓓ [4] **GEMMCDS9073(2)**

6a, 6b K. Ricciarelli, L. Pavarotti, Parma Teatro Regio Orch, G. Patanè (pp1976)
(5/94) (DECC) Ⓓ [2] **443 018-2DF2**

6a, 6b G. Zenatello, E. Mazzoleni, orch (r1911)
(5/94) (PEAR) Ⓓ [4] **GEMMCDS9074(1)**

6a, 6b T. Ralf, T. Lemnitz, Berlin St Op Orch, B. Seidler-Winkler (r1939: Ger)
(10/94) (PREI) Ⓓ **89077**

6a, 6b, 14a, 14b F. Merli, C. Muzio, orch, L. Molajoli (r1935) (PREI) Ⓓ **89091**

6a, 6b, 21. K. Ricciarelli, P. Domingo, Santa Cecilia Academy Orch, G. Gavazzeni
(12/87) (RCA) Ⓓ **GD86534**

6a(pt), 10c, 11. F. Völker, V. Ursuleac, J. von Manowarda, Vienna St Op Orch, C. Krauss (pp1933: Ger) (9/95) (SCHW) Ⓓ [2] **314662**

6a, 15, 23. V. Atlantov, K. Te Kanawa, P. Cappuccilli, Verona Arena Chor, Verona Arena Orch, Z. Peskó (CAST) ▣ **CVI2068**

6b A. Paoli, F. Chiesa, orch (r1911)
(PREI) Ⓓ **89998**

6b C. Muzio, F. Merli, orch, L. Molajoli (r1935)
(4/91) (NIMB) Ⓓ **NI7814**
(4/91) (NIMB) ▭ **NC7814**

7. T. Gobbi, Rome Op Orch, T. Serafin (r1960)
(4/94) (RCA) Ⓓ [6] **09026 61580-2(6)**

7a-c, 8a, 10b, 10c, 11, 12a-c L. Tibbett, G. Martinelli, A. de Paolis, NY Met Op Orch, E. Panizza (pp1941)
(3/91) (PEAR) Ⓓ [2] **GEMMCDS9452**

7a-c, 8a, 11. T. Gobbi, NHK Sym Chor, NHK SO, A. Erede (pp1959)
(MEMO) Ⓓ [2] **HR4376/7**

7b, 7c B. Weikl, Munich RO, H. Wallberg
(ACAN) Ⓓ **43 327**

7b, 7c T. Gobbi, Philh, A. Erede (r1963)
(10/89) (EMI) Ⓓ **CDM7 63109-2**

7b, 7c T. Gobbi, Philh, J. Robertson (r1950)
(8/93) (TEST) Ⓓ **SBT1019**

7c J. Schwarz, orch (Ger: r1916)
(PREI) Ⓓ **89033**

7c G. Evans, SRO, B. Balkwill
(DECC) Ⓓ **433 221-2DWO**
(DECC) ▭ **433 221-4DWO**

7c A. Orda, Polish RSO, K. Missona (bp1977)
(SYMP) Ⓓ **SYMCD1117**

7c P. Amato, orch, W.B. Rogers (r1911)
(PREI) Ⓓ **89064**

7c J. Herrmann, Leipzig RSO, R. Merten (r1941: Ger) (PREI) Ⓓ **89076**

7c P. Amato, orch, W.B. Rogers (r1911)
(PEAR) Ⓓ **GEMMCD9104**

7c S. Milnes, F. Becerra, Minería SO, H. de la Fuente (r1981) (IMP) Ⓓ **PCD1109**

7c R. Raimondi, Paris Op Orch, E. Tchakarov (r1981) (ERAT) Ⓓ **4509-98503-2**

7c A. Granforte, orch, G.W. Byng (r1925)
(PREI) Ⓓ **89105**

7c H. Schlusnus, orch (r1921: Ger)
(PREI) Ⓓ **89110**

7c C. Formichi, orch (r1928) (PREI) Ⓓ **89995**

7c G. Kaschmann, S. Cottone (r1903)
(12/89) (SYMP) Ⓓ **SYMCD1065**

7c T. Ruffo, orch, W.B. Rogers (r1914)
(11/90) (NIMB) Ⓓ **NI7810**
(NIMB) ▭ **NC7810**

7c C. Tagliabue, Turin EIAR Orch, A. la Rosa Parodi (r1942) (11/90) (PREI) Ⓓ **89015**

7c A. Endrèze, orch, G. Cloëz (French: r c1932)
(11/92) (MSCM) Ⓓ **MM30451**

7c I. Caley, S. Milnes, LPO, S. Varviso (1972)
(10/93) (DECC) Ⓓ **436 464-2DM**

7c C. Formichi, orch, A. Ketèlbey (r1924)
(11/94) (PREI) Ⓓ **89055**

7c E. Giraldoni, orch (r1905)
(10/95) (NIMB) Ⓓ **NI7867**

7c, 11. H. Hotter, Bavarian St Orch, H. Hollreiser (r1943: Ger) (PREI) Ⓓ **90200**

7c, 11. A. Sved, Radio Italiana SO, A. Simonetto (r1947) (PREI) Ⓓ **89096**

7c, 11. G. Bechi, Santa Cecilia Academy Orch, A. Votto (r1946) (2/90) (PREI) Ⓓ **89009**

7c, 11. P. Schoeffler, LPO, K. Rankl (r1947)
(1/95) (PREI) Ⓓ **90190**

7c, 12a, 12c T. Ruffo, E. Caruso, orch, W.B. Rogers (r1914) (PEAR) Ⓓ **GEMMCD9088**

7c, 12c T. Ruffo, E. Caruso, orch (r1914)
(2/93) (PREI) Ⓓ [3] **89303(1)**

7c, 12c, 21. P. Cappuccilli, V. Atlantov, K. Te Kanawa, Verona Arena Orch, Z. Peskó
(CAST) ▣ **CASH5052**

8a(pt), 10c, 12b, 12c, 15, 16b, 23. G. Zenatello, G. Noto, L. Cilla, E. Cotreil, M. Sampieri, orch, V. Bellezza (pp1926) (5/94) (PEAR) Ⓓ [4] **GEMMCDS9074(2)**
10a, 10c, 12c J. Lotrič, I. Morozov, Slovak RSO, J. Wildner (r1994) (2/95) (NAXO) Ⓓ **8 553030**
10b A. Paoli, orch (r1909) (PREI) Ⓓ **89998**
10b, 10c F. Völker, Berlin Staatskapelle, J. Schüler (r1937: Ger) (8/94) (PREI) Ⓓ **89070**
10b, 10c, 15. C. Vezzani, orch (r1933; French) (MSCM) Ⓓ **MM30377**
10b, 10c, 12c G. Zenatello, P. Amato, orch (r1909) (5/94) (PEAR) Ⓓ [4] **GEMMCDS9073(2)**
10c E. Caruso, orch (r1910) (RCA) Ⓓ **09026 61242-2**
10c M. Gilion, orch (r c1909) (BONG) Ⓓ **GB1076-2**
10c E. Caruso, orch (r1910) (5/89) (PEAR) Ⓓ **GEMMCD9309**
10c F. Merli, orch, L. Molajoli (r1927) (1/91) (PREI) Ⓓ **89026**
10c E. Caruso, orch (r1910) (3/91) (PEAR) Ⓓ [3] **EVC2**
10c E. Caruso, orch (r1910) (7/91) (RCA) Ⓓ [12] **GD60495(3)**
10c G. Zenatello, orch, V. Bellezza (pp1926) (7/92) (PEAR) Ⓓ [3] **GEMMCDS9925(2)**
10c G.B. de Negri, anon (r1902) (11/92) (MEMO) Ⓓ [2] **HR4408/9(1)**
10c A. Paoli, anon (r1907) (11/92) (MEMO) Ⓓ [2] **HR4408/9(2)**
10c G. Zenatello, orch (r1909) (12/93) (SYMP) Ⓓ **SYMCD1148**
10c E. Caruso, orch (r1910) (9/94) (NIMB) Ⓓ **NI7856**
10c L. Escalais, anon (r1906: Fr) (12/94) (SYMP) Ⓓ **SYMCD1128**
10c, 23. G.B. de Negri, anon (r1902) (12/89) (SYMP) Ⓓ **SYMCD1065**
10c, 23. G.B. De Negri, anon (r1902) (4/94) (EMI) Ⓓ [3] **CHS7 64860-2(1)**
11. T. Ruffo, orch, J. Pasternack (r1920) (PEAR) Ⓓ **GEMMCD9088**
11. A. Granforte, orch, G.W. Byng (r1926) (PREI) Ⓓ **89105**
11. H. Schlusnus, orch (r1925: Ger) (PREI) Ⓓ **89110**
11. T. Gobbi, RPO, A. Erede (r1948) (10/89) (EMI) Ⓓ **CDM7 63109-2**
11. T. Ruffo, orch, J. Pasternack (r1920) (11/90) (NIMB) Ⓓ **NI7810** (NIMB) ▭ **NC7810**
11. M. Sammarco, orch (r1908) (7/92) (PEAR) Ⓓ [3] **GEMMCDS9924(2)**
11. V. Maurel, anon (r1904) (7/92) (PEAR) Ⓓ [3] **GEMMCDS9923(1)**
11. V. Maurel, anon (r1903) (10/92) (SYMP) Ⓓ **SYMCD1101**
11. T. Ruffo, orch (r1920) (2/93) (PREI) Ⓓ [3] **89303(1)**
11. M. Ancona, orch (r1907) (7/93) (NIMB) Ⓓ [2] **NI7840/1**
11. V. Maurel, anon (r1904) (4/94) (EMI) Ⓓ [3] **CHS7 64860-2(1)**
11. V. Maurel, anon (r1905) (12/94) (SYMP) Ⓓ **SYMCD1128**
11, 12a, 12b, 12c J. Vickers, T. Gobbi, Rome Op Orch, T. Serafin (r1960) (RCA) Ⓓ **09026 62689-2**
12a-c C. Bergonzi, D. Fischer-Dieskau, BRSO, J. López-Cobos (ORFE) Ⓓ **C028821A**
12a-c G. Taddei, P. Domingo, Vienna St Op Orch, A. Fischer (pp1982) (ACAN) Ⓓ **49 402**
12a-c E. Caruso, T. Ruffo, orch, W.B. Rogers (r1914) (RCA) Ⓓ **09026 61242-2**
12a-c J. Björling, R. Merrill, RCA Victor SO, R. Cellini (2/89) (RCA) Ⓓ **GD87799** (RCA) ▭ **GK87799**
12b, 12c P. Domingo, S. Milnes, LSO, A. Guadagno (RCA) Ⓓ [2] **GD60866** (RCA) ▭ [2] **GK60866**
12b, 12c P. Domingo, S. Milnes, LSO, A. Guadagno (RCA) Ⓓ **09026 62699-2** (RCA) ▭ **09026 62699-4**
12b, 12c H. Schlusnus, R. Hutt, orch (r1921: Ger) (PREI) Ⓓ **89110**
12b, 12c P. Domingo, S. Milnes, LSO, A. Guadagno (r1970) (RCA) Ⓓ **09026 62595-2**
12c R. Stracciari, N. Fusati, orch (r1928) (PEAR) Ⓓ **GEMMCD9178**
12c E. Caruso, T. Ruffo, orch (r1914) (5/89) (PEAR) Ⓓ **GEMMCD9309**
12c A. Pertile, B. Franci, La Scala Orch, C. Sabajno (r1928) (9/90) (PREI) Ⓓ **89007**
12c E. Caruso, T. Ruffo, orch, W.B. Rogers (r1914) (11/90) (NIMB) Ⓓ **NI7810** (NIMB) ▭ **NC7810**
12c E. Caruso, T. Ruffo, orch, W.B. Rogers (r1914) (7/91) (RCA) Ⓓ [12] **GD60495(5)**
12c E. Caruso, T. Ruffo, orch, W.B. Rogers (r1914) (10/91) (PEAR) Ⓓ [3] **EVC3(1)**
12c G. Zenatello, P. Amato, orch (r1909) (12/93) (SYMP) Ⓓ **SYMCD1148**
12c R. Vinay, G. Valdengo, A. Toscanini, NBC SO (r1947) (4/94) (RCA) Ⓓ [6] **09026 61580-2(6)**
12c T. Ralf, J. Herrmann, Saxon St Orch, K. Böhm (r1941: Ger) (10/94) (PREI) Ⓓ **89077**
14a, 14b G. Cigna, A. Pertile, La Scala Orch, A. Erede (r1942) (11/90) (LYRC) Ⓓ **SRO805**
15. G. Zenatello, orch (r1908) (7/92) (PEAR) Ⓓ [3] **GEMMCDS9924(2)**
15. R. Zanelli, orch, J. Barbirolli (r1928) (7/92) (PEAR) Ⓓ [3] **GEMMCDS9926(1)**
15. L. Escalais, anon (r1905) (12/93) (SYMP) Ⓓ **SYMCD1126**
15. L. Escalais, anon (Fr: r1906) (12/93) (SYMP) Ⓓ **SYMCD1126**
15, 23. C. Bergonzi, New Philh, N. Santi (PHIL) Ⓓ [3] **432 486-2PM3**
15, 23. A. Paoli, orch (r1911) (PREI) Ⓓ **89998**
15, 23. J. Vickers, Rome Op Orch, T. Serafin (r1961) (VAI) Ⓓ **VAIA1016**
15, 23. L. Melchior, New SO, J. Barbirolli (r1930: Ger) (PREI) Ⓓ **89086**
15, 23. F. Merli, orch, L. Molajoli (r1935) (PREI) Ⓓ **89091**
15, 23. M. Lorenz, Vienna St Op Orch, K. Böhm (pp1942: Ger) (PREI) Ⓓ [2] **90230**
15, 23. L. Melchior, New SO, J. Barbirolli (Ger: r1930) (8/88) (DANA) Ⓓ [2] **DACOCD315/6**
15, 23. G. Zenatello, orch, Rosario Bourdon (r1928) (11/91) (CLUB) Ⓓ **CL99-025**
15, 23. G. Zenatello, orch, Rosario Bourdon (r1928) (11/91) (PREI) Ⓓ **89038**
15, 23. G. Zenatello, orch (r1908) (12/93) (SYMP) Ⓓ **SYMCD1148**
15, 23. G. Zenatello, orch (r1908) (5/94) (PEAR) Ⓓ [4] **GEMMCDS9073(1)**
15, 23. G. Zenatello, orch, B. Reibold (r1928) (5/94) (PEAR) Ⓓ [4] **GEMMCDS9074(2)**
15, 23. G. Zenatello, orch (r1916) (5/94) (PEAR) Ⓓ [4] **GEMMCDS9074(2)**
15, 23. T. Ralf, Berlin St Op Orch, H.U. Müller (r1941: Ger) (10/94) (PREI) Ⓓ **89077**
16a, 23. L. Tibbett, G. Martinelli, N. Massue, orch, W. Pelletier (r1939) (7/92) (PEAR) Ⓓ [3] **GEMMCDS9926(2)**
18c, 20c E. Burzio, orch (r c1907) (1/91) (CLUB) Ⓓ [2] **CL99-587/8**
19. Bologna Teatro Comunale Orch, R. Chailly (DECC) Ⓓ **436 475-2DM**
19. LSO, A. de Almeida (r1972) (PHIL) Ⓓ [2] **442 550-2PM2**
19. NY Met Op Orch, James Levine (r1992) (6/94) (SONY) Ⓓ **SK52489**
20a Sofia SO, V. Stefanov (LASE) Ⓓ **15 519** (LASE) ▭ **79 519**
20a-c, 21. M. Major, M. Findley, NZ SO, J. Matheson (KIWI) Ⓓ **CDTRL075**
20a, 20b, 20c, 21. L. Price, C. Vozza, RCA Italiana Op Orch, F. Molinari-Pradelli (12/92) (RCA) Ⓓ [4] **09026 61236-2**
20b R. Tebaldi, NY Met Op Orch, F. Stiedry (pp1955) (MEMO) Ⓓ [2] **HR4235/6**
20b, 20c J. Sutherland, ROHO, F. Molinari-Pradelli (1/90) (DECC) Ⓓ [2] **425 493-2DM2**
20b, 20c R. Scotto, National PO, James Levine (r1978) (4/94) (RCA) Ⓓ [6] **09026 61580-2(8)**
20b, 20c, 21. L. Price, RCA Italiana Op Orch, F. Molinari-Pradelli (RCA) Ⓓ **RD87016**
20b, 20c, 21. M. Freni, S. Malagù, VPO, H. von Karajan (pp1970) (MEMO) Ⓓ [2] **HR4277/8**
20b, 20c, 21. F. Weathers, Vienna Op Orch, A. Quadri (DECC) Ⓓ **433 624-2DSP**
20b, 20c, 21. R. Tebaldi, L. Ribacchi, Santa Cecilia Academy Orch, A. Erede (r1954) (DECC) Ⓓ **440 408-2DM**
20b, 20c, 21. R. Tebaldi, A. R. Satre, VPO, H. von Karajan (r1961) (DECC) Ⓓ **443 377-2DM**
20b, 20c, 21. M. Callas, Paris Cons, N. Rescigno (9/87) (EMI) Ⓓ **CDC7 47943-2**
20b, 20c, 21. R. Tebaldi, A.R. Satre, VPO, H. von Karajan (8/91) (DECC) Ⓓ [2] **430 481-2DX2**
20c R. Crespin, ROHO, E. Downes (r1961) (DECC) Ⓓ **433 442-2DA**
20c R. Tebaldi, Santa Cecilia Academy Orch, A. Erede (BELA) Ⓓ **450 133-2** (BELA) ▭ **450 133-4**
20c M. Seinemeyer, orch, F. Weissmann (r1926: Ger) (PEAR) Ⓓ **GEMMCD9082**
20c R. Ponselle, orch, Rosario Bourdon (r1924) (1/90) (RCA) Ⓓ **GD87810**
20c Lotte Lehmann, Berlin St Op Orch, G. Szell (Ger: r1924) (6/92) (PREI) Ⓓ [3] **89302**
20c N. Melba, orch, V. Bellezza (pp1926) (7/92) (PEAR) Ⓓ [3] **GEMMCDS9925(2)**
20c, 21. A. Tomowa-Sintow, Sofia PO, R. Raichev (r1970s) (FORL) Ⓓ **UCD16742**
20c, 21. J. Barstow, ENO Orch, M. Elder (1/89) (TER) Ⓓ **CDVIR8307** (1/89) (TER) ▭ **ZCVIR8307**
20c, 21. R. Ponselle, orch, Rosario Bourdon (r1924) (10/89) (NIMB) Ⓓ **NI7805** (NIMB) ▭ **NC7805**
20c, 21. T. Lemnitz, Berlin St Op Orch, B. Seidler-Winkler (Ger: r1938) (10/90) (PREI) Ⓓ **89025**
20c, 21. E. Norena, orch, F. Ruhlmann (r1938) (3/91) (PREI) Ⓓ **89041**
20c, 21. D. Giannini, La Scala Orch, C. Sabajno (r1932) (4/93) (PREI) Ⓓ **89044**
20c, 21. R. Ponselle, orch, Rosario Bourdon (r1924) (11/94) (ROMO) Ⓓ [2] **81006-2**
20c, 21. N. Melba, orch, W.B. Rogers (r1909) (5/95) (ROMO) Ⓓ [3] **81011-2(1)**
20c, 21. N. Melba, orch, W.B. Rogers (r1910) (5/95) (ROMO) Ⓓ [3] **81011-2(2)**
20c, 21. E. Rethberg, Victor SO, Rosario Bourdon (r1930) (10/95) (ROMO) Ⓓ [2] **81014-2**
20, 21. M. Caballé, E. Bainbridge, RPO, A. Guadagno (10/88) (EMI) Ⓓ **CDM7 69500-2**
20, 21. V. de los Angeles, G. Borelli, Rome Op Orch, G. Morelli (r1954) (8/90) (EMI) Ⓓ **CDH7 63495-2**
21. R. Ponselle, orch (r1922) (PEAR) Ⓓ [2] **GEMMCDS9964**
21. M. Caballé, RPO, A. Guadagno (CFP) Ⓓ **CD-CFP4575** (CFP) ▭ **TC-CFP4575**
21. R. Scotto, National PO, G. Gavazzeni (SONY) Ⓓ **SBK46548** (SONY) ▭ **SBT46548**
21. M. Caballé, NY Met Op Orch, Z. Mehta (pp1967) (MEMO) Ⓓ [2] **HR4279/80**
21. S. Murphy, WNO Orch, J. Smith (COLL) Ⓓ **Coll3025-2**
21. E. Grümmer, Berlin Deutsche Op Orch, R. Kraus (r1957: Ger) (CFP) Ⓓ **CD-CFP4616**
21. M. Hayward Segal, K. Bowyer (r1993) (SYMP) Ⓓ **SYMCD1175**
21. C. Muzio, orch (r1917) (PEAR) Ⓓ **GEMMCD9143**
21. M. Favero, orch, A. Sabino (r1941) (VAI) Ⓓ **VAIA1071**
21. M. Favero, orch, A. Sabino (r1941) (BONG) Ⓓ **GB1078-2**
21. V. de los Angeles, Rome Op Orch, G. Morelli (r1954) (EMI) Ⓓ **CDM5 65579-2**
21. E. Burzio, orch (r1913) (1/91) (CLUB) Ⓓ [2] **CL99-587/8**
21. E. Eames, orch (r1906) (7/92) (PEAR) Ⓓ [3] **GEMMCDS9923(1)**
21. M. Gauci, Belgian Rad & TV Orch, A. Rahbari (11/92) (NAXO) Ⓓ **8 550606**
21. N. Melba, orch, W.B. Rogers (r1910) (9/93) (RCA) Ⓓ **09026 61412-2**
21. E. Eames, orch (r1906: two vers) (11/93) (ROMO) Ⓓ [2] **81001-2**
21. K. Ricciarelli, Rome PO, G. Gavazzeni (r1972) (4/94) (RCA) Ⓓ [6] **09026 61580-2(8)**
21. A. Roocroft, LPO, F. Welser-Möst (10/94) (EMI) Ⓓ **CDC5 55090-2** (10/94) (EMI) ▭ **EL5 55090-4**
21. C. Muzio, orch (r1917) (1/95) (ROMO) Ⓓ [2] **81010-2**
21. E. Rethberg, orch (r1929) (2/95) (ROMO) Ⓓ [2] **81012-2**
21-23. Cincinnati Pops, E. Kunzel (r1994; arr & orch Kunzel & Beck) (TELA) Ⓓ **CD80364** (TELA) ▭ **CS30364**
23. J. Carreras, Barcelona SO, G. Navarro (11/92) (RCA) ▭ **09026 61204-4**
23. G. Martinelli, NY Met Op Orch, W. Pelletier (r1939) (MMOI) Ⓓ **CDMOIR405** (MMOI) ▭ **CMOIR405**
23. M. Lanza, Rome Op Orch, C. Callinicos (r1957) (RCA) Ⓓ **GD60516**
23. L. Slezak, Berlin St Op Orch, M. Gurlitt (r1928: Ger) (PREI) Ⓓ [2] **89203**
23. J. Carreras, Barcelona SO, G. Navarro (RCA) **ꝏ 09026 61204-5**

23. M. del Monaco, Santa Cecilia Academy Chor, Santa Cecilia Academy Orch, A. Erede (r1954) (DECC) ⦶ **440 407-2DM**
23. M. del Monaco, Milan SO, A. Quadri (r1951) (TEST) ⦶ **SBT1039**
23. M. del Monaco, Santa Cecilia Academy Chor, Santa Cecilia Academy Orch, A. Erede (r1954) (DECC) ⦶ **443 379-2DM**
23. P. Domingo, ROHO, J. Barker (pp1988) (9/89) (EMI) ⦶ **CDC7 49811-2**
23. F. Völker, Berlin St Op Orch, H. Weigert (r1930: Ger) (2/90) (PREI) ⦶ **89005**
23. G. Zenatello, L. Cilla, E. Cotreil, M. Sampieri, orch, V. Bellezza (pp1926) (7/92) (PEAR) ⦶ [3] **GEMMCDS9926(1)**
23. N. Zerola, orch (r1908) (11/92) (MEMO) ⦶ [2] **HR4408/9(2)**
23. A. Aramburo, anon (r1902) (11/92) (MEMO) ⦶ [2] **HR4408/9(1)**
23. G. Zenatello, anon (r1907) (12/93) (SYMP) ⦶ **SYMCD1148**
23. F. Merli, orch, L. Molajoli (r1935) (4/94) (EMI) ⦶ [3] **CHS7 64864-2(2)**
23. G. Oxilia, anon (r1902) (4/94) (EMI) ⦶ [3] **CHS7 64860-2(1)**
23. F. Tamagno, anon (r1904) (4/94) (EMI) ⦶ [3] **CHS7 64860-2(1)**
23. G. Zenatello, anon (r1907) (5/94) (PEAR) ⦶ [4] **GEMMCDS9073(1)**
23. G. Zenatello, orch (r1911) (5/94) (PEAR) ⦶ [4] **GEMMCDS9074(1)**
23. P. Domingo, ROHO, J. Barker (pp1988) (6/94) (EMI) ⦶ **CDC5 55017-2**
23. H. Roswaenge, BPO, E. Orthmann (r1933: Ger) (4/95) (PREI) ⦶ [2] **89209**

Rigoletto– opera: 3 acts (1851—Venice) (Lib. F Piave)

EXCERPTS: 1. Prelude. ACT 1: 2a. Della mia bella incognita borghese; 2b. Questa o quella; 3. Partite? Crudele!; 4. Gran nuova! gran nuova!; 5. Ch'io gli parli; 6. Quel vecchio maledivami; 7. Pari siamo!; 8. Figlia!...Mio padre!; 9. Ah! veglia, o donna; 10a. Signor nè principe; 10b. T'amo! T'amo; 10c. È il sol dell'anima; 10d. Addio, addio; 11a. Gualtier Maldè; 11b. Caro nome; 12a. Silenzio; 12b. Zitti, zitti. ACT 2: 13a. Ella mi fu rapita!; 13b. Parmi veder le lagrime; 13c. Scorrendo uniti remota; 13d. Possente amor mi chiama; 14a. Povero Rigoletto!; 14b. Cortigiani, vil razza dannata; 15a. Mio padre!...Tuttle le feste al tempio; 15b. Ah! Solo per me; 15c. Piangi, fanciulla; 15d. Sì, vendetta. ACT 3: 16. E l'ami?; 17. La donna è mobile; 18a. Un dì, se ben rammentomi; 18b. Bella figlia dell'amore; 19a. M'odi! ritorna a casa; 19b. Ah, più non ragioni!; 19c. Storm Music; 20. Della vendetta alfin giunge l'istante; 21a. Chi è la?; 21b. V'ho ingannato; 21c. Lassù in cielo. APPENDIX: 22. Prends pité de sa jeunesse (aria—Maddalena: comp for Paris production).

Rigoletto T. Gobbi
Gilda L. Pagliughi
Duke M. Filippeschi
Sparafucile G. Neri
Maddalena A.M. Canali
Monterone M. Giorda
Borsa R. Bruni
Marullo V. Gottardi
Count Ceprano G. Varni
Rome Op Chor, Rome Op Orch, T. Serafin, C. Gallone (r1947)
(7/90) (IMP) ■ **SL1056**

Rigoletto C. MacNeil
Gilda R. Grist
Duke N. Gedda
Sparafucile A. Ferrin
Maddalena A. di Stasio
Monterone R. Raimondi
Giovanna L. Leoni
Borsa F. Ricciardi
Marullo B. di Bella
Countess Ceprano M. Fiorentini
Count Ceprano A. Giacomotti
Rome Op Chor, Rome Op Orch, F. Molinari-Pradelli (r1967)
(CFP) ⦶ [2] **CD-CFPD4700**
(3/87) (CFP) ▭ [2] **TC-CFPD4700**

Rigoletto R. Merrill
Gilda R. Peters
Duke J. Björling
Sparafucile G. Tozzi
Maddalena A.M. Rota
Monterone V. Tatozzi
Giovanna S. Celli
Borsa T. Frascati
Marullo A. la Porta
Countess Ceprano L. Grandi
Count Ceprano L. Monreale
Page S. Chissari
Usher A. Mineo
Rome Op Chor, Rome Op Orch, J. Perlea (r1956)
(RCA) ⦶ [2] **GD60172**

Rigoletto R. Massard
Gilda R. Doria
Duke A. Vanzo
Sparafucile A. Legros
Maddalena D. Scharley
Monterone J-P. Laffage
Giovanna; Page A. Adam
Borsa C. Rouquetty
Marullo M. Forel
Countess Ceprano M. Dupré
Count Ceprano J. Scellier
chor, orch, J. Etcheverry (French: r1961)
(MSCM) ⦶ [2] **MM30323**

Rigoletto K. Paskalis
Gilda R. Scotto
Duke L. Pavarotti
Sparafucile P. Washington
Maddalena B. Bortoluzzi
Monterone P. Clabassi
Giovanna C. Vozza
Borsa F. Iacopucci
Marullo A. la Porta
Countess Ceprano N. Pragranza
Count Ceprano G. Ciavola
Page F. Carotenuto
Usher E. Titta
Rome Op Chor, Rome Op Orch, C.M. Giulini (pp1966)
(BUTT) ⦶ [2] **BMCD001**
(BUTT) ▭ [2] **BMK001**

Rigoletto E. Sundquist
Gilda E. Prytz
Duke J. Björling
Sparafucile S-E. Jacobsson
Maddalena K. Meyer
Monterone G. Svedenbrant
Giovanna B. Ericson
Borsa O. Sivall
Marullo C-A. Hallgren
Countess Ceprano J. Garellick
Count Ceprano I. Wixell
Page C. Nilsson
Usher B. Alstergård
Stockholm Royal Op Chor, Stockholm Royal Op Orch, K. Bendix (pp1957)
(BLUE) ⦶ [2] **ABCD044**

Rigoletto C. MacNeil
Gilda J. Sutherland
Duke R. Cioni
Sparafucile C. Siepi
Maddalena S. Malagù
Monterone F. Corena
Giovanna A. di Stasio
Borsa A. Mercuriali
Marullo G. Morresi
Countess Ceprano L. Valle
Count Ceprano G. Corti
Page M. Fiori
Santa Cecilia Academy Chor, Santa Cecilia Academy Orch, N. Sanzogno (r1961)
(DECC) ⦶ [2] **443 853-2DF2**

Rigoletto L. Piazza
Gilda L. Pagliughi
Duke T. Folgar
Sparafucile S. Baccaloni
Maddalena V. de Cristoff
Monterone; Marullo A. Baracchi
Giovanna; Countess Ceprano L. Brambilla
Borsa G. Nessi
Count Ceprano G. Menni
La Scala Chor, La Scala Orch, C. Sabajno (r1927/8)
(VAI) ⦶ [2] **VAIA1097**

Rigoletto L. Piazza
Gilda L. Pagliughi
Duke T. Folgar
Sparafucile S. Baccaloni
Maddalena V. De Cristoff
Monterone; Marullo A. Baracchi
Giovanna; Countess Ceprano L. Brambilla
Borsa G. Nessi
Count Ceprano G. Menni
La Scala Chor, La Scala Orch, C. Sabajno (r1927/8)
(PEAR) ⦶ [2] **GEMMCDS9180**

Rigoletto R. Bruson
Gilda A. Rost
Duke R. Alagna
Sparafucile D. Kavrakos
Maddalena M. Pentcheva
Monterone G. Giuseppini
Giovanna A. Trevisan
Borsa E. Gavazzi
Marullo S. Sammaritano
Countess Ceprano N. Zanini
Count Ceprano A. de Gobbi
Page M. Laurenza
Usher E. Panariello
La Scala Chor, La Scala Orch, R. Muti (pp1994)
(SONY) ⦶ [2] **S2K66314**

Rigoletto S. Milnes
Gilda J. Sutherland
Duke L. Pavarotti
Sparafucile M. Talvela
Maddalena H. Tourangeau
Monterone C. Grant
Giovanna G. Knight
Borsa R. Cassinelli
Marullo C. du Plessis
Countess Ceprano K. Te Kanawa
Count Ceprano J. Gibbs
Page J. Clément
Ambrosian Op Chor, LSO, R. Bonynge
(7/85) (DECC) ⦶ [2] **414 269-2DH2**

Rigoletto P. Cappuccilli
Gilda I. Cotrubas
Duke P. Domingo
Sparafucile N. Ghiaurov
Maddalena E. Obraztsova
Monterone K. Moll
Giovanna H. Schwarz
Borsa W. Gullino
Marullo L. de Corato
Countess Ceprano O. Fredricks
Count Ceprano D. Sagemüller
Page A. Michael
Vienna St Op Chor, VPO, C.M. Giulini
(11/85) (DG) ⦶ [2] **415 288-2GH2**

Rigoletto R. Bruson
Gilda E. Gruberová
Duke N. Shicoff
Sparafucile R. Lloyd
Maddalena B. Fassbaender
Monterone K. Rydl
Giovanna J. Rigby
Borsa W. Matteuzzi
Marullo A. Gabba
Countess Ceprano; Page M.G. Pittavini
Count Ceprano G. Moses
Santa Cecilia Academy Chor, Santa Cecilia Academy Orch, G. Sinopoli
(1/86) (PHIL) ⦶ [2] **412 592-2PH2**

Rigoletto T. Gobbi
Gilda M. Callas
Duke G. di Stefano
Sparafucile N. Zaccaria
Maddalena A. Lazzarini
Monterone P. Clabassi
Giovanna G. Gerbino
Borsa R. Ercolani
Marullo W. Dickie
Countess Ceprano E. Galassi
Count Ceprano C. Forti
Page L. Mandelli
Usher V. Tatozzi
La Scala Chor, La Scala Orch, T. Serafin (r1955)
(2/87) (EMI) ⦶ [2] **CDS7 47469-8**

Rigoletto R. Merrill
Gilda A. Moffo
Duke Alfredo Kraus
Sparafucile E. Flagello
Maddalena R. Elias
Monterone D. Ward
Giovanna A. di Stasio
Borsa P. de Palma
Marullo R. Kerns
Countess Ceprano C. Vozza
Count Ceprano M. Rinaudo
Page T. Toscano
Usher E. Titta
RCA Italiana Op Chor, RCA Italiana Op Orch, G. Solti
(9/88) (RCA) ⦶ [2] **GD86506**

Rigoletto I. Wixell
Gilda E. Gruberová
Duke L. Pavarotti
Sparafucile F. Furlanetto
Maddalena V. Vergara
Monterone I. Wixell
Giovanna F. Barbieri
Borsa R. Corazza
Marullo B. Weikl
Countess Ceprano K. Kuhlmann

Count Ceprano R. Bracht
Vienna St Op Chor, VPO, R. Chailly, J-P. Ponnelle
(10/88) (DECC) ◖ [2] **071 401-1DH2**
(DECC) ▣ **071 401-3DH**
Rigoletto G. Zancanaro
Gilda D. Dessì
Duke V. La Scola
Sparafucile P. Burchuladze
Maddalena M. Senn
Monterone G. Surian
Giovanna F. Franci
Borsa E. Gavazzi
Marullo L. Gallo
Countess Ceprano N. Curiel
Count Ceprano M. Pertusi
Page V. Esposito
Usher E. Panariello
La Scala Chor, La Scala Orch, R. Muti (r1988)
(11/89) (EMI) ① [2] **CDS7 49605-2**
Rigoletto L. Nucci
Gilda J. Anderson
Duke L. Pavarotti
Sparafucile N. Ghiaurov
Maddalena S. Verrett
Monterone N. de Carolis
Giovanna V. Mosca
Borsa P. de Palma
Marullo R. Scaltriti
Countess Ceprano A.C. Antonacci
Count Ceprano C. de Bortoli
Page M. Laurenza
Bologna Teatro Comunale Chor, Bologna Teatro Comunale Orch, R. Chailly
(1/90) (DECC) ① [2] **425 864-2DH2**
Rigoletto D. Fischer-Dieskau
Gilda R. Scotto
Duke C. Bergonzi
Sparafucile I. Vinco
Maddalena F. Cossotto
Monterone L. Testi
Giovanna M. Fiorentini
Borsa P. de Palma
Marullo V. Carbonari
Countess Ceprano; Page C. Alda
Count Ceprano A. Giacomotti
Usher G. Morresi
La Scala Chor, La Scala Orch, R. Kubelík (r1964)
(9/91) (DG) ① [2] **437 704-2GX2**
Rigoletto E. Tumagian
Gilda A. Ferrarini
Duke Y. Ramiro
Sparafucile J. Špaček
Monterone L. Neshyba
Maddalena J. Saparová
Giovanna A. Michalková
Borsa J. Abel
Marullo P. Šubert
Countess Ceprano I. Neshybová
Count Ceprano R. Szücs
Slovak Phil Chor, Bratislava RSO, A. Rahbari
(3/92) (NAXO) ① [2] **8 660013/4**
Rigoletto A. Agache
Gilda L. Vaduva
Duke R. Leech
Sparafucile S. Ramey
Maddalena J. Larmore
Monterone A. Miles
Giovanna P. Bardon
Borsa B. Banks
Marullo P. Sidhom
Countess Ceprano R. Evans
Count Ceprano G. Moses
Page P. Bradbury
Usher F. Visentin
WNO Chor, WNO Orch, C. Rizzi (r1993)
(11/93) (TELD) ① [2] **4509-90851-2**
Rigoletto A. Protti
Gilda H. Gueden
Duke M. del Monaco
Sparafucile C. Siepi
Maddalena G. Simionato
Monterone F. Corena
Giovanna L. Ribacchi
Borsa P. de Palma
Countess Ceprano M. L. Castelli
Count Ceprano D. Caselli
Page L. Rossi
Usher P. Poldi
Santa Cecilia Academy Chor, Santa Cecilia Academy Orch, A. Erede (r1954)
(7/94) (LOND) ① [2] **440 242-2LF2**
Rigoletto H. Hasslo
Gilda M. Hallin
Duke N. Gedda
Sparafucile A. Tyrén
Monterone G. Svedenbrant
Maddalena K. Meyer
Giovanna B. Ericson
Borsa O. Sivall
Marullo A. Näslund
Countess Ceprano I. Kjellgren
Count Ceprano I. Wixell
Page B. Nordin
Stockholm Royal Op Chor, Stockholm Royal Op Orch, S. Ehrling (pp1959)
(8/94) (BIS) ① [2] **BIS-CD296**
Rigoletto B. Weikl
Gilda L. Popp
Duke G. Aragall
Sparafucile J-H. Rootering
Maddalena K. Takács
Monterone A. Malta
Giovanna H. Jungwirth
Borsa A. Ionita
Marullo R. Riener
Countess Ceprano R. Freyer
Count Ceprano G. Auer
Page K. Hautermann
Bavarian Rad Chor, Munich RO, L. Gardelli (r1984)
(10/95) (RCA) ① [2] **74321 25286-2**
Act 3. L. Pavarotti, L. Nucci, C. Studer, N. Ghiaurov, B. Svendén, NY Met Op Chor, NY Met Op Orch, James Levine
(DG) ◖ [2] **072 428-1GH2**
(DG) ▣ **072 428-3GH**
Excs P. Cappuccilli, M. Rinaldi, L. Pavarotti, A. Lazzarini, N. Zaccaria, P. Clabassi, M. Benetti, T. Rovetta, L. Monreale, F. Iacopucci, L. Stabile, Turin RAI Chor, Turin RAI Orch, M. Rossi (pp1967) (BUTT) ① **BMCD018**
(BUTT) ▭ **BMK018**
Excs G. Zancanaro, D. Dessì, V. La Scola, P. Burchuladze, La Scala Chor, La Scala Orch, R. Muti (EMI) ① **CDC7 54495-2**
Excs E. Johnson, J. Drake (arr Bassi)
(ASV) ① **CDDCA800**
(ASV) ▭ **ZCDCA800**
1. Sofia SO, V. Stefanov (LASE) ① **15 519**
(LASE) ▭ **79 519**
1. Mexico St SO, E. Bátiz (r1990s)
(ASV) ① **CDDCA856**
(ASV) ▭ **ZCDCA856**
1. Hungarian St Op Orch, P.G. Morandi (r1994)
(NAXO) ① **8 553089**
1. BPO, H. von Karajan
(10/87) (DG) ① **419 622-2GH**
1. BPO, H. von Karajan
(1/95) (DG) ① **439 972-2GGA2**
1, 2a, 2b, 4, 5, 7, 8, 9(pt), 10a, 10b, 11a, 11b, 12b, 13a, 13b, 13d, 14a, 14b, 15a(pt), 15c(pt), 15d, 17, 18a, 18b, 21b A. Agache, R. Leech, L. Vaduva, J. Larmore, S. Ramey, WNO Chor, WNO Orch, C. Rizzi (r1993)
(TELD) ① **4509-97508-2**
1, 2b, 7, 8, 11a, 11b, 13a, 13b, 14a, 14b, 15a, 15d, 17, 18a, 18b, 21b, 21c P. Domingo, P. Cappuccilli, I. Cotrubas, N. Ghiaurov, E. Obraztsova, H. Schwarz, K. Moll, Vienna St Op Chor, VPO, C.M. Giulini (DG) ① **423 114-2GH**
1, 2b, 7-9, 10c, 11a, 11b, 12b, 13a, 13b, 14a, 14b, 15a-d, 17, 18a, 18b, 21b, 21c R. Merrill, A. Moffo, Alfredo Kraus, R. Elias, E. Flagello, RCA Italiana Op Chor, RCA Italiana Op Orch, G. Solti
(RCA) ① **GD60203**
(RCA) ▭ **GK60203**
1, 2b, 17. P. Dvorský, Bratislava RSO, O. Lenárd
(5/92) (NAXO) ① **8 550343**
2a, 2b, 10a-d, 13a, 13b, 17, 18a, 18b Alfredo Kraus, Trieste Teatro Verdi Orch, F. Molinari-Pradelli (pp1961) (MEMO) ① [2] **HR4233/4**
2a, 2b, 10a, 10b, 10c, 13a, 13b, 17, 18a, 18b J. Björling, E. Prytz, B. Ericson, K. Meyer, O. Sivall, E. Sundquist, Stockholm Royal Op Orch, K. Bendix (pp1957) (BLUE) ① **ABCD002**
2a, 2b, 13a, 13b, 17. M. Lanza, RCA Victor Orch, C. Callinicos (r1950) (RCA) ① **GD60049**
(RCA) ▭ **GK60049**
2b T. Schipa, orch (r1926)
(PEAR) ① **GEMMCD9364**
2b P. Domingo, New Philh, L. Price
(RCA) ① **GD84265**
2b L. Pavarotti, LSO, R. Bonynge
(DECC) ① **430 470-2DH**
(DECC) ▭ **430 470-4DH**
2b P. Domingo, New Philh, N. Santi
(RCA) ① [2] **GD60866**
(RCA) ▭ [2] **GK60866**
2b L. Pavarotti, LSO, R. Bonynge
(DECC) ① **433 069-2DWO**
(DECC) ▭ **433 069-4DWO**
2b M. Lanza, RCA Victor Orch, C. Callinicos (r1950) (RCA) ① [3] **GD60889(2)**
2b A. Paoli, orch (r1909) (PREI) ① **89998**
2b J. Björling, orch, N. Grevillius (r1930: Swed)
(NIMB) ① **NI7835**
2b J. Schmidt, BPO, Berlin City Op Orch (r1931)
(RELI) ① **CR921036**
2b J. Björling, orch, N. Grevillius (r1930: Swed)
(PEAR) ① **GEMMCD9043**
2b J. McCormack, orch (r1913)
(ASV) ① **CDAJA5137**
(ASV) ▭ **ZCAJA5137**
2b F. de Lucia, orch (r1917)
(BONG) ① [2] **GB1064/5-2**
2b E. Caruso, S. Cottone (r1902)
(5/89) (EMI) ① **CDH7 61046-2**
2b E. Caruso, orch (r1908)
(10/89) (NIMB) ① **NI7803**
(NIMB) ▭ **NC7803**
2b T. Schipa, orch, Rosario Bourdon (r1926)
(10/90) (MSCM) ① [2] **MM30231**
(MSCM) ▭ [2] **MM40086**
2b F. Marconi, anon (r1907)
(10/90) (SYMP) ① **SYMCD1069**
2b F. Marconi, S. Cottone (r1903)
(10/90) (SYMP) ① **SYMCD1069**
2b E. Caruso, S. Cottone (r1902)
(12/90) (PEAR) ① [3] **EVC1(1)**
2b E. Caruso, S. Cottone (r1902)
(7/91) (RCA) ① [12] **GD60495(1)**
2b A. Bonci, anon (r1905)
(7/92) (PEAR) ① [3] **GEMMCDS9923(2)**
2b A. Piccaver, orch (r1912)
(7/92) (PEAR) ① [3] **GEMMCDS9925(2)**
2b J. McCormack, orch (r1913)
(7/92) (PEAR) ① [3] **GEMMCDS9924(2)**
2b H. Lázaro, orch (r1916)
(11/92) (MEMO) ① [2] **HR4408/9(2)**
2b J. Björling, orch, N. Grevillius (r1944)
(10/93) (EMI) ① **CDH7 64707-2**
2b H. Lázaro, orch (r1911)
(4/94) (EMI) ① [3] **CHS7 64860-2(2)**
2b J. Björling, orch, N. Grevillius (r1941)
(9/94) (CONI) ① **CDHD214**
(9/94) (CONI) ▭ **MCHD214**
2b, 7, 8, 10c, 11a, 11b, 13b, 14a, 14b, 15a-c, 17, 18b, 21b, 21c S. Milnes, J. Sutherland, L. Pavarotti, M. Talvela, H. Tourangeau, G. Knight, J. Gibbs, C. du Plessis, R. Cassinelli, J. Clément, Ambrosian Op Chor, LSO, R. Bonynge
(DECC) ① **421 303-2DA**
(DECC) ▭ **421 303-4DA**
2b, 7, 8, 9, 10c, 11a, 11b, 13a-d, 14a, 14b, 15a, 17, 18a, 21b L. Pavarotti, L. Nucci, J. Anderson, N. Ghiaurov, S. Verrett, Bologna Teatro Comunale Chor, Bologna Teatro Comunale Orch, R. Chailly (r1988)
(DECC) ① **436 097-2DH**
2b, 7, 8, 9, 10c, 11a, 11b, 13a-d, 14a, 14b, 15a, 17, 18a, 21b L. Pavarotti, L. Nucci, J. Anderson, N. Ghiaurov, S. Verrett, Bologna Teatro Comunale Chor, Bologna Teatro Comunale Orch, R. Chailly (r1988)
(DECC) OO **436 097-5DH**
2b, 9(pt), 10b, 10c, 10d, 13a, 13b, 17. I. Kozlovsky, E. Shumskaya, USSR SO, Anon (cond) (r1930-50) (MYTO) ① **1MCD921.55**
2b, 10c P. Domingo, I. Cotrubas, VPO, C.M. Giulini (6/94) (BELA) ① **450 121-2**
(6/94) (BELA) ▭ **450 121-4**
2b, 11b, 17, 18a Cincinnati Pops, E. Kunzel (r1994; arr & orch Kunzel & Beck)
(TELA) ① **CD80364**
(TELA) ▭ **CS30364**
2b, 13a, 13b, 17. P. Domingo, P. Cappuccilli, N. Ghiaurov, VPO, C.M. Giulini
(DG) ▭ **419 091-4GW**
2b, 13a, 13b T. Schipa, orch, Anon (cond) (pp1928) (MEMO) ① [2] **HR4220/1**
2b, 13a, 13b, 17. C. Bergonzi, New Philh, N. Santi (PHIL) ① [3] **432 486-2PM3**
2b, 13a, 13b, 17. A. Cortis, La Scala Orch, C. Sabajno (r1930) (10/91) (PREI) ① **89043**
2b, 13a, 13b, 17. A. Cortis, La Scala Orch, C. Sabajno (r1930) (3/94) (NIMB) ① **NI7850**
2b, 13a, 13b, 17. L. Pavarotti, Turin SO, M. Rossi (pp1967)
(10/95) (RCA) ① **09026 68014-2**
2b, 13b, 17. A. Piccaver, orch (r1912)
(8/93) (PREI) ① **89060**
2b, 17. R. Tucker, Orch, E. Buckley (bp1963)
(VAI) ▣ **VAI69109**

2b, 17. T. Burke, orch (r1920/1) (PEAR) ⦶ **GEMMCD9411**
2b, 17. F. Wunderlich, Berlin SO, B. Klobučar (Ger) (EMI) ⦶ [3] **CZS7 62993-2**
2b, 17. L. Pavarotti, Orch (EDL) ⦶ **EDL2562-2** (EDL) ⊙ **EDL2562-1** ▭ **EDL2562-4**
2b, 17. E. Caruso, orch (r1908) (RCA) ⦶ **09026 61242-2**
2b, 17. J. Schmidt, BPO, Berlin City Op Orch (r1930: Ger) (RELI) ⦶ **CR921036**
2b, 17. R. Tucker, Naples San Carlo Op Orch, F. Molinari-Pradelli (PHIL) ⦶ **442 602-2PM** (PHIL) ▭ **442 602-4PM**
2b, 17. L. Pavarotti, Toscanini SO, E. Buckley (SONY) ⦶ **MDK47176** (SONY) ▭ **MDT47176**
2b, 17. A. Bonci, orch (r1913) (PEAR) ⦶ **GEMMCD9168**
2b, 17. L. Pavarotti, LSO, R. Bonynge (7/86) (DECC) ⦶ [2] **417 011-2DH2**
2b, 17. E. Caruso, orch (r1908) (5/89) (PEAR) ⦶ **GEMMCD9309**
2b, 17. R. Tauber, orch (Ger: r1927) (7/89) (PEAR) ⦶ **GEMMCD9327**
2b, 17. E. Caruso, anon (r1904) (12/90) (PEAR) ⦶ [3] **EVC1(1)**
2b, 17. L. Slezak, orch (Ger: r1907) (2/91) (PREI) ⦶ **89020**
2b, 17. E. Caruso, orch (r1908) (3/91) (PEAR) ⦶ [3] **EVC2**
2b, 17. E. Caruso, orch (r1908) (7/91) (RCA) ⦶ [12] **GD60495(2)**
2b, 17. E. Caruso, anon (r1904) (7/91) (RCA) ⦶ [12] **GD60495(1)**
2b, 17. H. Roswaenge, orch (r1928: Ger) (2/92) (PREI) ⦶ [2] **89201**
2b, 17. H. Nash, orch, C. Raybould (r1932: Eng) (2/95) (DUTT) ⦶ **CDLX7012**
6. G. Bechi, T. Pasero, Rome Op Orch, L. Ricci (r1943) (2/90) (PREI) ⦶ **89009**
6. A. Granforte, F. Zaccarini, La Scala Orch, C. Sabajno (r1930) (12/91) (PREI) ⦶ **89048**
6. C. Galeffi, E. Dominici, La Scala Orch, L. Molajoli (r1928) (2/92) (PREI) ⦶ **89040**
6. T. Pasero, G. Bechi, Rome Teatro Reale Orch, L. Ricci (r1943) (4/95) (PREI) ⦶ **89074**
7. A. Scotti, orch (r1906) (PEAR) ⦶ **GEMMCD9937**
7. T. Ruffo, orch, C. Sabajno (r1907) (PEAR) ⦶ **GEMMCD9088**
7. G. De Luca, anon (r1907) (PEAR) ⦶ [3] **GEMMCDS9159(1)**
7. T. Ruffo, orch, J. Pasternack (r1920) (11/90) (NIMB) ⦶ **NI7810** (NIMB) ▭ **NC7810**
7. C. Tagliabue, La Scala Orch, U. Berrettoni (r1946) (11/90) (PREI) ⦶ **89015**
7. A. Granforte, La Scala Orch, G. Nastrucci (r1930) (12/91) (PREI) ⦶ **89048**
7. C. Galeffi, La Scala Orch, L. Molajoli (r1926) (2/92) (PREI) ⦶ **89040**
7. M. Sammarco, orch (r1908) (7/92) (PEAR) ⦶ [3] **GEMMCDS9924(1)**
7. G. De Luca, anon (r1907) (7/92) (PEAR) ⦶ [3] **GEMMCDS9925(1)**
7. T. Ruffo, orch (r1908) (11/92) (MEMO) ⦶ [2] **HR4408/9(1)**
7. T. Ruffo, orch (r1920) (2/93) (PREI) ⦶ [3] **89303(1)**
7. T. Gobbi, Philh, W. Susskind (r1950) (8/93) (TEST) ⦶ **SBT1019**
7. C. Formichi, orch, A. Ketèlbey (r1924) (11/94) (PREI) ⦶ **89055**
7. C. Galeffi, orch (r1926) (10/95) (NIMB) ⦶ **NI7867**
7, 14b A. Sved, Berlin St Op Orch, C. Krauss (r1936) (PREI) ⦶ **89096**
7, 14b H. Schlusnus, Berlin St Op Orch, J. Heidenreich (r1927) (PREI) ⦶ [2] **89212**
7, 14b A. Granforte, orch, G.W. Byng (r1925) (PREI) ⦶ **89105**
7, 14b D. Fischer-Dieskau, BPO, A. Erede (r1959) (EMI) ⦶ [2] **CMS5 65621-2**
7, 14b E. Tumagian, Bratislava RSO, A. Rahbari (r1991) (12/94) (NAXO) ⦶ **8 550684**
7, 14b F.M. Bonini, anon (r1904/5) (12/94) (BONG) ⦶ **GB1043-2**
7, 14b, 15a-d, 18b L. Warren, A. Tokatyan, J. Dickenson, L. Alvary, L. Browning, chor, orch, W. Pelletier (r1940) (8/93) (VAI) ⦶ **VAIA1017**
7, 8(pt), 14b, 15b J. Schwarz, C. Dux, orch (Ger: r1916) (PREI) ⦶ **89033**
8(pt) J. Schwarz, C. Dux, orch (Ger: r1918) (PREI) ⦶ **89033**
8. P. Amato, F. Hempel, orch (r1914) (PREI) ⦶ **89064**
8(pt) L. Pons, G. De Luca, orch, W. Pelletier (r1940) (RCA) ⦶ **09026 61411-2**
8(pt) H. Schlusnus, S. Kurz, orch (r1923: Ger) (PREI) ⦶ **89110**
8. F. Hempel, P. Amato, orch (r1914) (3/94) (NIMB) ⦶ **NI7849**
8(pt) T. Ruffo, G. Finzi-Magrini, orch (r1912) (4/94) (EMI) ⦶ [3] **CHS7 64860-2(2)**
8. C. Formichi, I.M. Ferraris, orch (r1916) (11/94) (PREI) ⦶ **89055**
8-11. H. Schymberg, L. Warren, T. Altman, J. Peerce, NY Met Op Chor, NY Met Op Orch, C. Sodero (pp1947) (ALTN) ⦶ **CDAN3**
9. L. Pons, G. De Luca, orch, W. Pelletier (r1940) (PEAR) ⦶ [3] **GEMMCDS9159(2)**
9. A. Granforte, A. Saraceni, I. Mannarini, La Scala Orch, C. Sabajno (r1930) (12/91) (PREI) ⦶ **89048**
9, 15c A. Galli-Curci, G. De Luca, orch (r1927) (PEAR) ⦶ [3] **GEMMCDS9160(2)**
9, 15c A. Galli-Curci, G. De Luca, NY Met Op Orch, G. Setti (r1927) (3/94) (CONI) ⦶ **CDHD201** (3/94) (CONI) ▭ **MCHD201**
9, 15c G. De Luca, A. Galli-Curci, NY Met Op Orch, G. Setti (r1927) (10/94) (PREI) ⦶ **89073**
9, 15d T. Ruffo, M. Galvany, orch (r1907) (PEAR) ⦶ **GEMMCD9088**
10. J. Anderson, Alfredo Kraus, Paris Op Orch, M. Veltri (pp1987) (12/88) (EMI) ⦶ **CDC7 49067-2**
10a-d M. Callas, G. di Stefano, G. Gerbino, C. Forti, R. Ercolani, La Scala Orch, T. Serafin (10/88) (EMI) ⦶ **CDM7 69543-2**
10a, 10b, 10c F. Wunderlich, E. Köth, Munich RO, K. Eichhorn (Ger: bp) (DG) ⦶ [5] **435 145-2GX5(1)**
10a, 10c G. Pareto, L. Bergamini, orch (r1918) (PEAR) ⦶ **GEMMCD9117**
10a, 10c J. Hislop, L. Schöne, orch, P. Coppola (r1927) (1/93) (PEAR) ⦶ **GEMMCD9956**
10b, 10c L. Pavarotti, M. Rinaldi, M. Benetti, L. Monreale, F. Iacopucci, Turin RAI Orch, M. Rossi (pp1967) (BUTT) ⦶ **BMCD015** (BUTT) ▭ **BMK015**
10c T. Schipa, A. Galli-Curci, orch (r1930) (PEAR) ⦶ **GEMMCD9364**
10c A. Moffo, Philh, Colin Davis (CFP) ⦶ **CD-CFP4575** (CFP) ▭ **TC-CFP4575**
10c J. Sutherland, G. Knight, L. Pavarotti, R. Cassinelli, J. Gibbs, LSO, R. Bonynge (r1971) (DECC) ⦶ **436 313-2DA** (DECC) ▭ **436 313-4DA**
10c J. Hislop, L. Schöne, orch, P. Coppola (r1927) (PEAR) ⦶ **GEMMCD9129**
10c E. Berger, J. Patzak, Berlin St Op Orch, Wolfgang Martin (r1936: Ger) (PREI) ⦶ **89092**
10c F. de Lucia, J. Huguet, anon (r1906) (BONG) ⦶ [2] **GB1064/5-2**
10c J. Björling, H. Schymberg, orch, N. Grevillius (r1941) (8/92) (BLUE) ⦶ **ABCD016**
10c F. Wunderlich, E. Köth, Munich RO, K. Eichhorn (Ger) (5/93) (DG) ⦶ **431 110-2GB**
10c J. Björling, H. Schymberg, orch, N. Grevillius (r1941) (10/93) (NIMB) ⦶ **NI7842**
10c J. Björling, H. Schymberg, orch, N. Grevillius (r1941) (10/93) (EMI) ⦶ **CDH7 64707-2**
10c A. Galli-Curci, T. Schipa, orch, Rosario Bourdon (r1928) (3/94) (CONI) ⦶ **CDHD201** (3/94) (CONI) ▭ **MCHD201**
10c A. Galli-Curci, T. Schipa, orch, Rosario Bourdon (r1924) (8/94) (ROMO) ⦶ [2] **81004-2**
10c J. Björling, H. Schymberg, orch, N. Grevillius (r1941) (9/94) (CONI) ⦶ **CDHD214** (9/94) (CONI) ▭ **MCHD214**
10c F. de Lucia, J. Huguet, anon (r1906) (1/95) (SYMP) ⦶ **SYMCD1149**
10c H. Roswaenge, M. Korjus, Berlin St Op Orch, B. Seidler-Winkler (r1936: Ger) (4/95) (PREI) ⦶ [2] **89209**
10c, 11b, 15a M. Korjus, Berlin St Op Orch, E. Nick, B. Seidler-Winkler (r1934/6: Ger) (DANT) ⦶ **LYS001**
11. M. Callas, R. Ercolani, C. Forti, W. Dickie, La Scala Chor, La Scala Orch, T. Serafin (r1955) (EMI) ⦶ **CDC7 49502-2**
11. J. Sutherland, ROH Chor, ROHO, F. Molinari-Pradelli (DECC) ⦶ **433 624-2DSP**
11a, 11b J. Sutherland, ROH Chor, ROHO, R. Bonynge (DECC) ⦶ **433 064-2DWO**
11a, 11b J. Sutherland, LSO, R. Bonynge (DECC) ⦶ **433 221-2DWO** (DECC) ▭ **433 221-4DWO**
11a, 11b J. Sutherland, ROH Chor, ROHO, F. Molinari-Pradelli (r1960) (DECC) ⦶ **433 442-2DA**
11a, 11b J. Sutherland, ROHO, F. Molinari-Pradelli (BELA) ⦶ **450 133-2** (BELA) ▭ **450 133-4**
11a, 11b G. Pareto, orch (r1907) (PEAR) ⦶ **GEMMCD9117**
11a, 11b L. Price, Philh, H. Lewis (r1979) (RCA) ⦶ **09026 62596-2**
11a, 11b J. Sutherland, ROHO, F. Molinari-Pradelli (1/90) (DECC) ⦶ [2] **425 493-2DM2**
11a, 11b E. Berger, Berlin St Op Orch, C. Schmalstich (r1932; Ger) (12/91) (PREI) ⦶ **89035**
11a, 11b L. Pons, orch, Rosario Bourdon (r1931) (4/92) (MSOU) ⦶ **DFCDI-111**
11a, 11b L. Price, Philh, H. Lewis (r1979) (12/92) (RCA) ⦶ [4] **09026 61236-2**
11a, 11b A. Galli-Curci, orch, J. Pasternack (r1916/7: two vers) (3/94) (ROMO) ⦶ [2] **81003-2**
11a, 11b S. Jo, Monte Carlo PO, P. Olmi (r1994) (6/95) (ERAT) ⦶ **4509-97239-2**
11b M. Caballé, Barcelona SO, G-F. Masini (11/92) (RCA) ▭ [2] **RK61044**
11b R. Miloia, Timişoara Romanian Op Orch, M. Beleavcenco (ELCT) ⦶ **ELCD109**
11b I. Cotrubas, New Philh, J. Pritchard (SONY) ⦶ **SBK46548** (SONY) ▭ **SBT46548**
11b L. Pons, Orch, Rosario Bourdon (r1929) (MSCM) ⦶ **MM30446**
11b V. Loukjanetz, P. Lerebours (AUVI) ⦶ **V4662**
11b M. Foley, Orch (r1949-53) (ODE) ⦶ **CDODE1062**
11b M. Callas, La Scala Orch, T. Serafin (r1955) (EMI) ⦶ **CDC7 54702-2** (EMI) ▭ **EL754702-4**
11b M. Mesplé, Paris Op Orch, G-F. Masini (r1974) (EMI) ⦶ [2] **CZS7 67813-2**
11b A. Moffo, RCA Italiana Op Orch, G. Solti (RCA) ⦶ **09026 61886-2** (RCA) ▭ **09026 61886-4**
11b M. Ivogün, orch (r1916: Ger) (PREI) ⦶ **89094**
11b G. Bréjean-Silver, anon (r1905: Fr) (SYMP) ⦶ **SYMCD1173**
11b E. Berger, Berlin St Op Orch, L. Blech (r1935: Ger) (PREI) ⦶ **89092**
11b N. Melba, orch, W. B. Rogers (r1907) (RCA) ⦶ **74321 24284-2** (RCA) ▭ **74321 24284-4**
11b A. Galli-Curci, orch (r1916) (2/89) (PEAR) ⦶ **GEMMCD9308**
11b N. Melba, orch, L. Ronald (r1904) (3/89) (LARR) ⦶ **CDLRH221**
11b L. Tetrazzini, orch (r1911) (10/89) (NIMB) ⦶ **NI7802** (NIMB) ▭ **NC7802**
11b L. Tetrazzini, orch (r1911) (10/90) (NIMB) ⦶ **NI7808** (10/90) (NIMB) ▭ **NC7808**
11b E. Norena, orch, H. Defosse (French: r1929) (3/91) (PREI) ⦶ **89041**
11b N. Melba, orch, L. Ronald (r1904) (7/92) (PEAR) ⦶ [3] **GEMMCDS9923(1)**
11b L. Lipkowska, orch (Russ: r1914) (7/92) (PEAR) ⦶ [3] **GEMMCDS9925(1)**
11b L. Tetrazzini, orch (r1907) (7/92) (PEAR) ⦶ [3] **GEMMCDS9924(2)**
11b Dilbèr, Estonia Op Orch, E. Klas (9/92) (ONDI) ⦶ **ODE768-2**
11b L. Tetrazzini, orch, P. Pitt (r1907) (9/92) (EMI) ⦶ [3] **CHS7 63802-2(1)**
11b L. Tetrazzini, anon (r c1904) (9/92) (PEAR) ⦶ **GEMMCD9225**
11b L. Tetrazzini, orch, P. Pitt (r1907) (9/92) (PEAR) ⦶ **GEMMCD9221**
11b L. Tetrazzini, orch (r1911) (9/92) (PEAR) ⦶ **GEMMCD9224**
11b N. Melba, orch, W.B. Rogers (r1907) (9/93) (RCA) ⦶ **09026 61412-2**
11b M. Korjus, Berlin St Op Orch, E. Nick (Ger: r1934) (10/93) (PREI) ⦶ **89054**
11b M. Ivogün, orch (r c1924) (1/94) (CLUB) ⦶ **CL99-020**
11b F. Hempel, orch (r1910: Ger) (3/94) (NIMB) ⦶ **NI7849**
11b L. Tetrazzini, orch (r1911) (4/94) (RCA) ⦶ [6] **09026 61580-2(2)**
11b G. Pareto, orch (r1907) (4/94) (EMI) ⦶ [3] **CHS7 64860-2(2)**
11b A. Galli-Curci, orch (r1917) (8/94) (NIMB) ⦶ **NI7852**

17. Alfredo Kraus, RCA Italiana Op Orch, G. Solti (r1962) (RCA) Ⓓ **74321 25817-2**
(RCA) ▭ **74321 25817-4**
17. Capitol SO, C. Dragon (r1958: arr Dragon) (EMI) Ⓓ **CDM5 65430-2**
17. B. Gigli, La Scala Orch, F. Ghione (r1934) (PEAR) Ⓓ [2] **GEMMCDS9176**
17. F. de Lucia, orch (r1918) (BONG) Ⓓ [2] **GB1064/5-2**
17. R. Alagna, LPO, R. Armstrong (EMI) Ⓓ **CDC5 55540-2**
(EMI) ▭ **EL5 55540-4**
17. P. Domingo, VPO, C.M. Giulini (7/86) (DG) Ⓓ **415 366-2GH**
17. B. Gigli, La Scala Orch, F. Ghione (r1934) (9/88) (EMI) Ⓓ **CDH7 61051-2**
17. M. André, Toulouse Capitole Orch, M. Plasson (arr tpt) (1/89) (EMI) Ⓓ **CDC7 49219-2**
17. H. Nash, orch (Eng: r1926) (8/89) (PEAR) Ⓓ **GEMMCD9319**
17. M. Fleta, orch (r1924) (2/90) (PREI) Ⓓ **89002**
17. L. Pavarotti, LSO, R. Bonynge (7/90) (DECC) Ⓓ [2] **425 681-2DM2**
(7/90) (DECC) ▭ [2] **425 681-4DM2**
17. D. Smirnov, orch (r1921) (7/90) (CLUB) Ⓓ **CL99-031**
17. E. Barham, RPO, R. Stapleton (10/90) (IMP) Ⓓ **MCD15**
(10/90) (IMP) ▭ **MCC15**
17. E. Caruso, anon (r1903) (12/90) (PEAR) Ⓓ [3] **EVC1(1)**
17. E. Caruso, anon (r1903) (7/91) (RCA) Ⓓ [12] **GD60495(1)**
17. E. Caruso, orch (r1908) (7/91) (MSCM) Ⓓ **MM30352**
17. E. Caruso, orch (r1908) (7/92) (PEAR) Ⓓ [3] **GEMMCDS9923(2)**
17. J. Björling, orch (r1936) (10/92) (TEST) Ⓓ **SBT1005**
17. G. Martinelli, orch, Rosario Bourdon (r1926) (3/93) (PREI) Ⓓ **89062**
17. L. Sobinov, anon (r1901: Russ) (6/93) (PEAR) Ⓓ [3] **GEMMCDS9997/9(1)**
17. D. Yuzhin, anon (r1902: Russ) (6/93) (PEAR) Ⓓ [3] **GEMMCDS9001/3(1)**
17. B. Gigli, La Scala Orch, F. Ghione (r1934) (6/93) (MMOI) Ⓓ **CDMOIR417**
17. J. Björling, orch, N. Grevillius (r1936) (10/93) (NIMB) Ⓓ **NI7842**
17. J. Björling, orch, N. Grevillius (r1936) (10/93) (EMI) Ⓓ **CDH7 64707-2**
17. Alfredo Kraus, RCA Italiana Op Orch, G. Solti (r1963) (4/94) (RCA) Ⓓ [6] **09026 61580-2(8)**
17. M. Fleta, orch, C. Sabajno (r1923) (4/94) (EMI) Ⓓ [3] **CHS7 64864-2(1)**
17. J. Björling, orch, N. Grevillius (r1936) (9/94) (IMP) Ⓓ **GLRS103**
17. J. Carreras, P. Domingo, L. Pavarotti, Los Angeles Music Center Op Chor, Los Angeles PO, Z. Mehta (pp1994) (12/94) (TELD) Ⓓ **4509-96200-2**

(12/94) (TELD) ⊙ **4509-96200-1** ▭ **4509-96200-4**

17. F. de Lucia, anon (r1903) (1/95) (SYMP) Ⓓ **SYMCD1149**
17. E. Caruso, orch (r1908) (7/95) (NIMB) Ⓓ **NI7866**
17, 18b L. Pavarotti, J. Sutherland, H. Tourangeau, S. Milnes, M. Talvela, LSO, R. Bonynge (r1971) (DECC) Ⓓ **433 440-2DA**
(DECC) ▭ **433 440-4DA**
17, 18b J. Sutherland, R. Cioni, S. Malagù, C. MacNeil, C. Siepi, Santa Cecilia Academy Orch, N. Sanzogno (BELA) Ⓓ **450 133-2**
(BELA) ▭ **450 133-4**
18a K. Ricciarelli, L.V. Terrani, Alfredo Kraus, P. Coni, Madrid SO, G.P. Sanzogno (RNE) Ⓓ [2] **650004**
18a, 18b K. Ricciarelli, L.V. Terrani, Alfredo Kraus, P. Coni, Madrid SO, G.P. Sanzogno (pp1991) (IMP) Ⓓ [2] **DPCD998**
18a, 18b J. Rodgers, C. Powell, D.M. Anderson, K. Latham, English Northern Philh, P. Daniel (r1992) (EMI) Ⓓ **CDC7 54785-2**
18b E. Steber, B. Sullivan, R. Stevens, T.L. Thomas, Orch, Anon (cond) (bp1953) (VAI) ▬ **VAI69112**
18b J. Sutherland, H. Tourangeau, L. Pavarotti, S. Milnes, LSO, R. Bonynge (DECC) Ⓓ **433 822-2DH**
(DECC) ▭ **433 822-4DH**
18b J. Sutherland, H. Tourangeau, L. Pavarotti, S. Milnes, LSO, R. Bonynge (r1971) (DECC) Ⓓ **433 065-2DWO**
(DECC) ▭ **433 065-4DWO**
18b Classic Buskers (arr Copley) (SEAV) Ⓓ **CD007365**
18b J. Sutherland, H. Tourangeau, L. Pavarotti, S. Milnes, LSO, R. Bonynge (DECC) Ⓓ **433 221-2DWO**
(DECC) ▭ **433 221-4DWO**
18b M. Sembrich, G. Severina, E. Caruso, A. Scotti, orch, W.B. Rogers (r1908) (NIMB) Ⓓ **NI7834**
(NIMB) ▭ **NC7834**
18b J. Sutherland, I. Jones, L. Pavarotti, L. Nucci, NY Met Op Orch, R. Bonynge (DECC) ● **071 142-1DH**
(DECC) ▬ **071 142-3DH**
18b L. Pavarotti, R. Scotto, B. Bortoluzzi, K. Paskalis, Rome Op Orch, C.M. Giulini (pp1966) (BUTT) Ⓓ **BMCD015**
(BUTT) ▭ **BMK015**
18b E. Caruso, L. Tetrazzini, J. Jacoby, P. Amato, orch, W.B. Rogers (r1912) (RCA) Ⓓ **09026 61242-2**
18b A. Galli-Curci, F. Perini, E. Caruso, G. de Luca, orch, J. Pasternack (r1917) (MCI) Ⓓ **MCCD086**
(MCI) ▭ **MCTC086**
18b A. Galli-Curci, L. Homer, B. Gigli, G. De Luca, NY Met Op Orch, G. Setti (r1927) (CONI) Ⓓ **CDHD227**
(CONI) ▭ **MCHD227**
18b H. Schymberg, A. Hegert-Tibell, T. Ralf, S. Björling, Swedish RSO, T. Mann (bp1939) (ALTN) Ⓓ **CDAN3**
18b E. Berger, M. Wittrisch, M. Klose, W. Domgraf-Fassbaender, Berlin City Op Orch, F. Zweig (r1932: Ger) (PREI) Ⓓ **89092**
18b A. Galli-Curci, F. Perini, E. Caruso, G. De Luca, orch, J. Pasternack (r1917) (PEAR) Ⓓ [3] **GEMMCDS9159(2)**
18b A. Galli-Curci, L. Homer, B. Gigli, G. De Luca, orch (r1927) (PEAR) Ⓓ [3] **GEMMCDS9160(2)**
18b A. Galli-Curci, L. Homer, B. Gigli, G. De Luca, orch, G. Setti (r1927) (PEAR) Ⓓ [3] **GEMMCDS9159(2)**
18b L. Bori, J. Jacoby, J. McCormack, R. Werrenrath, Victor Orch, W.B. Rogers (r1914) (ROMO) Ⓓ [2] **81016-2**
18b A. Galli-Curci, L. Homer, G. De Luca, B. Gigli, NY Met Op Orch, G. Setti (r1927) (9/88) (EMI) Ⓓ **CDH7 61051-2**
18b G. De Luca, A. Galli-Curci, B. Gigli, L. Homer, NY Met Op Orch, G. Setti (r1927) (9/88) (PEAR) Ⓓ **GEMMCD9316**
18b L. Tetrazzini, J. Jacoby, E. Caruso, P. Amato, orch, W.B. Rogers (r1912) (7/90) (CLUB) Ⓓ **CL99-060**
18b L. Tetrazzini, J. Jacoby, E. Caruso, P. Amato, orch (r1912) (10/90) (NIMB) Ⓓ **NI7808**
(10/90) (NIMB) ▭ **NC7808**
18b(2 vers) B. Abott, L. Homer, E. Caruso, A. Scotti, orch (r1907) (12/90) (PEAR) Ⓓ [3] **EVC1(2)**
18b M. Sembrich, G. Severina, E. Caruso, A. Scotti, orch, W.B. Rogers (r1908) (12/90) (PEAR) Ⓓ [3] **EVC1(2)**
18b M. Sembrich, G. Severina, E. Caruso, A. Scotti, orch, W.B. Rogers (r1908) (7/91) (RCA) Ⓓ [12] **GD60495(2)**
18b B. Abott, L. Homer, E. Caruso, A. Scotti, orch (r1907) (7/91) (RCA) Ⓓ [12] **GD60495(2)**
18b(opening) E. Caruso, orch, J. Pasternack (r1917) (7/91) (RCA) Ⓓ [12] **GD60495(6)**
18b L. Tetrazzini, J. Jacoby, E. Caruso, P. Amato, orch, W.B. Rogers (r1912) (7/91) (RCA) Ⓓ [12] **GD60495(4)**
18b A. Galli-Curci, F. Perini, E. Caruso, G. De Luca, orch, J. Pasternack (r1917) (7/91) (RCA) Ⓓ [12] **GD60495(6)**
18b A. Galli-Curci, F. Perini, E. Caruso, G. De Luca, orch (r1917) (7/91) (MSCM) Ⓓ **MM30352**
18b L. Tetrazzini, J. Jacoby, E. Caruso, P. Amato, orch, W.B. Rogers (r1912) (10/91) (PEAR) Ⓓ [3] **EVC3(1)**
18b(opening) E. Caruso, orch, J. Pasternack (r1917) (10/91) (PEAR) Ⓓ [3] **EVC4(1)**
18b A. Galli-Curci, F. Perini, E. Caruso, G. De Luca, orch, J. Pasternack (r1917) (10/91) (PEAR) Ⓓ [3] **EVC4(1)**
18b F. Hüni-Mihacsek, E. Leisner, H. Roswaenge, T. Scheidl, orch (r1928: Ger) (2/92) (PREI) Ⓓ [2] **89201**
18b L. Tetrazzini, E. Caruso, P. Amato, M. Journet, orch (r1912) (9/92) (PEAR) Ⓓ **GEMMCD9224**
18b R. Pinkert, G. Lukacewska, A. Bonci, A. Magini-Coletti, anon (r1905) (12/93) (SYMP) Ⓓ **SYMCD1113**
18b A. Galli-Curci, F. Perini, E. Caruso, G. De Luca, orch, J. Pasternack (r1917) (3/94) (ROMO) Ⓓ [2] **81003-2**
18b A. Galli-Curci, F. Perini, E. Caruso, G. De Luca, orch, W.B. Rogers (r1917/92) (5/94) (CLAR) Ⓓ **CDGSE78-50-52**
18b A. Galli-Curci, L. Homer, B. Gigli, G. De Luca, NY Met Op Orch, G. Setti (r1927) (8/94) (NIMB) Ⓓ **NI7852**
18b H. Roswaenge, P. Yoder, L. Kindermann, H. Reinmar, Berlin St Op Orch, S. Meyrowitz (r1932: Ger) (4/95) (PREI) Ⓓ [2] **89209**
18b M. Licette, M. Brunskill, H. Nash, D. Noble, orch (r1931: Eng) (11/95) (PEAR) Ⓓ **GEMMCD9175**
21a-c(pt) G. De Luca, A. Galli-Curci, orch (r1918) (1/92) (PREI) Ⓓ **89036**

Simon Boccanegra– opera: prologue & 3 acts (1857 rev 1881—Venice) (Lib. F Piave, rev A Boito)

O. PROLOGUE: EXCERPTS: PROLOGUE: 1a. A te l'estremo addio; 1b. Il lacerato spirito; 2. Suona ogni labbro il mio nome; 3. Oh de' Fieschi implacata. ACT 1: 4. Come in quest'ora bruna; 5a. Orfanella il tetto umile; 5b. Figlia! a tal nome io palpito; 6. Plebe! Patrizi!. ACT 2: 7. Quei due vedesti; 8a. O inferno! Amelia qui!; 8b. Sento avvampar nell'anima; 9a. Oh! Amelia, ami un nemico; 9b. Perdon, Amelia. ACT 3: 10a. M'ardon le tempia; 10b. Come un fantasima; 11. Piango, perchè mi parla in te.

Simon Boccanegra	P. Cappuccilli
Amelia	M. Freni
Gabriele	J. Carreras
Fiesco	N. Ghiaurov
Paolo	J. Van Dam
Pietro	G. Foiani
Captain	A. Savastano

La Scala Chor, La Scala Orch, C. Abbado (r1977) (9/86) (DG) Ⓓ [2] **415 692-2GH2**

Simon Boccanegra	P. Cappuccilli
Amelia	K. Ricciarelli
Gabriele	P. Domingo
Fiesco	R. Raimondi
Paolo	G-P. Mastromei
Pietro	M. Mazzieri
Captain	P. de Palma
Maid	O. Jachetti

RCA Chor, RCA Orch, G. Gavazzeni (9/87) (RCA) Ⓓ [2] **RD70729**

Simon Boccanegra	L. Nucci
Amelia	K. Te Kanawa
Gabriele	G. Aragall
Fiesco	P. Burchuladze
Paolo	P. Coni
Pietro	C. Colombara
Captain	E. Gavazzi
Maid	A. Zoroberto

La Scala Chor, La Scala Orch, G. Solti (r1988) (12/89) (DECC) Ⓓ [2] **425 628-2DH2**

Simon Boccanegra	T. Gobbi
Amelia	V. de los Angeles
Gabriele	G. Campora
Fiesco	B. Christoff
Paolo	W. Monachesi
Pietro	P. Dari
Captain	P. Caroli
Maid	S. Bertona

Rome Op Chor, Rome Op Orch, G. Santini (r1957) (9/90) (EMI) Ⓓ [2] **CMS7 63513-2**

Simon Boccanegra	J. Van Dam
Amelia	N. Gustafson
Gabriele	A. Cupido
Fiesco	D. Pittsinger
Paolo	W. Stone
Pietro	C. Krause
Captain	A. Gregoire

Brussels Théâtre de la Monnaie Chor, Brussels Théâtre de la Monnaie Orch, S. Cambreling (pp1990) (1/92) (RICE) Ⓓ [2] **RIS093070/1**

Simon Boccanegra	A. Agache
Amelia	K. Te Kanawa
Gabriele	M. Sylvester
Fiesco	R. Scandiuzzi

Paolo A. Opie
Pietro M. Beesley
Captain R. Gibson
Maid E. Sikora
ROH Chor, ROHO, G. Solti, B. Large
(5/93) (DECC) ● [2] **071 423-1DH2**
(5/93) (DECC) ▣ **071 423-3DH**
Simon Boccanegra E. Tumagian
Amelia M. Gauci
Gabriele G. Aragall
Fiesco P. Mikuláš
Paolo V. Sardinero
Pietro V. de Kanel
Captain G. Tomckowiack
Maid M. Pieck
Brussels BRT Phil Chor, Brussels BRT PO, A. Rahbari (r1994)
(2/95) (DINT) ① [2] **DICD920225/6**
Prelude La Scala Orch, C. Abbado
(6/87) (CBS) ① **CD37228**
1. A. Silvestrelli, Berlin RSO, R. Buckley
(SCHW) ① [2] **314052**
1. E. Pinza, orch, C. Sabajno (r1923)
(2/89) (PEAR) ① **GEMMCD9306**
1. A. Kipnis, Berlin St Op Orch, E. Orthmann (r1931) (10/91) (PEAR) ① **GEMMCD9451**
1a T. Pasero, SO, D. Marzollo (r1944)
(4/95) (PREI) ① **89074**
1a, 1b C. Airizer, Timişoara Romanian Op Orch, I. Iancu (ELCT) ① **ELCD109**
1a, 1b P. Kang, S. Katz (SCHW) ① **312642**
1a, 1b B. Christoff, Rome Op Chor, Rome Op Orch, V. Gui (r1955) (EMI) ① **CDH5 65500-2**
1a, 1b E. Pinza, NY Met Op Chor, NY Met Op Orch, E. Panizza (bp1939)
(7/91) (MMOI) ① **CDMOIR404**
(MMOI) ▭ **CMOIR404**
1a, 1b E. Pinza, R. Shaw Chorale, RCA Victor Orch, E. Leinsdorf (r1951)
(9/93) (RCA) ① **09026 61245-2**
1b C. Siepi, Santa Cecilia Academy Orch, A. Erede (r1954) (DECC) ① **440 418-2DM**
1b G. Gravina, anon (r1902)
(12/89) (SYMP) ① **SYMCD1065**
1b E. Pinza, NY Met Op Orch, F. Cleva (r1946)
(4/90) (CBS) ① **CD45693**
1b A. Kipnis, chor, Berlin St Op Orch, E. Orthmann (r1931) (12/90) (PREI) ① **89019**
1b M. Salminen, Lahti SO, E. Klas
(8/92) (BIS) ① **BIS-CD520**
1b V. Arimondi, orch (r1907)
(11/92) (MEMO) ① [2] **HR4408/9(1)**
1b M. Reizen, Bolshoi Th Orch, V. Nebolsin (r1953: Russ) (2/95) (PREI) ① **89080**
2, 3, 6, 10a, 10b L. Tibbett, E. Rethberg, G. Martinelli, L. Warren, E. Pinza, NY Met Op Chor, NY Met Op Orch, E. Panizza (pp1939)
(3/91) (PEAR) ① [2] **GEMMCDS9452**
2, 6. M. Freni, G. Foiani, F. Schiavi, G. Raimondi, P. Cappuccilli, N. Ghiaurov, La Scala Chor, La Scala Orch, C. Abbado (pp1971)
(MEMO) ① [2] **HR4273/4**
4. L. Price, LSO, E. Downes (r1960s-70)
(RCA) ① **09026 62596-2**
4. L. Price, LSO, E. Downes
(12/92) (RCA) ① [4] **09026 61236-2**
5b L. Tibbett, R. Bampton, Orch, W. Pelletier (r1939) (3/90) (RCA) ① **GD87808**
6. H. Schlusnus, Berlin St Op Orch, A. Melichar (r1933: Ger) (PREI) ① [2] **89212**
6. T. Gobbi, Philh, A. Erede (r1963)
(10/89) (EMI) ① **CDM7 63109-2**
6. H. Schlusnus, Berlin St Op Orch, A. Melichar (Ger: r c1931) (9/90) (PREI) ① **89006**
8a, 8b P. Domingo, RPO, E. Downes
(RCA) ① [2] **GD60866**
(RCA) ▭ [2] **GK60866**
8a, 8b C. Bergonzi, New Philh, N. Santi
(PHIL) ① [3] **432 486-2PM3**
8a, 8b G. Aragall, P. Coni, La Scala Orch, G. Solti (r1988) (10/93) (DECC) ① **436 463-2DM**
(10/93) (DECC) ▭ **436 463-4DM**
8a, 8b J. Johnston, ROHO, M. Mudie (r1948: Eng) (4/95) (TEST) ① **SBT1058**

Stiffelio– opera: 3 acts (1950—Trieste) (Lib. F. Piave)

EXCERPTS: 1. Overture. ACT 1: 2. Oh santo libro; 3. Di qua varcando; 4a. Son quanti giorno?; 4b. Colla cenere disperso; 4c. Viva Stiffelio!; 5a. Non ha per me un accento!; 5b. Vidi dovunque gemere; 5c. Ah! v'appare in fronte scritto; 6. Tosto ei disse!; 7a. Verrà Dovrò risponder!; 7b. Dite che il fallo a tergere; 7c. Ed io pure in faccia agli uomini; 7d. Or meco venite; 8. M'evitan; 9. Plaudiam!; 10. Cugino, pensaste al sermone?; 11. Oh qual m'invade ed agita; 12. Nol volete?. ACT 2: 13a. Oh cielo! dove son io!; 13b. Ah, dagli scanni eterei; 13c. Perder dunque voi volete; 14. Io resto; 15a. Qual rumore!; 15b. Santo è il loco; 15c. Ah no, è impossibile!; 16. Dessa non è. ACT 3: 17a. Ei fugge!; 17b. Lina, pensai che un angelo; 17c. Ah, si finisca; 17d. In questo teto uno di noi morrà; 18. Dite ai fratei che al tempio; 19a. Inevitabil fu questo colloquio; 19b. Opposto è il calle; 19c. Non allo sposo volgomi; 19d. Egli un patto proponeva; 19e. Ah sì, voliamo al tempio; 20. Non punirmi, Signor; 21. Stiffelio! Eccomi.

Stiffelio J. Carreras
Lina C. Malfitano
Stankar G. Yurisch
Jorg G. Howell
Raffaele R. Leggate
Dorotea A. Paxton
Federico L. Atkinson
ROH Chor, ROHO, E. Downes, E. Moshinsky
(9/93) (CGP) ▣ **CVI1719**
Stiffelio J. Carreras
Lina C. Malfitano
Stankar G. Yurisch
Jorg G. Howell
Raffaele R. Leggate
Dorotea A. Paxton
Federico L. Atkinson
ROH Chor, ROHO, E. Downes, E. Moshinsky
(PION) ● **PLMCB00861**
Stiffelio J. Carreras
Lina S. Sass
Stankar M. Manuguerra
Jorg W. Ganzarolli
Raffaele E. di Cesare
Dorotea M. Venuti
Federico T. Moser
Austrian Rad Chor, Austrian RSO, L. Gardelli (r1979)
(3/90) (PHIL) ① [2] **422 432-2PM2**

La **Traviata– opera: 3 acts (1853—Venice) (Lib. F Piave, after A Dumas)**

EXCERPTS; 1. Prelude. ACT 1: 2. Dell'invito trascora è già l'ora; 3. Libiamo, ne' lieti calci (Brindisi); 4a. Che è ciò?; 4b. Un dì, felice; 5. Si ridesta in ciel; 6a. È strano! È strano!; 6b. Ah, fors'è lui; 6c. Follie! Sempra libera. ACT 2: 7a. Lunge da lei; 7b. De' miei bollenti spiriti; 7c. O mio romorso!; 8a. Madamigella Valery?; 8b. Pura siccome un angelo; 8c. Bella voi siete; 8d. Dite alla giovine; 9a. Morrò! La mia memoria; 9b. Dammi tu forza; 10a. Ah, vive sol quel core; 10b. Di Provenza il mar; 10c. Ne rispondi; 11. Avrem lieta; 12a. Noi siamo zingarelle; 12b. Di Madride noi siam Mattadori; 13. Alfredo! Voi!; 14a. Ogni suo aver tal femmina; 14b. Di Sprezzo degno! ACT 3: 15. Prelude; 16a. Annina? Commandate?; 16b. Teneste la promessa; 16c. Addio del passato; 17. Largo al quadrupede; 18a. Signora, Che t'accade; 18b. Parigi, o cara; 18c. Gran Dio! morir sì giovine; 19. Ah! Violetta.

Violetta B. Sills
Alfredo H. Price
Germont R. Fredericks
Flora F. Rakusin
Annina E. Petros
Gaston N. Rosenshein
Baron R. Orth
Marquis K. Kibler
Giuseppe R. Lucas
Wolf Trap Comp Chor, Filene Center Orch, J. Rudel, K. Browning (r1976)
(VAI) ▣ **VAI69079**
Violetta A. Gheorghiu
Alfredo F. Lopardo
Germont L. Nucci
Flora L-M. Jones
Annina G. Knight
Gaston R. Leggate
Baron R. Van Allan
Marquis R. Earle
Doctor M. Beesley
Giuseppe N. Griffiths
Messenger B. Secombe
Servant R. Gibson
ROH Chor, ROHO, G. Solti, R. Eyre (pp1994)
(9/95) (DECC) ▣ **071 431-3DH**
Violetta M. McLaughlin
Alfredo W. MacNeil
Germont B. Ellis
Flora J. Turner
Annina E. Hartle
Gaston D. Hillman
Baron G. Sandison
Marquis C. Thornton-Holmes
Doctor J. Hall
Giuseppe M. Harrison
Messenger C. Kerry
Glyndebourne Fest Chor, LPO, B. Haitink, P. Hall (r1987)
(7/90) (IMP) ▣ **SL2006**
Violetta J. Sutherland
Alfredo L. Pavarotti
Germont M. Manuguerra
Flora D. Jones
Annina M. Lambriks
Gaston A. Oliver
Baron J. Summers
Marquis J. Tomlinson
Doctor G. Tadeo
Giuseppe W. Elvin
Messenger D. Wilson-Johnson
London Op Chor, National PO, R. Bonynge (r1979)
(DECC) ① [2] **430 491-2DH2**
(DECC) ▭ [2] **430 491-4DH**
Violetta M. Krause
Alfredo Y. Ramiro
Germont G. Tichy
Flora R. Braga
Annina I. Neshybová
Gaston P. Oswald
Baron P. Maurery
Marquis; Messenger L. Neshyba
Doctor J. Špaček
Giuseppe P. Šubert
Slovak Phil Chor, Bratislava RSO, A. Rahbari (r1990)
(NAXO) ① [2] **8 660011/2**
Violetta R. Scotto
Alfredo L. Pavarotti
Germont P. Glossop
Flora N. Berry
Annina N. Roberts
Gaston J. Dobson
Baron D. Wicks
Marquis R. Best
Doctor D. Kelly
Giuseppe R. Vaughn
Messenger K. Reddish
ROH Chor, ROHO, C.F. Cillario (pp1965)
(MEMO) ① [2] **HR4404/5**
Violetta J. Sutherland
Alfredo L. Pavarotti
Germont S. Milnes
Flora F. von Stade
Annina L. di Franco
Gaston L. Goeke
Baron R. Gibbs
Marquis G. Boucher
Doctor L. Sgarro
Giuseppe L. Marcella
Messenger J. Trehy
NY Met Op Chor, NY Met Op Orch, R. Bonynge (pp1970)
(BUTT) ① [2] **BMCD002**
(BUTT) ▭ [2] **BMK002**
Violetta V. de los Angeles
Alfredo C. del Monte
Germont M. Sereni
Flora S. Chissari
Annina S. Bertona
Gaston S. Tedesco
Baron V. Polotto
Marquis S. Maionica
Doctor B. Giaiotti
Giuseppe R. Ercolani
Rome Op Chor, Rome Op Orch, T. Serafin (r1959)
(CFP) ① [2] **CD-CFPD4450**
(12/85) (CFP) ▭ [2] **TC-CFPD4450**
Violetta T. Stratas
Alfredo F. Wunderlich
Germont H. Prey
Flora M.L. Gilles
Annina B. Fassbaender
Gaston F. Lenz
Baron J. Knapp
Marquis H.B. Ernst
Doctor G. Missenhardt
Giuseppe H. Weber
Bavarian St Op Chor, Bavarian St Orch, G. Patanè (pp1965)
(ORFE) ① [2] **C344932I**
Violetta R. Scotto
Alfredo G. Raimondi
Germont E. Bastianini
Flora G. Tavolaccini
Annina A. Bonato
Gaston F. Ricciardi
Baron; Messenger G. Morresi
Marquis V. Carbonari

Doctor S. Maionica
Giuseppe A. Mercuriali
La Scala Chor, La Scala Orch, A. Votto (r1962)
(DG) Ⓓ [2] **439 720-2GX2**
Violetta A. Rozsa
Alfredo A. Ziliani
Germont L. Borgonovo
Flora; Annina O. de Franco
Gastone G. Callegari
Baron A. Lenzi
Marquis; Doctor A. Gelli
La Scala Chor, La Scala Orch, C. Sabajno (r1930)
(VAI) Ⓓ [2] **VAIA1108**
Violetta V. Masterson
Alfredo J. Brecknock
Germont C. du Plessis
Flora D. Jones
Annina S. Squires
Gaston G. Pogson
Baron J. Gibbs
Marquis D. Dowling
Doctor R. Earle
ENO Chor, ENO Orch, C. Mackerras (r1980: Eng)
(CFP) Ⓓ [2] **CD-CFPSD4799**
Violetta I. Cotrubas
Alfredo P. Domingo
Germont S. Milnes
Flora S. Malagù
Annina H. Jungwirth
Gaston W. Gullino
Baron B. Grella
Marquis A. Giacomotti
Doctor G. Foiani
Giuseppe W. Gullino
Messenger P. Winter
Servant P. Friess
Bavarian St Op Chor, Bavarian St Orch, C. Kleiber (r1977)
(3/86) (DG) Ⓓ [2] **415 132-2GH2**
Violetta M. Callas
Alfredo Alfredo Kraus
Germont M. Sereni
Flora L. Zannini
Annina M.C. de Castro
Gaston P. de Palma
Baron A. Malta
Marquis V. Susca
Doctor A. Maddalena
Messenger M. Leitao
Lisbon San Carlos Nat Th Chor, Lisbon San Carlos Nat Th Orch, F. Ghione (pp1958)
(11/87) (EMI) Ⓓ [2] **CDS7 49187-8**
Violetta R. Scotto
Alfredo Alfredo Kraus
Germont R. Bruson
Flora Sarah Walker
Annina C. Buchan
Gaston S. Mariategui
Baron H. Newman
Marquis R. Van Allan
Doctor R. Kennedy
Giuseppe M-R. Cosotti
Messenger C. Keyte
Ambrosian Op. Chor, Royal Marines Band, Philh, R. Muti (r1980)
(11/87) (EMI) Ⓓ [2] **CDS7 47538-8**
Violetta M. Caballé
Alfredo C. Bergonzi
Germont S. Milnes
Flora D. Krebill
Annina N. Stokes
Gaston F. Iacopucci
Baron G. Boucher
Marquis T. Jamerson
Doctor H. Enns
Giuseppe C. Sforza
Messenger F. Ruta
Servant F. Tasin
RCA Italiana Op Chor, RCA Italiana Op Orch, G. Prêtre (r1967)
(9/88) (RCA) Ⓓ [2] **RD86180**
Violetta R. Ponselle
Alfredo F. Jagel
Germont L. Tibbett
Flora E. Vettori
Annina H. Wakefield
Gaston A. Bada
Baron A. Gandolfi
Marquis M. Picco
Doctor P. Ananian
NY Met Op Chor, NY Met Op Orch, E. Panizza (pp1935)
(1/89) (PEAR) Ⓓ [2] **GEMMCD9317**
Violetta J. Sutherland
Alfredo C. Bergonzi
Germont R. Merrill
Flora M.T. Pace
Annina D. Carral
Gaston P. de Palma
Baron P. Pedani
Marquis S. Maionica
Doctor G. Foiani
Giuseppe A. Mercuriali
Messenger M. Frosini
MMF Chor, MMF Orch, J. Pritchard (r1962)
(2/89) (DECC) Ⓓ [2] **411 877-2DM2**
Violetta L. Aliberti
Alfredo P. Dvorský
Germont R. Bruson
Flora F. Mochiki
Annina S. Sawa
Gaston H. Mochiki
Baron H. Okayama
Marquis A. Shikano
Doctor Y. Yanagisawa
Fujiwara Op Chor, Tokyo PO, R. Paternostro (pp1988)
(9/89) (CAPR) Ⓓ [2] **10 274/5**
Violetta M. Callas
Alfredo G. di Stefano
Germont E. Bastianini
Flora S. Zanolli
Annina L. Mandelli
Gaston G. Zampieri
Baron A. la Porta
Marquis A. Zerbini
Doctor S. Maionica
Giuseppe F. Ricciardi
La Scala Chor, La Scala Orch, C.M. Giulini (pp1955)
(2/91) (EMI) Ⓓ [2] **CMS7 63628-2**
Violetta R. Tebaldi
Alfredo G. Poggi
Germont A. Protti
Flora A. Vercelli
Annina R. Cavallari
Gaston P. de Palma
Baron A. Sacchetti
Marquis D. Caselli
Doctor I. Sardi
Giuseppe M. Bianchi
Messenger L. Mancini
Santa Cecilia Academy Chor, Santa Cecilia Academy Orch, F. Molinari-Pradelli
(8/91) (DECC) Ⓓ [2] **430 250-2DM2**
Violetta L. Albanese
Alfredo J. Peerce
Germont R. Merrill
Flora M. Stellman
Annina J. Moreland
Gaston J. Garris
Baron G. Cehanovsky
Marquis P. Dennis
Doctor A. Newman
Chor, NBC SO, A. Toscanini (bp1946)
(4/92) (RCA) Ⓓ [2] **GD60303**
Violetta C. Studer
Alfredo L. Pavarotti
Germont J. Pons
Flora W. White
Annina S. Kelly
Gaston A. Laciura
Baron B. Pola
Marquis J. Wells
Doctor J. Robbins
Giuseppe J. Hanriot
Messenger M. Sendrowitz
Servant R. Crolius
NY Met Op Chor, NY Met Op Orch, James Levine
(11/92) (DG) Ⓓ [2] **435 797-2GH2**
Violetta E. Gruberová
Alfredo N. Shicoff
Germont G. Zancanaro
Flora P. Spence
Annina M. Bacelli
Gaston K. Begley
Baron P. Sidhom
Marquis D. Barrell
Doctor A. Miles
Giuseppe P. Bronder
Messenger N. Folwell
Servant F. Visentin
Ambrosian Sngrs, LSO, C. Rizzi
(2/93) (TELD) Ⓓ [2] **9031-76348-2**
Violetta M. McLaughlin
Alfredo W. MacNeil
Germont B. Ellis
Flora J. Turner
Annina E. Hartle
Gaston D. Hillman
Baron G. Sandison
Marquis C. Thornton-Holmes
Doctor J. Hall
Messenger C. Kerry
Glyndebourne Fest Chor, LPO, B. Haitink, P. Hall
(3/93) (PION) ◐ **PLMCC00291**
Violetta T. Fabbricini
Alfredo R. Alagna
Germont P. Coni
Flora N. Curiel
Annina A. Trevisan
Gastone E. Cossutta
Baron O. Mori
Marquis E. Capuano
Doctor F. Musinu
Giuseppe E. Gavazzi
Servant E. Panariello
Messenger S. Sammaritano
La Scala Chor, La Scala Orch, R. Muti (pp1992)
(10/93) (SONY) Ⓓ [2] **S2K52486**
Violetta T. Fabbricini
Alfredo R. Alagna
Germont P. Coni
Flora N. Curiel
Annina A. Trevisan
Gastone E. Cossutta
Baron O. Mori
Marquis E. Capuano
Doctor F. Musinu
Giuseppe E. Gavazz
Servant E. Panariello
Messenger S. Sammaritano
La Scala Chor, La Scala Orch, R. Muti (pp1992)
(10/93) (SONY) ◐ [2] **S2LV48353**
(10/93) (SONY) ▭ **SHV48353**
Violetta K. Te Kanawa
Alfredo Alfredo Kraus
Germont D. Hvorostovsky
Flora S. Mazzoni
Annina O. Borodina
Gaston B. Banks
Baron R. Scaltriti
Marquis G. Gatti
Doctor D. Di Stefano
Giuseppe M. La Guardia
Messenger A. Calama
MMF Chor, MMF Orch, Z. Mehta (r1992)
(12/93) (PHIL) Ⓓ [2] **438 238-2PH2**
Violetta P. Lorenga
Alfredo G. Aragal
Germont D. Fischer-Dieskau
Flora S. Malagù
Annina M. Fiorentini
Gastone P. F. Po
Baron V. Carbonari
Marquis S. Maionica
Dotor G. Foiani
Giuseppe A. Losa
Berlin Deutsche Op Chor, Berlin Deutsche Op Orch, L. Maazel (r1968)
(5/94) (DECC) Ⓓ [2] **443 000-2DF2**
Violetta M. Callas
Alfredo F. Albanese
Germont U. Savarese
Flora E.M. Gandolfo
Annina I. Mariet
Gaston M. Caruso
Baron A. Albertini
Marquis; Doctor M. Zorgniotti
Giuseppe T. Sole
Chor, Turin RAI Orch, G. Santini (r1953)
(2/95) (FONI) Ⓓ [2] **CDO**
Violetta A. Gheorghiu
Alfredo F. Lopardo
Germont L. Nucci
Flora L-M. Jones
Annina G. Knight
Gaston R. Leggate
Baron R. Van Allan
Marquis R. Earle
Doctor M. Beesley
Giuseppe N. Griffiths
Messenger B. Secombe
Servant R. Gibson
ROH Chor, ROHO, G. Solti (pp1994)
(8/95) (DECC) Ⓓ [2] **448 119-2DHO**
A. Moffo, R. Tucker, Rome Op Chor, Rome Op Orch, F. Previtali (r1960)
(RCA) Ⓓ **74321 25817-**
(RCA) ▭ **74321 25817-**
Excs P. Domingo (CAST) ▭ **CVI202**

Excs Grimethorpe Colliery Band, E. Howarth (arr Greenwood) (12/92) (DOYE) Ⓓ **DOYCD013**
(12/92) (DOYE) ▭ **DOYMC013**
excs NBC SO, A. Toscanini (r1946)
(4/95) (TELD) ◐ **4509-95038-6**
(4/95) (TELD) ▣ **4509-95038-3**
Excs P. Gallois, London Fest Orch, R. Pople (r1993: arr fl: Genin/Guiot)
(5/95) (DG) Ⓓ **445 822-2GH**
1. Sofia SO, V. Stefanov (LASE) Ⓓ **15 519**
(LASE) ▭ **79 519**
1. National PO, R. Bonynge
(DECC) Ⓓ **425 848-2DWO**
(DECC) ▭ **425 848-4DWO**
1. MMF Orch, J. Pritchard (r1962)
(DECC) Ⓓ **433 221-2DWO**
(DECC) ▭ **433 221-4DWO**
1. Munich Brass (arr brass ens)
(ORFE) Ⓓ **C247911A**
1. LSO, V. Tausky (IMP) Ⓓ [3] **TCD1070**
1. LSO, C. Rizzi (ERAT) Ⓓ **4509-94358-2**
(ERAT) ▭ **4509-94358-4**
1. Philh, R. Muti (EMIL) Ⓓ **CDZ102**
(EMIL) ▭ **LZ102**
1. RPO, A. Ceccato (r1972)
(CFP) Ⓓ **CD-CFP4658**
(CFP) ▭ **TC-CFP4658**
1. BPO, H. von Karajan
(DG) Ⓓ [2] **447 364-2GDB2**
1. South-West German RSO, K. Arp (r1994)
(PIER) Ⓓ **PV730050**
1. BPO, H. von Karajan
(10/87) (DG) Ⓓ **419 622-2GH**
1. BPO, H. von Karajan
(5/90) (DG) Ⓓ **429 164-2GR**
1. BPO, H. von Karajan
(1/95) (DG) Ⓓ **439 972-2GGA2**
1, 15. Mexico St SO, E. Bátiz (r1990s)
(ASV) Ⓓ **CDDCA856**
(ASV) ▭ **ZCDCA856**
1, 15. Hungarian St Op Orch, P.G. Morandi (r1994) (NAXO) Ⓓ **8 553018**
1, 15. LSO, A. Dorati (r1957)
(MERC) Ⓓ **434 345-2MM**
1, 15. RPO, T. Serafin (r1959)
(EMI) Ⓓ [2] **CES5 68541-2**
1, 15. RPO, Y. Simonov (r1994)
(TRIN) Ⓓ **TRP030**
1, 15. La Scala Orch, A. Guarnieri (r1927)
(BONG) Ⓓ **GB1039-2**
1, 15. NYPSO, A. Toscanini (r1929)
(3/90) (PEAR) Ⓓ [3] **GEMMCDS9373**
1, 15. Gothenburg SO, N. Järvi
(6/90) (DG) Ⓓ **429 494-2GDC**
(6/90) (DG) ▭ **429 494-4GDC**
1, 15. NYPSO, A. Toscanini (r1929)
(11/92) (RCA) Ⓓ **GD60318**
1, 15. Berlin RIAS Orch, F. Fricsay (r1953)
(11/94) (DG) Ⓓ **445 406-2GDO**
1, 15. I. Seefried, M. Forrester, E. Haefliger, D. Fischer-Dieskau, Berlin St Hedwig's Cath Ch, BPO, F. Fricsay, H. Krebs, T. Varga, Berlin RIAS Chbr Ch, Berlin RIAS Orch, H. Geusser, W. Fugmann, M. Weber, G. Herzog, Berlin RSO, VPO, E. Grümmer, G. Pitzinger, H. Hotter, Y. Menuhin (r1953)
(11/94) (DG) Ⓓ [11] **445 400-2GDO10**
1, 15. Santa Cecilia Academy Orch, V. de Sabata (r1948)
(9/95) (EMI) Ⓓ [2] **CHS5 65506-2**
1, 3. J. Sutherland, C. Bergonzi, MMF Chor, MMF Orch, J. Pritchard
(DECC) Ⓓ **433 069-2DWO**
(DECC) ▭ **433 069-4DWO**
1, 3. J. Sutherland, C. Bergonzi, MMF Chor, MMF Orch, J. Pritchard (BELA) Ⓓ **450 133-2**
(BELA) ▭ **450 133-4**
1-3, 4a, 4b, 6c, 10b Cincinnati Pops, E. Kunzel (r1994; arr & orch Kunzel & Beck)
(TELA) Ⓓ **CD80364**
(TELA) ▭ **CS30364**
1-3, 4b, 6a-c, 7a-c, 8d, 10b, 14a, 16b, 17, 18a-c, 19. C. Studer, L. Pavarotti, J. Pons, NY Met Op Chor, NY Met Op Orch, James Levine (r1991) (DG) Ⓓ **437 726-2GH**
1-3, 4b, 6a-c, 7a-c, 8d, 10b, 14a, 16b, 17, 18a-c, 19. C. Studer, L. Pavarotti, J. Pons, NY Met Op Chor, NY Met Op Orch, James Levine (r1991) (DG) ꝏ **437 726-5GH**
1, 3, 4b, 6a-c, 7a, 7b, 8b, 8d, 10b, 14a, 14b, 16b, 16c, 18b, 19. Berlin City Op Orch, Berlin Deutsche Op Chor, L. Maazel
(BELA) Ⓓ **450 101-2**
(BELA) ▭ **450 101-4**
1, 3, 4b, 6a, c, 7a-c, 8b, d, 10b, 15, 16b, c, 18b, 19. K. Te Kanawa, S. Mazzoni, O. Borodina, Alfredo Kraus, B. Banks, D. Hvorostovsky, R. Scaltriti, G. Gatti, D. Di Stefano, MMF Chor, MMF Orch, Z. Mehta (r1992)
(PHIL) Ⓓ **442 440-2PH**
1, 3, 4b, 6, 7b, 8d, 10b, 12a, 15, 16c, 18b, 19. R. Scotto, Alfredo Kraus, R. Bruson, Sarah Walker, C. Buchan, S. Mariategui, H. Newman, R. Van Allan, R. Kennedy, Ambrosian Op. Chor, Royal Marines Band, Philh, R. Muti (r1980)
(EMI) Ⓓ **CDM7 63088-2**
1, 3, 4b, 6, 7, 8b, 10b, 16b, 16c, 18b, 19. J. Sutherland, L. Pavarotti, M. Manuguerra, D. Jones, M. Lambriks, A. Oliver, J. Summers, J. Tomlinson, G. Tadeo, London Op. Chor, National PO, R. Bonynge
(3/83) (DECC) Ⓓ **400 057-2DH**
1-3, 6a-c, 7a-c, 8b-d, 10a, 10b, 11, 12a, 12b, 15, 16a-c, 18a-c, 19. I. Cotrubas, P. Domingo, S. Milnes, S. Malagù, H. Jungwirth, W. Gullino, B. Grella, A. Giacomotti, G. Foiani, Bavarian St Op Chor, Bavarian St Orch, C. Kleiber (r1976)
(DG) Ⓓ **439 421-2GCL**
(DG) ▭ **439 421-4GCL**
1, 3, 6a, 6c, 7a, 7b, 8b, 8d, 10b, 12a, 15, 16b, 16c, 18b, 19. E. Gruberová, N. Shicoff, G. Zancanaro, P. Spence, M. Bacelli, K. Begley, P. Sidhom, D. Barrell, A. Miles, Ambrosian Sngrs, LSO, C. Rizzi (r1992) (TELD) Ⓓ **4509-91975-2**
3. B. Sills, N. Gedda, John Alldis Ch, RPO, A. Ceccato (CFP) Ⓓ **CD-CFP4575**
(CFP) ▭ **TC-CFP4575**
3. R. Scotto, Alfredo Kraus, Ambrosian Op Chor, Philh, R. Muti (EMI) Ⓓ [2] **CDEMTVD59**
(EMI) ⊙ [2] **EMTVD59**
3. J. Barstow, A. Davies, ROH Chor, RPO, R. Stapleton (RPO) Ⓓ **CDRPO7009**
(RPO) ▭ **ZCRPO7009**
3. J. Sutherland, L. Pavarotti, London Op Chor, National PO, R. Bonynge
(DECC) Ⓓ **430 470-2DH**
(DECC) ▭ **430 470-4DH**
3. J. Sutherland, C. Bergonzi, MMF Orch, J. Pritchard (r1962) (DECC) Ⓓ **433 221-2DWO**
(DECC) ▭ **433 221-4DWO**
3. E. Malbin, M. Lanza, J. Alexander Ch, RCA Victor Orch, C. Callinicos (r1950)
(RCA) Ⓓ [3] **GD60889(1)**
3. P. Domingo, P. Lavirgen, T. Berganza, Alfredo Kraus, J. Pons, G. Aragall, M. Caballé, P. Lorengar, J. Carreras, Seville SO, L.A. Garcia-Navarro (pp1991) (RCA) Ⓓ **RD61191**
3. P. Domingo, P. Lavirgen, T. Berganza, Alfredo Kraus, J. Pons, G. Aragall, M. Caballé, P. Lorengar, J. Carreras, Seville SO, L.A. Garcia-Navarro (pp1991) (RCA) ꝏ **09026 61191-5**
3. E. Caruso, A. Gluck, NY Met Op Chor, orch (r1914) (RCA) Ⓓ **09026 61242-2**
3. L. Pavarotti, R. Kabaivanska, G. Furlanetto, P. Pace, E. Dara, G. Sabbatini, P. Cappuccilli, P. Coni, S. Verrett, J. Anderson, Bologna Teatro Comunale Orch, L. Magiera (pp1991)
(DECC) ◐ **071 140-1DH**
(DECC) ▣ **071 140-3DH**
3. S. McCulloch, J. Oakman, Czech PO, J. Bigg (with instr track for singing)
(IMP) Ⓓ [2] **DPCD1015**
(IMP) ▭ **CIMPCD1015**
3. J. Carreras, A. Baltsa, K. Ricciarelli, R. Raimondi, Orch, Anon Cond (pp1991)
(MCI) Ⓓ **MCCD090**
(MCI) ▭ **MCTC090**
3. V. de los Angeles, C. del Monte, Rome Op Chor, Rome Op Orch, T. Serafin (r1959)
(CFP) Ⓓ **CD-CFP4602**
(CFP) ▭ **TC-CFP4602**
3. J. Barstow, A. Davies, ROH Chor, RPO, R. Stapleton (r1991) (RPO) Ⓓ [2] **CDRPD9006**
(RPO) ▭ [2] **ZCRPD9006**
3. C. Baker, D.M. Anderson, Op North Chor, English Northern Philh, P. Daniel (r1992)
(EMI) Ⓓ **CDC7 54785-2**
3. S. McCulloch, Czech PO, J. Bigg (r1992)
(IMP) Ⓓ **PCD1043**
3. J. Sutherland, J. Carreras, National PO, R. Bonynge (r1980) (DECC) Ⓓ **440 947-2DH**
(DECC) ▭ **440 947-4DH**
3. C. Bergonzi, J. Sutherland, MMF Chor, MMF Orch, J. Pritchard (r1962)
(DECC) Ⓓ **433 440-2DA**
(DECC) ▭ **433 440-4DA**
3. A. Moffo, R. Tucker, Rome Op Chor, Rome Op Orch, F. Previtali (RCA) Ⓓ **09026 61440-2**
(RCA) ▭ **09026 61440-4**
3. S. McCulloch, J. Oakman, Prague Phil Chor, Czech SO, J. Bigg (IMP) Ⓓ [3] **TCD1070**
3. A. Baltsa, J. Carreras, Tallis Chbr Ch, LSO, P. Domingo (r1990-91) (SONY) Ⓓ **SK53968**
3. Alfredo Kraus, R. Scotto, Philh, R. Muti
(EMIL) Ⓓ **CDZ103**
(EMIL) ▭ **LZ103**
3. G. Pareto, L. Bergamini, chor, orch (r1918)
(PEAR) Ⓓ **GEMMCD9117**
3. J. Carreras, P. Domingo, L. Pavarotti, Los Angeles Music Center Op Chor, Los Angeles PO, Z. Mehta (pp1994)
(TELD) ꝏ **4509-96200-5**
3. J. Carreras, P. Domingo, L. Pavarotti, Los Angeles Music Center Op Chor, Los Angeles PO, Z. Mehta (pp1994)
(TELD) ✪ **4509-96200-8**
3. M. Wittrisch, M. Teschemacher, chor, Berlin St Op Orch, F. Zweig (r1932: Ger)
(PEAR) Ⓓ **GEMMCD9129**
3. R. Tauber, orch (r1926: Ger)
(PEAR) Ⓓ **GEMMCD9145**
3. L. Pavarotti, N. Gustafson, A. Bocelli, Giorgia, B. Adams, A. Vollenweider, Bologna Teatro Comunale Orch, L. Magiera (pp1994)
(DECC) Ⓓ **444 460-2DH**
(DECC) ▭ **444 460-4DH**
3. C. Studer, P. Domingo, ROHO, J. Barker (pp1988) (9/89) (EMI) Ⓓ **CDC7 49811-2**
3. A. Gluck, E. Caruso, NY Met Op Chor, NY Met Op Orch (r1914)
(7/91) (RCA) Ⓓ [12] **GD60495(5)**
3. E. Caruso, A. Gluck, NY Met Op Chor, NY Met Op Orch (r1914) (7/91) (MSCM) Ⓓ **MM30352**
3. E. Caruso, A. Gluck, NY Met Op Chor, NY Met Op Orch (r1914)
(10/91) (PEAR) Ⓓ [3] **EVC3(1)**
3. J. Sutherland, L. Pavarotti, National PO, R. Bonynge (12/91) (DECC) Ⓓ **430 724-2DM**
3. M. Caniglia, B. Gigli, ROH Chor, LPO, P. Cimara (pp1939)
(7/92) (PEAR) Ⓓ [3] **GEMMCDS9926(2)**
3. M. Freni, L. Pavarotti, Ater Orch, L. Magiera (pp) (5/94) (DECC) Ⓓ [2] **443 018-2DF2**
3. J. Carreras, P. Domingo, L. Pavarotti, Los Angeles Music Center Op Chor, Los Angeles PO, Z. Mehta (pp1994)
(12/94) (TELD) Ⓓ **4509-96200-2**
(12/94) (TELD) ⊙ **4509-96200-1** ▭ **4509-96200-4**
3, 10a Capitol SO, C. Dragon (r1958: arr Dragon) (EMI) Ⓓ **CDM5 65430-2**
3, 14b, 18b T. Schipa, N. Garelli, A. Galli-Curci, orch, Anon (cond) (pp1913,1928)
(MEMO) Ⓓ [2] **HR4220/1**
3, 18b F. Wunderlich, H. Gueden, Bavarian Rad Chor, BRSO, B. Bartoletti (Ger)
(DG) Ⓓ [5] **435 145-2GX5(1)**
3, 18b L. Pavarotti, M. Freni, Ater Orch, L. Magiera (pp1980) (BELA) Ⓓ **450 002-2**
(BELA) ▭ **450 002-4**
3, 18b F. Wunderlich, H. Gueden, Bavarian Rad Chor, BRSO, B. Bartoletti (Ger)
(5/93) (DG) Ⓓ **431 110-2GB**
3, 4a, 4b, 7a, 7b, 13, 14a, 14b, 18a, 18b C. Valletti, ROHO, N. Rescigno (pp1958)
(MEMO) Ⓓ [2] **HR4191/2**
3, 4b, 7a, 7b, 18b Alfredo Kraus, Lisbon San Carlos Nat Th Orch, F. Ghione (pp1958)
(MEMO) Ⓓ [2] **HR4233/4**
3, 4b, 18b L. Pavarotti, J. Sutherland, L. Goeke, NY Met Op Chor, NY Met Op Orch, R. Bonynge (pp1970) (BUTT) Ⓓ **BMCD015**
(BUTT) ▭ **BMK015**
3, 6a, 6b, 6c, 7a, 7b, 8b, 8d, 9b, 10b, 13, 14b, 16b, 16c, 19. J. Sutherland, C. Bergonzi, R. Merrill, M.T. Pace, D. Carral, P. de Palma, P. Pedani, S. Maionica, G. Foiani, MMF Chor, MMF Orch, J. Pritchard (DECC) Ⓓ **421 325-2DA**
3, 6b, 6c, 18c E. Steber, A. Tokatyan, orch, W. Pelletier (r1940) (11/95) (VAI) Ⓓ **VAIA1072**
3, 6, 7, 8b, 8c, 9b, 10b, 13, 14, 16b, 16c, 19. J. Sutherland, C. Bergonzi, D. Carral, R. Merrill, P. Pedani, M.T. Pace, P. de Palma, G. Foiani, S. Maionica, MMF Chor, MMF Orch, J. Pritchard
(DECC) ▭ **417 331-4DA**
3, 7a-c P. Domingo, I. Cotrubas, Bavarian St Op Chor, Bavarian St Orch, C. Kleiber
(5/93) (DG) Ⓓ **431 104-2GB**
4a, 4b, 7a, 7b, 14a, 18b M. Callas, G. di Stefano, La Scala Chor, La Scala Orch, C.M. Giulini (pp1955) (MEMO) Ⓓ **HR4372/3**
4b J. Sutherland, L. Pavarotti, National PO, R. Bonynge (DECC) Ⓓ **433 066-2DWO**
(DECC) ▭ **433 066-4DWO**

4b J. Sutherland, C. Bergonzi, MMF Orch, J. Pritchard (r1963) (BELA) ① **450 006-2** (BELA) ▭ **450 006-4**
4b A. Galli-Curci, T. Schipa, orch, Rosario Bourdon (r1928) (12/89) (RCA) ① **GD87969**
4b G. Zenatello, anon (r1903) (6/90) (SYMP) ① **SYMCD1073**
4b E. Ventura, anon (r1904) (11/92) (MEMO) ① [2] **HR4408/9(1)**
4b G. Zenatello, anon (r1903) (5/94) (PEAR) ① [4] **GEMMCDS9073(1)**
4b F. de Lucia, anon (r1904) (1/95) (SYMP) ① **SYMCD1149**
4b, 7a, 7b, 9b(pt), 18b M. Moralès, L. Simoneau, Lamoureux Orch, P. Dervaux (r1953) (11/94) (PHIL) ① [2] **438 953-2PM2**
4b, 7a, 7b, 18b D. Borgioli, E. Surinach, orch (r c1924) (PEAR) ① **GEMMCD9091**
4b, 18b A. Galli-Curci, T. Schipa, orch (r1924) (PEAR) ① **GEMMCD9450**
4b, 18b J. Zoon, H. de Vries, London Studio SO (arr Vrijens) (PHIL) ① **438 940-2PH**
4b, 18b A. Galli-Curci, T. Schipa, orch (r1930) (2/89) (PEAR) ① **GEMMCD9322**
4b, 18b F. Hempel, H. Jadlowker, orch (Ger: r1900s) (12/91) (CLUB) ① **CL99-042**
4b, 18b J. Sutherland, L. Pavarotti, National PO, R. Bonynge (r1979) (12/93) (DECC) ① **433 439-2DA** (DECC) ▭ **433 439-4DA**
4b, 18b A. Galli-Curci, T. Schipa, orch (r1924) (3/94) (CONI) ① **CDHD201** (3/94) (CONI) ▭ **MCHD201**
4b, 18b A. Galli-Curci, T. Schipa, orch (r1928) (8/94) (NIMB) ① **NI7852**
4b, 18b A. Galli-Curci, T. Schipa, orch, Rosario Bourdon (r1924) (8/94) (ROMO) ① [2] **81004-2**
4b, 18b H. Roswaenge, M. Perras, Berlin St Op Orch, B. Seidler-Winkler (r1936: Ger) (4/95) (PREI) ① [2] **89209**
4c, 5, 6. M. Callas, Alfredo Kraus, P. de Palma, Lisbon San Carlos Nat Th Chor, Lisbon San Carlos Nat Th Orch, F. Ghione (pp1958) (2/90) (EMI) ① [4] **CMS7 63244-2**
4, 6. J. Anderson, Alfredo Kraus, Paris Op Orch, M. Veltri (pp1987) (12/88) (EMI) ① **CDC7 49067-2**
5, 12a Slovak Phil Chor, Bratislava RSO, O. Dohnányi (4/91) (NAXO) ① **8 550241**
6. M. Callas, Alfredo Kraus, Lisbon San Carlos Nat Th Orch, F. Ghione (pp1958) (EMI) ① **CDC7 49502-2**
6. L. Bori, orch (r1928) (PEAR) ① **GEMMCD9458**
6. C. Gonzales, E. Ferretti, Berlin RSO, R. Buckley (SCHW) ① [2] **314052**
6. E. Gruberová, L.M. Vodička, Czech PO, F. Haider (SUPR) ① **11 0345-2**
6. K. Te Kanawa, LPO, J. Pritchard (5/85) (CBS) ① **MK37298** (CBS) ▭ **40-37298**
6. A. Galli-Curci, orch (r1919) (2/89) (PEAR) ① **GEMMCD9308**
6. M. Freni, Rome Op Orch, F. Ferraris (10/89) (EMI) ① **CDM7 63110-2**
6. L. Tetrazzini, orch (r1907/8) (7/92) (PEAR) ① [3] **GEMMCDS9924(2)**
6. L. Tetrazzini, orch (r1911) (9/92) (EMI) ① [3] **CHS7 63802-2(1)**
6. L. Tetrazzini, orch, P. Pitt (r1907/8) (9/92) (EMI) ① [3] **CHS7 63802-2(1)**
6. L. Tetrazzini, orch, P. Pitt (r1907/8) (9/92) (PEAR) ① **GEMMCD9221**
6a R. Tebaldi, MMF Orch, T. Serafin (pp1956) (MEMO) ① [2] **HR4235/6**
6a A. Tomowa-Sintow, Sofia PO, R. Raichev (r1970s) (FORL) ① **UCD16742**
6a-c K. Te Kanawa, LPO, J. Pritchard (CBS) ① **CD39208**
6a-c A. Moffo, Munich RO, K. Eichhorn (EURO) ① **GD69113**
6a-c G. Pareto, orch, P. Pitt (r1920) (PEAR) ① **GEMMCD9117**
6a-c E. Steber, RCA Victor Orch, W. Pelletier (r1940) (RCA) ① **74321 24284-2** (RCA) ▭ **74321 24284-4**
6a-c V. de los Angeles, C. del Monte, Rome Op Orch, T. Serafin (r1959) (EMI) ① **CDM5 65579-2**
6a-c J. Sutherland, ROHO, F. Molinari-Pradelli (1/90) (DECC) ① [2] **425 493-2DM2**
6a-c M. Ivogün, orch (r1916: Ger) (8/92) (NIMB) ① **NI7832** (8/92) (NIMB) ▭ **NC7832**
6a-c A. Galli-Curci, orch, J. Pasternack (r1919) (3/94) (ROMO) ① [2] **81003-2**
6a-c, 8d, 9a, 16c, 19. R. Scotto, ROH Chor, ROHO, C.F. Cillario (pp1965) (MEMO) ① [2] **HR4291/2**
6a-c, 16b, 16c J. Varady, L. Odinius, Bavarian St Orch, D. Fischer-Dieskau (r1995) (ORFE) ① **C186951**
6a, 6b M. Ivogün, orch (r1916: Ger) (PREI) ① **89094**
6a, 6b E. Gruberová, LSO, C. Rizzi (TELD) ① **4509-93691-2**
6a, 6b M. Kuznetsova, orch (r1904: Russ) (6/93) (PEAR) ① [3] **GEMMCDS9004/6(1)**
6a, 6b, 6c A. Moffo, Philh, Colin Davis (CFP) ① **CD-CFP4575** (CFP) ▭ **TC-CFP4575**
6a, 6b, 6c M. Callas, N. Rescigno, Turin RAI Orch, G. Santini (r1953) (MEMO) ① **HR4293/4**
6a, 6b, 6c M. Dragoni, Munich RSO, G. Kuhn (r1991) (ORFE) ① **C261921A**
6a, 6b, 6c, 16c M. Callas, Turin RAI Orch, G. Santini (r1953) (FONI) ① **CDO104**
6a, 6c M. Caballé, RCA Italiana Op Chor, RCA Italiana Op Orch, G. Prêtre (11/92) (RCA) ▭ [2] **RK61044**
6a, 16b A. Pendachanska, Sofia SO, M. Angelov (r1994) (CAPR) ① **10 706**
6b M. Foley, Orch (r1949-53) (ODE) ① **CDODE1062**
6b G. Bellincioni, S. Cottone (r1903) (6/90) (SYMP) ① **SYMCD1073**
6b M. Sembrich, orch (r1908) (7/92) (PEAR) ① [3] **GEMMCDS9923(1)**
6b A. Nezhdanova, U. Masetti (r1906: Russ) (6/93) (PEAR) ① [3] **GEMMCDS9007/9(1)**
6b M. Kuznetsova, anon (Russ: r1905) (7/93) (SYMP) ① **SYMCD1105**
6b M. Garden, orch (r1911: Fr) (8/93) (SYMP) ① **SYMCD1136**
6b F. Hempel, orch (r1914) (3/94) (NIMB) ① **NI7849**
6b G. Bellincioni, S. Cottone (r1903) (4/94) (EMI) ① [3] **CHS7 64860-2(1)**
6b-d M. Caballé, RCA Italiana Op Orch, G. Prêtre (r1966) (RCA) ① **74321 25817-2** (RCA) ▭ **74321 25817-4**
6b, 6c M. Caballé, RCA Italiana Op Orch, G. Prêtre (RCA) ① **09026 61886-2** (RCA) ▭ **09026 61886-4**
6b, 6c E. Berger, Berlin City Op Orch, H. Schmidt-Isserstedt (r1940: Ger) (PREI) ① **89092**
6b, 6c H. Gueden, Santa Cecilia Academy Orch, A. Erede (r1954) (PREI) ① **90227**
6b, 6c N. Melba, orch, W.B. Rogers (r1910) (3/89) (LARR) ① **CDLRH221**
6b, 6c L. Tetrazzini, orch (r1911) (9/92) (PEAR) ① **GEMMCD9222**
6b, 6c L. Tetrazzini, orch (r1911) (9/92) (PEAR) ① **GEMMCD9223**
6b, 6c E. Orel, anon (Russ: r c1902) (7/93) (SYMP) ① **SYMCD1105**
6b, 6c N. Melba, orch, W.B. Rogers (r1910) (9/93) (RCA) ① **09026 61412-2**
6b, 6c N. Melba, orch, W.B. Rogers (r1907) (5/95) (ROMO) ① [3] **81011-2(1)**
6b, 6c N. Melba, orch, W.B. Rogers (r1910) (5/95) (ROMO) ① [3] **81011-2(2)**
6c C. Studer, L. Pavarotti, NY Met Op Orch, James Levine (DG) ▭ **439 153-4GMA**
6c D. Bryant, J. Pruett, RTBF SO, R. Zollman (r1990) (PRES) ① **PCOM1109**
6c V. de los Angeles, C. del Monte, Rome Op Orch, T. Serafin (EMI) ① **CDM7 64359-2**
6c M. Callas, Alfredo Kraus, Lisbon San Carlos Nat Th Orch, F. Ghione (pp1958) (EMI) ① **CDC7 54702-2** (EMI) ▭ **EL754702-4**
6c H. Schymberg, Swedish RSO, T. Mann (bp1945) (ALTN) ① **CDAN3**
6c G. Farrar, orch (r1906) (IRCC) ① **IRCC-CD805**
6c A. Galli-Curci, orch, J. Pasternack (r1919) (5/90) (NIMB) ① **NI7806** (NIMB) ▭ **NC7806**
6c I. Bohuss, anon (r1902: Pol) (6/93) (PEAR) ① [3] **GEMMCDS9004/6(1)**
6c A. Nezhdanova, orch (r1912: Russ) (6/93) (PEAR) ① [3] **GEMMCDS9007/9(1)**
6c G. Bréjean-Silver, anon (r1905) (12/94) (SYMP) ① **SYMCD1172**
6c A. Nezhdanova, orch (r1912: Russ) (3/95) (NIMB) ① **NI7865**
7. P. Domingo, Bavarian St Orch, C. Kleiber (DG) ▭ **419 091-4GW**
7. G. di Stefano, LSO, A. Erede (r1947) (EMI) ① **CDM7 63105-2**
7. H. Buff-Giessen, anon (r1906: Ger) (SYMP) ① **SYMCD1085**
7. P. Domingo, Bavarian St Orch, C. Kleiber (7/86) (DG) ① **415 366-2GH**
7. B. Gigli, orch, Rosario Bourdon (r1928) (9/88) (PEAR) ① **GEMMCD9316**
7. J. McCormack, orch (r1910) (4/94) (RCA) ① [6] **09026 61580-2(2)**
7, Oh, mio rimorso Alfredo Kraus, Philh, R. Muti (10/89) (EMI) ① **CDM7 63104-2**
7a B. Gigli, orch, Rosario Bourdon (r1928) (CONI) ① **CDHD170**
7a Alfredo Kraus, Madrid SO, G.P. Sanzogno (RNE) ① [2] **650004**
7a-c P. Domingo, Bavarian St Orch, C. Kleiber (DG) ① [3] **427 708-2GX3**
7a-c Alfredo Kraus, Madrid SO, G.P. Sanzogno (pp1991) (IMP) ① [2] **DPCD998**
7a-c D. Carral, C. Bergonzi, Santa Cecilia Academy Orch, J. Pritchard (r1962) (DECC) ① **440 417-2DM**
7a-c L. Pavarotti, National PO, R. Bonynge (7/90) (DECC) ① [2] **425 681-2DM2** (7/90) (DECC) ▭ [2] **425 681-4DM2**
7a, 7b B. Gigli, orch, Rosario Bourdon (r1928) (NIMB) ① **NI7817** (NIMB) ▭ **NC7817**
7a, 7b P. Domingo, New Philh, S. Milnes (RCA) ① [2] **GD60866** (RCA) ▭ [2] **GK60866**
7a, 7b J. Schmidt, BPO, S. Meyrowitz (r1931: Ger) (RELI) ① **CR921036**
7a, 7b Alfredo Kraus, MMF Orch, Z. Mehta (PHIL) ① **442 602-2PM** (PHIL) ▭ **442 602-4PM**
7a, 7b P. Domingo, NYPO, Z. Mehta (SONY) ① **MDK47176** (SONY) ▭ **MDT47176**
7a, 7b T. Beltrán, RPO, R. Stapleton (r1994) (SILV) ① **SILKD6005** (SILV) ▭ **SILKC6005**
7a, 7b R. Tucker, Rome Op Chor, Rome Op Orch, F. Previtali (r1960) (RCA) ① **09026 62550-2**
7a, 7b G. Martinelli, orch, J. Pasternack (r1917) (10/89) (NIMB) ① **NI7804** (NIMB) ▭ **NC7804**
7a, 7b G. Aragall, Berlin Deutsche Op Orch, L. Maazel (r1968) (10/93) (DECC) ① **436 463-2DM** (10/93) (DECC) ▭ **436 463-4DM**
7a, 7b L. Pavarotti, Parma Teatro Regio Orch, G. Patanè (pp1976) (5/94) (DECC) ① [2] **443 018-2DF2**
7a, 7b G. Zenatello, orch (r1916) (5/94) (PEAR) ① [4] **GEMMCDS9074(1)**
7a, 7b G. Thill, orch, E. Bigot (r1927: Fr) (8/95) (FORL) ① **UCD16727**
7a, 7b L. Pavarotti, Modena Teatro Comunale Orch, L. Magiera (pp1965) (10/95) (RCA) ① **09026 68014-2**
7a, 7b, 14a G. Zenatello, chor, orch (r1908) (5/94) (PEAR) ① [4] **GEMMCDS9073(1)**
7a, 7b, 14a G. Zenatello, chor, anon (r1906) (5/94) (PEAR) ① [4] **GEMMCDS9073(1)**
7a, 7b, 18a, 18b I. Kozlovsky, E. Shumskaya, USSR SO, Anon (cond) (r1930-50) (MYTO) ① **1MCD921.5**
7b G. Thill, orch, F. Heurteur (r c1925: Fr) (PEAR) ① **GEMMCD9947**
7b M. Wittrisch, Berlin St Op Orch, F. Zweig (Ger: r1932) (PREI) ① **8902**
7b L. Muratore, orch (r1905; French) (MSCM) ① **MM3037**
7b L. Pavarotti, Parma Teatro Regio Orch, G. Patanè (pp1980) (BELA) ① **450 002-** (BELA) ▭ **450 002-**
7b R. Tauber, orch (r1925: Ger) (PEAR) ① **GEMMCD914**
7b J. Patzak, orch, M. Gurlitt (Ger: r1929) (3/90) (PEAR) ① **GEMMCD938**
7b D. Smirnov, orch (r1913) (7/90) (CLUB) ① **CL99-03**
7b H. Roswaenge, orch (r1928: Ger) (2/92) (PREI) ① [2] **8920**
7b H. Roswaenge, Berlin St Op Orch, B. Seidler-Winkler (r1935: Ger) (10/93) (NIMB) ① **NI784**
7b F. de Lucia, anon (r1906) (1/95) (SYMP) ① **SYMCD114**
7b D. Smirnov, orch (r1910: Russ) (3/95) (NIMB) ① **NI786**
7b H. Roswaenge, Berlin St Op Orch, B. Seidler-Winkler (r1937: Ger) (4/95) (PREI) ① [2] **8920**

7b H. Roswaenge, BPO, E. Orthmann (r1933: Ger) (4/95) (PREI) Ⓓ [2] **89209**
7b G. Anselmi, Bettinelli (r1910) (7/95) (SYMP) Ⓓ **SYMCD1170**
7b, 7c F. de la Mora, WNO Orch, C. Mackerras (r1994-5) (TELA) Ⓓ **CD80411**
7b, 14a G. Zenatello, chor, orch (r1908) (12/93) (SYMP) Ⓓ **SYMCD1138**
7b, 14a G. Zenatello, chor, anon (r1906) (12/93) (SYMP) Ⓓ **SYMCD1138**
8a-d G. Taddei, B. Daniels, Vienna St Op Orch, A. Guadagno (pp1984) (ACAN) Ⓓ **49 402**
8a-d, 10b E. Bastianini, M. Callas, La Scala Chor, La Scala Orch, C.M. Giulini (pp1955) (MEMO) Ⓓ [2] **HR4400/1**
8a, 8b M. Battistini, M. Mokrzycka, orch, C. Sabajno (r1912) (10/92) (NIMB) Ⓓ **NI7831** (10/92) (NIMB) ⊟ **NC7831**
8b M. Battistini, M. Mokrzycka, orch, C. Sabajno (r1912) (10/92) (PEAR) Ⓓ **GEMMCD9936**
8b, 10b P. Lisitsian, E. Shumskaya, Bolshoi Th Orch, A. Orlov (r1947: Russ) (8/93) (PREI) Ⓓ **89061**
8b, 14b L. Warren, E. Steber, A. Tokatyan, chor, orch, W. Pelletier (r1940) (8/93) (VAI) Ⓓ **VAIA1017**
8d P. Amato, F. Hempel, orch (r1914) (PREI) Ⓓ **89064**
8d G. Pareto, M. Dragoni, orch (r1918) (PEAR) Ⓓ **GEMMCD9117**
8d A. Galli-Curci, G. De Luca, orch (r1927) (PEAR) Ⓓ [3] **GEMMCDS9160(2)**
8d A. Galli-Curci, G. De Luca, orch, J. Pasternack (r1918) (PEAR) Ⓓ [3] **GEMMCDS9159(2)**
8d N. Melba, J. Brownlee, H. Craxton (r1926) (3/89) (LARR) Ⓓ **CDLRH221**
8d A. Galli-Curci, G. De Luca, orch, J. Pasternack (r1918) (5/90) (NIMB) Ⓓ **NI7806** (NIMB) ⊟ **NC7806**
8d A. Granforte, A. Rozsa, La Scala Orch, C. Sabajno (r1930) (12/91) (PREI) Ⓓ **89048**
8d A. Galli-Curci, G. De Luca, orch, J. Pasternack (r1918) (3/94) (ROMO) Ⓓ [2] **81003-2**
8d G. De Luca, A. Galli-Curci, NY Met Op Orch, G. Setti (r1927) (10/94) (PREI) Ⓓ **89073**
9b(pt) C. Muzio, G. Tommasini, orch (r1911) (1/94) (ROMO) Ⓓ [2] **81005-2**
10a, 10b G. Aragall, D. Fischer-Dieskau, Berlin Deutsche Op Orch, L. Maazel (r1968) (10/93) (DECC) Ⓓ **436 464-2DM**
10b B. Weikl, Munich RO, H. Wallberg (ACAN) Ⓓ **43 327**
10b R. Bruson, Philh, R. Muti (CFP) Ⓓ **CD-CFP4575** (CFP) ⊟ **TC-CFP4575**
10b J. Schwarz, orch (Ger: r1916) (PREI) Ⓓ **89033**
10b D. Fischer-Dieskau, Berlin Deutsche Op Orch, L. Maazel (DECC) Ⓓ **433 069-2DWO** (DECC) ⊟ **433 069-4DWO**
10b P. Amato, orch, W.B. Rogers (r1911) (PREI) Ⓓ **89064**
10b D. Fischer-Dieskau, Berlin Deutsche Op Orch, L. Maazel (r1968) (DECC) Ⓓ **440 409-2DM**
10b D. Fischer-Dieskau, Berlin Deutsche Op Orch, L. Maazel (r1968) (DECC) Ⓓ **433 442-2DA**
10b G. Laperrière, Three Rivers SO, G. Bellemare (r1991) (CBC) Ⓓ **SMCD5127**
10b M. Maksakov, anon (r1901: Russ) (PEAR) Ⓓ [3] **GEMMCDS9111(2)**
10b S. Milnes, Minería SO, H. de la Fuente (r1981) (IMP) Ⓓ **PCD1109**
10b H. Schlusnus, Berlin St Op Orch, J. Prüwer (r1928: Ger) (PREI) Ⓓ [2] **89212**
10b H. Schlusnus, Berlin St Op Orch, J. Schüler (r1937: Ger) (PREI) Ⓓ [2] **89212**
10b G. De Luca, orch (r1917) (PEAR) Ⓓ [3] **GEMMCDS9160(1)**
10b G. De Luca, orch (r1929) (PEAR) Ⓓ [3] **GEMMCDS9160(2)**
10b G. De Luca, anon (r1907) (PEAR) Ⓓ [3] **GEMMCDS9159(2)**
10b G. Danise, orch (r1926) (PREI) Ⓓ **89995**
10b R. Stracciari, orch, G. Polacco (r1917) (PEAR) Ⓓ **GEMMCD9178**
10b H. Schlusnus, orch (r1921: Ger) (PREI) Ⓓ **89110**
10b L. Melchior, Orch (Danish: r1913) (8/88) (DANA) Ⓓ [2] **DACOCD311/2**
10b J. Hynninen, Estonian SO, E. Klas (4/90) (ONDI) Ⓓ **ODE731-2**
10b D. Hvorostovsky, Rotterdam PO, V. Gergiev (7/90) (PHIL) Ⓓ **426 740-2PH**
10b H. Schlusnus, Berlin St Op Orch, J. Schüler (Ger: r1937) (9/90) (PREI) Ⓓ **89006**
10b T. Ruffo, orch, C. Sabajno (r1907) (11/90) (NIMB) Ⓓ **NI7810** (NIMB) ⊟ **NC7810**
10b M. Battistini, orch (r1911) (2/92) (PREI) Ⓓ **89045**
10b R. Stracciari, anon (r1906) (7/92) (PEAR) Ⓓ [3] **GEMMCDS9924(1)**
10b M. Battistini, orch, C. Sabajno (r1911) (7/92) (PEAR) Ⓓ [3] **GEMMCDS9923(1)**
10b M. Battistini, orch, C. Sabajno (r1911) (10/92) (PEAR) Ⓓ **GEMMCD9936**
10b T. Gobbi, Philh, W. Susskind (r1950) (8/93) (TEST) Ⓓ **SBT1019**
10b G. De Luca, NY Met Op Orch, G. Setti (r1929) (4/94) (RCA) Ⓓ [6] **09026 61580-2(2)**
10b R. Stracciari, anon (r1906) (4/94) (EMI) Ⓓ [3] **CHS7 64860-2(2)**
10b G. De Luca, NY Met Op Orch, G. Setti (r1929) (10/94) (PREI) Ⓓ **89073**
10b C. Formichi, orch (r1920) (11/94) (PREI) Ⓓ **89055**
10b M. Battistini, orch (r1911) (10/95) (NIMB) Ⓓ **NI7867**
12a, 12. RCA Italiana Op Chor, RCA Italiana Op Orch, James Levine (r1966) (RCA) Ⓓ **74321 24209-2**
12a, 12b D. Krebill, RCA Italiana Op Chor, RCA Italiana Op Orch, G. Prêtre (RCA) Ⓓ **GD60205**
12a, 12b Chicago Sym Chor, Chicago SO, G. Solti (DECC) **OO** **430 226-5DH**
12a, 12b Ambrosian Op Chor, Philh, R. Muti (r1980) (EMI) Ⓓ [2] **CZS5 68559-2**
12a, 12b Chicago Sym Chor, Chicago SO, G. Solti (4/91) (DECC) Ⓓ **430 226-2DH**
15. Philh, I. Westrip (r1993) (IMP) Ⓓ **PCD1075**
15. BPO, H. von Karajan (10/87) (DG) Ⓓ [3] **419 257-2GH3**
15. NYPSO, A. Toscanini (r1929) (4/92) (PEAR) Ⓓ [3] **GEMMCDS9922**
15. La Scala Orch, A. Toscanini (r1951) (4/94) (EMI) Ⓓ [3] **CHS7 64864-2(2)**
16b, 16c M. Callas, Lisbon San Carlos Nat Th Orch, F. Ghione (pp1958) (EMI) Ⓓ **CDC5 55016-2**
16b, 16c C. Muzio, orch, L. Molajoli (r1935) (4/91) (NIMB) Ⓓ **NI7814** (4/91) (NIMB) ⊟ **NC7814**
16b, 16c L. Price, RCA Italiana Op Orch, F. Molinari-Pradelli (12/92) (RCA) Ⓓ [4] **09026 61236-2**
16b, 16c G. Dalla Rizza, orch (r1928) (4/94) (EMI) Ⓓ [3] **CHS7 64864-2(1)**
16c L. Price, RCA Italiana Op Orch, F. Molinari-Pradelli (RCA) Ⓓ **RD87016**
16c J. Sutherland, Sydney Eliz Orch, R. Bonynge (DECC) ◐ **071 149-1DH** (DECC) ▣ **071 149-3DH**
16c A. Galli-Curci, orch, J. Pasternack (r1920) (5/90) (NIMB) Ⓓ **NI7806** (NIMB) ⊟ **NC7806**
16c L. Tetrazzini, orch (r1913) (10/90) (NIMB) Ⓓ **NI7808** (10/90) (NIMB) ⊟ **NC7808**
16c K. Te Kanawa, LSO, Myung-Whun Chung (11/90) (EMI) Ⓓ **CDC7 54062-2**
16c E. Berger, Berlin St Op Orch (Ger: r1935) (12/91) (PREI) Ⓓ **89035**
16c L. Tetrazzini, orch (r1913) (9/92) (EMI) Ⓓ [3] **CHS7 63802-2(2)**
16c L. Tetrazzini, orch (r1913) (9/92) (PEAR) Ⓓ **GEMMCD9223**
16c A. Galli-Curci, orch, J. Pasternack (r1920) (3/94) (ROMO) Ⓓ [2] **81003-2**
16c A. Moffo, Rome Op Orch, F. Previtali (r1960) (4/94) (RCA) Ⓓ [6] **09026 61580-2(7)**
16c C. Muzio, orch (r1918) (1/95) (ROMO) Ⓓ [2] **81010-2**
16c I. Galante, Latvian Nat SO, A. Vilumanis (r1994) (11/95) (CAMP) Ⓓ **RRCD1335** (11/95) (CAMP) ⊟ **RRMC8035**
16c, 18b L. Bori, J. McCormack, Victor Orch, W.B. Rogers (r1914) (ROMO) Ⓓ [2] **81016-2**
18a-c K. Battle, P. Domingo, NY Met Op Orch, James Levine (pp1988) (DG) Ⓓ **445 552-2GMA** (DG) ⊟ **445 552-4GMA**
18b F. Yeend, M. Lanza, Hollywood Bowl SO, E. Ormandy (pp1947) (IMP) Ⓓ **PWKS4230**
18b J. Sutherland, L. Pavarotti, ROHO, R. Bonynge (DECC) ◐ **071 149-1DH** (DECC) ▣ **071 149-3DH**
18b G. Groves, J. Watson, J. Partridge (r1994) (ASV) Ⓓ **CDWHL2088**
18b M. Ivogün, K. Erb, orch (r1917: Ger) (PREI) Ⓓ **89094**
18b J. McCormack, L. Bori, orch (r1914) (ASV) Ⓓ **CDAJA5137** (ASV) ⊟ **ZCAJA5137**
18b M. Caballé, C. Bergonzi, RCA Italiana Op Orch, G. Prêtre (RCA) Ⓓ **09026 62699-2** (RCA) ⊟ **09026 62699-4**
18b E. Berger, J. Patzak, Berlin St Op Orch, Wolfgang Martin (r1936: Ger) (PREI) Ⓓ **89092**
18b F. de Lucia, J. Huguet, orch (r1906) (BONG) Ⓓ [2] **GB1064/5-2**
18b J. McCormack, L. Bori, orch (r1914) (5/93) (MMOI) Ⓓ **CDMOIR418**
18b M. Ivogün, K. Erb, orch (r c1918: Ger) (1/94) (CLUB) Ⓓ **CL99-020**
18b G. Zenatello, E. Mazzoleni, orch (r1911) (5/94) (PEAR) Ⓓ [4] **GEMMCDS9074(1)**
18b M. Freni, L. Pavarotti, Ater Orch, L. Magiera (pp) (5/94) (DECC) Ⓓ [2] **443 018-2DF2**
18b F. de Lucia, J. Huguet, anon (r1906) (1/95) (SYMP) Ⓓ **SYMCD1149**
18b A. Davies, S. Bullock, A. Bryn Parri (r1994) (11/95) (SAIN) Ⓓ **SCDC2085**
18b, 18c G. Zenatello, L. Cannetti, orch (r c1911) (12/93) (SYMP) Ⓓ **SYMCD1138**

Il Trovatore– opera: 4 acts (1853—Rome) (Lib. S. Cammarano, after A G Gutiérrez)

EXCERPTS. ACT 1: 1a. Introduction; 1b. All'erta!; 1c. Di due figli; 1d. Abbietta zingara; 2a. Che più t'arresti?; 2b. Come d'aurato; 2c. Tacea la notte placida; 2d. Di tale amor (Cabaletta); 3a. Tace la notte!; 3b. Deserto sulla terra; 3c. Non m'inganno; 3d. Ah! dalle tenebre; 3e. Di geloso amor. ACT 2: 4a. Vedi! le fosche (Anvil Chorus); 4b. Stride la vampa!; 5a. Soli or siamo; 5b. Condotta ell'era in ceppi; 6a. Non son tuo figlio?; 6b. Mal reggendo; 6c. Perigliarti ancor languente; 7a. Tutto è deserto; 7b. Il balen del suo sorriso; 7c. Per me ora fatale; 8a. Ah! se l'error; 8b. Perchè piangete?; 8c. Degg'io volgermi; 8d. E deggio (Finale). ACT 3: 9a. Or co' dadi (Soldiers' Chorus); 9b. Squilli, echeggi; 9c. Ballabile; 10a. In bracciò al mio rival!; 10b. Giorni poveri; 10c. Deh! rallentate; 11a. Quale d'armi fragor; 11b. Ah! sì, ben mio; 11c. Di quella pira. ACT 4: 12a. Timor di me?; 12b. D'amor sull'ali rosee; 12c. Miserere...Ah, che la morte ognora; 12d. Tu vedrai che amore; 13a. Udiste? Come albeggi; 13b. Qual voce!; 13c. Mira, d'acerbe lagrime; 13d. Vivrà! Contende il giubilo; 14a. Madre, non dormi?; 14b. Se m'ami ancor; 14c. Ai nostri monti; 14d. Che! Non m'inganno!; 14e. Parlar non vuoi?; 14f. Ti scosta!.

Manrico F. Bonisolli
Leonora R. Plowright
Conte di Luna G. Zancanaro
Azucena F. Cossotto
Verona Arena Chor, Verona Arena Orch, R Giovaninetti, G.P. Griffi (CAST) ▣ **CVI2005**

Manrico F. Corelli
Leonora G. Tucci
Conte di Luna R. Merrill
Azucena G. Simionato
Ferrando F. Mazzoli
Inez L. Moneta
Ruiz; Messenger A. Mercuriali
Old Gypsy M. Rinaudo
Rome Op Chor, Rome Op Orch, T. Schippers (EMI) Ⓓ [2] **CMS7 63640-2**

Manrico J. Björling
Leonora H. Schymberg
Conte di Luna H. Hasslo
Azucena K. Meyer
Ferrando E. Saedén
Ines I. Kjellgren
Ruiz O. Sivall
Old Gypsy B. Alstergård
Messenger S. Ingebretzen
Stockholm Royal Op Chor, Stockholm Royal Op Orch, H. Sandberg (pp1960) (BLUE) Ⓓ [2] **ABCD045**

Manrico J. Björling
Leonora N. Greco
Conte di Luna F. Valentino
Azucena B. Castagna
Ferrando N. Moscona
Ines M. Stellman
Ruiz L. Oliviero
Old Gypsy A. Kent
NY Met Op Chor, NY Met Op Orch, F. Calusio (pp1941) (FORT) Ⓓ [2] **FT1507/8**

Manrico J. Carreras
Leonora K. Ricciarelli
Conte di Luna Y. Mazurok
Azucena S. Toczyska
Ferrando R. Lloyd
Ines P. Cannan
Ruiz R. Leggate
Old Gypsy R. Earle
Messenger J. Treleaven
ROH Chor, ROHO, Colin Davis (r1980)
(PHIL) Ⓓ [2] **446 151-2PM2**

Manrico C. Bergonzi
Leonora A. Stella
Conte di Luna E. Bastianini
Azucena F. Cossotto
Ferrando I. Vinco
Ines A. Bonato
Ruiz F. Ricciardi
Old Gypsy G. Morresi
Messenger A. Mercuriali
La Scala Chor, La Scala Orch, T. Serafin (r1962)
(DG) Ⓓ [2] **445 451-2GX2**

Manrico P. Domingo
Leonora R. Plowright
Conte di Luna G. Zancanaro
Azucena B. Fassbaender
Ferrando E. Nesterenko
Ines A. di Stasio
Ruiz W. Gullino
Old Gypsy A. Giacomotti
Messenger A. Verrecchia
Santa Cecilia Academy Chor, Santa Cecilia Academy Orch, C.M. Giulini
(2/85) (DG) Ⓓ [2] **423 858-2GH2**

Manrico L. Pavarotti
Leonora J. Sutherland
Conte di Luna I. Wixell
Azucena M. Horne
Ferrando N. Ghiaurov
Ines N. Burrowes
Ruiz G. Clark
Old Gypsy P. Knapp
Messenger W. Evans
London Op Chor, National PO, R. Bonynge (r1976)
(3/87) (DECC) Ⓓ [2] **417 137-2DH2**

Manrico G. di Stefano
Leonora M. Callas
Conte di Luna R. Panerai
Azucena F. Barbieri
Ferrando N. Zaccaria
Ines L. Villa
Ruiz R. Ercolani
Old Gypsy G. Mauri
Messenger R. Ercolani
La Scala Chor, La Scala Orch, H. von Karajan (r1956)
(12/87) (EMI) Ⓓ [2] **CDS7 49347-2**

Manrico P. Domingo
Leonora L. Price
Conte di Luna S. Milnes
Azucena F. Cossotto
Ferrando B. Giaiotti
Ines E. Bainbridge
Ruiz R. Davies
Old Gypsy S. Riley
Messenger N. Taylor
Ambrosian Op Chor, New Philh, Z. Mehta (r1970)
(8/88) (RCA) Ⓓ [2] **RD86194**

Manrico J. Björling
Leonora Z. Milanov
Conte di Luna L. Warren
Azucena F. Barbieri
Ferrando N. Moscona
Ines M. Roggero
Ruiz P. Franke
Old Gypsy G. Cehanovsky
Messenger N. Sprinzena
R. Shaw Chorale, RCA Victor Orch, R. Cellini (r1952)
(8/88) (RCA) Ⓓ [2] **GD86643**

Manrico L. Pavarotti
Leonora E. Marton
Conte di Luna S. Milnes
Azucena D. Zajick
Ferrando J. Wells
Ines L. di Franco
Ruiz M. Baker
Old Gypsy R. Morrison
Messenger J. Bills
NY Met Op Chor, NY Met Op Orch, James Levine, F. Melano
(2/92) (DG) ◖ [2] **072 413-1GH2**
(DG) ▣ **072 413-3GH**

Manrico J. Björling
Leonora G. Cigna
Conte di Luna M. Basiola I
Azucena G. Wettergren
Ferrando C. Zambelli
Ines M. Huder
Ruiz O. Dua
Old Gypsy L. Horsman
Messenger G. Zammit
ROH Chor, LPO, V. Gui (pp1939)
(2/94) (LYRC) Ⓓ [2] **LCD173**

Manrico P. Domingo
Leonora A. Millo
Conte di Luna V. Chernov
Azucena D. Zajick
Ferrando J. Morris
Ines S. Kelly
Ruiz A. Laciura
Old Gipsy G. Bater
Messenger T. Willson
NY Met Op Chor, NY Met Op Orch, James Levine (r1991)
(6/94) (SONY) Ⓓ [2] **S2K48070**

Manrico Gordon Wilson
Leonora S. Bisatt
Conte di Luna G. Quinn
Azucena S. Grevelle
Ferrando P. Parfitt
Ines P. Shaw
Ruiz E. Rahme
Tallis Chbr Ch, European Chbr Op Orch, European Chbr Op Chor, D. Hinnells (r1992)
(10/94) (ASV) Ⓓ [2] **CDDCS225**

Manrico L. Pavarotti
Leonora A. Banaudi
Conte di Luna L. Nucci
Azucena S. Verrett
Ferrando F. E. d'Artegna
Inez B. Frittoli
Ruiz P. de Palma
Old Gipsy R. Scaltriti
Messenger E. Facini
MMF Chor, MMF Orch, Z. Mehta (r1990)
(7/95) (DECC) Ⓓ [2] **430 694-2DHO2**

Manrico F. Bonisolli
Leonora L. Price
Conte di Luna P. Cappuccilli
Azucena E. Obraztsova
Ferrando R. Raimondi
Inez M. Venuti
Ruiz; Messenger H. Nitsche
Old Gypsy M. Egel
Berlin Deutsche Op Chor, BPO, H. von Karajan (r1977)
(9/95) (EMI) Ⓓ [2] **CMS7 69311-2**

Manrico F. Corelli
Leonora L. Price
Conte di Luna E. Bastianini
Azucena G. Simionato
Ferrando N. Zaccaria
Inez L. Dutoit
Ruiz S. R. Frese
Old Gypsy R. Zimmer
Messenger K. Equiluz
Salzburg Fest Chbr Ch, Vienna St Op Chor, VPO, H. von Karajan (pp1962)
(9/95) (DG) Ⓓ [2] **447 659-2GX2**

Excs J. Sutherland, Orch, Anon (cond), D. Bailey (11/92) (DECC) ◖ **071 135-1DH**
1. R. Raimondi, N. Ghiaurov, BPO, H. von Karajan (10/88) (EMI) Ⓓ **CDM7 69549-2**
1b-d, 2a-d, 3a-e, 4a, 4b, 7b, 11b, 11c, 12b, 12c, 14a, 14b R. Plowright, A. di Stasio, B. Fassbaender, P. Domingo, W. Gullino, G. Zancanaro, E. Nesterenko, Santa Cecilia Academy Chor, Santa Cecilia Academy Orch, C.M. Giulini (10/85) (DG) Ⓓ **415 285-2GH**
1c T. Pasero, orch, L. Molajoli (r1927) (6/90) (PREI) Ⓓ **89010**
1c, 1d E. Pinza, Chor, orch, C. Sabajno (r1923) (2/89) (PEAR) Ⓓ **GEMMCD9306**
1d E. Pinza, NY Met Op Chor, NY Met Op Orch, G. Setti (r1930) (3/92) (PREI) Ⓓ **89050**
1d E. Pinza, NY Met Op Chor, NY Met Op Orch, G. Setti (r1930) (9/93) (RCA) Ⓓ **09026 61245-2**
2a-c, 12a-c, 14d, 14e M. Caballé, MMF Chor, MMF Orch, T. Schippers (pp1969) (MEMO) Ⓓ [2] **HR4279/80**
2a(pt), 2b, 2c E. Urbanová, J. Svobodová, Prague SO, J. Bělohlávek (r1993) (SUPR) Ⓓ **11 1851-2**
2a, 2c, 4a, 4b, 7a, 7b, 9a, 9b, 11b, 11c, 12a-c, 14f L. Pavarotti, I. Wixell, J. Sutherland, M. Horne, N. Ghiaurov, G. Clark, N. Burrowes, P. Knapp, London Op Chor, National PO, R. Bonynge (DECC) Ⓓ **421 310-2DA**
(DECC) ⊟ **421 310-4DA**
2b, 2c A. Galli-Curci, orch (r1923) (PEAR) Ⓓ **GEMMCD9450**
2b, 2c A. Galli-Curci, orch (r1923) (8/94) (NIMB) Ⓓ **NI7852**
2c R. Ponselle, orch (r1922) (PEAR) Ⓓ [2] **GEMMCDS9964**
2c C. Muzio, orch (r1917) (PEAR) Ⓓ **GEMMCD9143**
2c G. Bumbry, Stuttgart RSO, S. Soltesz (11/86) (ORFE) Ⓓ **C081841A**
2c H. Spani, La Scala Orch, C. Sabajno (r1927) (9/90) (CLUB) Ⓓ [2] **CL99-509/10**
2c G. Arangi-Lombardi, La Scala Orch, L. Molajoli (r1932) (10/90) (PREI) Ⓓ **89013**
2c L. Tetrazzini, orch (r c1912) (10/90) (NIMB) Ⓓ **NI7808**
(10/90) (NIMB) ⊟ **NC7808**
2c K. Te Kanawa, LSO, Myung-Whun Chung (11/90) (EMI) Ⓓ **CDC7 54062-2**
2c C. Muzio, orch, L. Molajoli (r1935) (4/91) (NIMB) Ⓓ **NI7814**
(4/91) (NIMB) ⊟ **NC7814**
2c F. Leider, orch (r1926: Ger) (5/91) (PREI) Ⓓ [3] **89301**
2c H. Spani, La Scala Orch, C. Sabajno (r1927) (12/92) (PREI) Ⓓ **89037**
2c C. Muzio, orch (r1935) (4/94) (EMI) Ⓓ [3] **CHS7 64864-2(1)**
2c C. Muzio, orch (r1917) (1/95) (ROMO) Ⓓ [2] **81010-2**
2c, 2d L. Price, L. Londi, Rome Op Orch, A. Basile (r1959) (RCA) Ⓓ **09026 62689-2**
2c, 2d A. Galli-Curci, orch, Rosario Bourdon (r1923) (8/94) (ROMO) Ⓓ [2] **81004-2**
2c, 2d, 12a, 12b L. Gencer, Milan RAI SO, F. Previtali (pp1957) (MEMO) Ⓓ [2] **HR4239/40**
2c, 2d, 12a, 12b J. Varady, Bavarian St Orch, D. Fischer-Dieskau (r1995) (ORFE) Ⓓ **C186951**
2c, 2d, 12b M. Callas, Milan RAI SO, A. Votto (r1953) (SUIT) Ⓓ **CDS1-5001**
2c, 2d, 12b J. Sutherland, C. Johnston, Sydney Eliz Orch, R. Bonynge (DECC) ◖ **071 149-1DH**
(DECC) ▣ **071 149-3DH**
2c, 2d, 12b C. Muzio, orch (r1920) (5/90) (BOGR) Ⓓ [2] **BIM705-2**
2c, 12b L. Price, Rome Op Orch, A. Basile (RCA) Ⓓ **RD87016**
2c, 12b L. Tetrazzini, orch (r1913) (9/92) (PEAR) Ⓓ **GEMMCD9224**
2c, 12b C. Muzio, orch (r1920) (1/94) (ROMO) Ⓓ [2] **81005-2**
2c, 12b F. Litvinne, orch (r1907: Fr) (12/94) (SYMP) Ⓓ **SYMCD1128**
2c, 12c R. Plowright, F. Bonisolli, Verona Arena Chor, Verona Arena Orch, R. Giovaninetti (CAST) ▣ **CVI2068**
2d I. Abendroth, anon (r1902: Ger) (SYMP) Ⓓ **SYMCD1085**
3a, 3b G. Zenatello, P. Amato, orch (r1909) (12/93) (SYMP) Ⓓ **SYMCD1138**
3a, 3b, 11b, 11c M. Gilion, F.M. Bonini, anon (r1906) (BONG) Ⓓ **GB1076-2**
3a, 3b, 11c G. Zenatello, P. Amato, orch (r1909) (5/94) (PEAR) Ⓓ [4] **GEMMCDS9073(2)**
3b H. Winkelmann, anon (Ger: r1904) (7/91) (SYMP) Ⓓ **SYMCD1081**
3b F. Tamagno, anon (r1903) (7/92) (PEAR) Ⓓ [3] **GEMMCDS9923(2)**
3b, 11c J. Schmidt, M. Saal, chor, Berlin St. Op. Orch, C. Schmalstich (r1930: Ger) (EMI) Ⓓ [2] **CHS7 64673-2**
3b, 11c F. Tamagno, Anon (pf) (r1903-04) (2/92) (OPAL) Ⓓ **OPALCD9846**
3c G. Russ, L. Longobardi, G. Pacini, anon (r1904) (12/93) (SYMP) Ⓓ **SYMCD1113**
3c-e F. Leider, R. Hutt, H. Schlusnus, orch (r1925: Ger) (5/91) (PREI) Ⓓ [3] **89301**
3c, 3d, 3e, 11c, 12c H. Roswaenge, H. von Debička, F. Hüni-Mihacsek, T. Scheidl, orch (r1928: Ger) (2/92) (PREI) Ⓓ [2] **89201**
4a Ambrosian Op. Chor, Philh, R. Muti (EMI) Ⓓ **CDC7 47274-2**
4a Rome Op Chor, Rome Op Orch, T. Schippers (CFP) Ⓓ **CD-CFP4277**
4a R. Shaw Chorale, RCA Victor Orch, Robert Shaw (RCA) Ⓓ **GD60205**
4a La Scala Chor, La Scala Orch, L. von Matačić (CFP) Ⓓ **CD-CFP4575**
(CFP) ⊟ **TC-CFP4575**

4a Chicago Sym Chor, Chicago SO, G. Solti (DECC) Ⓓ **433 822-2DH** (DECC) ▭ **433 822-4DH**
4a London Op Chor, National PO, R. Bonynge (DECC) Ⓓ **433 068-2DWO** (DECC) ▭ **433 068-4DWO**
4a London Op Chor, National PO, R. Bonynge (r1976) (DECC) Ⓓ **433 221-2DWO** (DECC) ▭ **433 221-4DWO**
4a ROH Chor, ROHO, L. Gardelli (EMI) Ⓓ **CDM7 64356-2**
4a Berlin Deutsche Op Chor, Berlin Deutsche Op Orch, G. Sinopoli (DG) OO **415 283-5GH**
4a La Scala Chor, La Scala Orch, R. Muti (EMI) Ⓓ **CDC7 54484-2**
4a La Scala Chor, La Scala Orch, L. von Matačić (r1960) (CFP) Ⓓ **CD-CFP4602** (CFP) ▭ **TC-CFP4602**
4a ROH Chor, RPO, R. Stapleton (r1990) (RPO) Ⓓ [2] **CDRPD9006** (RPO) ▭ [2] **ZCRPD9006**
4a ROH Chor, ROHO, Colin Davis (r1981) (BELA) Ⓓ **450 052-2** (BELA) ▭ **450 052-4**
4a London Op Chor, National PO, R. Bonynge (r1976) (DECC) Ⓓ **433 443-2DA** (DECC) ▭ **433 443-4DA**
4a LSC, LSO, R. Hickox (r1987) (IMP) Ⓓ [3] **TCD1070**
4a LSC, LSO, R. Hickox (r1987/8) (IMP) Ⓓ [3] **TCD1073**
4a Berlin Deutsche Op Chor, Berlin Deutsche Op Orch, G. Sinopoli (10/85) (DG) Ⓓ **415 283-2GH**
4a Orphei Drängar Ch, Swedish RSO, E. Ericson, L. Segerstam (pp1978) (7/88) (BIS) Ⓓ **BIS-CD383**
4a LSC, LSO, R. Hickox (4/89) (IMP) Ⓓ **PCD908**
4a ROH Chor, ROHO, B. Haitink (12/89) (EMI) Ⓓ **CDC7 49849-2**
4a ROH Chor, RPO, R. Stapleton (10/90) (IMP) Ⓓ **MCD15** (10/90) (IMP) ▭ **MCC15**
4a, 4b, 11c R. Tebaldi, G. Simionato, M. del Monaco, A. Cesarini, MMF Chor, Geneva Grand Th Orch, A. Erede (BELA) Ⓓ **450 133-2** (BELA) ▭ **450 133-4**
4a, 5a, 5b G. Simionato, M. del Monaco, A. Balbi, MMF Chor, Geneva Grand Th Orch, A. Erede (r1956) (DECC) Ⓓ **443 378-2DM**
4a, 9a Fiesole School of Music Female Chor, MMF Chor, MMF Orch, M. Arena (ACAN) Ⓓ **43 540**
4a, 9a Slovak Phil Chor, Bratislava RSO, O. Dohnányi (4/91) (NAXO) Ⓓ **8 550241**
4a, 9b Chicago Sym Chor, Chicago SO, G. Solti (DECC) OO **430 226-5DH**
4a, 9b Ambrosian Op Chor, New Philh, Z. Mehta (r1969) (RCA) Ⓓ **74321 24209-2**
4a, 9b Berlin Deutsche Op Chor, BPO, H. von Karajan (r1977) (EMI) Ⓓ [2] **CZS5 68559-2**
4a, 9b Chicago Sym Chor, Chicago SO, G. Solti (4/91) (DECC) Ⓓ **430 226-2DH**
4a, 11c Cincinnati Pops, E. Kunzel (r1994; arr & orch Kunzel & Beck) (TELA) Ⓓ **CD80364** (TELA) ▭ **CS30364**
4b G. Simionato, Geneva Grand Th Orch, A. Erede (r1956) (DECC) Ⓓ **433 068-2DWO** (DECC) ▭ **433 068-4DWO**
4b M. Horne, National PO, R. Bonynge (r1976) (DECC) Ⓓ **433 221-2DWO** (DECC) ▭ **433 221-4DWO**
4b E. Randová, Brno St PO, O. Lenárd (pp1992) (SUPR) Ⓓ **11 1846-2**
4b E. Leisner, orch (r1916: Ger) (PREI) Ⓓ [2] **89210**
4b E. Stignani, EIAR Orch, A. la Rosa Parodi (r1940) (1/91) (PREI) Ⓓ **89014**
4b R. Anday, Vienna St Op Orch, K. Alwin (r1930) (5/92) (PREI) Ⓓ **89046**
4b K. Branzell, orch (Ger: r1927) (8/92) (PREI) Ⓓ **89039**
4b F. Cossotto, New Philh, Z. Mehta (r1969) (4/94) (RCA) Ⓓ [6] **09026 61580-2(8)**
4b I. Minghini-Cattaneo, La Scala Orch, C. Sabajno (r1930) (4/94) (EMI) Ⓓ [3] **CHS7 64864-2(1)**
4b, 5a, 5b G. Simionato, M. del Monaco, A. Balbi, MMF Chor, SRO, A. Erede (r1956) (DECC) Ⓓ **440 406-2DM**
4b, 5a, 5b I. Minghini-Cattaneo, A. Pertile, A. Gelli, La Scala Orch, C. Sabajno (r1930) (6/90) (PREI) Ⓓ **89008**
4b, 5a, 5b, 10a-c, 14a-c G. Simionato, F. Corelli, E. Bastianini, N. Zaccaria, Vienna St Op Chor, VPO, H. von Karajan (pp1962) (MEMO) Ⓓ [2] **HR4386/7**
4b, 5b M. Lipovšek, Munich RO, G. Patanè (6/90) (ORFE) Ⓓ **C179891A**
4b, 5b M. Klose, Berlin St Op Orch, B. Seidler-Winkler (r1937: Ger) (7/95) (PREI) Ⓓ **89082**
4b, 11c G. Simionato, R. Tebaldi, M. del Monaco, MMF Chor, Geneva Grand Th Orch, A. Erede (r1956) (DECC) Ⓓ **433 442-2DA**
4, 9a, 9b Forum Op Chor, Forum PO, G. Bellini (EURM) Ⓓ **350214**
5. M. Callas, Paris Cons, N. Rescigno (9/87) (EMI) Ⓓ **CDC7 47943-2**
5a, 5b, 6a, 6b, 6c A. Baltsa, J. Carreras, J. Howard, LSO, P. Domingo (r1990-91) (SONY) Ⓓ **SK53968**
5b F. Barbieri, M. Caruso, orch, A. Quadri (r1949) (4/92) (EMI) Ⓓ [7] **CHS7 69741-2(7)**
5b R. Anday, orch (Ger: r1926) (5/92) (PREI) Ⓓ **89046**
5b K. Branzell, orch (r1927) (8/92) (PREI) Ⓓ **89039**
5b E. Stignani, Rome Op Orch, L. Ricci (r1946) (4/94) (EMI) Ⓓ [3] **CHS7 64864-2(2)**
6a, 6b, 11a-c, 14d-f F. Corelli, VPO, H. von Karajan (pp1962) (MEMO) Ⓓ [2] **HR4204/5**
6a, 6b, 11a, 11b, 11c, 12c, 14a, 14c, 14d J. Björling, K. Meyer, O. Sivall, H. Schymberg, H. Hasslo, Stockholm Royal Op Chor, Stockholm Royal Op Orch, H. Sandberg (pp1960) (BLUE) Ⓓ **ABCD002**
6a, 6b, 11a-c J. Björling, N. Greco, B. Castagna, L. Oliviero, NY Met Op Chor, NY Met Op Orch, F. Calusio (pp1941) (2/94) (MYTO) Ⓓ [2] **2MCD90317**
6a, 6b, 14a-c, 18a, 18b L. Price, L. Dutoit, G. Simionato, E. Bastianini, F. Corelli, Vienna St Op Chor, VPO, H. von Karajan (pp1962) (MEMO) Ⓓ [2] **HR4396/7**
6b J. Patzak, G. Rünger, Berlin St Op Orch (Ger: r1936) (3/90) (PEAR) Ⓓ **GEMMCD9383**
6b G. Zenatello, E. Bruno, orch (r1911) (12/93) (SYMP) Ⓓ **SYMCD1138**
6b G. Zenatello, E. Bruno, orch (r1911) (5/94) (PEAR) Ⓓ [4] **GEMMCDS9073(2)**
6b, 14b, 14c L. Homer, E. Caruso, orch (r1910) (NIMB) Ⓓ **NI7834** (NIMB) ▭ **NC7834**
6b, 14b, 14c L. Homer, E. Caruso, orch (r1910) (7/91) (RCA) Ⓓ [12] **GD60495(3)**
6b, 14b, 14c E. Caruso, L. Homer, orch (r1910) (7/91) (MSCM) Ⓓ **MM30352**
6b, 14c E. Caruso, L. Homer, orch (r1910) (3/91) (PEAR) Ⓓ [3] **EVC2**
6c, 14b, 14c G. Zenatello, M. Gay, orch (r1911) (5/94) (PEAR) Ⓓ [4] **GEMMCDS9074(1)**
7a-c, 13b-d E. Bastianini, A. Stella, I. Vinco, La Scala Chor, La Scala Orch, G. Gavazzeni (pp1962) (MEMO) Ⓓ [2] **HR4400/1**
7a, 7b P. Cappuccilli, BPO, H. von Karajan (r1977) (CFP) Ⓓ **CD-CFP4656** (CFP) ▭ **TC-CFP4656**
7a, 7b D. Hvorostovsky, Rotterdam PO, V. Gergiev (7/90) (PHIL) Ⓓ **426 740-2PH**
7b R. Merrill, Orch, H. Barlow (bp1957) (VAI) ▣ **VAI69116**
7b B. Weikl, Munich RO, H. Wallberg (ACAN) Ⓓ **43 327**
7b J. Schwarz, orch (Ger: r1916) (PREI) Ⓓ **89033**
7b H. Schlusnus, Berlin St Op Orch, J. Schüler (r1937: Ger) (PREI) Ⓓ [2] **89212**
7b G. De Luca, orch (r1929) (PEAR) Ⓓ [3] **GEMMCDS9160(2)**
7b G. De Luca, anon (r1907) (PEAR) Ⓓ [3] **GEMMCDS9159(1)**
7b G. De Luca, orch (r1917) (PEAR) Ⓓ [3] **GEMMCDS9160(1)**
7b R. Stracciari, orch (r1917) (PEAR) Ⓓ **GEMMCD9178**
7b C. Tagliabue, orch (r1939) (PREI) Ⓓ **89995**
7b D. Fischer-Dieskau, BPO, A. Erede (r1959) (EMI) Ⓓ [2] **CMS5 65621-2**
7b L. Melchior, Orch (Danish: r1913) (8/88) (DANA) Ⓓ [2] **DACOCD311/2**
7b G. Bechi, La Scala Orch, U. Berrettoni (r1941) (2/90) (PREI) Ⓓ **89009**
7b J. Hynninen, Estonian SO, E. Klas (4/90) (ONDI) Ⓓ **ODE731-2**
7b H. Schlusnus, Berlin St Op Orch, J. Schüler (Ger: r1937) (9/90) (PREI) Ⓓ **89006**
7b C. Tagliabue, La Scala Orch, U. Berrettoni (r1946) (11/90) (PREI) Ⓓ **89015**
7b L. Tibbett, orch (pp1936) (3/91) (PEAR) Ⓓ [2] **GEMMCDS9452**
7b G. De Luca, orch (r1917) (1/92) (PREI) Ⓓ **89036**
7b C. Galeffi, La Scala Orch, L. Molajoli (r1926) (2/92) (PREI) Ⓓ **89040**
7b R. Stracciari, orch (r1909) (7/92) (PEAR) Ⓓ [3] **GEMMCDS9924(1)**
7b G. Pacini, anon (r1905) (11/92) (MEMO) Ⓓ [2] **HR4408/9(2)**
7b P. Lisitsian, Bolshoi Th Orch, V. Piradov (r1948: Russ) (8/93) (PREI) Ⓓ **89061**
7b H. Schlusnus, Berlin Staatskapelle, J. Schüler (r1937: Ger) (10/93) (NIMB) Ⓓ **NI7848**
7b G. Hüsch, W. Strienz, Berlin St Op Orch, H.U. Müller (r1935: Ger) (3/94) (PREI) Ⓓ **89071**
7b G. De Luca, orch, Rosario Bourdon (r1929) (10/94) (PREI) Ⓓ **89073**
7b, 7c H. Schlusnus, Berlin St Op Orch, J. Prüwer (r1928: Ger) (PREI) Ⓓ [2] **89212**
7b, 7c A. Granforte, La Scala Orch, C. Sabajno (r1928) (12/91) (PREI) Ⓓ **89048**
7c G. De Luca, NY Met Op Chor, NY Met Op Orch, G. Setti (r1930) (PEAR) Ⓓ [3] **GEMMCDS9160(2)**
7c B. Franci, G. Masini, La Scala Chor, La Scala Orch, C. Sabajno (r1928) (4/94) (EMI) Ⓓ [3] **CHS7 64864-2(1)**
7c G. De Luca, NY Met Op Chor, NY Met Op Orch, G. Setti (r1930) (10/94) (PREI) Ⓓ **89073**
9b London Op Chor, National PO, R. Bonynge (DECC) Ⓓ **433 069-2DWO** (DECC) ▭ **433 069-4DWO**
9b Dresden St Op Chor, Dresden St Op Orch, S. Varviso (r1985) (BELA) Ⓓ **450 052-2** (BELA) ▭ **450 052-4**
9b La Scala Chor, La Scala Orch, E. Panizza (pp1928) (4/94) (EMI) Ⓓ [3] **CHS7 64864-2(1)**
9c Monte Carlo Op Orch, A. de Almeida (r1973) (PHIL) Ⓓ [2] **442 550-2PM2**
11. A. Pertile, orch (r1925) (7/92) (PEAR) Ⓓ [3] **GEMMCDS9926(1)**
11a-c G. Flossmann, L. Pavarotti, P. Baillie, Vienna Op Chor, Vienna Volksoper Orch, N. Rescigno (7/90) (DECC) Ⓓ [2] **425 681-2DM2** (7/90) (DECC) ▭ [2] **425 681-4DM2**
11a, 11c G. Martinelli, G. Anthony, NY Met Op Chor, NY Met Op Orch, G. Setti (r1927) (3/93) (PREI) Ⓓ **89062**
11b C. Bergonzi, Santa Cecilia Academy Orch, G. Gavazzeni (DECC) Ⓓ **433 067-2DWO** (DECC) ▭ **433 067-4DWO**
11b A. Paoli, orch (r1911) (PREI) Ⓓ **89998**
11b E. Caruso, orch (r1908) (RCA) Ⓓ **09026 61242-2**
11b J. Schmidt, BPO, S. Meyrowitz (r1931: Ger) (RELI) Ⓓ **CR921036**
11b J. Vickers, Rome Op Orch, T. Serafin (r1961) (VAI) Ⓓ **VAIA1016**
11b B. Prevedi, ROHO, E. Downes (r1964) (DECC) Ⓓ **436 314-2DA** (DECC) ▭ **436 314-4DA**
11b C. Bergonzi, Santa Cecilia Academy Orch, G. Gavazzeni (r1957) (DECC) Ⓓ **440 417-2DM**
11b R. Tucker, Rome Op Chor, Rome Op Orch, A. Basile (r1959) (RCA) Ⓓ **09026 62550-2**
11b A. Piccaver, Berlin St Op Orch, J. Prüwer (r1928) (PREI) Ⓓ [2] **89217**
11b F. de Lucia, orch (r1917) (BONG) Ⓓ [2] **GB1064/5-2**
11b J. Björling, orch, N. Grevillius (r1939) (10/88) (EMI) Ⓓ **CDH7 61053-2**
11b E. Caruso, orch (r1908) (5/89) (PEAR) Ⓓ **GEMMCD9309**
11b F. Völker, Berlin St Op Orch, M. Gurlitt (r1928: Ger) (2/90) (PREI) Ⓓ **89005**
11b A. Pertile, La Scala Orch, C. Sabajno (r1927) (9/90) (PREI) Ⓓ **89007**
11b L. Slezak, orch (Ger: r1907) (2/91) (PREI) Ⓓ **89020**
11b E. Caruso, orch (r1908) (7/91) (RCA) Ⓓ [12] **GD60495(3)**
11b H. Roswaenge, orch (r1927: Ger) (2/92) (PREI) Ⓓ [2] **89201**
11b G. Martinelli, orch, W.B. Rogers (r1915) (10/92) (TEST) Ⓓ **SBT1005**
11b J. Johnston, orch, M. Mudie (r1948: Eng) (4/95) (TEST) Ⓓ **SBT1058**
11b E. Caruso, orch (r1908) (7/95) (NIMB) Ⓓ **NI7866**
11b, 11c P. Domingo, R. Wagner Chorale, Los Angeles PO, C.M. Giulini (DG) ▭ **419 091-4GW**

11b, 11c L. Escalais, anon (r1905; French) (MSCM) Ⓓ **MM30377**
11b, 11c C. Bergonzi, Ambrosian Sngrs, New Philh, N. Santi (PHIL) Ⓓ [3] **432 486-2PM3**
11b, 11c P. Domingo, L. Price, New Philh, Z. Mehta (RCA) Ⓓ [2] **GD60866** (RCA) ▭ [2] **GK60866**
11b, 11c H. Roswaenge, Philh Hungarica, Z. Rozsnyai (pp1959) (PREI) Ⓓ **90103**
11b, 11c J. Björling, orch, N. Grevillius (r1939) (NIMB) Ⓓ **NI7835**
11b, 11c R. Tebaldi, M. del Monaco, A. Cesarini, MMF Chor, SRO, A. Erede (r1956) (DECC) Ⓓ **440 407-2DM**
11b, 11c H. Roswaenge, Berlin St Op Orch, B. Seidler-Winkler (r1938: Ger) (PREI) Ⓓ [2] **89211**
11b, 11c P. Domingo, R. Wagner Chorale, Los Angeles PO, C.M. Giulini (r1980) (DG) Ⓓ **445 525-2GMA** (DG) ▭ **445 525-4GMA**
11b, 11c J. Sutherland, L. Pavarotti, National PO, R. Bonynge (7/86) (DECC) Ⓓ [2] **417 011-2DH2**
11b, 11c R. Tauber, orch (Ger: r1925/6) (7/89) (PEAR) Ⓓ **GEMMCD9327**
11b, 11c H. Roswaenge, Berlin St Op Orch, B. Seidler-Winkler (Ger: r1938) (5/90) (PEAR) Ⓓ **GEMMCD9394**
11b, 11c H. Roswaenge, Berlin St Op Orch, B. Seidler-Winkler (r1938: Ger) (5/90) (PREI) Ⓓ **89018**
11b, 11c A. Cortis, La Scala Orch, C. Sabajno (r1930) (10/91) (PREI) Ⓓ **89043**
11b, 11c J. Björling, orch, N. Grevillius (r1938) (8/92) (BLUE) Ⓓ **ABCD016**
11b, 11c G. Lauri-Volpi, orch (r1923) (7/93) (NIMB) Ⓓ **NI7845**
11b, 11c G. Flossmann, L. Pavarotti, P. Baillie, Vienna Op Chor, Vienna Op Orch, N. Rescigno (r1969) (12/93) (DECC) Ⓓ **433 437-2DA** (DECC) ▭ **433 437-4DA**
11b, 11c A. Cortis, La Scala Orch, C. Sabajno (r1930) (3/94) (NIMB) Ⓓ **NI7850**
11b, 11c J. Björling, orch, N. Grevillius (r1939) (9/94) (IMP) Ⓓ **GLRS103**
11b, 11c J. Björling, orch, N. Grevillius (r1939) (9/94) (CONI) Ⓓ **CDHD214** (9/94) (CONI) ▭ **MCHD214**
11b, 11c L. Escalais, anon (r1906: Fr) (12/94) (SYMP) Ⓓ **SYMCD1128**
11b, 11c G. Martinelli, orch, W.B. Rogers (r1915) (7/95) (MMOI) Ⓓ **CDMOIR428**
11b, 11c B. Heppner, Bavarian Rad Chor, Munich RO, R. Abbado (r1993/4) (11/95) (RCA) Ⓓ **09026 62504-2**
11b, 14c E. Caruso, L. Homer, orch (r1908) (3/91) (PEAR) Ⓓ [3] **EVC2**
11c L. Pavarotti, Vienna Op. Orch, N. Rescigno (7/75) (DECC) ▭ **400 053-4DH**
11c P. Domingo, L. Price, R. Davies, New Philh, Z. Mehta (RCA) Ⓓ **GD84265**
11c F. Bonisolli, Berlin Deutsche Op Chor, BPO, H. von Karajan (EMI) Ⓓ **CDC7 54016-2**
11c J. Carreras, K. Ricciarelli, ROH Chor, ROHO, Colin Davis (PHIL) Ⓓ **432 692-2PH** (PHIL) ▭ **432 692-4PH**
11c M. del Monaco, R. Tebaldi, MMF Chor, Geneva Grand Th Orch, A. Erede (r1956) (DECC) Ⓓ **433 069-2DWO** (DECC) ▭ **433 069-4DWO**
11c L. Pavarotti, National PO, R. Bonynge (r1976) (DECC) Ⓓ **433 221-2DWO** (DECC) ▭ **433 221-4DWO**
11c H. Roswaenge, Berlin RSO, A. Rother (Ger: bp1940s) (PREI) Ⓓ **90096**
11c J. Björling, orch, N. Grevillius (r1934: Swed) (NIMB) Ⓓ **NI7835**
11c T. Harper, Slovak Phil Chor, Bratislava RSO, M. Halász (NAXO) Ⓓ **8 550497**
11c E. Caruso, orch (r1906) (RCA) Ⓓ **09026 61242-2**
11c Deng, Württemberg PO, R. Paternostro (SINE) Ⓓ **39820222**
11c J. Carreras, ROHO, Colin Davis (r1980) (BELA) Ⓓ **450 059-2** (BELA) ▭ **450 059-4**
11c J. Björling, orch, N. Grevillius (r1934: Swed) (PEAR) Ⓓ **GEMMCD9043**
11c J. Björling, orch, N. Grevillius (r1939) (PEAR) Ⓓ **GEMMCD9043**
11c J. Schmidt, chor, orch, W. Goehr (r1934) (EMI) Ⓓ [2] **CHS7 64673-2**
11c J. Carreras, K. Ricciarelli, R. Leggate, ROH Chor, ROHO, Colin Davis (r1980) (PHIL) Ⓓ **442 600-2PH** (PHIL) ▭ **442 600-4PH**
11c E. Caruso, orch (r1906) (10/89) (NIMB) Ⓓ **NI7803** (NIMB) ▭ **NC7803**
11c J. Schmidt, chor, orch, W. Goehr (r1934) (4/90) (EMI) Ⓓ **CDM7 69478-2**
11c B. Gigli, orch, U. Berrettoni (r1940) (5/90) (EMI) Ⓓ **CDH7 61052-2**
11c A. Pertile, E. Lattuada, G. Nessi, La Scala Orch, C. Sabajno (r1928) (9/90) (PREI) Ⓓ **89007**
11c E. Caruso, orch (r1906) (12/90) (PEAR) Ⓓ [3] **EVC1(2)**
11c E. Caruso, orch (r1906) (7/91) (RCA) Ⓓ [12] **GD60495(2)**
11c E. Caruso, orch (r1906) (7/91) (MSCM) Ⓓ **MM30352**
11c D. Yuzhin, anon (r1902: Russ) (6/93) (PEAR) Ⓓ [3] **GEMMCDS9001/3(1)**
11c J. Björling, orch, N. Grevillius (r1939) (10/93) (EMI) Ⓓ **CDH7 64707-2**
11c L. Pavarotti, London Op Chor, National PO, R. Bonynge (r1976) (10/93) (DECC) Ⓓ **436 463-2DM** (10/93) (DECC) ▭ **436 463-4DM**
11c G. Zenatello, orch (r1909) (12/93) (SYMP) Ⓓ **SYMCD1138**
11c G. Zenatello, orch (r1911) (5/94) (PEAR) Ⓓ [4] **GEMMCDS9074(1)**
11c E. Caruso, orch (r1906) (7/95) (NIMB) Ⓓ **NI7866**
12. M. Callas, G. di Stefano, La Scala Chor, La Scala Orch, H. von Karajan (r1956) (2/90) (EMI) Ⓓ [4] **CMS7 63244-2**
12a-d M. Callas, Paris Cons, N. Rescigno (2/93) (EMI) Ⓓ **CDC7 54437-2**
12a, 12b A. Galli-Curci, orch (r1924) (PEAR) Ⓓ **GEMMCD9450**
12a, 12b M. Dragoni, Munich RSO, G. Kuhn (r1991) (ORFE) Ⓓ **C261921A**
12a, 12b E. Destinn, orch, W.B. Rogers (r1916) (PEAR) Ⓓ **GEMMCD9172**
12a, 12b K. Te Kanawa, LPO, J. Pritchard (5/85) (CBS) Ⓓ **MK37298** (CBS) ▭ **40-37298**
12a, 12b H. Spani, La Scala Orch, C. Sabajno (r1928) (9/90) (CLUB) Ⓓ [2] **CL99-509/10**
12a, 12b R. Tebaldi, A. Cesarini, Geneva Grand Th Orch, A. Erede (8/91) (DECC) Ⓓ [2] **430 481-2DX2**
12a, 12b Z. Milanov, orch, F. Weissmann (r1946) (4/92) (EMI) Ⓓ [7] **CHS7 69741-2(7)**
12a, 12b A. Galli-Curci, orch (r1924) (3/94) (CONI) Ⓓ **CDHD201** (3/94) (CONI) ▭ **MCHD201**
12a, 12b E. Destinn, orch, W.B. Rogers (r1916) (5/94) (SUPR) Ⓓ **11 1337-2**
12a, 12b A. Galli-Curci, orch (r1924) (8/94) (NIMB) Ⓓ **NI7852**
12a, 12b A. Galli-Curci, orch, Rosario Bourdon (r1924) (8/94) (ROMO) Ⓓ [2] **81004-2**
12a, 12b E. Destinn, orch, W.B Rogers (r1916) (12/94) (SUPR) Ⓓ [12] **11 2136-2(5)**
12a, 12b, 12d K. Ricciarelli, Rome PO, G. Gavazzeni (12/87) (RCA) Ⓓ **GD86534**
12a, 12b, 12c M. Callas, A. Lance, Paris Op Orch, G. Sébastian (pp1958) (11/91) (EMI) ◖ **LDB9 91258-1** (11/91) (EMI) ▣ **MVC9 91258-3**
12b R. Ponselle, orch (r1918) (PEAR) Ⓓ [2] **GEMMCDS9964**
12b M. Caballé, Barcelona SO, G-F. Masini (11/92) (RCA) ▭ [2] **RK61044**
12b M. Callas, Paris Op Chor, Paris Op Orch, G. Sébastian (pp1958) (MEMO) Ⓓ **HR4293/4**
12b M. Callas, La Scala Orch, H. von Karajan (r1956) (EMI) Ⓓ **CDC5 55216-2** (EMI) ▭ **EL555216-4**
12b C. Muzio, orch (r1918) (PEAR) Ⓓ **GEMMCD9143**
12b E. Turner, orch, T. Beecham (r1928) (9/89) (EMI) Ⓓ **CDH7 69791-2**
12b M. Németh, orch (r1927) (10/89) (NIMB) Ⓓ **NI7802** (NIMB) ▭ **NC7802**
12b F. Leider, orch (r1925: Ger) (5/91) (PREI) Ⓓ [3] **89301**
12b J. Gadski, orch (r1914) (7/91) (CLUB) Ⓓ **CL99-109**
12b E. Turner, orch, T. Beecham (r1928) (7/92) (PEAR) Ⓓ [3] **GEMMCDS9925(1)**
12b F. Leider, orch (Ger: r1922) (7/92) (PEAR) Ⓓ [3] **GEMMCDS9926(1)**
12b H. Spani, La Scala Orch, C. Sabajno (r1928) (12/92) (PREI) Ⓓ **89037**
12b R. Ponselle, orch, R. Romani (r1918) (10/93) (NIMB) Ⓓ **NI7846**
12b E. Destinn, orch, W.B. Rogers (r1916) (11/93) (ROMO) Ⓓ [2] **81002-2**
12b M. Németh, orch (Ger) (1/94) (CLUB) Ⓓ **CL99-007**
12b R. Raisa, orch (r1917) (1/94) (CLUB) Ⓓ **CL99-052**
12b E. Destinn, Odeon Orch, A. Pilz (r1908: Ger) (12/94) (SUPR) Ⓓ [12] **11 2136-2(2)**
12b C. Muzio, orch (r1918) (1/95) (ROMO) Ⓓ [2] **81010-2**
12b R. Ponselle, orch, R. Romani (r1918) (7/95) (MMOI) Ⓓ **CDMOIR428**
12c G. Tucci, F. Corelli, Rome Op Chor, Rome Op Orch, T. Schippers (CFP) Ⓓ **CD-CFP9013** (CFP) ▭ **TC-CFP4498**
12c J. Sutherland, L. Pavarotti, London Op Chor, National PO, R. Bonynge (DECC) Ⓓ **433 064-2DWO**
12c F. Alda, E. Caruso, NY Met Op Chor, orch, W.B. Rogers (r1910) (NIMB) Ⓓ **NI7834** (NIMB) ▭ **NC7834**
12c M. Callas, G. di Stefano, La Scala Chor, La Scala Orch, H. von Karajan (10/88) (EMI) Ⓓ **CDM7 69543-2**
12c E. Caruso, F. Alda, orch (r1910) (5/89) (PEAR) Ⓓ **GEMMCD9309**
12c R. Ponselle, G. Martinelli, NY Met Op Chor, NY Met Op Orch, G. Setti (r1928) (10/89) (NIMB) Ⓓ **NI7804** (NIMB) ▭ **NC7804**
12c E. Caruso, F. Alda, orch, W.B. Rogers (r1909) (7/90) (CLUB) Ⓓ **CL99-060**
12c E. Caruso, F. Alda, NY Met Op Chor, orch (r1910) (3/91) (PEAR) Ⓓ [3] **EVC2**
12c E. Caruso, F. Alda, orch (r1909) (3/91) (PEAR) Ⓓ [3] **EVC2**
12c F. Alda, E. Caruso, NY Met Op Chor, orch, W.B. Rogers (r1910) (7/91) (RCA) Ⓓ [12] **GD60495(3)**
12c F. Alda, E. Caruso, orch, W.B. Rogers (r1909) (7/91) (RCA) Ⓓ [12] **GD60495(3)**
12c R. Tauber, E. Bettendorf, Berlin St Op Chor, orch (Ger: r1922) (12/92) (NIMB) Ⓓ **NI7830** (12/92) (NIMB) ▭ **NC7830**
12c E. Destinn, G. Martinelli, orch, W.B. Rogers (r1915) (11/93) (ROMO) Ⓓ [2] **81002-2**
12c R. Raisa, A. Tokatyan, orch (r1923) (1/94) (CLUB) Ⓓ **CL99-052**
12c G. Zenatello, E. Destinn, chor, orch (r1912) (5/94) (PEAR) Ⓓ [4] **GEMMCDS9074(1)**
12c G. Zenatello, M. Rappold, chor, orch (r1916) (5/94) (PEAR) Ⓓ [4] **GEMMCDS9074(2)**
12c R. Ponselle, G. Martinelli, NY Met Op Chor, orch, G. Setti (r1928 (2 vers) (11/94) (ROMO) Ⓓ [2] **81007-2**
12c E. Destinn, G. Martinelli, chor, orch, W.B Rogers (r1915) (12/94) (SUPR) Ⓓ [12] **11 2136-2(5)**
12c E. Destinn, G. Zenatello, chor, orch (r1912) (12/94) (SUPR) Ⓓ [12] **11 2136-2(5)**
12c R. Ponselle, G. Martinelli, NY Met Op Chor, NY Met Op Orch, G. Setti (r1928) (7/95) (MMOI) Ⓓ **CDMOIR428**
12c H. Nash, M. Licette, chor, orch (r1931: Eng) (11/95) (PEAR) Ⓓ **GEMMCD9175**
13a-d F. Leider, R. Hutt, orch (Ger: r1925) (5/91) (PREI) Ⓓ [3] **89301**
13a, 13b, 13c, 13d G. Tucci, P. Cappuccilli, I. Vinco, La Scala Chor, La Scala Orch, G. Gavazzeni (pp1964) (MEMO) Ⓓ [2] **HR4273/4**
13b-d M. Battistini, E. Barbieri, orch (r1913) (PEAR) Ⓓ **GEMMCD9016**
13b, 13c E. Burzio, A. Magini-Coletti, orch (r1906) (1/91) (CLUB) Ⓓ [2] **CL99-587/8**
13c R. Ponselle, R. Stracciari, orch (r1920) (PEAR) Ⓓ [2] **GEMMCDS9964**
13c A. Sved, V. Ursuleac, Berlin St Op Orch, C. Krauss (r1936: Ger) (PREI) Ⓓ **89096**
13c H. Schlusnus, S. Kurz, orch (r1923: Ger) (PREI) Ⓓ **89110**
13c C. Galeffi, G. Arangi-Lombardi, La Scala Orch, L. Molajoli (r1928) (2/92) (PREI) Ⓓ **89040**
13c R. Raisa, G. Rimini, orch (r1929) (1/94) (CLUB) Ⓓ **CL99-052**
13c R. Ponselle, R. Stracciari, orch, R. Romani (r1920) (7/95) (MMOI) Ⓓ **CDMOIR428**
13c, 13d E. Eames, E. de Gogorza, orch (r1909) (11/93) (ROMO) Ⓓ [2] **81001-2**
13d J. Schwarz, C. Dux, orch (Ger: r1918) (PREI) Ⓓ **89033**

14a-c H. Roswaenge, F. Beckmann, Berlin St Op Orch, B. Seidler-Winkler (r1943: Ger) (PREI) Ⓓ [2] **89211**
14a, 14b, 14c L. Pavarotti, S. Verrett, Bologna Teatro Comunale Orch, L. Magiera (pp1991) (DECC) ◖ **071 140-1DH** (DECC) ▣ **071 140-3DH**
14b, 14c E. Caruso, E. Schumann-Heink, orch (r1913) (RCA) Ⓓ **09026 61242-2**
14b, 14c R. Elias, R. Tucker, Rome Op Orch, A. Basile (RCA) Ⓓ **09026 62699-2** (RCA) ▭ **09026 62699-4**
14b, 14c E. Caruso, L. Homer, orch (r1908) (7/90) (CLUB) Ⓓ **CL99-060**
14b, 14c L. Homer, E. Caruso, orch (r1908) (7/91) (RCA) Ⓓ [12] **GD60495(3)**
14b, 14c E. Schumann-Heink, E. Caruso, orch (r1913) (7/91) (RCA) Ⓓ [12] **GD60495(4)**
14b, 14c B. Gigli, C. Elmo, orch, U. Berrettoni (r1940) (4/92) (EMI) Ⓓ [7] **CHS7 69741-2(7)**
14c M. Wittrisch, M. Klose, Berlin St Op Orch, F. Zweig (Ger: r1932) (PREI) Ⓓ **89024**
14c G. Simionato, M. del Monaco, Geneva Grand Th Orch, A. Erede (r1959) (BELA) Ⓓ **450 006-2** (BELA) ▭ **450 006-4**
14c M. Gilion, N. Frascani, orch (r c1909) (BONG) Ⓓ **GB1076-2**
14c E. Leisner, R. Hutt, orch (r1921: Ger) (PREI) Ⓓ [2] **89210**
14c E. Caruso, E. Schumann-Heink, orch (r1913) (5/89) (PEAR) Ⓓ **GEMMCD9309**
14c C. Elmo, B. Gigli, orch, U. Berrettoni (r1940) (5/90) (EMI) Ⓓ **CDH7 61052-2**
14c E. Caruso, E. Schumann-Heink, orch (r1913) (10/91) (PEAR) Ⓓ [3] **EVC3(1)**
14c G. Zenatello, A. Parsi-Pettinella, anon (r1906) (12/93) (SYMP) Ⓓ **SYMCD1138**
14c G. Zenatello, A. Parsi-Pettinella, anon (r1906) (5/94) (PEAR) Ⓓ [4] **GEMMCDS9073(1)**
14c M. Klose, M. Wittrisch, Berlin St Op Orch, F. Zweig (r1932: Ger) (7/95) (PREI) Ⓓ **89082**
14d G. Zenatello, E. Bruno, E. Mazzoleni, orch (r c1908) (12/93) (SYMP) Ⓓ **SYMCD1138**
14d G. Zenatello, E. Mazzoleni, E. Bruno, orch (r1911) (5/94) (PEAR) Ⓓ [4] **GEMMCDS9074(1)**

Vespri Siciliani, '(The) Sicilian Vespers'– opera: 5 acts (1855—Paris) (Lib. Scribe and Duveyrier)

EXCERPTS: 1. Overture. ACT 1: 2a. In alto mare e battuto dai venti; 2b. Deh! tu calma, O Dio possente; 3. Arrigo...Non altro?. ACT 2: 4a. O patria; 4b. O tu, Palermo. ACT 3: 5. In braccio alle dovizie; 6a. Sogno, o son desto?; 6b. Quando al mio sen; 7. Ballet—'The Four Seasons'; 7a. Winter; 7b. Spring; 7c. Summer; 7d. Autumn. ACT 4: 8a. È di Monforte il cenno!; 8b. Giorno di pianto; 9a. O sdegni miei, tacete; 9b. Arrigo! Ah, parli. ACT 5: 10. Si celebri alfine; 11. Mercè, dilette amiche (Bolero); 12. A toi que j'ai chérie (Alternative aria for Act 4).

Elena C. Studer
Arrigo C. Merritt
Monforte G. Zancanaro
Procida F. Furlanetto
Ninetta G. Banditelli
Bethune E. Capuano
Vaudemont F. Musinu
Danieli E. Gavazzi
Tebaldo P. Barbacini
Robert M. Chingari
Manfredo F. Poggi
La Scala Chor, La Scala Orch, R. Muti (CAST) ▣ **CVI2228**

Elena S. Dunn
Arrigo V. Luchetti
Monteforte L. Nucci
Procida B. Giaiotti
Bologna Teatro Comunale Chor, Bologna Teatro Comunale Orch, R. Chailly, L. Ronconi (CAST) ▣ **CVI2034**

Elena M. Arroyo
Arrigo P. Domingo
Monforte S. Milnes
Procida R. Raimondi
Ninetta M. Ewing
Bethune T. Sharpe
Vaudemont R. Van Allan
Danieli L. Goeke
Tebaldo K. Collins
Robert J. Morris
Manfredo A. Byers
John Alldis Ch, New Philh, James Levine (r1973) (9/88) (RCA) Ⓓ [3] **RD80370**

A toi que j'ai chérie L. Pavarotti, La Scala Orch, C. Abbado (6/87) (CBS) Ⓓ **CD37228**
Quel est ton nom?...Henri T. Hampson, J. Hadley, WNO Orch, C. Rizzi (r1992) (TELD) Ⓓ **4509-98824-2**
Quel est ton nom?...Henri J. Hadley, T. Hampson, WNO Orch, C. Rizzi (r1992) (11/93) (TELD) Ⓓ **9031-73283-2**
1. New Philh, R. Muti (EMI) Ⓓ **CDC7 47274-2**
1. Sofia SO, V. Stefanov (LASE) Ⓓ **15 519** (LASE) ▭ **79 519**
1. Forum PO, G. Bellini (EURM) Ⓓ **350214**
1. Madrid SO, G.P. Sanzogno (pp1991) (IMP) Ⓓ [2] **DPCD998**
1. Madrid SO, G.P. Sanzogno (RNE) Ⓓ [2] **650004**
1. Philh, L. Magiera (DECC) **OO** **436 320-5DH**
1. Mexico St SO, E. Bátiz (r1990s) (ASV) Ⓓ **CDDCA856** (ASV) ▭ **ZCDCA856**
1. Hungarian St Op Orch, P.G. Morandi (r1994) (NAXO) Ⓓ **8 553018**
1. LSO, A. Dorati (r1957) (MERC) Ⓓ **434 345-2MM**
1. RPO, T. Serafin (r1959) (EMI) Ⓓ [2] **CES5 68541-2**
1. BPO, H. von Karajan (DG) Ⓓ [2] **447 364-2GDB2**
1. La Scala Orch, A. Guarnieri (r1927) (BONG) Ⓓ **GB1039-2**
1. RPO, A. Licata (r1994) (TRIN) Ⓓ **TRP044**
1. BPO, H. von Karajan (10/87) (DG) Ⓓ **419 622-2GH**
1. BPO, H. von Karajan (5/90) (DG) Ⓓ **429 164-2GR**
1. Philh, L. Magiera (11/91) (DECC) ◖ **071 150-1DH** (11/91) (DECC) ▣ **071 150-3DH**
1. La Scala Orch, A. Toscanini (r1951) (4/94) (EMI) Ⓓ [3] **CHS7 64860-2(1)**
1. Berlin RIAS Orch, F. Fricsay (r1952) (11/94) (DG) Ⓓ **445 406-2GDO**
1. I. Seefried, M. Forrester, E. Haefliger, D. Fischer-Dieskau, Berlin St Hedwig's Cath Ch, BPO, F. Fricsay, H. Krebs, T. Varga, Berlin RIAS Chbr Ch, Berlin RIAS Orch, H. Geusser, W. Fugmann, M. Weber, G. Herzog, Berlin RSO, VPO, E. Grümmer, G. Pitzinger, H. Hotter, Y. Menuhin (r1952) (11/94) (DG) Ⓓ [11] **445 400-2GDO10**
1. BPO, H. von Karajan (1/95) (DG) Ⓓ **439 972-2GGA2**
1. NYPO, L. Magiera (pp1993) (2/95) (DECC) Ⓓ **444 450-2DH** (2/95) (DECC) ▭ **444 450-4DH**
1. Santa Cecilia Academy Orch, V. de Sabata (r1947) (9/95) (EMI) Ⓓ [2] **CHS5 65506-2**
3, 6b J. Lotrič, I. Morozov, Slovak RSO, J. Wildner (r1994) (2/95) (NAXO) Ⓓ **8 553030**
4a, 4b R. Radford, orch, G.W. Byng (r1922: Eng) (PEAR) Ⓓ **GEMMCD9122**
4a, 4b E. Pinza, orch, Rosario Bourdon (r1927) (7/91) (MMOI) Ⓓ **CDMOIR404** (MMOI) ▭ **CMOIR404**
4b M. McEachern, orch (r1921) (PEAR) Ⓓ **GEMMCD9455**
4b B. Christoff, Philh, W. Schüchter (r1952) (EMI) Ⓓ **CDH5 65500-2**
4b E. Pinza, orch, Rosario Bourdon (r1927) (2/89) (PEAR) Ⓓ **GEMMCD9306**
4b E. Pinza, orch, Rosario Bourdon (r1927) (3/92) (PREI) Ⓓ **89050**
4b M. Reizen, Bolshoi Th Orch, V. Nebolsin (r1951) (2/95) (PREI) Ⓓ **89080**
5. G. Taddei, Naples San Carlo Op Orch, U. Rapalo (PREI) Ⓓ **90020**
5. H. Schlusnus, Berlin St Op Orch, A. Melichar (r1933: Ger) (PREI) Ⓓ [2] **89212**
5. H. Schlusnus, Berlin St Op Orch, A. Rother (r1943: Ger) (PREI) Ⓓ [2] **89212**
5. D. Fischer-Dieskau, BPO, A. Erede (r1959) (EMI) Ⓓ [2] **CMS5 65621-2**
5. H. Schlusnus, Berlin St Op Orch, A. Melichar (Ger: r c1931) (9/90) (PREI) Ⓓ **89006**
6a, 6b C. Bergonzi, D. Fischer-Dieskau, BRSO, J. López-Cobos (ORFE) Ⓓ **C028821A**
6a, 6b H. Roswaenge, H. Schlusnus, Berlin RSO, H. Steinkopf (bp1940s; Ger) (PREI) Ⓓ **90096**
6a, 6b P. Domingo, S. Milnes, LSO, A. Guadagno (r1970) (RCA) Ⓓ **09026 62595-2**
6a, 6b H. Roswaenge, H. Schlusnus, Berlin St Op Orch, A. Melichar (r1933: Ger) (4/95) (PREI) Ⓓ [2] **89209**
7. Bologna Teatro Comunale Orch, R. Chailly (DECC) Ⓓ **436 475-2DM**
7. Monte Carlo Op Orch, A. de Almeida (r1973) (PHIL) Ⓓ [2] **442 550-2PM2**
7. NY Met Op Orch, James Levine (r1992) (6/94) (SONY) Ⓓ **SK52489**
8a, 8b C. Bergonzi, New Philh, N. Santi (PHIL) Ⓓ [3] **432 486-2PM3**
8b P. Domingo, New Philh, James Levine (RCA) Ⓓ [2] **GD60866** (RCA) ▭ [2] **GK60866**
8b H. Roswaenge, Berlin St Op Orch, F.A. Schmidt (r1932: Ger) (4/95) (PREI) Ⓓ [2] **89209**
9b M. Callas, Paris Op Orch, N. Rescigno (r1969) (EMI) Ⓓ **CDC7 49428-2**
9b K. Ricciarelli, Rome PO, G. Gavazzeni (r1971) (RCA) Ⓓ **74321 24284-2** (RCA) ▭ **74321 24284-4**
9b M. Callas, Paris Cons, N. Rescigno (9/87) (EMI) Ⓓ **CDC7 47730-2**
9b K. Ricciarelli, Rome PO, G. Gavazzeni (12/87) (RCA) Ⓓ **GD86534**
9b M. Callas, Philh, A. Tonini (2/93) (EMI) Ⓓ **CDC7 54437-2**
11. R. Ponselle, orch (r1919) (PEAR) Ⓓ [2] **GEMMCDS9964**
11. M. Caballé, Barcelona SO, G-F. Masini (11/92) (RCA) ▭ [2] **RK61044**
11. M. Chiara, ROHO, N. Santi (DECC) Ⓓ **433 624-2DSP**
11. E. Gruberová, Smetana Th Chor, Czech PO, F. Haider (SUPR) Ⓓ **11 0345-2**
11. M. Chiara, ROHO, N. Santi (DECC) Ⓓ **433 069-2DWO** (DECC) ▭ **433 069-4DWO**
11. M. Chiara, ROHO, N. Santi (DECC) Ⓓ **433 221-2DWO** (DECC) ▭ **433 221-4DWO**
11. M. Korjus, Berlin St Op Orch, B. Seidler-Winkler (r1935) (DANT) Ⓓ **LYS001**
11. J. Sutherland, Paris Cons, N. Santi (r1959) (DECC) Ⓓ **440 404-2DM**
11. M. Callas, Philh, T. Serafin (r1954) (EMI) Ⓓ **CDC5 55016-2**
11. M. Major, NZ SO, B. Law (r1992) (KIWI) Ⓓ **CDSLD-82**
11. A. Cerquetti, MMF Orch, G. Gavazzeni (r1956) (DECC) Ⓓ **440 411-2DM**
11. C. Studer, La Scala Chor, La Scala Orch, R. Muti (pp1989) (EMI) Ⓓ **CDC5 55350-2**
11. J. Wiener-Chenisheva, Bulgarian RSO, S. Pennaci (r1970s) (FORL) Ⓓ **UCD16742**
11. M. Callas, Philh, T. Serafin (r1954) (11/86) (EMI) Ⓓ **CDC7 47282-2**
11. M. Callas, Philh, N. Rescigno (r1954) (2/90) (EMI) Ⓓ [4] **CMS7 63244-2**
11. C. Muzio, orch (r1924) (5/90) (BOGR) Ⓓ [2] **BIM705-2**
11. L. Tetrazzini, orch (r1914) (10/90) (NIMB) Ⓓ **NI7808** (10/90) (NIMB) ▭ **NC7808**
11. L. Tetrazzini, orch, P. Pitt (r1910) (9/92) (EMI) Ⓓ [3] **CHS7 63802-2(1)**
11. L. Tetrazzini, orch (r1914) (9/92) (PEAR) Ⓓ **GEMMCD9225**
11. L. Tetrazzini, orch, P. Pitt (r1910) (9/92) (PEAR) Ⓓ **GEMMCD9222**
11. A. Nezhdanova, orch (r1914: Russ) (6/93) (PEAR) Ⓓ [3] **GEMMCDS9007/9(2)**
11. M. Korjus, Berlin St Op Orch, B. Seidler-Winkler (r1935) (10/93) (PREI) Ⓓ **89054**
11. R. Raisa, orch (r1921) (1/94) (CLUB) Ⓓ **CL99-052**
11. C. Muzio, orch (r1924) (1/94) (ROMO) Ⓓ [2] **81005-2**
11. M. Freni, Ater Orch, L. Magiera (pp) (5/94) (DECC) Ⓓ [2] **443 018-2DF2**
11. C. Muzio, orch (r1918) (1/95) (ROMO) Ⓓ [2] **81010-2**
11. I. Galante, Latvian Nat SO, A. Vilumanis (r1994) (11/95) (CAMP) Ⓓ **RRCD1335** (11/95) (CAMP) ▭ **RRMC8035**

VERSTOVSKY , Alexey Nikolayevich *(1799–1862)* *Russia*

Askold's Grave– opera: 4 acts (1835—Moscow) (Lib. Zagoskin)
Drinking Song G. Nelepp, Moscow All-Union Rad Ch, Moscow All-Union RSO, V. Smirnov (r1952) (4/92) (EMI) Ⓓ [7] **CHS7 69741-2(6)**
In olden days our forefathers lived N. Shevelev, anon (r1901) (6/93) (PEAR) Ⓓ [3] **GEMMCDS9007/9(2)**
In olden days our forefathers lived L. Sibiriakov, chor, orch (r1910) (6/93) (PEAR) Ⓓ [3] **GEMMCDS9007/9(2)**
Near the town of Slavyansk A. Labinsky, anon (r1905) (7/93) (SYMP) Ⓓ **SYMCD1105**
Toropka's (3) arias G. Nelepp, orch (r c1950) (PREI) Ⓓ **89081**

VERT , Juan *(1890–1931)* *Spain*

La **leyenda del beso– zarzuela: 2 acts (1924—Madrid) (Lib. E Reoyo, Paso & S Arumburu)**
Amor mi raza sabe conquistar J. Carreras, I. Rey, ECO, E. Ricci (r1994) (2/95) (ERAT) Ⓓ **4509-95789-2** (2/95) (ERAT) ▭ **4509-95789-4**

VINCI, Leonardo *(1690–1730)* *Italy*

La **Caduta de' Decemvri– opera seria: 3 acts (1727—Naples) (Lib. Stampiglia)**
Nobil destrier feroce M.A. Peters, Italian International Orch, M. Carraro (pp1990) (MEMO) Ⓓ **DR3109**

Catone in Utica– opera seria: 3 acts (1728—Rome) (Lib. Metastasio)
EXCERPTS—ACT 1: 1. Chi in dolce amor condanna. ACT 2: 2. In che t'offende; 3. So che godendo vai. ACT 3: 4. Quell'amor che poco accende.
1-4. M.A. Peters, Italian International Orch, M. Carraro (pp1990) (MEMO) Ⓓ **DR3109**

Lo **Cecato fauzo– commedia musicali (1719—Naples) (Lib. Piscopo)**
Cecchimma Fauza M.A. Peters, Italian International Orch, M. Carraro (pp1990) (MEMO) Ⓓ **DR3109**

Didone abbandonata– opera series: 3 acts (1726—Rome) (Lib. Metastasio)
Ardi per me fedele M.A. Peters, Italian International Orch, M. Carraro (pp1990) (MEMO) Ⓓ **DR3109**

La **Festa di Bacco– commedia musicali (1722—Naples) (Lib. Tullio)**
Si mbè sò nzemprecella M.A. Peters, Italian International Orch, M. Carraro (pp1990) (MEMO) Ⓓ **DR3109**

La **Semiramide riconosciuta– opera seria (1729—Rome) (Lib. Metastasio)**
Tradita, sprezzata M.A. Peters, Italian International Orch, M. Carraro (pp1990) (MEMO) Ⓓ **DR3109**

VIVALDI, Antonio (Lucio) *(1678–1741)* *Italy*

RV numbers use in P. Ryom's Verzeichnis der Werke Antonio Vivaldi

L' **Atenaide o sia Gli affetti generosi– dramma per musica: 3 acts, RV702 (1728—Florence) (Lib. Zeno)**
EXCERPTS: 1. Un certo non so che; 2. Ferma, Teodosio.
1. M. Caballé, M. Zanetti (FORL) Ⓓ **UCD10902**
2. E. Kirkby, Brandenburg Consort, R. Goodman (r1994) (5/95) (HYPE) Ⓓ **CDA66745** (HYPE) ▭ **KA66745**

Bajazet (aka Tamerlano)– dramma per musica: 3 acts, RV703 (1735—Verona) (Lib. Piovene)
EXCERPTS: 1. Sinfonia; 2. Sposa son disprezzeta.
1. Brandenburg Consort, R. Goodman (r1994) (5/95) (HYPE) Ⓓ **CDA66745** (HYPE) ▭ **KA66745**
2. M. Caballé, M. Zanetti (FORL) Ⓓ **UCD10902**

Catone in Utica– dramma per musica: 3 acts, RV705 (1737—Verona) (Lib Metastasio: Act 1 lost)
EXCERPTS: 1. Se mai senti spirarti sul volto; 2. Se in campo armato.
1, 2. E. Kirkby, Brandenburg Consort, R. Goodman (r1994) (5/95) (HYPE) Ⓓ **CDA66745** (HYPE) ▭ **KA66745**

Dorilla in Tempe– dramma per musica: 3 acts, RV709 (1726—Venice) (Lib. Lucchini)

Dorilla	M. C. Kiehr
Elmiro	J. Elwes
Admeto	P. Cantor
Nomio/Apollo	J. Nirouët
Eudamia	C. Caroli
Filindo	L. Florentin

Nice Op Chor, Nice Baroque Ens, G. Bezzina (r1993) (2/95) (PIER) Ⓓ [2] **PV794092**

Ercole su'l Termodante– dramma per musica: 3 acts, RV710 (1723—Rome) (Lib. Bussani)
EXCERPTS: 1. Chiare onde.
1. M. Caballé, M. Zanetti (FORL) Ⓓ **UCD10902**

La **Fida ninfa– dramma per musica: 3 acts, RV714 (1732—Verona) (Lib. Maffei)**
EXCERPTS: 1. Alma oppressa.
1. K. Eckersley, Fiori Musicali, P. Rapson (10/90) (MERI) Ⓓ **CDE84195** (10/90) (MERI) ▭ **KE77195**

Griselda– dramma per musica: 3 acts, RV718 (1735—Venice) (Lib. Zeno, adapted by C. Goldoni)
EXCERPTS: 1. Sinfonia; 2. Agitata da due venti; 3. Ombre vane, ingiusti orrori.
1-3. E. Kirkby, Brandenburg Consort, R. Goodman (r1994) (5/95) (HYPE) Ⓓ **CDA66745** (HYPE) ▭ **KA66745**
2. M. Caballé, M. Zanetti (FORL) Ⓓ **UCD10902**
2. K. Eckersley, Fiori Musicali, P. Rapson (10/90) (MERI) Ⓓ **CDE84195** (10/90) (MERI) ▭ **KE77195**

L' **Incoronazione di Dario– dramma per musica: 3 acts, RV719 (1717—Venice) (Lib. Morselli)**
EXCERPTS: 1. Sinfonia; 2. Non mi lusinga vana speranza.
1. K. Eckersley, Fiori Musicali, P. Rapson (10/90) (MERI) Ⓓ **CDE84195** (10/90) (MERI) ▭ **KE77195**
2. E. Kirkby, Brandenburg Consort, R. Goodman (r1994) (5/95) (HYPE) Ⓓ **CDA66745** (HYPE) ▭ **KA66745**

Montezuma– pasticcio by J-C Malgoire after opera seria, RV723 (1733—Venice) (Lib. G. Giusti)

Montezuma	D. Visse
Mitrena	D. Borst
Teutile	I. Poulenard
Fernando	N. Rivenq
Ramiro	B. Balleys
Asprano	L. Masson

Voc Ens, Grande Ecurie, J-C. Malgoire (pp1992) (4/93) (ASTR) Ⓓ [2] **E8501**

L' **Olimpiade– dramma per musica: 3 acts (1734—Venice)**
EXCERPTS: 1. Overture.

Clistene	A.W. Schultze
Aristea	L. Meeuwsen
Argene	E. von Magnus
Megacle	M. van der Sluis
Licida	G. Lesne
Aminta	A. Christofellis
Alcandro	W. Oberholtzer

Cappella Voc Ens, Clemencic Consort, R. Clemenčič (pp1990) (NUOV) Ⓓ [2] **6932/3**
1. Freiburg Baroque Orch, T. Hengelbrock (r1992) (4/94) (DHM) Ⓓ **05472 77289-2**

Orlando (Furioso)– dramma per musica: 3 acts, RV728 (1727—Venice) (Lib. Braccioli)

Orlando	M. Horne
Angelica	S. Patterson
Alcina	K. Kuhlmann
Bradamante	Sandra Walker
Medoro	W. Matteuz
Ruggiero	J. G
Astolfo	K. Langa

San Francisco Op Chor, San Francisco Op Orch, R. Behr, P.L. Pizzi (MCEG) ▣ **VVD10**

Orlando	M. Horr
Angelica	V. de los Angel
Alcina	L.V. Terra
Bradamante	C. Gonzal
Medoro	L. Kozn
Ruggiero	S. Bruscant
Astolfo	N. Zaccar

Amici della Polifonia Chor, Solisti Veneti, C. Scimone (4/87) (ERAT) Ⓓ [3] **2292-45147**
Sol da te mio dolce amore J. Bowman, King's Consort, R. King (8/88) (IMP) Ⓓ **PCD8**

Ottone in Villa– dramma per musica: 3 acts, RV729 (1713—Vicenza) (Lib. Lalli)
EXCERPTS: 1. Sinfonia; 2. Vieni, vieni o mio diletto; 3. Gelosia, tu già rendi l'alma mia; 4. L'ombre, l'aure, e ancora il rio (duet).
1, 3, 4. E. Kirkby, L. Mazzarri, Brandenburg Consort, R. Goodman (r1994) (5/95) (HYPE) Ⓓ **CDA667** (HYPE) ▭ **KA667**
2. M. Caballé, M. Zanetti (FORL) Ⓓ **UCD109**

Tito Manlio– pasticcio, RV778 (1720—Rome) (collab with G. Boni & C. Giorgio; Lib della Pace)
EXCERPTS: 1. Non ti lusinghi la crudeltade.
1. E. Kirkby, Brandenburg Consort, R. Goodman (r1994) (5/95) (HYPE) Ⓓ **CDA667** (HYPE) ▭ **KA667**

VIVES, Amadeo *(1871–1932)* *Spain*

Bohemios– zarzuela: 1 act (1904) (Lib. G Perrin & M Palacios)

Cossette	A.M. Higuer
Roberto	P. Lavirg
Víctor	S. Garc
Bohemio	P. Farr
Pelagia	M. del Carmen Ramir
Cecilia	M. Or
Juana	M. Arag
Girard	L. Frut
Marcello	E. Fuent

Madrid Coros Cantores, Madrid Concerts Orch, P. Sorozábal (10/92) (HISP) Ⓓ [2] **CZS7 67322**

Cossette	M. Ba
Roberto	L. Lin
Víctor	S. S. Jeri
Bohemio	C. Alvar
Pelagia	R. M. Ys
Juana	M. J. Mart
Cecilia	I. Mon
Girard	A. Echever
Marcelo	E. Sánch

Laguna Uni Polyphonic Chor, Puerto de la Cruz Ch, Laguna Uni Ch, Tenerife SO, A. R. Marbà (r1993) (3/95) (AUVI) Ⓓ **V47**
No quiero que sepa que aquí vengo yo I. Rey, ECO, E. Ricci (r1994) (2/95) (ERAT) Ⓓ **4509-95789** (2/95) (ERAT) ▭ **4509-95789**

Doña Francisquita– zarzuela: 3 acts (1923—Madrid) (Lib. after Lope de Vega)

Doña Francisquita	T. Tour
Aurora la Beltrana	M. R. Gabr
Fernando	P. Lavirg
Cardona	S. Garc
Don Matías	J. Catar
Doña Francisca	C. Gimin
Lorenzo	L. Frut

Madrid Coros Cantores, Madrid Concerts Orch, P. Sorozábal (10/92) (HISP) Ⓓ [2] **CZS7 67322**

Doña Francisquita	M. Ba
Aurora la Beltrana	R. Piero
Fernando	Alfredo Kra
Cardona	S. S. Jeri
Don Matías	A. Echever
Doña Francisca	R. M. Ys
Lorenzo	I. Po

Laguna Uni Polyphonic Chor, Tenerife SO, A. R. Marbà (r1993) (9/94) (AUVI) Ⓓ [2] **V47**

Francisquita	A. Arte
Fernando	P. Doming

Aurora la Beltrana L. Mirabal
Cardona E. del Portal
Doña Francisca M. Perelstein
Lorenzo Pérez C. Alvarez
Don Matías C. Chausson
ordoba Grand Th Chor, Seville SO, M. Roa (r1994)
(4/95) (SONY) ① [2] **S2K66563**
Coro de Románticos chor, Madrid SO, E. G. Asensio (pp1991) (11/92) (IMP) ① **MCD45**
Mujer fatal A. Cortis, orch (r1925)
(3/94) (NIMB) ① **NI7850**
Por el humo P. Domingo, Barcelona SO, G. Navarro (ACAN) ① **49 390**

VIVIER , Claude *(1948–1983) Canada*

opernikus– ritual opera of death
Cpte Y. Parent, P. Vaillancourt, M-D. Parent, J. Fleury, D. Doane, M. Ducharme, Y. Saint-Amant, N. Forget, F. Martel, G. Plante, A. Moisan, L. Bouchard, A. Trudel, M. Bélanger, L. Vaillancourt
(CBC) ① **MVCD1047**

VOGLER , Georg Joseph *'1749–1814) Germany*

'win und Elmire– Singspiel: 1 act (1781) (Lib. Goethe)
Sono sposa e sono amante I. Siebert, D. Klöcker, South-West German RSO, K. Donath
(SCHW) ① **314018**

VAGNER , (Wilhelm) Richard *1813–1883) Germany*

escendons, descendons– chorus (1840) (for vaudeville 'La descente de la courtille')
Bamberg Sym Chor, Bamberg SO, K. A. Rickenbacher (r1993) (ORFE) ① **C312941A**

e Feen– opera: 3 acts (1888—Munich) (Lib. cpsr)
ACT 1: 1. Overture.
Ada L.E. Gray
Farzana K. Lövaas
Semina K. Laki
Arindal John Alexander
Lora J. Anderson
Morald R. Hermann
Fairy King K. Moll
Gernot J-H. Rootering
Drolla C. Studer
Groma R. Bracht
varian Rad Chor, BRSO, W. Sawallisch
(ORFE) ① [3] **C062833F**
Overture Philh, F. d'Avalos
(10/90) (ASV) ① **CDDCA704**

r Fliegende Holländer, '(The) Flying Dutchman'– opera: 3 acts (1843—Dresden) (Lib. cpsr)
1. Overture. ACT 1: 2. Hojohe!; 3. Mit Gewitter und Sturm; 4. Die Frist ist um; 5. He! Holla! Steuermann!; 6. Mein Schiff ist fest; 7. Blick hin, und überzeuge; 8. Wenn aus der Qualen; 9. Hei! Wie die Segel; 10. Interlude. ACT 2: 11. Summ und Brumm; 12. Du böses Kind; 13. Joho hoe! Traft ihr das Schiff; 14. Bleib, Senta!; 15. Ach möchtest du....Mein Kind, du siehst mich?; 16. Mögst du, mein Kind; 17. Wie aus der Ferne; 18. Verzeiht! Mein Volk hält; 19. Interlude. ACT 3: 20. Steuermann, lass die Wacht; 21. Jo ho ho hoe!; 22. Wass muss ich hören; 23. Willst jenes Tag's; 24. Verloren! Ach! Verloren!.
Holländer F. Crass
Senta Leonie Rysanek
Daland K. Ridderbusch
Erik C. Heater
Mary A.M. Bessel
Scala Chor, La Scala Orch, W. Sawallisch (pp1966)
(MEMO) ① [2] **HR4281/2**
Holländer S. Estes
Senta L. Balslev
Daland M. Salminen
Erik R. Schunk
Mary A. Schlemm
Steuermann G. Clark
yreuth Fest Chor, Bayreuth Fest Orch, W. Nelsson (pp1985)
(PHIL) ① [32] **434 420-2PM32(1)**
Holländer H. Hotter
Senta V. Ursuleac
Daland G. Hann
Erik K. Ostertag
Mary L. Willer
Steuermann F. Klarwein
Bavarian St Op Chor, Bavarian St Op Orch, C. Krauss (r1944)
(PILZ) ① [9] **442118-2**
Holländer T. Adam
Senta A. Silja
Daland M. Talvela
Erik E. Kozub
Mary A. Burmeister
Steuermann G. Unger
BBC Chor, New Philh, O. Klemperer (r1968)
(EMI) ① [2] **CDS5 55179-2**
Holländer F. Destal
Senta M. Lawrence
Daland A. Kipnis
Erik R. Maison
Mary I. Petina
Steuermann H. Fleischer
Buenos Aires Colón Th Orch, F. Busch (bp1936)
(PEAR) ① [2] **GEMMCDS9910**
Holländer J. Berglund
Senta M. Müller
Daland L. Hofmann
Erik F. Völker
Mary L. Asmus
Steuermann E. Zimmermann
Bayreuth Fest CHor, Bayreuth Fest Orch, R. Kraus (pp1942)
(PREI) ① [2] **90232**
Holländer H. Uhde
Senta A. Varnay
Daland L. Weber
Erik W. Windgassen
Mary E. Schärtel
Steuermann J. Traxel
Bayreuth Fest Chor, Bayreuth Fest Orch, H. Knappertsbusch (pp1955)
(MUSI) ① [2] **MACD-876**
Holländer H. Hotter
Senta V. Ursuleac
Daland G. Hann
Erik K. Ostertag
Mary L. Willer
Steuermann F. Klarwein
Bavarian St Op Chor, Bavarian St Op Orch, C. Krauss (r1944)
(PREI) ① [2] **90250**
Holländer S. Estes
Senta L. Balslev
Daland M. Salminen
Erik R. Schunk
Mary A. Schlemm
Steuermann G. Clark
Bayreuth Fest Chor, Bayreuth Fest Orch, W. Nelsson, H. Kupfer
(11/91) (PHIL) ☾ [2] **070 406-1PHE2**
(11/91) (PHIL) ▣ **070 406-3PH**
Holländer F. Grundheber
Senta H. Behrens
Daland M. Salminen
Erik R. Sirkiä
Mary A. Välkki
Steuermann J. Silvasti
Savonlinna Op Fest Chor, Savonlinna Op Fest Orch, L. Segerstam, I. Bäckmann
(11/91) (TELD) ☾ **9031-71486-6**
(11/91) (TELD) ▣ **9031-71486-3**
Holländer S. Estes
Senta L. Balslev
Daland M. Salminen
Erik R. Schunk
Mary A. Schlemm
Steuermann G. Clark
Bayreuth Fest Chor, Bayreuth Fest Orch, W. Nelsson (pp1985)
(10/92) (PHIL) ① [2] **434 599-2PH2**
Holländer R. Hale
Senta J. Varady
Daland J. Rhyänen
Erik P. Seiffert
Mary A. Schlemm
Steuermann U. Ress
Bavarian St Op Chor, Bavarian St Orch, W. Sawallisch
(3/93) (EMI) ☾ [2] **LDC99 1311-1**
(3/93) (EMI) ▣ **MVD99 1311-3**
Holländer J. van Dam
Senta D. Vejzovic
Daland K. Moll
Erik P. Hofmann
Mary K. Borris
Steuermann T. Moser
Vienna St Op Chor, BPO, H. von Karajan (r1981-3)
(7/93) (EMI) ① [2] **CMS7 64650-2**
Holländer T. Stewart
Senta G. Jones
Daland K. Ridderbusch
Erik H. Esser
Mary S. Wagner
Steuermann H. Ek
Bayreuth Fest Chor, Bayreuth Fest Orch, K. Böhm (pp1971)
(8/93) (DG) ① [2] **437 710-2GX2**
Holländer A. Muff
Senta I. Haubold
Daland E. Knodt
Erik P. Seiffert
Mary M. Schiml
Steuermann J. Hering
Austrian RSO, P. Steinberg
(9/93) (NAXO) ① [2] **8 660025/6**
Holländer R. Hale
Senta H. Behrens
Daland K. Rydl
Erik J. Protschka
Mary I. Vermillion
Steuermann U. Heilmann
Vienna St Op Concert Ch, VPO, C. von Dohnányi (r1991)
(4/94) (DECC) ① [2] **436 418-2DHO2**
Holländer D. Fischer-Dieskau
Senta M. Schech
Daland G. Frick
Erik R. Schock
Mary S. Wagner
Steuermann F. Wunderlich
Berlin Deutsche Op Chor, Berlin Deutsche Op Orch, F. Konwitschny (r1960)
(9/94) (BERL) ① [2] **BC2097-2**
Holländer F. Crass
Senta A. Silja
Daland J. Greindl
Erik F. Uhl
Mary R. Fischer
Steuermann G. Paskuda
Bayreuth Fest Chor, Bayreuth Fest Orch, W. Sawallisch (pp1961)
(9/94) (PHIL) ① [2] **442 103-2PM2**
Excs H. Hotter, J. von Manowarda, H. Braun, Vienna St Op Chor, Vienna St Op Orch, R. Moralt (pp1940) (SCHW) ① [2] **314722**
Excs A. Jerger, M. Németh, K. Norbert, J. Kalenberg, B. Paalen, Vienna St Op Chor, Vienna St Op Orch, R. Heger (pp1933)
(12/94) (SCHW) ① [2] **314542**
Excs W. Rode, J. von Manowarda, Vienna St Op Orch, L. Reichwein (pp1939)
(6/95) (SCHW) ① [2] **314632**
1. Chicago SO, G. Solti
(DECC) ▣ **071 101-3DH**
1. Seattle SO, G. Schwarz (DELO) ① **DE3053**
1. Budapest SO, G. Lehel (LASE) ① **15 521**
(LASE) ⊟ **79 521**
1. Cleveland Orch, G. Szell
(CBS) ① [2] **CD46466**
1. RPO, J. Horenstein
(CHES) ① **Chesky CD31**
1. LSO, B. Tuckwell (IMP) ① **PCDS6**
(IMP) ⊟ **PCDSC6**
1. BPO, R. Strauss (r1928)
(KOCH) ① **37119-2**
1. LPO, A. Boult (EMI) ① [2] **CZS7 62539-2**
1. BPO, H. von Karajan (r1974)
(EMI) ① **CDM7 64334-2**
1. BPO, S. Ozawa (PHIL) OO **426 271-5PH**
1. London Prom, Anon (cond)
(WORD) ① **FCD7409**
1. Philh, Y. Simonov (r1991)
(COLL) ① **Coll1294-2**
1. London Fest Orch, J. Armstrong
(ROSE) ① **3212**
1. NY Met Op Orch, James Levine (r1991)
(DG) OO **435 874-5GH**
1. VPO, H. Stein (r1974) (BELA) ① **450 025-2**
(BELA) ⊟ **450 025-4**
1. Chicago SO, G. Solti (r1976)
(DECC) ① **440 069-2DWO**
(DECC) ⊟ **440 069-4DWO**
1. NYPO, L. Bernstein (r1968)
(SONY) ① **SMK47643**
1. RPO, V. Handley (r1993) (TRIN) ① **TRP008**
(TRIN) ⊟ **MCTRP008**
1. J-F. Heisser, G. Pludermacher (r1993; trans Debussy 4 hands) (ERAT) ① **4509-93209-2**
1. BPO, R. Kempe (r1956)
(TEST) ① **SBT1035**

1. RPS Orch, B. Walter (r1926) (VAI) ① **VAIA1059**
1. Bayreuth Fest Orch, K. Böhm (pp1971) (DG) ① [2] **439 687-2GX2**
1. VPO, H. Knappertsbusch (r1953) (DECC) ① **440 062-2DM**
1. LPO, T. Beecham (r1937) (PEAR) ① **GEMMCD9094**
1. Cincinnati SO, J. López-Cobos (r1994) (TELA) ① **CD80379**
1. Bayreuth Fest Orch, K. Böhm (pp1971) (DG) ① **439 445-2GCL** (DG) ⊟ **439 445-4GCL**
1. Columbia SO, B. Walter (r1959) (SONY) ① [10] **SX10K66246**
1. Columbia SO, B. Walter (r1959) (SONY) ① [2] **SM2K64456**
1. VPO, G. Solti (r1961) (DECC) ① [2] **440 606-2DF2**
1. Bamberg SO, H. Löwlein (DG) ① [2] **447 364-2GDB2**
1. NYPO, G. Sinopoli (10/86) (DG) ① **419 169-2GH**
1. Columbia SO, B. Walter (r1959) (2/90) (CBS) ① **CD45701**
1. Philh, F. d'Avalos (10/90) (ASV) ① **CDDCA704**
1. Chicago SO, G. Solti (5/91) (DECC) ① **430 448-2DM**
1. NYPO, W. Mengelberg (r1925) (4/92) (PEAR) ① [3] **GEMMCDS9922**
1. NY Met Op Orch, James Levine (r1991) (10/93) (DG) ① **435 874-2GH**
1. Minnesota Orch, N. Marriner (r1983) (2/94) (TELA) ① **CD82005**
1. VPO, W. Furtwängler (r1949) (4/94) (EMI) ① [2] **CHS7 64935-2**
1. LPO, T. Beecham (r1937) (6/94) (DUTT) ① **CDLX7007**
1-4, 11, 13, 15(pt), 16, 17, 20, 23, 24. S. Estes, L. Balslev, M. Salminen, R. Schunk, A. Schlemm, G. Clark, Bayreuth Fest Chor, Bayreuth Fest Orch, W. Nelsson (pp1985) (PHIL) ① **446 618-2PM**
3. L. Melchior, Orch, H. Barlow (bp1950) (VAI) ▣ **VAI69107**
3. H.E. Groh, orch (r1932) (3/92) (PEAR) ① **GEMMCD9419**
3, 11, 20. Bayreuth Fest Chor, Bayreuth Fest Orch, W. Pitz (4/90) (DG) ① **429 169-2GR**
3, 20. L. Melchior, chor, Victor SO, E. McArthur (r1940) (PEAR) ① **GEMMCD9049**
3, 23. P. Anders, Berlin Deutsche Op Chor, Berlin Deutsche Op Orch, A. Grüber (r1939) (TELD) ① **4509-95512-2**
3, 4, 11, 13, 16, 17, 20, 22. J. van Dam, K. Moll, D. Vejzovic, P. Hofmann, T. Moser, K. Borris, Vienna St Op Chor, BPO, H. von Karajan (EMI) ① **CDM7 63449-2**
4. F. Schorr, Berlin St Op Orch, L. Blech (r1929) (PEAR) ① **GEMMCD9944**
4. J. Herrmann, VPO, R. Moralt (r1943) (PREI) ① **89076**
4. H. Hotter, Bavarian St Orch, H. Hollreiser (r1943) (PREI) ① **90200**
4. G. London, VPO, H. Knappertsbusch (r1958) (DECC) ① **443 380-2DM**
4. H. Hermann Nissen, Berlin SO, F. Zweig (r1928) (PREI) ① **89090**
4. A. Endrèze, SO, S. Meyrowitz (French: r1936) (1/92) (EMI) ① [4] **CMS7 64008-2(1)**
4. H. Hermann Nissen, Berlin St Op Orch, B. Seidler-Winkler (r1939) (1/92) (EMI) ① [4] **CMS7 64008-2(1)**
4. F. Schorr, Berlin St Op Orch, L. Blech (r1929) (7/92) (PEAR) ① [3] **GEMMCDS9925(2)**
4, 17. F. Schorr, Berlin St Op Orch, L. Blech (PREI) ① [2] **89214**
6. J. Herrmann, K. Böhme, orch (r1943) (PREI) ① **89076**
7(pt) F. Schorr, O. Helgers, orch (r1922) (PREI) ① **89052**
11, 20. Chicago Sym Chor, Chicago SO, G. Solti (DECC) ① **421 865-2DA**
12, 13, 20. T. Valjakka, A. Välkki, S. Ruohonen, R. Sirkiä, Savonlinna Op Fest Chor, Savonlinna Op Fest Orch, I. Mansnerus (BIS) ① [2] **BIS-CD373/4**
13. E. Rethberg, orch (r1930) (MSCM) ① [2] **MM30283** (MSCM) ⊟ [2] **MM40105**
13. E. Destinn, orch, B. Seidler-Winkler (r1906) (PEAR) ① **GEMMCD9172**
13. J. Norman, Ambrosian Op Chor, LPO, K. Tennstedt (r1987) (EMI) ① **CDM5 65576-2**
13. J. Norman, Ambrosian Op Chor, LPO, K. Tennstedt (11/88) (EMI) ① **CDC7 49759-2**
13. F. Leider, orch (r1925) (5/91) (PREI) ① [3] **89301**
13. S. Sedlmair, anon (r1904) (7/91) (SYMP) ① **SYMCD1081**
13. J. Gadski, orch (r1908) (7/91) (CLUB) ① **CL99-109**
13. M. Fuchs, F. Beckmann, Berlin St Op Orch, B. Seidler-Winkler (r1938) (1/92) (EMI) ① [4] **CMS7 64008-2(1)**
13. E. Rethberg, orch, Rosario Bourdon (r1930) (1/92) (EMI) ① [4] **CMS7 64008-2(1)**
13. E. Destinn, orch, B. Seidler-Winkler (r1906) (7/92) (PEAR) ① [3] **GEMMCDS9924(2)**
13. N. Ermolenko-Yuzhina, orch (r1911: Russ) (6/93) (PEAR) ① [3] **GEMMCDS9001/3(2)**
13. M. Németh, orch (1/94) (CLUB) ① **CL99-007**
13. J. Gadski, orch (r1908) (4/94) (RCA) ① [6] **09026 61580-2(1)**
13. M. Jeritza, orch (r1926) (4/94) (PREI) ① **89079**
13. E. Destinn, orch (r1911) (5/94) (SUPR) ① **11 1337-2**
13. E. Destinn, orch, B. Seidler-Winkler (r1906) (12/94) (SUPR) ① [12] **11 2136-2(1)**
13. E. Destinn, orch (r1911) (12/94) (SUPR) ① [12] **11 2136-2(4)**
13. E. Destinn, orch, F. Kark (r1906) (12/94) (SUPR) ① [12] **11 2136-2(1)**
13. E. Rethberg, Victor SO, Rosario Bourdon (r1930) (10/95) (ROMO) ① [2] **81014-2**
13, 17. Leonie Rysanek, S. Björling, ROH Chor, Philh, W. Schüchter (r1952) (2/95) (EMI) ① **CDH5 65201-2**
14(pt) F. Leider, C. Günther, orch (r1922) (5/91) (PREI) ① [3] **89301**
14(pt) F. Völker, I. Langhammer, Berlin Staatskapelle, G. Steeger (r1941) (8/94) (PREI) ① **89070**
14, 17, 23. J. Berglund, M. Németh, S. Svanholm, Vienna St Op Orch, L. Reichwein (pp1942) (SCHW) ① [2] **314692**
16. K. Moll, Munich RO, K. Eichhorn (r1981) (ORFE) ① **C009821A**
16. M. Schenk, Nuremberg SO, K. Seibel (12/91) (COLO) ① **COL34 9004**
16. M. Salminen, Lahti SO, E. Klas (8/92) (BIS) ① **BIS-CD520**
16. G. Hann, Berlin Deutsche Op Orch, A. Rother (r1942) (5/94) (PREI) ① **90168**
17. F. Schorr, M. Kurt, orch (r1921/2) (PREI) ① **89052**
17. F. Schorr, orch (r1921) (PEAR) ① [2] **GEMMCDS9121**
17. B. Nilsson, H. Hotter, Philh, L. Ludwig (1/92) (EMI) ① [4] **CMS7 64008-2(1)**
17. M. Müller, J. Prohaska, J. Greindl, Berlin RSO, A. Rother (bp1943) (6/92) (PREI) ① [3] **90043**
17. A. Marc, D. McIntyre, NZ SO, H. Wallberg (11/92) (ODE) ① **CDMANU1317**
17. F. Schorr, Berlin St Op Orch, L. Blech (r1927) (10/93) (NIMB) ① **NI7848**
17(pt) H. Braun, H. Hotter, Vienna St Op Orch, R. Moralt (pp1940) (6/94) (SCHW) ① **314502**
20. ROH Chor, RPO, R. Stapleton (RPO) ① **CDRPO7009** (RPO) ⊟ **ZCRPO7009**
20. ROH Chor, RPO, R. Stapleton (r1991) (RPO) ① [2] **CDRPD9006** (RPO) ⊟ [2] **ZCRPD9006**
20. Bayreuth Fest Chor, Bayreuth Fest Orch, W. Sawallisch (r1975) (BELA) ① **450 052-2** (BELA) ⊟ **450 052-4**
23. F. Völker, Berlin St Op Orch, J. Prüwer (r1928) (MSCM) ① [2] **MM30283** (MSCM) ⊟ [2] **MM40105**
23. M. Lorenz, Berlin St Op Orch, C. Schmalstich (r1930) (PREI) ① **89053**
23. P. Seiffert, Munich RO, J. Kout (r1992-3) (RCA) ① **09026 61214-2**
23. K. Erb, orch (r1917) (PREI) ① **89095**
23. F. Völker, Berlin St Op Orch, J. Prüwer (r1928) (2/90) (PREI) ① **89005**

Das **Liebesverbot– opera: 2 acts (1836—Munich) (Lib. cpsr, after Shakespeare)**

Overture Vienna SO, G. Prêtre (pp1989) (ORFE) ① **C237901A**
Overture Philh, F. d'Avalos (10/90) (ASV) ① **CDDCA70**

Lohengrin– opera: 3 acts (1850—Weimar) (Lib. cpsr)

EXCERPTS—; 1. Prelude. ACT 1: 2. Gott grüss' euch, liebe Männer; 3. Dank, König, dir; 4. Einsam in trüben Tagen (Elsa's Dream); 5a. Wer hier in Gotteskampf; 5b. In düst'rem Schweigen richtet Gott!...Du trugest zu ihm; 6. Nun sei bedankt; 7. Nie sollst du mich; 8. Mein Herr und Gott, nun ruf'ich Dich. ACT 2: 9. Erhebe dich, Genossin meiner Schmach; 10. Euch Lüften, die mein Klagen; 11. Elsa!...Wer ruft?; 12a. Entweihte Götter!; 12b. Ortrud! Wo bist du?; 12c. Du Ärmste; 13. Gesegnet soll sie schreiten (Procession); 14. O König; 15. Welch ein Geheimnis; 16. Mein Held. ACT 3: 17. Prelude; 18. Treulich geführt (Wedding March); 19a. Das süsse Lied verhallt; 19b. Atmest du nicht; 19c. Höchstes Vertraun; 20a. Heil König Heinrich!; 20b. Habt Dank; 21. In fernem Land; 22. Mein lieber Schwan!.

Lohengrin P. Doming
Elsa C. Stud
Ortrud D. Vejzov
Telramund H. Welk
King Henry R. Lloy
Herald G. Tich
Vienna St Op Chor, Vienna St Op Orch, C. Abbado, B. Large (MCEG) ▣ **VVD84**

Lohengrin L. Melchio
Elsa H. Traub
Ortrud A. Varna
Telramund H. Jansse
King Henry D. Ernst
Herald F. Guerrer
NY Met Op Chor, NY Met Op Orch, F. Stiedry (pp1950) (DANA) ① [3] **DACOCD322**

Lohengrin P. Fre
Elsa C. Stud
Ortrud G. Schna
Telramund E. Wlaschih
King Henry M. Scher
Herald E.W. Schul
Bayreuth Fest Chor, Bayreuth Fest Orch, P. Schneider (pp1990) (PHIL) ① [32] **434 420-2PM32(**

Lohengrin G. Vince
Elsa M. Schec
Ortrud M. Klos
Telramund A. Boeh
King Henry K. Böhm
Herald W. Wo
Bavarian St Op Chor, Bavarian St Op Orch, R. Kempe (r1951) (PILZ) ① [9] **442118-**

Lohengrin P. Fre
Elsa C. Stud
Ortrud G. Schna
Telramund E. Wlaschih
King Henry M. Scher
Herald E.W. Schul
Bayreuth Fest Chor, Bayreuth Fest Orch, P. Schneider, W. Herzog, B. Large (PHIL) ◖ [2] **070 436-1PH** (PHIL) ▣ [2] **070 436-3PH**

Lohengrin Jess Thoma
Elsa A. Sil
Ortrud A. Varna
Telramund R. Vina
King Henry F. Cras
Herald T. Kraus
Bayreuth Fest Chor, Bayreuth Fest Orch, W. Sawallisch (pp1962) (PHIL) ① [3] **446 337-2PM**

Lohengrin R. Schoc
Elsa M. Cuni
Ortrud M. Klos
Telramund J. Metternic
King Henry G. Fric
Herald H. Günte
NW German Rad Chor, Cologne Rad Chor, Hamburg RSO, W. Schüchter (r1953) (EMI) ① [3] **CHS5 65517-**

Lohengrin P. Doming
Elsa J. Norma
Ortrud E. Randov
Telramund S. Nimsge
King Henry H. Sot
Herald D. Fischer-Dieska
Vienna St Op Concert Ch, VPO, G. Solti (r1985/6) (10/87) (DECC) ① [4] **421 053-2DH**

Lohengrin Jess Thoma

Elsa E. Grümmer
Ortrud C. Ludwig
Telramund D. Fischer-Dieskau
King Henry G. Frick
Herald O. Wiener
Vienna St Op Chor, VPO, R. Kempe (r1962/3)
(2/88) (EMI) Ⓓ [3] **CDS7 49017-8**

Lohengrin R. Kollo
Elsa A. Tomowa-Sintow
Ortrud D. Vejzovic
Telramund S. Nimsgern
King Henry K. Ridderbusch
Herald R. Kerns
Berlin Deutsche Op Chor, BPO, H. von Karajan (r1975/6/81)
(8/88) (EMI) Ⓓ [4] **CMS7 69314-2**

Lohengrin P. Hofmann
Elsa K. Armstrong
Ortrud E. Connell
Telramund L. Roar
King Henry S. Vogel
Herald B. Weikl
Bayreuth Fest Chor, Bayreuth Fest Orch, W. Nelsson, G. Friedrich
(9/91) (PHIL) ● [2] **070 411-1PHG2**
(PHIL) ▭▭ [2] **070 411-3PHG2**

Lohengrin F. Völker
Elsa M. Müller
Ortrud M. Klose
Telramund J. Prohaska
King Henry L. Hofmann
Herald W. Grossmann
Berlin St Op Chor, Berlin St Op Orch, R. Heger (bp1942)
(6/92) (PREI) Ⓓ [3] **90043**

Lohengrin P. Frey
Elsa C. Studer
Ortrud G. Schnaut
Telramund E. Wlaschiha
King Henry M. Schenk
Herald E.W. Schulte
Bayreuth Fest Chor, Bayreuth Fest Orch, P. Schneider (pp1990)
(10/92) (PHIL) Ⓓ [4] **434 602-2PH4**

Lohengrin W. Windgassen
Elsa E. Steber
Telramund H. Uhde
Ortrud A. Varnay
King Henry J. Greindl
Herald H. Braun
Bayreuth Fest Chor, Bayreuth Fest Orch, J. Keilberth (pp1953)
(10/94) (TELD) Ⓓ [4] **4509-93674-2**

Lohengrin S. Jerusalem
Elsa C. Studer
Ortrud W. Meier
Telramund H. Welker
King Henry K. Moll
Herald A. Schmidt
Vienna St Op Concert Ch, VPO, C. Abbado (r1991/2)
(11/94) (DG) Ⓓ [3] **437 808-2GH3**

Lohengrin B. Heppner
Elsa S. Sweet
Ortrud E. Marton
Telramund S. Leiferkus
King Henry J-H. Rootering
Herald B. Terfel
Bavarian Rad Chor, BRSO, Colin Davis (r1994)
(11/95) (RCA) Ⓓ [3] **09026 62646-2**

Act 3. R. Berger, E. Destinn, Berlin Court Op Chor, Odeon Orch, A. Pilz (r1908)
(12/94) (SUPR) Ⓓ [12] **11 2136-2(3)**

Excs F. Völker, Z. Zika, J. von Manowarda, E. Schipper, G. Rünger, Vienna St Op Chor, Vienna St Op Orch, F. Ruhlmann (pp1933)
(9/95) (SCHW) Ⓓ [2] **314662**

1. Czech PO, K. Ančerl (SUPR) ▭ **11 0640-4**

1. NBC SO, A. Toscanini (pp1954)
(MUSI) Ⓓ **ATRA-3008**

1. Budapest SO, G. Lehel (LASE) Ⓓ **15 521**
(LASE) ▭ **79 521**

1. Cleveland Orch, G. Szell
(CBS) Ⓓ [2] **CD46466**

1. H. Bönisch, P. Bönisch, H. Herrmann (arr H.Bönisch) (MOTE) Ⓓ **CD20171**

1. BPO, H. von Karajan (r1974)
(EMI) Ⓓ **CDM7 64334-2**

1. BPO, S. Ozawa (PHIL) ⓄⓄ **426 271-5PH**

1. NBC SO, A. Toscanini (r1941)
(RCA) Ⓓ **GD60306**

1. London Fest Orch, J. Armstrong
(ROSE) Ⓓ **3212**

1. NYPO, L. Bernstein (r1968)
(SONY) Ⓓ **SMK47643**

1. Zurich Tonhalle Orch, H. Knappertsbusch (r1947) (PREI) Ⓓ **90189**

1. BPO, R. Kubelík (DG) Ⓓ [2] **439 687-2GX2**

1. BPO, R. Kubelík (r1963)
(DG) Ⓓ **439 445-2GCL**
(DG) ▭ **439 445-4GCL**

1. Columbia SO, B. Walter (r1959)
(SONY) Ⓓ [10] **SX10K66246**

1. Columbia SO, B. Walter (r1959)
(SONY) Ⓓ [2] **SM2K64456**

1. LSO, A. Dorati (r1960)
(MERC) Ⓓ **434 342-2MM**

1. VPO, G. Solti (r1985/6)
(DECC) Ⓓ [2] **440 606-2DF2**

1. Leningrad PO, E. Mravinsky (pp1978)
(MELO) Ⓓ **74321 25199-2**

1. Leningrad PO, E. Mravinsky (pp1978)
(MELO) Ⓓ [10] **74321 25189-2**

1. Philh, G. Simon
(3/87) (CALA) Ⓓ [2] **CACD0101**
(3/87) (CALA) ▭ [2] **CAMC0101**

1. Columbia SO, B. Walter (r1959)
(2/90) (CBS) Ⓓ **CD45701**

1. Concertgebouw, W. Mengelberg (r1927)
(7/90) (SYMP) Ⓓ **SYMCD1078**

1. BPO, W. Furtwängler (r1930)
(4/92) (KOCH) Ⓓ [2] **37073-2**

1. VPO, W. Furtwängler (r1954)
(4/94) (EMI) Ⓓ [2] **CHS7 64935-2**

1. NQHO, B. Wordsworth (r1995)
(6/95) (EYE) Ⓓ [2] **EOS5001**

1, 17. French Rad PO, M. Janowski (r1990)
(VIRG) ▭ **VJ7 59689-4**

1, 17. Seattle SO, G. Schwarz
(DELO) Ⓓ **DE3053**

1, 17. Concertgebouw, B. Haitink
(PHIL) Ⓓ **420 886-2PSL**

1, 17. New Philh, A. Boult
(EMI) Ⓓ [2] **CZS7 62539-2**

1, 17. Philh, Y. Simonov (r1991)
(COLL) Ⓓ **Coll1294-2**

1, 17. VPO, H. Stein (r1974)
(BELA) Ⓓ **450 025-2**
(BELA) ▭ **450 025-4**

1, 17. BPO, K. Tennstedt (r1982/3)
(EMI) Ⓓ [2] **CZS5 68616-2**

1, 17. NYPO, G. Sinopoli
(10/86) (DG) Ⓓ **419 169-2GH**

1, 17. LPO, K.A. Rickenbacher
(11/87) (CFP) Ⓓ **CD-CFP9008**

1, 17. Philh, F. d'Avalos
(3/90) (ASV) Ⓓ **CDDCA666**

1, 17. NYPSO, A. Toscanini (r1936)
(3/90) (PEAR) Ⓓ [3] **GEMMCDS9373**

1, 17. Philh, O. Klemperer
(11/90) (EMI) Ⓓ **CDM7 63617-2**

1, 17. Leningrad PO, E. Mravinsky (pp1973/pp)
(6/92) (ERAT) Ⓓ [11] **2292-45763-2**

1, 17. Leningrad PO, E. Mravinsky (pp1973/pp)
(6/92) (ERAT) Ⓓ **2292-45762-2**

1, 17. NBC SO, A. Toscanini (r1951)
(11/92) (RCA) Ⓓ **GD60305**

1, 17. NYPO, A. Toscanini (r1936)
(11/92) (RCA) Ⓓ **GD60318**

1, 17. Leningrad PO, E. Mravinsky (pp1967)
(3/94) (RUSS) Ⓓ **RDCD11166**

1, 2, 5b, 6, 7, 10, 12b, 17, 18, 19a-c, 21, 22. P. Frey, C. Studer, G. Schnaut, E. Wlaschiha, M. Schenk, Bayreuth Fest Chor, Bayreuth Fest Orch, P. Schneider (pp1990)
(PHIL) Ⓓ **438 500-2PH**

1(pt), 2, 5b, 6, 7(pt), 8(pt), 10, 12a, 12c, 13, 16(pt), 17, 19a(pt), 20a, 20b, 21(pt), 22(pt) J. von Manowarda, F. Völker, M. Müller, J. Prohaska, M. Klose, W. Grossmann, Berlin St Op Chor, Vienna St Op Chor, Vienna St Op Orch, H. Tietjen (pp1938)
(SCHW) Ⓓ [2] **314682**

1, 4, 5b, 6, 8, 10, 13, 17, 18, 19a-c, 21, 22. P. Frey, C. Studer, G. Schnaut, E. Wlaschiha, M. Schenk, E.W. Schulte, Bayreuth Fest Chor, Bayreuth Fest Orch, P. Schneider (pp1990)
(PHIL) Ⓓ **446 619-2PM**

1, 4, 6, 8, 9(pt), 10, 17, 18, 19a, 20a, 21, 22. S. Jerusalem, C. Studer, W. Meier, H. Welker, K. Moll, Vienna St Op Concert Ch, VPO, C. Abbado (r1991/2) (DG) Ⓓ **445 869-2GH**

2. I. Andrésen, orch, F. Zweig (r1930)
(PEAR) Ⓓ **GEMMCD9122**

2, 8, 20b I. Andrésen, E. Habich, Berlin St Op Orch, F. Weissmann (r1927)
(10/90) (PREI) Ⓓ **89028**

4. R. Ponselle, orch (r1923)
(PEAR) Ⓓ [2] **GEMMCDS9964**

4. E. Rethberg, Berlin St Op Orch, F. Zweig (r1927) (MSCM) Ⓓ [2] **MM30283**
(MSCM) ▭ [2] **MM40105**

4. C. Taha, Berlin RSO, J. Märkl (r1991)
(SCHW) Ⓓ [2] **312682**

4. K. Flagstad, orch, H. Lange (r1935)
(PEAR) Ⓓ **GEMMCD9049**

4. K. Flagstad, orch, H. Lange (r1935)
(IMP) Ⓓ **GLRS105**

4. A. Tomowa-Sintow, K. Ridderbusch, S. Nimsgern, Berlin Deutsche Op Chor, BPO, H. von Karajan (r1975/6/81)
(CFP) Ⓓ **CD-CFP4656**
(CFP) ▭ **TC-CFP4656**

4. F. Litvinne, anon (r1905: Fr)
(SYMP) Ⓓ **SYMCD1173**

4. K. Flagstad, VPO, H. Knappertsbusch (r1956)
(LOND) Ⓓ **440 495-2LM**

4. K. Flagstad, VPO, H. Knappertsbusch (r1956)
(LOND) Ⓓ [5] **440 490-2LM5(1)**

4. E. Schwarzkopf, Philh, W. Susskind (r1956)
(EMI) Ⓓ **CDM5 65577-2**

4. K. Flagstad, orch, H. Lange (r1935)
(SIMA) Ⓓ [3] **PSC1821(1)**

4. E. Schwarzkopf, Philh, W. Susskind
(10/88) (EMI) Ⓓ **CDM7 69501-2**

4. E. Turner, orch, J. Batten (r1933: Eng)
(9/89) (EMI) Ⓓ **CDH7 69791-2**

4. V. de los Angeles, Philh, A. Fistoulari (r1950)
(8/90) (EMI) Ⓓ **CDH7 63495-2**

4. H. Spani, La Scala Orch, C. Sabajno (Ital: r1928) (9/90) (CLUB) Ⓓ [2] **CL99-509/10**

4. K. Flagstad, Philadelphia, E. Ormandy (r1737)
(10/90) (RCA) Ⓓ **GD87915**

4. G. Lubin, orch, H. Defosse (French: r1929)
(5/91) (CLUB) Ⓓ **CL99-022**

4. G. Lubin, orch, H. Defosse (French: r1929)
(5/91) (EPM) Ⓓ **150 052**

4. S. Sedlmair, anon (r1904)
(7/91) (SYMP) Ⓓ **SYMCD1081**

4. E. Rethberg, Berlin St Op Orch, F. Zweig (r1927) (1/92) (EMI) Ⓓ [4] **CMS7 64008-2(1)**

4. G. Jones, Cologne RSO, R. Paternostro
(2/92) (CHAN) Ⓓ **CHAN8930**
(2/92) (CHAN) ▭ **ABTD1528**

4. H. Traubel, NYPSO, A. Rodzinski (r1945)
(4/92) (EMI) Ⓓ [7] **CHS7 69741-2(1)**

4. E. Destinn, orch, B. Seidler-Winkler (r1908)
(7/92) (PEAR) Ⓓ [3] **GEMMCDS9924(1)**

4. H. Spani, La Scala Orch, C. Sabajno (Ital: r1928) (12/92) (PREI) Ⓓ **89037**

4. F. Litvinne, anon (r1905: Fr)
(7/93) (NIMB) Ⓓ [2] **NI7840/1**

4. K. Flagstad, orch, H. Lange (r1935)
(7/93) (NIMB) Ⓓ **NI7847**

4. R. Pampanini, EIAR Orch, U. Tansini (Ital: r1940) (8/93) (PREI) Ⓓ **89063**

4. J. Norman, Vienna St Op Concert Ch, VPO, G. Solti (r1985)
(10/93) (DECC) Ⓓ **436 461-2DM**

4. R. Ponselle, orch, R. Romani (r1923)
(10/93) (NIMB) Ⓓ **NI7846**

4. A. Marc, Seattle SO, G. Schwarz (r1992)
(4/94) (DELO) Ⓓ **DE3120**

4. H. Traubel, RCA SO, B. Reibold (r1940)
(4/94) (RCA) Ⓓ [6] **09026 61580-2(4)**

4. E. Destinn, orch, B. Seidler-Winkler (r1906)
(5/94) (SUPR) Ⓓ **11 1337-2**

4. F. Litvinne, anon (r1905: Fr)
(12/94) (SYMP) Ⓓ **SYMCD1128**

4. E. Destinn, Odeon Orch, A. Pilz (r1908)
(12/94) (SUPR) Ⓓ [12] **11 2136-2(2)**

4. E. Rethberg, orch (r1928)
(2/95) (ROMO) Ⓓ [2] **81012-2**

4. E. Rethberg, Berlin SO, F. Zweig (r1927)
(10/95) (ROMO) Ⓓ [2] **81014-2**

4, 10. M. Favero, orch (r c1929: Ital)
(VAI) Ⓓ **VAIA1071**

4, 10. G. Janowitz, Berlin Deutsche Op Orch, F. Leitner (r1967) (DG) Ⓓ [2] **447 352-2GDB2**

4, 10. M. Favero, orch (r c1929: Ital)
(BONG) Ⓓ **GB1078-2**

4, 10. T. Lemnitz, Berlin St Op Orch, J. Schüler (r1937) (10/90) (PREI) Ⓓ **89025**

4, 10. Lotte Lehmann, orch (r1914)
(6/92) (PREI) Ⓓ [3] **89302**

4, 10. M. Reining, Berlin Deutsche Op Orch, W. Lutze (r1939) (9/92) (PREI) Ⓓ **90083**

4(2 vers), 10, 12c E. Destinn, orch, B. Seidler-Winkler (r1906)
(12/94) (SUPR) Ⓓ [12] **11 2136-2(1)**

4, 19a R. Bampton, A. Carron, N. Cordon, orch, W. Steinberg (r1940) (VAI) Ⓓ **VAIA1084**

4, 19a M. Teschemacher, M. Wittrisch, Berlin St Op Orch, F. Zaun (r1933)
(11/92) (PREI) Ⓓ **89049**

4, 6(pt), 10, 19a B. Nilsson, W. Windgassen, A. Varnay, H. Uhde, Bayreuth Fest Chor, Bayreuth Fest Orch, E. Jochum (pp1954)
(MEMO) Ⓓ [2] **HR4275/6**
4, 6, 8(pt), 9(pt), 17, 18, 19a, 21, 22. R. Kollo, A. Tomowa-Sintow, S. Nimsgern, D. Vejzovic, K. Ridderbusch, R. Kerns, Berlin Deutsche Op Chor, BPO, H. von Karajan
(EMI) Ⓓ **CDM7 63453-2**
5b(pt), 13, 18. Bayreuth Fest Chor, Bayreuth Fest Orch, W. Pitz
(4/90) (DG) Ⓓ **429 169-2GR**
6. A. Pertile, La Scala Chor, La Scala Orch, C. Sabajno (Ital: r1927)
(1/92) (EMI) Ⓓ [4] **CMS7 64008-2(1)**
6(pt), 19a A. Piccaver, M. Angerer, Berlin St Op Orch, M. Gurlitt (r1928) (PREI) Ⓓ [2] **89217**
6, 19c L. Slezak, orch (r1907)
(2/91) (PREI) Ⓓ **89020**
6, 21. A. Pertile, La Scala Orch, C. Sabajno (r1927: Ital) (10/94) (PREI) Ⓓ **89072**
6(pt), 7, 12c, 15(pt) P. Kötter, M. Teschemacher, H. Alsen, A. Konetzni, Vienna St Op Chor, Vienna St Op Orch, H. Knappertsbusch (pp1936)
(SCHW) Ⓓ [2] **314672**
7, 19a, 19c(pt) E. Destinn, E. Kraus, orch, B. Seidler-Winkler (r1906)
(12/94) (SUPR) Ⓓ [12] **11 2136-2(1)**
7, 19a, 22. F. de Lucia, J. Huguet, orch (r1907: Ital) (BONG) Ⓓ [2] **GB1064/5-2**
8. M. Journet, orch, Rosario Bourdon (r1926)
(PREI) Ⓓ **89021**
8. M. Journet, orch (r1913)
(MSCM) Ⓓ [2] **MM30283**
(MSCM) ▣ [2] **MM40105**
8. L. Hofmann, orch, J. Prüwer (r1929)
(PREI) Ⓓ **89102**
8. G. Hann, Berlin Deutsche Op Orch, A. Rother (r1942) (5/94) (PREI) Ⓓ **90168**
8(pt) T. Ralf, L. Helletsgruber, L. Hofmann, E. Schipper, A. Konetzni, Vienna St Op Chor, Vienna St Op Orch, H. Knappertsbusch (pp1936)
(7/94) (SCHW) Ⓓ [2] **314512**
8, 17, 18, 19a-c, 21, 22. M. Müller, M. Klose, F. Völker, J. Prohaska, J. von Manowarda, Bayreuth Fest Chor, Bayreuth Fest Orch, H. Tietjen (r1936) (8/93) (TELD) Ⓓ **9031-76442-2**
8, 20b E. List, orch (r1927) (PREI) Ⓓ **89083**
9. M. Lawrence, M. Singher, Pasdeloup Orch, P. Coppola (French: r1933)
(5/90) (PREI) Ⓓ **89011**
9. M. Lawrence, M. Singher, SO, P. Coppola (French: r1933)
(1/92) (EMI) Ⓓ [4] **CMS7 64008-2(1)**
10. Lotte Lehmann, Berlin St Op Orch, F. Weissmann (r1930) (MSCM) Ⓓ [2] **MM30283**
(MSCM) ▣ [2] **MM40105**
10. K. Flagstad, Philadelphia, E. Ormandy (r1937) (IMP) Ⓓ **GLRS105**
10. K. Flagstad, orch, E. Ormandy (r1938)
(PEAR) Ⓓ **GEMMCD9130**
10. E. Destinn, orch, B. Seidler-Winkler (r1906)
(PEAR) Ⓓ **GEMMCD9172**
10. K. Flagstad, Philadelphia, E. Ormandy (r1937) (SIMA) Ⓓ [3] **PSC1821(2)**
10. H. Spani, La Scala Orch, C. Sabajno (Ital: r1927) (9/90) (CLUB) Ⓓ [2] **CL99-509/10**
10. J. Gadski, orch (r1914)
(7/91) (CLUB) Ⓓ **CL99-109**
10. H. Spani, La Scala Orch, C. Sabajno (Ital: r1927) (1/92) (EMI) Ⓓ [4] **CMS7 64008-2(1)**
10. Lotte Lehmann, orch, F. Weissmann (r1930)
(1/92) (EMI) Ⓓ [4] **CMS7 64008-2(1)**
10. F. Saville, anon (r c1902)
(10/92) (SYMP) Ⓓ **SYMCD1093**
10. H. Spani, La Scala Orch, C. Sabajno (Ital: r1927) (12/92) (PREI) Ⓓ **89037**
10. K. Flagstad, Philadelphia, E. Ormandy (r1937) (7/93) (NIMB) Ⓓ **NI7847**
10. M. Jeritza, orch (r1922)
(4/94) (PREI) Ⓓ **89079**
10. E. Destinn, orch, F. Kark (r1906)
(12/94) (SUPR) Ⓓ [12] **11 2136-2(1)**
10. E. Rethberg, orch (r1927)
(2/95) (ROMO) Ⓓ [2] **81012-2**
10, 12a-c E. Schwarzkopf, C. Ludwig, Philh, H. Wallberg (10/88) (EMI) Ⓓ **CDM7 69501-2**
10, 12c E. Destinn, orch (r1911)
(12/94) (SUPR) Ⓓ [12] **11 2136-2(4)**
11. C. Studer, W. Meier, BPO, C. Abbado (pp1993) (5/94) (DG) Ⓓ **439 768-2GH**
(5/94) (DG) ▣ **439 768-4GH**
11. K. Thorborg, E. Rethberg, J. Huehn, NY Met Op Orch, E. Leinsdorf (bp1940)
(4/95) (PREI) Ⓓ **89084**

11, 12a-c M. Lawrence, Y. Brothier, Pasdeloup Orch, P. Coppola (French: r1933)
(5/90) (PREI) Ⓓ **89011**
11, 12a-c T. Lemnitz, M. Klose, Berlin St Op Orch, J. Schüler (r1948)
(1/92) (EMI) Ⓓ [4] **CMS7 64008-2(1)**
12a, 12b M. Klose, M. Müller, Vienna St Op Orch, H. Tietjen (pp1938)
(6/94) (SCHW) Ⓓ **314502**
12a, 17. E. Randová, Brno St PO, O. Lenárd (pp1992) (SUPR) Ⓓ **11 1846-2**
12c C. Ferrani, E. Ceresoli, anon (Ital: r1902)
(5/91) (SYMP) Ⓓ **SYMCD1077**
12c Lotte Lehmann, orch (r1916)
(6/92) (PREI) Ⓓ [3] **89302**
12c E. Eames, L. Homer, orch (r1908)
(11/93) (ROMO) Ⓓ [2] **81001-2**
12c E. Eames, L. Homer, orch (r1908)
(1/95) (NIMB) Ⓓ **NI7860**
13, 17, 18. Eastman Wind Ens, F. Fennell (r1959. arr Winterbottom; Caillet)
(MERC) Ⓓ **434 322-2MM**
13, 17, 18. Canadian Brass, BPO, Bayreuth Fest Orch, E. de Waart (r1991; arr Frackenpohl)
(PHIL) Ⓓ **434 109-2PH**
17. Philh, G. Simon (CALA) Ⓓ **CACD0001**
17. NBC SO, A. Toscanini, H. Keith (bp1948)
(RCA) ΘΘ **790 351**
17. Czech PO, Z. Chalabala
(SUPR) ▣ **11 0640-4**
17. BPO, K. Tennstedt (EMIL) Ⓓ **CDZ104**
(EMIL) ▣ **LZ104**
17. Philh, G. Simon (CALA) Ⓓ [6] **CACD0102**
17. Budapest SO, G. Lehel (LASE) Ⓓ **15 612**
(LASE) ▣ **79 612**
17. VPO, H. Stein (DECC) Ⓓ **425 853-2DWO**
(DECC) ▣ **425 853-4DWO**
17. Leningrad PO, E. Mravinsky (pp1965)
(OLYM) Ⓓ [6] **OCD5002**
17. LSO, B. Tuckwell (IMP) Ⓓ **PCDS8**
(IMP) ▣ **PCDSC8**
17. New SO, A. Gibson
(CHES) Ⓓ **Chesky CD62**
17. Classic Buskers, Chuckerbutty Ocarina Qt (arr Murray) (SEAV) Ⓓ **CD007366**
17. BPO, K. Tennstedt (EMI) Ⓓ **CDC2 53045-2**
(EMI) ▣ **EL2 53045-4**
17. Philadelphia, E. Ormandy
(SONY) Ⓓ **SBK39438**
17. NY Met Op Orch, James Levine (r1991)
(DG) ΘΘ **435 874-5GH**
17. D. Hill, B. Tuckwell (r1987)
(IMP) Ⓓ **PCDS20**
(IMP) ▣ **PCDSC20**
17. NYPO, L. Bernstein (r1967)
(SONY) Ⓓ **SMK47643**
17. RPO, V. Handley (r1993)
(TRIN) Ⓓ **TRP008**
(TRIN) ▣ **MCTRP008**
17. LPO, H. Knappertsbusch (r1947)
(PREI) Ⓓ **90189**
17. RPS Orch, B. Walter (r1926)
(VAI) Ⓓ **VAIA1059**
17. VPO, K. Böhm (DG) Ⓓ [2] **439 687-2GX2**
17. LPO, T. Beecham (r1935)
(PEAR) Ⓓ **GEMMCD9094**
17. Sydney SO, J. Serebrier
(IMG) Ⓓ **IMGCD1611**
17. RPO, A. Inglis (r1994)
(RPO) Ⓓ **CDRPO7025**
(RPO) ▣ **ZCRPO7025**
17. LSO, A. Dorati (r1959)
(MERC) Ⓓ **434 342-2MM**
17. Leningrad PO, E. Mravinsky (pp1965)
(MELO) Ⓓ [10] **74321 25189-2**
17. Leningrad PO, E. Mravinsky (pp1965)
(MELO) Ⓓ **74321 25199-2**
17. LPO, C. Mackerras
(11/87) (CFP) Ⓓ **CD-CFP9000**
17. Oslo PO, M. Jansons
(12/92) (EMI) Ⓓ **CDC7 54583-2**
17. NY Met Op Orch, James Levine (r1991)
(10/93) (DG) Ⓓ **435 874-2GH**
17. LPO, T. Beecham (r1935)
(6/94) (DUTT) Ⓓ **CDLX7007**
17. RCA Victor Orch, F. Reiner (r1950)
(8/94) (RCA) Ⓓ **09026 61792-2**
17. LCP, R. Norrington (r1994)
(11/95) (EMI) Ⓓ **CDC5 55479-2**
17, 18. Vienna St Op Chor, VPO, G. Solti
(DECC) Ⓓ **421 865-2DA**
17, 18. ROH Chor, RPO, R. Stapleton
(RPO) Ⓓ **CDRPO7009**
(RPO) ▣ **ZCRPO7009**

17, 18. ROH Chor, RPO, R. Stapleton (r1991)
(RPO) Ⓓ [2] **CDRPD900**
(RPO) ▣ [2] **ZCRPD900**
17, 18. Vienna St Op Chor, VPO, G. Solti (r1985)
(DECC) Ⓓ **440 069-2DW**
(DECC) ▣ **440 069-4DW**
17, 18. ROH Chor, RPO, R. Stapleton
(IMP) Ⓓ [3] **TCD107**
18. R. Shaw Chorale, RCA Victor Orch, Robert Shaw (RCA) Ⓓ **GD6020**
18. M. Austin (arr org) (CHAN) Ⓓ **CHAN651**
18. Mormon Tabernacle Ch, Philadelphia, E. Ormandy (SONY) Ⓓ **SBK3943**
18. J.E. Hansen (ERAT) Ⓓ **2292-45801-**
18. Ljubljana Rad Orch, Ljubljana Rad Chor, Anon (cond) (WORD) Ⓓ **FCD741**
18. Philh Chor, Philh, L. Magiera
(DECC) ΘΘ **436 320-5D**
18. A. Marsden-Thomas (r1992;arr Woods: org)
(CRAM) Ⓓ **CRACD**
18. S. Cleobury (arr Cunningham Wood)
(BELA) Ⓓ **450 013-**
(BELA) ▣ **450 013-**
18. Berlin Deutsche Op Chor, Berlin Deutsche Op Orch, G. Sinopoli (r1984)
(BELA) Ⓓ **450 052-**
(BELA) ▣ **450 052-**
18. Innsbruck SO, Innsbruck Chor, Robert Wagner (BELA) Ⓓ **450 126-**
(BELA) ▣ **450 126-**
18. F. Bayco (EMIL) Ⓓ **CDZ11**
(EMIL) ▣ **LZ11**
18. ROH Chor, ROHO, B. Haitink
(12/89) (EMI) Ⓓ **CDC7 49849-**
18. Philh Chor, Philh, L. Magiera
(11/91) (DECC) ◐ **071 150-1D**
(11/91) (DECC) ΘΘ **071 150-3D**
18. S. Cleobury (r1979: arr C Wood)
(6/93) (DECC) Ⓓ **436 402-2DW**
(6/93) (DECC) ▣ **436 402-4DW**
18. G. Thalben-Ball (r c1931: arr org)
(9/94) (BEUL) Ⓓ **1PD**
19a S. Sedlmair, E. Schmedes, anon (r1904)
(7/91) (SYMP) Ⓓ **SYMCD108**
19a T. Lemnitz, T. Ralf, Berlin Staatskapelle, L. Blech (r1939)
(7/92) (PEAR) Ⓓ [3] **GEMMCDS9926(**
19a T. Ralf, T. Lemnitz, Berlin St Op Orch, B. Seidler-Winkler (r1939)
(10/94) (PREI) Ⓓ **8907**
19a A. Pertile, I.A. Tellini, M.L. Fanelli, La Scala Orch, C. Sabajno (r1927/8: Ital)
(10/94) (PREI) Ⓓ **8907**
19a-c I. Kozlovsky, E. Shumskaya, USSR SO, Anon (cond) (r1930-50)
(MYTO) Ⓓ **1MCD921.5**
19a-c L. Melchior, E. Bettendorf, Berlin St Op Orch, F. Weissmann (r1926) (PREI) Ⓓ **8906**
19a-c E. Bettendorf, L. Melchior, orch, F. Weissmann (r1926)
(8/88) (DANA) Ⓓ [2] **DACOCD313/**
19a-c W. Widdop, G. Ljungberg, LSO, L. Collingwood (r1930)
(11/92) (CLAR) Ⓓ **CDGSE78-50-4**
19a, 19b K. Heidersbach, M. Lorenz, Berlin St Op Orch, C. Schmalstich (r1929)
(PREI) Ⓓ **8905**
19a, 21, 22. F. Völker, M. Müller, Bayreuth Fest Chor, Bayreuth Fest Orch, H. Tietjen (r1936)
(MSCM) Ⓓ [2] **MM3028**
(MSCM) ▣ [2] **MM4010**
19b E. Scaramberg, anon (r1905: Fr)
(SYMP) Ⓓ **SYMCD117**
19b F. Völker, Berlin St Op Orch, M. Gurlitt (r1928) (2/90) (PREI) Ⓓ **8900**
19b, 19c F. Ansseau, orch (Fr: r1924)
(1/91) (PREI) Ⓓ **8902**
19c L. Melchior, Berlin St Op Orch, L. Blech (r1928) (PREI) Ⓓ **8906**
19c L. Melchior, Berlin St Op Orch, L. Blech (r1928) (10/89) (EMI) Ⓓ **CDH7 69789-**
19c F. Merli, orch, L. Molajoli (Ital: r1926)
(1/91) (PREI) Ⓓ **8902**
19c H. Winkelmann, anon (r1904)
(7/91) (SYMP) Ⓓ **SYMCD108**
19c T. Ralf, M. Hussa, Vienna St Op Orch, J. Krips (pp1936) (7/94) (SCHW) Ⓓ [2] **31451**
19c, 21, 22. F. Völker, Berlin St Op Orch, J. Heidenreich (r1927) (2/90) (PREI) Ⓓ **8900**
19c, 22. P. Franz, orch (r1914: Fr)
(PREI) Ⓓ **8909**
19c, 22. L. Melchior, Berlin St Op Orch, L. Blech (r1928) (8/88) (DANA) Ⓓ [2] **DACOCD315/**
21. G. Thill, orch, E. Bigot (r c1930: Fr)
(PEAR) Ⓓ **GEMMCD994**

21. F. Völker, Bayreuth Fest Orch, H. Tietjen (r1936) (MMOI) ① **CDMOIR405** (MMOI) ⊟ **CMOIR405**
21. P. Domingo, RPO, E. Downes (RCA) ① [2] **GD60866** (RCA) ⊟ [2] **GK60866**
21. M. del Monaco, Milan SO, A. Quadri (r1948: Ital) (TEST) ① **SBT1039**
21. R. Crooks, orch (r1928) (CLAR) ① **CDGSE78-50-58**
21. P. Domingo, VPO, G. Solti (r1985/6) (DECC) ① **443 379-2DM**
21. P. Franz, orch (r1911: Fr) (PREI) ① **89099**
21. L. Melchior, Orch (Danish: r c1920) (8/88) (DANA) ① [2] **DACOCD311/2**
21. M. Wittrisch, Berlin St Op Orch, F. Zaun (r1933) (1/92) (EMI) ① [4] **CMS7 64008-2(1)**
21. R. Tauber, orch, N. Treep (bp1939) (2/92) (LYRC) ① [2] **SRO830**
21. F. Viñas, S. Cottone (Ital: r1903) (7/92) (PEAR) ① [3] **GEMMCDS9923(1)**
21. J. Hislop, orch, J. Barbirolli (Eng: r1929) (1/93) (PEAR) ① **GEMMCD9956**
21. P. Anders, Cologne RSO, R. Kraus (bp1951) (8/93) (ACAN) ① **43 268**
21. C. Kullman, orch, W. Goehr (r1938) (11/93) (PREI) ① **89057**
21. L. Suthaus, orch (3/94) (MYTO) ① [3] **3MCD93381**
21. S. Kónya, Boston SO, E. Leinsdorf (r1965) (4/94) (RCA) ① [6] **09026 61580-2(7)**
21. F. Viñas, S. Cottone (r1903: Ital) (4/94) (EMI) ① [3] **CHS7 64860-2(1)**
21. W. Widdop, orch, L. Collingwood (r1926: Eng) (5/94) (CLAR) ① **CDGSE78-50-52**
21. G. Thill, orch, E. Bigot (r1930: Fr) (8/95) (FORL) ① **UCD16727**
21, 22. L. Slezak, Berlin St Op Orch, M. Gurlitt (r1928) (PREI) ① [2] **89203**
21, 22. W. Lewis, RPO, G. Ötvös (RPO) ① **CDRPO7019**
21, 22. H. Roswaenge, VPO, R. Moralt (r1942) (PREI) ① [2] **89211**
21, 22. P. Domingo, J. Norman, E. Randová, H. Sotin, Vienna St Op Chor, VPO, G. Solti (r1985/6) (DECC) ① **440 410-2DM**
21, 22. A. Piccaver, Berlin St Op Orch, M. Gurlitt (r1929) (PREI) ① [2] **89217**
22. G. Thill, orch (r1931: Fr) (PEAR) ① **GEMMCD9947**
22. M. Lorenz, Berlin St Op Orch, C. Schmalstich (r1928) (PREI) ① **89053**
22. L. Melchior, Philadelphia, E. Ormandy (r1938) (PEAR) ① [2] **GEMMCDS9121**
22. L. Slezak, orch, M. Gurlitt (r1928) (PEAR) ① **GEMMCD9129**
22. K. Erb, orch (r1914) (PREI) ① **89095**
22. H. Roswaenge, VPO, R. Moralt (r1942) (1/92) (EMI) ① [4] **CMS7 64008-2(1)**
22. L. Melchior, Philadelphia, E. Ormandy (r1938) (10/92) (TEST) ① **SBT1005**
22. L. Sobinov, orch (r1910: Russ) (6/93) (PEAR) ① [3] **GEMMCDS9997/9(2)**
22. G. Borgatti, orch (r1919: Ital) (4/94) (EMI) ① [3] **CHS7 64860-2(1)**

Die Meistersinger von Nürnberg, '(The) Mastersingers of Nuremburg'– opera: 3 acts (1868—Munich) (Lib. cpsr)

EXCERPTS: 1. Prelude. ACT 1: 2. Da zu dir der Heiland kam; 3. Verweilt! Ein Wort! ein einzig Wort!; 4. Da bin ich! Wer ruft?; 5. David! Was stehst?; 6. Mein Herr! Der Singer Meisterschlag; 7. Der Meister Tön' und Weisen; 8. Damit, Herr Ritter, ist's so bewandt!; 9. So bleibt mir einzig der Meister-Lohn!; 10. Seid meiner Treue wohl versehen; 11a. Gott grüsst Euch, Meister; 11b. Zu einer Freiung und Zunftberatung; 12. Das schöne Fest, Johannistag (Pogner's address); 13. Vielleicht schon ginget ihr zu weit; 14a. Wohl, Meister, zur Tagesordnung kehrt; 14b. Dacht' ich mir's doch!; 15. Am stillen Herd; 16. Nun, Meister! Wenn's gefällt; 17. Was euch zum Liede Richt' und Schnur; 18. 'Fanget an'—So rief der Lenz (Trial Song); 19. Seid Ihr nun fertig?; 20. Halt! Meister! Nicht so geeilt! ACT 2: 21. Johannistag!; 22. Lass seh'n, ob Meister Sachs zu Haus?; 23a. Zeig' her, 's ist gut. Dort an die Tür'; 23b. Was duftet doch der Flieder (Fliedermonolog); 24. Gut'n Abend, Meister!; 25. Das dacht' ich wohl; 26. Da ist er!...Ja, ihr seid es; 27a. Geliebter, spare den Zorn; 27b. Hört, ihr Leut, und lasst euch sagen; 27c. Uble Dinge, die ich da merk; 28a. Tu's nicht!—Doch horch!; 28b. Jerum! Jerum!; 29a. Das Fenster geht auf; 29b. Freund Sachs! So hört doch nur ein Wort!; 30. Den Tag seh' ich erscheinen (Beckmesser's Serenade); 31. Mit den Schuhen ward ich fertig schier; 32. Zum Teufel mit dir, verdammter Kerl! ACT 3: 33. Prelude; 34. Gleich, Meister! Hier!; 35. Am Jordan Sankt Johannes stand; 36. Wahn! Wahn! Uberall Wahn! (Wahnmonolog); 37. Grüss Gott, mein Junker!; 38. Mein Freund! In holder Jugendzeit; 39. Morgenlich leuchtend (Prize song rehearsal); 40. Abendlich glühend; 41. Ein Werbelied! Von Sachs!; 42. Das Gedicht! hier liess ich's; 43a. So ganz boshaft doch keinen ich fand; 43b. Sieh Ev'chen!...Grüss Gott, mein Ev'chen; 44. Hat man mit dem Schuhwerk; 45. O Sachs! Mein Freund!; 46a. Mein Kind, von Tristan und Isolde; 46b. Aha! Da streicht die Lene; 46c. Ein Kind ward hier geboren; 47. Selig wie die Sonne (Quintet); 48. Sankt Krispin, lobet ihn! (Guild Choruses); 49. Ihr tanzt? (Dance of the Apprentices); 50. Entry of the Masters; 51. Wach auf! es nahet gen den Tag; 52. Euch macht ihr's leicht; 53. Nun denn, wenn's Meistern und Volk beliebt; 54. Morgen ich leuchte (Beckmesser); 55. Das Lied, für wahr, ist nicht von mir; 56. Morgenlich leuchtend (Prize Song); 57. Verachtet mir die Meister nicht (Sachs' Panegyric); 58. Ehrt eure deutche

Hans Sachs K. Ridderbusch
Walther J. Cox
Eva H. Bode
Pogner H. Sotin
Beckmesser K. Hirte
David F. Stricker
Magdalene A. Reynolds
Kothner G. Nienstedt
Vogelgesang H. Steinbach

Bayreuth Fest Chor, Bayreuth Fest Orch, S. Varviso (pp1974) (PHIL) ① [32] **434 420-2PM32(1)**

Hans Sachs D. Fischer-Dieskau
Walther P. Domingo
Eva C. Ligendza
Pogner P. Lagger
Beckmesser R. Hermann
David H. Laubenthal
Magdalene C. Ludwig
Kothner G. Feldhoff
Vogelgesang P. Maus
Nachtigall R. Bañuelas
Zorn L. Driscoll
Eisslinger K-E. Mercker
Moser M. Vantin
Ortel K. Lang
Schwarz I. Sardi
Foltz M. Nikolič
Nightwatchman V. von Halem

Berlin Deutsche Op Chor, Berlin Deutsche Op Orch, E. Jochum (r1976) (10/85) (DG) ① [4] **415 278-2GH4**

Hans Sachs N. Bailey
Walther R. Kollo
Eva H. Bode
Pogner K. Moll
Beckmesser B. Weikl
David A. Dallapozza
Magdalene J. Hamari
Kothner G. Nienstedt
Vogelgesang Adalbert Kraus
Nachtigall M. Egel
Zorn M. Schomberg
Eisslinger W. Appel
Moser M. Sénéchal
Ortel H. Berger-Tuna
Schwarz K. Rydl
Foltz R. Hartmann
Nightwatchman W. Klumlikboldt

Gumpoldskirchner Spatzen, Vienna St Op Chor, VPO, G. Solti (r1975/6) (7/87) (DECC) ① [4] **417 497-2DH4**

Hans Sachs T. Adam
Walther R. Kollo
Eva H. Donath
Pogner K. Ridderbusch
Beckmesser G. Evans
David P. Schreier
Magdalene R. Hesse
Kothner Z. Kélémen
Vogelgesang E. Büchner
Nachtigall H. Lunow
Zorn H.J. Rotzsch
Eisslinger P. Bindszus
Moser H. Hiestermann
Ortel H.C. Polster
Schwarz H. Reeh
Foltz S. Vogel
Nightwatchman K. Moll

Dresden St Op Chor, Leipzig Rad Chor, Staatskapelle Dresden, H. von Karajan (r1970) (7/88) (EMI) ① [4] **CDS7 49683-2**

Hans Sachs O. Wiener
Walther Jess Thomas
Eva C. Watson
Pogner H. Hotter
Beckmesser B. Kusche
David F. Lenz
Magdalene L. Benningsen
Kothner J. Metternich
Vogelgesang D. Thaw
Nachtigall C. Hoppe
Zorn W. Carnuth
Eisslinger F. Klarwein
Moser K. Ostertag
Ortel A. Keil
Schwarz G. Wieter
Foltz M. Proebstl
Nightwatchman H.B. Ernst

Bavarian St Op Chor, Bavarian St Op Orch, J. Keilberth (pp1963) (4/90) (EURO) ① [4] **GD69008**

Hans Sachs O. Edelmann
Walter H. Hopf
Eva E. Schwarzkopf
Pogner F. Dalberg
Beckmesser E. Kunz
David G. Unger
Magdalene I. Malaniuk
Kothner H. Pflanzl
Vogelgesang E. Majkut
Nachtigall H. Berg
Zorn J. Janko
Eisslinger K. Mikorey
Moser G. Stolze
Ortel H. Tandler
Schwarz H. Borst
Foltz A. Van Mill
Nightwatchman W. Faulhaber

Bayreuth Fest Chor, Bayreuth Fest Orch, H. von Karajan (pp1951) (9/90) (EMI) ① [4] **CHS7 63500-2**

Hans Sachs B. Weikl
Walther S. Jerusalem
Eva M.A. Häggander
Pogner M. Schenk
Beckmesser H. Prey
David G. Clark
Magdalene M. Schiml
Kothner J. Vermeersch
Vogelgesang A. Molnár
Nachtigall M. Egel
Zorn U. Holdorf
Eisslinger P. Maus
Moser H. Pampuch
Ortel S. Sólyom-Nagy
Schwarz H.K. Ecker
Foltz D. Schweikart
Nightwatchman M. Hölle

Bayreuth Fest Chor, Bayreuth Fest Orch, H. Stein, W. Wagner, B. Large (pp1984) (3/92) (PHIL) ● [3] **070 413-1PH3** (PHIL) ▭ **070 413-3PH2**

Hans Sachs K. Ridderbusch
Walther J. Cox
Eva H. Bode
Pogner H. Sotin
Beckmesser K. Hirte
David F. Stricker
Magdalene A. Reynolds
Kothner G. Nienstedt
Vogelgesang H. Steinbach
Nachtigall J. Dene
Zorn R. Licha
Eisslinger W. Appel
Moser N. Orth
Ortel H. Feldhoff
Schwarz H. Bauer
Foltz N. Hillebrand
Nightwatchman B. Weikl

Bayreuth Fest Chor, Bayreuth Fest Orch, S. Varviso (pp1974) (10/92) (PHIL) ① [4] **434 611-2PH4**

Hans Sachs F. Frantz
Walther R. Schock
Eva E. Grümmer
Pogner G. Frick
Beckmesser B. Kusche
David G. Unger
Magdalene M. Höffgen
Kothner G. Neidlinger
Vogelgesang H. Wilhelm
Nachtigall W. Stoll
Zorn M. Schmidt

Eisslinger L. Clam
Moser Herold Kraus
Ortel R. Koffmane
Schwarz A. Metternich
Foltz H. Pick
Nightwatchman H. Prey
Berlin St Hedwig's Cath Ch, Berlin Deutsche Op Chor, Berlin St Op Chor, BPO, R. Kempe (r1956)
(2/93) (EMI) Ⓓ [4] **CMS7 64154-2**
Hans Sachs P. Schoeffler
Walther L. Suthaus
Eva H. Scheppan
Pogner F. Dalberg
Beckmesser E. Kunz
David E. Witte
Magdalene C. Kallab
Kothner F. Krenn
Vogelgesang B. Arnold
Nachtigall H. Fehn
Zorn G. Witting
Eisslinger G. Rödin
Moser K. Krollmann
Ortel H. Gosebruch
Schwarz F. Sauer
Foltz A. Dome
Nightwatchman E. Pina
Bayreuth Fest Chor, Bayreuth Fest Orch, H. Abendroth (pp1943)
(2/94) (PREI) Ⓓ [4] **90174**
Hans Sachs B. Weikl
Walther B. Heppner
Eva C. Studer
Pogner K. Moll
Beckmesser S. Lorenz
David D. van der Walt
Magdalene C. Kallisch
Kothner H-J. Ketelsen
Vogelgesang M. Schade
Nachtigall H. Wilbrink
Zorn U. Ress
Eisslinger H. Sapell
Moser R. Wagenführer
Ortel R. Büse
Schwarz G. Götzen
Foltz F. Kunder
Nightwatchman R. Pape
Bavarian St Op Chor, Bavarian St Orch, W. Sawallisch (r1993)
(8/94) (EMI) Ⓓ [4] **CDS5 55142-2**
Hans Sachs P. Schoeffler
Walther G. Treptow
Eva H. Gueden
Pogner O. Edelmann
Beckmesser K. Dönch
David A. Dermota
Magdalene E. Schürhoff
Kothner A. Poell
Vogelgesang H. Meyer-Welfing
Nachtigall W. Felden
Zorn E. Majkut
Eisslinger W. Wernigk
Moser H. Gallos
Ortel; Nightwatchman H. Pröglhöf
Schwarz F. Bierbach
Foltz L. Pantscheff
Vienna St Op Chor, VPO, H. Knappertsbusch (r1950/1)
(10/94) (DECC) Ⓓ [4] **440 057-2DMO4**
Hans Sachs P. Schoeffler
Walther A. Seider
Eva I. Seefried
Pogner H. Alsen
Beckmesser E. Kunz
David P. Klein
Magdalene E. Schürhoff
Kothner F. Krenn
Vogelgesang A. Dermota
Nachtigall; Nightwatchman V. Madin
Zorn G. Maikl
Eisslinger J. Witt
Moser W. Wernigk
Ortel A. Muzzarelli
Schwarz A. Jerger
Foltz M. Rus
Vienna St Op Chor, VPO, K. Böhm (pp1944)
(6/95) (PREI) Ⓓ [4] **90234**

Act 2. G. Hann, H. Noort, T. Kempf, W. Schirp, E. Kunz, K. Wessely, M-L. Schilp, H. Heinz Nissen, A. Fügel, L. Windisch, H. Florian, W. Ulbricht, E. Schneider, E. Heyer, W. Lang, A. Will, Berlin Rad Chor, Berlin RO, A. Rother (bp1942) (5/94) (PREI) Ⓓ **90168**

Act 3. H. Hermann Nissen, T. Ralf, M. Teschemacher, S. Nilsson, E. Fuchs, M. Kremer, H. Jung, Dresden St Op Chor, Saxon St Orch, K. Böhm (r1938) (PEAR) Ⓓ [2] **GEMMCDS9121**

Exc A. Pinto, orch (r1914: Ital) (11/92) (MEMO) Ⓓ [2] **HR4408/9(2)**

Excs K. Kamann, H. Alsen, G. Maikl, G. Monthy, H. Wiedemann, F. Krenn, A. Arnold, E. Fritsch, R. Tomek, Walter Hellmich, H. Reich, K. Ettl, M. Lorenz, E. Zimmermann, M. Reining, E. Szánthó, Vienna St Op Chor, Vienna St Op Orch, W. Furtwängler (pp1937) (SCHW) Ⓓ [2] **314702**

Excs J. Prohaska, C. Reich, J. Kalenberg, H. Wiedemann, Vienna St Op Orch, J. Krips (pp1937) (11/94) (SCHW) Ⓓ [2] **314532**

Excs M. Lorenz, V. Ursuleac, A. Jerger, E. Zimmermann, B. Paalen, N. Zec, H. Gallos, H. Duhan, H. Wiedemann, V. Madin, A. Arnold, Wolken, W. Wernigk, A. Muzzarelli, H. Reich, K. Ettl, Vienna St Op Chor, Vienna St Op Orch, C. Krauss (pp1933) (1/95) (SCHW) Ⓓ [2] **314562**

Excs L. Hofmann, H. Alsen, G. Maikl, G. Monthy, H. Wiedemann, V. Madin, A. Arnold, E. Fritsch, R. Tomek, A. Muzzarelli, H. Reich, K. Ettl, J. Kalenberg, R. Sallaba, V. Mansinger, K. Thorborg, Vienna St Op Chor, Vienna St Op Orch, H. Knappertsbusch (pp1936) (3/95) (SCHW) Ⓓ [2] **314602**

Excs A. Jerger, V. Ursuleac, F. Völker, E. Zimmermann, E. Szánthó, Vienna St Op Chor, Vienna St Op Orch, C. Krauss (pp1934) (3/95) (SCHW) Ⓓ [2] **314602**

Excs R. Bockelmann, N. Zec, G. Maikl, H. Duhan, H. Wiedemann, V. Madin, A. Arnold, Wolken, R. Tomek, A. Muzzarelli, H. Reich, K. Ettl, E. Schipper, E. Zimmermann, V. Ursuleac, G. Rünger, Vienna St Op Chor, Vienna St Op Orch, C. Krauss (pp1933) (8/95) (SCHW) Ⓓ [2] **314642**

Suite French Rad PO, M. Janowski (r1990) (VIRG) ▭ **VJ7 59689-4**

1. RPO, T. Beecham (bp1959) (MUSI) Ⓓ **MACD-631**
1. LPO, E. Bátiz (MCI) Ⓓ **OQ0009**
1. Bavarian St Orch, W. Sawallisch (ORFE) Ⓓ **C161871A**
1. Concertgebouw, B. Haitink (PHIL) Ⓓ **420 886-2PSL**
1. NBC SO, A. Toscanini (pp1954) (MUSI) Ⓓ **ATRA-3008**
1. Vienna SO, Y. Ahronovitch (LASE) Ⓓ **15 514** (LASE) ▭ **79 514**
1. Vienna SO, Y. Ahronovitch (LASE) Ⓓ **15 521** (LASE) ▭ **79 521**
1. Cleveland Orch, G. Szell (CBS) Ⓓ [2] **CD46466**
1. LPO, K. Tennstedt (EMI) ◖ **LDB9 91234-1** (EMI) ▣ **MVD9 91234-3**
1. LSO, L. Stokowski (pp1972) (DECC) Ⓓ **433 639-2DSP** (DECC) ▭ **433 639-4DSP**
1. RPO, E. Bátiz (RPO) Ⓓ **CDRPO5006** (RPO) ▭ **ZCRPO5006**
1. BPO, H. von Karajan (r1974) (EMI) Ⓓ **CDM7 64334-2**
1. BPO, S. Ozawa (PHIL) OO **426 271-5PH**
1. Cleveland Orch, G. Szell (SONY) Ⓓ **SBK39438**
1. BBC PO, E. Downes (IMP) Ⓓ **PCD1023**
1. Philh, Y. Simonov (r1991) (COLL) Ⓓ **Coll1294-2**
1. London Fest Orch, J. Armstrong (ROSE) Ⓓ **3212**
1. D. Chorzempa (r1984: arr org) (PHIL) Ⓓ **438 309-2PM** (PHIL) ▭ **438 309-4PM**
1. W. Backhaus (r1929: arr Hutcheson: pf roll) (COND) Ⓓ **690.07.013**
1. NY Met Op Orch, James Levine (r1991) (DG) OO **435 874-5GH**
1. Basle SO, A. Jordan (r1983) (ERAT) Ⓓ **4509-92866-2**
1. VPO, H. Stein (r1974) (BELA) Ⓓ **450 025-2** (BELA) ▭ **450 025-4**
1. Chicago SO, G. Solti (r1972) (DECC) Ⓓ **440 069-2DWO** (DECC) ▭ **440 069-4DWO**
1. LSO, B. Tuckwell (IMP) Ⓓ [3] **TCD1070**
1. NYPO, L. Bernstein (r1964) (SONY) Ⓓ **SMK47643**
1. A. Partington (r1993; arr Westbrook) (PRIO) Ⓓ **PRCD479**
1. SRO, H. Knappertsbusch (r1947) (PREI) Ⓓ **9018**
1. G. Gould (r1973: trans pf: Gould) (SONY) Ⓓ **SMK5265**
1. Pittsburgh SO, W. Steinberg (r1956) (EMI) Ⓓ **CDM5 65208-**
1. VPO, K. Böhm (DG) Ⓓ [2] **439 687-2GX**
1. Sydney SO, J. Serebrier (IMG) Ⓓ **IMGCD161**
1. LPO, T. Beecham (r1936) (PEAR) Ⓓ **GEMMCD909**
1. Luxembourg RSO, L. de Froment (FORL) Ⓓ **FF02**
1. BPO, R. Kubelík (r1963) (DG) Ⓓ **439 445-2GCL** (DG) ▭ **439 445-4GCL**
1. Cincinnati SO, J. López-Cobos (r1994) (TELA) Ⓓ **CD8037**
1. Columbia SO, B. Walter (r1959) (SONY) Ⓓ [2] **SM2K6445**
1. Columbia SO, B. Walter (r1959) (SONY) Ⓓ [10] **SX10K6624**
1. LSO, A. Dorati (r1960) (MERC) Ⓓ **434 342-2M**
1. Leningrad PO, E. Mravinsky (pp1982) (MELO) Ⓓ [10] **74321 25189-**
1. Leningrad PO, E. Mravinsky (pp1982) (MELO) Ⓓ **74321 25199-**
1. BPO, R. Kubelík (DG) Ⓓ [2] **447 364-2GDB**
1. Solti Orchestral Project, G. Solti (pp1994) (DECC) Ⓓ **444 458-2D**
1. BPO, K. Tennstedt (r1982/3) (EMI) Ⓓ [2] **CZS5 68616-**
1. BBC PO, E. Downes (r1990) (IMP) Ⓓ **PCD204**
1. NYPO, G. Sinopoli (10/86) (DG) Ⓓ **419 169-2G**
1. T. Trotter (arr Lemare) (11/87) (HYPE) Ⓓ **CDA6621**
1. LSO, W. Morris (12/87) (CIRR) Ⓓ **CICD100**
1. Columbia SO, B. Walter (r1959) (2/90) (CBS) Ⓓ **CD4570**
1. Philh, F. d'Avalos (3/90) (ASV) Ⓓ **CDDCA66**
1. Chicago SO, G. Solti (5/91) (DECC) Ⓓ **430 448-2D**
1. VPO, R. Strauss (pp1944) (2/92) (DG) Ⓓ [12] **435 321-2GWP1**
1. VPO, R. Strauss (pp1944) (2/92) (DG) Ⓓ **435 333-2GW**
1. NBC SO, A. Toscanini (r1946) (11/92) (RCA) Ⓓ **GD6030**
1. Cleveland Orch, G. Szell (11/92) (SONY) Ⓓ **SBK4817**
1. Oslo PO, M. Jansons (12/92) (EMI) Ⓓ **CDC7 54583-**
1. NY Met Op Orch, James Levine (r1991) (10/93) (DG) Ⓓ **435 874-2G**
1. Minnesota Orch, N. Marriner (r1983) (2/94) (TELA) Ⓓ **CD8200**
1. Leningrad PO, E. Mravinsky (pp1967) (3/94) (RUSS) Ⓓ **RDCD1116**
1. LPO, T. Beecham (r1936) (6/94) (DUTT) Ⓓ **CDLX700**
1. Vienna St Op Orch, F. Weingartner (pp1935) (7/94) (SCHW) Ⓓ [2] **31451**
1. Chicago SO, F. Stock (r1926) (2/95) (BIDD) Ⓓ [2] **WHL021/**
1. BPO, W. Furtwängler (r1947) (4/95) (TELD) ◖ **4509-95038-** (4/95) (TELD) ▣ **4509-95038-**
1. NQHO, B. Wordsworth (r1995) (6/95) (EYE) Ⓓ [2] **EOS500**
1. NYPO, P. Boulez (r1972) (7/95) (SONY) Ⓓ **SMK6410**
1. LCP, R. Norrington (r1994) (11/95) (EMI) Ⓓ **CDC5 55479-**
1, 15, 23b, 28b-30, 31-33, 36, 41, 45, 48, 51, 55. J. Herrmann, K. Böhme, R. Sallaba, G. Monthy, E. Kunz, F. Krenn, E. Toriff, H. Gallos, W. Wernigk, H. Schweiger, R. Neumann, F. Worff, T. Ralf, P. Klein, M. Reining, M. Rohs, K. Ettl, Vienna St Op Chor, Vienna St Op Orch, K. Böhm (pp1944) (SCHW) Ⓓ [2] **31468**
1, 2. Vienna St Op Chor, VPO, G. Solti (r1975) (DECC) Ⓓ [2] **440 606-2DF**

1, 2, 12, 15, 18, 23b, 31, 33, 36, 47, 49, 51, 56, 57. F. Frantz, G. Frick, H. Wilhelm, W. Stoll, B. Kusche, G. Neidlinger, M. Schmidt, L. Clam, Herold Kraus, R. Koffmane, A. Metternich, H. Pick, R. Schock, G. Unger, E. Grümmer, M. Höffgen, H. Prey, Berlin St Hedwig's Cath Ch, Berlin Deutsche Op Chor, Berlin St Op Chor, BPO, R. Kempe (r1956)
(EMIN) Ⓓ **CD-EMX2228**
(EMIN) ⊟ **TC-EMX2228**

1, 2, 15, 18, 19, 23b, 35, 36, 39, 46c, 47, 57, 58. C. Ligendza, C. Ludwig, P. Domingo, H. Laubenthal, D. Fischer-Dieskau, R. Hermann, Berlin Deutsche Op Chor, Berlin Deutsche Op Orch, E. Jochum (r1976)
(DG) Ⓓ **445 470-2GMH**

1, 2, 20, 23b, 24, 28b, 29b(pt), 31(pt), 33, 36-38, 45, 46b, 46c, 47, 51, 52(pt), 55, 57, 58. R. Bockelmann, J. von Manowarda, J. Katona, E. Bürger, E. Fuchs, G. Hann, G. Heckel, K. Mikorey, J. Brombacher, W. Markgraf, A. von Diehl, H. Krenn, E. Laholm, E. Zimmermann, T. Lemnitz, R. Berglund, Vienna St Op Chor, Nuremberg Op Chor, Vienna St Op Orch, W. Furtwängler (pp1938)
(8/94) (SCHW) Ⓓ [2] **314522**

1, 23b B. Terfel, BPO, C. Abbado (pp1993)
(5/94) (DG) Ⓓ **439 768-2GH**
(5/94) (DG) ⊟ **439 768-4GH**

1-3, 15, 21, 23b, 33, 34, 36, 47, 51, 56-58. K. Ridderbusch, J. Cox, H. Bode, H. Sotin, K. Hirte, F. Stricker, A. Reynolds, G. Nienstedt, H. Steinbach, Bayreuth Fest Chor, Bayreuth Fest Orch, S. Varviso (pp1974)
(PHIL) Ⓓ **446 621-2PM**

1, 33. New Philh, A. Boult
(EMI) Ⓓ [2] **CZS7 62539-2**

1, 33, 49. VPO, W. Furtwängler (r1949/50)
(4/94) (EMI) Ⓓ [2] **CHS7 64935-2**

1, 33, 49, 50. Philadelphia, E. Ormandy
(RCA) Ⓓ **VD60493**

1, 33, 49, 50. G. Unger, Berlin St Hedwig's Cath Ch, Berlin Deutsche Op Chor, Berlin St Op Chor, BPO, R. Kempe (r1956) (TEST) Ⓓ **SBT1035**

1, 33, 49, 50. Chicago SO, F. Reiner (r1959)
(8/94) (RCA) Ⓓ **09026 61792-2**

1, 49. LPO, K.A. Rickenbacher
(11/87) (CFP) Ⓓ **CD-CFP9008**

1, 49. Philh, O. Klemperer (r1960)
(11/90) (EMI) Ⓓ **CDM7 63618-2**

2. Dresden St Op Chor, Dresden St Op Orch, S. Varviso (r1985) (BELA) Ⓓ **450 052-2**
(BELA) ⊟ **450 052-4**

2, 51, 56. T. Lemnitz, T. Ralf, ROH Chor, LPO, T. Beecham (pp1936)
(6/94) (DUTT) Ⓓ **CDLX7007**

6. J. Sacher, Berlin RSO, J. Märkl (r1991)
(SCHW) Ⓓ [2] **312682**

12. A. Kipnis, Berlin St Op Orch, C. Schmalstich (r1931) (MSCM) Ⓓ [2] **MM30283**
(MSCM) ⊟ [2] **MM40105**

12. I. Andrésen, orch (r1929)
(10/90) (PREI) Ⓓ **89028**

12. A. Kipnis, Berlin St Op Orch, E. Orthmann (r1931) (12/90) (PREI) Ⓓ **89019**

12. A. Kipnis, Berlin St Op Orch, E. Orthmann (r1931)
(7/92) (PEAR) Ⓓ [3] **GEMMCDS9926(1)**

12. W. Hesch, orch (r1906)
(7/93) (NIMB) Ⓓ [2] **NI7840/1**

15. M. Lorenz, Berlin St Op Orch, B. Seidler-Winkler (r1938) (PREI) Ⓓ **90213**

15. L. Melchior, LSO, L. Collingwood (r1931)
(8/88) (DANA) Ⓓ [2] **DACOCD315/6**

15. L. Melchior, LSO, L. Collingwood (r1931)
(10/89) (EMI) Ⓓ **CDH7 69789-2**

15. F. Völker, Berlin St Op Orch, J. Heidenreich (r1928) (2/90) (PREI) Ⓓ **89005**

15. G. Zenatello, anon (r1903: Ital)
(6/90) (SYMP) Ⓓ **SYMCD1073**

15. L. Melchior, LSO, L. Collingwood (r1931)
(10/92) (TEST) Ⓓ **SBT1005**

15. R. Tauber, Berlin St Op Orch, G. Szell (r1927) (12/92) (NIMB) Ⓓ **NI7830**
(12/92) (NIMB) ⊟ **NC7830**

15. M. Lorenz, Berlin St Op Orch, C. Schmalstich (r1930) (10/93) (NIMB) Ⓓ **NI7848**

15. G. Zenatello, orch (r1911: Ital)
(5/94) (SYMP) Ⓓ **SYMCD1168**

15. G. Zenatello, anon (r1903: Ital)
(5/94) (PEAR) Ⓓ [4] **GEMMCDS9073(1)**

15. G. Zenatello, orch (r1911: Ital)
(5/94) (PEAR) Ⓓ [4] **GEMMCDS9073(2)**

15, 18. M. Lorenz, Berlin St Op Orch, C. Schmalstich (r1928) (PREI) Ⓓ **89053**

15, 18. F. Giraud, anon (r1904: Ital)
(5/91) (SYMP) Ⓓ **SYMCD1077**

15, 18. P. Anders, H. Hotter, B. Kusche, ROHO, T. Beecham (bp1951) (8/93) (ACAN) Ⓓ **43 268**

15, 18, 40, 47, 51, 52, 56. P. Schoeffler, K. Böhme, R. Sallaba, G. Monthy, E. Kunz, F. Krenn, E. Toriff, H. Gallos, W. Wernigk, H. Schweiger, R. Neumann, K. Ettl, S. Svanholm, P. Klein, M. Reining, M. Rohs, Vienna St Op Chor, Vienna St Op Orch, K. Böhm (pp1943)
(SCHW) Ⓓ [2] **314692**

15, 56. H. Roswaenge, orch (r1935)
(MSCM) Ⓓ [2] **MM30283**
(MSCM) ⊟ [2] **MM40105**

15, 56. L. Slezak, Berlin St Op Orch, M. Gurlitt (r1928) (PREI) Ⓓ [2] **89203**

15, 56. L. Melchior, Philadelphia, E. Ormandy (r1939) (PEAR) Ⓓ **GEMMCD9049**

15, 56. A. Piccaver, Berlin St Op Orch, J. Prüwer (r1930) (PREI) Ⓓ [2] **89217**

15, 56. R. Tauber, orch (r1927)
(7/89) (PEAR) Ⓓ **GEMMCD9327**

15, 56. R. Tauber, Berlin St Op Orch, G. Szell (r1927) (3/92) (EMI) Ⓓ **CDH7 64029-2**

15, 56. H. Roswaenge, Berlin St Op Orch, F.A. Schmidt (r1932) (4/95) (PREI) Ⓓ [2] **89209**

18. G. Zenatello, orch (r1910: Ital)
(5/94) (PEAR) Ⓓ [4] **GEMMCDS9073(2)**

18. G. Zenatello, orch (r1910: Ital)
(5/94) (SYMP) Ⓓ **SYMCD1168**

18. T. Ralf, Berlin St Op Orch, H.U. Müller (r1941) (10/94) (PREI) Ⓓ **89077**

18, 56. F. Völker, Berlin St Op Orch, M. Gurlitt (r1928) (2/90) (PREI) Ⓓ **89005**

23b K. Moll, Munich RO, K. Eichhorn (r1981)
(ORFE) Ⓓ **C009821A**

23b H. Prey, Berlin Deutsche Op Orch, H. Hollreiser (EURO) Ⓓ **GD69019**

23b F. Schorr, Berlin St Op Orch, L. Blech (r1927) (MSCM) Ⓓ [2] **MM30283**
(MSCM) ⊟ [2] **MM40105**

23b J. Herrmann, Saxon St Orch, K. Böhm (r1941) (PREI) Ⓓ **89076**

23b H. Hotter, Berlin Deutsche Op Orch, A. Rother (r1942) (PREI) Ⓓ **90200**

23b L. Hofmann, Berlin St Op Orch, F.A. Schmidt (r1932) (PREI) Ⓓ [2] **90232**

23b F. Schorr, LSO, A. Coates (r1930)
(1/92) (EMI) Ⓓ [4] **CMS7 64008-2(1)**

23b P. Schoeffler, Zurich Tonhalle Orch, H. Knappertsbusch (r1947)
(1/95) (PREI) Ⓓ **90190**

23b, 28b, 37, 40, 46b F. Schorr, LSO, A. Coates
(PREI) Ⓓ [2] **89214**

23b, 28b, 47, 56, 57. J. Herrmann, E. Kunz, M. Lorenz, P. Klein, M. Reining, M. Rohs, Vienna St Op Chor, Vienna St Op Orch, K. Böhm (pp1943)
(SCHW) Ⓓ [2] **314732**

23b, 36. A. Sved, Radio Italiana SO, A. Simonetto (r1947) (PREI) Ⓓ **89096**

23b, 36. B. Weikl, Munich RO, H. Wallberg
(3/89) (ACAN) Ⓓ **43 266**

23b, 36. M. Schenk, Nuremberg SO, K. Seibel
(12/91) (COLO) Ⓓ **COL34 9004**

23b, 36, 57. F. Schorr, orch (r1921)
(PREI) Ⓓ **89052**

23b, 57. F. Schorr, Berlin St Op Orch, L. Blech (r1927) (PEAR) Ⓓ **GEMMCD9944**

23b, 57. J. von Manowarda, orch (r1922)
(PREI) Ⓓ **89069**

23b, 57. H. Hermann Nissen, Berlin SO, F. Zweig (r1929) (PREI) Ⓓ **89090**

23b, 57. L. Hofmann, Berlin St Op Orch, F.A. Schmidt (r1932) (PREI) Ⓓ **89102**

24. Lotte Lehmann, M. Bohnen, orch (r1916)
(6/92) (PREI) Ⓓ [3] **89302**

24. M. Reining, P. Schoeffler, Zurich Tonhalle Orch, H. Knappertsbusch (r1949)
(9/92) (PREI) Ⓓ **90083**

24. P. Schoeffler, M. Reining, Zurich Tonhalle Orch, H. Knappertsbusch (r1949)
(1/95) (PREI) Ⓓ **90190**

24, 52. F. Schorr, G. Ljungberg, LSO, L. Collingwood (r1931)
(PEAR) Ⓓ **GEMMCD9944**

24, 52. F. Schorr, LSO, L. Collingwood
(PREI) Ⓓ [2] **89214**

26. G. Thill, G. Martinelli, orch, E. Bigot (French: r1935) (1/92) (EMI) Ⓓ [4] **CMS7 64008-2(1)**

28b R. Bockelmann, Berlin St Op Orch, C. Schmalstich (r1931) (MSCM) Ⓓ [2] **MM30283**
(MSCM) ⊟ [2] **MM40105**

28b F. Schorr, orch (r1922) (PREI) Ⓓ **89052**

28b J. Herrmann, orch (r1943)
(PREI) Ⓓ **89076**

28b F. Schorr, LSO, A. Coates (r1930)
(9/91) (PEAR) Ⓓ **GEMMCD9398**

28b R. Bockelmann, Berlin St Op Orch, C. Schmalstich (r1930)
(1/92) (EMI) Ⓓ [4] **CMS7 64008-2(1)**

28b R. Bockelmann, Berlin St Op Orch, C. Schmalstich (r1930)
(7/92) (PEAR) Ⓓ [3] **GEMMCDS9926(2)**

28b A. Van Rooy, anon (r1902)
(3/93) (SYMP) Ⓓ **SYMCD1100**

28b, 46b F. Schorr, LSO, A. Coates (r1930)
(PEAR) Ⓓ **GEMMCD9944**

28b, 47. L. Hofmann, Lotte Lehmann, K. Thorborg, E. Laholm, W. Wernigk, H. Wiedemann, Vienna St Op Orch, F. Weingartner (pp1935) (11/95) (SCHW) Ⓓ [2] **314622**

33. BPO, R. Kempe (r1956)
(EMI) Ⓓ [2] **CHS5 65058-2**

33. Berlin Deutsche Op Orch, E. Jochum
(DG) Ⓓ [2] **439 687-2GX2**

33. NBC SO, A. Toscanini (r1951)
(11/92) (RCA) Ⓓ **GD60305**

33. Vienna St Op Orch, F. Weingartner (pp1934)
(7/94) (SCHW) Ⓓ [2] **314512**

33, 49, 50. Sofia Rad SO, V. Kazandjiev
(LASE) Ⓓ **15 612**
(LASE) ⊟ **79 612**

33, 49, 50. Seattle SO, G. Schwarz
(3/87) (DELO) Ⓓ **DE3040**

33, 49, 50. NYPO, J. Barbirolli (pp1938)
(3/95) (DUTT) Ⓓ **CDSJB1001**

33, 49, 50, 56. Canadian Brass, BPO, Bayreuth Fest Orch, E. de Waart (r1991: arr Frackenpohl)
(PHIL) Ⓓ **434 109-2PH**

36. F. Schorr, Berlin St Op Orch, L. Blech (r1929) (MSCM) Ⓓ [2] **MM30283**
(MSCM) ⊟ [2] **MM40105**

36. F. Schorr, Berlin St Op Orch, L. Blech (r1929) (PEAR) Ⓓ **GEMMCD9944**

36(pt) D. McIntyre, NZ SO, J. Matheson (r1975)
(KIWI) Ⓓ **CDSLD-82**

36. H. Hotter, Berlin Staatskapelle, R. Heger (r1942) (PREI) Ⓓ **90200**

36. J. Berglund, Stockholm Royal Orch, N. Grevillius (r1943) (PREI) Ⓓ [2] **90232**

36. H. Hermann Nissen, Berlin SO, F. Zweig (r1927) (PREI) Ⓓ **89090**

36. F. Schorr, Berlin St Op Orch, L. Blech (r1929) (1/92) (EMI) Ⓓ [4] **CMS7 64008-2(1)**

36. C. Whitehill, orch, P. Pitt (r1922)
(7/92) (PEAR) Ⓓ [3] **GEMMCDS9924(1)**

36. P. Schoeffler, National SO, K. Rankl (r1946)
(1/95) (PREI) Ⓓ **90190**

36, 37, 40. C. Doig, D. McIntyre, NZ SO, H. Wallberg (11/92) (ODE) Ⓓ **CDMANU1317**

36, 57. F. Schorr, Berlin St Op Orch, L. Blech
(PREI) Ⓓ [2] **89214**

37, 40. F. Schorr, R. Laubenthal, LSO, A. Coates (r1930) (PEAR) Ⓓ **GEMMCD9944**

39. P. Seiffert, Munich RO, J. Kout (r1992-3)
(RCA) Ⓓ **09026 61214-2**

40. L. Melchior, F. Schorr, LSO, R. Heger (r1931) (8/88) (DANA) Ⓓ [2] **DACOCD315/6**

43b, 44. F. Schorr, E. Rethberg, orch (r1930)
(PEAR) Ⓓ **GEMMCD9944**

43b, 44. F. Schorr, LSO, Rosario Bourdon
(PREI) Ⓓ [2] **89214**

43b, 44. E. Rethberg, F. Schorr, Victor SO, Rosario Bourdon (r1929)
(10/95) (ROMO) Ⓓ [2] **81014-2**

43b, 44, 45. E. Rethberg, F. Schorr, orch, Rosario Bourdon (r1929)
(4/94) (RCA) Ⓓ [6] **09026 61580-2(3)**

45. C. Studer, Bavarian St Orch, W. Sawallisch (r1993) (EMI) Ⓓ **CDC5 55350-2**

45. Lotte Lehmann, orch (r1921)
(6/92) (PREI) Ⓓ [3] **89302**

47. E. Schumann, G. Parr, L. Melchior, F. Schorr, B. Williams, LSO, J. Barbirolli (r1931)
(MSCM) Ⓓ [2] **MM30283**
(MSCM) ⊟ [2] **MM40105**

47. F. Schorr, E. Schumann, L. Melchior, B. Williams, G. Parr, LSO, J. Barbirolli (r1931)
(PEAR) Ⓓ **GEMMCD9944**

47. L. Hafgren, M. Olczewska, F. Soot, W. Henke, J. von Manowarda, orch (r1922)
(PREI) Ⓓ **89069**

47. F. Schorr, LSO, J. Barbirolli
(PREI) Ⓓ [2] **89214**

47. E. Schumann, G. Parr, L. Melchior, B. Williams, F. Schorr, LSO, J. Barbirolli (r1931)
(8/88) (DANA) Ⓓ [2] **DACOCD315/6**

47. E. Schumann, G. Parr, L. Melchior, B. Williams, F. Schorr, LSO, J. Barbirolli (r1931)
(1/92) (EMI) Ⓓ [4] **CMS7 64008-2(1)**

47. H. Roswaenge, P. Yoder, L. Kindermann, H. Reinmar, M. Kuttner, Berlin St Op Orch, S. Meyrowitz (r1932) (4/95) (PREI) Ⓓ [2] **89209**
48. Vienna St Op Chor, VPO, G. Solti (r1970s) (BELA) Ⓓ **450 117-2**
(BELA) ⊟ **450 117-4**
48-51. Vienna St Op Chor, VPO, G. Solti (r1975) (DECC) Ⓓ **421 865-2DA**
49. Leipzig Rad Chor, Dresden St Op Chor, Staatskapelle Dresden, H. von Karajan (r1970) (CFP) Ⓓ **CD-CFP4656**
(CFP) ⊟ **TC-CFP4656**
50, 51. Bayreuth Fest Chor, Bayreuth Fest Orch, W. Pitz (4/90) (DG) Ⓓ **429 169-2GR**
51. Timişoara Banatul Phil Chor, Timişoara Banatul PO, N. Boboc (ELCT) Ⓓ **ELCD109**
51. Vienna St Op Chor, Vienna St Op Orch, W. Furtwängler (pp1938) (6/94) (SCHW) Ⓓ **314502**
56. L. Melchior, Orch, H. Barlow (bp1950) (VAI) ▣ **VAI69107**
56. L. Melchior, orch (r1923) (PREI) Ⓓ **89032**
56. M. Elman, P. Kahn (r1910: arr Wilhelmj) (BIDD) Ⓓ **LAB035**
56. J. King, Vienna Op Orch, D. Bernet (r1967) (DECC) Ⓓ **433 065-2DWO**
(DECC) ⊟ **433 065-4DWO**
56. P. Casals, N. Mednikoff (r1926: arr Wilhelmj) (MSCM) Ⓓ **MM30428**
56. M. Lorenz, Berlin St Op Orch, C. Schmalstich (r1927) (PREI) Ⓓ **89053**
56. L. Melchior, LSO, J. Barbirolli (r1931) (BEUL) Ⓓ **2PD4**
56. G. Nelepp, Bolshoi Th Orch, N. Golovanov (r c1950: Russ) (PREI) Ⓓ **89081**
56. L. Melchior, Philadelphia, E. Ormandy (r1939) (NIMB) Ⓓ **NI7864**
56. R. Kollo, N. Bailey, Vienna St Op Chor, VPO, G. Solti (r1975) (DECC) Ⓓ **443 379-2DM**
56. L. Melchior, orch (r1923) (8/88) (DANA) Ⓓ [2] **DACOCD313/4**
56. L. Melchior, LSO, J. Barbirolli (r1931) (8/88) (DANA) Ⓓ [2] **DACOCD315/6**
56. L. Melchior, O. Helgers (r1926) (8/88) (DANA) Ⓓ [2] **DACOCD315/6**
56. L. Melchior, LSO, J. Barbirolli (r1931) (10/89) (EMI) Ⓓ **CDH7 69789-2**
56. F. Kreisler, H. Kreisler, C. Keith (r1923: arr Kreisler) (7/90) (BIDD) Ⓓ [2] **LAB009/10**
56(pt) H. Winkelmann, anon (r1904) (7/91) (SYMP) Ⓓ **SYMCD1081**
56. P. Casals, N. Mednikoff (r1926: arr vc/pf) (10/91) (BIDD) Ⓓ **LAB017**
56. T. Lemnitz, T. Ralf, R. Bockelmann, ROH Chor, LPO, T. Beecham (pp1936) (1/92) (EMI) Ⓓ [4] **CMS7 64008-2(1)**
56. H.E. Groh, orch (r1933) (3/92) (PEAR) Ⓓ **GEMMCD9419**
56. J. Hislop, orch, J. Barbirolli (r1929: Eng) (1/93) (PEAR) Ⓓ **GEMMCD9956**
56. B. Harrison, C. Salzedo, orch (r1915: arr vc/orch) (3/93) (CLAR) Ⓓ **CDGSE78-50-47**
56. P. Domingo, D. Fischer-Dieskau, P. Lagger, C. Ligendza, Berlin Deutsche Op Chor, Berlin Deutsche Op Orch, E. Jochum (5/93) (DG) Ⓓ **431 104-2GB**
56. C. Kullman, orch, W. Goehr (r1938) (11/93) (PREI) Ⓓ **89057**
56. S. Svanholm, RCA SO, F. Weissmann (r1947) (4/94) (RCA) Ⓓ [6] **09026 61580-2(6)**
56. R. Crooks, orch, Rosario Bourdon (r1928) (5/94) (CLAR) Ⓓ **CDGSE78-50-52**
56. P. Domingo, D. Fischer-Dieskau, P. Lagger, C. Ligendza, Berlin Deutsche Op Chor, Berlin Deutsche Op Orch, E. Jochum (6/94) (BELA) Ⓓ **450 121-2**
(6/94) (BELA) ⊟ **450 121-4**
56. R. Tauber, orch (r1927) (12/94) (MMOI) Ⓓ **CDMOIR425**
56. J. Johnston, ROHO, M. Mudie (r1948: Eng) (4/95) (TEST) Ⓓ **SBT1058**
57. A. Kipnis, Berlin St Op Orch, L. Blech (r1926) (10/91) (PEAR) Ⓓ **GEMMCD9451**

Parsifal– opera: 3 acts (1882—Bayreuth) (Lib. cpsr)

1. Prelude. ACT 1: 2. He! Ho! Waldhüter ihr; 3. Hei! Wie fliegen der Teufelsmähre; 4. Recht so! - Habt Dank!; 5. Wann alles ratlos steht; 6. Das ist ein and'res; 7. Titurel, der fromme Held; 8. Weh! Weh! Hoho! Auf!; 9. Unerhörtes Werk; 10. Den Vaterlosen gebar die Mutter; 11. So recht! So nach des Grales Gnade; 12a. Vom Bade kehrt der König heim; 12b. Transformation Scene; 13. Nun achte wohl....Zum letzten Liebesmahle; 14a. Mein Sohn Amfortas; 14b. Nein! Lasst ihn unenthüllt; 14c. Wehvolles Erbe; 15. 'Durch Mitleid wissend....'. ACT 2: 16. Prelude; 17. Die Zeit ist da; 18. Ach! Tiefe Nacht...Furchtbare Not!; 19. Hier war das Tosen!; 20. Komm; Komm; holder Knabe!; 21. Dies alles - hab' ich nun geträumt?; 22. Ich sah das Kind (Herzeleide); 23. Wehe! Wehe! Was tat ich?; 24. Amfortas! Die wunde!; 25. Grausamer! Fühlst du im Herzen; 26. Auf Ewigkeit. ACT 3: 27. Prelude; 28. Von dorther kam; 29. Heil dir, mein Gast!; 30. Zu ihm, des tiefe Klagen; 31. O Gnade! Höchstes Heil!; 32. Du wuchest mir die Füsse (Good Friday music); 33a. Transformation Scene; 33b. Geleiten wir im bergenden Schrein; 34. Ja, Wehe! Wehe! Weh' über mich!; 35. Nur eine Waffe taugt. 36. Good Friday music (concert version).

Parsifal R. Goldberg
Amfortas W. Schöne
Gurnemanz R. Lloyd
Kundry Y. Minton
Klingsor A. Haugland
Titurel H. Tschammer
Prague Phil Chor, Monte Carlo PO, A. Jordan, H.J. Syberberg (r1982) (ARTI) ▣ [2] **ARTOP1**

Parsifal P. Hofmann
Amfortas S. Estes
Gurnemanz H. Sotin
Kundry W. Meier
Klingsor F. Mazura
Titurel M. Salminen
Bayreuth Fest Chor, Bayreuth Fest Orch, James Levine (pp1985) (PHIL) Ⓓ [32] **434 420-2PM32(1)**

Parsifal S. Jerusalem
Amfortas B. Weikl
Gurnemanz H. Sotin
Kundry E. Randová
Klingsor L. Roar
Titurel M. Salminen
Knight I T. Krämer
Knight II H.K. Ecker
Squire I; Flower Maiden V M. Schiml
Squire II; Flower Maiden III; A Voice H. Schwarz
Squire III H. Pampuch
Squire IV M. Egel
Flower Maiden I N. Sharp
Flower Maiden II C. Richardson
Flower Maiden IV M.A. Häggander
Flower Maiden VI M. Neubauer
Bayreuth Fest Chor, Bayreuth Fest Orch, H. Stein, W. Wagner, B. Large (PHIL) ● [3] **070 410-1PHG3**

Parsifal W. Ellsworth
Amfortas P. Joll
Gurnemanz D. McIntyre
Kundry W. Meier
Klingsor N. Folwell
Titurel D. Gwynne
Knight I T. German
Knight II W. Mackie
Squire I Mary Davies
Squire II M. Morgan
Squire III J. Harris
Squire IV N. Ackerman
Flower Maiden I E. Ritchie
Flower Maiden II C. Teare
Flower Maiden III R. Cullis
Flower Maiden IV E. Collier
Flower Maiden V C. Bell
Flower Maiden VI; A Voice K. Harries
WNO Chor, WNO Orch, R. Goodall (r1984) (EMI) Ⓓ [4] **CMS5 65665-2**

Parsifal P. Hofmann
Amfortas J. Van Dam
Gurnemanz K. Moll
Kundry D. Vejzovic
Klingsor S. Nimsgern
Titurel V. von Halem
Knight I C.H. Ahnsjö
Knight II K. Rydl
Squire I M. Lambriks
Squire II A. Gjevang
Squire III H. Hopfner
Squire IV G. Tichy
Flower Maiden I B. Hendricks
Flower Maiden II J. Perry
Flower Maiden III D. Soffel
Flower Maiden IV I. Nielsen
Flower Maiden V A. Michael
Flower Maiden VI R. Yachmi-Caucig
A Voice H. Schwarz
Berlin Deutsche Op Chor, BPO, H. von Karajan (r1979/80) (10/84) (DG) Ⓓ [4] **413 347-2GH4**

Parsifal Jess Thomas
Amfortas G. London
Gurnemanz H. Hotter
Kundry I. Dalis
Klingsor G. Neidlinger
Titurel M. Talvela
Knight I N. Møller
Knight II G. Nienstedt
Squire I Š. Červená
Squire II U. Boese
Squire III G. Stolze
Squire IV G. Paskuda
Flower Maiden I G. Janowitz
Flower Maiden II A. Silja
Flower Maiden III E-M. Gardelli
Flower Maiden IV D. Siebert
Flower Maiden V R. Bartos
Flower Maiden VI Š. Červená
Bayreuth Fest Chor, Bayreuth Fest Orch, H. Knappertsbusch (pp1962) (6/86) (PHIL) Ⓓ [4] **416 390-2PH4**

Parsifal R. Kollo
Amfortas D. Fischer-Dieskau
Gurnemanz G. Frick
Kundry C. Ludwig
Klingsor Z. Kélémen
Titurel H. Hotter
Knight I R. Tear
Knight II H. Lackner
Squire I R. Hansmann
Squire II M. Schiml
Squire III H. Zednik
Squire IV E. Aichberger
Flower Maiden I L. Popp
Flower Miaden II A. Hargan
Flower Maiden III A. Howells
Flower Maiden IV K. Te Kanawa
Flower Maiden V G. Knight
Flower Maiden VI M. Lilowa
A Voice B. Finnilä
Vienna Boys' Ch, Vienna St Op Chor, VPO, G. Solti (r1971/2) (9/86) (DECC) Ⓓ [4] **417 143-2DH4**

Parsifal S. Jerusalem
Amfortas J. Van Dam
Gurnemanz M. Hölle
Kundry W. Meier
Klingsor G. von Kannen
Titurel J. Tomlinson
Knight I K. Schreibmayer
Knight II C. Hauptmann
Squire I M. Rørholm
Squire II A. Küttenbaum
Squire III H. Pampuch
Squire IV P. Maus
Flower Maiden I E. Wiens
Flower Maiden II C. Hauman
Flower Maiden III D. Bechly
Flower Maiden IV H. Leidland
Flower Maiden V P. Coburn
Flower Maiden VI S. Burgess
Voice W. Meier
Berlin St Op Chor, BPO, D. Barenboim (10/91) (TELD) Ⓓ [4] **9031-74448-2**

Parsifal R. Goldberg
Amfortas W. Schöne
Gurnemanz R. Lloyd
Kundry Y. Minton
Klingsor A. Haugland
Titurel H. Tschammer
Knight I P. Frey
Knight II G. Cachemaille
Squire I; Flower Maiden IV T. Herz
Squire II; Flower Maiden V H. Schaer
Squire III C. Bladin
Squire IV M. Roider
Flower Maiden I B-M. Aruhn
Flower Maiden II E. Saurova
Flower Maiden III G. Oertel
Flower Maiden VI J. Chamonin
Prague Phil Chor, Monte Carlo Op Orch, A. Jordan (9/92) (ERAT) Ⓓ [4] **2292-45662-2**

Parsifal J. King
Amfortas T. Stewart
Gurnemanz F. Crass
Kundry G. Jones
Klingsor D. McIntyre
Titurel K. Ridderbusch
Knight I H. Esser
Knight II B. Rundgren
Squire I E. Schwarzenberg
Squire II; Flower Maiden VI S. Wagner
Squire III D. Slembeck
Squire IV H. Zednik
Flower Maiden I H. Bode

Flower Maiden II M. Kyriaki
Flower Maiden III I. Paustian
Flower Maiden IV D. Siebert
Flower Maiden V W. Fine
Bayreuth Fest Chor, Bayreuth Fest Orch, P. Boulez (pp1970)
(9/92) (DG) Ⓓ [3] **435 718-2GX3**
Parsifal P. Hofmann
Amfortas S. Estes
Gurnemanz H. Sotin
Kundry W. Meier
Klingsor F. Mazura
Titurel M. Salminen
Knight I M. Pabst
Knight II M. Hölle
Squire I; A Voice R. Engert-Ely
Squire II S. Fues
Squire III H. Pampuch
Squire IV P. Maus
Flower Maiden I D. Sasson
Flower Maiden II S. Roberts
Flower Maiden III M. Schmitt
Flower Maiden IV A. Browner
Flower Maiden V H. Leidland
Flower Maiden VI M. Neubauer
Bayreuth Fest Chor, Bayreuth Fest Orch, James Levine (pp1985)
(10/92) (PHIL) Ⓓ [4] **434 616-2PH4**
Parsifal W. Windgassen
Amfortas G. London
Gurnemanz L. Weber
Kundry M. Mödl
Klingsor H. Uhde
Titurel A. Van Mill
Knight I W. Fritz
Knight II W. Faulhaber
Squire I; Flower Maiden III H. Ludwig
Squire II; Flower Maiden VI E. Wild
Squire III G. Baldauf
Squire IV G. Stolze
Flower Maiden I H. Schünemann
Flower Maiden II E. Zimmermann
Flower Maiden IV P. Brivkalne
Flower Maiden V M. Lacorn
A Voice R. Siewert
Bayreuth Fest Chor, Bayreuth Fest Orch, H. Knappertsbusch (pp1951)
(8/93) (TELD) Ⓓ [4] **9031-76047-2**
Parsifal R. Kollo
Amfortas T. Adam
Gurnemanz U. Cold
Kundry G. Schröter
Klingsor R. Bunger
Titurel F. Teschler
Knight I; Squire III H. Gebhardt
Knight II H.C. Polster
Squire I; Flower Maiden I E. Breul
Squire II; Flower Maiden III G. Pohl
Squire IV H-J. Wachsmuth
Flower Maiden II R. Werner
Flower Maiden IV H. Ambros
Flower Maiden V H. Terner
Flower Maiden VI I. Ludwig-Jahns
A Voice I. Springer
Leipzig Rad Chor, Berlin Rad Chor, Leipzig St Thomas Church Ch, Leipzig RSO, H. Kegel (pp1975)
(1/94) (SCHW) Ⓓ [4] **313482**
Parsifal S. Jerusalem
Amfortas B. Weikl
Gurnemanz K. Moll
Kundry W. Meier
Klingsor F. Mazura
Titurel J-H. Rootering
Knight 1 P. Groves
Knight II J. Wells
Squire I; Flower Maiden II H.G. Murphy
Squire II; Flower Maiden III J. Bunnell
Squire III J.H. Murray
Squire IV B. Fitch
Flower Maiden II K. Erickson
Flower Maiden IV K. Uecker
Flower Maiden V G. Geyer
Flower Maiden VI W. White
A Voice G. Bean
NY Met Op Chor, NY Met Op Orch, James Levine (r1992)
(11/94) (DG) ◐ [2] **072 435-1GH2**
(11/94) (DG) ▭▭ [2] **072 435-3GH2**
Parsifal P. Domingo
Amfortas J. Morris
Gurnemanz K. Moll
Kundry J. Norman
Klingsor E. Wlaschiha
Titurel J-H. Rootering
Knight I A. Glassman
Knight II J. Robbins
Squire I; Flower Maiden I H.G. Murphy
Squire II; Flower Maiden III J. Bunnell
Squire III P. Groves
Squire IV A. Laciura
Flower Maiden II K. Erickson
Flower Maiden IV K. Uecker
Flower Maiden V J. Guyer
Flower Maiden VI W. White
A Voice H. Katagiri
NY Met Op Chor, NY Met Op Orch, James Levine (r1991/2)
(11/94) (DG) Ⓓ [4] **437 501-2GH4**

Act 3 (abridged) G. Pistor, C. Bronsgeest, L. Hofmann, Berlin St Op Chor, Berlin St Op Orch, K. Muck (r1928)
(4/90) (OPAL) Ⓓ [2] **OPALCDS9843**
Excs H. Hotter, Vienna St Op Chor, Vienna St Op Orch, H. Knappertsbusch (pp1942)
(SCHW) Ⓓ [2] **314722**
Excs M. Lorenz, H. Braun, Vienna St Op Chor, Vienna St Op Orch, H. Knappertsbusch (pp1942)
(1/95) (SCHW) Ⓓ [2] **314562**
Excs M. Lorenz, P. Schoeffler, S. Roth, H. Braun, Adolf Vogel, Vienna St Op Chor, Vienna St Op Orch, L. Reichwein (pp1942)
(1/95) (SCHW) Ⓓ [2] **314562**
Excs H. Alsen, N. Zec, F. Destal, E. Nikolaidi, Vienna St Op Chor, Vienna St Op Orch, H. Knappertsbusch (pp1937)
(6/95) (SCHW) Ⓓ [2] **314632**
Excs G. Graarud, J. von Manowarda, E. Schipper, G. Rünger, H. Wiedemann, Vienna St Op Chor, Vienna St Op Orch, C. Krauss (pp1933) (8/95) (SCHW) Ⓓ [2] **314642**
Symphonic synthesis from Act 3. Philadelphia, L. Stokowski (arr Stokowski: r1934)
(2/91) (PEAR) Ⓓ **GEMMCD9448**
1. Concertgebouw, B. Haitink
(PHIL) Ⓓ **420 886-2PSL**
1. Budapest SO, G. Lehel (LASE) Ⓓ **15 521**
(LASE) ⊟ **79 521**
1. Monte Carlo PO, A. Jordan (r1982)
(ERAT) Ⓓ **4509-92866-2**
1. VPO, H. Knappertsbusch (r1950)
(DECC) Ⓓ **440 062-2DM**
1. VPO, G. Solti (r1972)
(DECC) Ⓓ [2] **440 606-2DF2**
1. BPO, W. Furtwängler (r1938)
(2/89) (ACAN) Ⓓ **43 121**
1. Berlin St Op Orch, K. Muck (r1927)
(4/90) (OPAL) Ⓓ [2] **OPALCDS9843**
1. Philh, O. Klemperer (r1961)
(11/90) (EMI) Ⓓ **CDM7 63618-2**
1. Philh, Y. Simonov
(10/91) (COLL) Ⓓ **Coll1207-2**
1. NYPSO, F. Reiner (r1938)
(4/92) (PEAR) Ⓓ [3] **GEMMCDS9922**
1. NQHO, B. Wordsworth (r1995)
(6/95) (EYE) Ⓓ [2] **EOS5001**
1. LCP, R. Norrington (r1994)
(11/95) (EMI) Ⓓ **CDC5 55479-2**
1, 12b, 27, 36. LSO, A. Boult
(EMI) Ⓓ [2] **CZS7 62539-2**
1, 13, 16, 19, 20, 24, 26(pt), 27, 32(pt), 33a, 33b, 35(pt) H. Grahl, H. Alsen, A. Konetzni, H. Wiedemann, Vienna St Op Chor, Vienna St Op Orch, H. Knappertsbusch (pp1939)
(8/94) (SCHW) Ⓓ [2] **314522**
1, 27, 28, 29, 32, 33a, 33b, 34, 35. E. Larcen, C. Hartmann, H. Reinmar, L. Weber, Berlin Deutsche Op Chor, Berlin Deutsche Op Orch, H. Knappertsbusch (pp1942)
(ACAN) Ⓓ [2] **44 2100-2**
1, 27, 36. Seattle SO, G. Schwarz
(DELO) Ⓓ **DE3053**
1, 28-35. G. Pistor, C. Bronsgeest, L. Hofmann, Berlin St Op Chor, Berlin St Op Orch, K. Muck (r1928) (OPAL) ⊙ [2] **OPAL837/8**
1, 36. Philh, F. d'Avalos (ASV) Ⓓ **CDDCA611**
1, 36. Pittsburgh SO, W. Steinberg (r1956)
(EMI) Ⓓ **CDM5 65208-2**
1, 36. BRSO, E. Jochum (r1950s)
(DG) Ⓓ [2] **439 687-2GX2**
1, 36. BRSO, E. Jochum (r1957)
(DG) Ⓓ **439 445-2GCL**
(DG) ⊟ **439 445-4GCL**
1, 36. Columbia SO, B. Walter (r1959)
(SONY) Ⓓ [2] **SM2K64456**
1, 36. Columbia SO, B. Walter (r1959)
(SONY) Ⓓ [10] **SX10K66246**
1, 36. Philadelphia, L. Stokowski (r1936)
(2/91) (PEAR) Ⓓ **GEMMCD9448**
1, 36. NBC SO, A. Toscanini (r1949)
(11/92) (RCA) Ⓓ **GD60305**
1, 36. BPO, W. Furtwängler (r1938)
(4/94) (EMI) Ⓓ [2] **CHS7 64935-2**
1, 36. BPO, W. Furtwängler (r1938)
(7/94) (BIDD) Ⓓ [2] **WHL006/7**
4, 12a, 12b, 13, 14a-c, 19-22, 31, 32, 33a, 33b P. Domingo, J. Morris, K. Moll, J. Norman, J-H. Rootering, A. Glassman, J. Robbins, H. G. Murphy, J. Bunnell, P. Groves, A. Laciura, J. Guyer, W. White, NY Met Op Chor, NY Met Op Orch, James Levine (r1991/2)
(DG) Ⓓ **445 868-2GH**
7, 32. I. Andrésen, Berlin St Op Orch, L. Blech (r1927) (10/90) (PREI) Ⓓ **89028**
12a, 12b, 13(pt), 15, 19. Bayreuth Fest Chor, Bayreuth Fest Orch, K. Muck (r1927)
(OPAL) ⊙ [2] **OPAL837/8**
12b, 15, 19. Bayreuth Fest Chor, Bayreuth Fest Orch, K. Muck (r1927)
(4/90) (OPAL) Ⓓ [2] **OPALCDS9843**
13. Vienna St Op Chor, VPO, G. Solti (r1971/2)
(DECC) Ⓓ **421 865-2DA**
13. J. Greindl, Bayreuth Fest Chor, Bayreuth Fest Orch, W. Pitz
(4/90) (DG) Ⓓ **429 169-2GR**
14a C. Whitehill, orch, T. Levy (r1914)
(4/94) (RCA) Ⓓ [6] **09026 61580-2(2)**
14b D. Fischer-Dieskau, C. Ludwig, Santa Cecilia Academy Orch, Vienna St Op Chor, G. Solti (r1971/2) (DECC) Ⓓ **440 409-2DM**
14b, 14c H. Hermann Nissen, Berlin SO, F. Zweig (r1928) (PREI) Ⓓ **89090**
14b, 34. D. Fischer-Dieskau, Bavarian Rad Chor, BRSO, R. Kubelík (r1977)
(EMI) Ⓓ [2] **CMS5 65621-2**
20. RPS Orch, B. Walter (r1925: arr orch)
(VAI) Ⓓ **VAIA1059**
21, 22. K. Flagstad, L. Melchior, RCA Victor SO, E. MacArthur (r1940)
(10/90) (RCA) Ⓓ **GD87915**
22. F. Leider, LSO, J. Barbirolli (r1931)
(MSCM) Ⓓ [2] **MM30285**
(MSCM) ⊟ [2] **MM40107**
22. K. Flagstad, VPO, H. Knappertsbusch (r1956) (LOND) Ⓓ [5] **440 490-2LM5(1)**
22. K. Flagstad, VPO, H. Knappertsbusch (r1956) (LOND) Ⓓ **440 495-2LM**
22. K. Flagstad, RCA Victor SO, E. McArthur (r1941) (SIMA) Ⓓ [3] **PSC1821(2)**
22. F. Leider, LSO, J. Barbirolli (r1931)
(11/89) (PEAR) Ⓓ **GEMMCD9331**
22. F. Leider, LSO, J. Barbirolli (r1931)
(2/90) (PREI) Ⓓ **89004**
22. F. Leider, orch (r1925)
(5/91) (PREI) Ⓓ [3] **89301**
22. F. Leider, LSO, J. Barbirolli (r1931)
(1/92) (EMI) Ⓓ [4] **CMS7 64008-2(2)**
22. F. Leider, LSO, J. Barbirolli (r1931)
(2/92) (MMOI) Ⓓ **CDMOIR408**
22. K. Thorborg, RCA SO, K. Riedel (r1940)
(4/95) (PREI) Ⓓ **89084**
24. L. Melchior, Berlin St Op Orch, P. Breisach (r1925) (PREI) Ⓓ **89068**
24. L. Melchior, Philadelphia, E. Ormandy (r1938) (PEAR) Ⓓ **GEMMCD9049**
24. L. Melchior, orch, P. Breisach (r1925)
(8/88) (DANA) Ⓓ [2] **DACOCD313/4**
24, 25. W. Lewis, RPO, G. Ötvös
(RPO) Ⓓ **CDRPO7019**
24, 35. L. Melchior, Philadelphia, E. Ormandy (r1938) (MSCM) Ⓓ [2] **MM30285**
(MSCM) ⊟ [2] **MM40107**
24(pt), 35. P. Franz, orch (r1914: Fr)
(PREI) Ⓓ **89099**
25(pt) K. Thorborg, Vienna St Op Orch, F. Weingartner (pp1936)
(7/94) (SCHW) Ⓓ [2] **314512**
31(pt), 32(pt) C. Doig, D. McIntyre, NZ SO, H. Wallberg (11/92) (ODE) Ⓓ **CDMANU1317**
32. A. Kipnis, F. Wolff, Bayreuth Fest Chor, Bayreuth Fest Orch, S. Wagner (r1927)
(MSCM) Ⓓ [2] **MM30285**
(MSCM) ⊟ [2] **MM40107**
32. Basle SO, A. Jordan (r1983)
(ERAT) Ⓓ **4509-92866-2**
32. F. Wolff, A. Kipnis, Bayreuth Fest Orch, S. Wagner (r1927)
(1/92) (EMI) Ⓓ [4] **CMS7 64008-2(2)**
34(pt) C. Whitehill, orch (r1914)
(IRCC) Ⓓ **IRCC-CD810**
35. L. Melchior, Berlin St Op Orch, P. Breisach (r1924) (PREI) Ⓓ **89068**
35. L. Melchior, orch, P. Breisach (r1924)
(8/88) (DANA) Ⓓ [2] **DACOCD313/4**

36. LSO, A. Dorati (r1960)
(MERC) Ⓓ **434 342-2MM**

Rienzi– opera: 5 acts (1842—Dresden) (Libr. cpsr)

ACT 1: 1. Overture; 2. Erstehe, hohe Roma, neu; 3. Ihr Römer, hort die Kunde; 4. Gerechter Gott...In seiner Blüthe; 5. Allmächt'ger Vater (Rienzi's prayer).

Rienzi R. Kollo
Irene S. Wennberg
Steffano Colonna N. Hillebrand
Adriano Colonna J. Martin
Paolo Orsini T. Adam
Raimondo S. Vogel
Baroncelli P. Schreier
Cecco del Vecchio G. Leib
Messenger of Peace I. Springer

Leipzig Rad Chor, Dresden St Op Chor, Staatskapelle Dresden, H. Hollreiser
(2/92) (EMI) Ⓓ [3] **CMS7 63980-2**

Excs M. Lorenz, H. Scheppan, R. von der Linde, M. Klose, J. Prohaska, G. Rödin, W. Hiller, Berlin St Op Chor, Berlin St Op Orch, J. Schüler (r1941) (PREI) Ⓓ **90223**

Excs F. Völker, R. Anday, H. Gallos, K. Ettl, Vienna St Op Chor, Vienna St Op Orch, J. Krips (pp1933) (9/95) (SCHW) Ⓓ [2] **314662**

1. Mexico St SO, E. Bátiz (MCI) Ⓓ **OQ0009**

1. Cleveland Orch, G. Szell
(CBS) Ⓓ [2] **CD46466**

1. LPO, K. Tennstedt (EMI) ◖ **LDB9 91234-1**
(EMI) ▭ **MVD9 91234-3**

1. VPO, H. Knappertsbusch (r1940)
(PREI) Ⓓ **90116**

1. London Fest Orch, J. Armstrong
(ROSE) Ⓓ **3212**

1. Philh, Y. Simonov (r1991)
(COLL) Ⓓ **Coll1294-2**

1. NY Met Op Orch, James Levine (r1991)
(DG) OO **435 874-5GH**

1. Canadian Brass, BPO, Bayreuth Fest Orch, E. de Waart (r1991; arr Frackenpohl)
(PHIL) Ⓓ **434 109-2PH**

1. NYPO, L. Bernstein (r1968)
(SONY) Ⓓ **SMK47643**

1. RPO, V. Handley (r1993) (TRIN) Ⓓ **TRP008**
(TRIN) ⊟ **MCTRP008**

1. LPO, H. Knappertsbusch (r1947)
(PREI) Ⓓ **90189**

1. VPO, K. Böhm (DG) Ⓓ [2] **439 687-2GX2**

1. VPO, H. Knappertsbusch (r1950)
(DECC) Ⓓ **440 062-2DM**

1. Bamberg SO, K. A. Rickenbacher (r1993)
(ORFE) Ⓓ **C312941A**

1. Cincinnati SO, J. López-Cobos (r1994)
(TELA) Ⓓ **CD80379**

1. VPO, G. Solti (r1961)
(DECC) Ⓓ [2] **440 606-2DF2**

1. BPO, K. Tennstedt (r1982/3)
(EMI) Ⓓ [2] **CZS5 68616-2**

1. Philh, F. d'Avalos
(10/90) (ASV) Ⓓ **CDDCA704**

1. Philh, O. Klemperer
(11/90) (EMI) Ⓓ **CDM7 63617-2**

1. Oslo PO, M. Jansons
(12/92) (EMI) Ⓓ **CDC7 54583-2**

1. NY Met Op Orch, James Levine (r1991)
(10/93) (DG) Ⓓ **435 874-2GH**

1. Minnesota Orch, N. Marriner (r1983)
(2/94) (TELA) Ⓓ **CD82005**

1. NYPO, J. Barbirolli (pp1938)
(3/95) (DUTT) Ⓓ **CDSJB1001**

1. NQHO, B. Wordsworth (r1995)
(6/95) (EYE) Ⓓ [2] **EOS5001**

1. LCP, R. Norrington (r1994)
(11/95) (EMI) Ⓓ **CDC5 55479-2**

2. F. Völker, Berlin St Op Orch, A. Melichar (r1933) (MSCM) Ⓓ [2] **MM30283**
(MSCM) ⊟ [2] **MM40105**

2. F. Völker, Berlin St Op Orch, A. Melichar (r1933) (2/90) (PREI) Ⓓ **89005**

2. F. Völker, Vienna St Op Chor, Vienna St Op Orch, J. Krips (pp1933)
(6/94) (SCHW) Ⓓ **314502**

2, 5. M. Lorenz, H. Scheppan, M. Klose, G. Rödin, W. Hiller, Berlin St Op Orch, J. Schüler (r1941) (PREI) Ⓓ **90213**

4. G. Janowitz, Berlin Deutsche Op Orch, F. Leitner (r1967) (DG) Ⓓ [2] **447 352-2GDB2**

4. M. Klose, Berlin RSO, A. Rother (r1942)
(PREI) Ⓓ **90223**

4. E. Schumann-Heink, orch (r1908)
(2/91) (NIMB) Ⓓ **NI7811**
(2/91) (NIMB) ⊟ **NC7811**

4. F. Leider, orch (r1922)
(5/91) (PREI) Ⓓ [3] **89301**

5. M. Lorenz, Berlin St Op Orch, C. Schmalstich (r1930) (MMOI) Ⓓ **CDMOIR405**
(MMOI) ⊟ **CMOIR405**

5. F. Völker, Berlin St Op Orch, H. Weigert (r1930) (MSCM) Ⓓ [2] **MM30283**
(MSCM) ⊟ [2] **MM40105**

5. L. Melchior, orch (r1923) (PREI) Ⓓ **89032**

5. M. Lorenz, Berlin St Op Orch, C. Schmalstich (r1930) (PREI) Ⓓ **89053**

5. W. Lewis, RPO, G. Ötvös
(RPO) Ⓓ **CDRPO7019**

5. L. Melchior, LSO, J. Barbirolli (r1930)
(PREI) Ⓓ **89086**

5. P. Seiffert, Munich RO, J. Kout (r1992-3)
(RCA) Ⓓ **09026 61214-2**

5. L. Melchior, orch (r1923)
(8/88) (DANA) Ⓓ [2] **DACOCD313/4**

5. L. Melchior, LSO, J. Barbirolli (r1930)
(8/88) (DANA) Ⓓ [2] **DACOCD315/6**

5. L. Melchior, LSO, J. Barbirolli (r1930)
(10/89) (EMI) Ⓓ **CDH7 69789-2**

5. F. Völker, Berlin St Op Orch, H. Weigert (r1930) (2/90) (PREI) Ⓓ **89005**

5. P. Domingo, National PO, E. Kohn
(11/90) (EMI) Ⓓ **CDC7 54053-2**

5. F. Völker, Berlin Staatskapelle, A. Melichar (r1930) (10/93) (NIMB) Ⓓ **NI7848**

5. F. Völker, Berlin Staatskapelle, G. Steeger (r1941) (8/94) (PREI) Ⓓ **89070**

Der **Ring des Nibelungen– explanation and analysis of Leitmotifs**

D. Cooke, Sols, VPO, G. Solti (r1958-67)
(5/95) (DECC) Ⓓ [2] **443 581-2DCS2**

Der **Ring des Nibelungen: Part 1, '(Das) Rheingold'– opera: 4 scenes (1869—Munich) (Lib. cpsr)**

EXCERPTS. SCENE 1: 1. Prelude; 2. Weia! Waga! Woge, du Welle; 3. He he! Ihr Nicker!; 4. Garstig glatter glitschriger Glimmer!; 5. Lugt, Schwestern; 6a. Der Welt Erbe; 6b. Spottet nur zu!; 7. orchestral interlude. SCENE 2: 8. Wotan! Gemahl! erwache!; 9. So schirme sie jetzt; 10. Sanft schloss Schlaf dein Aug'; 11. Du da, folge uns; 12. Endlich Loge!; 13. Immer ist Undank Loges Lohn; 14. Hör Wotan, der Harrenden Wort!; 15a. Schwester! Brüder! Rettet! Helft!; 15b. Uber stock und Stein; 16. Jetzt fand ich's; 17. Wotan, Gemahl, unsel'ger Mann!; 18a. Auf Loge hinab mit mir!; 18b. Nach! Nibelheim fahren wir nieder; 19. orchestral interlude (descent into Nibelheim). SCENE 3: 20. Hehe! hehe!; 21. Nibelheim hier; 22. Mit eurem Gefrage; 23. Was wollt ihr hier?; 24. Die in linder Lüfte Wehn da oben ihr lebt; 25. Riesenwurm winde sich ringeland!. SCENE 4: 26. Da, Vetter, sitze du fest!; 27. Wohlan, die Nibelheim rief ich mir nah; 28. Bin ich nun frei? (Alberich's curse); 29. Lauschtest du seinem Liebesgruss?; 30. Halt! Nicht sie berührt; 31. Nich so leicht und locker gefügt; 32. Freia, die Schöne; 33. Weiche, Wotan, weiche! (Erda's warning); 34. Hört, ihr Riesen!; 35. Halt, du Gieriger!; 36. Was gelicht, Wotan; 37. Schwüles Gedünst schwebt in der Luft; 38. Zur Burg führt die Brücke; 39. Abendlich strahlt; 40. Ihrem Ende; 41. Rheingold! Rheingold!; 42. Entrance of the Gods into Valhalla (orchestral version).

Wotan J. Morris
Fricka C. Ludwig
Loge S. Jerusalem
Mime H. Zednik
Alberich E. Wlaschiha
Freia M.A. Häggander
Froh M. Baker
Donner A. Held
Erda B. Svendén
Fasolt J-H. Rootering
Fafner M. Salminen
Woglinde K. Erickson
Wellgunde D. Kesling
Flosshilde M. Parsons

NY Met Op Orch, James Levine, O. Schenk, B. Large
(5/92) (DG) ▭ [7] **072 422-3GH7**

Wotan T. Adam
Fricka Y. Minton
Loge P. Schreier
Mime C. Vogel
Alberich S. Nimsgern
Freia M. Napier
Froh E. Büchner
Donner K-H. Stryczek
Erda O. Wenkel
Fasolt R. Bracht
Fafner M. Salminen
Woglinde L. Popp
Wellgunde U. Priew
Flosshilde H. Schwarz

Staatskapelle Dresden, M. Janowski
(EURO) Ⓓ [14] **GD69003**

Wotan D. McIntyre
Fricka H. Schwarz
Loge H. Zednik
Mime H. Pampuch
Alberich H. Becht
Freia C. Reppel
Froh S. Jerusalem
Donner M. Egel
Erda O. Wenkel

Bayreuth Fest Orch, P. Boulez (pp1980)
(PHIL) Ⓓ [32] **434 420-2PM32(2)**

Wotan J. Morris
Fricka C. Ludwig
Loge S. Jerusalem
Mime H. Zednik
Alberich E. Wlaschiha
Freia N. Gustafson
Froh M. Baker
Donner S. Lorenz
Erda B. Svendén
Fasolt K. Moll
Fafner J-H. Rootering
Woglinde H-K. Hong
Wellgunde D. Kesling
Flosshilde M. Parsons

NY Met Op Orch, James Levine (r1988)
(DG) Ⓓ [2] **445 295-2GH2**

Wotan G. London
Fricka K. Flagstad
Loge S. Svanholm
Mime P. Kuen
Alberich G. Neidlinger
Freia C. Watson
Froh W. Kmentt
Donner E. Waechter
Erda J. Madeira
Fasolt W. Kreppel
Fafner K. Böhme
Woglinde O. Balsborg
Wellgunde H. Plümacher
Flosshilde I. Malaniuk

VPO, G. Solti (r1958)
(10/84) (DECC) Ⓓ [3] **414 101-2DH3**

Wotan T. Adam
Fricka Y. Minton
Loge P. Schreier
Mime C. Vogel
Alberich S. Nimsgern
Freia M. Napier
Froh E. Büchner
Donner K-H. Stryczek
Erda O. Wenkel
Fasolt R. Bracht
Fafner M. Salminen
Woglinde L. Popp
Wellgunde U. Priew
Flosshilde H. Schwarz

Staatskapelle Dresden, M. Janowski
(10/84) (EURM) Ⓓ [2] **GD69004**

Wotan T. Adam
Fricka A. Burmeister
Loge W. Windgassen
Mime E. Wohlfahrt
Alberich G. Neidlinger
Freia A. Silja
Froh H. Esser
Donner G. Nienstedt
Erda V. Soukupová
Fasolt M. Talvela
Fafner K. Böhme
Woglinde D. Siebert
Wellgunde H. Dernesch
Flosshilde R. Hesse

Bayreuth Fest Orch, K. Böhm (pp1967)
(7/85) (PHIL) Ⓓ [2] **412 475-2PH2**

Wotan D. Fischer-Dieskau
Fricka J. Veasey
Loge G. Stolze
Mime E. Wohlfahrt
Alberich Z. Kélémen
Freia S. Mangelsdorff
Froh D. Grobe
Donner R. Kerns
Erda O. Dominguez
Fasolt M. Talvela
Fafner K. Ridderbusch
Woglinde H. Donath
Wellgunde E. Moser
Flosshilde A. Reynolds

BPO, H. von Karajan (r1967)
(7/85) (DG) Ⓓ [3] **415 141-2GH3**

Wotan H. Hotter
Fricka I. Malaniuk
Loge E. Witte
Mime P. Kuen
Alberich G. Neidlinger
Freia B. Falcon
Froh G. Stolze
Donner H. Uhde
Erda M. von Ilosvay
Fasolt L. Weber
Fafner J. Greindl
Woglinde E. Zimmermann
Wellgunde H. Plümacher
Flosshilde G. Litz
Bayreuth Fest Orch, C. Krauss (pp1953)
(6/88) (FOYE) ① [15] **15-CF2011**
Wotan H. Hotter
Fricka I. Malaniuk
Loge E. Witte
Mime P. Kuen
Alberich G. Neidlinger
Freia B. Falcon
Froh G. Stolze
Donner H. Uhde
Erda M. von Ilosvay
Fasolt L. Weber
Fafner J. Greindl
Woglinde E. Zimmermann
Wellgunde H. Plümacher
Flosshilde G. Litz
Bayreuth Fest Orch, C. Krauss (pp1953)
(6/88) (FOYE) ① [3] **3-CF2007**
Wotan H. Hotter
Donner H. Uhde
Froh G. Stolze
Loge E. Witte
Alberich G. Neidlinger
Mime P. Kuen
Fasolt L. Weber
Fafner J. Greindl
Fricka I. Malaniuk
Freia B. Falcon
Erda M. von Ilosvay
Woglinde E. Zimmermann
Wellgunde H. Plümacher
Flosshilde G. Litz
Bayreuth Fest Orch, C. Krauss (pp1953)
(6/88) (LAUD) ① [3] **LCD3 4002**
Wotan G. London
Fricka K. Flagstad
Loge S. Svanholm
Mime P. Kuen
Alberich G. Neidlinger
Freia C. Watson
Froh W. Kmentt
Donner E. Waechter
Erda J. Madeira
Fasolt W. Kreppel
Fafner K. Böhme
Woglinde O. Balsborg
Wellgunde H. Plümacher
Flosshilde I. Malaniuk
VPO, G. Solti (r1958)
(3/89) (DECC) ① [15] **414 100-2DM15**
Wotan J. Morris
Fricka M. Lipovšek
Loge H. Zednik
Mime P. Haage
Alberich T. Adam
Freia E. Johansson
Froh P. Seiffert
Donner A. Schmidt
Erda J. Rappé
Fasolt H. Tschammer
Fafner K. Rydl
Woglinde J. Kaufman
Wellgunde S. Herman
Flosshilde S. Quittmeyer
BRSO, B. Haitink (r1988)
(12/89) (EMI) ① [2] **CDS7 49853-2**
Wotan F. Frantz
Fricka I. Malaniuk
Loge W. Windgassen
Mime J. Patzak
Alberich G. Neidlinger
Freia E. Grümmer
Froh L. Fehenberger
Donner A. Poell
Erda R. Siewert
Fasolt J. Greindl
Fafner G. Frick
Woglinde S. Jurinac
Wellgunde M. Gabory
Flosshilde H. Rössl-Majdan
Rome RAI Orch, W. Furtwängler (bp1953)
(2/91) (EMI) ① [13] **CZS7 67123-2**

Wotan D. Fischer-Dieskau
Fricka J. Veasey
Loge G. Stolze
Mime E. Wohlfahrt
Alberich Z. Kélémen
Freia S. Mangelsdorff
Froh D. Grobe
Donner R. Kerns
Erda O. Dominguez
Fasolt M. Talvela
Fafner K. Ridderbusch
Woglinde H. Donath
Wellgunde E. Moser
Flosshilde A. Reynolds
BPO, H. von Karajan
(4/92) (DG) ① [15] **435 211-2GX15**
Wotan N. Bailey
Fricka K. Pring
Loge E. Belcourt
Mime G. Dempsey
Alberich D. Hammond-Stroud
Freia L. McDonall
Froh R. Ferguson
Donner N. Welsby
Erda A. Collins
Fasolt R. Lloyd
Fafner C. Grant
Woglinde V. Masterson
Wellgunde S. Squires
Flosshilde H. Attfield
ENO Orch, R. Goodall (Eng: pp1975)
(4/92) (EMI) ① [3] **CMS7 64110-2**
Wotan J. Morris
Fricka C. Ludwig
Loge S. Jerusalem
Mime H. Zednik
Alberich E. Wlaschiha
Freia M.A. Häggander
Froh M. Baker
Donner A. Held
Erda B. Svendén
Fasolt J-H. Rootering
Fafner M. Salminen
Woglinde K. Erickson
Wellgunde D. Kesling
Flosshilde M. Parsons
NY Met Op Orch, James Levine, O. Schenk, B. Large
(5/92) (DG) ◖ [2] **072 418-1GH2**
(5/92) (DG) ▭ **072 418-3GH**
Wotan D. McIntyre
Fricka H. Schwarz
Loge H. Zednik
Mime H. Pampuch
Alberich H. Becht
Freia C. Reppel
Froh S. Jerusalem
Donner M. Egel
Erda O. Wenkel
Fasolt M. Salminen
Fafner F. Hübner
Woglinde N. Sharp
Wellgunde I. Gramatzki
Flosshilde M. Schiml
Bayreuth Fest Orch, P. Boulez, P. Chéreau
(5/92) (PHIL) ◖ [2] **070 401-1PHE2**
(5/92) (PHIL) ▭ **070 401-3PHE**
Wotan R. Hale
Fricka M. Lipovšek
Loge R. Tear
Mime H. Pampuch
Alberich E. Wlaschiha
Freia N. Gustafson
Froh J. Hopferwieser
Donner F. Cerny
Erda H. Schwarz
Fasolt J-H. Rootering
Fafner K. Moll
Woglinde J. Kaufman
Wellgunde A.M. Blasi
Flosshilde B. Calm
Bavarian St Orch, W. Sawallisch (pp1989)
(5/92) (EMI) ◖ [2] **LDD9 91276-1**
(5/92) (EMI) ▭ [2] **MVB9 91276-3**
Wotan R. Hale
Fricka M. Lipovšek
Loge R. Tear
Mime H. Pampuch
Alberich E. Wlaschiha
Freia N. Gustafson
Froh J. Hopferwieser
Donner F. Cerny
Erda H. Schwarz
Fasolt J-H. Rootering
Fafner K. Moll
Woglinde J. Kaufman

Woglinde A.M. Blasi
Flosshilde B. Calm
Bavarian St Orch, W. Sawallisch (pp1989)
(5/92) (EMI) ◖ [10] **LDX9 91275-1**
(5/92) (EMI) ▭ [8] **MVX9 91275-3**
Wotan D. McIntyre
Fricka H. Schwarz
Loge H. Zednik
Mime H. Pampuch
Alberich H. Becht
Freia C. Reppel
Froh S. Jerusalem
Donner M. Egel
Erda O. Wenkel
Fasolt M. Salminen
Fafner F. Hübner
Woglinde N. Sharp
Wellgunde I. Gramatzki
Flosshilde M. Schiml
Bayreuth Fest Orch, P. Boulez (pp1980)
(10/92) (PHIL) ① [2] **434 421-2PH2**
Wotan J. Tomlinson
Fricka L. Finnie
Loge G. Clark
Mime H. Pampuch
Alberich G. von Kannen
Freia E. Johansson
Froh K. Schreibmayer
Donner B. Brinkmann
Erda B. Svendén
Fasolt M. Hölle
Fafner P. Kang
Woglinde H. Leidland
Wellgunde A. Küttenbaum
Flosshilde J. Turner
Bayreuth Fest Orch, D. Barenboim (pp1991)
(10/93) (TELD) ① [2] **4509-91185-2**
Wotan J. Tomlinson
Fricka L. Finnie
Loge G. Clark
Mime H. Pampuch
Alberich G. von Kannen
Freia E. Johansson
Froh K. Schreibmayer
Donner B. Brinkmann
Erda B. Svendén
Fasolt M. Hölle
Fafner P. Kang
Woglinde H. Leidland
Wellgunde A. Küttenbaum
Flosshilde J. Turner
Bayreuth Fest Orch, D. Barenboim, H. Kupfer, H.H. Hohlfeld (pp1991)
(10/93) (TELD) ◖ [2] **4509-91122-6**
(10/93) (TELD) ▭ **4509-91122-3**
Wotan J. Morris
Fricka C. Ludwig
Loge S. Jerusalem
Mime H. Zednik
Alberich E. Wlaschiha
Freia M.A. Häggander
Froh M. Baker
Donner S. Lorenz
Erda B. Svendén
Fasolt K. Moll
Fafner J-H. Rootering
Woglinde H-K. Hong
Wellgunde D. Kesling
Flosshilde M. Parsons
NY Met Op Orch, James Levine (r1988)
(10/94) (DG) ① [14] **445 354-2GX14**
Wotan T. Adam
Fricka A. Burmeister
Loge W. Windgassen
Mime E. Wohlfahrt
Alberich G. Neidlinger
Freia A. Silja
Froh H. Esser
Donner G. Nienstedt
Erda V. Soukupová
Fasolt M. Talvela
Fafner K. Böhme
Woglinde D. Siebert
Wellgunde H. Dernesch
Flosshilde R. Hesse
Bayreuth Fest Orch, K. Böhm (pp1966)
(10/94) (PHIL) ① [14] **446 057-2PB14**
Wotan R. Hale
Fricka H. Schwarz
Loge K. Begley
Mime P. Schreier
Alberich F-J. Kapellmann
Freia N. Gustafson
Froh T. Sunnegårdh
Donner E. W. Schulte
Erda E. Zaremba

Fasolt J-H. Rootering
Fafner W. Fink
Woglinde G. Fontana
Wellgunde I. Komlósi
Flosshilde M. Hintermeier
Cleveland Orch, C. von Dohnányi (r1993)
(11/95) (DECC) Ⓒ [2] **443 690-2DHO2**
Excs Philadelphia, L. Stokowski (r1933)
(PEAR) Ⓒ [2] **GEMMCDS9076**
Excs BPO, L. Maazel (without voices)
(10/88) (TELA) Ⓒ **CD80154**
Excs J. Prohaska, N. Zec, H. Alsen, A. Konetzni, Vienna St Op Orch, J. Krips (pp1937)
(8/95) (SCHW) Ⓒ [2] **314592**
Excs J. von Manowarda, B. Paalen, V. Ursuleac, G. Graarud, V. Madin, J. Kalenberg, E. Zimmermann, H. Wiedemann, F. Markhoff, L. Helletsgruber, D. With, E. Szánthó, Vienna St Op Orch, C. Krauss (pp1933)
(8/95) (SCHW) Ⓒ [2] **314642**
Leitmotifs LSO, L. Collingwood (r1931)
(4/95) (PEAR) Ⓒ [7] **GEMMCDS9137**
1, 2, 5, 6a, 7, 8, 14, 15b, 19, 20, 25, 27(pt), 28, 29, 33, 37. D. McIntyre, H. Schwarz, H. Zednik, H. Pampuch, H. Becht, C. Reppel, S. Jerusalem, M. Egel, O. Wenkel, Bayreuth Fest Orch, P. Boulez (pp1980) (PHIL) Ⓒ **446 613-2PM**
1, 2, 5, 6a, 10, 18b, 18b (pt), 28 (pt), 33, 37, 39-41. E. Johansson, H. Leidland, L. Finnie, B. Svendén, A. Küttenbaum, J. Turner, G. Clark, H. Pampuch, K. Schreibmayer, G. von Kannen, B. Brinkmann, P. Kang, J. Tomlinson, M. Hölle, Bayreuth Fest Orch, D. Barenboim (pp1991)
(TELD) Ⓒ **4509-97906-2**
1, 42. SO, A. Coates (r1926)
(11/91) (CLAR) Ⓒ [2] **CDGSE78-50-35/6**
1-5, 6a, 6b, 28-41. L. Otto, M. Muszely, S. Wagner, B. Kusche, R. Siewert, F. Frantz, J. Blatter, H. Melchert, J. Metternich, R. Schock, Berlin Staatskapelle, R. Kempe (r1959)
(10/94) (EMI) Ⓒ [4] **CMS5 65212-2**
1, 6b, 17. L. Trenton, E. Suddaby, N. Walker, W. Widdop, K. McKenna, H. Fry, A. Fear, LSO, A. Coates (r1926/8)
(4/95) (PEAR) Ⓒ [7] **GEMMCDS9137**
1, 7, 19, 42. Netherlands Rad PO, E. de Waart (r1992; arr Vlieger) (9/93) (FIDE) Ⓒ **9201**
5, 38. H-K. Hong, D. Kesling, M. Parsons, E. Wlaschiha, M. Baker, J. Morris, C. Ludwig, E. Wlaschiha (r1988) (DG) Ⓒ **437 825-2GH**
5, 38. Z. Kélémen, D. Grobe, D. Fischer-Dieskau, J. Veasey, G. Stolze, BPO, H. von Karajan (r1967) (3/94) (DG) Ⓒ **439 423-2GCL**
6b, 7, 17, 18a, 18b, 19. L. Trenton, E. Suddaby, N. Walker, W. Widdop, K. McKenna, H. Fry, A. Fear, LSO, A. Coates (r1928)
(11/91) (CLAR) Ⓒ [2] **CDGSE78-50-35/6**
13 (pt) W. Lewis, RPO, G. Ötvös
(RPO) Ⓒ **CDRPO7019**
13(pt) O. Briesemeister, anon (r1904)
(7/91) (SYMP) Ⓒ **SYMCD1081**
13, 16. K. Erb, orch (r1914) (PREI) Ⓒ **89095**
21(pt) H. Breuer, anon (r1904)
(7/91) (SYMP) Ⓒ **SYMCD1081**
33. R. Morloc, Berlin RSO, J. Märkl (r1991)
(SCHW) Ⓒ [2] **312682**
33. E. Schumann-Heink, H. Witherspoon, orch (r1907) (2/91) (NIMB) Ⓒ **NI7811**
(2/91) (NIMB) ▣ **NC7811**
33. E. Schumann-Heink, orch, Rosario Bourdon (r1919) (2/91) (NIMB) Ⓒ **NI7811**
(2/91) (NIMB) ▣ **NC7811**
33. E. Schumann-Heink, H. Witherspoon, orch (r1907)
(7/92) (PEAR) Ⓒ [3] **GEMMCDS9923(1)**
33. K. Branzell, orch (r1928)
(8/92) (PREI) Ⓒ **89039**
33. E. Feinhals, orch (r1908)
(12/93) (SYMP) Ⓒ **SYMCD1113**
33. K. Thorborg, RCA SO, K. Riedel (r1940)
(4/95) (PREI) Ⓒ **89084**
38. G. Guszalewicz, W. Henke, F. Schorr, Berlin St Op Orch, L. Blech (r1927)
(4/95) (PEAR) Ⓒ [7] **GEMMCDS9137**
38-41. D. Grobe, D. Fischer-Dieskau, J. Veasey, G. Stolze, H. Donath, E. Moser, A. Reynolds, BPO, H. von Karajan
(4/90) (DG) Ⓒ **429 168-2GR**
(4/90) (DG) ▣ **429 168-4GR**
39. E. Waechter, W. Kmentt, G. London, K. Flagstad, S. Svanholm, O. Balsborg, H. Plümacher, I. Malaniuk, VPO, G. Solti
(DECC) Ⓒ **421 313-2DA**
39. F. Schorr, W. Henke, G. Gusalewicz, Berlin St Op Orch, L. Blech (r1927)
(MSCM) Ⓒ [2] **MM30285**
(MSCM) ▣ [2] **MM40107**
39. R. Bockelmann, orch (r c1935)
(MSCM) Ⓒ [2] **MM30285**
(MSCM) ▣ [2] **MM40107**
39. J. von Manowarda, orch (r1922)
(PREI) Ⓒ **89069**
39. J. Herrmann, VPO, R. Moralt (r1943)
(PREI) Ⓒ **89076**
39. F. Schorr, Berlin St Op Orch, L. Blech
(PREI) Ⓒ [2] **89214**
39. L. Hofmann, E. Szánthó, Vienna St Op Orch, H. Knappertsbusch (pp1937)
(SCHW) Ⓒ [2] **314742**
39. T. Bertram, anon (r1904)
(7/91) (SYMP) Ⓒ **SYMCD1081**
39. F. Schorr, Berlin St Op Orch, L. Blech (r1927) (1/92) (EMI) Ⓒ [4] **CMS7 64008-2(2)**
39. T. Bertram, B. Seidler-Winkler (r1904)
(7/92) (PEAR) Ⓒ [3] **GEMMCDS9923(2)**
39. A. Van Rooy, anon (r1902)
(3/93) (SYMP) Ⓒ **SYMCD1100**
42. Sofia Rad SO, V. Kazandjiev
(LASE) Ⓒ **15 612**
(LASE) ▣ **79 612**
42. Cleveland Orch, G. Szell
(CBS) Ⓒ [2] **CD46466**
42. LSO, L. Stokowski
(DECC) Ⓒ **433 639-2DSP**
(DECC) ▣ **433 639-4DSP**
42. LPO, A. Boult (EMI) Ⓒ [2] **CZS7 62539-2**
42. VPO, G. Solti (DECC) OO **410 137-5DH**
42. Eastman Wind Ens, F. Fennell (r1959. arr Godfrey) (MERC) Ⓒ **434 322-2MM**
42. BPO, K. Tennstedt (r1980)
(EMI) Ⓒ [2] **CZS5 68616-2**
42. VPO, G. Solti
(11/83) (DECC) Ⓒ **410 137-2DH**
42. Seattle SO, G. Schwarz
(3/87) (DELO) Ⓒ **DE3040**
42. Philh, O. Klemperer (r1961)
(11/90) (EMI) Ⓒ **CDM7 63618-2**
42. Cleveland Orch, G. Szell
(11/92) (SONY) Ⓒ **SBK48175**
42. LSO, A. Coates (r1926)
(4/93) (KOCH) Ⓒ [2] **37704-2**

Der **Ring des Nibelungen: Part 2, '(Die) Walküre'– opera: 3 acts (1850—Weimar) (Lib. cpsr)**

EXCERPTS. ACT 1: 1. Prelude; 2. Wes Herd dies auch sei; 3. Müd am Herd fand ich den Mann; 4. Friedmund darf ich nicht heissen; 5. Ich weiss ein wildes Geschlecht; 6. Ein Schwert verheiss mir der Vater; 7. Schläfst du, Gast?; 8. Der Männer Sippe; 9. Winterstürme wichen dem Wonnemond; 10. Du bist der Lenz; 11. War Wälse dein Vater; 12. Siegmund heiss ich. ACT 2: 13. Prelude; 14. Nun zäume dein Ross; 15a. Hojotoho!; 15b. Dir rat ich, Vater; 16. Der alte Sturm; 17. So ist es denn aus; 18. Was verlangst du?; 19. Deiner ew'gen Gattin heilige Ehre; 20. Schimm, fürcht ich; 21. Als junger Liebe; 22. Ein andres ist's; 23a. Ihrem Willen muss ich gewähren; 23b. So nimmst du von Siegmund; 24. So sah ich Siegvater nie; 25. Raste nun hier; 26. Siegmund! Sieh auf mich! (Todesverkundigung); 27. Du sahest der Walküre; 28. Zauberfest bezähmt ein Schlaf; 29a. Der dort mich ruft; 29b. Kehrte der Vater nur heim!; 30a. Zu Ross, dass ich dich rette!; 30b. Geh hin, Knecht! ACT 3: 31. Hojotoho! (Ride of the Valkyries); 32. Schützt mich und helft; 33. Nicht sehre dich Sorgen; 34. Wo ist Brünnhild'; 35. Hier bin ich, Vater; 36. War es so schmählich; 37. Weil für dich im Auge; 38. So tatest du; 39a. Und das ich ihm in Stücken; 39b. Nicht streb, o Maid; 40. Leb wohl (Wotan's Farewell); 41. Der Augen leuchtendes Paar; 42. Loge, hör!; 43. Magic Fire Music; 44. Ride of the Valkyries (concert version).

Siegmund G. Lakes
Sieglinde J. Norman
Brünnhilde H. Behrens
Wotan J. Morris
Fricka C. Ludwig
Hunding K. Moll
Gerhilde P. Sellers
Helmwige K. Ikonomu
Ortlinde M. Thigpen
Waltraute J. Castle
Rossweisse J. Bower
Siegrune D. Kesling
Grimgerde W. Hillhouse
Schwertleite S. Kelly
NY Met Op Orch, James Levine, O. Schenk, B. Large
(5/92) (DG) ▬ [7] **072 422-3GH7**
Act 1. L. Melchior, Lotte Lehmann, E. List, VPO, B. Walter (r1935)
(DANA) Ⓒ [2] **DACOCD317/8**
Act 2. L. Melchior, Lotte Lehmann, M. Fuchs, E. Flesch, H. Hotter, A. Jerger, M. Klose, E. List, VPO, B. Walter, Berlin St Op Orch, B. Seidler-Winkler (Scenes 3 & 5 recorded Vienna 1935, balance Berlin 1938)
(DANA) Ⓒ [2] **DACOCD317/8**
Act 1. L. Melchior, D. Larsen, M. Wedel, Danish HSO, T. Jensen (bp1960)
(DANA) Ⓒ [3] **DACOCD319/21**
Siegmund S. Jerusalem
Sieglinde J. Norman
Brünnhilde J. Altmeyer
Wotan T. Adam
Fricka Y. Minton
Hunding K. Moll
Gerhilde E-M. Bundschuh
Helmwige R. Falcon
Ortlinde C. Studer
Waltraute O. Wenkel
Rossweisse U. Priew
Siegrune C. Borchers
Grimgerde K. Kuhlmann
Schwertleite A. Gjevang
Staatskapelle Dresden, M. Janowski
(EURO) Ⓒ [14] **GD69003**
Siegmund P. Hofmann
Sieglinde J. Altmeyer
Brünnhilde G. Jones
Wotan D. McIntyre
Fricka H. Schwarz
Hunding M. Salminen
Gerhilde C. Reppel
Helmwige K. Clarke
Ortlinde K. Middleton
Waltraute G. Schnaut
Rossweisse E. Glauser
Siegrune M. Schiml
Grimgerde I. Gramatzki
Schwertleite G. Killebrew
Bayreuth Fest Orch, P. Boulez (pp1980)
(PHIL) Ⓒ [32] **434 420-2PM32(2)**
Siegmund S. Jerusalem
Sieglinde J. Norman
Brünnhilde J. Altmeyer
Wotan T. Adam
Fricka Y. Minton
Hunding K. Moll
Gerhilde E-M. Bundschuh
Helmwige R. Falcon
Ortlinde C. Studer
Waltraute O. Wenkel
Rossweisse U. Priew
Siegrune C. Borchers
Grimgerde K. Kuhlmann
Schwertleite A. Gjevang
Staatskapelle Dresden, M. Janowski
(10/84) (EURO) Ⓒ [4] **GD69005**
Siegmund J. King
Sieglinde Leonie Rysanek
Brünnhilde B. Nilsson
Wotan T. Adam
Fricka; Siegrune A. Burmeister
Hunding G. Nienstedt
Gerhilde D. Mastilovic
Helmwige L. Synek
Ortlinde H. Dernesch
Waltraute G. Hopf
Rossweisse Š. Červená
Grimgerde E. Schärtel
Schwertleite S. Wagner
Bayreuth Fest Orch, K. Böhm (pp1967)
(2/85) (PHIL) Ⓒ [4] **412 478-2PH4**
Siegmund J. King
Sieglinde R. Crespin
Brünnhilde B. Nilsson
Wotan H. Hotter
Fricka C. Ludwig
Hunding G. Frick
Gerhilde V. Schlosser
Helmwige B. Lindholm
Ortlinde H. Dernesch
Waltraute B. Fassbaender
Rossweisse C. Hellmann
Siegrune V. Little
Grimgerde M. Tyler
Schwertleite H. Watts
VPO, G. Solti (r1965)
(4/85) (DECC) Ⓒ [4] **414 105-2DH4**
Siegmund J. Vickers

Sieglinde G. Janowitz
Brünnhilde R. Crespin
Wotan T. Stewart
Fricka J. Veasey
Hunding M. Talvela
Gerhilde L. Rebmann
Helmwige D. Mastilovic
Ortlinde C. Ordassy
Waltraute I. Steger
Rossweisse H. Jenckel
Siegrune B. Ericson
Grimgerde C. Ahlin
Schwertleite L. Brockhaus
BPO, H. von Karajan (r1966)
(7/85) (DG) Ⓓ [4] **415 145-2GH4**
Siegmund R. Vinay
Sieglinde R. Resnik
Brünnhilde A. Varnay
Wotan H. Hotter
Fricka I. Malaniuk
Hunding J. Greindl
Gerhilde B. Friedland
Helmwige L. Thomamüller
Ortlinde B. Falcon
Waltraute L. Sorrell
Rossweisse E. Schubert
Siegrune G. Litz
Grimgerde S. Plate
Schwertleite M. von Ilosvay
Bayreuth Fest Orch, C. Krauss (pp1953)
(6/88) (FOYE) Ⓓ [4] **4-CF2008**
Siegmund R. Vinay
Sieglinde R. Resnik
Brünnhilde A. Varnay
Wotan H. Hotter
Fricka I. Malaniuk
Hunding J. Greindl
Gerhilde B. Friedland
Helmwige L. Thomamüller
Ortlinde B. Falcon
Waltraute L. Sorrell
Rossweisse E. Schubert
Siegrune G. Litz
Grimgerde S. Plate
Schwertleite M. von Ilosvay
Bayreuth Fest Orch, C. Krauss (pp1953)
(6/88) (FOYE) Ⓓ [15] **15-CF2011**
Siegmund R. Vinay
Sieglinde R. Resnik
Brünnhilde A. Varnay
Wotan H. Hotter
Hunding J. Greindl
Fricka I. Malaniuk
Gerhilde B. Friedland
Ortlinde B. Falcon
Waltraute L. Sorrell
Schwertleite M. von Ilosvay
Helmwige L. Thomamüller
Siegrune G. Litz
Grimgerde S. Plate
Rossweisse E. Schubert
Bayreuth Fest Orch, C. Krauss (pp1953)
(6/88) (LAUD) Ⓓ [4] **LCD4 4003**
Siegmund G. Lakes
Sieglinde J. Norman
Brünnhilde H. Behrens
Wotan J. Morris
Fricka C. Ludwig
Hunding K. Moll
Gerhilde M. Napier
Helmwige L. Kelm
Ortlinde M. Mims
Waltraute R. Runkel
Rossweisse A. Wilkens
Siegrune D. Kesling
Grimgerde M. Parsons
Schwertleite R. Engert-Ely
NY Met Op Orch, James Levine
(11/88) (DG) Ⓓ [4] **423 389-2GH4**
Siegmund R. Goldberg
Sieglinde C. Studer
Brünnhilde E. Marton
Wotan J. Morris
Fricka W. Meier
Hunding M. Salminen
Gerhilde A. Soldh
Helmwige R. Falcon
Ortlinde S. Herman
Waltraute U. Walther
Rossweisse M. Lilowa
Siegrune M. Hintermeier
Grimgerde C. Watkinson
Schwertleite U. Kunz
BRSO, B. Haitink (r1988)
(12/88) (EMI) Ⓓ [4] **CDS7 49534-2**
Siegmund J. King

Sieglinde R. Crespin
Brünnhilde B. Nilsson
Wotan H. Hotter
Fricka C. Ludwig
Hunding G. Frick
Gerhilde V. Schlosser
Helmwige B. Lindholm
Ortlinde H. Dernesch
Waltraute B. Fassbaender
Rossweisse C. Hellmann
Siegrune V. Little
Grimgerde M. Tyler
Schwertleite H. Watts
VPO, G. Solti (r1965)
(3/89) (DECC) Ⓓ [15] **414 100-2DM15**
Siegmund L. Suthaus
Sieglinde Leonie Rysanek
Brünnhilde M. Mödl
Wotan F. Frantz
Fricka M. Klose
Hunding G. Frick
Gerhilde G. Schreyer
Helmwige E. Köth
Ortlinde J. Hellwig
Waltraute D. Schmedes
Rossweisse D. Hermann
Siegrune H. Töpper
Grimgerde J. Blatter
Schwertleite R. Siewert
VPO, W. Furtwängler (r1954)
(7/89) (EMI) Ⓓ [3] **CHS7 63045-2**
Siegmund W. Windgassen
Sieglinde H. Konetzni
Brünnhilde M. Mödl
Wotan F. Frantz
Fricka E. Cavelti
Hunding G. Frick
Gerhilde G. Scheyrer
Helmwige J. Hellwig
Ortlinde M. Gabory
Waltraute D. Schmedes
Rossweisse I. Malaniuk
Siegrune O. Bennings
Grimgerde E. Cavelti
Schwertleite H. Rössl-Majdan
Rome RAI Orch, W. Furtwängler (bp1953)
(2/91) (EMI) Ⓓ [13] **CZS7 67123-2**
Siegmund A. Remedios
Sieglinde M. Curphey
Brünnhilde R. Hunter
Wotan N. Bailey
Fricka A. Howard
Hunding C. Grant
Gerhilde K. Clarke
Helmwige Anne Evans
Ortlinde A. Conoley
Waltraute E. Connell
Rossweisse A. Collins
Siegrune Sarah Walker
Grimgerde S. Squires
Schwertleite H. Attfield
ENO Orch, R. Goodall (Eng: pp1975)
(7/91) (EMI) Ⓓ [4] **CMS7 63918-2**
Siegmund J. Vickers
Sieglinde G. Janowitz
Brünnhilde R. Crespin
Wotan T. Stewart
Fricka J. Veasey
Hunding M. Talvela
Gerhilde L. Rebmann
Helmwige D. Mastilovic
Ortlinde C. Ordassy
Waltraute I. Steger
Rossweisse H. Jenckel
Siegrune B. Ericson
Grimgerde C. Ahlin
Schwertleite L. Brockhaus
BPO, H. von Karajan
(4/92) (DG) Ⓓ [15] **435 211-2GX15**
Siegmund G. Lakes
Sieglinde J. Norman
Brünnhilde H. Behrens
Wotan J. Morris
Fricka C. Ludwig
Hunding K. Moll
Gerhilde P. Sellers
Helmwige K. Ikonomu
Ortlinde M. Thigpen
Waltraute J. Castle
Rossweisse J. Bower
Siegrune D. Kesling
Grimgerde W. Hillhouse

Schwertleite S. Kelly
NY Met Op Orch, James Levine, O. Schenk, B. Large
(5/92) (DG) ◐ [3] **072 419-1GH3**
(5/92) (DG) ▣ [2] **072 419-3GH2**
Siegmund P. Hofmann
Sieglinde J. Altmeyer
Brünnhilde G. Jones
Wotan D. McIntyre
Fricka H. Schwarz
Hunding M. Salminen
Gerhilde C. Reppel
Ortlinde K. Middleton
Helmwige K. Clarke
Waltraute G. Schnaut
Siegrune M. Schiml
Grimgerde I. Gramatzki
Schwertleite G. Killebrew
Rossweisse E. Glauser
Bayreuth Fest Orch, P. Boulez, P. Chéreau
(5/92) (PHIL) ◐ [3] **070 402-1PHE3**
(5/92) (PHIL) ▣ [2] **070 402-3PHE2**
Siegmund J. Vickers
Sieglinde G. Brouwenstijn
Brünnhilde B. Nilsson
Wotan G. London
Fricka R. Gorr
Hunding D. Ward
Gerhilde M. Collier
Helmwige Judith Pierce
Ortlinde J. Malyon
Waltraute M. Elkins
Rossweisse J. Veasey
Siegrune N. Berry
Grimgerde M. Guy
Schwertleite J. Edwards
LSO, E. Leinsdorf (r1961)
(5/92) (DECC) Ⓓ [3] **430 391-2DM3**
Siegmund R. Schunk
Sieglinde J. Varady
Brünnhilde H. Behrens
Wotan R. Hale
Fricka M. Lipovšek
Hunding K. Moll
Gerhilde A. Trauboth
Helmwige N. Gustafson
Ortlinde M. Seibel
Waltraute C. Wulkopf
Rossweisse G. Wewezow
Siegrune C. Borchers
Grimgerde B. Calm
Schwertleite A. Pellekoorne
Bavarian St Orch, W. Sawallisch (pp1989)
(5/92) (EMI) ◐ [10] **LDX9 91275-1**
(5/92) (EMI) ▣ [8] **MVX9 91275-3**
Siegmund R. Schunk
Sieglinde J. Varady
Brünnhilde H. Behrens
Wotan R. Hale
Fricka M. Lipovšek
Hunding K. Moll
Gerhilde A. Trauboth
Helmwige N. Gustafson
Ortlinde M. Seibel
Waltraute C. Wulkopf
Rossweisse G. Wewezow
Siegrune C. Borchers
Grimgerde B. Calm
Schwertleite A. Pellekoorne
Bavarian St Orch, W. Sawallisch (pp1989)
(5/92) (EMI) ◐ [3] **LDE9 91279-1**
(5/92) (EMI) ▣ [2] **MVB9 91279-3**
Siegmund P. Hofmann
Sieglinde J. Altmeyer
Brünnhilde G. Jones
Wotan D. McIntyre
Fricka H. Schwarz
Hunding M. Salminen
Gerhilde C. Reppel
Helmwige K. Clarke
Ortlinde K. Middleton
Waltraute G. Schnaut
Rossweisse E. Glauser
Siegrune M. Schiml
Grimgerde I. Gramatzki
Schwertleite G. Killebrew
Bayreuth Fest Orch, P. Boulez (pp1980)
(10/92) (PHIL) Ⓓ [3] **434 422-2PH3**
Seigmund P. Elming
Sieglinde N. Secunde
Brünnhilde Anne Evans
Wotan J. Tomlinson
Fricka; Siegrune L. Finnie
Hunding M. Hölle
Gerhilde E. Johansson
Helmwige E-M. Bundschuh

Ortlinde R. Floeren
Waltraute S. Close
Rossweisse H. Dijkstra
Waltraute S. Close
Grimgerde B. Svendén
Schwertleite H. Katagiri
Bayreuth Fest Orch, D. Barenboim (pp1992)
(10/93) (TELD) Ⓓ [4] **4509-91186-2**
Siegmund P. Elming
Sieglinde N. Secunde
Brünnhilde Anne Evans
Wotan J. Tomlinson
Fricka; Siegrune L. Finnie
Hunding M. Hölle
Gerhilde E. Johansson
Helmwige E-M. Bundschuh
Ortlinde R. Floeren
Waltraute S. Close
Rossweisse H. Dijkstra
Grimgerde B. Svendén
Schwertleite H. Katagiri
Bayreuth Fest Orch, D. Barenboim, H. Kupfer, H.H. Hohlfeld (pp1992)
(10/93) (TELD) ◐ [3] **4509-91123-6**
(10/93) (TELD) ▭▭ [2] **4509-91123-3**
Siegmund L. Suthaus
Sieglinde M. Müller
Brünnhilde P. Buchner
Wotan J. Herrmann
Fricka M. Klose
Hunding J. Greindl
Gerhilde I. Grunow
Helmwige F. Fleig
Ortlinde C. Breske
Waltraute F. Schmalz
Rossweisse E. Hufnagel
Siegrune H. Grohmann
Grimgerde E. Hagemann
Schwertleite C. Schäblen
Berlin City Op Orch, F. Fricsay (pp1951)
(3/94) (MYTO) Ⓓ [3] **3MCD93381**
Siegmund G. Lakes
Sieglinde J. Norman
Brünnhilde H. Behrens
Wotan J. Morris
Fricka C. Ludwig
Hunding K. Moll
Gerhilde M. Napier
Helmwige L. Kelm
Ortlinde M. Mims
Waltraute R. Runkel
Rossweisse A. Wilkens
Siegrune D. Kesling
Grimgerde M. Parsons
Schwertleite R. Engert-Ely
NY Met Op Orch, James Levine (r1987)
(10/94) (DG) Ⓓ [14] **445 354-2GX14**
Siegmund J. King
Sieglinde Leonie Rysanek
Brünnhilde B. Nilsson
Wotan T. Adam
Fricka; Siegrune A. Burmeister
Hunding G. Nienstedt
Gerhilde D. Mastilovic
Helmwige L. Synek
Ortlinde H. Dernesch
Waltraute G. Hopf
Rossweisse Š. Červená
Grimgerde E. Schärtel
Schwertleite S. Wagner
Bayreuth Fest Orch, K. Böhm (pp1967)
(10/94) (PHIL) Ⓓ [14] **446 057-2PB14**

Act 1. E. Moser, M. Lundberg, F. Olsen, Mecklenburg Staatskapelle, I. Törzs (pp1994) (CALI) Ⓓ **CAL50943**

Act 1. Lotte Lehmann, L. Melchior, E. List, VPO, B. Walter (r1935) (10/88) (EMI) Ⓓ **CDH7 61020-2**

Act 1. M. Lorenz, M. Teschemacher, K. Böhme, Saxon St Orch, K. Elmendorff (bp1944) (4/91) (PREI) Ⓓ **90015**

Act 1. K. König, S. Dunn, P. Meven, Pittsburgh SO, L. Maazel (7/91) (TELA) Ⓓ **CD80258**

Act 1. M. Reining, F. Krauss, J. von Manowarda, Stuttgart RSO, C. Leonhardt (bp1938) (11/93) (PREI) Ⓓ **90151**

Act 1. H. Dernesch, W. Cochran, H. Sotin, New Philh, O. Klemperer (r1969/70) (10/94) (EMI) Ⓓ [4] **CMS5 65212-2**

Act 1. J. King, Leonie Rysanek, G. Nienstedt, Bayreuth Fest Orch, K. Böhm (pp1967) (7/95) (PHIL) Ⓓ **442 640-2PM**

Act 2. L. Melchior, Lotte Lehmann, M. Fuchs, E. Flesch, H. Hotter, A. Jerger, M. Klose, E. List, VPO, B. Walter, Berlin St Op Orch, B. Seidler-Winkler (r1935/8) (5/92) (EMI) Ⓓ **CDH7 64255-2**

Act 2(abridged); Act 3. F. Krauss, M. Reining, E. Schlüter, R. Bockelmann, H. Jung, J. von Manowarda, I. Roster, T. Eipperle, P. Kapper, C. Carlsson, M. Kuhn-Liebel, M. Strack, E. Waldenau, P. Baumann, Stuttgart RSO, C. Leonhardt (pp1938) (PREI) Ⓓ [2] **90207**

Act 3. K. Flagstad, R. Bockelmann, M. Müller, M. Craven, E. Stenning, T. Bardsley, L. Seymour, E. Arden, E. Coates, G. Garside, G. Ripley, LPO, W. Furtwängler (pp1937) (GFON) Ⓓ **AB78512**

Act 3. A. Varnay, S. Björling, Leonie Rysanek, B. Friedland, L. Thomamüller, E. Wild, R. Siewert, E. Lausch, H. Töpper, I. Malaniuk, H. Ludwig, Bayreuth Fest Orch, H. von Karajan (pp1951) (10/93) (EMI) Ⓓ **CDH7 64704-2**

Excs L. Tibbett, Philadelphia, L. Stokowski (r1934) (PEAR) Ⓓ [2] **GEMMCDS9076**

Excs F. Völker, M. Müller, W. Grossmann, A. Konetzni, A. Jerger, L. Helletsgruber, E. Hadrabová, D. Komarek, R. Anday, A. Michalsky, D. With, B. Paalen, E. Szánthó, Vienna St Op Orch, W. Furtwängler (pp1936) (SCHW) Ⓓ [2] **314702**

Excs H. Hotter, H. Braun, M. Lorenz, H. Konetzni, D. Söderqvist, D. Ilitsch, E. Schulz, D. With, E. Schürhoff, E. Nikolaidi, O. Levko-Antosch, M. Frutschnigg, Vienna St Op Orch, H. Knappertsbusch (pp1943) (SCHW) Ⓓ [2] **314742**

Excs H. Hotter, H. Braun, Vienna St Op Orch, R. Moralt (pp1942) (SCHW) Ⓓ [2] **314722**

Excs P. Hofmann, J. Altmeyer, G. Jones, D. McIntyre, H. Schwarz, M. Salminen, C. Reppel, K. Clarke, K. Middleton, G. Schnaut, M. Schiml, I. Gramatzki, G. Killebrew, E. Glauser, Bayreuth Fest Orch, P. Boulez (pp1980) (PHIL) Ⓓ **446 614-2PM**

Excs BPO, L. Maazel (without voices) (10/88) (TELA) Ⓓ **CD80154**

Excs G. Ljungberg, L. Trenton, F. Austral, F. Leider, W. Widdop, H. Fry, F. Schorr, LSO, A. Coates, SO, L. Collingwood, Berlin St Op Orch, L. Blech (r1926/7) (11/91) (CLAR) Ⓓ [2] **CDGSE78-50-35/6**

Excs Grimethorpe Colliery Band, E. Howarth (arr Owen) (12/92) (DOYE) Ⓓ **DOYCD013**
(12/92) (DOYE) ⊟ **DOYMC013**

Excs L. Hofmann, F. Völker, H. Konetzni, R. Merker, H. Alsen, K. Thorborg, L. Helletsgruber, E. Flesch, M. Bokor, D. With, A. Michalsky, F. Stroinigg, B. Paalen, E. Weichert, Vienna St Op Orch, B. Walter (pp1936) (8/95) (SCHW) Ⓓ [2] **314592**

Excs F. Schorr, M. Jeritza, F. Hüni-Mihacsek, F. Völker, R. Mayr, L. Helletsgruber, E. Hadrabová, M. Bokor, R. Anday, A. Michalsky, D. With, B. Paalen, E. Szánthó, Vienna St Op Orch, C. Krauss (pp1933) (8/95) (SCHW) Ⓓ [2] **314642**

Excs G. Rünger, H. Konetzni, Vienna St Op Orch, H. Knappertsbusch (pp1938) (9/95) (SCHW) Ⓓ [2] **314662**

Excs F. Schorr, F. Völker, Lotte Lehmann, M. Jeritza, L. Helletsgruber, E. Hadrabová, M. Bokor, R. Anday, A. Michalsky, D. With, B. Paalen, E. Szánthó, Vienna St Op Orch, C. Krauss (pp1933) (11/95) (SCHW) Ⓓ [2] **314622**

Leitmotifs LSO, L. Collingwood (r1931) (4/95) (PEAR) Ⓓ [7] **GEMMCDS9137**

1, 2, 6-9, 12, 25, 26, 28, 30b G. Ljungberg, W. Widdop, F. Austral, L. Trenton, H. Fry, LSO, A. Coates (r1927) (4/95) (PEAR) Ⓓ [7] **GEMMCDS9137**

1, 4, 9-12, 26, 27, 31, 32, 38(pt), 39a, 40-42. N. Secunde, Anne Evans, E. Johansson, E-M. Bundschuh, R. Floeren, L. Finnie, S. Close, H. Dijkstra, B. Svendén, H. Katagiri, P. Elming, J. Tomlinson, M. Hölle, Bayreuth Fest Orch, D. Barenboim (pp1992) (TELD) Ⓓ **4509-97907-2**

2. M. Lorenz, H. Konetzni, Vienna St Op Orch, Wolfgang Martin (pp1930s/40s) (SCHW) Ⓓ [2] **314692**

2-4. C. Katsaris (r1994: freely arr: J Rubinstein) (SONY) Ⓓ **SK58973**

3(pt), 9. F. Völker, V. Ursuleac, R. Mayr, Vienna St Op Orch, C. Krauss (pp1933) (9/95) (SCHW) Ⓓ [2] **314662**

4, 6. L. Melchior, orch (r1923) (8/88) (DANA) Ⓓ [2] **DACOCD313/4**

4, 6, 10, 12. L. Melchior, F. Leider, orch (r1923) (PREI) Ⓓ **89032**

6. L. Melchior, Berlin St Op Orch, L. Blech (r1929) (PREI) Ⓓ **89086**

6. M. Lorenz, M. Reining, Berlin RSO, A. Rother (r1943) (PREI) Ⓓ **90213**

6. L. Melchior, Berlin St Op Orch, L. Blech (r1929) (8/88) (DANA) Ⓓ [2] **DACOCD315/6**

6. L. Melchior, Berlin St Op Orch, L. Blech (r1928) (8/88) (DANA) Ⓓ [2] **DACOCD315/6**

6. L. Melchior, Berlin St Op Orch, L. Blech (r1929) (7/92) (PEAR) Ⓓ [3] **GEMMCDS9925(2)**

6, 12. L. Melchior, G. Guszalewicz, Berlin St Op Orch, L. Blech (r1928) (PREI) Ⓓ **89068**

6, 12. L. Melchior, Berlin St Op Orch, L. Blech (r1929) (10/89) (EMI) Ⓓ **CDH7 69789-2**

6-12. H. Traubel, L. Melchior, NBC SO, A. Toscanini (bp1941) (12/91) (RCA) Ⓓ **GD60264**

6, 31, 40-43. J. Vickers, T. Stewart, BPO, H. von Karajan (4/90) (DG) Ⓓ **429 168-2GR**
(4/90) (DG) ⊟ **429 168-4GR**

6, 7, 8, 9. R. Kollo, I. Haubold, Berlin Deutsche Op Orch, C. Thielemann (5/93) (EMI) Ⓓ **CDC7 54776-2**

6, 9. F. Völker, Berlin Staatskapelle, J. Schüler (r1937) (8/94) (PREI) Ⓓ **89070**

7. C. Studer, R. Goldberg, BRSO, B. Haitink (r1988) (EMI) Ⓓ **CDC5 55350-2**

7, 10. K. Flagstad, NBC SO, E. McArthur (pp1955) (MUSI) Ⓓ **MACD-263**

8. J. Pölzer, H. Konetzni, Vienna St Op Orch, H. Knappertsbusch (pp1938) (SCHW) Ⓓ [2] **314692**

8. G. Lubin, orch, H. Defosse (French: r1929) (5/91) (CLUB) Ⓓ **CL99-022**

8. Lotte Lehmann, orch (r1921) (6/92) (PREI) Ⓓ [3] **89302**

8. M. Kurt, orch (r1911) (7/92) (PEAR) Ⓓ [3] **GEMMCDS9924(2)**

8, 10. K. Flagstad, VPO, H. Knappertsbusch (r1956) (LOND) Ⓓ **440 495-2LM**

8, 10. K. Flagstad, VPO, H. Knappertsbusch (r1956) (LOND) Ⓓ [5] **440 490-2LM5(1)**

8, 10. M. Seinemeyer, Berlin Staatskapelle, F. Weissmann (r1929) (1/92) (EMI) Ⓓ [4] **CMS7 64008-2(2)**

8, 12. G. Lubin, R. Verdière, orch, H. Defosse (French: r1929) (5/91) (EPM) Ⓓ **150 052**

8-12, 14, 15, 18, 29, 31, 33, 39b, 40-43. E. Marton, C. Studer, J. Morris, R. Goldberg, M. Salminen, W. Meier, A. Soldh, R. Falcon, U. Walther, U. Kunz, S. Herman, M. Hintermeier, C. Watkinson, M. Lilowa, BRSO, B. Haitink (EMI) Ⓓ **CDC7 54328-2**

8, 31, 41, 42. G. Janowitz, T. Stewart, BPO, H. von Karajan (r1966) (3/94) (DG) Ⓓ **439 423-2GCL**

8, 31, 41, 42, 43. J. Norman, M. Napier, L. Kelm, R. Runkel, R. Engert-Ely, M. Mims, D. Kesling, M. Parsons, A. Wilkens, J. Morris, NY Met Op Orch, James Levine (r1987) (DG) Ⓓ **437 825-2GH**

8(pt), 9, 10, 44. W. Meier, S. Jerusalem, BPO, C. Abbado (pp1993) (5/94) (DG) Ⓓ **439 768-2GH**
(5/94) (DG) ⊟ **439 768-4GH**

8(pt), 9-12. W. Widdop, G. Ljungberg, LSO, A. Coates, Orch, L. Collingwood (r1926/7) (11/92) (CLAR) Ⓓ **CDGSE78-50-46**

9. L. Melchior, Orch, H. Barlow (bp1951) (VAI) ▭▭ **VAI69107**

9. L. Melchior, Philadelphia, E. Ormandy (r1938) (MMOI) Ⓓ **CDMOIR405**
(MMOI) ⊟ **CMOIR405**

9. M. Müller, F. Völker, Bayreuth Fest Orch, H. Tietjen (r1936) (MSCM) Ⓓ [2] **MM30285**
(MSCM) ⊟ [2] **MM40107**

9. W. Lewis, RPO, G. Ötvös (RPO) Ⓓ **CDRPO7019**

9. L. Melchior, Philadelphia, E. Ormandy (r1938) (PEAR) Ⓓ **GEMMCD9049**

9. M. Gilion, orch (r c1909: Ital) (BONG) Ⓓ **GB1076-2**

9. L. Melchior, LSO, J. Barbirolli (r1931) (PREI) Ⓓ **89086**

9. P. Cornubert, anon (r1905: Fr) (SYMP) Ⓓ **SYMCD1173**

9. R. Tauber, orch (r c1920) (PEAR) Ⓓ **GEMMCD9145**

9. P. Franz, orch (r1914: Fr) (PREI) Ⓓ **89099**

9. L. Melchior, O. Helgers (r1926) (8/88) (DANA) Ⓓ [2] **DACOCD315/6**

9. L. Melchior, LSO, J. Barbirolli (r1931) (8/88) (DANA) Ⓓ [2] **DACOCD315/6**

9. L. Melchior, Orch (Danish: r c1921) (8/88) (DANA) Ⓓ [2] **DACOCD311/2**
9. L. Melchior, orch, P. Breisach (r1924) (8/88) (DANA) Ⓓ [2] **DACOCD313/4**
9. L. Melchior, LSO, J. Barbirolli (r1931) (10/89) (EMI) Ⓓ **CDH7 69789-2**
9. M. Lorenz, Berlin St Op Orch, E. Viebig (r1927) (1/92) (EMI) Ⓓ [4] **CMS7 64008-2(2)**
9. W. Hyde, orch, G.W. Byng (Eng: r1921) (7/92) (PEAR) Ⓓ [3] **GEMMCDS9924(2)**
9. P. Cornelius, orch (Danish: r1909) (7/92) (PEAR) Ⓓ [3] **GEMMCDS9924(2)**
9. W. Widdop, LSO, A. Coates (r1927) (7/92) (PEAR) Ⓓ [3] **GEMMCDS9926(1)**
9. G. Borgatti, orch (Ital: r1919) (11/92) (MEMO) Ⓓ [2] **HR4408/9(2)**
9. R. Tauber, orch (r1920) (12/92) (NIMB) Ⓓ **NI7830** (12/92) (NIMB) ▭ **NC7830**
9. G. Morskoi, anon (r1901: Russ) (6/93) (PEAR) Ⓓ [3] **GEMMCDS9001/3(1)**
9. J. Vickers, LSO, E. Leinsdorf (r1962) (10/93) (DECC) Ⓓ **436 463-2DM** (10/93) (DECC) ▭ **436 463-4DM**
9. S. Svanholm, Vienna St Op Orch, H. Knappertsbusch (pp1941) (6/94) (SCHW) Ⓓ **314502**
9. L. Melchior, LSO, J. Barbirolli (r1931) (9/94) (NIMB) Ⓓ **NI7856**
9. T. Ralf, Berlin St Op Orch, H.U. Müller (r1941) (10/94) (PREI) Ⓓ **89077**
9. E. Van Dyck, anon (r1905: Fr) (12/94) (SYMP) Ⓓ **SYMCD1172**
9. T. Hampson, Munich RO, F. Luisi (r1994) (9/95) (EMI) Ⓓ **CDC5 55233-2**
9, 10, 12. M. Müller, F. Völker, Bayreuth Fest Orch, H. Tietjen (r1936) (8/93) (TELD) Ⓓ **9031-76442-2**
9, 12. S. Svanholm, H. Konetzni, Vienna St Op Orch, H. Knappertsbusch (pp1941) (SCHW) Ⓓ [2] **314692**
9, 12. A. von Bary, anon (r1904) (7/91) (SYMP) Ⓓ **SYMCD1081**
10. Lotte Lehmann, Berlin St Op Orch, F. Weissmann (r1930) (PEAR) Ⓓ **GEMMCD9410**
10. J. Norman, NY Met Op Orch, James Levine (DG) ▭ **439 153-4GMA**
10. K. Flagstad, Philadelphia, E. Ormandy (r1937) (PEAR) Ⓓ **GEMMCD9049**
10. J. Norman, Staatskapelle Dresden, M. Janowski (RCA) Ⓓ **09026 61440-2** (RCA) ▭ **09026 61440-4**
10. K. Flagstad, Philadelphia, E. Ormandy (r1937) (IMP) Ⓓ **GLRS105**
10. G. Ljungberg, W. Widdop, orch (r1926) (PEAR) Ⓓ [2] **GEMMCDS9121**
10. K. Flagstad, Philadelphia, E. Ormandy (r1937) (SIMA) Ⓓ [3] **PSC1821(2)**
10. K. Flagstad, Philadelphia, E. Ormandy (r1937) (10/90) (RCA) Ⓓ **GD87915**
10. Lotte Lehmann, orch (r1917) (6/92) (PREI) Ⓓ [3] **89302**
10. G. Ljungberg, orch, L. Collingwood (r1926) (7/92) (PEAR) Ⓓ [3] **GEMMCDS9925(2)**
10. L. Price, LSO, E. Downes (12/92) (RCA) Ⓓ [4] **09026 61236-2**
10. K. Flagstad, Philadelphia, E. Ormandy (r1937) (7/93) (NIMB) Ⓓ **NI7847**
10. Lotte Lehmann, VPO, B. Walter (r1935) (12/93) (NIMB) Ⓓ **NI7851**
10. M. Jeritza, orch (r1922) (4/94) (PREI) Ⓓ **89079**
10. G. Ljungberg, W. Widdop, LSO, L. Collingwood (r1926) (4/95) (PEAR) Ⓓ [7] **GEMMCDS9137**
10-12. F. Leider, L. Melchior, orch (r1923) (8/88) (DANA) Ⓓ [2] **DACOCD313/4**
10-12. F. Leider, L. Melchior, orch (r1923) (5/91) (PREI) Ⓓ [3] **89301**
10, 33(pt) J. Gadski, orch (r1913) (7/91) (CLUB) Ⓓ **CL99-109**
12. C. Katsaris (r1994: arr pf: H Rupp) (SONY) Ⓓ **SK58973**
12. L. Melchior, Berlin St Op Orch, L. Blech (r1929) (8/88) (DANA) Ⓓ [2] **DACOCD315/6**
12. G. Guszalewicz, L. Melchior, Berlin St Op Orch, L. Blech (r1928) (8/88) (DANA) Ⓓ [2] **DACOCD315/6**
12, 28. F. Völker, V. Ursuleac, Vienna St Op Orch, C. Krauss (pp1934) (9/95) (SCHW) Ⓓ [2] **314662**
13, 14, 15a W. Grossmann, A. Konetzni, Vienna St Op Orch, W. Furtwängler (pp1936) (6/94) (SCHW) Ⓓ **314502**
13-15. M. Lawrence, J. Claverie, Pasdeloup Orch, P. Coppola (French: r1933) (5/90) (PREI) Ⓓ **89011**
14, 15a L. Hofmann, A. Konetzni, Vienna St Op Orch, H. Knappertsbusch (pp1937) (1/95) (SCHW) Ⓓ [2] **314562**
14, 15a, 20(pt), 23b(pt), 31, 34, 36, 40-42. F. Leider, E. Leisner, F. Schorr, G. Ljungberg, G. Guszalewicz, E. Marherr-Wagner, L. Kindermann, Berlin St Op Orch, L. Blech (r1927) (4/95) (PEAR) Ⓓ [7] **GEMMCDS9137**
14, 17, 34, 38(pt), 40. F. Schorr, Berlin St Op Orch, L. Blech (PREI) Ⓓ [2] **89214**
14, 36. F. Leider, F. Schorr, Berlin St Op Orch, L. Blech (r1927) (PREI) Ⓓ **89098**
15a K. Flagstad, orch, H. Lange (r1935) (IMP) Ⓓ **GLRS105**
15a H. Wildbrunn, orch (r1919: 2 vers) (PREI) Ⓓ **89097**
15a K. Flagstad, orch, H. Lange (r1935) (SIMA) Ⓓ [3] **PSC1821(1)**
15a K. Flagstad, orch, H. Lange (r1935) (10/90) (RCA) Ⓓ **GD87915**
15a S. Sedlmair, anon (r1904) (7/91) (SYMP) Ⓓ **SYMCD1081**
15a F. Litvinne, A. Cortot (r1902) (10/92) (SYMP) Ⓓ **SYMCD1101**
15a F. Litvinne, anon (r1903) (10/92) (SYMP) Ⓓ **SYMCD1101**
15a K. Flagstad, orch, H. Lange (r1935) (7/93) (NIMB) Ⓓ **NI7847**
15a, 26. B. Nilsson, J. Vickers, NY Met Op Orch, H. von Karajan (pp1969) (MEMO) Ⓓ [2] **HR4275/6**
16-18. E. Leisner, F. Schorr, LSO, J. Barbirolli (r1932) (4/95) (PEAR) Ⓓ [7] **GEMMCDS9137**
17. K. Thorborg, RCA SO, K. Riedel (r1940) (4/94) (RCA) Ⓓ [6] **09026 61580-2(4)**
17. K. Thorborg, RCA SO, K. Riedel (r1940) (4/95) (PREI) Ⓓ **89084**
17. M. Klose, Berlin St Op Orch, B. Seidler-Winkler (r1939) (7/95) (PREI) Ⓓ **89082**
26. F. Austral, W. Widdop, LSO, A. Coates (r1926) (PEAR) Ⓓ **GEMMCD9146**
26. F. Leider, F. Soot, orch (r1925) (5/91) (PREI) Ⓓ [3] **89301**
26. M. Kurt, J. Urlus, orch (r1910) (7/92) (PEAR) Ⓓ [3] **GEMMCDS9925(1)**
26. K. Flagstad, S. Svanholm, Philh, K. Böhm (r1949) (7/93) (TEST) Ⓓ **SBT1018**
26, 27. K. Flagstad, S. Svanholm, Philh, K. Böhm (r1949) (10/94) (EMI) Ⓓ [4] **CMS5 65212-2**
26-28. K. Flagstad, S. Svanholm, VPO, G. Solti (r1957) (LOND) Ⓓ [5] **440 490-2LM5(1)**
26-28. K. Flagstad, VPO, G. Solti (r1957) (LOND) Ⓓ **440 495-2LM**
31. V. Schlosser, B. Lindholm, B. Fassbaender, H. Watts, H. Dernesch, V. Little, M. Tyler, C. Hellmann, VPO, G. Solti (DECC) Ⓓ **433 067-2DWO** (DECC) ▭ **433 067-4DWO**
31. V. Schlosser, B. Lindholm, H. Dernesch, V. Little, M. Tyler, B. Fassbaender, H. Watts, C. Hellmann, VPO, G. Solti (r1965) (DECC) Ⓓ **436 300-2DX** (DECC) ▭ **436 300-4DX**
31. D. Chorzempa (r1984; arr org) (PHIL) Ⓓ **438 309-2PM** (PHIL) ▭ **438 309-4PM**
31. Canadian Brass, BPO, Bayreuth Fest Orch, E. de Waart (r1991; arr Frackenpohl) (PHIL) Ⓓ **434 109-2PH**
31. V. Schlosser, B. Lindholm, B. Fassbaender, H. Watts, H. Dernesch, V. Little, M. Tyler, C. Hellmann, VPO, G. Solti (r1965) (DECC) Ⓓ **440 069-2DWO** (DECC) ▭ **440 069-4DWO**
31. A. Partington (r1993; arr Lemare) (PRIO) Ⓓ **PRCD479**
31, 43. H. Hotter, V. Schlosser, B. Lindholm, B. Fassbaender, H. Watts, H. Dernesch, V. Little, M. Tyler, C. Hellmann, VPO, G. Solti (DECC) Ⓓ **421 313-2DA**
31, 43. Cleveland Orch, G. Szell (11/92) (SONY) Ⓓ **SBK48175**
31, 43. Netherlands Rad PO, E. de Waart (r1992; arr Vlieger) (9/93) (FIDE) Ⓓ **9201**
33(pt) F. Leider, G. Ljungberg, Berlin St Op Orch, L. Blech (r1927) (PREI) Ⓓ **89098**
36. M. Lawrence, Pasdeloup Orch, P. Coppola (French: r1933) (5/90) (PREI) Ⓓ **89011**
36. F. Leider, orch (r1925) (5/91) (PREI) Ⓓ [3] **89301**
36. J. Gadski, orch (r1910) (7/91) (CLUB) Ⓓ **CL99-109**
36. M. Lawrence, Pasdeloup Orch, P. Coppola (French: r1933) (1/92) (EMI) Ⓓ [4] **CMS7 64008-2(2)**
36. F. Leider, Berlin St Op Orch, L. Blech (r1927) (7/92) (PEAR) Ⓓ [3] **GEMMCDS9925(2)**
36-38, 39a, 39b, 40-43. B. Nilsson, H. Hotter, Philh, L. Ludwig (r1957) (10/94) (EMI) Ⓓ [4] **CMS5 65212-2**
36, 40. F. Leider, F. Schorr, Berlin St Op Orch, L. Blech (r1927) (MSCM) Ⓓ [2] **MM30285** (MSCM) ▭ [2] **MM40107**
40. F. Schorr, orch (r1921) (PREI) Ⓓ **89052**
40. J. von Manowarda, orch (r1922) (PREI) Ⓓ **89069**
40. J. Herrmann, VPO, R. Moralt (r1943) (PREI) Ⓓ **89076**
40. H. Hotter, Berlin Staatskapelle, R. Heger (r1942) (PREI) Ⓓ **90200**
40. H. Hermann Nissen, Berlin SO, F. Zweig (r1927) (PREI) Ⓓ **89090**
40. M. Schenk, Nuremberg SO, K. Seibel (12/91) (COLO) Ⓓ **COL34 9004**
40. M. Journet, SO, P. Coppola (French: r1928) (1/92) (EMI) Ⓓ [4] **CMS7 64008-2(2)**
40. R. Bockelmann, Berlin St Op Orch, C. Schmalstich (r1930) (1/92) (EMI) Ⓓ [4] **CMS7 64008-2(2)**
40. N. de Angelis, orch, L. Molajoli (Ital: r1929) (7/92) (PREI) Ⓓ **89042**
40. A. Van Rooy, anon (r1902) (7/92) (PEAR) Ⓓ [3] **GEMMCDS9923(2)**
40. F. Schorr, Berlin St Op Orch, L. Blech (r1927) (7/92) (PEAR) Ⓓ [3] **GEMMCDS9925(2)**
40(pt) C. Formichi, orch (Ital: r1920) (11/92) (MEMO) Ⓓ [2] **HR4408/9(2)**
40. A. Van Rooy, anon (r1902) (3/93) (SYMP) Ⓓ **SYMCD1100**
40. V. Sharonov, anon (Russ: r1903) (7/93) (SYMP) Ⓓ **SYMCD1105**
40. M. Journet, SO, P. Coppola (r1928: French) (1/94) (CLUB) Ⓓ **CL99-034**
40. G. Hann, Berlin Deutsche Op Orch, H. Steinkopf (bp1942) (5/94) (PREI) Ⓓ **90168**
40. C. Formichi, orch (r1920: Ital) (11/94) (PREI) Ⓓ **89055**
40. J-F. Delmas, anon (r1905: Fr) (12/94) (SYMP) Ⓓ **SYMCD1172**
40, 42. A. Kipnis, Berlin St Op Orch, L. Blech (r1926) (10/91) (PEAR) Ⓓ **GEMMCD9451**
40, 43. L. Tibbett, Philadelphia, L. Stokowski (r1934: arr Stokowski) (3/90) (RCA) Ⓓ **GD87808**
40-43. N. Bailey, New Philh, O. Klemperer (10/91) (EMI) Ⓓ [2] **CMS7 63835-2**
40, 43. Seattle SO, G. Schwarz (r1992) (4/94) (DELO) Ⓓ **DE3120**
40-43. D. Fischer-Dieskau, BRSO, R. Kubelík (r1977) (10/94) (EMI) Ⓓ [4] **CMS5 65212-2**
40-43. P. Schoeffler, LSO, K. Rankl (r1946) (1/95) (PREI) Ⓓ **90190**
40-43. M. Reizen, Bolshoi Th Orch, V. Nebolsin (r1950) (2/95) (PREI) Ⓓ **89080**
40, 43, 44. VPO, G. Solti (DECC) ƠƠ **410 137-5DH**
40, 43, 44. BPO, K. Tennstedt (r1980) (EMI) Ⓓ [2] **CZS5 68616-2**
40, 43, 44. VPO, G. Solti (11/83) (DECC) Ⓓ **410 137-2DH**
40, 43, 44. J. Tomlinson, Philh, F. d'Avalos (3/90) (ASV) Ⓓ **CDDCA666**
43. Boston SO, C. Munch (r1957) (RCA) Ⓓ **GD60686**
43. H. Hotter, VPO, G. Solti (DECC) Ⓓ **433 068-2DWO** (DECC) ▭ **433 068-4DWO**
43. NYPO, L. Bernstein (r1968) (SONY) Ⓓ **SMK47643**
43. Philadelphia, L. Stokowski (r1939) (PEAR) Ⓓ [2] **GEMMCDS9076**
43. J. Hofmann (r1923: arr pf: Brassin) (VAI) Ⓓ **VAIA1047**
43. LSO, A. Coates (r1926) (4/93) (KOCH) Ⓓ [2] **37704-2**
43, 44. Vienna SO, Y. Ahronovitch (LASE) Ⓓ **15 612** (LASE) ▭ **79 612**
43, 44. Cleveland Orch, G. Szell (CBS) Ⓓ [2] **CD46466**
43, 44. C. Katsaris (r1994: freely arr pf: L Brassin) (SONY) Ⓓ **SK58973**
44. NBC SO, A. Toscanini, H. Keith (bp1948) (RCA) ◘ **790 351**
44. LPO, A. Boult (EMI) Ⓓ **CDM7 69596-2**

44. H. Britton (arr Lemare) (ASV) ① **CDQS6028**
(ASV) ⊟ **ZCQS6028**
44. LPO, K. Tennstedt (EMI) ◖ **LDB9 91234-1**
(EMI) ▣ **MVD9 91234-3**
44. LSO, B. Tuckwell (IMP) ① **PCDS4**
(IMP) ⊟ **PCDSC4**
44. LSO, B. Tuckwell (IMP) ① **PCDS8**
(IMP) ⊟ **PCDSC8**
44. LSO, L. Stokowski (DECC) ① **433 639-2DSP**
(DECC) ⊟ **433 639-4DSP**
44. LPO, A. Boult (EMI) ① [2] **CZS7 62539-2**
44. Chicago SO, D. Barenboim (ERAT) ① **2292-45786-2**
44. BPO, K. Tennstedt (EMI) ① **CDC2 53045-2**
(EMI) ⊟ **EL2 53045-4**
44. NYPO, L. Bernstein (SONY) ① **SBK39438**
44. NBC SO, A. Toscanini (r1946) (RCA) ① **GD60306**
44. LSO, B. Tuckwell (IMP) ① **PCDS15**
(IMP) ⊟ **PCDSC15**
44. LPO, A. Boult (CFP) ① **CD-CFP4606**
(CFP) ⊟ **TC-CFP4606**
44. RPO, R. Stapleton (r1990) (RPO) ① [2] **CDRPD9006**
(RPO) ⊟ [2] **ZCRPD9006**
44. VPO, G. Solti (r1982) (DECC) ① **440 947-2DH**
(DECC) ⊟ **440 947-4DH**
44. National SO, A. Dorati (r1976) (BELA) ① **450 025-2**
(BELA) ⊟ **450 025-4**
44. NYPO, L. Bernstein (r1967) (SONY) ① **SMK47643**
44. RPO, V. Handley (r1993) (TRIN) ① **TRP008**
(TRIN) ⊟ **MCTRP008**
44. BPO, H. von Karajan (r1966) (DG) ① [2] **439 687-2GX2**
44. Sydney SO, J. Serebrier (IMG) ① **IMGCD1611**
44. VPO, H. Knappertsbusch (r1953) (DECC) ① **440 062-2DM**
44. BPO, K. Tennstedt (EMIL) ① **CDZ101**
(EMIL) ⊟ **LZ101**
44. Luxembourg RSO, L. de Froment (FORL) ① **FF020**
44. Luxembourg Rad & TV SO, P. Cao (FORL) ① **FF046**
44. Leningrad PO, E. Mravinsky (pp1965) (MELO) ① **74321 25199-2**
44. Leningrad PO, E. Mravinsky (pp1965) (MELO) ① [10] **74321 25189-2**
44. Los Angeles PO, E. Leinsdorf (r1977) (SHEF) ① **10052-2-G**
44. Staatskapelle Dresden, M. Janowski (r1990s) (RCA) ① **09026 62674-2**
44. Los Angeles PO, E. Leinsdorf (8/87) (SHEF) ① **CD-7/8**
44. LPO, K.A. Rickenbacher (11/87) (CFP) ① **CD-CFP9008**
44. LPO, W. Furtwängler (pp1937) (2/89) (ACAN) ① **43 121**
44. Cincinnati Pops, E. Kunzel (10/89) (TELA) ① **CD80170**
44. RPO, R. Stapleton (10/90) (IMP) ① **MCD15**
(10/90) (IMP) ⊟ **MCC15**
44. Philh, O. Klemperer (r1960) (11/90) (EMI) ① **CDM7 63618-2**
44. Philh, Y. Simonov (10/91) (COLL) ① **Coll1207-2**
44. NBC SO, A. Toscanini (r1952) (12/91) (RCA) ① **GD60264**
44. NYPO, W. Mengelberg (r1926) (4/92) (PEAR) ① [3] **GEMMCDS9922**
44. Leningrad PO, E. Mravinsky (pp1978) (6/92) (ERAT) ① **2292-45762-2**
44. Leningrad PO, E. Mravinsky (pp1978) (6/92) (ERAT) ① [11] **2292-45763-2**
44. Oslo PO, M. Jansons (12/92) (EMI) ① **CDC7 54583-2**
44. Leningrad PO, E. Mravinsky (pp1967) (3/94) (RUSS) ① **RDCD11166**
44. VPO, W. Furtwängler (r1949) (4/94) (EMI) ① [2] **CHS7 64935-2**
44. T. Trotter (r1992: trans org: E Lemare) (4/94) (DECC) ① **436 656-2DH**
44. Queen's Hall Orch, Henry Wood (r1935) (9/94) (DUTT) ① **CDAX8008**

Der **Ring des Nibelungen: Part 3, 'Siegfried'– opera: 3 acts (1876—Bayreuth) (Lib. cpsr)**

EXCERPTS. ACT 1: 1. Prelude; 2. Zwangvolle Plage!; 3. Hoiho! Hoiho! Hau ein!; 4. Als zullendes Kind; 5. Vieles lehrtest du, Mime; 6. Einst lag wimmernd ein Weib; 7. Soll ich der Kunde glauben; 8. Heil dir, weiser Schmied!; 9. Hier sitz' ich am Herd; 10. Auf wolkigen Höhn; 11. Was zu wissen dir frommt; 12. Verfluchtes Licht; 13. Bist du es, Kind?; 14. Fühltest du nie im finstren Wald; 15. Her mit den Stücken; 16. Nothung! Neidliches Schwert! (Forging Song); 17a. Hoho! Hoho! Hahei!; 17b. Schmiede, mein Hammer; 18. Den der Bruder schuf. ACT 2: 19. Prelude; 20. In Wald und Nacht; 21a. Wer naht dort schimmernd; 21b. Zur Neidhöhle fuhr ich; 22. Fafner, Fafner! Erwache, Wurm!; 23a. Ich lieg' und besitz; 23b. Nun, Alberich, das schlug fehl; 24. Wir sind zur Stelle!; 25a. Dass der mein Vater nicht ist (Forest murmurs); 25b. Forest murmurs (concert version); 26a. Meine Mutter, ein Menschenweib!; 26b. Du holdes Vöglein!; 27. Siegfried's horn-call; 28. Haha! Da hätte mein Lied; 29a. Da lieg, neidischer Kerl; 29b. Wer bist du, Kühner Knabe; 30. Zur Kunde taugt kein Toter; 31. Wohin schleichst du?; 32. Wilkommen, Siegfried!; 33. Neides Zoll zahlt Nothung; 34. Da lieg auch du, dunkler Wurm; 35. Freundliches Vöglein; 36a. Nun sing! Ich lausche; 36b. Hei! Siegfried erschlug nun den schlimmen Zwerg. ACT 3: 37. Prelude; 38. Wache, Wala! Erwach!; 39. Stark ruft das Lied; 40a. Weisst du, was Wotan will?; 40b. Dir Unweisen ruf' ich; 41. Dort seh' ich Siegfried nahn; 42. Mein Vöglein schwebte mir fort!; 43. Kenntest du mich, kühner Spross; 44. orchestral interlude. Scene 3: 45a. Selig Öde auf sonniger Höh!; 45b. Was ruht dort schlummernd; 46a. Dass ist kein Mann!; 46b. Brennender Zauber; 47. Heil dir, Sonne!; 48. O Siegfried! Seliger Held!; 49. Dort seh' ich Grane; 50. Ewig war ich, ewig bin ich.

Siegfried S. Jerusalem
Wanderer J. Morris
Brünnhilde H. Behrens
Mime H. Zednik
Alberich E. Wlaschiha
Erda B. Svendén
Fafner M. Salminen
Wood Bird D. Upshaw
NY Met Op Orch, James Levine, O. Schenk, B. Large
(5/92) (DG) ▣ [7] **072 422-3GH7**

Siegfried R. Kollo
Wanderer T. Adam
Brünnhilde J. Altmeyer
Mime P. Schreier
Alberich S. Nimsgern
Erda O. Wenkel
Fafner M. Salminen
Woodbird N. Sharp
Staatskapelle Dresden, M. Janowski
(EURO) ① [14] **GD69003**

Siegfried M. Jung
Wanderer D. McIntyre
Brünnhilde G. Jones
Mime H. Zednik
Alberich H. Becht
Erda O. Wenkel
Fafner F. Hübner
Woodbird N. Sharp
Bayreuth Fest Orch, P. Boulez (pp1980)
(PHIL) ① [32] **434 420-2PM32(2)**

Siegfried S. Jerusalem
Wanderer J. Tomlinson
Brünnhilde Anne Evans
Mime G. Clark
Alberich G. von Kannen
Erda B. Svendén
Fafner P. Kang
Woodbird H. Leidland
Bayreuth Fest Orch, D. Barenboim, H. Kupfer (pp1992)
(TELD) ◖ [3] **4509-94193-6**
(TELD) ▣ **4509-94193-3**

Siegfried R. Kollo
Wanderer T. Adam
Brünnhilde J. Altmeyer
Mime P. Schreier
Alberich S. Nimsgern
Erda O. Wenkel
Fafner M. Salminen
Woodbird N. Sharp
Staatskapelle Dresden, M. Janowski
(10/84) (EURO) ① [4] **GD69006**

Siegfried W. Windgassen
Wanderer H. Hotter
Brünnhilde B. Nilsson
Mime G. Stolze
Alberich G. Neidlinger
Erda M. Höffgen
Fafner K. Böhme
Woodbird J. Sutherland
VPO, G. Solti (r1962)
(12/84) (DECC) ① [4] **414 110-2DH4**

Siegfried Jess Thomas
Wanderer T. Stewart
Brünnhilde H. Dernesch
Mime G. Stolze
Alberich Z. Kélémen
Erda O. Dominguez
Fafner K. Ridderbusch
Woodbird C. Gayer
BPO, H. von Karajan (r1968/9)
(7/85) (DG) ① [4] **415 150-2GH4**

Siegfried W. Windgassen
Wanderer T. Adam
Brünnhilde B. Nilsson
Mime E. Wohlfahrt
Alberich G. Neidlinger
Erda V. Soukupová
Fafner K. Böhme
Woodbird E. Köth
Bayreuth Fest Orch, K. Böhm (pp1967)
(8/85) (PHIL) ① [4] **412 483-2PH4**

Siegfried W. Windgassen
Wanderer H. Hotter
Brünnhilde A. Varnay
Mime P. Kuen
Alberich G. Neidlinger
Erda M. von Ilosvay
Fafner J. Greindl
Woodbird R. Streich
Bayreuth Fest Orch, C. Krauss (pp1953)
(6/88) (FOYE) ① [15] **15-CF2011**

Siegfried W. Windgassen
Wanderer H. Hotter
Brünnhilde A. Varnay
Mime P. Kuen
Alberich G. Neidlinger
Erda M. von Ilosvay
Fafner J. Greindl
Woodbird R. Streich
Bayreuth Fest Orch, C. Krauss (pp1953)
(6/88) (FOYE) ① [4] **4-CF2009**

Siegfried W. Windgassen
Mime P. Kuen
Wanderer H. Hotter
Alberich G. Neidlinger
Brünnhilde A. Varnay
Erda M. von Ilosvay
Fafner J. Greindl
Woodbird R. Streich
Bayreuth Fest Orch, C. Krauss (pp1953)
(6/88) (LAUD) ① [4] **LCD4 4004**

Siegfried W. Windgassen
Wanderer H. Hotter
Brünnhilde B. Nilsson
Mime G. Stolze
Alberich G. Neidlinger
Erda M. Höffgen
Fafner K. Böhme
Woodbird J. Sutherland
VPO, G. Solti (r1962)
(3/89) (DECC) ① [15] **414 100-2DM15**

Siegfried L. Suthaus
Wanderer F. Frantz
Brünnhilde M. Mödl
Mime J. Patzak
Alberich A. Pernerstorfer
Erda M. Klose
Fafner J. Greindl
Woodbird R. Streich
Rome RAI Orch, W. Furtwängler (bp1953)
(2/91) (EMI) ① [13] **CZS7 67123-2**

Siegfried A. Remedios
Wanderer N. Bailey
Brünnhilde R. Hunter
Mime G. Dempsey
Alberich D. Hammond-Stroud
Erda A. Collins
Fafner C. Grant
Woodbird M. London
Sadler's Wells Op Orch, R. Goodall (Eng: pp1973)
(3/91) (EMI) ① [4] **CMS7 63595-2**

Siegfried S. Jerusalem
Wanderer J. Morris
Brünnhilde E. Marton
Mime P. Haage
Alberich T. Adam
Erda J. Rappé
Fafner K. Rydl
Woodbird K. Te Kanawa
BRSO, B. Haitink (r1990)
(11/91) (EMI) ① [4] **CDS7 54290-2**

Siegfried R. Goldberg

34, 35, 36a, 36b L. Melchior, N. Gruhn, LSO, A. Coates (r1929) (7/90) (CLAR) ⓒ **CDGSE78-50-33**
36a, 36b L. Melchior, N. Gruhn, LSO, A. Coates (r1929) (MSCM) ⓒ [2] **MM30285** (MSCM) ▭ [2] **MM40107**
37-39, 40a, 40b E. Schipper, M. Olczewska, Vienna St Op Orch, K. Alwin (r1927) (DANA) ⓒ [3] **DACOCD319/21**
37-39, 40b M. Olczewska, E. Schipper, Vienna St Op Orch, K. Alwin (r1928) (4/95) (PEAR) ⓒ [7] **GEMMCDS9137**
38. J. von Manowarda, orch (r1922) (PREI) ⓒ **89069**
39. M. Olczewska, E. Schipper, Vienna St Op Orch, K. Alwin (r1928) (1/92) (EMI) ⓒ [4] **CMS7 64008-2(2)**
43. L. Melchior, R. Bockelmann, LSO, A. Coates (r1929) (7/90) (CLAR) ⓒ **CDGSE78-50-33**
43, 44, 45a, 45b, 46a, 46b L. Melchior, R. Bockelmann, LSO, A. Coates, R. Heger (r1929/30) (DANA) ⓒ [3] **DACOCD319/21**
44. Rome RAI Orch, W. Furtwängler (bp1953) (2/89) (ACAN) ⓒ **43 121**
47. F. Leider, F. Soot, orch (r1925) (5/91) (PREI) ⓒ [3] **89301**
47, 48(pt), 50. J. Kalenberg, A. Konetzni, Vienna St Op Orch, H. Knappertsbusch (pp1936) (1/95) (SCHW) ⓒ [2] **314562**
47, 48, 50. F. Easton, L. Melchior, orch, R. Heger (r1932) (4/95) (PEAR) ⓒ [7] **GEMMCDS9137**
47-50. L. Melchior, F. Easton, ROHO, R. Heger (r1932) (DANA) ⓒ [3] **DACOCD319/21**
47-50. L. Melchior, F. Easton, LSO, R. Heger (r1932) (MSCM) ⓒ [2] **MM30285** (MSCM) ▭ [2] **MM40107**
47-50. F. Leider, R. Laubenthal, Berlin St Op Orch, L. Blech (r1927) (2/90) (PREI) ⓒ **89004**
47, 50. F. Leider, R. Laubenthal, Berlin St Op Orch, L. Blech (r1927) (1/92) (EMI) ⓒ [4] **CMS7 64008-2(2)**
47-50. K. Flagstad, S. Svanholm, Philh, G. Sébastian (r1951) (10/94) (EMI) ⓒ [4] **CMS5 65212-2**
50. H. Wildbrunn, orch (r1919/20: 2 vers) (PREI) ⓒ **89097**
50. K. Flagstad, S. Svanholm, Philh, G. Sébastian (r1951) (8/89) (EMI) ⓒ **CDH7 63030-2**
50. G. Lubin, orch, H. Defosse (French: r1929) (5/91) (CLUB) ⓒ **CL99-022**
50. G. Lubin, orch (French: r1929) (5/91) (EPM) ⓒ **150 052**
50. F. Leider, F. Soot, orch (r1925) (5/91) (PREI) ⓒ [3] **89301**
50. J. Gadski, orch (r1910) (7/91) (CLUB) ⓒ **CL99-109**
50. G. Lubin, orch, H. Defosse (French: r1930) (1/92) (EMI) ⓒ [4] **CMS7 64008-2(2)**

Der **Ring des Nibelungen: Part 4, 'Götterdämmerung'– opera: prologue & 3 acts (1876—Bayreuth) (Lib. cpsr)**

EXCERPTS. PROLOGUE: 1a. Introduction; 1b. Welch Licht leuchtet dort?; 2. orchestral interlude (Dawn); 3. Zu neuen Taten; 4. O heilige Götter!; 5. orchestral interlude (Siegfried's Rhine Journey). ACT 1: 6. Nun hör, Hagen; 7a. Was weckst du Zweifel und Zwist!; 7b. Brächte Siegfried die Braut; 8a. Heil! Siegfried, teurer Held!; 8b. Wer ist Gibichs, Sohn?; 9. Begrüsse froh, o Held; 10. Willkommen, Gast, in Gibichs Haus!; 11. Hast du, Gunther, ein Weib?; 12a. Blut-Brüderschaft schwöre ein Eid!; 12b. Blühenden Lebens labendes Blut; 13. Hier sitz' ich zur Wacht (Hagen's Watch); 14. orchestral interlude; 15. Altgewohntes Geräusch; 16a. Höre mit Sinn (Waltraute's Narration); 16b. Seit er von dir geschieden; 17. Da sann ich nach; 18. Welch banger Träume Mären; 19. Brünnhild! Ein Freier kam. ACT 2: 20. Prelude; 21. Schläfst du, Hagen, mein Sohn; 22. orchestral interlude; 23. Hoiho, Hagen! Müder Mann!; 24. Hoiho! Ihr Gibichsmannen; 25. Heil dir, Gunther; 26. Brünnhild', die hehrste Frau; 27a. Was ist ihr? Ist sie entrückt?; 27b. Was müht Brünnhildes Blick?; 28. Helle Wehr! Heilige Waffe!; 29. Welches Unholds List liegt hier verhohlen?; 30. Dir hilft kein Hirn. ACT 3: 31. Prelude; 32. Frau Sonne sendet lichte Strahlen; 33. Hoiho!; 34. Trink, Gunther, trink; 35. Mime heiss ein mürrischer Zwerg (Siegfried's Narration); 36. Brünnhilde, heilige Braut!; 37. Siegfried's funeral march; 38. War das sein Horn?; 39. Schweigt eures Jammers; 40. Starke Scheite (Brünnhildes's Immolation); 41. Mein Erbe nun nehm' ich zu eigen; 42. Fliegt heim, ihr Raben!; 43. Zurück vom Ring (orchestral finale); 44. Dawn and Siegfried's Rhine Journey (concert version).

Brünnhilde H. Behrens
Siegfried S. Jerusalem
Hagen M. Salminen
Alberich E. Wlaschiha
Gunther A. Raffell
Gutrune H. Lisowska
Waltraute C. Ludwig
Woglinde K. Erickson
Wellgunde D. Kesling
Flosshilde M. Parsons
Norn I G. Bean
Norn II J. Cactlo
Norn III A. Gruber
NY Met Op Chor, NY Met Op Orch, James Levine, O. Schenk, B. Large (5/92) (DG) ▭▭ [7] **072 422-3GH7**

Brünnhilde J. Altmeyer
Siegfried R. Kollo
Hagen M. Salminen
Alberich S. Nimsgern
Gunther H.G. Nöcker
Gutrune N. Sharp
Waltraute O. Wenkel
Woglinde L. Popp
Wellgunde U. Priew
Flosshilde H. Schwarz
Norn I A. Gjevang
Norn II D. Evangelatos
Norn III R. Falcon
Leipzig Rad Chor, Dresden St Op Chor, Staatskapelle Dresden, M. Janowski (EURO) ⓒ [14] **GD69003**

Brünnhilde G. Jones
Siegfried M. Jung
Hagen F. Hübner
Alberich H. Becht
Gunther F. Mazura
Gutrune J. Altmeyer
Waltraute G. Killebrew
Woglinde N. Sharp
Wellgunde I. Gramatzki
Flosshilde M. Schiml
Bayreuth Fest Chor, Bayreuth Fest Orch, P. Boulez (pp1979) (PHIL) ⓒ [32] **434 420-2PM32(1)**

Brünnhilde B. Nilsson
Siegfried B. Aldenhoff
Hagen G. Frick
Alberich O. Kraus
Gunther H. Uhde
Gutrune Leonie Rysanek
Waltraute I. Malaniuk
Woglinde G. Sommerschuh
Wellgunde E. Lindermeier
Flosshilde R. Michaelis
Norn I I. Barth
Norn II H. Töpper
Norn III M. Schech
Bavarian St Op Chor, Bavarian St Orch, H. Knappertsbusch (pp1955) (ORFE) ⓒ [4] **C356944L**

Brünnhilde J. Altmeyer
Siegfried R. Kollo
Hagen M. Salminen
Alberich S. Nimsgern
Gunther H.G. Nöcker
Gutrune N. Sharp
Waltraute O. Wenkel
Woglinde L. Popp
Wellgunde U. Priew
Flosshilde H. Schwarz
Norn I A. Gjevang
Norn II D. Evangelatos
Norn III R. Falcon
Leipzig Rad Chor, Dresden St Op Chor, Staatskapelle Dresden, M. Janowski (10/84) (EURO) ⓒ [4] **GD69007**

Brünnhilde B. Nilsson
Siegfried W. Windgassen
Hagen J. Greindl
Alberich G. Neidlinger
Gunther T. Stewart
Gutrune L. Dvořáková
Waltraute M. Mödl
Woglinde D. Siebert
Wellgunde H. Dernesch
Flosshilde S. Wagner
Norn I M. Höffgen
Norn II A. Burmeister
Norn III A. Silja
Bayreuth Fest Chor, Bayreuth Fest Orch, K. Böhm (pp1967) (5/85) (PHIL) ⓒ [4] **412 488-2PH4**

Brünnhilde B. Nilsson
Siegfried W. Windgassen
Hagen G. Frick
Alberich G. Neidlinger
Gunther D. Fischer-Dieskau
Gutrune C. Watson
Waltraute C. Ludwig
Woglinde L. Popp
Wellgunde G. Jones
Flosshilde M. Guy
Norn I H. Watts
Norn II G. Hoffman
Norn III A. Välkki
Vienna St Op Chor, VPO, G. Solti (r1964) (5/85) (DECC) ⓒ [4] **414 115-2DH4**

Brünnhilde H. Dernesch
Siegfried H. Brilioth
Hagen K. Ridderbusch
Alberich Z. Kélémen
Gunther T. Stewart
Gutrune G. Janowitz
Waltraute; Norn II C. Ludwig
Woglinde L. Rebmann
Wellgunde E. Moser
Flosshilde A. Reynolds
Norn I L. Chookasian
Norn III C. Ligendza
Berlin Deutsche Op Chor, BPO, H. von Karajan (r1969/70) (7/85) (DG) ⓒ [4] **415 155-2GH4**

Brünnhilde A. Varnay
Siegfried W. Windgassen
Hagen J. Greindl
Alberich G. Neidlinger
Gunther H. Uhde
Gutrune N. Hinsch-Gröndahl
Waltraute; Norn II I. Malaniuk
Woglinde E. Zimmermann
Wellgunde H. Plümacher
Flosshilde G. Litz
Norn I M. von Ilosvay
Norn III R. Resnik
Bayreuth Fest Chor, Bayreuth Fest Orch, C. Krauss (pp1953) (6/88) (FOYE) ⓒ [4] **4-CF2010**

Brünnhilde A. Varnay
Siegfried W. Windgassen
Hagen J. Greindl
Alberich G. Neidlinger
Gunther H. Uhde
Gutrune N. Hinsch-Gröndahl
Waltraute; Norn II I. Malaniuk
Woglinde E. Zimmermann
Wellgunde H. Plümacher
Flosshilde G. Litz
Norn I M. von Ilosvay
Norn III R. Resnik
Bayreuth Fest Chor, Bayreuth Fest Orch, C. Krauss (pp1953) (6/88) (FOYE) ⓒ [15] **15-CF2011**

Brünnhilde A. Varnay
Siegfried W. Windgassen
Hagen J. Greindl
Alberich G. Neidlinger
Gunther H. Uhde
Gutrune N. Hinsch-Gröndahl
Waltraute; Norn II I. Malaniuk
Woglinde E. Zimmermann
Wellgunde H. Plümacher
Flosshilde G. Litz
Norn I M. von Ilosvay
Norn III R. Resnik
Bayreuth Fest Chor, Bayreuth Fest Orch, C. Krauss (pp1953) (6/88) (LAUD) ⓒ [4] **LCD4 4005**

Brünnhilde B. Nilsson
Siegfried W. Windgassen
Hagen G. Frick
Alberich G. Neidlinger
Gunther D. Fischer-Dieskau
Gutrune C. Watson
Waltraute C. Ludwig
Woglinde L. Popp
Wellgunde G. Jones
Flosshilde M. Guy
Norn I H. Watts
Norn II G. Hoffman
Norn III A. Välkki
Vienna St Op Chor, VPO, G. Solti (r1964) (3/89) (DECC) ⓒ [15] **414 100-2DM15**

Brünnhilde M. Mödl
Siegfried L. Suthaus
Hagen J. Greindl
Alberich A. Pernerstorfer
Gunther A. Poell
Gutrune; Woglinde; Norn III S. Jurinac

Waltraute; Norn I M. Klose
Wellgunde M. Gabory
Flosshilde; Norn II H. Rössl-Majdan
Rome RAI Chor, Rome RAI Orch, W. Furtwängler (bp1953)
(2/91) (EMI) Ⓓ [13] **CZS7 67123-2**
Brünnhilde H. Behrens
Siegfried R. Goldberg
Hagen M. Salminen
Alberich E. Wlaschiha
Gunther B. Weikl
Gutrune C. Studer
Waltraute H. Schwarz
Woglinde H-K. Hong
Wellgunde D. Kesling
Flosshilde M. Parsons
Norn I H. Dernesch
Norn II T. Troyanos
Norn III A. Gruber
NY Met Op Chor, NY Met Op Orch, James Levine
(8/91) (DG) Ⓓ [4] **429 385-2GH4**
Brünnhilde H. Dernesch
Siegfried H. Brilioth
Hagen K. Ridderbusch
Alberich Z. Kélémen
Gunther T. Stewart
Gutrune G. Janowitz
Waltraute; Norn II C. Ludwig
Woglinde L. Rebmann
Wellgunde E. Moser
Flosshilde A. Reynolds
Norn I L. Chookasian
Norn III C. Ligendza
Berlin Deutsche Op Chor, BPO, H. von Karajan
(4/92) (DG) Ⓓ [15] **435 211-2GX15**
Brünnhilde H. Behrens
Siegfried S. Jerusalem
Hagen M. Salminen
Alberich E. Wlaschiha
Gunther A. Raffell
Gutrune H. Lisowska
Waltraute C. Ludwig
Woglinde K. Erickson
Wellgunde D. Kesling
Flosshilde M. Parsons
Norn I G. Bean
Norn II J. Castle
Norn III A. Gruber
NY Met Op Chor, NY Met Op Orch, James Levine, O. Schenk, B. Large
(5/92) (DG) ◖ [3] **072 421-1GH3**
(5/92) (DG) ▣ [2] **072 421-3GH2**
Brünnhilde G. Jones
Siegfried M. Jung
Hagen F. Hübner
Alberich H. Becht
Gunther F. Mazura
Gutrune J. Altmeyer
Waltraute G. Killebrew
Woglinde N. Sharp
Wellgunde I. Gramatzki
Flosshilde M. Schiml
Norn I O. Wenkel
Norn II G. Schnaut
Norn III K. Clarke
Bayreuth Fest Chor, Bayreuth Fest Orch, P. Boulez, P. Chéreau
(5/92) (PHIL) ◖ [3] **070 404-1PHE3**
(5/92) (PHIL) ▣ [2] **070 404-3PHE2**
Brünnhilde H. Behrens
Siegfried R. Kollo
Hagen M. Salminen
Alberich E. Wlaschiha
Gunther H.G. Nöcker
Gutrune L. Balslev
Waltraute W. Meier
Woglinde J. Kaufman
Wellgunde A.M. Blasi
Flosshilde B. Calm
Norn I M. Lipovšek
Norn II I. Karrasch
Norn III P. Thorn
Bavarian St Op Chor, Bavarian St Orch, W. Sawallisch (pp1989)
(5/92) (EMI) ◖ [3] **LDF9 91287-1**
(5/92) (EMI) ▣ [2] **MVD9 91287-3**
Brünnhilde H. Behrens
Siegfried R. Kollo
Hagen M. Salminen
Alberich E. Wlaschiha
Gunther H.G. Nöcker
Gutrune L. Balslev
Waltraute W. Meier
Woglinde J. Kaufman
Woglinde A.M. Blasi
Flosshilde B. Calm
Norn I M. Lipovšek
Norn II I. Karrasch
Norn III P. Thorn
Bavarian St Op Chor, Bavarian St Orch, W. Sawallisch (pp1989)
(5/92) (EMI) ◖ [10] **LDX9 91275-1**
(5/92) (EMI) ▣ [8] **MVX9 91275-3**
Brünnhilde E. Marton
Siegfried S. Jerusalem
Hagen J. Tomlinson
Alberich T. Adam
Gunther T. Hampson
Gutrune E-M. Bundschuh
Waltraute M. Lipovšek
Woglinde J. Kaufman
Wellgunde S. Herman
Flosshilde C. Hagen
Norn I J. van Nes
Norn II A.S. von Otter
Norn III J. Eaglen
Bavarian Rad Chor, BRSO, B. Haitink (r1991)
(9/92) (EMI) Ⓓ [4] **CDS7 54485-2**
Brünnhilde G. Jones
Siegfried M. Jung
Hagen F. Hübner
Alberich H. Becht
Gunther F. Mazura
Gutrune J. Altmeyer
Waltraute G. Killebrew
Woglinde N. Sharp
Wellgunde I. Gramatzki
Flosshilde M. Schiml
Norn I O. Wenkel
Norn II G. Schnaut
Norn III K. Clarke
Bayreuth Fest Chor, Bayreuth Fest Orch, P. Boulez (pp1979)
(10/92) (PHIL) Ⓓ [4] **434 424-2PH4**
Brünnhilde R. Hunter
Siegfried A. Remedios
Hagen A. Haugland
Alberich D. Hammond-Stroud
Gunther N. Welsby
Gutrune M. Curphey
Waltraute K. Pring
Woglinde V. Masterson
Wellgunde S. Squires
Flosshilde H. Attfield
Norn I A. Collins
Norn II G. Knight
Norn III Anne Evans
ENO Chor, ENO Orch, R. Goodall (Eng: pp1977)
(11/92) (EMI) Ⓓ [5] **CMS7 64244-2**
Brünnhilde M. Fuchs
Siegfried S. Svanholm
Hagen F. Dalberg
Alberich R. Burg
Gunther E. Koch
Gutrune E. Fischer
Waltraute; Norn I C. Kallab
Woglinde H. Scheppan
Wellgunde I. Langhammer
Flosshilde M. Booth
Norn II H. Jachnow
Norn III C. Siewart
Bayreuth Fest Chor, Bayreuth Fest Orch, K. Elmendorff (pp1942)
(1/94) (PREI) Ⓓ [4] **90164**
Brünnhilde H. Behrens
Siegfried R. Goldberg
Hagen M. Salminen
Alberich E. Wlaschiha
Gunther B. Weikl
Gutrune C. Studer
Waltraute H. Schwarz
Woglinde H-K. Hong
Wellgunde D. Kesling
Flosshilde M. Parsons
Norn I H. Dernesch
Norn II T. Troyanos
Norn III A. Gruber
NY Met Op Chor, NY Met Op Orch, James Levine (r1989)
(10/94) (DG) Ⓓ [14] **445 354-2GX14**
Brünnhilde Anne Evans
Siegfried S. Jerusalem
Hagen P. Kang
Alberich G. von Kannen
Gunther B. Brinkmann
Gutrune E-M. Bundschuh
Waltraute W. Meier
Woglinde H. Leidland
Wellgunde A. Küttenbaum
Flosshilde J. Turner
Norn I B. Svendén
Norn II L. Finnie
Norn III U. Priew
Bayreuth Fest Chor, Bayreuth Fest Orch, D. Barenboim (pp1991)
(10/94) (TELD) Ⓓ [4] **4509-94194-2**
Brünnhilde B. Nilsson
Siegfried W. Windgassen
Hagen J. Greindl
Alberich G. Neidlinger
Gunther T. Stewart
Gutrune L. Dvořáková
Waltraute M. Mödl
Woglinde D. Siebert
Wellgunde H. Dernesch
Flosshilde S. Wagner
Norn I M. Höffgen
Norn II A. Burmeister
Norn III A. Silja
Bayreuth Fest Chor, Bayreuth Fest Orch, K. Böhm (pp1967)
(10/94) (PHIL) Ⓓ [14] **446 057-2PB14**

Act 2, Sc 4/5. F. Leider, A. von Stosch, L. Melchior, H. Janssen, W. Schirp, ROH Chor, ROHO, W. Furtwängler (pp1938)
(11/89) (PEAR) Ⓓ **GEMMCD9331**

Act 3, Sc 2/3. R. Hunter, A. Remedios, C. Grant, N. Bailey, M. Curphey, Sadler's Wells Op Chor, Sadler's Wells Op Orch, R. Goodall (r1972; Eng)
(11/93) (CHAN) Ⓓ **CHAN6593**

Excs H. Behrens, R. Goldberg, M. Salminen, NY Met Op Chor, NY Met Op Orch, James Levine
(DG) Ⓓ **435 489-2GH**

Excs M. Lorenz, A. Konetzni, F. Destal, J. Prohaska, W. Achsel, B. Paalen, R. Anday, L. Helletsgruber, A. Michalsky, D. With, Vienna St Op Chor, Vienna St Op Orch, H. Knappertsbusch (pp1937)
(SCHW) Ⓓ [2] **314742**

Excs BPO, L. Maazel (without voices)
(10/88) (TELA) Ⓓ **CD80154**

Excs W. Widdop, R. Laubenthal, A. Fear, D. Zádor, F. Collier, I. Andrésen, E. List, F. Austral, G. Ljungberg, M. Offers, G. Palmer, E. Arden, N. Eadie, T. de Garmo, L. Kindermann, E. Marherr-Wagner, Berlin St Op Chor, LSO, A. Coates, SO, Berlin St Op Orch, L. Collingwood, L. Blech (r1926/8)
(11/91) (CLAR) Ⓓ [2] **CDGSE78-50-37/8**

Excs J. Kalenberg, H. Trundt, E. Schipper, E. Schipper, J. von Manowarda, M. Angerer, Vienna St Op Chor, Vienna St Op Orch, J. Krips (pp1933) (11/94) (SCHW) Ⓓ [2] **314532**

Excs M. Bugarinovic, D. With, E. Réthy, Vienna St Op Orch, H. Knappertsbusch (pp1938)
(3/95) (SCHW) Ⓓ [2] **314602**

Excs G. Kappel, J. Kalenberg, E. Schipper, W. Achsel, R. Anday, J. von Manowarda, G. Rünger, B. Paalen, E. Szánthó, Vienna St Op Orch, R. Heger (pp1933)
(8/95) (SCHW) Ⓓ [2] **314592**

Excs J. Kalenberg, H. Trundt, R. Anday, J. von Manowarda, E. Schipper, E. Szánthó, R. Anday, E. Hadrabová, Vienna St Op Orch, C. Krauss (pp1933) (8/95) (SCHW) Ⓓ [2] **314642**

Excs J. Pölzer, A. Konetzni, J. von Manowarda, E. Schipper, E. Szánthó, R. Anday, G. Rünger, Vienna St Op Orch, J. Krips (pp1933)
(9/95) (SCHW) Ⓓ [2] **314662**

Excs J. von Manowarda, E. Schipper, E. Szánthó, R. Anday, G. Rünger, Vienna St Op Chor, Vienna St Op Orch, C. Krauss (pp1934)
(9/95) (SCHW) Ⓓ [2] **314662**

Leitmotifs LSO, L. Collingwood (r1931)
(4/95) (PEAR) Ⓓ [7] **GEMMCDS9137**

1b, 2, 3, 5, 9, 16b, 28, 29, 37, 43. N. Eadie, E. Arden, G. Palmer, F. Austral, W. Widdop, A. Fear, F. Collier, G. Ljungberg, M. Offers, chor, LSO, A. Coates (r1926/9)
(4/95) (PEAR) Ⓓ [7] **GEMMCDS9137**

1b(pt), 3, 23. A. Konetzni, S. Svanholm, H. Alsen, D. Söderqvist, E. Schürhoff, P. Tutsek, H. Konetzni, Vienna St Op Orch, H. Knappertsbusch (pp1943)
(SCHW) Ⓓ [2] **314672**

1b(pt), 39. A. Konetzni, A. Kipnis, W. Achsel, E. Szánthó, R. Anday, Vienna St Op Orch, H. Knappertsbusch (pp1937)
(SCHW) Ⓓ [2] **314742**

2, 3(pt), 4, 5, 16a, 24, 25, 36, 37, 40-43. Anne Evans, E-M. Bundschuh, H. Leidland, W. Meier, A. Küttenbaum, J. Turner, B. Svendén, L. Finnie, U. Priew, S. Jerusalem, P. Kang, G. von Kannen, B. Brinkmann, Bayreuth Fest Chor, Bayreuth Fest Orch, D. Barenboim (pp1991)
(TELD) Ⓓ **4509-97909-2**

2, 3, 5, 37, 40-43. R. Hunter, A. Remedios, LPO, C. Mackerras (r1972) (CFP) Ⓓ **CD-CFP4670**
(CFP) ▭ **TC-CFP4670**
2, 36, 37, 40. Seattle SO, G. Schwarz (3/87) (DELO) Ⓓ **DE3040**
2, 5. NBC SO, A. Toscanini (pp1954) (MUSI) Ⓓ **ATRA-3008**
2-5. H. Traubel, L. Melchior, NBC SO, A. Toscanini (bp1941) (RCA) Ⓓ **GD60304**
2, 5, 35, 37, 40. Netherlands Rad PO, E. de Waart (r1992; arr Vlieger) (9/93) (FIDE) Ⓓ **9201**
2, 5, 37, 40. D. Polaski, Chicago SO, D. Barenboim (ERAT) Ⓓ **2292-45786-2**
2-5, 7b(pt), 8a, 10, 19-21, 36, 37, 40-43. G. Jones, M. Jung, F. Hübner, H. Becht, F. Mazura, J. Altmeyer, Bayreuth Fest Orch, P. Boulez (pp1979) (PHIL) Ⓓ **446 616-2PM**
3. F. Austral, T. Davies, orch, A. Coates (r1922: Eng) (PEAR) Ⓓ **GEMMCD9146**
3. K. Flagstad, L. Melchior, San Francisco SO, E. McArthur (r1939) (SIMA) Ⓓ [3] **PSC1821(2)**
3. F. Leider, F. Soot, orch (r1925) (6/90) (LYRC) Ⓓ [2] **LCD146**
3. K. Flagstad, L. Melchior, San Francisco Op Orch, E. MacArthur (r1939) (10/90) (RCA) Ⓓ **GD87915**
3. F. Leider, F. Soot, orch (r1925) (5/91) (PREI) Ⓓ [3] **89301**
3. J. Gadski, orch (r1912) (7/91) (CLUB) Ⓓ **CL99-109**
3. F. Austral, W. Widdop, LSO, A. Coates (r1928) (1/92) (EMI) Ⓓ [4] **CMS7 64008-2(2)**
3. F. Austral, W. Widdop, LSO, A. Coates (r1928) (7/92) (PEAR) Ⓓ [3] **GEMMCDS9925(1)**
3. W. Widdop, F. Austral, LSO, A. Coates (r1928) (11/92) (CLAR) Ⓓ **CDGSE78-50-46**
3. G. Rünger, J. Pölzer, Vienna St Op Orch, H. Knappertsbusch (pp1938) (9/95) (SCHW) Ⓓ [2] **314662**
3(pt), 28. L. Melchior, A. Konetzni, J. von Manowarda, Vienna St Op Chor, Vienna St Op Orch, F. Weingartner (pp1934) (7/94) (SCHW) Ⓓ [2] **314512**
3, 4. K. Flagstad, S. Svanholm, Philh, G. Sébastian (r1951) (10/94) (EMI) Ⓓ [4] **CMS5 65212-2**
3, 40, 44. Anne Evans, Philh, F. d'Avalos (2/88) (ASV) Ⓓ **CDDCA595**
5. Vienna SO, Y. Ahronovitch (LASE) Ⓓ **15 612**
(LASE) ▭ **79 612**
5. VPO, H. Knappertsbusch (pp1940) (ACAN) Ⓓ [2] **44 2100-2**
5. Basle SO, A. Jordan (r1983) (ERAT) Ⓓ **4509-92866-2**
5. RPS Orch, B. Walter (r1927) (VAI) Ⓓ **VAIA1059**
5. BPO, H. von Karajan (r1969) (DG) Ⓓ [2] **439 687-2GX2**
5. LSO, W. Morris (12/87) (CIRR) Ⓓ **CICD1005**
5. La Scala Orch, W. Furtwängler (pp1950) (2/89) (ACAN) Ⓓ **43 121**
5. Philh, O. Klemperer (r1961) (11/90) (EMI) Ⓓ **CDM7 63618-2**
5. Minnesota Orch, N. Marriner (r1983) (2/94) (TELA) Ⓓ **CD82005**
5. Vienna St Op Orch, C. Krauss (pp1933) (6/94) (SCHW) Ⓓ **314502**
5. National SO, Sidney Beer (r1944) (5/95) (DUTT) Ⓓ **CDK1200**
5, 37. VPO, H. Knappertsbusch (r1942) (PREI) Ⓓ **90116**
5, 37. Philh, Y. Simonov (10/91) (COLL) Ⓓ **Coll1207-2**
5, 37. LSO, A. Coates (r1926) (4/93) (KOCH) Ⓓ [2] **37704-2**
5, 37. VPO, W. Furtwängler (r1954) (4/94) (EMI) Ⓓ [2] **CHS7 64935-2**
5, 37. Chicago SO, F. Reiner (r1959) (8/94) (RCA) Ⓓ **09026 61792-2**
5, 37. Philh, W. Sawallisch (r1958) (10/94) (EMI) Ⓓ [4] **CMS5 65212-2**
5, 37. Berlin St Op Orch, K. Muck (r1927) (4/95) (PEAR) Ⓓ [7] **GEMMCDS9137**
5, 37, 43. Vienna SO, G. Prêtre (pp1989) (ORFE) Ⓓ **C237901A**
5, 37, 44. Cleveland Orch, G. Szell (11/92) (SONY) Ⓓ **SBK48175**
11. F. Schorr, Berlin St Op Orch, L. Blech (PREI) Ⓓ [2] **89214**
11. L. Melchior, F. Schorr, L. Topas, R. Watzke, Berlin St Op Orch, L. Blech (r1929) (8/88) (DANA) Ⓓ [2] **DACOCD315/6**
13. E. List, Berlin St Op Orch, E. Mörike (r1928) (PEAR) Ⓓ **GEMMCD9122**
13-15, 16a, 16b, 17-19, 23-26, 27a, 27b, 28-30. F. Leider, L. Melchior, K. Thorborg, L. Weber, H. Janssen, M. Nedzadel, ROH Chor, LPO, T. Beecham (pp1936) (6/90) (LYRC) Ⓓ [2] **LCD146**
13, 24. H. Janssen, L. Weber, ROH Chor, LPO, T. Beecham (pp1936) (6/94) (DUTT) Ⓓ **CDLX7007**
13, 24. G. Frick, Berlin Deutsche Op Chor, Berlin Deutsche Op Orch, F. Konwitschny (r1959) (10/94) (EMI) Ⓓ [4] **CMS5 65212-2**
13, 24, 32, 35, 36. I. Andrésen, R. Laubenthal, T. de Garmo, L. Kindermann, E. Marherr-Wagner, D. Zádor, E. List, Berlin St Op Chor, Berlin St Op Orch, L. Blech (r1928) (4/95) (PEAR) Ⓓ [7] **GEMMCDS9137**
13, 33. E. List, Berlin St Op Chor, Berlin St Op Orch, E. Mörike (r1928) (PREI) Ⓓ **89083**
16a E. Schumann-Heink, orch, Rosario Bourdon (r1919) (2/91) (NIMB) Ⓓ **NI7811**
(2/91) (NIMB) ▭ **NC7811**
16a C. Ludwig, VPO, G. Solti (r1964) (10/93) (DECC) Ⓓ **436 462-2DM**
16a, 16b B. Fassbaender, Stuttgart RSO, H. Graf (11/86) (ORFE) Ⓓ **C096841A**
16b R. Anday, Berlin St Op Orch, J. Prüwer (r1928) (5/92) (PREI) Ⓓ **89046**
16b K. Thorborg, RCA SO, K. Riedel (r1940) (4/95) (PREI) Ⓓ **89084**
18(pt) S. Sedlmair, anon (r1904) (7/91) (SYMP) Ⓓ **SYMCD1081**
23. E. List, Berlin Staatskapelle Chor, Berlin Staatskapelle, E. Mörike (r1928) (1/92) (EMI) Ⓓ [4] **CMS7 64008-2(2)**
24. Bayreuth Fest Chor, Bayreuth Fest Orch, W. Pitz (4/90) (DG) Ⓓ **429 169-2GR**
24. I. Andrésen, Berlin St Op Orch, L. Blech (r1927) (10/90) (PREI) Ⓓ **89028**
24(pt)-26. L. Weber, H. Janssen, ROH Chor, LPO, T. Beecham (pp1936) (1/92) (EMI) Ⓓ [4] **CMS7 64008-2(2)**
26. D. Fischer-Dieskau, Vienna St Op Chor, VPO, G. Solti (r1964) (DECC) Ⓓ **440 409-2DM**
28. K. Flagstad, S. Svanholm, Philh, H. Weigert (r1951) (10/94) (EMI) Ⓓ [4] **CMS5 65212-2**
32(pt), 33, 35, 36. S. Svanholm, H. Alsen, P. Schoeffler, E. Rutgers, E. Schürhoff, M. Bugarinovic, Vienna St Op Chor, Vienna St Op Orch, H. Knappertsbusch (pp1941) (SCHW) Ⓓ [2] **314692**
35. L. Melchior, O. Helgers, LSO, R. Heger (r1930) (PREI) Ⓓ **89086**
35, 36. Orch, LSO (r1930) (8/88) (DANA) Ⓓ [2] **DACOCD315/6**
35(pt), 36. M. Lorenz, P. Schoeffler, J. von Manowarda, Vienna St Op Orch, L. Reichwein (pp1942) (1/95) (SCHW) Ⓓ [2] **314562**
36. L. Melchior, LSO, R. Heger (r1930) (MSCM) Ⓓ [2] **MM30285**
(MSCM) ▭ [2] **MM40107**
36. W. Lewis, RPO, G. Ötvös (RPO) Ⓓ **CDRPO7019**
36. L. Melchior, LSO, R. Heger (r1930) (10/89) (EMI) Ⓓ **CDH7 69789-2**
36, 37. H. Brilioth, BPO, H. von Karajan (4/90) (DG) Ⓓ **429 168-2GR**
(4/90) (DG) ▭ **429 168-4GR**
37. Sofia Rad SO, V. Kazandjiev (LASE) Ⓓ **15 612**
(LASE) ▭ **79 612**
37. Leningrad PO, E. Mravinsky (pp1978) (OLYM) Ⓓ [6] **OCD5002**
37. LPO, A. Boult (EMIL) Ⓓ **CDZ7 67253-2**
37. BPO, W. Furtwängler (r1933) (SYMP) Ⓓ **SYMCD1043**
37. NBC SO, A. Toscanini (r1941) (RCA) Ⓓ **GD60304**
37. NBC SO, A. Toscanini (r1952) (RCA) Ⓓ **GD60306**
37. Canadian Brass, BPO, Bayreuth Fest Orch, E. de Waart (r1991; arr Frackenpohl) (PHIL) Ⓓ **434 109-2PH**
37. British SO, B. Walter (r1931) (VAI) Ⓓ **VAIA1059**
37. C. Katsaris (r1994: arr pf: F Busoni) (SONY) Ⓓ **SK58973**
37. VPO, G. Solti (r1964) (DECC) Ⓓ [2] **440 606-2DF2**
37. Leningrad PO, E. Mravinsky (pp1978) (MELO) Ⓓ **74321 25199-2**
37. Leningrad PO, E. Mravinsky (pp1978) (MELO) Ⓓ [10] **74321 25189-2**
37. Los Angeles PO, E. Leinsdorf (r1977) (SHEF) Ⓓ **10052-2-G**
37. Los Angeles PO, E. Leinsdorf (8/87) (SHEF) Ⓓ **CD-7/8**
37. orch, A. Coates (r1926) (7/90) (CLAR) Ⓓ **CDGSE78-50-33**
37. Philh, O. Klemperer (r1960) (11/90) (EMI) Ⓓ **CDM7 63618-2**
37. BPO, W. Furtwängler (r1933) (4/92) (KOCH) Ⓓ [2] **37073-2**
37. Leningrad PO, E. Mravinsky (pp1968) (6/92) (ERAT) Ⓓ [11] **2292-45763-2**
37. Leningrad PO, E. Mravinsky (pp1968) (6/92) (ERAT) Ⓓ **2292-45762-2**
37. Oslo PO, M. Jansons (12/92) (EMI) Ⓓ **CDC7 54583-2**
37. Leningrad PO, E. Mravinsky (pp1967) (3/94) (RUSS) Ⓓ **RDCD11166**
37, 39, 40. F. Austral, LSO, L. Collingwood (r1927) (4/95) (PEAR) Ⓓ [7] **GEMMCDS9137**
37, 40. B. Nilsson, G. Frick, VPO, G. Solti (DECC) Ⓓ **421 313-2DA**
37, 40-44. A. Davis, Philadelphia, L. Stokowski (r1933) (PEAR) Ⓓ [2] **GEMMCDS9076**
37, 42. B. Nilsson, G. Frick, VPO, G. Solti (r1964) (DECC) Ⓓ **440 069-2DWO**
(DECC) ▭ **440 069-4DWO**
37, 42, 43. H. Dernesch, K. Ridderbusch, BPO, H. von Karajan (r1969/70) (3/94) (DG) Ⓓ **439 423-2GCL**
37, 43. VPO, G. Solti (DECC) OO **410 137-5DH**
37, 43. H. Behrens, M. Salminen, NY Met Op Orch, James Levine (r1989) (DG) Ⓓ **437 825-2GH**
37, 43. VPO, G. Solti (11/83) (DECC) Ⓓ **410 137-2DH**
37, 44. Cleveland Orch, G. Szell (CBS) Ⓓ [2] **CD46466**
37, 44. LPO, K. Tennstedt (EMI) ◖ **LDB9 91234-1**
(EMI) ▣ **MVD9 91234-3**
37, 44. LSO, L. Stokowski (DECC) Ⓓ **433 639-2DSP**
(DECC) ▭ **433 639-4DSP**
37, 44. LPO, A. Boult (EMI) Ⓓ [2] **CZS7 62539-2**
37, 44. BPO, K. Tennstedt (r1980) (EMI) Ⓓ [2] **CZS5 68616-2**
37, 44. LPO, K.A. Rickenbacher (11/87) (CFP) Ⓓ **CD-CFP9008**
39-42. F. Leider, E. Marherr-Wagner, Berlin St Op Orch, L. Blech (r1928) (PREI) Ⓓ **89098**
39-43. H. Braun, D. Söderqvist, J. von Manowarda, Vienna St Op Orch, L. Reichwein (pp1942) (SCHW) Ⓓ [2] **314722**
39-43. F. Leider, E. Marherr-Wagner, Berlin St Op Orch, L. Blech (r1928) (11/89) (PEAR) Ⓓ **GEMMCD9331**
39-43. F. Leider, E. Marherr-Wagner, Berlin St Op Orch, L. Blech (r1928) (6/90) (LYRC) Ⓓ [2] **LCD146**
40. K. Flagstad, NBC SO, E. McArthur (pp1955) (MUSI) Ⓓ **MACD-263**
40. E. Farrell, Boston SO, C. Munch (r1957) (RCA) Ⓓ **GD60686**
40. Buenos Aires Colón Th Chor, Buenos Aires Colón Th Orch, E. Kleiber (bp1948) (PEAR) Ⓓ [2] **GEMMCDS9910**
40. H. Wildbrunn, orch (r1924: 2 vers of side 1) (PREI) Ⓓ **89097**
40. K. Flagstad, San Francisco Op Orch, E. McArthur (r1939) (7/93) (NIMB) Ⓓ **NI7847**
40-42. K. Flagstad, Oslo PO, Norwegian Rad Orch, Ø. Fjeldstad (r1956) (LOND) Ⓓ **440 495-2LM**
40-42. K. Flagstad, VPO, Oslo PO, A. Boult (r1956) (LOND) Ⓓ [5] **440 490-2LM5(1)**
40-42. K. Flagstad, Vienna St Op Orch, F. Weingartner (pp1936) (7/94) (SCHW) Ⓓ [2] **314512**
40-43. F. Leider, Berlin St Op Orch, L. Blech (r1928) (MSCM) Ⓓ [2] **MM30285**
(MSCM) ▭ [2] **MM40107**
40-43. H. Traubel, NBC SO, A. Toscanini (r1941) (RCA) Ⓓ **GD60304**
40-43. M. Mödl, Berlin City Op Orch, A. Rother (r1954) (PREI) Ⓓ **90136**
40-43. E. Farrell, NYPO, L. Bernstein (r1961) (SONY) Ⓓ **SMK47644**
40-43. C. Ludwig, Berlin Deutsche Op Orch, H. Hollreiser (r1963-4) (TESS) Ⓓ **049-2**
40-43. J. Norman, LPO, K. Tennstedt (11/88) (EMI) Ⓓ **CDC7 49759-2**

40-43. K. Flagstad, Philh, W. Furtwängler (r1948) (8/89) (EMI) ⓓ **CDH7 63030-2**
40-43. M. Lawrence, Pasdeloup Orch, P. Coppola (French: r1933) (5/90) (PREI) ⓓ **89011**
40-43. G. Lubin, orch, H. Defosse (French: r1929) (5/91) (EPM) ⓓ **150 052**
40-43. M. Lawrence, Pasdeloup Orch, P. Coppola (French: r1933) (1/92) (EMI) ⓓ [4] **CMS7 64008-2(2)**
40-43. G. Jones, Cologne RSO, R. Paternostro (2/92) (CHAN) ⓓ **CHAN8930**
(2/92) (CHAN) ▭ **ABTD1528**
40-43. K. Flagstad, Philh, W. Furtwängler (r1952) (4/94) (EMI) ⓓ [2] **CHS7 64935-2**
40-43. K. Flagstad, Philh, W. Furtwängler (r1948) (10/94) (EMI) ⓓ [4] **CMS5 65212-2**
41. M. Saltzmann-Stevens, orch, P. Pitt (Eng: r1909) (7/92) (PEAR) ⓓ [3] **GEMMCDS9924(2)**
41-43. K. Flagstad, San Francisco Op Orch, E. MacArthur (r1939) (10/90) (RCA) ⓓ **GD87915**
42, 43. H. Behrens, NY Met Op Orch, James Levine (DG) ▭ **439 153-4GMA**
43. Philadelphia, L. Stokowski (r1927) (PEAR) ⓓ [2] **GEMMCDS9076**
44. NBC SO, A. Toscanini, H. Keith (bp1948) (RCA) ▣ **790 351**
44. NBC SO, A. Toscanini (arr Toscanini: r1949) (RCA) ⓓ **GD60306**
44. BPO, R. Kempe (r1956) (TEST) ⓓ **SBT1035**
44. G. Gould (r1973: trans pf: Gould) (SONY) ⓓ **SMK52650**
44. NYPSO, A. Toscanini (r1936) (3/90) (PEAR) ⓓ [3] **GEMMCDS9373**
44. NBC SO, A. Toscanini (r1941) (11/92) (RCA) ⓓ **GD60296**
44. NYPO, A. Toscanini (r1936) (11/92) (RCA) ⓓ **GD60318**

Tannhäuser– opera: 3 acts (1845—Dresden) (Lib. cpsr)

ACT 1: 1. Overture; 2. Venusberg Music; 3. Geliebter, sag, wo weilt dein Sinn?; 4. Dir töne Lob; 5. Geliebter, komm! Sieh dort die Grotte; 6. Stets soll nur dir, nur dir mein Lied ertönen!; 7. Frau Holda kam aus dem Berg hervor; 8. Zu dir wall ich; 9. Als du in kuhnem Sange. ACT 2: 10. Dich teure Halle (Elisabeth's Greeting); 11. O Fürstin! Gott! Stehet auf!; 12. Entry of the Guests (Grand March); 13. Freudig begrüssen; 14. Gar viel und schön (Landgrave's address); 15. Blick ich umher; 16. Heraus zum kampfe mit uns allen; 17. O Himmel! Lass dich jetzt; 18. Zurück; 19. Ein Engel; 20. Ein furchbares Verbrechen. ACT 3: 21. Prelude; 22. Wohl wüsst ich hier sie im Gebet zu finden; 23. Beglückt darf nun (Pilgrims' Chorus); 24. Allmächt'ge Jungfrau (Elisabeth's Prayer); 25a. Wie Todesahnung; 25b. O du mein holder Abendstern; 26. Ich hörte Harfenschlag; 27. Inbrunst im Herzen (Rome Narration). 28. Willkommen, ungetreuer Mann!.

Tannhäuser S. Wenkoff
Elisabeth, Venus G. Jones
Wolfram B. Weikl
Hermann H. Sotin
Walther R. Schunk
Biterolf F. Mazura
Heinrich J. Pickering
Reinmar H. Feldhoff
Shepherd K. Brettschneider
L. Charles
K. Haigen
Bayreuth Fest Chor, Bayreuth Fest Orch, Colin Davis, G. Friedrich (PHIL) ◖ [2] **070 412-1PH2**
(PHIL) ▣ [2] **070 412-3PH2**

Tannhäuser S. Pilinszky
Elisabeth M. Müller
Wolfram H. Janssen
Venus R. Jost-Arden
Hermann I. Andrésen
Walther G. Belti-Pilinszky
Biterolf G. von Tschurtschenthaler
Heinrich J. Sattler
Reinmar C. Stralendorf
Shepherd E. Berger
Bayreuth Fest Chor, Bayreuth Fest Orch, K. Elmendorff (r1930) (PEAR) ⓓ [2] **GEMMCDS9941**

Tannhäuser W. Windgassen
Elisabeth A. Silja
Wolfram E. Waechter
Venus G. Bumbry
Hermann J. Greindl
Walther G. Stolze
Biterolf F. Crass
Heinrich G. Paskuda
Reinmar G. Nienstedt
Shepherd E-M. Gardelli
Bayreuth Fest Chor, Bayreuth Fest Orch, W. Sawallisch (pp1962) (PHIL) ⓓ [32] **434 420-2PM32(2)**

Tannhäuser A. Seider
Elisabeth M. Schech
Wolfram K. Paul
Venus M. Bäumer
Hermann O. von Rohr
Walther F. Klarwein
Biterolf B. Kusche
Heinrich K. Ostertag
Reinmar R. Wünzer
Shepherd R. Streich
Bavarian St Op Chor, Bavarian St Op Orch, R. Heger (r1951) (PILZ) ⓓ [9] **442118-2**

Tannhäuser R. Versalle
Elisabeth C. Studer
Wolfram W. Brendel
Venus R. Engert-Ely
Hermann H. Sotin
Walther W. Pell
Biterolf S. Vogel
Heinrich C. Bieber
Reinmar S. Sólyom-Nagy
Shepherd J. Robinson
Bayreuth Fest Chor, Bayreuth Fest Orch, G. Sinopoli, W. Wagner, B. Large (PHIL) ◖ [2] **070 435-1PH2**
(PHIL) ▣ [2] **070 435-3PH2**

Abridged E. Laholm, K. Flagstad, H. Janssen, R. Pauly, E. List, J. Carter, M. Harrell, M. Stellman, NY Met Op Chor, NY Met Op Orch, E. Leinsdorf (pp1939) (SYMP) ⓓ [2] **SYMCD1178/9**

Tannhäuser K. König
Elisabeth L. Popp
Wolfram B. Weikl
Venus W. Meier
Hermann K. Moll
Walther S. Jerusalem
Biterolf W. Groenroos
Heinrich D. Litaker
Reinmar R. Scholze
Shepherd G. Sima
Bavarian Rad Chor, BRSO, B. Haitink (2/86) (EMI) ⓓ [3] **CDS7 47296-8**

Tannhäuser R. Kollo
Elisabeth H. Dernesch
Wolfram V. Braun
Venus C. Ludwig
Hermann H. Sotin
Walther W. Hollweg
Biterolf M. Jungwirth
Heinrich K. Equiluz
Reinmar N. Bailey
Vienna Boys' Ch, Vienna St Op Chor, VPO, G. Solti (Paris vers) (2/86) (DECC) ⓓ [3] **414 581-2DH3**

Tannhäuser P. Domingo
Elisabeth C. Studer
Wolfram A. Schmidt
Venus A. Baltsa
Hermann M. Salminen
Walther W. Pell
Biterolf K. Rydl
Heinrich C. Biber
Reinmar O. Hillebrandt
Shepherd B. Bonney
ROH Chor, Philh, G. Sinopoli (Paris vers) (9/89) (DG) ⓓ [3] **427 625-2GH3**

Tannhäuser H. Hopf
Elisabeth E. Grümmer
Wolfram D. Fischer-Dieskau
Venus M. Schech
Hermann G. Frick
Walther F. Wunderlich
Biterolf R. Gonszar
Heinrich G. Unger
Reinmar R. Süss
Shepherd L. Otto
Berlin St Op Chor, Berlin St Op Orch, F. Konwitschny (10/90) (EMI) ⓓ [3] **CMS7 63214-2**

Tannhäuser W. Windgassen
Elisabeth A. Silja
Wolfram E. Waechter
Venus G. Bumbry
Hermann J. Greindl
Walther G. Stolze
Biterolf F. Crass
Heinrich G. Paskuda
Reinmar G. Nienstedt
Shepherd E-M. Gardelli
Bayreuth Fest Chor, Bayreuth Fest Orch, W. Sawallisch (pp1962) (10/92) (PHIL) ⓓ [3] **434 607-2PH3**
Orch, H. Barlow (bp1949) (VAI) ▣ **VAI69110**
Excs P. Domingo, C. Studer, A. Baltsa, M. Salminen, A. Schmidt, W. Pell, K. Rydl, C. Biber, O. Hillebrandt, B. Bonney, ROH Chor, Philh, G. Sinopoli (DG) ⓓ **429 789-2GH**
Excs M. Lorenz, M. Müller, Vienna St Op Chor, Vienna St Op Orch, W. Furtwängler (pp1936) (SCHW) ⓓ [2] **314702**
Excs Lotte Lehmann, J. Kalenberg, R. Mayr, F. Schorr, G. Maikl, F. Markhoff, W. Wernigk, K. Ettl, Vienna St Op Chor, Vienna St Op Orch, R. Heger (pp1933) (11/95) (SCHW) ⓓ [2] **314622**
Symphonic synthesis Pittsburgh Mendelssohn Ch, Pittsburgh SO, L. Maazel (arr Maazel) (4/92) (SONY) ⓓ **SK47178**
1. Chicago SO, G. Solti (DECC) ▣ **071 101-3DH**
1. French Rad PO, M. Janowski (r1990) (VIRG) ▭ **VJ7 59689-4**
1. BPO, H. von Karajan (r1975) (DG) ▣ **072 196-3GH**
1. LPO, E. Bátiz (MCI) ⓓ **OQ0009**
1. Budapest SO, G. Lehel (LASE) ⓓ **15 521**
(LASE) ▭ **79 521**
1. J. Sándor, LSO (LASE) ⓓ **15 514**
(LASE) ▭ **79 514**
1. Leningrad PO, E. Mravinsky (r1968) (OLYM) ⓓ [6] **OCD5002**
1. Cleveland Orch, G. Szell (CBS) ⓓ [2] **CD46466**
1. New Philh, A. Boult (EMI) ⓓ [2] **CZS7 62539-2**
1. BPO, S. Ozawa (PHIL) **OO 426 271-5PH**
1. LPO, A. Scholz (ROSE) ⓓ **3212**
1. BPO, E. Jochum (r1933) (TELD) ⓓ **9031-76444-2**
1. Philh, Y. Simonov (r1991) (COLL) ⓓ **Coll1294-2**
1. RPO, R. Leibowitz (r1962) (CHES) ⓓ **Chesky CD96**
1. LSO, B. Tuckwell (IMP) ⓓ [3] **TCD1070**
1. NYPO, L. Bernstein (r1967) (SONY) ⓓ **SMK47644**
1. RPO, V. Handley (r1993) (TRIN) ⓓ **TRP008**
(TRIN) ▭ **MCTRP008**
1. Berlin Deutsche Op Orch, O. Gerdes (DG) ⓓ [2] **439 687-2GX2**
1. Philh, M. Janowski (TELD) ⓓ **4509-96035-2**
(TELD) ▭ **4509-96035-4**
1. Luxembourg RSO, L. de Froment (FORL) ⓓ **FF020**
1. Minería SO, H. de la Fuente (r1987) (IMP) ⓓ **PCD1109**
1. Berlin Deutsche Op Orch, O. Gerdes (r1968) (DG) ⓓ **439 445-2GCL**
(DG) ▭ **439 445-4GCL**
1. Cincinnati SO, J. López-Cobos (r1994) (TELA) ⓓ **CD80379**
1. Turin RAI Orch, O. de Fabritiis (bp1953) (FONI) ⓓ **CDMR5003**
1. Leningrad PO, E. Mravinsky (pp1978) (MELO) ⓓ **74321 25199-2**
1. Leningrad PO, E. Mravinsky (pp1978) (MELO) ⓓ [10] **74321 25189-2**
1. Lamoureux Orch, I. Markevitch (DG) ⓓ [2] **447 364-2GDB2**
1. BPO, K. Tennstedt (r1982/3) (EMI) ⓓ [2] **CZS5 68616-2**
1. LSO, W. Morris (12/87) (CIRR) ⓓ **CICD1005**
1. VPO, H. von Karajan (pp1987) (8/88) (DG) ⓓ **423 613-2GH**
1. VPO, W. Furtwängler (r1952) (2/89) (ACAN) ⓓ **43 121**
1. Philh, O. Klemperer (11/90) (EMI) ⓓ **CDM7 63617-2**
1. Chicago SO, G. Solti (5/91) (DECC) ⓓ **430 448-2DM**
1. Leningrad PO, E. Mravinsky (pp1973) (6/92) (ERAT) ⓓ **2292-45762-2**
1. Oslo PO, M. Jansons (12/92) (EMI) ⓓ **CDC7 54583-2**
1. Leningrad PO, E. Mravinsky (pp1967) (3/94) (RUSS) ⓓ **RDCD11166**
1. VPO, W. Furtwängler (r1952) (4/94) (EMI) ⓓ [2] **CHS7 64935-2**
1. Concertgebouw, W. Mengelberg (pp1940) (7/94) (MUSI) ⓓ [4] **MACD-780**
1. SO, A. Coates (r1926) (2/95) (CLAR) ⓓ **CDGSE78-50-54**

14. M. Schenk, Nuremberg SO, K. Seibel (12/91) (COLO) Ⓓ **COL34 9004**
14. L. Weber, Philh, I. Dobroven (r1951) (4/92) (EMI) Ⓓ [7] **CHS7 69741-2(4)**
14. L. Hofmann, Vienna St Op Orch, W. Furtwängler (pp1935) (3/95) (SCHW) Ⓓ [2] **314602**
14, 20. W. Schirp, Vienna St Op Orch, L. Reichwein (pp1939) (6/95) (SCHW) Ⓓ [2] **314632**
15. R. Bockelmann, orch (r1936) (MSCM) Ⓓ [2] **MM30283**
(MSCM) ⊟ [2] **MM40105**
15. G. Hüsch, Berlin St Op Orch, F. Weissmann (r1928) (PEAR) Ⓓ [2] **GEMMCDS9121**
15. F. Schorr, LSO, A. Coates (r1930) (9/91) (PEAR) Ⓓ **GEMMCD9398**
15. H. Janssen, Bayreuth Fest Orch, K. Elmendorff (r1930) (1/92) (EMI) Ⓓ [4] **CMS7 64008-2(1)**
15. J. Berglund, orch, L. Blech (r c1946) (4/92) (EMI) Ⓓ [7] **CHS7 69741-2(5)**
15. H. Janssen, Bayreuth Fest Orch, K. Elmendorff (r1930) (7/92) (PEAR) Ⓓ [3] **GEMMCDS9926(1)**
15. M. Battistini, anon (Ital: r1911) (10/92) (PEAR) Ⓓ **GEMMCD9936**
15. A. Endrèze, orch, F. Ruhlmann (French: r c1932) (11/92) (MSCM) Ⓓ **MM30451**
15. A. Van Rooy, anon (r1902) (3/93) (SYMP) Ⓓ **SYMCD1100**
15, 25a, 25b B. Weikl, Munich RO, H. Wallberg (3/89) (ACAN) Ⓓ **43 266**
15, 25a, 25b H. Schlusnus, Berlin St Op Orch, L. Blech (r1935) (9/90) (PREI) Ⓓ **89006**
15, 25b H. Schlusnus, Berlin St Op Orch, L. Blech (r1935) (PREI) Ⓓ [2] **89212**
15, 25b G. Hüsch, Berlin St Op Orch, H.U. Müller (r1936) (3/94) (PREI) Ⓓ **89071**
18(pt) E. Destinn, orch (r1910) (12/94) (SUPR) Ⓓ [12] **11 2136-2(4)**
20. I. Andrésen, orch (r1929) (10/90) (PREI) Ⓓ **89028**
21. Philadelphia, L. Stokowski (arr Stokowski: r1936) (2/91) (PEAR) Ⓓ **GEMMCD9448**
21. SO, A. Coates (r1925) (2/95) (CLAR) Ⓓ **CDGSE78-50-54**
22. C. Whitehill, anon (r1904) (7/91) (SYMP) Ⓓ **SYMCD1081**
22, 25a, 25b G. Hüsch, Berlin St Op Orch, H.U. Müller (r1936) (1/92) (EMI) Ⓓ [4] **CMS7 64008-2(1)**
23. Vienna St Op Chor, VPO, G. Solti (DECC) Ⓓ **421 865-2DA**
23. ROH Chor, RPO, R. Stapleton (RPO) Ⓓ **CDRPO7009**
(RPO) ⊟ **ZCRPO7009**
23. V. Braun, H. Dernesch, Vienna St Op Chor, VPO, G. Solti (r1970) (DECC) Ⓓ **433 065-2DWO**
(DECC) ⊟ **433 065-4DWO**
23. H. Dernesch, V. Braun, Vienna St Op Chor, VPO, G. Solti (r1971) (DECC) Ⓓ **436 300-2DX**
(DECC) ⊟ **436 300-4DX**
23. Mormon Tabernacle Ch, Philadelphia, E. Ormandy (SONY) Ⓓ **SBK39438**
23. ROH Chor, RPO, R. Stapleton (r1991) (RPO) Ⓓ [2] **CDRPD9006**
(RPO) ⊟ [2] **ZCRPD9006**
23. D. Chorzempa (r1984; arr org) (PHIL) Ⓓ **438 309-2PM**
(PHIL) ⊟ **438 309-4PM**
23. Dresden St Op Chor, Dresden St Op Orch, S. Varviso (r1985) (BELA) Ⓓ **450 052-2**
(BELA) ⊟ **450 052-4**
23. H. Dernesch, V. Braun, Vienna St Op Chor, VPO, G. Solti (r1970) (DECC) Ⓓ **433 443-2DA**
(DECC) ⊟ **433 443-4DA**
23. H. Dernesch, V. Braun, Vienna St Op Chor, VPO, G. Solti (r1970) (DECC) Ⓓ **440 069-2DWO**
(DECC) ⊟ **440 069-4DWO**
23. ROH Chor, RPO, R. Stapleton (IMP) Ⓓ [3] **TCD1070**
23. Ambrosian Sngrs, Philh, M. Janowski (ERAT) Ⓓ **4509-91715-2**
(ERAT) ⊟ **4509-91715-4**
23. Capitol SO, C. Dragon (r1958: arr Dragon) (EMI) Ⓓ **CDM5 65430-2**
23. S. Preston (trans org: arr. Lemare) (6/91) (DECC) Ⓓ **430 091-2DWO**
(6/91) (DECC) ⊟ **430 091-4DWO**
23. T. Trotter (r1992: trans org: E Lemare) (4/94) (DECC) Ⓓ **436 656-2DH**
23(pt), 25a, 25b, 27(pt), 28(pt) J. Kalenberg, R. Bockelmann, G. Rünger, Vienna St Op Chor, Vienna St Op Orch, R. Heger (pp1933) (7/94) (SCHW) Ⓓ [2] **314512**
24. Lotte Lehmann, Berlin St Op Orch, F. Weissmann (r1930) (MSCM) Ⓓ [2] **MM30283**
(MSCM) ⊟ [2] **MM40105**
24. K. Flagstad, Philh, I. Dobroven (r1948) (8/89) (EMI) Ⓓ **CDH7 63030-2**
24. J. Gadski, orch (r1906) (7/91) (CLUB) Ⓓ **CL99-109**
24. K. Flagstad, Philh, I. Dobroven (r1948) (1/92) (EMI) Ⓓ [4] **CMS7 64008-2(1)**
24. E. Destinn, orch (r1914) (11/93) (ROMO) Ⓓ [2] **81002-2**
24. M. Reining, Berlin RSO, A. Rother (bp1943) (9/94) (PREI) Ⓓ **89065**
24. E. Destinn, orch, W.B Rogers (r1914) (12/94) (SUPR) Ⓓ [12] **11 2136-2(5)**
24. E. Rethberg, orch (r1928) (2/95) (ROMO) Ⓓ [2] **81012-2**
25a F. Schorr, orch (r1921) (PREI) Ⓓ **89052**
25a, 25b T. Krause, Vienna Op Orch, A. Quadri (DECC) Ⓓ **433 067-2DWO**
(DECC) ⊟ **433 067-4DWO**
25a, 25b T. Krause, Vienna Op Orch, A. Quadri (r1965) (DECC) Ⓓ **443 380-2DM**
25a, 25b L. Tibbett, orch, N. Shilkret (r1934) (3/91) (PEAR) Ⓓ [2] **GEMMCDS9452**
25a, 25b T. Hampson, Munich RO, F. Luisi (r1994) (9/95) (EMI) Ⓓ **CDC5 55233-2**
25b W. Thomas, Munich CO, H. Stadlmair (arr. Thomas) (ORFE) Ⓓ **C131851A**
25b M. Journet, orch, Rosario Bourdon (Ital: r1926) (PREI) Ⓓ **89021**
25b G. Hüsch, Berlin St Op Orch, H.U. Müller (r1936) (MSCM) Ⓓ [2] **MM30283**
(MSCM) ⊟ [2] **MM40105**
25b P. Casals, N. Mednikoff (arr vc/pf: r1926) (MSCM) Ⓓ **MM30428**
25b A. Ivanov, Bolshoi Th Orch, S. Samosud (r1940s: Russ) (PREI) Ⓓ **89067**
25b G. Hüsch, Berlin St Op Orch, H.U. Müller (r1936) (PEAR) Ⓓ [2] **GEMMCDS9121**
25b F. Schorr, Berlin St Op Orch, L. Blech (PREI) Ⓓ [2] **89214**
25b A. Sved, Radio Italiana SO, A. Simonetto (r1947) (PREI) Ⓓ **89096**
25b V. Fox (r1959: arr org) (EMI) Ⓓ **CDM5 65426-2**
25b Hollywood Bowl SO, C. Dragon (r1956: arr Dragon) (EMI) Ⓓ **CDM5 65430-2**
25b G. De Luca, anon (r1907: Ital) (PEAR) Ⓓ [3] **GEMMCDS9159(2)**
25b R. Stracciari, orch (r1925: Ital) (2/90) (PREI) Ⓓ **89003**
25b E. Giraldoni, anon (Ital: r1902) (6/90) (SYMP) Ⓓ **SYMCD1073**
25b C. Tagliabue, orch, U. Berrettoni (Ital: r1946) (11/90) (PREI) Ⓓ **89015**
25b F. Schorr, Berlin St Op Orch, L. Blech (r c1928) (9/91) (PEAR) Ⓓ **GEMMCD9398**
25b P. Casals, N. Mednikoff (arr vc/pf: r1926) (10/91) (BIDD) Ⓓ **LAB017**
25b A. Granforte, La Scala Orch, C. Sabajno (Ital: r1928) (12/91) (PREI) Ⓓ **89048**
25b M. Renaud, anon (r1902) (3/93) (SYMP) Ⓓ **SYMCD1100**
25b J. Schwarz, orch (r c1918) (10/95) (NIMB) Ⓓ **NI7867**
26. M. Lorenz, K. Schmitt-Walter, Berlin RSO, A. Rother (r1942) (PREI) Ⓓ **90213**
26, 27. L. Slezak, T. Scheidl, Berlin St Op Orch, M. Gurlitt (r1928) (PREI) Ⓓ [2] **89203**
27. M. Lorenz, Berlin St Op Orch, H. Schmidt-Isserstedt (r1936) (MSCM) Ⓓ [2] **MM30283**
(MSCM) ⊟ [2] **MM40105**
27. L. Melchior, orch (r1923) (PREI) Ⓓ **89032**
27. M. Lorenz, VPO, H. Knappertsbusch (r1942) (PREI) Ⓓ **90116**
27. W. Lewis, RPO, G. Ötvös (RPO) Ⓓ **CDRPO7019**
27. L. Melchior, Berlin St Op Orch, L. Blech (r1928) (PREI) Ⓓ **89068**
27. L. Melchior, LSO, A. Coates (r1929) (PREI) Ⓓ **89086**
27. K. Erb, orch (r1914) (PREI) Ⓓ **89095**
27. P. Franz, orch (r1914: Fr) (PREI) Ⓓ **89099**
27. L. Melchior, LSO, A. Coates (r1929) (8/88) (DANA) Ⓓ [2] **DACOCD315/6**
27. L. Melchior, orch (r1923-26) (8/88) (DANA) Ⓓ [2] **DACOCD313/4**
27. L. Melchior, LSO, A. Coates (r1929) (10/89) (EMI) Ⓓ **CDH7 69789-2**
27. L. Melchior, LSO, A. Coates (r1929) (7/90) (CLAR) Ⓓ **CDGSE78-50-33**
27. L. Melchior, LSO, A. Coates (r1929) (7/92) (PEAR) Ⓓ [3] **GEMMCDS9926(1)**
27. L. Melchior, LSO, A. Coates (r1929) (10/93) (NIMB) Ⓓ **NI7848**
27. L. Suthaus, orch (3/94) (MYTO) Ⓓ [3] **3MCD93381**
27. F. Völker, Berlin Staatskapelle, A. Melichar (r1933) (8/94) (PREI) Ⓓ **89070**
27. L. Melchior, LSO, A. Coates (r1929) (2/95) (CLAR) Ⓓ **CDGSE78-50-54**
27, 28. S. Svanholm, A. Poell, P. Tutsek, Vienna St Op Chor, Vienna St Op Orch, L. Reichwein (pp1942) (SCHW) Ⓓ [2] **314692**

Tristan und Isolde– music drama: 3 acts (1865—Munich) (Lib. cpsr)

ACT 1: 1. Prelude; 2. Hab acht, Tristan; 3. Doch nun von Tristan!; 4. Wie lachend sie (Isolde's Narrative and Curse); 5. So reihte sie die Mutter; 6. Begehrt, Herrin. ACT 2: 7. Prelude; 8a. Isolde! Geliebte! Tristan! geliebter; 8b. O eitler Tagesknecht!; 8c. O sink hernieder; 9a. Einsam wachend (Brangäne's Warning); 9b. Lausch Geliebter!; 9c. So starben wir; 9d. Lass' mich sterben!; 10. Tatest du's wirklich? (King Marke's monologue); 11. O König...Wohin nun Tristan scheidet. ACT 3: 12. Prelude; 13. Die alte Weise; 14. Dünkt dich das?; 15. Wie sie selig; 16. O diese Sonne!; 17. Ha! Ich bin's, ich bin's; 18. Mild und leise (Liebestod). 19. Prelude and Liebestod (concert version: arr. Humperdinck).

Tristan W. Windgassen
Isolde B. Nilsson
Brangäne C. Ludwig
King Marke M. Talvela
Kurwenal E. Waechter
Melot C. Heater
Bayreuth Fest Chor, Bayreuth Fest Orch, K. Böhm (pp1966)
(PHIL) Ⓓ [32] **434 420-2PM32(2)**

Tristan R. Kollo
Isolde J. Meier
Brangäne H. Schwarz
King Marke M. Salminen
Kurwenal H. Becht
Melot; Sailor R. Schunk
Shepherd H. Pampuch
Helmsman M. Egel
Bayreuth Fest Chor, Bayreuth Fest Orch, D. Barenboim, J-P. Ponnelle
(PHIL) ◐ [3] **070 409-1PHE3**

Tristan P. Hofmann
Isolde H. Behrens
Brangäne Y. Minton
King Marke H. Sotin
Kurwenal B. Weikl
Melot H. Steinbach
Shepherd H. Zednik
Helmsman R. Grumbach
Sailor T. Moser
Bavarian Rad Chor, BRSO, L. Bernstein (pp1981)
(PHIL) Ⓓ [4] **438 241-2PH4**

Tristan L. Suthaus
Isolde K. Flagstad
Brangäne B. Thebom
King Marke J. Greindl
Kurwenal D. Fischer-Dieskau
Melot E. Evans
Shepherd; Sailor R. Schock
Helmsman R. Davies
ROH Chor, Philh, W. Furtwängler (r1952)
(5/86) (EMI) Ⓓ [4] **CDS7 47322-8**

Tristan R. Kollo
Isolde M. Price
Brangäne B. Fassbaender
King Marke K. Moll
Kurwenal D. Fischer-Dieskau
Melot W. Götz
Shepherd A. Dermota
Helmsman Wolfgang Hellmich
Sailor E. Büchner
Leipzig Rad Chor, Staatskapelle Dresden, C. Kleiber
(11/86) (DG) Ⓓ [4] **413 315-2GH4**

Tristan J. Vickers
Isolde H. Dernesch
Brangäne C. Ludwig
King Marke K. Ridderbusch
Kurwenal W. Berry
Melot B. Weikl
Shepherd P. Schreier
Helmsman M. Vantin
Sailor P. Schreier
Berlin Deutsche Op Chor, BPO, H. von Karajan (r1971/2)
(7/88) (EMI) Ⓓ [4] **CMS7 69319-2**

Tristan L. Melchior
Isolde K. Flagstad
Brangäne K. Thorborg
King Marke E. List
Kurwenal J. Huehn
Melot G. Cehanovsky
Helmsman D. Beattie
Sailor A. Marlowe
NY Met Op Chor, NY Met Op Orch, E. Leinsdorf (pp1940)
(7/91) (MUSI) Ⓓ [3] **MACD-647**

Tristan L. Melchior
Isolde K. Flagstad
Brangäne M. Klose
Brangäne S. Kalter
King Marke S. Nilsson
King Marke E. List
Kurwenal H. Janssen
Melot B. Hitchin
Melot F. Sale
Shepherd O. Dua
Helmsman L. Horsman
Sailor Parry Jones
Sailor R. Devereux
ROH Chor, LPO, F. Reiner, T. Beecham (pp1936/7)
(1/92) (EMI) Ⓓ [3] **CHS7 64037-2**

Tristan W. Windgassen
Isolde B. Nilsson
Brangäne C. Ludwig
King Marke M. Talvela
Kurwenal E. Waechter
Melot C. Heater
Shepherd E. Wohlfahrt
Helmsman G. Nienstedt
Sailor P. Schreier
Bayreuth Fest Chor, Bayreuth Fest Orch, K. Böhm (pp1966)
(10/92) (PHIL) Ⓓ [3] **434 425-2PH3**

Tristan L. Melchior
Isolde K. Flagstad
Brangäne S. Kalter
King Marke E. List
Kurwenal H. Janssen
Melot F. Sale
Shepherd O. Dua
Helmsman L. Horsman
Sailor R. Devereux
ROH Chor, LPO, F. Reiner (pp1936)
(1/93) (VAI) Ⓓ [3] **VAIA1004**

Tristan G. Treptow
Isolde H. Braun
Brangäne M. Klose
King Marke F. Frantz
Kurwenal P. Schoeffler
Melot A. Peter
Shepherd; Sailor P. Kuen
Helmsman F.R. Bender
Bavarian St Op Chor, Bavarian St Orch, H. Knappertsbusch (pp1950)
(5/95) (ORFE) Ⓓ [3] **C355943D**

Tristan J. Mitchinson
Isolde L. E. Gray
Brangäne A. Wilkens
King Marke G. Howell
Kurwenal P. Joll
Melot N. Folwell
Shepherd A. Davies
Helmsman G. Moses
Sailor J. Harris
WNO Chor, WNO Orch, R. Goodall (r1980/1)
(5/95) (DECC) Ⓓ [4] **443 682-2DMO4**

Tristan M. Lorenz
Isolde P. Buchner
Brangäne M. Klose
King Marke L. Hofmann
Kurwenal J. Prohaska
Melot E. Fuchs
Shepherd E. Zimmermann
Helmsman F. Fleischer
Sailor B. Arnold
Berlin St Op Chor, Berlin Staatskapelle, R. Heger (bp1943)
(9/95) (PREI) Ⓓ [3] **90243**

Tristan S. Jerusalem
Isolde W. Meier
Brangäne M. Lipovšek
King Marke M. Salminen
Kurwenal F. Struckmann
Melot J. Botha
Shepherd P. Maus
Helmsman R. Trekel
Sailor U. Heilmann
Berlin St Op Chor, BPO, D. Barenboim (r1994)
(9/95) (TELD) Ⓓ [4] **4509-94568-2**

Act 3 (abridged) W. Widdop, G. Ljungberg, G. Guszalewicz, I. Andrésen, H. Fry, C. Victor, E. Habich, M. Noe, K. McKenna, SO, LSO, Berlin St Op Orch, A. Coates, L. Blech, L. Collingwood (r1926/7) (7/89) (CLAR) Ⓓ **CDGSE78-50-26**
Cor anglais solo (Act 3) N. Daniel (LEMA) Ⓓ **LC42801**
Dein werk J. Gadski, orch (r1909) (7/91) (CLUB) Ⓓ **CL99-109**
Dein Werk? O thör'ge Maid! N. Larsen-Todsen, A. Helm, Bayreuth Fest Orch, K. Elmendorff (r1928) (1/92) (EMI) Ⓓ [4] **CMS7 64008-2(2)**
Excs P. Hofmann, H. Behrens, Y. Minton, B. Weikl, Bavarian Rad Chor, BRSO, L. Bernstein (pp1981) (PHIL) Ⓓ **438 501-2PH**
Excs W. Windgassen, B. Nilsson, C. Ludwig, M. Talvela, E. Waechter, C. Heater, Bayreuth Fest Chor, Bayreuth Fest Orch, K. Böhm (pp1966) (PHIL) Ⓓ **446 617-2PM**
Excs M. Lorenz, A. Konetzni, M. Klose, H. Alsen, P. Schoeffler, G. Monthy, H. Gallos, K. Ettl, W. Franter, Vienna St Op Chor, Vienna St Op Orch, W, Furtwängler (pp1941/3) (5/95) (SCHW) Ⓓ [2] **314612**
1. French Rad PO, M. Janowski (r1990) (VIRG) ⊟ **VJ7 59689-4**
1. BPO, R. Strauss (r1928) (KOCH) Ⓓ **37119-2**
1. New Philh, A. Boult (EMI) Ⓓ [2] **CZS7 62539-2**
1. Philh, W. Furtwängler (r1952) (EMI) Ⓓ [2] **CHS5 65058-2**
1. VPO, G. Solti (r1960) (DECC) Ⓓ [2] **440 606-2DF2**
1. Los Angeles PO, E. Leinsdorf (r1977) (SHEF) Ⓓ **10052-2-G**
1. Los Angeles PO, E. Leinsdorf (8/87) (SHEF) Ⓓ **CD-7/8**
1. BPO, W. Furtwängler (r1938) (2/89) (ACAN) Ⓓ **43 121**
1. SO, A. Coates (r1926) (7/89) (CLAR) Ⓓ **CDGSE78-50-26**
1. I. Paderewski (arr Schelling: r1930) (3/93) (RCA) Ⓓ **GD60923**
1. I. Paderewski (arr Schelling: r1930) (3/93) (PEAR) Ⓓ **GEMMCD9943**
1, 12. Bayreuth Fest Orch, K. Böhm (pp1966) (DG) Ⓓ [2] **439 687-2GX2**
1, 18. E. Farrell, Boston SO, C. Munch (r1957) (RCA) Ⓓ **GD60686**
1, 18. E. Randová, Brno St PO, O. Lenárd (pp1992) (SUPR) Ⓓ **11 1846-2**
1, 18. J. Norman, LSO, Colin Davis (8/85) (PHIL) Ⓓ **412 655-2PH**
1, 18. J. Norman, VPO, H. von Karajan (pp1987) (8/88) (DG) Ⓓ **423 613-2GH**
1, 18. J. Norman, LPO, K. Tennstedt (11/88) (EMI) Ⓓ **CDC7 49759-2**
1, 18. G. Jones, Cologne RSO, R. Paternostro (2/92) (CHAN) Ⓓ **CHAN8930**
(2/92) (CHAN) ⊟ **ABTD1528**
1, 18. C. Studer, Staatskapelle Dresden, G. Sinopoli (7/94) (DG) Ⓓ **439 865-2GH**
1, 18. J. Eaglen, LCP, R. Norrington (r1994) (11/95) (EMI) Ⓓ **CDC5 55479-2**
1-3, 8c, 9a-d, 12, 15, 18. W. Windgassen, B. Nilsson, E. Waechter, C. Ludwig, P. Schreier, Bayreuth Fest Chor, Bayreuth Fest Orch, K. Böhm (pp1966) (DG) Ⓓ **439 469-2GCL**
1, 9a, 12, 18. A. Marc, Seattle SO, G. Schwarz (r1992) (4/94) (DELO) Ⓓ **DE3120**
3. F. Leider, E. Marherr-Wagner, Berlin St Op Orch, L. Blech (r1929) (MSCM) Ⓓ [2] **MM30283**
(MSCM) ⊟ [2] **MM40105**
3. F. Leider, E. Marherr-Wagner, Berlin St Op Orch, L. Blech (r1928) (PREI) Ⓓ **89098**
3. F. Leider, E. Marherr-Wagner, Berlin St Op Orch, L. Blech (r1928) (1/92) (EMI) Ⓓ [4] **CMS7 64008-2(2)**
3. F. Leider, E. Marherr-Wagner, Berlin St Op Orch, L. Blech (r1928) (10/93) (NIMB) Ⓓ **NI7848**
3, 4. K. Flagstad, E. Höngen, Philh, I. Dobroven (r1948) (8/89) (EMI) Ⓓ **CDH7 63030-2**
3, 8a-c, 9b-d, 18. M. Mödl, J. Blatter, W. Windgassen, Berlin City Op Orch, A. Rother (r1952/4) (5/95) (TELD) Ⓓ **4509-95516-2**
4. F. Leider, E. Marherr-Wagner, Berlin St Op Orch, L. Blech (r1928) (11/89) (PEAR) Ⓓ **GEMMCD9331**
4. F. Leider, E. Marherr-Wagner, Berlin St Op Orch, L. Blech (r1928) (6/90) (LYRC) Ⓓ [2] **LCD146**
6(pt) E. Ferrari-Fontana, orch (r1915: Ital) (4/94) (EMI) Ⓓ [3] **CHS7 64860-2(2)**

6(pt), 8c, 11, 18. R. Bampton, L. Summers, A. Carron, orch, W. Steinberg (r1940) (VAI) Ⓓ **VAIA108**
8. F. Leider, L. Melchior, Berlin St Op Orch, A. Coates (r1929) (8/88) (DANA) Ⓓ [2] **DACOCD315/**
8. L. Melchior, F. Leider, Berlin St Op Orch, LSO, A. Coates (r1929) (7/89) (CLAR) Ⓓ **CDGSE78-50-2**
8. F. Leider, L. Melchior, LSO, Berlin St Op Orch, A. Coates (r1929) (6/90) (LYRC) Ⓓ [2] **LCD14**
8a F. Leider, L. Melchior, Berlin St Op Orch, A. Coates (r1929) (1/92) (EMI) Ⓓ [4] **CMS7 64008-2(**
8a-c F. Leider, L. Melchior, Berlin St Op Orch, LSO, A. Coates (r1929) (MSCM) Ⓓ [2] **MM3028**
(MSCM) ⊟ [2] **MM4010**
8a-c F. Leider, L. Melchior, Berlin St Op Orch, LSO, A. Coates (r1929) (2/90) (PREI) Ⓓ **8900**
8a, 8c F. Leider, F. Soot, orch (r1925) (5/91) (PREI) Ⓓ [3] **8930**
8c H. Dernesch, J. Vickers, BPO, H. von Karajan (r1971/2) (CFP) Ⓓ **CD-CFP465**
(CFP) ⊟ **TC-CFP465**
8c F. Austral, T. Davies, orch, A. Coates (r1923: Eng) (PEAR) Ⓓ **GEMMCD914**
8c K. Flagstad, L. Melchior, San Francisco SO, E. McArthur (r1939) (SIMA) Ⓓ [3] **PSC1821(**
8c S. Sedlmair, E. Schmedes, anon (r1904) (7/91) (SYMP) Ⓓ **SYMCD108**
8c F. Leider, L. Melchior, LSO, A. Coates (r1929) (1/92) (EMI) Ⓓ [4] **CMS7 64008-2(**
8c K. Flagstad, C. Shacklock, S. Svanholm, Philh, K. Böhm (r1949) (7/93) (TEST) Ⓓ **SBT101**
8c, 9a, 9c M. Lorenz, A. Konetzni, M. Klose, Vienna St Op Orch, W. Furtwängler (pp1941) (1/95) (SCHW) Ⓓ [2] **3145**
9a E. Leisner, orch (r1922) (PREI) Ⓓ [2] **892**
9a R. Anday, orch (r1926) (5/92) (PREI) Ⓓ **8904**
9a K. Thorborg, RCA SO, K. Riedel (r1940) (4/95) (PREI) Ⓓ **8908**
10. A. Kipnis, orch (r c1916) (10/91) (PEAR) Ⓓ **GEMMCD945**
10. M. Schenk, Nuremberg SO, K. Seibel (12/91) (COLO) Ⓓ **COL34 90**
10. J. von Manowarda, J. Sattler, Vienna SO, H. Weisbach (pp1940) (11/93) (PREI) Ⓓ **901**
11, 15. L. Melchior, LSO, R. Heger (r1930) (MSCM) Ⓓ [2] **MM302**
(MSCM) ⊟ [2] **MM401**
11, 15. L. Melchior, LSO, R. Heger (r1930) (PREI) Ⓓ **890**
11, 15. L. Melchior, LSO, R. Heger (r1930) (8/88) (DANA) Ⓓ [2] **DACOCD315**
11, 15. L. Melchior, LSO, R. Heger (r1930) (10/89) (EMI) Ⓓ **CDH7 69789**
11, 15. L. Melchior, LSO, R. Heger (r1930) (1/92) (EMI) Ⓓ [4] **CMS7 64008-2(**
12. LPO, A. Boult (EMI) Ⓓ [2] **CZS7 62539**
12. Berlin St Op Orch, W. Furtwängler (pp1947) (2/89) (ACAN) Ⓓ **43 1**
12. Sym of the Air, L. Stokowski (r1961) (3/94) (RCA) Ⓓ **09026 61503**
12. NQHO, B. Wordsworth (r1995) (6/95) (EYE) Ⓓ [2] **EOS50**
12, 18. K. Flagstad, NBC SO, E. McArthur (pp1955) (MUSI) Ⓓ **MACD-2**
14. R. Kollo, Berlin Deutsche Op Orch, C. Thielemann (5/93) (EMI) Ⓓ **CDC7 54776**
15. M. Lorenz, Berlin St Op Orch, R. Heger (r1942) (PREI) Ⓓ **902**
15, 16. W. Widdop, G. Ljungberg, C. Victor, LSO, A. Coates (r1927) (11/92) (CLAR) Ⓓ **CDGSE78-50-**
18. Lotte Lehmann, Berlin St Op Orch, F. Weissmann (r1930) (PEAR) Ⓓ **GEMMCD94**
18. M. Callas, Athens Fest Orch, A. Votto (Ital: pp1957) (EMI) Ⓓ **CDC7 49428**
18. E. Wild (trans Moszkowski: pp1981) (AUDI) Ⓓ [2] **CD720**
18. K. Flagstad, SO, H. Lange (r1930s) (MSCM) Ⓓ [2] **MM302**
(MSCM) ⊟ [2] **MM401**
18. B. Nilsson, Bayreuth Fest Orch, K. Böhm (pp1966) (MEMO) Ⓓ [2] **HR427**
18. M. Caballé, NYPO, Z. Mehta (SONY) Ⓓ **SMK481**
(SONY) ⊟ **SMT481**

18. B. Nilsson, VPO, H. Knappertsbusch
(DECC) Ⓓ **433 068-2DWO**
(DECC) ▣ **433 068-4DWO**
18. M. Callas, Turin RAI Orch, A. Basile (Ital: r1949) (SUIT) Ⓓ **CDS1-5001**
18. BPO, W. Furtwängler (pp1942)
(MUSI) Ⓓ **MACD-730**
18. Philadelphia, E. Ormandy
(SONY) Ⓓ **SBK39438**
18. M. Mödl, Berlin City Op Orch, A. Rother (r1952) (PREI) Ⓓ **90136**
18. M. Korjus, orch, Anon (cond) (r1941)
(DANT) Ⓓ **LYS001**
18. M. Caballé, NYPO, Z. Mehta ( )
(SONY) ◘ **SM48155**
18. K. Flagstad, orch, H. Lange (r1935)
(PEAR) Ⓓ **GEMMCD9049**
18. B. Nilsson, VPO, G. Solti (r1960)
(DECC) Ⓓ **440 069-2DWO**
(DECC) ▣ **440 069-4DWO**
18. Hollywood Bowl SO, J. Mauceri (r1993: arr Stokowski: ed Mauceri)
(PHIL) Ⓓ **438 867-2PH**
(PHIL) ▣ **438 867-4PH**
18. L. Price, Philh, H. Lewis
(RCA) Ⓓ **09026 61886-2**
(RCA) ▣ **09026 61886-4**
18. K. Flagstad, orch, H. Lange (r1935)
(IMP) Ⓓ **GLRS105**
18. VPO, K. Böhm (DG) Ⓓ [2] **439 687-2GX2**
18. VPO, R. Kempe (r1958)
(CFP) Ⓓ **CD-CFP4658**
(CFP) ▣ **TC-CFP4658**
18. M. Callas, Turin RAI Orch, A. Basile (r1949: Ital) (FONI) Ⓓ **CDO104**
18. L. Price, Philh, H. Lewis
(RCA) Ⓓ **74321 25817-2**
(RCA) ▣ **74321 25817-4**
18. H. Wildbrunn, orch (r1919: 2 vers)
(PREI) Ⓓ **89097**
18. L. Price, Philh, H. Lewis (r1979)
(RCA) Ⓓ **09026 62596-2**
18. C. Studer, BRSO, J. Tate (r1988)
(EMI) Ⓓ **CDC5 55350-2**
18. La Scala Orch, A. Guarnieri (r1927)
(BONG) Ⓓ **GB1039-2**
18. J. Norman, LPO, K. Tennstedt (r1987)
(EMI) Ⓓ **CDM5 65576-2**
18. K. Flagstad, orch, H. Lange (r1935)
(SIMA) Ⓓ [3] **PSC1821(1)**
18. G. Saba (trs. Moszkowski)
(10/87) (IMP) Ⓓ **PCD858**
18. K. Flagstad, Philh, I. Dobroven (r1948)
(8/89) (EMI) Ⓓ **CDH7 63030-2**
18. F. Leider, LSO, J. Barbirolli (r1931)
(11/89) (PEAR) Ⓓ **GEMMCD9331**
18. F. Leider, LSO, J. Barbirolli (r1931)
(2/90) (PREI) Ⓓ **89004**
18. F. Leider, LSO, J. Barbirolli (r1931)
(6/90) (LYRC) Ⓓ [2] **LCD146**
18. K. Flagstad, San Francisco Op Orch, E. MacArthur (r1939) (10/90) (RCA) Ⓓ **GD87915**
18. C. Curley (arr Curley)
(2/91) (ARGO) Ⓓ **430 200-2ZH**
18. G. Lubin, orch, H. Defosse (French: r1930)
(5/91) (CLUB) Ⓓ **CL99-022**
18. F. Leider, orch (r1921)
(5/91) (PREI) Ⓓ [3] **89301**
18. G. Lubin, orch, H. Defosse (French: r1930)
(5/91) (EPM) Ⓓ **150 052**
18. M. Seinemeyer, Berlin St Op Orch, F. Weissmann (r1928)
(1/92) (EMI) Ⓓ [4] **CMS7 64008-2(2)**
18. G. Lubin, Paris Cons, P. Gaubert (French: r1938) (1/92) (EMI) Ⓓ [4] **CMS7 64008-2(2)**
18. K. Flagstad, orch, H. Lange (r1935)
(7/92) (PEAR) Ⓓ [3] **GEMMCDS9926(2)**
18. O. Fremstad, orch (r1913)
(7/92) (PEAR) Ⓓ [3] **GEMMCDS9923(2)**
18. C. Ludwig, Philh, O. Klemperer
(9/92) (EMI) Ⓓ [4] **CMS7 64074-2(2)**
18. F. Litvinne, anon (Fr: r1903)
(10/92) (SYMP) Ⓓ **SYMCD1101**
18. F. Litvinne, A. Cortot (Fr: r1902)
(10/92) (SYMP) Ⓓ **SYMCD1101**
18. L. Price, Philh, H. Lewis (r1979)
(12/92) (RCA) Ⓓ [4] **09026 61236-2**
8. K. Flagstad, orch, H. Lange (r1935)
(7/93) (NIMB) Ⓓ **NI7847**
8. K. Flagstad, orch, H. Lange (r1935)
(12/93) (NIMB) Ⓓ **NI7851**
8. M. Jeritza, orch (r1927)
(4/94) (PREI) Ⓓ **89079**
8. K. Flagstad, orch, H. Lange (r1936)
(4/94) (RCA) Ⓓ [6] **09026 61580-2(4)**

18. E. Destinn, orch (r1910)
(12/94) (SUPR) Ⓓ [12] **11 2136-2(4)**
18. E. Destinn, orch (r1911)
(12/94) (SUPR) Ⓓ [12] **11 2136-2(4)**
19. Chicago SO, G. Solti
(DECC) ▣ **071 101-3DH**
19. Philh, F. d'Avalos (ASV) Ⓓ **CDDCA611**
19. LPO, E. Bátiz (MCI) Ⓓ **OQ0009**
19. Concertgebouw, B. Haitink
(PHIL) Ⓓ **420 886-2PSL**
19. Budapest SO, G. Lehel (LASE) Ⓓ **15 521**
(LASE) ▣ **79 521**
19. Stockholm PO, W. Furtwängler (pp1942)
(BIS) Ⓓ [8] **BIS-CD421/4(2)**
19. Leningrad PO, E. Mravinsky (pp1965)
(OLYM) Ⓓ [6] **OCD5002**
19. Philadelphia, E. Ormandy
(RCA) Ⓓ **VD60493**
19. Cleveland Orch, G. Szell
(CBS) Ⓓ [2] **CD46466**
19. BPO, H. von Karajan (r1974)
(EMI) Ⓓ **CDM7 64334-2**
19. BPO, S. Ozawa (PHIL) OO **426 271-5PH**
19. NBC SO, A. Toscanini (r1942)
(RCA) Ⓓ **GD60306**
19. Prague RSO, V. Talich (r1953)
(MULT) Ⓓ **310151-2**
19. Bamberg SO, T. Guschlbauer (r1976)
(ERAT) Ⓓ **4509-92866-2**
19. VPO, H. Stein (r1974) (BELA) Ⓓ **450 025-2**
(BELA) ▣ **450 025-4**
19. South-West German RSO, M. Gielen (r1989)
(INTE) Ⓓ **INT860 908**
19. NYPO, L. Bernstein (r1967)
(SONY) Ⓓ **SMK47644**
19. Philh, F. d'Avalos (ASV) Ⓓ **CDQS6126**
19. Los Angeles PO, E. Leinsdorf (r1961)
(EMI) Ⓓ **CDM5 65208-2**
19. Sydney SO, J. Serebrier
(IMG) Ⓓ **IMGCD1611**
19. Cincinnati SO, J. López-Cobos (r1994)
(TELA) Ⓓ **CD80379**
19. LSO, A. Dorati (r1959)
(MERC) Ⓓ **434 342-2MM**
19. M. Caballé, Strasbourg PO, A. Lombard (r1976) (ERAT) Ⓓ **4509-98499-2**
19. Leningrad PO, E. Mravinsky (pp1978)
(MELO) Ⓓ **74321 25199-2**
19. Leningrad PO, E. Mravinsky (pp1965)
(MELO) Ⓓ [10] **74321 25189-2**
19. LSO, W. Morris
(12/87) (CIRR) Ⓓ **CICD1005**
19. Philh, O. Klemperer
(11/90) (EMI) Ⓓ **CDM7 63617-2**
19. Chicago SO, G. Solti
(5/91) (DECC) Ⓓ **430 448-2DM**
19. Philh, Y. Simonov
(10/91) (COLL) Ⓓ **Coll1207-2**
19. NBC SO, A. Toscanini (r1952)
(12/91) (RCA) Ⓓ **GD60264**
19. BPO, W. Furtwängler (r1930)
(4/92) (KOCH) Ⓓ [2] **37073-2**
19. Frankfurt RSO, E. Inbal
(6/92) (DENO) Ⓓ **CO-77715**
19. Leningrad PO, E. Mravinsky (pp1978)
(6/92) (ERAT) Ⓓ [11] **2292-45763-2**
19. Leningrad PO, E. Mravinsky (pp1978)
(6/92) (ERAT) Ⓓ **2292-45762-2**
19. BPO, V. de Sabata (r1939)
(11/92) (KOCH) Ⓓ **37126-2**
19. Cleveland Orch, G. Szell
(11/92) (SONY) Ⓓ **SBK48175**
19. Oslo PO, M. Jansons
(12/92) (EMI) Ⓓ **CDC7 54583-2**
19. Leningrad PO, E. Mravinsky (pp1967)
(3/94) (RUSS) Ⓓ **RDCD11166**
19. BPO, W. Furtwängler (r1938)
(4/94) (EMI) Ⓓ [2] **CHS7 64935-2**
19. BPO, W. Furtwängler (r1938)
(7/94) (BIDD) Ⓓ [2] **WHL006/7**
19. NYPO, J. Barbirolli (pp1938)
(3/95) (DUTT) Ⓓ **CDSJB1001**
19. BPO, W. Furtwängler (pp1942)
(3/95) (TAHR) Ⓓ [4] **FURT1004/7**
19. NYPO, P. Boulez (r1973)
(7/95) (SONY) Ⓓ **SMK64108**

WAGNER , Siegfried (Helferich Richard) *(1869–1930)* Germany

An allem ist Hütchen schuld– opera: 3 acts, Op. 11 (1917—Stuttgart) (Lib. cpsr)
EXCERPTS: 1. Prelude; 2. Waltz; 3. Forest Scene.
1, 2, 3. Rhineland-Pfalz State PO, W. A. Albert (r1994) (CPO) Ⓓ **CPO999 300-2**

Der Bärenhäuter– opera: 3 acts, Op. 1 (1899) (Lib. cpsr)
EXCERPTS: 1. Overture. ACT 3: 2. Introduction; 3. Devil's Waltz (concert vers of Act 1 Finale).

Hans Kraft	V. Horn
Melchior Fröhlich	H. Kiichli
Lene	K. Lukic
Gunda	T. Koon
Luise	B. Johanning
Pastor Wippenbeck	L. Hübel
Nikolaus Spitz	A. Feilhaber
Anna	K. Quandt
Colonel Muffel; Corporal	N. Barowski
Kaspar Wild	R. Hartmann
The stranger	A. Wenhold
The devil	A. Waller

Thüringian Landestheater Chor, Thüringian SO, K. Bach (r1993)
(6/95) (MARC) Ⓓ [2] **8 223713/4**
1, 2, 3. Rhineland-Pfalz State PO, W. A. Albert (r1994) (CPO) Ⓓ **CPO999 300-2**

Des Flüchlein, das jeder mitbekam– opera: 3 acts, Op. 18 (Lib. cpsr: work unfinished: cpted H P Mohr, 1983)
EXCERPTS: 1. Prelude.
1. Rhineland-Pfalz State PO, W. A. Albert (r1994) (CPO) Ⓓ **CPO999 300-2**

Der Friedensengel– opera: 3 acts, Op. 10 (1926—Karlsruhe) (Lib. cpsr)
EXCERPTS: 1. Prelude.
1. Rhineland-Pfalz State PO, W. A. Albert (r1994) (CPO) Ⓓ **CPO999 003-2**

Die heilige Lind– opera: 3 acts (1924—Bayreuth) (Lib. cpsr. Only Prelude given in 1924)
EXCERPTS: 1. Prelude.
1. Rhineland-Pfalz State PO, W. A. Albert (r1994) (CPO) Ⓓ **CPO999 003-2**

Herzog Wildfang– opera: 3 acts, Op. 2 (1901—Munich) (Lib. cpsr)
EXCERPTS: 1. Overture.
1. Rhineland-Pfalz State PO, W. A. Albert (r1994) (CPO) Ⓓ **CPO999 003-2**

Der Schmied von Marienburg– opera: 3 acts (1923—Rostock) (Lib. cpsr)
EXCERPTS: 1. Overture.
1. Rhineland-Pfalz State PO, W. A. Albert (r1994) (CPO) Ⓓ **CPO999 003-2**

Schwarzschwanenreich, 'Kingdom of the Black Swan'– opera: 3 acts, Op. 7 (1918—Karlsruhe) (Lib. cpsr)

Linda	B. Johanning
Ludwig	W. Raffeiner
Ursula	K. Quandt
Oswald	A. Wenhold
Zina	J. M. Schmitz
Tempter, Priest	R. Hartmann
Boy	L. Chioreanu
Girl	K. Lukic

Thüringian Landestheater Chor, Thüringian SO, K. Bach (pp1994)
(11/95) (MARC) Ⓓ [2] **8 223777/8**

WALLACE, Stewart *(b 1960)* USA

Kabbalah– opera: 7 movements (1989) (Lib. M. Korie)
Cpte K. Holvik, E. Means, R. Wong, A. Montano, P. Warrick-Smith, E. Bowers, J. Godfrey, H. Munday, M. Sokol, R. Osborne, I. Crawford, T. Christensen, A. Sterman, C. Paisner, T. Gilson, B. Ruyle, M. Barrett (KOCH) Ⓓ **37048-2**

WALLACE, (William) Vincent *(1812–1865)* Ireland

Maritana– opera: 3 acts (1845—London) (Lib. Fitzball)
EXCERPTS: 1. Overture. ACT 1: 3. 'Tis the harp in the air; 4. The Angelus; 5. Of fairy wand had I the power; 7. Pretty Gitana. ACT 2: 9. Alas! Those chimes; 11. Turn on, old time; 12. Yes, let me like a soldier fall; 13. In happy moments day by day; 17. Hear me, gentle Maritana; 18. There is a flower that bloometh; 19. What mystery? (Finale). ACT 3: 21. Scenes that are brightest; 22. I am the King of Spain; 24. Oh Maritana!; 25. Sainted Mother.

12. H. Nash, orch (r1931)
(8/89) (PEAR) Ⓓ **GEMMCD9319**
12. W. Widdop, Orch, L. Collingwood (r1930)
(11/92) (CLAR) Ⓓ **CDGSE78-50-46**
21. R. Ponselle, orch (r1921)
(PEAR) Ⓓ [2] **GEMMCDS9964**
21. J. Sutherland, LSO, R. Bonynge (r1962)
(DECC) Ⓓ **425 048-2DX**
(DECC) ▭ **425 048-4DX**
21. S. Murphy, WNO Orch, Julian Smith (r1992)
(SONY) Ⓓ **474364-2**

WALTON , Sir William (Turner) *(1902–1983) England*

The **Bear– extravaganza: 1 act (1967—Aldeburgh) (Lib. I P Dehn, after Chekhov)**
Madame Popova D. Jones
Smirnov A. Opie
Luka J. Shirley-Quirk
Northern Sinfonia, R. Hickox (r1993)
(1/94) (CHAN) Ⓓ **CHAN9245**

Troilus and Cressida– opera: 3 acts (1954—London) (Lib. C Hassall, after G Chaucer: rev 1976)
EXCERPTS: ACT 1: 1. Is Cressida a slave?; 2. Slowly it all comes back. ACT 2: 3. How can I sleep?; 4. Is anyone there?; 5. If one last doubt; 6. Now close your arms; 7. Interlude; 8. From isle to isle chill waters. ACT 3: 9. All's well; 10. Diomede!...Father!.
Troilus A. Davies
Cressida J. Howarth
Pandarus N. Robson
Evadne Y. Howard
Antenor J. Thornton
Calkas C. Bayley
Horaste D. Owen-Lewis
Diomede A. Opie
Priest P. Bodenham
Soldier K. Mills
Watchman I B. Budd
Watchman II S. Dowson
Watchman III B. Cookson
Op North Chor, English Northern Philh, R. Hickox (r1995)
(5/95) (CHAN) Ⓓ [2] **CHAN9370/1**
Troilus R. Cassilly
Cressida J. Baker
Pandarus G. English
Evadne E. Bainbridge
Antenor M. Rivers
Calkas R. Van Allan
Horaste R. Lloyd
Diomede B. Luxon
Priest G. Macpherson
Soldier G. Sullivan
Watchman I H. Thomas
Watchman II Alan Jones II
Watchman III D. McCoshan
ROH Chor, ROHO, L. Foster (pp1976)
(7/95) (EMI) Ⓓ [2] **CMS5 65550-2**
Interlude LPO, Carl Davis (r1986)
(EMI) Ⓓ **CDM5 65585-2**
1-3, 5-10. E. Schwarzkopf, M. Sinclair, Richard Lewis, L. Thomas, G. Walls, J. Hauxvell, Philh, W. Walton (r1955)
(1/94) (EMI) Ⓓ **CDM7 64199-2**
4. M. Collier, P. Pears, ROHO, W. Walton (r1968) (1/94) (EMI) Ⓓ **CDM7 64199-2**

Troilus and Cressida– concert suite from opera (1987) (arr C. Palmer)
1. Prelude and Seascape; 2. Scherzo; 3. The Lovers; 4. Finale.
LPO, B. Thomson
(7/90) (CHAN) Ⓓ **CHAN8772**
(7/90) (CHAN) ▭ **ABTD1410**

WARD , Robert *(b 1917) USA*

Abelard and Heloise– opera: 3 acts (1981—Charlotte) (Lib. J Hartman)
Condemn not, o woeful man W. Stone, T. Warburton (BAY) Ⓓ **BCD-1029**

Claudia Legare– opera: 4 acts (1973—Minneapolis) (Lib. Stambler, after Ibsen)
Lament for Aunt Renie;The South must industrialize W. Stone, T. Warburton
(BAY) Ⓓ **BCD-1029**

The **Crucible– opera: 4 acts (1961—New York) (Lib. B. Stambler, after A. Miller)**
Betty Parris J. Ebert
Revd. Samuel Parris N. Kelly
Tituba G. Wynder
Abigail Williams P. Brooks
Ann Putnam; Sarah Good N. Farr
Thomas Putnam P. Ukena
Rebecca Nurse E. Alberts
Francis Nurse S. Malas
Giles Corey M. Stern
John Proctor C. Ludgin
Revd. John Hale J. Macurdy
Elizabeth Proctor F. Bible
Mary Warren N. Foster
Ezekiel Cheever R. Krause
Judge Janforth J. DeLon
Ruth Putnam L. Ceniceros
Susanna Walcott H. Guile
Martha Sheldon M. Kova
Mercy Lewis E. Schwering
Bridget Booth B. Evans
NYC Op Orch, E. Buckley
(6/90) (ALBA) Ⓓ [2] **TROY025/6-2**
It's a good time is springtime;I am John Proctor W. Stone, T. Warburton
(BAY) Ⓓ **BCD-1029**

He who gets Slapped (Pantalon)– opera: 3 acts (1955 rev 1973—New York) (Lib. B. Stambler, after Andneyev)
Pantaloon's Ballad W. Stone, T. Warburton
(BAY) Ⓓ **BCD-1029**

The **Lady from Colorado– opera: 2 acts (1964—Central City) (Lib. Stambler, after H. Croy)**
Law and Order;I ride along;State Senator, Jack Spaniard!;I hail this land W. Stone, T. Warburton (BAY) Ⓓ **BCD-1029**

Minutes till Midnight– opera: 3 acts (1978-82—Miami) (Lib. Lang and cpsr)
O Cosmos, with your myriad stars W. Stone, T. Warburton (BAY) Ⓓ **BCD-1029**

WEBER, Carl Maria (Friedrich Ernst) von *(1786–1826) Germany*

J numbers used in F. W. Jahn's thematic catalogue

Abu Hassan– Singspiel: 1 act, J106 (1811—Munich) (Lib. Hiemer, after The 1001 Nights)
Abu Hassan E. Witte
Fatime E. Schwarzkopf
Omar M. Bohnen
chor, Berlin RSO, L. Ludwig (bp1944: omits dialogue)
(PREI) Ⓓ [2] **90209**
Abu Hassan E. Witte
Fatime E. Schwarzkopf
Omar M. Bohnen
chor, Berlin RSO, L. Ludwig (bp1944)
(9/89) (FORL) Ⓓ **UCD16572**
Overture Staatskapelle Dresden, G. Kuhn
(CAPR) Ⓓ **10 052**
(CAPR) ▭ **CC27 076**
Overture Paris Op Orch, H. Scherchen
(ADES) Ⓓ **13203-2**
Overture Hallé, S. Skrowaczewski
(IMP) Ⓓ **PCD1105**
Overture LSO, C. Mackerras (r1961)
(MERC) Ⓓ **434 352-2MM**
Overture BPO, H. von Karajan
(6/88) (DG) Ⓓ **419 070-2GGA**
Overture Hanover Band, R. Goodman
(6/89) (NIMB) Ⓓ **NI5154**
(NIMB) ▭ **NC5154**
Overture Philh, W. Sawallisch
(1/90) (EMI) Ⓓ **CDM7 69572-2**
Overture Philh, N. Järvi
(4/93) (CHAN) Ⓓ **CHAN9066**

Die **drei Pintos– comic opera: unfinished, JAnh5 (cpted Mahler)**
EXCERPTS: 1. Entr'acte (arr/reworked Mahler).
1. Queensland PO, J. Georgiadis (r1994)
(2/95) (NAXO) Ⓓ **8 550928**

Euryanthe– opera: 3 acts, J291 (1823—Vienna) (Lib. von Chezy)
Overture Staatskapelle Dresden, G. Kuhn
(CAPR) Ⓓ **10 052**
(CAPR) ▭ **CC27 076**
Overture Paris Op Orch, H. Scherchen
(ADES) Ⓓ **13203-2**
Overture BPO, R. Strauss (r1928)
(KOCH) Ⓓ **37119-2**
Overture NBC SO, A. Toscanini (r1951)
(RCA) Ⓓ **GD6029**
Overture Hallé, S. Skrowaczewski
(IMP) Ⓓ **PCD110**
Overture USSR SO, E. Mravinsky (pp1959)
(RUSS) Ⓓ **RDCD1090**
Overture BPO, H. von Karajan
(6/88) (DG) Ⓓ **419 070-2GG**
Overture Hanover Band, R. Goodman
(6/89) (NIMB) Ⓓ **NI515**
(NIMB) ▭ **NC515**
Overture Philh, W. Sawallisch
(1/90) (EMI) Ⓓ **CDM7 69572-**
Overture Philh, N. Järvi
(1/90) (CHAN) Ⓓ **CHAN876**
(1/90) (CHAN) ▭ **ABTD140**
Overture NBC SO, A. Toscanini, D. Rodgers
(9/91) (RCA) **780 35**
(12/90) (RCA) **790 35**
Overture Philh, N. Järvi
(4/93) (CHAN) Ⓓ **CHAN906**
Overture NYPO, L. Bernstein (r1968)
(9/93) (SONY) Ⓓ **SMK4760**
So bin ich nun verlassen...Hier dicht am Quell J. Norman, Staatskapelle Dresden, M. Janowski
(EMI) Ⓓ **CDM7 69256-**
Unter blüh'nden Mandelbäumen; Wehen mir Lüfte Ruh' K. Erb, orch (r1911)
(PREI) Ⓓ **8909**
Unter blüh'nden Mandelbäumen L. Slezak, orch (r1908) (2/91) (PREI) Ⓓ **8902**
Wo berg' ich mich? F. Schorr, orch (r1922)
(PREI) Ⓓ **8905**
Wo berg' ich mich? B. Weikl, Munich RO, H. Wallberg (3/89) (ACAN) Ⓓ **43 26**
Wo berg' ich mich? F. Schorr, orch (r1921)
(9/91) (PEAR) Ⓓ **GEMMCD939**
Wo berg' ich mich?...So weih' ich mich den Rachgewalten T. Hampson, Munich RO, F. Luisi (r1994) (9/95) (EMI) Ⓓ **CDC5 55233-**

Der **Freischütz– opera: 3 acts (1821—Berlin) (Lib. Kind)**
1. Overture. ACT 1: 2. Glück zu, Bauer!...Ah! Viktoria!; 3. Procession of villagers; 4. Schau der Herr mich an als König; 5. O diese Sonne!; 6. Mein Sohn, nur Mut; 7a. Nein! länger trag' ich nicht die Qualen; 7b. Durch die Wälder; 8. Hier im ird'schen Jammertal; 9. Schweig, schweig. ACT 2: 10. Schelm! Halt fest!; 11. Kommt ein schlanker Bursch; 12a. Wie nahte mir der Schlummer; 12b. Leise, leise, fromme Weise; 12c. Alles pflegt; 13. Wie? Was? Entsetzen!; 14. Milch des Mondes (Wolf's Glen Scene). ACT 3: 15. Entracte; 16. Und ob die Wolke; 17. Einst träumte meiner sel'gen Base; 18. Wir winden dir den Jungfernkranz; 19. Was gleicht wohl auf Erden (Huntsmen's Chorus); 20a. Genug nun der Freuden des Mahles; 20b. Schaut! O schaut!; 21. Leicht kann des Frommen Herz (Hermit's Aria); 22. Dein Wort genüget mir; 23. Die Zukunft soll mein Herz.
Agathe C. Ligendz
Max T. Kräme
Aennchen R. Viljakaine
Kaspar W. Prob
Württemberg St Op Chor, Württemberg St Op Orch, D.R. Davies, A. Freyer
(CAST) **CVI203**
Agathe G. Janowi
Max P. Schrei
Aennchen E. Math
Kaspar T. Ada
Ottokar B. Wei
Hermit F. Cras
Kuno S. Vog
Samiel G. Pa
Kilian G. Lie
Leipzig Rad Chor, Staatskapelle Dresden, C. Kleiber (with dialogue)
(11/86) (DG) Ⓓ [2] **415 432-2GH**
Agathe E. Grümm
Max R. Schoc
Aennchen L. Ot
Kaspar K.C. Kol
Ottokar H. Pr
Hermit G. Fri
Kuno E. Wiemar
Samiel F. Hopp
Kilian W.W. Dic
Berlin Deutsche Op Chor, BPO, J. Keilberth (r1958: with dialogue)
(9/89) (EMI) Ⓓ [2] **CMS7 69342**
Agathe I. Seefri
Max Richard Hol
Aennchen R. Strei
Kaspar K. Böhr

Ottokar	E. Waechter
Hermit	W. Kreppel
Kuno	A. Peter
Samiel	E. Ginsberg
Kilian	P. Kuen

Bavarian Rad Chor, BRSO, E. Jochum (r1959)
(12/94) (DG) ① [2] **439 717-2GX2**

Agathe	S. Sweet
Max	P. Seiffert
Aennchen	R. Ziesak
Kaspar	K. Rydl
Ottokar	A. Schmidt
Hermit	M. Hölle
Kuno	A. Scharinger
Samiel	P. Matić
Kilian	R. Trekel

Berlin Rad Chor, Berlin RO, M. Janowski (r1994; with dialogue)
(1/95) (RCA) ① [2] **09026 62538-2**

Agathe	C. Watson
Max	R. Schock
Aennchen	L. Schädle
Kaspar	G. Frick
Ottokar	C. Nicolai
Hermit	K. Böhme
Kuno	F. Ollendorff
Samiel	K. Meisel
Kilian	K. Lang

Berlin Deutsche Op Chor, Berlin Deutsche Op Orch, L. von Matačić (r1967; with dialogue)
(6/95) (RCA) ① [2] **74321 25287-2**

Agathe	H. Behrens
Max	R. Kollo
Aennchen	H. Donath
Kaspar	P. Meven
Ottakar	W. Brendel
Hermit	K. Moll
Kuno	R. Grumbach
Samiel	R. Boysen
Kilian	H. Sapell

Bavarian Rad Chor, BRSO, R. Kubelík (r1979)
(8/95) (DECC) ① [2] **443 672-2DMO2**

Excs Horreaux-Trehard Duo (arr 2 gtrs) (CALL) ① **CAL9218**

Excs Consortium Classicum (arr. Sedlak for wind ens) (3/88) (MDG) ① **L3267**

Young Brides' Chorus BRSO, BRS Chor, E. Jochum (BELA) ① **450 126-2** (BELA) ▭ **450 126-4**

1. Philh, W. Boughton (NIMB) ① **NI5120** (NIMB) ▭ **NC5120**

1. Czech PO, Z. Chalabala (SUPR) ▭ **11 0640-4**

1. Staatskapelle Dresden, G. Kuhn (CAPR) ① **10 052** (CAPR) ▭ **CC27 076**

1. BRSO, R. Kubelík (DG) ① **415 840-2GGA**

1. BPO, W. Furtwängler (r1926) (SYMP) ① **SYMCD1043**

1. NBC SO, A. Toscanini (r1945) (RCA) ① **GD60310**

1. NBC SO, A. Toscanini (r1952) (RCA) ① **GD60292**

1. BPO, H. von Karajan (EMI) ① **CDM7 64629-2**

1. BPO, H. von Karajan, H. Burton (r1985) (SONY) ◐ **SLV46402** (SONY) ▭ **SHV46402**

1. NY Harmonie Ens, S. Richman (r1992: arr K Flachs) (MUSI) ① **MACD-797**

1. Hallé, S. Skrowaczewski (IMP) ① **PCD1105**

1. BPO, W. Furtwängler (r1944) (MUSI) ① **MACD-826**

1. Bavarian Nat Orch, E. Jochum (DG) ① [2] **447 364-2GDB2**

1. BPO, H. von Karajan (6/88) (DG) ① **419 070-2GGA**

1. Hanover Band, R. Goodman (6/89) (NIMB) ① **NI5154** (NIMB) ▭ **NC5154**

1. Philh, W. Sawallisch (1/90) (EMI) ① **CDM7 69572-2**

1. Philh, N. Järvi (1/90) (CHAN) ① **CHAN8766** (1/90) (CHAN) ▭ **ABTD1404**

1. BPO, W. Furtwängler (r1926) (4/92) (KOCH) ① [2] **37059-2**

1. Philh, N. Järvi (4/93) (CHAN) ① **CHAN9066**

1. NYPO, L. Bernstein (r1968) (9/93) (SONY) ① **SMK47601**

1. LPO, T. Beecham (r1936) (10/94) (DUTT) ① **CDLX7009**

1. Paris SO, F. Weingartner (r1932) (4/95) (TELD) ◐ **4509-95038-6** (4/95) (TELD) ▭ **4509-95038-3**

1. Philh, C. P. Flor (r1993) (11/95) (RCA) ① **09026 62712-2**

1, 15. BPO, W. Furtwängler (r1935) (4/92) (KOCH) ① [2] **37073-2**

1, 2, 14, 15, 19, 20b(pt) M. Reining, E. Rutgers, J. Pölzer, H. Alsen, A. Muzzarelli, G. Monthy, K. Ettl, Vienna St Op Chor, Vienna St Op Orch, R. Moralt (pp1939) (6/95) (SCHW) ① [2] **314632**

1, 2, 4, 7a, 7b, 8, 10, 11, 12, 12a, 12b, 14, 16, 18, 19, 23. K. Mattila, F. Araiza, E. Lind, E. Wlaschiha, S. Lorenz, K. Moll, T. Thomaschke, W. Quadflieg, A. Scheibner, Leipzig Rad Chor, Staatskapelle Dresden, Colin Davis (r1990) (PHIL) ① **438 497-2PH**

1, 2, 7a, 7b, 9-11, 12a, 12b, 14, 16, 18, 19. G. Janowitz, E. Mathis, P. Schreier, T. Adam, G. Leib, G. Paul, Leipzig Rad Chor, Staatskapelle Dresden, C. Kleiber (r1973) (DG) ① **439 440-2GCL**

5. S. Svanholm, F. Normann, M. Rus, Vienna St Op Chor, Vienna St Op Orch, H. Knappertsbusch (pp1941) (SCHW) ① [2] **314692**

5, 7a, 7b, 8, 12a, 12b, 16, 18. F. Völker, E. Rethberg, J. von Manowarda, K. Ettl, Vienna St Op Chor, Vienna St Op Orch, J. Krips (pp1933) (11/94) (SCHW) ① [2] **314532**

5, 8, 9, 12a, 14(pt), 16. C. Bissuti, T. Lemnitz, E. Rutgers, M. Bohnen, F. Völker, V. Soetber, W. Franter, Vienna St Op Chor, Vienna St Op Orch, H. Knappertsbusch (pp1939) (SCHW) ① [2] **314672**

7. H. Roswaenge, Berlin St Op Orch, B. Seidler-Winkler (r1937) (5/90) (PEAR) ① **GEMMCD9394**

7. P. Anders, Berlin Deutsche Op Orch, A. Rother (r1952) (4/92) (EMI) ① [7] **CHS7 69741-2(4)**

7a, 7b A. Dermota, Ljubljana RSO, S. Hubad (r1950s) (PREI) ① **90022**

7a, 7b P. Anders, Berlin Deutsche Op Orch, J. Schüler (r1937) (TELD) ① **4509-95512-2**

7a, 7b P. Anders, South-West German RSO, O. Ackermann (bp1952) (8/93) (ACAN) ① **43 268**

7a, 7b F. Völker, Berlin Staatskapelle, G. Steeger (r1938) (8/94) (PREI) ① **89070**

7a, 7b H. Roswaenge, Berlin St Op Orch, B. Seidler-Winkler (r1936) (4/95) (PREI) ① [2] **89209**

7b P. Seiffert, Munich RO, J. Kout (r1992-3) (RCA) ① **09026 61214-2**

7b R. Tauber, orch, N. Treep (bp1939) (2/92) (LYRC) ① [2] **SRO830**

8. J. Herrmann, Berlin St Op Orch, B. Seidler-Winkler (r1942) (PREI) ① **89076**

8. E. List, Berlin St Op Orch, F. Weissmann (r1930) (PREI) ① **89083**

8. A. Kipnis, Berlin St Op Orch, C. Schmalstich (r1930) (12/90) (PREI) ① **89019**

8. J. Herrmann, Berlin St Op Orch, B. Seidler-Winkler (r1942) (4/92) (EMI) ① [7] **CHS7 69741-2(4)**

8. N. de Angelis, orch, L. Molajoli (Ital: r1927) (7/92) (PREI) ① **89042**

8, 9. K. Moll, Munich RO, K. Eichhorn (r1981) (ORFE) ① **C009821A**

11. M. Michailova, orch, B. Seidler-Winkler (r1905: Russ) (PEAR) ① [3] **GEMMCDS9111(1)**

12a E. Destinn, orch (r1910) (PEAR) ① **GEMMCD9172**

12a G. Lubin, orch (French: r1927) (5/91) (EPM) ① **150 052**

12a Lotte Lehmann, orch (r1917) (6/92) (PREI) ① [3] **89302**

12a M. Jeritza, orch (r1926) (4/94) (PREI) ① **89079**

12a-c T. Lemnitz, Berlin St Op Orch, B. Seidler-Winkler (r1939) (10/90) (PREI) ① **89025**

12a-c E. Destinn, orch (r1912) (12/94) (SUPR) ① [12] **11 2136-2(4)**

12a-c, 16. M. Seinemeyer, orch, F. Weissmann (r1926) (PEAR) ① **GEMMCD9082**

12a-c, 16. I. Seefried, BRSO, E. Jochum (r1959) (9/93) (DG) ① [2] **437 677-2GDO2**

12a, 12b P. Lorengar, Vienna St Op Orch, W. Weller (r1970) (DECC) ① **443 931-2DM**

12a, 12b E. Schwarzkopf, Philh, W. Susskind (r1956) (EMI) ① **CDM5 65577-2**

12a, 12b H. Konetzni, Berlin Deutsche Op Orch, H. Schmidt-Isserstedt (r1937) (1/95) (PREI) ① **90078**

12a, 12b E. Rethberg, orch (r1929) (2/95) (ROMO) ① [2] **81012-2**

12a, 12b, 16. G. Janowitz, Berlin Deutsche Op Orch, F. Leitner (r1967) (DG) ① [2] **447 352-2GDB2**

12a, 12b, 16. E. Destinn, orch, F. Kark (r1908) (12/94) (SUPR) ① [12] **11 2136-2(2)**

12a, 16. E. Destinn, orch (r1910) (12/94) (SUPR) ① [12] **11 2136-2(4)**

12c E. Destinn, orch (r1912) (PEAR) ① **GEMMCD9172**

12c Lotte Lehmann, orch (r1916) (6/92) (PREI) ① [3] **89302**

12c(pt) E. Destinn, orch, F. Kark (r1908) (5/94) (SUPR) ① **11 1337-2**

12, 12b L. Price, RCA Italiana Op Orch, F. Molinari-Pradelli (12/92) (RCA) ① [4] **09026 61236-2**

12, 16. E. Schwarzkopf, Philh, W. Susskind (10/88) (EMI) ① **CDM7 69501-2**

16. J. Sutherland, LSO, R. Bonynge (r1963) (DECC) ① **421 881-2DA**

16. A. Tomowa-Sintow, Munich RO, P. Sommer (11/86) (ORFE) ① **C106841A**

16. T. Lemnitz, Berlin St Op Orch, L. Blech (r1935) (10/90) (PREI) ① **89025**

16. Lotte Lehmann, orch (r1921) (6/92) (PREI) ① [3] **89302**

16. M. Teschemacher, Berlin City Op Orch, H.U. Müller (r1934) (11/92) (PREI) ① **89049**

19. ROH Chor, RPO, R. Stapleton (RPO) ① **CDRPO7009** (RPO) ▭ **ZCRPO7009**

19. Berlin Deutsche Op Chor, Berlin Deutsche Op Orch, G. Sinopoli (DG) **OO 415 283-5GH**

19. ROH Chor, RPO, R. Stapleton (r1991) (RPO) ① [2] **CDRPD9006** (RPO) ▭ [2] **ZCRPD9006**

19. ROH Male Chor, R. Stapleton (r1991) (IMP) ① **PCDS21** (IMP) ▭ **PCDSC21**

19. ROH Chor, RPO, R. Stapleton (IMP) ① [3] **TCD1070**

19. Berlin Deutsche Op Chor, Berlin Deutsche Op Orch, G. Sinopoli (10/85) (DG) ① **415 283-2GH**

19. ROH Chor, ROHO, B. Haitink (12/89) (EMI) ① **CDC7 49849-2**

21. F. Schorr, New SO, A. Coates (r1930) (2/95) (CLAR) ① **CDGSE78-50-54**

Oberon– romantic opera: 3 acts, J306 (1826—London) (Lib. Planché)

1. Overture. ACT 1: 2. Von Jugend auf schon in Kampfgefild. ACT 2: 7. Arabiens einsam Kind; 9. Über die blauen Wogen; 11. O wie wogt es sich schön; 13. Vater! Hör mich flehn zu dir!; 14. Ozean du Ungheuer! ACT 3: 16. Arabien, mein Heimatland; 17. Traure, mein Herz; 18. An den Strande der Garonne; 20. March.

Oberon	D. Grobe
Rezia	B. Nilsson
Hüon	P. Domingo
Scherasmin	H. Prey
Fatime	J. Hamari
Puck	M. Schiml
Mermaid	A. Auger

Bavarian Rad Chor, BRSO, R. Kubelík (with dialogue)
(12/91) (DG) ① [2] **419 038-2GX2**

Oberon	G. Lakes
Rezia	D. Voigt
Huon	B. Heppner
Scherasmin	D. Croft
Fatime	D. Ziegler
Puck	V. Livengood
Mermaid	M. Obata

Cologne Op Chor, Cologne Gürzenich Orch, J. Conlon (r1992: with narration)
(6/93) (EMI) ① [2] **CDS7 54739-2**

Seit frühster Jugend H. Roswaenge, Philh Hungarica, Z. Rozsnyai (pp1959) (PREI) ① **90103**

1. Staatskapelle Dresden, G. Kuhn (CAPR) ① **10 052** (CAPR) ▭ **CC27 076**

1. BRSO, R. Kubelík (DG) ① **415 840-2GGA**

1. Paris Op Orch, H. Scherchen (ADES) ① **13203-2**

1. NBC SO, A. Toscanini (r1952) (RCA) ① **GD60292**

1. Polish Chmbr PO, W. Rajski (INTE) ① **INT830 899**

1. LPO, T. Beecham (r1938) (PEAR) ① **GEMMCD9094**

1. Hallé, S. Skrowaczewski (IMP) ① **PCD1105**

1. Leningrad PO, E. Mravinsky (pp1978) (MELO) ① [10] **74321 25189-2**

1. Leningrad PO, E. Mravinsky (pp1978) (MELO) ① **74321 25190-2**

1. Leningrad PO, E. Mravinsky (pp1961) (RUSS) ① **RDCD10907**

1. BPO, H. von Karajan
(6/88) (DG) Ⓓ **419 070-2GGA**
1. Hanover Band, R. Goodman
(6/89) (NIMB) Ⓓ **NI5154**
(NIMB) ▭ **NC5154**
1. Philh, W. Sawallisch
(1/90) (EMI) Ⓓ **CDM7 69572-2**
1. Philh, N. Järvi (1/90) (CHAN) Ⓓ **CHAN8766**
(1/90) (CHAN) ▭ **ABTD1404**
1. NYPO, W. Mengelberg (r1923)
(7/90) (SYMP) Ⓓ **SYMCD1078**
1(pt) SO, T. Beecham (r1912)
(11/91) (SYMP) Ⓓ [2] **SYMCD1096/7**
1. Philh, N. Järvi (4/93) (CHAN) Ⓓ **CHAN9066**
1. LSO, A. Coates (r1926)
(4/93) (KOCH) Ⓓ [2] **37704-2**
1. Black Dyke Mills Band, P. Parkes (arr brass band: P Parkes) (9/93) (CHAN) Ⓓ **CHAN4514**
(9/93) (CHAN) ▭ **BBTD4514**
1. NYPO, L. Bernstein (r1968)
(9/93) (SONY) Ⓓ **SMK47601**
1. LPO, T. Beecham (r1938)
(10/94) (DUTT) Ⓓ **CDLX7009**
1. Luxembourg Rad & TV SO, L. de Froment
(11/94) (FORL) Ⓓ **FF009**
1. NBC SO, B. Walter (pp1939)
(2/95) (PEAR) Ⓓ **GEMMCD9131**
2. H. Roswaenge, Berlin St Op Orch, B. Seidler-Winkler (r1936) (5/90) (PREI) Ⓓ **89018**
2, 13. P. Domingo, BRSO, R. Kubelík
(6/94) (BELA) Ⓓ **450 121-2**
(6/94) (BELA) ▭ **450 121-4**
2, 13. H. Roswaenge, Berlin St Op Orch, B. Seidler-Winkler (r1936)
(4/95) (PREI) Ⓓ [2] **89209**
14. M. Callas, Paris Cons, N. Rescigno
(EMI) Ⓓ **CDC7 49005-2**
14(pt) A. Bahr-Mildenburg, anon (r1904)
(SYMP) Ⓓ **SYMCD1085**
14. R. Horna, Concertgebouw, W. Mengelberg (r1930s/40s) (ARHI) Ⓓ **ADCD109**
14. K. Flagstad, Philadelphia, E. Ormandy (r1937) (IMP) Ⓓ **GLRS105**
14. H. Wildbrunn, orch (r1923)
(PREI) Ⓓ **89097**
14. K. Flagstad, Philadelphia, E. Ormandy (r1937) (SIMA) Ⓓ [3] **PSC1821(2)**
14. F. Leider, orch (r1921)
(5/91) (PREI) Ⓓ [3] **89301**
14. M. Teschemacher, Stuttgart Op Orch, G. Görlich (bp1936)
(2/92) (MMOI) Ⓓ **CDMOIR408**
14. Lotte Lehmann, orch (r1919)
(6/92) (PREI) Ⓓ [3] **89302**
14. M. Teschemacher, Berlin St Op Orch, B. Seidler-Winkler (r1937)
(11/92) (PREI) Ⓓ **89049**
14. L. Price, Philh, H. Lewis (r1979)
(12/92) (RCA) Ⓓ [4] **09026 61236-2**
14. M. Callas, Philh, A. Tonini (Eng)
(2/93) (EMI) Ⓓ **CDC7 54437-2**
14. K. Flagstad, Philadelphia, E. Ormandy (r1937) (7/93) (NIMB) Ⓓ **NI7847**
14. M. Németh, orch (r1920s)
(1/94) (CLUB) Ⓓ **CL99-007**
14. H. Konetzni, Vienna SO, L. Ludwig
(8/94) (PREI) Ⓓ [2] **90195**
14, 17. G. Janowitz, Berlin Deutsche Op Orch, F. Leitner (r1967) (DG) Ⓓ [2] **447 352-2GDB2**

Peter Schmoll und seine Nachburn– opera: 2 acts, J8 (1803—Augsburg) (Lib. J. Türk(e), after C. G. Crämer)

Peter Schmoll	R. Busching
Martin Schmoll	J. Schmidt
Minette	A. Pfeffer
Karl Pikner	S. Basa
Hans Bast	H. J. Porcher
Niklas	H-J. Schöpflin

Hagen PO, G. Markson (r1993)
(4/94) (MARC) Ⓓ [2] **8 223592/3**
Ja, Gottes Erde ist doch schön J. Herrmann, orch (r1943) (PREI) Ⓓ **89076**
Overture Paris Op Orch, H. Scherchen
(ADES) Ⓓ **13203-2**
Overture Hallé, S. Skrowaczewski
(IMP) Ⓓ **PCD1105**
Overture BPO, H. von Karajan
(6/88) (DG) Ⓓ **419 070-2GGA**
Overture Hanover Band, R. Goodman
(6/89) (NIMB) Ⓓ **NI5154**
(NIMB) ▭ **NC5154**
Overture Philh, N. Järvi
(4/93) (CHAN) Ⓓ **CHAN9066**

Silvana– opera: 3 acts, J87 (1810—Frankfurt-am-Main) (Lib. F C Hiemer, after 'Das Waldmädchen' text)
EXCERPTS: 1. Overture; 2. Tanz der Edelknaben; 3. Fackel Tanz.
Soll denn dies Herz nie Liebe finden A. Piccaver, orch (r1920) (8/93) (PREI) Ⓓ **89060**
1. Philh, N. Järvi (4/93) (CHAN) Ⓓ **CHAN9066**
2, 3. Queensland PO, J. Georgiadis (r1994)
(2/95) (NAXO) Ⓓ **8 550928**

WEILL, Kurt (Julian) *(1900–1950) Germany/USA*

Aufstieg und Fall der Stadt Mahagonny, 'Rise and Fall of the City of Mahagonny'– opera: 3 acts (1930—Leipzig) (Lib. B Brecht & cpsr)
1a. Prelude. ACT 1: 1b. Melodrama (Fatty, Moses, Begbick); 1c. Darum lasst uns hier eine Stadt gründen (Begbick); 1d. Sie soll sein wie ein Netz (Begbick); 1e. Aber dieses ganze Mahgonny (Begbick, Fatty, Moses); 2. Alabama Song (Jenny, girls); 3a. Wir wohnen in den Städchen (chorus); 3b. Fern vom Getriebe der Welt (Fatty, Moses); 4. Auf nach Mahagonny (Jim, Jack, Bill, Joe); 5a. Wenn man an einem fremden Strand kommt (Jim, Jack, Bill, Joe); 5b. Ach, meine Herren, willkommen zu Hause (Begbick); 5c. Heraus, ihr Schönen von Mahagonny (Jim, Jack, Bill, Joe, Jenny, girls); 5d. Ach bedenken Sie, Herr Jack O'Brien (Jenny); 5e. Ich kenn' die Jimmys aus Alaska schon (Jenny, Jim, ensemble); 6a. Ich habe gelernt (jenny, Jim); 6b. Bitte, Jenny (Jenny, Jim); 7a. Ach deises ganze Mahagonny (Begbick, Fatty, Moses); 7b. Auch ich bein einmal Mauer gestanden (Begbick); 8a. Melodrama (Jim, Jack, Bill, Joe); 8b. Wunderbar ist das Heraufkommen des Abends (Jack, Bill, Joe); 8c. Ich glaube, ich will meinen Hut aufess'n (Jim); 9a. The Maiden's Prayer (piano solo); 9b. Tief in Alaskas schneeweissen Wäldern (Jim); 9c. Sieben Jahre (Jim, full ensemble); 10a. Fugato (orchestra); 10b. Oh furchtbares Ereignis (ensemble, chorus); 10c. Ach mit eurem ganzen Mahagonny (Jim); 11a. Haltet euch aufrecht (male chorus); 11b. On Moon of Alabama (Jenny, girls): Es nutzt nichts (Jake); 11c. Siehst du, so ist die Welt (Jim); 11d. Wenn es etwas gibt, das du haben kannst für Geld (Jim); 11e. Zerstört ist Pensacola (Fatty, Begbick, Jim, ensemble); 11f. Denn wie man sich bettet, so liegt man (Jim, full ensemble).

Jenny	L. Lenya
Jim Mahoney	H. Sauerbaum
Trinity Moses	H. Günter
Leokadja Begbick	G. Litz
Fatty, the book-keeper	P. Markwort
Jake Schmidt	F. Göllnitz
Alaska Wolf Joe	S. Roth
Pennybank Bill	G. Mund
Toby Higgins	F. Göllnitz

NW German Rad Chor, NW German RO, W. Brückner-Rüggeberg
(8/88) (CBS) Ⓓ [2] **CD77341**

Jenny	A. Silja
Jim Mahoney	W. Neumann
Trinity Moses	K. Hirte
Leokadja Begbick	A. Schlemm
Fatty, the book-keeper	T. Lehrberger
Jake Schmidt	F. Mayer
Alaska Wolf Joe	H. Franzen
Pennybank Bill	P. Wolfrum
Toby Higgins	F. Mayer

Cologne Pro Musica, Cologne RSO, J. Latham-König
(8/88) (CAPR) Ⓓ [2] **10 160/1**
2. A. Réaux, R. Kapilow
(6/92) (KOCH) Ⓓ [2] **37087-2**
2, 19l U. Lemper, Berlin Rad Ens, J. Mauceri
(3/89) (DECC) Ⓓ **425 204-2DNL**
2, 5a-e, 11f G. May, Studio Orch, H. Krtschil
(8/89) (CAPR) Ⓓ **10 180**
(8/89) (CAPR) ▭ **CC27 180**
2, 5d, 11f C. Farley, R. Vignoles
(6/92) (ASV) Ⓓ **CDDCA790**

Down in the Valley– folk opera: 1 act (1948—Indiana) (Lib. A. Sundgaard)

Jennie Parsons	I. Davidson
Brack Weaver	M. Acito
The Leader	D. Collup
Thomas Bouché	J. Mabry
Jennie's Father	D.P. Lang

Fredonia Chbr Sngrs, Dortmund Univ Chbr Ch, Buffalo College Wind Plyrs, Westphalia CO, W. Gundlach
(4/92) (CAPR) Ⓓ **60 020-1**

Der **Dreigroschenoper, '(The) Threepenny Opera'– play with music: 3 acts (1928—Berlin) (Lib. B. Brecht, after Gay's 'The Beggars's Opera')**
EXCERPTS: 1. Overture. PROLOGUE: 2. Moritat vom Mackie Messer (Eng: Ballad of Mack the Knife). ACT 1: 3. Morgenchoral des Peachum; 4. Anstatt-dass-Song (Mr and Mrs Peachum); 5. Hochzeitslied (chorus); 6. Seeräuberjenny (Polly); 7. Kanonen Song (Macheath, Brown); 8. Liebeslied (Polly, Macheath); 9. Barbara Song (Polly); 10. Erste Dreigroschenfinale (Polly, Peachum, Mrs Peachum). ACT 2: 11a. Hübsch als es wärhte—Melodrama (Macheath); 11b. Polly's Lied; 12. Ballade von der sexuellen Hörigkeit (Mrs Peachum); 13. Zuhälterballade (Macheath, Jenny); 14. Ballade vom angenehmen Leben (Macheath); 15. Eifersuchtsduett (Lucy, Polly); 16. Zweite Dreigroschenfinale (Macheath. Mrs Peachum and chorus). ACT 3: 17. Lied von der Unzulänglichkeit menschlichen Strebens; 18. Salomon Song (Jenny); 19. Ruf aus der Gruft (Macheath); 20a. Grabschrift (Macheath); 20b. Gang zum Galgen (orchestra); 21. Dritte Dreigroschenoperfinale.

Macheath	R. Kollo
Polly Peachum	U. Lempe
Jenny Smith	Milva
Peachum	M. Ador
Frau Peachum	H. Demesch
Brown	W. Reichmann
Lucy Brown	S. Trempe
Street Singer	R. Boyse

Berlin RIAS Chbr Ch, Berlin RIAS Sinfonietta, J. Mauceri
(3/90) (DECC) Ⓓ **430 075-2D**

Jenny	A. Shoumanova
Macheath	M. Jung
Mr Peachum	H. Bech
Mrs Peachum	A. Herrman
Polly Peachum	S. Myszal
Tiger Brown	E. Demerdjie
Lucy	N. Afeya
Street Singer	W. Kment

Bulgarian TV & Rad Mixed Chor, Bulgarian TV & Rad SO, V.C. Symonette
(2/91) (KOCH) Ⓓ **37006-**
1, 12, 18. U. Lemper, W. Meyer, Berlin Rad Ens, J. Mauceri (3/89) (DECC) Ⓓ **425 204-2DN**
1, 2, 4, 7, 11b, 13, 14. Tetra (r1989-91; arr Goss: gtr qt) (11/93) (CONI) Ⓓ **CDCF90**
(11/93) (CONI) ▭ **MCFC90**
2. J. Heifetz, E. Bay (r1945)
(11/94) (RCA) Ⓓ [65] **09026 61778-2(19**
2, 6, 9, 12, 17, 18. G. May, M. Samko, Studio Orch, H. Krtschil (8/89) (CAPR) Ⓓ **10 18**
(8/89) (CAPR) ▭ **CC27 18**
2, 7, 11b, 13, 14, 17, 18. Stanislas Ens (arr Frenkel) (GALL) Ⓓ **CD-67**
7. Canadian Brass (r1990; arr McNeff)
(PHIL) Ⓓ **432 571-2P**
7. Canadian Brass (r1990; arr McNeff)
(PHIL) **OO** **432 571-5P**
9, 18. A. Réaux, R. Kapilow
(6/92) (KOCH) Ⓓ [2] **37087-**
11a, 12. C. Farley, R. Vignoles
(6/92) (ASV) Ⓓ **CDDCA79**
12. C. Berberian, Juilliard Ens, L. Berio (r1968; arr Berio) (7/95) (RCA) Ⓓ **09026 62540-**

Firebrand of Florence– operetta: 2 acts (1945—Boston) (Book E J Mayer, lyrics I Gershwin)
1. Prelude. ACT 1: 2. The bell of doom is clanging (Hangman, assistants); 2b. Come to Florence (Hangman, chorus); 2c. Life, Love, and Laughter (Cellini, chorus); 3. Our Master is Free Again (Emilia, Ascanio); 4. I had just been pardoned (Cellini); 5. You're far too near me (Cellini, Angela); 6. Alessandro the Wise (Duke, chorus); 7. Finaletto (Angela, Emilia, Ottavino, Cellini, Duke, chorus); 8. Duchess's Entrance (Blackamoor); 9. Sing Me Not a Ballad (Duchess, courtiers); 10. When the Duchess is Away (Captain of the Guard, Duke, Emilia, chorus); 11. Life, Love, and Laughter (Angela, Cellini); 12. The Nozy Cook (Angela, Duke, Cellini); 13. Finale alla Tarantella (Emilia, Angela, Duke, Duchess, Cellini); 14. The Duchess's Letter (Cellini); 15. The Little Naked

Boy (Angela and models); 16. We're Soldiers of the Duchy (Just in Case—March chorus); 17. A Rhyme for Angela (Duke, Poets, Ladies-in-Waiting); 18. Procession; 19. Love is my Enemy (Cellini, Angela); 19a. Hear Ye! Hear Ye! (Clerk); 19b. The World is Full of Villains (three judges); 19c. You Have to Do What You Do Do (Cellini, Duke, chorus); 19d. How wonderfully fortunate (Angela); 19e. Love is my Enemy (Cellini, Angela); 20. Come to Paris (Marquis, two girls, chorus); 21. Finale; 21a. Sarabande (orch version of 19e); 21b. Come to Florence (full company).

9. A. Réaux, R. Kapilow (6/92) (KOCH) Ⓓ [2] **37087-2**

Happy End– comedy with music: 3 acts (1929—Berlin) (Book E Hauptmann, wds. B Brecht)

1. Bilbao Song (Bill); 2. Der kleine Leutnant des lieben Gottes (Lilian); 3. Heilsarmeelied I (Lilian, Salvationists); 4. Matrosen-Tango (Lilian); 5. Heilsarmeelied II—Bruder, gib dir einem Stoss; 6. Heilsarmeelied III—Fürchte dich nicht; 7. Heilsarmeelied IV—In der Jugend gold'nem Schimmer; 8. Das Lied vom Branntweinhändler (Hannibal Jackson); 9. Mandelay Song (Sam Worlitzer); 10. Surabaya-Johnny (Lilian); 11. Das Lied von der harten Nuss (Bill); 12. Die Ballade von der Höllen-Lili (Lady in Grey); 13. Hosianna Rockefeller (full cast).

Bill Cracker; Hannibal Jackson W. Raffeiner
Sam Wurlitzer S. Kimbrough
Lilian Holiday G. Ramm
Lady in Grey K. Ploog
Cologne Pro Musica, König Ens, J. Latham-König (9/90) (CAPR) Ⓓ **60 015-1**

Cpte L. Lenya, chor, orch, W. Brückner-Rüggeberg (4/91) (CBS) Ⓓ **CD45886**
1, 10, 11. A.S. von Otter, N German RSO, J.E. Gardiner (12/94) (DG) Ⓓ **439 894-2GH** (12/94) (DG) ▭ **439 894-4GH**
1, 4, 8, 9, 10. U. Lemper, J. Cohen, Berlin RIAS Sinfonietta, J. Mauceri (r1991-2) (7/93) (DECC) Ⓓ **436 417-2DH** (7/93) (DECC) ▭ **436 417-4DH**
1, 4, 9, 10, 11, 12. G. May, Studio Orch, H. Krtschil (8/89) (CAPR) Ⓓ **10 180** (8/89) (CAPR) ▭ **CC27 180**
4, 6, 7, 12. C. Farley, R. Vignoles (6/92) (ASV) Ⓓ **CDDCA790**
10. C. Berberian, B. Canino (7/89) (WERG) Ⓓ **WER60054-50**
10. C. Berberian, Juilliard Ens, L. Berio (r1968; arr Berio) (7/95) (RCA) Ⓓ **09026 62540-2**
10, 11. A. Réaux, R. Kapilow (6/92) (KOCH) Ⓓ [2] **37087-2**

Der Jasager– school opera: 2 acts (1930—Berlin) (Lib. B. Brecht)

Boy T. Schmeisser
Mother H. Helling
Teacher U. Schütte
Student T. Bräutigam
Student T. Fischer
Student M. Knöppel
Fredonia Chbr Sngrs, Dortmund Univ Chbr Ch, Buffalo College Wind Plyrs, Westphalia CO, W. Gundlach (4/92) (CAPR) Ⓓ **60 020-1**

Johnny Johnson– musical play: 3 acts (1936—New York) (Lib. P. Green)

Cowboy Song; Captain Valentine's Song H.K. Gruber, Modern Ens (LARG) Ⓓ **Largo 5114**
My Friend M. Marshall, W. Marshall (MEL) Ⓓ **MELCD022-2**

Knickerbocker Holiday– musical play: 2 acts (1938—New York) (Book and lyrics M. Anderson)

5. It never was you (Brom, Tina); 15. September Song (Stuyvesant).
5. K. Colson, London Sinfonietta, J. McGlinn (8/93) (EMI) Ⓓ **CDC7 54586-2**
5. J. Gomez, J. Constable (6/88) (UNIC) Ⓓ **DKPCD9055** (6/88) (UNIC) ▭ **DKPC9055**
5. A. Réaux, R. Kapilow (6/92) (KOCH) Ⓓ [2] **37087-2**
5. R. Merrill, Orch, H. Barlow (bp1957) (VAI) ▣ **VAI69116**
5. E. Steber, orch, H. Barlow (bp1951) (VAI) ▣ **VAI69102**
5. M. Marshall, W. Marshall (MEL) Ⓓ **MELCD022-2**
15. T. Johns, B. Kellock (r1994: arr hn/pf) (DIVI) Ⓓ **2-4102** (DIVI) ▭ **4-4102**
15. J. Norman, J.T. Williams (r1987) (4/92) (PHIL) Ⓓ **422 401-2PH**
15. R. Merrill, NY Met Op Orch, J. Conlon (pp1991) (6/93) (RCA) Ⓓ **09026 61509-2**
15. E. Pinza, Johnny Green Orch, J. Green (r1950) (9/93) (RCA) Ⓓ **09026 61245-2**

Der Kuhhandel– operetta: 2 acts (1934) (Lib. R Vambery: incomplete)

Excs L. Peacock, E. Büchner, C. Schotenröhr, W. Raffeiner, U. Holdorf, O. Hillebrandt, D. Niemirowicz, I. Most, F. Mayer, R. Zimmermann, R. Röttger, F. Gerihsen, H. Heidbüchel, J. Wagner, Cologne Rad Chor, Cologne RSO, J. Latham-König (1/93) (CAPR) Ⓓ **60 013**

Lady in the Dark– musical play: 2 acts (1940—Boston) (Book M. Hart, lyrics I. Gershwin)

3. One Life to Live (Liza, Beckmann); 13. The Saga of Jenny (Liza); 17. My Ship.
3, 13, 17. U. Lemper, J. Cohen, London Voices, Berlin RIAS Sinfonietta, J. Mauceri (r1991-2) (7/93) (DECC) Ⓓ **436 417-2DH** (7/93) (DECC) ▭ **436 417-4DH**
3, 17. A.S. von Otter, N German RSO, J.E. Gardiner (12/94) (DG) Ⓓ **439 894-2GH** (12/94) (DG) ▭ **439 894-4GH**
13. M. Marshall, W. Marshall (MEL) Ⓓ **MELCD022-2**
13. C. Farley, R. Vignoles (6/92) (ASV) Ⓓ **CDDCA790**
13, 17. D. Upshaw, orch, E. Stern (r1993: orch L Wilcox & D Troob arr E Stern) (12/94) (NONE) Ⓓ **7559-79345-2** (NONE) ▭ **7559-79345-4**
17. J. Gomez, J. Constable (6/88) (UNIC) Ⓓ **DKPCD9055** (6/88) (UNIC) ▭ **DKPC9055**
17. J. Norman, J.T. Williams (r1987) (4/92) (PHIL) Ⓓ **422 401-2PH**
17. A. Réaux, R. Kapilow (6/92) (KOCH) Ⓓ [2] **37087-2**

Lost in the Stars– musical tragedy (1949—New York) (Book and lyrics M. Anderson)

EXCERPTS: 1. The Hills of Ixopo; 2. Thousand of Miles; 2a. The Little Tin God (replaced in final version); 3. Train to Johannesburg; 4. The Search; 5. The Little Gray House; 6. Who'll buy?; 7. Gold; 8. Trouble Man (Irina); 9. Murder in Parkworld; 10. Fear!; 11. The Shadowy Glass; 12. Lost in the Stars (Stephen, chorus); 13. Entr'acte; 14. The Wild Justice; 15. O Trixo, Help Me; 16. Stay Well; 17. Cry the Beloved Country; 18. Big Mole; 19. A Bird of Passage; 20. Four o'clock; 21. Finale: Thousands of Miles (reprise).

Leader G. Hopkins
Stephen Kumalo A. Woodley
Absalom; John; Man; Villager R. Pindell
Irina C. Clarey
Linda C. Woods
Alex J. Howard
Stationmaster; Judge R. Vogt
NY Concert Chorale, St Luke's Orch, J. Rudel (r1992) (11/93) (MUSM) Ⓓ **67100-2**

12. S. Ramey, London Studio SO, E. Stratta (r1993) (TELD) Ⓓ **4509-90865-2**
16. D. Upshaw, orch, E. Stern (r1993: orch L Wilcox) (12/94) (NONE) Ⓓ **7559-79345-2** (NONE) ▭ **7559-79345-4**

Love Life– vaudeville: 2 parts (1948—Boston) (Book & lyrics A J Lerner)

7b. Green-up Time (Susan, women); 22. Is it him or is it me? (Susan); 25. This is the life.
22. C. Farley, R. Vignoles (6/92) (ASV) Ⓓ **CDDCA790**
22. A. Réaux, R. Kapilow (6/92) (KOCH) Ⓓ [2] **37087-2**
25. S. Kimbrough, D. Baldwin (11/88) (ARAB) Ⓓ **Z6579** (ARAB) ▭ **ABQC6579**

Mahagonny-Gesänge– Songspiel: 3 parts (1927—Baden-Baden) (Lib. B Brecht)

1. Auf nach Mahagonny; 2. Kleiner Marsch (orchestra); 3. Alabama Song; 4. Vivace (orchestra); 5. Wer in Mahagonny blieb; 6. Vivace assai (orchestra); 7. Benares Song; 8. Choral (orchestra); 9. Gott in Mahagonny; 10. Finale: Dieses ganze Mahagonny.

Cpte U. Lemper, H. Wildhaber, P. Haage, T. Mohr, M. Jungwirth, S. Tremper, Berlin RIAS Sinfonietta, J. Mauceri (r1989) (4/91) (DECC) Ⓓ **430 168-2DH**
Cpte T. Schmidt, G. Ramm, H. Hiestermann, P.N. Kante, W. Raffeiner, H. Franzen, König Ens, J. Latham-König (r1991) (12/93) (CAPR) Ⓓ **60 028**

Die Sieben Todsünden, '(The) Seven Deadly Sins'– spectacle: 9 scenes (1933—Paris) (Wds. B. Brecht)

1a. Introduction: Meine Schwester und ich stammen aus Louisiana; 1b. Faulheit (Sloth): Müssiggang ist aller Laster Anfang; 2. Stolz (Pride): Als wir aber ausgestattet waren; 3. Zorn (Anger): Das geht nicht vorwärts; 4. Völlerei (Gluttony): Das ist ein Brief aus Philadelphia; 5. Unzucht (Lechery): Und wir fanden einen Mann; 6. Habsucht (Avarice): Wie hier in der Zeitung steht; 7a. Neid (Envy): Und die letzte Stadt; 7b. Finaletto: Darauf kehrten wir zurück nach Louisiana.

Cpte J. Migenes, R. Tear, S. Kale, A. Opie, R. Kennedy, LSO, M. Tilson Thomas (arr Brückner-Rüggeberg) (3/89) (CBS) ▭ **40-44529**
Cpte A. Silja, D. George, V. Vogel, J. Gottschick, F-J. Kapellmann, Cleveland Orch, C. von Dohnányi (pp1992) (CLOR) Ⓓ [10] **TCO93-75**
Cpte L. Lenya, male qt, orch, W. Brückner-Rüggeberg (r1956) (4/91) (CBS) Ⓓ **CD45886**
Cpte U. Lemper, H. Wildhaber, P. Haage, T. Mohr, M. Jungwirth, Berlin RIAS Sinfonietta, J. Mauceri (r1989) (4/91) (DECC) Ⓓ **430 168-2DH**
Cpte B. Fassbaender, K-H. Brandt, H. Sojer, H. Komatsu, I. Urbas, Hanover Rad PO, C. Garben (r1992) (12/93) (HARM) Ⓓ **HMC90 1420**
Cpte D. Bierett, D. Ellenbeck, K. Markus, C. Feller, M. Smith, Cologne RSO, L. Zagrosek (r1978) (12/93) (CAPR) Ⓓ **60 028**
Cpte A. Réaux, Hudson Shad, NYPO, K. Masur (12/94) (TELD) Ⓓ **4509-95029-2**
Cpte A.S. von Otter, N German RSO, J.E. Gardiner (12/94) (DG) Ⓓ **439 894-2GH** (12/94) (DG) ▭ **439 894-4GH**
E. Ross, A. Rolfe Johnson, I. Caley, M. Rippon, J. Tomlinson, CBSO, S. Rattle (r1982) (12/93) (EMI) Ⓓ **CDM7 64739-2**

Street Scene– American opera: 2 acts (1946—Philadelphia) (Book E. Rice, lyrics L. Hughes)

ACT 1: 7. Ice-Cream Sextet; 10. Lonely house (Sam); 12. What good would the moon be? (Rose). ACT 2: 14. Remember that I care (Sam and Rose); 17. A Boy Like You (Mrs Maurrant).

Anna Kristine Ciesinski
Frank R. Van Allan
Rose J. Kelly
Sam B. Bottone
Nursemaid 1 F. Doria
Nursemaid 2 J. Douglas
Jenny C. Daniels
Abraham Timothy Jenkins
Emma M. Dickinson
Olga A. Hickey
ENO Chor, ENO Orch, Carl Davis (TER) Ⓓ [2] **CDTER2 1185** (TER) ▭ [2] **ZCTER2 1185**

7. M. O'Flynn, P. Pancella, J. Hadley, P. Groves, Daniel Smith, J. Mattsey, NY Met Op Orch, J. Conlon (pp1991) (6/93) (RCA) Ⓓ **09026 61509-2**
10. M. Marshall, W. Marshall (MEL) Ⓓ **MELCD022-2**
10. J. Gomez, J. Constable (6/88) (UNIC) Ⓓ **DKPCD9055** (6/88) (UNIC) ▭ **DKPC9055**
10, 14. A. Réaux, R. Kapilow (6/92) (KOCH) Ⓓ [2] **37087-2**
12. L. Garrett, Philh, I. Bolton (SILV) Ⓓ **SONGCD907** (SILV) ▭ **SONGC907**

Zar lässt sich Photographieren– opera buffa: 1 act, Op. 21 (1928—Leipzig) (Lib. G. Kaiser)

Tsar B. McDaniel
Angèle C. Pohl
Assistant T. Lehrberger
Boy U. Tocha
False Angèle M. Napier
False assistant H. Kruse
False boy H. Helling
Leader M. Brell

Tsar's equerry H. Franzen
Cologne Rad Chor, Cologne RSO, J. Latham-König
(5/90) (CAPR) Ⓓ **10 147**

WEINBERGER, Jaromír *(1896–1967) Bohemia/USA*

Schwanda the Bagpiper– folk opera: 2 acts (1927—Prague) (Lib. Brod and Kareš)
1. Polka; 2. Fugue.
BBC SO, V. Tausky (pp1976)
(BBCR) Ⓓ **BBCRD9103**
1. BPO, A. von Zemlinsky (r c1930)
(SCHW) Ⓓ **310037**
1, 2. Cincinnati Pops, E. Kunzel
(9/86) (TELA) Ⓓ **CD80115**
1, 2. Chicago SO, F. Reiner (r1956)
(8/95) (RCA) Ⓓ **09026 62587-2**

WEINGARTNER, (Paul) Felix *(1863–1942) Austria*

Dame Kobold– opera: 3 acts, Op. 57 (1916—Darmstadt) (Lib. cpsr, after Calderón)
Wie voll das weisse Mondlicht K. Erb, orch (r1917) (PREI) Ⓓ **89095**

WEIR, Judith *(b 1954) Scotland*

Blond Eckbert– opera: 2 acts (1994—London) (Lib. cpsr)
Bird N. Jones
Berthe A-M. Owens
Walther; Hugh; Old Woman C. Ventris
Blond Eckbert N. Folwell
ENO Chor, ENO Orch, S. Edwards (pp1994)
(7/95) (COLL) Ⓓ **Coll1461-2**

King Harald's Saga– 'grand opera': 2 acts (1979—Dumfries) (after 'Heimskoingla Saga')
J. Manning (r1989) (UNIT) Ⓓ **88040-2**
J. Manning (r1989)
(3/90) (NOVE) Ⓓ **NVLCD109**

WEYSE, Christoph Ernst Friedrich *(1774–1842) Denmark*

An **Adventure in Rosenborg Gardens (Et eventyr i Rosenborg Have)– operetta: 1 act (1827—Copenhagen) (Lib. J L Heiberg)**
EXCERPTS: 1. A declaration of love (En elskovserklaering).
1. A.B. Garde, H. Wellejus
(DANA) Ⓓ **DACOCD348**

Feast at Kenilworth, 'Festen påa Kenilworth'– opera: 3 acts (1836—Copenhagen) (Lib. Andersen, after W Scott)
Gypsy Dances Odense SO, O. Schmidt
(1/87) (UNIC) ▭ **DKPC9036**

Ludlam's Cave (Ludlam's hule)– opera: 4 acts (1816—Copenhagen) (Lib. A. Oehlenschläger)
EXCERPTS: 1. Tom Thumb (Tommeliden).
1. A.B. Garde, H. Wellejus
(DANA) Ⓓ **DACOCD348**

The **Sleeping-Draught (Sovedrikken)– opera: 2 acts (1809—Copenhagen) (Lib. A. Oehlenschläger, after C F Bretzner)**
EXCERPTS: 1. The clear waves rolled (De Klare bølger rulled).
1. A.B. Garde, H. Wellejus
(DANA) Ⓓ **DACOCD348**

WILLE, Rudolf *(fl 1939) Austria*

Königsballade– operetta
Euren König will ich preisen; Ewig muss ich dein gedenken H. Roswaenge, Berlin St Op Orch, B. Seidler-Winkler (r1938)
(PREI) Ⓓ [2] **89211**
Euren König will ich preisen; Ewig muss ich dein gedenken H. Roswaenge, Berlin St Op Orch, B. Seidler-Winkler (r1938)
(5/90) (PREI) Ⓓ **89018**

WILLIAMSON, Malcolm (Benjamin Graham Christopher) *(b 1931) Australia*

The **Red Sea– opera: 1 act (1972—Darlington)**
exc S. Michelow, M. Williamson (r1984;arr voc & pf) (JEWI) ▭ **BB 002**

WINTER, Peter *(1754–1825) Germany*

Maometto II– opera: 2 acts (1817—Milan) (Lib. F. Romani)
Dei che piangendo imploro B. Mills, A. Mason, C. du Plessis, Philh, D. Parry
(10/90) (OPRA) Ⓓ [3] **ORCH103**

WOLF, Hugo (Filipp Jakob) *(1860–1903) Austria*

Der **Corregidor– opera: 4 acts (1896—Mannheim) (Lib. Mayreder, after Alarcon)**
Corregidor W. Hollweg
Donna Mercedes H. Donath
Tio Lucas D. Fischer-Dieskau
Frasquita D. Soffel
Juan Lopez K. Moll
Repela V. von Halem
Tonuelo, Nightwatchman H. Berger-Tuna
Pedro P. Maus
Manuela G. Schreckenbach
Berlin RIAS Chbr Ch, Berlin RSO, G. Albrecht (r1985)
(12/87) (SCHW) Ⓓ [2] **314010**

Manuel Venegas– opera: 3 acts (1903—Mannheim) (Lib. M Hoernes, after Alarcon. 5 scenes only cpted)
M. Shirai, J. Protschka, C. Hauptmann, C. Späth, O. Widmer, K-J. Dusseljee, Württemberg Chbr Ch, H. Höll (5/91) (CAPR) Ⓓ **10 362**

WOLF-FERRARI, Ermanno *(1876–1948) Italy*

L' **Amore medico, 'Doctor Love'– opera: 2 acts (1913—Dresden) (cl)**
EXCERPTS: 1. Overture; 2. Intermezzo.
1. RPO, J. Serebrier
(9/93) (ASV) Ⓓ **CDDCA861**
1, 2. ASMF, N. Marriner
(3/93) (EMI) Ⓓ **CDC7 54585-2**

Il **Campiello– comic opera: 3 acts (1936—Milan) (Lib. Ghisalberti, after de Vega)**
EXCERPTS: 1. Introduzione. ACT 1: 2. Ancuo zé una zornada cuzzì bela; 3. Anzoleto, mio Anzoleto; 4. Várdelo qua?; 5. Aghi de fiandra!; 6. Oe, Lucieta?; 7. Via, l'amante è partito; 8. No son più una putela; 9. Vòi scoar sto campielo; 10. Voria, mi sposarme; 11. Anca mi, se ò da dir la verità; 12. Io per tutte le donne ho del rispetto; 13. Gnese, quel fior me l'ástu donà ti?; 14. Che 'l diga quel che 'l vuol; 15. Brava in ogni maniera; 16. Intermezzo. ACT 2: 17. I muci i vòi far mi!; 18. Ma cos'e stato?; 19. Volemo i risi co la castradina; 20. Ve femo reverenza; 21. A tola! A tola! Dài!... 22. Balletto: 22a. Le tose; 22b. I Peociosi; 22c. Serenata de Peociosi; 22d. La Polenta; 23. Uff! Non ne posso più... 24. Signor; 25. Soldi...Soldi!; 26. Ma cozza zé zto ztrepito; 27. El Cavalier Aztolfi?; 28. Sol sol sol sol!; 29. Ritornello. ACT 3: 30. E ze la caza non me piaze a mi?; 31. Bravi! Pulito!; 32. Fai massaria?; 33. Ah! parcossa me dàlo; 34. Baron, me vustu ben?; 35. Coss'è ste baronae?; 36. Se lo saveva avanti; 37. Oh! per Dio! La finite?; 38. Cara la mia Venezia.
Gasparina D. Mazzucato
Cate U. Benelli
Lucieta G. Devinu
Pasqua M-R. Cosotti
Gnese M. Bolgan
Orsola C. de Mola
Zorzeto M. Comencini
Anzoleto I. d'Arcangelo
Astolfi M. Biscotti
Fabrizio C. Striuli
Sansuga G. Principin
Trieste Teatro Verdi Chor, Trieste Teatro Verdi Orch, N. Bareza (pp1992)
(FONI) Ⓓ [2] **RFCD2014**
16, 29. ASMF, N. Marriner
(3/93) (EMI) Ⓓ **CDC7 54585-2**
16, 29. RPO, J. Serebrier
(9/93) (ASV) Ⓓ **CDDCA861**
29. La Scala Orch, G. Marinuzzi (r1936)
(4/94) (EMI) Ⓓ [3] **CHS7 64864-2(2)**

La **Dama boba– opera: 3 acts (1939—Milan) (Lib. Ghisalberti, after de Vega)**
EXCERPTS: 1. Overture.
1. ASMF, N. Marriner
(3/93) (EMI) Ⓓ **CDC7 54585-2**
1. RPO, J. Serebrier
(9/93) (ASV) Ⓓ **CDDCA861**

Le **Donne Curiose– opera: 3 acts (1906—Munich) (Lib Sugana, after Goldini)**
Rimprovera la mia curiosità...Tutto per te G. Farrar, orch (r1912) (IRCC) Ⓓ **IRCC-CD805**
Rimprovera la mia curiosita...Tutta per te G. Farrar, orch (r1912) (10/94) (NIMB) Ⓓ **NI7857**
Se in voi cotanto...Il cor nel contento G. Farrar, H. Jadlowker, orch (r1912)
(IRCC) Ⓓ **IRCC-CD805**
Se in voi cotanto...Il cor nel contento G. Farrar, H. Jadlowker, orch (r1912)
(4/94) (RCA) Ⓓ [6] **09026 61580-2(2)**

I **Gioielli della Madonna, '(The) Jewels of the Madonna'– opera: 3 acts (1911—Berlin) (Lib. Golisciani and Zangarini)**
1. Festa popolare; 2. Intermezzo, Act 2; 3. Serenata; 4. Danza napolitana.
Aprila, o bella G. De Luca, NY Met Op Chor, NY Met Op Orch, G. Setti (r1930)
(PEAR) Ⓓ [3] **GEMMCDS9160(2)**
Aprila, o bella G. De Luca, NY Met Op Orch, G. Setti (r1929) (10/94) (PREI) Ⓓ **89073**
Excs N. Ardelli, M. Bokor, A. Jerger, G. Maikl, K. Ettl, Vienna St Op Chor, Vienna St Op Orch, H. Knappertsbusch (pp1937: Ger)
(SCHW) Ⓓ [2] **314672**
Intermezzo, Act 1; 2. National SO, B. Neel (r1944) (5/95) (DUTT) Ⓓ **CDK1200**
1, 2, 3, 4. RPO, J. Serebrier
(9/93) (ASV) Ⓓ **CDDCA861**
1-4. ASMF, N. Marriner
(3/93) (EMI) Ⓓ **CDC7 54585-2**
2. orch, W. Pelletier (bp1963)
(VAI) ▣ **VAI69100**
2. Orch, H. Barlow (bp1951)
(VAI) ▣ **VAI69103**
2. BPO, H. von Karajan
(10/87) (DG) Ⓓ [3] **419 257-2GH3**
2. Gothenburg SO, N. Järvi
(6/90) (DG) Ⓓ **429 494-2GDC**
(6/90) (DG) ▭ **429 494-4GDC**
3. T. Gobbi, Rome Op Orch, O. de Fabritiis (r1955) (10/89) (EMI) Ⓓ **CDM7 63109-2**

I **Quattro Rusteghi, '(The) Four Ruffians'– opera: 3 acts (1906—Munich) (Lib. L Sugana & G Pizzolato, after Goldoni)**
EXCERPTS: 1. Overture; 2. Intermezzo.
Luceta xe un bel nôme Ferruccio Tagliavini, EIAR Orch, U. Tansini (r1940)
(3/94) (CENT) Ⓓ **CRC2164**
1, 2. ASMF, N. Marriner
(3/93) (EMI) Ⓓ **CDC7 54585-2**
1, 2. RPO, J. Serebrier
(9/93) (ASV) Ⓓ **CDDCA861**
2. Santa Cecilia Academy Orch, V. de Sabata (r1948) (9/95) (EMI) Ⓓ [2] **CHS5 65506-2**

Il **Segreto di Susanna, 'Susanna's Secret'– opera: 1 act (1909—Munich) (Lib. Golisciani)**
O gioia, la nube leggera C. Muzio, orch (r1917)
(PEAR) Ⓓ **GEMMCD9143**
O gioia, la nube leggera L. Bori, Victor Orch, J. Pasternack (r1921) (ROMO) Ⓓ [2] **81016-2**
O gioia, la nube leggera G. Farrar, orch (r1913)
(10/94) (NIMB) Ⓓ **NI7857**
O gioia, la nube leggera C. Muzio, orch (r1917)
(1/95) (ROMO) Ⓓ [2] **81010-2**
Overture La Scala Orch, A. Toscanini (r1921)
(11/92) (RCA) Ⓓ **GD60315**
Overture RPO, J. Serebrier
(9/93) (ASV) Ⓓ **CDDCA861**
Overture NBC SO, A. Toscanini (bp1946)
(5/94) (ATS) Ⓓ [2] **ATCD100**
Overture Santa Cecilia Academy Orch, V. de Sabata (r1948)
(9/95) (EMI) Ⓓ [2] **CHS5 65506-2**

Overture; Intermezzo ASMF, N. Marriner
(3/93) (EMI) ① **CDC7 54585-2**

Sly– opera: 3 acts (1927—Milan) (Lib. Forzano, after Shakespeare)
Un orso in musoliera; Io non sono un buffone F. Merli, orch, L. Molajoli (r1928)
(PREI) ① **89091**

XENAKIS, Iannis *(b 1922) Romania/France*

Orestia– drama (1966-87)
S. Sakkas
S. Gualda
Strasbourg Univ Music Dept Chor, Colmar Women's Voices, Anjou Voc Ens, Basse-Normandie Ens, D. Debart
(9/90) (SALA) ① **SCD8906**

YVAIN, Maurice *(1891–1965) France*

Au soleil du Mexique– opérette (1935—Paris) (Lib. Mouëzy-Éon & A Willemetz)
Marche de Nino; On croit toujours; J'ai peur A. Baugé, S. Laydeker, orch, G. Andolfi
(EMI) ① [2] **CZS5 68292-2**
On croit toujours A. Baugé, orch (r1930s)
(FORL) ① **UCD19022**

ZANDONAI , Riccardo *(1883–1944) Italy*

Francesca da Rimini– opera: 4 acts (1914—Turin) (Lib. d'Annunzio, arr T. Ricordi)
EXCERPTS: ACT 1: 1. Allegretto mosso; 2. Adonella, Adonella; 3. Meravigliosamente... 4. So le storie; 5. Come Morgana; 6. Or venuta che fue; 7. Che fai qui manigoldo; 8. Egli era si povero in arnese; 9. Allegretto mosso (Oimè, Oimè); 10. Francesca, dove andrai; 11. Verraà in breve anche il tuo giorno; 12. Madonna Francesca!; 13. O dattero fronzuto; 14. Portami nella stanza; 15. Largo (Per la terra di maggio). ACT 2: 16. Grave e pesante (È ancora sgombro il campo del comune?); 17. Paolo! Francesca!; 18. Ecco l'elmetto ch'io vi dono; 19. Questo cimento; 20. Ah non mi muoio!; 21. Viva, viva Giovanni Malatesta; 22. Orsù bisogna manganare una botte grande; 23. O sciagura, sciagura!; 24. La botte! La botte! ACT 3: 25. Allegro non troppo; 26. E Galeotto dice... 27. 'Nova in calen di marzo'; 28. Smaragdi, non torna?; 29. O dama, non ti disperare!; 30. Marzo è giunto; 31. Agitato e più mosso; 32. Benvenuto, signore mio cognato; 33. Paolo, datemi pace!; 34. Inghirlandata di violette; 35. Nemica ebbi la luce; 36. E Galeotto dice... ACT 4: 37. Agitato (Perchè tanto sei strano?); 38. Mia cara donna; 39. Torna Malatestino; 40. Era teco la tua moglie; 41. E se il fratello vede; 42. Allegretto triste; 43. L'ha colta il sonno, Dorme; 44. Oh! No, no! Non son io!; 45. O Biancofiore, piccola tu sei!; 46. Smaragdi! Smaragdi!; 47. Vieni, vieni, Francesca.
16, 17, 18, 19, 20, 31, 32, 33, 34, 35, 36, 45, 46, 47. M. Olivero, M. del Monaco, V. Carbonari, A. Gasparini, A. Cesarini, Monte Carlo Nat Op Orch, N. Rescigno
(3/92) (DECC) ① [2] **433 033-2DM2**
32. K. Ricciarelli, P. Domingo, Santa Cecilia Academy Orch, G. Gavazzeni (r1972)
(RCA) ① **09026 62595-2**
33. M. Freni, Venice La Fenice Orch, R. Abbado
(9/92) (DECC) ① **433 316-2DH**
33. L. Price, RCA Italiana Op Orch, F. Molinari-Pradelli (12/92) (RCA) ① [4] **09026 61236-2**
34, 35, 36. R. Tebaldi, F. Corelli, Leman Chor, SRO, A. Guadagno (r1972)
(10/93) (DECC) ① **436 301-2DA**

Giuliano– opera: prologue, 2 acts & epilogue (1928—Naples) (Lib. A Rosato, after J da Varagine)
La dolce madre che mi benedisse F. Merli, orch, L. Molajoli (r1928) (PREI) ① **89091**
La dolce nenia del vago usignolo R. Pampanini, orch, L. Molajoli (r1928)
(8/93) (PREI) ① **89063**

Giulietta e Romeo– opera: 3 acts (1922—Rome) (Lib. A. Rossato, after da Porto & Shakespeare)
Giulietta! son io! M. Fleta, orch (r1922)
(2/90) (PREI) ① **89002**

ZELEŃSKI , Władysław *(1837–1921) Poland*

Konrad Wallenrod– opera: 4 acts (1885—Lwów) (Lib. after A. Michiewicz)
Grand Commander's aria A. Orda, Polish RSO, S. Rachoń (bp1963) (SYMP) ① **SYMCD1117**

ZELLER , Carl (Johann Adam) *(1842–1898) Austria*

Der **Obersteiger, '(The) Master Miner'– operetta: 3 acts (1894—Vienna) (Lib. West & Held)**
EXCERPTS: 1a. Wo sie war die Müllerin; 1b. 'Sei nicht bös, es kann nicht sein'; 2. Ja dort in den Bergen.
Sei nicht bös E. Schumann, orch, L. Collingwood (r1930) (MMOI) ① **CDMOIR419**
(MMOI) ▭ **CMOIR419**
1a, 1b E. Schwarzkopf, Philh, O. Ackermann
(CFP) ① **CD-CFP4277**
1a, 1b H. Gueden, Vienna Operetta Chor, Vienna St Op Orch, R. Stolz
(DECC) ① **425 852-2DWO**
(DECC) ▭ **425 852-4DWO**
1a, 1b R. Karczykowski, Polish Nat RSO, R. Bibl
(POLS) ① **PNCD087**
1a, 1b H. Gueden, Vienna Operetta Chor, Vienna St Op Orch, R. Stolz (r1961)
(DECC) ① **436 316-2DA**
(DECC) ▭ **436 316-4DA**
1a, 1b M. Hill Smith, Chandos Concert Orch, S. Barry (Eng) (6/85) (CHAN) ① **CHAN8362**
(6/85) (CHAN) ▭ **LBTD013**
1a, 1b E. Schwarzkopf, Philh, O. Ackermann
(1/86) (EMI) ① **CDC7 47284-2**
1a, 1b L. Popp, ASMF, N. Marriner
(6/88) (EMI) ① **CDC7 49700-2**
1b E. Schumann, orch, L. Collingwood (r1930)
(ROMO) ① **81019-2**
2. L. Schöne, orch (r1925)
(12/92) (NIMB) ① **NI7833**
(12/92) (NIMB) ▭ **NC7833**

Der **Vogelhändler, '(The) Bird Catcher'– operetta: 3 acts (1891—Vienna) (Lib. West and Held)**
EXCERPTS: 1a. Prelude. ACT 1: 1b. Introduction; 2. Grüss euch Gott, alle miteinander; 3. Als dir die Welt voll Rosen ning (Duet); 4. Fröhlich Pfalz; 5. Ich bin die Christel von der Post; 6. Ach, ihre Reputation; 7c. Schenkt man sich Rosen in Tirol; ACT 2: 8. Introduction; 9. Ich bin der Prodekan; 10. Bescheiden, mit verschämten Wangen; 11. Mir scheint, ich kenn' dich, spröde Fee!; 12b. Wie mein Ahn'l zwanzig Jahr, 'Nightingale song'; 12c. Also fangt's an, Gott'snam'!; ACT 3: 13. Introduction; 14. Als geblüht der Kirschenbaum; 15. Kämpfenie mit Frau'n.

Kurfürstin Marie	A. Rothenberger
Adelaide	G. Litz
Baron Weps	W. Berry
Graf Stanislaus	G. Unger
Süffle	J. Förster
Würmchen	K. Dönch
Adam	A. Dallapozza
Christel	R. Holm
Schneck	W. Anheisser

Vienna St Op Chor, Vienna SO, W. Boskovsky
(7/89) (EMI) ① [2] **CMS7 69357-2**
Excs E. Köth, R. Holm, R. Schock, K-E. Mercker, K. Herford, R. Glawitsch, E. Pauly, Günther Arndt Ch, Berlin SO, F. Fox
(2/91) (EURO) ① **GD69026**
Hast du schon einmal zu gleich H.E. Groh, orch (r1932) (3/92) (PEAR) ① **GEMMCD9419**
Noch a-mal, noch a-mal R. Karczykowski, Polish Nat RSO, R. Bibl (POLS) ① **PNCD087**
2, 12b F. Wunderlich, R. Lamy Sngrs, Munich RO, W. Schmidt-Boelcke (EURO) ① **GD69018**
(EURO) ▭ **GK69018**
5. L. Schöne, orch (r1925)
(12/92) (NIMB) ① **NI7833**
(12/92) (NIMB) ▭ **NC7833**
5, 7c E. Schwarzkopf, Philh, O. Ackermann
(1/86) (EMI) ① **CDC7 47284-2**
7c P. Lorengar, Vienna Op Chor, Vienna Op Orch, W. Weller (r1970)
(LOND) ① **436 898-2DM**
7c P. Domingo, ECO, J. Rudel
(2/87) (EMI) ① **CDC7 47398-2**
7c Raphaele Concert Orch, P. Walden (arr Waldenmaier) (5/91) (MOZA) ① **MECD1002**
7c H.E. Groh, E. Bettendorf, orch (r1931)
(3/92) (PEAR) ① **GEMMCD9419**
7c B. Hendricks, Philh, L. Foster (r1992)
(8/93) (EMI) ① **CDC7 54626-2**
12b B. Weikl, Austrian RSO, K. Eichhorn
(ORFE) ① **C077831A**
12b K. Schmitt-Walter, Berlin Deutsche Op Orch, W. Lutze (r1939) (MMOI) ① **CDMOIR419**
(MMOI) ▭ **CMOIR419**
12b E. Schumann, orch, L. Collingwood (r1930: Eng) (NIMB) ① **NI7864**
12b R. Tauber, orch (r1928)
(PEAR) ① **GEMMCD9145**
12b E. Schumann, Vienna St Op Orch, K. Alwin (r1929) (ROMO) ① **81019-2**
12b E. Schumann, orch, L. Collingwood (r1930: Eng) (ROMO) ① **81019-2**
12b R. Tauber, Orch, E. Hauke (r1928)
(12/89) (EMI) ① **CDH7 69787-2**
12b E. Kunz, VPO, O. Ackermann (r1951)
(9/95) (TEST) ① **SBT1059**

ZEMLINSKY, Alexander von *(1871–1942) Austria*

Es war einmal– opera: prologue & 3 acts (1900—Vienna) (Lib. M Singer, after H Drachmann)

Princess	E. Johansson
Prince	K. Westi
Kasper	P-A. Wahlgren
King	A. Haugland
Suitor	O. Hedegaard
Commissionaire	G. Paevatalu
Commander; Herald	C. Christiansen
First Lady-in-Waiting	S. Lillesøe

Danish Nat Rad Chor, Danish Nat RSO, H. Graf
(5/91) (CAPR) ① [2] **60 019-2**

Eine **Florentinische Tragödie– opera: 1 act, Op. 16 (1917—Stuttgart) (Lib. Wilde trans Meyerfeld)**
D. Soffel, K. Riegel, G. Sarabia, Berlin RSO, G. Albrecht (12/85) (SCHW) ① **314012**

Der **Geburtstag der Infantin (aka 'Der Zwerg')– opera, Op. 17 (1922—Cologne) (Lib. Klaren, after Klaren)**

Donna Clara	I. Nielsen
Dwarf	K. Riegel
Ghita	B. Haldas
Major-Domo	D. Weller
First Maid	C. Studer
Second Maid	O. Fredricks
Third Maid	M. Hirsti

Berlin RSO, G. Albrecht
(4/86) (SCHW) ① **314013**

Kleider machen Leute– comic opera: 2 acts (1910—Vienna) (Lib. Feld, after Keller)

Wenzel Strapinski	H. Winkler
Nettchen	E. Mathis
Melchior Böhni	W. Slabbert
Adam Litumlei	H. Franzen
Frau Litumlei	S. Kaluza
Polykarpus Federspiel	V. Vogel
Master tailor	U. Hunziker
First apprentice, Servant	B. Jensson
Second apprentice	U.S. Eggimann
Magistrate	R. Hartmann
Häberlein's elder son	P. Keller
Frau Häberlein	R. Rohner
Häberlein's younger son	J. Will
Innkeeper	R. Scholze
Innkeeper's wife	R. Lenhart
Cook	K. Justus
Boy servant	S. Salminen
Coachman	C. Otelli
Prologue	U. Peter

Zurich Op Hse Chor, Zurich Op Orch, R. Weikert (pp1990)
(1/92) (SCHW) ① [2] **314069**

Der **König Kandaules– opera: 3 acts (1935-36) (Lib. Gide: orch unfinished)**
EXCERPTS: ACT 3: 1. Prelude; 2. Gyges's monologue.

1, 2. F. Grundheber, Hamburg PO, G. Albrecht (r1992; orch Beaumont)
(3/94) (CAPR) ⓓ **10 448**

Der **Kreidekreis– opera: 3 acts (1933—Zurich) (Lib. Klabund (Alfred Henschke)**

Tschang-Haitang R. Behle
Mrs Tschang G. Schreckenbach
Ma R. Hermann
Tschao S. Lorenz
Emperor Pao R. Goldberg
Tong U. Peter
Tschang-Ling H. Helm
Mrs Ma G. Ottenthal
Midwife K. Borris
Soldier G. Saks
A girl C. Lindsley
Berlin RSO, S. Soltesz
(1/92) (CAPR) ⓓ [2] **60 016-2**

Die **Traumgörge– opera: 2 acts & epilogue (1904-06) (Lib. L. Feld)**

Princess Gertraud J. Martin
Görge J. Protschka
Grete P. Coburn
Hans; Kaspar H. Welker
Minister M. Blasius
Innkeeper P. Haage
Miller V. von Halem
Zungl H. Kruse
Innkeeper's Wife B. Calm
Marei G.M. Ronge
Hesse Rad Ch, Frankfurt RSO, G. Albrecht
(3/89) (CAPR) ⓓ [2] **10 241/2**

ZIEHRER, C(arl) M(ichael) *(1843–1922) Austria*

Der **Fremdenführer– operetta: prelude & 3 acts (1902—Vienna) (Lib. L. Krenn and C. Lindau)**

Military Life! P. Morrison, Chandos Concert Orch, S. Barry (7/88) (CHAN) ⓓ **CHAN8561**
(7/88) (CHAN) ⊟ **LBTD019**

O Wien, mein liebes Wien E. List, O. Schulhof (r1951) (PREI) ⓓ **89083**

O Wien, mein liebes Wien E. Schumann, orch, W. Goehr (r1937) (ROMO) ⓓ **81019-2**

Prelude Steiermark Military Band, R. Bodingbauer (KOCH) ⓓ **321 759**

Die **Landstreicher– operetta: prelude & 2 acts (1899—Vienna) (Lib. L. Krenn and C. Lindau)**

EXCERPTS: 1. Overture; 2. Sei gepreisen, du lauschige Nacht.

2. Steiermark Military Band, R. Bodingbauer
(KOCH) ⓓ **321 759**

2. E. Schumann, orch, W. Goehr (r1937)
(ROMO) ⓓ **81019-2**

Die **Schätzmeister, '(The) Pawnbroker's Valuer'– operetta: 3 acts (1904—Vienna) (Lib. Engel & Horst)**

(ACT 1); 1. Do re mi fa sol la si.

O let me hold your tiny little hand M. Hill Smith, P. Morrison, Chandos Concert Orch, S. Barry (7/88) (CHAN) ⓓ **CHAN856**
(7/88) (CHAN) ⊟ **LBTD01**

1. M. Hill Smith, Chandos Concert Orch, S. Barry (Eng: arr. F. Bauer)
(6/85) (CHAN) ⓓ **CHAN836**
(6/85) (CHAN) ⊟ **LBTD01**

Die **Verliebte Eskadron– operetta: 3 acts (1931—Vienna) (posth arr K Pauspertl. Lib. Sterk, after B Buchbinder)**

So schön, wie's einmal war; Süsse melodie Steiermark Military Band, R. Bodingbauer
(KOCH) ⓓ **321 75**

ZIMMERMANN , Udo *(b 1943) Germany*

Weisse Rose– opera: 8 scenes (1967-68) (Lib. I. Zimmermann)

Sophie Scholl G. Fontan
Hans Scholl L-M. Harde
Inst. Ens, U. Zimmermann
(9/88) (ORFE) ⓓ **C162871**

Artist index

AACHEN YOUTH CHOIR
cond J. VAN IMMERSEEL
Mendelssohn: Hochzeit des Camacho (Cpte)

AADLAND, Eivind (cond)
see ECCO

AALBERS, Dieuwke (sop)
(PART) **Part1132-2** Schubert—Lieder

AARONSON, Cynthia (sop)
A. Davis: X (Cpte)

ABBADO, Claudio (cond)
see BPO
COE
La Scala Orch
LSO
Vienna St Op Orch
VPO

ABBADO, Roberto (cond)
see Munich RO
Munich RSO
Venice La Fenice Orch
Vienna St Op Orch

ABBEY ROAD ENSEMBLE
cond L. FOSTER
(EMI) **CDC5 55475-2** Itzhak Perlman - À la carte

ABBONDANZA, Roberto (bar)
Handel: Poro (Cpte)

ABBOTT, Drew (ten)
Spohr: Faust (Cpte)

ABDOUN, Georges (bass-bar)
(MONT) **TCE8760** Stravinsky: Stage Works

ABEL, Josef (ten)
Puccini: Madama Butterfly (Cpte)
Verdi: Rigoletto (Cpte)

ABENDROTH, Hermann (cond)
see Bayreuth Fest Orch

ABENDROTH, Irene (sop)
(SYMP) **SYMCD1085** The Harold Wayne Collection, Vol.6

ABENDROTH, Martin (bass)
(PREI) **89301** The Art of Frida Leider
(PREI) **90103** Helge Roswaenge Recital (1959)

ABOTT, Bessie (sop)
(PEAR) **EVC1(2)** The Caruso Edition, Vol.1 (pt 2)
(RCA) **GD60495(2)** The Complete Caruso Collection (pt 2)

ABUMRADI, Eduardo (bass)
Bizet: Pêcheurs de Perles (Cpte)

ACADEMY OF ANCIENT MUSIC
(CHAN) **CHAN0540** J.C.Bach—Orchestral Works
(L'OI) **443 201-2OM** Popular Baroque Works
(L'OI) **444 620-2OH** The Glory of Purcell
cond C. HOGWOOD
Handel: Orlando (Cpte)
Mozart: Clemenza di Tito (Cpte)
Purcell: Dido (Cpte)
(DECC) **448 300-2DH** Cecilia Bartoli—A Portrait
(L'OI) **410 553-2OH** 18th Century Orchestral Works
(L'OI) **425 835-2OH** Mozart—Concert and Opera Arias
(L'OI) **436 132-2OH** Emma Kirkby sings Mrs Arne
(L'OI) **443 267-2OX2** Christopher Hogwood - A Profile
(PHIL) **434 992-2PH** The Sorceress—Original Soundtrack
(PHIL) **446 081-2PH** The Echoing Air—The Music of Henry Purcell
(PHIL) **070 155-1PH (PHIL)** The Sorceress—Original Soundtrack

ACADEMY OF ANCIENT MUSIC CHORUS
(L'OI) **444 620-2OH** The Glory of Purcell
cond C. HOGWOOD
Mozart: Clemenza di Tito (Cpte)
Purcell: Dido (Cpte)

ACADEMY OF ST MARTIN IN THE FIELDS CHAMBER ENSEMBLE
(CHAN) **CHAN9131** Enescu/Shostakovich/Strauss—Chamber Works
(CHAN) **CHAN9216** Academy Classics

ACADEMY OF ST MARTIN IN THE FIELDS CHORUS
cond N. MARRINER
Sullivan: Yeomen of the Guard (exc)

ACADEMY OF ST MARTIN IN THE FIELDS
(CALA) **CACD0106** The London Viola Sound
(EMI) **MVP99 1042 2** The Academy of St Martin in the Fields at Longleat
cond COLIN DAVIS
Mozart: Entführung (Cpte)
(PHIL) **422 523-2PME8(2)** The Complete Mozart Edition Vol 23 (pt 2)
cond R. LEPPARD
(DECC) **444 543-2DF2** Essential Handel
cond N. MARRINER
Mozart: Così fan tutte (Cpte), Don Giovanni (exc), Nozze di Figaro (Cpte), Zauberflöte (Cpte)
Rossini: Barbiere di Siviglia (exc), Cenerentola (Cpte), Turco in Italia (Cpte)
Sullivan: Yeomen of the Guard (Cpte)
(BELA) **450 130-2** Romeo & Juliet
(CFP) **CD-CFP4557** Baroque Favourites
(CFP) **CD-CFP4613** Favourite TV Classics
(CFP) **CD-CFP4616** Ave Maria
(CFP) **CD-CFP4660** Everlasting Peace
(DECC) **417 778-2DM** English Orchestral Music
(DECC) **430 261-2DM** Handel—Orchestral Works
(DECC) **430 500-2DWO** World of Handel
(DECC) **440 323-2DWO** World of British Classics, Volume V
(DECC) **443 334-2LRX** Music for Relaxation, Vol 9 - A Touch of Romance
(DECC) **444 388-2DWO** The World of Baroque Favourites
(DECC) **444 543-2DF2** Essential Handel
(DECC) **433 870-4DWO** Classical Favourites
(EMI) **MDC7 47014-8** Mozart: Opera Overtures
(EMI) **CDC5 55095-2** Prima Diva
(EMI) **CDC5 55396-2** Amanda Roocroft - Mozart and his Contemporaries
(EMI) **CDC7 47014-2** Mozart: Opera Overtures
(EMI) **CDC7 49155-2** Rossini: Overtures
(EMI) **CDC7 49179-2** Handel—Arias
(EMI) **CDC7 49700-2** Lucia Popp sings Viennese Operetta
(EMI) **CDC7 54056-2** Suppé—Overtures
(EMI) **CDC7 54438-2** Cherubini—Overtures
(EMI) **CDC7 54585-2** Wolf-Ferrari—Overtures & Intermezzi
(EMI) **CDEMTVD59** Classic Experience 3
(EMI) **CZS7 67425-2** Baroque Passion
(EMI) **CZS7 67440-2** The Best of Rossini
(EMI) **DCC7 47014-5** Mozart: Opera Overtures
(EMIL) **CDZ103** Best Loved Classics 4
(EMIL) **CDZ104** Best Loved Classics 5
(LOND) **421 390-2LM** Delius: Orchestral Works
(LOND) **825 126-2** Amadeus - Original Soundtrack
(LOND) **827 267-2** More Amadeus - Original Soundtrack
(PHIL) **422 523-2PME8(2)** The Complete Mozart Edition Vol 23 (pt 2)
(PHIL) **434 016-2PM3** Rossini—Overtures
(PHIL) **434 173-2PM** Arie Amorose
(PHIL) **434 916-2PH** Gilbert & Sullivan—Overtures
(PHIL) **438 166-2PH** Best of the Classical Bits
(PHIL) **442 313-2PM6** Sir Neville Marriner—A Birthday Celebration
(PHIL) **442 410-2PM** Queen of the Night—Cheryl Studer sings Mozart
(PHIL) **446 196-2PM** Rossini—Overtures
(PHIL) **434 916-5PH** Gilbert & Sullivan—Overtures
(WIEN) **WNR2037** Desert Island Discs
cond K. SILLITO
(CAPR) **10 420** Handel—Overtures

ACCARDO, Salvatore (vn)
(FONE) **94F04** Homage to Fritz Kreisler, Volume 1

ACERBI, Giuseppe (ten)
(CLUB) **CL99-587/8** Eugenia Burzio (1872-1922)

ACHATZ, Dag (pf)
(BIS) **BIS-CD352** Bernstein: Piano Arrangements

ACHSEL, Wanda (sop)
(SCHW) **314592** Vienna State Opera Live, Vol.9
(SCHW) **314602** Vienna State Opera Live, Vol.10
(SCHW) **314662** Vienna State Opera Live, Vol.16
(SCHW) **314742** Vienna State Opera Live, Vol.24

ACITO, Marc (ten)
Weill: Down in the Valley (Cpte)

ACKERMAN, Neville (ten)
Wagner: Parsifal (Cpte)

ACKERMANN, Otto (cond)
see Philh
South-West German RSO
VPO

ACS, Janos (cond)
see Budapest Concert Orch

ADAM, Agnes (sop)
Verdi: Rigoletto (Cpte)

ADAM, Gunter (bass)
R. Strauss: Ariadne auf Naxos (Cpte)

ADAM, Theo (bass-bar)
Beethoven: Fidelio (Cpte)
Einem: Dantons Tod (Cpte)
Mozart: Clemenza di Tito (Cpte), Idomeneo (Cpte), Zauberflöte (Cpte)
R. Strauss: Ariadne auf Naxos (Cpte), Rosenkavalier (Cpte)
Schoeck: Penthesilea (Cpte)
Wagner: Fliegende Holländer (Cpte), Götterdämmerung (Cpte), Meistersinger (Cpte), Parsifal (Cpte), Rheingold (Cpte), Rienzi (Cpte), Siegfried (Cpte), Walküre (Cpte)
Weber: Freischütz (exc)
(EURO) **GD69003** Wagner—Der Ring des Nibelungen
(PHIL) **422 525-2PME2** The Complete Mozart Edition Vol 25
(PHIL) **446 057-2PB14** Wagner—The Ring Cycle - Bayreuth Festival 1967

ADAMI, Mariella (pf)
Puccini: Bohème (exc)

ADAMS, Bryan (sngr)
(DECC) **444 460-2DH** Pavarotti and Friends II

ADAMS, Donald (bass)
Janáček: Káťa Kabanová (Cpte)
Sullivan: Cox and Box (Cpte), HMS Pinafore (Cpte), Iolanthe (Cpte), Mikado (Cpte), Patience (Cpte), Pirates of Penzance (Cpte), Princess Ida (Cpte), Ruddigore (Cpte), Sorcerer (Cpte), Trial by Jury (Cpte), Yeomen of the Guard (Cpte)
(DECC) **430 095-2DWO** The World of Gilbert & Sullivan, Vol.1
(DECC) **433 868-2DWO** The World of Gilbert & Sullivan - Volume 2

ADAMS, Glyn (ten)
Offenbach: Orphée aux enfers (exc)

ADAMS, John (bar)
Massenet: Cid (Cpte)

ADAMS, Suzanne (sop)
(SYMP) **SYMCD1100** Harold Wayne Collection, Vol.8

ADANI, Mariella (sop)
Puccini: Bohème (Cpte)
(EMI) **CDM7 69596-2** The Movies go to the Opera

ADE-JESEMANN, Ingrid (sop)
Nono: Prometeo (Cpte)
(SONY) **SK53978** Prometheus

ADELAIDE SYMPHONY ORCHESTRA
cond J. SEREBRIER
(MCI) **OQ0008** Tchaikovsky & Gounod—Ballet music
(MCI) **OQ0011** A Baroque Collection

ADINI, Ada (sop)
(SYMP) **SYMCD1172** The Harold Wayne Collection, Vol.21

ADLER, Kurt Herbert (cond)
see National PO
NY Met Op Orch
RPO

ADLER, Peter Herman (cond)
see New Philh

ADLER, Stephen (bar)
G. Lloyd: John Socman (exc)

ADORF, Mario (sngr)
Weill: Dreigroschenoper (Cpte)

ADORNI, Claudio (ten)
Donizetti: Don Pasquale (Cpte)

ADRIAN, Max (sngr)
Bernstein: Candide (1956) (exc)

AFEYAN, Natalia (sngr)
Weill: Dreigroschenoper (Cpte)

AFFRE, Augustarello (ten)
(IRCC) **IRCC-CD800** Souvenirs from Meyerbeer Operas
(IRCC) **IRCC-CD802** Souvenirs of Rare French Opera

AFONSO, Helena (sop)
Monteverdi: Orfeo (Cpte)

AGACHE, Alexander (bar)
Bretan: Arald (Cpte), Golem (Cpte)
Donizetti: Lucia di Lammermoor (exc)
Gounod: Faust (Cpte)
Verdi: Rigoletto (Cpte), Simon Boccanegra (Cpte)
(TELD) **4509-93691-2** Queen of Coloratura

AGHOVA, Livia (sop)
Dvořák: Dimitrij (Cpte)

AGNETTI, Mario (ten)
Shostakovich: Lady Macbeth of Mtsensk (Cpte)

AGNEW, Paul (ten)
Blow: Venus and Adonis (Cpte)
Purcell: Dioclesian, Z627 (Cpte)

AHLERSMEYER, Mathieu (bar)
Mozart: Nozze di Figaro (Cpte)
Verdi: Macbeth (Cpte)
(SCHW) **314502** Vienna State Opera—Live Recordings (sampler)
(SCHW) **314562** Vienna State Opera Live, Vol.6
(SCHW) **314582** Vienna State Opera Live, Vol.8
(SCHW) **314602** Vienna State Opera Live, Vol.10

AHLIN, Cvetka (mez)
Mozart: Zauberflöte (exc)
R. Strauss: Elektra (Cpte), Rosenkavalier (Cpte)
Wagner: Walküre (Cpte)
(DG) **435 211-2GX15** Wagner—Der Ring des Nibelungen

AHLSTEDT, Douglas (ten)
Mysliveček: Bellerofonte (Cpte)

AHNSJÖ, Claes Hakon (ten)
Donizetti: Lucia di Lammermoor (Cpte)
Gluck: Rencontre imprévue (Cpte)
Haydn: Armida (Cpte), Orlando Paladino (Cpte)
Massenet: Chérubin (Cpte)
Mozart: Nozze di Figaro (Cpte), Sogno di Scipione (Cpte)
Puccini: Turandot (Cpte)
Verdi: Macbeth (Cpte)
Wagner: Parsifal (Cpte)
(PHIL) **432 416-2PH3** Haydn—L'incontro improvviso/Arias

AHRONOVITCH, Yuri (cond)
see LSO
Vienna SO

AICHBERGER, Ewald (ten)
R. Strauss: Frau ohne Schatten (Cpte), Rosenkavalier (Cpte)
Wagner: Parsifal (Cpte)

AIKIN, Laura (sop)
(SCHW) **312682** Opera Gala with Young Artists - Volume II

AINSLEY, John Mark (ten)
Berlioz: Troyens (Cpte)
Blow: Venus and Adonis (Cpte)
Britten: Gloriana (Cpte)
Monteverdi: Orfeo (Cpte)
Mozart: Don Giovanni (Cpte)
Purcell: Dido (Cpte), Dioclesian, Z627 (exc), Fairy Queen, Z629 (Cpte)
Sullivan: Pirates of Penzance (Cpte)
(EMI) **CDC7 49849-2** Famous Opera Choruses
(HYPE) **CDA66569** Vaughan Williams—Choral Works
(HYPE) **CDA67061/2** Britten—Purcell Realizations

AIRINEN, Kai (ten)
Madetoja: Juha (Cpte)

AIRIZER, Csaba (bass)
(ELCT) **ELCD109** Timisoara Memorial

AITKEN, Herbert (ten)
Sullivan: Gondoliers (Cpte)

AITKEN, Robert (fl)
(BIS) **BIS-CD166** The Virtuoso Flute
(IMP) **PCD1091** Jeux à deux

AIX-EN-PROVENCE FESTIVAL CHORUS
cond A. CLUYTENS
Gounod: Mireille (Cpte)
cond H. ROSBAUD
Mozart: Don Giovanni (Cpte), Nozze di Figaro (Cpte)

ÅKERLUND, Lina (sop)
Carvalho: Testoride Argonauta (Cpte)
Fux: Dafne in Lauro (Cpte)
Keiser: Croesus (Cpte)

ALAGNA, Roberto (ten)
Donizetti: Elisir d'amore (Cpte)
Gounod: Roméo et Juliette (Cpte)
Verdi: Rigoletto (Cpte), Traviata (Cpte)
(DECC) **436 261-2DHO3** Puccini—Il Trittico
(EMI) **CDC5 55540-2** Roberto Alagna sings Operatic Arias

ALAIMO, Simone (bar)
Bellini: Zaira (Cpte)
Donizetti: Maria Stuarda (Cpte)
Mozart: Don Giovanni (exc)
Rossini: Barbiere di Siviglia (Cpte), Cenerentola (Cpte), Ermione (Cpte), Turco in Italia (Cpte)
Verdi: Masnadieri (Cpte)

ALAIMO, Vincenzo (sngr)
Donizetti: Maria di Rohan (Cpte)

ALAMIKKOTERVO, Aki (ten)
(BIS) **BIS-CD373/4** Opera Scenes from Savaonlinna

ALAN, Hervey (bass)
Britten: Billy Budd (Cpte)
Purcell: King Arthur, Z628 (Cpte)
Rossini: Cenerentola (Cpte)
(DECC) **443 393-2DWO** The World of Henry Purcell

ALARIE, Pierrette (sop)
Bizet: Pêcheurs de Perles (Cpte)
Gluck: Orphée (Cpte)
R. Strauss: Schweigsame Frau (Cpte)
(PHIL) **438 953-2PM2** Alarie/Simoneau - Arias & Duets

ALBANESE, Francesco (ten)
Verdi: Traviata (Cpte)

ALBANESE, Licia (sop)
Bizet: Carmen (Cpte)
Puccini: Bohème (Cpte), Manon Lescaut (Cpte)
Verdi: Traviata (Cpte)
(EMI) **CHS7 64864-2(2)** La Scala Edition - Vol.2, 1915-46 (pt 2)
(RCA) **GD87799** The Pearl Fishers Duet plus Duets and Scenes
(RCA) **09026 61580-2(5)** RCA/Met 100 Singers, 100 Years (pt 5)
(RCA) **74321 24284-2** Opera's Greatest Heroines

ALBANI, Emma (sop)
(SYMP) **SYMCD1093** The Harold Wayne Collection, Vol.7

ALBERGONI, Angelo (cond)
see orch

ALBERS, Henri (bar)
(IRCC) **IRCC-CD802** Souvenirs of Rare French Opera

ALBERT, Donnie Ray (bar)
Gershwin: Porgy and Bess (Cpte)

ALBERT, Thomas (cond)
see Fiori Musicali

ALBERT, Werner Andreas (cond)
see Hanover Rad PO
Melbourne SO
Rhineland-Pfalz State PO

ALBERTI, Walter (bar)
Leoncavallo: Pagliacci (Cpte)

ALBERTINI, Alberto (bar)
Puccini: Gianni Schicchi (Cpte)
Verdi: Traviata (Cpte)

ALBERTS, Eunice (contr)
R. Ward: Crucible (Cpte)
(VANG) **08.4016.71** Music of Samuel Barber

ALBRECHT, Gerd (cond)
see Austrian RSO
Berlin Deutsches SO
Berlin RSO
Cologne RSO
Czech PO
Frankfurt RSO
Hamburg PO
Hamburg St Op Orch

ALCANTARA, Lynette (sop)
Lehár: Lustige Witwe (Cpte)

ALCHEVSKY, Ivan (ten)
(SYMP) **SYMCD1105** The Harold Wayne Collection, Vol.10

ALDA, Catarina (mez)
Verdi: Rigoletto (Cpte)

ALDA, Frances (sop)
(CLUB) **CL99-060** Enrico Caruso—Opera & Song Recital
(KIWI) **CDSLD-82** Southern Voices—NZ International Opera Singers
(NIMB) **NI7834** Caruso in Ensemble
(PEAR) **EVC2** The Caruso Edition, Vol.2—1908-12
(PEAR) **EVC3(1)** The Caruso Edition, Vol.3 (pt 1)
(PEAR) **GEMMCD9309** Enrico Caruso - Opera and Song Recital
(RCA) **GD60495(3)** The Complete Caruso Collection (pt 3)
(RCA) **GD60495(4)** The Complete Caruso Collection (pt 4)
(RCA) **GD60495(5)** The Complete Caruso Collection (pt 5)
(RCA) **09026 61242-2** Caruso Sings Verdi
(RCA) **09026 61580-2(2)** RCA/Met 100 Singers, 100 Years (pt 2)

ALDEBURGH FESTIVAL CHOIR
cond S. BEDFORD
Gay: Beggar's Opera (Cpte)

ALDEBURGH FESTIVAL ENSEMBLE
cond S. BEDFORD
Britten: Turn of the Screw (Cpte)

ALDEBURGH FESTIVAL ORCHESTRA
cond S. BEDFORD
Gay: Beggar's Opera (Cpte)

ALDENHOFF, Bernd (ten)
Wagner: Götterdämmerung (Cpte)

ALDERSON, Richard (sngr)
Rapchak: Lifework of Juan Diaz (Cpte)

ALER, John (ten)
Bizet: Pêcheurs de Perles (Cpte)
Gazzaniga: Don Giovanni (Cpte)
Gluck: Iphigénie en Aulide (Cpte), Iphigénie en Tauride (Cpte)
Handel: Sosarme (Cpte)
Lehár: Lustige Witwe (Cpte)
Mozart: Così fan tutte (Cpte)
Offenbach: Belle Hélène (Cpte)
Rossini: Comte Ory (Cpte)
(CFP) **CD-CFP4606** Favourite Movie Classics
(EMI) **CDM5 65576-2** Jessye Norman
(EMI) **CZS5 68113-2** Vive Offenbach!
(ERAT) **4509-99607-2** Gluck—Operas; Schubert—Symphonies Nos 8 & 9
(SONY) **SK45965** Esa-Pekka Salonen conducts Stravinsky

ALESSANDRINI, Mario (ten)
Verdi: Ballo in maschera (Cpte)

ALESSANDRO STRADELLA CONSORT
cond E. VELARDI
Stradella: Moro per amore (Cpte)

ALESSIO, Robert d' (ten)
Verdi: Falstaff (Cpte)

ALEXANDER, Carlos (bar)
Orff: Antigonae (Cpte)

ALEXANDER, John (ten)
Bellini: Norma (exc)
Wagner: Feen (Cpte)

ALEXANDER, Peter (bar)
Benatzky: Im weissen Rössl (exc)

ALEXANDER, Roberta (sop)
B. Goldschmidt: Gewaltige Hahnrei (Cpte)
Gluck: Paride ed Elena (Cpte)
Handel: Giulio Cesare (exc)
Janáček: Jenufa (Cpte)
Mozart: Don Giovanni (Cpte), Idomeneo (Cpte)
(ETCE) **KTC1037** Bernstein: Songs
(ETCE) **KTC1145** Barber—Scenes and Arias
(SONY) **S2K66836** Goldschmidt—Beatrice Cenci, etc
(TELD) **4509-96231-2** Gardening Classics
(TELD) **4509-97444-2** Gershwin—Orchestral Works

ALEXANDER, Stephen (treb)
Britten: Noye's Fludde (Cpte)
(DECC) **436 990-2DWO** The World of Benjamin Britten

(JEFF) ALEXANDER CHOIR
cond C. CALLINICOS
(RCA) **GD60889(1)** The Mario Lanza Collection
cond H. RENÉ
(RCA) **GD60720** Mario Lanza—Be my love
(RCA) **GD60889(1)** The Mario Lanza Collection
(RCA) **74321 18574-2** Mario Lanza - The Ultimate Collection

ALEXANDERSSON, Sven-Erik (ten)
Haeffner: Electra (Cpte)
Rameau: Castor et Pollux (Cpte)

ALEXANDRIDIS, Michal (treb)
Krása: Brundibár (Cpte)

ALEXASHKIN, Sergei (bass)
Prokofiev: War and Peace (Cpte)
Rimsky-Korsakov: Sadko (Cpte)
Tchaikovsky: Queen of Spades (Cpte)

ALEXEEV, Valery (bar)
Mussorgsky: Khovanshchina (Cpte)

ALFÖLDI, Zsuzsa (sop)
Schoeck: Venus (Cpte)

ALGORTA, Jorge (bass)
Verdi: Otello (Cpte)

ALGOS, Angelo (bass)
(SYMP) **SYMCD1126** The Harold Wayne Collection, Vol.14

ALIBERTI, Lucia (sop)
Verdi: Macbeth (Cpte), Traviata (Cpte)
(CAPR) **10 247** The Art of Bel Canto
(ORFE) **C119841A** Lucia Aliberti: Famous Opera Arias

ALLAIN, Jean (cond)
see Pasdeloup Ass Orch

(JOHN) ALLDIS CHOIR
Berlioz: Béatrice et Bénédict (Cpte)
Bizet: Carmen (Cpte)
Giordano: Andrea Chénier (Cpte)
Leoncavallo: Pagliacci (Cpte)
Massenet: Esclarmonde (Cpte), Thaïs (Cpte)
Mozart: Così fan tutte (Cpte), Entführung (Cpte), Nozze di Figaro (Cpte)
Puccini: Bohème (Cpte), Tabarro (Cpte), Tosca (Cpte), Turandot (Cpte)
Tchaikovsky: Eugene Onegin (Cpte)
Verdi: Aida (Cpte), Forza del destino (Cpte), Vespri Siciliani (Cpte)
(CFP) **CD-CFP4575** Verdi Arias
(DECC) **425 681-2DM2** Tutto Pavarotti
(DECC) **433 064-2DWO** Your Hundred Best Opera Tunes Volume I
(DECC) **433 067-2DWO** Your Hundred Best Opera Tunes IV
(DECC) **433 822-2DH** Essential Opera
(DECC) **436 317-2DA** Puccini—Famous Arias
(DECC) **436 406-2DWO** The World of Tchaikovsky
(DECC) **440 410-2DM** Plácido Domingo
(DECC) **443 378-2DM** Ten Top Mezzos 2
(DECC) **443 928-2DM** Montserrat Caballé sings Opera Arias
(DECC) **444 555-2DF2** Essential Puccini
(DECC) **400 053-4DH** World's Best Loved Tenor Arias
(RCA) **GD60205** Opera Choruses
(RCA) **GD60866** The Placido Domingo Album
(RCA) **GD84265** Con Amore
(RCA) **VD60535** Borodin—Orchestral Works
(RCA) **09026 61356-2** Domingo Sings Caruso
(RCA) **09026 61634-2** Verdi & Puccini Duets
(RCA) **74321 24209-2** Italian Opera Choruses

ALLEGRI, Maria Garcia (contr)
Donizetti: Linda di Chamounix (Cpte)
(DG) **419 257-2GH3** 'Cav' and 'Pag', etc

ALLEMANO, Carlo (ten)
Gazzaniga: Don Giovanni (Cpte)
Mozart: Nozze di Figaro (Cpte)

ALLEN, Betty (mez)
Joplin: Treemonisha (Cpte)

ALLEN, Thomas (bar)
Berlioz: Béatrice et Bénédict (Cpte)
Bizet: Carmen (Cpte)
Britten: Billy Budd (Cpte), Peter Grimes (Cpte)
Donizetti: Don Pasquale (Cpte)
Gluck: Iphigénie en Tauride (Cpte)
Gounod: Faust (exc)
Janáček: Cunning Little Vixen (Cpte)
Leoncavallo: Pagliacci (Cpte)
Massenet: Werther (Cpte)
Mozart: Così fan tutte (Cpte), Don Giovanni (exc), Nozze di Figaro (exc), Zauberflöte (exc)
Puccini: Bohème (Cpte), Manon Lescaut (Cpte)
Purcell: Dido (Cpte)
Rossini: Barbiere di Siviglia (exc)
Sullivan: HMS Pinafore (Cpte), Yeomen of the Guard (exc)
Tchaikovsky: Eugene Onegin (Cpte)
(CAST) **CASH5051** Puccini Favourites from Covent Garden and the Arena di Verona
(CAST) **CVI2065** Highlights from the Royal Opera House, Covent Garden
(CAST) **CVI2070** Great Puccini Love Scenes from Covent Garden, La Scala and Verona
(DECC) **433 067-2DWO** Your Hundred Best Opera Tunes IV
(DG) **431 601-2GCE10** Tchaikovsky Compact Edition
(EMI) **CDC7 49811-2** Covent Garden Gala Concert
(EMI) **CDH5 65072-2** Glyndebourne Recorded - 1934-1994
(EMI) **CDM5 65575-2** Montserrat Caballé
(EMI) **CDM7 69500-2** Montserrat Caballé sings Bellini & Verdi Arias
(EMIL) **CDZ7 67015-2** Mozart—Opera Arias
(EMIL) **CDZ100** Best Loved Classics 1
(EMIL) **CDZ104** Best Loved Classics 5
(EMIL) **CDZ105** Best Loved Classics 6
(GAMU) **GAMD506** An Anthology Of English Song
(TELD) **9031-77676-6(TELD)** My World of Opera - Kiri Te Kanawa
(TER) **CDVIR8317** If I Loved You - Love Duets from the Musicals

ALLERS, Franz (cond)
see Graunke SO

ALLEYN'S SCHOOL CHOIR
cond B. BRITTEN
(LOND) **436 393-2LM** Britten—The Little Sweep, etc

ALLIN, Norman (bass)
Mozart: Nozze di Figaro (Cpte)
(PEAR) **GEMMCDS9925(1)** Covent Garden on Record—Vol.3 (pt 1)

ALLIOT-LUGAZ, Colette (sop)
Debussy: Pelléas et Mélisande (Cpte)
Fauré: Pénélope (Cpte)
Gluck: Iphigénie en Tauride (Cpte)
Lully: Alceste (Cpte)
M-A. Charpentier: David et Jonathas (Cpte)
Massenet: Manon (Cpte)
Messager: Fortunio (Cpte)
Monteverdi: Orfeo (Cpte)
Offenbach: Belle Hélène (Cpte), Brigands (Cpte)
Prokofiev: Love for 3 Oranges (Cpte)
(DECC) **440 333-2DH** Ravel—Vocal Works
(EMI) **CZS5 68113-2** Vive Offenbach!

ALLISTER, Jean (mez)
Cavalli: Ormindo (Cpte)
Sullivan: Mikado (Cpte), Pirates of Penzance (exc), Ruddigore (Cpte), Sorcerer (Cpte)
(DECC) **430 095-2DWO** The World of Gilbert & Sullivan, Vol.1
(DECC) **433 868-2DWO** The World of Gilbert & Sullivan - Volume 2
(IMP) **PWK1157** Gilbert & Sullivan Spectacular

ALLMAN, Robert (bar)
Beethoven: Fidelio (Cpte)
(DECC) **071 149-1DH (DECC)** The Essential Sutherland

ALLOUBA, Nivine (sop)
Mozart: Don Giovanni (Cpte), Nozze di Figaro (Cpte)

ALL-UNION RADIO ORCHESTRA
cond A. ORLOV
(ARLE) **ARL23/5** Rimsky-Korsakov—Sadko

ALMEIDA, Antonio de (cond)
see Camerata de Provence Orch
LPO
LSO
Monte Carlo Op Orch
Philh

ALMGREN, Lars (cond)
see Stockholm Palm Court Orch

ALONSO, Francisco (bass)
(MEMO) **HR4372/3** Great Voices Giuseppe Di Stefano

ALONSO, Ramon (bass)
Barbieri: Barberillo de Lavapiès (Cpte)
Usandizaga: Golondrinas (Cpte)

ALONSO, Virginia (mez)
(DG) **072 110-1GH** Hommage a Sevilla—Placido Domingo in scenes from various operas
(DG) **072 187-1GH (DG)** Hommage a Sevilla

ALPAR, Gitta (sop)
(MMOI) **CDMOIR419** Vienna Nights - Golden Age of Operetta

ALSEN, Herbert (bass)
Beethoven: Fidelio (Cpte)
Verdi: Macbeth (Cpte)
Wagner: Meistersinger (Cpte), Parsifal (exc), Tristan und Isolde (exc)
(PREI) **90237** R Strauss—Daphne
(PREI) **90249** Mozart in tempore belli
(SCHW) **314532** Vienna State Opera Live, Vol.3
(SCHW) **314542** Vienna State Opera Live, Vol.4
(SCHW) **314552** Vienna State Opera Live, Vol.5
(SCHW) **314562** Vienna State Opera Live, Vol.6
(SCHW) **314572** Vienna State Opera Live, Vol.7
(SCHW) **314592** Vienna State Opera Live, Vol.9
(SCHW) **314602** Vienna State Opera Live, Vol.10
(SCHW) **314632** Vienna State Opera Live, Vol.13
(SCHW) **314652** Vienna State Opera Live, Vol.15
(SCHW) **314672** Vienna State Opera Live, Vol.17
(SCHW) **314692** Vienna State Opera Live, Vol.19
(SCHW) **314702** Vienna State Opera Live, Vol.20
(SCHW) **314712** Vienna State Opera Live, Vol.21

ALSINA, Estrella (sngr)
Moreno Torroba: Luisa Fernanda (Cpte)

ALSOP, Marin (cond)
see Concordia

ALSTERGÅRD, Bertil (bar)
Verdi: Rigoletto (Cpte), Trovatore (Cpte)

ALTENA, Marius van (ten)
Mozart: Thamos, K345 (Cpte)

ALTHOUSE, Paul (ten)
(IRCC) **IRCC-CD810** American Singers, Volume 1
(RCA) **09026 61580-2(2)** RCA/Met 100 Singers, 100 Years (pt 2)

ALTMAN, Thelma (sop)
(ALTN) **CDAN3** Hjördis Schymberg

ALTMEYER, Jeannine (sop)
Beethoven: Fidelio (Cpte)
Wagner: Götterdämmerung (Cpte), Siegfried (Cpte), Walküre (Cpte)
(EURO) **GD69003** Wagner—Der Ring des Nibelungen
(PHIL) **434 420-2PM32(1)** Richard Wagner Edition (Pt.1)

ALTMEYER, Theo (ten)
Monteverdi: Orfeo (Cpte)
Schultze: Schwarzer Peter (Cpte)

ALTRICHTER, Petr (cond)
see Prague SO

ALVA, Luigi (ten)
Donizetti: Elisir d'amore (Cpte)
Handel: Alcina (Cpte)
Mozart: Così fan tutte (Cpte), Don Giovanni (exc)
Rossini: Barbiere di Siviglia (Cpte), Cenerentola (Cpte), Italiana in Algeri (Cpte)
Verdi: Falstaff (Cpte)
(EMI) **CDH5 65072-2** Glyndebourne Recorded - 1934-1994
(MEMO) **HR4300/1** Great Voices—Sesto Bruscantini

ALVA, Robert (bass)
(DUTT) **CDLX7012** The Incomparable Heddle Nash
(PEAR) **GEMMCDS9926(2)** Covent Garden on Record—Vol.4 (pt 2)
(PEAR) **GEMMCD9473** Heddle Nash—Vol.2

ALVAREZ, Albert (ten)
(PEAR) **GEMMCDS9923(1)** Covent Garden on Record, Vol.1 (pt 1)

ALVAREZ, Carlos (bass)
Penella: Gato Montés (Cpte)
Shostakovich: Lady Macbeth of Mtsensk (Cpte)
Vives: Bohemios (Cpte), Doña Francisquita (Cpte)
(CAPR) **10 704** Young Voices of the Opera-Michele Pertusi

ALVARY, Lorenzo (bass)
R. Strauss: Frau ohne Schatten (Cpte)
(VAI) **VAIA1017** Leonard Warren—Early Recordings

ALVI, Bernard (ten)
Adam: Si j'étais roi (Cpte)
Terrasse: Travaux d'Hercule (Cpte)

ALWIN, Karl (cond)
see orch
Vienna St Op Orch
VPO

AMADE, Raymond (ten)
Adam: Toréador (Cpte)
Ganne: Saltimbanques (exc)
Offenbach: Chanson de Fortunio (Cpte), Contes d'Hoffmann (Cpte), Madame l'Archiduc (Cpte)
(EMI) **CZS5 68113-2** Vive Offenbach!
(EMI) **CZS7 67872-2** Lehár—Operettas (highlights in French)

AMADEUS ENSEMBLE
cond J. RUDEL
(MUSM) **67118-2** Mozart—Harmoniemusik

AMADI, Alberto (ten)
(IRCC) **IRCC-CD808** Souvenirs of 19th Century Italian Opera

AMADUCCI, Bruno (cond)
see Svizzera Italiana Orch
Warmia Nat PO

AMARA, Lucine (sop)
Leoncavallo: Pagliacci (Cpte)
Puccini: Bohème (Cpte)
Verdi: Aida (exc), Don Carlo (Cpte)

AMATO, Pasquale (bar)
(CLUB) **CL99-060** Enrico Caruso—Opera & Song Recital
(EMI) **CHS7 64860-2(2)** La Scala Edition - Vol.1, 1878-1914 (pt 2)
(IRCC) **IRCC-CD808** Souvenirs of 19th Century Italian Opera
(NIMB) **NI7808** Luisa Tetrazzini—Opera & Song Recital
(NIMB) **NI7834** Caruso in Ensemble
(NIMB) **NI7849** Frieda Hempel (1885-1955)
(NIMB) **NI7867** Legendary Baritones
(NIMB) **NI7872** Geraldine Farrar in French Opera
(PEAR) **EVC2** The Caruso Edition, Vol.2—1908-12
(PEAR) **EVC3(1)** The Caruso Edition, Vol.3 (pt 1)
(PEAR) **GEMMCDS9073(1)** Giovanni Zenatello, Vol.1 (pt 1)
(PEAR) **GEMMCDS9073(2)** Giovanni Zenatello, Vol.1 (pt 2)
(PEAR) **GEMMCDS9924(1)** Covent Garden on Record, Vol.2 (pt 1)
(PEAR) **GEMMCD9104** Pasquale Amato (1878-1942)
(PEAR) **GEMMCD9224** Luisa Tetrazzini—Vol.4
(PREI) **89064** Pasquale Amato (1878-1942)
(PREI) **89995** Famous Italian Baritones
(RCA) **GD60495(4)** The Complete Caruso Collection (pt 4)
(RCA) **09026 61242-2** Caruso Sings Verdi
(RCA) **09026 61580-2(2)** RCA/Met 100 Singers, 100 Years (pt 2)
(SYMP) **SYMCD1138** The Harold Wayne Collection, Vol.16
(SYMP) **SYMCD1148** The Harold Wayne Collection, Vol.17

AMBROS, Hermi (sop)
R. Strauss: Elektra (Cpte)
Wagner: Parsifal (Cpte)

AMBROSIAN CHORUS
cond J.O. EDWARDS
Romberg: Student Prince (Cpte)

AMBROSIAN LIGHT OPERA CHORUS
cond R. BONYNGE
(DECC) **417 780-2DM** Joan Sutherland's Greatest Hits
(DECC) **425 048-2DX** Joan Sutherland - Home Sweet Home
(DECC) **433 223-2DWO** The World of Operetta
(DECC) **436 316-2DA** Golden Operetta

AMBROSIAN OPERA CHORUS
cond C. ABBADO
Rossini: Barbiere di Siviglia (Cpte)
cond A. DE ALMEIDA
A. Thomas: Hamlet (Cpte)
Halévy: Juive (Cpte)
cond J. BARBIROLLI
Verdi: Otello (Cpte)

(PEAR) **GEMMCDS9925(1)** Covent Garden on Record—Vol.3 (pt 1)
(PEAR) **GEMMCDS9997/9(1)** Singers of Imperial Russia, Vol.1 (pt 1)
(PEAR) **GEMMCDS9997/9(2)** Singers of Imperial Russia, Vol.1 (pt 2)
(PEAR) **GEMMCD9016** Mattia Battistini, Vol.3
(PEAR) **GEMMCD9091** Dino Borgioli
(PEAR) **GEMMCD9161** Edmond Clément (1867-1928)
(PEAR) **GEMMCD9172** Emmy Destinn (1878-1930)
(PEAR) **GEMMCD9225** Luisa Tetrazzini—Vol.5
(PEAR) **GEMMCD9309** Enrico Caruso - Opera and Song Recital
(PEAR) **GEMMCD9411** Tom Burke—A Centenary Tribute
(PEAR) **GEMMCD9497** Pol Plançon
(PEAR) **GEMMCD9936** Mattia Battistini, Vol.1
(PEAR) **GEMMCD9937** Antonio Scotti
(PREI) **89996** Kyra Vayne (b.1916)
(PREI) **89998** Antonio Paoli (1871-1946)
(RCA) **GD60495(1)** The Complete Caruso Collection (pt 1)
(RCA) **09026 61243-2** Caruso sings Verismo Arias
(RCA) **09026 61580-2(1)** RCA/Met 110 Singers, 100 Years (pt 1)
(RECO) **TRC3** The Art of Aristodemo Giorgini
(ROMO) **81001-2** Emma Eames (1865-1952)
(ROMO) **81005-2** Claudia Muzio (1889-1936)
(ROMO) **82001-2** Pol Plançon—Complete Victor Recordings
(ROMO) **82002-2** Edmond Clément (1867-1928)
(SUPR) **11 2136-2(1)** Emmy Destinn—Complete Edition, Discs 1 & 2
(SYMP) **SYMCD1065** The Harold Wayne Collection, Vol.1
(SYMP) **SYMCD1069** The Harold Wayne Collection, Vol.2
(SYMP) **SYMCD1073** The Harold Wayne Collection, Vol.3
(SYMP) **SYMCD1077** The Harold Wayne Collection, Vol.4
(SYMP) **SYMCD1081** The Harold Wayne Collection, Vol.5
(SYMP) **SYMCD1085** The Harold Wayne Collection, Vol.6
(SYMP) **SYMCD1089** Historic Baritones of the French School
(SYMP) **SYMCD1093** The Harold Wayne Collection, Vol.7
(SYMP) **SYMCD1100** Harold Wayne Collection, Vol.8
(SYMP) **SYMCD1101** The Harold Wayne Collection, Vol.9
(SYMP) **SYMCD1105** The Harold Wayne Collection, Vol.10
(SYMP) **SYMCD1111** The Harold Wayne Collection, Vol.11
(SYMP) **SYMCD1113** The Harold Wayne Collection, Vol.13
(SYMP) **SYMCD1123** Sullivan—Sesquicentenial Commemorative Issue
(SYMP) **SYMCD1125** Lucien Fugère—Opera & Song Recital
(SYMP) **SYMCD1126** The Harold Wayne Collection, Vol.14
(SYMP) **SYMCD1128** The Harold Wayne Collection, Vol.15
(SYMP) **SYMCD1138** The Harold Wayne Collection, Vol.16
(SYMP) **SYMCD1148** The Harold Wayne Collection, Vol.17
(SYMP) **SYMCD1149** Fernando De Lucia
(SYMP) **SYMCD1158** The Harold Wayne Collection, Vol.18
(SYMP) **SYMCD1168** The Harold Wayne Collection, Vol.19
(SYMP) **SYMCD1170** The Harold Wayne Collection, Vol.20
(SYMP) **SYMCD1172** The Harold Wayne Collection, Vol.21
(SYMP) **SYMCD1173** The Harold Wayne Collection, Vol.22
(TEST) **SBT1008** Viva Rossini

ANONYMOUS TREBLE (treb)
Debussy: Pelléas et Mélisande (Cpte)
Monteverdi: Incoronazione di Poppea (Cpte)

ANONYMOUS TRUMPET PERFORMERS (tpt)
(BONG) **GB1043-2** Italian Baritones of the Acoustic Era

ANONYMOUS VIOLIN PERFORMERS (vn)
(PEAR) **GEMMCDS9007/9(1)** Singers of Imperial Russia, Vol.4 (pt 1)

ANSELMI, Giuseppe (ten)
(EMI) **CHS7 64860-2(2)** La Scala Edition - Vol.1, 1878-1914 (pt 2)
(PEAR) **GEMMCDS9923(2)** Covent Garden on Record, Vol.1 (pt 2)
(PEAR) **GEMMCDS9924(1)** Covent Garden on Record, Vol.2 (pt 1)
(PEAR) **GEMMCDS9924(2)** Covent Garden on Record, Vol.2 (pt 2)
(SYMP) **SYMCD1170** The Harold Wayne Collection, Vol.20

ANSELMI, Susanna (sop)
Handel: Giulio Cesare (Cpte)
Verdi: Luisa Miller (Cpte)

ANSERMET, Ernest (cond)
see SRO

ANSSEAU, Fernand (ten)
(CONI) **CDHD235** The Puccini Album
(IRCC) **IRCC-CD802** Souvenirs of Rare French Opera
(MSCM) **MM30377** 18 Tenors d'Expression Française
(PEAR) **GEMMCDS9926(1)** Covent Garden on Record—Vol.4 (pt 1)
(PEAR) **GEMMCD9129** Great Tenors, Vol.2
(PREI) **89021** Marcel Journet (1867-1933)
(PREI) **89022** Fernand Ansseau (1890-1972)

ANTAROVA, Konkordiya (mez)
Tchaikovsky: Eugene Onegin (Cpte)

ANTHONI, Gretje (sop)
(CPO) **CPO999 104-2** Mozart—Lo Sposo Deluso/L'Oca del Cairo

ANTHONY, Charles (ten)
Puccini: Fanciulla del West (Cpte)
Verdi: Aida (exc), Ernani (Cpte)
(DG) **072 428-1GH2(DG)** The Metropolitan Opera Gala

ANTHONY, Grace (sop)
(NIMB) **NI7804** Giovanni Martinelli—Opera Recital
(NIMB) **NI7851** Legendary Voices
(PEAR) **GEMMCDS9160(2)** De Luca Edition, Vol.2 (pt 2)
(PREI) **89062** Giovanni Martinelli (1885-1969)
(PREI) **89073** Giuseppe de Luca (1876-1950) - II

ANTHONY, Trevor (bass)
Purcell: King Arthur, Z628 (Cpte)
Sullivan: Patience (Cpte)
(DECC) **436 990-2DWO** The World of Benjamin Britten
(DECC) **443 393-2DWO** The World of Henry Purcell
(LOND) **436 393-2LM** Britten—The Little Sweep, etc

ANTHONY, Trevor (spkr)
Britten: Noye's Fludde (Cpte)

ANTINORI, Nazzareno (ten)
Puccini: Madama Butterfly (Cpte)
(CAST) **CVI2070** Great Puccini Love Scenes from Covent Garden, La Scala and Verona

ANTOINE, Bernadette (sop)
Delibes: Lakmé (Cpte)

ANTOLIČOVÁ, Eva (sop)
Bellini: Sonnambula (Cpte)
Suchoň: Whirlpool (Cpte)

ANTONACCI, Anna Caterina (sop)
Mozart: Così fan tutte (Cpte), Nozze di Figaro (Cpte)
Puccini: Madama Butterfly (Cpte)
Verdi: Macbeth (Cpte), Rigoletto (Cpte)

ANTONIAK, Mieczyslaw (ten)
Verdi: Due Foscari (Cpte)

ANTONICELLI, Giuseppe (cond)
see La Scala Orch
orch

ANTONINI, Giovanni (bass)
Rossini: Armida (Cpte)
(BUTT) **BMCD015** Pavarotti Collection - Duets and Scenes

ANTONIOU, John (bar)
Delius: Village Romeo and Juliet (Cpte)

ANTONIOZZI, Alfonso (bar)
Mozart: Nozze di Figaro (Cpte)
Rossini: Signor Bruschino (Cpte)

ANTONOVA, Elizaveta (mez)
(ARLE) **ARL23/5** Rimsky-Korsakov—Sadko

ANTONUCCI, Stefano (bar)
Mercadante: Bravo (Cpte)
Puccini: Bohème (Cpte)
Rossini: Torvaldo e Dorliska (Cpte)

ANTUNES, Celso (ten)
Hindemith: Neues vom Tage (Cpte)

AP ROBERT, Elen (sop)
(SAIN) **SCDC2002** Elen AP Robert - Soprano

APARICI, Montserrat (sop)
Verdi: Lombardi (Cpte)
(PHIL) **442 602-2PM** 3 x 3 Tenors

APOLLO CHORUS
cond ROSARIO BOURDON
(CLUB) **CL99-025** Giovanni Zenatello (1876-1949)
(PEAR) **GEMMCDS9074(2)** Giovanni Zenatello, Vol.2 (pt 2)
(PREI) **89038** Giovanni Zenatello (1876-1949)

APOLLONI, Anita (sop)
(PREI) **89023** Conchita Supervia (1895-1936)

APOSTOLU, Giovanni (ten)
(SYMP) **SYMCD1077** The Harold Wayne Collection, Vol.4

APPEL, Wolfgang (ten)
Wagner: Meistersinger (Cpte)

APPELGREN, Curt (bass)
Beethoven: Fidelio (Cpte)
Britten: Midsummer Night's Dream (Cpte)
Lidholm: Dream Play (Cpte)

APPELT, Hans-Dieter (bass)
Puccini: Bohème (Cpte)

APPLETON, Colin (ten)
Shostakovich: Lady Macbeth of Mtsensk (Cpte)

APREA, Bruno (cond)
see Italian International Orch

ARAGALL, Giacomo (ten)
Bellini: Capuleti (Cpte)
Donizetti: Lucrezia Borgia (Cpte)
Gounod: Faust (Cpte)
Mascagni: Cavalleria Rusticana (Cpte)
Massenet: Esclarmonde (Cpte)
Puccini: Bohème (Cpte), Tosca (exc)
Verdi: Rigoletto (Cpte), Simon Boccanegra (Cpte), Traviata (Cpte)
(CAST) **CASH5051** Puccini Favourites from Covent Garden and the Arena di Verona
(CAST) **CVI2068** Opera Highlights from Verona 1
(CAST) **CVI2070** Great Puccini Love Scenes from Covent Garden, La Scala and Verona
(DECC) **421 896-2DA** Puccini—Great Operatic Duets
(DECC) **430 724-2DM** Great Operatic Duets
(DECC) **436 463-2DM** Ten Top Tenors
(DECC) **436 464-2DM** Ten Top Baritones & Basses
(DECC) **436 472-2DM** Great Opera Arias
(ERAT) **2292-45797-2** The Ultimate Opera Collection
(NAXO) **8 550684** Duets and Arias from Italian Operas
(RCA) **RD61191** Gala Lirica
(RCA) **09026 61204-4** From the Official Barcelona Games Ceremony
(RCA) **09026 61191-5** Gala Lirica
(RCA) **09026 61204-5** From the Official Barcelona Games Ceremony

ARAGON, Maria (sngr)
Vives: Bohemios (Cpte)

ARAIZA, Francisco (ten)
Catalani: Wally (Cpte)
Donizetti: Don Pasquale (Cpte), Maria Stuarda (Cpte)
Gounod: Faust (Cpte)
Monteverdi: Orfeo (Cpte)
Mozart: Così fan tutte (Cpte), Don Giovanni (Cpte), Entführung (Cpte), Idomeneo (Cpte), Zauberflöte (exc)
Offenbach: Contes d'Hoffmann (Cpte)
Puccini: Bohème (Cpte), Turandot (Cpte)
R. Strauss: Rosenkavalier (Cpte)
Rossini: Barbiere di Siviglia (Cpte), Cenerentola (Cpte), Italiana in Algeri (exc), Viaggio a Reims (Cpte)
Spontini: Vestale (Cpte)
Verdi: Alzira (Cpte)
Weber: Freischütz (exc)
(EMIL) **CDZ7 67015-2** Mozart—Opera Arias
(EURO) **VD69256** Mozart—Opera Arias
(ORFE) **C394301B** Great Mozart Singers Series, Vol. 3
(PHIL) **442 602-2PM** 3 x 3 Tenors
(RCA) **09026 61163-2** The Romantic Tenor
(RCA) **09026 62550-2** Ten Tenors in Love

ARÁMBARRI, Jésus (cond)
see Madrid Concerts Orch

ARAMBURO, Antonio (ten)
(MEMO) **HR4408/9(1)** Singers in Genoa, Vol.1 (disc 1)

ARANGI-LOMBARDI, Giannina (sop)
Verdi: Aida (Cpte)
(EMI) **CHS7 64864-2(1)** La Scala Edition - Vol.2, 1915-46 (pt 1)
(PREI) **89013** Giannina Arangi-Lombardi (1890-1951)
(PREI) **89026** Francesco Merli (1887-1976) - I
(PREI) **89040** Carlo Galeffi (1884-1961)

ARAPIAN, Armand (ten)
Campra: Tancrède (exc)
Massenet: Chérubin (Cpte)

ARÁVALO, Carlos (voc)
M. Monk: Atlas (Cpte)

ARBACE, Libero (bass)
Puccini: Tosca (Cpte)
Verdi: Otello (Cpte)
(DECC) **440 417-2DM** Carlo Bergonzi

ARBÓS, Enrique Fernández (cond)
see Madrid SO

ARCADIAN ACADEMY
(HARM) **HMU90 7167** Purcell & Blow—Songs & Intrumental Music

ARCANGELO, Ildebrando d' (bass)
Mozart: Don Giovanni (Cpte), Nozze di Figaro (Cpte)
Rossini: Armida (Cpte), Semiramide (Cpte)
Verdi: Otello (Cpte)
Wolf-Ferrari: Campiello (Cpte)

ARCHER, Neill (ten)
Beethoven: Fidelio (Cpte)
Debussy: Pelléas et Mélisande (Cpte)
Mayr: Medea (Cpte)

ARDAM, Elzbieta (mez)
R. Strauss: Frau ohne Schatten (Cpte)
Verdi: Otello (exc)

ARDELLI, Norbert (bar)
(SCHW) **314602** Vienna State Opera Live, Vol.10
(SCHW) **314672** Vienna State Opera Live, Vol.17

ARDEN, Evelyn (mez)
Wagner: Götterdämmerung (exc), Walküre (exc)
(PEAR) **GEMMCDS9137** Wagner—Der Ring des Nibelungen

ARDUINI, Remo (cond)
see Rome Op Orch

ARENA, Maurizio (cond)
see MMF Orch
Verona Arena Orch

ARÉVALO, Octavio (ten)
Rossini: Semiramide (Cpte), Signor Bruschino (Cpte)

ARGENTA, Nancy (sop)
Blow: Venus and Adonis (Cpte)
Gluck: Iphigénie en Tauride (Cpte), Orfeo ed Euridice (Cpte)
Handel: Floridante (exc), Tamerlano (Cpte)
Haydn: Infedeltà delusa (Cpte)
Monteverdi: Orfeo (Cpte)
Mozart: Così fan tutte (Cpte), Don Giovanni (Cpte), Nozze di Figaro (Cpte), Zauberflöte (Cpte)
Purcell: Dioclesian, Z627 (Cpte), Fairy Queen, Z629 (Cpte), King Arthur, Z628 (Cpte)
(HARM) **HMP390 807** Great Baroque Masters—Purcell
(VIRG) **VC7 59324-2** Purcell—O Solitude - Songs and Airs

ARIÉ, Raffaele (bass)
Donizetti: Lucia di Lammermoor (Cpte)
Mozart: Don Giovanni (Cpte)
Puccini: Bohème (Cpte)
(EMI) **CHS7 69741-2(7)** Record of Singing, Vol.4—Italian School
(EMI) **CMS7 63244-2** The Art of Maria Callas

ARIÈGE-PYRÉNÉES VOCAL ENSEMBLE
cond D. DONDEYNE
Fauré: Prométhée (Cpte)

ARIMONDI, Vittorio (bass)
(MEMO) **HR4408/9(1)** Singers in Genoa, Vol.1 (disc 1)
(PEAR) **GEMMCDS9924(1)** Covent Garden on Record, Vol.2 (pt 1)

ARION ENSEMBLE
cond A. LASCAE
(PART) **Part1118-2** Arion Ensemble Recital

ARIOSTINI, Armando (bar)
Mascagni: Amico Fritz (Cpte)

ARIZMENDI, Elena (sop)
(EMI) **CHS7 69741-2(7)** Record of Singing, Vol.4—Italian School

ARKADIEV, I.P. (cond)
see orch

ARKADIEV, O.I. (cond)
see orch

ARKEL, Teresa (sop)
(EMI) **CHS7 64860-2(1)** La Scala Edition - Vol.1, 1878-1914 (pt 1)
(MEMO) **HR4408/9(1)** Singers in Genoa, Vol.1 (disc 1)

ARKHIPOV, Alexander (ten)
Rachmaninov: Miserly knight (Cpte)
Rimsky-Korsakov: Kashchey (Cpte)
Shostakovich: Gamblers (Cpte)

ARKHIPOVA, Irina (mez)
Rimsky-Korsakov: Tsar's Bride (Cpte)
Tchaikovsky: Eugene Onegin (exc), Queen of Spades (exc)

ARKOR, André d' (ten)
(TEST) **SBT1008** Viva Rossini

ARMAN, Howard (cond)
see Halle Op House Handel Fest Orch

ARMANINI, Giuseppe (ten)
(SYMP) **SYMCD1113** The Harold Wayne Collection, Vol.13

ARMATO, Amanda (sngr)
Rapchak: Lifework of Juan Diaz (Cpte)

ARMENIAN, Raffi (cond)
see Kitchener-Waterloo SO

ARMENIAN PHILHARMONIC ORCHESTRA
cond L. TJEKNAVORIAN
(ASV) **CDDCA771** Rimsky-Korsakov—Orchestral Works
(ASV) **CDDCA772** Rimsky-Korsakov—Orchestral Works
(ASV) **CDDCA886** Prokofiev—Orchestral Works
(ASV) **CDQS6106** Nocturne
(ASV) **CDQS6116** The Four Seasons, Volume 4 - Winter

ARMENTIA, Alicia (sngr)
Bretón: Verbena de la Paloma (Cpte)

ARMITSTEAD, Melanie (sop)
Fénelon: Chevalier Imaginaire (Cpte)

ARMSTRONG, Julian (cond)
see London Fest Orch

ARMSTRONG, Karan (sop)
Henze: Bassariden (Cpte)
Verdi: Falstaff (Cpte)
Wagner: Lohengrin (Cpte)

ARMSTRONG, Richard (cond)
see ECO
LPO
Scottish CO

ARMSTRONG, Sheila (sop)
Purcell: Dido (Cpte)
Vaughan Williams: Hugh the Drover (Cpte), Pilgrim's Progress (Cpte)
(DG) **439 474-2GCL** Purcell—Opera & Choral Works

(GÜNTHER) ARNDT CH
cond F. FOX
Fall: Rose von Stambul (exc)
Millöcker: Dubarry (exc)
Suppé: Boccaccio (exc)
Zeller: Vogelhändler (exc)
cond W. SCHMIDT-BOELCKE
Abraham: Blume von Hawaii (exc), Viktoria und ihr Husar (exc)
cond R. STOLZ
Lehár: Land des Lächelns (exc)
(EURO) **GD69022** Oscar Straus: Operetta excerpts
cond F. WALTER
(EMI) **CZS7 62993-2** Fritz Wunderlich—Great German Tenor

ARNDT-OBER, Margarethe (mez)
Humperdinck: Hänsel und Gretel (Cpte)
(PREI) **89032** Lauritz Melchior (1890-1973) - I

ARNELL, Johann (cond)
see Stockholm PO

ARNOLD, Anton (ten)
(SCHW) **314562** Vienna State Opera Live, Vol.6
(SCHW) **314572** Vienna State Opera Live, Vol.7
(SCHW) **314602** Vienna State Opera Live, Vol.10
(SCHW) **314642** Vienna State Opera Live, Vol.14
(SCHW) **314702** Vienna State Opera Live, Vol.20

ARNOLD, Benno (ten)
Wagner: Meistersinger (Cpte), Tristan und Isolde (Cpte)

ARNOLDSON, Sigrid (sop)
(PEAR) **GEMMCDS9923(1)** Covent Garden on Record, Vol.1 (pt 1)

ARNONE, Francesca (sop)
Paisiello: Don Chisciotte (Cpte)

ARNOULT, Louis (ten)
Ravel: Heure espagnole (Cpte)

ARP, Klaus (cond)
see Kaiserslautern Rad Orch
South-West German RSO

ARPIN, John (pf)
(PRO) **CDD585** The French Connection

ARRAU, Claudio (pf)
(PEAR) **GEMMCD9928** The Young Claudio Arrau

ARRAUZAU, Francine (mez)
Offenbach: Contes d'Hoffmann (exc)

ARROYO, Martina (sop)
Beethoven: Fidelio (exc)
Mascagni: Cavalleria Rusticana (Cpte)
Meyerbeer: Huguenots (Cpte)
Mozart: Don Giovanni (Cpte)
Verdi: Ballo in maschera (Cpte), Forza del destino (Cpte), Vespri Siciliani (Cpte)
(EMI) **CDM7 69549-2** Ruggero Raimondi: Italian Opera Arias

ARS NOVA ENSEMBLE
cond A. SIRANOSSIAN
(ARIO) **ARN68195** Milhaud—Sonatas; Trois Operas-Minute

ARSEGUET, Lise (sngr)
Audran: Miss Helyett (Cpte)

ARTALE, Sergio (ten)
(MEMO) **HR4223/4** Nicolai Ghiaurov

ARTEGNA, Francesco Ellero d' (bass)
Bellini: Puritani (Cpte)
Catalani: Wally (Cpte)
Cilea: Adriana Lecouvreur (Cpte)
Donizetti: Maria Stuarda (Cpte)
Puccini: Bohème (Cpte), Fanciulla del West (Cpte)
Verdi: Aida (Cpte), Falstaff (Cpte), Nabucco (Cpte), Trovatore (Cpte)

ARTETA, Aïnhoa (sop)
Vives: Doña Francisquita (Cpte)

ARTHARS, Rosemarie (mez)
Offenbach: Orphée aux enfers (Cpte)

ARTHARS, Rosemarie (sop)
J. Strauss II: Fledermaus (Cpte)

ARTHUR, Juliet (sop)
Sullivan: Pirates of Penzance (exc)

ARTHUR, Maurice (ten)
Donizetti: Ugo, Conte di Parigi (Cpte)
Offenbach: Christopher Columbus (Cpte)
(OPRA) **ORC003** Donizetti—Gabriella di Vergy

(LES) ARTS FLORISSANTS CHORUS
cond W. CHRISTIE
Campra: Idoménée (exc)
Lully: Atys (Cpte)
M-A. Charpentier: Médée (Cpte)
Montéclair: Jephté (Cpte)
Purcell: Fairy Queen, Z629 (Cpte), King Arthur, Z628 (Cpte)
Rameau: Castor et Pollux (Cpte), Indes galantes (Cpte)
(HARM) **HMP390 805** Great Baroque Masters—Lully
(HARM) **HMP390 807** Great Baroque Masters—Purcell

(LES) ARTS FLORISSANTS INSTRUMENTAL ENSEMBLE
cond W. CHRISTIE
M-A. Charpentier: Actéon (Cpte), Arts Florissants (Cpte), Comtesse d'Escarbagnas Ov, H494, David et Jonathas (Cpte)
Purcell: Dido (Cpte)
Rossi: Orfeo (Cpte)
(HARM) **HMP390 802** Great Baroque Masters: Charpentier
(HARM) **HMX290 1528/33(1)** A Purcell Companion (pt 1)

(LES) ARTS FLORISSANTS ORCHESTRA
cond W. CHRISTIE
Campra: Idoménée (exc)
Lully: Atys (exc)
M-A. Charpentier: Médée (Cpte)
Montéclair: Jephté (Cpte)
Purcell: Fairy Queen, Z629 (Cpte), King Arthur, Z628 (Cpte)
Rameau: Castor et Pollux (exc), Indes galantes (Cpte)
(HARM) **HMP390 805** Great Baroque Masters—Lully
(HARM) **HMP390 807** Great Baroque Masters—Purcell

(LES) ARTS FLORISSANTS VOCAL ENSEMBLE
cond W. CHRISTIE
M-A. Charpentier: Actéon (Cpte), Arts Florissants (Cpte), David et Jonathas (Cpte)
Purcell: Dido (Cpte)
Rossi: Orfeo (Cpte)
(HARM) **HMP390 802** Great Baroque Masters: Charpentier
(HARM) **HMX290 1528/33(1)** A Purcell Companion (pt 1)

ARTY, Mady (contr)
(MSCM) **MM30451** Mascagni—Cavalleria Rusticana, etc

ARUHN, Britt-Marie (sop)
Mozart: Finta Giardiniera (Cpte), Lucio Silla (Cpte)
Nørgård: Gilgamesh (Cpte)
Wagner: Parsifal (Cpte)

ASENSIO, Enrique Garcia (cond)
see Madrid SO

ASHE, Rosemary (sop)
Coward: Bitter Sweet (exc)
Gay: Beggar's Opera (Cpte)
Offenbach: Christopher Columbus (Cpte)
Romberg: Student Prince (exc)

ASHFORD, Rupert (spkr)
R. Strauss: Intermezzo (Cpte)

ASHKENAZY, Vladimir (cond)
see Philh
RPO
Swedish RSO

ASHLEY, Robert (sngr)
Ashley: Improvement (Cpte)

ASHLEY, Sam (sngr)
Ashley: Improvement (Cpte)

ASHMAN, David (bar)
(OPRA) **ORCH104** A Hundred Years of Italian Opera: 1820-1830

ASHTON, Caroline (sop)
Purcell: Dido (Cpte)

ASHTON, Margarette (sop)
(GEOR) **GR002** Country House Musick

ASKO ENSEMBLE
cond P. EÖTVÖS
Maderna: Hyperion (Cpte)

ASMUS, Lilo (mez)
(PREI) **90232** Wagner—Der Fliegende Holländer

ASMUS, Rudolf (narr)
R. Strauss: Ariadne auf Naxos (Cpte)

ASSANDRI, Virginio (ten)
Verdi: Aida (Cpte), Otello (Cpte)
(RCA) **GD60326** Verdi—Operas & Choral Works

ASSOCIAZIONE TEATRI EMILIA ROMAGNA ORCHESTRA
cond L. MAGIERA
(BELA) **450 002-2** Pavarotti Live
(DECC) **443 018-2DF2** Pavarotti/Freni/Ricciarelli—Live

ATANASOVA, Rosiza (contr)
Pfitzner: Herz (Cpte)

ATHANASSOVA, Claudia (sop)
Kalomiris: Mother's Ring (Cpte)

ATHENA ENSEMBLE
Mozart: Don Giovanni (exc)

ATHENS FESTIVAL ORCHESTRA
cond A. VOTTO
(EMI) **CDC7 49428-2** Maria Callas - The Unknown Recordings
(MEMO) **HR4293/4** The very best of Maria Callas

ATHERTON, David (cond)
see London Sinfonietta
LSO
RLPO

ATHERTON, James (ten)
R. Strauss: Rosenkavalier (Cpte)
V. Thomson: Mother of us all (Cpte)

ATKINSON, Lynton (ten)
Beethoven: Fidelio (Cpte)
Vaughan Williams: Hugh the Drover (Cpte)
Verdi: Stiffelio (Cpte)

ATLANTA SYMPHONY CHAMBER CHORUS
cond ROBERT SHAW
(TELA) **ECHOCD2** Absolute Heaven

ATLANTA SYMPHONY CHORUS
cond ROBERT SHAW
Borodin: Prince Igor (exc)
(TELA) **CD80109** Berlioz: Requiem, etc
(TELA) **CD80152** Verdi: Requiem & Opera Choruses
(TELA) **ECHOCD2** Absolute Heaven

ATLANTA SYMPHONY ORCHESTRA
cond Y. LEVI
(TELA) **CD80296** Mussorgsky—Orchestral Works
(TELA) **CD80334** Rossini—Overtures
cond ROBERT SHAW
Borodin: Prince Igor (exc)
(TELA) **CD80109** Berlioz: Requiem, etc
(TELA) **CD80152** Verdi: Requiem & Opera Choruses
(TELA) **ECHOCD2** Absolute Heaven

ATLANTOV, Vladimir (ten)
Leoncavallo: Pagliacci (Cpte)
Mussorgsky: Khovanshchina (Cpte)
Rimsky-Korsakov: Tsar's Bride (Cpte)
Tchaikovsky: Eugene Onegin (Cpte), Queen of Spades (Cpte)
Verdi: Otello (Cpte)
(CAST) **CASH5052** Verdi Operatic Favourites
(CAST) **CVI2068** Opera Highlights from Verona 1
(TELD) **9031-77676-6(TELD)** My World of Opera - Kiri Te Kanawa

ATTFIELD, Helen (sop)
Wagner: Götterdämmerung (Cpte), Rheingold (Cpte), Walküre (Cpte)

ATTROT, Ingrid (sop)
Handel: Floridante (exc)
(CHAN) **CHAN9392** Vaughan Williams—Riders to the Sea etc.

ATZMON, Moshe (cond)
see Basle SO

AUBERT, J. (bar)
Ravel: Heure espagnole (Cpte)

AUBERT, Pascal (ten)
Mercadante: Giuramento (Cpte)

AUBIN, Tony (cond)
see French Rad Lyric Orch

AUDOLI, Jean-Walter (cond)
see Ile de France CO

AUER, Gerhard (bass)
Mozart: Nozze di Figaro (Cpte), Zauberflöte (Cpte)
Puccini: Gianni Schicchi (Cpte)
Verdi: Rigoletto (Cpte)
(EURO) **GD69043** Puccini: Il Trittico

AUGER, Arleen (sop)
Bizet: Carmen (Cpte)
Cimarosa: Matrimonio segreto (Cpte)
Handel: Alcina (Cpte), Orlando (Cpte)
Haydn: Orlando Paladino (Cpte)
Humperdinck: Hänsel und Gretel (Cpte)
Meyerbeer: Huguenots (Cpte)
Mozart: Apollo et Hyacinthus (Cpte), Ascanio in Alba (Cpte), Don Giovanni (Cpte), Entführung (Cpte), Lucio Silla (Cpte), Mitridate (Cpte), Nozze di Figaro (exc), Schauspieldirektor (Cpte)
R. Strauss: Capriccio (Cpte), Rosenkavalier (Cpte)
Ravel: Enfant et les sortilèges (Cpte)
Verdi: Don Carlos (Cpte)
Weber: Oberon (Cpte)
(DECC) **433 437-2DA** Pavarotti—King of the High Cs
(DECC) **440 414-2DM** Arleen Auger
(DELO) **DE3026** A. Auger - Bach and Handel arias
(DELO) **DE3029** Love Songs
(HYPE) **CDJ33009** Schubert: Complete Lieder, Vol.9

AUGSBURG CATHEDRAL BOYS' CHOIR
cond R. ABBADO
Puccini: Turandot (Cpte)
(RCA) **74321 24209-2** Italian Opera Choruses

AUREL, Geneviève (sngr)
Lecocq: Jour et la Nuit (Cpte)
(MUSD) **20239-2** Delibes—Opéras-Comiques

AURIA, Anna d' (sop)
Verdi: Nabucco (exc)

AURIA, Diego d' (ten)
Donizetti: Imelda (Cpte)
Rossini: Bianca e Falliero (Cpte)

AUSENSI, Manuel (bar)
Rossini: Barbiere di Siviglia (Cpte)

AUSTIN, Anson (ten)
J. Strauss II: Fledermaus (Cpte)
Lehár: Lustige Witwe (Cpte)
Meyerbeer: Huguenots (Cpte)
Mozart: Così fan tutte (Cpte)
(DECC) **071 149-1DH (DECC)** The Essential Sutherland
(KIWI) **CDSLD-82** Southern Voices—NZ International Opera Singers

AUSTIN, Charles (bass-bar)
Puccini: Tosca (exc)

AUSTIN, Michael (organ)
(CHAN) **CHAN6518** Organ Classics

AUSTRAL, Florence (sop)
Wagner: Götterdämmerung (exc)
(CLAR) **CDGSE78-50-35/6** Wagner—Historical recordings
(CLAR) **CDGSE78-50-46** Walter Widdop (1892-1949)
(EMI) **CMS7 64008-2(2)** Wagner Singing on Record (pt 2)
(PEAR) **GEMMCDS9137** Wagner—Der Ring des Nibelungen
(PEAR) **GEMMCDS9925(1)** Covent Garden on Record—Vol.3 (pt 1)
(PEAR) **GEMMCD9146** Florence Austral
(PREI) **89002** Miguel Fleta (1893-1938)

AUSTRALIAN OPERA AND BALLET ORCHESTRA
Meyerbeer: Huguenots (Cpte)
cond R. BONYNGE
(DECC) **071 149-1DH (DECC)** The Essential Sutherland
(KIWI) **CDSLD-82** Southern Voices—NZ International Opera Singers

AUSTRALIAN OPERA CHORUS
cond R. BONYNGE
Bellini: Norma (Cpte)
Donizetti: Lucia di Lammermoor (Cpte)
J. Strauss II: Fledermaus (Cpte)
Lehár: Lustige Witwe (Cpte)
Meyerbeer: Huguenots (Cpte)

AUSTRALIAN OPERA DANCE ENSEMBLE
cond R. BONYNGE
Meyerbeer: Huguenots (Cpte)

AUSTRIAN RADIO CHORUS
cond G. ALBRECHT
Schoeck: Penthesilea (Cpte)
cond L. GARDELLI
Verdi: Battaglia di Legnano (Cpte), Due Foscari (Cpte), Stiffelio (Cpte)
cond M. GIELEN
Schoenberg: Moses und Aron (Cpte)
cond E. HOWARTH
Ligeti: Grand Macabre (Cpte)
cond L. ZAGROSEK
Einem: Dantons Tod (Cpte)

AUSTRIAN RADIO SYMPHONY ORCHESTRA
Delius: Village Romeo and Juliet (Cpte)
cond G. ALBRECHT
Schoeck: Penthesilea (Cpte)
cond L. BERNSTEIN
(DG) **439 251-2GY** The Leonard Bernstein Album
(DG) **439 251-5GY** The Leonard Bernstein Album
cond K. EICHHORN
(ORFE) **C077831A** Bernd Weikl sings Operetta
cond L. GARDELLI
Verdi: Battaglia di Legnano (Cpte), Due Foscari (Cpte), Stiffelio (Cpte)
cond M. GIELEN
Schoenberg: Moses und Aron (Cpte)
cond E. HOWARTH
Ligeti: Grand Macabre (Cpte)
cond C. MACKERRAS
Delius: Village Romeo and Juliet (Cpte)
cond G. NAVARRO
(SONY) **MK39210** Zarzuela Arias and Duets
cond M. SCHÖNHERR
(CAMB) **CD-1066** Korngold in Vienna
cond P. STEINBERG
Bellini: Beatrice di Tenda (Cpte)
Wagner: Fliegende Holländer (Cpte)
cond L. ZAGROSEK
Einem: Dantons Tod (Cpte)
(ORFE) **C335931A** Salzburg Festival highlights (1956-85)

AUSTRIAN STATE RADIO ORCHESTRA
cond G. KASSOWITZ
(CAMB) **CD-1032** From the Operas of Erich Wolfgang Korngold
cond E. KORNGOLD
(CAMB) **CD-1032** From the Operas of Erich Wolfgang Korngold
cond W. LOIBNER
(CAMB) **CD-1032** From the Operas of Erich Wolfgang Korngold
cond J. STROBL
(CAMB) **CD-1032** From the Operas of Erich Wolfgang Korngold

AUSTRO-HUNGARIAN HAYDN ORCHESTRA
cond A. FISCHER
(NIMB) **NI5341** Haydn—Orchestral Works

AUTENRIETH, Claire (sop)
R. Strauss: Elektra (Cpte)

AUTRAN, Victor (bar)
Gounod: Faust (Cpte)

AUVINEN, Ritva (sop)
(BIS) **BIS-CD373/4** Opera Scenes from Savaonlinna

AUZEVILLE, Maurice (ten)
Gounod: Roméo et Juliette (Cpte)

AVALOS, Francesco d' (cond)
see Philh

AVANTI CHAMBER ORCHESTRA
Kortekangas: Grand Hotel

AVDEYEVA, Larissa (mez)
Tchaikovsky: Eugene Onegin (Cpte)

AVIS, Marjorie (sop)
Delius: Village Romeo and Juliet (Cpte)

AVKSENTIEV, Boris (balalaika)
Shostakovich: Nose Suite

AVOGADRO, Liana (sop)
Puccini: Gianni Schicchi (Cpte)

AYARS, Ann (sop)
Gluck: Orfeo ed Euridice (exc)

AYLDON, John (bass)
Sullivan: Mikado (Cpte), Ruddigore (Cpte), Zoo (Cpte)
(BELA) **461 006-2** Gilbert & Sullivan—Songs and Snatches
(LOND) **436 813-2LM2** Sullivan—The Grand Duke. Overture Di Ballo. Henry VIII
(LOND) **436 816-2LM2** Sullivan—Utopia Ltd. Macbeth & Marmion Ovs etc

AZÉMA, Anne (sop)
Machover: Valis (Cpte)

AZESBERGER, Kurt (ten)
Lehár: Lustige Witwe (Cpte)

AZZIMONTI, Giovanni (bass)
Puccini: Tosca (Cpte)

BABA, Michael (ten)
Corghi: Divara (Cpte)

BABIKIN, Anatoli (bass)
Serov: Judith (Cpte)
Shostakovich: Gamblers (Cpte)
Tchaikovsky: Maid of Orleans (Cpte)

BACCALONI, Salvatore (bass)
Mozart: Don Giovanni (Cpte)
Puccini: Bohème (Cpte)
Verdi: Aida (Cpte), Falstaff (Cpte), Rigoletto (Cpte)
(EMI) **CDH5 65072-2** Glyndebourne Recorded - 1934-1994
(EMI) **CHS7 64864-2(1)** La Scala Edition - Vol.2, 1915-46 (pt 1)
(MSCM) **MM30276** Rossini—Barbiere di Siviglia, etc
(PEAR) **GEMMCDS9180** Verdi—Rigoletto, etc
(PEAR) **GEMMCD9122** 20 Great Basses sing Great Arias

BACELLI, Monica (mez)
Mozart: Così fan tutte (Cpte), Finta Giardiniera (Cpte), Nozze di Figaro (Cpte)
Rossini: Occasione fa il ladro (Cpte)
Verdi: Traviata (exc)
(SCHW) **314052** Opera Gala

BACH, Gottfried (organ)
(FSM) **FCD91114** Virtuoso Chamber Music with Guitar

BACH, Konrad (cond)
see Thüringian SO

BACH, Mechthild (sop)
Telemann: Don Quichotte (Cpte), Pimpinone (Cpte)

BACHMANN, Hermann (bar)
(SUPR) **11 2136-2(3)** Emmy Destinn—Complete Edition, Discs 5 to 8

BACIU, Ion (cond)
see Iaşi Moldova PO

BACKES, Constanze (mez)
Lehár: Lustige Witwe (Cpte)

BACKES, Constanze (sop)
Mozart: Nozze di Figaro (Cpte)

BACKHAUS, Wilhelm (pf)
(COND) **690.07.013** Wilhelm Backhaus—Piano Rolls

BACQUIER, Gabriel (bar)
Berlioz: Béatrice et Bénédict (Cpte)
Bizet: Jolie fille de Perth (Cpte)
Debussy: Pelléas et Mélisande (Cpte)
Delibes: Lakmé (Cpte)
Donizetti: Don Pasquale (Cpte), Favorita (Cpte)
G. Charpentier: Louise (Cpte)
Gounod: Roméo et Juliette (Cpte)
Massenet: Don Quichotte (Cpte), Werther (Cpte)
Meyerbeer: Huguenots (Cpte)
Mozart: Don Giovanni (Cpte), Nozze di Figaro (Cpte)
Offenbach: Belle Hélène (Cpte), Contes d'Hoffmann (exc), Périchole (Cpte)
Prokofiev: Love for 3 Oranges (Cpte)
Ravel: Heure espagnole (Cpte)
Rossini: Guillaume Tell (Cpte)
Verdi: Falstaff (Cpte), Forza del destino (Cpte), Otello (Cpte)
(DECC) **433 068-2DWO** Your Hundred Best Opera Tunes V
(DECC) **443 762-2DF2** The Essential Mozart
(EMI) **CZS5 68113-2** Vive Offenbach!
(GALL) **CD-816** Mozart—Concert Arias

BADA, Angelo (ten)
Verdi: Traviata (Cpte)
(CONI) **CDHD227** Gigli in Opera and Song

Mozart: Ascanio in Alba (Cpte), Don Giovanni (Cpte), Idomeneo (Cpte), Mitridate (Cpte), Nozze di Figaro (exc), Zauberflöte (exc)
Offenbach: Contes d'Hoffmann (Cpte)
Ponchielli: Gioconda (Cpte)
R. Strauss: Ariadne auf Naxos (Cpte), Rosenkavalier (exc)
Rossini: Barbiere di Siviglia (Cpte), Cenerentola (Cpte), Italiana in Algeri (Cpte)
Saint-Saëns: Samson et Dalila (Cpte)
Verdi: Aida (Cpte), Don Carlo (Cpte), Forza del destino (exc)
Wagner: Tannhäuser (Cpte)
(CAST) **CVI2065** Highlights from the Royal Opera House, Covent Garden
(CFP) **CD-CFP4612** Favourite Mozart
(CFP) **CD-CFP4656** Herbert von Karajan conducts Opera
(DECC) **430 724-2DM** Great Operatic Duets
(DECC) **436 462-2DM** Ten Top Mezzos
(DECC) **443 378-2DM** Ten Top Mezzos 2
(DECC) **443 928-2DM** Montserrat Caballé sings Opera Arias
(DG) **439 153-4GMA** Mad about Sopranos
(EMI) **CDC7 54524-2** The José Carreras Album
(EMI) **CDM7 63111-2** José Carreras sings Opera & Operetta Arias
(EMIL) **CDZ7 67015-2** Mozart—Opera Arias
(MCI) **MCCD090** Carreras & Friends sing Opera Arias & Songs
(ORFE) **C394301B** Great Mozart Singers Series, Vol. 3
(SONY) **SK53968** Opera Duets

BALTZER, Erwin (cond)
see Berlin St Op Orch
Vienna St Op Orch

BALZER, Wolfgang (cond)
see Rhenish PO

BAMBER, Peter (ten)
G. Charpentier: Louise (Cpte)

BAMBERG SYMPHONY CHORUS
cond K. A. RICKENBACHER
(ORFE) **C312941A** Wagner—Cantatas and Overtures

BAMBERG SYMPHONY ORCHESTRA
cond C.P. FLOR
(RCA) **RD87905** Mendelssohn—Overtures
cond H. GIERSTER
(DG) **431 110-2GB** Great Voices - Fritz Wunderlich
(DG) **435 145-2GX5(1)** Fritz Wunderlich—Opera Arias, Lieder, etc (part 1)
cond T. GUSCHLBAUER
(ERAT) **4509-92866-2** Wagner—Famous Overtures
cond E. JOCHUM
(RCA) **09026 61212-2** Beethoven—Overtures
cond R. KEMPE
(EMI) **CZS7 62993-2** Fritz Wunderlich—Great German Tenor
cond F. LEITNER
(DG) **447 361-2GDB2** French Orchestral Music
cond H. LÖWLEIN
(DG) **447 364-2GDB2** Great Opera Overtures
cond U. MUND
Suder: Kleider machen Leute (Cpte)
cond G. PATANÈ
(RCA) **09026 62674-2** Fortissimo!
cond G. PRÊTRE
Bizet: Carmen Suites
cond K. A. RICKENBACHER
(ORFE) **C312941A** Wagner—Cantatas and Overtures
(VIRG) **CUV5 61128-2** Humperdinck—Fairy-tale Music
(VIRG) **CUV5 61201-2** Hindemith—Orchestral Works
cond A. ROTHER
(FINL) **4509-95606-2** Kim Borg - Songs and Arias
cond C. STEPP
(DG) **437 677-2GDO2** Irmgard Seefried - Opera Recital

BAMBINI DI PRAGA
cond M. KLEMENS
(ROMA) **RR1941** Terezín - The Music 1941-44

BAMPTON, Rose (sop)
Beethoven: Fidelio (Cpte)
Mozart: Don Giovanni (Cpte)
(EMI) **CHS7 69741-2(1)** Record of Singing, Vol.4—Anglo-American School (pt 1)
(RCA) **GD60280** Toscanini Collection
(RCA) **GD87808** Lawrence Tibbett sings Opera Arias
(RCA) **09026 61580-2(4)** RCA/Met 100 Singers, 100 Years (pt 4)
(VAI) **VAIA1017** Leonard Warren—Early Recordings
(VAI) **VAIA1084** Rose Bampton sings Verdi and Wagner

BANAUDI, Antonella (sop)
Verdi: Trovatore (Cpte)

BANCROFT SCHOOL BOYS' CHOIR
cond H. VON KARAJAN
R. Strauss: Rosenkavalier (Cpte)

BANCROFT'S SCHOOL CHORUS
cond H. VON KARAJAN
Humperdinck: Hänsel und Gretel (Cpte)

BANDA CLASSICA
cond C. SIEGMANN
(SCHW) **310110** Banda Classica - Harmoniemusik

BANDELLI, Antonella (mez)
Verdi: Don Carlo (Cpte)

BANDEMEHR, Stefan (treb)
Mozart: Zauberflöte (Cpte)

BANDERA, Claudia Nicole (mez)
Puccini: Manon Lescaut (Cpte)

BANDITELLI, Gloria (contr)
Cavalli: Giasone (Cpte)
Gluck: Cinesi (Cpte)
Handel: Agrippina (Cpte), Poro (Cpte)
Rossini: Barbiere di Siviglia (exc), Cenerentola (exc)
Verdi: Vespri Siciliani (Cpte)

BANIEWICZ, Wiera (contr)
Mussorgsky: Boris Godunov (Cpte)
Puccini: Gianni Schicchi (Cpte)
(EURO) **GD69043** Puccini: Il Trittico

BANKL, Wolfgang (bass)
R. Strauss: Rosenkavalier (Cpte)

BANKS, Anna Victoria (mez)
Paisiello: Serva Padrona (Cpte)

BANKS, Barry (ten)
Britten: Billy Budd (Cpte)
Cavalli: Calisto (Cpte)
Puccini: Bohème (Cpte)
Verdi: Rigoletto (Cpte), Traviata (Cpte)

BANKS-MARTIN, George (bass)
Purcell: Fairy Queen, Z629 (Cpte)

BANNATYNE-SCOTT, Brian (bass)
Purcell: Dioclesian, Z627 (Cpte), King Arthur, Z628 (Cpte)
Smyth: Wreckers (Cpte)

BAÑUELAS, Roberto (ten)
Wagner: Meistersinger (Cpte)

BAQUERIZO, Enrique (bass)
Bretón: Verbena de La Paloma (Cpte)

BÄR, Olaf (bar)
J. Strauss II: Fledermaus (Cpte)
Mozart: Zauberflöte (Cpte)
R. Strauss: Ariadne auf Naxos (Cpte)

BARABAS, Sari (sop)
Rossini: Comte Ory (Cpte)
(EMI) **CDH5 65072-2** Glyndebourne Recorded - 1934-1994

BARACCHI, Aristide (bar)
Puccini: Bohème (Cpte)
Verdi: Rigoletto (Cpte)
(EMI) **CHS7 64864-2(1)** La Scala Edition - Vol.2, 1915-46 (pt 1)
(PEAR) **GEMMCDS9180** Verdi—Rigoletto, etc
(PREI) **89023** Conchita Supervia (1895-1936)

BÁRÁNY, Pál László (bar)
Respighi: Belfagor (Cpte)

BARASORDA, Antonio (ten)
Verdi: Macbeth (Cpte)

BARATTI, Giuseppe (ten)
Bellini: Pirata (Cpte)
Donizetti: Lucrezia Borgia (Cpte)
(EMI) **CDM7 69500-2** Montserrat Caballé sings Bellini & Verdi Arias

BARATTI, Walter (treb)
Puccini: Tosca (exc)

BARBACINI, Paolo (ten)
Donizetti: Ajo nell'imbarazzo (Cpte)
Paisiello: Don Chisciotte (Cpte)
Rossini: Barbiere di Siviglia (exc), Pietra del paragone (Cpte), Turco in Italia (exc)
Verdi: Falstaff (Cpte), Vespri Siciliani (Cpte)

BARBAOSA-LIMA, Carlos (gtr)
(CCOR) **CCD42012** Arrangements for Two Guitars

BARBAUX, Christine (sop)
Bizet: Carmen (exc)
Debussy: Pelléas et Mélisande (Cpte)
Fauré: Pénélope (Cpte)
Massenet: Werther (exc)
Mozart: Clemenza di Tito (Cpte), Lucio Silla (Cpte), Nozze di Figaro (Cpte)
(EMI) **CDM7 64687-2** French Works inspired by Edgar Allan Poe

BARBER, Kimberley (sop)
Delius: Village Romeo and Juliet (Cpte)

BARBER, Lynn (mez)
Kálmán: Gräfin Mariza (exc)

BARBESI, Attilio (bass)
Verdi: Macbeth (Cpte)

BARBIER, Jean-Claude (bar)
Massenet: Don Quichotte (Cpte)

BARBIERI, Elvira (sop)
(PEAR) **GEMMCD9016** Mattia Battistini, Vol.3

BARBIERI, Fedora (mez)
Donizetti: Linda di Chamounix (Cpte)
Mascagni: Cavalleria Rusticana (Cpte)
Verdi: Aida (Cpte), Ballo in maschera (Cpte), Falstaff (Cpte), Rigoletto (Cpte), Trovatore (Cpte)
(EMI) **CHS7 69741-2(7)** Record of Singing, Vol.4—Italian School
(EMI) **CMS7 64165-2** Puccini—Trittico
(PHIL) **442 602-2PM** 3 x 3 Tenors

BARBIERI, Gianni (bass)
Verdi: Due Foscari (Cpte)

BARBIERI, Hector (bass)
Verdi: Otello (Cpte)

BARBIROLLI, Sir John (cond)
see ECO
Hallé
LSO
New Philh
New SO
NYPO
orch
Rome Op Orch

BARCELONA SYMPHONY ORCHESTRA
cond C.F. CILLARIO
(RCA) **RK61044** Eternal Caballé
cond E.M. MARCO
(RCA) **RK61044** Eternal Caballé
cond G-F. MASINI
(RCA) **RK61044** Eternal Caballé
cond G. NAVARRO
(ACAN) **49 390** Placido Domingo sings Zarzuela Arias
(RCA) **09026 62550-2** Ten Tenors in Love
(RCA) **09026 61204-4** From the Official Barcelona Games Ceremony
(RCA) **09026 61204-5** From the Official Barcelona Games Ceremony

BARDON, Patricia (mez)
Tchaikovsky: Eugene Onegin (Cpte)
Verdi: Rigoletto (Cpte)
(ASV) **CDDCA758** Falla, Milhaud & Stravinsky—Operas

BARDSLEY, Thelma (sop)
Wagner: Walküre (exc)

BARENBOIM, Daniel (cond)
see Bayreuth Fest Orch
Berlin CO
BPO
Chicago SO
ECO
LPO
Paris Orch

BAREVA, Rumiana (sop)
Tchaikovsky: Queen of Spades (Cpte)

BAREZA, Nikša (cond)
see Trieste Teatro Verdi Orch
Vienna St Op Orch

BARHAM, Edmund (ten)
Mozart: Zauberflöte (Cpte)
(EMI) **CDC7 54785-2** Harry Enfield's Guide to Opera
(IMP) **MCD15** Opera Spectacular
(IMP) **TCD1070** Invitation to the Opera
(RPO) **CDRPD9006** Opera Spectacular 1 & 2

BARIKOVA, L'uba (contr)
Suchoň: Whirlpool (Cpte)

BARILI, Alfredo (pf)
(EMI) **CHS7 64860-2(1)** La Scala Edition - Vol.1, 1878-1914 (pt 1)
(NIMB) **NI7840/1** The Era of Adelina Patti
(PEAR) **GEMMCDS9923(1)** Covent Garden on Record, Vol.1 (pt 1)
(PEAR) **GEMMCD9312** Adelina Patti

BARIONI, Daniele (ten)
Puccini: Rondine (Cpte)
(RCA) **09026 61236-2** Leontyne Price - Prima Donna Collection

BARKER, John (cond)
see ROHO

BARLOW, Howard (cond)
see orch

BARLOW, Jeremy (cond)
see Broadside Band

BARNABEE, Henry Clay (sngr)
(PEAR) **GEMMCDS9050/2(1)** Music from the New York Stage, Vol. 1 (part 1)

BARNHILL, Paul (spkr)
J. Strauss II: Fledermaus (Cpte)

BARONI, Enrico (ten)
(PEAR) **GEMMCDS9074(2)** Giovanni Zenatello, Vol.2 (pt 2)

BARONTI, Duilio (bass)
Puccini: Bohème (Cpte)

BAROQUE INSTRUMENTAL ENSEMBLE
cond R. JACOBS
Cesti: Orontea (Cpte)

BAROVÁ, Anna (contr)
Dvořák: Kate and the Devil (Cpte), Rusalka (Cpte)
Fibich: Šárka (Cpte)
Foerster: Eva (Cpte)
Janáček: Fate (Cpte), Jenufa (Cpte)
Martinů: Alexandre Bis (Cpte), Comedy on the Bridge (Cpte), Miracles of Mary (Cpte)
(KOCH) **34036-2** A Pageant of Opera
(SUPR) **11 1878-2** The Unknown Janáček

BAROWSKI, Nikolai (sngr)
S. Wagner: Bärenhäuter (Cpte)

BARR, Frank (bass)
Janáček: Jenufa (Cpte)

BARRARD, Marc (bar)
Gounod: Faust (Cpte)
Mercadante: Giuramento (Cpte)
Ravel: Enfant et les sortilèges (Cpte)

BARRELL, David (bar)
Verdi: Traviata (Cpte)

BARRETT, David (bar)
Verdi: Ballo in maschera (Cpte)

BARRETT, Toby (bass)
Sullivan: Gondoliers (Cpte)

BARRIENTOS, Maria (sop)
(MEMO) **HR4408/9(2)** Singers in Genoa, Vol.1 (disc 2)
(PEAR) **GEMMCDS9073(1)** Giovanni Zenatello, Vol.1 (pt 1)
(PEAR) **GEMMCD9178** Riccardo Stracciari
(SYMP) **SYMCD1113** The Harold Wayne Collection, Vol.13
(SYMP) **SYMCD1168** The Harold Wayne Collection, Vol.19
(TEST) **SBT1008** Viva Rossini

BARRIO, Amalia (sngr)
Penella: Gato Montés (Cpte)

BARRUECO, Manuel (gtr)
(EMI) **CDC7 54057-2** J. Strauss II—Vocal Arrangements

BARRY, Stuart (cond)
see Chandos Concert Orch

BARSCHA, Monique (sop)
Offenbach: Brigands (Cpte)

BARSHAI, Rudolf (cond)
see Moscow CO

BARSOVA, Valeria (sop)
(DANT) **LYS013/5** Tchaikovsky—The Queen of Spades
(PREI) **89081** Georgi Nelepp (1904-1957)

BARSTOW, Josephine (sop)
Britten: Gloriana (Cpte)
Mozart: Idomeneo (Cpte)
Tippett: Knot Garden (Cpte)
Verdi: Ballo in maschera (Cpte), Macbeth (Cpte)
(IMP) **TCD1070** Invitation to the Opera
(RPO) **CDRPD9006** Opera Spectacular 1 & 2
(RPO) **CDRPO7009** Opera Spectacular II
(TER) **CDVIR8307** Josephine Barstow sings Verdi Arias

BARTH, Irmgard (mez)
Orff: Antigonae (Cpte)
R. Strauss: Salome (Cpte)
Wagner: Götterdämmerung (Cpte)

BARTHA, Clarry (sop)
(TELD) **9031-76372-6(TELD)** Tchaikovsky —Women and Fate

BARTHOLOMÉE, Pierre (cond)
see Liège PO

BARTLER, Annika (mez)
Nørgård: Gilgamesh (Cpte)

BARTLETT, Peta (sngr)
G. Charpentier: Louise (Cpte)

BARTOLETTI, Bruno (cond)
see BRSO
Buenos Aires Colón Th Orch
MMF Orch
National PO
New Philh
New PO
Rome RAI Orch
Santa Cecilia Academy Orch

BARTOLI, Cecilia (mez)
Mozart: Clemenza di Tito (Cpte), Così fan tutte (Cpte), Lucio Silla (Cpte), Nozze di Figaro (Cpte)
Puccini: Manon Lescaut (Cpte)
Rossini: Barbiere di Siviglia (exc), Cenerentola (exc), Scala di seta (Cpte)
(CAPR) **10 810** Mozart—Opera Highlights
(DECC) **425 430-2DH** Cecilia Bartoli sings Rossini Arias
(DECC) **430 513-2DH** Mozart—Arias
(DECC) **436 075-2DH** Rossini Heroines
(DECC) **436 133-2DWO** World of Rossini
(DECC) **436 267-2DH** Arie Antiche—Bartoli
(DECC) **436 462-2DM** Ten Top Mezzos
(DECC) **440 947-2DH** Essential Opera II
(DECC) **443 378-2DM** Ten Top Mezzos 2
(DECC) **443 452-2DH** Mozart Portraits—Bartoli
(DECC) **448 300-2DH** Cecilia Bartoli—A Portrait
(DECC) **071 141-1DH (DECC)** Cecilia Bartoli - A Portrait
(DECC) **436 075-5DH** Rossini Heroines
(ERAT) **4509-91715-2** The Ultimate Opera Collection 2
(TELD) **4509-97507-2** Mozart—Famous Opera Arias

BARTOLINI, Lando (ten)
Respighi: Semirama (Cpte)

BARTOS, Rita (sop)
Wagner: Parsifal (Cpte)

BARY, Alfred von (ten)
(SYMP) **SYMCD1081** The Harold Wayne Collection, Vol.5

BASA, Sibrand (ten)
Weber: Peter Schmoll (Cpte)

BASI, Leonildo (bar)
Leoncavallo: Pagliacci (Cpte)

BASILE, Arturo (cond)
see Milan RAI SO
Orch
RCA SO
Rome Op Orch
Rome RAI Orch
Turin RAI Orch

BASIOLA I, Mario (bar)
Leoncavallo: Pagliacci (Cpte)
Verdi: Trovatore (Cpte)
(NIMB) **NI7853** Lauri-Volpi sings Verdi
(PREI) **89995** Famous Italian Baritones

BASIOLA II, Mario (bar)
Puccini: Bohème (exc), Rondine (Cpte)
Verdi: Ballo in maschera (Cpte)

BASKERVILLE, Priscilla (sop)
A. Davis: X (Cpte)

BASKI, Sergio (bass)
Giordano: Fedora (Cpte)

BASKOV, Konstantin (ten)
Rimsky-Korsakov: Tsar's Bride (Cpte)
Tchaikovsky: Queen of Spades (Cpte)

BASLE BOYS' CHOIR
cond M. VENZAGO
Schoeck: Venus (Cpte)

BASLE SYMPHONY ORCHESTRA
cond M. ATZMON
(RCA) **74321 29237-2** Mozart—Overtures
cond A. JORDAN
(ERAT) **4509-92866-2** Wagner—Famous Overtures
cond H. ZENDER
Holliger: Magische Tänzer (Cpte)

BASLE THEATRE CHOIR
cond H. ZENDER
Holliger: Magische Tänzer (Cpte)

BASS, Robert (cond)
see Collegiate Orch

BASSANO PRO ARTE ORCHESTRA
cond M. PANNI
Handel: Giulio Cesare (Cpte)

BASSE-NORMANDIE ENSEMBLE
cond D. DEBART
Xenakis: Orestia (Cpte)

BASTIAN, Gert (bar)
Nielsen: Maskarade (Cpte)

BASTIANINI, Ettore (bar)
Giordano: Andrea Chénier (Cpte)
J. Strauss II: Fledermaus (Cpte)
Mascagni: Cavalleria Rusticana (Cpte)
Ponchielli: Gioconda (Cpte)
Puccini: Bohème (exc)
Rossini: Barbiere di Siviglia (Cpte)
Verdi: Don Carlo (Cpte), Traviata (Cpte), Trovatore (Cpte)
(BELA) **450 007-2** Puccini Favourites
(DECC) **433 068-2DWO** Your Hundred Best Opera Tunes V
(DECC) **436 315-2DA** Great Operatic Duets
(DECC) **436 464-2DM** Ten Top Baritones & Basses
(DECC) **440 411-2DM** Anita Cerquetti
(DECC) **444 555-2DF2** Essential Puccini
(MEMO) **HR4386/7** Great Voices - Giulietta Simionato
(MEMO) **HR4396/7** Great Voices—Leontyne Price
(MEMO) **HR4400/1** Great Voices - Ettore Bastianini

BASTIN, Jules (bass)
Auber: Fra Diavolo (Cpte)
Berg: Lulu (Cpte)
Berlioz: Benvenuto Cellini (Cpte), Béatrice et Bénédict (Cpte)
Debussy: Rodrigue et Chimène (Cpte)
Grétry: Caravane du Caire (Cpte), Jugement de Midas (exc)
Massenet: Cendrillon (Cpte), Jongleur de Notre Dame (Cpte), Werther (Cpte)
Meyerbeer: Prophète (Cpte)
Mozart: Così fan tutte (Cpte), Nozze di Figaro (exc)
Offenbach: Périchole (Cpte)
Prokofiev: Love for 3 Oranges (Cpte)
R. Strauss: Rosenkavalier (Cpte), Salomé (Cpte)
Ravel: Enfant et les sortilèges (Cpte)
Verdi: Attila (Cpte)
(ERAT) **2292-45797-2** The Ultimate Opera Collection

BATER, Glenn (bass)
Verdi: Trovatore (Cpte)

BATH FESTIVAL ORCHESTRA
cond Y. MENUHIN
(EMI) **CDM5 65341-2** Purcell—Theatre Music
(EMI) **CZS7 67425-2** Baroque Passion

BATHORI, Jane (mez)
(EPM) **150 122** Milhaud—Historic Recordings 1928-1948

BÁTHY, Anna (sop)
(SCHW) **314702** Vienna State Opera Live, Vol.20

BATIC, Polly (sop)
Einem: Prozess (Cpte)

BÁTIZ, Enrique (cond)
see LPO
Mexico City PO
Mexico St SO
Philh
RPO

BÁTOR, Tamás (bass)
Giordano: Andrea Chénier (Cpte)

BATTAGLIA, Elisabetta (sop)
Bellini: Sonnambula (Cpte)

BATTEDOU, André (ten)
Chabrier: Roi malgré lui (Cpte)

BATTEN, Joseph (cond)
see orch

BATTISTINI, Mattia (bar)
(EMI) **CHS7 64860-2(1)** La Scala Edition - Vol.1, 1878-1914 (pt 1)
(NIMB) **NI7831** Mattia Battistini (1856-1928)
(NIMB) **NI7840/1** The Era of Adelina Patti
(NIMB) **NI7867** Legendary Baritones
(PEAR) **GEMMCDS9923(1)** Covent Garden on Record, Vol.1 (pt 1)
(PEAR) **GEMMCDS9924(1)** Covent Garden on Record, Vol.2 (pt 1)
(PEAR) **GEMMCD9016** Mattia Battistini, Vol.3
(PEAR) **GEMMCD9936** Mattia Battistini, Vol.1
(PREI) **89045** Mattia Battistini (1856-1928)
(PREI) **89995** Famous Italian Baritones

BATTLE, Kathleen (sop)
Donizetti: Elisir d'amore (Cpte)
Mozart: Don Giovanni (Cpte), Entführung (Cpte), Nozze di Figaro (exc), Zauberflöte (Cpte)
R. Strauss: Ariadne auf Naxos (Cpte)
Rossini: Barbiere di Siviglia (Cpte), Italiana in Algeri (Cpte), Signor Bruschino (Cpte)
Verdi: Ballo in maschera (Cpte), Don Carlo (Cpte)
Wagner: Siegfried (Cpte)
(DECC) **425 681-2DM2** Tutto Pavarotti
(DECC) **436 461-2DM** Ten Top Sopranos
(DECC) **443 377-2DM** Ten Top Sopranos 2
(DG) **419 237-2GH** Schubert: Lieder
(DG) **435 440-2GH** Kathleen Battle at Carnegie Hall
(DG) **435 866-2GH** Kathleen Battle sings Italian Opera Arias
(DG) **437 787-2GH** Honey and Rue-Kathleen Battle
(DG) **437 825-2GH** Wagner—Der Ring des Nibelungen - Highlights
(DG) **445 354-2GX14** Wagner—Der Ring des Nibelungen
(DG) **445 524-2GMA** Battle in Salzburg
(DG) **445 552-2GMA** Battle and Domingo
(DG) **439 153-4GMA** Mad about Sopranos
(DG) **072 428-1GH2(DG)** The Metropolitan Opera Gala
(DG) **072 189-3GH** Kathleen Battle at the Metropolitan Museum
(DG) **435 866-5CH** Kathleen Battle sings Italian Opera Arias
(EMI) **CDC5 55095-2** Prima Diva
(EMI) **CDC7 47355-2** Mozart—Concert Arias
(EMI) **CDC7 49179-2** Handel—Arias
(ORFE) **C394301B** Great Mozart Singers Series, Vol. 3
(SONY) **SK46672** Baroque Duets
(SONY) **SK48235** A Carnegie Hall Christmas Concert
(SONY) **SK52565** New Year's Eve Concert 1992
(SONY) **SLV48361(SONY)** A Carnegie Hall Christmas

BATURIN, Alexandr (bass-bar)
(DANT) **LYS013/5** Tchaikovsky—The Queen of Spades

BAUCOMONT, Janette (sop)
Berio: Laborintus II

BAUDO, Serge (cond)
see BRSO
Czech PO
Lyon Op Orch

BAUDOZ, Germaine (mez)
Boïeldieu: Dame blanche (Cpte)
Offenbach: Périchole (Cpte)

BAUER, Hartmut (bass)
Wagner: Meistersinger (Cpte)

BAUER-THEUSSL, Franz (cond)
see Vienna Volksoper Chor
Vienna Volksoper Orch

BAUGÉ, André (bar)
(EMI) **CZS5 68292-2** Operetta Arias and Duets
(FORL) **UCD19022** The unforgettable André Baugé

BAUMANN, Ludwig (bass)
Lehár: Giuditta (Cpte)
Puccini: Fanciulla del West (Cpte)
R. Strauss: Daphne (Cpte)

BAUMANN, Paula (sop)
Wagner: Walküre (exc)

BÄUMER, Margarete (sop)
(PILZ) **442118-2** Wagner—Operas in Historical Recordings

BAUMGARTNER, Christian (treb)
Mozart: Zauberflöte (Cpte)

BAUMONT, Olivier (hpd)
(REM) **REM310990** Harpsichord Works

BAUR, Markus (treb)
Mozart: Zauberflöte (Cpte)

BAUR, Wilhelm (bar)
Puccini: Tosca (Cpte)

BAVARIAN NATIONAL ORCHESTRA
cond F. FRICSAY
(DG) **447 364-2GDB2** Great Opera Overtures
cond E. JOCHUM
(DG) **447 364-2GDB2** Great Opera Overtures

BAVARIAN RADIO CHORUS
cond R. ABBADO
Donizetti: Don Pasquale (Cpte)
Puccini: Turandot (Cpte)
(RCA) **09026 62504-2** Great Tenor Arias - Ben Heppner
(RCA) **09026 62674-2** Fortissimo!
cond F. ALLERS
Millöcker: Bettelstudent (Cpte)
cond B. BARTOLETTI
(DG) **431 110-2GB** Great Voices - Fritz Wunderlich
(DG) **435 145-2GX5(1)** Fritz Wunderlich—Opera Arias, Lieder, etc (part 1)
cond S. BAUDO
Gluck: Alceste (1776) (exc)
cond L. BERNSTEIN
Wagner: Tristan und Isolde (exc)
cond T. BUGAJ
Gluck: Corona (Cpte)
cond COLIN DAVIS
Gounod: Faust (Cpte)
Mozart: Idomeneo (Cpte), Nozze di Figaro (Cpte)
Saint-Saëns: Samson et Dalila (Cpte)
Verdi: Falstaff (Cpte)
Wagner: Lohengrin (Cpte)
cond P. DOMINGO
J. Strauss II: Fledermaus (Cpte)
cond K. EICHHORN
Orff: Mond (Cpte), Orpheus (Cpte), Tanz der Spröden (Cpte)
Suppé: Schöne Galathee (exc)
(ACAN) **44 2085-2** Carl Orff Collection
(RCA) **74321 24790-2** Carl Orff 100 Years Edition
cond L. GARDELLI
Bizet: Djamileh (Cpte)
Gluck: Iphigénie en Tauride (Cpte)
Leoncavallo: Pagliacci (Cpte)
Mascagni: Cavalleria Rusticana (Cpte)
Verdi: Alzira (Cpte), Oberto (Cpte), Rigoletto (Cpte)
cond H. GIERSTER
(DG) **431 110-2GB** Great Voices - Fritz Wunderlich
(DG) **435 145-2GX5(1)** Fritz Wunderlich—Opera Arias, Lieder, etc (part 1)
cond L. HAGER
Haydn: Anima del filosofo (Cpte)
cond B. HAITINK
Mozart: Zauberflöte (Cpte)
R. Strauss: Daphne (Cpte)
Wagner: Götterdämmerung (Cpte), Tannhäuser (Cpte)
cond M. HONECK
(CAPR) **10 481** R.Strauss—Opera Concert
cond M. JANOWSKI
Korngold: Violanta (Cpte)
(ACAN) **43 266** Bernd Weikl—Operatic Recital
cond E. JOCHUM
Weber: Freischütz (Cpte)
cond J. KROMBHOLC
Smetana: Bartered Bride (Cpte)
cond R. KUBELÍK
Hindemith: Mathis der Maler (Cpte)
Mozart: Don Giovanni (Cpte)
Pfitzner: Palestrina (Cpte)
Weber: Freischütz (Cpte), Oberon (Cpte)
(EMI) **CMS5 65621-2** Fischer-Dieskau - The Opera Singer
cond G. KUHN
Spontini: Vestale (Cpte)
cond E. LEINSDORF
Korngold: Tote Stadt (Cpte)
cond F. LEITNER
Busoni: Doktor Faust (Cpte)
Orff: Antigonae (Cpte)
cond F. LUISI
Bellini: Puritani (Cpte)
cond W. MATTES
Benatzky: Im weissen Rössl (Cpte)
Lehár: Land des Lächelns (Cpte), Lustige Witwe (exc)
cond U. MUND
Suder: Kleider machen Leute (Cpte)
cond G. PATANÈ
Donizetti: Maria Stuarda (Cpte)
Puccini: Gianni Schicchi (Cpte)
(EURO) **GD69043** Puccini: Il Trittico
cond W. SAWALLISCH
R. Strauss: Elektra (Cpte)
Wagner: Feen (Cpte)
(EMI) **CDC5 55350-2** Cheryl Studer - A Portrait
cond L. SLATKIN
Puccini: Fanciulla del West (Cpte)
cond S. SOLTESZ
Gazzaniga: Don Giovanni (Cpte)
cond P. STEINBERG
Catalani: Wally (Cpte)
cond H. WALLBERG
Donizetti: Don Pasquale (Cpte), Elisir d'amore (Cpte)
Egk: Peer Gynt (Cpte)
Flotow: Martha (Cpte)
Humperdinck: Königskinder (Cpte)
Leoncavallo: Bohème (Cpte)
Mozart: Entführung (Cpte)

BAVARIAN RADIO MALE CHORUS
cond COLIN DAVIS
Stravinsky: Oedipus rex (Cpte)

BAVARIAN RADIO SYMPHONY CHORUS
cond COLIN DAVIS
(BELA) **450 052-2** Great Opera Choruses
cond E. JOCHUM
(BELA) **450 126-2** Favourite Wedding Music II

BAVARIAN RADIO SYMPHONY ORCHESTRA
(BELA) **450 126-2** Favourite Wedding Music II
cond B. BARTOLETTI
(DG) **431 110-2GB** Great Voices - Fritz Wunderlich
(DG) **435 145-2GX5(1)** Fritz Wunderlich—Opera Arias, Lieder, etc (part 1)
cond S. BAUDO
Gluck: Alceste (1776) (Cpte)
cond L. BERNSTEIN
Wagner: Tristan und Isolde (Cpte)
cond K. BÖHM
R. Strauss: Capriccio (Cpte)
(DG) **439 467-2GCL** R. Strauss—Vocal and Orchestral Works
cond COLIN DAVIS
Gounod: Faust (Cpte)
Mozart: Idomeneo (Cpte), Nozze di Figaro (Cpte)
Saint-Saëns: Samson et Dalila (exc)
Stravinsky: Oedipus rex (Cpte)
Verdi: Falstaff (Cpte)
Wagner: Lohengrin (Cpte)
(BELA) **450 052-2** Great Opera Choruses
(PHIL) **422 545-2PME3** The Complete Mozart Edition Vol.45
(PHIL) **434 725-2PM** Kiri Te Kanawa - Classics
(RCA) **09026 61440-2** Opera's Greatest Moments
(RCA) **09026 61886-2** Operas Greatest Love Songs
(SONY) **SMK66927** Beethoven—Symphonies Nos 1 and 2;Overture-Leonore
cond H. FRICKE
K. A. Hartmann: Simplicius Simplicissimus (Cpte)
cond F. FRICSAY
(BELA) **450 139-2** An Invitation to the Dance
cond L. GARDELLI
Gluck: Iphigénie en Tauride (Cpte)
cond B. HAITINK
Mozart: Zauberflöte (Cpte)
R. Strauss: Daphne (Cpte)
Wagner: Götterdämmerung (Cpte), Rheingold (Cpte), Siegfried (Cpte), Tannhäuser (Cpte), Walküre (Cpte)
(CFP) **CD-CFP4612** Favourite Mozart
(EMI) **CDC5 55350-2** Cheryl Studer - A Portrait
cond E. JOCHUM
Mozart: Entführung (Cpte)
Weber: Freischütz (Cpte)
(DG) **437 677-2GDO2** Irmgard Seefried - Opera Recital
(DG) **439 445-2GCL** Wagner—Overtures and Preludes
(DG) **439 687-2GX2** Wagner—Overtures and Preludes
cond B. KLEE
Mendelssohn: Hochzeit des Camacho (Cpte)
cond R. KUBELÍK
Hindemith: Mathis der Maler (Cpte)
Mozart: Don Giovanni (Cpte)
Pfitzner: Palestrina (Cpte)
Weber: Freischütz (Cpte), Oberon (Cpte)
(BELA) **450 121-2** Plácido Domingo
(DG) **415 840-2GGA** Mendelssohn & Weber—Orchestral Works
(DG) **435 145-2GX5(1)** Fritz Wunderlich—Opera Arias, Lieder, etc (part 1)
(EMI) **CMS5 65212-2** Wagner—Les introuvables du Ring
(EMI) **CMS5 65621-2** Fischer-Dieskau - The Opera Singer
(RCA) **09026 62699-2** Opera's Greatest Duets
cond F. LEITNER
Busoni: Doktor Faust (Cpte)
Orff: Antigonae (Cpte)
cond J. LÓPEZ-COBOS
(ORFE) **C028821A** Famous Operatic Duets
cond L. MAAZEL
(RCA) **09026 68225-2** R. Strauss—Orchestral Works
cond D. RUNNICLES
Humperdinck: Hänsel und Gretel (Cpte)
cond W. SAWALLISCH
R. Strauss: Elektra (Cpte), Frau ohne Schatten (exc), Intermezzo (Cpte)
Wagner: Feen (Cpte)
(EMI) **CDC5 55350-2** Cheryl Studer - A Portrait
(EMI) **CMS5 65621-2** Fischer-Dieskau - The Opera Singer
(ORFE) **C168881A** Pfitzner: Overtures and Entr'actes
cond J. TATE
Humperdinck: Hänsel und Gretel (exc)
(EMI) **CDC5 55350-2** Cheryl Studer - A Portrait

BAVARIAN STATE OPERA BALLET
cond C. KLEIBER
J. Strauss II: Fledermaus (Cpte)

BAVARIAN STATE OPERA CHORUS
cond K. BÖHM
Mozart: Entführung (Cpte)
cond F. FRICSAY
Beethoven: Fidelio (Cpte)
cond R. HEGER
Flotow: Martha (Cpte)
Nicolai: Lustigen Weiber von Windsor (Cpte)
(PILZ) **442118-2** Wagner—Operas in Historical Recordings
cond E. JOCHUM
Mozart: Entführung (Cpte)
cond J. KEILBERTH
Janáček: Excursions of Mr Brouček (Cpte)
R. Strauss: Arabella (Cpte)
Wagner: Meistersinger (Cpte)
cond R. KEMPE
(PILZ) **442118-2** Wagner—Operas in Historical Recordings
cond C. KLEIBER
J. Strauss II: Fledermaus (Cpte)
R. Strauss: Rosenkavalier (Cpte)
Verdi: Traviata (exc)
(DG) **431 104-2GB** Great Voices - Plácido Domingo
cond H. KNAPPERTSBUSCH
Wagner: Götterdämmerung (Cpte), Tristan und Isolde (Cpte)
cond C. KRAUSS
Wagner: Fliegende Holländer (Cpte)
(PILZ) **442118-2** Wagner—Operas in Historical Recordings
cond W. MATTES
Lehár: Graf von Luxemburg (Cpte)
(EMI) **CMS7 64309-2** Kálmán—Best-loved Melodies
cond G. PATANÈ
Verdi: Traviata (Cpte)
cond W. SAWALLISCH
Mozart: Zauberflöte (Cpte)
Wagner: Fliegende Holländer (Cpte), Götterdämmerung (Cpte), Meistersinger (Cpte)
(EMI) **LDX9 91275-1(EMI)** Sawallisch conducts Wagner's Ring
cond G. SOLTI
Orff: Antigonae (Cpte)
cond P. STEINBERG
Massenet: Chérubin (Cpte)
cond H. WALLBERG
Millöcker: Gasparone (Cpte)

BAVARIAN STATE OPERA ORCHESTRA
J. Strauss II: Fledermaus (Cpte)
Mozart: Zauberflöte (Cpte)
R. Strauss: Rosenkavalier (Cpte)
cond O. GERDES
(DG) **431 110-2GB** Great Voices - Fritz Wunderlich
(DG) **435 145-2GX5(1)** Fritz Wunderlich—Opera Arias, Lieder, etc (part 1)
cond R. HEGER
(PILZ) **442118-2** Wagner—Operas in Historical Recordings
cond E. JOCHUM
(DG) **435 145-2GX5(1)** Fritz Wunderlich—Opera Arias, Lieder, etc (part 1)
(DG) **447 364-2GDB2** Great Opera Overtures
cond J. KEILBERTH
Wagner: Meistersinger (Cpte)
cond R. KEMPE
(PILZ) **442118-2** Wagner—Operas in Historical Recordings
cond C. KRAUSS
Wagner: Fliegende Holländer (Cpte)
(MYTO) **1MCD943104** R. Strauss—Capriccio (highlights) & Lieder
(PILZ) **442118-2** Wagner—Operas in Historical Recordings
(SCHW) **314712** Vienna State Opera Live, Vol.21
cond H. MÜLLER-KRAY
(CFP) **CD-CFP4616** Ave Maria
cond W. SAWALLISCH
Mozart: Zauberflöte (Cpte)
(CFP) **CD-CFP4602** Favourite Opera
(EMI) **CMS5 65621-2** Fischer-Dieskau - The Opera Singer
(EMIL) **CDZ7 67015-2** Mozart—Opera Arias

BAVARIAN STATE ORCHESTRA
Janáček: Excursions of Mr Brouček (Cpte)
Mozart: Entführung (Cpte)
cond W. EGK
Egk: Verlobung in San Domingo (Cpte)
cond D. FISCHER-DIESKAU
(ORFE) **C186951** Verdi—Heroines, Vol. 1
cond F. FRICSAY
Beethoven: Fidelio (Cpte)
(DG) **437 677-2GDO2** Irmgard Seefried - Opera Recital
cond R. HEGER
Flotow: Martha (Cpte)
Nicolai: Lustigen Weiber von Windsor (Cpte)
(CFP) **CD-CFP4616** Ave Maria
(EMI) **CZS7 62993-2** Fritz Wunderlich—Great German Tenor
cond H. HOLLREISER
(PREI) **90200** Hans Hotter in Early Recordings
cond E. JOCHUM
(DG) **431 110-2GB** Great Voices - Fritz Wunderlich
cond J. KEILBERTH
R. Strauss: Arabella (Cpte), Salome (Cpte)
cond C. KLEIBER
Verdi: Traviata (exc)
(DG) **415 366-2GH** Placido Domingo Recital
(DG) **427 708-2GX3** The Best of Domingo
(DG) **431 104-2GB** Great Voices - Plácido Domingo
(DG) **447 364-2GDB2** Great Opera Overtures
(DG) **419 091-4GW** Placido Domingo sings Favourite Arias, Songs and Tangos

cond H. KNAPPERTSBUSCH
Wagner: Götterdämmerung (Cpte), Tristan und Isolde (Cpte)
cond H. MOLTKAU
(EMI) **CMS7 64309-2** Kálmán—Best-loved Melodies
(EMI) **CZS7 62993-2** Fritz Wunderlich—Great German Tenor
cond H. MÜLLER-KRAY
(EMI) **CZS7 62993-2** Fritz Wunderlich—Great German Tenor
cond G. PATANÈ
Verdi: Traviata (Cpte)
cond W. SAWALLISCH
Wagner: Fliegende Holländer (Cpte), Götterdämmerung (Cpte), Meistersinger (Cpte), Rheingold (Cpte), Siegfried (Cpte), Walküre (Cpte)
(EMI) **CDC5 55350-2** Cheryl Studer - A Portrait
(EMI) **CZS7 67546-2** Entry of the Gladiators—Famous Marches
(EMI) **LDX9 91275-1(EMI)** Sawallisch conducts Wagner's Ring
(ORFE) **C161871A** Famous Overtures
cond G. SOLTI
Orff: Antigonae (Cpte)
cond R. STRAUSS
(PREI) **90205** Strauss conducts Strauss, Vol.1
cond M. VON ZALLINGER
(EMI) **CZS7 62993-2** Fritz Wunderlich—Great German Tenor
(NIMB) **NI7851** Legendary Voices

BAXA, Pavol (cond)
see Musica aeterna

BAXTER, Pamela (mez)
Offenbach: Orphée aux enfers (Cpte)
Sullivan: Gondoliers (Cpte)

BAY, Emanuel (pf)
(APR) **APR7015** The Auer Legacy, Vol.1
(APR) **APR7016** The Auer Legacy, Vol.2
(EMI) **CHS7 64929-2** Jascha Heifetz
(RCA) **09026 61778-2(03)** The Heifetz Collection, Vol. 3
(RCA) **09026 61778-2(06)** The Heifetz Collection, Vol. 6
(RCA) **09026 61778-2(19)** The Heifetz Collection, Vol. 19

BAYCO, Frederic (organ)
(EMIL) **CDZ112** Music for Weddings

BAYLEY, Clive (bar)
Bernstein: Candide (1988) (Cpte)
Britten: Billy Budd (Cpte)
M. Berkeley: Baa Baa Black Sheep (Cpte)
Walton: Troilus and Cressida (Cpte)

BAYLEY, Clive (bass)
(OPRA) **ORCH104** A Hundred Years of Italian Opera: 1820-1830

BAYLISS, Peter (sngr)
Gay: Beggar's Opera (Cpte)

BAYO, Maria (sop)
Bretón: Verbena de La Paloma (Cpte)
Cavalli: Calisto (Cpte)
Rossini: Occasione fa il ladro (Cpte)
Vives: Bohemios (Cpte), Doña Francisquita (Cpte)
(CLAV) **CD50-9023** Maria Bayo—Arie Antiche

BAYOD, Antonio Perez (sngr)
Bretón: Verbena de la Paloma (Cpte)

BAYREUTH FESTIVAL CHORUS
cond H. ABENDROTH
Wagner: Meistersinger (Cpte)
cond D. BARENBOIM
Wagner: Götterdämmerung (exc), Tristan und Isolde (Cpte)
cond P. BOULEZ
Wagner: Götterdämmerung (Cpte), Parsifal (Cpte)
(PHIL) **434 420-2PM32(1)** Richard Wagner Edition (Pt.1)
cond K. BÖHM
Wagner: Fliegende Holländer (Cpte), Götterdämmerung (Cpte), Tristan und Isolde (exc)
(PHIL) **434 420-2PM32(2)** Richard Wagner Edition (pt 2)
(PHIL) **446 057-2PB14** Wagner—The Ring Cycle - Bayreuth Festival 1967
cond COLIN DAVIS
Wagner: Tannhäuser (Cpte)
cond K. ELMENDORFF
Wagner: Götterdämmerung (Cpte), Tannhäuser (Cpte)
(MSCM) **MM30283** Great Wagnerian Singers, Vol.1
cond JAMES LEVINE
Wagner: Parsifal (Cpte)
(PHIL) **434 420-2PM32(1)** Richard Wagner Edition (Pt.1)
cond E. JOCHUM
(MEMO) **HR4275/6** Birgit Nilsson—Public Performances 1954-1969
cond H. VON KARAJAN
Wagner: Meistersinger (Cpte)
cond J. KEILBERTH
Wagner: Lohengrin (Cpte)
cond H. KNAPPERTSBUSCH
Wagner: Fliegende Holländer (Cpte), Parsifal (Cpte)
cond R. KRAUS
(PREI) **90232** Wagner—Der Fliegende Holländer
cond C. KRAUSS
Wagner: Götterdämmerung (Cpte)
(FOYE) **15-CF2011** Wagner—Der Ring de Nibelungen
cond K. MUCK
Wagner: Parsifal (exc)
(OPAL) **OPALCDS9843** Karl Muck conducts Wagner
cond W. NELSSON
Wagner: Fliegende Holländer (Cpte), Lohengrin (Cpte)
(BELA) **450 052-2** Great Opera Choruses
(PHIL) **434 420-2PM32(1)** Richard Wagner Edition (Pt.1)
cond W. PITZ
(BELA) **450 052-2** Great Opera Choruses
(DG) **429 169-2GR** Wagner—Choruses
cond W. SAWALLISCH
Wagner: Fliegende Holländer (Cpte), Lohengrin (Cpte), Tannhäuser (exc)
(BELA) **450 052-2** Great Opera Choruses
(PHIL) **434 420-2PM32(2)** Richard Wagner Edition (pt 2)
cond P. SCHNEIDER
Wagner: Lohengrin (Cpte)
(PHIL) **434 420-2PM32(1)** Richard Wagner Edition (Pt.1)
cond G. SINOPOLI
Wagner: Tannhäuser (Cpte)
cond H. STEIN
Wagner: Meistersinger (Cpte), Parsifal (Cpte)
cond H. TIETJEN
(MSCM) **MM30283** Great Wagnerian Singers, Vol.1
(TELD) **9031-76442-2** Wagner—Excerpts from the 1936 Bayreuth Festival
cond S. VARVISO
Wagner: Meistersinger (exc)
(PHIL) **434 420-2PM32(1)** Richard Wagner Edition (Pt.1)
cond S. WAGNER
(MSCM) **MM30285** Great Wagnerian Singers, Vol.2

BAYREUTH FESTIVAL ORCHESTRA
Wagner: Fliegende Holländer (Cpte), Götterdämmerung (Cpte), Lohengrin (Cpte), Meistersinger (Cpte), Parsifal (Cpte), Rheingold (Cpte), Siegfried (Cpte), Tannhäuser (Cpte), Tristan und Isolde (Cpte), Walküre (Cpte)
cond H. ABENDROTH
Wagner: Meistersinger (Cpte)
cond D. BARENBOIM
Wagner: Götterdämmerung (Cpte), Rheingold (Cpte), Siegfried (Cpte), Walküre (Cpte)
cond P. BOULEZ
Wagner: Götterdämmerung (Cpte), Parsifal (Cpte), Rheingold (exc), Siegfried (Cpte), Walküre (Cpte)
(PHIL) **434 420-2PM32(1)** Richard Wagner Edition (Pt.1)
cond K. BÖHM
Wagner: Fliegende Holländer (Cpte), Götterdämmerung (Cpte), Rheingold (Cpte), Siegfried (Cpte), Tristan und Isolde (exc), Walküre (exc)
(DG) **439 445-2GCL** Wagner—Overtures and Preludes
(DG) **439 687-2GX2** Wagner—Overtures and Preludes
(MEMO) **HR4275/6** Birgit Nilsson—Public Performances 1954-1969
(PHIL) **434 420-2PM32(2)** Richard Wagner Edition (pt 2)
(PHIL) **446 057-2PB14** Wagner—The Ring Cycle - Bayreuth Festival 1967
cond K. ELMENDORFF
Wagner: Götterdämmerung (Cpte), Tannhäuser (Cpte)
(EMI) **CMS7 64008-2(1)** Wagner Singing on Record (pt 1)
(EMI) **CMS7 64008-2(2)** Wagner Singing on Record (pt 2)
(MSCM) **MM30283** Great Wagnerian Singers, Vol.1
(PEAR) **GEMMCDS9926(1)** Covent Garden on Record—Vol.4 (pt 1)
cond JAMES LEVINE
Wagner: Parsifal (Cpte)
(PHIL) **434 420-2PM32(1)** Richard Wagner Edition (Pt.1)
cond E. JOCHUM
(MEMO) **HR4275/6** Birgit Nilsson—Public Performances 1954-1969
cond H. VON KARAJAN
Wagner: Meistersinger (Cpte), Walküre (exc)
cond J. KEILBERTH
Wagner: Lohengrin (Cpte)
cond H. KNAPPERTSBUSCH
Wagner: Fliegende Holländer (Cpte), Parsifal (Cpte)
cond R. KRAUS
(PREI) **90232** Wagner—Der Fliegende Holländer
cond C. KRAUSS
Wagner: Götterdämmerung (Cpte), Rheingold (Cpte), Siegfried (Cpte), Walküre (Cpte)
(FOYE) **15-CF2011** Wagner—Der Ring de Nibelungen
cond K. MUCK
Wagner: Parsifal (exc)
(OPAL) **OPALCDS9843** Karl Muck conducts Wagner
cond W. NELSSON
Wagner: Fliegende Holländer (Cpte)
(BELA) **450 052-2** Great Opera Choruses
(PHIL) **434 420-2PM32(1)** Richard Wagner Edition (Pt.1)
cond W. PITZ
(BELA) **450 052-2** Great Opera Choruses
(DG) **429 169-2GR** Wagner—Choruses
cond W. SAWALLISCH
Wagner: Fliegende Holländer (Cpte), Lohengrin (Cpte), Tannhäuser (Cpte)
(BELA) **450 052-2** Great Opera Choruses
(PHIL) **434 420-2PM32(2)** Richard Wagner Edition (pt 2)
cond P. SCHNEIDER
Wagner: Lohengrin (exc)
(PHIL) **434 420-2PM32(1)** Richard Wagner Edition (Pt.1)
cond H. TIETJEN
(MMOI) **CDMOIR405** Great Tenors
(MSCM) **MM30283** Great Wagnerian Singers, Vol.1
(MSCM) **MM30285** Great Wagnerian Singers, Vol.2
(TELD) **9031-76442-2** Wagner—Excerpts from the 1936 Bayreuth Festival
cond S. VARVISO
Wagner: Meistersinger (Cpte)
(PHIL) **434 420-2PM32(1)** Richard Wagner Edition (Pt.1)
cond E. DE WAART
(PHIL) **434 109-2PH** Wagner for Brass
cond S. WAGNER
(EMI) **CMS7 64008-2(2)** Wagner Singing on Record (pt 2)
(MSCM) **MM30285** Great Wagnerian Singers, Vol.2

BAZEMORE, Raymond (voc)
A. Davis: X (Cpte)
Joplin: Treemonisha (Cpte)

BAZOLA-MINORI, François (bar)
Handel: Teseo (Cpte)
Montéclair: Jephté (Cpte)
Purcell: Fairy Queen, Z629 (Cpte), King Arthur, Z628 (Cpte)

BAZSINKA, Zsuzsanna (sop)
Mascagni: Lodoletta (Cpte)

BBC CHOIR
cond T. BEECHAM
Gounod: Faust (Cpte)

BBC CHORUS
cond O. ACKERMANN
Lehár: Land des Lächelns (Cpte), Lustige Witwe (Cpte)
cond T. BEECHAM
(BBCR) **DMCD98** BBC Proms - The Centenary: 1895-1995
(PEAR) **GEMMCD9473** Heddle Nash—Vol.2
(SONY) **SMK58934** Delius—Orchestral Works
cond COLIN DAVIS
Mozart: Nozze di Figaro (Cpte)
cond O. KLEMPERER
Wagner: Fliegende Holländer (Cpte)

BBC CONCERT ORCHESTRA
cond G. LLOYD
G. Lloyd: Iernin
cond E. RICCI
(TELD) **4509-96080-6(TELD)** Carreras—A Tribute to Mario Lanza

BBC NORTHERN SYMPHONY ORCHESTRA
cond N. DEL MAR
(BBCR) **BBCRD9129** Bridge/Britten/Pärt—Orchestral Works

BBC PHILHARMONIC ORCHESTRA
cond E. DOWNES
(IMP) **PCDS21** Music of the World—Danube Dreams
(IMP) **PCD1023** Favourite Overtures
(IMP) **PCD2045** Favourite Overtures
(IMP) **TCD1070** Invitation to the Opera
cond S. GUNZENHAUSER
(NAXO) **8 550600** Dvořák—Overtures
cond G. LLOYD
(ALBA) **TROY015-2** G. Lloyd—Orchestral Works
cond O. DE LA MARTINEZ
Smyth: Wreckers (Cpte)
cond P. MAXWELL DAVIES
Maxwell Davies: Lighthouse (Cpte), Resurrection (Cpte)
(COLL) **Coll1444-2** Maximum Max—Music of Maxwell Davies
cond Y. P. TORTELIER
(CHAN) **CHAN9060** Hindemith—Orchestral Works

BBC SCOTTISH SYMPHONY ORCHESTRA
cond M. BRABBINS
(HYPE) **CDA66764** Alexander Mackenzie—Orchestral Music
cond J. Y. OSSONCE
Chabrier: Briséïs (Cpte)

BBC SINGERS
cond P. BOULEZ
Schoenberg: Moses und Aron (Cpte)
Stravinsky: Nightingale (Cpte)
(ERAT) **4509-98955-2** Boulez conducts Stravinsky
(SONY) **SMK48464** Boulez conducts Schoenberg - Volume 2
cond G. LLOYD
G. Lloyd: Iernin

BBC SYMPHONY CHORUS
cond COLIN DAVIS
Mozart: Nozze di Figaro (exc)
cond G. SIMON
(CALA) **CACD1011** Borodin—Orchestral Works

BBC SYMPHONY ORCHESTRA
(CALA) **CACD0106** The London Viola Sound
cond L. BERNSTEIN
(DG) **413 490-2GH** Elgar: Orchestral Works
cond P. BOULEZ
Schoenberg: Moses und Aron (Cpte)
Stravinsky: Nightingale (Cpte)
(ERAT) **4509-98955-2** Boulez conducts Stravinsky

(SONY) **SMK48464** Boulez conducts Schoenberg - Volume 2
(SONY) **SMK48466** Boulez conducts Schoenberg—Volume 3
cond A. BOULT
(BEUL) **1PD12** Boult's BBC Years
cond COLIN DAVIS
Berlioz: Benvenuto Cellini (Cpte)
Mozart: Nozze di Figaro (exc)
(BELA) **461 001-2** Popular Overtures
(PHIL) **422 269-4PMI** Best of Mozart
cond A. DAVIS
(TELD) **4509-90845-2** Delius—Orchestral Works
(TELD) **4509-96231-2** Gardening Classics
(TELD) **4509-97868-2** The Last Night of the Proms 1994
(TELD) **4509-97869-3** The Last Night of the Proms 1994
(VIRG) **VC7 59618-2** Nielsen—Orchestral Works
cond M. SARGENT
(KIWI) **CDSLD-82** Southern Voices—NZ International Opera Singers
(MEMO) **HR4293/4** The very best of Maria Callas
cond L. STOKOWSKI
(TELD) **4509-95038-6(TELD)** The Art of Conducting—Great Conductors of the Past
cond V. TAUSKY
(BBCR) **BBCRD9103** Classic Encores
cond A. TOSCANINI
(BIDD) **WHL008/9** Toscanini conducts the BBC Symphony Orchestra
(TEST) **SBT1015** Toscanini—Unpublished HMV Recordings, 1935/38

BBC SYMPHONY ORCHESTRA CELLOS
cond G. SIMON
(CALA) **CACD0104** The London Cello Sound

BBC THEATRE CHORUS
cond R. GOODALL
(EMI) **CMS7 64727-2** Britten—Opera excerpts and Folksongs

BBC WELSH SYMPHONY ORCHESTRA
cond T. OTAKA
(NIMB) **NI5235** R. Strauss: Orchestral Works

BBC WIRELESS MILITARY BAND
cond B.W. O'DONNELL
(BEUL) **2PD4** 78 Classics - Volume Two

BEAN, Gweneth (contr)
R. Strauss: Ariadne auf Naxos (Cpte)
Tchaikovsky: Eugene Onegin (Cpte)
Wagner: Götterdämmerung (Cpte), Parsifal (Cpte)
(DG) **072 422-3GH7** Levine conducts Wagner's Ring

BEARDSLEY, Karen (sop)
Knussen: Where the Wild Things are (Cpte)

BEASLEY, Marco (ten)
Stradella: Moro per amore (Cpte)

BEATON, Morag (sop)
Herrmann: Wuthering Heights (Cpte)

BEATTIE, Douglas (bar)
Wagner: Tristan und Isolde (Cpte)

BEATTIE, Herbert (bass)
(SONY) **SM22K46290(4)** Stravinsky—The Complete Edition (pt 4)

BEAUPRÉ, Odette (mez)
(DECC) **440 333-2DH** Ravel—Vocal Works

BEAVAN, David (bass)
Puccini: Rondine (Cpte)
Shostakovich: Lady Macbeth of Mtsensk (Cpte)

BEAVAN, Nigel (bass)
Giordano: Andrea Chénier (Cpte)
Purcell: King Arthur, Z628 (Cpte)
(HARM) **HMX290 1528/33(2)** A Purcell Companion (pt 2)

BECCARIA, Bruno (ten)
Verdi: Nabucco (Cpte)

BECERRA, Flavio (ten)
(IMP) **PCD1109** Overtures and Arias from Opera

BECHI, Gino (bar)
Mascagni: Cavalleria Rusticana (Cpte)
Verdi: Aida (Cpte)
(EMI) **CHS7 64864-2(2)** La Scala Edition - Vol.2, 1915-46 (pt 2)
(EMI) **CHS7 69741-2(7)** Record of Singing, Vol.4—Italian School
(NIMB) **NI7853** Lauri-Volpi sings Verdi
(PREI) **89009** Gino Bechi (b. 1913)
(PREI) **89074** Tancredi Pasero (1893-1983) - II
(PREI) **89995** Famous Italian Baritones

BECHLY, Daniela (sop)
Wagner: Parsifal (Cpte)

BECHT, Hermann (bar)
Wagner: Götterdämmerung (Cpte), Rheingold (Cpte), Siegfried (Cpte), Tristan und Isolde (Cpte)
Weill: Dreigroschenoper (Cpte)
(PHIL) **434 420-2PM32(1)** Richard Wagner Edition (Pt.1)

BECK, Walter (ten)
(PREI) **89092** Erna Berger (1900-1990) - II

BECK, William (bar)
Handel: Giulio Cesare (Cpte)

(MARTIN) BECK THEATER CHORUS
cond S. KRACHMALNICK
Bernstein: Candide (1956) (exc)

(MARTIN) BECK THEATER ORCHESTRA
cond S. KRACHMALNICK
Bernstein: Candide (1956) (exc)

BECKER, Georg (spkr)
Rihm: Eroberung von Mexico (Cpte)

BECKER, Gerhard (cond)
see Berlin SO

BECKER, Josef (bass)
Hindemith: Nusch-Nuschi (Cpte)
Mendelssohn: Hochzeit des Camacho (Cpte)
Schreker: Gezeichneten (Cpte)
Spontini: Olimpie (Cpte)

BECKER, Valerie J. (pf)
(ASV) **CDWHL2085** Saxophone Serenade

BECKERBAUER, Stefan (treb)
Gluck: Orfeo ed Euridice (Cpte)

BECKMANN, Friedel (mez)
(EMI) **CMS7 64008-2(1)** Wagner Singing on Record (pt 1)
(PREI) **89077** Torsten Ralf (1901-1954)
(PREI) **89211** Helge Roswaenge (1897-1972) - III

BEDAIR, Sobhi (ten)
Mozart: Don Giovanni (Cpte), Nozze di Figaro (Cpte)

BEDEX, Henri (sngr)
Lecocq: Jour et la Nuit (Cpte)
Messager: Monsieur Beaucaire (Cpte)

BEDFORD, Peter (bass)
G. Charpentier: Louise (Cpte)

BEDFORD, Steuart (cond)
see Aldeburgh Fest Ens
Aldeburgh Fest Orch
ECO
LSO

BEDNÁŘ, Václav (bar)
Dvořák: Rusalka (Cpte)

BEDNÁŘ, Vaclav (bass)
Martinů: Julietta (Cpte)
Smetana: Devil's Wall (Cpte)

BEECHAM, Sir Thomas (cond)
see BPO
FRNO
LPO
orch
RCA Victor Orch
RCA Victor SO
ROHO
RPO
RPS Orch
SO

BEECHAM CHORAL SOCIETY
cond T. BEECHAM
Borodin: Prince Igor (exc)
(EMI) **CHS7 63715-2** Mozart: Die Entführung, etc
cond J. HORENSTEIN
Wagner: Tannhäuser (exc)

BEER, Sidney (cond)
see National SO

BEESLEY, Mark (bar)
Beethoven: Fidelio (Cpte)
Verdi: Otello (Cpte), Simon Boccanegra (Cpte), Traviata (Cpte)

BEESLEY, Shauna (mez)
Purcell: Dido (Cpte)

BEGALI, Ottorino (ten)
Puccini: Manon Lescaut (Cpte)

BEGG, Heather (mez)
Berlioz: Troyens (Cpte)
Britten: Little Sweep (Cpte)
J. Strauss II: Fledermaus (Cpte)
Mozart: Nozze di Figaro (Cpte)
Sullivan: Iolanthe (exc)
(DECC) **071 149-1DH (DECC)** The Essential Sutherland

BEGLEY, Kim (ten)
Bellini: Norma (Cpte)
R. Strauss: Rosenkavalier (Cpte), Salome (Cpte)
Verdi: Traviata (exc)
Wagner: Rheingold (Cpte)

BÈGUELIN, Jean-Noël (bass)
(EMI) **CDM7 63104-2** Alfredo Krauss - Opera Recital

BEHLE, Renate (sop)
Rihm: Eroberung von Mexico (Cpte)
Schumann: Genoveva (Cpte)
Spohr: Jessonda (Cpte)
Zemlinsky: Kreidekreis (Cpte)

BEHM, Gisela (sop)
(PREI) **90103** Helge Roswaenge Recital (1959)

BEHR, Randall (cond)
see Philh

BEHRENS, Hildegard (sop)
Berg: Wozzeck (Cpte)
Humperdinck: Hänsel und Gretel (Cpte)
Puccini: Tosca (Cpte)
R. Strauss: Elektra (Cpte), Frau ohne Schatten (Cpte)
Wagner: Fliegende Holländer (Cpte), Götterdämmerung (Cpte), Siegfried (Cpte), Tristan und Isolde (Cpte), Walküre (Cpte)
Weber: Freischütz (Cpte)
(DECC) **436 472-2DM** Great Opera Arias
(DG) **437 825-2GH** Wagner—Der Ring des Nibelungen - Highlights
(DG) **445 354-2GX14** Wagner—Der Ring des Nibelungen
(DG) **439 153-4GMA** Mad about Sopranos
(DG) **072 422-3GH7** Levine conducts Wagner's Ring
(EMI) **LDX9 91275-1(EMI)** Sawallisch conducts Wagner's Ring

BEIER, Mikael (fl)
(DANA) **DACOCD306** Mikael Beier plays popular music for Flute and Harp

BEILKE, Irma (sop)
Mozart: Nozze di Figaro (Cpte), Zauberflöte (Cpte)
(ORFE) **C394101B** Great Mozart Singers Series, Vol. 1
(PREI) **89049** Margarete Teschemacher (1903-1959)
(SCHW) **314722** Vienna State Opera Live, Vol.22

BEIRER, Hans (ten)
Mozart: Zauberflöte (Cpte)
R. Strauss: Elektra (Cpte), Salome (Cpte)

BEISSEL, Heribert (cond)
see Bratislava RSO

BEKAERT, Herman (bar)
(CPO) **CPO999 104-2** Mozart—Lo Sposo Deluso/L'Oca del Cairo

(THE) BEKOVA SISTERS
(CHAN) **CHAN9364** Elegy

BELA, Dajos (cond)
see orch

BELAMARIC, Neven (sngr)
Schreker: Irrelohe (Cpte)

BÉLANGER, Marc (vn)
Vivier: Kopernikus (Cpte)

BELANOVÁ, Květa (sop)
Janáček: Jenufa (Cpte)

BELARSKY, Sidor (bass)
Beethoven: Fidelio (Cpte)

BELCOURT, Emile (ten)
Delibes: Lakmé (Cpte)
Offenbach: Orphée aux enfers (exc)
Wagner: Rheingold (Cpte)

BELEAVCENCO, Mihai (cond)
see Timişoara Romanian Op Orch

BELGIAN RADIO AND TELEVISION ORCHESTRA
cond A. RAHBARI
(NAXO) **8 550606** Soprano Arias from Italian Operas

BELGRADE NATIONAL OPERA CHORUS
cond O. DANON
(BELA) **450 117-2** Great Opera Chorus II

BELGRADE NATIONAL OPERA ORCHESTRA
cond O. DANON
(BELA) **450 117-2** Great Opera Chorus II

BELINCK, Susan (sop)
(SONY) **SM22K46290(3)** Stravinsky—The Complete Edition (pt 3)

BELL, Catriona (mez)
Janáček: Fate (Cpte)
Wagner: Parsifal (Cpte)

BELL, Donald (ten)
Britten: Midsummer Night's Dream (Cpte)

BELL, Donaldson (bar)
Herrmann: Wuthering Heights (Cpte)
Massenet: Werther (Cpte)

BELL, Galloway (sngr)
Saxton: Caritas (Cpte)

BELL, Joshua (vn)
(DECC) **433 519-2DH** Works for Violin and Orchestra
(DECC) **433 519-5DH** Works for Violin and Orchestra

BELLA, Benito di (bar)
Mascagni: Amico Fritz (Cpte)
Verdi: Rigoletto (Cpte)

BELLAMY, Marcia (mez)
Busoni: Arlecchino (Cpte)

BELLANTONI, Giuseppe (bar)
(BONG) **GB1043-2** Italian Baritones of the Acoustic Era
(MEMO) **HR4408/9(2)** Singers in Genoa, Vol.1 (disc 2)

BELLEAU, Marc (bass)
Berlioz: Troyens (Cpte)

BELLEMARE, Gilles (cond)
see Three Rivers SO

BELLERI, L. M. (sop)
(RCA) **GD87808** Lawrence Tibbett sings Opera Arias

BELLEZZA, Vincenzo (cond)
see Naples San Carlo Op Orch
orch
ROHO
Rome Academy Orch
Rome Op Orch
Santa Cecilia Academy Orch

BELLINCIONI, Gemma (sop)
(EMI) **CHS7 64860-2(1)** La Scala Edition - Vol.1, 1878-1914 (pt 1)
(MEMO) **HR4408/9(2)** Singers in Genoa, Vol.1 (disc 2)
(PEAR) **GEMMCDS9923(1)** Covent Garden on Record, Vol.1 (pt 1)
(SYMP) **SYMCD1073** The Harold Wayne Collection, Vol.3

BELLINI, Gabriele (cond)
see ENO Orch
Forum PO

BELLINI THEATRE CHORUS
cond A. LICATA
Bellini: Adelson e Salvini (Cpte), Bianca e Fernando (Cpte)

BELLINI THEATRE ORCHESTRA
cond A. LICATA
Bellini: Adelson e Salvini (Cpte), Bianca e Fernando (Cpte)

BELLO, Angela (sop)
R. Strauss: Rosenkavalier (Cpte)

BELLO, Vincenzo (ten)
Donizetti: Lucia di Lammermoor (Cpte)
Leoncavallo: Pagliacci (exc)
Verdi: Due Foscari (Cpte)

BELLON, Wolfgang (ten)
Mozart: Zaïde (Cpte)

BELLUGI, Piero (cond)
see Turin RAI Orch

BELMAS, Xenia (sop)
(MMOI) **CDMOIR422** Great Voices in Tchaikovsky
(PREI) **89047** Xenia Belmas (1890-1981)

BĚLOHLÁVEK, Jiří (cond)
see Czech PO
Prague SO

BELOV, Evgeny (bar)
Tchaikovsky: Eugene Onegin (Cpte)

BELTI-PILINSZKY, Geza (ten)
Wagner: Tannhäuser (Cpte)

BELTRÁN, Tito (ten)
(SILV) **SILKD6005** Tito-Tito Beltrán

BENACKA, Stanislav (bass)
Puccini: Bohème (Cpte), Tosca (Cpte)

BEŇAČKOVÁ, Gabriela (sop)
Beethoven: Fidelio (Cpte)
Boito: Mefistofele (Cpte)
Dvořák: Rusalka (exc)
Fibich: Bride of Messina (Cpte)
Janáček: Cunning Little Vixen (Cpte), Jenufa (Cpte)
Smetana: Bartered Bride (Cpte), Libuše (Cpte)
Suchoň: Whirlpool (Cpte)
(KOCH) **34036-2** A Pageant of Opera

BEŇAČKOVÁ, Marta (mez)
Patzelt: Castor et Pollux (Cpte)

BENCE, Margaret (contr)
Egk: Verlobung in San Domingo (Cpte)
Smetana: Bartered Bride (Cpte)

BENDA, Hans von (cond)
see orch

BENDAZZI-GARULLI, Ernestina (sop)
(SYMP) **SYMCD1077** The Harold Wayne Collection, Vol.4

BENDE, Zsolt (bar)
(DECC) **443 488-2DF2** Kodály—Háry János; Psalmus Hungaricus etc

BENDER, Fritz Richard (bar)
Wagner: Tristan und Isolde (Cpte)

BENDIX, Kurt (cond)
see Berlin St Op Orch
Stockholm Royal Op Orch

BENEGAS, Marta (sop)
Gluck: Iphigénie en Tauride (Cpte)

BENELLI, Ugo (ten)
Leoncavallo: Pagliacci (exc)
Meyerbeer: Crociato in Egitto (Cpte)
Mozart: Nozze di Figaro (Cpte)
Prokofiev: Love for 3 Oranges (Cpte)
Rossini: Barbiere di Siviglia (Cpte), Elisabetta (Cpte)
Wolf-Ferrari: Campiello (Cpte)
(DG) **419 257-2GH3** 'Cav' and 'Pag', etc
(OPRA) **ORR201** 19th Century Heroines-Yvonne Kenny

BENET, Josep (alto)
Keiser: Croesus (Cpte)

BENETTI, Margherita (sop)
Verdi: Rigoletto (exc)
(BUTT) **BMCD015** Pavarotti Collection - Duets and Scenes

BENI, Gimi (bass)
Puccini: Bohème (Cpte)
(DG) **439 151-2GMA** Mad about Puccini

BENINTENDE-NEGLIA, Tomaso (cond)
see Milan SO
Philh

BEŇAČKA, Stanislav (bass)
Puccini: Bohème (Cpte)
Suchoň: Whirlpool (Cpte)

BENNERT, Karl H. (bar)
Millöcker: Bettelstudent (Cpte)

BENNETT, Brenda (sop)
Sullivan: Mikado (Cpte)
(MMOI) **CDMOIR413** The Very Best of Gilbert & Sullivan

BENNETT, Donna (sop)
Henze: English Cat (Cpte)

BENNETT, Mavis (sop)
Sullivan: Gondoliers (Cpte)

BENNETT, Robert Russell (cond)
see RCA Victor Orch

BENNETT, Stephen (ten)
Meyerbeer: Huguenots (Cpte)

BENNETT, William (fl)
(ASV) **CDDCA652** Celebration for Flute & Orchestra
(BRAV) **BVA8634** Encores for Flute and Piano

BENNINGS, Olga (mez)
(EMI) **CZS7 67123-2** Wagner: Der Ring des Nibelungen

BENNINGSEN, Lilian (contr)
Janáček: Excursions of Mr Brouček (Cpte)
Mozart: Nozze di Figaro (Cpte)
Wagner: Meistersinger (Cpte)

BEN-NUN, Efrat (sop)
Monteverdi: Orfeo (Cpte)

BENOIT, Jean-Christoph (bar)
Bizet: Carmen (Cpte)
Delibes: Lakmé (Cpte)
Hahn: Ciboulette (exc)
Massenet: Werther (Cpte)
Offenbach: Contes d'Hoffmann (Cpte)
(EMI) **CDM5 65155-2** Chabrier—Une Education manquée; Mélodies
(EMI) **CZS5 68113-2** Vive Offenbach!
(EMI) **CZS5 68295-2** Messager/Lecocq—Operetta Highlights
(EMI) **CZS7 62877-2** Les inspirations insolites d'Erik Satie
(EMI) **CZS7 67869-2** J. Strauss II—Operetta Highlights
(EMI) **CZS7 67872-2** Lehár—Operettas (highlights in French)

BENSON, Catherine (sop)
Britten: Little Sweep (Cpte)

BENSON, Clifford (pf)
(BRAV) **BVA8634** Encores for Flute and Piano

BENSON, Lindsay (bar)
Bernstein: Candide (1988) (Cpte), West Side Story (Cpte)
Puccini: Rondine (Cpte)

BENTLEY, Anna (sop)
MacMillan: Búsqueda (Cpte)

BENZI, Roberto (cond)
see Bordeaux Aquitaine Orch
ECO
Lamoureux Concerts Orch
LSO
Paris Op Orch
RPO

BEN-ZVI, Eva (sop)
G. Fried: Diary of Anne Frank (Cpte)

BERBERIAN, Ara (bass)
Bizet: Carmen (Cpte)

BERBERIAN, Cathy (mez)
Monteverdi: Incoronazione di Poppea (Cpte), Orfeo (Cpte)
(RCA) **09026 62540-2** Cathy Berberian sings Berio & Weill
(WERG) **WER60054-50** Magnificathy—the many voices of Cathy Berberian

BERBIÉ, Guy (ten)
Bizet: Carmen (Cpte)

BERBIÉ, Jane (mez)
Auber: Fra Diavolo (Cpte)
Berlioz: Benvenuto Cellini (Cpte)
Bizet: Carmen (Cpte)
Boïeldieu: Dame blanche (Cpte)
Cavalli: Ormindo (Cpte)
Delibes: Lakmé (Cpte)
G. Charpentier: Louise (Cpte)
Martinů: Comedy on the Bridge (Cpte)
Massenet: Cendrillon (Cpte)
Mozart: Nozze di Figaro (exc)
Offenbach: Orphée aux enfers (Cpte)
Ravel: Enfant et les sortilèges (Cpte), Heure espagnole (Cpte)
Rossini: Turco in Italia (Cpte)
Roussel: Padmâvatî (Cpte)
Verdi: Otello (Cpte)
(CFP) **CD-CFP4602** Favourite Opera
(DECC) **433 066-2DWO** Your Hundred Best Opera Tunes III
(DECC) **433 067-2DWO** Your Hundred Best Opera Tunes IV
(DECC) **433 440-2DA** Golden Opera
(DECC) **436 315-2DA** Great Operatic Duets
(DECC) **440 947-2DH** Essential Opera II
(EMI) **CDC5 55016-2** Maria Callas - La Divina 2
(EMI) **CDM5 65155-2** Chabrier—Une Education manquée; Mélodies
(EMI) **CDM7 63182-2** The Incomparable Callas
(EMI) **CZS5 68113-2** Vive Offenbach!

BERDINI, Amedeo (sngr)
Mussorgsky: Khovanshchina (Cpte)

BEREZOWSKI, Nicolai (cond)
see RCA SO
Victor SO

BERG, Elisabeth (sop)
Mozart: Zauberflöte (Cpte)

BERG, Hans (bass)
Wagner: Meistersinger (Cpte)

BERG, Nathan (bass)
Purcell: Dido (Cpte), Dioclesian, Z627 (exc)

BERGAMINI, Lamberto (ten)
(PEAR) **GEMMCD9117** Graziella Pareto

BERGANZA, Teresa (mez)
Bizet: Carmen (Cpte)
Falla: Vida breve (Cpte)
Handel: Alcina (Cpte)
J. Strauss II: Fledermaus (Cpte)
Massenet: Don Quichotte (Cpte)
Mozart: Clemenza di Tito (Cpte), Don Giovanni (Cpte), Finta semplice (Cpte), Nozze di Figaro (Cpte)
Offenbach: Périchole (Cpte)
Penella: Gato Montés (Cpte)
Puccini: Madama Butterfly (Cpte)
Rossini: Barbiere di Siviglia (Cpte), Cenerentola (Cpte), Italiana in Algeri (Cpte)
(DECC) **421 899-2DA** Teresa Berganza - Mozart Arias
(DECC) **433 065-2DWO** Your Hundred Best Opera Tunes Volume II
(DECC) **433 067-2DWO** Your Hundred Best Opera Tunes IV
(DECC) **433 068-2DWO** Your Hundred Best Opera Tunes V
(DECC) **436 300-2DX** Opera Gala Sampler
(DECC) **436 462-2DM** Ten Top Mezzos
(DECC) **443 378-2DM** Ten Top Mezzos 2
(DECC) **443 762-2DF2** The Essential Mozart
(DG) **431 104-2GB** Great Voices - Plácido Domingo
(DG) **439 153-4GMA** Mad about Sopranos
(EMI) **CDM7 63111-2** José Carreras sings Opera & Operetta Arias
(EMI) **CDM7 64359-2** Gala de España
(EMI) **CZS5 68113-2** Vive Offenbach!
(ERAT) **4509-98498-2** Recital—Teresa Berganza
(MEMO) **HR4300/1** Great Voices—Sesto Bruscantini
(RCA) **RD61191** Gala Lirica
(RCA) **09026 61440-2** Opera's Greatest Moments
(RCA) **74321 25821-2** Café Classics—Music of Spain
(RCA) **09026 61204-4** From the Official Barcelona Games Ceremony
(RCA) **09026 61191-5** Gala Lirica
(RCA) **09026 61204-5** From the Official Barcelona Games Ceremony

BERGASA, Carlos (bar)
Puccini: Bohème (Cpte)

BERGASA, Carlos (sngr)
Penella: Gato Montés (Cpte)

BERGEN SYMPHONY ORCHESTRA
cond C. GARAGULY
(BLUE) **ABCD006** Jussi Björling Live - Holland 1939, Norway 1954
cond K. INGEBRETSEN
Bibalo: Gespenster (Cpte)

BERGER, Elsa (spkr)
Fauré: Prométhée (Cpte)

BERGER, Erna (sop)
Humperdinck: Hänsel und Gretel (Cpte)
Mozart: Don Giovanni (Cpte), Zauberflöte (Cpte)
Wagner: Tannhäuser (Cpte)
(ACAN) **43 268** Peter Anders sings German Opera Arias
(NIMB) **NI7848** Great Singers at the Berlin State Opera
(PREI) **89035** Erna Berger (1900-1990) - I
(PREI) **89057** Charles Kullmann (1903-1982)
(PREI) **89092** Erna Berger (1900-1990) - II
(PREI) **89212** Heinrich Schlusnus (1888-1952)
(RCA) **09026 61580-2(5)** RCA/Met 100 Singers, 100 Years (pt 5)
(SCHW) **314672** Vienna State Opera Live, Vol.17

BERGER, Rudolf (ten)
(SUPR) **11 2136-2(3)** Emmy Destinn—Complete Edition, Discs 5 to 8

BERGER-TUNA, Helmut (bass)
Einem: Dantons Tod (Cpte)
K. A. Hartmann: Simplicius Simplicissimus (Cpte)
Puccini: Fanciulla del West (Cpte)
Wagner: Meistersinger (Cpte)
Wolf: Corregidor (Cpte)

BERGGOLD, Christiane (mez)
B. Goldschmidt: Gewaltige Hahnrei (Cpte)

Gurlitt: Wozzeck (Cpte)
Schreker: Gezeichneten (Cpte)
Schulhoff: Plameny (Cpte)

BERGLUND, Joel (bar)
(EMI) **CHS7 69741-2(5)** Record of Singing, Vol.4—Scandinavian School
(PREI) **90232** Wagner—Der Fliegende Holländer
(SCHW) **314622** Vienna State Opera Live, Vol.12
(SCHW) **314692** Vienna State Opera Live, Vol.19

BERGLUND, Rut (contr)
Mozart: Zauberflöte (Cpte)
Wagner: Meistersinger (exc)

BERGMANN, Walter (hpd)
(EMI) **CDH5 65501-2** Alfred Deller - HMV Recordings, 1949-54
(VANG) **08.2003.72** Purcell—Celebrated Songs,Sacred Airs and Concert Pieces

BERGONZI, Carlo (ten)
Bellini: Norma (Cpte)
Cilea: Adriana Lecouvreur (Cpte)
Donizetti: Lucia di Lammermoor (Cpte)
Ponchielli: Gioconda (Cpte)
Puccini: Bohème (exc), Edgar (Cpte), Madama Butterfly (exc), Tosca (Cpte)
Verdi: Aida (exc), Attila (Cpte), Ballo in maschera (Cpte), Due Foscari (Cpte), Ernani (Cpte), Forza del destino (Cpte), Luisa Miller (Cpte), Macbeth (Cpte), Masnadieri (Cpte), Oberto (Cpte), Rigoletto (Cpte), Traviata (Cpte), Trovatore (Cpte)
(BELA) **450 005-2** Famous Tenor Arias
(BELA) **450 006-2** Famous Opera Duets
(BELA) **450 007-2** Puccini Favourites
(BELA) **450 133-2** Verdi Favourites
(CFP) **CD-CFP9013** Duets from Famous Operas
(DECC) **417 686-2DC** Puccini—Operatic Arias
(DECC) **430 481-2DX2** Renata Tebaldi sings Opera Arias
(DECC) **433 064-2DWO** Your Hundred Best Opera Tunes Volume I
(DECC) **433 066-2DWO** Your Hundred Best Opera Tunes III
(DECC) **433 067-2DWO** Your Hundred Best Opera Tunes IV
(DECC) **433 068-2DWO** Your Hundred Best Opera Tunes V
(DECC) **433 069-2DWO** Your Hundred Best Opera Tunes VI
(DECC) **433 221-2DWO** The World of Verdi
(DECC) **433 440-2DA** Golden Opera
(DECC) **433 442-2DA** Verdi—Famous Arias
(DECC) **433 623-2DSP** Famous Tenor Arias
(DECC) **433 636-2DSP** Puccini—Famous Arias
(DECC) **433 865-2DWO** The World of Puccini
(DECC) **436 300-2DX** Opera Gala Sampler
(DECC) **436 314-2DA** Great Tenor Arias
(DECC) **436 315-2DA** Great Operatic Duets
(DECC) **436 463-2DM** Ten Top Tenors
(DECC) **440 406-2DM** Giulietta Simionato
(DECC) **440 408-2DM** Renata Tebaldi
(DECC) **440 417-2DM** Carlo Bergonzi
(DECC) **443 379-2DM** Ten Top Tenors 2
(DECC) **444 555-2DF2** Essential Puccini
(DG) **419 257-2GH3** 'Cav' and 'Pag', etc
(EMI) **CDC7 54016-2** Tenorissimo!
(MCI) **MCCD099** Opera's Greatest Arias
(ORFE) **C028821A** Famous Operatic Duets
(PHIL) **432 486-2PM3** Verdi—31 Tenor Arias
(PHIL) **442 602-2PM** 3 x 3 Tenors
(RCA) **09026 61457-2** Shirley Verrett in Opera
(RCA) **09026 61580-2(7)** RCA/Met 100 Singers, 100 Years (pt 7)
(RCA) **09026 62689-2** The Voices of Living Stereo, Volume 1
(RCA) **09026 62699-2** Opera's Greatest Duets

BERGQUIST, Eleanor (sop)
Massenet: Cid (Cpte)

BERGSMA, Deanne (mute)
Offenbach: Contes d'Hoffmann (Cpte)

BERGSTRÖM, Anders (bar)
Lidholm: Dream Play (Cpte)

BERIO, Luciano (cond)
see Juilliard Ens
Musique Vivante Ens

BERKELEY-STEELE, Richard (ten)
Henze: English Cat (Cpte)
Mozart: Zauberflöte (Cpte)

BERKES, Kálmán (cond)
see Budapest Wind Ens

BERKMAN, Louis (bar)
Alman: King Ahaz (exc)

BERLIN BAROCK COMPAGNEY
(CAPR) **10 459** Music from Charlottenburg Castle

BERLIN CHAMBER ORCHESTRA
cond D. BARENBOIM
Mozart: Don Giovanni (exc)
cond M. POMMER
(CAPR) **10 113** Berlin Opera Composers

BERLIN CHARLOTTENBURG STÄDTISCHEN OPER ORCHESTRA
cond J. HEIDENREICH
(PEAR) **GEMMCD9451** Alexander Kipnis
cond A. VON ZEMLINSKY
(SCHW) **310037** Alexander von Zemlinsky conducts

BERLIN CITY OPERA ORCHESTRA
Verdi: Traviata (exc)
cond F. FRICSAY
(MYTO) **3MCD93381** Wagner—Die Walküre, etc
cond M. GURLITT
(PREI) **89102** Ludwig Hofmann (1895-1963)
cond W. LADWIG
(PREI) **89088** Walther Ludwig (1902-1981)
cond H. LÖWLEIN
(PREI) **90136** Martha Mödl sings
cond S. MEYROWITZ
(RELI) **CR921036** Joseph Schmidt—Opera and Operetta Arias
cond H.U. MÜLLER
(PREI) **89049** Margarete Teschemacher (1903-1959)
cond W.F. REUSS
(PREI) **89035** Erna Berger (1900-1990) - I
cond A. ROTHER
Wagner: Tristan und Isolde (exc)
(PREI) **90136** Martha Mödl sings
cond H. SCHMIDT-ISSERSTEDT
(PREI) **89092** Erna Berger (1900-1990) - II
cond F. WEISSMANN
(EMI) **CHS7 64673-2** Joseph Schmidt - Complete EMI Recordings Volume 1
cond A. VON ZEMLINSKY
(PREI) **89057** Charles Kullmann (1903-1982)
(PREI) **89071** Gerhard Hüsch (1901-1984) - II
cond F. ZWEIG
(PEAR) **GEMMCD9409** Lotte Lehmenn—Vol.1
(PEAR) **GEMMCD9410** Lotte Lehmann—Vol.2
(PREI) **89057** Charles Kullmann (1903-1982)
(PREI) **89092** Erna Berger (1900-1990) - II

BERLIN COURT OPERA CHORUS
cond A. PILZ
(SUPR) **11 2136-2(3)** Emmy Destinn—Complete Edition, Discs 5 to 8
cond B. SEIDLER-WINKLER
(SUPR) **11 2136-2(3)** Emmy Destinn—Complete Edition, Discs 5 to 8

BERLIN DEUTSCHE OPER CHORUS
cond G. ALBRECHT
Spontini: Olimpie (Cpte)
cond K. BÖHM
Berg: Wozzeck (Cpte)
Mozart: Nozze di Figaro (exc)
cond C. VON DOHNÁNYI
Henze: Junge Lord (Cpte)
cond A. GRÜBER
(TELD) **4509-95512-2** Mozart/Weber/Wagner—Opera Arias
cond H. HOLLREISER
(TESS) **049-2** R. Strauss/Wagner—Opera Scenes
cond E. JOCHUM
Wagner: Meistersinger (Cpte)
(BELA) **450 121-2** Plácido Domingo
(DG) **431 104-2GB** Great Voices - Plácido Domingo
cond H. VON KARAJAN
Beethoven: Fidelio (Cpte)
Debussy: Pelléas et Mélisande (Cpte)
Lehár: Lustige Witwe (exc)
Mozart: Don Giovanni (Cpte), Zauberflöte (exc)
Puccini: Bohème (Cpte), Tosca (exc)
Verdi: Don Carlo (Cpte), Otello (Cpte), Trovatore (Cpte)
Wagner: Götterdämmerung (Cpte), Lohengrin (exc), Parsifal (Cpte), Tristan und Isolde (Cpte)
(CFP) **CD-CFP4656** Herbert von Karajan conducts Opera
(DG) **435 211-2GX15** Wagner—Der Ring des Nibelungen
(DG) **435 712-2GX2** Lehár—The Merry Widow. Suppé—Overtures
(EMI) **CDC7 54016-2** Tenorissimo!
(EMI) **CDM7 63111-2** José Carreras sings Opera & Operetta Arias
(EMI) **CDM7 64334-2** Wagner—Orchestral Works
(EMI) **CZS5 68559-2** Italian Opera Choruses
cond J. KEILBERTH
Weber: Freischütz (Cpte)
cond R. KEMPE
Wagner: Meistersinger (exc)
(TEST) **SBT1035** Rudolf Kempe conducts Wagner
cond H. KNAPPERTSBUSCH
Wagner: Parsifal (exc)
cond F. KONWITSCHNY
Wagner: Fliegende Holländer (Cpte)
(EMI) **CMS5 65212-2** Wagner—Les introuvables du Ring
cond W. LUTZE
(TELD) **4509-95512-2** Mozart/Weber/Wagner—Opera Arias
cond L. MAAZEL
Bizet: Carmen (Cpte)
Verdi: Traviata (exc)
cond L. VON MATAČIĆ
Weber: Freischütz (Cpte)
cond R. PETERS
(DG) **435 748-2GDO2** Arias and Waltzes - Rita Streich
cond A. ROTHER
Humperdinck: Hänsel und Gretel (Cpte)
cond N. SANTI
(ERAT) **2292-45797-2** The Ultimate Opera Collection
cond W. SCHMIDT-BOELCKE
Raymond: Maske in Blau (exc)
cond W. SCHÜCHTER
(EMI) **CDH5 65201-2** Leonie Rysanek - Operatic Recital
(EMI) **CHS7 69741-2(4)** Record of Singing, Vol.4—German School
(EMI) **CMS5 65621-2** Fischer-Dieskau - The Opera Singer
cond G. SINOPOLI
Verdi: Macbeth (Cpte), Nabucco (exc)
(BELA) **450 052-2** Great Opera Choruses
(DG) **415 283-2GH** Opera Choruses
(DG) **445 525-2GMA** Domingo Favourites
(DG) **415 283-5GH** Opera Choruses
cond G. SOLTI
Verdi: Falstaff (Cpte)
cond R. STOLZ
Lehár: Zarewitsch (exc)

BERLIN DEUTSCHE OPER ORCHESTRA
R. Strauss: Salome (Cpte)
Verdi: Macbeth (Cpte)
cond K. BÖHM
Berg: Lulu (Cpte), Wozzeck (Cpte)
Mozart: Nozze di Figaro (Cpte)
(DG) **447 364-2GDB2** Great Opera Overtures
cond C. VON DOHNÁNYI
Henze: Junge Lord (Cpte)
cond O. GERDES
(DG) **439 445-2GCL** Wagner—Overtures and Preludes
(DG) **439 687-2GX2** Wagner—Overtures and Preludes
cond A. GRÜBER
(ACAN) **43 268** Peter Anders sings German Opera Arias
(TELD) **4509-95512-2** Mozart/Weber/Wagner—Opera Arias
cond H. HOLLREISER
(EURO) **GD69019** Hermann Prey—Recital
(TESS) **049-2** R. Strauss/Wagner—Opera Scenes
cond P. HÜHN
(MMOI) **CDMOIR419** Vienna Nights - Golden Age of Operetta
cond E. JOCHUM
Wagner: Meistersinger (Cpte)
(BELA) **450 121-2** Plácido Domingo
(DG) **431 104-2GB** Great Voices - Plácido Domingo
(DG) **439 687-2GX2** Wagner—Overtures and Preludes
cond H. KNAPPERTSBUSCH
Wagner: Parsifal (exc)
cond F. KONWITSCHNY
Wagner: Fliegende Holländer (Cpte)
(EMI) **CMS5 65212-2** Wagner—Les introuvables du Ring
cond R. KRAUS
(CFP) **CD-CFP4616** Ave Maria
cond F. LEITNER
(DG) **447 352-2GDB2** A Portrait of Gundula Janowitz
cond W. LUTZE
(MMOI) **CDMOIR419** Vienna Nights - Golden Age of Operetta
(PREI) **90083** Maria Reining
(TELD) **4509-95512-2** Mozart/Weber/Wagner—Opera Arias
cond L. MAAZEL
Bizet: Carmen (Cpte)
Verdi: Traviata (Cpte)
(DECC) **433 069-2DWO** Your Hundred Best Opera Tunes VI
(DECC) **433 442-2DA** Verdi—Famous Arias
(DECC) **436 463-2DM** Ten Top Tenors
(DECC) **436 464-2DM** Ten Top Baritones & Basses
(DECC) **440 409-2DM** Dietrich Fischer-Dieskau
cond L. VON MATAČIĆ
Weber: Freischütz (Cpte)
cond R. PETERS
(DG) **435 748-2GDO2** Arias and Waltzes - Rita Streich
cond H-M. RABENSTEIN
(EURO) **GD69019** Hermann Prey—Recital
cond A. ROTHER
(EMI) **CHS7 69741-2(4)** Record of Singing, Vol.4—German School
(PREI) **90168** Wagner—Die Meistersinger, Act 2, etc
(PREI) **90200** Hans Hotter in Early Recordings
cond N. SANTI
(ERAT) **4509-91715-2** The Ultimate Opera Collection 2
(TELD) **4509-96231-2** Gardening Classics
cond H. SCHMIDT-ISSERSTEDT
(PREI) **90078** Hilde Konetzni
(TELD) **4509-95512-2** Mozart/Weber/Wagner—Opera Arias
cond N. SCHULTZE
(MMOI) **CDMOIR419** Vienna Nights - Golden Age of Operetta
cond W. SCHÜCHTER
(EMI) **CHS7 69741-2(4)** Record of Singing, Vol.4—German School
cond J. SCHÜLER
(TELD) **4509-95512-2** Mozart/Weber/Wagner—Opera Arias
cond G. SINOPOLI
R. Strauss: Salome (Cpte)
Verdi: Macbeth (Cpte), Nabucco (exc)
(BELA) **450 052-2** Great Opera Choruses
(DG) **415 283-2GH** Opera Choruses
(DG) **445 525-2GMA** Domingo Favourites
(DG) **415 283-5GH** Opera Choruses
cond G. STEEGER
(PREI) **89082** Margarete Klose (1902-1968)
cond H. STEINKOPF
(PREI) **90168** Wagner—Die Meistersinger, Act 2, etc

cond C. THIELEMANN
(EMI) **CDC7 54776-2** René Kollo sings Wagner and Strauss

BERLIN DEUTSCHES SYMPHONY ORCHESTRA
cond G. ALBRECHT
Gurlitt: Wozzeck (Cpte)
cond J. MAUCERI
Schulhoff: Plameny (Cpte)
cond L. ZAGROSEK
B. Goldschmidt: Gewaltige Hahnrei (Cpte)
Schreker: Gezeichneten (Cpte)
(SONY) **S2K66836** Goldschmidt—Beatrice Cenci, etc

BERLIN ENSEMBLE
(ORFE) **C126901A** Salonmusik

BERLIN FFB ORCHESTRA
cond W. SCHMIDT-BOELCKE
(EMI) **CDM7 69475-2** Rudolf Schock sings Operetta and Songs

BERLIN KÜNSTLERTHEATER ORCHESTRA
cond E. HAUKE
(EMI) **CDH7 69787-2** Richard Tauber sings Operetta Arias
(MMOI) **CDMOIR425** Three Tenors, Volume 2
(NIMB) **NI7833** Schöne & Tauber in Operetta

BERLIN MOTET CHOIR
cond F. FRICSAY
Gluck: Orfeo ed Euridice (Cpte)

BERLIN PHILHARMONIC CELLISTS (12)
(TELD) **4509-92014-2** Sensual Classics II

BERLIN PHILHARMONIC ORCHESTRA
Verdi: Don Carlo (Cpte)
(DG) **445 400-2GDO10** Ferenc Fricsay - A Portrait
(PHIL) **434 109-2PH** Wagner for Brass
(RELI) **CR921036** Joseph Schmidt—Opera and Operetta Arias
(SONY) **SLV46401(SONY)** New Year's Eve Concert 1983
(SONY) **SLV46402(SONY)** New Year's Eve Concert 1985
cond C. ABBADO
Mussorgsky: Boris Godunov (Cpte)
Rossini: Viaggio a Reims (Cpte)
(DG) **435 617-2GH** Beethoven in Berlin—New Year's Eve Concert
(DG) **439 768-2GH** Wagner—Gala - New Year's Eve Concert 1993
(DG) **445 238-2GH** Mussorgsky—Orchestral and Choral Works
(DG) **072 124-3GH** Beethoven in Berlin - New Year's Concert
(SONY) **SK52565** New Year's Eve Concert 1992
(SONY) **SK53978** Prometheus
(SONY) **SLV46405(SONY)** Music for Europe
cond D. BARENBOIM
Mozart: Così fan tutte (exc), Don Giovanni (Cpte), Nozze di Figaro (exc)
Wagner: Parsifal (Cpte), Tristan und Isolde (Cpte)
(ERAT) **4509-91715-2** The Ultimate Opera Collection 2
(SONY) **SHV498602** Das Konzert—November 1989
cond T. BEECHAM
Mozart: Zauberflöte (Cpte)
(DUTT) **CDLX7009** Beecham conducts Favourite Overtures, Volume 2
(MMOI) **CDMOIR406** Mozart—Historical Recordings
(MMOI) **CDMOIR408** Great Sopranos
(PEAR) **GEMMCD9122** 20 Great Basses sing Great Arias
(PREI) **89025** Tiana Lemnitz (b. 1897)
(PREI) **89092** Erna Berger (1900-1990) - II
(PREI) **89211** Helge Roswaenge (1897-1972) - III
cond K. BÖHM
Mozart: Zauberflöte (exc)
(BELA) **450 139-2** An Invitation to the Dance
(DG) **431 110-2GB** Great Voices - Fritz Wunderlich
(DG) **435 145-2GX5(1)** Fritz Wunderlich—Opera Arias, Lieder, etc (part 1)
(DG) **447 364-2GDB2** Great Opera Overtures
cond A. EREDE
(EMI) **CMS5 65621-2** Fischer-Dieskau - The Opera Singer
(TEST) **SBT1036** Lisa Della Casa sings Richard Strauss
cond F. FRICSAY
Beethoven: Leonore (exc)
cond W. FURTWÄNGLER
Wagner: Tristan und Isolde (exc)
(ACAN) **43 121** Wagner: Orchestral Works
(BIDD) **WHL006/7** Furtwängler—Pre-war HMV Recordings
(EMI) **CHS5 65513-2** Furtwängler conducts Brahms & Beethoven
(EMI) **CHS7 64935-2** Wagner—Opera Excerpts
(KOCH) **37059-2** Furtwängler—The Early Recordings
(KOCH) **37073-2** Furtwängler—Early Recordings 1926-1937
(MUSI) **MACD-826** Furtwängler conducts World War II Concerts
(SYMP) **SYMCD1043** Furtwängler Conducts
(TAHR) **FURT1004/7** Furtwängler conducts the Berlin Philharmonic
(TELD) **9031-76435-2** Furtwängler conducts Orchestral Works
(TELD) **4509-95038-6(TELD)** The Art of Conducting—Great Conductors of the Past
cond J. HORENSTEIN
(KOCH) **37054-2** Horenstein and the Berlin Philharmonic
cond JAMES LEVINE
(DG) **429 724-2GH2** Berlioz—Requiem, etc
cond E. JOCHUM
Wagner: Tannhäuser (exc)
(DG) **413 145-2GW2** Beethoven—Orchestral Works
(DG) **437 677-2GDO2** Irmgard Seefried - Opera Recital
cond H. VON KARAJAN
Beethoven: Fidelio (exc), Leonore (exc)
Bizet: Carmen (Cpte)
Borodin: Prince Igor (exc)
Debussy: Pelléas et Mélisande (Cpte)
Lehár: Lustige Witwe (exc)
Mozart: Don Giovanni (Cpte), Zauberflöte (exc)
Puccini: Bohème (Cpte), Tosca (Cpte)
Smetana: Bartered Bride (exc)
Tchaikovsky: Eugene Onegin (exc)
Verdi: Don Carlo (Cpte), Otello (exc), Trovatore (Cpte)
Wagner: Fliegende Holländer (exc), Götterdämmerung (Cpte), Lohengrin (exc), Parsifal (Cpte), Rheingold (Cpte), Siegfried (Cpte), Tristan und Isolde (Cpte), Walküre (Cpte)
(BELA) **450 137-2** Meditation
(CFP) **CD-CFP4656** Herbert von Karajan conducts Opera
(DECC) **417 011-2DH2** Pavarotti's Greatest Hits
(DECC) **421 896-2DA** Puccini—Great Operatic Duets
(DECC) **425 681-2DM2** Tutto Pavarotti
(DECC) **425 850-2DWO** Your Hundred Best Tunes, Vol.4
(DECC) **430 470-2DH** Essential Pavarotti II
(DECC) **433 064-2DWO** Your Hundred Best Opera Tunes Volume I
(DECC) **433 066-2DWO** Your Hundred Best Opera Tunes III
(DECC) **433 068-2DWO** Your Hundred Best Opera Tunes V
(DECC) **433 437-2DA** Pavarotti—King of the High Cs
(DECC) **433 439-2DA** Great Love Duets
(DECC) **433 822-2DH** Essential Opera
(DECC) **433 865-2DWO** The World of Puccini
(DECC) **436 300-2DX** Opera Gala Sampler
(DECC) **436 317-2DA** Puccini—Famous Arias
(DECC) **436 461-2DM** Ten Top Sopranos
(DECC) **436 463-2DM** Ten Top Tenors
(DECC) **440 412-2DM** Mirella Freni
(DECC) **440 947-2DH** Essential Opera II
(DECC) **400 053-4DH** World's Best Loved Tenor Arias
(DG) **400 044-2GH** Offenbach: Overtures
(DG) **413 309-2GH** Baroque Favourites
(DG) **413 432-2GW2** J. Strauss II—Overtures, Polkas & Waltzes
(DG) **415 276-2GH** Beethoven—Orchestral Works
(DG) **415 853-2GGA** R. Strauss: Orchestral Works
(DG) **415 855-2GGA** Tchaikovsky: Orchestral works
(DG) **419 051-2GGA** Beethoven: Orchestral Works
(DG) **419 070-2GGA** Weber: Orchestral Works
(DG) **419 257-2GH3** 'Cav' and 'Pag', etc
(DG) **419 622-2GH** Verdi: Overtures & Preludes
(DG) **427 256-2GGA2** Beethoven—Overtures
(DG) **429 089-2GSE6** Beethoven: Symphonies, etc
(DG) **429 164-2GR** Rossini & Verdi: Overtures & Preludes
(DG) **429 168-2GR** Wagner: Excerpts from Der Ring
(DG) **431 160-2GR** Bizet & Offenbach—Orchestral Works
(DG) **435 211-2GX15** Wagner—Der Ring des Nibelungen
(DG) **435 712-2GX2** Lehár—The Merry Widow. Suppé—Overtures
(DG) **437 404-2GX2** Famous Ballet Works
(DG) **439 005-2GHS** Beethoven—Orchestral Works
(DG) **439 200-2GH6** Beethoven—Symphonies and Overtures
(DG) **439 415-2GCL** Rossini—Overtures
(DG) **439 423-2GCL** Wagner—Der Ring des Nibelungen (highlights)
(DG) **439 687-2GX2** Wagner—Overtures and Preludes
(DG) **439 972-2GGA2** Verdi—Overtures & Preludes
(DG) **447 364-2GDB2** Great Opera Overtures
(DG) **447 441-2GOR** R. Strauss—Tone Poems
(DG) **439 153-4GMA** Mad about Sopranos
(DG) **072 196-3GH** Karajan—The Best on Video
(DG) **439 005-5GHS** Beethoven—Orchestral Works
(EMI) **CDC7 54016-2** Tenorissimo!
(EMI) **CDC7 54524-2** The José Carreras Album
(EMI) **CDM7 63111-2** José Carreras sings Opera & Operetta Arias
(EMI) **CDM7 64334-2** Wagner—Orchestral Works
(EMI) **CDM7 64629-2** Popular Orchestral Works
(EMI) **CDM7 69549-2** Ruggero Raimondi: Italian Opera Arias
(EMI) **CZS5 68559-2** Italian Opera Choruses
cond J. KEILBERTH
Weber: Freischütz (Cpte)
cond R. KEMPE
Wagner: Meistersinger (Cpte)
(EMI) **CES5 68518-2** Beethoven—Orchestral Works
(EMI) **CHS5 65058-2** The Great German Tradition
(TEST) **SBT1035** Rudolf Kempe conducts Wagner
cond E. KLEIBER
(ARCI) **ARC102** Kleiber conducts Waltzes and Overtures
(BIDD) **WHL002** E. Kleiber conducts Viennese Music
(TELD) **4509-95513-2** Viennese Dance Music
cond R. KUBELÍK
Beethoven: Leonore (exc)
(DG) **437 395-2GX2** Schumann—Complete Symphonies, etc
(DG) **439 445-2GCL** Wagner—Overtures and Preludes
(DG) **439 687-2GX2** Wagner—Overtures and Preludes
(DG) **447 364-2GDB2** Great Opera Overtures
cond L. MAAZEL
(DG) **435 594-2GGA** Rachmaninov—Orchestral Works
(TELA) **CD80154** Wagner: The 'Ring' without Words
cond S. MEYROWITZ
(RELI) **CR921036** Joseph Schmidt—Opera and Operetta Arias
cond E. ORTHMANN
(PREI) **89209** Helge Roswaenge (1897-1972) - II
cond S. OZAWA
(PHIL) **426 271-5PH** Wagner: Overtures & Preludes
cond V. DE SABATA
(KOCH) **37126-2** Victor de Sabata conducts the BPO
cond F.A. SCHMIDT
(PREI) **89209** Helge Roswaenge (1897-1972) - II
cond W. SCHÜCHTER
(EMI) **CDH5 65201-2** Leonie Rysanek - Operatic Recital
(EMI) **CMS5 65621-2** Fischer-Dieskau - The Opera Singer
cond B. SEIDLER-WINKLER
(PREI) **89025** Tiana Lemnitz (b. 1897)
(PREI) **89092** Erna Berger (1900-1990) - II
cond R. STRAUSS
(KOCH) **37119-2** Richard Strauss Conducts
cond K. TENNSTEDT
(EMI) **CDC2 53045-2** Heavy Classix
(EMI) **CZS5 68616-2** Wagner—Orchestral Works from Operas
(EMIL) **CDZ101** Best Loved Classics 2
(EMIL) **CDZ104** Best Loved Classics 5
cond H. VON KARAJAN
(DG) **445 282-2GH** Adagio Karajan
cond A. VON ZEMLINSKY
(SCHW) **310037** Alexander von Zemlinsky conducts

BERLIN PHILHARMONIC WIND QUINTET
cond H. VON KARAJAN
(DG) **439 346-2GX2** Prussian and Austrian Marches

BERLIN RADIO CHAMBER CHOIR
cond G. ALBRECHT
Henze: Bassariden (Cpte)
Hindemith: Cardillac (Cpte)

BERLIN RADIO CHILDREN'S CHOIR
cond G. ALBRECHT
Gurlitt: Wozzeck (Cpte)
cond B. KLEE
Lortzing: Wildschütz (Cpte)

BERLIN RADIO CHORUS
cond C. ABBADO
Mussorgsky: Boris Godunov (Cpte)
Rossini: Viaggio a Reims (Cpte)
cond G. ALBRECHT
Schreker: Ferne Klang (Cpte)
cond HANS HAENCHEN
Gluck: Orfeo ed Euridice (Cpte)
cond M. JANOWSKI
Weber: Freischütz (Cpte)
cond H. KEGEL
Wagner: Parsifal (Cpte)
cond B. KLEE
Lortzing: Wildschütz (Cpte)
(PHIL) **422 525-2PME2** The Complete Mozart Edition Vol 25
cond J. MAUCERI
Korngold: Wunder der Heliane (Cpte)
cond A. ROTHER
(PREI) **90168** Wagner—Die Meistersinger, Act 2, etc
cond L. ZAGROSEK
B. Goldschmidt: Gewaltige Hahnrei (Cpte)
Schreker: Gezeichneten (Cpte)
(SONY) **S2K66836** Goldschmidt—Beatrice Cenci, etc

BERLIN RADIO ENSEMBLE
cond J. MAUCERI
(DECC) **425 204-2DNL** Ute Lemper sings Kurt Weill

BERLIN RADIO MEN'S CHORUS
cond K. MASUR
Beethoven: Fidelio (Cpte)

BERLIN RADIO ORCHESTRA
cond M. JANOWSKI
Weber: Freischütz (Cpte)
cond C. KRAUSS
(PREI) **89092** Erna Berger (1900-1990) - II
cond J. MÜLLER
(PREI) **89054** Miliza Korjus (1912-1980)
cond A. ROTHER
(PREI) **90168** Wagner—Die Meistersinger, Act 2, etc

BERLIN RADIO SYMPHONY ORCHESTRA
cond G. ALBRECHT
Busoni: Arlecchino (Cpte), Turandot (Cpte)
Henze: Bassariden (Cpte)
Hindemith: Cardillac (Cpte), Mörder, Hoffnung der Frauen (Cpte), Nusch-Nuschi (Cpte), Sancta Susanna (Cpte)
Schreker: Ferne Klang (Cpte)
Spontini: Olimpie (Cpte)

(PREI) **89217** Alfred Piccaver—The Complete Electric Recordings 1928-1930
cond R. HEGER
Wagner: Lohengrin (Cpte)
(PREI) **90213** Max Lorenz sings Wagner
cond J. HEIDENREICH
(PREI) **89005** Franz Völker (1899-1965) - I
(PREI) **89212** Heinrich Schlusnus (1888-1952)
cond P. HÜHN
(MMOI) **CDMOIR419** Vienna Nights - Golden Age of Operetta
cond R. JÄGER
(MSCM) **MM30285** Great Wagnerian Singers, Vol.2
(PEAR) **GEMMCD9410** Lotte Lehmann—Vol.2
cond O. KLEMPERER
(KOCH) **37053-2** The Young Otto Klemperer
(SCHW) **311162** World Famous Conductors from Silesia
(SYMP) **SYMCD1042** Otto Klemperer and the Kroll Years
cond F. KONWITSCHNY
Wagner: Tannhäuser (Cpte)
cond C. KRAUSS
(NIMB) **NI7848** Great Singers at the Berlin State Opera
(PREI) **89035** Erna Berger (1900-1990) - I
(PREI) **89096** Alexander Svéd (1906-1979)
(PREI) **89212** Heinrich Schlusnus (1888-1952)
cond E. KÜNNEKE
(PREI) **89209** Helge Roswaenge (1897-1972) - II
cond F. LEHÁR
(EMI) **CDM7 69476-2** Richard Tauber - A Portrait
(PEAR) **GEMMCD9310** Franz Lehár conducts Richard Tauber
cond H. LÖWLEIN
(PREI) **90103** Helge Roswaenge Recital (1959)
cond A. MELICHAR
(MMOI) **CDMOIR419** Vienna Nights - Golden Age of Operetta
(MMOI) **CDMOIR422** Great Voices in Tchaikovsky
(MSCM) **MM30283** Great Wagnerian Singers, Vol.1
(PEAR) **GEMMCD9383** Julius Patzak—Opera & Operetta Recital
(PREI) **89005** Franz Völker (1899-1965) - I
(PREI) **89006** Heinrich Schlusnus (1888-1952) - I
(PREI) **89035** Erna Berger (1900-1990) - I
(PREI) **89209** Helge Roswaenge (1897-1972) - II
(PREI) **89212** Heinrich Schlusnus (1888-1952)
cond S. MEYROWITZ
(PREI) **89209** Helge Roswaenge (1897-1972) - II
cond E. MÖRIKE
(PEAR) **GEMMCD9122** 20 Great Basses sing Great Arias
(PREI) **89083** Emanuel List (1890-1967)
cond K. MUCK
Wagner: Parsifal (exc)
(OPAL) **OPALCDS9843** Karl Muck conducts Wagner
(PEAR) **GEMMCDS9137** Wagner—Der Ring des Nibelungen
cond H.U. MÜLLER
(EMI) **CMS7 64008-2(1)** Wagner Singing on Record (pt 1)
(MSCM) **MM30283** Great Wagnerian Singers, Vol.1
(NIMB) **NI7848** Great Singers at the Berlin State Opera
(PEAR) **GEMMCDS9121** Wagner—Die Meistersinger, Act 3, etc
(PREI) **89024** Marcel Wittrisch (1901-1955)
(PREI) **89071** Gerhard Hüsch (1901-1984) - II
(PREI) **89077** Torsten Ralf (1901-1954)
cond E. NICK
(DANT) **LYS001** La Colorature des Colorarures - Volume 1
(PREI) **89054** Miliza Korjus (1912-1980)
cond E. ORTHMANN
(BEUL) **2PD4** 78 Classics - Volume Two
(CLUB) **CL99-020** Maria Ivogün & Lotte Schöne—Opera Recital
(MMOI) **CDMOIR405** Great Tenors
(NIMB) **NI7848** Great Singers at the Berlin State Opera
(NIMB) **NI7851** Legendary Voices
(PEAR) **GEMMCDS9926(1)** Covent Garden on Record—Vol.4 (pt 1)
(PEAR) **GEMMCD9451** Alexander Kipnis
(PREI) **89019** Alexander Kipnis (1891-1978)
(PREI) **89024** Marcel Wittrisch (1901-1955)
(PREI) **89057** Charles Kullmann (1903-1982)
cond H. PFITZNER
(EMI) **CDC5 55225-2** Pfitzner plays and conducts Pfitzner
cond J. PRÜWER
(MSCM) **MM30283** Great Wagnerian Singers, Vol.1
(PEAR) **GEMMCD9383** Julius Patzak—Opera & Operetta Recital
(PREI) **89005** Franz Völker (1899-1965) - I
(PREI) **89046** Rosette Anday (1903-1977)
(PREI) **89212** Heinrich Schlusnus (1888-1952)
(PREI) **89217** Alfred Piccaver—The Complete Electric Recordings 1928-1930
cond A. ROTHER
(EMI) **CHS7 69741-2(4)** Record of Singing, Vol.4—German School
(PREI) **89212** Heinrich Schlusnus (1888-1952)
(PREI) **90022** Anton Dermota
cond C. SCHMALSTICH
(CLAR) **CDGSE78-50-52** Three Tenors
(EMI) **CDM7 69478-2** A Portrait of Joseph Schmidt
(EMI) **CHS7 64673-2** Joseph Schmidt - Complete EMI Recordings Volume 1

(EMI) **CMS7 64008-2(1)** Wagner Singing on Record (pt 1)
(EMI) **CMS7 64008-2(2)** Wagner Singing on Record (pt 2)
(MMOI) **CDMOIR405** Great Tenors
(MMOI) **CDMOIR406** Mozart—Historical Recordings
(MMOI) **CDMOIR419** Vienna Nights - Golden Age of Operetta
(MSCM) **MM30283** Great Wagnerian Singers, Vol.1
(NIMB) **NI7848** Great Singers at the Berlin State Opera
(PEAR) **GEMMCDS9926(2)** Covent Garden on Record—Vol.4 (pt 2)
(PEAR) **GEMMCD9093** The Artistry of Richard Crooks, Volume 1
(PREI) **89019** Alexander Kipnis (1891-1978)
(PREI) **89024** Marcel Wittrisch (1901-1955)
(PREI) **89035** Erna Berger (1900-1990) - I
(PREI) **89044** Dusolina Giannini (1902-1986)
(PREI) **89053** Max Lorenz (1901-1975)
(PREI) **89057** Charles Kullmann (1903-1982)
cond F.A. SCHMIDT
(PREI) **89025** Tiana Lemnitz (b. 1897)
(PREI) **89082** Margarete Klose (1902-1968)
(PREI) **89102** Ludwig Hofmann (1895-1963)
(PREI) **89209** Helge Roswaenge (1897-1972) - II
(PREI) **90232** Wagner—Der Fliegende Holländer
cond H. SCHMIDT-ISSERSTEDT
(MMOI) **CDMOIR406** Mozart—Historical Recordings
(MSCM) **MM30283** Great Wagnerian Singers, Vol.1
(PREI) **90078** Hilde Konetzni
cond F. SCHÖNBAUMSFELD
(DANT) **LYS001** La Colorature des Colorarures - Volume 1
(PREI) **89054** Miliza Korjus (1912-1980)
cond J. SCHÜLER
Wagner: Rienzi (exc)
(ACAN) **43 268** Peter Anders sings German Opera Arias
(EMI) **CMS7 64008-2(1)** Wagner Singing on Record (pt 1)
(PREI) **89006** Heinrich Schlusnus (1888-1952) - I
(PREI) **89025** Tiana Lemnitz (b. 1897)
(PREI) **89212** Heinrich Schlusnus (1888-1952)
(PREI) **90213** Max Lorenz sings Wagner
cond W. SCHÜTZE
(PREI) **89035** Erna Berger (1900-1990) - I
cond B. SEIDLER-WINKLER
(DANT) **LYS001** La Colorature des Colorarures - Volume 1
(EMI) **CHS7 69741-2(4)** Record of Singing, Vol.4—German School
(EMI) **CMS7 64008-2(1)** Wagner Singing on Record (pt 1)
(EMI) **CMS7 64008-2(2)** Wagner Singing on Record (pt 2)
(MMOI) **CDMOIR405** Great Tenors
(NIMB) **NI7817** Beniamino Gigli—Vol.2
(NIMB) **NI7848** Great Singers at the Berlin State Opera
(PEAR) **GEMMCDS9176** Gigli - Arias, Duets & Songs, 1926-1937
(PEAR) **GEMMCDS9926(2)** Covent Garden on Record—Vol.4 (pt 2)
(PEAR) **GEMMCD9394** Helge Roswaenge—Operatic Recital
(PREI) **89018** Helge Rosvaenge (1897-1972)
(PREI) **89024** Marcel Wittrisch (1901-1955)
(PREI) **89025** Tiana Lemnitz (b. 1897)
(PREI) **89049** Margarete Teschemacher (1903-1959)
(PREI) **89054** Miliza Korjus (1912-1980)
(PREI) **89076** Josef Herrmann (1903-1955)
(PREI) **89077** Torsten Ralf (1901-1954)
(PREI) **89082** Margarete Klose (1902-1968)
(PREI) **89088** Walther Ludwig (1902-1981)
(PREI) **89209** Helge Roswaenge (1897-1972) - II
(PREI) **89211** Helge Roswaenge (1897-1972) - III
(PREI) **90213** Max Lorenz sings Wagner
(TEST) **SBT1005** Ten Top Tenors
cond G. STEEGER
(PREI) **89006** Heinrich Schlusnus (1888-1952) - I
(PREI) **89088** Walther Ludwig (1902-1981)
(PREI) **89212** Heinrich Schlusnus (1888-1952)
cond R. STRAUSS
(KOCH) **37119-2** Richard Strauss Conducts
cond G. SZELL
(EMI) **CDH7 64029-2** Richard Tauber - Opera Recital
(NIMB) **NI7830** Richard Tauber in Opera
(PREI) **89302** The Young Lotte Lehmann
cond E. VIEBIG
(EMI) **CMS7 64008-2(2)** Wagner Singing on Record (pt 2)
cond H. WEIGERT
(MSCM) **MM30283** Great Wagnerian Singers, Vol.1
(NIMB) **NI7833** Schöne & Tauber in Operetta
(NIMB) **NI7864** More Legendary Voices
(PEAR) **GEMMCD9383** Julius Patzak—Opera & Operetta Recital
(PEAR) **GEMMCD9410** Lotte Lehmann—Vol.2
(PREI) **89005** Franz Völker (1899-1965) - I
(PREI) **89209** Helge Roswaenge (1897-1972) - II
(PREI) **89212** Heinrich Schlusnus (1888-1952)
(PREI) **89302** The Young Lotte Lehmann
cond F. WEISSMANN
(ARLE) **ARL23/5** Rimsky-Korsakov—Sadko
(EMI) **CDM7 69478-2** A Portrait of Joseph Schmidt
(EMI) **CHS7 64673-2** Joseph Schmidt - Complete EMI Recordings Volume 1
(EMI) **CMS7 64008-2(2)** Wagner Singing on Record (pt 2)

(MMOI) **CDMOIR408** Great Sopranos
(MMOI) **CDMOIR412** Great Voices of the Century Sing Puccini
(MSCM) **MM30283** Great Wagnerian Singers, Vol.1
(NIMB) **NI7867** Legendary Baritones
(PEAR) **GEMMCDS9121** Wagner—Die Meistersinger, Act 3, etc
(PEAR) **GEMMCDS9925(2)** Covent Garden on Record—Vol.3 (pt 2)
(PEAR) **GEMMCD9394** Helge Roswaenge—Operatic Recital
(PEAR) **GEMMCD9409** Lotte Lehmenn—Vol.1
(PEAR) **GEMMCD9410** Lotte Lehmann—Vol.2
(PREI) **89028** Ivar Andresen (1896-1940)
(PREI) **89029** Meta Seinemeyer (1895-1929)
(PREI) **89068** Lauritz Melchior (1890-1973) - II
(PREI) **89083** Emanuel List (1890-1967)
(PREI) **89084** Kerstin Thorborg (1896-1970)
cond WOLFGANG MARTIN
(MMOI) **CDMOIR422** Great Voices in Tchaikovsky
(PREI) **89092** Erna Berger (1900-1990) - II
cond F. ZAUN
(EMI) **CMS7 64008-2(1)** Wagner Singing on Record (pt 1)
(PREI) **89049** Margarete Teschemacher (1903-1959)
(PREI) **89088** Walther Ludwig (1902-1981)
cond A. VON ZEMLINSKY
(SCHW) **310037** Alexander von Zemlinsky conducts
cond F. ZWEIG
(CLUB) **CL99-020** Maria Ivogün & Lotte Schöne—Opera Recital
(EMI) **CMS7 64008-2(1)** Wagner Singing on Record (pt 1)
(MMOI) **CDMOIR406** Mozart—Historical Recordings
(MMOI) **CDMOIR408** Great Sopranos
(MSCM) **MM30283** Great Wagnerian Singers, Vol.1
(NIMB) **NI7848** Great Singers at the Berlin State Opera
(NIMB) **NI7853** Lauri-Volpi sings Verdi
(PEAR) **GEMMCDS9926(1)** Covent Garden on Record—Vol.4 (pt 1)
(PEAR) **GEMMCD9129** Great Tenors, Vol.2
(PEAR) **GEMMCD9409** Lotte Lehmenn—Vol.1
(PREI) **89024** Marcel Wittrisch (1901-1955)
(PREI) **89028** Ivar Andresen (1896-1940)
(PREI) **89035** Erna Berger (1900-1990) - I
(PREI) **89082** Margarete Klose (1902-1968)
(PREI) **90034** Maria Cebotari (1910-49)

BERLIN SYMPHONY ORCHESTRA
cond G. BECKER
(EURO) **GD69018** Fritz Wunderlich—Recital
cond O. DOBRINDT
(EMI) **CHS7 64673-2** Joseph Schmidt - Complete EMI Recordings Volume 1
cond C.P. FLOR
(RCA) **RD60119** Nineteenth Century Orchestral Works
cond F. FOX
Fall: Rose von Stambul (exc)
Millöcker: Dubarry (exc)
Suppé: Boccaccio (exc)
Zeller: Vogelhändler (exc)
cond B. KLOBUČAR
(EMI) **CZS7 62993-2** Fritz Wunderlich—Great German Tenor
cond F. LEHÁR
(PEAR) **GEMMCD9310** Franz Lehár conducts Richard Tauber
cond A. MELICHAR
(EURO) **GD69018** Fritz Wunderlich—Recital
(RCA) **09026 62550-2** Ten Tenors in Love
cond H-M. RABENSTEIN
(EURO) **GD69019** Hermann Prey—Recital
cond A. ROTHER
(EURO) **GD69018** Fritz Wunderlich—Recital
cond W. SCHMIDT-BOELCKE
Abraham: Blume von Hawaii (exc), Viktoria und ihr Husar (exc)
Jessel: Schwarzwaldmädel (exc)
Künneke: Vetter aus Dingsda (exc)
Lehár: Schön ist die Welt (exc)
Raymond: Maske in Blau (exc)
(EMI) **CZS7 62993-2** Fritz Wunderlich—Great German Tenor
cond W. SCHÜCHTER
(EMI) **CDH5 65201-2** Leonie Rysanek - Operatic Recital
(EMI) **CHS7 69741-2(4)** Record of Singing, Vol.4—German School
(EMI) **CMS5 65621-2** Fischer-Dieskau - The Opera Singer
cond H. STEIN
(EMI) **CMS7 64074-2(2)** Christa Ludwig—Recital (pt 2)
(EMI) **CZS7 62993-2** Fritz Wunderlich—Great German Tenor
cond R. STOLZ
Lehár: Land des Lächelns (exc), Zarewitsch (exc)
(EURO) **GD69022** Oscar Straus: Operetta excerpts
cond F. WALTER
(EMI) **CZS7 62993-2** Fritz Wunderlich—Great German Tenor
cond F. WEISSMANN
(EMI) **CDM7 69478-2** A Portrait of Joseph Schmidt
(ROMO) **81014-2** Elisabeth Rethberg (1894-1976)
cond H. ZANOTELLI
(EMI) **CZS7 62993-2** Fritz Wunderlich—Great German Tenor
cond F. ZWEIG
(PREI) **89090** Hans Hermann Nissen (1893-1980)
(ROMO) **81014-2** Elisabeth Rethberg (1894-1976)

BERLIN VOLKSOPER ORCHESTRA
cond B. SEIDLER-WINKLER
(PREI) **89211** Helge Roswaenge (1897-1972) - III

BERMAN, Karel (bass)
Dvořák: Jacobin (Cpte)
Janáček: From the House of the Dead (Cpte), Jenufa (Cpte), Makropulos Affair (Cpte)
Martinů: Julietta (Cpte)
Smetana: Devil's Wall (Cpte)
(KOCH) **34036-2** A Pageant of Opera

BERMEJO, Julita (sngr)
Bretón: Verbena de la Paloma (Cpte)
Moreno Torroba: Luisa Fernanda (Cpte)

BERMINGHAM, Jennifer (mez)
Meyerbeer: Huguenots (Cpte)

BERNADET, Andrée (mez)
Massenet: Manon (Cpte)
(NIMB) **NI7836/7** Conchita Supervia (1895-1936)

BERNARD, Annabelle (sop)
(TESS) **049-2** R. Strauss/Wagner—Opera Scenes

BERNARD, Anthony (cond)
see RPO

BERNARDI, Giuliano (ten)
Verdi: Macbeth (Cpte)

BERNARDI, Mario (cond)
see Calgary PO

BERNARDINI, Don (ten)
Bellini: Beatrice di Tenda (Cpte)
Donizetti: Linda di Chamounix (Cpte), Roberto Devereux (Cpte)
Paisiello: Nina (Cpte)
Puccini: Bohème (Cpte)

BERNART, Massimo de (cond)
see Italian International Op Orch
Lugano Rad & TV Orch
Naples San Carlo Op Orch

BERNAS, Richard (cond)
see Ens

BERNE STATE ORCHESTRA
cond H. MÜLLER-KRAY
(ACAN) **43 267** Fritz Wunderlich sings Opera Arias

BERNE SYMPHONY ORCHESTRA
cond P. MAAG
(IMP) **PCD824** Mendelssohn—Orchestral Works
(IMP) **PCD2003** Mendelssohn—Symphony No. 4; Overtures

BERNELLI, Gina (sop)
(PREI) **89009** Gino Bechi (b. 1913)
(PREI) **89074** Tancredi Pasero (1893-1983) - II

BERNET, Dietfried (cond)
see Vienna Op Orch

BERNHARD, Kurt (bass)
R. Strauss: Rosenkavalier (Cpte)

BERNHEIMER, Julia (mez)
Mozart: Zauberflöte (Cpte)

BERNIUS, Frieder (cond)
see Tafelmusik

BERNOLD, Philippe (fl)
Mozart: Clemenza di Tito (Cpte)

BERNSTEIN, Alexander (spkr)
Bernstein: West Side Story (Cpte)

BERNSTEIN, Leonard (cond)
see Austrian RSO
BBC SO
Broadway Orch
BRSO
chor
Columbia Wind Ens
FNO
La Scala Orch
Los Angeles PO
LSO
NY Met Op Orch
NYPO
orch
Santa Cecilia Academy Orch
VPO

BERNSTEIN, Nina (narr)
Bernstein: West Side Story (Cpte)

BERNTSEN, Anne-Lise (sop)
Bibalo: Gespenster (Cpte)

BERONESI, Debora (sop)
(DECC) **436 261-2DHO3** Puccini—Il Trittico

BERRETTONI, Umberto (cond)
see La Scala Orch
orch

BERRY, Nicholas (treb)
Britten: Noye's Fludde (Cpte)

BERRY, Noreen (contr)
Verdi: Traviata (Cpte)
Wagner: Walküre (Cpte)

BERRY, Walter (bass-bar)
Bartók: Duke Bluebeard's castle (Cpte)
Beethoven: Fidelio (Cpte)
Einem: Prozess (Cpte)
Handel: Giulio Cesare (Cpte)
Humperdinck: Hänsel und Gretel (Cpte)
J. Strauss II: Fledermaus (Cpte)
Korngold: Violanta (Cpte)
Lehár: Giuditta (exc)
Mozart: Così fan tutte (Cpte), Don Giovanni (Cpte), Nozze di Figaro (Cpte), Zauberflöte (Cpte)
R. Strauss: Ariadne auf Naxos (Cpte), Frau ohne Schatten (Cpte), Rosenkavalier (Cpte), Salome (Cpte)
Rossini: Cenerentola (Cpte)
Smetana: Bartered Bride (Cpte)
Wagner: Tristan und Isolde (Cpte)
Zeller: Vogelhändler (Cpte)
(CFP) **CD-CFP4499** Strauss—Champagne and Laughter
(CFP) **CD-CFP4602** Favourite Opera
(DECC) **440 854-2DH** Ullmann—Der Kaiser von Atlantis
(EMIL) **CDZ7 67015-2** Mozart—Opera Arias
(ORFE) **C365941A** Christa Ludwig - Salzburg Festival highlights
(ORFE) **C394201B** Great Mozart Singers Series, Vol. 2
(ORFE) **C394301B** Great Mozart Singers Series, Vol. 3
(TESS) **049-2** R. Strauss/Wagner—Opera Scenes

BERSIERI, Mario (ten)
Verdi: Due Foscari (Cpte)

BERTELSEN, Lars Thodberg (bar)
(KONT) **32203** Nielsen—Orchestral Works

BERTHOLD, Charlotte (mez)
Humperdinck: Hänsel und Gretel (Cpte)

BERTHON, Mireille (sop)
Gounod: Faust (Cpte)
(CLUB) **CL99-034** Marcel Journet (1867-1933)

BERTI, Marco (ten)
Franchetti: Cristoforo Colombo (Cpte)
Mozart: Don Giovanni (Cpte)
Puccini: Manon Lescaut (Cpte)

BERTIN, Pascal (alto)
Handel: Amadigi di Gaula (Cpte)
(HARM) **HMC90 1552** The Three Countertenors

BERTIN, Pierre (narr)
(EMI) **CZS7 62877-2** Les inspirations insolites d'Erik Satie

BERTINI, Gary (cond)
see Frankfurt Op Orch
Vienna SO

BERTINI, Rossana (sop)
Handel: Poro (Cpte)

BERTOCCHI, Sergio (ten)
Mercadante: Bravo (Cpte)
Puccini: Fanciulla del West (Cpte)

BERTOCCI, Aldo (ten)
Verdi: Due Foscari (Cpte)

BERTOLI, Fulvia (sngr)
Mascagni: Rantzau (Cpte)

BERTOLO, Aldo (ten)
Donizetti: Don Pasquale (Cpte)
Rossini: Adelaide di Borgogna (Cpte)
(NUOV) **6905** Donizetti—Great Love Duets

BERTON, Liliane (sngr)
Adam: Si j'étais roi (Cpte)

BERTON, Liliane (sop)
Gounod: Faust (exc)
Lecocq: Jour et la Nuit (Cpte)
Poulenc: Dialogues des Carmélites (Cpte)
(EMI) **CDM5 65155-2** Chabrier—Une Education manquée; Mélodies
(EMI) **CZS5 68295-2** Messager/Lecocq—Operetta Highlights
(EMI) **CZS7 67515-2** Offenbach—Operetta highlights
(EMI) **CZS7 67869-2** J. Strauss II—Operetta Highlights
(EMI) **CZS7 67872-2** Lehár—Operettas (highlights in French)

BERTONA, Sylvia (sop)
Puccini: Madama Butterfly (Cpte)
Verdi: Simon Boccanegra (Cpte), Traviata (Cpte)
(EMI) **CMS7 64165-2** Puccini—Trittico

BERTRAM, Theodor (bar)
(PEAR) **GEMMCDS9923(2)** Covent Garden on Record, Vol.1 (pt 2)
(SYMP) **SYMCD1081** The Harold Wayne Collection, Vol.5

BERTRAND, Loïc (cond)
see Paris RSO

BERUILLY, Édouard (cond)
see orch

BESANÇON, Aimé (ten)
Offenbach: Périchole (Cpte)

BESANÇON, Maurice (bass)
Bizet: Carmen (Cpte)

BESL, Karl (cond)
see Berlin St Op Orch
orch

BESSEL, Anne Marie (mez)
Wagner: Fliegende Holländer (Cpte)

BESSES O' THE BARN BAND
(CHAN) **CHAN4513** British Bandsman Centenary Concert
cond R. NEWSOME
(CHAN) **CHAN6571/2** Around the World with the Besses

BEST, Jonathan (bass)
Maxwell Davies: Resurrection (Cpte)
Purcell: King Arthur, Z628 (Cpte)
Saxton: Caritas (Cpte)
(HYPE) **CDA66569** Vaughan Williams—Choral Works
(OPRA) **ORCH103** Italian Opera—1810-20

BEST, Matthew (cond)
see CLS
Corydon Orch

BEST, Matthew (bass)
Rossini: Barbiere di Siviglia (Cpte)
Saint-Saëns: Samson et Dalila (Cpte)
Stravinsky: Rake's Progress (Cpte)
Verdi: Don Carlo (Cpte)
(ASV) **CDDCA758** Falla, Milhaud & Stravinsky—Operas
(NIMB) **NI5217** Tippett conducts Tippett

BEST, Michael (ten)
Puccini: Fanciulla del West (Cpte)

BEST, Ronald (bass)
Verdi: Traviata (Cpte)

BETHELL, Anna (mez)
Sullivan: Sorcerer (Cpte)

BETLEY-SIERADZKA, Bozena (sop)
Mozart: Idomeneo (Cpte)

BETNER, Clara (mez)
Mascagni: Piccolo Marat (Cpte)

BETTENDORF, Emmy (sop)
(DANA) **DACOCD313/4** Lauritz Melchior Anthology - Vol. 2
(MMOI) **CDMOIR419** Vienna Nights - Golden Age of Operetta
(NIMB) **NI7830** Richard Tauber in Opera
(PEAR) **GEMMCD9130** Great Sopranos, Vol.2
(PEAR) **GEMMCD9398** Friedrich Schorr
(PEAR) **GEMMCD9419** Herbert Ernst Groh—Opera Recital
(PREI) **89032** Lauritz Melchior (1890-1973) - I
(PREI) **89052** Friederich Schorr (1889-1953)
(PREI) **89068** Lauritz Melchior (1890-1973) - II

BETTI, Freda (contr)
Lecocq: Jour et la Nuit (Cpte)
Offenbach: Chanson de Fortunio (Cpte)
Planquette: Rip van Winkle (Cpte)
(EMI) **CZS5 68295-2** Messager/Lecocq—Operetta Highlights
(EMI) **CZS7 67515-2** Offenbach—Operetta highlights

BETTINELLI (pf)
(SYMP) **SYMCD1170** The Harold Wayne Collection, Vol.20

BETTONI, Vincenzo (bass)
(CLUB) **CL99-074** Conchita Supervia (1895-1936)
(MEMO) **HR4408/9(2)** Singers in Genoa, Vol.1 (disc 2)
(MSCM) **MM30276** Rossini—Barbiere di Siviglia, etc

BEUACHEMIN, Michel (bass)
Berlioz: Troyens (Cpte)

BEUDERT, Mark (ten)
Bernstein: Candide (1988) (exc)

BEVACQUA, Antonio (ten)
Puccini: Turandot (Cpte)
Verdi: Otello (Cpte)

BEVAN, Maurice (bar)
Monteverdi: L'Arianna (exc)
Purcell: Dido (Cpte), Indian Queen, Z630 (Cpte), King Arthur, Z628 (Cpte)
(HARM) **HMP390 807** Great Baroque Masters—Purcell
(HARM) **HMX290 1528/33(2)** A Purcell Companion (pt 2)

BEVAN, Rachel (sop)
Purcell: Dido (Cpte)
(PAUL) **PACD56** Nielsen: Songs

BEVAN, Stanley (ten)
Sullivan: Iolanthe (exc)

BEYER, Bernd (ten)
R. Strauss: Rosenkavalier (Cpte)

BEYER, Reinhard (bass)
Schreker: Gezeichneten (Cpte)
(SONY) **S2K66836** Goldschmidt—Beatrice Cenci, etc

BEYLE, Léon (ten)
(IRCC) **IRCC-CD802** Souvenirs of Rare French Opera

BEZHKO, Boris (bar)
Glinka: Life for the Tsar (Cpte)

BEZINIAN, Ruth (mez)
Donizetti: Maria Stuarda (Cpte)

BEZRODNY, Sergei (hpd)
(RCA) **RD60861** It ain't necessarily so & other violin miniatures

BEZUBENKOV, Gennadi (bass)
Rimsky-Korsakov: Sadko (Cpte)
Tchaikovsky: Queen of Spades (Cpte)

BEZZINA, Gilbert (cond)
see Nice Baroque Ens

BIAGIONI, Lola (sop)
Verdi: Don Carlo (Cpte)

BIANCHI, Mario (ten)
Verdi: Traviata (Cpte)

BIANCHINI, Giovanni (treb)
Puccini: Tosca (Cpte)

BIANCO, René (bar)
Adam: Si j'étais roi (Cpte)
Bizet: Pêcheurs de Perles (Cpte)
Poulenc: Dialogues des Carmélites (Cpte)
(PHIL) **442 272-2PM2** The Best of Bizet

BIASINI, Piero (bar)
Mascagni: Cavalleria rusticana (Cpte)

BIBER, Clemens (ten)
Wagner: Tannhäuser (exc)

BIBL, Rudolf (cond)
see Polish Nat RSO

BIBLE, Frances (mez)
R. Ward: Crucible (Cpte)

BICKLEY, Susan (mez)
Purcell: Dido (Cpte), Fairy Queen, Z629 (Cpte)
(ASV) **CDDCA758** Falla, Milhaud & Stravinsky—Operas
(OPRA) **ORCH103** Italian Opera—1810-20

BIEBER, Clemens (ten)
Mendelssohn: Hochzeit des Camacho (Cpte)
Mozart: Zauberflöte (Cpte)
R. Strauss: Salome (Cpte)
Wagner: Tannhäuser (Cpte)

BIEL, Ann Christine (sop)
Mozart: Così fan tutte (Cpte), Finta Giardiniera (Cpte), Idomeneo (Cpte), Nozze di Figaro (Cpte), Zauberflöte (Cpte)

BIELECKI, André (ten)
Mussorgsky: Boris Godunov (Cpte)

BIELEFELD CITY THEATRE CHORUS
cond D. DE VILLIERS
Krenek: Sprüng über den Schatten (Cpte)

BIELEFELD OPERA CHORUS
cond G. MOULL
Spohr: Faust (Cpte)

BIELEFELD PHILHARMONIC ORCHESTRA
cond G. MOULL
Spohr: Faust (Cpte)
cond D. DE VILLIERS
Krenek: Sprüng über den Schatten (Cpte)

BIERBACH, Franz (bass)
Beethoven: Fidelio (Cpte)
Mozart: Zauberflöte (Cpte)
R. Strauss: Rosenkavalier (Cpte)
Verdi: Otello (Cpte)
Wagner: Meistersinger (Cpte)
(DECC) **425 959-2DM** Lisa della Casa sings R. Strauss

BIERBAUM, Andrea (contr)
Cesti: Orontea (Cpte)

BIERETT, Doris (sop)
Weill: Sieben Todsünden (Cpte)

BIGG, Julian (cond)
see Czech PO
Czech SO

BIGGAR, Marjorie (mez)
Cavalli: Calisto (Cpte)

BIGOT, Eugène (cond)
see orch
ORTF Lyric Orch

BILANDZIJA, Beate (sop)
Delius: Village Romeo and Juliet (Cpte)
Schillings: Mona Lisa (Cpte)

BILGRAM, Hedwig (organ)
(EMI) **CDC7 54330-2** Arrangements for Trumpet and Organ

BILLINGS, James (bar)
Bernstein: Candide (1982) (Cpte)

BILLS, John (ten)
Verdi: Luisa Miller (Cpte), Trovatore (Cpte)

BIMA, Jeanne Marie (sop)
Rossini: Italiana in Algeri (exc)

BINDELS, Paul (ten)
R. Strauss: Rosenkavalier (Cpte)

BINDER, Peter (bar)
Giordano: Fedora (Cpte)

BINDI, Jean-Louis (bass)
Mouret: Amours de Ragonde (Cpte)

BINDSZUS, Peter (ten)
Wagner: Meistersinger (Cpte)

BINI, Carlo (ten)
Verdi: Lombardi (Cpte)

BINZER, Kim von (ten)
Kuhlau: Lulu (Cpte)

BIONDI, Fabio (cond)
see Europa Galante

BIRCHALL, Pauline (sngr)
Sullivan: Pirates of Penzance (exc)

BIRCHALL, Simon (bass)
Monteverdi: Orfeo (Cpte)
Mozart: Zauberflöte (Cpte)
Purcell: Dioclesian, Z627 (Cpte)
(CHAN) **CHAN8865** Rossini: Opera Arias

BIRET, Idil (pf)
(MARC) **8 223452** Kempff—Piano Works
(NAXO) **8 550958** Brahms—Transciptions for piano

BISATT, Susan (sop)
Lampe: Pyramus and Thisbe (Cpte)
Verdi: Trovatore (Cpte)

BISCHOF, Lisa (sop)
R. Strauss: Elektra (Cpte)

BISCHOFF, Romain (bass)
M-A. Charpentier: David et Jonathas (Cpte)
(CPO) **CPO999 104-2** Mozart—Lo Sposo Deluso/L'Oca del Cairo

BISCOTTI, Manrico (bar)
Wolf-Ferrari: Campiello (Cpte)
(SCHW) **314052** Opera Gala

BISE, Juliette (sop)
Monteverdi: Orfeo (Cpte)
(DECC) **433 400-2DM2** Ravel & Debussy—Stage Works

BISH, Diane (organ)
(PHIL) **426 057-2PH** Glorious Pipes
(PHIL) **426 057-5PH** Glorious Pipes

BISHOP, Elizabeth (sngr)
Schuman: Question of Taste (Cpte)

BISPHAM, David (bass)
(SYMP) **SYMCD1093** The Harold Wayne Collection, Vol.7
(SYMP) **SYMCD1123** Sullivan—Sesquicentenial Commemorative Issue

BISSMEIER, Joachim (spkr)
Mozart: Entführung (Cpte)

BISSON, Yves (bar)
Gounod: Roméo et Juliette (Cpte)
Massenet: Jongleur de Notre Dame (Cpte)
Offenbach: Contes d'Hoffmann (exc)
R. Strauss: Salomé (Cpte)

BISSUTI, Carl (bass)
(SCHW) **314532** Vienna State Opera Live, Vol.3
(SCHW) **314542** Vienna State Opera Live, Vol.4
(SCHW) **314652** Vienna State Opera Live, Vol.15
(SCHW) **314672** Vienna State Opera Live, Vol.17

BITTER, Sabine (sop)
Hindemith: Neues vom Tage (Cpte)

BITTNER, Jack (bar)
D. Moore: Carry Nation (Cpte)

BJARNASON, Olafur (sngr)
(RCA) **09026 62547-2** Divas in Song—Marilyn Horne's 60th Birthday

BJÖRKER, Leon (bass)
Puccini: Bohème (exc)

BJÖRLIN, Ulf (cond)
see RPO

BJÖRLING, Anna-Lisa (sop)
(BLUE) **ABCD016** Jussi Björling—Rare Records & Alternative Takes
(EMI) **CDH7 61053-2** Jussi Björling sings Operatic Arias
(EMI) **CDH7 64707-2** Jussi Björling, Vol.2
(VAI) **VAI69101** Jussi Björling in Opera and Song Vol 1

BJÖRLING, Bette (mez)
(BLUE) **ABCD028** Jussi Björling live at the Stockholm Opera

BJÖRLING, Jussi (ten)
Gounod: Roméo et Juliette (exc)
J. Strauss II: Fledermaus (Cpte)
Leoncavallo: Pagliacci (Cpte)
Mascagni: Cavalleria Rusticana (Cpte)
Puccini: Bohème (Cpte), Madama Butterfly (Cpte), Manon Lescaut (Cpte), Tosca (exc), Turandot (Cpte)
Verdi: Aida (Cpte), Rigoletto (Cpte), Trovatore (Cpte)
(ALTN) **CDAN3** Hjördis Schymberg
(BLUE) **ABCD006** Jussi Björling Live - Holland 1939, Norway 1954
(BLUE) **ABCD016** Jussi Björling—Rare Records & Alternative Takes
(BLUE) **ABCD028** Jussi Björling live at the Stockholm Opera
(BLUE) **ABCD042** Björling - The Stockholm Tivoli Recordings, Vol.1: 1958-60
(BLUE) **ABCD057** Björling—Gröna Lund Recordings, Volume 2
(CFP) **CD-CFP9013** Duets from Famous Operas
(CONI) **CDHD214** Jussi Björling - Arias, Lieder and Songs
(CONI) **CDHD235** The Puccini Album
(DECC) **417 686-2DC** Puccini—Operatic Arias
(DECC) **433 064-2DWO** Your Hundred Best Opera Tunes Volume I
(DECC) **433 066-2DWO** Your Hundred Best Opera Tunes III
(DECC) **433 069-2DWO** Your Hundred Best Opera Tunes VI
(DECC) **433 636-2DSP** Puccini—Famous Arias
(DECC) **436 300-2DX** Opera Gala Sampler
(DECC) **436 314-2DA** Great Tenor Arias
(DECC) **436 316-2DA** Golden Operetta
(DECC) **436 463-2DM** Ten Top Tenors
(DECC) **443 379-2DM** Ten Top Tenors 2
(DECC) **443 930-2DM** Jussi Björling sings Opera Arias
(DECC) **444 555-2DF2** Essential Puccini
(EMI) **CDC7 54016-2** Tenorissimo!
(EMI) **CDH7 61053-2** Jussi Björling sings Operatic Arias
(EMI) **CDH7 64707-2** Jussi Björling, Vol.2
(EMI) **CDM5 65579-2** Victoria de los Angeles
(EMI) **CHS7 69741-2(5)** Record of Singing, Vol.4—Scandinavian School
(IMP) **GLRS103** The Magnificent Björling
(MMOI) **CDMOIR405** Great Tenors
(MMOI) **CDMOIR409** Three Tenors—Björling, Gigli & Tauber
(MMOI) **CDMOIR412** Great Voices of the Century Sing Puccini
(MMOI) **CDMOIR419** Vienna Nights - Golden Age of Operetta
(MMOI) **CDMOIR425** Three Tenors, Volume 2
(MYTO) **2MCD90317** Verdi—Un Ballo in maschera
(NIMB) **NI7835** Jussi Björling—The first ten years
(NIMB) **NI7842** Jussi Björling, Vol.2
(NIMB) **NI7851** Legendary Voices
(NIMB) **NI7856** Legendary Tenors
(PEAR) **GEMMCD9043** Jussi Björling - Songs and Arias, Volume 3
(PEAR) **GEMMCD9129** Great Tenors, Vol.2
(RCA) **GD87799** The Pearl Fishers Duet plus Duets and Scenes
(RCA) **GK85277** Legendary Performers - Björling
(RCA) **09026 61440-2** Opera's Greatest Moments
(RCA) **09026 61580-2(5)** RCA/Met 100 Singers, 100 Years (pt 5)
(RCA) **09026 61580-2(7)** RCA/Met 100 Singers, 100 Years (pt 7)
(RCA) **09026 61886-2** Operas Greatest Love Songs
(RCA) **09026 62550-2** Ten Tenors in Love
(RCA) **09026 62689-2** The Voices of Living Stereo, Volume 1
(RCA) **74321 25817-2** Café Classics - Operatic
(SCHW) **314542** Vienna State Opera Live, Vol.4
(TEST) **SBT1005** Ten Top Tenors
(VAI) **VAI69101** Jussi Björling in Opera and Song Vol 1
(VAI) **VAI69111** Jussi Björling in Opera and Song Vol 2

BJÖRLING, Sigurd (bar)
Wagner: Walküre (exc)
(ALTN) **CDAN3** Hjördis Schymberg
(EMI) **CDH5 65201-2** Leonie Rysanek - Operatic Recital
(SCHW) **314542** Vienna State Opera Live, Vol.4

BLACHUT, Beno (ten)
Dvořák: Jacobin (exc)
Janáček: Cunning Little Vixen (Cpte), From the House of the Dead (Cpte), Káta Kabanová (Cpte), Makropulos Affair (Cpte)
Smetana: Bartered Bride (Cpte)
(DECC) **430 375-2DH2** Janáček—Operatic and Orchestral Works
(EMI) **CHS7 69741-2(6)** Record of Singing, Vol.4—Russian & Slavonic Schools
(KOCH) **34036-2** A Pageant of Opera

BLACK, Frank (cond)
see orch

BLACK, Lynton (bar)
J. Strauss II: Fledermaus (Cpte)

BLACK DYKE MILLS BAND
(CHAN) **CHAN4513** British Bandsman Centenary Concert
cond G. BRAND
(CHAN) **CHAN6539** Classic Brass
(RSR) **RSRD1002** Black Dyke Mills Band, Vol.2 - Sovereign Heritage
cond D. HURST
(CHAN) **CHAN4514** Black Dyke Mills Band play Overtures
cond R. NEWSOME
(CHAN) **CHAN4528** The Lion and the Eagle
cond P. PARKES
(CHAN) **CHAN4501** The World's Most Beautiful Melodies
(CHAN) **CHAN4505** Black Dyke plays Rossini
(CHAN) **CHAN4507** A Tribute to Elgar, Delius and Vaughan Williams
(CHAN) **CHAN4513** British Bandsman Centenary Concert
(CHAN) **CHAN4514** Black Dyke Mills Band play Overtures
cond T. WALMSLEY
(CHAN) **CHAN4505** Black Dyke plays Rossini
cond J. WATSON
(POLY) **QPRL053D** Slavonic Brass

BLACKBURN, David (sngr)
Rorem: Miss Julie (Cpte)

BLACKBURN, Harold (bass)
Britten: Curlew River (Cpte)
(EMI) **CMS7 64412-2** Gilbert & Sullivan—Ruddigore/Shakespeare Music

BLACKBURN, Olivia (sop)
MacMillan: Visitatio Sepulchri (Cpte)

BLACKWELL, Derek (ten)
Berlioz: Benvenuto Cellini (Cpte)

BLACKWELL, George (sngr)
Bernstein: Candide (1956) (exc)

BLACKWELL, Harolyn (sop)
Gershwin: Porgy and Bess (Cpte)

BLADIN, Christer (ten)
Braunfels: Verkündigung (Cpte)
Wagner: Parsifal (Cpte)

BLAIR, Isla (sngr)
Gay: Beggar's Opera (Cpte)

BLAKE, Rockwell (ten)
Rossini: Barbiere di Siviglia (Cpte)
(ARAB) **Z6582** The Rossini Tenor
(ARAB) **Z6598** Rockwell Blake, the Mozart Tenor
(ARAB) **Z6612** Rossini: Opera Arias
(EMI) **CDC7 54643-2** Rossini—Bicentenary Gala Concert
(EMI) **LDB491007-1 (EMI)** Rossini Bicentennial Birthday Gala
(NUOV) **6820** Luciana Serra—Opera Recital

BLANC, Ernst (bar)
Bizet: Carmen (Cpte), Pêcheurs de perles (Cpte)
Gounod: Faust (Cpte)
Offenbach: Contes d'Hoffmann (Cpte)
Saint-Saëns: Samson et Dalila (exc)
(CFP) **CD-CFP4602** Favourite Opera
(CFP) **CD-CFP9013** Duets from Famous Operas
(EMI) **CDEMTVD59** Classic Experience 3
(EMI) **CDM7 69596-2** The Movies go to the Opera

BLANCAS, Angeles (treb)
Penella: Gato Montés (Cpte)

(ROGER) BLANCHARD VOCAL ENSEMBLE cond H. ROSBAUD
Gluck: Orphée (Cpte)

BLANCHART, Ramon (bar)
(MEMO) **HR4408/9(1)** Singers in Genoa, Vol.1 (disc 1)

BLAND, Elsa (sop)
(PREI) **89020** Leo Slezak (1873-1946)

BLANKENHEIM, Toni (bar)
Berg: Lulu (Cpte)

BLANKENSHIP, William (ten)
(DECC) **440 415-2DM** Marilyn Horne

BLAREAU, Richard (cond)
see Chor
orch

BLASI, Angela Maria (sop)
Puccini: Bohème (Cpte)
Wagner: Götterdämmerung (Cpte), Rheingold (Cpte)
(EMI) **LDX9 91275-1(EMI)** Sawallisch conducts Wagner's Ring

BLASIUS, Martin (bass)
Kreutzer: Nachtlager in Granada (Cpte)
Zemlinsky: Traumgörge (Cpte)

BLAS-NET (pf)
(PEAR) **GEMMCD9128** Pablo Casals - Bow and Baton

BLATTER, Johanna (mez)
Wagner: Tristan und Isolde (exc), Walküre (Cpte)
(EMI) **CMS5 65212-2** Wagner—Les introuvables du Ring

BLAZSÓ, Sándor (bass)
Giordano: Fedora (Cpte)

BLECH, Harry (cond)
see LMP

BLECH, Leo (cond)
see Berlin St Op Orch
Berlin Staatskapelle
orch

BLEGEN, Judith (sop)
Mozart: Nozze di Figaro (Cpte), Zaïde (Cpte)
Puccini: Bohème (Cpte)

BLIER, Steven (pf)
(KOCH) **37028-2** Gershwin—Songs & Duets
(KOCH) **37050-2** Blitzstein—Songs

BLOCHWITZ, Hans-Peter (ten)
Beethoven: Fidelio (Cpte)
Mozart: Don Giovanni (Cpte), Finta semplice (Cpte), Zauberflöte (Cpte)
(PHIL) **422 523-2PME8(2)** The Complete Mozart Edition Vol 23 (pt 2)
(TELD) **4509-97507-2** Mozart—Famous Opera Arias

BLOM, Inger (contr)
Mozart: Zauberflöte (Cpte)

BLOOM, Sara Lambert (ob)
(CENT) **CRC2084** Music from Cranberry Isles

BLUMENTHAL, Daniel (pf)
(SCHW) **313772** Franck—Pieces for two pianos and piano for four hands

BOATWRIGHT, McHenry (bar)
Gershwin: Porgy and Bess (exc)

BOBILLIER, Gisèle (sop)
(DECC) **433 400-2DM2** Ravel & Debussy—Stage Works

BOBOC, Nicolae (cond)
see Timişoara Banatul PO

BOCELLI, Andrea (sngr)
(DECC) **444 460-2DH** Pavarotti and Friends II

BOCKELMANN, Rudolf (bass-bar)
Wagner: Meistersinger (exc), Walküre (exc)
(CLAR) **CDGSE78-50-33** Lauritz Melchior & Albert Coates
(DANA) **DACOCD319/21** The Lauritz Melchior Anthology - Vol.5
(EMI) **CMS7 64008-2(1)** Wagner Singing on Record (pt 1)
(EMI) **CMS7 64008-2(2)** Wagner Singing on Record (pt 2)
(MSCM) **MM30283** Great Wagnerian Singers, Vol.1
(MSCM) **MM30285** Great Wagnerian Singers, Vol.2
(PEAR) **GEMMCDS9137** Wagner—Der Ring des Nibelungen
(PEAR) **GEMMCDS9926(2)** Covent Garden on Record—Vol.4 (pt 2)
(SCHW) **314512** Vienna State Opera Live, Vol.1
(SCHW) **314642** Vienna State Opera Live, Vol.14

BODANZKY, Artur (cond)
see NY Met Op Orch

BODE, Hannelore (sop)
Wagner: Meistersinger (Cpte), Parsifal (Cpte)
(PHIL) **434 420-2PM32(1)** Richard Wagner Edition (Pt.1)

BODENHAM, Peter (ten)
Walton: Troilus and Cressida (Cpte)

BODENSTEIN, Christoph (ten)
R. Strauss: Rosenkavalier (Cpte)

BODINGBAUER, Rudolf (cond)
see Steiermark Military Band

BODRA SMYANA CHILDREN'S CHOIR cond E. TCHAKAROV
Mussorgsky: Boris Godunov (Cpte)

BODUROV, Lyubomir (ten)
Mussorgsky: Khovanshchina (Cpte)

BOEHM, Andreas (bar)
(PILZ) **442118-2** Wagner—Operas in Historical Recordings

BOEMI, A. (bar)
(CLUB) **CL99-025** Giovanni Zenatello (1876-1949)
(PEAR) **GEMMCDS9074(2)** Giovanni Zenatello, Vol.2 (pt 2)
(PREI) **89038** Giovanni Zenatello (1876-1949)

BOEMIA DEL NORD PHILHARMONIC CHAMBER ORCHESTRA cond D. SANFILIPPO
A. Scarlatti: Lesbina e Adolfo (Cpte)
Salieri: Prima la musica (Cpte)

BOERNER, Eva (contr)
Mozart: Zauberflöte (Cpte)

BOESCH, Christian (bar)
J. Strauss II: Fledermaus (exc)
Monteverdi: Orfeo (Cpte)
Mozart: Zauberflöte (Cpte)
(ORFE) **C394301B** Great Mozart Singers Series, Vol. 3
(TELD) **0630-11470-2** The Best of Barbara Bonney

BOESCH, Ruthilde (mez)
J. Strauss II: Nacht in Venedig (Cpte)
Mozart: Zauberflöte (Cpte)

BOESE, Ursula (mez)
Berg: Lulu (Cpte)
R. Strauss: Salome (Cpte)
Wagner: Parsifal (Cpte)

BOETTCHER, Else (mez)
Verdi: Macbeth (Cpte)
(SCHW) **314552** Vienna State Opera Live, Vol.5
(SCHW) **314712** Vienna State Opera Live, Vol.21

BOGACHEV, Vladimir (ten)
Shostakovich: Gamblers (Cpte)
(CHAN) **CHAN9149** Rimsky-Korsakov/Glinka—Vocal Works

BOGACHEVA, Irina (mez)
Prokofiev: War and Peace (exc)

BOGARDE, Sir Dirk (narr)
Lehár: Lustige Witwe (Cpte)

BOGARDUS, Stephen (voc)
Bernstein: West Side Story (Cpte)

BOGART, John (alto)
(SCHW) **313772** Franck—Pieces for two pianos and piano for four hands

BOGART, John Paul (bass)
Bizet: Carmen (exc)
Puccini: Turandot (exc)

BOGDAN, Thomas (ten)
M. Monk: Atlas (Cpte)
Machover: Valis (Cpte)

BOGDANOV, Ilya (bar)
(ARLE) **ARL23/5** Rimsky-Korsakov—Sadko

BOGDANOVICH, Aleksandr (ten)
(PEAR) **GEMMCDS9007/9(1)** Singers of Imperial Russia, Vol.4 (pt 1)
(PEAR) **GEMMCDS9111(2)** Singers of Imperial Russia, Vol.5 (pt 2)

BOGUET, Jean (pf)
(MSCM) **MM30373** Gounod—Mélodies

BOHÁČOVÁ, Marta (sop)
Janáček: Jenufa (Cpte)

BOHAN, Edmund (ten)
(IMP) **PWK1157** Gilbert & Sullivan Spectacular

BOHÉE, Philippe (bar)
Chabrier: Roi malgré lui (Cpte)
Saint-Saëns: Henry VIII (Cpte)

BÖHEIM, Franz (buffo)
Lehár: Lustige Witwe (Cpte)

BÖHM, Karl (cond)
see Bayreuth Fest Orch
Berlin Deutsche Op Orch
Berlin RSO
BPO
BRSO
Dresden St Op Orch
Hamburg St Op Orch
Orch
Philh
Prague Nat Th Orch
Saxon St Orch
Staatskapelle Dresden
Stuttgart RO
Vienna SO
Vienna St Op Orch
VPO

BÖHME, Kurt (bass)
Janáček: Excursions of Mr Brouček (Cpte)
Lehár: Graf von Luxemburg (Cpte)
Mozart: Don Giovanni (Cpte), Entführung (Cpte), Nozze di Figaro (Cpte), Zauberflöte (Cpte)
Orff: Antigonae (Cpte), Kluge (Cpte)
R. Strauss: Elektra (Cpte)
Wagner: Meistersinger (exc), Rheingold (Cpte), Siegfried (Cpte), Walküre (exc)
Weber: Freischütz (Cpte)
(ACAN) **43 267** Fritz Wunderlich sings Opera Arias
(DECC) **414 100-2DM15** Wagner: Der Ring des Nibelungen
(DG) **437 677-2GDO2** Irmgard Seefried - Opera Recital
(EMI) **CMS7 64309-2** Kálmán—Best-loved Melodies
(PHIL) **446 057-2PB14** Wagner—The Ring Cycle - Bayreuth Festival 1967
(PILZ) **442118-2** Wagner—Operas in Historical Recordings
(PREI) **89076** Josef Herrmann (1903-1955)
(RCA) **74321 24790-2** Carl Orff 100 Years Edition
(SCHW) **314692** Vienna State Opera Live, Vol.19

BOHN, James (bar)
Britten: Paul Bunyan (Cpte)
Copland: Tender Land (Cpte)

BOHNEN, Michael (bass)
Weber: Abu Hassan (Cpte)
(PREI) **89302** The Young Lotte Lehmann
(RELI) **CR921036** Joseph Schmidt—Opera and Operetta Arias
(SCHW) **314672** Vienna State Opera Live, Vol.17

BOHUSS, Irena (sop)
(PEAR) **GEMMCDS9004/6(1)** Singers of Imperial Russia, Vol.3 (pt 1)

BOITSOV, Evgeni (ten)
Tchaikovsky: Queen of Spades (Cpte)

BOITSOV, Yevgeny (ten)
Mussorgsky: Boris Godunov (Cpte)
Rimsky-Korsakov: Sadko (Cpte)

BOKATTI, Aron (sngr)
Giordano: Fedora (Cpte)

BOKOR, Jutta (contr)
Giordano: Fedora (Cpte)

BOKOR, Margit (sop)
(ORFE) **C394101B** Great Mozart Singers Series, Vol. 1
(SCHW) **314542** Vienna State Opera Live, Vol.4
(SCHW) **314552** Vienna State Opera Live, Vol.5
(SCHW) **314572** Vienna State Opera Live, Vol.7
(SCHW) **314592** Vienna State Opera Live, Vol.9
(SCHW) **314622** Vienna State Opera Live, Vol.12
(SCHW) **314642** Vienna State Opera Live, Vol.14
(SCHW) **314652** Vienna State Opera Live, Vol.15
(SCHW) **314672** Vienna State Opera Live, Vol.17

BOKSTEDT, Bertil (pf)
(BLUE) **ABCD042** Björling - The Stockholm Tivoli Recordings, Vol.1: 1958-60
(BLUE) **ABCD057** Björling—Gröna Lund Recordings, Volume 2

BOKY, Colette (sop)
Bizet: Carmen (Cpte)

BOLDIN, Leonid (bar)
Kabalevsky: Colas Breugnon (Cpte)

BOLDRINI, Giancarlo (bass)
Mascagni: Rantzau (Cpte)

BOLGAN, Marina (sop)
Paisiello: Nina (Cpte)
Wolf-Ferrari: Campiello (Cpte)

BOLLE, James (cond)
see Budapest SO
Monadnock Fest Orch

BOLLEN, Ria (contr)
Handel: Alessandro (Cpte)

BOLLHAMMER, Karl (ten)
(SCHW) **314602** Vienna State Opera Live, Vol.10

BOLLMAN, Hans Heinz (ten)
(PEAR) **GEMMCD9310** Franz Lehár conducts Richard Tauber

BOLLONGINO, Ellen (sop)
Schreker: Gezeichneten (Cpte)

BOLOGNA TEATRO COMUNALE CHORUS
cond R. BONYNGE
Donizetti: Favorita (Cpte), Maria Stuarda (Cpte)
cond B. CAMPANELLA
(NUOV) **6892** William Matteuzzi sings Opera Arias
(NUOV) **6905** Donizetti—Great Love Duets
cond R. CHAILLY
Puccini: Manon Lescaut (Cpte)
Rossini: Cenerentola (Cpte)
Verdi: Giovanna d'Arco (Cpte), Macbeth (Cpte), Rigoletto (exc), Vespri Siciliani (Cpte)
(DECC) **448 300-2DH** Cecilia Bartoli—A Portrait
cond D. GATTI
Rossini: Armida (Cpte)
cond G. PATANÈ
Rossini: Barbiere di Siviglia (Cpte)

BOLOGNA TEATRO COMUNALE ORCHESTRA
Verdi: Giovanna d'Arco (Cpte), Macbeth (Cpte), Vespri Siciliani (Cpte)
cond R. BONYNGE
Donizetti: Favorita (Cpte), Maria Stuarda (Cpte)
(DECC) **417 011-2DH2** Pavarotti's Greatest Hits
(DECC) **425 037-2DM** Pavarotti in Concert
(DECC) **433 069-2DWO** Your Hundred Best Opera Tunes VI
(DECC) **436 313-2DA** Sutherland/Pavarotti—Operatic Duets
(DECC) **436 462-2DM** Ten Top Mezzos
cond B. CAMPANELLA
(NUOV) **6820** Luciana Serra—Opera Recital
(NUOV) **6892** William Matteuzzi sings Opera Arias
(NUOV) **6905** Donizetti—Great Love Duets
cond R. CHAILLY
Puccini: Manon Lescaut (Cpte)
Rossini: Cenerentola (Cpte)
Verdi: Rigoletto (Cpte)
(DECC) **421 896-2DA** Puccini—Great Operatic Duets
(DECC) **430 724-2DM** Great Operatic Duets
(DECC) **433 822-2DH** Essential Opera
(DECC) **436 463-2DM** Ten Top Tenors
(DECC) **436 472-2DM** Great Opera Arias
(DECC) **436 475-2DM** Dance of the Hours: ballet music from the opera
(DECC) **443 380-2DM** Ten Top Baritones & Basses 2
(DECC) **444 555-2DF2** Essential Puccini
(DECC) **448 300-2DH** Cecilia Bartoli—A Portrait
cond O. DE FABRITIIS
(MEMO) **HR4239/40** Opera Arias—Leyla Gencer
cond G. FERRO
Rossini: Scala di seta (Cpte)
cond D. GATTI
Rossini: Armida (Cpte)
cond H. VON KARAJAN
(DECC) **440 412-2DM** Mirella Freni
cond L. MAGIERA
(DECC) **444 460-2DH** Pavarotti and Friends II
(DECC) **071 140-1DH (DECC)** Pavarotti—30th Anniversary Gala Concert
(RCA) **09026 62699-2** Opera's Greatest Duets
cond G. PATANÈ
Rossini: Barbiere di Siviglia (Cpte)
(DECC) **433 822-2DH** Essential Opera
(DECC) **436 133-2DWO** World of Rossini
(DECC) **436 462-2DM** Ten Top Mezzos
(DECC) **436 464-2DM** Ten Top Baritones & Basses
(DECC) **436 472-2DM** Great Opera Arias
(DECC) **440 947-2DH** Essential Opera II
cond A. ZEDDA
Rossini: Semiramide (Cpte)

OLOGNESI, Mario (ten)
Monteverdi: Orfeo (Cpte)
Paisiello: Don Chisciotte (Cpte)
Puccini: Manon Lescaut (Cpte), Tosca (Cpte)
Rossini: Ermione (Cpte)
Verdi: Don Carlo (Cpte)

OLSHAKOV, Nikolai (ten)
(PEAR) **GEMMCDS9111(2)** Singers of Imperial Russia, Vol.5 (pt 2)

OLSHOI BALLET
cond A. LAZAREV
Rimsky-Korsakov: Mlada (Cpte)

OLSHOI SYMPHONY ORCHESTRA
Glinka: Life for the Tsar (Cpte)
Rimsky-Korsakov: Mlada (Cpte)
Tchaikovsky: Maid of Orleans (Cpte)
cond A. LAZAREV
(ERAT) **2292-45964-2** Tchaikovsky—Ballet Suites II
(ERAT) **4509-91723-2** Russian Opera Choruses
(ERAT) **4509-94808-2** Rimsky-Korsakov—Orchestral Works
(ERAT) **4509-96529-2** Ultimate Ballet

OLSHOI THEATRE CHORUS
cond A. CHISTIAKOV
(CDM) **LDC288 022** Popular Scenes from Russian Operas
cond M. ERMLER
Tchaikovsky: Eugene Onegin (Cpte), Queen of Spades (Cpte)
cond N. GOLOVANOV
(ARLE) **ARL23/5** Rimsky-Korsakov—Sadko
cond B. KHAIKIN
Tchaikovsky: Eugene Onegin (Cpte)
cond A. LAZAREV
Glinka: Life for the Tsar (Cpte)
Mussorgsky: Boris Godunov (Cpte)
Rimsky-Korsakov: Mlada (Cpte)
Tchaikovsky: Maid of Orleans (Cpte)
(ERAT) **4509-91723-2** Russian Opera Choruses
cond F. MANSOROV
Rimsky-Korsakov: Tsar's Bride (Cpte)
cond V. NEBOLSIN
Rimsky-Korsakov: Tale of Tsar Saltan (Cpte)
Tchaikovsky: Eugene Onegin (Cpte)
cond S. SAMOSUD
(DANT) **LYS013/5** Tchaikovsky—The Queen of Spades

BOLSHOI THEATRE ORCHESTRA
Mussorgsky: Boris Godunov (Cpte)
cond O. BRON
(PREI) **89061** Pavel Lisitian (born 1911)
cond A. CHISTIAKOV
G. Fried: Diary of Anne Frank (Cpte)
Rachmaninov: Francesca da Rimini (Cpte), Miserly knight (Cpte)
Rimsky-Korsakov: Kashchey (Cpte), Tsar's Bride (Cpte)
Serov: Judith (Cpte)
(CDM) **LDC288 022** Popular Scenes from Russian Operas
(CDM) **LDC288 053** Overtures & Orchestral Scenes from Russian Opera
cond M. ERMLER
Rimsky-Korsakov: Mozart and Salieri (Cpte)
Tchaikovsky: Eugene Onegin (exc), Queen of Spades (Cpte)
cond N. GOLOVANOV
(ARLE) **ARL23/5** Rimsky-Korsakov—Sadko
(EMI) **CHS7 69741-2(6)** Record of Singing, Vol.4—Russian & Slavonic Schools
(PREI) **89059** Mark Reizen (1895-1992) - I
(PREI) **89061** Pavel Lisitian (born 1911)
(PREI) **89078** Alexander Pirogov (1899-1964)
(PREI) **89080** Mark Reizen (1895-1992) - II
(PREI) **89081** Georgi Nelepp (1904-1957)
cond B. KHAIKIN
Tchaikovsky: Eugene Onegin (Cpte)
cond K. KONDRASHIN
(PREI) **89067** Andrei Ivanov (1900-1970)
cond A. LAZAREV
(ARLE) **ARL23/5** Rimsky-Korsakov—Sadko
cond F. MANSOROV
Rimsky-Korsakov: Tsar's Bride (Cpte)
cond A. MELIK-PASHAYEV
(PREI) **89059** Mark Reizen (1895-1992) - I
(PREI) **89061** Pavel Lisitian (born 1911)
(PREI) **89067** Andrei Ivanov (1900-1970)
(PREI) **89078** Alexander Pirogov (1899-1964)
(PREI) **89081** Georgi Nelepp (1904-1957)
cond V. NEBOLSIN
Rimsky-Korsakov: Tale of Tsar Saltan (Cpte)
Tchaikovsky: Eugene Onegin (Cpte)
(ARLE) **ARL23/5** Rimsky-Korsakov—Sadko
(PREI) **89059** Mark Reizen (1895-1992) - I
(PREI) **89061** Pavel Lisitian (born 1911)
(PREI) **89078** Alexander Pirogov (1899-1964)
(PREI) **89080** Mark Reizen (1895-1992) - II
(PREI) **89081** Georgi Nelepp (1904-1957)
cond A. ORLOV
(EMI) **CHS7 69741-2(6)** Record of Singing, Vol.4—Russian & Slavonic Schools
(PREI) **89061** Pavel Lisitian (born 1911)
(PREI) **89067** Andrei Ivanov (1900-1970)
cond V. PIRADOV
(PREI) **89061** Pavel Lisitian (born 1911)
cond S. SAMOSUD
(ARLE) **ARL23/5** Rimsky-Korsakov—Sadko
(DANT) **LYS013/5** Tchaikovsky—The Queen of Spades
(EMI) **CHS7 69741-2(6)** Record of Singing, Vol.4—Russian & Slavonic Schools
(PREI) **89059** Mark Reizen (1895-1992) - I
(PREI) **89061** Pavel Lisitian (born 1911)
(PREI) **89067** Andrei Ivanov (1900-1970)
(PREI) **89078** Alexander Pirogov (1899-1964)
(PREI) **89080** Mark Reizen (1895-1992) - II
(PREI) **89081** Georgi Nelepp (1904-1957)
cond L. STEINBERG
(ARLE) **ARL23/5** Rimsky-Korsakov—Sadko
cond G. ZHEMCHUZHIN
(PILZ) **441002-2** Original Bolshoi Theatre Orchestra

BOLTON, Andrea (sop)
(OPRA) **ORCH103** Italian Opera—1810-20

BOLTON, Ivor (cond)
see City of London Baroque Sinfonia
Philh
Scottish CO
St James's Baroque Plyrs

BÖMCHES, Helge Von (bass)
Mozart: Zauberflöte (Cpte)

BONA, Jacques (bar)
Campra: Tancrède (exc)
Lully: Atys (exc)
M-A. Charpentier: Médée (Cpte)
Montéclair: Jephté (Cpte)
Rameau: Zoroastre (Cpte)

BONATO, Armanda (mez)
Verdi: Traviata (Cpte), Trovatore (Cpte)

BONAVOLONTÀ, Nino (cond)
see Rome SO

BONAZZI, Elaine (mez)
(SONY) **SM22K46290(4)** Stravinsky—The Complete Edition (pt 4)

BONCI, Alessandro (ten)
(EMI) **CHS7 64860-2(1)** La Scala Edition - Vol.1, 1878-1914 (pt 1)
(MEMO) **HR4408/9(1)** Singers in Genoa, Vol.1 (disc 1)
(NIMB) **NI7856** Legendary Tenors
(PEAR) **GEMMCDS9923(2)** Covent Garden on Record, Vol.1 (pt 2)
(PEAR) **GEMMCDS9924(2)** Covent Garden on Record, Vol.2 (pt 2)
(PEAR) **GEMMCD9168** Alessandro Bonci
(SYMP) **SYMCD1113** The Harold Wayne Collection, Vol.13

BONCOMPAGNI, Elio (cond)
see Turin RAI Orch

BOND, Dorothy (sop)
Delius: Village Romeo and Juliet (Cpte)

BONDO, Niels Juul (bar)
Nielsen: Maskarade (Cpte)

BONELL, Carlos (gtr)
(ASV) **CDQS6038** Fandango

BONIFACCIO, Maddalena (sop)
Pergolesi: Serva Padrona

BONILLA, Daniel (bass)
Verdi: Alzira (Cpte)

BONINI, Francesco Maria (bar)
(BONG) **GB1043-2** Italian Baritones of the Acoustic Era
(BONG) **GB1076-2** Mario Gilion - Opera Arias

BONINSEGNA, Celestina (sop)
(EMI) **CHS7 64860-2(2)** La Scala Edition - Vol.1, 1878-1914 (pt 2)
(IRCC) **IRCC-CD808** Souvenirs of 19th Century Italian Opera
(PEAR) **GEMMCDS9924(1)** Covent Garden on Record, Vol.2 (pt 1)
(PEAR) **GEMMCD9130** Great Sopranos, Vol.2
(SYMP) **SYMCD1149** Fernando De Lucia
(TEST) **SBT1008** Viva Rossini

BÖNISCH, Hans (organ)
(MOTE) **CD20171** Romantic Organ Music

BÖNISCH, Peter (tpt)
(MOTE) **CD20171** Romantic Organ Music

BONISOLLI, Franco (ten)
Bizet: Djamileh (Cpte)
Giordano: Andrea Chénier (Cpte)
Gluck: Iphigénie en Tauride (Cpte)
Leoncavallo: Bohème (Cpte)
Mascagni: Cavalleria Rusticana (Cpte)
Verdi: Masnadieri (Cpte), Trovatore (Cpte)
(ACAN) **49 384** Puccini: Opera Arias and Duets
(CAST) **CVI2068** Opera Highlights from Verona 1
(EMI) **CDC7 54016-2** Tenorissimo!
(MCI) **MCCD099** Opera's Greatest Arias

BONITZ, Birgit (sop)
R. Strauss: Rosenkavalier (Cpte)

BONNAFOUS, Jean-Claude (ten)
Offenbach: Orphée aux enfers (Cpte)

BONNEAU, Paul (cond)
see New SO
Paris Champs-Élysées Orch
SO

BONNEMA, Albert (sngr)
Schillings: Mona Lisa (Cpte)

BONNER, Tessa (sop)
Monteverdi: Orfeo (Cpte)
Mozart: Zauberflöte (Cpte)
Purcell: Dido (Cpte), Indian Queen, Z630 (Cpte)

BONNET, Cécile (sop)
Essyad: Collier des Ruses (Cpte)

BONNEY, Barbara (sop)
Beethoven: Fidelio (Cpte)
Bernstein: West Side Story (Cpte)
Humperdinck: Hänsel und Gretel (Cpte)
J. Strauss II: Fledermaus (exc)
Lehár: Lustige Witwe (Cpte)
Mozart: Clemenza di Tito (Cpte), Don Giovanni (Cpte), Nozze di Figaro (Cpte), Zauberflöte (Cpte)
Purcell: Fairy Queen, Z629 (Cpte)
R. Strauss: Ariadne auf Naxos (Cpte), Rosenkavalier (Cpte)
Schoenberg: Moses und Aron (Cpte)
Verdi: Falstaff (Cpte)
Wagner: Tannhäuser (Cpte)
(CAST) **CVI2065** Highlights from the Royal Opera House, Covent Garden
(TELD) **0630-11470-2** The Best of Barbara Bonney
(TELD) **4509-97507-2** Mozart—Famous Opera Arias
(TELD) **4509-98824-2** Thomas Hampson Collection,Vol III-Operatic Scenes
(TELD) **9031-77676-6(TELD)** My World of Opera - Kiri Te Kanawa

BONTE, Raymond (ten)
Mussorgsky: Boris Godunov (Cpte)

BONYNGE, Richard (cond)
see Ambrosian Op Chor
Australian Op & Ballet Orch
Bologna Teatro Comunale Orch
Catania Teatro Massimo Bellini Orch
ECO
English Concert Orch
Ireland National SO
London Sym Chor
LPO
LSO
MMF Orch
Monte Carlo Nat Op Orch
Monte Carlo Op Orch
National PO
National SO
New Philh
New PO
New SO
NY Met Op Orch
NYC Op Orch
Orch
ROHO
Rovigo Venezze Cons Orch
Santa Cecilia Academy Orch
SRO
Sydney Eliz Orch
Sydney Eliz PO
WNO Orch

BONYNGE, Richard (pf)
(DECC) **436 202-2DM** Italian Songs

BOOTH, Margery (mez)
Wagner: Götterdämmerung (Cpte)

BOOTH, Philip (bass)
V. Thomson: Mother of us all (Cpte)
Verdi: Ballo in maschera (Cpte)

BOOTH, Thomas (ten)
G. Lloyd: John Socman (exc)

BOOTH, Webster (ten)
(EMI) **CHS7 69741-2(2)** Record of Singing, Vol.4—Anglo-American School (pt 2)
(PEAR) **GEMMCD9024** German—Orchestral and Vocal Music

BOOTH, William (ten)
Lehár: Lustige Witwe (exc)
Sullivan: Gondoliers (Cpte)

BOOTHBY, Richard (va da gamba)
(VIRG) **VC7 59324-2** Purcell—O Solitude - Songs and Airs

BOOTH-JONES, Christopher (bar)
Bizet: Carmen (Cpte)
Britten: Billy Budd (Cpte)
Handel: Giulio Cesare (Cpte)

BOOZER, Brenda (mez)
Verdi: Falstaff (Cpte)
(CAST) **CASH5052** Verdi Operatic Favourites

BORCHERS, Christel (contr)
Wagner: Walküre (Cpte)
(EMI) **LDX9 91275-1(EMI)** Sawallisch conducts Wagner's Ring
(EURO) **GD69003** Wagner—Der Ring des Nibelungen

BORDEAUX AQUITAINE ORCHESTRA
cond R. BENZI
(EMI) **CZS5 68113-2** Vive Offenbach!
cond A. LOMBARD
Bizet: Carmen (Cpte)
Ravel: Enfant et les sortilèges (Cpte)

BORDEAUX CNR CHILDREN'S CHOIR
cond A. LOMBARD
Bizet: Carmen (Cpte)

BORDEAUX THEATRE CHORUS
cond A. LOMBARD
Bizet: Carmen (Cpte)
Ravel: Enfant et les sortilèges (Cpte)

BORDEN, Barbara (sop)
Purcell: Dido (Cpte)
(HARM) **HMX290 1528/33(1)** A Purcell Companion (pt 1)

BORDONALI, Attilio (bar)
(MSCM) **MM30276** Rossini—Barbiere di Siviglia, etc

BORDONI, Franco (bar)
Verdi: Ballo in maschera (Cpte)

BORELLI, Giannella (mez)
(EMI) **CDH7 63495-2** Victoria de los Angeles—Early Recordings

BORG, Kim (bass)
Mozart: Zauberflöte (Cpte)
Mussorgsky: Boris Godunov (Cpte)
Orff: Antigonae (Cpte)
(FINL) **4509-95606-2** Kim Borg - Songs and Arias

BORGATO, Maria (mez)
Verdi: Macbeth (Cpte)

BORGATTI, Giuseppe (ten)
(EMI) **CHS7 64860-2(1)** La Scala Edition - Vol.1, 1878-1914 (pt 1)
(MEMO) **HR4408/9(2)** Singers in Genoa, Vol.1 (disc 2)

BORGHESE, Simone (mez)
Offenbach: Contes d'Hoffmann (Cpte)

BORGIOLI, Armando (bar)
Verdi: Aida (Cpte)

BORGIOLI, Dino (ten)
(CLUB) **CL99-014** Dino Borgioli (1891-1960)
(EMI) **CHS7 64864-2(1)** La Scala Edition - Vol.2, 1915-46 (pt 1)
(MSCM) **MM30276** Rossini—Barbiere di Siviglia, etc
(PEAR) **GEMMCDS9925(2)** Covent Garden on Record—Vol.3 (pt 2)
(PEAR) **GEMMCDS9926(1)** Covent Garden on Record—Vol.4 (pt 1)
(PEAR) **GEMMCD9091** Dino Borgioli
(PREI) **89063** Rosetta Pampanini (1896-1973)
(TEST) **SBT1008** Viva Rossini

BORGONOVA, Otello (bar)
Leoncavallo: Pagliacci (Cpte)

BORGONOVO, Luigi (bar)
Verdi: Traviata (Cpte)
(CONI) **CDHD235** The Puccini Album
(MMOI) **CDMOIR412** Great Voices of the Century Sing Puccini
(NIMB) **NI7845** Giacomo Lauri-Volpi (1892-1979)
(PREI) **89012** Giacomo Lauri-Volpi (1894-1979)

BORI, Lucrezia (sop)
(ASV) **CDAJA5137** The Three Tenors of the Century
(CONI) **CDHD170** Gigli—Centenary Tribute
(CONI) **CDHD235** The Puccini Album
(MMOI) **CDMOIR418** Great Voices of the Century—John McCormack
(PEAR) **GEMMCDS9160(1)** De Luca Edition, Vol.2 (pt 1)
(PEAR) **GEMMCD9130** Great Sopranos, Vol.2
(PEAR) **GEMMCD9364** Beethoven—Concertos
(PEAR) **GEMMCD9458** Lucrezia Bori—Opera & Song Recital
(PREI) **89002** Miguel Fleta (1893-1938)
(PREI) **89036** Giuseppe de Luca (1876-1950) - I
(RCA) **GD87811** Beniamino Gigli—Operatic Arias
(RCA) **09026 61580-2(2)** RCA/Met 100 Singers, 100 Years (pt 2)
(ROMO) **81016-2** Lucrezia Bori (1887-1960)

BORISENKO, Veronica (mez)
Rimsky-Korsakov: Tsar's Bride (Cpte)

BORISOVA, Galina (mez)
Rachmaninov: Aleko (Cpte)
Rimsky-Korsakov: Mlada (Cpte), Tsar's Bride (Cpte)
Tchaikovsky: Queen of Spades (Cpte)

BORK, Hanneke van (sop)
Cavalli: Ormindo (Cpte)
Mozart: Zauberflöte (exc)

BORKH, Inge (sop)
Orff: Antigonae (Cpte)
Puccini: Turandot (Cpte)
R. Strauss: Elektra (Cpte), Salome (Cpte)
(EMI) **CHS7 69741-2(4)** Record of Singing, Vol.4—German School
(RCA) **GD60874** R. Strauss—Scenes from Elektra & Salome

BORMIDA, Ida (mez)
Mascagni: Cavalleria Rusticana (Cpte)
(DECC) **425 681-2DM2** Tutto Pavarotti

BORODINA, Olga (mez)
Borodin: Prince Igor (Cpte)
Mussorgsky: Boris Godunov (Cpte), Khovanshchina (Cpte)
Prokofiev: War and Peace (Cpte)
Tchaikovsky: Eugene Onegin (exc), Queen of Spades (Cpte)
Verdi: Traviata (exc)

BORONAT, Olimpia (sop)
(NIMB) **NI7865** Great Singers at the Mariinsky Theatre

BOROWSKA, Joanna (sop)
Mozart: Così fan tutte (Cpte)
Mussorgsky: Khovanshchina (Cpte)
R. Strauss: Elektra (Cpte)

BOROWSKI, Nikolai (bar)
Pfitzner: Herz (Cpte)

BORRIELLO, Mario (bar)
Mozart: Così fan tutte (exc)
Puccini: Madama Butterfly (Cpte), Manon Lescaut (Cpte), Turandot (Cpte)

BORRIS, Kaja (mez)
R. Strauss: Elektra (Cpte)
Schmidt: Notre Dame (Cpte)
Schreker: Gezeichneten (Cpte)
Schulhoff: Plameny (Cpte)
Wagner: Fliegende Holländer (exc)
Zemlinsky: Kreidekreis (Cpte)

BORSKÝ, Miroslav (bar)
Hába: Mother (Cpte)

BORSÒ, Umberto (ten)
Mascagni: Piccolo Marat (Cpte)

BORST, Danielle (sop)
Fauré: Pénélope (Cpte)
Monteverdi: Incoronazione di Poppea (Cpte), Orfeo (Cpte)
Vivaldi: Montezuma (Cpte)

BORST, Heinz (bass)
Wagner: Meistersinger (Cpte)

BORST, Martina (mez)
Hindemith: Neues vom Tage (Cpte)
Spohr: Faust (Cpte)
(CAPR) **10 481** R.Strauss—Opera Concert

BORSTLAP, Freek (va da gamba)
(ETCE) **KTC1013** Purcell: Songs

BORTHAYRE, Jean (bass)
Gounod: Faust (Cpte)
(BELA) **450 006-2** Famous Opera Duets
(DECC) **433 066-2DWO** Your Hundred Best Opera Tunes III

BORTOLI, Carlo de (bass)
Ponchielli: Lituani (Cpte)
Verdi: Rigoletto (Cpte)

BORTOLUZZI, Bianca (mez)
Verdi: Rigoletto (Cpte)
(BUTT) **BMCD015** Pavarotti Collection - Duets and Scenes

BOSCHI, Hélène (pf)
(CHNT) **LDC278 1068** Chabrier—Une Education Manquée/Mélodies

BOSCHKOWÁ, Nelly (mez)
Puccini: Madama Butterfly (Cpte)

BOSCO, Carlo del (bass)
Puccini: Manon Lescaut (Cpte)
Verdi: Macbeth (Cpte)
(CBS) **CD79312** Puccini: Il Trittico

BOSI, Carlo (ten)
Mascagni: Amico Fritz (Cpte), Rantzau (Cpte)
Paisiello: Nina (Cpte)
Puccini: Fanciulla del West (Cpte)
Rossini: Armida (Cpte)

BOSKOVSKY, Willi (cond)
see Munich RO
Vienna SO
VJSO
VPO

BOSTOCK, Angela (sop)
Donizetti: Maria Stuarda (Cpte)

BOSTON POPS ORCHESTRA
cond A. FIEDLER
(RCA) **GD60700** Fiedler's Favourite Marches
(RCA) **09026 61207-2** Handel—Orchestral Works
(RCA) **09026 61249-2** Marches in Hi-Fi
(RCA) **09026 61429-2** Offenbach in America
(RCA) **09026 61497-2** Hi-Fi Fiedler
(RCA) **09026 68132-2** Pops Caviar—Russian Orchestral Fireworks
cond J.T. WILLIAMS
(SONY) **SK48224** John Williams—The Green Album
(SONY) **SK48232** Joy to the World

BOSTON SYMPHONY ORCHESTRA
cond A. COPLAND
(RCA) **GD86802** Copland—Suites
(RCA) **09026 61505-2** Copland/Gould - Composers Conduct
cond S. KOUSSEVITZKY
(EMI) **CHS7 69741-2(1)** Record of Singing, Vol.4—Anglo-American School (pt 1)
(PEAR) **GEMMCD9179** The Art of Serge Koussevitzk
cond E. LEINSDORF
(RCA) **GD60398** Leontyne Price sings Strauss arias
(RCA) **09026 61580-2(7)** RCA/Met 100 Singers, 100 Years (pt 7)
cond C. MUNCH
(RCA) **GD60682** Brahms—Symphony No.2/Tragic Overture
(RCA) **GD60686** Wagner—Opera Excerpts
(RCA) **GD86805** Orchestral Works
(RCA) **09026 61400-2** Berlioz/Saint-Saëns—Orchestral Works
cond S. OZAWA
R. Strauss: Elektra (Cpte)
Tchaikovsky: Queen of Spades (Cpte)
(RCA) **09026 61440-2** Opera's Greatest Moments
(SONY) **SLV53488(SONY)** Dvořák in Prague - A Celebration

BOSTRIDGE, Ian (ten)
Purcell: Dioclesian, Z627 (exc)
(SONY) **S2K66836** Goldschmidt—Beatrice Cenci, etc

BOTHA, Johan (ten)
Wagner: Tristan und Isolde (Cpte)
(ROH) **75605 55013-2** The Puccini Experience

BOTT, Catherine (sop)
Blow: Venus and Adonis (Cpte)
Monteverdi: Orfeo (Cpte)
Purcell: Dido (Cpte), Fairy Queen, Z629, Indian Queen, Z630 (Cpte)
(CHAN) **CHAN0571** A Purcell Miscellany
(L'OI) **444 620-2OH** The Glory of Purcell

BOTTAZZO, Pietro (ten)
Rossini: Armida (Cpte)

BÖTTCHER, Else (sop)
(SCHW) **314532** Vienna State Opera Live, Vol.3

BOTTCHER, Ron (bar)
Verdi: Forza del destino (Cpte)

BOTTINI, Giuseppe (treb)
Puccini: Tosca (Cpte)

BOTTION, Aldo (ten)
Puccini: Fanciulla del West (Cpte)
Verdi: Due Foscari (Cpte), Otello (Cpte)

BOTTONE, Bonaventura (ten)
Bernstein: Candide (1988) (exc)
Donizetti: Lucia di Lammermoor (Cpte)
J. Strauss II: Fledermaus (Cpte)
Offenbach: Orphée aux enfers (exc)
Romberg: Student Prince (Cpte)
Sullivan: Mikado (exc)
Tippett: Ice Break (Cpte)
Vaughan Williams: Hugh the Drover (Cpte)
Verdi: Otello (Cpte)
Weill: Street Scene (Cpte)

BOTTONE, Robert (pf)
(MERI) **CDE84162** Vocal Music for Choir

3OTVAY, Károly (cond)
see Budapest Stgs

3OUCHARD, Lise (tpt)
Vivier: Kopernikus (Cpte)

3OUCHER, Gene (bar)
Verdi: Traviata (Cpte)

3OUÉ, Géori (sop)
Offenbach: Contes d'Hoffmann (Cpte)

3OUGHTON, Ian (bar)
Boughton: Bethlehem (Cpte)
(CALA) **CACD1011** Borodin—Orchestral Works

3OUGHTON, William (cond)
see English SO
English Stg Orch
Philh

3OULEZ, Pierre (cond)
see Bayreuth Fest Orch
BBC SO
NYPO
Paris InterContemporain Ens
Paris Op. Orch
ROHO

OULIN, Sophie (sop)
Gluck: Echo et Narcisse (Cpte)
Handel: Alessandro (Cpte)
M-A. Charpentier: Médée (Cpte)
Marais: Alcyone (Cpte)

OULT, Sir Adrian (cond)
see BBC SO
LPO
LSO
New Philh
Oslo PO
ROHO

OULTON, Sophie (mez)
Gluck: Iphigénie en Tauride (Cpte)

OUR, Ernest (cond)
see FRNO

OURDIN, Roger (bar)
Offenbach: Contes d'Hoffmann (Cpte)

OURDON, Rosario (cond)
see LSO
orch
SO
Victor Orch
Victor SO

OURGOGNE CHORUS
cond S. BAUDO
Debussy: Pelléas et Mélisande (Cpte)

AURICE) BOURGUE WIND ENSEMBLE
(PIER) **PV730005** The Most Beautiful Operatic Arias
(PIER) **PV787033** Mozart—Opera Excerpts (arr Wind)

OURNEMOUTH MUNICIPAL ORCHESTRA
cond D. GODFREY
(BEUL) **1PD4** 78 Classics - Volume One

OURNEMOUTH SINFONIETTA
cond G. HURST
(CHAN) **CHAN6544** Elgar—Orchestral Favourites
(CHAN) **CHAN6545** Vaughan Williams—Orchestral Works
(CHAN) **CHAN8432** Elgar/Vaughan Williams—Orchestral Works

OURNEMOUTH SYMPHONY ORCHESTRA
cond J. FARRER
(IMP) **MCD75** Copland/Gershwin—Orchestral Works
cond R. HICKOX
Tippett: New Year Suite
(CHAN) **CHAN9355** Delius—Orchestral Works
cond A. LITTON
(VIRG) **VMT7 59699-2** Tchaikovsky—Symphonies, Vol.1

URSIN, Denise (sop)
Boïeldieu: Voitures Versées (Cpte)

URVIL (ten)
Offenbach: Contes d'Hoffmann (Cpte)
(EMI) **CZS5 68113-2** Vive Offenbach!

USQUET, Eugène (bass)
Mussorgsky: Boris Godunov (Cpte)

UTET, Benoît (bass)
Donizetti: Roberto Devereux (Cpte)

UTET, Benoit (ten)
Janáček: Makropulos Affair (Cpte)

BOUVET, Maximilien-Nicolas (bar)
(SYMP) **SYMCD1089** Historic Baritones of the French School

BOUVIER, Hélène (mez)
Saint-Saëns: Samson et Dalila (Cpte)
(EMI) **CHS7 69741-2(3)** Record of Singing, Vol.4—French School

BOVE, H. (fl)
(MSCM) **MM30446** Lily Pons - Recital

BOVET, Martina (sop)
Monteverdi: Incoronazione di Poppea (Cpte)

BOVINO, Maria (sop)
Britten: Albert Herring (Cpte), Peter Grimes (Cpte)
(OPRA) **ORCH103** Italian Opera—1810-20

BOVY, Vina (sop)
Offenbach: Contes d'Hoffmann (Cpte)

BOWDEN, Pamela (contr)
Herrmann: Wuthering Heights (Cpte)
(CFP) **CD-CFP4582** Flowers in Music
(EMI) **CMS7 64412-2** Gilbert & Sullivan—Ruddigore/Shakespeare Music

BOWEN, John (ten)
Boughton: Bethlehem (Cpte)

BOWEN, Kenneth (ten)
Britten: Death in Venice (Cpte)

BOWER, Jacalyn (mez)
Wagner: Walküre (Cpte)
(DG) **072 422-3GH7** Levine conducts Wagner's Ring

BOWERS, Evan (ten)
S. Wallace: Kabbalah (Cpte)

BOWKUN, Helena (pf)
(MSOU) **DFCDI-012** Art of Ofra Harnoy

BOWMAN, Brian (euphonium)
(KLVI) **KCD11060** American Variations

BOWMAN, David (bar)
(DECC) **436 990-2DWO** The World of Benjamin Britten

BOWMAN, James (alto)
Britten: Death in Venice (Cpte), Midsummer Night's Dream (Cpte)
Cavalli: Calisto (Cpte)
Gluck: Orfeo ed Euridice (Cpte)
Handel: Ariodante (Cpte), Giulio Cesare (Cpte), Orlando (Cpte), Ottone (Cpte)
Purcell: Dido (Cpte), Dioclesian, Z627 (exc), Fairy Queen, Z629 (Cpte)
(HYPE) **CDA66288** 'Mr Henry Purcell's Most Admirable Composure's'
(HYPE) **CDA66483** Handel—Heroic Arias
(HYPE) **KING2** Essential Purcell
(IMP) **ORCD11010** Baroque Beauties
(IMP) **PCD894** Great Baroque Arias, Part I

BOWMAN, Robert (ten)
(EMI) **LDB4 91283-1(EMI)** Maria Callas at Covent Garden

BOWYER, Kevin (organ)
(SYMP) **SYMCD1175** Ave Maria

BOYER, Antonio (bar)
Alfano: Risurrezione (Cpte)

BOYER, Marie (mez)
Campra: Idoménée (exc)
Rossi: Orfeo (Cpte)

BOYSEN, Rolf (spkr)
Mozart: Entführung (Cpte)
Weber: Freischütz (Cpte)
Weill: Dreigroschenoper (Cpte)

BRABBINS, Martyn (cond)
see BBC Scottish SO

BRACHT, Roland (bass)
Gluck: Alceste (1776) (Cpte)
Mozart: Entführung (Cpte), Zauberflöte (Cpte)
Stravinsky: Oedipus rex (Cpte)
Verdi: Rigoletto (Cpte)
Wagner: Feen (Cpte), Rheingold (Cpte)
(EURO) **GD69003** Wagner—Der Ring des Nibelungen

BRADBURY, Paula (sop)
Verdi: Rigoletto (Cpte)

BRADLEY, Gwendolyn (sop)
R. Strauss: Arabella (Cpte)

BRADSHAW, Claire (mez)
Vaughan Williams: Pilgrim's Progress (Cpte)

BRADSHAW, Dawn (sop)
Sullivan: Gondoliers (Cpte), Iolanthe (Cpte)

BRADSHAW, Sally (sop)
Handel: Agrippina (Cpte)

BRAFIELD, Mark (organ)
(CNTI) **CCD1054** Delius—Complete partsongs

BRAGA, Rannveig (mez)
R. Strauss: Salome (Cpte)
Verdi: Traviata (Cpte)

BRAHAM, Jean (sop)
Schoenberg: Moses und Aron (Cpte)

BRAIN, Dennis (hn)
(TEST) **SBT1012** Cantelli conducts Wagner & Brahms

BRAITHWAITE, Warwick (cond)
see LSO
orch
Philh
Sadlers Wells Op Orch

BRAMALL, Anthony (cond)
see Slovak PO

BRAMANTE, Aldo (bass)
Cherubini: Lodoïska (Cpte)
Puccini: Fanciulla del West (Cpte), Manon Lescaut (Cpte)
Spontini: Vestale (Cpte)
Verdi: Due Foscari (Cpte)

BRAMBILLA, Hugues (ten)
Offenbach: Orphée aux enfers (Cpte), Périchole (Cpte)

BRAMBILLA, Linda (mez)
Verdi: Rigoletto (Cpte)
(PEAR) **GEMMCDS9180** Verdi—Rigoletto, etc

BRAMMER, Philipp (spkr)
R. Strauss: Intermezzo (Cpte)

BRANCO KRSMANOVITCH CHORUS
cond J-C. CASADESUS
Ancelin: Filius Hominis (Cpte)

BRAND, Adrian (ten)
Rameau: Castor et Pollux (Cpte)

BRAND, Geoffrey (cond)
see Black Dyke Mills Band
Britannia Building Soc Band

(THE) BRANDENBURG CONSORT
cond R. GOODMAN
(HYPE) **CDA66600** Rondeaux Royaux - Baroque Pops
(HYPE) **CDA66745** Vivaldi—Opera Arias and Sinfonias

BRANDES, Christine (sop)
Purcell: Dido (Cpte)
(HARM) **HMU90 7167** Purcell & Blow—Songs & Intrumental Music

BRANDT, Karl-Heinz (ten)
Telemann: Don Quichotte (Cpte)
(HARM) **HMC90 1420** Weill—The Seven Deadly Sins; Songs

BRANDT, Marianne (sop/mez)
(SYMP) **SYMCD1085** The Harold Wayne Collection, Vol.6

BRANISTEANU, Horiana (sop)
Mozart: Don Giovanni (Cpte)

BRANNIGAN, Owen (bass)
Britten: Albert Herring (Cpte), Midsummer Night's Dream (Cpte), Noye's Fludde (Cpte), Peter Grimes (Cpte)
Cavalli: Calisto (Cpte)
Gay: Beggar's Opera (Cpte)
Purcell: Fairy Queen, Z629 (Cpte)
Sullivan: Gondoliers (Cpte), HMS Pinafore (Cpte), Iolanthe (Cpte), Mikado (Cpte), Pirates of Penzance (Cpte), Trial by Jury (Cpte), Yeomen of the Guard (Cpte)
(CFP) **CD-CFP4238** Gilbert and Sullivan
(CFP) **CD-CFP4609** Favourite Gilbert & Sullivan
(DECC) **430 095-2DWO** The World of Gilbert & Sullivan, Vol.1
(DECC) **436 990-2DWO** The World of Benjamin Britten
(EMI) **CMS7 64409-2** Sullivan—Pirates of Penzance & Orch. Works
(EMI) **CMS7 64412-2** Gilbert & Sullivan—Ruddigore/Shakespeare Music

BRANS, Werner (bar)
Puccini: Bohème (Cpte)

BRANZELL, Karin (contr)
(EMI) **CDH7 69787-2** Richard Tauber sings Operetta Arias
(PEAR) **GEMMCD9409** Lotte Lehmenn—Vol.1
(PREI) **89039** Karin Branzell (1891-1974)

(ELISABETH) BRASSEUR CHOIR
cond J. FOURNET
Bizet: Pêcheurs de Perles (Cpte)

BRASSUS CHORALE
cond R. BONYNGE
(DECC) **440 410-2DM** Plácido Domingo

BRATHWAITE, Maureen (mez)
Gershwin: Porgy and Bess (exc)

BRATISLAVA CHILDREN'S CHOIR
cond W. HUMBURG
Puccini: Bohème (Cpte)
cond O. LENÁRD
Puccini: Bohème (Cpte)
cond C. MACKERRAS
Janáček: Cunning Little Vixen (Cpte)

BRATISLAVA CITY CHORUS
cond J. WILDNER
J. Strauss II: Fledermaus (exc)

BRATISLAVA NATIONAL OPERA CHORUS
cond O. LENÁRD
Puccini: Bohème (Cpte)

BRATISLAVA PHILHARMONIC CHOIR
cond B. APREA
Mercadante: Bravo (Cpte)

cond F. LUISI
(NUOV) **6905** Donizetti—Great Love Duets

BRATISLAVA PHILHARMONIC ORCHESTRA
cond K. WÖSS
(CAPR) **10 810** Mozart—Opera Highlights

BRATISLAVA RADIO SYMPHONY ORCHESTRA
(MARC) **8 223369** Humperdinck—Orchestral Works
(OPUS) **9156 1824** Dvorský sings Operatic Arias
cond H. BEISSEL
(MARC) **8 223162** Pfitzner: Orchestral Works
cond M. DITTRICH
(MARC) **8 223381** Salieri—Overtures
cond O. DOHNÁNYI
(NAXO) **8 550241** Verdi—Opera Choruses
cond M. HALÁSZ
(NAXO) **8 550497** Thomas Harper—Opera Recital
cond W. HUMBURG
Puccini: Bohème (Cpte)
(NAXO) **8 550605** Favourite Soprano Arias
cond D. JOHANOS
(NAXO) **8 550486** Rimsky-Korsakov—Orchestral Works
cond A. LEAPER
(MARC) **8 223419** Edward German—Orchestral Works
(MARC) **8 223446** Holbrooke—Orchestral Works
cond O. LENÁRD
Bellini: Sonnambula (Cpte)
Puccini: Bohème (Cpte)
Suchoň: Whirlpool (Cpte)
(NAXO) **8 550080** The Best of French Ballet
(NAXO) **8 550081** Invitation to the Dance
(NAXO) **8 550098** Rimsky-Korsakov—Orchestral Works
(NAXO) **8 550343** Italian and French Opera Arias
cond A. RAHBARI
Leoncavallo: Pagliacci (Cpte)
Mascagni: Cavalleria Rusticana (Cpte)
Puccini: Madama Butterfly (Cpte), Tosca (Cpte)
Verdi: Rigoletto (Cpte), Traviata (Cpte)
(NAXO) **8 550684** Duets and Arias from Italian Operas
cond R. STANKOVSKY
(MARC) **8 223400** Cui—Orchestral Works
cond J. WILDNER
J. Strauss II: Fledermaus (exc)

BRAUER, Herbert (bar)
J. Strauss II: Fledermaus (Cpte)

BRAUN, Hans (bar)
Beethoven: Fidelio (Cpte)
R. Strauss: Daphne (Cpte)
Wagner: Lohengrin (Cpte)

BRAUN, Heinz (ten)
(PREI) **90103** Helge Roswaenge Recital (1959)

BRAUN, Helena (sop)
Mozart: Nozze di Figaro (Cpte)
Wagner: Tristan und Isolde (Cpte)
(ORFE) **C394101B** Great Mozart Singers Series, Vol. 1
(SCHW) **314502** Vienna State Opera—Live Recordings (sampler)
(SCHW) **314562** Vienna State Opera Live, Vol.6
(SCHW) **314692** Vienna State Opera Live, Vol.19
(SCHW) **314712** Vienna State Opera Live, Vol.21
(SCHW) **314722** Vienna State Opera Live, Vol.22
(SCHW) **314742** Vienna State Opera Live, Vol.24

BRAUN, Mel (bar)
Handel: Floridante (exc)

BRAUN, Victor (bar)
R. Strauss: Capriccio (Cpte)
Wagner: Tannhäuser (Cpte)
(DECC) **433 065-2DWO** Your Hundred Best Opera Tunes Volume II
(DECC) **433 443-2DA** Great Opera Choruses
(DECC) **436 300-2DX** Opera Gala Sampler
(DECC) **440 069-2DWO** The World of Wagner

BRAUNER, Hilde (contr)
Lehár: Graf von Luxemburg (exc)
O. Straus: Walzertraum (exc)
(KOCH) **399 225** Operetta Highlights 3

BRÄUTIGAM, Thomas (ten)
Weill: Jasager (Cpte)

BRAVURA, Giuseppe (bar)
Puccini: Turandot (Cpte)

BRAY CHORAL SOCIETY
cond R. SACCANI
Verdi: Aida (Cpte)

BREAM, Julian (gtr)
(RCA) **09026 61450-2** Together - Julian Bream & John Williams
(RCA) **09026 61583-2(5)** Julian Bream Edition (pt 5)
(RCA) **09026 61601-2** J. Bream Edition, Vol.18: Music for Voice & Gtr
(RCA) **74321 25821-2** Café Classics—Music of Spain

BREBION, Jean (cond)
see French Rad Lyric Orch
ORTF Lyric Orch

BRECKNOCK, John (ten)
Offenbach: Robinson Crusoé (Cpte)
Verdi: Traviata (Cpte)

BREDY, Rosine (sngr)
Offenbach: Madame l'Archiduc (Cpte)

BREESE, Timothy (bar)
Mussorgsky: Khovanshchina (Cpte)

BREGA, Marthe (sop)
(EPM) **150 122** Milhaud—Historic Recordings 1928-1948

BREGENZ FESTIVAL CHORUS
cond A. PAULIK
J. Strauss II: Nacht in Venedig (Cpte)

BREGONZI, Alec (ten)
Offenbach: Christopher Columbus (Cpte)

BREISACH, Paul (cond)
see Berlin St Op Orch
orch

BRÉJEAN-SILVER, Georgette (sop)
(PEAR) **GEMMCDS9923(2)** Covent Garden on Record, Vol.1 (pt 2)
(SYMP) **SYMCD1113** The Harold Wayne Collection, Vol.13
(SYMP) **SYMCD1172** The Harold Wayne Collection, Vol.21
(SYMP) **SYMCD1173** The Harold Wayne Collection, Vol.22

BREKKE, Ingeborg Marie (contr)
Braein: Anne Pedersdotter (Cpte)

BRELL, Mario (ten)
Weill: Zar lässt sich Photographieren (Cpte)

BREMAR, Jacquelin (sop)
Henze: English Cat (Cpte)

BREMEN VOCAL ENSEMBLE FOR ANCIENT MUSIC
cond T. ALBERT
Keiser: Masagniello furioso (Cpte)
cond M. SCHNEIDER
Telemann: Don Quichotte (Cpte)

BREMS, Elsa (mez)
(SCHW) **314572** Vienna State Opera Live, Vol.7

BRENDEL, Wolfgang (bar)
J. Strauss II: Fledermaus (exc)
Leoncavallo: Pagliacci (Cpte)
Mozart: Zauberflöte (Cpte)
Saint-Saëns: Samson et Dalila (Cpte)
Tchaikovsky: Eugene Onegin (Cpte)
Wagner: Tannhäuser (Cpte)
Weber: Freischütz (Cpte)

BRENNAN, David (bar)
Lehár: Lustige Witwe (Cpte)

BRENNER, Janis (voc)
M. Monk: Atlas (Cpte)

BRESKE, Claire (sop)
(MYTO) **3MCD93381** Wagner—Die Walküre, etc

BRET, Gustave (cond)
see orch

BRETT, Charles (alto)
Purcell: Fairy Queen, Z629 (Cpte)

BRETT, Kathleen (sop)
Janáček: Makropulos Affair (Cpte)

BRETTSCHNEIDER, Klaus (treb)
Monteverdi: Incoronazione di Poppea (Cpte)
Wagner: Tannhäuser (Cpte)

BREUER, Hans (ten)
(SYMP) **SYMCD1081** The Harold Wayne Collection, Vol.5

BREUL, Elisabeth (sop)
Wagner: Parsifal (Cpte)

BREVIARIO, Giovanni (ten)
Bellini: Norma (Cpte)
Mascagni: Cavalleria rusticana (Cpte)

BREVIG, Per-Christian (treb)
Mozart: Zauberflöte (Cpte)

BREWER, Aline (hp)
(COLL) **Coll1008-2** Romantic works for flute and harp

BREWER, Bruce (ten)
Henze: Boulevard Solitude (Cpte)
Offenbach: Orphée aux enfers (Cpte)
Verdi: Aida (Cpte)

BREWER, Christine (sop)
(TELA) **ECHOCD2** Absolute Heaven

BREWER CHAMBER CHORUS
cond R. PALMER
Handel: Imeneo (Cpte)

BREWER CHAMBER ORCHESTRA
cond R. PALMER
Handel: Imeneo (Cpte), Siroe, Rè di Persia (Cpte)
(NEWP) **NPD85540** Handel/Bononcini—Muzio Scevola
(NEWP) **NPD85568** Handel—Arias

BRIC, Ion (bass)
Spohr: Faust (Cpte)

BRICE, Carol (mez)
Gershwin: Porgy and Bess (exc)

BRIERCLIFFE, Nellie (sop)
Sullivan: HMS Pinafore (Cpte), Patience (Cpte), Pirates of Penzance (Cpte)
(MMOI) **CDMOIR413** The Very Best of Gilbert & Sullivan

BRIESEMEISTER, Otto (ten)
(SYMP) **SYMCD1081** The Harold Wayne Collection, Vol.5

BRIGGS, David (organ)
(MAYH) **KMCD1007** Great Organ Transcriptions-David Briggs

BRIGHAM-DIMIZIANI, Sylvia (sop)
Puccini: Rondine (Cpte)

BRIGHTON FESTIVAL CHORUS
cond CARL DAVIS
(RPO) **CDRPO7018** Leeds Castle Classics

BRILIOTH, Helge (ten)
Wagner: Götterdämmerung (Cpte)
(DG) **429 168-2GR** Wagner: Excerpts from Der Ring
(DG) **435 211-2GX15** Wagner—Der Ring des Nibelungen

BRINK, Frank van den (cl)
(PART) **Part1132-2** Schubert—Lieder

BRINKMANN, Bodo (bar)
K. A. Hartmann: Simplicius Simplicissimus (Cpte)
Wagner: Götterdämmerung (exc), Rheingold (Cpte)

BRISCIK, Barbara (sop)
Donizetti: Elisir d'amore (Cpte)

BRISSOT, Irène (hp)
(MARC) **8 223774** Ropartz—Choral Works

BRITANNIA BUILDING SOCIETY BAND
cond G. BRAND
(POLY) **QPRL049D** Boosey & Hawkes National Brass Band Gala Concert 1991
cond H. SNELL
(DOYE) **DOYCD004** Rule Brittania

BRITANNY ORCHESTRA
cond C. SCHNITZLER
(TIMP) **1C1021** Le Flem—Orchestral Works

BRITISH NATIONAL OPERA COMPANY CHORUS
cond A. BUESST
(PEAR) **GEMMCD9175** Heddle Nash - Serenade

BRITISH NATIONAL OPERA COMPANY ORCHESTRA
cond A. BUESST
(CLAR) **CDGSE78-50-52** Three Tenors
(PEAR) **GEMMCD9175** Heddle Nash - Serenade
cond E. GOOSSENS
(PEAR) **GEMMCD9319** Heddle Nash sings Opera Arias & Songs

BRITISH SYMPHONY ORCHESTRA
cond B. WALTER
(VAI) **VAIA1059** Walter—Early Electrical Recordings (1925-1931)

BRITTEN, Anthony (treb)
Debussy: Pelléas et Mélisande (Cpte)

BRITTEN, Benjamin (cond)
see ECO
EOG Orch
LSO
ROHO

BRITTON, Harold (organ)
(ASV) **CDQS6028** The Royal Albert Hall Organ Spectacular
(ASV) **CDWHL2064** Organ Extravaganza

BRIVKALNE, Paula (sop)
Wagner: Parsifal (Cpte)

BRNO JANÁČEK CHAMBER OPERA ORCHESTRA
cond F. JÍLEK
Martinů: Comedy on the Bridge (Cpte)

BRNO JANÁČEK OPERA CHORUS
cond J. ŠTYCH
Fibich: Šárka (Cpte)
cond F. JÍLEK
Janáček: Fate (Cpte), Jenufa (Cpte)
cond J. PINKAS
Dvořák: Kate and the Devil (Cpte)
cond F. VAJNAR
Smetana: Kiss (Cpte)

BRNO JANÁČEK OPERA ORCHESTRA
cond F. JÍLEK
Janáček: Fate (Cpte), Jenufa (Cpte)
Martinů: Alexandre Bis (Cpte), Comedy on the Bridge (Cpte)
(KOCH) **34036-2** A Pageant of Opera
cond J. PINKAS
Dvořák: Kate and the Devil (Cpte)
(KOCH) **34036-2** A Pageant of Opera
cond F. VAJNAR
Smetana: Kiss (Cpte)

BRNO RADIO CHORUS
cond B. BAKALA
Janáček: Šárka (Cpte)

BRNO RADIO SYMPHONY ORCHESTRA
cond B. BAKALA
Janáček: Šárka (Cpte)

BRNO STATE PHILHARMONIC ORCHESTRA
cond J. ŠTYCH
Fibich: Šárka (Cpte)
cond O. LENÁRD
(SUPR) **11 1846-2** Emmy Destinn Opera Gala
cond C. MACKERRAS
Martinů: Greek Passion (Cpte)
(KOCH) **34036-2** A Pageant of Opera

cond Y. MENUHIN
(SUPR) **11 1837-2** Menuhin conducting Czech Music
cond J. PINKAS
Dvořák: Jacobin (Cpte)
cond J. SEREBRIER
(IMG) **IMGCD1617** Tchaikovsky—Gala 2
cond L. SVÁROVSKÝ
(SUPR) **11 1878-2** The Unknown Janáček
cond P. VRONSKÝ
(SUPR) **11 0388-2** Berlioz—Overtures
cond I. YINON
(SCHW) **314372** Schulhoff—Orchestral Works

BROAD, John (bass)
Sullivan: Mikado (Cpte)
(LOND) **436 816-2LM2** Sullivan—Utopia Ltd. Macbeth & Marmion Ovs etc

BROADBENT, Ernest (pf)
(EMI) **CDP7 98844-2** Josef Locke—Hear My Song

BROADSIDE BAND
cond J. BARLOW
Gay: Beggar's Opera (Cpte)
(HARM) **HMA190 1039** Popular 17th Century English Tunes
(SAYD) **CD-SDL400** English National Songs

BROADWAY CAST
(PEAR) **GEMMCDS9050/2(1)** Music from the New York Stage, Vol. 1 (part 1)

BROADWAY CHORUS
cond L. BERNSTEIN
Bernstein: West Side Story (exc)

BROADWAY ORCHESTRA
cond L. BERNSTEIN
Bernstein: West Side Story (Cpte)

BRÖCHELER, John (bass)
Braunfels: Verkündigung (Cpte)
Donizetti: Lucrezia Borgia (Cpte)
R. Strauss: Arabella (Cpte)

BROCKHAUS, Lilo (mez)
Wagner: Walküre (Cpte)
(DG) **435 211-2GX15** Wagner—Der Ring des Nibelungen

BRODARD, Michel (bar)
Debussy: Pelléas et Mélisande (Cpte)

BRODERSEN, Edith (sop)
Nielsen: Maskarade (Cpte)

BRODIE, Isla (sop)
Cavalli: Calisto (Cpte)

BRODSKY QUARTET
(TELD) **2292-46015-2** Brodsky Unlimited - Encores

BROGLIA, Lauren (sop)
Puccini: Bohème (Cpte)

BROHM, Sabine (sop)
R. Strauss: Rosenkavalier (Cpte)

BROISSIN, Nicole (sop)
Ganne: Hans (Cpte)
Messager: Monsieur Beaucaire (Cpte)
(EMI) **CZS5 68295-2** Messager/Lecocq—Operetta Highlights

BROITMAN, Ruben (ten)
R. Strauss: Friedenstag (Cpte)

BROKMEIER, Willi (ten)
Korngold: Tote Stadt (Cpte)
Lehár: Graf von Luxemburg (Cpte)
Millöcker: Gasparone (Cpte)
Mozart: Nozze di Figaro (Cpte), Zauberflöte (Cpte)
(EMI) **CMS7 64309-2** Kálmán—Best-loved Melodies

BROMAN, Sten (cond)
see Stockholm PO

BROMBACHER, Julius (ten)
Wagner: Meistersinger (exc)

BRON, Onissim (cond)
see Bolshoi Th Orch
USSR Rad Orch

BRONDER, Peter (ten)
Cilea: Adriana Lecouvreur (Cpte)
Janáček: Fate (Cpte)
Rossini: Turco in Italia (Cpte)
Verdi: Traviata (Cpte)
(ARAB) **Z6612** Rossini: Opera Arias

BRONHILL, June (sop)
German: Merrie England (Cpte)
Lehár: Lustige Witwe (exc)

BRONK-ZDUNOWSKA, Katarzina (pf)
(REM) **REM11036** Chailley—Songs

BRONSGEEST, Cornelius (bar)
Wagner: Parsifal (exc)
(OPAL) **OPALCDS9843** Karl Muck conducts Wagner

BRONSKAYA, Eugenia (sop)
(NIMB) **NI7865** Great Singers at the Mariinsky Theatre
(PEAR) **GEMMCDS9111(1)** Singers of Imperial Russia, Vol.5 (pt 1)

BROOK, Delith (spkr)
R. Strauss: Intermezzo (Cpte)

BROOK, Mathew (bass)
Purcell: Dioclesian, Z627 (exc)

BROOKS, Patricia (sop)
Dittersdorf: Arcifanfano (Cpte)

R. Ward: Crucible (Cpte)

BROOME, Oliver (bass)
G. Charpentier: Louise (Cpte)
Puccini: Rondine (Cpte)
Shostakovich: Lady Macbeth of Mtsensk (Cpte)
Vaughan Williams: Hugh the Drover (Cpte)

BROTHIER, Yvonne (mez)
Debussy: Pelléas et Mélisande (exc)
(DANT) **LYS003/4** Charles Panzéra - Song Recital
(PREI) **89011** Marjorie Lawrence (1909-1979)

BROTT, Boris (cond)
see Hamilton PO

BROUWENSTIJN, Gré (sop)
Wagner: Walküre (Cpte)
(EMI) **CHS7 69741-2(4)** Record of Singing, Vol.4—German School

BROWN, Debria (sngr)
Maderna: Satyricon (Cpte)

BROWN, Donna (sop)
Debussy: Rodrigue et Chimène (Cpte)

BROWN, Gaye (sngr)
Gay: Beggar's Opera (Cpte)

BROWN, Ian (pf)
(CNTI) **CCD1025** Delius & Dyson—Music for Cello & Piano
(IMP) **PCDS22** Music of the World—La Douce France

BROWN, Joanna (sop)
Britten: Noye's Fludde (Cpte)
G. Charpentier: Louise (Cpte)

BROWN, Justin (cond)
see Scottish Op Orch
SNO

BROWN, Kerry Elizabeth (sop)
Meyerbeer: Huguenots (Cpte)

BROWN, Mark (bar)
G. Charpentier: Louise (Cpte)
(SONY) **SM3K47154** Bernstein—Theatre Works Volume 1

BROWN, Timothy (cond)
see Cambridge Univ Chbr Ch

BROWN, Trevor (ten)
Bellini: Norma (Cpte)

BROWN, Wilfred (ten)
Purcell: Indian Queen, Z630 (exc), King Arthur, Z628 (Cpte)

BROWN, William (ten)
Gershwin: Porgy and Bess (Cpte)

BROWNE, Sandra (mez)
Albinoni: Nascimento dell'Aurora (Cpte)
Offenbach: Robinson Crusoé (Cpte)
Rossini: Mosè in Egitto (Cpte)

BROWNER, Alison (mez)
Verdi: Oberto (Cpte)
Wagner: Parsifal (Cpte)

BROWNING, Lucielle (mez)
(VAI) **VAIA1017** Leonard Warren—Early Recordings

BROWNLEE, John (bar)
Donizetti: Lucia di Lammermoor (Cpte)
Mozart: Così fan tutte (Cpte), Don Giovanni (Cpte)
(DUTT) **CDLX7012** The Incomparable Heddle Nash
(EMI) **CDH5 65072-2** Glyndebourne Recorded - 1934-1994
(LARR) **CDLRH221** Dame Nellie Melba - Opera and Song Recital
(PEAR) **GEMMCDS9925(2)** Covent Garden on Record—Vol.3 (pt 2)
(PEAR) **GEMMCDS9926(2)** Covent Garden on Record—Vol.4 (pt 2)
(PEAR) **GEMMCD9473** Heddle Nash—Vol.2

BRUA, Claire (sop)
Jommelli: Armida abbandonata (Cpte)
Montéclair: Jephté (Cpte)
Purcell: Dido (Cpte)
Rameau: Castor et Pollux (exc)

BRUCK, Charles (cond)
see French Rad Lyric Orch
Netherlands Op Orch
Orch

BRÜCKNER-RÜGGEBERG, Wilhelm (cond)
see NW German RO
orch

BRÜGGEMANN, Christian (sngr)
Braunfels: Verkündigung (Cpte)

BRÜGGEN, Frans (cond)
see Eighteenth Century Orch

BRUMAIRE, Jacqueline (sop)
Milhaud: Malheurs d'Orphée (Cpte), Pauvre matelot (Cpte)
Tomasi: Don Juan de Mañara (Cpte)
(EMI) **CZS7 67869-2** J. Strauss II—Operetta Highlights

BRUN, Jean (bar)
Gounod: Faust (Cpte)

BRUN-BARAŃSKA, Bożena (contr)
Mussorgsky: Boris Godunov (Cpte)

BRUNELLE, Philip (cond)
see ECO
Plymouth Music Series Orch

BRUNELLI, Gianni (bass)
Puccini: Madama Butterfly (Cpte)

BRUNET, Sylvie (sop)
Gluck: Iphigénie en Tauride (Cpte)

BRUNETTI, Vito Maria (bass)
Donizetti: Lucrezia Borgia (Cpte), Pazzi per progetto (Cpte)

BRUNI, Roberto (ten)
Verdi: Rigoletto (Cpte)

BRÜNING, Thomas (sngr)
Krenek: Sprüng über den Schatten (Cpte)

BRUNNER, Richard (ten)
Mozart: Nozze di Figaro (exc)

BRÜNNER, Richard (ten)
Mozart: Don Giovanni (exc)

BRUNNER, Wolfgang (cond)
see Salzburg Hofmusik

BRUNO, Elisa (mez)
(EMI) **CHS7 64860-2(2)** La Scala Edition - Vol.1, 1878-1914 (pt 2)
(PEAR) **GEMMCDS9073(2)** Giovanni Zenatello, Vol.1 (pt 2)
(PEAR) **GEMMCDS9074(1)** Giovanni Zenatello, Vol.2 (pt 1)
(SYMP) **SYMCD1138** The Harold Wayne Collection, Vol.16
(SYMP) **SYMCD1148** The Harold Wayne Collection, Vol.17

BRUNSKILL, Muriel (contr)
Gounod: Faust (Cpte)
(PEAR) **GEMMCD9175** Heddle Nash - Serenade

BRUNSSEN, Karen (contr)
Schoenberg: Moses und Aron (Cpte)

BRUSCANTINI, Sesto (bar)
Donizetti: Don Pasquale (exc), Elisir d'amore (Cpte), Emilia di Liverpool (Cpte), Eremitaggio di Liverpool (Cpte), Favorita (Cpte)
Massenet: Werther (Cpte)
Mozart: Così fan tutte (Cpte), Nozze di Figaro (Cpte)
Puccini: Bohème (exc)
Rossini: Barbiere di Siviglia (Cpte), Cenerentola (Cpte)
Verdi: Forza del destino (exc)
Vivaldi: Orlando Furioso (Cpte)
(BUTT) **BMCD015** Pavarotti Collection - Duets and Scenes
(EMI) **CDH5 65072-2** Glyndebourne Recorded - 1934-1994
(MEMO) **HR4277/8** Mirella Freni—Public Performances 1963-1970
(MEMO) **HR4300/1** Great Voices—Sesto Bruscantini

BRUSON, Renato (bar)
Donizetti: Don Pasquale (Cpte), Fausta (Cpte), Linda di Chamounix (Cpte), Lucia di Lammermoor (Cpte), Martyrs (Cpte), Poliuto (Cpte)
Franchetti: Cristoforo Colombo (Cpte)
Giordano: Andrea Chénier (Cpte)
Mascagni: Cavalleria Rusticana (Cpte)
Mozart: Don Giovanni (Cpte)
Puccini: Manon Lescaut (Cpte), Tosca (Cpte)
Saint-Saëns: Samson et Dalila (Cpte)
Verdi: Alzira (Cpte), Ballo in maschera (Cpte), Due Foscari (Cpte), Ernani (Cpte), Falstaff (Cpte), Forza del destino (Cpte), Giovanna d'Arco (Cpte), Luisa Miller (Cpte), Macbeth (Cpte), Nabucco (Cpte), Otello (Cpte), Rigoletto (Cpte), Traviata (exc)
(CAPR) **10 247** The Art of Bel Canto
(CAPR) **10 348** Mozart Gala—Suntory Hall, Tokyo
(CAPR) **10 810** Mozart—Opera Highlights
(CAST) **CASH5052** Verdi Operatic Favourites
(CAST) **CVI2065** Highlights from the Royal Opera House, Covent Garden
(CAST) **CVI2067** Opera Highlights from La Scala
(CFP) **CD-CFP4575** Verdi Arias
(CHAN) **CHAN6551** Renato Bruson at the Wigmore Hall
(DG) **445 525-2GMA** Domingo Favourites

BRUSSELS BELGIAN RADIO & TV PHILHARMONIC CHORUS
cond A. RAHBARI
Puccini: Bohème (Cpte), Manon Lescaut (Cpte), Tabarro (Cpte)
Verdi: Simon Boccanegra (Cpte)

BRUSSELS BELGIAN RADIO & TV PHILHARMONIC ORCHESTRA
cond A. RAHBARI
Puccini: Bohème (Cpte), Gianni Schicchi (Cpte), Manon Lescaut (Cpte), Suor Angelica (Cpte), Tabarro (Cpte)
Verdi: Simon Boccanegra (Cpte)

BRUSSELS NATIONAL OPERA CHORUS
cond S. CAMBRELING
Offenbach: Contes d'Hoffmann (exc)

BRUSSELS NATIONAL OPERA ORCHESTRA
cond S. CAMBRELING
Offenbach: Contes d'Hoffmann (Cpte)

BUNGER, Reid (bar)
Wagner: Parsifal (Cpte)
(DECC) **433 437-2DA** Pavarotti—King of the High Cs

BUNNELL, Jane (mez)
Barber: Antony and Cleopatra (Cpte)
Rossini: Scala di seta (Cpte)
Verdi: Don Carlo (exc)
Wagner: Parsifal (Cpte)

BUNNING, Christine (mez)
Janáček: Káťa Kabanová (Cpte)
MacMillan: Visitatio Sepulchri (Cpte)

BUNSE, Rüdiger (bass)
Schreker: Ferne Klang (Cpte)

BÜNTEN, Wolfgang (treb)
Mozart: Zauberflöte (Cpte)
Puccini: Tosca (Cpte)

3URCHULADZE, Paata (bass)
Borodin: Prince Igor (Cpte)
Mozart: Don Giovanni (Cpte)
Mussorgsky: Khovanshchina (Cpte)
Puccini: Bohème (Cpte)
Rossini: Barbiere di Siviglia (Cpte)
Saint-Saëns: Samson et Dalila (Cpte)
Tchaikovsky: Eugene Onegin (exc)
Verdi: Aida (exc), Forza del destino (exc), Nabucco (Cpte), Rigoletto (Cpte), Simon Boccanegra (Cpte)
(CAST) **CVI2067** Opera Highlights from La Scala
(DECC) **436 464-2DM** Ten Top Baritones & Basses
(DG) **431 601-2GCE10** Tchaikovsky Compact Edition

3URG, Robert (bar)
Wagner: Götterdämmerung (Cpte)

3URG, Susanna von der (sop)
Corghi: Divara (Cpte)

3ÜRGER, Erich (bass)
Wagner: Meistersinger (exc)

3URGESS, Sally (mez)
Bernstein: West Side Story (Cpte)
Offenbach: Orphée aux enfers (exc)
Purcell: Dido (Cpte)
Rossini: Barbiere di Siviglia (Cpte)
Vaughan Williams: Hugh the Drover (Cpte)
Wagner: Parsifal (Cpte)
(TER) **CDVIR8307** Josephine Barstow sings Verdi Arias

URGSTALLER, Alfred (bar)
Ponchielli: Gioconda (Cpte)

URGUERAS, Manuel (pf)
(RCA) **09026 62547-2** Divas in Song—Marilyn Horne's 60th Birthday

URKE, Thomas (ten)
(PEAR) **GEMMCD9411** Tom Burke—A Centenary Tribute

URKEY, Samuel (treb)
Debussy: Pelléas et Mélisande (Cpte)

URLAK, I. (bar)
(MYTO) **1MCD921.55** Ivan Kozlovsky Recital

URLES, Charles (ten)
Delibes: Lakmé (Cpte)
Gounod: Roméo et Juliette (Cpte)
Massenet: Manon (Cpte)
Offenbach: Belle Hélène (Cpte), Orphée aux enfers (Cpte)
Rossini: Guillaume Tell (Cpte)
Roussel: Padmâvatî (Cpte)
(EMI) **CDS7 49361-2** Offenbach: Operettas
(EMI) **CZS5 68113-2** Vive Offenbach!

URMEISTER, Annelies (mez)
Mozart: Nozze di Figaro (Cpte)
R. Strauss: Ariadne auf Naxos (Cpte)
Wagner: Fliegende Holländer (Cpte), Götterdämmerung (Cpte), Rheingold (Cpte), Walküre (Cpte)
(PHIL) **446 057-2PB14** Wagner—The Ring Cycle - Bayreuth Festival 1967

JRNS, Thomas (bar)
(RCA) **GD61175** The Glory of the Human Voice-Florence Foster Jenkins

JRROWES, Norma (sop)
Bizet: Carmen (Cpte)
Handel: Ariodante (Cpte)
Haydn: Armida (Cpte)
Holst: Wandering Scholar (Cpte)
Massenet: Thaïs (Cpte)
Mozart: Entführung (Cpte)
Purcell: Fairy Queen, Z629 (Cpte)
R. Strauss: Ariadne auf Naxos (Cpte)
Vaughan Williams: Pilgrim's Progress (Cpte)
Verdi: Trovatore (exc)
(DECC) **433 067-2DWO** Your Hundred Best Opera Tunes IV
(EMI) **CDM7 64730-2** Vaughan Williams—Riders to the Sea; Epithalamion, etc

JRROWS, Stuart (ten)
Mozart: Clemenza di Tito (Cpte), Don Giovanni (Cpte), Entführung (Cpte), Zauberflöte (exc)
Tchaikovsky: Eugene Onegin (Cpte)
Tippett: Midsummer Marriage (Cpte)
(DECC) **433 223-2DWO** The World of Operetta
(DECC) **436 406-2DWO** The World of Tchaikovsky

RT, Michael (bass)
Henze: Bassariden (Cpte)

BURT, Robert (ten)
Tchaikovsky: Queen of Spades (Cpte)

BURTON, Amy (sop)
(EMI) **CDC7 54851-2** Gershwin—Blue Monday, etc

BURTON, Humphrey (prod)
(DG) **072 189-3GH** Kathleen Battle at the Metropolitan Museum

BURTON, Miriam (mez)
Gershwin: Porgy and Bess (exc)

BURZIO, Eugenia (sop)
(CLUB) **CL99-587/8** Eugenia Burzio (1872-1922)
(EMI) **CHS7 64860-2(2)** La Scala Edition - Vol.1, 1878-1914 (pt 2)
(PEAR) **GEMMCDS9073(1)** Giovanni Zenatello, Vol.1 (pt 1)
(PEAR) **GEMMCDS9159(2)** De Luca Edition, Vol.1 (pt 2)
(SYMP) **SYMCD1138** The Harold Wayne Collection, Vol.16

BUSCH, Adolf (vn)
(SYMP) **SYMCD1109** Great Violinists, Vol.5 - Adolf Busch

BUSCH, David (alto)
(PHIL) **422 527-2PME** The Complete Mozart Edition Vol 27

BUSCH, Fritz (cond)
see Berlin St Op Orch
Buenos Aires Colón Th Orch
Danish RSO
Glyndebourne Fest Orch
Staatskapelle Dresden

BUSCHING, Marianna (mez)
Verdi: Aroldo (Cpte)

BUSCHING, Rupert (bar)
Weber: Peter Schmoll (Cpte)

BÜSE, Rainer (bass)
Wagner: Meistersinger (Cpte)

BUSHER, Andrew (sngr)
Bernstein: West Side Story (Cpte)

BUSHKIN, Isser (bass)
Giordano: Andrea Chénier (Cpte)

BUSKIRK, John van (pf)
Rorem: Three Sisters Who Are Not Sisters (Cpte)

BUSSER, Henri (cond)
see orch
Paris Op Orch
SO

BÜSSER, Henri (cond)
see Paris Op Orch

BÜSSER, Henri (pf)
(EMI) **CZS5 68113-2** Vive Offenbach!

BUSTERUD, James (bar)
Puccini: Bohème (Cpte)
(DG) **439 151-2GMA** Mad about Puccini

BUTIENINA, Maria (mez)
Tchaikovsky: Eugene Onegin (Cpte)

BUTLER, Antonia (sop)
G. Charpentier: Louise (Cpte)
(SONY) **SM3K47154** Bernstein—Theatre Works Volume 1

BUTT, Dame Clara (contr)
(PEAR) **GEMMCDS9925(1)** Covent Garden on Record—Vol.3 (pt 1)

BUTT, Yondani (cond)
see RPO

BWV TRIO
Mozart: Clemenza di Tito (Cpte)

BYCHKOV, Semyon (cond)
see Paris Orch

BYDGOSZCZ PHILHARMONIC SYMPHONY ORCHESTRA
cond R. SATANOWSKI
(CPO) **CPO999 113-2** Moniuszko—Overtures

BYERS, Alan (ten)
Puccini: Bohème (Cpte), Madama Butterfly (Cpte), Rondine (Cpte)
Shostakovich: Lady Macbeth of Mtsensk (Cpte)
Verdi: Vespri Siciliani (Cpte)

BYLES, Edward (ten)
Britten: Billy Budd (Cpte), Peter Grimes (Cpte)
Dvořák: Rusalka (Cpte)
Offenbach: Orphée aux enfers (exc)

BYNG, George W. (cond)
see orch

BYRDING, Holger (bass)
Nielsen: Maskarade (Cpte)

BYRNE, Richard (bar)
A. Davis: X (Cpte)

BYRNE CAMP CHORALE
cond E. QUELER
Massenet: Cid (Cpte)

CABALLÉ, Montserrat (sop)
Bellini: Norma (Cpte), Pirata (Cpte)
Boito: Mefistofele (Cpte)
Donizetti: Caterina Cornaro (Cpte), Lucia di Lammermoor (Cpte), Lucrezia Borgia (Cpte), Maria Stuarda (Cpte)
Giordano: Andrea Chénier (Cpte)
Gounod: Faust (Cpte)
Leoncavallo: Pagliacci (Cpte)
Mascagni: Cavalleria rusticana (Cpte)
Mozart: Così fan tutte (Cpte)
Ponchielli: Gioconda (Cpte)
Puccini: Bohème (Cpte), Manon Lescaut (Cpte), Tosca (Cpte), Turandot (exc)
R. Strauss: Salome (Cpte)
Rossini: Elisabetta (Cpte), Guillaume Tell (Cpte), Turco in Italia (exc)
Verdi: Aida (Cpte), Aroldo (Cpte), Ballo in maschera (Cpte), Corsaro (Cpte), Don Carlo (exc), Giovanna d'Arco (Cpte), Luisa Miller (Cpte), Masnadieri (Cpte), Traviata (Cpte)
(CFP) **CD-CFP4569** Puccini: Arias
(CFP) **CD-CFP4575** Verdi Arias
(CFP) **CD-CFP4606** Favourite Movie Classics
(CFP) **CD-CFP4608** Favourite Classics 1
(DECC) **430 724-2DM** Great Operatic Duets
(DECC) **433 822-2DH** Essential Opera
(DECC) **436 300-2DX** Opera Gala Sampler
(DECC) **436 317-2DA** Puccini—Famous Arias
(DECC) **436 461-2DM** Ten Top Sopranos
(DECC) **436 472-2DM** Great Opera Arias
(DECC) **440 947-2DH** Essential Opera II
(DECC) **443 377-2DM** Ten Top Sopranos 2
(DECC) **443 928-2DM** Montserrat Caballé sings Opera Arias
(DECC) **444 555-2DF2** Essential Puccini
(DG) **431 103-2GB** Great Voices—Montserrat Caballé
(DG) **431 104-2GB** Great Voices - Plácido Domingo
(EMI) **CDC5 55017-2** Domingo Opera Classics
(EMI) **CDC5 55095-2** Prima Diva
(EMI) **CDC7 47841-2** Puccini: Opera Recital
(EMI) **CDM5 65575-2** Montserrat Caballé
(EMI) **CDM7 63104-2** Alfredo Krauss - Opera Recital
(EMI) **CDM7 64359-2** Gala de España
(EMI) **CDM7 69500-2** Montserrat Caballé sings Bellini & Verdi Arias
(EMI) **CDM7 69596-2** The Movies go to the Opera
(EMI) **CZS7 67440-2** The Best of Rossini
(EMIL) **CDZ104** Best Loved Classics 5
(EMIL) **CDZ105** Best Loved Classics 6
(EMIN) **CD-EMX9519** Great Sopranos of Our Time
(ERAT) **2292-45797-2** The Ultimate Opera Collection
(ERAT) **4509-91715-2** The Ultimate Opera Collection 2
(ERAT) **4509-98499-2** Recital—Montserrat Caballé
(FORL) **UCD10902** The Art of Montserrat Caballé, Vol. 1
(MEMO) **HR4273/4** Great Voices—Pietro Cappuccilli
(MEMO) **HR4279/80** Montserrat Caballè—Opera Arias
(PHIL) **434 986-2PM** Duetti Amorosi
(RCA) **GD60818** Great Operatic Duets
(RCA) **GD60941** Rarities - Montserrat Caballé
(RCA) **RD61191** Gala Lirica
(RCA) **RK61044** Eternal Caballé
(RCA) **09026 61440-2** Opera's Greatest Moments
(RCA) **09026 61580-2(8)** RCA/Met 100 Singers, 100 Years (pt 8)
(RCA) **09026 61886-2** Operas Greatest Love Songs
(RCA) **09026 62547-2** Divas in Song—Marilyn Horne's 60th Birthday
(RCA) **09026 62699-2** Opera's Greatest Duets
(RCA) **74321 24284-2** Opera's Greatest Heroines
(RCA) **74321 25817-2** Café Classics - Operatic
(RCA) **09026 61204-4** From the Official Barcelona Games Ceremony
(RCA) **09026 61191-5** Gala Lirica
(RCA) **09026 61204-5** From the Official Barcelona Games Ceremony
(SONY) **SM48155** Carreras and Caballe sing Souvenirs
(SONY) **SMK48155** Carreras and Caballe sing Souvenirs

CABAN, František (bar)
Janáček: Fate (Cpte)

CABANEL, Paul (bass)
Saint-Saëns: Samson et Dalila (Cpte)
Tomasi: Don Juan de Mañara (Cpte)
(EMI) **CHS7 61038-2** Debussy—Pelléas et Mélisande, etc

CABERO, Joan (ten)
Falla: Retablo de maese Pedro (Cpte)

CABERO, Xavier (treb)
Falla: Retablo de maese Pedro (Cpte)

CABLE, Margaret (mez)
G. Charpentier: Louise (Cpte)
(CBS) **CD79312** Puccini: Il Trittico

CACHEMAILLE, Gilles (bar)
Berlioz: Béatrice et Bénédict (Cpte)
Chausson: Roi Arthus (Cpte)
Debussy: Pelléas et Mélisande (Cpte)
Gluck: Iphigénie en Aulide (Cpte), Rencontre imprévue (Cpte)
Gounod: Faust (Cpte)
Messager: Fortunio (Cpte)
Mozart: Clemenza di Tito (Cpte), Così fan tutte (exc), Don Giovanni (Cpte), Zauberflöte (Cpte)
Rossini: Comte Ory (Cpte)
Wagner: Parsifal (Cpte)
(ERAT) **4509-99607-2** Gluck—Operas; Schubert—Symphonies Nos 8 & 9

CADDY, Ian (bass)
Gay: Beggar's Opera (Cpte)
R. Strauss: Intermezzo (Cpte)
Rameau: Naïs (Cpte)
Verdi: Macbeth (Cpte)

CADELO, Cettina (sop)
Cesti: Orontea (Cpte)

ČADIKOVIČOVÁ, Milada (contr)
Martinů: Julietta (Cpte)
(KOCH) **34036-2** A Pageant of Opera

CADIOT, Olivier (bass)
Dusapin: Romeo and Juliet (Cpte)

CADONI, Fernanda (mez)
Cilea: Adriana Lecouvreur (Cpte)
Rossini: Cenerentola (Cpte)

CAETANI, Oleg (cond)
see Vienna SO

CAFORIO, Armando (bass)
Bellini: Bianca e Fernando (Cpte)
Rossini: Adelaide di Borgogna (Cpte)

CAHIER, Sarah (contr)
(IRCC) **IRCC-CD800** Souvenirs from Meyerbeer Operas

CAHILL, Teresa (sop)
Britten: Peter Grimes (Cpte)
Cavalli: Calisto (Cpte)
Massenet: Cendrillon (Cpte)
Mozart: Zauberflöte (Cpte)

CAIRNS, Janice (sop)
Britten: Peter Grimes (Cpte)
(EMI) **CDC7 54785-2** Harry Enfield's Guide to Opera

CALABRESE, Franco (bass)
Mozart: Nozze di Figaro (Cpte)
Puccini: Gianni Schicchi (Cpte), Manon Lescaut (Cpte), Tosca (Cpte)
Rossini: Turco in Italia (Cpte)
Verdi: Otello (Cpte)
(EMI) **CDH5 65072-2** Glyndebourne Recorded - 1934-1994
(EMI) **CMS7 63244-2** The Art of Maria Callas

CALABRO, Suzanne (sop)
Monteverdi: Incoronazione di Poppea (Cpte), Orfeo (Cpte)

CALAMAI, Alessandro (bar)
Verdi: Traviata (Cpte)

CALDER, David (sngr)
Gay: Beggar's Opera (Cpte)

CALÈS, Claude (bar)
Bizet: Carmen (Cpte)
Delibes: Lakmé (exc)
Gounod: Roméo et Juliette (Cpte)
(ARIO) **ARN68195** Milhaud—Sonatas; Trois Operas-Minute

CALEY, Ian (ten)
Beethoven: Fidelio (Cpte)
Donizetti: Maria Padilla (Cpte)
Massenet: Esclarmonde (Cpte)
Meyerbeer: Dinorah (Cpte)
R. Strauss: Intermezzo (Cpte)
Rameau: Naïs (Cpte)
Stravinsky: Nightingale (Cpte)
Verdi: Macbeth (Cpte)
Weill: Sieben Todsünden
(DECC) **436 464-2DM** Ten Top Baritones & Basses
(ERAT) **4509-98955-2** Boulez conducts Stravinsky

CALGARY PHILHARMONIC ORCHESTRA
cond M. BERNARDI
(CBC) **SMCD5125** Glitter and Be Gay—Coloratura Soprano Arias

CALIX, Ariane (sop)
J. Strauss II: Fledermaus (Cpte)

CALLANWOLDE YOUNG SINGERS
cond ROBERT SHAW
(TELA) **CD80109** Berlioz: Requiem, etc

CALLAS, Maria (sop)
Bellini: Norma (Cpte), Pirata (exc), Puritani (Cpte), Sonnambula (Cpte)
Bizet: Carmen (exc)
Cherubini: Medea (Cpte)
Donizetti: Anna Bolena (Cpte), Lucia di Lammermoor (Cpte)
Leoncavallo: Pagliacci (Cpte)
Mascagni: Cavalleria Rusticana (Cpte)
Ponchielli: Gioconda (Cpte)
Puccini: Bohème (Cpte), Madama Butterfly (Cpte), Manon Lescaut (Cpte), Tosca (Cpte), Turandot (Cpte)
Rossini: Barbiere di Siviglia (Cpte), Turco in Italia (Cpte)
Verdi: Aida (Cpte), Ballo in maschera (Cpte), Forza del destino (Cpte), Macbeth (Cpte), Rigoletto (Cpte), Traviata (Cpte), Trovatore (Cpte)
(CFP) **CD-CFP4277** These you have Loved
(CFP) **CD-CFP4602** Favourite Opera
(CFP) **CD-CFP9013** Duets from Famous Operas
(EMI) **CDC5 55016-2** Maria Callas - La Divina 2
(EMI) **CDC5 55095-2** Prima Diva
(EMI) **CDC5 55216-2** Maria Callas - La Divina 3
(EMI) **CDC7 47282-2** Maria Callas - Operatic Recital
(EMI) **CDC7 47283-2** Maria Callas - Mad Scenes & Bel Canto Arias
(EMI) **CDC7 47730-2** Maria Callas sings Verdi Arias, Vol.1
(EMI) **CDC7 47943-2** Maria Callas sings Verdi Arias, Vol.2
(EMI) **CDC7 47966-2** Puccini and Bellini Arias
(EMI) **CDC7 49005-2** Maria Callas - Operatic Arias
(EMI) **CDC7 49059-2** Callas à Paris
(EMI) **CDC7 49428-2** Maria Callas - The Unknown Recordings
(EMI) **CDC7 49502-2** Maria Callas—The Voice of the Century
(EMI) **CDC7 54016-2** Tenorissimo!
(EMI) **CDC7 54437-2** Callas Rarities
(EMI) **CDC7 54702-2** Maria Callas - La Divina
(EMI) **CDM7 63182-2** The Incomparable Callas
(EMI) **CDM7 69543-2** Maria Callas and Giuseppe Di Stefano - Duets
(EMI) **CDM7 69596-2** The Movies go to the Opera
(EMI) **CHS7 69741-2(7)** Record of Singing, Vol.4—Italian School
(EMI) **CMS7 63244-2** The Art of Maria Callas
(EMI) **CZS7 67440-2** The Best of Rossini
(EMI) **LDB4 91283-1(EMI)** Maria Callas at Covent Garden
(EMI) **LDB9 91258-1(EMI)** Maria Callas at the Paris Opera December 1958
(EMIL) **CDZ100** Best Loved Classics 1
(EMIL) **CDZ105** Best Loved Classics 6
(EMIN) **CD-EMX2123** Maria Callas sings Operatic Arias
(EMIN) **CD-EMX9519** Great Sopranos of Our Time
(FONI) **CDO104** Maria Callas
(MEMO) **HR4293/4** The very best of Maria Callas
(MEMO) **HR4372/3** Great Voices Giuseppe Di Stefano
(MEMO) **HR4400/1** Great Voices - Ettore Bastianini
(NIMB) **NI7864** More Legendary Voices
(SUIT) **CDS1-5001** Maria Callas - La divina

CALLATAŸ, Marie-Noëlle de (sop)
Grétry: Caravane du Caire (Cpte)

CALLEGARI, Giordano (bass)
Verdi: Traviata (Cpte)
(MSCM) **MM30231** Don Pasquale & Tito Schipa Recital

CALLEJA, Icilio (ten)
(MEMO) **HR4408/9(2)** Singers in Genoa, Vol.1 (disc 2)
(SYMP) **SYMCD1113** The Harold Wayne Collection, Vol.13

CALLINICOS, Constantin (pf)
(RCA) **GD60889(2)** The Mario Lanza Collection
(RCA) **09026 61884-2** Mario Lanza—Live in London

CALLINICOS, Constantine (cond)
see orch
RCA Victor Orch
RCA Victor SO
Rome Op Orch

CALM, Birgit (mez)
Catalani: Wally (Cpte)
R. Strauss: Elektra (Cpte)
Wagner: Götterdämmerung (Cpte), Rheingold (Cpte), Walküre (Cpte)
Zemlinsky: Traumgörge (Cpte)
(EMI) **LDX9 91275-1(EMI)** Sawallisch conducts Wagner's Ring
(EURO) **GD69043** Puccini: Il Trittico

CALUSDIAN, George (pf)
(ENTR) **ESCD6502** Erich Wolfgang Korngold: Songs and Arias

CALUSIO, Ferruccio (cond)
see NY Met Op Orch

CALVÉ, Emma (sop)
(MSCM) **MM30221** 18 French Divas
(NIMB) **NI7840/1** The Era of Adelina Patti
(PEAR) **GEMMCDS9923(1)** Covent Garden on Record, Vol.1 (pt 1)
(PEAR) **GEMMCDS9924(1)** Covent Garden on Record, Vol.2 (pt 1)
(RCA) **09026 61580-2(1)** RCA/Met 110 Singers, 100 Years (pt 1)
(SYMP) **SYMCD1100** Harold Wayne Collection, Vol.8

CALVI, Caterina (sop)
Handel: Rinaldo (Cpte)

CALVINO, Michele (bar)
Puccini: Madama Butterfly (Cpte)

CAMARGUE PHILHARMONIC ORCHESTRA
cond REINHARDT WAGNER
(HARM) **HMC90 1552** The Three Countertenors

CAMBIATA, Remo (bar)
(DECC) **436 301-2DA** Renata Tebaldi & Franco Corelli—Arias & Duets

CAMBON, Charles (bass)
Gounod: Roméo et Juliette (Cpte)
Offenbach: Contes d'Hoffmann (Cpte)
Saint-Saëns: Samson et Dalila (Cpte)

CAMBRELING, Sylvain (cond)
see Brussels Nat Op Orch
Brussels Théâtre de la Monnaie Orch
LPO

CAMBRIDGE BAROQUE CAMERATA
cond J. HELLYER JONES
(PLAN) **PLCD076** Principia Musica

CAMBRIDGE UNIVERSITY CHAMBER CHOIR
cond T. BROWN
(GAMU) **GAMCD535** Barber—Choral Music

CAMERATA ACADEMICA
cond B. PAUMGARTNER
(ORFE) **C394401B** Great Mozart Singers Series, Vol. 4

CAMERATA DE PROVENCE CHORUS
Boïeldieu: Calife de Bagdad (Cpte)

CAMERATA DE PROVENCE ORCHESTRA
cond A. DE ALMEIDA
Boïeldieu: Calife de Bagdad (Cpte)

CAMERATA MUSICALE ORCHESTRA
cond C. DESDERI
Rossini: Pietra del paragone (Cpte)

CAMERON, Basil (cond)
see CBO

CAMERON, John (bar)
Britten: Billy Budd (Cpte)
Gay: Beggar's Opera (Cpte)
Purcell: King Arthur, Z628 (Cpte)
Sullivan: Gondoliers (Cpte), HMS Pinafore (Cpte), Iolanthe (Cpte), Mikado (Cpte), Patience (Cpte), Trial by Jury (Cpte)
(CFP) **CD-CFP4238** Gilbert and Sullivan
(CFP) **CD-CFP4609** Favourite Gilbert & Sullivan
(EMI) **CMS7 64409-2** Sullivan—Pirates of Penzance & Orch. Works

CAMERON, Patricia (sop)
Sullivan: Pirates of Penzance (exc)

CAMINADA, Anita (mez)
Bellini: Puritani (Cpte)

CAMPAGNOLA, Leon (ten)
(MSCM) **MM30377** 18 Tenors d'Expression Française

CAMPANARI, Giuseppe (bar)
(RCA) **09026 61580-2(1)** RCA/Met 110 Singers, 100 Years (pt 1)

CAMPANELLA, Bruno (cond)
see Bologna Teatro Comunale Orch
LPO
PAO
Paris Op Orch
Turin Teatro Regio Orch
Venice La Fenice Orch

CAMPBELL, Colin (bar)
Boughton: Bethlehem (Cpte)

CAMPBELL, Craig (sngr)
(PEAR) **GEMMCDS9053/5** Music from the New York Stage, Vol. 2: 1908—1913

CAMPBELL, Richard (va da gamba)
(L'OI) **417 123-2OH** Purcell: Songs and Airs
(L'OI) **444 620-2OH** The Glory of Purcell

CAMPI, Enrico (bass)
Massenet: Werther (Cpte)
Puccini: Madama Butterfly (Cpte), Manon Lescaut (Cpte)
Rossini: Italiana in Algeri (Cpte)
(RCA) **09026 61580-2(5)** RCA/Met 100 Singers, 100 Years (pt 5)

CAMPO, Antonio (bar)
Mozart: Don Giovanni (Cpte)

CAMPO, Giuseppe del (cond)
see Vienna St Op Orch

CAMPO, Maria-Rosa del (sop)
Verdi: Don Carlo (Cpte)

CAMPORA, Giuseppe (ten)
Puccini: Madama Butterfly (Cpte), Tosca (Cpte)
Verdi: Simon Boccanegra (Cpte)
(CFP) **CD-CFP4569** Puccini: Arias

CAMPORELLI, Maria (sop)
(SYMP) **SYMCD1113** The Harold Wayne Collection, Vol.13

CAMPOS, Rafael (sngr)
Moreno Torroba: Luisa Fernanda (Cpte)

CANADA NATIONAL BALLET
Lehár: Lustige Witwe (exc)
Tchaikovsky: Eugene Onegin (exc)
cond E. FLORIO
Lehár: Lustige Witwe (Cpte)

CANADA NATIONAL BALLET ORCHESTRA
Lehár: Lustige Witwe (Cpte)

CANADIAN BRASS
(PHIL) **432 571-2PH** Essential Canadian Brass
(PHIL) **432 571-5PH** Essential Canadian Brass
cond E. DE WAART
(PHIL) **434 109-2PH** Wagner for Brass

CANADIAN OPERA CHORUS, TORONTO
cond B. KLOBUČAR
Janáček: Makropulos Affair (Cpte)

CANADIAN OPERA ORCHESTRA, TORONTO
Janáček: Makropulos Affair (Cpte)

CANALI, Anna Maria (mez)
Donizetti: Lucia di Lammermoor (Cpte)
Mascagni: Cavalleria Rusticana (Cpte)
Verdi: Falstaff (Cpte), Rigoletto (Cpte)
(EMI) **CMS7 63244-2** The Art of Maria Callas
(EMI) **CMS7 64165-2** Puccini—Trittico

:ANCELA, José Luis (sngr)
Bretón: Verbena de la Paloma (Cpte)

:ANDIA, Roberto de (sngr)
Bellini: Zaira (Cpte)

'ANELLO, Giorgio (sngr)
Mussorgsky: Khovanshchina (Cpte)

:ANIGLIA, Maria (sop)
Verdi: Aida (Cpte)
(CONI) **CDHD235** The Puccini Album
(EMI) **CDH7 61051-2** Beniamino Gigli - Operatic Arias
(EMI) **CHS7 64864-2(2)** La Scala Edition - Vol.2, 1915-46 (pt 2)
(NIMB) **NI7853** Lauri-Volpi sings Verdi
(PEAR) **GEMMCDS9176** Gigli - Arias, Duets & Songs, 1926-1937
(PEAR) **GEMMCDS9926(2)** Covent Garden on Record—Vol.4 (pt 2)

:ANINO, Bruno (pf)
(ORFE) **C048831A** Kreisler: Famous Transcriptions for Violin and Piano
(WERG) **WER60054-50** Magnificathy—the many voices of Cathy Berberian

ANNAN, Phyllis (mez)
Britten: Turn of the Screw (Cpte)
Dvořák: Rusalka (Cpte)
Offenbach: Contes d'Hoffmann (Cpte)
Verdi: Trovatore (Cpte)

ANNELL, Helen (mez)
Janáček: Jenufa (Cpte)

ANNE-MEIJER, Cora (mez)
Rossini: Comte Ory (Cpte)
(EMI) **CDH5 65072-2** Glyndebourne Recorded - 1934-1994

ANNETTI, Linda (sop)
(PEAR) **GEMMCDS9073(2)** Giovanni Zenatello, Vol.1 (pt 2)
(SYMP) **SYMCD1138** The Harold Wayne Collection, Vol.16
(SYMP) **SYMCD1158** The Harold Wayne Collection, Vol.18

ANONICI, Luca (ten)
Bellini: Sonnambula (Cpte)
Donizetti: Don Pasquale (Cpte), Favorita (Cpte)
Rossini: Signor Bruschino (Cpte)
(ERAT) **2292-45797-2** The Ultimate Opera Collection
(ERAT) **4509-91715-2** The Ultimate Opera Collection 2

ANTABILE SINGERS
cond R. SACCANI
Verdi: Aida (Cpte)

ANTELLI, Guido (cond)
see Philh
Santa Cecilia Academy Orch

ANTELO, April (sop)
Britten: Albert Herring (Cpte)
Purcell: Indian Queen, Z630 (exc)
Sullivan: Iolanthe (Cpte)
(DECC) **436 315-2DA** Great Operatic Duets
(DECC) **443 335-2LRX** Music for Relaxation, Vol 10 - The Night Before
(LOND) **436 393-2LM** Britten—The Little Sweep, etc

ANTEMUS
cond M. DE BERNART
Rossini: Torvaldo e Dorliska (Cpte)

ANTOR, Philippe (ten)
M-A. Charpentier: Arts Florissants (Cpte), Comtesse d'Escarbagnas Ov, H494, Médée (Cpte)
Purcell: Dido (Cpte)
Rameau: Zoroastre (Cpte)
Vivaldi: Dorilla in Tempe (Cpte)
(HARM) **HMX290 1528/33(1)** A Purcell Companion (pt 1)

ANTORIA CHILDREN'S CHOIR
cond E. COHEN
Massenet: Werther (Cpte)

O, Pierre (cond)
see Luxembourg Rad & TV SO

PASSO, Camille (treb)
R. Strauss: Salome (Cpte)

PECCHI, Renato (bar)
Donizetti: Don Pasquale (Cpte), Elisir d'amore (Cpte), Linda di Chamounix (Cpte)
Mozart: Idomeneo (Cpte), Nozze di Figaro (Cpte)
Puccini: Bohème (Cpte), Gianni Schicchi (Cpte), Tosca (Cpte)
Rossini: Cenerentola (Cpte)
Verdi: Forza del destino (Cpte)
(DECC) **433 706-2DMO3** Bellini—Beatrice di Tenda; Operatic Arias
(EMI) **CDM7 63103-2** Placido Domingo sings Opera Arias

PELLA AGOSTINO STEFFANI
cond L. ROVATKAY
Steffani: Henrico Leone (Cpte)

PELLA BRUGENSIS
Rossini: Tancredi (Cpte)

PELLA CLEMENTINA
cond H. MÜLLER-BRÜHL
Hasse: Piramo e Tisbe (Cpte)

CAPELLA CRACOVIENSIS
cond K.A. RICKENBACHER
(SCHW) **311392** Milhaud—Little Symphonies and Little Operas

CAPELLA ISTROPOLITANA
cond J. WILDNER
Mozart: Così fan tutte (Cpte)
(NAXO) **8 550383** Mozart—Tenor Arias
(NAXO) **8 550435** Mozart—Arias and Duets

(LA) CAPELLA REIAL INSTRUMENTAL ENSEMBLE
cond J. SAVALL
(ASTR) **E8532** Arriaga—Orchestral Works

CAPELLA SAVARIA
cond N. MCGEGAN
Handel: Agrippina (Cpte), Floridante (Cpte)

CAPITOL SYMPHONY ORCHESTRA
cond C. DRAGON
(EMI) **CDM5 65430-2** The Orchestra Sings

CAPOUL, Victor (ten)
(SYMP) **SYMCD1172** The Harold Wayne Collection, Vol.21

CAPPELLA COLONIENSIS
cond W. CHRISTIE
Hasse: Cleofide (Cpte)
cond G. FERRO
Rossini: Cenerentola (exc), Italiana in Algeri (exc)
cond F. LEITNER
Gluck: Orfeo ed Euridice (Cpte)

(LA) CAPPELLA VOCAL ENSEMBLE
cond R. CLEMENČIĆ
Fux: Dafne in Lauro (Cpte)
Keiser: Croesus (Cpte)
Vivaldi: Olimpiade (Cpte)

CAPPELLINO, Lucia (sop)
Giordano: Fedora (Cpte)

CAPPUCCILLI, Piero (bar)
Bellini: Beatrice di Tenda (Cpte), Pirata (Cpte), Puritani (Cpte)
Bizet: Carmen (Cpte)
Catalani: Wally (Cpte)
Donizetti: Lucia di Lammermoor (Cpte)
Giordano: Andrea Chénier (Cpte)
Mascagni: Cavalleria Rusticana (Cpte)
Mozart: Don Giovanni (exc), Nozze di Figaro (Cpte)
Ponchielli: Gioconda (Cpte)
Verdi: Aida (exc), Ballo in maschera (Cpte), Don Carlo (Cpte), Due Foscari (Cpte), Forza del destino (Cpte), Macbeth (Cpte), Masnadieri (Cpte), Nabucco (exc), Otello (Cpte), Rigoletto (exc), Simon Boccanegra (Cpte), Trovatore (Cpte)
(CAST) **CASH5052** Verdi Operatic Favourites
(CAST) **CVI2057** Il Trittico live from La Scala, 1983
(CAST) **CVI2067** Opera Highlights from La Scala
(CAST) **CVI2068** Opera Highlights from Verona 1
(CAST) **CVI2070** Great Puccini Love Scenes from Covent Garden, La Scala and Verona
(CFP) **CD-CFP4656** Herbert von Karajan conducts Opera
(DECC) **443 380-2DM** Ten Top Baritones & Basses 2
(DECC) **071 140-1DH (DECC)** Pavarotti—30th Anniversary Gala Concert
(DG) **419 091-4GW** Placido Domingo sings Favourite Arias, Songs and Tangos
(EMI) **CDC7 54524-2** The José Carreras Album
(EMI) **CDM7 63111-2** José Carreras sings Opera & Operetta Arias
(MEMO) **HR4223/4** Nicolai Ghiaurov
(MEMO) **HR4273/4** Great Voices—Pietro Cappuccilli

CAPRICCIO STRAVAGANTE
(DHM) **RD77252** Purcell—Airs and Instrumental Music

CAPRONI, Bruno (bar)
Bizet: Carmen (Cpte)

CAPSIR, Mercedes (sop)
(MSCM) **MM30276** Rossini—Barbiere di Siviglia, etc

CAPUANA, Franco (cond)
see La Scala Orch
MMF Orch
Santa Cecilia Academy Orch

CAPUANA, Maria (mez)
Verdi: Aida (Cpte)

CAPUANO, Enzo (bass)
Cherubini: Lodoïska (Cpte)
Verdi: Traviata (Cpte), Vespri Siciliani (Cpte)

CARAVAGGIO ENSEMBLE
(ASV) **CDWHL2078** Bravo Bassoon

CARBONARI, Virgilio (bass)
Giordano: Fedora (Cpte)
Puccini: Bohème (exc), Madama Butterfly (Cpte)
Verdi: Forza del destino (Cpte), Rigoletto (Cpte), Traviata (Cpte)
Zandonai: Francesca da Rimini (exc)

CARDONA, Robert (ten)
Gounod: Roméo et Juliette (Cpte)

CARECCIA, Franco (ten)
Puccini: Gianni Schicchi (Cpte)

CARELLA, Giuliano (cond)
see Loire PO

CARELLI, Emma (sop)
(EMI) **CHS7 64860-2(1)** La Scala Edition - Vol.1, 1878-1914 (pt 1)
(MEMO) **HR4408/9(2)** Singers in Genoa, Vol.1 (disc 2)
(SYMP) **SYMCD1111** The Harold Wayne Collection, Vol.11

CARELLI, Gabor (ten)
Haydn: Orlando Paladino (Cpte)
Verdi: Falstaff (Cpte)
(RCA) **GD60326** Verdi—Operas & Choral Works

CAREWE, John (cond)
see Nice PO

CAREWE, Mary (sngr)
Bernstein: West Side Story (Cpte)

CAREY, Thomas (bar)
Tippett: Knot Garden (Cpte)

CARIVEN, Marcel (cond)
see French Rad Lyric Orch
orch
ORTF Lyric Orch

CARL PHILIP EMANUEL BACH ORCHESTRA
cond HANS HAENCHEN
Gluck: Orfeo ed Euridice (Cpte)
cond HARTMUT HAENCHEN
(CAPR) **80 213** Handel and Mozart Arias for Countertenor
(CAPR) **10 213** Handel and Mozart Arias for Countertenor
(CAPR) **10 810** Mozart—Opera Highlights
(CAPR) **70 213** Handel and Mozart Arias for Countertenor
cond P. SCHREIER
Mozart: Finta semplice (Cpte), Oca del Cairo (Cpte)

CARLIN, Mario (ten)
Donizetti: Lucia di Lammermoor (Cpte)
Mascagni: Iris (Cpte)
Puccini: Madama Butterfly (Cpte), Manon Lescaut (Cpte), Tosca (Cpte), Turandot (Cpte)
Rossini: Barbiere di Siviglia (Cpte)
Verdi: Aida (Cpte), Otello (Cpte)
(BELA) **450 007-2** Puccini Favourites
(RCA) **09026 62689-2** The Voices of Living Stereo, Volume 1

CARLO, John Del (bass)
Ponchielli: Gioconda (Cpte)
Rossini: Cenerentola (Cpte)

CARLSEN, Svein (bass)
Braein: Anne Pedersdotter (Cpte)

CARLSEN, Toril (sop)
(UNIC) **UKCD2056** Grieg—Stage Works

CARLSON, Claudine (mez)
Berlioz: Troyens (Cpte)
Debussy: Pelléas et Mélisande (Cpte)
(DECC) **440 333-2DH** Ravel—Vocal Works
(ERAT) **4509-96971-2** Marcel Landowski—Edition

CARLSSON, Carin (sop)
Wagner: Walküre (exc)

CARLYLE, Joan (sop)
Tippett: Midsummer Marriage (Cpte)
(DG) **419 257-2GH3** 'Cav' and 'Pag', etc
(EMI) **CDM5 65341-2** Purcell—Theatre Music

CARMASSI, Bruno (bass)
(EMI) **CDH7 69791-2** Dame Eva Turner sings Opera Arias and Songs

CARMELI, Boris (bass)
Meyerbeer: Prophète (Cpte)

CARMEN ANDRES, Maria del (sngr)
Bretón: Verbena de la Paloma (Cpte)

CARMEN RAMIREZ, Maria del (sngr)
Vives: Bohemios (Cpte)

CARNUTH, Walter (ten)
Wagner: Meistersinger (Cpte)

CAROL CASE, John (bar)
Sullivan: Yeomen of the Guard (Cpte)
Vaughan Williams: Pilgrim's Progress (Cpte)

CAROLI, Consuelo (mez)
Prokofiev: Love for 3 Oranges (Cpte)
Vivaldi: Dorilla in Tempe (Cpte)

CAROLI, Paolo (ten)
Bellini: Norma (Cpte)
Puccini: Madama Butterfly (Cpte)
Verdi: Don Carlo (Cpte), Simon Boccanegra (Cpte)

CAROLIS, Natale De (bass-bar)
Handel: Rinaldo (Cpte)
Mozart: Don Giovanni (exc)
Puccini: Manon Lescaut (Cpte)
Rossini: Inganno felice (Cpte), Occasione fa il ladro (Cpte), Scala di seta (Cpte), Signor Bruschino (Cpte)
Verdi: Rigoletto (Cpte)
(CLAV) **CD50-9120** Mozart—Opera and Concert Arias

CARON, Rose (sop)
(IRCC) **IRCC-CD802** Souvenirs of Rare French Opera
(SYMP) **SYMCD1172** The Harold Wayne Collection, Vol.21

CARON, Willy (bass)
Mozart: Nozze di Figaro (Cpte)

CARONNA, Ernesto (bar)
(IRCC) **IRCC-CD808** Souvenirs of 19th Century Italian Opera

CAROSI, Ubaldo (bass)
Puccini: Tosca (Cpte)
(MEMO) **HR4273/4** Great Voices—Pietro Cappuccilli

CAROSIO, Margherita (sop)
(CONI) **CDHD226** Chaliapin—Bass of the Century
(EMI) **CHS7 64864-2(2)** La Scala Edition - Vol.2, 1915-46 (pt 2)
(EMI) **CHS7 69741-2(7)** Record of Singing, Vol.4—Italian School
(FONI) **CDMR5003** Martini & Rossi Festival, Volume 3
(IRCC) **IRCC-CD808** Souvenirs of 19th Century Italian Opera

CAROTENUTO, Fausto (treb)
Verdi: Rigoletto (Cpte)

CARPIO, Selica Perez (sngr)
Sorozábal: Katiuska (Cpte)

CARR, Robert (bass)
Gounod: Faust (Cpte)

CARRAL, Dora (sop)
Cilea: Adriana Lecouvreur (Cpte)
Verdi: Nabucco (Cpte), Traviata (exc)
(DECC) **411 665-2DM3** Puccini: Il trittico
(DECC) **440 417-2DM** Carlo Bergonzi

CARRARO, Massimiliano (cond)
see Italian International Orch

CARRÉ, Marguerite (sop)
(IRCC) **IRCC-CD802** Souvenirs of Rare French Opera

CARRERAS, José (ten)
Bernstein: West Side Story (Cpte)
Bizet: Carmen (Cpte)
Donizetti: Caterina Cornaro (Cpte), Elisir d'amore (Cpte), Lucia di Lammermoor (Cpte), Maria Stuarda (Cpte)
Falla: Vida breve (Cpte)
Giordano: Andrea Chénier (Cpte), Fedora (Cpte)
Halévy: Juive (Cpte)
Leoncavallo: Pagliacci (exc)
Mascagni: Cavalleria rusticana (Cpte)
Massenet: Werther (Cpte)
Offenbach: Périchole (Cpte)
Puccini: Bohème (Cpte), Madama Butterfly (Cpte), Manon Lescaut (Cpte), Tosca (Cpte), Turandot (exc)
R. Strauss: Rosenkavalier (Cpte)
Rossini: Elisabetta (Cpte), Otello (Cpte)
Saint-Saëns: Samson et Dalila (Cpte)
Verdi: Aida (Cpte), Ballo in maschera (Cpte), Battaglia di Legnano (Cpte), Corsaro (Cpte), Don Carlo (Cpte), Due Foscari (Cpte), Forza del destino (Cpte), Lombardi (Cpte), Macbeth (Cpte), Simon Boccanegra (Cpte), Stiffelio (Cpte), Trovatore (Cpte)
(BELA) **450 059-2** Carreras—Memories
(CAST) **CASH5052** Verdi Operatic Favourites
(CAST) **CVI2067** Opera Highlights from La Scala
(CFP) **CD-CFP4656** Herbert von Karajan conducts Opera
(DECC) **421 896-2DA** Puccini—Great Operatic Duets
(DECC) **430 433-2DH** Carreras, Domingo and Pavarotti in Concert
(DECC) **430 724-2DM** Great Operatic Duets
(DECC) **433 822-2DH** Essential Opera
(DECC) **436 463-2DM** Ten Top Tenors
(DECC) **436 472-2DM** Great Opera Arias
(DECC) **440 280-2DH** Kiri on Broadway
(DECC) **440 947-2DH** Essential Opera II
(DECC) **444 555-2DF2** Essential Puccini
(DECC) **071 123-1DH (DECC)** Carreras, Domingo and Pavarotti in Concert
(DECC) **430 433-5DH** Carreras, Domingo and Pavarotti in Concert
(DG) **439 151-2GMA** Mad about Puccini
(DG) **439 251-2GY** The Leonard Bernstein Album
(DG) **439 251-5GY** The Leonard Bernstein Album
(EDL) **EDL2562-2** Carreras, Domingo, Pavarotti Greatest Hits
(EMI) **CDC7 54016-2** Tenorissimo!
(EMI) **CDC7 54524-2** The José Carreras Album
(EMI) **CDEMTVD59** Classic Experience 3
(EMI) **CDM5 65575-2** Montserrat Caballé
(EMI) **CDM7 63111-2** José Carreras sings Opera & Operetta Arias
(EMI) **CDM7 64359-2** Gala de España
(EMI) **CDM7 69549-2** Ruggero Raimondi: Italian Opera Arias
(EMI) **CDM7 69596-2** The Movies go to the Opera
(ERAT) **2292-45797-2** The Ultimate Opera Collection
(ERAT) **4509-91715-2** The Ultimate Opera Collection 2
(ERAT) **4509-95789-2** Zarzuelas-The Passion of Spain
(KIWI) **CDSLD-82** Southern Voices—NZ International Opera Singers
(MCI) **MCCD090** Carreras & Friends sing Opera Arias & Songs
(PHIL) **416 973-2PM** Jose Carreras sings Musicals
(PHIL) **432 692-2PH** The Essential José Carreras
(PHIL) **434 152-2PM** Jose Carreras - Classics
(PHIL) **434 926-2PH** The Pleasure of Love
(PHIL) **434 986-2PM** Duetti Amorosi
(PHIL) **442 600-2PH** The Great Carreras
(PHIL) **442 602-2PM** 3 x 3 Tenors
(PHIL) **434 926-5PH** The Pleasure of Love
(RCA) **RD61191** Gala Lirica
(RCA) **09026 61204-4** From the Official Barcelona Games Ceremony
(RCA) **09026 61191-5** Gala Lirica
(RCA) **09026 61204-5** From the Official Barcelona Games Ceremony
(SONY) **SM48155** Carreras and Caballe sing Souvenirs
(SONY) **MDK47176** Favourite Arias by the World's Favourite Tenors
(SONY) **SK48094** Favourite Puccini Arias
(SONY) **SK53968** Opera Duets
(SONY) **SMK48155** Carreras and Caballe sing Souvenirs
(TELD) **4509-96200-8** The Three Tenors 1994
(TELD) **4509-92369-2** With a Song in my Heart - Tribute to Mario Lanza
(TELD) **4509-96200-2** The Three Tenors 1994
(TELD) **4509-96080-6(TELD)** Carreras—A Tribute to Mario Lanza
(TELD) **9031-77676-6(TELD)** My World of Opera - Kiri Te Kanawa
(TELD) **4509-96200-5** The Three Tenors 1994
(VAI) **VAIA1009** Ilona Tokody. Portrait of the Artist

CARRERAS, Nicole (sop)
Offenbach: Belle Hélène (Cpte)

CARROLI, Silvano (bar)
Donizetti: Lucia di Lammermoor (Cpte)
Puccini: Fanciulla del West (Cpte), Tosca (Cpte)
Verdi: Attila (Cpte), Lombardi (Cpte)
(CAST) **CVI2067** Opera Highlights from La Scala

CARROLL, Frank (bar)
(NIMB) **NI5224** Bellini & Donizetti: Arias

CARRON, Arthur (ten)
(VAI) **VAIA1017** Leonard Warren—Early Recordings
(VAI) **VAIA1084** Rose Bampton sings Verdi and Wagner

CARTA, Nino (bar)
Puccini: Bohème (Cpte)

CARTER, John (sngr)
Gay: Beggar's Opera (Cpte)

CARTER, John (ten)
Wagner: Tannhäuser (Cpte)
(MYTO) **2MCD90317** Verdi—Un Ballo in maschera

CARTERI, Rosanna (sop)
Donizetti: Elisir d'amore (Cpte)
(EMI) **CDM7 63105-2** Giuseppe di Stefano sings Opera Arias & Songs
(FONI) **CDMR5014** Martini & Rossi Festival, Volume 14

CARTIER, John (bar)
Sullivan: Patience (Cpte)

CARTON, Pauline (sngr)
Hahn: Ciboulette (exc)

CARTURAN, Gabriella (mez)
Donizetti: Anna Bolena (Cpte)
Puccini: Fanciulla del West (Cpte)
Rossini: Barbiere di Siviglia (Cpte)
Verdi: Luisa Miller (Cpte)

CARTY, Nicole (sngr)
Bernstein: West Side Story (Cpte)

CARUSO, Enrico (ten)
(ASV) **CDAJA5112** Twenty Gramophone All-Time Greats
(ASV) **CDAJA5137** The Three Tenors of the Century
(CLAR) **CDGSE78-50-52** Three Tenors
(CLUB) **CL99-060** Enrico Caruso—Opera & Song Recital
(EMI) **CDC7 54016-2** Tenorissimo!
(EMI) **CDH7 61046-2** Enrico Caruso: Opera Arias and Songs - 1902-1904
(EMI) **CHS7 64860-2(1)** La Scala Edition - Vol.1, 1878-1914 (pt 1)
(EMI) **CHS7 64860-2(2)** La Scala Edition - Vol.1, 1878-1914 (pt 2)
(LARR) **CDLRH221** Dame Nellie Melba - Opera and Song Recital
(MCI) **MCCD086** The Essential Caruso
(MEMO) **HR4408/9(1)** Singers in Genoa, Vol.1 (disc 1)
(MSCM) **MM30352** Caruso—Italian Opera Arias
(NIMB) **NI7801** Great Singers, Vol.1
(NIMB) **NI7803** Enrico Caruso—Opera Recital
(NIMB) **NI7808** Luisa Tetrazzini—Opera & Song Recital
(NIMB) **NI7809** Caruso in Song
(NIMB) **NI7810** Titta Ruffo—Opera Recital
(NIMB) **NI7834** Caruso in Ensemble
(NIMB) **NI7851** Legendary Voices
(NIMB) **NI7856** Legendary Tenors
(NIMB) **NI7857** Farrar in Italian Opera
(NIMB) **NI7859** Caruso, Farrar & Journet in French Opera
(NIMB) **NI7866** Caruso in Opera, Volume 2
(PEAR) **EVC1(1)** The Caruso Edition, Vol.1 (pt 1)
(PEAR) **EVC1(2)** The Caruso Edition, Vol.1 (pt 2)
(PEAR) **EVC2** The Caruso Edition, Vol.2—1908-12
(PEAR) **EVC3(1)** The Caruso Edition, Vol.3 (pt 1)
(PEAR) **EVC3(2)** The Caruso Edition, Vol.3 (pt 2)
(PEAR) **EVC4(1)** The Caruso Edition, Vol.4 (pt 1)
(PEAR) **EVC4(2)** The Caruso Edition, Vol.4 (pt 2)
(PEAR) **GEMMCDS9159(2)** De Luca Edition, Vol.1 (p 2)
(PEAR) **GEMMCDS9160(1)** De Luca Edition, Vol.2 (p 1)
(PEAR) **GEMMCDS9923(2)** Covent Garden on Record, Vol.1 (pt 2)
(PEAR) **GEMMCDS9924(1)** Covent Garden on Record, Vol.2 (pt 1)
(PEAR) **GEMMCD9088** Titta Ruffo (1877-1953)
(PEAR) **GEMMCD9104** Pasquale Amato (1878-1942)
(PEAR) **GEMMCD9129** Great Tenors, Vol.2
(PEAR) **GEMMCD9224** Luisa Tetrazzini—Vol.4
(PEAR) **GEMMCD9309** Enrico Caruso - Opera and Song Recital
(PREI) **89303(1)** Titta Ruffo Edition (pt 1)
(RCA) **GD60495(1)** The Complete Caruso Collection (pt 1)
(RCA) **GD60495(2)** The Complete Caruso Collection (pt 2)
(RCA) **GD60495(3)** The Complete Caruso Collection (pt 3)
(RCA) **GD60495(4)** The Complete Caruso Collection (pt 4)
(RCA) **GD60495(5)** The Complete Caruso Collection (pt 5)
(RCA) **GD60495(6)** The Complete Caruso Collection (pt 6)
(RCA) **09026 61242-2** Caruso Sings Verdi
(RCA) **09026 61243-2** Caruso sings Verismo Arias
(RCA) **09026 61244-2** Caruso sings French Opera Arias
(RCA) **09026 61580-2(1)** RCA/Met 110 Singers, 100 Years (pt 1)
(RCA) **09026 62550-2** Ten Tenors in Love
(ROMO) **81002-2** Emmy Destinn (1878-1930)
(ROMO) **81003-2** Galli-Curci—Acoustic Recordings, Vol.1
(ROMO) **81011-2(1)** Dame Nellie Melba (pt 1)
(SUPR) **11 2136-2(5)** Emmy Destinn—Complete Edition, Discs 11 & 12
(TEST) **SBT1005** Ten Top Tenors

CARUSO, Mariano (ten)
Giordano: Andrea Chénier (Cpte)
Verdi: Falstaff (Cpte), Otello (Cpte), Traviata (Cpte)
(EMI) **CHS7 69741-2(7)** Record of Singing, Vol.4—Italian School

CASA, Lisa della (sop)
Einem: Prozess (Cpte)
Mozart: Così fan tutte (Cpte), Don Giovanni (Cpte), Nozze di Figaro (Cpte)
R. Strauss: Arabella (Cpte), Ariadne auf Naxos (Cpte), Elektra (Cpte)
(DECC) **425 959-2DM** Lisa della Casa sings R. Strauss
(ORFE) **C335931A** Salzburg Festival highlights (195 85)
(ORFE) **C394201B** Great Mozart Singers Series, Vol 2
(TEST) **SBT1036** Lisa Della Casa sings Richard Strauss

CASADESUS, Jean-Claude (cond)
see Lille Nat Orch

CASALS, Pablo (cond)
see London Musicum Collegium

CASALS, Pablo (vc)
(BIDD) **LAB017** Casals—The Victor Recordings
(MSCM) **MM30428** Pablo Casals - Recital
(PEAR) **GEMMCD9128** Pablo Casals - Bow and Baton
(SONY) **SMK66573** Encores

CASARINI, Gianfranco (bass)
Meyerbeer: Africaine (Cpte)
Puccini: Manon Lescaut (Cpte)
Verdi: Macbeth (Cpte), Otello (Cpte)

CASAS, Esther (sop)
Verdi: Aida (Cpte)

CASELLATO, Renzo (ten)
Donizetti: Lucia di Lammermoor (Cpte)

CASELLI, Dario (bass)
Giordano: Andrea Chénier (Cpte)
Puccini: Manon Lescaut (Cpte), Tosca (Cpte)
Verdi: Aida (Cpte), Forza del destino (Cpte), Macbet (Cpte), Otello (Cpte), Rigoletto (Cpte), Traviata (Cpte)

CASERTANO, Angelo (ten)
Puccini: Bohème (Cpte), Turandot (Cpte)

CASEY, Brian (sngr)
Handel: Giulio Cesare (Cpte)

CASEY, Isabel (mez)
Verdi: Otello (Cpte)

CASHMORE, John (bar)
(OPRA) **ORCH103** Italian Opera—1810-20

CASONI, Biancamaria (mez)
Donizetti: Campanello di notte (Cpte)
Verdi: Forza del destino (Cpte)
(CFP) **CD-CFP4575** Verdi Arias
(EMI) **CDM7 64356-2** Opera Choruses

CASPARI, Sergio (sngr)
Giordano: Fedora (Cpte)

CASSARA, Frank (perc)
Glass: Hydrogen Jukebox (Cpte)

ASSILLY, Richard (ten)
Berlioz: Troyens (Cpte)
R. Strauss: Friedenstag (Cpte), Salome (Cpte)
Schoenberg: Moses und Aron (Cpte)
Walton: Troilus and Cressida (Cpte)

ASSIMATIS, Irenie (sop)
Lehár: Lustige Witwe (Cpte)

ASSINELLI, Antonio (bass)
Puccini: Fanciulla del West (Cpte)

ASSINELLI, Riccardo (ten)
Giordano: Fedora (Cpte)
Offenbach: Brigands (Cpte), Contes d'Hoffmann (Cpte)
Puccini: Turandot (Cpte)
Rossini: Guillaume Tell (Cpte)
Verdi: Attila (Cpte), Macbeth (Cpte), Rigoletto (exc)
(DECC) **436 261-2DHO3** Puccini—Il Trittico
(DECC) **436 313-2DA** Sutherland/Pavarotti—Operatic Duets

ASSIS, Alessandro (bar)
Boito: Nerone (Cpte)
Ponchielli: Lituani (Cpte)

ASTAGNA, Bruna (mez)
Ponchielli: Gioconda (Cpte)
Verdi: Trovatore (Cpte)
(MYTO) **2MCD90317** Verdi—Un Ballo in maschera
(RCA) **09026 61580-2(4)** RCA/Met 100 Singers, 100 Years (pt 4)

ASTAING, Danièle (mez)
Offenbach: Orphée aux enfers (Cpte)

ASTALDI, Peter (sngr)
Rorem: Childhood Miracle (Cpte)

ASTEJÓN, Jesús (bass-bar)
Bretón: Verbena de La Paloma (Cpte)

ASTEJON, Rafael (sngr)
Bretón: Verbena de La Paloma (Cpte)

ASTEL, Nico (ten)
Bizet: Carmen (Cpte)
Puccini: Bohème (Cpte)
R. Strauss: Ariadne auf Naxos (Cpte)

ASTELLAT, Jean (spkr)
Fauré: Prométhée (Cpte)

ASTELLI, Christiane (sop)
(CHNT) **LDC278 1068** Chabrier—Une Education Manquée/Mélodies

ASTELLI, Maria Luisa (mez)
Verdi: Rigoletto (Cpte)

ASTETS, Maryse (sop)
Bizet: Carmen (Cpte)
Rossini: Comte Ory (Cpte)

ASTLE, Joyce (mez)
Bernstein: Candide (1982) (Cpte)
Wagner: Götterdämmerung (Cpte), Walküre (Cpte)
(DG) **072 422-3GH7** Levine conducts Wagner's Ring

ASTRO, Maria Cristina de (sop)
Verdi: Traviata (Cpte)

ASULA, Maria (sop)
Donizetti: Elisir d'amore (Cpte)
Mozart: Nozze di Figaro (Cpte)
Salieri: Prima la musica (Cpte)

TALANI, Nestore (bass)
Puccini: Madama Butterfly (Cpte), Tosca (Cpte)

TALUCCI, Gabriele (cond)
see Sassari SO

TANIA, Julio (bar)
Vives: Doña Francisquita (Cpte)

TANIA TEATRO MASSIMO BELLINI ORCHESTRA
cond R. BONYNGE
Bellini: Puritani (Cpte)
Paisiello: Nina (Cpte)
(NUOV) **6892** William Matteuzzi sings Opera Arias
cond P. OLMI
Bellini: Zaira (Cpte)
cond R. BONYNGE
Bellini: Puritani (Cpte)
Paisiello: Nina (Cpte)
(NUOV) **6892** William Matteuzzi sings Opera Arias
cond P. OLMI
Bellini: Zaira (Cpte)
cond A. QUADRI
(RCA) **09026 62541-2** Pavarotti - The Early Years, Vol.1

TLEY, Gwen (sop)
(EMI) **CHS7 69741-2(1)** Record of Singing, Vol.4—Anglo-American School (pt 1)

TNTARINI, Teresa (mez)
(EMI) **CMS7 64165-2** Puccini—Trittico

TTELANI, Aurora (sop)
Bellini: Puritani (Cpte)
Verdi: Don Carlo (Cpte)

UDLE, Theresa (cond)
see London Cornett and Sackbutt Ens

ULI, Arturo (bar)
Mozart: Don Giovanni (Cpte)
Spontini: Vestale (Cpte)

UN, Karenna (sop)
Vaughan Williams: Pilgrim's Progress (Cpte)

CAURAT, Albert (sngr)
Ganne: Hans (Cpte)

CAVA, Carlo (bass)
Donizetti: Linda di Chamounix (Cpte)
Puccini: Tosca (Cpte)
Rossini: Barbiere di Siviglia (Cpte)
Verdi: Nabucco (Cpte)
(MEMO) **HR4392/3** Great Voices - Marilyn Horne

CAVALIERI, Lina (sop)
(MEMO) **HR4408/9(2)** Singers in Genoa, Vol.1 (disc 2)

CAVALLARI, Rina (mez)
Bellini: Norma (Cpte)
Rossini: Barbiere di Siviglia (Cpte)
Verdi: Forza del destino (Cpte), Traviata (Cpte)

CAVALLI, Floriana (sop)
Boito: Mefistofele (Cpte)
(CFP) **CD-CFP4569** Puccini: Arias
(CFP) **CD-CFP4575** Verdi Arias

CAVALLIER, Nicolas (bass)
Handel: Radamisto (Cpte)
(ASV) **CDDCA758** Falla, Milhaud & Stravinsky—Operas

CAVELTI, Elsa (mez)
(EMI) **CZS7 67123-2** Wagner: Der Ring des Nibelungen

CAVENDISH, David (ten)
Offenbach: Orphée aux enfers (Cpte)
Sullivan: Gondoliers (Cpte)

CAYA, Patricia Ann (mez)
Delius: Village Romeo and Juliet (Cpte)

CAZZANIGA, Renato (ten)
Bellini: Puritani (Cpte)
Cherubini: Lodoïska (Cpte)
Verdi: Due Foscari (Cpte)
(DECC) **443 380-2DM** Ten Top Baritones & Basses 2

CAZZATO, Michele (bar)
Giordano: Andrea Chénier (Cpte)
Puccini: Madama Butterfly (Cpte)

CBC SYMPHONY ORCHESTRA
cond I. STRAVINSKY
(SONY) **SM22K46290(3)** Stravinsky—The Complete Edition (pt 3)

CEBOTARI, Maria (sop)
Mozart: Nozze di Figaro (Cpte)
(NIMB) **NI7848** Great Singers at the Berlin State Opera
(ORFE) **C394101B** Great Mozart Singers Series, Vol. 1
(PREI) **89211** Helge Roswaenge (1897-1972) - III
(PREI) **90034** Maria Cebotari (1910-49)
(PREI) **90096** Helge Roswaenge sings Verdi & Puccini
(PREI) **90222** Maria Cebotari sings Richard Strauss
(SCHW) **314602** Vienna State Opera Live, Vol.10
(SCHW) **314712** Vienna State Opera Live, Vol.21

CECCARINI, Giancarlo (bar)
Puccini: Turandot (Cpte)

CECCATO, Aldo (cond)
see RPO

CECCHELE, Gianfranco (ten)
Verdi: Aroldo (Cpte)

CECCHETTI, Mario (ten)
Salieri: Axur (Cpte)

CECIL, Lionello (ten)
(PREI) **89008** Irene Minghini-Cattaneo (1892-1944)

CEDERLÖF, Rolf (bass)
Lidholm: Dream Play (Cpte)

CEGILE, Berta (sop)
Paisiello: Nina (Cpte)

CEHANOVSKY, George (bar)
Barber: Vanessa (Cpte)
Bizet: Carmen (Cpte)
Puccini: Bohème (Cpte)
Verdi: Ballo in maschera (Cpte), Otello (Cpte), Traviata (Cpte), Trovatore (Cpte)
Wagner: Tristan und Isolde (Cpte)
(RCA) **09026 61580-2(5)** RCA/Met 100 Singers, 100 Years (pt 5)
(VAI) **VAIA1072** Eleanor Steber Collection, Volume 1

CÉLINE, Annette (mez)
Verdi: Luisa Miller (Cpte)

CELLI, Silvana (mez)
Verdi: Rigoletto (Cpte)

CELLINI, Renato (cond)
see Mexico Palacio Orch
RCA Orch
RCA SO
RCA Victor Orch
RCA Victor SO

CENCIC, Max Emanuel (treb)
Mozart: Zauberflöte (Cpte)

CENICEROS, Lorna (sop)
R. Ward: Crucible (Cpte)

CENTRE D'ACTION MUSICALE DE L'OUEST ORCHESTRA
cond J. PERRAS
Rossini: Tancredi (Cpte)

CERESOLI, Elvira (mez)
(PEAR) **GEMMCDS9159(1)** De Luca Edition, Vol.1 (pt 1)
(SYMP) **SYMCD1077** The Harold Wayne Collection, Vol.4
(SYMP) **SYMCD1111** The Harold Wayne Collection, Vol.11

CERNAY, Germaine (mez)
(EMI) **CHS7 61038-2** Debussy—Pelléas et Mélisande, etc
(MSCM) **MM30451** Mascagni—Cavalleria Rusticana, etc

CERNY, Florian (bar)
Wagner: Rheingold (Cpte)
(EMI) **LDX9 91275-1(EMI)** Sawallisch conducts Wagner's Ring

CERONI, Aronne (ten)
Donizetti: Linda di Chamounix (Cpte)
Verdi: Nabucco (Cpte)

CERQUETTI, Anita (sop)
Ponchielli: Gioconda (Cpte)
(DECC) **417 686-2DC** Puccini—Operatic Arias
(DECC) **433 069-2DWO** Your Hundred Best Opera Tunes VI
(DECC) **433 442-2DA** Verdi—Famous Arias
(DECC) **433 636-2DSP** Puccini—Famous Arias
(DECC) **440 411-2DM** Anita Cerquetti
(FONI) **CDMR5014** Martini & Rossi Festival, Volume 14
(MEMO) **HR4400/1** Great Voices - Ettore Bastianini

ČERVENÁ, Šona (mez)
Wagner: Parsifal (Cpte), Walküre (Cpte)
(PHIL) **446 057-2PB14** Wagner—The Ring Cycle - Bayreuth Festival 1967

CERVI-CAROLI, Erside (sop)
(BONG) **GB1076-2** Mario Gilion - Opera Arias
(PEAR) **GEMMCDS9073(1)** Giovanni Zenatello, Vol.1 (pt 1)
(SYMP) **SYMCD1168** The Harold Wayne Collection, Vol.19

ČERVINKA, Pavel (bar)
Smetana: Libuše (Cpte)

ČERVINKOVÁ, Ludmila (sop)
Smetana: Bartered Bride (Cpte)

CESARE, Ezio di (ten)
Mozart: Finta Giardiniera (Cpte)
Pergolesi: Frate 'nnamorato (Cpte)
Verdi: Otello (exc), Stiffelio (Cpte)

CESARI, Renato (bar)
Bretón: Verbena de la Paloma (Cpte)
Chapí: Revoltosa (Cpte)
Moreno Torroba: Luisa Fernanda (Cpte)
Puccini: Bohème (exc), Madama Butterfly (Cpte)
Rossini: Barbiere di Siviglia (Cpte)
Sorozábal: Katiuska (Cpte)
(BELA) **450 007-2** Puccini Favourites
(DECC) **444 555-2DF2** Essential Puccini
(GME) **GME221** Falla—Orchestral Works

CESARINI, Athos (ten)
Giordano: Fedora (Cpte)
Ponchielli: Gioconda (Cpte)
Verdi: Aida (Cpte), Otello (Cpte)
Zandonai: Francesca da Rimini (exc)
(BELA) **450 133-2** Verdi Favourites
(DECC) **430 481-2DX2** Renata Tebaldi sings Opera Arias
(DECC) **433 443-2DA** Great Opera Choruses
(DECC) **440 407-2DM** Mario del Monaco
(MEMO) **HR4400/1** Great Voices - Ettore Bastianini

CHABAY, Leslie (ten)
Verdi: Otello (Cpte)

CHABRIER, Nadyne (spkr)
Massenet: Amadis (Cpte)

CHACKSFIELD, Frank (cond)
see orch

CHAGNON, Pierre (cond)
see orch

CHAIGNAUD, Jean-Luc (bar)
Gazzaniga: Don Giovanni (Cpte)
Offenbach: Contes d'Hoffmann (Cpte)
Verdi: Ballo in maschera (Cpte)

CHAILLY, Riccardo (cond)
see Berlin RSO
Bologna Teatro Comunale Orch
Cologne RSO
La Scala Orch
London Sinfonietta
National PO
Rome Op Orch

CHAKARIS, George (sngr)
(SONY) **SB2K64391** Leonard Bernstein - Man of Music

CHALABALA, Zdeněk (cond)
see Czech PO
Prague Nat Th Orch

CHALIAPIN, Feodor (bass)
(ARLE) **ARL23/5** Rimsky-Korsakov—Sadko
(CONI) **CDHD226** Chaliapin—Bass of the Century
(EMI) **CDH7 61009-2** Chaliapin sings Russian Opera Arias
(EMI) **CHS7 64860-2(2)** La Scala Edition - Vol.1, 1878-1914 (pt 2)
(NIMB) **NI7864** More Legendary Voices
(PEAR) **GEMMCDS9925(2)** Covent Garden on Record—Vol.3 (pt 2)
(PEAR) **GEMMCDS9926(1)** Covent Garden on Record—Vol.4 (pt 1)
(PEAR) **GEMMCD9122** 20 Great Basses sing Great Arias
(PEAR) **GEMMCD9146** Florence Austral
(PEAR) **GEMMCD9314** Feodor Chaliapin - Aria and Song Recital
(PREI) **89030** Feodor Chaliapin (1873-1938)
(SYMP) **SYMCD1105** The Harold Wayne Collection, Vol.10

CHALMERS, Thomas (bar)
(PEAR) **GEMMCDS9074(2)** Giovanni Zenatello, Vol.2 (pt 2)

CHALUDE, Jacques (bass)
Milhaud: Christophe Colomb (Cpte)

CHAMBER ORCHESTRA OF EUROPE
cond C. ABBADO
Rossini: Barbiere di Siviglia (Cpte), Viaggio a Reims (Cpte)
Schubert: Fierrabras (Cpte)
(DG) **431 653-2GH** Rossini—Overtures
(DG) **439 932-2GH** Haydn—Symphonies, etc
cond N. HARNONCOURT
Beethoven: Fidelio (Cpte)
cond J. JUDD
(IMP) **PCDS23** Music of the World—Italy & Spain—The Latin Quarter
(IMP) **PCD805** Music of the Masters
(IMP) **TCD1070** Invitation to the Opera
cond M. POLLINI
Rossini: Donna del Lago (Cpte)

CHAMINÉ, Jorge (bar)
Pendleton: Miracle of the Nativity (Cpte)
Tchaikovsky: Queen of Spades (Cpte)

CHAMONIN, Jocelyne (mez)
Wagner: Parsifal (Cpte)

CHANCE, Michael (alto)
Britten: Death in Venice (Cpte)
Cavalli: Giasone (Cpte)
Gluck: Orfeo ed Euridice (Cpte)
Handel: Giustino (Cpte), Tamerlano (Cpte)
Landi: Mort d'Orfeo (Cpte)
Monteverdi: Orfeo (Cpte)
Mozart: Ascanio in Alba (Cpte)
Purcell: Dido (Cpte), Fairy Queen, Z629 (Cpte)
(DHM) **05472 77295-2** Handel/Purcell—Works

CHANDOS CONCERT ORCHESTRA
cond S. BARRY
(CHAN) **CHAN8362** Treasures of Operetta
(CHAN) **CHAN8561** Treasures of Operetta, Vol. 2
(CHAN) **CHAN8759** Treasures of Operetta III
(CHAN) **CHAN8978** Marilyn Hill Smith sings Kálmán & Lehár

CHANDOS SINGERS
cond S. BARRY
(CHAN) **CHAN8759** Treasures of Operetta III

CHANG, Sarah (vn)
(EMI) **CDC7 54352-2** Sarah Chang - Debut

(LA) CHAPELLE ROYALE CHOIR
cond M. CORBOZ
Monteverdi: Orfeo (Cpte)
cond P. HERREWEGHE
Lully: Armide

(LA) CHAPELLE ROYALE ORCHESTRA
cond P. HERREWEGHE
Dusapin: Medeamaterial (Cpte)
Lully: Armide

CHAPMAN, William (sngr)
Bernstein: Candide (1956) (exc)

CHARLES, Lynne (dncr)
Wagner: Tannhäuser (Cpte)

CHARNOCK, Helen (sop)
Turnage: Greek (Cpte)

CHARON, Jacques (ten)
Offenbach: Contes d'Hoffmann (Cpte)

CHARVÁT, J (pf)
(EMI) **CHS7 69741-2(6)** Record of Singing, Vol.4—Russian & Slavonic Schools

CHÂTEAU, Christiane (sop)
(EMI) **CZS5 68113-2** Vive Offenbach!

CHATEAUNEUF, Paula (theorbo)
(L'OI) **444 620-2OH** The Glory of Purcell

CHATEL, Liliane (sop)
(EMI) **CZS5 68113-2** Vive Offenbach!

CHAUNDY, Stephen (ten)
Vaughan Williams: Pilgrim's Progress (Cpte)

CHAUSSON, Carlos (bass)

CHAUSSON, Carlos (bass-bar)
Puccini: Bohème (Cpte)
Penella: Gato Montés (Cpte)
Rossini: Barbiere di Siviglia (Cpte)
Vives: Doña Francisquita (Cpte)

CHAUVET, Guy (ten)
Gluck: Iphigénie en Tauride (Cpte)
Massenet: Hérodiade (exc)
(EMI) **CZS7 67869-2** J. Strauss II—Operetta Highlights

CHEDEL, Arlette (contr)
Ravel: Enfant et les sortilèges (Cpte)

CHEEK, John (bass)
Puccini: Tosca (Cpte)
Stravinsky: Rake's Progress (Cpte)
(MUSM) **67078-2** Stravinsky The Composer - Volume 1
(TELA) **CD80109** Berlioz: Requiem, etc
(TELA) **ECHOCD2** Absolute Heaven

CHEE-YUN (vn)
(DENO) **CO-75118** Violin Show Pieces

CHEKERLISKI, Constantin (bar)
(EMI) **CMS7 63386-2** Borodin—Prince Igor & Complete Solo Songs

CHEKIN, P (ten)
Rimsky-Korsakov: Tale of Tsar Saltan (Cpte)

CHELLET, Germaine (sop)
Bizet: Carmen (Cpte)

CHELSEA CHAMBER ENSEMBLE
cond T. ROLEK
(ALBA) **TROY023-2** Music of Joseph Fennimore

CHELSEA OPERA GROUP CHORUS
cond H. WILLIAMS
Bridge: Christmas Rose (Cpte)

CHELSEA OPERA GROUP ORCHESTRA
cond W. SOUTHGATE
(KIWI) **CDSLD-82** Southern Voices—NZ International Opera Singers
cond H. WILLIAMS
Bridge: Christmas Rose (Cpte)

CHEN, Shi-Zheng (voc)
M. Monk: Atlas (Cpte)

CHENETTE, Stephen (cond)
see Hannaford St Silver Band

CHENI, Elena (sop)
(PREI) **89042** Nazzareno de Angelis (1881-1962)

CHERICI, Laura (sop)
Mozart: Così fan tutte (Cpte)
(DECC) **436 261-2DHO3** Puccini—Il Trittico

CHERIEZ, Claudine (mez)
Boïeldieu: Calife de Bagdad (Cpte)

CHERNOV, Vladimir (bar)
Tchaikovsky: Queen of Spades (exc)
Verdi: Don Carlo (exc), Luisa Miller (exc), Trovatore (Cpte)

CHERNOZHUKOV, Mikhail (bass)
Mussorgsky: Khovanshchina (Cpte)

CHESSOR, Derek (sngr)
Bernstein: West Side Story (Cpte)

CHESTER, Kenn (sngr)
Schuman: Mighty Casey (Cpte)

CHESTER, Kenn (ten)
Floyd: Susannah (Cpte)

CHEVALIER, Valerie (sop)
Offenbach: Brigands (Cpte)

CHEVY CHASE SCHOOL CHOIR
cond M. ROSTROPOVICH
Mussorgsky: Boris Godunov (Cpte)

CHIARA, Maria (sop)
Verdi: Aida (exc), Attila (Cpte)
(BELA) **450 007-2** Puccini Favourites
(BELA) **450 015-2** Cinema Classics
(BELA) **450 133-2** Verdi Favourites
(CAST) **CASH5052** Verdi Operatic Favourites
(DECC) **417 686-2DC** Puccini—Operatic Arias
(DECC) **433 067-2DWO** Your Hundred Best Opera Tunes IV
(DECC) **433 069-2DWO** Your Hundred Best Opera Tunes VI
(DECC) **433 221-2DWO** The World of Verdi
(DECC) **433 624-2DSP** Great Soprano Arias
(DECC) **433 636-2DSP** Puccini—Famous Arias
(DECC) **433 865-2DWO** The World of Puccini
(DECC) **436 317-2DA** Puccini—Famous Arias
(DECC) **444 555-2DF2** Essential Puccini

CHIAROSCURO
Monteverdi: Orfeo (Cpte)

CHICAGO CHAMBER OPERA ORCHESTRA
cond L. RAPCHAK
Rapchak: Lifework of Juan Diaz (Cpte)

CHICAGO CITY BALLET
cond B. BARTOLETTI
Tchaikovsky: Eugene Onegin (Cpte)

CHICAGO LYRIC OPERA CHORUS
cond B. BARTOLETTI
Tchaikovsky: Eugene Onegin (Cpte)
cond F. REINER
(RCA) **GD60874** R. Strauss—Scenes from Elektra & Salome
cond A. VOTTO
(MEMO) **HR4376/7** Tito Gobbi—Opera Arias

CHICAGO LYRIC OPERA ORCHESTRA
Tchaikovsky: Eugene Onegin (Cpte)
cond A. VOTTO
(MEMO) **HR4376/7** Tito Gobbi—Opera Arias

CHICAGO SYMPHONY CHORUS
cond G. SOLTI
Beethoven: Fidelio (Cpte)
Schoenberg: Moses und Aron (Cpte)
Verdi: Otello (exc)
(DECC) **421 865-2DA** Wagner—Opera Choruses
(DECC) **430 226-2DH** Verdi—Choruses
(DECC) **433 443-2DA** Great Opera Choruses
(DECC) **433 822-2DH** Essential Opera
(DECC) **443 756-2DF2** The Essential Beethoven
(DECC) **430 226-5DH** Verdi—Choruses

CHICAGO SYMPHONY ORCHESTRA
cond D. BARENBOIM
Rimsky-Korsakov: Tale of Tsar Saltan (exc)
(DG) **415 851-2GGA** Popular Orchestral Works
(ERAT) **2292-45786-2** Der Ring des Nibelungen - Excerpts
(ERAT) **2292-45998-2** Strauss—Waltzes & Polkas
cond N. JÄRVI
(CHAN) **CHAN8877** Kodály—Orchestral Works
cond S. OZAWA
(EMI) **CDC2 53045-2** Heavy Classix
cond F. REINER
(RCA) **GD60176** Prokofiev: Vocal & Orchestral Works
(RCA) **GD60387** Rossini—Overtures
(RCA) **GD60874** R. Strauss—Scenes from Elektra & Salome
(RCA) **VD60484** Mozart: Orchestral Works
(RCA) **09026 60930-2** R. Strauss—Orchestral Works
(RCA) **09026 60962-2** Beethoven—Orchestral Works
(RCA) **09026 61792-2** Reiner conducts Wagner & Humperdinck
(RCA) **09026 61958-2** Russian Showpieces
(RCA) **09026 62587-2** Dvořák/Smetana/Weinberger—Orchestral Works
cond G. SOLTI
Beethoven: Fidelio (Cpte)
Schoenberg: Moses und Aron (Cpte)
Verdi: Otello (Cpte)
(DECC) **421 865-2DA** Wagner—Opera Choruses
(DECC) **430 226-2DH** Verdi—Choruses
(DECC) **430 448-2DM** The Solti Collection—Wagner Overtures
(DECC) **430 792-2DC6** Beethoven—Complete Symphonies, etc
(DECC) **433 443-2DA** Great Opera Choruses
(DECC) **433 822-2DH** Essential Opera
(DECC) **436 472-2DM** Great Opera Arias
(DECC) **440 069-2DWO** The World of Wagner
(DECC) **443 444-2DH** Hungarian Connections
(DECC) **443 756-2DF2** The Essential Beethoven
(DECC) **071 101-3DH** Solti plays Berlioz and Wagner
(DECC) **430 226-5DH** Verdi—Choruses
cond F. STOCK
(BIDD) **WHL021/2** Frederick Stock and the Chicago Symphony Orchestra

CHIESA, Fernanda (sop)
(PREI) **89998** Antonio Paoli (1871-1946)

CHIESA, Vivian della (sop)
(RCA) **GD60276** Toscanini conducts Boito & Verdi

CHILDREN'S CHOIR
cond L. BERNSTEIN
Puccini: Bohème (Cpte)
cond O. HOLT
Probst: Maximilien Kolbe (Cpte)

CHILDREN'S CHORUS
cond I. ANGUELOV
Henze: Boulevard Solitude (Cpte)
cond W. SAWALLISCH
Orff: Mond (Cpte)

CHILDS, Lucinda (narr)
Glass: Einstein on the Beach (Cpte)

CHILDS, Nicholas (euphonium)
(POLY) **QPRL049D** Boosey & Hawkes National Brass Band Gala Concert 1991

CHILDS, Robert (euphonium)
(POLY) **QPRL049D** Boosey & Hawkes National Brass Band Gala Concert 1991

CHILES, Torin (ten)
(CBC) **SMCD5139** A Gilbert & Sullivan Gala

CHINCHILLA
cond L. ZAGROSEK
Krenek: Jonny spielt auf (Cpte)

CHINGARI, Mario (bar)
Puccini: Fanciulla del West (Cpte)
Verdi: Vespri Siciliani (Cpte)
(CAPR) **10 810** Mozart—Opera Highlights

CHIOLDI, Michael (bass-bar)
Moran: Dracula Diary (Cpte)

CHIOREANU, Lucian (ten)
Pfitzner: Herz (Cpte)
S. Wagner: Schwarzschwanenreich (Cpte)

CHISSARI, Santa (sop)
Verdi: Rigoletto (Cpte), Traviata (Cpte)
(EMI) **CMS7 64165-2** Puccini—Trittico

CHISTIAKOV, Andrey (cond)
see Bolshoi Th Orch
Orch

CHOEURS RUSSES DE PARIS
cond I. DOBROVEN
Mussorgsky: Boris Godunov (Cpte)

CHOI, Hans (bar)
(TELD) **9031-72674-3** The Winners' Gala Concert, International Tchaikovsky Comp. 1990

CHOOKASIAN, Lilli (mez)
Wagner: Götterdämmerung (Cpte)
(DG) **435 211-2GX15** Wagner—Der Ring des Nibelungen

CHORALE EXPÉRIMENTALE
cond L. BERIO
Berio: Laborintus II

CHORALE MADRIGAL
cond C. BRUCK
Martinů: Julietta (Cpte)

CHORUS
Ashley: Improvement (Cpte)
(EMI) **CHS7 63802-2(1)** Tetrazzini—The London Records (pt 1)
(EMI) **CHS7 64860-2(2)** La Scala Edition - Vol.1, 1878-1914 (pt 2)
(IRCC) **IRCC-CD800** Souvenirs from Meyerbeer Operas
(MMOI) **CDMOIR405** Great Tenors
(PEAR) **GEMMCDS9001/3(1)** Singers of Imperial Russia, Vol.2 (pt 1)
(PEAR) **GEMMCDS9004/6(2)** Singers of Imperial Russia, Vol.3 (pt 2)
(PEAR) **GEMMCDS9007/9(1)** Singers of Imperial Russia, Vol.4 (pt 1)
(PEAR) **GEMMCDS9007/9(2)** Singers of Imperial Russia, Vol.4 (pt 2)
(PEAR) **GEMMCDS9073(1)** Giovanni Zenatello, Vol.1 (pt 1)
(PEAR) **GEMMCDS9073(2)** Giovanni Zenatello, Vol.1 (pt 2)
(PEAR) **GEMMCDS9074(1)** Giovanni Zenatello, Vol.2 (pt 1)
(PEAR) **GEMMCDS9074(2)** Giovanni Zenatello, Vol.2 (pt 2)
(PEAR) **GEMMCDS9180** Verdi—Rigoletto, etc
(PEAR) **GEMMCDS9923(2)** Covent Garden on Record, Vol.1 (pt 2)
(PEAR) **GEMMCDS9925(1)** Covent Garden on Record—Vol.3 (pt 1)
(PEAR) **GEMMCD9093** The Artistry of Richard Crooks, Volume 1
(PEAR) **GEMMCD9104** Pasquale Amato (1878-1942)
(PEAR) **GEMMCD9117** Graziella Pareto
(PEAR) **GEMMCD9122** 20 Great Basses sing Great Arias
(PEAR) **GEMMCD9175** Heddle Nash - Serenade
(PEAR) **GEMMCD9222** Luisa Tetrazzini—Vol.2
(PEAR) **GEMMCD9455** Malcolm McEachern—Song Recital
(PREI) **89052** Friederich Schorr (1889-1953)
(PREI) **89064** Pasquale Amato (1878-1942)
(SUPR) **11 2136-2(5)** Emmy Destinn—Complete Edition, Discs 11 & 12
(SYMP) **SYMCD1138** The Harold Wayne Collection, Vol.16
(TEST) **SBT1008** Viva Rossini
cond O. ACKERMANN
J. Strauss II: Nacht in Venedig (Cpte)
(EMI) **CDC7 47284-2** Elisabeth Schwarzkopf sings Operetta
cond ANON
(BELA) **450 052-2** Great Opera Choruses
cond E. G. ASENSIO
(IMP) **MCD45** Spanish Royal Gala
cond J. BARBIROLLI
(PEAR) **GEMMCDS9926(1)** Covent Garden on Record—Vol.4 (pt 1)
cond T. BEECHAM
Delius: Village Romeo and Juliet (Cpte)
cond L. BERNSTEIN
(DG) **439 251-2GY** The Leonard Bernstein Album
(DG) **439 251-5GY** The Leonard Bernstein Album
cond E. BIGOT
(MMOI) **CDMOIR405** Great Tenors
cond R. BLAREAU
Adam: Si j'étais roi (Cpte)
cond R. BONYNGE
(BELA) **450 014-2** Sutherland sings Coward
cond W. BRÜCKNER-RÜGGEBERG
Weill: Happy End (Cpte)
cond H. BUSSER
Gounod: Faust (Cpte)
cond C. CALLINICOS
(RCA) **GD60048** Mario Lanza sings Songs from The Student Prince & The Desert Song
(RCA) **GD60516** Mario Lanza—For the first time
(RCA) **09026 68130-2** Mario Lanza at his Best
(RCA) **74321 18574-2** Mario Lanza - The Ultimate Collection
cond M. CARIVEN
(FORL) **UCD19053** L'Incomparable Tino Rossi
cond C.F. CILLARIO
(RCA) **RK61044** Eternal Caballé
cond G. CLOËZ
(MSCM) **MM30451** Mascagni—Cavalleria Rusticana, etc
cond A. COATES
(CLAR) **CDGSE78-50-54** Coates conducts Wagner, Weber & Mendelssohn
(PEAR) **GEMMCDS9137** Wagner—Der Ring des Nibelungen
cond P. DERVAUX
Ganne: Saltimbanques (exc)
cond J.O. EDWARDS
Bernstein: West Side Story (Cpte)
cond J. ETCHEVERRY
Verdi: Rigoletto (Cpte)
cond J. FEHRING
Benatzky: Im weissen Rössl (exc)
cond A. GALLIERA
Rossini: Barbiere di Siviglia (exc)
cond P. GAUBERT
(PEAR) **GEMMCDS9926(1)** Covent Garden on Record—Vol.4 (pt 1)
cond G. GELMETTI
Rossini: Barbiere di Siviglia (Cpte)
cond W. GOEHR
(EMI) **CDM7 69478-2** A Portrait of Joseph Schmidt
(EMI) **CHS7 64673-2** Joseph Schmidt - Complete EMI Recordings Volume 1
cond J. GREEN
(SONY) **SB2K64391** Leonard Bernstein - Man of Music
cond M. GURLITT
(PEAR) **GEMMCD9409** Lotte Lehmenn—Vol.1
cond F. GÜNTHER
(EMI) **CHS7 64676-2** Joseph Schmidt - Complete EMI Recordings Volume 2
cond E. HAUKE
(EMI) **CDH7 64029-2** Richard Tauber - Opera Recital
(NIMB) **NI7830** Richard Tauber in Opera
cond P. HERREWEGHE
Dusapin: Medeamaterial (Cpte)
cond H. VON KARAJAN
Mozart: Così fan tutte (Cpte)
Verdi: Falstaff (Cpte)
(MEMO) **HR4223/4** Nicolai Ghiaurov
cond C. KEENE
Puccini: Turandot (exc)
cond E. KHACHATURIAN
Karetnikov: Till Eulenspiegel (Cpte)
cond E. LEINSDORF
Cornelius: Barbier von Bagdad (Cpte)
cond R. LEPPARD
Purcell: Dido (Cpte)
cond L. LUDWIG
Weber: Abu Hassan (Cpte)
cond C. MANDEAL
Bretan: Golem (Cpte)
cond N. DEL MAR
Britten: Noye's Fludde (Cpte)
cond E. MCARTHUR
(PEAR) **GEMMCD9049** Flagstad and Melchior sing Wagner
cond C. MEDLAM
Blow: Venus and Adonis (Cpte)
cond A. MELICHAR
(PREI) **89070** Franz Völker (1899-1965) - II
cond F. MOLINARI-PRADELLI
(RCA) **09026 68014-2** Pavarotti - The Early Years, Vol.2
cond R. MUTI
(RCA) **09026 68014-2** Pavarotti - The Early Years, Vol.2
cond E. ORTHMANN
(PREI) **89019** Alexander Kipnis (1891-1978)
cond W. PELLETIER
(VAI) **VAIA1017** Leonard Warren—Early Recordings
(VAI) **VAIA1084** Rose Bampton sings Verdi and Wagner
cond M. RIESMAN
Glass: Einstein on the Beach (Cpte)
cond S. ROBINSON
(EMI) **CDH7 61052-2** Beniamino Gigli—Arias and Duets (1932-1949)
cond W.B ROGERS
(SUPR) **11 2136-2(5)** Emmy Destinn—Complete Edition, Discs 11 & 12
cond R. ROMANI
(NIMB) **NI7846** Rosa Ponselle, Vol.2
cond ROSARIO BOURDON
(NIMB) **NI7846** Rosa Ponselle, Vol.2
(PEAR) **GEMMCDS9074(2)** Giovanni Zenatello, Vol.2 (pt 2)
(ROMO) **81007-2** Rosa Ponselle—Victor Recordings 1926-1929
cond C. SABAJNO
(EMI) **CHS7 64864-2(1)** La Scala Edition - Vol.2, 1915-46 (pt 1)
(PEAR) **GEMMCDS9925(1)** Covent Garden on Record—Vol.3 (pt 1)
(PEAR) **GEMMCD9088** Titta Ruffo (1877-1953)
(PEAR) **GEMMCD9117** Graziella Pareto
(PEAR) **GEMMCD9306** Ezio Pinza—Opera Recital
cond G. SANTINI
Verdi: Traviata (Cpte)
(EMI) **CHS7 64864-2(1)** La Scala Edition - Vol.2, 1915-46 (pt 1)
cond M. SARGENT
(PEAR) **GEMMCD9468** Vaughan Williams
cond C. SCHMALSTICH
(EMI) **CHS7 64673-2** Joseph Schmidt - Complete EMI Recordings Volume 1
(PREI) **89019** Alexander Kipnis (1891-1978)
cond G. SETTI
(NIMB) **NI7804** Giovanni Martinelli—Opera Recital
cond H. STEINKOPF
(MYTO) **2MCD943103** Lortzing—Zar und Zimmermann
cond L. STOKOWSKI
(RCA) **09026 61503-2** Stokowski Favourites
cond P. STOLL
(SYMP) **SYMCD1103** Renée Doria—Opera Recital
cond A. TOSCANINI
Beethoven: Fidelio (Cpte)
Puccini: Bohème (Cpte)
Verdi: Otello (Cpte), Traviata (Cpte)
cond T. VETÖ
Nørgård: Gilgamesh (Cpte)
cond F. WEISSMANN
(EMI) **CDH7 69787-2** Richard Tauber sings Operetta Arias
(PREI) **89028** Ivar Andresen (1896-1940)
cond F. ZWEIG
(PEAR) **GEMMCD9129** Great Tenors, Vol.2
(PREI) **89028** Ivar Andresen (1896-1940)

CHORZEMPA, Daniel (organ)
(PHIL) **438 309-2PM** A Romantic Organ Extravaganza

CHRIST, Rudolf (ten)
Cornelius: Barbier von Bagdad (Cpte)
Kálmán: Csárdásfürstin (exc)
Lehár: Graf von Luxemburg (exc), Paganini (exc)
O. Straus: Walzertraum (exc)
Orff: Kluge (Cpte), Mond (Cpte)
R. Strauss: Capriccio (Cpte)
(CAMB) **CD-1032** From the Operas of Erich Wolfgang Korngold

CHRISTENSEN, Jacob (gtr)
(KONT) **32044** Cantos de España—Jacob Christensen and Michaela Fukačová

CHRISTENSEN, Tom (ww)
S. Wallace: Kabbalah (Cpte)

CHRISTIAN, Lesley (mez)
(SILV) **FILMCD127** Vampire Circus—The Essential Vampire Theme Collection

CHRISTIANSEN, Christian (bass)
Heise: Drot og Marsk (Cpte)
Nielsen: Saul and David (Cpte)
Nørgård: Siddhartha (Cpte)
Zemlinsky: Es war einmal (Cpte)

CHRISTIE, Nan (sop)
(OPRA) **ORH102** A Hundred Years of Italian Opera

CHRISTIE, William (cond)
see Arts Florissants Instr Ens
Arts Florissants Orch
Cappella Coloniensis

CHRISTIE, William (hpd)
(HARM) **HMC90 249** Purcell: Music for a while
(HARM) **HMP390 807** Great Baroque Masters—Purcell
(HARM) **HMX290 1528/33(2)** A Purcell Companion (pt 2)

CHRISTIN, Judith (mez)
Boito: Mefistofele (Cpte)
Corigliano: Ghosts of Versailles (Cpte)
Mozart: Zauberflöte (Cpte)
(ALBA) **TROY068-2** William Mayer—Voices from Lost Realms

CHRISTOFELLIS, Aris (alto)
Vivaldi: Olimpiade (Cpte)
(EMI) **CDC5 55250-2** Farinelli and his Time
(EMI) **CDC5 55259-2** The Age of the Castrato

CHRISTOFF, Boris (bass)
Boito: Mefistofele (Cpte)
Gounod: Faust (exc)
Massenet: Don Quichotte (Cpte)
Mussorgsky: Boris Godunov (Cpte), Khovanshchina (Cpte)
Verdi: Aida (Cpte), Don Carlo (Cpte), Simon Boccanegra (Cpte)
(EMI) **CDH5 65500-2** Boris Christoff - Italian Opera Arias
(EMI) **CDH7 64252-2** Christoff sings Russian Arias & Songs
(EMI) **CHS7 63025-2** Mussorgsky—Songs
(EMI) **CHS7 69741-2(6)** Record of Singing, Vol.4—Russian & Slavonic Schools
(EMI) **CMS7 63386-2** Borodin—Prince Igor & Complete Solo Songs
(FORL) **UCD16651** Boris Christoff - Recital
(FORL) **UCD16741** Bulgarian Voices, Vol. 1

CHRISTOPH, Ingo (ten)
Pfitzner: Herz (Cpte)

CHRISTOPHER, Russell (ten)
Bizet: Carmen (Cpte)
Puccini: Tosca (Cpte)

CHRISTOPHERS, Harry (cond)
see The Sixteen Orch

CHRISTOV, Nicolaï (bass)
Rossini: Guillaume Tell (Cpte)
Verdi: Ballo in maschera (Cpte)

CHUBIENKO, Nadezhda (sop)
(DANT) **LYS013/5** Tchaikovsky—The Queen of Spades

(THE) CHUCKERBUTTY OCARINA QUARTET
(SEAV) **CD007366** The Ocarina is no Trombone

CHUNG, Kyung-Wha (vn)
(DECC) **417 289-2DH** Con amore

CHUNG, Myung-Whun (cond)
see Gothenburg SO
LSO
Paris Bastille Orch
Paris Opéra-Bastille Orch

CIAMPOLINI, Daniel (perc)
Machover: Valis (Cpte)

CIAPARELLI-VIAFORA, Gina (mez)
(NIMB) **NI7834** Caruso in Ensemble
(NIMB) **NI7857** Farrar in Italian Opera
(PEAR) **EVC1(2)** The Caruso Edition, Vol.1 (pt 2)
(RCA) **GD60495(2)** The Complete Caruso Collection (pt 2)
(RCA) **09026 61243-2** Caruso sings Verismo Arias

CIAVOLA, Giovanni (bass)
Verdi: Rigoletto (Cpte)

CIBELLI, Signor **(mndl)**
(PEAR) **GEMMCD9306** Ezio Pinza—Opera Recital
(RCA) **09026 61580-2(3)** RCA/Met 100 Singers, 100 Years (pt 3)

CICOGNA, Adriana (mez)
Donizetti: Pazzi per progetto (Cpte)

CID, Manuel (ten)
Falla: Vida breve (Cpte)

CIDONI, Mary (sngr)
Rorem: Childhood Miracle (Cpte)

CIESINSKI, Katherine (mez)
Prokofiev: War and Peace (Cpte)
Tchaikovsky: Queen of Spades (Cpte)

CIESINSKI, Kristine (sop)
Shostakovich: Lady Macbeth of Mtsensk (Cpte)
Weill: Street Scene (Cpte)

CIESLEWICZ, Phillipe (treb)
Mozart: Apollo et Hyacinthus (Cpte)

CIGNA, Gina (sop)
Bellini: Norma (Cpte)
Puccini: Turandot (Cpte)
Verdi: Forza del destino (exc), Otello (exc), Trovatore (Cpte)
(EMI) **CHS7 64864-2(2)** La Scala Edition - Vol.2, 1915-46 (pt 2)
(LYRC) **SRO805** Gina Cigna—Opera Recital
(PREI) **89010** Tancredi Pasero (1893-1983) - I
(PREI) **89014** Ebe Stignani (1903-1974)
(PREI) **89016** Gina Cigna (b. 1900)
(PREI) **89042** Nazzareno de Angelis (1881-1962)

CILEA, Francesco (pf)
(EMI) **CDH7 61046-2** Enrico Caruso: Opera Arias and Songs - 1902-1904
(PEAR) **EVC1(1)** The Caruso Edition, Vol.1 (pt 1)
(PEAR) **GEMMCDS9159(1)** De Luca Edition, Vol.1 (pt 1)
(RCA) **GD60495(1)** The Complete Caruso Collection (pt 1)
(SYMP) **SYMCD1111** The Harold Wayne Collection, Vol.11

CILIENTO, Nicoletta (mez)
Rossini: Torvaldo e Dorliska (Cpte)

CILLA, Luigi (bass)
(PEAR) **GEMMCDS9926(1)** Covent Garden on Record—Vol.4 (pt 1)

CILLA, Luigi (ten)
(PEAR) **GEMMCDS9074(2)** Giovanni Zenatello, Vol.2 (pt 2)

CILLARIO, Carlo Felice (cond)
see Barcelona SO
LPO
LSO
Milan RAI SO
orch
RCA Italiana Op Orch
ROHO

CIMARA, Pietro (cond)
see Columbia SO
LPO
orch

CIMARELLA, Maria (contr)
R. Strauss: Aegyptische Helena (Cpte)

CINCINNATI POPS ORCHESTRA
cond E. KUNZEL
(TELA) **CD80115** Orchestral Spectaculars
(TELA) **CD80117** Copland—Orchestral Works
(TELA) **CD80170** Symphonic Spectacular
(TELA) **CD80260** Pops Plays Puccini
(TELA) **CD80294** Gaîté Parisienne
(TELA) **CD80364** Verdi without Words
(TELA) **CD80401** The Very Best of Erich Kunzel
(TELA) **CD80407** Divine Sopranos

CINCINNATI SYMPHONY ORCHESTRA
cond E. KUNZEL
(TELA) **CD80041** Tchaikovsky: Orchestral Works
cond J. LÓPEZ-COBOS
Falla: Vida breve (Cpte)
(TELA) **CD80149** Falla—Theatre Music
(TELA) **CD80224** Bizet—Orchestral Works
(TELA) **CD80371** R. Strauss—Der Rosenkavalier Suite, etc
(TELA) **CD80379** Wagner—Overtures in Surround Sound

CINCINNATI UNIVERSITY SINGERS
cond E. RIVERS
(NEW) **80221-2** I Wants to be a Actor Lady

CINCINNATI UNIVERSITY THEATRE ORCHESTRA
cond E. RIVERS
(NEW) **80221-2** I Wants to be a Actor Lady

CINCINNATI WIND SYMPHONY
cond E. CORPORON
(KLVI) **KCD11060** American Variations

CINGOLANI, F. (sop)
(RCA) **GD87808** Lawrence Tibbett sings Opera Arias

CINISELLI, Fernandino (ten)
(EMI) **CDH7 69791-2** Dame Eva Turner sings Opera Arias and Songs
(PREI) **89063** Rosetta Pampanini (1896-1973)

CIONI, Renato (ten)
Donizetti: Lucia di Lammermoor (Cpte)
Verdi: Rigoletto (Cpte)
(BELA) **450 133-2** Verdi Favourites
(EMI) **LDB4 91283-1(EMI)** Maria Callas at Covent Garden

CITY OF BIRMINGHAM ORCHESTRA
cond B. CAMERON
(DUTT) **CDLX7013** The Unforgettable Isobel Baillie
(PEAR) **GEMMCD9934** Dame Isobel Baillie
cond L. HEWARD
(EMI) **CHS5 65590-2** CBSO 75th Anniversary Set
(SAIN) **SCDC2076** David Lloyd-Early Recordings, 1940-1941
(TEST) **SBT1013** Dame Joan Hammond—A Celebration
cond G. WELDON
(EMI) **CHS5 65590-2** CBSO 75th Anniversary Set

CITY OF BIRMINGHAM SYMPHONY ORCHESTRA
cond L. FRÉMAUX
(EMI) **CDM5 65150-2** Massenet/Charpentier—Orchestral Works
(KLVI) **KCD11040** Offenbach—Overtures
cond S. RATTLE
Weill: Sieben Todsünden
(EMI) **CDC5 55212-2** Schoenberg—Orchestral Works

CITY OF LONDON BAROQUE SINFONIA
cond I. BOLTON
(VIRG) **VJ7 59644-2** Handel—Favourite Arias
cond R. HICKOX
Handel: Alcina (Cpte)

CITY OF LONDON SINFONIA
cond M. BEST
(HYPE) **CDA66569** Vaughan Williams—Choral Works
cond R. HICKOX
Britten: Midsummer Night's Dream (Cpte), Noye's Fludde (Cpte), Rape of Lucretia (Cpte)
Holst: Sávitri (Cpte)
(CHAN) **CHAN8840** La flûte enchantée
(CHAN) **CHAN8865** Rossini: Opera Arias
cond A. MELVILLE
Boughton: Bethlehem (Cpte)

(THE) CITY WAITES
cond A. ROOLEY
Purcell: Don Quixote: The Musical (Cpte)

CIURCA, Cleopatra (mez)
Cilea: Adriana Lecouvreur (Cpte)

CIVIL, Pablo (ten)
(PREI) **89010** Tancredi Pasero (1893-1983) - I
(PREI) **89016** Gina Cigna (b. 1900)

CLABASSI, Plinio (bass)
Donizetti: Anna Bolena (Cpte)
Puccini: Gianni Schicchi (Cpte), Madama Butterfly (Cpte)
Rossini: Mosè (Cpte)
Verdi: Aida (exc), Don Carlo (Cpte), Forza del destino (Cpte), Otello (Cpte), Rigoletto (Cpte)
(EMI) **CMS7 64165-2** Puccini—Trittico
(MEMO) **HR4386/7** Great Voices - Giulietta Simionato

CLACK, Caroline (sop)
Britten: Noye's Fludde (Cpte)
Lehár: Lustige Witwe (Cpte)
(DECC) **436 990-2DWO** The World of Benjamin Britten

CLAESSENS, Huub (bass)
Mascagni: Piccolo Marat (Cpte)
Mozart: Così fan tutte (Cpte)

CLAM, Leopold (ten)
Berg: Lulu (Cpte)
Wagner: Meistersinger (exc)

CLARE COLLEGE CHOIR, CAMBRIDGE
Purcell: Dido (Cpte)

CLAREY, Cynthia (sop)
Berg: Lulu (Cpte)
Gershwin: Porgy and Bess (Cpte)
Monteverdi: Incoronazione di Poppea (Cpte)
Tippett: Ice Break (Cpte)
Weill: Lost in the Stars (Cpte)

CLARION MUSIC SOCIETY
cond N. JENKINS
Dittersdorf: Arcifanfano (Cpte)

CLARK, Gordon (treb)
Britten: Midsummer Night's Dream (Cpte)

CLARK, Graham (ten)
Berg: Lulu (Cpte)
Corigliano: Ghosts of Versailles (Cpte)
Donizetti: Lucrezia Borgia (Cpte), Maria Padilla (Cpte)
Gay: Beggar's Opera (Cpte)
Janáček: Makropulos Affair (Cpte)
Massenet: Esclarmonde (Cpte)
Mozart: Nozze di Figaro (Cpte)
R. Strauss: Rosenkavalier (Cpte)
Verdi: Trovatore (Cpte)
Wagner: Fliegende Holländer (exc), Meistersinger (Cpte), Rheingold (exc), Siegfried (exc)
(PHIL) **434 420-2PM32(1)** Richard Wagner Edition (Pt.1)

CLARK, Michael (ten)
G. Charpentier: Louise (Cpte)
(SONY) **SM3K47154** Bernstein—Theatre Works Volume 1

CLARK, Patricia (sop)
G. Charpentier: Louise (Cpte)
Korngold: Tote Stadt (Cpte)
Purcell: Dido (Cpte)
Rossini: Semiramide (Cpte)

CLARK, Stanley (bar)
(EBS) **EBS6023** Contrasts - Music for Trombone & Piano

CLARKE, Katie (sop)
Wagner: Götterdämmerung (Cpte), Walküre (Cpte)
(PHIL) **434 420-2PM32(2)** Richard Wagner Edition (pt 2)

CLARKE, Paul Charles (ten)
Gounod: Roméo et Juliette (Cpte)

CLARKSON, Julian (bass)
Lehár: Lustige Witwe (Cpte)
Mozart: Don Giovanni (Cpte), Nozze di Figaro (Cpte)

(THE) CLASSIC BUSKERS
(SEAV) **CD007365** The Classic Buskers-Omnibusk
(SEAV) **CD007366** The Ocarina is no Trombone

CLAVENSY, Charles (bass-bar)
Adam: Toréador (Cpte)
Martin: Mystère de la Nativité
Ravel: Heure espagnole (Cpte)

CLAVERIE, Jean (bar)
(PREI) **89011** Marjorie Lawrence (1909-1979)

CLEMENČIĆ, René (cond)
see Clemencic Consort
Clemencic Consort Baroque Orch

CLEMENCIC, René (hpd/dir)
Salieri: Axur (Cpte)

CLEMENCIC CONSORŢ
cond R. CLEMENČIĆ
Fux: Dafne in Lauro (Cpte)
Keiser: Croesus (Cpte)
Vivaldi: Olimpiade (Cpte)

CLEMENCIC CONSORŢ BAROQUE ORCHESTRA
cond R. CLEMENČIĆ
Carvalho: Testoride Argonauta (Cpte)

CLÉMENT, Edmond (ten)
(IRCC) **IRCC-CD800** Souvenirs from Meyerbeer Operas
(NIMB) **NI7856** Legendary Tenors
(NIMB) **NI7872** Geraldine Farrar in French Opera
(PEAR) **GEMMCD9129** Great Tenors, Vol.2
(PEAR) **GEMMCD9161** Edmond Clément (1867-1928)
(ROMO) **82002-2** Edmond Clément (1867-1928)

CLÉMENT, Josephte (sop)
Delibes: Lakmé (exc)
Meyerbeer: Huguenots (Cpte)
Verdi: Rigoletto (exc)

CLEMENT, Maris (mez)
Bernstein: Candide (1982) (Cpte)

CLEMENT, Richard (ten)
Tchaikovsky: Queen of Spades (Cpte)

CLÉMENT, Willy (bar)
Hahn: Ciboulette (exc)
Messager: Monsieur Beaucaire (Cpte)
(EMI) **CZS5 68295-2** Messager/Lecocq—Operetta Highlights
(EMI) **CZS7 67515-2** Offenbach—Operetta highlights

CLEMENTIS, Tamás (bass)
Respighi: Semirama (Cpte)

CLEMMONS, François (ten)
Gershwin: Porgy and Bess (Cpte)

CLEOBURY, Nicholas (cond)
see ECO
New Belgian CO
RPO

CLEOBURY, Stephen (organ)
(BELA) **450 013-2** Favourite Wedding Music
(DECC) **436 402-2DWO** The World of Wedding Music

CLEVA, Fausto (cond)
see LSO
Monte Carlo Nat Op Orch
Monte Carlo Op Orch
NY Met Op Orch
RCA Italiana Op Orch

CLEVELAND, M. (sngr)
Barber: Antony and Cleopatra (Cpte)

CLEVELAND ORCHESTRA
cond C. VON DOHNÁNYI
Beethoven: Leonore (exc)
Tchaikovsky: Eugene Onegin (exc)
Wagner: Rheingold (Cpte)
(CLOR) **TCO93-75** The Cleveland Orchestra-75th Anniversary CD Edition
cond E. LEINSDORF
(CLOR) **TCO93-75** The Cleveland Orchestra-75th Anniversary CD Edition
cond L. MAAZEL
Gershwin: Porgy and Bess (Cpte)
cond G. SZELL
Beethoven: Fidelio (exc)
(CBS) **CD46466** Wagner: Orchestral Music
(IMP) **DUET 15CD** Mozart: Favourites
(SONY) **SBK39436** Mozart—Greatest Hits
(SONY) **SBK39438** Wagner—Greatest Hits
(SONY) **SBK48162** Popular Orchestral Works
(SONY) **SBK48175** George Szell conducts Wagner
(SONY) **SBK48279** Offenbach/Rachmaninov/Smetana—Orchestral Works
(SONY) **SB5K48396** Beethoven— Symphonies and Overtures

CLEVELAND ORCHESTRA CHILDREN'S CHORUS
cond L. MAAZEL
Gershwin: Porgy and Bess (Cpte)

CLEVELAND ORCHESTRA CHORUS
cond L. MAAZEL
Gershwin: Porgy and Bess (Cpte)

CLIFFORD, Grahame (bass)
(LYRC) **SRO830** Smetana—The Bartered Bride, etc

CLINTON, Gordon (bar)
Delius: Village Romeo and Juliet (Cpte)

CLOËZ, Gustav (cond)
see orch
Paris Opéra-Comique Orch

CLOSE, Shirley (mez)
R. Strauss: Elektra (Cpte)
Wagner: Walküre (Cpte)

CLOSEL, Amaury du (cond)
see Versailles Camerata

CLOUGH, John (euphonium)
(CHAN) **CHAN4505** Black Dyke plays Rossini

CLUYTENS, André (cond)
see FNO
FRNO
Paris Cons
Paris Op Orch
Paris Opéra-Comique Orch
VPO

COADOU, Luc (bass)
Lully: Armide

COADOU, Luc (ten)
Rameau: Hippolyte et Aricie (Cpte)

COATES, Albert (cond)
see Berlin St Op Orch
LSO
National SO
New SO
orch
SO

COATES, Edith (mez)
Donizetti: Fille du régiment (Cpte)
Wagner: Walküre (exc)

COATES, John (ten)
(SYMP) **SYMCD1123** Sullivan—Sesquicentenial Commemorative Issue
(SYMP) **SYMCD1130** Joseph Holbrooke—Historic Recordings

COBB, Cheryl (sngr)
Handel: Giulio Cesare (Cpte)

COBELLI, Giuseppina (sop)
(EMI) **CHS7 64864-2(1)** La Scala Edition - Vol.2, 1915-46 (pt 1)

COBURN, Pamela (sop)
Beethoven: Fidelio (exc)
Gazzaniga: Don Giovanni (Cpte)
Gounod: Faust (Cpte)
J. Strauss II: Fledermaus (Cpte), Zigeunerbaron (Cpte)
Mozart: Oca del Cairo (Cpte), Zauberflöte (Cpte)
Suder: Kleider machen Leute (Cpte)
Wagner: Parsifal (Cpte)
Zemlinsky: Traumgörge (Cpte)
(CAPR) **10 481** R.Strauss—Opera Concert

COCHRAN, William (ten)
Busoni: Doktor Faust (Cpte)
Hindemith: Mathis der Maler (Cpte)
Schreker: Gezeichneten (Cpte)
(EMI) **CMS5 65212-2** Wagner—Les introuvables du Ring

COCKERILL, John (hp)
(EMI) **CHS7 69741-2(2)** Record of Singing, Vol.4—Anglo-American School (pt 2)

COCTEAU, Jean (narr)
(MONT) **TCE8760** Stravinsky: Stage Works

CODA, Eraldo (bar)
Puccini: Bohème (Cpte)
(DECC) **436 464-2DM** Ten Top Baritones & Basses

COERTSE, Mimi (sop)
R. Strauss: Arabella (Cpte), Ariadne auf Naxos (Cpte)

COGAN, Dmitriy (pf)
(ERAT) **4509-98481-2** Violin Encores

COGNET, André (bass-bar)
Auber: Manon Lescaut (Cpte)

COHEN, Elie (cond)
see orch
Paris Opéra-Comique Orch

COHEN, Jeff (pf)
(DECC) **436 417-2DH** Ute Lemper sings Kurt Weill, Vol.2

COHN, Richard (bar)
Schoenberg: Moses und Aron (Cpte)
Verdi: Otello (Cpte)

COIFFIER, Marthe (sop)
Gounod: Faust (Cpte)

COLAFELICE, Giacomo (bass)
Donizetti: Maria di Rohan (Cpte)

COLAIANNI, Domenico (sngr)
Mascagni: Rantzau (Cpte)

COLAS, Sylvie (sop)
Montéclair: Jephté (Cpte)

COLAZZA, Luigi (ten)
(IRCC) **IRCC-CD808** Souvenirs of 19th Century Italian Opera
(NIMB) **NI7831** Mattia Battistini (1856-1928)
(PREI) **89045** Mattia Battistini (1856-1928)

COLD, Ulrik (bass)
Kuhlau: Lulu (Cpte)
Mendelssohn: Hochzeit des Camacho (Cpte)
Verdi: Falstaff (Cpte)
Wagner: Parsifal (Cpte)

COLE, Joanna (sop)
Meyerbeer: Huguenots (Cpte)

COLE, Steven (ten)
Barber: Antony and Cleopatra (Cpte)
Floyd: Susannah (Cpte)

COLE, Vinson (ten)
R. Strauss: Rosenkavalier (exc)
(SONY) **SK45855** Mozart: Bastien und Bastienne

COLELLA, Alfredo (bass)
Verdi: Lombardi (Cpte)

COLEMAN, Barrington (ten)
Gershwin: Porgy and Bess (exc)

COLES, Mark (bass)
Corghi: Divara (Cpte)
Henze: English Cat (Cpte)
Puccini: Bohème (Cpte)

COLES, Priti (sop)
Mozart: Così fan tutte (Cpte)

COLICOS, Nicolas (sngr)
Romberg: Student Prince (Cpte)

COLLADO, José (cond)
see Philh

COLLARD, Jeannine (mez)
Debussy: Pelléas et Mélisande (Cpte)
Milhaud: Malheurs d'Orphée (Cpte)
Offenbach: Contes d'Hoffmann (Cpte)
(CFP) **CD-CFP4602** Favourite Opera
(EMI) **CZS5 68113-2** Vive Offenbach!

COLLART, Claudine (sop)
Audran: Miss Helyett (Cpte)
Bazin: Voyage en Chine (Cpte)
Boïeldieu: Voitures Versées (Cpte)
Gounod: Roméo et Juliette (Cpte)
Martinů: Alexandre Bis (Cpte)
Messager: Coups de Roulis (Cpte), Passionêment (Cpte), P'tites Michu (exc)
Milhaud: Malheurs d'Orphée (Cpte)
Planquette: Rip van Winkle (Cpte)
(CHNT) **LDC278 1068** Chabrier—Une Education Manquée/Mélodies
(EMI) **CZS7 67515-2** Offenbach—Operetta highlights
(EMI) **CZS7 67872-2** Lehár—Operettas (highlights in French)

COLLEGIATE CHORALE
cond R. BASS
R. Strauss: Friedenstag (Cpte)
cond J. CONLON
(RCA) **09026 61509-2** A Salute to American Music

COLLEGIATE ORCHESTRA
cond R. BASS
R. Strauss: Friedenstag (Cpte)

COLLEGIUM ACADEMICUM ORCHESTRE
cond R. DUNAND
(GALL) **CD-816** Mozart—Concert Arias

COLLEGIUM AUREUM
Pergolesi: Serva Padrona
cond G. LEONHARDT
Rameau: Indes galantes (exc)
cond R. PETERS
Rameau: Dardanus (exc)

COLLEGIUM INSTRUMENTALE BRUGENSE
cond A. ZEDDA
Rossini: Tancredi (Cpte)

COLLEGIUM MUSICUM 90
cond R. HICKOX
Purcell: Dido (Cpte), Dioclesian, Z627 (exc)

COLLEGIUM MUSICUM 90 CHORUS
cond R. HICKOX
Purcell: Dido (Cpte), Dioclesian, Z627 (Cpte)

COLLEGIUM VOCALE
cond N. HARNONCOURT
Mozart: Thamos, K345 (Cpte)
(TELD) **4509-97505-2** Mozart—Famous Opera Choruses
cond P. HERREWEGHE
Dusapin: Medeamaterial (Cpte)
Lully: Armide

COLLIER, Elizabeth (sop)
Bizet: Carmen (Cpte)
Wagner: Parsifal (Cpte)

COLLIER, Frederick (bass)
Wagner: Götterdämmerung (exc)
(PEAR) **GEMMCDS9137** Wagner—Der Ring des Nibelungen
(PEAR) **GEMMCD9468** Vaughan Williams

COLLIER, Marie (sop)
Puccini: Madama Butterfly (exc)
R. Strauss: Elektra (Cpte)
Wagner: Walküre (Cpte)
Walton: Troilus and Cressida (exc)

COLLINGWOOD, Lawrance (cond)
see LSO
orch
Philh
ROHO

COLLINS, Anne (contr)
Gay: Beggar's Opera (Cpte)
Mozart: Zauberflöte (exc)
Sullivan: Yeomen of the Guard (Cpte)
Wagner: Götterdämmerung (Cpte), Rheingold (Cpte), Siegfried (Cpte), Walküre (Cpte)

COLLINS, Kenneth (ten)
Bellini: Norma (Cpte)
Verdi: Ballo in maschera (Cpte), Nabucco (exc), Vespri Siciliani (Cpte)
(EMI) **CDM7 64356-2** Opera Choruses

COLLINS, Martha (sop)
(CFP) **CD-CFP4569** Puccini: Arias

COLLINS, Michael (cond)
see M. Collins Orch
Orch

(MICHAEL) COLLINS ORCHESTRA
cond M. COLLINS
German: Merrie England (Cpte)

COLLINS-WHITE, David (ten)
Meyerbeer: Huguenots (Cpte)

CÖLLN SALON ORCHESTRA
(EMI) **CDC7 49819-2** Christmas Salon
(EURO) **GD69295** Salon Music
(EURO) **GD69296** Paris Salon Music
(EURO) **GD69297** Vienna Salon Music

COLLUP, Donald (bar)
Weill: Down in the Valley (Cpte)

COLMAR WOMEN'S VOICES
cond D. DEBART
Xenakis: Orestia (Cpte)

COLOGNE CHILDREN'S CHOIR
cond N. SCHULTZE
Schultze: Schwarzer Peter (Cpte)

COLOGNE CONCERTO
cond R. JACOBS
Handel: Giulio Cesare (exc)

COLOGNE GÜRZENICH ORCHESTRA
cond J. CONLON
Weber: Oberon (Cpte)
cond J. PRITCHARD
Humperdinck: Hänsel und Gretel (Cpte)
(CBS) **CD39208** A Portrait of Kiri te Kanawa

COLOGNE OPERA CHILDREN'S CHOIR
cond J. PRITCHARD
Humperdinck: Hänsel und Gretel (Cpte)

COLOGNE OPERA CHORUS
cond J. CONLON
Weber: Oberon (Cpte)

COLOGNE PRO MUSICA
cond J. LATHAM-KÖNIG
Hindemith: Neues vom Tage (Cpte)
Weill: Happy End (Cpte), Mahagonny (Cpte)

COLOGNE RADIO CHORUS
cond G. ALBRECHT
Hindemith: Mathis der Maler (Cpte)
Schoeck: Massimilla Doni (Cpte)
cond K. EICHHORN
Lortzing: Undine (Cpte)
cond H. FROSCHAUER
Kreutzer: Nachtlager in Granada (Cpte)
cond N. JÄRVI
Mozart: Don Giovanni (Cpte)
cond J. KEILBERTH
Hindemith: Cardillac (Cpte)

cond J. LATHAM-KÖNIG
Weill: Kuhhandel (exc), Zar lässt sich Photographieren (Cpte)
cond F. LEITNER
Gluck: Orfeo ed Euridice (Cpte)
cond W. SCHÜCHTER
Wagner: Lohengrin (Cpte)

COLOGNE RADIO SYMPHONY ORCHESTRA
cond G. ALBRECHT
Hindemith: Mathis der Maler (Cpte)
Schoeck: Massimilla Doni (Cpte)
cond R. CHAILLY
(BELA) **450 121-2** Plácido Domingo
cond K. EICHHORN
Lortzing: Undine (Cpte)
cond H. FROSCHAUER
Kreutzer: Nachtlager in Granada (Cpte)
cond N. JÄRVI
Mozart: Don Giovanni (Cpte)
cond J. KEILBERTH
Hindemith: Cardillac (Cpte)
cond R. KRAUS
(ACAN) **43 268** Peter Anders sings German Opera Arias
cond J. LATHAM-KÖNIG
Hindemith: Neues vom Tage (Cpte)
Weill: Kuhhandel (exc), Mahagonny (Cpte), Zar lässt sich Photographieren (Cpte)
cond F. LEITNER
Orff: Prometheus (Cpte)
(ACAN) **44 2085-2** Carl Orff Collection
cond O. MAGA
(THOR) **CTH2044** Music Between the World Wars
cond R. PATERNOSTRO
(CHAN) **CHAN8930** Wagner—Arias
cond N. SCHULTZE
Schultze: Schwarzer Peter (Cpte)
cond E. SMOLA
(CAPR) **10 705** Theo Mackeben—Film Music
cond P. STEINBERG
(LASE) **15 504** Sabre Dance
cond L. ZAGROSEK
Weill: Sieben Todsünden (Cpte)

COLOGNE SYMPHONY ORCHESTRA
cond D.R. DAVIES
Braunfels: Verkündigung (Cpte)

COLOGNE SYMPHONY ORCHESTRA CHORUS
cond D.R. DAVIES
Braunfels: Verkündigung (Cpte)

COLOMBARA, Carlo (bass)
Handel: Rinaldo (Cpte)
Verdi: Simon Boccanegra (Cpte)

COLOMER, Edmon (cond)
see Seville SO

COLONNE CONCERTS ORCHESTRA
cond J. PERNOO
(EMI) **CZS5 68295-2** Messager/Lecocq—Operetta Highlights

COLSON, Kevin (bar)
(EMI) **CDC7 54586-2** Broadway Showstoppers

COLUMBIA CHAMBER ENSEMBLE
cond I. STRAVINSKY
(SONY) **SM3K46291** Stravinsky—Ballets, Vol.1
(SONY) **SM22K46290(4)** Stravinsky—The Complete Edition (pt 4)

COLUMBIA CHAMBER ORCHESTRA
cond F. WALDMAN
Beeson: Hello Out There (Cpte)

COLUMBIA SYMPHONY ORCHESTRA
(SONY) **SK45816** Humoresque—Favourite Violin Encores
cond P. CIMARA
(CBS) **CD45694** Lily Pons—Opera & Song Recital
cond A. KOSTELANETZ
(CBS) **CD45694** Lily Pons—Opera & Song Recital
cond C. OGERMAN
(SONY) **SM33452** Classical Barbra
(SONY) **SK33452** Classical Barbra
cond I. STRAVINSKY
(SONY) **SM22K46290(3)** Stravinsky—The Complete Edition (pt 3)
cond B. WALTER
(CBS) **CD45701** Bruno Walter conducts Wagner Overtures
(IMP) **DUET 15CD** Mozart: Favourites
(SONY) **SMK64467** J. Strauss II/Brahms/Smetana—Orchestral Works
(SONY) **SM2K64456** Wagner—Orchestral Music
(SONY) **SM3K47211** Mozart Legendary Interpretations—Opera and Concert Arias
(SONY) **SX10K66246** The Bruno Walter Edition, Volume I

COLUMBIA WIND ENSEMBLE
cond L. BERNSTEIN
(SONY) **SM3K47154** Bernstein—Theatre Works Volume 1

COLUMBUS BOYCHOIR
cond T. BEECHAM
Puccini: Bohème (Cpte)
cond R. CELLINI
Leoncavallo: Pagliacci (Cpte)
cond A. TOSCANINI
(RCA) **GD60276** Toscanini conducts Boito & Verdi

COLUSSO, Flavio (cond)
see Seicentonovecento Ens

COMBATTIMENTO
(MERI) **CDE84196** Rossini—Songs

COMBERTI, Sebastian (vc)
Mozart: Zauberflöte (exc)

COMBEY, Julien (bass)
Dusapin: Romeo and Juliet (Cpte)

COMBOY, Ian (bass)
Maxwell Davies: Lighthouse (Cpte)
(COLL) **Coll1444-2** Maximum Max—Music of Maxwell Davies

COMEAUX, Elisabeth (sop)
Copland: Tender Land (Cpte)

COMENCINI, Maurizio (ten)
Piccinni: Pescatrice (Cpte)
Rossini: Siège de Corinthe (Cpte)
Wolf-Ferrari: Campiello (Cpte)

COMISSIONA, Sergiu (cond)
see Helsinki PO
Houston SO

COMMAND, Michèle (sop)
Debussy: Pelléas et Mélisande (Cpte)
Fauré: Pénélope (Cpte)
Gounod: Faust (Cpte), Sapho (Cpte)
Massenet: Don Quichotte (Cpte), Grisélidis (Cpte)
Offenbach: Orphée aux enfers (Cpte), Périchole (Cpte)
Saint-Saëns: Henry VIII (Cpte)
(CFP) **CD-CFP4582** Flowers in Music
(EMI) **CZS5 68113-2** Vive Offenbach!

COMMICHAU, Jürgen (bass)
R. Strauss: Salome (Cpte)

COMO CITY CHORUS
cond M. VIOTTI
Bellini: Sonnambula (exc)

COMPAGNIE BAROCCO
cond J-C. MALGOIRE
Lully: Alceste (Cpte)

COMPANEEZ, Irene (contr)
Mussorgsky: Khovanshchina (Cpte)
Ponchielli: Gioconda (Cpte)

CONCERT ARTS SYMPHONY ORCHESTRA
cond E. LEINSDORF
(EMI) **CDM5 65208-2** Wagner—Orchestral Works from the Operas

(LE) CONCERT DES NATIONS
(ASTR) **E8532** Arriaga—Orchestral Works
cond J. SAVALL
Marais: Alcyone (exc)

CONCERT ROYAL
(GEOR) **GR002** Country House Musick

(LE) CONCERT SPIRITUEL ORCHESTRA
cond H. NIQUET
Rameau: Temple de la gloire (exc)

(ROYAL) CONCERTGEBOUW ORCHESTRA, AMSTERDAM
(TELD) **4509-95523-2** Mozart—Overtures
cond B. HAITINK
(PHIL) **420 886-2PSL** Wagner: Opera Preludes and Siegfried Idyll
(PHIL) **442 079-2PB2** Schumann—Complete Symphonies, etc
cond N. HARNONCOURT
J. Strauss II: Fledermaus (exc)
Mozart: Così fan tutte (Cpte), Don Giovanni (Cpte), Nozze di Figaro (Cpte), Schauspieldirektor (Cpte), Thamos, K345 (Cpte)
(ERAT) **4509-91715-2** The Ultimate Opera Collection 2
(TELD) **0630-11470-2** The Best of Barbara Bonney
(TELD) **4509-93691-2** Queen of Coloratura
(TELD) **4509-97463-2** A Portrait of Thomas Hampson-Arias and Songs
(TELD) **4509-97505-2** Mozart—Famous Opera Choruses
(TELD) **4509-97507-2** Mozart—Famous Opera Arias
(TELD) **4509-98824-2** Thomas Hampson Collection,Vol III-Operatic Scenes
(TELD) **9031-74785-2** Schubert/Mozart—Orchestral Works
(TELD) **9031-74786-2** Johann Strauss II—Orchestral Works
cond E. JOCHUM
(PHIL) **442 281-2PM2** R. Strauss—Five Great Tone Poems
cond W. MENGELBERG
(ARHI) **ADCD109** Mengelberg Edition - Volume 3
(ARHI) **ADCD111** Mengelberg Edition - Volume 5
(ARHI) **ADCD115** Mengelberg Edition, Volume 9
(KOCH) **37011-2** Legendary Conductors
(MUSI) **MACD-780** The Mengelberg Legacy
(SYMP) **SYMCD1078** Willem Mengelberg conducts
cond N. RESCIGNO
Bellini: Pirata (exc)
(EMI) **CDC7 49428-2** Maria Callas - The Unknown Recordings
cond E. DE WAART
(PHIL) **442 550-2PM2** Verdi—Complete Ballet Music &c

CONCERTO ARMONICO
cond J. GRIMBERT
Mozart: Ascanio in Alba (Cpte)

CONCERTO COLOGNE
cond R. JACOBS
Gluck: Echo et Narcisse (Cpte)

CONCERTO VOCALE
Cavalli: Giasone (Cpte)
(HARM) **HMC90 1129** Monteverdi and Ferrari vocal works
cond R. JACOBS
Cavalli: Calisto (Cpte)
Monteverdi: Incoronazione di Poppea (Cpte), Orfeo (Cpte)
(HARM) **HMP390 806** Great Baroque Masters: Monteverdi

CONCORDIA
cond M. ALSOP
(EMI) **CDC7 54851-2** Gershwin—Blue Monday, etc

CONDE, Carlos (sngr)
Schuman: Mighty Casey (Cpte)

CONDÒ, Nucci (mez)
Alfano: Risurrezione (Cpte)
Boito: Mefistofele (Cpte)
Mozart: Nozze di Figaro (Cpte)
Prokofiev: Love for 3 Oranges (Cpte)
Rossini: Otello (Cpte)
Verdi: Falstaff (Cpte)

CONI, Paolo (bar)
Donizetti: Favorita (Cpte), Maria di Rohan (Cpte)
Leoncavallo: Pagliacci (Cpte)
Puccini: Manon Lescaut (Cpte)
Verdi: Don Carlo (Cpte), Simon Boccanegra (Cpte), Traviata (Cpte)
(DECC) **436 463-2DM** Ten Top Tenors
(DECC) **071 140-1DH (DECC)** Pavarotti—30th Anniversary Gala Concert
(IMP) **DPCD998** Opera Stars in Concert
(NUOV) **6905** Donizetti—Great Love Duets
(RNE) **650004** Opera Stars in Concert

CONLON, James (cond)
see Cologne Gürzenich Orch
FNO
NY Met Op Orch
Rotterdam PO

CONNELL, Elizabeth (sop)
Donizetti: Poliuto (Cpte)
Rossini: Guillaume Tell (Cpte)
Schreker: Gezeichneten (Cpte)
Verdi: Due Foscari (Cpte)
Wagner: Lohengrin (Cpte), Walküre (Cpte)

CONNELL, John (bass)
Britten: Billy Budd (Cpte)
Tchaikovsky: Eugene Onegin (Cpte)
(TER) **CDVIR8307** Josephine Barstow sings Verdi Arias

CONNORS, Anne-Marie (sop)
Massenet: Thaïs (Cpte)

CONNORS, Ursula (sop)
G. Charpentier: Louise (Cpte)
Puccini: Rondine (Cpte)
(CBS) **CD79312** Puccini: Il Trittico

CONOLEY, Ann (sop)
Wagner: Walküre (Cpte)

CONQUET, Elisabeth (sop)
Mozart: Zauberflöte (Cpte)

CONRAD, Andreas (ten)
R. Strauss: Ariadne auf Naxos (Cpte)

CONRAD, Barbara (mez)
A. Thomas: Hamlet (Cpte)
Gershwin: Porgy and Bess (Cpte)

CONRAD, Margrit (contr)
Monteverdi: Orfeo (Cpte)

CONRAD, Richard (ten)
Handel: Giulio Cesare (exc)
(DECC) **421 881-2DA** The Age of Bel Canto - Sutherland

CONROY-WARD, James (ten)
(LOND) **436 813-2LM2** Sullivan—The Grand Duke. Overture Di Ballo. Henry VIII
(LOND) **436 816-2LM2** Sullivan—Utopia Ltd. Macbeth & Marmion Ovs etc

CONSORT OF LONDON
cond R. HAYDON CLARK
(COLL) **Coll3008-2** Favourite Trumpet Concertos

CONSORT OF MUSICKE
cond A. ROOLEY
Purcell: Don Quixote: The Musical (Cpte)
(IMP) **PCD881** Monteverdi—Solos and Duets

CONSORTIUM CLASSICUM
cond D. KLÖCKER
Mozart: Clemenza di Tito (exc), Nozze di Figaro (exc)

CONSTABLE, John (pf)
Britten: Little Sweep (Cpte)
(GAMU) **GAMD506** An Anthology Of English Song
(UNIC) **DKPCD9055** Cabaret Classics

CONTI, Max (bar)
Poulenc: Dialogues des Carmélites (Cpte)

CONTRERAS, Ramon (voc)
Falla: Vida breve (Cpte)

CONWAY, Clive (fl)
(MERI) **CDE84241** Music for Flute & Harp

CONWELL, Judy (sop)
Mozart: Finta Giardiniera (Cpte)

COOK, Barbara (sop)
Bernstein: Candide (1956) (exc)

COOK, Deborah (sop)
Meyerbeer: Dinorah (Cpte)
R. Strauss: Ariadne auf Naxos (Cpte)

COOK, George (bass)
Sullivan: Gondoliers (Cpte), HMS Pinafore (exc), Pirates of Penzance (exc), Princess Ida (Cpte)
(DECC) **433 868-2DWO** The World of Gilbert & Sullivan - Volume 2

COOK, Jane (sop)
R. Strauss: Elektra (Cpte)

COOK, Terry (bass)
R. Strauss: Friedenstag (Cpte)
Verdi: Aida (exc)

COOKE, Deryck (narr)
Wagner: Ring des Nibelungen Introduction

COOKE, Max (pf)
Puccini: Fanciulla del West (Cpte)

COOKSON, Brian (ten)
M. Berkeley: Baa Baa Black Sheep (Cpte)
Saxton: Caritas (Cpte)
Walton: Troilus and Cressida (Cpte)

COOPER, Anna (mez)
Puccini: Manon Lescaut (Cpte)

COOPER, Emil (cond)
see NY Met Op Orch

COOPERATIVA ARTISTI ASSOCIATI CHORUS
cond A. PINZAUTI
Mascagni: Amico Fritz (Cpte)

COOTE, Alice (mez)
Vaughan Williams: Hugh the Drover (Cpte)

COOTE, Alice (sop)
Vaughan Williams: Pilgrim's Progress (Cpte)

COPLAND, Aaron (cond)
see Boston SO
Czech PO

COPPENS, Matthijs (ten)
R. Strauss: Rosenkavalier (Cpte)

COPPOLA, Piero (cond)
see orch
Paris Op Orch
Pasdeloup Orch
SO

COPPOLA, Piero (pf)
(PEAR) **GEMMCD9912** Vanni Marcoux—Recital

COPPOLA, Walter (ten)
Bellini: Bianca e Fernando (Cpte)

CORATO, Luigi de (bar)
Verdi: Luisa Miller (Cpte), Rigoletto (Cpte)

CORAZZA, Remy (ten)
Auber: Fra Diavolo (Cpte)
Puccini: Turandot (Cpte)
Saint-Saëns: Samson et Dalila (Cpte)
Verdi: Rigoletto (Cpte)
(EMI) **CZS7 67869-2** J. Strauss II—Operetta Highlights
(ERAT) **4509-96971-2** Marcel Landowski—Edition

CORBELLI, Alessandro (bar)
Cherubini: Lodoïska (Cpte)
Donizetti: Ajo nell'imbarazzo (Cpte), Don Pasquale (Cpte)
Mozart: Così fan tutte (Cpte), Nozze di Figaro (Cpte)
Pergolesi: Frate 'nnamorato (Cpte)
Rossini: Barbiere di Siviglia (Cpte), Cenerentola (Cpte), Italiana in Algeri (Cpte), Occasione fa il ladro (Cpte), Scala di seta (Cpte), Signor Bruschino (Cpte), Turco in Italia (Cpte)

CORBOZ, Michel (cond)
see English Bach Fest Baroque Orch
Lausanne Instr Ens
Lyon Op Orch

CORDES, Marcel (bar)
Orff: Kluge (Cpte)
(EMI) **CZS7 62993-2** Fritz Wunderlich—Great German Tenor

CORDIER, David (alto)
Handel: Rodelinda (Cpte)
Hasse: Cleofide (Cpte)
Keiser: Masagniello furioso (Cpte)
Landi: Mort d'Orfeo (Cpte)

CORDOBA GRAND THEATRE CHORUS
cond L. A. GARCIA-NAVARRO
(RCA) **09026 61440-2** Opera's Greatest Moments
cond M. ROA
Vives: Doña Francisquita (Cpte)

CORDON, Norman (bass)
Mozart: Don Giovanni (Cpte)
(MYTO) **2MCD90317** Verdi—Un Ballo in maschera
(VAI) **VAIA1017** Leonard Warren—Early Recordings
(VAI) **VAIA1084** Rose Bampton sings Verdi and Wagner

CORDONE, Mario (cond)
see orch
SO

CORDOVA, Alvaro (treb)
Puccini: Tosca (Cpte)

CORELLI, Franco (ten)
Bellini: Norma (exc)
Bizet: Carmen (exc)
Giordano: Andrea Chénier (Cpte)
Gounod: Faust (Cpte), Roméo et Juliette (Cpte)
Leoncavallo: Pagliacci (Cpte)
Mascagni: Cavalleria Rusticana (Cpte)
Puccini: Tosca (Cpte), Turandot (Cpte)
Verdi: Aida (Cpte), Don Carlo (Cpte), Ernani (Cpte), Trovatore (Cpte)
(CFP) **CD-CFP4277** These you have Loved
(CFP) **CD-CFP4569** Puccini: Arias
(CFP) **CD-CFP9013** Duets from Famous Operas
(DECC) **433 064-2DWO** Your Hundred Best Opera Tunes Volume I
(DECC) **433 065-2DWO** Your Hundred Best Opera Tunes Volume II
(DECC) **433 439-2DA** Great Love Duets
(DECC) **433 440-2DA** Golden Opera
(DECC) **436 300-2DX** Opera Gala Sampler
(DECC) **436 301-2DA** Renata Tebaldi & Franco Corelli—Arias & Duets
(DECC) **436 317-2DA** Puccini—Famous Arias
(DECC) **436 463-2DM** Ten Top Tenors
(DECC) **443 379-2DM** Ten Top Tenors 2
(DECC) **444 108-2DA** Ballet Music from Opera
(EMI) **CDC7 54016-2** Tenorissimo!
(EMI) **CDC7 54437-2** Callas Rarities
(EMIL) **CDZ103** Best Loved Classics 4
(FONI) **CDMR5014** Martini & Rossi Festival, Volume 14
(MEMO) **HR4204/5** Franco Corelli—Opera Arias
(MEMO) **HR4235/6** Great Voices-Renata Tebaldi
(MEMO) **HR4275/6** Birgit Nilsson—Public Performances 1954-1969
(MEMO) **HR4386/7** Great Voices - Giulietta Simionato
(MEMO) **HR4396/7** Great Voices—Leontyne Price
(MEMO) **HR4400/1** Great Voices - Ettore Bastianini
(RCA) **09026 61580-2(7)** RCA/Met 100 Singers, 100 Years (pt 7)
(RCA) **09026 61886-2** Operas Greatest Love Songs
(RCA) **09026 62689-2** The Voices of Living Stereo, Volume 1
(VAI) **VAI69100** Renata Tebaldi and Franco Corelli

CORENA, Fernando (bass)
Donizetti: Don Pasquale (Cpte), Elisir d'amore (Cpte)
Giordano: Andrea Chénier (Cpte)
J. Strauss II: Fledermaus (Cpte)
Mozart: Don Giovanni (Cpte), Entführung (Cpte), Nozze di Figaro (Cpte)
Puccini: Bohème (Cpte), Gianni Schicchi (Cpte), Madama Butterfly (Cpte), Manon Lescaut (Cpte), Tosca (exc), Turandot (Cpte)
Rossini: Barbiere di Siviglia (Cpte), Italiana in Algeri (Cpte)
Verdi: Aida (Cpte), Otello (Cpte), Rigoletto (Cpte)
(BELA) **450 007-2** Puccini Favourites
(DECC) **411 665-2DM3** Puccini: Il trittico
(DECC) **433 706-2DMO3** Bellini—Beatrice di Tenda; Operatic Arias
(DECC) **436 464-2DM** Ten Top Baritones & Basses
(DECC) **440 407-2DM** Mario del Monaco
(DECC) **440 417-2DM** Carlo Bergonzi
(DECC) **444 555-2DF2** Essential Puccini
(RCA) **GK85277** Legendary Performers - Björling

CORMAN, David (sngr)
Schuman: Mighty Casey (Cpte), Question of Taste (Cpte)

CORNELIUS, Peter (ten)
(PEAR) **GEMMCDS9924(2)** Covent Garden on Record, Vol.2 (pt 2)

CORNOLDI, Claudio (ten)
(EMI) **CMS7 64165-2** Puccini—Trittico

CORNUBERT, Pierre (ten)
(SYMP) **SYMCD1173** The Harold Wayne Collection, Vol.22

CORPORON, Eugene (cond)
see Cincinnati Wind Sym

CORRADETTI, Ferrucio (bar)
(BONG) **GB1043-2** Italian Baritones of the Acoustic Era
(IRCC) **IRCC-CD808** Souvenirs of 19th Century Italian Opera
(PEAR) **GEMMCDS9159(1)** De Luca Edition, Vol.1 (pt 1)
(PEAR) **GEMMCDS9159(2)** De Luca Edition, Vol.1 (pt 2)
(SYMP) **SYMCD1113** The Harold Wayne Collection, Vol.13
(SYMP) **SYMCD1126** The Harold Wayne Collection, Vol.14

CORRADI, Giampaolo (ten)
Boito: Nerone (Cpte)
Puccini: Turandot (Cpte)
Verdi: Aida (Cpte)
(MEMO) **HR4223/4** Nicolai Ghiaurov

CORRÉAS, Jérôme (bass)
Campra: Idoménée (exc)
Purcell: Fairy Queen, Z629 (Cpte)
Rameau: Castor et Pollux (Cpte), Indes galantes (Cpte)
Rossi: Orfeo (Cpte)

CORSI, Emilia (sop)
(MEMO) **HR4408/9(1)** Singers in Genoa, Vol.1 (disc 1)
(NIMB) **NI7831** Mattia Battistini (1856-1928)
(PEAR) **GEMMCDS9924(1)** Covent Garden on Record, Vol.2 (pt 1)
(PEAR) **GEMMCD9016** Mattia Battistini, Vol.3
(PREI) **89045** Mattia Battistini (1856-1928)

CORSI, Rina (contr)
Mascagni: Cavalleria Rusticana (Cpte)

CORSI, Rina (sop)
Donizetti: Linda di Chamounix (Cpte)
(DECC) **443 930-2DM** Jussi Björling sings Opera Arias

CORTEZ, Viorica (mez)
Bizet: Carmen (Cpte)
Tchaikovsky: Iolanta (Cpte)

CORTI, Giulio (bass)
Verdi: Rigoletto (Cpte)

CORTIS, Antonio (ten)
(CONI) **CDHD235** The Puccini Album
(MMOI) **CDMOIR412** Great Voices of the Century Sing Puccini
(NIMB) **NI7850** Antonio Cortis (1891-1952)
(PEAR) **GEMMCDS9926(2)** Covent Garden on Record—Vol.4 (pt 2)
(PREI) **89043** Antonio Cortis (1891-1952)

CORTIS, Marcello (bar)
Gounod: Mireille (Cpte)
Mozart: Don Giovanni (Cpte), Nozze di Figaro (Cpte)
Rossini: Italiana in Algeri (Cpte)

CORTOT, Alfred (pf)
(SYMP) **SYMCD1101** The Harold Wayne Collection, Vol.9

CORYDON ORCHESTRA
cond M. BEST
Vaughan Williams: Hugh the Drover (Cpte)

CORYDON SINGERS
cond M. BEST
Vaughan Williams: Hugh the Drover (Cpte)
(HYPE) **CDA66569** Vaughan Williams—Choral Works

CORYN, Franck (db)
Rossini: Tancredi (Cpte)

COSOTTI, Max-René (ten)
Rossini: Barbiere di Siviglia (Cpte)
Verdi: Falstaff (Cpte), Traviata (Cpte)
Wolf-Ferrari: Campiello (Cpte)

COSSA, Dominic (bar)
Donizetti: Elisir d'amore (Cpte)
Handel: Giulio Cesare (Cpte)
Meyerbeer: Huguenots (Cpte)

COSSINS, James (sngr)
Gay: Beggar's Opera (Cpte)

COSSOTTO, Fiorenza (mez)
Bellini: Norma (Cpte), Sonnambula (Cpte)
Donizetti: Favorita (Cpte)
Giordano: Andrea Chénier (Cpte)
Mozart: Nozze di Figaro (Cpte)
Ponchielli: Gioconda (Cpte)
Puccini: Madama Butterfly (Cpte), Manon Lescaut (Cpte)
Verdi: Aida (Cpte), Ballo in maschera (Cpte), Don Carlo (Cpte), Forza del destino (Cpte), Macbeth (Cpte), Rigoletto (Cpte), Trovatore (Cpte)
(CAST) **CASH5052** Verdi Operatic Favourites
(DECC) **433 069-2DWO** Your Hundred Best Opera Tunes VI
(DECC) **433 865-2DWO** The World of Puccini
(DECC) **436 462-2DM** Ten Top Mezzos
(DECC) **443 378-2DM** Ten Top Mezzos 2
(DECC) **444 555-2DF2** Essential Puccini
(DG) **419 257-2GH3** 'Cav' and 'Pag', etc
(EMIL) **CDZ7 67015-2** Mozart—Opera Arias
(MEMO) **HR4300/1** Great Voices—Sesto Bruscantini
(RCA) **09026 61580-2(8)** RCA/Met 100 Singers, 100 Years (pt 8)

COSSUTTA, Carlo (ten)
Verdi: Otello (Cpte)
(DECC) **433 439-2DA** Great Love Duets

COSSUTTA, Enrico (ten)
Puccini: Manon Lescaut (Cpte)
Verdi: Traviata (Cpte)

COSTA, Fernanda (sop)
Rossini: Cenerentola (exc)

COSTA, Jean-Claude (ten)
Shostakovich: Lady Macbeth of Mtsensk (Cpte)

COSTA, Mary (sop)
Puccini: Bohème (Cpte)

COSTANTINO, Antonio (ten)
Puccini: Fanciulla del West (Cpte)

COSTARIOL, Giuseppe (bar)
Puccini: Fanciulla del West (Cpte)

COSTE, Sharon (sop)
Gounod: Sapho (Cpte)

COSTER, Janet (mez)
Meyerbeer: Huguenots (Cpte)

COTOGNI, Antonio (bar)
(MEMO) **HR4408/9(1)** Singers in Genoa, Vol.1 (disc 1)

COTREIL, Eduard (bass)
(PEAR) **GEMMCDS9074(2)** Giovanni Zenatello, Vol.2 (pt 2)
(PEAR) **GEMMCDS9926(1)** Covent Garden on Record—Vol.4 (pt 1)

COTRUBAS, Ileana (sop)
Bizet: Carmen (exc), Pêcheurs de Perles (Cpte)
Britten: Midsummer Night's Dream (Cpte)
Cavalli: Calisto (Cpte)
Donizetti: Favorita (Cpte)
G. Charpentier: Louise (Cpte)
Humperdinck: Hänsel und Gretel (Cpte)
Massenet: Manon (Cpte)
Mozart: Così fan tutte (Cpte), Finta Giardiniera (Cpte), Mitridate (Cpte), Nozze di Figaro (exc), Schauspieldirektor (Cpte), Sposo deluso (Cpte), Zauberflöte (Cpte)
Offenbach: Contes d'Hoffmann (Cpte)
Puccini: Bohème (Cpte)
Verdi: Alzira (Cpte), Don Carlo (Cpte), Rigoletto (Cpte), Traviata (exc)
(BELA) **450 121-2** Plácido Domingo
(CAST) **CASH5051** Puccini Favourites from Covent Garden and the Arena di Verona
(CAST) **CVI2065** Highlights from the Royal Opera House, Covent Garden
(CAST) **CVI2070** Great Puccini Love Scenes from Covent Garden, La Scala and Verona
(CBS) **CD79312** Puccini: Il Trittico
(DG) **431 104-2GB** Great Voices - Plácido Domingo
(EMIN) **CD-EMX9519** Great Sopranos of Our Time
(EURO) **VD69256** Mozart—Opera Arias
(IMP) **MCD42** Three Sopranos
(ORFE) **C394301B** Great Mozart Singers Series, Vol. 3
(RCA) **09026 61440-2** Opera's Greatest Moments
(SONY) **SBK46548** Opera Arias
(SONY) **SMK39030** Placido Domingo sings Great Love Scenes
(TELD) **9031-77676-6(TELD)** My World of Opera - Kiri Te Kanawa

COTTON, William (ten)
Mozart: Nozze di Figaro (Cpte)

COTTONE, Salvatore (pf)
(CLUB) **CL99-060** Enrico Caruso—Opera & Song Recital
(EMI) **CDC7 54016-2** Tenorissimo!
(EMI) **CDH7 61046-2** Enrico Caruso: Opera Arias and Songs - 1902-1904
(EMI) **CHS7 64860-2(1)** La Scala Edition - Vol.1, 1878-1914 (pt 1)
(EMI) **CHS7 64860-2(2)** La Scala Edition - Vol.1, 1878-1914 (pt 2)
(PEAR) **EVC1(1)** The Caruso Edition, Vol.1 (pt 1)
(PEAR) **GEMMCDS9923(1)** Covent Garden on Record, Vol.1 (pt 1)
(PEAR) **GEMMCDS9997/9(2)** Singers of Imperial Russia, Vol.1 (pt 2)
(RCA) **GD60495(1)** The Complete Caruso Collection (pt 1)
(SYMP) **SYMCD1065** The Harold Wayne Collection, Vol.1
(SYMP) **SYMCD1069** The Harold Wayne Collection, Vol.2
(SYMP) **SYMCD1073** The Harold Wayne Collection, Vol.3
(SYMP) **SYMCD1111** The Harold Wayne Collection, Vol.11

COTTRET, Bernard (bass-bar)
(MONT) **TCE8760** Stravinsky: Stage Works

COUDERC, Florence (sngr)
Lully: Phaëton (Cpte)

COURT, Carol (sop)
Henze: English Cat (Cpte)

COURTIS, Jean-Philippe (bass)
A. Thomas: Hamlet (Cpte)
Berlioz: Troyens (Cpte)
Bizet: Carmen (Cpte), Pêcheurs de Perles (Cpte)
Debussy: Pelléas et Mélisande (Cpte)
Massenet: Esclarmonde (Cpte), Grisélidis (Cpte)
Messiaen: Saint François d'Assise (Cpte)
Rameau: Dardanus (Cpte)
Saint-Saëns: Samson et Dalila (Cpte)
(HARM) **HMP390 1293** Berlioz—Choral Works

COURTNEY, James (bass)
Corigliano: Ghosts of Versailles (Cpte)
Mozart: Zauberflöte (Cpte)
Puccini: Fanciulla del West (Cpte), Manon Lescaut (Cpte), Tosca (Cpte)
Verdi: Falstaff (Cpte)

COUTURE, Michelle (sop)
Rorem: Childhood Miracle (Cpte)

COUTURIER, François (pf)
(HARM) **HMC90 1552** The Three Countertenors

COVA, Mila (mez)
Verdi: Forza del destino (Cpte)

COVENT GARDEN SINGERS
cond M. PLASSON
Massenet: Werther (Cpte)

COVEY-CRUMP, Rogers (ten)
Blow: Venus and Adonis (Cpte)
Monteverdi: Orfeo (Cpte)
Purcell: Dioclesian, Z627 (exc), Indian Queen, Z630 (Cpte)
(ERAT) **4509-96371-2** Gardiner—The Purcell Collection

COVIELLO, Roberto (bar)
Bellini: Adelson e Salvini (Cpte)
Rossini: Gazza ladra (Cpte), Scala di seta (Cpte)

COWAN, Richard (bar)
Puccini: Bohème (Cpte)

COWAN, Sigmund (bar)
Mascagni: Piccolo Marat (Cpte)
Schreker: Gezeichneten (Cpte)

COWARD, Sir Noel (sngr)
(BELA) **450 014-2** Sutherland sings Coward

COWDRICK, Kathryn (contr)
Barber: Antony and Cleopatra (Cpte)
Janáček: Jenufa (Cpte)

COWLES, Eugene (sngr)
(PEAR) **GEMMCDS9050/2(1)** Music from the New York Stage, Vol. 1 (part 1)

COWLEY, Deidre (contr)
Janáček: Jenufa (Cpte)

COX, Jean (ten)
Wagner: Meistersinger (exc)
(PHIL) **434 420-2PM32(1)** Richard Wagner Edition (Pt.1)

COX, Kenneth (bass)
Debussy: Pelléas et Mélisande (Cpte)

COZETTE, Michel (bar)
Gounod: Faust (Cpte)
(CLUB) **CL99-034** Marcel Journet (1867-1933)
(CLUB) **CL99-101** Vanni Marcoux (1877-1962)
(CONI) **CDHD226** Chaliapin—Bass of the Century
(PEAR) **GEMMCD9314** Feodor Chaliapin - Aria and Song Recital
(PEAR) **GEMMCD9912** Vanni Marcoux—Recital
(PREI) **89021** Marcel Journet (1867-1933)

CRABTREE, Libby (sop)
Blow: Venus and Adonis (Cpte)

CRACOW BOYS' CHOIR
cond J. SEMKOW
Mussorgsky: Boris Godunov (Cpte)

CRACOW PHILHARMONIC BOYS' CHORUS
cond K. STRYJA
Szymanowski: King Roger (Cpte)

CRACOW POLISH RADIO CHORUS
cond J. SEMKOW
Mussorgsky: Boris Godunov (Cpte)

CRACOW RADIO SYMPHONY ORCHESTRA
cond J. SEMKOW
Mussorgsky: Boris Godunov (Cpte)

CRAFT, Jean (mez)
Tchaikovsky: Eugene Onegin (Cpte)

CRAFT, Robert (cond)
see St Luke's Orch

CRAIG, Charles (ten)
Puccini: Madama Butterfly (exc)
Verdi: Otello (Cpte)
(CFP) **CD-CFP4569** Puccini: Arias
(CFP) **CD-CFP4575** Verdi Arias
(CFP) **CD-CFP4602** Favourite Opera

CRAMER, Heinz (bar)
Orff: Prometheus (Cpte)
Puccini: Tosca (Cpte)
(ACAN) **44 2085-2** Carl Orff Collection

CRASS, Franz (bass)
Beethoven: Fidelio (Cpte)
Mozart: Don Giovanni (Cpte), Zauberflöte (exc)
Orff: Mond (Cpte)
Wagner: Fliegende Holländer (Cpte), Lohengrin (Cpte), Parsifal (Cpte), Tannhäuser (exc)
Weber: Freischütz (Cpte)
(ORFE) **C365941A** Christa Ludwig - Salzburg Festival highlights
(PHIL) **434 420-2PM32(2)** Richard Wagner Edition (pt 2)
(RCA) **74321 24790-2** Carl Orff 100 Years Edition

CRAVEN, Mae (sop)
Wagner: Walküre (exc)

CRAWFORD, Iain (bass)
S. Wallace: Kabbalah (Cpte)

CRAXTON, Harold (pf)
(BIDD) **LAB014** Jacques Thibaud—1922-24 Recordings
(BIDD) **LAB024** Jacques Thibaud—1924-27 Recordings
(LARR) **CDLRH221** Dame Nellie Melba - Opera and Song Recital

CREASEY, Philip (ten)
Sullivan: Gondoliers (Cpte), Iolanthe (Cpte), Pirates of Penzance (Cpte)

CREDICO, Oslavio di (ten)
Donizetti: Martyrs (Cpte)
Rossini: Donna del Lago (Cpte), Gazza ladra (Cpte), Scala di seta (Cpte), Signor Bruschino (Cpte)
Salieri: Locandiera (Cpte)

CREECH, Philip (ten)
(ALBA) **TROY023-2** Music of Joseph Fennimore

CREES, Eric (cond)
see LSO Brass Ens

CREFFIELD, Rosanne (mez)
Rossini: Elisabetta (Cpte)

CRESPIN, Régine (sop)
Gluck: Iphigénie en Tauride (Cpte)
Massenet: Don Quichotte (Cpte)
Offenbach: Périchole (Cpte)
Poulenc: Dialogues des Carmélites (Cpte)
R. Strauss: Rosenkavalier (Cpte)
Wagner: Walküre (Cpte)
(DECC) **414 100-2DM15** Wagner: Der Ring des Nibelungen
(DECC) **433 440-2DA** Golden Opera
(DECC) **433 442-2DA** Verdi—Famous Arias
(DECC) **433 624-2DSP** Great Soprano Arias
(DECC) **436 316-2DA** Golden Operetta
(DECC) **436 461-2DM** Ten Top Sopranos
(DECC) **440 416-2DM** Régine Crespin
(DG) **435 211-2GX15** Wagner—Der Ring des Nibelungen
(EMI) **CZS5 68113-2** Vive Offenbach!

CRESWELL, Brad (ten)
R. Strauss: Elektra (Cpte)

CREUS, Emile de (ten)
Massenet: Manon (Cpte)

CRIDER, Michèle (sop)
(CAPR) **10 481** R.Strauss—Opera Concert

CRIMI, G. (ten)
(CLUB) **CL99-052** Rosa Raisa (1893-1963)

CRISTOFF, Vera de (mez)
Verdi: Rigoletto (Cpte)
(PEAR) **GEMMCDS9180** Verdi—Rigoletto, etc

CROFT, Dwayne (bar)
Puccini: Manon Lescaut (Cpte)

CROFT, Dwayne (bass)
Puccini: Fanciulla del West (Cpte)
Verdi: Don Carlo (Cpte)
Weber: Oberon (Cpte)
(DG) **072 428-1GH2(DG)** The Metropolitan Opera Gala

CROFT, Richard (ten)
Mozart: Entführung (Cpte), Finta Giardiniera (Cpte)
(DG) **435 866-2GH** Kathleen Battle sings Italian Opera Arias
(DG) **435 866-5CH** Kathleen Battle sings Italian Opera Arias

CROISIER, Marcelle (mez)
Bizet: Carmen (Cpte)

CROIZA, Claire (mez)
Debussy: Pelléas et Mélisande (exc)

CROLIUS, Ross (bass)
Verdi: Traviata (Cpte)

CROMMEN, Els (sop)
Grétry: Caravane du Caire (Cpte)

CRONE, Tan (pf)
(ETCE) **KTC1007** Carolyn Watkinson recital
(ETCE) **KTC1037** Bernstein: Songs

CROOK, Howard (ten)
Lully: Alceste (Cpte), Armide, Phaëton (Cpte)
Purcell: Fairy Queen, Z629 (Cpte)
Rameau: Castor et Pollux (Cpte), Indes galantes (Cpte)
Traetta: Buovo d'Antona (Cpte)
(DHM) **RD77252** Purcell—Airs and Instrumental Music

CROOK, Paul (ten)
Bellini: Norma (Cpte)
Cilea: Adriana Lecouvreur (Cpte)
Massenet: Cendrillon (Cpte), Werther (Cpte)
Menotti: Boy who grew too fast (Cpte)
Offenbach: Contes d'Hoffmann (Cpte)
Puccini: Bohème (Cpte), Fanciulla del West (exc)
R. Strauss: Rosenkavalier (Cpte)
Verdi: Otello (Cpte)

CROOKS, Richard (ten)
(CLAR) **CDGSE78-50-50** Richard Crooks sings Ballads & Sacred Songs
(CLAR) **CDGSE78-50-52** Three Tenors
(CLAR) **CDGSE78-50-58** Richard Crooks (1900-1972)
(PEAR) **GEMMCD9093** The Artistry of Richard Crooks, Volume 1
(RCA) **09026 61580-2(4)** RCA/Met 100 Singers, 100 Years (pt 4)

CROSBY, Bing (sngr)
(RCA) **09026 61778-2(19)** The Heifetz Collection, Vol. 19

CROSS, Gregory (ten)
Berlioz: Troyens (Cpte)
(DECC) **440 947-2DH** Essential Opera II

CROSS, Joan (sop)
Britten: Turn of the Screw (Cpte)
(EMI) **CMS7 64727-2** Britten—Opera excerpts and Folksongs
(PEAR) **GEMMCDS9926(2)** Covent Garden on Record—Vol.4 (pt 2)

CROSS, Richard (bass)
Bellini: Norma (exc)
(DECC) **433 706-2DMO3** Bellini—Beatrice di Tenda; Operatic Arias

CROWDEN, Graham (spkr)
Gay: Beggar's Opera (Cpte)

CROWSON, Lamar (pf)
(DG) **447 349-2GDB2** Homage to Pierre Fournier

CRYER, Doreen (sop)
(CBS) **CD79312** Puccini: Il Trittico

CSÁNYI, Tamás (contr)
Giordano: Fedora (Cpte)

CSAPÓ, Eva (sop)
Schoenberg: Moses und Aron (Cpte)

CSENGERY, Adrienne (sop)
V. Thomson: Lord Byron (Cpte)

CSERE, László (sngr)
Lehár: Lustige Witwe (exc)

CUBEIRO, Josefina (sngr)
Usandizaga: Golondrinas (Cpte)

CUBERLI, Lella (sop)
Mozart: Così fan tutte (exc), Don Giovanni (Cpte), Lucio Silla (Cpte), Nozze di Figaro (exc)
Rossini: Tancredi (Cpte), Viaggio a Reims (Cpte)

CUE, Colin (ten)
Cilea: Adriana Lecouvreur (Cpte)
(DECC) **436 261-2DHO3** Puccini—Il Trittico

CUÉNOD, Hugues (ten)
Berlioz: Benvenuto Cellini (Cpte)
Cavalli: Calisto (Cpte), Ormindo (Cpte)
Giordano: Andrea Chénier (Cpte)
Martin: Mystère de la Nativité
Mozart: Nozze di Figaro (Cpte)
Offenbach: Contes d'Hoffmann (exc)
Puccini: Turandot (Cpte)
R. Strauss: Ariadne auf Naxos (Cpte)
(DECC) **433 400-2DM2** Ravel & Debussy—Stage Works

CUKA, Frances (sngr)
Gay: Beggar's Opera (Cpte)

CULBERT, Tom (ten)
(EMI) **CMS7 64727-2** Britten—Opera excerpts and Folksongs

CULLEN, Bernadette (sop)
Balfe: Bohemian Girl (Cpte)

CULLIS, Rita (sop)
Martinů: Greek Passion (Cpte)
Wagner: Parsifal (Cpte)
(KOCH) **34036-2** A Pageant of Opera
(NIMB) **NI5217** Tippett conducts Tippett

CULVER, Andrew (dir)
Cage: Europera 3, Europera 4

CULWICK CHORAL SOCIETY
cond R. SACCANI
Verdi: Aida (Cpte)

CUMMINGS, Claudia (sop)
Glass: Satyagraha (Cpte)

CUNDARI, Emilia (sop)
Rossini: Inganno felice (Cpte)

CUNITZ, Maud (sop)
Wagner: Lohengrin (Cpte)

CUNNINGHAM, Anthony (bar)
Britten: Billy Budd (Cpte)

CUNNINGHAM, Roberta (sop)
Pfitzner: Herz (Cpte)

CUNNINGHAM, Sarah (va da gamba)
(ARCA) **A02** Purcell—Ayres and Songs from Orpheus Britannicus

CUPIDO, Alberto (ten)
Donizetti: Maria di Rudenz (Cpte)
Verdi: Due Foscari (Cpte), Macbeth (Cpte), Simon Boccanegra (Cpte)
(DENO) **CO-79785** Donizetti—10 Opera Arias
(MCI) **MCCD099** Opera's Greatest Arias

CURIEL, Glauco (cond)
see Philh

CURIEL, Nicoletta (mez)
Mozart: Nozze di Figaro (Cpte)
Pergolesi: Frate 'nnamorato (Cpte)
Rossini: Signor Bruschino (Cpte)
Verdi: Rigoletto (Cpte), Traviata (Cpte)
(DECC) **436 261-2DHO3** Puccini—Il Trittico

CURLEY, Carlo (organ)
(ARGO) **430 200-2ZH** The Emperor's Fanfare
(ARGO) **436 260-2ZH** Carlo Curley—Organ Fantasia

CURPHEY, Margaret (sop)
Wagner: Götterdämmerung (Cpte), Walküre (Cpte)

CURRENDE VOCAL ENSEMBLE
Landi: Mort d'Orfeo (Cpte)

CURROS, Abelardo (sngr)
Moreno Torroba: Luisa Fernanda (Cpte)

CURRY, William Henry (cond)
see St. Luke's Orch

CURTIS, Alan (cond)
see Teatro la Fenice Orch

CURTIS, Alan (hpd/dir)
Handel: Floridante (exc)

CURTIS, Josephine (mez)
Sullivan: Mikado (Cpte)

CURTIS, Mark (ten)
Lehár: Lustige Witwe (exc)
Puccini: Madama Butterfly (Cpte), Manon Lescaut (exc)
Tippett: King Priam (Cpte)
Verdi: Forza del destino (Cpte)
(CAST) **CVI2070** Great Puccini Love Scenes from Covent Garden, La Scala and Verona
(NIMB) **NI5217** Tippett conducts Tippett

CURTIS VERNA, Maria (sop)
Verdi: Aida (Cpte)

CURZI, Cesare (ten)
J. Strauss II: Fledermaus (exc)

CUSICK, Russell (sngr)
Schuman: Mighty Casey (Cpte)

CUSSAC, Jean (bass)
Milhaud: Malheurs d'Orphée (Cpte)

CVEJIC, Biserka (contr)
Mussorgsky: Boris Godunov (Cpte)

CZAKOVÁ, Anna (mez)
Janáček: Makropulos Affair (Cpte)

CZECH PHILHARMONIC CHORUS
cond G. ALBRECHT
Dvořák: Dimitrij (Cpte)
cond F. JÍLEK
Janáček: Excursions of Mr Brouček (Cpte)
cond Z. KOŠLER
Smetana: Bartered Bride (Cpte)
cond C. MACKERRAS
Martinů: Greek Passion (Cpte)
(KOCH) **34036-2** A Pageant of Opera
cond V. NEUMANN
Janáček: Cunning Little Vixen (Cpte), From the House of the Dead (Cpte)
(KOCH) **34036-2** A Pageant of Opera
cond Z. PESKÓ
Mysliveček: Bellerofonte (Cpte)

CZECH PHILHARMONIC ORCHESTRA
cond G. ALBRECHT
Dvořák: Dimitrij (Cpte)
(KOCH) **34036-2** A Pageant of Opera
cond K. ANČERL
(ORFE) **C395951B** Dvořák—Violin Concerto; Symphony No. 9
(PRAG) **PR254 005** Edition Live Karel Ančerl
(SUPR) **11 0572-2** Popular Classics
(SUPR) **11 1935-2** Mozart—Orchestral Works
(SUPR) **11 0640-4** Famous Opera Overtures
cond S. BAUDO
Debussy: Pelléas et Mélisande (exc)
cond J. BĚLOHLÁVEK
(CHAN) **CHAN9080** Janáček—Orchestral Works
cond J. BIGG
(IMP) **DPCD1015** Karaoke Opera
(IMP) **PCD1043** Opera Favourites
cond Z. CHALABALA
(SUPR) **11 0640-4** Famous Opera Overtures
cond A. COPLAND
(ROMA) **RR1973** An American in Prague
cond F. HAIDER
(SUPR) **11 0345-2** Edith Gruberová - Operatic Recital
cond F. JÍLEK
Janáček: Excursions of Mr Brouček (Cpte)
(SUPR) **C37-7303** Janáček: Operatic Orchestral Suites
cond Z. KOŠLER
Smetana: Bartered Bride (Cpte)
(KOCH) **34036-2** A Pageant of Opera
cond B. LIŠKA
(SUPR) **11 0640-4** Famous Opera Overtures
cond V. NEUMANN
Dvořák: Rusalka (Cpte)
Janáček: Cunning Little Vixen (Cpte), From the House of the Dead (Cpte)
Martinů: Ariane (Cpte)
(KOCH) **34036-2** A Pageant of Opera
(ORFE) **C180891A** Popular Czech Music
(PHIL) **422 387-2PH** Dvořák—Orchestral Works
(SUPR) **11 0624-2** Bohemian & Czech orchestral music
(SUPR) **11 0724-2** Famous Operetta Overtures
(SUPR) **11 1287-2** Gala Concert from Prague
cond G. ROZHDESTVENSKY
Shostakovich: Nose Suite
cond V. TALICH
(MULT) **310151-2** Mozart/Smetana/Wagner—Vocal and Orchestral Works
(SUPR) **11 1905-2** Czech Orchestral Works
cond F. VAJNAR
(SUPR) **11 1118-2** Beethoven—Overtures

CZECH RADIO SYMPHONY ORCHESTRA
cond O. LENÁRD
(OPUS) **9156 1824** Dvorský sings Operatic Arias

CZECH SINGERS CHORUS
cond K. BÖHM
Mozart: Don Giovanni (Cpte)

CZECH SYMPHONY ORCHESTRA
cond J. BIGG
(IMP) **PCDS23** Music of the World—Italy & Spain—The Latin Quarter
(IMP) **TCD1070** Invitation to the Opera
cond A. KRIEGER
(IMP) **MCD42** Three Sopranos

CZERNY, Henrik (sngr)
Schreker: Gezeichneten (Cpte)

CZERNY, Werner (bass)
R. Strauss: Rosenkavalier (Cpte)

CZERWENKA, Oscar (bass)
Cornelius: Barbier von Bagdad (Cpte)
Einem: Prozess (Cpte)
Mozart: Nozze di Figaro (Cpte)
R. Strauss: Ariadne auf Naxos (Cpte), Salome (Cpte)

CZIDRA, László (rec)
(NAXO) **8 550700** Handel—Recorder Sonatas

CZIFFRA, György (pf)
(EMI) **CDM5 65253-2** Cziffra Edition, Volume 4
(EMI) **CDM5 65255-2** Cziffra Edition, Volume 6

DACHARY, Lina (sop)
Audran: Miss Helyett (Cpte)
Bazin: Voyage en Chine (Cpte)
Boïeldieu: Voitures Versées (Cpte)
Lecocq: Jour et la Nuit (Cpte)
Messager: Coups de Roulis (Cpte), Monsieur Beaucaire (Cpte), Passionêment (Cpte)
Offenbach: Chanson de Fortunio (Cpte), Madame l'Archiduc (Cpte)
Planquette: Rip van Winkle (Cpte)
Terrasse: Fiancée du Scaphandrier (Cpte), Travaux d'Hercule (Cpte)
(EMI) **CZS7 67515-2** Offenbach—Operetta highlights
(MUSD) **20239-2** Delibes—Opéras-Comiques

DADDI, Francesco (ten)
(NIMB) **NI7834** Caruso in Ensemble
(PEAR) **EVC1(2)** The Caruso Edition, Vol.1 (pt 2)
(RCA) **GD60495(2)** The Complete Caruso Collection (pt 2)

DAGUERRESSAR, Charles (bar)
Messager: Coups de Roulis (Cpte)
Planquette: Rip van Winkle (Cpte)
Terrasse: Travaux d'Hercule (Cpte)

DAHL, Tim (ten)
Britten: Paul Bunyan (Cpte)

DAHL, Tracy (sop)
Corigliano: Ghosts of Versailles (Cpte)
(CBC) **SMCD5125** Glitter and Be Gay—Coloratura Soprano Arias
(CBC) **SMCD5139** A Gilbert & Sullivan Gala

DAHLBERG, Stefan (ten)
Busoni: Arlecchino (Cpte), Turandot (Cpte)
Mozart: Zauberflöte (Cpte)

DÄHLER, Jörg Ewald (cond)
see ECO

DÄHLER, Jörg Ewald (hpd)
(CLAV) **CD50-0705** Purcell—Songs

DAHN, Felix (bar)
(SUPR) **11 2136-2(3)** Emmy Destinn—Complete Edition, Discs 5 to 8

DAKIN, Richard (treb)
Britten: Midsummer Night's Dream (Cpte)

DALBERG, Frederick (bass)
Britten: Billy Budd (Cpte)
Wagner: Götterdämmerung (Cpte), Meistersinger (Cpte)

DALE, Clamma (sop)
Gershwin: Porgy and Bess (exc)

DALE, Laurence (ten)
Auber: Gustav III (Cpte)
Boïeldieu: Calife de Bagdad (Cpte)
Debussy: Rodrigue et Chimène (Cpte)
Monteverdi: Orfeo (Cpte)
Purcell: Fairy Queen, Z629 (Cpte)
Rossini: Cenerentola (Cpte), Maometto II (Cpte)
Roussel: Padmâvatî (Cpte)
(CAST) **CVI2071** Highlights from Glyndebourne
(ERAT) **2292-45984-2** Monteverdi—Ballet Music
(ERAT) **4509-99713-2** Baroque Works
(TELD) **9031-77676-6(TELD)** My World of Opera - Kiri Te Kanawa

DALES, Ellen (sop)
Purcell: Dido (Cpte)

DALIS, Irene (mez)
Verdi: Ballo in maschera (Cpte)
Wagner: Parsifal (Cpte)

DALLAPOZZA, Adolf (ten)
Beethoven: Fidelio (Cpte)
Humperdinck: Königskinder (Cpte)
Mozart: Idomeneo (Cpte)
R. Strauss: Intermezzo (Cpte)
Wagner: Meistersinger (Cpte)
Zeller: Vogelhändler (Cpte)
(EMI) **CMS7 64309-2** Kálmán—Best-loved Melodies

DALLAS SYMPHONY ORCHESTRA
cond ANON
(WORD) **FCD7406** Best of Tchaikovsky

DAWES, Christopher (ten)
Lehár: Lustige Witwe (Cpte)

DAWSON, Anna (sop)
Offenbach: Christopher Columbus (Cpte)

DAWSON, Anne (sop)
Boughton: Immortal Hour (Cpte)
Gay: Beggar's Opera (Cpte)
Mozart: Nozze di Figaro (Cpte)
(EMI) **CDC7 54785-2** Harry Enfield's Guide to Opera

DAWSON, John (treb)
Mozart: Zauberflöte (Cpte)

DAWSON, Julian (hpd)
Mozart: Zauberflöte (exc)

DAWSON, Lynne (sop)
Blow: Venus and Adonis (Cpte)
Gluck: Iphigénie en Aulide (Cpte), Orfeo ed Euridice (Cpte), Rencontre imprévue (Cpte)
Monteverdi: Orfeo (Cpte)
Mozart: Don Giovanni (Cpte)
Purcell: Dioclesian, Z627 (exc), Fairy Queen, Z629 (Cpte)
(CHAN) **CHAN9392** Vaughan Williams—Riders to the Sea etc.
(ERAT) **4509-96371-2** Gardiner—The Purcell Collection
(ERAT) **4509-99607-2** Gluck—Operas; Schubert—Symphonies Nos 8 & 9

DAWSON, Peter (bass-bar)
Sullivan: Pirates of Penzance (Cpte)
(PEAR) **GEMMCD9122** 20 Great Basses sing Great Arias
(PEAR) **GEMMCD9384** Songs of the Sea—Peter Dawson
(PEAR) **GEMMCD9468** Vaughan Williams
(SYMP) **SYMCD1123** Sullivan—Sesquicentenial Commemorative Issue

DAYMOND, Karl Morgan (bar)
Purcell: Dido (Cpte)
Vaughan Williams: Hugh the Drover (Cpte)
(CHAN) **CHAN9392** Vaughan Williams—Riders to the Sea etc.
(OPRA) **ORCH104** A Hundred Years of Italian Opera: 1820-1830

DAZELEY, William (bar)
M. Berkeley: Baa Baa Black Sheep (Cpte)

DEAM, Donna (sop)
Purcell: Dido (Cpte)

DEAN, Michael (bass-bar)
Handel: Agrippina (Cpte), Ottone (Cpte), Radamisto (Cpte)
Purcell: Dido (Cpte)

DEAN, Robert (bass)
Rossini: Barbiere di Siviglia (Cpte)

DEAN, Stafford (bass)
Britten: Burning Fiery Furnace (Cpte), Peter Grimes (Cpte)
Delius: Village Romeo and Juliet (Cpte)
Gay: Beggar's Opera (Cpte)
Mozart: Don Giovanni (Cpte)
Stravinsky: Rake's Progress (Cpte)
Sullivan: Yeomen of the Guard (Cpte)
Tippett: Midsummer Marriage (Cpte)
Verdi: Lombardi (Cpte), Otello (Cpte)

DEANE, Christopher (bar)
Gershwin: Porgy and Bess (Cpte)

DEARNLEY, Christopher (organ)
(GUIL) **GMCD7102** Coronation Music from St Paul's
(IMP) **ORCD11009** The Magnificent Organ

DEARTH, Harry (bass)
(SYMP) **SYMCD1123** Sullivan—Sesquicentenial Commemorative Issue

DEBART, Dominique (cond)
see Basse-Normandie Ens

DEBICH, H. (cond)
see Polish RSO

DEBIČKA, Hedwig von (sop)
(PEAR) **GEMMCD9394** Helge Roswaenge—Operatic Recital
(PREI) **89201** Helge Roswaenge (1897-1972) - I
(PREI) **89209** Helge Roswaenge (1897-1972) - II

DEBUSSY, Claude (pf)
(EMI) **CHS7 61038-2** Debussy—Pelléas et Mélisande, etc
(SYMP) **SYMCD1093** The Harold Wayne Collection, Vol.7

DECKER, Franz-Paul (cond)
see Quebec Cons Orch

DECKER, Richard (ten)
Mozart: Così fan tutte (Cpte)

DEDIEU-VIDAL, Marcelle (pf)
(REM) **REM311151** Schubert—Lieder

DEFOSSE, Henri (cond)
see orch

DEGAETANI, Jan (mez)
Birtwistle: Punch and Judy (Cpte)

DEGELIN, Bernadette (sop)
Puccini: Suor Angelica (Cpte)

DELACÔTE, Jacques (cond)
see Munich RO
ROHO

DELAGE, Roger (cond)
see Strasbourg Collegium Musicum Orch

DELAHAYE, Hélène (sop)
Offenbach: Contes d'Hoffmann (Cpte)

DELANGE, Pierrette (sop)
Offenbach: Périchole (Cpte)

DELAVAN, Mark (bar)
Meyerbeer: Africaine (Cpte)

DELDI, Pierre (bar)
(MSCM) **MM30377** 18 Tenors d'Expression Française

DELESCLUSE, Jean (sngr)
Debussy: Rodrigue et Chimène (Cpte)

DELÉTRÉ, Bernard (bass)
Campra: Idoménée (exc)
Cavalli: Giasone (Cpte)
Gluck: Iphigénie en Aulide (Cpte)
Lully: Armide, Atys (exc)
M-A. Charpentier: David et Jonathas (Cpte), Médée (Cpte)
Marais: Alcyone (Cpte)
Purcell: Fairy Queen, Z629 (Cpte)
Rameau: Indes galantes (Cpte), Platée (Cpte)
Rossi: Orfeo (Cpte)
(ERAT) **4509-99607-2** Gluck—Operas; Schubert—Symphonies Nos 8 & 9
(HARM) **HMP390 805** Great Baroque Masters—Lully
(HARM) **HMP390 807** Great Baroque Masters—Purcell

DELFS, Andreas (cond)
see Swiss YSO

DELILLE, Jany (sop)
Gluck: Orphée (Cpte)

DELL, Patti (sop)
R. Strauss: Aegyptische Helena (Cpte)

DELLER, Alfred (cond)
see King's Musick

DELLER, Alfred (alto)
Britten: Midsummer Night's Dream (Cpte)
Purcell: Indian Queen, Z630 (Cpte), King Arthur, Z628 (Cpte)
(DECC) **443 393-2DWO** The World of Henry Purcell
(EMI) **CDH5 65501-2** Alfred Deller - HMV Recordings, 1949-54
(HARM) **HMC90 249** Purcell: Music for a while
(HARM) **HMP390 807** Great Baroque Masters—Purcell
(HARM) **HMX290 1528/33(2)** A Purcell Companion (pt 2)
(INA) **262004** Alfred Deller—Renaissance and Baroque songs
(VANG) **08.2003.72** Purcell—Celebrated Songs,Sacred Airs and Concert Pieces
(VANG) **08.5069.71** Bach—Cantatas; Handel—Airs

DELLER, Alfred (alto/dir)
Monteverdi: L'Arianna (exc)
Purcell: Fairy Queen, Z629 (Cpte)
(HARM) **HMA190 214** Purcell—Theatre Music and Sacred Songs

DELLER, Mark (alto)
Purcell: Indian Queen, Z630 (Cpte), King Arthur, Z628 (Cpte)
(HARM) **HMX290 1528/33(2)** A Purcell Companion (pt 2)

DELLER CHOIR
cond A. DELLER
Purcell: Indian Queen, Z630 (Cpte), King Arthur, Z628 (Cpte)
(HARM) **HMX290 1528/33(2)** A Purcell Companion (pt 2)

DELLER CONSORT
Monteverdi: L'Arianna (exc)
Purcell: Fairy Queen, Z629 (Cpte)
(HARM) **HMA190 214** Purcell—Theatre Music and Sacred Songs
cond A. DELLER
Purcell: King Arthur, Z628 (exc)
(HARM) **HMP390 807** Great Baroque Masters—Purcell

DELLOW, Carl Magnus (spkr)
Börtz: Bacchae (Cpte)

DELMAS, Jean-François (bass-bar)
(IRCC) **IRCC-CD800** Souvenirs from Meyerbeer Operas
(SYMP) **SYMCD1172** The Harold Wayne Collection, Vol.21

DELNA, Marie (mez)
(PEAR) **GEMMCDS9923(1)** Covent Garden on Record, Vol.1 (pt 1)

DELON, Jack (ten)
R. Ward: Crucible (Cpte)

DELUNSCH, Mireille (sop)
(ARIO) **ARN68252** Chabrier—Trois opérettes

DEMAIN, John (cond)
see Houston Grand Op Orch
Rio de Janeiro Municipal Th Orch

DEMENTIEV, Yuri (bass)
Tchaikovsky: Queen of Spades (Cpte)

DEMERDJIEV, Eugene (sngr)
Weill: Dreigroschenoper (Cpte)

DEMERS, Robert Lucien (bar)
Delius: Village Romeo and Juliet (Cpte)

DEMEYERE, Ewald (hpd)
Rossini: Tancredi (Cpte)

DEMIGNY, Bernard (bass)
Bizet: Carmen (Cpte)
Boïeldieu: Voitures Versées (Cpte)
Martinů: Comedy on the Bridge (Cpte), Julietta (Cpte)
Milhaud: Malheurs d'Orphée (Cpte)
Tomasi: Don Juan de Mañara (Cpte)
(EMI) **CZS7 67515-2** Offenbach—Operetta highlights

DEMPSEY, Gregory (ten)
Wagner: Rheingold (Cpte), Siegfried (Cpte)
(DECC) **436 990-2DWO** The World of Benjamin Britten

DEMUTH, Leopold (bar)
(PREI) **89020** Leo Slezak (1873-1946)

DENE, Jószef (bass)
Wagner: Meistersinger (Cpte)

DENG (ten)
(SCHW) **312642** Unicef Gala 1991
(SINE) **39820222** Deng - Tenor

DENIZE, Nadine (mez)
Debussy: Pelléas et Mélisande (Cpte)
Gounod: Faust (Cpte)

DENLEY, Catherine (mez)
Handel: Ottone (Cpte)
Monteverdi: Orfeo (Cpte)
Mozart: Zauberflöte (Cpte)

DENNING, Angela (sop)
Rossini: Cenerentola (Cpte)

DENNIS, Paul (bass)
Verdi: Traviata (Cpte)

DENNISON, John (bass)
Berlioz: Troyens (Cpte)

DENNISON, Kenneth (cond)
see Fairey Band

DENS, Michel (bar)
Bizet: Carmen (Cpte), Pêcheurs de Perles (Cpte)
Ganne: Hans (Cpte)
Gounod: Mireille (Cpte)
Lully: Alceste (Cpte)
(EMI) **CZS5 68295-2** Messager/Lecocq—Operetta Highlights
(EMI) **CZS7 67872-2** Lehár—Operettas (highlights in French)

DĚPOLTOVÁ, Eva (sop)
Fibich: Šárka (Cpte)
Foerster: Eva (Cpte)
Martinů: Miracles of Mary (Cpte)
Smetana: Kiss (Cpte), Libuše (Cpte)

DEPRAZ, Xavier (bass)
Bizet: Carmen (Cpte), Pêcheurs de Perles (Cpte)
Gounod: Roméo et Juliette (Cpte)
Milhaud: Christophe Colomb (Cpte), Pauvre matelot (Cpte)
Poulenc: Dialogues des Carmélites (Cpte)
(CHNT) **LDC278 1068** Chabrier—Une Education Manquée/Mélodies

DEPREIST, James (cond)
see Malmö SO
Stockholm PO

DERENNE, Paul (ten)
(DECC) **433 400-2DM2** Ravel & Debussy—Stage Works

DERICK, Peter van (bar)
R. Strauss: Friedenstag (Cpte)

DERMOTA, Anton (ten)
Beethoven: Fidelio (Cpte)
J. Strauss II: Fledermaus (Cpte)
Mozart: Così fan tutte (Cpte), Don Giovanni (Cpte), Zauberflöte (Cpte)
R. Strauss: Arabella (Cpte), Rosenkavalier (Cpte)
Verdi: Otello (Cpte)
Wagner: Meistersinger (Cpte), Tristan und Isolde (Cpte)
(CAMB) **CD-1032** From the Operas of Erich Wolfgang Korngold
(EMI) **CHS7 69741-2(4)** Record of Singing, Vol.4—German School
(ORFE) **C394201B** Great Mozart Singers Series, Vol. 2
(PREI) **90022** Anton Dermota
(PREI) **90237** R Strauss—Daphne
(PREI) **90249** Mozart in tempore belli
(SCHW) **314532** Vienna State Opera Live, Vol.3
(SCHW) **314552** Vienna State Opera Live, Vol.5
(SCHW) **314572** Vienna State Opera Live, Vol.7
(SCHW) **314582** Vienna State Opera Live, Vol.8
(SCHW) **314602** Vienna State Opera Live, Vol.10
(SCHW) **314652** Vienna State Opera Live, Vol.15
(SCHW) **314712** Vienna State Opera Live, Vol.21

DERNESCH, Helga (sop/mez)
Beethoven: Fidelio (exc)
Schoeck: Penthesilea (Cpte)

Wagner: Götterdämmerung (Cpte), Rheingold (Cpte), Siegfried (Cpte), Tannhäuser (Cpte), Tristan und Isolde (Cpte), Walküre (Cpte)
Weill: Dreigroschenoper (Cpte)
(CFP) **CD-CFP4656** Herbert von Karajan conducts Opera
(DECC) **414 100-2DM15** Wagner: Der Ring des Nibelungen
(DECC) **421 313-2DA** Wagner: Der Ring des Nibelungen - Great Scenes
(DECC) **433 065-2DWO** Your Hundred Best Opera Tunes Volume II
(DECC) **433 067-2DWO** Your Hundred Best Opera Tunes IV
(DECC) **433 443-2DA** Great Opera Choruses
(DECC) **436 300-2DX** Opera Gala Sampler
(DECC) **440 069-2DWO** The World of Wagner
(DG) **429 168-2GR** Wagner: Excerpts from Der Ring
(DG) **435 211-2GX15** Wagner—Der Ring des Nibelungen
(DG) **439 423-2GCL** Wagner—Der Ring des Nibelungen (highlights)
(DG) **445 354-2GX14** Wagner—Der Ring des Nibelungen
(EMI) **CMS5 65212-2** Wagner—Les introuvables du Ring
(PHIL) **446 057-2PB14** Wagner—The Ring Cycle - Bayreuth Festival 1967

DEROO, Lieven (bass)
Landi: Mort d'Orfeo (Cpte)

DERVAUX, Pierre (cond)
see Lamoureux Orch
Loire PO
orch
ORTF PO
Paris Op Orch
Paris Opéra-Comique Orch
Paris Orch

DÉRY, Andràs (cond)
see Budapest SO

DERZHINSKAYA, Xenia (sop)
(DANT) **LYS013/5** Tchaikovsky—The Queen of Spades

DESANA, Tina (sop)
(IRCC) **IRCC-CD808** Souvenirs of 19th Century Italian Opera

DESBOROUGH SCHOOL CHOIR
cond L. MAAZEL
(CBS) **CD79312** Puccini: Il Trittico

DESCOMBES, Paul (spkr)
Massenet: Amadis (Cpte)

DESDERI, Claudio (cond)
see Camerata Musicale Orch

DESDERI, Claudio (bar)
Mozart: Così fan tutte (Cpte), Don Giovanni (Cpte), Nozze di Figaro (Cpte)
Rossini: Barbiere di Siviglia (Cpte), Cenerentola (Cpte), Signor Bruschino (Cpte)
(CFP) **CD-CFP4612** Favourite Mozart
(EMI) **CDH5 65072-2** Glyndebourne Recorded - 1934-1994
(EMIL) **CDZ7 67015-2** Mozart—Opera Arias
(TELD) **9031-77676-6(TELD)** My World of Opera - Kiri Te Kanawa

DESFORD COLLIERY CATERPILLAR BAND
cond J. WATSON
(POLY) **QPRL049D** Boosey & Hawkes National Brass Band Gala Concert 1991

DESMOUTIERS, Gisèle (sop)
Poulenc: Dialogues des Carmélites (Cpte)

DESNOUES, Brigitte (sop)
Massenet: Grisélidis (Cpte)
Messager: Fortunio (Cpte)
Verdi: Luisa Miller (Cpte)
(ARIO) **ARN68252** Chabrier—Trois opérettes

DESORMIÈRE, Roger (cond)
see orch
SO

DESROCHERS, Isabelle (sop)
Lully: Atys (exc)
Purcell: Fairy Queen, Z629 (Cpte)

DESROCHES, Gérard (ten)
Offenbach: Belle Hélène (Cpte)

DESSAY, Nathalie (sop)
Offenbach: Contes d'Hoffmann (Cpte)

DESSÌ, Daniella (sop)
Leoncavallo: Pagliacci (Cpte)
Mozart: Così fan tutte (Cpte)
Verdi: Don Carlo (Cpte), Falstaff (Cpte), Rigoletto (Cpte)

DESTAIN, R. (sngr)
Offenbach: Chanson de Fortunio (Cpte)

DESTAL, Fred (bar)
Wagner: Fliegende Holländer (Cpte)
(SCHW) **314572** Vienna State Opera Live, Vol.7
(SCHW) **314632** Vienna State Opera Live, Vol.13
(SCHW) **314742** Vienna State Opera Live, Vol.24

DESTINN, Emmy (sop)
(PEAR) **EVC3(1)** The Caruso Edition, Vol.3 (pt 1)
(PEAR) **GEMMCDS9074(1)** Giovanni Zenatello, Vol.2 (pt 1)
(PEAR) **GEMMCDS9924(1)** Covent Garden on Record, Vol.2 (pt 1)
(PEAR) **GEMMCDS9924(2)** Covent Garden on Record, Vol.2 (pt 2)
(PEAR) **GEMMCD9130** Great Sopranos, Vol.2
(PEAR) **GEMMCD9172** Emmy Destinn (1878-1930)
(RCA) **GD60495(5)** The Complete Caruso Collection (pt 5)
(RCA) **09026 61580-2(2)** RCA/Met 100 Singers, 100 Years (pt 2)
(ROMO) **81002-2** Emmy Destinn (1878-1930)
(SUPR) **11 1337-2** Emmy Destinn (1878-1930)
(SUPR) **11 2136-2(1)** Emmy Destinn—Complete Edition, Discs 1 & 2
(SUPR) **11 2136-2(2)** Emmy Destinn—Complete Edition, Discs 3 & 4
(SUPR) **11 2136-2(3)** Emmy Destinn—Complete Edition, Discs 5 to 8
(SUPR) **11 2136-2(4)** Emmy Destinn—Complete Edition, Discs 9 & 10
(SUPR) **11 2136-2(5)** Emmy Destinn—Complete Edition, Discs 11 & 12

DETROIT SYMPHONY ORCHESTRA
cond A. DORATI
Gershwin: Porgy and Bess Suite
R. Strauss: Aegyptische Helena (Cpte)
cond N. JÄRVI
(CHAN) **CHAN9227** Encore!
cond P. PARAY
(MERC) **434 303-2MM** Chabrier/Roussel—Orchestral Works
(MERC) **434 309-2MM** Suppé/Auber—Overtures
(MERC) **434 321-2MM** Bizet/Thomas—Orchestral Works
(MERC) **434 332-2MM** French Marches & Overtures

DEUTEKOM, Cristina (sop)
Donizetti: Lucia di Lammermoor (Cpte)
Mozart: Zauberflöte (exc)
Rossini: Armida (Cpte)
Verdi: Attila (Cpte), Lombardi (Cpte)

DEUTSCH, Helmut (pf)
(KOCH) **321 214** Wiener Sängerknaben - Kein Schöner Land

DEVER, Barbara (mez)
Verdi: Aida (Cpte)

DEVEREUX, Roy (ten)
Wagner: Tristan und Isolde (Cpte)

DEVIA, Mariella (sop)
Bellini: Puritani (Cpte), Sonnambula (exc)
Cherubini: Lodoïska (Cpte)
Donizetti: Elisabetta (Cpte), Elisir d'amore (Cpte)
Rossini: Adelaide di Borgogna (Cpte), Signor Bruschino (Cpte)
(BONG) **GB2513-2** Mariella Devia—Opera Arias
(NUOV) **6892** William Matteuzzi sings Opera Arias

DEVINU, Giusy (sngr)
Wolf-Ferrari: Campiello (Cpte)

DEVLIN, Michael (bass-bar)
Handel: Giulio Cesare (Cpte)
Meyerbeer: Africaine (Cpte)
Mozart: Zauberflöte (Cpte)
R. Strauss: Salome (Cpte)
Rameau: Dardanus (Cpte)
(PHIL) **432 416-2PH3** Haydn—L'incontro improvviso/Arias

DEVOL, Luana (sop)
Schreker: Irrelohe (Cpte)

DEVOS, Claude (ten)
Messager: P'tites Michu (exc)
(EMI) **CZS7 67515-2** Offenbach—Operetta highlights
(EMI) **CZS7 67872-2** Lehár—Operettas (highlights in French)

DEVOS, Louis (ten)
Martin: Mystère de la Nativité
Schoenberg: Moses und Aron (Cpte)

DEVRIÈS, David (ten)
(NIMB) **NI7856** Legendary Tenors

DEYCK, Lucienne van (mez)
Puccini: Tabarro (Cpte)

DIAKOV, Anton (bass)
Mussorgsky: Boris Godunov (Cpte)
Saint-Saëns: Samson et Dalila (Cpte)

DIAZ, Justino (bass)
Catalani: Wally (Cpte)
Falla: Retablo de maese Pedro (Cpte)
Meyerbeer: Africaine (Cpte)
Offenbach: Contes d'Hoffmann (Cpte)
Rossini: Siège de Corinthe (Cpte)
Verdi: Otello (Cpte)
(ASV) **CDQS6065** The Mozart Miracle
(DG) **072 428-1GH2(DG)** The Metropolitan Opera Gala

DICKENSON, Jean (sop)
(VAI) **VAIA1017** Leonard Warren—Early Recordings

DICKERSON, Bernard (ten)
Mozart: Nozze di Figaro (Cpte)
Offenbach: Contes d'Hoffmann (Cpte)
Puccini: Manon Lescaut (Cpte)
Vaughan Williams: Pilgrim's Progress (Cpte)
Verdi: Falstaff (Cpte)

DICKIE, John (ten)
J. Strauss II: Fledermaus (Cpte)
Mozart: Così fan tutte (Cpte)
(NAXO) **8 550383** Mozart—Tenor Arias

DICKIE, Murray (ten)
Busoni: Arlecchino (Cpte)
Lehár: Giuditta (exc)
Monteverdi: Ritorno d'Ulisse in Patria (Cpte)
Mozart: Nozze di Figaro (Cpte)
R. Strauss: Ariadne auf Naxos (Cpte), Frau ohne Schatten (Cpte), Rosenkavalier (Cpte)

DICKIE, William (bar)
Verdi: Rigoletto (Cpte)
(EMI) **CDC7 49502-2** Maria Callas—The Voice of the Century

DICKINSON, Meriel (mez)
G. Charpentier: Louise (Cpte)
Weill: Street Scene (Cpte)

DICKS, Wilhelm Walter (bar)
Berg: Lulu (Cpte)
Weber: Freischütz (Cpte)

DICKSON, Muriel (sop)
Sullivan: Sorcerer (Cpte)

DICKSON, Stephen (bar)
Puccini: Bohème (Cpte)
R. Strauss: Ariadne auf Naxos (Cpte)

DIDIER GAMBARDELLA, Laura (mez)
Mascagni: Amico Fritz (Cpte)

DIDUR, Adam (bass)
(CLUB) **CL99-089** Adamo Didur (1874-1946)
(EMI) **CHS7 64860-2(2)** La Scala Edition - Vol.1, 1878-1914 (pt 2)
(MMOI) **CDMOIR422** Great Voices in Tchaikovsky
(PEAR) **GEMMCDS9073(1)** Giovanni Zenatello, Vol.1 (pt 1)
(PEAR) **GEMMCDS9925(1)** Covent Garden on Record—Vol.3 (pt 1)
(PEAR) **GEMMCDS9997/9(2)** Singers of Imperial Russia, Vol.1 (pt 2)
(SYMP) **SYMCD1168** The Harold Wayne Collection, Vol.19
(TEST) **SBT1008** Viva Rossini

DIDUSCH, Margot (sop)
Beethoven: Fidelio (Cpte)

DIDUSCH, Reinhard (sngr)
Mozart: Mitridate (Cpte)

DIEBERITZ, Gerd W. (narr)
Millöcker: Gasparone (Cpte)

DIEDRICH, Cyril (cond)
see Montpellier PO

DIEDRICH, Michael (treb)
Mozart: Zauberflöte (Cpte)

DIEHL, André von (bass)
Wagner: Meistersinger (exc)

DIEKEN, Joseph (spkr)
Nono: Intolleranza 1960 (Cpte)

DIELEMAN, Marianne (sop)
R. Strauss: Rosenkavalier (Cpte)

DIETRICH, Marie (sop)
(SUPR) **11 2136-2(3)** Emmy Destinn—Complete Edition, Discs 5 to 8

DIETSCHY, Véronique (sop)
Rameau: Dardanus (Cpte)

DIEZ, Ramon (sngr)
Chapí: Revoltosa (Cpte)

DIGIORGIO, Arturo (bar)
(IRCC) **IRCC-CD808** Souvenirs of 19th Century Italian Opera

DIJKSTRA, Hebe (mez)
Wagner: Walküre (Cpte)

DILBÈR (sop)
(ONDI) **ODE768-2** Dilbèr sings Coloratura Arias

DILOVA, Penka (mez)
Mussorgsky: Boris Godunov (Cpte)
Tchaikovsky: Queen of Spades (Cpte)

DIMCHEWSKA, Martya (sop)
Mussorgsky: Khovanshchina (Cpte)

DIMITROVA, Ghena (sop)
Puccini: Turandot (exc)
Verdi: Aida (Cpte), Lombardi (Cpte), Nabucco (Cpte), Oberto (Cpte)
(CAST) **CASH5051** Puccini Favourites from Covent Garden and the Arena di Verona
(CAST) **CASH5052** Verdi Operatic Favourites
(CAST) **CVI2067** Opera Highlights from La Scala
(CAST) **CVI2068** Opera Highlights from Verona 1
(FORL) **UCD16742** Bulgarian Voices, Vol. 2

D'INTINO, Luciana (mez)
Rossini: Gazza ladra (exc)
Verdi: Don Carlo (Cpte)

DIOZZI, Gianna (mez)
Puccini: Madama Butterfly (Cpte)

DIRKS, Math (bar)
Mascagni: Piccolo Marat (Cpte)
Schreker: Gezeichneten (Cpte)

DISMAN RADIO CHILDREN'S CHOIR
cond J. KARAS
Krása: Brundibár (Cpte)

DISMAN RADIO CHILDREN'S ORCHESTRA
cond J. KARAS
Krása: Brundibár (Cpte)

DISNEY, Agnes (mez)
Delibes: Lakmé (Cpte)

DITTRICH, Michael (cond)
see Bratislava RSO

DIVERTIMENTO ENSEMBLE
cond S. GORLI
Maderna: Satyricon (Cpte)

DIVES, Tamsin (mez)
MacMillan: Visitatio Sepulchri (Cpte)
Maxwell Davies: Martyrdom of St Magnus (Cpte)

DIWIAK, Dantes (ten)
Steffani: Henrico Leone (Cpte)

DIXEY, Amilia (mez)
Offenbach: Christopher Columbus (Cpte)

DIXON, Beryl (mez)
Sullivan: Mikado (Cpte)

DOANE, David (ten)
Vivier: Kopernikus (Cpte)

DOBIE, Elizabeth (sop)
Delius: Village Romeo and Juliet (Cpte)

DOBRIANOVA, Nadezhda (sop)
Mussorgsky: Boris Godunov (Cpte)

DOBRIANSKY, Andrij (bass)
(DG) **072 428-1GH2(DG)** The Metropolitan Opera Gala

DOBRINDT, Otto (cond)
see Berlin SO
Berlin St Op Orch
orch

DOBROVEN, Issay (cond)
see FRNO
Philh

DOBSON, John (ten)
Britten: Peter Grimes (Cpte)
Donizetti: Don Pasquale (Cpte)
Giordano: Andrea Chénier (Cpte)
J. Strauss II: Fledermaus (Cpte)
Janáček: Cunning Little Vixen (Cpte)
Menotti: Amahl and the Night Visitors (Cpte)
Puccini: Fanciulla del West (Cpte)
R. Strauss: Rosenkavalier (Cpte)
Saint-Saëns: Samson et Dalila (Cpte)
Stravinsky: Rake's Progress (Cpte)
Verdi: Falstaff (Cpte), Traviata (Cpte)
(CAST) **CASH5052** Verdi Operatic Favourites

DODS, Marcus (cond)
see London Concert Orch

DOGHAN, Phillip (ten)
Fénelon: Chevalier Imaginaire (Cpte)
(OPRA) **ORCH103** Italian Opera—1810-20
(OPRA) **ORH102** A Hundred Years of Italian Opera
(OPRA) **ORR201** 19th Century Heroines-Yvonne Kenny

DOHMEN, Albert (bar)
Mozart: Così fan tutte (Cpte), Don Giovanni (Cpte)
R. Strauss: Frau ohne Schatten (Cpte)

DOHNÁNYI, Christoph von (cond)
see Berlin Deutsche Op Orch
Cleveland Orch
VPO

DOHNÁNYI, Oliver (cond)
see Bratislava RSO
Prague Nat Th Orch

DOIG, Christopher (ten)
Einem: Dantons Tod (Cpte)
R. Strauss: Elektra (Cpte)
(ODE) **CDMANU1317** Wagner—Opera Excerpts

DOIKOV, Roumen (ten)
Mussorgsky: Khovanshchina (Cpte)

DOLBASHIAN, Gregory (narr)
Glass: Einstein on the Beach (Cpte)

DOLEŽAL, Vladimír (ten)
Martinů: Ariane (Cpte)
(SUPR) **11 1878-2** The Unknown Janáček

DOLTON, Geoffrey (bar)
Donizetti: Emilia di Liverpool (Cpte), Eremitaggio di Liverpool (Cpte)
(OPRA) **ORCH103** Italian Opera—1810-20
(OPRA) **ORCH104** A Hundred Years of Italian Opera: 1820-1830

DOLUKHANOVA, Zara (mez)
(EMI) **CHS7 69741-2(6)** Record of Singing, Vol.4—Russian & Slavonic Schools
(PREI) **89066** Zara Dolukhanova
(RUSS) **RDCD11341** Prokofiev/Stravinsky—Songs and Arias
(RUSS) **RDCD15023** Zara Dolukhanova sings

DOMANÍNSKÁ, Libuše (sop)
Janáček: Cunning Little Vixen (Cpte), Jenufa (Cpte)
Smetana: Devil's Wall (Cpte)

DOME, Alfred (bass)
Wagner: Meistersinger (Cpte)

DOMENICO, Dino di (ten)
Mercadante: Bravo (Cpte)

DOMGRAF-FASSBAENDER, Willi (bar)
Mozart: Così fan tutte (Cpte), Nozze di Figaro (Cpte)
(EMI) **CDH5 65072-2** Glyndebourne Recorded - 1934-1994
(MMOI) **CDMOIR406** Mozart—Historical Recordings
(NIMB) **NI7848** Great Singers at the Berlin State Opera
(ORFE) **C394101B** Great Mozart Singers Series, Vol. 1
(PREI) **89047** Xenia Belmas (1890-1981)
(PREI) **89092** Erna Berger (1900-1990) - II

DOMINANTE CHOIR
cond U. SÖDERBLOM
Bergman: Singing Tree (Cpte)

DOMINGO, Alvaro (treb)
(CBS) **CD79312** Puccini: Il Trittico

DOMINGO, Plácido (cond)
see LSO
Munich RO
ROHO
Seville SO

DOMINGO, Plácido (ten)
Bellini: Norma (Cpte)
Bizet: Carmen (exc)
Boito: Mefistofele (Cpte)
Bretón: Verbena de La Paloma (Cpte)
Cilea: Adriana Lecouvreur (Cpte)
Donizetti: Lucia di Lammermoor (Cpte)
G. Charpentier: Louise (Cpte)
Giordano: Andrea Chénier (Cpte)
Gounod: Faust (Cpte)
J. Strauss II: Fledermaus (Cpte)
Leoncavallo: Pagliacci (exc)
Mascagni: Cavalleria Rusticana (Cpte)
Massenet: Cid (Cpte)
Meyerbeer: Africaine (Cpte)
Offenbach: Contes d'Hoffmann (exc)
Penella: Gato Montés (Cpte)
Ponchielli: Gioconda (Cpte)
Puccini: Bohème (Cpte), Fanciulla del West (Cpte), Madama Butterfly (Cpte), Manon Lescaut (Cpte), Rondine (Cpte), Tabarro (Cpte), Tosca (exc), Turandot (Cpte), Villi (Cpte)
R. Strauss: Frau ohne Schatten (Cpte), Rosenkavalier (Cpte)
Rossini: Barbiere di Siviglia (Cpte)
Saint-Saëns: Samson et Dalila (Cpte)
Verdi: Aida (exc), Ballo in maschera (Cpte), Don Carlo (exc), Don Carlos (exc), Ernani (Cpte), Forza del destino (Cpte), Giovanna d'Arco (Cpte), Lombardi (Cpte), Luisa Miller (Cpte), Macbeth (Cpte), Nabucco (exc), Otello (Cpte), Rigoletto (Cpte), Simon Boccanegra (Cpte), Traviata (exc), Trovatore (exc), Vespri Siciliani (Cpte)
Vives: Doña Francisquita (Cpte)
Wagner: Lohengrin (Cpte), Meistersinger (exc), Parsifal (Cpte), Tannhäuser (exc)
Weber: Oberon (Cpte)
(ABMU) **95542** Symphony for the Spire
(ACAN) **49 390** Placido Domingo sings Zarzuela Arias
(ACAN) **49 402** Giuseppe Taddei—Recital
(BELA) **450 036-2** Domingo—Love Songs and Tangos
(BELA) **450 121-2** Plácido Domingo
(CAST) **CASH5051** Puccini Favourites from Covent Garden and the Arena di Verona
(CAST) **CVI2021** A year in the life of Placido Domingo
(CAST) **CVI2065** Highlights from the Royal Opera House, Covent Garden
(CAST) **CVI2067** Opera Highlights from La Scala
(CAST) **CVI2070** Great Puccini Love Scenes from Covent Garden, La Scala and Verona
(CBS) **CD79312** Puccini: Il Trittico
(CFP) **CD-CFP4575** Verdi Arias
(CFP) **CD-CFP4602** Favourite Opera
(CFP) **CD-CFP4608** Favourite Classics 1
(DECC) **430 433-2DH** Carreras, Domingo and Pavarotti in Concert
(DECC) **433 067-2DWO** Your Hundred Best Opera Tunes IV
(DECC) **433 822-2DH** Essential Opera
(DECC) **436 300-2DX** Opera Gala Sampler
(DECC) **436 463-2DM** Ten Top Tenors
(DECC) **440 410-2DM** Plácido Domingo
(DECC) **440 947-2DH** Essential Opera II
(DECC) **443 379-2DM** Ten Top Tenors 2
(DECC) **071 123-1DH (DECC)** Carreras, Domingo and Pavarotti in Concert
(DECC) **071 142-1DH (DECC)** Essential Opera
(DECC) **430 433-5DH** Carreras, Domingo and Pavarotti in Concert
(DG) **413 451-2GH** Be My Love
(DG) **415 366-2GH** Placido Domingo Recital
(DG) **427 708-2GX3** The Best of Domingo
(DG) **431 103-2GB** Great Voices—Montserrat Caballé
(DG) **431 104-2GB** Great Voices - Plácido Domingo
(DG) **439 151-2GMA** Mad about Puccini
(DG) **445 525-2GMA** Domingo Favourites
(DG) **445 552-2GMA** Battle and Domingo
(DG) **419 091-4GW** Placido Domingo sings Favourite Arias, Songs and Tangos
(DG) **072 110-1GH** Hommage a Sevilla—Placido Domingo in scenes from various operas
(DG) **072 187-1GH (DG)** Hommage a Sevilla
(DG) **072 428-1GH2(DG)** The Metropolitan Opera Gala
(EDL) **EDL2562-2** Carreras, Domingo, Pavarotti Greatest Hits
(EMI) **CDC5 55017-2** Domingo Opera Classics
(EMI) **CDC5 55018-2** Domingo sings and conducts Tchaikovsky
(EMI) **CDC7 47398-2** Placido Domingo: Vienna, City of My Dreams
(EMI) **CDC7 49148-2** Romanzas de Zarzuelas
(EMI) **CDC7 49811-2** Covent Garden Gala Concert
(EMI) **CDC7 54016-2** Tenorissimo!
(EMI) **CDC7 54053-2** Roman Heroes
(EMI) **CDC7 54266-2** Domingo and Perlman—Together
(EMI) **CDC7 54329-2** Domingo sings Mozart Arias
(EMI) **CDM7 63103-2** Placido Domingo sings Opera Arias
(EMI) **CDM7 64359-2** Gala de España
(EMI) **CMS7 64309-2** Kálmán—Best-loved Melodies
(EMIL) **CDZ102** Best Loved Classics 3
(EMIL) **CDZ104** Best Loved Classics 5
(ERAT) **2292-45797-2** The Ultimate Opera Collection
(ERAT) **4509-91715-2** The Ultimate Opera Collection 2
(EURO) **VD69256** Mozart—Opera Arias
(IMP) **MCD43** Domingo Live from Miami
(IMP) **MCD45** Spanish Royal Gala
(MEMO) **HR4275/6** Birgit Nilsson—Public Performances 1954-1969
(PHIL) **442 602-2PM** 3 x 3 Tenors
(RCA) **GD60866** The Placido Domingo Album
(RCA) **GD84265** Con Amore
(RCA) **GD86534** Verdi Arias and Duets
(RCA) **RD61191** Gala Lirica
(RCA) **09026 61356-2** Domingo Sings Caruso
(RCA) **09026 61440-2** Opera's Greatest Moments
(RCA) **09026 61580-2(7)** RCA/Met 100 Singers, 100 Years (pt 7)
(RCA) **09026 61580-2(8)** RCA/Met 100 Singers, 100 Years (pt 8)
(RCA) **09026 61634-2** Verdi & Puccini Duets
(RCA) **09026 61886-2** Operas Greatest Love Songs
(RCA) **09026 62550-2** Ten Tenors in Love
(RCA) **09026 62595-2** Opera Duets
(RCA) **09026 62699-2** Opera's Greatest Duets
(RCA) **74321 25817-2** Café Classics - Operatic
(RCA) **09026 61204-4** From the Official Barcelona Games Ceremony
(RCA) **09026 61191-5** Gala Lirica
(RCA) **09026 61204-5** From the Official Barcelona Games Ceremony
(SONY) **MDK47176** Favourite Arias by the World's Favourite Tenors
(SONY) **MK39210** Zarzuela Arias and Duets
(SONY) **SBK46548** Opera Arias
(SONY) **SK48094** Favourite Puccini Arias
(SONY) **SMK39030** Placido Domingo sings Great Love Scenes
(SONY) **SLV48362(SONY)** Concert for the Planet Earth
(TELD) **4509-96200-8** The Three Tenors 1994
(TELD) **4509-96200-2** The Three Tenors 1994
(TELD) **4509-96231-2** Gardening Classics
(TELD) **9031-77676-6(TELD)** My World of Opera - Kiri Te Kanawa
(TELD) **4509-96200-5** The Three Tenors 1994

DOMINGO, Plácido (treb)
Puccini: Tosca (Cpte)

DOMINGO JNR, Plácido (ten)
(EMI) **CDC7 54053-2** Roman Heroes

DOMINGUEZ, Oralia (mez)
Ponchielli: Gioconda (Cpte)
Puccini: Tabarro (Cpte)
Wagner: Rheingold (Cpte), Siegfried (Cpte)
(DG) **435 211-2GX15** Wagner—Der Ring des Nibelungen

DOMINICI, Ernesto (bass)
(PREI) **89040** Carlo Galeffi (1884-1961)

DOMMER, Barbara (spkr)
Braunfels: Verkündigung (Cpte)

DONAGGIO, Luciano (bass)
Verdi: Falstaff (exc)
(EMI) **CHS7 64864-2(2)** La Scala Edition - Vol.2, 1915-46 (pt 2)

DONALD, Robin (ten)
Donizetti: Lucia di Lammermoor (Cpte)

DONAT, Zdisława (sop)
Mozart: Zauberflöte (Cpte)

DONATH, Helen (sop)
Beethoven: Fidelio (exc)
Bizet: Carmen (Cpte)
Britten: Turn of the Screw (Cpte)
Gluck: Orfeo ed Euridice (Cpte)
Haydn: Anima del filosofo (Cpte)
Hindemith: Sancta Susanna (Cpte)
Humperdinck: Hänsel und Gretel (Cpte), Königskinder (Cpte)
K. A. Hartmann: Simplicius Simplicissimus (Cpte)
Monteverdi: Incoronazione di Poppea (Cpte)
Mozart: Finta Giardiniera (Cpte), Finta semplice (Cpte), Lucio Silla (Cpte), Nozze di Figaro (Cpte)
Pfitzner: Palestrina (Cpte)
Puccini: Gianni Schicchi (Cpte)
R. Strauss: Rosenkavalier (Cpte)
Verdi: Ballo in maschera (Cpte)
Wagner: Meistersinger (Cpte), Rheingold (Cpte)
Weber: Freischütz (Cpte)
Wolf: Corregidor (Cpte)
(CFP) **CD-CFP4602** Favourite Opera

(CFP) **CD-CFP4656** Herbert von Karajan conducts Opera
(DG) **429 168-2GR** Wagner: Excerpts from Der Ring
(DG) **435 211-2GX15** Wagner—Der Ring des Nibelungen
(EMIL) **CDZ7 67015-2** Mozart—Opera Arias
(EURO) **GD69043** Puccini: Il Trittico
(ORFE) **C394301B** Great Mozart Singers Series, Vol. 3
(RCA) **09026 61440-2** Opera's Greatest Moments
(RCA) **09026 62547-2** Divas in Song—Marilyn Horne's 60th Birthday
(RCA) **74321 25817-2** Café Classics - Operatic

DONATH, Klaus (cond)
see South-West German RSO

DONATH, Klaus (pf)
(RCA) **09026 62547-2** Divas in Song—Marilyn Horne's 60th Birthday

DÖNCH, Karl (bar)
J. Strauss II: Nacht in Venedig (Cpte)
Lehár: Giuditta (exc), Lustige Witwe (exc)
Mozart: Nozze di Figaro (Cpte)
R. Strauss: Ariadne auf Naxos (Cpte), Schweigsame Frau (Cpte)
Smetana: Bartered Bride (Cpte)
Wagner: Meistersinger (Cpte)
Zeller: Vogelhändler (Cpte)
(ORFE) **C394201B** Great Mozart Singers Series, Vol. 2

DONDEYNE, Désiré (cond)
see Midi-Pyrénées Regional Orch

DONECKER, Thomas (bar)
Hindemith: Neues vom Tage (Cpte)

DONIAT, Aimé (bar)
Audran: Miss Helyett (Cpte)
Boïeldieu: Dame blanche (Cpte), Voitures Versées (Cpte)
Martinů: Alexandre Bis (Cpte)
Messager: Basoche (Cpte), Coups de Roulis (Cpte), Passionêment (Cpte)
Offenbach: Chanson de Fortunio (Cpte), Madame l'Archiduc (Cpte)
(EMI) **CZS7 67515-2** Offenbach—Operetta highlights

DONLAN, Brian (bar)
Puccini: Bohème (Cpte)
R. Strauss: Intermezzo (Cpte)
Verdi: Macbeth (Cpte)

DONNARIEIX, G. (sngr)
(MUSD) **20239-2** Delibes—Opéras-Comiques

DONNELLY, Malcolm (bar)
Britten: Gloriana (Cpte)
Donizetti: Lucia di Lammermoor (Cpte)
Mozart: Nozze di Figaro (Cpte)
(DECC) **071 149-1DH (DECC)** The Essential Sutherland

DONNELLY, Patrick (bass)
(ASV) **CDDCA758** Falla, Milhaud & Stravinsky—Operas

DONOHUE, Carl (bar)
Offenbach: Orphée aux enfers (Cpte)

DORATI, Antál (cond)
see Detroit SO
Lamoureux Concerts Orch
Lausanne CO
LSO
Minneapolis SO
National SO
Philh Hungarica
Philomusica of London
RCA Victor Orch
RPO
Stockholm PO

DORIA, Fiametta (sop)
Weill: Street Scene (Cpte)

DORIA, Renée (sop)
Massé: Noces de Jeannette (Cpte)
Offenbach: Contes d'Hoffmann (Cpte)
Verdi: Rigoletto (Cpte)
(MSCM) **MM30221** 18 French Divas
(MSCM) **MM30373** Gounod—Mélodies
(SYMP) **SYMCD1103** Renée Doria—Opera Recital

DORMOY, Claude (ten)
Debussy: Pelléas et Mélisande (Cpte)

DORO, Mina (mez)
(EMI) **CMS7 64165-2** Puccini—Trittico

DOROW, Dorothy (sop)
Holliger: Magische Tänzer (Cpte)
Purcell: Dido (Cpte)

DÖRPINGHANS, Eleonore (mez)
Mozart: Zauberflöte (Cpte)

DORTMUND UNIVERSITY CHAMBER CHOIR
cond W. GUNDLACH
Weill: Down in the Valley (Cpte), Jasager (Cpte)

DÖSE, Helena (sop)
Mozart: Così fan tutte (Cpte), Don Giovanni (Cpte)

DOSS, Mark S. (bass)
(DG) **435 866-2GH** Kathleen Battle sings Italian Opera Arias
(DG) **435 866-5CH** Kathleen Battle sings Italian Opera Arias

DOUBEK, Jindřich (bass)
Janáček: Fate (Cpte)

DOUBLEDAY, Elizabeth (sop)
(RCA) **GD60048** Mario Lanza sings Songs from The Student Prince & The Desert Song
(RCA) **GD60889(1)** The Mario Lanza Collection

DOUGHERTY, Celius (pf)
(PEAR) **GEMMCDS9095(1)** Povla Frijsh (pt 1)

DOUGLAS, Judith (mez)
Weill: Street Scene (Cpte)

DOUGLAS, Nigel (ten)
R. Strauss: Salome (Cpte)
(LOND) **433 200-2LHO2** Britten—Owen Wingrave, etc.

DOUSSARD, Jean (cond)
see French Rad Lyric Orch
ORTF Lyric Orch

DOWLING, Denis (bar)
Delius: Village Romeo and Juliet (Cpte)
Lehár: Lustige Witwe (exc)
Sullivan: Iolanthe (exc), Mikado (Cpte), Yeomen of the Guard (Cpte)
Verdi: Traviata (Cpte)
(EMI) **CMS7 64727-2** Britten—Opera excerpts and Folksongs

DOWNES, Sir Edward (cond)
see BBC PO
English Concert Orch
LSO
New Philh
New SO
ROHO
RPO
Vienna Op Orch
VPO

DOWNSIDE SCHOOL BOYS' CHOIR
cond B. BRITTEN
Britten: Midsummer Night's Dream (Cpte)

DOWSON, Stephen (bass-bar)
Walton: Troilus and Cressida (Cpte)
(EMI) **CDC7 54785-2** Harry Enfield's Guide to Opera

D'OYLY CARTE OPERA CHORUS
cond J. O. EDWARDS
J. Strauss II: Fledermaus (Cpte)
Offenbach: Orphée aux enfers (Cpte)
Sullivan: Yeomen of the Guard (Cpte)
cond I. GODFREY
Sullivan: Gondoliers (Cpte), HMS Pinafore (exc), Iolanthe (Cpte), Mikado (Cpte), Patience (Cpte), Pirates of Penzance (Cpte), Ruddigore (Cpte), Sorcerer (Cpte)
(DECC) **425 850-2DWO** Your Hundred Best Tunes, Vol.4
(DECC) **430 095-2DWO** The World of Gilbert & Sullivan, Vol.1
(DECC) **433 868-2DWO** The World of Gilbert & Sullivan - Volume 2
(MMOI) **CDMOIR413** The Very Best of Gilbert & Sullivan
cond R. NASH
Sullivan: Mikado (Cpte), Zoo (Cpte)
(DECC) **430 095-2DWO** The World of Gilbert & Sullivan, Vol.1
(DECC) **433 868-2DWO** The World of Gilbert & Sullivan - Volume 2
(LOND) **436 813-2LM2** Sullivan—The Grand Duke. Overture Di Ballo. Henry VIII
(LOND) **436 816-2LM2** Sullivan—Utopia Ltd. Macbeth & Marmion Ovs etc
cond H. NORRIS
Sullivan: Gondoliers (Cpte), Trial by Jury (Cpte)
(MMOI) **CDMOIR413** The Very Best of Gilbert & Sullivan
cond J. PRYCE-JONES
Sullivan: Gondoliers (Cpte), Iolanthe (Cpte), Mikado (Cpte), Pirates of Penzance (Cpte)
cond M. SARGENT
Sullivan: Gondoliers (Cpte), HMS Pinafore (Cpte), Mikado (Cpte), Patience (Cpte), Pirates of Penzance (Cpte), Princess Ida (Cpte), Yeomen of the Guard (Cpte)
(BELA) **461 006-2** Gilbert & Sullivan—Songs and Snatches
(DECC) **430 095-2DWO** The World of Gilbert & Sullivan, Vol.1
(DECC) **433 868-2DWO** The World of Gilbert & Sullivan - Volume 2
(MMOI) **CDMOIR413** The Very Best of Gilbert & Sullivan

D'OYLY CARTE OPERA ORCHESTRA
(DECC) **425 850-2DWO** Your Hundred Best Tunes, Vol.4
cond J. O. EDWARDS
J. Strauss II: Fledermaus (Cpte)
Offenbach: Orphée aux enfers (Cpte)
Sullivan: Yeomen of the Guard (exc)
(TER) **CDVIR8316** Sullivan—Overtures
cond J. PRYCE-JONES
Sullivan: Gondoliers (Cpte), Iolanthe (Cpte), Mikado (Cpte), Pirates of Penzance (Cpte), Thespis (exc)
(TER) **CDVIR8315** Carousel Waltz
(TER) **CDVIR8316** Sullivan—Overtures

DR RADIO CHOIR
cond D. KITAIENKO
Mussorgsky: Boris Godunov (Cpte)

DR RADIO SYMPHONY ORCHESTRA
cond D. KITAIENKO
Mussorgsky: Boris Godunov (Cpte)

DRABOWICZ, Wojciech (ten)
Mussorgsky: Boris Godunov (Cpte)

DRAGON, Carmen (cond)
see Capitol SO
Hollywood Bowl SO

DRAGONI, Maria (sop)
Verdi: Aida (Cpte)
(ORFE) **C261921A** Maria Dragoni sings Famous Opera Arias

DRAGONI, Matteo (bar)
(PEAR) **GEMMCD9117** Graziella Pareto

DRAKE, Bryan (bar)
Britten: Billy Budd (Cpte), Burning Fiery Furnace (Cpte), Curlew River (Cpte), Prodigal Son (Cpte), Rape of Lucretia (Cpte)
(KIWI) **CDSLD-82** Southern Voices—NZ International Opera Singers

DRAKE, Julius (pf)
(ASV) **CDDCA800** Encores - Emma Johnson
(REGE) **REGCD104** The Bel Canto Bassoon

DRAKE, Susan (hp)
(OPRA) **ORCH103** Italian Opera—1810-20

DRAKSLER, Sonja (mez)
R. Strauss: Elektra (Cpte)

DRAN, Thierry (ten)
Auber: Fra Diavolo (Cpte)
Chausson: Roi Arthus (Cpte)
Messager: Fortunio (Cpte)
Offenbach: Brigands (Cpte), Contes d'Hoffmann (exc)

DRAPAL, Otto (treb)
(SCHW) **314602** Vienna State Opera Live, Vol.10

DREIER, Per (cond)
see LSO

DRESDEN CATHEDRAL HIGH CHURCH BOYS' CHOIR
cond H. KEGEL
Schoenberg: Moses und Aron (Cpte)

DRESDEN KREUZCHOR CHILDREN'S VOICES
cond B. HAITINK
R. Strauss: Rosenkavalier (Cpte)

DRESDEN PHILHARMONIC ORCHESTRA
cond H. KEGEL
(LASE) **15 523** Beethoven: Orchestral Works
(LASE) **15 622** Famous Classical Overtures
(LASE) **15 625** Meditation
cond J-P. WEIGLE
(PHIL) **422 523-2PME8(2)** The Complete Mozart Edition Vol 23 (pt 2)

DRESDEN STATE OPERA CHORUS
Beethoven: Fidelio (exc)
Humperdinck: Hänsel und Gretel (exc)
R. Strauss: Elektra (Cpte), Rosenkavalier (exc)
Wagner: Götterdämmerung (Cpte), Meistersinger (Cpte), Rienzi (Cpte)
(BELA) **450 052-2** Great Opera Choruses
(CFP) **CD-CFP4656** Herbert von Karajan conducts Opera
(DG) **437 677-2GDO2** Irmgard Seefried - Opera Recital
(EURO) **GD69003** Wagner—Der Ring des Nibelungen
(PEAR) **GEMMCDS9121** Wagner—Die Meistersinger, Act 3, etc

DRESDEN STATE OPERA ORCHESTRA
cond K. BÖHM
(PREI) **90237** R Strauss—Daphne
cond S. VARVISO
(BELA) **450 052-2** Great Opera Choruses
(BELA) **450 126-2** Favourite Wedding Music II

DRESSEL, Ina (narr)
J. Strauss II: Fledermaus (exc)

DRESSEN, Dan (ten)
Britten: Paul Bunyan (exc)
Copland: Tender Land (Cpte)

DRESSEN, Elvira (mez)
Schulhoff: Plameny (Cpte)

DRESSLER, Robert (spkr)
Pfitzner: Herz (Cpte)

DREWS, Richard (ten)
Corigliano: Ghosts of Versailles (Cpte)

DREYER, Derek (sngr)
Schuman: Mighty Casey (Cpte)

DREYER, Jelle (bar)
Keiser: Masagniello furioso (Cpte)

DRISCOLL, Loren (ten)
Berg: Lulu (Cpte)
Henze: Junge Lord (Cpte)
Wagner: Meistersinger (Cpte)
(SONY) **SM3K46291** Stravinsky—Ballets, Vol.1
(SONY) **SM22K46290(3)** Stravinsky—The Complete Edition (pt 3)
(SONY) **SM22K46290(4)** Stravinsky—The Complete Edition (pt 4)

DROBKOVÁ, Drahomira (contr)
Dvořák: Dimitrij (Cpte), Rusalka (exc)

DROFOVÁ, Barbora (sop)
Krása: Brundibár (Cpte)

DROTTNINGHOLM BAROQUE ENSEMBLE
Mozart: Don Giovanni (Cpte)
cond A. ÖHRWALL
(PROP) **PRCD9008** Anne Sofie Von Otter — Recital
cond T. SCHUBACK
Haeffner: Electra (Cpte)

DROTTNINGHOLM COURT THEATRE CHORUS
cond A. ÖSTMAN
Mozart: Così fan tutte (Cpte), Don Giovanni (Cpte), Entführung (Cpte), Finta Giardiniera (Cpte), Idomeneo (Cpte), Nozze di Figaro (Cpte), Zauberflöte (Cpte)

DROTTNINGHOLM COURT THEATRE ORCHESTRA
Mozart: Così fan tutte (Cpte), Don Giovanni (Cpte), Entführung (Cpte), Finta Giardiniera (Cpte), Idomeneo (Cpte), Nozze di Figaro (Cpte), Zauberflöte (Cpte)
cond A. ÖSTMAN
Mozart: Don Giovanni (Cpte), Nozze di Figaro (Cpte), Zauberflöte (Cpte)
(DECC) **440 414-2DM** Arleen Auger

DROUET, Jean-Pierre (perc)
Bernstein: West Side Story Symphonic Dances

DRUIETT, Michael (bass)
Floyd: Susannah (Cpte)
(ROH) **75605 55013-2** The Puccini Experience

DRUMMOND-GRANT, Ann (contr)
Sullivan: Mikado (Cpte)

DRUZHIAKINA, Sofia (sop)
(ARLE) **ARL23/5** Rimsky-Korsakov—Sadko

DRY, Marion (mez)
V. Thomson: Lord Byron (Cpte)

DU BRASSUS CHOIR
cond R. BONYNGE
Offenbach: Contes d'Hoffmann (exc)

DUA, Octave (ten)
Verdi: Trovatore (Cpte)
Wagner: Tristan und Isolde (Cpte)
(PEAR) **GEMMCDS9926(1)** Covent Garden on Record—Vol.4 (pt 1)

DUBBINI, Agnese (mez)
Puccini: Gianni Schicchi (Cpte)

DUBERNET, Gilles (bar)
Auber: Gustav III (Cpte), Manon Lescaut (Cpte)

DUBLIN COUNTY CHOIR
cond R. SACCANI
Verdi: Aida (Cpte)

DUBOIS, Mark (ten)
(CBC) **SMCD5126** A Night in Venice & Other Operetta Excerpts

DUBOSC, Catherine (sop)
Berlioz: Troyens (Cpte)
Cavalli: Giasone (Cpte)
Gluck: Rencontre imprévue (Cpte)
Mussorgsky: Boris Godunov (Cpte)
Poulenc: Dialogues des Carmélites (Cpte)
Prokofiev: Love for 3 Oranges (Cpte)
(DECC) **440 333-2DH** Ravel—Vocal Works
(ERAT) **4509-99607-2** Gluck—Operas; Schubert—Symphonies Nos 8 & 9

DUCAREL, Michael (bar)
Sullivan: Mikado (Cpte)

DUCHARME, Michel (bar)
Vivier: Kopernikus (Cpte)

DUCHÊNE, Maria (mez)
(NIMB) **NI7834** Caruso in Ensemble
(PEAR) **EVC3(1)** The Caruso Edition, Vol.3 (pt 1)
(RCA) **GD60495(5)** The Complete Caruso Collection (pt 5)
(ROMO) **81002-2** Emmy Destinn (1878-1930)
(SUPR) **11 2136-2(5)** Emmy Destinn—Complete Edition, Discs 11 & 12

DUCKENS, Dorceal (voc)
Joplin: Treemonisha (Cpte)

(RENÉ) DUCLOS CHOIR
cond A. CLUYTENS
Offenbach: Contes d'Hoffmann (Cpte)
(CFP) **CD-CFP4602** Favourite Opera
(EMI) **CZS5 68113-2** Vive Offenbach!
cond A. LOMBARD
(EMI) **CZS7 67869-2** J. Strauss II—Operetta Highlights
cond I. MARKEVITCH
(EMI) **CZS5 68113-2** Vive Offenbach!
cond J-P. MARTY
(EMI) **CZS5 68113-2** Vive Offenbach!
cond F. NUVOLONE
(EMI) **CZS5 68113-2** Vive Offenbach!
cond F. POURCEL
(EMI) **CZS7 67869-2** J. Strauss II—Operetta Highlights
(EMI) **CZS7 67872-2** Lehár—Operettas (highlights in French)
cond G. PRÊTRE
Bizet: Carmen (exc)
Saint-Saëns: Samson et Dalila (exc)
(CFP) **CD-CFP4602** Favourite Opera
(EMI) **CDC5 55016-2** Maria Callas - La Divina 2
(EMIL) **CDZ100** Best Loved Classics 1
(EMIN) **CD-EMX2123** Maria Callas sings Operatic Arias

DUDAREV, Georgy (bass)
Kabalevsky: Colas Breugnon (Cpte)

DUDZIAK, Francis (bar)
(ARIO) **ARN68252** Chabrier—Trois opérettes

DUDZIAK, Francis (ten)
Berg: Lulu (Cpte)
Gluck: Rencontre imprévue (Cpte)
Messager: Fortunio (Cpte)
Offenbach: Brigands (Cpte)
Rossini: Comte Ory (Cpte)
(ERAT) **4509-99607-2** Gluck—Operas; Schubert—Symphonies Nos 8 & 9

DUESING, Dale (bar)
Britten: Midsummer Night's Dream (Cpte)
Monteverdi: Incoronazione di Poppea (Cpte)
Mozart: Così fan tutte (Cpte), Don Giovanni (exc)
Offenbach: Contes d'Hoffmann (exc)
(EMI) **CDM5 65576-2** Jessye Norman

DUETSCHLER, Ursula (hpd)
(CLAV) **CD50-9023** Maria Bayo—Arie Antiche

DUFALLO, Richard (cond)
see Netherlands Wind Ens

DUFEK, Jaroslav (narr)
Martinů: Comedy on the Bridge (Cpte)

DUFFY, Tony (sngr)
Menotti: Boy who grew too fast (Cpte)

DUFOUR, Olivier (ten)
Monteverdi: Orfeo (Cpte)

DUFRANNE, Hector (bass)
Debussy: Pelléas et Mélisande (exc)
Ravel: Heure espagnole (Cpte)

DUGAY, Richard (ten)
Campra: Idoménée (exc)

DUGDALE, Sandra (sop)
(OPRA) **ORH102** A Hundred Years of Italian Opera

DUHAN, Hans (cond)
see Vienna St Op Orch

DUHAN, Hans (bar)
Lehár: Giuditta (exc), Lustige Witwe (exc)
(ORFE) **C394101B** Great Mozart Singers Series, Vol. 1
(SCHW) **314562** Vienna State Opera Live, Vol.6
(SCHW) **314642** Vienna State Opera Live, Vol.14

DULGUEROV, Kiril (ten)
(EMI) **CMS7 63386-2** Borodin—Prince Igor & Complete Solo Songs

DUMAINE, Olympe (sop)
(EMI) **CDS7 49361-2** Offenbach: Operettas

DUMAY, Augustin (vn)
(EMI) **CDC7 47544-2** French music for violin and orchestra

DUMINY, Philippe (bass)
Shostakovich: Lady Macbeth of Mtsensk (Cpte)
Verdi: Otello (exc)

DUMONT, Fernand (bar)
R. Strauss: Salomé (Cpte)
Tchaikovsky: Iolanta (Cpte)

DUN LAOGHAIRE CHORAL SOCIETY
cond R. SACCANI
Verdi: Aida (Cpte)

DUNAND, Robert (cond)
see Collegium Academicum Orch

DUNDEKOVA, Evghenia (mez)
Giordano: Andrea Chénier (Cpte)

DUNLOP, Fergus (bar)
Mozart: Nozze di Figaro (Cpte)

DUNN, Darcy (sngr)
Horem: Childhood Miracle (Cpte)

DUNN, Mignon (mez)
G. Charpentier: Louise (Cpte)
R. Strauss: Salome (Cpte)
V. Thomson: Mother of us all (Cpte)

DUNN, Susan (sop)
Verdi: Giovanna d'Arco (Cpte), Vespri Siciliani (Cpte)
Wagner: Walküre (exc)
(DECC) **436 472-2DM** Great Opera Arias

DUPOUY, Jean (ten)
Massenet: Jongleur de Notre Dame (Cpte)
Meyerbeer: Prophète (Cpte)
R. Strauss: Salomé (Cpte)

DUPRÉ, Lily (sngr)
(IRCC) **IRCC-CD802** Souvenirs of Rare French Opera

DUPRÉ, Micheline (sop)
Verdi: Rigoletto (Cpte)

DUPUY, Martine (mez)
Handel: Giulio Cesare (Cpte)
Poulenc: Dialogues des Carmélites (Cpte)
Rossini: Adelaide di Borgogna (Cpte)

DUR, John (bass)
Grétry: Caravane du Caire (Cpte)

DURCO, Jan (bass)
Puccini: Tosca (Cpte)

DURDEN, Richard (spkr)
Gay: Beggar's Opera (Cpte)

DÜREN, Margarete (sop)
(PREI) **89076** Josef Herrmann (1903-1955)

DÜRMÜLLER, Jörg (ten)
Krenek: Sprüng über den Schatten (Cpte)

DUSSAUT, Catherine (sop)
Campra: Tancrède (exc)
M-A. Charpentier: Arts Florissants (Cpte)

DUSSELJEE, Kor-Jan (ten)
Wolf: Manuel Venegas

DUTCH RADIO PHILHARMONIC CHORUS
cond E. DE WAART
Schreker: Gezeichneten (Cpte)

DUTCH RADIO PHILHARMONIC ORCHESTRA
cond E. DE WAART
Schreker: Gezeichneten (Cpte)

DUTERTRE, Annick (sop)
Massenet: Don Quichotte (Cpte)
Rameau: Dardanus (Cpte)

DUTOIT, Charles (cond)
see French Rad New PO
Monte Carlo PO
Montreal SO

DUTOIT, Laurence (sop)
R. Strauss: Rosenkavalier (Cpte)
Verdi: Trovatore (Cpte)
(MEMO) **HR4396/7** Great Voices—Leontyne Price

DUVAL, Denise (sop)
Poulenc: Dialogues des Carmélites (Cpte), Mamelles de Tirésias (Cpte), Voix Humaine (Cpte)
Ravel: Heure espagnole (Cpte)

DUVAL, Pierre (ten)
Donizetti: Lucia di Lammermoor (Cpte)
(DECC) **433 706-2DMO3** Bellini—Beatrice di Tenda; Operatic Arias

DUVALEIX (ten)
Audran: Poupée (exc)
Bazin: Voyage en Chine (Cpte)
(EMI) **CZS7 67515-2** Offenbach—Operetta highlights

DUX, Claire (sop)
(PREI) **89033** Joseph Schwarz (1880-1926)

DUXBURY, John (ten)
Offenbach: Christopher Columbus (Cpte)

DVOŘÁKOVÁ, Ludmila (sop)
Wagner: Götterdämmerung (Cpte)
(MULT) **310151-2** Mozart/Smetana/Wagner—Vocal and Orchestral Works
(PHIL) **446 057-2PB14** Wagner—The Ring Cycle - Bayreuth Festival 1967

DVORSKÝ, Miroslav (ten)
Leoncavallo: Pagliacci (Cpte)
Puccini: Tosca (Cpte)

DVORSKÝ, Peter (ten)
Donizetti: Elisir d'amore (Cpte)
Janáček: Jenufa (Cpte), Makropulos Affair (Cpte)
Puccini: Bohème (Cpte), Madama Butterfly (Cpte), Manon Lescaut (Cpte)
Smetana: Bartered Bride (Cpte)
Suchoň: Whirlpool (Cpte)
Tchaikovsky: Eugene Onegin (Cpte)
Verdi: Otello (Cpte), Traviata (Cpte)
(ACAN) **43 123** Peter Dvorský sings Puccini Arias
(DECC) **421 852-2DH2** Janáček: Operatic & Chamber Works
(KOCH) **34036-2** A Pageant of Opera
(MCI) **MCCD099** Opera's Greatest Arias
(NAXO) **8 550343** Italian and French Opera Arias
(OPUS) **9156 1824** Dvorský sings Operatic Arias

DYADKOVA, Larissa (mez)
Mussorgsky: Boris Godunov (Cpte)
Rimsky-Korsakov: Sadko (Cpte)
Tchaikovsky: Mazeppa (Cpte)

DYER, Lorely (sop)
Delius: Village Romeo and Juliet (Cpte)

DYER, Olive (sop)
Britten: Turn of the Screw (Cpte)

DYMIT, Thomas (ten)
Schoenberg: Moses und Aron (Cpte)

DYMOVSKI, Alexander (bass)
Beethoven: Fidelio (Cpte)

DYSON, Sally Cooper (sop)
(NIMB) **NI5224** Bellini & Donizetti: Arias

EADIE, Noel (sop)
Wagner: Götterdämmerung (exc)
(PEAR) **GEMMCDS9137** Wagner—Der Ring des Nibelungen

EAGLEN, Jane (sop)
Bellini: Norma (Cpte)
Mayr: Medea (Cpte)
Schulhoff: Plameny (Cpte)
Wagner: Götterdämmerung (Cpte)
(EMI) **CDC5 55479-2** Wagner—Orchestral Works

EALES, Margaret (sop)
Sullivan: Yeomen of the Guard (Cpte)

EAMES, Emma (sop)
(NIMB) **NI7860** Emma Eames & Pol Plançon

(PEAR) **GEMMCDS9923(1)** Covent Garden on Record, Vol.1 (pt 1)
(RCA) **09026 61580-2(1)** RCA/Met 110 Singers, 100 Years (pt 1)
(ROMO) **81001-2** Emma Eames (1865-1952)
(ROMO) **82001-2** Pol Plançon—Complete Victor Recordings

EARLE, Roderick (bass)
Bizet: Carmen (Cpte)
Donizetti: Maria Padilla (Cpte)
Meyerbeer: Dinorah (Cpte)
Puccini: Manon Lescaut (Cpte)
Purcell: Tempest, Z631 (Cpte)
R. Strauss: Rosenkavalier (Cpte)
Verdi: Otello (Cpte), Traviata (Cpte), Trovatore (Cpte)
(ERAT) **4509-96371-2** Gardiner—The Purcell Collection

EARLY INSTRUMENTS CHAMBER ENSEMBLE
cond M. VENHODA
(CAMP) **RRCD1323** Welcome Ev'ry Guest - John Blow/Henry Purcell Songs

EAST SUFFOLK CHILDREN'S ORCHESTRA
cond N. DEL MAR
Britten: Noye's Fludde (Cpte)
(DECC) **436 990-2DWO** The World of Benjamin Britten

EASTER, Allison (voc)
M. Monk: Atlas (Cpte)

EASTMAN WIND ENSEMBLE
cond F. FENNELL
(MERC) **434 322-2MM** Works for Wind Ensemble
cond D. HUNSBERGER
(SONY) **SM42137** Carnaval—Wynton Marsalis
(SONY) **MK42137** Carnaval—Wynton Marsalis

EASTMAN-DRYDEN ORCHESTRA
cond D. HUNSBERGER
(ARAB) **Z6547** Herbert—L'Encore

EASTON, Florence (sop)
(DANA) **DACOCD319/21** The Lauritz Melchior Anthology - Vol.5
(MSCM) **MM30285** Great Wagnerian Singers, Vol.2
(PEAR) **GEMMCDS9137** Wagner—Der Ring des Nibelungen

EASTON, Robert (bass)
Gounod: Faust (Cpte)
(DUTT) **CDLX7012** The Incomparable Heddle Nash
(PEAR) **GEMMCDS9926(2)** Covent Garden on Record—Vol.4 (pt 2)
(PEAR) **GEMMCD9473** Heddle Nash—Vol.2

EATHORNE, Wendy (sop)
Bridge: Christmas Rose (Cpte)
Vaughan Williams: Pilgrim's Progress (Cpte)

EATON, Michèle A (sop)
Glass: Hydrogen Jukebox (Cpte)

EBEL, Gudrun (sop)
Mozart: Entführung (Cpte)

EBELING, Gertrud (mez)
R. Strauss: Salome (Cpte)

EBERT, Harry (pf)
(BLUE) **ABCD042** Björling - The Stockholm Tivoli Recordings, Vol.1: 1958-60
(BLUE) **ABCD057** Björling—Gröna Lund Recordings, Volume 2

EBERT, Joyce (mez)
R. Ward: Crucible (Cpte)

EBNET, Lisolette (sop)
Abraham: Blume von Hawaii (exc), Viktoria und ihr Husar (exc)

EBRAHIM, Omar (bar)
Tippett: King Priam (Cpte)

ECHEVERRIA, Alfonso (bass)
Vives: Bohemios (Cpte), Doña Francisquita (Cpte)

ECKER, Heinz Klaus (bass)
Wagner: Meistersinger (Cpte), Parsifal (Cpte)

ECKERSLEY, Kate (sop)
(MERI) **CDE84195** Vivaldi: Orchestral and Vocal Works

ECKHOFF, Ranveig (sop)
Nørgård: Gilgamesh (Cpte)

EDA-PIERRE, Christiane (sop)
Berlioz: Benvenuto Cellini (Cpte), Béatrice et Bénédict (Cpte)
Messiaen: Saint François d'Assise (Cpte)
Mozart: Entführung (Cpte)
Rameau: Dardanus (Cpte)

EDEIKEN, Louise (sop)
Bernstein: West Side Story (Cpte)
(DG) **439 251-2GY** The Leonard Bernstein Album
(DG) **439 251-5GY** The Leonard Bernstein Album

EDELMANN, Otto (bass)
Beethoven: Fidelio (Cpte)
Mozart: Don Giovanni (Cpte)
R. Strauss: Arabella (Cpte), Rosenkavalier (exc)
Wagner: Meistersinger (Cpte)
(ORFE) **C335931A** Salzburg Festival highlights (1956-85)

EDER, Claudia (mez)
Offenbach: Contes d'Hoffmann (Cpte)

EDERVEEN, Regina (hp)
(SAGA) **SCD9023** Melodies for Flute and Harp

EDGAR-WILSON, Richard (ten)
Purcell: Dioclesian, Z627 (Cpte)

EDINBURGH FESTIVAL CHORUS
cond I. KERTÉSZ
(DECC) **443 488-2DF2** Kodály—Háry János; Psalmus Hungaricus etc
cond C. MACKERRAS
Mozart: Così fan tutte (Cpte)

EDLERS, Ellen Margrethe (sop)
Nielsen: Maskarade (Cpte)

EDMEADS, Adrian (sngr)
Bernstein: West Side Story (Cpte)

EDVINA, Louise (sop)
(PEAR) **GEMMCDS9925(1)** Covent Garden on Record—Vol.3 (pt 1)

EDWARDS, Anne (sop)
Donizetti: Caterina Cornaro (Cpte)
Verdi: Nabucco (exc)

EDWARDS, Catherine (pf)
(CONI) **CDCF905** Karen Jones—The Flute Album

EDWARDS, Cheryl (sop)
Janáček: Fate (Cpte)

EDWARDS, Jack (spkr)
Lampe: Pyramus and Thisbe (Cpte)

EDWARDS, Joan (contr)
Wagner: Walküre (Cpte)

EDWARDS, John Owen (cond)
see D'Oyly Carte Op Orch
National SO
Philh

EDWARDS, Ronald (ten)
A. Davis: X (Cpte)

EDWARDS, Sian (cond)
see ENO Orch
LPO

EDWARDS, Terry (bass)
Monteverdi: Orfeo (Cpte)

EDWARDS, Terry (ten)
Machover: Valis (Cpte)

EEN, Robert (voc)
M. Monk: Atlas (Cpte)
(ECM) **437 439-2** Meredith Monk—Facing North and other works

EFFENBERKOVÁ, Božena (sop)
Fibich: Šárka (Cpte)
Janáček: Cunning Little Vixen (Cpte), Jenufa (Cpte)
Smetana: Kiss (Cpte)

EGEL, Martin (bass)
Verdi: Trovatore (Cpte)
Wagner: Meistersinger (Cpte), Parsifal (Cpte), Rheingold (exc), Tristan und Isolde (Cpte)
(PHIL) **434 420-2PM32(2)** Richard Wagner Edition (pt 2)

EGENER, Minnie (mez)
(MSCM) **MM30352** Caruso—Italian Opera Arias
(PEAR) **EVC4(1)** The Caruso Edition, Vol.4 (pt 1)
(PEAR) **GEMMCDS9159(2)** De Luca Edition, Vol.1 (pt 2)
(RCA) **GD60495(6)** The Complete Caruso Collection (pt 6)
(ROMO) **81003-2** Galli-Curci—Acoustic Recordings, Vol.1

EGERTON, Francis (ten)
Bizet: Carmen (Cpte)
Borodin: Prince Igor (Cpte)
Mozart: Nozze di Figaro (Cpte)
Offenbach: Contes d'Hoffmann (Cpte)
Puccini: Bohème (Cpte), Fanciulla del West (Cpte), Tosca (Cpte)
Tchaikovsky: Eugene Onegin (Cpte)
Verdi: Falstaff (Cpte)
(CAST) **CASH5052** Verdi Operatic Favourites
(ROH) **75605 55013-2** The Puccini Experience

EGGARS, Walter (sngr)
R. Strauss: Rosenkavalier (Cpte)

EGGIMANN, Ulrich Simon (sngr)
Zemlinsky: Kleider machen Leute (Cpte)

EGGLESTON, Anne (sop)
(LOND) **436 813-2LM2** Sullivan—The Grand Duke. Overture Di Ballo. Henry VIII

EGK, Werner (cond)
see Bavarian St Orch

EGMOND, Max van (bass)
Monteverdi: Orfeo (Cpte), Ritorno d'Ulisse in Patria (Cpte)

EGO, Constantino (bar)
Bellini: Pirata (Cpte)

EGUCHI, Akira (pf)
(DENO) **CO-75118** Violin Show Pieces

EHRLING, Sixten (cond)
see Stockholm Royal Op Orch

EHRSTEDT, Caj (ten)
Braein: Anne Pedersdotter (Cpte)

EIAR ORCHESTRA
cond V. GUI
(PREI) **89014** Ebe Stignani (1903-1974)
cond G. MARINUZZI
(PREI) **89014** Ebe Stignani (1903-1974)
cond A. LA ROSA PARODI
(PREI) **89014** Ebe Stignani (1903-1974)
cond U. TANSINI
(CENT) **CRC2164** Ferruccio Tagliavini—Early Operatic Recordings
(PREI) **89014** Ebe Stignani (1903-1974)
(PREI) **89016** Gina Cigna (b. 1900)
(PREI) **89063** Rosetta Pampanini (1896-1973)
(PREI) **89074** Tancredi Pasero (1893-1983) - II

EICHHORN, Kurt (cond)
see Austrian RSO
Cologne RSO
Munich RO
Munich RSO
Stuttgart RSO

EICHSTAEDT, Karin (sop)
(PHIL) **422 525-2PME2** The Complete Mozart Edition Vol 25

EICHWALDER, Martin (bass)
Spohr: Faust (Cpte)

EINHORN, Aviva (cond)
see Musicholiers

EIPPERLE, Trude (sop)
Mozart: Zauberflöte (Cpte)
Wagner: Walküre (exc)
(ACAN) **43 268** Peter Anders sings German Opera Arias

EISINGER, Irene (sop)
Mozart: Così fan tutte (Cpte)
(RELI) **CR921036** Joseph Schmidt—Opera and Operetta Arias

EISLER, David (ten)
Bernstein: Candide (1982) (Cpte)

EISNER, Maurice (pf)
(BIDD) **LAB019** Fritz Kreisler—Early Victors

EK, Harald (ten)
Wagner: Fliegende Holländer (Cpte)

EKEBERG, Kjersti (sop)
Braein: Anne Pedersdotter (Cpte)

EKLÖF, Marianne (mez)
Marschner: Hans Heiling (Cpte)

EL DIN, Tahia Shams (sop)
Mozart: Don Giovanni (Cpte)

EL HAGE, Robert (bass)
Donizetti: Lucrezia Borgia (Cpte)
Puccini: Rondine (Cpte), Tabarro (Cpte)
(RCA) **09026 61236-2** Leontyne Price - Prima Donna Collection
(RCA) **09026 61457-2** Shirley Verrett in Opera

ELBURN, Beatrice (mez)
Sullivan: Gondoliers (Cpte)

ELDER, Mark (cond)
see ENO Orch

ELENKOV, Stefan (bass)
Mussorgsky: Khovanshchina (Cpte)
(EMI) **CDM5 65575-2** Montserrat Caballé
(EMI) **CDM7 63104-2** Alfredo Krauss - Opera Recital

ELGAR, Sir Edward (cond)
see LSO

ELIAS, Rosalind (mez)
Barber: Vanessa (Cpte)
Puccini: Madama Butterfly (Cpte)
Stravinsky: Rake's Progress (Cpte)
Verdi: Falstaff (Cpte), Rigoletto (Cpte)
(RCA) **09026 61580-2(5)** RCA/Met 100 Singers, 100 Years (pt 5)
(RCA) **09026 62689-2** The Voices of Living Stereo, Volume 1
(RCA) **09026 62699-2** Opera's Greatest Duets

ELIASSON, Sven Olof (sngr)
Monteverdi: Ritorno d'Ulisse in Patria (Cpte)

ELIZABETHAN SINGERS
cond B. HERRMANN
Herrmann: Wuthering Heights (Cpte)

ELKINS, Margreta (mez)
Bellini: Norma (Cpte)
Donizetti: Lucia di Lammermoor (Cpte), Maria Stuarda (Cpte)
Gounod: Faust (Cpte)
Handel: Giulio Cesare (exc)
Wagner: Walküre (Cpte)
(DECC) **433 064-2DWO** Your Hundred Best Opera Tunes Volume I
(DECC) **433 443-2DA** Great Opera Choruses
(DECC) **433 706-2DMO3** Bellini—Beatrice di Tenda; Operatic Arias
(EMI) **CDM7 63182-2** The Incomparable Callas
(OPRA) **ORC004** Donizetti—Ne m'oubliez pas; Arias
(RCA) **GD60941** Rarities - Montserrat Caballé

ELLENBECK, Dieter (ten)
Weill: Sieben Todsünden (Cpte)

ELLIOTT, Elizabeth (sop)
Sullivan: Gondoliers (Cpte)

ELLIOTT, Paul (ten)
Purcell: Dido (Cpte), Dioclesian, Z627 (exc), Indian Queen, Z630 (Cpte), King Arthur, Z628 (Cpte)
(ERAT) **4509-96371-2** Gardiner—The Purcell Collection
(HARM) **HMX290 1528/33(2)** A Purcell Companion (pt 2)

ELLIS, Brent (bar)
Verdi: Traviata (Cpte)

ELLIS, Roger (cond)
see French Rad Lyric Orch

ELLISON, Jon (bar)
(LOND) **436 813-2LM2** Sullivan—The Grand Duke. Overture Di Ballo. Henry VIII
(LOND) **436 816-2LM2** Sullivan—Utopia Ltd. Macbeth & Marmion Ovs etc

ELLSWORTH, Warren (ten)
Wagner: Parsifal (Cpte)

(GLEN) ELLYN CHILDREN'S CHORUS
cond G. SOLTI
Schoenberg: Moses und Aron (Cpte)

ELMAN, Mischa (vn)
(BIDD) **LAB035** Mischa Elman—Solo Recordings 1910-1911
(VANG) **08.8029.71** Mischa Elman - Favourite Encores

ELMENDORFF, Karl (cond)
see Bayreuth Fest Orch
Saxon St Orch

ELMING, Poul (ten)
Heise: Drot og Marsk (Cpte)
Nørgård: Siddhartha (Cpte)
Wagner: Walküre (Cpte)

ELMO, Cloe (mez)
Verdi: Falstaff (Cpte)
(EMI) **CDH7 61052-2** Beniamino Gigli—Arias and Duets (1932-1949)
(EMI) **CHS7 69741-2(7)** Record of Singing, Vol.4—Italian School
(LYRC) **SRO805** Gina Cigna—Opera Recital
(PREI) **89016** Gina Cigna (b. 1900)
(RCA) **GD60326** Verdi—Operas & Choral Works

ELMS, Lauris (mez)
Britten: Peter Grimes (Cpte)

ELOIR, Cécile (mez)
Rossi: Orfeo (Cpte)

ELQUIST, Martin (cond)
see Danish Rad Concert Orch

ELVIN, William (bar)
Puccini: Bohème (Cpte), Fanciulla del West (Cpte), Tosca (Cpte)
Verdi: Ballo in maschera (Cpte), Forza del destino (Cpte), Masnadieri (Cpte), Traviata (Cpte)
(PHIL) **434 986-2PM** Duetti Amorosi

ELVIRA, Pablo (bar)
Mascagni: Cavalleria Rusticana (Cpte)

ELWES, John (ten)
Cavalli: Xerse (Cpte)
Grétry: Jugement de Midas (exc)
Landi: Mort d'Orfeo (Cpte)
Purcell: Indian Queen, Z630 (Cpte), Tempest, Z631 (Cpte)
Rameau: Zoroastre (Cpte)
Vaughan Williams: Pilgrim's Progress (Cpte)
Vivaldi: Dorilla in Tempe (Cpte)
(ERAT) **4509-96371-2** Gardiner—The Purcell Collection

ELY, Dean (sngr)
Handel: Giustino (Cpte)

ELYSIAN SINGERS OF LONDON
cond M. GREENALL
(CNTI) **CCD1054** Delius—Complete partsongs

EMANUEL SCHOOL BOYS' CHOIR
cond B. BRITTEN
Britten: Midsummer Night's Dream (Cpte)

EMERSON, Dina (voc)
M. Monk: Atlas (Cpte)

EMILI, Romano (ten)
Leoncavallo: Bohème (Cpte)
(DECC) **436 261-2DHO3** Puccini—Il Trittico

EMILIA ROMAGNA 'TOSCANINI' SYMPHONY ORCHESTRA
cond E. BUCKLEY
(SONY) **MDK47176** Favourite Arias by the World's Favourite Tenors
cond F. LUISI
Salieri: Locandiera (Cpte)
cond B. RIGACCI
Donizetti: Pazzi per progetto (Cpte)
cond H. SOUDANT
Donizetti: Elisir d'amore (Cpte)
(MEMO) **HR4300/1** Great Voices—Sesto Bruscantini
(NUOV) **6905** Donizetti—Great Love Duets

EMMERSON, Steven (bass)
Shostakovich: Lady Macbeth of Mtsensk (Cpte)

EMPIRE BRASS
(TELA) **CD80305** Classical Brass II - On the Edge

EMPIRE BRASS QUINTET
(TELA) **CD80303** Empire Brass on Broadway

ENDRÈZE, Arthur (bar)
Puccini: Tosca (exc)
(EMI) **CMS7 64008-2(1)** Wagner Singing on Record (pt 1)
(MSCM) **MM30451** Mascagni—Cavalleria Rusticana, etc

ENGELMAN, Wilfred (bass)
Ponchielli: Gioconda (Cpte)

ENGEN, Kieth (bass)
Beethoven: Fidelio (Cpte)
Janáček: Excursions of Mr Brouček (Cpte)
Nicolai: Lustigen Weiber von Windsor (Cpte)
Orff: Antigonae (Cpte), Prometheus (Cpte)
(ACAN) **44 2085-2** Carl Orff Collection

ENGERT-ELY, Ruthild (mez)
Prokofiev: Fiery Angel (Cpte)
Tchaikovsky: Eugene Onegin (Cpte)
Wagner: Parsifal (Cpte), Tannhäuser (Cpte), Walküre (Cpte)
(DG) **437 825-2GH** Wagner—Der Ring des Nibelungen - Highlights
(DG) **445 354-2GX14** Wagner—Der Ring des Nibelungen

ENGLISH, Gerald (ten)
Vaughan Williams: Pilgrim's Progress (Cpte)
Walton: Troilus and Cressida (Cpte)

ENGLISH BACH FESTIVAL BAROQUE ORCHESTRA
cond M. CORBOZ
M-A. Charpentier: David et Jonathas (Cpte)
cond C. FARNCOMBE
Rameau: Castor et Pollux (Cpte)

ENGLISH BACH FESTIVAL CHORUS
cond C. FARNCOMBE
Rameau: Castor et Pollux (Cpte)
cond N. MCGEGAN
Rameau: Naïs (Cpte)

ENGLISH BACH FESTIVAL ORCHESTRA
cond N. MCGEGAN
Rameau: Naïs (Cpte)

ENGLISH BAROQUE SOLOISTS
Gay: Beggar's Opera (Cpte)
Monteverdi: Orfeo (Cpte)
Mozart: Così fan tutte (Cpte), Nozze di Figaro (Cpte)
cond J.E. GARDINER
Gluck: Orfeo ed Euridice (Cpte)
Handel: Tamerlano (Cpte)
Mozart: Clemenza di Tito (Cpte), Così fan tutte (exc), Don Giovanni (Cpte), Entführung (Cpte), Idomeneo (Cpte), Nozze di Figaro (Cpte), Thamos, K345 (Cpte)
Purcell: Dido (Cpte), Dioclesian, Z627 (exc), Fairy Queen, Z629 (Cpte), Indian Queen, Z630 (Cpte), King Arthur, Z628 (exc)
(DG) **439 474-2GCL** Purcell—Opera & Choral Works
(ERAT) **2292-45984-2** Monteverdi—Ballet Music
(ERAT) **4509-96371-2** Gardiner—The Purcell Collection
(ERAT) **4509-99713-2** Baroque Works

ENGLISH CHAMBER ORCHESTRA
(SONY) **SMK58936** A Musical Heritage
cond R. ARMSTRONG
(ABMU) **95542** Symphony for the Spire
cond J. BARBIROLLI
Purcell: Dido (Cpte)
(EMI) **CDM5 65341-2** Purcell—Theatre Music
(EMIL) **CDZ7 67253-2** Funeral Music
cond D. BARENBOIM
Cimarosa: Matrimonio segreto (Cpte)
Mozart: Nozze di Figaro (Cpte)
(CFP) **CD-CFP4602** Favourite Opera
(EMI) **CDM7 64359-2** Gala de España
(EMIL) **CDZ7 67015-2** Mozart—Opera Arias
cond S. BEDFORD
Britten: Death in Venice (Cpte), Death in Venice Suite (Cpte)
Holst: Wandering Scholar (Cpte)
(ASV) **CDDCA652** Celebration for Flute & Orchestra
(COLL) **Coll1102-2** Britten & Saxton: Orchestral Works
cond R. BENZI
(PHIL) **416 973-2PM** Jose Carreras sings Musicals
(PHIL) **434 152-2PM** Jose Carreras - Classics
(PHIL) **442 602-2PM** 3 x 3 Tenors
cond R. BONYNGE
Donizetti: Elisir d'amore (Cpte)
(DECC) **417 011-2DH2** Pavarotti's Greatest Hits
(DECC) **425 681-2DM2** Tutto Pavarotti
(DECC) **433 068-2DWO** Your Hundred Best Opera Tunes V
(DECC) **436 313-2DA** Sutherland/Pavarotti—Operatic Duets
(DECC) **440 679-2DH** Carnaval!
(DECC) **443 762-2DF2** The Essential Mozart
(DECC) **444 543-2DF2** Essential Handel
cond B. BRITTEN
Britten: Albert Herring (Cpte), Rape of Lucretia (Cpte)
Purcell: Fairy Queen, Z629 (Cpte)
(DECC) **443 393-2DWO** The World of Henry Purcell
(LOND) **433 200-2LHO2** Britten—Owen Wingrave, etc.
cond P. BRUNELLE
Britten: Paul Bunyan (exc)
cond N. CLEOBURY
(PHIL) **412 231-2PH** Travels with my Cello
cond J.E. DÄHLER
(CLAV) **CD50-8305** Ernst Haefliger sings Mozart Arias
cond G. FISCHER
(EMI) **CDM7 69546-2** Lucia Popp
cond L. HAGER
(NOVA) **150 041-2** Mozart—Overtures
cond J. JUDD
(NOVA) **150 044-2** Classical Masterpieces
cond R. LEPPARD
Handel: Ariodante (Cpte)
Purcell: Dido (Cpte)
(EMI) **CZS7 67425-2** Baroque Passion
(PHIL) **426 450-2PBQ** Handel—Arias
(SONY) **SMK66940** Baroque Music
cond A. LEWIS
Purcell: Dido (Cpte)
(DECC) **436 462-2DM** Ten Top Mezzos
(DECC) **443 393-2DWO** The World of Henry Purcell
cond J. LOCKHART
(RCA) **09026 61635-2** Margaret Price sings Mozart
(RCA) **74321 24284-2** Opera's Greatest Heroines
cond C. MACKERRAS
Purcell: Indian Queen, Z630 (exc)
(NOVA) **150 108-2** Handel—Orchestral Works from Operas and Oratorios
cond N. DEL MAR
(DECC) **436 990-2DWO** The World of Benjamin Britten
cond I. MARIN
Rossini: Signor Bruschino (Cpte)
cond G-F. MASINI
(DECC) **443 380-2DM** Ten Top Baritones & Basses 2
cond A. MELVILLE
Boughton: Immortal Hour (Cpte)
cond Y. MENUHIN
(EMIN) **CD-EMX2227** Holst—Orchestral Works
cond E. RICCI
(ERAT) **4509-95789-2** Zarzuelas-The Passion of Spain
cond J. RUDEL
(EMI) **CDC7 47398-2** Placido Domingo: Vienna, City of My Dreams
(EMI) **CMS7 64309-2** Kálmán—Best-loved Melodies
cond E. STRATTA
(ASV) **CDQS6065** The Mozart Miracle
cond V. SUTEJ
(PHIL) **434 926-2PH** The Pleasure of Love
(PHIL) **434 926-5PH** The Pleasure of Love
cond J. TATE
(EMI) **CDC5 55095-2** Prima Diva
(EMI) **CDC7 47122-2** Mozart: Concert and Operatic Arias
(PHIL) **420 950-2PH** Kiri te Kanawa sings Mozart arias
(PHIL) **434 725-2PM** Kiri Te Kanawa - Classics
cond P. TORTELIER
(VIRG) **VC7 59668-2** French Impressions
(VIRG) **VJ5 61109-2** French Connections
cond M. VIOTTI
Donizetti: Elisir d'amore (Cpte)
Rossini: Inganno felice (Cpte), Occasione fa il ladro (Cpte)
(CLAV) **CD50-9202** Donizetti/Rossini—Tenor Arias
cond A. ZEDDA
(PHIL) **442 602-2PM** 3 x 3 Tenors

ENGLISH CHAMBER ORCHESTRA CHORUS
cond R. LEPPARD
Purcell: Dido (Cpte)

ENGLISH CHORALE
cond M. DODS
(IMP) **PWK1157** Gilbert & Sullivan Spectacular

(THE) ENGLISH CONCERT
cond T. PINNOCK
Purcell: Dioclesian, Z627 (Cpte), King Arthur, Z628 (Cpte)

(THE) ENGLISH CONCERT CHOIR
cond T. PINNOCK
Purcell: Dioclesian, Z627 (Cpte), King Arthur, Z628 (Cpte)

ENGLISH CONCERT CHORUS
cond E. RICCI
(TELD) **4509-96080-6(TELD)** Carreras—A Tribute to Mario Lanza

ENGLISH CONCERT ORCHESTRA
cond R. BONYNGE
(DECC) **421 818-2DH2** Ballet Gala
cond E. DOWNES
(DECC) **436 464-2DM** Ten Top Baritones & Basses

ENGLISH GUITAR QUARTET
(SAYD) **CD-SDL386** Baroque Guitar Quartets
(SAYD) **CD-SDL399** Spanish Guitar Quartets

ENGLISH NATIONAL OPERA CHORUS
cond D. ATHERTON
Britten: Billy Budd (Cpte), Peter Grimes (Cpte)
cond G. BELLINI
Rossini: Barbiere di Siviglia (Cpte)
cond CARL DAVIS
Weill: Street Scene (Cpte)
cond S. EDWARDS
Weir: Blond Eckbert (Cpte)
cond M. ELDER
Britten: Gloriana (Cpte)
Dvořák: Rusalka (Cpte)
Offenbach: Orphée aux enfers (exc)
Verdi: Otello (Cpte)

cond R. GOODALL
Wagner: Götterdämmerung (Cpte)
cond C. MACKERRAS
Donizetti: Maria Stuarda (Cpte)
Handel: Giulio Cesare (Cpte)
Verdi: Traviata (Cpte)
cond PETER ROBINSON
Sullivan: Mikado (exc)

ENGLISH NATIONAL OPERA NORTH CHORUS
cond J. PRYCE-JONES
(MAX) **MSCB3** English Nat Opera North Chorus recital

ENGLISH NATIONAL OPERA ORCHESTRA
Britten: Billy Budd (Cpte), Gloriana (Cpte), Peter Grimes (Cpte)
Donizetti: Maria Stuarda (Cpte)
Dvořák: Rusalka (Cpte)
Handel: Giulio Cesare (Cpte)
cond G. BELLINI
Rossini: Barbiere di Siviglia (Cpte)
cond CARL DAVIS
Weill: Street Scene (Cpte)
cond S. EDWARDS
Weir: Blond Eckbert (Cpte)
cond M. ELDER
Offenbach: Orphée aux enfers (exc)
Verdi: Otello (Cpte)
(TER) **CDVIR8307** Josephine Barstow sings Verdi Arias
cond L. FRIEND
Britten: Rape of Lucretia (Cpte)
cond R. GOODALL
Wagner: Götterdämmerung (Cpte), Rheingold (Cpte), Walküre (Cpte)
cond C. MACKERRAS
Handel: Giulio Cesare (Cpte)
Verdi: Traviata (Cpte)
cond PETER ROBINSON
Sullivan: Mikado (exc)
cond G. SIMON
(CALA) **CACD0106** The London Viola Sound

ENGLISH NORTHERN PHILHARMONIA
cond P. DANIEL
M. Berkeley: Baa Baa Black Sheep (Cpte)
(EMI) **CDC7 54785-2** Harry Enfield's Guide to Opera
cond R. HICKOX
Walton: Troilus and Cressida (Cpte)
cond D. MASSON
Saxton: Caritas (Cpte)
cond M. TIPPETT
(NIMB) **NI5217** Tippett conducts Tippett

ENGLISH OPERA GROUP CHAMBER ORCHESTRA
cond R. GOODALL
(EMI) **CMS7 64727-2** Britten—Opera excerpts and Folksongs

ENGLISH OPERA GROUP CHORUS
cond S. BEDFORD
Britten: Death in Venice (Cpte)
cond B. BRITTEN
Britten: Burning Fiery Furnace (Cpte), Curlew River (Cpte), Prodigal Son (Cpte)

ENGLISH OPERA GROUP ORCHESTRA
cond B. BRITTEN
Britten: Burning Fiery Furnace (Cpte), Curlew River (Cpte), Prodigal Son (Cpte), Turn of the Screw (Cpte)
(KIWI) **CDSLD-82** Southern Voices—NZ International Opera Singers
(LOND) **436 393-2LM** Britten—The Little Sweep, etc
cond N. DEL MAR
Britten: Noye's Fludde (Cpte)

ENGLISH SINFONIA
cond C. GROVES
(IMP) **BOXD9** Essential Mozart—Symphonies and Overtures
(IMP) **PCDS11** English Sinfonia - 30th Anniversary
(IMP) **PCD939** Mozart: Orchestral Works
(IMP) **PCD967** Schubert—Orchestral Works
(IMP) **PCD968** Schubert—Orchestral Works
(IMP) **TCD1014** An Invitation to the Classics
(IMP) **TCD1070** Invitation to the Opera

ENGLISH STRING ORCHESTRA
cond W. BOUGHTON
(NIMB) **NC5008** Elgar: Music for Strings

ENGLISH SYMPHONY ORCHESTRA
cond W. BOUGHTON
(NIMB) **NI5295** Britten—Orchestral Works

ENGLISH TRUMPET VIRTUOSI
(MOSC) **070979** Sound the Trumpets from Shore to Shore

ENNS, Harold (bass)
Verdi: Traviata (Cpte)
(RCA) **GD60205** Opera Choruses

ENOT, Marcel (sngr)
Ganne: Hans (Cpte)
Messager: Monsieur Beaucaire (Cpte)

ENS, Phillip (bass)
Debussy: Pelléas et Mélisande (Cpte)

(ANONYMOUS) ENSEMBLE
J. Moran: Manson Family (Cpte)
(UNIC) **DKPCD9138** Britten/Cole Porter—Blues & Cabaret Songs
cond R. BERNAS
Turnage: Greek (Cpte)

cond R. JACOBS
Cavalli: Xerse (Cpte)
cond P. NAHON
Essyad: Collier des Ruses (Cpte)

ENSEMBLE 415
cond R. JACOBS
Handel: Flavio (Cpte)
(HARM) **HMP390 804** Great Baroque Masters: Handel

EÖTVÖS, Peter (cond)
see Asko Ens
Paris InterContemporain Ens

EPISTEME
cond W.H. CURRY
A. Davis: X (Cpte)

EQUILUZ, Kurt (ten)
Lehár: Giuditta (exc), Lustige Witwe (Cpte), Paganini (exc)
Monteverdi: Orfeo (Cpte), Ritorno d'Ulisse in Patria (Cpte)
Mozart: Idomeneo (Cpte), Nozze di Figaro (Cpte)
R. Strauss: Ariadne auf Naxos (Cpte), Daphne (Cpte), Rosenkavalier (Cpte)
Verdi: Otello (Cpte), Trovatore (Cpte)
Wagner: Tannhäuser (Cpte)
(KOCH) **399 225** Operetta Highlights 3

EQUINOXE
cond D. DONDEYNE
Fauré: Prométhée (Cpte)

ERASSOVA, Natalia (sop)
Rachmaninov: Aleko (Cpte)

ERB, Karl (ten)
(CLUB) **CL99-020** Maria Ivogün & Lotte Schöne—Opera Recital
(PREI) **89094** Maria Ivogün (1891-1987)
(PREI) **89095** Karl Erb (1877-1958)

ERBE, Tom (tape op)
Ashley: Improvement (Cpte)

ERBNER, Fritz (bass)
R. Strauss: Rosenkavalier (Cpte)

ERCOLANI, Renato (ten)
Mozart: Nozze di Figaro (exc)
Ponchielli: Gioconda (Cpte)
Puccini: Fanciulla del West (Cpte), Madama Butterfly (Cpte), Tosca (exc), Turandot (Cpte)
Verdi: Ballo in maschera (Cpte), Falstaff (Cpte), Rigoletto (Cpte), Traviata (Cpte), Trovatore (Cpte)
(BELA) **450 007-2** Puccini Favourites
(DECC) **411 665-2DM3** Puccini: Il trittico
(EMI) **CDC7 49502-2** Maria Callas—The Voice of the Century
(EMI) **CDM7 69543-2** Maria Callas and Giuseppe Di Stefano - Duets

ERDMANN, Hildegard (sop)
Humperdinck: Hänsel und Gretel (Cpte)

EREDE, Alberto (cond)
see BPO
Geneva Grand Th Orch
La Scala Orch
LSO
MMF Orch
New SO
NHK SO
orch
Paris Cons
Paris Op Orch
Philh
RPO
Santa Cecilia Academy Orch
SRO
Vienna St Op Orch
VPO

ERIAN, Nabila (sop)
Mozart: Don Giovanni (Cpte), Nozze di Figaro (Cpte)

ERICKSON, Kaaren (sop)
Gluck: Cinesi (Cpte)
Wagner: Götterdämmerung (Cpte), Parsifal (Cpte), Rheingold (Cpte)
(DG) **072 422-3GH7** Levine conducts Wagner's Ring

ERICKSON, Raymond (hpd)
(ALBA) **TROY127-2** Purcell—From Rosy Bow'rs

ERICSON, Barbro (mez)
Verdi: Rigoletto (Cpte)
Wagner: Walküre (Cpte)
(DG) **435 211-2GX15** Wagner—Der Ring des Nibelungen

ERICSON, Eric (cond)
see Swedish RSO

ERIKSEN, Randi (contr)
Braein: Anne Pedersdotter (Cpte)

ERIKSSON, Birger (bass)
Nørgård: Gilgamesh (Cpte)

ERIKSSON, Marie (hp)
(DANA) **DACOCD306** Mikael Beier plays popular music for Flute and Harp

ERKKILÄ, Eero (ten)
Madetoja: Juha (Cpte)

ERMLER, Mark (cond)
see Bolshoi Th Orch
RPO

ERMOLENKO-YUZHINA, Natalia (sop)
(PEAR) **GEMMCDS9001/3(2)** Singers of Imperial Russia, Vol.2 (pt 2)

ERMOLLI, Francesca Russo (sop)
Traetta: Buovo d'Antona (Cpte)

ERNI, Daniel (gtr)
(ORFE) **C189891A** Music for Two Guitars

ERNST, Hans Bruno (bass)
Handel: Giulio Cesare (Cpte)
Verdi: Traviata (Cpte)
Wagner: Meistersinger (Cpte)

ERNSTER, Deszö (bass)
Mozart: Così fan tutte (Cpte), Don Giovanni (Cpte)
Wagner: Lohengrin (Cpte)

ERNSTER, Judd (bass)
Rorem: Miss Julie (Cpte)

ERNST-SENFF CHAMBER CHORUS
cond R. BUCKLEY
(SCHW) **314052** Opera Gala

ERRANTE, Valerie (sop)
Puccini: Gianni Schicchi (Cpte)
(EURO) **GD69043** Puccini: Il Trittico

ERSHOV, Ivan (ten)
(PEAR) **GEMMCDS9997/9(1)** Singers of Imperial Russia, Vol.1 (pt 1)

ERWEN, Keith (ten)
Verdi: Giovanna d'Arco (Cpte), Lombardi (Cpte), Macbeth (Cpte)
(EMI) **CDM7 69544-2** Berlioz: Vocal Works

ESCALAIS, Léon (ten)
(EMI) **CHS7 64860-2(1)** La Scala Edition - Vol.1, 1878-1914 (pt 1)
(IRCC) **IRCC-CD802** Souvenirs of Rare French Opera
(MSCM) **MM30377** 18 Tenors d'Expression Française
(SYMP) **SYMCD1126** The Harold Wayne Collection, Vol.14
(SYMP) **SYMCD1128** The Harold Wayne Collection, Vol.15

ESCHENBRENNER, Isabelle (sop)
Gluck: Iphigénie en Aulide (Cpte)
(ERAT) **4509-99607-2** Gluck—Operas; Schubert—Symphonies Nos 8 & 9

ESHAM, Faith (sop)
Bizet: Carmen (exc)
Mozart: Nozze di Figaro (Cpte)

ESLOVACA PHILHARMONICA ORCHESTRA
cond K. LEITNER
(IMP) **PCDS21** Music of the World—Danube Dreams

ESPOSITO, Andrée (sop)
Martinů: Julietta (Cpte)

ESPOSITO, Valeria (sop)
Verdi: Rigoletto (Cpte)
(DECC) **436 261-2DHO3** Puccini—Il Trittico
(SCHW) **312682** Opera Gala with Young Artists - Volume II

ESSER, Hermin (ten)
Wagner: Fliegende Holländer (Cpte), Parsifal (Cpte), Rheingold (Cpte)
(PHIL) **446 057-2PB14** Wagner—The Ring Cycle - Bayreuth Festival 1967

ESSEX, Violet (sop)
(SYMP) **SYMCD1123** Sullivan—Sesquicentenial Commemorative Issue

ESSO, Rachel (sop)
Fauré: Prométhée (Cpte)

ESSWOOD, Paul (alto)
Glass: Akhnaten (Cpte)
M-A. Charpentier: David et Jonathas (Cpte)
Monteverdi: Incoronazione di Poppea (Cpte), Ritorno d'Ulisse in Patria (Cpte)
Purcell: Dido (Cpte)
(HYPE) **CDA66070** Purcell: Songs
(SONY) **SK64133** The Essential Philip Glass

ESTEP, Craig (ten)
(EMI) **CDC7 54643-2** Rossini—Bicentenary Gala Concert
(EMI) **LDB491007-1 (EMI)** Rossini Bicentennial Birthday Gala

ESTES, Simon (bass)
Bizet: Carmen (Cpte)
Mozart: Idomeneo (Cpte)
R. Strauss: Salome (Cpte)
Saint-Saëns: Samson et Dalila (Cpte)
Verdi: Don Carlo (Cpte)
Wagner: Fliegende Holländer (Cpte), Parsifal (Cpte)
(EMI) **CDM7 63103-2** Placido Domingo sings Opera Arias
(PHIL) **434 420-2PM32(1)** Richard Wagner Edition (Pt.1)
(SONY) **S2K66836** Goldschmidt—Beatrice Cenci, etc

ESTONIA OPERA CHORUS
cond P. LILJE
Tubin: Barbara von Tisenhusen (Cpte)

ESTONIA OPERA ORCHESTRA
cond E. KLAS
(ONDI) **ODE768-2** Dilbèr sings Coloratura Arias
cond P. LILJE
Tubin: Barbara von Tisenhusen (Cpte)

ESTONIAN SYMPHONY ORCHESTRA
cond E. KLAS
(ONDI) **ODE731-2** Jorma Hynninen sings Opera Arias

ESTOURELLE, Catherine (sop)
Auber: Manon Lescaut (Cpte)
Berg: Lulu (Cpte)

ETCHEVERRY, Henri (bar)
(EMI) **CHS7 61038-2** Debussy—Pelléas et Mélisande, etc

ETCHEVERRY, Jesus (cond)
see FRNO
orch
Paris ORTF Lyric Orch
Paris Sols Orch

ETELÄVUORI, Paula (contr)
Sallinen: Kullervo (Cpte)

ETHERIDGE, Brian (bass)
Massenet: Thaïs (Cpte)

ETTL, Karl (bass)
Verdi: Macbeth (Cpte)
Wagner: Meistersinger (exc), Tristan und Isolde (exc)
(EMI) **CHS7 64487-2** R. Strauss—Der Rosenkavalier & Lieder
(PEAR) **GEMMCDS9365** R. Strauss: Der Rosenkavalier (abridged), etc
(SCHW) **314532** Vienna State Opera Live, Vol.3
(SCHW) **314542** Vienna State Opera Live, Vol.4
(SCHW) **314562** Vienna State Opera Live, Vol.6
(SCHW) **314572** Vienna State Opera Live, Vol.7
(SCHW) **314602** Vienna State Opera Live, Vol.10
(SCHW) **314622** Vienna State Opera Live, Vol.12
(SCHW) **314632** Vienna State Opera Live, Vol.13
(SCHW) **314642** Vienna State Opera Live, Vol.14
(SCHW) **314662** Vienna State Opera Live, Vol.16
(SCHW) **314672** Vienna State Opera Live, Vol.17
(SCHW) **314692** Vienna State Opera Live, Vol.19
(SCHW) **314702** Vienna State Opera Live, Vol.20

EUBA, Wolf (spkr)
K. A. Hartmann: Simplicius Simplicissimus (Cpte)

EUPANI, Silvio (sngr)
Donizetti: Maria di Rudenz (Cpte)

(L')EUROPA GALANTE
cond F. BIONDI
Handel: Poro (Cpte)

EUROPEAN CHAMBER OPERA CHORUS
cond D. HINNELLS
Verdi: Trovatore (Cpte)

EUROPEAN CHAMBER OPERA ORCHESTRA
cond D. HINNELLS
Verdi: Trovatore (Cpte)

EUROPEAN COMMUNITY CHAMBER ORCHESTRA
cond E. AADLAND
(ASV) **CDDCA766** Handel—Works for Soprano and Orchestra

EUSTRATI, Diana (contr)
Mozart: Zauberflöte (Cpte)

EVANGELATOS, Daphne (contr)
Mozart: Zauberflöte (Cpte)
R. Strauss: Elektra (Cpte)
Rossini: Cenerentola (Cpte)
Wagner: Götterdämmerung (Cpte)
(EURO) **GD69003** Wagner—Der Ring des Nibelungen

EVANGELIDES, Petros (ten)
Bizet: Carmen (Cpte)
Monteverdi: Incoronazione di Poppea (Cpte)

EVANS, Anne (sop)
Wagner: Götterdämmerung (exc), Siegfried (exc), Walküre (exc)

EVANS, Beverly (sop)
R. Ward: Crucible (Cpte)

EVANS, Damon (ten)
Gershwin: Porgy and Bess (exc)

EVANS, Edgar (ten)
Britten: Albert Herring (Cpte)
Wagner: Tristan und Isolde (Cpte)

EVANS, Edith (sop)
(SYMP) **SYMCD1123** Sullivan—Sesquicentenial Commemorative Issue

EVANS, Sir Geraint (bar)
Britten: Billy Budd (Cpte), Peter Grimes (Cpte)
Busoni: Arlecchino (Cpte)
Donizetti: Don Pasquale (Cpte)
Mozart: Così fan tutte (Cpte), Don Giovanni (Cpte), Nozze di Figaro (Cpte)
Offenbach: Contes d'Hoffmann (Cpte)
Sullivan: Gondoliers (Cpte), Mikado (Cpte), Yeomen of the Guard (Cpte)
Verdi: Falstaff (Cpte), Forza del destino (Cpte)
Wagner: Meistersinger (Cpte)
(CFP) **CD-CFP4238** Gilbert and Sullivan
(CFP) **CD-CFP4582** Flowers in Music
(CFP) **CD-CFP4609** Favourite Gilbert & Sullivan
(DECC) **433 221-2DWO** The World of Verdi
(DECC) **443 380-2DM** Ten Top Baritones & Basses 2
(MEMO) **HR4223/4** Nicolai Ghiaurov

EVANS, Greek (sngr)
(PEAR) **GEMMCDS9059/61** Music from the New York Stage, Vol. 4: 1917-20

EVANS, Nancy (contr)
(EMI) **CMS7 64727-2** Britten—Opera excerpts and Folksongs
(LOND) **436 393-2LM** Britten—The Little Sweep, etc

EVANS, Rebecca (sop)
Mozart: Nozze di Figaro (Cpte)
Purcell: Dido (Cpte)
Sullivan: HMS Pinafore (Cpte), Pirates of Penzance (Cpte)
Vaughan Williams: Hugh the Drover (Cpte)
Verdi: Rigoletto (Cpte)

EVANS, Robert (bass)
Boughton: Bethlehem (Cpte)
Monteverdi: Orfeo (Cpte)

EVANS, Wynford (ten)
Puccini: Rondine (Cpte)
Purcell: Fairy Queen, Z629 (Cpte)
Vaughan Williams: Hugh the Drover (Cpte), Pilgrim's Progress (Cpte)
Verdi: Trovatore (Cpte)

EVITTS, David (bar)
Mozart: Nozze di Figaro (Cpte)

EVITTS, David (bass)
(MUSM) **67110-2** Stravinsky—The Composer, Volume V

EVSTATIEVA, Stefka (sop)
Borodin: Prince Igor (Cpte)
Mascagni: Cavalleria Rusticana (Cpte)
Tchaikovsky: Queen of Spades (Cpte)

EWER, Graeme (ten)
Donizetti: Lucrezia Borgia (Cpte)
J. Strauss II: Fledermaus (Cpte)
Lehár: Lustige Witwe (Cpte)
(DECC) **071 149-1DH (DECC)** The Essential Sutherland

EWING, Alan (bass)
Puccini: Bohème (Cpte)

EWING, Maria (sop)
Bizet: Carmen (Cpte)
Debussy: Pelléas et Mélisande (Cpte)
Giordano: Andrea Chénier (Cpte)
Monteverdi: Incoronazione di Poppea (Cpte)
Mozart: Don Giovanni (Cpte), Nozze di Figaro (Cpte)
Purcell: Dido (Cpte)
R. Strauss: Salome (Cpte)
Rossini: Barbiere di Siviglia (Cpte)
Shostakovich: Lady Macbeth of Mtsensk (Cpte)
Verdi: Vespri Siciliani (Cpte)
(CAST) **CVI2071** Highlights from Glyndebourne
(EMIL) **CDZ7 67015-2** Mozart—Opera Arias

EYRE, Emily (voc)
M. Monk: Atlas (Cpte)

EYRE, Marjorie (mez)
Sullivan: Mikado (Cpte), Patience (Cpte)
(MMOI) **CDMOIR413** The Very Best of Gilbert & Sullivan

EYRON, Jan (pf)
(BIS) **BIS-CD017** Söderström and Meyer sing Duets

FABBRI, Guerrina (contr)
(SYMP) **SYMCD1065** The Harold Wayne Collection, Vol.1

FABBRICINI, Tiziana (sop)
Verdi: Traviata (Cpte)

FABBRIS, Guido (ten)
Donizetti: Don Pasquale (Cpte)

FABBRY, Ernst (ten)
Mozart: Zauberflöte (Cpte)

FABRITIIS, Oliviero De (cond)
see Bologna Teatro Comunale Orch
La Scala Orch
Livorno Teatro La Gran Guardia Orch
Milan RAI SO
National PO
New Philh
New PO
NHK SO
Rome Op Orch
Rome RAI Orch
Turin RAI Orch

FABRY, Rachel (mez)
Puccini: Gianni Schicchi (Cpte), Suor Angelica (Cpte)

FACINI, Enrico (ten)
Verdi: Trovatore (Cpte)

FACINI, Francesco (bass)
Rossini: Siège de Corinthe (Cpte)

FAGIUS, Hans (organ)
(BIS) **BIS-CD555** Saint-Saëns—Orchestral Works

FAGOTTO, Gianpaolo (ten)
Cavalli: Giasone (Cpte)
Handel: Flavio (Cpte)
Traetta: Buovo d'Antona (Cpte)

FAHBERG, Antonia (sop)
Janáček: Excursions of Mr Brouček (Cpte)
Mozart: Zauberflöte (exc)

FAIREY BAND
cond K. DENNISON
(CHAN) **CHAN6530** Brass Favourites

FAIRHURST, Robin (treb)
(LOND) **436 393-2LM** Britten—The Little Sweep, etc

FALCK, Jorma (ten)
(BIS) **BIS-CD373/4** Opera Scenes from Savaonlinna

FALCON, Bruni (sop)
Wagner: Rheingold (Cpte), Walküre (Cpte)
(FOYE) **15-CF2011** Wagner—Der Ring de Nibelungen

FALCON, Ruth (sop)
Wagner: Götterdämmerung (Cpte), Walküre (exc)
(EURO) **GD69003** Wagner—Der Ring des Nibelungen

FALEWICZ, Magdalena (sop)
Gluck: Orfeo ed Euridice (Cpte)

FALK, Juliana (contr)
Mascagni: Cavalleria Rusticana (Cpte)

FALKENSTEIN, George (pf)
(BIDD) **LAB019** Fritz Kreisler—Early Victors

FALKMAN, Carl-Johan (bar)
Henze: Boulevard Solitude (Cpte)

FALLISI, Guiseppe (sngr)
Rossini: Adelaide di Borgogna (Cpte)

FANCOURT, Darrell (bass)
Sullivan: HMS Pinafore (Cpte), Mikado (Cpte), Patience (Cpte), Sorcerer (Cpte)
(MMOI) **CDMOIR413** The Very Best of Gilbert & Sullivan

FANELLI, Gaetano (ten)
Puccini: Turandot (Cpte)

FANELLI, Maria Luisa (sop)
(PREI) **89072** Aureliano Pertile (1885-1952) - II

FARDILHA, José (bass)
Rossini: Barbiere di Siviglia (Cpte)

FARELL, Marita (sop)
Beethoven: Fidelio (Cpte)

FARIS, Alexander (cond)
see Sadlers Wells Op Orch
Scottish CO

FARKAS, Andor (pseudonym of Andor Foldes) (pf)
(SONY) **MPK52569** Joseph Szigeti Recital

FARKAS, Evá (contr)
Boito: Mefistofele (Cpte)
Giordano: Andrea Chénier (Cpte)

FARKAS, Katalin (sop)
Handel: Floridante (Cpte)

FARLEY, Carole (sop)
Menotti: Telephone (Cpte)
Poulenc: Voix Humaine (Cpte)
R. Strauss: Capriccio (exc), Daphne (exc)
(ASV) **CDDCA790** Weill—Songs
(IMP) **MCD64** Tchaikovsky—Soprano Arias
(IMP) **PCD1055** Tchaikovsky—Glorious Melodies, Volume 1
(IMP) **TCD1070** Invitation to the Opera

FARNCOMBE, Charles (cond)
see English Bach Fest Baroque Orch

FARNETI, Maria (sop)
(CONI) **CDHD235** The Puccini Album
(MEMO) **HR4408/9(1)** Singers in Genoa, Vol.1 (disc 1)

FARNON, Robert (cond)
see orch
R. Farnon Orch

(ROBERT) FARNON ORCHESTRA
cond R. FARNON
(BELA) **450 059-2** Carreras—Memories
(PHIL) **434 152-2PM** Jose Carreras - Classics

FARR, Naomi (sop)
R. Ward: Crucible (Cpte)

FARRAR, Geraldine (sop)
(BIDD) **LAB022** Fritz Kreisler—Duets with McCormack & Farrar
(CLUB) **CL99-060** Enrico Caruso—Opera & Song Recital
(IRCC) **IRCC-CD805** Geraldine Farrar - 60th Anniversary Issue
(MCI) **MCCD086** The Essential Caruso
(NIMB) **NI7834** Caruso in Ensemble
(NIMB) **NI7857** Farrar in Italian Opera
(NIMB) **NI7859** Caruso, Farrar & Journet in French Opera
(NIMB) **NI7872** Geraldine Farrar in French Opera
(PEAR) **EVC1(2)** The Caruso Edition, Vol.1 (pt 2)
(PEAR) **EVC2** The Caruso Edition, Vol.2—1908-12
(PEAR) **EVC3(1)** The Caruso Edition, Vol.3 (pt 1)
(PEAR) **GEMMCDS9160(1)** De Luca Edition, Vol.2 (pt 1)
(PEAR) **GEMMCD9130** Great Sopranos, Vol.2
(PEAR) **GEMMCD9161** Edmond Clément (1867-1928)
(PEAR) **GEMMCD9937** Antonio Scotti
(RCA) **GD60495(2)** The Complete Caruso Collection (pt 2)
(RCA) **GD60495(3)** The Complete Caruso Collection (pt 3)
(RCA) **GD60495(4)** The Complete Caruso Collection (pt 4)

(RCA) **09026 61243-2** Caruso sings Verismo Arias
(RCA) **09026 61244-2** Caruso sings French Opera Arias
(RCA) **09026 61580-2(2)** RCA/Met 100 Singers, 100 Years (pt 2)
(ROMO) **82002-2** Edmond Clément (1867-1928)

FARRELL, Eileen (sop)
(RCA) **GD60686** Wagner—Opera Excerpts
(SONY) **SMK47644** Wagner—Orchestral and Vocal Works

FARRER, John (cond)
see Bournemouth SO

FARRÉS, Pedro (bar)
Penella: Gato Montés (Cpte)
Vives: Bohemios (Cpte)

FARRUGGIA, Michele (ten)
Donizetti: Favorita (Cpte)
Rossini: Adelaide di Borgogna (Cpte), Signor Bruschino (Cpte)

FASANO, Renato (cond)
see Virtuosi di Roma

FASSBAENDER, Brigitte (mez)
Berg: Lulu (Cpte)
Flotow: Martha (Cpte)
Gounod: Faust (Cpte)
J. Strauss II: Fledermaus (exc)
Mozart: Così fan tutte (Cpte), Finta Giardiniera (Cpte), Mitridate (Cpte), Zauberflöte (Cpte)
Pfitzner: Palestrina (Cpte)
Puccini: Manon Lescaut (Cpte)
R. Strauss: Elektra (Cpte), Rosenkavalier (Cpte)
Verdi: Rigoletto (Cpte), Traviata (Cpte), Trovatore (exc)
Wagner: Tristan und Isolde (Cpte), Walküre (Cpte)
(CFP) **CD-CFP4499** Strauss—Champagne and Laughter
(DECC) **414 100-2DM15** Wagner: Der Ring des Nibelungen
(DECC) **421 313-2DA** Wagner: Der Ring des Nibelungen - Great Scenes
(DECC) **430 498-2DWO** The World of Mozart
(DECC) **433 064-2DWO** Your Hundred Best Opera Tunes Volume I
(DECC) **433 066-2DWO** Your Hundred Best Opera Tunes III
(DECC) **433 067-2DWO** Your Hundred Best Opera Tunes IV
(DECC) **433 440-2DA** Golden Opera
(DECC) **436 300-2DX** Opera Gala Sampler
(DECC) **440 069-2DWO** The World of Wagner
(DECC) **440 947-2DH** Essential Opera II
(DECC) **443 335-2LRX** Music for Relaxation, Vol 10 - The Night Before
(HARM) **HMC90 1420** Weill—The Seven Deadly Sins; Songs
(ORFE) **C096841A** Famous Opera Arias
(ORFE) **C394301B** Great Mozart Singers Series, Vol. 3

FASSBENDER, Hedwig (mez)
Schoeck: Venus (Cpte)

FAUCHÉ, François (bass)
Cavalli: Xerse (Cpte)
Rameau: Zoroastre (Cpte)

FAUCHEY, Michel (sngr)
Messager: Coups de Roulis (Cpte)
Offenbach: Madame l'Archiduc (Cpte)
Terrasse: Travaux d'Hercule (Cpte)

FAULHABER, Werner (bass)
Wagner: Meistersinger (Cpte), Parsifal (Cpte)

FAULKNER, Julie (sop)
Mozart: Zauberflöte (Cpte)
R. Strauss: Elektra (Cpte), Rosenkavalier (Cpte)
Rossini: Semiramide (Cpte)
Schumann: Genoveva (Cpte)

FAULL, Ellen (sop)
D. Moore: Carry Nation (Cpte)

FAULSTICH, Gerhard (bar)
Steffani: Henrico Leone (Cpte)

FAURE, Jean Baptiste (bar)
(SYMP) **SYMCD1089** Historic Baritones of the French School

FAURE, Renée (mez)
Offenbach: Contes d'Hoffmann (Cpte)

FAURY, Eric (ten)
Gounod: Sapho (Cpte)

FAVANO, Eugenio (ten)
Rossini: Signor Bruschino (Cpte)

FAVAT, Dominique (mez)
Rossi: Orfeo (Cpte)

FAVERO, Mafalda (sop)
(BONG) **GB1078-2** Mafalda Favero
(EMI) **CDH7 63200-2** Tito Schipa—Recital
(EMI) **CHS7 64864-2(2)** La Scala Edition - Vol.2, 1915-46 (pt 2)
(MEMO) **HR4220/1** Great Voices-Tito Schipa
(MMOI) **CDMOIR412** Great Voices of the Century Sing Puccini
(NIMB) **NI7801** Great Singers, Vol.1
(VAI) **VAIA1071** Mafalda Favero (1903-1981)

FAVRES SOLISTEN VEREINIGUNG
cond T. BEECHAM
Mozart: Zauberflöte (Cpte)

FAYT, Marie-Paul (sop)
Grétry: Caravane du Caire (Cpte)

FEAR, Arthur (bass)
Wagner: Götterdämmerung (exc)
(CLAR) **CDGSE78-50-35/6** Wagner—Historical recordings
(PEAR) **GEMMCDS9137** Wagner—Der Ring des Nibelungen

FECKLER, Heribert (bass)
Hindemith: Neues vom Tage (Cpte)

FEDERICI, Francesco (bar)
(RECO) **TRC3** The Art of Aristodemo Giorgini

FEDERICI, Franco (bass)
Bellini: Puritani (Cpte)
Donizetti: Poliuto (Cpte)
Giordano: Andrea Chénier (Cpte)
Puccini: Gianni Schicchi (Cpte), Manon Lescaut (Cpte), Tosca (Cpte)
(EURO) **GD69043** Puccini: Il Trittico

FEDIN, Alexander (ten)
Mussorgsky: Boris Godunov (Cpte)
Rimsky-Korsakov: Mozart and Salieri (Cpte)

FEDOSEYEV, Andrei (bar)
Tchaikovsky: Queen of Spades (Cpte)

FEDOSEYEV, Vladimir (cond)
see Moscow RSO
USSR RSO

FEDOTOV, Yevgeny (bass)
Mussorgsky: Boris Godunov (Cpte), Khovanshchina (Cpte)

FEHENBERGER, Lorenz (ten)
Janáček: Excursions of Mr Brouček (Cpte)
R. Strauss: Salome (Cpte)
(EMI) **CZS7 67123-2** Wagner: Der Ring des Nibelungen

FEHN, Helmut (bass)
Wagner: Meistersinger (Cpte)

FEHRING, Johannes (cond)
see SO

FEIGHAN, Thérèse (sop)
Rameau: Hippolyte et Aricie (Cpte)

FEILHABER, Alfred (ten)
S. Wagner: Bärenhäuter (Cpte)

FEINHALS, Elise (mez)
(SYMP) **SYMCD1113** The Harold Wayne Collection, Vol.13

FEINSTEIN, Michael (bar)
(EMI) **EG749768-2** Cabaret Songs—Michael Finstein

FEKETE, Zoltán (cond)
see Prague SO

FELBERMAYER, Anny (sop)
Humperdinck: Hänsel und Gretel (Cpte)
Mozart: Nozze di Figaro (Cpte)
R. Strauss: Ariadne auf Naxos (Cpte), Elektra (Cpte), Rosenkavalier (Cpte)
(EMI) **CDH7 61001-2** R. Strauss—Lieder & Arias

FELDEN, Wilhelm (bass)
Mozart: Nozze di Figaro (Cpte)
Wagner: Meistersinger (Cpte)

FELDER, Linda (sop)
Bazin: Maître Pathelin (Cpte)

FELDHOFF, Gerd (bass)
Berg: Lulu (Cpte)
Hindemith: Mathis der Maler (Cpte)
Wagner: Meistersinger (Cpte)

FELDHOFF, Heinz (bass)
Wagner: Meistersinger (Cpte), Tannhäuser (Cpte)

FELDMAN, Jill (sop)
Cavalli: Xerse (Cpte)
Cesti: Orontea (Cpte)
M-A. Charpentier: Actéon (Cpte), Arts Florissants (Cpte), Médée (Cpte)
Mozart: Ascanio in Alba (Cpte)
Purcell: Dido (Cpte)
(ARCA) **A02** Purcell—Ayres and Songs from Orpheus Britannicus
(HARM) **HMX290 1528/33(1)** A Purcell Companion (pt 1)
(LINN) **CKD005** Udite Amanti—17th Century Italian Love Songs

FELINAU, Pelz von (narr)
Lehár: Zarewitsch (exc)

FÉLIX, Thierry (bar)
A. Thomas: Hamlet (Cpte)

FELLE, Amelia (sop)
Pergolesi: Frate 'nnamorato (Cpte)
Rossini: Barbiere di Siviglia (Cpte), Guillaume Tell (exc), Inganno felice (Cpte), Signor Bruschino (Cpte)

FELLER, Carlos (bass)
Mozart: Così fan tutte (Cpte), Nozze di Figaro (Cpte)
R. Strauss: Rosenkavalier (Cpte)
Rossini: Signor Bruschino (Cpte)
Weill: Sieben Todsünden (Cpte)

FELTSMAN, Vladimir (pf)
(SONY) **SMK64243** Prokofiev—Orchestral & Piano Works

FELTY, Janice (mez)
Glass: Belle et la Bête (Cpte)
Machover: Valis (Cpte)

FELUMB, Sven (cond)
see Tivoli Concert Orch

FENBY, Eric (cond)
see RPO

FENNELL, Frederick (cond)
see Eastman Wind Ens

FENOYER, Marinette (mez)
Massenet: Manon (Cpte)

FÉRALDY, Germaine (sop)
Gluck: Orphée (Cpte)
Massenet: Manon (exc), Werther (Cpte)
(EMI) **CDM7 69548-2** Georges Thill sings French Opera Arias
(IRCC) **IRCC-CD802** Souvenirs of Rare French Opera
(MSCM) **MM30221** 18 French Divas

FERENC, Tibor (cond)
see Hungarian Nat PO

FERGUSON, Robert (ten)
Wagner: Rheingold (Cpte)

FERNANDEZ, Ana Maria (sngr)
Sorozábal: Katiuska (Cpte)

FERNANDEZ, Anita (sngr)
Bretón: Verbena de la Paloma (Cpte)
Moreno Torroba: Luisa Fernanda (Cpte)

FERNANDI, Eugenio (ten)
Puccini: Turandot (Cpte)
Verdi: Don Carlo (Cpte)

FERRANI, Cesira (sop)
(MEMO) **HR4408/9(1)** Singers in Genoa, Vol.1 (disc 1)
(MSCM) **MM30276** Rossini—Barbiere di Siviglia, etc
(SYMP) **SYMCD1077** The Harold Wayne Collection, Vol.4

FERRANTI, Nick (sngr)
Bernstein: West Side Story (Cpte)

FERRARA, Mario (ten)
Donizetti: Lucia di Lammermoor (Cpte)
Puccini: Madama Butterfly (Cpte), Tosca (Cpte)

FERRARI, Renza (sop)
Puccini: Gianni Schicchi (Cpte)

FERRARI, Riccardo (bass)
Verdi: Aida (Cpte)

FERRARI-FONTANA, Edoardo (ten)
(EMI) **CHS7 64860-2(2)** La Scala Edition - Vol.1, 1878-1914 (pt 2)

FERRARINI, Alida (sop)
Verdi: Rigoletto (Cpte)

FERRARIS, Franco (cond)
see Orch
Rome Op Orch

FERRARIS, Ines Maria (sop)
(CLUB) **CL99-074** Conchita Supervia (1895-1936)
(EMI) **CHS7 64864-2(1)** La Scala Edition - Vol.2, 1915-46 (pt 1)
(PREI) **89023** Conchita Supervia (1895-1936)
(PREI) **89055** Cesare Formichi (1883-1949)

FERRARO, Pier Miranda (ten)
Bellini: Pirata (Cpte)
Ponchielli: Gioconda (Cpte)

FERRAS, Christian (vn)
(BELA) **461 003-2** Romantic Violin
(EMIL) **CDZ114** Best of Baroque

FERRETTI, Elio (ten)
(SCHW) **314052** Opera Gala

FERRIER, Kathleen (contr)
Gluck: Orfeo ed Euridice (exc)
(DECC) **430 096-2DWO** The World of Kathleen Ferrier
(DECC) **433 470-2DM** Ferrier Edition - Volume 3
(DECC) **433 473-2DM** Ferrier Edition - Volume 6
(EMI) **CDH7 61003-2** Kathleen Ferrier sings Opera and Songs

FERRIN, Agostino (bass)
Boito: Nerone (Cpte)
Donizetti: Lucia di Lammermoor (Cpte)
Meyerbeer: Africaine (Cpte)
Verdi: Rigoletto (Cpte)
(BUTT) **BMCD015** Pavarotti Collection - Duets and Scenes
(EMI) **CDM5 65575-2** Montserrat Caballé
(EMI) **CDM7 63104-2** Alfredo Krauss - Opera Recital
(EMI) **CDM7 69500-2** Montserrat Caballé sings Bellini & Verdi Arias

FERRIN, Gaetano (bass)
Bellini: Capuleti (Cpte)
(RCA) **09026 68014-2** Pavarotti - The Early Years, Vol.2

FERRO, Gabriele (cond)
see Bologna Teatro Comunale Orch
Cappella Coloniensis
Lyon Op Orch
Munich RO
WNO Orch

FERRO, Leonardo del (ten)
Donizetti: Lucia di Lammermoor (exc)

FERRONI, Maria Gabriella (sop)
(EURO) **GD69043** Puccini: Il Trittico

FEUERMANN, Emanuel (vc)
(PEAR) **GEMMCD9442** Feuermann—The Columbia Records, Vol.1
(PEAR) **GEMMCD9443** Feuermann—The Columbia Records, Vol.2

FEUGE, Emilie (sop)
(SYMP) **SYMCD1081** The Harold Wayne Collection, Vol.5

FEYBLI, Walter (gtr)
(ORFE) **C189891A** Music for Two Guitars

FIDELIO ENSEMBLE
(GALL) **CD-674** Fidelio Ensemble play Bizet, Gounod & D'Indy

FIDLEROVÁ, Miloslava (sop)
Smetana: Brandenburgers in Bohemia (Cpte)

FIEDLER, Arthur (cond)
see Boston Pops Orch

FIEDLER, Hans Herbert (bar)
Mozart: Nozze di Figaro (Cpte)

FIEHL, Horst (bar)
Schreker: Ferne Klang (Cpte)

FIELD, Helen (sop)
Boughton: Bethlehem (Cpte)
Delius: Village Romeo and Juliet (Cpte)
Janáček: Fate (Cpte)
Martinů: Greek Passion (Cpte)
(EMI) **CDC7 49849-2** Famous Opera Choruses
(KOCH) **34036-2** A Pageant of Opera
(NIMB) **NI5123** Baroque Arias for Soprano and Trumpet
(TELD) **9031-76372-6(TELD)** Tchaikovsky —Women and Fate

FIELD, Margaret (sop)
(CALA) **CACD1011** Borodin—Orchestral Works

FIELD, Pamela (sop)
(LOND) **436 816-2LM2** Sullivan—Utopia Ltd. Macbeth & Marmion Ovs etc

FIELDSEND, David (ten)
J. Strauss II: Fledermaus (Cpte)
Offenbach: Orphée aux enfers (Cpte)
Sullivan: Gondoliers (Cpte), Yeomen of the Guard (Cpte)

FIESOLE SCHOOL OF MUSIC FEMALE CHORUS
cond M. ARENA
(ACAN) **43 540** Opera Choruses

FIGNER, Nicolai (ten)
(PEAR) **GEMMCDS9997/9(1)** Singers of Imperial Russia, Vol.1 (pt 1)

FILABER, Rev Andrzej (cond)
see Warsaw Cath Ch

FILATOVA, Ludmila (mez)
Mussorgsky: Boris Godunov (Cpte)
Tchaikovsky: Queen of Spades (Cpte)

FILENE CENTER ORCHESTRA
Verdi: Traviata (Cpte)

FILIMONIVA, Tatiana (sop)
Tchaikovsky: Queen of Spades (Cpte)

FILIPPESCHI, Mario (ten)
Bellini: Norma (Cpte)
Rossini: Mosè (Cpte)
Verdi: Don Carlo (Cpte), Rigoletto (Cpte)
(EMI) **CMS7 63244-2** The Art of Maria Callas

FILM SYMPHONY ORCHESTRA
cond Š. KONÍČEK
(SUPR) **11 1865-2** Alois Hába—Centenary

FINCHLEY CHILDREN'S MUSIC GROUP
cond B. BARTOLETTI
Ponchielli: Gioconda (Cpte)
cond R. BONYNGE
Massenet: Esclarmonde (Cpte)
cond L. GARDELLI
Verdi: Attila (Cpte)
cond P. LEDGER
Britten: Little Sweep (Cpte)
cond G. PATANÈ
Leoncavallo: Pagliacci (exc)

FINDLAY, Jane (sop)
Handel: Tamerlano (Cpte)

FINDLEY, Margaret (mez)
(KIWI) **CDTRL075** Malvina Major—Opera Recital

FINE, Wendy (sop)
Wagner: Parsifal (Cpte)

FINE ARTS BRASS ENSEMBLE
cond M. SHEPHERD
(BIRM) **BBCCD2** There shall a star

FINEL, Paul (ten)
Poulenc: Dialogues des Carmélites (Cpte)

FINESCHI, Onelia (sop)
Leoncavallo: Pagliacci (Cpte)

FINK, Bernarda (contr)
Handel: Amadigi di Gaula (Cpte), Flavio (Cpte), Giulio Cesare (Cpte), Poro (Cpte)
Monteverdi: Orfeo (Cpte)
Rameau: Hippolyte et Aricie (Cpte)
Rossini: Zelmira (Cpte)

FINK, Walter (bass)
Wagner: Rheingold (Cpte)

FINKE, Martin (ten)
Lehár: Giuditta (Cpte)
Millöcker: Gasparone (Cpte)
R. Strauss: Ariadne auf Naxos (Cpte), Intermezzo (Cpte)

FINLEY, Gerald (bar)
Britten: Death in Venice (Cpte)
Maxwell Davies: Resurrection (Cpte)
Mozart: Don Giovanni (Cpte)
Purcell: King Arthur, Z628 (Cpte)
(CHAN) **CHAN8865** Rossini: Opera Arias

FINNIE, Linda (mez)
Puccini: Rondine (Cpte)
Ravel: Enfant et les sortilèges (Cpte)
Tchaikovsky: Eugene Onegin (Cpte)
Wagner: Götterdämmerung (exc), Rheingold (Cpte), Walküre (Cpte)
(CHAN) **CHAN9392** Vaughan Williams—Riders to the Sea etc.

FINNILÄ, Birgit (mez)
Mozart: Nozze di Figaro (Cpte)
Shostakovich: Lady Macbeth of Mtsensk (Cpte)
Wagner: Parsifal (Cpte)

FINNISH CHAMBER CHOIR
cond O. POHJOLA
Kortekangas: Grand Hotel

FINNISH NATIONAL OPERA CHORUS
cond F. MANCHUROV
Rautavaara: Vincent (Cpte)
cond U. SÖDERBLOM
Sallinen: Kullervo (Cpte)

FINNISH NATIONAL OPERA ORCHESTRA
cond F. MANCHUROV
Rautavaara: Vincent (Cpte)
cond U. SÖDERBLOM
Bergman: Singing Tree (Cpte)
Sallinen: Kullervo (Cpte)

FINNISH RADIO SYMPHONY ORCHESTRA
cond J. JALAS
Madetoja: Juha (Cpte)
cond J-P. SARASTE
(FINL) **4509-96867-2** Madetoja—Orchestral Works

FINNISH RADIO YOUTH CHOIR
cond J. JALAS
Madetoja: Juha (Cpte)

FINZI-MAGRINI, Giuseppina (sop)
(EMI) **CHS7 64860-2(2)** La Scala Edition - Vol.1, 1878-1914 (pt 2)

FIORAVANTI, Giulio (bar)
Cilea: Adriana Lecouvreur (Cpte)
Puccini: Manon Lescaut (Cpte)

FIORE, John (cond)
see Munich RSO

FIORENTINI, Mirella (mez)
Verdi: Aida (Cpte), Rigoletto (Cpte)

FIORENTINO, Mirelle (sop)
Verdi: Traviata (Cpte)

FIORI, Maria (sop)
Verdi: Rigoletto (Cpte)

FIORI MUSICALI
(MERI) **CDE84195** Vivaldi: Orchestral and Vocal Works
cond T. ALBERT
Keiser: Masagniello furioso (Cpte)

(THE) FIRES OF LONDON
cond P. MAXWELL DAVIES
Maxwell Davies: Miss Donnithorne's Maggot

FISCHER, Adám (cond)
see Austro-Hungarian Haydn Orch
Hungarian St Orch
Hungarian St SO
Vienna St Op Orch

FISCHER, Andreas (treb)
Mozart: Zauberflöte (Cpte)

FISCHER, Else (sop)
Wagner: Götterdämmerung (Cpte)

FISCHER, György (cond)
see ECO
Vienna CO

FISCHER, György (pf)
(DECC) **436 267-2DH** Arie Antiche—Bartoli
(DECC) **071 141-1DH (DECC)** Cecilia Bartoli - A Portrait

FISCHER, Hanne (mez)
Delius: Village Romeo and Juliet (Cpte)

FISCHER, Res (contr)
Mozart: Nozze di Figaro (Cpte)
Wagner: Fliegende Holländer (Cpte)
(ORFE) **C394101B** Great Mozart Singers Series, Vol. 1
(SCHW) **314722** Vienna State Opera Live, Vol.22

FISCHER, Susanne (contr)
(PREI) **89082** Margarete Klose (1902-1968)

FISCHER, Thomas (ten)
Weill: Jasager (Cpte)

FISCHER-DIESKAU, Dietrich (cond)
see Bavarian St Orch

FISCHER-DIESKAU, Dietrich (bar)
Beethoven: Fidelio (exc)
Berg: Lulu (Cpte), Wozzeck (Cpte)
Busoni: Doktor Faust (Cpte)
Cimarosa: Matrimonio segreto (Cpte)
Gluck: Iphigénie en Tauride (Cpte), Orfeo ed Euridice (Cpte)
Hindemith: Cardillac (Cpte), Mathis der Maler (exc)
Humperdinck: Hänsel und Gretel (Cpte)
Mozart: Così fan tutte (Cpte), Don Giovanni (Cpte), Nozze di Figaro (Cpte), Oca del Cairo (Cpte), Zauberflöte (exc)
Pfitzner: Palestrina (Cpte)
Puccini: Tosca (Cpte)
R. Strauss: Arabella (Cpte), Ariadne auf Naxos (Cpte), Capriccio (Cpte), Elektra (Cpte), Intermezzo (Cpte), Salome (Cpte)
Spohr: Jessonda (Cpte)
Spontini: Olimpie (Cpte)
Verdi: Macbeth (Cpte), Otello (Cpte), Rigoletto (Cpte), Traviata (Cpte)
Wagner: Fliegende Holländer (Cpte), Götterdämmerung (Cpte), Lohengrin (Cpte), Meistersinger (exc), Parsifal (Cpte), Rheingold (Cpte), Tannhäuser (Cpte), Tristan und Isolde (Cpte)
Wolf: Corregidor (Cpte)
(BELA) **450 121-2** Plácido Domingo
(CASC) **VEL2001** Martin—Orchestral Works
(CFP) **CD-CFP4499** Strauss—Champagne and Laughter
(DECC) **414 100-2DM15** Wagner: Der Ring des Nibelungen
(DECC) **433 069-2DWO** Your Hundred Best Opera Tunes VI
(DECC) **433 442-2DA** Verdi—Famous Arias
(DECC) **436 315-2DA** Great Operatic Duets
(DECC) **436 464-2DM** Ten Top Baritones & Basses
(DECC) **440 409-2DM** Dietrich Fischer-Dieskau
(DG) **429 168-2GR** Wagner: Excerpts from Der Ring
(DG) **431 104-2GB** Great Voices - Plácido Domingo
(DG) **435 211-2GX15** Wagner—Der Ring des Nibelungen
(DG) **437 677-2GDO2** Irmgard Seefried - Opera Recital
(DG) **439 423-2GCL** Wagner—Der Ring des Nibelungen (highlights)
(DG) **445 400-2GDO10** Ferenc Fricsay - A Portrait
(EMI) **CMS5 65061-2(2)** The Fabulous Victoria de los Angeles (pt 2)
(EMI) **CMS5 65212-2** Wagner—Les introuvables du Ring
(EMI) **CMS5 65621-2** Fischer-Dieskau - The Opera Singer
(ORFE) **C028821A** Famous Operatic Duets
(ORFE) **C335931A** Salzburg Festival highlights (1956-85)
(ORFE) **C394201B** Great Mozart Singers Series, Vol. 2

FISCHER-DIESKAU, Manuel (vc)
(MARC) **8 223369** Humperdinck—Orchestral Works

FISCHER-SANDT, Siegfried (ten)
Puccini: Tosca (Cpte)

FISEISKY, Alexei (organ)
(ETCE) **KTC2019** 200 years of Russian Music for Organ

FISELIER, Frans (ten)
R. Strauss: Rosenkavalier (Cpte)

FISH, Matthew Adam (treb)
Mussorgsky: Boris Godunov (Cpte)

FISHER, Gillian (sop)
Purcell: Dioclesian, Z627 (exc), Fairy Queen, Z629 (Cpte), Indian Queen, Z630 (Cpte), King Arthur, Z628 (exc)
Rameau: Castor et Pollux (Cpte)
(ERAT) **4509-96371-2** Gardiner—The Purcell Collection
(HYPE) **KING2** Essential Purcell
(IMP) **PCDS19** Music of the World - This Sceptred Isle
(IMP) **PCD894** Great Baroque Arias, Part I

FISHER, John (cond)
see Venice La Fenice Orch

FISHER, Sylvia (sop)
Britten: Albert Herring (Cpte)
(LOND) **433 200-2LHO2** Britten—Owen Wingrave, etc.

FISICHELLA, Salvatore (ten)
Rossini: Mosè in Egitto (Cpte), Otello (Cpte)
(MCI) **MCCD099** Opera's Greatest Arias

FISSORE, Enrico (bar)
Donizetti: Gianni di Parigi (Cpte)
Monteverdi: Incoronazione di Poppea (Cpte)

Puccini: Bohème (Cpte), Fanciulla del West (Cpte), Manon Lescaut (Cpte)
Verdi: Rigoletto (Cpte)
(EMI) **CDC7 49502-2** Maria Callas—The Voice of the Century
(EMI) **CDC7 54016-2** Tenorissimo!
(EMI) **CDM7 69543-2** Maria Callas and Giuseppe Di Stefano - Duets
(EMI) **CMS7 63244-2** The Art of Maria Callas

FORTUNA, Maria (sop)
(EMI) **CDC7 54643-2** Rossini—Bicentenary Gala Concert
(EMI) **LDB491007-1 (EMI)** Rossini Bicentennial Birthday Gala

FORTUNATO, D'Anna (contr)
Handel: Imeneo (Cpte), Siroe, Rè di Persia (Cpte), Sosarme (Cpte)
V. Thomson: Lord Byron (Cpte)
(NEWP) **NPD85540** Handel/Bononcini—Muzio Scevola
(NEWP) **NPD85595** Haydn—La canterina

FORTUNATO, Scilly (sop)
(CBS) **CD79312** Puccini: Il Trittico

FORTUNE, George (bass)
Spontini: Olimpie (Cpte)

FORUM OPERA CHORUS
cond G. BELLINI
(EURM) **350214** Verdi—Sinfonie & Cori

FORUM PHILHARMONIC ORCHESTRA
cond G. BELLINI
(EURM) **350214** Verdi—Sinfonie & Cori

FOSTER, Lawrence (cond)
see *Abbey Road Ens*
Lyon Op Orch
Monte Carlo PO
Philh
ROHO

FOSTER, Nancy (sop)
R. Ward: Crucible (Cpte)

FOSTER, Norman (bass)
Verdi: Don Carlo (Cpte)

FOSTER-JENKINS, Florence (sop)
(RCA) **GD61175** The Glory of the Human Voice-Florence Foster Jenkins

FOTI, Clara (mez)
Donizetti: Elisabetta (Cpte)
Rossini: Italiana in Algeri (Cpte)

FOUCHÉCOURT, Jean-Paul (ten)
Campra: Idoménée (Cpte)
Debussy: Rodrigue et Chimène (Cpte)
Lully: Atys (Cpte), Phaëton (Cpte)
M-A. Charpentier: David et Jonathas (Cpte)
Marais: Alcyone (Cpte)
Mondonville: Titon et l'Aurore (Cpte)
Mouret: Amours de Ragonde (Cpte)
Purcell: Dido (Cpte), Fairy Queen, Z629 (Cpte)
Rameau: Hippolyte et Aricie (Cpte), Indes galantes (Cpte)
Rossi: Orfeo (Cpte)
(HARM) **HMP390 805** Great Baroque Masters—Lully
(HARM) **HMP390 807** Great Baroque Masters—Purcell

FOUCHER, Patrick (ten)
Auber: Gustav III (Cpte)
Montéclair: Jephté (Cpte)

FOURCADE, Philippe (bass)
Gounod: Faust (Cpte)

FOURESTIER, Louis (cond)
see *Paris Op Orch*
Paris Opéra-Comique Orch

FOURNET, Anne (narr)
Stravinsky: Perséphone (Cpte)

FOURNET, Jean (cond)
see *Lamoureux Concerts Orch*
Lamoureux Orch

FOURNIER, Brigitte (sop)
Gluck: Orphée (Cpte)
Poulenc: Dialogues des Carmélites (Cpte)
Prokofiev: Love for 3 Oranges (Cpte)

FOURNIER, Pierre (vc)
(DG) **447 349-2GDB2** Homage to Pierre Fournier

FOURNILLIER, Patrick (cond)
see *Budapest F. Liszt SO*
Budapest Liszt SO
Paris Op Orch
Picardy Regional Orch
Saint-Étienne Nouvel Orch

FOURRIER, Janine (sop)
Poulenc: Dialogues des Carmélites (Cpte)

FOWLER, Bruce (ten)
Rossini: Armida (Cpte)

FOX, Frank (cond)
see *Berlin SO*

FOX, Virgil (organ)
(EMI) **CDM5 65426-2** The Art of Virgil Fox

FRACKER, Richard (ten)
Glass: Hydrogen Jukebox (Cpte)

FRANC, Tugomir (bass)
R. Strauss: Elektra (Cpte)

(DECC) **436 315-2DA** Great Operatic Duets

(MARTINA) FRANCA FESTIVAL ORCHESTRA
cond A. ZEDDA
Rossini: Adelaide di Borgogna (Cpte)

FRANCEK, Josef (cond)
see *VJSO*

FRANCESCHETTO, Romano (sngr)
Paisiello: Don Chisciotte (Cpte)

FRANCI, Benvenuto (bar)
(BONG) **GB1064/5-2** Fernando de Lucia
(CLUB) **CL99-014** Dino Borgioli (1891-1960)
(EMI) **CHS7 64864-2(1)** La Scala Edition - Vol.2, 1915-46 (pt 1)
(PEAR) **GEMMCDS9925(2)** Covent Garden on Record—Vol.3 (pt 2)
(PREI) **89007** Aureliano Pertile (1885-1952) - I
(PREI) **89995** Famous Italian Baritones

FRANCI, Carlo (cond)
see *Naples RAI Orch*
Naples San Carlo Op Orch
Santa Cecilia Academy Orch
Turin RAI Orch
Venice La Fenice Orch

FRANCI, Francesca (mez)
Donizetti: Maria di Rohan (Cpte)
Verdi: Rigoletto (Cpte)

FRANCIS, Alun (cond)
see *LMP*
LSO
New Philh
RPO

FRANCIS, Hannah (sop)
Rossini: Tancredi (Cpte)

FRANCIS, Jeffrey (ten)
Rossini: Armida (Cpte)

FRANCK, Hannerle (sop)
Mozart: Nozze di Figaro (Cpte)

FRANCK, Joseph (ten)
Mussorgsky: Boris Godunov (Cpte)
R. Strauss: Ariadne auf Naxos (Cpte)

FRANCK, Walter (spkr)
Mozart: Entführung (Cpte)

FRANCO, Loretta di (sop)
Rossini: Barbiere di Siviglia (Cpte)
Verdi: Traviata (Cpte), Trovatore (Cpte)

FRANCO, Olga de (contr)
Mascagni: Cavalleria rusticana (Cpte)

FRANCO, Olga De (mez)
Verdi: Traviata (Cpte)

FRANDSEN, Birgit Louise (sop)
Mozart: Zauberflöte (Cpte)

FRANDSEN, John (cond)
see *Danish RSO*

FRANK, Susan Storey (sop)
(CENT) **CRC2084** Music from Cranberry Isles

FRANKE, Paul (ten)
Leoncavallo: Pagliacci (Cpte)
Verdi: Trovatore (Cpte)

FRANKFURT OPERA ORCHESTRA
cond G. BERTINI
(WERG) **WER6173-2** T.W.Adorno—Chamber & Choral Works

FRANKFURT RADIO SYMPHONY ORCHESTRA
cond G. ALBRECHT
Zemlinsky: Traumgörge (Cpte)
cond E. INBAL
Bartók: Duke Bluebeard's castle (Cpte)
Wagner: Tristan und Isolde (exc)
(TELD) **4509-94530-2** Virtuoso Orchestra
cond M. VIOTTI
Franchetti: Cristoforo Colombo (Cpte)
Giordano: Andrea Chénier (Cpte)
Puccini: Fanciulla del West (Cpte)

FRANKLIN, David (bass)
Mozart: Don Giovanni (Cpte)

FRANKS, Dobbs (cond)
see *Tasmanian SO*

FRANSSON, Göran (ten)
R. Strauss: Arabella (Cpte)

FRANTER, Willy (ten)
Verdi: Macbeth (Cpte)
Wagner: Tristan und Isolde (exc)
(SCHW) **314652** Vienna State Opera Live, Vol.15
(SCHW) **314672** Vienna State Opera Live, Vol.17
(SCHW) **314692** Vienna State Opera Live, Vol.19
(SCHW) **314712** Vienna State Opera Live, Vol.21

FRANTZ, Ferdinand (bass-bar)
Wagner: Meistersinger (Cpte), Tristan und Isolde (Cpte), Walküre (Cpte)
(EMI) **CMS5 65212-2** Wagner—Les introuvables du Ring
(EMI) **CZS7 67123-2** Wagner: Der Ring des Nibelungen

FRANZ, Paul (ten)
(PEAR) **GEMMCDS9925(1)** Covent Garden on Record—Vol.3 (pt 1)
(PREI) **89099** Paul Franz (1876-1950)

FRANZ LISZT SYMPHONY ORCHESTRA, BUDAPEST
cond P. FOURNILLIER
Massenet: Grisélidis (Cpte)

FRANZEN, Hans (bass)
Monteverdi: Orfeo (Cpte)
Mozart: Zauberflöte (Cpte)
R. Strauss: Frau ohne Schatten (Cpte)
Weill: Mahagonny (Cpte), Mahagonny-Gesänge (Cpte), Zar lässt sich Photographieren (Cpte)
Zemlinsky: Kleider machen Leute (Cpte)

FRASCANI, Nini (mez)
(BONG) **GB1076-2** Mario Gilion - Opera Arias
(PEAR) **GEMMCDS9073(1)** Giovanni Zenatello, Vol.1 (pt 1)
(SYMP) **SYMCD1138** The Harold Wayne Collection, Vol.16

FRASCATI, Tommaso (ten)
Massenet: Don Quichotte (Cpte)
Puccini: Turandot (Cpte)
Verdi: Rigoletto (Cpte)
(RCA) **GD87799** The Pearl Fishers Duet plus Duets and Scenes

FRASER, Andrew (ten)
Vaughan Williams: Pilgrim's Progress (Cpte)

FRASS, Dorothea (mez)
R. Strauss: Salome (Cpte)

FRATE, Ines de (sop)
(MEMO) **HR4408/9(1)** Singers in Genoa, Vol.1 (disc 1)

FRATI, Augusto (ten)
Mascagni: Piccolo Marat (Cpte)

FREDERICKS, Richard (bar)
Verdi: Traviata (Cpte)

FREDMAN, Myer (cond)
see *NZ SO*

FREDONIA CHAMBER SINGERS
cond W. GUNDLACH
Weill: Down in the Valley (Cpte), Jasager (Cpte)

FREDRICKS, Helena (sngr)
(PEAR) **GEMMCDS9050/2(1)** Music from the New York Stage, Vol. 1 (part 1)

FREDRICKS, Olive (sop)
Ligeti: Grand Macabre (Cpte)
Verdi: Rigoletto (Cpte)
Zemlinsky: Geburtstag der Infantin (Cpte)
(ADES) **14122-2** Music of our Time

FREDRIKSSON, Karl-Magnus (bar)
Lehár: Lustige Witwe (Cpte)

FREEMAN, Carroll (ten)
Mozart: Don Giovanni (Cpte)

FREEMAN, Colenton (ten)
Gershwin: Porgy and Bess (Cpte)

FREIBURG BAROQUE ORCHESTRA
Handel: Radamisto (Cpte)
cond G. VON DER GOLTZ
(DHM) **05472 77295-2** Handel/Purcell—Works
cond T. HENGELBROCK
(DHM) **RD77231** Purcell—Instrumental Music
(DHM) **05472 77289-2** Bach/Vivaldi—Orchestral Works
cond N. MCGEGAN
Handel: Giustino (Cpte), Ottone (Cpte)

FREIBURG SOLOISTS CHOIR
cond C. ABBADO
(SONY) **SK53978** Prometheus
cond I. METZMACHER
Nono: Prometeo (Cpte)

FREITAS BRANCO, Pedro de (cond)
see *Madrid Concerts Orch*

FRELLESVIG, Anne (sngr)
Kuhlau: Lulu (Cpte)
Nørgård: Siddhartha (Cpte)

FRÉMAUX, Louis (cond)
see *CBSO*
Monte Carlo Nat Op Orch

FRÉMEAU, Jean-Marie (bar)
Gounod: Roméo et Juliette (Cpte)
Massenet: Don Quichotte (Cpte), Manon (Cpte)
(EMI) **CDS7 49361-2** Offenbach: Operettas

FRÉMONT, Louis (narr)
Bizet: Carmen (Cpte)

FREMSTAD, Olive (mez)
(PEAR) **GEMMCDS9923(2)** Covent Garden on Record, Vol.1 (pt 2)

FRENCH ARMY CHORUS
cond M. PLASSON
Gounod: Faust (Cpte)

FRENCH LYRIQUE ORCHESTRA
cond A. GUINGAL
Saint-Saëns: Henry VIII (Cpte)
cond M. SWIERCZEWSKI
Auber: Gustav III (Cpte)

FRENCH MUSIC THEATRE CHORUS
cond P. FOURNILLIER
Auber: Manon Lescaut (Cpte)

FRENCH NATIONAL ORCHESTRA
cond L. BERNSTEIN
(DG) **431 103-2GB** Great Voices—Montserrat Caballé
cond A. CLUYTENS
(MONT) **TCE8760** Stravinsky: Stage Works
cond J. CONLON
Puccini: Bohème (Cpte)
(ERAT) **2292-45797-2** The Ultimate Opera Collection
(ERAT) **4509-91715-2** The Ultimate Opera Collection 2
cond J. HORENSTEIN
(MUSI) **MACD-784** Horenstein in Paris - November 1956
cond D-E. INGHELBRECHT
Debussy: Pelléas et Mélisande (Cpte)
cond A. JORDAN
(ERAT) **4509-96370-2** Chabrier—España
cond L. MAAZEL
Bizet: Carmen (exc)
(ERAT) **2292-45797-2** The Ultimate Opera Collection
(ERAT) **4509-91715-2** The Ultimate Opera Collection 2
(TELD) **4509-90055-2** Sensual Classics
cond P. MONTEUX
(MONT) **TCE8740** Pieree Monteux conducts...
cond C. MUNCH
(MONT) **MUN2011** Berlioz—Symphonie fantastique; Overtures
cond S. OZAWA
Bizet: Carmen (exc)
Offenbach: Contes d'Hoffmann (exc)
(DG) **439 153-4GMA** Mad about Sopranos
cond M. ROSTROPOVICH
Prokofiev: War and Peace (Cpte)
cond I. STRAVINSKY
(MONT) **TCE8760** Stravinsky: Stage Works
cond J. TATE
Berg: Lulu (Cpte)
cond H. TOMASI
Tomasi: Don Juan de Mañara (Cpte)

FRENCH RADIO AND TV CHORUS
cond A. CLUYTENS
(MONT) **TCE8760** Stravinsky: Stage Works
cond I. STRAVINSKY
(MONT) **TCE8760** Stravinsky: Stage Works

FRENCH RADIO CHORUS
cond T. BEECHAM
Bizet: Carmen (Cpte)
cond J. CONLON
(ERAT) **2292-45797-2** The Ultimate Opera Collection
(ERAT) **4509-91715-2** The Ultimate Opera Collection 2
cond C. DUTOIT
Chabrier: Roi malgré lui (Cpte)
cond J. GRESSIER
Ganne: Hans (Cpte)
cond A. JORDAN
Chausson: Roi Arthus (Cpte)
cond L. MAAZEL
Bizet: Carmen (exc)
(ERAT) **2292-45797-2** The Ultimate Opera Collection
(ERAT) **4509-91715-2** The Ultimate Opera Collection 2
cond S. OZAWA
Bizet: Carmen (exc)
Offenbach: Contes d'Hoffmann (exc)
(DG) **439 153-4GMA** Mad about Sopranos
cond G. PRÊTRE
Bizet: Jolie fille de Perth (Cpte)
cond M. ROSENTHAL
Milhaud: Christophe Colomb (Cpte)
cond M. ROSTROPOVICH
Prokofiev: War and Peace (Cpte)
cond H. TOMASI
Tomasi: Don Juan de Mañara (Cpte)

FRENCH RADIO LYRIC CHORUS
cond T. AUBIN
Messager: Basoche (Cpte)
cond J. BREBION
Bazin: Maître Pathelin (Cpte)
cond M. CARIVEN
Audran: Poupée (exc)
Bazin: Voyage en Chine (Cpte)
Planquette: Rip van Winkle (Cpte)
Terrasse: Travaux d'Hercule (Cpte)
cond A. GIRARD
(MUSD) **20239-2** Delibes—Opéras-Comiques
cond J. GRESSIER
Messager: Monsieur Beaucaire (Cpte)
cond J-C. HARTEMANN
Massenet: Navarraise (Cpte)

FRENCH RADIO LYRIC ORCHESTRA
cond T. AUBIN
Messager: Basoche (Cpte)
cond J. BREBION
Bazin: Maître Pathelin (Cpte)
Boïeldieu: Voitures Versées (Cpte)
cond C. BRUCK
Martinů: Julietta (Cpte)
cond M. CARIVEN
Audran: Poupée (exc)
Bazin: Voyage en Chine (Cpte)
Planquette: Rip van Winkle (Cpte)
Terrasse: Travaux d'Hercule (Cpte)
cond J. DOUSSARD
Martinů: Alexandre Bis (Cpte)
cond R. ELLIS
Lecocq: Jour et la Nuit (Cpte)
Messager: P'tites Michu (exc)
cond H. GALLOIS
Gounod: Philémon et Baucis (Cpte)
cond A. GIRARD
(MUSD) **20239-2** Delibes—Opéras-Comiques
cond J. GRESSIER
Ganne: Hans (Cpte)
Messager: Monsieur Beaucaire (Cpte)
cond J-C. HARTEMANN
Massenet: Navarraise (Cpte)
cond M. ROSENTHAL
Martinů: Comedy on the Bridge (Cpte)
Milhaud: Christophe Colomb (Cpte)

FRENCH RADIO NATIONAL CHORUS
cond T. BEECHAM
(EMI) **CDM7 64359-2** Gala de España
cond E. BOUR
Ravel: Enfant et les sortilèges (Cpte)
cond J. CONLON
Puccini: Bohème (Cpte)
cond D-E. INGHELBRECHT
Debussy: Pelléas et Mélisande (Cpte)
cond G. TZIPINE
Bizet: Ivan IV (exc)

FRENCH RADIO NATIONAL MAÎTRISE
cond J. CONLON
Puccini: Bohème (Cpte)
cond J. ETCHEVERRY
Massenet: Werther (Cpte)

FRENCH RADIO NATIONAL ORCHESTRA
cond T. BEECHAM
Bizet: Carmen (Cpte)
(CFP) **CD-CFP4659** Everlasting Happiness
(EMI) **CDM5 65579-2** Victoria de los Angeles
(EMI) **CDM7 63379-2** Beecham conducts French Orchestral Works
(EMI) **CDM7 63401-2** French Favourites
(EMI) **CDM7 64359-2** Gala de España
cond E. BOUR
Ravel: Enfant et les sortilèges (Cpte)
cond A. CLUYTENS
Debussy: Pelléas et Mélisande (Cpte)
cond I. DOBROVEN
Mussorgsky: Boris Godunov (Cpte)
cond J. ETCHEVERRY
Massenet: Werther (Cpte)
cond L. MAAZEL
Ravel: Heure espagnole (Cpte)
cond J. MARTINON
(EMI) **CDM7 63160-2** Dukas: Orchestral works
cond G. PRÊTRE
(EMI) **CDC5 55016-2** Maria Callas - La Divina 2
(EMI) **CDC7 49059-2** Callas à Paris
(EMI) **CDC7 54016-2** Tenorissimo!
(EMI) **CDC7 54702-2** Maria Callas - La Divina
(EMI) **CDM7 63182-2** The Incomparable Callas
(EMIL) **CDZ100** Best Loved Classics 1
(EMIL) **CDZ105** Best Loved Classics 6
(EMIN) **CD-EMX2123** Maria Callas sings Operatic Arias
(MEMO) **HR4293/4** The very best of Maria Callas
cond G. TZIPINE
Bizet: Ivan IV (exc)

FRENCH RADIO NEW PHILHARMONIC ORCHESTRA
cond G. AMY
(ADES) **14122-2** Music of our Time
cond C. DUTOIT
Chabrier: Roi malgré lui (Cpte)
cond A. JORDAN
Chausson: Roi Arthus (Cpte)
cond G. PRÊTRE
Bizet: Jolie fille de Perth (Cpte)
(EMI) **CDM7 63104-2** Alfredo Krauss - Opera Recital

FRENCH RADIO PHILHARMONIC ORCHESTRA
cond M. JANOWSKI
(VIRG) **VJ7 59689-4** Wagner—Orchestral Works

FRENI, Mirella (sop)
Bizet: Carmen (exc)
Boito: Mefistofele (Cpte)
Donizetti: Don Pasquale (Cpte)
Gounod: Faust (exc), Roméo et Juliette (Cpte)
Handel: Alcina (Cpte)
Leoncavallo: Pagliacci (exc)
Mascagni: Amico Fritz (Cpte)
Massenet: Manon (Cpte)
Mozart: Don Giovanni (Cpte), Nozze di Figaro (exc)
Puccini: Bohème (Cpte), Madama Butterfly (Cpte), Manon Lescaut (Cpte), Tosca (exc), Turandot (exc)
Rossini: Guillaume Tell (Cpte)
Tchaikovsky: Eugene Onegin (exc), Queen of Spades (Cpte)
Verdi: Aida (Cpte), Don Carlo (Cpte), Ernani (Cpte), Falstaff (Cpte), Forza del destino (Cpte), Otello (exc), Simon Boccanegra (Cpte)
(ACAN) **49 384** Puccini: Opera Arias and Duets
(BELA) **450 002-2** Pavarotti Live
(BUTT) **BMCD015** Pavarotti Collection - Duets and Scenes
(CAST) **CASH5052** Verdi Operatic Favourites
(CAST) **CVI2067** Opera Highlights from La Scala
(CFP) **CD-CFP4569** Puccini: Arias
(CFP) **CD-CFP4602** Favourite Opera
(CFP) **CD-CFP4656** Herbert von Karajan conducts Opera
(CFP) **CD-CFP9013** Duets from Famous Operas
(DECC) **421 896-2DA** Puccini—Great Operatic Duets
(DECC) **430 470-2DH** Essential Pavarotti II
(DECC) **433 064-2DWO** Your Hundred Best Opera Tunes Volume I
(DECC) **433 068-2DWO** Your Hundred Best Opera Tunes V
(DECC) **433 069-2DWO** Your Hundred Best Opera Tunes VI
(DECC) **433 316-2DH** Verismo Arias - Mirella Freni
(DECC) **433 439-2DA** Great Love Duets
(DECC) **433 822-2DH** Essential Opera
(DECC) **433 865-2DWO** The World of Puccini
(DECC) **436 261-2DHO3** Puccini—Il Trittico
(DECC) **436 300-2DX** Opera Gala Sampler
(DECC) **436 315-2DA** Great Operatic Duets
(DECC) **436 317-2DA** Puccini—Famous Arias
(DECC) **436 461-2DM** Ten Top Sopranos
(DECC) **436 472-2DM** Great Opera Arias
(DECC) **440 412-2DM** Mirella Freni
(DECC) **440 947-2DH** Essential Opera II
(DECC) **443 018-2DF2** Pavarotti/Freni/Ricciarelli—Live
(DECC) **443 377-2DM** Ten Top Sopranos 2
(DECC) **444 555-2DF2** Essential Puccini
(DECC) **071 142-1DH (DECC)** Essential Opera
(DG) **431 601-2GCE10** Tchaikovsky Compact Edition
(DG) **439 151-2GMA** Mad about Puccini
(DG) **445 525-2GMA** Domingo Favourites
(DG) **439 153-4GMA** Mad about Sopranos
(DG) **072 428-1GH2(DG)** The Metropolitan Opera Gala
(EMI) **CDC7 54484-2** Verdi—Opera Choruses
(EMI) **CDC7 54524-2** The José Carreras Album
(EMI) **CDM7 63103-2** Placido Domingo sings Opera Arias
(EMI) **CDM7 63110-2** Mirella Freni: Opera Recital
(EMI) **CDM7 63111-2** José Carreras sings Opera & Operetta Arias
(EMI) **CDM7 69596-2** The Movies go to the Opera
(EMIN) **CD-EMX9519** Great Sopranos of Our Time
(MEMO) **HR4223/4** Nicolai Ghiaurov
(MEMO) **HR4273/4** Great Voices—Pietro Cappuccilli
(MEMO) **HR4277/8** Mirella Freni—Public Performances 1963-1970
(ORFE) **C394301B** Great Mozart Singers Series, Vol. 3
(RCA) **09026 61580-2(8)** RCA/Met 100 Singers, 100 Years (pt 8)
(RCA) **09026 62541-2** Pavarotti - The Early Years, Vol.1
(RCA) **09026 62699-2** Opera's Greatest Duets
(RCA) **09026 68014-2** Pavarotti - The Early Years, Vol.2
(TELD) **9031-77676-6(TELD)** My World of Opera - Kiri Te Kanawa

FRENKEL, Paul (pf)
(BIDD) **LAB077/8** Huberman—Complete Brunwick Recordings

FRESCHI, Ledo (bass)
Puccini: Manon Lescaut (Cpte)

FRESE, Siegfried Rudolf (bass)
Beethoven: Fidelio (Cpte)
Mussorgsky: Boris Godunov (Cpte)
Puccini: Madama Butterfly (Cpte)
R. Strauss: Rosenkavalier (Cpte)
Verdi: Trovatore (Cpte)

FREY, Dorothea (sop)
Gluck: Paride ed Elena (Cpte)

FREY, Hans Joachim (spkr)
Rihm: Eroberung von Mexico (Cpte)

FREY, Inge (mez)
Nielsen: Saul and David (Cpte)

FREY, Paul (ten)
R. Strauss: Ariadne auf Naxos (Cpte)
Wagner: Lohengrin (exc), Parsifal (Cpte)
(PHIL) **434 420-2PM32(1)** Richard Wagner Edition (Pt.1)

FREYER, Renate (mez)
Korngold: Violanta (Cpte)
Pfitzner: Palestrina (Cpte)
Verdi: Rigoletto (Cpte)

FRIANT, Charles (ten)
(MSCM) **MM30377** 18 Tenors d'Expression Française
(PEAR) **GEMMCD9948** Ninon Vallin in Opera and Song

FRIBOE, Brigitte (sngr)
Kuhlau: Lulu (Cpte)

FRICK, Gottlob (bass)
Beethoven: Fidelio (Cpte)
Mozart: Don Giovanni (Cpte), Entführung (Cpte), Zauberflöte (exc)
Nicolai: Lustigen Weiber von Windsor (Cpte)
Orff: Kluge (Cpte)
Wagner: Fliegende Holländer (Cpte), Götterdämmerung (Cpte), Lohengrin (Cpte), Meistersinger (Cpte), Parsifal (Cpte), Tannhäuser (Cpte), Walküre (Cpte)
Weber: Freischütz (Cpte)
(CFP) **CD-CFP4612** Favourite Mozart
(DECC) **414 100-2DM15** Wagner: Der Ring des Nibelungen
(DECC) **421 313-2DA** Wagner: Der Ring des Nibelungen - Great Scenes
(DECC) **440 069-2DWO** The World of Wagner
(EMI) **CHS7 63715-2** Mozart: Die Entführung, etc
(EMI) **CHS7 69741-2(4)** Record of Singing, Vol.4—German School

(EMI) **CMS5 65212-2** Wagner—Les introuvables du Ring
(EMI) **CMS5 65621-2** Fischer-Dieskau - The Opera Singer
(EMI) **CZS7 62993-2** Fritz Wunderlich—Great German Tenor
(EMI) **CZS7 67123-2** Wagner: Der Ring des Nibelungen
(EMIL) **CDZ7 67015-2** Mozart—Opera Arias
(RCA) **74321 24790-2** Carl Orff 100 Years Edition

FRICKE, Heinz (cond)
see Berlin RSO
BRSO
Munich RO

FRICSAY, Ferenc (cond)
see Bavarian Nat Orch
Bavarian St Orch
Berlin City Op Orch
Berlin RIAS Orch
Berlin RSO
BPO
BRSO
VPO

FRIED, Theodora (sop)
Rorem: Miss Julie (Cpte)

FRIEDAUER, Harry (ten)
Lehár: Land des Lächelns (Cpte)

FRIEDLAND, Brünnhilde (sop)
Wagner: Walküre (Cpte)
(FOYE) **15-CF2011** Wagner—Der Ring de Nibelungen

FRIEDMAN, Ignaz (pf)
(PEAR) **IF2000(1)** Ignaz Friedman—Solo Recordings (discs 1-3)

FRIEDMAN, Maria (sngr)
Romberg: Student Prince (Cpte)

FRIEDMAN, Stephanie (mez)
J. Adams: Death of Klinghoffer (Cpte)

FRIEDMANN, Gérard (ten)
Bazin: Maître Pathelin (Cpte)
Chausson: Roi Arthus (Cpte)
Fauré: Pénélope (Cpte)
Martinů: Alexandre Bis (Cpte), Comedy on the Bridge (Cpte)
Messager: Passionêment (Cpte)
Mozart: Nozze di Figaro (Cpte)
Offenbach: Contes d'Hoffmann (Cpte), Périchole (Cpte)
Saint-Saëns: Samson et Dalila (Cpte)
Terrasse: Fiancée du Scaphandrier (Cpte)

FRIEDRICH, Fritz (bass)
R. Strauss: Salome (Cpte)

FRIEDRICH, Heinz (bar)
Orff: Kluge (Cpte), Mond (Cpte)
(RCA) **74321 24790-2** Carl Orff 100 Years Edition

FRIEDRICH, Karl (ten)
J. Strauss II: Nacht in Venedig (Cpte)
R. Strauss: Rosenkavalier (Cpte)
(PREI) **90237** R Strauss—Daphne
(SCHW) **314572** Vienna State Opera Live, Vol.7

FRIEDRICH, Wolf Matthias (bar)
Kreutzer: Nachtlager in Granada (Cpte)

FRIEND, Lionel (cond)
see ENO Orch

FRIESS, Paul (bass)
Schreker: Ferne Klang (Cpte)
Verdi: Traviata (Cpte)

FRIGARA, Maurice (cond)
see Orch

FRIJSH, Povla (sop)
(PEAR) **GEMMCDS9095(1)** Povla Frijsh (pt 1)
(PEAR) **GEMMCDS9095(2)** Povla Frijsh (pt 2)

FRIMMER, Monika (sop)
Handel: Radamisto (Cpte)
Steffani: Henrico Leone (Cpte)

FRISTAD, Merle (bass)
Britten: Paul Bunyan (Cpte)
Copland: Tender Land (Cpte)

FRITSCH, Eduard (ten)
(SCHW) **314602** Vienna State Opera Live, Vol.10
(SCHW) **314702** Vienna State Opera Live, Vol.20

FRITTOLI, Barbara (sop)
Rossini: Barbiere di Siviglia (Cpte)
Verdi: Trovatore (Cpte)
(DECC) **436 261-2DHO3** Puccini—Il Trittico
(SCHW) **312682** Opera Gala with Young Artists - Volume II

FRITZ, Walther (ten)
Wagner: Parsifal (Cpte)

FRÖHLICH, Christian (cond)
see Berlin RSO

FROMENT, Louis de (cond)
see Luxembourg Rad & TV SO
Luxembourg RSO

FRONTALI, Roberto (bar)
Verdi: Falstaff (Cpte)

FRONTALINI, Silvano (cond)
see Minsk PO
Moldava SO

FROSCHAUER, Helmuth (cond)
see Cologne RSO

FROSINI, Mario (bass)
Mascagni: Piccolo Marat (Cpte)
Verdi: Traviata (Cpte)

FROUMENTY, Pierre (bass)
Debussy: Pelléas et Mélisande (Cpte)

FROZIER-MARROT, Georgette (mez)
(MSCM) **MM30221** 18 French Divas

FRÜHBECK DE BURGOS, Rafael (cond)
see LSO
New Philh
Paris Cons
Paris Op Orch
Sinfonia of London
Spanish Nat Orch

FRUTOS, Luis (bass)
Barbieri: Barberillo de Lavapiès (Cpte)
Vives: Bohemios (Cpte), Doña Francisquita (Cpte)

FRUTSCHNIGG, Melanie (contr)
R. Strauss: Ariadne auf Naxos (Cpte)
(PREI) **90237** R Strauss—Daphne
(SCHW) **314552** Vienna State Opera Live, Vol.5
(SCHW) **314742** Vienna State Opera Live, Vol.24

FRY, Howard (bar)
(CLAR) **CDGSE78-50-26** Wagner: Tristan und Isolde excerpts
(CLAR) **CDGSE78-50-35/6** Wagner—Historical recordings
(PEAR) **GEMMCDS9137** Wagner—Der Ring des Nibelungen

FRY, Tristan (perc)
Britten: Little Sweep (Cpte)

FRYATT, John (ten)
Mozart: Idomeneo (Cpte), Nozze di Figaro (Cpte), Zauberflöte (Cpte)
Puccini: Manon Lescaut (Cpte)
Stravinsky: Rake's Progress (Cpte)
Tchaikovsky: Eugene Onegin (Cpte)
Vaughan Williams: Hugh the Drover (Cpte)
Verdi: Falstaff (Cpte)

FRYDLEWICZ, Miroslav (ten)
Janáček: Cunning Little Vixen (Cpte)

FU, Haijing (bar)
Bellini: Bianca e Fernando (Cpte)

FUCHS, Eugen (bar)
Wagner: Meistersinger (exc), Tristan und Isolde (Cpte)

FUCHS, Eugen (bass)
(PEAR) **GEMMCDS9121** Wagner—Die Meistersinger, Act 3, etc
(PREI) **89057** Charles Kullmann (1903-1982)
(PREI) **89071** Gerhard Hüsch (1901-1984) - II

FUCHS, Gabriele (sop)
Korngold: Tote Stadt (Cpte)
Millöcker: Gasparone (Cpte)
R. Strauss: Intermezzo (Cpte)

FUCHS, Marta (sop)
Wagner: Götterdämmerung (Cpte), Walküre (exc)
(ACAN) **43 268** Peter Anders sings German Opera Arias
(EMI) **CMS7 64008-2(1)** Wagner Singing on Record (pt 1)

FUENTE, Herrera de la (cond)
see Minería SO
Xalapa SO

FUENTES, Eduardo (sngr)
Vives: Bohemios (Cpte)

FUES, Sabine (sop)
Wagner: Parsifal (Cpte)

FÜGEL, Alfons (ten)
(PREI) **90168** Wagner—Die Meistersinger, Act 2, etc

FUGELLE, Jacquelyn (sop)
Mozart: Mitridate (Cpte)

FUGÈRE, Lucien (bar)
(IRCC) **IRCC-CD800** Souvenirs from Meyerbeer Operas
(NIMB) **NI7840/1** The Era of Adelina Patti
(NIMB) **NI7867** Legendary Baritones
(SYMP) **SYMCD1089** Historic Baritones of the French School
(SYMP) **SYMCD1125** Lucien Fugère—Opera & Song Recital

FUGISS, Carmen (sop)
Rihm: Eroberung von Mexico (Cpte)

FUJIWARA OPERA CHORUS
cond G KUHN
Verdi: Otello (Cpte)
cond G. KUHN
Verdi: Macbeth (Cpte)
cond R. PATERNOSTRO
Verdi: Traviata (Cpte)

FUKAČOVÁ, Michaela (vc)
(KONT) **32044** Cantos de España—Jacob Christensen and Michaela Fukačová

FULKERSON, Gregory (vn)
Glass: Einstein on the Beach (Cpte)
(NEW) **80313-2** Copland/Glass/Ornstein/Wernick—Chamber Works

FÜLÖP, Attila (ten)
Giordano: Fedora (Cpte)

FURLAN, Jean-Pierre (ten)
A. Thomas: Hamlet (Cpte)

FURLANETTO, Ferruccio (bass)
Donizetti: Martyrs (Cpte)
Gazzaniga: Don Giovanni (Cpte)
Halévy: Juive (Cpte)
Mozart: Così fan tutte (Cpte), Don Giovanni (Cpte), Nozze di Figaro (Cpte)
Rossini: Armida (Cpte), Barbiere di Siviglia (Cpte), Gazza ladra (Cpte)
Verdi: Don Carlo (exc), Rigoletto (Cpte), Vespri Siciliani (Cpte)
(DG) **072 428-1GH2(DG)** The Metropolitan Opera Gala
(SONY) **SK47192** Ferruccio Furlanetto sings Mozart

FURLANETTO, Giovanni (bar)
(DECC) **071 140-1DH (DECC)** Pavarotti—30th Anniversary Gala Concert

FÜRST, Janos (cond)
see Helsinki PO

FURTWÄNGLER, Wilhelm (cond)
see Berlin St Op Orch
BPO
La Scala Orch
LPO
Philh
ROHO
Rome RAI Orch
Stockholm PO
Vienna St Op Orch
VPO

FUSATI, Nicola (ten)
(BONG) **GB1043-2** Italian Baritones of the Acoustic Era
(PEAR) **GEMMCD9178** Riccardo Stracciari

FUSCO, Elisabetta (sop)
Mozart: Nozze di Figaro (Cpte)

FUTRAL, Elizabeth (sop)
Glass: Hydrogen Jukebox (Cpte)

FYSON, Leslie (bar)
Puccini: Bohème (Cpte)

FYSON, Leslie (ten)
G. Charpentier: Louise (Cpte)
Rossini: Semiramide (Cpte), Zelmira (Cpte)
Shostakovich: Lady Macbeth of Mtsensk (Cpte)
Vaughan Williams: Hugh the Drover (Cpte)
Verdi: Macbeth (Cpte)

GABARAIN, Marina de (mez)
Rossini: Cenerentola (Cpte)
(EMI) **CDH5 65072-2** Glyndebourne Recorded - 1934-1994

GABBA, Armando (bar)
Verdi: Rigoletto (Cpte)

GABELLE, Guy (bar)
Massenet: Esclarmonde (Cpte)

GABOR, Arnold (bar)
Beethoven: Fidelio (Cpte)

GABORY, Magda (sop)
(EMI) **CZS7 67123-2** Wagner: Der Ring des Nibelungen

GABRIEL, Alain (ten)
Auber: Manon Lescaut (Cpte)
Saint-Saëns: Henry VIII (Cpte)

GABRIEL, Andrée (mez)
Adam: Si j'étais roi (Cpte)
R. Strauss: Salomé (Cpte)

GABRIEL, Maria Reyes (sngr)
Chapí: Revoltosa (Cpte)
Vives: Dona Francisquita (Cpte)

GABRIELE, Leyna (sop)
Beeson: Hello Out There (Cpte)

GABRY, Edith (sngr)
Mozart: Ascanio in Alba (Cpte), Mitridate (Cpte)

GADD, Stephen (bass)
Purcell: Dioclesian, Z627 (Cpte)

GADJEV, Zdravko (ten)
Mussorgsky: Khovanshchina (Cpte)

GADSKI, Johanna (sop)
(CLUB) **CL99-109** Johanna Gadski (1871-1932)
(MSCM) **MM30352** Caruso—Italian Opera Arias
(NIMB) **NI7834** Caruso in Ensemble
(PEAR) **EVC2** The Caruso Edition, Vol.2—1908-12
(PEAR) **GEMMCDS9923(2)** Covent Garden on Record, Vol.1 (pt 2)
(PEAR) **GEMMCD9104** Pasquale Amato (1878-1942)
(RCA) **GD60495(3)** The Complete Caruso Collection (pt 3)
(RCA) **09026 61242-2** Caruso Sings Verdi
(RCA) **09026 61580-2(1)** RCA/Met 110 Singers, 100 Years (pt 1)

GAEBEL, Kurt (cond)
see Berlin RSO

GAETANO, Colleen (mez)
Tchaikovsky: Iolanta (Cpte)

(PEAR) **GEMMCD9130** Great Sopranos, Vol.2
(ROMO) **81008-2** Mary Garden (1874-1967)
(SYMP) **SYMCD1093** The Harold Wayne Collection, Vol.7
(SYMP) **SYMCD1136** Opera in Chicago, Vol.1

GARDINER, John Eliot (cond)
see EBS
His Majesties Sagbutts and Cornetts
Lyon Op Orch
Monte Carlo Op Orch
Monteverdi Orch
N German RSO
VPO

GARDINO, Jolanda (mez)
Rossini: Turco in Italia (Cpte)

GARDNER, Jake (bar)
Massenet: Cid (Cpte)

GARDOW, Helrun (mez)
Monteverdi: Incoronazione di Poppea (Cpte)
Purcell: Dido (Cpte)

GARELLI, Nina (sop)
(MEMO) **HR4220/1** Great Voices-Tito Schipa

GARELLICK, Judith (mez)
Verdi: Rigoletto (Cpte)

GARETTI, Hélène (sop)
Massenet: Chérubin (Cpte)
Rameau: Dardanus (Cpte)

GARI, Suzanne (sop)
Grétry: Jugement de Midas (exc)
Hasse: Piramo e Tisbe (Cpte)

GARINO, Gérard (ten)
A. Thomas: Hamlet (Cpte)
Bizet: Carmen (Cpte)
(ARIO) **ARN68195** Milhaud—Sonatas; Trois Operas-Minute

GARMO, Tilly de (sop)
Wagner: Götterdämmerung (exc)
(PEAR) **GEMMCDS9137** Wagner—Der Ring des Nibelungen
(PREI) **89201** Helge Roswaenge (1897-1972) - I

GARRARD, Don (bass)
Stravinsky: Rake's Progress (Cpte)
(SONY) **SM22K46290(4)** Stravinsky—The Complete Edition (pt 4)

GARRETT, Eric (bar)
Borodin: Prince Igor (Cpte)
Donizetti: Fille du régiment (Cpte)
J. Strauss II: Fledermaus (Cpte)
Menotti: Boy who grew too fast (Cpte)
Offenbach: Contes d'Hoffmann (Cpte)
Puccini: Fanciulla del West (Cpte)
(DECC) **417 011-2DH2** Pavarotti's Greatest Hits
(DECC) **433 437-2DA** Pavarotti—King of the High Cs
(ROH) **75605 55013-2** The Puccini Experience

GARRETT, Lesley (sop)
Monteverdi: Incoronazione di Poppea (Cpte)
Sullivan: Mikado (exc)
(SILV) **FILMCD127** Vampire Circus—The Essential Vampire Theme Collection
(SILV) **SILKD6004** Simple Gifts—Lesley Garrett
(SILV) **SONGCD903** Diva! A Soprano at the Movies
(SILV) **SONGCD907** Lesley Garrett—Prima Donna
(SILV) **SILVACD105(SILV)** Flower Duet from Lakme - Lesley Garrett

GARRETT, Margo (pf)
(DG) **435 440-2GH** Kathleen Battle at Carnegie Hall

GARRIS, John (ten)
Verdi: Traviata (Cpte)

GARRISON, Jon (ten)
Stravinsky: Rake's Progress (Cpte)
(MUSM) **67078-2** Stravinsky The Composer - Volume 1
(NEWP) **NPD85595** Haydn—La canterina

GARSIDE, Gwladys (mez)
Delius: Village Romeo and Juliet (Cpte)
Wagner: Walküre (exc)

GARTNER, Jane (sop)
Monteverdi: Incoronazione di Poppea (Cpte)

GARTSIDE, Joyce (sop)
(TEST) **SBT1058** James Johnston - Opera Arias and Songs

GARULLI, Alfonso (ten)
(SYMP) **SYMCD1077** The Harold Wayne Collection, Vol.4

GAS, Manuel (sngr)
Sorozábal: Katiuska (Cpte)

GASDIA, Cecilia (sop)
Gounod: Faust (Cpte)
Handel: Rinaldo (Cpte)
Puccini: Turandot (Cpte)
Rossini: Armida (Cpte), Ermione (Cpte), Viaggio a Reims (Cpte), Zelmira (Cpte)
(CAST) **CVI2057** Il Trittico live from La Scala, 1983
(CAST) **CVI2068** Opera Highlights from Verona 1

GASKELL, Elizabeth (sop)
Janáček: Fate (Cpte)

GASPARINI, Annamaria (mez)
Zandonai: Francesca da Rimini (exc)

GASSIEV, Nikolai (ten)
Borodin: Prince Igor (Cpte)
Mussorgsky: Khovanshchina (Cpte)
Rimsky-Korsakov: Sadko (Cpte)
Tchaikovsky: Queen of Spades (Cpte)

GASZTECKI, Marek (bass)
Schillings: Mona Lisa (Cpte)

GÁTI, Istvan (bar)
Handel: Floridante (Cpte)
Mozart: Nozze di Figaro (Cpte)
Puccini: Tosca (Cpte)
(ACAN) **43 123** Peter Dvorský sings Puccini Arias

GATTA, Dora (sop)
Massenet: Werther (Cpte)
Mozart: Nozze di Figaro (exc)

GATTI, Daniele (cond)
see Bologna Teatro Comunale Orch

GATTI, Giorgio (bar)
A. Scarlatti: Lesbina e Adolfo (Cpte)
Piccinni: Pescatrice (Cpte)
Puccini: Tosca (Cpte)
Sacchini: Contadina in Corte (Cpte)
Salieri: Prima la musica (Cpte)
Verdi: Traviata (Cpte)

GATTO, Armando (cond)
see Verona Arena Orch

GATTOZZI, Vittorio (ten)
Bellini: Sonnambula (Cpte)

GAUBERT, Philippe (cond)
see orch
Paris Cons

GAUCI, Miriam (sop)
Leoncavallo: Pagliacci (Cpte)
Puccini: Bohème (Cpte), Gianni Schicchi (Cpte), Madama Butterfly (Cpte), Manon Lescaut (Cpte), Suor Angelica (Cpte)
Verdi: Simon Boccanegra (Cpte)
(NAXO) **8 550606** Soprano Arias from Italian Operas

GAUDEL, Christiane (mez)
G. Charpentier: Louise (exc)

GAUDIN, André (bar)
Massenet: Manon (Cpte)

GAUDIOSO, Gerardo (bar)
Puccini: Bohème (Cpte), Gianni Schicchi (Cpte)

GAUK, Alexander (cond)
see USSR Rad Orch

GAUK, Rachel (gtr)
(MARQ) **ERAD137** Danzas y Canciones

GAUTIER, Georges (ten)
Messiaen: Saint François d'Assise (Cpte)
Offenbach: Brigands (Cpte), Contes d'Hoffmann (Cpte)
Prokofiev: Love for 3 Oranges (Cpte)
Rameau: Dardanus (Cpte)
(DECC) **440 333-2DH** Ravel—Vocal Works

GAVAZZENI, Gianandrea (cond)
see La Scala Orch
LSO
Milan RAI SO
MMF Orch
National PO
National SO
RCA Orch
ROHO
Rome Op Orch
Rome PO
Rome RAI Orch
Santa Cecilia Academy Orch
Turin RAI Orch
Venice La Fenice Orch

GAVAZZI, Ernesto (ten)
Bellini: Norma (Cpte)
Donizetti: Favorita (Cpte)
Leoncavallo: Pagliacci (Cpte)
Mozart: Nozze di Figaro (exc)
Puccini: Fanciulla del West (Cpte), Madama Butterfly (Cpte)
Rossini: Bianca e Falliero (Cpte), Guillaume Tell (Cpte)
Tchaikovsky: Queen of Spades (Cpte)
Verdi: Aida (Cpte), Attila (Cpte), Falstaff (Cpte), Forza del destino (Cpte), Rigoletto (Cpte), Simon Boccanegra (Cpte), Traviata (Cpte), Vespri Siciliani (Cpte)

GAVRILOVA, Maria (sop)
Rimsky-Korsakov: Mlada (Cpte)
Tchaikovsky: Maid of Orleans (Cpte)

GAY, Maria (mez)
(CLUB) **CL99-025** Giovanni Zenatello (1876-1949)
(PEAR) **GEMMCDS9074(1)** Giovanni Zenatello, Vol.2 (pt 1)
(PEAR) **GEMMCDS9074(2)** Giovanni Zenatello, Vol.2 (pt 2)
(PEAR) **GEMMCDS9924(2)** Covent Garden on Record, Vol.2 (pt 2)
(PREI) **89038** Giovanni Zenatello (1876-1949)

GAYER, Catherine (sop)
Wagner: Siegfried (Cpte)
(DG) **435 211-2GX15** Wagner—Der Ring des Nibelungen
(DG) **439 423-2GCL** Wagner—Der Ring des Nibelungen (highlights)

GAYRAUD, Christiane (contr)
Gounod: Mireille (Cpte)
Mozart: Nozze di Figaro (Cpte)
Offenbach: Contes d'Hoffmann (Cpte)
(EMI) **CZS7 67869-2** J. Strauss II—Operetta Highlights
(MONT) **TCE8760** Stravinsky: Stage Works

GEAY, Robert (bass)
Bizet: Carmen (Cpte)
Offenbach: Contes d'Hoffmann (Cpte)

GEBER, Klaus (bar)
Suder: Kleider machen Leute (Cpte)

GEBHARDT, Bernd (bar)
Delius: Village Romeo and Juliet (Cpte)

GEBHARDT, Bernd (sngr)
Schillings: Mona Lisa (Cpte)

GEBHARDT, Horst (ten)
Wagner: Parsifal (Cpte)

GEDDA, Nicolai (ten)
Auber: Fra Diavolo (Cpte)
Barber: Vanessa (Cpte)
Berlioz: Benvenuto Cellini (Cpte)
Bernstein: Candide (1988) (Cpte)
Bizet: Carmen (exc), Pêcheurs de perles (Cpte)
Cornelius: Barbier von Bagdad (Cpte)
Flotow: Martha (Cpte)
G. Charpentier: Louise (Cpte)
Gluck: Alceste (1776) (Cpte)
Gounod: Faust (exc), Mireille (Cpte)
J. Strauss II: Nacht in Venedig (Cpte)
Korngold: Wunder der Heliane (Cpte)
Lehár: Giuditta (Cpte), Graf von Luxemburg (Cpte), Land des Lächelns (Cpte), Lustige Witwe (Cpte)
Massenet: Cendrillon (Cpte), Thaïs (Cpte), Werther (Cpte)
Meyerbeer: Prophète (Cpte)
Millöcker: Bettelstudent (Cpte)
Mozart: Così fan tutte (Cpte), Don Giovanni (Cpte), Entführung (Cpte), Idomeneo (Cpte), Zauberflöte (exc)
Mussorgsky: Boris Godunov (Cpte)
Offenbach: Contes d'Hoffmann (Cpte)
Pfitzner: Palestrina (Cpte)
Prokofiev: War and Peace (Cpte)
Puccini: Bohème (Cpte), Madama Butterfly (Cpte)
R. Strauss: Capriccio (Cpte), Rosenkavalier (Cpte)
Rossini: Guillaume Tell (Cpte), Turco in Italia (Cpte)
Roussel: Padmâvatî (Cpte)
Shostakovich: Lady Macbeth of Mtsensk (Cpte)
Tchaikovsky: Eugene Onegin (Cpte), Iolanta (Cpte)
Verdi: Rigoletto (Cpte)
(BLUE) **ABCD014** Viennese Delights
(CFP) **CD-CFP4499** Strauss—Champagne and Laughter
(CFP) **CD-CFP4569** Puccini: Arias
(CFP) **CD-CFP4575** Verdi Arias
(CFP) **CD-CFP4582** Flowers in Music
(CFP) **CD-CFP4602** Favourite Opera
(CFP) **CD-CFP4613** Favourite TV Classics
(CFP) **CD-CFP4616** Ave Maria
(CFP) **CD-CFP9013** Duets from Famous Operas
(EMI) **CDC5 55216-2** Maria Callas - La Divina 3
(EMI) **CDC7 54016-2** Tenorissimo!
(EMI) **CDEMTVD59** Classic Experience 3
(EMI) **CDH5 65352-2** Nicolai Gedda Lieder Recital
(EMI) **CDM7 69596-2** The Movies go to the Opera
(EMI) **CHS7 69741-2(5)** Record of Singing, Vol.4—Scandinavian School
(EMI) **CMS5 65621-2** Fischer-Dieskau - The Opera Singer
(EMI) **CMS7 63244-2** The Art of Maria Callas
(EMI) **CMS7 64309-2** Kálmán—Best-loved Melodies
(EMI) **CZS5 68113-2** Vive Offenbach!
(EMI) **CZS7 67440-2** The Best of Rossini
(EMI) **CZS7 67813-2** Opera Arias and Duets
(EMIL) **CDZ7 67015-2** Mozart—Opera Arias
(EMIN) **CD-EMX2123** Maria Callas sings Operatic Arias
(MEMO) **HR4392/3** Great Voices - Marilyn Horne
(RCA) **09026 61580-2(5)** RCA/Met 100 Singers, 100 Years (pt 5)
(RCA) **09026 62689-2** The Voices of Living Stereo, Volume 1

GEDDA, Tania (sop)
Tchaikovsky: Iolanta (Cpte)
(BLUE) **ABCD014** Viennese Delights

GEEHL, Henry (cond)
see orch

GEHRMAN, Shura (bass)
(NIMB) **NI5214** Mirages - Songs by Fauré, Gounod & Ravel

GEISEN, Erik (ten)
Romberg: Student Prince (exc)

GEISSINGER, Katie (mez)
M. Monk: Atlas (Cpte)

GELIOT, Michael (spkr)
Martinů: Greek Passion (Cpte)

GELLI, Antonio (bass)
Puccini: Tosca (Cpte)
Verdi: Traviata (Cpte)
(PREI) **89008** Irene Minghini-Cattaneo (1892-1944)

GELLING, Philip (bass)
A. Thomas: Hamlet (Cpte)
Britten: Peter Grimes (Cpte)
Offenbach: Contes d'Hoffmann (Cpte)

GELMETTI, Gianluigi (cond)
see Stuttgart RSO
Turin RSO
Tuscan Orch
Venice La Fenice Orch

GEMIGNANI, Paul (cond)
see American Th Orch

GENCER, Leyla (sop)
Donizetti: Martyrs (Cpte)
(MEMO) **HR4239/40** Opera Arias—Leyla Gencer
(MEMO) **HR4273/4** Great Voices—Pietro Cappuccilli

GENDRON, Maurice (vc)
(PHIL) **438 960-2PM3** Maurice Gendron

GENEST, Corinna (sngr)
Schultze: Schwarzer Peter (Cpte)

GÉNETAY, Claude (cond)
see Stockholm Nat Museum CO
Swedish Nat Museum CO

GENEVA GRAND THEATRE CHORUS
cond A. LOMBARD
(DECC) **440 416-2DM** Régine Crespin
cond J. LÓPEZ-COBOS
Rossini: Barbiere di Siviglia (Cpte)
cond T. SCHIPPERS
Bizet: Carmen (Cpte)
(BELA) **450 006-2** Famous Opera Duets

GENEVA GRAND THEATRE ORCHESTRA
cond A. EREDE
(BELA) **450 006-2** Famous Opera Duets
(BELA) **450 133-2** Verdi Favourites
(DECC) **430 481-2DX2** Renata Tebaldi sings Opera Arias
(DECC) **433 068-2DWO** Your Hundred Best Opera Tunes V
(DECC) **433 069-2DWO** Your Hundred Best Opera Tunes VI
(DECC) **433 442-2DA** Verdi—Famous Arias
(DECC) **443 378-2DM** Ten Top Mezzos 2

GENEVA MOTET CHOIR
cond E. ANSERMET
Martin: Mystère de la Nativité
(DECC) **433 400-2DM2** Ravel & Debussy—Stage Works
(DECC) **443 464-2DF2** Rimsky-Korsakov—Scheherazade, etc

GENEVA OPERA CHORUS
cond H. LEWIS
(DECC) **421 891-2DA** Marilyn Horne sings Rossini, Bellini & Donizetti
(DECC) **440 415-2DM** Marilyn Horne

GÉNIO (sngr)
Audran: Poupée (exc)
Ganne: Hans (Cpte)
Messager: Basoche (Cpte), Coups de Roulis (Cpte)

GENNARI, Oreste (ten)
(PEAR) **GEMMCDS9159(1)** De Luca Edition, Vol.1 (pt 1)

GENOA TEATRO CARLO FELICE CHORUS
cond P. OLMI
Rossini: Siège de Corinthe (Cpte)

GENOA TEATRO CARLO FELICE ORCHESTRA
cond P. OLMI
Rossini: Siège de Corinthe (Cpte)

GENOA TEATRO COMUNALE CHORUS
cond D. OREN
Puccini: Turandot (Cpte)

GENOA TEATRO COMUNALE ORCHESTRA
cond D. OREN
Puccini: Turandot (exc)

GENOVA, Tiha (sop)
Kalomiris: Mother's Ring (Cpte)

GENS, Véronique (sop)
Jommelli: Armida abbandonata (Cpte)
Lully: Alceste (Cpte), Armide, Atys (Cpte), Phaëton (Cpte)
Marais: Alcyone (Cpte)
Purcell: Dido (Cpte), Fairy Queen, Z629 (Cpte), King Arthur, Z628 (Cpte)
Rameau: Castor et Pollux (exc), Hippolyte et Aricie (Cpte), Platée (Cpte)

GENT, Willemijn van (sop)
Purcell: Fairy Queen, Z629 (Cpte)

GENTILE, Maria (sop)
(PEAR) **GEMMCD9091** Dino Borgioli
(PREI) **89040** Carlo Galeffi (1884-1961)

GENTNER-FISCHER, Else (sop)
(PREI) **89053** Max Lorenz (1901-1975)

GEORG, Mechthild (mez)
Puccini: Gianni Schicchi (Cpte)
(EURO) **GD69043** Puccini: Il Trittico

GEORGE, Donald (ten)
Puccini: Manon Lescaut (Cpte)
Verdi: Alzira (Cpte)
(CLOR) **TCO93-75** The Cleveland Orchestra-75th Anniversary CD Edition

GEORGE, Michael (bass)
Blow: Venus and Adonis (Cpte)
Chabrier: Briséïs (Cpte)
G. Lloyd: John Socman (exc)
Handel: Ottone (Cpte)
Holst: At the Boar's Head (Cpte)
Monteverdi: Orfeo (Cpte)
Purcell: Dioclesian, Z627 (exc), Fairy Queen, Z629 (Cpte)
Stravinsky: Nightingale (Cpte)
(ERAT) **4509-96371-2** Gardiner—The Purcell Collection
(ERAT) **4509-98955-2** Boulez conducts Stravinsky

GEORGEL, Jean-Louis (bar)
(ARIO) **ARN68252** Chabrier—Trois opérettes

GEORGEL, Jean-Louis (ten)
Rameau: Hippolyte et Aricie (Cpte)

GEORGES, Philippe (ten)
Gounod: Sapho (Cpte)
Massenet: Cléopâtre (Cpte)

GEORGIADIS, John (cond)
see LSO
Queensland PO

GEORGIADIS, John (vn)
(IMP) **PCD902** An Evening in Vienna
(RPO) **CDRPO5006** Orchestral Lollipops

GEORGIEV, Stoil (bar)
Borodin: Prince Igor (Cpte)
Glinka: Life for the Tsar (Cpte)
Mussorgsky: Khovanshchina (Cpte)
Tchaikovsky: Eugene Onegin (Cpte), Queen of Spades (Cpte)

GERBER-CANDY, Audrey (sop)
R. Strauss: Elektra (Cpte)

GERBINO, Giuse (mez)
Verdi: Rigoletto (Cpte)
(EMI) **CDM7 69543-2** Maria Callas and Giuseppe Di Stefano - Duets

GERDES, Otto (cond)
see Bavarian St Op Orch
Berlin Deutsche Op Orch

GERDESITS, Ferenc (ten)
Puccini: Tosca (Cpte)

GERELO, Vassili (bar)
Mussorgsky: Khovanshchina (Cpte)
Prokofiev: War and Peace (exc)

GERGALOV, Alexander (bar)
Prokofiev: War and Peace (Cpte)
Rimsky-Korsakov: Sadko (Cpte)
Tchaikovsky: Queen of Spades (Cpte)

GERGIEV, Valery (cond)
see Kirov Th Orch
Leningrad Kirov Th Orch
Rotterdam PO

GERHARD, Maria (sop)
(SCHW) **314502** Vienna State Opera—Live Recordings (sampler)

GERHARDT, Charles (cond)
see National PO
Phil Pops Orch
RCA SO
RPO

GERHART, Maria (sop)
(ORFE) **C394101B** Great Mozart Singers Series, Vol. 1
(SCHW) **314512** Vienna State Opera Live, Vol.1

GERIHSEN, Franz (bar)
Weill: Kuhhandel (exc)

GÉRIMON, Paul (bass)
Monteverdi: Orfeo (Cpte)
Probst: Maximilien Kolbe (Cpte)

GERMAIN, John (bar)
Lehár: Lustige Witwe (Cpte)

GERMAIN, Pierre (bar)
Martinů: Julietta (Cpte)
Milhaud: Christophe Colomb (Cpte)
(EMI) **CZS5 68295-2** Messager/Lecocq—Operetta Highlights
(EMI) **CZS7 67872-2** Lehár—Operettas (highlights in French)

GERMAN, Timothy (ten)
Balfe: Bohemian Girl (Cpte)
Janáček: Fate (Cpte)
Wagner: Parsifal (Cpte)

GERMAN FESTIVAL ORCHESTRA
cond A. SCHOLZ
(CAVA) **CAVCD017** Classical Concert, Vol.1
(CAVA) **CAVCD018** Classical Concert, Vol.2

GERMAN NATIONAL YOUTH ORCHESTRA
cond C. PRICK
(ARSM) **AMP5014-2**
Schumann/Ravel/R.Strauss—Orchestral Works

GERSON, Therese (sop)
(PREI) **89082** Margarete Klose (1902-1968)

GERSTENHABER, Cyrille (sop)
Dusapin: Romeo and Juliet (Cpte)

GESSENDORF, Mechtild (sop)
Busoni: Turandot (Cpte)
Schoeck: Penthesilea (Cpte)

GESTER, Kurt (narr)
Busoni: Arlecchino (Cpte)

GESZTY, Sylvia (sop)
Lehár: Schön ist die Welt (exc)
R. Strauss: Ariadne auf Naxos (Cpte)

GEUER, Wolf (ten)
Hindemith: Neues vom Tage (Cpte)

GEYER, Gwynne (sop)
Wagner: Parsifal (Cpte)

GHASNE, Alexis (bar)
(IRCC) **IRCC-CD802** Souvenirs of Rare French Opera
(SYMP) **SYMCD1089** Historic Baritones of the French School

GHAZARIAN, Sona (sop)
Beethoven: Fidelio (Cpte)
Mozart: Don Giovanni (Cpte)
R. Strauss: Arabella (Cpte)
Verdi: Ballo in maschera (Cpte)
(CAPR) **10 348** Mozart Gala—Suntory Hall, Tokyo
(CAPR) **10 810** Mozart—Opera Highlights
(PHIL) **434 986-2PM** Duetti Amorosi

GHENT COLLEGIUM VOCALE
cond S. KUIJKEN
Gluck: Orfeo ed Euridice (Cpte)
Rameau: Zoroastre (Cpte)

GHEORGHIU, Angela (sop)
Verdi: Traviata (Cpte)
(ROH) **75605 55013-2** The Puccini Experience

GHIAUROV, Nicolai (bass)
Bellini: Puritani (Cpte), Sonnambula (Cpte)
Boito: Mefistofele (Cpte)
Borodin: Prince Igor (Cpte)
Donizetti: Favorita (Cpte), Lucia di Lammermoor (exc)
Gounod: Faust (Cpte)
Janáček: From the House of the Dead (Cpte)
Massenet: Don Quichotte (Cpte), Roi de Lahore (Cpte)
Mozart: Don Giovanni (Cpte)
Mussorgsky: Boris Godunov (Cpte), Khovanshchina (Cpte)
Ponchielli: Gioconda (Cpte)
Puccini: Bohème (Cpte), Turandot (Cpte)
Rossini: Barbiere di Siviglia (Cpte), Guillaume Tell (Cpte)
Tchaikovsky: Eugene Onegin (Cpte)
Verdi: Aida (Cpte), Don Carlo (Cpte), Don Carlos (Cpte), Ernani (Cpte), Macbeth (Cpte), Nabucco (exc), Rigoletto (exc), Simon Boccanegra (Cpte), Trovatore (Cpte)
(CAST) **CVI2067** Opera Highlights from La Scala
(DECC) **417 011-2DH2** Pavarotti's Greatest Hits
(DECC) **425 849-2DWO** Your hundred best tunes vol 3
(DECC) **433 064-2DWO** Your Hundred Best Opera Tunes Volume I
(DECC) **433 067-2DWO** Your Hundred Best Opera Tunes IV
(DECC) **433 069-2DWO** Your Hundred Best Opera Tunes VI
(DECC) **433 439-2DA** Great Love Duets
(DECC) **433 440-2DA** Golden Opera
(DECC) **433 443-2DA** Great Opera Choruses
(DECC) **433 822-2DH** Essential Opera
(DECC) **433 865-2DWO** The World of Puccini
(DECC) **436 300-2DX** Opera Gala Sampler
(DECC) **436 317-2DA** Puccini—Famous Arias
(DECC) **436 464-2DM** Ten Top Baritones & Basses
(DECC) **436 472-2DM** Great Opera Arias
(DECC) **440 947-2DH** Essential Opera II
(DECC) **443 380-2DM** Ten Top Baritones & Basses 2
(DECC) **443 585-2DF2** Your Hundred Best Tunes - Top 20
(DECC) **444 108-2DA** Ballet Music from Opera
(DECC) **444 389-2DWO** The World of Borodin
(DECC) **444 555-2DF2** Essential Puccini
(DG) **419 091-4GW** Placido Domingo sings Favourite Arias, Songs and Tangos
(DG) **072 428-1GH2(DG)** The Metropolitan Opera Gala
(EMI) **CDM7 69549-2** Ruggero Raimondi: Italian Opera Arias
(FORL) **FF060** Famous Russian Operatic Choruses
(FORL) **UCD16741** Bulgarian Voices, Vol. 1
(FORL) **UCD16743** Bulgarian Voices, Vol. 3
(MEMO) **HR4223/4** Nicolai Ghiaurov
(MEMO) **HR4273/4** Great Voices—Pietro Cappuccilli
(MEMO) **HR4277/8** Mirella Freni—Public Performances 1963-1970
(MEMO) **HR4300/1** Great Voices—Sesto Bruscantini
(MEMO) **HR4386/7** Great Voices - Giulietta Simionato
(ORFE) **C394301B** Great Mozart Singers Series, Vol. 3

GHIONE, Franco (cond)
see La Scala Orch
Lisbon San Carlos Nat Th Orch
Santa Cecilia Academy Orch
Turin EIAR Orch

GHIONE, Susanna (sngr)
Ponchielli: Lituani (Cpte)

GHIRARDINI, Emilio (bar)
Verdi: Falstaff (Cpte), Forza del destino (exc)

GHIUSELEV, Nikola (bass)
Borodin: Prince Igor (Cpte)
Meyerbeer: Huguenots (Cpte)
Mozart: Don Giovanni (Cpte)
Mussorgsky: Boris Godunov (Cpte), Khovanshchina (Cpte)
Offenbach: Contes d'Hoffmann (Cpte)
Ponchielli: Gioconda (Cpte)
Prokofiev: War and Peace (Cpte)
Puccini: Bohème (exc)
Tchaikovsky: Eugene Onegin (Cpte)
Verdi: Battaglia di Legnano (Cpte)
(FORL) **UCD16741** Bulgarian Voices, Vol. 1
(FORL) **UCD16743** Bulgarian Voices, Vol. 3

GIACOMINI, Giuseppe (ten)
Bellini: Norma (Cpte)
Donizetti: Fausta (Cpte)
Mascagni: Cavalleria Rusticana (Cpte)
Puccini: Tosca (Cpte)
(DECC) **436 261-2DHO3** Puccini—Il Trittico

GIACOMOTTI, Alfredo (bass)
Bellini: Capuleti (Cpte)
Cherubini: Medea (Cpte)
Donizetti: Don Pasquale (Cpte)
Meyerbeer: Prophète (Cpte)
Puccini: Turandot (Cpte)
Verdi: Ernani (Cpte), Otello (Cpte), Rigoletto (Cpte), Traviata (Cpte), Trovatore (Cpte)
(CBS) **CD37228** Pavarotti sings Verdi
(RCA) **09026 68014-2** Pavarotti - The Early Years, Vol.2

GIAIOTTI, Bonaldo (bass)
Puccini: Madama Butterfly (Cpte), Turandot (Cpte)
Verdi: Aida (Cpte), Ballo in maschera (Cpte), Forza del destino (Cpte), Luisa Miller (Cpte), Traviata (Cpte), Trovatore (Cpte), Vespri Siciliani (Cpte)
(BUTT) **BMCD015** Pavarotti Collection - Duets and Scenes
(DECC) **443 928-2DM** Montserrat Caballé sings Opera Arias
(MEMO) **HR4277/8** Mirella Freni—Public Performances 1963-1970
(MEMO) **HR4300/1** Great Voices—Sesto Bruscantini
(RCA) **09026 68014-2** Pavarotti - The Early Years, Vol.2

IANNINI, Dusolina (sop)
Verdi: Aida (Cpte)
(EMI) **CDH7 61052-2** Beniamino Gigli—Arias and Duets (1932-1949)
(MMOI) **CDMOIR417** Great Voices of the Century—Beniamino Gigli
(PEAR) **GEMMCDS9176** Gigli - Arias, Duets & Songs, 1926-1937
(PREI) **89044** Dusolina Giannini (1902-1986)

IANNOTTI, Armando (ten)
Puccini: Turandot (Cpte)

IANNOTTI, Pierre (ten)
G. Charpentier: Louise (Cpte)

IBAND, Félix (bass)
Gounod: Philémon et Baucis (Cpte)

IBBONS, Jack (pf)
(ASV) **CDWHL2082** The Authentic Gershwin, Volume 3
(ASV) **CDWLS328** The Authentic Gershwin, Vols. 1-3

IBBS, John (bar)
Gay: Beggar's Opera (Cpte)
Meyerbeer: Huguenots (Cpte)
Puccini: Bohème (Cpte), Tosca (Cpte)
R. Strauss: Rosenkavalier (Cpte)
Verdi: Rigoletto (Cpte), Traviata (Cpte)
(DECC) **436 313-2DA** Sutherland/Pavarotti—Operatic Duets

IBBS, Raymond (bar)
Bizet: Carmen (Cpte)
Verdi: Traviata (Cpte)

BIN, João (ten)
Puccini: Fanciulla del West (Cpte)

BSON, Sir Alexander (cond)
see LSO
New SO
ROHO
SNO

BSON, Barbara (sop)
(RCA) **GD60280** Toscanini Collection

BSON, Jon (sax)
(PNT) **434 873-2PTH** Jon Gibson—In Good Company

BSON, Lee (sngr)
Bernstein: West Side Story (Cpte)

BSON, Rodney (ten)
Verdi: Simon Boccanegra (Cpte), Traviata (Cpte)

BSON, Sian wyn (sop)
Offenbach: Orphée aux enfers (Cpte)

EBEL, Agnes (sop)
Mozart: Zauberflöte (Cpte)

ELEN, Michael (cond)
see Austrian RSO
South-West German RSO

GIENGER, Stefan (treb)
Mozart: Zauberflöte (Cpte)

GIEPEL, Dorothea (sop)
R. Strauss: Elektra (Cpte)

GIERSTER, Hans (cond)
see Bamberg SO

GIESEN, Hubert (pf)
(BIDD) **LAB032** The young Yehudi Menuhin, Vol.2
(TEST) **SBT1003** The Young Menuhin—Encores, Vol.1

GIFFORD, Gerald (hpd)
(LIBR) **LRCD156** Georgian Harpsichord Music

GIGLI, Beniamino (ten)
Leoncavallo: Pagliacci (Cpte)
Mascagni: Cavalleria Rusticana (Cpte)
Puccini: Bohème (Cpte)
Verdi: Aida (Cpte)
(ASV) **CDAJA5137** The Three Tenors of the Century
(CONI) **CDHD149** Gigli Favourites
(CONI) **CDHD170** Gigli—Centenary Tribute
(CONI) **CDHD227** Gigli in Opera and Song
(CONI) **CDHD235** The Puccini Album
(EMI) **CDC7 54016-2** Tenorissimo!
(EMI) **CDH7 61051-2** Beniamino Gigli - Operatic Arias
(EMI) **CDH7 61052-2** Beniamino Gigli—Arias and Duets (1932-1949)
(EMI) **CHS7 64864-2(1)** La Scala Edition - Vol.2, 1915-46 (pt 1)
(EMI) **CHS7 64864-2(2)** La Scala Edition - Vol.2, 1915-46 (pt 2)
(EMI) **CHS7 69741-2(7)** Record of Singing, Vol.4—Italian School
(IMP) **GLRS102** The Magnificent Gigli
(MMOI) **CDMOIR405** Great Tenors
(MMOI) **CDMOIR409** Three Tenors—Björling, Gigli & Tauber
(MMOI) **CDMOIR412** Great Voices of the Century Sing Puccini
(MMOI) **CDMOIR417** Great Voices of the Century—Beniamino Gigli
(MMOI) **CDMOIR425** Three Tenors, Volume 2
(NIMB) **NI7801** Great Singers, Vol.1
(NIMB) **NI7807** Beniamino Gigli—Vol. 1: 1918-24
(NIMB) **NI7810** Titta Ruffo—Opera Recital
(NIMB) **NI7817** Beniamino Gigli—Vol.2
(NIMB) **NI7852** Galli-Curci, Vol.2
(NIMB) **NI7856** Legendary Tenors
(NIMB) **NI7864** More Legendary Voices
(PEAR) **GEMMCDS9159(2)** De Luca Edition, Vol.1 (pt 2)
(PEAR) **GEMMCDS9160(2)** De Luca Edition, Vol.2 (pt 2)
(PEAR) **GEMMCDS9176** Gigli - Arias, Duets & Songs, 1926-1937
(PEAR) **GEMMCDS9926(2)** Covent Garden on Record—Vol.4 (pt 2)
(PEAR) **GEMMCD9129** Great Tenors, Vol.2
(PEAR) **GEMMCD9316** Beniamino Gigli
(PEAR) **GEMMCD9367** Gigli—Arias and Duets
(PEAR) **GEMMCD9458** Lucrezia Bori—Opera & Song Recital
(PREI) **89073** Giuseppe de Luca (1876-1950) - II
(PREI) **89303(2)** Titta Ruffo Edition (pt 2)
(RCA) **GD87811** Beniamino Gigli—Operatic Arias
(RCA) **09026 61580-2(3)** RCA/Met 100 Singers, 100 Years (pt 3)
(ROMO) **81014-2** Elisabeth Rethberg (1894-1976)
(ROMO) **81016-2** Lucrezia Bori (1887-1960)
(SCHW) **314632** Vienna State Opera Live, Vol.13
(TEST) **SBT1005** Ten Top Tenors

GILBERT, David (cond)
see MSM Op Orch

GILFRY, Rodney (bar)
Ancelin: Filius Hominis (Cpte)
Mozart: Così fan tutte (exc), Don Giovanni (Cpte), Nozze di Figaro (Cpte)

GILHOFER, Eva (contr)
Holliger: Magische Tänzer (Cpte)

GILIBERT, Gabrielle (mez)
(PEAR) **EVC2** The Caruso Edition, Vol.2—1908-12

GILILOV, Pavel (pf)
(DG) **431 544-2GH** Meditation
(DG) **431 544-5GH** Meditation

GILION, Mario (ten)
(BONG) **GB1076-2** Mario Gilion - Opera Arias

GILJE, Tor (ten)
Braein: Anne Pedersdotter (Cpte)

GILL, Dorothy (contr)
Sullivan: Gondoliers (Cpte), Pirates of Penzance (Cpte), Sorcerer (Cpte)

GILLASPIE, Jon (fp)
(PEAR) **SHECD9613** Jane Austen Songs

GILLES, Marie Louise (contr)
Verdi: Traviata (Cpte)

GILLES, Raoul (ten)
Ravel: Heure espagnole (Cpte)

GILLESSEN, Dieter (bass)
Hindemith: Neues vom Tage (Cpte)

GILLETT, Christopher (ten)
Gay: Beggar's Opera (Cpte)
Maxwell Davies: Martyrdom of St Magnus (Cpte)
Sullivan: HMS Pinafore (Cpte)
Tippett: King Priam (Cpte)

GILLY, Dinh (bar)
(PEAR) **GEMMCDS9925(1)** Covent Garden on Record—Vol.3 (pt 1)
(PEAR) **GEMMCD9956** Joseph Hislop (1884-1977)
(SUPR) **11 2136-2(4)** Emmy Destinn—Complete Edition, Discs 9 & 10

GILMORE, Peter (sngr)
Gay: Beggar's Opera (Cpte)

GILSON, Tom (pf/hpd)
S. Wallace: Kabbalah (Cpte)

GIMENEZ, Edoardo (ten)
Mozart: Nozze di Figaro (Cpte)
Rossini: Armida (Cpte), Viaggio a Reims (Cpte)

GIMÉNEZ, Raúl (ten)
Mayr: Medea (Cpte)
Mysliveček: Bellerofonte (Cpte)
Rossini: Barbiere di Siviglia (exc), Cenerentola (Cpte), Turco in Italia (Cpte), Viaggio a Reims (Cpte)
(NIMB) **NI5106** Rossini—Opera Arias
(NIMB) **NI5224** Bellini & Donizetti: Arias
(NIMB) **NI5300** Mozart Arias—Raúl Giménez

GIMINEZ, Charito (mez)
Vives: Doña Francisquita (Cpte)

GIMPEL, Jakob (pf)
(RCA) **RD86218** Mario Lanza—The Legendary Tenor

GINN, Michael (treb)
Britten: Turn of the Screw (Cpte)

GINROD, Friedrich (bar)
(SCHW) **314542** Vienna State Opera Live, Vol.4

GINSBERG, Allen (narr)
Glass: Hydrogen Jukebox (Cpte)

GINSBERG, Ernst (spkr)
Weber: Freischütz (Cpte)

GINZEL, Reinhard (ten)
Gurlitt: Wozzeck (Cpte)
Schreker: Gezeichneten (Cpte)

GINZER, Frances (sop)
Cilea: Adriana Lecouvreur (Cpte)

GIOMBI, Claudio (bar)
Puccini: Bohème (Cpte), Fanciulla del West (Cpte), Madama Butterfly (Cpte)

GIORDA, Marcello (bar)
Verdi: Rigoletto (Cpte)

GIORDANO, Ezio (bass)
Puccini: Turandot (Cpte)
Verdi: Ballo in maschera (Cpte)

GIORDANO, Umberto (pf)
(EMI) **CDH7 61046-2** Enrico Caruso: Opera Arias and Songs - 1902-1904
(MCI) **MCCD086** The Essential Caruso
(PEAR) **EVC1(1)** The Caruso Edition, Vol.1 (pt 1)
(RCA) **GD60495(1)** The Complete Caruso Collection (pt 1)

GIORGETTI, Giorgio (bar)
Ponchielli: Gioconda (Cpte)
Puccini: Bohème (exc)
Verdi: Ballo in maschera (Cpte)
(DECC) **436 261-2DHO3** Puccini—Il Trittico

GIORGIA (sngr)
(DECC) **444 460-2DH** Pavarotti and Friends II

GIORGINI, Aristodemo (ten)
Puccini: Bohème (Cpte)
(RECO) **TRC3** The Art of Aristodemo Giorgini

GIOVANINETTI, Reynald (cond)
see New Philh
Verona Arena Orch

GIOVANNETTI, Julien (bar)
Massenet: Werther (Cpte)
Offenbach: Contes d'Hoffmann (exc)
Planquette: Rip van Winkle (Cpte)

GIRALDONI, Eugenio (bar)
(EMI) **CHS7 64860-2(1)** La Scala Edition - Vol.1, 1878-1914 (pt 1)
(EMI) **CHS7 64860-2(2)** La Scala Edition - Vol.1, 1878-1914 (pt 2)
(MEMO) **HR4408/9(2)** Singers in Genoa, Vol.1 (disc 2)
(NIMB) **NI7867** Legendary Baritones
(PEAR) **GEMMCDS9073(1)** Giovanni Zenatello, Vol.1 (pt 1)
(SYMP) **SYMCD1073** The Harold Wayne Collection, Vol.3
(SYMP) **SYMCD1168** The Harold Wayne Collection, Vol.19

GIRARD, André (cond)
see French Rad Lyric Orch

GIRARD, Valerie (sop)
(DINT) **DICD920204** Mozart—Concert Arias

GIRARDI, Piero (ten)
(PREI) **89048** Apollo Granforte (1886-1975) - I

GIRAUD, Fiorello (ten)
(MEMO) **HR4408/9(1)** Singers in Genoa, Vol.1 (disc 1)
(SYMP) **SYMCD1073** The Harold Wayne Collection, Vol.3

(SYMP) **SYMCD1077** The Harold Wayne Collection, Vol.4

GIRAUDEAU, Jean (ten)
Martinů: Comedy on the Bridge (Cpte), Julietta (Cpte)
Milhaud: Christophe Colomb (Cpte), Pauvre matelot (Cpte)
Offenbach: Contes d'Hoffmann (exc)
Poulenc: Mamelles de Tirésias (Cpte)
Ravel: Heure espagnole (Cpte)
(MONT) **TCE8760** Stravinsky: Stage Works

GIROD, Vincent (alto)
Monteverdi: Orfeo (Cpte)

GISMONDO, Giuseppe (ten)
Alfano: Risurrezione (Cpte)

GIULINI, Carlo Maria (cond)
see La Scala Orch
Los Angeles PO
Milan RAI SO
Philh
ROHO
Rome Op Orch
Rome RAI Orch
Santa Cecilia Academy Orch
VPO

GIURANNA, Bruno (cond)
see Venice and Padua CO

GIUSEPPINI, Giorgio (bass)
Verdi: Rigoletto (Cpte)

GJEVANG, Anne (mez)
Mozart: Mitridate (Cpte)
Nielsen: Saul and David (Cpte)
Wagner: Götterdämmerung (Cpte), Parsifal (Cpte), Walküre (Cpte)
(DG) **437 523-2GH** Grieg—Dramatic Works with Orchestra
(DG) **437 842-2GH6** Grieg—Complete Music with Orchestra
(EURO) **GD69003** Wagner—Der Ring des Nibelungen

GLANVILLE, Mark (bass)
(OPRA) **ORCH104** A Hundred Years of Italian Opera: 1820-1830

GLASGOW CWS BAND
cond R. TENNANT
(DOYE) **DOYCD005** Flower of Scotland

GLASS, Philip (pf)
Glass: Hydrogen Jukebox (Cpte)

(PHILIP) GLASS ENSEMBLE
cond M. RIESMAN
Glass: Belle et la Bête (Cpte), Einstein on the Beach (Cpte)

GLASSMAN, Allan (ten)
Puccini: Turandot (Cpte)
R. Strauss: Ariadne auf Naxos (Cpte)
Wagner: Parsifal (Cpte)
(DECC) **071 142-1DH (DECC)** Essential Opera

GLAUSER, Elisabeth (contr)
Wagner: Walküre (Cpte)
(PHIL) **434 420-2PM32(2)** Richard Wagner Edition (pt 2)

GLAWITSCH, Rupert (ten)
Suppé: Boccaccio (exc)
Zeller: Vogelhändler (exc)

GLEMSER, Bernd (pf)
(NAXO) **8 550785** Le Grand Tango

GLENN, Bonita (sop)
(SCHW) **312642** Unicef Gala 1991

GLENNIE, Evelyn (perc)
Bizet: Carmen Suites
(RCA) **RD60242** Evelyn Glennie - Rhythm Song

GLENNON, Jean (sngr)
Floyd: Susannah (Cpte)

GLICK, David (treb)
Britten: Little Sweep (Cpte)

GLOSSOP, Peter (bar)
Berlioz: Troyens (Cpte)
German: Merrie England (Cpte)
Purcell: Dido (Cpte)
Verdi: Otello (Cpte), Traviata (Cpte)
(DECC) **436 990-2DWO** The World of Benjamin Britten

GLOVER, Jane (cond)
see LMP
RPO

GLOVER, Lawrence (pf)
(LINN) **CKD008** Scotland's Music

GLUBOKY, Pyotr (bass)
Karetnikov: Till Eulenspiegel (Cpte)
Rachmaninov: Miserly knight (Cpte)
Rimsky-Korsakov: Tsar's Bride (Cpte)
Serov: Judith (Cpte)
(CDM) **LDC288 005/6** Bass Arias from Russian Opera

GLUCK, Alma (sop)
(MSCM) **MM30352** Caruso—Italian Opera Arias
(PEAR) **EVC3(1)** The Caruso Edition, Vol.3 (pt 1)
(PEAR) **GEMMCD9130** Great Sopranos, Vol.2
(RCA) **GD60495(5)** The Complete Caruso Collection (pt 5)
(RCA) **09026 61242-2** Caruso Sings Verdi
(RCA) **09026 61580-2(2)** RCA/Met 100 Singers, 100 Years (pt 2)

GLYNDEBOURNE FESTIVAL CHORUS
cond F. BUSCH
Mozart: Così fan tutte (Cpte), Don Giovanni (Cpte), Nozze di Figaro (Cpte)
(EMI) **CDH5 65072-2** Glyndebourne Recorded - 1934-1994
cond S. CAMBRELING
Rossini: Barbiere di Siviglia (Cpte)
cond A. DAVIS
Janáček: Jenufa (Cpte), Káťa Kabanová (Cpte)
Tchaikovsky: Queen of Spades (Cpte)
cond GRAEME JENKINS
Britten: Death in Venice (Cpte)
cond V. GUI
Mozart: Nozze di Figaro (Cpte)
Rossini: Barbiere di Siviglia (Cpte), Cenerentola (Cpte), Comte Ory (Cpte)
(EMI) **CDH5 65072-2** Glyndebourne Recorded - 1934-1994
cond B. HAITINK
Beethoven: Fidelio (Cpte)
Bizet: Carmen (Cpte)
Britten: Midsummer Night's Dream (Cpte)
Mozart: Così fan tutte (Cpte), Don Giovanni (Cpte), Idomeneo (Cpte), Nozze di Figaro (Cpte), Zauberflöte (Cpte)
Prokofiev: Love for 3 Oranges (Cpte)
R. Strauss: Arabella (Cpte)
Stravinsky: Rake's Progress (Cpte)
Verdi: Traviata (Cpte)
cond G. KUHN
Mozart: Entführung (Cpte)
R. Strauss: Intermezzo (Cpte)
cond R. LEPPARD
Cavalli: Calisto (Cpte)
Gluck: Orfeo ed Euridice (Cpte)
Monteverdi: Incoronazione di Poppea (Cpte)
(ERAT) **2292-45797-2** The Ultimate Opera Collection
cond J. PRITCHARD
Mozart: Così fan tutte (Cpte), Idomeneo (Cpte), Nozze di Figaro (Cpte)
Verdi: Falstaff (Cpte), Macbeth (Cpte)
cond S. RATTLE
Gershwin: Porgy and Bess (Cpte)
cond D. RENZETTI
Rossini: Cenerentola (Cpte)
(CAST) **CVI2071** Highlights from Glyndebourne
cond M. SARGENT
Sullivan: Gondoliers (Cpte), HMS Pinafore (Cpte), Iolanthe (Cpte), Mikado (Cpte), Patience (Cpte), Trial by Jury (Cpte), Yeomen of the Guard (Cpte)
(CFP) **CD-CFP4238** Gilbert and Sullivan
(CFP) **CD-CFP4582** Flowers in Music
(CFP) **CD-CFP4609** Favourite Gilbert & Sullivan
(EMI) **CMS7 64409-2** Sullivan—Pirates of Penzance & Orch. Works
(EMI) **CMS7 64412-2** Gilbert & Sullivan—Ruddigore/Shakespeare Music
cond F. STIEDRY
Gluck: Orfeo ed Euridice (exc)
cond F. WELSER-MÖST
Lehár: Lustige Witwe (Cpte)

GLYNDEBOURNE FESTIVAL ORCHESTRA
cond F. BUSCH
Mozart: Così fan tutte (Cpte), Don Giovanni (Cpte), Nozze di Figaro (Cpte)
(DUTT) **CDLX7012** The Incomparable Heddle Nash
(EMI) **CDH5 65072-2** Glyndebourne Recorded - 1934-1994
(EMI) **CDH7 63199-2** Sena Jurinac—Opera and Song Recital
(EMI) **CHS5 65058-2** The Great German Tradition
(MMOI) **CDMOIR406** Mozart—Historical Recordings
(PEAR) **GEMMCD9122** 20 Great Basses sing Great Arias
cond V. GUI
Mozart: Nozze di Figaro (Cpte)
Rossini: Cenerentola (Cpte), Comte Ory (Cpte)
(EMI) **CDH5 65072-2** Glyndebourne Recorded - 1934-1994
(EMIN) **CD-EMX9519** Great Sopranos of Our Time
cond R. LEPPARD
(TELD) **9031-77676-6(TELD)** My World of Opera - Kiri Te Kanawa
cond J. PRITCHARD
Busoni: Arlecchino (Cpte)
(EMI) **CDH5 65072-2** Glyndebourne Recorded - 1934-1994

GLYNNE, Howell (bass)
German: Merrie England (Cpte)
Lehár: Lustige Witwe (exc)

GLYNNE, Walter (ten)
(SYMP) **SYMCD1123** Sullivan—Sesquicentenial Commemorative Issue

GNEUER, Herbert (ten)
R. Strauss: Rosenkavalier (Cpte)

GOBBI, Antonio de (bass)
Verdi: Rigoletto (Cpte)

GOBBI, Tito (bar)
Donizetti: Lucia di Lammermoor (Cpte)
Giordano: Fedora (Cpte)
Leoncavallo: Pagliacci (Cpte)
Puccini: Bohème (exc), Tosca (Cpte), Villi (Cpte)
Rossini: Barbiere di Siviglia (exc)
Verdi: Aida (Cpte), Ballo in maschera (Cpte), Don Carlo (Cpte), Falstaff (Cpte), Nabucco (exc), Otello (Cpte), Rigoletto (Cpte), Simon Boccanegra (Cpte)
(CBS) **CD79312** Puccini: Il Trittico
(CFP) **CD-CFP4602** Favourite Opera
(CFP) **CD-CFP4613** Favourite TV Classics
(CFP) **CD-CFP4656** Herbert von Karajan conducts Opera
(CFP) **CD-CFP9013** Duets from Famous Operas
(DECC) **436 464-2DM** Ten Top Baritones & Basses
(EMI) **CDC5 55216-2** Maria Callas - La Divina 3
(EMI) **CDM7 63109-2** Tito Gobbi - Opera Aria Recital
(EMI) **CHS7 64864-2(2)** La Scala Edition - Vol.2, 1915-46 (pt 2)
(EMI) **CHS7 69741-2(7)** Record of Singing, Vol.4—Italian School
(EMI) **CMS7 64165-2** Puccini—Trittico
(EMI) **CZS7 67440-2** The Best of Rossini
(EMI) **LDB4 91283-1(EMI)** Maria Callas at Covent Garden
(EMI) **LDB9 91258-1(EMI)** Maria Callas at the Paris Opera December 1958
(EMIL) **CDZ101** Best Loved Classics 2
(MEMO) **HR4376/7** Tito Gobbi—Opera Arias
(NIMB) **NI7851** Legendary Voices
(PREI) **89995** Famous Italian Baritones
(RCA) **09026 61580-2(6)** RCA/Met 100 Singers, 100 Years (pt 6)
(RCA) **09026 62689-2** The Voices of Living Stereo, Volume 1
(TEST) **SBT1019** Tito Gobbi - Opera Arias & Songs

GOBBI, Vito (ten)
Donizetti: Ajo nell'imbarazzo (Cpte)
Rossini: Signor Bruschino (Cpte)

GOBLE, Theresa (mez)
(OPRA) **ORCH104** A Hundred Years of Italian Opera: 1820-1830

GODDING, Emile (bass)
Schreker: Gezeichneten (Cpte)

GODES, Pacual (cond)
see orch

GODFREY, Batyah (contr)
V. Thomson: Mother of us all (Cpte)

GODFREY, Sir Dan (cond)
see Bournemouth Municipal Orch

GODFREY, Graham (ten)
Menotti: Boy who grew too fast (Cpte)

GODFREY, Isidore (cond)
see New SO
ROHO
RPO
SO

GODFREY, Jerry (bar)
S. Wallace: Kabbalah (Cpte)

GODIN, Emmerich (ten)
(SCHW) **314602** Vienna State Opera Live, Vol.10

GODIN, Guy (sngr)
(EMI) **CZS5 68295-2** Messager/Lecocq—Operetta Highlights
(EMI) **CZS7 67872-2** Lehár—Operettas (highlights in French)

GOEDHARDT, Wouter (ten)
R. Strauss: Rosenkavalier (Cpte)

GOEHR, Walter (cond)
see LSO
orch

GOEKE, Leo (ten)
Leoncavallo: Pagliacci (Cpte)
Mozart: Don Giovanni (Cpte), Idomeneo (Cpte), Zauberflöte (Cpte)
Stravinsky: Rake's Progress (Cpte)
Verdi: Don Carlo (Cpte), Traviata (Cpte), Vespri Siciliani (Cpte)
(BUTT) **BMCD015** Pavarotti Collection - Duets and Scenes

GOERKE, Amo (sngr)
Schultze: Schwarzer Peter (Cpte)

GOETHE INSTITUT CHOIR
cond R. SACCANI
Verdi: Aida (Cpte)

GOETZEN, Vittorio de (sngr)
(PREI) **89998** Antonio Paoli (1871-1946)

GOGORZA, Emilio de (bar)
(NIMB) **NI7860** Emma Eames & Pol Plançon
(ROMO) **81001-2** Emma Eames (1865-1952)

GOLDBERG, Reiner (ten)
Beethoven: Fidelio (Cpte)
Mozart: Zauberflöte (Cpte)
R. Strauss: Daphne (Cpte)
Schoenberg: Moses und Aron (Cpte)
Wagner: Götterdämmerung (Cpte), Parsifal (Cpte), Siegfried (Cpte), Walküre (exc)
Zemlinsky: Kreidekreis (Cpte)
(DG) **437 825-2GH** Wagner—Der Ring des Nibelungen - Highlights
(DG) **445 354-2GX14** Wagner—Der Ring des Nibelungen
(EMI) **CDC5 55350-2** Cheryl Studer - A Portrait

GOLDRAY, Martin (kybd)
Glass: Hydrogen Jukebox (Cpte)

GOLDRAY, Martin (pf)
(PNT) **434 873-2PTH** Jon Gibson—In Good Company

GOLDSACK, Christopher (treb)
R. Strauss: Salomé (Cpte)

GOLDSTONE, Anthony (pf)
(AMPH) **PHICD123** Celebration of Piano Music from Castle Howard

GOLFIER, Françoise (sop)
Debussy: Pelléas et Mélisande (Cpte)

GOLL, Axelle (sop)
Mascagni: Cavalleria Rusticana (Cpte)

GÖLLNITZ, Fritz (ten)
R. Strauss: Elektra (Cpte)
Weill: Mahagonny (Cpte)

GOLOVANOV, Nikolai (cond)
see Bolshoi Th Orch

GOLOVSHIN, Igor (cond)
see Moscow St SO

GOLSCHMANN, Vladimir (cond)
see Sym of the Air
Vienna St Op Orch

GOLTZ, Christel (sop)
Mozart: Zauberflöte (Cpte)
Orff: Antigonae (Cpte)
(VAI) **VAIA1012** Eleanor Sterber sings R. Strauss

GOLTZ, Gottfried von der (cond)
see Freiburg Baroque Orch

GOMEZ, Jill (sop)
Alwyn: Miss Julie (Cpte)
Britten: Midsummer Night's Dream (Cpte)
Tippett: Knot Garden (Cpte)
(UNIC) **DKPCD9055** Cabaret Classics

GONDA, Anna (mez)
Berg: Wozzeck (Cpte)
Mozart: Zauberflöte (Cpte)
R. Strauss: Rosenkavalier (Cpte)
Rossini: Italiana in Algeri (Cpte)

GONDEK, Juliana (sop)
Handel: Giustino (Cpte), Ottone (Cpte), Radamisto (Cpte)
Mozart: Zauberflöte (Cpte)

GONSZAR, Rudolph (bass)
Wagner: Tannhäuser (Cpte)

GONTCHARENKO, Bernard (bass)
Bizet: Carmen (Cpte)

GONZAGA, Aida (sop)
(PEAR) **GEMMCDS9159(2)** De Luca Edition, Vol.1 (pt 2)

GONZALES, Carmen (mez)
Mascagni: Cavalleria Rusticana (Cpte)
Puccini: Bohème (Cpte)
Vivaldi: Orlando Furioso (Cpte)
(SCHW) **314052** Opera Gala

GONZALEZ, Ching (voc)
M. Monk: Atlas (Cpte)

GONZALEZ, Dalmacio (ten)
Halévy: Juive (Cpte)
Rossini: Donna del Lago (Cpte), Signor Bruschino (Cpte)
Verdi: Falstaff (Cpte)
(CAST) **CASH5052** Verdi Operatic Favourites
(CAST) **CVI2065** Highlights from the Royal Opera House, Covent Garden

GONZALEZ, Fabienne (sop)
Essyad: Collier des Ruses (Cpte)

GOODALL, David (gtr)
(NIMB) **NI5106** Rossini—Opera Arias

GOODALL, Sir Reginald (cond)
see ENO Orch
EOGCO
ROHO
Sadler's Wells Op Orch
WNO Orch

GOODALL, Valorie (sop)
Lehár: Land des Lächelns (exc)

GOODING, Julia (sop)
Blow: Venus and Adonis (Cpte)
Handel: Teseo (Cpte)
Monteverdi: Orfeo (Cpte)
Purcell: King Arthur, Z628 (Cpte)
Vaughan Williams: Hugh the Drover (Cpte)

GOODMAN, Al (cond)
see orch

GOODMAN, Erica (hp)
(IMP) **PCD1091** Jeux à deux

GOODMAN, Roy (cond)
see Brandenburg Consort
Hanover Band
Parley of Instr

GOOSSENS, Sir Eugene (cond)
see BNOC Orch
orch

GORALSKI, Jan (bar)
Mussorgsky: Boris Godunov (Cpte)

GORCHAKOVA, Galina (sop)
Borodin: Prince Igor (Cpte)
Tchaikovsky: Mazeppa (Cpte)

GORDON, Sybil (mez)
Sullivan: Gondoliers (Cpte)

GORIN, Igor (bar)
(NIMB) **NI7867** Legendary Baritones

GORLI, Sandro (cond)
see Divertimento Ens

GÖRLICH, Gustav (cond)
see Stuttgart Op Orch

GÖRNE, Matthias (bass-bar)
Schreker: Gezeichneten (Cpte)

GÖRNER, Anne (sop)
Delius: Village Romeo and Juliet (Cpte)

GOROKHOVSKAYA, Yevgenia (mez)
Mussorgsky: Boris Godunov (Cpte)

GORR, Rita (mez)
Gounod: Faust (exc)
Massenet: Werther (Cpte)
Poulenc: Dialogues des Carmélites (Cpte)
Saint-Saëns: Samson et Dalila (Cpte)
Verdi: Aida (exc)
Wagner: Walküre (Cpte)
(EMI) **CHS7 69741-2(3)** Record of Singing, Vol.4—French School

GORTON, Susan (contr)
Britten: Peter Grimes (Cpte)
Sullivan: Mikado (Cpte), Pirates of Penzance (Cpte)

GÓRZYŃSKA, Halina (sop)
Gluck: Corona (Cpte)
Rossini: Signor Bruschino (Cpte)

GOSEBRUCH, Herbert (bass)
Wagner: Meistersinger (Cpte)

GOSS, Julia (sop)
Sullivan: Zoo (Cpte)
(BELA) **461 006-2** Gilbert & Sullivan—Songs and Snatches
(LOND) **436 813-2LM2** Sullivan—The Grand Duke. Overture Di Ballo. Henry VIII
(LOND) **436 816-2LM2** Sullivan—Utopia Ltd. Macbeth & Marmion Ovs etc

GOSSAGE, Julie (mez)
Sullivan: Pirates of Penzance (Cpte)

GÖSSLING, Christhard (euphonium/tuba)
(SONY) **SK53978** Prometheus

GOSTIC, Joseph (ten)
Mozart: Zauberflöte (Cpte)

GOTHENBURG CONCERT HALL CHOIR
cond N. JÄRVI
Sibelius: Maiden in the Tower (Cpte)

GOTHENBURG PRO MUSICA CHAMBER CHOIR
cond N. JÄRVI
Prokofiev: Fiery Angel (Cpte)

GOTHENBURG SYMPHONY CHORUS
cond N. JÄRVI
(DG) **429 984-2GH** Russian Orchestral Works
(DG) **435 757-2GH2** Borodin—Orchestral Works
(DG) **437 523-2GH** Grieg—Dramatic Works with Orchestra
(DG) **437 842-2GH6** Grieg—Complete Music with Orchestra
(DG) **429 984-5GH** Russian Orchestral Works

GOTHENBURG SYMPHONY ORCHESTRA
cond N. JÄRVI
Prokofiev: Fiery Angel (Cpte)
Sibelius: Maiden in the Tower (Cpte)
Tchaikovsky: Mazeppa (Cpte)
(DG) **429 494-2GDC** Intermezzo
(DG) **429 984 2GH** Russian Orchestral Works
(DG) **435 757-2GH2** Borodin—Orchestral Works
(DG) **437 523-2GH** Grieg—Dramatic Works with Orchestra
(DG) **437 842-2GH6** Grieg—Complete Music with Orchestra
(DG) **439 152-2GMA** Mad about Romance
(DG) **429 984-5GH** Russian Orchestral Works
cond T. MANN
(CPRI) **CAP22032** Berwald X 2—Historic Recordings, Vol.4
cond MYUNG-WHUN CHUNG
(BIS) **BIS-CD321** Nielsen—Orchestral Works

GOTTARDI, Virgilio (bar)
Verdi: Rigoletto (Cpte)

GOTTLIEB, Elizabeth (mez)
Schoenberg: Moses und Aron (Cpte)

GOTTLIEB, Henriette (sop)
(NIMB) **NI7848** Great Singers at the Berlin State Opera

GOTTLIEB, Peter (bar)
Cavalli: Calisto (Cpte)

GÖTTLING, Karin (sop)
J. Strauss II: Fledermaus (Cpte)

GOTTSCHICK, Jörg (bass)
Gurlitt: Wozzeck (Cpte)
Schreker: Gezeichneten (Cpte)
(CLOR) **TCO93-75** The Cleveland Orchestra-75th Anniversary CD Edition

GÖTZ, Werner (ten)
Wagner: Tristan und Isolde (Cpte)

GÖTZE, Marie (contr)
(SUPR) **11 2136-2(3)** Emmy Destinn—Complete Edition, Discs 5 to 8

GÖTZEN, Guido (bass)
Wagner: Meistersinger (Cpte)

GOULD, Glenn (pf)
(SONY) **SMK52650** Glenn Gould conducts and plays Wagner
(SONY) **SLV48433(SONY)** Glenn Gould's Greatest Hits
(SONY) **S6LV48400(2)(SONY)** Glenn Gould Collection (Part 2)

GOULDING, Charles (ten)
Sullivan: HMS Pinafore (Cpte)

GOUSLARCHE BOYS' CHOIR
cond E. TCHAKAROV
Tchaikovsky: Queen of Spades (Cpte)

GOWRIE, Gladys (mez)
Sullivan: Gondoliers (Cpte)

GRAARUD, Gunnar (ten)
(SCHW) **314622** Vienna State Opera Live, Vol.12
(SCHW) **314642** Vienna State Opera Live, Vol.14

GRACE, Nickolas (bar)
Bernstein: Candide (1988) (exc)
Sullivan: HMS Pinafore (exc)

GRACIA, Oscar Garcia de (bar)
Hindemith: Neues vom Tage (Cpte)

GRACIS, Ettore (cond)
see Bulgarian RSO
La Scala Orch

GRAEME, James (sngr)
Bernstein: West Side Story (Cpte)

GRAF, Hans (cond)
see Danish Nat RSO
Salzburg Mozarteum Orch
Stuttgart RSO

GRAF, Peter-Lukas (fl)
(JECK) **JD506-2** Flute Concertos

GRAFFIN, Philippe (vn)
(ETCE) **KTC1125** Showpieces for Violin & Orchestra

GRAHAM, Edna (sop)
Sullivan: Gondoliers (Cpte)
(CFP) **CD-CFP4238** Gilbert and Sullivan

GRAHAM, Susan (sop)
Berlioz: Béatrice et Bénédict (Cpte)
Verdi: Falstaff (Cpte)

GRAHAM-HALL, John (ten)
Britten: Albert Herring (Cpte), Midsummer Night's Dream (Cpte)
Janáček: Káta Kabanová (Cpte)

GRAHL, Hans (ten)
Wagner: Parsifal (exc)

GRAMATZKI, Ilse (mez)
Mozart: Zauberflöte (Cpte)
Wagner: Götterdämmerung (Cpte), Rheingold (Cpte), Walküre (Cpte)
(PHIL) **434 420-2PM32(1)** Richard Wagner Edition (Pt.1)

GRAML, Helmut (bar)
Orff: Mond (Cpte)

GRAMM, Donald (bass)
Bizet: Carmen (Cpte)
Verdi: Falstaff (Cpte)
(SONY) **SM3K46291** Stravinsky—Ballets, Vol.1
(SONY) **SM22K46290(3)** Stravinsky—The Complete Edition (pt 3)
(SONY) **SM22K46290(4)** Stravinsky—The Complete Edition (pt 4)

GRANCHER, Micheline (sop)
Debussy: Pelléas et Mélisande (Cpte)

(LA) GRANDE ECURIE ET LA CHAMBRE DU ROY
Lully: Alceste (Cpte)
cond J-C. MALGOIRE
Gluck: Orfeo ed Euridice (Cpte)
Vivaldi: Montezuma (Cpte)
(SONY) **SBK48285** Handel—Orchestral Works

GRANDI, Lidia (sop)
Verdi: Rigoletto (Cpte)

GRANDI, Margherita (sop)
(EMI) **CHS7 69741-2(7)** Record of Singing, Vol.4—Italian School

GRANDIS, Franco de (bass)
Mozart: Don Giovanni (Cpte), Nozze di Figaro (exc)
Rossini: Barbiere di Siviglia (Cpte), Guillaume Tell (exc)
Spontini: Vestale (Cpte)
Verdi: Don Carlo (Cpte)
(DECC) **436 261-2DHO3** Puccini—Il Trittico

GRANDJEAN, Andrée (mez)
Hahn: Ciboulette (exc)
(EMI) **CZS7 67515-2** Offenbach—Operetta highlights

GRANFORTE, Apollo (bar)
Leoncavallo: Pagliacci (Cpte)
Puccini: Tosca (Cpte)
(CLUB) **CL99-025** Giovanni Zenatello (1876-1949)

(CLUB) **CL99-509/10** Hina Spani (1896-1969)
(CONI) **CDHD235** The Puccini Album
(PEAR) **GEMMCDS9074(2)** Giovanni Zenatello, Vol.2 (pt 2)
(PEAR) **GEMMCD9956** Joseph Hislop (1884-1977)
(PREI) **89008** Irene Minghini-Cattaneo (1892-1944)
(PREI) **89037** Hina Spani (1896-1969)
(PREI) **89038** Giovanni Zenatello (1876-1949)
(PREI) **89048** Apollo Granforte (1886-1975) - I
(PREI) **89072** Aureliano Pertile (1885-1952) - II
(PREI) **89105** Apollo Granforte (1886-1975) - II
(PREI) **89995** Famous Italian Baritones

GRANT, Clifford (bass)
Bellini: Norma (Cpte)
Donizetti: Lucia di Lammermoor (Cpte)
Massenet: Esclarmonde (Cpte)
Meyerbeer: Huguenots (Cpte)
Mozart: Nozze di Figaro (Cpte), Schauspieldirektor (Cpte), Sposo deluso (Cpte)
Puccini: Tosca (Cpte)
Verdi: Corsaro (Cpte), Lombardi (Cpte), Rigoletto (Cpte)
Wagner: Götterdämmerung (exc), Rheingold (Cpte), Siegfried (Cpte), Walküre (Cpte)
(DECC) **071 149-1DH (DECC)** The Essential Sutherland

GRANT, Donnalynn (mez)
(CBC) **SMCD5139** A Gilbert & Sullivan Gala

GRANT, Simon (bass)
Blow: Venus and Adonis (Cpte)
Monteverdi: Orfeo (Cpte)

GRANT-MURPHY, Heidi (sop)
Mozart: Nozze di Figaro (Cpte)

GRANVILLE, Sydney (bar)
Sullivan: Gondoliers (Cpte), HMS Pinafore (Cpte), Mikado (Cpte)
(MMOI) **CDMOIR413** The Very Best of Gilbert & Sullivan

GRASSI, Rinaldo (ten)
(EMI) **CHS7 64860-2(2)** La Scala Edition - Vol.1, 1878-1914 (pt 2)

GRAUDAN, Joanna (pf)
(BIDD) **LAB059/60** Henri Temianka—Recital

GRAUNKE SYMPHONY ORCHESTRA
cond F. ALLERS
Millöcker: Bettelstudent (Cpte)
cond W. MATTES
Lehár: Graf von Luxemburg (Cpte), Land des Lächelns (Cpte), Lustige Witwe (exc)
(EMI) **CMS7 64309-2** Kálmán—Best-loved Melodies
cond C. MICHALSKI
(EMI) **CZS7 62993-2** Fritz Wunderlich—Great German Tenor
cond C. WILDMANN
(EMI) **CMS7 64309-2** Kálmán—Best-loved Melodies

GRAVES, Denyce (mez)
A. Thomas: Hamlet (Cpte)
Spontini: Vestale (Cpte)
Verdi: Otello (Cpte)
(SONY) **SLV48362(SONY)** Concert for the Planet Earth

GRAVINA, Giovanni (bass)
(SYMP) **SYMCD1065** The Harold Wayne Collection, Vol.1

GRAY, Fenton (bar)
Sullivan: Yeomen of the Guard (Cpte)

GRAY, James (hpd)
(AUVI) **AV6833** Madrigals and Laments

GRAY, Julian (gtr)
(DORI) **DOR90209** Baroque Inventions

GRAY, Linda Esther (sop)
Wagner: Feen (Cpte), Tristan und Isolde (Cpte)

GRAY, Lissa (sop)
Offenbach: Christopher Columbus (Cpte)

GRAYSON, Robert (ten)
Barber: Antony and Cleopatra (Cpte)

GREAGER, Richard (ten)
Donizetti: Lucia di Lammermoor (Cpte)
(KIWI) **CDSLD-82** Southern Voices—NZ International Opera Singers

GRECO, Norina (sop)
Verdi: Trovatore (Cpte)
(MYTO) **2MCD90317** Verdi—Un Ballo in maschera

GREEN, Adolf (sngr)
Bernstein: Candide (1988) (exc)

GREEN, Johnny (cond)
see Johnny Green Orch
orch
Orig Film Cast

GREEN, Martyn (bar)
Sullivan: Mikado (Cpte), Patience (Cpte)
(MMOI) **CDMOIR413** The Very Best of Gilbert & Sullivan

GREEN, Simon (sngr)
Romberg: Student Prince (Cpte)

GREENAN, Andrew (bass)
Britten: Peter Grimes (Cpte)

GREENAWALT, Roger (sngr)
J. Moran: Manson Family (Cpte)

GREENBERG, Sylvia (sop)
Haydn: Anima del filosofo (Cpte)

GREENE, Leon (bass)
Romberg: Student Prince (Cpte)
Sullivan: Iolanthe (exc)

GREENE, Patrick (sngr)
Rorem: Childhood Miracle (Cpte)

GREENWOOD, Anthony (cond)
see Philh

GREENWOOD, Clifford (cond)
see orch

GREEVY, Bernadette (mez)
(DECC) **444 543-2DF2** Essential Handel
(EMI) **CDM7 69544-2** Berlioz: Vocal Works

GREFE, Gustav (bass)
Puccini: Tosca (Cpte)

GREGER, Emmy (mez)
(EMI) **CDS7 49361-2** Offenbach: Operettas

GREGG SMITH SINGERS
cond R. CRAFT
Stravinsky: Rake's Progress (Cpte)

(JAAK) GREGGOOR CHORUS
cond A. RAHBARI
Puccini: Suor Angelica (Cpte)

GREGOIRE, André (ten)
Verdi: Simon Boccanegra (Cpte)

(JACK) GREGOOR CHOIR
cond A. RAHBARI
Puccini: Manon Lescaut (Cpte), Tabarro (Cpte)

GREGOR, Bohumil (cond)
see Prague Nat Th Orch

GREGOR, József (bass)
Giordano: Andrea Chénier (Cpte), Fedora (Cpte)
Puccini: Tosca (exc)

GREGORIAN, Gegam (ten)
Prokofiev: War and Peace (Cpte)

GREGORIG, Anna (sop)
(SCHW) **314572** Vienna State Opera Live, Vol.7

GREINDL, Josef (bass)
Beethoven: Fidelio (Cpte)
Berg: Lulu (Cpte)
Mozart: Entführung (Cpte), Zauberflöte (Cpte)
Orff: Prometheus (Cpte)
R. Strauss: Elektra (Cpte)
Verdi: Otello (Cpte)
Wagner: Fliegende Holländer (Cpte), Götterdämmerung (Cpte), Lohengrin (Cpte), Rheingold (Cpte), Siegfried (Cpte), Tannhäuser (Cpte), Tristan und Isolde (Cpte), Walküre (Cpte)
(ACAN) **44 2085-2** Carl Orff Collection
(DG) **429 169-2GR** Wagner—Choruses
(EMI) **CZS7 67123-2** Wagner: Der Ring des Nibelungen
(FOYE) **15-CF2011** Wagner—Der Ring de Nibelungen
(MYTO) **3MCD93381** Wagner—Die Walküre, etc
(PHIL) **434 420-2PM32(2)** Richard Wagner Edition (pt 2)
(PHIL) **446 057-2PB14** Wagner—The Ring Cycle - Bayreuth Festival 1967

GREINDL-ROSNER, Gudrun (sop)
R. Strauss: Intermezzo (Cpte)

GREISS, Renate (fl)
(FSM) **FCD91114** Virtuoso Chamber Music with Guitar

GRELLA, Bruno (bar)
Puccini: Tosca (Cpte)
Verdi: Traviata (Cpte)

GRENADIER GUARDS BAND
Sullivan: Iolanthe (Cpte)

GRESSE, André (bass)
(IRCC) **IRCC-CD800** Souvenirs from Meyerbeer Operas

GRESSIER, Jules (cond)
see French Rad Lyric Orch
Lamoureux Concerts Orch
Lamoureux Orch

GREVELLE, Sarian (mez)
Verdi: Trovatore (Cpte)

GREVILLIUS, Nils (cond)
see orch
Stockholm Concert Soc Orch
Stockholm Royal Op Orch
Stockholm Royal Orch

GRICOLO, Vittorio (alto)
Puccini: Tosca (Cpte)

GRIER, Francis (pf)
Britten: Little Sweep (Cpte)

GRIFFEL, Kay (sop/mez)
Verdi: Falstaff (Cpte)

GRIFFETT, James (ten)
(CAMP) **RRCD1323** Welcome Ev'ry Guest - John Blow/Henry Purcell Songs

GRIFFIN, Elsie (sop)
Sullivan: HMS Pinafore (Cpte), Pirates of Penzance (Cpte)
(MMOI) **CDMOIR413** The Very Best of Gilbert & Sullivan

GRIFFITH, David (ten)
Rossini: Scala di seta (Cpte)
Verdi: Macbeth (Cpte)

GRIFFITHS, Barry (vn)
(EMI) **CDC7 47355-2** Mozart—Concert Arias

GRIFFITHS, Gwyn (bar)
Mozart: Nozze di Figaro (Cpte)
Puccini: Madama Butterfly (exc)
R. Strauss: Salome (Cpte)

GRIFFITHS, Justine (mez)
(PEAR) **GEMMCD9175** Heddle Nash - Serenade

GRIFFITHS, Neil (ten)
Verdi: Traviata (Cpte)

GRIFFITHS, Rosalind (sop)
(LOND) **436 816-2LM2** Sullivan—Utopia Ltd. Macbeth & Marmion Ovs etc

GRIFFITHS, Wyn (bass-bar)
Vaughan Williams: Pilgrim's Progress (Cpte)

GRIGORESCU, Elena (sop)
Schreker: Ferne Klang (Cpte)

GRIGORIAN, Gegam (ten)
Borodin: Prince Igor (Cpte)
Prokofiev: War and Peace (exc)
Rimsky-Korsakov: Sadko (Cpte)
Tchaikovsky: Queen of Spades (Cpte)

GRIGORIEVA, Nina (mez)
Tchaikovsky: Queen of Spades (Cpte)

GRIGORIOU, Christos (bar)
Gounod: Roméo et Juliette (Cpte)
Massenet: Werther (Cpte)

GRIGOROVA, Petya (sop)
Keiser: Croesus (Cpte)

GRILLI, Umberto (ten)
Verdi: Lombardi (Cpte)

GRIMBERT, Jacques (cond)
see Concerto Armonico

GRIMETHORPE COLLIERY BAND
cond E. HOWARTH
(DOYE) **DOYCD013** A Night at the Opera

GRIMINELLI, Andrea (fl)
(DECC) **071 150-1DH (DECC)** Pavarotti in Hyde Park
(DECC) **436 320-5DH** Pavarotti in Hyde Park

GRIMM, Hans Günter (bass)
Lehár: Graf von Luxemburg (Cpte)

GRIMSHAW, Katherine (contr)
R. Strauss: Aegyptische Helena (Cpte)

GRIPEKOVEN, Margot (sop)
(MYTO) **2MCD943103** Lortzing—Zar und Zimmermann

GRIPPE, Solwig (sop)
Nørgård: Gilgamesh (Cpte)

GRIST, Reri (sop)
Donizetti: Elisir d'amore (Cpte)
Mozart: Così fan tutte (exc), Don Giovanni (Cpte), Entführung (Cpte), Nozze di Figaro (Cpte), Schauspieldirektor (Cpte)
Verdi: Ballo in maschera (Cpte), Rigoletto (Cpte)
(BUTT) **BMCD015** Pavarotti Collection - Duets and Scenes
(EMI) **CDC5 55017-2** Domingo Opera Classics
(SONY) **SM22K46290(4)** Stravinsky—The Complete Edition (pt 4)

GRITTON, Susan (sop)
(HYPE) **CDA67061/2** Britten—Purcell Realizations

GRITZIUK, Grigory (bar)
Shostakovich: Lady Macbeth of Mtsensk (Cpte)

GRIZZELL, Paul (bass)
Schoenberg: Moses und Aron (Cpte)

GROBE, Donald (ten)
Berg: Lulu (Cpte)
Henze: Junge Lord (Cpte)
Hindemith: Cardillac (Cpte), Mathis der Maler (Cpte)
Lehár: Lustige Witwe (exc)
Wagner: Rheingold (Cpte)
Weber: Oberon (Cpte)
(DG) **429 168-2GR** Wagner: Excerpts from Der Ring
(DG) **435 211-2GX15** Wagner—Der Ring des Nibelungen
(DG) **435 712-2GX2** Lehár—The Merry Widow. Suppé—Overtures
(DG) **439 423-2GCL** Wagner—Der Ring des Nibelungen (highlights)

GROENROOS, Walton (bar)
Gluck: Iphigénie en Tauride (Cpte)
Tchaikovsky: Iolanta (Cpte)
Wagner: Tannhäuser (Cpte)
(BIS) **BIS-CD373/4** Opera Scenes from Savaonlinna

GROH, Herbert Ernst (ten)
(MMOI) **CDMOIR419** Vienna Nights - Golden Age of Operetta
(PEAR) **GEMMCD9419** Herbert Ernst Groh—Opera Recital

GROHMANN, Hilde (mez)
(MYTO) **3MCD93381** Wagner—Die Walküre, etc

GROHOWSKI, Elizabeth (sngr)
Schuman: Question of Taste (Cpte)

GRØNDAHL, Launy (cond)
see Danish RSO

GROOP, Monica (mez)
Donizetti: Linda di Chamounix (Cpte)
Mozart: Così fan tutte (Cpte)

GROOTE, Hilda de (sop)
R. Strauss: Ariadne auf Naxos (Cpte)

GRÖSCHEL, Werner (bass)
Monteverdi: Orfeo (Cpte)

GROSSBERGER, Dina (mez)
Puccini: Suor Angelica (Cpte)

GROSSMANN, Walter (bass)
Mozart: Zauberflöte (Cpte)
Wagner: Lohengrin (Cpte)
(PREI) **89057** Charles Kullmann (1903-1982)
(PREI) **89082** Margarete Klose (1902-1968)
(PREI) **89092** Erna Berger (1900-1990) - II
(SCHW) **314502** Vienna State Opera—Live Recordings (sampler)
(SCHW) **314702** Vienna State Opera Live, Vol.20

GROUPE VOCAL DE FRANCE
cond L. PFAFF
Dusapin: Romeo and Juliet (Cpte)
cond M. ROSTROPOVICH
Tchaikovsky: Iolanta (Cpte)

ROVE, Jill (mez)
Moran: Dracula Diary (Cpte)

ROVES, Sir Charles (cond)
see English Sinfonia
RLPO
RPO

ROVES, Glenys (sop)
J. Strauss II: Fledermaus (Cpte)
Janáček: Cunning Little Vixen (Cpte)
(ASV) **CDWHL2088** Trumpet and Soprano in Duet

ROVES, Paul (ten)
Puccini: Manon Lescaut (Cpte)
Wagner: Parsifal (exc)
(RCA) **09026 61509-2** A Salute to American Music

ROVES, Travis Paul (sngr)
Schuman: Question of Taste (Cpte)

RUBER, Andrea (sop)
Wagner: Götterdämmerung (Cpte)
(DG) **445 354-2GX14** Wagner—Der Ring des Nibelungen
(DG) **072 422-3GH7** Levine conducts Wagner's Ring

RÜBER, Arthur (cond)
see Berlin Deutsche Op Orch

RUBER, Ferry (ten)
Abraham: Blume von Hawaii (exc), Viktoria und ihr Husar (exc)
J. Strauss II: Fledermaus (Cpte), Wiener Blut (exc)
Lehár: Land des Lächelns (exc)
Orff: Kluge (Cpte), Mond (Cpte)
R. Strauss: Rosenkavalier (Cpte)
Suppé: Schöne Galathee (exc)
(EURO) **GD69022** Oscar Straus: Operetta excerpts
(RCA) **74321 24790-2** Carl Orff 100 Years Edition

RUBER, Heinz Karl (bar)
(LARG) **Largo 5114** Weill—Berlin im licht

RUBER, Josef Leo (cond)
see Vienna Volksoper Orch

RUBEROVÁ, Edita (sop)
Bellini: Beatrice di Tenda (Cpte), Capuleti (Cpte), Puritani (Cpte)
Donizetti: Linda di Chamounix (Cpte), Lucia di Lammermoor (Cpte), Maria Stuarda (Cpte), Roberto Devereux (Cpte)
Gluck: Orfeo ed Euridice (Cpte)
Humperdinck: Hänsel und Gretel (Cpte)
J. Strauss II: Fledermaus (exc)
Mozart: Don Giovanni (Cpte), Entführung (Cpte), Finta Giardiniera (Cpte), Idomeneo (Cpte), Lucio Silla (Cpte), Mitridate (Cpte), Sogno di Scipione (Cpte), Zauberflöte (Cpte)
Offenbach: Contes d'Hoffmann (exc)
R. Strauss: Arabella (Cpte), Ariadne auf Naxos (Cpte)
Verdi: Don Carlo (Cpte), Rigoletto (Cpte), Traviata (Cpte)
(CFP) **CD-CFP4612** Favourite Mozart
(CFP) **CD-CFP4656** Herbert von Karajan conducts Opera
(DG) **439 153-4GMA** Mad about Sopranos
(EMI) **CZS7 67440-2** The Best of Rossini
(EMIN) **CD-EMX2234** French and Italian Operatic Arias
(EMIN) **CD-EMX9519** Great Sopranos of Our Time
(EURO) **VD69256** Mozart—Opera Arias
(NIGH) **NC090560-2** The Anniversary Concert - Gruberova
(ORFE) **C072831A** The Art of the Coloratura
(ORFE) **C101841A** Famous Operatic Arias
(ORFE) **C394301B** Great Mozart Singers Series, Vol. 3
(SONY) **SK45855** Mozart: Bastien und Bastienne
(SUPR) **11 0345-2** Edith Gruberová - Operatic Recital
(TELD) **4509-93691-2** Queen of Coloratura
(TELD) **4509-97507-2** Mozart—Famous Opera Arias

GRUDGIONZ FESTIVAL CHORUS
cond G-F. MASINI
(RCA) **09026 68014-2** Pavarotti - The Early Years, Vol.2

GRUDGIONZ FESTIVAL ORCHESTRA
cond G-F. MASINI
(RCA) **09026 68014-2** Pavarotti - The Early Years, Vol.2

GRUHN, Nora (sop)
(CLAR) **CDGSE78-50-33** Lauritz Melchior & Albert Coates
(DANA) **DACOCD319/21** The Lauritz Melchior Anthology - Vol.5
(EMI) **CDH7 69789-2** Melchior sings Wagner
(MSCM) **MM30285** Great Wagnerian Singers, Vol.2
(PEAR) **GEMMCDS9137** Wagner—Der Ring des Nibelungen

GRUMBACH, Raimund (bass)
Leoncavallo: Bohème (Cpte)
Orff: Mond (Cpte)
R. Strauss: Intermezzo (Cpte)
Wagner: Tristan und Isolde (Cpte)
Weber: Freischütz (Cpte)
(RCA) **74321 24790-2** Carl Orff 100 Years Edition

GRÜMMER, Elisabeth (sop)
Humperdinck: Hänsel und Gretel (Cpte)
Mozart: Don Giovanni (Cpte), Idomeneo (Cpte)
Wagner: Lohengrin (Cpte), Meistersinger (exc), Tannhäuser (Cpte)
Weber: Freischütz (Cpte)
(CFP) **CD-CFP4616** Ave Maria
(EMI) **CDH5 65201-2** Leonie Rysanek - Operatic Recital
(EMI) **CDM7 63657-2** Schwarzkopf sings Opera Arias
(EMI) **CZS7 62993-2** Fritz Wunderlich—Great German Tenor
(EMI) **CZS7 67123-2** Wagner: Der Ring des Nibelungen
(ORFE) **C394201B** Great Mozart Singers Series, Vol. 2

GRUMMET, Adey (sop)
J. Strauss II: Fledermaus (Cpte)

GRUNDEN, Per (ten)
Lehár: Lustige Witwe (exc)

GRUNDHEBER, Franz (bar)
Berg: Wozzeck (Cpte)
Busoni: Doktor Faust (Cpte)
Hindemith: Mörder, Hoffnung der Frauen (Cpte)
Humperdinck: Hänsel und Gretel (Cpte)
R. Strauss: Elektra (Cpte), Rosenkavalier (exc), Salome (Cpte)
Wagner: Fliegende Holländer (Cpte)
(CAPR) **10 448** Zemlinsky—Orchestral Works and Songs

GRUNDY, Owen (bass)
Sullivan: Mikado (Cpte)

GRUNOW, Irina (sop)
(MYTO) **3MCD93381** Wagner—Die Walküre, etc

GRYCHNIK, Henryk (ten)
Szymanowski: King Roger (Cpte)

GRYZUNOV, Ivan (bar)
(ARLE) **ARL23/5** Rimsky-Korsakov—Sadko
(PEAR) **GEMMCDS9111(2)** Singers of Imperial Russia, Vol.5 (pt 2)

GUADAGNO, Anton (cond)
see LSO
New Philh
RCA Italiana Op Orch
RPO
SRO
Verona Arena Orch
Vienna St Op Orch

GUAGNI, Enzo (ten)
Puccini: Bohème (exc)

GUALDA, Silvio (perc)
Bernstein: West Side Story Symphonic Dances
Xenakis: Orestia (Cpte)

GUARNERA, Piero (bar)
Salieri: Locandiera (Cpte)

GUARNIERI, Antonio (cond)
see La Scala Orch

GUARRERA, Frank (bar)
Verdi: Falstaff (Cpte)
(RCA) **GD60326** Verdi—Operas & Choral Works

GUBER, Carola (contr)
Steffani: Henrico Leone (Cpte)

GUDBJÖRNSSON, Gunnar (ten)
(IMP) **TCD1070** Invitation to the Opera
(PHIL) **422 523-2PME8(2)** The Complete Mozart Edition Vol 23 (pt 2)
(RPO) **CDRPD9001** Classical Spectacular
(RPO) **CDRPO5010** Classical Spectacular 2

GUEDEN, Hilde (sop)
Donizetti: Elisir d'amore (Cpte)
J. Strauss II: Fledermaus (Cpte), Wiener Blut (exc)
Lehár: Giuditta (exc), Graf von Luxemburg (exc), Lustige Witwe (exc), Zarewitsch (exc)
Mozart: Don Giovanni (Cpte), Nozze di Figaro (Cpte), Zauberflöte (Cpte)
Puccini: Bohème (Cpte)
R. Strauss: Arabella (Cpte), Ariadne auf Naxos (Cpte), Daphne (Cpte), Rosenkavalier (Cpte), Schweigsame Frau (Cpte)
Verdi: Rigoletto (Cpte)
Wagner: Meistersinger (Cpte)
(DECC) **425 852-2DWO** Your hundred best tunes vol 6
(DECC) **425 959-2DM** Lisa della Casa sings R. Strauss
(DECC) **436 316-2DA** Golden Operetta
(DG) **431 110-2GB** Great Voices - Fritz Wunderlich
(DG) **435 145-2GX5(1)** Fritz Wunderlich—Opera Arias, Lieder, etc (part 1)
(ORFE) **C394201B** Great Mozart Singers Series, Vol. 2
(ORFE) **C394401B** Great Mozart Singers Series, Vol. 4
(PREI) **90227** Hilde Gueden - As The World Knew Her

GUELFI, Giangiacomo (bar)
Donizetti: Lucia di Lammermoor (Cpte)
Meyerbeer: Africaine (Cpte)
Verdi: Aida (Cpte), Due Foscari (Cpte)
(DG) **419 257-2GH3** 'Cav' and 'Pag', etc
(MEMO) **HR4235/6** Great Voices-Renata Tebaldi

GUÉNOT, L. (bass)
Massenet: Manon (Cpte), Werther (Cpte)

GUERRERA, Frank (bar)
Wagner: Lohengrin (Cpte)

GUERRINI, Barbara (mez)
(DECC) **436 261-2DHO3** Puccini—Il Trittico

GUERRINI, Virginia (mez)
(EMI) **CHS7 64860-2(2)** La Scala Edition - Vol.1, 1878-1914 (pt 2)
(MEMO) **HR4408/9(2)** Singers in Genoa, Vol.1 (disc 2)

GUGGENHEIM, Janet Goodman (pf)
(EMI) **CDC7 54108-2** Tchaikovsky—Violin Works
(EMI) **LDB9 91243-1(EMI)** Itzak Perlman Live in Russia

GUGGIA, Mario (ten)
Donizetti: Martyrs (Cpte)
R. Strauss: Rosenkavalier (Cpte)

GUGLIELMI, Margherita (sop)
Rossini: Cenerentola (Cpte)

GUGLIELMO, Roberto (pf)
(MDIT) **MED92102** Airs, Dances and Prayers

GUI, Henri (bar)
Gounod: Roméo et Juliette (Cpte)

GUI, Vittorio (cond)
see EIAR Orch
Glyndebourne Fest Orch
LPO
Rome Op Orch
RPO
Turin EIAR Orch
Vienna St Op Orch

GUIDI, Amelia (mez)
Giordano: Andrea Chénier (Cpte)

GUIDO D'AREZZO CHOIR
Salieri: Axur (Cpte)

GUIGUE, Paul (bar)
Fauré: Pénélope (Cpte)
Offenbach: Périchole (Cpte)
(EMI) **CZS5 68113-2** Vive Offenbach!

GUILDHALL STRING ENSEMBLE
(RCA) **09026 61275-2** Strings! The Definitive Collection
(RCA) **74321 25819-2** Café Classics - Strings

GUILE, Helen (contr)
R. Ward: Crucible (Cpte)

GUILLAUME, Edith (mez)
Nørgård: Siddhartha (Cpte)

GUILLEAUME, Margot (sop)
Mozart: Zauberflöte (Cpte)

GUINGAL, Alain (cond)
see French Lyrique Orch

GUIOMAR, Julien (narr)
Bizet: Carmen (Cpte)

GUIOT, Andréa (sop)
Bizet: Carmen (exc)
Offenbach: Contes d'Hoffmann (exc)

GUITTON, Lyliane (mez)
G. Charpentier: Louise (Cpte)

GULDBAEK, Ruth (sop)
Nielsen: Maskarade (Cpte), Saul and David (Cpte)

GULEGINA, Maria (sop)
Giordano: Andrea Chénier (Cpte)
Tchaikovsky: Queen of Spades (Cpte)
Verdi: Otello (Cpte)

GÜLKE, Peter (cond)
see Vienna SO

GULLINO, Walter (ten)
Verdi: Rigoletto (Cpte), Traviata (exc), Trovatore (exc)

GUMPOLDSKIRCHNER SPATZEN
cond E. HOWARTH
Ligeti: Grand Macabre (Cpte)

cond G. SOLTI
Wagner: Meistersinger (Cpte)

GUNDLACH, Willi (cond)
see Westphalia CO

GUNSON, Ameral (mez)
Britten: Rape of Lucretia (Cpte)
(CBS) **CD79312** Puccini: Il Trittico

GÜNTER, Horst (bar)
R. Strauss: Arabella (Cpte)
Wagner: Lohengrin (Cpte)
Weill: Mahagonny (Cpte)

GÜNTHER, Carl (ten)
Mozart: Apollo et Hyacinthus (Cpte), Zauberflöte (Cpte)
(PREI) **89301** The Art of Frida Leider

GÜNTHER, Felix (cond)
see orch

GÜNTHER, Hans (spkr)
Lehár: Graf von Luxemburg (Cpte)

GUNZENHAUSER, Stephen (cond)
see BBC PO
Slovak PO

GURA, Hedy (mez)
R. Strauss: Elektra (Cpte)

GURLITT, Manfred (cond)
see Berlin City Op Orch
Berlin St Op Orch
Berlin Staatskapelle
orch

GURTU, Trilok (perc)
Bernstein: West Side Story Symphonic Dances

GUSAK-GRIN, Marina (pf)
(CHAN) **CHAN8500** Russian Music for Violin and Piano

GUSALEWICZ, Genia (contr)
(MSCM) **MM30285** Great Wagnerian Singers, Vol.2

GUSCHLBAUER, Theodore (cond)
see Bamberg SO

GUSTAFSON, Nancy (sop)
J. Strauss II: Fledermaus (Cpte)
Janáček: Káťa Kabanová (Cpte)
Puccini: Bohème (Cpte)
Tchaikovsky: Queen of Spades (Cpte)
Verdi: Simon Boccanegra (Cpte)
Wagner: Rheingold (Cpte), Walküre (Cpte)
(DECC) **444 460-2DH** Pavarotti and Friends II
(EMI) **LDX9 91275-1(EMI)** Sawallisch conducts Wagner's Ring

GUSTAVSON, Eva (mez)
Verdi: Aida (Cpte)
(RCA) **GD60326** Verdi—Operas & Choral Works

GUSZALEWICZ, Genia (sop)
(CLAR) **CDGSE78-50-26** Wagner: Tristan und Isolde excerpts
(DANA) **DACOCD315/6** Lauritz Melchior Anthology - Vol. 3
(PEAR) **GEMMCDS9137** Wagner—Der Ring des Nibelungen
(PREI) **89068** Lauritz Melchior (1890-1973) - II

GUTH, Peter (cond)
see Vienna Strauss Festival Orch

GUTHRIE, Anne (sop)
(BELA) **461 006-2** Gilbert & Sullivan—Songs and Snatches

GUTOROVICH, Nikolai (ten)
Kabalevsky: Colas Breugnon (Cpte)

GUTSTEIN, Ernst (bar)
Berg: Lulu (Cpte)
Nicolai: Lustigen Weiber von Windsor (Cpte)
R. Strauss: Rosenkavalier (Cpte)

GUY, Maureen (mez)
Wagner: Götterdämmerung (Cpte), Walküre (Cpte)
(DECC) **414 100-2DM15** Wagner: Der Ring des Nibelungen

GUY-BROMLEY, Phillip (bass)
Britten: Billy Budd (Cpte)
(OPRA) **ORCH103** Italian Opera—1810-20

GUYER, Joyce (sop)
Wagner: Parsifal (Cpte)
(NEWP) **NPD85595** Haydn—La canterina

GUZELIMIAN, Armen (pf)
(EMI) **EG749768-2** Cabaret Songs—Michael Finstein

GWYNNE, David (bass)
Martinů: Greek Passion (Cpte)
Saxton: Caritas (Cpte)
Wagner: Parsifal (Cpte)

GYÁRTÓ, Stefan (cond)
see Hamburg St Op Orch

GYLDENFELDT, Graciela de (mez)
R. Strauss: Rosenkavalier (Cpte)

GYTON, Paul (ten)
(PHIL) **442 785-2PH** The Incomparable Alfredo Kraus

HAAGE, Pater (ten)
Ligeti: Grand Macabre (Cpte)
Schreker: Schatzgräber (Cpte)
Spohr: Jessonda (Cpte)
Wagner: Rheingold (Cpte), Siegfried (Cpte)
Weill: Mahagonny-Gesänge (Cpte), Sieben Todsünden (Cpte)
Zemlinsky: Traumgörge (Cpte)
(ADES) **14122-2** Music of our Time

HAAN, John David de (ten)
Korngold: Wunder der Heliane (Cpte)
(SONY) **S2K66836** Goldschmidt—Beatrice Cenci, etc

HAAN, Remco de (gtr)
(OTTA) **OTRC48710** Spanish Dances

HAAN, Richard (bass)
Janáček: From the House of the Dead (Cpte)

HAARLEM, Renée van (sop)
R. Strauss: Rosenkavalier (Cpte)

HAARTTI, Kristina (mez)
Madetoja: Juha (Cpte)

HAATANEN, Kyösti (cond)
see Savonlinna Op Fest Orch

HABERDASHERS' ASKE'S SCHOOL CHOIR
cond B. HAITINK
(EMI) **CDC7 49849-2** Famous Opera Choruses
cond H. LEWIS
Meyerbeer: Prophète (Cpte)
cond G. SOLTI
Bizet: Carmen (Cpte)

HABERDASHERS' ASKE'S SCHOOL GIRLS CHOIR
cond R. MUTI
Verdi: Ballo in maschera (Cpte)

HABICH, Eduard (bass)
Wagner: Siegfried (Cpte)
(CLAR) **CDGSE78-50-26** Wagner: Tristan und Isolde excerpts
(DANA) **DACOCD319/21** The Lauritz Melchior Anthology - Vol.5
(PEAR) **GEMMCDS9137** Wagner—Der Ring des Nibelungen
(PREI) **89028** Ivar Andresen (1896-1940)

HACKETT, Charles (ten)
(PEAR) **GEMMCDS9964** Rosa Ponselle - Columbia Acoustics
(PEAR) **GEMMCD9178** Riccardo Stracciari

HACQUARD, Mario (bar)
Massenet: Cléopâtre (Cpte)

HADDEN, Nancy (fl)
Mozart: Zauberflöte (exc)

HADICS, László (sngr)
Lehár: Lustige Witwe (exc)

HADJIEVA, Ludmila (sop)
Mussorgsky: Boris Godunov (Cpte)

HADLEY, Jerry (ten)
Bernstein: Candide (1988) (exc)
Floyd: Susannah (Cpte)
Gounod: Faust (Cpte)
Mozart: Così fan tutte (exc), Idomeneo (Cpte), Zauberflöte (Cpte)
Puccini: Bohème (Cpte)
Rossini: Barbiere di Siviglia (Cpte)
(CAST) **CVI2071** Highlights from Glyndebourne
(DG) **439 151-2GMA** Mad about Puccini
(DG) **439 251-2GY** The Leonard Bernstein Album
(DG) **439 251-5GY** The Leonard Bernstein Album
(RCA) **09026 61509-2** A Salute to American Music
(RCA) **09026 62681-2** Mr Jerry Hadley—Golden Days
(TELD) **4509-97463-2** A Portrait of Thomas Hampson-Arias and Songs
(TELD) **4509-98824-2** Thomas Hampson Collection,Vol III-Operatic Scenes
(TELD) **9031-73283-2** Hampson and Hadley

HADRABOVÁ, Eva (mez)
(SCHW) **314502** Vienna State Opera—Live Recordings (sampler)
(SCHW) **314512** Vienna State Opera Live, Vol.1
(SCHW) **314622** Vienna State Opera Live, Vol.12
(SCHW) **314642** Vienna State Opera Live, Vol.14
(SCHW) **314702** Vienna State Opera Live, Vol.20

HAEFLIGER, Ernst (ten)
Beethoven: Fidelio (Cpte)
Mozart: Don Giovanni (Cpte), Entführung (Cpte), Idomeneo (Cpte), Zauberflöte (Cpte)
Orff: Antigonae (Cpte)
(CLAV) **CD50-8305** Ernst Haefliger sings Mozart Arias
(DG) **437 677-2GDO2** Irmgard Seefried - Opera Recital
(DG) **445 400-2GDO10** Ferenc Fricsay - A Portrait

HAENCHEN, Hans (cond)
see CPE Bach Orch

HAENCHEN, Hartmut (cond)
see CPE Bach Orch

HAENDEL, Ida (vn)
(PEAR) **GEMMCD9939** Josef Hassid & Ida Haendel - 1940-42 Recordings

HAENEN, Anne (sngr)
Maderna: Satyricon (Cpte)

HAENEN, Tom (sngr)
Maderna: Satyricon (Cpte)

HAENGEL, Aracelly (mez)
Donizetti: Ajo nell'imbarazzo (Cpte)

HAFGREN, Lilly (sop)
(PREI) **89069** Josef von Manowarda (1890-1942)

HAGAN, Samuel (ten)
Gershwin: Porgy and Bess (Cpte)

HAGEGÅRD, Erland (ten)
Sibelius: Maiden in the Tower (Cpte)

HAGEGÅRD, Håkan (bar)
Corigliano: Ghosts of Versailles (Cpte)
Lidholm: Dream Play (Cpte)
Mozart: Don Giovanni (Cpte), Nozze di Figaro (Cpte), Zauberflöte (Cpte)
Puccini: Bohème (Cpte)
R. Strauss: Capriccio (Cpte)
Rossini: Barbiere di Siviglia (Cpte)
Wagner: Tannhäuser (exc)
(DG) **437 523-2GH** Grieg—Dramatic Works with Orchestra
(DG) **437 842-2GH6** Grieg—Complete Music with Orchestra

HAGEMANN, Emmi (mez)
(MYTO) **3MCD93381** Wagner—Die Walküre, etc

HAGEN, Christine (mez)
Wagner: Götterdämmerung (Cpte)

HAGEN OPERA CHORUS
cond M. HALÁSZ
Schreker: Ferne Klang (Cpte)

HAGEN PHILHARMONIC ORCHESTRA
cond M. HALÁSZ
Schreker: Ferne Klang (Cpte)
cond G. MARKSON
Weber: Peter Schmoll (Cpte)

HAGEN QUARTET
(DG) **447 069-2GH** Verdi/Puccini/Muzio—Works for String Quartet

HÄGER, Klaus (bass)
Lortzing: Undine (Cpte)

HAGER, Leopold (cond)
see ECO
Luxembourg RSO
Munich RO
RTL SO
Salzburg Mozarteum Orch

HAGER, Robert (bar)
R. Strauss: Elektra (Cpte)

HÄGGANDER, Mari Anne (sop)
Sibelius: Maiden in the Tower (Cpte)
Wagner: Meistersinger (Cpte), Parsifal (Cpte), Rheingold (Cpte)
(DG) **445 354-2GX14** Wagner—Der Ring des Nibelungen
(DG) **072 422-3GH7** Levine conducts Wagner's Ring

HÄGGSTAM, Alf (bass)
Haeffner: Electra (Cpte)

HAGLEY, Alison (sop)
Debussy: Pelléas et Mélisande (Cpte)
Janáček: Jenufa (Cpte)
Mozart: Nozze di Figaro (Cpte)

(THE) HAGUE PHILHARMONIC ORCHESTRA
cond E. SPANJAARD
(OLYM) **OCD507** 400 Years of Dutch Music, Volume 8
(OLYM) **OCD5008** 400 years of Dutch Music

HAHN, Werner (bar)
Schreker: Ferne Klang (Cpte)

HAIDER, Friederich (cond)
see Czech PO
Strasbourg PO
Swedish RSO
Tokyo PO

HAIGEN, Kevin (dncr)
Wagner: Tannhäuser (Cpte)

HAITINK, Bernard (cond)
see BRSO
Concertgebouw
LPO
ROHO
Staatskapelle Dresden

HAJÓSSYOVÁ, Magdaléna (sop)
Dvořák: Dimitrij (Cpte)
Janáček: Cunning Little Vixen (Cpte), Fate (Cpte)
Marschner: Hans Heiling (Cpte)
(KOCH) **34036-2** A Pageant of Opera
(OPUS) **9156 1824** Dvorský sings Operatic Arias

HAKEN, Eduard (bass)
Dvořák: Rusalka (Cpte)
Smetana: Brandenburgers in Bohemia (Cpte), Kiss (Cpte)

HALÁSZ, Michael (cond)
see Bratislava RSO
Budapest Failoni Orch
Hagen PO
Zagreb PO

HALDAS, Béatrice (sop)
Hindemith: Mörder, Hoffnung der Frauen (Cpte)
Zemlinsky: Geburtstag der Infantin (Cpte)

HALE, Robert (bass-bar)
R. Strauss: Frau ohne Schatten (Cpte)
Wagner: Fliegende Holländer (Cpte), Rheingold (Cpte), Siegfried (Cpte), Walküre (Cpte)
(EMI) **LDX9 91275-1(EMI)** Sawallisch conducts Wagner's Ring

HALEM, Victor von (bass)
Hindemith: Mathis der Maler (Cpte), Mörder, Hoffnung der Frauen (Cpte), Nusch-Nuschi (Cpte)
Mozart: Don Giovanni (Cpte), Zauberflöte (Cpte)
Pfitzner: Palestrina (Cpte)
Puccini: Tosca (exc)
R. Strauss: Rosenkavalier (Cpte)
Schreker: Ferne Klang (Cpte)
Wagner: Meistersinger (Cpte), Parsifal (Cpte)
Wolf: Corregidor (Cpte)
Zemlinsky: Traumgörge (Cpte)
(MEMO) **HR4223/4** Nicolai Ghiaurov

HALFVARSON, Eric (bass-bar)
Barber: Antony and Cleopatra (Cpte)

HALGRIMSON, Amanda (sop)
Mozart: Don Giovanni (Cpte)

HALÍŘ, Václav (bass)
Janáček: Jenufa (Cpte)

HALJÁKOVÁ, Sidónia (sop)
Puccini: Bohème (Cpte)
(OPUS) **9156 1824** Dvorský sings Operatic Arias

HALL, Berniece (sop)
Gershwin: Porgy and Bess (exc)

HALL, Carol (sop)
Gay: Beggar's Opera (Cpte)
Purcell: Tempest, Z631 (Cpte)
(ERAT) **4509-96371-2** Gardiner—The Purcell Collection

HALL, Janice (sop)
Rossini: Signor Bruschino (Cpte)

HALL, John (bar)
R. Strauss: Arabella (Cpte)
Verdi: Traviata (Cpte)

HALL, Meredith (sop)
Rameau: Hippolyte et Aricie (Cpte)

HALL, Peter (ten)
Holst: At the Boar's Head (Cpte)
Nono: Prometeo (Cpte)
Verdi: Ballo in maschera (Cpte)
(SONY) **SK53978** Prometheus

HALL, Robert (bass)
Purcell: Fairy Queen, Z629 (Cpte)

HALLACKER, Klaus-Peter (bar)
Delius: Village Romeo and Juliet (Cpte)

HALLAND, Edward (bass)
(CLAR) **CDGSE78-50-54** Coates conducts Wagner, Weber & Mendelssohn

HALLASCHKA, Heike (sop)
Telemann: Don Quichotte (Cpte)

HALLAWELL, Rachael (mez)
Henze: English Cat (Cpte)

HALLE CANTAMUS CHAMBER CHOIR
cond N. MCGEGAN
Handel: Giustino (Cpte)

HALLE OPERA HOUSE HANDEL FESTIVAL ORCHESTRA
cond H. ARMAN
(CAPR) **10 547** Handel—Arias

HALLÉ ORCHESTRA
cond J. BARBIROLLI
(BBCR) **DMCD98** BBC Proms - The Centenary: 1895-1995
(EMI) **CMS5 65119-2** Delius—Orchestral Works
cond M. HANDFORD
(CFP) **CD-CFP4543** Encores you love
(CFP) **CD-CFP4658** Everlasting Love
(CFP) **CD-CFP4661** Everlasting Tranquillity
cond H. HARTY
(BEUL) **1PD4** 78 Classics - Volume One
(PEAR) **GEMMCD9485** Harty conducts Berlioz
cond L. HEWARD
(CONI) **CDHD235** The Puccini Album
(DUTT) **CDAX8010** Hallé Orchestra Wartime Recordings
(MMOI) **CDMOIR412** Great Voices of the Century Sing Puccini
(TEST) **SBT1013** Dame Joan Hammond—A Celebration
cond C. LAMBERT
(TEST) **SBT1014** Delius—Orchestral Works
cond J. LOUGHRAN
(CFP) **CD-CFPSD4751** Berlioz—Orchestral Works
cond S. SKROWACZEWSKI
(IMP) **PCD1105** Weber—Overtures
cond B. TOVEY
(CFP) **CD-CFP4577** A Viennese Evening

HALLER, Andreas (bass-bar)
Schreker: Ferne Klang (Cpte)

HALLETT, Alfred (ten)
Bizet: Carmen (Cpte)

HALLGREN, Carl-Axel (bar)
Verdi: Rigoletto (Cpte)

HALLHUBER, Erich (sngr)
Schultze: Schwarzer Peter (Cpte)

HALLIN, Margareta (sop)
Verdi: Rigoletto (Cpte)

HALLON, Ladislav (ten)
Puccini: Bohème (Cpte)

HALLSTEIN, Ingeborg (sop)
Beethoven: Fidelio (Cpte)
Benatzky: Im weissen Rössl (exc)
(DG) **431 110-2GB** Great Voices - Fritz Wunderlich
(DG) **435 145-2GX5(1)** Fritz Wunderlich—Opera Arias, Lieder, etc (part 1)

HALSTEAD, Anthony (cond)
see Hanover Band

HALSTEAD, Patrick (bass)
G. Charpentier: Louise (Cpte)

HAMARI, Júlia (mez)
Cimarosa: Matrimonio segreto (Cpte)
J. Strauss II: Zigeunerbaron (Cpte)
Mascagni: Cavalleria rusticana (Cpte)
R. Strauss: Salome (Cpte)
Tchaikovsky: Eugene Onegin (Cpte)
Verdi: Ernani (Cpte)
Wagner: Meistersinger (Cpte)
Weber: Oberon (Cpte)
(EMI) **CDC7 54524-2** The José Carreras Album
(EMI) **CDM5 65575-2** Montserrat Caballé

HAMBOURG, Mark (pf)
(OPAL) **OPALCD9839** Pupils of Theodore Leschetizky

HAMBURG MONTEVERDI CHOIR
cond C. MACKERRAS
Purcell: Dido (Cpte)
(DG) **439 474-2GCL** Purcell—Opera & Choral Works

HAMBURG NDR CHAMBER ORCHESTRA
cond C. MACKERRAS
Purcell: Dido (Cpte)
(DG) **439 474-2GCL** Purcell—Opera & Choral Works

HAMBURG PHILHARMONIC ORCHESTRA
cond G. ALBRECHT
Beethoven: Leonore (exc)
Schumann: Genoveva (Cpte)
Spohr: Jessonda (Cpte)
(CAPR) **10 448** Zemlinsky—Orchestral Works and Songs
cond E. JOCHUM
R. Strauss: Elektra (Cpte)
cond L. MAGIERA
(ACAN) **49 384** Puccini: Opera Arias and Duets
cond I. METZMACHER
Rihm: Eroberung von Mexico (Cpte)

HAMBURG RADIO CHOIR
cond H. ROSBAUD
(STDV) **STR10022** La nuova musica, Vol.5

HAMBURG RADIO ORCHESTRA
(STDV) **STR10022** La nuova musica, Vol.5

HAMBURG RADIO SYMPHONY ORCHESTRA
cond W. SCHÜCHTER
Wagner: Lohengrin (Cpte)

HAMBURG STATE OPERA CHORUS
cond G. ALBRECHT
Schreker: Schatzgräber (Cpte)
Schumann: Genoveva (Cpte)
Spohr: Jessonda (Cpte)
cond S. GYÁRTÓ
Romberg: Student Prince (exc)
cond R. JACOBS
Gluck: Echo et Narcisse (Cpte)
cond E. JOCHUM
R. Strauss: Elektra (Cpte)
cond I. METZMACHER
Rihm: Eroberung von Mexico (Cpte)

HAMBURG STATE OPERA ORCHESTRA
cond G. ALBRECHT
Schreker: Schatzgräber (Cpte)
cond K. BÖHM
R. Strauss: Salome (Cpte)
cond S. GYÁRTÓ
Romberg: Student Prince (exc)
cond A. ROTHER
(EURO) **GD69018** Fritz Wunderlich—Recital
(RCA) **09026 62550-2** Ten Tenors in Love

HAMEL, Michel (ten)
Auber: Fra Diavolo (Cpte)
Audran: Miss Helyett (Cpte)
Bazin: Maître Pathelin (Cpte)
Bizet: Carmen (Cpte)
Hahn: Ciboulette (exc)
Lecocq: Jour et la Nuit (Cpte)
Offenbach: Chanson de Fortunio (Cpte)
Terrasse: Fiancée du Scaphandrier (Cpte)
(DECC) **433 400-2DM2** Ravel & Debussy—Stage Works
(EMI) **CDS7 49361-2** Offenbach: Operettas
(EMI) **CZS5 68113-2** Vive Offenbach!
(EMI) **CZS7 67515-2** Offenbach—Operetta highlights
(MONT) **TCE8760** Stravinsky: Stage Works
(MUSD) **20239-2** Delibes—Opéras-Comiques

HAMER, Ralph (bass)
Giordano: Andrea Chénier (Cpte)

HAMILTON, David (bar)
Barber: Antony and Cleopatra (Cpte)
Rossini: Barbiere di Siviglia (Cpte)

HAMILTON, Tom (tape op)
Ashley: Improvement (Cpte)

HAMILTON PHILHARMONIC ORCHESTRA
cond B. BROTT
(CBC) **SMCD5111** Gershwin—Orchestral Works

HAMMARSTRÖM, Kristina (mez)
Börtz: Bacchae (Cpte)

HAMMER, Gusta (mez)
R. Strauss: Elektra (Cpte)

HAMMERSMITH COUNTY SCHOOL GIRLS' CHOIR
cond J. BARBIROLLI
Verdi: Otello (Cpte)

HAMMES, Karl (bar)
(SCHW) **314662** Vienna State Opera Live, Vol.16

HAMMOND, Arthur (cond)
see orch

HAMMOND, Dame Joan (sop)
(CONI) **CDHD235** The Puccini Album
(EMI) **CHS5 65590-2** CBSO 75th Anniversary Set
(EMI) **CHS7 69741-2(1)** Record of Singing, Vol.4—Anglo-American School (pt 1)
(MMOI) **CDMOIR412** Great Voices of the Century Sing Puccini
(SAIN) **SCDC2076** David Lloyd-Early Recordings, 1940-1941
(TEST) **SBT1013** Dame Joan Hammond—A Celebration

HAMMOND-STROUD, Derek (bar)
Britten: Albert Herring (Cpte)
Prokofiev: Love for 3 Oranges (Cpte)
R. Strauss: Rosenkavalier (Cpte)
Verdi: Forza del destino (Cpte)
Wagner: Götterdämmerung (Cpte), Rheingold (Cpte), Siegfried (Cpte)

HAMMONS, Thomas (bar)
J. Adams: Death of Klinghoffer (Cpte)

HAMPE, Christiane (sop)
Lortzing: Undine (Cpte)

HAMPEL, Alfréd (ten)
Smetana: Bartered Bride (Cpte), Two Widows (Cpte)

HAMPSON, Thomas (bar)
A. Thomas: Hamlet (Cpte)
Delius: Village Romeo and Juliet (Cpte)
Gounod: Faust (exc)
Lehár: Lustige Witwe (Cpte)
Mozart: Così fan tutte (exc), Don Giovanni (Cpte), Nozze di Figaro (Cpte), Schauspieldirektor (Cpte), Zauberflöte (Cpte)
Puccini: Bohème (Cpte)
Rossini: Barbiere di Siviglia (Cpte)
Schubert: Fierrabras (Cpte)
Tchaikovsky: Eugene Onegin (Cpte)
Wagner: Götterdämmerung (Cpte)
(DG) **439 151-2GMA** Mad about Puccini
(DG) **072 428-1GH2(DG)** The Metropolitan Opera Gala
(EMI) **CDC5 55233-2** German Opera Arias
(EMI) **CDC7 54643-2** Rossini—Bicentenary Gala Concert
(EMI) **LDB491007-1 (EMI)** Rossini Bicentennial Birthday Gala
(ERAT) **4509-91715-2** The Ultimate Opera Collection 2
(TELD) **4509-97463-2** A Portrait of Thomas Hampson-Arias and Songs
(TELD) **4509-97507-2** Mozart—Famous Opera Arias
(TELD) **4509-98824-2** Thomas Hampson Collection,Vol III-Operatic Scenes
(TELD) **9031-73283-2** Hampson and Hadley

HANAK, Dorit (sop)
(SCHW) **312732** Lehár—Der Zarewitsch (excs)

HANAKOVA, Olga (contr)
Suchoň: Whirlpool (Cpte)

HANCHARD, Dana (sop)
Handel: Radamisto (Cpte)
M. Monk: Atlas (Cpte)

HANCOCK, John (bar)
Lully: Armide

HANCORN, John (bar)
Rameau: Castor et Pollux (Cpte)
Tippett: King Priam (Cpte)

HANDEL FESTIVAL ORCHESTRA
cond A. LEWIS
(VANG) **08.5069.71** Bach—Cantatas; Handel—Airs

HANDFORD, Maurice (cond)
see Hallé

HANDL, Herma (sop)
R. Strauss: Arabella (Cpte)

HANDLEY, Vernon (cond)
see LPO
RPO

HANDLOS, Franz (bass)
Verdi: Battaglia di Legnano (Cpte), Due Foscari (Cpte)

HANDT, Herbert (ten)
Mussorgsky: Khovanshchina (Cpte)

HANKIN, Wayne (cond)
see Orch

HANLEY, Regina (contr)
Sullivan: Gondoliers (Cpte), Iolanthe (Cpte)

HANN, Alexandra (sop)
Sullivan: Ruddigore (Cpte)

HANN, Georg (bass)
Mozart: Zauberflöte (Cpte)
R. Strauss: Arabella (Cpte)
Wagner: Fliegende Holländer (Cpte), Meistersinger (exc)
(ACAN) **43 268** Peter Anders sings German Opera Arias
(MYTO) **1MCD943104** R. Strauss—Capriccio (highlights) & Lieder
(MYTO) **2MCD943103** Lortzing—Zar und Zimmermann
(PILZ) **442118-2** Wagner—Operas in Historical Recordings
(PREI) **90168** Wagner—Die Meistersinger, Act 2, etc
(SCHW) **314582** Vienna State Opera Live, Vol.8

HANNAFORD STREET SILVER BAND
cond S. CHENETTE
(CBC) **SMCD5103** The Hannaford Street Silver Band

HANNAN, Eilene (sop)
Dvořák: Rusalka (Cpte)
Tchaikovsky: Eugene Onegin (exc)

HANNULA, Kaisa (sop)
Bergman: Singing Tree (Cpte)

HANNULA, Tero (bar)
Glass: Akhnaten (Cpte)

HANOVER BAND
cond R. GOODMAN
(NIMB) **NI5154** Weber: Orchestral Works
(RCA) **09026 61205-2** Handel—Opera Arias
(RCA) **09026 68139-2** Rossini—Overtures
cond A. HALSTEAD
(CPO) **CPO999 129-2** J. C. Bach—Opera Overtures, Vol. 1

HANOVER RADIO PHILHARMONIC ORCHESTRA
cond W.A. ALBERT
(CPO) **CPO999 076-2** Goetz—Orchestral Works
cond C. GARBEN
(HARM) **HMC90 1420** Weill—The Seven Deadly Sins; Songs

HANRIOT, John (ten)
Verdi: Traviata (Cpte)

HANSEN, Ib (bass-bar)
Nielsen: Maskarade (Cpte)

HANSEN, Jørgen Ernst (organ)
(ERAT) **2292-45801-2** Wedding Music

HANSEN, Kai (ten)
Monteverdi: Ritorno d'Ulisse in Patria (Cpte)

HANSEN, Ove Verner (bar)
Nielsen: Maskarade (Cpte)

HANSEN, Paul (ten)
Egk: Peer Gynt (Cpte)
Haydn: Anima del filosofo (Cpte)
Korngold: Violanta (Cpte)

HANSEN, Pia (mez)
Mozart: Zauberflöte (Cpte)

HANSKOV, Mette (db)
(DANA) **DACOCD378** Mette Hanskov plays music for Double Bass

HANSLI, Asbjørn (bar)
(UNIC) **UKCD2056** Grieg—Stage Works

HANSMANN, Rotraud (sop)
Monteverdi: Incoronazione di Poppea (Cpte), Orfeo (Cpte), Ritorno d'Ulisse in Patria (Cpte)
Wagner: Parsifal (Cpte)

HANSSEN, Vessa (mez)
Braein: Anne Pedersdotter (Cpte)
(UNIC) **UKCD2056** Grieg—Stage Works

HANUŠ, Karel (bass)
Fibich: Bride of Messina (Cpte)
Janáček: Cunning Little Vixen (Cpte), Excursions of Mr Brouček (Cpte)
Smetana: Bartered Bride (Cpte), Kiss (Cpte)

HANZALÍKOVÁ, Ludmila (mez)
Martinů: Julietta (Cpte)

HARBELL, Christiane (sop)
Bazin: Maître Pathelin (Cpte)
Messager: Passionêment (Cpte), P'tites Michu (exc)
Terrasse: Travaux d'Hercule (Cpte)
(MUSD) **20239-2** Delibes—Opéras-Comiques

HARBO, Erik (sngr)
Kuhlau: Lulu (Cpte)
Mussorgsky: Boris Godunov (Cpte)
Nørgård: Siddhartha (Cpte)

HARBOUR, Dennis (bass)
Verdi: Aida (Cpte)
(RCA) **GD60326** Verdi—Operas & Choral Works

HARDER, Lutz-Michael (ten)
U. Zimmermann: Weisse Rose (Cpte)

HARDY, Janis (mez)
Britten: Paul Bunyan (Cpte)
Copland: Tender Land (Cpte)

HARDY, Robert (spkr)
Gay: Beggar's Opera (Cpte)

HARDY, Rosemary (sop)
Knussen: Higglety Pigglety Pop! (Cpte), Where the Wild Things are (Cpte)
Purcell: Indian Queen, Z630 (Cpte), King Arthur, Z628 (Cpte), Tempest, Z631 (Cpte)
(ERAT) **4509-96371-2** Gardiner—The Purcell Collection
(HARM) **HMP390 807** Great Baroque Masters—Purcell
(HARM) **HMX290 1528/33(2)** A Purcell Companion (pt 2)

HARGAN, Alison (sop)
Wagner: Parsifal (Cpte)

HARISMENDY, François (sngr)
Saint-Saëns: Samson et Dalila (Cpte)

HARJANNE, Jouko (tpt)
(FINL) **4509-95583-2** Virtuoso Trumpet

HARJU, Marianne (sop)
Bergman: Singing Tree (Cpte)

HARLING, Stuart (bar)
Bizet: Carmen (Cpte)
Giordano: Andrea Chénier (Cpte)

HARMAN, Gerda (sop)
Mozart: Don Giovanni (exc)

HARMS, Kirsti (mez)
Meyerbeer: Huguenots (Cpte)

HARNEY, Ben (voc)
Joplin: Treemonisha (Cpte)

HARNISCH, Monika (mez)
R. Strauss: Rosenkavalier (Cpte)

HARNONCOURT, Nikolaus (cond)
see *COE*
Concertgebouw
VCM
Vienna SO
Zurich Op Hse Mozart Orch
Zurich Op Orch

HARNOY, Ofra (vc)
(MSOU) **DFCDI-012** Art of Ofra Harnoy
(RCA) **RD60697** Ofra Harnoy—Salut D'Amour
(RCA) **RD60758** Tchaikovsky—Cello Works
(RCA) **09026 60758-5** Tchaikovsky—Cello Works

HARPER, Daniel (ten)
Boito: Mefistofele (Cpte)
Puccini: Bohème (Cpte)
Schoenberg: Moses und Aron (Cpte)
(ETCE) **KTC1041** Nelly Miricioiu—Recital

HARPER, David (pf)
(ETCE) **XTC1041** Nelly Miricioiu at Wigmore Hall

HARPER, Heather (sop)
Britten: Midsummer Night's Dream (Cpte), Peter Grimes (Cpte), Rape of Lucretia (Cpte), Turn of the Screw (Cpte)
Mozart: Nozze di Figaro (Cpte)
Purcell: Dido (Cpte), King Arthur, Z628 (Cpte)
Sullivan: Iolanthe (Cpte), Patience (Cpte)
Tippett: Ice Break (Cpte)
(DECC) **443 393-2DWO** The World of Henry Purcell
(EMI) **CDM5 65341-2** Purcell—Theatre Music
(EMI) **CMS7 64409-2** Sullivan—Pirates of Penzance & Orch. Works
(LOND) **433 200-2LHO2** Britten—Owen Wingrave, etc.
(PHIL) **442 602-2PM** 3 x 3 Tenors

HARPER, Thomas (ten)
Schreker: Ferne Klang (Cpte)
(NAXO) **8 550497** Thomas Harper—Opera Recital

HARRÉ, Clive (bar)
Offenbach: Christopher Columbus (Cpte)

HARRELL, Mack (bar)
Mozart: Don Giovanni (Cpte)
Wagner: Tannhäuser (Cpte)

HARRELL, Ray Evans (cond)
see Magic Circle CO

HARRELL, Richard (voc)
Bernstein: West Side Story (Cpte)

HARRER, Uwe (pf)
(KOCH) **321 214** Wiener Sängerknaben - Kein Schöner Land

HARRER, Uwe Christian (cond)
see Vienna Boys' Ch
Vienna SO

HARRHY, Eiddwen (sop)
Donizetti: Assedio di Calais (Cpte), Ugo, Conte di Parigi (Cpte)
Handel: Alcina (Cpte), Amadigi di Gaula (Cpte)
Lehár: Lustige Witwe (exc)
Purcell: Fairy Queen, Z629 (Cpte)
(DG) **439 474-2GCL** Purcell—Opera & Choral Works
(OPRA) **ORCH103** Italian Opera—1810-20
(OPRA) **ORCH104** A Hundred Years of Italian Opera: 1820-1830
(OPRA) **ORC003** Donizetti—Gabriella di Vergy
(OPRA) **ORH102** A Hundred Years of Italian Opera
(VIRG) **VC7 59022-2** Smyth—Vocal and Orchestral Works

HARRHY, Paul (ten)
(ASV) **CDDCA758** Falla, Milhaud & Stravinsky—Operas

HARRIES, Kathryn (sop)
Britten: Rape of Lucretia (Cpte)
Chabrier: Briséïs (Cpte)
Janáček: Fate (Cpte)
Massenet: Cléopâtre (Cpte)
Nono: Intolleranza 1960 (Cpte)
Wagner: Parsifal (Cpte)

HARRIS, Brenda (sop)
(NEWP) **NPD85595** Haydn—La canterina

HARRIS, Diana (sop)
Purcell: Indian Queen, Z630 (Cpte)
(EMI) **CDC7 47355-2** Mozart—Concert Arias
(ERAT) **4509-96371-2** Gardiner—The Purcell Collection

HARRIS, Hilda (mez)
A. Davis: X (Cpte)

HARRIS, John (ten)
Martinů: Greek Passion (Cpte)
Verdi: Masnadieri (Cpte)
Wagner: Parsifal (Cpte), Tristan und Isolde (Cpte)

HARRISON, Beatrice (vc)
(CLAR) **CDGSE78-50-47** The Harrison Sisters—An English Musical Heritage

HARRISON, Julius (cond)
see orch

HARRISON, Martyn (ten)
Verdi: Traviata (Cpte)

HARRISON, Stephen (pf)
(SCHW) **312642** Unicef Gala 1991

HARROLD, Jack (ten)
Bernstein: Candide (1982) (Cpte)

HART, Mary Ann (mez)
Glass: Hydrogen Jukebox (Cpte)

HART, Robin (sngr)
Romberg: Student Prince (Cpte)

HART, Simon (treb)
Britten: Midsummer Night's Dream (Cpte)

HARTEMANN, Jean-Claude (cond)
see French Rad Lyric Orch
ORTF Lyric Orch
Paris Cons
Paris Sols Orch

HARTFIEL, Jurgen (ten)
Offenbach: Contes d'Hoffmann (Cpte)
Tchaikovsky: Eugene Onegin (exc)
(DG) **431 601-2GCE10** Tchaikovsky Compact Edition

HARTLE, Enid (mez)
Cavalli: Calisto (Cpte)
Offenbach: Robinson Crusoé (Cpte)
R. Strauss: Arabella (Cpte), Ariadne auf Naxos (Cpte)
Tchaikovsky: Eugene Onegin (Cpte), Queen of Spades (Cpte)
Tippett: King Priam (Cpte)
Verdi: Traviata (Cpte)

HARTLEY, Fred (cond)
see orch

HARTLIEP, Nikki Li (mez)
Janáček: Jenufa (Cpte)

HARTMAN, Vernon (bar)
Bizet: Carmen (Cpte)
Puccini: Fanciulla del West (Cpte)

HARTMANN, Carl (ten)
Wagner: Parsifal (exc)

HARTMANN, Roland (bar)
S. Wagner: Bärenhäuter (Cpte), Schwarzschwanenreich (Cpte)

HARTMANN, Rudolf (bass)
Monteverdi: Orfeo (Cpte)
Wagner: Meistersinger (Cpte)
Zemlinsky: Kleider machen Leute (Cpte)

HARTMANN, Willy (ten)
R. Strauss: Salome (Cpte)

HARTY, Sir Hamilton (cond)
see Hallé
LPO
orch

HARVARD GLEE CLUB
cond P. GEMIGNANI
(RCA) **09026 62681-2** Mr Jerry Hadley—Golden Days

HARVEY, Peter (bass)
Purcell: Dido (Cpte), Indian Queen, Z630 (Cpte)

HARWOOD, Elizabeth (sop)
Britten: Midsummer Night's Dream (Cpte)
Lehár: Lustige Witwe (exc)
Puccini: Bohème (exc)
Sullivan: Iolanthe (exc), Patience (Cpte), Princess Ida (Cpte), Yeomen of the Guard (Cpte)
Tippett: Midsummer Marriage (Cpte)
(BBCR) **BBCRD9103** Classic Encores
(DECC) **430 095-2DWO** The World of Gilbert & Sullivan, Vol.1
(DECC) **433 068-2DWO** Your Hundred Best Opera Tunes V
(DECC) **433 865-2DWO** The World of Puccini
(DECC) **433 868-2DWO** The World of Gilbert & Sullivan - Volume 2
(DECC) **436 317-2DA** Puccini—Famous Arias
(DG) **435 712-2GX2** Lehár—The Merry Widow. Suppé—Overtures
(EMI) **CMS7 64412-2** Gilbert & Sullivan—Ruddigore/Shakespeare Music

HASEL, Michael (bass fl)
(SONY) **SK53978** Prometheus

HASELBÖCK, Martin (cond)
see Vienna Academy Orch

HASELEU, Werner (spkr)
Schoenberg: Moses und Aron (Cpte)

HASHIMOTO, Kyoko (pf)
(INTU) **INT3113-2** Zapateado - Suzy Whang

HASKIN, Howard (ten)
Tippett: King Priam (Cpte)

HASKINS, Virginia (sop)
Verdi: Ballo in maschera (Cpte)

HASS, Sabine (sop)
Hindemith: Mathis der Maler (Cpte)

HASSID, Josef (vn)
(PEAR) **GEMMCD9939** Josef Hassid & Ida Haendel - 1940-42 Recordings
(TEST) **SBT1010** Ginette Neveu & Josef Hassid

HASSLO, Hugo (bar)
Verdi: Rigoletto (Cpte), Trovatore (exc)
(BLUE) **ABCD028** Jussi Björling live at the Stockholm Opera
(EMI) **CHS7 69741-2(5)** Record of Singing, Vol.4—Scandinavian School

HASSON, Maurice (vn)
(IMP) **PCDS22** Music of the World—La Douce France

HATTEY, Philip (bass-bar)
Delius: Village Romeo and Juliet (Cpte)

HAUBOLD, Ingrid (sop)
Wagner: Fliegende Holländer (Cpte)
(EMI) **CDC7 54776-2** René Kollo sings Wagner and Strauss

HAUGAN, Björn (ten)
Nørgård: Gilgamesh (Cpte)

HAUGLAND, Aage (bass)
Berg: Wozzeck (Cpte)
Heise: Drot og Marsk (Cpte)
Mozart: Zauberflöte (exc)
Mussorgsky: Boris Godunov (Cpte), Khovanshchina (Cpte)
Nielsen: Maskarade (Cpte), Saul and David (Cpte)
Nørgård: Siddhartha (Cpte)
R. Strauss: Rosenkavalier (Cpte)
Schoenberg: Moses und Aron (Cpte)
Shostakovich: Lady Macbeth of Mtsensk (Cpte)
Wagner: Götterdämmerung (Cpte), Parsifal (Cpte)
Zemlinsky: Es war einmal (Cpte)
(CHAN) **CHAN9336/8** Mussorgsky—Songs

HAUKE, Ernst (cond)
see Berlin Künstlertheater Orch
Berlin Schauspielhaus Orch
Berlin Staatskapelle
orch

HAUMAN, Constance (sop)
Wagner: Parsifal (Cpte)

HAUPTMANN, Cornelius (bass)
Glass: Akhnaten (Cpte)
Kreutzer: Nachtlager in Granada (Cpte)
Mozart: Clemenza di Tito (Cpte), Entführung (Cpte), Idomeneo (Cpte), Zauberflöte (Cpte)
Wagner: Parsifal (Cpte)
Wolf: Manuel Venegas

HAUTERMANN, Karin (mez)
Korngold: Violanta (Cpte)
Verdi: Rigoletto (Cpte)
(EURO) **GD69043** Puccini: Il Trittico

HAUTERMANN, Karin (spkr)
R. Strauss: Intermezzo (Cpte)

HAUTS-DE-SEINE MAÎTRISE
cond P. FOURNILLIER
Massenet: Amadis (Cpte)
cond MYUNG-WHUN CHUNG
Verdi: Otello (exc)

HAUXVELL, John (bar)
Walton: Troilus and Cressida (exc)

AVENITH, Raimund (pf)
(MARC) **8 223403** Virtuoso Cello Encores

AVERINEN, Margareta (sop)
Madetoja: Juha (Cpte)

AVLÁK, Lubomír (ten)
Hába: Mother (Cpte)

AWKINS, Ossie (bar)
Bizet: Carmen (Cpte)
Verdi: Macbeth (Cpte)

AWKSLEY, Deborah (mez)
J. Strauss II: Fledermaus (Cpte)

AWLATA, Franz (bass)
Puccini: Fanciulla del West (Cpte)
Spohr: Faust (Cpte)
(CAPR) **10 481** R.Strauss—Opera Concert

AYASHI, Yasuko (sop)
Ponchielli: Lituani (Cpte)
Puccini: Madama Butterfly (Cpte)

HAYDN PHILHARMONIA
cond E. ROJATTI
(NUOV) **6726** Italian Overtures

HAYDON CLARK, Robert (cond)
see Consort of London

HAYES, Quentin (bass)
Turnage: Greek (Cpte)

HAYMON, Cynthia (sop)
Gershwin: Porgy and Bess (exc)
R. Strauss: Elektra (Cpte)
(EMI) **CDH5 65072-2** Glyndebourne Recorded - 1934-1994

HAYWARD SEGAL, Marie (sop)
Vaughan Williams: Pilgrim's Progress (Cpte)
(SYMP) **SYMCD1175** Ave Maria

HAYWOOD, Lorna (sop)
Menotti: Amahl and the Night Visitors (Cpte)

HAZART, Jean (bass)
(EPM) **150 122** Milhaud—Historic Recordings 1928-1948

HAZELL, Hy (sngr)
Gay: Beggar's Opera (Cpte)

HAZELL, Richard (bass)
Puccini: Bohème (Cpte)

HEARD, Daphne (spkr)
Gay: Beggar's Opera (Cpte)

HEATER, Claude (ten)
Wagner: Fliegende Holländer (Cpte), Tristan und Isolde (exc)
(PHIL) **434 420-2PM32(2)** Richard Wagner Edition (pt 2)

HECKEL, Georg (ten)
Wagner: Meistersinger (exc)

HEDEGAARD, Ole (ten)
Heise: Drot og Marsk (Cpte)
Zemlinsky: Es war einmal (Cpte)

HEDLUND, Klas (ten)
Donizetti: Linda di Chamounix (Cpte)
Haeffner: Electra (Cpte)

HEFNI, Ratibael El (sop)
Mozart: Così fan tutte (Cpte)

HEGARTY, Mary (sop)
Offenbach: Orphée aux enfers (Cpte)

HEGER, Robert (cond)
see Bavarian St Op Orch
Bavarian St Orch
Berlin St Op Orch
Berlin Staatskapelle
LSO
orch
ROHO
Vienna St Op Orch
VPO

HEGERT-TIBELL, Anna (mez)
(ALTN) **CDAN3** Hjördis Schymberg

HEGGEN, Almar (bass)
Bibalo: Gespenster (Cpte)

HEICHELE, Hildegard (sop)
J. Strauss II: Fledermaus (Cpte)

HEIDBÜCHEL, Heinz (ten)
Weill: Kuhhandel (exc)

HEIDELBERG CHAMBER CHOIR
cond M. VENZAGO
Schoeck: Venus (Cpte)

HEIDENREICH, Johannes (cond)
see Berlin Charlottenburg Op Orch
Berlin St Op Orch

HEIDERSBACH, Kathe (sop)
(MSCM) **MM30285** Great Wagnerian Singers, Vol.2
(PEAR) **GEMMCD9410** Lotte Lehmann—Vol.2
(PREI) **89053** Max Lorenz (1901-1975)

HEIFETZ, Jascha (vn)
(APR) **APR7015** The Auer Legacy, Vol.1
(EMI) **CHS7 64929-2** Jascha Heifetz
(RCA) **09026 61778-2(02)** The Heifetz Collection, Vol.2 - 1925-34
(RCA) **09026 61778-2(03)** The Heifetz Collection, Vol. 3
(RCA) **09026 61778-2(06)** The Heifetz Collection, Vol. 6
(RCA) **09026 61778-2(19)** The Heifetz Collection, Vol. 19
(RCA) **09026 61778-2(35)** The Heifetz Collection, Vol. 35
(RCA) **09026 61778-2(40)** The Heifetz Collection, Vol. 40
(RCA) **09026 62706-3** Heifetz in Performance

HEIGL, Michael (ten)
R. Strauss: Rosenkavalier (Cpte)

HEILMANN, Uwe (ten)
Beethoven: Fidelio (Cpte)
Mozart: Clemenza di Tito (Cpte), Don Giovanni (Cpte), Finta Giardiniera (Cpte), Idomeneo (Cpte), Zauberflöte (exc)
Wagner: Fliegende Holländer (Cpte), Tristan und Isolde (Cpte)
(DG) **072 428-1GH2(DG)** The Metropolitan Opera Gala

HEINIKARI, Matti (ten)
Rautavaara: Vincent (Cpte)
Sallinen: Kullervo (Cpte)

HEISSER, Jean-François (pf)
(ERAT) **4509-93209-2** Debussy—Transcriptions for Piano - Four hands & Piano Duet

HÉJA, Benedek (treb)
Puccini: Tosca (Cpte)

HELD, Alan (bar)
Wagner: Rheingold (Cpte)
(DG) **072 422-3GH7** Levine conducts Wagner's Ring

HELDY, Fanny (sop)
(CLUB) **CL99-034** Marcel Journet (1867-1933)
(PEAR) **GEMMCDS9926(1)** Covent Garden on Record—Vol.4 (pt 1)
(PEAR) **GEMMCD9129** Great Tenors, Vol.2
(PREI) **89022** Fernand Ansseau (1890-1972)

HELGERS, Otto (bass)
(DANA) **DACOCD315/6** Lauritz Melchior Anthology - Vol. 3
(PREI) **89052** Friederich Schorr (1889-1953)
(PREI) **89086** Lauritz Melchior (1890-1973) - III
(PREI) **89301** The Art of Frida Leider

HELLEKANT, Charlotta (contr)
Bergman: Singing Tree (Cpte)

HELLELAND, Arild (ten)
Braein: Anne Pedersdotter (Cpte)
Lidholm: Dream Play (Cpte)

HELLER, Helmut (vn)
(PEAR) **GEMMCD9367** Gigli—Arias and Duets

HELLETSGRUBER, Luise (sop)
Mozart: Così fan tutte (Cpte), Don Giovanni (Cpte), Nozze di Figaro (Cpte)
(EMI) **CDH5 65072-2** Glyndebourne Recorded - 1934-1994
(MMOI) **CDMOIR406** Mozart—Historical Recordings
(ORFE) **C394101B** Great Mozart Singers Series, Vol. 1
(SCHW) **314512** Vienna State Opera Live, Vol.1
(SCHW) **314532** Vienna State Opera Live, Vol.3
(SCHW) **314592** Vienna State Opera Live, Vol.9
(SCHW) **314602** Vienna State Opera Live, Vol.10
(SCHW) **314622** Vienna State Opera Live, Vol.12
(SCHW) **314642** Vienna State Opera Live, Vol.14
(SCHW) **314702** Vienna State Opera Live, Vol.20
(SCHW) **314742** Vienna State Opera Live, Vol.24

HELLING, Hilke (contr)
Weill: Jasager (Cpte), Zar lässt sich Photographieren (Cpte)

HELLMANN, Claudia (mez)
Orff: Antigonae (Cpte)
Puccini: Tosca (Cpte)
Wagner: Walküre (Cpte)
(DECC) **414 100-2DM15** Wagner: Der Ring des Nibelungen
(DECC) **421 313-2DA** Wagner: Der Ring des Nibelungen - Great Scenes
(DECC) **433 067-2DWO** Your Hundred Best Opera Tunes IV
(DECC) **436 300-2DX** Opera Gala Sampler
(DECC) **440 069-2DWO** The World of Wagner

HELLMICH, Walter (bass)
(SCHW) **314702** Vienna State Opera Live, Vol.20

HELLMICH, Wolfgang (bar)
Wagner: Tristan und Isolde (Cpte)

HELLSTROM, Elisabeth (sop)
Mozart: Entführung (Cpte)

HELLWIG, Judith (sop)
Mozart: Zauberflöte (Cpte)
R. Strauss: Elektra (Cpte), Rosenkavalier (Cpte)
Wagner: Walküre (Cpte)
(EMI) **CZS7 67123-2** Wagner: Der Ring des Nibelungen

HELLYER JONES, Jonathan (cond)
see Cambridge Baroque Camerata

HELM, Anny (sop)
(EMI) **CMS7 64008-2(2)** Wagner Singing on Record (pt 2)

HELM, Hans (bar)
Giordano: Andrea Chénier (Cpte)
Puccini: Madama Butterfly (Cpte)
R. Strauss: Arabella (Cpte), Frau ohne Schatten (Cpte)
Schmidt: Notre Dame (Cpte)
Schreker: Ferne Klang (Cpte), Schatzgräber (Cpte)
Verdi: Otello (Cpte)
Zemlinsky: Kreidekreis (Cpte)

HELM, Karl (bass)
Mozart: Zauberflöte (Cpte)

HELSINKI PHILHARMONIC ORCHESTRA
cond S. COMISSIONA
(PRO) **CDS580** Tempest - The Classic Storms
cond J. FÜRST
(KONT) **32153/4** Kodály—Symphonic Works

HELTAU, Michael (spkr)
Mozart: Entführung (Cpte)

HEMINGWAY, Doris (sop)
Sullivan: Gondoliers (Cpte)

HEMM, Manfred (bar)
Mozart: Zauberflöte (Cpte)
R. Strauss: Frau ohne Schatten (Cpte)

HEMMINGS, David (treb)
Britten: Turn of the Screw (Cpte)

(LOND) **436 393-2LM** Britten—The Little Sweep, etc

HEMPEL, Frieda (sop)
(CLUB) **CL99-042** Frieda Hempel (1885-1955) & Hermann Jadlowker (1877-1953)
(IRCC) **IRCC-CD800** Souvenirs from Meyerbeer Operas
(NIMB) **NI7802** Divas 1906-1935
(NIMB) **NI7834** Caruso in Ensemble
(NIMB) **NI7849** Frieda Hempel (1885-1955)
(PEAR) **EVC3(1)** The Caruso Edition, Vol.3 (pt 1)
(PREI) **89064** Pasquale Amato (1878-1942)
(RCA) **GD60495(5)** The Complete Caruso Collection (pt 5)
(RCA) **09026 61242-2** Caruso Sings Verdi

HEMSLEY, Thomas (bar)
Britten: Midsummer Night's Dream (Cpte)
Mozart: Idomeneo (Cpte)
Purcell: Dido (Cpte)
Tippett: Knot Garden (Cpte)

HENA, Alice (mez)
(MSCM) **MM30451** Mascagni—Cavalleria Rusticana, etc

HENCHE, José Ramon (sngr)
Bretón: Verbena de la Paloma (Cpte)
Moreno Torroba: Luisa Fernanda (Cpte)

HENDERSON, Kerry (bar)
Meyerbeer: Huguenots (Cpte)

HENDERSON, Roald (ten)
Schoenberg: Moses und Aron (Cpte)

HENDERSON, Roy (bar)
Mozart: Don Giovanni (Cpte), Nozze di Figaro (Cpte)
(EMI) **CDH5 65072-2** Glyndebourne Recorded - 1934-1994

HENDERSON, Skitch (cond)
see RCA Victor Orch
RCA Victor SO

HENDRICKS, Barbara (sop)
Bizet: Pêcheurs de Perles (Cpte)
Chabrier: Roi malgré lui (Cpte)
Donizetti: Don Pasquale (Cpte)
Gershwin: Porgy and Bess (Cpte)
Gluck: Orphée (Cpte)
Humperdinck: Hänsel und Gretel (exc)
Mozart: Finta semplice (Cpte), Idomeneo (Cpte), Nozze di Figaro (Cpte), Zauberflöte (exc)
Offenbach: Contes d'Hoffmann (Cpte)
Puccini: Bohème (Cpte), Turandot (Cpte)
R. Strauss: Aegyptische Helena (Cpte), Rosenkavalier (exc)
Verdi: Don Carlo (Cpte), Falstaff (Cpte)
Wagner: Parsifal (Cpte)
(CAST) **CASH5052** Verdi Operatic Favourites
(CAST) **CVI2065** Highlights from the Royal Opera House, Covent Garden
(DG) **439 153-4GMA** Mad about Sopranos
(EMI) **CDC5 55095-2** Prima Diva
(EMI) **CDC5 55151-2** Operetta Duets
(EMI) **CDC7 47122-2** Mozart: Concert and Operatic Arias
(EMI) **CDC7 54004-2** Chabrier: Vocal & Orchestral Works
(EMI) **CDC7 54626-2** Operetta Arias
(ERAT) **2292-45797-2** The Ultimate Opera Collection
(ERAT) **4509-91715-2** The Ultimate Opera Collection 2
(PHIL) **416 460-2PH** Barbara Hendricks sings Gershwin
(PHIL) **422 545-2PME3** The Complete Mozart Edition Vol.45
(TELA) **CD80407** Divine Sopranos

HENDRIKS, Alwin (ten)
Beethoven: Fidelio (Cpte)

HENDRIKX, Louis (bass)
Rossini: Guillaume Tell (Cpte)

HENGELBROCK, Thomas (cond)
see Freiburg Baroque Orch

HENKE, Waldemar (ten)
(MSCM) **MM30285** Great Wagnerian Singers, Vol.2
(PEAR) **GEMMCDS9137** Wagner—Der Ring des Nibelungen
(PREI) **89069** Josef von Manowarda (1890-1942)

HENNEBERG, Matthias (bar)
R. Strauss: Salome (Cpte)

HENNECKE, Daniela (mez)
Carvalho: Testoride Argonauta (Cpte)

HENNEQUIN, Hervé (bass-bar)
Berg: Lulu (Cpte)
Tchaikovsky: Eugene Onegin (Cpte)

HENNETIER, Huguette (mez)
Audran: Poupée (exc)
Boïeldieu: Voitures Versées (Cpte)
Terrasse: Travaux d'Hercule (Cpte)

HENRI, Louie (sop)
(SYMP) **SYMCD1123** Sullivan—Sesquicentenial Commemorative Issue

HENRY, Didier (bar)
Debussy: Pelléas et Mélisande (Cpte)
Mascagni: Piccolo Marat (Cpte)
Massenet: Amadis (Cpte), Cléopâtre (Cpte), Grisélidis (Cpte)
Prokofiev: Love for 3 Oranges (Cpte)
(DECC) **440 333-2DH** Ravel—Vocal Works
(MARC) **8 223774** Ropartz—Choral Works

HENSCHEL, Dietrich (bar)
Delius: Village Romeo and Juliet (Cpte)

HENSON, Robert (ten)
Gershwin: Porgy and Bess (exc)

HEPPE, Leo (ten)
R. Strauss: Elektra (Cpte), Rosenkavalier (Cpte)

HEPPNER, Ben (ten)
Puccini: Turandot (Cpte)
Wagner: Lohengrin (Cpte), Meistersinger (Cpte)
Weber: Oberon (Cpte)
(CBC) **SMCD5142** Ben Heppner sings Richard Strauss
(RCA) **09026 61440-2** Opera's Greatest Moments
(RCA) **09026 62504-2** Great Tenor Arias - Ben Heppner
(RCA) **09026 62550-2** Ten Tenors in Love
(RCA) **74321 25817-2** Café Classics - Operatic

HÉRAL, Pierre (bass)
Adam: Si j'étais roi (Cpte)
Boïeldieu: Dame blanche (Cpte)

HERBER, Sue (mez)
Britten: Paul Bunyan (Cpte)
Copland: Tender Land (Cpte)

HERBERT, Victor (cond)
see Orig Broadway Cast

HERBIG, Günther (cond)
see RPO

HERDENBERG, Sven (bar)
Puccini: Bohème (exc)

HÉRENT, René (ten)
Ravel: Heure espagnole (Cpte)
(EMI) **CZS5 68295-2** Messager/Lecocq—Operetta Highlights

HERFORD, Henry (bar)
Bridge: Christmas Rose (Cpte)
Britten: Midsummer Night's Dream (Cpte)
G. Lloyd: Iernin
Maxwell Davies: Resurrection (Cpte)
Rameau: Castor et Pollux (Cpte)

HERFORD, Karl (ten)
Zeller: Vogelhändler (exc)

HERIBAN, Josef (bass)
Smetana: Bartered Bride (Cpte)

HERINCX, Raimund (bass)
Berlioz: Benvenuto Cellini (Cpte), Troyens (Cpte)
Lehár: Lustige Witwe (exc)
Purcell: Dido (Cpte)
Tippett: Knot Garden (Cpte), Midsummer Marriage (Cpte)
Vaughan Williams: Pilgrim's Progress (Cpte)

HERING, Jörg (ten)
Wagner: Fliegende Holländer (Cpte)

HERMAN, Silvia (sop)
Wagner: Götterdämmerung (Cpte), Rheingold (Cpte), Walküre (Cpte)

HERMANN, Dagmar (mez)
Lehár: Graf von Luxemburg (exc)
Mozart: Così fan tutte (Cpte)
O. Straus: Walzertraum (exc)
R. Strauss: Salome (Cpte)
Wagner: Walküre (Cpte)

HERMANN, Roland (bar)
Egk: Peer Gynt (Cpte)
Gurlitt: Wozzeck (Cpte)
Hindemith: Mathis der Maler (Cpte)
Monteverdi: Orfeo (Cpte)
Orff: Prometheus (Cpte)
Schoeck: Massimilla Doni (Cpte)
Schoenberg: Moses und Aron (Cpte)
Schreker: Ferne Klang (Cpte)
Wagner: Feen (Cpte), Meistersinger (exc)
Zemlinsky: Kreidekreis (Cpte)
(ACAN) **44 2085-2** Carl Orff Collection

HERNANDEZ, Marta (sngr)
Chapí: Revoltosa (Cpte)

HERNDL, Johanna (contr)
R. Strauss: Rosenkavalier (Cpte)

(FRANÇOISE) HERR VOCAL ENSEMBLE
cond M. MINKOWSKI
Mondonville: Titon et l'Aurore (Cpte)
Rameau: Platée (Cpte)

HERREWEGHE, Philippe (cond)
see Chapelle Royale Orch

HERRFURTH, Annelis (sop)
Jessel: Schwarzwaldmädel (exc)

HERRICK, Christopher (organ)
(HYPE) **CDA66605** Organ Fireworks, Vol.4

HERRMANN, Anita (sngr)
Weill: Dreigroschenoper (Cpte)

HERRMANN, Bernard (cond)
see PAO

HERRMANN, Heiko (tpt)
(MOTE) **CD20171** Romantic Organ Music

HERRMANN, Josef (bar)
Wagner: Meistersinger (exc)
(EMI) **CHS7 69741-2(4)** Record of Singing, Vol.4—German School
(MYTO) **3MCD93381** Wagner—Die Walküre, etc
(PREI) **89076** Josef Herrmann (1903-1955)
(PREI) **89077** Torsten Ralf (1901-1954)
(SCHW) **314552** Vienna State Opera Live, Vol.5

HERWIN, Carrie (contr)
(SYMP) **SYMCD1123** Sullivan—Sesquicentenial Commemorative Issue

HERZ, Ottó (pf)
(BIDD) **LAB045** Hubay & Flesch —HMV Recordings

HERZ, Tamara (sop)
Wagner: Parsifal (Cpte)

HESCH, Wilhelm (bass)
(NIMB) **NI7840/1** The Era of Adelina Patti
(PREI) **89020** Leo Slezak (1873-1946)

HESSE, Ruth (mez)
Henze: Junge Lord (Cpte)
Korngold: Violanta (Cpte)
R. Strauss: Frau ohne Schatten (Cpte)
Wagner: Meistersinger (Cpte), Rheingold (Cpte)
(PHIL) **446 057-2PB14** Wagner—The Ring Cycle - Bayreuth Festival 1967

HESSE RADIO CHOIR
cond G. ALBRECHT
Zemlinsky: Traumgörge (Cpte)

HETHERINGTON, Hugh (ten)
Knussen: Where the Wild Things are (Cpte)
Prokofiev: Love for 3 Oranges (Cpte)
(ASV) **CDDCA758** Falla, Milhaud & Stravinsky—Operas

HEURTEFEUX, Christine (gtr)
(MAND) **MAN4806** Music for Guitar and Cello

HEURTEUR, Fernand (cond)
see Orch

HEWARD, Leslie (cond)
see CBO
Hallé

HEWETSON, Polly (sop)
Britten: Noye's Fludde (Cpte)

HEYER, Edwin (bass)
(PREI) **90168** Wagner—Die Meistersinger, Act 2, etc

HEYER, Edwin (ten)
J. Strauss II: Fledermaus (Cpte)

HEYNIS, Aafje (contr)
Martin: Mystère de la Nativité

HIBBARD, David (ten)
Meyerbeer: Huguenots (Cpte)

HIBBERD, Linda (sngr)
Saxton: Caritas (Cpte)

HICKEY, Angela (mez)
Weill: Street Scene (Cpte)

HICKOX, David (ten)
Barber: Antony and Cleopatra (Cpte)

HICKOX, Richard (cond)
see Bournemouth SO
City of London Baroque Sinfonia
CLS
Collegium Musicum 90
English Northern Philh
LSC
LSO
Northern Sinfonia
Richard Hickox Orch

(RICHARD) HICKOX ORCHESTRA
cond R. HICKOX
(DECC) **425 848-2DWO** Your hundred best tunes vol 2

(RICHARD) HICKOX SINGERS
cond R. HICKOX
Holst: Sávitri (Cpte)
(CHAN) **CHAN8865** Rossini: Opera Arias

HICKS, Kenneth (voc)
Joplin: Treemonisha (Cpte)

HIDALGO, Elvira de (sop)
(EMI) **CHS7 64864-2(1)** La Scala Edition - Vol.2, 1915-46 (pt 1)

HIELSCHER, Ulrich (bass)
Hindemith: Mathis der Maler (Cpte)

HIERONIMUS (sngr)
Messager: Passionêment (Cpte)

HIESTERMANN, Horst (ten)
Einem: Dantons Tod (Cpte)
Hindemith: Neues vom Tage (Cpte)
Mozart: Zauberflöte (Cpte)
R. Strauss: Salome (Cpte)
Schoeck: Penthesilea (Cpte)
Wagner: Meistersinger (Cpte)
Weill: Mahagonny-Gesänge (Cpte)

HIGUERAS, Ana Maria (sop)
Chapí: Revoltosa (Cpte)
Vives: Bohemios (Cpte)

HILDEBRAND, Herman (bass)
Handel: Giulio Cesare (Cpte)
Mozart: Nozze di Figaro (Cpte)

HILDMANN, Hanslutz (spkr)
Corghi: Divara (Cpte)

HOLEŠOVSKÝ, Jiří (ten)
Janáček: Fate (Cpte)

HÖLL, Hartmut (pf)
Wolf: Manuel Venegas

HOLL, Robert (bass)
Mozart: Don Giovanni (Cpte), Finta semplice (Cpte), Zaïde (Cpte)
Schubert: Fierrabras (Cpte)
(TELD) **4509-98824-2** Thomas Hampson Collection,Vol III-Operatic Scenes

HOLLAND, Eric (ten)
Beethoven: Fidelio (Cpte)

HOLLAND, Lyndsie (contr)
Sullivan: Mikado (Cpte)
(DECC) **433 868-2DWO** The World of Gilbert & Sullivan - Volume 2
(LOND) **436 813-2LM2** Sullivan—The Grand Duke. Overture Di Ballo. Henry VIII
(LOND) **436 816-2LM2** Sullivan—Utopia Ltd. Macbeth & Marmion Ovs etc

HOLLAND, Mark (bar)
Janáček: Fate (Cpte)
M. Berkeley: Baa Baa Black Sheep (Cpte)

HOLLANDER, Adrian E. (sngr)
J. Strauss II: Fledermaus (Cpte)

HÖLLE, Matthias (bass)
R. Strauss: Daphne (Cpte)
Wagner: Meistersinger (Cpte), Parsifal (Cpte), Rheingold (Cpte), Walküre (Cpte)
Weber: Freischütz (Cpte)

HOLLOWAY, David (bar)
Bizet: Carmen (Cpte)

HOLLREISER, Heinrich (cond)
see Bavarian St Orch
Berlin Deutsche Op Orch
Staatskapelle Dresden
VPO

HOLLWEG, Ilse (sop)
(EMI) **CHS7 63715-2** Mozart: Die Entführung, etc
(EMIL) **CDZ7 67015-2** Mozart—Opera Arias

HOLLWEG, Werner (ten)
Beethoven: Fidelio (exc)
Einem: Dantons Tod (Cpte)
J. Strauss II: Fledermaus (exc)
Lehár: Lustige Witwe (exc)
Mozart: Finta Giardiniera (Cpte), Idomeneo (Cpte), Mitridate (Cpte), Nozze di Figaro (Cpte), Zaïde (Cpte)
Wagner: Tannhäuser (Cpte)
Wolf: Corregidor (Cpte)
(DG) **435 712-2GX2** Lehár—The Merry Widow. Suppé—Overtures
(TELD) **4509-97507-2** Mozart—Famous Opera Arias

HOLLYWOOD BOWL ORCHESTRA
cond J. MAUCERI
(PHIL) **438 663-2PH** American Classics
(PHIL) **446 403-2PH** Journey to the Stars - A Sci-Fi Fantasy Adventure

HOLLYWOOD BOWL SYMPHONY ORCHESTRA
cond ALFRED NEWMAN
(EMI) **CDM5 65430-2** The Orchestra Sings
cond C. DRAGON
(CFP) **CD-CFP4660** Everlasting Peace
(EMI) **CDM5 65430-2** The Orchestra Sings
cond J. MAUCERI
(PHIL) **438 685-2PH** The Great Waltz
(PHIL) **438 867-2PH** Songs of the Earth
cond E. ORMANDY
(IMP) **PWKS4230** Mario Lanza in Concert
cond F. SLATKIN
(EMI) **CMS7 64123-2** The Art of Michael Rabin (1936-1972)
cond L. SLATKIN
(EMIN) **CD-EMX2175** Music of Gershwin

HOLM, Michael (spkr)
Corghi: Divara (Cpte)

HOLM, Renate (sop)
J. Strauss II: Fledermaus (exc)
Künneke: Vetter aus Dingsda (exc)
Lehár: Graf von Luxemburg (exc), Land des Lächelns (Cpte), Zarewitsch (exc)
Millöcker: Bettelstudent (Cpte)
Mozart: Zauberflöte (exc)
O. Straus: Walzertraum (exc)
Suppé: Boccaccio (exc)
Zeller: Vogelhändler (exc)
(CFP) **CD-CFP4499** Strauss—Champagne and Laughter
(DECC) **436 316-2DA** Golden Operetta
(LOND) **436 897-2DM** Lehár Gala
(LOND) **436 898-2DM** Operetta Gala

HOLM, Richard (ten)
Egk: Verlobung in San Domingo (Cpte)
Weber: Freischütz (Cpte)

HOLMAN, Peter (cond)
see Opera Restor'd
Parley of Instr

HOLMES, Eugene B. (bar)
(SCHW) **312642** Unicef Gala 1991

HOLMES, John (bass)
Sullivan: Mikado (Cpte)

HOLMES, Ralph (vn)
(DECC) **433 220-2DWO** The World of the Violin

HOLMGREN, Carl Gustaf (bar)
Prokofiev: Fiery Angel (Cpte)

HOLMQUIST, Ward (cond)
see Houston Op Studio

HOLST, Grace (sop)
(PREI) **89055** Cesare Formichi (1883-1949)

HOLST SINGERS
cond A. MELVILLE
Boughton: Bethlehem (Cpte)

HOLT, Olivier (cond)
see Inst Ens

HOLTON, Ruth (sop)
Purcell: Dido (Cpte)

HOLTZMANN, Thomas (spkr)
Mozart: Entführung (Cpte)

HOLVIK, Karen (sop)
S. Wallace: Kabbalah (Cpte)
(KOCH) **37050-2** Blitzstein—Songs

HOLZAPFEL, Helmut (ten)
Glass: Akhnaten (Cpte)

HOLZER, Robert (spkr)
Mozart: Zauberflöte (Cpte)

HOLZHERR, Wolfgang (ten)
R. Strauss: Rosenkavalier (Cpte)

HÖLZLIN, Heinrich (bass)
(MYTO) **2MCD943103** Lortzing—Zar und Zimmermann

HOLZMAIR, Wolfgang (bar)
Busoni: Arlecchino (Cpte), Turandot (Cpte)
J. Strauss II: Zigeunerbaron (Cpte)

HOMBERGER, Christophe (ten)
Monteverdi: Incoronazione di Poppea (Cpte)

HOMER, Louise (contr)
(CLUB) **CL99-060** Enrico Caruso—Opera & Song Recital
(CONI) **CDHD227** Gigli in Opera and Song
(EMI) **CDH7 61051-2** Beniamino Gigli - Operatic Arias
(IRCC) **IRCC-CD800** Souvenirs from Meyerbeer Operas
(IRCC) **IRCC-CD810** American Singers, Volume 1
(MSCM) **MM30352** Caruso—Italian Opera Arias
(NIMB) **NI7834** Caruso in Ensemble
(NIMB) **NI7852** Galli-Curci, Vol.2
(NIMB) **NI7860** Emma Eames & Pol Plançon
(PEAR) **EVC1(2)** The Caruso Edition, Vol.1 (pt 2)
(PEAR) **EVC2** The Caruso Edition, Vol.2—1908-12
(PEAR) **EVC4(2)** The Caruso Edition, Vol.4 (pt 2)
(PEAR) **GEMMCDS9159(2)** De Luca Edition, Vol.1 (pt 2)
(PEAR) **GEMMCDS9160(2)** De Luca Edition, Vol.2 (pt 2)
(PEAR) **GEMMCDS9923(2)** Covent Garden on Record, Vol.1 (pt 2)
(PEAR) **GEMMCD9130** Great Sopranos, Vol.2
(PEAR) **GEMMCD9316** Beniamino Gigli
(PEAR) **GEMMCD9367** Gigli—Arias and Duets
(RCA) **GD60495(2)** The Complete Caruso Collection (pt 2)
(RCA) **GD60495(3)** The Complete Caruso Collection (pt 3)
(RCA) **GD60495(4)** The Complete Caruso Collection (pt 4)
(RCA) **GD60495(6)** The Complete Caruso Collection (pt 6)
(RCA) **09026 61244-2** Caruso sings French Opera Arias
(RCA) **09026 61580-2(1)** RCA/Met 110 Singers, 100 Years (pt 1)
(ROMO) **81001-2** Emma Eames (1865-1952)

HONECK, Manfred (cond)
see Munich RSO

HONEGGER, Arthur (cond)
see Odeon Grand Orch

HONEYMAN, Ian (ten)
Gay: Beggar's Opera (Cpte)

HONG, Hei-Kyung (sop)
Verdi: Aida (Cpte)
Wagner: Götterdämmerung (Cpte), Rheingold (Cpte)
(DG) **437 825-2GH** Wagner—Der Ring des Nibelungen - Highlights
(DG) **445 354-2GX14** Wagner—Der Ring des Nibelungen

HONG KONG PHILHARMONIC ORCHESTRA
cond K. JEAN
(MARC) **8 223354** Massenet—Orchestral Suites
cond K. SCHERMERHORN
(IMP) **PCDS4** Discover the Classics—Master Disc
(IMP) **PCDS6** Discover the Classics—Myths and Legends
(IMP) **PCD827** The Art of the Coloratura
(IMP) **TCD1070** Invitation to the Opera
(MARC) **8 220323** R. Strauss: Rarely heard orchestral works

HÖNGEN, Elisabeth (contr)
Humperdinck: Hänsel und Gretel (Cpte)
Mozart: Nozze di Figaro (Cpte)
Verdi: Don Carlo (exc), Macbeth (Cpte)
(EMI) **CDH7 63030-2** Kirsten Flagstad - Wagner Opera Arias
(PREI) **90249** Mozart in tempore belli
(SCHW) **314552** Vienna State Opera Live, Vol.5

HÖNIG, Dieter (bass-bar)
Romberg: Student Prince (exc)

HOOD, Ann (sop)
Sullivan: Princess Ida (Cpte), Sorcerer (Cpte), Trial by Jury (Cpte), Yeomen of the Guard (Cpte)
(DECC) **433 868-2DWO** The World of Gilbert & Sullivan - Volume 2

HOOD, Dorothy (sop)
Janáček: Fate (Cpte)

HOOGLAND, Stanley (fp)
(PART) **Part1132-2** Schubert—Lieder

HOOPER, James (bar)
(PHIL) **432 416-2PH3** Haydn—L'incontro improvviso/Arias

HOPF, Gertraud (mez)
Wagner: Walküre (Cpte)
(PHIL) **446 057-2PB14** Wagner—The Ring Cycle - Bayreuth Festival 1967

HOPF, Hans (ten)
Egk: Peer Gynt (Cpte)
Wagner: Meistersinger (Cpte), Tannhäuser (Cpte)

HOPFERWIESER, Josef (ten)
J. Strauss II: Fledermaus (Cpte)
Wagner: Rheingold (Cpte)
(EMI) **LDX9 91275-1(EMI)** Sawallisch conducts Wagner's Ring

HOPFNER, Heiner (ten)
Egk: Peer Gynt (Cpte)
Mozart: Zauberflöte (Cpte)
Wagner: Parsifal (Cpte)

HÖPFNER, Otto (sngr)
Schultze: Schwarzer Peter (Cpte)

HOPKINS, Gregory (ten)
Weill: Lost in the Stars (Cpte)
(EMI) **CDC7 54851-2** Gershwin—Blue Monday, etc

HOPPE, Carl (bass)
Nicolai: Lustigen Weiber von Windsor (Cpte)
R. Strauss: Arabella (Cpte), Salome (Cpte)
Wagner: Meistersinger (Cpte)

HOPPE, Fritz (bar)
Henze: Junge Lord (Cpte)

HOPPE, Fritz (narr)
J. Strauss II: Fledermaus (Cpte)
Weber: Freischütz (Cpte)

HOPPE, Heinz (ten)
(CAMB) **CD-1032** From the Operas of Erich Wolfgang Korngold

HOPPE, Leo (bass)
R. Strauss: Rosenkavalier (Cpte)

HORÁČEK, Jaroslav (bass)
Dvořák: Kate and the Devil (Cpte)
Fibich: Bride of Messina (Cpte)
Janáček: From the House of the Dead (Cpte)
Martinů: Julietta (Cpte)
Smetana: Bartered Bride (Cpte), Dalibor (Cpte), Two Widows (Cpte)
(KOCH) **34036-2** A Pageant of Opera

HORÁČEK, Pavel (bass)
(SUPR) **11 0345-2** Edith Gruberová - Operatic Recital

HORÁČKOVÁ, Dora (sop)
Krása: Brundibár (Cpte)

HORDERN, Michael (spkr)
Gay: Beggar's Opera (Cpte)

HORENSTEIN, Jascha (cond)
see BPO
FNO
RPO
Vienna St Op Orch

HÖRICKE, Friedrich (pf)
(MDG) **MDG611 0547-2** Rachmaninov—Piano Transcriptions; Piano Sonata No 2

HORN, Robert (ten)
Britten: Midsummer Night's Dream (Cpte)

HORN, Volker (ten)
Mendelssohn: Hochzeit des Camacho (Cpte)
Mozart: Zauberflöte (Cpte)
Pfitzner: Herz (Cpte)
S. Wagner: Bärenhäuter (Cpte)
Verdi: Don Carlo (Cpte), Nabucco (exc)

HORNA, Ruth (sop)
(ARHI) **ADCD109** Mengelberg Edition - Volume 3

HORNBLOW, Philip (ten)
(KIWI) **CDTRL075** Malvina Major—Opera Recital

HORNE, Marilyn (mez)
Bellini: Norma (exc)
Bernstein: West Side Story (Cpte)
Bizet: Carmen (Cpte)
Corigliano: Ghosts of Versailles (Cpte)
Donizetti: Lucrezia Borgia (Cpte)
Gluck: Orfeo ed Euridice (Cpte)
Handel: Giulio Cesare (exc), Rinaldo (Cpte)
J. Strauss II: Fledermaus (Cpte)

Meyerbeer: Prophète (Cpte)
Ponchielli: Gioconda (Cpte)
R. Strauss: Elektra (Cpte)
Rossini: Barbiere di Siviglia (Cpte), Bianca e Falliero (Cpte), Italiana in Algeri (Cpte), Semiramide (exc), Tancredi (Cpte)
Roussel: Padmâvatî (Cpte)
Verdi: Falstaff (Cpte), Trovatore (exc)
Vivaldi: Orlando Furioso (Cpte)
(CBS) **CD79312** Puccini: Il Trittico
(DECC) **421 306-2DA** Marilyn Horne sings Rossini
(DECC) **421 881-2DA** The Age of Bel Canto - Sutherland
(DECC) **421 891-2DA** Marilyn Horne sings Rossini, Bellini & Donizetti
(DECC) **425 854-2DWO** Youtr Hundred Best Tunes, Vol. 8
(DECC) **430 500-2DWO** World of Handel
(DECC) **433 064-2DWO** Your Hundred Best Opera Tunes Volume I
(DECC) **433 065-2DWO** Your Hundred Best Opera Tunes Volume II
(DECC) **433 067-2DWO** Your Hundred Best Opera Tunes IV
(DECC) **433 221-2DWO** The World of Verdi
(DECC) **433 440-2DA** Golden Opera
(DECC) **436 133-2DWO** World of Rossini
(DECC) **436 300-2DX** Opera Gala Sampler
(DECC) **436 315-2DA** Great Operatic Duets
(DECC) **436 462-2DM** Ten Top Mezzos
(DECC) **436 472-2DM** Great Opera Arias
(DECC) **440 415-2DM** Marilyn Horne
(DECC) **443 334-2LRX** Music for Relaxation, Vol 9 - A Touch of Romance
(DECC) **443 378-2DM** Ten Top Mezzos 2
(DECC) **444 543-2DF2** Essential Handel
(DECC) **444 552-2DF2** Essential Saint-Saëns
(DECC) **071 149-1DH (DECC)** The Essential Sutherland
(EMI) **CDC7 54643-2** Rossini—Bicentenary Gala Concert
(EMI) **LDB491007-1 (EMI)** Rossini Bicentennial Birthday Gala
(ERAT) **2292-45186-2** Marilyn Horne sings Handel Opera Arias
(ERAT) **2292-45797-2** The Ultimate Opera Collection
(ERAT) **4509-91715-2** The Ultimate Opera Collection 2
(ERAT) **4509-98501-2** Recital—Marilyn Horne
(MCEG) **VVD780** Sydney Opera House Gala Concert
(MEMO) **HR4392/3** Great Voices - Marilyn Horne
(RCA) **09026 61580-2(8)** RCA/Met 100 Singers, 100 Years (pt 8)
(RCA) **09026 62647-2** Marilyn Horne - The Men in My Life
(RCA) **09026 62699-2** Opera's Greatest Duets

HORNIK, Gottfried (bar)
Lortzing: Wildschütz (Cpte)
Mozart: Zauberflöte (Cpte)
Puccini: Tosca (exc), Turandot (Cpte)
R. Strauss: Frau ohne Schatten (Cpte), Rosenkavalier (exc)
(DG) **072 428-1GH2(DG)** The Metropolitan Opera Gala

HOROWITZ, Vladimir (pf)
(EMI) **CHS7 63538-2** Horowitz—The HMV Recordings, 1930-51

HORREAUX-TREHARD DUO
(CALL) **CAL9218** Two Guitars at the Opera

HORSMAN, Leslie (bar)
Verdi: Trovatore (Cpte)
Wagner: Tristan und Isolde (Cpte)

HORST, Steven (bass)
Janáček: Makropulos Affair (Cpte)

HOSKING, Arthur (bar)
Sullivan: Gondoliers (Cpte), Trial by Jury (Cpte)

HOSKINS, Andrew (tpt/dir)
(MOSC) **070979** Sound the Trumpets from Shore to Shore

HOSKINS, Bob (spkr)
Gay: Beggar's Opera (Cpte)

HOSKINS, Mark (tpt/dir)
(MOSC) **070979** Sound the Trumpets from Shore to Shore

HOTTER, Hans (bass-bar)
Berg: Lulu (Cpte)
Mozart: Nozze di Figaro (Cpte), Zauberflöte (Cpte)
Orff: Mond (Cpte)
R. Strauss: Arabella (Cpte), Capriccio (Cpte), Salome (Cpte), Schweigsame Frau (Cpte)
Verdi: Don Carlo (exc)
Wagner: Fliegende Holländer (Cpte), Meistersinger (Cpte), Parsifal (Cpte), Rheingold (Cpte), Siegfried (Cpte), Walküre (Cpte)
(ACAN) **43 268** Peter Anders sings German Opera Arias
(DECC) **414 100-2DM15** Wagner: Der Ring des Nibelungen
(DECC) **421 313-2DA** Wagner: Der Ring des Nibelungen - Great Scenes
(DECC) **433 068-2DWO** Your Hundred Best Opera Tunes V
(EMI) **CMS5 65212-2** Wagner—Les introuvables du Ring
(EMI) **CMS7 64008-2(1)** Wagner Singing on Record (pt 1)
(FOYE) **15-CF2011** Wagner—Der Ring de Nibelungen
(MYTO) **1MCD943104** R. Strauss—Capriccio (highlights) & Lieder
(ORFE) **C394101B** Great Mozart Singers Series, Vol. 1
(PILZ) **442118-2** Wagner—Operas in Historical Recordings
(PREI) **90200** Hans Hotter in Early Recordings
(SCHW) **314502** Vienna State Opera—Live Recordings (sampler)
(SCHW) **314532** Vienna State Opera Live, Vol.3
(SCHW) **314582** Vienna State Opera Live, Vol.8
(SCHW) **314652** Vienna State Opera Live, Vol.15
(SCHW) **314712** Vienna State Opera Live, Vol.21
(SCHW) **314722** Vienna State Opera Live, Vol.22
(SCHW) **314742** Vienna State Opera Live, Vol.24

HOUSTON GRAND OPERA CHORUS
cond J. DEMAIN
Gershwin: Porgy and Bess (exc)
cond G. SCHULLER
Joplin: Treemonisha (Cpte)

HOUSTON GRAND OPERA ORCHESTRA
cond J. DEMAIN
Gershwin: Porgy and Bess (Cpte)
cond G. SCHULLER
Joplin: Treemonisha (Cpte)

HOUSTON OPERA STUDIO
cond W. HOLMQUIST
Moran: Dracula Diary (Cpte)

HOUSTON SYMPHONY ORCHESTRA
cond S. COMISSIONA
(PRO) **CDS584** Tchaikovsky—Waltzes

HOUTMANN, Jacques (cond)
see Lorraine PO

HOVENCAMP, Robert (sngr)
Rapchak: Lifework of Juan Diaz (Cpte)

HOVORA, Daria (pf)
(FORL) **FF038** Cello for Happy Days

HOWARD, Ann (contr)
Bernstein: Candide (1988) (exc)
Britten: Peter Grimes (Cpte)
Dvořák: Rusalka (Cpte)
Wagner: Walküre (Cpte)
(CBS) **CD79312** Puccini: Il Trittico

HOWARD, Christopher (sngr)
Bernstein: West Side Story (Cpte)

HOWARD, Jamal (treb)
Weill: Lost in the Stars (Cpte)

HOWARD, Jason (bar)
Romberg: Student Prince (Cpte)
(IMP) **TCD1070** Invitation to the Opera
(RPO) **CDRPD9001** Classical Spectacular
(RPO) **CDRPO5010** Classical Spectacular 2
(SONY) **SK53968** Opera Duets

HOWARD, Kathleen (mez)
(ROMO) **81010-2** Claudia Muzio—Complete Pathé Recordings, 1917-8

HOWARD, Leslie (pf)
(HYPE) **CDA66090** Rare piano encores

HOWARD, Yvonne (mez)
Walton: Troilus and Cressida (Cpte)

HOWARD, Yvonne (spkr)
R. Strauss: Intermezzo (Cpte)

HOWARTH, Elgar (cond)
see Austrian RSO
Grimethorpe Colliery Band

HOWARTH, Judith (sop)
Bizet: Carmen (Cpte)
J. Strauss II: Fledermaus (Cpte)
Menotti: Boy who grew too fast (Cpte)
Smyth: Wreckers (Cpte)
Sullivan: Yeomen of the Guard (exc)
Walton: Troilus and Cressida (Cpte)

HOWELL, Gwynne (bass)
Beethoven: Fidelio (Cpte)
Bellini: Capuleti (Cpte)
Janáček: Cunning Little Vixen (Cpte)
Offenbach: Contes d'Hoffmann (Cpte)
Puccini: Bohème (Cpte), Fanciulla del West (Cpte), Manon Lescaut (Cpte)
Rossini: Guillaume Tell (Cpte), Siège de Corinthe (Cpte)
Saint-Saëns: Samson et Dalila (Cpte)
Verdi: Ballo in maschera (Cpte), Luisa Miller (Cpte), Stiffelio (Cpte)
Wagner: Tristan und Isolde (Cpte)
(CAST) **CVI2065** Highlights from the Royal Opera House, Covent Garden
(CAST) **CVI2070** Great Puccini Love Scenes from Covent Garden, La Scala and Verona
(EMI) **CDM7 69544-2** Berlioz: Vocal Works
(PHIL) **434 986-2PM** Duetti Amorosi
(TELD) **9031-77676-6(TELD)** My World of Opera - Kiri Te Kanawa

HOWELLS, Anne (mez)
Berlioz: Troyens (Cpte)
Cavalli: Ormindo (Cpte)
Floyd: Susannah (Cpte)
R. Strauss: Rosenkavalier (Cpte)
Sullivan: Mikado (Cpte)
Wagner: Parsifal (Cpte)
(CAST) **CVI2065** Highlights from the Royal Opera House, Covent Garden
(LOND) **825 126-2** Amadeus - Original Soundtrack
(TELD) **9031-77676-6(TELD)** My World of Opera - Kiri Te Kanawa

HOWLETT, Neil (bar)
Britten: Billy Budd (Cpte), Gloriana (Cpte)
Giordano: Andrea Chénier (Cpte)
R. Strauss: Salome (Cpte)
Stravinsky: Nightingale (Cpte)
Verdi: Otello (Cpte)
(DECC) **440 400-2DM** Luciano Pavarotti
(ERAT) **4509-98955-2** Boulez conducts Stravinsky

HR-BRASS
cond J. WHIGHAM
(CAPR) **10 429** Bernstein/Gershwin—HR-Brass

HUBAD, Samo (cond)
see Ljubljana RSO

HUBAY, Jenö (vn)
(BIDD) **LAB045** Hubay & Flesch —HMV Recordings

HUBBARD, Bruce (bar)
Bizet: Carmen (Cpte)
Gershwin: Porgy and Bess (exc)

HUBBARD, Leonard (ten)
Sullivan: Gondoliers (Cpte)

HÜBEL, Lars (bass)
Pfitzner: Herz (Cpte)
S. Wagner: Bärenhäuter (Cpte)

HUBER, Marcus (treb)
Mozart: Zauberflöte (Cpte)
Saint-Saëns: Samson et Dalila (Cpte)

HUBERMAN, Bronislaw (vn)
(BIDD) **LAB077/8** Huberman—Complete Brunwick Recordings

HUBERTY, Lucien (bar)
Massé: Noces de Jeannette (Cpte)

HÜBNER, Fritz (bass)
Wagner: Götterdämmerung (Cpte), Rheingold (Cpte), Siegfried (Cpte)
(PHIL) **434 420-2PM32(1)** Richard Wagner Edition (Pt.1)

HUDD, Roy (spkr/bar)
Purcell: Don Quixote: The Musical (Cpte)

HUDDERSFIELD CHORAL SOCIETY
cond O. DE LA MARTINEZ
Smyth: Wreckers (Cpte)

HUDER, Maria (mez)
Verdi: Aida (Cpte), Trovatore (Cpte)
(CENT) **CRC2164** Ferruccio Tagliavini—Early Operatic Recordings
(EMI) **CMS7 64165-2** Puccini—Trittico

HUDSON, Paul (bass)
Cilea: Adriana Lecouvreur (Cpte)
Mozart: Nozze di Figaro (Cpte)
Puccini: Fanciulla del West (Cpte), Tosca (exc)

HUDSON SHAD
cond K. MASUR
Weill: Sieben Todsünden (Cpte)

HUEHN, Julius (bar)
Wagner: Tristan und Isolde (Cpte)
(PREI) **89084** Kerstin Thorborg (1896-1970)

HUEHNS, Colin (treb)
Britten: Little Sweep (Cpte)

HUFFMAN, Ted (treb)
Mozart: Zauberflöte (Cpte)
(NEWP) **NPD85514** The Treble Boys - Wonder Solos & Duets

HUFFSTODT, Karen (sop)
R. Strauss: Salomé (Cpte)
Spontini: Vestale (Cpte)

HUFNAGEL, Elisabeth (mez)
(MYTO) **3MCD93381** Wagner—Die Walküre, etc

HUFNAGEL, Wilhelm (bass)
Benatzky: Im weissen Rössl (exc)

HUGHES, David (ten)
Mozart: Idomeneo (Cpte)
(EMI) **CDM7 64356-2** Opera Choruses
(EMI) **CZS5 68559-2** Italian Opera Choruses

HUGHES, Janet (sop)
Cavalli: Calisto (Cpte)

HUGHES, Owain Arwel (cond)
see Philh

HUGUET, Giuseppina (sop)
(IRCC) **IRCC-CD800** Souvenirs from Meyerbeer Operas
(TEST) **SBT1008** Viva Rossini

HUGUET, Josefina (sop)
(BONG) **GB1064/5-2** Fernando de Lucia
(NIMB) **NI7840/1** The Era of Adelina Patti
(SYMP) **SYMCD1149** Fernando De Lucia

HÜHN, Paul (cond)
see Berlin Deutsche Op Orch
Berlin St Op Orch

HUISMAN, Wilhelm (bass)
R. Strauss: Rosenkavalier (Cpte)

HULSE, Eileen (sop)
Britten: Turn of the Screw (Cpte)

Dvořák: Rusalka (Cpte)
M. Berkeley: Baa Baa Black Sheep (Cpte)

HUMBERT, Jacqueline (sngr)
Ashley: Improvement (Cpte)

HUMBURG, Will (cond)
see Bratislava RSO
Failoni CO
Münster SO

HUME, Doreen (sop)
Sullivan: Yeomen of the Guard (Cpte)

HUMPHREY, Jon (ten)
(MUSM) **67078-2** Stravinsky The Composer - Volume 1

HUMPHRIES, Linda (sop)
Massenet: Werther (Cpte)

HUNGARIAN CHAMBER ORCHESTRA
cond V. TÁTRAI
(LASE) **15 511** Mozart: Symphonies and Overtures

HUNGARIAN FESTIVAL CHORUS
cond M. HALÁSZ
Mozart: Zauberflöte (Cpte)

HUNGARIAN NATIONAL PHILHARMONIC ORCHESTRA
cond T. FERENC
(IMP) **PCDS24** Music of the World—Scandinavia & Eastern Europe—Forests & Fjords

HUNGARIAN RADIO AND TELEVISION CHORUS
cond L. GARDELLI
Respighi: Belfagor (Cpte), Semirama (Cpte)
cond G. PATANÈ
Giordano: Andrea Chénier (Cpte), Fedora (Cpte)
cond C. ROSEKRANS
Mascagni: Lodoletta (Cpte)
cond M. TILSON THOMAS
Puccini: Tosca (Cpte)

HUNGARIAN RADIO AND TELEVISION ORCHESTRA
cond G. PATANÈ
Giordano: Fedora (Cpte)

HUNGARIAN RADIO CHORUS
cond W. HUMBURG
Rossini: Barbiere di Siviglia (Cpte)
cond M. VIOTTI
Franchetti: Cristoforo Colombo (Cpte)
Giordano: Andrea Chénier (Cpte)
Puccini: Fanciulla del West (Cpte)

HUNGARIAN STATE OPERA CHILDREN'S CHORUS
cond C. ROSEKRANS
Mascagni: Lodoletta (Cpte)

HUNGARIAN STATE OPERA ORCHESTRA
(LASE) **15 611** Suppé—Overtures
cond E. LUKÁCS
(CAPR) **10 810** Mozart—Opera Highlights
cond P.G. MORANDI
(NAXO) **8 553018** Verdi—Overtures, Volume 1
(NAXO) **8 553089** Verdi—Overtures, Volume 2
cond G. PATANÈ
(SONY) **SM48155** Carreras and Caballe sing Souvenirs
(SONY) **SMK48155** Carreras and Caballe sing Souvenirs
cond M. TILSON THOMAS
(SONY) **SM48155** Carreras and Caballe sing Souvenirs
(SONY) **SMK48155** Carreras and Caballe sing Souvenirs

HUNGARIAN STATE ORCHESTRA
cond A. FISCHER
(NIMB) **NI5284** Kodaly—Orchestral works
cond L. GARDELLI
Respighi: Belfagor (Cpte), Semirama (Cpte)
cond G. PATANÈ
Boito: Mefistofele (Cpte)
Giordano: Andrea Chénier (Cpte)
(SONY) **MDK47176** Favourite Arias by the World's Favourite Tenors
cond C. ROSEKRANS
Mascagni: Lodoletta (Cpte)
cond M. TILSON THOMAS
Puccini: Tosca (Cpte)
(SONY) **MDK47176** Favourite Arias by the World's Favourite Tenors
(SONY) **SK48094** Favourite Puccini Arias

HUNGARIAN STATE SYMPHONY ORCHESTRA
cond A. FISCHER
(NIMB) **NI7010** Meditations at Sunset

HUNGAROTON OPERA CHORUS
cond G. PATANÈ
Boito: Mefistofele (Cpte)

HÜNI-MIHACSEK, Felicie (sop)
(PREI) **89201** Helge Roswaenge (1897-1972) - I
(SCHW) **314642** Vienna State Opera Live, Vol.14

HUNSBERGER, Donald (cond)
see Eastman Wind Ens
Eastman-Dryden Orch

HUNT, Lorraine (sop)
Handel: Giulio Cesare (Cpte)
M-A. Charpentier: Médée (Cpte)
Mozart: Don Giovanni (Cpte)
Purcell: Dido (Cpte), Fairy Queen, Z629 (Cpte)
(HARM) **HMU90 7056** Handel—Arias for Durastanti
(HARM) **HMU90 7149** Handel—Arias

HUNTER, Rita (sop)
Wagner: Götterdämmerung (exc), Siegfried (Cpte), Walküre (Cpte)
(ABCC) **8 7000 10** Rita Hunter—Opera Arias

HUNZIKER, Ueli (sngr)
Zemlinsky: Kleider machen Leute (Cpte)

HURDLEY, Bryan (cond)
see Sun Life Band

HURST, David (cond)
see Black Dyke Mills Band

HURST, George (cond)
see Bournemouth Sinfonietta

HURTEAU, Jean-Pierre (bass)
Saint-Saëns: Samson et Dalila (Cpte)
(EMI) **LDB9 91258-1(EMI)** Maria Callas at the Paris Opera December 1958

HURWITZ CHAMBER ENSEMBLE
cond J.T. WILLIAMS
(CHAN) **CHAN6560** Jubilate - Music for the Kings & Queens of England

HÜSCH, Gerhard (bar)
Mozart: Zauberflöte (Cpte)
(EMI) **CMS7 64008-2(1)** Wagner Singing on Record (pt 1)
(MMOI) **CDMOIR406** Mozart—Historical Recordings
(MSCM) **MM30283** Great Wagnerian Singers, Vol.1
(NIMB) **NI7848** Great Singers at the Berlin State Opera
(NIMB) **NI7867** Legendary Baritones
(PEAR) **GEMMCDS9121** Wagner—Die Meistersinger, Act 3, etc
(PEAR) **GEMMCD9394** Helge Roswaenge—Operatic Recital
(PEAR) **GEMMCD9419** Herbert Ernst Groh—Opera Recital
(PREI) **89024** Marcel Wittrisch (1901-1955)
(PREI) **89071** Gerhard Hüsch (1901-1984) - II
(PREI) **89088** Walther Ludwig (1902-1981)
(PREI) **89211** Helge Roswaenge (1897-1972) - III

HUSSA, Maria (sop)
(SCHW) **314512** Vienna State Opera Live, Vol.1

HUTT, Robert (ten)
(PREI) **89110** Heinrich Schlusnus (1888-1952) - II
(PREI) **89210** The Art of Emmi Leisner
(PREI) **89301** The Art of Frida Leider
(PREI) **89302** The Young Lotte Lehmann

HUTTENLOCHER, Philippe (bar)
Busoni: Arlecchino (Cpte)
Debussy: Pelléas et Mélisande (Cpte)
Fauré: Pénélope (Cpte)
Gounod: Faust (Cpte)
Grétry: Caravane du Caire (Cpte)
Lully: Phaëton (Cpte)
M-A. Charpentier: David et Jonathas (Cpte)
Marais: Alcyone (Cpte)
Mondonville: Titon et l'Aurore (Cpte)
Monteverdi: Incoronazione di Poppea (Cpte), Orfeo (Cpte)
Mozart: Così fan tutte (Cpte)
Rameau: Castor et Pollux (Cpte)
Ravel: Enfant et les sortilèges (Cpte)
(CLAV) **CD50-0705** Purcell—Songs
(ERAT) **4509-96971-2** Marcel Landowski—Edition

HUTTON, Adrian (bass)
Vaughan Williams: Hugh the Drover (Cpte)

HVIID, Jørgen (ten)
Nørgård: Gilgamesh (Cpte)

HVOROSTOVSKY, Dmitri (bar)
Mascagni: Cavalleria Rusticana (Cpte)
Tchaikovsky: Eugene Onegin (Cpte), Queen of Spades (Cpte)
Verdi: Traviata (Cpte)
(PHIL) **426 740-2PH** Dmitri Hvorostovsky sings Tchaikovsky & Verdi Arias
(PHIL) **434 912-2PH** Bel Canto Arias
(PHIL) **438 872-2PH** Songs and Dances of Death
(RCA) **09026 61440-2** Opera's Greatest Moments

HYDE, Philippa (sop)
Lampe: Pyramus and Thisbe (Cpte)

HYDE, Walter (ten)
(PEAR) **GEMMCDS9924(2)** Covent Garden on Record, Vol.2 (pt 2)

HYLDGAARD, Tove (sop)
Nielsen: Maskarade (Cpte)

HYNNINEN, Jorma (bar)
Madetoja: Juha (Cpte)
Mozart: Nozze di Figaro (exc)
R. Strauss: Elektra (Cpte)
Rautavaara: Vincent (Cpte)
Sallinen: Kullervo (Cpte)
Sibelius: Maiden in the Tower (Cpte)
(BIS) **BIS-CD373/4** Opera Scenes from Savaonlinna
(ONDI) **ODE731-2** Jorma Hynninen sings Opera Arias

IACOPUCCI, Fernando (ten)
Donizetti: Lucrezia Borgia (Cpte)
Puccini: Rondine (Cpte)
Verdi: Ballo in maschera (Cpte), Ernani (Cpte), Lombardi (Cpte), Rigoletto (exc), Traviata (Cpte)
(BUTT) **BMCD015** Pavarotti Collection - Duets and Scenes

IANCU, Ion (cond)
see Timişoara Romanian Op Orch

IAŞI MOLDOVA PHILHARMONIC ORCHESTRA
cond I. BACIU
(ELCT) **ELCD104** Caudella—Orchestral works

ICELAND SYMPHONY ORCHESTRA
cond I. BUKETOFF
Rachmaninov: Monna Vanna (exc)
cond P. SAKARI
(CHAN) **CHAN9036** Madetoja—Orchestral Works

ICELANDIC OPERA CHORUS
cond I. BUKETOFF
Rachmaninov: Monna Vanna (exc)

ICHIHARA, Taro (ten)
Verdi: Luisa Miller (Cpte)

IDLE, Eric (bar)
Sullivan: Mikado (exc)

IGNAL, Madeleine (sop)
Gounod: Mireille (Cpte)
Mozart: Nozze di Figaro (Cpte)

IGNATOWICZ, Ewa (sop)
Gluck: Danza (Cpte)

IHLOFF, Jutta-Renate (sop)
Mozart: Finta Giardiniera (Cpte), Finta semplice (Cpte)
Verdi: Falstaff (Cpte)

IKAIA-PURDY, Keith (ten)
R. Strauss: Rosenkavalier (Cpte)

IKONOMU, Katarina (sop)
Wagner: Walküre (Cpte)
(DG) **072 422-3GH7** Levine conducts Wagner's Ring

ILE DE FRANCE CHAMBER ORCHESTRA
cond J-W. AUDOLI
Pendleton: Miracle of the Nativity (Cpte)

ILE DE FRANCE VITTORIA REGIONAL CHOIR
cond M. PIQUEMAL
(MARC) **8 223774** Ropartz—Choral Works

ILES, John Henry (cond)
see Massed Brass Bands

ILGENFRITZ, McNair (pf)
(COND) **690.07.004** Saint-Saëns - Piano Rolls

ILITSCH, Daniza (sop)
(SCHW) **314562** Vienna State Opera Live, Vol.6
(SCHW) **314582** Vienna State Opera Live, Vol.8
(SCHW) **314712** Vienna State Opera Live, Vol.21
(SCHW) **314742** Vienna State Opera Live, Vol.24

ILLAVSKÝ, Ladislav (bar)
Schoenberg: Moses und Aron (Cpte)

ILOSFALVY, Robert (ten)
Lehár: Lustige Witwe (exc)

ILOSVAY, Maria von (mez)
Humperdinck: Hänsel und Gretel (Cpte)
R. Strauss: Elektra (Cpte)
Wagner: Götterdämmerung (Cpte), Rheingold (Cpte), Siegfried (Cpte), Walküre (Cpte)
(FOYE) **15-CF2011** Wagner—Der Ring de Nibelungen

IM THURN, Paul (bar)
Vaughan Williams: Hugh the Drover (Cpte)

IMBERT, M. (sngr)
(IRCC) **IRCC-CD802** Souvenirs of Rare French Opera

IMBODEM, Stephan (bass)
Pendleton: Miracle of the Nativity (Cpte)

IMMERSEEL, Jos van (cond)
see Anima Eterna

IMMLER, Christian (alto)
Mozart: Zauberflöte (Cpte)

INBAL, Eliahu (cond)
see Frankfurt RSO
Venice La Fenice Orch

INDERMÜHLE, Thomas (ob)
(EURO) **GD69298** Music from Opera and Operetta

INGEBRETSEN, Kjell (cond)
see Bergen SO
Stockholm Royal Orch

INGEBRETZEN, Sture (ten)
Verdi: Trovatore (Cpte)

INGELSE, Christiaan (organ)
(LIND) **LBCD23** Mozart/Haydn/Beethoven—Organ Works

INGHELBRECHT, Désiré-Emile (cond)
see FNO

INGHILLERI, Giovanni (bar)
Puccini: Bohème (Cpte), Madama Butterfly (Cpte)
Verdi: Aida (Cpte)
(PEAR) **GEMMCDS9926(1)** Covent Garden on Record—Vol.4 (pt 1)

INGLIS, Anthony (cond)
see RPO

INGRAM, Clinton (ten)
Massenet: Cid (Cpte)

INGRAM, Michael (treb)
(LOND) **436 393-2LM** Britten—The Little Sweep, etc

INGRAM, Paula (mez)
Gershwin: Porgy and Bess (exc)

IÑIGO, Paloma Perez (sop)
Falla: Vida breve (Cpte)

INNOCENT, Harold (bar)
Sullivan: Ruddigore (Cpte)

INNOCENTI, Angelo dell' (sngr)
Donizetti: Poliuto (Cpte)

INNSBRUCK CHORUS
cond ROBERT WAGNER
(BELA) **450 126-2** Favourite Wedding Music II

INNSBRUCK POSTMUSIK
cond F. PEDARNIG
Lortzing: Waffenschmied (exc)

INNSBRUCK SALON QUINTET
(SCHW) **310212** Innsbrucker Salonquintett

INNSBRUCK SYMPHONY ORCHESTRA
(BELA) **450 126-2** Favourite Wedding Music II

INSTRUMENTAL ENSEMBLE
Cocteau: Bel indifférent
(DECC) **436 316-2DA** Golden Operetta
(DECC) **443 930-2DM** Jussi Björling sings Opera Arias
(EMI) **CDC5 55259-2** The Age of the Castrato
(SYMP) **SYMCD1123** Sullivan—Sesquicentenial Commemorative Issue
cond O. HOLT
Probst: Maximilien Kolbe (Cpte)
cond B. TETU
(HARM) **HMP390 1293** Berlioz—Choral Works
cond U. ZIMMERMANN
U. Zimmermann: Weisse Rose (Cpte)

INTERMEZZO VOCAL ENSEMBLE
cond M. SWIERCZEWSKI
Auber: Gustav III (Cpte)

INTINO, Luciana d' (sop)
Pergolesi: Frate 'nnamorato (Cpte)
Rossini: Gazza ladra (Cpte), Guillaume Tell (Cpte)

INVERNIZZI, Roberta (sop)
Stradella: Moro per amore (Cpte)

IONITA, Alexandru (ten)
Leoncavallo: Pagliacci (Cpte)
Stravinsky: Oedipus rex (Cpte)
Verdi: Alzira (Cpte), Rigoletto (Cpte)

IRELAND NATIONAL SYMPHONY ORCHESTRA
cond R. BONYNGE
Balfe: Bohemian Girl (Cpte)
(KIWI) **CDSLD-82** Southern Voices—NZ International Opera Singers
cond R. SACCANI
Verdi: Aida (Cpte)

IRISH ARMY BAND
Verdi: Aida (Cpte)

IRVING, Robert (cond)
see orch
Sinfonia of London

ISAKOVA, N. (sop)
Kabalevsky: Colas Breugnon (Cpte)

ISBIN, Sharon (gtr)
(CCOR) **CCD42012** Arrangements for Two Guitars

ISHERWOOD, Nicholas (bass)
Dusapin: Romeo and Juliet (Cpte)
Handel: Agrippina (Cpte)
Rossi: Orfeo (Cpte)

ISLANDI, Stefan (ten)
(EMI) **CHS7 69741-2(5)** Record of Singing, Vol.4—Scandinavian School

ISOKOSKI, Soile (sop)
Mozart: Così fan tutte (Cpte), Don Giovanni (Cpte)

ISON, Daniel (treb)
Mozart: Zauberflöte (Cpte)

ISRAEL PHILHARMONIC ORCHESTRA
cond I. KERTÉSZ
(DECC) **443 015-2DF2** Smetana/Dvořák—Orchestral Works

ITALIAN INTERNATIONAL OPERA ORCHESTRA
cond M. DE BERNART
Donizetti: Maria di Rohan (Cpte)

ITALIAN INTERNATIONAL ORCHESTRA
cond B. APREA
Mercadante: Bravo (Cpte)
cond M. CARRARO
(MEMO) **DR3109** Vinci—Opera Arias
cond F. LUISI
Donizetti: Favorita (Cpte)
(NUOV) **6905** Donizetti—Great Love Duets
cond C. PIANTINI
Bizet: Pêcheurs de Perles (Cpte)

ITHACA COLLEGE CONCERT CHOIR
cond I. STRAVINSKY
(SONY) **SM22K46290(3)** Stravinsky—The Complete Edition (pt 3)

IVALDI, Jean-Marc (bar)
Massenet: Chérubin (Cpte)
Puccini: Fanciulla del West (Cpte)

IVANOV, Andrei (bar)
Rimsky-Korsakov: Tale of Tsar Saltan (Cpte)
(EMI) **CHS7 69741-2(6)** Record of Singing, Vol.4—Russian & Slavonic Schools
(PREI) **89067** Andrei Ivanov (1900-1970)

IVANOV, Emil (ten)
(MCI) **MCCD099** Opera's Greatest Arias

IVANOVSKY, Vladimir (ten)
Rimsky-Korsakov: Tale of Tsar Saltan (Cpte)

IVES, Gene (bar)
V. Thomson: Mother of us all (Cpte)

IVOGÜN, Maria (sop)
(CLUB) **CL99-020** Maria Ivogün & Lotte Schöne—Opera Recital
(NIMB) **NI7832** Maria Ivogün (1891-1987)
(PEAR) **GEMMCDS9925(2)** Covent Garden on Record—Vol.3 (pt 2)
(PEAR) **GEMMCDS9926(1)** Covent Garden on Record—Vol.4 (pt 1)
(PREI) **89094** Maria Ivogün (1891-1987)

JACHETTI, Ornella (sop)
Verdi: Simon Boccanegra (Cpte)

JACHNOW, Hildegard (mez)
Wagner: Götterdämmerung (Cpte)

JACKSON, Francis (organ)
(AMPH) **PHI120** Organ at Sledmere House, played by Francis Jackson

JACKSON, Richard (bass)
Gay: Beggar's Opera (Cpte)
Rameau: Naïs (Cpte)

JACKSON, Stephen (bar)
G. Lloyd: Iernin

JACKSON, Thomas (treb)
Vaughan Williams: Pilgrim's Progress (Cpte)

JACOBS, Jane (spkr)
Gay: Beggar's Opera (Cpte)

JACOBS, René (cond)
see Baroque Instr Ens
Cologne Concerto
Concerto Cologne
Concerto Vocale
Ens
Ens 415
SCB

JACOBS, René (alto)
Campra: Europe galante
Cavalli: Giasone (Cpte), Xerse (Cpte)
Cesti: Orontea (Cpte)
Gluck: Orfeo ed Euridice (Cpte)
Handel: Alessandro (Cpte), Partenope (Cpte)
M-A. Charpentier: David et Jonathas (Cpte)
(ACCE) **ACC57802D** Purcell: Songs and Elegies
(HARM) **HMA190 1183** Works for Lute and Voice

JACOBSEN, Marius (ten)
Nielsen: Maskarade (Cpte)

JACOBSSON, John-Eric (bar)
Mozart: Idomeneo (Cpte)

JACOBSSON, Sven-Erik (bass)
Verdi: Rigoletto (Cpte)

JACOBY, Josephine (mez)
(CLUB) **CL99-060** Enrico Caruso—Opera & Song Recital
(NIMB) **NI7808** Luisa Tetrazzini—Opera & Song Recital
(NIMB) **NI7834** Caruso in Ensemble
(NIMB) **NI7857** Farrar in Italian Opera
(PEAR) **EVC2** The Caruso Edition, Vol.2—1908-12
(PEAR) **EVC3(1)** The Caruso Edition, Vol.3 (pt 1)
(PEAR) **GEMMCD9224** Luisa Tetrazzini—Vol.4
(RCA) **GD60495(4)** The Complete Caruso Collection (pt 4)
(RCA) **09026 61242-2** Caruso Sings Verdi
(ROMO) **81016-2** Lucrezia Bori (1887-1960)

JACOPUCCI, Ferdinando (ten)
Rossini: Inganno felice (Cpte)

JACQUES, Roland (bass)
Offenbach: Contes d'Hoffmann (Cpte)

JACQUIN, Christiane (sop)
Gounod: Mireille (Cpte)
Terrasse: Fiancée du Scaphandrier (Cpte)
(MUSD) **20239-2** Delibes—Opéras-Comiques

JADLOWKER, Herman (ten)
(CLUB) **CL99-042** Frieda Hempel (1885-1955) & Hermann Jadlowker (1877-1953)
(IRCC) **IRCC-CD805** Geraldine Farrar - 60th Anniversary Issue
(RCA) **09026 61580-2(2)** RCA/Met 100 Singers, 100 Years (pt 2)

JAGEL, Frederick (ten)
Donizetti: Lucia di Lammermoor (Cpte)
Verdi: Traviata (Cpte)
(PEAR) **GEMMCDS9076** Stokowski conducts Wagner, Volume III

JÄGER, Richard (cond)
see Berlin St Op Orch

JAGUSZ, Maria (spkr)
R. Strauss: Intermezzo (Cpte)

JAHN, Gertrud (mez)
Berg: Wozzeck (Cpte)
Janáček: Cunning Little Vixen (Cpte)
Mozart: Ascanio in Alba (Cpte)
R. Strauss: Frau ohne Schatten (Cpte)
(DECC) **421 852-2DH2** Janáček: Operatic & Chamber Works

JAKOBI, Regina (mez)
Monteverdi: Incoronazione di Poppea (Cpte)

JAKOBSEN, Hjørdis (sngr)
Kuhlau: Lulu (Cpte)

JAKOBSON, Anna-Lisa (mez)
Bergman: Singing Tree (Cpte)
Sallinen: Kullervo (Cpte)

JALAS, Jussi (cond)
see Finnish RSO

JAMERSON, Thomas (bar)
Verdi: Traviata (Cpte)
(RCA) **GD60205** Opera Choruses

JAMES, David (alto)
Cesti: Orontea (Cpte)
Handel: Giulio Cesare (Cpte)

JAMES, Eirian (mez)
Bridge: Christmas Rose (Cpte)
Handel: Teseo (Cpte)
Mozart: Così fan tutte (Cpte), Don Giovanni (Cpte), Zauberflöte (Cpte)

JAMES, Elmore (bar)
Mozart: Così fan tutte (exc), Don Giovanni (Cpte)

JAMES, Rhianon (mez)
Purcell: Dido (Cpte)

JANČI, Štefan (bass)
Puccini: Bohème (Cpte)

JANDÓ, Jenö (pf)
(NAXO) **8 550306** Violin Miniatures

JANIGRO, Antonio (vc)
(ARCI) **ARC112/3** Dinu Lipatti—Les Inédits

JANKEN, Kim (sngr)
Nørgård: Siddhartha (Cpte)

JANKO, Josef (ten)
Wagner: Meistersinger (Cpte)

JANKOBSKÝ, Zdeněk (ten)
Smetana: Kiss (Cpte)

JANKOVIC, Eleonora (mez)
Bellini: Adelson e Salvini (Cpte), Puritani (Cpte)
Puccini: Madama Butterfly (Cpte)

JANNI, Attilia (sop)
(PEAR) **GEMMCD9016** Mattia Battistini, Vol.3

JANOUŠEK, Jiří (ten)
Hába: Mother (Cpte)

JANOWITZ, Gundula (sop)
Beethoven: Fidelio (Cpte)
J. Strauss II: Fledermaus (exc)
Mozart: Così fan tutte (exc), Don Giovanni (Cpte), Idomeneo (Cpte), Nozze di Figaro (exc), Zauberflöte (Cpte)
R. Strauss: Arabella (Cpte), Ariadne auf Naxos (Cpte), Capriccio (Cpte)
Wagner: Götterdämmerung (Cpte), Parsifal (Cpte), Walküre (Cpte)
Weber: Freischütz (exc)
(CAMB) **CD-1032** From the Operas of Erich Wolfgang Korngold
(DECC) **436 316-2DA** Golden Operetta
(DG) **435 211-2GX15** Wagner—Der Ring des Nibelungen
(DG) **439 423-2GCL** Wagner—Der Ring des Nibelungen (highlights)
(DG) **439 467-2GCL** R. Strauss—Vocal and Orchestral Works
(DG) **447 352-2GDB2** A Portrait of Gundula Janowitz
(ORFE) **C394301B** Great Mozart Singers Series, Vol. 3

JANOWSKI, Marek (cond)
see Berlin RO
French Rad PO
Munich RO
Philh
Staatskapelle Dresden

JANSEN, Jacques (bar)
Debussy: Pelléas et Mélisande (Cpte)
(EMI) **CHS7 61038-2** Debussy—Pelléas et Mélisande, etc

JANSEN, Rudolf (pf)
(CBC) **MVCD1053** Schubert—Lieder

JANSKÁ, Jaroslava (sop)
Fibich: Šárka (Cpte)
Janáček: Fate (Cpte), Jenufa (Cpte)
(DECC) **430 375-2DH2** Janáček—Operatic and Orchestral Works
(SUPR) **11 1878-2** The Unknown Janáček

JANSONS, Mariss (cond)
see Oslo PO

JANSSEN, Herbert (bar)
Beethoven: Fidelio (Cpte)
Wagner: Lohengrin (Cpte), Tannhäuser (Cpte), Tristan und Isolde (Cpte)
(DUTT) **CDLX7007** Beecham conducts Wagner
(EMI) **CMS7 64008-2(1)** Wagner Singing on Record (pt 1)
(EMI) **CMS7 64008-2(2)** Wagner Singing on Record (pt 2)
(LYRC) **LCD146** Frida Leider sings Wagner

(PEAR) **GEMMCDS9926(1)** Covent Garden on Record—Vol.4 (pt 1)
(PEAR) **GEMMCD9331** Frida Leider sings Wagner

JANSSEN, John (bar)
Lortzing: Undine (Cpte)

JARESCH, August (ten)
Cornelius: Barbier von Bagdad (Cpte)
Mozart: Zauberflöte (Cpte)
R. Strauss: Ariadne auf Naxos (Cpte), Rosenkavalier (Cpte)
Verdi: Otello (Cpte)

JARRED, Mary (contr)
(LYRC) **SRO830** Smetana—The Bartered Bride, etc

JARRY, Michel (sngr)
Bazin: Maître Pathelin (Cpte)

JÄRVEFELT, Göran (prod)
Mozart: Don Giovanni (Cpte)

JÄRVI, Neeme (cond)
see Chicago SO
Cologne RSO
Danish Nat RSO
Detroit SO
Gothenburg SO
LSO
Philh
SNO

JARVIS, Joyce (sop)
G. Charpentier: Louise (Cpte)

JASPER, Bella (sop)
Henze: Junge Lord (Cpte)

JASZKOWSKI, Bogumit (bass)
Rossini: Signor Bruschino (Cpte)

JAUMILLOT, Irene (sngr)
Messager: Basoche (Cpte)

JAY, Isabel (sop)
(SYMP) **SYMCD1123** Sullivan—Sesquicentenial Commemorative Issue

JAZZ ENSEMBLE
(SONY) **SK44995** Maureen McGovern sings Gershwin

JEAN, Christian (ten)
Offenbach: Brigands (Cpte)

JEAN, Kenneth (cond)
see Hong Kong PO
Polish St PO

JEANTET, Robert (bar)
Gounod: Faust (Cpte)
Poulenc: Mamelles de Tirésias (Cpte)

JEDENÁCTÍK, Vladimír (bass)
Hába: Mother (Cpte)
Martinů: Julietta (Cpte)

JEDLIČKA, Dalibor (bass)
Janáček: Cunning Little Vixen (Cpte), Jenufa (Cpte), Makropulos Affair (Cpte)
Martinů: Julietta (Cpte), Miracles of Mary (Cpte)
Smetana: Dalibor (Cpte), Two Widows (Cpte)
(DECC) **421 852-2DH2** Janáček: Operatic & Chamber Works
(DECC) **430 375-2DH2** Janáček—Operatic and Orchestral Works

JEDLIČKA, Rudolf (bar)
Janáček: Káťa Kabanová (Cpte)

JEFFES, Peter (ten)
Chabrier: Roi malgré lui (Cpte)
Rameau: Castor et Pollux (Cpte)
Rossini: Tancredi (Cpte)
(ARAB) **Z6612** Rossini: Opera Arias

JEFFREYS, Celia (sop)
Romberg: Student Prince (exc)

JELINEK, Friedrich (ten)
R. Strauss: Ariadne auf Naxos (Cpte)
(SCHW) **314652** Vienna State Opera Live, Vol.15
(SCHW) **314712** Vienna State Opera Live, Vol.21

JELÍNKOVÁ, Štěpánka (sngr)
Martinů: Julietta (Cpte)

JELOSITS, Peter (ten)
Mozart: Nozze di Figaro (Cpte), Zauberflöte (Cpte)
R. Strauss: Rosenkavalier (Cpte)

JENCKEL, Helga (mez)
Wagner: Walküre (Cpte)
(DG) **435 211-2GX15** Wagner—Der Ring des Nibelungen

JENIS, Dalibor (bar)
Franchetti: Cristoforo Colombo (Cpte)
(DECC) **436 261-2DHO3** Puccini—Il Trittico

JENKIN, Nicola (sop)
Purcell: Dido (Cpte)

JENKINS, Neil (ten)
Bernstein: Candide (1988) (Cpte)
Britten: Peter Grimes (Cpte)
G. Charpentier: Louise (Cpte)
Knussen: Higglety Pigglety Pop! (Cpte)
Lehár: Graf von Luxemburg (exc)
Maxwell Davies: Resurrection (Cpte)
Mozart: Nozze di Figaro (Cpte)
Ponchielli: Gioconda (Cpte)
Romberg: Student Prince (exc)
Rossini: Elisabetta (Cpte)
Tippett: King Priam (Cpte)
Vaughan Williams: Hugh the Drover (Cpte)

JENKINS, Newell (cond)
see Clarion Music Soc

JENKINS, Timothy (ten)
Mozart: Idomeneo (Cpte)
Weill: Street Scene (Cpte)

JENNINGS, Diane (mez)
Spohr: Faust (Cpte)
(EURO) **GD69043** Puccini: Il Trittico

JENNINGS, Gloria (mez)
G. Charpentier: Louise (Cpte)
Vaughan Williams: Pilgrim's Progress (Cpte)
(CBS) **CD79312** Puccini: Il Trittico

JENSEN, Thomas (cond)
see Danish RSO
Danish St RSO

JENSON, Julian (ten)
Sullivan: Yeomen of the Guard (exc)

JENSSON, Björn (sngr)
Zemlinsky: Kleider machen Leute (Cpte)

JEPSON, Helen (sop)
(RCA) **09026 61580-2(4)** RCA/Met 100 Singers, 100 Years (pt 4)

JERGER, Alfred (bass-bar)
J. Strauss II: Nacht in Venedig (Cpte)
R. Strauss: Rosenkavalier (Cpte)
Wagner: Meistersinger (Cpte), Walküre (exc)
(SCHW) **314502** Vienna State Opera—Live Recordings (sampler)
(SCHW) **314542** Vienna State Opera Live, Vol.4
(SCHW) **314552** Vienna State Opera Live, Vol.5
(SCHW) **314562** Vienna State Opera Live, Vol.6
(SCHW) **314572** Vienna State Opera Live, Vol.7
(SCHW) **314602** Vienna State Opera Live, Vol.10
(SCHW) **314632** Vienna State Opera Live, Vol.13
(SCHW) **314652** Vienna State Opera Live, Vol.15
(SCHW) **314662** Vienna State Opera Live, Vol.16
(SCHW) **314672** Vienna State Opera Live, Vol.17
(SCHW) **314692** Vienna State Opera Live, Vol.19
(SCHW) **314702** Vienna State Opera Live, Vol.20
(SCHW) **314712** Vienna State Opera Live, Vol.21

JERICO, Santiago S. (bar)
Vives: Bohemios (Cpte), Doña Francisquita (Cpte)

JERITZA, Maria (sop)
(MMOI) **CDMOIR422** Great Voices in Tchaikovsky
(NIMB) **NI7864** More Legendary Voices
(PEAR) **GEMMCDS9925(2)** Covent Garden on Record—Vol.3 (pt 2)
(PEAR) **GEMMCD9130** Great Sopranos, Vol.2
(PREI) **89079** Maria Jeritza (1887-1982)
(RCA) **09026 61580-2(3)** RCA/Met 100 Singers, 100 Years (pt 3)
(SCHW) **314502** Vienna State Opera—Live Recordings (sampler)
(SCHW) **314622** Vienna State Opera Live, Vol.12
(SCHW) **314642** Vienna State Opera Live, Vol.14

JEROME, Marcus (ten)
Mercadante: Orazi e Curiazi (Cpte)

JERUSALEM, Siegfried (ten)
Beethoven: Fidelio (Cpte)
Flotow: Martha (Cpte)
Korngold: Violanta (Cpte)
Mozart: Zauberflöte (Cpte)
Wagner: Götterdämmerung (Cpte), Lohengrin (exc), Meistersinger (Cpte), Parsifal (Cpte), Rheingold (exc), Siegfried (Cpte), Tannhäuser (Cpte), Tristan und Isolde (Cpte), Walküre (Cpte)
(DG) **439 768-2GH** Wagner—Gala - New Year's Eve Concert 1993
(DG) **445 354-2GX14** Wagner—Der Ring des Nibelungen
(DG) **072 422-3GH7** Levine conducts Wagner's Ring
(EURO) **GD69003** Wagner—Der Ring des Nibelungen
(PHIL) **434 420-2PM32(2)** Richard Wagner Edition (pt 2)

JESSERER, Gertraud (narr)
Mozart: Zauberflöte (Cpte)

JETTE, Maria (sop)
Britten: Paul Bunyan (Cpte)
Copland: Tender Land (Cpte)

JEUNES DE L'EGLISE CHOIR
cond E. ANSERMET
Martin: Mystère de la Nativité

JEUNES SOLOISTS VOCAL ENSEMBLE
cond P. EÖTVÖS
Maderna: Hyperion (Cpte)

(KENNETH) JEWELL CHORALE
cond A. DORATI
R. Strauss: Aegyptische Helena (Cpte)

JEŽIL, Miloš (ten)
Dvořák: Kate and the Devil (Cpte)

JÍLEK, František (cond)
see Brno Janáček Chbr Op Orch
Brno Janáček Op Orch
Czech PO
Prague Nat Th Orch

JÍLKOVÁ, Milena (sop)
Janáček: Fate (Cpte)

JINDRÁK, Jindřich (bar)
Janáček: From the House of the Dead (Cpte), Jenufa (Cpte)
Martinů: Julietta (Cpte), Miracles of Mary (Cpte)
Shostakovich: Nose Suite
Smetana: Bartered Bride (Cpte), Brandenburgers in Bohemia (Cpte), Dalibor (Cpte)

JIRGLOVÁ, Milada (sop)
Janáček: From the House of the Dead (Cpte)

JIROUŠ, Jiří (cond)
see Prague Nat Th Orch

JISKROVÁ, Jana (mez)
(SUPR) **11 1878-2** The Unknown Janáček

JO, Sumi (sop)
Mozart: Zauberflöte (exc)
R. Strauss: Frau ohne Schatten (Cpte)
Rossini: Comte Ory (Cpte), Tancredi (Cpte), Turco in Italia (Cpte)
Verdi: Ballo in maschera (Cpte)
(CAPR) **10 810** Mozart—Opera Highlights
(DECC) **440 679-2DH** Carnaval!
(DECC) **443 377-2DM** Ten Top Sopranos 2
(ERAT) **2292-45797-2** The Ultimate Opera Collection
(ERAT) **4509-97239-2** Virtuoso Arias

JOACHIM, Iréne (sop)
(EMI) **CHS7 61038-2** Debussy—Pelléas et Mélisande, etc

JOBIN, Raoul (ten)
Bizet: Carmen (Cpte)
Gounod: Roméo et Juliette (Cpte)
Offenbach: Contes d'Hoffmann (Cpte)
Tomasi: Don Juan de Mañara (Cpte)
(EMI) **CHS7 69741-2(3)** Record of Singing, Vol.4—French School

JOCHENS, Wilfried (ten)
Hasse: Piramo e Tisbe (Cpte)
Keiser: Masagniello furioso (Cpte)
Landi: Mort d'Orfeo (Cpte)

JOCHUM, Eugen (cond)
see Bamberg SO
Bavarian Nat Orch
Bavarian St Op Orch
Bavarian St Orch
Bayreuth Fest Orch
Berlin Deutsche Op Orch
BPO
BRS Chor
BRSO
Concertgebouw
Hamburg PO

JÕGEVA, Mare (mez)
Tubin: Barbara von Tisenhusen (Cpte)

JOHANN STRAUSS ORCHESTRA OF VIENNA
cond W. BOSKOVSKY
(CFP) **CD-CFP4607** Favourite Strauss
(EMI) **CDC7 47020-2** Lehár: Waltzes
(EMI) **CZS7 62751-2** The Strausses of Vienna
cond J. FRANCEK
(LASE) **15 619** Johann Strauss II—Famous Overtures

JOHANNING, Beth (sop)
Pfitzner: Herz (Cpte)
S. Wagner: Bärenhäuter (Cpte), Schwarzschwanenreich (Cpte)

JOHANNSSON, Kristjan (ten)
Verdi: Aida (Cpte)

JOHANOS, Donald (cond)
see Bratislava RSO
NZ SO

JOHANSEN, Ronnie (bass)
Heise: Drot og Marsk (Cpte)

JOHANSSON, Eva (sop)
Heise: Drot og Marsk (Cpte)
Wagner: Rheingold (Cpte), Walküre (exc)
Zemlinsky: Es war einmal (Cpte)

JOHN, Keith (organ)
(PRIO) **PRCD370** Great European Organs, No 26

JOHN, Kevin (ten)
(OPRA) **ORCH103** Italian Opera—1810-20
(OPRA) **ORH102** A Hundred Years of Italian Opera

JOHN, Lindsay (mez)
Mozart: Zauberflöte (Cpte)

JOHNNY GREEN ORCHESTRA
cond J. GREEN
(RCA) **09026 61245-2** Ezio Pinza - Recital

JOHNS, Stratford (sngr)
Gay: Beggar's Opera (Cpte)

JOHNS, Terry (hn)
(DIVI) **2-4102** The Classic and Romantic Horn

JOHNSON, Camelia (mez)
Britten: Noye's Fludde (Cpte)
Gershwin: Porgy and Bess (Cpte)

JOHNSON, Cora (voc)
Joplin: Treemonisha (Cpte)

JOHNSON, David (bar)
Mozart: Oca del Cairo (Cpte)

JOHNSON, Douglas (ten)
Gazzaniga: Don Giovanni (Cpte)
Mozart: Finta semplice (Cpte)

JOHNSON, Edward (ten)
(RCA) **09026 61580-2(3)** RCA/Met 100 Singers, 100 Years (pt 3)

JOHNSON, Emma (cl)
(ASV) **CDDCA800** Encores - Emma Johnson

JOHNSON, Graham (pf)
(EMI) **CDC7 54411-2** On Wings of Song
(HYPE) **CDA67061/2** Britten—Purcell Realizations
(HYPE) **CDJ33009** Schubert: Complete Lieder, Vol.9

JOHNSON, Jeffrey (ten)
Stravinsky: Rake's Progress (Cpte)

JOHNSON, Katherine (sop)
Janáček: Jenufa (Cpte)

JOHNSON, Patricia (mez)
Berg: Lulu (Cpte)
Britten: Albert Herring (Cpte)
Giordano: Andrea Chénier (Cpte)
Henze: Junge Lord (Cpte)
Mozart: Nozze di Figaro (Cpte)
Purcell: Dido (Cpte)
(DG) **439 474-2GCL** Purcell—Opera & Choral Works
(EMI) **CDM5 65341-2** Purcell—Theatre Music

JOHNSON, Richard (bass)
V. Thomson: Lord Byron (Cpte)

JOHNSON, Robert (ten)
Beethoven: Fidelio (Cpte)
(DECC) **433 443-2DA** Great Opera Choruses

JOHNSON, Samuel (narr)
Glass: Einstein on the Beach (Cpte)

JOHNSON, William (bar)
Gershwin: Porgy and Bess (Cpte)

JOHNSSON, Hillary (mez)
(ALBA) **TROY023-2** Music of Joseph Fennimore

JOHNSTON, Cynthia (sop)
(DECC) **071 149-1DH (DECC)** The Essential Sutherland

JOHNSTON, David (ten)
Beethoven: Fidelio (Cpte)
Vaughan Williams: Hugh the Drover (Cpte)

JOHNSTON, James (ten)
(EMI) **CHS7 69741-2(2)** Record of Singing, Vol.4—Anglo-American School (pt 2)
(TEST) **SBT1058** James Johnston - Opera Arias and Songs

JOHNSTON, Suzanne (mez)
Meyerbeer: Huguenots (Cpte)

JOLL, Phillip (bass-bar)
Martinů: Greek Passion (Cpte)
Wagner: Parsifal (Cpte), Tristan und Isolde (Cpte)

JONASON, Louisa (sop)
V. Thomson: Lord Byron (Cpte)

JONÁŠOVÁ, Jana (sop)
Dvořák: Rusalka (Cpte)
Janáček: Excursions of Mr Brouček (Cpte), Jenufa (Cpte)
Martinů: Greek Passion (Cpte)
Smetana: Bartered Bride (Cpte), Two Widows (Cpte)

JONES, Alan (ten)
Donizetti: Fille du régiment (Cpte)
Walton: Troilus and Cressida (Cpte)

JONES, Alonzo (ten)
Gershwin: Porgy and Bess (exc)

JONES, Bessie (sop)
(CLAR) **CDGSE78-50-54** Coates conducts Wagner, Weber & Mendelssohn

JONES, Ceinwen (mez)
Sullivan: Gondoliers (Cpte)

JONES, Della (mez)
Alwyn: Miss Julie (Cpte)
Bellini: Sonnambula (Cpte)
Bernstein: Candide (1988) (exc)
Boito: Mefistofele (Cpte)
Britten: Gloriana (Cpte), Midsummer Night's Dream (Cpte)
Donizetti: Assedio di Calais (Cpte), Maria Padilla (Cpte), Ugo, Conte di Parigi (Cpte)
Floyd: Susannah (Cpte)
Handel: Alcina (Cpte), Giulio Cesare (Cpte), Teseo (Cpte)
Maxwell Davies: Resurrection (Cpte)
Meyerbeer: Crociato in Egitto (Cpte), Dinorah (Cpte)
Mozart: Clemenza di Tito (Cpte), Don Giovanni (Cpte), Nozze di Figaro (Cpte)
Purcell: Dido (Cpte)
Rossini: Barbiere di Siviglia (Cpte), Guillaume Tell (Cpte)
Verdi: Traviata (exc)
Walton: Bear (Cpte)
(CBS) **CD79312** Puccini: Il Trittico
(CHAN) **CHAN8865** Rossini: Opera Arias
(OPRA) **ORCH103** Italian Opera—1810-20
(OPRA) **ORCH104** A Hundred Years of Italian Opera: 1820-1830
(OPRA) **ORC003** Donizetti—Gabriella di Vergy
(OPRA) **ORH102** A Hundred Years of Italian Opera
(OPRA) **ORR201** 19th Century Heroines-Yvonne Kenny
(PHIL) **432 416-2PH3** Haydn—L'incontro improvviso/Arias
(SONY) **S2K66836** Goldschmidt—Beatrice Cenci, etc

JONES, Emlyn (ten)
Britten: Billy Budd (Cpte)

JONES, Gareth (bar)
Offenbach: Orphée aux enfers (Cpte)
Sullivan: Mikado (Cpte), Pirates of Penzance (Cpte)

JONES, Geraint (cond)
see Mermaid Orch

JONES, Gordon (bass)
Blow: Venus and Adonis (Cpte)

JONES, Granville (cond)
see Philomusica of London

JONES, Dame **Gwyneth (sop)**
Beethoven: Fidelio (Cpte)
Humperdinck: Hänsel und Gretel (exc)
Puccini: Fanciulla del West (Cpte)
R. Strauss: Aegyptische Helena (Cpte), Rosenkavalier (Cpte), Salome (Cpte)
Schmidt: Notre Dame (Cpte)
Verdi: Don Carlo (exc), Macbeth (Cpte), Otello (Cpte)
Wagner: Fliegende Holländer (Cpte), Götterdämmerung (Cpte), Parsifal (Cpte), Siegfried (Cpte), Tannhäuser (Cpte), Walküre (exc)
(CHAN) **CHAN8930** Wagner—Arias
(DECC) **414 100-2DM15** Wagner: Der Ring des Nibelungen
(DECC) **433 221-2DWO** The World of Verdi
(DECC) **433 624-2DSP** Great Soprano Arias
(PHIL) **434 420-2PM32(1)** Richard Wagner Edition (Pt.1)

JONES, Isola (mez)
Gershwin: Porgy and Bess (Cpte)
Mascagni: Cavalleria Rusticana (Cpte)
(DECC) **071 142-1DH (DECC)** Essential Opera

JONES, Joela (pf)
Gershwin: Porgy and Bess (Cpte)

JONES, Karen (fl)
(CONI) **CDCF905** Karen Jones—The Flute Album

JONES, Leah-Marian (mez)
Verdi: Traviata (Cpte)

JONES, Louise (vn)
(SAIN) **SCD4058** Louise Jones—Violin Recital

JONES, Morgan (ten)
Mozart: Nozze di Figaro (Cpte)

JONES, Nerys (sop)
Weir: Blond Eckbert (Cpte)

JONES, Parry (ten)
Wagner: Tristan und Isolde (Cpte)

JONES, Peggy Ann (mez)
Sullivan: Mikado (Cpte)
(BELA) **461 006-2** Gilbert & Sullivan—Songs and Snatches
(DECC) **430 095-2DWO** The World of Gilbert & Sullivan, Vol.1
(DECC) **433 868-2DWO** The World of Gilbert & Sullivan - Volume 2

JONES, Philip Blake (ten)
Sullivan: Iolanthe (exc)

JONES, Stephen (treb)
Britten: Midsummer Night's Dream (Cpte)

JONES, Warren (pf)
(DG) **072 189-3GH** Kathleen Battle at the Metropolitan Museum
(RCA) **09026 62547-2** Divas in Song—Marilyn Horne's 60th Birthday

JONES, Yolande (sop)
Janáček: Fate (Cpte)

(PHILIP) JONES BRASS ENSEMBLE
(CLAV) **CD50-8503** Philip Jones Brass Ensemble Lollipops

JONES-HUDSON, Eleanor (sop)
(SYMP) **SYMCD1123** Sullivan—Sesquicentenial Commemorative Issue

JORAN, Jiří (bass)
Janáček: Makropulos Affair (Cpte)
Smetana: Brandenburgers in Bohemia (Cpte)

JORDAN, Armin (cond)
see Basle SO
FNO
French Rad New PO
Monte Carlo Nat Op Orch
Monte Carlo Op Orch
Monte Carlo PO
Paris Orch Ens

JORDIS, Eelco von (bass)
Spohr: Faust (Cpte)

JORGENSON, Phil (ten)
Britten: Paul Bunyan (Cpte)

JORIS, Jan (bar)
Puccini: Bohème (Cpte), Gianni Schicchi (Cpte)

JÖRN, Karl (ten)
(IRCC) **IRCC-CD805** Geraldine Farrar - 60th Anniversary Issue
(SUPR) **11 2136-2(2)** Emmy Destinn—Complete Edition, Discs 3 & 4
(SUPR) **11 2136-2(3)** Emmy Destinn—Complete Edition, Discs 5 to 8

JOSEPHSON, Kim (bar)
Puccini: Fanciulla del West (Cpte)

JOSHUA, Rosemary (sop)
Humperdinck: Hänsel und Gretel (Cpte)

JOSSOUD, Hélène (mez)
Debussy: Rodrigue et Chimène (Cpte)
Offenbach: Contes d'Hoffmann (Cpte)
R. Strauss: Salomé (Cpte)

JOST-ARDEN, Ruth (mez)
Wagner: Tannhäuser (Cpte)

JOURINA, Irina (sop)
Rimsky-Korsakov: Kashchey (Cpte)

JOURNET, Marcel (bass)
Gounod: Faust (Cpte)
(CLUB) **CL99-034** Marcel Journet (1867-1933)
(EMI) **CHS7 64864-2(1)** La Scala Edition - Vol.2, 1915-46 (pt 1)
(EMI) **CMS7 64008-2(2)** Wagner Singing on Record (pt 2)
(IRCC) **IRCC-CD800** Souvenirs from Meyerbeer Operas
(MSCM) **MM30283** Great Wagnerian Singers, Vol.1
(MSCM) **MM30352** Caruso—Italian Opera Arias
(MSCM) **MM30377** 18 Tenors d'Expression Française
(NIMB) **NI7834** Caruso in Ensemble
(NIMB) **NI7859** Caruso, Farrar & Journet in French Opera
(PEAR) **EVC1(2)** The Caruso Edition, Vol.1 (pt 2)
(PEAR) **EVC2** The Caruso Edition, Vol.2—1908-12
(PEAR) **EVC3(1)** The Caruso Edition, Vol.3 (pt 1)
(PEAR) **EVC4(1)** The Caruso Edition, Vol.4 (pt 1)
(PEAR) **EVC4(2)** The Caruso Edition, Vol.4 (pt 2)
(PEAR) **GEMMCDS9159(2)** De Luca Edition, Vol.1 (pt 2)
(PEAR) **GEMMCDS9923(2)** Covent Garden on Record, Vol.1 (pt 2)
(PEAR) **GEMMCDS9924(2)** Covent Garden on Record, Vol.2 (pt 2)
(PEAR) **GEMMCD9104** Pasquale Amato (1878-1942)
(PEAR) **GEMMCD9122** 20 Great Basses sing Great Arias
(PEAR) **GEMMCD9129** Great Tenors, Vol.2
(PEAR) **GEMMCD9161** Edmond Clément (1867-1928)
(PEAR) **GEMMCD9224** Luisa Tetrazzini—Vol.4
(PREI) **89021** Marcel Journet (1867-1933)
(RCA) **GD60495(2)** The Complete Caruso Collection (pt 2)
(RCA) **GD60495(3)** The Complete Caruso Collection (pt 3)
(RCA) **GD60495(4)** The Complete Caruso Collection (pt 4)
(RCA) **GD60495(6)** The Complete Caruso Collection (pt 6)
(RCA) **09026 61242-2** Caruso Sings Verdi
(RCA) **09026 61244-2** Caruso sings French Opera Arias
(RCA) **09026 61580-2(1)** RCA/Met 110 Singers, 100 Years (pt 1)
(ROMO) **81003-2** Galli-Curci—Acoustic Recordings, Vol.1
(ROMO) **82002-2** Edmond Clément (1867-1928)

JOUVE, André (cond)
see Lamoureux Orch
Paris Champs-Élysées Orch

JOYCE, Donald (organ)
(CATA) **09026 61825-2** Glass—Organ Works

JUDD, James (cond)
see COE
ECO
Philh

JUFFINGER, Andreas (organ)
(SCHW) **312642** Unicef Gala 1991
(SCHW) **314073** Canzone Sacre

JUILLIARD CHORUS
cond L. BERNSTEIN
Beethoven: Fidelio (exc)

JUILLIARD ENSEMBLE
cond L. BERIO
(RCA) **09026 62540-2** Cathy Berberian sings Berio & Weill

JUILLIARD OPERA CENTER
cond G. SCHWARZ
Schuman: Mighty Casey (Cpte), Question of Taste (Cpte)

JUILLIARD ORCHESTRA
cond G. SCHWARZ
Schuman: Mighty Casey (Cpte), Question of Taste (Cpte)

JULIIS, Gabriele De (ten)
Verdi: Otello (Cpte)

JULLIA, Gilbert (sngr)
Poulenc: Mamelles de Tirésias (Cpte)

JULLIOT, Marguerite (mez)
Massenet: Manon (Cpte)

JUNE, Ava (sop)
Britten: Turn of the Screw (Cpte)

JUNG, Helene (mez)
Wagner: Walküre (exc)

(PEAR) **GEMMCDS9121** Wagner—Die Meistersinger, Act 3, etc
(PREI) **89029** Meta Seinemeyer (1895-1929)

JUNG, Jürgen (narr)
Lehár: Giuditta (Cpte)

JUNG, Manfred (ten)
Wagner: Götterdämmerung (Cpte), Siegfried (exc)
Weill: Dreigroschenoper (Cpte)
(PHIL) **434 420-2PM32(1)** Richard Wagner Edition (Pt.1)

JUNGE KANTOREI
cond N. HARNONCOURT
Monteverdi: Ritorno d'Ulisse in Patria (Cpte)

JUNGHÄNEL, Konrad (lte)
(HARM) **HMA190 1183** Works for Lute and Voice

JUNGHÄNEL, Konrad (theorbo)
(ACCE) **ACC57802D** Purcell: Songs and Elegies

JUNGWIRTH, Helena (sop)
Verdi: Rigoletto (Cpte), Traviata (Cpte)

JUNGWIRTH, Manfred (bass)
Beethoven: Fidelio (Cpte)
R. Strauss: Ariadne auf Naxos (Cpte), Rosenkavalier (Cpte)
Wagner: Tannhäuser (Cpte)
Weill: Mahagonny-Gesänge (Cpte), Sieben Todsünden (Cpte)

JUON, Julia (mez)
Schreker: Ferne Klang (Cpte)

JURANEK, Lidia (sop)
Gluck: Corona (Cpte)

JUREČKA, Antonín (ten)
Janáček: Fate (Cpte), Šárka (Cpte)

JÜRGENS, Curd (narr)
Mozart: Entführung (Cpte)

JURINAC, Sena (sop)
Beethoven: Fidelio (Cpte)
Gluck: Orfeo ed Euridice (Cpte)
Mozart: Così fan tutte (exc), Don Giovanni (Cpte), Nozze di Figaro (Cpte), Zauberflöte (Cpte)
R. Strauss: Ariadne auf Naxos (Cpte), Rosenkavalier (Cpte)
Verdi: Don Carlo (Cpte)
(EMI) **CDH5 65072-2** Glyndebourne Recorded - 1934-1994
(EMI) **CDH7 63199-2** Sena Jurinac—Opera and Song Recital
(EMI) **CHS7 69741-2(4)** Record of Singing, Vol.4—German School
(EMI) **CZS7 67123-2** Wagner: Der Ring des Nibelungen
(ORFE) **C394301B** Great Mozart Singers Series, Vol. 3

JUSTUS, Kimberly (sngr)
Zemlinsky: Kleider machen Leute (Cpte)

JÜTEN, Grit van (sop)
Benatzky: Im weissen Rössl (Cpte)
Schultze: Schwarzer Peter (Cpte)

JUYOL, Suzanne (mez)
(EMI) **CHS7 69741-2(3)** Record of Singing, Vol.4—French School

KAASCH, Donald (ten)
Rossini: Armida (Cpte)

KABAIVANSKA, Raina (sop)
Donizetti: Fausta (Cpte)
Puccini: Madama Butterfly (Cpte), Tosca (Cpte)
Verdi: Falstaff (Cpte), Otello (Cpte)
(CAST) **CASH5051** Puccini Favourites from Covent Garden and the Arena di Verona
(CAST) **CVI2070** Great Puccini Love Scenes from Covent Garden, La Scala and Verona
(DECC) **071 140-1DH (DECC)** Pavarotti—30th Anniversary Gala Concert
(DECC) **071 142-1DH (DECC)** Essential Opera
(FORL) **UCD16741** Bulgarian Voices, Vol. 1
(FORL) **UCD16742** Bulgarian Voices, Vol. 2

KAHN, Percy (pf)
(BIDD) **LAB035** Mischa Elman—Solo Recordings 1910-1911
(LYRC) **SRO830** Smetana—The Bartered Bride, etc

KAIDANOV, K.E. (bass)
(PEAR) **GEMMCDS9004/6(2)** Singers of Imperial Russia, Vol.3 (pt 2)
(PEAR) **GEMMCD9106** Dmitri Smirnov

KAISERSLAUTERN RADIO ORCHESTRA
cond K. ARP
Spohr: Faust (Cpte)

KAJIYAMA, Akemi (sngr)
Braunfels: Verkündigung (Cpte)

KAL, Berthe (mez)
Martinů: Alexandre Bis (Cpte), Julietta (Cpte)

KALAŠ, Karel (bass)
Martinů: Julietta (Cpte)
Smetana: Bartered Bride (Cpte), Brandenburgers in Bohemia (Cpte)
(KOCH) **34036-2** A Pageant of Opera

KALE, Stuart (ten)
Berg: Lulu (Cpte)
Britten: Peter Grimes (Cpte)
Floyd: Susannah (Cpte)
Janáček: Fate (Cpte)
Mozart: Finta Giardiniera (Cpte), Idomeneo (Cpte)
Offenbach: Orphée aux enfers (exc)
Rossini: Occasione fa il ladro (Cpte)
Verdi: Otello (Cpte)
Weill: Sieben Todsünden (Cpte)

KALENBERG, Josef (ten)
(SCHW) **314512** Vienna State Opera Live, Vol.1
(SCHW) **314532** Vienna State Opera Live, Vol.3
(SCHW) **314542** Vienna State Opera Live, Vol.4
(SCHW) **314562** Vienna State Opera Live, Vol.6
(SCHW) **314592** Vienna State Opera Live, Vol.9
(SCHW) **314602** Vienna State Opera Live, Vol.10
(SCHW) **314622** Vienna State Opera Live, Vol.12
(SCHW) **314642** Vienna State Opera Live, Vol.14
(SCHW) **314742** Vienna State Opera Live, Vol.24

KALENDOCSKY, Jirí (bass)
Smetana: Dalibor (Cpte)

KALES, Elisabeth (sop)
Mozart: Zauberflöte (Cpte)

KALLAB, Camilla (mez)
Wagner: Götterdämmerung (Cpte), Meistersinger (Cpte)

KALLISCH, Cornelia (contr)
Mozart: Nozze di Figaro (Cpte)
Wagner: Meistersinger (Cpte)

KALM, Stephen (voc)
M. Monk: Atlas (Cpte)

KÁLMÁNDI, Mihály (bar)
Mascagni: Lodoletta (Cpte)

KALMÁR, Magda (sop)
Respighi: Belfagor (Cpte)

KALTER, Sabine (contr)
Wagner: Tristan und Isolde (Cpte)
(LYRC) **SRO830** Smetana—The Bartered Bride, etc

KALUDOV, Kaludi (ten)
Borodin: Prince Igor (Cpte)
Mussorgsky: Khovanshchina (Cpte)
Puccini: Manon Lescaut (Cpte)

KALUZA, Stefania (mez)
Zemlinsky: Kleider machen Leute (Cpte)

KAMANN, Karl (bass)
(SCHW) **314652** Vienna State Opera Live, Vol.15
(SCHW) **314702** Vienna State Opera Live, Vol.20

KAMAS, Pavel (bass)
Dvořák: Kate and the Devil (Cpte)
Janáček: From the House of the Dead (Cpte)

KAMI, Hassan (ten)
Mozart: Così fan tutte (Cpte)

KAMIONSKY, Oskar (bar)
(PEAR) **GEMMCDS9001/3(1)** Singers of Imperial Russia, Vol.2 (pt 1)

KAMMERSPIEL
(TIMB) **DMHCD1** Kammerspiel

KAMP, Harry van der (bass)
Cavalli: Giasone (Cpte)
Keiser: Masagniello furioso (Cpte)
Landi: Mort d'Orfeo (Cpte)
Mozart: Schauspieldirektor (Cpte), Thamos, K345 (Cpte)

KANDBLINDER, Roland (ten)
Puccini: Fanciulla del West (Cpte)

KANEL, Vladimir de (bass-bar)
Prokofiev: War and Peace (Cpte)
Verdi: Simon Boccanegra (Cpte)

KANG, Philip (bar)
Wagner: Götterdämmerung (Cpte), Rheingold (Cpte), Siegfried (Cpte)
(SCHW) **312642** Unicef Gala 1991

KANNEN, Günter von (bar)
Gazzaniga: Don Giovanni (Cpte)
Mozart: Nozze di Figaro (exc)
Wagner: Götterdämmerung (Cpte), Parsifal (Cpte), Rheingold (Cpte), Siegfried (Cpte)

KANTE, Peter Nikolaus (ten)
Schreker: Ferne Klang (Cpte)
Weill: Mahagonny-Gesänge (Cpte)

KANTILÉNA CHILDREN'S CHORUS
cond J. PINKAS
Dvořák: Jacobin (exc)

KANTSCHIEDER, Paul (cond)
see Masurian PO
Mazovian PO

KANUNNIKOVA, Ludmilla (contr)
Prokofiev: War and Peace (Cpte)

KAPELLMANN, Franz-Josef (bass)
B. Goldschmidt: Gewaltige Hahnrei (Cpte)
Wagner: Rheingold (Cpte)
(CLOR) **TCO93-75** The Cleveland Orchestra-75th Anniversary CD Edition

KAPILOW, Robert (pf)
(KOCH) **37087-2** Songs of Kurt Weill

KAPPAUN, Lothar (bar)
Delius: Village Romeo and Juliet (Cpte)

KAPPEL, Gertrude (sop)
(SCHW) **314592** Vienna State Opera Live, Vol.9

KAPPER, Paula (sop)
Wagner: Walküre (exc)

KAPTAIN, Laurence (cimbalom)
(DECC) **443 444-2DH** Hungarian Connections

KARADJIAN, Michaela (mez)
Puccini: Suor Angelica (Cpte)

KARAJAN, Herbert von (cond)
see Bayreuth Fest Orch
Berlin Phil Wind Qnt
Berlin RIAS Orch
Berlin RSO
Bologna Teatro Comunale Orch
BPO
La Scala Orch
NY Met Op Orch
Philh
Staatskapelle Dresden
VPO

KARAKASH, Mikhail (bar)
(NIMB) **NI7865** Great Singers at the Mariinsky Theatre
(PEAR) **GEMMCDS9111(2)** Singers of Imperial Russia, Vol.5 (pt 2)

KARAS, Joža (cond)
see Disman Rad Children's Orch

KARASYOV, Grigory (bass)
Mussorgsky: Boris Godunov (Cpte)

KARCZYKOWSKI, Ryszard (ten)
(POLS) **PNCD087** Famous Operetta Arias

KARENINOVÁ, Zdenka (sop)
Janáček: Fate (Cpte)

KARK, Friedrich (cond)
see orch

KARLSRUD, Edmond (bar)
Verdi: Aida (exc)

KAROLIDIS, Paul (bass)
Mussorgsky: Boris Godunov (Cpte)

KAROUSATOS, Nickolas (bass)
Rachmaninov: Monna Vanna (exc)

KARP, Benjamin (vc)
(CENT) **CRC2084** Music from Cranberry Isles

KARPÍŠEK, Milan (ten)
Janáček: From the House of the Dead (Cpte), Makropulos Affair (Cpte)

KARR, Isidore (cond)
see SRO

KARRASCH, Ingrid (mez)
Wagner: Götterdämmerung (Cpte)
(EMI) **LDX9 91275-1(EMI)** Sawallisch conducts Wagner's Ring

KARWAUTZ, Brigitte (sop)
J. Strauss II: Fledermaus (exc)

KASAROVA, Vesselina (mez)
Bellini: Beatrice di Tenda (Cpte)

KASCHMANN, Giuseppe (bar)
(EMI) **CHS7 64860-2(1)** La Scala Edition - Vol.1, 1878-1914 (pt 1)
(MEMO) **HR4408/9(1)** Singers in Genoa, Vol.1 (disc 1)
(SYMP) **SYMCD1065** The Harold Wayne Collection, Vol.1

KASEMANN, Franz (ten)
Mozart: Nozze di Figaro (Cpte)
R. Strauss: Rosenkavalier (Cpte)

KASHIWAGI, Hiroko (mez)
(SCHW) **312642** Unicef Gala 1991

KASKAS, Anna (contr)
Ponchielli: Gioconda (Cpte)

KASPSZYK, Jacek (cond)
see Warsaw Chbr Op Orch

KASSAI, István (pf)
(MARC) **8 223318** Erkel—Opera Transcriptions

KASSNER, Danielle (gtr)
(PRES) **PCOM1120** Duo Kassner-Quer—Tambor de granaderos

KASSOWITZ, Gottfried (cond)
see Austrian St Rad Orch

KASTORSKY, Vladimir (bass)
(MMOI) **CDMOIR422** Great Voices in Tchaikovsky
(NIMB) **NI7865** Great Singers at the Mariinsky Theatre
(PEAR) **GEMMCDS9001/3(1)** Singers of Imperial Russia, Vol.2 (pt 1)

KASTU, Matti (ten)
R. Strauss: Aegyptische Helena (Cpte)

KATAGIRI, Hitomi (mez)
Wagner: Parsifal (Cpte), Walküre (Cpte)

KATANOSAKA, Eiko (sop)
Monteverdi: Orfeo (Cpte)

KATIMS, Milton (va)
(SONY) **SK45816** Humoresque—Favourite Violin Encores

KATONA, Julius (ten)
Wagner: Meistersinger (exc)

KATOWICE RADIO SYMPHONY ORCHESTRA
cond G. FITELBERG
(OLYM) **OCD386** Moniuszko—Overtures

cond J. KRENZ
(OLYM) **OCD386** Moniuszko—Overtures

KATOWICE STATE PHILHARMONIC CHORUS
cond K. STRYJA
Szymanowski: King Roger (Cpte)

KATOWICE STATE PHILHARMONIC ORCHESTRA
cond K. STRYJA
Szymanowski: King Roger (Cpte)

KATRAMA, Jorma (db)
(FINL) **4509-95605-2** Contrabasso con amroe
(FINL) **4509-97894-2** Contrabasso con Sentimento

KATSARIS, Cyprien (pf)
(SONY) **SK58973** Wagneriana—Wagner Transcriptions

KATSAROVA, Wesselina (mez)
Tchaikovsky: Queen of Spades (Cpte)

KATULSKAYA, Elena (sop)
(ARLE) **ARL23/5** Rimsky-Korsakov—Sadko
(NIMB) **NI7865** Great Singers at the Mariinsky Theatre
(PEAR) **GEMMCDS9111(1)** Singers of Imperial Russia, Vol.5 (pt 1)
(PEAR) **GEMMCDS9111(2)** Singers of Imperial Russia, Vol.5 (pt 2)

KATZ, Eberhard (ten)
Hindemith: Cardillac (Cpte)

KATZ, Florence (sop)
Rameau: Hippolyte et Aricie (Cpte)

KATZ, Shelley (pf)
(SCHW) **312642** Unicef Gala 1991

KAUFMAN, Jolanta (sop)
Catalani: Wally (Cpte)
Gazzaniga: Don Giovanni (Cpte)
Gluck: Rencontre imprévue (Cpte)
R. Strauss: Ariadne auf Naxos (Cpte)
Wagner: Götterdämmerung (Cpte), Rheingold (Cpte), Siegfried (Cpte)
(EMI) **LDX9 91275-1(EMI)** Sawallisch conducts Wagner's Ring

KAUFMAN, Louis (vn)
(CAMB) **CD-1063** Louis Kaufman - Violin Works

KAUFMANN, Erich (bass)
(SCHW) **314572** Vienna State Opera Live, Vol.7

KAUFMANN, Julie (sop)
Verdi: Falstaff (Cpte)

KAUPOVÁ, Helena (sop)
Smetana: Libuše (Cpte)

KAVRAKOS, Dimitri (bass)
Bellini: Norma (Cpte)
Mozart: Don Giovanni (Cpte)
Spontini: Vestale (Cpte)
Verdi: Aida (Cpte), Battaglia di Legnano (Cpte), Otello (Cpte), Rigoletto (Cpte)

KAWAHARA, Yasunori (db)
(LARG) **Largo 5105** Elegia: Works for Double-bass and Piano

KAYE, Judy (sop)
(KOCH) **37028-2** Gershwin—Songs & Duets

KAYE, Milton (pf)
(RCA) **09026 61778-2(19)** The Heifetz Collection, Vol. 19

KAYEVCHENKO, Valentina (sop)
Kabalevsky: Colas Breugnon (Cpte)

KAZANDJIEV, Vassil (cond)
see Sofia Rad SO

KAZARAS, Peter (ten)
Corigliano: Ghosts of Versailles (Cpte)
Janáček: Jenufa (Cpte)

KAZBEK, Merih (bass)
Donizetti: Roberto Devereux (Cpte)

KAZIMIERCZUK, Angela (sop)
Lehár: Lustige Witwe (Cpte)

KEEBLE, Gaynor (sop)
Janáček: Fate (Cpte)

KEEN, Catherine (mez)
Falla: Vida breve (Cpte)

KEENE, Christopher (cond)
see NYC Op Orch
orch

KEENLYSIDE, Simon (bar)
Britten: Peter Grimes (Cpte)
Cavalli: Calisto (Cpte)
Chabrier: Briséïs (Cpte)
R. Strauss: Capriccio (Cpte)

KEGEL, Herbert (cond)
see Dresden PO
Leipzig RSO

KEGLER, Helmut (bass)
Spohr: Faust (Cpte)

KEIL, Adolf (bass)
R. Strauss: Salome (Cpte)
Wagner: Meistersinger (Cpte)

KEILBERTH, Joseph (cond)
see Bavarian St Op Chor
Bavarian St Op Orch
Bavarian St Orch
Bayreuth Fest Orch
BPO
Cologne RSO
Stuttgart RO
VPO

KEITH, Charlton (pf)
(BIDD) **LAB009/10** The Kreisler Collection

KÉLÉMEN, Zoltan (bar)
Beethoven: Fidelio (exc)
Lehár: Lustige Witwe (exc)
Mozart: Nozze di Figaro (exc)
Mussorgsky: Boris Godunov (Cpte)
Wagner: Götterdämmerung (Cpte), Meistersinger (Cpte), Parsifal (Cpte), Rheingold (Cpte), Siegfried (Cpte)
(DG) **435 211-2GX15** Wagner—Der Ring des Nibelungen
(DG) **435 712-2GX2** Lehár—The Merry Widow. Suppé—Overtures
(DG) **439 423-2GCL** Wagner—Der Ring des Nibelungen (highlights)

KELEN, Péter (ten)
Mascagni: Lodoletta (Cpte)

KELLER, Peter (ten)
Monteverdi: Incoronazione di Poppea (Cpte), Orfeo (Cpte)
Mozart: Zauberflöte (Cpte)
Zemlinsky: Kleider machen Leute (Cpte)

KELLEY, Frank (ten)
Mozart: Nozze di Figaro (Cpte)

KELLOCK, Brian (pf)
(DIVI) **2-4102** The Classic and Romantic Horn

KELLS, Iris (sop)
Britten: Peter Grimes (Cpte)

KELLY, Claire (contr)
Sullivan: Gondoliers (Cpte)

KELLY, David (bass)
Britten: Midsummer Night's Dream (Cpte)
Verdi: Traviata (Cpte)

KELLY, Denise (hp)
Britten: Peter Grimes (Cpte)
Herrmann: Wuthering Heights (Cpte)
R. Strauss: Salome (Cpte)

KELLY, Janis (sop)
Weill: Street Scene (Cpte)

KELLY, Norman (ten)
R. Ward: Crucible (Cpte)

KELLY, Sondra (contr)
Puccini: Fanciulla del West (Cpte)
Verdi: Traviata (Cpte), Trovatore (Cpte)
Wagner: Walküre (Cpte)
(DG) **072 428-1GH2(DG)** The Metropolitan Opera Gala
(DG) **072 422-3GH7** Levine conducts Wagner's Ring

KELM, Linda (sop)
Puccini: Turandot (exc)
Wagner: Walküre (Cpte)
(DG) **437 825-2GH** Wagner—Der Ring des Nibelungen - Highlights
(DG) **445 354-2GX14** Wagner—Der Ring des Nibelungen

KEMENY, Lynda (sop)
Krenek: Sprüng über den Schatten (Cpte)

KEMPE, Rudolf (cond)
see Bamberg SO
Bavarian St Op Orch
Berlin Staatskapelle
BPO
Staatskapelle Dresden
VPO

KEMPF, Thea (sop)
(PREI) **90168** Wagner—Die Meistersinger, Act 2, etc

KEMPFF, Wilhelm (pf)
(DG) **439 108-2GGA** Bach/Gluck/Handel—Keyboard Works & trans by Wilhelm Kempff
(DG) **439 672-2GX2** Bach/Gluck—Piano Works & Transcriptions

KENDA, Gerd (bass)
Biber: Arminio (Cpte)

KENNAWAY, Igor (cond)
see RNCM Op Orch

KENNEDY, Laurie (vc)
(LOND) **827 267-2** More Amadeus - Original Soundtrack

KENNEDY, Louisa (sop)
Henze: English Cat (Cpte)

KENNEDY, Nigel (vn)
Massenet: Thaïs (exc)
(DECC) **425 849-2DWO** Your hundred best tunes vol 3
(DECC) **433 220-2DWO** The World of the Violin
(DECC) **443 585-2DF2** Your Hundred Best Tunes - Top 20

KENNEDY, Roderick (bass)
Boughton: Immortal Hour (Cpte)

Donizetti: Maria Padilla (Cpte)
Mozart: Idomeneo (Cpte)
Offenbach: Robinson Crusoé (Cpte)
Rossini: Cenerentola (Cpte)
Verdi: Traviata (exc)
Weill: Sieben Todsünden (Cpte)
(TELD) **9031-77676-6(TELD)** My World of Opera - Kiri Te Kanawa

KENNEY, Margherita (mez)
Mozart: Zauberflöte (Cpte)

KENNY, Jonathan Peter (alto)
Purcell: Dido (Cpte)

KENNY, Yvonne (sop)
Bizet: Carmen (Cpte)
Britten: Gloriana (Cpte)
Donizetti: Emilia di Liverpool (Cpte), Eremitaggio di Liverpool (Cpte), Ugo, Conte di Parigi (Cpte)
Gay: Beggar's Opera (Cpte)
Mayr: Medea (Cpte)
Meyerbeer: Crociato in Egitto (Cpte)
Mozart: Entführung (Cpte), Idomeneo (Cpte), Lucio Silla (Cpte), Mitridate (Cpte), Nozze di Figaro (Cpte), Zauberflöte (Cpte)
Offenbach: Robinson Crusoé (Cpte)
(CAST) **CVI2071** Highlights from Glyndebourne
(OPRA) **ORCH103** Italian Opera—1810-20
(OPRA) **ORCH104** A Hundred Years of Italian Opera: 1820-1830
(OPRA) **ORH102** A Hundred Years of Italian Opera
(OPRA) **ORR201** 19th Century Heroines-Yvonne Kenny
(TELD) **4509-97507-2** Mozart—Famous Opera Arias

KENT, Arthur (bar)
Verdi: Trovatore (Cpte)
(MYTO) **2MCD90317** Verdi—Un Ballo in maschera

KENT OPERA CHORUS
cond R. NORRINGTON
Tippett: King Priam (Cpte)

KENT OPERA ORCHESTRA
Tippett: King Priam (Cpte)

KENTISH, John (ten)
Lehár: Lustige Witwe (exc)

KENTON, Peter (sngr)
Gay: Beggar's Opera (Cpte)

KER, Thora (mez)
Sullivan: Mikado (Cpte)

KERN, Adele (sop)
(SCHW) **314582** Vienna State Opera Live, Vol.8
(SCHW) **314652** Vienna State Opera Live, Vol.15
(SCHW) **314742** Vienna State Opera Live, Vol.24

KERN, Patricia (mez)
Britten: Albert Herring (Cpte)
German: Merrie England (Cpte)
Massenet: Thaïs (Cpte)
Monteverdi: Incoronazione di Poppea (Cpte)
Purcell: Dido (Cpte)
Sullivan: Iolanthe (exc), Mikado (Cpte)

KERNS, Robert (bar)
Puccini: Madama Butterfly (exc), Turandot (exc)
Verdi: Otello (Cpte), Rigoletto (Cpte)
Wagner: Lohengrin (Cpte), Rheingold (Cpte)
(DG) **435 211-2GX15** Wagner—Der Ring des Nibelungen

KERRY, Charles (bar)
Verdi: Traviata (Cpte)

KERTESI, Ingrid (sop)
Mozart: Nozze di Figaro (Cpte)
Rossini: Barbiere di Siviglia (Cpte)

KERTÉSZ, István (cond)
see Israel PO
LSO
Vienna Haydn Orch
Vienna Op Orch
Vienna St Op Orch
VPO

KESLING, Diane (mez)
Bizet: Carmen (Cpte)
R. Strauss: Elektra (Cpte)
Wagner: Götterdämmerung (Cpte), Rheingold (Cpte), Walküre (Cpte)
(DG) **437 825-2GH** Wagner—Der Ring des Nibelungen - Highlights
(DG) **445 354-2GX14** Wagner—Der Ring des Nibelungen
(DG) **072 422-3GH7** Levine conducts Wagner's Ring

KESTEREN, John van (ten)
Mozart: Nozze di Figaro (Cpte)
Orff: Mond (Cpte)
Pfitzner: Palestrina (Cpte)
R. Strauss: Rosenkavalier (Cpte)
(RCA) **74321 24790-2** Carl Orff 100 Years Edition

KETÈLBEY, Albert (cond)
see orch

KETELSEN, Hans-Joachim (bar)
Wagner: Meistersinger (Cpte)

KETTLEWELL, Alison (contr)
Vaughan Williams: Pilgrim's Progress (Cpte)

KEYES, John (ten)
Verdi: Otello (Cpte)

KEYTE, Christopher (bass)
Maxwell Davies: Lighthouse (Cpte)
Puccini: Madama Butterfly (Cpte)
Purcell: Indian Queen, Z630 (exc)
Vaughan Williams: Pilgrim's Progress (Cpte)
Verdi: Traviata (Cpte)
(COLL) **Coll1444-2** Maximum Max—Music of Maxwell Davies

KHACHATURIAN, Emin (cond)
see Soviet Cinema Orch

KHAIKIN, Boris (cond)
see Bolshoi Th Orch

KHANAYEV, Nikhandr (ten)
(DANT) **LYS013/5** Tchaikovsky—The Queen of Spades

KHARA, Joan (contr)
R. Strauss: Elektra (Cpte)

KHARITONOV, Dimitri (bass)
Tchaikovsky: Queen of Spades (Cpte)

KHRAMTSOV, Andrei (bass)
Mussorgsky: Khovanshchina (Cpte)

KHRULEV, Vladimir (bar)
Mussorgsky: Marriage (Cpte)

KHYLE, Magnus (ten)
Mozart: Zauberflöte (Cpte)

KIBERG, Tina (sop)
Kuhlau: Lulu (Cpte)
Nielsen: Saul and David (Cpte)
Nørgård: Siddhartha (Cpte)

KIBLER, Keith (bass)
Verdi: Traviata (Cpte)

KIEFER, Günter (bar)
Corghi: Divara (Cpte)

KIEHR, Maria Cristina (sop)
Monteverdi: Incoronazione di Poppea (Cpte)
Vivaldi: Dorilla in Tempe (Cpte)

KIEL OPERA CHORUS
cond K. SEIBEL
Delius: Village Romeo and Juliet (Cpte)
Schillings: Mona Lisa (Cpte)

KIEL PHILHARMONIC ORCHESTRA
cond K. SEIBEL
Delius: Village Romeo and Juliet (Cpte)
Schillings: Mona Lisa (Cpte)

KIENER, Maximilian (treb)
(WERG) **WER6173-2** T.W.Adorno—Chamber & Choral Works

KIEPURA, Jan (ten)
(PEAR) **GEMMCD9409** Lotte Lehmenn—Vol.1
(SCHW) **314602** Vienna State Opera Live, Vol.10

KIESEL, Lena-Luis (organ)
(MERI) **DUOCD89009** The Romantic Englishman

KIICHLI, Henry (bass)
S. Wagner: Bärenhäuter (Cpte)

KILBEY, Reginald (cond)
see R. Kilbey Stgs

KILDUFF, Barbara (sop)
Mozart: Zauberflöte (Cpte)
(DG) **072 428-1GH2(DG)** The Metropolitan Opera Gala

KILLEBREW, Gwendoline (mez)
Giordano: Andrea Chénier (Cpte)
Haydn: Orlando Paladino (Cpte)
Puccini: Edgar (Cpte)
Wagner: Götterdämmerung (Cpte), Walküre (Cpte)
(PHIL) **434 420-2PM32(2)** Richard Wagner Edition (pt 2)

KILPELÄINEN, Heikki (bar)
(BIS) **BIS-CD373/4** Opera Scenes from Savaonlinna

KIM, Ettore (bar)
Bellini: Puritani (Cpte)
Donizetti: Linda di Chamounix (Cpte), Roberto Devereux (Cpte)

KIM, Hak-Nam (mez)
Puccini: Madama Butterfly (Cpte)

KIMBROUGH, Steven (bar)
Weill: Happy End (Cpte)
(ARAB) **Z6579** Kurt Weill: Songs

KIMM, Fiona (mez)
Dvořák: Rusalka (Cpte)
M. Berkeley: Baa Baa Black Sheep (Cpte)
Mozart: Zauberflöte (Cpte)
Offenbach: Orphée aux enfers (exc)
Prokofiev: Love for 3 Oranges (Cpte)
Turnage: Greek (Cpte)
(OPRA) **ORCH104** A Hundred Years of Italian Opera: 1820-1830
(SONY) **S2K66836** Goldschmidt—Beatrice Cenci, etc

KINASZ, Bożena (mez)
Mussorgsky: Boris Godunov (Cpte)

KINCSES, Veronika (sop)
Giordano: Fedora (Cpte)
Puccini: Bohème (Cpte)
Respighi: Semirama (Cpte)
(MARC) **8 223596** O. Strauss—His Most Popular Works
(OPUS) **9156 1824** Dvorský sings Operatic Arias

KINDERMANN, Lydia (mez)
Wagner: Götterdämmerung (exc)
(PEAR) **GEMMCDS9137** Wagner—Der Ring des Nibelungen
(PREI) **89209** Helge Roswaenge (1897-1972) - II

KING, Andrew (ten)
Blow: Venus and Adonis (Cpte)
Monteverdi: Orfeo (Cpte)

KING, Gibner (pf)
(SUPR) **11 1491-2** Jarmila Novotna sings Czech Songs and Arias

KING, James (ten)
Beethoven: Fidelio (Cpte)
Hindemith: Mathis der Maler (Cpte)
Mozart: Zauberflöte (Cpte)
R. Strauss: Ariadne auf Naxos (Cpte), Daphne (Cpte), Elektra (Cpte), Frau ohne Schatten (Cpte), Salome (Cpte)
Schmidt: Notre Dame (Cpte)
Wagner: Parsifal (Cpte), Walküre (Cpte)
(DECC) **414 100-2DM15** Wagner: Der Ring des Nibelungen
(DECC) **433 065-2DWO** Your Hundred Best Opera Tunes Volume II
(ORFE) **C365941A** Christa Ludwig - Salzburg Festival highlights
(PHIL) **446 057-2PB14** Wagner—The Ring Cycle - Bayreuth Festival 1967

KING, John (bar)
Sullivan: HMS Pinafore (Cpte)

KING, Malcolm (bass)
Giordano: Andrea Chénier (Cpte)
Massenet: Werther (Cpte)
Mozart: Don Giovanni (Cpte)
Puccini: Fanciulla del West (Cpte), Madama Butterfly (Cpte), Tosca (Cpte)
Verdi: Ballo in maschera (Cpte), Forza del destino (Cpte), Otello (Cpte)
(DECC) **425 681-2DM2** Tutto Pavarotti

KING, Mary (mez)
Janáček: Cunning Little Vixen (Cpte)
Knussen: Where the Wild Things are (Cpte)
Machover: Valis (Cpte)

KING, Robert (cond)
see King's Consort

KING, Robert (treb/dir)
(IMP) **PCDS19** Music of the World - This Sceptred Isle

KING, Stuart (treb)
Britten: Midsummer Night's Dream (Cpte)

KING, Thea (cl)
(HYPE) **CDJ33009** Schubert: Complete Lieder, Vol.9

KING'S COLLEGE CHOIR, CAMBRIDGE
cond P. LEDGER
Britten: Little Sweep (Cpte)

KING'S CONSORT
(IMP) **PCDS19** Music of the World - This Sceptred Isle
cond R. KING
Handel: Ottone (Cpte)
(HYPE) **CDA66288** 'Mr Henry Purcell's Most Admirable Composure's'
(HYPE) **CDA66483** Handel—Heroic Arias
(HYPE) **KING 1** Music of the King's Consort
(HYPE) **KING2** Essential Purcell
(IMP) **ORCD11010** Baroque Beauties
(IMP) **PCD894** Great Baroque Arias, Part I

(THE) KING'S MUSICK
cond A. DELLER
Purcell: Indian Queen, Z630 (Cpte), King Arthur, Z628 (Cpte)
(HARM) **HMP390 807** Great Baroque Masters—Purcell
(HARM) **HMX290 1528/33(2)** A Purcell Companion (pt 2)

KING'S SINGERS
(EMI) **CDC7 54057-2** J. Strauss II—Vocal Arrangements
(RCA) **09026 61885-2** Here's A Howdy Do—A Gilbert & Sullivan Festival

KINZEL, Margit (sop)
Gazzaniga: Don Giovanni (Cpte)

KIPNIS, Alexander (bass)
Mozart: Don Giovanni (Cpte)
Mussorgsky: Boris Godunov (exc)
Wagner: Fliegende Holländer (Cpte)
(BEUL) **2PD4** 78 Classics - Volume Two
(EMI) **CMS7 64008-2(2)** Wagner Singing on Record (pt 2)
(MMOI) **CDMOIR406** Mozart—Historical Recordings
(MSCM) **MM30283** Great Wagnerian Singers, Vol.1
(MSCM) **MM30285** Great Wagnerian Singers, Vol.2
(NIMB) **NI7848** Great Singers at the Berlin State Opera
(NIMB) **NI7851** Legendary Voices
(ORFE) **C394101B** Great Mozart Singers Series, Vol. 1
(PEAR) **GEMMCDS9926(1)** Covent Garden on Record—Vol.4 (pt 1)
(PEAR) **GEMMCD9122** 20 Great Basses sing Great Arias
(PEAR) **GEMMCD9451** Alexander Kipnis
(PREI) **89019** Alexander Kipnis (1891-1978)
(RCA) **GD60522** Alexander Kipnis—Opera & Song Recital

(RCA) **09026 61580-2(5)** RCA/Met 100 Singers, 100 Years (pt 5)
(SCHW) **314542** Vienna State Opera Live, Vol.4
(SCHW) **314602** Vienna State Opera Live, Vol.10
(SCHW) **314632** Vienna State Opera Live, Vol.13
(SCHW) **314742** Vienna State Opera Live, Vol.24

KIRILOVÁ, Ida (mez)
(OPUS) **9356 2047** Romantic Operatic Duets

KIRKBY, Emma (sop)
Handel: Orlando (Cpte)
Hasse: Cleofide (Cpte)
Monteverdi: Orfeo (Cpte)
Purcell: Dido (Cpte), Don Quixote: The Musical (Cpte)
(HYPE) **CDA66056** Purcell: Songs and Dialogues
(HYPE) **CDA66745** Vivaldi—Opera Arias and Sinfonias
(L'OI) **417 123-2OH** Purcell: Songs and Airs
(L'OI) **425 835-2OH** Mozart—Concert and Opera Arias
(L'OI) **436 132-2OH** Emma Kirkby sings Mrs Arne
(L'OI) **444 620-2OH** The Glory of Purcell
(MOSC) **070979** Sound the Trumpets from Shore to Shore

KIRKBY, Neil (bar)
Lehár: Lustige Witwe (Cpte)
Meyerbeer: Huguenots (Cpte)

KIRKBY-LUNN, Louise (mez)
(PEAR) **GEMMCDS9924(1)** Covent Garden on Record, Vol.2 (pt 1)
(PEAR) **GEMMCDS9924(2)** Covent Garden on Record, Vol.2 (pt 2)
(SUPR) **11 2136-2(4)** Emmy Destinn—Complete Edition, Discs 9 & 10

KIRKLAND, Glenda (mez)
R. Strauss: Aegyptische Helena (Cpte)

KIRKWOOD, William (bass)
Schoenberg: Moses und Aron (Cpte)

KIROV BALLET
cond V. GERGIEV
Mussorgsky: Khovanshchina (Cpte)
Rimsky-Korsakov: Sadko (Cpte)

KIROV THEATRE CHORUS
cond V. GERGIEV
Borodin: Prince Igor (Cpte)
Mussorgsky: Boris Godunov (Cpte), Khovanshchina (Cpte)
Prokofiev: War and Peace (exc)
Rimsky-Korsakov: Sadko (Cpte)
Tchaikovsky: Queen of Spades (Cpte)
(PHIL) **442 011-2PH** Russian Orchestral Works
(PHIL) **442 775-2PH** Russian Spectacular

KIROV THEATRE ORCHESTRA
Mussorgsky: Boris Godunov (Cpte), Khovanshchina (Cpte)
Rimsky-Korsakov: Sadko (Cpte)
Tchaikovsky: Queen of Spades (Cpte)
cond V. GERGIEV
Borodin: Prince Igor (Cpte)
Prokofiev: War and Peace (Cpte)
Rimsky-Korsakov: Sadko (Cpte)
Tchaikovsky: Queen of Spades (exc)
(PHIL) **438 872-2PH** Songs and Dances of Death
(PHIL) **442 011-2PH** Russian Orchestral Works
(PHIL) **442 775-2PH** Russian Spectacular
(PHIL) **070 166-1PH (PHIL)** Essential Ballet - Stars of Russian Dance

KIRSCHBICHLER, Theodore (bass)
R. Strauss: Salome (Cpte)

KIRSCHSTEIN, Leonore (sop)
Hindemith: Cardillac (Cpte)
Mozart: Zauberflöte (Cpte)
(TEST) **SBT1036** Lisa Della Casa sings Richard Strauss

KIRSTEN, Dorothy (sop)
(EMI) **CHS7 69741-2(1)** Record of Singing, Vol.4—Anglo-American School (pt 1)
(RCA) **09026 61580-2(6)** RCA/Met 100 Singers, 100 Years (pt 6)

KIT, Mikhail (bar)
Borodin: Prince Igor (Cpte)
Mussorgsky: Boris Godunov (Cpte)
Prokofiev: War and Peace (Cpte)

KITAIENKO, Dmitri (cond)
see DR RSO
Moscow PO

KITCHEN, Linda (sop)
Meyerbeer: Crociato in Egitto (Cpte)
Monteverdi: Incoronazione di Poppea (Cpte)
(EMI) **CDC7 54785-2** Harry Enfield's Guide to Opera
(HYPE) **CDA66569** Vaughan Williams—Choral Works
(OPRA) **ORCH104** A Hundred Years of Italian Opera: 1820-1830
(OPRA) **ORR201** 19th Century Heroines-Yvonne Kenny

KITCHENER-WATERLOO SYMPHONY ORCHESTRA
cond R. ARMENIAN
(CBC) **SMCD5126** A Night in Venice & Other Operetta Excerpts

KITCHINER, John (bar)
Handel: Giulio Cesare (Cpte)
Herrmann: Wuthering Heights (Cpte)

KITE, Celia (sop)
Offenbach: Christopher Columbus (Cpte)

KITSCHIN, Alexander (cond)
see orch

KITZINGER, Fritz (pf)
(RCA) **09026 61245-2** Ezio Pinza - Recital

KJELLGREN, Ingeborg (mez)
Verdi: Rigoletto (Cpte), Trovatore (Cpte)

KLÁN, Josef (bass)
Fibich: Šárka (Cpte)

KLARE, Susanne (mez)
Albinoni: Nascimento dell'Aurora (Cpte)
Gluck: Iphigénie en Tauride (Cpte)
Suder: Kleider machen Leute (Cpte)

KLARWEIN, Franz (ten)
Mozart: Zauberflöte (Cpte)
Wagner: Fliegende Holländer (Cpte), Meistersinger (Cpte)
(MYTO) **1MCD943104** R. Strauss—Capriccio (highlights) & Lieder
(PILZ) **442118-2** Wagner—Operas in Historical Recordings

KLAS, Eri (cond)
see Estonia Op Orch
Estonian SO
Lahti SO

KLEBER, Manfred (ten)
Hindemith: Nusch-Nuschi (Cpte)

KLEE, Bernhard (cond)
see Berlin Staatskapelle
BRSO

KLEIBER, Carlos (cond)
see Bavarian St Orch
Staatskapelle Dresden
VPO

KLEIBER, Erich (cond)
see BPO
Buenos Aires Colón Th Orch
VPO

KLEIN, Adam (sngr)
Ashley: Improvement (Cpte)

KLEIN, Peter (ten)
Beethoven: Fidelio (Cpte)
Einem: Prozess (Cpte)
J. Strauss II: Fledermaus (Cpte), Nacht in Venedig (Cpte)
Lehár: Lustige Witwe (exc)
Mozart: Zauberflöte (Cpte)
R. Strauss: Ariadne auf Naxos (Cpte), Rosenkavalier (Cpte)
Verdi: Otello (Cpte)
Wagner: Meistersinger (exc)
(DECC) **443 530-2LF2** Mozart—Die Entführung aus dem Serail
(PREI) **90249** Mozart in tempore belli
(SCHW) **314692** Vienna State Opera Live, Vol.19

KLEMENS, Mario (cond)
see Prague FISYO

KLEMPERER, Otto (cond)
see Berlin St Op Orch
New Philh
Philh

KLEPPER, Regina (sop)
Kreutzer: Nachtlager in Granada (Cpte)
(CAPR) **10 481** R.Strauss—Opera Concert
(SCHW) **314002** Early songs by famous composers

KLETZKI, Paul (cond)
see Philh

KLIEGEL, Maria (vc)
(MARC) **8 223403** Virtuoso Cello Encores
(NAXO) **8 550785** Le Grand Tango

KLIETMANN, Martin (ten)
Fux: Dafne in Lauro (Cpte)
Keiser: Croesus (Cpte)

KLINE, Olive (sop)
(NIMB) **NI7864** More Legendary Voices

KLINT, Jørgen (bass)
Nielsen: Maskarade (Cpte), Saul and David (Cpte)
(PAUL) **PACD56** Nielsen: Songs

KLOBUČAR, Berislav (cond)
see Berlin SO
Buenos Aires Colón Th Orch
Vienna St Op Orch

KLÖCKER, Dieter (cond)
see Consortium Classicum

KLÖCKER, Dieter (cl)
(SCHW) **314018** Virtuoso Operatic Arias for Soprano and Clarinet

KLÖPPER, Robert (ten)
Delius: Village Romeo and Juliet (Cpte)

KLOS, Friedemann (treb)
Mozart: Zauberflöte (Cpte)

KLOSE, Margarete (mez)
Mozart: Zauberflöte (Cpte)
Wagner: Lohengrin (Cpte), Rienzi (exc), Tristan und Isolde (exc), Walküre (exc)
(EMI) **CMS7 64008-2(1)** Wagner Singing on Record (pt 1)
(EMI) **CZS7 67123-2** Wagner: Der Ring des Nibelungen
(MYTO) **3MCD93381** Wagner—Die Walküre, etc
(PILZ) **442118-2** Wagner—Operas in Historical Recordings
(PREI) **89024** Marcel Wittrisch (1901-1955)
(PREI) **89082** Margarete Klose (1902-1968)
(PREI) **89092** Erna Berger (1900-1990) - II
(PREI) **90213** Max Lorenz sings Wagner
(SCHW) **314502** Vienna State Opera—Live Recordings (sampler)
(SCHW) **314562** Vienna State Opera Live, Vol.6
(TELD) **9031-76442-2** Wagner—Excerpts from the 1936 Bayreuth Festival

KLUMLIKBOLDT, Werner (bar)
Wagner: Meistersinger (Cpte)

KMENTT, Waldemar (ten)
J. Strauss II: Fledermaus (Cpte)
Lehár: Giuditta (exc), Graf von Luxemburg (exc), Lustige Witwe (exc), Zarewitsch (exc)
Mozart: Così fan tutte (Cpte), Idomeneo (Cpte), Zauberflöte (Cpte)
Puccini: Turandot (Cpte)
R. Strauss: Arabella (Cpte), Rosenkavalier (Cpte), Salome (Cpte)
Wagner: Rheingold (Cpte)
Weill: Dreigroschenoper (Cpte)
(DECC) **414 100-2DM15** Wagner: Der Ring des Nibelungen
(DECC) **421 313-2DA** Wagner: Der Ring des Nibelungen - Great Scenes
(DECC) **436 316-2DA** Golden Operetta

KNAPP, Josef (bar)
Lehár: Lustige Witwe (Cpte)
R. Strauss: Schweigsame Frau (Cpte)
Verdi: Traviata (Cpte)

KNAPP, Michael (ten)
(CAPR) **10 810** Mozart—Opera Highlights

KNAPP, Peter (bass)
Verdi: Trovatore (exc)
(DECC) **433 908-2DM2** Falla—Orchestral Music

KNAPPERTSBUSCH, Hans (cond)
see Bavarian St Orch
Bayreuth Fest Orch
Berlin Deutsche Op Orch
LPO
SRO
Vienna St Op Orch
VPO
Zurich Tonhalle Orch

KNIBBS, Jean (contr)
Purcell: King Arthur, Z628 (Cpte)
(HARM) **HMX290 1528/33(2)** A Purcell Companion (pt 2)

KNIGHT, Andrew (bass)
Lampe: Pyramus and Thisbe (Cpte)
(HYPE) **CDA66608** Dibdin—Three Operas

KNIGHT, Gillian (mez)
Janáček: Cunning Little Vixen (Cpte)
Puccini: Madama Butterfly (Cpte), Rondine (Cpte)
R. Strauss: Salome (Cpte)
Schoenberg: Moses und Aron (Cpte)
Sullivan: Gondoliers (Cpte), HMS Pinafore (exc), Iolanthe (Cpte), Patience (Cpte), Pirates of Penzance (Cpte), Ruddigore (Cpte), Yeomen of the Guard (Cpte)
Verdi: Forza del destino (Cpte), Rigoletto (Cpte), Traviata (Cpte)
Wagner: Götterdämmerung (Cpte), Parsifal (Cpte)
(CBS) **CD79312** Puccini: Il Trittico
(DECC) **430 095-2DWO** The World of Gilbert & Sullivan, Vol.1
(DECC) **433 868-2DWO** The World of Gilbert & Sullivan - Volume 2
(DECC) **436 313-2DA** Sutherland/Pavarotti—Operatic Duets
(SONY) **SK48094** Favourite Puccini Arias

KNIGHT, Peter (cond)
see Orch

KNIPLOVÁ, Naděžda (sop)
Janáček: Jenufa (Cpte)
Smetana: Dalibor (Cpte)
(DECC) **421 852-2DH2** Janáček: Operatic & Chamber Works

KNOBLICH, Hans Georg (sngr)
Flotow: Martha (Cpte)
Schultze: Schwarzer Peter (Cpte)

KNODT, Erich (bass)
Wagner: Fliegende Holländer (Cpte)

KNOLL, Rudolf (bar)
Mozart: Don Giovanni (exc)

KNOOP, Laura (sop)
Moran: Dracula Diary (Cpte)

KNÖPPEL, Michael (bass)
Weill: Jasager (Cpte)

KNÜPFER, Paul (bass)
(PEAR) **GEMMCD9122** 20 Great Basses sing Great Arias
(SUPR) **11 2136-2(3)** Emmy Destinn—Complete Edition, Discs 5 to 8

KNUSSEN, Oliver (cond)
see London Sinfonietta

KNUTSON, David (alto)
Hindemith: Nusch-Nuschi (Cpte)

KOBAYASHI, Marie (mez)
Berg: Lulu (Cpte)

KOBAYASHI, Osamu (ten)
R. Strauss: Rosenkavalier (Cpte)

KOBERA, Walter (cond)
see Vienna Amadeus Ens

KÖBERLE, Ulrich (ten)
Delius: Village Romeo and Juliet (Cpte)
Schillings: Mona Lisa (Cpte)

KOBLITZ, Ingo (ten)
R. Strauss: Rosenkavalier (Cpte)

KOCH, Egmont (bar)
Wagner: Götterdämmerung (Cpte)

KOCHERGA, Anatoly (bass)
Mussorgsky: Boris Godunov (Cpte), Khovanshchina (Cpte)
Shostakovich: Lady Macbeth of Mtsensk (Cpte)
Tchaikovsky: Mazeppa (Cpte)

KOČÍ, Přemysl (bass)
Hába: Mother (Cpte)
Janáček: Makropulos Affair (Cpte)

KOČÍ, Viktor (ten)
Janáček: From the House of the Dead (Cpte), Káťa Kabanová (Cpte), Makropulos Affair (Cpte)

KOCIÁN, Vojtech (ten)
Martinů: Miracles of Mary (Cpte)

KOFFMANE, Robert (bar)
Wagner: Meistersinger (exc)

KOGEL, Richard (bass)
Orff: Kluge (Cpte), Mond (Cpte)
(RCA) **74321 24790-2** Carl Orff 100 Years Edition

KOHAMA, Taemi (sop)
Verdi: Macbeth (Cpte)

KÖHLER, Annette (mez)
Telemann: Don Quichotte (Cpte)

KÖHLER, Axel (alto)
Monteverdi: Incoronazione di Poppea (Cpte)
(CAPR) **10 470** Monteverdi—Arie e Duetti
(CAPR) **10 547** Handel—Arias

KÖHLER, Markus (bar)
Schreker: Gezeichneten (Cpte)

KOHN, Andreas (bass)
Mozart: Don Giovanni (Cpte)

KOHN, Eugene (cond)
see Miami SO
Munich RO
National PO

KOHN, Karl Christian (bass)
Berg: Wozzeck (Cpte)
Busoni: Doktor Faust (Cpte)
Egk: Verlobung in San Domingo (Cpte)
Handel: Giulio Cesare (Cpte)
Hindemith: Cardillac (Cpte)
Mozart: Don Giovanni (Cpte)
R. Strauss: Arabella (Cpte), Capriccio (Cpte)
Weber: Freischütz (Cpte)

KOHT, Maja (sop)
Delius: Village Romeo and Juliet (Cpte)

KOKAS, Lászlo (sngr)
Lehár: Lustige Witwe (exc)

KOLASSI, Irma (mez)
Martinů: Julietta (Cpte)

KOLK, Stanley (ten)
Mozart: Mitridate (Cpte)
(SONY) **SM22K46290(3)** Stravinsky—The Complete Edition (pt 3)

KOLLEK, Peter (sngr)
Rihm: Eroberung von Mexico (Cpte)

KOLLER, Dagmar (sop)
Lehár: Land des Lächelns (exc)
(SCHW) **312732** Lehár—Der Zarewitsch (excs)

KOLLO, Ants (ten)
Tubin: Barbara von Tisenhusen (Cpte)

KOLLO, René (ten)
Beethoven: Fidelio (exc)
Korngold: Tote Stadt (Cpte)
Lehár: Lustige Witwe (exc)
R. Strauss: Arabella (Cpte), Ariadne auf Naxos (Cpte), Frau ohne Schatten (exc)
Smetana: Bartered Bride (Cpte)
Suppé: Schöne Galathee (exc)
Wagner: Götterdämmerung (Cpte), Lohengrin (Cpte), Meistersinger (Cpte), Parsifal (Cpte), Rienzi (Cpte), Siegfried (Cpte), Tannhäuser (exc), Tristan und Isolde (Cpte)
Weber: Freischütz (Cpte)
Weill: Dreigroschenoper (Cpte)
(ACAN) **43 266** Bernd Weikl—Operatic Recital
(DECC) **443 379-2DM** Ten Top Tenors 2
(DG) **435 712-2GX2** Lehár—The Merry Widow. Suppé—Overtures
(EMI) **CDC7 54776-2** René Kollo sings Wagner and Strauss
(EMI) **LDX9 91275-1(EMI)** Sawallisch conducts Wagner's Ring

(EURO) **GD69003** Wagner—Der Ring des Nibelungen

KOLMAKOVA, Loudmila (mez)
Mussorgsky: Marriage (Cpte)

KOLNIAK, Angela (sop)
Mozart: Nozze di Figaro (Cpte)

KOLOMYJEC, Joanne (sop)
(CBC) **SMCD5126** A Night in Venice & Other Operetta Excerpts

KOLOWRATNIK, Karl (sngr)
(SCHW) **314632** Vienna State Opera Live, Vol.13

KOLTYPIN, Sergei (bass)
(ARLE) **ARL23/5** Rimsky-Korsakov—Sadko

KOMANCOVÁ, Ludmila (contr)
Janáček: Káta Kabanová (Cpte)

KOMAREK, Dora (sop)
(SCHW) **314572** Vienna State Opera Live, Vol.7
(SCHW) **314602** Vienna State Opera Live, Vol.10
(SCHW) **314632** Vienna State Opera Live, Vol.13
(SCHW) **314652** Vienna State Opera Live, Vol.15
(SCHW) **314702** Vienna State Opera Live, Vol.20

KOMARNICZKY, Zita (sop)
Respighi: Belfagor (Cpte)

KOMATSU, Hidenori (bar)
Puccini: Madama Butterfly (Cpte)
(HARM) **HMC90 1420** Weill—The Seven Deadly Sins; Songs

KOMLÓSI, Ildikó (mez)
Wagner: Rheingold (Cpte)

KOMLÓSSY, Erzsébet (contr)
(DECC) **443 488-2DF2** Kodály—Háry János; Psalmus Hungaricus etc

KONDINA, Olga (sop)
Mussorgsky: Boris Godunov (Cpte)

KONDRASHIN, Kyrill (cond)
see Bolshoi Th Orch
USSR RSO

KONETZNI, Anny (sop)
Wagner: Parsifal (exc), Tristan und Isolde (exc)
(SCHW) **314502** Vienna State Opera—Live Recordings (sampler)
(SCHW) **314512** Vienna State Opera Live, Vol.1
(SCHW) **314532** Vienna State Opera Live, Vol.3
(SCHW) **314562** Vienna State Opera Live, Vol.6
(SCHW) **314592** Vienna State Opera Live, Vol.9
(SCHW) **314632** Vienna State Opera Live, Vol.13
(SCHW) **314652** Vienna State Opera Live, Vol.15
(SCHW) **314662** Vienna State Opera Live, Vol.16
(SCHW) **314672** Vienna State Opera Live, Vol.17
(SCHW) **314702** Vienna State Opera Live, Vol.20
(SCHW) **314742** Vienna State Opera Live, Vol.24

KONETZNI, Hilde (sop)
Beethoven: Fidelio (Cpte)
Verdi: Don Carlo (exc), Otello (Cpte)
Weber: Oberon (exc)
(EMI) **CZS7 67123-2** Wagner: Der Ring des Nibelungen
(LYRC) **SRO830** Smetana—The Bartered Bride, etc
(PREI) **90078** Hilde Konetzni
(PREI) **90249** Mozart in tempore belli
(SCHW) **314502** Vienna State Opera—Live Recordings (sampler)
(SCHW) **314552** Vienna State Opera Live, Vol.5
(SCHW) **314582** Vienna State Opera Live, Vol.8
(SCHW) **314592** Vienna State Opera Live, Vol.9
(SCHW) **314602** Vienna State Opera Live, Vol.10
(SCHW) **314662** Vienna State Opera Live, Vol.16
(SCHW) **314672** Vienna State Opera Live, Vol.17
(SCHW) **314692** Vienna State Opera Live, Vol.19
(SCHW) **314742** Vienna State Opera Live, Vol.24

KONÍČEK, Štěpán (cond)
see Film SO

KÖNIG, Klaus (ten)
Beethoven: Fidelio (Cpte)
K. A. Hartmann: Simplicius Simplicissimus (Cpte)
Suder: Kleider machen Leute (Cpte)
Wagner: Tannhäuser (Cpte), Walküre (exc)

KÖNIG ENSEMBLE
cond J. LATHAM-KÖNIG
Weill: Happy End (Cpte), Mahagonny-Gesänge (Cpte)

KONSULOV, Ivan (bar)
Puccini: Bohème (Cpte)
Tchaikovsky: Queen of Spades (Cpte)
(OPUS) **9156 1824** Dvorský sings Operatic Arias

KONTARSKY, Bernhard (cond)
see Stuttgart Op Orch

KONVALINKA, Miloš (cond)
see Prague SO

KONWITSCHNY, Franz (cond)
see Berlin Deutsche Op Orch
Berlin St Op Orch

KÓNYA, Sándor (ten)
(RCA) **09026 61580-2(7)** RCA/Met 100 Singers, 100 Years (pt 7)

KOOIJMANS, Ad (bar)
R. Strauss: Rosenkavalier (Cpte)

KOON, Theresa (sop)
S. Wagner: Bärenhäuter (Cpte)

KOOPMAN, Ton (cond)
see Amsterdam Baroque Orch

KOPČÁK, Sergej (bass)
Mozart: Don Giovanni (Cpte)
(OPUS) **9156 1824** Dvorský sings Operatic Arias

KOPP, Miroslav (ten)
Janáček: From the House of the Dead (Cpte)
Martinů: Ariane (Cpte)
Smetana: Bartered Bride (Cpte), Dalibor (Cpte)
(SUPR) **11 1878-2** The Unknown Janáček

KORD, Kazimierz (cond)
see SRO

KORÉH, Endre (bass)
Einem: Prozess (Cpte)
(DECC) **443 530-2LF2** Mozart—Die Entführung aus dem Serail

KORJUS, Miliza (sop)
(DANT) **LYS001** La Colorature des Colorature - Volume 1
(PREI) **89024** Marcel Wittrisch (1901-1955)
(PREI) **89054** Miliza Korjus (1912-1980)
(PREI) **89209** Helge Roswaenge (1897-1972) - II

KORN, Artur (bass)
Mozart: Nozze di Figaro (Cpte)
R. Strauss: Arabella (Cpte), Ariadne auf Naxos (Cpte)

KÖRNER, Ewald (cond)
see Slovak PO

KORNGOLD, Erich (cond)
see Austrian St Rad Orch
Odeon Künstlerorchester
orch

KORNILOV, D.G. (pf)
(PEAR) **GEMMCDS9997/9(2)** Singers of Imperial Russia, Vol.1 (pt 2)

KÓRODI, András (cond)
see Budapest PO

KOROLEWICZ-WAYDA, Janina (sop)
(PEAR) **GEMMCDS9004/6(1)** Singers of Imperial Russia, Vol.3 (pt 1)

KOROMANTZOU, Maria (sop)
Kalomiris: Mother's Ring (Cpte)

KOROTKOV, G. (bass)
(PREI) **89081** Georgi Nelepp (1904-1957)

KORSOFF, Lucette (sop)
(IRCC) **IRCC-CD802** Souvenirs of Rare French Opera
(MSCM) **MM30221** 18 French Divas

KOSBAHN, Gerda (sop)
Schillings: Mona Lisa (Cpte)

KOSHETZ, Nina (sop)
(ARLE) **ARL23/5** Rimsky-Korsakov—Sadko
(NIMB) **NI7802** Divas 1906-1935

KOŠLER, Zdeněk (cond)
see Czech PO
Prague Nat Th Orch
Slovak PO

KOSLOWSKY, Johanna (sop)
Landi: Mort d'Orfeo (Cpte)

KOSTELANETZ, André (cond)
see Columbia SO
NYPO
orch
RCA SO

KOSTIA, Raili (contr)
Mozart: Zauberflöte (exc)

KÖSTLINGER, Josef (ten)
Purcell: Dido (Cpte)

KOSZUT, Ursula (sop)
Hindemith: Mathis der Maler (Cpte)
Nono: Intolleranza 1960 (Cpte)

KÖTH, Erika (sop)
Benatzky: Im weissen Rössl (exc)
Fall: Rose von Stambul (exc)
J. Strauss II: Fledermaus (Cpte)
Lehár: Lustige Witwe (exc)
Millöcker: Dubarry (exc)
Mozart: Entführung (Cpte)
Wagner: Siegfried (Cpte), Walküre (Cpte)
Zeller: Vogelhändler (exc)
(DG) **431 110-2GB** Great Voices - Fritz Wunderlich
(DG) **435 145-2GX5(1)** Fritz Wunderlich—Opera Arias, Lieder, etc (part 1)
(EMI) **CDH5 65201-2** Leonie Rysanek - Operatic Recital
(EMI) **CDM7 69475-2** Rudolf Schock sings Operetta and Songs
(EMI) **CHS7 69741-2(4)** Record of Singing, Vol.4—German School
(EURO) **VD69256** Mozart—Opera Arias
(ORFE) **C394201B** Great Mozart Singers Series, Vol. 2
(PHIL) **446 057-2PB14** Wagner—The Ring Cycle - Bayreuth Festival 1967

KOTILAINEN, Juha (bar)
Sallinen: Kullervo (Cpte)

KOTOSKI, Dawn (sop)
Handel: Giustino (Cpte)

KOTOWSKA, Adela (pf)
(PEAR) **GEMMCD9939** Josef Hassid & Ida Haendel - 1940-42 Recordings

KÖTTER, Paul (ten)
(SCHW) **314672** Vienna State Opera Live, Vol.17

KOULOUMBIS, Andreas (bar)
Kalomiris: Mother's Ring (Cpte)

KOUSNIETZOFF, Marie (sop)
(PEAR) **GEMMCDS9924(2)** Covent Garden on Record, Vol.2 (pt 2)

KOUSSEVITZKY, Serge (cond)
see Boston SO

KOUT, Jiří (cond)
see Munich RO

KOVA, Marija (sop)
R. Ward: Crucible (Cpte)

KOVÁCS, Attila (bass)
Delius: Village Romeo and Juliet (Cpte)

KOVÁCS, Pál (bar)
Giordano: Fedora (Cpte)

KOVALENKO, I. (ten)
Tchaikovsky: Eugene Onegin (Cpte)

KOVALENKO, Maria (sop)
(NIMB) **NI7865** Great Singers at the Mariinsky Theatre
(PREI) **89030** Feodor Chaliapin (1873-1938)

KOVALYOV, Aleksei (cond)
see USSR Rad Orch

KOVÁTS, Kolos (bass)
Giordano: Fedora (Cpte)
Rossini: Guillaume Tell (Cpte)

KÖVES, Péter (bass)
Mozart: Zauberflöte (Cpte)

KOVES, Toni (cimbalom)
(SONY) **SM3K46291** Stravinsky—Ballets, Vol.1
(SONY) **SM22K46290(4)** Stravinsky—The Complete Edition (pt 4)

KOWALSKI, Jochen (alto)
Gluck: Orfeo ed Euridice (Cpte)
J. Strauss II: Fledermaus (Cpte)
Mozart: Mitridate (Cpte)
(CAPR) **80 213** Handel and Mozart Arias for Countertenor
(CAPR) **80 416** Jochen Kowalski sings Opera Arias
(CAPR) **10 113** Berlin Opera Composers
(CAPR) **10 213** Handel and Mozart Arias for Countertenor
(CAPR) **10 416** Jochen Kowalski sings Opera Arias
(CAPR) **10 810** Mozart—Opera Highlights
(CAPR) **70 213** Handel and Mozart Arias for Countertenor
(CAPR) **70 416** Jochen Kowalski sings Opera Arias

KOWALSKI, Stanislaw (ten)
Szymanowski: King Roger (Cpte)

KOWOLLIK, Maria (mez)
Spohr: Faust (Cpte)

KOZLOVSKY, Ivan (ten)
(ARLE) **ARL23/5** Rimsky-Korsakov—Sadko
(EMI) **CHS7 69741-2(6)** Record of Singing, Vol.4—Russian & Slavonic Schools
(MMOI) **CDMOIR405** Great Tenors
(MYTO) **1MCD921.55** Ivan Kozlovsky Recital
(PEAR) **GEMMCD9129** Great Tenors, Vol.2
(PREI) **89078** Alexander Pirogov (1899-1964)

KOZMA, Lajos (ten)
Monteverdi: Orfeo (Cpte)
Vivaldi: Orlando Furioso (Cpte)
(RCA) **GD60941** Rarities - Montserrat Caballé

KOZNOWSKI, Zenon (bass)
R. Strauss: Salome (Cpte)

KOZUB, Ernst (ten)
Wagner: Fliegende Holländer (Cpte)

KRAAK, Meinard (ten)
Maderna: Satyricon (Cpte)

KRACHMALNICK, Samuel (cond)
see M. Beck Th Orch
NYC Op Orch

KRAEMMER, Hans (bar)
Mozart: Nozze di Figaro (Cpte)
R. Strauss: Arabella (Cpte)

KRAFT, Jean (mez)
Giordano: Andrea Chénier (Cpte)
Mascagni: Cavalleria Rusticana (Cpte)
Verdi: Otello (Cpte)

KRAHMER, Renate (sop)
Schoenberg: Moses und Aron (Cpte)

KRÄMER, Toni (ten)
Wagner: Parsifal (Cpte)
Weber: Freischütz (Cpte)

KRÄMMER, Hans (bar)
J. Strauss II: Fledermaus (Cpte)

KRASA, Rudolf (bar)
(SUPR) **11 2136-2(3)** Emmy Destinn—Complete Edition, Discs 5 to 8

KRASOVSKY, Sergei (bass)
(ARLE) **ARL23/5** Rimsky-Korsakov—Sadko

(PEAR) **GEMMCD9122** 20 Great Basses sing Great Arias

KRASTEVA, Svetla (sop)
Gluck: Iphigénie en Tauride (Cpte)

KRATĚNOVÁ, Jana (sop)
Krása: Brundibár (Cpte)

KRÁTKÁ, Jarmila (sop)
Janáček: Fate (Cpte)
Martinů: Comedy on the Bridge (Cpte)

KRATOCHVÍLOVÁ, Anna (sop)
Martinů: Miracles of Mary (Cpte)

KRAUS, Adalbert (ten)
Pfitzner: Palestrina (Cpte)
Wagner: Meistersinger (Cpte)

KRAUS, Alfredo (ten)
Bizet: Jolie fille de Perth (Cpte)
Donizetti: Favorita (Cpte), Linda di Chamounix (Cpte), Lucia di Lammermoor (Cpte), Lucrezia Borgia (Cpte)
Gounod: Roméo et Juliette (Cpte)
Massenet: Manon (Cpte), Werther (exc)
Mozart: Così fan tutte (Cpte), Don Giovanni (Cpte)
Puccini: Bohème (Cpte)
Sorozábal: Katiuska (Cpte)
Verdi: Falstaff (Cpte), Rigoletto (Cpte), Traviata (Cpte)
Vives: Doña Francisquita (Cpte)
(BONG) **GB1060-2** Virginia Zeani - Various opera arias
(EMI) **CDC7 49067-2** Opera Arias and Duets
(EMI) **CDC7 49502-2** Maria Callas—The Voice of the Century
(EMI) **CDC7 54016-2** Tenorissimo!
(EMI) **CDC7 54702-2** Maria Callas - La Divina
(EMI) **CDEMTVD59** Classic Experience 3
(EMI) **CDM5 65575-2** Montserrat Caballé
(EMI) **CDM7 63104-2** Alfredo Krauss - Opera Recital
(EMI) **CDM7 64359-2** Gala de España
(EMI) **CMS7 63244-2** The Art of Maria Callas
(EMIL) **CDZ103** Best Loved Classics 4
(IMP) **DPCD998** Opera Stars in Concert
(MEMO) **HR4233/4** Alfredo Kraus—Public Performances
(MEMO) **HR4273/4** Great Voices—Pietro Cappuccilli
(MEMO) **HR4300/1** Great Voices—Sesto Bruscantini
(NIMB) **NI5102** Alfredo Kraus sings Arie Antiche
(PHIL) **442 602-2PM** 3 x 3 Tenors
(PHIL) **442 785-2PH** The Incomparable Alfredo Kraus
(RCA) **RD61191** Gala Lirica
(RCA) **09026 61440-2** Opera's Greatest Moments
(RCA) **09026 61580-2(8)** RCA/Met 100 Singers, 100 Years (pt 8)
(RCA) **74321 25817-2** Café Classics - Operatic
(RCA) **09026 61191-5** Gala Lirica
(RNE) **650004** Opera Stars in Concert

KRAUS, Ernst (ten)
(SUPR) **11 2136-2(1)** Emmy Destinn—Complete Edition, Discs 1 & 2

KRAUS, Herold (ten)
Wagner: Meistersinger (exc)

KRAUS, Michael (ten)
B. Goldschmidt: Gewaltige Hahnrei (Cpte)
Busoni: Turandot (Cpte)
Krenek: Jonny spielt auf (Cpte)
Mozart: Zauberflöte (Cpte)
R. Strauss: Rosenkavalier (Cpte)
(DECC) **440 854-2DH** Ullmann—Der Kaiser von Atlantis
(DECC) **440 947-2DH** Essential Opera II

KRAUS, Otakar (bar)
Lehár: Land des Lächelns (Cpte), Lustige Witwe (Cpte)
Wagner: Götterdämmerung (Cpte)

KRAUS, Peter (ten)
Benatzky: Im weissen Rössl (Cpte)

KRAUS, Philip (bar)
Beethoven: Fidelio (Cpte)
(DECC) **433 443-2DA** Great Opera Choruses

KRAUS, Richard (cond)
see Bayreuth Fest Orch
Berlin Deutsche Op Orch
Berlin RSO
Cologne RSO

KRAUSE, Carlos (bass)
Verdi: Simon Boccanegra (Cpte)

KRAUSE, Monika (sop)
Lortzing: Undine (Cpte)
Puccini: Bohème (Cpte)
Verdi: Traviata (Cpte)

KRAUSE, Richard (ten)
R. Ward: Crucible (Cpte)

KRAUSE, Tom (bar)
Beethoven: Fidelio (Cpte)
Bizet: Carmen (exc)
Donizetti: Don Pasquale (Cpte)
Giordano: Andrea Chénier (Cpte)
Gluck: Alceste (1776) (exc)
J. Strauss II: Fledermaus (exc)
Mozart: Nozze di Figaro (Cpte)
Puccini: Turandot (Cpte)
R. Strauss: Elektra (Cpte), Salome (Cpte)
Tchaikovsky: Iolanta (Cpte)
Verdi: Otello (Cpte)
Wagner: Lohengrin (Cpte)
(BIS) **BIS-CD373/4** Opera Scenes from Savaonlinna
(DECC) **430 498-2DWO** The World of Mozart
(DECC) **433 066-2DWO** Your Hundred Best Opera Tunes III
(DECC) **433 067-2DWO** Your Hundred Best Opera Tunes IV
(DECC) **433 068-2DWO** Your Hundred Best Opera Tunes V
(DECC) **433 440-2DA** Golden Opera
(DECC) **433 443-2DA** Great Opera Choruses
(DECC) **433 822-2DH** Essential Opera
(DECC) **436 317-2DA** Puccini—Famous Arias
(DECC) **440 947-2DH** Essential Opera II
(DECC) **443 380-2DM** Ten Top Baritones & Basses 2
(DECC) **444 555-2DF2** Essential Puccini

KRAUSS, Clemens (cond)
see Bavarian St Op Orch
Bayreuth Fest Orch
Berlin RO
Berlin St Op Orch
National SO
Vienna St Op Orch
VPO

KRAUSS, Fritz (ten)
Wagner: Walküre (exc)

KRÄUTLER, Walter (ten)
Verdi: Nabucco (exc)
(DECC) **436 464-2DM** Ten Top Baritones & Basses

KRAVTSOVA, Tatiana (sop)
Mussorgsky: Khovanshchina (Cpte)

KREBILL, Dorothy (mez)
Verdi: Traviata (Cpte)
(RCA) **GD60205** Opera Choruses

KREBS, Helmut (ten)
Henze: Junge Lord (Cpte)
J. Strauss II: Fledermaus (Cpte)
R. Strauss: Ariadne auf Naxos (Cpte)

KREDER, Jean-Paul (cond)
see ORTF Lyric Orch

KREEN, Uno (bass)
Tubin: Barbara von Tisenhusen (Cpte)

KREIDER, Paul (bass)
Puccini: Bohème (Cpte)

KREISLER, Fritz (pf)
(BIDD) **LAB009/10** The Kreisler Collection

KREISLER, Fritz (vn)
(BIDD) **LAB009/10** The Kreisler Collection
(BIDD) **LAB019** Fritz Kreisler—Early Victors
(BIDD) **LAB021** Fritz Kreisler—Acoustic Victors
(BIDD) **LAB022** Fritz Kreisler—Duets with McCormack & Farrar
(BIDD) **LAB040** Kreisler Collection
(BIDD) **LAB049/50** Kreisler - The Berlin HMV Recordings (1926-7)
(BIDD) **LAB068/9** The Kreisler Collection—1921-25
(BIDD) **LAB075** Kreisler—1926-1927 Victor Recordings
(BIDD) **LAB080** Kreisler—1928 Victor Recordings
(EMI) **CDH7 64701-2** Kreisler plays Kreisler
(IMP) **GLRS106** Kreisler plays Kreisler
(PEAR) **GEMMCD9315** Kreisler/McCormack Duets
(PEAR) **GEMMCD9324** Fritz Kreisler plays Encores

KREISLER, Hugo (vc)
(BIDD) **LAB009/10** The Kreisler Collection

KREJČÍK, Vladimír (ten)
Janáček: Cunning Little Vixen (Cpte), Excursions of Mr Brouček (Cpte), Fate (Cpte), Jenufa (Cpte), Makropulos Affair (Cpte)
Martinů: Alexandre Bis (Cpte), Comedy on the Bridge (Cpte)
(DECC) **421 852-2DH2** Janáček: Operatic & Chamber Works
(DECC) **430 375-2DH2** Janáček—Operatic and Orchestral Works
(KOCH) **34036-2** A Pageant of Opera

KREKOW, Ude (bass)
Ligeti: Grand Macabre (Cpte)
Schreker: Schatzgräber (Cpte)

KREMER, Martin (ten)
(PEAR) **GEMMCDS9121** Wagner—Die Meistersinger, Act 3, etc

KRENN, Fritz (bass)
Wagner: Meistersinger (Cpte)
(LYRC) **SRO830** Smetana—The Bartered Bride, etc
(SCHW) **314692** Vienna State Opera Live, Vol.19
(SCHW) **314702** Vienna State Opera Live, Vol.20

KRENN, Hans (bass)
Wagner: Meistersinger (exc)

KRENN, Werner (ten)
Lehár: Lustige Witwe (exc)
Mozart: Ascanio in Alba (Cpte), Lucio Silla (Cpte)
Shostakovich: Lady Macbeth of Mtsensk (Cpte)
(DECC) **433 223-2DWO** The World of Operetta
(DECC) **436 316-2DA** Golden Operetta
(DG) **435 712-2GX2** Lehár—The Merry Widow. Suppé—Overtures
(LOND) **436 897-2DM** Lehár Gala
(LOND) **436 898-2DM** Operetta Gala

KRENZ, Jan (cond)
see Katowice RSO

KREPPEL, Walter (bass)
Mozart: Don Giovanni (Cpte)
Wagner: Rheingold (Cpte)
Weber: Freischütz (Cpte)
(DECC) **414 100-2DM15** Wagner: Der Ring des Nibelungen

KRIEG, Christopher (spkr)
Corghi: Divara (Cpte)

KRIEGER, Armando (cond)
see Czech SO

KRIEGER, Jeanne (sop)
Ravel: Heure espagnole (Cpte)

KRILOVÁ, Věra (contr)
Dvořák: Rusalka (Cpte)
Smetana: Bartered Bride (Cpte)

KRINGELBORN, Solveig (sop)
(VIRG) **VC5 45051-2** Grieg—Choral Works

KRIPS, Josef (cond)
see LSO
Philh
Vienna St Op Orch
VPO
Zurich Tonhalle Orch

KRISTJANSSON, Einar (ten)
Mozart: Zauberflöte (Cpte)

KRIŠTOFOVÁ, Petra (treb)
Krása: Brundibár (Cpte)

KRIVINE, Emmanuel (cond)
see Lyon Nat Orch
Sinfonia Varsovia

KŘÍŽ, Vratislav (bar)
Smetana: Dalibor (Cpte), Libuše (Cpte)

KROESE, Myra (contr)
Landi: Mort d'Orfeo (Cpte)

KROGEN, Hanne (mez)
Gluck: Echo et Narcisse (Cpte)

KROLLMANN, Karl (ten)
Wagner: Meistersinger (Cpte)

KROMBHOLC, Jaroslav (cond)
see Munich RSO
Prague Nat Th Orch
Prague RSO

KRONENBERG, Karl (bar)
(MYTO) **1MCD943104** R. Strauss—Capriccio (highlights) & Lieder
(SCHW) **314582** Vienna State Opera Live, Vol.8
(SCHW) **314712** Vienna State Opera Live, Vol.21

KROPAT, Tamara (gtr)
(CHNN) **CG9103** Guitar Duets

KROUPA, Zdeněk (bar)
Janáček: Jenufa (Cpte), Káťa Kabanová (Cpte)

KRTSCHIL, Henry (cond)
see Studio Orch

KRUGLIKOVA, Elena (sop)
(PREI) **89067** Andrei Ivanov (1900-1970)

KRUKOWSKI, Ernst (bass)
Henze: Junge Lord (Cpte)
Künneke: Vetter aus Dingsda (exc)
Suppé: Boccaccio (exc)

KRÜLL, Rolf-Dieter (spkr)
Braunfels: Verkündigung (Cpte)

KRUMBIEGEL, Ulrike (spkr)
(SONY) **SK53978** Prometheus

KRUMEICH, Theo (gtr)
(CHNN) **CG9103** Guitar Duets

KRUSE, Heiner (sngr)
Schultze: Schwarzer Peter (Cpte)

KRUSE, Heinz (ten)
Hindemith: Mathis der Maler (Cpte)
Krenek: Jonny spielt auf (Cpte)
Lortzing: Undine (Cpte)
Mozart: Zauberflöte (exc)
Schreker: Gezeichneten (Cpte), Schatzgräber (Cpte)
Schultze: Schwarzer Peter (Cpte)
Weill: Zar lässt sich Photographieren (Cpte)
Zemlinsky: Traumgörge (Cpte)

KRUSE, Tone (contr)
Sibelius: Maiden in the Tower (Cpte)

KRUTIKOV, Mikhail (bass)
Mussorgsky: Boris Godunov (Cpte)
Rachmaninov: Miserly knight (Cpte)
Serov: Judith (Cpte)
Shostakovich: Gamblers (Cpte)
Tchaikovsky: Maid of Orleans (Cpte)

KUBANKOVA, Alzbeta (contr)
Suchoň: Whirlpool (Cpte)

KUBELÍK, Jan (vn)
(BIDD) **LAB033/4** Jan Kubelík—The Acoustic Recordings (1902-13)
(RCA) **09026 61412-2** Nellie Melba - Recital
(ROMO) **81011-2(2)** Dame Nellie Melba (pt 2)

KUBELÍK, Rafael (cond)
see BPO
BRSO
La Scala Orch

KUBIAK, Teresa (sop)
Cavalli: Calisto (Cpte)
Tchaikovsky: Eugene Onegin (Cpte)

KUBLER, Françoise (mez)
Dusapin: Romeo and Juliet (Cpte)

KUBOVČIK, Vladimir (bass)
Puccini: Madama Butterfly (Cpte)
Suchoň: Whirlpool (Cpte)

KUCHAR, Erich (bar)
J. Strauss II: Fledermaus (exc)

KUCHAREK, Helen (sop)
Lehár: Lustige Witwe (exc)

KUDO, Shigenori (fl)
(DINT) **DICD920141** French Music for Flute and Harp

KUDRIASHOV, Vladimir (ten)
Rachmaninov: Miserly knight (Cpte)
Rimsky-Korsakov: Mlada (Cpte), Tsar's Bride (Cpte)
Serov: Judith (Cpte)

KUDRIAVCHENKO, Ekaterina (sop)
Rimsky-Korsakov: Tsar's Bride (Cpte)

KUDRIAVTSEV, Boris (bar)
Karetnikov: Till Eulenspiegel (Cpte)

KUEBLER, David (ten)
Beethoven: Fidelio (Cpte)
Mozart: Idomeneo (Cpte), Mitridate (Cpte)
R. Strauss: Capriccio (Cpte)
Rossini: Scala di seta (Cpte), Signor Bruschino (Cpte)

KUEN, Paul (ten)
Janáček: Excursions of Mr Brouček (Cpte)
Mozart: Nozze di Figaro (Cpte)
Orff: Antigonae (Cpte), Kluge (Cpte), Mond (Cpte)
R. Strauss: Rosenkavalier (Cpte)
Wagner: Rheingold (Cpte), Siegfried (Cpte), Tristan und Isolde (Cpte)
Weber: Freischütz (Cpte)
(DECC) **414 100-2DM15** Wagner: Der Ring des Nibelungen
(FOYE) **15-CF2011** Wagner—Der Ring de Nibelungen

KUETHER, John (bass)
Glass: Belle et la Bête (Cpte)

KUETTENBAUM, Annette (mez)
Mozart: Zauberflöte (Cpte)

KUHLMANN, Kathleen (mez)
Donizetti: Lucia di Lammermoor (Cpte)
Giordano: Andrea Chénier (Cpte)
Handel: Alcina (Cpte)
Rossini: Cenerentola (Cpte)
Verdi: Rigoletto (Cpte)
Vivaldi: Orlando Furioso (Cpte)
Wagner: Walküre (Cpte)
(CAST) **CVI2071** Highlights from Glyndebourne
(EMI) **CDC7 54643-2** Rossini—Bicentenary Gala Concert
(EMI) **LDB491007-1 (EMI)** Rossini Bicentennial Birthday Gala
(EURO) **GD69003** Wagner—Der Ring des Nibelungen
(TELD) **9031-77676-6(TELD)** My World of Opera - Kiri Te Kanawa

KUHN, Alfred (bass)
R. Strauss: Elektra (Cpte)

KUHN, Gustav (cond)
see Marchigiano PO
Munich RO
Munich RSO
RPO
Staatskapelle Dresden
Tokyo PO

KÜHN CHILDREN'S CHORUS
cond C. MACKERRAS
Martinů: Greek Passion (Cpte)
cond V. NEUMANN
Janáček: Cunning Little Vixen (Cpte)

KÜHN CHORUS
cond J. PINKAS
Dvořák: Jacobin (exc)

KUHN-LIEBEL, Martha (mez)
Wagner: Walküre (exc)

KUIJKEN, Barthold (fl)
(SONY) **SK48045** Flute Concertos

KUIJKEN, Sigiswald (cond)
see Petite Bande

KUIJKEN, Wieland (va da gamba)
(ACCE) **ACC57802D** Purcell: Songs and Elegies
(ASTR) **E8757** Purcell—Songs from Orpheus Britannicus
(HARM) **HMC90 249** Purcell: Music for a while
(HARM) **HMP390 807** Great Baroque Masters—Purcell
(HARM) **HMX290 1528/33(2)** A Purcell Companion (pt 2)

KULKO, Oleg (ten)
Rimsky-Korsakov: Mlada (Cpte)
Tchaikovsky: Maid of Orleans (Cpte)

KULLENBO, Lars (ten)
Lidholm: Dream Play (Cpte)

KULLMAN, Charles (ten)
Mozart: Don Giovanni (Cpte)
(MMOI) **CDMOIR429** Charles Kullman - Serenade
(PREI) **89057** Charles Kullmann (1903-1982)
(SCHW) **314512** Vienna State Opera Live, Vol.1

KUNC, František (bass)
Janáček: Šárka (Cpte)

KUNDE, Gregory (ten)
A. Thomas: Hamlet (Cpte)
Bellini: Bianca e Fernando (Cpte)
Rossini: Armida (Cpte), Semiramide (Cpte)

KUNDER, Friedmann (bass)
Wagner: Meistersinger (Cpte)

KUNDLÁK, Jozef (ten)
Bellini: Sonnambula (Cpte)
Donizetti: Elisabetta (Cpte)
Mozart: Così fan tutte (Cpte)
Suchoň: Whirlpool (Cpte)

KÜNNEKE, Eduard (cond)
see Berlin St Op Orch

KUNZ, Claudio (treb)
Puccini: Gianni Schicchi (Cpte)
(EURO) **GD69043** Puccini: Il Trittico

KUNZ, Erich (bar)
J. Strauss II: Fledermaus (Cpte), Nacht in Venedig (Cpte), Wiener Blut (exc)
Lehár: Land des Lächelns (Cpte), Lustige Witwe (Cpte)
Mozart: Così fan tutte (Cpte), Nozze di Figaro (Cpte), Zauberflöte (Cpte)
R. Strauss: Ariadne auf Naxos (Cpte)
Wagner: Meistersinger (Cpte)
(EMI) **CDH5 65072-2** Glyndebourne Recorded - 1934-1994
(EMI) **CHS7 69741-2(4)** Record of Singing, Vol.4—German School
(ORFE) **C335931A** Salzburg Festival highlights (1956-85)
(ORFE) **C394101B** Great Mozart Singers Series, Vol. 1
(ORFE) **C394201B** Great Mozart Singers Series, Vol. 2
(PREI) **90168** Wagner—Die Meistersinger, Act 2, etc
(PREI) **90249** Mozart in tempore belli
(SCHW) **314532** Vienna State Opera Live, Vol.3
(SCHW) **314692** Vienna State Opera Live, Vol.19
(SCHW) **314712** Vienna State Opera Live, Vol.21
(SCHW) **314722** Vienna State Opera Live, Vol.22
(TEST) **SBT1059** Erich Kunz (b. 1909)

KUNZ, Erich (spkr)
J. Strauss II: Fledermaus (Cpte)
R. Strauss: Ariadne auf Naxos (Cpte)

KUNZ, Ursula (mez)
Wagner: Walküre (exc)

KUNZEL, Erich (cond)
see Cincinnati Pops
Cincinnati SO

KUPPER, Anneliese (sop)
R. Strauss: Elektra (Cpte)

KURCHUMOV, Pavel (ten)
(FORL) **UCD16743** Bulgarian Voices, Vol. 3

KURFÜRST, Bohumil (bass)
Janáček: Fate (Cpte)

KURFÜRST, Bohumir (spkr)
Martinů: Comedy on the Bridge (Cpte)

KURMANGALIEV, Erik (alto)
(MEZH) **MK417047** Erik Kurmangaliev - Recital

KURT, Melanie (sop)
(IRCC) **IRCC-CD800** Souvenirs from Meyerbeer Operas
(PEAR) **GEMMCDS9924(2)** Covent Garden on Record, Vol.2 (pt 2)
(PEAR) **GEMMCDS9925(1)** Covent Garden on Record—Vol.3 (pt 1)
(PREI) **89052** Friederich Schorr (1889-1953)

KURTZ, Efrem (cond)
see Philh

KURZ, Selma (sop)
(PEAR) **GEMMCDS9924(1)** Covent Garden on Record, Vol.2 (pt 1)
(PREI) **89110** Heinrich Schlusnus (1888-1952) - II

KUSAKA, Keiko (hp)
(PRES) **PCOM1109** Le Maître de Musique—Original Soundtrack

KUSCHE, Benno (bar)
J. Strauss II: Fledermaus (Cpte), Wiener Blut (exc)
Orff: Antigonae (Cpte), Kluge (Cpte), Mond (Cpte)
R. Strauss: Rosenkavalier (Cpte)
Wagner: Meistersinger (exc)
(ACAN) **43 268** Peter Anders sings German Opera Arias
(EMI) **CMS5 65212-2** Wagner—Les introuvables du Ring
(EMI) **CMS7 64309-2** Kálmán—Best-loved Melodies
(PILZ) **442118-2** Wagner—Operas in Historical Recordings
(RCA) **74321 24790-2** Carl Orff 100 Years Edition

KUSNJER, Iván (bar)
Dvořák: Dimitrij (Cpte)
Martinů: Miracles of Mary (Cpte)
Smetana: Dalibor (Cpte)

KÜTTENBAUM, Annette (mez)
Schoeck: Massimilla Doni (Cpte)
Wagner: Götterdämmerung (exc), Parsifal (Cpte), Rheingold (Cpte)

KUTTNER, Max (ten)
(PREI) **89209** Helge Roswaenge (1897-1972) - II

KUUSK, Ivo (ten)
Tubin: Barbara von Tisenhusen (Cpte)

KUZMA, Sue Ellen (sop)
Mozart: Nozze di Figaro (Cpte)

KUZNETSOV, Leo (ten)
Serov: Judith (Cpte)
Tchaikovsky: Eugene Onegin (Cpte)

KUZNETSOVA, Maria (sop)
(PEAR) **GEMMCDS9004/6(1)** Singers of Imperial Russia, Vol.3 (pt 1)
(SYMP) **SYMCD1105** The Harold Wayne Collection, Vol.10

KWEKSILBER, Marjanne (sop)
Campra: Europe galante
Gluck: Orfeo ed Euridice (Cpte)

KWELLA, Patrizia (sop)
Handel: Alcina (Cpte)
Monteverdi: Orfeo (Cpte)

KWON, Hellen (sop)
Mozart: Zauberflöte (Cpte)

KYRIAKI, Margarita (sop)
Wagner: Parsifal (Cpte)

LA BARBARA, Joan (sngr)
Ashley: Improvement (Cpte)

LA FORGE, Frank (pf)
(NIMB) **NI7856** Legendary Tenors
(PEAR) **GEMMCD9161** Edmond Clément (1867-1928)
(ROMO) **82002-2** Edmond Clément (1867-1928)

LA GUARDIA, Massimo (ten)
Verdi: Traviata (Cpte)

LA PORTA, Arturo (bar)
Rossini: Barbiere di Siviglia (Cpte)

LA PORTA, Arturo (bass)
Puccini: Gianni Schicchi (Cpte), Madama Butterfly (Cpte)
Verdi: Rigoletto (Cpte), Traviata (Cpte)

LA ROSA PARODI, Armando (cond)
see EIAR Orch
Milan RAI SO
Turin EIAR Orch

LA SCOLA, Vincenzo (ten)
Bellini: Beatrice di Tenda (Cpte), Norma (Cpte)
Verdi: Giovanna d'Arco (Cpte), Rigoletto (Cpte)

LABBETTE, Dora (sop)
(DUTT) **CDLX7012** The Incomparable Heddle Nash
(PEAR) **GEMMCDS9926(2)** Covent Garden on Record—Vol.4 (pt 2)
(PEAR) **GEMMCD9473** Heddle Nash—Vol.2

LABELLE, Dominique (sop)
Mozart: Don Giovanni (Cpte)
R. Strauss: Elektra (Cpte)
Tchaikovsky: Queen of Spades (Cpte)

LABÈQUE, Katia (pf)
Bernstein: West Side Story (exc), West Side Story Symphonic Dances
(PHIL) **416 460-2PH** Barbara Hendricks sings Gershwin
(PHIL) **438 938-2PH** España!
(SONY) **SK48381** Encore - Katia & Marielle Labeque

LABÈQUE, Marielle (pf)
Bernstein: West Side Story (exc), West Side Story Symphonic Dances
(PHIL) **416 460-2PH** Barbara Hendricks sings Gershwin
(PHIL) **438 938-2PH** España!
(SONY) **SK48381** Encore - Katia & Marielle Labeque

LABINSKY, Aleksandr (sngr)
(PEAR) **GEMMCDS9111(2)** Singers of Imperial Russia, Vol.5 (pt 2)

LABINSKY, Alexandre (cond)
see orch

LABINSKY, Alexandre (pf)
(EMI) **CHS7 63025-2** Mussorgsky—Songs

LABINSKY, Andrei (ten)
(NIMB) **NI7865** Great Singers at the Mariinsky Theatre
(PEAR) **GEMMCDS9001/3(1)** Singers of Imperial Russia, Vol.2 (pt 1)
(PEAR) **GEMMCDS9007/9(2)** Singers of Imperial Russia, Vol.4 (pt 2)
(SYMP) **SYMCD1105** The Harold Wayne Collection, Vol.10

LABÒ, Flaviano (ten)
Bellini: Pirata (Cpte)
Verdi: Don Carlo (Cpte)

LACIURA, Anthony (ten)
Bizet: Carmen (Cpte)
Donizetti: Lucia di Lammermoor (Cpte)
Mozart: Nozze di Figaro (Cpte)

Puccini: Fanciulla del West (Cpte), Madama Butterfly (Cpte), Manon Lescaut (Cpte), Tosca (Cpte), Turandot (Cpte)
R. Strauss: Ariadne auf Naxos (Cpte)
Verdi: Falstaff (Cpte), Traviata (Cpte), Trovatore (Cpte)
Wagner: Parsifal (exc)
(DECC) **071 142-1DH (DECC)** Essential Opera
(DG) **439 151-2GMA** Mad about Puccini

LACKNER, Christopher (bar)
Verdi: Otello (Cpte)

LACKNER, Herbert (bass)
R. Strauss: Rosenkavalier (Cpte)
Wagner: Parsifal (Cpte)
(DECC) **433 437-2DA** Pavarotti—King of the High Cs

LACORN, Maria (sop)
Wagner: Parsifal (Cpte)

LACZÓ, András (ten)
Mascagni: Lodoletta (Cpte)

LADEROUTE, Joseph (ten)
Beethoven: Fidelio (Cpte)

LADWIG, Werner (cond)
see Berlin City Op Orch

ŁADYSZ, Bernard (bass)
Donizetti: Lucia di Lammermoor (Cpte)

LAFARGUE, Marie (sop)
(IRCC) **IRCC-CD800** Souvenirs from Meyerbeer Operas

LAFAYE, Suzanne (mez)
(EMI) **CZS5 68113-2** Vive Offenbach!

LAFFAGE, Jean-Pierre (bar)
Offenbach: Contes d'Hoffmann (Cpte)
Verdi: Rigoletto (Cpte)

LAFON, Brigitte (mez)
Auber: Gustav III (Cpte), Manon Lescaut (Cpte)

LAFONT, Jean-Philippe (bar)
Bizet: Carmen (Cpte), Djamileh (Cpte)
Chabrier: Roi malgré lui (Cpte)
Gluck: Rencontre imprévue (Cpte)
Lully: Alceste (Cpte)
Massenet: Werther (Cpte)
Offenbach: Belle Hélène (Cpte), Orphée aux enfers (Cpte)
(EMI) **CDM7 64687-2** French Works inspired by Edgar Allan Poe
(EMI) **CDS7 49361-2** Offenbach: Operettas
(EMI) **CZS5 68113-2** Vive Offenbach!
(ERAT) **4509-99607-2** Gluck—Operas; Schubert—Symphonies Nos 8 & 9

(JEAN) LAFORGE CHORAL ENSEMBLE
(EMI) **CDS7 49361-2** Offenbach: Operettas
cond C. DUTOIT
Fauré: Pénélope (Cpte)
cond A. SIRANOSSIAN
(ARIO) **ARN68195** Milhaud—Sonatas; Trois Operas-Minute
cond M. SOUSTROT
Auber: Fra Diavolo (Cpte)

LAGERSPETZ, Juhani (pf)
(FINL) **4509-95583-2** Virtuoso Trumpet

LAGGER, Peter (bass)
Mozart: Nozze di Figaro (exc)
Orff: Mond (Cpte)
Wagner: Meistersinger (Cpte)
(BELA) **450 121-2** Plácido Domingo
(DG) **431 104-2GB** Great Voices - Plácido Domingo

LAGHEZZA, Rosa (mez)
Mascagni: Cavalleria Rusticana (Cpte)

LAGOYA, Alexandre (gtr)
(BELA) **450 146-2** Romantic Guitar
(PHIL) **422 979-2PCC** Romantic Music for Two Guitars

LAGRANGE, Michèle (sop)
Prokofiev: Love for 3 Oranges (Cpte)
Ravel: Enfant et les sortilèges (Cpte)

(LA) LAGUNA UNIVERSITY CHOIR
cond A. R. MARBÀ
Vives: Bohemios (Cpte)

(LA) LAGUNA UNIVERSITY POLYPHONIC CHORUS
cond A. R. MARBÀ
Vives: Bohemios (Cpte), Doña Francisquita (Cpte)

LAHOLM, Eyvind (ten)
Wagner: Meistersinger (exc), Tannhäuser (Cpte)
(SCHW) **314622** Vienna State Opera Live, Vol.12

LAHTI SYMPHONY ORCHESTRA
cond E. KLAS
(BIS) **BIS-CD520** Matti Salminen - Opera Recital
cond O. VÄNSKÄ
(BIS) **BIS-CD498** Kokkonen—Complete Orchestral Music, Vol.3

LAITER, Alexandre (ten)
Auber: Manon Lescaut (Cpte)
Chausson: Roi Arthus (Cpte)
Saint-Saëns: Henry VIII (Cpte)

LAJARRIGE, Christine (pf)
(MARC) **8 223774** Ropartz—Choral Works

LAKES, Gary (ten)
Berlioz: Troyens (Cpte)
R. Strauss: Ariadne auf Naxos (Cpte)
Wagner: Walküre (Cpte)
Weber: Oberon (Cpte)
(DG) **445 354-2GX14** Wagner—Der Ring des Nibelungen
(DG) **072 422-3GH7** Levine conducts Wagner's Ring

LAKI, Krisztina (sop)
Einem: Dantons Tod (Cpte)
Handel: Partenope (Cpte)
Mozart: Schauspieldirektor (Cpte)
Mysliveček: Bellerofonte (Cpte)
Wagner: Feen (Cpte)

LALÁK, Bohumír (bass)
Martinů: Julietta (Cpte)

LALLOUETTE, Olivier (bass)
Bizet: Carmen (Cpte)
Fauré: Prométhée (Cpte)
Handel: Giulio Cesare (Cpte), Scipione (Cpte)
Lully: Alceste (Cpte)

LAM, Basil (hpd)
(EMI) **CDH5 65501-2** Alfred Deller - HMV Recordings, 1949-54

LAMASSE, Aleth (vc)
(FORL) **FF038** Cello for Happy Days

LAMB, Timothy (treb)
Britten: Noye's Fludde (Cpte)

LAMBERT, Constant (cond)
see Hallé
RLPO

LAMBERTI, Giorgio (ten)
Puccini: Tosca (Cpte)
Respighi: Belfagor (Cpte)
(EURO) **GD69043** Puccini: Il Trittico

LAMBRECHT, Heinz (cond)
see Vienna Volksoper Orch

LAMBRIKS, Marjon (mez)
Verdi: Traviata (exc)
Wagner: Parsifal (Cpte)

LAMON, Jeanne (cond)
see Tafelmusik

LAMOUREUX CONCERTS ORCHESTRA
cond R. BENZI
(BELA) **461 001-2** Popular Overtures
cond A. DORATI
(PHIL) **442 272-2PM2** The Best of Bizet
cond J. FOURNET
Bizet: Pêcheurs de Perles (Cpte)
(PHIL) **442 272-2PM2** The Best of Bizet
cond J. GRESSIER
(EMI) **CZS5 68295-2** Messager/Lecocq—Operetta Highlights
cond I. MARKEVITCH
Bizet: Carmen Suites

LAMOUREUX ORCHESTRA
cond P. DERVAUX
(PHIL) **438 953-2PM2** Alarie/Simoneau - Arias & Duets
cond J. FOURNET
(DG) **437 677-2GDO2** Irmgard Seefried - Opera Recital
cond J. GRESSIER
(EMI) **CZS7 67515-2** Offenbach—Operetta highlights
cond A. JOUVE
(PHIL) **438 953-2PM2** Alarie/Simoneau - Arias & Duets
cond I. MARKEVITCH
(DG) **447 364-2GDB2** Great Opera Overtures
(DG) **447 406-2GOR** Berlioz—Symphonie fantastique etc
(EMI) **CZS5 68113-2** Vive Offenbach!
cond J-P. MARTY
(EMI) **CZS5 68113-2** Vive Offenbach!
cond H. ROSBAUD
Gluck: Orphée (Cpte)
(PHIL) **442 602-2PM** 3 x 3 Tenors

LAMPRECHT, Doris (mez)
Handel: Scipione (Cpte)

LAMSON, Carl (pf)
(BIDD) **LAB068/9** The Kreisler Collection—1921-25
(BIDD) **LAB075** Kreisler—1926-1927 Victor Recordings
(BIDD) **LAB080** Kreisler—1928 Victor Recordings
(IMP) **GLRS106** Kreisler plays Kreisler
(PEAR) **GEMMCD9324** Fritz Kreisler plays Encores

(R.) LAMY SINGERS
cond W. SCHMIDT-BOELCKE
(EURO) **GD69018** Fritz Wunderlich—Recital

LANCE, Albert (ten)
Massenet: Werther (Cpte)
Offenbach: Contes d'Hoffmann (exc)
(EMI) **LDB9 91258-1(EMI)** Maria Callas at the Paris Opera December 1958
(PHIL) **442 272-2PM2** The Best of Bizet

LANDAUER, Bernhard (alto)
Biber: Arminio (Cpte)

LANDER, Thomas (bass)
Purcell: Fairy Queen, Z629 (Cpte)

LANDOUZY, Lise (sop)
(IRCC) **IRCC-CD800** Souvenirs from Meyerbeer Operas

LANDOWSKA, Wanda (hpd)
(BIDD) **LHW016** Landowska—The Early Recordings 1923-1930

LANDY, Tonny (ten)
Nielsen: Maskarade (Cpte)

LANE, Betty (sop)
Gershwin: Porgy and Bess (Cpte)
R. Strauss: Aegyptische Helena (Cpte)

LANE, Clifford (sngr)
J. Moran: Manson Family (Cpte)

LANE, Gloria (mez)
(MEMO) **HR4223/4** Nicolai Ghiaurov

LANE, Jennifer (mez)
Handel: Giustino (Cpte), Sosarme (Cpte)
(NEWP) **NPD85540** Handel/Bononcini—Muzio Scevola

LANG, Donald P. (voc)
Weill: Down in the Valley (Cpte)

LANG, Frieder (ten)
Schoeck: Venus (Cpte)
Schreker: Gezeichneten (Cpte)

LANG, Klaus (bar)
Lehár: Zarewitsch (exc)
R. Strauss: Salome (Cpte)
Wagner: Meistersinger (Cpte)
Weber: Freischütz (Cpte)

LANG, Petra (mez)
Mozart: Nozze di Figaro (Cpte)
(TELD) **4509-97507-2** Mozart—Famous Opera Arias

LANG, Rosemarie (contr)
Prokofiev: Fiery Angel (Cpte)
Tchaikovsky: Eugene Onegin (exc)

LANG, Wilhelm (bass)
(PREI) **90168** Wagner—Die Meistersinger, Act 2, etc

LANG, William (cornet)
(CHAN) **CHAN4513** British Bandsman Centenary Concert

LANGAN, Kevin (bass)
Mozart: Nozze di Figaro (Cpte)
Saint-Saëns: Samson et Dalila (Cpte)
Vivaldi: Orlando Furioso (Cpte)

LANGDON, Michael (bass)
Beethoven: Fidelio (Cpte)
Britten: Billy Budd (Cpte)
Holst: Wandering Scholar (Cpte)
Mozart: Nozze di Figaro (Cpte)
Rossini: Semiramide (Cpte)

LANGDON-DAVIES, Michael (cl)
(COLN) **VAN201** Carnival of Venice

LANGE, Hans (cond)
see orch
SO

LANGE, Hans (ten)
(PEAR) **GEMMCD9409** Lotte Lehmann—Vol.1
(RCA) **09026 61580-2(4)** RCA/Met 100 Singers, 100 Years (pt 4)

LANGE, Käthe (sop)
R. Strauss: Elektra (Cpte)

LANGHAMMER, Irmgard (sop)
Wagner: Götterdämmerung (Cpte)
(PREI) **89070** Franz Völker (1899-1965) - II

LANGRIDGE, Philip (ten)
Berg: Wozzeck (Cpte)
Birtwistle: Punch and Judy (Cpte)
Britten: Billy Budd (Cpte), Gloriana (Cpte), Peter Grimes (Cpte), Turn of the Screw (Cpte)
Gay: Beggar's Opera (Cpte)
Holliger: Magische Tänzer (Cpte)
Holst: At the Boar's Head (Cpte), Sávitri (Cpte)
Janáček: Fate (Cpte), From the House of the Dead (Cpte), Jenufa (Cpte)
Massenet: Werther (Cpte)
Monteverdi: Incoronazione di Poppea (Cpte)
Mozart: Clemenza di Tito (Cpte), Idomeneo (Cpte), Nozze di Figaro (Cpte)
Mussorgsky: Boris Godunov (Cpte)
Purcell: Dido (Cpte)
Ravel: Enfant et les sortilèges (Cpte)
Schoenberg: Moses und Aron (Cpte)
Shostakovich: Lady Macbeth of Mtsensk (Cpte)
Stravinsky: Rake's Progress (Cpte)
(CAST) **CVI2071** Highlights from Glyndebourne
(TELD) **4509-97507-2** Mozart—Famous Opera Arias

LANGSTON, John (ten)
Bernstein: Candide (1982) (Cpte)

LANIGAN, John (ten)
Britten: Peter Grimes (Cpte)
Verdi: Falstaff (Cpte)
(BELA) **450 117-2** Great Opera Chorus II
(EMI) **CDC7 47283-2** Maria Callas - Mad Scenes & Bel Canto Arias
(EMI) **CMS7 63244-2** The Art of Maria Callas

LANNERBÄCK, Helge (bar)
Nørgård: Gilgamesh (Cpte)

LANSBURY, Angela (mez)
Gay: Beggar's Opera (Cpte)

LANTIERI, Rita (sop)
Mascagni: Rantzau (Cpte)

LANZA, Mario (ten)
(IMP) **PWKS4230** Mario Lanza in Concert
(RCA) **GD60048** Mario Lanza sings Songs from The Student Prince & The Desert Song
(RCA) **GD60049** 'The Great Caruso' and other Caruso favourites
(RCA) **GD60516** Mario Lanza—For the first time
(RCA) **GD60720** Mario Lanza—Be my love
(RCA) **GD60889(1)** The Mario Lanza Collection
(RCA) **GD60889(2)** The Mario Lanza Collection
(RCA) **RD86218** Mario Lanza—The Legendary Tenor
(RCA) **09026 61420-2** Mario Lanza - Don't Forget Me
(RCA) **09026 61440-2** Opera's Greatest Moments
(RCA) **09026 61884-2** Mario Lanza—Live in London
(RCA) **09026 62550-2** Ten Tenors in Love
(RCA) **09026 62681-2** Mr Jerry Hadley—Golden Days
(RCA) **09026 68130-2** Mario Lanza at his Best
(RCA) **74321 18574-2** Mario Lanza - The Ultimate Collection
(RCA) **74321 25817-2** Café Classics - Operatic

LAPELLETRIE, René (ten)
Offenbach: Contes d'Hoffmann (Cpte)

LAPERRIÈRE, Gaétan (bar)
(CBC) **SMCD5127** Great Baritone Arias

LAPIERRE, Gabriel (pf)
(RCA) **09026 61412-2** Nellie Melba - Recital
(ROMO) **81011-2(2)** Dame Nellie Melba (pt 2)

LAPINA, Marina (sop)
Rachmaninov: Francesca da Rimini (Cpte)

LAPITINO, Francis (hp)
(NIMB) **NI7804** Giovanni Martinelli—Opera Recital
(PEAR) **EVC4(1)** The Caruso Edition, Vol.4 (pt 1)
(RCA) **GD60495(3)** The Complete Caruso Collection (pt 3)
(RCA) **GD60495(5)** The Complete Caruso Collection (pt 5)
(RCA) **09026 61243-2** Caruso sings Verismo Arias
(RCA) **09026 61244-2** Caruso sings French Opera Arias

LAPLÉNIE, Michel (ten)
Lully: Atys (Cpte)
M-A. Charpentier: Comtesse d'Escarbagnas Ov, H494
Purcell: Dido (Cpte)
(HARM) **HMP390 805** Great Baroque Masters—Lully
(HARM) **HMX290 1528/33(1)** A Purcell Companion (pt 1)

LARA, Christian (ten)
(ARIO) **ARN68195** Milhaud—Sonatas; Trois Operas-Minute

LARCEN, Elsa (sop)
Wagner: Parsifal (exc)

LARCHER, Claire (mez)
Massenet: Grisélidis (Cpte)

LAREDO, Jaime (cond)
see Scottish CO

LAREDO, Jaime (vn/dir)
(IMP) **PCD802** String Masterpieces

LARGE, Brian (prod)
(DECC) **071 119-1DH (DECC)** Pavarotti and Levine in Recital at the Met

LARIN, Sergei (bass)
Shostakovich: Lady Macbeth of Mtsensk (Cpte)

LARIN, Sergei (ten)
Mussorgsky: Boris Godunov (Cpte)
Tchaikovsky: Mazeppa (Cpte)

LARIONOVA, Nina (mez)
Rimsky-Korsakov: Tsar's Bride (Cpte)

LARMORE, Jennifer (mez)
Donizetti: Lucia di Lammermoor (Cpte)
Handel: Giulio Cesare (Cpte)
Humperdinck: Hänsel und Gretel (Cpte)
Monteverdi: Incoronazione di Poppea (Cpte), Orfeo (Cpte)
Rossini: Barbiere di Siviglia (Cpte), Cenerentola (Cpte), Semiramide (Cpte), Signor Bruschino (Cpte)
Verdi: Rigoletto (exc)
(TELD) **4509-96800-2** Jennifer Larmore—Where Shall I Fly?

LAROZE, André (ten)
G. Charpentier: Louise (Cpte)

LARREA, Vicente (sngr)
Moreno Torroba: Luisa Fernanda (Cpte)

LARRIEU, Maxence (fl)
(DENO) **C37-7301** Duo Recital

LARROCHA, Alicia de (pf)
(EMI) **CDM7 64527-2** Falla—Piano Works
(RCA) **09026 61389-2** Goyescas Andaluza Alicia de Larrocha

LARSEN, Dorothy (sop)
(DANA) **DACOCD319/21** The Lauritz Melchior Anthology - Vol.5

LARSEN, John (ten)
Lehár: Lustige Witwe (exc)

LARSEN-TODSEN, Nanny (sop)
(EMI) **CMS7 64008-2(2)** Wagner Singing on Record (pt 2)

LARSON, Susan (mez)
Handel: Giulio Cesare (Cpte)
Mozart: Nozze di Figaro (Cpte)

LARSSON, Ann-Christine (sop)
Mozart: Zauberflöte (Cpte)

LARSSON, Birgitta (sop)
Mozart: Nozze di Figaro (Cpte), Zauberflöte (Cpte)

LASCAE, Alexandru (cond)
see Arion Ens

LASSALLE, Jean (bar)
(PEAR) **GEMMCDS9923(1)** Covent Garden on Record, Vol.1 (pt 1)
(SYMP) **SYMCD1089** Historic Baritones of the French School

LÁSZLÓ, Magda (sop)
(EMI) **CDH5 65072-2** Glyndebourne Recorded - 1934-1994

LÁSZLÓ, Margit (sop)
(DECC) **443 488-2DF2** Kodály—Háry János; Psalmus Hungaricus etc

LATHAM, Keith (bar)
(EMI) **CDC7 54785-2** Harry Enfield's Guide to Opera

LATHAM-KÖNIG, Jan (cond)
see Cologne RSO
Danish Nat RSO
König Ens
Milan RAI SO
Rome Op Chor
Turin Fenice Orch

LATINUCCI, Pier Luigi (bass)
Puccini: Gianni Schicchi (Cpte)
Verdi: Otello (Cpte)

LATTUADA, Emma (sop)
(PREI) **89007** Aureliano Pertile (1885-1952) - I

LATVIAN NATIONAL SYMPHONY ORCHESTRA
cond A. VILUMANIS
(CAMP) **RRCD1335** Inese Galante - Début Recital

LAUBENTHAL, Hansgeorg (spkr)
(EMI) **CHS7 63715-2** Mozart: Die Entführung, etc

LAUBENTHAL, Horst (ten)
Beethoven: Fidelio (Cpte)
Berg: Wozzeck (Cpte)
Korngold: Violanta (Cpte)
Schmidt: Notre Dame (Cpte)
Wagner: Meistersinger (exc)
(CFP) **CD-CFP4656** Herbert von Karajan conducts Opera

LAUBENTHAL, Rudolf (ten)
Wagner: Götterdämmerung (exc)
(EMI) **CMS7 64008-2(2)** Wagner Singing on Record (pt 2)
(PEAR) **GEMMCDS9137** Wagner—Der Ring des Nibelungen
(PEAR) **GEMMCD9944** Friedrich Schorr sings Wagner
(PREI) **89004** Frida Leider (1888-1975) - I

LAUFKÖTTER, Karl (ten)
Beethoven: Fidelio (Cpte)
Wagner: Siegfried (Cpte)

LAURENCE, Elisabeth (mez)
Floyd: Susannah (Cpte)
Stravinsky: Nightingale (Cpte)
(ERAT) **4509-98955-2** Boulez conducts Stravinsky

LAURENS, Guillemette (mez)
Gluck: Iphigénie en Aulide (Cpte)
Lully: Armide, Atys (Cpte)
M-A. Charpentier: Actéon (Cpte), Arts Florissants (Cpte)
Monteverdi: Incoronazione di Poppea (Cpte), Orfeo (Cpte)
Purcell: Dido (Cpte)
Rameau: Platée (Cpte)
(ERAT) **4509-99607-2** Gluck—Operas; Schubert—Symphonies Nos 8 & 9
(HARM) **HMP390 805** Great Baroque Masters—Lully
(HARM) **HMP390 807** Great Baroque Masters—Purcell
(HARM) **HMX290 1528/33(1)** A Purcell Companion (pt 1)
(TELD) **4509-91181-2** Lettera Amorosa

LAURENTI, Mario (bar)
(BOGR) **BIM705-2** Muzio—The Published Edisons, 1920-25
(ROMO) **81005-2** Claudia Muzio (1889-1936)

LAURENZA, Marilena (sop)
Donizetti: Favorita (Cpte)
Verdi: Don Carlo (Cpte), Rigoletto (Cpte)

LAURIKAINEN, Kauko (spkr)
Kortekangas: Grand Hotel

LAURI-VOLPI, Giacomo (ten)
(CONI) **CDHD235** The Puccini Album
(EMI) **CHS7 64864-2(2)** La Scala Edition - Vol.2, 1915-46 (pt 2)
(MMOI) **CDMOIR405** Great Tenors
(MMOI) **CDMOIR412** Great Voices of the Century Sing Puccini
(NIMB) **NI7801** Great Singers, Vol.1
(NIMB) **NI7845** Giacomo Lauri-Volpi (1892-1979)
(NIMB) **NI7853** Lauri-Volpi sings Verdi
(PEAR) **GEMMCDS9159(2)** De Luca Edition, Vol.1 (pt 2)
(PEAR) **GEMMCDS9925(2)** Covent Garden on Record—Vol.3 (pt 2)
(PEAR) **GEMMCDS9926(2)** Covent Garden on Record—Vol.4 (pt 2)
(PEAR) **GEMMCD9129** Great Tenors, Vol.2
(PREI) **89009** Gino Bechi (b. 1913)
(PREI) **89012** Giacomo Lauri-Volpi (1894-1979)
(RCA) **09026 61580-2(3)** RCA/Met 100 Singers, 100 Years (pt 3)
(ROMO) **81014-2** Elisabeth Rethberg (1894-1976)
(SCHW) **314512** Vienna State Opera Live, Vol.1

LAUSANNE CHAMBER ORCHESTRA
cond A. DORATI
Haydn: Armida (Cpte), Orlando Paladino (Cpte)
(PHIL) **420 084-2PH** Frederica von Stade sings Haydn, Mozart & Rossini Arias
(PHIL) **432 416-2PH3** Haydn—L'incontro improvviso/Arias
cond J. LÓPEZ-COBOS
Rossini: Barbiere di Siviglia (exc)
(TELD) **4509-96800-2** Jennifer Larmore—Where Shall I Fly?

LAUSANNE INSTRUMENTAL ENSEMBLE
cond M. CORBOZ
Monteverdi: Orfeo (Cpte)

LAUSANNE OPERA CHORUS
cond I. ANGUELOV
Henze: Boulevard Solitude (Cpte)

LAUSANNE PRO ARTE CHOIR
cond R. BONYNGE
Offenbach: Contes d'Hoffmann (exc)
(DECC) **433 067-2DWO** Your Hundred Best Opera Tunes IV
(DECC) **433 440-2DA** Golden Opera
(DECC) **433 822-2DH** Essential Opera
(DECC) **436 300-2DX** Opera Gala Sampler
(DECC) **436 315-2DA** Great Operatic Duets
(DECC) **436 463-2DM** Ten Top Tenors
(DECC) **443 335-2LRX** Music for Relaxation, Vol 10 - The Night Before
cond A. JORDAN
(ERAT) **2292-45797-2** The Ultimate Opera Collection

LAUSANNE VOCAL ENSEMBLE
cond M. CORBOZ
Monteverdi: Orfeo (Cpte)

LAUSCH, Eleanor (sop)
Wagner: Walküre (exc)

LAUSNAY, Georges de (pf)
(APR) **APR7028** Jacques Thibaud—Complete Solo Recordings 1929-36
(MSCM) **MM30321** Jacques Thibaud—Violin Recital

LAUTTEN COMPAGNEY
(CAPR) **10 470** Monteverdi—Arie e Duetti

LAUWERS, Henk (bass)
Puccini: Manon Lescaut (Cpte)

LAVENDER, Justin (ten)
Bellini: Puritani (Cpte)
Mozart: Mitridate (Cpte)
Smyth: Wreckers (Cpte)

LAVIRGEN, Pedro (ten)
Moreno Torroba: Luisa Fernanda (Cpte)
Vives: Bohemios (Cpte), Doña Francisquita (Cpte)
(GME) **GME221** Falla—Orchestral Works
(RCA) **RD61191** Gala Lirica
(RCA) **09026 61191-5** Gala Lirica

LAW, Brian (cond)
see NZ SO

LAWLESS, James (spkr)
Britten: Paul Bunyan (Cpte)

LAWLOR, Thomas (bar)
Mozart: Nozze di Figaro (Cpte)
Stravinsky: Rake's Progress (Cpte)
Sullivan: HMS Pinafore (Cpte), Ruddigore (Cpte), Yeomen of the Guard (Cpte)
(BELA) **461 006-2** Gilbert & Sullivan—Songs and Snatches
(DECC) **433 868-2DWO** The World of Gilbert & Sullivan - Volume 2

LAWRENCE, Amy (sop)
Schillings: Mona Lisa (Cpte)

LAWRENCE, Helen (sop)
Alman: King Ahaz (exc)
B. Goldschmidt: Gewaltige Hahnrei (Cpte)
Verdi: Macbeth (Cpte)

LAWRENCE, Marjorie (sop)
Wagner: Fliegende Holländer (Cpte)
(EMI) **CMS7 64008-2(1)** Wagner Singing on Record (pt 1)
(EMI) **CMS7 64008-2(2)** Wagner Singing on Record (pt 2)
(PREI) **89011** Marjorie Lawrence (1909-1979)

LAWRENCE, Robert (cond)
see American Op Soc Orch

LAWSON, Winifred (sop)
Sullivan: Gondoliers (Cpte), Patience (Cpte), Trial by Jury (Cpte)
(MMOI) **CDMOIR413** The Very Best of Gilbert & Sullivan

LAWTON, Jeffrey (ten)
Martinů: Greek Passion (Cpte)

LAYDEKER, Suzanne (sop)
(EMI) **CZS5 68292-2** Operetta Arias and Duets

LAZAR, Hans-Jürgen (ten)
J. Strauss II: Zigeunerbaron (Cpte)

LAZAREV, Alexander (cond)
see Bolshoi SO
Bolshoi Th Orch

LÁZARO, Hipolito (ten)
(EMI) **CHS7 64860-2(2)** La Scala Edition - Vol.1, 1878-1914 (pt 2)
(MEMO) **HR4408/9(2)** Singers in Genoa, Vol.1 (disc 2)

LAZZARA, Marco (alto)
Stradella: Moro per amore (Cpte)

LAZZARETTI, Bruno (ten)
Donizetti: Lucia di Lammermoor (Cpte), Poliuto (Cpte)
Rossini: Sigismondo (Cpte)
(CAPR) **10 380** Breezes from the Orient, Vol.2

LAZZARI, Agostino (ten)
Puccini: Gianni Schicchi (Cpte)
Rossini: Mosè (Cpte)
(BONG) **GB1060-2** Virginia Zeani - Various opera arias
(DECC) **411 665-2DM3** Puccini: Il trittico

LAZZARINI, Adriana (mez)
Mascagni: Cavalleria Rusticana (Cpte)
Verdi: Rigoletto (exc)

LE BLANC, Suzie (sop)
(TELD) **4509-95068-2** Purcell—Songs of Welcome & Farewell

LE BRETON, M. (sngr)
(MUSD) **20239-2** Delibes—Opéras-Comiques

LE BRIS, Michèle (sop)
Massenet: Hérodiade (exc)

LE BROCQ, Mark (alto)
Purcell: Fairy Queen, Z629 (Cpte)

LE COZ, Claudine (sngr)
Gluck: Rencontre imprévue (Cpte)
Lully: Alceste (Cpte)
(ERAT) **4509-99607-2** Gluck—Operas; Schubert—Symphonies Nos 8 & 9

LE HÉMONET, Pierre (bass)
Debussy: Pelléas et Mélisande (Cpte)

LE MAIGAT, Pierre-Yves (bass-bar)
Berg: Lulu (Cpte)
Offenbach: Brigands (Cpte)
(EMI) **CDM7 64687-2** French Works inspired by Edgar Allan Poe

LE PALUDIER, Christophe (alto)
Purcell: Fairy Queen, Z629 (Cpte)

LE ROUX, François (bar)
A. Thomas: Hamlet (Cpte)
Bizet: Carmen (exc)
Debussy: Pelléas et Mélisande (Cpte)
Fauré: Pénélope (Cpte)
Gounod: Roméo et Juliette (Cpte)
M-A. Charpentier: David et Jonathas (Cpte)
Monteverdi: Orfeo (Cpte)
Offenbach: Brigands (Cpte)
Poulenc: Dialogues des Carmélites (Cpte)
(EMI) **CDM7 64687-2** French Works inspired by Edgar Allan Poe

LE SAGE, Sally (sop)
Monteverdi: L'Arianna (exc)

LEA, Yvonne (mez)
Prokofiev: Love for 3 Oranges (Cpte)

LEANDERSON, Rolf (bar)
Nørgård: Gilgamesh (Cpte)
Rameau: Castor et Pollux (Cpte)

LEAPER, Adrian (cond)
see Bratislava RSO
RPO

LEAR, Evelyn (sop)
Berg: Lulu (Cpte), Wozzeck (Cpte)
Egk: Verlobung in San Domingo (Cpte)
Mozart: Zauberflöte (exc)
R. Strauss: Rosenkavalier (Cpte)
(CFP) **CD-CFP9013** Duets from Famous Operas
(ORFE) **C394301B** Great Mozart Singers Series, Vol. 3

LEATHERMAN, Alan (sngr)
Gershwin: Porgy and Bess (Cpte)

LEBED, Valery (bass)
Mussorgsky: Khovanshchina (Cpte)

LEBEDA, Andreas (bar)
Monteverdi: Incoronazione di Poppea (Cpte)

LEBEDEVA, Ludmila (sop)
Mussorgsky: Boris Godunov (Cpte)

LEBEDEVA, Neyla (sop)
Rimsky-Korsakov: Tsar's Bride (Cpte)
Tchaikovsky: Queen of Spades (Cpte)

LEBHERZ, Louis (bass)
Verdi: Aroldo (Cpte)

LEBLANC, Gyózó (sngr)
Lehár: Lustige Witwe (exc)

LEBRUN, Eric (organ)
(MARC) **8 223774** Ropartz—Choral Works

LECHLEITNER, Franz (ten)
(DECC) **440 062-2DM** Wagner—Overtures

LECHNER, Gabriele (sop)
R. Strauss: Elektra (Cpte)

LECOCQ, Michel (ten)
Hasse: Piramo e Tisbe (Cpte)
Tchaikovsky: Eugene Onegin (Cpte)
(EMI) **CZS7 67869-2** J. Strauss II—Operetta Highlights

LECOUVREUR, A. (contr)
G. Charpentier: Louise (exc)

LEDGER, Philip (cond)
see Medici Qt

LEDROIT, Henri (alto)
Monteverdi: Orfeo (Cpte)

LEECH, Richard (ten)
Gounod: Faust (exc)
J. Strauss II: Fledermaus (exc)
Puccini: Bohème (Cpte)
R. Strauss: Rosenkavalier (exc), Salome (Cpte)
Verdi: Rigoletto (Cpte)
(TELA) **CD80401** The Very Best of Erich Kunzel

LEEDS FESTIVAL CHORUS
cond T. BEECHAM
(DUTT) **CDLX7003** Vintage Beecham

LEEMING, Peter (bass)
Britten: Burning Fiery Furnace (Cpte), Death in Venice (Cpte)

LEFEBRE, Pierre (ten)
Rossini: Gazza ladra (Cpte)
Spontini: Vestale (Cpte)
Verdi: Giovanna d'Arco (Cpte)

LEFEBVRE, Philippe (organ)
Ancelin: Filius Hominis (Cpte)

LEFEBVRE, Pierre (ten)
Franchetti: Cristoforo Colombo (Cpte)
Giordano: Andrea Chénier (Cpte)
Puccini: Fanciulla del West (Cpte)

LEFORT, Marie-Françoise (sop)
(DECC) **440 333-2DH** Ravel—Vocal Works

LEGAY, Henri (ten)
Bizet: Ivan IV (exc), Pêcheurs de Perles (Cpte)
(EMI) **CZS5 68295-2** Messager/Lecocq—Operetta Highlights

LEGGATE, Robin (ten)
Boito: Mefistofele (Cpte)
Borodin: Prince Igor (Cpte)
Haydn: Armida (Cpte)
Offenbach: Contes d'Hoffmann (Cpte)
Puccini: Fanciulla del West (exc), Manon Lescaut (Cpte)
R. Strauss: Salome (Cpte)
Verdi: Ballo in maschera (Cpte), Otello (Cpte), Stiffelio (Cpte), Traviata (Cpte), Trovatore (Cpte)
(LOND) **825 126-2** Amadeus - Original Soundtrack
(OPRA) **ORCH103** Italian Opera—1810-20
(OPRA) **ORH102** A Hundred Years of Italian Opera
(PHIL) **442 600-2PH** The Great Carreras
(ROH) **75605 55013-2** The Puccini Experience

LEGOUHY, Marguérite (mez)
Poulenc: Mamelles de Tirésias (Cpte)
Ravel: Enfant et les sortilèges (Cpte)

LEGRAND, Christiane (sop)
Berio: Laborintus II

LEGROS, Adrien (bass)
Boïeldieu: Dame blanche (Cpte)
Massenet: Hérodiade (exc)
Verdi: Rigoletto (Cpte)

LEGUÉRINGEL, Franck (bar)
Auber: Gustav III (Cpte)
Bizet: Carmen (Cpte)

LEHANE, Maureen (mez)
Meyerbeer: Huguenots (Cpte)
R. Strauss: Elektra (Cpte)

LEHÁR, Franz (cond)
see Berlin SO
Berlin St Op Orch
Berlin Staatskapelle
Vienna SO
Vienna St Op Orch
VPO

LEHEL, György (cond)
see Budapest SO

LEHMANN, Lilli (sop)
(NIMB) **NI7840/1** The Era of Adelina Patti
(PEAR) **GEMMCDS9923(2)** Covent Garden on Record, Vol.1 (pt 2)

LEHMANN, Lotte (sop)
Wagner: Walküre (exc)
(EMI) **CDH7 64029-2** Richard Tauber - Opera Recital
(EMI) **CDH7 69787-2** Richard Tauber sings Operetta Arias
(EMI) **CHS7 64487-2** R. Strauss—Der Rosenkavalier & Lieder
(EMI) **CMS7 64008-2(1)** Wagner Singing on Record (pt 1)
(MMOI) **CDMOIR406** Mozart—Historical Recordings
(MMOI) **CDMOIR408** Great Sopranos
(MMOI) **CDMOIR412** Great Voices of the Century Sing Puccini
(MMOI) **CDMOIR422** Great Voices in Tchaikovsky
(MSCM) **MM30283** Great Wagnerian Singers, Vol.1
(MSCM) **MM30285** Great Wagnerian Singers, Vol.2
(NIMB) **NI7802** Divas 1906-1935
(NIMB) **NI7830** Richard Tauber in Opera
(NIMB) **NI7851** Legendary Voices
(PEAR) **GEMMCDS9365** R. Strauss: Der Rosenkavalier (abridged), etc
(PEAR) **GEMMCDS9925(2)** Covent Garden on Record—Vol.3 (pt 2)
(PEAR) **GEMMCDS9926(2)** Covent Garden on Record—Vol.4 (pt 2)
(PEAR) **GEMMCD9409** Lotte Lehmenn—Vol.1
(PEAR) **GEMMCD9410** Lotte Lehmann—Vol.2
(PREI) **89302** The Young Lotte Lehmann
(SCHW) **314622** Vienna State Opera Live, Vol.12

LEHR, LeRoy (bass)
Copland: Tender Land (Cpte)

LEHRBERGER, Thomas (ten)
Weill: Mahagonny (Cpte), Zar lässt sich Photographieren (Cpte)

LEIB, Günther (bass)
Beethoven: Fidelio (Cpte)
Wagner: Rienzi (Cpte)
Weber: Freischütz (exc)

LEIBOWITZ, René (cond)
see Paris Cons
RPO

LEICHT, Georg (bass)
Nielsen: Maskarade (Cpte)

LEIDER, Frida (sop)
(CLAR) **CDGSE78-50-26** Wagner: Tristan und Isolde excerpts
(CLAR) **CDGSE78-50-35/6** Wagner—Historical recordings
(DANA) **DACOCD313/4** Lauritz Melchior Anthology - Vol. 2
(DANA) **DACOCD315/6** Lauritz Melchior Anthology - Vol. 3
(EMI) **CMS7 64008-2(2)** Wagner Singing on Record (pt 2)
(LYRC) **LCD146** Frida Leider sings Wagner
(MMOI) **CDMOIR406** Mozart—Historical Recordings
(MMOI) **CDMOIR408** Great Sopranos
(MSCM) **MM30283** Great Wagnerian Singers, Vol.1
(MSCM) **MM30285** Great Wagnerian Singers, Vol.2
(NIMB) **NI7848** Great Singers at the Berlin State Opera
(PEAR) **GEMMCDS9137** Wagner—Der Ring des Nibelungen
(PEAR) **GEMMCDS9925(2)** Covent Garden on Record—Vol.3 (pt 2)
(PEAR) **GEMMCDS9926(1)** Covent Garden on Record—Vol.4 (pt 1)
(PEAR) **GEMMCD9331** Frida Leider sings Wagner
(PREI) **89004** Frida Leider (1888-1975) - I
(PREI) **89032** Lauritz Melchior (1890-1973) - I
(PREI) **89098** Frida Leider (1888-1975) - II
(PREI) **89301** The Art of Frida Leider

LEIDLAND, Hilde (sop)
Dusapin: Medeamaterial (Cpte)
Mozart: Nozze di Figaro (Cpte)
Wagner: Götterdämmerung (exc), Parsifal (Cpte), Rheingold (exc), Siegfried (exc)

LEIFERKUS, Sergei (bar)
Beethoven: Fidelio (Cpte)
Borodin: Prince Igor (Cpte)
Mussorgsky: Boris Godunov (Cpte)
Tchaikovsky: Mazeppa (Cpte), Queen of Spades (Cpte)
Verdi: Otello (Cpte)
Wagner: Lohengrin (Cpte)

LEIGHTON SMITH, Laurence (cond)
see Moscow PO

LEINMARK, Bo (ten)
Mozart: Nozze di Figaro (Cpte)

LEINSDORF, Erich (cond)
see Boston SO
Cleveland Orch
Concert Arts SO
Los Angeles PO
LSO
Munich RO
New Philh
NY Met Op Orch
Philh
RCA Italiana Op Orch
RCA Victor Orch
Rome Op Chor
Rome Op. Orch
VPO

LEIPNITZ, Harald (spkr)
Mozart: Entführung (Cpte)

LEIPZIG GEWANDHAUS ORCHESTRA
cond K. MASUR
Beethoven: Fidelio (Cpte)
R. Strauss: Ariadne auf Naxos (Cpte)
(PHIL) **438 706-2PM2** Beethoven—Overtures; Minuets; Dances
(TELD) **9031-76456-2** Tchaikovsky—Orchestral Works
cond V. NEUMANN
Gluck: Orfeo ed Euridice (Cpte)
cond L. ZAGROSEK
Krenek: Jonny spielt auf (Cpte)

(DECC) **440 854-2DH** Ullmann—Der Kaiser von Atlantis

LEIPZIG OPERA CHORUS
cond L. ZAGROSEK
Krenek: Jonny spielt auf (Cpte)

LEIPZIG RADIO CHORUS
Beethoven: Fidelio (Cpte)
Gluck: Orfeo ed Euridice (Cpte)
Mozart: Clemenza di Tito (Cpte), Entführung (Cpte), Idomeneo (Cpte), Zauberflöte (Cpte)
Offenbach: Contes d'Hoffmann (exc)
Schoenberg: Moses und Aron (Cpte)
Tchaikovsky: Eugene Onegin (Cpte)
Wagner: Götterdämmerung (Cpte), Meistersinger (Cpte), Parsifal (Cpte), Rienzi (Cpte), Tristan und Isolde (Cpte)
Weber: Freischütz (Cpte)
(CFP) **CD-CFP4656** Herbert von Karajan conducts Opera
(DG) **431 601-2GCE10** Tchaikovsky Compact Edition
(EURO) **GD69003** Wagner—Der Ring des Nibelungen

LEIPZIG RADIO SYMPHONY ORCHESTRA
cond H. KEGEL
Schoenberg: Moses und Aron (Cpte)
Wagner: Parsifal (Cpte)
cond R. MERTEN
(PREI) **89076** Josef Herrmann (1903-1955)
cond H. WEISBACH
(PREI) **90200** Hans Hotter in Early Recordings

LEIPZIG ST THOMAS CHURCH CHOIR
cond H. KEGEL
Wagner: Parsifal (Cpte)

LEISENHEIMER, Reinhard (ten)
Schreker: Ferne Klang (Cpte)

LEISNER, Emmi (contr)
(PEAR) **GEMMCDS9137** Wagner—Der Ring des Nibelungen
(PREI) **89201** Helge Roswaenge (1897-1972) - I
(PREI) **89210** The Art of Emmi Leisner

LEITAO, Manuel (ten)
Verdi: Traviata (Cpte)

LEITNER, Ferdinand (cond)
see Bamberg SO
Berlin Deutsche Op Orch
BRSO
Cappella Coloniensis
Cologne RSO
Munich PO
Vienna SO

LEITNER, Konrad (cond)
see Eslovaca Philharmonica Orch
Vienna Mozart Orch

LEITNER, Lotte (sop)
Mozart: Zauberflöte (Cpte)
R. Strauss: Rosenkavalier (Cpte)

LEITNER, Luise (sop)
Einem: Prozess (Cpte)
Mozart: Zauberflöte (Cpte)

LEITNER, Markus (alto)
Mozart: Zauberflöte (Cpte)

LEJEUNE-GILIBERT, Gabrielle (mez)
(RCA) **GD60495(3)** The Complete Caruso Collection (pt 3)
(RCA) **09026 61244-2** Caruso sings French Opera Arias

LELIO, Loretta di (sop)
Verdi: Don Carlo (Cpte)

LELIWA, Tadeusz (ten)
(CLUB) **CL99-089** Adamo Didur (1874-1946)

LEMAN CHORUS
cond A. GUADAGNO
(DECC) **436 301-2DA** Renata Tebaldi & Franco Corelli—Arias & Duets

LEMARIOVÁ, Marcela (mez)
Hába: Mother (Cpte)
Janáček: Káťa Kabanová (Cpte)
Martinů: Julietta (Cpte)

LEMESHEV, Sergei (ten)
Tchaikovsky: Eugene Onegin (Cpte)
(ARLE) **ARL23/5** Rimsky-Korsakov—Sadko

LEMKE, David (bass)
Meyerbeer: Huguenots (Cpte)

LEMMONÉ, John (fl)
(LARR) **CDLRH221** Dame Nellie Melba - Opera and Song Recital

LEMNITZ, Tiana (sop)
Mozart: Zauberflöte (Cpte)
Wagner: Meistersinger (exc)
(DUTT) **CDLX7007** Beecham conducts Wagner
(EMI) **CMS7 64008-2(1)** Wagner Singing on Record (pt 1)
(MMOI) **CDMOIR406** Mozart—Historical Recordings
(MMOI) **CDMOIR408** Great Sopranos
(NIMB) **NI7848** Great Singers at the Berlin State Opera
(PEAR) **GEMMCDS9926(2)** Covent Garden on Record—Vol.4 (pt 2)
(PREI) **89025** Tiana Lemnitz (b. 1897)
(PREI) **89035** Erna Berger (1900-1990) - I
(PREI) **89077** Torsten Ralf (1901-1954)
(PREI) **89209** Helge Roswaenge (1897-1972) - II
(PREI) **89211** Helge Roswaenge (1897-1972) - III
(PREI) **90222** Maria Cebotari sings Richard Strauss
(SCHW) **314672** Vienna State Opera Live, Vol.17

LEMPER, Ute (sop)
Weill: Dreigroschenoper (Cpte), Mahagonny-Gesänge (Cpte), Sieben Todsünden (Cpte)
(DECC) **425 204-2DNL** Ute Lemper sings Kurt Weill
(DECC) **436 417-2DH** Ute Lemper sings Kurt Weill, Vol.2

LENÁRD, Ondrej (cond)
see Bratislava RSO
Brno St PO
Czech RSO

LENCHNER, Paula (sop)
Bizet: Carmen (Cpte)

LENDI, Lucretia (mez)
Rossini: Tancredi (Cpte)

LENHART, Renate (sngr)
Monteverdi: Incoronazione di Poppea (Cpte)
Zemlinsky: Kleider machen Leute (Cpte)

LENINGRAD KIROV THEATRE CHORUS
cond V. GERGIEV
Mussorgsky: Khovanshchina (Cpte)

LENINGRAD KIROV THEATRE ORCHESTRA
cond V. GERGIEV
Mussorgsky: Khovanshchina (Cpte)

LENINGRAD PHILHARMONIC ORCHESTRA
cond E. MRAVINSKY
(ERAT) **2292-45757-2** Popular Russian Orchestral Works
(ERAT) **2292-45762-2** Orchestral Music from Wagner's Operas
(ERAT) **2292-45763-2** Mravinsky conducts... (including free CD interview & rehearsal)
(MELO) **74321 25189-2** Yevgeny Mravinsky Edition - Vols 1-10
(MELO) **74321 25190-2** Mravinsky Edition, Vol 1
(MELO) **74321 25191-2** Mravinsky Edition, Vol 2
(MELO) **74321 25199-2** Mravinsky Edition, Vol 10
(OLYM) **OCD5002** The Mravinsky Legacy—Volumes 1-6
(RUSS) **RDCD10905** The Mravinsky Collection
(RUSS) **RDCD10907** The Mravinsky Collection—Brahms/Sibelius/Weber
(RUSS) **RDCD11166** Wagner—Orchestral excerpts from Operas
cond G. ROZHDESTVENSKY
(RCA) **74321 29251-2** Janáček—Orchestral Works
cond Y. TEMIRKANOV
(RCA) **RD60739** Tchaikovsky Gala in Leningrad
(RCA) **09026 60739-5** Tchaikovsky Gala in Leningrad

LENNOX, David (ten)
Berlioz: Troyens (Cpte)
Mozart: Nozze di Figaro (Cpte)

LENOTY, René (ten)
Audran: Miss Helyett (Cpte), Poupée (exc)
Bazin: Voyage en Chine (Cpte)
Ganne: Hans (Cpte)
Messager: Coups de Roulis (Cpte), Monsieur Beaucaire (Cpte), Passionêment (Cpte)
Offenbach: Madame l'Archiduc (Cpte)
Planquette: Rip van Winkle (Cpte)
Terrasse: Travaux d'Hercule (Cpte)
(MUSD) **20239-2** Delibes—Opéras-Comiques

LENSKY, Margaret (contr)
Purcell: Dido (Cpte)
(DG) **439 474-2GCL** Purcell—Opera & Choral Works

LENYA, Lotte (sop)
Weill: Happy End (Cpte), Mahagonny (Cpte), Sieben Todsünden (Cpte)

LENZ, Friedrich (ten)
Beethoven: Fidelio (Cpte)
Egk: Peer Gynt (Cpte)
Humperdinck: Königskinder (Cpte)
Lehár: Giuditta (Cpte)
Leoncavallo: Bohème (Cpte)
Mozart: Entführung (Cpte), Nozze di Figaro (Cpte), Zauberflöte (Cpte)
Nicolai: Lustigen Weiber von Windsor (Cpte)
Pfitzner: Palestrina (Cpte)
R. Strauss: Rosenkavalier (Cpte)
Verdi: Traviata (Cpte)
Wagner: Meistersinger (Cpte)

LENZI, Arnoldo (bar)
Verdi: Traviata (Cpte)

LEO, Accurzio di (narr)
Bizet: Carmen (Cpte)

LEOLINI, Paola (sop)
Salieri: Locandiera (Cpte)

LEONARD, J. Michael (sax/cl)
(ASV) **CDWHL2085** Saxophone Serenade

LEONARD, Patricia (contr)
(LOND) **436 813-2LM2** Sullivan—The Grand Duke. Overture Di Ballo. Henry VIII

LEONCAVALLO, Ruggero (pf)
(SUPR) **11 2136-2(1)** Emmy Destinn—Complete Edition, Discs 1 & 2

LEONEL, Antonio (ten)
Puccini: Tabarro (Cpte)

LEONHARDT, Carl (cond)
see Stuttgart RSO

LEONHARDT, Gustav (cond)
see Collegium Aureum
Petite Bande

LEONHARDT, Gustav (hpd)
Grétry: Jugement de Midas (exc)

LEONI, Limbania (mez)
Verdi: Rigoletto (Cpte)

LEOZ, Alfonso (ten)
Rossini: Otello (Cpte)

LEPPARD, Raymond (cond)
see ASMF
ECO
F. Liszt CO
Glyndebourne Fest Orch
LPO
New Philh
Paris Op Orch
Santa Fé Op Orch
Scottish CO

LEPRIN, Frédéric (ten)
Bizet: Carmen (Cpte)
Poulenc: Mamelles de Tirésias (Cpte)

LEQUENNE, A. (sngr)
(MUSD) **20239-2** Delibes—Opéras-Comiques

LEREBOURS, Pascal (pf)
(AUVI) **V4662** International Competitions Prize-Winners

LERER, Norma (mez)
Fauré: Pénélope (Cpte)
Monteverdi: Ritorno d'Ulisse in Patria (Cpte)
Rameau: Castor et Pollux (Cpte)

LERNER, Mimi (mez)
Mozart: Zauberflöte (Cpte)
(EMI) **CDC7 54643-2** Rossini—Bicentenary Gala Concert
(EMI) **LDB491007-1 (EMI)** Rossini Bicentennial Birthday Gala

LEROUX, Xavier (pf)
(IRCC) **IRCC-CD802** Souvenirs of Rare French Opera

LESKAYA, Anna (sop)
(RCA) **GD60522** Alexander Kipnis—Opera & Song Recital

LESLEY-GREEN, Carol (sop)
Sullivan: Yeomen of the Guard (exc)

LESNE, Gérard (alto)
Fux: Dafne in Lauro (Cpte)
Handel: Poro (Cpte)
M-A. Charpentier: David et Jonathas (Cpte)
Vivaldi: Olimpiade (Cpte)

LESTELLY (ten)
Terrasse: Travaux d'Hercule (Cpte)

LESTER, Harold (hpd)
Purcell: Dido (Cpte)

LESTER, Harold (hpd/org)
(INA) **262004** Alfred Deller—Renaissance and Baroque songs

LESTER, Todd (voc)
Bernstein: West Side Story (Cpte)

LESTRIGANT, Etienne (ten)
Purcell: Dido (Cpte)
(HARM) **HMX290 1528/33(1)** A Purcell Companion (pt 1)

LEUTGEB, Johann (bar)
Ligeti: Grand Macabre (Cpte)

LEVALLIER, Adam (spkr)
Offenbach: Belle Hélène (Cpte)

LEVASSEUR, Jeanette (sngr)
Ganne: Hans (Cpte)
Offenbach: Madame l'Archiduc (Cpte)

LEVENTAL, Alexander (organ)
Knaifel: Canterville Ghost (exc)

LEVI, Yoel (cond)
see Atlanta SO

LEVIN, Mats (vc)
(BLUE) **ABCD038** 4 X Göran W. Nilson

LEVIN, Robert (pf)
(VICT) **VCD19037** Brynjar Hoff - Encores for Oboe

LEVIN, Sylvan (cond)
see RCA SO

LEVINE, James (cond)
see Bayreuth Fest Orch
BPO
LSO
National PO
New Philh
NY Met Op Orch
Philh
RCA Italiana Op Orch
Staatskapelle Dresden
VPO

LEVINE, James (pf)
(DECC) **071 119-1DH (DECC)** Pavarotti and Levine in Recital at the Met
(DG) **419 237-2GH** Schubert: Lieder

(DG) **445 524-2GMA** Battle in Salzburg

LEVINSKY, Ilya (ten)
Shostakovich: Lady Macbeth of Mtsensk (Cpte)

LEVITZKI, Mischa (pf)
(APR) **APR7014** Romantic Piano Rarities, Vol.2
(APR) **APR7020** Mischa Levitzki—The Complete HMV Recordings, 1927-33

LEVKO, Valentina (mez)
Tchaikovsky: Queen of Spades (Cpte)

LEVKO-ANTOSCH, Olga (sop)
(SCHW) **314572** Vienna State Opera Live, Vol.7
(SCHW) **314602** Vienna State Opera Live, Vol.10
(SCHW) **314632** Vienna State Opera Live, Vol.13
(SCHW) **314742** Vienna State Opera Live, Vol.24

LEVY, T. (cond)
see orch

LEWINGTON, James (ten)
G. Charpentier: Louise (Cpte)
Shostakovich: Lady Macbeth of Mtsensk (Cpte)

LEWIS, Sir **Anthony (cond)**
see ECO
Handel Fest Orch
Philomusica of London

LEWIS, Bertha (contr)
Sullivan: Gondoliers (Cpte), HMS Pinafore (Cpte), Patience (Cpte)
(MMOI) **CDMOIR413** The Very Best of Gilbert & Sullivan

LEWIS, Henry (cond)
see Munich RO
orch
Philh
ROHO
RPO
SRO
Turin RAI Orch
Vienna Cantata Orch
Vienna Op Orch

LEWIS, Keith (ten)
A. Thomas: Hamlet (Cpte)
Monteverdi: Incoronazione di Poppea (Cpte)
Mozart: Don Giovanni (Cpte)
R. Strauss: Arabella (Cpte)
Rossini: Mosè in Egitto (Cpte), Otello (Cpte), Tancredi (Cpte)
Schumann: Genoveva (Cpte)
(KIWI) **CDSLD-82** Southern Voices—NZ International Opera Singers

LEWIS, Mary (sop)
(BEUL) **1PD13** Sir Malcolm Sargent conducts British Music
(PEAR) **GEMMCD9468** Vaughan Williams

LEWIS, Michael (bass)
J. Strauss II: Fledermaus (Cpte)
Massenet: Werther (exc)
Puccini: Bohème (Cpte)

LEWIS, Richard (ten)
Mozart: Così fan tutte (exc), Idomeneo (Cpte)
R. Strauss: Salome (Cpte)
Sullivan: Gondoliers (Cpte), HMS Pinafore (Cpte), Mikado (Cpte), Trial by Jury (Cpte), Yeomen of the Guard (Cpte)
Walton: Troilus and Cressida (exc)
(CFP) **CD-CFP4238** Gilbert and Sullivan
(CFP) **CD-CFP4582** Flowers in Music
(CFP) **CD-CFP4609** Favourite Gilbert & Sullivan
(EMI) **CDH5 65072-2** Glyndebourne Recorded - 1934-1994
(EMI) **CMS7 64409-2** Sullivan—Pirates of Penzance & Orch. Works
(EMI) **CMS7 64412-2** Gilbert & Sullivan—Ruddigore/Shakespeare Music

LEWIS, Ronald (bar)
Britten: Billy Budd (Cpte)

LEWIS, William (ten)
Berlioz: Troyens (Cpte)
V. Thomson: Mother of us all (Cpte)
(RPO) **CDRPO7019** The Sword and The Grail
(VANG) **08.4016.71** Music of Samuel Barber

LICATA, Andrea (cond)
see Bellini Th Orch
RPO

LICETTE, Miriam (sop)
Gounod: Faust (Cpte)
(PEAR) **GEMMCDS9925(1)** Covent Garden on Record—Vol.3 (pt 1)
(PEAR) **GEMMCD9130** Great Sopranos, Vol.2
(PEAR) **GEMMCD9175** Heddle Nash - Serenade
(PEAR) **GEMMCD9319** Heddle Nash sings Opera Arias & Songs
(PEAR) **GEMMCD9473** Heddle Nash—Vol.2

LICHA, Robert (ten)
R. Strauss: Rosenkavalier (Cpte)
Wagner: Meistersinger (Cpte)

LICHTENBERGER, Hannes (bass)
R. Strauss: Rosenkavalier (Cpte)
Verdi: Battaglia di Legnano (Cpte)

LIEB, Günther (bar)
Weber: Freischütz (Cpte)

LIEBAN, Julius (ten)
(SUPR) **11 2136-2(3)** Emmy Destinn—Complete Edition, Discs 5 to 8

LIEBERMANN, Melinda (sop)
Glass: Akhnaten (Cpte)

LIEBESBERG, Else (sop)
Kálmán: Csárdásfürstin (exc)
Lehár: Graf von Luxemburg (exc), Paganini (exc)
O. Straus: Walzertraum (exc)

LIEBL, Karl (ten)
Mozart: Zauberflöte (Cpte)

LIEBMANN, Heike (contr)
R. Strauss: Rosenkavalier (Cpte)

LIECKE, Karl Rudolf (sngr)
Schultze: Schwarzer Peter (Cpte)

LIÈGE PHILHARMONIC ORCHESTRA
cond P. BARTHOLOMÉE
Lekeu: Burgraves
(RICE) **RIS084067** Lekeu—Symphonic Works

LIER, Ellen van (sop)
(EURO) **GD69043** Puccini: Il Trittico

LIEWEHR, Fred (narr)
J. Strauss II: Wiener Blut (exc)

LIEWEHR, Fred (ten)
Mozart: Zauberflöte (Cpte)

LIGABUE, Ilva (sop)
Boito: Nerone (Cpte)
Massenet: Werther (Cpte)
Verdi: Falstaff (Cpte)

LIGENDZA, Catarina (sop)
R. Strauss: Elektra (Cpte)
Wagner: Götterdämmerung (Cpte), Meistersinger (Cpte)
Weber: Freischütz (Cpte)
(BELA) **450 121-2** Plácido Domingo
(DG) **431 104-2GB** Great Voices - Plácido Domingo
(DG) **435 211-2GX15** Wagner—Der Ring des Nibelungen

LIGHTFOOT, Peter (bass-bar)
Massenet: Cid (Cpte)

LIGI, Josella (sop)
Handel: Giulio Cesare (Cpte)

LIGUORI, Maria Grazia (sop)
Stradella: Moro per amore (Cpte)

LIKA, Peter (bass)
Busoni: Arlecchino (Cpte)
Donizetti: Don Pasquale (Cpte)
Egk: Peer Gynt (Cpte)
Flotow: Martha (Cpte)
Gluck: Alceste (1776) (Cpte)

LILJE, Peeter (cond)
see Estonia Op Orch

LILJEFORS, Mats (cond)
see Swedish CO

LILLE NATIONAL ORCHESTRA
cond J-C. CASADESUS
Ancelin: Filius Hominis (Cpte)

LILLEQVIST, Torbjörn (ten)
Mozart: Nozze di Figaro (Cpte), Zauberflöte (Cpte)

LILLESØE, Susse (sop)
Mussorgsky: Boris Godunov (Cpte)
Zemlinsky: Es war einmal (Cpte)

LILLEY, Barbara (sop)
(LOND) **436 813-2LM2** Sullivan—The Grand Duke. Overture Di Ballo. Henry VIII

LILOWA, Margarita (mez)
Mozart: Nozze di Figaro (Cpte)
Mussorgsky: Boris Godunov (Cpte)
Offenbach: Contes d'Hoffmann (Cpte)
Ponchielli: Gioconda (Cpte)
R. Strauss: Arabella (Cpte), Elektra (Cpte), Rosenkavalier (Cpte)
Tchaikovsky: Eugene Onegin (Cpte)
Wagner: Parsifal (Cpte), Walküre (exc)

LIMA, Luis (ten)
Bizet: Carmen (Cpte)
Massenet: Roi de Lahore (Cpte)
Verdi: Don Carlo (Cpte)
Vives: Bohemios (Cpte)
(CAST) **CVI2065** Highlights from the Royal Opera House, Covent Garden

LIMBERG CATHEDRAL CHILDREN'S CHOIR
cond A. GUADAGNO
Puccini: Bohème (Cpte)

LIMPT, Adriaan van (ten)
R. Strauss: Rosenkavalier (Cpte)

LIN, Cho-Liang (vn)
(CBS) **CD39133** Bravura - Violin Showpieces

LINAY, Samuel (treb)
Delius: Village Romeo and Juliet (Cpte)
Janáček: Fate (Cpte)
(ASV) **CDDCA758** Falla, Milhaud & Stravinsky—Operas

LIND, Eva (sop)
Humperdinck: Hänsel und Gretel (Cpte)
J. Strauss II: Fledermaus (Cpte)
Mozart: Finta semplice (Cpte), Zauberflöte (Cpte)
Offenbach: Contes d'Hoffmann (exc)
R. Strauss: Ariadne auf Naxos (Cpte), Frau ohne Schatten (Cpte)
Weber: Freischütz (exc)

LIND, Joanna (sngr)
Rapchak: Lifework of Juan Diaz (Cpte)

LIND, Lane (sngr)
Kuhlau: Lulu (Cpte)

LINDBERG, Christian (tbn)
(BIS) **BIS-CD258** The Virtuoso Trombone
(BIS) **BIS-CD328** The Criminal Trombone
(BIS) **BIS-CD478** The Russian Trombone

LINDE, Robert von der (bass)
Wagner: Rienzi (exc)

LINDÉN, Magnus (bass)
Mozart: Così fan tutte (Cpte)

LINDENSTRAND, Sylvia (mez)
Börtz: Bacchae (Cpte)
Mozart: Così fan tutte (Cpte), Nozze di Figaro (Cpte)
Verdi: Falstaff (Cpte)

LINDERMEIER, Elisabeth (sop)
Wagner: Götterdämmerung (Cpte)

LINDGREN, Karl-Robert (bass)
Mozart: Nozze di Figaro (Cpte)

LINDHJEM, Thorbjøm (bar)
Bibalo: Gespenster (Cpte)

LINDHOLM, Berit (sop)
Berlioz: Troyens (Cpte)
Börtz: Bacchae (Cpte)
Wagner: Walküre (Cpte)
(DECC) **414 100-2DM15** Wagner: Der Ring des Nibelungen
(DECC) **421 313-2DA** Wagner: Der Ring des Nibelungen - Great Scenes
(DECC) **433 067-2DWO** Your Hundred Best Opera Tunes IV
(DECC) **436 300-2DX** Opera Gala Sampler
(DECC) **440 069-2DWO** The World of Wagner

LINDI, Aroldo (ten)
Verdi: Aida (Cpte)

LINDNER, Brigitte (sop)
Humperdinck: Königskinder (Cpte)
Lehár: Giuditta (Cpte)
Mozart: Zauberflöte (Cpte)
Suder: Kleider machen Leute (Cpte)

LINDROOS, Peter (ten)
Bergman: Singing Tree (Cpte)
Nielsen: Saul and David (Cpte)
(BIS) **BIS-CD373/4** Opera Scenes from Savaonlinna

LINDROOS, Petri (bass)
Bergman: Singing Tree (Cpte)

LINDSLEY, Celina (sop)
Busoni: Turandot (Cpte)
Gurlitt: Wozzeck (Cpte)
Henze: Bassariden (Cpte)
Hindemith: Nusch-Nuschi (Cpte)
Martinů: Ariane (Cpte)
Mysliveček: Bellerofonte (Cpte)
Schoeck: Massimilla Doni (Cpte)
Schulhoff: Plameny (Cpte)
Zemlinsky: Kreidekreis (Cpte)

LINK, Kurt (bar)
Schoenberg: Moses und Aron (Cpte)

LINOS, Glenys (sop)
Giordano: Andrea Chénier (Cpte)
Monteverdi: Orfeo (Cpte)

LINOS ENSEMBLE
Mozart: Così fan tutte (exc), Don Giovanni (exc), Entführung (exc), Nozze di Figaro (exc), Zauberflöte (exc)

LINTON, Charles (pf)
(RCA) **09026 61580-2(2)** RCA/Met 100 Singers, 100 Years (pt 2)

LINVAL, Monique (sop)
Bizet: Carmen (exc)
Delibes: Lakmé (Cpte)
(EMI) **CZS7 67872-2** Lehár—Operettas (highlights in French)
(RCA) **GD60205** Opera Choruses

LIONI, Elsa (sngr)
Maderna: Satyricon (Cpte)

LIOT, Raymond (sngr)
Ganne: Hans (Cpte)

LIPATTI, Dinu (pf)
(ARCI) **ARC112/3** Dinu Lipatti—Les Inédits

LIPKOWSKA, Lydia (sop)
(MMOI) **CDMOIR422** Great Voices in Tchaikovsky
(NIMB) **NI7865** Great Singers at the Mariinsky Theatre
(PEAR) **GEMMCDS9004/6(1)** Singers of Imperial Russia, Vol.3 (pt 1)
(PEAR) **GEMMCDS9925(1)** Covent Garden on Record—Vol.3 (pt 1)

LIPOVŠEK, Marjana (mez)
Einem: Dantons Tod (Cpte)
Gounod: Faust (Cpte)
Humperdinck: Hänsel und Gretel (Cpte)
J. Strauss II: Fledermaus (exc)
Mozart: Zauberflöte (Cpte)

Mussorgsky: Boris Godunov (Cpte), Khovanshchina (Cpte)
R. Strauss: Elektra (Cpte), Frau ohne Schatten (Cpte)
Schoeck: Penthesilea (Cpte)
Wagner: Götterdämmerung (Cpte), Rheingold (Cpte), Tristan und Isolde (Cpte), Walküre (Cpte)
(EMI) **LDX9 91275-1(EMI)** Sawallisch conducts Wagner's Ring
(EURO) **GD69043** Puccini: Il Trittico
(ORFE) **C179891A** Marjana Lipovšek sings Famous Opera Arias

LIPP, Wilma (sop)
J. Strauss II: Fledermaus (exc), Wiener Blut (exc)
Janáček: Excursions of Mr Brouček (Cpte)
Mozart: Zauberflöte (Cpte)
R. Strauss: Rosenkavalier (Cpte)
(DECC) **443 530-2LF2** Mozart—Die Entführung aus dem Serail
(EURO) **GD69022** Oscar Straus: Operetta excerpts
(ORFE) **C394201B** Great Mozart Singers Series, Vol. 2

LIPPERT, Herbert (ten)
J. Strauss II: Zigeunerbaron (Cpte)
Mozart: Zauberflöte (Cpte)
R. Strauss: Frau ohne Schatten (Cpte)
Schreker: Gezeichneten (Cpte)
(DECC) **440 854-2DH** Ullmann—Der Kaiser von Atlantis

LIPPI, Marcello (bass)
Bellini: Capuleti (Cpte)
Cavalli: Calisto (Cpte)
Rossini: Gazza ladra (Cpte), Siège de Corinthe (Cpte)

LIS, Sofia (sop)
Leoncavallo: Bohème (Cpte)
Verdi: Alzira (Cpte)

LISBON GULBENKIAN FOUNDATION ORCHESTRA
cond M. SWIERCZEWSKI
(NIMB) **NI5184/5** Méhul: Orchestral Works

LISBON SAN CARLOS NATIONAL THEATRE CHORUS
cond F. GHIONE
Verdi: Traviata (Cpte)
(EMI) **CMS7 63244-2** The Art of Maria Callas

LISBON SAN CARLOS NATIONAL THEATRE ORCHESTRA
cond F. GHIONE
Verdi: Traviata (Cpte)
(EMI) **CDC5 55016-2** Maria Callas - La Divina 2
(EMI) **CDC7 49502-2** Maria Callas—The Voice of the Century
(EMI) **CDC7 54702-2** Maria Callas - La Divina
(EMI) **CMS7 63244-2** The Art of Maria Callas
(MEMO) **HR4233/4** Alfredo Kraus—Public Performances

LISI, Leonardo de (sngr)
Mercadante: Bravo (Cpte)

LISITSIAN, Pavel (bar)
(ARLE) **ARL23/5** Rimsky-Korsakov—Sadko
(EMI) **CHS7 69741-2(6)** Record of Singing, Vol.4—Russian & Slavonic Schools
(PREI) **89061** Pavel Lisitian (born 1911)

LIŠKA, Bohumír (cond)
see Czech PO

LISO, Giovanna de (sop)
Mercadante: Giuramento (Cpte)

LISOWSKA, Hanna (sop)
Wagner: Götterdämmerung (Cpte)
(DG) **072 422-3GH7** Levine conducts Wagner's Ring

LISS, Rhonda (mez)
Glass: Satyagraha (Cpte)

LIST, Emanuel (bass)
Beethoven: Fidelio (Cpte)
Wagner: Götterdämmerung (exc), Siegfried (Cpte), Tannhäuser (Cpte), Tristan und Isolde (Cpte), Walküre (Cpte)
(EMI) **CMS7 64008-2(2)** Wagner Singing on Record (pt 2)
(PEAR) **GEMMCDS9137** Wagner—Der Ring des Nibelungen
(PEAR) **GEMMCD9122** 20 Great Basses sing Great Arias
(PREI) **89083** Emanuel List (1890-1967)

(FRANZ) LISZT CHAMBER ORCHESTRA
(TELD) **9031-74789-2** Canon and Gigue—Popular Classics
cond R. LEPPARD
(SONY) **SK45855** Mozart: Bastien und Bastienne

LITAKER, Donald (ten)
Wagner: Tannhäuser (Cpte)

LITTASY, György (bass)
Mozart: Idomeneo (Cpte)
R. Strauss: Elektra (Cpte)

LITTLE, Frank (ten)
Verdi: Otello (Cpte)

LITTLE, Vera (contr)
Henze: Junge Lord (Cpte)
R. Strauss: Daphne (Cpte)
Wagner: Walküre (Cpte)
(DECC) **414 100-2DM15** Wagner: Der Ring des Nibelungen
(DECC) **421 313-2DA** Wagner: Der Ring des Nibelungen - Great Scenes
(DECC) **433 067-2DWO** Your Hundred Best Opera Tunes IV
(DECC) **436 300-2DX** Opera Gala Sampler
(DECC) **440 069-2DWO** The World of Wagner

LITTLEJOHN, Hubert (bass)
Britten: Billy Budd (Cpte)

LITTON, Andrew (cond)
see Bournemouth SO
Philh
RPO

LITVINNE, Félia (sop)
(NIMB) **NI7840/1** The Era of Adelina Patti
(PEAR) **GEMMCDS9923(2)** Covent Garden on Record, Vol.1 (pt 2)
(SYMP) **SYMCD1101** The Harold Wayne Collection, Vol.9
(SYMP) **SYMCD1128** The Harold Wayne Collection, Vol.15
(SYMP) **SYMCD1173** The Harold Wayne Collection, Vol.22

LITZ, Gisela (mez)
Lehár: Graf von Luxemburg (Cpte)
Millöcker: Bettelstudent (Cpte)
Nicolai: Lustigen Weiber von Windsor (Cpte)
Wagner: Götterdämmerung (Cpte), Rheingold (Cpte), Walküre (Cpte)
Weill: Mahagonny (Cpte)
Zeller: Vogelhändler (Cpte)
(EMI) **CZS7 62993-2** Fritz Wunderlich—Great German Tenor
(FOYE) **15-CF2011** Wagner—Der Ring de Nibelungen

LIVENGOOD, Victoria (sop)
Weber: Oberon (Cpte)

LIVERPOOL PHILHARMONIC CHOIR
cond D. ATHERTON
Holst: At the Boar's Head (Cpte)

LIVERPOOL PHILHARMONIC ORCHESTRA
cond M. SARGENT
(PEAR) **GEMMCD9175** Heddle Nash - Serenade

LIVINGSTONE, David (voc)
Bernstein: West Side Story (Cpte)

LIVINGSTONE, Laureen (sop)
Kálmán: Gräfin Mariza (exc)

LIVORNO CEL-TEATRO CHORUS
cond B. RIGACCI
Mascagni: Rantzau (Cpte)

LIVORNO CEL-TEATRO ORCHESTRA
cond B. RIGACCI
Mascagni: Rantzau (Cpte)

LIVORNO TEATRO LA GRAN GUARDIA ORCHESTRA
cond O. DE FABRITIIS
Mascagni: Piccolo Marat (Cpte), Piccolo Marat (Cpte)

LJUBLJANA RADIO CHORUS
cond ANON
(WORD) **FCD7410** World's Greatest Choruses

LJUBLJANA RADIO ORCHESTRA
(WORD) **FCD7410** World's Greatest Choruses

LJUBLJANA RADIO SYMPHONY ORCHESTRA
cond S. HUBAD
(PREI) **90022** Anton Dermota
cond A. NANUT
(CAVA) **CAVCD003** Russian Orchestral Works

LJUNGBERG, Göta (sop)
Wagner: Götterdämmerung (exc)
(CLAR) **CDGSE78-50-26** Wagner: Tristan und Isolde excerpts
(CLAR) **CDGSE78-50-35/6** Wagner—Historical recordings
(CLAR) **CDGSE78-50-46** Walter Widdop (1892-1949)
(EMI) **CHS7 64673-2** Joseph Schmidt - Complete EMI Recordings Volume 1
(PEAR) **GEMMCDS9121** Wagner—Die Meistersinger, Act 3, etc
(PEAR) **GEMMCDS9137** Wagner—Der Ring des Nibelungen
(PEAR) **GEMMCDS9925(2)** Covent Garden on Record—Vol.3 (pt 2)
(PEAR) **GEMMCD9944** Friedrich Schorr sings Wagner
(PREI) **89098** Frida Leider (1888-1975) - II

LLOYD, David (ten)
Purcell: Dido (Cpte)
(SAIN) **SCDC2076** David Lloyd-Early Recordings, 1940-1941

LLOYD, George (cond)
see BBC Concert Orch
BBC PO
Philh

LLOYD, Robert (bass)
Beethoven: Fidelio (Cpte)
Berlioz: Benvenuto Cellini (Cpte), Béatrice et Bénédict (Cpte)
Bizet: Carmen (Cpte)
Britten: Little Sweep (Cpte)
Donizetti: Lucia di Lammermoor (Cpte)
Gay: Beggar's Opera (Cpte)
Gounod: Roméo et Juliette (Cpte)
Massenet: Esclarmonde (Cpte), Werther (Cpte)
Monteverdi: Incoronazione di Poppea (Cpte)
Mozart: Clemenza di Tito (Cpte), Don Giovanni (exc), Entführung (Cpte), Finta semplice (Cpte), Nozze di Figaro (exc), Zauberflöte (exc)
Mussorgsky: Boris Godunov (Cpte)
Offenbach: Contes d'Hoffmann (Cpte)
Puccini: Bohème (Cpte), Fanciulla del West (Cpte), Manon Lescaut (Cpte)
Rossini: Barbiere di Siviglia (Cpte), Siège de Corinthe (Cpte)
Saint-Saëns: Samson et Dalila (Cpte)
Sullivan: Yeomen of the Guard (exc)
Vaughan Williams: Hugh the Drover (Cpte), Pilgrim's Progress (Cpte)
Verdi: Ballo in maschera (Cpte), Don Carlo (Cpte), Giovanna d'Arco (Cpte), Macbeth (Cpte), Nabucco (exc), Rigoletto (Cpte), Trovatore (Cpte)
Wagner: Lohengrin (Cpte), Parsifal (Cpte), Rheingold (Cpte)
Walton: Troilus and Cressida (Cpte)
(CAST) **CVI2065** Highlights from the Royal Opera House, Covent Garden
(DECC) **425 681-2DM2** Tutto Pavarotti
(EMI) **CDM7 64356-2** Opera Choruses
(EMI) **CZS5 68559-2** Italian Opera Choruses
(PHIL) **434 986-2PM** Duetti Amorosi
(TELD) **9031-77676-6(TELD)** My World of Opera - Kiri Te Kanawa

LLOYD WEBBER, Julian (vc)
(PHIL) **412 231-2PH** Travels with my Cello
(PHIL) **416 698-2PH** Encore! Travels with my cello, Vol. 2

LLOYD-EVANS, Philip (bar)
Janáček: Fate (Cpte)
Sullivan: HMS Pinafore (Cpte)

LLOYD-JONES, Beti (mez)
Sullivan: Patience (Cpte)
(LOND) **436 813-2LM2** Sullivan—The Grand Duke. Overture Di Ballo. Henry VIII

LLOYD-ROBERTS, Jeffrey (ten)
Vaughan Williams: Pilgrim's Progress (Cpte)

LÖBL, Luděk (ten)
Shostakovich: Nose Suite

LOCHMANN, Daniel (treb)
Purcell: Dido (Cpte)

LOCK, Robert (sngr)
Romberg: Student Prince (Cpte)

LOCKE, Josef (ten)
(EMI) **CDP7 98844-2** Josef Locke—Hear My Song

LOCKE BRASS CONSORT
cond J. STOBART
(CRD) **CRD3402** Symphonic Marches for Concert Brass

LOCKHART, James (cond)
see ECO
Rhine State PO
RPO

LOGES, Karl-Heinz (cond)
see LSO

LOHNER, Helmut (bass)
J. Strauss II: Fledermaus (Cpte)

LOIBNER, Wilfriede (sop)
R. Strauss: Rosenkavalier (Cpte)

LOIBNER, Wilhelm (cond)
see Austrian St Rad Orch
Lower Austria Orch
Vienna St Op Orch

LOIRE PHILHARMONIC ORCHESTRA
cond G. CARELLA
Mercadante: Giuramento (Cpte)
cond P. DERVAUX
(EMI) **CDM7 63951-2** Rabaud—Orchestral Works
cond M. SOUSTROT
(FORL) **UCD16681** The Great Italian Arias
(PIER) **PV730022** Bizet—Symphony No 1; Offenbach—Overtures
(PIER) **PV792051** Chausson/Fauré—Orchestral Works

LOIRI, Vesa-Matti (sngr)
Sallinen: Kullervo (Cpte)

LOISEL, Jean-Marc (bass)
Saint-Saëns: Henry VIII (Cpte)

LOISELEUR DES LONGCHAMPS, Jacques-François (ten)
Rameau: Hippolyte et Aricie (Cpte)

LOJARRO, Daniela (sop)
(CAPR) **10 810** Mozart—Opera Highlights

LOKKA, Maija (sop)
Madetoja: Juha (Cpte)

LOMBANA, Sergio (ten)
Delius: Village Romeo and Juliet (Cpte)

LOMBARD, Alain (cond)
see Bordeaux Aquitaine Orch
Paris Op Orch
Paris Opéra-Comique Orch
Pasdeloup Ass Orch
SRO
Strasbourg PO
Vienna Volksoper Orch

LOMBARDO, Bernard (ten)
Cherubini: Lodoïska (Cpte)

Donizetti: Lucia di Lammermoor (exc)

LOMBARDO, Pasquale (bass)
Verdi: Due Foscari (Cpte)

LOMONOSOV, Aleksandr (ten)
Glinka: Life for the Tsar (Cpte)

LONDI, Laura (sop)
(RCA) **09026 62689-2** The Voices of Living Stereo, Volume 1

LONDON, George (bass-bar)
Mozart: Don Giovanni (Cpte), Nozze di Figaro (Cpte), Zauberflöte (Cpte)
Offenbach: Contes d'Hoffmann (Cpte)
Puccini: Tosca (Cpte)
R. Strauss: Arabella (Cpte)
Wagner: Parsifal (Cpte), Rheingold (Cpte), Walküre (Cpte)
(BELA) **450 007-2** Puccini Favourites
(DECC) **414 100-2DM15** Wagner: Der Ring des Nibelungen
(DECC) **421 313-2DA** Wagner: Der Ring des Nibelungen - Great Scenes
(DECC) **443 380-2DM** Ten Top Baritones & Basses 2
(EMI) **CHS7 69741-2(2)** Record of Singing, Vol.4—Anglo-American School (pt 2)
(SONY) **SM3K47211** Mozart Legendary Interpretations—Opera and Concert Arias

LONDON, Maurine (sop)
Wagner: Siegfried (Cpte)

LONDON BAROQUE
cond C. MEDLAM
Blow: Venus and Adonis (Cpte)
Monteverdi: Orfeo (Cpte)
(HARM) **HMA190 1244** Charpentier—Theatre Music; Sonatas

LONDON CAST
cond N. RHODEN
Gay: Beggar's Opera (Cpte)

LONDON CHORAL SOCIETY
cond A. INGLIS
(RPO) **CDRPO7025** Classical Spectacular 3
cond M. REED
(IMP) **TCD1070** Invitation to the Opera
(RPO) **CDRPD9001** Classical Spectacular
(RPO) **CDRPO5009** Classical Spectacular I

LONDON CLASSICAL PLAYERS
cond R. NORRINGTON
Mozart: Don Giovanni (Cpte), Zauberflöte (Cpte)
Purcell: Fairy Queen, Z629 (Cpte)
(EMI) **MDC7 54091-8** Rossini—Overtures
(EMI) **CDC5 55479-2** Wagner—Orchestral Works
(EMI) **CDC7 54091-2** Rossini—Overtures
(EMI) **DCC7 54091-5** Rossini—Overtures

(THE) LONDON CONCERT ARTISTS
(ASV) **CDWHL2070** Salut d'amour - Old Sweet Songs

LONDON CONCERT ORCHESTRA
cond M. DODS
(IMP) **PWK1157** Gilbert & Sullivan Spectacular

LONDON CORNETT AND SACKBUTT ENSEMBLE
cond T. CAUDLE
Monteverdi: Orfeo (Cpte)

LONDON FESTIVAL ORCHESTRA
cond J. ARMSTRONG
(ROSE) **3212** Wagner—Great Overtures
cond R. POPLE
(DG) **445 822-2GH** Une flûte à l'opéra
(HYPE) **CDH88030** Favourite Classics
cond K. REDEL
(INTR) **409 015-2** Mozart Edition, Vol.15

LONDON MOZART PLAYERS
cond H. BLECH
(TEST) **SBT1026** Irmgard Seefried
cond A. FRANCIS
Offenbach: Christopher Columbus (Cpte)
cond J. GLOVER
(ASV) **CDDCA683** Mozart—Arias

LONDON MUSICUM COLLEGIUM
cond P. CASALS
(MUSI) **MACD-689** Casals Festival at Prades, Volume II

LONDON OBOE BAND
cond P. GOODWIN
(HARM) **HMU90 7122** Lully/Philidor—Stage Works

LONDON OPERA CHORUS
Bellini: Sonnambula (Cpte)
Donizetti: Lucrezia Borgia (Cpte)
J. Adams: Death of Klinghoffer (Cpte)
Leoncavallo: Pagliacci (exc)
Mascagni: Cavalleria Rusticana (exc)
Mozart: Don Giovanni (Cpte), Nozze di Figaro (Cpte)
Ponchielli: Gioconda (Cpte)
Puccini: Tosca (exc)
Verdi: Ballo in maschera (Cpte), Luisa Miller (Cpte), Traviata (exc), Trovatore (Cpte)
(DECC) **425 681-2DM2** Tutto Pavarotti
(DECC) **430 470-2DH** Essential Pavarotti II
(DECC) **433 064-2DWO** Your Hundred Best Opera Tunes Volume I
(DECC) **433 065-2DWO** Your Hundred Best Opera Tunes Volume II
(DECC) **433 068-2DWO** Your Hundred Best Opera Tunes V
(DECC) **433 069-2DWO** Your Hundred Best Opera Tunes VI
(DECC) **433 221-2DWO** The World of Verdi
(DECC) **433 443-2DA** Great Opera Choruses
(DECC) **436 463-2DM** Ten Top Tenors
(DECC) **443 928-2DM** Montserrat Caballé sings Opera Arias
(DECC) **444 555-2DF2** Essential Puccini

LONDON ORCHESTRA NOVA
cond M. DAVIES
(EMI) **CDM7 64730-2** Vaughan Williams—Riders to the Sea; Epithalamion, etc

LONDON PHILHARMONIC CHOIR
cond A. BOULT
Vaughan Williams: Pilgrim's Progress (Cpte)
cond P. BRUNELLE
Britten: Paul Bunyan (exc)
cond K. NAGANO
Stravinsky: Perséphone (Cpte)

LONDON PHILHARMONIC ORCHESTRA CELLOS
cond G. SIMON
(CALA) **CACD0104** The London Cello Sound

LONDON PHILHARMONIC ORCHESTRA
Beethoven: Fidelio (Cpte)
Bizet: Carmen (Cpte)
Britten: Albert Herring (Cpte), Midsummer Night's Dream (Cpte)
Gershwin: Porgy and Bess (Cpte)
Gluck: Orfeo ed Euridice (Cpte)
Janáček: Jenufa (Cpte), Káta Kabanová (Cpte)
Monteverdi: Incoronazione di Poppea (Cpte)
Mozart: Così fan tutte (Cpte), Don Giovanni (Cpte), Entführung (Cpte), Idomeneo (Cpte), Nozze di Figaro (Cpte), Zauberflöte (Cpte)
Prokofiev: Love for 3 Oranges (Cpte)
R. Strauss: Arabella (Cpte), Intermezzo (Cpte)
Rossini: Barbiere di Siviglia (Cpte), Cenerentola (Cpte)
Stravinsky: Rake's Progress (Cpte)
Tchaikovsky: Queen of Spades (Cpte)
Verdi: Falstaff (Cpte), Macbeth (Cpte), Traviata (Cpte)
(CALA) **CACD0105** The London Violin Sound
(CALA) **CACD0106** The London Viola Sound
(LYRI) **SRCD209** Holst—Orchestral Works
cond A. DE ALMEIDA
A. Thomas: Hamlet (Cpte)
cond ANON
(WORD) **FCD7404** Best of Mozart
cond R. ARMSTRONG
Beethoven: Leonore (exc)
(EMI) **CDC5 55540-2** Roberto Alagna sings Operatic Arias
cond D. BARENBOIM
(CBS) **CD46465** Elgar—Orchestral Music
(SONY) **SBK48265** Elgar—Orchestral Works
cond E. BÁTIZ
(IMG) **IMGCD1603** Prokofiev—Orchestral Works
(MCI) **OQ0009** Wagner—Orchestral music from operas
cond T. BEECHAM
Gounod: Faust (exc)
(BEEC) **BEECHAM3** Delius—Vocal & Orchestral Works
(DUTT) **CDLX7001** Beecham conducts Favourite Overtures, Volume 1
(DUTT) **CDLX7003** Vintage Beecham
(DUTT) **CDLX7007** Beecham conducts Wagner
(DUTT) **CDLX7009** Beecham conducts Favourite Overtures, Volume 2
(DUTT) **CDLX7011** Beecham conducts Delius
(DUTT) **CDLX7012** The Incomparable Heddle Nash
(EMI) **CMS7 64008-2(1)** Wagner Singing on Record (pt 1)
(EMI) **CMS7 64008-2(2)** Wagner Singing on Record (pt 2)
(LYRC) **LCD146** Frida Leider sings Wagner
(LYRC) **SRO830** Smetana—The Bartered Bride, etc
(PEAR) **GEMMCD9065** Beecham conducts French Works
(PEAR) **GEMMCD9081** Sir Thomas Beecham and the LPO, Volume 3
(PEAR) **GEMMCD9084** Sir Thomas Beecham and the LPO, Volume 4
(PEAR) **GEMMCD9094** Beecham & the LPO, Vol.5
(PEAR) **GEMMCD9473** Heddle Nash—Vol.2
(SYMP) **SYMCD1096/7** Sir Thomas Beecham, Bart conducts Beecham SO & LPO
cond R. BONYNGE
(DECC) **421 881-2DA** The Age of Bel Canto - Sutherland
cond A. BOULT
Holst: Perfect Fool (exc)
Vaughan Williams: Pilgrim's Progress (Cpte)
(CFP) **CD-CFP4606** Favourite Movie Classics
(DECC) **440 318-2DWO** World of British Classics, Volume II
(DECC) **444 549-2DF2** Essential Holst
(EMI) **CDM7 69596-2** The Movies go to the Opera
(EMI) **CZS7 62539-2** Wagner—Overtures & Preludes
(EMIL) **CDZ7 67253-2** Funeral Music
cond S. CAMBRELING
(CAST) **CVI2071** Highlights from Glyndebourne
cond B. CAMPANELLA
(DG) **435 866-2GH** Kathleen Battle sings Italian Opera Arias
(DG) **435 866-5GH** Kathleen Battle sings Italian Opera Arias
cond CARL DAVIS
(EMI) **CDM5 65585-2** Walton—Film Music
(VIRG) **VJ7 59654-2** Fanfare for the Common Man
cond C.F. CILLARIO
Bellini: Norma (Cpte)
(RCA) **RK61044** Eternal Caballé
(RCA) **74321 24209-2** Italian Opera Choruses
(RCA) **74321 25817-2** Café Classics - Operatic
cond P. CIMARA
(PEAR) **GEMMCDS9926(2)** Covent Garden on Record—Vol.4 (pt 2)
cond S. EDWARDS
Tchaikovsky: Eugene Onegin (exc)
cond W. FURTWÄNGLER
Wagner: Walküre (exc)
(ACAN) **43 121** Wagner: Orchestral Works
cond L. GARDELLI
Verdi: Macbeth (Cpte)
(DECC) **433 443-2DA** Great Opera Choruses
(DECC) **440 409-2DM** Dietrich Fischer-Dieskau
cond V. GUI
Verdi: Trovatore (Cpte)
cond B. HAITINK
Mozart: Così fan tutte (Cpte), Don Giovanni (Cpte), Nozze di Figaro (Cpte)
(CAST) **CVI2071** Highlights from Glyndebourne
(CFP) **CD-CFP4606** Favourite Movie Classics
(CFP) **CD-CFP4612** Favourite Mozart
(EMI) **CDH5 65072-2** Glyndebourne Recorded - 1934-1994
(EMIL) **CDZ7 67015-2** Mozart—Opera Arias
(EMIL) **CDZ100** Best Loved Classics 1
(KIWI) **CDSLD-82** Southern Voices—NZ International Opera Singers
(PHIL) **432 512-2PSL** Mozart—Overtures
cond V. HANDLEY
(CFP) **CD-CFP4304** Delius: Orchestral Works
cond H. HARTY
(DUTT) **CDLX7016** The Art of Sir Hamilton Harty
(PEAR) **GEMMCD9485** Harty conducts Berlioz
cond H. KNAPPERTSBUSCH
(PREI) **90189** Knappertsbusch in London and Switzerland
cond M. PLASSON
Massenet: Werther (Cpte)
cond R. LEPPARD
Cavalli: Calisto (Cpte), Ormindo (Cpte)
Gluck: Orfeo ed Euridice (Cpte)
(BBCR) **DMCD98** BBC Proms - The Centenary: 1895-1995
(CAST) **CVI2071** Highlights from Glyndebourne
(ERAT) **2292-45797-2** The Ultimate Opera Collection
cond J. LÓPEZ-COBOS
(BELA) **450 059-2** Carreras—Memories
(PHIL) **434 152-2PM** Jose Carreras - Classics
cond C. MACKERRAS
Wagner: Götterdämmerung (exc)
(CFP) **CD-CFP9000** Orchestral Favourites
(RCA) **RD60758** Tchaikovsky—Cello Works
(RCA) **09026 60758-5** Tchaikovsky—Cello Works
cond Z. MEHTA
Puccini: Turandot (Cpte)
(DECC) **417 011-2DH2** Pavarotti's Greatest Hits
(DECC) **421 896-2DA** Puccini—Great Operatic Duets
(DECC) **425 681-2DM2** Tutto Pavarotti
(DECC) **433 064-2DWO** Your Hundred Best Opera Tunes Volume I
(DECC) **433 822-2DH** Essential Opera
(DECC) **436 300-2DX** Opera Gala Sampler
(DECC) **436 317-2DA** Puccini—Famous Arias
(DECC) **440 947-2DH** Essential Opera II
(DECC) **443 928-2DM** Montserrat Caballé sings Opera Arias
(DECC) **444 555-2DF2** Essential Puccini
(DECC) **400 053-4DH** World's Best Loved Tenor Arias
cond K. NAGANO
Stravinsky: Perséphone (Cpte)
cond M. PLASSON
Massenet: Werther (exc)
(EMI) **CDM7 63104-2** Alfredo Krauss - Opera Recital
cond J. PRITCHARD
Mozart: Idomeneo (Cpte)
(CBS) **CD39208** A Portrait of Kiri te Kanawa
(CBS) **MK37298** Puccini and Verdi Arias
(EMI) **CDH5 65072-2** Glyndebourne Recorded - 1934-1994
(KIWI) **CDSLD-82** Southern Voices—NZ International Opera Singers
(SONY) **SBK46548** Opera Arias
(SONY) **SK48094** Favourite Puccini Arias
cond A. RAHBARI
Beethoven: Leonore (exc)
cond C. RAINER
(INTR) **409 005-2** Mozart Edition, Vol.5
cond K. RANKL
(PREI) **90190** Paul Schoeffler—Recital
cond S. RATTLE
Gershwin: Porgy and Bess (exc)
(EMI) **CDH5 65072-2** Glyndebourne Recorded - 1934-1994
cond F. REINER
Wagner: Tristan und Isolde (Cpte)
cond D. RENZETTI
(CAST) **CVI2071** Highlights from Glyndebourne
cond K.A. RICKENBACHER
(CFP) **CD-CFP9008** Wagner Orchestral Works
cond M. ROSTROPOVICH
Shostakovich: Lady Macbeth of Mtsensk (Cpte)
(EMI) **CMS5 65716-2** Rostropovich as Accompanist

(DANA) **DACOCD319/21** The Lauritz Melchior Anthology - Vol.5
(EMI) **CDH7 69789-2** Melchior sings Wagner
(EMI) **CMS7 64008-2(1)** Wagner Singing on Record (pt 1)
(EMI) **CMS7 64008-2(2)** Wagner Singing on Record (pt 2)
(KOCH) **37700-2** Albert Coates Conducts, Vol.1 - Russian Favourites
(KOCH) **37704-2** Albert Coates conducts the LSO, Vol.2
(MSCM) **MM30283** Great Wagnerian Singers, Vol.1
(MSCM) **MM30285** Great Wagnerian Singers, Vol.2
(NIMB) **NI7848** Great Singers at the Berlin State Opera
(PEAR) **GEMMCDS9121** Wagner—Die Meistersinger, Act 3, etc
(PEAR) **GEMMCDS9137** Wagner—Der Ring des Nibelungen
(PEAR) **GEMMCDS9925(1)** Covent Garden on Record—Vol.3 (pt 1)
(PEAR) **GEMMCDS9926(1)** Covent Garden on Record—Vol.4 (pt 1)
(PEAR) **GEMMCD9146** Florence Austral
(PEAR) **GEMMCD9398** Friedrich Schorr
(PEAR) **GEMMCD9944** Friedrich Schorr sings Wagner
(PREI) **89004** Frida Leider (1888-1975) - I
(PREI) **89086** Lauritz Melchior (1890-1973) - III
(PREI) **89214** Friedrich Schorr sings Wagner

cond COLIN DAVIS
Berlioz: Béatrice et Bénédict (Cpte)
Mozart: Schauspieldirektor (Cpte), Sposo deluso (Cpte)
Wagner: Tristan und Isolde (exc)
(DECC) **436 315-2DA** Great Operatic Duets
(DECC) **443 335-2LRX** Music for Relaxation, Vol 10 - The Night Before
(PHIL) **411 148-2PH** Mozart: Opera Arias
(PHIL) **416 431-2PH** Works by Berlioz
(PHIL) **434 725-2PM** Kiri Te Kanawa - Classics

cond L. COLLINGWOOD
(CLAR) **CDGSE78-50-46** Walter Widdop (1892-1949)
(DANA) **DACOCD315/6** Lauritz Melchior Anthology - Vol. 3
(EMI) **CDH7 69789-2** Melchior sings Wagner
(PEAR) **GEMMCDS9137** Wagner—Der Ring des Nibelungen
(PEAR) **GEMMCD9944** Friedrich Schorr sings Wagner
(PREI) **89214** Friedrich Schorr sings Wagner
(TEST) **SBT1005** Ten Top Tenors

cond P. DOMINGO
(SONY) **SK53968** Opera Duets

cond A. DORATI
Bartók: Duke Bluebeard's castle (Cpte)
Berg: Wozzeck (exc)
(MERC) **434 308-2MM** Borodin/Rimsky-Korsakov—Suites
(MERC) **434 342-2MM** Wagner—Preludes and Overtures
(MERC) **434 345-2MM** Rossini/Verdi—Overtures

cond E. DOWNES
(DECC) **433 067-2DWO** Your Hundred Best Opera Tunes IV
(DECC) **433 069-2DWO** Your Hundred Best Opera Tunes VI
(DECC) **444 389-2DWO** The World of Borodin
(RCA) **09026 61236-2** Leontyne Price - Prima Donna Collection
(RCA) **09026 61357-2** Leontyne Price Sings Mozart
(RCA) **09026 62596-2** Prima Donna Collection - Higlights

cond P. DREIER
(UNIC) **UKCD2056** Grieg—Stage Works

cond E. ELGAR
(EMI) **CDS7 54564-2** The Elgar Edition, Vol.2

cond A. EREDE
(CFP) **CD-CFP4569** Puccini: Arias
(EMI) **CDM7 63105-2** Giuseppe di Stefano sings Opera Arias & Songs
(EMI) **CHS7 69741-2(7)** Record of Singing, Vol.4—Italian School

cond A. FRANCIS
Donizetti: Maria Padilla (Cpte)

cond R. FRÜHBECK DE BURGOS
Bizet: Carmen Suites (exc)
Kodály: Háry János Suite
(IMP) **PCDS8** Discover the Classics—Heroes and Heroines
(IMP) **PCDS15** Instruments of the Orchestra - Brass
(IMP) **PCDS012** Instruments of the Orchestra - Master Sampler
(IMP) **PCDS014** Instruments of the Orchestra - Woodwind
(IMP) **PCDS016** Instruments of the Orchestra - Percussion
(IMP) **PCDS018** Instruments of the Orchestra - The Orchestra
(IMP) **PCD924** Spanish Spectacular
(IMP) **TCD1014** An Invitation to the Classics

cond A. GALLIERA
(EMI) **CDM7 69501-2** Elisabeth Schwarzkopf—Romantic Heroines

cond P. GAMBA
(DECC) **433 606-2DSP** Rossini—Overtures

cond G. GAVAZZENI
(SONY) **SK48094** Favourite Puccini Arias
(SONY) **SK53549** Woody Allen Classics

cond J. GEORGIADIS
(IMP) **ORCD11015** Magic of Vienna
(IMP) **TCD1070** Invitation to the Opera

cond A. GIBSON
(DECC) **433 068-2DWO** Your Hundred Best Opera Tunes V
(EMI) **CDM7 69544-2** Berlioz: Vocal Works

cond W. GOEHR
(EMI) **CHS7 69741-2(7)** Record of Singing, Vol.4—Italian School

cond A. GUADAGNO
(RCA) **GD60866** The Placido Domingo Album
(RCA) **09026 62595-2** Opera Duets
(RCA) **09026 62699-2** Opera's Greatest Duets

cond R. HEGER
(DANA) **DACOCD315/6** Lauritz Melchior Anthology - Vol. 3
(DANA) **DACOCD319/21** The Lauritz Melchior Anthology - Vol.5
(EMI) **CDH7 69789-2** Melchior sings Wagner
(EMI) **CMS7 64008-2(2)** Wagner Singing on Record (pt 2)
(MSCM) **MM30283** Great Wagnerian Singers, Vol.1
(MSCM) **MM30285** Great Wagnerian Singers, Vol.2
(PEAR) **GEMMCDS9137** Wagner—Der Ring des Nibelungen
(PREI) **89086** Lauritz Melchior (1890-1973) - III

cond R. HICKOX
(IMP) **PCDS4** Discover the Classics—Master Disc
(IMP) **PCDS10** Discover the Classics—Power and Glory
(IMP) **PCDS15** Instruments of the Orchestra - Brass
(IMP) **PCDS23** Music of the World—Italy & Spain—The Latin Quarter
(IMP) **PCD908** Great Opera Choruses
(IMP) **TCD1070** Invitation to the Opera
(IMP) **TCD1073** The Best of Richard Hickox

cond L. HOLDRIDGE
Holdridge: Lazarus and His Beloved Suite
(KLVI) **CTD88104** Holdridge conducts Holdridge

cond JAMES LEVINE
Verdi: Forza del destino (Cpte), Giovanna d'Arco (Cpte)
(EMI) **CDM5 65575-2** Montserrat Caballé
(EMI) **CDM7 63103-2** Placido Domingo sings Opera Arias
(EMI) **CDM7 69549-2** Ruggero Raimondi: Italian Opera Arias
(EMI) **CZS5 68559-2** Italian Opera Choruses
(RCA) **GD60866** The Placido Domingo Album
(RCA) **74321 24209-2** Italian Opera Choruses

cond N. JÄRVI
Schumann: Genoveva (exc)
(CHAN) **CHAN6548** Schumann—Overtures

cond I. KERTÉSZ
Bartók: Duke Bluebeard's castle (Cpte)
(BELA) **461 012-2** Kodály—Orchestral Works
(DECC) **443 488-2DF2** Kodály—Háry János; Psalmus Hungaricus etc

cond J. KRIPS
(DECC) **443 530-2LF2** Mozart—Die Entführung aus dem Serail
(EMI) **CHS7 69741-2(7)** Record of Singing, Vol.4—Italian School

cond E. LEINSDORF
R. Strauss: Salome (Cpte)
Verdi: Aida (Cpte)
Wagner: Walküre (Cpte)
(DECC) **436 463-2DM** Ten Top Tenors
(RCA) **GD60205** Opera Choruses
(RCA) **GD60866** The Placido Domingo Album
(RCA) **GD84265** Con Amore
(RCA) **09026 61356-2** Domingo Sings Caruso
(RCA) **09026 61580-2(7)** RCA/Met 100 Singers, 100 Years (pt 7)
(RCA) **09026 61634-2** Verdi & Puccini Duets
(RCA) **74321 24209-2** Italian Opera Choruses

cond K-H. LOGES
(BELA) **450 036-2** Domingo—Love Songs and Tangos
(DG) **413 451-2GH** Be My Love
(DG) **427 708-2GX3** The Best of Domingo
(DG) **419 091-4GW** Placido Domingo sings Favourite Arias, Songs and Tangos

cond J. LÓPEZ-COBOS
(BELA) **450 059-2** Carreras—Memories
(PHIL) **432 692-2PH** The Essential José Carreras
(PHIL) **434 152-2PM** Jose Carreras - Classics

cond L. MAAZEL
Puccini: Rondine (Cpte)
(CBS) **CD79312** Puccini: Il Trittico
(SONY) **MDK47176** Favourite Arias by the World's Favourite Tenors
(SONY) **SMK39030** Placido Domingo sings Great Love Scenes

cond C. MACKERRAS
(CFP) **CD-CFP4606** Favourite Movie Classics
(CFP) **CD-CFP4608** Favourite Classics 1
(EMI) **CDC5 55095-2** Prima Diva
(EMI) **CDC7 47841-2** Puccini: Opera Recital
(EMI) **CDM5 65575-2** Montserrat Caballé
(EMI) **CDM7 64359-2** Gala de España
(EMI) **CDM7 69596-2** The Movies go to the Opera
(EMIL) **CDZ104** Best Loved Classics 5
(EMIL) **CDZ105** Best Loved Classics 6
(MERC) **434 352-2MM** Kaleidoscope

cond I. MARIN
Donizetti: Lucia di Lammermoor (Cpte)
Rossini: Semiramide (Cpte)

cond N. MARRINER
(PHIL) **426 640-2PSL** Prokofiev—Orchestral Works
(PHIL) **442 278-2PM2** Prokofiev—Favourite Orchestral Works
(PHIL) **446 198-2PM** Bizet—Orchestral Works

cond G-F. MASINI
Rossini: Elisabetta (Cpte)
(PHIL) **434 986-2PM** Duetti Amorosi

cond J. MAUCERI
(DECC) **084 474-3** The Essential Kiri

cond J. MCCARTHY
(ARAB) **Z6582** The Rossini Tenor

cond N. MCGEGAN
(ARAB) **Z6598** Rockwell Blake, the Mozart Tenor

cond W. MORRIS
(CIRR) **CICD1005** Wagner: Orchestral Works

cond MYUNG-WHUN CHUNG
(EMI) **CDC5 55095-2** Prima Diva
(EMI) **CDC7 54062-2** Kiri Te Kanawa—Italian Opera Arias
(EMI) **CDM5 65578-2** Kiri Te Kanawa

cond K. NAGANO
Puccini: Bohème (Cpte)

cond G. NAVARRO
Falla: Vida breve (Cpte)

cond E. PEDRAZZOLI
(CBC) **PSCD2001** Lois Marshall sings Oratorio & Operatic Arias

cond F. PETRACCHI
(ASV) **CDDCA907** Bottesini—Volume 3 - Passioni Amorose

cond A. PREVIN
Ravel: Enfant et les sortilèges (Cpte)
(EMI) **CDM7 64630-2** Berlioz—Orchestral Works
(EMI) **CDM7 64745-2** Berlioz—Orchestral Works
(EMI) **CMS7 64530-2** Rachmaninov—Orchestral Works
(RCA) **VD60487** Rimsky-Korsakov: Orchestral Works

cond J. PRITCHARD
(DECC) **421 899-2DA** Teresa Berganza - Mozart Arias
(DECC) **436 300-2DX** Opera Gala Sampler
(DECC) **443 762-2DF2** The Essential Mozart

cond K. RANKL
(PREI) **90190** Paul Schoeffler—Recital

cond C. RIZZI
Verdi: Traviata (Cpte)
(ERAT) **4509-94358-2** Stressbusters
(TELD) **4509-93691-2** Queen of Coloratura

cond S. ROBINSON
(EMI) **CHS7 69741-2(1)** Record of Singing, Vol.4—Anglo-American School (pt 1)

cond ROSARIO BOURDON
(PREI) **89214** Friedrich Schorr sings Wagner

cond J. RUDEL
(EMI) **CDC5 55017-2** Domingo Opera Classics
(EMI) **CDM5 65575-2** Montserrat Caballé
(EMI) **CDM7 63103-2** Placido Domingo sings Opera Arias
(EMI) **CZS5 68559-2** Italian Opera Choruses

cond N. SANTI
Leoncavallo: Pagliacci (Cpte)
(RCA) **GD60866** The Placido Domingo Album
(RCA) **GD84265** Con Amore
(RCA) **09026 61356-2** Domingo Sings Caruso
(RCA) **09026 61440-2** Opera's Greatest Moments
(RCA) **09026 61634-2** Verdi & Puccini Duets
(RCA) **09026 61886-2** Operas Greatest Love Songs
(RCA) **74321 24209-2** Italian Opera Choruses
(RCA) **74321 25817-2** Café Classics - Operatic

cond M. SARGENT
(DECC) **430 096-2DWO** The World of Kathleen Ferrier
(DECC) **433 470-2DM** Ferrier Edition - Volume 3

cond T. SCHIPPERS
Rossini: Siège de Corinthe (Cpte)
(EMI) **CZS5 68559-2** Italian Opera Choruses

cond G. SIMON
Smetana: Bartered Bride (exc)
(CALA) **CACD0002** Cala Series, Volume 2
(CALA) **CACD0101** Orchestral works
(CALA) **CACD0102** Orchestral Masterpieces - The Cala Series
(CHAN) **CHAN8310/1** Tchaikovsky—Orchestral Works
(CHAN) **CHAN8457** Falla—El amor brujo; Nights in the gardens of Spain
(CHAN) **CHAN9190** Tchaikovsky—Orchestral Works

cond G. SOLTI
(BELA) **450 017-2** Russian Masterpieces
(DECC) **444 389-2DWO** The World of Borodin

cond M. STEINMANN
(CONI) **CDHD226** Chaliapin—Bass of the Century
(EMI) **CDH7 61009-2** Chaliapin sings Russian Opera Arias
(PEAR) **GEMMCD9314** Feodor Chaliapin - Aria and Song Recital

cond E. STERN
(RCA) **09026 61790-2** Concerto! Stoltzman plays Copland etc.

cond L. STOKOWSKI
(DECC) **433 639-2DSP** Wagner—Orchestral Works

cond G. SZELL
(BELA) **450 001-2** Handel—Orchestral Works
(DECC) **425 851-2DWO** Your hundred best tunes vol 5
(DECC) **444 543-2DF2** Essential Handel

cond V. TAUSKY
(IMP) **TCD1070** Invitation to the Opera

cond M. TILSON THOMAS
Weill: Sieben Todsünden (Cpte)
(SONY) **SMK64243** Prokofiev—Orchestral & Piano Works

cond Y.P. TORTELIER
(CIRR) **CICD1001** Orchestral Favourites.

cond G. TOYE
(BEUL) **2PD4** 78 Classics - Volume Two

cond B. TUCKWELL
(IMP) **PCDS15** Instruments of the Orchestra - Brass
(IMP) **TCD1070** Invitation to the Opera
cond M. VALDES
(ARAB) **Z6612** Rossini: Opera Arias
cond B. WALTER
(DUTT) **CDLX7008** Bruno Walter conducts the LSO
cond B. WORDSWORTH
(COLL) **Coll1336-2** Delius—Orchestral Works

LONDON VOICES
cond R. BONYNGE
Gay: Beggar's Opera (Cpte)
Massenet: Roi de Lahore (Cpte)
cond G. GAVAZZENI
Mascagni: Cavalleria Rusticana (Cpte)
cond R. LEPPARD
Handel: Ariodante (Cpte)
cond G. LLOYD
G. Lloyd: John Socman (exc)
cond J. MAUCERI
(DECC) **436 417-2DH** Ute Lemper sings Kurt Weill, Vol.2
cond G. PATANÈ
Leoncavallo: Pagliacci (Cpte)
cond J. PERRAS
Rossini: Tancredi (Cpte)

LONG BEACH OPERA
Cage: Europera 3, Europera 4

LONGOBARDI, Luigi (ten)
(SYMP) **SYMCD1113** The Harold Wayne Collection, Vol.13

LONGUET, Dominique (bar)
Auber: Manon Lescaut (Cpte)

LØNSKOV, Tove (pf)
(CANZ) **CAN33009** Rachmaninov/R.Strauss—Cello Sonatas
(DANA) **DACOCD378** Mette Hanskov plays music for Double Bass

LOONEN, Bernard (ten)
Montéclair: Jephté (Cpte)
Purcell: Fairy Queen, Z629 (Cpte)
(CPO) **CPO999 104-2** Mozart—Lo Sposo Deluso/L'Oca del Cairo

LOOR, Friedl (sop)
(KOCH) **399 225** Operetta Highlights 3

LOOSE, Emmy (sop)
J. Strauss II: Nacht in Venedig (Cpte)
Lehár: Giuditta (exc), Land des Lächelns (Cpte), Lustige Witwe (exc)
Mozart: Così fan tutte (Cpte), Zauberflöte (Cpte)
R. Strauss: Ariadne auf Naxos (Cpte), Rosenkavalier (Cpte)
(DECC) **443 530-2LF2** Mozart—Die Entführung aus dem Serail
(PREI) **90237** R Strauss—Daphne
(PREI) **90249** Mozart in tempore belli
(SCHW) **314552** Vienna State Opera Live, Vol.5

LOOTENS, Lena (sop)
Handel: Flavio (Cpte)
Haydn: Infedeltà delusa (Cpte)
Monteverdi: Incoronazione di Poppea (Cpte)

LOPARDO, Frank (ten)
Donizetti: Don Pasquale (Cpte)
Mozart: Don Giovanni (Cpte)
Rossini: Barbiere di Siviglia (exc), Italiana in Algeri (Cpte), Semiramide (Cpte), Signor Bruschino (Cpte)
Verdi: Falstaff (Cpte), Traviata (Cpte)

LOPATTO, Dimitri (sngr)
Mussorgsky: Khovanshchina (Cpte)

LÓPEZ-COBOS, Jésus (cond)
see BRSO
Cincinnati SO
Lausanne CO
LPO
LSO
New Philh
Philh

LORAINE, Karol (mez)
R. Strauss: Elektra (Cpte)

LORAND, Colette (sop)
Orff: Prometheus (Cpte)
R. Strauss: Elektra (Cpte)
(ACAN) **44 2085-2** Carl Orff Collection

LORD, Bernadette (sop)
Britten: Albert Herring (Cpte)

LORD, Matthew (ten)
V. Thomson: Lord Byron (Cpte)

LOREAU, Jacques (bar)
Bizet: Carmen (Cpte)
Massenet: Don Quichotte (Cpte), Manon (Cpte)
Offenbach: Belle Hélène (Cpte), Brigands (Cpte)

LORENGAR, Pilar (sop)
Gluck: Iphigénie en Tauride (Cpte), Orfeo ed Euridice (Cpte)
Hindemith: Mathis der Maler (exc)
Mozart: Idomeneo (Cpte), Nozze di Figaro (Cpte), Zauberflöte (exc)
Sorozábal: Katiuska (Cpte)
Verdi: Traviata (Cpte)
(DECC) **425 853-2DWO** Your hundred best tunes vol 7
(DECC) **433 065-2DWO** Your Hundred Best Opera Tunes Volume II
(DECC) **436 316-2DA** Golden Operetta
(DECC) **443 765-2DF2** The Essential Dvořák
(DECC) **443 931-2DM** Pilar Lorengar sings Opera Arias
(EMI) **CZS7 62993-2** Fritz Wunderlich—Great German Tenor
(LOND) **436 897-2DM** Lehár Gala
(LOND) **436 898-2DM** Operetta Gala
(RCA) **RD61191** Gala Lirica
(RCA) **09026 61191-5** Gala Lirica
(SONY) **MK39210** Zarzuela Arias and Duets

LORENZ, Eberhard (ten)
Trojahn: Enrico (Cpte)

LORENZ, Max (ten)
Einem: Prozess (Cpte)
R. Strauss: Ariadne auf Naxos (Cpte), Elektra (Cpte), Salome (Cpte)
Verdi: Otello (exc)
Wagner: Meistersinger (exc), Rienzi (exc), Tristan und Isolde (exc), Walküre (exc)
(EMI) **CMS7 64008-2(1)** Wagner Singing on Record (pt 1)
(EMI) **CMS7 64008-2(2)** Wagner Singing on Record (pt 2)
(MMOI) **CDMOIR405** Great Tenors
(MSCM) **MM30283** Great Wagnerian Singers, Vol.1
(MSCM) **MM30285** Great Wagnerian Singers, Vol.2
(NIMB) **NI7848** Great Singers at the Berlin State Opera
(PREI) **89053** Max Lorenz (1901-1975)
(PREI) **89065** Maria Reining (1903-1991)
(PREI) **90116** Knappertsbuch conducts the Vienna Philharmonic
(PREI) **90213** Max Lorenz sings Wagner
(SCHW) **314502** Vienna State Opera—Live Recordings (sampler)
(SCHW) **314532** Vienna State Opera Live, Vol.3
(SCHW) **314562** Vienna State Opera Live, Vol.6
(SCHW) **314582** Vienna State Opera Live, Vol.8
(SCHW) **314602** Vienna State Opera Live, Vol.10
(SCHW) **314672** Vienna State Opera Live, Vol.17
(SCHW) **314692** Vienna State Opera Live, Vol.19
(SCHW) **314702** Vienna State Opera Live, Vol.20
(SCHW) **314742** Vienna State Opera Live, Vol.24
(TELD) **9031-76442-2** Wagner—Excerpts from the 1936 Bayreuth Festival

LORENZ, Siegfried (bar)
Busoni: Arlecchino (Cpte)
Mozart: Finta semplice (Cpte)
Prokofiev: Fiery Angel (Cpte)
Wagner: Meistersinger (Cpte), Rheingold (Cpte)
Weber: Freischütz (exc)
Zemlinsky: Kreidekreis (Cpte)
(DG) **445 354-2GX14** Wagner—Der Ring des Nibelungen
(SONY) **S2K66836** Goldschmidt—Beatrice Cenci, etc

LORENZI, Ermanno (ten)
Leoncavallo: Pagliacci (Cpte)
Puccini: Manon Lescaut (Cpte)

LORIMER, Malcolm (treb)
M. Berkeley: Baa Baa Black Sheep (Cpte)

LORRAINE PHILHARMONIC ORCHESTRA
cond J. HOUTMANN
Pierné: Ramuntcho (exc)

LOS ANGELES MASTER CHORALE
cond C.M. GIULINI
Verdi: Falstaff (Cpte)

LOS ANGELES MUSIC CENTER OPERA CHORUS
cond Z. MEHTA
(TELD) **4509-96200-8** The Three Tenors 1994
(TELD) **4509-96200-2** The Three Tenors 1994
(TELD) **4509-96200-5** The Three Tenors 1994

LOS ANGELES PHILHARMONIC ORCHESTRA
cond L. BERNSTEIN
(DG) **410 025-2GH** Bernstein and Gershwin
(DG) **439 251-2GY** The Leonard Bernstein Album
(DG) **439 251-5GY** The Leonard Bernstein Album
cond C.M. GIULINI
Verdi: Falstaff (Cpte)
(DG) **415 366-2GH** Placido Domingo Recital
(DG) **427 708-2GX3** The Best of Domingo
(DG) **445 525-2GMA** Domingo Favourites
(DG) **419 091-4GW** Placido Domingo sings Favourite Arias, Songs and Tangos
cond E. LEINSDORF
(EMI) **CDM5 65208-2** Wagner—Orchestral Works from the Operas
(SHEF) **CD-7/8** Prokofiev & Wagner: Orchestral Works
(SHEF) **10043-2-G** Leinsdorf Sessions, Volume 1
(SHEF) **10052-2-G** Leinsdorf Sessions, Volume 2
cond Z. MEHTA
(TELD) **4509-96200-8** The Three Tenors 1994
(TELD) **4509-96200-2** The Three Tenors 1994
(TELD) **4509-96200-5** The Three Tenors 1994
cond M. TILSON THOMAS
(SONY) **SK53549** Woody Allen Classics

LOSA, Alfonso (ten)
Verdi: Traviata (Cpte)

LOSCH, Liselotte (sop)
Mozart: Zauberflöte (Cpte)

LOTRIČ (TEN), Janez (ten)
(NAXO) **8 553030** Opera Duets

LOTT, Felicity (sop)
Britten: Midsummer Night's Dream (Cpte), Peter Grimes (Cpte), Turn of the Screw (Cpte)
Lehár: Lustige Witwe (Cpte)
Mozart: Così fan tutte (exc), Nozze di Figaro (Cpte), Zauberflöte (Cpte)
R. Strauss: Intermezzo (Cpte), Rosenkavalier (Cpte)
Stravinsky: Rake's Progress (Cpte)
(ASV) **CDDCA683** Mozart—Arias
(CHAN) **CHAN8758** R. Strauss—Opera Excerpts
(EMI) **CDC7 54411-2** On Wings of Song
(HYPE) **CDA67061/2** Britten—Purcell Realizations
(LOND) **825 126-2** Amadeus - Original Soundtrack

LOUGHRAN, James (cond)
see Hallé

LOUGHTON HIGH SCHOOL FOR GIRLS' CHOIR
cond H. VON KARAJAN
Humperdinck: Hänsel und Gretel (Cpte)
R. Strauss: Rosenkavalier (Cpte)

LOUKJANETZ, Victoria (vn)
(AUVI) **V4662** International Competitions Prize-Winners

LOUP, François (bass)
Chausson: Roi Arthus (Cpte)
Debussy: Pelléas et Mélisande (Cpte)
Lully: Alceste (Cpte)
Monteverdi: Orfeo (Cpte)

LOUVAY, Françoise (sop)
Boïeldieu: Dame blanche (Cpte)

LÖVAAS, Kari (sop)
Egk: Peer Gynt (Cpte)
R. Strauss: Rosenkavalier (Cpte)
Wagner: Feen (Cpte)

LOVANO, Lucien (bass)
Martinů: Comedy on the Bridge (Cpte), Julietta (Cpte)
Massenet: Navarraise (Cpte)
Messager: Basoche (Cpte), Monsieur Beaucaire (Cpte)
Milhaud: Christophe Colomb (Cpte)
Offenbach: Chanson de Fortunio (Cpte)
Planquette: Rip van Winkle (Cpte)
Terrasse: Travaux d'Hercule (Cpte)
(DECC) **433 400-2DM2** Ravel & Debussy—Stage Works
(MONT) **TCE8760** Stravinsky: Stage Works

LOVANO, Lucien (narr)
Milhaud: Christophe Colomb (Cpte)

LOVE, Shirley (mez)
Stravinsky: Rake's Progress (Cpte)

LOVERDE, Carol (sngr)
Rapchak: Lifework of Juan Diaz (Cpte)

LOWE, Marion (sop)
Lehár: Lustige Witwe (exc)

LOWER AUSTRIA ORCHESTRA
cond W. LOIBNER
(PREI) **89083** Emanuel List (1890-1967)

LOWERY, Melvin (ten)
Stravinsky: Rake's Progress (Cpte)

LÖWLEIN, Hans (cond)
see Bamberg SO
Berlin City Op Orch
Berlin St Op Orch

LOZANO, Fernando (cond)
see Mexico City PO

LSO BRASS ENSEMBLE
cond E. CREES
(COLL) **Coll1288-2** American Music for Brass

LUBIN, Germaine (sop)
(CLUB) **CL99-022** Germaine Lubin (1891-1979)
(EMI) **CMS7 64008-2(2)** Wagner Singing on Record (pt 2)
(EPM) **150 052** Germaine Lubin—Opera & Song Recital
(MSCM) **MM30221** 18 French Divas

LUBLIN, Eliane (sop)
Bizet: Carmen (Cpte)
G. Charpentier: Louise (Cpte)
Gounod: Roméo et Juliette (Cpte)
(EMI) **CZS5 68113-2** Vive Offenbach!

(NORMAN) LUBOFF CHOIR
cond L. STOKOWSKI
(RCA) **09026 61867-2** Christmas Treasures

LUCA, Giuseppe De (bar)
(CLAR) **CDGSE78-50-52** Three Tenors
(CLUB) **CL99-587/8** Eugenia Burzio (1872-1922)
(CONI) **CDHD149** Gigli Favourites
(CONI) **CDHD170** Gigli—Centenary Tribute
(CONI) **CDHD201** Galli-Curci in Opera and Song
(CONI) **CDHD227** Gigli in Opera and Song
(EMI) **CDH7 61051-2** Beniamino Gigli - Operatic Arias
(EMI) **CHS7 64860-2(2)** La Scala Edition - Vol.1, 1878-1914 (pt 2)
(IMP) **GLRS102** The Magnificent Gigli
(IRCC) **IRCC-CD808** Souvenirs of 19th Century Italian Opera
(MCI) **MCCD086** The Essential Caruso
(MMOI) **CDMOIR412** Great Voices of the Century Sing Puccini

(MMOI) **CDMOIR417** Great Voices of the Century—Beniamino Gigli
(MSCM) **MM30352** Caruso—Italian Opera Arias
(MSCM) **MM30446** Lily Pons - Recital
(MSOU) **DFCDI-111** The Art of the Coloratura
(NIMB) **NI7804** Giovanni Martinelli—Opera Recital
(NIMB) **NI7806** Galli-Curci—Opera & Song Recital
(NIMB) **NI7817** Beniamino Gigli—Vol.2
(NIMB) **NI7851** Legendary Voices
(NIMB) **NI7852** Galli-Curci, Vol.2
(NIMB) **NI7853** Lauri-Volpi sings Verdi
(NIMB) **NI7867** Legendary Baritones
(PEAR) **EVC4(1)** The Caruso Edition, Vol.4 (pt 1)
(PEAR) **EVC4(2)** The Caruso Edition, Vol.4 (pt 2)
(PEAR) **GEMMCDS9159(1)** De Luca Edition, Vol.1 (pt 1)
(PEAR) **GEMMCDS9159(2)** De Luca Edition, Vol.1 (pt 2)
(PEAR) **GEMMCDS9160(1)** De Luca Edition, Vol.2 (pt 1)
(PEAR) **GEMMCDS9160(2)** De Luca Edition, Vol.2 (pt 2)
(PEAR) **GEMMCDS9924(2)** Covent Garden on Record, Vol.2 (pt 2)
(PEAR) **GEMMCDS9925(1)** Covent Garden on Record—Vol.3 (pt 1)
(PEAR) **GEMMCD9316** Beniamino Gigli
(PEAR) **GEMMCD9367** Gigli—Arias and Duets
(PEAR) **GEMMCD9458** Lucrezia Bori—Opera & Song Recital
(PREI) **89012** Giacomo Lauri-Volpi (1894-1979)
(PREI) **89036** Giuseppe de Luca (1876-1950) - I
(PREI) **89062** Giovanni Martinelli (1885-1969)
(PREI) **89073** Giuseppe de Luca (1876-1950) - II
(PREI) **89995** Famous Italian Baritones
(RCA) **GD60495(6)** The Complete Caruso Collection (pt 6)
(RCA) **09026 61411-2** Lily Pons Recital
(RCA) **09026 61580-2(2)** RCA/Met 100 Singers, 100 Years (pt 2)
(ROMO) **81003-2** Galli-Curci—Acoustic Recordings, Vol.1
(ROMO) **81014-2** Elisabeth Rethberg (1894-1976)
(ROMO) **81016-2** Lucrezia Bori (1887-1960)
(SYMP) **SYMCD1111** The Harold Wayne Collection, Vol.11
(TEST) **SBT1008** Viva Rossini

UCA, Libero de (ten)
(BELA) **450 006-2** Famous Opera Duets
(DECC) **433 066-2DWO** Your Hundred Best Opera Tunes III

JCARINI, Bernadette (sngr)
Mozart: Don Giovanni (Cpte)
Paisiello: Don Chisciotte (Cpte)

JCAS, Roger (ten)
Schoenberg: Moses und Aron (Cpte)
Verdi: Traviata (Cpte)

JCCARDI, Giancarlo (bass)
Bellini: Puritani (Cpte)
Cilea: Adriana Lecouvreur (Cpte)
Monteverdi: Incoronazione di Poppea (Cpte)
Puccini: Tosca (Cpte)
(CBS) **CD79312** Puccini: Il Trittico
(DECC) **417 011-2DH2** Pavarotti's Greatest Hits

JCCIONI, José (ten)
Saint-Saëns: Samson et Dalila (Cpte)
(MSCM) **MM30377** 18 Tenors d'Expression Française

JCEY, Frances (sop)
Trojahn: Enrico (Cpte)

CHETTI, Veriano (ten)
Meyerbeer: Africaine (Cpte)
Verdi: Attila (Cpte), Macbeth (Cpte), Nabucco (exc), Vespri Siciliani (Cpte)

CIA, Fernando De (ten)
Rossini: Barbiere di Siviglia (exc)
(BONG) **GB1064/5-2** Fernando de Lucia
(EMI) **CHS7 64860-2(1)** La Scala Edition - Vol.1, 1878-1914 (pt 1)
(NIMB) **NI7840/1** The Era of Adelina Patti
(PEAR) **GEMMCDS9923(1)** Covent Garden on Record, Vol.1 (pt 1)
(PEAR) **GEMMCDS9923(2)** Covent Garden on Record, Vol.1 (pt 2)
(SYMP) **SYMCD1149** Fernando De Lucia
(TEST) **SBT1008** Viva Rossini

DGIN, Chester (bar)
R. Ward: Crucible (Cpte)

DHA, L'udovit (ten)
Suchoň: Whirlpool (Cpte)

DLOW, Howard (ten)
J. Strauss II: Fledermaus (Cpte)

DWIG, Christa (mez)
Bartók: Duke Bluebeard's castle (Cpte)
Beethoven: Fidelio (Cpte)
Bellini: Norma (Cpte)
Bernstein: Candide (1988) (Cpte)
Debussy: Pelléas et Mélisande (Cpte)
Giordano: Andrea Chénier (Cpte)
Handel: Giulio Cesare (Cpte)
Humperdinck: Hänsel und Gretel (Cpte)
J. Strauss II: Fledermaus (Cpte)
Mozart: Così fan tutte (Cpte), Don Giovanni (Cpte), Nozze di Figaro (Cpte), Zauberflöte (Cpte)
Offenbach: Contes d'Hoffmann (Cpte)
Puccini: Madama Butterfly (Cpte)
R. Strauss: Capriccio (Cpte), Elektra (Cpte), Rosenkavalier (exc)
Verdi: Aida (exc), Ballo in maschera (Cpte), Don Carlo (exc), Falstaff (Cpte)
Wagner: Götterdämmerung (Cpte), Lohengrin (Cpte), Meistersinger (Cpte), Parsifal (Cpte), Rheingold (Cpte), Tannhäuser (Cpte), Tristan und Isolde (Cpte), Walküre (Cpte)
(CFP) **CD-CFP4656** Herbert von Karajan conducts Opera
(DECC) **414 100-2DM15** Wagner: Der Ring des Nibelungen
(DECC) **433 439-2DA** Great Love Duets
(DECC) **436 315-2DA** Great Operatic Duets
(DECC) **436 462-2DM** Ten Top Mezzos
(DECC) **440 409-2DM** Dietrich Fischer-Dieskau
(DECC) **440 412-2DM** Mirella Freni
(DECC) **443 377-2DM** Ten Top Sopranos 2
(DG) **435 145-2GX5(1)** Fritz Wunderlich—Opera Arias, Lieder, etc (part 1)
(DG) **435 211-2GX15** Wagner—Der Ring des Nibelungen
(DG) **437 825-2GH** Wagner—Der Ring des Nibelungen - Highlights
(DG) **439 251-2GY** The Leonard Bernstein Album
(DG) **445 354-2GX14** Wagner—Der Ring des Nibelungen
(DG) **072 422-3GH7** Levine conducts Wagner's Ring
(DG) **439 251-5GY** The Leonard Bernstein Album
(EMI) **CDM7 69501-2** Elisabeth Schwarzkopf—Romantic Heroines
(EMI) **CMS7 64074-2(2)** Christa Ludwig—Recital (pt 2)
(ORFE) **C365941A** Christa Ludwig - Salzburg Festival highlights
(ORFE) **C394201B** Great Mozart Singers Series, Vol. 2
(PHIL) **434 420-2PM32(2)** Richard Wagner Edition (pt 2)
(TESS) **049-2** R. Strauss/Wagner—Opera Scenes

LUDWIG, Hanna (sop)
J. Strauss II: Nacht in Venedig (Cpte)
Wagner: Parsifal (Cpte), Walküre (exc)

LUDWIG, Leopold (cond)
see Berlin RSO
Philh
Vienna SO
Vienna St Op Orch

LUDWIG, Walther (ten)
Mozart: Zauberflöte (Cpte)
(DECC) **443 530-2LF2** Mozart—Die Entführung aus dem Serail
(EMI) **CHS7 69741-2(4)** Record of Singing, Vol.4—German School
(PREI) **89088** Walther Ludwig (1902-1981)

LUDWIG-JAHNS, Isle (mez)
Wagner: Parsifal (Cpte)

LUDWIGSHAFEN THEATRE CHORUS
cond M. HASELBÖCK
Mozart: Don Giovanni (Cpte)

LUGANO RADIO AND TELEVISION CHOIR
cond M. ANDREAE
Donizetti: Imelda (Cpte)
(NUOV) **6905** Donizetti—Great Love Duets
cond M. DE BERNART
Rossini: Torvaldo e Dorliska (Cpte)

LUGANO RADIO AND TELEVISION ORCHESTRA
cond M. ANDREAE
Donizetti: Imelda (Cpte)
(NUOV) **6905** Donizetti—Great Love Duets
cond M. DE BERNART
Rossini: Torvaldo e Dorliska (Cpte)

LUGO, Giuseppe (ten)
(EMI) **CHS7 64864-2(2)** La Scala Edition - Vol.2, 1915-46 (pt 2)
(PREI) **89034** Giuseppe Lugo (1900-1980)

LUISE, Melchiorre (bass)
Puccini: Bohème (Cpte), Madama Butterfly (Cpte), Tosca (Cpte)

LUISI, Fabio (cond)
see Italian International Orch
Munich RO
Toscanini SO

LUKACEWSKA, Giannina (mez)
(SYMP) **SYMCD1113** The Harold Wayne Collection, Vol.13

LUKÁCS, Ervin (cond)
see Hungarian St Op Orch

LUKAN, Sylvia (mez)
J. Strauss II: Fledermaus (exc)

LUKAS, Ralf (bass)
Mendelssohn: Hochzeit des Camacho (Cpte)
Puccini: Tosca (exc)
R. Strauss: Salome (Cpte)

LUKIC, Ksenija (sop)
S. Wagner: Bärenhäuter (Cpte), Schwarzschwanenreich (Cpte)

LUKIN, Márta (mez)
Respighi: Belfagor (Cpte)

LUKOMSKA, Halina (sop)
Mussorgsky: Boris Godunov (Cpte)

LUMSDEN, Norman (bass)
Britten: Midsummer Night's Dream (Cpte)
(EMI) **CMS7 64727-2** Britten—Opera excerpts and Folksongs

LUND, Elisabeth Cornelius (mez)
(VICT) **VCD19008** Wien, Wien, nur du allein

LUNDBERG, Mark (ten)
Wagner: Walküre (exc)

LUNDBORG, Bo (bass)
(BLUE) **ABCD028** Jussi Björling live at the Stockholm Opera

LUNGO, Laura del (mez)
(IRCC) **IRCC-CD808** Souvenirs of 19th Century Italian Opera

LUNOW, Horst (bass)
Wagner: Meistersinger (Cpte)

LUPERI, Mario (bass)
Cherubini: Lodoïska (Cpte)

LUPPI, Oreste (bass)
(EMI) **CHS7 64860-2(2)** La Scala Edition - Vol.1, 1878-1914 (pt 2)
(MEMO) **HR4408/9(1)** Singers in Genoa, Vol.1 (disc 1)
(PEAR) **GEMMCDS9924(2)** Covent Garden on Record, Vol.2 (pt 2)
(SYMP) **SYMCD1113** The Harold Wayne Collection, Vol.13
(SYMP) **SYMCD1126** The Harold Wayne Collection, Vol.14

LUSMANN, Stephen (bar)
R. Strauss: Friedenstag (Cpte)

LUSSAN, Zélie de (mez)
(IRCC) **IRCC-CD802** Souvenirs of Rare French Opera

LUTZE, Walter (cond)
see Berlin Deutsche Op Orch

LUXEMBOURG RADIO & TV SYMPHONY ORCHESTRA
cond P. CAO
(FORL) **FF027** Italian Dances and Overtures
(FORL) **FF046** Fantasia
cond L. DE FROMENT
(FORL) **FF009** Weber—Clarinet Concertos Nos 1 and 2; Oberon Overture
(FORL) **FF027** Italian Dances and Overtures
(FORL) **FF028** Musiques de Ballet
(FORL) **FF029** The Most Beautiful Promenade Concert
(FORL) **FF042** Gems of Baroque Music
(FORL) **FF044** French Overtures and Ballet Music
(FORL) **FF045** Grieg/Lalo—Orchestral Works
(FORL) **FF046** Fantasia

LUXEMBOURG RADIO SYMPHONY ORCHESTRA
cond L. DE FROMENT
(FORL) **FF020** Wagner/Liszt—Orchestral Works
cond L. HAGER
Smetana: Bartered Bride (exc)

LUXON, Benjamin (bar)
Alwyn: Miss Julie (Cpte)
Britten: Rape of Lucretia (Cpte)
Haydn: Orlando Paladino (Cpte)
J. Strauss II: Fledermaus (Cpte)
Korngold: Tote Stadt (Cpte)
Mozart: Don Giovanni (Cpte), Nozze di Figaro (Cpte), Zauberflöte (Cpte)
Verdi: Falstaff (Cpte)
Walton: Troilus and Cressida (Cpte)
(EMI) **CDM7 64730-2** Vaughan Williams—Riders to the Sea; Epithalamion, etc
(LOND) **433 200-2LHO2** Britten—Owen Wingrave, etc.
(PHIL) **432 416-2PH3** Haydn—L'incontro improvviso/Arias

LYON ENFANTS DE LA CIGALE CHOIR
cond M. CORBOZ
M-A. Charpentier: David et Jonathas (Cpte)

LYON LYCÉE MUSICAL CHOIR
cond M. CORBOZ
M-A. Charpentier: David et Jonathas (Cpte)

LYON NATIONAL CHOIR
cond P. FOURNILLIER
Massenet: Grisélidis (Cpte)
cond B. TETU
(HARM) **HMP390 1293** Berlioz—Choral Works

LYON NATIONAL ORCHESTRA
cond E. KRIVINE
Berlioz: Troyens (exc)

LYON OPÉRA CHORUS
cond M. ARENA
Verdi: Luisa Miller (Cpte)
cond M. CORBOZ
M-A. Charpentier: David et Jonathas (Cpte)
cond G. FERRO
Donizetti: Don Pasquale (Cpte)
(ERAT) **4509-91715-2** The Ultimate Opera Collection 2
(VIRG) **CUV5 61139-2** Rossini—Arias
cond P. FOURNILLIER
Massenet: Grisélidis (Cpte)
cond J.E. GARDINER
Messager: Fortunio (Cpte)
Offenbach: Brigands (Cpte)

Rossini: Comte Ory (Cpte)
(EMI) **CZS5 68113-2** Vive Offenbach!
cond C. GIBAULT
Offenbach: Brigands (Cpte)
cond K. NAGANO
Busoni: Arlecchino (Cpte), Turandot (Cpte)
Debussy: Rodrigue et Chimène (Cpte)
Floyd: Susannah (Cpte)
Offenbach: Contes d'Hoffmann (Cpte)
Poulenc: Dialogues des Carmélites (Cpte)
Prokofiev: Love for 3 Oranges (Cpte)
cond J. NELSON
Berlioz: Béatrice et Bénédict (Cpte)
cond P. VERROT
(ERAT) **2292-45797-2** The Ultimate Opera Collection
(ERAT) **4509-91715-2** The Ultimate Opera Collection 2

LYON OPERA ORCHESTRA
Offenbach: Brigands (Cpte)
Prokofiev: Love for 3 Oranges (Cpte)
Verdi: Luisa Miller (Cpte)
cond S. BAUDO
Debussy: Pelléas et Mélisande (Cpte)
cond M. CORBOZ
Monteverdi: Orfeo (Cpte)
cond G. FERRO
Donizetti: Don Pasquale (Cpte)
(ERAT) **4509-91715-2** The Ultimate Opera Collection 2
(VIRG) **CUV5 61139-2** Rossini—Arias
cond L. FOSTER
(EMI) **CDC5 55151-2** Operetta Duets
cond J.E. GARDINER
Gluck: Iphigénie en Aulide (Cpte), Iphigénie en Tauride (Cpte), Orphée (Cpte), Rencontre imprévue (Cpte)
Messager: Fortunio (Cpte)
Offenbach: Brigands (Cpte)
Rossini: Comte Ory (Cpte)
(EMI) **CZS5 68113-2** Vive Offenbach!
(ERAT) **4509-99607-2** Gluck—Operas; Schubert—Symphonies Nos 8 & 9
cond K. NAGANO
Busoni: Arlecchino (Cpte), Turandot (Cpte)
Debussy: Rodrigue et Chimène (Cpte)
Floyd: Susannah (Cpte)
J. Adams: Death of Klinghoffer (Cpte)
Offenbach: Contes d'Hoffmann (Cpte)
Poulenc: Dialogues des Carmélites (Cpte)
Prokofiev: Love for 3 Oranges (Cpte)
R. Strauss: Salomé (Cpte)
cond J. NELSON
Berlioz: Béatrice et Bénédict (Cpte)
cond P. VERROT
(ERAT) **2292-45797-2** The Ultimate Opera Collection
(ERAT) **4509-91715-2** The Ultimate Opera Collection 2

LYONS, Darius (fl)
(RCA) **09026 61580-2(1)** RCA/Met 110 Singers, 100 Years (pt 1)

LYTTING, Katia (mez)
Bellini: Puritani (Cpte)
Rossini: Signor Bruschino (Cpte)

LYTTON, Sir **Henry (bar)**
Sullivan: Gondoliers (Cpte), HMS Pinafore (Cpte)
(MMOI) **CDMOIR413** The Very Best of Gilbert & Sullivan
(SYMP) **SYMCD1123** Sullivan—Sesquicentenial Commemorative Issue

MAAG, Peter (cond)
see Berne SO
La Scala Orch
National PO
Veneto PO

MAAZEL, Lorin (cond)
see Berlin Deutsche Op Chor
Berlin Deutsche Op Orch
BPO
BRSO
Cleveland Orch
FNO
FRNO
La Scala Orch
LSO
National PO
New Philh
Paris Op Orch
Philh
Pittsburgh SO
ROHO
Santa Cecilia Academy Orch
Vienna St Op Orch
VPO

MABRY, James (sngr)
Weill: Down in the Valley (Cpte)

MACALLISTER, Scott (ten)
Mozart: Don Giovanni (Cpte)

MCALPINE, William (ten)
Britten: Billy Budd (Cpte)
German: Merrie England (Cpte)
Lehár: Lustige Witwe (exc)

MACANN, Rodney (bass)
Dvořák: Rusalka (Cpte)
Tippett: King Priam (Cpte)

MACARTHUR, Edwin (cond)
see RCA Victor SO
San Francisco Op Orch

MCARTHUR, Edwin (cond)
see NBC SO
RCA SO
RCA Victor SO
San Francisco Op Orch
San Francisco SO
Victor SO

MCASLAN, Lorraine (vn)
(LYRI) **SRCD209** Holst—Orchestral Works

MACAUX, Geneviève (sop)
Bizet: Carmen (exc)
(RCA) **GD60205** Opera Choruses

MCBRIDE, Brendan (ten)
(OPRA) **ORCH104** A Hundred Years of Italian Opera: 1820-1830

MCCAFFERTY, Frances (sop)
Offenbach: Orphée aux enfers (Cpte)

MCCANN, Paul (ten)
M. Berkeley: Baa Baa Black Sheep (Cpte)

MCCANN, Phillip (cornet)
(CHAN) **CHAN4501** The World's Most Beautiful Melodies
(CHAN) **CHAN4505** Black Dyke plays Rossini
(CHAN) **CHAN4513** British Bandsman Centenary Concert

MCCARTHY, John (cond)
see LSO

MCCAULEY, Barry (ten)
Bizet: Carmen (Cpte)
Janáček: From the House of the Dead (Cpte), Káťa Kabanová (Cpte)
(CAST) **CVI2071** Highlights from Glyndebourne

MACCHI, Maria de (sop)
(MEMO) **HR4408/9(2)** Singers in Genoa, Vol.1 (disc 2)

MACCHÌ, Mario (bass)
Verdi: Otello (Cpte)

MCCOLLUM, John (ten)
Dittersdorf: Arcifanfano (Cpte)

MCCORD, Catherine (mez)
Rossini: Barbiere di Siviglia (Cpte)

MCCORMACK, John (ten)
(ASV) **CDAJA5137** The Three Tenors of the Century
(BIDD) **LAB022** Fritz Kreisler—Duets with McCormack & Farrar
(MMOI) **CDMOIR418** Great Voices of the Century—John McCormack
(NIMB) **NI7801** Great Singers, Vol.1
(PEAR) **GEMMCDS9924(2)** Covent Garden on Record, Vol.2 (pt 2)
(PEAR) **GEMMCD9315** Kreisler/McCormack Duets
(RCA) **09026 61580-2(2)** RCA/Met 100 Singers, 100 Years (pt 2)
(ROMO) **81016-2** Lucrezia Bori (1887-1960)
(TEST) **SBT1005** Ten Top Tenors
(TEST) **SBT1008** Viva Rossini

MCCOSHAN, Daniel (ten)
Mozart: Nozze di Figaro (Cpte)
Walton: Troilus and Cressida (Cpte)
(EMI) **CDH5 65072-2** Glyndebourne Recorded - 1934-1994

MCCOY, Seth (ten)
Rachmaninov: Monna Vanna (exc)

MCCRACKEN, James (ten)
Bizet: Carmen (Cpte)
Meyerbeer: Prophète (Cpte)
Verdi: Otello (Cpte)
(BELA) **450 007-2** Puccini Favourites
(DECC) **433 066-2DWO** Your Hundred Best Opera Tunes III
(DECC) **433 443-2DA** Great Opera Choruses
(DECC) **433 865-2DWO** The World of Puccini
(DECC) **436 314-2DA** Great Tenor Arias

MCCUE, William (bass)
Mozart: Nozze di Figaro (Cpte)

MACCULI, Sabina (sop)
(DECC) **436 261-2DHO3** Puccini—Il Trittico

MCCULLOCH, Susan (sop)
Mozart: Nozze di Figaro (Cpte)
(IMP) **DPCD1015** Karaoke Opera
(IMP) **PCDS23** Music of the World—Italy & Spain—The Latin Quarter
(IMP) **PCD1043** Opera Favourites
(IMP) **TCD1070** Invitation to the Opera
(OPRA) **ORCH104** A Hundred Years of Italian Opera: 1820-1830

MCDANIEL, Barry (bar)
Bizet: Carmen (Cpte)
Henze: Junge Lord (Cpte)
Leoncavallo: Pagliacci (Cpte)
Mozart: Finta Giardiniera (Cpte)
Purcell: Dido (Cpte)
R. Strauss: Ariadne auf Naxos (Cpte)
Schultze: Schwarzer Peter (Cpte)
Weill: Zar lässt sich Photographieren (Cpte)
(DG) **439 474-2GCL** Purcell—Opera & Choral Works

MCDONALD, Anne-Maree (sop)
J. Strauss II: Fledermaus (Cpte)
Lehár: Lustige Witwe (Cpte)

MCDONALD, Christie (sngr)
(PEAR) **GEMMCDS9053/5** Music from the New York Stage, Vol. 2: 1908—1913
(PEAR) **GEMMCDS9056/8** Music from the New York Stage, Vol. 3: 1913-17

MACDONALD, Kenneth (ten)
Britten: Midsummer Night's Dream (Cpte)
Donizetti: Lucia di Lammermoor (Cpte)

MCDONALD, Robert (pf)
(SONY) **SK52568** Midori—Encore!

MACDONALD, W. H. (sngr)
(PEAR) **GEMMCDS9050/2(1)** Music from the New York Stage, Vol. 1 (part 1)

MCDONALL, Lois (sop)
Donizetti: Maria Padilla (Cpte)
Wagner: Rheingold (Cpte)

MCDONNELL, Tom (bar)
Puccini: Fanciulla del West (Cpte)
Rossini: Tancredi (Cpte)
(RCA) **GD60941** Rarities - Montserrat Caballé

MACDOUGALL, Jamie (ten)
Boughton: Bethlehem (Cpte)
Purcell: Dido (Cpte), King Arthur, Z628 (Cpte)

MCEACHERN, Malcolm (bass)
(PEAR) **GEMMCD9455** Malcolm McEachern—Song Recital

MCFADDEN, Claron (sop)
Gluck: Orfeo ed Euridice (Cpte), Paride ed Elena (Cpte)
Handel: Ottone (Cpte)
Purcell: King Arthur, Z628 (Cpte)
Rameau: Indes galantes (Cpte)

MCFARLAND, Robert (bar)
Glass: Satyagraha (Cpte)

MCFERRIN, Bobby (cond)
see St Paul CO

MCGEGAN, Nicholas (cond)
see Capella Savaria
English Bach Fest Orch
Freiburg Baroque Orch
LSO
Philh Baroque Orch

MCGEGAN, Nicholas (hpd/dir)
Handel: Radamisto (Cpte)
(HARM) **HMU90 7167** Purcell & Blow—Songs & Intrumental Music

MCGLINN, John (cond)
see London Sinfonietta
New Princess Th Orch

MCGOVERN, Mary (sop)
(SONY) **SK44995** Maureen McGovern sings Gershwin

MCGRATH, Bob (sngr)
J. Moran: Manson Family (Cpte)

MCGRAW, William (bar)
Falla: Vida breve (Cpte)

MACGREGOR, Alison (sngr)
G. Charpentier: Louise (Cpte)

MCGRUDER, Jasper (narr)
Glass: Einstein on the Beach (Cpte)

MACHELL, Alison (sngr)
Menotti: Boy who grew too fast (Cpte)

MACHI, Mario (bar)
Verdi: Otello (exc)

MACHOTKOVÁ, Marcela (sop)
Dvořák: Jacobin (exc)
Smetana: Two Widows (Cpte)

MACIAS, Reinaldo (ten)
Beethoven: Fidelio (Cpte)

MACIEJEWSKI, Stephan (bass)
Lully: Atys (Cpte)

MCINTYRE, Sir **Donald (bass-bar)**
Debussy: Pelléas et Mélisande (Cpte)
Wagner: Parsifal (Cpte), Rheingold (Cpte), Siegfried (Cpte), Walküre (Cpte)
(KIWI) **CDSLD-82** Southern Voices—NZ International Opera Singers
(ODE) **CDMANU1317** Wagner—Opera Excerpts
(PHIL) **434 420-2PM32(2)** Richard Wagner Edition (pt 2)

MACKAY, Ann (sop)
Rameau: Naïs (Cpte)

MCKAY, Marjory (sop)
Meyerbeer: Huguenots (Cpte)

MACKAY, Penelope (sop)
Britten: Death in Venice (Cpte)

MACKAY, Rita (sop)
Sullivan: Patience (Cpte)

MACKEBEN, Theo (cond)
see orch

MCKEE, Joseph (bass)
Britten: Paul Bunyan (Cpte)
Puccini: Bohème (Cpte)

V. Thomson: Mother of us all (Cpte)

ICKEEL, James (bar)
(ALBA) **TROY068-2** William Mayer—Voices from Lost Realms

ICKELLAR, Kenneth (ten)
(DECC) **425 849-2DWO** Your hundred best tunes vol 3
(DECC) **425 851-2DWO** Your hundred best tunes vol 5

ICKENNA, Kennedy (ten)
(CLAR) **CDGSE78-50-26** Wagner: Tristan und Isolde excerpts
(CLAR) **CDGSE78-50-35/6** Wagner—Historical recordings
(PEAR) **GEMMCDS9137** Wagner—Der Ring des Nibelungen

ICKERRACHER, Colin (sngr)
(OPRA) **ORR201** 19th Century Heroines-Yvonne Kenny

ACKERRAS, Sir Charles (cond)
see Austrian RSO
Brno St PO
ECO
ENO Orch
Hamburg NDR CO
LPO
LSO
OAE
Philh
RLPO
San Francisco Op Orch
Scottish CO
Vienna St Op Orch
VPO
WNO Orch

ACKIE, Neil (ten)
Maxwell Davies: Lighthouse (Cpte)
Sullivan: Yeomen of the Guard (Cpte)
(COLL) **Coll1444-2** Maximum Max—Music of Maxwell Davies

ACKIE, William (bass)
Wagner: Parsifal (Cpte)

CKINNON, Neil (ten)
Mozart: Zauberflöte (Cpte)

ACKINTOSH, Catherine (vn)
Mozart: Zauberflöte (exc)
(L'OI) **417 123-2OH** Purcell: Songs and Airs
(L'OI) **444 620-2OH** The Glory of Purcell

CKNIGHT, Anne (sop)
Puccini: Bohème (Cpte)

CLAUGHLIN, Marie (sop)
Beethoven: Fidelio (Cpte)
Bizet: Carmen (Cpte)
Mozart: Così fan tutte (Cpte), Don Giovanni (Cpte), Nozze di Figaro (Cpte), Zauberflöte (Cpte)
Purcell: Dido (Cpte)
Sullivan: Mikado (Cpte)
Verdi: Traviata (Cpte)
(DG) **439 153-4GMA** Mad about Sopranos
(TELA) **CD80407** Divine Sopranos

ACLEAN, Susan (mez)
Krenek: Sprung über den Schatten (Cpte)

CLEOD, Linda (mez)
Dvořák: Rusalka (Cpte)

CLEOD, Suzanne (mez)
Corghi: Divara (Cpte)

MAHON, Alan (spkr)
Lampe: Pyramus and Thisbe (Cpte)

CMAHON, Patricia (sop)
(LINN) **CKD008** Scotland's Music

CMILLAN, James (cond)
see Scottish CO

MOON, Cosme (pf)
(RCA) **GD61175** The Glory of the Human Voice-Florence Foster Jenkins

NAB, Eilidh (sop)
Purcell: Dido (Cpte)

NAIR, Sylvia (sop)
Berlioz: Béatrice et Bénédict (Cpte)
Gluck: Orfeo ed Euridice (Cpte)
Mozart: Clemenza di Tito (Cpte), Idomeneo (Cpte), Nozze di Figaro (Cpte)
Purcell: Fairy Queen, Z629 (Cpte)
Rossini: Viaggio a Reims (Cpte)
Sullivan: Yeomen of the Guard (Cpte)
(PHIL) **446 081-2PH** The Echoing Air—The Music of Henry Purcell

NAUGHTON, Tom (sngr)
(PEAR) **GEMMCDS9053/5** Music from the New York Stage, Vol. 2: 1908—1913

CNEIL, Cornell (bar)
Mascagni: Cavalleria Rusticana (Cpte)
Puccini: Tosca (Cpte)
Verdi: Aida (exc), Luisa Miller (Cpte), Rigoletto (Cpte)
(BELA) **450 133-2** Verdi Favourites

CNEIL, Walter (ten)
Verdi: Traviata (Cpte)

CPHERSON, George (bass)
Puccini: Manon Lescaut (Cpte)

Walton: Troilus and Cressida (Cpte)

MCSHANE, David (bar)
Delius: Village Romeo and Juliet (Cpte)

MACURDY, John (bass)
Mozart: Don Giovanni (Cpte)
R. Ward: Crucible (Cpte)
Verdi: Don Carlo (Cpte), Otello (exc)

MACWHERTER, Rod (ten)
Bellini: Norma (Cpte)
Verdi: Aida (exc), Don Carlo (Cpte)

MADASI, Antonio (ten)
Verdi: Falstaff (Cpte)
(RCA) **GD60326** Verdi—Operas & Choral Works

MADDALENA, Alessandro (bass)
Rossini: Armida (Cpte)
Verdi: Don Carlo (Cpte), Traviata (Cpte)

MADDALENA, James (bar)
Handel: Giulio Cesare (Cpte)
J. Adams: Death of Klinghoffer (Cpte)
Moran: Dracula Diary (Cpte)
Mozart: Nozze di Figaro (Cpte)

MADEIRA, Jean (mez)
R. Strauss: Elektra (Cpte)
Verdi: Ballo in maschera (Cpte)
Wagner: Rheingold (Cpte)
(DECC) **414 100-2DM15** Wagner: Der Ring des Nibelungen

MADERNA, Bruno (cond)
see Milan RAI SO
Rome RAI Orch

MADIN, Viktor (bar)
Verdi: Macbeth (Cpte), Otello (Cpte)
Wagner: Meistersinger (Cpte)
(EMI) **CHS7 64487-2** R. Strauss—Der Rosenkavalier & Lieder
(PEAR) **GEMMCDS9365** R. Strauss: Der Rosenkavalier (abridged), etc
(SCHW) **314562** Vienna State Opera Live, Vol.6
(SCHW) **314602** Vienna State Opera Live, Vol.10
(SCHW) **314622** Vienna State Opera Live, Vol.12
(SCHW) **314632** Vienna State Opera Live, Vol.13
(SCHW) **314642** Vienna State Opera Live, Vol.14
(SCHW) **314652** Vienna State Opera Live, Vol.15
(SCHW) **314672** Vienna State Opera Live, Vol.17

MADRID COMUNIDAD CHORUS
cond A. R. MARBÀ
Bretón: Verbena de La Paloma (Cpte)

MADRID CONCERTS ORCHESTRA
cond J. ARÁMBARRI
(GME) **GME225** Arriaga—String and Orchestral Works
cond P. DE FREITAS BRANCO
(GME) **GME221** Falla—Orchestral Works
cond F. MORENO TORROBA
Bretón: Verbena de la Paloma (Cpte)
Moreno Torroba: Luisa Fernanda (Cpte)
cond P. SOROZÁBAL
Chapí: Revoltosa (Cpte)
Sorozábal: Katiuska (Cpte)
Vives: Bohemios (Cpte), Doña Francisquita (Cpte)

MADRID COROS CANTORES
cond F. MORENO TORROBA
Barbieri: Barberillo de Lavapiès (Cpte)
Bretón: Verbena de la Paloma (Cpte)
Usandizaga: Golondrinas (Cpte)
cond P. SOROZÁBAL
Chapí: Revoltosa (Cpte)
Sorozábal: Katiuska (Cpte)
Vives: Bohemios (Cpte), Doña Francisquita (Cpte)

MADRID RONDALLA LÍRICA
cond M. MORENO-BUENDIA
(EMI) **CDC7 49148-2** Romanzas de Zarzuelas

MADRID SYMPHONY ORCHESTRA
cond E.F. ARBÓS
(VAI) **VAIA1046** Spanish Orchestral Favorites
cond E. G. ASENSIO
(IMP) **MCD45** Spanish Royal Gala
cond A. R. MARBÀ
Bretón: Verbena de La Paloma (Cpte)
cond M. MORENO-BUENDIA
(EMI) **CDC7 49148-2** Romanzas de Zarzuelas
(EMI) **CDM7 64359-2** Gala de España
cond M. ROA
Penella: Gato Montés (Cpte)
cond G.P. SANZOGNO
(IMP) **DPCD998** Opera Stars in Concert
(RNE) **650004** Opera Stars in Concert

MADRID ZARZUELA THEATRE CHORUS
cond M. MORENO-BUENDIA
(EMI) **CDC7 49148-2** Romanzas de Zarzuelas
cond M. ROA
Penella: Gato Montés (Cpte)
cond N. SANZOGNO
Puccini: Bohème (Cpte)

MADRID ZARZUELA THEATRE ORCHESTRA
cond G. RIVOLI
(MEMO) **HR4279/80** Montserrat Caballè—Opera Arias
cond N. SANZOGNO
Puccini: Bohème (Cpte)

MAERO, Philip (bar)
Puccini: Bohème (exc), Madama Butterfly (Cpte)
(VANG) **08.4016.71** Music of Samuel Barber

MAFFEO, Gianni (bar)
Puccini: Bohème (Cpte)
(DECC) **433 439-2DA** Great Love Duets
(DECC) **433 865-2DWO** The World of Puccini
(DECC) **440 947-2DH** Essential Opera II

MAGA, Othmar (cond)
see Cologne RSO

MAGALOFF, Nikita (pf)
(BIDD) **LAB007/8** The Art of Joseph Szigeti, Vol.2

MAGGIO MUSICALE FIORENTINO CHORUS
cond M. ARENA
(ACAN) **43 540** Opera Choruses
cond B. BARTOLETTI
(DECC) **436 261-2DHO3** Puccini—Il Trittico
cond R. BONYNGE
(DECC) **433 706-2DMO3** Bellini—Beatrice di Tenda; Operatic Arias
cond F. CAPUANA
Bellini: Pirata (Cpte)
(MEMO) **HR4273/4** Great Voices—Pietro Cappuccilli
(MEMO) **HR4279/80** Montserrat Caballè—Opera Arias
cond A. EREDE
Mascagni: Cavalleria Rusticana (Cpte)
Rossini: Barbiere di Siviglia (Cpte)
(BELA) **450 133-2** Verdi Favourites
(DECC) **433 069-2DWO** Your Hundred Best Opera Tunes VI
(DECC) **433 442-2DA** Verdi—Famous Arias
(DECC) **440 406-2DM** Giulietta Simionato
(DECC) **440 407-2DM** Mario del Monaco
(DECC) **443 378-2DM** Ten Top Mezzos 2
(DECC) **443 930-2DM** Jussi Björling sings Opera Arias
cond L. GARDELLI
(DECC) **411 665-2DM3** Puccini: Il trittico
cond G. GAVAZZENI
Ponchielli: Gioconda (Cpte)
(DECC) **440 411-2DM** Anita Cerquetti
(MEMO) **HR4291/2** Great Voices - Renata Scotto
cond Z. MEHTA
Mozart: Nozze di Figaro (Cpte)
Verdi: Traviata (exc), Trovatore (Cpte)
cond D. MITROPOULOS
(MEMO) **HR4400/1** Great Voices - Ettore Bastianini
cond F. MOLINARI-PRADELLI
Donizetti: Elisir d'amore (Cpte)
(DECC) **436 464-2DM** Ten Top Baritones & Basses
cond R. MUTI
Bellini: Norma (Cpte)
Leoncavallo: Pagliacci (Cpte)
Meyerbeer: Africaine (Cpte)
cond J. PRITCHARD
Verdi: Traviata (Cpte)
(BELA) **450 133-2** Verdi Favourites
(DECC) **433 069-2DWO** Your Hundred Best Opera Tunes VI
(DECC) **433 440-2DA** Golden Opera
cond T. SCHIPPERS
(MEMO) **HR4279/80** Montserrat Caballè—Opera Arias
cond T. SERAFIN
Donizetti: Lucia di Lammermoor (Cpte)
(EMI) **CMS7 63244-2** The Art of Maria Callas
cond S. VARVISO
Rossini: Italiana in Algeri (Cpte)
cond A. VOTTO
Puccini: Bohème (exc)

MAGGIO MUSICALE FIORENTINO ORCHESTRA
(DECC) **430 433-2DH** Carreras, Domingo and Pavarotti in Concert
(DECC) **440 410-2DM** Plácido Domingo
(DECC) **440 947-2DH** Essential Opera II
(DECC) **071 123-1DH (DECC)** Carreras, Domingo and Pavarotti in Concert
(DECC) **071 142-1DH (DECC)** Essential Opera
(DECC) **430 433-5DH** Carreras, Domingo and Pavarotti in Concert
cond M. ARENA
(ACAN) **43 540** Opera Choruses
cond B. BARTOLETTI
(DECC) **436 261-2DHO3** Puccini—Il Trittico
cond R. BONYNGE
(DECC) **433 706-2DMO3** Bellini—Beatrice di Tenda; Operatic Arias
cond F. CAPUANA
Bellini: Pirata (Cpte)
(MEMO) **HR4273/4** Great Voices—Pietro Cappuccilli
(MEMO) **HR4279/80** Montserrat Caballè—Opera Arias
cond A. EREDE
Mascagni: Cavalleria Rusticana (Cpte)
Rossini: Barbiere di Siviglia (Cpte)
(DECC) **417 686-2DC** Puccini—Operatic Arias
(DECC) **433 064-2DWO** Your Hundred Best Opera Tunes Volume I
(DECC) **433 066-2DWO** Your Hundred Best Opera Tunes III
(DECC) **433 069-2DWO** Your Hundred Best Opera Tunes VI
(DECC) **433 636-2DSP** Puccini—Famous Arias
(DECC) **436 300-2DX** Opera Gala Sampler
(DECC) **436 314-2DA** Great Tenor Arias
(DECC) **436 463-2DM** Ten Top Tenors
(DECC) **440 406-2DM** Giulietta Simionato
(DECC) **443 930-2DM** Jussi Björling sings Opera Arias
(DECC) **444 555-2DF2** Essential Puccini

cond L. GARDELLI
(DECC) **411 665-2DM3** Puccini: Il trittico
(DECC) **430 481-2DX2** Renata Tebaldi sings Opera Arias
(DECC) **433 065-2DWO** Your Hundred Best Opera Tunes Volume II
(DECC) **433 440-2DA** Golden Opera
(DECC) **433 624-2DSP** Great Soprano Arias
(DECC) **433 822-2DH** Essential Opera
(DECC) **436 317-2DA** Puccini—Famous Arias
(DECC) **440 408-2DM** Renata Tebaldi
(DECC) **444 555-2DF2** Essential Puccini
cond G. GAVAZZENI
Ponchielli: Gioconda (Cpte)
(DECC) **417 686-2DC** Puccini—Operatic Arias
(DECC) **433 069-2DWO** Your Hundred Best Opera Tunes VI
(DECC) **433 442-2DA** Verdi—Famous Arias
(DECC) **433 636-2DSP** Puccini—Famous Arias
(DECC) **440 407-2DM** Mario del Monaco
(DECC) **440 411-2DM** Anita Cerquetti
(MEMO) **HR4291/2** Great Voices - Renata Scotto
cond Z. MEHTA
Mozart: Nozze di Figaro (Cpte)
Verdi: Traviata (exc), Trovatore (Cpte)
(PHIL) **442 602-2PM** 3 x 3 Tenors
cond D. MITROPOULOS
(MEMO) **HR4400/1** Great Voices - Ettore Bastianini
cond F. MOLINARI-PRADELLI
Donizetti: Elisir d'amore (Cpte)
(DECC) **433 065-2DWO** Your Hundred Best Opera Tunes Volume II
(DECC) **436 464-2DM** Ten Top Baritones & Basses
(DECC) **440 403-2DM** Giuseppe di Stefano
(MEMO) **HR4239/40** Opera Arias—Leyla Gencer
cond R. MUTI
Bellini: Norma (Cpte)
Leoncavallo: Pagliacci (Cpte)
Meyerbeer: Africaine (Cpte)
cond F. PATANÈ
(DECC) **436 463-2DM** Ten Top Tenors
cond J. PRITCHARD
Verdi: Traviata (exc)
(BELA) **450 006-2** Famous Opera Duets
(BELA) **450 133-2** Verdi Favourites
(DECC) **433 069-2DWO** Your Hundred Best Opera Tunes VI
(DECC) **433 221-2DWO** The World of Verdi
(DECC) **433 440-2DA** Golden Opera
cond T. SCHIPPERS
(MEMO) **HR4279/80** Montserrat Caballè—Opera Arias
cond T. SERAFIN
Donizetti: Lucia di Lammermoor (Cpte)
(EMI) **CDC7 54437-2** Callas Rarities
(EMI) **CMS7 63244-2** The Art of Maria Callas
(MEMO) **HR4235/6** Great Voices-Renata Tebaldi
cond S. VARVISO
Rossini: Italiana in Algeri (Cpte)
cond A. VOTTO
Puccini: Bohème (exc)

MAGIC CIRCLE CHAMBER ORCHESTRA
cond R. EVANS HARRELL
Rorem: Childhood Miracle (Cpte), Three Sisters Who Are Not Sisters (Cpte)

MAGIERA, Leone (cond)
see Ater Orch
Bologna Teatro Comunale Orch
Hamburg PO
Modena Teatro Comunale Orch
National PO
New Philh
NYPO
Orch
Philh
RPO
Vienna Volksoper Orch

MAGINI-COLETTI, Antonio (bar)
(CLUB) **CL99-587/8** Eugenia Burzio (1872-1922)
(NIMB) **NI7867** Legendary Baritones
(PREI) **89995** Famous Italian Baritones
(SYMP) **SYMCD1113** The Harold Wayne Collection, Vol.13
(SYMP) **SYMCD1126** The Harold Wayne Collection, Vol.14

MAGLAGNINI, Mario (ten)
Leoncavallo: Bohème (Cpte)
(MCI) **MCCD099** Opera's Greatest Arias

MAGNANT, Philippe (spkr)
Berlioz: Béatrice et Bénédict (Cpte)

MAGNUS, Elisabeth von (sop)
Carvalho: Testoride Argonauta (Cpte)
J. Strauss II: Fledermaus (exc), Zigeunerbaron (Cpte)
Purcell: Dido (Cpte), Fairy Queen, Z629 (Cpte)
Vivaldi: Olimpiade (Cpte)
(TELD) **0630-11470-2** The Best of Barbara Bonney

MAGNUSSON, Bengt-Ola (ten)
Hindemith: Mörder, Hoffnung der Frauen (Cpte)

MAGNUSSON, Lars (ten)
Trojahn: Enrico (Cpte)

MAGRINI, Vera (mez)
Alfano: Risurrezione (Cpte)

MAGUENAT, Alfred (bar)
Debussy: Pelléas et Mélisande (exc)

MAGUIRE, Linda (mez)
Handel: Floridante (exc)

MAHÉ, Martine (mez)
Gounod: Faust (Cpte)
Massenet: Manon (Cpte)
Ravel: Enfant et les sortilèges (Cpte)

MAHLER, Jerzy (bass)
Rossini: Signor Bruschino (Cpte)

MAHSOORI, Khosrow (ten)
J. Strauss II: Fledermaus (Cpte)

MAIER, Franzjosef (vn/dir)
Pergolesi: Serva Padrona

MAIER, Fritz (bass)
R. Strauss: Rosenkavalier (Cpte)

MAIEVSKI, Maurice (ten)
Bizet: Carmen (Cpte)

MAIKL, Georg (ten)
Wagner: Meistersinger (Cpte)
(SCHW) **314572** Vienna State Opera Live, Vol.7
(SCHW) **314602** Vienna State Opera Live, Vol.10
(SCHW) **314622** Vienna State Opera Live, Vol.12
(SCHW) **314642** Vienna State Opera Live, Vol.14
(SCHW) **314672** Vienna State Opera Live, Vol.17
(SCHW) **314702** Vienna State Opera Live, Vol.20

MAIKL, Liselotte (sop)
Humperdinck: Hänsel und Gretel (Cpte)
R. Strauss: Ariadne auf Naxos (Cpte), Salome (Cpte)

MAINZ WIND ENSEMBLE
cond K.R. SCHÖLL
(WERG) **WER6174-2** Orff—Kleines Konzert

MAIONICA, Silvio (bass)
Cilea: Adriana Lecouvreur (Cpte)
Giordano: Andrea Chénier (Cpte), Fedora (Cpte)
Ponchielli: Gioconda (Cpte)
Puccini: Tosca (Cpte)
Verdi: Ballo in maschera (Cpte), Falstaff (Cpte), Traviata (exc)
(DECC) **411 665-2DM3** Puccini: Il trittico

MAIRENA, Manuel (bar)
Falla: Vida breve (Cpte)

MAISEY, Susan (sop)
R. Strauss: Rosenkavalier (Cpte)
Sullivan: Pirates of Penzance (exc)

MAISKY, Mischa (vc)
(DG) **431 544-2GH** Meditation
(DG) **431 544-5GH** Meditation

MAISON, René (ten)
Beethoven: Fidelio (Cpte)
Wagner: Fliegende Holländer (Cpte)
(MSCM) **MM30377** 18 Tenors d'Expression Française
(SCHW) **314542** Vienna State Opera Live, Vol.4

MAÎTRISE DE LA RADIOFFUSION FRANÇAISE
cond T. BEECHAM
Bizet: Carmen (Cpte)
cond E. BOUR
Ravel: Enfant et les sortilèges (Cpte)
cond P. DERVAUX
Massenet: Jongleur de Notre Dame (Cpte)
cond S. OZAWA
Bizet: Carmen (Cpte)
cond G. PRÊTRE
Massenet: Werther (Cpte)

(LA) MAÎTRISE DE LA RÉSURRECTION
cond J. RUDEL
G. Charpentier: Louise (Cpte)

MAJKUT, Erich (spkr)
(SCHW) **314602** Vienna State Opera Live, Vol.10

MAJKUT, Erich (ten)
Einem: Prozess (Cpte)
J. Strauss II: Fledermaus (Cpte)
Lehár: Giuditta (exc)
Mozart: Nozze di Figaro (Cpte), Zauberflöte (Cpte)
R. Strauss: Elektra (Cpte), Rosenkavalier (Cpte)
Wagner: Meistersinger (Cpte)

MAJOR, Malvina (sop)
Mascagni: Amico Fritz (Cpte)
(KIWI) **CDSLD-82** Southern Voices—NZ International Opera Singers
(KIWI) **CDTRL075** Malvina Major—Opera Recital

MAKAROVA, Aleksandra (sngr)
(PEAR) **GEMMCDS9111(2)** Singers of Imperial Russia, Vol.5 (pt 2)

MÄKELÄ, Pertti (ten)
Sallinen: Kullervo (Cpte)

MAKLÁRY, László (cond)
see Budapest Operetta Orch

MAKSAKOV, Max (bass-bar)
(MMOI) **CDMOIR422** Great Voices in Tchaikovsky
(PEAR) **GEMMCDS9111(2)** Singers of Imperial Russia, Vol.5 (pt 2)

MAKSAKOVA, Maria (mez)
(DANT) **LYS013/5** Tchaikovsky—The Queen of Spades

MAKSYMIUK, Jerzy (cond)
see Polish CO

MALACHOVSKÝ, Ondrej (bass)
Suchoň: Whirlpool (Cpte)

MALAGÙ, Stefania (mez)
Catalani: Wally (Cpte)
Giordano: Andrea Chénier (Cpte)
Rossini: Barbiere di Siviglia (Cpte)
Verdi: Macbeth (Cpte), Otello (Cpte), Rigoletto (Cpte), Traviata (Cpte)
(BELA) **450 133-2** Verdi Favourites
(CBS) **CD79312** Puccini: Il Trittico
(MEMO) **HR4277/8** Mirella Freni—Public Performances 1963-1970

MALAKOVA, Petra (mez)
Verdi: Otello (exc)

MALANIUK, Ira (contr)
Mozart: Così fan tutte (Cpte), Nozze di Figaro (Cpte)
R. Strauss: Arabella (Cpte)
Wagner: Götterdämmerung (Cpte), Meistersinger (Cpte), Rheingold (Cpte), Walküre (Cpte)
(DECC) **414 100-2DM15** Wagner: Der Ring des Nibelungen
(DECC) **421 313-2DA** Wagner: Der Ring des Nibelungen - Great Scenes
(EMI) **CZS7 67123-2** Wagner: Der Ring des Nibelungen
(FOYE) **15-CF2011** Wagner—Der Ring de Nibelunger

MALAS, Spiro (bass)
Donizetti: Elisir d'amore (Cpte), Fille du régiment (Cpte)
Handel: Giulio Cesare (Cpte)
Puccini: Tosca (Cpte)
R. Ward: Crucible (Cpte)
Rossini: Semiramide (Cpte)

MALAS-GODLEWSKA, Ewa (sop)
Jommelli: Armida abbandonata (Cpte)

MALASPINA, Giampiero (bar)
Mussorgsky: Khovanshchina (Cpte)
(EMI) **CHS7 69741-2(7)** Record of Singing, Vol.4—Italian School

MALBIN, Elaine (sop)
Busoni: Arlecchino (Cpte)
(RCA) **GD60889(1)** The Mario Lanza Collection

MALCHENKO, Vladimir (bass)
Rimsky-Korsakov: Tsar's Bride (Cpte)

MALCOLM, George (hpd)
(DECC) **444 390-2DWO** The World of The Harpsichord
(VANG) **08.2003.72** Purcell—Celebrated Songs,Sacred Airs and Concert Pieces

MALE CHAMBER CHOIR
cond A. CHISTIAKOV
Serov: Judith (Cpte)

MALE CHORUS
cond O. HOLT
Probst: Maximilien Kolbe (Cpte)

MALE QUARTET
cond W. BRÜCKNER-RÜGGEBERG
Weill: Sieben Todsünden (Cpte)

MALEWICZ-MADEY, Anna (contr)
Szymanowski: King Roger (Cpte)

MALFITANO, Catherine (sop)
Gounod: Roméo et Juliette (Cpte)
Puccini: Tosca (Cpte)
R. Strauss: Salome (Cpte)
Verdi: Stiffelio (Cpte)

MALGARINI, Pina (sop)
Massenet: Don Quichotte (Cpte)

MALGOIRE, Jean-Claude (cond)
see Compagnie Barocco
Grande Ecurie

MALIDOR, Lisette (sop)
Offenbach: Contes d'Hoffmann (Cpte)

MALIPIERO, Giovanni (ten)
(EMI) **CHS7 64864-2(2)** La Scala Edition - Vol.2, 1915-46 (pt 2)
(EMI) **CHS7 69741-2(7)** Record of Singing, Vol.4—Italian School

MALIPONTE, Adriana (sop)
Bizet: Carmen (Cpte)

MALKHASSIANTS, Yulia (mez)
Rimsky-Korsakov: Mlada (Cpte)

MALKO, Nicolai (cond)
see Philh

MALLABRERA, André (ten)
Adam: Si j'étais roi (Cpte)
Boïeldieu: Voitures Versées (Cpte)
Massenet: Werther (Cpte)
Offenbach: Orphée aux enfers (Cpte)

MALLERET, Béatrice (sop)
Rossi: Orfeo (Cpte)

MALMBERG, Urban (bar)
Mendelssohn: Hochzeit des Camacho (Cpte)
Offenbach: Contes d'Hoffmann (Cpte)
R. Strauss: Ariadne auf Naxos (Cpte)
Rossini: Barbiere di Siviglia (Cpte)
Saint-Saëns: Samson et Dalila (Cpte)
Schreker: Schatzgräber (Cpte)

MALMÖ SYMPHONY ORCHESTRA
cond J. DEPREIST
(BIS) **BIS-CD570** Malmö Symphony Orchestra

MALONE, Carol (sop)
Rossini: Cenerentola (Cpte)

MALTA, Alexander (bass)
Berg: Wozzeck (Cpte)
Bizet: Carmen (exc)
Hindemith: Mathis der Maler (Cpte)
Leoncavallo: Bohème (Cpte)
Mozart: Don Giovanni (Cpte)
Shostakovich: Lady Macbeth of Mtsensk (Cpte)
Smetana: Bartered Bride (Cpte)
Verdi: Rigoletto (Cpte), Traviata (Cpte)

MALVISI, Desdemona (sop)
Verdi: Lombardi (Cpte)

MALY, Alexander (bass)
Mozart: Zauberflöte (Cpte)
R. Strauss: Rosenkavalier (Cpte)

MALYON, Julia (sop)
Wagner: Walküre (Cpte)

MANCA DI NISSA, Bernadette (contr)
Pergolesi: Frate 'nnamorato (Cpte)
Rossini: Gazza ladra (Cpte), Tancredi (Cpte)
Verdi: Falstaff (Cpte)

MANCHAVIN, Yuri (bass)
Tchaikovsky: Eugene Onegin (Cpte)
(DANT) **LYS013/5** Tchaikovsky—The Queen of Spades

MANCHESTER CAMERATA
cond C. RIZZI
(MANC) **MCL20** Camerata Celebration 1972-1992

MANCHESTER CHILDREN'S CHOIR
cond H. HARTY
(BEUL) **1PD4** 78 Classics - Volume One

MANCHET, Éliane (sop)
Debussy: Pelléas et Mélisande (Cpte)
G. Charpentier: Louise (Cpte)

MANCHUROV, Fuat (cond)
see Finnish Nat Op Orch

MANCINI, Caterina (sop)
Rossini: Mosè (Cpte)

MANCINI, Jolanda (sngr)
Mussorgsky: Khovanshchina (Cpte)

MANCINI, Luigi (bass)
Verdi: Traviata (Cpte)

MANDALARI, Maria Teresa (mez)
Giordano: Andrea Chénier (Cpte)

MANDEAL, Cristian (cond)
see Moldova PO

MANDELLI, Luisa (sop)
Donizetti: Elisir d'amore (Cpte)
Verdi: Rigoletto (Cpte), Traviata (Cpte)

MANDIKIAN, Arda (mez)
Britten: Turn of the Screw (Cpte)
Purcell: Dido (Cpte)

MANFREDINI, Cécile (sngr)
Lecocq: Jour et la Nuit (Cpte)

MANFRINI, Luigi (bass)
Puccini: Bohème (Cpte)
Verdi: Aida (Cpte)
(NIMB) **NI7853** Lauri-Volpi sings Verdi

MANGA, Silvana (sngr)
Donizetti: Gianni di Parigi (Cpte)

MANGANOTTI, Gianfranco (ten)
Donizetti: Lucia di Lammermoor (exc)
Verdi: Ernani (Cpte)
(BUTT) **BMCD015** Pavarotti Collection - Duets and Scenes

MANGELSDORFF, Simone (sop)
Mozart: Ascanio in Alba (Cpte)
Wagner: Rheingold (Cpte)
(DG) **435 211-2GX15** Wagner—Der Ring des Nibelungen

MANG-HABASHI, Karin (mez)
Mozart: Nozze di Figaro (Cpte)

MANGIN, Noel (bass)
Puccini: Bohème (Cpte), Manon Lescaut (Cpte)
(KIWI) **CDSLD-82** Southern Voices—NZ International Opera Singers

MANHART, Emily (mez)
Bellini: Bianca e Fernando (Cpte)
Boito: Mefistofele (Cpte)

MANHATTAN OPERA CHORUS
cond L. BERNSTEIN
Bizet: Carmen (Cpte)

MANHATTAN SCHOOL OF MUSIC OPERA CHORUS
cond D. GILBERT
Rorem: Miss Julie (Cpte)

MANHATTAN SCHOOL OF MUSIC OPERA ORCHESTRA
cond D. GILBERT
Rorem: Miss Julie (Cpte)

MANN, Paul (spkr)
Glass: Einstein on the Beach (Cpte)

MANN, Tor (cond)
see Gothenburg SO
Stockholm PO
Swedish RSO

MANN, Werner (bass)
Schoenberg: Moses und Aron (Cpte)

MANNARINI, Ida (mez)
(PEAR) **GEMMCD9091** Dino Borgioli
(PREI) **89016** Gina Cigna (b. 1900)
(PREI) **89023** Conchita Supervia (1895-1936)
(PREI) **89042** Nazzareno de Angelis (1881-1962)
(PREI) **89048** Apollo Granforte (1886-1975) - I

MANNING, Frances (sop)
Janáček: Fate (Cpte)

MANNING, Jane (sop)
Berg: Lulu (Cpte)
Schoenberg: Moses und Aron (Cpte)
(CHAN) **CHAN6535** Stravinsky—Symphonies of Wind Instruments
(NMC) **NMCD011** Lutyens—Vocal and Chamber Works
(NOVE) **NVLCD109** Weir—Mini-Operas
(UNIT) **88040-2** Judith Weir—Three Operas

MANNING, Jean (mez)
Stravinsky: Rake's Progress (Cpte)
(SONY) **SM22K46290(4)** Stravinsky—The Complete Edition (pt 4)

MANNION, Rosa (sop)
Mozart: Ascanio in Alba (Cpte), Così fan tutte (exc)

MANNO, Vincenzo (ten)
Verdi: Aroldo (Cpte)

MANOWARDA, Josef von (bass)
Mozart: Zauberflöte (Cpte)
Wagner: Lohengrin (exc), Meistersinger (exc), Tristan und Isolde (exc), Walküre (exc)
(PREI) **89069** Josef von Manowarda (1890-1942)
(SCHW) **314512** Vienna State Opera Live, Vol.1
(SCHW) **314532** Vienna State Opera Live, Vol.3
(SCHW) **314562** Vienna State Opera Live, Vol.6
(SCHW) **314582** Vienna State Opera Live, Vol.8
(SCHW) **314592** Vienna State Opera Live, Vol.9
(SCHW) **314622** Vienna State Opera Live, Vol.12
(SCHW) **314632** Vienna State Opera Live, Vol.13
(SCHW) **314642** Vienna State Opera Live, Vol.14
(SCHW) **314662** Vienna State Opera Live, Vol.16
(SCHW) **314672** Vienna State Opera Live, Vol.17
(SCHW) **314722** Vienna State Opera Live, Vol.22
(TELD) **9031-76442-2** Wagner—Excerpts from the 1936 Bayreuth Festival

MANSINGER, Vera (sop)
(SCHW) **314602** Vienna State Opera Live, Vol.10

MANSNERUS, Ilpo (cond)
see Savonlinna Op Fest Orch

MANSOROV, Fuat (cond)
see Bolshoi Th Orch

MANSUETO, Gaudio (bass)
(EMI) **CHS7 64860-2(2)** La Scala Edition - Vol.1, 1878-1914 (pt 2)

MANTOVANI, Alessandro (sop)
Cavalli: Calisto (Cpte)

MANTOVANI, Dino (bar)
Giordano: Andrea Chénier (Cpte)
Puccini: Fanciulla del West (Cpte), Tosca (Cpte)
Rossini: Barbiere di Siviglia (Cpte)

MANUEL, Paul (sngr)
Bernstein: West Side Story (Cpte)

MANUEL, Peter (ten)
Suppé: Boccaccio (exc)

MANUGUERRA, Matteo (bar)
Mascagni: Cavalleria rusticana (exc)
Massenet: Werther (exc)
Ponchielli: Gioconda (Cpte)
Puccini: Bohème (Cpte)
Verdi: Battaglia di Legnano (Cpte), Masnadieri (Cpte), Nabucco (exc), Stiffelio (Cpte), Traviata (exc)
(EMI) **CDM7 69500-2** Montserrat Caballé sings Bellini & Verdi Arias

MANURITTA, Giovanni (ten)
(NIMB) **NI7836/7** Conchita Supervia (1895-1936)
(PEAR) **GEMMCD9117** Graziella Pareto
(PREI) **89023** Conchita Supervia (1895-1936)

MANZINI, Laura (pf)
(FONE) **94F04** Homage to Fritz Kreisler, Volume 1

MANZONI, Valeria (voc)
Distel: Stazione (Cpte)

MAR, Norman del (cond)
see BBC Northern SO
ECO
EOG Orch
RPO

MAŘÁK, Otakar (ten)
(SUPR) **11 2136-2(2)** Emmy Destinn—Complete Edition, Discs 3 & 4

MARANDON, Monique (sop)
Rameau: Dardanus (Cpte)

MARANI, Antonio (bass)
Rossini: Torvaldo e Dorliska (Cpte)

MARBÀ, Antoni Ros (cond)
see Madrid SO
Tenerife SO

MARC, Alessandra (sop)
Krenek: Jonny spielt auf (Cpte)
R. Strauss: Friedenstag (Cpte)
(DELO) **DE3108** Alessandra Marc—Opera Recital
(DELO) **DE3120** Wagner—Orchestral and Vocal Works
(ODE) **CDMANU1317** Wagner—Opera Excerpts

MARCANGELI, Anna (sop)
(EMI) **CMS7 64165-2** Puccini—Trittico

MARCELIN, Emile (ten)
(MSCM) **MM30377** 18 Tenors d'Expression Française

MARCELLA, Lou (ten)
Verdi: Traviata (Cpte)

MARCENO, Antonio (ten)
Verdi: Aida (Cpte)

MARC'HADOUR, Yvon le (bar)
Ravel: Enfant et les sortilèges (Cpte)

MARCHAT, Jean (narr)
Milhaud: Christophe Colomb (Cpte)

MARCHESI, Ruggero (vn)
(MDIT) **MED92102** Airs, Dances and Prayers

MARCHIGIANO PHILHARMONIC ORCHESTRA
cond G. KUHN
Mozart: Così fan tutte (Cpte), Don Giovanni (Cpte)

MARCHIGIANO VINCENZO BELLINI LYRIC CHORUS
cond G. KUHN
Mozart: Così fan tutte (Cpte), Don Giovanni (Cpte)

MARCO, Eugenio M. (cond)
see Barcelona SO

MARCONI, Francesco (ten)
(EMI) **CHS7 64860-2(1)** La Scala Edition - Vol.1, 1878-1914 (pt 1)
(NIMB) **NI7840/1** The Era of Adelina Patti
(PEAR) **GEMMCDS9923(1)** Covent Garden on Record, Vol.1 (pt 1)
(SYMP) **SYMCD1069** The Harold Wayne Collection, Vol.2
(SYMP) **SYMCD1073** The Harold Wayne Collection, Vol.3

MARCUCCI, Maria (mez)
Mascagni: Cavalleria Rusticana (Cpte)

MARDONES, José (bass)
(PEAR) **GEMMCDS9074(1)** Giovanni Zenatello, Vol.2 (pt 1)
(PEAR) **GEMMCDS9159(2)** De Luca Edition, Vol.1 (pt 2)
(PEAR) **GEMMCDS9160(1)** De Luca Edition, Vol.2 (pt 1)
(PEAR) **GEMMCD9122** 20 Great Basses sing Great Arias
(TEST) **SBT1008** Viva Rossini

MARE, Anthony de (sngr/pf)
(KOCH) **37104-2** Cage/Monk—Pianos and Voices

MARESTIN, Valérie (sop)
Auber: Gustav III (Cpte)

MARGIONO, Charlotte (sop)
Beethoven: Fidelio (Cpte)
Mozart: Così fan tutte (Cpte), Don Giovanni (Cpte), Finta Giardiniera (Cpte), Nozze di Figaro (Cpte)
(TELD) **4509-97507-2** Mozart—Famous Opera Arias
(TELD) **4509-98824-2** Thomas Hampson Collection,Vol III-Operatic Scenes

MARGISON, Richard (ten)
Janáček: Makropulos Affair (Cpte)
Tchaikovsky: Mazeppa (Cpte)

MARGITA, Štefan (ten)
Mysliveček: Bellerofonte (Cpte)

MARHERR-WAGNER, Elfriede (mez)
Mozart: Zauberflöte (Cpte)
Wagner: Götterdämmerung (exc)
(EMI) **CMS7 64008-2(2)** Wagner Singing on Record (pt 2)
(LYRC) **LCD146** Frida Leider sings Wagner
(MSCM) **MM30283** Great Wagnerian Singers, Vol.1
(NIMB) **NI7848** Great Singers at the Berlin State Opera
(PEAR) **GEMMCDS9137** Wagner—Der Ring des Nibelungen
(PEAR) **GEMMCD9331** Frida Leider sings Wagner
(PREI) **89098** Frida Leider (1888-1975) - II

MARI, Jean-Baptiste (cond)
see Paris Cons
Paris Op Orch

MARIATEGUI, Suso (ten)
Verdi: Traviata (Cpte)

MARIETTI, Ines (sop)
Verdi: Traviata (Cpte)

MARIMPIETRI, Lydia (sop)
Catalani: Wally (Cpte)
Cherubini: Medea (Cpte)
(EMI) **CMS7 64165-2** Puccini—Trittico

MARIN, Ion (cond)
see ECO
LSO
Philh
Venice La Fenice Orch
Vienna SO

MARIN, José (sngr)
Sorozábal: Katiuska (Cpte)

MARIN-DEGOR, Sophie (sop)
Gluck: Rencontre imprévue (Cpte)
Lully: Alceste (Cpte)
Mouret: Amours de Ragonde (Cpte)
Purcell: Dido (Cpte)
(ERAT) **4509-99607-2** Gluck—Operas; Schubert—Symphonies Nos 8 & 9

MARINOV, Ivan (cond)
see Bulgarian Nat Op Orch
Bulgarian RSO

MARINOV, Pali (bass)
M-A. Charpentier: David et Jonathas (Cpte)

MARINOVA, Sonya (sop)
Mussorgsky: Khovanshchina (Cpte)

MARINUZZI, Gino (cond)
see EIAR Orch
La Scala Orch
Turin EIAR Orch

MARION, Gloria (sop)
(CLUB) **CL99-025** Giovanni Zenatello (1876-1949)
(PEAR) **GEMMCDS9074(2)** Giovanni Zenatello, Vol.2 (pt 2)
(PREI) **89038** Giovanni Zenatello (1876-1949)

MARIOTTI, Alfredo (bass)
Catalani: Wally (Cpte)
Mozart: Don Giovanni (Cpte)
Puccini: Bohème (Cpte), Manon Lescaut (Cpte), Tosca (Cpte)
Verdi: Macbeth (Cpte)
(CBS) **CD79312** Puccini: Il Trittico
(DECC) **433 065-2DWO** Your Hundred Best Opera Tunes Volume II
(DECC) **433 440-2DA** Golden Opera
(DECC) **436 261-2DHO3** Puccini—Il Trittico
(DECC) **436 301-2DA** Renata Tebaldi & Franco Corelli—Arias & Duets
(DECC) **436 317-2DA** Puccini—Famous Arias

MARKELOV, Yury (ten)
Rimsky-Korsakov: Tsar's Bride (Cpte)

MARKERT, Annette (contr)
Handel: Floridante (Cpte)
R. Strauss: Salome (Cpte)

MARKEVITCH, Igor (cond)
see Lamoureux Concerts Orch
Lamoureux Orch
New Philh
Philh

MARKGRAF, Wolfgang (bass)
Wagner: Meistersinger (exc)

MARKHAM, Richard (pf)
(IMP) **MCD76** Nettle and Markham in America

MARKHOFF, Franz (bass)
(SCHW) **314622** Vienna State Opera Live, Vol.12
(SCHW) **314642** Vienna State Opera Live, Vol.14

MÄRKL, Jun (cond)
see Berlin RSO

MARKOV, Alexander (vn)
(ERAT) **4509-98481-2** Violin Encores

MARKOV, Sabin (bass)
Mussorgsky: Boris Godunov (Cpte)
Puccini: Turandot (Cpte)

MARKOVÁ, Jiřina (sop)
Dvořák: Rusalka (Cpte)
Janáček: Excursions of Mr Brouček (Cpte)
Martinů: Miracles of Mary (Cpte)
Smetana: Dalibor (Cpte)
(KOCH) **34036-2** A Pageant of Opera
(SUPR) **11 0345-2** Edith Gruberová - Operatic Recital

MARKOVICH, Alexander (pf)
(TELD) **4509-94554-2** Carmen Fantasy—Virtuoso Music for Trumpet
(TELD) **4509-96231-2** Gardening Classics
(TELD) **9031-77705-2** Works for Trumpet & Piano

MARKOW, Emil (bass)
(RCA) **GD87799** The Pearl Fishers Duet plus Duets and Scenes

MARKS, Alfred (bar)
Gay: Beggar's Opera (Cpte)

MARKSON, Gerhard (cond)
see Hagen PO

MARKUS, Karl (ten)
Marschner: Hans Heiling (Cpte)
Weill: Sieben Todsünden (Cpte)

MARKVART, Jan (ten)
Smetana: Libuše (Cpte)

MARKWORT, Peter (ten)
R. Strauss: Elektra (Cpte)
Weill: Mahagonny (Cpte)

MARLO, Erfried (ten)
Suppé: Boccaccio (exc)

MARLOWE, Anthony (ten)
Britten: Billy Budd (Cpte)
Wagner: Tristan und Isolde (Cpte)

MAROTO, Francisco (sngr)
Sorozábal: Katiuska (Cpte)

MÁROVÁ, Libuše (mez)
Fibich: Bride of Messina (Cpte)
Foerster: Eva (Cpte)
Janáček: Cunning Little Vixen (Cpte), Excursions of Mr Brouček (Cpte)
Smetana: Kiss (Cpte)
(DECC) **421 852-2DH2** Janáček: Operatic & Chamber Works

MARRINER, Sir Neville (cond)
see ASMF
LSO
Minnesota Orch
Stuttgart RSO

MARS, Jacques (bar)
Bizet: Carmen (exc), Pêcheurs de perles (Cpte)
Martinů: Comedy on the Bridge (Cpte)
Massenet: Navarraise (Cpte), Werther (Cpte)
Poulenc: Dialogues des Carmélites (Cpte)
(EMI) **LDB9 91258-1(EMI)** Maria Callas at the Paris Opera December 1958

MARSALIS, Wynton (cornet)
(SONY) **SM42137** Carnaval—Wynton Marsalis
(SONY) **MK42137** Carnaval—Wynton Marsalis

MARSALIS, Wynton (tpt)
(SONY) **SK46672** Baroque Duets

MARSCHALL, Werner (ten)
Hindemith: Nusch-Nuschi (Cpte)

MARSDEN, John (ten)
Vaughan Williams: Pilgrim's Progress (Cpte)

MARSDEN-THOMAS, Anne (organ)
(CRAM) **CRACD 1** Wedding Album

MARSH, Calvin (bar)
Rossini: Barbiere di Siviglia (Cpte)
Verdi: Ballo in maschera (Cpte)

MARSH, Jane (sop)
Schoeck: Penthesilea (Cpte)

MARSH, Lucy Isabelle (sop)
(IRCC) **IRCC-CD810** American Singers, Volume 1

MARSHALL, Larry (ten)
Gershwin: Porgy and Bess (Cpte)

MARSHALL, Lois (sop)
(CBC) **PSCD2001** Lois Marshall sings Oratorio & Operatic Arias
(EMI) **CHS7 63715-2** Mozart: Die Entführung, etc

MARSHALL, Margaret (sop)
Gluck: Orfeo ed Euridice (Cpte)
(CFP) **CD-CFP4612** Favourite Mozart
(EMIL) **CDZ7 67015-2** Mozart—Opera Arias
(ORFE) **C394301B** Great Mozart Singers Series, Vol. 3
(ORFE) **C394501B** Great Mozart Singers Series, Vol. 5
(PHIL) **432 416-2PH3** Haydn—L'incontro improvviso/Arias

MARSHALL, Melanie (mez)
Purcell: Dido (Cpte)
(MEL) **MELCD022-2** Soirée at Snape

MARSHALL, Wayne (pf)
Gershwin: Porgy and Bess (Cpte)
(MEL) **MELCD022-2** Soirée at Snape

MARŠÍK, Bohumil (bass)
Janáček: Excursions of Mr Brouček (Cpte)
Martinů: Miracles of Mary (Cpte)

MARŠÍK, Bohuslav (bass)
Smetana: Dalibor (Cpte)

MARTEL, François (cl)
Vivier: Kopernikus (Cpte)

MARTENSEN, Martha (sop)
Mozart: Zauberflöte (Cpte)

MARTI, Bernabé (ten)
Bellini: Pirata (Cpte)
(CFP) **CD-CFP4569** Puccini: Arias
(EMI) **CDM7 69500-2** Montserrat Caballé sings Bellini & Verdi Arias

MARTIN, Andrea (bar)
Donizetti: Imelda (Cpte)
J. Strauss II: Fledermaus (Cpte)
Keiser: Croesus (Cpte)
Mozart: Così fan tutte (Cpte)
Salieri: Axur (Cpte)
(NAXO) **8 550435** Mozart—Arias and Duets
(NUOV) **6905** Donizetti—Great Love Duets

MARTIN, Drew (ten)
(MUSM) **67110-2** Stravinsky—The Composer, Volume V

MARTIN, Ion (cond)
see Venice La Fenice Orch

MARTIN, Janis (sop)
Wagner: Rienzi (Cpte)
Zemlinsky: Traumgörge (Cpte)
(SONY) **SMK48466** Boulez conducts Schoenberg—Volume 3

MARTIN, János (bar)
Giordano: Fedora (Cpte)

MARTIN, Michel (alto)
Offenbach: Madame l'Archiduc (Cpte)

MARTIN, Milagros (sngr)
Bretón: Verbena de La Paloma (Cpte)

MARTIN, Ray (cond)
see orch

MARTIN, Wolfgang (cond)
see Berlin St Op Orch
Vienna St Op Orch

MARTINEAU, Annette (sngr)
Bazin: Voyage en Chine (Cpte)
Messager: Basoche (Cpte)
(MUSD) **20239-2** Delibes—Opéras-Comiques

MARTINELLI, Germaine (sop)
(EMI) **CMS7 64008-2(1)** Wagner Singing on Record (pt 1)
(MSCM) **MM30221** 18 French Divas

MARTINELLI, Giovanni (ten)
Ponchielli: Gioconda (Cpte)
Verdi: Otello (Cpte)
(MEMO) **HR4408/9(2)** Singers in Genoa, Vol.1 (disc 2)
(MMOI) **CDMOIR405** Great Tenors
(MMOI) **CDMOIR428** Rosa Ponselle and Giovanni Martinelli sing Verdi
(NIMB) **NI7804** Giovanni Martinelli—Opera Recital
(NIMB) **NI7805** Rosa Ponselle—Opera & Song Recital
(NIMB) **NI7846** Rosa Ponselle, Vol.2
(NIMB) **NI7856** Legendary Tenors
(NIMB) **NI7872** Geraldine Farrar in French Opera
(PEAR) **GEMMCDS9159(2)** De Luca Edition, Vol.1 (pt 2)
(PEAR) **GEMMCDS9160(1)** De Luca Edition, Vol.2 (pt 1)
(PEAR) **GEMMCDS9160(2)** De Luca Edition, Vol.2 (pt 2)
(PEAR) **GEMMCDS9452** The Emperor Tibbett
(PEAR) **GEMMCDS9925(1)** Covent Garden on Record—Vol.3 (pt 1)
(PEAR) **GEMMCDS9926(2)** Covent Garden on Record—Vol.4 (pt 2)
(PEAR) **GEMMCD9129** Great Tenors, Vol.2
(PEAR) **GEMMCD9306** Ezio Pinza—Opera Recital
(PREI) **89062** Giovanni Martinelli (1885-1969)
(RCA) **GD87810** Rosa Ponselle - Opera & Song Recital
(RCA) **09026 61580-2(2)** RCA/Met 100 Singers, 100 Years (pt 2)
(ROMO) **81002-2** Emmy Destinn (1878-1930)
(ROMO) **81006-2** Rosa Ponselle (1897-1981)
(ROMO) **81007-2** Rosa Ponselle—Victor Recordings 1926-1929
(SUPR) **11 2136-2(5)** Emmy Destinn—Complete Edition, Discs 11 & 12
(TEST) **SBT1005** Ten Top Tenors
(TEST) **SBT1008** Viva Rossini

MARTINEZ, Ana Maria (sop)
Glass: Belle et la Bête (Cpte)

MARTINEZ, Dominick (treb)
Puccini: Tosca (Cpte)

MARTINEZ, Ivo (treb)
Puccini: Tosca (Cpte)

MARTINEZ, Odaline de la (cond)
see BBC PO

MARTINEZ, Sébastien (sngr)
Gounod: Sapho (Cpte)

MARTINI, Juan E. (cond)
see orch

MARTINI, Luise (sop)
J. Strauss II: Fledermaus (Cpte)

MARTINIS, Dragica (sop)
Verdi: Otello (Cpte)

MARTINO, Adriane (mez)
Puccini: Bohème (Cpte)
(DG) **419 257-2GH3** 'Cav' and 'Pag', etc

MARTINO, Vito (ten)
Rossini: Siège de Corinthe (Cpte)

MARTINON, Jean (cond)
see FRNO

MARTINOTTI, Bruno (cond)
see Verona Arena Orch

MARTINOVICH, Boris (bass-bar)
Borodin: Prince Igor (Cpte)
Glinka: Life for the Tsar (Cpte)
Mussorgsky: Boris Godunov (Cpte)
Offenbach: Contes d'Hoffmann (Cpte)
(RCA) **09026 61236-2** Leontyne Price - Prima Donna Collection

MARTINPELTO, Hillevi (sop)
Haeffner: Electra (Cpte)
Lidholm: Dream Play (Cpte)
Mozart: Idomeneo (Cpte), Nozze di Figaro (Cpte)
Spohr: Faust (Cpte)

(BOHUSLAV) MARTINŮ PHILHARMONIC ORCHESTRA
cond P. TIBORIS
(ERIE) **GRK702** Beethoven edited Mahler

MARTINUCCI, Nicola (ten)
Donizetti: Poliuto (Cpte)
Leoncavallo: Pagliacci (Cpte)
Puccini: Tabarro (Cpte), Turandot (exc)
Verdi: Aida (Cpte)
(CAST) **CASH5051** Puccini Favourites from Covent Garden and the Arena di Verona
(CAST) **CASH5052** Verdi Operatic Favourites
(CAST) **CVI2057** Il Trittico live from La Scala, 1983
(CAST) **CVI2068** Opera Highlights from Verona 1
(CAST) **CVI2070** Great Puccini Love Scenes from Covent Garden, La Scala and Verona

MARTIS, Delia de (sop)
(PREI) **89008** Irene Minghini-Cattaneo (1892-1944)

MARTON, Eva (sop)
Boito: Mefistofele (Cpte)
Catalani: Wally (Cpte)
Giordano: Andrea Chénier (Cpte), Fedora (Cpte)
Korngold: Violanta (Cpte)
Ponchielli: Gioconda (Cpte)
Puccini: Fanciulla del West (Cpte), Tosca (Cpte), Turandot (Cpte)
R. Strauss: Elektra (Cpte), Frau ohne Schatten (Cpte)
Respighi: Semirama (Cpte)
Verdi: Trovatore (Cpte)
Wagner: Götterdämmerung (Cpte), Lohengrin (Cpte), Siegfried (Cpte), Walküre (exc)
(ACAN) **43 266** Bernd Weikl—Operatic Recital
(CAST) **CASH5051** Puccini Favourites from Covent Garden and the Arena di Verona
(CAST) **CVI2067** Opera Highlights from La Scala
(CAST) **CVI2068** Opera Highlights from Verona 1
(CAST) **CVI2070** Great Puccini Love Scenes from Covent Garden, La Scala and Verona
(EMI) **CDC5 55350-2** Cheryl Studer - A Portrait
(RCA) **09026 61440-2** Opera's Greatest Moments
(RCA) **09026 62674-2** Fortissimo!
(SONY) **SK48094** Favourite Puccini Arias

MARTOS, Maria José (sop)
Vives: Bohemios (Cpte)

MARTVON, Juraj (bar)
Suchoň: Whirlpool (Cpte)

MARTVONOVA, Anna (sop)
Suchoň: Whirlpool (Cpte)

MARTY, Jean-Pierre (cond)
see Lamoureux Orch
Paris Cons
Paris Op Orch

MARTYNOV, Alexei (ten)
Karetnikov: Till Eulenspiegel (Cpte)

MARUSIN, Yuri (ten)
Mussorgsky: Khovanshchina (Cpte)
Prokofiev: War and Peace (Cpte)
Tchaikovsky: Queen of Spades (Cpte)
(CAST) **CVI2057** Il Trittico live from La Scala, 1983

MARZOLLO, Dick (cond)
see SO

MAS, Margaret (sop)
(EMI) **CMS7 64165-2** Puccini—Trittico

MASCAGNI, Pietro (cond)
see La Scala Orch

MASCHERINI, Enzo (bar)
Puccini: Tosca (Cpte)
Verdi: Macbeth (Cpte)
(CENT) **CRC2164** Ferruccio Tagliavini—Early Operatic Recordings

MASCHERONI, Edoardo (pf)
(SYMP) **SYMCD1111** The Harold Wayne Collection, Vol.11

MASETTI, Umberto (pf)
(PEAR) **GEMMCDS9007/9(1)** Singers of Imperial Russia, Vol.4 (pt 1)

MASIMENKO, Eugene (bass-bar)
Kabalevsky: Colas Breugnon (Cpte)

MASINI, Galliano (ten)
Leoncavallo: Pagliacci (Cpte)
(EMI) **CHS7 64864-2(2)** La Scala Edition - Vol.2, 1915-46 (pt 2)

MASINI, Gian-Franco (cond)
see Barcelona SO
ECO
Grudgionz Fest Orch
LSO
Paris Op Orch

MASINI, Guglielmo (bass)
Verdi: Aida (Cpte)
(EMI) **CHS7 64864-2(1)** La Scala Edition - Vol.2, 1915-46 (pt 1)

MASINI, Mafalda (mez)
Rossini: Italiana in Algeri (Cpte)

MASINI, Paolo (ten)
(CLUB) **CL99-509/10** Hina Spani (1896-1969)

MASLENNIKOV, Alexei (ten)
Mussorgsky: Boris Godunov (Cpte)
Shostakovich: Gamblers (Cpte)
(DECC) **433 443-2DA** Great Opera Choruses

MASLENNIKOVA, Irina (sop)
(PREI) **89067** Andrei Ivanov (1900-1970)

MASLOV, Mikhail (bar)
Rimsky-Korsakov: Mlada (Cpte)

MASON, Anne (mez)
(OPRA) **ORCH104** A Hundred Years of Italian Opera: 1820-1830

MASON, Anne (sop)
Donizetti: Emilia di Liverpool (Cpte), Eremitaggio di Liverpool (Cpte)
Mayr: Medea (Cpte)
Mozart: Nozze di Figaro (Cpte)
Tippett: King Priam (Cpte)
(OPRA) **ORCH103** Italian Opera—1810-20

MASON, Barry (lte)
(AMON) **CD-SAR50** Now What is Love?

MASON, Edith (sop)
(ROMO) **81009-2** Edith Mason—Complete Recordings 1924-1928
(SYMP) **SYMCD1136** Opera in Chicago, Vol.1

MASON, Patrick (bar)
Machover: Valis (Cpte)

MASON, Ralph (ten)
Janáček: Fate (Cpte)
(BELA) **461 006-2** Gilbert & Sullivan—Songs and Snatches

MASON, William (bass)
G. Charpentier: Louise (Cpte)
Puccini: Bohème (Cpte)
Tchaikovsky: Eugene Onegin (Cpte)

MASOTTI, Giovanni (bass)
(SYMP) **SYMCD1126** The Harold Wayne Collection, Vol.14

MASQUELIN, Martine (sop)
(ARIO) **ARN68195** Milhaud—Sonatas; Trois Operas-Minute

MASSA, Fulvio (ten)
Rossini: Occasione fa il ladro (Cpte), Signor Bruschino (Cpte)

MASSARD, Robert (bar)
Audran: Poupée (exc)
Berlioz: Benvenuto Cellini (Cpte)
Bizet: Carmen (exc)
Ganne: Saltimbanques (exc)
Gluck: Iphigénie en Tauride (Cpte)
Gounod: Faust (Cpte)
Massenet: Hérodiade (exc), Jongleur de Notre Dame (Cpte)
Milhaud: Christophe Colomb (Cpte)
Offenbach: Contes d'Hoffmann (exc)
Verdi: Rigoletto (Cpte)
(CFP) **CD-CFP4602** Favourite Opera
(DECC) **433 064-2DWO** Your Hundred Best Opera Tunes Volume I
(DECC) **433 443-2DA** Great Opera Choruses
(EMIL) **CDZ100** Best Loved Classics 1

MASSED BRASS BANDS
cond J. H. ILES
(BEUL) **1PD2** Crystal Palace Champions

MASSELL, Deborah (sop)
Gluck: Echo et Narcisse (Cpte)

MASSENET FESTIVAL CHORUS
cond P. FOURNILLIER
Massenet: Cléopâtre (Cpte), Esclarmonde (Cpte)

MASSIS, Annick (sop)
Rameau: Hippolyte et Aricie (Cpte)

MASSIS, René (bass-bar)
Auber: Manon Lescaut (Cpte)
Chausson: Roi Arthus (Cpte)
Donizetti: Favorita (Cpte)
Gluck: Iphigénie en Tauride (Cpte)
Halévy: Juive (Cpte)

MASSOCCHI, Peter (bass)
Debussy: Pelléas et Mélisande (Cpte)

MASSON, Diego (cond)
see English Northern Philh

MASSON, Luis (bass)
Fénelon: Chevalier Imaginaire (Cpte)
Vivaldi: Montezuma (Cpte)
(EMI) **CZS5 68113-2** Vive Offenbach!

MASSOZ, Claude (bass)
Grétry: Caravane du Caire (Cpte)
Massenet: Cléopâtre (Cpte)

MASSUE, Nicholas (ten)
Verdi: Otello (Cpte)
(PEAR) **GEMMCDS9926(2)** Covent Garden on Record—Vol.4 (pt 2)

MASTERSON, Valerie (sop)
Coward: Bitter Sweet (exc)
Handel: Giulio Cesare (Cpte)
Mozart: Entführung (Cpte)
Rossini: Elisabetta (Cpte)
Sullivan: Mikado (Cpte), Pirates of Penzance (exc), Princess Ida (Cpte), Sorcerer (Cpte)
Verdi: Traviata (Cpte)
Wagner: Götterdämmerung (Cpte), Rheingold (Cpte)
(BELA) **461 006-2** Gilbert & Sullivan—Songs and Snatches
(DECC) **430 095-2DWO** The World of Gilbert & Sullivan, Vol.1
(DECC) **433 868-2DWO** The World of Gilbert & Sullivan - Volume 2
(IMP) **MCD15** Opera Spectacular
(IMP) **TCD1070** Invitation to the Opera
(PEAR) **SHECD9590** Valerie Masterson—Recital
(PHIL) **434 986-2PM** Duetti Amorosi
(RPO) **CDRPD9006** Opera Spectacular 1 & 2
(TER) **CDVIR8317** If I Loved You - Love Duets from the Musicals

MASTERTON-SMITH, Simon (bass)
Offenbach: Orphée aux enfers (exc)
Sullivan: Pirates of Penzance (exc)

MASTILOVIC, Daniza (sop)
Wagner: Walküre (Cpte)
(DG) **435 211-2GX15** Wagner—Der Ring des Nibelungen
(PHIL) **446 057-2PB14** Wagner—The Ring Cycle - Bayreuth Festival 1967

MASTROMEI, Gian-Piero (bar)
Verdi: Corsaro (Cpte), Otello (Cpte), Simon Boccanegra (Cpte)

MASUR, Kurt (cond)
see Leipzig Gewandhaus
NYPO

MASURIAN PHILHARMONIC ORCHESTRA
cond P. KANTSCHIEDER
Beethoven: Fidelio (Cpte), Leonore (exc)

MATA, Eduardo (cond)
see Dallas SO

MATACCHINI, Valeria (contr)
Stradella: Moro per amore (Cpte)

MATAČIĆ, Lovro von (cond)
see Berlin Deutsche Op Orch
La Scala Orch
Philh
Vienna St Op Orch
VPO

MATHESON, John (cond)
see NZ SO

MATHESON-BRUCE, Graeme (ten)
Boughton: Bethlehem (Cpte)
Tchaikovsky: Queen of Spades (Cpte)

MATHIS, Edith (sop)
Beethoven: Fidelio (Cpte)
Handel: Ariodante (Cpte)
Henze: Junge Lord (Cpte)
Lortzing: Wildschütz (Cpte)
Mozart: Apollo et Hyacinthus (Cpte), Ascanio in Alba (Cpte), Clemenza di Tito (Cpte), Don Giovanni (Cpte), Idomeneo (Cpte), Lucio Silla (Cpte), Nozze di Figaro (exc), Sogno di Scipione (Cpte), Zaïde (Cpte), Zauberflöte (exc)
Nicolai: Lustigen Weiber von Windsor (Cpte)
R. Strauss: Rosenkavalier (Cpte)
Schoeck: Massimilla Doni (Cpte)
Weber: Freischütz (Cpte)
Zemlinsky: Kleider machen Leute (Cpte)
(DG) **439 153-4GMA** Mad about Sopranos
(EMI) **CZS7 62993-2** Fritz Wunderlich—Great German Tenor
(ORFE) **C365941A** Christa Ludwig - Salzburg Festival highlights
(ORFE) **C394301B** Great Mozart Singers Series, Vol. 3
(RCA) **09026 62699-2** Opera's Greatest Duets

MATHIS, Joyce (sop)
Verdi: Aida (Cpte)

MATIĆ, Peter (spkr)
Weber: Freischütz (Cpte)

MATORIN, Vladimir (bass)
Rachmaninov: Aleko (Cpte), Francesca da Rimini (Cpte)
Rimsky-Korsakov: Kashchey (Cpte)

MATRIX ENSEMBLE
cond R. ZIEGLER
(ASV) **CDDCA758** Falla, Milhaud & Stravinsky—Operas

MATSUMOTO, Shigemi (sop)
Donizetti: Elisir d'amore (Cpte)

MATTEI, Peter (bar)
Börtz: Bacchae (Cpte)
Haeffner: Electra (Cpte)

MATTEINI, Giuliana (mez)
Meyerbeer: Africaine (Cpte)
Verdi: Don Carlo (Cpte)

MATTEIS, Giuseppe de (bass)
Handel: Giulio Cesare (Cpte)
Mercadante: Bravo (Cpte)

MATTEO, Vicenzo di (bar)
Rossini: Pietra del paragone (Cpte)

MATTERS, Arnold (bar)
(LYRC) **SRO830** Smetana—The Bartered Bride, etc

MATTES, Willy (cond)
see Graunke SO
Munich RO

MATTEUZZI, William (ten)
Bellini: Puritani (Cpte)
Puccini: Manon Lescaut (Cpte)

Rossini: Armida (Cpte), Barbiere di Siviglia (Cpte), Cenerentola (Cpte), Ermione (Cpte), Gazza ladra (Cpte), Scala di seta (Cpte), Viaggio a Reims (Cpte), Zelmira (Cpte)
Verdi: Rigoletto (Cpte)
Vivaldi: Orlando Furioso (Cpte)
(DECC) **436 463-2DM** Ten Top Tenors
(NUOV) **6820** Luciana Serra—Opera Recital
(NUOV) **6892** William Matteuzzi sings Opera Arias
(NUOV) **6905** Donizetti—Great Love Duets

MATTHES, Walter (bar)
R. Strauss: Arabella (Cpte)

MATTHEWS, Andrea (sop)
Handel: Siroe, Rè di Persia (Cpte)
Rorem: Three Sisters Who Are Not Sisters (Cpte)
(NEWP) **NPD85540** Handel/Bononcini—Muzio Scevola

MATTHEWS, Brian (bass)
R. Strauss: Elektra (Cpte)

MATTHEWS, Hubert (bass)
Vaughan Williams: Pilgrim's Progress (Cpte)

MATTILA, Karita (sop)
Mozart: Così fan tutte (Cpte), Don Giovanni (exc), Nozze di Figaro (Cpte)
Schubert: Fierrabras (Cpte)
Weber: Freischütz (exc)

MATTIOLI, Renata (sop)
(MEMO) **HR4300/1** Great Voices—Sesto Bruscantini

MATTIUCCI, Franca (mez)
Puccini: Rondine (Cpte)

MATTONI, André von (spkr)
Mozart: Zauberflöte (exc)

MATTSEY, Jeff (bar)
(RCA) **09026 61509-2** A Salute to American Music

MATTSSON, Per (spkr)
Börtz: Bacchae (Cpte)

MATZENAUER, Margarete (mez)
(IRCC) **IRCC-CD800** Souvenirs from Meyerbeer Operas
(PEAR) **GEMMCDS9074(2)** Giovanni Zenatello, Vol.2 (pt 2)
(PEAR) **GEMMCD9104** Pasquale Amato (1878-1942)
(PREI) **89064** Pasquale Amato (1878-1942)

MAUCERI, John (cond)
see Berlin Deutsches SO
Berlin Rad Ens
Berlin RIAS Sinfonietta
Berlin RSO
Hollywood Bowl Orch
Hollywood Bowl SO
LSO
NYC Op Orch

MAUCLERC, Guy (sngr)
(ARIO) **ARN68195** Milhaud—Sonatas; Trois Operas-Minute

MAURANE, Camille (bar)
Messager: Basoche (Cpte), P'tites Michu (exc)
Offenbach: Contes d'Hoffmann (Cpte)

MAUREL, Victor (bar)
(EMI) **CHS7 64860-2(1)** La Scala Edition - Vol.1, 1878-1914 (pt 1)
(MEMO) **HR4408/9(1)** Singers in Genoa, Vol.1 (disc 1)
(NIMB) **NI7840/1** The Era of Adelina Patti
(PEAR) **GEMMCDS9923(1)** Covent Garden on Record, Vol.1 (pt 1)
(SYMP) **SYMCD1101** The Harold Wayne Collection, Vol.9
(SYMP) **SYMCD1128** The Harold Wayne Collection, Vol.15

MAURERY, Pavol (bar)
Verdi: Traviata (Cpte)

MAURETTE, Jean-Luc (ten)
Berlioz: Troyens (Cpte)
Massenet: Cléopâtre (Cpte)
Offenbach: Brigands (Cpte)

MAURI, Giulio (bar)
Puccini: Turandot (Cpte)
Verdi: Trovatore (Cpte)

MAURO, Anna di (mez)
Mascagni: Cavalleria Rusticana (Cpte)
(NAXO) **8 550684** Duets and Arias from Italian Operas

MAURO, E. (ten)
(RCA) **GD60941** Rarities - Montserrat Caballé

MAUS, Peter (ten)
Hindemith: Nusch-Nuschi (Cpte)
Verdi: Falstaff (Cpte)
Wagner: Meistersinger (Cpte), Parsifal (Cpte), Tristan und Isolde (Cpte)
Wolf: Corregidor (Cpte)

MAXWELL, Donald (bar)
Britten: Midsummer Night's Dream (Cpte), Noye's Fludde (Cpte), Rape of Lucretia (Cpte)
Coward: Bitter Sweet (Cpte)
Debussy: Pelléas et Mélisande (Cpte)
Menotti: Amahl and the Night Visitors (Cpte)
Mozart: Nozze di Figaro (exc)
Romberg: Student Prince (Cpte)
Sullivan: Yeomen of the Guard (exc)
Tippett: Ice Break (Cpte)
(EMI) **CDC7 54785-2** Harry Enfield's Guide to Opera

MAXWELL, Linn (mez)
Purcell: Dido (Cpte)
V. Thomson: Mother of us all (Cpte)

MAXWELL DAVIES, Sir Peter (cond)
see BBC PO
Fires of London
Scottish CO

MAY, Gisela (mez)
Mysliveček: Bellerofonte (Cpte)
(CAPR) **10 180** Gisela May sings Weill

(MICHAEL) MAY FESTIVAL CHORUS
cond J. LÓPEZ-COBOS
Falla: Vida breve (Cpte)

MAYER, Emma (contr)
(MYTO) **2MCD943103** Lortzing—Zar und Zimmermann

MAYER, Frederic (ten)
Weill: Kuhhandel (exc), Mahagonny (Cpte)

MAYER-GÄNSBACHER, Hugo (ten)
J. Strauss II: Nacht in Venedig (Cpte)

MAYNARD, Ted (spkr)
Gershwin: Porgy and Bess (Cpte)

MAYNOR, Dorothy (sop)
(EMI) **CHS7 69741-2(1)** Record of Singing, Vol.4—Anglo-American School (pt 1)
(PEAR) **GEMMCD9179** The Art of Serge Koussevitzky

MAYO, Lydia (sop)
Boïeldieu: Calife de Bagdad (Cpte)

MAYR, Ingrid (mez)
Einem: Dantons Tod (Cpte)
Mozart: Zauberflöte (Cpte)
R. Strauss: Rosenkavalier (Cpte)

MAYR, Richard (bass)
(EMI) **CHS7 64487-2** R. Strauss—Der Rosenkavalier & Lieder
(ORFE) **C394101B** Great Mozart Singers Series, Vol. 1
(PEAR) **GEMMCDS9365** R. Strauss: Der Rosenkavalier (abridged), etc
(PEAR) **GEMMCDS9925(2)** Covent Garden on Record—Vol.3 (pt 2)
(PEAR) **GEMMCD9122** 20 Great Basses sing Great Arias
(SCHW) **314512** Vienna State Opera Live, Vol.1
(SCHW) **314622** Vienna State Opera Live, Vol.12
(SCHW) **314642** Vienna State Opera Live, Vol.14
(SCHW) **314652** Vienna State Opera Live, Vol.15
(SCHW) **314662** Vienna State Opera Live, Vol.16

MAZALOUBAUD, Jean-Pierre (bass)
Shostakovich: Lady Macbeth of Mtsensk (Cpte)

MAZAROFF, Todor (ten)
(SCHW) **314502** Vienna State Opera—Live Recordings (sampler)
(SCHW) **314542** Vienna State Opera Live, Vol.4
(SCHW) **314572** Vienna State Opera Live, Vol.7
(SCHW) **314632** Vienna State Opera Live, Vol.13
(SCHW) **314692** Vienna State Opera Live, Vol.19

MAZETTI, Umberto (pf)
(ARLE) **ARL23/5** Rimsky-Korsakov—Sadko

MAZO, Ekaterina (sop)
Karetnikov: Till Eulenspiegel (Cpte)

MAZOVIAN PHILHARMONIC ORCHESTRA
cond P. KANTSCHIEDER
(SCHW) **311155** Johann Strauss II—Waltzes, Polkas and Overtures

MAZURA, Franz (bar)
Berg: Lulu (Cpte)
Pfitzner: Palestrina (Cpte)
Schoenberg: Moses und Aron (Cpte)
Wagner: Götterdämmerung (Cpte), Parsifal (Cpte), Tannhäuser (Cpte)
(DECC) **440 854-2DH** Ullmann—Der Kaiser von Atlantis
(PHIL) **434 420-2PM32(1)** Richard Wagner Edition (Pt.1)

MAZUROK, Yuri (bar)
Tchaikovsky: Eugene Onegin (Cpte), Queen of Spades (Cpte)
Verdi: Trovatore (Cpte)

MAZZARIA, Lucia (sop)
Leoncavallo: Bohème (Cpte)

MAZZARRI, Liliana (sop)
(HYPE) **CDA66745** Vivaldi—Opera Arias and Sinfonias

MAZZEI, Enrico di (ten)
Puccini: Tosca (exc)

MAZZETTI, Sofia (sop)
(RCA) **09026 68014-2** Pavarotti - The Early Years, Vol.2

MAZZIERI, Maurizio (bass)
Donizetti: Caterina Cornaro (Cpte), Maria Stuarda (Cpte)
Haydn: Orlando Paladino (Cpte)
Verdi: Masnadieri (Cpte), Simon Boccanegra (Cpte)

MAZZINI, Guido (bass)
Donizetti: Poliuto (Cpte)
Puccini: Bohème (Cpte), Turandot (Cpte)

MAZZOLA, Denia (sop)
Donizetti: Elisabetta (Cpte), Lucia di Lammermoor (Cpte)
Massenet: Esclarmonde (Cpte)
(NUOV) **6905** Donizetti—Great Love Duets

MAZZOLA, Rudolf (bass)
Debussy: Pelléas et Mélisande (Cpte)
Mozart: Nozze di Figaro (Cpte)

MAZZOLENI, Ester (sop)
(EMI) **CHS7 64860-2(2)** La Scala Edition - Vol.1, 1878-1914 (pt 2)
(IRCC) **IRCC-CD808** Souvenirs of 19th Century Italian Opera
(PEAR) **GEMMCDS9073(2)** Giovanni Zenatello, Vol.1 (pt 2)
(PEAR) **GEMMCDS9074(1)** Giovanni Zenatello, Vol.2 (pt 1)
(SYMP) **SYMCD1113** The Harold Wayne Collection, Vol.13
(SYMP) **SYMCD1138** The Harold Wayne Collection, Vol.16
(SYMP) **SYMCD1148** The Harold Wayne Collection, Vol.17
(SYMP) **SYMCD1158** The Harold Wayne Collection, Vol.18
(SYMP) **SYMCD1168** The Harold Wayne Collection, Vol.19

MAZZOLI, Ferruccio (bass)
Donizetti: Lucrezia Borgia (Cpte)
Puccini: Bohème (exc), Gianni Schicchi (Cpte)
Rossini: Guillaume Tell (Cpte), Mosè (Cpte)
Verdi: Aida (Cpte), Ballo in maschera (Cpte), Otello (Cpte), Trovatore (Cpte)

MAZZONI, Silvia (mez)
Verdi: Traviata (Cpte)

MAZZUCATO, Daniela (sop)
Wolf-Ferrari: Campiello (Cpte)

MEAD, Andrew (treb)
Britten: Midsummer Night's Dream (Cpte)

MEANS, Edrie (sop)
S. Wallace: Kabbalah (Cpte)

MECHALY, Gaëlle (sop)
Purcell: Dido (Cpte)

MECHERA, Erika (sop)
Lehár: Paganini (exc)
R. Strauss: Daphne (Cpte)

MECKLENBURG STAATSKAPELLE SCHWEIN
cond I. TÖRZS
Wagner: Walküre (exc)

MEDICI, Domenico (sngr)
Puccini: Tosca (Cpte)

MEDICI QUARTET
R. Strauss: Capriccio (exc)
cond P. LEDGER
Britten: Little Sweep (Cpte)
cond R. MUTI
Verdi: Ballo in maschera (Cpte)

MEDLAM, Charles (cond)
see London Baroque

MEDLAM, Charles (va da gamba)
(HYPE) **CDA66070** Purcell: Songs

MEDNIKOFF, Nikolai (pf)
(BIDD) **LAB017** Casals—The Victor Recordings
(MSCM) **MM30428** Pablo Casals - Recital

MÉDUS, Henri (sngr)
Adam: Si j'étais roi (Cpte)

MEEK, James (sngr)
(OPRA) **ORR201** 19th Century Heroines-Yvonne Kenny

MEENS, Hein (ten)
Keiser: Masagniello furioso (Cpte)
Schreker: Gezeichneten (Cpte)

MEERSMAN, Mark (bass-bar)
Puccini: Gianni Schicchi (Cpte)

MEEUWSEN, Lucia (sop)
Carvalho: Testoride Argonauta (Cpte)
Vivaldi: Olimpiade (Cpte)

MEHLTRETTER, Florian (bar)
Biber: Arminio (Cpte)

MEHN, Christian (ten)
(ARIO) **ARN68252** Chabrier—Trois opérettes

MEHTA, Zubin (cond)
see Los Angeles PO
LPO
MMF Orch
New Philh
NY Met Op Orch
NYPO
ROHO
Rome Op Orch
Rome RAI Orch
Vienna Volksoper Orch
VPO

MEI, Eva (sop)
Bellini: Norma (Cpte)
Donizetti: Don Pasquale (Cpte)
Salieri: Axur (Cpte)

MEIER, Johanna (sop)
Wagner: Tristan und Isolde (Cpte)

MEIER, Waltraud (mez)
Mozart: Don Giovanni (Cpte)
Saint-Saëns: Samson et Dalila (Cpte)
Wagner: Götterdämmerung (Cpte), Lohengrin (exc), Parsifal (Cpte), Tannhäuser (Cpte), Tristan und Isolde (Cpte), Walküre (exc)
(DG) **439 768-2GH** Wagner—Gala - New Year's Eve Concert 1993
(EMI) **LDX9 91275-1(EMI)** Sawallisch conducts Wagner's Ring
(PHIL) **434 420-2PM32(1)** Richard Wagner Edition (Pt.1)

MEI-FIGNER, Medea (sop)
(PEAR) **GEMMCDS9997/9(1)** Singers of Imperial Russia, Vol.1 (pt 1)

MEIJER, Xenia (mez)
Biber: Arminio (Cpte)

MEINERTZHAGEN, Josef (sngr)
Schultze: Schwarzer Peter (Cpte)

MEINRAD, Josef (spkr)
J. Strauss II: Fledermaus (Cpte)

MEINRAD, Josef (ten)
(TELD) **9031-77676-6(TELD)** My World of Opera - Kiri Te Kanawa

MEISEL, Kurt (spkr)
Weber: Freischütz (Cpte)

MEISTER, Ine (mez)
Offenbach: Périchole (Cpte)

MELANDER, Anders (bass)
Donizetti: Linda di Chamounix (Cpte)

MELBA, Dame Nellie (sop)
(LARR) **CDLRH221** Dame Nellie Melba - Opera and Song Recital
(MEMO) **HR4408/9(1)** Singers in Genoa, Vol.1 (disc 1)
(NIMB) **NI7802** Divas 1906-1935
(NIMB) **NI7840/1** The Era of Adelina Patti
(NIMB) **NI7866** Caruso in Opera, Volume 2
(PEAR) **EVC1(2)** The Caruso Edition, Vol.1 (pt 2)
(PEAR) **GEMMCDS9923(1)** Covent Garden on Record, Vol.1 (pt 1)
(PEAR) **GEMMCDS9924(1)** Covent Garden on Record, Vol.2 (pt 1)
(PEAR) **GEMMCDS9925(2)** Covent Garden on Record—Vol.3 (pt 2)
(PEAR) **GEMMCD9130** Great Sopranos, Vol.2
(PEAR) **GEMMCD9309** Enrico Caruso - Opera and Song Recital
(RCA) **GD60495(2)** The Complete Caruso Collection (pt 2)
(RCA) **09026 61243-2** Caruso sings Verismo Arias
(RCA) **09026 61412-2** Nellie Melba - Recital
(RCA) **09026 61580-2(1)** RCA/Met 110 Singers, 100 Years (pt 1)
(RCA) **74321 24284-2** Opera's Greatest Heroines
(ROMO) **81011-2(1)** Dame Nellie Melba (pt 1)
(ROMO) **81011-2(2)** Dame Nellie Melba (pt 2)

MELBOURNE SYMPHONY ORCHESTRA
cond W.A. ALBERT
(CPO) **CPO999 007-2** Hindemith—Orchestral Works, Volume 4
cond J. SEREBRIER
(IMP) **MCD64** Tchaikovsky—Soprano Arias
(IMP) **PCD1055** Tchaikovsky—Glorious Melodies, Volume 1
(IMP) **TCD1070** Invitation to the Opera

MELBYE, Mikael (bar)
Bizet: Carmen (Cpte)
Mozart: Zauberflöte (exc)

MELCHERT, Helmut (ten)
Berg: Wozzeck (Cpte)
(EMI) **CMS5 65212-2** Wagner—Les introuvables du Ring

MELCHIOR, Lauritz (bar/ten)
Wagner: Lohengrin (Cpte), Siegfried (Cpte), Tristan und Isolde (Cpte), Walküre (Cpte)
(BEUL) **2PD4** 78 Classics - Volume Two
(CLAR) **CDGSE78-50-26** Wagner: Tristan und Isolde excerpts
(CLAR) **CDGSE78-50-33** Lauritz Melchior & Albert Coates
(CLAR) **CDGSE78-50-54** Coates conducts Wagner, Weber & Mendelssohn
(DANA) **DACOCD311/2** Lauritz Melchior Anthology - Vol.1
(DANA) **DACOCD313/4** Lauritz Melchior Anthology - Vol. 2
(DANA) **DACOCD315/6** Lauritz Melchior Anthology - Vol. 3
(DANA) **DACOCD319/21** The Lauritz Melchior Anthology - Vol.5
(EMI) **CDH7 69789-2** Melchior sings Wagner
(EMI) **CMS7 64008-2(1)** Wagner Singing on Record (pt 1)
(EMI) **CMS7 64008-2(2)** Wagner Singing on Record (pt 2)
(LYRC) **LCD146** Frida Leider sings Wagner
(MMOI) **CDMOIR405** Great Tenors
(MSCM) **MM30283** Great Wagnerian Singers, Vol.1
(MSCM) **MM30285** Great Wagnerian Singers, Vol.2
(NIMB) **NI7848** Great Singers at the Berlin State Opera
(NIMB) **NI7856** Legendary Tenors
(NIMB) **NI7864** More Legendary Voices
(PEAR) **GEMMCDS9121** Wagner—Die Meistersinger, Act 3, etc
(PEAR) **GEMMCDS9137** Wagner—Der Ring des Nibelungen
(PEAR) **GEMMCDS9925(2)** Covent Garden on Record—Vol.3 (pt 2)
(PEAR) **GEMMCDS9926(1)** Covent Garden on Record—Vol.4 (pt 1)
(PEAR) **GEMMCD9049** Flagstad and Melchior sing Wagner
(PEAR) **GEMMCD9331** Frida Leider sings Wagner
(PEAR) **GEMMCD9944** Friedrich Schorr sings Wagner
(PREI) **89004** Frida Leider (1888-1975) - I
(PREI) **89032** Lauritz Melchior (1890-1973) - I
(PREI) **89068** Lauritz Melchior (1890-1973) - II
(PREI) **89086** Lauritz Melchior (1890-1973) - III
(PREI) **89301** The Art of Frida Leider
(RCA) **GD60264** Wagner—Opera excerpts
(RCA) **GD60304** Toscanini Collection - Wagner
(RCA) **GD87915** Wagner: Arias and Duets
(RCA) **09026 61580-2(3)** RCA/Met 100 Singers, 100 Years (pt 3)
(SCHW) **314512** Vienna State Opera Live, Vol.1
(SIMA) **PSC1821(2)** Kirsten Flagstad, Vol.1 (pt 2)
(TEST) **SBT1005** Ten Top Tenors
(VAI) **VAI69107** Lauritz Melchior in Opera and Song

MELCHISSÉDEC, Léon (bar)
(SYMP) **SYMCD1089** Historic Baritones of the French School

MELETTI, Carlo (bar)
Verdi: Don Carlo (Cpte)

MELETTI, Saturno (bar)
Mascagni: Iris (Cpte)
(EMI) **CMS7 64165-2** Puccini—Trittico

MELICHAR, Alois (cond)
see Berlin SO
Berlin St Op Orch
Berlin Staatskapelle

MELIK-PASHAYEV, Alexsander (cond)
see Bolshoi Th Orch

MELIS, Carmen (sop)
Puccini: Tosca (Cpte)
(PEAR) **GEMMCDS9926(1)** Covent Garden on Record—Vol.4 (pt 1)

MELIS, György (bar)
(DECC) **443 488-2DF2** Kodály—Háry János; Psalmus Hungaricus etc

MELLE, Iris (sop)
Pfitzner: Herz (Cpte)

MELLERIO, Laura (contr)
(BONG) **GB1043-2** Italian Baritones of the Acoustic Era

MELLIES, Otto (spkr)
Mozart: Entführung (Cpte)

MELLIS, Andrea (sop)
Delius: Village Romeo and Juliet (Cpte)

MELLON, Agnès (sop)
Cavalli: Giasone (Cpte), Xerse (Cpte)
Hasse: Cleofide (Cpte)
Lully: Atys (exc)
M-A. Charpentier: Actéon (Cpte), Arts Florissants (Cpte), Médée (Cpte)
Purcell: Dido (Cpte)
Rameau: Castor et Pollux (Cpte), Zoroastre (Cpte)
Rossi: Orfeo (Cpte)
(ASTR) **E8757** Purcell—Songs from Orpheus Britannicus
(HARM) **HMX290 1528/33(1)** A Purcell Companion (pt 1)

MELONI, Claude (ten)
Berg: Lulu (Cpte)
Bizet: Carmen (Cpte)
Massenet: Cendrillon (Cpte), Jongleur de Notre Dame (Cpte)

MELVILLE, Alan G. (cond)
see CLS
ECO

MEMELSDORFF, Pedro (rec)
(DHM) **05472 77318-2** Delight in Disorder—English Consort of Two Parts, 1640-1680

MEMEO, Francesco (ten)
Puccini: Fanciulla del West (Cpte)

MENEGUZZER, Jolanda (sop)
Puccini: Bohème (exc)

MENENDEZ, Michèle Vilma (mez)
Donizetti: Maria Stuarda (Cpte)

MENGELBERG, Willem (cond)
see Concertgebouw
NYPO
NYPSO

MENICUCCI, Delfo (sngr)
Donizetti: Ajo nell'imbarazzo (Cpte)

MENNI, Giuseppe (bass)
Verdi: Rigoletto (Cpte)
(PEAR) **GEMMCDS9180** Verdi—Rigoletto, etc
(PREI) **89048** Apollo Granforte (1886-1975) - I

MENOTTI, Tatiana (sop)
Puccini: Bohème (Cpte)

MENTZER, Susanne (mez)
Busoni: Arlecchino (Cpte)
Gounod: Faust (Cpte)
Mozart: Don Giovanni (Cpte), Idomeneo (Cpte), Nozze di Figaro (Cpte)
Rossini: Barbiere di Siviglia (Cpte), Turco in Italia (Cpte)
(PHIL) **422 545-2PME3** The Complete Mozart Edition Vol.45

MENTZER, Susanne (narr)
Mozart: Don Giovanni (exc)

MENUHIN, Sir Yehudi (cond)
see Bath Fest Orch
Brno St PO
ECO
Menuhin FO
RPO

MENUHIN, Sir Yehudi (vn)
(BIDD) **LAB032** The young Yehudi Menuhin, Vol.2
(BIDD) **LAB046** The Young Yehudi Menuhin
(TEST) **SBT1003** The Young Menuhin—Encores, Vol.1

MENUHIN, Sir Yehudi (vn/dir)
(EMIL) **CDZ114** Best of Baroque

MENUHIN FESTIVAL ORCHESTRA
cond Y. MENUHIN
(EMI) **CES5 68523-2** Handel—Orchestral Works

MENZ, Sylvia (sop)
J. Strauss II: Fledermaus (Cpte)

MENZEL, Peter (bass)
Offenbach: Contes d'Hoffmann (exc)
Schreker: Gezeichneten (Cpte)

MERCER, Gregory (ten)
V. Thomson: Lord Byron (Cpte)
(ALBA) **TROY068-2** William Mayer—Voices from Lost Realms

MERCKER, Karl-Ernst (ten)
Berg: Lulu (Cpte)
Bizet: Carmen (Cpte)
Jessel: Schwarzwaldmädel (exc)
Künneke: Vetter aus Dingsda (exc)
Lehár: Zarewitsch (exc)
Raymond: Maske in Blau (exc)
Wagner: Meistersinger (Cpte)
Zeller: Vogelhändler (exc)

MERCURIALI, Angelo (ten)
Bellini: Puritani (Cpte)
Cilea: Adriana Lecouvreur (Cpte)
Donizetti: Don Pasquale (Cpte)
Giordano: Andrea Chénier (Cpte)
Puccini: Fanciulla del West (Cpte), Madama Butterfly (Cpte), Manon Lescaut (Cpte), Tosca (Cpte), Turandot (Cpte)
Verdi: Otello (Cpte), Rigoletto (Cpte), Traviata (Cpte), Trovatore (Cpte)
(EMI) **CDM7 69543-2** Maria Callas and Giuseppe Di Stefano - Duets

MERCZ, Nóra (hp)
(NAXO) **8 550741** Romantic Music for Flute and Harp

MERKER, Rose (sop)
(SCHW) **314592** Vienna State Opera Live, Vol.9

MERLI, Francesco (ten)
Puccini: Turandot (Cpte)
(EMI) **CHS7 64864-2(2)** La Scala Edition - Vol.2, 1915-46 (pt 2)
(LYRC) **SRO805** Gina Cigna—Opera Recital
(NIMB) **NI7814** Claudia Muzio—Opera Arias & Songs
(PREI) **89010** Tancredi Pasero (1893-1983) - I
(PREI) **89026** Francesco Merli (1887-1976) - I
(PREI) **89091** Francesco Merli (1887-1976) - II

MERMAID ORCHESTRA
cond GERAINT JONES
Purcell: Dido (Cpte)

MERMAID SINGERS
cond GERAINT JONES
Purcell: Dido (Cpte)

MERREM-NIKISCH, Greta (sop)
(EMI) **CDH7 69787-2** Richard Tauber sings Operetta Arias

MERRI, Judi (mez)
(LOND) **436 816-2LM2** Sullivan—Utopia Ltd. Macbeth & Marmion Ovs etc

MERRILL, Robert (bar)
Bizet: Carmen (exc)
Donizetti: Lucia di Lammermoor (Cpte)
Leoncavallo: Pagliacci (Cpte)
Mascagni: Cavalleria Rusticana (Cpte)
Ponchielli: Gioconda (Cpte)
Puccini: Bohème (exc), Manon Lescaut (Cpte)
Rossini: Barbiere di Siviglia (Cpte)
Verdi: Aida (exc), Ballo in maschera (Cpte), Falstaff (Cpte), Forza del destino (Cpte), Rigoletto (Cpte), Traviata (Cpte), Trovatore (Cpte)
(DECC) **411 665-2DM3** Puccini: Il trittico
(DECC) **417 780-2DM** Joan Sutherland's Greatest Hits
(DECC) **443 380-2DM** Ten Top Baritones & Basses 2
(EMI) **CHS7 69741-2(2)** Record of Singing, Vol.4—Anglo-American School (pt 2)
(RCA) **GD87799** The Pearl Fishers Duet plus Duets and Scenes

(RCA) **09026 61440-2** Opera's Greatest Moments
(RCA) **09026 61509-2** A Salute to American Music
(RCA) **09026 61580-2(6)** RCA/Met 100 Singers, 100 Years (pt 6)
(RCA) **09026 62689-2** The Voices of Living Stereo, Volume 1
(RCA) **74321 25817-2** Café Classics - Operatic
(VAI) **VAI69116** Robert Merrill in Opera and Song

MERRIMAN, Nan (mez)
Mozart: Così fan tutte (Cpte)
Verdi: Falstaff (Cpte), Otello (Cpte)
(DG) **437 677-2GDO2** Irmgard Seefried - Opera Recital
(RCA) **GD60276** Toscanini conducts Boito & Verdi
(RCA) **GD60280** Toscanini Collection
(RCA) **GD60326** Verdi—Operas & Choral Works

MERRITT, Chris (ten)
Donizetti: Elisir d'amore (Cpte), Emilia di Liverpool (Cpte), Eremitaggio di Liverpool (Cpte)
Glinka: Life for the Tsar (Cpte)
Rossini: Armida (Cpte), Bianca e Falliero (Cpte), Ermione (Cpte), Guillaume Tell (exc), Zelmira (Cpte)
Verdi: Vespri Siciliani (Cpte)
(EMI) **CDC7 54643-2** Rossini—Bicentenary Gala Concert
(EMI) **LDB491007-1 (EMI)** Rossini Bicentennial Birthday Gala
(MEMO) **HR4300/1** Great Voices—Sesto Bruscantini
(NUOV) **6905** Donizetti—Great Love Duets
(OPRA) **ORCH103** Italian Opera—1810-20
(PHIL) **434 102-2PH** The Heroic Bel Canto Tenor

MERRITT, Myra (mez)
Bizet: Carmen (Cpte)

MERTEN, Reinhold (cond)
see Leipzig RSO

MESCHERIAKOVA, Marina (sop)
Glinka: Life for the Tsar (Cpte)

MESPLÉ, Mady (sop)
Adam: Toréador (Cpte)
Auber: Fra Diavolo (Cpte)
Delibes: Lakmé (Cpte)
Massenet: Werther (Cpte)
Offenbach: Contes d'Hoffmann (exc), Orphée aux enfers (Cpte)
Rossini: Guillaume Tell (Cpte)
(CFP) **CD-CFP4582** Flowers in Music
(CFP) **CD-CFP4613** Favourite TV Classics
(EMI) **CDM7 69596-2** The Movies go to the Opera
(EMI) **CDS7 49361-2** Offenbach: Operettas
(EMI) **CZS5 68113-2** Vive Offenbach!
(EMI) **CZS7 62877-2** Les inspirations insolites d'Erik Satie
(EMI) **CZS7 67440-2** The Best of Rossini
(EMI) **CZS7 67813-2** Opera Arias and Duets
(RCA) **74321 25817-2** Café Classics - Operatic

MESROBIAN, Robert (sngr)
Bernstein: Candide (1956) (exc)

MESSNER, Joseph (cond)
see orch

MESSTHALER, Ulrich (bass)
Handel: Flavio (Cpte)

METCALFE, Jane (mez)
Sullivan: Zoo (Cpte)
(LOND) **436 813-2LM2** Sullivan—The Grand Duke. Overture Di Ballo. Henry VIII

METSOMÄKI, Maaria (sop)
Madetoja: Juha (Cpte)

METTERNICH, Anton (bass)
Wagner: Meistersinger (exc)

METTERNICH, Josef (bar)
Humperdinck: Hänsel und Gretel (Cpte)
R. Strauss: Salome (Cpte)
Wagner: Lohengrin (Cpte), Meistersinger (Cpte)
(EMI) **CDH7 61001-2** R. Strauss—Lieder & Arias
(EMI) **CDM5 65577-2** Elisabeth Schwarzkopf
(EMI) **CMS5 65212-2** Wagner—Les introuvables du Ring

METZGER, Julian (sngr)
Schreker: Gezeichneten (Cpte)

METZGER, Ottilie (contr)
(IRCC) **IRCC-CD800** Souvenirs from Meyerbeer Operas
(SUPR) **11 2136-2(3)** Emmy Destinn—Complete Edition, Discs 5 to 8

METZMACHER, Ingo (cond)
see Hamburg PO
Modern Ens

MEUCCI, Valerio (sngr)
(MEMO) **HR4300/1** Great Voices—Sesto Bruscantini

MEUNIER, Claudine (contr)
Berio: Laborintus II

MEUNIER, Jean-Louis (ten)
Debussy: Rodrigue et Chimène (Cpte)
Offenbach: Brigands (Cpte)
Rameau: Hippolyte et Aricie (Cpte)

MEUSBURGER, Friedl (mez)
Mozart: Zauberflöte (Cpte)

MEVEN, Peter (bass)
Beethoven: Fidelio (Cpte)
Debussy: Pelléas et Mélisande (Cpte)
Hindemith: Mathis der Maler (Cpte)
Pfitzner: Palestrina (Cpte)
Wagner: Walküre (exc)
Weber: Freischütz (Cpte)

MEXICO CITY PALACIO DEL BELLAS ARTES CHORUS
cond R. CELLINI
(MEMO) **HR4372/3** Great Voices Giuseppe Di Stefano

MEXICO CITY PALACIO DEL BELLAS ARTES ORCHESTRA
cond R. CELLINI
(MEMO) **HR4372/3** Great Voices Giuseppe Di Stefano
cond U. MUGNAI
(MEMO) **HR4372/3** Great Voices Giuseppe Di Stefano
cond G. PICCO
(MEMO) **HR4372/3** Great Voices Giuseppe Di Stefano

MEXICO CITY PHILHARMONIC ORCHESTRA
cond E. BÁTIZ
(ASV) **CDDCA735** Music of Spain
(ASV) **CDQS6089** Rimsky-Korsakov—Orchestral Works
(ASV) **CDQS6112** Serenade
(ASV) **CDQS6121** España!
(ASV) **CDQS6122** Gypsy
(ASV) **CDQS6133** Bizet—Carmen Suites
cond F. LOZANO
(FORL) **FF047** Falla/Ravel—Orchestral Works

MEXICO STATE SYMPHONY ORCHESTRA
cond E. BÁTIZ
Borodin: Prince Igor (exc)
(ASV) **CDDCA856** Verdi—Overtures and Preludes
(ASV) **CDDCA857** Rossini—Overtures
(ASV) **CDQS6119** Russia!
(IMG) **IMGCD1610** Borodin/Stravinsky—Orchestral Works
(IMP) **PCD2028** Falla—Ballet and Opera
(MCI) **OQ0009** Wagner—Orchestral music from operas

MEY, Guy de (ten)
Cavalli: Giasone (Cpte), Xerse (Cpte)
Cesti: Orontea (Cpte)
Gluck: Cinesi (Cpte), Rencontre imprévue (Cpte)
Grétry: Caravane du Caire (Cpte)
Handel: Alessandro (Cpte)
Lully: Atys (exc)
Monteverdi: Incoronazione di Poppea (Cpte), Orfeo (Cpte)
Mozart: Zauberflöte (Cpte)
Rameau: Platée (Cpte)
(ERAT) **4509-99607-2** Gluck—Operas; Schubert—Symphonies Nos 8 & 9

MEYER, Kerstin (mez)
R. Strauss: Elektra (Cpte), Rosenkavalier (Cpte)
Verdi: Rigoletto (Cpte), Trovatore (Cpte)
(BIS) **BIS-CD017** Söderström and Meyer sing Duets

MEYER, Wolfgang (harm)
(DECC) **425 204-2DNL** Ute Lemper sings Kurt Weill

MEYER-ESCHE, Corinna (sop)
Spohr: Jessonda (Cpte)

MEYERS, Anne Akiko (vn)
(RCA) **09026 61700-2** Works for Violin & Orchestra
(RCA) **09026 62546-2** Salut d'amour

MEYERSON, Mitzi (hpd)
(HARM) **HMU90 7035** Sweeter than Roses - Purcell Songs

MEYER-WELFING, Hugo (ten)
Mozart: Nozze di Figaro (Cpte)
Wagner: Meistersinger (Cpte)
(EMI) **CHS7 69741-2(4)** Record of Singing, Vol.4—German School

MEYROWITZ, Selmar (cond)
see Berlin City Op Orch
Berlin St Op Orch
BPO
SO

MEYSENBUG, Malwida (voc)
Distel: Stazione (Cpte)

MEZZETTI, Sofia (sop)
Verdi: Lombardi (Cpte)

MIAMI SYMPHONIC ORCHESTRA
cond E. KOHN
(IMP) **MCD43** Domingo Live from Miami

MICCO, Anna Maria di (sop)
Rossini: Tancredi (Cpte)

MICHAEL, Audrey (mez)
Monteverdi: Orfeo (Cpte)
Verdi: Luisa Miller (Cpte), Rigoletto (Cpte)
Wagner: Parsifal (Cpte)

MICHAELIS, Ruth (sop)
R. Strauss: Arabella (Cpte)
Wagner: Götterdämmerung (Cpte)

MICHAELS, Mark (sngr)
Bernstein: West Side Story (Cpte)

MICHAELS-MOORE, Anthony (bar)
J. Strauss II: Fledermaus (Cpte)
Mercadante: Orazi e Curiazi (Cpte)
Purcell: Fairy Queen, Z629 (Cpte)
Sullivan: Yeomen of the Guard (Cpte)
(EMI) **CDC7 54785-2** Harry Enfield's Guide to Opera
(IMP) **MCD15** Opera Spectacular
(IMP) **TCD1070** Invitation to the Opera
(ROH) **75605 55013-2** The Puccini Experience
(RPO) **CDRPD9006** Opera Spectacular 1 & 2

MICHAILOVA, Maria (sop)
(MMOI) **CDMOIR422** Great Voices in Tchaikovsky
(PEAR) **GEMMCDS9001/3(2)** Singers of Imperial Russia, Vol.2 (pt 2)
(PEAR) **GEMMCDS9007/9(2)** Singers of Imperial Russia, Vol.4 (pt 2)
(PEAR) **GEMMCDS9111(1)** Singers of Imperial Russia, Vol.5 (pt 1)
(PEAR) **GEMMCDS9111(2)** Singers of Imperial Russia, Vol.5 (pt 2)
(PREI) **89030** Feodor Chaliapin (1873-1938)

MICHALKOVÁ, Alzbeta (mez)
Mascagni: Cavalleria Rusticana (Cpte)
Puccini: Madama Butterfly (Cpte)
Suchoň: Whirlpool (Cpte)
Verdi: Rigoletto (Cpte)

MICHALSKI, Carl (cond)
see Graunke SO

MICHALSKY, Anne (sop)
(EMI) **CHS7 64487-2** R. Strauss—Der Rosenkavalier & Lieder
(PEAR) **GEMMCDS9365** R. Strauss: Der Rosenkavalier (abridged), etc
(SCHW) **314542** Vienna State Opera Live, Vol.4
(SCHW) **314592** Vienna State Opera Live, Vol.9
(SCHW) **314622** Vienna State Opera Live, Vol.12
(SCHW) **314642** Vienna State Opera Live, Vol.14
(SCHW) **314672** Vienna State Opera Live, Vol.17
(SCHW) **314702** Vienna State Opera Live, Vol.20
(SCHW) **314742** Vienna State Opera Live, Vol.24

MICHEAU, Janine (sop)
Bizet: Carmen (Cpte), Ivan IV (exc), Pêcheurs de perles (Cpte)
Ganne: Saltimbanques (exc)
Gounod: Roméo et Juliette (Cpte)
Milhaud: Christophe Colomb (Cpte)
O. Straus: Drei Walzer (exc)
(EMI) **CZS7 67869-2** J. Strauss II—Operetta Highlights
(MONT) **TCE8760** Stravinsky: Stage Works
(MUSD) **20239-2** Delibes—Opéras-Comiques

MICHEL, Solange (mez)
Bizet: Carmen (Cpte)
Debussy: Pelléas et Mélisande (Cpte)
G. Charpentier: Louise (Cpte)
Gounod: Faust (Cpte)
Martinů: Julietta (Cpte)
Offenbach: Contes d'Hoffmann (exc)
Ravel: Enfant et les sortilèges (Cpte)
(EMI) **CHS7 69741-2(3)** Record of Singing, Vol.4—French School

MICHEL-DANSAC, Donatienne (sop)
Rossi: Orfeo (Cpte)

MICHELETTI, Gaston (ten)
(MSCM) **MM30377** 18 Tenors d'Expression Française
(MSCM) **MM30451** Mascagni—Cavalleria Rusticana, etc
(NIMB) **NI7836/7** Conchita Supervia (1895-1936)

MICHELINI, Joëlle (sop)
Boïeldieu: Calife de Bagdad (Cpte)

MICHELOW, Sybil (mez)
(JEWI) **BB 002** Michelow and Williamson in Recital

MICHIELI, Jolanda (sop)
Verdi: Ernani (Cpte)

MICHNIEWSKI, Wojciech (cond)
see Warsaw PO

MICU, Ioan (ten)
(CPO) **CPO999 104-2** Mozart—Lo Sposo Deluso/L'Oca del Cairo

MIDBOE, David (bar)
Corghi: Divara (Cpte)

MIDDLETON, Arthur (bass)
(PEAR) **GEMMCDS9074(2)** Giovanni Zenatello, Vol.2 (pt 2)

MIDDLETON, Karen (sop)
Wagner: Walküre (Cpte)
(PHIL) **434 420-2PM32(2)** Richard Wagner Edition (pt 2)

MIDGLEY, Maryetta (sop)
G. Charpentier: Louise (Cpte)
Puccini: Rondine (Cpte)

MIDGLEY, Vernon (ten)
G. Charpentier: Louise (Cpte)
Puccini: Rondine (Cpte)
Rossini: Zelmira (Cpte)

MIDGLEY, Walter (ten)
(EMI) **CHS7 69741-2(2)** Record of Singing, Vol.4—Anglo-American School (pt 2)

MIDHOE, David (bar)
Delius: Village Romeo and Juliet (Cpte)

MIDI-PYRÉNÉES JUNIOR HARMONIE RÉGIONALE
cond D. DONDEYNE
Fauré: Prométhée (Cpte)

MIDI-PYRENEES REGIONAL CHOIR
cond M. PLASSON
Gounod: Roméo et Juliette (Cpte)

MIDORI, Miss (vn)
(SONY) **SK52568** Midori—Encore!

MIGENES (JOHNSON), Julia (sop)
Bizet: Carmen (exc)
Weill: Sieben Todsünden (Cpte)
(ERAT) **2292-45797-2** The Ultimate Opera Collection
(ERAT) **4509-91715-2** The Ultimate Opera Collection 2
(ERAT) **4509-92875-2** Vienna - Operetta Arias

MIGLIETTE, Adrienne (sop)
(DECC) **433 400-2DM2** Ravel & Debussy—Stage Works
(SYMP) **SYMCD1103** Renée Doria—Opera Recital

MIGUEL, Pablo (pf)
Offenbach: Madame l'Archiduc (Cpte)

MIHAILOV, Luben (ten)
(EMI) **CMS7 63386-2** Borodin—Prince Igor & Complete Solo Songs

MIHÁLY, Andras (cond)
see Budapest Op Orch

MIILBERG, Hans (bass)
Tubin: Barbara von Tisenhusen (Cpte)

MIKAELI CHAMBER CHOIR
cond F. HAIDER
Donizetti: Linda di Chamounix (Cpte)

MIKHAILOV, Igor (bass)
Tchaikovsky: Eugene Onegin (Cpte)

MIKHAILOV, Maxim (bass)
Serov: Judith (Cpte)
Tchaikovsky: Maid of Orleans (Cpte)
(ARLE) **ARL23/5** Rimsky-Korsakov—Sadko

MIKOREY, Karl (ten)
Wagner: Meistersinger (Cpte)

MÍKOVÁ, Alena (mez)
Dvořák: Rusalka (Cpte)
Janáček: From the House of the Dead (Cpte)

MIKULÁŠ, Peter (bass)
Bellini: Sonnambula (Cpte)
Dvořák: Dimitrij (Cpte)
Mozart: Così fan tutte (Cpte)
Patzelt: Castor et Pollux (Cpte)
Suchoň: Whirlpool (Cpte)
Verdi: Simon Boccanegra (Cpte)

MIKUS, Winfried (ten)
Keiser: Masagniello furioso (Cpte)

MILAN, Susan (fl)
(CHAN) **CHAN8840** La flûte enchantée

MILAN CHAMBER ORCHESTRA
cond P. VAGLIERI
Paisiello: Serva Padrona (Cpte)

MILAN LA SCALA CHORUS
(SYMP) **SYMCD1113** The Harold Wayne Collection, Vol.13
cond C. ABBADO
Bellini: Capuleti (Cpte)
Donizetti: Lucia di Lammermoor (Cpte)
Rossini: Barbiere di Siviglia (Cpte), Cenerentola (Cpte)
Verdi: Aida (exc), Don Carlos (Cpte), Macbeth (Cpte), Simon Boccanegra (Cpte)
(MEMO) **HR4273/4** Great Voices—Pietro Cappuccilli
(MEMO) **HR4291/2** Great Voices - Renata Scotto
(RCA) **09026 68014-2** Pavarotti - The Early Years, Vol.2
cond U. BERRETTONI
Puccini: Bohème (Cpte)
cond F. CAPUANA
Massenet: Werther (Cpte)
cond R. CHAILLY
Giordano: Andrea Chénier (Cpte)
Rossini: Barbiere di Siviglia (Cpte)
(CAST) **CVI2067** Opera Highlights from La Scala
cond A. EREDE
Verdi: Otello (exc)
cond G. GAVAZZENI
Donizetti: Anna Bolena (Cpte), Linda di Chamounix (Cpte)
Rossini: Turco in Italia (Cpte)
Verdi: Due Foscari (Cpte), Lombardi (Cpte)
(CAST) **CASH5052** Verdi Operatic Favourites
(CAST) **CVI2057** Il Trittico live from La Scala, 1983
(CAST) **CVI2067** Opera Highlights from La Scala
(MEMO) **HR4223/4** Nicolai Ghiaurov
(MEMO) **HR4273/4** Great Voices—Pietro Cappuccilli
(MEMO) **HR4275/6** Birgit Nilsson—Public Performances 1954-1969
(MEMO) **HR4386/7** Great Voices - Giulietta Simionato
(MEMO) **HR4400/1** Great Voices - Ettore Bastianini
cond F. GHIONE
Leoncavallo: Pagliacci (Cpte)
(EMI) **CDH7 63200-2** Tito Schipa—Recital
(MSCM) **MM30231** Don Pasquale & Tito Schipa Recital
cond C.M. GIULINI
Rossini: Italiana in Algeri (Cpte)
Verdi: Traviata (Cpte)
(MEMO) **HR4372/3** Great Voices Giuseppe Di Stefano
(MEMO) **HR4400/1** Great Voices - Ettore Bastianini
cond A. GUARNIERI
(BONG) **GB1039-2** Antonio Guarnieri
cond H. VON KARAJAN
Donizetti: Lucia di Lammermoor (Cpte)
Puccini: Bohème (Cpte), Madama Butterfly (Cpte)
Verdi: Trovatore (Cpte)
(DG) **419 257-2GH3** 'Cav' and 'Pag', etc
(EMI) **CDC7 49502-2** Maria Callas—The Voice of the Century
(EMI) **CDM7 69543-2** Maria Callas and Giuseppe Di Stefano - Duets
(EMI) **CMS7 63244-2** The Art of Maria Callas
(MEMO) **HR4277/8** Mirella Freni—Public Performances 1963-1970
(MEMO) **HR4372/3** Great Voices Giuseppe Di Stefano
cond R. KUBELÍK
Verdi: Rigoletto (Cpte)
cond P. MAAG
Massenet: Manon (Cpte)
(MEMO) **HR4277/8** Mirella Freni—Public Performances 1963-1970
cond L. MAAZEL
Puccini: Fanciulla del West (Cpte), Madama Butterfly (Cpte), Manon Lescaut (Cpte)
Verdi: Aida (Cpte), Otello (exc)
(DECC) **433 822-2DH** Essential Opera
cond P. MASCAGNI
Mascagni: Cavalleria Rusticana (Cpte)
cond L. VON MATAČIĆ
Leoncavallo: Pagliacci (Cpte)
Puccini: Fanciulla del West (Cpte)
(CFP) **CD-CFP4575** Verdi Arias
(CFP) **CD-CFP4602** Favourite Opera
cond L. MOLAJOLI
Verdi: Aida (Cpte), Falstaff (Cpte)
(EMI) **CDH7 69791-2** Dame Eva Turner sings Opera Arias and Songs
(MSCM) **MM30276** Rossini—Barbiere di Siviglia, etc
(PEAR) **GEMMCD9091** Dino Borgioli
cond R. MUTI
Cherubini: Lodoïska (Cpte)
Gluck: Iphigénie en Tauride (Cpte)
Mozart: Così fan tutte (Cpte), Don Giovanni (Cpte)
Rossini: Guillaume Tell (Cpte)
Spontini: Vestale (Cpte)
Verdi: Attila (Cpte), Don Carlo (Cpte), Ernani (Cpte), Falstaff (Cpte), Forza del destino (Cpte), Nabucco (Cpte), Rigoletto (Cpte), Traviata (Cpte), Vespri Siciliani (Cpte)
(CAST) **CVI2067** Opera Highlights from La Scala
(EMI) **CDC5 55350-2** Cheryl Studer - A Portrait
(EMI) **CDC7 54484-2** Verdi—Opera Choruses
(EMI) **CZS5 68559-2** Italian Opera Choruses
(TELD) **9031-77676-6(TELD)** My World of Opera - Kiri Te Kanawa
cond G. NASTRUCCI
(PREI) **89001** Toti dal Monte (1898-1975)
cond E. PANIZZA
(EMI) **CHS7 64864-2(1)** La Scala Edition - Vol.2, 1915-46 (pt 1)
cond G. PRÊTRE
Leoncavallo: Pagliacci (Cpte)
Mascagni: Cavalleria Rusticana (Cpte)
(BELA) **450 052-2** Great Opera Choruses
(MEMO) **HR4223/4** Nicolai Ghiaurov
(MEMO) **HR4277/8** Mirella Freni—Public Performances 1963-1970
(PHIL) **442 602-2PM** 3 x 3 Tenors
cond C. SABAJNO
Leoncavallo: Pagliacci (Cpte)
Mascagni: Cavalleria rusticana (Cpte)
Puccini: Bohème (Cpte), Tosca (Cpte)
Verdi: Aida (Cpte), Rigoletto (Cpte), Traviata (Cpte)
(EMI) **CHS7 64864-2(1)** La Scala Edition - Vol.2, 1915-46 (pt 1)
(EMI) **CMS7 64008-2(1)** Wagner Singing on Record (pt 1)
(MSCM) **MM30231** Don Pasquale & Tito Schipa Recital
(NIMB) **NI7831** Mattia Battistini (1856-1928)
(NIMB) **NI7853** Lauri-Volpi sings Verdi
(PEAR) **GEMMCDS9074(2)** Giovanni Zenatello, Vol.2 (pt 2)
(PEAR) **GEMMCDS9180** Verdi—Rigoletto, etc
(PEAR) **GEMMCDS9926(1)** Covent Garden on Record—Vol.4 (pt 1)
cond V. DE SABATA
Puccini: Tosca (Cpte)
Verdi: Falstaff (Cpte), Macbeth (Cpte)
(EMI) **CDM7 69543-2** Maria Callas and Giuseppe Di Stefano - Duets
(EMI) **CMS7 63244-2** The Art of Maria Callas
cond G. SANTINI
Verdi: Don Carlo (Cpte)
(PREI) **89001** Toti dal Monte (1898-1975)
cond N. SANZOGNO
(MEMO) **HR4277/8** Mirella Freni—Public Performances 1963-1970
(RCA) **09026 62541-2** Pavarotti - The Early Years, Vol.1
cond W. SAWALLISCH
Wagner: Fliegende Holländer (Cpte)
cond T. SERAFIN
Bellini: Norma (Cpte), Puritani (Cpte)
Cherubini: Medea (Cpte)
Donizetti: Elisir d'amore (Cpte)
Leoncavallo: Pagliacci (Cpte)
Mascagni: Cavalleria Rusticana (Cpte)
Puccini: Manon Lescaut (Cpte), Turandot (Cpte)
Verdi: Aida (Cpte), Forza del destino (Cpte), Rigoletto (Cpte), Trovatore (Cpte)
(EMI) **CDC5 55095-2** Prima Diva
(EMI) **CDC7 49502-2** Maria Callas—The Voice of the Century
(EMI) **CDC7 54016-2** Tenorissimo!
(EMI) **CDC7 54702-2** Maria Callas - La Divina
(EMI) **CMS7 63244-2** The Art of Maria Callas
cond G. SOLTI
Verdi: Simon Boccanegra (Cpte)
cond V. VENEZIANI
(EMI) **CHS7 64864-2(2)** La Scala Edition - Vol.2, 1915-46 (pt 2)
cond A. VOTTO
Bellini: Sonnambula (Cpte)
Ponchielli: Gioconda (Cpte)
Puccini: Bohème (Cpte)
Verdi: Ballo in maschera (Cpte), Traviata (Cpte)
(EMI) **CMS7 63244-2** The Art of Maria Callas
(MEMO) **HR4400/1** Great Voices - Ettore Bastianini

MILAN LA SCALA ORCHESTRA
Giordano: Andrea Chénier (Cpte)
Leoncavallo: Pagliacci (Cpte)
Mascagni: Cavalleria Rusticana (Cpte)
Mozart: Così fan tutte (Cpte), Don Giovanni (Cpte)
Puccini: Bohème (Cpte), Madama Butterfly (Cpte)
Rossini: Barbiere di Siviglia (Cpte), Cenerentola (Cpte), Guillaume Tell (exc)
Verdi: Aida (Cpte), Don Carlo (Cpte), Due Foscari (Cpte), Ernani (Cpte), Lombardi (Cpte), Nabucco (Cpte)
(CAST) **CVI2057** Il Trittico live from La Scala, 1983
(DECC) **430 470-2DH** Essential Pavarotti II
(PREI) **89001** Toti dal Monte (1898-1975)
cond C. ABBADO
Bellini: Capuleti (Cpte)
Donizetti: Lucia di Lammermoor (Cpte)
Verdi: Aida (exc), Don Carlos (Cpte), Macbeth (Cpte), Simon Boccanegra (Cpte)
(BELA) **450 121-2** Plácido Domingo
(CBS) **CD37228** Pavarotti sings Verdi
(DG) **415 366-2GH** Placido Domingo Recital
(DG) **427 708-2GX3** The Best of Domingo
(DG) **431 104-2GB** Great Voices - Plácido Domingo
(DG) **445 525-2GMA** Domingo Favourites
(DG) **419 091-4GW** Placido Domingo sings Favourite Arias, Songs and Tangos
(DG) **439 153-4GMA** Mad about Sopranos
(MEMO) **HR4273/4** Great Voices—Pietro Cappuccilli
(MEMO) **HR4291/2** Great Voices - Renata Scotto
(RCA) **09026 68014-2** Pavarotti - The Early Years, Vol.2
cond G. ANTONICELLI
(BONG) **GB1078-2** Mafalda Favero
(EMI) **CDH7 63200-2** Tito Schipa—Recital
(EMI) **CHS7 64864-2(2)** La Scala Edition - Vol.2, 1915-46 (pt 2)
(NIMB) **NI7801** Great Singers, Vol.1
(VAI) **VAIA1071** Mafalda Favero (1903-1981)
cond L. BERNSTEIN
(MEMO) **HR4191/2** Cesare Valletti—Public Performances
(MEMO) **HR4293/4** The very best of Maria Callas
cond U. BERRETTONI
Puccini: Bohème (Cpte)
(CONI) **CDHD227** Gigli in Opera and Song
(EMI) **CDH7 61052-2** Beniamino Gigli—Arias and Duets (1932-1949)
(EMI) **CDM7 63109-2** Tito Gobbi - Opera Aria Recital
(EMI) **CHS7 64864-2(2)** La Scala Edition - Vol.2, 1915-46 (pt 2)
(NIMB) **NI7851** Legendary Voices
(PEAR) **GEMMCDS9926(2)** Covent Garden on Record—Vol.4 (pt 2)
(PREI) **89009** Gino Bechi (b. 1913)
(PREI) **89015** Carlo Tagliabue (1898-1978)
(PREI) **89995** Famous Italian Baritones
(TEST) **SBT1019** Tito Gobbi - Opera Arias & Songs
cond F. CAPUANA
Massenet: Werther (Cpte)
cond R. CHAILLY
Rossini: Barbiere di Siviglia (Cpte)
(CAST) **CVI2067** Opera Highlights from La Scala
(TELD) **9031-77676-6(TELD)** My World of Opera - Kiri Te Kanawa
cond A. EREDE
Verdi: Falstaff (exc), Otello (exc)
(EMI) **CHS7 64864-2(2)** La Scala Edition - Vol.2, 1915-46 (pt 2)
(LYRC) **SRO805** Gina Cigna—Opera Recital
cond O. DE FABRITIIS
(EMI) **CDH7 61051-2** Beniamino Gigli - Operatic Arias
(MMOI) **CDMOIR425** Three Tenors, Volume 2
cond W. FURTWÄNGLER
(ACAN) **43 121** Wagner: Orchestral Works
cond G. GAVAZZENI
Donizetti: Anna Bolena (Cpte), Linda di Chamounix (Cpte)
Rossini: Turco in Italia (Cpte)
(CAST) **CASH5052** Verdi Operatic Favourites
(CAST) **CVI2067** Opera Highlights from La Scala
(CAST) **CVI2070** Great Puccini Love Scenes from Covent Garden, La Scala and Verona
(EMI) **CMS7 63244-2** The Art of Maria Callas
(MEMO) **HR4204/5** Franco Corelli—Opera Arias
(MEMO) **HR4223/4** Nicolai Ghiaurov
(MEMO) **HR4239/40** Opera Arias—Leyla Gencer
(MEMO) **HR4273/4** Great Voices—Pietro Cappuccilli
(MEMO) **HR4275/6** Birgit Nilsson—Public Performances 1954-1969

(MEMO) **HR4386/7** Great Voices - Giulietta Simionato
(MEMO) **HR4400/1** Great Voices - Ettore Bastianini
cond F. GHIONE
Leoncavallo: Pagliacci (Cpte)
(BONG) **GB1078-2** Mafalda Favero
(CONI) **CDHD227** Gigli in Opera and Song
(CONI) **CDHD235** The Puccini Album
(EMI) **CDH7 61051-2** Beniamino Gigli - Operatic Arias
(EMI) **CDH7 61052-2** Beniamino Gigli—Arias and Duets (1932-1949)
(EMI) **CDH7 63200-2** Tito Schipa—Recital
(EMI) **CHS7 64864-2(2)** La Scala Edition - Vol.2, 1915-46 (pt 2)
(MMOI) **CDMOIR405** Great Tenors
(MMOI) **CDMOIR409** Three Tenors—Björling, Gigli & Tauber
(MMOI) **CDMOIR412** Great Voices of the Century Sing Puccini
(MMOI) **CDMOIR417** Great Voices of the Century—Beniamino Gigli
(MMOI) **CDMOIR425** Three Tenors, Volume 2
(MSCM) **MM30231** Don Pasquale & Tito Schipa Recital
(NIMB) **NI7817** Beniamino Gigli—Vol.2
(NIMB) **NI7845** Giacomo Lauri-Volpi (1892-1979)
(NIMB) **NI7853** Lauri-Volpi sings Verdi
(PEAR) **GEMMCDS9176** Gigli - Arias, Duets & Songs, 1926-1937
(PEAR) **GEMMCDS9925(2)** Covent Garden on Record—Vol.3 (pt 2)
(PREI) **89012** Giacomo Lauri-Volpi (1894-1979)
(PREI) **89995** Famous Italian Baritones
(TEST) **SBT1005** Ten Top Tenors
(VAI) **VAIA1071** Mafalda Favero (1903-1981)
cond C.M. GIULINI
Rossini: Italiana in Algeri (Cpte)
Verdi: Traviata (Cpte)
(MEMO) **HR4372/3** Great Voices Giuseppe Di Stefano
(MEMO) **HR4400/1** Great Voices - Ettore Bastianini
cond E. GRACIS
(MEMO) **HR4279/80** Montserrat Caballè—Opera Arias
cond A. GUARNIERI
(BONG) **GB1039-2** Antonio Guarnieri
(EMI) **CHS7 64864-2(1)** La Scala Edition - Vol.2, 1915-46 (pt 1)
cond H. VON KARAJAN
Puccini: Madama Butterfly (Cpte)
Verdi: Trovatore (Cpte)
(DECC) **071 142-1DH (DECC)** Essential Opera
(DG) **419 257-2GH3** 'Cav' and 'Pag', etc
(DG) **447 364-2GDB2** Great Opera Overtures
(EMI) **CDC5 55216-2** Maria Callas - La Divina 3
(EMI) **CDC7 49502-2** Maria Callas—The Voice of the Century
(EMI) **CDM7 69543-2** Maria Callas and Giuseppe Di Stefano - Duets
(EMI) **CMS7 63244-2** The Art of Maria Callas
(MEMO) **HR4277/8** Mirella Freni—Public Performances 1963-1970
cond R. KUBELÍK
Berlioz: Troyens (exc)
Verdi: Rigoletto (Cpte)
cond P. MAAG
Massenet: Manon (Cpte)
(BUTT) **BMCD015** Pavarotti Collection - Duets and Scenes
(MEMO) **HR4277/8** Mirella Freni—Public Performances 1963-1970
(RCA) **09026 62541-2** Pavarotti - The Early Years, Vol.1
cond L. MAAZEL
Puccini: Fanciulla del West (Cpte), Manon Lescaut (Cpte)
Verdi: Aida (exc), Otello (Cpte)
(DECC) **433 822-2DH** Essential Opera
cond G. MARINUZZI
(EMI) **CHS7 64864-2(2)** La Scala Edition - Vol.2, 1915-46 (pt 2)
(NIMB) **NI7853** Lauri-Volpi sings Verdi
cond P. MASCAGNI
Mascagni: Cavalleria Rusticana (Cpte)
cond L. VON MATAČIĆ
Leoncavallo: Pagliacci (Cpte)
Puccini: Fanciulla del West (Cpte)
(CFP) **CD-CFP4575** Verdi Arias
(CFP) **CD-CFP4602** Favourite Opera
(EMIL) **CDZ103** Best Loved Classics 4
cond L. MOLAJOLI
(MEMO) **HR4408/9(2)** Singers in Genoa, Vol.1 (disc 2)
(MMOI) **CDMOIR412** Great Voices of the Century Sing Puccini
(MSCM) **MM30276** Rossini—Barbiere di Siviglia, etc
(PREI) **89007** Aureliano Pertile (1885-1952) - I
(PREI) **89013** Giannina Arangi-Lombardi (1890-1951)
(PREI) **89040** Carlo Galeffi (1884-1961)
cond R. MUTI
Cherubini: Lodoïska (Cpte)
Gluck: Iphigénie en Tauride (Cpte)
Pergolesi: Frate 'nnamorato (Cpte)
Rossini: Guillaume Tell (exc)
Spontini: Vestale (Cpte)
Verdi: Attila (Cpte), Don Carlo (Cpte), Ernani (Cpte), Falstaff (Cpte), Forza del destino (Cpte), Rigoletto (exc), Traviata (Cpte), Vespri Siciliani (Cpte)
(CAST) **CASH5052** Verdi Operatic Favourites
(CAST) **CVI2067** Opera Highlights from La Scala
(EMI) **CDC5 55017-2** Domingo Opera Classics
(EMI) **CDC5 55350-2** Cheryl Studer - A Portrait
(EMI) **CDC7 54484-2** Verdi—Opera Choruses
(EMI) **CZS5 68559-2** Italian Opera Choruses
(TELD) **9031-77676-6(TELD)** My World of Opera - Kiri Te Kanawa
cond G. NASTRUCCI
(CONI) **CDHD235** The Puccini Album
(PREI) **89007** Aureliano Pertile (1885-1952) - I
(PREI) **89048** Apollo Granforte (1886-1975) - I
(PREI) **89072** Aureliano Pertile (1885-1952) - II
cond D. OLIVIERI
(NIMB) **NI7817** Beniamino Gigli—Vol.2
cond E. PANIZZA
(EMI) **CHS7 64864-2(1)** La Scala Edition - Vol.2, 1915-46 (pt 1)
cond G. PRÊTRE
Leoncavallo: Pagliacci (Cpte)
Mascagni: Cavalleria rusticana (exc)
(BELA) **450 052-2** Great Opera Choruses
(DECC) **071 142-1DH (DECC)** Essential Opera
(MEMO) **HR4223/4** Nicolai Ghiaurov
(MEMO) **HR4277/8** Mirella Freni—Public Performances 1963-1970
(PHIL) **442 602-2PM** 3 x 3 Tenors
cond C. SABAJNO
Leoncavallo: Pagliacci (Cpte)
Mascagni: Cavalleria rusticana (Cpte)
Puccini: Bohème (Cpte), Tosca (Cpte)
Verdi: Aida (Cpte), Rigoletto (Cpte), Traviata (Cpte)
(CLUB) **CL99-025** Giovanni Zenatello (1876-1949)
(CLUB) **CL99-509/10** Hina Spani (1896-1969)
(CONI) **CDHD227** Gigli in Opera and Song
(CONI) **CDHD235** The Puccini Album
(EMI) **CDH7 61051-2** Beniamino Gigli - Operatic Arias
(EMI) **CDH7 61052-2** Beniamino Gigli—Arias and Duets (1932-1949)
(EMI) **CDH7 63200-2** Tito Schipa—Recital
(EMI) **CHS7 64860-2(2)** La Scala Edition - Vol.1, 1878-1914 (pt 2)
(EMI) **CHS7 64864-2(1)** La Scala Edition - Vol.2, 1915-46 (pt 1)
(EMI) **CHS7 64864-2(2)** La Scala Edition - Vol.2, 1915-46 (pt 2)
(EMI) **CMS7 64008-2(1)** Wagner Singing on Record (pt 1)
(MMOI) **CDMOIR405** Great Tenors
(MMOI) **CDMOIR408** Great Sopranos
(MMOI) **CDMOIR417** Great Voices of the Century—Beniamino Gigli
(MSCM) **MM30231** Don Pasquale & Tito Schipa Recital
(NIMB) **NI7850** Antonio Cortis (1891-1952)
(NIMB) **NI7853** Lauri-Volpi sings Verdi
(NIMB) **NI7856** Legendary Tenors
(NIMB) **NI7870** Tito Schipa in Song
(PEAR) **GEMMCDS9074(2)** Giovanni Zenatello, Vol.2 (pt 2)
(PEAR) **GEMMCDS9176** Gigli - Arias, Duets & Songs, 1926-1937
(PEAR) **GEMMCDS9180** Verdi—Rigoletto, etc
(PEAR) **GEMMCDS9925(2)** Covent Garden on Record—Vol.3 (pt 2)
(PEAR) **GEMMCDS9926(1)** Covent Garden on Record—Vol.4 (pt 1)
(PEAR) **GEMMCDS9926(2)** Covent Garden on Record—Vol.4 (pt 2)
(PEAR) **GEMMCD9129** Great Tenors, Vol.2
(PEAR) **GEMMCD9322** Tito Schipa sings Opera Arias and Songs
(PREI) **89001** Toti dal Monte (1898-1975)
(PREI) **89007** Aureliano Pertile (1885-1952) - I
(PREI) **89008** Irene Minghini-Cattaneo (1892-1944)
(PREI) **89030** Feodor Chaliapin (1873-1938)
(PREI) **89037** Hina Spani (1896-1969)
(PREI) **89038** Giovanni Zenatello (1876-1949)
(PREI) **89043** Antonio Cortis (1891-1952)
(PREI) **89044** Dusolina Giannini (1902-1986)
(PREI) **89048** Apollo Granforte (1886-1975) - I
(PREI) **89072** Aureliano Pertile (1885-1952) - II
(PREI) **89105** Apollo Granforte (1886-1975) - II
(PREI) **89995** Famous Italian Baritones
cond V. DE SABATA
Puccini: Tosca (Cpte)
Verdi: Falstaff (Cpte), Macbeth (Cpte)
(EMI) **CDM7 69543-2** Maria Callas and Giuseppe Di Stefano - Duets
(EMI) **CMS7 63244-2** The Art of Maria Callas
cond A. SABINO
(PREI) **89074** Tancredi Pasero (1893-1983) - II
cond G. SANTINI
Verdi: Don Carlo (Cpte)
(EMI) **CHS7 64864-2(1)** La Scala Edition - Vol.2, 1915-46 (pt 1)
cond N. SANZOGNO
(MEMO) **HR4233/4** Alfredo Kraus—Public Performances
(MEMO) **HR4277/8** Mirella Freni—Public Performances 1963-1970
(RCA) **09026 62541-2** Pavarotti - The Early Years, Vol.1
cond W. SAWALLISCH
Wagner: Fliegende Holländer (Cpte)
cond T. SCHIPPERS
(MEMO) **HR4392/3** Great Voices - Marilyn Horne
cond T. SERAFIN
Bellini: Norma (Cpte), Puritani (Cpte)
Cherubini: Medea (Cpte)
Donizetti: Elisir d'amore (Cpte)
Leoncavallo: Pagliacci (Cpte)
Mascagni: Cavalleria Rusticana (Cpte)
Puccini: Manon Lescaut (Cpte), Turandot (Cpte)
Verdi: Aida (Cpte), Forza del destino (Cpte), Rigoletto (Cpte), Trovatore (Cpte)
(EMI) **CDC5 55016-2** Maria Callas - La Divina 2
(EMI) **CDC5 55095-2** Prima Diva
(EMI) **CDC5 55216-2** Maria Callas - La Divina 3
(EMI) **CDC7 47282-2** Maria Callas - Operatic Recital
(EMI) **CDC7 47966-2** Puccini and Bellini Arias
(EMI) **CDC7 49502-2** Maria Callas—The Voice of the Century
(EMI) **CDC7 54016-2** Tenorissimo!
(EMI) **CDC7 54702-2** Maria Callas - La Divina
(EMI) **CDM7 63182-2** The Incomparable Callas
(EMI) **CDM7 63657-2** Schwarzkopf sings Opera Arias
(EMI) **CDM7 69543-2** Maria Callas and Giuseppe Di Stefano - Duets
(EMI) **CMS7 63244-2** The Art of Maria Callas
cond G. SOLTI
Verdi: Simon Boccanegra (Cpte)
(DECC) **436 463-2DM** Ten Top Tenors
cond E. TIERI
(EMI) **CHS7 69741-2(7)** Record of Singing, Vol.4—Italian School
(MEMO) **HR4372/3** Great Voices Giuseppe Di Stefano
cond A. TOSCANINI
(EMI) **CHS7 64860-2(1)** La Scala Edition - Vol.1, 1878-1914 (pt 1)
(EMI) **CHS7 64864-2(2)** La Scala Edition - Vol.2, 1915-46 (pt 2)
(NIMB) **NI7872** Geraldine Farrar in French Opera
(RCA) **GD60315** Toscanini Collection, Vol.71
cond V. VENEZIANI
(EMI) **CHS7 64864-2(2)** La Scala Edition - Vol.2, 1915-46 (pt 2)
cond A. VOTTO
Bellini: Sonnambula (Cpte)
Ponchielli: Gioconda (Cpte)
Puccini: Bohème (Cpte)
Verdi: Ballo in maschera (Cpte), Traviata (Cpte)
(EMI) **CDC5 55216-2** Maria Callas - La Divina 3
(EMI) **CDC7 49502-2** Maria Callas—The Voice of the Century
(EMI) **CDC7 54702-2** Maria Callas - La Divina
(EMI) **CDM7 63105-2** Giuseppe di Stefano sings Opera Arias & Songs
(EMI) **CDM7 63110-2** Mirella Freni: Opera Recital
(EMI) **CDM7 63182-2** The Incomparable Callas
(EMI) **CDM7 69543-2** Maria Callas and Giuseppe Di Stefano - Duets
(EMI) **CMS7 63244-2** The Art of Maria Callas
(MEMO) **HR4204/5** Franco Corelli—Opera Arias
(MEMO) **HR4239/40** Opera Arias—Leyla Gencer
(MEMO) **HR4372/3** Great Voices Giuseppe Di Stefano
(MEMO) **HR4376/7** Tito Gobbi—Opera Arias
(MEMO) **HR4400/1** Great Voices - Ettore Bastianini

MILAN RAI CHORUS

cond C.F. CILLARIO
Donizetti: Gianni di Parigi (Cpte)
cond G. GAVAZZENI
(MEMO) **HR4279/80** Montserrat Caballè—Opera Arias
(MEMO) **HR4386/7** Great Voices - Giulietta Simionato
cond C.M. GIULINI
Verdi: Due Foscari (Cpte)
cond J. LATHAM-KÖNIG
Donizetti: Elisabetta (Cpte)
cond B. MADERNA
Maderna: Satyricon (Cpte)
cond L. VON MATAČIĆ
(MEMO) **HR4235/6** Great Voices-Renata Tebaldi
cond D. RENZETTI
Donizetti: Favorita (Cpte)
cond N. SANZOGNO
Gounod: Philémon et Baucis (Cpte)
(MEMO) **HR4300/1** Great Voices—Sesto Bruscantini
cond A. SIMONETTO
Massenet: Don Quichotte (Cpte)

MILAN RAI SYMPHONY ORCHESTRA

cond A. BASILE
(FONI) **CDMR5014** Martini & Rossi Festival, Volume 14
(MEMO) **HR4233/4** Alfredo Kraus—Public Performances
cond C.F. CILLARIO
Donizetti: Gianni di Parigi (Cpte)
(NUOV) **6820** Luciana Serra—Opera Recital
cond O. DE FABRITIIS
(FONI) **CDMR5014** Martini & Rossi Festival, Volume 14
(MEMO) **HR4204/5** Franco Corelli—Opera Arias
cond G. GAVAZZENI
(MEMO) **HR4239/40** Opera Arias—Leyla Gencer
(MEMO) **HR4279/80** Montserrat Caballè—Opera Arias
(MEMO) **HR4386/7** Great Voices - Giulietta Simionato
cond C.M. GIULINI
Verdi: Due Foscari (Cpte)
cond A. LA ROSA PARODI
(MEMO) **HR4233/4** Alfredo Kraus—Public Performances
cond J. LATHAM-KÖNIG
Donizetti: Elisabetta (Cpte)
cond B. MADERNA
Maderna: Satyricon (Cpte)

cond F. PREVITALI
(MEMO) **HR4239/40** Opera Arias—Leyla Gencer
cond D. RENZETTI
Donizetti: Favorita (Cpte)
cond M. ROSSI
(MEMO) **HR4204/5** Franco Corelli—Opera Arias
cond N. SANZOGNO
Gounod: Philémon et Baucis (Cpte)
(FONI) **CDMR5023** Martini & Rossi Festival, Volume 23
(MEMO) **HR4300/1** Great Voices—Sesto Bruscantini
(MEMO) **HR4386/7** Great Voices - Giulietta Simionato
cond A. SIMONETTO
Massenet: Don Quichotte (Cpte)
(FONI) **CDO104** Maria Callas
(MEMO) **HR4293/4** The very best of Maria Callas
(MEMO) **HR4376/7** Tito Gobbi—Opera Arias
(SUIT) **CDS1-5001** Maria Callas - La divina
cond A. VOTTO
(SUIT) **CDS1-5001** Maria Callas - La divina

MILAN SYMPHONY ORCHESTRA
cond T. BENINTENDE-NEGLIA
(TEST) **SBT1039** Mario Del Monaco—The HMV Milan Recordings
cond L. MOLAJOLI
Verdi: Aida (Cpte), Falstaff (Cpte)
(PREI) **89013** Giannina Arangi-Lombardi (1890-1951)
cond A. QUADRI
(EMI) **CDC7 54016-2** Tenorissimo!
(EMI) **CHS7 69741-2(7)** Record of Singing, Vol.4—Italian School
(PREI) **89009** Gino Bechi (b. 1913)
(TEST) **SBT1039** Mario Del Monaco—The HMV Milan Recordings
cond A. TONINI
(EMI) **CDM7 63105-2** Giuseppe di Stefano sings Opera Arias & Songs

MILANOV, Zinka (sop)
Mascagni: Cavalleria Rusticana (Cpte)
Ponchielli: Gioconda (Cpte)
Puccini: Tosca (exc)
Verdi: Aida (Cpte), Trovatore (Cpte)
(EMI) **CHS7 69741-2(7)** Record of Singing, Vol.4—Italian School
(MYTO) **2MCD90317** Verdi—Un Ballo in maschera
(RCA) **GD60276** Toscanini conducts Boito & Verdi
(RCA) **GD87799** The Pearl Fishers Duet plus Duets and Scenes
(RCA) **09026 61580-2(5)** RCA/Met 100 Singers, 100 Years (pt 5)
(RCA) **09026 62689-2** The Voices of Living Stereo, Volume 1

MILASHKINA, Tamara (sop)
Tchaikovsky: Eugene Onegin (exc), Queen of Spades (Cpte)

MILCHEVA, Alexandrina (mez)
Borodin: Prince Igor (Cpte)
Gluck: Cinesi (Cpte)
Leoncavallo: Bohème (Cpte)
Mussorgsky: Khovanshchina (Cpte)
(FORL) **UCD16741** Bulgarian Voices, Vol. 1
(FORL) **UCD16743** Bulgarian Voices, Vol. 3

MILDENHALL, Pamela (sop)
Keiser: Croesus (Cpte)

MILDMAY, Audrey (sop)
Mozart: Don Giovanni (Cpte), Nozze di Figaro (Cpte)
(EMI) **CDH5 65072-2** Glyndebourne Recorded - 1934-1994

MILDONIAN, Susanna (hp)
(DENO) **C37-7301** Duo Recital

MILES, Alastair (bass)
Britten: Rape of Lucretia (Cpte)
Donizetti: Lucia di Lammermoor (Cpte)
Mayr: Medea (Cpte)
Mercadante: Orazi e Curiazi (Cpte)
Mozart: Don Giovanni (Cpte), Nozze di Figaro (Cpte), Thamos, K345 (Cpte), Zauberflöte (Cpte)
Rossini: Cenerentola (Cpte)
Verdi: Rigoletto (Cpte), Traviata (exc)
(EMI) **CDC7 49849-2** Famous Opera Choruses
(OPRA) **ORCH104** A Hundred Years of Italian Opera: 1820-1830
(TELD) **4509-93691-2** Queen of Coloratura

MILES, Gaynor (sngr)
Bernstein: Candide (1988) (exc)

MILHAUD, Darius (cond)
see Paris Op Orch
Pro Musica Ens

MILILOTTI, Bice (sop)
(SYMP) **SYMCD1069** The Harold Wayne Collection, Vol.2

MILINKOVIC, Georgine von (mez)
R. Strauss: Salome (Cpte), Schweigsame Frau (Cpte)

MILITANO, Filippo (bass)
Mascagni: Amico Fritz (Cpte)

MILJAKOVIC, Olivera (mez)
Mozart: Zauberflöte (Cpte)
Mussorgsky: Boris Godunov (Cpte)
R. Strauss: Ariadne auf Naxos (Cpte), Rosenkavalier (Cpte)

(DECC) **436 464-2DM** Ten Top Baritones & Basses
(EMI) **CMS7 64309-2** Kálmán—Best-loved Melodies

MILKOVSKY, Andrei (bar)
(EMI) **CMS7 63386-2** Borodin—Prince Igor & Complete Solo Songs

MILLER, Jenny (sop)
Monteverdi: Incoronazione di Poppea (Cpte)

MILLER, John (tpt)
(NIMB) **NI5123** Baroque Arias for Soprano and Trumpet

MILLER, Kevin (ten)
Stravinsky: Rake's Progress (Cpte)
(SONY) **SM22K46290(4)** Stravinsky—The Complete Edition (pt 4)

MILLER, Lajos (bar)
Mussorgsky: Boris Godunov (Cpte)
Prokofiev: War and Peace (Cpte)
Respighi: Belfagor (Cpte), Semirama (Cpte)

MILLET, Danielle (mez)
Delibes: Lakmé (exc)
(CFP) **CD-CFP4582** Flowers in Music
(CFP) **CD-CFP4613** Favourite TV Classics
(EMI) **CDM7 69596-2** The Movies go to the Opera
(RCA) **74321 25817-2** Café Classics - Operatic

MILLET, Danielle (sop)
(EMI) **CZS5 68113-2** Vive Offenbach!

MILLIGAN, James (bass-bar)
Sullivan: Gondoliers (Cpte), HMS Pinafore (Cpte)
(CFP) **CD-CFP4609** Favourite Gilbert & Sullivan
(EMI) **CMS7 64409-2** Sullivan—Pirates of Penzance & Orch. Works

MILLO, Aprile (sop)
Verdi: Aida (Cpte), Don Carlo (Cpte), Luisa Miller (Cpte), Trovatore (Cpte)
(DG) **072 428-1GH2(DG)** The Metropolitan Opera Gala

MILLO, Grace (sop)
(DG) **072 428-1GH2(DG)** The Metropolitan Opera Gala

MILLOT, Valérie (sop)
Fauré: Prométhée (Cpte)
Offenbach: Brigands (Cpte)

MILLS, Bronwen (sop)
Britten: Paul Bunyan (exc)
Donizetti: Emilia di Liverpool (Cpte), Eremitaggio di Liverpool (Cpte)
Gay: Beggar's Opera (Cpte)
(HYPE) **CDA66608** Dibdin—Three Operas
(OPRA) **ORCH103** Italian Opera—1810-20
(OPRA) **ORCH104** A Hundred Years of Italian Opera: 1820-1830

MILLS, Erie (sop)
Bernstein: Candide (1982) (Cpte)
(NEWP) **NPD85540** Handel/Bononcini—Muzio Scevola

MILLS, Keith (ten)
Walton: Troilus and Cressida (Cpte)

MILNE, Peter (spkr)
Lampe: Pyramus and Thisbe (Cpte)

MILNER, Howard (ten)
Britten: Billy Budd (Cpte)
Monteverdi: Orfeo (Cpte)
Mozart: Ascanio in Alba (Cpte)

MILNES, Sherrill (cond)
see New Philh

MILNES, Sherrill (bar)
A. Thomas: Hamlet (Cpte)
Bizet: Carmen (exc)
Cilea: Adriana Lecouvreur (Cpte)
Donizetti: Lucia di Lammermoor (exc)
Giordano: Andrea Chénier (Cpte)
Leoncavallo: Pagliacci (Cpte)
Massenet: Roi de Lahore (Cpte), Thaïs (Cpte)
Mozart: Così fan tutte (Cpte), Don Giovanni (exc)
Ponchielli: Gioconda (Cpte)
Puccini: Bohème (Cpte), Fanciulla del West (Cpte), Tabarro (Cpte), Tosca (Cpte)
R. Strauss: Salome (Cpte)
Rachmaninov: Monna Vanna (exc)
Rossini: Guillaume Tell (Cpte)
Verdi: Aida (Cpte), Attila (Cpte), Ballo in maschera (Cpte), Don Carlo (Cpte), Forza del destino (Cpte), Giovanna d'Arco (Cpte), Luisa Miller (Cpte), Macbeth (Cpte), Otello (Cpte), Rigoletto (exc), Traviata (Cpte), Trovatore (Cpte), Vespri Siciliani (Cpte)
(DECC) **430 724-2DM** Great Operatic Duets
(DECC) **433 064-2DWO** Your Hundred Best Opera Tunes Volume I
(DECC) **433 065-2DWO** Your Hundred Best Opera Tunes Volume II
(DECC) **433 221-2DWO** The World of Verdi
(DECC) **433 440-2DA** Golden Opera
(DECC) **433 822-2DH** Essential Opera
(DECC) **436 300-2DX** Opera Gala Sampler
(DECC) **436 317-2DA** Puccini—Famous Arias
(DECC) **436 464-2DM** Ten Top Baritones & Basses
(DECC) **443 380-2DM** Ten Top Baritones & Basses 2
(DECC) **443 928-2DM** Montserrat Caballé sings Opera Arias
(DECC) **444 555-2DF2** Essential Puccini

(DG) **072 428-1GH2(DG)** The Metropolitan Opera Gala
(EMI) **CDM5 65575-2** Montserrat Caballé
(EMI) **CDM7 63103-2** Placido Domingo sings Opera Arias
(EURO) **VD69256** Mozart—Opera Arias
(IMP) **PCD1109** Overtures and Arias from Opera
(RCA) **GD60866** The Placido Domingo Album
(RCA) **09026 61509-2** A Salute to American Music
(RCA) **09026 61580-2(8)** RCA/Met 100 Singers, 100 Years (pt 8)
(RCA) **09026 62595-2** Opera Duets
(RCA) **09026 62699-2** Opera's Greatest Duets

MILOIA, Rodica (sop)
(ELCT) **ELCD109** Timisoara Memorial

MILSTEIN, Nathan (vn)
(APR) **APR7016** The Auer Legacy, Vol.2
(EMI) **ZDMF7 64830-2** The Art of Nathan Milstein
(TELD) **4509-95998-2** Nathan Milstein - The Last Recital

MILVA (sngr)
Weill: Dreigroschenoper (Cpte)

MIMS, Marilyn (sop)
Wagner: Walküre (Cpte)
(DG) **437 825-2GH** Wagner—Der Ring des Nibelungen - Highlights
(DG) **445 354-2GX14** Wagner—Der Ring des Nibelungen

MINEO, Andrea (bar)
Donizetti: Lucrezia Borgia (Cpte)
Mussorgsky: Khovanshchina (Cpte)
Verdi: Rigoletto (Cpte)

MINERÍA SYMPHONY ORCHESTRA
(IMP) **PCD1057** Crazy for Gershwin
cond H. DE LA FUENTE
(IMP) **PCDS26** Music of the World—From the New World
(IMP) **PCD1109** Overtures and Arias from Opera

MINETTI, Hans-Peter (spkr)
Mozart: Entführung (Cpte)

MINETTO, Maria (contr)
Monteverdi: Incoronazione di Poppea (Cpte)
Puccini: Gianni Schicchi (Cpte)

MINEVA, Stefka (mez)
Mussorgsky: Boris Godunov (Cpte), Khovanshchina (Cpte)

MINGARDO, Sara (contr)
Handel: Giulio Cesare (Cpte)
Piccinni: Cecchina (Cpte)

MINGHINI-CATTANEO, Irene (mez)
Verdi: Aida (Cpte)
(EMI) **CHS7 64864-2(1)** La Scala Edition - Vol.2, 1915-46 (pt 1)
(NIMB) **NI7853** Lauri-Volpi sings Verdi
(PEAR) **GEMMCDS9926(1)** Covent Garden on Record—Vol.4 (pt 1)
(PREI) **89008** Irene Minghini-Cattaneo (1892-1944)

MINICH, Peter (ten)
Benatzky: Im weissen Rössl (Cpte)

MINKOWSKI, Marc (cond)
see Musiciens du Louvre
Ricercar Acad

MINNEAPOLIS SYMPHONY ORCHESTRA
cond A. DORATI
(MERC) **432 005-2MM** Orchestral Works
(MERC) **432 753-2MM** Prokofiev—Orchestral Works
(MERC) **434 305-2MM** Tchaikovsky—Orchestral Works
(MERC) **434 345-2MM** Rossini/Verdi—Overtures
(MERC) **434 348-2MM** Antal Dorati conducts Richard Strauss

MINNESOTA ORCHESTRA
cond ANON
(WORD) **FCD7409** World's Greatest Overtures
cond N. MARRINER
(TELA) **CD82005** Wagner—Orchestral Music from Operas
cond E. DE WAART
(VIRG) **CUV5 61194-2** Gershwin/Bernstein—Orchestral Works

MINSK PHILHARMONIC ORCHESTRA
cond S. FRONTALINI
(BONG) **GB2115-2** Ponchielli—Orchestral Works

MINTER, Drew (alto)
Handel: Agrippina (Cpte), Floridante (Cpte), Giulio Cesare (Cpte), Giustino (Cpte), Ottone (Cpte), Sosarme (Cpte)
(HARM) **HMC90 5183** Handel: Arias for Senesino
(HARM) **HMP390 804** Great Baroque Masters: Handel
(HARM) **HMU90 7035** Sweeter than Roses - Purcell Songs

MINTON, Yvonne (mez)
Bellini: Norma (Cpte)
Berg: Lulu (Cpte)
Bizet: Carmen (Cpte)
Debussy: Pelléas et Mélisande (Cpte)
Mozart: Clemenza di Tito (Cpte), Così fan tutte (Cpte), Nozze di Figaro (Cpte), Zauberflöte (exc)
R. Strauss: Elektra (Cpte), Rosenkavalier (Cpte)
Tippett: Knot Garden (Cpte)
Wagner: Parsifal (Cpte), Rheingold (Cpte), Tristan und Isolde (exc), Walküre (Cpte)

(EURO) **GD69003** Wagner—Der Ring des Nibelungen

MINTY, Shirley (mez)
G. Charpentier: Louise (Cpte)
Vaughan Williams: Hugh the Drover (Cpte)
(CBS) **CD79312** Puccini: Il Trittico

MINZHILKIEV, Bulat (bass)
Borodin: Prince Igor (Cpte)
Mussorgsky: Khovanshchina (Cpte)
Rimsky-Korsakov: Sadko (Cpte)

MIRA, Brigitte (sop)
Künneke: Vetter aus Dingsda (exc)
Schultze: Schwarzer Peter (Cpte)

MIRABAL, Linda (mez)
Vives: Doña Francisquita (Cpte)

MIRICIOIU, Nelly (sop)
Mercadante: Orazi e Curiazi (Cpte)
Puccini: Tosca (Cpte)
(ETCE) **KTC1041** Nelly Miricioiu—Recital
(ETCE) **XTC1041** Nelly Miricioiu at Wigmore Hall

MIRTSCH, Senta (mez)
R. Strauss: Elektra (Cpte)

MISCIANO, Alvinio (ten)
Gounod: Philémon et Baucis (Cpte)
Rossini: Barbiere di Siviglia (Cpte)

MISHCHEVSKI, Anatole (ten)
Kabalevsky: Colas Breugnon (Cpte)

MISHENKIN, Arkady (ten)
Rimsky-Korsakov: Tsar's Bride (Cpte)
Tchaikovsky: Maid of Orleans (Cpte)

MISSENHARDT, Günther (bar)
Mozart: Entführung (Cpte)
Verdi: Traviata (Cpte)

MISSONA, K. (cond)
see Polish RSO

MITCHELL, Billy J. (spkr)
Gershwin: Porgy and Bess (Cpte)

MITCHELL, Leona (sop)
Bizet: Carmen (Cpte)
Gershwin: Porgy and Bess (Cpte)
Puccini: Turandot (Cpte)
(BELA) **450 007-2** Puccini Favourites
(DECC) **433 865-2DWO** The World of Puccini
(DECC) **071 142-1DH (DECC)** Essential Opera

MITCHELL, Madeleine (sop)
Sullivan: Iolanthe (exc)

MITCHELL, Warren (spkr)
Gay: Beggar's Opera (Cpte)

(GEOFFREY) MITCHELL CHOIR
cond A. FRANCIS
Donizetti: Maria Padilla (Cpte), Ugo, Conte di Parigi (Cpte)
Offenbach: Christopher Columbus (Cpte), Robinson Crusoé (Cpte)
(OPRA) **ORC003** Donizetti—Gabriella di Vergy
cond J. JUDD
Meyerbeer: Dinorah (Cpte)
(OPRA) **ORC004** Donizetti—Ne m'oubliez pas; Arias
cond A. MELVILLE
Boughton: Immortal Hour (Cpte)
cond D. PARRY
Donizetti: Assedio di Calais (Cpte), Emilia di Liverpool (Cpte), Eremitaggio di Liverpool (Cpte)
Mayr: Medea (Cpte)
Mercadante: Orazi e Curiazi (Cpte)
Meyerbeer: Crociato in Egitto (Cpte)
(OPRA) **ORCH103** Italian Opera—1810-20
(OPRA) **ORCH104** A Hundred Years of Italian Opera: 1820-1830
(OPRA) **ORR201** 19th Century Heroines-Yvonne Kenny

MITCHINSON, John (ten)
Alwyn: Miss Julie (Cpte)
Martinů: Greek Passion (Cpte)
Purcell: Dido (Cpte)
Wagner: Tristan und Isolde (Cpte)
(KOCH) **34036-2** A Pageant of Opera

MITROPOULOS, Dimitri (cond)
see Florence Teatro Comunale Orch
MMF Orch
NY Met Op Orch
VPO

MITTEREGGER, Werner (spkr)
Benatzky: Im weissen Rössl (Cpte)

MIXOVÁ, Ivana (mez)
Dvořák: Jacobin (Cpte)
Janáček: Cunning Little Vixen (Cpte), Jenufa (Cpte), Káťa Kabanová (Cpte), Makropulos Affair (Cpte)
Martinů: Julietta (Cpte)
Smetana: Devil's Wall (Cpte)
(KOCH) **34036-2** A Pageant of Opera

MIXOVÁ, Ivana (sop)
Dvořák: Rusalka (Cpte)

MIZUGUSHI, Satoshi (bar)
Keiser: Croesus (Cpte)

MKRTCHIAN, Lina (contr)
Karetnikov: Till Eulenspiegel (Cpte)

MOBERG, Ruth (sop)
(BLUE) **ABCD028** Jussi Björling live at the Stockholm Opera

MOCHALOV, Alexei (bass)
Karetnikov: Till Eulenspiegel (Cpte)

MOCHIKI, Fumiko (mez)
Verdi: Traviata (Cpte)

MOCHIKI, Hiroshi (ten)
Verdi: Traviata (Cpte)

MODENA TEATRO COMUNALE ORCHESTRA
cond L. MAGIERA
(RCA) **09026 62541-2** Pavarotti - The Early Years, Vol.1
(RCA) **09026 68014-2** Pavarotti - The Early Years, Vol.2

MODENO TEATRO COMUNALE CHORUS
cond C. DESDERI
Rossini: Pietra del paragone (Cpte)

MODERN ENSEMBLE
(LARG) **Largo 5114** Weill—Berlin im licht
cond I. METZMACHER
Nono: Prometeo (Cpte)

MODESTI, Guiseppe (bass)
Cherubini: Medea (Cpte)
Donizetti: Linda di Chamounix (Cpte)
Giordano: Andrea Chénier (Cpte)
Puccini: Bohème (Cpte), Gianni Schicchi (Cpte)
Verdi: Aida (Cpte)

MÖDL, Martha (sop/mez)
Beethoven: Fidelio (Cpte)
R. Strauss: Arabella (Cpte)
Schultze: Schwarzer Peter (Cpte)
Wagner: Götterdämmerung (Cpte), Parsifal (Cpte), Tristan und Isolde (exc), Walküre (Cpte)
(EMI) **CZS7 67123-2** Wagner: Der Ring des Nibelungen
(PHIL) **446 057-2PB14** Wagner—The Ring Cycle - Bayreuth Festival 1967
(PREI) **90136** Martha Mödl sings

MODOS, Laszlo (bar)
Ligeti: Grand Macabre (Cpte)

MODUS NOVUS CHOIR
cond J. VAN IMMERSEEL
Mendelssohn: Hochzeit des Camacho (Cpte)

MOELLER, Jobst (bar)
Lehár: Land des Lächelns (Cpte)

MOFFO, Anna (sop)
Bizet: Carmen (Cpte)
Donizetti: Lucia di Lammermoor (Cpte)
Gluck: Orfeo ed Euridice (Cpte)
Humperdinck: Hänsel und Gretel (Cpte)
Mozart: Don Giovanni (Cpte), Nozze di Figaro (Cpte)
Puccini: Bohème (exc), Madama Butterfly (Cpte), Rondine (Cpte)
R. Strauss: Capriccio (Cpte)
Suppé: Schöne Galathee (exc)
Verdi: Falstaff (Cpte), Luisa Miller (Cpte), Rigoletto (exc)
(CFP) **CD-CFP4575** Verdi Arias
(EMIL) **CDZ7 67015-2** Mozart—Opera Arias
(EURO) **GD69113** Anna Moffo Recital
(RCA) **09026 61440-2** Opera's Greatest Moments
(RCA) **09026 61580-2(7)** RCA/Met 100 Singers, 100 Years (pt 7)
(RCA) **09026 61886-2** Operas Greatest Love Songs
(RCA) **09026 62689-2** The Voices of Living Stereo, Volume 1
(RCA) **74321 25817-2** Café Classics - Operatic
(VAI) **VAI69114** Anna Moffo in Opera and Song

MOGLUILEVSKY, Evgeny (pf)
(PAVA) **ADW7277** Prokofiev/Ravel/Schumann—Piano Works

MOGRELIA, Andrew (cond)
see Košice St PO

MOHR, Thomas (bar)
Busoni: Arlecchino (Cpte)
Marschner: Hans Heiling (Cpte)
Trojahn: Enrico (Cpte)
Weill: Mahagonny-Gesänge (Cpte), Sieben Todsünden (Cpte)

MOISAN, André (cl)
Vivier: Kopernikus (Cpte)

MOIZAN, Geneviève (sop)
Ganne: Saltimbanques (exc)
Massenet: Navarraise (Cpte)
(MONT) **TCE8760** Stravinsky: Stage Works

MOK, Warren (ten)
Mendelssohn: Hochzeit des Camacho (Cpte)

MOKRZYCKA (MOSCISCA), Maria (sop)
(NIMB) **NI7831** Mattia Battistini (1856-1928)
(PEAR) **GEMMCD9936** Mattia Battistini, Vol.1

MOLA, Cinzia de (contr)
Leoncavallo: Bohème (Cpte)
Wolf-Ferrari: Campiello (Cpte)

MOLAJOLI, Lorenzo (cond)
see La Scala Orch
Milan SO
orch

MOLDAVA SYMPHONY ORCHESTRA
cond S. FRONTALINI
(BONG) **GB2144-2** Mercandante—Overtures from the Operas

MOLDOVA PHILHARMONIC ORCHESTRA
cond C. MANDEAL
Bretan: Arald (Cpte), Golem (Cpte)

MOLDVAY, József (bass)
Giordano: Andrea Chénier (Cpte)
Handel: Floridante (Cpte)

MOLEDA, Krzysztof (ten)
Rossini: Signor Bruschino (Cpte)

MOLESE, Michele (ten)
(SONY) **SM22K46290(3)** Stravinsky—The Complete Edition (pt 3)

MOLINARI, Enrico (bar)
(PREI) **89013** Giannina Arangi-Lombardi (1890-1951)
(PREI) **89995** Famous Italian Baritones

MOLINARI-PRADELLI, Francesco (cond)
see London Sym Chor
MMF Orch
Naples San Carlo Op Orch
NY Met Op Orch
RCA Italiana Op Orch
ROHO
Rome Op Orch
Santa Cecilia Academy Orch
Trieste Teatro Verdi Orch
Turin RAI Orch
Turin SO
Vienna St Op Orch

MOLL, Kurt (bass)
Beethoven: Fidelio (Cpte)
Mozart: Don Giovanni (Cpte), Entführung (Cpte), Nozze di Figaro (Cpte), Schauspieldirektor (Cpte), Zauberflöte (Cpte)
Prokofiev: Fiery Angel (Cpte)
R. Strauss: Daphne (Cpte), Elektra (Cpte), Intermezzo (Cpte), Rosenkavalier (exc), Salome (Cpte)
Schmidt: Notre Dame (Cpte)
Shostakovich: Lady Macbeth of Mtsensk (Cpte)
Spohr: Jessonda (Cpte)
Verdi: Forza del destino (Cpte), Otello (Cpte), Rigoletto (Cpte)
Wagner: Feen (Cpte), Fliegende Holländer (exc), Lohengrin (Cpte), Meistersinger (Cpte), Parsifal (Cpte), Rheingold (Cpte), Siegfried (Cpte), Tannhäuser (Cpte), Tristan und Isolde (Cpte), Walküre (Cpte)
Weber: Freischütz (exc)
Wolf: Corregidor (Cpte)
(DG) **445 354-2GX14** Wagner—Der Ring des Nibelungen
(DG) **072 422-3GH7** Levine conducts Wagner's Ring
(EMI) **LDX9 91275-1(EMI)** Sawallisch conducts Wagner's Ring
(EURO) **GD69003** Wagner—Der Ring des Nibelungen
(ORFE) **C009821A** Famous Bass Arias

MOLL, Philip (pf)
(DECC) **417 289-2DH** Con amore

MOLLE, Giuseppina Dalle (mez)
Donizetti: Fausta (Cpte)

MØLLER, Annemarie (mez)
Mussorgsky: Boris Godunov (Cpte)

MØLLER, Niels (ten)
Nielsen: Saul and David (Cpte)
Wagner: Parsifal (Cpte)

MOLLET, Pierre (bar)
Gounod: Roméo et Juliette (Cpte)
Martin: Mystère de la Nativité
(CASC) **VEL2010** Memories of the Suisse Romande - Suzanne Danco
(DECC) **433 400-2DM2** Ravel & Debussy—Stage Works

MOLLIEN, Jean (bass)
Ganne: Hans (Cpte)
(MUSD) **20239-2** Delibes—Opéras-Comiques

MOLNÁR, András (ten)
Wagner: Meistersinger (Cpte)

MOLSBERGER, Friedrich (bass)
Busoni: Turandot (Cpte)
Mendelssohn: Hochzeit des Camacho (Cpte)
R. Strauss: Salome (Cpte)
Schreker: Gezeichneten (Cpte)

MOLTKAU, Hans (cond)
see Bavarian St Orch
Munich RO

MÔN, Elen (sop)
Vaughan Williams: Pilgrim's Progress (Cpte)

MONACHESI, Walter (bar)
Verdi: Simon Boccanegra (Cpte)

MONACO, Daniela del (contr)
Traetta: Buovo d'Antona (Cpte)

MONACO, Jerome lo (ten)
Verdi: Lombardi (Cpte)

MONACO, Mario Del (ten)
Berlioz: Troyens (exc)
Bizet: Carmen (Cpte)
Boito: Mefistofele (Cpte)
Catalani: Wally (Cpte)
Cilea: Adriana Lecouvreur (Cpte)
Giordano: Andrea Chénier (Cpte), Fedora (Cpte)

J. Strauss II: Fledermaus (Cpte)
Leoncavallo: Pagliacci (Cpte)
Mascagni: Cavalleria Rusticana (Cpte)
Ponchielli: Gioconda (Cpte)
Puccini: Manon Lescaut (Cpte), Tosca (Cpte), Turandot (Cpte)
Verdi: Aida (Cpte), Otello (Cpte), Rigoletto (Cpte)
Zandonai: Francesca da Rimini (exc)
(BELA) **450 006-2** Famous Opera Duets
(BELA) **450 007-2** Puccini Favourites
(BELA) **450 015-2** Cinema Classics
(BELA) **450 133-2** Verdi Favourites
(DECC) **411 665-2DM3** Puccini: Il trittico
(DECC) **433 067-2DWO** Your Hundred Best Opera Tunes IV
(DECC) **433 068-2DWO** Your Hundred Best Opera Tunes V
(DECC) **433 069-2DWO** Your Hundred Best Opera Tunes VI
(DECC) **433 442-2DA** Verdi—Famous Arias
(DECC) **433 443-2DA** Great Opera Choruses
(DECC) **436 314-2DA** Great Tenor Arias
(DECC) **436 315-2DA** Great Operatic Duets
(DECC) **436 463-2DM** Ten Top Tenors
(DECC) **440 406-2DM** Giulietta Simionato
(DECC) **440 407-2DM** Mario del Monaco
(DECC) **440 411-2DM** Anita Cerquetti
(DECC) **443 378-2DM** Ten Top Mezzos 2
(DECC) **443 379-2DM** Ten Top Tenors 2
(EMI) **CDC7 54016-2** Tenorissimo!
(EMI) **CHS7 69741-2(7)** Record of Singing, Vol.4—Italian School
(MEMO) **HR4400/1** Great Voices - Ettore Bastianini
(TEST) **SBT1039** Mario Del Monaco—The HMV Milan Recordings

MONADNOCK FESTIVAL CHORUS
cond J. BOLLE
V. Thomson: Lord Byron (Cpte)

MONADNOCK FESTIVAL ORCHESTRA
cond J. BOLLE
V. Thomson: Lord Byron (Cpte)

MONAR, Isabel (mez)
Vives: Bohemios (Cpte)

MONCK, Sam (treb)
Britten: Little Sweep (Cpte)

MONETA, Luciana (mez)
Giordano: Andrea Chénier (Cpte)
Verdi: Trovatore (Cpte)

MONGELLI, Andrea (bar)
Puccini: Fanciulla del West (Cpte)
(BONG) **GB1060-2** Virginia Zeani - Various opera arias

MONK, Allan (bar)
Giordano: Andrea Chénier (Cpte)
Verdi: Ballo in maschera (Cpte)

MONK, Meredith (voc)
M. Monk: Atlas (Cpte)

MONK, Meredith (voc/kybd)
(ECM) **437 439-2** Meredith Monk—Facing North and other works

MONMART, Berthe (sop)
G. Charpentier: Louise (Cpte)

MONOGAROVA, Tatiana (sop)
Knaifel: Canterville Ghost (exc)

MONOYIOS, Ann (sop)
Gluck: Iphigénie en Aulide (Cpte)
Hasse: Piramo e Tisbe (Cpte)
Mondonville: Titon et l'Aurore (Cpte)
Purcell: Dioclesian, Z627 (Cpte)
(CAPR) **10 459** Music from Charlottenburg Castle
(ERAT) **4509-99607-2** Gluck—Operas; Schubert—Symphonies Nos 8 & 9

MONREALE, Leonardo (bass)
Donizetti: Pazzi per progetto (Cpte)
Giordano: Fedora (Cpte)
Ponchielli: Gioconda (Cpte)
Puccini: Fanciulla del West (Cpte), Madama Butterfly (Cpte), Tosca (Cpte), Turandot (Cpte)
Verdi: Ballo in maschera (Cpte), Otello (Cpte), Rigoletto (exc)
(BUTT) **BMCD015** Pavarotti Collection - Duets and Scenes

MONTAGUD, Fermin (ten)
Puccini: Fanciulla del West (Cpte)

MONTAGUE, Diana (mez)
Bellini: Capuleti (Cpte), Norma (Cpte)
Donizetti: Lucia di Lammermoor (Cpte)
G. Lloyd: John Socman (exc)
Gluck: Iphigénie en Tauride (Cpte)
Janáček: Cunning Little Vixen (Cpte)
Meyerbeer: Crociato in Egitto (Cpte)
Monteverdi: Orfeo (Cpte)
Mozart: Clemenza di Tito (Cpte)
Romberg: Student Prince (exc)
Rossini: Comte Ory (Cpte)
(OPRA) **ORCH103** Italian Opera—1810-20
(OPRA) **ORCH104** A Hundred Years of Italian Opera: 1820-1830
(OPRA) **ORH102** A Hundred Years of Italian Opera
(OPRA) **ORR201** 19th Century Heroines-Yvonne Kenny

MONTAINE, Gary (bass)
Sullivan: Yeomen of the Guard (Cpte)

MONTALANT, Berthe Auguez de (sop)
(IRCC) **IRCC-CD800** Souvenirs from Meyerbeer Operas

MONTANO, Alexandra (mez)
S. Wallace: Kabbalah (Cpte)

MONTARSOLO, Paolo (bass)
Giordano: Andrea Chénier (Cpte)
Gounod: Philémon et Baucis (Cpte)
Mozart: Don Giovanni (Cpte), Nozze di Figaro (Cpte)
Puccini: Bohème (exc), Madama Butterfly (Cpte)
Rossini: Barbiere di Siviglia (Cpte), Cenerentola (Cpte), Inganno felice (Cpte), Italiana in Algeri (Cpte)
(EMI) **CMS7 64165-2** Puccini—Trittico

MONTE, Carlo del (ten)
Verdi: Traviata (Cpte)
(CFP) **CD-CFP4602** Favourite Opera
(EMI) **CDM5 65579-2** Victoria de los Angeles
(EMI) **CDM7 64359-2** Gala de España
(EMI) **CDM7 69596-2** The Movies go to the Opera
(EMI) **CMS7 64165-2** Puccini—Trittico

MONTE, George del (bar)
Puccini: Bohème (Cpte)

MONTE, Toti dal (sop)
(EMI) **CDH7 63200-2** Tito Schipa—Recital
(EMI) **CHS7 64864-2(1)** La Scala Edition - Vol.2, 1915-46 (pt 1)
(MEMO) **HR4220/1** Great Voices-Tito Schipa
(MMOI) **CDMOIR406** Mozart—Historical Recordings
(MMOI) **CDMOIR408** Great Sopranos
(MSCM) **MM30231** Don Pasquale & Tito Schipa Recital
(PEAR) **GEMMCDS9925(2)** Covent Garden on Record—Vol.3 (pt 2)
(PEAR) **GEMMCD9364** Beethoven—Concertos
(PREI) **89001** Toti dal Monte (1898-1975)
(RCA) **09026 61580-2(3)** RCA/Met 100 Singers, 100 Years (pt 3)
(SCHW) **314512** Vienna State Opera Live, Vol.1

MONTE CARLO NATIONAL OPERA ORCHESTRA
cond R. BONYNGE
(DECC) **433 066-2DWO** Your Hundred Best Opera Tunes III
(DECC) **433 440-2DA** Golden Opera
(DECC) **436 315-2DA** Great Operatic Duets
cond F. CLEVA
Catalani: Wally (Cpte)
(DECC) **430 481-2DX2** Renata Tebaldi sings Opera Arias
(DECC) **433 066-2DWO** Your Hundred Best Opera Tunes III
(DECC) **433 440-2DA** Golden Opera
(DECC) **433 822-2DH** Essential Opera
(DECC) **440 408-2DM** Renata Tebaldi
cond L. FRÉMAUX
(BELA) **450 139-2** An Invitation to the Dance
(DG) **447 364-2GDB2** Great Opera Overtures
cond L. GARDELLI
Giordano: Fedora (Cpte)
cond A. JORDAN
Debussy: Pelléas et Mélisande (Cpte)
cond N. RESCIGNO
Zandonai: Francesca da Rimini (exc)
cond A. ZEDDA
Bellini: Beatrice di Tenda (Cpte)

MONTE CARLO OPERA CHORUS
cond R. BONYNGE
Delibes: Lakmé (Cpte)
cond L. GARDELLI
Giordano: Fedora (Cpte)
cond A. JORDAN
Debussy: Pelléas et Mélisande (Cpte)

MONTE CARLO OPERA ORCHESTRA
cond A. DE ALMEIDA
(PHIL) **442 550-2PM2** Verdi—Complete Ballet Music &c
cond R. BONYNGE
Delibes: Lakmé (exc)
cond F. CLEVA
(DECC) **436 461-2DM** Ten Top Sopranos
cond J.E. GARDINER
(ERAT) **2292-45859-2** Massenet—Orchestral Works
cond A. JORDAN
Wagner: Parsifal (Cpte)

MONTE CARLO PHILHARMONIC ORCHESTRA
Wagner: Parsifal (Cpte)
(EMI) **CDC7 47544-2** French music for violin and orchestra
(EMI) **CDS7 49361-2** Offenbach: Operettas
cond C. DUTOIT
Fauré: Pénélope (Cpte)
cond L. FOSTER
(ERAT) **2292-45860-2** Famous Romances and Adagios
(ERAT) **4509-91715-2** The Ultimate Opera Collection 2
(ERAT) **4509-98501-2** Recital—Marilyn Horne
cond A. JORDAN
(ERAT) **4509-92866-2** Wagner—Famous Overtures
cond P. OLMI
(ERAT) **4509-97239-2** Virtuoso Arias
cond G. PRÊTRE
(EMI) **CDM7 64687-2** French Works inspired by Edgar Allan Poe

cond M. ROSENTHAL
(EMI) **CZS5 68113-2** Vive Offenbach!
cond C. SCIMONE
Rossini: Ermione (Cpte)
cond M. SOUSTROT
Auber: Fra Diavolo (Cpte)

MONTEIL, Denise (sop)
Bizet: Carmen (Cpte)

MONTESANTO, Luigi (bar)
(BONG) **GB1043-2** Italian Baritones of the Acoustic Era
(MEMO) **HR4408/9(2)** Singers in Genoa, Vol.1 (disc 2)
(PREI) **89995** Famous Italian Baritones
(SCHW) **314512** Vienna State Opera Live, Vol.1

MONTEUX, Pierre (cond)
see FNO
Paris Opéra-Comique Orch
Rome Op Orch
San Francisco SO

MONTEVERDI CHOIR
cond J.E. GARDINER
Gluck: Iphigénie en Aulide (Cpte), Iphigénie en Tauride (Cpte), Orfeo ed Euridice (Cpte), Orphée (Cpte)
Monteverdi: Orfeo (Cpte)
Mozart: Clemenza di Tito (Cpte), Così fan tutte (Cpte), Don Giovanni (Cpte), Entführung (Cpte), Idomeneo (Cpte), Nozze di Figaro (Cpte), Thamos, K345 (Cpte)
Purcell: Dido (Cpte), Dioclesian, Z627 (exc), Fairy Queen, Z629 (Cpte), Indian Queen, Z630 (Cpte), King Arthur, Z628 (exc), Tempest, Z631 (Cpte)
(DG) **439 474-2GCL** Purcell—Opera & Choral Works
(ERAT) **2292-45984-2** Monteverdi—Ballet Music
(ERAT) **4509-96371-2** Gardiner—The Purcell Collection
(ERAT) **4509-99607-2** Gluck—Operas; Schubert—Symphonies Nos 8 & 9
(ERAT) **4509-99713-2** Baroque Works

MONTEVERDI ORCHESTRA
cond J.E. GARDINER
Purcell: Tempest, Z631 (Cpte)

MONTEYROL, Laurence (sop)
(AUVI) **V4682** L'accompagnatrice - Original Fim Score

MONTFORT, Jeanne (mez)
Gounod: Faust (Cpte)

MONTGOMERY, Brian (bar)
Puccini: Fanciulla del West (Cpte)

MONTHY, Georg (bass)
Verdi: Otello (Cpte)
Wagner: Meistersinger (exc), Tristan und Isolde (exc)
(PREI) **90237** R Strauss—Daphne
(SCHW) **314542** Vienna State Opera Live, Vol.4
(SCHW) **314552** Vienna State Opera Live, Vol.5
(SCHW) **314572** Vienna State Opera Live, Vol.7
(SCHW) **314602** Vienna State Opera Live, Vol.10
(SCHW) **314632** Vienna State Opera Live, Vol.13
(SCHW) **314652** Vienna State Opera Live, Vol.15
(SCHW) **314692** Vienna State Opera Live, Vol.19
(SCHW) **314702** Vienna State Opera Live, Vol.20

MONTI, Hilda (sop)
(PREI) **89105** Apollo Granforte (1886-1975) - II

MONTI, Nicola (ten)
Bellini: Sonnambula (Cpte)
Leoncavallo: Pagliacci (Cpte)
(DECC) **433 706-2DMO3** Bellini—Beatrice di Tenda; Operatic Arias
(EMI) **CDM7 63109-2** Tito Gobbi - Opera Aria Recital

MONTICONE, Rita (mez)
Verdi: Falstaff (Cpte)

MONTMOLLIN, Marie-Luise de (mez)
(DECC) **433 400-2DM2** Ravel & Debussy—Stage Works

MONTPELLIER LANGUEDOC-ROUSSILLON PHILHARMONIC ORCHESTRA
cond C. DIEDERICH
Berlioz: Benvenuto Cellini (exc)
(ERAT) **4509-98502-2** Recital-Françoise Pollet

MONTPELLIER OPERA CHORUS
cond M. ARENA
Verdi: Luisa Miller (Cpte)

MONTREAL I MUSICI
cond Y. TUROVSKY
(CHAN) **CHAN9149** Rimsky-Korsakov/Glinka—Vocal Works
(CHAN) **CHAN9304** Lullabies

MONTREAL SYMPHONY ORCHESTRA
cond C. DUTOIT
Berlioz: Troyens (Cpte)
Bizet: Carmen Suites
Debussy: Pelléas et Mélisande (Cpte)
Falla: Retablo de maese Pedro (Cpte)
Gounod: Faust (exc)
(DECC) **414 408-2DH** Suppé Overtures
(DECC) **421 527-2DH** Fête à la française
(DECC) **436 475-2DM** Dance of the Hours: ballet music from the opera
(DECC) **440 331-2DH** Prokofiev—Orchestral Works
(DECC) **440 333-2DH** Ravel—Vocal Works
(DECC) **440 947-2DH** Essential Opera II

(DECC) **444 552-2DF2** Essential Saint-Saëns
(DECC) **440 331-5DH** Prokofiev—Orchestral Works

MONTREAL SYMPHONY ORCHESTRA CHORUS
Berlioz: Troyens (Cpte)
Debussy: Pelléas et Mélisande (Cpte)

MOOR, Chris de (bass)
Chabrier: Roi malgré lui (Cpte)

MOOR, Frank de (ten)
Puccini: Bohème (Cpte)

MOORE, Anthony Michaels (ten)
Spontini: Vestale (Cpte)

MOORE, Darron (bar)
Vaughan Williams: Pilgrim's Progress (Cpte)

MOORE, Gerald (pf)
(APR) **APR7016** The Auer Legacy, Vol.2
(EMI) **CDH7 61003-2** Kathleen Ferrier sings Opera and Songs
(EMI) **CDM7 63654-2** Schwarzkopf Encores
(EMI) **CHS7 69741-2(4)** Record of Singing, Vol.4—German School
(EMI) **CMS5 65061-2(2)** The Fabulous Victoria de los Angeles (pt 2)
(EMI) **CZS5 68485-2** Les Introuvables de János Starker
(PEAR) **GEMMCD9443** Feuermann—The Columbia Records, Vol.2
(PEAR) **GEMMCD9939** Josef Hassid & Ida Haendel - 1940-42 Recordings
(TEST) **SBT1010** Ginette Neveu & Josef Hassid

MOORE, Grace (sop)
(ARHI) **ADCD109** Mengelberg Edition - Volume 3
(PEAR) **GEMMCDS9926(2)** Covent Garden on Record—Vol.4 (pt 2)
(PEAR) **GEMMCD9130** Great Sopranos, Vol.2
(RCA) **09026 61580-2(4)** RCA/Met 100 Singers, 100 Years (pt 4)

MOORE, Susan (sop)
Prokofiev: Love for 3 Oranges (Cpte)

MOPIN, Anne (sop)
Campra: Idoménée (Cpte)

MORA, Barry (bar)
Delius: Village Romeo and Juliet (Cpte)
Janáček: Fate (Cpte)

MORA, Fernando de la (ten)
Donizetti: Lucia di Lammermoor (Cpte)
(TELA) **CD80411** The Artistry of Fernando de la Mora

MORALÈS, Maria (sop)
(PHIL) **438 953-2PM2** Alarie/Simoneau - Arias & Duets

MORALT, Rudolf (cond)
see Vienna SO
Vienna St Op Orch
VPO

MORAN, John (sngr)
J. Moran: Manson Family (Cpte)

MORANDI, Pier Giorgio (cond)
see Hungarian St Op Orch
Rome Op Orch

MORDKOVITCH, Lydia (vn)
(CHAN) **CHAN8500** Russian Music for Violin and Piano

MOREHOUSE-SPELMAN CHORUS
cond ROBERT SHAW
(TELA) **CD80109** Berlioz: Requiem, etc
(TELA) **ECHOCD2** Absolute Heaven

MOREL, Jean-Paul (cond)
see RCA Orch
RCA SO
RCA Victor Orch

MORELAND, Johanne (sop)
Verdi: Traviata (Cpte)

MORELLE, Maureen (mez)
Menotti: Boy who grew too fast (Cpte)

MORELLI, Carlo (bar)
Ponchielli: Gioconda (Cpte)

MORELLI, Giuseppe (cond)
see Rome Op Orch

MORENO, Gabriel (bar)
Falla: Vida breve (Cpte)

MORENO, Myrna (mez)
(OPRA) **ORCH103** Italian Opera—1810-20
(OPRA) **ORH102** A Hundred Years of Italian Opera

MORENO TORROBA, Federico (cond)
see Madrid Concerts Orch
Spanish Lyric Orch

MORENO-BUENDIA, Manuel (cond)
see Madrid SO

MORESE, Giovanni (bass)
Puccini: Tosca (Cpte)

MOREY, Cynthia (sop)
Sullivan: Iolanthe (exc)

MORGAN, Arwel Huw (bass)
A. Thomas: Hamlet (Cpte)

MORGAN, Bengt-Ola (ten)
Mozart: Entführung (Cpte)

MORGAN, Gaynor (sop)
(ASV) **CDDCA758** Falla, Milhaud & Stravinsky—Operas

MORGAN, Margaret (sop)
Wagner: Parsifal (Cpte)

MORGAN, Morris (bar)
Suder: Kleider machen Leute (Cpte)

MORGAN, Tim (bar)
Sullivan: Gondoliers (Cpte)

MORI, Orazio (bass)
Puccini: Fanciulla del West (Cpte), Tosca (exc), Turandot (Cpte)
Verdi: Otello (Cpte), Traviata (Cpte)
(DECC) **436 261-2DHO3** Puccini—Il Trittico

MORIGI, Gabriella (sop)
Piccinni: Cecchina (Cpte)

MÖRIKE, Eduard (cond)
see Berlin St Op Orch
Berlin Staatskapelle

MORINO, Giuseppe (ten)
Bizet: Pêcheurs de Perles (Cpte)
Donizetti: Favorita (Cpte), Gianni di Parigi (Cpte), Lucia di Lammermoor (Cpte), Maria di Rohan (Cpte)
Mercadante: Giuramento (Cpte)
Piccinni: Cecchina (Cpte)
(NUOV) **6851** Giuseppe Morino—King of Bel Canto
(NUOV) **6905** Donizetti—Great Love Duets

MORISON, Elsie (sop)
Gay: Beggar's Opera (Cpte)
Purcell: King Arthur, Z628 (Cpte)
Sullivan: Gondoliers (Cpte), HMS Pinafore (Cpte), Iolanthe (Cpte), Mikado (Cpte), Patience (Cpte), Trial by Jury (Cpte), Yeomen of the Guard (Cpte)
(CFP) **CD-CFP4238** Gilbert and Sullivan
(CFP) **CD-CFP4609** Favourite Gilbert & Sullivan
(EMI) **CMS7 64409-2** Sullivan—Pirates of Penzance & Orch. Works
(EMI) **CMS7 64412-2** Gilbert & Sullivan—Ruddigore/Shakespeare Music

MORLING, Carina (mez)
Börtz: Bacchae (Cpte)

MORLOC, Renée (contr)
(SCHW) **312682** Opera Gala with Young Artists - Volume II

MORMON TABERNACLE CHOIR
cond E. ORMANDY
(SONY) **SBK39438** Wagner—Greatest Hits
cond J. RUDEL
(LOND) **443 381-2LM** Hallelujah! - Great Choral Classics
cond J. SILVERSTEIN
(DECC) **436 284-2DH** A Song of Thanksgiving
(LOND) **443 381-2LM** Hallelujah! - Great Choral Classics

MOROZOV, Alexandr (bass)
Mussorgsky: Boris Godunov (Cpte)
Prokofiev: War and Peace (Cpte)

MOROZOV, Boris (bass)
Rimsky-Korsakov: Tsar's Bride (Cpte)

MOROZOV, Igor (bar)
Bellini: Beatrice di Tenda (Cpte)
(NAXO) **8 553030** Opera Duets

MORPHY, Derek (bar)
(CBC) **SMCD5139** A Gilbert & Sullivan Gala

MORPURGO, Nelly (sop)
Prokofiev: Love for 3 Oranges (Cpte)
R. Strauss: Rosenkavalier (Cpte)

MORRESI, Giuseppe (bass)
Bellini: Sonnambula (Cpte)
Giordano: Andrea Chénier (Cpte)
Massenet: Manon (Cpte)
Puccini: Fanciulla del West (Cpte), Madama Butterfly (Cpte), Manon Lescaut (Cpte), Turandot (Cpte)
Verdi: Macbeth (Cpte), Rigoletto (Cpte), Traviata (Cpte), Trovatore (Cpte)
(CBS) **CD37228** Pavarotti sings Verdi
(RCA) **09026 62541-2** Pavarotti - The Early Years, Vol.1

MORRIS, Andrew (bar)
Vaughan Williams: Pilgrim's Progress (Cpte)

MORRIS, Ivor (ten)
Offenbach: Orphée aux enfers (exc)

MORRIS, James (bass)
A. Thomas: Hamlet (Cpte)
Donizetti: Maria Stuarda (Cpte)
Gay: Beggar's Opera (Cpte)
Massenet: Roi de Lahore (Cpte)
Offenbach: Contes d'Hoffmann (Cpte)
R. Strauss: Salome (Cpte)
Verdi: Aida (exc), Macbeth (Cpte), Trovatore (Cpte), Vespri Siciliani (Cpte)
Wagner: Parsifal (exc), Rheingold (Cpte), Siegfried (Cpte), Walküre (Cpte)
(DG) **437 825-2GH** Wagner—Der Ring des Nibelungen - Highlights
(DG) **445 354-2GX14** Wagner—Der Ring des Nibelungen
(DG) **072 422-3GH7** Levine conducts Wagner's Ring
(ORFE) **C394301B** Great Mozart Singers Series, Vol. 3

MORRIS, Joan (mez)
Offenbach: Contes d'Hoffmann (exc)

MORRIS, Richard (bar)
Maxwell Davies: Martyrdom of St Magnus (Cpte)

MORRIS, Wyn (cond)
see LSO

MORRISON, Peter (bar)
(CHAN) **CHAN8362** Treasures of Operetta
(CHAN) **CHAN8561** Treasures of Operetta, Vol. 2
(CHAN) **CHAN8759** Treasures of Operetta III

MORRISON, Ray (bar)
Verdi: Trovatore (Cpte)

MORSKOI, Gavriil (ten)
(ARLE) **ARL23/5** Rimsky-Korsakov—Sadko
(PEAR) **GEMMCDS9001/3(1)** Singers of Imperial Russia, Vol.2 (pt 1)

MORTENSEN, Gert (perc)
Nørgård: Siddhartha (Cpte)

MORTIMER, Harry (cond)
see Yorkshire Imperial Band

MORYN, Gilbert (sngr)
Lecocq: Jour et la Nuit (Cpte)
Messager: Monsieur Beaucaire (Cpte)

MOSCA, Vitalba (mez)
Verdi: Rigoletto (Cpte)

MOSCONA, Nicola (bass)
Beethoven: Fidelio (Cpte)
Mussorgsky: Boris Godunov (exc)
Ponchielli: Gioconda (Cpte)
Puccini: Bohème (Cpte)
Verdi: Ballo in maschera (Cpte), Otello (Cpte), Trovatore (Cpte)
(MYTO) **2MCD90317** Verdi—Un Ballo in maschera
(RCA) **GD60276** Toscanini conducts Boito & Verdi

MOSCOW ALL-UNION RADIO CHOIR
(EMI) **CHS7 69741-2(6)** Record of Singing, Vol.4—Russian & Slavonic Schools

MOSCOW ALL-UNION RADIO SYMPHONY ORCHESTRA
cond V. SMIRNOV
(EMI) **CHS7 69741-2(6)** Record of Singing, Vol.4—Russian & Slavonic Schools

MOSCOW CHAMBER ORCHESTRA
cond R. BARSHAI
(PREI) **89066** Zara Dolukhanova

MOSCOW CONTEMPORARY MUSIC ENSEMBLE
cond A. VINOGRADOV
(CDM) **LDC288 060** Contemporary Listening—Kasparov

MOSCOW FORUM THEATRE ORCHESTRA
cond M. YUROVSKY
Knaifel: Canterville Ghost (exc)

MOSCOW IMPERIAL OPERA CHORUS
(PEAR) **GEMMCDS9001/3(2)** Singers of Imperial Russia, Vol.2 (pt 2)

MOSCOW IMPERIAL OPERA ORCHESTRA
cond M.I. SEMENOV
(PREI) **89030** Feodor Chaliapin (1873-1938)

MOSCOW 'MALY' SYMPHONY ORCHESTRA
cond V. PONKIN
(MEZH) **MK417047** Erik Kurmangaliev - Recital

MOSCOW PHILHARMONIC ORCHESTRA
cond D. KITAIENKO
(TELD) **9031-72674-3** The Winners' Gala Concert, International Tchaikovsky Comp. 1990
cond L. LEIGHTON SMITH
(SHEF) **CD25** The Moscow Sessions - I
cond G. STOLAROV
(RUSS) **RDCD15023** Zara Dolukhanova sings

MOSCOW RADIO SYMPHONY ORCHESTRA
Tchaikovsky: Eugene Onegin (exc)
cond V. FEDOSEYEV
(CANY) **EC3687-2** Prokofiev—Orchestral Suites
(NOVA) **150 079-2** Borodin—Orchestral Works

MOSCOW STANISLAVSKY TH CHORUS
cond G. ZHEMCHUZHIN
Kabalevsky: Colas Breugnon (Cpte)

MOSCOW STANISLAVSKY TH ORCHESTRA
cond G. ZHEMCHUZHIN
Kabalevsky: Colas Breugnon (Cpte)

MOSCOW STATE SYMPHONY ORCHESTRA
cond I. GOLOVSHIN
Rubinstein: Feramors

MOSCOW VIRTUOSI
cond V. SPIVAKOV
(RCA) **09026 68185-2** Encore!

MOSCUCCI, Orietta (sop)
Boito: Mefistofele (Cpte)
Verdi: Don Carlo (Cpte)

MOSELEY-MORGAN, Rebecca (sop)
Janáček: Fate (Cpte)

MOSER, Edda (sop)
Lehár: Giuditta (Cpte)
Mozart: Don Giovanni (Cpte), Idomeneo (Cpte), Zauberflöte (Cpte)
Orff: Prometheus (Cpte)
Wagner: Götterdämmerung (Cpte), Rheingold (Cpte), Walküre (exc)

(ACAN) **44 2085-2** Carl Orff Collection
(DG) **429 168-2GR** Wagner: Excerpts from Der Ring
(DG) **435 211-2GX15** Wagner—Der Ring des Nibelungen
(EMI) **CMS7 64309-2** Kálmán—Best-loved Melodies

MOSER, Thomas (ten)
Cherubini: Lodoïska (Cpte)
Gluck: Cinesi (Cpte)
Mozart: Don Giovanni (Cpte), Finta Giardiniera (Cpte), Finta semplice (Cpte), Sogno di Scipione (Cpte), Zaïde (Cpte), Zauberflöte (Cpte)
R. Strauss: Frau ohne Schatten (Cpte)
Schreker: Ferne Klang (Cpte)
Spohr: Jessonda (Cpte)
Stravinsky: Oedipus rex (Cpte)
Verdi: Aida (Cpte), Stiffelio (Cpte)
Wagner: Fliegende Holländer (Cpte), Tristan und Isolde (Cpte)

MOSES, Geoffrey (bass)
Martinů: Greek Passion (Cpte)
R. Strauss: Arabella (Cpte)
Verdi: Rigoletto (Cpte)
Wagner: Tristan und Isolde (Cpte)

MOSLEY, George (bar)
M. Berkeley: Baa Baa Black Sheep (Cpte)

MOSLEY, George (bass)
Purcell: Dido (Cpte)

MOST, Ingeborg (contr)
Lortzing: Undine (Cpte)
Weill: Kuhhandel (exc)

MOSTLY MOZART ORCHESTRA
cond G. SCHWARZ
(DELO) **DE3026** A. Auger - Bach and Handel arias

MOULL, Geoffrey (cond)
see Bielefeld PO

MOXON, Alice (sop)
Sullivan: Sorcerer (Cpte)

MOYLE, Julian (bar)
Kálmán: Gräfin Mariza (exc)
Lehár: Lustige Witwe (exc)
Sullivan: Iolanthe (exc)

MOZART WIND ENSEMBLE
Mozart: Don Giovanni (exc)

MRAVINSKY, Evgeny (cond)
see Leningrad PO
USSR SO

MRÁZ, Ladislav (bar)
Smetana: Bartered Bride (Cpte), Devil's Wall (Cpte)

MRÁZOVÁ, Marie (contr)
Janáček: Cunning Little Vixen (Cpte), Jenufa (Cpte)
Martinů: Miracles of Mary (Cpte)
Smetana: Bartered Bride (Cpte)

MRÓZ, Leonard Andrzej (bass)
Mussorgsky: Boris Godunov (Cpte)
Schoenberg: Moses und Aron (Cpte)
Shostakovich: Lady Macbeth of Mtsensk (Cpte)
Szymanowski: King Roger (Cpte)

MUCK, Karl (cond)
see Bayreuth Fest Orch
Berlin St Op Orch

MUDIE, Michael (cond)
see orch
Philh
ROHO

MUELLER, Hartje (bass)
Verdi: Ernani (Cpte)

MUFF, Alfred (bass)
Einem: Dantons Tod (Cpte)
R. Strauss: Frau ohne Schatten (exc)
Schreker: Gezeichneten (Cpte)
Wagner: Fliegende Holländer (Cpte)
(EMI) **CDC5 55350-2** Cheryl Studer - A Portrait

MUGNAI, Umberto (cond)
see Mexico Palacio Orch

MÜHLBERGER, Erna (sop)
R. Strauss: Rosenkavalier (Cpte)

MÜHLE, Anne-Marie (sop)
Börtz: Bacchae (Cpte)
Monteverdi: Ritorno d'Ulisse in Patria (Cpte)
Mozart: Thamos, K345 (Cpte)

MUKK, József (ten)
Mascagni: Lodoletta (Cpte)

MULHOLLAND, Declan (sngr)
Gay: Beggar's Opera (Cpte)

MÜLLER, Anneliese (mez)
J. Strauss II: Fledermaus (Cpte)

MÜLLER, Bruno (bass)
(MYTO) **2MCD943103** Lortzing—Zar und Zimmermann

MÜLLER, Charlotte (mez)
(PREI) **89035** Erna Berger (1900-1990) - I

MÜLLER, Hanns Udo (cond)
see Berlin City Op Orch
Berlin St Op Orch
Prussian St Orch

MÜLLER, Johannes (cond)
see Berlin RO
Berlin RSO

MÜLLER, Maria (sop)
Wagner: Fliegende Holländer (exc), Lohengrin (Cpte), Tannhäuser (Cpte), Walküre (exc)
(EMI) **CMS7 64008-2(1)** Wagner Singing on Record (pt 1)
(MSCM) **MM30283** Great Wagnerian Singers, Vol.1
(MSCM) **MM30285** Great Wagnerian Singers, Vol.2
(MYTO) **3MCD93381** Wagner—Die Walküre, etc
(PREI) **90232** Wagner—Der Fliegende Holländer
(SCHW) **314502** Vienna State Opera—Live Recordings (sampler)
(SCHW) **314702** Vienna State Opera Live, Vol.20
(TELD) **9031-76442-2** Wagner—Excerpts from the 1936 Bayreuth Festival

MÜLLER, Rufus (ten)
Mozart: Zauberflöte (Cpte)

MÜLLER, Vladimir (mute)
Britten: Turn of the Screw (Cpte)

MÜLLER-BRUHL, Helmut (cond)
see Capella Clementina

MÜLLER-HEUSER, Franz (bar)
Schultze: Schwarzer Peter (Cpte)

MÜLLER-KRAY, Hans (cond)
see Bavarian St Op Orch
Bavarian St Orch
Berne St Orch
Stuttgart RSO

MÜLLER-MOLINARI, Helga (contr)
Cesti: Orontea (Cpte)
Rossini: Pietra del paragone (Cpte)

MÜLLER-MOLINARI, Helga (mez)
Handel: Partenope (Cpte)
R. Strauss: Ariadne auf Naxos (Cpte), Rosenkavalier (Cpte)

MULLIGAN, Mark (ten)
Rorem: Miss Julie (Cpte)

MUNCH, Charles (cond)
see Boston SO
FNO

MÜNCHINGER, Karl (cond)
see Stuttgart CO

MUND, Georg (bar)
Weill: Mahagonny (Cpte)

MUND, Uwe (cond)
see Bamberg SO

MUNDAY, Hugo (bar)
S. Wallace: Kabbalah (Cpte)

MUNDT, Richard (bass)
Verdi: Ballo in maschera (Cpte)

MUNICH BACH ORCHESTRA
cond K. RICHTER
(DG) **447 364-2GDB2** Great Opera Overtures

MUNICH BRASS
(ORFE) **C247911A** Works for Brass Ensemble

MUNICH CHAMBER ORCHESTRA
cond H. STADLMAIR
(ORFE) **C131851A** Virtuoso cello arrangements

MUNICH CHILDREN'S CHOIR
cond W. MATTES
Benatzky: Im weissen Rössl (Cpte)

MUNICH CONCERT CHOIR
cond H. FRICKE
K. A. Hartmann: Simplicius Simplicissimus (Cpte)

MUNICH CONCERT CHORUS
cond W. BOSKOVSKY
Lehár: Giuditta (Cpte)

MUNICH PHILHARMONIC ORCHESTRA
cond F. LEITNER
Handel: Giulio Cesare (Cpte)
(DG) **435 145-2GX5(1)** Fritz Wunderlich—Opera Arias, Lieder, etc (part 1)
cond A. ROTHER
(FINL) **4509-95606-2** Kim Borg - Songs and Arias

MUNICH PRO ARTE ORCHESTRA
cond K. REDEL
(FORL) **FF051** Les Immortels

MUNICH RADIO CHORUS
cond R. ABBADO
(RCA) **74321 24209-2** Italian Opera Choruses

MUNICH RADIO ORCHESTRA
cond R. ABBADO
Donizetti: Don Pasquale (Cpte)
Puccini: Turandot (Cpte)
(RCA) **09026 62504-2** Great Tenor Arias - Ben Heppner
(RCA) **09026 62550-2** Ten Tenors in Love
(RCA) **09026 62674-2** Fortissimo!
(RCA) **74321 24209-2** Italian Opera Choruses
cond W. BOSKOVSKY
Lehár: Giuditta (Cpte)
cond J. DELACÔTE
(EMI) **CZS7 67440-2** The Best of Rossini
cond P. DOMINGO
J. Strauss II: Fledermaus (Cpte)
(EMI) **CDEMTVD59** Classic Experience 3
cond K. EICHHORN
Humperdinck: Hänsel und Gretel (Cpte)
Orff: Kluge (Cpte), Mond (Cpte)
Suppé: Schöne Galathee (exc)
(CAPR) **10 109** Josef Protschka sings Mozart arias
(CAPR) **10 810** Mozart—Opera Highlights
(DG) **431 110-2GB** Great Voices - Fritz Wunderlich
(DG) **435 145-2GX5(1)** Fritz Wunderlich—Opera Arias, Lieder, etc (part 1)
(EURO) **GD69113** Anna Moffo Recital
(ORFE) **C009821A** Famous Bass Arias
(RCA) **74321 24790-2** Carl Orff 100 Years Edition
cond G. FERRO
(EMI) **CDC5 55350-2** Cheryl Studer - A Portrait
cond H. FRICKE
(ACAN) **43 266** Bernd Weikl—Operatic Recital
cond L. GARDELLI
Bizet: Djamileh (Cpte)
Gluck: Cinesi (Cpte)
Leoncavallo: Pagliacci (Cpte)
Mascagni: Cavalleria Rusticana (Cpte)
Verdi: Alzira (Cpte), Oberto (Cpte), Rigoletto (Cpte)
(ORFE) **C101841A** Famous Operatic Arias
(ORFE) **C119841A** Lucia Aliberti: Famous Opera Arias
cond L. HAGER
Gluck: Rencontre imprévue (Cpte)
Haydn: Anima del filosofo (Cpte)
cond M. JANOWSKI
Korngold: Violanta (Cpte)
(ACAN) **43 266** Bernd Weikl—Operatic Recital
cond E. KOHN
(EMI) **CDC5 55017-2** Domingo Opera Classics
(EMI) **CDC7 54329-2** Domingo sings Mozart Arias
cond J. KOUT
(RCA) **09026 61214-2** German Opera Arias
cond G. KUHN
(EMI) **CZS7 67440-2** The Best of Rossini
(EMIN) **CD-EMX2234** French and Italian Operatic Arias
(EMIN) **CD-EMX9519** Great Sopranos of Our Time
cond E. LEINSDORF
Korngold: Tote Stadt (Cpte)
cond H. LEWIS
(RCA) **74321 25817-2** Café Classics - Operatic
cond F. LUISI
Bellini: Puritani (Cpte)
(EMI) **CDC5 55233-2** German Opera Arias
cond W. MATTES
Benatzky: Im weissen Rössl (Cpte)
cond H. MOLTKAU
(DG) **431 110-2GB** Great Voices - Fritz Wunderlich
(DG) **435 145-2GX5(1)** Fritz Wunderlich—Opera Arias, Lieder, etc (part 1)
cond G. PATANÈ
Donizetti: Maria Stuarda (Cpte)
Puccini: Gianni Schicchi (Cpte)
(EURO) **GD69043** Puccini: Il Trittico
(ORFE) **C179891A** Marjana Lipovšek sings Famous Opera Arias
(RCA) **74321 25817-2** Café Classics - Operatic
(SONY) **MDK47176** Favourite Arias by the World's Favourite Tenors
(SONY) **SK48094** Favourite Puccini Arias
cond K. REDEL
(PIER) **PV786104** Great French Overtures
cond W. SCHMIDT-BOELCKE
(EURO) **GD69018** Fritz Wunderlich—Recital
cond L. SLATKIN
(EMI) **CDC7 47019-2** Mozart—Opera Arias
cond S. SOLTESZ
Gazzaniga: Don Giovanni (Cpte)
(CFP) **CD-CFP4606** Favourite Movie Classics
(EMI) **CDC7 49319-2** Lucia Popp sings Slavonic Opera Arias
cond P. SOMMER
(ORFE) **C106841A** Famous Opera Arias
cond H. STEIN
(DG) **431 110-2GB** Great Voices - Fritz Wunderlich
(DG) **435 145-2GX5(1)** Fritz Wunderlich—Opera Arias, Lieder, etc (part 1)
cond P. STEINBERG
Catalani: Wally (Cpte)
cond H. WALLBERG
Donizetti: Elisir d'amore (Cpte)
Egk: Peer Gynt (Cpte)
Flotow: Martha (Cpte)
Humperdinck: Königskinder (Cpte)
Leoncavallo: Bohème (Cpte)
Millöcker: Gasparone (Cpte)
Mozart: Entführung (Cpte)
(ACAN) **43 266** Bernd Weikl—Operatic Recital
(ACAN) **43 327** Bernd Weikl—Operatic Arias
(EMI) **CMS5 65621-2** Fischer-Dieskau - The Opera Singer
cond R. WEIKERT
(RCA) **09026 62550-2** Ten Tenors in Love

MUNICH RADIO SYMPHONY ORCHESTRA
cond R. ABBADO
(RCA) **09026 61440-2** Opera's Greatest Moments
(RCA) **09026 61886-2** Operas Greatest Love Songs
cond K. EICHHORN
Humperdinck: Hänsel und Gretel (Cpte)
Orff: Orpheus (Cpte), Tanz der Spröden (Cpte)
(ACAN) **44 2085-2** Carl Orff Collection
cond J. FIORE
(PHIL) **434 102-2PH** The Heroic Bel Canto Tenor
cond M. HONECK
(CAPR) **10 481** R.Strauss—Opera Concert
cond J. KROMBHOLC
Smetana: Bartered Bride (Cpte)
cond G. KUHN
Spontini: Vestale (Cpte)
(ORFE) **C261921A** Maria Dragoni sings Famous Opera Arias

cond G. PATANÈ
(RCA) **09026 61440-2** Opera's Greatest Moments
cond L. SLATKIN
Puccini: Fanciulla del West (Cpte)
cond P. STEINBERG
Massenet: Chérubin (Cpte)
(RCA) **09026 61440-2** Opera's Greatest Moments
(RCA) **09026 61886-2** Operas Greatest Love Songs
cond H. WALLBERG
Donizetti: Don Pasquale (Cpte)
cond J-P. WEIGLE
(PHIL) **422 523-2PME8(2)** The Complete Mozart Edition Vol 23 (pt 2)
cond R. WEIKERT
(RCA) **09026 61163-2** The Romantic Tenor

MUNICH ROCOCO SOLOISTS
Rossini: Barbiere di Siviglia (exc)

MUNICH ST WOLFGANG CHILDREN'S CHOIR
cond R. HEGER
(CFP) **CD-CFP4616** Ave Maria
cond H. MÜLLER-KRAY
(EMI) **CZS7 62993-2** Fritz Wunderlich—Great German Tenor

MUNICH WIND ENSEMBLE
Mozart: Zauberflöte (exc)

MUNIER, Alain (ten)
Chabrier: Roi malgré lui (Cpte)

MUÑIZ, Ricardo (ten)
Penella: Gato Montés (Cpte)

MUNKITTRICK, Mark (bass)
Puccini: Edgar (Cpte)

MUNRO, Donald (bar)
Delius: Village Romeo and Juliet (Cpte)

MUNRO, Jeremy (bar)
Knussen: Where the Wild Things are (Cpte)
R. Strauss: Arabella (Cpte)

MUNSEL, Patrice (sop)
(MMOI) **CDMOIR406** Mozart—Historical Recordings
(RCA) **09026 61580-2(6)** RCA/Met 100 Singers, 100 Years (pt 6)

MÜNSTER CITY THEATRE CHORUS
cond W. HUMBURG
Corghi: Divara (Cpte)

MÜNSTER SYMPHONY ORCHESTRA
cond W. HUMBURG
Corghi: Divara (Cpte)

MUNTEANU, Petre (ten)
Donizetti: Don Pasquale (Cpte)

MURA, Bernard-Jean (sngr)
(ARIO) **ARN68195** Milhaud—Sonatas; Trois Operas-Minute

MURATORE, Lucien (ten)
(IRCC) **IRCC-CD802** Souvenirs of Rare French Opera
(MSCM) **MM30377** 18 Tenors d'Expression Française

MURGATROYD, Andrew (ten)
Britten: Paul Bunyan (exc)
Purcell: Dido (Cpte)

MURGU, Corneliu (ten)
Puccini: Fanciulla del West (Cpte)
Verdi: Otello (Cpte)

MURO, Bernardo De (ten)
(EMI) **CHS7 64860-2(2)** La Scala Edition - Vol.1, 1878-1914 (pt 2)

MURPHY, Heidi Grant (mez)
Wagner: Parsifal (Cpte)

MURPHY, Maureen (sop)
Vaughan Williams: Pilgrim's Progress (Cpte)

MURPHY, Maurice (cornet)
(CHAN) **CHAN4513** British Bandsman Centenary Concert

MURPHY, Maurice (tpt)
(COLL) **Coll3008-2** Favourite Trumpet Concertos

MURPHY, Suzanne (sop)
Mozart: Nozze di Figaro (Cpte)
(COLL) **Coll3025-2** Puccini & Verdi Heroines
(SONY) **474364-2** Suzanne Murphy: There is an Isle

MURPHY, William (bar)
(SONY) **SM3K46291** Stravinsky—Ballets, Vol.1
(SONY) **SM22K46290(4)** Stravinsky—The Complete Edition (pt 4)

MURRAY, Ann (mez)
Bellini: Norma (Cpte)
Cilea: Adriana Lecouvreur (Cpte)
Donizetti: Lucia di Lammermoor (Cpte)
Gay: Beggar's Opera (Cpte)
Gounod: Roméo et Juliette (Cpte)
Humperdinck: Hänsel und Gretel (exc)
Massenet: Thaïs (Cpte)
Mozart: Clemenza di Tito (Cpte), Don Giovanni (Cpte), Finta semplice (Cpte), Lucio Silla (Cpte), Mitridate (Cpte), Nozze di Figaro (exc), Zauberflöte (Cpte)
Offenbach: Contes d'Hoffmann (Cpte)
Puccini: Madama Butterfly (Cpte), Tosca (Cpte)
Purcell: Dido (Cpte), Fairy Queen, Z629 (Cpte)
Rossini: Cenerentola (Cpte)
Verdi: Battaglia di Legnano (Cpte), Don Carlos (Cpte)
(EMI) **CDC7 54411-2** On Wings of Song
(EMI) **CDM5 65576-2** Jessye Norman
(FORL) **UCD16738** Great Handel Arias
(TELD) **4509-97507-2** Mozart—Famous Opera Arias

MURRAY, Doreen (sop)
G. Charpentier: Louise (Cpte)

MURRAY, John Horton (bar)
Verdi: Don Carlo (exc)
Wagner: Parsifal (Cpte)

MURRAY, Thomas (organ)
(PRIO) **PRCD338** The Symphonic Organ, Volume 1

MURRAY, William (bass)
Henze: Bassariden (Cpte)
Mendelssohn: Hochzeit des Camacho (Cpte)
R. Strauss: Salome (Cpte)

MUSACCHIO, Martina (sop)
(REM) **REM311151** Schubert—Lieder

MUSELLA, Laura (mez)
Bellini: Sonnambula (Cpte)

MUSICA AETERNA
cond P. BAXA
Patzelt: Castor et Pollux (Cpte)

MUSICA SACRA SINGERS
cond R. SACCANI
Verdi: Aida (Cpte)

(LES) MUSICHOLIERS
cond A. EINHORN
(ARIO) **ARN68067** Rameau—The Glory of 18th Century Dance Music

(LES) MUSICIENS DU LOUVRE
cond M. MINKOWSKI
Handel: Amadigi di Gaula (Cpte), Teseo (Cpte)
Lully: Phaëton (Cpte)
Marais: Alcyone (Cpte)
Mondonville: Titon et l'Aurore (Cpte)
Mouret: Amours de Ragonde (Cpte)
Rameau: Hippolyte et Aricie (Cpte), Platée (Cpte)

MUSILOVÁ, Milada (contr)
Janáček: Makropulos Affair (Cpte)

MUSINU, Francesco (bass)
Paisiello: Nina (Cpte)
Rossini: Gazza ladra (Cpte)
Verdi: Traviata (Cpte), Vespri Siciliani (Cpte)

MUSINU, Giuseppe (bass)
(NUOV) **6892** William Matteuzzi sings Opera Arias

MUSIQUE VIVANTE ENSEMBLE
cond L. BERIO
Berio: Laborintus II

MUSY, Louis (bar)
Gounod: Faust (Cpte)
Offenbach: Contes d'Hoffmann (Cpte)

MUSY, Louis (bass)
G. Charpentier: Louise (Cpte)

MUSZELY, Melitta (sop)
(EMI) **CMS5 65212-2** Wagner—Les introuvables du Ring
(EMI) **CZS7 62993-2** Fritz Wunderlich—Great German Tenor

MUTI, Riccardo (cond)
see *La Scala Orch*
MMF Orch
Naples Scarlatti Orch
New Philh
Philadelphia
Philh
ROHO
Rome RAI Orch
Rome SO
VPO

MUTIS, Andre (sngr)
Romberg: Student Prince (Cpte)

MUTTER, Anne-Sophie (vn)
(DG) **437 544-2GH** Carmen-Fantasie
(DG) **437 544-5GH** Carmen-Fantasie
(EMI) **CDM7 64629-2** Popular Orchestral Works

MUXENEDER, Franz (bass)
J. Strauss II: Fledermaus (Cpte)

MUZIO, Claudia (sop)
(BOGR) **BIM705-2** Muzio—The Published Edisons, 1920-25
(CONI) **CDHD235** The Puccini Album
(EMI) **CHS7 64864-2(1)** La Scala Edition - Vol.2, 1915-46 (pt 1)
(MMOI) **CDMOIR412** Great Voices of the Century Sing Puccini
(NIMB) **NI7802** Divas 1906-1935
(NIMB) **NI7814** Claudia Muzio—Opera Arias & Songs
(NIMB) **NI7864** More Legendary Voices
(PEAR) **GEMMCDS9925(1)** Covent Garden on Record—Vol.3 (pt 1)
(PEAR) **GEMMCD9130** Great Sopranos, Vol.2
(PEAR) **GEMMCD9143** Claudia Muzio, Volume 2
(PREI) **89091** Francesco Merli (1887-1976) - II
(ROMO) **81005-2** Claudia Muzio (1889-1936)
(ROMO) **81010-2** Claudia Muzio—Complete Pathé Recordings, 1917-8

MUZZARELLI, Alfred (bass)
Wagner: Meistersinger (Cpte)
(SCHW) **314562** Vienna State Opera Live, Vol.6
(SCHW) **314602** Vienna State Opera Live, Vol.10
(SCHW) **314642** Vienna State Opera Live, Vol.14

MUZZARELLI, Alfred (spkr)
R. Strauss: Ariadne auf Naxos (Cpte)
(SCHW) **314632** Vienna State Opera Live, Vol.13
(SCHW) **314652** Vienna State Opera Live, Vol.15

MYERS, Raymond (bar)
Gounod: Faust (Cpte)
Verdi: Macbeth (Cpte)

MYHUS, M. (mez)
Mussorgsky: Boris Godunov (Cpte)

MYRLAK, Kazimierz (ten)
Gluck: Danza (Cpte)
Rossini: Signor Bruschino (Cpte)

MYSZAK, Stephanie (sngr)
Weill: Dreigroschenoper (Cpte)

NACHBAUER, Bernd (bass)
Suder: Kleider machen Leute (Cpte)

NADLER, Sheila (mez)
J. Adams: Death of Klinghoffer (Cpte)

NADOR, Magda (sop)
Mozart: Schauspieldirektor (Cpte)

NAFÉ, Alicia (mez)
Bellini: Adelson e Salvini (Cpte)
Bizet: Carmen (exc)
Falla: Vida breve (Cpte)
Mozart: Nozze di Figaro (Cpte)

NAGANO, Kent (cond)
see *LPO*
LSO
Lyon Op Orch

NAGANO, Yonako (mez)
(TESS) **049-2** R. Strauss/Wagner—Opera Scenes

NAGLIA, Sandro (ten)
Handel: Poro (Cpte)

NAGY, Robert (ob)
Barber: Vanessa (Cpte)

NAGY, Robert (ten)
Verdi: Ballo in maschera (Cpte)

NAHON, Philippe (cond)
see *Ens*

NAHR, William (ten)
Puccini: Bohème (Cpte)

NAKARJAKOV, Sergei (tpt)
(TELD) **4509-94554-2** Carmen Fantasy—Virtuoso Music for Trumpet
(TELD) **4509-96231-2** Gardening Classics
(TELD) **9031-77705-2** Works for Trumpet & Piano

NAM, Lyudmila (mez)
Rimsky-Korsakov: Mlada (Cpte)

NAMARA, Marguerite (sop)
(IRCC) **IRCC-CD802** Souvenirs of Rare French Opera

NAMUR CHAMBER CHOIR
cond J-C. MALGOIRE
Gluck: Orfeo ed Euridice (Cpte)
cond M. MINKOWSKI
Grétry: Caravane du Caire (Cpte)

NANCY SYMPHONY ORCHESTRA
cond M. PIQUEMAL
(MARC) **8 223774** Ropartz—Choral Works

NANNI, Oscar (bass)
Puccini: Madama Butterfly (Cpte)

NANTES OPERA CHORUS
cond G. CARELLA
Mercadante: Giuramento (Cpte)

NANUT, Anton (cond)
see *Ljubljana RSO*

NAOURI, Laurent (bar)
Lully: Phaëton (Cpte)
Rameau: Hippolyte et Aricie (Cpte)

NAPIER, Marita (sop)
R. Strauss: Elektra (Cpte)
Wagner: Rheingold (Cpte), Walküre (Cpte)
Weill: Zar lässt sich Photographieren (Cpte)
(DG) **437 825-2GH** Wagner—Der Ring des Nibelungen - Highlights
(DG) **445 354-2GX14** Wagner—Der Ring des Nibelungen
(EURO) **GD69003** Wagner—Der Ring des Nibelungen

NAPLES RAI ORCHESTRA
cond C. FRANCI
Rossini: Inganno felice (Cpte)

NAPLES SAN CARLO OPERA CHORUS
cond V. BELLEZZA
Leoncavallo: Pagliacci (Cpte)
cond M. DE BERNART
Donizetti: Lucia di Lammermoor (Cpte)
(NUOV) **6905** Donizetti—Great Love Duets
cond C. FRANCI
Donizetti: Lucia di Lammermoor (Cpte)
cond F. MOLINARI-PRADELLI
Donizetti: Don Pasquale (Cpte)
Puccini: Bohème (Cpte), Gianni Schicchi (Cpte)
cond M. ROSSI
(MEMO) **HR4273/4** Great Voices—Pietro Cappuccilli
(MEMO) **HR4400/1** Great Voices - Ettore Bastianini

cond N. SANZOGNO
(MEMO) **HR4273/4** Great Voices—Pietro Cappuccilli
cond S. SASSANO
Rossini: Barbiere di Siviglia (exc)
cond T. SERAFIN
Donizetti: Linda di Chamounix (Cpte)
Rossini: Mosè (Cpte)

NAPLES SAN CARLO OPERA ORCHESTRA
cond V. BELLEZZA
Leoncavallo: Pagliacci (Cpte)
cond M. DE BERNART
Donizetti: Lucia di Lammermoor (Cpte)
(NUOV) **6905** Donizetti—Great Love Duets
cond C. FRANCI
Donizetti: Lucia di Lammermoor (Cpte)
cond F. MOLINARI-PRADELLI
Donizetti: Don Pasquale (Cpte)
Puccini: Bohème (Cpte), Gianni Schicchi (Cpte)
(PHIL) **442 602-2PM** 3 x 3 Tenors
cond F. PREVITALI
(BONG) **GB1060-2** Virginia Zeani - Various opera arias
cond U. RAPALO
(PREI) **90020** Giuseppe Taddei sings Arias and Neapolitan Songs
cond M. ROSSI
(MEMO) **HR4204/5** Franco Corelli—Opera Arias
(MEMO) **HR4273/4** Great Voices—Pietro Cappuccilli
(MEMO) **HR4400/1** Great Voices - Ettore Bastianini
cond N. SANZOGNO
(MEMO) **HR4273/4** Great Voices—Pietro Cappuccilli
cond S. SASSANO
Rossini: Barbiere di Siviglia (exc)
cond T. SERAFIN
Donizetti: Linda di Chamounix (Cpte)
Rossini: Mosè (Cpte)

NAPLES SCARLATTI CHORUS
cond R. MUTI
(MEMO) **HR4300/1** Great Voices—Sesto Bruscantini
cond N. SANZOGNO
(MEMO) **HR4277/8** Mirella Freni—Public Performances 1963-1970
(MEMO) **HR4300/1** Great Voices—Sesto Bruscantini
cond S. VARVISO
Rossini: Barbiere di Siviglia (Cpte)

NAPLES SCARLATTI ORCHESTRA
cond R. MUTI
(MEMO) **HR4300/1** Great Voices—Sesto Bruscantini
cond N. SANZOGNO
(MEMO) **HR4277/8** Mirella Freni—Public Performances 1963-1970
(MEMO) **HR4300/1** Great Voices—Sesto Bruscantini
cond S. VARVISO
Rossini: Barbiere di Siviglia (Cpte)

APOLI, Catherine (sop)
Grétry: Caravane du Caire (Cpte)
Handel: Teseo (Cpte)
Mondonville: Titon et l'Aurore (Cpte)

ARÇON, Armand (bass)
Debussy: Pelléas et Mélisande (exc)
Massenet: Werther (Cpte)
(EMI) **CHS7 61038-2** Debussy—Pelléas et Mélisande, etc

ARKÉ, Victor de (bass)
Gluck: Iphigénie en Tauride (Cpte)

ASEBAND, Dennis (treb)
Mozart: Zauberflöte (Cpte)

ASH, Damien (spkr)
Britten: Midsummer Night's Dream (Cpte)

ASH, Dorothy (sop)
Sullivan: Mikado (Cpte)

ASH, Heddle (ten)
Gounod: Faust (Cpte)
Mozart: Così fan tutte (Cpte), Nozze di Figaro (Cpte)
(ASV) **CDAJA5112** Twenty Gramophone All-Time Greats
(DUTT) **CDLX7012** The Incomparable Heddle Nash
(EMI) **CDH5 65072-2** Glyndebourne Recorded - 1934-1994
(MMOI) **CDMOIR405** Great Tenors
(MMOI) **CDMOIR406** Mozart—Historical Recordings
(PEAR) **GEMMCDS9926(1)** Covent Garden on Record—Vol.4 (pt 1)
(PEAR) **GEMMCDS9926(2)** Covent Garden on Record—Vol.4 (pt 2)
(PEAR) **GEMMCD9175** Heddle Nash - Serenade
(PEAR) **GEMMCD9319** Heddle Nash sings Opera Arias & Songs
(PEAR) **GEMMCD9473** Heddle Nash—Vol.2

ASH, John Heddle (bar)
Sullivan: Mikado (Cpte)

ASH, Royston (cond)
see New SO
RPO

ASHMAN, Laura (fl)
(PRO) **CDD585** The French Connection

ASLUND, Anders (bar)
Verdi: Rigoletto (Cpte)

ASRAWI, Douglas (ten)
Lully: Alceste (Cpte)

ASSERI, Hamid (sngr)
Egk: Verlobung in San Domingo (Cpte)

NAST, Minnie (sop)
(SUPR) **11 2136-2(3)** Emmy Destinn—Complete Edition, Discs 5 to 8

NASTRUCCI, Gino (cond)
see La Scala Chor
La Scala Orch
orch

NATALI, Valiano (ten)
Donizetti: Lucia di Lammermoor (Cpte)

NATIONAL PHILHARMONIC ORCHESTRA
cond K.H. ADLER
(BELA) **450 007-2** Puccini Favourites
(BELA) **450 015-2** Cinema Classics
(DECC) **433 624-2DSP** Great Soprano Arias
(DECC) **433 865-2DWO** The World of Puccini
(SONY) **SMK39030** Placido Domingo sings Great Love Scenes
cond B. BARTOLETTI
Ponchielli: Gioconda (Cpte)
(DECC) **430 724-2DM** Great Operatic Duets
(DECC) **436 475-2DM** Dance of the Hours: ballet music from the opera
(DECC) **443 331-2LRX** Music for Relaxation, Vol 6 - The Morning After
(DECC) **443 378-2DM** Ten Top Mezzos 2
(DECC) **443 928-2DM** Montserrat Caballé sings Opera Arias
cond R. BONYNGE
Bellini: Sonnambula (Cpte)
Donizetti: Lucrezia Borgia (Cpte)
Gay: Beggar's Opera (Cpte)
Massenet: Cid (exc), Esclarmonde (Cpte), Roi de Lahore (Cpte), Thaïs (exc)
Verdi: Traviata (exc), Trovatore (Cpte)
(DECC) **417 011-2DH2** Pavarotti's Greatest Hits
(DECC) **417 645-2DH** Kiri - Portrait
(DECC) **425 681-2DM2** Tutto Pavarotti
(DECC) **425 848-2DWO** Your hundred best tunes vol 2
(DECC) **425 849-2DWO** Your hundred best tunes vol 3
(DECC) **430 470-2DH** Essential Pavarotti II
(DECC) **430 724-2DM** Great Operatic Duets
(DECC) **433 064-2DWO** Your Hundred Best Opera Tunes Volume I
(DECC) **433 066-2DWO** Your Hundred Best Opera Tunes III
(DECC) **433 068-2DWO** Your Hundred Best Opera Tunes V
(DECC) **433 069-2DWO** Your Hundred Best Opera Tunes VI
(DECC) **433 220-2DWO** The World of the Violin
(DECC) **433 221-2DWO** The World of Verdi
(DECC) **433 223-2DWO** The World of Operetta
(DECC) **433 439-2DA** Great Love Duets
(DECC) **433 443-2DA** Great Opera Choruses
(DECC) **436 463-2DM** Ten Top Tenors
(DECC) **440 947-2DH** Essential Opera II
(DECC) **444 108-2DA** Ballet Music from Opera
(DECC) **444 110-2DA** Massenet/ Meyerbeer/ Delibes/ Thomas—Ballet Music
cond R. CHAILLY
Giordano: Andrea Chénier (Cpte)
Rossini: Guillaume Tell (Cpte), Turco in Italia (exc)
(DECC) **425 852-2DWO** Your hundred best tunes vol 6
(DECC) **436 133-2DWO** World of Rossini
(DECC) **436 472-2DM** Great Opera Arias
(DECC) **440 400-2DM** Luciano Pavarotti
(DECC) **440 412-2DM** Mirella Freni
(DECC) **443 377-2DM** Ten Top Sopranos 2
(DECC) **443 850-2DF2** Rossini—Overtures
(DECC) **443 928-2DM** Montserrat Caballé sings Opera Arias
(DECC) **400 049-5DH** Rossini: Overtures
(SONY) **SM48155** Carreras and Caballe sing Souvenirs
(SONY) **SMK48155** Carreras and Caballe sing Souvenirs
cond O DE FABRITIIS
(DECC) **440 412-2DM** Mirella Freni
cond O. DE FABRITIIS
Boito: Mefistofele (Cpte)
(DECC) **425 681-2DM2** Tutto Pavarotti
(DECC) **430 470-2DH** Essential Pavarotti II
(DECC) **436 317-2DA** Puccini—Famous Arias
(DECC) **436 472-2DM** Great Opera Arias
(DECC) **440 400-2DM** Luciano Pavarotti
(DECC) **443 928-2DM** Montserrat Caballé sings Opera Arias
cond G. GAVAZZENI
Mascagni: Cavalleria Rusticana (Cpte)
(DECC) **425 681-2DM2** Tutto Pavarotti
(DECC) **425 848-2DWO** Your hundred best tunes vol 2
(DECC) **433 065-2DWO** Your Hundred Best Opera Tunes Volume II
(DECC) **433 822-2DH** Essential Opera
(SONY) **SBK46548** Opera Arias
cond C. GERHARDT
(CHES) **Chesky CD108** Light Classics, Volume II
(RCA) **GD60924** James Galway - Man with the Golden Flute
cond JAMES LEVINE
Bellini: Norma (Cpte)
Giordano: Andrea Chénier (Cpte)
Mascagni: Cavalleria Rusticana (Cpte)
Puccini: Bohème (Cpte)
Verdi: Otello (Cpte)
(CFP) **CD-CFP4569** Puccini: Arias
(EMI) **CDM7 63104-2** Alfredo Krauss - Opera Recital
(RCA) **GD60866** The Placido Domingo Album
(RCA) **09026 61580-2(8)** RCA/Met 100 Singers, 100 Years (pt 8)
(RCA) **74321 24209-2** Italian Opera Choruses
(SONY) **SBK46548** Opera Arias
cond E. KOHN
(EMI) **CDC5 55017-2** Domingo Opera Classics
(EMI) **CDC7 54053-2** Roman Heroes
cond P. MAAG
Verdi: Luisa Miller (Cpte)
(DECC) **443 928-2DM** Montserrat Caballé sings Opera Arias
cond L. MAAZEL
Puccini: Villi (Cpte)
cond L. MAGIERA
(DECC) **440 412-2DM** Mirella Freni
cond G. PATANÈ
Leoncavallo: Pagliacci (exc)
(DECC) **417 011-2DH2** Pavarotti's Greatest Hits
(DECC) **433 066-2DWO** Your Hundred Best Opera Tunes III
(DECC) **440 412-2DM** Mirella Freni
(DECC) **440 947-2DH** Essential Opera II
cond N. RESCIGNO
Puccini: Tosca (Cpte)
(DECC) **417 011-2DH2** Pavarotti's Greatest Hits
(DECC) **425 681-2DM2** Tutto Pavarotti
(DECC) **430 470-2DH** Essential Pavarotti II
(DECC) **433 439-2DA** Great Love Duets
(DECC) **436 300-2DX** Opera Gala Sampler
(DECC) **440 412-2DM** Mirella Freni
(DECC) **444 555-2DF2** Essential Puccini
cond G. SOLTI
Puccini: Tosca (exc)
Verdi: Ballo in maschera (Cpte)
(DECC) **417 645-2DH** Kiri - Portrait
(DECC) **421 896-2DA** Puccini—Great Operatic Duets
(DECC) **425 681-2DM2** Tutto Pavarotti
(DECC) **430 724-2DM** Great Operatic Duets
(DECC) **433 066-2DWO** Your Hundred Best Opera Tunes III
(DECC) **433 822-2DH** Essential Opera
(DECC) **436 461-2DM** Ten Top Sopranos
(DECC) **436 472-2DM** Great Opera Arias
cond R. STAPLETON
(DECC) **425 849-2DWO** Your hundred best tunes vol 3
(DECC) **433 223-2DWO** The World of Operetta
cond L. STOKOWSKI
(EMI) **CDM7 64140-2** Stokowski Showcase
(SONY) **SFK47279** Passport to Spain
cond L. TJEKNAVORIAN
(RCA) **VD60535** Borodin—Orchestral Works
cond B. WORDSWORTH
(RCA) **RD60242** Evelyn Glennie - Rhythm Song

NATIONAL SYMPHONY ORCHESTRA
cond R. BONYNGE
(DECC) **443 585-2DF2** Your Hundred Best Tunes - Top 20
cond A. COATES
(BEUL) **2PD11** Russian Masters
cond A. DORATI
(BELA) **450 025-2** Essential Wagner
cond J.O. EDWARDS
Bernstein: West Side Story (Cpte)
(TER) **CDVIR8315** Carousel Waltz
cond A. FISTOULARI
(DUTT) **CDK1200** This is Full Frequency Range Recording
cond G. GAVAZZENI
(DECC) **443 585-2DF2** Your Hundred Best Tunes - Top 20
cond C. KRAUSS
(PREI) **90190** Paul Schoeffler—Recital
cond B. NEEL
(DUTT) **CDK1200** This is Full Frequency Range Recording
cond K. RANKL
(PREI) **90190** Paul Schoeffler—Recital
cond SIDNEY BEER
(DUTT) **CDK1200** This is Full Frequency Range Recording
cond R. STAPLETON
(DECC) **443 585-2DF2** Your Hundred Best Tunes - Top 20

NATZKE, Oscar (bass)
(EMI) **CHS7 69741-2(2)** Record of Singing, Vol.4—Anglo-American School (pt 2)
(KIWI) **CDSLD-82** Southern Voices—NZ International Opera Singers
(ODE) **CDODE1365** Oscar Natzke - A Legend in His Time

NAUMENKO, Alexander (bass)
Shostakovich: Gamblers (Cpte)

NAVARINI, Francesco (bass)
(EMI) **CHS7 64860-2(1)** La Scala Edition - Vol.1, 1878-1914 (pt 1)
(MEMO) **HR4408/9(1)** Singers in Genoa, Vol.1 (disc 1)
(PEAR) **GEMMCDS9923(1)** Covent Garden on Record, Vol.1 (pt 1)

NAVARRO, Garcia (cond)
see Austrian RSO
Barcelona SO
LSO
Seville SO
Württemberg St Orch

NAZARETH, Daniel (cond)
see Slovak PO

NBC SYMPHONY ORCHESTRA
Weber: Euryanthe (exc)
(RCA) **790 351** Toscanini conducts Wagner from NBC Studio 8-H, 1948
cond E. MCARTHUR
(MUSI) **MACD-263** Flagstad sings Wagner—1955 New York Farewell Concert
cond A. TOSCANINI
Beethoven: Fidelio (Cpte), Leonore (exc)
Puccini: Bohème (Cpte)
Verdi: Aida (Cpte), Ballo in maschera (Cpte), Falstaff (Cpte), Otello (Cpte), Traviata (Cpte)
(ATS) **ATCD100** Toscanini conducts Italian Music
(DELL) **CDDA9020** Toscanini conducts music by his contemporaries
(DELL) **CDDA9021** Toscanini conducts French Works
(MUSI) **ATRA-3008** Toscanini's Farewell Concert
(RCA) **GD60255** Beethoven: Orchestral Works
(RCA) **GD60264** Wagner—Opera excerpts
(RCA) **GD60267** Toscanini Collection, Vol.45
(RCA) **GD60274** Berlioz—Roméo et Juliette/Bizet—Suites
(RCA) **GD60276** Toscanini conducts Boito & Verdi
(RCA) **GD60278** Cherubini/Cimarosa—Orchestral Works
(RCA) **GD60279** Toscanini Collection, Vol.24
(RCA) **GD60280** Toscanini Collection
(RCA) **GD60286** Toscanini Collection - Mozart
(RCA) **GD60289** Toscanini Collection - Rossini Overtures
(RCA) **GD60292** Schumann/Weber—Orchestral Works
(RCA) **GD60296** Toscanini Collection, Vol.31
(RCA) **GD60299** Verdi: Requiem, etc
(RCA) **GD60304** Toscanini Collection - Wagner
(RCA) **GD60305** Toscanini Collection - Wagner
(RCA) **GD60306** Wagner—Orchestral Works
(RCA) **GD60308** Toscanini Collection, Vol.40
(RCA) **GD60310** Various Overtures and Preludes
(RCA) **GD60322** Toscanini Collection, Vol.39
(RCA) **GD60324** Beethoven—Complete Symphonies
(RCA) **GD60326** Verdi—Operas & Choral Works
(RCA) **790 353** Toscanini—Carnegie Hall Concert, 15/03/52
(RELI) **CR1861** Beethoven—Symphonies Nos 1 & 4; Fidelio—Ov
(TELD) **4509-95038-6(TELD)** The Art of Conducting—Great Conductors of the Past
cond B. WALTER
(PEAR) **GEMMCD9131** Bruno Walter live

NEALE, John (bass)
Vaughan Williams: Pilgrim's Progress (Cpte)

NEALLEY, Ralph (sngr)
Gershwin: Porgy and Bess (Cpte)

NEBLETT, Carol (sop)
Korngold: Tote Stadt (Cpte)
Puccini: Bohème (Cpte), Fanciulla del West (Cpte)
(BELA) **450 121-2** Plácido Domingo
(CAST) **CVI2070** Great Puccini Love Scenes from Covent Garden, La Scala and Verona

NEBOLSIN, Vassily (cond)
see Bolshoi Th Orch

NEDZADEL, Maria (sop)
(LYRC) **LCD146** Frida Leider sings Wagner

NEEL, Boyd (cond)
see National SO

NEGRI, Giovanni Battista de (ten)
(EMI) **CHS7 64860-2(1)** La Scala Edition - Vol.1, 1878-1914 (pt 1)
(MEMO) **HR4408/9(1)** Singers in Genoa, Vol.1 (disc 1)
(SYMP) **SYMCD1065** The Harold Wayne Collection, Vol.1

NEIDLINGER, Gustav (bass-bar)
Mozart: Nozze di Figaro (Cpte)
Orff: Kluge (Cpte)
R. Strauss: Elektra (Cpte)
Wagner: Götterdämmerung (Cpte), Meistersinger (exc), Parsifal (Cpte), Rheingold (Cpte), Siegfried (Cpte)
(DECC) **414 100-2DM15** Wagner: Der Ring des Nibelungen
(EMI) **CZS7 67123-2** Wagner: Der Ring des Nibelungen
(FOYE) **15-CF2011** Wagner—Der Ring de Nibelungen
(ORFE) **C394101B** Great Mozart Singers Series, Vol. 1
(PHIL) **446 057-2PB14** Wagner—The Ring Cycle - Bayreuth Festival 1967
(SCHW) **314722** Vienna State Opera Live, Vol.22

NEILL, Hallie (sop)
Glass: Belle et la Bête (Cpte)

NEILL, William (voc)
Maderna: Satyricon (Cpte)

NEILZ, Jacques (vc)
(EMI) **CMS5 65621-2** Fischer-Dieskau - The Opera Singer

NEISER, Holger (treb)
(WERG) **WER6173-2** T.W.Adorno—Chamber & Choral Works

NELEPP, Georgi (ten)
(ARLE) **ARL23/5** Rimsky-Korsakov—Sadko
(DANT) **LYS013/5** Tchaikovsky—The Queen of Spades
(EMI) **CHS7 69741-2(6)** Record of Singing, Vol.4—Russian & Slavonic Schools
(PREI) **89080** Mark Reizen (1895-1992) - II
(PREI) **89081** Georgi Nelepp (1904-1957)

NELLI, Herva (sop)
Verdi: Aida (Cpte), Ballo in maschera (Cpte), Falstaff (Cpte), Otello (Cpte)
(RCA) **GD60326** Verdi—Operas & Choral Works

NELSON, Elisabeth Comeaux (sop)
Britten: Paul Bunyan (Cpte)

NELSON, John (cond)
see Lyon Op Orch
St Luke's Orch

NELSON, Judith (sop)
Cavalli: Xerse (Cpte)
Purcell: Dido (Cpte), Fairy Queen, Z629 (Cpte)
(DG) **439 474-2GCL** Purcell—Opera & Choral Works

NELSON, Marty (voc)
Bernstein: West Side Story (Cpte)

NELSSON, Woldemar (cond)
see Bayreuth Fest Orch

NÉMET, János (boy alto)
Puccini: Tosca (Cpte)

NÉMETH, József (bar)
Giordano: Fedora (Cpte)
Puccini: Tosca (exc)

NÉMETH, Maria (sop)
(CLUB) **CL99-007** Maria Nemeth/Tiana Lemnitz
(NIMB) **NI7802** Divas 1906-1935
(PEAR) **GEMMCDS9926(2)** Covent Garden on Record—Vol.4 (pt 2)
(SCHW) **314542** Vienna State Opera Live, Vol.4
(SCHW) **314572** Vienna State Opera Live, Vol.7
(SCHW) **314602** Vienna State Opera Live, Vol.10
(SCHW) **314632** Vienna State Opera Live, Vol.13
(SCHW) **314692** Vienna State Opera Live, Vol.19

NÉMETH, Sándor (bar)
Lehár: Lustige Witwe (exc)

NENADOVSKY, Alexander (bar)
Tchaikovsky: Eugene Onegin (exc)

NENTWIG, Franz Ferdinand (bass-bar)
R. Strauss: Ariadne auf Naxos (Cpte)
Schreker: Schatzgräber (Cpte)

NÉQUECAUR, Pierre (bar)
Gounod: Philémon et Baucis (Cpte)

NERALIČ, Tomislav (bar)
Beethoven: Fidelio (Cpte)
Verdi: Otello (Cpte)
(SCHW) **314552** Vienna State Opera Live, Vol.5
(SCHW) **314712** Vienna State Opera Live, Vol.21

NERI, Giulio (bass)
Mascagni: Iris (Cpte)
Verdi: Aida (Cpte), Don Carlo (Cpte), Rigoletto (Cpte)

NERONI, Luciano (bass)
Puccini: Turandot (Cpte)

NEROZZI, Lidia (mez)
Puccini: Madama Butterfly (Cpte)

NES, Jard van (contr)
Mozart: Zauberflöte (exc)
Wagner: Götterdämmerung (Cpte)

NESHYBA, Ladislav (bass)
Marschner: Hans Heiling (Cpte)
Verdi: Rigoletto (Cpte), Traviata (Cpte)

NESHYBOVÁ, Ivica (mez)
Verdi: Rigoletto (Cpte), Traviata (Cpte)

NESPOULOUS, Marthe (sop)
Debussy: Pelléas et Mélisande (exc)

NESSI, Giuseppe (ten)
Leoncavallo: Pagliacci (Cpte)
Puccini: Bohème (Cpte), Turandot (Cpte)
Verdi: Aida (Cpte), Falstaff (exc), Rigoletto (Cpte)
(EMI) **CHS7 64864-2(1)** La Scala Edition - Vol.2, 1915-46 (pt 1)
(EMI) **CHS7 64864-2(2)** La Scala Edition - Vol.2, 1915-46 (pt 2)
(PEAR) **GEMMCDS9180** Verdi—Rigoletto, etc
(PREI) **89007** Aureliano Pertile (1885-1952) - I
(PREI) **89023** Conchita Supervia (1895-1936)

NESTERENKO, Evgeny (bass)
Donizetti: Don Pasquale (Cpte), Elisir d'amore (Cpte)
Glinka: Life for the Tsar (Cpte)
Gounod: Faust (Cpte)
Mussorgsky: Boris Godunov (Cpte)
Rimsky-Korsakov: Mozart and Salieri (Cpte), Tsar's Bride (Cpte)
Tchaikovsky: Eugene Onegin (Cpte)
Verdi: Attila (Cpte), Nabucco (Cpte), Trovatore (Cpte)
(RUSS) **RDCD11372** Tchaikovsky—Romances; Rachmaninov—Aleko Aria

NETHERLANDS CHAMBER CHOIR
cond N. HARNONCOURT
Mozart: Thamos, K345 (Cpte)
(TELD) **4509-97505-2** Mozart—Famous Opera Choruses

NETHERLANDS CHAMBER ORCHESTRA
cond D. ZINMAN
(PHIL) **422 525-2PME2** The Complete Mozart Edition Vol 25

NETHERLANDS OPERA CHORUS
cond C. BRUCK
(EMI) **CDH7 61003-2** Kathleen Ferrier sings Opera and Songs
cond N. HARNONCOURT
J. Strauss II: Fledermaus (exc)
Mozart: Così fan tutte (Cpte), Don Giovanni (Cpte), Nozze di Figaro (Cpte)
(TELD) **4509-97505-2** Mozart—Famous Opera Choruses
(TELD) **4509-98824-2** Thomas Hampson Collection,Vol III-Operatic Scenes
cond E. DE WAART
R. Strauss: Rosenkavalier (Cpte)

NETHERLANDS OPERA ORCHESTRA
cond C. BRUCK
(EMI) **CDH7 61003-2** Kathleen Ferrier sings Opera and Songs

NETHERLANDS PHILHARMONIC ORCHESTRA
cond E. DE WAART
(ETCE) **KTC1145** Barber—Scenes and Arias

NETHERLANDS RADIO CHORUS
cond K. BAKELS
Mascagni: Piccolo Marat (Cpte)

NETHERLANDS RADIO PHILHARMONIC ORCHESTRA
cond E. DE WAART
(FIDE) **9201** Wagner—The Ring - An orchestral adventure

NETHERLANDS RADIO SYMPHONY ORCHESTRA
cond K. BAKELS
Mascagni: Piccolo Marat (Cpte)

NETHERLANDS WIND ENSEMBLE
(PHIL) **422 545-2PME3** The Complete Mozart Edition Vol.45
cond R. DUFALLO
(CHAN) **CHAN9210** Twentieth-Century American Music

NETT, Willi (bar)
Hindemith: Cardillac (Cpte)

NETTLE, David (pf)
(IMP) **MCD76** Nettle and Markham in America

NEUBAUER, Margit (mez)
Wagner: Parsifal (Cpte)

NEUBURG, Amy X. (sngr)
Ashley: Improvement (Cpte)

NEUDAHM, Arthur (bass)
(SUPR) **11 2136-2(3)** Emmy Destinn—Complete Edition, Discs 5 to 8

NEUGEBAUER, Alfred (narr)
R. Strauss: Ariadne auf Naxos (Cpte)

NEUGEBAUER, Karl (bass)
R. Strauss: Rosenkavalier (Cpte)

NEUKIRCH, Harald (ten)
Mozart: Entführung (Cpte)

NEUMANN, Astrid (sop)
(DANA) **DACOCD311/2** Lauritz Melchior Anthology - Vol.1

NEUMANN, Clara (sngr)
Milhaud: Malheurs d'Orphée (Cpte)

NEUMANN, Roland (bass)
Verdi: Otello (Cpte)
Wagner: Meistersinger (exc)
(SCHW) **314552** Vienna State Opera Live, Vol.5
(SCHW) **314692** Vienna State Opera Live, Vol.19

NEUMANN, Václav (cond)
see Czech PO
Leipzig Gewandhaus

NEUMANN, Wolfgang (ten)
Weill: Mahagonny (Cpte)

NEURY, André (bar)
Offenbach: Contes d'Hoffmann (Cpte)

NEUWEILER, Ulrich (ten)
Krenek: Sprüng über den Schatten (Cpte)
Spohr: Faust (Cpte)

NEVES, Susan (sop)
Mascagni: Piccolo Marat (Cpte)

NEVEU, Ginette (vn)
(PEAR) **GEMMCD9125** 20 Great Violinists plays 20 Masterpieces
(TEST) **SBT1010** Ginette Neveu & Josef Hassid

NEVILLE, John (spkr)
Gay: Beggar's Opera (Cpte)

NEW YORK METROPOLITAN OPERA BALLET
cond JAMES LEVINE
Bizet: Carmen (Cpte)
Corigliano: Ghosts of Versailles (Cpte)
Puccini: Turandot (Cpte)
Verdi: Aida (Cpte)
(DECC) **071 142-1DH (DECC)** Essential Opera

NEW YORK METROPOLITAN OPERA CHILDREN'S CHOIR
cond L. BERNSTEIN
Bizet: Carmen (Cpte)

NEW YORK METROPOLITAN OPERA CHORUS
cond G. SOLTI
Verdi: Otello (Cpte)
(MSCM) **MM30352** Caruso—Italian Opera Arias
(NIMB) **NI7803** Enrico Caruso—Opera Recital
(PEAR) **EVC2** The Caruso Edition, Vol.2—1908-12
(PEAR) **EVC3(1)** The Caruso Edition, Vol.3 (pt 1)
(PEAR) **GEMMCDS9160(2)** De Luca Edition, Vol.2 (pt 2)
(PEAR) **GEMMCD9104** Pasquale Amato (1878-1942)
(PREI) **89064** Pasquale Amato (1878-1942)
(RCA) **GD60495(4)** The Complete Caruso Collection (pt 4)
(RCA) **GD60495(5)** The Complete Caruso Collection (pt 5)
(RCA) **09026 61242-2** Caruso Sings Verdi
cond A. BODANZKY
Beethoven: Fidelio (Cpte)
cond R. BONYNGE
Bellini: Norma (Cpte)
Verdi: Traviata (Cpte)
(BUTT) **BMCD015** Pavarotti Collection - Duets and Scenes
cond F. CALUSIO
Verdi: Trovatore (Cpte)
(MYTO) **2MCD90317** Verdi—Un Ballo in maschera
cond F. CLEVA
Verdi: Aida (exc)
cond E. COOPER
(CBS) **CD45693** Portrait—Ezio Pinza
cond JAMES LEVINE
Bizet: Carmen (Cpte)
Corigliano: Ghosts of Versailles (Cpte)
Donizetti: Elisir d'amore (exc)
Mozart: Nozze di Figaro (exc), Zauberflöte (Cpte)
Puccini: Manon Lescaut (Cpte), Turandot (Cpte)
Verdi: Aida (exc), Don Carlo (Cpte), Falstaff (Cpte), Luisa Miller (exc), Traviata (exc), Trovatore (Cpte)
Wagner: Götterdämmerung (Cpte), Parsifal (Cpte)
(DECC) **071 142-1DH (DECC)** Essential Opera
(DG) **445 354-2GX14** Wagner—Der Ring des Nibelungen
(DG) **072 428-1GH2(DG)** The Metropolitan Opera Gala
(DG) **072 422-3GH7** Levine conducts Wagner's Ring
cond E. LEINSDORF
Rossini: Barbiere di Siviglia (Cpte)
Verdi: Macbeth (Cpte)
Wagner: Tannhäuser (Cpte), Tristan und Isolde (Cpte)
(RCA) **74321 24209-2** Italian Opera Choruses
cond D. MITROPOULOS
Barber: Vanessa (Cpte)
(RCA) **GD87911** Marian Anderson - Opera, Oratorio & Song Recital
(RCA) **74321 24284-2** Opera's Greatest Heroines
cond F. MOLINARI-PRADELLI
Verdi: Don Carlo (Cpte)
cond E. PANIZZA
Ponchielli: Gioconda (Cpte)
Verdi: Otello (Cpte), Traviata (Cpte)
(MMOI) **CDMOIR404** Ezio Pinza—Recital
(MYTO) **2MCD90317** Verdi—Un Ballo in maschera
(PEAR) **GEMMCDS9452** The Emperor Tibbett
cond G. PAPI
Donizetti: Lucia di Lammermoor (Cpte)
cond J. PASTERNACK
(PEAR) **EVC4(1)** The Caruso Edition, Vol.4 (pt 1)
(RCA) **GD60495(5)** The Complete Caruso Collection (pt 5)
(RCA) **09026 61244-2** Caruso sings French Opera Arias
cond W.B. ROGERS
(NIMB) **NI7834** Caruso in Ensemble
(PEAR) **GEMMCD9104** Pasquale Amato (1878-1942)
(RCA) **GD60495(3)** The Complete Caruso Collection (pt 3)
cond J. RUDEL
Handel: Giulio Cesare (Cpte)
cond N. SANTI
Verdi: Ballo in maschera (Cpte)
(MEMO) **HR4400/1** Great Voices - Ettore Bastianini
cond G. SCHICK
(MEMO) **HR4275/6** Birgit Nilsson—Public Performances 1954-1969
cond T. SCHIPPERS
Verdi: Ernani (Cpte)
(MEMO) **HR4279/80** Montserrat Caballé—Opera Arias
(MEMO) **HR4396/7** Great Voices—Leontyne Price
cond G. SCOGNAMIGLIO
(NIMB) **NI7834** Caruso in Ensemble
(PEAR) **EVC3(1)** The Caruso Edition, Vol.3 (pt 1)
(RCA) **GD60495(5)** The Complete Caruso Collection (pt 5)
(RCA) **09026 61242-2** Caruso Sings Verdi
cond G. SETTI
Bellini: Norma (exc)
(CONI) **CDHD149** Gigli Favourites
(CONI) **CDHD227** Gigli in Opera and Song
(IMP) **GLRS102** The Magnificent Gigli
(MMOI) **CDMOIR404** Ezio Pinza—Recital
(MMOI) **CDMOIR412** Great Voices of the Century Sing Puccini
(MMOI) **CDMOIR428** Rosa Ponselle and Giovanni Martinelli sing Verdi
(NIMB) **NI7801** Great Singers, Vol.1
(NIMB) **NI7804** Giovanni Martinelli—Opera Recital
(NIMB) **NI7805** Rosa Ponselle—Opera & Song Recital
(NIMB) **NI7845** Giacomo Lauri-Volpi (1892-1979)
(NIMB) **NI7851** Legendary Voices
(PEAR) **GEMMCDS9160(2)** De Luca Edition, Vol.2 (pt 2)
(PEAR) **GEMMCDS9452** The Emperor Tibbett
(PEAR) **GEMMCDS9924(1)** Covent Garden on Record, Vol.2 (pt 1)
(PEAR) **GEMMCDS9926(2)** Covent Garden on Record—Vol.4 (pt 2)
(PEAR) **GEMMCD9104** Pasquale Amato (1878-1942)
(PEAR) **GEMMCD9306** Ezio Pinza—Opera Recital
(PREI) **89012** Giacomo Lauri-Volpi (1894-1979)
(PREI) **89050** Ezio Pinza (1892-1957)
(PREI) **89062** Giovanni Martinelli (1885-1969)
(PREI) **89064** Pasquale Amato (1878-1942)
(PREI) **89073** Giuseppe de Luca (1876-1950) - II
(RCA) **GD87808** Lawrence Tibbett sings Opera Arias
(RCA) **GD87810** Rosa Ponselle - Opera & Song Recital
(RCA) **GD87811** Beniamino Gigli—Operatic Arias
(RCA) **09026 61245-2** Ezio Pinza - Recital
(RCA) **09026 61580-2(3)** RCA/Met 100 Singers, 100 Years (pt 3)
(ROMO) **81007-2** Rosa Ponselle—Victor Recordings 1926-1929
cond G. SINOPOLI
Puccini: Tosca (Cpte)
cond L. SLATKIN
Puccini: Fanciulla del West (Cpte)
cond C. SODERO
(ALTN) **CDAN3** Hjördis Schymberg
cond F. STIEDRY
Wagner: Lohengrin (Cpte)
cond G. SZELL
Mussorgsky: Boris Godunov (exc)
cond B. WALTER
Mozart: Don Giovanni (Cpte)
(MMOI) **CDMOIR404** Ezio Pinza—Recital
cond R. WEIKERT
Rossini: Barbiere di Siviglia (Cpte)

NEW YORK METROPOLITAN OPERA ORCHESTRA
Bizet: Carmen (Cpte)
Corigliano: Ghosts of Versailles (Cpte)
Donizetti: Elisir d'amore (Cpte)
Mozart: Zauberflöte (Cpte)
Puccini: Fanciulla del West (Cpte), Tosca (Cpte), Turandot (Cpte)
R. Strauss: Ariadne auf Naxos (Cpte)
Verdi: Aida (Cpte), Falstaff (Cpte), Trovatore (Cpte)
Wagner: Götterdämmerung (Cpte), Rheingold (Cpte), Siegfried (Cpte), Walküre (Cpte)
(DG) **072 422-3GH7** Levine conducts Wagner's Ring
(RCA) **09026 61580-2(3)** RCA/Met 100 Singers, 100 Years (pt 3)
cond K.H. ADLER
(MEMO) **HR4204/5** Franco Corelli—Opera Arias
cond L. BERNSTEIN
Bizet: Carmen (Cpte)
cond A. BODANZKY
Beethoven: Fidelio (Cpte)
Wagner: Siegfried (Cpte)
cond R. BONYNGE
Bellini: Norma (Cpte)
Verdi: Traviata (Cpte)
(BUTT) **BMCD015** Pavarotti Collection - Duets and Scenes
(DECC) **071 142-1DH (DECC)** Essential Opera
(MEMO) **HR4392/3** Great Voices - Marilyn Horne
cond F. CALUSIO
Verdi: Trovatore (Cpte)
(MYTO) **2MCD90317** Verdi—Un Ballo in maschera
cond F. CLEVA
Verdi: Aida (exc)
(CBS) **CD45693** Portrait—Ezio Pinza
cond J. CONLON
(RCA) **09026 61509-2** A Salute to American Music
cond E. COOPER
(CBS) **CD45693** Portrait—Ezio Pinza
(EMI) **CHS7 69741-2(2)** Record of Singing, Vol.4—Anglo-American School (pt 2)
cond JAMES LEVINE
Donizetti: Elisir d'amore (exc)
Mozart: Nozze di Figaro (Cpte)
Puccini: Manon Lescaut (Cpte)
Schoenberg: Erwartung (Cpte)
Verdi: Aida (exc), Don Carlo (Cpte), Luisa Miller (Cpte), Traviata (exc), Trovatore (Cpte)
Wagner: Götterdämmerung (Cpte), Parsifal (Cpte), Rheingold (Cpte), Siegfried (Cpte), Walküre (Cpte)
(DECC) **071 142-1DH (DECC)** Essential Opera
(DG) **431 103-2GB** Great Voices—Montserrat Caballé
(DG) **431 104-2GB** Great Voices - Plácido Domingo
(DG) **435 874-2GH** Wagner—Overtures and Preludes
(DG) **437 825-2GH** Wagner—Der Ring des Nibelungen - Highlights
(DG) **439 150-2GMA** Mad about Mozart
(DG) **445 354-2GX14** Wagner—Der Ring des Nibelungen
(DG) **445 552-2GMA** Battle and Domingo
(DG) **439 153-4GMA** Mad about Sopranos
(DG) **072 428-1GH2(DG)** The Metropolitan Opera Gala
(DG) **435 874-5GH** Wagner—Overtures and Preludes
(RCA) **09026 62699-2** Opera's Greatest Duets
(SONY) **SK52489** Verdi—Ballet Music from the Operas
cond H. VON KARAJAN
(MEMO) **HR4275/6** Birgit Nilsson—Public Performances 1954-1969
cond E. LEINSDORF
Rossini: Barbiere di Siviglia (exc)
Verdi: Macbeth (Cpte)
Wagner: Tannhäuser (Cpte), Tristan und Isolde (Cpte)
(PREI) **89084** Kerstin Thorborg (1896-1970)
(RCA) **09026 61440-2** Opera's Greatest Moments
(RCA) **09026 61580-2(6)** RCA/Met 100 Singers, 100 Years (pt 6)
(RCA) **09026 61580-2(7)** RCA/Met 100 Singers, 100 Years (pt 7)
(RCA) **09026 62689-2** The Voices of Living Stereo, Volume 1
(RCA) **74321 24209-2** Italian Opera Choruses
cond Z. MEHTA
(MEMO) **HR4279/80** Montserrat Caballè—Opera Arias
cond D. MITROPOULOS
Barber: Vanessa (Cpte)
(MEMO) **HR4235/6** Great Voices-Renata Tebaldi
(MEMO) **HR4293/4** The very best of Maria Callas
(RCA) **GD87911** Marian Anderson - Opera, Oratorio & Song Recital
(RCA) **09026 61580-2(5)** RCA/Met 100 Singers, 100 Years (pt 5)
(RCA) **09026 61580-2(6)** RCA/Met 100 Singers, 100 Years (pt 6)
(RCA) **09026 62689-2** The Voices of Living Stereo, Volume 1
(RCA) **74321 24284-2** Opera's Greatest Heroines
cond F. MOLINARI-PRADELLI
Verdi: Don Carlo (Cpte)
cond E. PANIZZA
Ponchielli: Gioconda (Cpte)
Verdi: Otello (Cpte), Traviata (Cpte)
(MMOI) **CDMOIR404** Ezio Pinza—Recital
(MYTO) **2MCD90317** Verdi—Un Ballo in maschera
(PEAR) **GEMMCDS9452** The Emperor Tibbett
cond G. PAPI
Donizetti: Lucia di Lammermoor (Cpte)
cond W. PELLETIER
(MMOI) **CDMOIR404** Ezio Pinza—Recital
(MMOI) **CDMOIR405** Great Tenors
(RCA) **GD87808** Lawrence Tibbett sings Opera Arias
cond J. RUDEL
Handel: Giulio Cesare (Cpte)
cond N. SANTI
Verdi: Ballo in maschera (Cpte)
(MEMO) **HR4400/1** Great Voices - Ettore Bastianini
cond G. SCHICK
(MEMO) **HR4275/6** Birgit Nilsson—Public Performances 1954-1969
cond T. SCHIPPERS
Verdi: Ernani (Cpte)
(MEMO) **HR4204/5** Franco Corelli—Opera Arias
(MEMO) **HR4279/80** Montserrat Caballè—Opera Arias
(MEMO) **HR4396/7** Great Voices—Leontyne Price
cond G. SETTI
Bellini: Norma (exc)
(CONI) **CDHD149** Gigli Favourites
(CONI) **CDHD170** Gigli—Centenary Tribute
(CONI) **CDHD201** Galli-Curci in Opera and Song
(CONI) **CDHD227** Gigli in Opera and Song
(EMI) **CDH7 61051-2** Beniamino Gigli - Operatic Arias
(IMP) **GLRS102** The Magnificent Gigli
(MMOI) **CDMOIR404** Ezio Pinza—Recital
(MMOI) **CDMOIR412** Great Voices of the Century Sing Puccini
(MMOI) **CDMOIR428** Rosa Ponselle and Giovanni Martinelli sing Verdi
(NIMB) **NI7801** Great Singers, Vol.1
(NIMB) **NI7804** Giovanni Martinelli—Opera Recital
(NIMB) **NI7805** Rosa Ponselle—Opera & Song Recital
(NIMB) **NI7817** Beniamino Gigli—Vol.2
(NIMB) **NI7845** Giacomo Lauri-Volpi (1892-1979)
(NIMB) **NI7851** Legendary Voices
(NIMB) **NI7852** Galli-Curci, Vol.2
(PEAR) **GEMMCDS9160(2)** De Luca Edition, Vol.2 (pt 2)
(PEAR) **GEMMCDS9452** The Emperor Tibbett
(PEAR) **GEMMCDS9926(2)** Covent Garden on Record—Vol.4 (pt 2)
(PEAR) **GEMMCD9306** Ezio Pinza—Opera Recital
(PEAR) **GEMMCD9316** Beniamino Gigli
(PEAR) **GEMMCD9367** Gigli—Arias and Duets
(PREI) **89012** Giacomo Lauri-Volpi (1894-1979)
(PREI) **89050** Ezio Pinza (1892-1957)
(PREI) **89062** Giovanni Martinelli (1885-1969)
(PREI) **89064** Pasquale Amato (1878-1942)
(PREI) **89073** Giuseppe de Luca (1876-1950) - II
(RCA) **GD87808** Lawrence Tibbett sings Opera Arias

(RCA) **GD87810** Rosa Ponselle - Opera & Song Recital
(RCA) **GD87811** Beniamino Gigli—Operatic Arias
(RCA) **09026 61245-2** Ezio Pinza - Recital
(RCA) **09026 61580-2(2)** RCA/Met 100 Singers, 100 Years (pt 2)
cond C. SODERO
(ALTN) **CDAN3** Hjördis Schymberg
cond F. STIEDRY
Wagner: Lohengrin (Cpte)
(MEMO) **HR4235/6** Great Voices-Renata Tebaldi
cond G. SZELL
Mussorgsky: Boris Godunov (exc)
cond B. WALTER
Mozart: Don Giovanni (Cpte)
(CBS) **CD45693** Portrait—Ezio Pinza
(MMOI) **CDMOIR404** Ezio Pinza—Recital
(PEAR) **GEMMCDS9926(2)** Covent Garden on Record—Vol.4 (pt 2)
(SONY) **SM3K47211** Mozart Legendary Interpretations—Opera and Concert Arias
cond R. WEIKERT
Rossini: Barbiere di Siviglia (Cpte)
(DECC) **071 142-1DH (DECC)** Essential Opera

NEW YORK NATIONAL SYMPHONY ORCHESTRA
cond W. DAMROSCH
(SCHW) **311162** World Famous Conductors from Silesia

NEW YORK OPERA ORCHESTRA
cond E. QUELER
Janáček: Jenufa (Cpte)
Massenet: Cid (Cpte)
Puccini: Edgar (Cpte)
Verdi: Aroldo (Cpte)
(SONY) **SM48155** Carreras and Caballe sing Souvenirs
(SONY) **MDK47176** Favourite Arias by the World's Favourite Tenors
(SONY) **SMK48155** Carreras and Caballe sing Souvenirs

NEW YORK ORATORIO SOCIETY
cond E. QUELER
Verdi: Aroldo (Cpte)

NEW YORK PHILHARMONIC ORCHESTRA
cond J. BARBIROLLI
(DUTT) **CDSJB1001** Barbirolli in New York - 1938 Wagner Concert
cond L. BERNSTEIN
Beethoven: Fidelio (exc)
Bizet: Carmen Suites (exc)
(SONY) **SBK39438** Wagner—Greatest Hits
(SONY) **SBK39448** Bernstein—Greatest Hits
(SONY) **SFK47279** Passport to Spain
(SONY) **SMK47521** Beethoven—Orchestral Works
(SONY) **SMK47525** Berlioz—Orchestral Works
(SONY) **SMK47529** Bernstein conducts Bernstein
(SONY) **SMK47532** Bizet/Offenbach/Suppé—Orchestral Works
(SONY) **SMK47600** Ballet Music from Famous Operas
(SONY) **SMK47601** Opera Overtures
(SONY) **SMK47606** Rossini/Suppé—Overtures
(SONY) **SMK47607** Russian Orchestral Pieces
(SONY) **SMK47609** Schubert/Schumann—Orchestral Works
(SONY) **SMK47625** R. Strauss—Orchestral Works
(SONY) **SMK47636** Tchaikovsky—Ballet Music
(SONY) **SMK47643** Wagner—Opera Orchestral Music
(SONY) **SMK47644** Wagner—Orchestral and Vocal Works
(SONY) **SM3K47154** Bernstein—Theatre Works Volume 1
cond P. BOULEZ
(SONY) **SMK64108** Wagner—Orchestral Music
(SONY) **SM3K64103** Berlioz—Orchestral and Vocal Works
cond A. KOSTELANETZ
(SONY) **SBK39448** Bernstein—Greatest Hits
(SONY) **SFK47279** Passport to Spain
cond L. MAGIERA
(DECC) **444 450-2DH** Pavarotti in Central Park
cond K. MASUR
Weill: Sieben Todsünden (Cpte)
(TELD) **4509-94571-2** Tchaikovsky—Famous Waltzes
cond Z. MEHTA
(SONY) **SM48155** Carreras and Caballe sing Souvenirs
(SONY) **MDK47176** Favourite Arias by the World's Favourite Tenors
(SONY) **SMK48155** Carreras and Caballe sing Souvenirs
(TELD) **4509-96231-2** Gardening Classics
(TELD) **4509-97444-2** Gershwin—Orchestral Works
cond W. MENGELBERG
(PEAR) **GEMMCDS9922** New York Philharmonic - 150th Anniversary
(SYMP) **SYMCD1078** Willem Mengelberg conducts
cond F. REINER
Mussorgsky: Boris Godunov (exc)
cond G. SINOPOLI
(DG) **419 169-2GH** Wagner—Orchestral Works
cond J. STRANSKY
(PEAR) **GEMMCDS9922** New York Philharmonic - 150th Anniversary
cond A. TOSCANINI
(RCA) **GD60318** Toscanini Collection, Vol.66
cond B. WALTER
(CBS) **CD47682** Songs and Waltzes from Vienna

NEW YORK PHILHARMONIC SYMPHONY ORCHESTRA
cond W. MENGELBERG
(ARHI) **AD105/6** Willem Mengelberg conducts
(PEAR) **GEMMCD9474** Mengelberg conducts the NYPSO
cond F. REINER
(PEAR) **GEMMCDS9922** New York Philharmonic - 150th Anniversary
cond A. RODZINSKI
(EMI) **CHS7 69741-2(1)** Record of Singing, Vol.4—Anglo-American School (pt 1)
cond A. TOSCANINI
(PEAR) **GEMMCDS9373** Toscanini & the NYPSO—1926-36
(PEAR) **GEMMCDS9922** New York Philharmonic - 150th Anniversary
(RCA) **GD60318** Toscanini Collection, Vol.66

NEW YORK SCHOLA CANTORUM
cond E. QUELER
Janáček: Jenufa (Cpte)
Puccini: Edgar (Cpte)

NEW YORK STADIUM SYMPHONY ORCHESTRA
cond L. STOKOWSKI
(EVER) **EVC9004** R. Strauss/Canning—Orchestral Works

NEW YORK STUDIO ORCHESTRA
cond J. TUNICK
(EMI) **CDC7 54266-2** Domingo and Perlman—Together

NEW ZEALAND SYMPHONY ORCHESTRA
cond M. FREDMAN
(NAXO) **8 553001** Delius—Orchestral Works
cond P. GAMBA
(KIWI) **CDTRL075** Malvina Major—Opera Recital
cond D. JOHANOS
(NAXO) **8 553027** Bizet—Orchestral Works
cond B. LAW
(KIWI) **CDSLD-82** Southern Voices—NZ International Opera Singers
cond J. MATHESON
(KIWI) **CDSLD-82** Southern Voices—NZ International Opera Singers
(KIWI) **CDTRL075** Malvina Major—Opera Recital
cond J-Y. OSSONCE
(NAXO) **8 553124** Massenet—Heródiade Orchestral Suites Nos 1-3
cond C. ROLLER
(KIWI) **CDSLD-82** Southern Voices—NZ International Opera Singers
cond A. SCHENCK
(KOCH) **37005-2** Menotti/Barber—Orchestral Works
cond H. WALLBERG
(DELO) **DE3108** Alessandra Marc—Opera Recital
(ODE) **CDMANU1317** Wagner—Opera Excerpts

NEWAY, Patricia (sop)
(VANG) **08.4016.71** Music of Samuel Barber

(THE) NEWBERRY CONSORT
cond M. SPRINGFELS
(HARM) **HMU90 7022** Spanish Songs & Theatre Music

NEWMAN, Alfred (cond)
see Hollywood Bowl SO
Twentieth Cent Fox SO

NEWMAN, Arthur (bar)
Verdi: Otello (Cpte), Traviata (Cpte)

NEWMAN, Daisy (sop)
(IMP) **PCDS26** Music of the World—From the New World
(IMP) **PCD1057** Crazy for Gershwin

NEWMAN, Henry (bass)
M. Berkeley: Baa Baa Black Sheep (Cpte)
Vaughan Williams: Hugh the Drover (Cpte)
Verdi: Traviata (Cpte)

NEWMAN, Paul (narr)
(MUSM) **67078-2** Stravinsky The Composer - Volume 1

NEWMAN, Yvonne (mez)
Sullivan: Iolanthe (Cpte), Patience (Cpte)

NEWSOME, Roy (cond)
see Besses o' the Barn Band
Black Dyke Mills Band
Sun Life Band

NEZHDANOVA, Antonina (sop)
(ARLE) **ARL23/5** Rimsky-Korsakov—Sadko
(NIMB) **NI7865** Great Singers at the Mariinsky Theatre
(PEAR) **GEMMCDS9007/9(1)** Singers of Imperial Russia, Vol.4 (pt 1)
(PEAR) **GEMMCDS9007/9(2)** Singers of Imperial Russia, Vol.4 (pt 2)

NGUYEN-HUU, Ingo (sngr)
Schreker: Gezeichneten (Cpte)

NHK (TOKYO) CHAMBER SOLOISTS
cond R. PATERNOSTRO
(CAPR) **10 348** Mozart Gala—Suntory Hall, Tokyo
(CAPR) **10 810** Mozart—Opera Highlights

NHK (TOKYO) ITALIAN OPERA CHORUS
cond O. DE FABRITIIS
Donizetti: Favorita (Cpte)

NHK (TOKYO) SYMPHONY CHORUS
cond A. EREDE
Verdi: Otello (Cpte)
(MEMO) **HR4376/7** Tito Gobbi—Opera Arias

NHK (TOKYO) SYMPHONY ORCHESTRA
cond A. EREDE
Verdi: Otello (Cpte)
(MEMO) **HR4376/7** Tito Gobbi—Opera Arias
cond O. DE FABRITIIS
Donizetti: Favorita (Cpte)
(MEMO) **HR4300/1** Great Voices—Sesto Bruscantini

NICE BAROQUE ENSEMBLE
cond G. BEZZINA
Vivaldi: Dorilla in Tempe (Cpte)
cond G. SCHMIDT-GADEN
Mozart: Apollo et Hyacinthus (Cpte)

NICE OPERA CHORUS
cond G. BEZZINA
Vivaldi: Dorilla in Tempe (Cpte)
cond J. CAREWE
Debussy: Pelléas et Mélisande (Cpte)

NICE PHILHARMONIC ORCHESTRA
cond J. CAREWE
Debussy: Pelléas et Mélisande (Cpte)
cond K. REDEL
(FORL) **UCD16584** Mozart Orchestral Works

NICHITEANU, Liliana (mez)
Mussorgsky: Boris Godunov (Cpte)

NICHOL, Harry (ten)
(OPRA) **ORCH103** Italian Opera—1810-20

NICHOLL, Harry (ten)
(CHAN) **CHAN8865** Rossini: Opera Arias

NICHOLLS, Christopher (cond)
see orch

NICHOLS, Mary (mez)
Monteverdi: Orfeo (Cpte)

NICHOLSON, Pamela (pf)
(ASV) **CDDCA698** Violin Virtuoso
(ASV) **CDQS6114** The Four Seasons, Volume 2 - Summer
(ASV) **CDQS6126** Romeo and Juliet

NICHOLSON, Paul (hpd/org)
(VIRG) **VC7 59324-2** Purcell—O Solitude - Songs and Airs

NICK, Edmund (cond)
see Berlin St Op Orch

NICKELL-LEAN, Elizabeth (contr)
Sullivan: Mikado (Cpte)
(MMOI) **CDMOIR413** The Very Best of Gilbert & Sullivan

NICOLAI, Claudio (bar)
Hindemith: Neues vom Tage (Cpte)
J. Strauss II: Fledermaus (exc)
Künneke: Vetter aus Dingsda (exc)
Mozart: Così fan tutte (Cpte), Zauberflöte (Cpte)
Orff: Kluge (Cpte)
Weber: Freischütz (Cpte)
(RCA) **74321 24790-2** Carl Orff 100 Years Edition

NICOLAI, Elena (mez)
Verdi: Don Carlo (Cpte), Forza del destino (Cpte)

NICOLAI, Theodor (bass)
Humperdinck: Königskinder (Cpte)
Smetana: Bartered Bride (Cpte)

NICOLESCO, Mariana (sop)
Bellini: Beatrice di Tenda (Cpte)
Donizetti: Maria di Rohan (Cpte)
Mozart: Nozze di Figaro (exc)
Puccini: Rondine (Cpte)

NICOLL, Harry (ten)
Lehár: Graf von Luxemburg (exc)
Vaughan Williams: Hugh the Drover (Cpte)

NIEL, H. (ten)
Massenet: Werther (Cpte)

NIELSEN, Alice (sngr)
(PEAR) **GEMMCDS9050/2(1)** Music from the New York Stage, Vol. 1 (part 1)

NIELSEN, Alice (sop)
(PEAR) **GEMMCDS9074(1)** Giovanni Zenatello, Vol.2 (pt 1)
(SYMP) **SYMCD1168** The Harold Wayne Collection, Vol.19

NIELSEN, Flora (mez)
(EMI) **CMS7 64727-2** Britten—Opera excerpts and Folksongs

NIELSEN, Inge (sop)
Heise: Drot og Marsk (Cpte)
Mozart: Oca del Cairo (Cpte)
Wagner: Parsifal (Cpte)
Zemlinsky: Geburtstag der Infantin (Cpte)
(ADES) **14122-2** Music of our Time

NIEMIROWICZ, Dariusz (bass)
Puccini: Bohème (Cpte)
Rossini: Signor Bruschino (Cpte)
Weill: Kuhhandel (exc)

NIENSTEDT, Gerd (bass)
Berg: Lulu (Cpte)
Pfitzner: Palestrina (Cpte)

Wagner: Meistersinger (Cpte), Parsifal (Cpte), Rheingold (Cpte), Tannhäuser (Cpte), Tristan und Isolde (Cpte), Walküre (exc)
(PHIL) **434 420-2PM32(1)** Richard Wagner Edition (Pt.1)
(PHIL) **446 057-2PB14** Wagner—The Ring Cycle - Bayreuth Festival 1967

NIESSNER, Anton (bar)
Lehár: Lustige Witwe (Cpte)
(KOCH) **399 225** Operetta Highlights 3

NIGL, Georg (treb)
(PHIL) **422 527-2PME** The Complete Mozart Edition Vol 27

NIGOGHOSSIAN, Sonia (mez)
Bellini: Bianca e Fernando (Cpte)
Offenbach: Périchole (Cpte)

NIKITIN, Kirill (sngr)
Rimsky-Korsakov: Mlada (Cpte)

NIKITINA, Galina (mez)
(PEAR) **GEMMCDS9007/9(2)** Singers of Imperial Russia, Vol.4 (pt 2)
(PEAR) **GEMMCDS9111(2)** Singers of Imperial Russia, Vol.5 (pt 2)

NIKITINA, Larissa (mez)
Rimsky-Korsakov: Tale of Tsar Saltan (Cpte)

NIKODEM, Zdzisław (ten)
Szymanowski: King Roger (Cpte)

NIKOLAIDI, Elena (mez)
Verdi: Otello (Cpte)
(PREI) **90249** Mozart in tempore belli
(SCHW) **314562** Vienna State Opera Live, Vol.6
(SCHW) **314572** Vienna State Opera Live, Vol.7
(SCHW) **314582** Vienna State Opera Live, Vol.8
(SCHW) **314602** Vienna State Opera Live, Vol.10
(SCHW) **314632** Vienna State Opera Live, Vol.13
(SCHW) **314652** Vienna State Opera Live, Vol.15
(SCHW) **314712** Vienna State Opera Live, Vol.21
(SCHW) **314742** Vienna State Opera Live, Vol.24

NIKOLAU, Stepan (bass)
(ARLE) **ARL23/5** Rimsky-Korsakov—Sadko

NIKOLIČ, Miomir (bass)
Verdi: Macbeth (Cpte)
Wagner: Meistersinger (Cpte)

NIKOLOV, Bojidar (ten)
Janáček: From the House of the Dead (Cpte)

NIKOLOV, Nikola (ten)
(FORL) **UCD16741** Bulgarian Voices, Vol. 1

NIKOLOVA, Milkana (mez)
R. Strauss: Elektra (Cpte)
(FORL) **UCD16742** Bulgarian Voices, Vol. 2

NIKOLSKY, Gleb (bass)
Mussorgsky: Boris Godunov (Cpte)
Rimsky-Korsakov: Mlada (Cpte)
Tchaikovsky: Maid of Orleans (Cpte)

NILON, Paul (ten)
Mayr: Medea (Cpte)
Mercadante: Orazi e Curiazi (Cpte)
(OPRA) **ORCH103** Italian Opera—1810-20
(OPRA) **ORCH104** A Hundred Years of Italian Opera: 1820-1830

NILSON, Göran W. (cond)
see Örebro CO

NILSSON, Birgit (sop)
J. Strauss II: Fledermaus (Cpte)
Mozart: Don Giovanni (Cpte)
Puccini: Fanciulla del West (Cpte), Tosca (Cpte), Turandot (Cpte)
R. Strauss: Elektra (Cpte), Frau ohne Schatten (Cpte), Salome (Cpte)
Verdi: Aida (Cpte)
Wagner: Götterdämmerung (Cpte), Siegfried (Cpte), Tristan und Isolde (exc), Walküre (Cpte)
Weber: Oberon (Cpte)
(DECC) **414 100-2DM15** Wagner: Der Ring des Nibelungen
(DECC) **421 313-2DA** Wagner: Der Ring des Nibelungen - Great Scenes
(DECC) **433 068-2DWO** Your Hundred Best Opera Tunes V
(DECC) **436 317-2DA** Puccini—Famous Arias
(DECC) **436 461-2DM** Ten Top Sopranos
(DECC) **440 069-2DWO** The World of Wagner
(EMI) **CMS5 65212-2** Wagner—Les introuvables du Ring
(EMI) **CMS7 64008-2(1)** Wagner Singing on Record (pt 1)
(MEMO) **HR4275/6** Birgit Nilsson—Public Performances 1954-1969
(PHIL) **434 420-2PM32(2)** Richard Wagner Edition (pt 2)
(PHIL) **446 057-2PB14** Wagner—The Ring Cycle - Bayreuth Festival 1967
(RCA) **09026 61580-2(7)** RCA/Met 100 Singers, 100 Years (pt 7)
(RCA) **09026 62689-2** The Voices of Living Stereo, Volume 1

NILSSON, Carrie (mez)
Verdi: Rigoletto (Cpte)

NILSSON, Gunvor (mez)
Henze: English Cat (Cpte)

NILSSON, Raymond (ten)
Britten: Peter Grimes (Cpte)

NILSSON, Sven (bass)
Wagner: Tristan und Isolde (Cpte)
(PEAR) **GEMMCDS9121** Wagner—Die Meistersinger, Act 3, etc

NIMSGERN, Siegmund (bass-bar)
Beethoven: Fidelio (Cpte)
Braunfels: Verkündigung (Cpte)
Flotow: Martha (Cpte)
Gluck: Alceste (1776) (Cpte)
Hindemith: Cardillac (Cpte)
Humperdinck: Hänsel und Gretel (Cpte)
Mozart: Nozze di Figaro (Cpte)
Offenbach: Contes d'Hoffmann (Cpte)
Pergolesi: Serva Padrona
Puccini: Turandot (Cpte)
Rossini: Mosè in Egitto (Cpte)
Schreker: Ferne Klang (Cpte)
Stravinsky: Oedipus rex (Cpte)
Wagner: Götterdämmerung (Cpte), Lohengrin (exc), Parsifal (Cpte), Rheingold (Cpte), Siegfried (Cpte)
(CFP) **CD-CFP4656** Herbert von Karajan conducts Opera
(EURO) **GD69003** Wagner—Der Ring des Nibelungen
(EURO) **GD69043** Puccini: Il Trittico
(SONY) **SMK48464** Boulez conducts Schoenberg - Volume 2

NINNO, Antonio di (ten)
(DECC) **411 665-2DM3** Puccini: Il trittico

NIQUET, Hervé (cond)
see Concert Spirituel Orch

NIROUËT, Jean (alto)
Cavalli: Xerse (Cpte)
Handel: Alessandro (Cpte)
Vivaldi: Dorilla in Tempe (Cpte)

NISHIZAKI, Takako (vn)
(NAXO) **8 550306** Violin Miniatures

NISSEN, Hanns Heinz (bass)
Humperdinck: Hänsel und Gretel (Cpte)
(PREI) **90168** Wagner—Die Meistersinger, Act 2, etc

NISSEN, Hans Hermann (bass)
(EMI) **CMS7 64008-2(1)** Wagner Singing on Record (pt 1)
(EMI) **CMS7 64008-2(2)** Wagner Singing on Record (pt 2)
(PEAR) **GEMMCDS9121** Wagner—Die Meistersinger, Act 3, etc
(PREI) **89090** Hans Hermann Nissen (1893-1980)

NITRANOVÁ, Marta (mez)
(OPUS) **9156 1824** Dvorský sings Operatic Arias

NITSCHE, Horst (bass)
Mozart: Zauberflöte (Cpte)
R. Strauss: Rosenkavalier (Cpte)
Verdi: Don Carlo (Cpte), Trovatore (Cpte)

NIVETTE, Juste (bass)
(PEAR) **GEMMCDS9924(2)** Covent Garden on Record, Vol.2 (pt 2)

NIXON, Leigh (ten)
Purcell: King Arthur, Z628 (Cpte)
(HARM) **HMX290 1528/33(2)** A Purcell Companion (pt 2)

NIXON, Marnie (sngr)
Bernstein: West Side Story (Cpte)

NIZINENKO, Nikolai (bass)
Rimsky-Korsakov: Tsar's Bride (Cpte)
Shostakovich: Gamblers (Cpte)

NOACK, Erwin (sngr)
Krenek: Jonny spielt auf (Cpte)

NOBILE, Alfredo (ten)
Massenet: Don Quichotte (Cpte)

NOBLE, Anthony (hpd)
(HERA) **HAVPCD181** The Age of Elegance

NOBLE, Dennis (bar)
(DUTT) **CDLX7012** The Incomparable Heddle Nash
(PEAR) **GEMMCDS9925(1)** Covent Garden on Record—Vol.3 (pt 1)
(PEAR) **GEMMCD9175** Heddle Nash - Serenade
(PEAR) **GEMMCD9319** Heddle Nash sings Opera Arias & Songs

NOBLE, John (bar)
Britten: Albert Herring (Cpte)
G. Charpentier: Louise (Cpte)
Massenet: Cendrillon (Cpte)
Meyerbeer: Huguenots (Cpte)
Puccini: Bohème (Cpte)
Schoenberg: Moses und Aron (Cpte)
Shostakovich: Lady Macbeth of Mtsensk (Cpte)
Vaughan Williams: Pilgrim's Progress (Cpte)
Verdi: Corsaro (Cpte), Don Carlo (Cpte), Macbeth (Cpte)

NOCENTINI, Maria Costanza (sop)
Rossini: Pietra del paragone (Cpte)

NÖCKER, Hans Günter (bass-bar)
Egk: Verlobung in San Domingo (Cpte)
Handel: Giulio Cesare (Cpte)
Trojahn: Enrico (Cpte)
Wagner: Götterdämmerung (Cpte)
(ACAN) **43 267** Fritz Wunderlich sings Opera Arias

(EMI) **LDX9 91275-1(EMI)** Sawallisch conducts Wagner's Ring
(EURO) **GD69003** Wagner—Der Ring des Nibelungen

NOE, Marcel (bar)
(CLAR) **CDGSE78-50-26** Wagner: Tristan und Isolde excerpts

NOGUERA, Louis (bass)
Bizet: Ivan IV (exc), Pêcheurs de Perles (Cpte)
Messager: Basoche (Cpte)
(EMI) **CZS5 68113-2** Vive Offenbach!
(EMI) **CZS7 67872-2** Lehár—Operettas (highlights in French)

NOLAN, David (vn)
(IMP) **PCD1075** Opera Intermezzi; Bizet—Carmen Suites Nos 1 & 2

NOLAN, Joanna (sop)
(CNTI) **CCD1054** Delius—Complete partsongs

NOLI, Alberto (bass)
Puccini: Bohème (Cpte)
Rossini: Guillaume Tell (Cpte)

NOLI, Rosetta (sop)
Leoncavallo: Pagliacci (Cpte)

NOLTE, Raimund (bass)
Telemann: Don Quichotte (Cpte)

NONI, Alda (sop)
Mozart: Così fan tutte (exc)
R. Strauss: Ariadne auf Naxos (Cpte)
Rossini: Cenerentola (Cpte)
Verdi: Falstaff (Cpte)
(EMI) **CHS7 69741-2(7)** Record of Singing, Vol.4—Italian School
(SCHW) **314582** Vienna State Opera Live, Vol.8
(SCHW) **314712** Vienna State Opera Live, Vol.21

NOORMAN, Jantina (mez)
Purcell: Dido (Cpte)

NOORT, Henk (ten)
(PREI) **90168** Wagner—Die Meistersinger, Act 2, etc

NORBERG-SCHULZ, Elizabeth (sop)
Mozart: Zauberflöte (Cpte)
Pergolesi: Frate 'nnamorato (Cpte)
R. Strauss: Frau ohne Schatten (Cpte)

NORBERT, Karl (bass)
(SCHW) **314542** Vienna State Opera Live, Vol.4

NØRBY, Einar (bar)
Nielsen: Maskarade (Cpte)

NORDICA, Lillian (sop)
(NIMB) **NI7840/1** The Era of Adelina Patti

NORDIN, Birgit (sop)
Mozart: Don Giovanni (Cpte)
Verdi: Rigoletto (Cpte)

NORDMO-LØVBERG, Aase (sop)
(BLUE) **ABCD028** Jussi Björling live at the Stockholm Opera

NORENA, Eidé (sop)
(IRCC) **IRCC-CD800** Souvenirs from Meyerbeer Operas
(NIMB) **NI7802** Divas 1906-1935
(PREI) **89041** Eidé Norena (1884-1968)

NORMAN, Jessye (sop)
Beethoven: Fidelio (exc)
Bizet: Carmen (exc)
Fauré: Pénélope (Cpte)
Gluck: Alceste (1776) (Cpte)
Haydn: Armida (Cpte)
Mascagni: Cavalleria Rusticana (Cpte)
Meyerbeer: Africaine (Cpte)
Mozart: Finta Giardiniera (Cpte), Nozze di Figaro (Cpte)
Offenbach: Belle Hélène (Cpte), Contes d'Hoffmann (exc)
Purcell: Dido (Cpte)
R. Strauss: Ariadne auf Naxos (Cpte), Salome (Cpte)
Schoenberg: Erwartung (Cpte)
Stravinsky: Oedipus rex (Cpte)
Verdi: Corsaro (Cpte)
Wagner: Lohengrin (Cpte), Parsifal (Cpte), Tristan und Isolde (exc), Walküre (Cpte)
(DECC) **436 461-2DM** Ten Top Sopranos
(DECC) **440 410-2DM** Plácido Domingo
(DG) **423 613-2GH** Wagner—Opera excerpts
(DG) **437 825-2GH** Wagner—Der Ring des Nibelungen - Highlights
(DG) **439 251-2GY** The Leonard Bernstein Album
(DG) **445 354-2GX14** Wagner—Der Ring des Nibelungen
(DG) **439 153-4GMA** Mad about Sopranos
(DG) **072 422-3GH7** Levine conducts Wagner's Ring
(DG) **439 251-5GY** The Leonard Bernstein Album
(EMI) **CDC5 55095-2** Prima Diva
(EMI) **CDC7 49759-2** Wagner: Opera Scenes and Arias
(EMI) **CDM5 65576-2** Jessye Norman
(EMI) **CDM7 69256-2** L'incomparable Jessye Norman
(EMI) **CZS5 68113-2** Vive Offenbach!
(EURO) **GD69003** Wagner—Der Ring des Nibelungen
(MEMO) **HR4271** Jessye Norman—Florence Recital, 1971
(PHIL) **422 048-2PH** Jessye Norman—Song Recital

(PHIL) **422 235-2PH** Jessye Norman—European Tour, 1987
(PHIL) **422 401-2PH** Jessye Norman - Lucky To Be Me
(RCA) **RD60739** Tchaikovsky Gala in Leningrad
(RCA) **09026 61440-2** Opera's Greatest Moments
(RCA) **09026 60739-5** Tchaikovsky Gala in Leningrad

NORMAND, Antoine (ten)
Offenbach: Brigands (Cpte)

NORMANN, Franz (bass)
Mozart: Nozze di Figaro (Cpte)
(SCHW) **314692** Vienna State Opera Live, Vol.19
(SCHW) **314712** Vienna State Opera Live, Vol.21
(SCHW) **314722** Vienna State Opera Live, Vol.22

NORRICK, Cécilia (sngr)
(ARIO) **ARN68195** Milhaud—Sonatas; Trois Operas-Minute

NORRINGTON, Roger (cond)
see LCP
St Luke's Orch

NORRIS, Harry (cond)
see orch
SO

NORSKA, Éva (sop)
(REM) **REM11036** Chailley—Songs

NORTH, Nigel (lte)
(ARCA) **A02** Purcell—Ayres and Songs from Orpheus Britannicus
(LINN) **CKD005** Udite Amanti—17th Century Italian Love Songs

NORTH, Nigel (lte/gtr)
(VIRG) **VC7 59324-2** Purcell—O Solitude - Songs and Airs

NORTH GERMAN RADIO CHORUS
cond G. ALBRECHT
Hindemith: Mathis der Maler (Cpte)
cond H. SCHMIDT-ISSERSTEDT
Mozart: Finta Giardiniera (Cpte)

NORTH GERMAN RADIO SYMPHONY ORCHESTRA
(MEMO) **HR4293/4** The very best of Maria Callas
cond J.E. GARDINER
(DG) **439 894-2GH** Speak Low - Songs by Kurt Weill
cond N. RESCIGNO
(MEMO) **HR4293/4** The very best of Maria Callas
cond H. SCHMIDT-ISSERSTEDT
Mozart: Finta Giardiniera (Cpte)
(ACAN) **43 268** Peter Anders sings German Opera Arias
cond G. WAND
Beethoven: Leonore (exc)
(RCA) **RD60827** Modern Pictures - Günter Wand

NORTHERN SINFONIA
cond R. HICKOX
Walton: Bear (Cpte)
(CHAN) **CHAN9354** R Strauss/Wagner—Orchestral and Vocal Works
(CHAN) **CHAN9392** Vaughan Williams—Riders to the Sea etc.
(EMI) **CDM5 65067-2** Delius—Orchestral Miniatures

NORTH-WEST GERMAN PHILHARMONIC ORCHESTRA
cond M. YUROVSKY
Shostakovich: Gamblers (Cpte)

NORTH-WEST GERMAN RADIO CHORUS
cond W. BRÜCKNER-RÜGGEBERG
Weill: Mahagonny (Cpte)
cond W. SCHÜCHTER
Wagner: Lohengrin (Cpte)

NORTH-WEST GERMAN RADIO ORCHESTRA
cond W. BRÜCKNER-RÜGGEBERG
Weill: Mahagonny (Cpte)

NORTON, Angela (sngr)
Schuman: Question of Taste (Cpte)

NORTSOV, Panteleimon (bar)
Tchaikovsky: Eugene Onegin (Cpte)
(DANT) **LYS013/5** Tchaikovsky—The Queen of Spades

ORUP, Bent (bar)
Heise: Drot og Marsk (Cpte)

NORWEGIAN NATIONAL OPERA CHORUS
cond P. Å. ANDERSSON
Braein: Anne Pedersdotter (Cpte)

NORWEGIAN NATIONAL OPERA ORCHESTRA
cond P. Å. ANDERSSON
Braein: Anne Pedersdotter (Cpte)

NORWEGIAN RADIO ORCHESTRA
cond Ø. FJELDSTAD
(LOND) **440 495-2LM** Kirsten Flagstad Edition, Vol. 5

OSOTTI, Angelo (bass)
Mozart: Nozze di Figaro (Cpte)

OSSEK, Carola (sop)
Beethoven: Fidelio (Cpte)

OTARE, Karen (sop)
Falla: Vida breve (Cpte)

OTARISTEFANI, Virginia de (sop)
Puccini: Rondine (Cpte)

NOTÉ, Jean (bar)
(SYMP) **SYMCD1089** Historic Baritones of the French School

NOTO, Giuseppe (bass)
(CONI) **CDHD227** Gigli in Opera and Song
(PEAR) **GEMMCDS9074(2)** Giovanni Zenatello, Vol.2 (pt 2)

NOTTI, Raymonde (sop)
Bizet: Carmen (Cpte)

NOVA, Ettore (bass)
Salieri: Axur (Cpte)

NOVA SCOTIA SYMPHONY ORCHESTRA
cond G. TINTNER
(CBC) **SMCD5134** Delius—Intermezzi & Pieces for Small Orchestra

NOVAES, Guiomar (pf)
(VOX) **CDX2 5501** Novaes/Klemperer

NOVÁK, Richard (bass)
Dvořák: Kate and the Devil (Cpte), Rusalka (Cpte)
Janáček: Cunning Little Vixen (Cpte), Excursions of Mr Brouček (Cpte), Fate (Cpte), From the House of the Dead (Cpte)
Martinů: Alexandre Bis (Cpte), Ariane (Cpte), Comedy on the Bridge (Cpte)
Puccini: Bohème (Cpte)
Smetana: Bartered Bride (Cpte)
(DECC) **430 375-2DH2** Janáček—Operatic and Orchestral Works

NOVÁKOVÁ, Alena (sop)
Janáček: Šárka (Cpte)

NOVELLI, Francesco (bar)
Rossini: Barbiere di Siviglia (exc)

NOVIKOVA, Claudia (mez)
(EMI) **CHS7 69741-2(6)** Record of Singing, Vol.4—Russian & Slavonic Schools

NOVIKOVA, Tatiana (sop)
Borodin: Prince Igor (Cpte)

NOVOTNÁ, Jarmila (sop)
Mozart: Don Giovanni (Cpte)
(EMI) **CDC7 54838-2** Franz Lehár
(ORFE) **C394101B** Great Mozart Singers Series, Vol. 1
(PEAR) **GEMMCD9310** Franz Lehár conducts Richard Tauber
(PREI) **90150** Lehár conducts Lehár
(RCA) **09026 61580-2(5)** RCA/Met 100 Singers, 100 Years (pt 5)
(SCHW) **314512** Vienna State Opera Live, Vol.1
(SUPR) **11 1491-2** Jarmila Novotna sings Czech Songs and Arias

NOVOTNÝ, Břetislav (cond)
see Prague CO

NOVOYENIN, M. (ten)
(DANT) **LYS013/5** Tchaikovsky—The Queen of Spades

NOWICKA, Barbara (mez)
Gluck: Corona (Cpte)

NOWSKI, Angelika (mez)
Gluck: Iphigénie en Tauride (Cpte)

NUCCI, Leo (bar)
Cilea: Adriana Lecouvreur (Cpte)
Donizetti: Don Pasquale (Cpte), Elisir d'amore (Cpte), Maria di Rudenz (Cpte)
Giordano: Andrea Chénier (Cpte)
Mozart: Idomeneo (Cpte)
Puccini: Rondine (Cpte), Tosca (exc), Villi (Cpte)
Rossini: Barbiere di Siviglia (Cpte), Turco in Italia (Cpte), Viaggio a Reims (Cpte)
Verdi: Aida (Cpte), Ballo in maschera (Cpte), Don Carlos (Cpte), Falstaff (Cpte), Macbeth (Cpte), Otello (Cpte), Rigoletto (exc), Simon Boccanegra (Cpte), Traviata (Cpte), Trovatore (Cpte), Vespri Siciliani (Cpte)
(CAST) **CASH5052** Verdi Operatic Favourites
(DECC) **433 822-2DH** Essential Opera
(DECC) **436 133-2DWO** World of Rossini
(DECC) **436 261-2DHO3** Puccini—Il Trittico
(DECC) **436 464-2DM** Ten Top Baritones & Basses
(DECC) **436 472-2DM** Great Opera Arias
(DECC) **443 380-2DM** Ten Top Baritones & Basses 2
(DECC) **071 142-1DH (DECC)** Essential Opera
(DG) **072 428-1GH2(DG)** The Metropolitan Opera Gala

NUREMBERG OPERA CHORUS
cond W. FURTWÄNGLER
Wagner: Meistersinger (exc)

NUREMBERG SYMPHONY ORCHESTRA
cond K. SEIBEL
(COLO) **COL34 9004** Manfred Schenk sings Wagner
(COLO) **COL34 9007** Mendelssohn: Overtures, Vol.1

NURMELA, Kari (bar)
Leoncavallo: Pagliacci (Cpte)

NUVOLONE, Félix (cond)
see Paris Cons

NYGÅRD, Roald (spkr)
Braein: Anne Pedersdotter (Cpte)

NYHUS, Minna (contr)
Nørgård: Siddhartha (Cpte)

NYIREGYHÁZI BOYS' CHOIR
cond G. PATANÈ
Boito: Mefistofele (Cpte)

NYMAN, Tom (ten)
Bergman: Singing Tree (Cpte)

NYSTROM, Bradley (bar)
Schoenberg: Moses und Aron (Cpte)

OAKMAN, John (ten)
(IMP) **DPCD1015** Karaoke Opera
(IMP) **PCDS23** Music of the World—Italy & Spain—The Latin Quarter
(IMP) **PCD1043** Opera Favourites
(IMP) **TCD1070** Invitation to the Opera

OBATA, Machiko (sop)
Weber: Oberon (Cpte)

OBER, Margarete (contr)
(DANA) **DACOCD313/4** Lauritz Melchior Anthology - Vol. 2
(IRCC) **IRCC-CD810** American Singers, Volume 1
(RCA) **09026 61580-2(2)** RCA/Met 100 Singers, 100 Years (pt 2)

OBERHOLTZER, William (bar)
Vivaldi: Olimpiade (Cpte)

OBRAZTSOVA, Elena (mez)
Cilea: Adriana Lecouvreur (Cpte)
Mascagni: Cavalleria Rusticana (Cpte)
Saint-Saëns: Samson et Dalila (Cpte)
Verdi: Aida (Cpte), Luisa Miller (Cpte), Nabucco (exc), Rigoletto (Cpte), Trovatore (Cpte)
(CFP) **CD-CFP4575** Verdi Arias
(CFP) **CD-CFP4602** Favourite Opera
(IMP) **MCD42** Three Sopranos
(PHIL) **442 602-2PM** 3 x 3 Tenors

O'BRIEN, Vincent (pf)
(BIDD) **LAB022** Fritz Kreisler—Duets with McCormack & Farrar
(PEAR) **GEMMCD9315** Kreisler/McCormack Duets

OBROWSKY, Elfrided (contr)
Schoenberg: Moses und Aron (Cpte)

OBUKHOVA, Nadezhda (mez)
(ARLE) **ARL23/5** Rimsky-Korsakov—Sadko
(DANT) **LYS013/5** Tchaikovsky—The Queen of Spades

OCCIDENTAL COLLEGE CONCERT CHOIR
cond B. WALTER
(CBS) **CD45701** Bruno Walter conducts Wagner Overtures
(SONY) **SM2K64456** Wagner—Orchestral Music
(SONY) **SX10K66246** The Bruno Walter Edition, Volume I

OCHAGAVIA, José (ten)
Shostakovich: Lady Macbeth of Mtsensk (Cpte)

OCHMAN, Wiesław (ten)
Dvořák: Rusalka (exc)
Janáček: Jenufa (Cpte)
Moniuszko: Halka (Cpte)
Mozart: Idomeneo (Cpte)
Prokofiev: War and Peace (Cpte)
R. Strauss: Salome (Cpte)
Szymanowski: King Roger (Cpte)
Tchaikovsky: Queen of Spades (Cpte)

O'CONNOR, Caroline (sop)
Bernstein: West Side Story (Cpte)

O'CONOR, John (pf)
(TELA) **CD80391** Autumn Songs

OCTOPHOROS
Beethoven: Fidelio (exc)

ODENSE SYMPHONY ORCHESTRA
cond O. SCHMIDT
(UNIC) **DKPC9036** Music inspired by Hans Christian Andersen
cond E. SEROV
(KONT) **32117** Rimsky-Korsakov—Opera Suites, Vol.
(KONT) **32157** Nielsen—Orchestral Works
(KONT) **32178** Nielsen—Orchestral Works
(KONT) **32203** Nielsen—Orchestral Works
(UNIC) **DKPCD9132** Kuhlau—Theatre Music

ODEON GRAND ORCHESTRA
cond A. HONEGGER
(MUSI) **MACD-767** Honegger conducts Honegger

ODEON KÜNSTLERORCHESTER
cond E. KORNGOLD
(NIMB) **NI7833** Schöne & Tauber in Operetta
cond F. WEISSMANN
(EMI) **CDH7 69787-2** Richard Tauber sings Operetta Arias

ODEON ORCHESTRA
cond A. PILZ
(SUPR) **11 2136-2(2)** Emmy Destinn—Complete Edition, Discs 3 & 4
(SUPR) **11 2136-2(3)** Emmy Destinn—Complete Edition, Discs 5 to 8

O'DETTE, Paul (lte)
(HARM) **HMU90 7035** Sweeter than Roses - Purcell Songs

ODINIUS, Lothar (ten)
(ORFE) **C186951** Verdi—Heroines, Vol. 1

O'DONNELL, B. Walton (cond)
see BBC Wireless Military Band

O'DONOVAN, Eileen (sop)
Britten: Noye's Fludde (Cpte)
(DECC) **436 990-2DWO** The World of Benjamin Britten

OEGGL, Georg (bar)
Verdi: Don Carlo (exc)

OELKE, Alice (mez)
Berg: Lulu (Cpte), Wozzeck (Cpte)
Suppé: Boccaccio (exc)

OELZE, Christiane (sop)
Humperdinck: Hänsel und Gretel (Cpte)
J. Strauss II: Zigeunerbaron (Cpte)
(DECC) **440 854-2DH** Ullmann—Der Kaiser von Atlantis

OERTEL, Gertrud (sop)
Wagner: Parsifal (Cpte)

OFFENBACH, Jamie J. (bass-bar)
(EMI) **CDC7 54851-2** Gershwin—Blue Monday, etc

OFFERS, Maartje (mez)
Wagner: Götterdämmerung (exc)
(PEAR) **GEMMCDS9137** Wagner—Der Ring des Nibelungen

O'FLYNN, Maureen (sop)
Verdi: Falstaff (Cpte)
(RCA) **09026 61509-2** A Salute to American Music

OGÉAS, Françoise (sop)
Debussy: Pelléas et Mélisande (Cpte)
Hahn: Ciboulette (exc)

OGERMAN, Claus (cond)
see Columbia SO

OGNOVENKO, Vladimir (bass)
Borodin: Prince Igor (Cpte)
Mussorgsky: Boris Godunov (Cpte)
Rimsky-Korsakov: Sadko (Cpte)

O'GRADY, Jenny (sngr)
Bernstein: West Side Story (Cpte)

OGSTON, Bruce (bar)
Puccini: Rondine (Cpte)
Vaughan Williams: Hugh the Drover (Cpte)

(GÖSTA) OHLIN VOCAL ENSEMBLE
cond N. JÄRVI
Prokofiev: Fiery Angel (Cpte)

ÖHRWALL, Anders (cond)
see Drottningholm Baroque Ens

OKADA, Kiyoko (sop)
Rameau: Hippolyte et Aricie (Cpte)

OKAMURA, Takao (bass)
Verdi: Otello (Cpte)

OKAYAMA, Hiroyuki (bass)
Verdi: Traviata (Cpte)

OKE, Alan (bar)
Lehár: Lustige Witwe (exc)
MacMillan: Visitatio Sepulchri (Cpte)
Sullivan: Gondoliers (Cpte)

OKHOTNIKOV, Nikolai (bass)
Mussorgsky: Khovanshchina (Cpte)
Prokofiev: War and Peace (Cpte)

OKLAHOMA CITY AMBASSADORS CHOIR
cond H. DE LA FUENTE
(IMP) **PCD1057** Crazy for Gershwin

OKOLYCHEVA, Elena (contr)
Rimsky-Korsakov: Tsar's Bride (Cpte)

ØLAFIMIHAN, Tinuke (sop)
Bernstein: West Side Story (Cpte)

ØLAND, Bodil (sngr)
Kuhlau: Lulu (Cpte)

OLCZEWSKA, Maria (mez)
(DANA) **DACOCD319/21** The Lauritz Melchior Anthology - Vol.5
(EMI) **CHS7 64487-2** R. Strauss—Der Rosenkavalier & Lieder
(EMI) **CMS7 64008-2(2)** Wagner Singing on Record (pt 2)
(PEAR) **GEMMCDS9137** Wagner—Der Ring des Nibelungen
(PEAR) **GEMMCDS9365** R. Strauss: Der Rosenkavalier (abridged), etc
(PREI) **89069** Josef von Manowarda (1890-1942)

OLDHAM, Derek (ten)
Sullivan: Gondoliers (Cpte), Mikado (Cpte), Patience (Cpte), Pirates of Penzance (Cpte), Sorcerer (Cpte), Trial by Jury (Cpte)
(MMOI) **CDMOIR413** The Very Best of Gilbert & Sullivan

OLEINICHENKO, Galina (sop)
Rimsky-Korsakov: Tale of Tsar Saltan (Cpte)

OLEJNÍČEK, Jiří (ten)
Janáček: Excursions of Mr Brouček (Cpte), Fate (Cpte)

OLIVA, Amalia (sop)
Mascagni: Iris (Cpte)

OLIVER, Alexander (ten)
Britten: Albert Herring (Cpte)
Handel: Ariodante (Cpte)
Janáček: From the House of the Dead (Cpte)
Meyerbeer: Dinorah (Cpte)
Monteverdi: Incoronazione di Poppea (Cpte)
Mozart: Idomeneo (Cpte), Nozze di Figaro (Cpte)
Offenbach: Contes d'Hoffmann (Cpte), Robinson Crusoé (Cpte)
Verdi: Ballo in maschera (Cpte), Corsaro (Cpte), Traviata (exc)
(DECC) **433 908-2DM2** Falla—Orchestral Music
(LOND) **825 126-2** Amadeus - Original Soundtrack
(OPRA) **ORC004** Donizetti—Ne m'oubliez pas; Arias

OLIVERI, Liliana (sop)
Maderna: Satyricon (Cpte)

OLIVERO, Magda (sop)
Alfano: Risurrezione (Cpte)
Giordano: Fedora (Cpte)
Mascagni: Iris (Cpte)
Puccini: Manon Lescaut (Cpte), Turandot (Cpte)
Zandonai: Francesca da Rimini (exc)
(CENT) **CRC2164** Ferruccio Tagliavini—Early Operatic Recordings
(MEMO) **HR4400/1** Great Voices - Ettore Bastianini

OLIVIERI, Dino (cond)
see La Scala Orch
orch
Rome Op Orch

OLIVIERO, Lodovico (ten)
Verdi: Trovatore (Cpte)
(MYTO) **2MCD90317** Verdi—Un Ballo in maschera

OLLENDORFF, Fritz (bass)
Busoni: Arlecchino (Cpte)
Jessel: Schwarzwaldmädel (exc)
R. Strauss: Ariadne auf Naxos (Cpte)
Rossini: Barbiere di Siviglia (Cpte)
Weber: Freischütz (Cpte)

OLLI, Kalevi (bass)
Madetoja: Juha (Cpte)

OLLMANN, Kurt (bar)
Bernstein: Candide (1988) (exc), West Side Story (exc)
Gounod: Roméo et Juliette (Cpte)

OLMEDA, Martine (mez)
Bizet: Carmen (Cpte)
Massenet: Cléopâtre (Cpte)
Mercadante: Giuramento (Cpte)

OLMI, Paolo (cond)
see Catania Teatro Massimo Bellini Orch
Genoa Carlo Felice Th Orch
Monte Carlo PO

OLSEN, Derrik (bar)
Martin: Mystère de la Nativité

OLSEN, Frode (bass)
R. Strauss: Salome (Cpte)
Wagner: Walküre (exc)

OLSEN, Stanford (ten)
Mozart: Entführung (Cpte)
Rossini: Tancredi (Cpte)

OLTRABELLA, Augusta (sop)
(EMI) **CHS7 64864-2(2)** La Scala Edition - Vol.2, 1915-46 (pt 2)

OLVIS, William (ten)
Bernstein: Candide (1956) (exc)
Verdi: Macbeth (Cpte)

O'MARA, Joseph (sngr)
(PEAR) **GEMMCDS9050/2(1)** Music from the New York Stage, Vol. 1 (part 1)

O'MARA, Joseph (ten)
(SYMP) **SYMCD1093** The Harold Wayne Collection, Vol.7

OMBUENA, Vicente (ten)
Franchetti: Cristoforo Colombo (Cpte)
Puccini: Fanciulla del West (Cpte)
(SCHW) **312682** Opera Gala with Young Artists - Volume II

OMMERLÉ, Jeanne (sop)
Mozart: Nozze di Figaro (Cpte)
V. Thomson: Lord Byron (Cpte)

ONCINA, Juan (ten)
Donizetti: Don Pasquale (Cpte)
Rossini: Cenerentola (Cpte), Comte Ory (Cpte)
(EMI) **CDH5 65072-2** Glyndebourne Recorded - 1934-1994

ONDRAČKA, Vít (treb)
Krása: Brundibár (Cpte)

O'NEAL, James (ten)
Schoeck: Venus (Cpte)

ONEGIN, Sigrid (contr)
(PREI) **89027** Sigrid Onegin (1889-1943)

O'NEILL, Dennis (ten)
Boito: Mefistofele (Cpte)
J. Strauss II: Fledermaus (Cpte)
Puccini: Fanciulla del West (Cpte)
Verdi: Macbeth (Cpte)

ONESTI, Giorgio (bass)
Puccini: Bohème (Cpte), Gianni Schicchi (Cpte)

OOSTERKAMP, Wout (bass)
Schreker: Gezeichneten (Cpte)

OOSTWOUD, Roelof (ten)
(SCHW) **312642** Unicef Gala 1991

OPALACH, Jan (bass)
Handel: Imeneo (Cpte)
(EMI) **CDC7 54643-2** Rossini—Bicentenary Gala Concert
(EMI) **LDB491007-1 (EMI)** Rossini Bicentennial Birthday Gala

OPERA ATELIER
cond C. DUTOIT
Falla: Retablo de maese Pedro (Cpte)

OPERA NORTH CHORUS
cond P. DANIEL
M. Berkeley: Baa Baa Black Sheep (Cpte)
(EMI) **CDC7 54785-2** Harry Enfield's Guide to Opera
cond R. HICKOX
Walton: Troilus and Cressida (Cpte)
cond M. TIPPETT
(NIMB) **NI5217** Tippett conducts Tippett

OPERA RESTOR'D
cond P. HOLMAN
Lampe: Pyramus and Thisbe (Cpte)
(HYPE) **CDA66608** Dibdin—Three Operas

OPERA STAGE CHORUS
cond R. HICKOX
Handel: Alcina (Cpte)

OPIE, Alan (bar)
Boughton: Bethlehem (Cpte)
Britten: Albert Herring (Cpte), Death in Venice (Cpte), Gloriana (Cpte), Peter Grimes (Cpte), Rape of Lucretia (Cpte)
Donizetti: Maria Stuarda (Cpte)
Meyerbeer: Huguenots (Cpte)
Offenbach: Christopher Columbus (Cpte), Robinson Crusoé (Cpte)
Rossini: Barbiere di Siviglia (Cpte)
Vaughan Williams: Hugh the Drover (Cpte)
Verdi: Otello (Cpte), Simon Boccanegra (Cpte)
Walton: Bear (Cpte), Troilus and Cressida (Cpte)
Weill: Sieben Todsünden (Cpte)
(HYPE) **CDA66569** Vaughan Williams—Choral Works

OPTHOF, Cornelius (bar)
Janáček: Makropulos Affair (Cpte)
(DECC) **433 706-2DMO3** Bellini—Beatrice di Tenda; Operatic Arias

ORADEA PHILHARMONIC ORCHESTRA
cond R. RÎMBU
(OLYM) **OCD485** M Haydn—Symphonies, Volume 4

ORAIN, Marie-Thérèse (sop)
Auber: Manon Lescaut (Cpte)

ORAN, Maria (sop)
Puccini: Bohème (Cpte)
Vives: Bohemios (Cpte)

ORAVEZ, Edith (sop)
Mozart: Zauberflöte (Cpte)

ORAZI, Attilio d' (bar)
Puccini: Bohème (exc)

ØRBAEK, Hanne Mari (sop)
Monteverdi: Incoronazione di Poppea (Cpte)

(ANONYMOUS) ORCHESTRA
Adam: Si j'étais roi (Cpte)
(CFP) **CD-CFP4569** Puccini: Arias
(DANA) **DACOCD315/6** Lauritz Melchior Anthology - Vol. 3
(DECC) **071 135-1DH** La Stupenda - A Portrait of Dame Joan Sutherland
(DG) **439 251-2GY** The Leonard Bernstein Album
(DG) **439 251-5GY** The Leonard Bernstein Album
(MMOI) **CDMOIR412** Great Voices of the Century Sing Puccini
(NIMB) **NI7802** Divas 1906-1935
(PREI) **89034** Giuseppe Lugo (1900-1980)
(RCA) **09026 61580-2(1)** RCA/Met 110 Singers, 100 Years (pt 1)
(RCA) **09026 61580-2(3)** RCA/Met 100 Singers, 100 Years (pt 3)
(RCA) **09026 61580-2(4)** RCA/Met 100 Singers, 100 Years (pt 4)
(RCA) **74321 24284-2** Opera's Greatest Heroines
cond A. ALBERGONI
(CLUB) **CL99-074** Conchita Supervia (1895-1936)
(EMI) **CHS7 64864-2(1)** La Scala Edition - Vol.2, 1915-46 (pt 1)
(NIMB) **NI7836/7** Conchita Supervia (1895-1936)
(NIMB) **NI7864** More Legendary Voices
(PEAR) **GEMMCDS9926(2)** Covent Garden on Record—Vol.4 (pt 2)
(PREI) **89023** Conchita Supervia (1895-1936)
(PREI) **89063** Rosetta Pampanini (1896-1973)
(TEST) **SBT1008** Viva Rossini
cond K. ALWIN
(MMOI) **CDMOIR419** Vienna Nights - Golden Age of Operetta
(PEAR) **GEMMCDS9926(2)** Covent Garden on Record—Vol.4 (pt 2)
(PEAR) **GEMMCD9445** Elisabeth Schumann—Vol.2
(ROMO) **81019-2** Elisabeth Schumann
cond G. ANDOLFI
(EMI) **CZS5 68292-2** Operetta Arias and Duets
cond ANON
(BELA) **450 052-2** Great Opera Choruses
(DANT) **LYS001** La Colorature des Coloratures - Volume 1
(MCI) **MCCD090** Carreras & Friends sing Opera Arias & Songs
(MEMO) **HR4220/1** Great Voices-Tito Schipa
(VAI) **VAIA1009** Ilona Tokody. Portrait of the Artist
(VAI) **VAI69112** Eleanor Steber in Opera and Song Vol 2

cond W.B. ROGERS
(BIDD) **LAB022** Fritz Kreisler—Duets with McCormack & Farrar
(CLAR) **CDGSE78-50-52** Three Tenors
(CLUB) **CL99-060** Enrico Caruso—Opera & Song Recital
(LARR) **CDLRH221** Dame Nellie Melba - Opera and Song Recital
(MCI) **MCCD086** The Essential Caruso
(MMOI) **CDMOIR418** Great Voices of the Century—John McCormack
(MMOI) **CDMOIR428** Rosa Ponselle and Giovanni Martinelli sing Verdi
(NIMB) **NI7801** Great Singers, Vol.1
(NIMB) **NI7802** Divas 1906-1935
(NIMB) **NI7804** Giovanni Martinelli—Opera Recital
(NIMB) **NI7810** Titta Ruffo—Opera Recital
(NIMB) **NI7834** Caruso in Ensemble
(NIMB) **NI7859** Caruso, Farrar & Journet in French Opera
(NIMB) **NI7872** Geraldine Farrar in French Opera
(PEAR) **EVC1(2)** The Caruso Edition, Vol.1 (pt 2)
(PEAR) **EVC3(1)** The Caruso Edition, Vol.3 (pt 1)
(PEAR) **EVC3(2)** The Caruso Edition, Vol.3 (pt 2)
(PEAR) **GEMMCD9088** Titta Ruffo (1877-1953)
(PEAR) **GEMMCD9104** Pasquale Amato (1878-1942)
(PEAR) **GEMMCD9172** Emmy Destinn (1878-1930)
(PREI) **89064** Pasquale Amato (1878-1942)
(RCA) **GD60495(2)** The Complete Caruso Collection (pt 2)
(RCA) **GD60495(3)** The Complete Caruso Collection (pt 3)
(RCA) **GD60495(4)** The Complete Caruso Collection (pt 4)
(RCA) **GD60495(5)** The Complete Caruso Collection (pt 5)
(RCA) **09026 61242-2** Caruso Sings Verdi
(RCA) **09026 61243-2** Caruso sings Verismo Arias
(RCA) **09026 61244-2** Caruso sings French Opera Arias
(RCA) **09026 61412-2** Nellie Melba - Recital
(RCA) **09026 61580-2(2)** RCA/Met 100 Singers, 100 Years (pt 2)
(RCA) **74321 24284-2** Opera's Greatest Heroines
(ROMO) **81002-2** Emmy Destinn (1878-1930)
(ROMO) **81011-2(1)** Dame Nellie Melba (pt 1)
(ROMO) **81011-2(2)** Dame Nellie Melba (pt 2)
(SUPR) **11 1337-2** Emmy Destinn (1878-1930)
(SUPR) **11 2136-2(5)** Emmy Destinn—Complete Edition, Discs 11 & 12
(TEST) **SBT1005** Ten Top Tenors
cond R. ROMANI
(MMOI) **CDMOIR428** Rosa Ponselle and Giovanni Martinelli sing Verdi
(NIMB) **NI7846** Rosa Ponselle, Vol.2
(NIMB) **NI7851** Legendary Voices
cond L. RONALD
(LARR) **CDLRH221** Dame Nellie Melba - Opera and Song Recital
(PEAR) **GEMMCDS9923(1)** Covent Garden on Record, Vol.1 (pt 1)
cond ROSARIO BOURDON
(CLAR) **CDGSE78-50-52** Three Tenors
(CLUB) **CL99-025** Giovanni Zenatello (1876-1949)
(CONI) **CDHD170** Gigli—Centenary Tribute
(CONI) **CDHD201** Galli-Curci in Opera and Song
(CONI) **CDHD227** Gigli in Opera and Song
(CONI) **CDHD235** The Puccini Album
(EMI) **CMS7 64008-2(1)** Wagner Singing on Record (pt 1)
(MMOI) **CDMOIR404** Ezio Pinza—Recital
(MMOI) **CDMOIR406** Mozart—Historical Recordings
(MMOI) **CDMOIR408** Great Sopranos
(MMOI) **CDMOIR411** Sacred Songs and Arias
(MMOI) **CDMOIR412** Great Voices of the Century Sing Puccini
(MMOI) **CDMOIR417** Great Voices of the Century—Beniamino Gigli
(MMOI) **CDMOIR419** Vienna Nights - Golden Age of Operetta
(MMOI) **CDMOIR428** Rosa Ponselle and Giovanni Martinelli sing Verdi
(MSCM) **MM30231** Don Pasquale & Tito Schipa Recital
(MSCM) **MM30446** Lily Pons - Recital
(MSOU) **DFCDI-111** The Art of the Coloratura
(NIMB) **NI7801** Great Singers, Vol.1
(NIMB) **NI7804** Giovanni Martinelli—Opera Recital
(NIMB) **NI7805** Rosa Ponselle—Opera & Song Recital
(NIMB) **NI7806** Galli-Curci—Opera & Song Recital
(NIMB) **NI7807** Beniamino Gigli—Vol. 1: 1918-24
(NIMB) **NI7810** Titta Ruffo—Opera Recital
(NIMB) **NI7811** Ernestine Schumann-Heink—Opera & Song Recital
(NIMB) **NI7817** Beniamino Gigli—Vol.2
(NIMB) **NI7845** Giacomo Lauri-Volpi (1892-1979)
(NIMB) **NI7846** Rosa Ponselle, Vol.2
(NIMB) **NI7851** Legendary Voices
(NIMB) **NI7853** Lauri-Volpi sings Verdi
(NIMB) **NI7864** More Legendary Voices
(PEAR) **GEMMCDS9074(2)** Giovanni Zenatello, Vol.2 (pt 2)
(PEAR) **GEMMCDS9159(2)** De Luca Edition, Vol.1 (pt 2)
(PEAR) **GEMMCDS9176** Gigli - Arias, Duets & Songs, 1926-1937
(PEAR) **GEMMCDS9452** The Emperor Tibbett
(PEAR) **GEMMCDS9925(2)** Covent Garden on Record—Vol.3 (pt 2)
(PEAR) **GEMMCDS9926(2)** Covent Garden on Record—Vol.4 (pt 2)
(PEAR) **GEMMCD9122** 20 Great Basses sing Great Arias
(PEAR) **GEMMCD9129** Great Tenors, Vol.2
(PEAR) **GEMMCD9161** Edmond Clément (1867-1928)
(PEAR) **GEMMCD9306** Ezio Pinza—Opera Recital
(PEAR) **GEMMCD9314** Feodor Chaliapin - Aria and Song Recital
(PEAR) **GEMMCD9316** Beniamino Gigli
(PEAR) **GEMMCD9367** Gigli—Arias and Duets
(PREI) **89012** Giacomo Lauri-Volpi (1894-1979)
(PREI) **89021** Marcel Journet (1867-1933)
(PREI) **89027** Sigrid Onegin (1889-1943)
(PREI) **89038** Giovanni Zenatello (1876-1949)
(PREI) **89050** Ezio Pinza (1892-1957)
(PREI) **89062** Giovanni Martinelli (1885-1969)
(PREI) **89073** Giuseppe de Luca (1876-1950) - II
(RCA) **GD87808** Lawrence Tibbett sings Opera Arias
(RCA) **GD87810** Rosa Ponselle - Opera & Song Recital
(RCA) **GD87811** Beniamino Gigli—Operatic Arias
(RCA) **GD87969** Tito Schipa - Opera & Song Recital
(RCA) **09026 61245-2** Ezio Pinza - Recital
(RCA) **09026 61411-2** Lily Pons Recital
(RCA) **09026 61580-2(2)** RCA/Met 100 Singers, 100 Years (pt 2)
(RCA) **09026 61580-2(3)** RCA/Met 100 Singers, 100 Years (pt 3)
(RCA) **09026 61580-2(4)** RCA/Met 100 Singers, 100 Years (pt 4)
(RCA) **74321 24284-2** Opera's Greatest Heroines
(ROMO) **81004-2** Galli-Curci—Acoustic Recordings, Vol.2
(ROMO) **81006-2** Rosa Ponselle (1897-1981)
(ROMO) **81007-2** Rosa Ponselle—Victor Recordings 1926-1929
(ROMO) **81008-2** Mary Garden (1874-1967)
(ROMO) **82002-2** Edmond Clément (1867-1928)
(TEST) **SBT1005** Ten Top Tenors
cond F. RUHLMANN
(MMOI) **CDMOIR408** Great Sopranos
(MSCM) **MM30451** Mascagni—Cavalleria Rusticana, etc
(PEAR) **GEMMCD9948** Ninon Vallin in Opera and Song
(PREI) **89041** Eidé Norena (1884-1968)
cond C. SABAJNO
(CLUB) **CL99-509/10** Hina Spani (1896-1969)
(EMI) **CDC7 54016-2** Tenorissimo!
(EMI) **CDH7 63200-2** Tito Schipa—Recital
(EMI) **CHS7 64860-2(1)** La Scala Edition - Vol.1, 1878-1914 (pt 1)
(EMI) **CHS7 64860-2(2)** La Scala Edition - Vol.1, 1878-1914 (pt 2)
(EMI) **CHS7 64864-2(1)** La Scala Edition - Vol.2, 1915-46 (pt 1)
(MMOI) **CDMOIR412** Great Voices of the Century Sing Puccini
(NIMB) **NI7807** Beniamino Gigli—Vol. 1: 1918-24
(NIMB) **NI7810** Titta Ruffo—Opera Recital
(NIMB) **NI7831** Mattia Battistini (1856-1928)
(NIMB) **NI7864** More Legendary Voices
(PEAR) **GEMMCDS9923(1)** Covent Garden on Record, Vol.1 (pt 1)
(PEAR) **GEMMCDS9924(1)** Covent Garden on Record, Vol.2 (pt 1)
(PEAR) **GEMMCDS9925(1)** Covent Garden on Record—Vol.3 (pt 1)
(PEAR) **GEMMCD9088** Titta Ruffo (1877-1953)
(PEAR) **GEMMCD9117** Graziella Pareto
(PEAR) **GEMMCD9306** Ezio Pinza—Opera Recital
(PEAR) **GEMMCD9936** Mattia Battistini, Vol.1
cond A. SABINO
(BONG) **GB1078-2** Mafalda Favero
(PREI) **89074** Tancredi Pasero (1893-1983) - II
(VAI) **VAIA1071** Mafalda Favero (1903-1981)
cond M. SARGENT
Sullivan: HMS Pinafore (Cpte)
(BEUL) **1PD13** Sir Malcolm Sargent conducts British Music
(CLAR) **CDGSE78-50-52** Three Tenors
(PEAR) **GEMMCD9112** Walter Widdop
(PEAR) **GEMMCD9468** Vaughan Williams
cond C. SCHMALSTICH
(EMI) **CHS7 64673-2** Joseph Schmidt - Complete EMI Recordings Volume 1
cond F. SCHÖNBAUMSFELD
(EMI) **CDH7 69787-2** Richard Tauber sings Operetta Arias
cond W. SCHÜCHTER
(EMI) **CDM7 69475-2** Rudolf Schock sings Operetta and Songs
cond G. SCOGNAMIGLIO
(NIMB) **NI7834** Caruso in Ensemble
(PEAR) **EVC3(1)** The Caruso Edition, Vol.3 (pt 1)
(RCA) **GD60495(5)** The Complete Caruso Collection (pt 5)
(RCA) **09026 61242-2** Caruso Sings Verdi
cond G. SCOTT-WOOD
(EMI) **CDP7 98844-2** Josef Locke—Hear My Song
cond B. SEIDLER-WINKLER
(ARLE) **ARL23/5** Rimsky-Korsakov—Sadko
(PEAR) **GEMMCDS9001/3(1)** Singers of Imperial Russia, Vol.2 (pt 1)
(PEAR) **GEMMCDS9111(1)** Singers of Imperial Russia, Vol.5 (pt 1)
(PEAR) **GEMMCDS9924(1)** Covent Garden on Record, Vol.2 (pt 1)
(PEAR) **GEMMCDS9924(2)** Covent Garden on Record, Vol.2 (pt 2)
(PEAR) **GEMMCD9172** Emmy Destinn (1878-1930)
(SUPR) **11 1337-2** Emmy Destinn (1878-1930)
(SUPR) **11 2136-2(1)** Emmy Destinn—Complete Edition, Discs 1 & 2
(SUPR) **11 2136-2(2)** Emmy Destinn—Complete Edition, Discs 3 & 4
(SUPR) **11 2136-2(3)** Emmy Destinn—Complete Edition, Discs 5 to 8
cond G. SETTI
(NIMB) **NI7804** Giovanni Martinelli—Opera Recital
(PEAR) **GEMMCDS9159(2)** De Luca Edition, Vol.1 (pt 2)
(PEAR) **GEMMCDS9924(1)** Covent Garden on Record, Vol.2 (pt 1)
(PEAR) **GEMMCD9104** Pasquale Amato (1878-1942)
(ROMO) **81007-2** Rosa Ponselle—Victor Recordings 1926-1929
cond N. SHILKRET
(BEUL) **1PD4** 78 Classics - Volume One
(BIDD) **LHW016** Landowska—The Early Recordings 1923-1930
(CLAR) **CDGSE78-50-52** Three Tenors
(NIMB) **NI7804** Giovanni Martinelli—Opera Recital
(NIMB) **NI7817** Beniamino Gigli—Vol.2
(PEAR) **GEMMCDS9159(2)** De Luca Edition, Vol.1 (pt 2)
(PEAR) **GEMMCDS9452** The Emperor Tibbett
(PEAR) **GEMMCD9130** Great Sopranos, Vol.2
(PEAR) **GEMMCD9367** Gigli—Arias and Duets
(RCA) **GD87808** Lawrence Tibbett sings Opera Arias
(ROMO) **81008-2** Mary Garden (1874-1967)
cond R. SINATRA
(IMP) **PWKS4230** Mario Lanza in Concert
(RCA) **GD60720** Mario Lanza—Be my love
(RCA) **GD60889(1)** The Mario Lanza Collection
(RCA) **09026 61420-2** Mario Lanza - Don't Forget Me
(RCA) **09026 62550-2** Ten Tenors in Love
(RCA) **74321 18574-2** Mario Lanza - The Ultimate Collection
cond E. SIVIERI
(RCA) **GD87811** Beniamino Gigli—Operatic Arias
cond A. SMALLENS
(PEAR) **GEMMCDS9452** The Emperor Tibbett
(RCA) **GD87808** Lawrence Tibbett sings Opera Arias
cond W. STEINBERG
(VAI) **VAIA1084** Rose Bampton sings Verdi and Wagner
cond E. STERN
(NONE) **7559-79330-2** Patinkin—Experiment
(NONE) **7559-79345-2** I Wish It So - Dawn Upshaw
cond P. STOLL
(SYMP) **SYMCD1103** Renée Doria—Opera Recital
cond I. STRAVINSKY
(ARHI) **ADCD110** Mengelberg Edition - Volume 4
cond G. SZELL
(EMI) **CDH7 64029-2** Richard Tauber - Opera Recital
(NIMB) **NI7830** Richard Tauber in Opera
(TEST) **SBT1005** Ten Top Tenors
cond J. SZYFER
(EMI) **CDM7 69548-2** Georges Thill sings French Opera Arias
cond F. TOURS
(NIMB) **NI7867** Legendary Baritones
cond N. TREEP
(LYRC) **SRO830** Smetana—The Bartered Bride, etc
cond G. TRUC
Debussy: Pelléas et Mélisande (exc)
cond M. DI VEROLI
(MMOI) **CDMOIR412** Great Voices of the Century Sing Puccini
cond E. VITALE
(EMI) **CHS7 64860-2(2)** La Scala Edition - Vol.1, 1878-1914 (pt 2)
cond D. VOORHEES
(MMOI) **CDMOIR404** Ezio Pinza—Recital
cond G.I. WAHRLICH
(PEAR) **GEMMCDS9111(1)** Singers of Imperial Russia, Vol.5 (pt 1)
cond A. WALLENSTEIN
(SUPR) **11 1491-2** Jarmila Novotna sings Czech Songs and Arias
cond B. WALTER
(PEAR) **GEMMCDS9925(2)** Covent Garden on Record—Vol.3 (pt 2)
(SONY) **SM3K47211** Mozart Legendary Interpretations—Opera and Concert Arias
cond H. WEIGERT
(NIMB) **NI7830** Richard Tauber in Opera
cond F. WEISSMANN
(DANA) **DACOCD313/4** Lauritz Melchior Anthology - Vol. 2
(EMI) **CHS7 64673-2** Joseph Schmidt - Complete EMI Recordings Volume 1
(EMI) **CHS7 69741-2(7)** Record of Singing, Vol.4—Italian School
(EMI) **CMS7 64008-2(1)** Wagner Singing on Record (pt 1)
(PEAR) **GEMMCDS9926(2)** Covent Garden on Record—Vol.4 (pt 2)
(PEAR) **GEMMCD9082** Meta Seinemeyer
(PEAR) **GEMMCD9419** Herbert Ernst Groh—Opera Recital
cond A. WOLFF
(MSCM) **MM30221** 18 French Divas
(PREI) **89034** Giuseppe Lugo (1900-1980)

cond V. YOUNG
(RCA) **09026 61778-2(19)** The Heifetz Collection, Vol. 19
cond R. ZAMBONI
(EMI) **CDH7 61052-2** Beniamino Gigli—Arias and Duets (1932-1949)
cond F. ZWEIG
(PEAR) **GEMMCDS9926(2)** Covent Garden on Record—Vol.4 (pt 2)
(PEAR) **GEMMCD9122** 20 Great Basses sing Great Arias

ORCHESTRA OF THE AGE OF ENLIGHTENMENT
cond C. MACKERRAS
(FORL) **UCD16738** Great Handel Arias

ORCHESTRA OF THE EIGHTEENTH CENTURY
cond F. BRÜGGEN
Rameau: Abaris (exc), Dardanus (exc)
(PHIL) **426 714-2PH** Rameau & Purcell: Orchestral Works

ORCHESTRE DE LA BASTILLE (PARIS)
cond MYUNG-WHUN CHUNG
(DG) **431 778-2GH** Bizet—Orchestral Works

ORCHESTRE DE L'ASSOCIATION DES CONCERTS PASDELOUP
cond P. COPPOLA
(EMI) **CMS7 64008-2(2)** Wagner Singing on Record (pt 2)
(PREI) **89011** Marjorie Lawrence (1909-1979)

ORCHESTRE DE PARIS
cond D. BARENBOIM
Saint-Saëns: Samson et Dalila (Cpte)
(DG) **415 847-2GGA** Saint-Saëns—Orchestral Works
(EMI) **CDM7 64869-2** Bizet—Orchestral Works
(SONY) **SBK53255** Berlioz—Orchestral Works
cond S. BYCHKOV
Bizet: Carmen Suites
Mascagni: Cavalleria Rusticana (Cpte)
Tchaikovsky: Eugene Onegin (Cpte)
cond P. DERVAUX
(EMI) **CZS7 62877-2** Les inspirations insolites d'Erik Satie
cond G. PRÊTRE
Massenet: Werther (Cpte)
cond M. ROSTROPOVICH
Tchaikovsky: Iolanta (Cpte)

ORCIANI, Patrizia (sop)
Handel: Giulio Cesare (Cpte)
Rossini: Bianca e Falliero (Cpte), Signor Bruschino (Cpte)

ORDA, Alfred (bar)
(SYMP) **SYMCD1117** Alfred Orda—Opera Recital

ORDASSY, Carlotta (sop)
Bellini: Norma (Cpte)
Verdi: Ernani (Cpte), Macbeth (Cpte)
Wagner: Walküre (Cpte)
(DG) **435 211-2GX15** Wagner—Der Ring des Nibelungen
(RCA) **09026 61580-2(7)** RCA/Met 100 Singers, 100 Years (pt 7)

ORDÓÑEZ, Antonio (ten)
Falla: Vida breve (Cpte)

ÖREBRO CHAMBER ORCHESTRA
cond G.W. NILSON
(BLUE) **ABCD038** 4 X Göran W. Nilson

ORECCHIA, Paolo (bass)
Gluck: Rencontre imprévue (Cpte)

OREL, Ekaterina (sop)
(SYMP) **SYMCD1105** The Harold Wayne Collection, Vol.10

OREN, Daniel (cond)
see Genoa Teatro Comunale Orch
Rome Op Orch
Verona Arena Orch

ORFÉON DONOSTIARRA
cond M. PLASSON
Roussel: Padmâvatî (Cpte)

ORFF, Carl (narr)
Orff: Orpheus (Cpte)
(ACAN) **44 2085-2** Carl Orff Collection

ORGONÁŠOVÁ, Luba (sop)
Mozart: Don Giovanni (Cpte), Entführung (Cpte), Mitridate (Cpte)
Puccini: Bohème (Cpte)
(NAXO) **8 550605** Favourite Soprano Arias

ORIADEY, Patrick (sngr)
Planquette: Rip van Winkle (Cpte)

ORIANA CONCERT CHOIR
cond A. DELLER
Purcell: Dido (Cpte)

ORIANA CONCERT ORCHESTRA
Purcell: Dido (Cpte)

ORIESCHNIG, Dominik (treb)
(PHIL) **422 527-2PME** The Complete Mozart Edition Vol 27

ORIGINAL BROADWAY CAST
cond V. HERBERT
(PEAR) **GEMMCDS9059/61** Music from the New York Stage, Vol. 4: 1917-20

ORIGINAL FILM CAST
cond J. GREEN
Bernstein: West Side Story (Cpte)

ORIGINAL VOLGA COSSACKS CHORUS
cond E-G. SCHERZER
(SCHW) **312732** Lehár—Der Zarewitsch (excs)

ORLANDINI, Gino (bar)
Massenet: Werther (Cpte)

ORLIAC, Jean-Claude (ten)
Gounod: Philémon et Baucis (Cpte)

ORLOV, Alexander (cond)
see All-Union Rad Orch
Bolshoi Th Orch

ORLOV, Polikarp (bar)
(PEAR) **GEMMCDS9001/3(1)** Singers of Imperial Russia, Vol.2 (pt 1)

ORMANDY, Eugene (cond)
see Hollywood Bowl SO
orch
Philadelphia
Stockholm PO

ORMISTON, Linda (mez)
Britten: Noye's Fludde (Cpte)
Janáček: Jenufa (Cpte), Káta Kabanová (Cpte)
Saxton: Caritas (Cpte)
Sullivan: HMS Pinafore (exc), Ruddigore (Cpte)

ORPHEI DRÄNGAR CHOIR
cond E. ERICSON
(BIS) **BIS-CD383** Works for Male Chorus

ORPHEUS BOYS' CHOIR
cond P. BOULEZ
Schoenberg: Moses und Aron (Cpte)

ORREGO, Rodrigo (ten)
Spohr: Faust (Cpte)

ORTF CHORUS
cond P. DERVAUX
Massenet: Jongleur de Notre Dame (Cpte)

ORTF LYRIC CHORALE
cond M. CARIVEN
Audran: Miss Helyett (Cpte)
Messager: Coups de Roulis (Cpte)
cond J-C. HARTEMANN
Offenbach: Madame l'Archiduc (Cpte)

ORTF LYRIC ORCHESTRA
cond E. BIGOT
Adam: Toréador (Cpte)
cond J. BREBION
(MUSD) **20239-2** Delibes—Opéras-Comiques
cond M. CARIVEN
Audran: Miss Helyett (Cpte)
Messager: Coups de Roulis (Cpte)
cond J. DOUSSARD
Terrasse: Fiancée du Scaphandrier (Cpte)
cond J-C. HARTEMANN
Offenbach: Chanson de Fortunio (Cpte), Madame l'Archiduc (Cpte)
cond J-P. KREDER
Messager: Passionêment (Cpte)

ORTF PHILHARMONIC ORCHESTRA
cond P. DERVAUX
Massenet: Jongleur de Notre Dame (Cpte)

ORTH, Norbert (ten)
Benatzky: Im weissen Rössl (Cpte)
Leoncavallo: Bohème (Cpte)
Mozart: Entführung (Cpte), Zauberflöte (Cpte)
R. Strauss: Rosenkavalier (Cpte)
Wagner: Meistersinger (Cpte)

ORTH, Robert (bass)
Janáček: Makropulos Affair (Cpte)
Verdi: Traviata (Cpte)

ORTHMANN, Erich (cond)
see Berlin St Op Orch
BPO

ØRVAD, Hanne (sngr)
Kuhlau: Lulu (Cpte)

OSBORNE, Robert (bass-bar)
M. Monk: Atlas (Cpte)
S. Wallace: Kabbalah (Cpte)

OSKARSSON, GuØjon (bass)
Braein: Anne Pedersdotter (Cpte)

OSLO PHILHARMONIC CHORUS
cond P. DREIER
(UNIC) **UKCD2056** Grieg—Stage Works

OSLO PHILHARMONIC ORCHESTRA
(LOND) **440 495-2LM** Kirsten Flagstad Edition, Vol. 5
cond A. BOULT
(LOND) **440 490-2LM5(1)** Kirsten Flagstad Edition
cond M. JANSONS
(EMI) **CDC7 49797-2** Mussorgsky—Orchestral Works
(EMI) **CDC7 54583-2** Wagner—Overtures and Orchestral Works

OSSER, Glen (cond)
see Orch

OSSONCE, Jean Yves (cond)
see BBC Scottish SO

OSSONCE, Jean-Yves (cond)
see NZ SO

OSSWALD, Max (ten)
Mozart: Zauberflöte (Cpte)

OSTAPIUK, Jerzy (bass)
Beethoven: Fidelio (Cpte)
Moniuszko: Halka (Cpte)
Szymanowski: King Roger (Cpte)

OSTENDORF, John (bass)
Handel: Imeneo (Cpte), Siroe, Rè di Persia (Cpte)
Telemann: Pimpinone (Cpte)
(MUSM) **67078-2** Stravinsky The Composer - Volume 1
(NEWP) **NPD85540** Handel/Bononcini—Muzio Scevola

ÖSTERBERG, Eva (sop)
Börtz: Bacchae (Cpte)

OSTERTAG, Karl (ten)
Janáček: Excursions of Mr Brouček (Cpte)
Orff: Antigonae (Cpte)
Wagner: Fliegende Holländer (Cpte), Meistersinger (Cpte)
(PILZ) **442118-2** Wagner—Operas in Historical Recordings

ÖSTMAN, Arnold (cond)
see Drottningholm Court Th Chor
Drottningholm Court Th Orch

OSTROMOV, Sergei (ten)
(DANT) **LYS013/5** Tchaikovsky—The Queen of Spades

OSWALD, Hermann (ten)
Biber: Arminio (Cpte)

OSWALD, Peter (ten)
Patzelt: Castor et Pollux (Cpte)
Verdi: Traviata (Cpte)

OTAKA, Tadaaki (cond)
see BBC Welsh SO

OTAVA, Zdeněk (bar)
Martinů: Julietta (Cpte)
Smetana: Brandenburgers in Bohemia (Cpte)

OTELLI, Claudio (bar)
B. Goldschmidt: Gewaltige Hahnrei (Cpte)
Giordano: Andrea Chénier (Cpte)
Mozart: Don Giovanni (exc)
Puccini: Fanciulla del West (Cpte)
R. Strauss: Elektra (Cpte)
Schreker: Ferne Klang (Cpte)
Zemlinsky: Kleider machen Leute (Cpte)
(CAPR) **10 810** Mozart—Opera Highlights

OTEY, Louis (bar)
J. Strauss II: Fledermaus (Cpte)

OTT, Karin (sop)
Mozart: Zauberflöte (exc)
(CPO) **CPO999 044-2** Viardot-Garcia—Songs
(DG) **439 153-4GMA** Mad about Sopranos

OTTAVI (sop)
(PREI) **89048** Apollo Granforte (1886-1975) - I

OTTENTHAL, Gertrud von (mez)
Lortzing: Wildschütz (Cpte)

OTTENTHAL, Getrud (sop)
Mozart: Don Giovanni (Cpte)
R. Strauss: Rosenkavalier (Cpte)
Zemlinsky: Kreidekreis (Cpte)
(CAPR) **10 810** Mozart—Opera Highlights

OTTER, Anne Sofie von (mez)
Gluck: Cinesi (Cpte), Iphigénie en Aulide (Cpte), Orphée (Cpte)
Humperdinck: Hänsel und Gretel (Cpte)
Monteverdi: Orfeo (Cpte)
Mozart: Clemenza di Tito (Cpte), Così fan tutte (Cpte), Idomeneo (Cpte), Nozze di Figaro (Cpte)
Offenbach: Contes d'Hoffmann (Cpte)
R. Strauss: Rosenkavalier (exc)
Tchaikovsky: Eugene Onegin (Cpte)
Wagner: Götterdämmerung (Cpte)
(DG) **431 601-2GCE10** Tchaikovsky Compact Edition
(DG) **439 894-2GH** Speak Low - Songs by Kurt Weill
(DG) **072 428-1GH2(DG)** The Metropolitan Opera Gala
(ERAT) **4509-99607-2** Gluck—Operas; Schubert—Symphonies Nos 8 & 9
(PROP) **PRCD9008** Anne Sofie Von Otter — Recital

OTTEVAERE, Daniel (bass)
Henze: Boulevard Solitude (Cpte)

OTTO, Carsten (spkr)
Nono: Intolleranza 1960 (Cpte)

OTTO, Lisa (sop)
Henze: Junge Lord (Cpte)
Mozart: Così fan tutte (exc), Zauberflöte (exc)
R. Strauss: Ariadne auf Naxos (Cpte), Elektra (Cpte)
Wagner: Tannhäuser (Cpte)
Weber: Freischütz (Cpte)
(EMI) **CMS5 65212-2** Wagner—Les introuvables du Ring
(EMI) **CZS7 62993-2** Fritz Wunderlich—Great German Tenor
(TEST) **SBT1036** Lisa Della Casa sings Richard Strauss

OTTO, Susanne (contr)
Rihm: Eroberung von Mexico (Cpte)
(SONY) **SK53978** Prometheus

ÖTVÖS, Gabor (cond)
see RPO

OUROUSSOV, Olga (sop)
(SYMP) **SYMCD1093** The Harold Wayne Collection, Vol.7

OUTIN, Regis (spkr)
Bizet: Carmen (Cpte)

OVČAČÍKOVÁ, Marie (contr)
Dvořák: Rusalka (Cpte)

OWEN, Chloe (sop)
(IRCC) **IRCC-CD808** Souvenirs of 19th Century Italian Opera

OWEN, Handel (ten)
Puccini: Fanciulla del West (Cpte)

OWEN, Louise (mez)
Sullivan: Iolanthe (exc)

OWEN, Stephen (bass)
V. Thomson: Lord Byron (Cpte)

OWEN-LEWIS, David (bass)
Walton: Troilus and Cressida (Cpte)

OWENS, Anne-Marie (mez)
Britten: Rape of Lucretia (Cpte)
Monteverdi: Incoronazione di Poppea (Cpte)
Smyth: Wreckers (Cpte)
Weir: Blond Eckbert (Cpte)
(IMP) **DPCD1015** Karaoke Opera
(IMP) **PCD1043** Opera Favourites
(IMP) **TCD1070** Invitation to the Opera

OXFORD CITY ORCHESTRA
cond M. PAPADOPOULOS
(IMP) **PCD1104** Baroque Encores

OXILIA, Giuseppe (ten)
(EMI) **CHS7 64860-2(1)** La Scala Edition - Vol.1, 1878-1914 (pt 1)

OZAWA, Seiji (cond)
see Boston SO
BPO
Chicago SO
FNO
Paris Op Orch
San Francisco SO
Staatskapelle Dresden
VPO

OZEROV, Nikolai (ten)
(ARLE) **ARL23/5** Rimsky-Korsakov—Sadko

PAALEN, Bella (contr)
(EMI) **CHS7 64487-2** R. Strauss—Der Rosenkavalier & Lieder
(PEAR) **GEMMCDS9365** R. Strauss: Der Rosenkavalier (abridged), etc
(PEAR) **GEMMCD9122** 20 Great Basses sing Great Arias
(SCHW) **314512** Vienna State Opera Live, Vol.1
(SCHW) **314542** Vienna State Opera Live, Vol.4
(SCHW) **314562** Vienna State Opera Live, Vol.6
(SCHW) **314592** Vienna State Opera Live, Vol.9
(SCHW) **314622** Vienna State Opera Live, Vol.12
(SCHW) **314642** Vienna State Opera Live, Vol.14
(SCHW) **314672** Vienna State Opera Live, Vol.17
(SCHW) **314702** Vienna State Opera Live, Vol.20
(SCHW) **314742** Vienna State Opera Live, Vol.24

PABST, Michael (ten)
Kreutzer: Nachtlager in Granada (Cpte)
Schreker: Irrelohe (Cpte)
Wagner: Parsifal (Cpte)

PACE, Miti Truccato (mez)
Puccini: Madama Butterfly (Cpte)
Rossini: Italiana in Algeri (Cpte)
Verdi: Traviata (exc)
(DECC) **411 665-2DM3** Puccini: Il trittico

PACE, Patrizia (sop)
Alfano: Risurrezione (Cpte)
Debussy: Pelléas et Mélisande (Cpte)
Mozart: Don Giovanni (Cpte), Nozze di Figaro (exc)
Rossini: Italiana in Algeri (Cpte)
(DECC) **071 140-1DH (DECC)** Pavarotti—30th Anniversary Gala Concert

PACETTI, Iva (sop)
Leoncavallo: Pagliacci (Cpte)
(CONI) **CDHD227** Gigli in Opera and Song
(EMI) **CDH7 61052-2** Beniamino Gigli—Arias and Duets (1932-1949)
(PEAR) **GEMMCDS9176** Gigli - Arias, Duets & Songs, 1926-1937

PACETTI, Sandra (sop)
Mascagni: Amico Fritz (Cpte)
Puccini: Bohème (Cpte)

PACI, Leone (bar)
Leoncavallo: Pagliacci (Cpte)
(EMI) **CDH7 69791-2** Dame Eva Turner sings Opera Arias and Songs

PACINI, Giuseppe (bar)
(EMI) **CHS7 64860-2(1)** La Scala Edition - Vol.1, 1878-1914 (pt 1)
(MEMO) **HR4408/9(2)** Singers in Genoa, Vol.1 (disc 2)
(SYMP) **SYMCD1113** The Harold Wayne Collection, Vol.13

PADEREWSKI, Ignace Jan (pf)
(PEAR) **GEMMCD9943** The Art of Paderewski, Vol.2
(RCA) **GD60923** Legendary Performers - Paderewski

PADMORE, Mark (ten)
Chabrier: Briséïs (Cpte)
Handel: Giustino (Cpte)
Lampe: Pyramus and Thisbe (Cpte)
M-A. Charpentier: Médée (Cpte)
Montéclair: Jephté (Cpte)
Purcell: Dioclesian, Z627 (Cpte), Fairy Queen, Z629 (Cpte), King Arthur, Z628 (Cpte)
Rameau: Castor et Pollux (exc)
(HYPE) **CDA66608** Dibdin—Three Operas

PADOAN, Silvana (mez)
Puccini: Madama Butterfly (Cpte)

PAEVATALU, Guido (bar)
Mussorgsky: Boris Godunov (Cpte)
Zemlinsky: Es war einmal (Cpte)

PAGE, Carolann (sop)
Tippett: Ice Break (Cpte)

PAGE, Steven (bar)
Romberg: Student Prince (exc)
(IMP) **DPCD1015** Karaoke Opera
(IMP) **PCD1043** Opera Favourites

PAGLIUCA, Silvano (bass)
Donizetti: Lucia di Lammermoor (Cpte)
Leoncavallo: Bohème (Cpte)

PAGLIUGHI, Lina (sop)
Verdi: Rigoletto (Cpte)
(EMI) **CHS7 64864-2(2)** La Scala Edition - Vol.2, 1915-46 (pt 2)
(PEAR) **GEMMCDS9180** Verdi—Rigoletto, etc
(PEAR) **GEMMCDS9926(2)** Covent Garden on Record—Vol.4 (pt 2)
(TEST) **SBT1008** Viva Rossini

PAIGE, Autris (ten)
Gershwin: Porgy and Bess (exc)

PAINTER, Christopher (bar)
Menotti: Amahl and the Night Visitors (Cpte)

PAINTER, Eleanor (sngr)
(PEAR) **GEMMCDS9056/8** Music from the New York Stage, Vol. 3: 1913-17

PAISNER, Caryl (vc)
S. Wallace: Kabbalah (Cpte)

PÁL, Tamás (cond)
see Budapest SO

PALACIO, Ernesto (ten)
Handel: Rinaldo (Cpte)
Rossini: Ermione (Cpte), Italiana in Algeri (Cpte), Maometto II (Cpte), Mosè in Egitto (Cpte), Tancredi (Cpte), Torvaldo e Dorliska (Cpte), Turco in Italia (exc)
Sacchini: Contadina in Corte (Cpte)

PALAI, Nello (ten)
Leoncavallo: Pagliacci (Cpte)
Puccini: Bohème (Cpte), Tosca (Cpte)
(PREI) **89048** Apollo Granforte (1886-1975) - I

PALATCHI, Stefano (bass)
Donizetti: Linda di Chamounix (Cpte)

PALERINI, Ernesto (treb)
Puccini: Tosca (Cpte)

PALERMO TEATRO MASSIMO CHORUS
cond N. SANZOGNO
(MEMO) **HR4291/2** Great Voices - Renata Scotto

PALERMO TEATRO MASSIMO ORCHESTRA
cond N. SANZOGNO
(MEMO) **HR4291/2** Great Voices - Renata Scotto
(MEMO) **HR4372/3** Great Voices Giuseppe Di Stefano

PALET, José (ten)
(MEMO) **HR4408/9(2)** Singers in Genoa, Vol.1 (disc 2)

PALIVCOVÁ, Jarmila (sop)
Janáček: Fate (Cpte)
Smetana: Bartered Bride (Cpte)

PALLINI, Rina (mez)
Puccini: Manon Lescaut (Cpte)

PALM, Mati (bass)
Tubin: Barbara von Tisenhusen (Cpte)

PALMA, Piero De (ten)
Bellini: Norma (Cpte), Sonnambula (Cpte)
Boito: Mefistofele (Cpte)
Donizetti: Favorita (Cpte), Linda di Chamounix (Cpte), Lucia di Lammermoor (Cpte), Lucrezia Borgia (Cpte)
Giordano: Andrea Chénier (Cpte), Fedora (Cpte)
Leoncavallo: Pagliacci (Cpte)
Ponchielli: Gioconda (Cpte)
Puccini: Bohème (exc), Gianni Schicchi (Cpte), Madama Butterfly (Cpte), Manon Lescaut (Cpte), Rondine (Cpte), Tabarro (Cpte), Tosca (Cpte), Turandot (Cpte)
Rossini: Guillaume Tell (Cpte), Mosè (Cpte), Turco in Italia (Cpte)
Verdi: Aida (exc), Ballo in maschera (Cpte), Don Carlo (Cpte), Falstaff (Cpte), Forza del destino (Cpte), Luisa Miller (Cpte), Otello (Cpte), Rigoletto (Cpte), Simon Boccanegra (Cpte), Traviata (Cpte), Trovatore (Cpte)
(BELA) **450 007-2** Puccini Favourites
(DECC) **433 066-2DWO** Your Hundred Best Opera Tunes III
(DECC) **436 261-2DHO3** Puccini—Il Trittico
(DECC) **436 317-2DA** Puccini—Famous Arias
(DECC) **444 555-2DF2** Essential Puccini
(EMI) **CMS7 63244-2** The Art of Maria Callas
(EMI) **CMS7 64165-2** Puccini—Trittico
(EURO) **VD69256** Mozart—Opera Arias
(MEMO) **HR4392/3** Great Voices - Marilyn Horne
(PHIL) **434 986-2PM** Duetti Amorosi
(RCA) **GD87799** The Pearl Fishers Duet plus Duets and Scenes
(RCA) **09026 61236-2** Leontyne Price - Prima Donna Collection
(RCA) **09026 61357-2** Leontyne Price Sings Mozart

PALMER, Christene (contr)
Sullivan: Pirates of Penzance (exc), Princess Ida (Cpte), Sorcerer (Cpte)
(BELA) **461 006-2** Gilbert & Sullivan—Songs and Snatches
(DECC) **433 868-2DWO** The World of Gilbert & Sullivan - Volume 2

PALMER, David (ten)
Sullivan: Princess Ida (Cpte), Sorcerer (Cpte), Yeomen of the Guard (Cpte)

PALMER, Felicity (sop/mez)
Britten: Albert Herring (Cpte)
Holst: At the Boar's Head (Cpte), Sávitri (Cpte)
Janáček: Káťa Kabanová (Cpte)
Mozart: Idomeneo (exc), Nozze di Figaro (Cpte), Sposo deluso (Cpte)
Offenbach: Contes d'Hoffmann (exc)
Purcell: Dido (Cpte)
Rossini: Cenerentola (Cpte)
Schoenberg: Moses und Aron (Cpte)
Stravinsky: Nightingale (Cpte)
Sullivan: HMS Pinafore (Cpte), Mikado (exc)
Tchaikovsky: Queen of Spades (Cpte)
(ERAT) **4509-98955-2** Boulez conducts Stravinsky

PALMER, Gladys (contr)
Wagner: Götterdämmerung (exc)
(PEAR) **GEMMCDS9137** Wagner—Der Ring des Nibelungen

PALMER, Rudolph (cond)
see Brewer CO
Palmer CO
St Luke's Baroque Orch

PALMER CHAMBER ORCHESTRA
cond R. PALMER
(NEWP) **NPD85595** Haydn—La canterina

PALMIERI, Giovanni Battista (ten)
Bellini: Zaira (Cpte)
Salieri: Axur (Cpte)

PALÓCZ, László (bass-bar)
(DECC) **443 488-2DF2** Kodály—Háry János; Psalmus Hungaricus etc

PALOMBINI, Vittoria (mez)
Puccini: Gianni Schicchi (Cpte)
Verdi: Falstaff (exc)

PALTRINIERI, Giordano (ten)
Ponchielli: Gioconda (Cpte)

PAMPANINI, Rosetta (sop)
(CLUB) **CL99-014** Dino Borgioli (1891-1960)
(EMI) **CHS7 64864-2(1)** La Scala Edition - Vol.2, 1915-46 (pt 1)
(MMOI) **CDMOIR412** Great Voices of the Century Sing Puccini
(PEAR) **GEMMCDS9926(1)** Covent Garden on Record—Vol.4 (pt 1)
(PEAR) **GEMMCD9091** Dino Borgioli
(PREI) **89063** Rosetta Pampanini (1896-1973)

PAMPUCH, Helmut (ten)
Berg: Lulu (Cpte)
Wagner: Meistersinger (Cpte), Parsifal (Cpte), Rheingold (Cpte), Siegfried (Cpte), Tristan und Isolde (Cpte)
(EMI) **LDX9 91275-1(EMI)** Sawallisch conducts Wagner's Ring
(PHIL) **434 420-2PM32(2)** Richard Wagner Edition (pt 2)

PANAGULIAS, Ana (sop)
(IMP) **MCD43** Domingo Live from Miami

PANARIELLO, Ernesto (bass)
Cherubini: Lodoïska (Cpte)
Puccini: Fanciulla del West (Cpte), Manon Lescaut (Cpte)
Verdi: Rigoletto (Cpte), Traviata (Cpte)

PANCELLA, Phyllis (mez)
Mozart: Nozze di Figaro (Cpte)
(RCA) **09026 61509-2** A Salute to American Music

PANDANO, Vittorio (ten)
Donizetti: Lucia di Lammermoor (Cpte)
Massenet: Werther (Cpte)
Puccini: Bohème (Cpte)

PANDOLFINI, Angelica (sop)
(MEMO) **HR4408/9(1)** Singers in Genoa, Vol.1 (disc 1)
(SYMP) **SYMCD1073** The Harold Wayne Collection, Vol.3

PANE, Tullio (ten)
Donizetti: Fausta (Cpte)
Giordano: Andrea Chénier (Cpte)
Puccini: Gianni Schicchi (Cpte), Turandot (Cpte)
(EURO) **GD69043** Puccini: Il Trittico

PANERAI, Rolando (bar)
Bellini: Puritani (Cpte)
Donizetti: Elisir d'amore (Cpte), Lucia di Lammermoor (Cpte)
Gounod: Philémon et Baucis (Cpte)
Leoncavallo: Pagliacci (Cpte)
Mascagni: Cavalleria Rusticana (Cpte)
Mozart: Così fan tutte (exc), Don Giovanni (Cpte), Nozze di Figaro (Cpte)
Puccini: Bohème (Cpte), Gianni Schicchi (Cpte), Madama Butterfly (Cpte)
Rossini: Italiana in Algeri (Cpte)
Verdi: Falstaff (Cpte), Oberto (Cpte), Trovatore (Cpte)
(DECC) **421 896-2DA** Puccini—Great Operatic Duets
(DECC) **433 068-2DWO** Your Hundred Best Opera Tunes V
(DECC) **433 439-2DA** Great Love Duets
(DECC) **433 865-2DWO** The World of Puccini
(DECC) **436 317-2DA** Puccini—Famous Arias
(DECC) **440 947-2DH** Essential Opera II
(DG) **419 257-2GH3** 'Cav' and 'Pag', etc
(EMI) **CDM7 69543-2** Maria Callas and Giuseppe Di Stefano - Duets
(EMI) **CMS7 63244-2** The Art of Maria Callas
(EURO) **GD69043** Puccini: Il Trittico
(ORFE) **C365941A** Christa Ludwig - Salzburg Festival highlights

PANINA, Antonina (mez)
(PEAR) **GEMMCDS9001/3(2)** Singers of Imperial Russia, Vol.2 (pt 2)

PANIZZA, Ettore (cond)
see La Scala Orch
NY Met Op Orch
orch

PANKOV, Georgi (bass)
Tchaikovsky: Eugene Onegin (Cpte)

PANNI, Marcello (cond)
see Bassano Pro Arte Orch

PANTALEONI, Mimma (mez)
Mascagni: Cavalleria rusticana (Cpte)

PANTSCHEFF, Ljubomir (bass)
Beethoven: Fidelio (Cpte)
Lehár: Lustige Witwe (exc)
Mozart: Zauberflöte (Cpte)
R. Strauss: Ariadne auf Naxos (Cpte), Rosenkavalier (Cpte)
Wagner: Meistersinger (Cpte)

PANZARELLA, Anna Maria (sop)
Gounod: Roméo et Juliette (Cpte)

PANZENBÖCK, Gerhard (bass)
R. Strauss: Rosenkavalier (Cpte)

PANZÉRA, Charles (bar)
Debussy: Pelléas et Mélisande (exc)
(DANT) **LYS003/4** Charles Panzéra - Song Recital

PAOLETTI, Alberto (cond)
see Rome RAI Orch
Santa Cecilia Academy Orch

PAOLI, Antonio (ten)
(EMI) **CHS7 64860-2(2)** La Scala Edition - Vol.1, 1878-1914 (pt 2)
(MEMO) **HR4408/9(2)** Singers in Genoa, Vol.1 (disc 2)
(PREI) **89998** Antonio Paoli (1871-1946)

PAOLILLO, Silvano (ten)
Donizetti: Lucia di Lammermoor (Cpte)

PAOLIS, Alessio de (ten)
Bizet: Carmen (Cpte)
Mussorgsky: Boris Godunov (exc)
Puccini: Turandot (Cpte)
(PEAR) **GEMMCDS9452** The Emperor Tibbett

PAP, Robert (treb)
Mozart: Zauberflöte (Cpte)

PAPADJIAKOU, Alexandra (contr)
Bellini: Zaira (Cpte)

PAPADOPOULOS, Marios (cond)
see Oxford City Orch

PAPE, René (bass)
Busoni: Arlecchino (Cpte), Turandot (Cpte)
Korngold: Wunder der Heliane (Cpte)
Wagner: Meistersinger (Cpte)

PAPI, Gennaro (cond)
see NY Met Op Orch

PAPIS, Christian (ten)
Bizet: Carmen (Cpte)
Gounod: Sapho (Cpte)
Massenet: Don Quichotte (Cpte)
Saint-Saëns: Samson et Dalila (Cpte)
(MARC) **8 223774** Ropartz—Choral Works

PAPROCKI, Bohdan (ten)
Mussorgsky: Boris Godunov (Cpte)

PARAMOR, Norrie (cond)
see orch

PARAT, Germaine (sngr)
Ganne: Hans (Cpte)
Messager: Basoche (Cpte)
Terrasse: Travaux d'Hercule (Cpte)
(MUSD) **20239-2** Delibes—Opéras-Comiques

PARATORE, Anthony (pf)
(SCHW) **310115** Classics To Broadway

PARATORE, Joseph (pf)
(SCHW) **310115** Classics To Broadway

PARAY, Paul (cond)
see Detroit SO

PARBS, Grete (mez)
(SUPR) **11 2136-2(3)** Emmy Destinn—Complete Edition, Discs 5 to 8

PARENT, Marie-Danielle (mez)
Vivier: Kopernikus (Cpte)

PARENT, Yolande (sop)
Vivier: Kopernikus (Cpte)

PARETO, Graziella (sop)
(EMI) **CHS7 64860-2(2)** La Scala Edition - Vol.1, 1878-1914 (pt 2)
(PEAR) **GEMMCDS9925(1)** Covent Garden on Record—Vol.3 (pt 1)
(PEAR) **GEMMCD9117** Graziella Pareto

PARFITT, Paul (bar)
Lehár: Lustige Witwe (exc)
Sullivan: HMS Pinafore (exc)
Verdi: Trovatore (Cpte)

PARFITT, Wyndham (bar)
Offenbach: Robinson Crusoé (Cpte)

PARIS CHAMPS-ÉLYSÉES THEATRE CHORUS
cond P. BONNEAU
Hahn: Ciboulette (exc)

PARIS CHAMPS-ÉLYSÉES THEATRE ORCHESTRA
cond P. BONNEAU
Hahn: Ciboulette (exc)
cond A. JOUVE
(EMI) **CHS7 63715-2** Mozart: Die Entführung, etc

PARIS CHAPELLE ROYALE CHORUS
Grétry: Jugement de Midas (exc)

PARIS CONSERVATOIRE ORCHESTRA
(CFP) **CD-CFP9013** Duets from Famous Operas
cond A. CLUYTENS
Gounod: Mireille (Cpte)
Offenbach: Contes d'Hoffmann (Cpte)
(CFP) **CD-CFP4602** Favourite Opera
(CFP) **CD-CFP9013** Duets from Famous Operas
(EMI) **CDM7 69110-2** Russian Music
(EMI) **CZS5 68113-2** Vive Offenbach!
cond A. EREDE
(BELA) **450 006-2** Famous Opera Duets
(DECC) **433 066-2DWO** Your Hundred Best Opera Tunes III
cond R. FRÜHBECK DE BURGOS
(EMI) **CZS7 67474-2** Viva España!
cond P. GAUBERT
(EMI) **CMS7 64008-2(2)** Wagner Singing on Record (pt 2)
cond J-C. HARTEMANN
(EMI) **CDM5 65155-2** Chabrier—Une Education manquée; Mélodies
cond R. LEIBOWITZ
(CHES) **Chesky CD57** A Portrait Of France
(CHES) **Chesky CD61** Rene Leibowitz—An Evening of Opera
cond J-B. MARI
(MAND) **MAN4805** Light Music: The French Touch
cond J-P. MARTY
(EMI) **CZS5 68113-2** Vive Offenbach!
cond F. NUVOLONE
(EMI) **CZS5 68113-2** Vive Offenbach!
cond F. POURCEL
(EMI) **CZS7 67872-2** Lehár—Operettas (highlights in French)
cond G. PRÊTRE
Puccini: Tosca (Cpte)
(CFP) **CD-CFP4277** These you have Loved
(CFP) **CD-CFP4602** Favourite Opera
(EMI) **CDC5 55216-2** Maria Callas - La Divina 3
(EMI) **CDC7 49005-2** Maria Callas - Operatic Arias
(EMI) **CDC7 49059-2** Callas à Paris
(EMI) **CDC7 49502-2** Maria Callas—The Voice of the Century
(EMI) **CDC7 54016-2** Tenorissimo!
(EMI) **CDC7 54702-2** Maria Callas - La Divina
(EMI) **CDM7 63182-2** The Incomparable Callas
(EMI) **CMS7 63244-2** The Art of Maria Callas
(EMIN) **CD-EMX2123** Maria Callas sings Operatic Arias
cond N. RESCIGNO
(EMI) **CDC5 55016-2** Maria Callas - La Divina 2
(EMI) **CDC7 47283-2** Maria Callas - Mad Scenes & Bel Canto Arias
(EMI) **CDC7 47730-2** Maria Callas sings Verdi Arias, Vol.1
(EMI) **CDC7 47943-2** Maria Callas sings Verdi Arias, Vol.2
(EMI) **CDC7 49005-2** Maria Callas - Operatic Arias
(EMI) **CDC7 54437-2** Callas Rarities
(EMI) **CDC7 54702-2** Maria Callas - La Divina
(EMI) **CDM7 63182-2** The Incomparable Callas
(EMI) **CZS7 67440-2** The Best of Rossini
cond H. ROSBAUD
Mozart: Don Giovanni (Cpte), Nozze di Figaro (Cpte)
cond N. SANTI
(DECC) **436 300-2DX** Opera Gala Sampler
(DECC) **436 461-2DM** Ten Top Sopranos
(DECC) **440 404-2DM** Joan Sutherland
cond C. SILVESTRI
(EMI) **CZS5 68229-2** Constantin Silvestri—A profile
cond B. WALTER
(PEAR) **GEMMCD9945** Bruno Walter conducts Haydn, Schubert & J.Strauss II

PARIS INTERCONTEMPORAIN ENSEMBLE
cond P. BOULEZ
(DG) **431 751-2GC** Stravinsky—Songs
cond P. EÖTVÖS
Fénelon: Chevalier Imaginaire (Cpte)

PARIS OPERA CHORUS
cond H. BUSSER
(CONI) **CDHD226** Chaliapin—Bass of the Century
cond H. BÜSSER
(PEAR) **GEMMCD9314** Feodor Chaliapin - Aria and Song Recital
cond B. CAMPANELLA
(EMI) **CDM7 63104-2** Alfredo Krauss - Opera Recital
cond A. CLUYTENS
Gounod: Faust (exc)
cond P. DERVAUX
Poulenc: Dialogues des Carmélites (Cpte)
(EMI) **CZS7 62877-2** Les inspirations insolites d'Erik Satie
cond A. EREDE
Gounod: Roméo et Juliette (Cpte)
cond L. FOURESTIER
Saint-Saëns: Samson et Dalila (Cpte)
cond P. FOURNILLIER
Massenet: Amadis (Cpte)
cond R. FRÜHBECK DE BURGOS
Bizet: Carmen (Cpte)
cond H. VON KARAJAN
Bizet: Carmen (exc)
cond R. LEPPARD
Rameau: Dardanus (Cpte)
cond A. LOMBARD
Gounod: Roméo et Juliette (Cpte)
cond L. MAAZEL
Mozart: Don Giovanni (Cpte)
cond S. OZAWA
Messiaen: Saint François d'Assise (Cpte)
cond G. PRÊTRE
Bizet: Pêcheurs de Perles (Cpte)
Gounod: Faust (Cpte)
Puccini: Tosca (exc)
(CFP) **CD-CFP4602** Favourite Opera
cond J. RUDEL
G. Charpentier: Louise (Cpte)
cond N. SANTI
(DECC) **436 461-2DM** Ten Top Sopranos
(DECC) **440 404-2DM** Joan Sutherland
cond G. SÉBASTIAN
(EMI) **LDB9 91258-1(EMI)** Maria Callas at the Paris Opera December 1958
(MEMO) **HR4293/4** The very best of Maria Callas

PARIS OPERA ORCHESTRA
cond R. BENZI
(PHIL) **442 272-2PM2** The Best of Bizet
cond P. BOULEZ
Berg: Lulu (Cpte)
cond H. BUSSER
(CONI) **CDHD226** Chaliapin—Bass of the Century
cond H. BÜSSER
(PEAR) **GEMMCD9314** Feodor Chaliapin - Aria and Song Recital
cond B. CAMPANELLA
(EMI) **CDM7 63104-2** Alfredo Krauss - Opera Recital
cond A. CLUYTENS
Gounod: Faust (exc)
(EMI) **CDM5 65579-2** Victoria de los Angeles
cond P. COPPOLA
(MSCM) **MM30377** 18 Tenors d'Expression Française
cond P. DERVAUX
Poulenc: Dialogues des Carmélites (Cpte)
(EMI) **CZS5 68113-2** Vive Offenbach!
(EMI) **CZS7 67813-2** Opera Arias and Duets
cond A. EREDE
Gounod: Roméo et Juliette (Cpte)
cond L. FOURESTIER
Saint-Saëns: Samson et Dalila (Cpte)
(EMI) **CHS7 69741-2(3)** Record of Singing, Vol.4—French School
cond P. FOURNILLIER
Massenet: Amadis (Cpte)
cond R. FRÜHBECK DE BURGOS
Bizet: Carmen (Cpte)
(EMI) **CDC7 54016-2** Tenorissimo!
cond R. LEPPARD
Rameau: Dardanus (Cpte)
cond A. LOMBARD
Gounod: Roméo et Juliette (Cpte)
cond L. MAAZEL
Mozart: Don Giovanni (Cpte)
(CBS) **CD39208** A Portrait of Kiri te Kanawa
(SONY) **SBK46548** Opera Arias
cond J-B. MARI
Pierné: Ramuntcho
cond J-P. MARTY
(EMI) **CZS7 67813-2** Opera Arias and Duets
cond G-F. MASINI
(EMI) **CZS7 67440-2** The Best of Rossini
(EMI) **CZS7 67813-2** Opera Arias and Duets
cond D. MILHAUD
Milhaud: Malheurs d'Orphée (Cpte), Pauvre matelot (Cpte)
cond S. OZAWA
Messiaen: Saint François d'Assise (Cpte)

cond G. PRÊTRE
Bizet: Carmen (exc), Pêcheurs de Perles (Cpte)
Gounod: Faust (Cpte)
Saint-Saëns: Samson et Dalila (Cpte)
(CFP) **CD-CFP4582** Flowers in Music
(CFP) **CD-CFP4602** Favourite Opera
(EMI) **CDC5 55016-2** Maria Callas - La Divina 2
(EMI) **CDC5 55017-2** Domingo Opera Classics
(EMI) **CDC5 55216-2** Maria Callas - La Divina 3
(EMI) **CDC7 49502-2** Maria Callas—The Voice of the Century
(EMI) **CDC7 54016-2** Tenorissimo!
(EMI) **CDC7 54437-2** Callas Rarities
(EMI) **CDM7 63103-2** Placido Domingo sings Opera Arias
(EMI) **CDM7 63182-2** The Incomparable Callas
(EMI) **CDM7 64359-2** Gala de España
(EMI) **CDM7 69112-2** Best of Saint-Saëns
(EMIL) **CDZ100** Best Loved Classics 1
(EMIN) **CD-EMX2123** Maria Callas sings Operatic Arias
(EMIN) **CD-EMX9519** Great Sopranos of Our Time
cond N. RESCIGNO
(EMI) **CDC7 47943-2** Maria Callas sings Verdi Arias, Vol.2
(EMI) **CDC7 49428-2** Maria Callas - The Unknown Recordings
cond J. RUDEL
G. Charpentier: Louise (Cpte)
cond H. SCHERCHEN
(ADES) **13203-2** Weber—Overtures
cond G. SÉBASTIAN
(EMI) **LDB9 91258-1(EMI)** Maria Callas at the Paris Opera December 1958
(MEMO) **HR4293/4** The very best of Maria Callas
cond E. TCHAKAROV
(ERAT) **4509-98503-2** Recital—Ruggero Raimondi
cond M. VELTRI
(EMI) **CDC7 49067-2** Opera Arias and Duets
(EMI) **CZS7 67440-2** The Best of Rossini

ARIS OPÉRA-BASTILLE CHORUS
cond MYUNG-WHUN CHUNG
Saint-Saëns: Samson et Dalila (Cpte)
Shostakovich: Lady Macbeth of Mtsensk (Cpte)
Verdi: Otello (exc)

ARIS OPÉRA-BASTILLE ORCHESTRA
cond MYUNG-WHUN CHUNG
Saint-Saëns: Samson et Dalila (Cpte)
Shostakovich: Lady Macbeth of Mtsensk (Cpte)
Verdi: Otello (exc)

ARIS OPÉRA-COMIQUE CHORUS
cond G. CLOËZ
Puccini: Tosca (exc)
cond A. CLUYTENS
Bizet: Carmen (Cpte), Pêcheurs de Perles (Cpte)
Offenbach: Contes d'Hoffmann (Cpte)
Poulenc: Mamelles de Tirésias (Cpte)
cond E. COHEN
Massenet: Manon (Cpte), Werther (Cpte)
cond P. DERVAUX
Bizet: Pêcheurs de perles (Cpte)
cond A. LOMBARD
Delibes: Lakmé (exc)

ARIS OPÉRA-COMIQUE ORCHESTRA
cond G. CLOËZ
Puccini: Tosca (exc)
cond A. CLUYTENS
Bizet: Carmen (Cpte), Pêcheurs de Perles (Cpte)
Offenbach: Contes d'Hoffmann (Cpte)
Poulenc: Mamelles de Tirésias (Cpte)
Ravel: Heure espagnole (Cpte)
(EMI) **CHS7 69741-2(3)** Record of Singing, Vol.4—French School
(EMI) **CZS5 68113-2** Vive Offenbach!
cond E. COHEN
Massenet: Manon (Cpte), Werther (Cpte)
cond P. DERVAUX
Bizet: Pêcheurs de perles (Cpte)
(CFP) **CD-CFP4602** Favourite Opera
(CFP) **CD-CFP9013** Duets from Famous Operas
(EMI) **CDEMTVD59** Classic Experience 3
(EMI) **CDM7 69596-2** The Movies go to the Opera
cond L. FOURESTIER
(EMI) **CHS7 69741-2(3)** Record of Singing, Vol.4—French School
cond A. LOMBARD
Delibes: Lakmé (Cpte)
(CFP) **CD-CFP4582** Flowers in Music
(CFP) **CD-CFP4613** Favourite TV Classics
(EMI) **CDM7 69596-2** The Movies go to the Opera
(RCA) **74321 25817-2** Café Classics - Operatic
cond P. MONTEUX
(EMI) **CDM5 65579-2** Victoria de los Angeles
cond G. PRÊTRE
Poulenc: Voix Humaine (Cpte)

RIS ORCHESTRA CHORUS
cond D. BARENBOIM
Saint-Saëns: Samson et Dalila (Cpte)
cond S. BYCHKOV
Mascagni: Cavalleria Rusticana (Cpte)

RIS ORCHESTRAL ENSEMBLE
cond A. JORDAN
(ERAT) **2292-45797-2** The Ultimate Opera Collection
(ERAT) **4509-97239-2** Virtuoso Arias
cond J-P. WALLEZ
(NOVA) **150 014-2** Mozart—Gala Concert

PARIS ORCHESTRE DES SOLOISTES
cond J. ETCHEVERRY
(SYMP) **SYMCD1103** Renée Doria—Opera Recital
cond J-C. HARTEMANN
(SYMP) **SYMCD1103** Renée Doria—Opera Recital

PARIS ORTF LYRIC CHORUS
cond N. SANTI
Donizetti: Maria Stuarda (Cpte)

PARIS ORTF LYRIC ORCHESTRA
cond J. ETCHEVERRY
Massenet: Hérodiade (exc)
cond N. SANTI
Donizetti: Maria Stuarda (Cpte)

PARIS RADIO SYMPHONY ORCHESTRA
cond L. BERTRAND
(ROSE) **3201** Ravel/Bizet—Orchestral Works
(ROSE) **3229** Popular Orchestral Works

PARIS RUSSIAN OPERA CHORUS
cond M. STEINMANN
(EMI) **CDH7 61009-2** Chaliapin sings Russian Opera Arias
cond O. TCHERNOYAROV
(PEAR) **GEMMCD9314** Feodor Chaliapin - Aria and Song Recital

PARIS RUSSIAN OPERA ORCHESTRA
(EMI) **CDH7 61009-2** Chaliapin sings Russian Opera Arias

PARIS SORBONNE UNIVERSITY CHOIR
cond J. GRIMBERT
Mozart: Ascanio in Alba (Cpte)

PARIS SYMPHONY CHORUS
cond P. STOLL
Boïeldieu: Dame blanche (Cpte)

PARIS SYMPHONY ORCHESTRA
cond P. STOLL
Boïeldieu: Dame blanche (Cpte)
cond H. TOMASI
Gluck: Orphée (exc)
cond F. WEINGARTNER
(TELD) **4509-95038-6(TELD)** The Art of Conducting—Great Conductors of the Past

PARISI, Vittorio (cond)
see Teatro La Fenice Orch

PARKER, Christine (sngr)
G. Charpentier: Louise (Cpte)

PARKER, Patricia (mez)
Mozart: Zauberflöte (Cpte)

PARKER-SMITH, Jane (organ)
(EMI) **CDM7 69062-2** Trumpet and Organ Works
(EMIL) **CDZ112** Music for Weddings

PARKES, Peter (cond)
see Black Dyke Mills Band

PARKIN, Eric (pf)
(CLOU) **ACN6002** Gershwin: Piano Works

PARKMAN, Stefan (cond)
see Uppsala Univ Chmbr Ch

PARKS, Andrew (sngr)
Schuman: Mighty Casey (Cpte)

(THE) PARLEY OF INSTRUMENTS
(HYPE) **CDA66255** Italian Baroque Trumpet Music
cond R. GOODMAN
(HYPE) **CDA66108** Purcell's London: English Consort Music
cond P. HOLMAN
(HYPE) **CDA66667** Four and Twenty Fiddlers

(THE) PARLEY OF INSTRUMENTS BAROQUE ORCHESTRA
(HYPE) **CDA67001/3** Purcell—Complete Ayres for the Theatre

PARMA TEATRO REGIO CHORUS
cond R. CHAILLY
Verdi: Giovanna d'Arco (Cpte)
cond H. SOUDANT
Donizetti: Elisir d'amore (Cpte)
(MEMO) **HR4300/1** Great Voices—Sesto Bruscantini
(NUOV) **6905** Donizetti—Great Love Duets

PARMA TEATRO REGIO ORCHESTRA
cond G. PATANÈ
(BELA) **450 002-2** Pavarotti Live
(DECC) **443 018-2DF2** Pavarotti/Freni/Ricciarelli—Live

PARNASSUS ORCHESTRA
cond M. STENZ
Henze: English Cat (Cpte)

PARNIS, William (ten)
(PEAR) **GEMMCD9956** Joseph Hislop (1884-1977)

PARR, Gladys (contr)
(DANA) **DACOCD315/6** Lauritz Melchior Anthology - Vol. 3
(EMI) **CMS7 64008-2(1)** Wagner Singing on Record (pt 1)
(MSCM) **MM30283** Great Wagnerian Singers, Vol.1
(PEAR) **GEMMCD9944** Friedrich Schorr sings Wagner

PARR, Stephen (bass)
Vaughan Williams: Pilgrim's Progress (Cpte)

PARROTT, Andrew (cond)
see Taverner Plyrs

PARRY, David (cond)
see G. Mitchell Ch
Philh
RPO

PARRY, Marjorie (sop)
(PEAR) **GEMMCD9175** Heddle Nash - Serenade

PARSI-PETTINELLA, Armida (mez)
(EMI) **CHS7 64860-2(1)** La Scala Edition - Vol.1, 1878-1914 (pt 1)
(IRCC) **IRCC-CD800** Souvenirs from Meyerbeer Operas
(PEAR) **GEMMCDS9073(1)** Giovanni Zenatello, Vol.1 (pt 1)
(SYMP) **SYMCD1113** The Harold Wayne Collection, Vol.13
(SYMP) **SYMCD1138** The Harold Wayne Collection, Vol.16

PARSONS, Brian (ten)
Rameau: Castor et Pollux (Cpte), Naïs (Cpte)

PARSONS, Geoffrey (pf)
(COLL) **Coll1247-2** An Evening with Victoria De Los Angeles
(ORFE) **C363941B** Lucia Popp - Lieder Recital
(PHIL) **422 048-2PH** Jessye Norman—Song Recital
(PHIL) **422 235-2PH** Jessye Norman—European Tour, 1987

PARSONS, Meredith (contr)
Wagner: Götterdämmerung (Cpte), Rheingold (Cpte), Walküre (Cpte)
(DG) **437 825-2GH** Wagner—Der Ring des Nibelungen - Highlights
(DG) **445 354-2GX14** Wagner—Der Ring des Nibelungen
(DG) **072 422-3GH7** Levine conducts Wagner's Ring

PARTAMIAN, Maro (mez)
Janáček: Jenufa (Cpte)

PARTINGTON, Adrian (organ)
(PRIO) **PRCD479** The Symphonic Organ, Volume 2

PARTRIDGE, Ian (ten)
Berlioz: Troyens (Cpte)
Puccini: Manon Lescaut (Cpte)
Purcell: Fairy Queen, Z629 (Cpte), Indian Queen, Z630 (exc)
Vaughan Williams: Pilgrim's Progress (Cpte)

PARTRIDGE, Jennifer (pf)
(ASV) **CDWHL2070** Salut d'amour - Old Sweet Songs
(ASV) **CDWHL2088** Trumpet and Soprano in Duet

PARVIS, Taurino (bar)
(BONG) **GB1043-2** Italian Baritones of the Acoustic Era
(MEMO) **HR4408/9(2)** Singers in Genoa, Vol.1 (disc 2)

PASCO, Richard (spkr)
Britten: Noye's Fludde (Cpte)

PASDELOUP CONCERT ASSOCIATION ORCHESTRA
cond J. ALLAIN
Massé: Noces de Jeannette (Cpte)
(SYMP) **SYMCD1103** Renée Doria—Opera Recital
cond A. LOMBARD
(EMI) **CZS7 67869-2** J. Strauss II—Operetta Highlights

PASELLA, Guido (ten)
Donizetti: Don Pasquale (Cpte)

PASERO, Tancredi (bass)
Bellini: Norma (Cpte)
Verdi: Aida (Cpte)
(EMI) **CHS7 64864-2(1)** La Scala Edition - Vol.2, 1915-46 (pt 1)
(EMI) **CHS7 69741-2(7)** Record of Singing, Vol.4—Italian School
(PREI) **89009** Gino Bechi (b. 1913)
(PREI) **89010** Tancredi Pasero (1893-1983) - I
(PREI) **89016** Gina Cigna (b. 1900)
(PREI) **89074** Tancredi Pasero (1893-1983) - II

PASHINSKY, Vladislav (bass)
Rimsky-Korsakov: Tsar's Bride (Cpte)

PASHLEY, Anne (sop)
Britten: Albert Herring (Cpte), Peter Grimes (Cpte)

PASINI-VITALE, Lina (sop)
(PEAR) **GEMMCDS9073(2)** Giovanni Zenatello, Vol.1 (pt 2)
(SYMP) **SYMCD1113** The Harold Wayne Collection, Vol.13
(SYMP) **SYMCD1148** The Harold Wayne Collection, Vol.17

PASINO, Gisella (mez)
Franchetti: Cristoforo Colombo (Cpte)
Giordano: Andrea Chénier (Cpte)
Puccini: Fanciulla del West (Cpte)
Spontini: Vestale (Cpte)
Verdi: Otello (Cpte)
(CAPR) **10 810** Mozart—Opera Highlights

PASKALIS, Kostas (bar)
Bizet: Carmen (Cpte)
Verdi: Don Carlo (exc), Macbeth (Cpte), Rigoletto (Cpte)
(BUTT) **BMCD015** Pavarotti Collection - Duets and Scenes

PASKUDA, Georg (ten)
R. Strauss: Arabella (Cpte), Rosenkavalier (Cpte)

Wagner: Fliegende Holländer (Cpte), Parsifal (Cpte), Tannhäuser (Cpte)
(PHIL) **434 420-2PM32(2)** Richard Wagner Edition (pt 2)

PASQUALINI, Serena (mez)
(SCHW) **314052** Opera Gala

PASSMORE, Walter (bar)
(SYMP) **SYMCD1123** Sullivan—Sesquicentenial Commemorative Issue

PASTERNACK, Josef (cond)
see orch
Victor Orch

PASTERNAK, Wassili (ten)
Mussorgsky: Boris Godunov (Cpte)

PASTINE, Gianfranco (ten)
Rossini: Otello (Cpte)
(MCI) **MCCD099** Opera's Greatest Arias

PASTOR, Michel (ten)
Verdi: Luisa Miller (Cpte)

PATAKI, Antál (ten)
Boito: Mefistofele (Cpte)

PATAKY, Koloman von (ten)
Mozart: Don Giovanni (Cpte)
(EMI) **CDH5 65072-2** Glyndebourne Recorded - 1934-1994
(SCHW) **314512** Vienna State Opera Live, Vol.1
(SCHW) **314542** Vienna State Opera Live, Vol.4

PATANÈ, Franco (cond)
see MMF Orch
Santa Cecilia Academy Orch
Stuttgart Op Orch
Zurich Tonhalle Orch

PATANÈ, Giuseppe (cond)
see Bamberg SO
Bavarian St Orch
Berlin RSO
Bologna Teatro Comunale Orch
Hungarian Radio & TV Orch
Hungarian St Op Orch
Hungarian St Orch
Munich RO
Munich RSO
National PO
Parma Teatro Regio Orch
Philh
ROHO
San Francisco Op Orch
Santa Cecilia Academy Orch
Vienna Volksoper Orch
Zurich Tonhalle Orch

PATERNINA, Federico (voc)
Distel: Stazione (Cpte)

PATERNOSTRO, Robert (cond)
see Berlin RSO
Cologne RSO
NHK Chbr Sols
Tokyo PO
Württemberg PO

PATINKIN, Mandy (ten)
(NONE) **7559-79330-2** Patinkin—Experiment

PATON, Iain (ten)
Purcell: King Arthur, Z628 (Cpte)

PATON, Julie (sngr)
Bernstein: West Side Story (Cpte)

PATRICK, Julian (bar)
D. Moore: Carry Nation (Cpte)

PATRICK, Julian (bass-bar)
(SONY) **SM3K47154** Bernstein—Theatre Works Volume 1

PATRICK, Yvonne (sngr)
Sullivan: Gondoliers (Cpte), Iolanthe (Cpte), Mikado (Cpte)

PATTERSON, Barry (ten)
Offenbach: Orphée aux enfers (Cpte)

PATTERSON, James (bass)
Mozart: Don Giovanni (Cpte)

PATTERSON, Susan (sop)
Rossini: Occasione fa il ladro (Cpte)
Vivaldi: Orlando Furioso (Cpte)

PATTI, Adelina (sop)
(EMI) **CHS7 64860-2(1)** La Scala Edition - Vol.1, 1878-1914 (pt 1)
(NIMB) **NI7840/1** The Era of Adelina Patti
(PEAR) **GEMMCDS9923(1)** Covent Garden on Record, Vol.1 (pt 1)
(PEAR) **GEMMCD9130** Great Sopranos, Vol.2
(PEAR) **GEMMCD9312** Adelina Patti

PATTI, Gino Martinez (ten)
(BONG) **GB1043-2** Italian Baritones of the Acoustic Era

PATTIERA, Tino (ten)
(PEAR) **GEMMCD9082** Meta Seinemeyer
(PREI) **89029** Meta Seinemeyer (1895-1929)

PATZAK, Julius (ten)
Beethoven: Fidelio (Cpte)
R. Strauss: Arabella (Cpte)
(EMI) **CZS7 67123-2** Wagner: Der Ring des Nibelungen
(MMOI) **CDMOIR406** Mozart—Historical Recordings
(MMOI) **CDMOIR419** Vienna Nights - Golden Age of Operetta
(MMOI) **CDMOIR422** Great Voices in Tchaikovsky
(NIMB) **NI7856** Legendary Tenors
(PEAR) **GEMMCD9383** Julius Patzak—Opera & Operetta Recital
(PREI) **89092** Erna Berger (1900-1990) - II
(SCHW) **314712** Vienna State Opera Live, Vol.21

PAUCKER, Georg (bass)
R. Strauss: Salome (Cpte)

PAUL, Charles (bar)
Poulenc: Dialogues des Carmélites (Cpte)

PAUL, Gerhard (narr)
Weber: Freischütz (exc)

PAUL, Karl (bar)
(PILZ) **442118-2** Wagner—Operas in Historical Recordings

PAULEY, Wilbur (bass)
M. Monk: Atlas (Cpte)
(MUSM) **67110-2** Stravinsky—The Composer, Volume V

PAULI, Dietrich (ten)
Suder: Kleider machen Leute (Cpte)

PAULI, Piero (ten)
Puccini: Tosca (Cpte)

PAULIK, Anton (cond)
see Vienna SO
Vienna St Op Orch
Vienna Th an der Wien Orch
Vienna Th Orch
Vienna Volksoper Orch

PAULSEN, Thomas (treb)
Mozart: Zauberflöte (Cpte)

PAULY, Ernst (ten)
Zeller: Vogelhändler (exc)

PAULY, Rose (sop)
Wagner: Tannhäuser (Cpte)
(PEAR) **GEMMCDS9365** R. Strauss: Der Rosenkavalier (abridged), etc
(SCHW) **314512** Vienna State Opera Live, Vol.1
(SCHW) **314672** Vienna State Opera Live, Vol.17

PAUMGARTNER, Bernhard (cond)
see Camerata Academica
Salzburg Mozarteum Camerata Academica
Vienna SO

PAUNOV, Milen (ten)
Mussorgsky: Boris Godunov (Cpte)

PAUNOVA, Mariana (contr)
Prokofiev: War and Peace (Cpte)

PAUSTIAN, Inger (sop)
Wagner: Parsifal (Cpte)

PAUT, Françoise (sop)
M-A. Charpentier: Actéon (Cpte)

PAVAROTTI, Fernando (ten)
Verdi: Luisa Miller (Cpte)

PAVAROTTI, Luciano (ten)
Bellini: Capuleti (Cpte), Norma (Cpte), Puritani (Cpte), Sonnambula (Cpte)
Boito: Mefistofele (Cpte)
Donizetti: Elisir d'amore (Cpte), Favorita (Cpte), Fille du régiment (Cpte), Lucia di Lammermoor (Cpte), Maria Stuarda (Cpte)
Giordano: Andrea Chénier (Cpte)
J. Strauss II: Fledermaus (Cpte)
Leoncavallo: Pagliacci (Cpte)
Mascagni: Amico Fritz (Cpte), Cavalleria Rusticana (Cpte)
Massenet: Manon (Cpte)
Mozart: Idomeneo (Cpte)
Ponchielli: Gioconda (Cpte)
Puccini: Bohème (Cpte), Madama Butterfly (Cpte), Manon Lescaut (Cpte), Tosca (Cpte), Turandot (Cpte)
R. Strauss: Rosenkavalier (Cpte)
Rossini: Guillaume Tell (Cpte)
Verdi: Aida (exc), Ballo in maschera (Cpte), Don Carlo (Cpte), Lombardi (Cpte), Luisa Miller (Cpte), Macbeth (Cpte), Otello (exc), Rigoletto (Cpte), Traviata (Cpte), Trovatore (exc)
(ACAN) **49 402** Giuseppe Taddei—Recital
(BELA) **450 002-2** Pavarotti Live
(BUTT) **BMCD015** Pavarotti Collection - Duets and Scenes
(CBS) **CD37228** Pavarotti sings Verdi
(CFP) **CD-CFP4602** Favourite Opera
(DECC) **417 011-2DH2** Pavarotti's Greatest Hits
(DECC) **417 796-2DM** Luciano Pavarotti—'Mattinata'
(DECC) **421 896-2DA** Puccini—Great Operatic Duets
(DECC) **425 037-2DM** Pavarotti in Concert
(DECC) **425 681-2DM2** Tutto Pavarotti
(DECC) **425 848-2DWO** Your hundred best tunes vol 2
(DECC) **425 849-2DWO** Your hundred best tunes vol 3
(DECC) **425 850-2DWO** Your Hundred Best Tunes, Vol.4
(DECC) **430 433-2DH** Carreras, Domingo and Pavarotti in Concert
(DECC) **430 470-2DH** Essential Pavarotti II
(DECC) **430 716-2DM** Pavarotti—Gala Concert at the Albert Hall
(DECC) **430 724-2DM** Great Operatic Duets
(DECC) **433 064-2DWO** Your Hundred Best Opera Tunes Volume I
(DECC) **433 065-2DWO** Your Hundred Best Opera Tunes Volume II
(DECC) **433 066-2DWO** Your Hundred Best Opera Tunes III
(DECC) **433 068-2DWO** Your Hundred Best Opera Tunes V
(DECC) **433 069-2DWO** Your Hundred Best Opera Tunes VI
(DECC) **433 221-2DWO** The World of Verdi
(DECC) **433 437-2DA** Pavarotti—King of the High Cs
(DECC) **433 439-2DA** Great Love Duets
(DECC) **433 440-2DA** Golden Opera
(DECC) **433 442-2DA** Verdi—Famous Arias
(DECC) **433 706-2DMO3** Bellini—Beatrice di Tenda; Operatic Arias
(DECC) **433 710-2DH** O Holy Night
(DECC) **433 822-2DH** Essential Opera
(DECC) **433 865-2DWO** The World of Puccini
(DECC) **436 300-2DX** Opera Gala Sampler
(DECC) **436 313-2DA** Sutherland/Pavarotti—Operatic Duets
(DECC) **436 314-2DA** Great Tenor Arias
(DECC) **436 315-2DA** Great Operatic Duets
(DECC) **436 317-2DA** Puccini—Famous Arias
(DECC) **436 461-2DM** Ten Top Sopranos
(DECC) **436 463-2DM** Ten Top Tenors
(DECC) **436 472-2DM** Great Opera Arias
(DECC) **440 400-2DM** Luciano Pavarotti
(DECC) **440 412-2DM** Mirella Freni
(DECC) **440 947-2DH** Essential Opera II
(DECC) **443 018-2DF2** Pavarotti/Freni/Ricciarelli—Live
(DECC) **443 377-2DM** Ten Top Sopranos 2
(DECC) **443 379-2DM** Ten Top Tenors 2
(DECC) **443 585-2DF2** Your Hundred Best Tunes - Top 20
(DECC) **443 928-2DM** Montserrat Caballé sings Opera Arias
(DECC) **444 450-2DH** Pavarotti in Central Park
(DECC) **444 460-2DH** Pavarotti and Friends II
(DECC) **444 555-2DF2** Essential Puccini
(DECC) **400 053-4DH** World's Best Loved Tenor Arias
(DECC) **071 119-1DH (DECC)** Pavarotti and Levine in Recital at the Met
(DECC) **071 123-1DH (DECC)** Carreras, Domingo and Pavarotti in Concert
(DECC) **071 140-1DH (DECC)** Pavarotti—30th Anniversary Gala Concert
(DECC) **071 142-1DH (DECC)** Essential Opera
(DECC) **071 149-1DH (DECC)** The Essential Sutherland
(DECC) **071 150-1DH (DECC)** Pavarotti in Hyde Park
(DECC) **430 433-5DH** Carreras, Domingo and Pavarotti in Concert
(DECC) **436 320-5DH** Pavarotti in Hyde Park
(DG) **439 153-4GMA** Mad about Sopranos
(DG) **072 428-1GH2(DG)** The Metropolitan Opera Gala
(EDL) **EDL2562-2** Carreras, Domingo, Pavarotti Greatest Hits
(MEMO) **HR4277/8** Mirella Freni—Public Performances 1963-1970
(PHIL) **442 602-2PM** 3 x 3 Tenors
(RCA) **09026 61886-2** Operas Greatest Love Songs
(RCA) **09026 62541-2** Pavarotti - The Early Years, Vol.1
(RCA) **09026 62550-2** Ten Tenors in Love
(RCA) **09026 62699-2** Opera's Greatest Duets
(RCA) **09026 68014-2** Pavarotti - The Early Years, Vol.2
(SONY) **MDK47176** Favourite Arias by the World's Favourite Tenors
(TELD) **4509-96200-8** The Three Tenors 1994
(TELD) **4509-96200-2** The Three Tenors 1994
(TELD) **4509-96200-5** The Three Tenors 1994

PAVLOVÁ, Jitka (sop)
Fibich: Šárka (Cpte)
(DECC) **421 852-2DH2** Janáček: Operatic & Chamber Works
(SUPR) **11 1878-2** The Unknown Janáček

PAWELS, Jürgen von (narr)
Lehár: Giuditta (Cpte)

PAXTON, Adele (sop)
Verdi: Stiffelio (Cpte)

PAY, Sam (treb)
Britten: Turn of the Screw (Cpte)

PAYEN, Paul (bar)
Massenet: Manon (Cpte)

PAYNE, Patricia (mez)
Britten: Peter Grimes (Cpte)
Verdi: Ballo in maschera (Cpte)
(CBS) **CD79312** Puccini: Il Trittico
(KIWI) **CDSLD-82** Southern Voices—NZ International Opera Singers
(LOND) **825 126-2** Amadeus - Original Soundtrack

PEACHEY, Richard (treb)
Britten: Albert Herring (Cpte)

PEACOCK, Adrian (bass)
Boughton: Bethlehem (Cpte)

PEACOCK, Lucy (sop)
Hindemith: Mörder, Hoffnung der Frauen (Cpte)
Weill: Kuhhandel (exc)

PEARCE, John (ten)
Vaughan Williams: Hugh the Drover (Cpte)

PEARL, David (treb)
Puccini: Tosca (Cpte)

PEARL, Ronald (gtr)
(DORI) **DOR90209** Baroque Inventions

PEARN, Michael (sngr)
Bernstein: West Side Story (Cpte)

PEARS, Sir Peter (ten)
Britten: Albert Herring (Cpte), Billy Budd (Cpte), Burning Fiery Furnace (Cpte), Curlew River (Cpte), Death in Venice (Cpte), Midsummer Night's Dream (Cpte), Peter Grimes (Cpte), Prodigal Son (Cpte), Rape of Lucretia (Cpte), Turn of the Screw (Cpte)
Puccini: Turandot (Cpte)
Purcell: Fairy Queen, Z629 (Cpte)
Walton: Troilus and Cressida (exc)
(EMI) **CMS7 64727-2** Britten—Opera excerpts and Folksongs
(LOND) **433 200-2LHO2** Britten—Owen Wingrave, etc.
(LOND) **436 393-2LM** Britten—The Little Sweep, etc
(RCA) **09026 61583-2(5)** Julian Bream Edition (pt 5)
(RCA) **09026 61601-2** J. Bream Edition, Vol.18: Music for Voice & Gtr

PEARSON, Barbara (sop)
Schoenberg: Moses und Aron (Cpte)

PEARSON, Leslie (organ)
(LDR) **LDRCD1006** Well-Tempered Trumpet

PEARSON, Leslie (hpd)
(EMI) **CDC7 47122-2** Mozart: Concert and Operatic Arias

PEASE, James (bar)
Britten: Peter Grimes (Cpte)

PECHNER, Gerhard (bar)
Verdi: Macbeth (Cpte)
(RCA) **09026 61580-2(7)** RCA/Met 100 Singers, 100 Years (pt 7)

PECHOVÁ, Jarmila (sop)
Smetana: Bartered Bride (Cpte)

PECHURIA, Tatiana (mez)
Rimsky-Korsakov: Mlada (Cpte), Tsar's Bride (Cpte)

PECK, Richard (ten sax)
Glass: Hydrogen Jukebox (Cpte)

PEDACI, Francesca (sngr)
Cherubini: Lodoïska (Cpte)
Mozart: Don Giovanni (Cpte)

PEDANI, Paolo (bar)
Giordano: Andrea Chénier (Cpte)
Verdi: Traviata (Cpte)
(CFP) **CD-CFP9013** Duets from Famous Operas

PEDARNIG, Florian (cond)
see *Innsbruck Postmusik*

PEDERSON, Monte (bar)
Beethoven: Fidelio (Cpte)
Janáček: From the House of the Dead (Cpte)
Schreker: Gezeichneten (Cpte), Irrelohe (Cpte)
Tchaikovsky: Mazeppa (Cpte)

PEDICONI, Fiorella (sop)
Paisiello: Nina (Cpte)
Rossini: Torvaldo e Dorliska (Cpte)

PEDLEY, Anthony (sngr)
Gay: Beggar's Opera (Cpte)

PEDRAZZOLI, Eduardo (cond)
see *LSO*

PEDRONI, Augusto (ten)
Donizetti: Favorita (Cpte)
(MEMO) **HR4300/1** Great Voices—Sesto Bruscantini

PEDRONI, Gina (mez)
(PEAR) **GEMMCD9091** Dino Borgioli

PEEL, Ruth (contr)
Vaughan Williams: Pilgrim's Progress (Cpte)

PEERCE, Jan (ten)
Beethoven: Fidelio (Cpte)
Bizet: Carmen (Cpte)
Puccini: Bohème (Cpte)
R. Strauss: Ariadne auf Naxos (Cpte)
Verdi: Ballo in maschera (Cpte), Traviata (Cpte)
(ALTN) **CDAN3** Hjördis Schymberg
(EMI) **CHS7 69741-2(2)** Record of Singing, Vol.4—Anglo-American School (pt 2)
(RCA) **GD60276** Toscanini conducts Boito & Verdi
(RCA) **GD60299** Verdi: Requiem, etc
(RCA) **GD60326** Verdi—Operas & Choral Works
(RCA) **09026 61580-2(5)** RCA/Met 100 Singers, 100 Years (pt 5)
(RCA) **09026 62550-2** Ten Tenors in Love
(VAI) **VAI69117** Jan Peerce in Opera and Song

PETERS, Harry (bass)
Janáček: From the House of the Dead (Cpte)
Monteverdi: Orfeo (Cpte)
Mozart: Idomeneo (Cpte), Zauberflöte (Cpte)
R. Strauss: Salome (Cpte)

PEKINEL, Güher (pf)
(TELD) **4509-92143-2** 20th Century Piano Works

PEKINEL, Süher (pf)
(TELD) **4509-92143-2** 20th Century Piano Works

PELIZZONI, Rinaldo (ten)
Donizetti: Lucia di Lammermoor (Cpte)
(DECC) **417 780-2DM** Joan Sutherland's Greatest Hits

PELL, William (ten)
Wagner: Tannhäuser (Cpte)

PELLE, Nadia (sop)
(CHAN) **CHAN9304** Lullabies

PELLEGRINO, Liliana (mez)
Verdi: Due Foscari (Cpte)

PELLEKOORNE, Anne (contr)
Wagner: Walküre (Cpte)
(EMI) **LDX9 91275-1(EMI)** Sawallisch conducts Wagner's Ring

PELLERIN, Raymond (alto)
Handel: Sosarme (Cpte)

PELLETIER, Wilfrid (cond)
see *NY Met Op Orch*
orch
RCA SO
RCA Victor Orch
Victor SO

PELON, Caroline (sop)
Rossi: Orfeo (Cpte)

PÉNA, Michèle (sop)
Offenbach: Orphée aux enfers (Cpte)
(EMI) **CZS5 68113-2** Vive Offenbach!

PENDACHANSKA, Alexandrina (sop)
Glinka: Life for the Tsar (Cpte)
(CAPR) **10 706** Young Voices of the Opera-Alexandrina Pendatchanska

PENDARVIS, Janice (voc)
(SONY) **SK64133** The Essential Philip Glass

PENDERGAST, Glynis (sop)
(LOND) **436 813-2LM2** Sullivan—The Grand Duke. Overture Di Ballo. Henry VIII

PENKOVA, Reni (mez)
Verdi: Falstaff (Cpte)
(EMI) **CMS7 63386-2** Borodin—Prince Igor & Complete Solo Songs

PENNACI, Sergio (cond)
see *Bulgarian RSO*

PENNICCHI, Marinella (sop)
Piccinni: Pescatrice (Cpte)

PENNO, Gino (ten)
Verdi: Macbeth (Cpte)

PENNY, Andrew (cond)
see *RTE Concert Orch*
Ukraine National SO

PENROSE, Timothy (alto)
Purcell: Fairy Queen, Z629 (Cpte)
(CAMP) **RRCD1323** Welcome Ev'ry Guest - John Blow/Henry Purcell Songs
(DG) **439 474-2GCL** Purcell—Opera & Choral Works

PENTCHEVA, Mariana (contr)
Verdi: Rigoletto (Cpte)

PEPER, Uwe (ten)
Lehár: Lustige Witwe (Cpte)
Mozart: Entführung (Cpte)

PEREA, Emilio (ten)
(MEMO) **HR4408/9(2)** Singers in Genoa, Vol.1 (disc 2)

PEREGUDOV, Alexandr (ten)
(ARLE) **ARL23/5** Rimsky-Korsakov—Sadko

PEREIRA, Malvina (sop)
(PEAR) **GEMMCDS9074(1)** Giovanni Zenatello, Vol.2 (pt 1)

PERELSTEIN, Mabel (contr)
Penella: Gato Montés (Cpte)
Puccini: Gianni Schicchi (Cpte)
Vives: Doña Francisquita (Cpte)

PEREZ, Dolores (sngr)
Barbieri: Barberillo de Lavapiès (Cpte)

PEREZ INIGO, Paloma (sop)
(IMP) **MCD45** Spanish Royal Gala

PÉREZ-QUER, Guillem (gtr)
(PRES) **PCOM1120** Duo Kassner-Quer—Tambor de granaderos

PERGOLA, Luciano della (ten)
Verdi: Macbeth (Cpte)

PERICK, Christof (cond)
see *Berlin RSO*

PERILLO, Linda (sop)
Purcell: King Arthur, Z628 (Cpte)

PERINI, Flora (mez)
(CLAR) **CDGSE78-50-52** Three Tenors
(MCI) **MCCD086** The Essential Caruso
(MSCM) **MM30352** Caruso—Italian Opera Arias
(PEAR) **EVC4(1)** The Caruso Edition, Vol.4 (pt 1)
(PEAR) **GEMMCDS9159(2)** De Luca Edition, Vol.1 (pt 2)
(RCA) **GD60495(6)** The Complete Caruso Collection (pt 6)
(ROMO) **81003-2** Galli-Curci—Acoustic Recordings, Vol.1

PERLASOVA, Evgenia (mez)
Borodin: Prince Igor (Cpte)
Mussorgsky: Boris Godunov (Cpte)
Tchaikovsky: Queen of Spades (Cpte)

PERLEA, Jonel (cond)
see *RCA Italiana Op Orch*
Rome Op Chor
Rome Op Orch

PERLMAN, Itzhak (bass)
Puccini: Tosca (Cpte)

PERLMAN, Itzhak (vn)
(EMI) **CDC5 55475-2** Itzhak Perlman - À la carte
(EMI) **CDC7 47467-2** My Favourite Kreisler
(EMI) **CDC7 54108-2** Tchaikovsky—Violin Works
(EMI) **CDC7 54266-2** Domingo and Perlman—Together
(EMI) **CZS4 83177-2(2)** Itzhak Perlman Edition (pt 2)
(EMI) **LDB9 91243-1(EMI)** Itzak Perlman Live in Russia

PERNERSTORFER, Alois (bass-bar)
Einem: Prozess (Cpte)
R. Strauss: Elektra (Cpte), Schweigsame Frau (Cpte)
Verdi: Don Carlo (exc)
(EMI) **CZS7 67123-2** Wagner: Der Ring des Nibelungen
(SCHW) **314572** Vienna State Opera Live, Vol.7

PERNET, André (bass)
G. Charpentier: Louise (exc)
Offenbach: Contes d'Hoffmann (Cpte)

PERNOO, Jacques (cond)
see *Colonne Concerts Orch*

PERRAGUIN, Hélène (mez)
Berlioz: Troyens (Cpte)
Massenet: Amadis (Cpte), Esclarmonde (Cpte)
Prokofiev: Love for 3 Oranges (Cpte)
R. Strauss: Salomé (Cpte)

PERRAS, John (cond)
see *Centre d'Action Musicale de l'Ouest Orch*

PERRAS, Margherita (sop)
(NIMB) **NI7848** Great Singers at the Berlin State Opera
(ORFE) **C394101B** Great Mozart Singers Series, Vol. 1
(PEAR) **GEMMCD9394** Helge Roswaenge—Operatic Recital
(PREI) **89082** Margarete Klose (1902-1968)
(PREI) **89088** Walther Ludwig (1902-1981)
(PREI) **89209** Helge Roswaenge (1897-1972) - II
(SCHW) **314632** Vienna State Opera Live, Vol.13

PERRIERS, Daniele (sop)
Mozart: Così fan tutte (Cpte)

PERRIN, Cécile (sop)
Jommelli: Armida abbandonata (Cpte)

PERRIN, Yvonne (sop)
Monteverdi: Orfeo (Cpte)

PERRIS, Adriana (sop)
Bellini: Norma (Cpte)

PERRY, Douglas (ten)
Glass: Satyagraha (Cpte)
V. Thomson: Mother of us all (Cpte)
(SONY) **SK64133** The Essential Philip Glass

PERRY, Eugene (bar)
A. Davis: X (Cpte)
J. Adams: Death of Klinghoffer (Cpte)
Mozart: Don Giovanni (Cpte)

PERRY, Herbert (bass)
A. Davis: X (Cpte)
Mozart: Don Giovanni (Cpte)

PERRY, Janet (sop)
Egk: Peer Gynt (Cpte)
J. Strauss II: Fledermaus (Cpte)
Mercadante: Bravo (Cpte)
Monteverdi: Incoronazione di Poppea (Cpte)
Mozart: Nozze di Figaro (Cpte), Thamos, K345 (Cpte), Zauberflöte (exc)
R. Strauss: Rosenkavalier (Cpte)
Smetana: Bartered Bride (Cpte)
Verdi: Falstaff (Cpte)
Wagner: Parsifal (Cpte)
(DG) **439 153-4GMA** Mad about Sopranos

PERT, Jill (contr)
Offenbach: Orphée aux enfers (Cpte)
Sullivan: Gondoliers (Cpte), Iolanthe (Cpte), Yeomen of the Guard (Cpte)

PERTILE, Aureliano (ten)
Verdi: Aida (Cpte), Otello (exc)
(CONI) **CDHD235** The Puccini Album
(EMI) **CHS7 64864-2(1)** La Scala Edition - Vol.2, 1915-46 (pt 1)
(EMI) **CMS7 64008-2(1)** Wagner Singing on Record (pt 1)
(LYRC) **SRO805** Gina Cigna—Opera Recital
(MMOI) **CDMOIR405** Great Tenors
(NIMB) **NI7856** Legendary Tenors
(PEAR) **GEMMCDS9925(2)** Covent Garden on Record—Vol.3 (pt 2)
(PEAR) **GEMMCDS9926(1)** Covent Garden on Record—Vol.4 (pt 1)
(PEAR) **GEMMCD9129** Great Tenors, Vol.2
(PREI) **89007** Aureliano Pertile (1885-1952) - I

PHILHARMONIA HUNGARICA
cond A. DORATI
(DECC) **425 034-2DM** Kodály—Orchestral Works
(DECC) **443 006-2DF2** Kodály—Orchestral Works
cond Z. ROZSNYAI
(PREI) **90103** Helge Roswaenge Recital (1959)

PHILHARMONIA ORCHESTRA
(EMI) **CDC7 54626-2** Operetta Arias
(EMI) **CDM7 69501-2** Elisabeth Schwarzkopf—Romantic Heroines
cond O. ACKERMANN
J. Strauss II: Fledermaus (Cpte), Nacht in Venedig (Cpte)
Lehár: Land des Lächelns (Cpte), Lustige Witwe (Cpte)
(CFP) **CD-CFP4277** These you have Loved
(EMI) **CDC7 47284-2** Elisabeth Schwarzkopf sings Operetta
(EMI) **CDH7 61001-2** R. Strauss—Lieder & Arias
(EMI) **CDM5 65577-2** Elisabeth Schwarzkopf
(EMI) **CDM7 63657-2** Schwarzkopf sings Opera Arias
(TEST) **SBT1059** Erich Kunz (b. 1909)
cond A. DE ALMEIDA
Halévy: Juive (Cpte)
(PHIL) **442 403-2PM** Offenbach—Ballet Music
cond F. D'AVALOS
Wagner: Götterdämmerung (exc), Tannhäuser (exc)
(ASV) **CDDCA611** Wagner—Orchestral Music, Vol. 2
(ASV) **CDDCA666** D'Avalos conducts Wagner, Vol 3
(ASV) **CDDCA704** Wagner—Overtures & Preludes
(ASV) **CDQS6126** Romeo and Juliet
(IMP) **MCD81** Mendelssohn—Orchestral Works
(IMP) **MCD88** Mendelssohn—Symphonies and Overtures
cond E. BÁTIZ
Rimsky-Korsakov: Tale of Tsar Saltan (exc)
cond R. BEHR
(EMI) **CDC5 55018-2** Domingo sings and conducts Tchaikovsky
cond T. BENINTENDE-NEGLIA
(EMI) **CHS7 69741-2(7)** Record of Singing, Vol.4—Italian School
cond I. BOLTON
(SILV) **SONGCD907** Lesley Garrett—Prima Donna
cond W. BOUGHTON
Holst: Perfect Fool (exc)
(NIMB) **NI5120** Popular Operatic Overtures
(NIMB) **NI5387** Kelly's Classic Challenge II
(NIMB) **NI5450/3** Spirit of England II
cond K. BÖHM
Mozart: Così fan tutte (Cpte)
(EMI) **CDM5 65577-2** Elisabeth Schwarzkopf
(EMI) **CDM7 63104-2** Alfredo Krauss - Opera Recital
(EMI) **CDM7 64359-2** Gala de España
(EMI) **CMS5 65212-2** Wagner—Les introuvables du Ring
(EMIL) **CDZ7 67015-2** Mozart—Opera Arias
(EMIN) **CD-EMX9519** Great Sopranos of Our Time
(TEST) **SBT1018** Kirsten Flagstad
cond W. BRAITHWAITE
(EMI) **CDH7 63199-2** Sena Jurinac—Opera and Song Recital
(EMI) **CDH7 63708-2** Mozart—Opera Arias
(EMI) **CHS7 69741-2(5)** Record of Singing, Vol.4—Scandinavian School
(TEST) **SBT1018** Kirsten Flagstad
cond G. CANTELLI
(TEST) **SBT1034** Guido Cantelli conducts Rossini, Mendelssohn & Beethoven
cond COLIN DAVIS
(CFP) **CD-CFP4575** Verdi Arias
cond J. COLLADO
(RCA) **RK61044** Eternal Caballé
cond L. COLLINGWOOD
(EMI) **CDH7 63199-2** Sena Jurinac—Opera and Song Recital
(EMI) **CHS7 69741-2(3)** Record of Singing, Vol.4—French School
(EMI) **CHS7 69741-2(4)** Record of Singing, Vol.4—German School
(TEST) **SBT1013** Dame Joan Hammond—A Celebration
cond G. CURIEL
(TEST) **SBT1013** Dame Joan Hammond—A Celebration
cond I. DOBROVEN
(EMI) **CDH5 65500-2** Boris Christoff - Italian Opera Arias
(EMI) **CDH7 63030-2** Kirsten Flagstad - Wagner Opera Arias
(EMI) **CDH7 64252-2** Christoff sings Russian Arias & Songs
(EMI) **CHS7 69741-2(4)** Record of Singing, Vol.4—German School
(EMI) **CMS7 64008-2(1)** Wagner Singing on Record (pt 1)
cond J.O. EDWARDS
Romberg: Student Prince (Cpte)
(TER) **CDVIR8314** Is it really me?
(TER) **CDVIR8315** Carousel Waltz
(TER) **CDVIR8317** If I Loved You - Love Duets from the Musicals
cond A. EREDE
(EMI) **CDM7 63109-2** Tito Gobbi - Opera Aria Recital
(EMI) **CHS7 64864-2(2)** La Scala Edition - Vol.2, 1915-46 (pt 2)
cond A. FISTOULARI
(EMI) **CDH5 65500-2** Boris Christoff - Italian Opera Arias
(EMI) **CDH7 63495-2** Victoria de los Angeles—Early Recordings
(EMI) **CDH7 64028-2** Victoria de los Angeles sings Spanish Songs
(EMI) **CHS7 69741-2(2)** Record of Singing, Vol.4—Anglo-American School (pt 2)
(EMI) **CHS7 69741-2(7)** Record of Singing, Vol.4—Italian School
cond C. P. FLOR
(RCA) **09026 62712-2** Weber—Symphonies, etc
cond L. FOSTER
(EMI) **CDC7 54626-2** Operetta Arias
cond W. FURTWÄNGLER
Wagner: Tristan und Isolde (Cpte)
(EMI) **CDH7 63030-2** Kirsten Flagstad - Wagner Opera Arias
(EMI) **CHS5 65058-2** The Great German Tradition
(EMI) **CHS7 64935-2** Wagner—Opera Excerpts
(EMI) **CMS5 65212-2** Wagner—Les introuvables du Ring
cond A. GALLIERA
Rossini: Barbiere di Siviglia (exc)
(CFP) **CD-CFP4602** Favourite Opera
(CFP) **CD-CFP4613** Favourite TV Classics
(CFP) **CD-CFP9013** Duets from Famous Operas
(EMI) **CDC5 55095-2** Prima Diva
(EMI) **CDC5 55216-2** Maria Callas - La Divina 3
(EMI) **CDM5 65577-2** Elisabeth Schwarzkopf
(EMI) **CDM7 69596-2** The Movies go to the Opera
(EMI) **CES5 68541-2** Rossini/Verdi/Bellini/Donizetti—Overtures
(EMI) **CHS7 69741-2(4)** Record of Singing, Vol.4—German School
(EMI) **CHS7 69741-2(5)** Record of Singing, Vol.4—Scandinavian School
(EMI) **CZS7 67440-2** The Best of Rossini
(EMIL) **CDZ101** Best Loved Classics 2
(EMIN) **CD-EMX2123** Maria Callas sings Operatic Arias
cond P. GAMBA
(DECC) **417 796-2DM** Luciano Pavarotti—'Mattinata'
(DECC) **433 710-2DH** O Holy Night
cond C.M. GIULINI
Mozart: Don Giovanni (exc), Nozze di Figaro (Cpte)
(CFP) **CD-CFP4602** Favourite Opera
(CFP) **CD-CFP4606** Favourite Movie Classics
(CFP) **CD-CFP9013** Duets from Famous Operas
(EMI) **CDC5 55095-2** Prima Diva
(EMI) **CDM5 65577-2** Elisabeth Schwarzkopf
(EMI) **CDM7 69042-2** Rossini—Overtures
(EMI) **CDM7 69596-2** The Movies go to the Opera
(EMI) **CZS7 67440-2** The Best of Rossini
(EMIL) **CDZ7 67015-2** Mozart—Opera Arias
(EMIN) **CD-EMX9519** Great Sopranos of Our Time
cond A. GREENWOOD
Joseph James: Scarlet Letter (exc)
(SILV) **FILMCD127** Vampire Circus—The Essential Vampire Theme Collection
(SILV) **SONGCD903** Diva! A Soprano at the Movies
(SILV) **SILVACD105(SILV)** Flower Duet from Lakme - Lesley Garrett
cond O.A. HUGHES
(ASV) **CDDCA627** Delius—A Song of Summer
(ASV) **CDQS6126** Romeo and Juliet
cond JAMES LEVINE
Cilea: Adriana Lecouvreur (Cpte)
Puccini: Tosca (Cpte)
(EMI) **CDC5 55017-2** Domingo Opera Classics
(EMI) **CDM7 63103-2** Placido Domingo sings Opera Arias
(EMI) **CDM7 64359-2** Gala de España
(EMIL) **CDZ102** Best Loved Classics 3
(SONY) **MDK47176** Favourite Arias by the World's Favourite Tenors
(SONY) **SMK39030** Placido Domingo sings Great Love Scenes
cond M. JANOWSKI
Wagner: Tannhäuser (exc)
(ERAT) **4509-91715-2** The Ultimate Opera Collection 2
(TELD) **4509-96035-2** Tracks Across Europe
cond N. JÄRVI
(CHAN) **CHAN8766** Hindemith & Weber: Orchestral Works
(CHAN) **CHAN9066** Weber—Overtures
(CHAN) **CHAN9081** Rachmaninov—Orchestral Works
(CHAN) **CHAN9096** Prokofiev—Orchestral Works
cond J. JUDD
Meyerbeer: Dinorah (Cpte)
(OPRA) **ORC004** Donizetti—Ne m'oubliez pas; Arias
cond H. VON KARAJAN
Humperdinck: Hänsel und Gretel (Cpte)
Mozart: Così fan tutte (exc)
R. Strauss: Ariadne auf Naxos (Cpte), Rosenkavalier (exc)
Verdi: Falstaff (Cpte)
(CFP) **CD-CFP4656** Herbert von Karajan conducts Opera
(EMI) **CDH5 65500-2** Boris Christoff - Italian Opera Arias
(EMI) **CDH7 63201-2** Elisabeth Schwarzkopf—Early Recordings
(EMI) **CDH7 64252-2** Christoff sings Russian Arias & Songs
(EMI) **CDM5 65577-2** Elisabeth Schwarzkopf
(EMI) **CDM7 63113-2** Rossini—Overtures
(EMI) **CDM7 63657-2** Schwarzkopf sings Opera Arias
(EMI) **CZS5 68550-2** Russian Music
(EMIL) **CDZ101** Best Loved Classics 2
cond O. KLEMPERER
Beethoven: Fidelio (Cpte), Leonore (exc)
Mozart: Zauberflöte (exc)
(EMI) **CDM7 63350-2** R. Strauss—Orchestral Works
(EMI) **CDM7 63611-2** Klemperer conducts Beethoven Overtures
(EMI) **CDM7 63617-2** Wagner—Orchestral Works, Vol. 1
(EMI) **CDM7 63618-2** Wagner—Orchestral Works, Vol.2
(EMI) **CDM7 63619-2** Mozart-Overtures; Serenade, K477 & Masonic Funeral Music
(EMI) **CDM7 64143-2** Klemperer conducts Gluck/Beethoven/Berlioz
(EMI) **CDM7 64144-2** Klemperer conducts Mendelssohn/Liszt/J.Strauss II
(EMI) **CMS7 64074-2(2)** Christa Ludwig—Recital (pt 2)
(EMIL) **CDZ7 67015-2** Mozart—Opera Arias
cond P. KLETZKI
(EMI) **CZS5 68098-2** Rimsky-Korsakov—Orchestral Works
(EMI) **CZS7 67726-2** Paul Kletzki—A Profile
cond J. KRIPS
(EMI) **CDH7 69793-2** Elisabeth Schwarzkopf & Irmgard Seefried sing Duets
(EMI) **CHS7 69741-2(4)** Record of Singing, Vol.4—German School
(ORFE) **C394101B** Great Mozart Singers Series, Vol. 1
(PREI) **90034** Maria Cebotari (1910-49)
cond E. KURTZ
(EMI) **CZS5 68098-2** Rimsky-Korsakov—Orchestral Works
(EMI) **CZS7 67729-2** Efrem Kurtz - A profile
cond E. LEINSDORF
Cornelius: Barbier von Bagdad (Cpte)
cond H. LEWIS
(RCA) **09026 61236-2** Leontyne Price - Prima Donna Collection
(RCA) **09026 61886-2** Operas Greatest Love Songs
(RCA) **09026 62596-2** Prima Donna Collection - Higlights
(RCA) **74321 25817-2** Café Classics - Operatic
cond A. LITTON
(RCA) **09026 61700-2** Works for Violin & Orchestra
cond G. LLOYD
G. Lloyd: John Socman (exc)
cond J. LÓPEZ-COBOS
Rossini: Otello (Cpte)
(PHIL) **442 600-2PH** The Great Carreras
cond L. LUDWIG
(EMI) **CMS5 65212-2** Wagner—Les introuvables du Ring
(EMI) **CMS7 64008-2(1)** Wagner Singing on Record (pt 1)
cond L. MAAZEL
Puccini: Madama Butterfly (Cpte)
(SONY) **MDK47176** Favourite Arias by the World's Favourite Tenors
(SONY) **SBK46548** Opera Arias
(SONY) **SK48094** Favourite Puccini Arias
(SONY) **SMK39030** Placido Domingo sings Great Love Scenes
cond C. MACKERRAS
(EMI) **CZS5 68098-2** Rimsky-Korsakov—Orchestral Works
(EMI) **CZS5 68550-2** Russian Music
cond L. MAGIERA
(DECC) **071 150-1DH (DECC)** Pavarotti in Hyde Park
(DECC) **436 320-5DH** Pavarotti in Hyde Park
cond N. MALKO
(CFP) **CD-CFP4523** Prokofiev—Orchestral Works
(EMI) **CDH5 65500-2** Boris Christoff - Italian Opera Arias
(EMI) **CDH7 64252-2** Christoff sings Russian Arias & Songs
(TEST) **SBT1062** Nicolai Malko
cond I. MARIN
(PHIL) **434 912-2PH** Bel Canto Arias
cond I. MARKEVITCH
(TEST) **SBT1060** Igor Markevitch
cond L. VON MATAČIĆ
Lehár: Lustige Witwe (Cpte)
(EMI) **CDC5 55095-2** Prima Diva
(EMI) **CDH7 61001-2** R. Strauss—Lieder & Arias
(EMI) **CDM5 65577-2** Elisabeth Schwarzkopf
(EMI) **CZS5 68550-2** Russian Music
cond M. MUDIE
(TEST) **SBT1058** James Johnston - Opera Arias and Songs
cond R. MUTI
Donizetti: Don Pasquale (Cpte)
Gluck: Orfeo ed Euridice (Cpte)
Leoncavallo: Pagliacci (exc)
Mascagni: Cavalleria rusticana (Cpte)
Verdi: Nabucco (exc), Traviata (Cpte)
(CFP) **CD-CFP4575** Verdi Arias
(CFP) **CD-CFP4613** Favourite TV Classics
(EMI) **CDC7 47274-2** Verdi: Opera Choruses
(EMI) **CDC7 54524-2** The José Carreras Album
(EMI) **CDEMTVD59** Classic Experience 3
(EMI) **CDM5 65575-2** Montserrat Caballé
(EMI) **CDM7 63104-2** Alfredo Krauss - Opera Recital
(EMI) **CDM7 63111-2** José Carreras sings Opera & Operetta Arias
(EMI) **CDM7 64359-2** Gala de España
(EMI) **CDM7 69500-2** Montserrat Caballé sings Bellini & Verdi Arias
(EMI) **CDM7 69596-2** The Movies go to the Opera
(EMI) **CZS5 68559-2** Italian Opera Choruses

(SCHW) **314572** Vienna State Opera Live, Vol.7

PIEROTTI, Raquel (mez)
Bretón: Verbena de La Paloma (Cpte)
Handel: Giulio Cesare (Cpte)
Rossini: Barbiere di Siviglia (Cpte), Comte Ory (Cpte)
Verdi: Nabucco (Cpte)
Vives: Doña Francisquita (Cpte)

PIERRE, Gregory (treb)
Britten: Midsummer Night's Dream (Cpte)

PIERRE, Joelle (sngr)
Planquette: Rip van Winkle (Cpte)

PIERSON, Edward (bar)
D. Moore: Carry Nation (Cpte)

PIERSON, Edward (voc)
Joplin: Treemonisha (Cpte)

PIETSCH, Gernot (ten)
Puccini: Bohème (Cpte)

PIGLIUCCI, Giannicola (bar)
Verdi: Otello (Cpte)

PIHA, Etela (mez)
Bellini: Norma (Cpte)

PIKE, Julian (ten)
Henze: English Cat (Cpte)

PILAR ALONSO, Maria del (sngr)
Bretón: Verbena de la Paloma (Cpte)

PILARCZYK, Helga (sop)
Berg: Wozzeck (exc)

PILARL, Erica (sngr)
Schreker: Ferne Klang (Cpte)

PILAT, Eva (sop)
Mozart: Finta Giardiniera (Cpte)

PILINSZKY, Sigismund (ten)
Wagner: Tannhäuser (Cpte)

PILTTI, Lea (sop)
Mozart: Zauberflöte (Cpte)

PILZ, August (cond)
see Odeon Orch
orch

INA, Erich (bass)
Wagner: Meistersinger (Cpte)

INA, Filippo (ten)
Rossini: Sigismondo (Cpte)

INDELL, Reginald (bar)
Weill: Lost in the Stars (Cpte)

INEAU, Jacques (spkr)
Bizet: Djamileh (Cpte)

INEDO, Joe (ten)
Verdi: Ballo in maschera (Cpte)

INI, Amalia (contr)
Boito: Mefistofele (Cpte)

INI-CORSI, Antonio (bar)
(BONG) **GB1064/5-2** Fernando de Lucia
(EMI) **CHS7 64860-2(2)** La Scala Edition - Vol.1, 1878-1914 (pt 2)
(MEMO) **HR4408/9(1)** Singers in Genoa, Vol.1 (disc 1)
(NIMB) **NI7840/1** The Era of Adelina Patti
(PEAR) **GEMMCDS9923(1)** Covent Garden on Record, Vol.1 (pt 1)
(SYMP) **SYMCD1149** Fernando De Lucia
(TEST) **SBT1008** Viva Rossini

INI-CORSI, Gaetano (ten)
(PEAR) **GEMMCDS9159(1)** De Luca Edition, Vol.1 (pt 1)

INKAS, Jiří (cond)
see Brno Janáček Op Orch
Brno St PO

INKERT, Regina (sop)
(MEMO) **HR4408/9(1)** Singers in Genoa, Vol.1 (disc 1)
(PEAR) **GEMMCDS9923(1)** Covent Garden on Record, Vol.1 (pt 1)
(SYMP) **SYMCD1113** The Harold Wayne Collection, Vol.13

NNOCK, Trevor (cond)
see English Concert

NTO, Amelia (sop)
(EMI) **CHS7 64860-2(2)** La Scala Edition - Vol.1, 1878-1914 (pt 2)
(IRCC) **IRCC-CD808** Souvenirs of 19th Century Italian Opera
(MEMO) **HR4408/9(2)** Singers in Genoa, Vol.1 (disc 2)
(SYMP) **SYMCD1111** The Harold Wayne Collection, Vol.11

NTO, David (treb)
Britten: Noye's Fludde (Cpte)
(DECC) **436 990-2DWO** The World of Benjamin Britten

NTO, Marie-Thérèse (sop)
Britten: Noye's Fludde (Cpte)
(DECC) **436 990-2DWO** The World of Benjamin Britten

NZA, Ezio (bass)
Donizetti: Lucia di Lammermoor (Cpte)
Mozart: Don Giovanni (Cpte)
(CBS) **CD45693** Portrait—Ezio Pinza
(CONI) **CDHD227** Gigli in Opera and Song
(CONI) **CDHD235** The Puccini Album
(EMI) **CDH7 61051-2** Beniamino Gigli - Operatic Arias
(EMI) **CHS7 64864-2(1)** La Scala Edition - Vol.2, 1915-46 (pt 1)
(IMP) **GLRS102** The Magnificent Gigli
(MMOI) **CDMOIR404** Ezio Pinza—Recital
(MMOI) **CDMOIR406** Mozart—Historical Recordings
(MMOI) **CDMOIR428** Rosa Ponselle and Giovanni Martinelli sing Verdi
(NIMB) **NI7804** Giovanni Martinelli—Opera Recital
(NIMB) **NI7805** Rosa Ponselle—Opera & Song Recital
(NIMB) **NI7851** Legendary Voices
(NIMB) **NI7852** Galli-Curci, Vol.2
(ORFE) **C394101B** Great Mozart Singers Series, Vol. 1
(PEAR) **GEMMCDS9160(2)** De Luca Edition, Vol.2 (pt 2)
(PEAR) **GEMMCDS9452** The Emperor Tibbett
(PEAR) **GEMMCDS9926(2)** Covent Garden on Record—Vol.4 (pt 2)
(PEAR) **GEMMCD9122** 20 Great Basses sing Great Arias
(PEAR) **GEMMCD9306** Ezio Pinza—Opera Recital
(PEAR) **GEMMCD9367** Gigli—Arias and Duets
(PREI) **89050** Ezio Pinza (1892-1957)
(PREI) **89062** Giovanni Martinelli (1885-1969)
(RCA) **GD87810** Rosa Ponselle - Opera & Song Recital
(RCA) **GD87811** Beniamino Gigli—Operatic Arias
(RCA) **09026 61245-2** Ezio Pinza - Recital
(RCA) **09026 61580-2(3)** RCA/Met 100 Singers, 100 Years (pt 3)
(ROMO) **81007-2** Rosa Ponselle—Victor Recordings 1926-1929
(ROMO) **81014-2** Elisabeth Rethberg (1894-1976)
(SCHW) **314512** Vienna State Opera Live, Vol.1
(SONY) **SM3K47211** Mozart Legendary Interpretations—Opera and Concert Arias
(TEST) **SBT1008** Viva Rossini

PINZAUTI, Alessandro (cond)
see Tuscan Accademia Strumentale Orch

PIOLINO, François (ten)
Purcell: Fairy Queen, Z629 (Cpte)

PIPAL, Hans (sngr)
R. Strauss: Rosenkavalier (Cpte)

PIQUEMAL, Michel (cond)
see Nancy SO

(MICHEL) PIQUEMAL VOCAL ENSEMBLE
cond J-W. AUDOLI
Pendleton: Miracle of the Nativity (Cpte)

PIRADOV, Vladimir (cond)
see Bolshoi Th Orch

PIRAZZINI, Miriam (mez)
Cherubini: Medea (Cpte)
Puccini: Madama Butterfly (Cpte)
Verdi: Aida (Cpte), Otello (Cpte)
(EMI) **CMS7 64165-2** Puccini—Trittico

PIRILLO, Vincent (ten)
Delius: Village Romeo and Juliet (Cpte)

PIROGOV, Alexandr (bass)
Tchaikovsky: Eugene Onegin (Cpte)
(PEAR) **GEMMCD9122** 20 Great Basses sing Great Arias
(PREI) **89078** Alexander Pirogov (1899-1964)

PISANI, Bernard (ten)
Offenbach: Brigands (Cpte)

PISTOR, Gotthelf (ten)
Wagner: Parsifal (exc)
(OPAL) **OPALCDS9843** Karl Muck conducts Wagner

PITA, Jorge (ten)
Ponchielli: Gioconda (Cpte)

PITOUR, Sylvaine (sop)
Montéclair: Jephté (Cpte)

PITT, Percy (cond)
see orch

PITT, Percy (pf)
(EMI) **CHS7 63802-2(2)** Tetrazzini—The London Records (pt 2)

PITTAVINI, Maria Grazia (sop)
Verdi: Rigoletto (Cpte)

PITTSBURGH MENDELSSOHN CHOIR
cond L. MAAZEL
Wagner: Tannhäuser (exc)

PITTSBURGH SYMPHONY ORCHESTRA
cond L. MAAZEL
Wagner: Tannhäuser (exc), Walküre (exc)
(SONY) **SK52491** Popular American Music
cond W. STEINBERG
(EMI) **CDM5 65204-2** Orchestral Masterworks
(EMI) **CDM5 65208-2** Wagner—Orchestral Works from the Operas
(EMI) **CDM5 65424-2** Rimsky-Korsakov/Prokofiev—Orchestral Works

PITTSINGER, David (bass)
Cavalli: Calisto (Cpte)
Floyd: Susannah (Cpte)
Verdi: Simon Boccanegra (Cpte)

PITZ, Wilhelm (cond)
see Bayreuth Fest Orch

PIVA, Franco (ten)
Verdi: Don Carlo (Cpte)

PIZZERI, Luigi (bar)
Puccini: Madama Butterfly (Cpte)

PLANÇON, Pol (bass)
(NIMB) **NI7840/1** The Era of Adelina Patti
(NIMB) **NI7860** Emma Eames & Pol Plançon
(PEAR) **GEMMCDS9923(1)** Covent Garden on Record, Vol.1 (pt 1)
(PEAR) **GEMMCDS9923(2)** Covent Garden on Record, Vol.1 (pt 2)
(PEAR) **GEMMCD9122** 20 Great Basses sing Great Arias
(PEAR) **GEMMCD9497** Pol Plançon
(ROMO) **81001-2** Emma Eames (1865-1952)
(ROMO) **82001-2** Pol Plançon—Complete Victor Recordings
(SYMP) **SYMCD1100** Harold Wayne Collection, Vol.8

PLANEL, Jean (ten)
(EPM) **150 122** Milhaud—Historic Recordings 1928-1948

PLANT, Andrew (sngr)
Menotti: Boy who grew too fast (Cpte)

PLANTE, Gilles (cl)
Vivier: Kopernikus (Cpte)

PLANTÉ, Walter (ten)
Puccini: Fanciulla del West (Cpte)

PLANTEY, Bernard (bass)
Bazin: Maître Pathelin (Cpte)
Bizet: Carmen (Cpte)
(MUSD) **20239-2** Delibes—Opéras-Comiques

PLASSON, Michel (cond)
see LPO
Toulouse Capitole Orch

PLATE, Sibylla (contr)
Wagner: Walküre (Cpte)
(FOYE) **15-CF2011** Wagner—Der Ring de Nibelungen

PLATE, Wilfried (ten)
Suder: Kleider machen Leute (Cpte)

PLATT, Ian (bar)
Henze: English Cat (Cpte)
Meyerbeer: Crociato in Egitto (Cpte)
(OPRA) **ORCH104** A Hundred Years of Italian Opera: 1820-1830
(OPRA) **ORR201** 19th Century Heroines-Yvonne Kenny

PLAZAS, Mary (sop)
Purcell: Dido (Cpte)

PLEASANTS, Victoria (pf)
(EMI) **CHS7 69741-2(2)** Record of Singing, Vol.4—Anglo-American School (pt 2)

PLECH, Linda (sop)
Busoni: Turandot (Cpte)

PLESNER, Gurli (contr)
Nielsen: Maskarade (Cpte)

PLESSIS, Christian du (bar)
Donizetti: Assedio di Calais (Cpte), Maria Padilla (Cpte), Ugo, Conte di Parigi (Cpte)
Massenet: Cendrillon (Cpte)
Meyerbeer: Dinorah (Cpte), Prophète (Cpte)
Offenbach: Christopher Columbus (Cpte)
Verdi: Rigoletto (Cpte), Traviata (Cpte)
(OPRA) **ORCH103** Italian Opera—1810-20
(OPRA) **ORC003** Donizetti—Gabriella di Vergy
(OPRA) **ORC004** Donizetti—Ne m'oubliez pas; Arias

PLETNEV, Mikhail (cond)
see Russian Nat Orch

PLISHKA, Paul (bass)
Bellini: Norma (Cpte)
Gounod: Faust (Cpte)
Massenet: Cid (Cpte)
Mozart: Nozze di Figaro (Cpte)
Mussorgsky: Boris Godunov (Cpte)
Offenbach: Contes d'Hoffmann (Cpte)
Puccini: Bohème (Cpte), Tosca (Cpte), Turandot (Cpte)
Rossini: Cenerentola (Cpte)
Verdi: Don Carlo (exc), Falstaff (Cpte), Forza del destino (exc), Luisa Miller (Cpte), Otello (Cpte)
(DECC) **071 142-1DH (DECC)** Essential Opera
(DG) **439 151-2GMA** Mad about Puccini
(DG) **072 428-1GH2(DG)** The Metropolitan Opera Gala
(EMI) **CDC7 54524-2** The José Carreras Album
(RCA) **GD60866** The Placido Domingo Album

PLOOG, Karin (sop)
Weill: Happy End (Cpte)

PLOVDIV PHILHARMONIC ORCHESTRA
cond R. RAYCHEV
(HARM) **HMP390 466** Rossini—Overtures
(HARM) **HMC40 466** Rossini—Overtures
(LASE) **15 506** Rossini: Overtures
(LASE) **15 520** Rossini: Overtures
(LASE) **15 621** Famous Marches and Dances
cond V. STEFANOV
(FORL) **UCD16743** Bulgarian Voices, Vol. 3

cond E. TCHAKAROV
(FORL) **UCD16743** Bulgarian Voices, Vol. 3

PLOWRIGHT, Rosalind (sop)
Donizetti: Maria Stuarda (Cpte)
Offenbach: Contes d'Hoffmann (exc)
Spontini: Vestale (Cpte)
Verdi: Forza del destino (Cpte), Otello (Cpte), Trovatore (Cpte)
(CAST) **CVI2057** Il Trittico live from La Scala, 1983
(CAST) **CVI2068** Opera Highlights from Verona 1

PLUDERMACHER, Georges (pf)
(ERAT) **4509-93209-2** Debussy—Transcriptions for Piano - Four hands & Piano Duet
(TELD) **4509-95998-2** Nathan Milstein - The Last Recital

PLÜMACHER, Hetty (contr)
Mozart: Zauberflöte (exc)
Orff: Antigonae (Cpte)
R. Strauss: Schweigsame Frau (Cpte)
Wagner: Götterdämmerung (Cpte), Rheingold (Cpte)
(DECC) **414 100-2DM15** Wagner: Der Ring des Nibelungen
(DECC) **421 313-2DA** Wagner: Der Ring des Nibelungen - Great Scenes
(FOYE) **15-CF2011** Wagner—Der Ring de Nibelungen

PLUZHNIKOV, Konstantin (ten)
Borodin: Prince Igor (Cpte)
Mussorgsky: Khovanshchina (Cpte)

PLYMOUTH MUSIC SERIES CHORUS
cond P. BRUNELLE
Britten: Paul Bunyan (Cpte)
Copland: Tender Land (Cpte)

PLYMOUTH MUSIC SERIES ORCHESTRA
cond P. BRUNELLE
Britten: Paul Bunyan (Cpte)
Copland: Tender Land (Cpte)
(VIRG) **VC7 59022-2** Smyth—Vocal and Orchestral Works

POCHAPSKY, Viacheslav (bass-bar)
Rachmaninov: Aleko (Cpte)

POCHON, Virginie (sngr)
Lully: Phaëton (Cpte)

PODBOLOTOV, Alexandre (ten)
Mussorgsky: Marriage (Cpte)

PODLES, Ewa (contr)
Rossini: Tancredi (Cpte)
(DECC) **436 261-2DHO3** Puccini—Il Trittico

PODSKALSKÝ, Miroslav (bass)
Smetana: Libuše (Cpte)

POELL, Alfred (bar)
Beethoven: Fidelio (Cpte)
Einem: Prozess (Cpte)
Mozart: Nozze di Figaro (Cpte)
R. Strauss: Arabella (Cpte), Ariadne auf Naxos (Cpte), Rosenkavalier (Cpte)
Wagner: Meistersinger (Cpte)
(CAMB) **CD-1032** From the Operas of Erich Wolfgang Korngold
(DECC) **425 959-2DM** Lisa della Casa sings R. Strauss
(EMI) **CZS7 67123-2** Wagner: Der Ring des Nibelungen
(SCHW) **314552** Vienna State Opera Live, Vol.5
(SCHW) **314652** Vienna State Opera Live, Vol.15
(SCHW) **314692** Vienna State Opera Live, Vol.19
(SCHW) **314712** Vienna State Opera Live, Vol.21

POGGI, Ferrero (ten)
Verdi: Vespri Siciliani (Cpte)

POGGI, Gianni (ten)
Puccini: Bohème (Cpte)
Verdi: Traviata (Cpte)

POGSON, Geoffrey (ten)
Bizet: Carmen (Cpte)
G. Lloyd: Iernin
Tchaikovsky: Queen of Spades (Cpte)
Verdi: Traviata (Cpte)

POHJOLA, Olli (cond)
see Tapiola Chbr Ch

POHL, Carla (sop)
Weill: Zar lässt sich Photographieren (Cpte)

POHL, Gisela (contr)
Hindemith: Nusch-Nuschi (Cpte)
Schoenberg: Moses und Aron (Cpte)
Wagner: Parsifal (Cpte)
(PHIL) **422 525-2PME2** The Complete Mozart Edition Vol 25

POHL, Hans-Dietrich (bar)
Puccini: Bohème (Cpte)

PÓKA, Balázs (bar)
Puccini: Bohème (Cpte)

POKHITONOV, Daniil (pf)
(ARLE) **ARL23/5** Rimsky-Korsakov—Sadko

POKORNÁ, Jindra (mez)
Janáček: Jenufa (Cpte)

POKORNÁ, Jindra (sop)
Janáček: Fate (Cpte)

POLA, Bruno (bar)
Verdi: Falstaff (Cpte), Traviata (Cpte)

POLACCO, Giorgio (cond)
see orch

POLÁŠEK, Oldřich (ten)
Dvořák: Kate and the Devil (Cpte)

POLASKI, Deborah (sop)
(ERAT) **2292-45786-2** Der Ring des Nibelungen - Excerpts

POLÁŠKOVÁ, Magda (sop)
Janáček: Fate (Cpte)

POLDI, Piero (ten)
Verdi: Rigoletto (Cpte)

POLGÁR, László (bass)
Beethoven: Fidelio (Cpte)
Mascagni: Lodoletta (Cpte)
Mozart: Clemenza di Tito (Cpte), Don Giovanni (Cpte), Zauberflöte (Cpte)
Respighi: Belfagor (Cpte), Semirama (Cpte)
Schreker: Gezeichneten (Cpte)
Schubert: Fierrabras (Cpte)
(SONY) **SK45855** Mozart: Bastien und Bastienne
(TELD) **4509-98824-2** Thomas Hampson Collection,Vol III-Operatic Scenes

POLI, Afro (bar)
Leoncavallo: Pagliacci (Cpte)
Mascagni: Piccolo Marat (Cpte)
Puccini: Bohème (Cpte), Turandot (Cpte)
Verdi: Falstaff (exc)
(EMI) **CHS7 64864-2(2)** La Scala Edition - Vol.2, 1015 46 (pt 2)
(MSCM) **MM30231** Don Pasquale & Tito Schipa Recital

POLI, Piero Francesco (ten)
Donizetti: Lucia di Lammermoor (exc)
Puccini: Turandot (Cpte)
Verdi: Ballo in maschera (Cpte), Traviata (Cpte)
(DECC) **436 317-2DA** Puccini—Famous Arias
(DECC) **444 555-2DF2** Essential Puccini

POLIDORI, Graziano (bar)
Donizetti: Pazzi per progetto (Cpte)
Puccini: Turandot (Cpte)
Salieri: Prima la musica (Cpte)

POLI-RANDACCIO, Tina (sop)
(EMI) **CHS7 64860-2(2)** La Scala Edition - Vol.1, 1878-1914 (pt 2)

POLISH CHAMBER ORCHESTRA
cond J. MAKSYMIUK
(CFP) **CD-CFP4608** Favourite Classics 1
(EMI) **CES5 68541-2** Rossini/Verdi/Bellini/ Donizetti—Overtures

POLISH CHAMBER PHILHARMONIC ORCHESTRA
cond W. RAJSKI
(INTE) **INT830 899** Virtuoso Orchestral Music

POLISH NATIONAL RADIO ORCHESTRA
cond Y. EL SISI
Mozart: Così fan tutte (Cpte), Don Giovanni (Cpte), Nozze di Figaro (Cpte)
cond A. WIT
(POLS) **PNCD020** Penderecki: Orchestral Works

POLISH NATIONAL RADIO SYMPHONY ORCHESTRA
cond R. BIBL
(POLS) **PNCD087** Famous Operetta Arias
cond J. WILDNER
(NAXO) **8 550608** Schumann—Overtures

POLISH RADIO SYMPHONY ORCHESTRA
cond H. DEBICH
(SYMP) **SYMCD1117** Alfred Orda—Opera Recital
cond K. MISSONA
(SYMP) **SYMCD1117** Alfred Orda—Opera Recital
cond S. RACHOŃ
(SYMP) **SYMCD1117** Alfred Orda—Opera Recital

POLISH STATE PHILHARMONIC ORCHESTRA (KATOWICE)
cond K. JEAN
(NAXO) **8 550231** Berlioz: Orchestral Works

POLITKOVSKY, Vladimir (bar)
(DANT) **LYS013/5** Tchaikovsky—The Queen of Spades

POLÍVKOVÁ, Jana (sop)
Hába: Mother (Cpte)

POLLAK, Anna (mez)
Gay: Beggar's Opera (Cpte)
Purcell: Dido (Cpte)

POLLARD, Emma (contr)
Vaughan Williams: Pilgrim's Progress (Cpte)

POLLET, Françoise (sop)
Berlioz: Troyens (Cpte)
(ERAT) **4509-98502-2** Recital-Françoise Pollet

POLLINI, Maurizio (cond)
see COE

POLOTTO, Vico (bar)
Giordano: Andrea Chénier (Cpte)
Verdi: Traviata (Cpte)

POLOZOV, Vyacheslav (ten)
Mussorgsky: Boris Godunov (Cpte)

POLSTER, Hermann Christian (bass)
Schoenberg: Moses und Aron (Cpte)
Wagner: Meistersinger (Cpte), Parsifal (Cpte)

(PHIL) **422 525-2PME2** The Complete Mozart Edition Vol 25

POLVERELLI, Laura (mez)
Jommelli: Armida abbandonata (Cpte)
Rossini: Cenerentola (Cpte)

PÖLZER, Julius (ten)
(SCHW) **314512** Vienna State Opera Live, Vol.1
(SCHW) **314632** Vienna State Opera Live, Vol.13
(SCHW) **314662** Vienna State Opera Live, Vol.16
(SCHW) **314692** Vienna State Opera Live, Vol.19

POMMER, Max (cond)
see Berlin CO

POMMERS, Leon (pf)
(EMI) **CMS7 64123-2** The Art of Michael Rabin (1936-1972)
(EMI) **ZDMF7 64830-2** The Art of Nathan Milstein

POMPONI, Franco (sngr)
Schuman: Mighty Casey (Cpte)

PONKIN, Vladimir (cond)
see Moscow Maly SO

PONS, Ismael (sngr)
Vives: Doña Francisquita (Cpte)

PONS, Josep (cond)
see Teatre Iliure CO

PONS, Juan (bar)
Donizetti: Elisir d'amore (Cpte), Lucia di Lammermoor (Cpte)
Falla: Vida breve (Cpte)
Leoncavallo: Pagliacci (Cpte)
Penella: Gato Montés (Cpte)
Puccini: Fanciulla del West (Cpte), Madama Butterfly (Cpte), Tosca (exc)
Verdi: Aida (Cpte), Aroldo (Cpte), Falstaff (Cpte), Forza del destino (Cpte), Traviata (exc)
(CAST) **CVI2057** Il Trittico live from La Scala, 1983
(DECC) **436 261-2DHO3** Puccini—Il Trittico
(DG) **439 151-2GMA** Mad about Puccini
(RCA) **RD61191** Gala Lirica
(RCA) **09026 61204-4** From the Official Barcelona Games Ceremony
(RCA) **09026 61191-5** Gala Lirica
(RCA) **09026 61204-5** From the Official Barcelona Games Ceremony

PONS, Lily (sop)
Donizetti: Lucia di Lammermoor (Cpte)
(CBS) **CD45694** Lily Pons—Opera & Song Recital
(MSCM) **MM30221** 18 French Divas
(MSCM) **MM30446** Lily Pons - Recital
(MSOU) **DFCDI-111** The Art of the Coloratura
(PEAR) **GEMMCDS9159(2)** De Luca Edition, Vol.1 (pt 2)
(PEAR) **GEMMCDS9160(2)** De Luca Edition, Vol.2 (pt 2)
(RCA) **09026 61411-2** Lily Pons Recital
(RCA) **09026 61580-2(4)** RCA/Met 100 Singers, 100 Years (pt 4)
(RCA) **74321 24284-2** Opera's Greatest Heroines
(SONY) **SM3K47211** Mozart Legendary Interpretations—Opera and Concert Arias

PONSEELE, Marcel (cond)
see Ricercar Acad

PONSELLE, Carmela (mez)
(PEAR) **GEMMCDS9964** Rosa Ponselle - Columbia Acoustics

PONSELLE, Rosa (sop)
Bellini: Norma (exc)
Verdi: Traviata (Cpte)
(MMOI) **CDMOIR408** Great Sopranos
(MMOI) **CDMOIR428** Rosa Ponselle and Giovanni Martinelli sing Verdi
(NIMB) **NI7801** Great Singers, Vol.1
(NIMB) **NI7802** Divas 1906-1935
(NIMB) **NI7804** Giovanni Martinelli—Opera Recital
(NIMB) **NI7805** Rosa Ponselle—Opera & Song Recital
(NIMB) **NI7846** Rosa Ponselle, Vol.2
(NIMB) **NI7851** Legendary Voices
(PEAR) **GEMMCDS9926(1)** Covent Garden on Record—Vol.4 (pt 1)
(PEAR) **GEMMCDS9926(2)** Covent Garden on Record—Vol.4 (pt 2)
(PEAR) **GEMMCDS9964** Rosa Ponselle - Columbia Acoustics
(RCA) **GD87810** Rosa Ponselle - Opera & Song Recital
(RCA) **09026 61580-2(3)** RCA/Met 100 Singers, 100 Years (pt 3)
(RCA) **74321 24284-2** Opera's Greatest Heroines
(ROMO) **81006-2** Rosa Ponselle (1897-1981)
(ROMO) **81007-2** Rosa Ponselle—Victor Recordings 1926-1929

PONTI, Raffaele Delle (pf)
(EMI) **CHS7 64860-2(2)** La Scala Edition - Vol.1, 1878-1914 (pt 2)
(PEAR) **GEMMCDS9073(1)** Giovanni Zenatello, Vol.1 (pt 1)
(PEAR) **GEMMCDS9159(1)** De Luca Edition, Vol.1 (pt 1)

PONTIGGIA, Luigi (ten)
Mascagni: Amico Fritz (Cpte)

PÖNTINEN, Roland (pf)
(BIS) **BIS-CD258** The Virtuoso Trombone
(BIS) **BIS-CD300** Music for a Rainy Day

cond J. BĚLOHLÁVEK
Martinů: Miracles of Mary (Cpte)
(KOCH) **34036-2** A Pageant of Opera
(SUPR) **11 0377-2** Smetana Festival
(SUPR) **11 1851-2** Famous Opera Arias
cond Z. FEKETE
(SUPR) **11 1116-2** Berlioz & d'Indy—Orchestral Works
cond M. KONVALINKA
(PRAG) **PR254 045** Dvořák—Orchestral Works
cond V. SMETÁČEK
Rimsky-Korsakov: Invisible city of Kitezh
(SUPR) **11 1107-2** Rimsky-Korsakov—Suites from the Operas
cond V. VÁLEK
(SUPR) **11 1823-2** Fibich—Orchestral Works

PRAGUE VIRTUOSI
cond O. VLČEK
(DINT) **DICD920201** Mozart—Orchestral Works
(DINT) **DICD920204** Mozart—Concert Arias

PRANDELLI, Francesco Molinari (cond)
see Trieste Teatro Verdi Orch

PRANDELLI, Giacinto (ten)
Boito: Mefistofele (Cpte)
Puccini: Bohème (Cpte)
(EMI) **CHS7 69741-2(7)** Record of Singing, Vol.4—Italian School
(EMI) **CMS7 64165-2** Puccini—Trittico
(FONI) **CDMR5023** Martini & Rossi Festival, Volume 23

PRATA, Gabrielle (contr)
Janáček: Makropulos Affair (Cpte)

PRATICÒ, Bruno (bar)
Bizet: Pêcheurs de Perles (Cpte)
Donizetti: Elisir d'amore (Cpte)
Leoncavallo: Bohème (Cpte)
Paisiello: Don Chisciotte (Cpte)
Piccinni: Cecchina (Cpte)
Rossini: Barbiere di Siviglia (Cpte), Signor Bruschino (Cpte)

PRATO VOCI BIANCHE GUIDO MONACO CHOR
cond B. BARTOLETTI
(DECC) **436 261-2DHO3** Puccini—Il Trittico

PRATSCHSKE, Sébastien (treb)
Mozart: Apollo et Hyacinthus (Cpte)

PRATT, Peter (bar)
Sullivan: Mikado (Cpte)

PRECHT, Ulrika (sop)
Donizetti: Linda di Chamounix (Cpte)

PRÉGARDIEN, Christoph (ten)
Handel: Rodelinda (Cpte)
Haydn: Infedeltà delusa (Cpte)
Mozart: Don Giovanni (Cpte)

PREGER, Kurt (bar)
J. Strauss II: Nacht in Venedig (Cpte)
R. Strauss: Ariadne auf Naxos (Cpte)

PREIN, Johann Werner (bass)
Busoni: Turandot (Cpte)
Schreker: Ferne Klang (Cpte)
Schulhoff: Plameny (Cpte)

PREIS, Manfred (bass cl)
(SONY) **SK53978** Prometheus

PREISIG, Lilly (sop)
Mozart: Zauberflöte (Cpte)

PREOBRAZHENSKY, Sergei (bass)
(PEAR) **GEMMCDS9111(2)** Singers of Imperial Russia, Vol.5 (pt 2)

PRESCOTT, Jonathan (bass)
(PHIL) **432 416-2PH3** Haydn—L'incontro improvviso/Arias

PRESTEL, Kurt (cond)
see Salzburg Mozarteum Orch

PRESTI, Ida (gtr)
(BELA) **450 146-2** Romantic Guitar
(PHIL) **422 979-2PCC** Romantic Music for Two Guitars

PRESTIA, Giacomo (bass)
Puccini: Tosca (Cpte)
Rossini: Sigismondo (Cpte)
Verdi: Otello (exc)

PRESTON, Simon (organ)
(DECC) **430 091-2DWO** The World of the Organ

PRESTON, Stephen (fl)
(L'OI) **410 553-2OH** 18th Century Orchestral Works

PRESTON-ROBERTS, Michael (bar)
Janáček: Fate (Cpte)

PRESTON'S POCKET
(AMON) **CD-SAR11** Music for Two Flutes

PRÊTRE, Georges (cond)
see Bamberg SO
French Rad New PO
FRNO
La Scala Chor
La Scala Orch
Monte Carlo PO
New Philh
Paris Cons
Paris Op Orch
Paris Opéra-Comique Orch
Paris Orch
RCA Italiana Op Orch
ROHO
Rome RAI Orch
Vienna SO

PREVEDI, Bruno (ten)
Boito: Nerone (Cpte)
Verdi: Nabucco (Cpte)
(BELA) **450 005-2** Famous Tenor Arias
(BELA) **450 007-2** Puccini Favourites
(DECC) **417 686-2DC** Puccini—Operatic Arias
(DECC) **433 623-2DSP** Famous Tenor Arias
(DECC) **433 636-2DSP** Puccini—Famous Arias
(DECC) **433 865-2DWO** The World of Puccini
(DECC) **436 314-2DA** Great Tenor Arias
(MEMO) **HR4273/4** Great Voices—Pietro Cappuccilli

PREVIATI, Fabio (bar)
Bellini: Adelson e Salvini (Cpte)
Franchetti: Cristoforo Colombo (Cpte)
Puccini: Bohème (Cpte)
Rossini: Inganno felice (Cpte), Occasione fa il ladro (Cpte)

PREVIN, André (cond)
see LSO
Orch
RPO
St Luke's Orch
VPO

PREVITALI, Fernando (cond)
see Milan RAI SO
Naples San Carlo Op Orch
Rome Op Orch
Santa Cecilia Academy Orch

PREY, Hermann (bar)
Cornelius: Barbier von Bagdad (Cpte)
Flotow: Martha (Cpte)
Humperdinck: Königskinder (Cpte)
J. Strauss II: Fledermaus (Cpte)
Korngold: Tote Stadt (Cpte)
Kreutzer: Nachtlager in Granada (Cpte)
Millöcker: Bettelstudent (Cpte), Gasparone (Cpte)
Mozart: Così fan tutte (Cpte), Finta Giardiniera (Cpte), Nozze di Figaro (exc), Zauberflöte (exc)
Orff: Kluge (Cpte), Orpheus (Cpte)
Pfitzner: Palestrina (Cpte)
R. Strauss: Ariadne auf Naxos (Cpte), Capriccio (Cpte), Schweigsame Frau (Cpte)
Rossini: Barbiere di Siviglia (Cpte)
Verdi: Traviata (Cpte)
Wagner: Meistersinger (exc)
Weber: Freischütz (Cpte), Oberon (Cpte)
(ACAN) **44 2085-2** Carl Orff Collection
(CAPR) **10 810** Mozart—Opera Highlights
(DENO) **CO-1741** Mozart: Operatic Arias
(DG) **431 110-2GB** Great Voices - Fritz Wunderlich
(DG) **435 145-2GX5(1)** Fritz Wunderlich—Opera Arias, Lieder, etc (part 1)
(DG) **072 428-1GH2(DG)** The Metropolitan Opera Gala
(EMI) **CZS7 62993-2** Fritz Wunderlich—Great German Tenor
(EURO) **GD69019** Hermann Prey—Recital
(ORFE) **C335931A** Salzburg Festival highlights (1956-85)

PREZIOSA, Vincenzo (bass)
Puccini: Tosca (Cpte)

PŘIBILOVÁ, Gabriela (sop)
Krása: Brundibár (Cpte)

PŘIBYL, Vilém (ten)
Dvořák: Jacobin (exc)
Fibich: Šárka (Cpte)
Janáček: Excursions of Mr Brouček (Cpte), Fate (Cpte), From the House of the Dead (Cpte), Jenufa (Cpte)
Smetana: Dalibor (Cpte)

PRICE, Henry (ten)
Verdi: Traviata (Cpte)

PRICE, Janet (sop)
Donizetti: Ugo, Conte di Parigi (Cpte)
Tippett: King Priam (Cpte)

PRICE, Leontyne (sop)
Bizet: Carmen (exc)
Gershwin: Porgy and Bess (exc)
J. Strauss II: Fledermaus (Cpte)
Mozart: Così fan tutte (Cpte)
Puccini: Madama Butterfly (Cpte), Tabarro (Cpte), Tosca (Cpte)
R. Strauss: Ariadne auf Naxos (Cpte)
Verdi: Aida (Cpte), Ballo in maschera (Cpte), Ernani (Cpte), Forza del destino (Cpte), Trovatore (Cpte)
(DECC) **433 067-2DWO** Your Hundred Best Opera Tunes IV
(DECC) **433 442-2DA** Verdi—Famous Arias
(DECC) **436 461-2DM** Ten Top Sopranos
(DECC) **440 402-2DM** Leontyne Price
(EURO) **VD69256** Mozart—Opera Arias
(MEMO) **HR4396/7** Great Voices—Leontyne Price
(MEMO) **HR4400/1** Great Voices - Ettore Bastianini
(RCA) **GD60205** Opera Choruses
(RCA) **GD60398** Leontyne Price sings Strauss arias
(RCA) **GD60866** The Placido Domingo Album
(RCA) **GD84265** Con Amore
(RCA) **RD87016** Leontyne Price sings Verdi Arias
(RCA) **09026 61236-2** Leontyne Price - Prima Donna Collection
(RCA) **09026 61357-2** Leontyne Price Sings Mozart
(RCA) **09026 61440-2** Opera's Greatest Moments
(RCA) **09026 61580-2(7)** RCA/Met 100 Singers, 100 Years (pt 7)
(RCA) **09026 61634-2** Verdi & Puccini Duets
(RCA) **09026 61886-2** Operas Greatest Love Songs
(RCA) **09026 61983-2** Leontyne Price sings Barber
(RCA) **09026 62596-2** Prima Donna Collection - Higlights
(RCA) **09026 62689-2** The Voices of Living Stereo, Volume 1
(RCA) **09026 62699-2** Opera's Greatest Duets
(RCA) **74321 24284-2** Opera's Greatest Heroines
(RCA) **74321 25817-2** Café Classics - Operatic

PRICE, Dame Margaret (sop)
Mozart: Così fan tutte (Cpte), Don Giovanni (Cpte), Nozze di Figaro (exc), Zauberflöte (Cpte)
Puccini: Turandot (Cpte)
Verdi: Ballo in maschera (Cpte), Otello (Cpte)
Wagner: Tristan und Isolde (Cpte)
(DECC) **430 724-2DM** Great Operatic Duets
(DECC) **433 439-2DA** Great Love Duets
(EMI) **CDH5 65072-2** Glyndebourne Recorded - 1934-1994
(EMI) **CDM7 64730-2** Vaughan Williams—Riders to the Sea; Epithalamion, etc
(EMIL) **CDZ7 67015-2** Mozart—Opera Arias
(RCA) **09026 61635-2** Margaret Price sings Mozart
(RCA) **09026 61886-2** Operas Greatest Love Songs
(RCA) **74321 24284-2** Opera's Greatest Heroines

PRICE, Mr (cond)
see orch

PRICE, Olwen (mez)
(TEST) **SBT1058** James Johnston - Opera Arias and Songs

PRICE, Patricia (mez)
Donizetti: Lucia di Lammermoor (Cpte)
Rossini: Tancredi (Cpte)
(DECC) **071 149-1DH (DECC)** The Essential Sutherland

PRICE, Timothy Deryl (ten)
A. Davis: X (Cpte)

PRICK, Christof (cond)
see German Nat Youth Orch

PRIDAY, Elizabeth (sop)
Purcell: Dido (Cpte), King Arthur, Z628 (exc)
(DG) **439 474-2GCL** Purcell—Opera & Choral Works
(ERAT) **4509-96371-2** Gardiner—The Purcell Collection

PRIES, Ronald (ten)
Hindemith: Neues vom Tage (Cpte)

PRIESTMAN, Brian (cond)
see Vienna RSO

PRIEW, Uta (contr)
Wagner: Götterdämmerung (Cpte), Rheingold (Cpte), Walküre (Cpte)
(EURO) **GD69003** Wagner—Der Ring des Nibelungen

PRIGENT, Maurice (ten)
Ravel: Enfant et les sortilèges (Cpte)

PRIKOPA, Herbert (bar)
Kálmán: Csárdásfürstin (exc)
Lehár: Graf von Luxemburg (exc)
Ligeti: Grand Macabre (Cpte)
O. Straus: Walzertraum (exc)
R. Strauss: Rosenkavalier (Cpte)

PRINCIPINI, Giuseppe (sngr)
Wolf-Ferrari: Campiello (Cpte)

PRING, Katherine (mez)
Wagner: Götterdämmerung (Cpte), Rheingold (Cpte)

PRING, Sarah (sop)
Britten: Peter Grimes (Cpte)
Janáček: Jenufa (Cpte)

PRINGLE, John (bass)
Meyerbeer: Huguenots (Cpte)
Prokofiev: Love for 3 Oranges (Cpte)
R. Strauss: Intermezzo (Cpte)

PRINTEMPS, Yvonne (sop)
(EMI) **CZS5 68113-2** Vive Offenbach!

PRIOR, Beniamino (ten)
Donizetti: Lucia di Lammermoor (Cpte)

PRIOR, John (treb)
Britten: Midsummer Night's Dream (Cpte)

PRITCHARD, Sir John (cond)
see Cologne Gürzenich Orch
Glyndebourne Fest Orch
LPO
LSO
MMF Orch
New Philh
Philh
ROHO
RPO
Santa Cecilia Academy Orch
VPO

PRO ARTE CHOIR
cond R. BONYNGE
(DECC) **440 410-2DM** Plácido Domingo

PRO ARTE CHORUS
cond M. SARGENT
Gay: Beggar's Opera (Cpte)

PRO ARTE ORCHESTRA
cond B. CAMPANELLA
Piccinni: Cecchina (Cpte)
cond B. HERRMANN
Herrmann: Wuthering Heights (Cpte)
cond M. SARGENT
Gay: Beggar's Opera (Cpte)
Sullivan: Gondoliers (Cpte), HMS Pinafore (Cpte), Iolanthe (Cpte), Mikado (Cpte), Patience (Cpte), Trial by Jury (Cpte), Yeomen of the Guard (Cpte)
(CFP) **CD-CFP4238** Gilbert and Sullivan
(CFP) **CD-CFP4529** Gilbert & Sullivan: Overtures
(CFP) **CD-CFP4582** Flowers in Music
(CFP) **CD-CFP4609** Favourite Gilbert & Sullivan
(EMI) **CMS7 64409-2** Sullivan—Pirates of Penzance & Orch. Works
(EMI) **CMS7 64412-2** Gilbert & Sullivan—Ruddigore/Shakespeare Music

PRO MUSICA ENSEMBLE
cond D. MILHAUD
(EPM) **150 122** Milhaud—Historic Recordings 1928-1948

PROBST, Wolfgang (bar)
Nono: Intolleranza 1960 (Cpte)
Suder: Kleider machen Leute (Cpte)

PROBST, Wolfram (sngr)
Weber: Freischütz (Cpte)

PROCHÁZKOVÁ, Jaroslava (mez)
Janáček: Jenufa (Cpte), Makropulos Affair (Cpte)
Martinů: Julietta (Cpte)

PROCURONOFF, Elizabeth (sngr)
Mercadante: Giuramento (Cpte)

PROEBSTL, Max (bass)
Handel: Giulio Cesare (Cpte)
R. Strauss: Salome (Cpte)
Wagner: Meistersinger (Cpte)

PROENZA, Pedro di (ten)
(DECC) **436 300-2DX** Opera Gala Sampler
(DECC) **440 410-2DM** Plácido Domingo

PRÖGLHÖF, Harald (bass)
Lehár: Giuditta (exc)
Mozart: Nozze di Figaro (Cpte), Zauberflöte (Cpte)
R. Strauss: Arabella (Cpte), Ariadne auf Naxos (Cpte), Daphne (Cpte), Rosenkavalier (Cpte), Salome (Cpte)
Wagner: Meistersinger (Cpte)

PROHASKA, Felix (cond)
see VPO

PROHASKA, Jaro (bar)
Wagner: Fliegende Holländer (exc), Lohengrin (exc), Rienzi (exc), Tristan und Isolde (Cpte)
(SCHW) **314532** Vienna State Opera Live, Vol.3
(SCHW) **314592** Vienna State Opera Live, Vol.9
(SCHW) **314742** Vienna State Opera Live, Vol.24
(TELD) **9031-76442-2** Wagner—Excerpts from the 1936 Bayreuth Festival

PROKINA, Jelena (sop)
Mussorgsky: Khovanshchina (Cpte)

PROKINA, Yelena (sop)
Prokofiev: War and Peace (exc)

PROTSCHKA, Josef (ten)
Beethoven: Fidelio (Cpte)
Busoni: Turandot (Cpte)
Hindemith: Cardillac (Cpte), Mathis der Maler (Cpte)
J. Strauss II: Fledermaus (exc)
Lortzing: Undine (Cpte)
R. Strauss: Ariadne auf Naxos (Cpte)
Schoeck: Massimilla Doni (Cpte)
Schreker: Schatzgräber (Cpte)
Schubert: Fierrabras (Cpte)
Wagner: Fliegende Holländer (Cpte)
Wolf: Manuel Venegas
Zemlinsky: Traumgörge (Cpte)
(CAPR) **10 109** Josef Protschka sings Mozart arias
(CAPR) **10 810** Mozart—Opera Highlights

PROTTI, Aldo (bar)
Verdi: Aida (Cpte), Otello (Cpte), Rigoletto (Cpte), Traviata (Cpte)
(BONG) **GB1060-2** Virginia Zeani - Various opera arias
(DECC) **433 443-2DA** Great Opera Choruses
(MEMO) **HR4372/3** Great Voices Giuseppe Di Stefano

PROVENCE INSTRUMENTAL ENSEMBLE
cond C. ZAFFINI
Campra: Tancrède (exc)

PROVENCE VOCAL ENSEMBLE
cond C. ZAFFINI
Campra: Tancrède (exc)

PROVVISIONATO, Francesca (mez)
Donizetti: Elisir d'amore (Cpte)
Rossini: Occasione fa il ladro (Cpte), Siège de Corinthe (Cpte)

PRUDENT, Jean (ten)
Bizet: Carmen (exc)

PRUDON, Huguette (sngr)
(EMI) **CZS7 67515-2** Offenbach—Operetta highlights

PRUETT, Jérôme (ten)
Henze: Boulevard Solitude (Cpte)
(PRES) **PCOM1109** Le Maître de Musique—Original Soundtrack

PRŮŠA, Karel (bass)
Dvořák: Jacobin (exc)
Janáček: Cunning Little Vixen (Cpte), From the House of the Dead (Cpte)
Martinů: Miracles of Mary (Cpte)
Smetana: Libuše (Cpte)

PRUSSIAN STATE ORCHESTRA
cond H.U. MÜLLER
(PREI) **89065** Maria Reining (1903-1991)

PRUVOST, Jacques (bar)
Audran: Poupée (exc)
Bizet: Carmen (Cpte)
Messager: Coups de Roulis (Cpte), Monsieur Beaucaire (Cpte)
Offenbach: Chanson de Fortunio (Cpte), Madame l'Archiduc (Cpte)
Planquette: Rip van Winkle (Cpte)
(EMI) **CZS7 67869-2** J. Strauss II—Operetta Highlights
(EMI) **CZS7 67872-2** Lehár—Operettas (highlights in French)

PRÜWER, Julius (cond)
see Berlin St Op Orch
orch

PRUZHANSKY, Arkady (ten)
Karetnikov: Till Eulenspiegel (Cpte)

PRYCE-JONES, John (cond)
see D'Oyly Carte Op Orch

PRYLOVÁ, Libuše (sop)
Janáček: Makropulos Affair (Cpte)

PRYTZ, Eva (sop)
Verdi: Rigoletto (Cpte)

PSAROS, Georgetta (sop)
(RCA) **GD60866** The Placido Domingo Album
(RCA) **GD84265** Con Amore
(RCA) **09026 61356-2** Domingo Sings Caruso

PUERTO DE LA CRUZ 'REYES BARTLET' CHOIR
cond A. R. MARBÀ
Vives: Bohemios (Cpte)

PUGH, William (ten)
Spohr: Faust (Cpte)

PUGLIESE, James (perc)
Glass: Hydrogen Jukebox (Cpte)

PUHLMANN-RICHTER, Christa (mez)
Ligeti: Grand Macabre (Cpte)

PUJOL, Roger (bass)
Auber: Gustav III (Cpte)

PULLEN, Joanne (sop)
Offenbach: Orphée aux enfers (Cpte)

PUMA, Salvatore (ten)
Mascagni: Iris (Cpte)

PURCELL, Pat (sop)
Janáček: Cunning Little Vixen (Cpte)

PURCELL QUARTET
(CHAN) **CHAN0571** A Purcell Miscellany

(THE) PURCELL SIMFONY
Purcell: Indian Queen, Z630 (Cpte)
cond A. ROOLEY
Purcell: Don Quixote: The Musical (Cpte)

(THE) PURCELL SIMFONY VOICES
Purcell: Indian Queen, Z630 (Cpte)

PURNHAGEN, Gregory (bar)
Glass: Belle et la Bête (Cpte), Hydrogen Jukebox (Cpte)

PURVIS, Jennifer (pf)
(CLRI) **CC0006** Clarinet Virtuosi of the Past—Hermstedt

PUSHEE, Graham (alto)
Cavalli: Calisto (Cpte)

PUSTELAK, Kazimierz (ten)
Mussorgsky: Boris Godunov (Cpte)

PUTILIN, Nikolai (bar)
Rimsky-Korsakov: Sadko (Cpte)
Tchaikovsky: Queen of Spades (exc)

PUTKONEN, Matti (bass)
Rautavaara: Vincent (Cpte)
Sallinen: Kullervo (Cpte)

PUTNAM, Ashley (sop)
Puccini: Bohème (Cpte)
R. Strauss: Arabella (Cpte)
V. Thomson: Mother of us all (Cpte)

PUTTAR, Nada (mez)
(TEST) **SBT1036** Lisa Della Casa sings Richard Strauss

PUTTEN, Thea van der (contr)
R. Strauss: Rosenkavalier (Cpte)

PUTZ, Hans (spkr)
Benatzky: Im weissen Rössl (Cpte)

PÜTZ, Ruth-Margret (sop)
Gluck: Orfeo ed Euridice (Cpte)
Mozart: Zauberflöte (exc)
Nicolai: Lustigen Weiber von Windsor (Cpte)

PUURA, Väino (bar)
Tubin: Barbara von Tisenhusen (Cpte)

PYLE, Thomas (sngr)
Bernstein: Candide (1956) (exc)

QUADFLIEG, Will (narr)
Mozart: Entführung (Cpte)
Weber: Freischütz (exc)

QUADRI, Argeo (cond)
see Catania Teatro Massimo Bellini Orch
Milan SO
orch
Vienna Op Orch

QUANDT, Kerstin (contr)
Pfitzner: Herz (Cpte)
S. Wagner: Bärenhäuter (Cpte), Schwarzschwanenreich (Cpte)

QUARTARARO, Florence (sop)
(EMI) **CHS7 69741-2(1)** Record of Singing, Vol.4—Anglo-American School (pt 1)

QUASTHOFF, Thomas (bar)
Haydn: Anima del filosofo (Cpte)

QUEBEC CONSERVATOIRE ORCHESTRA
cond F-P. DECKER
(REM) **REM311120** Orchestre du Conservatiore du Quebec -Concert 1989

QUEEN'S HALL ORCHESTRA
cond HENRY WOOD
(BEUL) **1PD3** Sir Henry's Themes and Variations
(DUTT) **CDAX8008** Sir Henry Wood conducts Proms Favourites

QUEENSLAND PHILHARMONIC ORCHESTRA
cond J. GEORGIADIS
(NAXO) **8 550928** Weber—Orchestral Works

QUELER, Eve (cond)
see NY Op Orch

QUESTA, Angelo (cond)
see Turin RAI Orch
Turin RSO

QUILICO, Gino (bar)
Berlioz: Troyens (Cpte)
Bizet: Carmen (Cpte), Jolie fille de Perth (Cpte), Pêcheurs de Perles (Cpte)
Chabrier: Roi malgré lui (Cpte)
Chausson: Roi Arthus (Cpte)
Corigliano: Ghosts of Versailles (Cpte)
Donizetti: Don Pasquale (Cpte)
Gounod: Roméo et Juliette (Cpte)
Massenet: Manon (Cpte)
Monteverdi: Orfeo (Cpte)
Puccini: Bohème (Cpte), Manon Lescaut (Cpte)
Rossini: Cenerentola (Cpte), Comte Ory (Cpte)
(DECC) **440 947-2DH** Essential Opera II
(EMI) **CDC5 55151-2** Operetta Duets
(ERAT) **4509-91715-2** The Ultimate Opera Collection 2

QUILICO, Louis (bar)
Massenet: Esclarmonde (Cpte)

QUILLEVÉRÉ, Marcel (ten)
(EMI) **CDS7 49361-2** Offenbach: Operettas

QUINN, Gerard (bar)
Verdi: Trovatore (Cpte)

QUITTMEYER, Susan (mez)
Verdi: Falstaff (Cpte)
Wagner: Rheingold (Cpte)

QUIVAR, Florence (contr)
Gershwin: Porgy and Bess (Cpte)
Verdi: Ballo in maschera (Cpte), Luisa Miller (Cpte)

RAAMAT, Helvi (sop)
Tubin: Barbara von Tisenhusen (Cpte)

RAANOJA, Pia (sop)
(BIS) **BIS-CD373/4** Opera Scenes from Savaonlinna

RABENSTEIN, Hans-Martin (cond)
see Berlin Deutsche Op Orch
Berlin SO

RABIN, Michael (vn)
(EMI) **CMS7 64123-2** The Art of Michael Rabin (1936-1972)

RABINER, Ellen (mez)
Purcell: Dido (Cpte)

RABOL, Georges (pf)
(O111) **OPS30-64** Classics of the Americas, Vol.6

RACEWICZ, Ryszarda (mez)
Moniuszko: Halka (Cpte)
Szymanowski: King Roger (Cpte)

RACHMANINOV, Sergei (pf)
(DECC) **425 964-2DM** Rachmaninov from Ampico Piano Rolls
(DECC) **440 066-2DM** Ampico Piano Roll Recordings (1919-1929)
(RCA) **GD87766** Rachmaninov plays Rachmaninov
(RCA) **09026 61265-2(1)** Rachmaninov—The Complete Recordings (pt 1)
(RCA) **09026 61265-2(2)** Rachmaninov—The Complete Recordings (pt 2)

RACHOŃ, Stefan (cond)
see Polish RSO

RADFORD, Robert (bass)
(PEAR) **GEMMCD9122** 20 Great Basses sing Great Arias

RADFORD, Winifred (sop)
Mozart: Nozze di Figaro (Cpte)

RADI, Afaf (sop)
Mozart: Così fan tutte (Cpte), Nozze di Figaro (Cpte)

RADIO ITALIANA SYMPHONY ORCHESTRA
cond A. SIMONETTO
(PREI) **89096** Alexander Svéd (1906-1979)

RAFFALLI, Tibère (ten)
Offenbach: Brigands (Cpte)
Verdi: Don Carlos (Cpte)
(EMI) **CZS5 68113-2** Vive Offenbach!

RAFFANELLI, Flora (sop)
Bellini: Pirata (Cpte)
Donizetti: Lucia di Lammermoor (Cpte)
Verdi: Otello (Cpte)
(EMI) **CDM7 69500-2** Montserrat Caballé sings Bellini & Verdi Arias

RAFFANTI, Dano (ten)
Bellini: Capuleti (Cpte)
Rossini: Donna del Lago (Cpte), Siège de Corinthe (Cpte)

RAFFEINER, Walter (ten)
Berg: Wozzeck (Cpte)
R. Strauss: Salome (Cpte)
S. Wagner: Schwarzschwanenreich (Cpte)
Weill: Happy End (Cpte), Kuhhandel (exc), Mahagonny-Gesänge (Cpte)

RAFFELL, Anthony (bass)
Berlioz: Troyens (Cpte)
Sullivan: Princess Ida (Cpte), Trial by Jury (Cpte), Yeomen of the Guard (Cpte)
Wagner: Götterdämmerung (Cpte)
(DECC) **433 868-2DWO** The World of Gilbert & Sullivan - Volume 2
(DG) **072 422-3GH7** Levine conducts Wagner's Ring

RAFFERTY, Michael (cond)
see Scottish Chbr Op Ens

RAFTERY, J. Patrick (ten)
Spontini: Vestale (Cpte)

RAGATZU, Rosella (sop)
Franchetti: Cristoforo Colombo (Cpte)
Rossini: Sigismondo (Cpte)
(SCHW) **314052** Opera Gala

RAGGETT, Keith (ten)
Britten: Midsummer Night's Dream (Cpte)

RAGIN, Derek Lee (alto)
Gluck: Orfeo ed Euridice (Cpte)
Handel: Flavio (Cpte), Giulio Cesare (Cpte), Scipione (Cpte), Tamerlano (Cpte), Teseo (Cpte)
Hasse: Cleofide (Cpte)
Purcell: Dido (Cpte)
(HARM) **HMP390 804** Great Baroque Masters: Handel

RAGON, Gilles (ten)
Cavalli: Calisto (Cpte)
Debussy: Rodrigue et Chimène (Cpte)
Grétry: Caravane du Caire (Cpte)
Jommelli: Armida abbandonata (Cpte)
Lully: Alceste (Cpte), Armide, Atys (exc)
M-A. Charpentier: Médée (Cpte)
Marais: Alcyone (Cpte)
Mouret: Amours de Ragonde (Cpte)
Rameau: Platée (Cpte)
(HARM) **HMP390 805** Great Baroque Masters—Lully

RAHBARI, Alexander (cond)
see Belgian Rad & TV Orch
Bratislava RSO
Brussels BRT PO
LPO

RAHKONEN, Margit (pf)
(FINL) **4509-95605-2** Contrabasso con amroe
(FINL) **4509-97894-2** Contrabasso con Sentimento

RAHME, Edmondo (ten)
Verdi: Trovatore (Cpte)

RAICHEV, Rouslan (cond)
see Bulgarian RSO
Sofia National Op Orch
Sofia PO

RAIMONDI, Gianni (ten)
Donizetti: Anna Bolena (Cpte), Lucia di Lammermoor (Cpte)
Puccini: Bohème (Cpte)
Verdi: Traviata (Cpte)
(DECC) **071 142-1DH (DECC)** Essential Opera
(MEMO) **HR4223/4** Nicolai Ghiaurov
(MEMO) **HR4273/4** Great Voices—Pietro Cappuccilli
(MEMO) **HR4277/8** Mirella Freni—Public Performances 1963-1970

RAIMONDI, Ruggero (bass)
Bellini: Norma (Cpte), Pirata (Cpte)
Bizet: Carmen (Cpte)
Debussy: Pelléas et Mélisande (Cpte)
Donizetti: Favorita (Cpte)
Mozart: Don Giovanni (Cpte), Nozze di Figaro (Cpte)
Mussorgsky: Boris Godunov (Cpte)
Puccini: Bohème (Cpte), Tosca (Cpte), Turandot (Cpte)
Rossini: Barbiere di Siviglia (Cpte), Cenerentola (Cpte), Italiana in Algeri (Cpte), Mosè in Egitto (Cpte), Viaggio a Reims (Cpte)
Verdi: Aida (Cpte), Attila (Cpte), Don Carlo (Cpte), Don Carlos (exc), Forza del destino (Cpte), Lombardi (Cpte), Macbeth (Cpte), Masnadieri (Cpte), Rigoletto (Cpte), Simon Boccanegra (Cpte), Trovatore (Cpte), Vespri Siciliani (Cpte)
(EMI) **CDC7 54524-2** The José Carreras Album
(EMI) **CDM5 65575-2** Montserrat Caballé
(EMI) **CDM7 64356-2** Opera Choruses
(EMI) **CDM7 69549-2** Ruggero Raimondi: Italian Opera Arias
(ERAT) **2292-45797-2** The Ultimate Opera Collection
(ERAT) **4509-98503-2** Recital—Ruggero Raimondi
(IMP) **DPCD998** Opera Stars in Concert
(MCI) **MCCD090** Carreras & Friends sing Opera Arias & Songs
(RNE) **650004** Opera Stars in Concert

RAINBIRD, James (treb)
Menotti: Amahl and the Night Visitors (Cpte)

RAINE, Nic (synths)
(SILV) **SILVACD105(SILV)** Flower Duet from Lakme - Lesley Garrett

RAINER, Christian (cond)
see LPO

RAINERO, Ruth (sop)
Purcell: Dido (Cpte)

RAISA, Rosa (sop)
(CLUB) **CL99-052** Rosa Raisa (1893-1963)

RAISBECK, Rosina (sop)
Lehár: Lustige Witwe (Cpte)

RAITZIN, Misha (ten)
Mussorgsky: Boris Godunov (Cpte)

RAJSKI, Wojciech (cond)
see Polish Chmbr PO

RAKUSIN, Fredda (mez)
Verdi: Traviata (Cpte)

RALF, Torsten (ten)
Beethoven: Fidelio (Cpte)
Verdi: Otello (Cpte)
Wagner: Meistersinger (exc)
(ALTN) **CDAN3** Hjördis Schymberg
(DUTT) **CDLX7007** Beecham conducts Wagner
(EMI) **CMS7 64008-2(1)** Wagner Singing on Record (pt 1)
(PEAR) **GEMMCDS9121** Wagner—Die Meistersinger, Act 3, etc
(PEAR) **GEMMCDS9926(2)** Covent Garden on Record—Vol.4 (pt 2)
(PREI) **89077** Torsten Ralf (1901-1954)
(PREI) **90237** R Strauss—Daphne
(SCHW) **314512** Vienna State Opera Live, Vol.1
(SCHW) **314552** Vienna State Opera Live, Vol.5

RALLIER, Serge (ten)
Poulenc: Mamelles de Tirésias (Cpte)

RAMBERT, Mlle (sop)
Massenet: Manon (Cpte)

RAMEY, Samuel (bass)
A. Thomas: Hamlet (Cpte)
Bellini: Norma (Cpte)
Bizet: Carmen (Cpte)
Boito: Mefistofele (Cpte)
Donizetti: Lucia di Lammermoor (Cpte)
Floyd: Susannah (Cpte)
Gounod: Faust (Cpte)
Handel: Ariodante (Cpte)
Haydn: Armida (Cpte)
Massenet: Chérubin (Cpte)
Mozart: Don Giovanni (Cpte), Nozze di Figaro (exc), Zauberflöte (exc)
Mussorgsky: Boris Godunov (Cpte)
Offenbach: Contes d'Hoffmann (exc)
Puccini: Tosca (Cpte)
Rossini: Barbiere di Siviglia (Cpte), Donna del Lago (Cpte), Gazza ladra (Cpte), Italiana in Algeri (Cpte), Maometto II (Cpte), Otello (Cpte), Semiramide (Cpte), Signor Bruschino (Cpte), Turco in Italia (Cpte), Viaggio a Reims (Cpte)
Saint-Saëns: Samson et Dalila (Cpte)
Stravinsky: Rake's Progress (Cpte)
Verdi: Aida (exc), Attila (Cpte), Don Carlo (Cpte), Due Foscari (Cpte), Macbeth (Cpte), Masnadieri (Cpte), Rigoletto (exc)
(BELA) **450 117-2** Great Opera Chorus II
(DECC) **436 464-2DM** Ten Top Baritones & Basses
(DECC) **440 947-2DH** Essential Opera II
(DECC) **443 380-2DM** Ten Top Baritones & Basses 2
(DG) **072 428-1GH2(DG)** The Metropolitan Opera Gala
(EMI) **CDC5 55350-2** Cheryl Studer - A Portrait
(EMI) **CDC7 54643-2** Rossini—Bicentenary Gala Concert
(EMI) **CZS7 67440-2** The Best of Rossini
(EMI) **LDB491007-1 (EMI)** Rossini Bicentennial Birthday Gala
(LOND) **825 126-2** Amadeus - Original Soundtrack
(PHIL) **432 692-2PH** The Essential José Carreras
(RCA) **09026 61509-2** A Salute to American Music
(TELD) **4509-90865-2** So in Love - Samuel Ramey on Broadway
(TELD) **9031-73242-2** Rossini—Arias

RAMIREZ, Alejandro (ten)
Hindemith: Nusch-Nuschi (Cpte)
Mozart: Nozze di Figaro (exc)

RAMIREZ, Mari Carmen (sngr)
Barbieri: Barberillo de Lavapiès (Cpte)

RAMIRO, Yordi (ten)
Puccini: Gianni Schicchi (Cpte), Madama Butterfly (Cpte)
R. Strauss: Rosenkavalier (Cpte)
Verdi: Rigoletto (Cpte), Traviata (Cpte)

RAMM, Gabriele (sop)
Weill: Happy End (Cpte), Mahagonny-Gesänge (Cpte)

RAMPAL, Jean-Pierre (fl)
(EMI) **CMS5 65621-2** Fischer-Dieskau - The Opera Singer

RAMPY, David (ten)
Nono: Intolleranza 1960 (Cpte)

RANCZAK, Hildegard (sop)
(PREI) **90096** Helge Roswaenge sings Verdi & Puccini

RANDLE, Thomas (ten)
Purcell: Fairy Queen, Z629 (Cpte)
Tippett: Ice Break (Cpte)

RANDOVÁ, Eva (mez)
Fibich: Šárka (Cpte)
Janáček: Cunning Little Vixen (Cpte), Jenufa (Cpte)
Schreker: Irrelohe (Cpte)
Wagner: Lohengrin (Cpte), Parsifal (Cpte)
(DECC) **440 410-2DM** Plácido Domingo
(EMI) **CDC7 49811-2** Covent Garden Gala Concert
(SUPR) **11 1846-2** Emmy Destinn Opera Gala

RANDS, Leslie (bar)
Sullivan: Gondoliers (Cpte), Mikado (Cpte), Patience (Cpte), Sorcerer (Cpte)

RANKIN, Bruce (sngr)
Romberg: Student Prince (Cpte)

RANKIN, Nell (mez)
Berlioz: Troyens (exc)
Puccini: Madama Butterfly (Cpte)

RANKL, Karl (cond)
see LPO
LSO
National SO
ROHO

RANSOM, Dwight (voc)
Joplin: Treemonisha (Cpte)

RANSOME, Antony (bar)
Rameau: Naïs (Cpte)

RAPALO, Ugo (cond)
see Naples San Carlo Op Orch

RAPCHAK, Lawrence (cond)
see Chicago Chbr Op Orch

RAPHAEL ENSEMBLE
(HYPE) **CDA66704** Bruckner/R. Strauss—Chamber Works

RAPHAELE CONCERT ORCHESTRA
cond E. RONDELL
(MOZA) **MECD1002** Operetta Melodies
cond P. WALDEN
(MOZA) **MECD1002** Operetta Melodies

RAPHANEL, Ghyslaine (sop)
Bizet: Carmen (Cpte)
Massenet: Manon (Cpte)
Offenbach: Brigands (Cpte)
(EMI) **CZS5 68113-2** Vive Offenbach!

RAPISARDI, Grete (sop)
Puccini: Gianni Schicchi (Cpte)

RAPPÉ, Jadwiga (contr)
Wagner: Rheingold (Cpte), Siegfried (Cpte)

RAPPOLD, Marie (sop)
(CLUB) **CL99-025** Giovanni Zenatello (1876-1949)
(IRCC) **IRCC-CD802** Souvenirs of Rare French Opera
(PEAR) **GEMMCDS9074(2)** Giovanni Zenatello, Vol.2 (pt 2)

RAPSON, Penelope (hpd)
(MERI) **CDE84195** Vivaldi: Orchestral and Vocal Works

RAPTIS, Paulos (ten)
Mussorgsky: Boris Godunov (Cpte)

RASA, Lina Bruna (sop)
Mascagni: Cavalleria Rusticana (Cpte)
(PREI) **89040** Carlo Galeffi (1884-1961)

(SUPR) **11 1491-2** Jarmila Novotna sings Czech Songs and Arias

RCA VICTOR SYMPHONY ORCHESTRA
cond T. BEECHAM
Puccini: Bohème (Cpte)
cond C. CALLINICOS
(RCA) **09026 61440-2** Opera's Greatest Moments
cond R. CELLINI
(RCA) **GD87799** The Pearl Fishers Duet plus Duets and Scenes
(RCA) **09026 61440-2** Opera's Greatest Moments
cond S. HENDERSON
(RCA) **09026 62699-2** Opera's Greatest Duets
cond E. MACARTHUR
(RCA) **GD87915** Wagner: Arias and Duets
cond E. MCARTHUR
(SIMA) **PSC1821(2)** Kirsten Flagstad, Vol.1 (pt 2)
cond L. STOKOWSKI
(RCA) **09026 61503-2** Stokowski Favourites

REA, Sean (bass)
Verdi: Otello (Cpte)

READ, David (bass)
Vaughan Williams: Hugh the Drover (Cpte)

REARDON, John (bar)
Beeson: Hello Out There (Cpte)
Puccini: Bohème (Cpte)
Stravinsky: Rake's Progress (Cpte)
(SONY) **SM3K47154** Bernstein—Theatre Works Volume 1
(SONY) **SM22K46290(3)** Stravinsky—The Complete Edition (pt 3)
(SONY) **SM22K46290(4)** Stravinsky—The Complete Edition (pt 4)

REAUTSCHNIGG, Johann (ten)
R. Strauss: Rosenkavalier (Cpte)

RÉAUX, Angelina (sop)
Bernstein: West Side Story (Cpte)
Puccini: Bohème (Cpte)
Weill: Sieben Todsünden (Cpte)
(DG) **439 151-2GMA** Mad about Puccini
(KOCH) **37087-2** Songs of Kurt Weill

REAVILLE, Richard (ten)
Britten: Billy Budd (Cpte)

REBMANN, Liselotte (sop)
Wagner: Götterdämmerung (Cpte), Walküre (Cpte)
(DG) **435 211-2GX15** Wagner—Der Ring des Nibelungen

RECHETNIAK, Nikolai (bar)
Rachmaninov: Francesca da Rimini (Cpte)

REDDISH, Keith (bar)
Verdi: Traviata (Cpte)

REDEL, Kurt (cond)
see London Fest Orch
Munich Pro Arte Orch
Munich RO
Nice PO
Rhineland-Pfalz State PO
Slovak PO

REDGRAVE, Michael (bar)
(EMI) **CDH5 65072-2** Glyndebourne Recorded - 1934-1994

REDKIN, Vladimir (bar)
Tchaikovsky: Maid of Orleans (Cpte)

REED, David (bass)
Verdi: Macbeth (Cpte)

REED, John (bar)
Sullivan: Gondoliers (Cpte), HMS Pinafore (exc), Iolanthe (Cpte), Mikado (exc), Patience (Cpte), Pirates of Penzance (Cpte), Princess Ida (Cpte), Ruddigore (Cpte), Sorcerer (Cpte), Trial by Jury (Cpte), Yeomen of the Guard (Cpte)
(BELA) **461 006-2** Gilbert & Sullivan—Songs and Snatches
(DECC) **430 095-2DWO** The World of Gilbert & Sullivan, Vol.1
(DECC) **433 868-2DWO** The World of Gilbert & Sullivan - Volume 2
(LOND) **436 813-2LM2** Sullivan—The Grand Duke. Overture Di Ballo. Henry VIII
(LOND) **436 816-2LM2** Sullivan—Utopia Ltd. Macbeth & Marmion Ovs etc

REED, Michael (cond)
see New Sadler's Wells Op Orch
RPO
Welsh Guards Band

REEH, Horst (bass)
Mozart: Zauberflöte (Cpte)
Wagner: Meistersinger (Cpte)

REES, Deborah (sop)
Knussen: Higglety Pigglety Pop! (Cpte)
Sullivan: Mikado (Cpte)
(LOND) **825 126-2** Amadeus - Original Soundtrack

REES, Judith (sop)
Purcell: Dido (Cpte)
Rameau: Castor et Pollux (Cpte)

REEVE, Scott (bass)
Bernstein: Candide (1982) (Cpte)
Glass: Satyagraha (Cpte)

REGENSBURG CATHEDRAL CHOIR
cond J. KEILBERTH
Mozart: Zauberflöte (Cpte)

REGINALD KILBEY STRINGS
cond R. KILBEY
(EMIL) **CDZ114** Best of Baroque

REHFUSS, Heinz (bar)
Dittersdorf: Arcifanfano (Cpte)
Gounod: Roméo et Juliette (Cpte)
Mozart: Nozze di Figaro (Cpte)
(DECC) **433 400-2DM2** Ravel & Debussy—Stage Works

REIBOLD, Bruno (cond)
see orch
RCA SO
Victor SO

REICH, Cäcilie (sop)
R. Strauss: Arabella (Cpte)
(SCHW) **314532** Vienna State Opera Live, Vol.3

REICH, Günter (narr)
Schoenberg: Moses und Aron (Cpte)

REICH, Günter (spkr)
Schoenberg: Moses und Aron (Cpte)

REICH, Hermann (bass)
(SCHW) **314562** Vienna State Opera Live, Vol.6
(SCHW) **314602** Vienna State Opera Live, Vol.10
(SCHW) **314642** Vienna State Opera Live, Vol.14
(SCHW) **314702** Vienna State Opera Live, Vol.20

(GOTTFRIED) REICHE CONSORT
(AMBI) **amb97865** English Renaissance & Baroque Works

REICHENBERGER, Hugo (cond)
see Vienna St Op Orch

REICHERT, Willy (sngr)
Jessel: Schwarzwaldmädel (exc)

REICHMANN, Wolfgang (narr)
Mozart: Entführung (Cpte)
Weill: Dreigroschenoper (Cpte)

REICHWEIN, Leopold (cond)
see Vienna St Op Orch

REID, Lesley (sop)
G. Charpentier: Louise (Cpte)

REID, Meston (ten)
Sullivan: Zoo (Cpte)
(LOND) **436 813-2LM2** Sullivan—The Grand Duke. Overture Di Ballo. Henry VIII
(LOND) **436 816-2LM2** Sullivan—Utopia Ltd. Macbeth & Marmion Ovs etc

REID, William (cond)
see Sadler's Wells Op Orch

REIMER, Eva-Christine (sop)
Schillings: Mona Lisa (Cpte)

REIMER, Eva-Christine (sop)
Delius: Village Romeo and Juliet (Cpte)

REINBOLD, Véronique (mez)
Essyad: Collier des Ruses (Cpte)

REINECKE, Renate (sop)
R. Strauss: Elektra (Cpte)

REINER, Charles (pf)
(MERC) **434 351-2MM** Szeryng plays Kreisler

REINER, Fritz (cond)
see Chicago SO
LPO
NYPO
NYPSO
RCA SO
RCA Victor Orch

REINHART, Gregory (bass)
Cesti: Orontea (Cpte)
Lully: Alceste (Cpte)
M-A. Charpentier: Arts Florissants (Cpte)
Prokofiev: Love for 3 Oranges (Cpte)
Rameau: Zoroastre (Cpte)

REINING, Maria (sop)
R. Strauss: Arabella (Cpte), Ariadne auf Naxos (Cpte), Rosenkavalier (Cpte)
Wagner: Meistersinger (exc), Walküre (exc)
(EMI) **CDC7 54838-2** Franz Lehár
(EMI) **CHS7 69741-2(4)** Record of Singing, Vol.4—German School
(EMI) **CMS7 64008-2(1)** Wagner Singing on Record (pt 1)
(PREI) **89065** Maria Reining (1903-1991)
(PREI) **90083** Maria Reining
(PREI) **90150** Lehár conducts Lehár
(PREI) **90190** Paul Schoeffler—Recital
(PREI) **90213** Max Lorenz sings Wagner
(PREI) **90237** R Strauss—Daphne
(SCHW) **314502** Vienna State Opera—Live Recordings (sampler)
(SCHW) **314542** Vienna State Opera Live, Vol.4
(SCHW) **314552** Vienna State Opera Live, Vol.5
(SCHW) **314602** Vienna State Opera Live, Vol.10
(SCHW) **314632** Vienna State Opera Live, Vol.13
(SCHW) **314672** Vienna State Opera Live, Vol.17
(SCHW) **314692** Vienna State Opera Live, Vol.19
(SCHW) **314702** Vienna State Opera Live, Vol.20

REINMAR, Hans (bar)
Wagner: Parsifal (exc)
(PREI) **89209** Helge Roswaenge (1897-1972) - II

REINPRECHT, Johann (ten)
R. Strauss: Rosenkavalier (Cpte)

REISS, Albert (ten)
(CLAR) **CDGSE78-50-33** Lauritz Melchior & Albert Coates
(DANA) **DACOCD319/21** The Lauritz Melchior Anthology - Vol.5
(EMI) **CDH7 69789-2** Melchior sings Wagner
(PEAR) **GEMMCDS9121** Wagner—Die Meistersinger, Act 3, etc
(PEAR) **GEMMCDS9137** Wagner—Der Ring des Nibelungen
(PREI) **89086** Lauritz Melchior (1890-1973) - III

REITER, Alfred (bass)
Spohr: Faust (Cpte)

REITER, Helga (sop)
Rameau: Castor et Pollux (Cpte)

REITH, Maria (sop)
Mozart: Zauberflöte (Cpte)

REIZEN, Mark (bass)
(ARLE) **ARL23/5** Rimsky-Korsakov—Sadko
(PEAR) **GEMMCD9122** 20 Great Basses sing Great Arias
(PREI) **89059** Mark Reizen (1895-1992) - I
(PREI) **89080** Mark Reizen (1895-1992) - II

REMEDIOS, Alberto (ten)
Tippett: Midsummer Marriage (Cpte)
Wagner: Götterdämmerung (exc), Siegfried (Cpte), Walküre (Cpte)

REMEDIOS, Ramon (ten)
Kálmán: Gräfin Mariza (exc)
Verdi: Otello (Cpte)

REMIGIO, Carmela (sngr)
Bellini: Norma (Cpte)

REMOR, Michela (mez)
Gluck: Iphigénie en Tauride (Cpte)

RENAISSANCE QUARTET
(MSCM) **MM30446** Lily Pons - Recital

RENAISSANCE QUINTET
(RCA) **09026 61411-2** Lily Pons Recital

RENAISSANCE SINGERS
(CHAN) **CHAN6608** Violin Favourites

RENARD, Paul (spkr)
Bizet: Carmen (Cpte)

RENAUD, Maurice (bar)
(IRCC) **IRCC-CD802** Souvenirs of Rare French Opera
(NIMB) **NI7840/1** The Era of Adelina Patti
(NIMB) **NI7867** Legendary Baritones
(PEAR) **GEMMCDS9923(2)** Covent Garden on Record, Vol.1 (pt 2)
(SYMP) **SYMCD1089** Historic Baritones of the French School
(SYMP) **SYMCD1100** Harold Wayne Collection, Vol.8

RENAUX, Nadine (sop)
(EMI) **CZS5 68295-2** Messager/Lecocq—Operetta Highlights
(EMI) **CZS7 67515-2** Offenbach—Operetta highlights

RENCONTRES MUSICALES ORCHESTRA
cond I. ANGUELOV
Henze: Boulevard Solitude (Cpte)

RENDALL, David (ten)
Donizetti: Maria Stuarda (Cpte)
Handel: Ariodante (Cpte)
Mozart: Così fan tutte (Cpte)
Puccini: Rondine (Cpte)
Romberg: Student Prince (exc)

RENÉ, Henri (cond)
see orch

RENÉE, Madelyn (sop)
Verdi: Aida (Cpte)

RENTON, Frank (cond)
see Kneller Hall Band

RENTON, Lavinia (sop)
Sullivan: Gondoliers (Cpte)

RENZETTI, Donato (cond)
see London Sinf Op Orch
LPO
Milan RAI SO
Turin RAI Orch
Tuscany Rad & TV Orch

RENZI, Emilio (ten)
Bellini: Norma (Cpte)

REPPEL, Carmen (sop)
R. Strauss: Elektra (Cpte)
Wagner: Rheingold (exc), Walküre (Cpte)
(PHIL) **434 420-2PM32(2)** Richard Wagner Edition (pt 2)

RESCH, Rudolf (ten)
R. Strauss: Rosenkavalier (Cpte)

RESCIGNO, Nicola (cond)
see American Op Soc Orch
Concertgebouw
Monte Carlo Nat Op Orch
N German RSO
National PO
Paris Cons
Paris Op Orch
Philh
ROHO
RPO
Vienna Op. Orch
Vienna Volksoper Orch

RESEMBA, Maria (sop)
Rossini: Barbiere di Siviglia (exc)

RESICK, Georgine (sop)
Hindemith: Nusch-Nuschi (Cpte)
Lortzing: Wildschütz (Cpte)
Mozart: Nozze di Figaro (Cpte)

RESNIK, Regina (mez)
Barber: Vanessa (Cpte)
Berlioz: Troyens (Cpte)
Bizet: Carmen (Cpte)
Gay: Beggar's Opera (Cpte)
J. Strauss II: Fledermaus (Cpte)
R. Strauss: Elektra (Cpte), Salome (Cpte)
Verdi: Ballo in maschera (Cpte)
Wagner: Götterdämmerung (Cpte), Walküre (Cpte)
(BELA) **450 006-2** Famous Opera Duets
(DECC) **433 068-2DWO** Your Hundred Best Opera Tunes V
(DECC) **436 462-2DM** Ten Top Mezzos
(FOYE) **15-CF2011** Wagner—Der Ring de Nibelungen
(RCA) **09026 61580-2(5)** RCA/Met 100 Singers, 100 Years (pt 5)
(RCA) **09026 62689-2** The Voices of Living Stereo, Volume 1

RESS, Ulrich (ten)
Gluck: Rencontre imprévue (Cpte)
Hindemith: Mathis der Maler (Cpte)
Puccini: Turandot (Cpte)
R. Strauss: Elektra (Cpte)
Schoeck: Massimilla Doni (Cpte)
Verdi: Falstaff (Cpte)
Wagner: Fliegende Holländer (Cpte), Meistersinger (Cpte)

RESZKE, Edouard de (bass)
(NIMB) **NI7840/1** The Era of Adelina Patti
(PEAR) **GEMMCDS9923(1)** Covent Garden on Record, Vol.1 (pt 1)

RETHBERG, Elisabeth (sop)
Verdi: Otello (Cpte)
(CONI) **CDHD227** Gigli in Opera and Song
(EMI) **CDH7 64029-2** Richard Tauber - Opera Recital
(EMI) **CMS7 64008-2(1)** Wagner Singing on Record (pt 1)
(MMOI) **CDMOIR419** Vienna Nights - Golden Age of Operetta
(MSCM) **MM30283** Great Wagnerian Singers, Vol.1
(NIMB) **NI7853** Lauri-Volpi sings Verdi
(ORFE) **C394101B** Great Mozart Singers Series, Vol. 1
(PEAR) **GEMMCDS9159(2)** De Luca Edition, Vol.1 (pt 2)
(PEAR) **GEMMCDS9452** The Emperor Tibbett
(PEAR) **GEMMCDS9925(2)** Covent Garden on Record—Vol.3 (pt 2)
(PEAR) **GEMMCDS9926(2)** Covent Garden on Record—Vol.4 (pt 2)
(PEAR) **GEMMCD9367** Gigli—Arias and Duets
(PEAR) **GEMMCD9944** Friedrich Schorr sings Wagner
(PREI) **89012** Giacomo Lauri-Volpi (1894-1979)
(PREI) **89051** Elisabeth Rethberg (1894-1976)
(PREI) **89073** Giuseppe de Luca (1876-1950) - II
(PREI) **89084** Kerstin Thorborg (1896-1970)
(RCA) **GD87811** Beniamino Gigli—Operatic Arias
(RCA) **09026 61580-2(3)** RCA/Met 100 Singers, 100 Years (pt 3)
(ROMO) **81012-2** Elisabeth Rethberg— Brunswick Recordings 1924-1929
(ROMO) **81014-2** Elisabeth Rethberg (1894-1976)
(SCHW) **314532** Vienna State Opera Live, Vol.3

RÉTHY, Esther (sop)
J. Strauss II: Nacht in Venedig (Cpte)
(EMI) **CDC7 54838-2** Franz Lehár
(PREI) **90150** Lehár conducts Lehár
(SCHW) **314532** Vienna State Opera Live, Vol.3
(SCHW) **314542** Vienna State Opera Live, Vol.4
(SCHW) **314572** Vienna State Opera Live, Vol.7
(SCHW) **314582** Vienna State Opera Live, Vol.8
(SCHW) **314602** Vienna State Opera Live, Vol.10
(SCHW) **314692** Vienna State Opera Live, Vol.19
(SCHW) **314712** Vienna State Opera Live, Vol.21

RETTORE, Aurore (sop)
(PEAR) **GEMMCD9091** Dino Borgioli
(PEAR) **GEMMCD9178** Riccardo Stracciari

REUSS, Wilhelm Franz (cond)
see Berlin City Op Orch

REUTER, Rolf (cond)
see Thüringian SO

REVELL, Geoffrey (organ)
(APPL) **APC003** Classical Organ Music

REVERS, Anna de (sop)
(BONG) **GB1043-2** Italian Baritones of the Acoustic Era

REVILL, Clive (bar)
Sullivan: Mikado (Cpte)

REVOIL, Fanély (mez)
Offenbach: Contes d'Hoffmann (Cpte)

RÉVOIL, Fanély (sop)
(EMI) **CZS5 68292-2** Operetta Arias and Duets
(MSCM) **MM30221** 18 French Divas

REX, Sheila (mez)
Britten: Albert Herring (Cpte), Noye's Fludde (Cpte)
Purcell: Dido (Cpte)

REY, Gaston (bar)
Audran: Miss Helyett (Cpte)
Bazin: Voyage en Chine (Cpte)
Ganne: Hans (Cpte)
Lecocq: Jour et la Nuit (Cpte)
Messager: Coups de Roulis (Cpte)
Offenbach: Madame l'Archiduc (Cpte)
Terrasse: Travaux d'Hercule (Cpte)
(EMI) **CZS7 67515-2** Offenbach—Operetta highlights

REY, Isabel (sop)
Mozart: Nozze di Figaro (Cpte)
(ERAT) **4509-95789-2** Zarzuelas-The Passion of Spain

REYGHERE, Greta de (sop)
Grétry: Caravane du Caire (Cpte)
Rameau: Zoroastre (Cpte)

REYNOLDS, Anna (mez)
Mozart: Zauberflöte (Cpte)
Tchaikovsky: Eugene Onegin (Cpte)
Verdi: Luisa Miller (Cpte)
Wagner: Götterdämmerung (Cpte), Meistersinger (Cpte), Rheingold (Cpte)
(DG) **429 168-2GR** Wagner: Excerpts from Der Ring
(DG) **435 211-2GX15** Wagner—Der Ring des Nibelungen
(PHIL) **434 420-2PM32(1)** Richard Wagner Edition (Pt.1)

RHENISH PHILHARMONIC ORCHESTRA
cond W. BALZER
(EBS) **EBS6071** Bruch—Orchestral Works

RHINE OPERA CHORUS
cond F. HAIDER
Donizetti: Roberto Devereux (Cpte)
cond A. LOMBARD
Gounod: Faust (Cpte)
Mozart: Così fan tutte (Cpte)
Offenbach: Périchole (Cpte)
Puccini: Turandot (Cpte)
(EMI) **CDC7 54016-2** Tenorissimo!
(EMI) **CDC7 54524-2** The José Carreras Album
(EMI) **CDM5 65575-2** Montserrat Caballé
(EMI) **CDM7 63111-2** José Carreras sings Opera & Operetta Arias
(EMI) **CDM7 64359-2** Gala de España
(EMI) **CDM7 69596-2** The Movies go to the Opera
(EMI) **CZS5 68559-2** Italian Opera Choruses
(ERAT) **2292-45797-2** The Ultimate Opera Collection
(ERAT) **4509-91715-2** The Ultimate Opera Collection 2
(ERAT) **4509-96971-2** Marcel Landowski—Edition

RHINE STATE PHILHARMONIC ORCHESTRA
cond J. LOCKHART
(MARC) **8 223498** Bruneau—Orchestral Highlights

RHINELAND-PFALZ STATE PHILHARMONIC ORCHESTRA
cond W. A. ALBERT
(CPO) **CPO999 003-2** Siegfried Wagner—Complete Overtures, Volume 1
(CPO) **CPO999 300-2** Siegfried Wagner—Overtures, Vol. 2
cond K. REDEL
(FORL) **FF058** An Evening in Moscow
cond L. SEGERSTAM
(MARC) **8 223503** Rabaud—Orchestral Works

RHIN-MULHOUSE SYMPHONY ORCHESTRA
cond L. PFAFF
Dusapin: Romeo and Juliet (Cpte)

RHODEN, Neil (cond)
see London Cast

RHODES, Jane (mez)
Offenbach: Orphée aux enfers (Cpte)
(EMI) **CZS5 68113-2** Vive Offenbach!
(PHIL) **442 272-2PM2** The Best of Bizet

RHODES, Paul (pf)
(ASV) **CDDCA739** Summer Works
(ASV) **CDWHL2072** Walking in the Air - Favourites for Flute

RHYÄNEN, Jaakko (bass)
Wagner: Fliegende Holländer (Cpte)
(BIS) **BIS-CD373/4** Opera Scenes from Savaonlinna

RHYS-DAVIES, Gareth (bar)
Janáček: Fate (Cpte)

RHYS-DAVIES, Jennifer (sop)
Mercadante: Orazi e Curiazi (Cpte)
Rossini: Barbiere di Siviglia (Cpte)
(OPRA) **ORCH104** A Hundred Years of Italian Opera: 1820-1830

RHYS-EVANS, Huw (ten)
Boïeldieu: Calife de Bagdad (Cpte)
Mendelssohn: Hochzeit des Camacho (Cpte)

RHYS-WILLIAMS, Stephen (bass-bar)
Knussen: Where the Wild Things are (Cpte)

RIALLAND, Louis (ten)
G. Charpentier: Louise (Cpte)
Gounod: Roméo et Juliette (Cpte)
Poulenc: Dialogues des Carmélites (Cpte)
(EMI) **LDB9 91258-1(EMI)** Maria Callas at the Paris Opera December 1958

RIBACCHI, Luisa (mez)
Puccini: Manon Lescaut (Cpte)
Verdi: Otello (Cpte), Rigoletto (Cpte)
(DECC) **440 408-2DM** Renata Tebaldi

RIBASENKO, Vladimir (bass)
Mussorgsky: Marriage (Cpte)

RICCI, Enrique (cond)
see BBC Concert Orch
ECO

RICCI, Gian Luca (bar)
Paisiello: Serva Padrona (Cpte)

RICCI, Luigi (cond)
see Rome Op Orch
Rome Teatro Reale Orch

RICCIARDI, Franco (ten)
Bellini: Sonnambula (Cpte)
Cilea: Adriana Lecouvreur (Cpte)
Donizetti: Lucia di Lammermoor (exc), Lucrezia Borgia (Cpte)
Massenet: Manon (Cpte)
Puccini: Bohème (Cpte), Manon Lescaut (Cpte), Turandot (Cpte)
Verdi: Aida (Cpte), Rigoletto (Cpte), Traviata (Cpte), Trovatore (Cpte)
(BUTT) **BMCD015** Pavarotti Collection - Duets and Scenes

RICCIARELLI, Katia (sop)
Bellini: Capuleti (Cpte), Zaira (Cpte)
Bizet: Carmen (exc)
Donizetti: Elisir d'amore (Cpte), Maria di Rudenz (Cpte)
Puccini: Bohème (Cpte), Tosca (exc), Turandot (Cpte)
Rossini: Bianca e Falliero (Cpte), Donna del Lago (Cpte), Gazza ladra (exc), Viaggio a Reims (Cpte)
Verdi: Aida (Cpte), Battaglia di Legnano (Cpte), Don Carlos (Cpte), Due Foscari (Cpte), Falstaff (Cpte), Luisa Miller (Cpte), Otello (exc), Simon Boccanegra (Cpte), Trovatore (Cpte)
(BELA) **450 002-2** Pavarotti Live
(BELA) **450 121-2** Plácido Domingo
(CAST) **CASH5052** Verdi Operatic Favourites
(CAST) **CVI2065** Highlights from the Royal Opera House, Covent Garden
(DECC) **443 018-2DF2** Pavarotti/Freni/Ricciarelli—Live
(DG) **439 151-2GMA** Mad about Puccini
(DG) **439 153-4GMA** Mad about Sopranos
(ERMI) **ERM151** Katia Ricciarelli in Recital
(IMP) **DPCD998** Opera Stars in Concert
(MCI) **MCCD090** Carreras & Friends sing Opera Arias & Songs
(PHIL) **432 692-2PH** The Essential José Carreras
(PHIL) **442 600-2PH** The Great Carreras
(RCA) **GD60866** The Placido Domingo Album
(RCA) **GD86534** Verdi Arias and Duets
(RCA) **09026 61580-2(8)** RCA/Met 100 Singers, 100 Years (pt 8)
(RCA) **09026 62595-2** Opera Duets
(RCA) **74321 24284-2** Opera's Greatest Heroines
(RNE) **650004** Opera Stars in Concert
(VIRG) **CUV5 61139-2** Rossini—Arias

RICE, JoAnn (cond)
see New Calliope Sngrs

RICERCAR ACADEMY
cond M. MINKOWSKI
Grétry: Caravane du Caire (Cpte)
cond M. PONSEELE
(RICE) **RIC126114** Rossini—Overtures (arr Wind Ens)

RICERCAR CONSORT
(RICE) **RIC93001** Compendium of Baroque Musical Instruments

RICHARD, Lawrence (bass)
Lehár: Graf von Luxemburg (exc)
Sullivan: Iolanthe (Cpte)

RICHARDS, Angela (sngr)
Gay: Beggar's Opera (Cpte)

RICHARDSON, Carol (sop)
Wagner: Parsifal (Cpte)

RICHARDSON, Linda (mez)
G. Charpentier: Louise (Cpte)
Massenet: Werther (exc)
Ravel: Enfant et les sortilèges (Cpte)
Shostakovich: Lady Macbeth of Mtsensk (Cpte)
Vaughan Williams: Hugh the Drover (Cpte)

RICHARDSON, Marilyn (sop)
Britten: Billy Budd (Cpte)
Mozart: Zauberflöte (Cpte)

RICHARDSON, Mark (bar)
Britten: Peter Grimes (Cpte)
Sullivan: Mikado (exc)

RICHARDSON, Stephen (bar)
Knussen: Higglety Pigglety Pop! (Cpte), Where the Wild Things are (Cpte)
MacMillan: Visitatio Sepulchri (Cpte)

RICHERT, François (bass)
Donizetti: Roberto Devereux (Cpte)

RICHMAN, Steven (cond)
see NY Harmonie Ens

RICHTER, Carl (bar)
Puccini: Bohème (exc)

RICHTER, Caspar (cond)
see Berlin RSO

RICHTER, Ernst Theo (bar)
Busoni: Arlecchino (Cpte)

RICHTER, Karl (cond)
see Munich Bach Orch

RICHTER, Maximilian (treb)
Mozart: Zauberflöte (Cpte)

RICKARDS, Steven (alto)
Handel: Siroe, Rè di Persia (Cpte)

RICKENBACHER, Karl Anton (cond)
see Bamberg SO
Capella Cracoviensis
LPO

RICQUIER, Odette (sop)
Gounod: Roméo et Juliette (Cpte)
(CLUB) **CL99-101** Vanni Marcoux (1877-1962)
(PEAR) **GEMMCD9912** Vanni Marcoux—Recital

RIDDER, Anton de (ten)
Beethoven: Fidelio (Cpte)
Busoni: Doktor Faust (Cpte)
Korngold: Tote Stadt (Cpte)
R. Strauss: Capriccio (Cpte), Rosenkavalier (Cpte)

RIDDERBUSCH, Karl (bass)
Beethoven: Fidelio (exc)
Flotow: Martha (Cpte)
Humperdinck: Königskinder (Cpte)
Orff: Orpheus (Cpte), Tanz der Spröden (Cpte)
Pfitzner: Palestrina (Cpte)
R. Strauss: Capriccio (Cpte)
Wagner: Fliegende Holländer (Cpte), Götterdämmerung (Cpte), Lohengrin (Cpte), Meistersinger (Cpte), Parsifal (Cpte), Rheingold (Cpte), Siegfried (Cpte), Tristan und Isolde (Cpte)
(ACAN) **44 2085-2** Carl Orff Collection
(CFP) **CD-CFP4656** Herbert von Karajan conducts Opera
(DG) **435 211-2GX15** Wagner—Der Ring des Nibelungen
(DG) **439 423-2GCL** Wagner—Der Ring des Nibelungen (highlights)
(PHIL) **434 420-2PM32(1)** Richard Wagner Edition (Pt.1)

RIDEOUT, Gary (ten)
Janáček: Makropulos Affair (Cpte)

RIDEOUT, Patricia (sop)
(SONY) **SM22K46290(3)** Stravinsky—The Complete Edition (pt 3)

RIEDEL, Bernd (bar)
Lortzing: Wildschütz (Cpte)

RIEDEL, Karl (cond)
see RCA SO

RIEDELBAUCH, Wolfgang (ten)
Mozart: Zauberflöte (Cpte)

RIEDIKER, Hans (bass)
Holliger: Magische Tänzer (Cpte)

RIEDL, Franz (bass)
R. Strauss: Rosenkavalier (Cpte)

RIEGEL, Kenneth (ten)
Berg: Lulu (Cpte)
Henze: Bassariden (Cpte)
Messiaen: Saint François d'Assise (Cpte)
Mozart: Don Giovanni (Cpte)
Mussorgsky: Boris Godunov (Cpte)
R. Strauss: Salome (Cpte)
Zemlinsky: Florentinische Tragödie, Geburtstag der Infantin (Cpte)

RIEGLER, Friedl (sop)
Mozart: Zauberflöte (Cpte)

RIENER, Robert (bar)
Puccini: Gianni Schicchi (Cpte)
Verdi: Rigoletto (Cpte)
(EURO) **GD69043** Puccini: Il Trittico

RIESMAN, Michael (cond)
see Philip Glass Ens

RIESMAN, Michael (kybds)
(PNT) **434 873-2PTH** Jon Gibson—In Good Company

RIGACCI, Bruno (cond)
see Livorno Cel-Teatro Orch
Toscanini SO

RIGACCI, Susanna (sop)
Donizetti: Elisir d'amore (Cpte), Pazzi per progetto (Cpte)
Sacchini: Contadina in Corte (Cpte)

RIGBY, Jean (mez)
Bizet: Carmen (exc)
Britten: Albert Herring (Cpte), Gloriana (Cpte), Rape of Lucretia (Cpte)
Sullivan: Mikado (exc), Yeomen of the Guard (exc)
Verdi: Forza del destino (exc), Rigoletto (Cpte)

RILEY, Stanley (bass)
Sullivan: Ruddigore (Cpte), Sorcerer (Cpte)
Verdi: Trovatore (Cpte)

RÎMBU, Romeo (cond)
see Oradea PO

RIME, Noémi (sop)
Lully: Armide, Atys (Cpte)
M-A. Charpentier: Médée (Cpte)
Mouret: Amours de Ragonde (Cpte)
Purcell: Fairy Queen, Z629 (Cpte)
Rameau: Indes galantes (Cpte)
Rossi: Orfeo (Cpte)

RIMINI, Giacomo (bar)
Verdi: Falstaff (Cpte)
(CLUB) **CL99-052** Rosa Raisa (1893-1963)

RINALDI, Alberto (bar)
Cimarosa: Matrimonio segreto (Cpte)
Leoncavallo: Pagliacci (Cpte)
Rossini: Cenerentola (Cpte), Scala di seta (Cpte), Signor Bruschino (Cpte)
(TELD) **9031-77676-6(TELD)** My World of Opera - Kiri Te Kanawa

RINALDI, Margherita (sop)
Donizetti: Linda di Chamounix (Cpte)
Meyerbeer: Prophète (Cpte)
Verdi: Rigoletto (exc)
(BUTT) **BMCD015** Pavarotti Collection - Duets and Scenes

RINALDI-MILIANI, Stefano (bar)
Giordano: Andrea Chénier (Cpte)
Mozart: Don Giovanni (Cpte)

RINAUDO, Mario (bass)
Donizetti: Lucia di Lammermoor (Cpte)
Meyerbeer: Africaine (Cpte)
Puccini: Bohème (Cpte), Madama Butterfly (Cpte)
Verdi: Forza del destino (Cpte), Lombardi (Cpte), Rigoletto (Cpte), Trovatore (Cpte)

RINGART, Anna (mez)
Berg: Lulu (Cpte)

RINGEISSEN, Bernard (pf)
(ADES) **14166-2** Piano Music by the Group of Five

RINGHOLZ, Teresa (sop)
(ARAB) **Z6547** Herbert—L'Encore

RINTZLER, Marius (bass)
Busoni: Doktor Faust (Cpte)
Mozart: Nozze di Figaro (Cpte)
Puccini: Madama Butterfly (Cpte)

RIO DE JANEIRO MUNICIPAL THEATRE CHORUS

RIO DE JANEIRO MUNICIPAL THEATRE ORCHESTRA
(SONY) **SLV48362(SONY)** Concert for the Planet Earth
cond J. DEMAIN
(SONY) **SLV48362(SONY)** Concert for the Planet Earth

RIORDAN, Joseph (ten)
Sullivan: Cox and Box (Cpte), Gondoliers (Cpte)

RIPLEY, Gladys (contr)
Wagner: Walküre (exc)

RIPOLLES, Dolores (sngr)
Bretón: Verbena de la Paloma (Cpte)

RIPPON, Michael (bass)
Herrmann: Wuthering Heights (Cpte)
Holst: Wandering Scholar (Cpte)
Puccini: Tosca (Cpte)
R. Strauss: Salome (Cpte)
Schoenberg: Moses und Aron (Cpte)
Vaughan Williams: Hugh the Drover (Cpte)
Weill: Sieben Todsünden

RISCHNER, Alfons (cond)
see Stuttgart RSO

RISTORI, Gabrielle (mez)
Audran: Miss Helyett (Cpte), Poupée (exc)

RISTORI, Riccardo (bass)
Stradella: Moro per amore (Cpte)

RITCHIE, Elizabeth (sop)
Sullivan: HMS Pinafore (exc)
Wagner: Parsifal (Cpte)
(CLRI) **CC0006** Clarinet Virtuosi of the Past—Hermstedt

RITCHIE, Margaret (sop)
Delius: Village Romeo and Juliet (Cpte)
(EMI) **CMS7 64727-2** Britten—Opera excerpts and Folksongs

RITTER-CIAMPI, Gabriella (sop)
(MSCM) **MM30221** 18 French Divas

RIVA, Ambrogio (bass)
Mercadante: Bravo (Cpte)
Ponchielli: Lituani (Cpte)
Rossini: Bianca e Falliero (Cpte)

RIVA, Giuseppe (bass)
Bellini: Sonnambula (Cpte)

RIVAS, Isabel (sngr)
Usandizaga: Golondrinas (Cpte)

RIVENQ, Nicolas (bar)
Bizet: Carmen (Cpte)
Massenet: Don Quichotte (Cpte)
Messager: Fortunio (Cpte)
Monteverdi: Orfeo (Cpte)
Montéclair: Jephté (Cpte)
Rameau: Indes galantes (Cpte)
Rossini: Comte Ory (Cpte)
Vivaldi: Montezuma (Cpte)

RIVERS, Earl (cond)
see Cincinnati Uni Th Orch

RIVERS, Malcolm (bass-bar)
Britten: Billy Budd (Cpte)
G. Lloyd: Iernin, John Socman (exc)
Puccini: Fanciulla del West (Cpte)
Sullivan: Mikado (Cpte), Pirates of Penzance (exc)
Verdi: Otello (Cpte)
Walton: Troilus and Cressida (Cpte)

RIVERS, Sandra (pf)
(CBS) **CD39133** Bravura - Violin Showpieces
(EMI) **CDC7 54352-2** Sarah Chang - Debut
(RCA) **09026 62546-2** Salut d'amour

RIVOLI, Gianfranco (cond)
see Madrid Zarzuela Orch

RIZZA, Gilda dalla (sop)
(EMI) **CHS7 64864-2(1)** La Scala Edition - Vol.2, 1915-46 (pt 1)
(PEAR) **GEMMCDS9925(1)** Covent Garden on Record—Vol.3 (pt 1)

RIZZI, Carlo (cond)
see LSO
Manchester Camerata
ROHO
Sassari SO
WNO Orch

RIZZI, Lucia (contr)
Bellini: Adelson e Salvini (Cpte)
Rossini: Italiana in Algeri (exc)

RIZZOLI, Bruna (sop)
Donizetti: Don Pasquale (Cpte)
Puccini: Bohème (Cpte), Gianni Schicchi (Cpte)
Rossini: Mosè (Cpte)
Verdi: Aida (Cpte)

ROA, Miguel (cond)
see Madrid SO
Seville SO

ROACH, Jeanette (contr)
Sullivan: Gondoliers (Cpte)

ROAR, Leif (bass)
Wagner: Lohengrin (Cpte), Parsifal (Cpte)

ROARK-STRUMMER, Linda (sop)
Verdi: Due Foscari (Cpte)

ROBARTS, Jonathon (bass)
G. Lloyd: Iernin

ROBBIN, Catherine (mez)
Berlioz: Béatrice et Bénédict (Cpte)
Handel: Floridante (exc), Orlando (Cpte)
Mozart: Clemenza di Tito (Cpte)

ROBBINS, Julien (bass)
Puccini: Fanciulla del West (Cpte)
Verdi: Traviata (Cpte)
Wagner: Parsifal (exc)

ROBERTS, Eric (bar)
Sullivan: Mikado (Cpte), Pirates of Penzance (exc)

ROBERTS, Joy (sop)
Offenbach: Christopher Columbus (Cpte)

ROBERTS, Noëlle (sop)
Verdi: Traviata (Cpte)

ROBERTS, Rachel (spkr)
Gay: Beggar's Opera (Cpte)

ROBERTS, Rebecca (sop)
Offenbach: Périchole (Cpte)

ROBERTS, Stephen (bar)
Birtwistle: Punch and Judy (Cpte)

ROBERTS, Susan (sop)
Wagner: Parsifal (Cpte)

ROBERTSON, Christopher (bar)
Bellini: Puritani (Cpte)
(NUOV) **6892** William Matteuzzi sings Opera Arias

ROBERTSON, Duncan (ten)
Rossini: Barbiere di Siviglia (Cpte)
(EMI) **CDC7 47283-2** Maria Callas - Mad Scenes & Bel Canto Arias
(EMI) **CMS7 63244-2** The Art of Maria Callas

ROBERTSON, James (cond)
see Philh

ROBERTSON, John (ten)
Mozart: Nozze di Figaro (Cpte)

ROBERTSON, Nicholas (ten)
Monteverdi: Orfeo (Cpte)

ROBERTSON, Stuart (bar)
Sullivan: Gondoliers (Cpte), HMS Pinafore (Cpte), Pirates of Penzance (Cpte), Sorcerer (Cpte)

ROBEV, Georgi (cond)
see Sofia PO

(EMI) **CDM7 63110-2** Mirella Freni: Opera Recital
cond G. GAVAZZENI
Verdi: Lombardi (Cpte)
(BUTT) **BMCD015** Pavarotti Collection - Duets and Scenes
(MEMO) **HR4291/2** Great Voices - Renata Scotto
(RCA) **09026 68014-2** Pavarotti - The Early Years, Vol.2
cond C.M. GIULINI
Verdi: Rigoletto (Cpte)
(BUTT) **BMCD015** Pavarotti Collection - Duets and Scenes
cond V. GUI
Boito: Mefistofele (Cpte)
(EMI) **CDH5 65500-2** Boris Christoff - Italian Opera Arias
(EMI) **CHS7 69741-2(6)** Record of Singing, Vol.4—Russian & Slavonic Schools
cond E. LEINSDORF
Puccini: Bohème (exc), Madama Butterfly (Cpte), Tosca (Cpte), Turandot (Cpte)
(RCA) **GD60205** Opera Choruses
(RCA) **GD87799** The Pearl Fishers Duet plus Duets and Scenes
(RCA) **GK85277** Legendary Performers - Björling
(RCA) **09026 61580-2(5)** RCA/Met 100 Singers, 100 Years (pt 5)
(RCA) **09026 61580-2(7)** RCA/Met 100 Singers, 100 Years (pt 7)
(RCA) **09026 61886-2** Operas Greatest Love Songs
(RCA) **09026 62689-2** The Voices of Living Stereo, Volume 1
cond Z. MEHTA
Verdi: Aida (Cpte)
(DECC) **430 433-2DH** Carreras, Domingo and Pavarotti in Concert
(DECC) **440 410-2DM** Plácido Domingo
(DECC) **440 947-2DH** Essential Opera II
(DECC) **071 123-1DH (DECC)** Carreras, Domingo and Pavarotti in Concert
(DECC) **071 142-1DH (DECC)** Essential Opera
(DECC) **430 433-5DH** Carreras, Domingo and Pavarotti in Concert
cond F. MOLINARI-PRADELLI
Puccini: Turandot (Cpte)
Verdi: Rigoletto (Cpte)
(CFP) **CD-CFP4277** These you have Loved
cond P. MONTEUX
(RCA) **09026 62689-2** The Voices of Living Stereo, Volume 1
cond P.G. MORANDI
Paisiello: Don Chisciotte (Cpte)
cond G. MORELLI
(EMI) **CDH7 63495-2** Victoria de los Angeles—Early Recordings
(EMI) **CDM5 65579-2** Victoria de los Angeles
cond D. OLIVIERI
(EMI) **CHS7 64864-2(2)** La Scala Edition - Vol.2, 1915-46 (pt 2)
cond D. OREN
Donizetti: Fausta (Cpte)
Puccini: Tosca (Cpte)
(RCA) **09026 61886-2** Operas Greatest Love Songs
(RCA) **09026 62550-2** Ten Tenors in Love
cond J. PERLEA
Puccini: Manon Lescaut (Cpte)
Verdi: Aida (Cpte), Rigoletto (Cpte)
(RCA) **GD87799** The Pearl Fishers Duet plus Duets and Scenes
(RCA) **GK85277** Legendary Performers - Björling
(RCA) **09026 61886-2** Operas Greatest Love Songs
(RCA) **09026 62550-2** Ten Tenors in Love
cond F. PREVITALI
(MEMO) **HR4239/40** Opera Arias—Leyla Gencer
(RCA) **09026 61440-2** Opera's Greatest Moments
(RCA) **09026 61580-2(7)** RCA/Met 100 Singers, 100 Years (pt 7)
(RCA) **09026 62550-2** Ten Tenors in Love
(RCA) **74321 25817-2** Café Classics - Operatic
cond L. RICCI
(EMI) **CHS7 64864-2(2)** La Scala Edition - Vol.2, 1915-46 (pt 2)
(PREI) **89009** Gino Bechi (b. 1913)
cond G. SANTINI
Giordano: Andrea Chénier (Cpte)
Mascagni: Cavalleria Rusticana (Cpte)
Puccini: Madama Butterfly (Cpte)
Verdi: Don Carlo (Cpte), Simon Boccanegra (Cpte)
(CFP) **CD-CFP4569** Puccini: Arias
(CFP) **CD-CFP4602** Favourite Opera
(CFP) **CD-CFP9013** Duets from Famous Operas
(EMI) **CDC5 55095-2** Prima Diva
(EMI) **CDC7 54016-2** Tenorissimo!
(EMI) **CDM5 65579-2** Victoria de los Angeles
(EMI) **CDM7 63109-2** Tito Gobbi - Opera Aria Recital
(EMI) **CDM7 69596-2** The Movies go to the Opera
(EMI) **CMS7 64165-2** Puccini—Trittico
cond T. SCHIPPERS
Puccini: Bohème (Cpte)
Verdi: Trovatore (Cpte)
(CFP) **CD-CFP4277** These you have Loved
(CFP) **CD-CFP4602** Favourite Opera
(CFP) **CD-CFP9013** Duets from Famous Operas
(EMI) **CDM7 69596-2** The Movies go to the Opera
(EMIN) **CD-EMX9519** Great Sopranos of Our Time
cond T. SERAFIN
Verdi: Aida (Cpte), Otello (Cpte), Traviata (Cpte)
(BELA) **450 106-2** Rossini—Overtures
(CFP) **CD-CFP4602** Favourite Opera
(EMI) **CDM5 65579-2** Victoria de los Angeles
(EMI) **CDM7 64359-2** Gala de España
(EMI) **CHS7 64864-2(2)** La Scala Edition - Vol.2, 1915-46 (pt 2)
(EMI) **CMS7 64165-2** Puccini—Trittico
(RCA) **09026 61580-2(6)** RCA/Met 100 Singers, 100 Years (pt 6)
(RCA) **09026 61580-2(7)** RCA/Met 100 Singers, 100 Years (pt 7)
(RCA) **09026 62689-2** The Voices of Living Stereo, Volume 1
(VAI) **VAIA1016** Jon Vickers - Italian Opera Arias
cond G. SOLTI
Verdi: Aida (Cpte)
(DECC) **433 067-2DWO** Your Hundred Best Opera Tunes IV
(DECC) **433 221-2DWO** The World of Verdi
(DECC) **433 442-2DA** Verdi—Famous Arias
(DECC) **440 402-2DM** Leontyne Price

ROME ORCHESTRA
cond S. VARVISO
(DECC) **433 068-2DWO** Your Hundred Best Opera Tunes V
(DECC) **433 624-2DSP** Great Soprano Arias
(DECC) **440 405-2DM** Elena Souliotis

ROME PHILHARMONIC ORCHESTRA
cond G. GAVAZZENI
(RCA) **GD86534** Verdi Arias and Duets
(RCA) **09026 61580-2(8)** RCA/Met 100 Singers, 100 Years (pt 8)
(RCA) **74321 24284-2** Opera's Greatest Heroines

ROME POLYPHONIC CHORUS
cond R. FASANO
Gluck: Orfeo ed Euridice (Cpte)
cond G. GAVAZZENI
(RCA) **GD86534** Verdi Arias and Duets

ROME RAGAZZA DEL COLOSSEO CHORUS
cond L. GARDELLI
(DECC) **433 066-2DWO** Your Hundred Best Opera Tunes III

ROME RAI CHORUS
cond O. DE FABRITIIS
Verdi: Forza del destino (exc)
(MEMO) **HR4300/1** Great Voices—Sesto Bruscantini
cond W. FURTWÄNGLER
(EMI) **CZS7 67123-2** Wagner: Der Ring des Nibelungen
cond G. GAVAZZENI
Bellini: Pirata (Cpte)
(EMI) **CDM7 69500-2** Montserrat Caballé sings Bellini & Verdi Arias
(EMI) **CZS5 68559-2** Italian Opera Choruses
cond C.M. GIULINI
(MEMO) **HR4300/1** Great Voices—Sesto Bruscantini
cond Z. MEHTA
Puccini: Tosca (Cpte)
cond R. MUTI
(BUTT) **BMCD015** Pavarotti Collection - Duets and Scenes
(MEMO) **HR4277/8** Mirella Freni—Public Performances 1963-1970
(MEMO) **HR4279/80** Montserrat Caballè—Opera Arias
(MEMO) **HR4300/1** Great Voices—Sesto Bruscantini
cond G. PRÊTRE
(MEMO) **HR4392/3** Great Voices - Marilyn Horne
cond A. RODZINSKI
Mussorgsky: Khovanshchina (Cpte)
cond W. SAWALLISCH
(MEMO) **HR4223/4** Nicolai Ghiaurov
cond T. SCHIPPERS
Puccini: Bohème (exc)
(MEMO) **HR4273/4** Great Voices—Pietro Cappuccilli

ROME RAI ORCHESTRA
cond B. BARTOLETTI
(MEMO) **HR4279/80** Montserrat Caballè—Opera Arias
cond A. BASILE
(FONI) **CDMR5023** Martini & Rossi Festival, Volume 23
(MEMO) **HR4235/6** Great Voices-Renata Tebaldi
cond O. DE FABRITIIS
Verdi: Forza del destino (exc)
(MEMO) **HR4300/1** Great Voices—Sesto Bruscantini
cond W. FURTWÄNGLER
(ACAN) **43 121** Wagner: Orchestral Works
(EMI) **CZS7 67123-2** Wagner: Der Ring des Nibelungen
cond G. GAVAZZENI
Bellini: Pirata (Cpte)
(EMI) **CDM5 65575-2** Montserrat Caballé
(EMI) **CDM7 69500-2** Montserrat Caballé sings Bellini & Verdi Arias
(EMI) **CZS5 68559-2** Italian Opera Choruses
cond C.M. GIULINI
(MEMO) **HR4300/1** Great Voices—Sesto Bruscantini
cond B. MADERNA
(BONG) **GB1060-2** Virginia Zeani - Various opera arias
cond Z. MEHTA
Puccini: Tosca (Cpte)
cond R. MUTI
(BUTT) **BMCD015** Pavarotti Collection - Duets and Scenes
(MEMO) **HR4277/8** Mirella Freni—Public Performances 1963-1970
(MEMO) **HR4279/80** Montserrat Caballè—Opera Arias
(MEMO) **HR4300/1** Great Voices—Sesto Bruscantini
cond A. PAOLETTI
(MEMO) **HR4235/6** Great Voices-Renata Tebaldi
cond G. PRÊTRE
(MEMO) **HR4392/3** Great Voices - Marilyn Horne
cond A. RODZINSKI
Mussorgsky: Khovanshchina (Cpte)
cond W. SAWALLISCH
(MEMO) **HR4223/4** Nicolai Ghiaurov
cond T. SCHIPPERS
Puccini: Bohème (exc)
(BUTT) **BMCD015** Pavarotti Collection - Duets and Scenes
(MEMO) **HR4223/4** Nicolai Ghiaurov
(MEMO) **HR4273/4** Great Voices—Pietro Cappuccilli
cond A. SIMONETTO
(EMI) **CDC7 54437-2** Callas Rarities
(EMI) **CHS7 69741-2(7)** Record of Singing, Vol.4—Italian School
(MEMO) **HR4293/4** The very best of Maria Callas

ROME SYMPHONY ORCHESTRA
cond N. BONAVOLONTÀ
(RCA) **09026 62541-2** Pavarotti - The Early Years, Vol.1
(RCA) **09026 68014-2** Pavarotti - The Early Years, Vol.2
cond R. MUTI
(RCA) **09026 68014-2** Pavarotti - The Early Years, Vol.2

ROME TEATRO REALE OPERA ORCHESTRA
cond L. RICCI
(PREI) **89074** Tancredi Pasero (1893-1983) - II

ROMERO, Angelo (bar)
Donizetti: Campanello di notte (Cpte), Elisir d'amore (Cpte), Gianni di Parigi (Cpte)
Rossini: Barbiere di Siviglia (Cpte)

ROMERO, Celedonio (gtr)
(PHIL) **442 781-2PH** Spanish Guitar Favourites

ROMERO, Celín (gtr)
(PHIL) **434 727-2PM** Pepe Romero - Guitar Solos
(PHIL) **442 781-2PH** Spanish Guitar Favourites

ROMERO, Celino (gtr)
(PHIL) **442 781-2PH** Spanish Guitar Favourites

ROMERO, Pepe (gtr)
(PHIL) **434 727-2PM** Pepe Romero - Guitar Solos
(PHIL) **442 781-2PH** Spanish Guitar Favourites

ROMM, Avis (pf)
(EBS) **EBS6023** Contrasts - Music for Trombone & Piano

RONALD, Sir Landon (cond)
see orch

RONALD, Sir Landon (pf)
(NIMB) **NI7840/1** The Era of Adelina Patti
(PEAR) **GEMMCD9130** Great Sopranos, Vol.2
(PEAR) **GEMMCD9312** Adelina Patti

RONCATO, Massimiliano (treb)
Mozart: Mitridate (Cpte)

RONDELL, Erwin (cond)
see Raphaele Concert Orch

RONGE, Gabriele Maria (sop)
Zemlinsky: Traumgörge (Cpte)

RONI, Luigi (bass)
Bellini: Zaira (Cpte)
Donizetti: Fausta (Cpte)
Mozart: Don Giovanni (Cpte)
Puccini: Fanciulla del West (Cpte), Manon Lescaut (Cpte)
Rossini: Barbiere di Siviglia (Cpte)
Verdi: Aida (Cpte), Due Foscari (Cpte), Falstaff (Cpte)

RONO, Luigi (bass)
Rossini: Guillaume Tell (exc)

ROOCROFT, Amanda (sop)
Mozart: Così fan tutte (Cpte)
(EMI) **CDC5 55090-2** Amanda Roocroft—Recital
(EMI) **CDC5 55396-2** Amanda Roocroft - Mozart and his Contemporaries

ROOLEY, Anthony (cond)
see Consort of Musicke
Purcell Simfony

ROOLEY, Anthony (chitarrone)
(MOSC) **070974** King of the Low Seas

ROOLEY, Anthony (lte)
(HYPE) **CDA66056** Purcell: Songs and Dialogues
(L'OI) **417 123-2OH** Purcell: Songs and Airs
(L'OI) **444 620-2OH** The Glory of Purcell
(MOSC) **070971** The Scyence of Luytinge

ROOTERING, Jan-Hendrik (bass)
Gluck: Rencontre imprévue (Cpte)
Mozart: Don Giovanni (Cpte), Zauberflöte (Cpte)
Puccini: Fanciulla del West (Cpte), Turandot (Cpte)
Rossini: Semiramide (Cpte)
Suder: Kleider machen Leute (Cpte)
Verdi: Alzira (Cpte), Luisa Miller (exc), Rigoletto (Cpte)
Wagner: Feen (Cpte), Lohengrin (Cpte), Parsifal (Cpte), Rheingold (Cpte)
(DG) **445 354-2GX14** Wagner—Der Ring des Nibelungen
(DG) **072 422-3GH7** Levine conducts Wagner's Ring
(EMI) **LDX9 91275-1(EMI)** Sawallisch conducts Wagner's Ring

ROQUE, Marcel (bar)
Massenet: Werther (Cpte)

ROQUETTY, Camille (bar)
Gounod: Roméo et Juliette (Cpte)

RØRHOLM, Marianne (contr)
Handel: Giulio Cesare (Cpte)
Puccini: Madama Butterfly (Cpte)
R. Strauss: Ariadne auf Naxos (Cpte), Salome (Cpte)
Wagner: Parsifal (Cpte)

ROSBAUD, Hans (cond)
see Hamburg Rad Ch
Lamoureux Orch
Paris Cons

ROSCA, Marcel (bass)
Puccini: Bohème (Cpte), Gianni Schicchi (Cpte), Manon Lescaut (Cpte), Tabarro (Cpte)

RÖSCHMANN, Dorothea (sop)
Handel: Giustino (Cpte)
Keiser: Masagniello furioso (Cpte)

ROSE, Leonard (vc)
(SONY) **SMK47609** Schubert/Schumann—Orchestral Works

ROSE, Peter (bass)
Mozart: Nozze di Figaro (exc)
R. Strauss: Salome (Cpte)
Rossini: Barbiere di Siviglia (Cpte)
(SONY) **S2K66836** Goldschmidt—Beatrice Cenci, etc

ROSEKRANS, Charles (cond)
see Hungarian St Orch

ROSEN, Carole (mez)
Alman: King Ahaz (exc)

ROSENBAUM, Poul (pf)
(CHAN) **CHAN9336/8** Mussorgsky—Songs

ROSENBAUM, Susan (sngr)
Schuman: Mighty Casey (Cpte)

ROSENBERG, Berle Sanford (ten)
(OLYM) **OCD370** Berle Sanford Rosenberg Live From Budapest

ROSENSHEIN, Neil (ten)
Corigliano: Ghosts of Versailles (Cpte)
Tchaikovsky: Eugene Onegin (Cpte)
Verdi: Traviata (Cpte)

ROSENTHAL, Manuel (cond)
see French Rad Lyric Orch
Monte Carlo PO

ROSENTHAL, Moriz (pf)
(EMI) **CDS7 49361-2** Offenbach: Operettas

ROSNER, Anton (ten)
Gazzaniga: Don Giovanni (Cpte)

ROSS, Christopher (bass)
Britten: Billy Budd (Cpte)
Rossini: Barbiere di Siviglia (Cpte)

ROSS, Elise (sop)
Holst: At the Boar's Head (Cpte)
Weill: Sieben Todsünden

ROSS, Gill (sop)
Purcell: King Arthur, Z628 (Cpte)
(ERAT) **4509-96371-2** Gardiner—The Purcell Collection

ROSS, Lesley Echo (sop)
Sullivan: Gondoliers (Cpte), Yeomen of the Guard (Cpte)

ROSSDEUTSCHER, Cedric (treb)
Mozart: Zauberflöte (Cpte)

ROSSI, Alessandra (sop)
Mascagni: Amico Fritz (Cpte)

ROSSI, Annabella (sop)
Paisiello: Don Chisciotte (Cpte)

ROSSI, Arcangelo (bass)
(TEST) **SBT1008** Viva Rossini

ROSSI, Giulio (bass)
(SYMP) **SYMCD1077** The Harold Wayne Collection, Vol.4

ROSSI, John Carmen (ten)
Verdi: Ballo in maschera (Cpte), Falstaff (Cpte)
(RCA) **GD60326** Verdi—Operas & Choral Works

ROSSI, Lina (mez)
Verdi: Rigoletto (Cpte)

ROSSI, Mario (cond)
see Milan RAI SO
Naples San Carlo Op Orch
Turin RAI Orch
Turin SO

ROSSI, Tino (ten)
(FORL) **UCD19053** L'Incomparable Tino Rossi

ROSSIGNOL, Martial (sngr)
Ganne: Hans (Cpte)

ROSSI-LEMENI, Nicola (bass)
Bellini: Norma (Cpte), Puritani (Cpte)
Donizetti: Anna Bolena (Cpte)
Mascagni: Piccolo Marat (Cpte)
Rossini: Mosè (Cpte), Turco in Italia (Cpte)
Verdi: Forza del destino (Cpte)
(BONG) **GB1060-2** Virginia Zeani - Various opera arias
(EMI) **CDC7 54016-2** Tenorissimo!
(EMI) **CHS7 69741-2(7)** Record of Singing, Vol.4—Italian School
(EMI) **CMS7 63244-2** The Art of Maria Callas

RÖSSL-MAJDAN, Hilde (mez)
Mozart: Nozze di Figaro (Cpte), Zauberflöte (Cpte)
R. Strauss: Ariadne auf Naxos (Cpte), Rosenkavalier (Cpte)
(EMI) **CZS7 67123-2** Wagner: Der Ring des Nibelungen

ROSSMANITH, Gabriele (sop)
Hindemith: Mathis der Maler (Cpte)

ROST, Andrea (sop)
Janáček: From the House of the Dead (Cpte)
Mozart: Nozze di Figaro (Cpte)
R. Strauss: Frau ohne Schatten (Cpte)
Verdi: Rigoletto (Cpte)

ROST, Monika (gtr)
(LASE) **15 602** Spanish Guitar Music

ROSTER, Irma (sop)
Wagner: Walküre (exc)

ROSTROPOVICH, Mstislav (cond)
see FNO
LPO
Paris Orch
Washington NSO

ROSWAENGE, Helge (ten)
Mozart: Zauberflöte (Cpte)
(EMI) **CMS7 64008-2(1)** Wagner Singing on Record (pt 1)
(MMOI) **CDMOIR405** Great Tenors
(MSCM) **MM30283** Great Wagnerian Singers, Vol.1
(NIMB) **NI7848** Great Singers at the Berlin State Opera
(NIMB) **NI7856** Legendary Tenors
(ORFE) **C394101B** Great Mozart Singers Series, Vol. 1
(PEAR) **GEMMCDS9926(2)** Covent Garden on Record—Vol.4 (pt 2)
(PEAR) **GEMMCD9129** Great Tenors, Vol.2
(PEAR) **GEMMCD9394** Helge Roswaenge—Operatic Recital
(PREI) **89018** Helge Rosvaenge (1897-1972)
(PREI) **89201** Helge Roswaenge (1897-1972) - I
(PREI) **89209** Helge Roswaenge (1897-1972) - II
(PREI) **89211** Helge Roswaenge (1897-1972) - III
(PREI) **90096** Helge Roswaenge sings Verdi & Puccini
(PREI) **90103** Helge Roswaenge Recital (1959)
(SCHW) **314502** Vienna State Opera—Live Recordings (sampler)
(SCHW) **314552** Vienna State Opera Live, Vol.5
(SCHW) **314622** Vienna State Opera Live, Vol.12
(TEST) **SBT1005** Ten Top Tenors

ROSWAENGE, Ilonka (sop)
(PREI) **89209** Helge Roswaenge (1897-1972) - II

ROTA, Anna Maria (contr)
Puccini: Manon Lescaut (Cpte)
Verdi: Rigoletto (Cpte)
(MEMO) **HR4273/4** Great Voices—Pietro Cappuccilli

ROTA, Marcello (cond)
see Svizzera Italiana Orch

ROTA, Rinaldo (bar)
Mascagni: Piccolo Marat (Cpte)

ROTH, Sigmund (bass)
Weill: Mahagonny (Cpte)
(SCHW) **314562** Vienna State Opera Live, Vol.6
(SCHW) **314582** Vienna State Opera Live, Vol.8
(SCHW) **314692** Vienna State Opera Live, Vol.19
(SCHW) **314712** Vienna State Opera Live, Vol.21

ROTHENBERGER, Anneliese (sop)
Benatzky: Im weissen Rössl (Cpte)
Flotow: Martha (Cpte)
Gluck: Orfeo ed Euridice (Cpte)
Humperdinck: Hänsel und Gretel (Cpte)
Lehár: Land des Lächelns (Cpte), Lustige Witwe (exc)
Millöcker: Gasparone (Cpte)
Mozart: Entführung (Cpte), Idomeneo (Cpte), Zauberflöte (Cpte)
R. Strauss: Arabella (Cpte)
Verdi: Ballo in maschera (Cpte), Don Carlo (Cpte)
Zeller: Vogelhändler (Cpte)
(CFP) **CD-CFP4499** Strauss—Champagne and Laughter
(EMI) **CMS7 64309-2** Kálmán—Best-loved Melodies
(EMI) **CZS7 62993-2** Fritz Wunderlich—Great German Tenor
(EMIL) **CDZ7 67015-2** Mozart—Opera Arias
(ORFE) **C394301B** Great Mozart Singers Series, Vol. 3

ROTHER, Artur (cond)
see Bamberg SO
Berlin City Op Orch
Berlin Deutsche Op Orch
Berlin RO
Berlin RSO
Berlin SO
Berlin St Op Orch
Berlin Staatskapelle
Hamburg St Op Orch
Munich PO

ROTHIER, Léon (bass)
(NIMB) **NI7834** Caruso in Ensemble
(PEAR) **EVC3(1)** The Caruso Edition, Vol.3 (pt 1)
(RCA) **GD60495(5)** The Complete Caruso Collection (pt 5)
(RCA) **09026 61242-2** Caruso Sings Verdi

ROTHMÜLLER, Marko (bar)
(EMI) **CHS7 69741-2(4)** Record of Singing, Vol.4—German School
(LYRC) **SRO830** Smetana—The Bartered Bride, etc

ROTHSCHILD, Charlotte de (sop)
(NATI) **NTCD006** Voice and Harp Recital

ROTMAN, Hans (cond)
see Transparant Chbr Op Orch

ROTTERDAM PHILHARMONIC ORCHESTRA
cond J. CONLON
Mussorgsky: Khovanshchina (exc)
cond V. GERGIEV
(PHIL) **426 740-2PH** Dmitri Hvorostovsky sings Tchaikovsky & Verdi Arias
cond J. TATE
(EMI) **CDC7 54581-2** R.Strauss—Orchestral Music from Operas
cond E. DE WAART
R. Strauss: Rosenkavalier (Cpte)
(PHIL) **420 084-2PH** Frederica von Stade sings Haydn, Mozart & Rossini Arias
(PHIL) **442 600-2PH** The Great Carreras
cond D. ZINMAN
(PHIL) **438 763-2PM2** Chopin/Delibes/Gounod—Ballet Music

RÖTTGER, Renate (sop)
Weill: Kuhhandel (exc)

ROTZSCH, Hans Joachim (ten)
R. Strauss: Ariadne auf Naxos (Cpte)
Wagner: Meistersinger (Cpte)

ROUCHON, Jean-Philippe (cond)
see Philh
Vienna Ravel Orch

ROUEN THÉÂTRE DES ARTS CHORUS
cond A. GUINGAL
Saint-Saëns: Henry VIII (Cpte)

ROUGEL CHORUS
cond E. BIGOT
G. Charpentier: Louise (exc)

ROUILLON, Philippe (bar)
Saint-Saëns: Henry VIII (Cpte)

ROULEAU, Joseph (bass)
A. Thomas: Hamlet (Cpte)
Meyerbeer: Africaine (Cpte)
Rossini: Semiramide (Cpte)
Verdi: Don Carlo (Cpte)
(BELA) **450 117-2** Great Opera Chorus II
(EMI) **CDC7 47283-2** Maria Callas - Mad Scenes & Bel Canto Arias
(EMI) **CMS7 63244-2** The Art of Maria Callas
(EMI) **CMS7 64412-2** Gilbert & Sullivan—Ruddigore/Shakespeare Music

ROUND, Thomas (ten)
Lehár: Lustige Witwe (exc)
Sullivan: Gondoliers (Cpte), HMS Pinafore (exc), Iolanthe (Cpte), Mikado (Cpte), Ruddigore (Cpte), Trial by Jury (Cpte)
(DECC) **425 850-2DWO** Your Hundred Best Tunes, Vol.4
(DECC) **430 095-2DWO** The World of Gilbert & Sullivan, Vol.1
(DECC) **433 868-2DWO** The World of Gilbert & Sullivan - Volume 2

ROUNSEVILLE, Robert (ten)
Bernstein: Candide (1956) (exc)
(VAI) **VAI69112** Eleanor Steber in Opera and Song Vol 2

ROUQUETTY, Camille (ten)
Verdi: Rigoletto (Cpte)

ROUSKOVÁ, Anna (contr)
Janáček: Jenufa (Cpte)

ROUSSEAU, Emile (bar)
Poulenc: Mamelles de Tirésias (Cpte)
(EMI) **CHS7 61038-2** Debussy—Pelléas et Mélisande, etc

ROUSSEAU, Eugene (sax)
(DELO) **DE1007** Saxophone Colors

ROUSSELIÈRE, Charles (ten)
(IRCC) **IRCC-CD802** Souvenirs of Rare French Opera

ROUSSET, Christophe (cond)
see Talens Lyriques

ROUSSET, Christophe (hpd)
(ASTR) **E8757** Purcell—Songs from Orpheus Britannicus

ROUTLEDGE, Patricia (sngr)
Gay: Beggar's Opera (Cpte)

ROUX, Michel (bar)
Bizet: Carmen (Cpte), Ivan IV (exc)
Debussy: Pelléas et Mélisande (Cpte)
Ganne: Saltimbanques (exc)
Rossini: Comte Ory (Cpte)
(EMI) **CZS7 67515-2** Offenbach—Operetta highlights
(EMI) **CZS7 67869-2** J. Strauss II—Operetta Highlights
(MONT) **TCE8760** Stravinsky: Stage Works

ROVATKAY, Lajos (cond)
see Capella A. Steffani

ROVERO, Ornella (sop)
Massenet: Don Quichotte (Cpte)
Puccini: Gianni Schicchi (Cpte)

ROVETTA, Teodore (bar)
Verdi: Rigoletto (exc)

ROVIGO VENEZZE CONSERVATORY ORCHESTRA
cond R. BONYNGE
Rossini: Sigismondo (Cpte)

ROWADER, Darrell (sngr)
Rapchak: Lifework of Juan Diaz (Cpte)

ROWICKI, Witold (cond)
see Warsaw Nat PO

ROYAL BALLET
cond B. HAITINK
Borodin: Prince Igor (Cpte)

ROYAL COLLEGE OF MUSIC JUNIOR DEPARTMENT CHORUS
cond G. SOLTI
Verdi: Ballo in maschera (Cpte)

ROYAL LIVERPOOL PHILHARMONIC ORCHESTRA
cond D. ATHERTON
Holst: At the Boar's Head (Cpte)
cond CARL DAVIS
(CFP) **CD-CFP4601** Musicals - Volume 2
cond C. GROVES
(CFP) **CD-CFP4515** Meditation
(EMIL) **CDZ114** Best of Baroque
cond C. LAMBERT
(TEST) **SBT1013** Dame Joan Hammond—A Celebration
cond C. MACKERRAS
Holst: Perfect Fool (exc)
(VIRG) **CUV5 61135-2** Mussorgsky—Orchestral Works
cond L. PEŠEK
(VIRG) **VC7 59285-2** Favourite Czech Orchestral Works
cond T. YUASA
(EMIN) **CD-EMX2231** Britten—Orchestral Works

ROYAL MARINES BAND
cond R. MUTI
Verdi: Traviata (exc)

ROYAL MILITARY SCHOOL OF MUSIC BAND, KNELLER HALL
cond F. RENTON
(BAND) **BNA5067** Sullivan Salute

ROYAL NORTHERN COLLEGE OF MUSIC OPERA CHORUS
cond I. KENNAWAY
Vaughan Williams: Pilgrim's Progress (Cpte)

ROYAL NORTHERN COLLEGE OF MUSIC OPERA ORCHESTRA
cond I. KENNAWAY
Vaughan Williams: Pilgrim's Progress (Cpte)

ROYAL OPERA HOUSE CHORUS, COVENT GARDEN
Menotti: Amahl and the Night Visitors (Cpte)
cond T. BEECHAM
(DUTT) **CDLX7007** Beecham conducts Wagner
(EMI) **CMS7 64008-2(1)** Wagner Singing on Record (pt 1)
(EMI) **CMS7 64008-2(2)** Wagner Singing on Record (pt 2)
(LYRC) **LCD146** Frida Leider sings Wagner
(LYRC) **SRO830** Smetana—The Bartered Bride, etc
cond V. BELLEZZA
(CONI) **CDHD226** Chaliapin—Bass of the Century
(EMI) **CDH7 61009-2** Chaliapin sings Russian Opera Arias
cond R. BONYNGE
Bellini: Puritani (Cpte)
Donizetti: Fille du régiment (Cpte), Lucia di Lammermoor (Cpte)
J. Strauss II: Fledermaus (Cpte)
(DECC) **417 011-2DH2** Pavarotti's Greatest Hits
(DECC) **417 780-2DM** Joan Sutherland's Greatest Hits
(DECC) **433 064-2DWO** Your Hundred Best Opera Tunes Volume I
(DECC) **433 437-2DA** Pavarotti—King of the High Cs
(DECC) **436 300-2DX** Opera Gala Sampler
cond P. BOULEZ
Debussy: Pelléas et Mélisande (Cpte)
cond B. BRITTEN
Britten: Billy Budd (Cpte), Peter Grimes (Cpte)
cond C.F. CILLARIO
Verdi: Traviata (Cpte)
(EMI) **LDB4 91283-1(EMI)** Maria Callas at Covent Garden
(MEMO) **HR4291/2** Great Voices - Renata Scotto
(MEMO) **HR4376/7** Tito Gobbi—Opera Arias
cond P. CIMARA
(PEAR) **GEMMCDS9926(2)** Covent Garden on Record—Vol.4 (pt 2)
cond COLIN DAVIS
Berlioz: Benvenuto Cellini (Cpte), Troyens (Cpte)
Britten: Peter Grimes (Cpte)
Mozart: Clemenza di Tito (Cpte), Così fan tutte (Cpte), Don Giovanni (Cpte)
Puccini: Bohème (Cpte), Tosca (Cpte)
Saint-Saëns: Samson et Dalila (Cpte)
Tippett: Midsummer Marriage (Cpte)
Verdi: Ballo in maschera (Cpte), Trovatore (Cpte)
(BELA) **450 052-2** Great Opera Choruses
(KIWI) **CDSLD-82** Southern Voices—NZ International Opera Singers
(PHIL) **432 692-2PH** The Essential José Carreras
(PHIL) **434 986-2PM** Duetti Amorosi
(PHIL) **442 600-2PH** The Great Carreras
(PHIL) **442 602-2PM** 3 x 3 Tenors
cond I. DOBROVEN
(EMI) **CDH7 64252-2** Christoff sings Russian Arias & Songs
cond C. VON DOHNÁNYI
Beethoven: Fidelio (Cpte)
cond P. DOMINGO
J. Strauss II: Fledermaus (Cpte)
cond E. DOWNES
Verdi: Stiffelio (Cpte)
(BELA) **450 117-2** Great Opera Chorus II
(ROH) **75605 55013-2** The Puccini Experience
cond L. FOSTER
Walton: Troilus and Cressida (Cpte)
cond W. FURTWÄNGLER
Wagner: Tristan und Isolde (Cpte)
(PEAR) **GEMMCD9331** Frida Leider sings Wagner
cond L. GARDELLI
Puccini: Bohème (Cpte)
(CFP) **CD-CFP4569** Puccini: Arias
(EMI) **CDM7 64356-2** Opera Choruses
(EMI) **CZS5 68559-2** Italian Opera Choruses
(EMIL) **CDZ101** Best Loved Classics 2
(EMIL) **CDZ102** Best Loved Classics 3
cond G. GAVAZZENI
Mascagni: Amico Fritz (Cpte)
cond C.M. GIULINI
Verdi: Falstaff (Cpte)
(CAST) **CASH5052** Verdi Operatic Favourites
cond V. GUI
Verdi: Trovatore (Cpte)
cond B. HAITINK
Borodin: Prince Igor (Cpte)
Britten: Peter Grimes (Cpte)
Verdi: Don Carlo (Cpte)
(EMI) **CDC7 49849-2** Famous Opera Choruses
cond HARTMUT HAENCHEN
Gluck: Orfeo ed Euridice (Cpte)
cond L. MAAZEL
Verdi: Luisa Miller (Cpte)
cond C. MACKERRAS
Gounod: Roméo et Juliette (Cpte)
cond Z. MEHTA
Bizet: Carmen (Cpte)
Puccini: Fanciulla del West (Cpte)
cond F. MOLINARI-PRADELLI
(DECC) **425 493-2DM2** Joan Sutherland: The Art of the Prima Donna
(DECC) **433 442-2DA** Verdi—Famous Arias
(DECC) **433 624-2DSP** Great Soprano Arias
(DECC) **440 404-2DM** Joan Sutherland
cond M. MUDIE
(EMI) **CHS7 69741-2(7)** Record of Singing, Vol.4—Italian School
cond R. MUTI
Bellini: Capuleti (Cpte)
Verdi: Aida (Cpte), Ballo in maschera (Cpte)
(EMI) **CDC5 55017-2** Domingo Opera Classics
(EMI) **CDC7 47274-2** Verdi: Opera Choruses
(EMI) **CZS5 68559-2** Italian Opera Choruses
cond G. PRÊTRE
Offenbach: Contes d'Hoffmann (Cpte)
cond J. PRITCHARD
(SONY) **SBK46548** Opera Arias
cond S. RATTLE
Janáček: Cunning Little Vixen (Cpte)
cond F. REINER
Wagner: Tristan und Isolde (Cpte)
cond C. RIZZI
Rossini: Cenerentola (Cpte)
cond J. RUDEL
Giordano: Andrea Chénier (Cpte)
cond N. SANTI
Puccini: Fanciulla del West (Cpte)
cond W. SCHÜCHTER
(EMI) **CDH5 65201-2** Leonie Rysanek - Operatic Recital
cond G. SINOPOLI
Puccini: Manon Lescaut (Cpte), Tosca (Cpte)
Wagner: Tannhäuser (exc)
cond G. SOLTI
Gluck: Orfeo ed Euridice (Cpte)
R. Strauss: Rosenkavalier (Cpte)
Verdi: Otello (Cpte), Simon Boccanegra (Cpte), Traviata (Cpte)
(DECC) **436 315-2DA** Great Operatic Duets
cond R. STAPLETON
(IMP) **MCD15** Opera Spectacular
(IMP) **TCD1070** Invitation to the Opera
(RPO) **CDRPD9006** Opera Spectacular 1 & 2
(RPO) **CDRPO7009** Opera Spectacular II

ROYAL OPERA HOUSE, COVENT GARDEN CHILDREN'S CHORUS
cond G. SOLTI
Puccini: Tosca (exc)

ROYAL OPERA HOUSE, COVENT GARDEN MALE CHORUS
cond R. STAPLETON
(IMP) **PCDS21** Music of the World—Danube Dreams

ROYAL OPERA HOUSE ORCHESTRA, COVENT GARDEN
Beethoven: Fidelio (Cpte)
Bizet: Carmen (Cpte)
Borodin: Prince Igor (Cpte)
Britten: Peter Grimes (Cpte), Turn of the Screw (Cpte)
Giordano: Andrea Chénier (Cpte)
Gluck: Orfeo ed Euridice (Cpte)
Gounod: Roméo et Juliette (Cpte)
J. Strauss II: Fledermaus (Cpte)
Menotti: Amahl and the Night Visitors (Cpte), Boy who grew too fast (Cpte)
Offenbach: Contes d'Hoffmann (Cpte)
Puccini: Bohème (Cpte), Fanciulla del West (Cpte), Manon Lescaut (Cpte)
R. Strauss: Rosenkavalier (Cpte), Salome (Cpte)
Saint-Saëns: Samson et Dalila (Cpte)
Tchaikovsky: Eugene Onegin (Cpte)
Verdi: Don Carlo (Cpte), Falstaff (Cpte), Otello (Cpte), Simon Boccanegra (Cpte), Stiffelio (Cpte), Traviata (Cpte)
(EMI) **LDB4 91283-1(EMI)** Maria Callas at Covent Garden
cond J. BARKER
(EMI) **CDC5 55017-2** Domingo Opera Classics
(EMI) **CDC5 55095-2** Prima Diva
(EMI) **CDC7 49811-2** Covent Garden Gala Concert
cond T. BEECHAM
(ACAN) **43 268** Peter Anders sings German Opera Arias
cond V. BELLEZZA
(EMI) **CDH7 61009-2** Chaliapin sings Russian Opera Arias
cond R. BONYNGE
Donizetti: Fille du régiment (Cpte), Lucia di Lammermoor (exc)
(DECC) **417 011-2DH2** Pavarotti's Greatest Hits
(DECC) **417 780-2DM** Joan Sutherland's Greatest Hits
(DECC) **433 064-2DWO** Your Hundred Best Opera Tunes Volume I
(DECC) **433 437-2DA** Pavarotti—King of the High Cs
(DECC) **436 300-2DX** Opera Gala Sampler
(DECC) **436 313-2DA** Sutherland/Pavarotti—Operatic Duets
(DECC) **436 315-2DA** Great Operatic Duets
(DECC) **071 149-1DH (DECC)** The Essential Sutherland
cond P. BOULEZ
Debussy: Pelléas et Mélisande (Cpte)
cond A. BOULT
(DECC) **425 851-2DWO** Your hundred best tunes vol 5
cond B. BRITTEN
Britten: Billy Budd (Cpte), Peter Grimes (Cpte)
(DECC) **436 990-2DWO** The World of Benjamin Britten
(LOND) **425 659-2LM** Britten: Orchestral Works
cond C.F. CILLARIO
Verdi: Traviata (Cpte)
(MEMO) **HR4291/2** Great Voices - Renata Scotto
(MEMO) **HR4376/7** Tito Gobbi—Opera Arias
cond COLIN DAVIS
Berlioz: Troyens (Cpte)
Britten: Peter Grimes (Cpte)
Massenet: Werther (Cpte)
Mozart: Clemenza di Tito (Cpte), Così fan tutte (Cpte), Don Giovanni (Cpte)
Puccini: Bohème (Cpte), Tosca (Cpte)
Tippett: Knot Garden (Cpte), Midsummer Marriage (Cpte)
Verdi: Ballo in maschera (Cpte), Trovatore (Cpte)
(BELA) **450 052-2** Great Opera Choruses
(BELA) **450 059-2** Carreras—Memories
(BELA) **461 001-2** Popular Overtures
(KIWI) **CDSLD-82** Southern Voices—NZ International Opera Singers
(PHIL) **411 448-2PH** Tchaikovsky Orchestral Works
(PHIL) **432 692-2PH** The Essential José Carreras
(PHIL) **434 152-2PM** Jose Carreras - Classics
(PHIL) **434 986-2PM** Duetti Amorosi
(PHIL) **442 600-2PH** The Great Carreras
(PHIL) **442 602-2PM** 3 x 3 Tenors
cond L. COLLINGWOOD
(TEST) **SBT1058** James Johnston - Opera Arias and Songs
cond P. DANIEL
Mozart: Mitridate (Cpte)
cond J. DELACÔTE
(EMI) **CDC7 54524-2** The José Carreras Album
(EMI) **CDM7 64359-2** Gala de España
cond P. DOMINGO
(TELD) **9031-77676-6(TELD)** My World of Opera - Kiri Te Kanawa
cond E. DOWNES
(BELA) **450 005-2** Famous Tenor Arias
(BELA) **450 007-2** Puccini Favourites
(BELA) **450 117-2** Great Opera Chorus II
(CFP) **CD-CFP4569** Puccini: Arias
(CFP) **CD-CFP4575** Verdi Arias
(DECC) **417 686-2DC** Puccini—Operatic Arias
(DECC) **433 440-2DA** Golden Opera
(DECC) **433 442-2DA** Verdi—Famous Arias
(DECC) **433 623-2DSP** Famous Tenor Arias
(DECC) **433 624-2DSP** Great Soprano Arias
(DECC) **433 636-2DSP** Puccini—Famous Arias
(DECC) **433 865-2DWO** The World of Puccini
(DECC) **436 314-2DA** Great Tenor Arias
(DECC) **436 461-2DM** Ten Top Sopranos
(DECC) **436 462-2DM** Ten Top Mezzos
(ROH) **75605 55013-2** The Puccini Experience
cond L. FOSTER
Walton: Troilus and Cressida (Cpte)

cond Y. MENUHIN
(ETCE) **KTC1125** Showpieces for Violin & Orchestra
cond R. NASH
Sullivan: Mikado (Cpte), Zoo (Cpte)
(DECC) **430 095-2DWO** The World of Gilbert & Sullivan, Vol.1
(LOND) **436 813-2LM2** Sullivan—The Grand Duke. Overture Di Ballo. Henry VIII
(LOND) **436 816-2LM2** Sullivan—Utopia Ltd. Macbeth & Marmion Ovs etc
cond D. PARRY
Meyerbeer: Crociato in Egitto (Cpte)
(OPRA) **ORR201** 19th Century Heroines-Yvonne Kenny
cond A. PREVIN
Rimsky-Korsakov: Tale of Tsar Saltan (exc)
(EMI) **CDC7 47355-2** Mozart—Concert Arias
(TELA) **CD80126** Works by Britten and Prokofiev
cond J. PRITCHARD
(EMI) **CDH5 65072-2** Glyndebourne Recorded - 1934-1994
cond M. REED
(IMP) **ORCD11006** Classical Masterpieces
(IMP) **PCDS22** Music of the World—La Douce France
(IMP) **PCDS23** Music of the World—Italy & Spain—The Latin Quarter
(IMP) **PCDS018** Instruments of the Orchestra - The Orchestra
(IMP) **TCD1014** An Invitation to the Classics
(IMP) **TCD1070** Invitation to the Opera
(RPO) **CDRPD9001** Classical Spectacular
(RPO) **CDRPO5010** Classical Spectacular 2
cond N. RESCIGNO
Donizetti: Lucia di Lammermoor (Cpte)
(EMI) **CDM7 63104-2** Alfredo Krauss - Opera Recital
(EMI) **CZS5 68559-2** Italian Opera Choruses
cond P. ROBINSON
(SILV) **SILKD6004** Simple Gifts—Lesley Garrett
cond S. SANDERLING
(TRIN) **TRP021** Haydn—Orchestral Works
cond M. SARGENT
Sullivan: Princess Ida (Cpte), Yeomen of the Guard (Cpte)
(BELA) **461 006-2** Gilbert & Sullivan—Songs and Snatches
(DECC) **430 095-2DWO** The World of Gilbert & Sullivan, Vol.1
cond C. SEAMAN
(TRIN) **TRP036** Delius—Orchestral Works
cond T. SERAFIN
(EMI) **CES5 68541-2** Rossini/Verdi/Bellini/Donizetti—Overtures
cond J. SEREBRIER
(ASV) **CDDCA861** Wolf-Ferrari—Overtures & Intermezzos
cond Y. SIMONOV
(TRIN) **TRP015** Tchaikovsky—Orchestral Works
(TRIN) **TRP030** 19th Century Orchestral Music
cond R. STAPLETON
(IMP) **MCD15** Opera Spectacular
(IMP) **PCDS23** Music of the World—Italy & Spain—The Latin Quarter
(IMP) **TCD1070** Invitation to the Opera
(RPO) **CDRPD9006** Opera Spectacular 1 & 2
(RPO) **CDRPO7009** Opera Spectacular II
(SILV) **SILKD6005** Tito-Tito Beltrán
cond L. STOKOWSKI
(DECC) **433 625-2DSP** Stokowski conducts Famous Russian Works
cond I. STRAVINSKY
Stravinsky: Rake's Progress (Cpte)
(SONY) **SM22K46290(4)** Stravinsky—The Complete Edition (pt 4)
cond Y. TEMIRKANOV
(RCA) **RD60195** Mussorgsky—Orchestral & Vocal Works
(RCA) **09026 61203-2** Berlioz—Symphonie fantastique
cond B. TOVEY
(RPO) **CDRPO7010** Ballet Spectacular
cond VLADIMIR ASHKENAZY
(DECC) **430 370-2DH** R. Strauss—Works for Horn
(RPO) **CDRPO7014** Ashkenazy Live in Moscow
cond J. WALKER
(BELA) **461 006-2** Gilbert & Sullivan—Songs and Snatches
cond B. WORDSWORTH
Bernstein: West Side Story (Cpte)

ROYAL PHILHARMONIC ORCHESTRA CELLOS
cond G. SIMON
(CALA) **CACD0104** The London Cello Sound

ROYAL PHILHARMONIC SOCIETY ORCHESTRA
cond T. BEECHAM
(BEEC) **BEECHAM3** Delius—Vocal & Orchestral Works
cond B. WALTER
(VAI) **VAIA1059** Walter—Early Electrical Recordings (1925-1931)

ROYAL PROMENADE ORCHESTRA
cond ANON
(WORD) **FCD7411** World's Greatest Waltzes

ROYAL SCOTTISH ORCHESTRA
cond J. BROWN
Bernstein: Candide (1988) (exc)
cond A. GIBSON
Elgar: Crown of India (Cpte)
(CFP) **CD-CFP4635** Music of the Four Countries
(CHAN) **CHAN8316** Berlioz: Overtures
(CHAN) **CHAN8379** Scottish Overtures
(CHAN) **CHAN8429** Elgar—Orchestral Works
cond N. JÄRVI
(CHAN) **CHAN6511** Russian Masterpieces
(CHAN) **CHAN6598** Russian Dances
(CHAN) **CHAN7000/1** Shostakovich—Orchestral Works
(CHAN) **CHAN8327/9** Rimsky-Korsakov—Suites
(CHAN) **CHAN8587** Shostakovich: Orchestral Works
(CHAN) **CHAN8729** Prokofiev—Ballet & Opera Suites
(CHAN) **CHAN8758** R. Strauss—Opera Excerpts
(CHAN) **CHAN8834** R. Strauss: Orchestral and Vocal Works

ROZARIO, Patricia (sop)
Britten: Rape of Lucretia (Cpte)
Purcell: Dido (Cpte)

ROZHDESTVENSKY, Gennadi (cond)
see Czech PO
Leningrad PO
Stockholm PO
USSR Ministry of Culture SO

ROZOVA, Natalia (pf)
(MEZH) **MK417030** Fine Night with Alexander Shirinsky

ROZSA, Anna (sop)
Verdi: Traviata (Cpte)
(PREI) **89007** Aureliano Pertile (1885-1952) - I
(PREI) **89043** Antonio Cortis (1891-1952)
(PREI) **89048** Apollo Granforte (1886-1975) - I

ROZSNYAI, Zoltán (cond)
see Philh Hungarica

ROZSOS, István (ten)
Giordano: Andrea Chénier (Cpte), Fedora (Cpte)

RTBF NEW SYMPHONY ORCHESTRA
cond J. SEREBRIER
R. Strauss: Capriccio (exc), Daphne (exc)

RTBF SYMPHONY ORCHESTRA
cond R. ZOLLMAN
(PRES) **PCOM1109** Le Maître de Musique—Original Soundtrack

RTE CHAMBER CHOIR
cond R. SACCANI
Verdi: Aida (Cpte)

RTE CONCERT ORCHESTRA
cond A. PENNY
Sullivan: Thespis (exc)
(MARC) **8 223461** Sullivan—Incidental Music

RTE PHILHARMONIC CHOIR
cond R. BONYNGE
Balfe: Bohemian Girl (Cpte)
cond R. SACCANI
Verdi: Aida (Cpte)

RTL SYMPHONY ORCHESTRA
cond L. HAGER
(LASE) **15 504** Sabre Dance

RUBADI, Erminia (mez)
(EMI) **CDH7 69791-2** Dame Eva Turner sings Opera Arias and Songs

RUBINSTEIN, Artur (pf)
(COND) **690.07.007** Artur Rubinstein - Piano Rolls
(RCA) **RD85666** Works for Piano and Orchestra
(RCA) **09026 61863-2** Saint-Saëns/Falla/Franck—Piano Works

(ARTUR) RUBINSTEIN PHILHARMONIC ORCHESTRA
cond I. STUPEL
(DANA) **DACOCD410** Langaard—Complete Symphonies, Vol.7

RUBSTEIN, Ariel (mez)
Janáček: Jenufa (Cpte)

RUCKER, Helmut (fl)
(LASE) **15 625** Meditation

RUCKER, Mark (bar)
Verdi: Aida (Cpte)

RUDEL, Julius (cond)
see Amadeus Ens
ECO
LSO
NY Met Op Orch
Paris Op Orch
Philh
St Luke's Orch
Utah SO

RUDOLF, Leopold (narr)
Mozart: Entführung (Cpte)

RUDOLF KIERMEYER CHILDREN'S CHOIR
cond K. EICHHORN
Orff: Mond (Cpte)
(RCA) **74321 24790-2** Carl Orff 100 Years Edition

RUFFINI, Alessandra (sop)
Bizet: Pêcheurs de Perles (Cpte)
Donizetti: Favorita (Cpte)
Piccinni: Cecchina (Cpte)
Salieri: Locandiera (Cpte)

RUFFO, Titta (bar)
(EMI) **CHS7 64860-2(2)** La Scala Edition - Vol.1, 1878-1914 (pt 2)
(MEMO) **HR4408/9(1)** Singers in Genoa, Vol.1 (disc 1)
(NIMB) **NI7810** Titta Ruffo—Opera Recital
(NIMB) **NI7864** More Legendary Voices
(NIMB) **NI7867** Legendary Baritones
(PEAR) **EVC3(1)** The Caruso Edition, Vol.3 (pt 1)
(PEAR) **GEMMCDS9176** Gigli - Arias, Duets & Songs, 1926-1937
(PEAR) **GEMMCDS9923(2)** Covent Garden on Record, Vol.1 (pt 2)
(PEAR) **GEMMCD9088** Titta Ruffo (1877-1953)
(PEAR) **GEMMCD9309** Enrico Caruso - Opera and Song Recital
(PEAR) **GEMMCD9367** Gigli—Arias and Duets
(PREI) **89303(1)** Titta Ruffo Edition (pt 1)
(PREI) **89303(2)** Titta Ruffo Edition (pt 2)
(PREI) **89995** Famous Italian Baritones
(RCA) **GD60495(5)** The Complete Caruso Collection (pt 5)
(RCA) **GD87811** Beniamino Gigli—Operatic Arias
(RCA) **09026 61242-2** Caruso Sings Verdi
(RCA) **09026 61580-2(3)** RCA/Met 100 Singers, 100 Years (pt 3)
(TEST) **SBT1008** Viva Rossini

RÜGGEBERG, Claudia (sngr)
Braunfels: Verkündigung (Cpte)

RÜGGEBERG, Erika (spkr)
R. Strauss: Intermezzo (Cpte)

RUGGERI, Miriam (sop)
Lully: Alceste (Cpte)
Rameau: Indes galantes (Cpte)

RUHLMANN, François (cond)
see orch
Vienna St Op Orch

RUHRSEITZ, Kurt (pf)
(ROMO) **81014-2** Elisabeth Rethberg (1894-1976)

RUMBO, Luigi (ten)
Donizetti: Anna Bolena (Cpte)

RUMETZ, Paolo (bass)
Rossini: Pietra del paragone (Cpte)

RUMMEL, Hedwig (sngr)
Kuhlau: Lulu (Cpte)

RUNDGREN, Bengt (bass)
Mozart: Don Giovanni (Cpte)
R. Strauss: Salome (Cpte)
Wagner: Parsifal (Cpte)
(BIS) **BIS-CD373/4** Opera Scenes from Savaonlinna

RUNEY, Henry (bass-bar)
(EMI) **CDC7 54643-2** Rossini—Bicentenary Gala Concert
(EMI) **LDB491007-1 (EMI)** Rossini Bicentennial Birthday Gala

RUNGE, Peter-Christoph (bar)
Cavalli: Ormindo (Cpte)
Prokofiev: Love for 3 Oranges (Cpte)

RÜNGER, Gertrud (mez)
(PEAR) **GEMMCD9383** Julius Patzak—Opera & Operetta Recital
(SCHW) **314512** Vienna State Opera Live, Vol.1
(SCHW) **314592** Vienna State Opera Live, Vol.9
(SCHW) **314642** Vienna State Opera Live, Vol.14
(SCHW) **314652** Vienna State Opera Live, Vol.15
(SCHW) **314662** Vienna State Opera Live, Vol.16

RUNKEL, Reinhild (contr)
Korngold: Wunder der Heliane (Cpte)
R. Strauss: Frau ohne Schatten (Cpte)
Wagner: Walküre (Cpte)
(DG) **437 825-2GH** Wagner—Der Ring des Nibelungen - Highlights
(DG) **445 354-2GX14** Wagner—Der Ring des Nibelungen

RUNNICLES, Donald (cond)
see BRSO
San Francisco Op Orch

RUNSWICK, Daryl (bar)
Machover: Valis (Cpte)

RUOHONEN, Seppo (ten)
(BIS) **BIS-CD373/4** Opera Scenes from Savaonlinna

RUOTOLO, Ines (hp)
(BONG) **GB1078-2** Mafalda Favero
(VAI) **VAIA1071** Mafalda Favero (1903-1981)

RÜPING, Martina (sngr)
Schreker: Gezeichneten (Cpte)

RUPP, Franz (pf)
(BIDD) **LAB040** Kreisler Collection
(EMI) **CDH7 64701-2** Kreisler plays Kreisler
(IMP) **GLRS106** Kreisler plays Kreisler

RUS, Marjan (bass)
Lehár: Lustige Witwe (exc)
Mozart: Nozze di Figaro (Cpte)
R. Strauss: Ariadne auf Naxos (Cpte)
Wagner: Meistersinger (Cpte)
(SCHW) **314532** Vienna State Opera Live, Vol.3
(SCHW) **314552** Vienna State Opera Live, Vol.5
(SCHW) **314582** Vienna State Opera Live, Vol.8
(SCHW) **314692** Vienna State Opera Live, Vol.19

RUSHTON, Lorna (sop)
Vaughan Williams: Pilgrim's Progress (Cpte)

RUSS, Giannina (sop)
(EMI) **CHS7 64860-2(2)** La Scala Edition - Vol.1, 1878-1914 (pt 2)
(MEMO) **HR4408/9(2)** Singers in Genoa, Vol.1 (disc 2)

(PEAR) **GEMMCDS9923(2)** Covent Garden on Record, Vol.1 (pt 2)
(PEAR) **GEMMCDS9924(2)** Covent Garden on Record, Vol.2 (pt 2)
(SYMP) **SYMCD1113** The Harold Wayne Collection, Vol.13

RUSS, Karsten (ten)
Delius: Village Romeo and Juliet (Cpte)
Schillings: Mona Lisa (Cpte)

RUSSEL, Christofer (bass)
Verdi: Ernani (Cpte)

RUSSELL, Anna (sop)
Dittersdorf: Arcifanfano (Cpte)

RUSSELL, James (sngr)
Schuman: Mighty Casey (Cpte)

RUSSELL, Linda (sop)
Rameau: Naïs (Cpte)

RUSSIAN ACADEMIC CHAMBER CHORUS
cond A. CHISTIAKOV
Serov: Judith (Cpte)

RUSSIAN FEDERATION STATE SYMPHONY ORCHESTRA
cond E. SVETLANOV
(CANY) **EC3657-2** Russian Orchestral Works

RUSSIAN NATIONAL ORCHESTRA
cond M. PLETNEV
(DG) **439 892-2GH** Russian Overtures

RUSSIAN PHILHARMONIC ORCHESTRA
Salieri: Axur (Cpte)

RUSSIAN STATE CHOIR
cond A. CHISTIAKOV
Rachmaninov: Aleko (Cpte), Francesca da Rimini (Cpte)

RUSSIAN STATE SYMPHONY ORCHESTRA
cond E. SVETLANOV
(RCA) **09026 61674-2** Borodin—Orchestral Works
(RCA) **09026 62684-2** Rimsky-Korsakov—Symphony No 3, etc

RUTA, Eva (mez)
Donizetti: Lucia di Lammermoor (Cpte)

RUTA, Franco (bass)
Donizetti: Lucrezia Borgia (Cpte)
Verdi: Traviata (Cpte)

RUTGERS, Elisabeth (sop)
R. Strauss: Ariadne auf Naxos (Cpte)
(PREI) **90249** Mozart in tempore belli
(SCHW) **314632** Vienna State Opera Live, Vol.13
(SCHW) **314652** Vienna State Opera Live, Vol.15
(SCHW) **314672** Vienna State Opera Live, Vol.17
(SCHW) **314692** Vienna State Opera Live, Vol.19
(SCHW) **314712** Vienna State Opera Live, Vol.21

RUTISHAUSER, Johanna (sop)
Beethoven: Fidelio (Cpte)

RUUD, Ole Kristian (cond)
see Trondheim SO

RUUTTUNEN, Esa (bar)
Sallinen: Kullervo (Cpte)

RUYLE, Bill (perc)
S. Wallace: Kabbalah (Cpte)

RUZICZKA, Else (mez)
(NIMB) **NI7848** Great Singers at the Berlin State Opera
(PEAR) **GEMMCD9451** Alexander Kipnis
(PREI) **89019** Alexander Kipnis (1891-1978)

RYDL, Kurt (bass)
Beethoven: Fidelio (Cpte)
Einem: Dantons Tod (Cpte)
Gluck: Alceste (1776) (Cpte)
J. Strauss II: Fledermaus (Cpte)
Mozart: Nozze di Figaro (exc), Zauberflöte (Cpte)
Offenbach: Contes d'Hoffmann (Cpte)
Ponchielli: Gioconda (Cpte)
Puccini: Madama Butterfly (Cpte), Manon Lescaut (Cpte), Turandot (exc)
R. Strauss: Arabella (Cpte), Ariadne auf Naxos (Cpte), Rosenkavalier (Cpte)
Verdi: Ballo in maschera (Cpte), Nabucco (exc), Rigoletto (Cpte)
Wagner: Fliegende Holländer (Cpte), Meistersinger (Cpte), Parsifal (Cpte), Rheingold (Cpte), Siegfried (Cpte), Tannhäuser (Cpte)
Weber: Freischütz (Cpte)

RYSANEK, Leonie (sop)
Beethoven: Fidelio (Cpte)
Janáček: Jenufa (Cpte)
R. Strauss: Ariadne auf Naxos (Cpte), Elektra (Cpte), Frau ohne Schatten (Cpte), Salome (Cpte)
Verdi: Ballo in maschera (Cpte), Don Carlo (exc), Macbeth (Cpte), Otello (Cpte)
Wagner: Fliegende Holländer (Cpte), Götterdämmerung (Cpte), Walküre (exc)
(EMI) **CDH5 65201-2** Leonie Rysanek - Operatic Recital
(EMI) **CHS7 69741-2(4)** Record of Singing, Vol.4—German School
(PHIL) **446 057-2PB14** Wagner—The Ring Cycle - Bayreuth Festival 1967
(RCA) **09026 61580-2(7)** RCA/Met 100 Singers, 100 Years (pt 7)
(RCA) **09026 62689-2** The Voices of Living Stereo, Volume 1

RYSANEK, Lotte (sop)
Kálmán: Csárdásfürstin (exc)
R. Strauss: Frau ohne Schatten (Cpte)

SAAL, Max (hp)
(EMI) **CHS7 64673-2** Joseph Schmidt - Complete EMI Recordings Volume 1

SAARINEN, Eeva-Liisa (mez)
Kortekangas: Grand Hotel
Rautavaara: Vincent (Cpte)
Sallinen: Kullervo (Cpte)

SAARMAN, Risto (ten)
Kuhlau: Lulu (Cpte)

SABA, Geoffrey (pf)
(IMP) **PCDS6** Discover the Classics—Myths and Legends
(IMP) **PCD858** Piano Transcriptions

SABAJNO, Carlo (cond)
see La Scala Orch
orch

SABAJNO, Carlo (pf)
(NIMB) **NI7831** Mattia Battistini (1856-1928)
(PEAR) **GEMMCDS9923(1)** Covent Garden on Record, Vol.1 (pt 1)
(SYMP) **SYMCD1069** The Harold Wayne Collection, Vol.2

SABATA, Victor de (cond)
see BPO
La Scala Orch
Santa Cecilia Academy Orch
Vienna St Op Orch

SABATANO, Nina (sop)
Rossini: Barbiere di Siviglia (exc)

SABBATINI, Giuseppe (ten)
Mozart: Don Giovanni (Cpte)
(CAPR) **10 247** The Art of Bel Canto
(CAPR) **10 348** Mozart Gala—Suntory Hall, Tokyo
(CAPR) **10 810** Mozart—Opera Highlights
(DECC) **071 140-1DH (DECC)** Pavarotti—30th Anniversary Gala Concert
(SCHW) **314073** Canzone Sacre

SABEL, Jakob (ten)
(SCHW) **314532** Vienna State Opera Live, Vol.3

SABINO, Antonio (cond)
see La Scala Orch
orch

SABO, Katja (mez)
R. Strauss: Salome (Cpte)

SABROWSKI, Jörg (bar)
Delius: Village Romeo and Juliet (Cpte)

SABROWSKI, Jörg (sngr)
Schillings: Mona Lisa (Cpte)

SACCANI, Rico (cond)
see Ireland National SO

SACCHETTI, Antonio (bass)
Puccini: Madama Butterfly (Cpte), Manon Lescaut (Cpte), Tosca (Cpte)
Verdi: Traviata (Cpte)

SACCHI, Franca (contr)
Ponchielli: Gioconda (Cpte)

SACCOMANI, Lorenzo (bar)
Donizetti: Caterina Cornaro (Cpte)
Leoncavallo: Pagliacci (exc)
Puccini: Madama Butterfly (Cpte)

SACHER, Jürgen (ten)
(SCHW) **312682** Opera Gala with Young Artists - Volume II

SACK, Erna (sop)
(DANT) **LYS2** Erna Sack—A German Nightingale

SADLER'S WELLS OPERA CHORUS
cond A. FARIS
Sullivan: Iolanthe (exc), Mikado (Cpte)
(KIWI) **CDSLD-82** Southern Voices—NZ International Opera Singers
cond R. GOODALL
Wagner: Götterdämmerung (exc)
cond W. REID
Lehár: Lustige Witwe (exc)
cond I. STRAVINSKY
Stravinsky: Rake's Progress (Cpte)
(SONY) **SM22K46290(4)** Stravinsky—The Complete Edition (pt 4)

SADLER'S WELLS OPERA ORCHESTRA
cond B. BALKWILL
Puccini: Madama Butterfly (exc)
cond W. BRAITHWAITE
(PEAR) **GEMMCDS9925(1)** Covent Garden on Record—Vol.3 (pt 1)
cond A. FARIS
Sullivan: Iolanthe (exc), Mikado (Cpte)
(KIWI) **CDSLD-82** Southern Voices—NZ International Opera Singers
cond R. GOODALL
Wagner: Götterdämmerung (exc), Siegfried (Cpte)
cond W. REID
Lehár: Lustige Witwe (exc)

SADLO, Peter (perc)
(TELD) **4509-92143-2** 20th Century Piano Works

SAEDÉN, Erik (bar)
Mozart: Don Giovanni (Cpte), Nozze di Figaro (Cpte)
Verdi: Trovatore (Cpte)

SAFFER, Lisa (sop)
Handel: Agrippina (Cpte), Ottone (Cpte), Radamisto (Cpte)
Purcell: Dido (Cpte)
(HARM) **HMU90 7036** Handel—Arias for Cuzzoni

SAFIULIN, Anatoly (bass)
(CDM) **LDC288 005/6** Bass Arias from Russian Opera

SAGEMÜLLER, Dirk (bar)
Verdi: Rigoletto (Cpte)

SAGITTARIUS VOCAL ENSEMBLE
cond J-C. MALGOIRE
Lully: Alceste (Cpte)
cond M. MINKOWSKI
Lully: Phaëton (Cpte)
Rameau: Hippolyte et Aricie (Cpte)

SAGI-VELA, Luis (sngr)
Barbieri: Barberillo de Lavapiès (Cpte)

SAIDULA, Hermine (mez)
R. Strauss: Rosenkavalier (Cpte)

SAINT PAUL CHAMBER ORCHESTRA
cond B. MCFERRIN
(SONY) **SK64600** Bobby McFerrin-Paper Music

SAINT-AMANT, Yves (bass)
Vivier: Kopernikus (Cpte)

SAINT-ETIENNE LYRIC CHORUS
cond P. FOURNILLIER
Gounod: Sapho (Cpte)

SAINT-ETIENNE NOUVEL ORCHESTRA
cond P. FOURNILLIER
Gounod: Sapho (Cpte)
Massenet: Cléopâtre (Cpte)

SAINT-PALAIS, Mary (sop)
Campra: Idoménée (Cpte)
Montéclair: Jephté (Cpte)

SAKARI, Petri (cond)
see Iceland SO

SAKHAROVA, G (sop)
(PREI) **89066** Zara Dolukhanova

SAKKAS, Spiros (bar)
Xenakis: Orestia (Cpte)

SAKS, Gidon (bass)
Schreker: Ferne Klang (Cpte)
Zemlinsky: Kreidekreis (Cpte)
(SCHW) **314052** Opera Gala

SALA, Giuseppe (ten)
(PREI) **89998** Antonio Paoli (1871-1946)
(SYMP) **SYMCD1126** The Harold Wayne Collection, Vol.14

SALE, Frank (ten)
Wagner: Tristan und Isolde (Cpte)

SALLABA, Richard (ten)
R. Strauss: Ariadne auf Naxos (Cpte)
Wagner: Meistersinger (exc)
(PREI) **90237** R Strauss—Daphne
(SCHW) **314602** Vienna State Opera Live, Vol.10
(SCHW) **314652** Vienna State Opera Live, Vol.15
(SCHW) **314692** Vienna State Opera Live, Vol.19

SALLAY, Linnea (mez)
Mozart: Zauberflöte (Cpte)

SALMINEN, Matti (bass)
Monteverdi: Incoronazione di Poppea (Cpte)
Mozart: Don Giovanni (Cpte), Entführung (Cpte), Zauberflöte (Cpte)
Sallinen: Kullervo (Cpte)
Verdi: Don Carlo (Cpte)
Wagner: Fliegende Holländer (exc), Götterdämmerung (Cpte), Parsifal (Cpte), Rheingold (Cpte), Siegfried (Cpte), Tannhäuser (exc), Tristan und Isolde (Cpte), Walküre (Cpte)
(BIS) **BIS-CD373/4** Opera Scenes from Savaonlinna
(BIS) **BIS-CD520** Matti Salminen - Opera Recital
(DG) **437 825-2GH** Wagner—Der Ring des Nibelungen - Highlights
(DG) **445 354-2GX14** Wagner—Der Ring des Nibelungen
(DG) **072 422-3GH7** Levine conducts Wagner's Ring
(EMI) **LDX9 91275-1(EMI)** Sawallisch conducts Wagner's Ring
(EURO) **GD69003** Wagner—Der Ring des Nibelungen
(PHIL) **434 420-2PM32(1)** Richard Wagner Edition (Pt.1)
(TELD) **4509-97505-2** Mozart—Famous Opera Choruses

SALMINEN, Sarianna (sngr)
Zemlinsky: Kleider machen Leute (Cpte)

SALMON, Philip (ten)
Lehár: Lustige Witwe (Cpte)

SALOMAA, Petteri (bass)
Bergman: Singing Tree (Cpte)
Mozart: Finta Giardiniera (Cpte), Nozze di Figaro (exc), Zauberflöte (Cpte)
Prokofiev: Fiery Angel (Cpte)
Puccini: Madama Butterfly (Cpte)
Purcell: King Arthur, Z628 (Cpte)
Schreker: Gezeichneten (Cpte)

Verdi: Forza del destino (exc), Macbeth (Cpte)

SALONEN, Esa-Pekka (cond)
see London Sinfonietta
Swedish RSO

(I) SALONISTI
(EURO) **GD69298** Music from Opera and Operetta
(EURO) **GD69299** Serenata

SALTARIN, Maurizio (ten)
Verdi: Otello (Cpte)

SALTER, Richard (bar)
Rihm: Eroberung von Mexico (Cpte)
Schoenberg: Moses und Aron (Cpte)
Trojahn: Enrico (Cpte)

SALTER, Robert (vn/dir)
(RCA) **09026 61275-2** Strings! The Definitive Collection
(RCA) **74321 25819-2** Café Classics - Strings

SALTZMANN-STEVENS, Minnie (sop)
(PEAR) **GEMMCDS9924(2)** Covent Garden on Record, Vol.2 (pt 2)

SALVADORI, Antonio (bar)
Bellini: Capuleti (Cpte)
Puccini: Fanciulla del West (Cpte)

SALVATINI, Mafalda (sop)
(PREI) **89102** Ludwig Hofmann (1895-1963)

SALZBURG BALLET SCHOOL
cond H. VON KARAJAN
Verdi: Falstaff (Cpte)

SALZBURG CHAMBER CHOIR
cond L. HAGER
Mozart: Apollo et Hyacinthus (Cpte), Ascanio in Alba (Cpte), Sogno di Scipione (Cpte)
cond H. VON KARAJAN
Verdi: Don Carlo (Cpte)

SALZBURG CHILDREN'S CHOIR
cond G. SOLTI
R. Strauss: Frau ohne Schatten (Cpte)

SALZBURG FESTIVAL CHAMBER CHOIR
cond L. HAGER
Mozart: Ascanio in Alba (Cpte)
cond H. VON KARAJAN
Verdi: Trovatore (Cpte)

SALZBURG HOFMUSIK
cond W. BRUNNER
Biber: Arminio (Cpte)

SALZBURG MOZARTEUM CAMERATA ACADEMICA
cond B. PAUMGARTNER
(DG) **431 875-2GDO** Rita Streich sings Mozart Arias

SALZBURG MOZARTEUM CHORUS
cond L. HAGER
Mozart: Lucio Silla (Cpte)
cond K. PRESTEL
Mozart: Don Giovanni (exc)

SALZBURG MOZARTEUM ORCHESTRA
cond H. GRAF
(CAPR) **10 253** Mozart: Marches
(CAPR) **10 809** Mozart—Overtures, Dances & Marches
cond L. HAGER
Mozart: Apollo et Hyacinthus (Cpte), Ascanio in Alba (Cpte), Finta Giardiniera (Cpte), Finta semplice (Cpte), Lucio Silla (Cpte), Mitridate (Cpte), Sogno di Scipione (Cpte), Zaïde (Cpte)
cond K. PRESTEL
Mozart: Don Giovanni (exc)
cond R. WEIKERT
(ORFE) **C394501B** Great Mozart Singers Series, Vol. 5
cond B. WEIL
(DENO) **CO-1741** Mozart: Operatic Arias

SALZBURG RADIO CHORUS
cond L. HAGER
Mozart: Lucio Silla (Cpte)

SALZEDO, Carlos (hp)
(CLAR) **CDGSE78-50-47** The Harrison Sisters—An English Musical Heritage

SALZER, Ernst (bar)
Ligeti: Grand Macabre (Cpte)

SALZMANN, Jean-Marc (bar)
Henze: Boulevard Solitude (Cpte)
M-A. Charpentier: Médée (Cpte)
Rossi: Orfeo (Cpte)

SAMKO, Milan (harm)
(CAPR) **10 180** Gisela May sings Weill

SAMMARCO, Mario (bar)
(EMI) **CHS7 64860-2(1)** La Scala Edition - Vol.1, 1878-1914 (pt 1)
(EMI) **CHS7 64860-2(2)** La Scala Edition - Vol.1, 1878-1914 (pt 2)
(PEAR) **GEMMCDS9073(2)** Giovanni Zenatello, Vol.1 (pt 2)
(PEAR) **GEMMCDS9924(1)** Covent Garden on Record, Vol.2 (pt 1)
(PEAR) **GEMMCDS9924(2)** Covent Garden on Record, Vol.2 (pt 2)
(PREI) **89995** Famous Italian Baritones
(SYMP) **SYMCD1111** The Harold Wayne Collection, Vol.11
(SYMP) **SYMCD1113** The Harold Wayne Collection, Vol.13
(SYMP) **SYMCD1158** The Harold Wayne Collection, Vol.18
(TEST) **SBT1008** Viva Rossini

SAMMARITANO, Silvestro (bass)
Puccini: Manon Lescaut (Cpte), Tosca (Cpte)
Rossini: Barbiere di Siviglia (exc)
Spontini: Vestale (Cpte)
Verdi: Forza del destino (exc), Rigoletto (Cpte), Traviata (Cpte)

SAMOSUD, Samuel (cond)
see Bolshoi Th Orch

SAMPIERI, Michele (bar)
(PEAR) **GEMMCDS9074(2)** Giovanni Zenatello, Vol.2 (pt 2)
(PEAR) **GEMMCDS9926(1)** Covent Garden on Record—Vol.4 (pt 1)

SAMUEL, Harold (pf)
(KOCH) **37137-2** The Art of Harold Samuel

SAMUELSON, Mikael (bar)
Haeffner: Electra (Cpte)
Mozart: Nozze di Figaro (Cpte), Zauberflöte (Cpte)

SAN DIEGO MASTER CHORALE
cond Y. TALMI
Berlioz: Troyens (exc)

SAN DIEGO SYMPHONY ORCHESTRA
cond Y. TALMI
Berlioz: Troyens (exc)
(NAXO) **8 550999** Berlioz—Overtures

SAN FRANCISCO OPERA BALLET
cond M. ARENA
Meyerbeer: Africaine (Cpte)

SAN FRANCISCO OPERA CHORUS
cond M. ARENA
Boito: Mefistofele (Cpte)
Meyerbeer: Africaine (Cpte)
cond R. BEHR
Vivaldi: Orlando Furioso (Cpte)
cond C. MACKERRAS
Verdi: Ballo in maschera (Cpte)
cond G. PATANÈ
Donizetti: Elisir d'amore (Cpte)
cond J. RUDEL
Saint-Saëns: Samson et Dalila (Cpte)
cond T. SEVERINI
Puccini: Bohème (Cpte)

SAN FRANCISCO OPERA ORCHESTRA
Boito: Mefistofele (Cpte)
Meyerbeer: Africaine (Cpte)
Puccini: Bohème (Cpte)
Saint-Saëns: Samson et Dalila (Cpte)
Vivaldi: Orlando Furioso (Cpte)
cond E. MACARTHUR
(RCA) **GD87915** Wagner: Arias and Duets
cond C. MACKERRAS
Verdi: Ballo in maschera (Cpte)
cond E. MCARTHUR
(NIMB) **NI7847** Kirsten Flagstad (1895-1962)
cond G. PATANÈ
Donizetti: Elisir d'amore (Cpte)
(BUTT) **BMCD015** Pavarotti Collection - Duets and Scenes
cond D. RUNNICLES
R. Strauss: Capriccio (Cpte)

SAN FRANCISCO SYMPHONY ORCHESTRA
cond E. MCARTHUR
(SIMA) **PSC1821(2)** Kirsten Flagstad, Vol.1 (pt 2)
cond P. MONTEUX
(RCA) **09026 61893-2** Pierre Monteux Edition
cond S. OZAWA
(DG) **413 851-2GW2** Modern American Favourites
(DG) **439 425-2GCL** Music from America - Gershwin and Bernstein

SÁNCHEZ, Emilio (sngr)
Vives: Bohemios (Cpte)

SANCHEZ, Guadalupe (sop)
(IMP) **MCD45** Spanish Royal Gala

SANCHIONI, Nunu (sop)
(PREI) **89048** Apollo Granforte (1886-1975) - I

SAND, Annemarie (mez)
Smyth: Wreckers (Cpte)

SANDBERG, Herbert (cond)
see Stockholm Royal Op Orch

SANDERLING, Stefan (cond)
see RPO

SANDERS, Samuel (pf)
(EMI) **CDC7 47467-2** My Favourite Kreisler
(EMI) **CZS4 83177-2(2)** Itzhak Perlman Edition (pt 2)

SANDERSON, Michael (ten)
Lampe: Pyramus and Thisbe (Cpte)

SANDFORD, Kenneth (bar)
Sullivan: Gondoliers (Cpte), Iolanthe (Cpte), Mikado (exc), Patience (Cpte), Princess Ida (Cpte), Ruddigore (Cpte), Trial by Jury (Cpte), Yeomen of the Guard (Cpte), Zoo (Cpte)
(BELA) **461 006-2** Gilbert & Sullivan—Songs and Snatches
(DECC) **433 868-2DWO** The World of Gilbert & Sullivan - Volume 2
(LOND) **436 813-2LM2** Sullivan—The Grand Duke. Overture Di Ballo. Henry VIII
(LOND) **436 816-2LM2** Sullivan—Utopia Ltd. Macbeth & Marmion Ovs etc

SANDISON, Gordon (bar)
Bizet: Carmen (Cpte)
J. Strauss II: Fledermaus (Cpte)
Janáček: Jenufa (Cpte)
Sullivan: HMS Pinafore (exc), Ruddigore (Cpte)
Verdi: Traviata (Cpte)

SANDLUND, Staffan (bass)
Lidholm: Dream Play (Cpte)

SANDNER, Arwed (bass)
Hindemith: Neues vom Tage (Cpte)

SÁNDOR, Arpad (pf)
(BIDD) **LAB049/50** Kreisler - The Berlin HMV Recordings (1926-7)
(RCA) **09026 61778-2(02)** The Heifetz Collection, Vol.2 - 1925-34
(SUPR) **11 1491-2** Jarmila Novotna sings Czech Songs and Arias

SÁNDOR, János (cond)
see Budapest PO

SANDOR, John (ten)
Verdi: Masnadieri (Cpte)
(LASE) **15 611** Suppé—Overtures

SÁNDOR, Judit (mez)
(LASE) **14 012** Mussorgsky—Orchestral Works
(LASE) **15 514** Most Famous Overtures
(LASE) **15 616** French Ballet Music
(LASE) **15 621** Famous Marches and Dances
(LASE) **15 622** Famous Classical Overtures

SANDOZ, May (sop)
Mozart: Zauberflöte (Cpte)

ŞANDRU, Sanda (sop)
Bretan: Arald (Cpte), Golem (Cpte)

SANDTNEROVÁ, Marta (mez)
Hába: Mother (Cpte)

SANDVE, Kjell Magnus (ten)
Bibalo: Gespenster (Cpte)
Braein: Anne Pedersdotter (Cpte)

SANFILIPPO, Domenico (cond)
see Boemia del Nord Phil CO

SANFORD, Sally (sop)
(ALBA) **TROY127-2** Purcell—From Rosy Bow'rs

SANGUINETI, Edoardo (narr)
Berio: Laborintus II

SANSO, Vincenzo (ten)
Probst: Maximilien Kolbe (Cpte)

SANSOM, Mary (sop)
Sullivan: Gondoliers (Cpte), Iolanthe (Cpte), Patience (Cpte), Ruddigore (Cpte)
(DECC) **433 868-2DWO** The World of Gilbert & Sullivan - Volume 2

SANSONNETTI, Marcelle (sngr)
Ganne: Hans (Cpte)

SÁNTA, Jolán (mez)
Mascagni: Lodoletta (Cpte)

SANTA CECILIA ACADEMY CHORUS, ROME
cond B. BARTOLETTI
Verdi: Ballo in maschera (Cpte)
cond L. BERNSTEIN
Puccini: Bohème (Cpte)
cond F. CAPUANA
Cilea: Adriana Lecouvreur (Cpte)
cond A. EREDE
Puccini: Bohème (Cpte), Madama Butterfly (Cpte), Tosca (Cpte), Turandot (Cpte)
Verdi: Aida (Cpte), Otello (Cpte), Rigoletto (Cpte)
(BELA) **450 007-2** Puccini Favourites
(DECC) **440 407-2DM** Mario del Monaco
(DECC) **443 379-2DM** Ten Top Tenors 2
cond C. FRANCI
(BELA) **450 117-2** Great Opera Chorus II
(BELA) **450 133-2** Verdi Favourites
(DECC) **425 849-2DWO** Your hundred best tunes vol 3
(DECC) **433 069-2DWO** Your Hundred Best Opera Tunes VI
(DECC) **433 443-2DA** Great Opera Choruses
(DECC) **443 585-2DF2** Your Hundred Best Tunes - Top 20
cond L. GARDELLI
Ponchielli: Gioconda (Cpte)
(DECC) **433 066-2DWO** Your Hundred Best Opera Tunes III
(DECC) **433 443-2DA** Great Opera Choruses
cond G. GAVAZZENI
Giordano: Andrea Chénier (Cpte)
cond C.M. GIULINI
Verdi: Trovatore (Cpte)
cond L. MAAZEL
Puccini: Tosca (Cpte)
(DECC) **440 409-2DM** Dietrich Fischer-Dieskau
cond F. MOLINARI-PRADELLI
Puccini: Manon Lescaut (Cpte), Tosca (Cpte)
Verdi: Traviata (Cpte)
(BELA) **450 007-2** Puccini Favourites
(DECC) **440 406-2DM** Giulietta Simionato
cond A. PAOLETTI
(DECC) **440 406-2DM** Giulietta Simionato
cond J. PRITCHARD
Donizetti: Lucia di Lammermoor (Cpte)

(DECC) **417 780-2DM** Joan Sutherland's Greatest Hits
cond N. SANZOGNO
Verdi: Rigoletto (Cpte)
cond T. SERAFIN
Boito: Mefistofele (Cpte)
Mascagni: Cavalleria Rusticana (Cpte)
Puccini: Bohème (exc), Madama Butterfly (Cpte)
(BELA) **450 007-2** Puccini Favourites
(BELA) **450 117-2** Great Opera Chorus II
(DECC) **433 865-2DWO** The World of Puccini
(DECC) **440 403-2DM** Giuseppe di Stefano
(DECC) **444 555-2DF2** Essential Puccini
cond G. SINOPOLI
Verdi: Rigoletto (Cpte)
cond G. SOLTI
(DECC) **440 406-2DM** Giulietta Simionato
(DECC) **440 417-2DM** Carlo Bergonzi

SANTA CECILIA ACADEMY ORCHESTRA, ROME
(DECC) **433 865-2DWO** The World of Puccini
(DECC) **440 409-2DM** Dietrich Fischer-Dieskau
(TELD) **4509-96035-2** Tracks Across Europe
cond B. BARTOLETTI
Verdi: Ballo in maschera (Cpte)
cond V. BELLEZZA
(PREI) **89009** Gino Bechi (b. 1913)
cond L. BERNSTEIN
Puccini: Bohème (Cpte)
(DG) **439 151-2GMA** Mad about Puccini
cond R. BONYNGE
(DECC) **436 301-2DA** Renata Tebaldi & Franco Corelli—Arias & Duets
cond G. CANTELLI
(TEST) **SBT1017** Orchestral Works - Cantelli
cond F. CAPUANA
Cilea: Adriana Lecouvreur (Cpte)
(DECC) **433 067-2DWO** Your Hundred Best Opera Tunes IV
(DECC) **440 407-2DM** Mario del Monaco
(DECC) **440 408-2DM** Renata Tebaldi
cond A. EREDE
Puccini: Bohème (Cpte), Madama Butterfly (Cpte), Tosca (Cpte), Turandot (Cpte)
Verdi: Aida (Cpte), Otello (Cpte), Rigoletto (Cpte)
(BELA) **450 007-2** Puccini Favourites
(BELA) **450 133-2** Verdi Favourites
(DECC) **430 481-2DX2** Renata Tebaldi sings Opera Arias
(DECC) **440 407-2DM** Mario del Monaco
(DECC) **440 408-2DM** Renata Tebaldi
(DECC) **440 418-2DM** Cesare Siepi
(DECC) **443 379-2DM** Ten Top Tenors 2
(PREI) **90227** Hilde Gueden - As The World Knew Her
cond C. FRANCI
(BELA) **450 117-2** Great Opera Chorus II
(BELA) **450 133-2** Verdi Favourites
(DECC) **425 849-2DWO** Your hundred best tunes vol 3
(DECC) **433 069-2DWO** Your Hundred Best Opera Tunes VI
(DECC) **433 443-2DA** Great Opera Choruses
(DECC) **443 585-2DF2** Your Hundred Best Tunes - Top 20
cond L. GARDELLI
Ponchielli: Gioconda (Cpte)
(BELA) **450 007-2** Puccini Favourites
(DECC) **433 066-2DWO** Your Hundred Best Opera Tunes III
(DECC) **433 443-2DA** Great Opera Choruses
(DECC) **440 417-2DM** Carlo Bergonzi
(DECC) **443 378-2DM** Ten Top Mezzos 2
cond G. GAVAZZENI
Giordano: Andrea Chénier (Cpte)
(BELA) **450 005-2** Famous Tenor Arias
(BELA) **450 133-2** Verdi Favourites
(DECC) **417 686-2DC** Puccini—Operatic Arias
(DECC) **430 481-2DX2** Renata Tebaldi sings Opera Arias
(DECC) **433 066-2DWO** Your Hundred Best Opera Tunes III
(DECC) **433 067-2DWO** Your Hundred Best Opera Tunes IV
(DECC) **433 068-2DWO** Your Hundred Best Opera Tunes V
(DECC) **433 069-2DWO** Your Hundred Best Opera Tunes VI
(DECC) **433 221-2DWO** The World of Verdi
(DECC) **433 442-2DA** Verdi—Famous Arias
(DECC) **433 623-2DSP** Famous Tenor Arias
(DECC) **433 636-2DSP** Puccini—Famous Arias
(DECC) **436 300-2DX** Opera Gala Sampler
(DECC) **436 314-2DA** Great Tenor Arias
(DECC) **436 463-2DM** Ten Top Tenors
(DECC) **440 407-2DM** Mario del Monaco
(DECC) **440 408-2DM** Renata Tebaldi
(DECC) **440 417-2DM** Carlo Bergonzi
(DECC) **440 418-2DM** Cesare Siepi
(DECC) **443 379-2DM** Ten Top Tenors 2
(RCA) **GD60866** The Placido Domingo Album
(RCA) **GD86534** Verdi Arias and Duets
(RCA) **09026 62595-2** Opera Duets
cond F. GHIONE
(DECC) **440 406-2DM** Giulietta Simionato
cond C.M. GIULINI
Verdi: Trovatore (Cpte)
cond L. MAAZEL
Puccini: Tosca (Cpte)
(DECC) **433 065-2DWO** Your Hundred Best Opera Tunes Volume II
(DECC) **433 440-2DA** Golden Opera
(DECC) **436 300-2DX** Opera Gala Sampler
(DECC) **436 463-2DM** Ten Top Tenors
(DECC) **440 409-2DM** Dietrich Fischer-Dieskau
cond F. MOLINARI-PRADELLI
Puccini: Manon Lescaut (Cpte), Tosca (Cpte)
Verdi: Traviata (Cpte)
(BELA) **450 006-2** Famous Opera Duets
(BELA) **450 007-2** Puccini Favourites
(DECC) **430 481-2DX2** Renata Tebaldi sings Opera Arias
(DECC) **433 068-2DWO** Your Hundred Best Opera Tunes V
(DECC) **433 624-2DSP** Great Soprano Arias
(DECC) **436 315-2DA** Great Operatic Duets
(DECC) **436 463-2DM** Ten Top Tenors
(DECC) **436 464-2DM** Ten Top Baritones & Basses
(DECC) **440 406-2DM** Giulietta Simionato
(DECC) **440 407-2DM** Mario del Monaco
(DECC) **440 408-2DM** Renata Tebaldi
cond A. PAOLETTI
(DECC) **440 406-2DM** Giulietta Simionato
cond F. PATANÈ
(BELA) **450 005-2** Famous Tenor Arias
(BELA) **450 007-2** Puccini Favourites
(DECC) **417 686-2DC** Puccini—Operatic Arias
(DECC) **433 623-2DSP** Famous Tenor Arias
(DECC) **433 636-2DSP** Puccini—Famous Arias
(DECC) **433 865-2DWO** The World of Puccini
(DECC) **440 403-2DM** Giuseppe di Stefano
(DECC) **443 379-2DM** Ten Top Tenors 2
cond G. PATANÈ
(DECC) **425 853-2DWO** Your hundred best tunes vol 7
(DECC) **433 065-2DWO** Your Hundred Best Opera Tunes Volume II
(DECC) **443 765-2DF2** The Essential Dvořák
(DECC) **443 931-2DM** Pilar Lorengar sings Opera Arias
cond F. PREVITALI
(BELA) **450 006-2** Famous Opera Duets
(DECC) **440 403-2DM** Giuseppe di Stefano
(DECC) **440 406-2DM** Giulietta Simionato
cond J. PRITCHARD
Donizetti: Lucia di Lammermoor (Cpte)
(DECC) **417 780-2DM** Joan Sutherland's Greatest Hits
(DECC) **440 417-2DM** Carlo Bergonzi
cond V. DE SABATA
(EMI) **CHS5 65506-2** Victor de Sabata conducts
cond N. SANZOGNO
Verdi: Rigoletto (Cpte)
(BELA) **450 133-2** Verdi Favourites
cond T. SERAFIN
Boito: Mefistofele (Cpte)
Mascagni: Cavalleria Rusticana (Cpte)
Puccini: Bohème (exc), Madama Butterfly (exc)
(BELA) **450 006-2** Famous Opera Duets
(BELA) **450 007-2** Puccini Favourites
(BELA) **450 117-2** Great Opera Chorus II
(DECC) **417 686-2DC** Puccini—Operatic Arias
(DECC) **425 847-2DWO** Your hunded best tunes vol. 1
(DECC) **430 481-2DX2** Renata Tebaldi sings Opera Arias
(DECC) **433 064-2DWO** Your Hundred Best Opera Tunes Volume I
(DECC) **433 065-2DWO** Your Hundred Best Opera Tunes Volume II
(DECC) **433 636-2DSP** Puccini—Famous Arias
(DECC) **433 865-2DWO** The World of Puccini
(DECC) **436 300-2DX** Opera Gala Sampler
(DECC) **440 403-2DM** Giuseppe di Stefano
(DECC) **440 408-2DM** Renata Tebaldi
(DECC) **440 418-2DM** Cesare Siepi
(DECC) **444 555-2DF2** Essential Puccini
cond G. SINOPOLI
Verdi: Rigoletto (Cpte)
cond G. SOLTI
(DECC) **440 406-2DM** Giulietta Simionato
cond A. VOTTO
(PREI) **89009** Gino Bechi (b. 1913)

SANTA CECILIA ORCHESTRA DA CAMERA
cond A. VLAD
(EURM) **350262** Pergolesi—Sinfonie

SANTA FÉ OPERA CHORUS
cond R. LEPPARD
V. Thomson: Mother of us all (Cpte)

SANTA FÉ OPERA ORCHESTRA
cond R. LEPPARD
V. Thomson: Mother of us all (Cpte)

SANTAFE, Ildebrando (bass)
Puccini: Bohème (Cpte)

SANTE, Sophia van (mez)
Orff: Prometheus (Cpte)
R. Strauss: Rosenkavalier (Cpte)
(ACAN) **44 2085-2** Carl Orff Collection

SANTI, Nello (cond)
see *Berlin Deutsche Op Chor*
Berlin Deutsche Op Orch
LSO
New Philh
NY Met Op Orch
Paris Cons
Paris ORTF Lyric Orch
ROHO
Verona Arena Orch
Vienna Op Orch
Vienna Volksoper Orch

SANTINI, Angelo (ten)
(IRCC) **IRCC-CD808** Souvenirs of 19th Century Italian Opera

SANTINI, Gabriele (cond)
see *La Scala Chor*
La Scala Orch
Rome Op Orch
Turin RAI Orch

SANTLEY, Sir Charles (bar)
(SYMP) **SYMCD1093** The Harold Wayne Collection, Vol.7

SANZIO, Delia (sop)
Mascagni: Cavalleria rusticana (Cpte)

SANZOGNO, Gian Paolo (cond)
see *Madrid SO*

SANZOGNO, Nino (cond)
see *La Scala Orch*
Madrid Zarzuela Orch
Milan RAI SO
Naples San Carlo Op Orch
Naples Scarlatti Orch
Palermo Teatro Massimo Orch
Santa Cecilia Academy Orch
Turin RAI Orch

SAPAROVÁ, Jikta (mez)
Bellini: Sonnambula (Cpte)
Patzelt: Castor et Pollux (Cpte)
Verdi: Rigoletto (Cpte)

SAPELL, Hermann (bar)
Wagner: Meistersinger (Cpte)
Weber: Freischütz (Cpte)

SARABIA, Guillermo (bar)
Bizet: Pêcheurs de Perles (Cpte)
Zemlinsky: Florentinische Tragödie

SARACENI, Adelaide (sop)
Leoncavallo: Pagliacci (Cpte)
(MSCM) **MM30231** Don Pasquale & Tito Schipa Recital
(PREI) **89048** Apollo Granforte (1886-1975) - I

SARAGOSSE, Jean-Claude (bass)
Montéclair: Jephté (Cpte)

SARASTE, Jukka-Pekka (cond)
see *Finnish RSO*

SARDI, Ivan (bass)
Henze: Junge Lord (Cpte)
Mozart: Don Giovanni (Cpte), Nozze di Figaro (Cpte)
Verdi: Traviata (Cpte)
Wagner: Meistersinger (Cpte)
(DG) **437 677-2GDO2** Irmgard Seefried - Opera Recital

SARDINERO, Vicente (bar)
Donizetti: Lucia di Lammermoor (Cpte)
Mascagni: Amico Fritz (Cpte)
Puccini: Bohème (Cpte), Edgar (Cpte), Manon Lescaut (Cpte), Turandot (exc)
Usandizaga: Golondrinas (Cpte)
Verdi: Simon Boccanegra (Cpte)

SARFATY, Regina (contr)
Beethoven: Fidelio (exc)
Bellini: Pirata (Cpte)
Berlioz: Troyens (Cpte)
R. Strauss: Arabella (Cpte)
Stravinsky: Rake's Progress (Cpte)
(SONY) **SM22K46290(4)** Stravinsky—The Complete Edition (pt 4)

SARGENT, Sir Malcolm (cond)
see *BBC SO*
D'Oyly Carte Op Chor
Liverpool PO
LPO
LSO
New SO
orch
PAO
RPO
SO
VPO

SÁRKÁNY, Kázmér (bass)
Giordano: Andrea Chénier (Cpte)
Rossini: Barbiere di Siviglia (Cpte)

SARPLE, Adrian (sngr)
Bernstein: West Side Story (Cpte)

SARRAGOSSE, Jean-Claude (bass)
Campra: Idoménée (Cpte)
Rameau: Castor et Pollux (exc)

SARRAZIN, Lionel (bass)
Bizet: Carmen (Cpte)
Gounod: Sapho (Cpte)
(DECC) **440 333-2DH** Ravel—Vocal Works

SARRI, Gino (ten)
Donizetti: Lucia di Lammermoor (Cpte)
(EMI) **CMS7 63244-2** The Art of Maria Callas

SARRIS, Heather (mez)
Rorem: Miss Julie (Cpte)

SARROCA, Suzanne (sop)
Offenbach: Contes d'Hoffmann (exc)

SARTI, Gastone (bar)
Cesti: Orontea (Cpte)
Donizetti: Imelda (Cpte), Pazzi per progetto (Cpte)

Salieri: Locandiera (Cpte)
Verdi: Macbeth (Cpte)

SARTI, Laura (mez)
Monteverdi: Orfeo (Cpte)
Rossini: Barbiere di Siviglia (Cpte)

SASAKI, Noriko (sop)
R. Strauss: Elektra (Cpte)

SASS, Sylvia (sop)
Mozart: Don Giovanni (Cpte)
Respighi: Belfagor (Cpte)
Verdi: Stiffelio (Cpte)
(CAPR) **10 810** Mozart—Opera Highlights
(CAST) **CVI2057** Il Trittico live from La Scala, 1983
(CAST) **CVI2070** Great Puccini Love Scenes from Covent Garden, La Scala and Verona

SASSANO, Salvatore (cond)
see Naples San Carlo Op Orch

SASSARI SYMPHONY ORCHESTRA
cond G. CATALUCCI
Sacchini: Contadina in Corte (Cpte)
cond C. RIZZI
Piccinni: Pescatrice (Cpte)

SASSON, Deborah (sop)
Wagner: Parsifal (Cpte)

SATANOWSKI, Robert (cond)
see Bydgoszcz PSO
Warsaw Wiekl Th Orch
Wielki Th Orch

SATRE, Ana Raquel (mez)
Donizetti: Lucia di Lammermoor (Cpte)
Mascagni: Cavalleria Rusticana (Cpte)
Verdi: Otello (Cpte)
(DECC) **430 481-2DX2** Renata Tebaldi sings Opera Arias
(DECC) **443 377-2DM** Ten Top Sopranos 2

SATTLER, Joachim (ten)
Wagner: Tannhäuser (Cpte), Tristan und Isolde (exc)
(SCHW) **314532** Vienna State Opera Live, Vol.3
(SCHW) **314722** Vienna State Opera Live, Vol.22

SAUER, Franz (bass)
Wagner: Meistersinger (Cpte)

SAUERBAUM, Heinz (ten)
Weill: Mahagonny (Cpte)

SAUGEY, Pierre (bar)
Messager: Basoche (Cpte), Coups de Roulis (Cpte)
Offenbach: Chanson de Fortunio (Cpte)
(MUSD) **20239-2** Delibes—Opéras-Comiques

SAUNDERS, Arlene (sop)
Alman: King Ahaz (exc)

SAUNDERS, Dominic (pf)
(NEWP) **NPD85551** Eugene Fodor—Virtuoso Violin

SAUNDERS, Iris (sop)
Britten: Death in Venice (Cpte)

SAUNDERS, Jenny (sop)
Vaughan Williams: Hugh the Drover (Cpte)

SAURA, Francisco (sngr)
Barbieri: Barberillo de Lavapiès (Cpte)

SAUROVA, Eva (sop)
Offenbach: Périchole (Cpte)
Wagner: Parsifal (Cpte)

SAUSY, Pascal (bar)
Dusapin: Romeo and Juliet (Cpte)

SAUTEREAU, Nadine (sop)
Bizet: Carmen (exc)
Martinů: Comedy on the Bridge (Cpte)
Messager: Basoche (Cpte)
Ravel: Enfant et les sortilèges (Cpte)
(CFP) **CD-CFP4602** Favourite Opera
(DECC) **440 404-2DM** Joan Sutherland
(EMI) **CDC5 55016-2** Maria Callas - La Divina 2
(EMI) **CDM7 63182-2** The Incomparable Callas
(EMI) **CZS7 67872-2** Lehár—Operettas (highlights in French)

SAVAGE, Richard (bar)
Lehár: Lustige Witwe (Cpte)

SAVALL, Jordi (cond)
see Capella Reial Instr Ens
Concert des Nations

SAVARESE, Ugo (bar)
Verdi: Traviata (Cpte)

SAVASTANO, Antonio (ten)
Verdi: Don Carlos (Cpte), Macbeth (Cpte), Simon Boccanegra (Cpte)
(CBS) **CD37228** Pavarotti sings Verdi

SAVIGNOL, Jean (ten)
Shostakovich: Lady Macbeth of Mtsensk (Cpte)

SAVIGNOL, Pierre (bass)
Bizet: Ivan IV (exc)

SAVILLE, Frances (sop)
(SYMP) **SYMCD1093** The Harold Wayne Collection, Vol.7

SAVIO, Giuseppe (ten)
Puccini: Gianni Schicchi (Cpte)

SAVOIARDO, Giovanni (bar)
Puccini: Fanciulla del West (Cpte)

SAVONLINNA OPERA FESTIVAL CHORUS
cond K. HAATANEN
(BIS) **BIS-CD373/4** Opera Scenes from Savonlinna
cond I. MANSNERUS
(BIS) **BIS-CD373/4** Opera Scenes from Savonlinna
cond L. SEGERSTAM
Wagner: Fliegende Holländer (Cpte)
(BIS) **BIS-CD373/4** Opera Scenes from Savonlinna
cond U. SÖDERBLOM
(BIS) **BIS-CD373/4** Opera Scenes from Savonlinna

SAVONLINNA OPERA FESTIVAL ORCHESTRA
Wagner: Fliegende Holländer (Cpte)
cond K. HAATANEN
(BIS) **BIS-CD373/4** Opera Scenes from Savonlinna
cond I. MANSNERUS
(BIS) **BIS-CD373/4** Opera Scenes from Savonlinna
cond L. SEGERSTAM
(BIS) **BIS-CD373/4** Opera Scenes from Savonlinna
cond U. SÖDERBLOM
(BIS) **BIS-CD373/4** Opera Scenes from Savonlinna

SAVORY, Catherine (mez)
Martinů: Greek Passion (Cpte)

SAWA, Shigeru (mez)
Verdi: Traviata (Cpte)

SAWALLISCH, Wolfgang (cond)
see Bavarian St Op Orch
Bavarian St Orch
Bayreuth Fest Orch
BRSO
La Scala Orch
Philh
Rome RAI Orch
Vienna SO
VPO

SAWKA, Johann (sngr)
(SCHW) **314632** Vienna State Opera Live, Vol.13

SAXON STATE ORCHESTRA
cond K. BÖHM
(PEAR) **GEMMCDS9121** Wagner—Die Meistersinger, Act 3, etc
(PREI) **89049** Margarete Teschemacher (1903-1959)
(PREI) **89076** Josef Herrmann (1903-1955)
(PREI) **89077** Torsten Ralf (1901-1954)
cond K. ELMENDORFF
Wagner: Walküre (exc)

SAYÃO, Bidù (sop)
Mozart: Don Giovanni (Cpte)
(IRCC) **IRCC-CD808** Souvenirs of 19th Century Italian Opera
(RCA) **09026 61580-2(4)** RCA/Met 100 Singers, 100 Years (pt 4)
(VAI) **VAI69103** Bidù Sayão in Opera and Song

SCACCIATI, Bianca (sop)
(PREI) **89010** Tancredi Pasero (1893-1983) - I
(PREI) **89091** Francesco Merli (1887-1976) - II

SCALAVINO, Umberto (sngr)
Puccini: Fanciulla del West (Cpte)

SCALCHI, Gloria (mez)
Donizetti: Favorita (Cpte)
Rossini: Semiramide (Cpte)
(DECC) **436 261-2DHO3** Puccini—Il Trittico

SCALTRITI, Roberto (bar)
Rossini: Pietra del paragone (Cpte)
Verdi: Rigoletto (Cpte), Traviata (exc), Trovatore (Cpte)

SCAMPINI, Augusto (ten)
(IRCC) **IRCC-CD808** Souvenirs of 19th Century Italian Opera

SCANDIUZZI, Roberto (bass)
Franchetti: Cristoforo Colombo (Cpte)
Puccini: Bohème (Cpte), Turandot (Cpte)
Verdi: Macbeth (Cpte), Simon Boccanegra (Cpte)

SCANDOLA, Giuseppe (bar)
Verdi: Aida (Cpte)
(CAST) **CASH5052** Verdi Operatic Favourites

SCANO, Gaetano (ten)
Rossini: Siège de Corinthe (Cpte)

SCARABELLI, Adelina (sop)
Donizetti: Elisir d'amore (Cpte)
Mozart: Così fan tutte (Cpte)
Rossini: Cenerentola (Cpte)
(MEMO) **HR4300/1** Great Voices—Sesto Bruscantini
(NUOV) **6892** William Matteuzzi sings Opera Arias
(NUOV) **6905** Donizetti—Great Love Duets

SCARAMBERG, Emile (ten)
(MSCM) **MM30377** 18 Tenors d'Expression Française
(PEAR) **GEMMCDS9923(2)** Covent Garden on Record, Vol.1 (pt 2)
(SYMP) **SYMCD1113** The Harold Wayne Collection, Vol.13
(SYMP) **SYMCD1173** The Harold Wayne Collection, Vol.22

SCARPINATI, Nicolas (bass)
(PHIL) **432 416-2PH3** Haydn—L'incontro improvviso/Arias

SCATARZI, Simone (treb)
Puccini: Tosca (Cpte)

SCATTOLA, Carlo (bass)
Puccini: Bohème (Cpte)

(NIMB) **NI7836/7** Conchita Supervia (1895-1936)

SCELLIER, Jacques (bass)
Messager: Basoche (Cpte)
Verdi: Rigoletto (Cpte)
(MUSD) **20239-2** Delibes—Opéras-Comiques

SCHAAF, Jerrold van der (ten)
Nono: Intolleranza 1960 (Cpte)

SCHÄBLEN, Charlotte (mez)
(MYTO) **3MCD93381** Wagner—Die Walküre, etc

SCHADE, Michael (ten)
Sullivan: HMS Pinafore (Cpte)
Verdi: Otello (Cpte)
Wagner: Meistersinger (Cpte)

SCHÄDLE, Lotte (sop)
Jessel: Schwarzwaldmädel (exc)
Mozart: Entführung (Cpte)
Weber: Freischütz (Cpte)

SCHADOCK, Mathias (spkr)
(SONY) **SK53978** Prometheus

SCHAER, Hanna (mez)
Wagner: Parsifal (Cpte)

SCHÄFER, Christine (sop)
Humperdinck: Hänsel und Gretel (Cpte)

SCHÄFER, Markus (ten)
Busoni: Turandot (Cpte)
Haydn: Infedeltà delusa (Cpte)
Mozart: Apollo et Hyacinthus (Cpte), Così fan tutte (Cpte)

SCHAFFER, Emmerich (spkr)
Mozart: Entführung (Cpte)

SCHARINGER, Anton (bass)
Gazzaniga: Don Giovanni (Cpte)
Gurlitt: Wozzeck (Cpte)
J. Strauss II: Fledermaus (exc)
Mozart: Don Giovanni (Cpte), Finta Giardiniera (Cpte), Nozze di Figaro (Cpte), Oca del Cairo (Cpte), Zauberflöte (Cpte)
Purcell: Dido (Cpte)
Weber: Freischütz (Cpte)
(TELD) **4509-97507-2** Mozart—Famous Opera Arias

SCHARLEY, Denise (mez)
Massenet: Hérodiade (exc)
Poulenc: Dialogues des Carmélites (Cpte)
Ravel: Enfant et les sortilèges (Cpte)
Verdi: Rigoletto (Cpte)

SCHÄRTEL, Elisabeth (mez)
Wagner: Fliegende Holländer (Cpte), Walküre (Cpte)
(DG) **429 169-2GR** Wagner—Choruses
(PHIL) **446 057-2PB14** Wagner—The Ring Cycle - Bayreuth Festival 1967

SCHARY, Elke (mez)
Benatzky: Im weissen Rössl (Cpte)
Puccini: Madama Butterfly (Cpte)

SCHASCHING, Rudolf (ten)
J. Strauss II: Zigeunerbaron (Cpte)
Lehár: Lustige Witwe (Cpte)

SCHATZBERGER, Lesley (basset-hn)
(DECC) **448 300-2DH** Cecilia Bartoli—A Portrait

SCHAUWECKER, Frederic (pf)
(PEAR) **GEMMCD9093** The Artistry of Richard Crooks, Volume 1

SCHECH, Marianne (sop)
Mozart: Zauberflöte (Cpte)
Orff: Antigonae (Cpte)
R. Strauss: Elektra (Cpte)
Wagner: Fliegende Holländer (Cpte), Götterdämmerung (Cpte), Tannhäuser (Cpte)
(DG) **437 677-2GDO2** Irmgard Seefried - Opera Recital
(PILZ) **442118-2** Wagner—Operas in Historical Recordings

SCHECK, Gustav (fl)
(ACAN) **43 801** Elisabeth Schwarzkopf—Wartime Recordings

SCHEEBEN, Christoph (bar)
Hindemith: Neues vom Tage (Cpte)

SCHEELE-MÜLLER, Ida von (contr)
(SUPR) **11 2136-2(3)** Emmy Destinn—Complete Edition, Discs 5 to 8

SCHEIBNER, Andreas (bar)
Weber: Freischütz (exc)

SCHEIDEMANTEL, Karl (bar)
(SYMP) **SYMCD1085** The Harold Wayne Collection, Vol.6

SCHEIDER, Wolfgang (bar)
R. Strauss: Rosenkavalier (Cpte)

SCHEIDL, Theodor (bar)
(PREI) **89201** Helge Roswaenge (1897-1972) - I
(PREI) **89203** Leo Slezak (1873-1946)
(PREI) **89217** Alfred Piccaver—The Complete Electric Recordings 1928-1930

SCHÉLE, Märta (sop)
Rameau: Castor et Pollux (Cpte)

SCHELLENBERG, Arno (bar)
(SCHW) **314672** Vienna State Opera Live, Vol.17

SCHELLENBERGER, Dagmar (sop)
Gluck: Orfeo ed Euridice (Cpte)

Mozart: Ascanio in Alba (Cpte), Clemenza di Tito (Cpte), Così fan tutte (exc), Don Giovanni (Cpte), Entführung (Cpte), Idomeneo (Cpte), Lucio Silla (Cpte), Oca del Cairo (Cpte), Schauspieldirektor (Cpte), Sogno di Scipione (Cpte), Zaïde (Cpte), Zauberflöte (Cpte)
R. Strauss: Ariadne auf Naxos (Cpte), Capriccio (Cpte), Daphne (Cpte)
Wagner: Meistersinger (Cpte), Rheingold (Cpte), Rienzi (Cpte), Siegfried (Cpte), Tristan und Isolde (exc)
Weber: Freischütz (Cpte)
(EURO) **GD69003** Wagner—Der Ring des Nibelungen
(EURO) **VD69256** Mozart—Opera Arias
(ORFE) **C335931A** Salzburg Festival highlights (1956-85)
(ORFE) **C394301B** Great Mozart Singers Series, Vol. 3

SCHREIER, Peter (ten/dir)
(PHIL) **422 523-2PME8(2)** The Complete Mozart Edition Vol 23 (pt 2)

SCHRENKEL, Vojtech (ten)
Bellini: Sonnambula (Cpte)
Puccini: Bohème (Cpte)

SCHREYER, Gerda (sop)
R. Strauss: Elektra (Cpte)
Wagner: Walküre (Cpte)

SCHROETER, Joachim (bass)
R. Strauss: Rosenkavalier (Cpte)

SCHRÖTER, Gisela (mez)
Wagner: Parsifal (Cpte)

SCHUBACK, Thomas (cond)
see Drottningholm Baroque Ens

SCHUBERT, Claudia (contr)
Handel: Rodelinda (Cpte)

SCHUBERT, Erika (mez)
Wagner: Walküre (Cpte)
(FOYE) **15-CF2011** Wagner—Der Ring de Nibelungen

SCHUBERT, Hedwig (sop)
J. Strauss II: Fledermaus (Cpte)

SCHUBERT, Peter (cond)
see New Calliope Sngrs

SCHUBERT, Richard (ten)
(SCHW) **314592** Vienna State Opera Live, Vol.9

SCHÜCHTER, Wilhelm (cond)
see Berlin Deutsche Op Orch
Berlin SO
BPO
Hamburg RSO
orch
Philh

SCHUDEL, Regina (sop)
Gurlitt: Wozzeck (Cpte)
Mendelssohn: Hochzeit des Camacho (Cpte)
Schreker: Gezeichneten (Cpte)
Schulhoff: Plameny (Cpte)

SCHÜLER, Johannes (cond)
see Berlin Deutsche Op Orch
Berlin St Op Orch
Berlin Staatskapelle

SCHULHOF, Otto (pf)
(PREI) **89083** Emanuel List (1890-1967)

SCHULLER, Gunther (cond)
see Houston Grand Op Orch

SCHULTE, Eike Wilm (bar)
Wagner: Lohengrin (Cpte), Rheingold (Cpte)
(PHIL) **434 420-2PM32(1)** Richard Wagner Edition (Pt.1)

SCHULTZ, Carl (bar)
R. Strauss: Salome (Cpte)
Schreker: Schatzgräber (Cpte)
Schumann: Genoveva (Cpte)

SCHULTZE, Andrew Walker (bass)
Vivaldi: Olimpiade (Cpte)

SCHULTZE, Norbert (cond)
see Berlin Deutsche Op Orch
Cologne RSO

SCHULZ, Christian (treb)
Mozart: Zauberflöte (Cpte)

SCHULZ, Else (sop)
(SCHW) **314532** Vienna State Opera Live, Vol.3
(SCHW) **314552** Vienna State Opera Live, Vol.5
(SCHW) **314572** Vienna State Opera Live, Vol.7
(SCHW) **314652** Vienna State Opera Live, Vol.15
(SCHW) **314742** Vienna State Opera Live, Vol.24

SCHULZ, Wolfgang (fl)
(DG) **439 150-2GMA** Mad about Mozart

SCHUMACHER, Marten (spkr)
Hindemith: Nusch-Nuschi (Cpte)

SCHUMAN, Patricia (sop)
Rossini: Tancredi (Cpte)

SCHUMANN, Elisabeth (sop)
(BEUL) **2PD4** 78 Classics - Volume Two
(DANA) **DACOCD315/6** Lauritz Melchior Anthology - Vol. 3
(EMI) **CHS7 64487-2** R. Strauss—Der Rosenkavalier & Lieder
(EMI) **CHS7 69741-2(4)** Record of Singing, Vol.4—German School
(EMI) **CMS7 64008-2(1)** Wagner Singing on Record (pt 1)
(MMOI) **CDMOIR406** Mozart—Historical Recordings
(MMOI) **CDMOIR408** Great Sopranos
(MMOI) **CDMOIR419** Vienna Nights - Golden Age of Operetta
(MSCM) **MM30283** Great Wagnerian Singers, Vol.1
(NIMB) **NI7864** More Legendary Voices
(ORFE) **C394101B** Great Mozart Singers Series, Vol. 1
(PEAR) **GEMMCDS9365** R. Strauss: Der Rosenkavalier (abridged), etc
(PEAR) **GEMMCDS9925(2)** Covent Garden on Record—Vol.3 (pt 2)
(PEAR) **GEMMCDS9926(2)** Covent Garden on Record—Vol.4 (pt 2)
(PEAR) **GEMMCD9445** Elisabeth Schumann—Vol.2
(PEAR) **GEMMCD9944** Friedrich Schorr sings Wagner
(PREI) **89031** Elisabeth Schumann (1885-1952)
(ROMO) **81019-2** Elisabeth Schumann
(SCHW) **314622** Vienna State Opera Live, Vol.12
(SCHW) **314632** Vienna State Opera Live, Vol.13
(SCHW) **314672** Vienna State Opera Live, Vol.17
(SCHW) **314742** Vienna State Opera Live, Vol.24

SCHUMANN-HEINK, Ernestine (contr)
(NIMB) **NI7801** Great Singers, Vol.1
(NIMB) **NI7811** Ernestine Schumann-Heink—Opera & Song Recital
(PEAR) **EVC3(1)** The Caruso Edition, Vol.3 (pt 1)
(PEAR) **GEMMCDS9923(1)** Covent Garden on Record, Vol.1 (pt 1)
(PEAR) **GEMMCD9309** Enrico Caruso - Opera and Song Recital
(RCA) **GD60495(4)** The Complete Caruso Collection (pt 4)
(RCA) **09026 61242-2** Caruso Sings Verdi
(RCA) **09026 61580-2(1)** RCA/Met 110 Singers, 100 Years (pt 1)

SCHÜNEMANN, Hildegard (sop)
Wagner: Parsifal (Cpte)

SCHUNK, Robert (ten)
Hindemith: Cardillac (Cpte)
Wagner: Fliegende Holländer (Cpte), Tannhäuser (Cpte), Tristan und Isolde (Cpte), Walküre (Cpte)
(EMI) **LDX9 91275-1(EMI)** Sawallisch conducts Wagner's Ring
(PHIL) **434 420-2PM32(1)** Richard Wagner Edition (Pt.1)

SCHÜRHOFF, Else (mez)
Humperdinck: Hänsel und Gretel (Cpte)
Mozart: Zauberflöte (Cpte)
Wagner: Meistersinger (Cpte)
(PREI) **89083** Emanuel List (1890-1967)
(SCHW) **314532** Vienna State Opera Live, Vol.3
(SCHW) **314672** Vienna State Opera Live, Vol.17
(SCHW) **314692** Vienna State Opera Live, Vol.19
(SCHW) **314712** Vienna State Opera Live, Vol.21
(SCHW) **314742** Vienna State Opera Live, Vol.24

SCHURICHT, Carl (cond)
see Stuttgart RSO

SCHÜTTE, Ulrich (bar)
Weill: Jasager (Cpte)

SCHÜTZE, Walter (cond)
see Berlin St Op Orch

SCHWAIGER, Rosl (sop)
Mozart: Nozze di Figaro (Cpte), Zauberflöte (exc)
R. Strauss: Rosenkavalier (Cpte)
(CAMB) **CD-1032** From the Operas of Erich Wolfgang Korngold

SCHWALBÉ, Michel (vn)
(BELA) **450 137-2** Meditation

SCHWANBECK, Bodo (bass)
Berg: Lulu (Cpte)
R. Strauss: Rosenkavalier (Cpte)

SCHWARTS, Robert (ten)
Corghi: Divara (Cpte)

SCHWARTZ, Magali (mez)
Monteverdi: Orfeo (Cpte)

SCHWARZ, Arturo (voc)
Distel: Stazione (Cpte)

SCHWARZ, Gerard (cond)
see Juilliard Orch
Mostly Mozart Orch
Seattle SO

SCHWARZ, Gotthold (bass)
Biber: Arminio (Cpte)
Busoni: Turandot (Cpte)
Handel: Rodelinda (Cpte)
Schreker: Gezeichneten (Cpte)

SCHWARZ, Hanna (mez)
Berg: Lulu (Cpte)
Humperdinck: Hänsel und Gretel (Cpte), Königskinder (Cpte)
Mozart: Apollo et Hyacinthus (Cpte), Zauberflöte (exc)
Orff: Tanz der Spröden (Cpte)
R. Strauss: Frau ohne Schatten (exc), Salome (Cpte)
Verdi: Rigoletto (Cpte)
Wagner: Götterdämmerung (Cpte), Parsifal (Cpte), Rheingold (Cpte), Siegfried (Cpte), Tristan und Isolde (Cpte), Walküre (Cpte)
(ACAN) **44 2085-2** Carl Orff Collection
(DG) **445 354-2GX14** Wagner—Der Ring des Nibelungen
(EMI) **LDX9 91275-1(EMI)** Sawallisch conducts Wagner's Ring
(EURO) **GD69003** Wagner—Der Ring des Nibelungen
(PHIL) **434 420-2PM32(2)** Richard Wagner Edition (pt 2)

SCHWARZ, Irmgard (sop)
Delius: Village Romeo and Juliet (Cpte)

SCHWARZ, Joseph (bar)
(NIMB) **NI7867** Legendary Baritones
(PREI) **89033** Joseph Schwarz (1880-1926)

SCHWARZ, Vera (sop)
(EMI) **CDC7 54838-2** Franz Lehár
(EMI) **CDH7 69787-2** Richard Tauber sings Operetta Arias
(EMI) **CDM7 69476-2** Richard Tauber - A Portrait
(PEAR) **GEMMCD9310** Franz Lehár conducts Richard Tauber
(PEAR) **GEMMCD9327** The Vocal Prime of Richard Tauber

SCHWARZENBERG, Elisabeth (sop)
Wagner: Parsifal (Cpte)

SCHWARZER, Regina (mez)
Biber: Arminio (Cpte)

SCHWARZKOPF, Dame **Elisabeth (sop)**
Beethoven: Fidelio (Cpte)
Cornelius: Barbier von Bagdad (Cpte)
Humperdinck: Hänsel und Gretel (Cpte)
J. Strauss II: Nacht in Venedig (Cpte)
Lehár: Land des Lächelns (Cpte), Lustige Witwe (Cpte)
Mozart: Così fan tutte (Cpte), Don Giovanni (Cpte), Nozze di Figaro (Cpte), Zauberflöte (Cpte)
Offenbach: Contes d'Hoffmann (Cpte)
Orff: Kluge (Cpte)
Puccini: Turandot (Cpte)
Purcell: Dido (Cpte)
R. Strauss: Ariadne auf Naxos (Cpte), Capriccio (Cpte), Rosenkavalier (Cpte)
Verdi: Falstaff (Cpte)
Wagner: Meistersinger (Cpte)
Walton: Troilus and Cressida (exc)
Weber: Abu Hassan (Cpte)
(ACAN) **43 801** Elisabeth Schwarzkopf—Wartime Recordings
(CFP) **CD-CFP4277** These you have Loved
(CFP) **CD-CFP4602** Favourite Opera
(CFP) **CD-CFP4656** Herbert von Karajan conducts Opera
(EMI) **CDC5 55095-2** Prima Diva
(EMI) **CDC7 47284-2** Elisabeth Schwarzkopf sings Operetta
(EMI) **CDH7 61001-2** R. Strauss—Lieder & Arias
(EMI) **CDH7 63201-2** Elisabeth Schwarzkopf—Early Recordings
(EMI) **CDH7 63708-2** Mozart—Opera Arias
(EMI) **CDH7 69793-2** Elisabeth Schwarzkopf & Irmgard Seefried sing Duets
(EMI) **CDM5 65577-2** Elisabeth Schwarzkopf
(EMI) **CDM7 63654-2** Schwarzkopf Encores
(EMI) **CDM7 63657-2** Schwarzkopf sings Opera Arias
(EMI) **CDM7 69501-2** Elisabeth Schwarzkopf—Romantic Heroines
(EMI) **CHS7 69741-2(4)** Record of Singing, Vol.4—German School
(EMI) **CZS5 68113-2** Vive Offenbach!
(EMIN) **CD-EMX9519** Great Sopranos of Our Time
(ORFE) **C335931A** Salzburg Festival highlights (1956-85)
(ORFE) **C394201B** Great Mozart Singers Series, Vol. 2

SCHWEIGER, Hans (bar)
Beethoven: Fidelio (Cpte)
R. Strauss: Ariadne auf Naxos (Cpte)
Wagner: Meistersinger (exc)
(PREI) **90237** R Strauss—Daphne
(SCHW) **314532** Vienna State Opera Live, Vol.3
(SCHW) **314692** Vienna State Opera Live, Vol.19

SCHWEIKART, Dieter (bass)
Wagner: Meistersinger (Cpte)

SCHWEIKERT, Sally (sop)
Schoenberg: Moses und Aron (Cpte)

SCHWEIZER, Verena (sop)
Hindemith: Cardillac (Cpte), Nusch-Nuschi (Cpte)

SCHWERING, Elizabeth (sop)
R. Ward: Crucible (Cpte)

SCHWIER, Elisabeth (sop)
R. Strauss: Elektra (Cpte)

SCHYMBERG, Hjördis (sop)
Gounod: Roméo et Juliette (exc)
Puccini: Bohème (exc)
Verdi: Trovatore (exc)
(ALTN) **CDAN3** Hjördis Schymberg
(BLUE) **ABCD016** Jussi Björling—Rare Records & Alternative Takes
(BLUE) **ABCD028** Jussi Björling live at the Stockholm Opera
(CONI) **CDHD214** Jussi Björling - Arias, Lieder and Songs

SEIGER, Joe (pf)
(VANG) **08.8029.71** Mischa Elman - Favourite Encores

SEINEMEYER, Meta (sop)
(EMI) **CMS7 64008-2(2)** Wagner Singing on Record (pt 2)
(MMOI) **CDMOIR408** Great Sopranos
(MMOI) **CDMOIR412** Great Voices of the Century Sing Puccini
(PEAR) **GEMMCD9082** Meta Seinemeyer
(PREI) **89029** Meta Seinemeyer (1895-1929)
(PREI) **89083** Emanuel List (1890-1967)

SELEZNIEV, Georgy (bass)
Borodin: Prince Igor (Cpte)

SELIG, Franz-Josef (bass)
Busoni: Turandot (Cpte)

SELIMSKI, Assen (bar)
Mussorgsky: Khovanshchina (Cpte)

SELIVANOV, Piotr (bar)
(DANT) **LYS013/5** Tchaikovsky—The Queen of Spades
(MYTO) **1MCD921.55** Ivan Kozlovsky Recital

SELLAR, David (treb)
Puccini: Tosca (Cpte)
(CHES) **Chesky CD108** Light Classics, Volume II

SELLERS, Pyramid (sop)
Wagner: Walküre (Cpte)
(DG) **072 422-3GH7** Levine conducts Wagner's Ring

SELLS, Michael (ten)
Verdi: Falstaff (Cpte)

SEMBRICH, Marcella (sop)
(NIMB) **NI7834** Caruso in Ensemble
(NIMB) **NI7840/1** The Era of Adelina Patti
(NIMB) **NI7860** Emma Eames & Pol Plançon
(PEAR) **EVC1(2)** The Caruso Edition, Vol.1 (pt 2)
(PEAR) **GEMMCDS9923(1)** Covent Garden on Record, Vol.1 (pt 1)
(PEAR) **GEMMCD9130** Great Sopranos, Vol.2
(PEAR) **GEMMCD9937** Antonio Scotti
(RCA) **GD60495(2)** The Complete Caruso Collection (pt 2)
(RCA) **09026 61580-2(1)** RCA/Met 110 Singers, 100 Years (pt 1)
(ROMO) **81001-2** Emma Eames (1865-1952)

SEMELLAZ, François (sop)
Lully: Atys (Cpte)

SEMENOV, M.I. (cond)
see Moscow Imperial Op Orch

SEMKOW, Jerzy (cond)
see Cracow RSO
Sofia National Op Orch

SEMPÉ, Skip (hpd/dir)
(DHM) **RD77252** Purcell—Airs and Instrumental Music

SEMPERE, José (ten)
Massenet: Esclarmonde (Cpte)
(MCI) **MCCD099** Opera's Greatest Arias

SENATOR, Boaz (bass)
Puccini: Bohème (Cpte)
Rossini: Zelmira (Cpte)

SENDROWITZ, Mitchell (bar)
Verdi: Traviata (Cpte)

SÉNÉCHAL, Michel (ten)
Bazin: Voyage en Chine (Cpte)
Bizet: Carmen (Cpte), Ivan IV (exc)
Boïeldieu: Dame blanche (Cpte)
Cilea: Adriana Lecouvreur (Cpte)
G. Charpentier: Louise (Cpte)
Giordano: Andrea Chénier (Cpte)
Massenet: Chérubin (Cpte)
Messiaen: Saint François d'Assise (Cpte)
Offenbach: Contes d'Hoffmann (Cpte), Orphée aux enfers (Cpte), Périchole (Cpte)
Poulenc: Dialogues des Carmélites (Cpte)
Puccini: Bohème (exc), Madama Butterfly (Cpte), Tosca (Cpte), Turandot (exc)
R. Strauss: Capriccio (Cpte)
Ravel: Heure espagnole (Cpte)
Tchaikovsky: Eugene Onegin (Cpte)
Verdi: Forza del destino (Cpte), Otello (exc)
Wagner: Meistersinger (Cpte)
(CBS) **CD79312** Puccini: Il Trittico
(DECC) **433 068-2DWO** Your Hundred Best Opera Tunes V
(DECC) **433 865-2DWO** The World of Puccini
(DECC) **436 317-2DA** Puccini—Famous Arias
(DECC) **444 555-2DF2** Essential Puccini
(EMI) **CZS5 68113-2** Vive Offenbach!
(EMI) **CZS5 68295-2** Messager/Lecocq—Operetta Highlights
(MUSD) **20239-2** Delibes—Opéras-Comiques
(SYMP) **SYMCD1103** Renée Doria—Opera Recital

SENGER, Alexander (ten)
R. Strauss: Daphne (Cpte)

SENIGLOVÁ, Eva (sop)
Marschner: Hans Heiling (Cpte)

SENN, Martha (mez)
Leoncavallo: Bohème (Cpte)
Mascagni: Cavalleria Rusticana (Cpte)
Mozart: Clemenza di Tito (Cpte)
Verdi: Rigoletto (Cpte)

SEPHIRA ENSEMBLE, STUTTGART
(BAYE) **BR100083** Glanz des Rokoko

SERAFIN, Tullio (cond)
see La Scala Orch
MMF Orch
Naples San Carlo Op Orch
Philh
Rome Op Orch
RPO
Santa Cecilia Academy Orch

SEREBRIER, José (cond)
see Adelaide SO
Brno St PO
Melbourne SO
RPO
RTBF New SO
Sicilian SO
Sydney SO

SERENI, Mario (bar)
Donizetti: Lucia di Lammermoor (Cpte)
Giordano: Andrea Chénier (Cpte)
Mascagni: Cavalleria Rusticana (Cpte)
Puccini: Bohème (Cpte), Madama Butterfly (Cpte), Rondine (Cpte), Turandot (Cpte)
Verdi: Aida (Cpte), Ernani (Cpte), Traviata (Cpte)
(CFP) **CD-CFP4602** Favourite Opera
(CFP) **CD-CFP9013** Duets from Famous Operas
(RCA) **GD87799** The Pearl Fishers Duet plus Duets and Scenes

SERGE, John (ten)
Rossini: Semiramide (Cpte)

SERKOYAN, Gérard (bass)
Offenbach: Contes d'Hoffmann (exc)
Saint-Saëns: Henry VIII (Cpte)
(MONT) **TCE8760** Stravinsky: Stage Works

SEROV, Eduard (cond)
see Odense SO

SERRA, Enrique (bass)
Donizetti: Caterina Cornaro (Cpte), Maria Stuarda (Cpte)

SERRA, Luciana (sop)
Donizetti: Ajo nell'imbarazzo (Cpte), Don Pasquale (Cpte), Gianni di Parigi (Cpte)
Gazzaniga: Don Giovanni (Cpte)
Mozart: Zauberflöte (exc)
Offenbach: Contes d'Hoffmann (Cpte)
Rossini: Scala di seta (Cpte), Siège de Corinthe (Cpte), Viaggio a Reims (Cpte)
(CAST) **CVI2065** Highlights from the Royal Opera House, Covent Garden
(NUOV) **6820** Luciana Serra—Opera Recital
(NUOV) **6905** Donizetti—Great Love Duets

SERRAIOCCO, Danilo (bass-bar)
Cherubini: Lodoïska (Cpte)
Puccini: Fanciulla del West (Cpte), Tosca (Cpte)
Rossini: Inganno felice (Cpte)
(DECC) **436 261-2DHO3** Puccini—Il Trittico

SERRANO, Enriqueta (sngr)
Sorozábal: Katiuska (Cpte)

SERRE, Jean-Louis (bar)
Mouret: Amours de Ragonde (Cpte)

SERVILE, Roberto (bar)
Rossini: Barbiere di Siviglia (Cpte)
(CAPR) **10 380** Breezes from the Orient, Vol.2

SESSIONS, John (bass)
J. Strauss II: Fledermaus (Cpte)

SETTI, Giulio (cond)
see NY Met Op Chor
NY Met Op Orch
orch

SETTMACHER, Ferdinand (bass)
R. Strauss: Rosenkavalier (Cpte)

SETZER, Franz (ten)
R. Strauss: Rosenkavalier (Cpte)

SEVENICH, Stefan (sngr)
Braunfels: Verkündigung (Cpte)

SEVERIN, Ulla (sop)
Mozart: Così fan tutte (Cpte)

SEVERINA, Gina (mez)
(NIMB) **NI7834** Caruso in Ensemble
(PEAR) **EVC1(2)** The Caruso Edition, Vol.1 (pt 2)
(RCA) **GD60495(2)** The Complete Caruso Collection (pt 2)

SEVILLE SYMPHONY ORCHESTRA
cond E. COLOMER
(RCA) **RD61191** Gala Lirica
(RCA) **09026 61191-5** Gala Lirica
cond P. DOMINGO
(RCA) **RD61191** Gala Lirica
(RCA) **09026 61191-5** Gala Lirica
cond E. GARCIA-ASENSIO
(RCA) **RD61191** Gala Lirica
(RCA) **09026 61191-5** Gala Lirica
cond L.A. GARCIA-NAVARRO
(RCA) **RD61191** Gala Lirica
(RCA) **09026 61440-2** Opera's Greatest Moments
(RCA) **09026 61191-5** Gala Lirica
cond G. NAVARRO
(RCA) **74321 25821-2** Café Classics—Music of Spain
cond M. ROA
Vives: Doña Francisquita (Cpte)

SEWEN, Marek (cond)
see Warsaw CO

SEYMOUR, Linda (contr)
Wagner: Walküre (exc)

SEYMOUR, Valerie (sop)
Sullivan: HMS Pinafore (Cpte)

SFEKAS-KARVELAS, Joan (mez)
Kalomiris: Mother's Ring (Cpte)

SFORZA, Camillo (ten)
Donizetti: Lucrezia Borgia (Cpte)
Verdi: Traviata (Cpte)

SGARRO, Louis (bar)
Verdi: Traviata (Cpte)

SHACKLOCK, Constance (mez)
Gay: Beggar's Opera (Cpte)
(TEST) **SBT1018** Kirsten Flagstad

SHAFFER, Thomas (bar)
Britten: Paul Bunyan (Cpte)

SHAGIDULLIN, Albert (bass)
Mussorgsky: Boris Godunov (Cpte)

SHAKESNIDER, Wilma (sop)
Gershwin: Porgy and Bess (exc)

SHARLING, Elayne (sngr)
Gay: Beggar's Opera (Cpte)

SHARONOV, Vasili (bar)
(PEAR) **GEMMCDS9001/3(1)** Singers of Imperial Russia, Vol.2 (pt 1)
(SYMP) **SYMCD1105** The Harold Wayne Collection, Vol.10

SHARP, Frederick (bar)
Delius: Village Romeo and Juliet (Cpte)
(EMI) **CMS7 64727-2** Britten—Opera excerpts and Folksongs

SHARP, Norma (sop)
Egk: Peer Gynt (Cpte)
Wagner: Götterdämmerung (Cpte), Parsifal (Cpte), Rheingold (Cpte), Siegfried (Cpte)
(EURO) **GD69003** Wagner—Der Ring des Nibelungen
(PHIL) **434 420-2PM32(1)** Richard Wagner Edition (Pt.1)

SHARP, William (bar)
(EMI) **CDC7 54851-2** Gershwin—Blue Monday, etc
(KOCH) **37028-2** Gershwin—Songs & Duets
(KOCH) **37050-2** Blitzstein—Songs

SHARPE, Ivan (ten)
(OPRA) **ORCH104** A Hundred Years of Italian Opera: 1820-1830

SHARPE, Terence (bar)
Giordano: Andrea Chénier (Cpte)
Sullivan: Yeomen of the Guard (exc)
Vaughan Williams: Hugh the Drover (Cpte), Pilgrim's Progress (Cpte)
Verdi: Vespri Siciliani (Cpte)

SHARQAWI, Awatef El (mez)
Mozart: Così fan tutte (Cpte), Nozze di Figaro (Cpte)

SHAW, Geoffrey (bass)
Monteverdi: Orfeo (Cpte)
Vaughan Williams: Pilgrim's Progress (Cpte)

SHAW, John (bar)
Sullivan: Patience (Cpte)
(CFP) **CD-CFP4609** Favourite Gilbert & Sullivan
(DECC) **071 149-1DH (DECC)** The Essential Sutherland

SHAW, Kenneth (ten)
Janáček: Jenufa (Cpte)

SHAW, Penny (sop)
Verdi: Trovatore (Cpte)

SHAW, Robert (cond)
see Atlanta SO
orch
RCA Victor Orch

SHAW, Teresa (mez)
Purcell: Dido (Cpte)

(ROBERT) SHAW CHORALE
cond R. CELLINI
Leoncavallo: Pagliacci (Cpte)
Mascagni: Cavalleria Rusticana (Cpte)
Verdi: Trovatore (Cpte)
(RCA) **GD60205** Opera Choruses
cond E. LEINSDORF
(RCA) **09026 61245-2** Ezio Pinza - Recital
cond F. REINER
Bizet: Carmen (Cpte)
cond ROBERT SHAW
(RCA) **GD60205** Opera Choruses
(RCA) **74321 24209-2** Italian Opera Choruses
cond A. TOSCANINI
Verdi: Aida (Cpte), Ballo in maschera (Cpte), Falstaff (Cpte)
(RCA) **GD60276** Toscanini conducts Boito & Verdi
(RCA) **GD60280** Toscanini Collection
(RCA) **GD60326** Verdi—Operas & Choral Works

SHEARER, Mary (sop)
Ancelin: Filius Hominis (Cpte)

SHEFFIELD, Leo (bar)
Sullivan: Gondoliers (Cpte), Pirates of Penzance (Cpte), Trial by Jury (Cpte)
(MMOI) **CDMOIR413** The Very Best of Gilbert & Sullivan

SHEFFIELD, Philip (ten)
G. Lloyd: John Socman (exc)
M. Berkeley: Baa Baa Black Sheep (Cpte)

SHELBY, Karen (mez)
Janáček: Cunning Little Vixen (Cpte)

SHELLEY, Elizabeth (mez)
(EMI) **CDM7 64356-2** Opera Choruses
(EMI) **CZS5 68559-2** Italian Opera Choruses

SHELLEY, Howard (pf)
(HYPE) **CDA66486** Rachmaninov—Piano Transcriptions
(HYPE) **CDS44041/8** Rachmaninov—Complete Piano Music

SHEMCHUK, Ludmila (mez)
Mussorgsky: Khovanshchina (Cpte)
Ponchielli: Gioconda (Cpte)

SHENDEROVICH, Evgeni (pf)
(RUSS) **RDCD11372** Tchaikovsky—Romances; Rachmaninov—Aleko Aria

SHEPHERD, James (cornet)
(CHAN) **CHAN4513** British Bandsman Centenary Concert

SHEPHERD, Muriel (cond)
see Fine Arts Brass Ens

SHEPPARD, Craig (pf)
(CHAN) **CHAN6551** Renato Bruson at the Wigmore Hall

SHEPPARD, Honor (sop)
Monteverdi: L'Arianna (exc)
Purcell: Dido (Cpte), Indian Queen, Z630 (Cpte), King Arthur, Z628 (Cpte)
(HARM) **HMX290 1528/33(2)** A Purcell Companion (pt 2)

SHERIDAN, Margaret (sop)
(CONI) **CDHD235** The Puccini Album
(PEAR) **GEMMCDS9925(2)** Covent Garden on Record—Vol.3 (pt 2)
(PREI) **89072** Aureliano Pertile (1885-1952) - II

SHERNIKH, Lydia (sop)
Tchaikovsky: Eugene Onegin (exc)

SHEVELEV, Nikolai (bar)
(PEAR) **GEMMCDS9007/9(2)** Singers of Imperial Russia, Vol.4 (pt 2)

SHICOFF, Neil (ten)
Bizet: Carmen (Cpte)
Donizetti: Lucia di Lammermoor (exc)
Offenbach: Contes d'Hoffmann (exc)
Puccini: Bohème (Cpte)
Tchaikovsky: Eugene Onegin (Cpte)
Verdi: Attila (Cpte), Macbeth (Cpte), Rigoletto (Cpte), Traviata (Cpte)
(CAST) **CASH5051** Puccini Favourites from Covent Garden and the Arena di Verona
(CAST) **CVI2065** Highlights from the Royal Opera House, Covent Garden
(CAST) **CVI2070** Great Puccini Love Scenes from Covent Garden, La Scala and Verona
(DG) **431 601-2GCE10** Tchaikovsky Compact Edition
(EMI) **CDC7 54016-2** Tenorissimo!
(EMI) **CDM5 65576-2** Jessye Norman

SHIKANO, Akihito (bass)
Verdi: Traviata (Cpte)

SHILKRET, Nathaniel (cond)
see orch
Victor Orch

SHILLING, Eric (bar)
Sullivan: Iolanthe (exc)

SHIMELL, William (bar)
Cherubini: Lodoïska (Cpte)
Mozart: Don Giovanni (exc)

SHIN, Young Ok (sop)
Bellini: Bianca e Fernando (Cpte)

SHIRAI, Mitsuko (mez)
Wolf: Manuel Venegas

SHIRASAKA-TERATANI, Chieko (sngr)
Braunfels: Verkündigung (Cpte)

SHIRINKSY, Alexander (vn)
(MEZH) **MK417030** Fine Night with Alexander Shirinsky

SHIRLEY, George (ten)
Debussy: Pelléas et Mélisande (Cpte)
Haydn: Orlando Paladino (Cpte)
Mozart: Così fan tutte (Cpte)
R. Strauss: Friedenstag (Cpte)
(SONY) **SM3K46291** Stravinsky—Ballets, Vol.1
(SONY) **SM22K46290(3)** Stravinsky—The Complete Edition (pt 3)
(SONY) **SM22K46290(4)** Stravinsky—The Complete Edition (pt 4)

SHIRLEY-QUIRK, John (bar)
Britten: Burning Fiery Furnace (Cpte), Curlew River (Cpte), Death in Venice (Cpte), Gloriana (Cpte), Midsummer Night's Dream (Cpte), Prodigal Son (Cpte), Rape of Lucretia (Cpte)
Purcell: Fairy Queen, Z629 (Cpte)
Vaughan Williams: Pilgrim's Progress (Cpte)
Walton: Bear (Cpte)
(LOND) **433 200-2LHO2** Britten—Owen Wingrave, etc.

SHITKOVA, Albina (sop)
Kabalevsky: Colas Breugnon (Cpte)

SHOPLAND, Martin (ten)
Chabrier: Roi malgré lui (Cpte)

SHORE, Andrew (bass-bar)
Rossini: Barbiere di Siviglia (Cpte)

SHORT, Kevin (bar)
Puccini: Fanciulla del West (Cpte)

SHOUMANOVA, Anelia (sngr)
Weill: Dreigroschenoper (Cpte)

SHOVELTON, Geoffrey (spkr)
Sullivan: Zoo (Cpte)

SHUARD, Amy (sop)
(CFP) **CD-CFP4569** Puccini: Arias
(CFP) **CD-CFP4575** Verdi Arias
(TEST) **SBT1058** James Johnston - Opera Arias and Songs

SHULMAN, Andrew (vn)
(CNTI) **CCD1025** Delius & Dyson—Music for Cello & Piano

SHUMILOVA, E (sop)
Rimsky-Korsakov: Tale of Tsar Saltan (Cpte)
(PREI) **89081** Georgi Nelepp (1904-1957)

SHUMSKAYA, Elizaveta (sop)
(ARLE) **ARL23/5** Rimsky-Korsakov—Sadko
(MYTO) **1MCD921.55** Ivan Kozlovsky Recital
(PREI) **89061** Pavel Lisitian (born 1911)

SHUTOVA, Marina (mez)
Serov: Judith (Cpte)

SIBILLE, Madeleine (contr)
(PEAR) **GEMMCD9948** Ninon Vallin in Opera and Song

SIBIRIAKOV, Lev (bass)
(NIMB) **NI7865** Great Singers at the Mariinsky Theatre
(PEAR) **GEMMCDS9001/3(2)** Singers of Imperial Russia, Vol.2 (pt 2)
(PEAR) **GEMMCDS9007/9(2)** Singers of Imperial Russia, Vol.4 (pt 2)
(PEAR) **GEMMCDS9111(1)** Singers of Imperial Russia, Vol.5 (pt 1)
(PEAR) **GEMMCDS9111(2)** Singers of Imperial Russia, Vol.5 (pt 2)
(PEAR) **GEMMCDS9925(1)** Covent Garden on Record—Vol.3 (pt 1)

SICA, Gennaro (ten)
Mozart: Nozze di Figaro (Cpte)

SICILIAN SYMPHONY ORCHESTRA
cond J. SEREBRIER
(IMP) **MCD64** Tchaikovsky—Soprano Arias

SIDERER, Mathilde (sngr)
Lecocq: Jour et la Nuit (Cpte)
Terrasse: Travaux d'Hercule (Cpte)

SIDHOM, Peter (bar)
Gounod: Roméo et Juliette (Cpte)
Smyth: Wreckers (Cpte)
Verdi: Rigoletto (Cpte), Traviata (exc)

SIEBER, Gudrun (sop)
Hindemith: Nusch-Nuschi (Cpte)
Mozart: Zauberflöte (Cpte)

SIEBERT, Dorothea (sop)
Mozart: Zauberflöte (Cpte)
Wagner: Götterdämmerung (Cpte), Parsifal (Cpte), Rheingold (Cpte)
(PHIL) **446 057-2PB14** Wagner—The Ring Cycle - Bayreuth Festival 1967

SIEBERT, Isolde (sop)
(SCHW) **314018** Virtuoso Operatic Arias for Soprano and Clarinet

SIEDEN, Cyndia (sop)
Gluck: Orfeo ed Euridice (Cpte)
Mozart: Entführung (Cpte)
(EMI) **CDC5 55350-2** Cheryl Studer - A Portrait

SIEGEL, Hermann (bass)
R. Strauss: Elektra (Cpte)

SIEGEL, Laurenc (cond)
see Philh

SIEGELE, Dankwart (bass)
Bellini: Puritani (Cpte)

SIEGHART, Martin (cond)
see Stuttgart CO

SIEGLAND CANTATA CHOIR
cond N. SCHULTZE
Schultze: Schwarzer Peter (Cpte)

SIEGMANN, Christian (cond)
see Banda Classica

SIEMS, Margarete (sop)
(PEAR) **GEMMCDS9925(1)** Covent Garden on Record—Vol.3 (pt 1)

SIEPI, Cesare (bass)
Bellini: Norma (Cpte)
Boito: Mefistofele (Cpte)
Donizetti: Lucia di Lammermoor (Cpte)
Mozart: Don Giovanni (Cpte), Nozze di Figaro (Cpte)
Ponchielli: Gioconda (Cpte)
Puccini: Bohème (Cpte)
Rossini: Barbiere di Siviglia (Cpte)
Verdi: Don Carlo (Cpte), Ernani (Cpte), Rigoletto (Cpte)
(BELA) **450 007-2** Puccini Favourites
(BELA) **450 133-2** Verdi Favourites
(DECC) **417 780-2DM** Joan Sutherland's Greatest Hits
(DECC) **440 403-2DM** Giuseppe di Stefano
(DECC) **440 418-2DM** Cesare Siepi
(DECC) **444 555-2DF2** Essential Puccini
(ORFE) **C394201B** Great Mozart Singers Series, Vol. 2

SIEWART, Charlotte (sop)
Wagner: Götterdämmerung (Cpte)

SIEWERT, Ruth (contr)
Wagner: Parsifal (Cpte), Walküre (exc)
(EMI) **CMS5 65212-2** Wagner—Les introuvables du Ring
(EMI) **CZS7 67123-2** Wagner: Der Ring des Nibelungen

SIEYES, Maurice (bar)
Chabrier: Roi malgré lui (Cpte)
Massenet: Grisélidis (Cpte)

SIGHELE, Mietta (sop)
Leoncavallo: Pagliacci (Cpte)
Meyerbeer: Africaine (Cpte)
Verdi: Aida (Cpte)

SIGMUNDSSON, Kristin (bass)
Mozart: Don Giovanni (Cpte), Zauberflöte (Cpte)
Schreker: Gezeichneten (Cpte)

SIGNOR, Franco (bass)
Donizetti: Martyrs (Cpte)

SIGNORE, Gino del (ten)
Puccini: Gianni Schicchi (Cpte), Turandot (Cpte)
Verdi: Forza del destino (Cpte)

SIGNORETTI, Leopoldo (ten)
(SYMP) **SYMCD1065** The Harold Wayne Collection, Vol.1

SIGNORINI, Francesco (ten)
(MEMO) **HR4408/9(1)** Singers in Genoa, Vol.1 (disc 1)

SIKIRA, Alisa (sop)
Delius: Village Romeo and Juliet (Cpte)

SIKON, James Scott (bass-bar)
Moran: Dracula Diary (Cpte)

SIKORA, Elizabeth (sop)
Verdi: Simon Boccanegra (Cpte)

SILBANO, Silvana (mez)
Bellini: Zaira (Cpte)

SILD, Tarmo (bar)
Tubin: Barbara von Tisenhusen (Cpte)

SILESIAN CHAMBER MUSIC CHOIR
cond Y. EL SISI
Mozart: Così fan tutte (Cpte), Don Giovanni (Cpte), Nozze di Figaro (Cpte)

SILJA, Anja (sop)
Berg: Wozzeck (Cpte)
Janáček: Jenufa (Cpte)
Schoenberg: Erwartung (Cpte)
Wagner: Fliegende Holländer (Cpte), Götterdämmerung (Cpte), Lohengrin (Cpte), Parsifal (Cpte), Rheingold (Cpte), Tannhäuser (Cpte)
Weill: Mahagonny (Cpte)
(BELA) **450 052-2** Great Opera Choruses
(CLOR) **TCO93-75** The Cleveland Orchestra-75th Anniversary CD Edition
(PHIL) **434 420-2PM32(2)** Richard Wagner Edition (pt 2)
(PHIL) **446 057-2PB14** Wagner—The Ring Cycle - Bayreuth Festival 1967

SILLICH, Aristodemo (bass)
(NIMB) **NI7831** Mattia Battistini (1856-1928)
(PREI) **89045** Mattia Battistini (1856-1928)

SILLITO, Kenneth (cond)
see ASMF

SILLS, Beverly (sop)
G. Charpentier: Louise (Cpte)
Handel: Giulio Cesare (Cpte)
Massenet: Thaïs (Cpte)
Rossini: Siège de Corinthe (Cpte)
Verdi: Traviata (Cpte)
(CFP) **CD-CFP4575** Verdi Arias

SILOTI, Alexander (pf)
(PEAR) **GEMMCD9993** Arthur Friedheim—complete recordings, etc

SILVASTI, Jorma (ten)
Sallinen: Kullervo (Cpte)
Wagner: Fliegende Holländer (Cpte)
(BIS) **BIS-CD373/4** Opera Scenes from Savaonlinna

SILVER, Mark (ten)
(TELD) **9031-76372-6(TELD)** Tchaikovsky —Women and Fate

SILVERI, Paolo (bar)
Verdi: Falstaff (Cpte)

(EMI) **CHS7 69741-2(7)** Record of Singing, Vol.4—Italian School

SILVERSTEIN, Joseph (cond)
see Utah SO

SILVESTRELLI, Andrea (bass)
Mozart: Don Giovanni (Cpte)
Verdi: Don Carlo (Cpte)
(SCHW) **314052** Opera Gala

SILVESTRI, Constantin (cond)
see Paris Cons
Philh

SIMA, Gabriele (sop)
Busoni: Turandot (Cpte)
Einem: Dantons Tod (Cpte)
Mozart: Nozze di Figaro (Cpte), Zauberflöte (exc)
R. Strauss: Elektra (Cpte), Rosenkavalier (Cpte)
Rossini: Barbiere di Siviglia (Cpte)
Schoeck: Penthesilea (Cpte)
Wagner: Tannhäuser (Cpte)

SIMÁNDY, József (ten)
(VAI) **VAIA1009** Ilona Tokody. Portrait of the Artist

IMIC, Goran (bass)
Ponchielli: Gioconda (Cpte)
R. Strauss: Elektra (Cpte)
Schreker: Irrelohe (Cpte)
Verdi: Ballo in maschera (Cpte)

IMIONATO, Giulietta (mez)
Berlioz: Troyens (exc)
Cilea: Adriana Lecouvreur (Cpte)
Donizetti: Anna Bolena (Cpte)
Gluck: Orfeo ed Euridice (Cpte)
J. Strauss II: Fledermaus (Cpte)
Mascagni: Cavalleria Rusticana (Cpte)
Massenet: Werther (Cpte)
Ponchielli: Gioconda (Cpte)
Rossini: Barbiere di Siviglia (Cpte), Italiana in Algeri (Cpte)
Verdi: Aida (Cpte), Don Carlo (Cpte), Falstaff (Cpte), Rigoletto (Cpte), Trovatore (Cpte)
(BELA) **450 006-2** Famous Opera Duets
(BELA) **450 133-2** Verdi Favourites
(DECC) **411 665-2DM3** Puccini: Il trittico
(DECC) **433 068-2DWO** Your Hundred Best Opera Tunes V
(DECC) **433 442-2DA** Verdi—Famous Arias
(DECC) **440 406-2DM** Giulietta Simionato
(DECC) **440 411-2DM** Anita Cerquetti
(DECC) **443 378-2DM** Ten Top Mezzos 2
(EMI) **CHS7 69741-2(7)** Record of Singing, Vol.4—Italian School
(MEMO) **HR4386/7** Great Voices - Giulietta Simionato
(MEMO) **HR4396/7** Great Voices—Leontyne Price

MKOWSKY, Nikolaus (ten)
Monteverdi: Orfeo (Cpte), Ritorno d'Ulisse in Patria (Cpte)
R. Strauss: Rosenkavalier (Cpte)

MMONS, Mary (mez)
(SONY) **SM22K46290(3)** Stravinsky—The Complete Edition (pt 3)

MON, Geoffrey (cond)
see ENO Orch
LPO
LSO
Philh
Philh Vcs

MON, Monique (sop)
Rameau: Hippolyte et Aricie (Cpte)

MONE, Bruno de (bar)
Pergolesi: Frate 'nnamorato (Cpte)
Puccini: Turandot (Cpte)

MONEAU, Léopold (ten)
Bizet: Pêcheurs de Perles (Cpte)
Gluck: Orphée (Cpte)
Mozart: Così fan tutte (exc), Don Giovanni (Cpte), Zauberflöte (Cpte)
(EMI) **CDH5 65072-2** Glyndebourne Recorded - 1934-1994
(EMI) **CHS7 63715-2** Mozart: Die Entführung, etc
(MONT) **TCE8760** Stravinsky: Stage Works
(ORFE) **C394201B** Great Mozart Singers Series, Vol. 2
(PHIL) **438 953-2PM2** Alarie/Simoneau - Arias & Duets
(PHIL) **442 272-2PM2** The Best of Bizet
(PHIL) **442 602-2PM** 3 x 3 Tenors

MONETTI, Riccardo (bar)
Vaughan Williams: Pilgrim's Progress (Cpte)

MONETTO, Alfredo (cond)
see Milan RAI SO
Radio Italiana SO
Rome RAI Orch
Turin RAI Orch

MONOV, Yuri (cond)
see Philh
RPO

MPSON, Glenda (mez)
AMON) **CD-SAR50** Now What is Love?

MPSON, Marietta (mez)
Gershwin: Porgy and Bess (exc)

NATRA, Ray (cond)
see orch

SINCLAIR, Bernard (bar)
(EMI) **CZS5 68113-2** Vive Offenbach!

SINCLAIR, Jeannette (sop)
Mozart: Nozze di Figaro (Cpte)
Rossini: Comte Ory (Cpte)
Sullivan: Mikado (Cpte)
(CFP) **CD-CFP4609** Favourite Gilbert & Sullivan

SINCLAIR, Monica (contr)
Delibes: Lakmé (exc)
Donizetti: Fille du régiment (Cpte)
Gay: Beggar's Opera (Cpte)
German: Merrie England (Cpte)
Gounod: Faust (Cpte)
Handel: Alcina (Cpte), Giulio Cesare (exc)
Mozart: Nozze di Figaro (Cpte)
Purcell: Dido (Cpte)
Rossini: Comte Ory (Cpte)
Sullivan: Gondoliers (Cpte), HMS Pinafore (Cpte), Iolanthe (Cpte), Mikado (Cpte), Patience (Cpte), Yeomen of the Guard (Cpte)
Walton: Troilus and Cressida (exc)
(CFP) **CD-CFP4238** Gilbert and Sullivan
(CFP) **CD-CFP4609** Favourite Gilbert & Sullivan
(DECC) **433 064-2DWO** Your Hundred Best Opera Tunes Volume I
(DECC) **433 443-2DA** Great Opera Choruses
(EMI) **CDC7 47283-2** Maria Callas - Mad Scenes & Bel Canto Arias
(EMI) **CDH5 65072-2** Glyndebourne Recorded - 1934-1994
(EMI) **CMS7 63244-2** The Art of Maria Callas
(EMI) **CMS7 64409-2** Sullivan—Pirates of Penzance & Orch. Works
(EMI) **CMS7 64412-2** Gilbert & Sullivan—Ruddigore/Shakespeare Music

SINFONIA
cond D. VERMEULEN
(DINT) **DICD920289** Haydn—Symphonies Nos 44 and 45;Sinfonia-Acide e Galatea

SINFONIA OF LONDON
cond R. FRÜHBECK DE BURGOS
(EMI) **CDM7 69502-2** On Wings of Song
cond R. IRVING
(CFP) **CD-CFP4606** Favourite Movie Classics
(EMI) **CDEMTVD59** Classic Experience 3

SINFONIA VARSOVIA
cond E. KRIVINE
(DENO) **CO-75372** Mozart—Overtures

SINGER, Mark (sngr)
Rorem: Three Sisters Who Are Not Sisters (Cpte)

SINGH, Werner (spkr)
Benatzky: Im weissen Rössl (Cpte)

SINGHER, Martial (bar)
Berlioz: Troyens (Cpte)
(EMI) **CMS7 64008-2(1)** Wagner Singing on Record (pt 1)
(PREI) **89011** Marjorie Lawrence (1909-1979)

SINIMBERGHI, Gino (ten)
Leoncavallo: Pagliacci (Cpte)
(NIMB) **NI7848** Great Singers at the Berlin State Opera
(PREI) **89092** Erna Berger (1900-1990) - II

SINNONE, Aldo (ten)
(SCHW) **314512** Vienna State Opera Live, Vol.1

SINOPOLI, Giuseppe (cond)
see Berlin Deutsche Op Orch
NYPO
Philh
ROHO
Santa Cecilia Academy Orch
Staatskapelle Dresden

SINYAVSKAYA, Tamara (mez)
Mussorgsky: Boris Godunov (Cpte)
Tchaikovsky: Eugene Onegin (Cpte)

SIPPOLA, Ulla (mez)
(BIS) **BIS-CD373/4** Opera Scenes from Savaonlinna

SIRANOSSIAN, Alexandre (cond)
see Ars Nova Ens

SIRKIÄ, Raimo (ten)
Wagner: Fliegende Holländer (Cpte)
(BIS) **BIS-CD373/4** Opera Scenes from Savaonlinna

SIROTA, Leo (pf)
(PEAR) **GEMMCD9156** Busoni and his Circle, Volume 2

SISI, Yousef El (cond)
see Polish Nat RO

SITKOVETSKY, Dmitry (vn)
(ORFE) **C048831A** Kreisler: Famous Transcriptions for Violin and Piano

SIVALL, Olle (ten)
Verdi: Rigoletto (exc), Trovatore (exc)

SIVIERI, Enrico (cond)
see orch

(THE) SIXTEEN
cond H. CHRISTOPHERS
Purcell: Fairy Queen, Z629 (Cpte)

(THE) SIXTEEN ORCHESTRA
cond H. CHRISTOPHERS
Purcell: Fairy Queen, Z629 (Cpte)

SJÖSTEDT, Margareta (mez)
R. Strauss: Elektra (Cpte)

SKEAPING, Lucie (mez)
(SAYD) **CD-SDL400** English National Songs

SKEAPING, Roderick (vn)
(HARM) **HMC90 249** Purcell: Music for a while
(HARM) **HMX290 1528/33(2)** A Purcell Companion (pt 2)

SKINNER, John York (alto)
Handel: Partenope (Cpte)

SKINNER, Philip (bass)
Meyerbeer: Africaine (Cpte)

SKITCH, Jeffrey (bar)
Sullivan: Gondoliers (Cpte), HMS Pinafore (Cpte), Princess Ida (Cpte)
(DECC) **430 095-2DWO** The World of Gilbert & Sullivan, Vol.1
(DECC) **433 868-2DWO** The World of Gilbert & Sullivan - Volume 2

SKOGLUND, Annika (mez)
Mozart: Finta Giardiniera (Cpte)

SKOKAN, Franz (bass)
(SCHW) **314602** Vienna State Opera Live, Vol.10

SKÖLD, Olle (bass)
Mozart: Idomeneo (Cpte), Zauberflöte (Cpte)

SKOVHUS, Boje (bar)
Beethoven: Fidelio (Cpte)
Lehár: Lustige Witwe (Cpte)
Leoncavallo: Pagliacci (Cpte)
Mozart: Nozze di Figaro (Cpte)
Schoeck: Venus (Cpte)
Spohr: Faust (Cpte)
(CAPR) **10 481** R.Strauss—Opera Concert

SKRAM, Knut (bar)
Mozart: Nozze di Figaro (Cpte)

ŠKROBÁNEK, Josef (ten)
Janáček: Fate (Cpte)

SKROWACZEWSKI, Stanislaw (cond)
see Hallé

SKULSKI, Florian (bar)
Szymanowski: King Roger (Cpte)

SLABBERT, Wicus (sngr)
Zemlinsky: Kleider machen Leute (Cpte)

SLANIA, Czesława (contr)
R. Strauss: Rosenkavalier (Cpte)

SLATER, Andrew (bass)
Tchaikovsky: Queen of Spades (Cpte)

SLATINARU, Maria (sop)
Puccini: Tabarro (Cpte)

SLATKIN, Felix (cond)
see Hollywood Bowl SO

SLATKIN, Leonard (cond)
see Hollywood Bowl SO
Munich RO
Munich RSO
St Louis SO

SLEMBECK, Dieter (ten)
Wagner: Parsifal (Cpte)

SLEZAK, Leo (ten)
(NIMB) **NI7856** Legendary Tenors
(PEAR) **GEMMCDS9924(2)** Covent Garden on Record, Vol.2 (pt 2)
(PEAR) **GEMMCD9129** Great Tenors, Vol.2
(PREI) **89020** Leo Slezak (1873-1946)
(PREI) **89203** Leo Slezak (1873-1946)
(SYMP) **SYMCD1081** The Harold Wayne Collection, Vol.5

SLOVAK PHILHARMONIC CHORUS
cond C. ABBADO
Mussorgsky: Boris Godunov (Cpte), Khovanshchina (Cpte)
cond M. DE BERNART
Donizetti: Maria di Rohan (Cpte)
cond O. DOHNÁNYI
(NAXO) **8 550241** Verdi—Opera Choruses
cond M. HALÁSZ
(NAXO) **8 550497** Thomas Harper—Opera Recital
cond W. HUMBURG
Puccini: Bohème (Cpte)
cond E. KÖRNER
Marschner: Hans Heiling (Cpte)
cond O. LENÁRD
Bellini: Sonnambula (Cpte)
Suchoň: Whirlpool (Cpte)
cond F. LUISI
Donizetti: Favorita (Cpte)
cond C. PIANTINI
Bizet: Pêcheurs de Perles (Cpte)
cond A. RAHBARI
Leoncavallo: Pagliacci (Cpte)
Mascagni: Cavalleria Rusticana (Cpte)
Puccini: Madama Butterfly (Cpte), Tosca (Cpte)
Verdi: Rigoletto (Cpte), Traviata (Cpte)
cond J. WILDNER
Mozart: Così fan tutte (Cpte)

SLOVAK PHILHARMONIC ORCHESTRA
cond A. BRAMALL
Bizet: Carmen Suites (exc)
cond S. GUNZENHAUSER
(NAXO) **8 550072** Beethoven—Overtures

cond Z. KOŠLER
(NAXO) **8 550342** R. Strauss: Orchestral Works
cond E. KÖRNER
Marschner: Hans Heiling (Cpte)
cond D. NAZARETH
(NAXO) **8 550051** Borodin & Mussorgsky—Orchestral Works
cond K. REDEL
(PIER) **PV730023** Ballets from the Great Operas

SLOVAK RADIO SYMPHONY ORCHESTRA
(NAXO) **8 553030** Opera Duets
cond J. WILDNER
(NAXO) **8 553030** Opera Duets

SLOVAK STATE PHILHARMONIC ORCHESTRA, KOŠICE
cond A. MOGRELIA
(NAXO) **8 550381** Prokofiev—Orchestral Suites
cond U. SCHNEIDER
(MARC) **8 223638** Raff—Orchestral Works
cond R. STANKOVSKY
(MARC) **8 223272** Dvořák—Opera Overtures
cond P. VRONSKÝ
(OPUS) **9356 2047** Romantic Operatic Duets
cond A. WALTER
(MARC) **8 223324** Von Schillings—Orchestral Works
(MARC) **8 223342** Marschner—Overtures
(MARC) **8 223647** Suppé—Overtures, Vol. 1
(MARC) **8 223648** Suppé—Overtures, Volume 2
(MARC) **8 223683** Suppé—Overtures, Volume 3
(NAXO) **8 550468** Famous Operetta Overtures

SŁOWAKIEWICZ, Alicia (sop)
Gluck: Corona (Cpte)
Rossini: Signor Bruschino (Cpte)

SLUIS, Mieke van der (sop)
Fux: Dafne in Lauro (Cpte)
Grétry: Jugement de Midas (exc)
Keiser: Croesus (Cpte)
Rameau: Zoroastre (Cpte)
Vivaldi: Olimpiade (Cpte)
(CAPR) **10 470** Monteverdi—Arie e Duetti

SMALES, Kathleen (mez)
Offenbach: Christopher Columbus (Cpte)

SMALLENS, Alexander (cond)
see Orch
RCA SO

SMALLS, Alexander B. (ten)
Gershwin: Porgy and Bess (exc)

SMATI, Xavier (bass)
Bizet: Carmen (Cpte)

SMETÁČEK, Václav (cond)
see Prague SO

SMETANA THEATRE CHORUS
cond F. HAIDER
(SUPR) **11 0345-2** Edith Gruberová - Operatic Recital

SMID, Ernst Daniel (bar)
Schreker: Gezeichneten (Cpte)

SMIRNOV, Dmitri (ten)
(ARLE) **ARL23/5** Rimsky-Korsakov—Sadko
(CLUB) **CL99-031** Dmitri Smirnov—Opera & Song Recital
(MMOI) **CDMOIR422** Great Voices in Tchaikovsky
(NIMB) **NI7856** Legendary Tenors
(NIMB) **NI7865** Great Singers at the Mariinsky Theatre
(PEAR) **GEMMCDS9004/6(1)** Singers of Imperial Russia, Vol.3 (pt 1)
(PEAR) **GEMMCDS9004/6(2)** Singers of Imperial Russia, Vol.3 (pt 2)
(PEAR) **GEMMCD9106** Dmitri Smirnov
(PEAR) **GEMMCD9129** Great Tenors, Vol.2

SMIRNOV, V. (cond)
see Moscow All-Union RSO

SMIT, Henk (bass)
R. Strauss: Rosenkavalier (Cpte)

SMITH, Alma Jean (sop)
Gluck: Iphigénie en Tauride (Cpte)

SMITH, Amanda (vn)
(MCI) **MCCD090** Carreras & Friends sing Opera Arias & Songs

SMITH, Andrew (bar)
Gershwin: Porgy and Bess (Cpte)

SMITH, Angus (ten)
Britten: Paul Bunyan (exc)

SMITH, Brooks (pf)
(RCA) **09026 61778-2(35)** The Heifetz Collection, Vol. 35
(RCA) **09026 61778-2(40)** The Heifetz Collection, Vol. 40
(RCA) **09026 62706-3** Heifetz in Performance

SMITH, Carol (mez)
Mascagni: Cavalleria Rusticana (Cpte)
(CHAN) **CHAN8865** Rossini: Opera Arias

SMITH, Craig (cond)
see Piano Circus Band

SMITH, Daniel (bar)
(RCA) **09026 61509-2** A Salute to American Music

SMITH, Daniel (bn)
(ASV) **CDWHL2078** Bravo Bassoon

SMITH, David (bar)
Dittersdorf: Arcifanfano (Cpte)

SMITH, Donald George (ten)
Saint-Saëns: Samson et Dalila (exc)

SMITH, Jeffrey (treb)
Puccini: Tosca (Cpte)

SMITH, Jennifer (sop)
Handel: Amadigi di Gaula (Cpte), Ottone (Cpte)
Lully: Phaëton (Cpte)
Marais: Alcyone (Cpte)
Mondonville: Titon et l'Aurore (Cpte)
Monteverdi: Orfeo (Cpte)
Purcell: Fairy Queen, Z629 (Cpte), Indian Queen, Z630 (Cpte), King Arthur, Z628 (exc), Tempest, Z631 (Cpte)
Rameau: Castor et Pollux (Cpte), Naïs (Cpte), Platée (Cpte)
(COLL) **Coll3025-2** Puccini & Verdi Heroines
(DECC) **433 908-2DM2** Falla—Orchestral Music
(DG) **439 474-2GCL** Purcell—Opera & Choral Works
(ERAT) **4509-96371-2** Gardiner—The Purcell Collection

SMITH, Julian (cond)
see WNO Orch

SMITH, Kenneth (bass)
Berlioz: Troyens (Cpte)
(SONY) **SM22K46290(4)** Stravinsky—The Complete Edition (pt 4)

SMITH, Kenneth (fl)
(ASV) **CDDCA739** Summer Works
(ASV) **CDWHL2072** Walking in the Air - Favourites for Flute

SMITH, Kevin (alto)
Ligeti: Grand Macabre (Cpte)

SMITH, Malcolm (bass)
Prokofiev: War and Peace (Cpte)
Weill: Sieben Todsünden (Cpte)
(ACAN) **49 402** Giuseppe Taddei—Recital

SMITH, Martin (sngr)
Coward: Bitter Sweet (exc)

SMOLA, Emmerich (cond)
see Cologne RSO
South-West German RSO

SMOLENSKAYA, Elena (sop)
Rimsky-Korsakov: Tale of Tsar Saltan (Cpte)

SMOLYANINOVA, Zoya (sop)
Tchaikovsky: Maid of Orleans (Cpte)

SMUDA, Agnes (sngr)
Copland: Tender Land (Cpte)

SMYTHE, Russell (bar)
Britten: Rape of Lucretia (Cpte)
Donizetti: Assedio di Calais (Cpte), Don Pasquale (Cpte)
Menotti: Telephone (Cpte)
Rameau: Hippolyte et Aricie (Cpte)
(OPRA) **ORCH103** Italian Opera—1810-20
(OPRA) **ORCH104** A Hundred Years of Italian Opera: 1820-1830
(OPRA) **ORH102** A Hundred Years of Italian Opera
(OPRA) **ORR201** 19th Century Heroines-Yvonne Kenny

SNARSKI, Andréa (bar)
Probst: Maximilien Kolbe (Cpte)

SNASHALL, Mark (treb)
Herrmann: Wuthering Heights (Cpte)

SNELL, Howard (cond)
see Britannia Building Soc Band

SNELL, Martin (bar)
Vaughan Williams: Pilgrim's Progress (Cpte)

SNELL, Paige (sngr)
J. Moran: Manson Family (Cpte)

SNIPP, Peter (bar)
Rossini: Barbiere di Siviglia (Cpte)

SNOOK, Robert (sngr)
Gershwin: Porgy and Bess (Cpte)

SOAMES, René (ten)
Delius: Village Romeo and Juliet (Cpte)

SOAMES, Victoria (cl)
(CLRI) **CC0006** Clarinet Virtuosi of the Past—Hermstedt

SOBINOV, Leonid (ten)
(EMI) **CHS7 64860-2(2)** La Scala Edition - Vol.1, 1878-1914 (pt 2)
(MMOI) **CDMOIR422** Great Voices in Tchaikovsky
(NIMB) **NI7856** Legendary Tenors
(NIMB) **NI7865** Great Singers at the Mariinsky Theatre
(PEAR) **GEMMCDS9997/9(1)** Singers of Imperial Russia, Vol.1 (pt 1)
(PEAR) **GEMMCDS9997/9(2)** Singers of Imperial Russia, Vol.1 (pt 2)
(PEAR) **GEMMCD9129** Great Tenors, Vol.2

SOCIÉTÉ DES CONCERTS DU CONSERVATOIRE ORCH
cond F. POURCEL
(EMI) **CZS7 67869-2** J. Strauss II—Operetta Highlights

SÖDERBLOM, Ulf (cond)
see Finnish Nat Op Orch
Savonlinna Op Fest Orch

SODERO, Cesare (cond)
see NY Met Op Orch

SÖDERQVIST, Daga (sop)
(SCHW) **314672** Vienna State Opera Live, Vol.17
(SCHW) **314722** Vienna State Opera Live, Vol.22
(SCHW) **314742** Vienna State Opera Live, Vol.24

SÖDERSTRÖM, Elisabeth (sop)
Beethoven: Fidelio (Cpte)
Debussy: Pelléas et Mélisande (Cpte)
Gluck: Orfeo ed Euridice (Cpte)
Hindemith: Cardillac (Cpte)
Humperdinck: Hänsel und Gretel (Cpte)
Janáček: Jenufa (Cpte), Makropulos Affair (Cpte)
Monteverdi: Incoronazione di Poppea (Cpte)
Mozart: Nozze di Figaro (Cpte)
(BIS) **BIS-CD017** Söderström and Meyer sing Duets
(DECC) **421 852-2DH2** Janáček: Operatic & Chamber Works

SOETBER, Volker (spkr)
(SCHW) **314672** Vienna State Opera Live, Vol.17

SOFFEL, Doris (mez)
Flotow: Martha (Cpte)
J. Strauss II: Fledermaus (Cpte)
Lortzing: Wildschütz (Cpte)
Mozart: Zauberflöte (Cpte)
Wagner: Parsifal (Cpte)
Wolf: Corregidor (Cpte)
Zemlinsky: Florentinische Tragödie
(CPRI) **CAP21428** Virtuoso Arias - Soffel

SOFIA FESTIVAL ORCHESTRA
cond E. TCHAKAROV
Borodin: Prince Igor (Cpte)
Glinka: Life for the Tsar (Cpte)
Mussorgsky: Boris Godunov (Cpte)
Tchaikovsky: Eugene Onegin (Cpte), Queen of Spades (Cpte)

SOFIA NATIONAL OPERA CHORUS
cond A. CLUYTENS
(CFP) **CD-CFP9013** Duets from Famous Operas
cond R. RAICHEV
Mussorgsky: Khovanshchina (Cpte)
cond J. SEMKOW
(EMI) **CMS7 63386-2** Borodin—Prince Igor & Complete Solo Songs
cond E. TCHAKAROV
Borodin: Prince Igor (Cpte)
Glinka: Life for the Tsar (Cpte)
Mussorgsky: Boris Godunov (Cpte), Khovanshchina (Cpte)
Tchaikovsky: Eugene Onegin (Cpte)

SOFIA NATIONAL OPERA ORCHESTRA
cond R. RAICHEV
Mussorgsky: Khovanshchina (Cpte)
cond J. SEMKOW
(EMI) **CMS7 63386-2** Borodin—Prince Igor & Complete Solo Songs
cond E. TCHAKAROV
Mussorgsky: Khovanshchina (Cpte)

SOFIA PHILHARMONIC ORCHESTRA
cond Y. DARAS
Kalomiris: Mother's Ring (Cpte)
cond R. RAICHEV
(FORL) **FF060** Famous Russian Operatic Choruses
(FORL) **UCD16742** Bulgarian Voices, Vol. 2
cond G. ROBEV
(CAPR) **10 810** Mozart—Opera Highlights
cond E. TABAKOV
(CAPR) **10 704** Young Voices of the Opera-Michele Pertusi
cond E. TCHAKAROV
(FORL) **FF060** Famous Russian Operatic Choruses
(FORL) **UCD16743** Bulgarian Voices, Vol. 3

SOFIA RADIO CHORUS
cond H. VON KARAJAN
Mussorgsky: Boris Godunov (Cpte)
(DECC) **436 464-2DM** Ten Top Baritones & Basses

SOFIA RADIO SYMPHONY ORCHESTRA
cond V. KAZANDJIEV
(LASE) **15 612** Wagner - Magic Fire Music

SOFIA SYMPHONY ORCHESTRA
cond M. ANGELOV
(CAPR) **10 706** Young Voices of the Opera-Alexandrina Pendatchanska
cond V. STEFANOV
(LASE) **15 519** Verdi Overtures

SOIX, Charles (bass)
Offenbach: Contes d'Hoffmann (Cpte)

SOJER, Hans (ten)
R. Strauss: Ariadne auf Naxos (Cpte)
(HARM) **HMC90 1420** Weill—The Seven Deadly Sins; Songs

SOKOL, Michael (bar)
S. Wallace: Kabbalah (Cpte)

SOKOLOV, Andrei (ten)
Rimsky-Korsakov: Tsar's Bride (Cpte)
Tchaikovsky: Eugene Onegin (Cpte), Queen of Spades (Cpte)

SOLDH, Anita (sop)
Börtz: Bacchae (Cpte)

Mozart: Don Giovanni (Cpte), Idomeneo (Cpte), Zauberflöte (Cpte)
Wagner: Walküre (Cpte)

OLEY, Tommaso (ten)
Verdi: Traviata (Cpte)

) SOLISTI ITALIANI
(DENO) **CO-73335** Celebrated Baroque Pieces

) SOLISTI VENETI
cond C. SCIMONE
Albinoni: Nascimento dell'Aurora (Cpte)
Rossini: Armida (Cpte), Italiana in Algeri (Cpte), Zelmira (Cpte)
Vivaldi: Orlando Furioso (Cpte)
(ERAT) **2292-45186-2** Marilyn Horne sings Handel Opera Arias
(ERAT) **2292-45797-2** The Ultimate Opera Collection
(ERAT) **4509-91715-2** The Ultimate Opera Collection 2
(RCA) **09026 61580-2(8)** RCA/Met 100 Singers, 100 Years (pt 8)

OLODOVNIKOV, Vladimir (ten)
Mussorgsky: Boris Godunov (Cpte)
Tchaikovsky: Queen of Spades (exc)

OLOMAN, Donald (bar)
Lehár: Lustige Witwe (Cpte)

OLOVIANENKO, Anatoly (ten)
(MCI) **MCCD099** Opera's Greatest Arias

OLTESZ, Stefan (cond)
see Berlin RSO
Munich RO
Stuttgart RSO

OLTI, Sir Georg (cond)
see Bavarian St Orch
Chicago SO
La Scala Orch
LPO
LSO
National PO
RCA Italiana Op Orch
ROHO
Rome Op Chor
Rome Op Orch
Santa Cecilia Academy Chor
Santa Cecilia Academy Orch
Solti Orchestral Project
Vienna St Op Chor
VPO

HE) SOLTI ORCHESTRAL PROJECT, CARNEGIE HALL
cond G. SOLTI
(DECC) **444 458-2DH** Solti—Carnegie Hall Project

OLYOM-NAGY, Sándor (bar)
Wagner: Meistersinger (Cpte), Tannhäuser (Cpte)

OMARY, Johannes (cond)
see Amor Artis Orch

OMMER, Peter (cond)
see Munich RO

OMMERSCHUH, Gerda (sop)
Mozart: Nozze di Figaro (Cpte)
Wagner: Götterdämmerung (Cpte)
(ORFE) **C394101B** Great Mozart Singers Series, Vol. 1
(SCHW) **314722** Vienna State Opera Live, Vol.22

ONNENSCHEIN, Susanne (sop)
R. Strauss: Rosenkavalier (Cpte)

ONNENSCHMIDT, Rosina (sop)
(BAYE) **BR100083** Glanz des Rokoko

ONNLEITNER, Johann (hpd)
(HYPE) **CDA66070** Purcell: Songs

OOT, Fritz (ten)
(LYRC) **LCD146** Frida Leider sings Wagner
(PREI) **89069** Josef von Manowarda (1890-1942)
(PREI) **89301** The Art of Frida Leider

OPHER, Joseph (ten)
Dittersdorf: Arcifanfano (Cpte)

ORDELLO, Enzo (bar)
Puccini: Fanciulla del West (Cpte), Madama Butterfly (Cpte)

ORENSEN, Christian (ten)
Nielsen: Maskarade (Cpte)

ORMOVÁ, Naďa (sop)
Fibich: Bride of Messina (Cpte)
Smetana: Two Widows (Cpte)

OROZÁBAL, Pablo (cond)
see Madrid Concerts Orch

ORRELL, Lise (mez)
Wagner: Walküre (Cpte)
(FOYE) **15-CF2011** Wagner—Der Ring de Nibelungen

ORTOMME, Richard (va)
J. Moran: Manson Family (Cpte)

OSKIN, Gabrielle (sop)
(LOND) **436 393-2LM** Britten—The Little Sweep, etc

OTIN, Hans (bass)
Beethoven: Fidelio (Cpte)
Busoni: Doktor Faust (Cpte)
Lortzing: Wildschütz (Cpte)
Mozart: Così fan tutte (Cpte)
R. Strauss: Salome (Cpte)
Verdi: Aida (Cpte)

Wagner: Lohengrin (Cpte), Meistersinger (Cpte), Parsifal (Cpte), Tannhäuser (Cpte), Tristan und Isolde (Cpte)
(DECC) **440 410-2DM** Plácido Domingo
(EMI) **CMS5 65212-2** Wagner—Les introuvables du Ring
(PHIL) **434 420-2PM32(1)** Richard Wagner Edition (Pt.1)

SOUČEK, Jaroslav (bar)
Foerster: Eva (Cpte)
Janáček: Cunning Little Vixen (Cpte), Excursions of Mr Brouček (Cpte), Fate (Cpte), From the House of the Dead (Cpte)
(DECC) **421 852-2DH2** Janáček: Operatic & Chamber Works
(DECC) **430 375-2DH2** Janáček—Operatic and Orchestral Works

SOUDANT, Hubert (cond)
see Toscanini SO

SOUEZ, Ina (sop)
Mozart: Così fan tutte (Cpte), Don Giovanni (Cpte)
(DUTT) **CDLX7012** The Incomparable Heddle Nash
(EMI) **CDH5 65072-2** Glyndebourne Recorded - 1934-1994
(MMOI) **CDMOIR406** Mozart—Historical Recordings

SOUKUPOVÁ, Věra (mez)
Dvořák: Rusalka (exc)
Janáček: Jenufa (Cpte)
Martinů: Julietta (Cpte)
Smetana: Brandenburgers in Bohemia (Cpte), Libuše (Cpte)
Wagner: Rheingold (Cpte), Siegfried (Cpte)
(KOCH) **34036-2** A Pageant of Opera
(PHIL) **446 057-2PB14** Wagner—The Ring Cycle - Bayreuth Festival 1967

SOULACROIX, Gabriel (bar)
(SYMP) **SYMCD1089** Historic Baritones of the French School

SOULIÉ, François (spkr)
Fauré: Prométhée (Cpte)

SOUMAR, Jan (bass)
Smetana: Bartered Bride (Cpte)

ŠOUNOVÁ-BROUKOVÁ, Daniela (sop)
Dvořák: Jacobin (Cpte), Rusalka (Cpte)
Martinů: Alexandre Bis (Cpte)
Smetana: Two Widows (Cpte)

SOUŠEK, Zdeněk (ten)
(DECC) **430 375-2DH2** Janáček—Operatic and Orchestral Works

SOUSTROT, Marc (cond)
see Loire PO
Monte Carlo PO

SOUTH GERMAN RADIO CHORUS
cond G. ALBRECHT
Henze: Bassariden (Cpte)

SOUTHEND BOYS' CHOIR
cond R. HICKOX
(IMP) **PCD908** Great Opera Choruses
(IMP) **TCD1073** The Best of Richard Hickox
cond R. MUTI
Leoncavallo: Pagliacci (exc)
Mascagni: Cavalleria rusticana (Cpte)

SOUTHERN FESTIVAL ORCHESTRA
cond R. WHITE
(CHAN) **CHAN9110** Edwardian Echoes

SOUTHERN PHILHARMONIC ORCHESTRA
cond F. STIEDRY
Gluck: Orfeo ed Euridice (exc)

SOUTHGATE, William (cond)
see Chelsea Op Group Orch

SOUTH-WEST GERMAN RADIO SYMPHONY ORCHESTRA
cond O. ACKERMANN
(ACAN) **43 268** Peter Anders sings German Opera Arias
cond K. ARP
(PIER) **PV730050** Overtures
cond K. DONATH
(SCHW) **314018** Virtuoso Operatic Arias for Soprano and Clarinet
cond M. GIELEN
Wagner: Tristan und Isolde (exc)
(INTE) **INT860 912** Beethoven—Orchestral Works
cond E. SMOLA
(DG) **431 110-2GB** Great Voices - Fritz Wunderlich
(DG) **435 145-2GX5(1)** Fritz Wunderlich—Opera Arias, Lieder, etc (part 1)

SOUZAY, Gérard (bar)
Debussy: Pelléas et Mélisande (Cpte)
Rameau: Castor et Pollux (Cpte)
(DECC) **440 419-2DM** Gérard Souzay

SOVIERO, Diana (sop)
(TELA) **CD80407** Divine Sopranos

SOVIET CINEMA ORCHESTRA
cond E. KHACHATURIAN
Karetnikov: Till Eulenspiegel (Cpte)
(CDM) **LDC288 005/6** Bass Arias from Russian Opera

SOVILLA, Floriana (sop)
Donizetti: Imelda (Cpte)
(NUOV) **6905** Donizetti—Great Love Duets

SOYER, Roger (bass)
Berlioz: Benvenuto Cellini (Cpte), Troyens (Cpte)
Bizet: Pêcheurs de Perles (Cpte)
Debussy: Pelléas et Mélisande (Cpte)
Delibes: Lakmé (Cpte)
Donizetti: Maria Stuarda (Cpte)
M-A. Charpentier: David et Jonathas (Cpte)
Massenet: Werther (Cpte)
Offenbach: Contes d'Hoffmann (exc)
Rameau: Dardanus (Cpte)
(CFP) **CD-CFP4602** Favourite Opera
(EMIL) **CDZ7 67015-2** Mozart—Opera Arias

SPACAGNA, Maria (sop)
Mascagni: Lodoletta (Cpte)

ŠPAČEK, Jozef (bass)
Puccini: Madama Butterfly (Cpte), Tosca (Cpte)
Verdi: Rigoletto (Cpte), Traviata (Cpte)

SPADA, Pietro (pf)
(ASV) **CDDCA921** Catalani—Complete Piano Music

SPAGLI, Renato (bar)
Mascagni: Piccolo Marat (Cpte)

SPAGNOLI, Pietro (bar)
Donizetti: Elisir d'amore (Cpte)
Handel: Giulio Cesare (Cpte)
Leoncavallo: Bohème (Cpte)
Mozart: Don Giovanni (Cpte)
Piccinni: Cecchina (Cpte)
Puccini: Fanciulla del West (Cpte)
Rossini: Signor Bruschino (Cpte), Tancredi (Cpte)
Verdi: Giovanna d'Arco (Cpte)

SPANELLYS, Georgette (sop)
Bizet: Carmen (exc)

SPANI, Hina (sop)
(CLUB) **CL99-509/10** Hina Spani (1896-1969)
(CONI) **CDHD235** The Puccini Album
(EMI) **CHS7 64864-2(2)** La Scala Edition - Vol.2, 1915-46 (pt 2)
(EMI) **CMS7 64008-2(1)** Wagner Singing on Record (pt 1)
(MMOI) **CDMOIR408** Great Sopranos
(MMOI) **CDMOIR412** Great Voices of the Century Sing Puccini
(PEAR) **GEMMCDS9074(2)** Giovanni Zenatello, Vol.2 (pt 2)
(PREI) **89037** Hina Spani (1896-1969)
(PREI) **89038** Giovanni Zenatello (1876-1949)

SPANISH LYRIC ORCHESTRA
cond F. MORENO TORROBA
Barbieri: Barberillo de Lavapiès (Cpte)
Usandizaga: Golondrinas (Cpte)

SPANISH NATIONAL ORCHESTRA
cond R. FRÜHBECK DE BURGOS
(EMI) **CDM5 65579-2** Victoria de los Angeles
(EMI) **CDM7 64359-2** Gala de España
(EMI) **CMS7 64467-2** Classical Music of Spain, Vol.2

SPANJAARD, Ed (cond)
see Hague PO

SPATAFORA, Manuel (bar)
Puccini: Bohème (Cpte)
(EMI) **CDM7 69543-2** Maria Callas and Giuseppe Di Stefano - Duets

SPATARO, Tomaso (ten)
Verdi: Falstaff (Cpte)

SPÄTH, Christoph (ten)
Mozart: Nozze di Figaro (Cpte)
Spohr: Faust (Cpte)
Wolf: Manuel Venegas

SPÄTHE, Frank-Peter (bar)
Beethoven: Fidelio (Cpte)

SPEISER, Elisabeth (sop)
Gluck: Orfeo ed Euridice (Cpte)

SPENCE, Patricia (mez)
Handel: Ottone (Cpte)
Meyerbeer: Africaine (Cpte)
Verdi: Traviata (exc)
(OPRA) **ORCH104** A Hundred Years of Italian Opera: 1820-1830

SPERRY, Paul (ten)
Maderna: Satyricon (Cpte)

SPERTI, Cesare Masini (ten)
Mascagni: Piccolo Marat (Cpte)

SPIESS, Ludovic (ten)
Mussorgsky: Boris Godunov (Cpte)

(DIE) SPILAR SCHRAMMELN
cond R. STOLZ
(DG) **435 145-2GX5(2)** Fritz Wunderlich—Opera Arias, Lieder, etc, (part 2)

SPINA, Mario (ten)
Leoncavallo: Pagliacci (Cpte)

SPINA, Pietro (sngr)
Cherubini: Lodoïska (Cpte)

SPINK, Charlotte (sop)
MacMillan: Búsqueda (Cpte)

SPISAR, Oldřich (ten)
Hába: Mother (Cpte)

SPIVAKOV, Vladimir (cond)
see Moscow Virtuosi

SPIVAKOV, Vladimir (vn)
(RCA) **RD60861** It ain't necessarily so & other violin miniatures

SPLETTER, Carla (sop)
Mozart: Zauberflöte (Cpte)

SPOLETO FESTIVAL ORCHESTRA
cond C. BADEA
Barber: Antony and Cleopatra (Cpte)

SPORSÉN, Torgny (bass)
(DG) **429 984-2GH** Russian Orchestral Works
(DG) **429 984-5GH** Russian Orchestral Works

SPRINGER, Ingeborg (mez)
Wagner: Parsifal (Cpte), Rienzi (Cpte)

SPRINGFELS, Mary (cond)
see Newberry Consort

SPRINGFELS, Mary (va da gamba)
(HARM) **HMU90 7035** Sweeter than Roses - Purcell Songs

SPRINZENA, Nathaniel (ten)
Verdi: Trovatore (Cpte)

SPURR, Phyllis (pf)
(DECC) **433 473-2DM** Ferrier Edition - Volume 6

SQUIRES, Shelagh (mez)
Offenbach: Orphée aux enfers (exc)
Verdi: Otello (Cpte), Traviata (Cpte)
Wagner: Götterdämmerung (Cpte), Rheingold (Cpte), Walküre (Cpte)

SRAMEK, Alfred (bar)
Beethoven: Fidelio (Cpte)
Mozart: Don Giovanni (Cpte)
Ponchielli: Gioconda (Cpte)
R. Strauss: Ariadne auf Naxos (Cpte), Rosenkavalier (Cpte)

ST ANTHONY SINGERS
cond A. LEWIS
Purcell: Dido (Cpte), King Arthur, Z628 (Cpte)
(DECC) **436 462-2DM** Ten Top Mezzos
(DECC) **443 393-2DWO** The World of Henry Purcell
cond C. MACKERRAS
Purcell: Indian Queen, Z630 (exc)

ST CLEMENT DANES SCHOOL CHOIR
cond JAMES LEVINE
Puccini: Tosca (Cpte)
cond K. NAGANO
Puccini: Bohème (Cpte)

ST HEDWIG'S CATHEDRAL CHOIR, BERLIN
cond F. FRICSAY
(DG) **445 400-2GDO10** Ferenc Fricsay - A Portrait
cond R. KEMPE
Wagner: Meistersinger (exc)
(TEST) **SBT1035** Rudolf Kempe conducts Wagner
cond C. PERICK
Schmidt: Notre Dame (Cpte)

ST HILL, Krister (ten)
Krenek: Jonny spielt auf (Cpte)

ST JAMES'S BAROQUE PLAYERS
cond I. BOLTON
Purcell: Dido (Cpte)

ST JAMES'S SINGERS
cond I. BOLTON
Purcell: Dido (Cpte)

ST LOUIS SYMPHONY ORCHESTRA
cond L. SLATKIN
Bizet: Carmen Suites (exc)
(RCA) **RD87716** Classic Marches
(TELA) **CD80072** Russian Orchestral Works

ST LUKE'S BAROQUE ORCHESTRA
cond R. PALMER
Telemann: Pimpinone (Cpte)

ST LUKE'S ORCHESTRA
cond R. CRAFT
Stravinsky: Rake's Progress (Cpte)
(MUSM) **67078-2** Stravinsky The Composer - Volume 1
(MUSM) **67110-2** Stravinsky—The Composer, Volume V
cond W.H. CURRY
A. Davis: X (Cpte)
cond J. NELSON
(SONY) **SK46672** Baroque Duets
cond R. NORRINGTON
(EMI) **CDC7 54643-2** Rossini—Bicentenary Gala Concert
(EMI) **LDB491007-1 (EMI)** Rossini Bicentennial Birthday Gala
cond A. PREVIN
(DG) **437 787-2GH** Honey and Rue-Kathleen Battle
(SONY) **SLV48361(SONY)** A Carnegie Hall Christmas
cond J. RUDEL
Weill: Lost in the Stars (Cpte)

ST PAUL'S CATHEDRAL CHOIR
cond C. GROVES
Vaughan Williams: Hugh the Drover (Cpte)

ST PETER AD VINCULA CHOIR (TOWER OF LONDON)
cond J.T. WILLIAMS
(CHAN) **CHAN6560** Jubilate - Music for the Kings & Queens of England

ST PETERSBURG CHAMBER CHOIR
cond S. BYCHKOV
Tchaikovsky: Eugene Onegin (Cpte)

ST PETERSBURG PHILHARMONIC ORCHESTRA
cond Y. TEMIRKANOV
(RCA) **09026 62710-2** Rachmaninov—Orchestral Works

ST PETERSBURG STATE SYMPHONY ORCHESTRA
cond A. ANICHANOV
(MARC) **8 223675** Glière—Orchestral Works

STAATSKAPELLE DRESDEN
Handel: Giulio Cesare (Cpte)
cond K. BÖHM
Beethoven: Fidelio (Cpte)
Mozart: Clemenza di Tito (Cpte), Entführung (Cpte), Idomeneo (Cpte), Schauspieldirektor (Cpte)
R. Strauss: Elektra (Cpte)
(DG) **413 145-2GW2** Beethoven—Orchestral Works
(DG) **427 194-2GR** Beethoven—Symphony No 3 & Overtures
(DG) **437 677-2GDO2** Irmgard Seefried - Opera Recital
(DG) **437 928-2GX2** Beethoven—Symphonies & Overtures
cond F. BUSCH
(TELD) **4509-95038-6(TELD)** The Art of Conducting—Great Conductors of the Past
cond COLIN DAVIS
Humperdinck: Hänsel und Gretel (exc)
Mozart: Zauberflöte (Cpte)
Weber: Freischütz (exc)
(PHIL) **446 067-2PH6** Beethoven—Complete Symphonies
cond B. HAITINK
Beethoven: Fidelio (exc)
R. Strauss: Rosenkavalier (Cpte)
(EMI) **CDM5 65578-2** Kiri Te Kanawa
cond H. HOLLREISER
Wagner: Rienzi (Cpte)
cond JAMES LEVINE
Tchaikovsky: Eugene Onegin (Cpte)
(DG) **431 601-2GCE10** Tchaikovsky Compact Edition
(DG) **447 364-2GDB2** Great Opera Overtures
cond M. JANOWSKI
Wagner: Götterdämmerung (Cpte), Rheingold (Cpte), Siegfried (Cpte), Walküre (Cpte)
(EMI) **CDM7 69256-2** L'incomparable Jessye Norman
(EURO) **GD69003** Wagner—Der Ring des Nibelungen
(RCA) **09026 61440-2** Opera's Greatest Moments
(RCA) **09026 62674-2** Fortissimo!
cond H. VON KARAJAN
Wagner: Meistersinger (Cpte)
(CFP) **CD-CFP4656** Herbert von Karajan conducts Opera
cond R. KEMPE
R. Strauss: Ariadne auf Naxos (Cpte)
(EMI) **CMS7 64346-2** R. Strauss—Orchestral Works, Vol.2
(EMI) **CZS5 68110-2** R. Strauss—Orchestral Works
cond C. KLEIBER
Wagner: Tristan und Isolde (Cpte)
Weber: Freischütz (Cpte)
cond G. KUHN
(CAPR) **10 052** Weber: Overtures
cond S. OZAWA
R. Strauss: Salome (Cpte)
cond H. SCHMIDT-ISSERSTEDT
Mozart: Idomeneo (Cpte)
cond G. SINOPOLI
(DG) **439 865-2GH** Cheryl Studer sings Strauss and Wagner
cond O. SUITNER
(BELA) **461 001-2** Popular Overtures
cond J. TATE
Offenbach: Contes d'Hoffmann (Cpte)
cond S. VARVISO
(PHIL) **442 550-2PM2** Verdi—Complete Ballet Music &c
cond H. VONK
(CAPR) **10 070** Mozart: Overtures
(CAPR) **10 809** Mozart—Overtures, Dances & Marches
(CAPR) **10 810** Mozart—Opera Highlights
(LASE) **15 504** Sabre Dance
(LASE) **15 610** Tchaikovsky - Favourite Waltzes
(LASE) **15 622** Famous Classical Overtures

STABILE, Leonarda (sop)
Verdi: Rigoletto (exc)

STABILE, Mariano (bar)
Rossini: Turco in Italia (Cpte)
Verdi: Falstaff (Cpte)
(EMI) **CHS7 64864-2(2)** La Scala Edition - Vol.2, 1915-46 (pt 2)
(PEAR) **GEMMCDS9926(1)** Covent Garden on Record—Vol.4 (pt 1)
(PREI) **89995** Famous Italian Baritones

STADE, Frederica Von (mez)
Debussy: Pelléas et Mélisande (Cpte)
Humperdinck: Hänsel und Gretel (Cpte)
Massenet: Cendrillon (Cpte), Chérubin (Cpte), Werther (Cpte)
Mozart: Clemenza di Tito (Cpte), Così fan tutte (Cpte), Nozze di Figaro (exc)
R. Strauss: Rosenkavalier (Cpte)
Rameau: Dardanus (Cpte)
Rossini: Cenerentola (Cpte), Otello (Cpte)
Verdi: Don Carlo (Cpte), Traviata (Cpte)
(DECC) **433 822-2DH** Essential Opera
(DECC) **436 284-2DH** A Song of Thanksgiving
(DECC) **436 462-2DM** Ten Top Mezzos
(DECC) **436 472-2DM** Great Opera Arias
(DG) **072 428-1GH2(DG)** The Metropolitan Opera Gala
(EMI) **CDC7 54643-2** Rossini—Bicentenary Gala Concert
(EMI) **LDB491007-1 (EMI)** Rossini Bicentennial Birthday Gala
(ERAT) **2292-45797-2** The Ultimate Opera Collection
(ERAT) **4509-98504-2** Recital—Frederica Von Stade
(PHIL) **420 084-2PH** Frederica von Stade sings Haydn, Mozart & Rossini Arias
(PHIL) **442 600-2PH** The Great Carreras
(RCA) **09026 61509-2** A Salute to American Music
(SONY) **SK48235** A Carnegie Hall Christmas Concert
(SONY) **SK52565** New Year's Eve Concert 1992
(SONY) **SLV48361(SONY)** A Carnegie Hall Christmas
(SONY) **SLV53488(SONY)** Dvořák in Prague - A Celebration

STADER, Maria (sop)
Gluck: Orfeo ed Euridice (Cpte)
Mozart: Don Giovanni (Cpte), Entführung (Cpte), Nozze di Figaro (Cpte), Zauberflöte (Cpte)

STADLMAIR, Hans (cond)
see Munich CO

STAEGEMANN, Waldemar (ten)
(EMI) **CDH7 69787-2** Richard Tauber sings Operetta Arias
(PEAR) **GEMMCD9409** Lotte Lehmann—Vol.1

STAEMPFLI, Jakob (bass)
Monteverdi: Orfeo (Cpte)

STAEMPFLI, Wally (sop)
Monteverdi: Orfeo (Cpte)

STAERN, Camilla (contr)
Börtz: Bacchae (Cpte)

STAFFORD, Ashley (alto)
Purcell: Fairy Queen, Z629 (Cpte), Indian Queen, Z630 (Cpte), King Arthur, Z628 (exc)
(ERAT) **4509-96371-2** Gardiner—The Purcell Collection

(LA) STAGIONE
cond M. SCHNEIDER
Gluck: Paride ed Elena (Cpte)
Handel: Rodelinda (Cpte)
Hasse: Piramo e Tisbe (Cpte)
Telemann: Don Quichotte (Cpte), Pimpinone (Cpte)

(LA) STAGIONE VOCAL ENSEMBLE
cond M. SCHNEIDER
Gluck: Paride ed Elena (Cpte)

STAHLMAN, Sylvia (sop)
(DECC) **440 417-2DM** Carlo Bergonzi

STAIER, Andreas (hpd)
(DHM) **05472 77318-2** Delight in Disorder—English Consort of Two Parts, 1640-1680

STAMM, Harald (bass)
Hindemith: Cardillac (Cpte), Mathis der Maler (Cpte), Nusch-Nuschi (Cpte)
Offenbach: Contes d'Hoffmann (Cpte)
Schoeck: Massimilla Doni (Cpte)
Schreker: Schatzgräber (Cpte)
Schumann: Genoveva (Cpte)

STANCHEV, Dimiter (bass)
Mussorgsky: Khovanshchina (Cpte)
Tchaikovsky: Eugene Onegin (Cpte)

STANCHIEV, Nikola (ten)
(FORL) **UCD16651** Boris Christoff - Recital

STANDAGE, Simon (vn)
(PHIL) **446 081-2PH** The Echoing Air—The Music of Henry Purcell

STANDAGE, Simon (vn/dir)
(CHAN) **CHAN0540** J.C.Bach—Orchestral Works

STANĚK, Tomás (treb)
Krása: Brundibár (Cpte)

STANISLAS ENSEMBLE
(GALL) **CD-676** Stanislas Ensemble - 20th Cent Chamber Works

STANKOVSKY, Robert (cond)
see Bratislava RSO
Košice St PO

STAPF, Silke (sop)
Telemann: Don Quichotte (Cpte)

STAPLETON, Robin (cond)
see National PO
National SO
Philh
ROH Male Chor
RPO

STAPP, Olivia (mez)
(OPUS) **9356 2047** Romantic Operatic Duets

STARKER, János (vc)
(EMI) **CZS5 68485-2** Les Introuvables de János Starker

STARTZ, Drago (ten)
(BELA) **450 117-2** Great Opera Chorus II

STASIO, Anna di (mez)
Alfano: Risurrezione (Cpte)

Boito: Nerone (Cpte)
Donizetti: Lucia di Lammermoor (exc)
Giordano: Andrea Chénier (Cpte)
Mascagni: Cavalleria Rusticana (Cpte)
Puccini: Madama Butterfly (Cpte)
Verdi: Lombardi (Cpte), Otello (Cpte), Rigoletto (Cpte), Trovatore (Cpte)
(BUTT) **BMCD015** Pavarotti Collection - Duets and Scenes
(CBS) **CD79312** Puccini: Il Trittico
(CFP) **CD-CFP4582** Flowers in Music
(DECC) **411 665-2DM3** Puccini: Il trittico
(DECC) **440 405-2DM** Elena Souliotis
(MEMO) **HR4277/8** Mirella Freni—Public Performances 1963-1970

STATNIK, Yuri (sngr)
Rimsky-Korsakov: Mlada (Cpte)

STAUDE, Hans-Jörg (bass)
R. Strauss: Rosenkavalier (Cpte)

ŠTÁVA, Aleš (bass)
Dvořák: Kate and the Devil (Cpte)

STAVAD, Hanne (contr)
(DANI) **DCD8143** Hanne Stavad - Song Recital

STAVROVSKAYA, Ludmilla (mez)
(DANT) **LYS013/5** Tchaikovsky—The Queen of Spades

STEAR, Ronald (bass)
Sullivan: Gondoliers (Cpte)

STEBER, Eleanor (sop)
Barber: Vanessa (Cpte)
Beethoven: Fidelio (Cpte)
Berlioz: Troyens (Cpte)
Dittersdorf: Arcifanfano (Cpte)
Wagner: Lohengrin (Cpte)
(EMI) **CHS7 69741-2(1)** Record of Singing, Vol.4—Anglo-American School (pt 1)
(RCA) **09026 61580-2(5)** RCA/Met 100 Singers, 100 Years (pt 5)
(RCA) **09026 62689-2** The Voices of Living Stereo, Volume 1
(RCA) **74321 24284-2** Opera's Greatest Heroines
(SONY) **SM3K47211** Mozart Legendary Interpretations—Opera and Concert Arias
(VAI) **VAIA1012** Eleanor Sterber sings R. Strauss
(VAI) **VAIA1017** Leonard Warren—Early Recordings
(VAI) **VAIA1072** Eleanor Steber Collection, Volume 1
(VAI) **VAI69102** Eleanor Steber in Opera and Song Vol 1
(VAI) **VAI69110** Leonard Warren in Opera and Song Vol 2
(VAI) **VAI69112** Eleanor Steber in Opera and Song Vol 2

STEBLIANKO, Alexei (ten)
Borodin: Prince Igor (Cpte)
Mussorgsky: Boris Godunov (Cpte), Khovanshchina (Cpte)

STEEGER, Gerhard (cond)
see Berlin Deutsche Op Orch
Berlin St Op Orch
Berlin Staatskapelle

STEELE-PERKINS, Crispian (tpt)
(HYPE) **CDA66255** Italian Baroque Trumpet Music
(LDR) **LDRCD1006** Well-Tempered Trumpet
(PHIL) **446 081-2PH** The Echoing Air—The Music of Henry Purcell

STEFANO, Donato Di (bar)
Verdi: Traviata (exc)

STEFANO, Giuseppe di (ten)
Bellini: Puritani (Cpte)
Donizetti: Elisir d'amore (Cpte), Lucia di Lammermoor (Cpte)
Lehár: Land des Lächelns (exc)
Leoncavallo: Pagliacci (Cpte)
Mascagni: Cavalleria Rusticana (Cpte)
Puccini: Bohème (Cpte), Manon Lescaut (Cpte), Tosca (Cpte)
Verdi: Ballo in maschera (Cpte), Rigoletto (Cpte), Traviata (Cpte), Trovatore (Cpte)
(BELA) **450 005-2** Famous Tenor Arias
(BELA) **450 006-2** Famous Opera Duets
(BELA) **450 007-2** Puccini Favourites
(DECC) **417 686-2DC** Puccini—Operatic Arias
(DECC) **433 065-2DWO** Your Hundred Best Opera Tunes Volume II
(DECC) **433 066-2DWO** Your Hundred Best Opera Tunes III
(DECC) **433 623-2DSP** Famous Tenor Arias
(DECC) **433 636-2DSP** Puccini—Famous Arias
(DECC) **433 865-2DWO** The World of Puccini
(DECC) **436 314-2DA** Great Tenor Arias
(DECC) **436 463-2DM** Ten Top Tenors
(DECC) **440 403-2DM** Giuseppe di Stefano
(DECC) **443 379-2DM** Ten Top Tenors 2
(EMI) **CDC5 55216-2** Maria Callas - La Divina 3
(EMI) **CDC7 54016-2** Tenorissimo!
(EMI) **CDM7 63105-2** Giuseppe di Stefano sings Opera Arias & Songs
(EMI) **CDM7 69543-2** Maria Callas and Giuseppe Di Stefano - Duets
(EMI) **CHS7 69741-2(7)** Record of Singing, Vol.4—Italian School
(EMI) **CMS7 63244-2** The Art of Maria Callas
(FONI) **CDMR5003** Martini & Rossi Festival, Volume 3
(MEMO) **HR4235/6** Great Voices-Renata Tebaldi
(MEMO) **HR4372/3** Great Voices Giuseppe Di Stefano
(MEMO) **HR4396/7** Great Voices—Leontyne Price
(RCA) **09026 61580-2(6)** RCA/Met 100 Singers, 100 Years (pt 6)
(SCHW) **312732** Lehár—Der Zarewitsch (excs)

STEFANONI, Marco (bass)
Alfano: Risurrezione (Cpte)
Verdi: Don Carlo (Cpte)

STEFANOV, Vassil (cond)
see Bulgarian RSO
Plovdiv PO
Sofia SO

STEFFAN, Katherine (mez)
(CHAN) **CHAN8865** Rossini: Opera Arias

STEFFEK, Hanny (sop)
Gluck: Orfeo ed Euridice (Cpte)
Lehár: Lustige Witwe (Cpte)
Mozart: Così fan tutte (Cpte), Zauberflöte (Cpte)

STEFFEK, Ronald (bass)
R. Strauss: Rosenkavalier (Cpte)

STEFFENSEN, Ingeborg (mez)
Nielsen: Maskarade (Cpte)

STEGER, Ingrid (mez)
Wagner: Walküre (Cpte)
(DG) **435 211-2GX15** Wagner—Der Ring des Nibelungen

STEHLE, Adelina (sop)
(MEMO) **HR4408/9(1)** Singers in Genoa, Vol.1 (disc 1)
(SYMP) **SYMCD1113** The Harold Wayne Collection, Vol.13

STEIERMARK MILITARY BAND cond R. BODINGBAUER
(KOCH) **321 759** Ziehrer—Militärmusik Steiermark

STEIGER, Anna (sop)
Mozart: Così fan tutte (Cpte)
(ASV) **CDDCA758** Falla, Milhaud & Stravinsky—Operas

STEIN, Andreas (alto)
Mozart: Zauberflöte (Cpte)

STEIN, Horst (cond)
see Berlin RSO
Berlin SO
Munich RO
VPO

STEINBACH, Heribert (ten)
Pfitzner: Palestrina (Cpte)
Wagner: Meistersinger (Cpte), Tristan und Isolde (Cpte)
(PHIL) **434 420-2PM32(1)** Richard Wagner Edition (Pt.1)

STEINBEISSER, Irene (sngr)
J. Strauss II: Fledermaus (Cpte)

STEINBERG, Lev (cond)
see Bolshoi Th Orch

STEINBERG, Pinchas (cond)
see Austrian RSO
Cologne RSO
Munich RO
Munich RSO

STEINBERG, William (cond)
see orch
Pittsburgh SO

STEINER, Elisabeth (mez)
J. Strauss II: Fledermaus (exc)

STEINEROVÁ, Marie (contr)
Janáček: Fate (Cpte)

STEINGRUBER, Ilona (sop)
R. Strauss: Elektra (Cpte)
(CAMB) **CD-1032** From the Operas of Erich Wolfgang Korngold
(DG) **437 677-2GDO2** Irmgard Seefried - Opera Recital
(VAI) **VAIA1012** Eleanor Sterber sings R. Strauss

STEINKOPF, Hanns (cond)
see Berlin Deutsche Op Orch
Berlin RSO

STEINMANN, Max (cond)
see LSO

STEINMASSL, Hermine (sop)
Mozart: Zauberflöte (Cpte)

STEINSKY, Eva (sop)
Gazzaniga: Don Giovanni (Cpte)

STEINSKY, Ulrike (sop)
J. Strauss II: Fledermaus (Cpte)
Mozart: Zauberflöte (Cpte)

STELLA, Antonietta (sop)
Donizetti: Linda di Chamounix (Cpte)
Giordano: Andrea Chénier (Cpte)
Puccini: Bohème (Cpte)
Verdi: Don Carlo (Cpte), Trovatore (Cpte)
(CFP) **CD-CFP4569** Puccini: Arias
(CFP) **CD-CFP9013** Duets from Famous Operas
(MEMO) **HR4400/1** Great Voices - Ettore Bastianini

STELLMAN, Maxine (mez)
Verdi: Traviata (Cpte), Trovatore (Cpte)
Wagner: Tannhäuser (Cpte)

STEMME, Nina (sop)
Lidholm: Dream Play (Cpte)

STENDORO, Giorgio (bar)
Puccini: Madama Butterfly (Cpte)

STENE, Randi (contr)
R. Strauss: Salome (Cpte)
(DG) **435 866-2GH** Kathleen Battle sings Italian Opera Arias
(DG) **437 523-2GH** Grieg—Dramatic Works with Orchestra
(DG) **437 842-2GH6** Grieg—Complete Music with Orchestra
(DG) **435 866-5CH** Kathleen Battle sings Italian Opera Arias
(VIRG) **VC5 45051-2** Grieg—Choral Works

STENNING, Elsa (sop)
Wagner: Walküre (exc)

STENSVOLD, Terje (bass)
Braein: Anne Pedersdotter (Cpte)

STENZ, Markus (cond)
see Parnassus Orch

STEPANOVA, Elena (sop)
(ARLE) **ARL23/5** Rimsky-Korsakov—Sadko

STEPHEN, Pamela Helen (mez)
Mozart: Nozze di Figaro (Cpte)
Purcell: Dido (Cpte)
(CHAN) **CHAN9392** Vaughan Williams—Riders to the Sea etc.

STEPHENSON, Elinor (sngr)
Bernstein: West Side Story (Cpte)

STEPHENSON, Emma (pf/kybd)
Machover: Valis (Cpte)

STĘPIEŃ, Jozef (ten)
Beethoven: Fidelio (Cpte)

STEPP, Christoph (cond)
see Bamberg SO

STERMAN, Andrew (reeds)
S. Wallace: Kabbalah (Cpte)

STERMAN, Andrew (sop sax/bass cl)
Glass: Hydrogen Jukebox (Cpte)

STERN, Eric (cond)
see LSO
orch

STERN, Eric (pf)
(NONE) **7559-79345-2** I Wish It So - Dawn Upshaw

STERN, Isaac (vn)
(SONY) **SK45816** Humoresque—Favourite Violin Encores

STERN, Maurice (ten)
R. Ward: Crucible (Cpte)

STERNBERG, Harold (bass)
Verdi: Macbeth (Cpte)

STERNECK, Berthold (bass)
(SCHW) **314622** Vienna State Opera Live, Vol.12
(SCHW) **314672** Vienna State Opera Live, Vol.17

STEVENS, Garry (sngr)
Bernstein: West Side Story (Cpte)

STEVENS, Pauline (mez)
(EMI) **CDM7 64730-2** Vaughan Williams—Riders to the Sea; Epithalamion, etc

STEVENS, Risë (mez)
Bizet: Carmen (Cpte)
Mozart: Nozze di Figaro (Cpte)
(RCA) **09026 61580-2(5)** RCA/Met 100 Singers, 100 Years (pt 5)
(RCA) **09026 62689-2** The Voices of Living Stereo, Volume 1
(VAI) **VAI69106** Risë Stevens in Opera and Song
(VAI) **VAI69112** Eleanor Steber in Opera and Song Vol 2

STEVENS, Ronald (ten)
Bellini: Norma (Cpte)
Lehár: Lustige Witwe (Cpte)
(DECC) **071 149-1DH (DECC)** The Essential Sutherland

STEVENSON, Juliet (spkr)
MacMillan: Búsqueda (Cpte)

STEWART, Maeretha (sop)
Gershwin: Porgy and Bess (exc)

STEWART, Sylvie (mez)
Messager: Fortunio (Cpte)

STEWART, Thomas (bar)
Orff: Kluge (Cpte)
Wagner: Fliegende Holländer (Cpte), Götterdämmerung (Cpte), Parsifal (Cpte), Siegfried (Cpte), Walküre (Cpte)
(DG) **429 168-2GR** Wagner: Excerpts from Der Ring
(DG) **435 211-2GX15** Wagner—Der Ring des Nibelungen
(DG) **439 423-2GCL** Wagner—Der Ring des Nibelungen (highlights)
(PHIL) **446 057-2PB14** Wagner—The Ring Cycle - Bayreuth Festival 1967
(RCA) **74321 24790-2** Carl Orff 100 Years Edition

STEYER, Arlette (sop)
Lully: Atys (Cpte)

(EMI) **CDM7 69596-2** The Movies go to the Opera
(EMI) **CZS5 68559-2** Italian Opera Choruses
(ERAT) **2292-45797-2** The Ultimate Opera Collection
(ERAT) **2292-45925-2** Berlioz—Orchestral Works
(ERAT) **4509-91715-2** The Ultimate Opera Collection 2
(ERAT) **4509-96971-2** Marcel Landowski—Edition
(ERAT) **4509-98499-2** Recital—Montserrat Caballé
(ERAT) **4509-98504-2** Recital—Frederica Von Stade
(RCA) **09026 61580-2(8)** RCA/Met 100 Singers, 100 Years (pt 8)

STRASBOURG UNIVERSITY MUSIC DEPARTMENT CHORUS
cond D. DEBART
Xenakis: Orestia (Cpte)

STRATAS, Teresa (sop)
Berg: Lulu (Cpte)
Corigliano: Ghosts of Versailles (Cpte)
Lehár: Lustige Witwe (exc)
Leoncavallo: Pagliacci (exc)
Mozart: Così fan tutte (Cpte)
R. Strauss: Salome (Cpte)
Smetana: Bartered Bride (Cpte)
Verdi: Traviata (Cpte)
(DG) **435 712-2GX2** Lehár—The Merry Widow. Suppé—Overtures

STRATTA, Ettore (cond)
see ECO
London Studio SO

STRAUSS, Richard (cond)
see Bavarian St Orch
Berlin St Op Orch
BPO
Tivoli Augmented Orch
Vienna St Op Orch
VPO

STRAUSS-SMITH, Lloyd (ten)
Delius: Village Romeo and Juliet (Cpte)

STRAVINSKY, Igor (cond)
see CBC SO
Columbia Chbr Ens
Columbia SO
FNO
orch
RPO
Washington Op Soc Orch

STREETON, Jane (sop)
(HYPE) **CDA66608** Dibdin—Three Operas

STREICH, Rita (sop)
Gluck: Orfeo ed Euridice (Cpte)
J. Strauss II: Fledermaus (Cpte)
Millöcker: Bettelstudent (Cpte)
Mozart: Don Giovanni (Cpte), Entführung (Cpte), Nozze di Figaro (Cpte), Zauberflöte (Cpte)
R. Strauss: Ariadne auf Naxos (Cpte), Daphne (Cpte)
Wagner: Siegfried (Cpte)
Weber: Freischütz (Cpte)
(DG) **431 875-2GDO** Rita Streich sings Mozart Arias
(DG) **435 748-2GDO2** Arias and Waltzes - Rita Streich
(DG) **437 677-2GDO2** Irmgard Seefried - Opera Recital
(DG) **437 680-2GDO2** Rita Streich - Lieder Recital
(EMI) **CMS5 65621-2** Fischer-Dieskau - The Opera Singer
(EMI) **CZS7 67123-2** Wagner: Der Ring des Nibelungen
(FOYE) **15-CF2011** Wagner—Der Ring de Nibelungen
(PILZ) **442118-2** Wagner—Operas in Historical Recordings

STREIFF, Danièle (sop)
Massenet: Amadis (Cpte), Cléopâtre (Cpte)

STREISAND, Barbra (voc)
(SONY) **SM33452** Classical Barbra
(SONY) **SK33452** Classical Barbra

STREIT, Kurt (ten)
Gluck: Echo et Narcisse (Cpte)
Mozart: Così fan tutte (exc), Entführung (exc), Zauberflöte (Cpte)
Sullivan: Yeomen of the Guard (Cpte)

STRICKER, Frieder (ten)
Wagner: Meistersinger (Cpte)
(PHIL) **434 420-2PM32(1)** Richard Wagner Edition (Pt.1)

STRIENZ, Wilhelm (bass)
Mozart: Zauberflöte (Cpte)
(MYTO) **2MCD943103** Lortzing—Zar und Zimmermann
(PEAR) **GEMMCD9122** 20 Great Basses sing Great Arias
(PREI) **89024** Marcel Wittrisch (1901-1955)
(PREI) **89071** Gerhard Hüsch (1901-1984) - II
(PREI) **89211** Helge Roswaenge (1897-1972) - III

STŘÍŠKA, Jaroslav (ten)
Janáček: From the House of the Dead (Cpte)
Martinů: Julietta (Cpte)

STRIULI, Carlo (sngr)
Donizetti: Elisabetta (Cpte)
Wolf-Ferrari: Campiello (Cpte)

STRÖBERG, Helena (sop)
Börtz: Bacchae (Cpte)

STROBL, Joseph (cond)
see Austrian St Rad Orch

STROHBAUER, Hans (ten)
Lehár: Lustige Witwe (Cpte)

STROINIGG, Frieda (mez)
(SCHW) **314592** Vienna State Opera Live, Vol.9

STRUCKMANN, Falk (bar)
Bartók: Duke Bluebeard's castle (Cpte)
Beethoven: Fidelio (Cpte)
Busoni: Turandot (Cpte)
Wagner: Tristan und Isolde (Cpte)

STRYCZEK, Karl-Heinz (bar)
Schoenberg: Moses und Aron (Cpte)
Wagner: Rheingold (Cpte)
(EURO) **GD69003** Wagner—Der Ring des Nibelungen

STRYJA, Karol (cond)
see Katowice St Phil Orch

STUART, Richard (bar)
Sullivan: Iolanthe (exc)

STUART-ROBERTS, Deborah (mez)
Cilea: Adriana Lecouvreur (Cpte)

STUBBS, Stephen (lte)
Landi: Mort d'Orfeo (Cpte)

STÜCKL, Annelies (contr)
Mozart: Zauberflöte (Cpte)

STUDER, Cheryl (sop)
Donizetti: Lucia di Lammermoor (Cpte)
Floyd: Susannah (Cpte)
Gounod: Faust (Cpte)
Lehár: Lustige Witwe (Cpte)
Mozart: Don Giovanni (Cpte), Entführung (Cpte), Nozze di Figaro (Cpte), Zauberflöte (exc)
Offenbach: Contes d'Hoffmann (Cpte)
R. Strauss: Elektra (Cpte), Frau ohne Schatten (exc), Salome (Cpte)
Rossini: Guillaume Tell (exc), Semiramide (Cpte), Viaggio a Reims (Cpte)
Schubert: Fierrabras (Cpte)
Verdi: Attila (Cpte), Otello (exc), Traviata (Cpte), Vespri Siciliani (Cpte)
Wagner: Feen (Cpte), Götterdämmerung (Cpte), Lohengrin (exc), Meistersinger (Cpte), Tannhäuser (Cpte), Walküre (Cpte)
Zemlinsky: Geburtstag der Infantin (Cpte)
(DG) **439 768-2GH** Wagner—Gala - New Year's Eve Concert 1993
(DG) **439 865-2GH** Cheryl Studer sings Strauss and Wagner
(DG) **445 354-2GX14** Wagner—Der Ring des Nibelungen
(DG) **439 153-4GMA** Mad about Sopranos
(DG) **072 428-1GH2(DG)** The Metropolitan Opera Gala
(EMI) **CDC5 55095-2** Prima Diva
(EMI) **CDC5 55350-2** Cheryl Studer - A Portrait
(EMI) **CDC7 49811-2** Covent Garden Gala Concert
(EURO) **GD69003** Wagner—Der Ring des Nibelungen
(PHIL) **434 420-2PM32(1)** Richard Wagner Edition (Pt.1)
(PHIL) **442 410-2PM** Queen of the Night—Cheryl Studer sings Mozart
(SONY) **SLV46405(SONY)** Music for Europe

STUDHOLME, Marion (sop)
Britten: Peter Grimes (Cpte)
Sullivan: Mikado (Cpte)
(IMP) **PWK1157** Gilbert & Sullivan Spectacular

STUDIO ORCHESTRA
cond H. KRTSCHIL
(CAPR) **10 180** Gisela May sings Weill

STUMPER, Rudolf (bass)
R. Strauss: Rosenkavalier (Cpte)

STUMPHIUS, Annegeer (sop)
Gluck: Rencontre imprévue (Cpte)

STUPEL, Ilya (cond)
see Rubinstein PO

STURROCK, Kathron (pf)
(SAIN) **SCD4058** Louise Jones—Violin Recital

STUTTGART CHAMBER CHOIR
cond F. BERNIUS
Gluck: Orfeo ed Euridice (Cpte)
cond B. WEIL
Gazzaniga: Don Giovanni (Cpte)

STUTTGART CHAMBER ORCHESTRA
cond K. MÜNCHINGER
(DECC) **417 781-2DM** Eighteenth Century Miniatures
(DECC) **433 631-2DSP** Baroque Favourites
cond M. SIEGHART
(ORFE) **C223911A** Fagotto Concertante

STUTTGART OPERA CHORUS
cond D.R. DAVIES
Glass: Akhnaten (Cpte)
cond B. KONTARSKY
Nono: Intolleranza 1960 (Cpte)
cond F. PATANÈ
Puccini: Tosca (Cpte)

STUTTGART OPERA ORCHESTRA
cond D.R. DAVIES
Glass: Akhnaten (Cpte)
cond G. GÖRLICH
(MMOI) **CDMOIR408** Great Sopranos
cond B. KONTARSKY
Nono: Intolleranza 1960 (Cpte)
cond F. PATANÈ
Puccini: Tosca (Cpte)

STUTTGART RADIO CHORUS
cond K. ARP
Spohr: Faust (Cpte)
cond K. BÖHM
Mozart: Nozze di Figaro (Cpte)
cond J. KEILBERTH
Mozart: Zauberflöte (Cpte)
cond F. LEITNER
Handel: Giulio Cesare (Cpte)
cond H. MÜLLER-KRAY
(ACAN) **43 267** Fritz Wunderlich sings Opera Arias
cond A. RISCHNER
(ACAN) **43 267** Fritz Wunderlich sings Opera Arias
cond B. ZIMMERMANN
(MYTO) **2MCD943103** Lortzing—Zar und Zimmermann

STUTTGART RADIO ORCHESTRA
cond K. BÖHM
Mozart: Nozze di Figaro (Cpte)
cond J. KEILBERTH
Mozart: Zauberflöte (Cpte)
cond B. ZIMMERMANN
(MYTO) **2MCD943103** Lortzing—Zar und Zimmermann

STUTTGART RADIO SYMPHONY ORCHESTRA
Rossini: Scala di seta (Cpte), Signor Bruschino (Cpte)
cond D. R. DAVIES
Trojahn: Enrico (Cpte)
cond K. EICHHORN
(ORFE) **C072831A** The Art of the Coloratura
cond G. GELMETTI
Rossini: Occasione fa il ladro (Cpte)
cond H. GRAF
(ORFE) **C096841A** Famous Opera Arias
cond C. LEONHARDT
Wagner: Walküre (exc)
cond N. MARRINER
(CAPR) **10 369** R. Strauss—Orchestral Works
(CAPR) **10 466** American Classics - Volume 2
(CFP) **CD-CFP4658** Everlasting Love
(CFP) **CD-CFP4661** Everlasting Tranquillity
(EMIL) **CDZ102** Best Loved Classics 3
cond H. MÜLLER-KRAY
(ACAN) **43 267** Fritz Wunderlich sings Opera Arias
cond A. RISCHNER
(ACAN) **43 267** Fritz Wunderlich sings Opera Arias
cond C. SCHURICHT
(ACAN) **43 267** Fritz Wunderlich sings Opera Arias
cond S. SOLTESZ
(ORFE) **C081841A** Grace Bumbry: Famous Opera Arias

STUTTGART SCHOLA CANTORUM
cond H. ZENDER
Holliger: Magische Tänzer (Cpte)

STUTTGART STATE CHORUS
(SONY) **SK64133** The Essential Philip Glass

STUTTGART STATE ORCHESTRA
(SONY) **SK64133** The Essential Philip Glass

STUTZMANN, Nathalie (contr)
Handel: Amadigi di Gaula (Cpte)
(RCA) **09026 61205-2** Handel—Opera Arias

ŠTYCH, Jan (cond)
see Brno St PO

STYLER, Alan (bar)
Sullivan: Cox and Box (Cpte), Gondoliers (Cpte), Iolanthe (Cpte), Mikado (Cpte), Sorcerer (Cpte)
(DECC) **430 095-2DWO** The World of Gilbert & Sullivan, Vol.1
(DECC) **433 868-2DWO** The World of Gilbert & Sullivan - Volume 2

SUAREZ, Cesar Antonio (ten)
Rossini: Guillaume Tell (Cpte)

SUART, Richard (bass)
Bernstein: Candide (1988) (Cpte)
Britten: Midsummer Night's Dream (Cpte)
Holst: At the Boar's Head (Cpte)
Offenbach: Orphée aux enfers (Cpte)
Purcell: Fairy Queen, Z629 (Cpte)
Sullivan: Gondoliers (Cpte), HMS Pinafore (Cpte), Iolanthe (Cpte), Mikado (Cpte), Pirates of Penzance (Cpte)
Tippett: King Priam (Cpte)
Turnage: Greek (Cpte)
(CBC) **SMCD5139** A Gilbert & Sullivan Gala

ŠUBERT, Peter (bar)
Verdi: Rigoletto (Cpte), Traviata (Cpte)

ŠUBRTOVÁ, Milada (sop)
Dvořák: Rusalka (Cpte)
Smetana: Brandenburgers in Bohemia (Cpte), Devil's Wall (Cpte)

SUDDABY, Elsie (sop)
(CLAR) **CDGSE78-50-35/6** Wagner—Historical recordings
(PEAR) **GEMMCDS9137** Wagner—Der Ring des Nibelungen

SUHONEN, Antti (bass)
Mozart: Zauberflöte (Cpte)

SUISSE ROMANDE CHAMBER CHOIR
cond A. JORDAN
(ERAT) **2292-45797-2** The Ultimate Opera Collection

SUISSE ROMANDE ORCHESTRA
(DECC) **436 316-2DA** Golden Operetta
cond E. ANSERMET
Martin: Mystère de la Nativité
(BELA) **450 132-2** Rimsky-Korsakov—Scheherazade
(CASC) **VEL2001** Martin—Orchestral Works
(CASC) **VEL2010** Memories of the Suisse Romande - Suzanne Danco
(DECC) **417 771-2DM** de Falla: Orchestral & Stage Works
(DECC) **425 848-2DWO** Your hundred best tunes vol 2
(DECC) **433 400-2DM2** Ravel & Debussy—Stage Works
(DECC) **433 908-2DM2** Falla—Orchestral Music
(DECC) **443 464-2DF2** Rimsky-Korsakov—Scheherazade, etc
cond B. BALKWILL
(DECC) **433 221-2DWO** The World of Verdi
(DECC) **443 380-2DM** Ten Top Baritones & Basses 2
cond R. BONYNGE
Offenbach: Contes d'Hoffmann (Cpte)
(DECC) **433 067-2DWO** Your Hundred Best Opera Tunes IV
(DECC) **433 440-2DA** Golden Opera
(DECC) **433 822-2DH** Essential Opera
(DECC) **436 300-2DX** Opera Gala Sampler
(DECC) **436 315-2DA** Great Operatic Duets
(DECC) **436 316-2DA** Golden Operetta
(DECC) **436 463-2DM** Ten Top Tenors
(DECC) **440 410-2DM** Plácido Domingo
(DECC) **443 335-2LRX** Music for Relaxation, Vol 10 - The Night Before
(DECC) **433 870-4DWO** Classical Favourites
(DG) **415 366-2GH** Placido Domingo Recital
(DG) **427 708-2GX3** The Best of Domingo
cond A. EREDE
(DECC) **440 406-2DM** Giulietta Simionato
(DECC) **440 407-2DM** Mario del Monaco
(EMI) **CHS7 69741-2(7)** Record of Singing, Vol.4—Italian School
cond A. GUADAGNO
(DECC) **433 439-2DA** Great Love Duets
(DECC) **436 301-2DA** Renata Tebaldi & Franco Corelli—Arias & Duets
cond I. KARR
(CASC) **VEL2010** Memories of the Suisse Romande - Suzanne Danco
cond H. KNAPPERTSBUSCH
(PREI) **90189** Knappertsbusch in London and Switzerland
cond K. KORD
Massenet: Don Quichotte (Cpte)
cond H. LEWIS
(DECC) **421 306-2DA** Marilyn Horne sings Rossini
(DECC) **421 891-2DA** Marilyn Horne sings Rossini, Bellini & Donizetti
(DECC) **436 133-2DWO** World of Rossini
(DECC) **436 300-2DX** Opera Gala Sampler
(DECC) **440 415-2DM** Marilyn Horne
cond A. LOMBARD
(DECC) **436 316-2DA** Golden Operetta
(DECC) **440 416-2DM** Régine Crespin
cond T. SCHIPPERS
Bizet: Carmen (Cpte)
(BELA) **450 006-2** Famous Opera Duets
(DECC) **433 068-2DWO** Your Hundred Best Opera Tunes V

SUISSE ROMANDE RADIO CHOIR
cond R. BONYNGE
Offenbach: Contes d'Hoffmann (Cpte)
(DECC) **433 067-2DWO** Your Hundred Best Opera Tunes IV
(DECC) **433 440-2DA** Golden Opera
(DECC) **436 315-2DA** Great Operatic Duets

SUISSE ROMANDE RADIO CHORUS
cond R. BONYNGE
(DECC) **433 822-2DH** Essential Opera
(DECC) **436 463-2DM** Ten Top Tenors
(DECC) **440 410-2DM** Plácido Domingo
(DECC) **443 335-2LRX** Music for Relaxation, Vol 10 - The Night Before
cond K. KORD
Massenet: Don Quichotte (Cpte)

SUITNER, Otmar (cond)
see Berlin Staatskapelle
Staatskapelle Dresden

SUKIS, Lilian (sop)
Mozart: Ascanio in Alba (Cpte), Finta Giardiniera (Cpte)

ŠULCOVÁ, Brigita (sop)
Dvořák: Kate and the Devil (Cpte)

SULEYMANOV, Stanislav (bass)
Knaifel: Canterville Ghost (exc)
Serov: Judith (Cpte)
Shostakovich: Gamblers (Cpte)

SULIOTIS, Elena (sop)
Verdi: Macbeth (Cpte), Nabucco (exc)
(DECC) **433 068-2DWO** Your Hundred Best Opera Tunes V
(DECC) **433 624-2DSP** Great Soprano Arias
(DECC) **436 261-2DHO3** Puccini—Il Trittico
(DECC) **436 300-2DX** Opera Gala Sampler
(DECC) **440 405-2DM** Elena Souliotis

SULLIVAN, Brian (ten)
(VAI) **VAI69112** Eleanor Steber in Opera and Song Vol 2

SULLIVAN, Daniel (ten)
Verdi: Ballo in maschera (Cpte)

SULLIVAN, Gwynne (ten)
Walton: Troilus and Cressida (Cpte)

SULZENKO, Jirí (bass)
Puccini: Bohème (Cpte)

SUMEGI, Daniel (bass)
Bellini: Beatrice di Tenda (Cpte)

SUMMERS, Jonathan (bar)
Balfe: Bohemian Girl (Cpte)
Britten: Gloriana (Cpte), Peter Grimes (Cpte)
Giordano: Andrea Chénier (Cpte)
Leoncavallo: Bohème (Cpte)
Puccini: Fanciulla del West (Cpte), Madama Butterfly (Cpte)
R. Strauss: Rosenkavalier (Cpte)
Saint-Saëns: Samson et Dalila (exc)
Verdi: Ballo in maschera (Cpte), Battaglia di Legnano (Cpte), Traviata (exc)
(PHIL) **442 602-2PM** 3 x 3 Tenors

SUMMERS, Lydia (mez)
(VAI) **VAIA1017** Leonard Warren—Early Recordings
(VAI) **VAIA1084** Rose Bampton sings Verdi and Wagner

(THE) SUN LIFE BAND
cond B. HURDLEY
(GRAS) **GRCD41** Avondale - The Sun Life Band
cond R. NEWSOME
(GRAS) **GRCD41** Avondale - The Sun Life Band

SUNARA, Maja (mez)
(RCA) **GD60941** Rarities - Montserrat Caballé

SUNDINE, Stephanie (sop)
Janáček: Makropulos Affair (Cpte)

SUNDQUIST, Erik (bar)
Verdi: Rigoletto (Cpte)

SUNNEGÅRDH, Thomas (ten)
Wagner: Rheingold (Cpte)

SUPERVIA, Conchita (mez)
(CLUB) **CL99-074** Conchita Supervia (1895-1936)
(EMI) **CHS7 64864-2(1)** La Scala Edition - Vol.2, 1915-46 (pt 1)
(NIMB) **NI7801** Great Singers, Vol.1
(NIMB) **NI7836/7** Conchita Supervia (1895-1936)
(NIMB) **NI7864** More Legendary Voices
(PEAR) **GEMMCDS9926(2)** Covent Garden on Record—Vol.4 (pt 2)
(PEAR) **GEMMCD9130** Great Sopranos, Vol.2
(PREI) **89023** Conchita Supervia (1895-1936)
(TEST) **SBT1008** Viva Rossini

SURIAN, Giorgio (bar)
Donizetti: Favorita (Cpte), Maria di Rudenz (Cpte)
Gluck: Iphigénie en Tauride (Cpte)
Paisiello: Nina (Cpte)
Rossini: Bianca e Falliero (Cpte), Guillaume Tell (Cpte), Viaggio a Reims (Cpte)
Verdi: Attila (Cpte), Forza del destino (Cpte), Rigoletto (Cpte)

SURINACH, E. (sop)
(CLUB) **CL99-014** Dino Borgioli (1891-1960)
(PEAR) **GEMMCD9091** Dino Borgioli

SURYOVÁ, Daniela (contr)
Dvořák: Kate and the Devil (Cpte)
Fibich: Šárka (Cpte)
Janáček: Fate (Cpte), Jenufa (Cpte)

SUSCA, Vito (bass)
Verdi: Traviata (Cpte)

SÜSS, Reiner (bar)
Lortzing: Wildschütz (Cpte)
Mozart: Zaïde (Cpte)
Wagner: Tannhäuser (Cpte)

SUSSKIND, Walter (cond)
see LPO
Philh

SUTEJ, Vjeksolav (cond)
see ECO

SUTHAUS, Ludwig (ten)
Wagner: Meistersinger (Cpte), Tristan und Isolde (Cpte), Walküre (Cpte)
(EMI) **CZS7 67123-2** Wagner: Der Ring des Nibelungen
(MYTO) **3MCD93381** Wagner—Die Walküre, etc

SUTHERLAND, Dame Joan (sop)
A. Thomas: Hamlet (Cpte)
Bellini: Norma (Cpte), Puritani (Cpte), Sonnambula (Cpte)
Bizet: Carmen (exc)
Cilea: Adriana Lecouvreur (Cpte)
Delibes: Lakmé (exc)
Donizetti: Elisir d'amore (Cpte), Fille du régiment (Cpte), Lucia di Lammermoor (Cpte), Lucrezia Borgia (Cpte), Maria Stuarda (Cpte)
Gay: Beggar's Opera (Cpte)
Gounod: Faust (Cpte)
Handel: Alcina (Cpte), Giulio Cesare (exc)
J. Strauss II: Fledermaus (Cpte)
Lehár: Lustige Witwe (Cpte)
Massenet: Esclarmonde (Cpte), Roi de Lahore (Cpte)
Meyerbeer: Huguenots (Cpte)
Mozart: Don Giovanni (Cpte)
Offenbach: Contes d'Hoffmann (Cpte)
Puccini: Turandot (Cpte)
Rossini: Semiramide (exc)
Verdi: Masnadieri (Cpte), Rigoletto (Cpte), Traviata (Cpte), Trovatore (exc)
Wagner: Siegfried (Cpte)
(BELA) **450 006-2** Famous Opera Duets
(BELA) **450 007-2** Puccini Favourites
(BELA) **450 014-2** Sutherland sings Coward
(BELA) **450 117-2** Great Opera Chorus II
(BELA) **450 133-2** Verdi Favourites
(BUTT) **BMCD015** Pavarotti Collection - Duets and Scenes
(CFP) **CD-CFP4602** Favourite Opera
(DECC) **414 100-2DM15** Wagner: Der Ring des Nibelungen
(DECC) **417 011-2DH2** Pavarotti's Greatest Hits
(DECC) **417 780-2DM** Joan Sutherland's Greatest Hits
(DECC) **421 881-2DA** The Age of Bel Canto - Sutherland
(DECC) **421 896-2DA** Puccini—Great Operatic Duets
(DECC) **425 048-2DX** Joan Sutherland - Home Sweet Home
(DECC) **425 493-2DM2** Joan Sutherland: The Art of the Prima Donna
(DECC) **425 850-2DWO** Your Hundred Best Tunes, Vol.4
(DECC) **430 470-2DH** Essential Pavarotti II
(DECC) **430 724-2DM** Great Operatic Duets
(DECC) **433 064-2DWO** Your Hundred Best Opera Tunes Volume I
(DECC) **433 065-2DWO** Your Hundred Best Opera Tunes Volume II
(DECC) **433 066-2DWO** Your Hundred Best Opera Tunes III
(DECC) **433 067-2DWO** Your Hundred Best Opera Tunes IV
(DECC) **433 068-2DWO** Your Hundred Best Opera Tunes V
(DECC) **433 069-2DWO** Your Hundred Best Opera Tunes VI
(DECC) **433 221-2DWO** The World of Verdi
(DECC) **433 223-2DWO** The World of Operetta
(DECC) **433 439-2DA** Great Love Duets
(DECC) **433 440-2DA** Golden Opera
(DECC) **433 442-2DA** Verdi—Famous Arias
(DECC) **433 624-2DSP** Great Soprano Arias
(DECC) **433 706-2DMO3** Bellini—Beatrice di Tenda; Operatic Arias
(DECC) **433 822-2DH** Essential Opera
(DECC) **433 865-2DWO** The World of Puccini
(DECC) **436 133-2DWO** World of Rossini
(DECC) **436 227-2DM2** Handel—Acis and Galatea; Baroque Arias
(DECC) **436 300-2DX** Opera Gala Sampler
(DECC) **436 313-2DA** Sutherland/Pavarotti—Operatic Duets
(DECC) **436 315-2DA** Great Operatic Duets
(DECC) **436 316-2DA** Golden Operetta
(DECC) **436 317-2DA** Puccini—Famous Arias
(DECC) **436 461-2DM** Ten Top Sopranos
(DECC) **436 472-2DM** Great Opera Arias
(DECC) **440 404-2DM** Joan Sutherland
(DECC) **440 947-2DH** Essential Opera II
(DECC) **443 335-2LRX** Music for Relaxation, Vol 10 - The Night Before
(DECC) **443 377-2DM** Ten Top Sopranos 2
(DECC) **444 555-2DF2** Essential Puccini
(DECC) **071 135-1DH** La Stupenda - A Portrait of Dame Joan Sutherland
(DECC) **071 142-1DH (DECC)** Essential Opera
(DECC) **071 149-1DH (DECC)** The Essential Sutherland
(EMI) **CDC5 55095-2** Prima Diva
(EMIN) **CD-EMX9519** Great Sopranos of Our Time
(MCEG) **VVD780** Sydney Opera House Gala Concert
(MEMO) **HR4392/3** Great Voices - Marilyn Horne
(VAI) **VAI69108** Presenting Joan Sutherland

SUTTON, Sheryl (narr)
Glass: Einstein on the Beach (Cpte)

SUTTON, Vern (ten)
Britten: Paul Bunyan (Cpte)
Copland: Tender Land (Cpte)

SUZUKI, Azuko (sop)
Haydn: Anima del filosofo (Cpte)

SUZUKI, Kai (treb)
Mozart: Zauberflöte (Cpte)

SVAB, Alessandro (bar)
Rossini: Pietra del paragone (Cpte)

SVANHOLM, Set (ten)
Wagner: Götterdämmerung (Cpte), Rheingold (Cpte)
(DECC) **414 100-2DM15** Wagner: Der Ring des Nibelungen
(DECC) **421 313-2DA** Wagner: Der Ring des Nibelungen - Great Scenes
(EMI) **CDH7 63030-2** Kirsten Flagstad - Wagner Opera Arias
(EMI) **CMS5 65212-2** Wagner—Les introuvables du Ring
(LOND) **440 490-2LM5(1)** Kirsten Flagstad Edition

(RCA) **09026 61580-2(6)** RCA/Met 100 Singers, 100 Years (pt 6)
(SCHW) **314502** Vienna State Opera—Live Recordings (sampler)
(SCHW) **314582** Vienna State Opera Live, Vol.8
(SCHW) **314652** Vienna State Opera Live, Vol.15
(SCHW) **314672** Vienna State Opera Live, Vol.17
(SCHW) **314692** Vienna State Opera Live, Vol.19
(SCHW) **314742** Vienna State Opera Live, Vol.24
(TEST) **SBT1018** Kirsten Flagstad
(VAI) **VAIA1012** Eleanor Sterber sings R. Strauss

SVARFVAR, Sven-Ole (vn)
(BLUE) **ABCD038** 4 X Göran W. Nilson

SVÁROVSKÝ, Leoš (cond)
see Brno St PO

SVED, Alexander (bar)
(EMI) **CHS7 64864-2(2)** La Scala Edition - Vol.2, 1915-46 (pt 2)
(MYTO) **2MCD90317** Verdi—Un Ballo in maschera
(PREI) **89096** Alexander Svéd (1906-1979)
(SCHW) **314542** Vienna State Opera Live, Vol.4
(SCHW) **314572** Vienna State Opera Live, Vol.7
(SCHW) **314622** Vienna State Opera Live, Vol.12
(SCHW) **314632** Vienna State Opera Live, Vol.13
(TEST) **SBT1008** Viva Rossini

SVEDENBRANT, Georg (bass)
Verdi: Rigoletto (Cpte)
(BLUE) **ABCD028** Jussi Björling live at the Stockholm Opera

ŠVEHLA, Zdeněk (ten)
Janáček: Makropulos Affair (Cpte)
Martinů: Julietta (Cpte)
Smetana: Dalibor (Cpte), Two Widows (Cpte)
(DECC) **421 852-2DH2** Janáček: Operatic & Chamber Works
(DECC) **430 375-2DH2** Janáček—Operatic and Orchestral Works

ŠVEJDA, Miroslav (ten)
Fibich: Bride of Messina (Cpte)
Janáček: Excursions of Mr Brouček (Cpte), From the House of the Dead (Cpte)
Smetana: Two Widows (Cpte)

SVENDÉN, Brigitta (mez)
Wagner: Götterdämmerung (Cpte), Rheingold (Cpte), Siegfried (exc), Walküre (Cpte)
(DG) **445 354-2GX14** Wagner—Der Ring des Nibelungen
(DG) **072 428-1GH2(DG)** The Metropolitan Opera Gala
(DG) **072 422-3GH7** Levine conducts Wagner's Ring

SVENDSEN, Otte (ten)
Nielsen: Saul and David (Cpte)

SVENSSON, Peter (ten)
Mozart: Zauberflöte (Cpte)

SVESHNIKOV RUSSIAN ACADEMY CHOIR
cond A. CHISTIAKOV
Rimsky-Korsakov: Tsar's Bride (Cpte)

SVETLANOV, Evgeni (cond)
see Philh
Russian Federation St SO
Russian St SO
USSR Academy SO
USSR SO

SVETLANOVA, Nina (pf)
(RUSS) **RDCD11341** Prokofiev/Stravinsky—Songs and Arias

SVETLEV, Mikhail (ten)
Mussorgsky: Boris Godunov (Cpte)

SVETOSLAV OBRETENOV NATIONAL CHORUS
cond E. TCHAKAROV
Tchaikovsky: Queen of Spades (Cpte)

SVIZZERA ITALIANA ORCHESTRA
cond B. AMADUCCI
(ERMI) **ERM151** Katia Ricciarelli in Recital
cond M. ROTA
(BONG) **GB2513-2** Mariella Devia—Opera Arias

SVOBODOVÁ, Jitka (sop)
(SUPR) **11 1851-2** Famous Opera Arias

SVOBODOVÁ-JANKŮ, Hana (sop)
Smetana: Dalibor (Cpte)

ŠVORC, Antonín (bass)
Smetana: Dalibor (Cpte), Libuše (Cpte)
(DECC) **430 375-2DH2** Janáček—Operatic and Orchestral Works

SWANSON, Catherine (sop)
Mendelssohn: Hochzeit des Camacho (Cpte)

SWAROWSKY, Hans (cond)
see Vienna SO

SWARTHOUT, Gladys (mez)
(RCA) **09026 61580-2(4)** RCA/Met 100 Singers, 100 Years (pt 4)

(ROYAL) SWEDISH CHAMBER ORCHESTRA
cond M. LILJEFORS
(CPRI) **CAP21428** Virtuoso Arias - Soffel

SWEDISH NATIONAL MUSEUM CHAMBER ORCHESTRA
cond C. GÉNETAY
(MSVE) **MSCD412** Music from the Age of Liberty

SWEDISH RADIO SYMPHONY ORCHESTRA
cond E. ERICSON
(BIS) **BIS-CD383** Works for Male Chorus
cond F. HAIDER
Donizetti: Linda di Chamounix (Cpte)
cond T. MANN
(ALTN) **CDAN3** Hjördis Schymberg
cond E-P. SALONEN
(SONY) **SK53276** Nielsen—Orchestral Works
cond T. VETÖ
Nørgård: Gilgamesh (Cpte)
cond VLADIMIR ASHKENAZY
(TELD) **9031-76372-6(TELD)** Tchaikovsky —Women and Fate

SWEET, Sharon (sop)
Mozart: Don Giovanni (exc)
Verdi: Falstaff (Cpte)
Wagner: Lohengrin (Cpte)
Weber: Freischütz (Cpte)

SWENSEN, Robert (ten)
Gazzaniga: Don Giovanni (Cpte)
Haydn: Anima del filosofo (Cpte)
Puccini: Fanciulla del West (Cpte), Turandot (Cpte)
Saint-Saëns: Samson et Dalila (exc)
Spohr: Faust (Cpte)

SWENSON, Ruth Ann (sop)
Meyerbeer: Africaine (Cpte)

SWIERCZEWSKI, Michel (cond)
see French Lyrique Orch
Lisbon Gulbenkian Orch

(THE) SWINGLE SINGERS
(VIRG) **VC7 59617-2** A capella Mozart

SWISS WORKSHOP PHILHARMONIC ORCHESTRA
cond M. VENZAGO
Schoeck: Venus (Cpte)

SWISS YOUTH SYMPHONY ORCHESTRA
cond A. DELFS
Schoeck: Penthesilea (exc)

SYDNEY ELIZABETHAN ORCHESTRA
Bellini: Norma (Cpte)
Donizetti: Lucia di Lammermoor (Cpte)
J. Strauss II: Fledermaus (Cpte)
cond R. BONYNGE
(DECC) **071 149-1DH (DECC)** The Essential Sutherland
(MCEG) **VVD780** Sydney Opera House Gala Concert

SYDNEY ELIZABETHAN PHILHARMONIC ORCHESTRA
Lehár: Lustige Witwe (Cpte)
cond R. BONYNGE
(DECC) **071 149-1DH (DECC)** The Essential Sutherland

SYDNEY SYMPHONY ORCHESTRA
cond R. PICKLER
(CHAN) **CHAN6587** Berlioz—Ballet Music
cond J. SEREBRIER
(IMG) **IMGCD1611** Wagner/Mussorgsky/Beethoven—Orchestral Works

SYKES, Peter (organ)
(CENT) **CRC2084** Music from Cranberry Isles

SYLVAN, Sanford (bar)
J. Adams: Death of Klinghoffer (Cpte)
Mozart: Nozze di Figaro (Cpte)
Tippett: Ice Break (Cpte)

SYLVEST, Nils (vc)
(CANZ) **CAN33009** Rachmaninov/R.Strauss—Cello Sonatas

SYLVESTER, Michael (ten)
Verdi: Don Carlo (exc), Simon Boccanegra (Cpte)

SYMONETTE, Victor C. (cond)
see Bulgarian TV & Rad SO

SYMPHONY OF THE AIR (NEW YORK)
cond V. GOLSCHMANN
(VANG) **08.4016.71** Music of Samuel Barber
cond L. STOKOWSKI
(EMI) **ZDMB5 65427-2** Stokowski's United Artists Recordings
(RCA) **09026 61503-2** Stokowski Favourites

SYMPHONY ORCHESTRA
(CLAR) **CDGSE78-50-26** Wagner: Tristan und Isolde excerpts
cond T. BEECHAM
Gounod: Faust (Cpte)
(PEAR) **GEMMCD9473** Heddle Nash—Vol.2
(SYMP) **SYMCD1096/7** Sir Thomas Beecham, Bart conducts Beecham SO & LPO
cond P. BONNEAU
O. Straus: Drei Walzer (exc)
cond H. BUSSER
(CLUB) **CL99-034** Marcel Journet (1867-1933)
cond A. COATES
(CLAR) **CDGSE78-50-26** Wagner: Tristan und Isolde excerpts
(CLAR) **CDGSE78-50-35/6** Wagner—Historical recordings
(CLAR) **CDGSE78-50-54** Coates conducts Wagner, Weber & Mendelssohn
cond P. COPPOLA
(CLUB) **CL99-034** Marcel Journet (1867-1933)
(DANT) **LYS003/4** Charles Panzéra - Song Recital
(EMI) **CMS7 64008-2(1)** Wagner Singing on Record (pt 1)
(EMI) **CMS7 64008-2(2)** Wagner Singing on Record (pt 2)
(MSCM) **MM30377** 18 Tenors d'Expression Française
cond M. CORDONE
(NIMB) **NI7845** Giacomo Lauri-Volpi (1892-1979)
cond R. DESORMIÈRE
(EMI) **CHS7 61038-2** Debussy—Pelléas et Mélisande, etc
cond J. FEHRING
Benatzky: Im weissen Rössl (exc)
cond I. GODFREY
Sullivan: Sorcerer (Cpte)
(MMOI) **CDMOIR413** The Very Best of Gilbert & Sullivan
cond H. LANGE
(MSCM) **MM30283** Great Wagnerian Singers, Vol.1
cond D. MARZOLLO
(PREI) **89074** Tancredi Pasero (1893-1983) - II
cond S. MEYROWITZ
(EMI) **CMS7 64008-2(1)** Wagner Singing on Record (pt 1)
cond H. NORRIS
(MMOI) **CDMOIR413** The Very Best of Gilbert & Sullivan
cond C. POWELL
(SYMP) **SYMCD1130** Joseph Holbrooke—Historic Recordings
cond ROSARIO BOURDON
(CLUB) **CL99-034** Marcel Journet (1867-1933)
cond M. SARGENT
Sullivan: Gondoliers (Cpte), HMS Pinafore (Cpte), Mikado (Cpte), Patience (Cpte), Pirates of Penzance (Cpte)
(MMOI) **CDMOIR413** The Very Best of Gilbert & Sullivan
cond G. TRUC
Ravel: Heure espagnole (Cpte)

SYNEK, Liane (sop)
Wagner: Walküre (Cpte)
(PHIL) **446 057-2PB14** Wagner—The Ring Cycle - Bayreuth Festival 1967

SYROMATNIKOV, Mikhail (ten)
Kabalevsky: Colas Breugnon (Cpte)

SYRUS, David (pf)
Menotti: Amahl and the Night Visitors (Cpte), Boy who grew too fast (Cpte)

SZAMEIT, Sabine (sop)
Steffani: Henrico Leone (Cpte)

SZÁNTHÓ, Enid (mez)
(SCHW) **314572** Vienna State Opera Live, Vol.7
(SCHW) **314592** Vienna State Opera Live, Vol.9
(SCHW) **314602** Vienna State Opera Live, Vol.10
(SCHW) **314622** Vienna State Opera Live, Vol.12
(SCHW) **314642** Vienna State Opera Live, Vol.14
(SCHW) **314662** Vienna State Opera Live, Vol.16
(SCHW) **314702** Vienna State Opera Live, Vol.20
(SCHW) **314742** Vienna State Opera Live, Vol.24

SZÉKELY, Mihály (bass)
Bartók: Duke Bluebeard's castle (Cpte)

SZELL, George (cond)
see Berlin St Op Orch
Cleveland Orch
LSO
NY Met Op Orch
orch
VPO

SZEMERE, László (ten)
Einem: Prozess (Cpte)
R. Strauss: Salome (Cpte)

SZENDRÉNYI, Katalin (sop)
Bartók: Duke Bluebeard's castle (Cpte)

SZERYNG, Henryk (vn)
(MERC) **434 351-2MM** Szeryng plays Kreisler

SZIGETI, Joseph (vn)
(BIDD) **LAB007/8** The Art of Joseph Szigeti, Vol.2
(BIDD) **LAB070/1** Szigeti recordings with Bartók and Foldes
(SONY) **MPK52569** Joseph Szigeti Recital

SZILÁGYI, Béla (bass)
Handel: Agrippina (Cpte)

SZILÁGYI, Károly (bar)
Mascagni: Lodoletta (Cpte)

SZIRMAY, Márta (contr)
Verdi: Falstaff (Cpte)

SZKOKAN, Franz (spkr)
R. Strauss: Arabella (Cpte)
(SCHW) **314632** Vienna State Opera Live, Vol.13

SZMYTKA, Elzbieta (sop)
Gazzaniga: Don Giovanni (Cpte)
Janáček: From the House of the Dead (Cpte)
Lehár: Lustige Witwe (Cpte)
Mozart: Così fan tutte (Cpte), Entführung (Cpte)
(PHIL) **422 523-2PME8(2)** The Complete Mozart Edition Vol 23 (pt 2)

SZÖNYI, Olga (sop)
Bartók: Duke Bluebeard's castle (Cpte)
(DECC) **443 488-2DF2** Kodály—Háry János; Psalmus Hungaricus etc

SZÜCS, Robert (bass)
Puccini: Madama Butterfly (Cpte)
Verdi: Rigoletto (Cpte)

SZULE, Tamas (bass)
Mozart: Entführung (Cpte)

SZYFER, J.F. (cond)
see Orch

TABAKOV, Emil (cond)
see Sofia PO

TABERY, Vanda (sop)
Handel: Scipione (Cpte)

TABIADON, Adelisa (mez)
Donizetti: Favorita (Cpte)
Mercadante: Bravo (Cpte)
(NUOV) **6905** Donizetti—Great Love Duets

TADDEI, Giuseppe (bar)
Donizetti: Elisir d'amore (Cpte), Linda di Chamounix (Cpte)
Mozart: Così fan tutte (Cpte), Don Giovanni (exc), Nozze di Figaro (Cpte)
Puccini: Bohème (Cpte), Gianni Schicchi (Cpte), Manon Lescaut (Cpte), Tosca (Cpte)
Rossini: Mosè (Cpte)
Verdi: Falstaff (Cpte)
(ACAN) **49 402** Giuseppe Taddei—Recital
(DECC) **433 066-2DWO** Your Hundred Best Opera Tunes III
(DG) **419 257-2GH3** 'Cav' and 'Pag', etc
(EMIL) **CDZ7 67015-2** Mozart—Opera Arias
(PREI) **89995** Famous Italian Baritones
(PREI) **90020** Giuseppe Taddei sings Arias and Neapolitan Songs

TADDEI, Marta (sop)
Rossini: Cenerentola (Cpte)
(TELD) **9031-77676-6(TELD)** My World of Opera - Kiri Te Kanawa

TADEO, Giorgio (bass)
Giordano: Andrea Chénier (Cpte)
Mozart: Nozze di Figaro (Cpte)
Puccini: Manon Lescaut (Cpte), Tosca (exc)
Rossini: Inganno felice (Cpte)
Verdi: Traviata (exc)

TAFELMUSIK
Handel: Floridante (exc)
cond F. BERNIUS
Gluck: Orfeo ed Euridice (Cpte)
cond J. LAMON
(SONY) **SK48045** Flute Concertos
cond B. WEIL
Gazzaniga: Don Giovanni (Cpte)
(SONY) **SK46695** Mozart—Overtures, etc
(SONY) **SK52498** Highlights on Period Instruments

TAGHADOSSI, Mario (bar)
Puccini: Fanciulla del West (Cpte)

TAGHKANIC CHORALE
cond J. SOMARY
Handel: Sosarme (Cpte)

TAGLIABUE, Carlo (bar)
Verdi: Forza del destino (Cpte)
(PREI) **89015** Carlo Tagliabue (1898-1978)
(PREI) **89995** Famous Italian Baritones

TAGLIASACCHI, Monica (sop)
Verdi: Due Foscari (Cpte)

TAGLIAVINI, Ferruccio (ten)
Donizetti: Lucia di Lammermoor (Cpte)
Massenet: Werther (Cpte)
Spontini: Olimpie (Cpte)
(CENT) **CRC2164** Ferruccio Tagliavini—Early Operatic Recordings
(EMI) **CHS7 69741-2(7)** Record of Singing, Vol.4—Italian School

TAHA, Claudia (sop)
Spohr: Faust (Cpte)
(SCHW) **312682** Opera Gala with Young Artists - Volume II

TAILLON, Jocelyne (mez)
Debussy: Pelléas et Mélisande (Cpte)
Fauré: Pénélope (Cpte)
Gounod: Faust (Cpte), Roméo et Juliette (Cpte)
Offenbach: Contes d'Hoffmann (Cpte)
Ravel: Enfant et les sortilèges (Cpte)
Rossini: Guillaume Tell (Cpte)

TAJO, Italo (bass)
Mozart: Nozze di Figaro (Cpte)
Puccini: Bohème (Cpte), Manon Lescaut (Cpte), Tosca (exc)
Verdi: Aida (Cpte), Macbeth (Cpte)
(DECC) **444 555-2DF2** Essential Puccini

TAKÁCS, Klára (contr)
Giordano: Andrea Chénier (Cpte)
Respighi: Belfagor (Cpte)
Verdi: Rigoletto (Cpte)

TAKÁCS, Tamara (mez)
Boito: Mefistofele (Cpte)
Giordano: Andrea Chénier (Cpte)

TALARICO, Rita (sop)
Puccini: Bohème (exc)
(BUTT) **BMCD015** Pavarotti Collection - Duets and Scenes

(LES) TALENS LYRIQUES
cond C. ROUSSET
Handel: Scipione (Cpte)
Jommelli: Armida abbandonata (Cpte)

TALEXIS, Amelia (sop)
(IRCC) **IRCC-CD802** Souvenirs of Rare French Opera
(PEAR) **GEMMCDS9924(2)** Covent Garden on Record, Vol.2 (pt 2)
(SYMP) **SYMCD1126** The Harold Wayne Collection, Vol.14

TALICH, Vaclav (cond)
see Czech PO
Prague RSO

TALITMAN, Rachel (hp)
(DINT) **DICD920141** French Music for Flute and Harp

TALLEY, Marian (sop)
(PEAR) **GEMMCD9367** Gigli—Arias and Duets

TALLIS CHAMBER CHOIR
cond P. DOMINGO
(SONY) **SK53968** Opera Duets
cond D. HINNELLS
Verdi: Trovatore (Cpte)
cond M. VIOTTI
Donizetti: Elisir d'amore (Cpte)

TALMI, Yoav (cond)
see San Diego SO

TALOLA, Pirkko (sop)
(BIS) **BIS-CD373/4** Opera Scenes from Savaonlinna

TALVELA, Martti (bass)
Beethoven: Fidelio (Cpte)
Mozart: Don Giovanni (Cpte), Entführung (Cpte), Zauberflöte (Cpte)
Mussorgsky: Boris Godunov (Cpte)
Verdi: Rigoletto (exc)
Wagner: Fliegende Holländer (Cpte), Parsifal (Cpte), Rheingold (Cpte), Tristan und Isolde (Cpte), Walküre (Cpte)
(BIS) **BIS-CD373/4** Opera Scenes from Savaonlinna
(DECC) **433 440-2DA** Golden Opera
(DECC) **436 464-2DM** Ten Top Baritones & Basses
(DG) **435 211-2GX15** Wagner—Der Ring des Nibelungen
(EURO) **VD69256** Mozart—Opera Arias
(ORFE) **C394301B** Great Mozart Singers Series, Vol. 3
(PHIL) **434 420-2PM32(2)** Richard Wagner Edition (pt 2)
(PHIL) **446 057-2PB14** Wagner—The Ring Cycle - Bayreuth Festival 1967
(RCA) **09026 61580-2(8)** RCA/Met 100 Singers, 100 Years (pt 8)

TAMAGNO, Francesco (ten)
(EMI) **CHS7 64860-2(1)** La Scala Edition - Vol.1, 1878-1914 (pt 1)
(EMI) **CHS7 64860-2(2)** La Scala Edition - Vol.1, 1878-1914 (pt 2)
(MEMO) **HR4408/9(1)** Singers in Genoa, Vol.1 (disc 1)
(NIMB) **NI7840/1** The Era of Adelina Patti
(NIMB) **NI7856** Legendary Tenors
(OPAL) **OPALCD9846** Francesco Tamagno—Complete Recordings
(PEAR) **GEMMCDS9923(2)** Covent Garden on Record, Vol.1 (pt 2)
(TEST) **SBT1008** Viva Rossini

TAMALET, Xavier (bass)
Debussy: Pelléas et Mélisande (Cpte)

TAMAR, Iano (sop)
Rossini: Semiramide (Cpte)

TAMARIN, Ilya (ten)
(RCA) **GD60522** Alexander Kipnis—Opera & Song Recital

TAMAYO, Pablo (sngr)
Moreno Torroba: Luisa Fernanda (Cpte)

TAMBLYN, Russ (sngr)
Bernstein: West Side Story (Cpte)

TANDLER, Heinz (bass)
Wagner: Meistersinger (Cpte)

TANDURA, Elisabetta (sop)
Rossini: Adelaide di Borgogna (Cpte), Ermione (Cpte)

TANGLEWOOD FESTIVAL CHORUS
cond S. OZAWA
R. Strauss: Elektra (Cpte)
Tchaikovsky: Queen of Spades (Cpte)
cond J.T. WILLIAMS
(SONY) **SK48224** John Williams—The Green Album

TANNENBERGEROVA, Yvette (sop)
Mozart: Nozze di Figaro (Cpte)
(SUPR) **11 1878-2** The Unknown Janáček

TANNER, Mark (pf)
(COLN) **VAN201** Carnival of Venice

TANSINI, Ugo (cond)
see EIAR Orch
Turin EIAR Orch

TAPIOLA CHAMBER CHOIR
cond O. POHJOLA
Kortekangas: Grand Hotel
cond U. SÖDERBLOM
Bergman: Singing Tree (Cpte)

TAPPY, Eric (ten)
Debussy: Pelléas et Mélisande (Cpte)
Martin: Mystère de la Nativité
Monteverdi: Incoronazione di Poppea (Cpte), Orfeo (Cpte)
Mozart: Zauberflöte (Cpte)
(ORFE) **C394301B** Great Mozart Singers Series, Vol. 3
(RCA) **09026 61886-2** Operas Greatest Love Songs

TARALLO, Nino (bar)
Puccini: Gianni Schicchi (Cpte)

TARASCHENKO, Vitaly (ten)
Rachmaninov: Aleko (Cpte), Francesca da Rimini (Cpte)

TARASSOVA, Marianna (mez)
Rimsky-Korsakov: Sadko (Cpte)

TARGLER, Ursula (sop)
Keiser: Croesus (Cpte)

TARRÈS, Enriqueta (sop)
Mozart: Idomeneo (Cpte)

TARTAKOV, Ioakim (bar)
(PEAR) **GEMMCDS9997/9(1)** Singers of Imperial Russia, Vol.1 (pt 1)

TASHIRO, Makoto (ten)
Verdi: Macbeth (Cpte)

TASIN, Flavio (bar)
Verdi: Traviata (Cpte)

TASMANIAN SYMPHONY ORCHESTRA
cond D. FRANKS
(ABCC) **8 7000 10** Rita Hunter—Opera Arias

TASSEL, Charles van (bar)
Schreker: Gezeichneten (Cpte)

TASSINARI, Pia (sop)
Verdi: Falstaff (Cpte)
(CENT) **CRC2164** Ferruccio Tagliavini—Early Operatic Recordings
(EMI) **CHS7 64864-2(2)** La Scala Edition - Vol.2, 1915-46 (pt 2)

TATE, Jeffrey (cond)
see BRSO
ECO
FNO
ROHO
Rotterdam PO
Staatskapelle Dresden

TATE, Richard (ten)
Saint-Saëns: Samson et Dalila (Cpte)

TATONE, Vito (ten)
Puccini: Manon Lescaut (Cpte)

TATOZZI, Vittorio (bar)
Verdi: Rigoletto (Cpte)

TÁTRAI, Vilmos (cond)
see Hungarian CO

TATTERMUSCHOVÁ, Helena (sop)
Janáček: Makropulos Affair (Cpte)

TAUBER, Richard (ten)
(ASV) **CDAJA5112** Twenty Gramophone All-Time Greats
(EMI) **CDC7 54838-2** Franz Lehár
(EMI) **CDH7 64029-2** Richard Tauber - Opera Recital
(EMI) **CDH7 69787-2** Richard Tauber sings Operetta Arias
(EMI) **CDM7 69476-2** Richard Tauber - A Portrait
(LYRC) **SRO830** Smetana—The Bartered Bride, etc
(MMOI) **CDMOIR405** Great Tenors
(MMOI) **CDMOIR406** Mozart—Historical Recordings
(MMOI) **CDMOIR409** Three Tenors—Björling, Gigli & Tauber
(MMOI) **CDMOIR419** Vienna Nights - Golden Age of Operetta
(MMOI) **CDMOIR425** Three Tenors, Volume 2
(NIMB) **NI7801** Great Singers, Vol.1
(NIMB) **NI7830** Richard Tauber in Opera
(NIMB) **NI7833** Schöne & Tauber in Operetta
(NIMB) **NI7856** Legendary Tenors
(NIMB) **NI7864** More Legendary Voices
(ORFE) **C394101B** Great Mozart Singers Series, Vol. 1
(PEAR) **GEMMCDS9926(2)** Covent Garden on Record—Vol.4 (pt 2)
(PEAR) **GEMMCD9129** Great Tenors, Vol.2
(PEAR) **GEMMCD9145** Richard Tauber - Operatic Arias
(PEAR) **GEMMCD9310** Franz Lehár conducts Richard Tauber
(PEAR) **GEMMCD9327** The Vocal Prime of Richard Tauber
(PEAR) **GEMMCD9409** Lotte Lehmenn—Vol.1
(PREI) **89051** Elisabeth Rethberg (1894-1976)
(PREI) **90150** Lehár conducts Lehár
(SCHW) **314512** Vienna State Opera Live, Vol.1
(TEST) **SBT1005** Ten Top Tenors

TAUBEROVÁ, Maria (sop)
Martinů: Julietta (Cpte)

TAUBMANN, Horst (ten)
R. Strauss: Arabella (Cpte)

TAUSKY, Vilem (cond)
see BBC SO
LSO
Philh

TAVERNER CHOIR
cond A. PARROTT
Purcell: Dido (Cpte)

(VIRG) **VC5 45116-2** The Pocket Purcell

TAVERNER PLAYERS
cond A. PARROTT
Purcell: Dido (Cpte)
(CHAN) **CHAN8301** The Special Sound of Chandos
(EMI) **CDM7 69853-2** Baroque Classics
(VIRG) **VC5 45116-2** The Pocket Purcell

TAVINI, Virgilio (ten)
Verdi: Otello (Cpte)

TAVOLACCINI, Giuliana (sop)
Rossini: Italiana in Algeri (Cpte)
Verdi: Traviata (Cpte)
(DECC) **411 665-2DM3** Puccini: Il trittico

TAWIL, Rima (sop)
Auber: Gustav III (Cpte)

TAYLOR, Gavin (bass)
Vaughan Williams: Pilgrim's Progress (Cpte)

TAYLOR, Janice (mez)
Tchaikovsky: Queen of Spades (Cpte)

TAYLOR, Neilson (bar)
Mozart: Idomeneo (Cpte)
Verdi: Macbeth (Cpte), Trovatore (Cpte)

TAYLOR, Patricia (contr)
Boughton: Immortal Hour (Cpte)

TAYLOR, Paul (ten)
Donizetti: Lucrezia Borgia (Cpte)

TAYLOR, Richard (bass)
Purcell: Fairy Queen, Z629 (Cpte)

TAYLOR-MORLEY, Ann (mez)
M. Berkeley: Baa Baa Black Sheep (Cpte)

TCHAKAROV, Emil (cond)
see *Paris Op Orch*
Plovdiv PO
Sofia Fest Orch
Sofia National Op Orch
Sofia PO

TCHERNOYAROV, O. (cond)
see *Balalaika Orch*

TE KANAWA, Dame **Kiri (sop)**
Bernstein: West Side Story (Cpte)
Bizet: Carmen (Cpte)
Gay: Beggar's Opera (Cpte)
Giordano: Fedora (Cpte)
Gounod: Faust (Cpte)
Humperdinck: Hänsel und Gretel (Cpte)
J. Strauss II: Fledermaus (Cpte)
Meyerbeer: Huguenots (Cpte)
Mozart: Così fan tutte (Cpte), Don Giovanni (Cpte), Nozze di Figaro (exc), Zauberflöte (exc)
Puccini: Bohème (Cpte), Manon Lescaut (Cpte), Rondine (Cpte), Tosca (Cpte)
R. Strauss: Capriccio (Cpte), Rosenkavalier (Cpte)
Tchaikovsky: Eugene Onegin (Cpte)
Verdi: Otello (exc), Rigoletto (Cpte), Simon Boccanegra (Cpte), Traviata (exc)
Wagner: Parsifal (Cpte), Siegfried (Cpte), Tannhäuser (exc)
(CAST) **CASH5051** Puccini Favourites from Covent Garden and the Arena di Verona
(CAST) **CASH5052** Verdi Operatic Favourites
(CAST) **CVI2065** Highlights from the Royal Opera House, Covent Garden
(CAST) **CVI2068** Opera Highlights from Verona 1
(CAST) **CVI2070** Great Puccini Love Scenes from Covent Garden, La Scala and Verona
(CBS) **CD39208** A Portrait of Kiri te Kanawa
(CBS) **MK37298** Puccini and Verdi Arias
(DECC) **417 645-2DH** Kiri - Portrait
(DECC) **421 896-2DA** Puccini—Great Operatic Duets
(DECC) **430 498-2DWO** The World of Mozart
(DECC) **430 724-2DM** Great Operatic Duets
(DECC) **433 064-2DWO** Your Hundred Best Opera Tunes Volume I
(DECC) **433 066-2DWO** Your Hundred Best Opera Tunes III
(DECC) **433 068-2DWO** Your Hundred Best Opera Tunes V
(DECC) **433 822-2DH** Essential Opera
(DECC) **436 300-2DX** Opera Gala Sampler
(DECC) **436 461-2DM** Ten Top Sopranos
(DECC) **436 472-2DM** Great Opera Arias
(DECC) **440 280-2DH** Kiri on Broadway
(DECC) **440 401-2DM** Kiri Te Kanawa — Mozart Arias
(DECC) **440 947-2DH** Essential Opera II
(DECC) **444 555-2DF2** Essential Puccini
(DECC) **084 474-3** The Essential Kiri
(DG) **439 251-2GY** The Leonard Bernstein Album
(DG) **439 153-4GMA** Mad about Sopranos
(DG) **439 251-5GY** The Leonard Bernstein Album
(EMI) **CDC5 55095-2** Prima Diva
(EMI) **CDC7 47454-2** Kiri sings Gershwin
(EMI) **CDC7 49863-2** French Opera Arias
(EMI) **CDC7 54062-2** Kiri Te Kanawa—Italian Opera Arias
(EMI) **CDM5 65578-2** Kiri Te Kanawa
(EMI) **LDA9 91242-1(EMI)** Kiri Te Kanawa—Live Mozart Recital
(ERAT) **2292-45797-2** The Ultimate Opera Collection
(ERAT) **4509-91715-2** The Ultimate Opera Collection 2
(KIWI) **CDSLD-82** Southern Voices—NZ International Opera Singers
(PHIL) **411 148-2PH** Mozart: Opera Arias
(PHIL) **420 950-2PH** Kiri te Kanawa sings Mozart arias
(PHIL) **434 725-2PM** Kiri Te Kanawa - Classics
(PHIL) **434 992-2PH** The Sorceress—Original Soundtrack
(PHIL) **070 155-1PH (PHIL)** The Sorceress—Original Soundtrack
(RCA) **09026 61580-2(8)** RCA/Met 100 Singers, 100 Years (pt 8)
(SONY) **SBK46548** Opera Arias
(SONY) **SK48094** Favourite Puccini Arias
(SONY) **SMK39030** Placido Domingo sings Great Love Scenes
(TELD) **9031-77676-6(TELD)** My World of Opera - Kiri Te Kanawa

TE WIATA, Inia (bass)
Britten: Billy Budd (Cpte)
(KIWI) **CDSLD-82** Southern Voices—NZ International Opera Singers

TEAR, Robert (ten)
Berg: Lulu (Cpte)
Berlioz: Béatrice et Bénédict (Cpte)
Britten: Burning Fiery Furnace (Cpte), Death in Venice (Cpte), Little Sweep (Cpte), Midsummer Night's Dream (Cpte), Prodigal Son (Cpte), Turn of the Screw (Cpte)
Henze: Bassariden (Cpte)
Holst: Wandering Scholar (Cpte)
Janáček: Cunning Little Vixen (Cpte)
Mozart: Entführung (Cpte), Idomeneo (Cpte), Nozze di Figaro (Cpte), Sposo deluso (Cpte), Zauberflöte (Cpte)
Offenbach: Contes d'Hoffmann (Cpte)
Puccini: Manon Lescaut (Cpte)
Purcell: Dido (Cpte), Indian Queen, Z630 (exc)
R. Strauss: Rosenkavalier (Cpte)
Shostakovich: Lady Macbeth of Mtsensk (Cpte)
Tippett: Knot Garden (Cpte)
Vaughan Williams: Hugh the Drover (Cpte)
Wagner: Parsifal (Cpte), Rheingold (Cpte)
Weill: Sieben Todsünden (Cpte)
(CAST) **CVI2065** Highlights from the Royal Opera House, Covent Garden
(EMI) **CMS5 65119-2** Delius—Orchestral Works
(EMI) **LDX9 91275-1(EMI)** Sawallisch conducts Wagner's Ring

TEARE, Christine (sop)
Janáček: Fate (Cpte)
Wagner: Parsifal (Cpte)

TEATRE LLIURE CHAMBER ORCHESTRA (BARCELONA)
cond J. PONS
Falla: Corregidor y la molinera

TEATRO LA FENICE CHORUS
cond V. PARISI
(NUOV) **6892** William Matteuzzi sings Opera Arias

TEATRO LA FENICE ORCHESTRA
cond A. CURTIS
Traetta: Buovo d'Antona (Cpte)
cond V. PARISI
(NUOV) **6892** William Matteuzzi sings Opera Arias

TEBALDI, Renata (sop)
Boito: Mefistofele (Cpte)
Catalani: Wally (Cpte)
Cilea: Adriana Lecouvreur (Cpte)
Giordano: Andrea Chénier (Cpte)
J. Strauss II: Fledermaus (Cpte)
Mascagni: Cavalleria Rusticana (Cpte)
Ponchielli: Gioconda (Cpte)
Puccini: Bohème (exc), Madama Butterfly (Cpte), Manon Lescaut (Cpte), Tosca (Cpte), Turandot (Cpte)
Verdi: Aida (Cpte), Ballo in maschera (Cpte), Falstaff (Cpte), Otello (Cpte), Traviata (Cpte)
(BELA) **450 006-2** Famous Opera Duets
(BELA) **450 007-2** Puccini Favourites
(BELA) **450 133-2** Verdi Favourites
(DECC) **411 665-2DM3** Puccini: Il trittico
(DECC) **417 686-2DC** Puccini—Operatic Arias
(DECC) **425 847-2DWO** Your hunded best tunes vol. 1
(DECC) **430 481-2DX2** Renata Tebaldi sings Opera Arias
(DECC) **433 064-2DWO** Your Hundred Best Opera Tunes Volume I
(DECC) **433 065-2DWO** Your Hundred Best Opera Tunes Volume II
(DECC) **433 066-2DWO** Your Hundred Best Opera Tunes III
(DECC) **433 067-2DWO** Your Hundred Best Opera Tunes IV
(DECC) **433 069-2DWO** Your Hundred Best Opera Tunes VI
(DECC) **433 439-2DA** Great Love Duets
(DECC) **433 440-2DA** Golden Opera
(DECC) **433 442-2DA** Verdi—Famous Arias
(DECC) **433 624-2DSP** Great Soprano Arias
(DECC) **433 636-2DSP** Puccini—Famous Arias
(DECC) **433 822-2DH** Essential Opera
(DECC) **433 865-2DWO** The World of Puccini
(DECC) **436 202-2DM** Italian Songs
(DECC) **436 300-2DX** Opera Gala Sampler
(DECC) **436 301-2DA** Renata Tebaldi & Franco Corelli—Arias & Duets
(DECC) **436 317-2DA** Puccini—Famous Arias
(DECC) **436 461-2DM** Ten Top Sopranos
(DECC) **440 407-2DM** Mario del Monaco
(DECC) **440 408-2DM** Renata Tebaldi
(DECC) **443 377-2DM** Ten Top Sopranos 2
(DECC) **443 930-2DM** Jussi Björling sings Opera Arias
(DECC) **444 555-2DF2** Essential Puccini
(EMI) **CHS7 69741-2(7)** Record of Singing, Vol.4—Italian School
(FONI) **CDMR5023** Martini & Rossi Festival, Volume 23
(MEMO) **HR4235/6** Great Voices-Renata Tebaldi
(MEMO) **HR4372/3** Great Voices Giuseppe Di Stefano
(MEMO) **HR4400/1** Great Voices - Ettore Bastianini
(RCA) **GD87799** The Pearl Fishers Duet plus Duets and Scenes
(RCA) **GK85277** Legendary Performers - Björling
(RCA) **09026 62689-2** The Voices of Living Stereo, Volume 1
(VAI) **VAI69100** Renata Tebaldi and Franco Corelli

TEDESCO, Alfio (ten)
(PEAR) **GEMMCDS9160(2)** De Luca Edition, Vol.2 (pt 2)
(PREI) **89073** Giuseppe de Luca (1876-1950) - II

TEDESCO, Sergio (ten)
Boito: Mefistofele (Cpte)
Verdi: Traviata (Cpte)

TEDESCO DUO
(SCHW) **310402** Guitar Music from the Age of Viennese Classicism

TELLINI, Ines Alfani (sop)
Verdi: Falstaff (Cpte)
(PREI) **89072** Aureliano Pertile (1885-1952) - II

TELVA, Marion (mez)
Bellini: Norma (exc)
(NIMB) **NI7805** Rosa Ponselle—Opera & Song Recital
(ROMO) **81007-2** Rosa Ponselle—Victor Recordings 1926-1929

TEMIANKA, Henri (vn)
(BIDD) **LAB059/60** Henri Temianka—Recital

TEMIRKANOV, Yuri (cond)
see *Leningrad PO*
RPO
St Petersburg PO

TEMPLE, Richard (bar)
(SYMP) **SYMCD1123** Sullivan—Sesquicentenial Commemorative Issue

TENERIFE SYMPHONY ORCHESTRA
cond A. R. MARBÀ
Vives: Bohemios (Cpte), Doña Francisquita (Cpte)

TENNANT, Raymond (cond)
see *Glasgow CWS Band*

TENNSTEDT, Klaus (cond)
see *BPO*
LPO

TENZI, Fausto (ten)
Donizetti: Imelda (Cpte)

TEODORINI, Elena (sop)
(EMI) **CHS7 64860-2(1)** La Scala Edition - Vol.1, 1878-1914 (pt 1)
(SYMP) **SYMCD1077** The Harold Wayne Collection, Vol.4

TEREKIN, Konstantin (bass)
(DANT) **LYS013/5** Tchaikovsky—The Queen of Spades

TERENTIEVA, Nina (mez)
Rimsky-Korsakov: Kashchey (Cpte), Tsar's Bride (Cpte)

TERFEL, Bryn (bass-bar)
Britten: Gloriana (Cpte)
Cilea: Adriana Lecouvreur (Cpte)
Lehár: Lustige Witwe (Cpte)
Mozart: Don Giovanni (Cpte), Nozze di Figaro (Cpte)
Prokofiev: Fiery Angel (Cpte)
Puccini: Tosca (Cpte)
R. Strauss: Frau ohne Schatten (Cpte), Salome (Cpte)
Sullivan: Yeomen of the Guard (Cpte)
Wagner: Lohengrin (Cpte)
(DG) **439 768-2GH** Wagner—Gala - New Year's Eve Concert 1993
(HYPE) **CDA66569** Vaughan Williams—Choral Works
(PHIL) **422 523-2PME8(2)** The Complete Mozart Edition Vol 23 (pt 2)

TERKAL, Karl (ten)
Beethoven: Fidelio (Cpte)
Einem: Dantons Tod (Cpte)
J. Strauss II: Fledermaus (Cpte)
Mozart: Zauberflöte (Cpte)
R. Strauss: Rosenkavalier (Cpte)
(KOCH) **399 225** Operetta Highlights 3

TERNER, Helga (sop)
Wagner: Parsifal (Cpte)

TERRANI, Lucia Valentini (mez)
Rossini: Cenerentola (exc), Donna del Lago (Cpte), Italiana in Algeri (exc), Viaggio a Reims (Cpte)
Verdi: Aida (Cpte), Don Carlos (exc), Falstaff (Cpte), Nabucco (exc)
Vivaldi: Orlando Furioso (Cpte)
(CAST) **CASH5052** Verdi Operatic Favourites
(IMP) **DPCD998** Opera Stars in Concert
(RNE) **650004** Opera Stars in Concert

TERRANOVA, Vittorio (ten)
Rossini: Guillaume Tell (Cpte)

TERROSI, Aldo (bar)
Puccini: Bohème (Cpte)

TERRY, Stephen (spkr)
Britten: Midsummer Night's Dream (Cpte)

TERRY, Stephen (treb)
Britten: Albert Herring (Cpte)

TERSSON, Eva Maria (mez)
Gluck: Echo et Narcisse (Cpte)

TERZAKIS, Zahos (ten)
Kalomiris: Mother's Ring (Cpte)

TERZIAN, Anita (mez)
Gounod: Faust (Cpte)

TESAROWICZ, Romuald (bass)
Mussorgsky: Boris Godunov (Cpte)
Rossini: Semiramide (Cpte)
Shostakovich: Lady Macbeth of Mtsensk (Cpte)
Verdi: Luisa Miller (Cpte)

TESCHEMACHER, Margarete (sop)
Mozart: Nozze di Figaro (Cpte)
Wagner: Walküre (exc)
(MMOI) **CDMOIR408** Great Sopranos
(PEAR) **GEMMCDS9121** Wagner—Die Meistersinger, Act 3, etc
(PEAR) **GEMMCD9129** Great Tenors, Vol.2
(PREI) **89024** Marcel Wittrisch (1901-1955)
(PREI) **89049** Margarete Teschemacher (1903-1959)
(PREI) **89211** Helge Roswaenge (1897-1972) - III
(PREI) **90237** R Strauss—Daphne
(SCHW) **314672** Vienna State Opera Live, Vol.17

TESCHLER, Fred (bass)
R. Strauss: Elektra (Cpte)
Wagner: Parsifal (Cpte)

TESSMER, Heinrich (ten)
Mozart: Zauberflöte (Cpte)
(DANA) **DACOCD319/21** The Lauritz Melchior Anthology - Vol.5
(LYRC) **SRO830** Smetana—The Bartered Bride, etc
(PEAR) **GEMMCDS9137** Wagner—Der Ring des Nibelungen
(PREI) **89076** Josef Herrmann (1903-1955)

TESTA, Arturo (ten)
Puccini: Madama Butterfly (Cpte)

TESTI, Lorenzo (bar)
Verdi: Rigoletto (Cpte)

TETRA
(CONI) **CDCF903** By Arrangement—Tetra Guitar Quartet

TETRAZZINI, Luisa (sop)
(BEUL) **1PD4** 78 Classics - Volume One
(CLUB) **CL99-060** Enrico Caruso—Opera & Song Recital
(EMI) **CHS7 63802-2(1)** Tetrazzini—The London Records (pt 1)
(EMI) **CHS7 63802-2(2)** Tetrazzini—The London Records (pt 2)
(NIMB) **NI7801** Great Singers, Vol.1
(NIMB) **NI7802** Divas 1906-1935
(NIMB) **NI7808** Luisa Tetrazzini—Opera & Song Recital
(NIMB) **NI7851** Legendary Voices
(PEAR) **EVC3(1)** The Caruso Edition, Vol.3 (pt 1)
(PEAR) **GEMMCDS9924(2)** Covent Garden on Record, Vol.2 (pt 2)
(PEAR) **GEMMCD9221** Luisa Tetrazzini—Vol.1
(PEAR) **GEMMCD9222** Luisa Tetrazzini—Vol.2
(PEAR) **GEMMCD9223** Luisa Tetrazzini—Vol.3
(PEAR) **GEMMCD9224** Luisa Tetrazzini—Vol.4
(PEAR) **GEMMCD9225** Luisa Tetrazzini—Vol.5
(RCA) **GD60495(4)** The Complete Caruso Collection (pt 4)
(RCA) **09026 61242-2** Caruso Sings Verdi
(RCA) **09026 61580-2(2)** RCA/Met 100 Singers, 100 Years (pt 2)
(TEST) **SBT1008** Viva Rossini

TETU, Bernard (cond)
see Inst Ens

TEXAS BOYS' CHOIR
cond I. STRAVINSKY
(SONY) **SM22K46290(3)** Stravinsky—The Complete Edition (pt 3)

TEXIER, Vincent le (bass-bar)
Berlioz: Béatrice et Bénédict (Cpte)
Bizet: Carmen (Cpte)
Debussy: Pelléas et Mélisande (Cpte), Rodrigue et Chimène (Cpte)
Grétry: Caravane du Caire (Cpte)
Marais: Alcyone (Cpte)
Prokofiev: Love for 3 Oranges (Cpte)
R. Strauss: Salomé (Cpte)
Rameau: Platée (Cpte)
Ravel: Enfant et les sortilèges (Cpte)
(MARC) **8 223774** Ropartz—Choral Works

TEYTE, Dame **Maggie (sop)**
(MMOI) **CDMOIR408** Great Sopranos

THALBEN-BALL, Sir **George (organ)**
(BEUL) **1PD5** Historic Organs, Volume 1

THALLAUG, Edith (mez)
Bibalo: Gespenster (Cpte)

THANE, Amanda (sop)
Meyerbeer: Huguenots (Cpte)

THARANDE, Jacques (sngr)
Terrasse: Fiancée du Scaphandrier (Cpte)

THAU, Pierre (bass)
Berlioz: Troyens (Cpte)
Bizet: Carmen (Cpte)
Debussy: Pelléas et Mélisande (Cpte)
Gounod: Roméo et Juliette (Cpte)
Massenet: Jongleur de Notre Dame (Cpte)
Mozart: Don Giovanni (Cpte)
Saint-Saëns: Samson et Dalila (Cpte)
(DECC) **433 067-2DWO** Your Hundred Best Opera Tunes IV

THAW, David (ten)
Mozart: Zauberflöte (Cpte)
R. Strauss: Capriccio (Cpte), Rosenkavalier (Cpte)
Wagner: Meistersinger (Cpte)

THAYSEN, Eva Hess (sop)
(KONT) **32203** Nielsen—Orchestral Works

THEBOM, Blanche (mez)
Mozart: Così fan tutte (exc)
Wagner: Tristan und Isolde (Cpte)
(EMI) **CDH5 65072-2** Glyndebourne Recorded - 1934-1994
(EMI) **CDH7 63199-2** Sena Jurinac—Opera and Song Recital
(EMI) **CHS7 69741-2(1)** Record of Singing, Vol.4—Anglo-American School (pt 1)

THEIMER, Uwe (cond)
see Vienna Op Ball Orch

THEODORIDOU, Sonia (sop)
Cavalli: Calisto (Cpte)

THERVEL, Gérard (bar)
Lully: Phaëton (Cpte)

THEURING, Günther (ten)
Monteverdi: Orfeo (Cpte)

THEYARD, Harry (ten)
Rossini: Siège de Corinthe (Cpte)

THIBAUD, Jacques (vn)
(APR) **APR7028** Jacques Thibaud—Complete Solo Recordings 1929-36
(BIDD) **LAB014** Jacques Thibaud—1922-24 Recordings
(BIDD) **LAB024** Jacques Thibaud—1924-27 Recordings
(MSCM) **MM30321** Jacques Thibaud—Violin Recital

THIELEMANN, Christian (cond)
see Berlin Deutsche Op Orch

THIGPEN, Martha (sop)
Wagner: Walküre (Cpte)
(DG) **072 422-3GH7** Levine conducts Wagner's Ring

THILL, Georges (ten)
G. Charpentier: Louise (exc)
Massenet: Werther (Cpte)
(EMI) **CDC7 54016-2** Tenorissimo!
(EMI) **CDM7 69548-2** Georges Thill sings French Opera Arias
(EMI) **CMS7 64008-2(1)** Wagner Singing on Record (pt 1)
(FORL) **UCD16727** L'Incomparable Georges Thill
(MMOI) **CDMOIR405** Great Tenors
(MMOI) **CDMOIR419** Vienna Nights - Golden Age of Operetta
(MSCM) **MM30377** 18 Tenors d'Expression Française
(NIMB) **NI7856** Legendary Tenors
(PEAR) **GEMMCDS9926(1)** Covent Garden on Record—Vol.4 (pt 1)
(PEAR) **GEMMCD9947** Georges Thill
(TEST) **SBT1005** Ten Top Tenors

THINGBOE, Eva Lillian (mez)
Corghi: Divara (Cpte)

THIRACHE, Julien (bar)
Bizet: Carmen (Cpte)
Poulenc: Mamelles de Tirésias (Cpte)

THIVEL, Benoît (alto)
Rossi: Orfeo (Cpte)

THOM, Peter (voc)
Bernstein: West Side Story (Cpte)

THOMAMÜLLER, Lieselotte (sop)
Wagner: Walküre (Cpte)
(FOYE) **15-CF2011** Wagner—Der Ring de Nibelungen

THOMAS, David (bass)
Handel: Orlando (Cpte)
Monteverdi: Orfeo (Cpte)
Purcell: Dido (Cpte), Don Quixote: The Musical (Cpte), Fairy Queen, Z629 (Cpte), Indian Queen, Z630 (Cpte), Tempest, Z631 (Cpte)
(DG) **439 474-2GCL** Purcell—Opera & Choral Works
(ERAT) **4509-96371-2** Gardiner—The Purcell Collection
(HARM) **HMP390 804** Great Baroque Masters: Handel
(HARM) **HMU90 7016** Handel: Arias for Montagnana
(HYPE) **CDA66056** Purcell: Songs and Dialogues
(MOSC) **070974** King of the Low Seas

THOMAS, Glynne (bar)
Meyerbeer: Huguenots (Cpte)
Verdi: Otello (Cpte)

THOMAS, Handel (bass)
Puccini: Manon Lescaut (Cpte)
Walton: Troilus and Cressida (Cpte)

THOMAS, Jeffrey (ten)
Purcell: Fairy Queen, Z629

THOMAS, Jess (ten)
Wagner: Lohengrin (Cpte), Meistersinger (Cpte), Parsifal (Cpte), Siegfried (Cpte)
(DG) **429 168-2GR** Wagner: Excerpts from Der Ring
(DG) **435 211-2GX15** Wagner—Der Ring des Nibelungen
(DG) **439 423-2GCL** Wagner—Der Ring des Nibelungen (highlights)

THOMAS, John Charles (bar)
(NIMB) **NI7867** Legendary Baritones

THOMAS, John Charles (sngr)
(PEAR) **GEMMCDS9059/61** Music from the New York Stage, Vol. 4: 1917-20

THOMAS, Kelvin (bass)
Maxwell Davies: Martyrdom of St Magnus (Cpte)

THOMAS, Lewis (ten)
Walton: Troilus and Cressida (exc)

THOMAS, Marjorie (contr)
Sullivan: Gondoliers (Cpte), HMS Pinafore (Cpte), Iolanthe (Cpte), Mikado (Cpte), Patience (Cpte), Yeomen of the Guard (Cpte)
(CFP) **CD-CFP4238** Gilbert and Sullivan
(CFP) **CD-CFP4609** Favourite Gilbert & Sullivan
(EMI) **CMS7 64409-2** Sullivan—Pirates of Penzance & Orch. Works

THOMAS, Mary (sop)
Maxwell Davies: Miss Donnithorne's Maggot
Puccini: Rondine (Cpte)
Purcell: Dido (Cpte), King Arthur, Z628 (Cpte)

THOMAS, Nova (sop)
Balfe: Bohemian Girl (Cpte)

THOMAS, Pascal (bass)
Debussy: Pelléas et Mélisande (Cpte)

THOMAS, Thomas L. (sngr)
(VAI) **VAI69112** Eleanor Steber in Opera and Song Vol 2

THOMAS, Werner (vc)
(ORFE) **C131851A** Virtuoso cello arrangements

THOMASCHKE, Thomas (bass)
Mozart: Thamos, K345 (Cpte), Zauberflöte (Cpte)
Weber: Freischütz (exc)

THOMPSON, Adrian (ten)
Britten: Midsummer Night's Dream (Cpte)
Gay: Beggar's Opera (Cpte)
(ASV) **CDDCA758** Falla, Milhaud & Stravinsky—Operas
(HYPE) **CDA66569** Vaughan Williams—Choral Works

THOMPSON, Arthur (bar)
Gershwin: Porgy and Bess (Cpte)
Puccini: Turandot (Cpte)

THOMPSON, Hugh (bar)
Bizet: Carmen (Cpte)

THOMPSON, Ian (ten)
G. Charpentier: Louise (Cpte)
(OPRA) **ORCH104** A Hundred Years of Italian Opera: 1820-1830

THOMPSON, Linda (sop)
Gershwin: Porgy and Bess (Cpte)

THOMSON, Bryden (cond)
see LPO

THOMSON, Paul (bar)
Maxwell Davies: Martyrdom of St Magnus (Cpte)
Sullivan: HMS Pinafore (Cpte)

THORBORG, Kerstin (mez)
Wagner: Siegfried (Cpte), Tristan und Isolde (Cpte)
(LYRC) **LCD146** Frida Leider sings Wagner
(PREI) **89084** Kerstin Thorborg (1896-1970)
(RCA) **09026 61580-2(4)** RCA/Met 100 Singers, 100 Years (pt 4)
(SCHW) **314512** Vienna State Opera Live, Vol.1
(SCHW) **314542** Vienna State Opera Live, Vol.4
(SCHW) **314572** Vienna State Opera Live, Vol.7
(SCHW) **314592** Vienna State Opera Live, Vol.9
(SCHW) **314602** Vienna State Opera Live, Vol.10
(SCHW) **314622** Vienna State Opera Live, Vol.12

THORBURN, Ashley (bass)
(OPRA) **ORCH104** A Hundred Years of Italian Opera: 1820-1830

THORN, Penelope (sop)
Wagner: Götterdämmerung (Cpte)
(EMI) **LDX9 91275-1(EMI)** Sawallisch conducts Wagner's Ring

THORNTON, Edna (contr)
(PEAR) **GEMMCDS9925(1)** Covent Garden on Record—Vol.3 (pt 1)
(PREI) **89002** Miguel Fleta (1893-1938)

THORNTON, James (bar)
Walton: Troilus and Cressida (Cpte)

THORNTON-HOLMES, Christopher (bar)
Donizetti: Emilia di Liverpool (Cpte), Eremitaggio di Liverpool (Cpte)
Tchaikovsky: Queen of Spades (Cpte)
Verdi: Traviata (Cpte)

THORPE, Catherine (sngr)
Schuman: Mighty Casey (Cpte)

THORSEN, Stein Arild (bar)
Braein: Anne Pedersdotter (Cpte)

THORSTEINSSON, Jon (ten)
Rachmaninov: Monna Vanna (exc)

THREE RIVERS SYMPHONY ORCHESTRA
cond G. BELLEMARE
(CBC) **SMCD5127** Great Baritone Arias

THÜRINGIAN LANDESTHEATER CHORUS
cond K. BACH
S. Wagner: Bärenhäuter (Cpte), Schwarzschwanenreich (Cpte)
cond R. REUTER
Pfitzner: Herz (Cpte)

THÜRINGIAN SYMPHONY ORCHESTRA
cond K. BACH
S. Wagner: Bärenhäuter (Cpte), Schwarzschwanenreich (Cpte)
cond R. REUTER
Pfitzner: Herz (Cpte)

THURSTON CLARINET QUARTET
(ASV) **CDWHL2076** Clarinet Masquerade

THYGESEN, Thyge (ten)
Nielsen: Maskarade (Cpte)

TIAN, Hao Jiang (bass)
Puccini: Fanciulla del West (Cpte)

TIBBETT, Lawrence (bar)
Verdi: Otello (Cpte), Traviata (Cpte)
(BEUL) **1PD4** 78 Classics - Volume One
(MMOI) **CDMOIR412** Great Voices of the Century Sing Puccini
(NIMB) **NI7801** Great Singers, Vol.1
(NIMB) **NI7867** Legendary Baritones
(PEAR) **GEMMCDS9076** Stokowski conducts Wagner, Volume III
(PEAR) **GEMMCDS9452** The Emperor Tibbett
(PEAR) **GEMMCDS9926(2)** Covent Garden on Record—Vol.4 (pt 2)
(RCA) **GD87808** Lawrence Tibbett sings Opera Arias
(RCA) **09026 61580-2(3)** RCA/Met 100 Singers, 100 Years (pt 3)

TIBBS, Gary (sngr)
Gay: Beggar's Opera (Cpte)

TIBELL, Lars (ten)
Mozart: Così fan tutte (Cpte), Idomeneo (Cpte)

TIBOLDI, Mária (sop)
Lehár: Lustige Witwe (exc)

TIBORIS, Peter (cond)
see *B. Martinů PO*

TICHÁ, Klára (sop)
Krása: Brundibár (Cpte)

TICHY, Georg (bass)
Mozart: Zauberflöte (Cpte)
Puccini: Madama Butterfly (Cpte)
R. Strauss: Ariadne auf Naxos (Cpte)
Verdi: Traviata (Cpte)
Wagner: Lohengrin (Cpte), Parsifal (Cpte)

TICHÝ, Jan Hus (cond)
see *Prague Nat Th Orch*

TICOZZI, Ebe (mez)
Mascagni: Cavalleria Rusticana (Cpte)
(EMI) **CDC7 54702-2** Maria Callas - La Divina
(EMI) **CMS7 63244-2** The Art of Maria Callas

TIEPPO, Giorgio (ten)
(MCI) **MCCD099** Opera's Greatest Arias

TIERI, Emidio (cond)
see *La Scala Orch*

TIERNAN, Lee (treb)
Puccini: Tosca (exc)

TIERNEY, Vivien (sop)
Joseph James: Scarlet Letter (exc)
Lehár: Graf von Luxemburg (exc)

TIETJEN, Heinz (cond)
see *Bayreuth Fest Orch*
Vienna St Op Orch

TIFFIN BOYS' SCHOOL CHOIR
cond K. NAGANO
Stravinsky: Perséphone (Cpte)

TIILIKAINEN, Sauli (bar)
Bergman: Singing Tree (Cpte)
Kortekangas: Grand Hotel

TIKALOVÁ, Drahomíra (sop)
Janáček: Cunning Little Vixen (Cpte), Káťa Kabanová (Cpte)
(KOCH) **34036-2** A Pageant of Opera

TILLI, Johann (bass)
Gazzaniga: Don Giovanni (Cpte)
Schumann: Genoveva (Cpte)
Shostakovich: Lady Macbeth of Mtsensk (Cpte)
(BIS) **BIS-CD373/4** Opera Scenes from Savaonlinna

TILSON THOMAS, Michael (cond)
see *Hungarian St Op Orch*
Hungarian St Orch
Los Angeles PO
LSO

TILVERN, Alan (spkr)
Gershwin: Porgy and Bess (Cpte)

TIMIŞOARA BANATUL PHILHARMONIC CHORUS
cond N. BOBOC
(ELCT) **ELCD109** Timisoara Memorial

TIMIŞOARA BANATUL PHILHARMONIC ORCHESTRA
cond N. BOBOC
(ELCT) **ELCD109** Timisoara Memorial

TIMIŞOARA ROMANIAN OPERA ORCHESTRA
cond M. BELEAVCENCO
(ELCT) **ELCD109** Timisoara Memorial
cond I. IANCU
(ELCT) **ELCD109** Timisoara Memorial

TIMM, Liane (sop)
Mozart: Nozze di Figaro (Cpte)
(SCHW) **314722** Vienna State Opera Live, Vol.22

TINDALL, Paul (ten)
Purcell: Dido (Cpte)

TINKLER, Mark (treb)
Bernstein: Candide (1988) (exc)

TINSLEY, Pauline (sop)
R. Strauss: Elektra (Cpte)
(EMI) **CDM7 64356-2** Opera Choruses
(EMI) **CZS5 68559-2** Italian Opera Choruses
(EMIL) **CDZ102** Best Loved Classics 3

TINTNER, Georg (cond)
see *Nova Scotia SO*

TIPPETT, Sir Michael (cond)
see *English Northern Philh*

TIRARD, Charlotte (mez)
(MSCM) **MM30221** 18 French Divas

TIRMONT, Dominique (bar)
Audran: Miss Helyett (Cpte)
Messager: Coups de Roulis (Cpte), Passionêment (Cpte)
Offenbach: Madame l'Archiduc (Cpte)
Terrasse: Travaux d'Hercule (Cpte)

TITTA, Enzo (bass)
Verdi: Rigoletto (Cpte)

TITUS, Alan (bar)
Catalani: Wally (Cpte)
Leoncavallo: Bohème (Cpte)
Mozart: Don Giovanni (Cpte), Nozze di Figaro (Cpte)
Puccini: Bohème (Cpte)
Schumann: Genoveva (Cpte)
Verdi: Falstaff (Cpte)
(EURO) **VD69256** Mozart—Opera Arias
(RCA) **09026 62699-2** Opera's Greatest Duets

TIVOLI AUGMENTED ORCHESTRA
cond R. STRAUSS
R. Strauss: Rosenkavalier film

TIVOLI CONCERT ORCHESTRA
cond S. FELUMB
(EMI) **CHS7 69741-2(5)** Record of Singing, Vol.4—Scandinavian School

TJEKNAVORIAN, Loris (cond)
see *Armenian PO*
National PO

TOBIASSON, Ingrid (contr)
Börtz: Bacchae (Cpte)
Lidholm: Dream Play (Cpte)

TOBIN, Eugene (ten)
Puccini: Tosca (Cpte)

TOCHA, Ulla (mez)
Weill: Zar lässt sich Photographieren (Cpte)

TOCZYSKA, Stefania (mez)
Bellini: Beatrice di Tenda (Cpte)
Glinka: Life for the Tsar (Cpte)
Mussorgsky: Boris Godunov (Cpte)
Prokofiev: War and Peace (Cpte)
Spontini: Olimpie (Cpte)
Tchaikovsky: Queen of Spades (Cpte)
Verdi: Trovatore (Cpte)

TODD, Philip (ten)
Monteverdi: L'Arianna (exc)

TODISCO, Nunzio (ten)
(MCI) **MCCD099** Opera's Greatest Arias

TODOROV, Todor (ten)
(EMI) **CMS7 63386-2** Borodin—Prince Igor & Complete Solo Songs

TODOROVITCH, Marie-Ange (sop)
Massenet: Don Quichotte (Cpte)
Tchaikovsky: Queen of Spades (Cpte)

TOKATYAN, Armand (ten)
(CLUB) **CL99-052** Rosa Raisa (1893-1963)
(VAI) **VAIA1017** Leonard Warren—Early Recordings
(VAI) **VAIA1072** Eleanor Steber Collection, Volume 1

TOKODY, Ilona (sop)
(EURO) **GD69043** Puccini: Il Trittico
(VAI) **VAIA1009** Ilona Tokody. Portrait of the Artist

TOKYO LITTLE SINGERS
cond G KUHN
Verdi: Otello (Cpte)

TOKYO PHILHARMONIC ORCHESTRA
cond F. HAIDER
(NIGH) **NC090560-2** The Anniversary Concert - Gruberova
cond G KUHN
Verdi: Otello (Cpte)
cond G. KUHN
Verdi: Macbeth (Cpte)
cond R. PATERNOSTRO
Verdi: Traviata (Cpte)

TOLZ BOYS' CHOIR
cond C. ABBADO
Mussorgsky: Boris Godunov (Cpte)
cond K. EICHHORN
Humperdinck: Hänsel und Gretel (Cpte)
cond L. GARDELLI
Leoncavallo: Pagliacci (Cpte)
cond B. HAITINK
Mozart: Zauberflöte (Cpte)
cond R. KUBELÍK
Pfitzner: Palestrina (Cpte)
cond E. LEINSDORF
Korngold: Tote Stadt (Cpte)
cond D. RUNNICLES
Humperdinck: Hänsel und Gretel (Cpte)
cond J. TATE
Humperdinck: Hänsel und Gretel (exc)
cond H. WALLBERG
Humperdinck: Königskinder (Cpte)

TOMASCHEK, Adolf (ten)
R. Strauss: Rosenkavalier (Cpte)
Verdi: Ballo in maschera (Cpte)

TOMASI, Henri (cond)
see *FNO*
Paris SO
Vlassof Orch

TOMASZEWSKI, Rolf (bar)
Offenbach: Contes d'Hoffmann (exc)
R. Strauss: Salome (Cpte)

TOMCKOWIACK, Gonzalo (ten)
Verdi: Simon Boccanegra (Cpte)

TOMEI, Giulio (bass)
(EMI) **CDH7 61052-2** Beniamino Gigli—Arias and Duets (1932-1949)
(MMOI) **CDMOIR412** Great Voices of the Century Sing Puccini

TOMEK, Richard (ten)
(SCHW) **314602** Vienna State Opera Live, Vol.10
(SCHW) **314622** Vienna State Opera Live, Vol.12
(SCHW) **314632** Vienna State Opera Live, Vol.13
(SCHW) **314642** Vienna State Opera Live, Vol.14
(SCHW) **314702** Vienna State Opera Live, Vol.20

TOMICICH, Aurio (bass)
Bellini: Adelson e Salvini (Cpte), Bianca e Fernando (Cpte)
Fénelon: Chevalier Imaginaire (Cpte)
Maderna: Satyricon (Cpte)

TOMLINSON, John (bass)
A. Thomas: Hamlet (Cpte)
Bellini: Capuleti (Cpte), Sonnambula (Cpte)
Birtwistle: Punch and Judy (Cpte)
Britten: Peter Grimes (Cpte)
Donizetti: Maria Stuarda (Cpte)
Handel: Alcina (Cpte), Giulio Cesare (Cpte)
Holst: At the Boar's Head (Cpte)
Martinů: Greek Passion (Cpte)
Monteverdi: Orfeo (Cpte)
Mozart: Così fan tutte (exc), Don Giovanni (exc), Nozze di Figaro (Cpte)
Puccini: Manon Lescaut (Cpte), Tosca (Cpte)
Rameau: Naïs (Cpte)
Rossini: Guillaume Tell (Cpte)
Saint-Saëns: Samson et Dalila (Cpte)
Stravinsky: Nightingale (Cpte)
Verdi: Forza del destino (Cpte), Macbeth (Cpte), Traviata (Cpte)
Wagner: Götterdämmerung (Cpte), Parsifal (Cpte), Rheingold (Cpte), Siegfried (exc), Walküre (Cpte)
Weill: Sieben Todsünden
(ASV) **CDDCA666** D'Avalos conducts Wagner, Vol 3
(ERAT) **4509-98955-2** Boulez conducts Stravinsky
(KOCH) **34036-2** A Pageant of Opera
(LOND) **825 126-2** Amadeus - Original Soundtrack
(OPRA) **ORC003** Donizetti—Gabriella di Vergy
(SONY) **SK45965** Esa-Pekka Salonen conducts Stravinsky

TOMMASINI, Giuseppe (ten)
(ROMO) **81005-2** Claudia Muzio (1889-1936)

TOMMASINI, Mario (bass)
Verdi: Macbeth (Cpte)

TOMMASO, Angelo (bass)
Rossini: Barbiere di Siviglia (exc)

TOMMASO, Salvatore de (ten)
Mascagni: Iris (Cpte)

TOMOWA-SINTOW, Anna (sop)
Borodin: Prince Igor (Cpte)
Giordano: Andrea Chénier (Cpte)
Korngold: Wunder der Heliane (Cpte)
Mozart: Don Giovanni (Cpte), Nozze di Figaro (Cpte), Zauberflöte (Cpte)
R. Strauss: Ariadne auf Naxos (Cpte), Rosenkavalier (Cpte)
Tchaikovsky: Eugene Onegin (Cpte)
Wagner: Lohengrin (exc)

TRINITY BOYS' CHOIR
cond O. DE FABRITIIS
Boito: Mefistofele (Cpte)
cond R. HICKOX
Britten: Midsummer Night's Dream (Cpte)
cond JAMES LEVINE
Puccini: Bohème (Cpte)
cond G. LLOYD
G. Lloyd: John Socman (exc)

TRO, Silvia (sop)
Bretón: Verbena de La Paloma (Cpte)

TROEVA-MIRCHEVA, Rossitza (contr)
Mussorgsky: Boris Godunov (Cpte)
Tchaikovsky: Eugene Onegin (Cpte)

TROFIMOV, Viacheslav (bar)
Mussorgsky: Khovanshchina (Cpte)

TROGU-RÖHRICH, Caterina (sop)
Traetta: Buovo d'Antona (Cpte)

TRONDHEIM SYMPHONY CHORUS
cond O.K. RUUD
(VIRG) **VC5 45051-2** Grieg—Choral Works

TRONDHEIM SYMPHONY ORCHESTRA
cond O.K. RUUD
(VIRG) **VC5 45051-2** Grieg—Choral Works

TROPIN, Robert (sngr)
Gounod: Mireille (Cpte)

TROST, Rainer (ten)
Lehár: Lustige Witwe (Cpte)
Mozart: Così fan tutte (Cpte)

TROTTA, Bernardino (sngr)
Rossini: Armida (Cpte)

TROTTER, Thomas (organ)
(DECC) **436 656-2DH** Organ Transcriptions - Thomas Trotter
(HYPE) **CDA66216** The Grand Organ

TROTTMANN, Barbara (sngr)
Corghi: Divara (Cpte)

TROUPOVA, Irena (sop)
Biber: Arminio (Cpte)

TROVARELLI, Antonella (mez)
Rossini: Pietra del paragone (Cpte)

TROY, Dermot (ten)
R. Strauss: Capriccio (Cpte)
Rossini: Comte Ory (Cpte)

TROYANOS, Tatiana (mez)
Bellini: Norma (Cpte)
Bernstein: West Side Story (Cpte)
Bizet: Carmen (Cpte)
Massenet: Werther (exc)
Mozart: Così fan tutte (Cpte), Finta Giardiniera (Cpte), Nozze di Figaro (exc)
Purcell: Dido (Cpte)
R. Strauss: Ariadne auf Naxos (Cpte), Capriccio (Cpte), Rosenkavalier (Cpte)
Wagner: Götterdämmerung (Cpte)
(DECC) **433 067-2DWO** Your Hundred Best Opera Tunes IV
(DECC) **440 410-2DM** Plácido Domingo
(DECC) **440 947-2DH** Essential Opera II
(DECC) **443 378-2DM** Ten Top Mezzos 2
(DG) **439 251-2GY** The Leonard Bernstein Album
(DG) **439 474-2GCL** Purcell—Opera & Choral Works
(DG) **445 354-2GX14** Wagner—Der Ring des Nibelungen
(DG) **439 251-5GY** The Leonard Bernstein Album
(ORFE) **C365941A** Christa Ludwig - Salzburg Festival highlights

TRUC, Georges (cond)
see orch
SO

TRUCCO, Victor (cond)
see RCA SO

TRUDEL, Alain (tbn)
Vivier: Kopernikus (Cpte)

TRUFFELLI, Romano (ten)
(RCA) **GD86534** Verdi Arias and Duets

TRUNDT, Henny (sop)
(SCHW) **314532** Vienna State Opera Live, Vol.3
(SCHW) **314642** Vienna State Opera Live, Vol.14

TRUPP, Maria (contr)
R. Strauss: Rosenkavalier (Cpte)

TSCHAMMER, Hans (bass-bar)
Beethoven: Fidelio (Cpte)
Wagner: Parsifal (Cpte), Rheingold (Cpte)

TSCHUPP, Räto (cond)
see Zurich Camerata

TSCHURTSCHENTHALER, Georg von (bass)
Wagner: Tannhäuser (Cpte)

TSELOVALNIK, Evgenia (sop)
Mussorgsky: Khovanshchina (Cpte)

TSHERNAKOV, Tikhon (ten)
(ARLE) **ARL23/5** Rimsky-Korsakov—Sadko

TSIDIPOVA, Valentina (sop)
Rimsky-Korsakov: Sadko (Cpte)

TSINGOPOULOS, Madeline (sngr)
Rorem: Childhood Miracle (Cpte), Three Sisters Who Are Not Sisters (Cpte)

TUAND, Carlo (ten)
Bellini: Puritani (Cpte)

TUBB, Evelyn (sop)
Mozart: Zauberflöte (Cpte)
Purcell: Don Quixote: The Musical (Cpte)
(IMP) **PCD881** Monteverdi—Solos and Duets

TUCCI, Gabriella (sop)
Verdi: Otello (Cpte), Trovatore (Cpte)
(CFP) **CD-CFP9013** Duets from Famous Operas
(MEMO) **HR4273/4** Great Voices—Pietro Cappuccilli

TUČEK, René (bar)
Dvořák: Jacobin (Cpte), Rusalka (Cpte)
Janáček: Excursions of Mr Brouček (Cpte)
Martinů: Alexandre Bis (Cpte), Comedy on the Bridge (Cpte)
Smetana: Libuše (Cpte)

TUCKER, Mark (ten)
Keiser: Croesus (Cpte)
Monteverdi: Orfeo (Cpte)
Purcell: King Arthur, Z628 (Cpte)

TUCKER, Richard (ten)
Leoncavallo: Pagliacci (Cpte)
Puccini: Bohème (exc), Madama Butterfly (Cpte)
Verdi: Aida (Cpte), Forza del destino (Cpte)
(EMI) **CHS7 69741-2(2)** Record of Singing, Vol.4—Anglo-American School (pt 2)
(MEMO) **HR4235/6** Great Voices-Renata Tebaldi
(PHIL) **442 602-2PM** 3 x 3 Tenors
(RCA) **GD60326** Verdi—Operas & Choral Works
(RCA) **09026 61440-2** Opera's Greatest Moments
(RCA) **09026 61580-2(6)** RCA/Met 100 Singers, 100 Years (pt 6)
(RCA) **09026 61886-2** Operas Greatest Love Songs
(RCA) **09026 62550-2** Ten Tenors in Love
(RCA) **09026 62689-2** The Voices of Living Stereo, Volume 1
(RCA) **09026 62699-2** Opera's Greatest Duets
(RCA) **74321 25817-2** Café Classics - Operatic
(VAI) **VAI69109** Richard Tucker in Opera and Song

TUCKWELL, Barry (cond)
see LSO

TUCKWELL, Barry (hn)
(DECC) **430 370-2DH** R. Strauss—Works for Horn
(IMP) **PCDS4** Discover the Classics—Master Disc
(IMP) **PCDS6** Discover the Classics—Myths and Legends
(IMP) **PCDS8** Discover the Classics—Heroes and Heroines

TUGARINOVA, Klavdila (contr)
(MMOI) **CDMOIR422** Great Voices in Tchaikovsky
(PEAR) **GEMMCDS9111(1)** Singers of Imperial Russia, Vol.5 (pt 1)

TUGARINOVA, Tatiana (mez)
Tchaikovsky: Eugene Onegin (Cpte)

TUMAGIAN, Eduard (bar)
Leoncavallo: Pagliacci (Cpte)
Mascagni: Cavalleria Rusticana (Cpte)
Prokofiev: War and Peace (Cpte)
Puccini: Gianni Schicchi (Cpte), Tabarro (Cpte), Turandot (Cpte)
Verdi: Luisa Miller (Cpte), Rigoletto (Cpte), Simon Boccanegra (Cpte)
(NAXO) **8 550684** Duets and Arias from Italian Operas

TUMAGIAN, Edward (bass)
Verdi: Otello (Cpte)

TUNICK, Jonathan (cond)
see NY Studio Orch

TUOMELA, Tuula-Marja (sop)
Bergman: Singing Tree (Cpte)

TURA, Gennaro De (ten)
(EMI) **CHS7 64860-2(2)** La Scala Edition - Vol.1, 1878-1914 (pt 2)

TURBAN, Dietlinde (sop)
Monteverdi: Orfeo (Cpte)

TURBA-RABIER, Odette (sop)
Ravel: Enfant et les sortilèges (Cpte)

TURCHETTA, Sonia (contr)
Salieri: Axur (Cpte)

TURCHETTI, Anna Maria (sop)
(TEST) **SBT1008** Viva Rossini

TURCO, Enrico (bass)
Franchetti: Cristoforo Colombo (Cpte)
Gluck: Iphigénie en Tauride (Cpte)
Mozart: Don Giovanni (Cpte)
Puccini: Fanciulla del West (Cpte)

TURGEON, Bernard (bar)
Sullivan: Trial by Jury (Cpte)

TURIN EIAR CHORUS
cond F. GHIONE
Puccini: Turandot (Cpte)
cond V. GUI
Bellini: Norma (Cpte)

TURIN EIAR ORCHESTRA
cond F. GHIONE
Puccini: Turandot (Cpte)
(LYRC) **SRO805** Gina Cigna—Opera Recital
cond V. GUI
Bellini: Norma (Cpte)
cond G. MARINUZZI
(PREI) **89015** Carlo Tagliabue (1898-1978)
cond A. LA ROSA PARODI
(PREI) **89015** Carlo Tagliabue (1898-1978)
cond U. TANSINI
(LYRC) **SRO805** Gina Cigna—Opera Recital
(PREI) **89015** Carlo Tagliabue (1898-1978)

TURIN LYRIC CHORUS
cond F. CLEVA
Catalani: Wally (Cpte)

TURIN PHILHARMONIC ORCHESTRA
cond M. VIOTTI
Rossini: Signor Bruschino (Cpte)

TURIN RADIO CHORUS
cond A. QUESTA
Verdi: Aida (Cpte)

TURIN RADIO SYMPHONY ORCHESTRA
cond G. GELMETTI
Rossini: Gazza ladra (Cpte)
cond A. QUESTA
Verdi: Aida (Cpte)

TURIN RAI CHORUS
cond E. BONCOMPAGNI
Alfano: Risurrezione (Cpte)
cond C. FRANCI
(MEMO) **HR4392/3** Great Voices - Marilyn Horne
cond G. GAVAZZENI
Boito: Nerone (Cpte)
Ponchielli: Lituani (Cpte)
cond H. LEWIS
Meyerbeer: Prophète (Cpte)
(MEMO) **HR4392/3** Great Voices - Marilyn Horne
cond F. MOLINARI-PRADELLI
Donizetti: Lucia di Lammermoor (exc)
(BUTT) **BMCD015** Pavarotti Collection - Duets and Scenes
cond A. QUESTA
Mascagni: Iris (Cpte)
cond M. ROSSI
Verdi: Rigoletto (exc)
cond N. SANZOGNO
(MEMO) **HR4300/1** Great Voices—Sesto Bruscantini
cond C. SCIMONE
Donizetti: Elisir d'amore (Cpte)

TURIN RAI ORCHESTRA
cond A. BASILE
(FONI) **CDO104** Maria Callas
(SUIT) **CDS1-5001** Maria Callas - La divina
cond P. BELLUGI
(MEMO) **HR4279/80** Montserrat Caballè—Opera Arias
cond E. BONCOMPAGNI
Alfano: Risurrezione (Cpte)
cond O. DE FABRITIIS
(FONI) **CDMR5003** Martini & Rossi Festival, Volume 3
(SUIT) **CDS1-5001** Maria Callas - La divina
cond C. FRANCI
(MEMO) **HR4392/3** Great Voices - Marilyn Horne
cond G. GAVAZZENI
Boito: Nerone (Cpte)
Ponchielli: Lituani (Cpte)
cond H. LEWIS
Meyerbeer: Prophète (Cpte)
(MEMO) **HR4392/3** Great Voices - Marilyn Horne
cond F. MOLINARI-PRADELLI
Donizetti: Lucia di Lammermoor (exc)
(BUTT) **BMCD015** Pavarotti Collection - Duets and Scenes
cond A. QUESTA
Mascagni: Iris (Cpte)
cond D. RENZETTI
Rossini: Signor Bruschino (Cpte)
cond M. ROSSI
Verdi: Rigoletto (exc)
(BONG) **GB1060-2** Virginia Zeani - Various opera arias
(BUTT) **BMCD015** Pavarotti Collection - Duets and Scenes
(MEMO) **HR4273/4** Great Voices—Pietro Cappuccilli
cond G. SANTINI
Verdi: Traviata (Cpte)
(FONI) **CDO104** Maria Callas
cond N. SANZOGNO
(MEMO) **HR4300/1** Great Voices—Sesto Bruscantini
cond C. SCIMONE
Donizetti: Elisir d'amore (Cpte)
(PHIL) **432 692-2PH** The Essential José Carreras
(PHIL) **442 600-2PH** The Great Carreras
cond A. SIMONETTO
Puccini: Gianni Schicchi (Cpte)
cond P. URBINI
(BONG) **GB1060-2** Virginia Zeani - Various opera arias
cond F. VERNIZZI
(BONG) **GB1060-2** Virginia Zeani - Various opera arias
cond A. VOTTO
(FONI) **CDO104** Maria Callas
(SUIT) **CDS1-5001** Maria Callas - La divina

TURIN SYMPHONY ORCHESTRA
cond F. MOLINARI-PRADELLI
(RCA) **09026 68014-2** Pavarotti - The Early Years, Vol.2
cond M. ROSSI
(RCA) **09026 68014-2** Pavarotti - The Early Years, Vol.2

VALDENASSI, Cecilia (sop)
Rossini: Donna del Lago (Cpte)

VALDENGO, Giuseppe (bar)
Donizetti: Don Pasquale (Cpte)
Verdi: Aida (Cpte), Falstaff (Cpte), Otello (Cpte)
(RCA) **GD60326** Verdi—Operas & Choral Works
(RCA) **09026 61580-2(6)** RCA/Met 100 Singers, 100 Years (pt 6)

VALDEPEÑAS, Joaquin (cl)
(CBC) **MVCD1053** Schubert—Lieder

VALDES, Maximiano (cond)
see LSO

VÁLEK, Vladimir (cond)
see Prague SO

VALENCIN, Anne (sop)
(EPM) **150 122** Milhaud—Historic Recordings 1928-1948

VALENTA, Leopold (bass)
Mozart: Zauberflöte (Cpte)

VALENTE, Alessandro (ten)
Leoncavallo: Pagliacci (Cpte)
(CONI) **CDHD235** The Puccini Album
(MMOI) **CDMOIR412** Great Voices of the Century Sing Puccini

VALENTE, Valentina (sop)
Mussorgsky: Boris Godunov (Cpte)

VALENTIK, Jan (spkr)
Suchoň: Whirlpool (Cpte)

VALENTINI, Fernando (bar)
(EMI) **CMS7 64165-2** Puccini—Trittico

VALENTINI, Massimo (bass)
Salieri: Axur (Cpte)

VALENTINO, Frank (bar)
Puccini: Bohème (Cpte)
Verdi: Trovatore (Cpte)

VALENTINO, Stefano (bass)
Rossini: Barbiere di Siviglia (exc)

VALENT1, Monica (sop)
Rossini: Semiramide (Cpte)

VALERO, Fernando (ten)
(EMI) **CHS7 64860-2(1)** La Scala Edition - Vol.1, 1878-1914 (pt 1)
(MEMO) **HR4408/9(1)** Singers in Genoa, Vol.1 (disc 1)
(PEAR) **GEMMCDS9923(2)** Covent Garden on Record, Vol.1 (pt 2)
(SYMP) **SYMCD1073** The Harold Wayne Collection, Vol.3

VALJAKKA, Taru (sop)
Shostakovich: Lady Macbeth of Mtsensk (Cpte)
(BIS) **BIS-CD373/4** Opera Scenes from Savaonlinna

VÁLKA, Josef (ten)
Janáček: Šárka (Cpte)

VÄLKKI, Anita (sop)
Madetoja: Juha (Cpte)
Wagner: Fliegende Holländer (Cpte), Götterdämmerung (Cpte)
(BIS) **BIS-CD373/4** Opera Scenes from Savaonlinna
(DECC) **414 100-2DM15** Wagner: Der Ring des Nibelungen

VALKOVA, Denca (sop)
Kalomiris: Mother's Ring (Cpte)

VALLE, Luisa (sop)
Verdi: Rigoletto (Cpte)

VALLETTI, Cesare (ten)
Donizetti: Linda di Chamounix (Cpte)
Puccini: Madama Butterfly (Cpte)
Rossini: Barbiere di Siviglia (Cpte), Italiana in Algeri (Cpte)
Verdi: Falstaff (Cpte)
(MEMO) **HR4191/2** Cesare Valletti—Public Performances
(MEMO) **HR4396/7** Great Voices—Leontyne Price
(RCA) **09026 61580-2(6)** RCA/Met 100 Singers, 100 Years (pt 6)

VALLIN, Ninon (sop)
G. Charpentier: Louise (exc)
Massenet: Werther (Cpte)
Puccini: Tosca (exc)
(EMI) **CZS5 68292-2** Operetta Arias and Duets
(FORL) **UCD19022** The unforgettable André Baugé
(MMOI) **CDMOIR408** Great Sopranos
(MSCM) **MM30221** 18 French Divas
(PEAR) **GEMMCD9948** Ninon Vallin in Opera and Song

VALORI, Eugenio (ten)
Verdi: Otello (Cpte)

VALTASAARI, Tapani (bass)
Madetoja: Juha (Cpte)

VALTRIANI, Jeda (sop)
(DECC) **411 665-2DM3** Puccini: Il trittico

VAN ALLAN, Richard (bass)
Boughton: Bethlehem (Cpte)
Britten: Albert Herring (Cpte), Billy Budd (Cpte), Gloriana (Cpte), Peter Grimes (Cpte), Rape of Lucretia (Cpte)
Cavalli: Ormindo (Cpte)
Donizetti: Lucrezia Borgia (Cpte)
Massenet: Thaïs (Cpte)
Mozart: Così fan tutte (Cpte), Don Giovanni (Cpte)
Offenbach: Contes d'Hoffmann (Cpte)
Prokofiev: Love for 3 Oranges (Cpte)
Puccini: Manon Lescaut (Cpte), Tosca (Cpte)
Rossini: Guillaume Tell (Cpte)
Stravinsky: Rake's Progress (Cpte)
Sullivan: HMS Pinafore (Cpte), Mikado (exc), Pirates of Penzance (Cpte)
Tchaikovsky: Eugene Onegin (Cpte)
Vaughan Williams: Hugh the Drover (Cpte)
Verdi: Ballo in maschera (Cpte), Forza del destino (exc), Luisa Miller (Cpte), Traviata (Cpte), Vespri Siciliani (Cpte)
Walton: Troilus and Cressida (Cpte)
Weill: Street Scene (Cpte)
(DECC) **433 439-2DA** Great Love Duets

VAN ALLAN, Richard (narr)
Berlioz: Béatrice et Bénédict (Cpte)

VAN BAASBANK, Adrian (bar)
Mozart: Lucio Silla (Cpte)

VAN DAM, José (bass-bar)
Beethoven: Fidelio (Cpte)
Bizet: Carmen (Cpte), Jolie fille de Perth (Cpte)
Debussy: Pelléas et Mélisande (Cpte), Rodrigue et Chimène (Cpte)
Fauré: Pénélope (Cpte)
G. Charpentier: Louise (Cpte)
Gluck: Iphigénie en Aulide (Cpte)
Gounod: Faust (Cpte), Roméo et Juliette (Cpte)
Massenet: Don Quichotte (Cpte), Manon (Cpte)
Messiaen: Saint François d'Assise (Cpte)
Mozart: Così fan tutte (Cpte), Don Giovanni (Cpte), Nozze di Figaro (Cpte), Zauberflöte (exc)
Offenbach: Contes d'Hoffmann (Cpte)
Poulenc: Dialogues des Carmélites (Cpte)
R. Strauss: Frau ohne Schatten (Cpte), Salomé (Cpte)
Rameau: Dardanus (Cpte)
Ravel: Heure espagnole (Cpte)
Roussel: Padmâvatî (Cpte)
Verdi: Aida (Cpte), Ballo in maschera (Cpte), Don Carlo (Cpte), Otello (Cpte), Simon Boccanegra (Cpte)
Wagner: Fliegende Holländer (Cpte), Parsifal (Cpte)
(CFP) **CD-CFP4612** Favourite Mozart
(DECC) **433 067-2DWO** Your Hundred Best Opera Tunes IV
(EMIL) **CDZ7 67015-2** Mozart—Opera Arias
(ERAT) **4509-96971-2** Marcel Landowski—Edition
(ERAT) **4509-99607-2** Gluck—Operas; Schubert—Symphonies Nos 8 & 9
(FORL) **UCD16681** The Great Italian Arias
(NOVA) **150 014-2** Mozart—Gala Concert
(ORFE) **C394301B** Great Mozart Singers Series, Vol. 3
(PRES) **PCOM1109** Le Maître de Musique—Original Soundtrack

VAN DE VOORDE, Oliver (treb)
Puccini: Gianni Schicchi (Cpte)

VAN DEN BOSCH, Betty (sop)
(ARHI) **ADCD109** Mengelberg Edition - Volume 3

VAN DER MEEL, Nico (ten)
Landi: Mort d'Orfeo (Cpte)
Mendelssohn: Hochzeit des Camacho (Cpte)
Mozart: Don Giovanni (Cpte)

VAN DER PAAL, Rolande (sop)
(CPO) **CPO999 104-2** Mozart—Lo Sposo Deluso/L'Oca del Cairo

VAN DER PAS, Theo (pf)
(PEAR) **GEMMCD9442** Feuermann—The Columbia Records, Vol.1

VAN DEYCK, Lucienne (contr)
Puccini: Manon Lescaut (Cpte), Suor Angelica (Cpte)

VAN DYCK, Ernest (ten)
(SYMP) **SYMCD1172** The Harold Wayne Collection, Vol.21

VAN DYCK, Stephan (ten)
Rameau: Hippolyte et Aricie (Cpte)

VAN DYCK, Stephen (treb)
(NEWP) **NPD85514** The Treble Boys - Wonder Solos & Duets

VAN EETVELDT, Frans (bass)
Puccini: Gianni Schicchi (Cpte)

VAN EVERA, Emily (sop)
Blow: Venus and Adonis (Cpte)
Purcell: Dido (Cpte)

VAN GIJSEGEM, Ludwig (ten)
Puccini: Manon Lescaut (Cpte)

VAN KEMPEN, Paul (cond)
see Hilversum RO

VAN MILL, Arnold (bass)
Verdi: Aida (Cpte)
Wagner: Meistersinger (Cpte), Parsifal (Cpte)

VAN ROOY, Anton (bass-bar)
(PEAR) **GEMMCDS9923(2)** Covent Garden on Record, Vol.1 (pt 2)
(SYMP) **SYMCD1100** Harold Wayne Collection, Vol.8

VANAUD, Marcel (bar)
Offenbach: Contes d'Hoffmann (exc)

VANCE, Marjorie (sop)
R. Strauss: Elektra (Cpte)

VANCONTI, Carlotta (sop)
(PEAR) **GEMMCD9145** Richard Tauber - Operatic Arias
(PEAR) **GEMMCD9310** Franz Lehár conducts Richard Tauber

VANDENBURG, Howard (ten)
Mozart: Zauberflöte (Cpte)

VANDERLINDE, Debra (sop)
V. Thomson: Lord Byron (Cpte)

VANDERSTEENE, Zeger (ten)
Rameau: Castor et Pollux (Cpte)

VANE, Doris (sop)
Gounod: Faust (Cpte)
(SYMP) **SYMCD1130** Joseph Holbrooke—Historic Recordings

VANELLI, Gino (bar)
(CLUB) **CL99-014** Dino Borgioli (1891-1960)
(PREI) **89026** Francesco Merli (1887-1976) - I
(PREI) **89091** Francesco Merli (1887-1976) - II

VANESS, Carol (sop)
Gluck: Iphigénie en Tauride (Cpte)
Mozart: Clemenza di Tito (Cpte), Così fan tutte (Cpte), Don Giovanni (Cpte), Idomeneo (Cpte), Nozze di Figaro (Cpte)
Puccini: Tosca (Cpte)
(CAST) **CVI2071** Highlights from Glyndebourne
(EMI) **CDC7 54329-2** Domingo sings Mozart Arias
(EMI) **CDH5 65072-2** Glyndebourne Recorded - 1934-1994
(EMIL) **CDZ7 67015-2** Mozart—Opera Arias
(RCA) **09026 61509-2** A Salute to American Music

VANESSA-MAE (vn)
(TRIT) **TCvan27102** My Favourite Things

VANHECKE, François (sop)
Grétry: Jugement de Midas (exc)

VANNI, Helen (mez)
V. Thomson: Mother of us all (Cpte)

VANNI-MARCOUX (bass)
Debussy: Pelléas et Mélisande (exc)
(CLUB) **CL99-101** Vanni Marcoux (1877-1962)
(PEAR) **GEMMCDS9924(2)** Covent Garden on Record, Vol.2 (pt 2)
(PEAR) **GEMMCD9122** 20 Great Basses sing Great Arias
(PEAR) **GEMMCD9912** Vanni Marcoux—Recital

VANNUCCINI, Enrico (bass)
(IRCC) **IRCC-CD808** Souvenirs of 19th Century Italian Opera

VÄNSKÄ, Osmo (cond)
see Lahti SO

VANTIN, Martin (ten)
Mozart: Entführung (Cpte), Nozze di Figaro (Cpte), Zauberflöte (Cpte)
Wagner: Meistersinger (Cpte), Tristan und Isolde (Cpte)

VANTONI, Carlotta (sop)
(EMI) **CDH7 69787-2** Richard Tauber sings Operetta Arias

VANZO, Alain (ten)
Bizet: Pêcheurs de Perles (Cpte)
Delibes: Lakmé (exc)
Fauré: Pénélope (Cpte)
Massenet: Jongleur de Notre Dame (Cpte), Navarraise (Cpte)
Offenbach: Périchole (Cpte)
Verdi: Rigoletto (Cpte)
(EMI) **CDC7 54016-2** Tenorissimo!

VARADY, Julia (sop)
Cimarosa: Matrimonio segreto (Cpte)
Halévy: Juive (Cpte)
Mascagni: Cavalleria Rusticana (exc)
Mozart: Clemenza di Tito (Cpte), Don Giovanni (Cpte), Idomeneo (Cpte), Lucio Silla (Cpte), Nozze di Figaro (Cpte)
R. Strauss: Ariadne auf Naxos (Cpte), Frau ohne Schatten (Cpte)
Spohr: Jessonda (Cpte)
Spontini: Olimpie (Cpte)
Wagner: Fliegende Holländer (Cpte), Walküre (Cpte)
(ACAN) **43 266** Bernd Weikl—Operatic Recital
(DECC) **425 681-2DM2** Tutto Pavarotti
(DECC) **433 065-2DWO** Your Hundred Best Opera Tunes Volume II
(EMI) **LDX9 91275-1(EMI)** Sawallisch conducts Wagner's Ring
(EURO) **VD69256** Mozart—Opera Arias
(ORFE) **C186951** Verdi—Heroines, Vol. 1
(ORFE) **C323941A** Puccini—Famous Opera Arias
(ORFE) **C394301B** Great Mozart Singers Series, Vol. 3
(RCA) **09026 61440-2** Opera's Greatest Moments
(RCA) **09026 61886-2** Operas Greatest Love Songs

VARCOE, Stephen (bar)
Blow: Venus and Adonis (Cpte)
Handel: Alessandro (Cpte), Partenope (Cpte)
Haydn: Infedeltà delusa (Cpte)
Holst: Sávitri (Cpte)
Monteverdi: Orfeo (Cpte)
Ponchielli: Gioconda (Cpte)

Purcell: Dioclesian, Z627 (exc), Fairy Queen, Z629 (Cpte), Indian Queen, Z630 (Cpte), King Arthur, Z628 (exc), Tempest, Z631 (Cpte)
(DG) **439 474-2GCL** Purcell—Opera & Choral Works
(ERAT) **4509-96371-2** Gardiner—The Purcell Collection

VARGAS, Milagr (contr)
Glass: Akhnaten (Cpte)
Maderna: Satyricon (Cpte)

VARGAS, Ramon (ten)
Bellini: Zaira (Cpte)
Puccini: Manon Lescaut (Cpte)
Rossini: Barbiere di Siviglia (Cpte)
Verdi: Falstaff (Cpte), Otello (Cpte)
(CLAV) **CD50-9202** Donizetti/Rossini—Tenor Arias

VARLA, Olga (sop)
R. Strauss: Elektra (Cpte)

VARNAY, Astrid (sop/mez)
Giordano: Andrea Chénier (Cpte)
Mascagni: Cavalleria rusticana (exc)
R. Strauss: Elektra (Cpte), Salome (Cpte)
Stravinsky: Rake's Progress (Cpte)
Wagner: Fliegende Holländer (Cpte), Götterdämmerung (Cpte), Lohengrin (Cpte), Siegfried (Cpte), Walküre (Cpte)
(EMI) **CDC7 54524-2** The José Carreras Album
(EMI) **CDM5 65575-2** Montserrat Caballé
(EMI) **CDM7 63111-2** José Carreras sings Opera & Operetta Arias
(EMI) **CHS7 69741-2(1)** Record of Singing, Vol.4—Anglo-American School (pt 1)
(FOYE) **15-CF2011** Wagner—Der Ring de Nibelungen
(MEMO) **HR4275/6** Birgit Nilsson—Public Performances 1954-1969

VARNI, Giuseppe (bass)
Verdi: Rigoletto (Cpte)

VARNIER, Jérome (bar)
Rameau: Hippolyte et Aricie (Cpte)

VARNIER, Jérôme (sngr)
Lully: Phaëton (Cpte)

VARVISO, Silvio (cond)
see Bayreuth Fest Orch
Dresden St Op Orch
LPO
MMF Orch
Naples Scarlatti Orch
Rome Orch
Staatskapelle Dresden

VÁSÁRI, Monika (sngr)
Lehár: Lustige Witwe (exc)

VASILEV, Nikola (bar)
Mussorgsky: Khovanshchina (Cpte)

VASILIEV, Nikolai (ten)
Rachmaninov: Francesca da Rimini (Cpte)

VASSAR, Frédéric (bass-bar)
Mascagni: Piccolo Marat (Cpte)

VASSILEVA, Liliana (sop)
(FORL) **UCD16741** Bulgarian Voices, Vol. 1

VASSILIEV, Nikolai (ten)
Serov: Judith (Cpte)

VASSILIEVA, Elena (sop)
Henze: Boulevard Solitude (Cpte)

VATER, Wolfgang (bass)
R. Strauss: Daphne (Cpte)

VAUGHAN, Elizabeth (sop)
Britten: Gloriana (Cpte)

VAUGHAN, Gareth (bar)
Sullivan: Gondoliers (Cpte)

VAUGHAN, Lyn (treb)
(LOND) **436 393-2LM** Britten—The Little Sweep, etc

VAUGHAN-LEWIS, David (bar)
Vaughan Williams: Pilgrim's Progress (Cpte)

VAUGHN, Robert (ten)
Verdi: Traviata (Cpte)

VAUQUELIN, Jean-Paul (bar)
Bizet: Carmen (Cpte)

VAVON, Andrée (sop)
Massenet: Manon (Cpte)
(NIMB) **NI7836/7** Conchita Supervia (1895-1936)

VAVRUŠKA, Jaromír (bass)
Martinů: Miracles of Mary (Cpte)

VAYNE, Kyra (sop)
(PREI) **89996** Kyra Vayne (b.1916)

VEASEY, Josephine (mez)
Berlioz: Troyens (Cpte)
Britten: Midsummer Night's Dream (Cpte)
Mozart: Zauberflöte (exc)
R. Strauss: Salome (Cpte)
Wagner: Rheingold (Cpte), Walküre (Cpte)
(DECC) **433 706-2DMO3** Bellini—Beatrice di Tenda; Operatic Arias
(DG) **429 168-2GR** Wagner: Excerpts from Der Ring
(DG) **435 211-2GX15** Wagner—Der Ring des Nibelungen
(DG) **439 423-2GCL** Wagner—Der Ring des Nibelungen (highlights)

VECCIA, Angelo (bar)
Gluck: Iphigénie en Tauride (Cpte)

Puccini: Tosca (exc)
(DG) **445 525-2GMA** Domingo Favourites

VEDDER, Rudolf (bar)
R. Strauss: Rosenkavalier (Cpte)

VEJZOVIC, Dunja (mez)
Wagner: Fliegende Holländer (Cpte), Lohengrin (Cpte), Parsifal (Cpte)
(CAST) **CVI2057** Il Trittico live from La Scala, 1983

VELARDI, Esteban (cond)
see A. Stradella Consort

VELAZQUEZ, Ruben (ten)
Fauré: Prométhée (Cpte)

VELE, Ludek (bass)
Dvořák: Dimitrij (Cpte)
Martinů: Ariane (Cpte)
Smetana: Libuše (Cpte)

VELICHKO, Olga (sngr)
Rimsky-Korsakov: Mlada (Cpte)

VELIS, Andrea (ten)
Bizet: Carmen (Cpte)
Puccini: Tosca (exc)
Verdi: Ballo in maschera (Cpte)

VELTRI, Michelangelo (cond)
see Paris Op Orch
Scottish CO

VENETO PHILHARMONIC ORCHESTRA
cond P. MAAG
(MARC) **8 223397** Malipiero—Orchestral Works

VENEZIANI, Vittore (cond)
see La Scala Orch

VENGEROV, Maxim (vn)
(CANY) **EC3655-2** Maxim Vengerov—Carmen Fantasy

VENHODA, Mirsolav (cond)
see Early Instr Chbr Ens

VENICE AND PADUA CHAMBER ORCHESTRA
cond B. GIURANNA
(CLAV) **CD50-9120** Mozart—Opera and Concert Arias

VENICE LA FENICE CHORUS
cond C. ABBADO
Rossini: Barbiere di Siviglia (Cpte)
cond B. CAMPANELLA
Bellini: Capuleti (Cpte)
cond C. FRANCI
Rossini: Armida (Cpte)
cond G. GELMETTI
Donizetti: Martyrs (Cpte)
cond E. INBAL
Donizetti: Maria di Rudenz (Cpte)
cond I. MARTIN
(DECC) **436 075-2DH** Rossini Heroines
(DECC) **436 075-5DH** Rossini Heroines
cond R. WEIKERT
Rossini: Tancredi (Cpte)

VENICE LA FENICE ORCHESTRA
cond R. ABBADO
(DECC) **433 316-2DH** Verismo Arias - Mirella Freni
(DG) **439 151-2GMA** Mad about Puccini
cond B. CAMPANELLA
Bellini: Capuleti (Cpte)
cond J. FISHER
Handel: Rinaldo (Cpte)
(MEMO) **HR4392/3** Great Voices - Marilyn Horne
cond C. FRANCI
Rossini: Armida (Cpte)
(MEMO) **HR4239/40** Opera Arias—Leyla Gencer
cond G. GAVAZZENI
(MEMO) **HR4239/40** Opera Arias—Leyla Gencer
cond G. GELMETTI
Donizetti: Martyrs (Cpte)
cond E. INBAL
Donizetti: Maria di Rudenz (Cpte)
cond I. MARIN
(DECC) **448 300-2DH** Cecilia Bartoli—A Portrait
cond I. MARTIN
(DECC) **436 075-2DH** Rossini Heroines
(DECC) **436 075-5DH** Rossini Heroines
cond R. WEIKERT
Rossini: Tancredi (Cpte)

VENTO, Marc (bass)
Gounod: Faust (exc)
Roussel: Padmâvatî (Cpte)

VENTRIGLIA, Franco (bass)
Puccini: Manon Lescaut (Cpte)

VENTRIS, Christopher (ten)
Britten: Death in Venice (Cpte)
Saxton: Caritas (Cpte)
Weir: Blond Eckbert (Cpte)

VENTURA, Enrico (ten)
(MEMO) **HR4408/9(1)** Singers in Genoa, Vol.1 (disc 1)
(MEMO) **HR4408/9(2)** Singers in Genoa, Vol.1 (disc 2)
(SYMP) **SYMCD1111** The Harold Wayne Collection, Vol.11

VENTURINI, Emilio (ten)
Verdi: Falstaff (Cpte)
(EMI) **CHS7 64864-2(1)** La Scala Edition - Vol.2, 1915-46 (pt 1)
(PREI) **89042** Nazzareno de Angelis (1881-1962)

VENUTI, Maria (sop)
Delius: Village Romeo and Juliet (Cpte)
Mozart: Zauberflöte (Cpte)
Verdi: Stiffelio (Cpte), Trovatore (Cpte)

VENZAGO, Mario (cond)
see Swiss Workshop PO

VERBIT, Marthanne (pf)
(ALBA) **TROY146-2** Antheil—Piano Works

VERBITSKAYA, Evgenya (mez)
Rimsky-Korsakov: Tale of Tsar Saltan (Cpte)
Tchaikovsky: Eugene Onegin (Cpte)

VERCELLI, Angela (mez)
Donizetti: Elisir d'amore (Cpte)
Verdi: Macbeth (Cpte), Traviata (Cpte)

VERDERA, Teresa (sop)
(IMP) **MCD45** Spanish Royal Gala

VERDIÈRE, René (ten)
(EPM) **150 052** Germaine Lubin—Opera & Song Recital
(MSCM) **MM30377** 18 Tenors d'Expression Française

VERDOODT, Diane (sop)
Puccini: Gianni Schicchi (Cpte), Suor Angelica (Cpte)

VERDUCCI, Alessandro (bass)
Bellini: Sonnambula (Cpte)
Donizetti: Favorita (Cpte)

VERESTNIKOV, Vladislav (bar)
Rachmaninov: Miserly knight (Cpte)
Rimsky-Korsakov: Kashchey (Cpte), Tsar's Bride (Cpte)
Shostakovich: Gamblers (Cpte)

VERGARA, Victoria (mez)
Verdi: Rigoletto (Cpte)
(DG) **072 110-1GH** Hommage a Sevilla—Placido Domingo in scenes from various operas
(DG) **072 187-1GH (DG)** Hommage a Sevilla

VERLET, Alice (sop)
(PEAR) **GEMMCDS9074(2)** Giovanni Zenatello, Vol.2 (pt 2)

VERMEERSCH, Jef (bar)
Wagner: Meistersinger (Cpte)

VERMEIL, Henry (spkr)
Tomasi: Don Juan de Mañara (Cpte)

VERMEULEN, Dirk (cond)
see Sinfonia

VERMILLION, Iris (mez)
Donizetti: Maria Stuarda (Cpte)
Gluck: Rencontre imprévue (Cpte)
Mozart: Zauberflöte (Cpte)
Schulhoff: Plameny (Cpte)
Wagner: Fliegende Holländer (Cpte)
(DECC) **440 854-2DH** Ullmann—Der Kaiser von Atlantis
(PHIL) **422 523-2PME8(2)** The Complete Mozart Edition Vol 23 (pt 2)

VERNET, Isabelle (sop)
Massenet: Don Quichotte (Cpte)
Offenbach: Contes d'Hoffmann (Cpte)

VERNEUIL, Claudine (sop)
Ravel: Enfant et les sortilèges (Cpte)

VERNIZZI, Fulvio (cond)
see Turin RAI Orch

VERNON, Richard (bass)
Puccini: Fanciulla del West (Cpte), Tosca (Cpte)

VEROLI, Manlio di (cond)
see orch

VERONA ARENA CHORUS
cond M. ARENA
Puccini: Madama Butterfly (Cpte), Turandot (Cpte)
Verdi: Nabucco (Cpte)
(CAST) **CASH5051** Puccini Favourites from Covent Garden and the Arena di Verona
(CAST) **CASH5052** Verdi Operatic Favourites
(CAST) **CVI2068** Opera Highlights from Verona 1
cond R. GIOVANINETTI
Verdi: Trovatore (Cpte)
(CAST) **CVI2068** Opera Highlights from Verona 1
cond A. GUADAGNO
Puccini: Bohème (Cpte)
Verdi: Aida (Cpte)
(CAST) **CASH5052** Verdi Operatic Favourites
cond D. OREN
Puccini: Tosca (Cpte)
(CAST) **CASH5051** Puccini Favourites from Covent Garden and the Arena di Verona
(CAST) **CVI2068** Opera Highlights from Verona 1
cond Z. PESKÓ
Verdi: Otello (Cpte)
(CAST) **CVI2068** Opera Highlights from Verona 1
cond N. SANTI
Puccini: Manon Lescaut (Cpte)
Verdi: Attila (Cpte)

VERONA ARENA CORPS DE BALLET
cond A. GUADAGNO
Verdi: Aida (Cpte)

VERONA ARENA ORCHESTRA
Puccini: Madama Butterfly (Cpte), Tosca (Cpte), Turandot (Cpte)

Verdi: Aida (Cpte), Attila (Cpte), Nabucco (Cpte), Otello (Cpte), Trovatore (Cpte)
cond M. ARENA
(CAST) **CASH5051** Puccini Favourites from Covent Garden and the Arena di Verona
(CAST) **CASH5052** Verdi Operatic Favourites
(CAST) **CVI2068** Opera Highlights from Verona 1
(CAST) **CVI2070** Great Puccini Love Scenes from Covent Garden, La Scala and Verona
cond A. GATTO
(BELA) **450 002-2** Pavarotti Live
cond R. GIOVANINETTI
(CAST) **CVI2068** Opera Highlights from Verona 1
cond A. GUADAGNO
Puccini: Bohème (Cpte)
(CAST) **CASH5052** Verdi Operatic Favourites
(MCI) **MCCD099** Opera's Greatest Arias
cond B. MARTINOTTI
(DECC) **443 018-2DF2** Pavarotti/Freni/Ricciarelli—Live
cond D. OREN
(CAST) **CASH5051** Puccini Favourites from Covent Garden and the Arena di Verona
(CAST) **CVI2068** Opera Highlights from Verona 1
(CAST) **CVI2070** Great Puccini Love Scenes from Covent Garden, La Scala and Verona
cond Z. PESKÓ
(CAST) **CASH5052** Verdi Operatic Favourites
(CAST) **CVI2068** Opera Highlights from Verona 1
(TELD) **9031-77676-6(TELD)** My World of Opera - Kiri Te Kanawa
cond N. SANTI
Puccini: Manon Lescaut (Cpte)

VERONELLI, Patrizio (treb)
Puccini: Tosca (Cpte)

VERRECCHIA, Aldo (ten)
Verdi: Trovatore (Cpte)

VERRETT, Shirley (mez)
Donizetti: Lucrezia Borgia (Cpte)
Gluck: Orfeo ed Euridice (Cpte)
Meyerbeer: Africaine (Cpte)
Rossini: Siège de Corinthe (Cpte)
Saint-Saëns: Samson et Dalila (Cpte)
Verdi: Ballo in maschera (Cpte), Don Carlo (exc), Forza del destino (Cpte), Luisa Miller (Cpte), Macbeth (Cpte), Rigoletto (exc), Trovatore (Cpte)
(DECC) **071 140-1DH (DECC)** Pavarotti—30th Anniversary Gala Concert
(RCA) **GD60818** Great Operatic Duets
(RCA) **09026 61457-2** Shirley Verrett in Opera
(RCA) **09026 61580-2(8)** RCA/Met 100 Singers, 100 Years (pt 8)
(RCA) **09026 62699-2** Opera's Greatest Duets
(RCA) **74321 24284-2** Opera's Greatest Heroines
(RCA) **74321 25817-2** Café Classics - Operatic
(SONY) **SM22K46290(3)** Stravinsky—The Complete Edition (pt 3)

VERRI, Nella (mez)
Puccini: Fanciulla del West (Cpte)

VERROT, Pascal (cond)
see Lyon Op Orch

VERSAILLES CAMERATA
cond A. DU CLOSEL
(FORL) **UCD16567** Haydn: Orchestral Works

VERSALLE, Richard (ten)
Wagner: Tannhäuser (Cpte)

VERSCHAEVE, Michel (bass)
Grétry: Jugement de Midas (exc)
Mouret: Amours de Ragonde (Cpte)
Rameau: Platée (Cpte), Zoroastre (Cpte)

VERY, Ray (ten)
Moran: Dracula Diary (Cpte)

VERZIER, Jacques (ten)
Offenbach: Contes d'Hoffmann (Cpte)

VERZOUB, Saül (ten)
Milhaud: Malheurs d'Orphée (Cpte)

VESCOVI, Pino de (bass)
Verdi: Otello (Cpte)

VESELÁ, Marie (sop)
Smetana: Bartered Bride (Cpte)

VESPASIANI, Ambra (mez)
Donizetti: Fausta (Cpte)
Salieri: Axur (Cpte)

VESPERMANN, Gerd (sngr)
Schultze: Schwarzer Peter (Cpte)

VESSARI, Ernesto (bar)
Mascagni: Piccolo Marat (Cpte)

VESSIÈRES, André (bass)
Debussy: Pelléas et Mélisande (Cpte)
Gounod: Mireille (Cpte)
Martin: Mystère de la Nativité
Milhaud: Malheurs d'Orphée (Cpte), Pauvre matelot (Cpte)
Mozart: Don Giovanni (Cpte), Nozze di Figaro (Cpte)
Offenbach: Contes d'Hoffmann (Cpte)
Ravel: Enfant et les sortilèges (Cpte)
Tomasi: Don Juan de Mañara (Cpte)
(CASC) **VEL2010** Memories of the Suisse Romande - Suzanne Danco
(DECC) **433 400-2DM2** Ravel & Debussy—Stage Works

VETÖ, Tamás (cond)
see Swedish RSO

VETTORI, Elda (mez)
Verdi: Traviata (Cpte)

VEVERKA, Jaroslav (bass)
Martinů: Julietta (Cpte)

VEVERKA, Josef (ten)
Janáček: From the House of the Dead (Cpte)

VEYRON-LACROIX, Robert (hpd)
(EMI) **CMS5 65621-2** Fischer-Dieskau - The Opera Singer

VEZZANI, César (ten)
Gounod: Faust (Cpte)
(CLUB) **CL99-034** Marcel Journet (1867-1933)
(MSCM) **MM30377** 18 Tenors d'Expression Française

VIALA, Jean-Luc (ten)
Berlioz: Béatrice et Bénédict (Cpte)
Gluck: Rencontre imprévue (Cpte)
Massenet: Grisélidis (Cpte)
Offenbach: Brigands (Cpte)
Poulenc: Dialogues des Carmélites (Cpte)
Prokofiev: Love for 3 Oranges (Cpte)
R. Strauss: Salomé (Cpte)
(EMI) **CZS5 68113-2** Vive Offenbach!
(ERAT) **4509-99607-2** Gluck—Operas; Schubert—Symphonies Nos 8 & 9

VICH, Bohumil (ten)
Smetana: Bartered Bride (Cpte), Brandenburgers in Bohemia (Cpte)
(KOCH) **34036-2** A Pageant of Opera

VÍCH, Bohumír (ten)
Janáček: Káťa Kabanová (Cpte)

VICHEY, Luben (bass)
Verdi: Ballo in maschera (Cpte)

VICKERS, Jon (ten)
Beethoven: Fidelio (Cpte)
Berlioz: Troyens (Cpte)
Bizet: Carmen (Cpte)
Britten: Peter Grimes (Cpte)
Saint-Saëns: Samson et Dalila (Cpte)
Verdi: Aida (exc), Otello (Cpte)
Wagner: Tristan und Isolde (Cpte), Walküre (Cpte)
(CFP) **CD-CFP4656** Herbert von Karajan conducts Opera
(DECC) **433 221-2DWO** The World of Verdi
(DECC) **433 442-2DA** Verdi—Famous Arias
(DECC) **436 463-2DM** Ten Top Tenors
(DG) **429 168-2GR** Wagner: Excerpts from Der Ring
(DG) **435 211-2GX15** Wagner—Der Ring des Nibelungen
(EMI) **CDC7 54016-2** Tenorissimo!
(MEMO) **HR4275/6** Birgit Nilsson—Public Performances 1954-1969
(PHIL) **442 602-2PM** 3 x 3 Tenors
(RCA) **09026 61580-2(7)** RCA/Met 100 Singers, 100 Years (pt 7)
(RCA) **09026 62689-2** The Voices of Living Stereo, Volume 1
(VAI) **VAIA1016** Jon Vickers - Italian Opera Arias

VICTOR, Charles (bar)
(CLAR) **CDGSE78-50-26** Wagner: Tristan und Isolde excerpts
(CLAR) **CDGSE78-50-46** Walter Widdop (1892-1949)

VICTOR CHORALE
cond N. BEREZOWSKI
(RCA) **GD60522** Alexander Kipnis—Opera & Song Recital

VICTOR ORCHESTRA
cond J. PASTERNACK
(ROMO) **81016-2** Lucrezia Bori (1887-1960)
cond W.B. ROGERS
(ROMO) **81016-2** Lucrezia Bori (1887-1960)
cond ROSARIO BOURDON
(ROMO) **81016-2** Lucrezia Bori (1887-1960)
cond N. SHILKRET
(ROMO) **81016-2** Lucrezia Bori (1887-1960)

VICTOR SYMPHONY ORCHESTRA
cond N. BEREZOWSKI
(RCA) **GD60522** Alexander Kipnis—Opera & Song Recital
cond E. MCARTHUR
(PEAR) **GEMMCD9049** Flagstad and Melchior sing Wagner
cond W. PELLETIER
(EMI) **CHS7 69741-2(1)** Record of Singing, Vol.4—Anglo-American School (pt 1)
cond B. REIBOLD
(NIMB) **NI7867** Legendary Baritones
cond ROSARIO BOURDON
(ROMO) **81014-2** Elisabeth Rethberg (1894-1976)
cond F. TOURS
(NIMB) **NI7867** Legendary Baritones

VIDAL, Elisabeth (sop)
Auber: Manon Lescaut (Cpte)
Ravel: Enfant et les sortilèges (Cpte)

VIDERAS, Sigfredo (sngr)
Moreno Torroba: Luisa Fernanda (Cpte)

VIDEV, Konstantin (bass)
Glinka: Life for the Tsar (Cpte)

VIEBIG, Ernst (cond)
see Berlin St Op Orch

VIENNA ACADEMY CHOIR
cond C. MACKERRAS
Gluck: Orfeo ed Euridice (Cpte)

VIENNA ACADEMY ORCHESTRA
cond M. HASELBÖCK
Mozart: Don Giovanni (Cpte)

VIENNA AMADEUS ENSEMBLE
cond W. KOBERA
(DIVE) **DIV31013** Mozart/Salieri—Arias for Countertenors

VIENNA BOYS' CHOIR
(KOCH) **321 214** Wiener Sängerknaben - Kein Schöner Land
cond C. ABBADO
Berg: Wozzeck (Cpte)
Mussorgsky: Khovanshchina (Cpte)
cond A. CLUYTENS
Humperdinck: Hänsel und Gretel (Cpte)
cond M. GIELEN
Schoenberg: Moses und Aron (Cpte)
cond U.C. HARRER
(PHIL) **426 307-2PH** Vienna Boys' Choir - Recital
(PHIL) **434 726-2PM** Vienna Boys' Choir - Portrait
cond H. VON KARAJAN
Bizet: Carmen (Cpte)
Mussorgsky: Boris Godunov (Cpte)
Puccini: Turandot (exc)
(RCA) **GD60205** Opera Choruses
cond L. MAAZEL
Puccini: Turandot (Cpte)
cond G. SOLTI
Mozart: Zauberflöte (exc)
R. Strauss: Frau ohne Schatten (Cpte)
Verdi: Otello (Cpte)
Wagner: Parsifal (Cpte), Tannhäuser (Cpte)

VIENNA CANTATA ORCHESTRA
cond H. LEWIS
(DECC) **430 500-2DWO** World of Handel
(DECC) **433 065-2DWO** Your Hundred Best Opera Tunes Volume II
(DECC) **440 415-2DM** Marilyn Horne
(DECC) **444 543-2DF2** Essential Handel

VIENNA CHAMBER CHOIR
cond R. MORALT
Mozart: Don Giovanni (Cpte)

VIENNA CHAMBER ORCHESTRA
cond G. FISCHER
(DECC) **430 513-2DH** Mozart—Arias
(DECC) **440 401-2DH** Kiri Te Kanawa — Mozart Arias
(DECC) **443 452-2DH** Mozart Portraits—Bartoli
(DECC) **448 300-2DH** Cecilia Bartoli—A Portrait

VIENNA CHILDREN'S CHOIR
cond H. VON KARAJAN
Verdi: Otello (Cpte)

VIENNA CONCENTUS MUSICUS
Mozart: Mitridate (Cpte)
(TELD) **4509-95498-2** Famous Handel Choruses
cond N. HARNONCOURT
Handel: Giulio Cesare (exc)
Monteverdi: Incoronazione di Poppea (Cpte), Orfeo (Cpte), Ritorno d'Ulisse in Patria (Cpte)
Mozart: Finta Giardiniera (Cpte), Lucio Silla (Cpte)
Purcell: Dido (Cpte), Fairy Queen, Z629 (Cpte)
Rameau: Castor et Pollux (Cpte)
(ERAT) **4509-91715-2** The Ultimate Opera Collection 2
(TELD) **4509-93691-2** Queen of Coloratura
(TELD) **4509-95523-2** Mozart—Overtures
(TELD) **4509-97505-2** Mozart—Famous Opera Choruses
(TELD) **4509-97507-2** Mozart—Famous Opera Arias

VIENNA ENSEMBLE
(SONY) **SK47187** A Vienna Souvenir

VIENNA HAYDN ORCHESTRA
cond I. KERTÉSZ
(DECC) **433 064-2DWO** Your Hundred Best Opera Tunes Volume I
(DECC) **433 066-2DWO** Your Hundred Best Opera Tunes III
(DECC) **433 067-2DWO** Your Hundred Best Opera Tunes IV
(DECC) **433 068-2DWO** Your Hundred Best Opera Tunes V
(DECC) **433 440-2DA** Golden Opera
(DECC) **440 947-2DH** Essential Opera II
(DECC) **443 377-2DM** Ten Top Sopranos 2
(DECC) **443 762-2DF2** The Essential Mozart

VIENNA JEUNESSE CHOIR
cond P. STEINBERG
Bellini: Beatrice di Tenda (Cpte)

VIENNA MOZART ORCHESTRA
cond K. LEITNER
(NAXO) **8 550435** Mozart—Arias and Duets
cond R. PETERS
(DECC) **440 409-2DM** Dietrich Fischer-Dieskau

VIENNA OPERA BALL ORCHESTRA
cond U. THEIMER
(DENO) **CO-77949** J. Strauss II—Operetta Highlights
(VICT) **VCD19008** Wien, Wien, nur du allein

VIENNA OPERA CHORUS
cond N. RESCIGNO
(DECC) **425 681-2DM2** Tutto Pavarotti
(DECC) **433 437-2DA** Pavarotti—King of the High Cs
(DECC) **443 379-2DM** Ten Top Tenors 2

cond W. WELLER
(LOND) **436 898-2DM** Operetta Gala

VIENNA OPERA ORCHESTRA
(DECC) **440 415-2DM** Marilyn Horne
cond D. BERNET
(DECC) **433 065-2DWO** Your Hundred Best Opera Tunes Volume II
(DECC) **436 314-2DA** Great Tenor Arias
cond E. DOWNES
(DECC) **425 681-2DM2** Tutto Pavarotti
(DECC) **433 065-2DWO** Your Hundred Best Opera Tunes Volume II
(DECC) **433 437-2DA** Pavarotti—King of the High Cs
(DECC) **436 314-2DA** Great Tenor Arias
cond L. GARDELLI
(DECC) **425 847-2DWO** Your hunded best tunes vol. 1
(DECC) **433 065-2DWO** Your Hundred Best Opera Tunes Volume II
(DECC) **436 300-2DX** Opera Gala Sampler
(DECC) **436 464-2DM** Ten Top Baritones & Basses
(DECC) **440 405-2DM** Elena Souliotis
(DECC) **443 585-2DF2** Your Hundred Best Tunes - Top 20
cond I. KERTÉSZ
(DECC) **430 498-2DWO** The World of Mozart
cond H. LEWIS
(DECC) **425 854-2DWO** Youtr Hundred Best Tunes, Vol. 8
(DECC) **433 064-2DWO** Your Hundred Best Opera Tunes Volume I
(DECC) **433 067-2DWO** Your Hundred Best Opera Tunes IV
(DECC) **433 440-2DA** Golden Opera
(DECC) **440 415-2DM** Marilyn Horne
(DECC) **443 334-2LRX** Music for Relaxation, Vol 9 - A Touch of Romance
(DECC) **444 552-2DF2** Essential Saint-Saëns
cond A. QUADRI
(BELA) **450 007-2** Puccini Favourites
(BELA) **450 015-2** Cinema Classics
(DECC) **417 686-2DC** Puccini—Operatic Arias
(DECC) **433 067-2DWO** Your Hundred Best Opera Tunes IV
(DECC) **433 069-2DWO** Your Hundred Best Opera Tunes VI
(DECC) **433 221-2DWO** The World of Verdi
(DECC) **433 624-2DSP** Great Soprano Arias
(DECC) **433 636-2DSP** Puccini—Famous Arias
(DECC) **443 380-2DM** Ten Top Baritones & Basses 2
cond N. RESCIGNO
(DECC) **433 437-2DA** Pavarotti—King of the High Cs
(DECC) **433 440-2DA** Golden Opera
(DECC) **443 379-2DM** Ten Top Tenors 2
(DECC) **400 053-4DH** World's Best Loved Tenor Arias
cond N. SANTI
(DECC) **444 555-2DF2** Essential Puccini
cond W. WELLER
(LOND) **436 897-2DM** Lehár Gala
(LOND) **436 898-2DM** Operetta Gala

VIENNA OPERETTA CHORUS
cond E-G. SCHERZER
(SCHW) **312732** Lehár—Der Zarewitsch (excs)
cond R. STOLZ
(DECC) **425 852-2DWO** Your hundred best tunes vol 6
(DECC) **436 316-2DA** Golden Operetta

VIENNA OPERETTA ORCHESTRA
(SCHW) **312732** Lehár—Der Zarewitsch (excs)

VIENNA PHILHARMONIC ORCHESTRA
Janáček: From the House of the Dead (Cpte)
Mozart: Don Giovanni (Cpte), Nozze di Figaro (Cpte)
Puccini: Madama Butterfly (Cpte)
R. Strauss: Arabella (Cpte), Ariadne auf Naxos (Cpte), Elektra (Cpte), Frau ohne Schatten (Cpte), Rosenkavalier (Cpte)
Rossini: Cenerentola (Cpte)
Verdi: Falstaff (Cpte), Rigoletto (Cpte)
Wagner: Walküre (Cpte)
(DG) **072 146-3GH** New Year's Concert in Vienna 1989
(LOND) **440 490-2LM5(1)** Kirsten Flagstad Edition
(PHIL) **070 152-3PH** New Year's Concert 1992
cond C. ABBADO
Berg: Wozzeck (Cpte)
Debussy: Pelléas et Mélisande (Cpte)
Mozart: Nozze di Figaro (Cpte)
Rossini: Italiana in Algeri (Cpte)
Wagner: Lohengrin (Cpte)
(DG) **423 662-2GH** New Year's Day Concert, Vienna, 1988
(DG) **427 306-2GH6** Beethoven: Complete Symphonies
(DG) **429 762-2GH2** Beethoven: Overtures
(DG) **431 628-2GH** Vienna New Year's Concert, 1991
(DG) **072 175-1GH (DG)** New Year's Concert in Vienna 1991
cond O. ACKERMANN
(EMI) **CHS7 69741-2(4)** Record of Singing, Vol.4—German School
(TEST) **SBT1059** Erich Kunz (b. 1909)
cond K. ALWIN
(ORFE) **C394101B** Great Mozart Singers Series, Vol. 1
cond L. BERNSTEIN
Beethoven: Fidelio (Cpte)
R. Strauss: Rosenkavalier (Cpte)
(DG) **423 481-2GX6** Beethoven: Complete Symphonies
(DG) **435 091-2GCE10** DG Beethoven Edition
(SONY) **MDK47176** Favourite Arias by the World's Favourite Tenors
cond W. BOSKOVSKY
(DECC) **417 747-2DM** Johann Strauss Favourites
(DG) **435 335-2GWP2** VPO plays Johann & Josef Strauss
(LOND) **436 781-2LM** Wiener Tanzgala 1
(LOND) **436 785-2LM** Wiener Tanzgala 5
cond K. BÖHM
Einem: Prozess (Cpte)
J. Strauss II: Fledermaus (exc)
Mozart: Così fan tutte (Cpte), Don Giovanni (exc), Zauberflöte (Cpte)
R. Strauss: Arabella (Cpte), Ariadne auf Naxos (Cpte), Rosenkavalier (Cpte), Salome (Cpte), Schweigsame Frau (Cpte)
Wagner: Meistersinger (Cpte)
(BELA) **450 117-2** Great Opera Chorus II
(DECC) **436 316-2DA** Golden Operetta
(DG) **439 687-2GX2** Wagner—Overtures and Preludes
(EMI) **CHS7 69741-2(4)** Record of Singing, Vol.4—German School
(ORFE) **C335931A** Salzburg Festival highlights (1956-85)
(ORFE) **C365941A** Christa Ludwig - Salzburg Festival highlights
(ORFE) **C394201B** Great Mozart Singers Series, Vol. 2
(ORFE) **C394301B** Great Mozart Singers Series, Vol. 3
(PREI) **90237** R Strauss—Daphne
(PREI) **90249** Mozart in tempore belli
cond A. CLUYTENS
Humperdinck: Hänsel und Gretel (Cpte)
cond C. VON DOHNÁNYI
Beethoven: Fidelio (Cpte)
Berg: Wozzeck (Cpte)
R. Strauss: Salome (Cpte)
Schoenberg: Erwartung (Cpte)
Wagner: Fliegende Holländer (Cpte)
cond E. DOWNES
(DECC) **443 380-2DM** Ten Top Baritones & Basses 2
cond A. EREDE
(PREI) **90227** Hilde Gueden - As The World Knew Her
cond F. FRICSAY
Mozart: Idomeneo (Cpte)
cond W. FURTWÄNGLER
Beethoven: Fidelio (Cpte), Leonore (exc)
Mozart: Don Giovanni (Cpte), Zauberflöte (Cpte)
Verdi: Otello (Cpte)
Wagner: Walküre (Cpte)
(ACAN) **43 121** Wagner: Orchestral Works
(DG) **435 321-2GWP12** 150 Years - Vienna Philharmonic
(DG) **435 324-2GWP** VPO under Wilhelm Furtwängler
(EMI) **CDM7 63657-2** Schwarzkopf sings Opera Arias
(EMI) **CHS7 64935-2** Wagner—Opera Excerpts
(ORFE) **C394201B** Great Mozart Singers Series, Vol. 2
cond L. GARDELLI
(DECC) **433 443-2DA** Great Opera Choruses
cond J. E. GARDINER
Lehár: Lustige Witwe (Cpte)
cond C.M. GIULINI
Verdi: Rigoletto (exc)
(BELA) **450 121-2** Plácido Domingo
(DG) **415 366-2GH** Placido Domingo Recital
(DG) **427 708-2GX3** The Best of Domingo
(DG) **419 091-4GW** Placido Domingo sings Favourite Arias, Songs and Tangos
cond R. HEGER
(EMI) **CHS7 64487-2** R. Strauss—Der Rosenkavalier & Lieder
(PEAR) **GEMMCDS9365** R. Strauss: Der Rosenkavalier (abridged), etc
(PEAR) **GEMMCD9122** 20 Great Basses sing Great Arias
cond H. HOLLREISER
(DECC) **425 959-2DM** Lisa della Casa sings R. Strauss
cond JAMES LEVINE
Mozart: Zauberflöte (Cpte)
R. Strauss: Ariadne auf Naxos (Cpte)
Smetana: Bartered Bride (exc)
(DECC) **071 142-1DH (DECC)** Essential Opera
(DG) **437 544-2GH** Carmen-Fantasie
(DG) **439 153-4GMA** Mad about Sopranos
(DG) **072 110-1GH** Hommage a Sevilla—Placido Domingo in scenes from various operas
(DG) **072 187-1GH (DG)** Hommage a Sevilla
(DG) **437 544-5GH** Carmen-Fantasie
(ORFE) **C394301B** Great Mozart Singers Series, Vol. 3
(RCA) **09026 61440-2** Opera's Greatest Moments
(RCA) **09026 61580-2(8)** RCA/Met 100 Singers, 100 Years (pt 8)
(RCA) **09026 61886-2** Operas Greatest Love Songs
cond H. VON KARAJAN
Bizet: Carmen (exc)
Gluck: Orfeo ed Euridice (Cpte)
J. Strauss II: Fledermaus (Cpte)
Mozart: Don Giovanni (Cpte), Nozze di Figaro (Cpte), Zauberflöte (Cpte)
Mussorgsky: Boris Godunov (Cpte)
Puccini: Madama Butterfly (exc), Tosca (Cpte), Turandot (exc)
R. Strauss: Rosenkavalier (exc)
Verdi: Aida (Cpte), Ballo in maschera (Cpte), Don Carlo (Cpte), Otello (Cpte), Trovatore (Cpte)
(CFP) **CD-CFP4656** Herbert von Karajan conducts Opera
(DECC) **430 481-2DX2** Renata Tebaldi sings Opera Arias
(DECC) **433 066-2DWO** Your Hundred Best Opera Tunes III
(DECC) **433 067-2DWO** Your Hundred Best Opera Tunes IV
(DECC) **433 069-2DWO** Your Hundred Best Opera Tunes VI
(DECC) **433 439-2DA** Great Love Duets
(DECC) **433 443-2DA** Great Opera Choruses
(DECC) **433 822-2DH** Essential Opera
(DECC) **436 315-2DA** Great Operatic Duets
(DECC) **436 317-2DA** Puccini—Famous Arias
(DECC) **436 464-2DM** Ten Top Baritones & Basses
(DECC) **440 402-2DM** Leontyne Price
(DECC) **440 408-2DM** Renata Tebaldi
(DECC) **440 947-2DH** Essential Opera II
(DECC) **443 377-2DM** Ten Top Sopranos 2
(DECC) **448 042-2DC9** Karajan - The Great Decca Recordings, 1959-1963
(DECC) **071 142-1DH (DECC)** Essential Opera
(DG) **415 366-2GH** Placido Domingo Recital
(DG) **423 613-2GH** Wagner—Opera excerpts
(DG) **427 708-2GX3** The Best of Domingo
(DG) **439 104-2GDO** Schubert—Symphony No 8; J.Strauss II—Waltzes
(DG) **439 151-2GMA** Mad about Puccini
(DG) **445 525-2GMA** Domingo Favourites
(DG) **439 153-4GMA** Mad about Sopranos
(EMI) **CDC7 54524-2** The José Carreras Album
(EMI) **CDH7 63708-2** Mozart—Opera Arias
(EMI) **CDH7 69793-2** Elisabeth Schwarzkopf & Irmgard Seefried sing Duets
(EMI) **CDM7 63111-2** José Carreras sings Opera & Operetta Arias
(EMI) **CDM7 63657-2** Schwarzkopf sings Opera Arias
(EMI) **CDM7 69549-2** Ruggero Raimondi: Italian Opera Arias
(MEMO) **HR4191/2** Cesare Valletti—Public Performances
(MEMO) **HR4204/5** Franco Corelli—Opera Arias
(MEMO) **HR4223/4** Nicolai Ghiaurov
(MEMO) **HR4233/4** Alfredo Kraus—Public Performances
(MEMO) **HR4277/8** Mirella Freni—Public Performances 1963-1970
(MEMO) **HR4386/7** Great Voices - Giulietta Simionato
(MEMO) **HR4396/7** Great Voices—Leontyne Price
(ORFE) **C394201B** Great Mozart Singers Series, Vol. 2
(ORFE) **C394301B** Great Mozart Singers Series, Vol. 3
(PREI) **90034** Maria Cebotari (1910-49)
(PREI) **90078** Hilde Konetzni
(RCA) **GD60205** Opera Choruses
(RCA) **09026 61580-2(7)** RCA/Met 100 Singers, 100 Years (pt 7)
(RCA) **09026 61580-2(8)** RCA/Met 100 Singers, 100 Years (pt 8)
(RCA) **09026 61886-2** Operas Greatest Love Songs
(RCA) **09026 62689-2** The Voices of Living Stereo, Volume 1
(RCA) **74321 24284-2** Opera's Greatest Heroines
(SONY) **SLV45985** Karajan - His Video Legacy. New Year's Concert 1987
(TEST) **SBT1059** Erich Kunz (b. 1909)
cond J. KEILBERTH
(ORFE) **C335931A** Salzburg Festival highlights (1956-85)
cond R. KEMPE
Wagner: Lohengrin (Cpte)
(CFP) **CD-CFP4658** Everlasting Love
(EMI) **CES5 68535-2** Strauss Family—Overtures, Waltzes, Polkas & Marches
cond I. KERTÉSZ
(DECC) **430 773-2DC4** Schubert—Complete Symphonies, etc
(ORFE) **C394301B** Great Mozart Singers Series, Vol. 3
cond C. KLEIBER
(SONY) **SK45938** Carlos Kleiber conducts Johann Strauss
(SONY) **SX3K53385** New Year's Concerts 1989 and 1992
cond E. KLEIBER
Mozart: Nozze di Figaro (Cpte)
R. Strauss: Rosenkavalier (Cpte)
(DECC) **440 418-2DM** Cesare Siepi
cond H. KNAPPERTSBUSCH
Wagner: Götterdämmerung (exc), Meistersinger (Cpte)
(DECC) **433 068-2DWO** Your Hundred Best Opera Tunes V
(DECC) **440 062-2DM** Wagner—Overtures
(DECC) **443 380-2DM** Ten Top Baritones & Basses 2
(LOND) **440 490-2LM5(1)** Kirsten Flagstad Edition
(LOND) **440 495-2LM** Kirsten Flagstad Edition, Vol. 5
(PREI) **90116** Knappertsbuch conducts the Vienna Philharmonic
cond C. KRAUSS
Mozart: Nozze di Figaro (Cpte)

(KOCH) **37129-2** Clemens Kraus Conducts
(ORFE) **C394101B** Great Mozart Singers Series, Vol. 1
(PREI) **90112** Clemens Krauss conducts the VPO
(PREI) **90139** Vienna Philharmonic on the way to New Year's Concerts
(PREI) **90227** Hilde Gueden - As The World Knew Her
cond J. KRIPS
Mozart: Don Giovanni (Cpte), Entführung (Cpte)
(CFP) **CD-CFP4612** Favourite Mozart
(DECC) **440 418-2DM** Cesare Siepi
(DECC) **443 530-2LF2** Mozart—Die Entführung aus dem Serail
(EMI) **CDH7 63708-2** Mozart—Opera Arias
(EMIL) **CDZ7 67015-2** Mozart—Opera Arias
(PREI) **90083** Maria Reining
cond F. LEHÁR
(EMI) **CDC7 54838-2** Franz Lehár
(EMI) **CDM7 69476-2** Richard Tauber - A Portrait
(EMI) **CHS7 69741-2(4)** Record of Singing, Vol.4—German School
(PEAR) **GEMMCD9310** Franz Lehár conducts Richard Tauber
(PREI) **89065** Maria Reining (1903-1991)
(PREI) **90150** Lehár conducts Lehár
cond E. LEINSDORF
R. Strauss: Ariadne auf Naxos (Cpte)
(DECC) **440 402-2DM** Leontyne Price
cond L. MAAZEL
(BELA) **450 117-2** Great Opera Chorus II
(DG) **429 562-2GX2** The Best of the New Year's Concerts in Vienna
(DG) **435 335-2GWP2** VPO plays Johann & Josef Strauss
(DG) **439 439-2GCL** J. Strauss II—Waltzes and Polkas
cond C. MACKERRAS
Janáček: Cunning Little Vixen (Cpte), Cunning Little Vixen Suite, Jenufa (Cpte), Makropulos Affair (Cpte)
(DECC) **421 852-2DH2** Janáček: Operatic & Chamber Works
(DECC) **430 375-2DH2** Janáček—Operatic and Orchestral Works
cond L. VON MATAČIĆ
(MEMO) **HR4386/7** Great Voices - Giulietta Simionato
(MEMO) **HR4396/7** Great Voices—Leontyne Price
(MEMO) **HR4400/1** Great Voices - Ettore Bastianini
cond Z. MEHTA
Mozart: Entführung (Cpte)
(SONY) **SK45808** New Year's Day Concert 1990
cond D. MITROPOULOS
Mozart: Don Giovanni (Cpte)
R. Strauss: Elektra (Cpte)
cond R. MORALT
(DECC) **425 959-2DM** Lisa della Casa sings R. Strauss
(EMI) **CHS7 69741-2(4)** Record of Singing, Vol.4—German School
(EMI) **CMS7 64008-2(1)** Wagner Singing on Record (pt 1)
(PREI) **89018** Helge Rosvaenge (1897-1972)
(PREI) **89065** Maria Reining (1903-1991)
(PREI) **89076** Josef Herrmann (1903-1955)
(PREI) **89211** Helge Roswaenge (1897-1972) - III
(PREI) **90213** Max Lorenz sings Wagner
(PREI) **90249** Mozart in tempore belli
(TEST) **SBT1059** Erich Kunz (b. 1909)
cond R. MUTI
Mozart: Clemenza di Tito (Cpte), Don Giovanni (Cpte), Nozze di Figaro (exc)
(CFP) **CD-CFP4612** Favourite Mozart
(EMI) **CDC5 55095-2** Prima Diva
(EMI) **CDC5 55350-2** Cheryl Studer - A Portrait
(EMIL) **CDZ7 67015-2** Mozart—Opera Arias
(ORFE) **C394301B** Great Mozart Singers Series, Vol. 3
(PHIL) **438 493-2PH** New Year's Concert 1993
cond S. OZAWA
(ORFE) **C394301B** Great Mozart Singers Series, Vol. 3
cond A. PREVIN
J. Strauss II: Fledermaus (Cpte)
(DG) **437 790-2GH** R. Strauss—Orchestral Works
(PHIL) **434 725-2PM** Kiri Te Kanawa - Classics
cond J. PRITCHARD
Mozart: Idomeneo (Cpte)
(DECC) **436 462-2DM** Ten Top Mezzos
(DECC) **440 401-2DM** Kiri Te Kanawa — Mozart Arias
cond F. PROHASKA
(PREI) **90034** Maria Cebotari (1910-49)
cond M. SARGENT
(EMI) **CES5 68541-2** Rossini/Verdi/Bellini/ Donizetti—Overtures
cond W. SAWALLISCH
(ORFE) **C335931A** Salzburg Festival highlights (1956-85)
cond G. SOLTI
Mozart: Entführung (Cpte), Zauberflöte (exc)
R. Strauss: Arabella (Cpte), Elektra (Cpte), Frau ohne Schatten (Cpte), Rosenkavalier (Cpte), Salome (Cpte)
Verdi: Otello (Cpte)
Wagner: Götterdämmerung (Cpte), Lohengrin (Cpte), Meistersinger (Cpte), Parsifal (Cpte), Rheingold (Cpte), Ring des Nibelungen Introduction, Siegfried (Cpte), Tannhäuser (Cpte), Walküre (Cpte)
(BELA) **450 117-2** Great Opera Chorus II
(DECC) **410 137-2DH** Wagner: Excerpts from The Ring
(DECC) **414 100-2DM15** Wagner: Der Ring des Nibelungen
(DECC) **417 011-2DH2** Pavarotti's Greatest Hits
(DECC) **421 313-2DA** Wagner: Der Ring des Nibelungen - Great Scenes
(DECC) **421 865-2DA** Wagner—Opera Choruses
(DECC) **425 853-2DWO** Your hundred best tunes vol 7
(DECC) **433 065-2DWO** Your Hundred Best Opera Tunes Volume II
(DECC) **433 067-2DWO** Your Hundred Best Opera Tunes IV
(DECC) **433 068-2DWO** Your Hundred Best Opera Tunes V
(DECC) **433 437-2DA** Pavarotti—King of the High Cs
(DECC) **433 439-2DA** Great Love Duets
(DECC) **433 443-2DA** Great Opera Choruses
(DECC) **436 300-2DX** Opera Gala Sampler
(DECC) **436 461-2DM** Ten Top Sopranos
(DECC) **436 462-2DM** Ten Top Mezzos
(DECC) **436 464-2DM** Ten Top Baritones & Basses
(DECC) **440 069-2DWO** The World of Wagner
(DECC) **440 409-2DM** Dietrich Fischer-Dieskau
(DECC) **440 410-2DM** Plácido Domingo
(DECC) **440 606-2DF2** Wagner—Orchestral Favourites
(DECC) **440 947-2DH** Essential Opera II
(DECC) **443 335-2LRX** Music for Relaxation, Vol 10 - The Night Before
(DECC) **443 377-2DM** Ten Top Sopranos 2
(DECC) **443 379-2DM** Ten Top Tenors 2
(DECC) **410 137-5DH** Wagner: Excerpts from The Ring
(LOND) **440 490-2LM5(1)** Kirsten Flagstad Edition
(LOND) **440 495-2LM** Kirsten Flagstad Edition, Vol. 5
(ORFE) **C394201B** Great Mozart Singers Series, Vol. 2
cond H. STEIN
(BELA) **450 025-2** Essential Wagner
(DECC) **425 853-2DWO** Your hundred best tunes vol 7
cond R. STRAUSS
(DG) **435 321-2GWP12** 150 Years - Vienna Philharmonic
(DG) **435 333-2GWP** VPO under Richard Strauss
cond G. SZELL
(ORFE) **C394201B** Great Mozart Singers Series, Vol. 2
cond A. TOSCANINI
(ORFE) **C394101B** Great Mozart Singers Series, Vol. 1
cond H. VON KARAJAN
Mozart: Zauberflöte (exc)
cond H. WALLBERG
(ORFE) **C394301B** Great Mozart Singers Series, Vol. 3
cond B. WALTER
Wagner: Walküre (Cpte)
(KOCH) **37011-2** Legendary Conductors
(NIMB) **NI7851** Legendary Voices
(ORFE) **C394101B** Great Mozart Singers Series, Vol. 1
(PREI) **90157** Beethoven/Wagner—Orchestral Works

VIENNA RADIO SYMPHONY ORCHESTRA
cond L. GARDELLI
(PHIL) **442 600-2PH** The Great Carreras
cond B. PRIESTMAN
(CBC) **PSCD2002** Maureen Forrester sings Handel Arias

VIENNA RAVEL ORCHESTRA
cond J-P. ROUCHON
(DIVE) **DIV31011** Various Orchestral Works

VIENNA SINGVEREIN
cond P. GÜLKE
Schreker: Irrelohe (Cpte)
cond N. HARNONCOURT
Mozart: Zauberflöte (Cpte)
cond H. VON KARAJAN
Mozart: Zauberflöte (Cpte)
Verdi: Aida (exc)
cond H. VON KARAJAN
Mozart: Zauberflöte (exc)

VIENNA STATE OPERA BALLET
cond H. VON KARAJAN
Verdi: Falstaff (Cpte)

VIENNA STATE OPERA CHORUS
cond C. ABBADO
Berg: Wozzeck (Cpte)
Debussy: Pelléas et Mélisande (Cpte)
Janáček: From the House of the Dead (Cpte)
Mozart: Nozze di Figaro (Cpte)
Mussorgsky: Khovanshchina (Cpte)
R. Strauss: Elektra (Cpte)
Rossini: Italiana in Algeri (Cpte)
Wagner: Lohengrin (Cpte)
cond K. ALWIN
(SCHW) **314512** Vienna State Opera Live, Vol.1
(SCHW) **314542** Vienna State Opera Live, Vol.4
(SCHW) **314632** Vienna State Opera Live, Vol.13
(SCHW) **314662** Vienna State Opera Live, Vol.16
cond N. BAREZA
(ACAN) **49 402** Giuseppe Taddei—Recital
cond L. BERNSTEIN
Beethoven: Fidelio (exc)
R. Strauss: Rosenkavalier (Cpte)
cond G. BERTINI
Donizetti: Campanello di notte (Cpte)
cond W. BOSKOVSKY
Zeller: Vogelhändler (Cpte)
(CFP) **CD-CFP4499** Strauss—Champagne and Laughter
cond K. BÖHM
Beethoven: Fidelio (Cpte)
Einem: Prozess (Cpte)
J. Strauss II: Fledermaus (exc)
Mozart: Così fan tutte (Cpte), Don Giovanni (exc), Nozze di Figaro (Cpte), Zauberflöte (Cpte)
R. Strauss: Arabella (Cpte), Daphne (Cpte), Elektra (Cpte), Frau ohne Schatten (Cpte), Rosenkavalier (Cpte), Schweigsame Frau (Cpte)
Verdi: Macbeth (Cpte), Otello (Cpte)
Wagner: Meistersinger (Cpte)
(BELA) **450 117-2** Great Opera Chorus II
(EMI) **CHS7 69741-2(4)** Record of Singing, Vol.4—German School
(PREI) **90237** R Strauss—Daphne
(PREI) **90249** Mozart in tempore belli
(SCHW) **314552** Vienna State Opera Live, Vol.5
(SCHW) **314582** Vienna State Opera Live, Vol.8
(SCHW) **314692** Vienna State Opera Live, Vol.19
cond G. DEL CAMPO
(SCHW) **314512** Vienna State Opera Live, Vol.1
cond R. CHAILLY
Rossini: Cenerentola (Cpte)
Verdi: Rigoletto (Cpte)
cond C. VON DOHNÁNYI
Berg: Wozzeck (Cpte)
cond A. FISCHER
Ponchielli: Gioconda (Cpte)
cond F. FRICSAY
Mozart: Idomeneo (Cpte)
cond W. FURTWÄNGLER
Beethoven: Fidelio (Cpte)
Mozart: Don Giovanni (Cpte), Zauberflöte (Cpte)
Verdi: Otello (Cpte)
Wagner: Meistersinger (exc)
(MEMO) **HR4376/7** Tito Gobbi—Opera Arias
(SCHW) **314502** Vienna State Opera—Live Recordings (sampler)
(SCHW) **314702** Vienna State Opera Live, Vol.20
cond W. FURTWÄNGLER
Wagner: Tristan und Isolde (exc)
cond L. GARDELLI
Verdi: Nabucco (Cpte)
(DECC) **425 847-2DWO** Your hunded best tunes vol. 1
(DECC) **433 065-2DWO** Your Hundred Best Opera Tunes Volume II
(DECC) **433 443-2DA** Great Opera Choruses
(DECC) **436 300-2DX** Opera Gala Sampler
(DECC) **443 585-2DF2** Your Hundred Best Tunes - Top 20
cond C.M. GIULINI
Verdi: Rigoletto (Cpte)
cond A. GUADAGNO
(ACAN) **49 402** Giuseppe Taddei—Recital
cond V. GUI
(SCHW) **314582** Vienna State Opera Live, Vol.8
cond R. HEGER
(EMI) **CHS7 64487-2** R. Strauss—Der Rosenkavalier & Lieder
(PEAR) **GEMMCDS9365** R. Strauss: Der Rosenkavalier (abridged), etc
(PEAR) **GEMMCD9122** 20 Great Basses sing Great Arias
(SCHW) **314512** Vienna State Opera Live, Vol.1
(SCHW) **314542** Vienna State Opera Live, Vol.4
(SCHW) **314622** Vienna State Opera Live, Vol.12
cond JAMES LEVINE
Mozart: Zauberflöte (Cpte)
cond H. VON KARAJAN
Bizet: Carmen (Cpte)
Gluck: Orfeo ed Euridice (Cpte)
J. Strauss II: Fledermaus (Cpte)
Mozart: Don Giovanni (Cpte), Nozze di Figaro (Cpte)
Mussorgsky: Boris Godunov (Cpte)
Puccini: Madama Butterfly (exc), Tosca (Cpte), Turandot (exc)
R. Strauss: Rosenkavalier (exc)
Verdi: Aida (Cpte), Ballo in maschera (Cpte), Don Carlo (Cpte), Falstaff (Cpte), Otello (Cpte), Trovatore (Cpte)
Wagner: Fliegende Holländer (exc)
(DECC) **433 066-2DWO** Your Hundred Best Opera Tunes III
(DECC) **433 443-2DA** Great Opera Choruses
(DECC) **436 464-2DM** Ten Top Baritones & Basses
(DECC) **440 947-2DH** Essential Opera II
(DG) **439 151-2GMA** Mad about Puccini
(DG) **445 525-2GMA** Domingo Favourites
(EMI) **CDM7 63111-2** José Carreras sings Opera & Operetta Arias
(EMI) **CDM7 69549-2** Ruggero Raimondi: Italian Opera Arias
(MEMO) **HR4386/7** Great Voices - Giulietta Simionato
(MEMO) **HR4396/7** Great Voices—Leontyne Price
(RCA) **GD60205** Opera Choruses
cond R. KEMPE
Wagner: Lohengrin (Cpte)
cond I. KERTÉSZ
Donizetti: Don Pasquale (Cpte)
cond C. KLEIBER
R. Strauss: Rosenkavalier (Cpte)
cond E. KLEIBER
Mozart: Nozze di Figaro (Cpte)
R. Strauss: Rosenkavalier (Cpte)

cond L. REICHWEIN
(SCHW) **311162** World Famous Conductors from Silesia
(SCHW) **314542** Vienna State Opera Live, Vol.4
(SCHW) **314562** Vienna State Opera Live, Vol.6
(SCHW) **314632** Vienna State Opera Live, Vol.13
(SCHW) **314692** Vienna State Opera Live, Vol.19
(SCHW) **314722** Vienna State Opera Live, Vol.22
cond F. RUHLMANN
(SCHW) **314662** Vienna State Opera Live, Vol.16
cond V. DE SABATA
(SCHW) **314512** Vienna State Opera Live, Vol.1
(SCHW) **314542** Vienna State Opera Live, Vol.4
cond R. STOLZ
Lehár: Lustige Witwe (exc)
(DECC) **425 852-2DWO** Your hundred best tunes vol 6
(DECC) **436 316-2DA** Golden Operetta
cond R. STRAUSS
(SCHW) **314532** Vienna State Opera Live, Vol.3
cond H. TIETJEN
Wagner: Lohengrin (exc)
(SCHW) **314502** Vienna State Opera—Live Recordings (sampler)
cond B. WALTER
(SCHW) **314502** Vienna State Opera—Live Recordings (sampler)
(SCHW) **314542** Vienna State Opera Live, Vol.4
(SCHW) **314572** Vienna State Opera Live, Vol.7
(SCHW) **314592** Vienna State Opera Live, Vol.9
(SCHW) **314602** Vienna State Opera Live, Vol.10
cond F. WEINGARTNER
(SCHW) **314512** Vienna State Opera Live, Vol.1
(SCHW) **314602** Vienna State Opera Live, Vol.10
(SCHW) **314622** Vienna State Opera Live, Vol.12
cond W. WELLER
(DECC) **443 931-2DM** Pilar Lorengar sings Opera Arias
cond WOLFGANG MARTIN
(SCHW) **314692** Vienna State Opera Live, Vol.19
cond R. ZELLER
(CBC) **PSCD2002** Maureen Forrester sings Handel Arias

VIENNA STRAUSS FESTIVAL ORCHESTRA
cond P. GUTH
(DINT) **DICD920149** The Magic of the Strauss Dynasty

VIENNA STRING SEXTET
(EMI) **CDC5 55108-2** R. Strauss/Mozart—Chamber Works

VIENNA SYMPHONY ORCHESTRA
Mozart: Nozze di Figaro (Cpte)
cond Y. AHRONOVITCH
(LASE) **15 514** Most Famous Overtures
(LASE) **15 521** Wagner Overtures and Preludes
(LASE) **15 612** Wagner - Magic Fire Music
cond G. BERTINI
Donizetti: Campanello di notte (Cpte)
cond W. BOSKOVSKY
Zeller: Vogelhändler (Cpte)
(CFP) **CD-CFP4499** Strauss—Champagne and Laughter
cond K. BÖHM
Mozart: Nozze di Figaro (Cpte)
R. Strauss: Daphne (Cpte)
cond O. CAETANI
(SONY) **SM48155** Carreras and Caballe sing Souvenirs
(SONY) **SMK48155** Carreras and Caballe sing Souvenirs
cond P. GÜLKE
Schreker: Irrelohe (Cpte)
cond N. HARNONCOURT
J. Strauss II: Zigeunerbaron (Cpte)
cond U.C. HARRER
(PHIL) **422 527-2PME** The Complete Mozart Edition Vol 27
cond F. LEHÁR
(EMI) **CDC7 54838-2** Franz Lehár
(PREI) **90150** Lehár conducts Lehár
cond F. LEITNER
(DG) **437 677-2GDO2** Irmgard Seefried - Opera Recital
cond L. LUDWIG
Weber: Oberon (exc)
cond I. MARIN
(SONY) **SK47192** Ferruccio Furlanetto sings Mozart
cond R. MORALT
Mozart: Così fan tutte (Cpte), Don Giovanni (Cpte)
R. Strauss: Salome (Cpte)
(PHIL) **442 602-2PM** 3 x 3 Tenors
cond A. PAULIK
J. Strauss II: Nacht in Venedig (Cpte)
cond B. PAUMGARTNER
(PHIL) **438 953-2PM2** Alarie/Simoneau - Arias & Duets
cond G. PRÊTRE
(ORFE) **C237901A** Wagner—Orchestral and Vocal works
cond W. SAWALLISCH
(ORFE) **C236901A** Music of the Strauss Family
cond R. STOLZ
J. Strauss II: Fledermaus (exc), Wiener Blut (exc)
(EURO) **258 665** Music of Vienna, Vol.10
(EURO) **258 667** Music of Vienna, Vol.12
cond H. SWAROWSKY
(PREI) **90078** Hilde Konetzni
cond B. WEIL
Mozart: Entführung (exc)
(SONY) **SK53288** Offenbach—Overtures
cond H. WEISBACH
Wagner: Tristan und Isolde (exc)

VIENNA SYMPHONY ORCHESTRA JOHANN STRAUSS ENSEMBLE
cond J. WILDNER
(ORFE) **C291931A** Soirée dansante

VIENNA THEATER AN DER WIEN ORCHESTRA
cond A. PAULIK
(NIMB) **NI7833** Schöne & Tauber in Operetta

VIENNA THEATRE ORCHESTRA
cond A. PAULIK
(TEST) **SBT1005** Ten Top Tenors

VIENNA VOLKSOPER CHORUS
cond F. BAUER-THEUSSL
Kálmán: Csárdásfürstin (exc)
Lehár: Graf von Luxemburg (exc), Paganini (exc)
O. Straus: Walzertraum (exc)
(KOCH) **399 225** Operetta Highlights 3
cond J.L. GRUBER
(KOCH) **399 225** Operetta Highlights 3
cond M. SCHÖNHERR
Lehár: Graf von Luxemburg (exc), Zarewitsch (exc)

VIENNA VOLKSOPER ORCHESTRA
(DG) **435 145-2GX5(2)** Fritz Wunderlich—Opera Arias, Lieder, etc, (part 2)
cond F. BAUER-THEUSSL
Kálmán: Csárdásfürstin (exc)
Lehár: Graf von Luxemburg (exc), Paganini (exc)
O. Straus: Walzertraum (exc)
cond J.L. GRUBER
(KOCH) **399 225** Operetta Highlights 3
cond H. LAMBRECHT
Lehár: Land des Lächelns (exc)
cond A. LOMBARD
(DECC) **436 316-2DA** Golden Operetta
(DECC) **440 416-2DM** Régine Crespin
cond L. MAGIERA
(DECC) **417 011-2DH2** Pavarotti's Greatest Hits
(DECC) **425 681-2DM2** Tutto Pavarotti
(DECC) **433 069-2DWO** Your Hundred Best Opera Tunes VI
(DECC) **433 440-2DA** Golden Opera
(DECC) **400 053-4DH** World's Best Loved Tenor Arias
cond Z. MEHTA
(DECC) **436 317-2DA** Puccini—Famous Arias
cond G. PATANÈ
(DECC) **425 430-2DH** Cecilia Bartoli sings Rossini Arias
(DECC) **436 133-2DWO** World of Rossini
(DECC) **443 378-2DM** Ten Top Mezzos 2
cond A. PAULIK
(DECC) **436 316-2DA** Golden Operetta
(LOND) **436 897-2DM** Lehár Gala
(LOND) **436 898-2DM** Operetta Gala
(TEST) **SBT1059** Erich Kunz (b. 1909)
cond N. RESCIGNO
(DECC) **425 681-2DM2** Tutto Pavarotti
cond N. SANTI
(BELA) **450 007-2** Puccini Favourites
(DECC) **417 686-2DC** Puccini—Operatic Arias
(DECC) **433 067-2DWO** Your Hundred Best Opera Tunes IV
(DECC) **433 624-2DSP** Great Soprano Arias
(DECC) **433 636-2DSP** Puccini—Famous Arias
(DECC) **433 865-2DWO** The World of Puccini
(DECC) **436 317-2DA** Puccini—Famous Arias
cond L. SCHIFRIN
(ERAT) **4509-92875-2** Vienna - Operetta Arias
cond M. SCHÖNHERR
Lehár: Graf von Luxemburg (exc), Zarewitsch (exc)
cond G. SÉBASTIAN
(DECC) **440 416-2DM** Régine Crespin
cond W. WELLER
(DECC) **436 316-2DA** Golden Operetta

VIER, Michael (bar)
Spohr: Faust (Cpte)

VIERA, Jonathan (bar)
(OPRA) **ORCH104** A Hundred Years of Italian Opera: 1820-1830

VIEUILLE, Jean (bar)
Bizet: Carmen (Cpte)
Debussy: Pelléas et Mélisande (Cpte)
Massenet: Manon (Cpte)
Ravel: Heure espagnole (Cpte)

VIGLIONE-BORGHESE, Domenico (bar)
(MEMO) **HR4408/9(2)** Singers in Genoa, Vol.1 (disc 2)
(PREI) **89995** Famous Italian Baritones

VIGNERON, Marcel (bass)
Debussy: Pelléas et Mélisande (Cpte)
Martinů: Alexandre Bis (Cpte)
Massenet: Navarraise (Cpte)
Offenbach: Madame l'Archiduc (Cpte)

VIGNOLES, Roger (pf)
(ASV) **CDDCA790** Weill—Songs
(PEAR) **SHECD9590** Valerie Masterson—Recital

VIGNON, Lucile (mez)
Fauré: Prométhée (Cpte)
Saint-Saëns: Henry VIII (Cpte)

VIHAVAINEN, Satu (sop)
Sallinen: Kullervo (Cpte)
(BIS) **BIS-CD373/4** Opera Scenes from Savaonlinna

VIITANEN, Usko (bar)
(BIS) **BIS-CD373/4** Opera Scenes from Savaonlinna

VILET, Patrick (bass)
Chabrier: Roi malgré lui (Cpte)

VILJAKAINEN, Raili (sop)
Weber: Freischütz (Cpte)
(BIS) **BIS-CD373/4** Opera Scenes from Savaonlinna

VILKE, Eeva-Kaarina (contr)
Bergman: Singing Tree (Cpte)

VILLA, Luisa (mez)
Donizetti: Lucia di Lammermoor (Cpte)
Puccini: Madama Butterfly (Cpte)
Verdi: Trovatore (Cpte)

VILLABELLA, Miguel (ten)
(MSCM) **MM30377** 18 Tenors d'Expression Française
(PEAR) **GEMMCD9948** Ninon Vallin in Opera and Song

VILLANUEVA, Leroy (bar)
Fénelon: Chevalier Imaginaire (Cpte)

VILLARROEL, Veronica (sop)
Penella: Gato Montés (Cpte)

VILLIER, Georges (bar)
Massenet: Manon (Cpte)

VILLIERS, David de (cond)
see Bielefeld PO

VILLISECH, Jacques (bass)
Messager: Basoche (Cpte)
Monteverdi: Orfeo (Cpte)
Rameau: Castor et Pollux (Cpte)

VILMA, Michèle (mez)
Gounod: Roméo et Juliette (Cpte)

VILUMANIS, Alexander (cond)
see Latvian Nat SO

VIÑAS, Francisco (ten)
(EMI) **CHS7 64860-2(1)** La Scala Edition - Vol.1, 1878-1914 (pt 1)
(IRCC) **IRCC-CD800** Souvenirs from Meyerbeer Operas
(MEMO) **HR4408/9(1)** Singers in Genoa, Vol.1 (disc 1)
(NIMB) **NI7840/1** The Era of Adelina Patti
(PEAR) **GEMMCDS9923(1)** Covent Garden on Record, Vol.1 (pt 1)
(PEAR) **GEMMCDS9924(1)** Covent Garden on Record, Vol.2 (pt 1)

VINAY, Ramon (ten)
Verdi: Otello (Cpte)
Wagner: Lohengrin (Cpte), Walküre (Cpte)
(FOYE) **15-CF2011** Wagner—Der Ring de Nibelungen
(RCA) **09026 61580-2(6)** RCA/Met 100 Singers, 100 Years (pt 6)

VINCENT, Catherine (sop)
Delius: Village Romeo and Juliet (Cpte)

VINCENT, George (ten)
(PILZ) **442118-2** Wagner—Operas in Historical Recordings

VINCENZI, Edda (sop)
Bellini: Norma (Cpte)

VINCO, Ivo (bass)
Mozart: Nozze di Figaro (exc)
Ponchielli: Gioconda (Cpte)
Puccini: Bohème (Cpte), Turandot (Cpte)
Verdi: Don Carlo (Cpte), Macbeth (Cpte), Rigoletto (Cpte), Trovatore (Cpte)
(CAST) **CVI2068** Opera Highlights from Verona 1
(MEMO) **HR4273/4** Great Voices—Pietro Cappuccilli
(MEMO) **HR4400/1** Great Voices - Ettore Bastianini

VINDEVOGEL, Judith (sop)
Cavalli: Calisto (Cpte)

VIÑES, Antonio (sngr)
Chapí: Revoltosa (Cpte)

VINOGRADOV, Alexei (cond)
see Moscow Contemp Music Ens

VINOGRADOV, Georgi (ten)
(EMI) **CHS7 69741-2(6)** Record of Singing, Vol.4—Russian & Slavonic Schools

VINZING, Ute (sop)
R. Strauss: Frau ohne Schatten (exc)
(EMI) **CDC5 55350-2** Cheryl Studer - A Portrait

VIOTTI, Marcello (cond)
see Berlin RSO
ECO
Frankfurt RSO
London Studio SO
Piacenza SO
Turin PO

VIRGILIO, Nicolas di (ten)
Beethoven: Fidelio (exc)

VIRTUOSI DI ROMA
cond R. FASANO
Gluck: Orfeo ed Euridice (Cpte)

VISENTIN, Fabrizio (bar)
Verdi: Rigoletto (Cpte), Traviata (Cpte)

VISHNEVSKAYA, Galina (sop)
Mussorgsky: Boris Godunov (Cpte)
Prokofiev: War and Peace (Cpte)

Rimsky-Korsakov: Tsar's Bride (Cpte)
Shostakovich: Lady Macbeth of Mtsensk (Cpte)
Tchaikovsky: Eugene Onegin (Cpte), Iolanta (Cpte)
(EMI) **CMS5 65716-2** Rostropovich as Accompanist

VISSE, Dominique (alto)
Cavalli: Calisto (Cpte), Giasone (Cpte), Xerse (Cpte)
Handel: Giulio Cesare (Cpte), Ottone (Cpte)
Hasse: Cleofide (Cpte)
M-A. Charpentier: Actéon (Cpte), Arts Florissants (Cpte), Comtesse d'Escarbagnas Ov, H494, David et Jonathas (Cpte)
Purcell: Dido (Cpte)
Vivaldi: Montezuma (Cpte)
(HARM) **HMC90 1552** The Three Countertenors
(HARM) **HMX290 1528/33(1)** A Purcell Companion (pt 1)

VISSER, Lieuwe (bass)
Britten: Midsummer Night's Dream (Cpte)
Donizetti: Lucrezia Borgia (Cpte)
Mascagni: Piccolo Marat (Cpte)

VITALE, Edoardo (cond)
see orch

VITALE, Maria (sop)
Verdi: Due Foscari (Cpte)

VITAPHONE ORCHESTRA
(PEAR) **GEMMCD9367** Gigli—Arias and Duets

VÍTKOVÁ, Blanka (contr)
Janáček: Makropulos Affair (Cpte)
Martinů: Miracles of Mary (Cpte)

VITTING, Eugene (ten)
(ARLE) **ARL23/5** Rimsky-Korsakov—Sadko
(NIMB) **NI7865** Great Singers at the Mariinsky Theatre
(PEAR) **GEMMCDS9111(1)** Singers of Imperial Russia, Vol.5 (pt 1)
(PEAR) **GEMMCDS9111(2)** Singers of Imperial Russia, Vol.5 (pt 2)

VITULLI, Thea (sop)
Puccini: Bohème (Cpte)

VIVALDA, Janette (sop)
Gounod: Mireille (Cpte)
(EMI) **CZS7 67872-2** Lehár—Operettas (highlights in French)

VIVIANI, Gaetano (bar)
(BONG) **GB1043-2** Italian Baritones of the Acoustic Era

VIVO, Graziano del (bass)
Meyerbeer: Africaine (Cpte)

VLACHOPOULOS, Zoë (sop)
Gluck: Orfeo ed Euridice (exc)

VLAD, Alessio (cond)
see Santa Cecilia Orch da Camera

VLASOV, Vitali (ten)
Tchaikovsky: Queen of Spades (Cpte)

(ALEXIS) VLASSOF CHORUS
cond H. TOMASI
Gluck: Orphée (exc)

(ALEXIS) VLASSOF ORCHESTRA
cond H. TOMASI
Gluck: Orphée (Cpte)

VLČEK, Oldřich (cond)
see Prague CO
Prague Virtuosi

VLIEGEN, Marianne (mez)
Puccini: Suor Angelica (Cpte)

VOCAL ENSEMBLE
cond J-C. MALGOIRE
Vivaldi: Montezuma (Cpte)

VOCAL ENSEMBLE
cond R. DELAGE
(ARIO) **ARN68252** Chabrier—Trois opérettes

VOCAL SOLOISTS (sngrs)
Wagner: Ring des Nibelungen Introduction

VODIČKA, Leo Marian (ten)
Dvořák: Dimitrij (Cpte)
Foerster: Eva (Cpte)
Smetana: Dalibor (Cpte), Kiss (Cpte), Libuše (Cpte)
(KOCH) **34036-2** A Pageant of Opera
(SUPR) **11 0345-2** Edith Gruberová - Operatic Recital

VOGEL, Adolf (bass)
R. Strauss: Salome (Cpte)
(SCHW) **314562** Vienna State Opera Live, Vol.6

VOGEL, Alfred (bass)
(SCHW) **314652** Vienna State Opera Live, Vol.15
(SCHW) **314712** Vienna State Opera Live, Vol.21.

VOGEL, Barbara (sop)
Mozart: Nozze di Figaro (exc)

VOGEL, Christian (bass)
Wagner: Rheingold (Cpte)
(EURO) **GD69003** Wagner—Der Ring des Nibelungen

VOGEL, Siegfried (bass)
Mozart: Idomeneo (Cpte)
R. Strauss: Ariadne auf Naxos (Cpte), Elektra (Cpte)
Wagner: Lohengrin (Cpte), Meistersinger (Cpte), Rienzi (Cpte), Tannhäuser (Cpte)
Weber: Freischütz (Cpte)

VOGEL, Volker (ten)
Zemlinsky: Kleider machen Leute (Cpte)
(CLOR) **TCO93-75** The Cleveland Orchestra-75th Anniversary CD Edition

VOGT, Annette (mez)
Delius: Village Romeo and Juliet (Cpte)

VOGT, Richard (spkr)
Weill: Lost in the Stars (Cpte)

VOIGT, Deborah (sop)
Berlioz: Troyens (Cpte)
Weber: Oberon (Cpte)
(EMI) **CDC7 54643-2** Rossini—Bicentenary Gala Concert
(EMI) **LDB491007-1 (EMI)** Rossini Bicentennial Birthday Gala
(TELD) **9031-72674-3** The Winners' Gala Concert, International Tchaikovsky Comp. 1990

VOINEAG, Ionel (ten)
Bretan: Arald (Cpte)

VOKETAITIS, Arnold (bar)
Massenet: Cid (Cpte)
Saint-Saëns: Samson et Dalila (Cpte)

VOKETAITIS, Arnold (bass-bar)
D. Moore: Carry Nation (Cpte)

VOLANTE, Gian Franco (treb)
Puccini: Tosca (Cpte)

VOLI, Albert (ten)
Bizet: Carmen (Cpte)

VÖLKER, Franz (ten)
Wagner: Lohengrin (exc)
(MMOI) **CDMOIR405** Great Tenors
(MSCM) **MM30283** Great Wagnerian Singers, Vol.1
(MSCM) **MM30285** Great Wagnerian Singers, Vol.2
(NIMB) **NI7848** Great Singers at the Berlin State Opera
(PEAR) **GEMMCD9383** Julius Patzak—Opera & Operetta Recital
(PREI) **89005** Franz Völker (1899-1965) - I
(PREI) **89070** Franz Völker (1899-1965) - II
(PREI) **90232** Wagner—Der Fliegende Holländer
(SCHW) **314502** Vienna State Opera—Live Recordings (sampler)
(SCHW) **314532** Vienna State Opera Live, Vol.3
(SCHW) **314552** Vienna State Opera Live, Vol.5
(SCHW) **314592** Vienna State Opera Live, Vol.9
(SCHW) **314602** Vienna State Opera Live, Vol.10
(SCHW) **314622** Vienna State Opera Live, Vol.12
(SCHW) **314642** Vienna State Opera Live, Vol.14
(SCHW) **314662** Vienna State Opera Live, Vol.16
(SCHW) **314672** Vienna State Opera Live, Vol.17
(SCHW) **314702** Vienna State Opera Live, Vol.20
(TELD) **9031-76442-2** Wagner—Excerpts from the 1936 Bayreuth Festival

VOLKOVÁ, Miroslava (contr)
Smetana: Libuše (Cpte)

VOLKOVA, Svetlana (mez)
Prokofiev: War and Peace (exc)

VOLLENWEIDER, Andreas (elec hp)
(DECC) **444 460-2DH** Pavarotti and Friends II

VOLLESTAD, Per (bar)
Mozart: Così fan tutte (Cpte)
(VIRG) **VC5 45051-2** Grieg—Choral Works

VONÁSEK, Rudolf (ten)
Janáček: Makropulos Affair (Cpte)
Smetana: Bartered Bride (Cpte)

VONK, Hans (cond)
see Staatskapelle Dresden

VOORHEES, Donald (cond)
see orch

VOTAVA, Antonín (ten)
Smetana: Brandenburgers in Bohemia (Cpte), Devil's Wall (Cpte)

VOTIPKA, Thelma (mez)
Donizetti: Lucia di Lammermoor (Cpte)
Verdi: Otello (Cpte)

VOTTO, Antonino (cond)
see Athens Fest Orch
Chicago Lyric Op Orch
La Scala Orch
Milan RAI SO
MMF Orch
Santa Cecilia Academy Orch
Turin RAI Orch

VOUTSINOS, Frangikos (bass)
Kalomiris: Mother's Ring (Cpte)
Monteverdi: Orfeo (Cpte)

VOZZA, Corinna (mez)
Boito: Nerone (Cpte)
Donizetti: Lucia di Lammermoor (Cpte)
Mascagni: Cavalleria Rusticana (Cpte)
Verdi: Forza del destino (Cpte), Rigoletto (Cpte)
(EMI) **CDM5 65579-2** Victoria de los Angeles
(EMI) **CMS7 64165-2** Puccini—Trittico
(RCA) **GD60941** Rarities - Montserrat Caballé
(RCA) **09026 61236-2** Leontyne Price - Prima Donna Collection
(RCA) **74321 24284-2** Opera's Greatest Heroines

VRACHOVSKI, Werther (ten)
Mussorgsky: Khovanshchina (Cpte)

VRENIOS, Anastasios (ten)
Meyerbeer: Huguenots (Cpte)

VRIEND, Jan Willem de (cond)
see Amsterdam Bach Sols

VRIES, Han de (ob)
(PHIL) **438 940-2PH** Opera Fantasy

VRONSKÝ, Petr (cond)
see Brno St PO
Košice St PO

VROOMAN, Richard van (ten)
Mozart: Ascanio in Alba (Cpte)

VYVYAN, Jennifer (sop)
Britten: Turn of the Screw (Cpte)
Purcell: Fairy Queen, Z629 (Cpte)
(LOND) **433 200-2LHO2** Britten—Owen Wingrave, etc.
(LOND) **436 393-2LM** Britten—The Little Sweep, etc

WAART, Edo de (cond)
see Bayreuth Fest Orch
Concertgebouw
Dutch Rad PO
Minnesota Orch
Netherlands PO
Netherlands Rad PO
Rotterdam PO

WAAS, Anneliese (sop)
R. Strauss: Rosenkavalier (Cpte)

WACHSMUTH, Hans-Jürgen (ten)
Wagner: Parsifal (Cpte)

WADDINGTON, Henry (bass)
Vaughan Williams: Pilgrim's Progress (Cpte)

WADSWORTH, Michael (bass-bar)
Falla: Vida breve (Cpte)

WAECHTER, Eberhard (bar)
Berg: Wozzeck (Cpte)
Cornelius: Barbier von Bagdad (Cpte)
J. Strauss II: Fledermaus (exc)
Lehár: Lustige Witwe (Cpte)
Mozart: Don Giovanni (exc), Idomeneo (Cpte), Nozze di Figaro (exc)
R. Strauss: Arabella (Cpte), Capriccio (Cpte), Rosenkavalier (exc), Salome (Cpte)
Wagner: Rheingold (Cpte), Tannhäuser (exc), Tristan und Isolde (exc)
Weber: Freischütz (Cpte)
(BELA) **450 052-2** Great Opera Choruses
(CFP) **CD-CFP4656** Herbert von Karajan conducts Opera
(CFP) **CD-CFP9013** Duets from Famous Operas
(DECC) **414 100-2DM15** Wagner: Der Ring des Nibelungen
(DECC) **421 313-2DA** Wagner: Der Ring des Nibelungen - Great Scenes
(ORFE) **C394201B** Great Mozart Singers Series, Vol. 2
(PHIL) **434 420-2PM32(2)** Richard Wagner Edition (pt 2)

WAGEMAN, Rose (mez)
Korngold: Tote Stadt (Cpte)
Orff: Orpheus (Cpte), Tanz der Spröden (Cpte)
(ACAN) **44 2085-2** Carl Orff Collection

WAGENFÜHRER, Roland (ten)
Wagner: Meistersinger (Cpte)

WAGMANN, Rose (mez)
Hindemith: Mathis der Maler (Cpte)
Suppé: Schöne Galathee (exc)

WAGNER, José (sngr)
Weill: Kuhhandel (exc)

WAGNER, Pop (bar)
Britten: Paul Bunyan (Cpte)

WAGNER, Reinhardt (cond)
see Camargue PO

WAGNER, Robert (cond)
see Innsbruck Chor

WAGNER, Siegfried (cond)
see Bayreuth Fest Orch

WAGNER, Sieglinde (mez)
Mozart: Zauberflöte (exc)
R. Strauss: Elektra (Cpte)
Verdi: Otello (Cpte)
Wagner: Fliegende Holländer (Cpte), Götterdämmerung (Cpte), Parsifal (Cpte), Walküre (Cpte)
(EMI) **CDH5 65201-2** Leonie Rysanek - Operatic Recital
(EMI) **CMS5 65212-2** Wagner—Les introuvables du Ring
(EMI) **CZS7 62993-2** Fritz Wunderlich—Great German Tenor
(PHIL) **446 057-2PB14** Wagner—The Ring Cycle - Bayreuth Festival 1967
(TESS) **049-2** R. Strauss/Wagner—Opera Scenes

(ROGER) WAGNER CHORALE
cond C.M. GIULINI
(DG) **445 525-2GMA** Domingo Favourites
(DG) **419 091-4GW** Placido Domingo sings Favourite Arias, Songs and Tangos

WAHLGREN, Per-Arne (bar)
Mozart: Nozze di Figaro (Cpte)
Zemlinsky: Es war einmal (Cpte)

WAHLUND, Sten (bar)
Börtz: Bacchae (Cpte)
Lidholm: Dream Play (Cpte)

WAHRLICH, G. I. (cond)
see orch

WAKEEL, Reda Al (bass)
Mozart: Così fan tutte (Cpte), Don Giovanni (Cpte), Nozze di Figaro (Cpte)

WAKEFIELD, Henrietta (sop)
Verdi: Traviata (Cpte)

WAKEFIELD, John (ten)
Cavalli: Ormindo (Cpte)
Meyerbeer: Huguenots (Cpte)
Sullivan: Mikado (Cpte)

WAKEHAM, Michael (bar)
Sullivan: Gondoliers (Cpte)

WALDEN, Peter (cond)
see Raphaele Concert Orch

WALDENAU, Elisabeth (mez)
Humperdinck: Hänsel und Gretel (Cpte)
Mozart: Nozze di Figaro (Cpte)
Wagner: Walküre (exc)

WALDMAN, Frederick (cond)
see Columbia CO

WALES, Pauline (mez)
Sullivan: Iolanthe (Cpte), Mikado (Cpte), Pirates of Penzance (Cpte)
(BELA) **461 006-2** Gilbert & Sullivan—Songs and Snatches
(DECC) **430 095-2DWO** The World of Gilbert & Sullivan, Vol.1
(DECC) **433 868-2DWO** The World of Gilbert & Sullivan - Volume 2

WALKER, Blythe (sop)
Rachmaninov: Monna Vanna (exc)

WALKER, Drummond (ten)
Spohr: Faust (Cpte)

WALKER, Gertrud (sop)
Humperdinck: Hänsel und Gretel (Cpte)

WALKER, Helen (sop)
Monteverdi: Incoronazione di Poppea (Cpte)
Purcell: Dido (Cpte)

WALKER, James (cond)
see RPO

WALKER, James (fl)
(DECC) **433 220-2DWO** The World of the Violin

WALKER, Kim (bn)
(REGE) **REGCD104** The Bel Canto Bassoon

WALKER, Malcolm (bar)
Bizet: Carmen (Cpte)
Chabriér: Roi malgré lui (Cpte)
Debussy: Pelléas et Mélisande (Cpte)
Gluck: Rencontre imprévue (Cpte)
(ASV) **CDDCA758** Falla, Milhaud & Stravinsky—Operas

WALKER, Nellie (contr)
Sullivan: Pirates of Penzance (Cpte)
(CLAR) **CDGSE78-50-35/6** Wagner—Historical recordings
(PEAR) **GEMMCDS9137** Wagner—Der Ring des Nibelungen
(PEAR) **GEMMCD9468** Vaughan Williams
(PEAR) **GEMMCD9934** Dame Isobel Baillie

WALKER, Nina (pf)
(NIMB) **NI5214** Mirages - Songs by Fauré, Gounod & Ravel

WALKER, Norman (bass)
(SYMP) **SYMCD1130** Joseph Holbrooke—Historic Recordings

WALKER, Penelope (mez)
Britten: Midsummer Night's Dream (Cpte)
Debussy: Pelléas et Mélisande (Cpte)
(OPRA) **ORCH103** Italian Opera—1810-20
(OPRA) **ORCH104** A Hundred Years of Italian Opera: 1820-1830
(OPRA) **ORH102** A Hundred Years of Italian Opera

WALKER, Richard (bass)
Sullivan: Gondoliers (Cpte)

WALKER, Sandra (mez)
Tchaikovsky: Eugene Onegin (Cpte)
Vivaldi: Orlando Furioso (Cpte)

WALKER, Sarah (mez)
Britten: Gloriana (Cpte), Peter Grimes (Cpte)
Gay: Beggar's Opera (Cpte)
Gounod: Roméo et Juliette (Cpte)
Handel: Giulio Cesare (Cpte)
Stravinsky: Rake's Progress (Cpte)
Tchaikovsky: Eugene Onegin (Cpte)
Tippett: Ice Break (Cpte), King Priam (Cpte)
Vaughan Williams: Hugh the Drover (Cpte)
Verdi: Traviata (Cpte)
Wagner: Walküre (Cpte)
(HYPE) **CDA67061/2** Britten—Purcell Realizations

WALKER, Zena (spkr)
Gay: Beggar's Opera (Cpte)

WALKLEY, Stephen (tbn)
(GRAS) **GRCD41** Avondale - The Sun Life Band

WALLACE, Ian (bass)
Busoni: Arlecchino (Cpte)
Gay: Beggar's Opera (Cpte)
Mozart: Nozze di Figaro (Cpte)
Rossini: Barbiere di Siviglia (Cpte), Cenerentola (Cpte), Comte Ory (Cpte)
Sullivan: Iolanthe (Cpte), Mikado (Cpte)
(CFP) **CD-CFP4238** Gilbert and Sullivan
(CFP) **CD-CFP4609** Favourite Gilbert & Sullivan
(EMI) **CDH5 65072-2** Glyndebourne Recorded - 1934-1994
(IMP) **PWK1157** Gilbert & Sullivan Spectacular

WALLACE, John (tpt)
(NIMB) **NI5017** John Wallace: Man - the measure of all things
(NIMB) **NI5123** Baroque Arias for Soprano and Trumpet

WALLACE, Mervyn (ten)
Gershwin: Porgy and Bess (Cpte)

WALLACE, Stephen (alto)
Vaughan Williams: Pilgrim's Progress (Cpte)

WALLBERG, Heinz (cond)
see Munich RO
Munich RSO
NZ SO
Philh
VPO

WALLDER, Daniel (sngr)
Menotti: Boy who grew too fast (Cpte)

WALLÉN, Martti (bass)
Bergman: Singing Tree (Cpte)

WALLENSTEIN, Alfred (cond)
see orch

WALLER, Adalbert (bass)
S. Wagner: Bärenhäuter (Cpte)

WALLEZ, Jean-Pierre (cond)
see Paris Orch Ens

WALLINGTON, Lawrence (bass)
Purcell: Dioclesian, Z627 (Cpte)
Rameau: Castor et Pollux (Cpte)

WALLIS, Delia (mez)
Puccini: Manon Lescaut (Cpte)
Rossini: Siège de Corinthe (Cpte)
Vaughan Williams: Pilgrim's Progress (Cpte)
Verdi: Don Carlo (Cpte)

WALLPRECHT, Klaus (bar)
Delius: Village Romeo and Juliet (Cpte)

WALLPRECHT, Klaus (bass-bar)
Schillings: Mona Lisa (Cpte)

WALLS, Geoffrey (bass-bar)
Walton: Troilus and Cressida (exc)

WALLSTRÖM, Tord (bass)
Mozart: Don Giovanni (Cpte)

WALMSLEY, Trevor (cond)
see Black Dyke Mills Band

WALMSLEY-CLARK, Penelope (sop)
Ligeti: Grand Macabre (Cpte)
Maderna: Hyperion (Cpte)

WALT, Deon van der (ten)
Beethoven: Fidelio (Cpte)
Mozart: Così fan tutte (Cpte)
Schoeck: Massimilla Doni (Cpte)
Wagner: Meistersinger (Cpte)
(TELD) **4509-97507-2** Mozart—Famous Opera Arias

WALTER, Alfred (cond)
see Budapest SO
Budapest Strauss SO
Košice St PO

WALTER, Bruno (cond)
see British SO
Columbia SO
LSO
NBC SO
NY Met Op Orch
NYPO
orch
Paris Cons
RPS Orch
Vienna St Op Orch
VPO

WALTER, Fried (cond)
see Berlin SO

WALTER, Gustav (ten)
(SYMP) **SYMCD1085** The Harold Wayne Collection, Vol.6

WALTEROVÁ, Virginie (mez)
(SUPR) **11 0345-2** Edith Gruberová - Operatic Recital

WALTHER, Ute (mez)
Wagner: Walküre (Cpte)

WALTON, Sir William (cond)
see Philh
ROHO

WAND, Betty (sngr)
(SONY) **SB2K64391** Leonard Bernstein - Man of Music

WAND, Günter (cond)
see N German RSO

WAND, Ulrich (ten)
Spohr: Faust (Cpte)

WANDSWORTH SCHOOL BOYS' CHOIR
cond B. BRITTEN
(LOND) **433 200-2LHO2** Britten—Owen Wingrave, etc.
cond COLIN DAVIS
Berlioz: Troyens (Cpte)
cond I. KERTÉSZ
(DECC) **443 488-2DF2** Kodály—Háry János; Psalmus Hungaricus etc
cond Z. MEHTA
Puccini: Tosca (Cpte), Turandot (Cpte)
cond N. RESCIGNO
Puccini: Tosca (Cpte)
(DECC) **444 555-2DF2** Essential Puccini
cond G. SOLTI
Puccini: Bohème (Cpte)

WARBURTON, Thomas (pf)
(BAY) **BCD-1029** Robert Ward—Arias and Songs

WARD, David (bass)
Debussy: Pelléas et Mélisande (Cpte)
Verdi: Rigoletto (Cpte)
Wagner: Walküre (Cpte)

WARD, Joseph (bar)
Bellini: Norma (Cpte)
Britten: Albert Herring (Cpte)
Herrmann: Wuthering Heights (Cpte)
Meyerbeer: Huguenots (Cpte)
Vaughan Williams: Pilgrim's Progress (Cpte)
(DECC) **433 706-2DMO3** Bellini—Beatrice di Tenda; Operatic Arias

WARE, Clifton (ten)
Britten: Paul Bunyan (Cpte)

WARFIELD, William (bar)
Gershwin: Porgy and Bess (exc)
(RCA) **09026 62699-2** Opera's Greatest Duets

WARMIA NATIONAL PHILHARMONIC ORCHESTRA
cond B. AMADUCCI
(NUOV) **6851** Giuseppe Morino—King of Bel Canto

WARNFORD, Nicholas (sngr)
Bernstein: West Side Story (Cpte)

WARR, Martin (treb)
Britten: Midsummer Night's Dream (Cpte)

WARREN, Leonard (bar)
Leoncavallo: Pagliacci (Cpte)
Puccini: Tosca (exc)
Verdi: Aida (Cpte), Macbeth (Cpte), Trovatore (Cpte)
(ALTN) **CDAN3** Hjördis Schymberg
(BELA) **450 006-2** Famous Opera Duets
(EMI) **CHS7 69741-2(2)** Record of Singing, Vol.4—Anglo-American School (pt 2)
(PEAR) **GEMMCDS9452** The Emperor Tibbett
(RCA) **GD60276** Toscanini conducts Boito & Verdi
(RCA) **09026 61580-2(5)** RCA/Met 100 Singers, 100 Years (pt 5)
(RCA) **09026 62689-2** The Voices of Living Stereo, Volume 1
(VAI) **VAIA1017** Leonard Warren—Early Recordings
(VAI) **VAIA1072** Eleanor Steber Collection, Volume 1
(VAI) **VAIA1084** Rose Bampton sings Verdi and Wagner
(VAI) **VAI69105** Leonard Warren in Opera and Song
(VAI) **VAI69110** Leonard Warren in Opera and Song Vol 2

WARREN-GREEN, Christopher (cond)
see Philh

WARRICK-SMITH, Pamela (contr)
S. Wallace: Kabbalah (Cpte)

WARRILOW, David (narr)
Glass: Akhnaten (Cpte)

WARSAW CATHEDRAL CHOIR
cond A. FILABER
(POLS) **PNCD132** Polish Religious Music

WARSAW CHAMBER OPERA ORCHESTRA
cond T. BUGAJ
Gluck: Corona (Cpte), Danza (Cpte)
cond J. KASPSZYK
Rossini: Signor Bruschino (Cpte)

WARSAW CHAMBER ORCHESTRA
cond M. SEWEN
(OLYM) **OCD382** 18th Century Polish Miniatures

WARSAW NATIONAL OPERA CHORUS
cond P. KANTSCHIEDER
Beethoven: Fidelio (Cpte)

WARSAW NATIONAL PHILHARMONIC ORCHESTRA
cond W. ROWICKI
(OLYM) **OCD386** Moniuszko—Overtures

WARSAW PHILHARMONIC ORCHESTRA
cond W. MICHNIEWSKI
(PAVA) **ADW7289** Mozart—Opera Arias; Exsultate, jubilate

WARSAW WIEKL THEATRE CHORUS
cond R. SATANOWSKI
Szymanowski: King Roger (Cpte)

WARSAW WIEKL THEATRE ORCHESTRA
cond R. SATANOWSKI
Szymanowski: King Roger (Cpte)

WASHINGTON, Daniel (bar)
Beethoven: Fidelio (Cpte)

WASHINGTON, Paolo (bass)
Bellini: Puritani (Cpte)
Puccini: Madama Butterfly (Cpte)
Verdi: Rigoletto (Cpte)
(DECC) **411 665-2DM3** Puccini: Il trittico
(NUOV) **6892** William Matteuzzi sings Opera Arias

WASHINGTON CHORAL ARTS SOCIETY cond M. ROSTROPOVICH
Mussorgsky: Boris Godunov (Cpte)

WASHINGTON NATIONAL SYMPHONY ORCHESTRA cond M. ROSTROPOVICH
Mussorgsky: Boris Godunov (Cpte)

WASHINGTON OPERA SOCIETY CHORUS cond I. STRAVINSKY
(SONY) **SM22K46290(3)** Stravinsky—The Complete Edition (pt 3)
(SONY) **SM22K46290(4)** Stravinsky—The Complete Edition (pt 4)

WASHINGTON OPERA SOCIETY ORCHESTRA cond I. STRAVINSKY
(SONY) **SM22K46290(3)** Stravinsky—The Complete Edition (pt 3)
(SONY) **SM22K46290(4)** Stravinsky—The Complete Edition (pt 4)

WASHINGTON ORATORIO SOCIETY cond M. ROSTROPOVICH
Mussorgsky: Boris Godunov (Cpte)

WATERS, Jan (sngr)
Gay: Beggar's Opera (Cpte)

WATERS, Susannah (sop)
Purcell: King Arthur, Z628 (Cpte)

WATKINS, David (hp)
(MERI) **CDE84241** Music for Flute & Harp
(NATI) **NTCD006** Voice and Harp Recital

WATKINSON, Carolyn (contr)
Monteverdi: Orfeo (Cpte)
Purcell: Dido (Cpte)
Wagner: Walküre (exc)
(ETCE) **KTC1007** Carolyn Watkinson recital
(ETCE) **KTC1064** Baroque Opera Arias

WATSON, Chester (bass)
Bellini: Pirata (Cpte)
Berlioz: Troyens (Cpte)
(SONY) **SM22K46290(3)** Stravinsky—The Complete Edition (pt 3)

WATSON, Claire (sop)
Britten: Peter Grimes (Cpte)
Mozart: Don Giovanni (Cpte)
Wagner: Götterdämmerung (Cpte), Meistersinger (Cpte), Rheingold (Cpte)
Weber: Freischütz (Cpte)
(DECC) **414 100-2DM15** Wagner: Der Ring des Nibelungen

WATSON, Curtis (bass)
Gershwin: Porgy and Bess (Cpte)
Menotti: Amahl and the Night Visitors (Cpte)

WATSON, James (cond)
see Black Dyke Mills Band
Desford Colliery Caterpillar Band

WATSON, James (tpt)
(ASV) **CDWHL2088** Trumpet and Soprano in Duet

WATSON, Janice (sop)
Britten: Gloriana (Cpte), Peter Grimes (Cpte)
G. Lloyd: John Socman (exc)
Sullivan: Mikado (Cpte)

WATSON, Laurelyn (sop)
Rorem: Miss Julie (Cpte)

WATSON, Lilian (sop)
Bizet: Carmen (Cpte)
Britten: Midsummer Night's Dream (Cpte), Turn of the Screw (Cpte)
Cilea: Adriana Lecouvreur (Cpte)
Donizetti: Don Pasquale (Cpte)
Janáček: Cunning Little Vixen (Cpte)
Mozart: Così fan tutte (Cpte), Entführung (Cpte), Mitridate (Cpte), Nozze di Figaro (Cpte), Zauberflöte (Cpte)
Offenbach: Orphée aux enfers (exc)
Puccini: Rondine (Cpte)

WATSON, Nathaniel (bar)
Glass: Hydrogen Jukebox (Cpte)
Handel: Sosarme (Cpte)

WATSON, Nicholas (treb)
Britten: Midsummer Night's Dream (Cpte)

(GEORGE) WATSON COLLEGE BOYS' CHORUS cond C. ABBADO
Bizet: Carmen (Cpte)

WATT, Alan (bass)
Henze: English Cat (Cpte)

WATTS, Helen (contr)
Berlioz: Béatrice et Bénédict (Cpte)
Britten: Midsummer Night's Dream (Cpte)
Purcell: Dido (Cpte)
R. Strauss: Elektra (Cpte)
Schoenberg: Moses und Aron (Cpte)
Sullivan: Gondoliers (Cpte)
Tippett: Midsummer Marriage (Cpte)
Vaughan Williams: Hugh the Drover (Cpte)
Wagner: Götterdämmerung (Cpte), Walküre (Cpte)
(DECC) **414 100-2DM15** Wagner: Der Ring des Nibelungen
(DECC) **421 313-2DA** Wagner: Der Ring des Nibelungen - Great Scenes
(DECC) **433 067-2DWO** Your Hundred Best Opera Tunes IV
(DECC) **436 300-2DX** Opera Gala Sampler
(DECC) **436 315-2DA** Great Operatic Duets
(DECC) **440 069-2DWO** The World of Wagner
(DECC) **443 335-2LRX** Music for Relaxation, Vol 10 - The Night Before
(EMI) **CDM7 64730-2** Vaughan Williams—Riders to the Sea; Epithalamion, etc

WATTS, Nathan (treb)
Mozart: Zauberflöte (exc)

WATZKE, Rudolf (bass)
(DANA) **DACOCD315/6** Lauritz Melchior Anthology - Vol. 3
(PREI) **89201** Helge Roswaenge (1897-1972) - I

WEARING, Catherine (sop)
Britten: Little Sweep (Cpte)

WEATHERS, Felicia (sop)
R. Strauss: Elektra (Cpte)
(BELA) **450 007-2** Puccini Favourites
(BELA) **450 015-2** Cinema Classics
(DECC) **417 686-2DC** Puccini—Operatic Arias
(DECC) **433 069-2DWO** Your Hundred Best Opera Tunes VI
(DECC) **433 624-2DSP** Great Soprano Arias
(DECC) **433 636-2DSP** Puccini—Famous Arias

WEAVER, K. (sngr)
Barber: Antony and Cleopatra (Cpte)

WEBB, Barbara (sop)
Britten: Curlew River (Cpte)
Gershwin: Porgy and Bess (exc)

WEBER, Heinrich (ten)
Egk: Peer Gynt (Cpte)
Korngold: Violanta (Cpte)
Puccini: Fanciulla del West (Cpte)
Verdi: Traviata (Cpte)

WEBER, Janice (pf)
(IMP) **PCD1051** Rachmaninov—Piano Transcriptions

WEBER, Ludwig (bass)
Mozart: Don Giovanni (Cpte), Zauberflöte (exc)
R. Strauss: Rosenkavalier (Cpte)
Wagner: Fliegende Holländer (Cpte), Parsifal (Cpte), Rheingold (Cpte)
(DUTT) **CDLX7007** Beecham conducts Wagner
(EMI) **CHS7 69741-2(4)** Record of Singing, Vol.4—German School
(EMI) **CMS7 64008-2(2)** Wagner Singing on Record (pt 2)
(FOYE) **15-CF2011** Wagner—Der Ring de Nibelungen
(LYRC) **LCD146** Frida Leider sings Wagner

WEBER, Peter (bass)
Schoeck: Penthesilea (Cpte)

WEBER, Peter (ten)
Mozart: Zauberflöte (Cpte)
R. Strauss: Ariadne auf Naxos (Cpte)
Verdi: Ballo in maschera (Cpte)

WEBSTER, Gillian (sop)
Britten: Peter Grimes (Cpte)
Gluck: Orfeo ed Euridice (Cpte)

WEDEL, Mogens (bass)
Nielsen: Saul and David (Cpte)
(DANA) **DACOCD319/21** The Lauritz Melchior Anthology - Vol.5

WEDIN, Lage (bass)
Haeffner: Electra (Cpte)

WEGNER, John (bar)
Meyerbeer: Huguenots (Cpte)

WEGNER, Walburga (sop)
R. Strauss: Salome (Cpte)
(ACAN) **43 268** Peter Anders sings German Opera Arias

WEHOFSCHITZ, Kurt (ten)
Beethoven: Fidelio (Cpte)

WEI, Xue (vn)
(ASV) **CDDCA698** Violin Virtuoso
(ASV) **CDQS6114** The Four Seasons, Volume 2 - Summer
(ASV) **CDQS6126** Romeo and Juliet

WEICHERT, Elsa (contr)
(SCHW) **314592** Vienna State Opera Live, Vol.9

WEICHERT, Matthias (bass)
Krenek: Jonny spielt auf (Cpte)

WEIDINGER, Christine (sop)
Handel: Rinaldo (Cpte)
Mozart: Mitridate (Cpte)

WEIGERT, Hermann (cond)
see Berlin St Op Orch
orch
Philh

WEIGLE, Jörg-Peter (cond)
see Dresden PO
Munich RSO

WEIKERT, Ralf (cond)
see Munich RO
Munich RSO
NY Met Op Orch
Salzburg Mozarteum Orch
Venice La Fenice Orch
Zurich Op Orch

WEIKL, Bernd (bar)
Donizetti: Don Pasquale (Cpte), Elisir d'amore (Cpte)
Gluck: Alceste (1776) (Cpte)
Humperdinck: Hänsel und Gretel (Cpte)
Leoncavallo: Bohème (Cpte), Pagliacci (Cpte)
Mascagni: Cavalleria Rusticana (Cpte)
Mozart: Don Giovanni (Cpte)
Pfitzner: Palestrina (Cpte)
R. Strauss: Arabella (Cpte), Elektra (Cpte), Salome (Cpte)
Tchaikovsky: Eugene Onegin (Cpte)
Verdi: Rigoletto (Cpte)
Wagner: Götterdämmerung (Cpte), Lohengrin (Cpte), Meistersinger (Cpte), Parsifal (Cpte), Tannhäuser (Cpte), Tristan und Isolde (Cpte)
Weber: Freischütz (Cpte)
(ACAN) **43 266** Bernd Weikl—Operatic Recital
(ACAN) **43 327** Bernd Weikl—Operatic Arias
(DECC) **433 822-2DH** Essential Opera
(DECC) **436 406-2DWO** The World of Tchaikovsky
(DG) **445 354-2GX14** Wagner—Der Ring des Nibelungen
(ORFE) **C077831A** Bernd Weikl sings Operetta

WEIL, Bruno (cond)
see Salzburg Mozarteum Orch
Tafelmusik
Vienna SO

WEIL, Terence (vc)
(EMI) **CDH5 65501-2** Alfred Deller - HMV Recordings, 1949-54

WEINGARTNER, Felix (cond)
see Paris SO
Vienna St Op Orch

WEIR, Scot (ten)
Mendelssohn: Hochzeit des Camacho (Cpte)

WEISBACH, Hans (cond)
see Leipzig RSO
Vienna SO

WEISS, Franz (narr)
(PREI) **89034** Giuseppe Lugo (1900-1980)

WEISS, Herbert (treb)
Puccini: Tosca (Cpte)

WEISSMANN, Frieder (cond)
see Berlin City Op Orch
Berlin SO
Berlin St Op Orch
Berlin Staatskapelle
Hilversum RO
Odeon Künstlerorchester
orch
RCA SO
RCA Victor Orch

WELCH, Jonathan (ten)
Puccini: Bohème (Cpte)

WELDON, George (cond)
see CBO
Philh

WELITSCH, Alexander (bass)
Mozart: Zauberflöte (Cpte)
Verdi: Don Carlo (exc)

WELITSCH, Ljuba (sop)
J. Strauss II: Fledermaus (Cpte)
R. Strauss: Rosenkavalier (Cpte)
(EMI) **CHS7 69741-2(4)** Record of Singing, Vol.4—German School

WELKER, Hartmut (bar)
Beethoven: Fidelio (Cpte)
Korngold: Wunder der Heliane (Cpte)
Schmidt: Notre Dame (Cpte)
Schubert: Fierrabras (Cpte)
Wagner: Lohengrin (Cpte)
Zemlinsky: Traumgörge (Cpte)

WELLEJUS, Henning (pf)
(DANA) **DACOCD348** Danish Songs

WELLER, Dieter (bass)
Flotow: Martha (Cpte)
Ligeti: Grand Macabre (Cpte)
Schreker: Schatzgräber (Cpte)
Zemlinsky: Geburtstag der Infantin (Cpte)
(ADES) **14122-2** Music of our Time

WELLER, Lawrence (bar)
Britten: Paul Bunyan (Cpte)

WELLER, Walter (cond)
see LPO
Vienna Op Orch
Vienna St Op Orch
Vienna Volksoper Orch

WELLS, Jeffrey (bass-bar)
Barber: Antony and Cleopatra (Cpte)
Verdi: Traviata (Cpte), Trovatore (Cpte)
Wagner: Parsifal (Cpte)

WELLS, Mary (sop)
Britten: Little Sweep (Cpte)

Purcell: Fairy Queen, Z629 (Cpte)

WELSBY, Norman (bar)
Wagner: Götterdämmerung (Cpte), Rheingold (Cpte)

WELSER-MÖST, Franz (cond)
see LPO

WELSH, Scott (sngr)
(PEAR) **GEMMCDS9059/61** Music from the New York Stage, Vol. 4: 1917-20

WELSH GUARDS BAND
(RPO) **CDRPD9001** Classical Spectacular
cond M. REED
(RPO) **CDRPO5009** Classical Spectacular I

WELSH NATIONAL OPERA CHORUS
cond R. ARMSTRONG
Donizetti: Don Pasquale (Cpte)
cond R. BONYNGE
A. Thomas: Hamlet (Cpte)
Bellini: Norma (Cpte)
Cilea: Adriana Lecouvreur (Cpte)
Verdi: Masnadieri (Cpte)
(BELA) **450 117-2** Great Opera Chorus II
cond P. BOULEZ
Debussy: Pelléas et Mélisande (Cpte)
cond R. CHAILLY
Giordano: Andrea Chénier (Cpte)
cond G. FERRO
(TELD) **9031-73242-2** Rossini—Arias
cond R. GOODALL
Wagner: Parsifal (Cpte), Tristan und Isolde (Cpte)
cond C. MACKERRAS
Britten: Gloriana (Cpte)
Janáček: Fate (Cpte)
Sullivan: HMS Pinafore (Cpte), Mikado (Cpte), Pirates of Penzance (Cpte)
Tchaikovsky: Eugene Onegin (Cpte)
(TELA) **CD80407** Divine Sopranos
cond C. RIZZI
Gounod: Faust (Cpte)
Verdi: Rigoletto (Cpte)
(PHIL) **442 785-2PH** The Incomparable Alfredo Kraus
cond G. SOLTI
Puccini: Tosca (Cpte)
cond L. STOKOWSKI
(DECC) **433 625-2DSP** Stokowski conducts Famous Russian Works

WELSH NATIONAL OPERA ORCHESTRA
Debussy: Pelléas et Mélisande (Cpte)
(COLL) **Coll3025-2** Puccini & Verdi Heroines
cond R. BONYNGE
A. Thomas: Hamlet (Cpte)
Bellini: Norma (Cpte)
Cilea: Adriana Lecouvreur (Cpte)
Verdi: Masnadieri (Cpte)
(BELA) **450 117-2** Great Opera Chorus II
cond G. FERRO
(TELD) **9031-73242-2** Rossini—Arias
cond R. GOODALL
Wagner: Parsifal (Cpte), Tristan und Isolde (Cpte)
cond JULIAN SMITH
(SONY) **474364-2** Suzanne Murphy: There is an Isle
cond C. MACKERRAS
Britten: Gloriana (Cpte)
Janáček: Fate (Cpte)
Sullivan: HMS Pinafore (Cpte), Mikado (Cpte), Pirates of Penzance (Cpte)
Tchaikovsky: Eugene Onegin (Cpte)
(EMI) **CDM5 65578-2** Kiri Te Kanawa
(EMI) **LDA9 91242-1(EMI)** Kiri Te Kanawa—Live Mozart Recital
(TELA) **CD80407** Divine Sopranos
(TELA) **CD80411** The Artistry of Fernando de la Mora
cond C. RIZZI
Gounod: Faust (Cpte)
Verdi: Rigoletto (Cpte)
(PHIL) **442 785-2PH** The Incomparable Alfredo Kraus
(TELD) **4509-97463-2** A Portrait of Thomas Hampson-Arias and Songs
(TELD) **4509-98824-2** Thomas Hampson Collection,Vol III-Operatic Scenes
(TELD) **9031-73283-2** Hampson and Hadley

ELSH PHILHARMONIA
Donizetti: Don Pasquale (Cpte)

ELTING, Ruth (sop)
Humperdinck: Hänsel und Gretel (Cpte)
Massenet: Cendrillon (Cpte)
Mozart: Schauspieldirektor (Cpte)
R. Strauss: Rosenkavalier (Cpte)

END, Flore (sop)
(DECC) **433 400-2DM2** Ravel & Debussy—Stage Works

ENDLER, Anton (ten)
J. Strauss II: Fledermaus (Cpte)

ENHOLD, André (bar)
Pfitzner: Herz (Cpte)
S. Wagner: Bärenhäuter (Cpte), Schwarzschwanenreich (Cpte)

ENKEL, Ortrun (contr)
Henze: Bassariden (Cpte)
Humperdinck: Königskinder (Cpte)
Mozart: Zauberflöte (Cpte)
R. Strauss: Daphne (Cpte)
Wagner: Götterdämmerung (Cpte), Rheingold (Cpte), Siegfried (Cpte), Walküre (Cpte)
(EURO) **GD69003** Wagner—Der Ring des Nibelungen
(PHIL) **434 420-2PM32(2)** Richard Wagner Edition (pt 2)

WENKOFF, Spas (ten)
Wagner: Tannhäuser (Cpte)

WENKOFF, Wenko (ten)
(SCHW) **314552** Vienna State Opera Live, Vol.5
(SCHW) **314712** Vienna State Opera Live, Vol.21

WENNBERG, Siv (sop)
Wagner: Rienzi (Cpte)

WENNING, Hermann (spkr)
Nono: Intolleranza 1960 (Cpte)

WERBA, Erik (pf)
(DG) **437 680-2GDO2** Rita Streich - Lieder Recital
(EMI) **CDH5 65352-2** Nicolai Gedda Lieder Recital
(SCHW) **314002** Early songs by famous composers

WERNER, Alfred (bar)
J. Strauss II: Fledermaus (exc)

WERNER, Regina (sop)
Wagner: Parsifal (Cpte)

WERNIGK, William (ten)
Mozart: Nozze di Figaro (Cpte)
Wagner: Meistersinger (exc)
(EMI) **CHS7 64487-2** R. Strauss—Der Rosenkavalier & Lieder
(SCHW) **314532** Vienna State Opera Live, Vol.3
(SCHW) **314552** Vienna State Opera Live, Vol.5
(SCHW) **314562** Vienna State Opera Live, Vol.6
(SCHW) **314572** Vienna State Opera Live, Vol.7
(SCHW) **314582** Vienna State Opera Live, Vol.8
(SCHW) **314602** Vienna State Opera Live, Vol.10
(SCHW) **314622** Vienna State Opera Live, Vol.12
(SCHW) **314632** Vienna State Opera Live, Vol.13
(SCHW) **314652** Vienna State Opera Live, Vol.15
(SCHW) **314692** Vienna State Opera Live, Vol.19
(SCHW) **314712** Vienna State Opera Live, Vol.21
(SCHW) **314722** Vienna State Opera Live, Vol.22

WERRENRATH, Reinald (bar)
(ROMO) **81016-2** Lucrezia Bori (1887-1960)

WERRES, Elisabeth (sop)
Hindemith: Neues vom Tage (Cpte)

WESSEL, Kai (alto)
Handel: Rodelinda (Cpte)

WESSELY, Karl (ten)
Mozart: Nozze di Figaro (Cpte)
(PREI) **90168** Wagner—Die Meistersinger, Act 2, etc

WESSNER, Erich (ten)
J. Strauss II: Fledermaus (Cpte)

WEST, Jayne (sop)
Mozart: Nozze di Figaro (Cpte)
Stravinsky: Rake's Progress (Cpte)
(ARGO) **436 128-2ZH** Moran—Vocal and Chamber Works

WEST, Jon Frederic (ten)
Puccini: Turandot (exc)

WEST GERMAN RADIO CHORUS
cond G. FERRO
Rossini: Cenerentola (Cpte), Italiana in Algeri (exc)
cond F. LEITNER
Orff: Prometheus (Cpte)
(ACAN) **44 2085-2** Carl Orff Collection

WESTBERG, Henrik (bar)
Lidholm: Dream Play (Cpte)

WESTBROCK, James (ten)
Britten: Paul Bunyan (Cpte)

WESTBROOK, John (spkr)
(SONY) **SM22K46290(3)** Stravinsky—The Complete Edition (pt 3)

WESTBROOK-GEHA, Mary (mez)
Handel: Giulio Cesare (Cpte)

WESTCHESTER CHORAL SOCIETY
cond E. QUELER
Verdi: Aroldo (Cpte)

WESTENHOLZ, Elisabeth (pf)
(BIS) **BIS-CD166** The Virtuoso Flute

WESTENHOLZ, Peter (pf)
(DANI) **DCD8143** Hanne Stavad - Song Recital

WESTERHOF, Erik (gtr)
(OTTA) **OTRC48710** Spanish Dances

WESTHEAD, Paul (bar)
Vaughan Williams: Pilgrim's Progress (Cpte)

WESTI, Kurt (ten)
Heise: Drot og Marsk (Cpte)
Nielsen: Saul and David (Cpte)
Schulhoff: Plameny (Cpte)
Zemlinsky: Es war einmal (Cpte)

WESTMINSTER ABBEY SCHOOL CHORISTERS
cond P. PICKETT
Blow: Venus and Adonis (Cpte)

WESTMINSTER CHOIR
cond C. BADEA
Barber: Antony and Cleopatra (Cpte)
cond A. TOSCANINI
(RCA) **GD60299** Verdi: Requiem, etc
(RCA) **GD60326** Verdi—Operas & Choral Works

WESTMINSTER SYMPHONIC CHOIR
cond R. MUTI
Leoncavallo: Pagliacci (Cpte)
Puccini: Tosca (exc)

WESTPHALIA CHAMBER ORCHESTRA
cond W. GUNDLACH
Weill: Down in the Valley (Cpte), Jasager (Cpte)

WESTRIP, Ian (cond)
see Philh

WESTROP, Stephen (organ)
(MAX) **MSCB3** English Nat Opera North Chorus recital

WETTERGREN, Gertrud (mez)
Verdi: Trovatore (Cpte)

WEWEL, Günter (bass)
Humperdinck: Königskinder (Cpte)
Lehár: Giuditta (Cpte)
Lortzing: Undine (Cpte)
Millöcker: Gasparone (Cpte)
Mozart: Zauberflöte (Cpte)

WEWEZOW, Gudrun (mez)
R. Strauss: Rosenkavalier (Cpte)
Smetana: Bartered Bride (Cpte)
Wagner: Walküre (Cpte)
(EMI) **LDX9 91275-1(EMI)** Sawallisch conducts Wagner's Ring

WHANG, Suzy (vn)
(INTU) **INT3113-2** Zapateado - Suzy Whang

WHARFEDALE, Mark (bass)
Vaughan Williams: Pilgrim's Progress (Cpte)

WHEELER, Victoria (sop)
R. Strauss: Elektra (Cpte)

WHELAN, David (bar)
Puccini: Bohème (Cpte)
Tippett: Midsummer Marriage (Cpte)

WHIGHAM, Jiggs (cond)
see HR-Brass

WHITE, Carolina (sop)
(IRCC) **IRCC-CD810** American Singers, Volume 1

WHITE, Jeremy (bass)
G. Lloyd: Iernin

WHITE, Robert (ten)
(VIRG) **VJ7 59644-2** Handel—Favourite Arias

WHITE, Robin (cond)
see Southern Fest Orch

WHITE, Wendy (mez)
Stravinsky: Rake's Progress (Cpte)
Verdi: Luisa Miller (Cpte), Traviata (Cpte)
Wagner: Parsifal (exc)
(DG) **439 251-2GY** The Leonard Bernstein Album
(DG) **439 251-5GY** The Leonard Bernstein Album
(MUSM) **67078-2** Stravinsky The Composer - Volume 1

WHITE, Willard (bass)
Britten: Gloriana (Cpte)
Gershwin: Porgy and Bess (exc)
Joplin: Treemonisha (Cpte)
Monteverdi: Orfeo (Cpte)
Mozart: Entführung (Cpte), Zauberflöte (Cpte)
Prokofiev: Love for 3 Oranges (Cpte)
R. Strauss: Aegyptische Helena (Cpte)
(EMI) **CDH5 65072-2** Glyndebourne Recorded - 1934-1994
(LOND) **825 126-2** Amadeus - Original Soundtrack

WHITEHILL, Clarence (bass-bar)
(IRCC) **IRCC-CD810** American Singers, Volume 1
(PEAR) **GEMMCDS9924(1)** Covent Garden on Record, Vol.2 (pt 1)
(RCA) **09026 61580-2(2)** RCA/Met 100 Singers, 100 Years (pt 2)
(SYMP) **SYMCD1081** The Harold Wayne Collection, Vol.5

WHITEHOUSE, Richard (bar)
Vaughan Williams: Pilgrim's Progress (Cpte)

WHITELEY, Franklyn (bass)
Puccini: Bohème (Cpte)

WHITING, Jonathan (treb)
Britten: Midsummer Night's Dream (Cpte)

WHITMER, Jason (sngr)
Rapchak: Lifework of Juan Diaz (Cpte)

WHITTINGHAM, Shelley (mez)
Monteverdi: Orfeo (Cpte)

WHITWORTH, John (alto)
Purcell: King Arthur, Z628 (Cpte)

WICKS, Dennis (bass)
Berlioz: Troyens (Cpte)
Debussy: Pelléas et Mélisande (Cpte)
Mozart: Idomeneo (Cpte)
R. Strauss: Salome (Cpte)
Schoenberg: Moses und Aron (Cpte)
Verdi: Traviata (Cpte)
(CBS) **CD79312** Puccini: Il Trittico
(EMI) **LDB4 91283-1(EMI)** Maria Callas at Covent Garden

WIDDOP, Walter (ten)
Wagner: Götterdämmerung (exc)
(CLAR) **CDGSE78-50-26** Wagner: Tristan und Isolde excerpts

(CLAR) **CDGSE78-50-35/6** Wagner—Historical recordings
(CLAR) **CDGSE78-50-46** Walter Widdop (1892-1949)
(CLAR) **CDGSE78-50-52** Three Tenors
(CLAR) **CDGSE78-50-54** Coates conducts Wagner, Weber & Mendelssohn
(EMI) **CMS7 64008-2(2)** Wagner Singing on Record (pt 2)
(PEAR) **GEMMCDS9121** Wagner—Die Meistersinger, Act 3, etc
(PEAR) **GEMMCDS9137** Wagner—Der Ring des Nibelungen
(PEAR) **GEMMCDS9925(1)** Covent Garden on Record—Vol.3 (pt 1)
(PEAR) **GEMMCDS9926(1)** Covent Garden on Record—Vol.4 (pt 1)
(PEAR) **GEMMCD9112** Walter Widdop
(PEAR) **GEMMCD9146** Florence Austral

WIDMER, Oliver (bar)
Mozart: Zauberflöte (Cpte)
Schreker: Gezeichneten (Cpte)
Wolf: Manuel Venegas

WIEDEMANN, Hermann (bass)
Wagner: Parsifal (exc)
(SCHW) **314532** Vienna State Opera Live, Vol.3
(SCHW) **314562** Vienna State Opera Live, Vol.6
(SCHW) **314602** Vienna State Opera Live, Vol.10
(SCHW) **314622** Vienna State Opera Live, Vol.12
(SCHW) **314642** Vienna State Opera Live, Vol.14
(SCHW) **314652** Vienna State Opera Live, Vol.15
(SCHW) **314702** Vienna State Opera Live, Vol.20

WIEDEMANN, Poul (bar)
Nielsen: Maskarade (Cpte)

WIEDENHOFER, Thomas (narr)
Lehár: Giuditta (Cpte)

WIELKI THEATRE CHORUS cond R. SATANOWSKI
Moniuszko: Halka (Cpte)

WIELKI THEATRE ORCHESTRA cond R. SATANOWSKI
Moniuszko: Halka (Cpte)

WIEMANN, Ernst (bass)
Weber: Freischütz (Cpte)

WIENER, Julia (sop)
(EMI) **CMS7 63386-2** Borodin—Prince Igor & Complete Solo Songs

WIENER, Otto (bass)
R. Strauss: Rosenkavalier (Cpte)
Wagner: Lohengrin (Cpte), Meistersinger (Cpte)
(VAI) **VAIA1012** Eleanor Sterber sings R. Strauss

WIENER TSCHUSCHENKAPELLE cond J. E. GARDINER
Lehár: Lustige Witwe (Cpte)

WIENER-CHENISHEVA, Julia (sop)
(FORL) **UCD16742** Bulgarian Voices, Vol. 2

WIENS, Edith (sop)
Mozart: Oca del Cairo (Cpte)
Wagner: Parsifal (Cpte)
(CBC) **MVCD1053** Schubert—Lieder
(PHIL) **422 523-2PME8(2)** The Complete Mozart Edition Vol 23 (pt 2)

WIETER, Georg (bass)
Mozart: Nozze di Figaro (Cpte)
Orff: Kluge (Cpte)
Wagner: Meistersinger (Cpte)
(MYTO) **1MCD943104** R. Strauss—Capriccio (highlights) & Lieder

WILBRINK, Hans (bar)
R. Strauss: Rosenkavalier (Cpte)
Wagner: Meistersinger (Cpte)

WILCOCK, Gordon (ten)
J. Strauss II: Fledermaus (Cpte)
Lehár: Lustige Witwe (Cpte)

WILD, Earl (pf)
(AUDI) **CD72008** The Art of the Transcription
(CHES) **Chesky CD32** Earl Wild plays his transcriptions of Gershwin

WILD, Elfriede (sop)
Wagner: Parsifal (Cpte), Walküre (exc)

WILD, Waldemar (bass)
Egk: Peer Gynt (Cpte)
Mendelssohn: Hochzeit des Camacho (Cpte)

WILDBRUNN, Helene (sop)
(PREI) **89097** Helene Wildbrunn (1882-1972)

WILDE, Scott (sngr)
Schuman: Question of Taste (Cpte)

WILDERMAN, William (bass)
R. Strauss: Friedenstag (Cpte)
Verdi: Falstaff (Cpte)
(CAST) **CASH5052** Verdi Operatic Favourites

WILDHABER, Helmut (ten)
Gazzaniga: Don Giovanni (Cpte)
Mozart: Zauberflöte (exc)
Mussorgsky: Boris Godunov (Cpte)
Puccini: Turandot (Cpte)
Schreker: Irrelohe (Cpte)
Weill: Mahagonny-Gesänge (Cpte), Sieben Todsünden (Cpte)
(ACAN) **49 402** Giuseppe Taddei—Recital

WILDMANN, Charles (cond)
see Graunke SO

WILDNER, Johannes (cond)
see Bratislava RSO
Capella Istropolitana
Polish Nat RSO
Slovak RSO
Vienna SO Strauss Ens

WILHELM, Horst (ten)
Millöcker: Dubarry (exc)
R. Strauss: Salome (Cpte)
Wagner: Meistersinger (exc)

WILI, Graham (ten)
Vaughan Williams: Pilgrim's Progress (Cpte)

WILKENS, Anne (mez)
Gay: Beggar's Opera (Cpte)
Puccini: Fanciulla del West (Cpte)
Wagner: Tristan und Isolde (Cpte), Walküre (Cpte)
(BELA) **450 121-2** Plácido Domingo
(DG) **437 825-2GH** Wagner—Der Ring des Nibelungen - Highlights
(DG) **445 354-2GX14** Wagner—Der Ring des Nibelungen

WILKIE, Neville (bass)
Meyerbeer: Huguenots (Cpte)

WILKINSON, Kathleen (contr)
Vaughan Williams: Pilgrim's Progress (Cpte)

WILL, Arthur (bass)
(PREI) **90168** Wagner—Die Meistersinger, Act 2, etc

WILL, Jacob (bass)
Zemlinsky: Kleider machen Leute (Cpte)

WILLER, Luise (mez)
Wagner: Fliegende Holländer (Cpte)
(PILZ) **442118-2** Wagner—Operas in Historical Recordings

WILLIAMS, Ben (ten)
(DANA) **DACOCD315/6** Lauritz Melchior Anthology - Vol. 3
(EMI) **CMS7 64008-2(1)** Wagner Singing on Record (pt 1)
(MSCM) **MM30283** Great Wagnerian Singers, Vol.1
(PEAR) **GEMMCD9944** Friedrich Schorr sings Wagner

WILLIAMS, Bradley (sngr)
Bellini: Adelson e Salvini (Cpte)

WILLIAMS, Harold (bar)
Gounod: Faust (Cpte)
(SYMP) **SYMCD1123** Sullivan—Sesquicentenial Commemorative Issue

WILLIAMS, Howard (cond)
see Chelsea Op Group Orch

WILLIAMS, Jenny (sop)
(RCA) **GD61175** The Glory of the Human Voice-Florence Foster Jenkins

WILLIAMS, Jenovora (mez)
Sullivan: Pirates of Penzance (Cpte)

WILLIAMS, John (gtr)
(RCA) **09026 61450-2** Together - Julian Bream & John Williams
(RCA) **74321 25821-2** Café Classics—Music of Spain

WILLIAMS, John Towner (cond)
see Boston Pops

WILLIAMS, John Towner (pf)
(PHIL) **422 401-2PH** Jessye Norman - Lucky To Be Me

WILLIAMS, Karen (sop)
R. Strauss: Friedenstag (Cpte)
(ALBA) **TROY023-2** Music of Joseph Fennimore

WILLIAMS, Laverne (sop)
Bernstein: West Side Story (Cpte)

WILLIAMS, Neville (bass-bar)
Britten: Death in Venice (Cpte)
Donizetti: Caterina Cornaro (Cpte)

WILLIAMS, Tom Emlyn (alto)
Handel: Giulio Cesare (Cpte)

(RITA) WILLIAMS SINGERS cond M. COLLINS
German: Merrie England (Cpte)

WILLIAMSON, Malcolm (pf)
(JEWI) **BB 002** Michelow and Williamson in Recital

WILLIS, Aimée Elizabeth (sop)
R. Strauss: Salome (Cpte)

WILLIS, Constance (mez)
Mozart: Nozze di Figaro (Cpte)
(EMI) **CDH5 65072-2** Glyndebourne Recorded - 1934-1994
(PEAR) **GEMMCD9468** Vaughan Williams

WILLIS, Katherine (sop)
Britten: Little Sweep (Cpte)

WILLIS, Nuala (mez)
Gay: Beggar's Opera (Cpte)
Stravinsky: Rake's Progress (Cpte)

WILLSON, Tim (ten)
Verdi: Trovatore (Cpte)

WILSING, Jörn W (bar)
Leoncavallo: Bohème (Cpte)
R. Strauss: Intermezzo (Cpte)
Smetana: Bartered Bride (Cpte)

WILSON, Catherine (mez)
Britten: Albert Herring (Cpte)
Purcell: Dido (Cpte)

WILSON, Catherine (pf)
(RCA) **RD60697** Ofra Harnoy—Salut D'Amour

WILSON, Gordon (ten)
Verdi: Trovatore (Cpte)

WILSON, Paul (ten)
Saxton: Caritas (Cpte)

WILSON HYDE, Eric (bar)
Sullivan: HMS Pinafore (Cpte)

WILSON-JOHNSON, David (bar)
Birtwistle: Punch and Judy (Cpte)
Boughton: Immortal Hour (Cpte)
Bridge: Christmas Rose (Cpte)
Britten: Peter Grimes (Cpte)
Donizetti: Lucrezia Borgia (Cpte)
G. Lloyd: John Socman (exc)
Holst: At the Boar's Head (Cpte)
Purcell: Fairy Queen, Z629 (Cpte)
Smyth: Wreckers (Cpte)
Tippett: Ice Break (Cpte)
Verdi: Traviata (Cpte)
(SONY) **SK45965** Esa-Pekka Salonen conducts Stravinsky

WILTSCHINSKY, Peter (gtr)
(TELD) **4509-94523-2** Virtuoso Guitar

WIMBERGER, Peter (bass-bar)
R. Strauss: Frau ohne Schatten (Cpte), Rosenkavalier (Cpte)

WINBERGH, Gösta (ten)
A. Thomas: Hamlet (Cpte)
Chausson: Roi Arthus (Cpte)
Donizetti: Don Pasquale (Cpte)
Gluck: Iphigénie en Tauride (Cpte)
Mozart: Clemenza di Tito (Cpte), Don Giovanni (Cpte), Entführung (Cpte), Mitridate (Cpte)

WINCENE, Carol (fl)
Glass: Hydrogen Jukebox (Cpte)

WINCHESTER QUIRISTERS cond JULIAN SMITH
(MERI) **CDE84162** Vocal Music for Choir

WINDGASSEN, Wolfgang (ten)
Beethoven: Fidelio (Cpte)
J. Strauss II: Fledermaus (exc)
Wagner: Fliegende Holländer (Cpte), Götterdämmerung (Cpte), Lohengrin (Cpte), Parsifal (Cpte), Rheingold (Cpte), Siegfried (Cpte), Tannhäuser (exc), Tristan und Isolde (exc)
(DECC) **414 100-2DM15** Wagner: Der Ring des Nibelungen
(DECC) **421 313-2DA** Wagner: Der Ring des Nibelungen - Great Scenes
(DECC) **440 069-2DWO** The World of Wagner
(EMI) **CZS7 67123-2** Wagner: Der Ring des Nibelungen
(FOYE) **15-CF2011** Wagner—Der Ring de Nibelunge
(MEMO) **HR4275/6** Birgit Nilsson—Public Performances 1954-1969
(PHIL) **434 420-2PM32(2)** Richard Wagner Edition (pt 2)
(PHIL) **446 057-2PB14** Wagner—The Ring Cycle - Bayreuth Festival 1967

WINDISCH, Ludwig (bass)
(PREI) **90168** Wagner—Die Meistersinger, Act 2, etc

WINDS, Erich-Alexander (spkr)
R. Strauss: Ariadne auf Naxos (Cpte)

WINDSOR, Lorna (sop)
Mozart: Ascanio in Alba (Cpte)

WINFIELD, John (ten)
G. Lloyd: John Socman (exc)
Schoenberg: Moses und Aron (Cpte)
(OPRA) **ORC003** Donizetti—Gabriella di Vergy

WINKELMANN, Hermann (ten)
(SYMP) **SYMCD1081** The Harold Wayne Collection, Vol.5

WINKLER, Hermann (ten)
Berg: Wozzeck (Cpte)
Hindemith: Mathis der Maler (Cpte)
Mozart: Idomeneo (Cpte), Zauberflöte (Cpte)
R. Strauss: Elektra (Cpte)
Schoeck: Massimilla Doni (Cpte)
Zemlinsky: Kleider machen Leute (Cpte)

WINNIPEG GILBERT & SULLIVAN SOCIETY cond B. TOVEY
(CBC) **SMCD5139** A Gilbert & Sullivan Gala

(THE) WINNIPEG SINGERS cond B. TOVEY
(CBC) **SMCD5139** A Gilbert & Sullivan Gala

WINNIPEG SYMPHONY ORCHESTRA cond B. TOVEY
(CBC) **SMCD5139** A Gilbert & Sullivan Gala

WINSAUER, Waltraud (mez)
Mozart: Zauberflöte (Cpte)
R. Strauss: Elektra (Cpte), Rosenkavalier (Cpte)

WINSKA, Aga (sop)
Mozart: Entführung (Cpte)

(PAVA) **ADW7289** Mozart—Opera Arias; Exsultate, jubilate

WINSLADE, Glenn (ten)
Lehár: Lustige Witwe (exc)
Mozart: Idomeneo (Cpte)
R. Strauss: Arabella (Cpte), Intermezzo (Cpte)

WINTER, Horst (ten)
(KOCH) **399 225** Operetta Highlights 3

WINTER, Louise (mez)
Janáček: Káťa Kabanová (Cpte)

WINTER, Paul (bar)
Verdi: Traviata (Cpte)

WION, G. (sngr)
(MUSD) **20239-2** Delibes—Opéras-Comiques

WIRKKALA, Merja (sop)
Madetoja: Juha (Cpte)

WIRTZ, Dorothea (sop)
R. Strauss: Daphne (Cpte)

WISE, Patricia (sop)
Berg: Lulu (Cpte)

WISNIEWSKA, Helga (sop)
Lehár: Zarewitsch (exc)

WISSICK, Brent (baroque vc)
(ALBA) **TROY127-2** Purcell—From Rosy Bow'rs

WISSICK, Brent (va da gamba)
(ALBA) **TROY127-2** Purcell—From Rosy Bow'rs

WISTREICH, Richard (bass)
Cavalli: Xerse (Cpte)
Mozart: Zauberflöte (Cpte)
Purcell: Fairy Queen, Z629 (Cpte)

WIT, Antoni (cond)
see Polish Nat RO

WITH, Dora (mez)
(SCHW) **314532** Vienna State Opera Live, Vol.3
(SCHW) **314592** Vienna State Opera Live, Vol.9
(SCHW) **314602** Vienna State Opera Live, Vol.10
(SCHW) **314622** Vienna State Opera Live, Vol.12
(SCHW) **314632** Vienna State Opera Live, Vol.13
(SCHW) **314642** Vienna State Opera Live, Vol.14
(SCHW) **314702** Vienna State Opera Live, Vol.20
(SCHW) **314742** Vienna State Opera Live, Vol.24

WITHERSPOON, Herbert (bar)
(NIMB) **NI7811** Ernestine Schumann-Heink—Opera & Song Recital
(PEAR) **GEMMCDS9923(1)** Covent Garden on Record, Vol.1 (pt 1)

WITT, Jannina de (sop)
(PEAR) **GEMMCD9016** Mattia Battistini, Vol.3

WITT, Josef (ten)
Mozart: Nozze di Figaro (Cpte)
R. Strauss: Arabella (Cpte), Ariadne auf Naxos (Cpte)
Verdi: Macbeth (Cpte), Otello (Cpte)
Wagner: Meistersinger (Cpte)
(ORFE) **C394101B** Great Mozart Singers Series, Vol. 1
(PREI) **90249** Mozart in tempore belli
(SCHW) **314532** Vienna State Opera Live, Vol.3
(SCHW) **314572** Vienna State Opera Live, Vol.7
(SCHW) **314582** Vienna State Opera Live, Vol.8
(SCHW) **314652** Vienna State Opera Live, Vol.15
(SCHW) **314712** Vienna State Opera Live, Vol.21
(SCHW) **314722** Vienna State Opera Live, Vol.22

WITT, Kerstin (mez)
R. Strauss: Salome (Cpte)

WITTE, Erich (ten)
Wagner: Meistersinger (Cpte), Rheingold (Cpte)
Weber: Abu Hassan (Cpte)
(FOYE) **15-CF2011** Wagner—Der Ring de Nibelungen

WITTE, Wolfgang (ten)
Verdi: Ballo in maschera (Cpte)

WITTGES, Herbert (bar)
Schoenberg: Moses und Aron (Cpte)

WITTGES, Max (bass-bar)
R. Strauss: Friedenstag (Cpte)

WITTING, Eugene (ten)
(PEAR) **GEMMCDS9004/6(2)** Singers of Imperial Russia, Vol.3 (pt 2)

WITTING, Gerhard (ten)
Wagner: Meistersinger (Cpte)

WITTRISCH, Marcel (ten)
(EMI) **CMS7 64008-2(1)** Wagner Singing on Record (pt 1)
(MMOI) **CDMOIR405** Great Tenors
(MMOI) **CDMOIR419** Vienna Nights - Golden Age of Operetta
(NIMB) **NI7848** Great Singers at the Berlin State Opera
(PEAR) **GEMMCD9129** Great Tenors, Vol.2
(PREI) **89024** Marcel Wittrisch (1901-1955)
(PREI) **89049** Margarete Teschemacher (1903-1959)
(PREI) **89082** Margarete Klose (1902-1968)
(PREI) **89092** Erna Berger (1900-1990) - II
(PREI) **90034** Maria Cebotari (1910-49)

WIXELL, Ingvar (bar)
Donizetti: Elisir d'amore (Cpte), Lucrezia Borgia (Cpte)
Leoncavallo: Pagliacci (exc)
Mozart: Don Giovanni (Cpte), Nozze di Figaro (exc), Zaïde (Cpte)
Puccini: Bohème (Cpte), Madama Butterfly (Cpte), Tosca (Cpte)
Verdi: Ballo in maschera (Cpte), Rigoletto (Cpte), Trovatore (exc)
(CAST) **CASH5051** Puccini Favourites from Covent Garden and the Arena di Verona
(CAST) **CVI2068** Opera Highlights from Verona 1
(CBS) **CD79312** Puccini: Il Trittico
(DECC) **433 066-2DWO** Your Hundred Best Opera Tunes III
(MSVE) **MSCD617** Swedish Ballads
(PHIL) **434 986-2PM** Duetti Amorosi
(SONY) **MDK47176** Favourite Arias by the World's Favourite Tenors
(SONY) **SBK46548** Opera Arias

WLASCHIHA, Ekkehard (bass)
Beethoven: Fidelio (Cpte)
Wagner: Götterdämmerung (Cpte), Lohengrin (exc), Parsifal (Cpte), Rheingold (Cpte), Siegfried (Cpte)
Weber: Freischütz (exc)
(DG) **437 825-2GH** Wagner—Der Ring des Nibelungen - Highlights
(DG) **445 354-2GX14** Wagner—Der Ring des Nibelungen
(DG) **072 422-3GH7** Levine conducts Wagner's Ring
(EMI) **LDX9 91275-1(EMI)** Sawallisch conducts Wagner's Ring
(PHIL) **434 420-2PM32(1)** Richard Wagner Edition (Pt.1)

WOCKE, Hans (bass)
J. Strauss II: Fledermaus (Cpte)

WODEHOUSE, Ian (treb)
Britten: Midsummer Night's Dream (Cpte)

WOESTER, Heinz (spkr)
(DECC) **443 530-2LF2** Mozart—Die Entführung aus dem Serail

WOHLERS, Rüdiger (ten)
Beethoven: Fidelio (Cpte)

WOHLFAHRT, Erwin (ten)
Mozart: Nozze di Figaro (Cpte)
Wagner: Rheingold (Cpte), Siegfried (Cpte), Tristan und Isolde (Cpte)
(DG) **435 211-2GX15** Wagner—Der Ring des Nibelungen
(PHIL) **446 057-2PB14** Wagner—The Ring Cycle - Bayreuth Festival 1967

WOHLFARTH, Brigitte (sop)
Spohr: Faust (Cpte)

WOICIECHOWSKI, Marek (bass)
Moniuszko: Halka (Cpte)

WOLAŃSKI, Jan (bass)
Rossini: Signor Bruschino (Cpte)

WOLANSKY, Raymond (bar)
Beethoven: Fidelio (Cpte)

WOLF, Gerd (bass)
R. Strauss: Ariadne auf Naxos (Cpte)
Schulhoff: Plameny (Cpte)

(THE) WOLF TRAP COMPANY CHORUS cond J. RUDEL
Verdi: Traviata (Cpte)

WOLFF, Albert (cond)
see orch

WOLFF, Beverly (mez)
D. Moore: Carry Nation (Cpte)
Handel: Giulio Cesare (Cpte)

WOLFF, Fritz (ten)
(EMI) **CMS7 64008-2(2)** Wagner Singing on Record (pt 2)
(MSCM) **MM30285** Great Wagnerian Singers, Vol.2

WOLFF, Willi (bar)
(PILZ) **442118-2** Wagner—Operas in Historical Recordings

WOLFGANG, Randall (ob)
(DG) **439 147-2GMA** Mad about Baroque

WOLFRUM, Paul (bar)
Weill: Mahagonny (Cpte)

WOLKEN (ten)
(SCHW) **314562** Vienna State Opera Live, Vol.6
(SCHW) **314622** Vienna State Opera Live, Vol.12
(SCHW) **314642** Vienna State Opera Live, Vol.14

WOLSTAD, Odd (bass)
Nielsen: Saul and David (Cpte)

WONG, Randall (sop)
Hasse: Cleofide (Cpte)
M. Monk: Atlas (Cpte)
S. Wallace: Kabbalah (Cpte)

WOOD, Sir Henry (cond)
see orch
Queen's Hall Orch

WOOD, Sir Henry (pf)
(SYMP) **SYMCD1093** The Harold Wayne Collection, Vol.7

WOOD, James (bass)
R. Strauss: Friedenstag (Cpte)

WOODALL, Richard (ten)
Offenbach: Orphée aux enfers (Cpte)

WOODLAND, Rae (sop)
R. Strauss: Intermezzo (Cpte)
Verdi: Macbeth (Cpte)

WOODLEY, Arthur (bass-bar)
Stravinsky: Rake's Progress (Cpte)
Weill: Lost in the Stars (Cpte)
(EMI) **CDC7 54851-2** Gershwin—Blue Monday, etc
(IMP) **PCD1057** Crazy for Gershwin

WOODMAN, Thomas (bar)
V. Thomson: Lord Byron (Cpte)

WOODROW, Alan (ten)
Britten: Peter Grimes (Cpte)
Shostakovich: Lady Macbeth of Mtsensk (Cpte)
(ERAT) **2292-45984-2** Monteverdi—Ballet Music
(ERAT) **4509-99713-2** Baroque Works

WOODS, Carol (sngr)
Weill: Lost in the Stars (Cpte)

WOODS, Denise (sop)
(RCA) **09026 61509-2** A Salute to American Music

WOODS, Jonathan (hpd)
(IMP) **PCD1086** Jonathan Woods plays Harpsichord

WOODS, Sheryl (sop)
Glass: Satyagraha (Cpte)

WOOLLETT, Elizabeth (sop)
Sullivan: Gondoliers (Cpte), Iolanthe (exc)

WORDEN, Marvin (ten)
Beeson: Hello Out There (Cpte)

WORDSWORTH, Barry (cond)
see LSO
National PO
New Sadler's Wells Op Orch
NQHO
ROHO
RPO

WORFF, Franz (bass)
Wagner: Meistersinger (exc)
(SCHW) **314582** Vienna State Opera Live, Vol.8
(SCHW) **314602** Vienna State Opera Live, Vol.10
(SCHW) **314712** Vienna State Opera Live, Vol.21

WORKMAN, Charles Herbert (bar)
Rossini: Armida (Cpte)
(SYMP) **SYMCD1123** Sullivan—Sesquicentenial Commemorative Issue

WÖRLE, Robert (ten)
B. Goldschmidt: Gewaltige Hahnrei (Cpte)
Busoni: Arlecchino (Cpte), Turandot (Cpte)
Gurlitt: Wozzeck (Cpte)
Mozart: Zauberflöte (Cpte)
Schreker: Ferne Klang (Cpte), Gezeichneten (Cpte)
(SCHW) **314052** Opera Gala

WORTHLEY, Max (ten)
Monteverdi: L'Arianna (exc)

WORTHY, Johnny (ten)
Gershwin: Porgy and Bess (Cpte)

WOSKA, Elisabeth (spkr)
R. Strauss: Intermezzo (Cpte)

WÖSS, Kurt (cond)
see Bratislava PO

WOTTRICH, Erich (ten)
B. Goldschmidt: Gewaltige Hahnrei (Cpte)
Gurlitt: Wozzeck (Cpte)
Schreker: Gezeichneten (Cpte)
(SONY) **S2K66836** Goldschmidt—Beatrice Cenci, etc

WRANA, Hans (bass)
(PREI) **90096** Helge Roswaenge sings Verdi & Puccini

WRAY, Margaret Jane (sop)
Shostakovich: Lady Macbeth of Mtsensk (Cpte)
Verdi: Aida (Cpte)

WRIGHT, Colin (ten)
Sullivan: Mikado (exc)
(DECC) **430 095-2DWO** The World of Gilbert & Sullivan, Vol.1
(DECC) **433 868-2DWO** The World of Gilbert & Sullivan - Volume 2
(LOND) **436 816-2LM2** Sullivan—Utopia Ltd. Macbeth & Marmion Ovs etc

WRIGHT, Joyce (mez)
Sullivan: Gondoliers (Cpte), HMS Pinafore (Cpte)
(DECC) **430 095-2DWO** The World of Gilbert & Sullivan, Vol.1
(DECC) **433 868-2DWO** The World of Gilbert & Sullivan - Volume 2

WRIGHT, Patricia (sop)
(PEAR) **SHECD9613** Jane Austen Songs

WRIGHT, Simon (cond)
see Philh

WULF, Martina (sop)
R. Strauss: Elektra (Cpte)

WULKOPF, Cornelia (mez)
Egk: Peer Gynt (Cpte)
Mozart: Apollo et Hyacinthus (Cpte), Zauberflöte (Cpte)
Puccini: Fanciulla del West (Cpte)
Wagner: Walküre (Cpte)
(EMI) **LDX9 91275-1(EMI)** Sawallisch conducts Wagner's Ring

WUNDERER, Gabriele (sop)
Corghi: Divara (Cpte)

WUNDERLICH, Fritz (ten)
Berg: Wozzeck (Cpte)
Egk: Verlobung in San Domingo (Cpte)
Handel: Giulio Cesare (Cpte)
Janáček: Excursions of Mr Brouček (Cpte)
Mozart: Entführung (Cpte), Zauberflöte (exc)
Nicolai: Lustigen Weiber von Windsor (Cpte)
R. Strauss: Daphne (Cpte), Schweigsame Frau (Cpte)
Verdi: Traviata (Cpte)
Wagner: Fliegende Holländer (Cpte), Tannhäuser (Cpte)
(ACAN) **43 267** Fritz Wunderlich sings Opera Arias
(CFP) **CD-CFP4616** Ave Maria
(DG) **431 110-2GB** Great Voices - Fritz Wunderlich
(DG) **435 145-2GX5(1)** Fritz Wunderlich—Opera Arias, Lieder, etc (part 1)
(DG) **435 145-2GX5(2)** Fritz Wunderlich—Opera Arias, Lieder, etc, (part 2)
(EMI) **CMS7 64309-2** Kálmán—Best-loved Melodies
(EMI) **CZS7 62993-2** Fritz Wunderlich—Great German Tenor
(EURO) **GD69018** Fritz Wunderlich—Recital
(EURO) **VD69256** Mozart—Opera Arias
(NIMB) **NI7851** Legendary Voices
(ORFE) **C394301B** Great Mozart Singers Series, Vol. 3
(RCA) **09026 62550-2** Ten Tenors in Love

WUNSCH, Douglas (ten)
Boito: Mefistofele (Cpte)

WÜNZER, Rudolf (bass)
(PILZ) **442118-2** Wagner—Operas in Historical Recordings

WÜRTTEMBERG CHAMBER CHOIR
Wolf: Manuel Venegas

WÜRTTEMBERG PHILHARMONIC ORCHESTRA cond R. PATERNOSTRO
(SINE) **39820222** Deng - Tenor

WÜRTTEMBERG STATE OPERA CHORUS (STUTTGART) cond D.R. DAVIES
Weber: Freischütz (Cpte)

WÜRTTEMBERG STATE OPERA ORCHESTRA (STUTTGART)
Weber: Freischütz (Cpte)

WÜRTTEMBERG STATE ORCHESTRA, STUTTGART cond G. NAVARRO
(CAPR) **10 461** Falla—Orchestral Works

WÜSTMANN, Erika (sop)
R. Strauss: Ariadne auf Naxos (Cpte)

WYATT, Frances (sop)
Berlioz: Troyens (Cpte)

WYATT, Walker (bass)
Monteverdi: Ritorno d'Ulisse in Patria (Cpte)

WYNBERG, Simon (gtr)
(CHAN) **CHAN6581** Summertime

WYNDER, Gloria (contr)
R. Ward: Crucible (Cpte)

WYNER, Susan Davenny (mez)
Ravel: Enfant et les sortilèges (Cpte)

WYN-ROGERS, Catherine (contr)
Gay: Beggar's Opera (Cpte)

WYSOCZANSKÁ, Jadwiga (sop)
Dvořák: Rusalka (Cpte)

WYZNER, Franz (bass)
Einem: Dantons Tod (Cpte)

XALAPA SYMPHONY ORCHESTRA cond H. DE LA FUENTE
(IMP) **PCD1109** Overtures and Arias from Opera

YACHMI-CAUCIG, Rohangiz (contr)
J. Strauss II: Fledermaus (exc)
Mozart: Così fan tutte (Cpte)
R. Strauss: Elektra (Cpte), Rosenkavalier (Cpte)
Wagner: Parsifal (Cpte)

YAHIA, Mino (bass)
Egk: Verlobung in San Domingo (Cpte)

YAHR, Carol (mez)
Debussy: Pelléas et Mélisande (Cpte)

YAKAR, Rachel (sop)
Campra: Europe galante
Debussy: Pelléas et Mélisande (Cpte)
Lully: Phaëton (Cpte)
Monteverdi: Incoronazione di Poppea (Cpte)
Mozart: Don Giovanni (Cpte), Idomeneo (exc), Zauberflöte (Cpte)
Poulenc: Dialogues des Carmélites (Cpte)
Purcell: Dido (Cpte)

YAKHONTOV, A. (bass)
Tchaikovsky: Eugene Onegin (Cpte)

YAMAJ, Yoshihisa (ten)
Albinoni: Nascimento dell'Aurora (Cpte)

YAN, Igor (ten)
Mussorgsky: Boris Godunov (Cpte)

YANIGISAWA, Yasuo (bass)
Verdi: Traviata (Cpte)

YANNISSIS, Yanni (bass)
Puccini: Fanciulla del West (Cpte)

YAPRIDZE, Anton (bass)
Tchaikovsky: Eugene Onegin (Cpte)

YAROSLAVTSEV, Valeri (bass)
Tchaikovsky: Eugene Onegin (Cpte), Queen of Spades (Cpte)

YEEND, Frances (sop)
(IMP) **PWKS4230** Mario Lanza in Concert
(RCA) **GD60874** R. Strauss—Scenes from Elektra & Salome

YELISEEV, Leo (ten)
Kabalevsky: Colas Breugnon (Cpte)

YINON, Israel (cond)
see Brno St PO

YODER, Pearl (sop)
(PREI) **89209** Helge Roswaenge (1897-1972) - II

YOKO, Nagashima (contr)
Steffani: Henrico Leone (Cpte)

YORKSHIRE IMPERIAL BAND cond H. MORTIMER
(CHAN) **CHAN4513** British Bandsman Centenary Concert

YOSHIDA, Hiroyuki (ten)
Verdi: Otello (Cpte)

YOUNG, Alexander (ten)
Gay: Beggar's Opera (Cpte)
Stravinsky: Rake's Progress (Cpte)
Sullivan: Gondoliers (Cpte), Iolanthe (Cpte), Patience (Cpte), Yeomen of the Guard (Cpte)
(CFP) **CD-CFP4238** Gilbert and Sullivan
(CFP) **CD-CFP4609** Favourite Gilbert & Sullivan
(EMI) **CDC7 47283-2** Maria Callas - Mad Scenes & Bel Canto Arias
(SONY) **SM22K46290(4)** Stravinsky—The Complete Edition (pt 4)

YOUNG, Christiane (mez)
Janáček: From the House of the Dead (Cpte)

YOUNG, Thomas J. (ten)
A. Davis: X (Cpte)
J. Adams: Death of Klinghoffer (Cpte)

YOUNG, Victor (cond)
see orch

YSAS, Rosa Maria (contr)
Vives: Bohemios (Cpte), Doña Francisquita (Cpte)

YU, Djong Victorin (cond)
see Philh

YUASA, Takuo (cond)
see RLPO

YURISCH, Gregory (bar)
J. Strauss II: Fledermaus (Cpte)
Mozart: Don Giovanni (Cpte)
Verdi: Stiffelio (Cpte)
(DECC) **071 149-1DH (DECC)** The Essential Sutherland

YURLOV RUSSIAN CHOIR cond A. CHISTIAKOV
Rimsky-Korsakov: Kashchey (Cpte)

YUROVSKY, Mikhail (cond)
see Moscow Forum Th Orch
NW German PO

YUZHIN, David (ten)
(NIMB) **NI7865** Great Singers at the Mariinsky Theatre
(PEAR) **GEMMCDS9001/3(1)** Singers of Imperial Russia, Vol.2 (pt 1)
(PEAR) **GEMMCDS9001/3(2)** Singers of Imperial Russia, Vol.2 (pt 2)

YVONNE GOUVERNÉ CHOIR cond R. DESORMIÈRE
(EMI) **CHS7 61038-2** Debussy—Pelléas et Mélisande, etc

ZABELA-VRUBEL, Nadezhda (sop)
(ARLE) **ARL23/5** Rimsky-Korsakov—Sadko
(PEAR) **GEMMCDS9004/6(1)** Singers of Imperial Russia, Vol.3 (pt 1)

ZACCARIA, Nicola (bass)
Bellini: Norma (exc), Sonnambula (Cpte)
Donizetti: Lucia di Lammermoor (Cpte), Lucrezia Borgia (Cpte)
Puccini: Bohème (Cpte), Fanciulla del West (Cpte), Turandot (Cpte)
Rossini: Barbiere di Siviglia (Cpte), Italiana in Algeri (Cpte), Tancredi (Cpte)
Verdi: Aida (Cpte), Ballo in maschera (Cpte), Don Carlo (Cpte), Falstaff (Cpte), Rigoletto (Cpte), Trovatore (Cpte)
Vivaldi: Orlando Furioso (Cpte)
(BELA) **450 007-2** Puccini Favourites
(EMI) **CDM7 69543-2** Maria Callas and Giuseppe Di Stefano - Duets
(MEMO) **HR4386/7** Great Voices - Giulietta Simionato
(MEMO) **HR4396/7** Great Voices—Leontyne Price

ZACCARINI, Franco (bass)
(PREI) **89048** Apollo Granforte (1886-1975) - I

ZACHRISSON, Gösta (ten)
Prokofiev: Fiery Angel (Cpte)

ZADEK, Hilde (sop)
Mozart: Don Giovanni (Cpte)

ZÁDOR, Deszö (bar)
Wagner: Götterdämmerung (exc)
(PEAR) **GEMMCDS9137** Wagner—Der Ring des Nibelungen
(SUPR) **11 2136-2(3)** Emmy Destinn—Complete Edition, Discs 5 to 8

ZÁDORI, Mária (sop)
Handel: Floridante (Cpte)

ZADVORNY, Sergei (bass)
Rossini: Armida (Cpte), Semiramide (Cpte)
Tchaikovsky: Eugene Onegin (Cpte)

ZAFFINI, Clément (cond)
see Provence Vocal Ens

ZAGONARA, Adelio (ten)
Puccini: Bohème (Cpte), Manon Lescaut (Cpte), Turandot (Cpte)
Verdi: Aida (Cpte)
(EMI) **CMS7 64165-2** Puccini—Trittico

ZAGÓRZANKA, Barbara (sop)
Moniuszko: Halka (Cpte)
Szymanowski: King Roger (Cpte)

ZAGREB PHILHARMONIC ORCHESTRA cond M. HALÁSZ
(NAXO) **8 550236** Rossini—Overtures

ZAGROSEK, Lothar (cond)
see Austrian RSO
Berlin Deutsches SO
Cologne RSO
Leipzig Gewandhaus

ZAHARIA, Constantin (ten)
Saint-Saëns: Samson et Dalila (Cpte)
Verdi: Otello (Cpte)

ZAHRADNÍČEK, Jiří (ten)
Smetana: Two Widows (Cpte)
(DECC) **430 375-2DH2** Janáček—Operatic and Orchestral Works

ZAIDAN, Raouf (bar)
Mozart: Così fan tutte (Cpte), Don Giovanni (Cpte), Nozze di Figaro (Cpte)

ZAJAC, Karen (contr)
Schoenberg: Moses und Aron (Cpte)

ZAJICK, Dolora (mez)
Verdi: Aida (Cpte), Don Carlo (Cpte), Forza del destino (Cpte), Trovatore (Cpte)
(EMI) **CDC7 54484-2** Verdi—Opera Choruses

ZAJÍČKOVÁ-VYSKOČILOVÁ, Kamila (sop)
Patzelt: Castor et Pollux (Cpte)

ZAKAI, Mira (contr)
Mussorgsky: Boris Godunov (Cpte)
Schoenberg: Moses und Aron (Cpte)

ZAKHAROVA, Daria (mez)
(PEAR) **GEMMCDS9111(2)** Singers of Imperial Russia, Vol.5 (pt 2)

ZAKOWSKY, Rainer (ten)
R. Strauss: Rosenkavalier (Cpte)

ZALEWSKI, Wlodzimierz (bar)
Mussorgsky: Boris Godunov (Cpte)

ZALLINGER, Meinhard von (cond)
see Bavarian St Orch

ZAMBALIS, Stella (mez)
Bernstein: West Side Story (Cpte)
Corigliano: Ghosts of Versailles (Cpte)

ZAMBELLI, Corrado (bass)
Verdi: Trovatore (Cpte)

ZAMBERG, Viktor (bass)
Kabalevsky: Colas Breugnon (Cpte)

ZAMBON, Giuseppe (ten)
Traetta: Buovo d'Antona (Cpte)

ZAMBONI, Maria (sop)
(EMI) **CHS7 64864-2(1)** La Scala Edition - Vol.2, 1915-46 (pt 1)
(PEAR) **GEMMCD9091** Dino Borgioli

ZAMBONI, Rinaldo (cond)
see orch
ROHO

ZAMFIR, Gheorghe (panpipes)
(PHIL) **426 057-2PH** Glorious Pipes
(PHIL) **426 057-5PH** Glorious Pipes

ZAMMIT, Giuseppe (ten)
Verdi: Trovatore (Cpte)

ZAMPIERI, Giuseppe (ten)
Donizetti: Lucia di Lammermoor (Cpte)
J. Strauss II: Fledermaus (Cpte)
Rossini: Barbiere di Siviglia (Cpte)
Verdi: Traviata (Cpte)

ZAMPIERI, Mara (sop)
Puccini: Fanciulla del West (Cpte)
Verdi: Macbeth (Cpte)

ZANASI, Furio (bass)
Handel: Giulio Cesare (exc)

ZANASI, Mario (bar)
Leoncavallo: Pagliacci (Cpte)

ZANAZZO, Alfredo (bass)
Verdi: Aida (Cpte)

ZANCANARO, Giorgio (bar)
Giordano: Andrea Chénier (Cpte)
Puccini: Madama Butterfly (Cpte), Tosca (Cpte)
Rossini: Guillaume Tell (exc)
Verdi: Attila (Cpte), Don Carlo (Cpte), Forza del destino (exc), Rigoletto (exc), Traviata (Cpte), Trovatore (exc), Vespri Siciliani (Cpte)
(CAST) **CVI2065** Highlights from the Royal Opera House, Covent Garden

ZANCU, Dan (bass)
Bretan: Arald (Cpte), Golem (Cpte)

ZANDER, Benjamin (cond)
see New England Conservatory Youth PO

ZANELLI, Renato (bar/ten)
(NIMB) **NI7856** Legendary Tenors
(NIMB) **NI7867** Legendary Baritones
(PEAR) **GEMMCDS9926(1)** Covent Garden on Record—Vol.4 (pt 1)

ZANETTI, Miguel (pf)
(FORL) **UCD10902** The Art of Montserrat Caballé, Vol. 1

ZANETTI, Monique (sop)
Campra: Idoménée (exc)
Lully: Atys (Cpte)
M-A. Charpentier: David et Jonathas (Cpte), Médée (Cpte)
Rossi: Orfeo (Cpte)

ZANETTI, Orfeo (ten)
Verdi: Don Carlo (Cpte)

ZANINI, Nicoletta (mez)
Rossini: Sigismondo (Cpte)
Verdi: Rigoletto (Cpte)

ZANNI, Maria Cristina (sop)
Mercadante: Bravo (Cpte)
Piccinni: Cecchina (Cpte)

ZANNINI, Laura (mez)
Berg: Lulu (Cpte)
Rossini: Cenerentola (Cpte)
Verdi: Traviata (Cpte)
(TELD) **9031-77676-6(TELD)** My World of Opera - Kiri Te Kanawa

ZANOLLI, Silvana (sop)
Verdi: Traviata (Cpte)

ZANOTELLI, Hans (cond)
see Berlin SO

ZARA, Meredith (sop)
Mozart: Mitridate (Cpte)

ZARDO, Carlo (bass)
Verdi: Aida (Cpte), Macbeth (Cpte)

ZAREMBA, Eléna (mez)
Borodin: Prince Igor (Cpte)
Glinka: Life for the Tsar (Cpte)
Mussorgsky: Boris Godunov (Cpte)
Serov: Judith (Cpte)
Shostakovich: Lady Macbeth of Mtsensk (Cpte)
Wagner: Rheingold (Cpte)

ZARESKA, Eugenia (mez)
Mussorgsky: Boris Godunov (Cpte)
(MONT) **TCE8760** Stravinsky: Stage Works

AUN, Fritz (cond)
see Berlin St Op Orch

BRUEVA, Evgenia (contr)
(NIMB) **NI7865** Great Singers at the Mariinsky Theatre
(PEAR) **GEMMCDS9004/6(2)** Singers of Imperial Russia, Vol.3 (pt 2)
(PEAR) **GEMMCDS9007/9(1)** Singers of Imperial Russia, Vol.4 (pt 1)
(PEAR) **GEMMCDS9111(2)** Singers of Imperial Russia, Vol.5 (pt 2)

EANI, Virginia (sop)
Mascagni: Piccolo Marat (Cpte)
(BONG) **GB1060-2** Virginia Zeani - Various opera arias
(DECC) **417 686-2DC** Puccini—Operatic Arias
(DECC) **433 636-2DSP** Puccini—Famous Arias
(DECC) **433 865-2DWO** The World of Puccini

EC, Nikolaus (bass)
(SCHW) **314542** Vienna State Opera Live, Vol.4
(SCHW) **314562** Vienna State Opera Live, Vol.6
(SCHW) **314592** Vienna State Opera Live, Vol.9
(SCHW) **314602** Vienna State Opera Live, Vol.10
(SCHW) **314632** Vienna State Opera Live, Vol.13
(SCHW) **314642** Vienna State Opera Live, Vol.14
(SCHW) **314652** Vienna State Opera Live, Vol.15
(SCHW) **314742** Vienna State Opera Live, Vol.24

ECCHILLO, Giuseppe (bass)
Puccini: Madama Butterfly (Cpte), Tosca (Cpte)

EDDA, Alberto (cond)
see Bologna Teatro Comunale Orch
Collegium Instr Brugense
ECO
M. Franca Fest Orch
Monte Carlo Nat Op Orch
Piacenza SO

EDNIK, Heinz (ten)
Berg: Wozzeck (Cpte)
Bizet: Carmen (exc)
Giordano: Andrea Chénier (Cpte)
J. Strauss II: Fledermaus (Cpte)
Janáček: From the House of the Dead (Cpte)
Lehár: Lustige Witwe (Cpte)
Mozart: Entführung (Cpte), Nozze di Figaro (Cpte), Zauberflöte (Cpte)
Mussorgsky: Boris Godunov (Cpte), Khovanshchina (Cpte)
Prokofiev: Fiery Angel (Cpte)
Puccini: Tosca (Cpte), Turandot (Cpte)
R. Strauss: Ariadne auf Naxos (Cpte), Rosenkavalier (Cpte)
Schreker: Irrelohe (Cpte)
Shostakovich: Lady Macbeth of Mtsensk (Cpte)
Smetana: Bartered Bride (Cpte)
Tchaikovsky: Mazeppa (Cpte)
Verdi: Falstaff (Cpte)
Wagner: Parsifal (Cpte), Rheingold (Cpte), Siegfried (Cpte), Tristan und Isolde (Cpte)
(DG) **445 354-2GX14** Wagner—Der Ring des Nibelungen
(DG) **072 422-3GH7** Levine conducts Wagner's Ring
(PHIL) **434 420-2PM32(2)** Richard Wagner Edition (pt 2)

ZEFFIRELLI, Franco (prod)
Leoncavallo: Pagliacci (Cpte)

ZEH, Walter (bar)
R. Strauss: Rosenkavalier (Cpte), Salome (Cpte)

ZELLER, Richard (bar)
V. Thomson: Lord Byron (Cpte)

ZELLER, Robert (cond)
see Vienna St Op Orch

ZEMLINSKY, Alexander von (cond)
see Berlin Charlottenburg Op Orch
Berlin City Op Orch
Berlin St Op Orch
BPO

ZEMPLÉNI, Mária (sop)
Respighi: Belfagor (Cpte)

ZENATELLO, Giovanni (ten)
(CLUB) **CL99-025** Giovanni Zenatello (1876-1949)
(CLUB) **CL99-509/10** Hina Spani (1896-1969)
(EMI) **CHS7 64860-2(2)** La Scala Edition - Vol.1, 1878-1914 (pt 2)
(IRCC) **IRCC-CD808** Souvenirs of 19th Century Italian Opera
(PEAR) **GEMMCDS9073(1)** Giovanni Zenatello, Vol.1 (pt 1)
(PEAR) **GEMMCDS9073(2)** Giovanni Zenatello, Vol.1 (pt 2)
(PEAR) **GEMMCDS9074(1)** Giovanni Zenatello, Vol.2 (pt 1)
(PEAR) **GEMMCDS9074(2)** Giovanni Zenatello, Vol.2 (pt 2)
(PEAR) **GEMMCDS9924(1)** Covent Garden on Record, Vol.2 (pt 1)
(PEAR) **GEMMCDS9924(2)** Covent Garden on Record, Vol.2 (pt 2)
(PEAR) **GEMMCDS9925(2)** Covent Garden on Record—Vol.3 (pt 2)
(PEAR) **GEMMCDS9926(1)** Covent Garden on Record—Vol.4 (pt 1)
(PREI) **89038** Giovanni Zenatello (1876-1949)
(SUPR) **11 2136-2(5)** Emmy Destinn—Complete Edition, Discs 11 & 12
(SYMP) **SYMCD1073** The Harold Wayne Collection, Vol.3
(SYMP) **SYMCD1138** The Harold Wayne Collection, Vol.16
(SYMP) **SYMCD1148** The Harold Wayne Collection, Vol.17
(SYMP) **SYMCD1158** The Harold Wayne Collection, Vol.18
(SYMP) **SYMCD1168** The Harold Wayne Collection, Vol.19

ZENDER, Hans (cond)
see Basle SO

ZENNARO, Iorio (ten)
Bellini: Beatrice di Tenda (Cpte)
Rossini: Armida (Cpte), Inganno felice (Cpte), Occasione fa il ladro (Cpte)

ZERBINI, Antonio (bass)
Boito: Nerone (Cpte)
Massenet: Manon (Cpte)
Verdi: Aida (Cpte), Forza del destino (Cpte), Traviata (Cpte)

ZEROLA, Nicola (ten)
(MEMO) **HR4408/9(2)** Singers in Genoa, Vol.1 (disc 2)

ZEUTHEN, Morten (vc)
(DANI) **DCD8143** Hanne Stavad - Song Recital

ZHADAN, Ivan (ten)
(EMI) **CHS7 69741-2(6)** Record of Singing, Vol.4—Russian & Slavonic Schools

ZHEMCHUZHIN, Georgy (cond)
see Bolshoi Th Orch
Moscow Stanislavsky Th Orch

ZHOU, Zheng (bar)
Glass: Belle et la Bête (Cpte)

ZHU, Ai Lan (sop)
Mozart: Don Giovanni (Cpte)

ZHUKOVSKAYA, Glafira (sop)
Tchaikovsky: Eugene Onegin (Cpte)

ZHURINA, Irina (sop)
Serov: Judith (Cpte)

ŽÍDEK, Ivo (ten)
Dvořák: Rusalka (Cpte)
Fibich: Bride of Messina (Cpte)
Janáček: From the House of the Dead (Cpte), Jenufa (Cpte), Makropulos Affair (Cpte)
Martinů: Julietta (Cpte)
Smetana: Brandenburgers in Bohemia (Cpte), Devil's Wall (Cpte)
(DECC) **430 375-2DH2** Janáček—Operatic and Orchestral Works
(KOCH) **34036-2** A Pageant of Opera

ZIEGLER, Benno (bar)
(PEAR) **GEMMCD9145** Richard Tauber - Operatic Arias
(PEAR) **GEMMCD9327** The Vocal Prime of Richard Tauber

ZIEGLER, Delores (mez)
Donizetti: Roberto Devereux (Cpte)
Mozart: Clemenza di Tito (Cpte), Così fan tutte (Cpte), Zauberflöte (Cpte)
Verdi: Falstaff (Cpte)
Weber: Oberon (Cpte)
(EMI) **CDH5 65072-2** Glyndebourne Recorded - 1934-1994
(TELD) **4509-98824-2** Thomas Hampson Collection,Vol III-Operatic Scenes

ZIEGLER, Robert (cond)
see Matrix Ens

ZIESAK, Ruth (sop)
Beethoven: Fidelio (Cpte)
Humperdinck: Hänsel und Gretel (Cpte)
Mozart: Clemenza di Tito (Cpte), Zauberflöte (Cpte)
Weber: Freischütz (Cpte)

ZIKA, Zdenka (sop)
(SCHW) **314662** Vienna State Opera Live, Vol.16

ZIKMUNDOVÁ, Eva (sop)
Hába: Mother (Cpte)
Janáček: Cunning Little Vixen (Cpte)
(DECC) **430 375-2DH2** Janáček—Operatic and Orchestral Works

ZILIANI, Alessandro (ten)
Verdi: Traviata (Cpte)
(BONG) **GB1078-2** Mafalda Favero
(EMI) **CHS7 64864-2(2)** La Scala Edition - Vol.2, 1915-46 (pt 2)
(MMOI) **CDMOIR412** Great Voices of the Century Sing Puccini
(VAI) **VAIA1071** Mafalda Favero (1903-1981)

ZILIO, Elena (mez)
Donizetti: Gianni di Parigi (Cpte), Linda di Chamounix (Cpte)
Paisiello: Don Chisciotte (Cpte)

ZIMBALIST, Efrem (vn)
(APR) **APR7016** The Auer Legacy, Vol.2

ZIMERMAN, Krystian (pf)
(DG) **431 469-2GGA** Works for Violin and Piano

ZIMMER, Rudolf (bar)
Verdi: Trovatore (Cpte)

ZIMMERMANN, Bernhard (cond)
see Stuttgart RO

ZIMMERMANN, Erich (ten)
Wagner: Meistersinger (exc), Tristan und Isolde (Cpte)
(PREI) **90232** Wagner—Der Fliegende Holländer
(SCHW) **314562** Vienna State Opera Live, Vol.6
(SCHW) **314592** Vienna State Opera Live, Vol.9
(SCHW) **314602** Vienna State Opera Live, Vol.10
(SCHW) **314642** Vienna State Opera Live, Vol.14
(SCHW) **314702** Vienna State Opera Live, Vol.20
(SCHW) **314742** Vienna State Opera Live, Vol.24
(TELD) **9031-76442-2** Wagner—Excerpts from the 1936 Bayreuth Festival

ZIMMERMANN, Erika (sop)
Wagner: Götterdämmerung (Cpte), Parsifal (Cpte), Rheingold (Cpte)
(FOYE) **15-CF2011** Wagner—Der Ring de Nibelungen

ZIMMERMANN, Margarita (mez)
Albinoni: Nascimento dell'Aurora (Cpte)

ZIMMERMANN, Mark (sngr)
Bizet: Jolie fille de Perth (Cpte)
Puccini: Manon Lescaut (Cpte)
Rossini: Ermione (Cpte), Maometto II (Cpte)

ZIMMERMANN, Renate (mez)
Weill: Kuhhandel (exc)

ZIMMERMANN, Udo (cond)
see Inst. Ens

ZINETTI, Giuseppina (sop)
(PREI) **89010** Tancredi Pasero (1893-1983) - I
(PREI) **89013** Giannina Arangi-Lombardi (1890-1951)

ZINKLER, Jan (bar)
Trojahn: Enrico (Cpte)

ZINMAN, David (cond)
see Baltimore SO
Netherlands CO
Rotterdam PO

ZÍTEK, Václav (bar)
Dvořák: Jacobin (Cpte)

Fibich: Bride of Messina (Cpte), Šárka (Cpte)
Janáček: Cunning Little Vixen (Cpte), Jenufa (Cpte), Makropulos Affair (Cpte)
Martinů: Miracles of Mary (Cpte)
Smetana: Kiss (Cpte), Libuše (Cpte)
(DECC) **430 375-2DH2** Janáček—Operatic and Orchestral Works
(KOCH) **34036-2** A Pageant of Opera

ZLATOGOROVA, Bronislava (mez)
Tchaikovsky: Eugene Onegin (Cpte)
(DANT) **LYS013/5** Tchaikovsky—The Queen of Spades
(PREI) **89080** Mark Reizen (1895-1992) - II

ZLESÁK, Antonin (ten)
Martinů: Julietta (Cpte)

ZOGHBY, Linda (sop)
(PHIL) **432 416-2PH3** Haydn—L'incontro improvviso/Arias

ZOLLMAN, Ronald (cond)
see RTBF SO

ZOON, Jacques (fl)
Maderna: Hyperion (Cpte)
(PHIL) **438 940-2PH** Opera Fantasy

ZORGNIOTTI, Mario (bass)
Verdi: Traviata (Cpte)

ZORINA, Verina (narr)
(ARHI) **ADCD110** Mengelberg Edition - Volume 4
(SONY) **SM22K46290(3)** Stravinsky—The Complete Edition (pt 3)

ZOROBERTO, Anna (sop)
Gluck: Iphigénie en Tauride (Cpte)
Verdi: Simon Boccanegra (Cpte)

ZOTTI, Marisa (sop)
Donizetti: Favorita (Cpte)
Puccini: Madama Butterfly (Cpte)

ZSCHAU, Marilyn (sop)
Puccini: Bohème (Cpte)
(CAST) **CASH5051** Puccini Favourites from Covent Garden and the Arena di Verona
(CAST) **CVI2065** Highlights from the Royal Opera House, Covent Garden
(CAST) **CVI2070** Great Puccini Love Scenes from Covent Garden, La Scala and Verona

ZUCCA, Donald (sngr)
Gershwin: Porgy and Bess (Cpte)

ZUKOFSKY, Paul (vn)
Glass: Einstein on the Beach (Cpte)

ZUMBRO, Nicholas (pf)
(CONC) **CACD9004** Zumbro plays Granados & Falla

ZURICH CAMERATA
cond R. TSCHUPP
(JECK) **JD506-2** Flute Concertos

ZURICH OPERA HOUSE CHORUS
cond N. HARNONCOURT
Mozart: Clemenza di Tito (Cpte), Entführung (Cpte), Idomeneo (Cpte), Zauberflöte (Cpte)
(TELD) **4509-97505-2** Mozart—Famous Opera Choruses
cond R. WEIKERT
Zemlinsky: Kleider machen Leute (Cpte)

ZURICH OPERA HOUSE MONTEVERDI ENSEMBLE
Monteverdi: Incoronazione di Poppea (Cpte), Orfeo (Cpte)

ZURICH OPERA HOUSE MOZART ORCHESTRA
(TELD) **4509-95523-2** Mozart—Overtures
cond N. HARNONCOURT
Mozart: Entführung (Cpte), Idomeneo (Cpte)
(TELD) **4509-97505-2** Mozart—Famous Opera Choruses
(TELD) **4509-97507-2** Mozart—Famous Opera Arias

ZURICH OPERA ORCHESTRA
(TELD) **4509-95523-2** Mozart—Overtures
cond N. HARNONCOURT
Mozart: Clemenza di Tito (Cpte), Zauberflöte (Cpte)
(TELD) **0630-11470-2** The Best of Barbara Bonney
(TELD) **4509-93691-2** Queen of Coloratura
(TELD) **4509-97505-2** Mozart—Famous Opera Choruses
(TELD) **4509-97507-2** Mozart—Famous Opera Arias
cond R. WEIKERT
Zemlinsky: Kleider machen Leute (Cpte)

ZURICH TONHALLE ORCHESTRA
cond H. KNAPPERTSBUSCH
(PREI) **90083** Maria Reining
(PREI) **90189** Knappertsbusch in London and Switzerland
(PREI) **90190** Paul Schoeffler—Recital
cond J. KRIPS
(ADES) **13225-2** Mozart—Overtures
cond F. PATANÈ
(BELA) **450 005-2** Famous Tenor Arias
(DECC) **433 066-2DWO** Your Hundred Best Opera Tunes III
(DECC) **433 623-2DSP** Famous Tenor Arias
(DECC) **436 463-2DM** Ten Top Tenors
(DECC) **440 403-2DM** Giuseppe di Stefano
cond G. PATANÈ
(DECC) **436 314-2DA** Great Tenor Arias

ZWEIG, Fritz (cond)
see Berlin City Op Orch
Berlin SO
Berlin St Op Orch
orch

ZYLIS-GARA, Teresa (sop)
Chausson: Roi Arthus (Cpte)
Mozart: Don Giovanni (Cpte)
R. Strauss: Ariadne auf Naxos (Cpte)
(MEMO) **HR4223/4** Nicolai Ghiaurov

Concert index

ABC Classics

Ⓓ **8 7000 10** (10/95)
Rita Hunter—Opera Arias
Verdi: Aida (exc); Macbeth (exc); Forza del destino (exc); Ballo in maschera (exc); *Ponchielli:* Gioconda (exc); *Puccini:* Madama Butterfly (exc); Tosca (exc); *Beethoven:* Fidelio (exc); *Mozart:* Idomeneo (exc); Nozze di Figaro (exc). (R. Hunter, Tasmanian SO/D. Franks)

Academy Collection

Ⓓ **ACDM6** ▭ **MC-ACDM6**
Beethoven—Symphony No 6.Leonore Overture
Beethoven: Symphony 6; Leonore (exc). (LPO/R. Armstrong)

Acanta

Ⓓ **ACAN44 2128-2** (7/93)
R. Strauss—Elektra
R. Strauss: Elektra (Cpte). (E. Schlüter, G. Hammer, A. Kupper, P. Markwort, R. Hager, G. Neidlinger, E. Schwier, K. Lange, F. Göllnitz, H. Siegel, C. Autenrieth, M. von Ilosvay, H. Gura, M. Wulf, L. Bischof, S. Mirtsch, Hamburg St Op Chor, Hamburg PO/E. Jochum)

Ⓓ **43 121** (2/89)
Wagner: Orchestral Works
Wagner: Tannhäuser (exc); Parsifal (exc); Walküre (exc); Siegfried (exc); Götterdämmerung (exc); Tristan und Isolde (exc); Tristan und Isolde (exc). (VPO, BPO, Rome RAI Orch, La Scala Orch, LPO, Berlin St Op Orch/W. Furtwängler)

Ⓓ **43 123**
Peter Dvorský sings Puccini Arias
Puccini: Bohème (exc); Manon Lescaut (exc); Turandot (exc); Tosca (exc); Tosca (exc); Madama Butterfly (exc). (F.I. d'Amico, P. Dvorský, I. Gáti, Berlin RSO, Budapest Op Orch/R. Paternostro/A. Mihály)

Ⓓ **43 266** (3/89)
Bernd Weikl—Operatic Recital
Wagner: Tannhäuser (exc); Meistersinger (exc); *Marschner:* Hans Heiling (exc); Vampyr (exc); *Weber:* Euryanthe (exc); *Lortzing:* Zar und Zimmermann (exc); *Albert:* Tiefland (exc); *R. Strauss:* Feuersnot (exc). (B. Weikl, Munich RO/H. Wallberg, E. Marton, R. Kollo, Bavarian Rad Chor/M. Janowski, J. Varady/H. Fricke)

Ⓓ **43 267** (10/89)
Fritz Wunderlich sings Opera Arias
Mozart: Zauberflöte (exc); Zaïde (exc); *Cornelius:* Barbier von Bagdad (exc); *Lortzing:* Undine (exc); Waffenschmied (exc); *Kienzl:* Kuhreigen (exc); *Schubert:* Fierrabras (exc); *Beethoven:* Fidelio (exc). (F. Wunderlich, K. Böhme, H.G. Nöcker, Stuttgart Rad Chor, Stuttgart RSO/C. Schuricht/A. Rischner/H. Müller-Kray, Berne St Orch)

43 268 (8/93)
Peter Anders sings German Opera Arias
Weber: Freischütz (exc); *Beethoven:* Fidelio (exc); Fidelio (exc); *Wagner:* Lohengrin (exc); *Mozart:* Zauberflöte (exc); Zauberflöte (exc); Entführung (exc); Entführung (exc); *Flotow:* Martha (exc); *Lortzing:* Undine (exc); *Nicolai:* Lustigen Weiber von Windsor (exc); *Kienzl:* Evangelimann (exc); *Wagner:* Meistersinger (exc). (P. Anders, W. Wegner, T. Eipperle, M. Fuchs, G. Hann, E. Berger, H. Hotter, B. Kusche, South-West German RSO, N German RSO, Berlin RSO, Cologne RSO, Berlin Deutsche Op Orch, Berlin Staatskapelle, Berlin St Op Orch, ROHO/O. Ackermann/H. Schmidt-Isserstedt/A. Rother/R. Kraus/A. Grüber/K. Schmidt/J. Schüler/T. Beecham/R. Heger)

Ⓓ **43 327**
Bernd Weikl—Operatic Arias
Verdi: Trovatore (exc); Forza del destino (exc); Traviata (exc); Don Carlo (exc); Otello (exc); Rigoletto (exc); Ballo in maschera (exc); Macbeth (exc). (B. Weikl, Munich RO/H. Wallberg)

Ⓓ **43 540**
Opera Choruses
Bellini: Norma (exc); *Donizetti:* Don Pasquale (exc); *Verdi:* Nabucco (exc); Lombardi (exc); Macbeth (exc); Trovatore (exc); *Puccini:* Madama Butterfly (exc); Turandot (exc); *Leoncavallo:* Pagliacci (exc); *Mascagni:* Cavalleria Rusticana (exc). (Fiesole School of Music Female Chor, MMF Chor, MMF Orch/M. Arena)

Ⓓ **43 801** (6/87)
Elisabeth Schwarzkopf—Wartime Recordings
Rameau: Hippolyte et Aricie (exc); *Leveridge:* Old English Melodies (exc); *M. Arne:* Lass with the Delicate Air; *G. Sammartini:* Weisse Schäfchen; *Gluck:* Rencontre imprévue (exc); *Mozart:* Oiseaux, si tous les ans, K307; Verschweigung, K518; *Beethoven:* Geheimnis, WoO145; *Schubert:* An den Frühling, D587; *Schumann:* Lieder und Gesänge, Op. 51 (exc); *Brahms:* Lieder, Op. 97 (exc); *Reger:* Wiegenlied, Op.142/1; *Verdi:* Romanze (1845) (exc); *R. Strauss:* Lieder, Op. 29 (exc); *Loewe:* Liedergabe, Op. 130 (exc); *Zilcher:* Rococo Suite; *Trunk:* Hemd; Allee; *Traditional:* 's Schätzli; O du liebs Ängeli; Beruhigte; Z' Lauterbach han; *Rossini:* Soirées musicales (exc). (E. Schwarzkopf, G. Scheck, P. Richartz, A. Steiner, M. Raucheisen)

Ⓓ **44 2085-2**
Carl Orff Collection
Orff: Carmina Burana; Catulli Carmina; Trionfo di Afrodite; Orpheus (Cpte); Klage der Ariadne; Tanz der Spröden (Cpte); Prometheus (Cpte). (R-M. Pütz, E. Tarrès, B. Dürrler, R. Wageman, D. Grobe, M. Cousins, B. McDaniel, R. Hermann, H. Laubenthal, H.G. Nöcker, H. Prey, L. Popp, R. Wageman, K. Ridderbusch, C. Orff, L. Popp, R. Wageman, K. Ridderbusch, H. Schwarz, R. Hermann, J. Greindl, H. Cramer, K. Engen, E. Moser, S. van Sante, C. Lorand, F. Uhl, Tolz Boys' Ch, Cologne Rad Chor, Bavarian Rad Chor, W German Rad Chor, Cologne RSO/F. Leitner, Munich RSO/K. Eichhorn)

Ⓓ **44 2089-2**
Orff—Orpheus
Orff: Orpheus (Cpte). (H. Prey, L. Popp, R. Wageman, K. Ridderbusch, C. Orff, Bavarian Rad Chor, Munich RSO/K. Eichhorn)

Ⓓ **44 2090-2**
Orff—Klage der Ariadne/Tanz de Spröden
Orff: Klage der Ariadne; Tanz der Spröden (Cpte). (R. Wagemann, L. Popp, R. Wageman, K. Ridderbusch, H. Schwarz, Bavarian Rad Chor, Munich RSO/K. Eichhorn)

Ⓓ **44 2099-2**
Orff—Prometheus
Orff: Prometheus (Cpte). (R. Hermann, J. Greindl, H. Cramer, K. Engen, E. Moser, S. van Sante, C. Lorand, F. Uhl, W German Rad Chor, Cologne RSO/F. Leitner)

Ⓓ **44 2100-2**
Knappertsbusch conducts Wagner
Wagner: Parsifal (exc); Götterdämmerung (exc). (E. Larcen, C. Hartmann, H. Reinmar, L. Weber, Berlin Deutsche Op Chor, Berlin Deutsche Op Orch, VPO/H. Knappertsbusch)

Ⓓ **49 384** (11/88)
Puccini: Opera Arias and Duets
Puccini: Gianni Schicchi (exc); Gianni Schicchi (exc); Manon Lescaut (exc); Manon Lescaut (exc); Bohème (exc); Bohème (exc); Madama Butterfly (exc); Madama Butterfly (exc); Turandot (exc). (M. Freni, F. Bonisolli, Hamburg PO/L. Magiera)

Ⓓ **49 390**
Placido Domingo sings Zarzuela Arias
Moreno Torroba: Luisa Fernanda (exc); Chulapona (exc); *Soriano:* Guitarrico (exc); *Soutullo:* Leyenda del beso (exc); Ultimo romantico (exc); *Serrano:* Los de Aragón (exc); Trust de los tenorios (exc); *Vives:* Doña Francisquita (exc); *Guerrero y Torres:* Huésped del Sevillano (exc); *Luna:* Pícara molinera (exc). (P. Domingo, Barcelona SO/G. Navarro)

Ⓓ **49 402**
Giuseppe Taddei—Recital
Donizetti: Elisir d'amore (exc); *Rossini:* Cenerentola (exc); *Mozart:* Nozze di Figaro (exc); *Verdi:* Luisa Miller (exc); Traviata (exc); Otello (exc); *Puccini:* Tosca (exc). (G. Taddei, L. Pavarotti, M. Smith, B. Daniels, H. Wildhaber, Vienna St Op Chor, Vienna St Op Orch/N. Bareza/R. Abbado/K. Böhm/A. Erede/A. Guadagno/A. Fischer, P. Domingo)

Accent

Ⓓ **ACC48223/4D** (1/90)
Gluck—Orfeo ed Euridice
Gluck: Orfeo ed Euridice (Cpte). (R. Jacobs, M. Kweksilber, M. Falewicz, Ghent Collegium Vocale, Petite Bande/S. Kuijken)

Ⓓ **ACC48434D** ▭ **MC-ACC8434**
Beethoven—Wind ensemble arrangements
Beethoven: Symphony 7; Fidelio (exc). (Octophoros)

Ⓓ **ACC57802D** (8/85)
Purcell: Songs and Elegies
Purcell: St Cecilia's Day Ode, Z328 (exc); Oedipus, Z583 (exc); King Richard II, Z581 (exc); Dioclesian, Z627 (exc); Pious Celinda, Z410; Queen's Epicedium, Z383; Ah! cruel nymph, Z352; Fatal hour comes on apace, Z421; Old Bachelor, Z607 (exc); Pausanias, Z585 (exc); I lov'd fair Celia, Z381; Young Thirsis' fate, Z473. (R. Jacobs, W. Kuijken, K. Junghänel)

Ⓓ **ACC8746/7D** (10/88)
Landi—Mort d'Orfeo
Landi: Mort d'Orfeo (Cpte). (J. Elwes, J. Koslowsky, D. Cordier, M. Chance, M. Kroese, W. Jochens, N. van der Meel, H. van der Kamp, L. Deroo, Currende Voc Ens, Tragicomedia, S. Stubbs)

Ⓓ **ACC9296/8D** (2/94)
Mozart—Così fan tutte
Mozart: Così fan tutte (Cpte). (S. Isokoski, M. Groop, N. Argenta, M. Schäfer, P. Vollestad, H. Claessens, Petite Bande Chor, Petite Bande/S. Kuijken)

Accord

Ⓓ **20116-2**
Dusapin—Romeo & Juliette
Dusapin: Romeo and Juliet (Cpte). (F. Kubler, N. Isherwood, C. Gerstenhaber, J. Combey, O. Cadiot, P. Sausy, France Groupe Vocal, Rhin-Mulhouse SO/L. Pfaff)

Ⓓ **20119-2**
Massé—Les Noces de Jeannette
Massé: Noces de Jeannette (Cpte). (R. Doria, L. Huberty, Pasdeloup Ass Orch/J. Allain)

Ⓓ **22086-2** (11/90)
Boïeldieu: La Dame Blanche
Boïeldieu: Dame blanche (Cpte). (A. Legros, F. Louvay, M. Sénéchal, A. Doniat, J. Berbié, G. Baudoz, P. Héral, Paris Sym Chor, Paris SO/P. Stoll)

Adès

Ⓓ **13203-2**
Weber—Overtures
Weber: Euryanthe (exc); Preciosa (exc); Jubel-Ouverture; Oberon (exc); Abu Hassan (exc); Peter Schmoll (exc). (Paris Op Orch/H. Scherchen)

Ⓓ **13208-2**
Offenbach—Les Contes d'Hoffmann
Offenbach: Contes d'Hoffmann (exc). (A. Lance, S. Sarroca, R. Massard, J. Giovannetti, S. Michel, R. Andreozzi, Y. Bisson, M. Mesplé, A. Guiot, G. Bacquier, G. Serkoyan, J. Giraudeau, R. Soyer, F. Arrauzau, orch/J. Etcheverry)

Ⓓ **13225-2**
Mozart—Overtures
Mozart: Nozze di Figaro (exc); Don Giovanni (exc); Schauspieldirektor (exc); Zauberflöte (exc); Entführung (exc); Clemenza di Tito (exc); Così fan tutte (exc); Finta Giardiniera (exc); Idomeneo (exc). (Zurich Tonhalle Orch/J. Krips)

Ⓓ **13284-2**
Milhaud—Malheurs d'Orphée/Pauvre matelot
Milhaud: Malheurs d'Orphée (Cpte); Pauvre matelot (Cpte). (J. Cussac, J. Brumaire, S. Verzoub, B. Demigny, A. Vessières, C. Collart, C. Neumann, J. Collard, J. Brumaire, J. Giraudeau, X. Depraz, A. Vessières, Paris Op Orch/D. Milhaud)

Ⓓ **14083-2**
Massenet—Werther
Massenet: Werther (Cpte). (A. Lance, R. Gorr, G. Bacquier, M. Mesplé, J. Giovannetti, R. Andreozzi, J. Mars, FNR Maîtrise, FRNO/J. Etcheverry)

Ⓓ **14122-2**
Music of our Time
Messiaen: Chronochromie; *Boulez:* Marteau sans Maître; *Cage:* Daughters of the Lonesome Isle (1945); *Schaeffer:* Symphonie pour un homme seul; *Xenakis:* Metastasis; Nuits; *Stockhausen:* Klavierstücke (exc); *Dutilleux:* Métaboles; *Ohana:* Sybille; *Berio:* Sinfonia; *Lutoslawski:* Livre pour Orchestre; *Boucourechliev:* Anarchipel; *Ligeti:* Grand Macabre (exc). (FNO/M. Rosenthal, J. Deroubaix, Inst Ens/P. Boulez, G. Fremy, P. Schaeffer, P. Henry, South-West German RSO/H. Rosbaud, ORTF Chor/M. Couraud, C.R. Alsina/J. Martinon, I. Garcisanz, B. Balet, Sinfonia Sngrs, PSO/L. Berio, Polish Radio & TV SO/J. Krenz, I. Nielsen, O. Fredricks, P. Haage, D. Weller, French Rad New PO/G. Amy)

Ⓓ **14166-2**
Piano Music by the Group of Five
Mussorgsky: Pictures; *Rimsky-Korsakov:* Tale of Tsar Saltan (exc); Pieces, Op. 11; B-A-C-H Variations, Op. 10; *Balakirev:* Islamey; *Borodin:* Petite Suite; *Cui:* Miniatures, Op. 39. (B. Ringeissen)

Akademia

Ⓓ **2CDAK123** (11/94)
Rossini—Torvaldo e Dorliska
Rossini: Torvaldo e Dorliska (Cpte). (E. Palacio, F. Pediconi, S. Antonucci, M. Buda, N. Ciliento, A. Marani, Cantemus, Lugano Rad & TV Ch, Lugano Rad & TV Orch/M. de Bernart)

Albany

Ⓓ **TROY015-2** (8/89) ▭ **TROY015-4**
G. Lloyd—Orchestral Works
G. Lloyd: Symphony 6; Symphony 10; John Socman (exc). (BBC PO, BBC Phil Brass/G. Lloyd)

Ⓓ **TROY017-2** (4/90)
Virgil Thomson—Vocal and Orchestral Works
V. Thomson: Symphony on a Hymn Tune; Symphony 2; Lord Byron (exc); Shipwreck and Love Scene; Solemn Music; Joyful Fugue. (M. Hill, Monadnock Fest Orch, Budapest SO/J. Bolle)

Ⓓ **TROY023-2**
Music of Joseph Fennimore
Fennimore: Eventide (Cpte); Berlitz; Inscape; Winterlove; Mary Weeps for Her Child; Snow Grew out of the Sky; Infant Joy; Now Death has Shut Your Eyes; My Heart. (K. Williams, H. Johnsson, P. Creech, Chelsea Chbr Ens/T. Rolek, K. Williams, J. Castle, J. Fennimore)

Ⓓ **TROY025/6-2** (6/90)
R. Ward—Crucible
R. Ward: Crucible (Cpte). (J. Ebert, N. Kelly, G. Wynder, P. Brooks, N. Farr, P. Ukena, E. Alberts, S. Malas, M. Stern, C. Ludgin, J. Macurdy, F. Bible, N. Foster, R. Krause, J. DeLon, L. Ceniceros, H. Guile, M. Kova, E. Schwering, B. Evans, NYC Op Orch/E. Buckley)

Ⓓ **TROY068-2**
William Mayer—Voices from Lost Realms
W. Mayer: Death in the Family (exc); Kyrie; First Song; Passage (exc); Madrigals; Abandoned Bells; Fern Hill; Belle Dame; Enter Ariel; One Christmas (exc); Inner and Outer Strings. (E. Poore, J. Bryden, J. Christin, M. Feinsinger, G. Mercer, J. McKeel, P. Dunkel, R. Goldsmith, C. Stier, M. Coid, P. Hosford, S. Mayer, S. Shames, Florilegium Chbr Ch, New Calliope Sngrs/P. Schubert/J. Rice, Music Today Stg Orch/G. Schwarz)

Ⓓ **TROY091-2**
Lawrence Rapchak—The Lifework of Juan Diaz
Rapchak: Lifework of Juan Diaz (Cpte). (R. Hovencamp, C. Loverde, R. Alderson, D. Rowader, J. Whitmer, A. Armato, J. Lind, Chicago Chbr Op Orch/L. Rapchak)

Ⓓ **TROY121/3** (9/94)
G. Lloyd—Iernin
G. Lloyd: Iernin. (M. Hill Smith, G. Pogson, H. Herford, M. Rivers, J. Robarts, J. White, S. Jackson, C. Powell, BBC Sngrs, BBC Concert Orch/G. Lloyd)

Ⓓ **TROY127-2** (10/95)
Purcell—From Rosy Bow'rs
Purcell: St Cecilia's Day Ode, Z328 (exc); Birthday Ode, Z323 (exc); Fairy Queen, Z629 (exc); Don Quixote, Z578 (exc); Dioclesian, Z627 (exc); Tyrannic Love, Z613 (exc); Tempest, Z631 (exc); Oedipus, Z583 (exc); Indian Queen, Z630 (exc); If music be the food of love, Z379/3; Blessed Virgin's Expostulation, Z196; Evening Hymn, Z193; Hornpipes (exc); Choice Collection of Lessons (exc); Musick's hand-maid, Part 2 (exc). (S. Sanford, B. Wissick, B. Wissick, R. Erickson, R. Erickson)

Ⓓ **TROY131-2** (1/95)
G.Lloyd—John Socman-Highlights
G. Lloyd: John Socman (exc). (D. Wilson-Johnson, T. Booth, J. Watson, D. Montague, J. Winfield, M. George, M. Rivers, P. Sheffield, S. Adler, London Voices, Trinity Boy's Ch, Philh/G. Lloyd)

Ⓓ **TROY146-2** (11/95)
Antheil—Piano Works
Antheil: Airplane Sonata; Sonata sauvage; Femme 100 Têtes (exc); Little Shimmy; Transatlantic (exc); Piano Sonata 4; Valentine Waltzes. (M. Verbit)

Alta Nova

Ⓓ **CDAN3**
Hjördis Schymberg
Mozart: Zauberflöte (exc); *Puccini:* Bohème (exc); Bohème (exc); *Mozart:* Nozze di Figaro (exc); *Massenet:* Manon (exc); *Verdi:* Rigoletto (exc); Rigoletto (exc); *J. Strauss II:* Frühlingsstimmen, Op. 410; *Puccini:* Madama Butterfly (exc); *Mozart:* Così fan tutte (exc); *Alfvén:* Songs, Op.28 (exc); *Verdi:* Traviata (exc). (H. Schymberg, J. Björling, L. Warren, T. Altman, J. Peerce, A. Hegert-Tibell, T. Ralf, S. Björling, NY Met Op Chor, NY Met Op Orch/C. Sodero, Swedish RSO, Stockholm Royal Orch/N. Grevillius/H. Alfvén/T. Mann)

Ambitus

Ⓓ **amb97865**
English Renaissance & Baroque Works
A. Holborne: Almain 'The Honiesuckle'; Mens innovata; Night Watch; Patiencia; Choise; *Farnaby:* Old Spagnoletta; His rest; Tell mee Daphne; Toye; Giles Farnaby - His Dreame; New Sa-hoo; *Coleman:* Sackbut Suite; *Henry VIII:* It is to me a ryght gret joy; Adew Madam et ma mastres; Pastyme with good companye; Departure is my chef payne; En vray amoure; *Purcell:* Funeral Sentences (exc); March and Canzona, Z860; Viola da gamba fantasias, Z732-4 (exc); Indian Queen, Z630 (exc); *Dowland:* Lachrimae (exc); *Locke:* Musick for His Majesty's Cornetts and Sackbutts; *Boyce:* Voluntaries (exc). (G. Reiche Consort)

Amon Ra

Ⓓ **CD-SAR11** ▭ **CSAR11** (5/84)
Music for Two Flutes
Bach: Trio Sonatas, BWV1036-9 (exc); *Handel:* Trio Sonatas, Op 2 (exc); *Haydn:* Flute Trio, HobIV/1; *Mozart:* Nozze di Figaro (exc); *Drouet:* Paisiello Variations; *Kohler:* Valse des fleurs, Op. 87. (Preston's Pocket)

Ⓓ **CD-SAR28** (3/88) ▭ **CSAR28**
John Playford's Popular Tunes
Playford: English Dancing Master, Part One (exc); English Dancing Master, Part Two (exc); English Dancing Master, Appendix (exc); Musick's Delight (exc); Musick's Recreation (exc); Musick's Hande-maide (exc); *Gay:* Beggar's Opera (exc). (Broadside Band)

Ⓓ **CD-SAR50**
Now What is Love?
Robert Jones: Second Booke of Songs (exc); *Rossi:* Guardatevi olà; *Anon:* Occhi Belli; *Piccinini:* Intavolatura di liuto libro primo (exc); *Striggio:* Se più del canto mio; *Dowland:* First Book of Songs (exc); Pavans (exc); *Danyel:* Songs for the Lute (exc); *Moulinié:* Enfin la beauté; *Bataille:* Ma bergère non légère; *Guédron:* Cessés mortels de soupirer; *Purcell:* Love arms himself, Z392; Fairy Queen, Z629 (exc); *N. Matteis I:* Suite in D. (G. Simpson, B. Mason, B. Mason, B. Mason)

Amphion

Ⓓ **PHICD123** ▭ **PHI123**
Celebration of Piano Music from Castle Howard
Chopin: Waltzes (exc); *Schumann:* Kinderszenen (exc); *Gershwin:* Preludes (exc); *Debussy:* Suite Bergamasque (exc); *Rossini:* Péchés de Vieillesse X (exc); *Granados:* Goyescas (exc); *MacDowell:* Woodland Sketches (exc); *Brahms:* Hungarian Dances (exc); *Beethoven:* Bagatelles (exc); *Joplin:* Elite Syncopations; *Grieg:* Folksongs, Op. 66 (exc); *Tchaikovsky:* Album for the young (exc); *Coleridge Taylor:* Negro Melodies (exc); *Liszt:* Années de pèlerinage 1 (exc); *Schubert:* Impromptus (exc); *Alkan:* Préludes, Op. 31 (exc); *Mendelssohn:* Songs without Words (exc); *Liadov:* Musical Snuffbox, Op. 32; *Mozart:* Minuet, K355; *Gottschalk:* Bananier; *Gluck:* Orfeo ed Euridice (exc); *Scriabin:* Etudes, Op. 8 (exc); *Daquin:* Premier livre de pièces de clavecin (exc). (A. Goldstone)

▭ **PHI120**
Organ at Sledmere House, played by Francis Jackson
Handel: Solomon (exc); Berenice (exc); Water Music (exc); *Vierne:* Pièces en stile libre (exc); Suite 3 (exc); Suite 2 (exc); *Schumann:* Pedal Studies, Op. 56 (exc); *Whitlock:* Pieces for organ; *Wolstenholme:* Handel Sonata. (F. Jackson)

Applecross Productions

Ⓓ **APC003**
Classical Organ Music
Mozart: Fantasia, K608; *Haydn:* Flute-clock pieces, HobXIX (exc); *C.P.E. Bach:* Organ Sonata, H87; *Clarke:* Suite in D (exc); *Purcell:* Choice Collection of Lessons (exc); *Bach:* Trio Sonatas, BWV525-530 (exc); *Handel:* Serse (exc); *Mozart:* Adagio and Allegro, K594. (G. Revell)

APR

Ⓓ **APR7014** (1/93)
Romantic Piano Rarities, Vol.2
Chopin: Mazurkas (exc); Preludes (exc); Etudes (exc); Etudes (exc); Waltzes (exc); Mazurkas (exc); Mazurkas (exc); Berceuse; Etudes (exc); Polonaises (exc); Impromptus (exc); Nocturnes (exc); *Liszt:* Concert Studies, S145 (exc); *Chopin:* Etudes (exc); Waltzes (exc); *Rachmaninov:* Polka de W.R.; *D. Scarlatti:* Keyboard Sonatas (exc); *Chopin:* Scherzos (exc); Impromptus (exc); Waltzes (exc); *Liszt:* Concert Studies, S144 (exc); Concert Studies, S145 (exc); *Scriabin:* Etudes, Op.8 (exc); *Gluck:* Orfeo ed Euridice (exc); *Chopin:* Waltzes (exc); Waltzes (exc); Etudes (exc); *Moszkowski:* Jongleuse, Op.52/4; *Liszt:* Hungarian Rhapsodies, S244 (exc); *Levitzki:* Valse, Op.1; Waltz, Op.2; *Tchaikovsky:* Seasons (exc); *Liszt:* Paganini Studies, S140 (exc); *D. Scarlatti:* Keyboard Sonatas (exc); *Chopin:* Mazurkas (exc); *Liszt:* Paganini Studies, S140 (exc); Valses oubliées, S215 (exc); *Debussy:* Children's Corner (exc); *Dohnányi:* Concert Etudes, Op.28 (exc); *Horowitz:* Moment exotique; Carmen Variations; *Chopin:* Piano Sonata 2 (exc). (I. Friedman, S. Barere, M. Levitzki, V. Horowitz)

Ⓓ **APR7015** (12/91)
The Auer Legacy, Vol.1
Tchaikovsky: Souvenir d'un lieu cher, Op.42 (exc); *Brahms:* Hungarian Dances (exc); *Paganini:* Moto perpetuo, Op.11; *Bach:* Suites, BWV1066-9 (exc); *Chopin:* Nocturnes (exc); *Halvorsen:* Danses norvégiennes (exc); Mosaïques (exc); *Brahms:* Hungarian Dances (exc); *Cui:* Suite Miniature 1 (exc); *Vieuxtemps:* Morceaux de salon, Op.32 (exc); *Wieniawski:* Kujawiak in A minor; *Hubay:* Scènes de la Csárda (exc); *Godard:* Morceaux, Op.128 (exc); *Brahms:* Hungarian Dances (exc); *Sarasate:* Danzas españolas (exc); *Fauré:* Berceuse, Op.16; *Hubay:* Scènes de la Csárda; *Schubert:* Violin Sonata, D408; *Hubay:* Blumenleben, Op.30 (exc); *C. Böhm:* Pieces, Op.314

(exc); *Wieniawski:* Souvenir de Moscou, Op.6; *Brüll:* Morceaux, Op.90 (exc); *Tchaikovsky:* Souvenir d'un lieu cher, Op.42 (exc); *Chopin:* Nocturnes (exc); *Drigo:* Arlekinda (exc); Arlekinda (exc); *Sammartini:* Sonatas, Op.1 (exc); *Schumann:* Waldszenen (exc); *Grieg:* Lyric Pieces, Op.54 (exc); *Beethoven:* Contredanses, WoO14 (exc); *T. Moore:* Irish Melodies (exc); *Dvořák:* Humoresques, Op.101 (exc); *F. Schubert II:* Bagatelles, Op.13 (exc); *Wieniawski:* Scherzo-tarantelle, Op.16; *Elgar:* Capricieuse; *Glazunov:* Méditation, Op.32; *Sarasate:* Danzas españolas (exc); *Bazzini:* Ronde des lutins; *Moszkowski:* Pieces, Op.45 (exc); *Clérambault:* Largo in C minor; *Godowsky:* Triakontameron (exc); *Rimsky-Korsakov:* Tale of Tsar Saltan (exc). (L. Auer, W. Bogutskahein, K. Parlow, Anon, C. Hansen, B. Zakharoff, I. Menges, H. Harty, E. Beattie, A. de Greef, M. Elman, P. Kahn, J. Bonime, A. Loesser, J. Heifetz, A. Benoist, E. Bay)

Ⓓ **APR7016** (7/93)
The Auer Legacy, Vol.2
Zimbalist: Slavonic Dances (exc); Slavonic Dances (exc); *Aulin:* Aquarelles (exc); *Cui:* Kaleydoskop (exc); *Saint-Saëns:* Déluge (exc); *Glinka:* Farewell to St Petersburg (exc); Ruslan and Lyudmila (exc); *Chopin:* Waltzes (exc); *Saint-Saëns:* Carnaval des animaux (exc); *Chopin:* Waltzes (exc); *Macmillen:* Causerie; *Randegger:* Bohemian Dance; Saltarello-caprice; *Henri:* Légende amoureuse; *Lederer:* Poèmes hongroise (exc); *Bach:* Solo Violin Partitas and Sonatas (exc); *Gluck:* Orfeo ed Euridice (exc); *Rimsky-Korsakov:* Tale of Tsar Saltan (exc); *Paganini:* Violin Concerto 2 (exc); *Chopin:* Nocturnes (exc); *Liszt:* Consolations, S172 (exc); *Smetana:* From the Homeland (exc); *Wieniawski:* Violin Concerto 2 (exc); Polonaise, Op.4; *Cui:* Kaleydoskop (exc); *Ambrosio:* Canzonetta 1; *Kreisler:* Liebesfreud; *Rimsky-Korsakov:* Scheherazade (exc); *Wagner:* Albumblatt; *Brahms:* Hungarian Dances (exc); *Provost:* Intermezzo; *Kuzdo:* Pieces, Op.25 (exc); *Durand:* Chaconne, Op.62; *Traditional:* Turkey in the straw; *MacDowell:* Woodland Sketches (exc); *Grieg:* Violin Sonata 2; *Handel:* Keyboard Suites Set I (exc); *Sarasate:* Navarra; *Léonard:* Scènes humoristiques (exc). (E. Zimbalist, F. Macmillen, N. Milstein, T. Seidel, E. Brown, F. Moore, M. Rabinovitch, E. Kusmiak, J. Zayde, C. Adler, B. Rabinof, orch, anon, S. Chotzinoff, E. Bay, G. Moore, L. Mittman, H. Kaufman, J. Bonime, M. Katims, M. Mischakoff, R. Totenberg)

Ⓓ **APR7020** (6/92)
Mischa Levitzki—The Complete HMV Recordings, 1927-33
Chopin: Preludes (exc); Waltzes (exc); Ballades (exc); Nocturnes (exc); Nocturnes (exc); Scherzos (exc); Polonaises (exc); *D. Scarlatti:* Keyboard Sonatas (exc); *Gluck:* Iphigénie en Aulide (exc); *Beethoven:* Ecossaise, WoO86; *Schubert:* Marches Militaires, D733 (exc); *Rubinstein:* Studies, Op.23 (exc); *Mendelssohn:* Rondo capriccioso; *Schumann:* Piano Sonata 2; *Liszt:* Piano Concerto 1; Preludes and Fugue, S462 (exc); Concert Studies, S144 (exc); Paganini Studies, S140 (exc); Hungarian Rhapsodies, S244 (exc); Hungarian Rhapsodies, S244 (exc); *Moszkowski:* Jongleuse, Op.52/4; *Rachmaninov:* Preludes (exc); *Levitzki:* Waltz, Op.2. (M. Levitzki, LSO/L. Ronald)

Ⓓ **APR7027** (8/95)
Egon Petri, Vol.3
Schubert: Divertissement, D823 (exc); *Chopin:* Preludes (exc); *Franck:* Prélude, choral et fugue; *Gluck:* Orfeo ed Euridice (exc); *Bach:* Applicatio, BWV841-843; Orgel-Büchlein, BWV599-644 (exc); Schübler Chorales, BWV645-650 (exc); Nun freut euch, BWV734a; *Busoni:* Bach Fantasia; *Mozart:* Don Giovanni (exc); *Busoni:* An die Jugend (exc); Sonatina 3; Sonatina 6; Indianisches Tagebuch; Albumblätter (exc); Elegien (exc). (E. Petri)

Ⓓ **APR7028** (12/94)
Jacques Thibaud—Complete Solo Recordings 1929-36
Saint-Saëns: Déluge (exc); *Falla:* Vida breve (exc); *Granados:* Danzas españolas (exc); *Falla:* Canciones populares españolas (exc); *Paradies:* Sicilienne; *Bach:* Concertos, BWV592-7 (exc); *Mozart:* Piano Concerto 21 (exc); *Lalo:* Fantaisie norvégienne; *H. Eccles:* Violin Sonata; *M. Marsick:* Violin Pieces, Op.6 (exc); *Albéniz:* España, Op.165 (exc); *Poldini:* Marionnettes (exc); *Szymanowski:* Myths, Op.30 (exc); *Saint-Saëns:* Havanaise; *Desplanes:* Intrada; *Vitali:* Ciacona; *Bach:* Solo Violin Partitas and Sonatas (exc); *Mozart:* Serenade, K250 (exc); *Veracini:* Violin Sonatas, Op.2 (exc); *Debussy:* Préludes (exc); *Fauré:* Berceuse, Op.16; *Lalo:* Symphonie espagnole. (J. Thibaud, G. de Lausnay, T. Janopoulo, A. Cortot, SRO/E. Ansermet)

Arabesque

Ⓓ **Z6547**
Herbert—L'Encore
Herbert: Babes in Toyland (exc); Only Girl (exc); Molly; Canzonetta; Fleurette; Punchinello; Royal Sec; Red Mill (exc); Encore; Sweethearts (exc); Veiled Prophet. (T. Ringholz, Eastman-Dryden Orch/D. Hunsberger)

Ⓓ **Z6579** (11/88) ▭ **ABQC6579**
Kurt Weill: Songs
Weill: Walt Whitman Songs (Cpte); Come up from the Fields, Father; Huckleberry Finn (exc); Propaganda Songs (exc); Love Life (exc); Im Volkston; Schöne Kind; Stundenbuch (exc). (S. Kimbrough, D. Baldwin)

Ⓓ **Z6582** (4/88) ▭ **ABQC6582** (4/88)
The Rossini Tenor
Rossini: Barbiere di Siviglia (exc); Comte Ory (exc); Italiana in Algeri (exc); Elisabetta (exc); Turco in Italia (exc); Donna del Lago (exc). (R. Blake, Ambrosian Sngrs, LSO/J. McCarthy)

Ⓓ **Z6598** (3/89) ▭ **ABQC6598** (3/89)
Rockwell Blake, the Mozart Tenor
Mozart: Mitridate (exc); Misero! o sogno, K431; Don Giovanni (exc); Idomeneo (exc); Entführung (exc); Così fan tutte (exc); Clemenza di Tito (exc). (R. Blake, LSO/N. McGegan)

Ⓓ **Z6612** (12/89) ▭ **ABQC6612** (12/89)
Rossini: Opera Arias
Rossini: Zelmira (exc); Ermione (exc); Semiramide (exc); Otello (exc); Gazza ladra (exc); Ricciardo e Zoriade (exc); Armida (exc). (R. Blake, P. Jeffes, P. Bronder, Ambrosian Sngrs, LSO/M. Valdes)

Ⓓ **Z8068-2** (11/87)
Sullivan—Pirates of Penzance & The Sorcerer
Sullivan: Pirates of Penzance (Cpte); Sorcerer (exc). (George Baker, P. Dawson, S. Robertson, D. Oldham, L. Sheffield, E. Griffin, N. Briercliffe, N. Walker, D. Gill, D'Oyly Carte Op Chor, SO/M. Sargent, D. Fancourt, D. Oldham, L. Rands, S. Robertson, George Baker, D. Gill, M. Dickson, A. Bethell, A. Moxon/I. Godfrey)

Ⓓ **Z8095-2** (7/89)
Sullivan—Patience & The Gondoliers
Sullivan: Patience (Cpte); Gondoliers (exc). (N. Briercliffe, R. Mackay, W. Lawson, M. Eyre, D. Fancourt, George Baker, L. Rands, D. Oldham, B. Lewis, M. Green, D'Oyly Carte Op Chor, SO/M. Sargent, George Baker, William Booth, S. Granville, D. Oldham, L. Rands, L. Hubbard, S. Robertson, E. Ackland, N. Walker, A. Moxon, M. Dickson, P. Evens, B. Elburn)

Arcana

Ⓓ **A02** (1/93)
Purcell—Ayres and Songs from Orpheus Britannicus
Purcell: Dido (exc); Don Quixote, Z578 (exc); Oedipus, Z583 (exc); Fly swift, ye hours, Z369; Birthday Ode, Z323 (exc); Pausanias, Z585 (exc); Indian Queen, Z630 (exc); Bess of Bedlam, Z370; Spanish Friar, Z610 (exc); What a sad fate is mine, Z428; Tyrannic Love, Z613 (exc); Dioclesian, Z627 (exc); Fairy Queen, Z629 (exc); St Cecilia's Day Ode, Z328 (exc); King Arthur, Z628 (exc); Tempest, Z631 (exc); Bonduca, Z574 (exc); Timon of Athens, Z632 (exc); If music be the food of love, Z379/3. (J. Feldman, N. North, S. Cunningham)

Archiphon

Ⓓ **ARC102** (5/94)
Kleiber conducts Waltzes and Overtures
Weber: Invitation to the Dance; *J. Strauss II:* Accelerationen, Op.234; Zigeunerbaron (exc); Du und Du, Op.367; Künstlerleben, Op. 316; *Rezniček:* Donna Diana (exc); *Heuberger:* Opernball (exc); *J. Strauss II:* Wein, Weib und Gesang; Kaiser, Op. 437; Blauen Donau, Op.314. (BPO, VPO, Berlin St Op Orch/E. Kleiber)

Ⓓ **ARC112/3** (10/95)
Dinu Lipatti—Les Inédits
Liszt: Piano Concerto 1; *Enescu:* Piano Sonata 1 (exc); *Brahms:* Piano Pieces, Op.117 (exc); Piano Pieces, Op.116 (exc); *Bach:* Cantata 147 (exc); *D. Scarlatti:* Keyboard Sonatas (exc); *Chopin:* Etudes (exc); *Schumann:* Symphonic Studies (exc); *Liszt:* Concert Studies, S145 (exc); Concert Studies, S144 (exc); *Fauré:* Songs, Op.7 (exc); *Ravel:* Pièce en forme de Habanera; *Rimsky-Korsakov:* Tale of Tsar Saltan (exc); *Chopin:* Etudes (exc); *Bartók:* Piano Concerto 3 (exc); *Lipatti:* Piano Concertino; Romanian Dances; Symphonie Concertante; Tziganes. (D. Lipatti, M. Lipatti, B. Siki, A. Janigro, SRO/E. Ansermet, SW German Rad Orch/P. Sacher, orch)

Archiv Produktion

Ⓓ **419 221-2AH2** (8/87)
Purcell—The Fairy Queen
Purcell: Fairy Queen, Z629 (Cpte). (E. Harrhy, J. Smith, J. Nelson, T. Penrose, A. Stafford, W. Evans, M. Hill, S. Varcoe, D. Thomas, Monteverdi Ch, EBS/J.E. Gardiner)

Ⓓ **419 250-2AH2** (12/87)
Monteverdi—Orfeo
Monteverdi: Orfeo (Cpte). (A. Rolfe Johnson, J. Baird, L. Dawson, A.S. von Otter, N. Argenta, M. Nichols, J. Tomlinson, D. Montague, W. White, M. Tucker, N. Robson, M. Chance, S. Birchall, H. Milner, N. Robertson, Monteverdi Ch, EBS, His Majesties Sagbutts and Cornetts/J.E. Gardiner)

Ⓓ **431 674-2AH3** (6/91)
Mozart—Idomeneo
Mozart: Idomeneo (Cpte). (A. Rolfe Johnson, A.S. von Otter, S. McNair, H. Martinpelto, N. Robson, G. Winslade, C. Hauptmann, Monteverdi Ch, EBS/J.E. Gardiner)

Ⓓ **431 806-2AH2** (12/91)
Mozart—La clemenza di Tito
Mozart: Clemenza di Tito (Cpte). (A. Rolfe Johnson, J. Varady, A.S. von Otter, C. Robbin, S. McNair, C. Hauptmann, Monteverdi Ch, EBS/J.E. Gardiner)

Ⓓ **435 490-2AH2** (9/92)
Purcell—King Arthur
Purcell: King Arthur, Z628 (Cpte). (N. Argenta, J. Gooding, L. Perillo, J. MacDougall, M. Tucker, B. Bannatyne-Scott, G. Finley, English Concert Ch, English Concert/T. Pinnock)

Ⓓ **435 857-2AH2** (12/92)
Mozart—Die Entführung aus dem Serail
Mozart: Entführung (Cpte). (L. Orgonášová, C. Sieden, S. Olsen, U. Peper, C. Hauptmann, H-P. Minetti, Monteverdi Ch, EBS/J.E. Gardiner)

Ⓓ **437 556-2AH** (2/94)
Mozart—Thamos, König in Agypten
Mozart: Thamos, K345 (Cpte). (A. Miles, Monteverdi Ch, EBS/J.E. Gardiner)

Ⓓ **437 829-2AH3** (2/94)
Mozart—Così fan tutte
Mozart: Così fan tutte (Cpte). (A. Roocroft, R. Mannion, E. James, R. Trost, R. Gilfry, C. Feller, Monteverdi Ch, EBS/J. E. Gardiner)

Ⓓ **437 994-2AH**
Mozart—Così fan tutte - Highlights
Mozart: Così fan tutte (exc). (A. Roocroft, R. Mannion, E. James, R. Trost, R. Gilfry, C. Nicolai, EBS/J. E. Gardiner)

Ⓓ **439 871-2AH3** (8/94)
Mozart—Le Nozze di Figaro
Mozart: Nozze di Figaro (Cpte). (B. Terfel, A. Hagley, R. Gilfry, H. Martinpelto, P. H. Stephen, S. McCulloch, C. Feller, F. Egerton, J. Clarkson, C. Backes, Monteverdi Ch, EBS/J. E. Gardiner)

Ⓓ **445 853-2AH3** (9/95)
Rameau—Hippolyte et Aricie
Rameau: Hippolyte et Aricie (Cpte). (J-P. Fouchécourt, V. Gens, B. Fink, R. Smythe, T. Feighan, A. Massis, L. Naouri, F. Katz, J-L. Georgel, L. Coadou, J-L. Meunier, J-F. Loiseleur des Longchamps, J. Varnier, M. Simon, S. van Dyck, K. Okada, M. Hall, Sagittarius Ens, Musiciens du Louvre/M. Minkowski)

Ⓓ **445 870-2AH3** (8/95)
Mozart—Don Giovanni
Mozart: Don Giovanni (Cpte). (R. Gilfry, L. Orgonášová, C. Margiono, E. James, C. Prégardien, I. D'Arcangelo, J. Clarkson, A. Silvestrelli, Monteverdi Ch, EBS/J. E. Gardiner)

Ⓓ **445 874-2AH**
Mozart—Le Nozze di Figaro - Highlights
Mozart: Nozze di Figaro (exc). (B. Terfel, A. Hagley, R. Gilfry, H. Martinpelto, P. H. Stephen, S. McCulloch, C. Feller, F. Egerton, J. Clarkson, C. Backes, Monteverdi Ch, EBS/J. E. Gardiner)

Ⓓ **447 071-2AH2**
Purcell—Dioclesian; Timon of Athens
Purcell: Dioclesian, Z627 (Cpte); Timon of Athens, Z632 (Cpte). (N. Argenta, A. Monoyios, P. Agnew, R. Edgar-Wilson, S. Gadd, S. Birchall, L. Wallington, B. Bannatyne-Scott, C. Foster, English Concert Ch, English Concert/T. Pinnock)

Ⓓ **447 148-2AP** (7/95)
Purcell—Dido and Aeneas
Purcell: Dido (Cpte). (T. Troyanos, B. McDaniel, S. Armstrong, P. Johnson, Margaret Baker, M. Lensky, P. Esswood, N. Rogers, Hamburg Monteverdi Ch, Hamburg NDR CO/C. Mackerras)

Archive Documents

Ⓓ **ADCD109**
Mengelberg Edition - Volume 3
Puccini: Madama Butterfly (exc); *Schubert:* Rosamunde

(exc); Claudine von Villa Bella (exc); Didone abbandonata, D510; *Mozart:* Exsultate jubilate, K165; *Weber:* Oberon (exc); *Bach:* St Matthew Passion, BWV244 (exc). (G. Moore, B. Van den Bosch, R. Ginster, R. Horna, J. Vincent, I. Durigo, K. Erb, W. Ravelli, Amsterdam Toonkunst Ch, Concertgebouw/W. Mengelberg)

Ⓓ **ADCD110** (12/93)
Mengelberg Edition - Volume 4
Stravinsky: Baiser de la Fée (exc); Choral Variations; Perséphone (exc); *Hindemith:* Violin Concerto. (Boston SO, Westminster Ch, V. Zorina, orch/I. Stravinsky, F. Helmann, Concertgebouw/W. Mengelberg)

Ⓓ **ADCD111** (12/93)
Mengelberg Edition - Volume 5
Beethoven: Symphony 7; *Cherubini:* Anacréon (exc); *Mendelssohn:* Midsummer Night's Dream (exc). (BBC SO, Berlin RO, Concertgebouw/W. Mengelberg)

Ⓓ **ADCD115**
Mengelberg Edition, Volume 9
Kodály: Háry János Suite; Peacock Variations; *Ravel:* Daphnis et Chloé Suites (exc). (Concertgebouw/W. Mengelberg)

⊙ **AD105/6** (7/90)
Willem Mengelberg conducts
Liszt: Hungarian Fantasia, S123; *Beethoven:* Symphony 1; Piano Concerto 5; *Schelling:* Victory Ball; *Tchaikovsky:* Marche slave; *Handel:* Alcina (exc). (Breslau RO, Concertgebouw, NYPSO/W. Mengelberg, W. Backhaus, C. de Groot, NYPO)

Argo

Ⓓ **430 200-2ZH** (2/91)
The Emperor's Fanfare
Soler: Emperor's Fanfare; *Wagner:* Tristan und Isolde (exc); *Jongen:* Pièces, Op. 37 (exc); *Bach:* Toccata and Fugue, BWV565; *Albinoni:* Adagio; *Alain:* Litanies; *Schubert:* Ave Maria, D839; *Karg-Elert:* Choral-Improvisationen, Op. 65 (exc); *Grieg:* Sigurd Jorsalfar (exc); *Guilmant:* March, Op. 15. (C. Curley)

Ⓓ **430 275-2ZH2** (12/90)
Delius—A Village Romeo & Juliet
Delius: Village Romeo and Juliet (Cpte). (B. Mora, S. Dean, S. Linay, A. Davies, H. Field, T. Hampson, E. Dobie, K. Barber, P.A. Caya, V. Pirillo, R.L. Demers, J. Antoniou, M. Venuti, S. Lombana, A. Mellis, D. McShane, A. Schoenberg Ch, Austrian RSO/C. Mackerras)

Ⓓ **433 324-2ZH2** (8/92)
Balfe—The Bohemian Girl
Balfe: Bohemian Girl (Cpte). (N. Thomas, P. Power, B. Cullen, J. Summers, T. German, RTE Phil Ch, Ireland National SO/R. Bonynge)

Ⓓ **436 128-2ZH** (8/92)
Moran—Vocal and Chamber Works
Moran: Desert of Roses (exc); Open Veins; Ten Miles High over Albania. (J. West, A. Balanescu, M. Falco, Piano Circus Band/C. Smith/R. Moran)

Ⓓ **436 260-2ZH**
Carlo Curley—Organ Fantasia
Bach: Prelude and fugue, BWV544; *Stanley:* Introduction and Trumpet Tune; *Franck:* Fantaisie in A; *Rubinstein:* Rocky Island (exc); *Beethoven:* Ruinen von Athen (exc); *Pierné:* Pièces, Op. 29; *Dupré:* Vêpres de la Vierge (exc); *Thalben-Ball:* Elegy; *Handel:* Serse (exc); *Holst:* Planets (exc); *Widor:* Symphony 5 (exc). (C. Curley)

Ⓓ **436 850-2ZHO2** (9/93)
Gay/Britten—The Beggar's Opera
Gay: Beggar's Opera (Cpte). (A. Murray, P. Langridge, Y. Kenny, J. Rawnsley, R. Lloyd, A. Collins, N. Willis, C. Gillett, D. Mulholland, Aldeburgh Fest Ch, Aldeburgh Fest Orch/S. Bedford)

Ⓓ **440 213-2ZHO2** (7/93)
Britten—Gloriana
Britten: Gloriana (Cpte). (J. Barstow, P. Langridge, D. Jones, J. Summers, A. Opie, Y. Kenny, R. Van Allan, B. Terfel, J. Watson, W. White, J. Shirley-Quirk, J.M. Ainsley, P. Hoare, WNO Chor, WNO Orch/C. Mackerras)

Ⓓ **440 368-2ZHO** (7/94) ▭ **440 368-4ZHO** (7/94)
Turnage—Greek
Turnage: Greek (Cpte). (Q. Hayes, R. Suart, F. Kimm, H. Charnock, Ens/R. Bernas)

Ⓓ **444 454-2ZH** (7/95)
Dance Mix
Bernstein: West Side Story Symphonic Dances (exc); *J. Adams:* Chairman Dances; *Kernis:* New Era Dance; *Schiff:* Stomp; *Larsen:* Collage: Boogie; *Harbison:* Remembering Gatsby; *Torke:* Black and White (exc); *Moran:* Points of Departure; *Argento:* Dream of Valentino (exc); *Daugherty:* Desi; *Rouse:* Bonham. (Baltimore SO/D. Zinman)

Arion

Ⓓ **ARN368200** (5/94)
Rossini—Tancredi
Rossini: Tancredi (Cpte). (P. Price, H. Francis, K. Lewis, T. McDonnell, E. Stokes, P. Jeffes, London Voices, Centre d'Action Musicale de l'Ouest Orch/J. Perras)

Ⓓ **ARN368220** (9/93)
Auber—Gustave III
Auber: Gustav III (Cpte). (L. Dale, R. Tawil, C. Treguier, B. Lafon, V. Marestin, R. Pujol, G. Dubernet, P. Foucher, F. Leguérinel, Intermezzo Voc Ens, French Lyrique Orch/M. Swierczewski)

Ⓓ **ARN68067**
Rameau—The Glory of 18th Century Dance Music
Rameau: Paladins (exc); Indes Galantes (exc); Platée (exc); Dardanus (exc); Castor et Pollux (exc). (Musicholiers/A. Einhorn)

Ⓓ **ARN68195**
Milhaud—Sonatas; Trois Operas-Minute
Milhaud: Violin Sonata 2; Flute Sonatina; Cello Sonata; Enlèvement d'Europe; Abandon d'Ariane; Déliverance de Thésée. (C. Bonaldi, S. Billier, K. Redel, N. Lee, P. Penassou, J. Robin, M. Masquelin, C. Norrick, C. Calès, G. Garino, B-J. Mura, G. Mauclerc, C. Lara, F. Raynal, J. Laforge Choral Ens, Ars Nova Ens/A. Siranossian)

Ⓓ **ARN68252**
Chabrier—Trois opérettes
Chabrier: Éducation manquée; Fisch-Ton-Kan; Vaucochard et Fils Ier. (M. Delunsch, B. Desnoues, J-L. Georgel, F. Dudziak, C. Mehn, Vocal Ens, Strasbourg Collegium Musicum Orch/R. Delage)

Arlecchino

Ⓓ **ARL23/5**
Rimsky-Korsakov—Sadko
Rimsky-Korsakov: Sadko (Cpte); Sadko (exc); Sadko (exc); Sadko (exc); Sadko (exc); Sadko (exc); Sadko (exc); Sadko (exc); Sadko (exc); Sadko (exc); Sadko (exc); Sadko (exc); Sadko (exc); Sadko (exc); Sadko (exc); Sadko (exc); Sadko (exc); Sadko (exc); Sadko (exc). (G. Nelepp, E. Shumskaya, S. Krasovsky, V. Davydova, E. Antonova, M. Reizen, I. Kozlovsky, P. Lisitsian, S. Koltypin, A. Peregudov, I. Bogdanov, T. Tshernakov, S. Nikolau, Bolshoi Th Chor, Bolshoi Th Orch/N. Golovanov, G. Morskoi, N. Zabela-Vrubel, V. Damaev, S. Druzhiakina, F. Chaliapin, D. Smirnov, I. Gryzunov, A. Nezhdanova, E. Vitting, E. Katulskaya, G. Pozemkovsky, N. Koshetz, N. Obukhova, N. Ozerov, M. Mikhailov, S. Lemeshev, D. Gamrekeli, E. Stepanova, V. Petrov, anon, orch, D. Pokhitonov/B. Seidler-Winkler, U. Mazetti/A. Labinsky, Berlin St Op Orch/F. Weissmann/B. Reibold/L. Steinberg/S. Samosud, All-Union Rad Orch/A. Orlov/V. Nebolsin/A. Lazarev)

Ars Musici

Ⓓ **AMP5014-2**
Schumann/Ravel/R.Strauss—Orchestral Works
Schumann: Symphony 3; *Ravel:* Rapsodie espagnole; Alborada del gracioso; *R. Strauss:* Salome (exc). (German Nat Youth Orch/C. Prick)

AS Discs

Ⓓ **AS311**
Fritz Busch Edition Vol. 1
Schubert: Symphony 9; *Mendelssohn:* Symphony 4; *Beethoven:* Leonore (exc). (Danish RSO/F. Busch)

Astrée

Ⓓ **E8501** (4/93)
Vivaldi—Montezuma
Vivaldi: Montezuma (Cpte). (D. Visse, D. Borst, I. Poulenard, N. Rivenq, B. Balleys, L. Masson, Voc Ens, Grande Ecurie/J-C. Malgoire)

Ⓓ **E8525** (2/95)
Marais—Alcione-Suites
Marais: Alcyone (exc). (Concert des Nations/J. Savall)

Ⓓ **E8527** (4/93)
Lully—Alceste
Lully: Alceste (Cpte). (C. Alliot-Lugaz, J-P. Lafont, H. Crook, S. Marin-Degor, G. Ragon, J-F. Gardeil, F. Loup, G. Reinhart, M. Dens, V. Gens, C. Le Coz, M. Ruggeri, O. Lallouette, D. Nasrawi, Grande Ecurie, Sagittarius Ens, Compagnie Baroccο/J-C. Malgoire)

Ⓓ **E8532** (10/95)
Arriaga—Orchestral Works
Arriaga: Symphony in D; Esclavos felices (exc); Overture, Op. 1. (Concert des Nations, Capella Reial Instr Ens/J. Savall)

Ⓓ **E8538** (1/95)
Gluck—Orfeo ed Euridice
Gluck: Orfeo ed Euridice (Cpte). (J. Bowman, L. Dawson, C. McFadden, Namur Chbr Ch, Grande Ecurie/J-C. Malgoire)

Ⓓ **E8757** (9/93)
Purcell—Songs from Orpheus Britannicus
Purcell: Rival Sisters, Z609 (exc); Fly swift, ye hours, Z369; Gentle Shepherds, Z464; Aureng-Zebe, Z573 (exc); Pausanias, Z585 (exc); I came, I saw, Z375; If music be the food of love, Z379/3; Bess of Bedlam, Z370; Timon of Athens, Z632 (exc); Don Quixote, Z578 (exc); King Arthur, Z628 (exc); Tyrannic Love, Z613 (exc); Fatal hour comes on apace, Z421; O Solitude, Z406; Dioclesian, Z627 (exc); Bonduca, Z574 (exc); Fairy Queen, Z629 (exc); Musick's Hand-maid Part 2 (exc); Grounds (exc); Hornpipes (exc); Choice Collection of Lessons (exc). (A. Mellon, W. Kuijken, C. Rousset)

ASV

Ⓓ **CDAJA5112** ▭ **ZCAJA5112**
Twenty Gramophone All-Time Greats
Leoncavallo: Pagliacci (exc); *Bishop:* Lo, here the gentle Lark; *Purcell:* Libertine, Z600 (exc); *Leoncavallo:* Mattinata; *Mendelssohn:* Hear my prayer; *C. Marshall:* I hear you calling me; *Elgar:* Salut d'amour; *J. Strauss II:* Casanova (exc); *Rachmaninov:* Preludes (exc); *Koenemann:* Song of the Volga Boatmen; *Kreisler:* Liebesfreud; *Moss:* Floral Dance; *Bach:* Cantata 147 (exc); *Handel:* Messiah (exc); *Saint-Saëns:* Samson et Dalila (exc); *Bizet:* Jolie fille de Perth (exc); *Chopin:* Waltzes (exc); *Lehár:* Land des Lächelns (exc); *Kern:* Show Boat (exc); *Sullivan:* Lost chord. (A. Galli-Curci, A. Frind, D. Labbette, M. Anderson, C. Butt, E. Lough, E. Caruso, B. Gigli, J. McCormack, H. Nash, R. Tauber, P. Dawson, F. Chaliapin, P. Robeson, M. Beringuer, F. Kreisler, E. Schneider, S. Rachmaninov, C. Lamson, G. Moore, M. Hess, A. Cortot, W. G. Webber, G. Thalben-Ball, Manchester Children's Ch, Temple Church Ch, Berlin Schauspielhaus Chor, SO, Victor Orch, Hallé, La Scala Orch, New SO, Berlin Schauspielhaus Orch, orch/H. Harty/F. Ghione/E. Elgar/E. Hauke/A. Coates/T. Beecham/J. Batten/R. Noble/L. Collingwood)

Ⓓ **CDAJA5137** ▭ **ZCAJA5137**
The Three Tenors of the Century
Leoncavallo: Pagliacci (exc); *Verdi:* Aida (exc); *Bizet:* Carmen (exc); Pêcheurs de perles (exc); *Mascagni:* Cavalleria Rusticana (exc); *Handel:* Serse (exc); *Di Capua:* O sole mio; *Donizetti:* Elisir d'amore (exc); *Verdi:* Rigoletto (exc); *Puccini:* Bohème (exc); *Verdi:* Traviata (exc); *Mozart:* Don Giovanni (exc); *Massenet:* Manon (exc); *Buzzi-Peccia:* Lolita; *Donizetti:* Favorita (exc); *Flotow:* Martha (exc); *Puccini:* Tosca (exc); *Gounod:* Roméo et Juliette (exc); *Giordano:* Andrea Chénier (exc); *Meyerbeer:* Africaine (exc); *Drigo:* Arlekinda (exc). (E. Caruso, J. McCormack, B. Gigli, M. Ancona, L. Bori, C. Marshall, orch)

Ⓓ **CDDCA595** (2/88)
Wagner—Orchestral music from Götterdämmerung & Tannhäuser
Wagner: Götterdämmerung (exc); Tannhäuser (exc). (Anne Evans, Philh/F. d'Avalos)

Ⓓ **CDDCA611**
Wagner—Orchestral Music, Vol. 2
Wagner: Parsifal (exc); Tristan und Isolde (exc); Siegfried (exc). (Philh/F. d'Avalos)

Ⓓ **CDDCA627** (12/88)
Delius—A Song of Summer
Delius: Song of Summer; Brigg Fair; In a Summer Garden; Song before Sunrise; Summer Night on the River; Village Romeo and Juliet (exc). (Philh/O.A. Hughes)

Ⓓ **CDDCA652** (10/89)
Celebration for Flute & Orchestra
Saint-Saëns: Odelette; Romance, Op. 37; Ascanio (exc); *Hüe:* Flute Fantasia; *Gaubert:* Nocturne; *Doppler:* Fantaisie, Op. 26; *Fauré:* Fantaisie; *Godard:* Suite, Op. 116. (W. Bennett, ECO/S. Bedford)

Ⓓ **CDDCA666** (3/90)
D'Avalos conducts Wagner, Vol 3
Wagner: Siegfried Idyll; Lohengrin (exc); Meistersinger (exc); Walküre (exc). (J. Tomlinson, Philh/F. d'Avalos)

Ⓓ **CDDCA683** (2/90)
Mozart—Arias
Mozart: Exsultate, jubilate, K165; Voi avete un cor fedele, K217; Vado, ma dove?, K583; Chi sà, K582; Nehmt

meinen Dank, K383; Bella mia fiamma, K528; Zaïde (exc); Mitridate (exc). (F. Lott, LMP/J. Glover)

Ⓓ **CDDCA698** (9/90)
Violin Virtuoso
Brahms: Hungarian Dances (exc); *Sarasate:* Danzas españolas (exc); *Elgar:* Capricieuse; *Mendelssohn:* Songs without words (exc); *Wieniawski:* Capriccio-valse, op 7; *Traditional:* Deep River; *Paradies:* Sicilienne; *Dinicu:* Hora Staccato; *Rachmaninov:* Songs, Op. 38 (exc); Songs, Op. 21 (exc); *Heuberger:* Opernball (exc); *Gluck:* Orfeo ed Euridice (exc); *Prokofiev:* Love for 3 Oranges Suite (exc); *Tchaikovsky:* Souvenir d'un lieu cher, op 42 (exc); *Gershwin:* Porgy and Bess (exc); *Castelnuovo-Tedesco:* Etudes d'ondes. (X. Wei, Pam Nicholson)

Ⓓ **CDDCA704** (10/90)
Wagner—Overtures & Preludes
Wagner: Faust Overture; Feen (exc); Liebesverbot (exc); Rienzi (exc); Fliegende Holländer (exc). (Philh/F. d'Avalos)

Ⓓ **CDDCA709** (10/90)
Lalo—Orchestral Works
Lalo: Roi d'Ys (exc); Scherzo; Symphony in G minor; Rapsodie norvégienne. (RPO/Y. Butt)

Ⓓ **CDDCA735** (9/91)
Music of Spain
Turina: Procesión del Rocio; Oración del torero; *Granados:* Danzas españolas (exc); Goyescas (exc); *Albéniz:* Catalonia; *Falla:* Amor Brujo (exc); Vida breve (exc). (Mexico City PO/E. Bátiz)

Ⓓ **CDDCA739** (1/91)
Summer Works
Delius: Koanga (exc); *Ranish:* Flute sonata; *R. R. Bennett:* Summer Music; *P. Lamb:* Flute sonata; *Elgar:* Nursery Suite (exc); *Dunhill:* Flute suite; *C. Scott:* Extatic Shepherd; *Arnold:* Flute sonata, Op. 121. (K. Smith, P. Rhodes)

Ⓓ **CDDCA758** (7/91)
Falla, Milhaud & Stravinsky—Operas
Falla: Retablo de maese Pedro (Cpte); *Milhaud:* Malheurs d'Orphée (Cpte); *Stravinsky:* Renard. (S. Linay, Adrian Thompson, M. Best, M. Walker, A. Steiger, P. Harrhy, P. Donnelly, M. Best, Gaynor Morgan, P. Bardon, S. Bickley, H. Hetherington, P. Harrhy, P. Donnelly, N. Cavallier, Matrix Ens/R. Ziegler)

Ⓓ **CDDCA766** (12/91)
Handel—Works for Soprano and Orchestra
Handel: Silete venti; Rinaldo (exc); Dunque sarà pur vero; Flavio (exc). (A. Mackay, ECCO/E. Aadland)

Ⓓ **CDDCA771** ▭ **ZCDCA771**
Rimsky-Korsakov—Orchestral Works
Rimsky-Korsakov: Scheherazade; Fairy Tale, Op. 29; Sadko; Sadko (exc). (Armenian PO/L. Tjeknavorian)

Ⓓ **CDDCA772** (9/92) ▭ **ZCDCA772** (9/92)
Rimsky-Korsakov—Orchestral Works
Rimsky-Korsakov: Golden Cockerel Suite (exc); Tale of Tsar Saltan (exc); Christmas Eve (exc). (Armenian PO/L. Tjeknavorian)

Ⓓ **CDDCA790** (6/92)
Weill—Songs
Weill: Huckleberry Finn (exc); One touch of Venus (exc); Love life (exc); Lady in the Dark (exc); Happy End (exc); Mahagonny (exc); Dreigroschenoper (exc); Schöne Kind; Berliner Requiem (exc); Reiterlied. (C. Farley, R. Vignoles)

Ⓓ **CDDCA800** ▭ **ZCDCA800**
Encores - Emma Johnson
Reade: Victorian Kitchen Garden; *Rimsky-Korsakov:* Tale of Tsar Saltan (exc); *Macdowell:* Woodland Sketches (exc); *Beethoven:* Variations, WoO28; *Paradies:* Sicilienne; *Gershwin:* Preludes; *P. Harvey:* Gershwin Suite (exc); *Granados:* Danzas españolas (exc); *Benjamin:* Jamaican Rumba; *Ravel:* Pièce en forme de habanera; *Mozart:* Zaïde (exc); *Verdi:* Rigoletto (exc); *Leó Weiner:* Two Movements. (E. Johnson, J. Drake, S. Kanga)

Ⓓ **CDDCA856** ▭ **ZCDCA856**
Verdi—Overtures and Preludes
Verdi: Forza del destino (exc); Vespri siciliani (exc); Aida (exc); Traviata (exc); Nabucco (exc); Rigoletto (exc); Aroldo (exc); Ballo in maschera (exc); Luisa Miller (exc). (Mexico St SO/E. Bátiz)

Ⓓ **CDDCA857** ▭ **ZCDCA857**
Rossini—Overtures
Rossini: Scala di seta (exc); Signor Bruschino (exc); Barbiere di Siviglia (exc); Siège de Corinthe (exc); Turco in Italia (exc); Italiana in Algeri (exc); Semiramide (exc); Guillaume Tell (exc). (Mexico St SO/E. Bátiz)

Ⓓ **CDDCA861** (9/93)
Wolf-Ferrari—Overtures & Intermezzos
Wolf-Ferrari: Gioielli della Madonna (exc); Quattro rusteghi (exc); Amore medico (exc); Campiello (exc); Dama Boba (exc); Segreto di Susanna (exc). (RPO/J. Serebrier)

Ⓓ **CDDCA886** ▭ **ZCDCA886**
Prokofiev—Orchestral Works
Prokofiev: Lt Kijé Suite; Cinderella Suite 3; Love for 3 Oranges Suite. (Armenian PO/L. Tjeknavorian)

Ⓓ **CDDCA895** (8/94)
Berlioz—Vocal & Orchestral Works
Berlioz: Béatrice et Bénédict (exc); Mort de Cléopâtre; King Lear; Herminie. (R. Plowright, Philh/J-P. Rouchon)

Ⓓ **CDDCA907** (3/95)
Bottesini—Volume 3 - Passioni Amorose
Bottesini: Ero e Leandro (exc); Concertino; Diavolo della Notte (exc); Passione Amorosa; Elegie in D; Alì Babà (exc); Duo Concertant on Bellini themes (exc). (T. Martin, M. Welsh, LSO, F. Petracchi/F. Petracchi/M. Gibson)

Ⓓ **CDDCA921**
Catalani—Complete Piano Music
Catalani: Impressioni; Se tu sapessi; Scherzo-tarantella; Aspirazione; Ricordo di Lugnano; A sera; Eleganza; Notturno; Contemplazione; Loreley (exc). (P. Spada)

Ⓓ **CDDCS225** (10/94)
Verdi—Il trovatore
Verdi: Trovatore (Cpte). (Gordon Wilson, S. Bisatt, G. Quinn, S. Grevelle, P. Parfitt, P. Shaw, E. Rahme, Tallis Chbr Ch, European Chbr Op Orch, European Chbr Op Chor/D. Hinnells)

Ⓓ **CDQS6018** ▭ **ZCQS6018** (9/88)
Borodin—Orchestral Music
Borodin: Symphony 2; Prince Igor (exc). (Mexico St SO/E. Bátiz)

Ⓓ **CDQS6028** ▭ **ZCQS6028**
The Royal Albert Hall Organ Spectacular
Suppé: Leichte Kavallerie (exc); *Lemare:* Andantino; *Verdi:* Aida (exc); *Albinoni:* Adagio; *Wagner:* Walküre (exc); *Bach:* Toccata and Fugue, BWV565; *Joplin:* Entertainer; *Tchaikovsky:* Songs, Op. 6 (exc); *Elgar:* Pomp and Circumstance Marches (exc); *Sousa:* Liberty Bell; *Widor:* Symphony 5 (exc). (H. Britton)

Ⓓ **CDQS6033** (11/89) ▭ **ZCQS6033** (11/89)
Mozart—Orchestral Works
Mozart: Symphony 31; Symphony 36; Nozze di Figaro (exc). (LPO, RPO/E. Bátiz)

Ⓓ **CDQS6038** ▭ **ZCQS6038**
Fandango
Purcell: Fairy Queen, Z629 (exc); *Bach:* Partita in C minor, BWV997; *Sanz:* Spanish Guitar Instruction I (exc); *Tárrega:* Capricho árabe; Maria; Gran Jota; *Sor:* Fantasia 13; *Pujol Vilarrubí:* Spanish Pieces (exc); *Rodrigo:* Piezas españolas (exc); Pequeñas piezas (exc). (C. Bonell)

Ⓓ **CDQS6065** ▭ **ZCQS6065**
The Mozart Miracle
Mozart: Serenade, K525 (exc); Serenade, K361 (exc); Exsultate, jubilate, K165 (exc); Piano Sonata, K331 (exc); Nozze di Figaro (exc); Nozze di Figaro (exc); Piano Concerto 24 (exc); Oboe Concerto, K314 (exc); Symphony 40 (exc); Horn Concerti (exc); Ave verum corpus, K618; Clarinet Concerto, K622 (exc); Requiem (exc); Symphony 41 (exc). (St John's Smith Square Orch/J. Lubbock, LMP/J. Glover, F. Lott, A. Schiller, RPO/E. Bátiz, J. Diaz, ECO/E. Stratta, J.F. Osorio, RPO, D. Boyd, COE/P. Berglund, J. Williams/A. Schneider, Oxford Christ Church Cath Ch/F. Grier, H. Bicket, E. Johnson/R. Leppard, BBC Sngrs)

Ⓓ **CDQS6076** ▭ **ZCQS6076**
Popular Overtures
Handel: Solomon (exc); *Beethoven:* Leonore (exc); *Mendelssohn:* Hebrides; *Brahms:* Academic Festival Overture; *Mozart:* Nozze di Figaro (exc); *Schubert:* Rosamunde (exc); *Rossini:* Gazza ladra (exc); *Berlioz:* Carnaval romain. (RPO/E. Bátiz)

Ⓓ **CDQS6089** ▭ **ZCQS6089**
Rimsky-Korsakov—Orchestral Works
Rimsky-Korsakov: Capriccio Espagnol; Sadko; May Night (exc); Russian Easter Festival Ov. (Mexico City PO/E. Bátiz)

Ⓓ **CDQS6106** ▭ **ZCQS6106**
Nocturne
Mendelssohn: Midsummer Night's Dream (exc); *Field:* Nocturnes (exc); *Vivaldi:* Concerti, Op. 10 (exc); *Raff:* Abends-Rhapsodie; *Chopin:* Nocturnes (exc); *Fauré:* Shylock Suite (exc); *Rimsky-Korsakov:* Christmas Eve (exc); *Grieg:* Lyric Suite, Op. 54 (exc); *Martucci:* Nocturne, Op. 70/1; *Debussy:* Nocturne; *Delius:* Summer Night on the River; *Gaubert:* Nocturne (exc); *Khachaturian:* Masquerade (exc). (W. Bennett, R. Stallman, Y. Boghosian, G. Ives, A. Schiller, P. Frankl, G. Fergus-Thompson, St John's Smith Square Orch/J. Lubbock, Philh/F. d'Avalos, Mexico City PO/E. Bátiz, Armenian PO/L. Tjeknavorian, RPO/Y. Butt, ECO/S. Bedford/O.A. Hughes)

Ⓓ **CDQS6112**
Serenade
Mozart: Serenade, K525 (exc); Serenade, K361 (exc); *Brahms:* Serenade 1 (exc); *Goldmark:* Rustic Wedding (exc); *Dvořák:* Serenade, Op. 22 (exc); Serenade, Op. 44 (exc); *Suk:* Serenade, Op. 6 (exc); *Tchaikovsky:* Serenade, Op. 48 (exc); Sérénade mélancolique; *Glazunov:* Serenade 1; *Bizet:* Jolie Fille de Perth Suite (exc); *Elgar:* Serenade; *Martucci:* Serenata, Op. 57/1; *Wolf:* Italian Serenade. (St John's Smith Square Orch/J. Lubbock, COE Wind Sols/A. Schneider, Philh/F. D'Avalos, RPO/Y. Butt, COE, Polish Radio CO/A. Duczmal, Scottish CO/J. Serebrier, X. Wei/S. Accardo, Mexico City PO/E. Bátiz, ASMF/N. Marriner, D. Poppen)

Ⓓ **CDQS6114**
The Four Seasons, Volume 2 - Summer
Anon: Sumer is icumen in; *Vivaldi:* Concerti, Op. 8; *Delius:* Song of Summer; *Coates:* Song of Summer; *Gershwin:* Porgy and Bess (exc); *Prokofiev:* Summer Day; *Rodrigo:* Concierto de estío; *R.R. Bennett:* Summer Music; *Reade:* Victorian Kitchen Garden (exc). (St George's Canzona/J. Sothcott, J-L. Garcia (vn/dir), ECO, Philh/O.A. Hughes, B. Rayner Cook, R. Terroni, X. Wei, Pam Nicholson, Scottish CO/J. Serebrier, M. Guttman, RPO, K. Smith, P. Rhodes, E. Johnson, S. Kanga)

Ⓓ **CDQS6116**
The Four Seasons, Volume 4 - Winter
Vivaldi: Concerti, Op. 8 (exc); *Prokofiev:* Winter Bonfire; *Debussy:* Préludes (exc); Children's Corner (exc); *Handel:* Messiah (exc); *Berlioz:* Enfance du Christ (exc); *Traditional:* Wexford Carol; *Ireland:* Holy Boy; *Britten:* Ceremony of Carols (exc); *Rimsky-Korsakov:* Christmas Eve (exc). (J-L. Garcia, ECO, Scottish CO/J. Serebrier, G. Fergus-Thompson, RPO/C. Mackerras, John Alldis Ch/P. Ledger, J. Lloyd Webber, J. McCabe, Galliard Brass Ens, Oxford Christ Church Cath Ch/F. Grier, Armenian PO/L. Tjeknavorian, Paisley Abbey Ch)

Ⓓ **CDQS6119**
Russia!
Prokofiev: Winter Bonfire (exc); *Borodin:* Prince Igor (exc); *Rimsky-Korsakov:* Russian Easter Festival Ov; *Rachmaninov:* Suite 1 (exc); *Ippolitov-Ivanov:* Caucasian Sketches (exc); *Tchaikovsky:* Nutcracker (exc); *Liadov:* Russian Folksongs, Op. 58 (exc); *Traditional:* Song of the Volga boatmen; *Glazunov:* Stenka Razin; *Khachaturian:* Gayaneh (exc); *Shostakovich:* Novorossiisk Chimes. (Scottish CO/J. Serebrier, Mexico City PO/E. Bátiz, Mexico St SO, Armenian PO/L. Tjeknavorian, RPO, F. Chaliapin, orch/A. Coates, LSO/Y. Butt, J. Ogdon, B. Lucas)

Ⓓ **CDQS6121**
España!
Chabrier: España; *Rodrigo:* Piezas españolas (exc); *Turina:* Oración del torero; *Bizet:* Carmen Suites (exc); *Albéniz:* España, Op. 165 (exc); Cantos de España (exc); Suite española 2 (exc); Suite española 2 (exc); *Granados:* Goyescas (exc); Tonadillas (exc); Danzas españolas (exc); Danzas españolas (exc); *Tárrega:* Gran Jota; *Falla:* Vida breve (exc); Canciones populares españolas (exc); Amor brujo (exc). (Mexico City PO/E. Bátiz, C. Bonell, A. Schiller, Pro Arte Gtr Trio, A. Petchersky, G. Fierens, S. Browne, M. Isidor, M. Garzón)

Ⓓ **CDQS6122**
Gypsy
Brahms: Hungarian Dances (exc); *Doppler:* Fantaisie, Op. 26; *Kreisler:* Gitana; *Bizet:* Carmen (exc); *Sarasate:* Zigeunerweisen; *Dvořák:* Slavonic Dances; *Monti:* Csárdás; *Leó Weiner:* Hungarian Rural Dances; Two Movements; *Bartók:* Romanian folkdances, Sz68; *Farkas:* Old Hungarian Dances (exc); *Dinicu:* Hora Staccato. (Philh/F. D'Avalos, W. Bennett, ECO/S. Bedford, O. Shumsky, M. Kaye, Mexico City PO/E. Bátiz, M. Hasson, St John's Smith Square Orch/J. Lubbock, COE Wind Sols, K. Smith, P. Rhodes, P. Frankl, E. Johnson, J. Drake, S. Stanzeleit, G. Fenyö, Thurston Cl Qt, X. Wei, Pam Nicholson)

Ⓓ **CDQS6126**
Romeo and Juliet
Tchaikovsky: Romeo and Juliet; *Delius:* Village Romeo and Juliet (exc); *Prokofiev:* Romeo and Juliet Suites (exc); *Ravel:* Daphnis et Chloé Suites (exc); *Fauré:* Pelléas et Mélisande Suite (exc); *Sibelius:* Pelleas and Melisande (exc); *Gershwin:* Porgy and Bess (exc); *Wagner:* Tristan und Isolde (exc). (LPO/J. Farrer, Philh/O.A. Hughes, English Brass Ens, LSO/G. Nowak, Mexico City PO/E. Bátiz, RPO/Y. Butt, X. Wei, Pam Nicholson/F. d'Avalos)

Athens

Atrium Records

Arturo Toscanini Society

Audiofon

Aurora

Auvidis

Bandleader

Bay Cities

Bayer

inganno; *Anon:* Sinfonia; *Gaelle:* Hymnus pro festo; Hymnus pro Nativitate; *Kraus:* Aure belle; *B. Ottani:* Son vezzosa e gentillina. (R. Sonnenschmidt, H. Hoeren, Sephira Ens)

⦶ **BR150004**
Romberg—The Student Prince excerpts
Romberg: Student Prince (exc). (C. Jeffreys, E. Geisen, D. Hönig, Hamburg St Op Chor, Hamburg St Op Orch/S. Gyártó)

BBC Radio Classics

⦶ **BBCRD9103**
Classic Encores
Walton: Crown Imperial; *Grainger:* Molly on the shore, BFMS1; *Smetana:* Má vlast (exc); *Millöcker:* Dubarry (exc); *Mackeben:* Bal paré (exc); *Dostal:* Clivia (exc); *Borodin:* Prince Igor (exc); *Arnold:* Harmonica Concerto; *Weinberger:* Schwanda the Bagpiper. (E. Harwood, T. Reilly, Goldsmith's Choral Union, Kneller Hall Trumpeters, BBC Concert Orch, BBC SO/H. Krips/V. Tausky)

⦶ **BBCRD9107** (3/95)
Brahms/Klemperer/Ravel/Vaughan Williams—Orchestral Works
Klemperer: Ziel (exc); *Vaughan Williams:* Tallis Fantasia; *Ravel:* Rapsodie espagnole; *Brahms:* Symphony 4. (New Philh/L. Stokowski)

⦶ **BBCRD9129** (10/95)
Bridge/Britten/Pärt—Orchestral Works
Bridge: Poems (1916); *Britten:* Gloriana Suite; Sinfonia da Requiem; Passacaglia, Op. 33b; *Pärt:* Cantus in memory of Benjamin Britten. (BBC Northern SO/N. Del Mar, BBC SO/G. Rozhdestvensky)

⦶ **DMCD98** (10/95)
BBC Proms - The Centenary: 1895-1995
Berlioz: Symphonie funèbre et triomphale (exc); *Tchaikovsky:* Nutcracker Suite; *Elgar:* Symphony 1; *Gluck:* Orfeo ed Euridice (exc); *Wagner:* Tannhäuser (exc); *R. Strauss:* Rosenkavalier (exc); *Janáček:* Sinfonietta; *Shostakovich:* Taiti trot. (J. Baker, BBC Chor, BBC SO, LPO, RPO, Hallé/J. Pritchard/M. Sargent/A. Boult/R. Leppard/T. Beecham/J. Barbirolli/R. Kempe/G. Rozhdestvensky)

Belart

⦶ **450 001-2** ▭ **450 001-4**
Handel—Orchestral Works
Handel: Water Music - Suite; Fireworks Music Suite; Faithful Shepherd (exc); Serse (exc). (LSO/G. Szell)

⦶ **450 002-2** ▭ **450 002-4**
Pavarotti Live
Verdi: Traviata (exc); *Massenet:* Werther (exc); *Donizetti:* Elisir d'amore (exc); *Ponchielli:* Gioconda (exc); *Meyerbeer:* Africaine (exc); *Puccini:* Turandot (exc); *Rossini:* Petite Messe Solennelle (exc); *Donizetti:* Messa da Requiem (exc); *Verdi:* Traviata (exc); Macbeth (exc); Lombardi (exc); Otello (exc). (L. Pavarotti, M. Freni, K. Ricciarelli, Ater Orch/L. Magiera, Verona Arena Orch/A. Gatto, L. Magiera, V. Rosetta/R. Gandolfi/G. Fackler, Parma Teatro Regio Orch/G. Patanè)

⦶ **450 005-2** ▭ **450 005-4**
Famous Tenor Arias
Verdi: Aida (exc); Luisa Miller (exc); Ballo in maschera (exc); *Meyerbeer:* Africaine (exc); *Bizet:* Carmen (exc); *Gounod:* Faust (exc); *Massenet:* Werther (exc); *Puccini:* Tosca (exc); *Giordano:* Andrea Chénier (exc); *Verdi:* Forza del Destino (exc); *Giordano:* Fedora (exc); *Mascagni:* Cavalleria Rusticana (exc); *Puccini:* Fanciulla del West (exc); Turandot (exc). (C. Bergonzi, G. Di Stefano, B. Prevedi, Santa Cecilia Academy Orch, Zurich Tonhalle Orch, ROHO/G. Gavazzeni/F. Patanè/E. Downes)

⦶ **450 006-2** ▭ **450 006-4**
Famous Opera Duets
Verdi: Traviata (exc); Trovatore (exc); Forza del Destino (exc); *Puccini:* Tosca (exc); Bohème (exc); Madama Butterfly (exc); *Bizet:* Pêcheurs de Perles (exc); Carmen (exc). (J. Sutherland, C. Bergonzi, MMF Orch, G. Simionato, M. del Monaco, Geneva Grand Th Orch/A. Erede, G. di Stefano, L. Warren, Santa Cecilia Academy Orch/F. Previtali, R. Tebaldi/F. Molinari-Pradelli/T. Serafin, L. de Luca, J. Borthayre, Paris Cons, R. Resnik, Geneva Grand Th Chor, SRO/T. Schippers/J. Pritchard)

⦶ **450 007-2** ▭ **450 007-4**
Puccini Favourites
Puccini: Bohème (exc); Gianni Schicchi (exc); Fanciulla del West (exc); Madama Butterfly (exc); Manon Lescaut (exc); Rondine (exc); Tosca (exc); Tosca (exc); Tosca (exc); Suor Angelica (exc); Turandot (exc); Turandot (exc). (R. Tebaldi, C. Bergonzi, R. Cesari, C. Siepi, E. Bastianini, Santa Cecilia Academy Orch/T. Serafin, L. Mitchell, National PO/K.H. Adler, B. Prevedi, ROHO/E. Downes, Santa Cecilia Academy Chor, M. Chiara, Vienna Volksoper Orch/N. Santi, G. London, P. de Palma/F. Molinari-Pradelli, J. Sutherland, New Philh/R. Bonynge, J. McCracken/L. Gardelli, F. Weathers, Vienna Op Orch/A. Quadri, M. del Monaco, N. Zaccaria, F. Corena, Mario Carlin, R. Ercolani/A. Erede, G. di Stefano/F. Patanè)

⦶ **450 013-2** ▭ **450 013-4**
Favourite Wedding Music
Mendelssohn: Midsummer Night's Dream (exc); *Bach:* Orgel-Büchlein, BWV599-644 (exc); Suites, BWV1066-9 (exc); Cantata 147 (exc); *Wagner:* Lohengrin (exc); *Handel:* Serse (exc); Water Music (exc); *Clarke:* Suite in D (exc); *Guilmant:* Grand Choeur in D; *S.S. Wesley:* Air and Gavotte; *Brahms:* Chorale Preludes, Op. 122 (exc); *Widor:* Symphony 5 (exc). (S. Cleobury)

⦶ **450 014-2** ▭ **450 014-4**
Sutherland sings Coward
Coward: Bitter Sweet (exc); Conversation Piece (exc); Operette (exc); After the Ball (exc); Pacific 1860 (exc). (J. Sutherland, N. Coward, chor, orch/R. Bonynge)

⦶ **450 015-2** ▭ **450 015-4**
Cinema Classics
R. Strauss: Also sprach Zarathustra (exc); *Barber:* Adagio for Strings; *Catalani:* Wally (exc); *Bach:* 2-Violin Concerto (exc); *Leoncavallo:* Pagliacci (exc); *Addinsell:* Warsaw Concerto; *Orff:* Carmina Burana (exc); *Mahler:* Symphony 5 (exc); *Puccini:* Gianni Schicchi (exc); *Handel:* Keyboard Suites Set II (exc); *Mozart:* Piano Concerto 21 (exc); Requiem (exc). (F. Weathers, M. Chiara, M. del Monaco, G. Jones, C. Pini, I. Vered, M. Rawicz, W. Landauer, C. Hogwood, Brighton Fest Chor, Vienna St Op Chor, Los Angeles PO, Stuttgart CO, National PO, Philomusica of London, Santa Cecilia Academy Orch, orch, RPO, Vienna Op Orch, VPO/Z. Mehta/K. Münchinger/K. H. Adler, T. Dart (hpd/dir)/F. Molinari-Pradelli/A. P. Mantovani/A. Dorati/A. Quadri/L. Foster/I. Kertész)

⦶ **450 016-2** ▭ **450 016-4**
Mascagni—Cavalleria Rusticana
Mascagni: Cavalleria Rusticana (Cpte). (G. Simionato, M. del Monaco, C. MacNeil, A.R. Satre, A. di Stasio, Santa Cecilia Academy Chor, Santa Cecilia Academy Orch/T. Serafin)

⦶ **450 017-2** ▭ **450 017-4**
Russian Masterpieces
Glinka: Ruslan and Lyudmila (exc); *Mussorgsky:* Khovanshchina (exc); Night on the Bare Mountain; *Borodin:* Prince Igor (exc). (London Sym Chor, LSO/G. Solti)

⦶ **450 025-2** ▭ **450 025-4**
Essential Wagner
Wagner: Fliegende Holländer (exc); Lohengrin (exc); Tristan und Isolde (exc); Walküre (exc); Meistersinger (exc). (VPO/H. Stein, National SO/A. Dorati)

⦶ **450 036-2** ▭ **450 036-4**
Domingo—Love Songs and Tangos
Cardillo: Core 'ngrato; *Lehár:* Land des Lächelns (exc); *Leoncavallo:* Mattinata; *Brodszky:* Toast of New Orleans (exc); *Grever:* Muñequita Linda; *Hardelot:* Because; *Simons:* Marta; *Loges:* Ich schenk dir eine neue Welt; *Filiberto:* Caminito; *Cobián:* Nostalgias; *Gardel:* Volver; *O. Fresedo:* Vida mía; *Gardel:* Día que me quieras; *J. A. Caruso:* Alma de Bohemio. (P. Domingo, LSO/K-H. Loges/M. Peeters, orch/R. Pansera)

⦶ **450 037-2** ▭ **450 037-4**
Beethoven—Symphony No 3; Leonora Overture
Beethoven: Symphony 3; Leonore (exc). (BPO/R. Kubelík)

⦶ **450 043-2** ▭ **450 043-4**
Bizet—Carmen and L'Arlésienne Suites
Bizet: Carmen Suites; Arlésienne Suites. (Lamoureux Concerts Orch/I. Markevitch)

⦶ **450 047-2** ▭ **450 047-4**
Mozart—Marriage of Figaro - Highlights
Mozart: Nozze di Figaro (exc). (M. Freni, J. Norman, Y. Minton, L. Watson, W. Ganzarolli, I. Wixell, BBC Sym Chor, BBC SO/Colin Davis)

⦶ **450 052-2** ▭ **450 052-4**
Great Opera Choruses
Verdi: Trovatore (exc); Trovatore (exc); Nabucco (exc); Nabucco (exc); Lombardi (exc); Lombardi (exc); *Leoncavallo:* Pagliacci (exc); *Gounod:* Faust (exc); *Wagner:* Fliegende Holländer (exc); Lohengrin (exc); Tannhäuser (exc); Meistersinger (exc); *Verdi:* Macbeth (exc); Aida (exc); Don Carlo (exc). (ROH Chor, ROHO/Colin Davis, Dresden St Op Chor, Dresden St Op Orch/S. Varviso, La Scala Chor, La Scala Orch/G. Prêtre, BRS Chor, BRSO, Bayreuth Fest Chor, Bayreuth Fest Orch, A. Silja, E. Waechter/W. Sawallisch/W. Nelsson, Berlin Deutsche Op Chor, Berlin Deutsche Op Orch/G. Sinopoli/W. Pitz, Chor, Orch/Anon)

⦶ **450 059-2** ▭ **450 059-4**
Carreras—Memories
Bernstein: West Side Story (exc); *Cilea:* Arlesiana (exc); *Lara:* Granada; *Leoncavallo:* Pagliacci (exc); Mattinata; *Donizetti:* Elisir d'amore (exc); *A. Lloyd Webber:* Cats (exc); *Massenet:* Werther (exc); *Di Capua:* 'O sole mio; *Puccini:* Tosca (exc); *Cardillo:* Core 'ngrato; *Verdi:* Trovatore (exc); *Cannio:* O surdato 'nnammurato; *Puccini:* Bohème (exc); *Bixio:* Parlami d'amore, Mariù; *Puccini:* Turandot (exc). (J. Carreras, R. Farnon Orch/R. Farnon, LSO, LPO/J. López-Cobos, ECO/E. Müller/E.G. Asensio/R. Benzi, ROHO/Colin Davis)

⦶ **450 080-2** (5/94) ▭ **450 080-4** (5/94)
Mozart—Don Giovanni (highlights)
Mozart: Don Giovanni (exc). (G. Harman, R. Brünner, R. Knoll, Salzburg Mozarteum Chor, Salzburg Mozarteum Orch/K. Prestel)

⦶ **450 101-2** ▭ **450 101-4**
Verdi—La traviata - excs
Verdi: Traviata (exc). (Berlin City Op Orch, Berlin Deutsche Op Chor/L. Maazel)

⦶ **450 106-2** ▭ **450 106-4**
Rossini—Overtures
Rossini: Gazza ladra (exc); Scala di Seta (exc); Guillaume Tell (exc); Barbiere di Siviglia (exc); Semiramide (exc). (Rome Op Orch/T. Serafin)

⦶ **450 114-2** ▭ **450 114-4**
Mozart—Così fan tutte (highlights)
Mozart: Così fan tutte (exc). (G. Janowitz, B. Fassbaender, R. Grist, P. Schreier, H. Prey, R. Panerai, Vienna St Op Chor, VPO/K. Böhm)

⦶ **450 117-2** ▭ **450 117-4**
Great Opera Chorus II
Verdi: Nabucco (exc); Otello (exc); *Puccini:* Madama Butterfly (exc); *Beethoven:* Fidelio (exc); *Mozart:* Zauberflöte (exc); *Tchaikovsky:* Eugene Onegin (exc); *Bellini:* Norma (exc); *Mascagni:* Cavalleria Rusticana (exc); *Verdi:* Attila (exc); *Mussorgsky:* Boris Godunov (exc); *Wagner:* Meistersinger (exc). (J. Sutherland, D. Startz, J. Lanigan, D. Popovich, S. Ramey, J. Rouleau, Santa Cecilia Academy Chor, Santa Cecilia Academy Orch, Vienna St Op Chor, VPO, Belgrade Nat Op Chor, Belgrade Nat Op Orch, WNO Chor, WNO Orch, ROH Chor, ROHO/C. Franci/L. Maazel/K. Böhm/O. Danon/R. Bonynge/T. Serafin/E. Downes/G. Solti)

⦶ **450 121-2** (6/94) ▭ **450 121-4** (6/94)
Plácido Domingo
Wagner: Meistersinger (exc); *Massenet:* Werther (exc); *Bizet:* Carmen (exc); *Verdi:* Luisa Miller (exc); Rigoletto (exc); *Weber:* Oberon (exc); *Verdi:* Ballo in maschera (exc); *Puccini:* Fanciulla del West (exc); *Berlioz:* Damnation de Faust (exc); *Verdi:* Macbeth (exc). (P. Domingo, D. Fischer-Dieskau, P. Lagger, C. Ligendza, K. Ricciarelli, C. Neblett, A. Wilkens, I. Cotrubas, Berlin Deutsche Op Chor, Berlin Deutsche Op Orch, Cologne RSO, LSO, ROHO, VPO, BRSO, La Scala Orch, Paris Orch/E. Jochum/R. Chailly/C. Abbado/L. Maazel/C.M. Giulini/R. Kubelík/Z. Mehta/D. Barenboim)

⦶ **450 126-2** ▭ **450 126-4**
Favourite Wedding Music II
Wagner: Lohengrin (exc); *Bach:* Toccata and Fugue, BWV565; *Albinoni:* Adagio; *Weber:* Freischütz (exc); *Grieg:* Peer Gynt (exc); *Bach:* Suites, BWV1066-9 (exc); *Mendelssohn:* Midsummer Night's Dream (exc); *Offenbach:* Contes d'Hoffmann (exc); *Beethoven:* Romances (exc); *Tchaikovsky:* Nutcracker (exc). (Innsbruck SO, Innsbruck Chor/Robert Wagner, W. Rübsam, I Musici, BRSO, BRS Chor/E. Jochum, Nordmark SO/H. Steiner, ECO/R. Leppard, Concertgebouw/G. Szell, Dresden St Op Orch/S. Varviso, A. Grumiaux, New PO/E. de Waart, LSO/A. Dorati)

⦶ **450 130-2** ▭ **450 130-4**
Romeo & Juliet
Tchaikovsky: Romeo and Juliet; *Delius:* Village Romeo and Juliet (exc); *Prokofiev:* Romeo and Juliet (exc); *Berlioz:* Roméo et Juliette (exc). (Vienna St Op Chor, VPO/L. Maazel, ASMF/N. Marriner, SRO/E. Ansermet)

⦶ **450 132-2** (6/94) ▭ **450 132-4**
Rimsky-Korsakov—Scheherazade
Rimsky-Korsakov: Scheherazade; May Night (exc); Sadko. (LSO/P. Monteux, SRO/E. Ansermet)

⦶ **450 133-2** ▭ **450 133-4**
Verdi Favourites
Verdi: Traviata (exc); Aida (exc); Aida (exc); Luisa Miller (exc); Otello (exc); Nabucco (exc); Rigoletto (exc); Rigoletto (exc); Trovatore (exc). (J. Sutherland, C. Bergonzi, M. Chiara, R. Tebaldi, R. Cioni, S. Malagù, C.

MacNeil, C. Siepi, G. Simionato, M. del Monaco, A. Cesarini, MMF Chor, Santa Cecilia Academy Chor, MMF Orch, Santa Cecilia Academy Orch, ROHO, Geneva Grand Th Orch/J. Pritchard/G. Gavazzeni/N. Santi/A. Erede/C. Franci/F. Molinari-Pradelli/N. Sanzogno)

Ⓓ **450 134-2** ⊟ **450 134-4**
Puccini—La Bohème-Highlights
Puccini: Bohème (exc). (R. Scotto, J. Meneguzzer, G. Poggi, E. Guagni, T. Gobbi, G. Giorgetti, V. Carbonari, G. Modesti, MMF Chor, MMF Orch/A. Votto)

Ⓓ **450 137-2** ⊟ **450 137-4**
Meditation
Bach: Suites, BWV1066-9 (exc); Violin Concerto, BWV1042 (exc); *Mozart:* Bassoon Concerto, K191; Andante, K315; *Bruch:* Violin Concerto 1 (exc); *Chopin:* Piano Concerto 2 (exc); *Massenet:* Thaïs (exc); *Dvořák:* Symphony 9 (exc). (A. Nicolet, Munich Bach Orch/K. Richter, Z. Francescatti, Lucerne Fest Strings/R. Baumgartner, D. Zeman, VPO/K. Böhm, K. Zoeller, ECO/B. Klee, Y. U. Kim, Bamberg SO/O. Kamu, T. Vásáry, BPO/J. Kulka, M. Schwalbé/H. von Karajan/R. Kubelík)

Ⓓ **450 139-2** ⊟ **450 139-4**
An Invitation to the Dance
Weber: Invitation to the Dance; *Gounod:* Faust (exc); *Borodin:* Prince Igor (exc); *Tchaikovsky:* Swan Lake (exc); Eugene Onegin (exc); Sleeping Beauty (exc); Nutcracker (exc); *R. Strauss:* Rosenkavalier (exc). (BRSO/F. Fricsay, Monte Carlo Nat Op Orch/L. Frémaux, Warsaw Nat PO/W. Rowicki, BPO/F. Leitner/K. Böhm)

Ⓓ **450 146-2** ⊟ **450 146-4**
Romantic Guitar
Carulli: Serenade, Op. 96/3; *Paganini:* Sonata concertata in A; *Granados:* Goyescas (exc); Danzas españolas (exc); *Albéniz:* Danza; España, Op. 165 (exc); *Sor:* Divertissement, Op. 34. (I. Presti, A. Lagoya)

Ⓓ **461 001-2** ⊟ **461 001-4**
Popular Overtures
Mozart: Don Giovanni (exc); *Rossini:* Gazza ladra (exc); *Bizet:* Carmen Suites (exc); *Verdi:* Forza del destino (exc); *Suppé:* Schöne Galathee (exc); *Weber:* Invitation to the dance; *Mozart:* Zauberflöte (exc); *Rossini:* Cenerentola (exc). (ROHO, Lamoureux Concerts Orch, New Philh, Staatskapelle Dresden, LSO, BBC SO/Colin Davis/R. Benzi/I. Markevitch/O. Suitner/C. Mackerras)

Ⓓ **461 003-2** ⊟ **461 003-4**
Romantic Violin
Kreisler: Liebesfreud; Liebesleid; *Schumann:* Kinderszenen (exc); *Schubert:* Ave Maria, D839; *Kreisler:* Beethoven Rondino; *Mendelssohn:* Songs without words (exc); *Dinicu:* Hora Staccato; *Dvořák:* Humoresques, Op. 101 (exc); *Kreisler:* Caprice Viennois; *Massenet:* Thaïs (exc); *Chaminade:* Sérénade espagnole; *Fauré:* Berceuse, Op. 16; *Rimsky-Korsakov:* Sadko (exc); *Sarasate:* Danzas españolas (exc); *Falla:* Vida Breve (exc); *Saint-Saëns:* Carnaval des animaux (exc); *Stravinsky:* Mavra (exc). (C. Ferras, J-C. Ambrosini)

Ⓓ **461 004-2** ⊟ **461 004-4**
March militaire
Elgar: Pomp and Circumstance Marches (exc); *Gounod:* Marche funèbre d'une marionette; *Meyerbeer:* Prophète (exc); *Berlioz:* Damnation de Faust (exc); *Schubert:* Marches militaires, D733 (exc); *J. Strauss II:* Jubel-Marsch, Op. 126; *Tchaikovsky:* Marche slave; *Grieg:* Sigurd Jorsalfar, Op. 56 (exc); *Mendelssohn:* Athalie (exc); *Tchaikovsky:* Nutcracker (exc); *J. Strauss I:* Radetzky March. (LSO, ROHO, SRO, VPO, National PO/A. Bliss/A. Gibson/R. Bonynge/E. Ansermet/H. Knappertsbusch/W. Boskovsky/L. Stokowski/C. von Dohnányi)

Ⓓ **461 006-2** ⊟ **461 006-4**
Gilbert & Sullivan—Songs and Snatches
Sullivan: Gondoliers (exc); Iolanthe (exc); Ruddigore (exc); Yeomen of the Guard (exc); Mikado (exc). (J. Reed, C. Palmer, J. Goss, P. Potter, A. Guthrie, R. Mason, P. Wales, T. Lawlor, J. Ayldon, K. Sandford, P.A. Jones, V. Masterson, D'Oyly Carte Op Chor, RPO/J. Walker/M. Sargent)

Ⓓ **461 012-2** ⊟ **461 012-4**
Kodály—Orchestral Works
Kodály: Háry János Suite; Galánta Dances; Peacock Variations. (LSO/I. Kertész)

Berlin Classics

Ⓓ **BC2097-2** (9/94)
Wagner—The Flying Dutchman
Wagner: Fliegende Holländer (Cpte). (D. Fischer-Dieskau, M. Schech, G. Frick, R. Schock, S. Wagner, F. Wunderlich, Berlin Deutsche Op Chor, Berlin Deutsche Op Orch/F. Konwitschny)

Ⓓ **0011 432BC**
Lortzing—Der Wildschütz
Lortzing: Wildschütz (Cpte). (G. Hornik, D. Soffel, P. Schreier, E. Mathis, G. von Ottenthal, H. Sotin, G. Resick, R. Süss, B. Riedel, Berlin Rad Children's Ch, Berlin Rad Chor, Berlin Staatskapelle/B. Klee)

Ⓓ **0011162BC**
Schoenberg—Moses und Aron
Schoenberg: Moses und Aron (Cpte). (W. Haseleu, R. Goldberg, L. Mróz, R. Krahmer, G. Pohl, A. Ude, H. C. Polster, K-H. Stryczek, Leipzig Rad Chor, Dresden Cath Boys' Ch, Leipzig RSO/H. Kegel)

Ⓓ **0090 332BC**
Gluck—Orfeo ed Eurydice
Gluck: Orfeo ed Euridice (Cpte). (G. Bumbry, A. Rothenberger, R-M. Pütz, Leipzig Rad Chor, Leipzig Gewandhaus/V. Neumann)

Beulah

Ⓓ **1PD12** (2/95)
Boult's BBC Years
Beethoven: Symphony 8; *Humperdinck:* Hänsel und Gretel (exc); *Tchaikovsky:* Capriccio italien; Serenade, Op. 48. (BBC SO/A. Boult)

Ⓓ **1PD13** (7/95)
Sir Malcolm Sargent conducts British Music
Holst: Perfect Fool (exc); *Britten:* Instruments of the Orchestra; *Vaughan Williams:* Hugh the Drover (exc); *Elgar:* I sing the birth; Pomp and Circumstance Marches (exc); *Coleridge Taylor:* Othello (exc); *Bax:* Coronation March. (Mary Lewis, T. Davies, RCS, LPO, LSO, New SO, orch/M. Sargent, M. Sargent)

Ⓓ **1PD2** (11/93)
Crystal Palace Champions
Ireland: Downland Suite; *Elgar:* Severn Suite (exc); *Bliss:* Kenilworth; *Meyerbeer:* Prophète (exc); *Holst:* Moorside Suite; *Bath:* Honour and Glory; *Iles:* Sing a song; Championship Medley 3; *Handel:* Messiah (exc); *Iles:* Homeland Melodies. (Fodens Motor Works Band, Massed Brass Bands, Black Dyke Mills Band, Wingates Temperance Band/F. Mortimer/J. H. Iles/W. Halliwell/H. Moss)

Ⓓ **1PD3** (1/94)
Sir Henry's Themes and Variations
Delius: Dance Rhapsody 1; *Holbrooke:* Blind Mice Variations; *Rameau:* Fêtes d'Hébé (exc); *Handel:* Rodrigo (exc); Almira (exc); *Dvořák:* Symphonic Variations; *Glinka:* Ruslan and Lyudmila (exc); *Bruckner:* Overture in G minor; *Dohnányi:* Symphonic Minuets, Op. 34; *Handel:* Samson (exc). (Queen's Hall Orch/Henry Wood)

Ⓓ **1PD4**
78 Classics - Volume One
Hérold: Zampa (exc); *Veracini:* Rosalinda (exc); *Senaillé:* Premier livre de Sonates (exc); *Schubert:* Heidenröslein, D257; *Elgar:* Capricieuse; *Tchaikovsky:* Mazeppa (exc); *Handel:* Messiah (exc); *Traditional:* Greensleeves (Alas! my love); *Delius:* First cuckoo; *Humperdinck:* Hänsel und Gretel (exc); *Bach:* Cantata 147 (exc); *Lanner:* Pesther-Walzer, Op. 93; *Wagner:* Albumblatt; *Rossini:* Barbiere di Siviglia (exc); *Chopin:* Ballades (exc); *Haydn:* Keyboard Trio 25 (exc); *Haydn Wood:* Roses of Picardy; *Wagner:* Tannhäuser (exc). (L. Tetrazzini, R. Tauber, L. Tibbett, P. Dawson, A. Kipnis, C. Dolmetsch, N. Dolmetsch, A. Camden, A. Campoli, J. Thibaud, P. Casals, M. Hess, A. Cortot, G. Moore, Anon, A. Dolmetsch, Manchester Children's Ch, Bournemouth Municipal Orch/D. Godfrey, orch, Hallé, LSO, Berlin St Op Orch, Massed Brass Bands/H. Harty/G. Toye/C. Schmalstich, BPO/H. Pfitzner/N. Shilkret, R. Zeiler)

Ⓓ **1PD5** (9/94)
Historic Organs, Volume 1
Saint-Saëns: Carnaval des animaux (exc); *Wagner:* Lohengrin (exc); *S.S. Wesley:* Holsworthy Church Bells; *Sibelius:* Finlandia; *Widor:* Symphony 8 (exc); *Elgar:* Organ Sonata 1 (exc); *MacDowell:* Woodland Sketches (exc); *Watling:* Cantilène in B minor; *Batiste:* Pilgrim's Song of Hope; *Bach:* Prelude and Fugue, BWV533; *Clérambault:* Premier livre d'Orgue (exc); *Daquin:* Nouveau livre de noëls (exc); *Franck:* Prélude, fugue et variation; *Saint-Saëns:* Préludes et fugues, Op.99 (exc); Carnaval des animaux (exc). (R. Goss-Custard, G. Thalben-Ball, G.D. Cunningham, J.A. Meale, A. Schweitzer, M. Dupré)

Ⓓ **2PD11**
Russian Masters
Stravinsky: Rite of Spring (Cpte); *Mussorgsky:* Night on the Bare Mountain; Fair at Sorochintsï (exc); *Rimsky-Korsakov:* Golden Cockerel (exc); Snow Maiden (exc). (Concertgebouw/E. van Beinum, LSO, National SO/A. Coates)

Ⓓ **2PD4**
78 Classics - Volume Two
Rossini: Tancredi (exc); *Sullivan:* Lost Chord; *J. Mohr:* Air varié; *Moreno Torroba:* Sonatina in A; *Chabrier:* España; *Smetana:* Kiss (exc); *Rubinstein:* Soirées, Op. 44 (exc); *Delius:* Village Romeo and Juliet (exc); *Purcell:* Libertine, Z600 (exc); *Litolff:* Concerto symphonique, Op. 102 (exc); *Mozart:* Vespers, K339 (exc); *Wagner:* Meistersinger (exc); *J. Strauss II:* Perpetuum mobile; *Handel:* Organ Concertos (exc); *Mozart:* Entführung (exc); *Elgar:* Imperial March. (E. Schumann, U. van Diemen, E. Caruso, L. Melchior, A. Kipnis, C. Draper, A. Segovia, I. Friedman, I. Scharrer, H. Dawson, BBC Wireless Military Band/B.W. O'Donnell, orch, LPO/T. Beecham, LSO/G. Toye, Manchester Children's Ch, Hallé/H. Harty/Henry Wood, Berlin Phil Ch, BPO/S. Ochs/J. Barbirolli, Concertgebouw/W. Mengelberg/A. Coates, Berlin St Op Orch/E. Orthmann, BBC SO/A. Boult, Anon)

Biddulph

Ⓓ **LAB007/8** (1/90)
The Art of Joseph Szigeti, Vol.2
Tartini: Violin Concerto, D96 (exc); *Handel:* Violin Sonatas (exc); *Mozart:* Violin Sonata, K304; *Weber:* Violin Sonatas, J99-104 (exc); *Schubert:* Piano Sonata, D850 (exc); *Brahms:* Violin Sonata 3; *Elgar:* Serenade; Adieu; *Warlock:* Capriol Suite (exc); *Lie:* Snow; *Chabrier:* Pièces pittoresques (exc); *Ravel:* Pièce en forme de habanera; *Falla:* Vida Breve (exc); *Rimsky-Korsakov:* Tale of Tsar Saltan (exc); *Scriabin:* Etudes, Op.8 (exc); *Prokofiev:* Symphony 1 (exc); *Stravinsky:* Pastorale; Petrushka (exc); *Szymanowski:* Myths, Op.30 (exc); *Hubay:* Scènes de la Csárda (exc); *Bartók:* Romanian Folkdances, Sz56; For Children (1908/09) (exc). (J. Szigeti, N. Magaloff, E. Petri, B. Bartók)

Ⓓ **LAB009/10** (7/90)
The Kreisler Collection
Bach: Solo Violin Partitas and Sonatas (exc); Suites, BWV1066-9 (exc); *Sulzer:* Sarabande, Op.8; *F. Schubert II:* Bagatelles, Op.13 (exc); *Tchaikovsky:* Souvenirs de Hapsal, Op.2 (exc); *Kreisler:* Couperin Aubade provençal; Chanson Louis XIII; Couperin précieuse; Dittersdorf Scherzo; Boccherini Allegretto; Cartier Chasse; Liebesfreud; Liebesleid; Tambourin chinois; Caprice viennois; *Bach:* Solo Violin Partitas and Sonatas (exc); *Brahms:* Hungarian Dances (exc); *Tchaikovsky:* Souvenirs de Hapsal, Op.2 (exc); *Cottenet:* Chanson méditation; *Marie:* Cinquantaine; *Rubinstein:* Melodies, Op.3 (exc); *Drigo:* Arlekinda (exc); *Chaminade:* Sérénade espagnole; *Kreisler:* Apple Blossoms (exc); Liebesleid; *H. Kreisler:* Viennese Folksong Fantasy; *Pergolesi:* Tre giorni son che Nina; *Beethoven:* Menuet, WoO10/2; Andante favori, WoO57; *Schumann:* Klavierstücke, Op.85 (exc); *Wagner:* Meistersinger (exc); *Jeral:* Sérénade viennois; *Kreisler:* Marche miniature viennoise; Syncopation; *Traditional:* Londonderry Air; *Mozart:* Violin Concerto, K218; *Bruch:* Violin Concerto 1. (F. Kreisler, anon, H. Squire, F. Kreisler, H. Kreisler, C. Keith, orch/L. Ronald, RAHO/E. Goossens)

Ⓓ **LAB014**
Jacques Thibaud—1922-24 Recordings
Rameau: Fêtes d'Hébé (exc); *Schubert:* Moments musicaux, D780 (exc); *Rode:* Violin Caprices (exc); *Vieuxtemps:* Voix Intimes, Op.45 (exc); *Wieniawski:* Etudes-Caprices, Op.18 (exc); *Dvořák:* Slavonic Dances (exc); *Rimsky-Korsakov:* Golden Cockerel (exc); *Granados:* Danzas españolas (exc); *Franck:* Violin Sonata; *Saint-Saëns:* Déluge (exc); Carnaval des Animaux (exc); *Debussy:* Petite Suite (exc); *Simonetti:* Madrigale. (J. Thibaud, H. Craxton, A. Cortot, J-M. Sanromá)

Ⓓ **LAB017** (10/91)
Casals—The Victor Recordings
Bach: Toccata, Adagio and Fugue, BWV564 (exc); English Suites, BWV806-811 (exc); *Schubert:* Moments musicaux, D780 (exc); *Chopin:* Preludes (exc); Nocturnes (exc); *Schumann:* Klavierstücke, Op.85 (exc); *Wagner:* Meistersinger (exc); Tannhäuser (exc); *Bruch:* Kol Nidrei; *Rubinstein:* Melodies, Op.3 (exc); *Popper:* Stücke, Op. 11 (exc); Vito, Op.54/5; *Hillemacher:* Gavotte tendre; *Sgambati:* Serenata napoletana, Op.24/2; *Godard:* Jocelyn (exc); *Saint-Saëns:* Carnaval des Animaux (exc); *Fauré:* Songs, Op.7 (exc); *Debussy:* Petite Suite (exc); *Granados:* Danzas españolas (exc); Goyescas (exc). (P. Casals, N. Mednikoff)

Ⓓ **LAB019**
Fritz Kreisler—Early Victors
Smetana: From the homeland (exc); *Massenet:* Thaïs (exc); *Dvořák:* Humoresques, Op.101 (exc); *Foster:* Old Folks at Home; *Kreisler:* Caprice viennois; Liebesfreud; Tartini's Corelli Variations; *Rameau:* Fêtes d'Hébé (exc); *Schubert:* Moments musicaux, D780 (exc); *Brahms:* Hungarian Dances (exc); *Tchaikovsky:* Souvenirs de

Hapsal, Op.2 (exc); *Cottenet:* Chanson méditation; *Bach:* Solo Violin Partitas and Sonatas (exc); Solo Violin Partitas and Sonatas (exc); *Gluck:* Orfeo ed Euridice (exc); *Kreisler:* Martini Andantino; Chanson Louis XIII; Liebesleid; Schön Rosmarin; *Townsend:* Berceuse; *Dvořák:* Violin Sonatina (exc); *Rameau:* Fêtes d'Hébé (exc); *Schubert:* Moments musicaux, D780 (exc); *Kreisler:* Austrian Hymn; *Dvořák:* Humoresques, Op.101 (exc). (F. Kreisler, G. Falkenstein, V. O'Brien, M. Eisner, F. Kreisler)

Ⓓ **LAB021**
Fritz Kreisler—Acoustic Victors
Bach: 2-Violin Concerto; *Tchaikovsky:* String Quartet 1 (exc); *Boccherini:* String Quintets, G271-6 (exc); *Kreisler:* Beethoven Rondino; *Bizet:* Arlésienne Suites (exc); *H. Spencer:* Underneath the Stars; *Hubbell:* Big Show (exc); *Schubert:* Rosamunde (exc); *Kreisler:* Polichinelle; *Paderewski:* Humoresques de Concert, Op.14 (exc); *Winternitz:* Dream of Youth; *Earl:* Beautiful Ohio; *Rimsky-Korsakov:* Sadko (exc); *Krakauer:* Im Paradies; *Kreisler:* Gitana; *Valdez:* Sérénade du Tzigane; *Koschat:* Forsaken; *C.C. White:* Bandana Sketches (exc); *Dvořák:* Humoresques, Op.101 (exc); *Kreisler:* Apple Blossoms (exc); *Hirsch:* Mary (exc); *Jacobi:* On Miami Shore. (F. Kreisler, E. Zimbalist, Stg Qt, Stg Trio, orch/J. Pasternack)

Ⓓ **LAB022**
Fritz Kreisler—Duets with McCormack & Farrar
G. Braga: Melodies (exc); *Leroux:* Nil; *Godard:* Jocelyn (exc); *Schubert:* Ave Maria, D839; Schwanengesang, D957 (exc); *Gounod:* Ave Maria; *Mascagni:* Cavalleria Rusticana (exc); *Moszkowski:* Klavierstücke, Op.15 (exc); *G.B. de Curtis:* Carmé; *Meyer-Helmund:* Fensterin, Op.73/2; *C. Böhm:* Lieder, Op.326 (exc); *Raff:* Serenade, Op.1; *Offenbach:* Contes d'Hoffmann (exc); *Rachmaninov:* Songs, Op.4 (exc); *Kramer:* Last Hour, Op.34/6; *J.W. Johnson:* Since you went away; *Kreisler:* Cradle Song; *Brandl:* Liebe Augustin (exc); *A. Thomas:* Mignon (exc); *E. Nevin:* Mighty lak' a rose; *Kreisler:* Apple Blossoms (exc). (F. Kreisler, V. O'Brien, L. Schwat, E. Schneider, J. McCormack, G. Farrar, orch/J. Pasternack/W.B. Rogers)

Ⓓ **LAB024**
Jacques Thibaud—1924-27 Recordings
Bach: Violin Concerto, BWV1042; *Desplanes:* Intrada; *Veracini:* Violin Sonatas, Op.2 (exc); *Mouret:* Triomphe de sens (exc); *Couperin:* Livre de clavecin IV (exc); *Leclair:* Violin Sonatas, Op.9 (exc); *Bach:* Suites, BWV1066-9 (exc); *Beethoven:* Romances (exc); *Brahms:* Waltzes, Op.39 (exc); *Rimsky-Korsakov:* Golden Cockerel (exc); *Debussy:* Children's Corner (exc); Préludes (exc); *Granados:* Danzas españolas (exc). (J. Thibaud, orch/R. Ortmans, H. Craxton, M. Adami)

Ⓓ **LAB032** (4/91)
The young Yehudi Menuhin, Vol.2
Bach: Solo Violin Partitas and Sonatas (exc); *Beethoven:* Violin Sonata 1; *Mozart:* Violin Sonata, K296 (exc); *Corelli:* Sonatas, Op.5 (exc); *Monsigny:* Aline, reine de Golconde (exc); *Nováček:* Concert caprices, Op. 5 (exc); *Rimsky-Korsakov:* Tsar's Bride (exc); *Paganini:* Violin Concerto 2 (exc). (Y. Menuhin, H. Giesen)

Ⓓ **LAB033/4** (6/91)
Jan Kubelík—The Acoustic Recordings (1902-13)
Ambrosio: Romance, Op.9; *Drdla:* Serenade 1; *Saint-Lubin:* Lucia Sextet; *Wieniawski:* Faust Fantaisie (exc); *Sarasate:* Carmen Fantasy (exc); *Paganini:* Paisiello's Introduction and Variations; *Bazzini:* Ronde des lutins; *Ambrosio:* Serenade, Op.4; *Nachéz:* Hungarian Dance 1; *Wieniawski:* Faust Fantaisie (exc); *Paganini:* God save the King variations; Moto Perpetuo, Op.11; *Saint-Lubin:* Lucia Sextet; *Drdla:* Serenade 1; *Schumann:* Kinderszenen (exc); *Bazzini:* Ronde des lutins; *Hubay:* Blumenleben, Op.30 (exc); *Wieniawski:* Scherzo-tarantelle, Op.16; *Raff:* Pieces, Op.85 (exc); *Drdla:* Visione; Souvenir; *Sarasate:* Zigeunerweisen; Danzas españolas (exc); *Fibich:* Moods, Op. 41, Part 2 (exc); *Sgambati:* Serenata napoletana, Op.24/2; *Drdla:* Berceuse, Op.56; *Saint-Saëns:* Carnaval des Animaux (exc); *Paganini:* Violin Concerto 1 (exc); Caprices, Op.1 (exc); *Randegger:* Pierrot sérénade; Pierrot sérénade; *Wieniawski:* Mazurkas, Op.19 (exc); *Sarasate:* Danzas españolas (exc); *F. Ries:* Suite, Op. 34 (exc); *Mozart:* Romanze, KAnh205; *Gluck:* Orfeo ed Euridice (exc); *Tchaikovsky:* Violin Concerto (exc); *Drdla:* Souvenir; *Dvořák:* Humoresques, Op.101 (exc); *Sarasate:* Zigeunerweisen; *Wieniawski:* Violin Concerto 2 (exc); *Sarasate:* Danzas españolas (exc); *Fiorillo:* Etude-caprices, Op. 3 (exc); *Rubinstein:* Soirées, Op. 44. (J. Kubelík, anon, G. Lapierre)

Ⓓ **LAB035**
Mischa Elman—Solo Recordings 1910-1911
Dvořák: Humoresques, Op.101 (exc); *Tchaikovsky:* Songs, Op.6 (exc); *Sarasate:* Caprice Basque; *Beethoven:* Menuet, WoO10/2; *Mozart:* Idomeneo (exc); *Wagner:* Meistersinger (exc); *Saint-Saëns:* Introduction and Rondo Capriccioso; *Tchaikovsky:* Souvenir d'un lieu cher, Op.42 (exc); *Wieniawski:* Souvenir de Moscou, Op.6; *Schubert:* Schwanengesang, D957 (exc); *Chopin:* Nocturnes (exc); *Dittersdorf:* Deutsche Tanz; *Gossec:* Rosine (exc); *Drigo:* Arlekinda (exc); *Pente:* Pieces, Op.12 (exc); *Haydn:* Minuet in F; *Wieniawski:* Faust Fantaisie (exc); *Kreisler:* Francoeur Siciliano and Rigaudon; *Bach:* Suites, BWV1066-9 (exc); *Monsigny:* Aline, reine de Golconde (exc); *Mendelssohn:* String Quartet 1 (exc); *Schumann:* Kinderszenen (exc); *Grétry:* Céphale et Procris (exc); *Gossec:* Camp du Grand Pré (exc); *Dvořák:* Humoresques, Op.101 (exc). (M. Elman, P. Kahn)

Ⓓ **LAB040**
Kreisler Collection
Bach: Solo Violin Partitas and Sonatas (exc); *Mozart:* Serenade, K250 (exc); *Chopin:* Mazurkas (exc); *Brahms:* Waltzes, Op.39 (exc); *Dvořák:* Humoresques, Op.101 (exc); *Tchaikovsky:* String Quartet 1 (exc); *Rimsky-Korsakov:* Golden Cockerel (exc); Sadko (exc); *Falla:* Vida Breve (exc); *Poldini:* Marionnettes (exc); *C. Scott:* Pieces, Op. 47 (exc); *Kreisler:* Caprice viennois; Tambourin chinois; Liebesfreud; Liebesleid; Schön Rosmarin; Beethoven Rondino; Gitana; *Traditional:* Londonderry Air. (F. Kreisler, F. Rupp)

Ⓓ **LAB045** (12/91)
Hubay & Flesch —HMV Recordings
Hubay: Cremona lutenist (exc); Berceuse, Op.79/7; Scènes de la Csárda (exc); Scènes de la Csárda (exc); *Bach:* Suites, BWV1066-9 (exc); *Handel:* Flute Sonatas (exc); *Hubay:* Ugy-e jani?; *Handel:* Dettingen Te Deum (exc); *Paganini:* Caprices, Op.1 (exc); *Handel:* Choice of Hercules (exc); *Fauré:* Berceuse, Op.16; *Falla:* Canciones populares españolas (exc); *Dobroven:* Melody hebraïque. (J. Hubay, O. Herz, Budapest Cons Orch/Mr Zsolt, M. Basilides, C. Flesch, I. Strasfogel)

Ⓓ **LAB046** (12/91)
The Young Yehudi Menuhin
Tartini: Devil's Trill Sonata; *Schubert:* Ave Maria, D839; *Wieniawski:* Scherzo-tarantelle, Op.16; *Moszkowski:* Pieces, Op.45 (exc); *Rimsky-Korsakov:* Tale of Tsar Saltan (exc); *Kreisler:* Francoeur Siciliano and Rigaudon; *Falla:* Vida Breve (exc); *Debussy:* Préludes (exc); *Ravel:* Tzigane; *Lalo:* Symphonie espagnole. (Y. Menuhin, A. Balsam, Paris SO/G. Enescu)

Ⓓ **LAB049/50** (9/92)
Kreisler - The Berlin HMV Recordings (1926-7)
Bach: Solo Violin Partitas and Sonatas (exc); *Beethoven:* Violin Concerto; *Mendelssohn:* Violin Concerto, Op.64; *Brahms:* Violin Concerto; *Mendelssohn:* Songs without words (exc); *Schumann:* Romanzen, Op.94 (exc); *Brahms:* Hungarian Dances (exc); *Debussy:* Préludes (exc); Petite Suite (exc); *Falla:* Vida breve (exc); Vida breve (exc); *C. Scott:* Pieces, Op. 47 (exc); *Corelli:* Trio Sonatas, Op.2 (exc); *Bizet:* Arlésienne Suites (exc); *Kreisler:* Marche miniature viennoise; Syncopation. (F. Kreisler, H. Kreisler, M. Raucheisen, A. Sándor, Berlin St Op Orch/L. Blech)

Ⓓ **LAB059/60** (2/93)
Henri Temianka—Recital
Pugnani: Violin Sonatas, Op.7 (exc); *Bach:* Violin Sonatas, BWV1014-19 (exc); *Handel:* Flute Sonatas (exc); *Schumann:* Romanzen, Op.94 (exc); *Wieniawski:* Polonaise, Op.21; Scherzo-Tarantelle, Op.16; *Sarasate:* Danzas españolas (exc); *Saint-Saëns:* Introduction and Rondo Capriccioso; *Szymanowski:* Romance; King Roger (exc); *Bridge:* Cradle Song, H96; Moto perpetuo, H4c; *Arensky:* Piano Trio 1; *Schubert:* Rondo, D438; *Sibelius:* Humoresques, Opp.87/89 (exc); *Wieniawski:* Polonaise, Op.21. (H. Temianka, J. Graudan, F. Reizenstein, A. Sala, E. Joyce, Temianka CO, H. Temianka (vn/dir), V. Topilin)

Ⓓ **LAB068/9** (9/93)
The Kreisler Collection—1921-25
Brahms: Waltzes, Op.39 (exc); *Grieg:* Lyric Pieces, Op.43 (exc); *Dawes:* Melody in A; *Drdla:* Souvenir; *Kreisler:* Aucassin and Nicolette; Toy Soldier; *Rimsky-Korsakov:* Golden Cockerel (exc); Scheherazade (exc); *F. Logan:* Pale Moon; *C. Scott:* Pieces, Op.47 (exc); Cherry Ripe; *Chopin:* Mazurkas (exc); *Paderewski:* Miscellanea, Op.16 (exc); *Heuberger:* Opernball (exc); *Kramer:* Entr'acte, Op.46/2; *Openshaw:* Love sends a little gift; *Seitz:* World is waiting; *Haydn:* Symphony 96 (exc); *Tchaikovsky:* Violin Concerto (exc); *Friedberg:* Old French Gavotte; *Schütt:* Morceaux, Op.53 (exc); *Poldini:* Marionnettes (exc); *Grainger:* Molly on the Shore; *Balogh:* Dirge of the North; *Korngold:* Tote Stadt (exc); *Handel:* Serse (exc); *Tchaikovsky:* Souvenirs de Hapsal, Op.2 (exc); *Bass:* Chansonette; *Brandl:* Liebe Augustin (exc); *Dawes:* Melody in A; *Herbert:* Orange Blossoms (exc); *Kreisler:* Caprice viennois; *Balogh:* Caprice antique; *Cadman:* Legend of the Canyon; *Lalo:* Symphonie espagnole (exc); *Bach:* Menuet, BWV Anh114; *L. Koželuch:* Ritrovata figlia (exc); *Kreisler:* Russian Folksong paraphrase; *Liliuokalani:* Aloha Oe; *Dvořák:* Symphony 9 (exc); *Cadman:* American Indian Songs, Op.45 (exc); *Traditional:* I saw from the beach; *Rachmaninov:* Songs, Op.26 (exc); *R. Strauss:* Lieder, Op.27 (exc); *Larchet:* Padriac the fiddler. (F. Kreisler, C. Lamson, J. McCormack, E. Schneider)

Ⓓ **LAB070/1** (7/94)
Szigeti recordings with Bartók and Foldes
Bach: Solo Violin Partitas and Sonatas (exc); *Corelli:* Sonatas, Op.5 (exc); *Schubert:* Violin Sonata, D384; Piano Sonata, D850 (exc); *Brahms:* Hungarian Dances (exc); *Dvořák:* Slavonic Dances (exc); *Hubay:* Scènes de la Csárda (exc); *Kodály:* Háry János Suite (exc); *Mussorgsky:* Fair at Sorochintsï (exc); *Lalo:* Roi d'Ys (exc); *Debussy:* Suite bergamasque (exc); Violin Sonata; *Falla:* Sombrero de tres picos Suites (exc); *Milhaud:* Saudades do Brasil (exc); *Bloch:* Baal Shem; *Ives:* Violin Sonata 4; *Bartók:* Rhapsody 1; Contrasts. (J. Szigeti, A. Foldes, B. Bartók, B. Goodman)

Ⓓ **LAB075** (12/93)
Kreisler—1926-1927 Victor Recordings
Romberg: Student Prince (exc); *Friml:* Rose Marie (exc); *Lemare:* Andantino; *Cadman:* At dawning; *Lehár:* Giuditta (exc); *E. Owen:* Invocation; *Rimsky-Korsakov:* Songs, Op.2 (exc); *Tchaikovsky:* Morceaux, Op.10 (exc); *Rachmaninov:* Songs, Op.38 (exc); *Lehár:* Frasquita (exc); *Kreisler:* Caprice viennois; Liebesfreud; Liebesleid; *Berlin:* Blue skies; *Friml:* Dance of the Maidens; *Kreisler:* Shepherd's Madrigal; Gypsy Caprice; Schön Rosmarin; *Falla:* Canciones populares españolas (exc); *Albéniz:* España, Op.165 (exc); *Dvořák:* Humoresques, Op.101 (exc). (F. Kreisler, C. Lamson)

Ⓓ **LAB077/8** (3/94)
Huberman—Complete Brunwick Recordings
Bach: Suites, BWV1066-9 (exc); *Gluck:* Orfeo ed Euridice (exc); *Beethoven:* Violin Sonata 9; *Mendelssohn:* Violin Concerto, Op.64 (exc); *Lalo:* Symphonie espagnole (exc); *Chopin:* Nocturnes (exc); *Tchaikovsky:* Souvenir d'un lieu cher, Op.42 (exc); Violin Concerto (exc); *Brahms:* Hungarian Dances (exc); Hungarian Dances (exc); *Bruch:* Kol Nidrei; *Elgar:* Capricieuse; *Paganini:* Violin Concerto 2 (exc); *Bazzini:* Ronde des lutins; *Vieuxtemps:* Ballade and Polonaise, Op.38; *Wieniawski:* Capriccio-Valse, Op.7; Violin Concerto 2 (exc); Mazurkas, Op.19 (exc); *Zarzycki:* Mazurka, Op.26; *Sarasate:* Danzas españolas (exc); Carmen Fantasy. (B. Huberman, P. Frenkel, S. Schultze)

Ⓓ **LAB080** (12/93)
Kreisler—1928 Victor Recordings
Dohnányi: Ruralia Hungarica; *Debussy:* Petite Suite (exc); Préludes (exc); *Drdla:* Souvenir; *Massenet:* Thaïs (exc); *E. Nevin:* Mighty lak' a rose; Rosary; *Foster:* Old Folks at Home; *Falla:* Vida breve (exc); *Albéniz:* España, Op.165 (exc); *Kreisler:* Tambourin chinois; *Winternitz:* Dance of the Marionettes; *Kreisler:* Beethoven Rondino; *Dvořák:* Slavonic Dances (exc); Violin Sonatina (exc); Gipsy Melodies (exc). (F. Kreisler, C. Lamson)

Ⓓ **LHW016**
Landowska—The Early Recordings 1923-1930
Handel: Keyboard Suites Set I (exc); *Bach:* English Suites, BWV806-811 (exc); *D. Scarlatti:* Keyboard Sonatas (exc); *Rameau:* Pièces de clavecin (exc); *Landowska:* Bourrée d'Auvergne 1; *Mozart:* Piano Sonata, K331 (exc); Don Giovanni (exc); *Rameau:* Pièces de clavecin (exc); *Daquin:* Premier livre de pièces de clavecin (exc); *Handel:* Keyboard Suites Set I (exc); *Mozart:* Piano Sonata, K331 (exc); *Byrd:* Wilson's Wild, BK37; *Daquin:* Premier livre de pièces de clavecin (exc); *Landowska:* Bourrée d'Auvergne 2; *Bach:* English Suites, BWV806-811 (exc); English Suites, BWV806-811 (exc); Fantasia, BWV906; *D. Scarlatti:* Keyboard Sonatas (exc); *Couperin:* Livre de clavecin III (exc); *Mozart:* Piano Sonata, K311. (W. Landowska, W. Landowska, orch/N. Shilkret)

Ⓓ **WHL002**
E. Kleiber conducts Viennese Music
Weber: Invitation to the Dance; *Jos Strauss:* Dorfschwalben aus Österreich; *J. Strauss II:* Zigeunerbaron (exc); Künstlerleben, Op. 316; Fledermaus (exc); Du und Du, Op. 367; Kaiser, Op. 437; *Heuberger:* Opernball (exc); *R. Strauss:* Rosenkavalier (exc). (BPO, VPO/E. Kleiber)

Ⓓ **WHL006/7** (7/94)
Furtwängler—Pre-war HMV Recordings
Beethoven: Symphony 5; *Wagner:* Tristan und Isolde (exc); Parsifal (exc); *Furtwängler:* Symphonic Concerto (exc); *Tchaikovsky:* Symphony 6. (Edwin Fischer, BPO/W. Furtwängler)

Ⓓ **WHL008/9** (5/94)
Toscanini conducts the BBC Symphony Orchestra
Mozart: Zauberflöte (exc); *Beethoven:* Symphony 1; Symphony 4; Symphony 6; Leonore (exc); *Rossini:* Scala di seta (exc); *Weber:* Invitation to the Dance; *Brahms:* Tragic Overture. (BBC SO/A. Toscanini)

Ⓓ **WHL011** (8/95)
Stokowski conducts French Music, Vol.1
Franck: Symphony; Grande pièce symphonique (exc); Panis Angelicus; *Satie:* Gymnopédies (exc); *Dukas:* Apprenti Sorcier; *A. Thomas:* Mignon (exc); *Berlioz:* Damnation de Faust (exc). (Philadelphia/L. Stokowski)

Ⓓ **WHL012** (8/95)
Stokowski conducts French Music, Vol.2
Bizet: Carmen Suites (exc); Arlésienne Suites (exc); *Saint-Saëns:* Danse macabre; Samson et Dalila (exc); Carnaval des animaux. (O. Barabini, M.B. Montgomery, Philadelphia/L. Stokowski)

Ⓓ **WHL021/2** (2/95)
Frederick Stock and the Chicago Symphony Orchestra
Wagner: Meistersinger (exc); *Brahms:* Hungarian Dances (exc); *Goldmark:* Im Frühling; *Suk:* Fairy Tale (exc); *Glazunov:* Ruses d'amour (exc); *Tchaikovsky:* Symphony 5; *Paganini:* Moto perpetuo, Op.11; *Walton:* Scapino; *Dohnányi:* Suite, Op. 19; *R. Strauss:* Also sprach Zarathustra; *Stock:* Waltz, Op.8. (Chicago SO/F. Stock)

Ⓓ **WHL027** (11/95)
Stokowski conducts Dvořák, Liszt, Chopin & Borodin
Dvořák: Symphony 9; *Liszt:* Hungarian Rhapsodies, S359 (exc); *Chopin:* Mazurkas (exc); Preludes (exc); *Borodin:* Prince Igor (exc). (Philadelphia/L. Stokowski)

Biographies in Music

Ⓓ **BIM705-2** (5/90)
Muzio—The Published Edisons, 1920-25
Bachelet: Chère nuit; *Bellini:* Bianca e Fernando (exc); *Bizet:* Carmen (exc); *Boito:* Mefistofele (exc); *Buzzi-Peccia:* Mal d'amore; *Catalani:* Wally (exc); Loreley (exc); *Cilea:* Adriana Lecouvreur (exc); *Giordano:* Andrea Chénier (exc); Madame Sans-Gêne (exc); *Chopin:* Aspiration; *Gluck:* Paride ed Elena (exc); *Gomes:* Salvator Rosa (exc); *Guagni-Benvenuti:* Guardami!; *Handel:* Rinaldo (exc); *Herbert:* Orange Blossoms (exc); *Leoncavallo:* Pagliacci (exc); Zazà (exc); *Mascagni:* Amico Fritz (exc); *A. Mascheroni:* Eternamente; *Massenet:* Hérodiade (exc); *Monahan:* Shepherd's love; *Meyerbeer:* Africaine (exc); *Offenbach:* Contes d'Hoffmann (exc); *Parisotti:* Se tu m'ami; *Puccini:* Bohème (exc); *Rossini:* Separazione; *Sodero:* Crisantemi; *Tchaikovsky:* Eugene Onegin (exc); *Verdi:* Trovatore (exc); Forza del Destino (exc); Lombardi (exc); Vespri Siciliani (exc). (C. Muzio, orch, Anon, M. Laurenti, A. Spalding, R. Gaylor)

Birmingham Bach Choir

Ⓓ **BBCCD2** (12/93)
There shall a star
Traditional: Torches; As with gladness; There shall a star; *Humperdinck:* Hänsel und Gretel (exc); *Prokofiev:* Lt Kijé Suite (exc); *Traditional:* Tomorrow shall be my dancing day; Away in a manger; Shepherds had an Angel; *M. Praetorius:* Es ist ein Ros'; *Traditional:* Benedicamus Domino; Bethlehem Down; What Cheer?; In dulci jubilo; Little child on the earth; In the bleak midwinter; Stille Nacht; Noël Nouvelet; Sing lullaby; Sussex carol; Nowell: Dieu vous garde. (Birmingham Bach Ch, Fine Arts Brass Ens/M. Shepherd, R. Dacey/P. Spicer)

BIS

Ⓓ **BIS-CD017** (9/93)
Söderström and Meyer sing Duets
Kodály: Bicinia hungarica (exc); *Tchaikovsky:* Duets, Op. 46 (exc); *Dvořák:* Moravian Duets, B62 (exc); Moravian Duets, B60 (exc); *Purcell:* Welcome Song, Z335; King Arthur, Z628 (exc); Indian Queen, Z630 (exc); *Wennerberg:* Sutlers; Girls; *Geijer:* Dance; *Rossini:* Soirées musicales (exc); Duetto buffo di due gatti. (E. Söderström, K. Meyer, J. Eyron)

Ⓓ **BIS-CD100**
Sun-Flute
Albinoni: Adagio; *Debussy:* Syrinx; *Gluck:* Orfeo ed Euridice (exc); *Molter:* Flauto d'amore Concerto; *Mozart:* Andante, K315; Rondo, KAnh184; *Nielsen:* Mother (exc); *Grieg:* Elegiac Melodies (exc); *Bach:* Suites, BWV1066-9 (exc). (G. von Bahr, Stockholm Chbr Ens/J-O. Wedin, W. Sundling, J-O. Wedin, L. Jonsson, L-O. Bergström, S. Westling, E. Nordenfelt, K. Langebo, K. Langebo, R. Östblom)

Ⓓ **BIS-CD166**
The Virtuoso Flute
Taffanel: Der Freischütz Fantasia; *Kuhlau:* Introduction and Rondo, Op. 98a; *Paganini:* Caprices, Op. 1 (exc); *Saint-Saëns:* Ascanio (exc); *T. Böhm:* Grande Polonaise; *Doppler:* Fantaisie, Op. 26; Berceuse, Op. 15; Souvenir du Rigi, Op. 38; Andante et Rondo, Op. 25. (R. Aitken, P. Øien, G.H. Braaten, E. Westenholz)

Ⓓ **BIS-CD250** (3/85)
Sibelius—The Maiden in the Tower; Karelia
Sibelius: Maiden in the Tower (Cpte); Karelia Suite. (M.A. Häggander, E. Hagegård, J. Hynninen, T. Kruse, Gothenburg Concert Hall Ch, Gothenburg SO/N. Järvi)

Ⓓ **BIS-CD258**
The Virtuoso Trombone
Rimsky-Korsakov: Tale of Tsar Saltan (exc); *Šulek:* Sonata (Vox Gabrieli); *Martin:* Trombone Ballade; *Monti:* Csárdás; *Kreisler:* Liebesleid; *Pryor:* Blue bells of Scotland; *Hindemith:* Trombone Sonata; *Berio:* Sequenza V. (C. Lindberg, R. Pöntinen)

Ⓓ **BIS-CD296** (8/94)
Verdi—Rigoletto
Verdi: Rigoletto (Cpte). (H. Hasslo, M. Hallin, N. Gedda, A. Tyrén, G. Svedenbrant, K. Meyer, B. Ericson, O. Sivall, A. Näslund, I. Kjellgren, I. Wixell, B. Nordin, Stockholm Royal Op Chor, Stockholm Royal Op Orch/S. Ehrling)

Ⓓ **BIS-CD300** (11/85)
Music for a Rainy Day
Satie: Gnossiennes; *Debussy:* Suite bergamasque (exc); *Seymer:* Sologa; *Prokofiev:* Love for 3 Oranges Suite (exc); *Grieg:* Lyric Pieces, Op. 65 (exc); *Schumann:* Kinderszenen (exc); *Stenhammar:* Fantasies, Op. 11 (exc); *Beethoven:* Bagatelles (exc); *Scriabin:* Poèmes, Op. 32 (exc); *Falla:* Amor Brujo (exc); *Chopin:* Nocturnes (exc); Preludes (exc). (R. Pöntinen)

Ⓓ **BIS-CD321** (8/86)
Nielsen—Orchestral Works
Nielsen: Symphony 3; Clarinet Concerto; Maskarade (exc). (P. Raanoja, K. Skram, O. Schill, Gothenburg SO/Myung-Whun Chung)

Ⓓ **BIS-CD328**
The Criminal Trombone
Rossini: Barbiere di Siviglia (exc); *Schumann:* Romanzen, Op. 94; *Mozart:* Variations, K265; *Albinoni:* Adagio; *Schubert:* Arpeggione Sonata, D821 (exc); *Bach:* Suites, BWV1066-9 (exc). (C. Lindberg, R. Pöntinen)

Ⓓ **BIS-CD352** (9/87)
Bernstein: Piano Arrangements
Bernstein: West Side Story Symphonic Dances; Fancy Free; Touches. (D. Achatz)

Ⓓ **BIS-CD373/4**
Opera Scenes from Savaonlinna
Beethoven: Fidelio (exc); *Mozart:* Zauberflöte (exc); *Wagner:* Fliegende Holländer (exc); *Mussorgsky:* Boris Godunov (exc); *Verdi:* Don Carlo (exc); Aida (exc). (R. Auvinen, S. Vihavainen, P. Lindroos, J. Silvasti, T. Krause, B. Rundgren, J. Hynninen, J. Falck, J. Rhyänen, T. Valjakka, A. Välkki, S. Ruohonen, R. Sirkiä, M. Talvela, U. Viitanen, H. Kilpeläinen, A. Alamikkotervo, M. Salminen, R. Viljakainen, P. Talola, P. Raanoja, U. Sippola, J. Tilli, W. Groenroos, Savonlinna Op Fest Chor, Savonlinna Op Fest Orch/U. Söderblom/I. Mansnerus/K. Haatanen/L. Segerstam)

Ⓓ **BIS-CD381** (8/88)
Pierné—Orchestral Music
Pierné: Ramuntcho (exc); Piano Concerto. (D. Achatz, Lorraine PO/J. Houtmann)

Ⓓ **BIS-CD383** (7/88)
Works for Male Chorus
Traditional: Hey, let's carouse; In our meadow; *Peterson-Berger:* On the fell in sunshine; *Söderman:* Peasant wedding (exc); *Wikander:* King Lily of the Valley; *Bartók:* Old Hungarian Folksongs, Sz50; *Tormis:* Songs of Hamlet; *Suchoň:* Slovakian Folksongs; *J. N. David:* Wir zogen in das Feld; *R. Strauss:* Männerchöre (1935) (exc); *Reger:* An das Meer; *Barber:* Stopwatch; *Bossi:* Brivido; *Milhaud:* Psaumes de David (exc); *Saint-Saëns:* Saltarelle; *Verdi:* Trovatore (exc); *Gounod:* Faust (exc). (Orphei Drängar Ch, Swedish RSO/E. Ericson/L. Segerstam)

Ⓓ **BIS-CD421/4(1)**
The Stockholm PO—1914-1989
Alfvén: Midsummer Vigil, Op. 19; Symphony 4 (exc); *Auber:* Gustav III (exc); *Bartók:* Duke Bluebeard's Castle (exc); Miraculous Mandarin (exc); *Beethoven:* Symphony 9 (exc); Symphony 9 (exc); Symphony 9 (exc); Symphony 9 (exc); Symphony 9 (exc); Symphony 9 (exc); Symphony 9 (exc); Symphony 9 (exc); Symphony 9 (exc); Symphony 9 (exc); Leonore (exc); Leonore (exc); *F. Berwald:* Symphony 1 (exc); Symphony 3 (exc); Symphony 3; *Brahms:* Symphony 1 (exc); Symphony 3 (exc); *Dvořák:* Symphony 6; Symphony 7 (exc); *Hindemith:* Concerto for Orchestra; Symphonic Metamorphosis (exc); *Kodály:* Psalmus hungaricus; *Larsson:* Symphony 2 (exc); *Mahler:* Lied von der Erde (exc); *Mozart:* Symphony 40; Symphony 40 (exc); *Mahler:* Symphony 6 (exc); *Nystroem:* Sinfonia Espressiva; *Orff:* Carmina burana. (Stockholm PO/P. Berglund/A. Dorati, S. Björling/B. Walter, A. Nordmo-Løvberg, H. Selin, R. Ulfung, Musikaliska Sällskapet/H. Schmidt-Isserstedt, G. Bäckelin/P. Kletzki/E. Kleiber/H. Abendroth, H. Schymberg, L. Tunell/W. Furtwängler, R. Althén, I. Aulin-Voghera, E. Krogh, J. Berglund/V. Talich/H. von Karajan/G. Schnéevoigt, K. Thorborg/F. Busch/N. Grevillius/T. Mann/C. von Garaguly, E. Söderström, S. Svanholm, Stockholm Univ Chor, J. Simándy/G. Rozhdestvensky/Y. Ahronovitch/E. Ormandy/I. Markevitch/P. Hindemith/R. Kubelík/O. Klemperer/J. Horenstein/A. Toscanini/L. Stokowski)

Ⓓ **BIS-CD421/4(2)**
The Stockholm PO, 1914-1989
Stenhammar: Serenade, Op. 31; Symphony 2 (exc); *Tchaikovsky:* Nutcracker Suite (exc); Suite 3 (exc); Symphony 5 (exc); *Wagner:* Tristan und Isolde (exc); *Wiklund:* Symphonic Prologue; *Pergament:* Rapsodie ebraica; *Pettersson:* Symphonic Movement; Symphony 16 (exc); *Ravel:* Daphnis et Chloé Suites (exc); *Rosenberg:* Concerto for Strings (1946) (exc); *Rossini:* Barbiere di Siviglia (exc); *Scriabin:* Symphony 2 (exc); *Shostakovich:* Bolt Suite (exc); *Sibelius:* Symphony 5 (exc); *Stenhammar:* Florez and Blanzeflor. (Stockholm PO/A. Dorati/T. Mann/D. Kaye/Y. Ahronovitch/F. Fricsay/W. Furtwängler/A. Wiklund/C. von Garaguly/A. Toscanini/G. Rozhdestvensky/H. von Karajan, J. Berglund/G. Schnéevoigt)

Ⓓ **BIS-CD449/50**
Janáček—Jenůfa
Janáček: Jenufa (Cpte). (G. Beňačková, W. Ochman, Leonie Rysanek, P. Kazaras, K. Cowdrick, B. Schramm, K. Shaw, F. Barr, N.L. Hartliep, M. Partamian, A. Rubstein, K. Johnson, NY Schola Cantorum, NY Op Orch/E. Queler)

Ⓓ **BIS-CD478**
The Russian Trombone
Goedicke: Improvisation; *Tchaikovsky:* Queen of Spades (exc); *H.G. Okunev:* Adagio and Scherzo; *Ewald:* Mélodie; *Prokofiev:* Romeo and Juliet Suites (exc); *Denisov:* Choral varié. (C. Lindberg, R. Pöntinen)

Ⓓ **BIS-CD498** (8/92)
Kokkonen—Complete Orchestral Music, Vol.3
Kokkonen: Inauguratio; Symphony 2; Last Temptations (exc); Erekhtheion. (S. Vihavainen, W. Groenroos, Academic Choral Soc, Lahti SO/O. Vänskä)

Ⓓ **BIS-CD520** (8/92)
Matti Salminen - Opera Recital
Mozart: Zauberflöte (exc); Entführung (exc); *Beethoven:* Fidelio (exc); *Verdi:* Macbeth (exc); Simon Boccanegra (exc); Don Carlo (exc); *Rossini:* Barbiere di Siviglia (exc); *Puccini:* Bohème (exc); *Tchaikovsky:* Eugene Onegin (exc); *Wagner:* Fliegende Holländer (exc); *R. Strauss:* Schweigsame Frau (exc). (M. Salminen, Lahti SO/E. Klas)

Ⓓ **BIS-CD555** (7/93)
Saint-Saëns—Orchestral Works
Saint-Saëns: Symphony 3; Danse macabre; Samson et Dalila (exc); Rhapsodies, Op. 7. (H. Fagius, Stockholm PO/J. DePreist)

Ⓓ **BIS-CD570** (1/93)
Malmö Symphony Orchestra
Rosenberg: Marionetter Overture and Suite; *Bizet:* Carmen Suites (exc); *Larsson:* Hours of the Day (exc); *Glinka:* Ruslan and Lyudmila (exc); *Satie:* Gymnopédies (exc); *Shostakovich:* Festive Overture; *Svendsen:* Romance, Op.26; *Alfvén:* Herdsmaiden's dance. (Malmö SO/J. DePreist)

Bluebell

Ⓓ **ABCD002**
Jussi Björling in Rigoletto & Il Trovatore
Verdi: Rigoletto (exc); Trovatore (exc). (J. Björling, E. Prytz, B. Ericson, K. Meyer, O. Sivall, E. Sundquist, Stockholm Royal Op Orch/K. Bendix, H. Schymberg, H. Hasslo, Stockholm Royal Op Chor/H. Sandberg)

Ⓓ **ABCD006** (8/88)
Jussi Björling Live - Holland 1939, Norway 1954
Verdi: Requiem (exc); *Meyerbeer:* Africaine (exc); *Bizet:* Carmen (exc); *Massenet:* Manon (exc); *Gounod:* Faust (exc); *Puccini:* Bohème (exc); *Handel:* Serse (exc); *Niedermeyer:* Pietà, Signore; *Verdi:* Requiem (exc); *Alfvén:* Songs, Op. 28 (exc); *Sibelius:* Songs, Op.36 (exc); *Grieg:* Melodies of the Heart, Op. 5 (exc); Songs, Op.25 (exc). (J. Björling, Hilversum RO/F. Weissmann, Bergen SO/C. Garaguly)

Ⓓ **ABCD011**
Uppsala Chamber Soloists
Tchaikovsky: Souvenir de Florence; *Wolf:* Italian Serenade; *R. Strauss:* Capriccio (exc). (Uppsala Chbr Sols)

Ⓓ **ABCD013** (3/92)
Björling & Schymberg sing Puccini & Gounod
Puccini: Bohème (exc); *Gounod:* Roméo et Juliette (exc). (H. Schymberg, J. Björling, S. Herdenberg, C. Richter, L. Björker, Stockholm Royal Op Orch/N. Grevillius)

Ⓓ **ABCD014**
Viennese Delights
J. Strauss II: Indigo-Marsch, Op. 349; Wiener Blut (exc); Nacht in Venedig (exc); Fledermaus Quadrille, Op. 363; Fledermaus (exc); Tausend und eine Nacht; *Lehár:* Paganini (exc); Gold und Silber; Lustige Witwe (exc); Weiber-Marsch. (N. Gedda, T. Gedda, Stockholm Palm Court Orch/L. Almgren)

Ⓓ **ABCD016** (8/92)
Jussi Björling—Rare Records & Alternative Takes
Borodin: Prince Igor (exc); *Dahl:* Bacchanal; *Nyblom:* Flaming Golden Stream; *O. Thiel:* Was it a dream?; *Enders:* Little Princess; *J. Strauss II:* Zigeunerbaron (exc); *Millöcker:* Bettelstudent (exc); *Offenbach:* Belle Hélène (exc); *Rossini:* Stabat mater (exc); *Verdi:* Trovatore (exc); Rigoletto (exc); *Mascagni:* Cavalleria rusticana (exc); *Gounod:* Roméo et Juliette (exc); *Foster:* Jeanie with the light brown hair; *Hardelot:* Because; *Puccini:* Manon Lescaut (exc); *Mascagni:* Cavalleria rusticana (exc); *Gounod:* Roméo et Juliette (exc); *Dresser:* On the Banks of the Wabash; *Traditional:* In Heaven; God's innocent Lamb; *Beneken:* Oh, how peacefully; *Wennerberg:* Psalm 4. (J. Björling, H. Schymberg, A-L. Björling, orch/N. Grevillius/S. Waldimir, Stockholm Royal Op Orch, Stockholm Concert Soc Orch, Inst Ens)

Ⓓ **ABCD028** (3/92)
Jussi Björling live at the Stockholm Opera
Puccini: Manon Lescaut (exc); *Mascagni:* Cavalleria Rusticana (exc); *Leoncavallo:* Pagliacci (exc). (H. Schymberg, J. Björling, H. Hasslo, B. Lundborg, A. Nordmo-Løvberg, B. Björling, M. Sehlmark, G. Svedenbrant, R. Moberg, Stockholm Royal Op Chor, Stockholm Royal Op Orch/N. Grevillius/K. Bendix/L. Gardelli)

Ⓓ **ABCD038**
4 X Göran W. Nilson
Debussy: Préludes (exc); *Söderlundh:* Haväng Suite; *Fibich:* Moods, Op. 41, Part 2 (exc); *Bizet:* Pêcheurs de Perles (exc); *Tchaikovsky:* Souvenirs de Hapsal, Op. 2 (exc); *Halvorsen:* Veslemöy's song; *Rimsky-Korsakov:* Tale of Tsar Saltan (exc); *Massenet:* Thaïs (exc); *Nilson:* Meditations; Swedish Folk Songs. (N-E Sparf, M. Levin, G.W. Nilson (pf/dir), S-O. Svarfvar, Örebro CO/G.W. Nilson)

Ⓓ **ABCD042**
Björling - The Stockholm Tivoli Recordings, Vol.1: 1958-60
Rachmaninov: Songs, Op. 4 (exc); *Bizet:* Carmen (exc); *Millöcker:* Bettelstudent (exc); *Mozart:* Zauberflöte (exc); *R. Strauss:* Lieder, Op. 29 (exc); Lieder, Op.27 (exc); *Körling:* Evening Mood; *Peterson-Berger:* Swedish Folk Ballads (exc); *Eklöf:* Morning; *Wolf:* Mörike Lieder (exc); *Liszt:* Es muss ein Wunderbares sein, S314; *R. Strauss:* Lieder, Op. 17 (exc); *Peterson-Berger:* Swedish Folk Ballads (exc); *Nordqvist:* Toward the sea; *Giordano:* Andrea Chénier (exc); *De Curtis:* Torna a Surriento; *Söderman:* Enchanted Lake; *Borodin:* Prince Igor (exc); *Tosti:* Ideale; *Althén:* Thou Blessed Land; *Hardelot:* Because. (J. Björling, H. Ebert, B. Bokstedt)

Ⓓ **ABCD044**
Verdi—Rigoletto
Verdi: Rigoletto (Cpte). (E. Sundquist, E. Prytz, J. Björling, S-E. Jacobsson, K. Meyer, G. Svedenbrant, B. Ericson, O. Sivall, C-A. Hallgren, J. Garellick, I. Wixell, C. Nilsson, B. Alstergård, Stockholm Royal Op Chor, Stockholm Royal Op Orch/K. Bendix)

Ⓓ **ABCD045**
Verdi—Il Trovatore
Verdi: Trovatore (Cpte). (J. Björling, H. Schymberg, H. Hasslo, K. Meyer, E. Saedén, I. Kjellgren, O. Sivall, B. Alstergård, S. Ingebretzen, Stockholm Royal Op Chor, Stockholm Royal Op Orch/H. Sandberg)

Ⓓ **ABCD057**
Björling—Gröna Lund Recordings, Volume 2
Leoncavallo: Pagliacci (exc); *Giordano:* Andrea Chénier (exc); *Meyerbeer:* Africaine (exc); *Schubert:* Schöne Müllerin (exc); *Tosti:* Alba separa; *Sjögren:* You are near in my dreams; Ich möchte schweben; *Puccini:* Turandot (exc); *Mascagni:* Cavalleria rusticana (exc); *Stenhammar:* Sweden; *Leoncavallo:* Mattinata; *Sjöberg:* Tonerna; *Peterson-Berger:* Maiden under the Linden Tree; *Verdi:* Aida (exc); *Flotow:* Martha (exc); *Sibelius:* Songs, Op.36 (exc); *Puccini:* Bohème (exc); *Verdi:* Rigoletto (exc); *Millöcker:* Bettelstudent (exc); *Ponchielli:* Gioconda (exc); *A. Thomas:* Mignon (exc); *Verdi:* Ballo in maschera (exc). (J. Björling, H. Ebert, B. Bokstedt)

BNL

Ⓓ **BNL112822**
Transcriptions for Piano
Liszt: Don Juan réminiscences, S418; *Gluck:* Orfeo ed Euridice (exc); *Liszt:* Chants polonais, S480 (exc); *Saint-Saëns:* Danse macabre; *Delibes:* Lakmé (exc); *Chopin:* Waltzes (exc); *Ravel:* Pièce en forme de Habanera; *Horowitz:* Carmen Variations; *Albéniz:* España, Op. 165 (exc); *Falla:* Amor brujo (exc); *Handel:* Lessons (exc). (E. Himy)

Bongiovanni

Ⓓ **GB1039-2**
Antonio Guarnieri
Spontini: Vestale (exc); *Rossini:* Gazza ladra (exc); Guillaume Tell (exc); *Verdi:* Traviata (exc); Vespri siciliani (exc); Otello (exc); *Wagner:* Tristan und Isolde (exc); *Bizet:* Carmen (exc); *Catalani:* Loreley (exc); *Mascagni:* Cavalleria rusticana (exc). (La Scala Chor, La Scala Orch/A. Guarnieri)

Ⓓ **GB1043-2** (12/94)
Italian Baritones of the Acoustic Era
Verdi: Rigoletto (exc); *Leoncavallo:* Roland von Berlin (exc); *Verdi:* Forza del destino (exc); *Petrella:* Jone (exc); *Donizetti:* Elisir d'amore (exc); *Robaudi:* Alla stella confidente; *Tirindelli:* Mistica; *Marchetti:* Ruy Blas (exc); *Gastaldon:* Musica proibita; Ti vorrei rapire; *Donizetti:* Favorita (exc); *Massenet:* Hérodiade (exc); *Tirindelli:* Myosotis; *Verdi:* Aida (exc); Forza del destino (exc); Forza del destino (exc); *Bizet:* Carmen (exc); *A. Thomas:* Hamlet (exc); *Gounod:* Faust (exc). (F.M. Bonini, F. Corradetti, T. Parvis, G. Bellantoni, G. Campanari, L. Montesanto, G. Viviani, E. Badini, G.M. Patti, N. Fusati, A. de Revers, L. Mellerio, anon, orch, anon)

Ⓓ **GB1060-2**
Virginia Zeani - Various opera arias
Bellini: Puritani (exc); *Donizetti:* Lucia di Lammermoor (exc); Elisir d'amore (exc); Anna Bolena (exc); *Verdi:* Forza del Destino (exc); Aida (exc); Don Carlo (exc); *Lehár:* Lustige Witwe (exc). (V. Zeani, A. Mongelli, A. Protti, Alfredo Kraus, N. Rossi-Lemeni, A. Lazzari, Trieste Teatro Verdi Orch, Piacenza SO, Turin RAI Orch, Naples San Carlo Op Orch, Rome RAI Orch/F. M. Prandelli/A. Zedda/F. Vernizzi/M. Rossi/F. Previtali/P. Urbini/B. Maderna)

Ⓓ **GB1064/5-2**
Fernando de Lucia
Massenet: Werther (exc); *Giordano:* Fedora (exc); *Mascagni:* Cavalleria Rusticana (exc); *Bizet:* Carmen (exc); Pêcheurs de perles (exc); *A. Thomas:* Mignon (exc); *Gounod:* Faust (exc); *Rossini:* Barbiere di Siviglia (exc); *Verdi:* Traviata (exc); *Bizet:* Pêcheurs de perles (exc); *Rossini:* Barbiere di Siviglia (exc); *Verdi:* Rigoletto (exc); *Wagner:* Lohengrin (exc); *Bizet:* Carmen (exc); *Bellini:* Sonnambula (exc); *Verdi:* Luisa Miller (exc); *Barthélemy:* Sulla bocca amorosa; *P.M. Costa:* Era di maggio; *Boito:* Mefistofele (exc); *Massenet:* Manon (exc); *Ponchielli:* Gioconda (exc); *Bizet:* Pêcheurs de perles (exc); *Verdi:* Rigoletto (exc); Aida (exc); *Meyerbeer:* Africaine (exc); *Puccini:* Bohème (exc); Tosca (exc); *Verdi:* Trovatore (exc); Forza del destino (exc); Ernani (exc); *Mascagni:* Amico Fritz (exc); *Gounod:* Ave Maria; *Verdi:* Rigoletto (exc); *Puccini:* Tosca (exc); *Ponchielli:* Gioconda (exc); *Mascagni:* Iris (exc). (F. de Lucia, A. Pini-Corsi, J. Huguet, M. Galvany, B. Franci, anon, orch)

Ⓓ **GB1076-2**
Mario Gilion - Opera Arias
Verdi: Trovatore (exc); *Rossini:* Guillaume Tell (exc); *Verdi:* Forza del destino (exc); *Mascagni:* Cavalleria Rusticana (exc); *Meyerbeer:* Africaine (exc); *Verdi:* Ballo in maschera (exc); *Bellini:* Norma (exc); *Bizet:* Carmen (exc); *Halévy:* Juive (exc); *Franchetti:* Germania (exc); *Meyerbeer:* Prophète (exc); *Verdi:* Otello (exc); *Meyerbeer:* Huguenots (exc); *Petrella:* Jone (exc); *Saint-Saëns:* Samson et Dalila (exc); *Wagner:* Walküre (exc); *Verdi:* Don Carlo (exc); *Wagner:* Tannhäuser (exc); *Verdi:* Trovatore (exc). (M. Gilion, F.M. Bonini, E. Cervi-Caroli, N. Frascani, anon, orch)

Ⓓ **GB1078-2**
Mafalda Favero
Mozart: Don Giovanni (exc); *Flotow:* Martha (exc); *Wagner:* Lohengrin (exc); *Boito:* Mefistofele (exc); Mefistofele (exc); *Verdi:* Otello (exc); *Mascagni:* Amico Fritz (exc); Amico Fritz (exc); *Leoncavallo:* Pagliacci (exc); *Puccini:* Manon Lescaut (exc); Bohème (exc); Bohème (exc); Bohème (exc); Madama Butterfly (exc); Madama Butterfly (exc); *Mascagni:* Lodoletta (exc); *Puccini:* Turandot (exc); Turandot (exc); *Bottacchiari:* Ombra (exc). (M. Favero, A. Ziliani, orch, La Scala Orch/A. Sabino/F. Ghione/G. Antonicelli, I. Ruotolo)

Ⓓ **GB1101/2-2**
Massenet—Werther
Massenet: Werther (Cpte). (Ferruccio Tagliavini, G. Simionato, G. Orlandini, D. Gatta, S. Bruscantini, V. Pandano, E. Campi, I. Ligabue, La Scala Chor, La Scala Orch/F. Capuana)

Ⓓ **GB2063/4-2**
Salieri and Scarlatti—Operas
Salieri: Prima la musica (Cpte); *A. Scarlatti:* Lesbina e Adolfo (Cpte). (G. Polidori, G. Gatti, M. Casula, K. Gamberucci, D. Uccello, G. Gatti, Boemia del Nord Phil CO/D. Sanfilippo)

Ⓓ **GB2070-2** (7/95)
Donizetti—I pazzi per progetto
Donizetti: Pazzi per progetto (Cpte). (L. Monreale, S. Rigacci, G. Polidori, A. Cicogna, V. M. Brunetti, E. Fissore, G. Sarti, Toscanini SO/B. Rigacci)

Ⓓ **GB2073/4-2**
Piccinni—La Pescatrice
Piccinni: Pescatrice (Cpte). (M. Pennicchi, M.L. Garbato, M. Comencini, G. Gatti, Sassari SO/C. Rizzi)

Ⓓ **GB2115-2** (1/94)
Ponchielli—Orchestral Works
Ponchielli: Garibaldi Elegia; Sinfonia; Sinfonia; Scena campestre; Lituani (exc); Promessi sposi (exc); Gavotte poudrée. (Minsk PO/S. Frontalini)

Ⓓ **GB2131/2-2**
Rossini—Sigismondo
Rossini: Sigismondo (Cpte). (S. Ganassi, R. Ragatzu, B. Lazzaretti, N. Zanini, G. Prestia, F. Pina, Trevigiano Autunno Chor, Rovigo Venezze Cons Orch/R. Bonynge)

Ⓓ **GB2144-2**
Mercandante—Overtures from the Operas
Mercadante: Elena da Feltre (exc); Normanni a Parigi (exc); Nitocri (exc); Schiava saracena (exc); Reggente (exc); Sciti (exc); 4-Cello Melodia. (Moldava SO/S. Frontalini)

Ⓓ **GB2145/6-2** (1/95)
Sacchini—La Contadina in Corte
Sacchini: Contadina in Corte (Cpte). (C. Forte, S. Rigacci, E. Palacio, G. Gatti, Sassari SO/G. Catalucci)

Ⓓ **GB2153/5-2**
Stradella—Moro per Amore
Stradella: Moro per amore (Cpte). (R. Ristori, R. Invernizzi, S. Piccollo, M. Lazzara, V. Matacchini, M. G. Liguori, M. Beasley, A. Stradella Consort/E. Velardi)

Ⓓ **GB2168/9-2**
Mascagni—Il Piccolo Marat
Mascagni: Piccolo Marat (Cpte). (D. Galvez-Vallejo, F. Vassar, S. Neves, C. Pfeiler, S. Cowan, H. Claessens, M. Dirks, L. Visser, D. Henry, Netherlands Rad Chor, Netherlands RSO/K. Bakels)

Ⓓ **GB2513-2** (10/94)
Mariella Devia—Opera Arias
Bellini: Capuleti (exc); Sonnambula (exc); Puritani (exc); *Donizetti:* Lucia di Lammermoor (exc); *Gounod:* Roméo et Juliette (exc); *G. Charpentier:* Louise (exc); *Delibes:* Lakmé (exc). (M. Devia, Svizzera Italiana Orch/M. Rota)

Bravura

Ⓓ **BVA8634** ▭ **BVA8632**
Encores for Flute and Piano
Pierné: Canzonetta; *Elgar:* Chanson de Matin; Salut d'Amour; Nursery Suite (exc); *Brahms:* Waltzes, op 39 (exc); *Caplet:* Rêverie et Petite Valse (exc); *Chopin:* Waltzes (exc); *Fauré:* Morceau de lecture; *Gounod:* Petite symphonie (exc); *Purcell:* Airs (exc); *F. Ries:* Capricciosa; *Donizetti:* Oboe Sonata (exc); *Drdla:* Serenade 1; *Flotow:* Martha (exc); *Genin:* Air Napolitain; *Hüe:* Petite Pièce; *Mendelssohn:* Shepherd's Song; *S. Robinson:* Moon Maiden; *Woodall:* Serenade. (W. Bennett, C. Benson)

Bridge

Ⓓ **BCD9007**
Machover—Valis
Machover: Valis (Cpte). (P. Mason, J. Felty, T. Edwards, T. Bogdan, M. King, D. Runswick, A. Azéma, D. Ciampolini, E. Stephenson/T. Machover)

Butterfly

Ⓓ **BMCD001** ▭ **BMK001**
Pavarotti Collection - Rigoletto
Verdi: Rigoletto (Cpte). (K. Paskalis, R. Scotto, L. Pavarotti, P. Washington, B. Bortoluzzi, P. Clabassi, C.

Vozza, F. Iacopucci, A. la Porta, N. Pragranza, G. Ciavola, F. Carotenuto, E. Titta, Rome Op Chor, Rome Op Orch/C.M. Giulini)

Ⓓ **BMCD002** ▭ **BMK002**
Pavarotti Collection - La Traviata
Verdi: Traviata (Cpte). (J. Sutherland, L. Pavarotti, S. Milnes, F. von Stade, L. di Franco, L. Goeke, R. Gibbs, G. Boucher, L. Sgarro, L. Marcella, J. Trehy, NY Met Op Chor, NY Met Op Orch/R. Bonynge)

Ⓓ **BMCD003** ▭ **BMK003**
Pavarotti Collection - Lucia di Lammermoor
Donizetti: Lucia di Lammermoor (Cpte). (C. Deutekom, L. Pavarotti, D. Trimarchi, S. Pagliuca, B. Sebastian, M. Ferrara, Naples San Carlo Op Chor, Naples San Carlo Op Orch/C. Franci)

Ⓓ **BMCD004** ▭ **BMK004**
Pavarotti Collection - Manon
Massenet: Manon (Cpte). (M. Freni, L. Pavarotti, W. Ganzarolli, A. Zerbini, G. Morresi, F. Ricciardi, La Scala Chor, La Scala Orch/P. Maag)

Ⓓ **BMCD006** ▭ **BMK006**
Pavarotti Collection - L'Elisir d'Amore
Donizetti: Elisir d'amore (Cpte). (R. Grist, L. Pavarotti, I. Wixell, S. Bruscantini, S. Matsumoto, San Francisco Op Chor, San Francisco Op Orch/G. Patanè)

Ⓓ **BMCD007** ▭ **BMK007**
Pavarotti Collection - La Boheme
Puccini: Bohème (Cpte). (M. Freni, L. Pavarotti, M. Oran, G. Taddei, N. Carta, R. Arié, Madrid Zarzuela Chor, Madrid Zarzuela Orch/N. Sanzogno)

Ⓓ **BMCD008** ▭ **BMK008**
Pavarotti Collection - I Lombardi
Verdi: Lombardi (Cpte). (R. Scotto, L. Pavarotti, R. Raimondi, U. Grilli, M. Rinaudo, A. Colella, S. Mezzetti, F. Iacopucci, A. di Stasio, Rome Op Chor, Rome Op Orch/G. Gavazzeni)

Ⓓ **BMCD010** ▭ **BMK010**
Pavarotti Collection - Idomeneo
Mozart: Idomeneo (Cpte). (Richard Lewis, L. Pavarotti, G. Janowitz, E. Tarrès, N. Taylor, D. Hughes, D. Wicks, Glyndebourne Fest Chor, LPO/J. Pritchard)

Ⓓ **BMCD012** ▭ **BMK012**
Pavarotti Collection - I Capuleti e I Montecchi
Bellini: Capuleti (Cpte). (R. Scotto, G. Aragall, L. Pavarotti, G. Ferrin, A. Giacomotti, La Scala Chor, La Scala Orch/C. Abbado)

Ⓓ **BMCD015** ▭ **BMK015**
Pavarotti Collection - Duets and Scenes
Verdi: Traviata (exc); *Donizetti:* Lucia di Lammermoor (exc); *Puccini:* Bohème (exc); *Verdi:* Lombardi (exc); *Massenet:* Manon (exc); *Verdi:* Rigoletto (exc); *Donizetti:* Elisir d'amore (exc); *Bellini:* Puritani (exc); *Verdi:* Rigoletto (exc). (L. Pavarotti, J. Sutherland, R. Scotto, M. Freni, S. Bruscantini, R. Talarico, L. Goeke, G. Manganotti, A. Ferrin, A. di Stasio, F. Ricciardi, F. Iacopucci, B. Bortoluzzi, K. Paskalis, R. Grist, B. Giaiotti, G. Antonini, M. Rinaldi, M. Benetti, L. Monreale, NY Met Op Chor, NY Met Op Orch, Turin RAI Orch, Rome RAI Orch, Turin RAI Chor, Rome Op Orch, La Scala Orch, San Francisco Op Orch/R. Bonynge/F. Molinari-Pradelli/T. Schippers/G. Gavazzeni/P. Maag/C.M. Giulini/G. Patanè/R. Muti/M. Rossi, Rome RAI Chor)

Ⓓ **BMCD016** ▭ **BMK016**
Pavarotti Collection - La bohème (highlights)
Puccini: Bohème (exc). (M. Freni, L. Pavarotti, R. Talarico, S. Bruscantini, G. Maffeo, N. Ghiuselev, Rome RAI Chor, Rome RAI Orch/T. Schippers)

Ⓓ **BMCD017** ▭ **BMK017**
Pavarotti Collection - Lucia Highlights
Donizetti: Lucia di Lammermoor (exc). (R. Scotto, L. Pavarotti, P. Cappuccilli, G. Manganotti, A. Ferrin, A. di Stasio, F. Ricciardi, Turin RAI Chor, Turin RAI Orch/F. Molinari-Pradelli)

Ⓓ **BMCD018** ▭ **BMK018**
Pavarotti Collection - Rigoletto (highlights)
Verdi: Rigoletto (exc). (P. Cappuccilli, M. Rinaldi, L. Pavarotti, A. Lazzarini, N. Zaccaria, P. Clabassi, M. Benetti, T. Rovetta, L. Monreale, F. Iacopucci, L. Stabile, Turin RAI Chor, Turin RAI Orch/M. Rossi)

Ⓓ **BMCD022** ▭ **BMK022**
Pavarotti Collection - Ballo in Maschera
Verdi: Ballo in maschera (Cpte). (M. Arroyo, L. Pavarotti, F. Bordoni, H. Donath, I. Dalis, R. Mundt, P. Booth, A. Monk, J. Pinedo, D. Sullivan, San Francisco Op Chor, San Francisco Op Orch/C. Mackerras)

Cala

Ⓓ **CACD0001**
Cala Series, Volume 1
Wagner: Lohengrin (exc); *Tchaikovsky:* Violin Concerto; *Beethoven:* Symphony 5. (N. Shkolnikova, Philh/G. Simon)

Ⓓ **CACD0002**
Cala Series, Volume 2
Rossini: Guillaume Tell (exc); *Debussy:* Après-midi; *Paganini:* Moses in Egypt Variations; *Gershwin:* Rhapsody in Blue; *Vaughan Williams:* Greensleeves Fantasia; *Rimsky-Korsakov:* Capriccio Espagnol. (G. Karr, J. Tocco, LSO/G. Simon)

Ⓓ **CACD0101** (3/87) ▭ **CAMC0101** (3/87)
Orchestral works
Wagner: Lohengrin (exc); *Tchaikovsky:* Violin Concerto; *Beethoven:* Symphony 5; *Rossini:* Guillaume Tell (exc); *Debussy:* Après-midi; *Paganini:* Moses in Egypt Variations; *Gershwin:* Rhapsody in Blue; *Vaughan Williams:* Greensleeves Fantasia; *Rimsky-Korsakov:* Capriccio espagnol. (N. Shkolnikova, G. Karr, J. Tocco, Philh, LSO/G. Simon)

Ⓓ **CACD0102**
Orchestral Masterpieces - The Cala Series
Wagner: Lohengrin (exc); *Tchaikovsky:* Violin Concerto; *Beethoven:* Symphony 5; *Rossini:* Guillaume Tell (exc); *Debussy:* Après-midi; *Paganini:* Moses in Egypt Variations; *Gershwin:* Rhapsody in Blue; *Vaughan Williams:* Greensleeves Fantasia; *Rimsky-Korsakov:* Capriccio Espagnol; *Josephs:* Fanfare; *Grieg:* Piano Concerto; *Dvořák:* Symphony 9; *J. Strauss II:* Frühlingsstimmen, Op. 410; Unter Donner und Blitz; *Sibelius:* Legends (exc); *Elgar:* Pomp and Circumstance Marches (exc); *Saint-Saëns:* Introduction and Rondo Capriccioso; *Barber:* Adagio for Strings; *Mussorgsky:* Night on the Bare Mountain; *Ravel:* Boléro; *Bach:* Brandenburg Concertos (exc); *Mozart:* Clarinet Concerto, K622; *Grieg:* Elegiac Melodies; *Schubert:* Symphony 5; *Bernstein:* Candide Overture; *Franck:* Symphonic Variations; *Holst:* Planets. (N. Shkolnikova, G. Karr, J. Tocco, M. Fingerhut, S. Chase, D. Glazer, H. Shelley, LSC, Philh, LSO, ECO/G. Simon)

Ⓓ **CACD0104** (9/95)
The London Cello Sound
Balcombe: Greensleeves Suite; *Bernstein:* West Side Story (exc); *Casals:* Sardana; *Rachmaninov:* Songs, Op. 34 (exc); *Saint-Saëns:* Carnaval des animaux (exc). (LPO Vcs, RPO Vcs, BBC SO Vcs, Philh Vcs/G. Simon)

◑ **CACD0105**
The London Violin Sound
Dvořák: Gipsy Melodies (exc); *Monti:* Csárdás; *Gershwin:* Porgy and Bess (exc); *Mascagni:* Cavalleria Rusticana (exc); *Khachaturian:* Gayaneh (exc); *Shostakovich:* Gadfly Suite (exc); *Debussy:* Préludes (exc); *Rachmaninov:* Pieces, Op. 6 (exc). (LPO, RPO, Philh)

◑ **CACD0106**
The London Viola Sound
Gershwin: Porgy and Bess (exc); *Weill:* Kiddush; *Shostakovich:* Moscow, Cherymushki (exc); *Dvořák:* Slavonic Dances (exc); *Grainger:* Arrival Platform Humlet; *Ravel:* Pavane pour une infante défunte; *Prokofiev:* War and Peace (exc); *Bacharach:* This guy's in love with you; *Strayhorn:* Take the 'A' Train. (R. Golani, ASMF, BBC SO, LPO, ENO Orch/G. Simon)

Ⓓ **CACD0501**
Stokowski conducts Philadelphia Rarities
Turina: Danzas gitanas, Op.55 (exc); *Anon:* Veni Creator Spiritus; Veni Emmanuel; Etenraku; *Eichheim:* Bali; Oriental Impressions (exc); *Dubensky:* Raven; *McDonald:* 2-Piano Concerto; Legend of the Arkansas Traveller; Festival of the Workers (exc); Symphony 2 (exc); *Sousa:* Manhattan Beach; Capitan; *Falla:* Vida breve (exc). (B. de Loache, J. Behrend, A. Kelberine, Philadelphia/L. Stokowski)

Ⓓ **CACD0502**
Stokowski - Previously Unpublished 78s
Various: National Anthems (exc); *Schubert:* Schwanengesang, D957 (exc); *La Monaca:* Saltarello; *Stokowski:* Balance Test March; *Foster:* Oh, Susanna; *Handel:* Messiah (exc); *R. Strauss:* Salome (exc); *Tchaikovsky:* Songs, Op.73 (exc); *R. Kelly:* Adironack Suite (exc); *Tchaikovsky:* Marche slave; *Scriabin:* Pieces, Op.2 (exc); *Schubert:* Deutsche Tänze, D783 (exc); *Tchaikovsky:* Romeo and Juliet. (Philadelphia, NBC SO, NY City SO/L. Stokowski)

Ⓓ **CACD1005** (11/91) ▭ **CAMC1005** (11/91)
Ravel—Orchestral Works, Vol.2
Ravel: Rapsodie espagnole; Gaspard de la nuit (exc); Enfant et les sortilèges (exc); Piano Concerto; Pavane; Pièce en forme de habanera; Daphnis et Chloé Suites (exc). (H. de Vries, G. Mok, Philh/G. Simon)

Ⓓ **CACD1011** (3/94) ▭ **CAMC1011** (3/94)
Borodin—Orchestral Works
Borodin: Prince Igor (exc); String Quartet 2 (exc); In the Steppes of Central Asia; Petite Suite; Requiem. (M. Field, I. Boughton, BBC Sym Chor, S. Chase, Philh/G. Simon)

Ⓓ **CACD1012** (11/93) ▭ **CAMC1012** (11/93)
Mussorgsky—Orchestral Works
Mussorgsky: Night on the Bare Mountain; Fair at Sorochintsï (exc); Pictures; On the southern shore of the Crimea; Khovanshchina (exc); From my tears; Scherzo in B flat. (T. Ungár, Philh/G. Simon)

Ⓓ **CACD1015** ▭ **CAMC1015**
Saint-Saëns—Volume 1
Saint-Saëns: Ascanio (exc); Africa, Op. 89; Parysatis (exc); Requiem, Op. 54; Sarabande et rigaudon, Op. 93; Suite algérienne (exc); Tarentelle, Op. 6. (T. Ølafimihan, C. Wyn-Rogers, A. Roden, S. Kirkbride, S. Milan, J. Campbell, G. Mok, Hertfordshire Chor, Harlow Chor, East London Chor, LPO/G. Simon)

Ⓓ **CACD1016** ▭ **CAMC1016**
Saint-Saëns—Volume 2
Saint-Saëns: Jota aragonese, Op. 64; Samson et Dalila (exc); Princesse jaune (exc); Muse et le poète; Danse macabre; Symphony 3. (A. Roden, S. Chase, R. Truman, J. O'Donnell, LPO/G. Simon)

Calig

Ⓓ **CAL50855**
Steffani—Enrico Leone
Steffani: Henrico Leone (Cpte). (R. Popken, M. Frimmer, D. Diwiak, S. Szameit, N. Yoko, G. Faulstich, C. Guber, Capella A. Steffani/L. Rovatkay)

Ⓓ **CAL50943**
Wagner—Die Walküre - Act 1
Wagner: Walküre (exc). (E. Moser, M. Lundberg, F. Olsen, Mecklenburg Staatskapelle/I. Törzs)

Calliope

Ⓓ **CAL9218**
Two Guitars at the Opera
Mozart: Don Giovanni (exc); *Bellini:* Pirata (exc); *Méhul:* Chasse de jeune Henri (exc); *Weber:* Freischütz (exc); *Rossini:* Semiramide (exc); *Spontini:* Fernand Cortez (exc). (Horreaux-Trehard Duo)

Cambria

Ⓓ **CD-1032** (5/92)
From the Operas of Erich Wolfgang Korngold
Korngold: Ring des Polykrates (exc); Violanta (exc); Tote Stadt (exc); Tote Stadt (exc); Wunder der Heliane (exc); Kathrin (exc); Kathrin (exc); Kathrin (exc); Kathrin (exc); Kathrin (exc); Kathrin (exc). (G. Janowitz, H. Hoppe, H. Hillebrecht, I. Steingruber, A. Dermota, A. Poell, R. Schwaiger, R. Christ, Austrian St Rad Orch/W. Loibner/J. Strobl/E. Korngold/G. Kassowitz)

Ⓓ **CD-1063** (8/92)
Louis Kaufman - Violin Works
Martinů: Violin Concerto 2; *Khachaturian:* Violin Concerto; *Achron:* Stimmungen, Op.32; *Rimsky-Korsakov:* Golden Cockerel (exc); *Traditional:* Londonderry Air; *Tchaikovsky:* String Quartet 1 (exc). (L. Kaufman, P. Ulanowsky, French Rad and TV Orch/J.M. Leconte, Santa Monica Orch/J. Rachmilovich, Columbia SO/B. Herrmann)

Ⓓ **CD-1066** (3/93)
Korngold in Vienna
Korngold: Much Ado About Nothing Suite; Tomorrow; Schneemann (exc); Violanta (exc); Theme and Variations, Op. 42. (Austrian RSO/M. Schönherr)

Campion

Ⓓ **RRCD1323**
Welcome Ev'ry Guest - John Blow/Henry Purcell Songs
Blow: Welcome, every guest; Ah, Heav'n; Loving above himself; If my Celia could persuade; Fair lover and his black mistress; Why weeps Asteria?; Spheres; Hark! how the waken'd strings resound; *Purcell:* Indian Queen, Z630 (exc); If prayers and tears, Z380; Yorkshire Feast Song, Z333 (exc); St Cecilia's Day Ode, Z328 (exc); Fairy Queen, Z629 (exc); Birthday Ode, Z321 (exc); Ode, Z327 (exc). (T. Penrose, J. Griffett, Early Instr Chbr Ens/M. Venhoda)

Ⓓ **RRCD1325**
Pendleton—The Miracle of the Nativity
Pendleton: Miracle of the Nativity (Cpte). (S. Bullock, S.

Imbodem, D. Robinson, J. Chaminé, M. Piquemal Voc Ens, Ile de France CO/J-W. Audoli)

Ⓓ **RRCD1335** (11/95) ▭ **RRMC8035** (11/95)
Inese Galante - Début Recital
Bellini: Norma (exc); *Gounod:* Roméo et Juliette (exc); *Puccini:* Rondine (exc); *Bizet:* Carmen (exc); *Leoncavallo:* Pagliacci (exc); *Puccini:* Bohème (exc); *Verdi:* Traviata (exc); *Caccini:* Ave Maria; *Gounod:* Ave Maria; *Franck:* Panis angelicus; *Mozart:* Zauberflöte (exc); *Verdi:* Vespri Siciliani (exc); *Boito:* Mefistofele (exc); *Puccini:* Gianni Schicchi (exc); *Villa-Lobos:* Bachianas Brasileiras 5. (I. Galante, Latvian Nat SO/A. Vilumanis)

Ⓓ **RR2CD1311/2** (11/90) ▭ **WL2M411/2** (11/90)
Suchoň—The Whirlpool
Suchoň: Whirlpool (Cpte). (P. Dvorský, G. Beňačková, O. Malachovský, V. Kubovčik, A. Michalková, J. Sedlarova, O. Hanakova, E. Antoličová, L. Barikova, J. Valásková, J. Kundlák, J. Martvon, P. Mikuláš, S. Benňačka, A. Kubankova, L. Ludha, A. Martvonova, J. Valentik, Slovak Phil Chor, Bratislava RSO/O. Lenárd)

Canyon Classics

Ⓓ **EC3655-2**
Maxim Vengerov—Carmen Fantasy
Beethoven: Violin Sonata 7; *Schubert:* Fantasie, D934; *Bach:* Solo Violin Partitas and Sonatas (exc); *Bizet:* Carmen (exc). (M. Vengerov, I. Vinogradova)

Ⓓ **EC3657-2**
Russian Orchestral Works
Glinka: Ruslan and Lyudmila (exc); *Borodin:* Prince Igor (exc); In the Steppes of Central Asia; *Rimsky-Korsakov:* Capriccio espagnol; *Khachaturian:* Gayaneh (exc); *Mussorgsky:* Night on the Bare Mountain; Khovanshchina (exc). (Russian Federation St SO/E. Svetlanov)

Ⓓ **EC3687-2**
Prokofiev—Orchestral Suites
Prokofiev: Romeo and Juliet (exc); Love for 3 Oranges (exc); Lt. Kijé Suite. (Moscow RSO/V. Fedoseyev)

Canzone

Ⓓ **CAN33009**
Rachmaninov/R.Strauss—Cello Sonatas
R. Strauss: Cello Sonata; *Rachmaninov:* Cello Sonata; Songs, Op. 34 (exc); *R. Strauss:* Ariadne auf Naxos (exc). (N. Sylvest, T. Lønskov)

Capriccio

Ⓓ **10 052** ▭ **CC27 076**
Weber: Overtures
Weber: Oberon (exc); Euryanthe (exc); Preciosa (exc); Abu Hassan (exc); Beherrscher der Geister; Freischütz (exc); Jubel-Ouverture. (Staatskapelle Dresden/G. Kuhn)

Ⓓ **10 070** ▭ **CC27 086**
Mozart: Overtures
Mozart: Zauberflöte (exc); Nozze di Figaro (exc); Ascanio in Alba (exc); Idomeneo (exc); Schauspieldirektor (exc); Così fan tutte (exc); Entführung (exc); Finta giardiniera (exc); Lucio Silla (exc); Clemenza di Tito (exc); Don Giovanni (exc). (Staatskapelle Dresden/H. Vonk)

Ⓓ **10 109** (3/89)
Josef Protschka sings Mozart arias
Mozart: Zauberflöte (exc); Entführung (exc); Finta giardiniera (exc); Clemenza di Tito (exc); Così fan tutte (exc); Don Giovanni (exc); Mitridate (exc); Idomeneo (exc). (J. Protschka, Munich RO/K. Eichhorn)

Ⓓ **10 113** (9/88) ▭ **CC27 127** (9/88)
Berlin Opera Composers
C.H. Graun: Rodelinda (exc); Artaserse (exc); Cleopatra e Cesare (exc); *Telemann:* Flavius Bertaridus (exc); *Bononcini:* Polifemo (exc); Griselda (exc); *Hasse:* Lucio Papirio (exc); Clemenza di Tito (exc); *Frederick the Great:* Ré pastore (exc); *J.F. Agricola:* Achille in Sciro (exc). (J. Kowalski, Berlin CO/M. Pommer)

Ⓓ **10 147** (5/90)
Weill—Zar lässt sich Photographieren
Weill: Zar lässt sich Photographieren (Cpte). (B. McDaniel, C. Pohl, T. Lehrberger, U. Tocha, M. Napier, H. Kruse, H. Helling, M. Brell, H. Franzen, Cologne Rad Chor, Cologne RSO/J. Latham-König)

Ⓓ **10 160/1** (8/88)
Weill—Mahagonny
Weill: Mahagonny (Cpte). (A. Silja, W. Neumann, K. Hirte, A. Schlemm, T. Lehrberger, F. Mayer, H. Franzen, P. Wolfrum, F. Mayer, Cologne Pro Musica, Cologne RSO/J. Latham-König)

Ⓓ **10 180** (8/89) ▭ **CC27 180** (8/89)
Gisela May sings Weill
Weill: Happy End (exc); Berliner Requiem (exc); Dreigroschenoper (exc); Mahagonny (exc). (G. May, W. Eberhardt, H. Dittmann, W. Dersch, M. Schmieder, G. Sonsalla, S. Lotz, M. Samko, Studio Orch/H. Krtschil)

Ⓓ **10 193/6** (2/88)
Hasse—Cleofide
Hasse: Cleofide (Cpte). (E. Kirkby, A. Mellon, D.L. Ragin, D. Visse, R. Wong, D. Cordier, Cappella Coloniensis/W. Christie)

Ⓓ **10 213** (3/88) ▭ **CC27 213** (3/88)
Handel and Mozart Arias for Countertenor
Handel: Rinaldo (exc); Giulio Cesare (exc); Serse (exc); Giustino (exc); Alcina (exc); Rodelinda (exc); *Mozart:* Mitridate (exc); Ombra felice, K255. (J. Kowalski, CPE Bach Orch/Hartmut Haenchen)

Ⓓ **10 241/2** (3/89)
Zemlinsky—Traumgörge
Zemlinsky: Traumgörge (Cpte). (J. Martin, J. Protschka, P. Coburn, H. Welker, M. Blasius, P. Haage, V. von Halem, H. Kruse, B. Calm, G.M. Ronge, Hesse Rad Ch, Frankfurt RSO/G. Albrecht)

Ⓓ **10 247** (10/89) ▭ **CC27 247** (10/89)
The Art of Bel Canto
Bellini: Puritani (exc); Puritani (exc); *Donizetti:* Messa da Requiem (exc); Caterina Cornaro (exc); Don Pasquale (exc); Don Pasquale (exc); Dom Sébastien (exc); Favorita (exc); Gemma di Vergy (exc). (L. Aliberti, G. Sabbatini, R. Bruson, Berlin RSO/R. Paternostro)

Ⓓ **10 248/9** (5/89)
Schmidt—Notre Dame
Schmidt: Notre Dame (Cpte). (G. Jones, J. King, H. Laubenthal, H. Welker, K. Moll, H. Helm, K. Borris, Berlin St Hedwig's Cath Ch, Berlin RIAS Chbr Ch, Berlin RSO/C. Perick)

Ⓓ **10 253** (11/89) ▭ **CC27 253** (11/89)
Mozart: Marches
Mozart: March, K62; March, K189; March, K214; March, K215; Idomeneo (exc); March, K248; March, K249; Nozze di Figaro (exc); Marches, K335; Marches, K408; March, K445. (Salzburg Mozarteum Orch/H. Graf)

Ⓓ **10 274/5** (9/89)
Verdi—(La) Traviata
Verdi: Traviata (Cpte). (L. Aliberti, P. Dvorský, R. Bruson, F. Mochiki, S. Sawa, H. Mochiki, H. Okayama, A. Shikano, Y. Yanagisawa, Fujiwara Op Chor, Tokyo PO/R. Paternostro)

Ⓓ **10 348** (10/91)
Mozart Gala—Suntory Hall, Tokyo
Mozart: Nozze di Figaro (exc); Nozze di Figaro (exc); Idomeneo (exc); Idomeneo (exc); Così fan tutte (exc); Don Giovanni (exc); Don Giovanni (exc); Don Giovanni (exc); Clemenza di Tito (exc). (S. Ghazarian, G. Sabbatini, R. Bruson, NHK Chbr Sols/R. Paternostro)

Ⓓ **10 362** (5/91)
Wolf: Vocal Works
Wolf: Spanisches Liederbuch (exc); Manuel Venegas. (M. Shirai, J. Protschka, H. Höll, C. Hauptmann, C. Späth, O. Widmer, K-J. Dusseljee, Württemberg Chbr Ch)

Ⓓ **10 369** (9/92)
R. Strauss—Orchestral Works
R. Strauss: Don Juan; Capriccio (exc); Till Eulenspiegel; Rosenkavalier (exc). (Stuttgart RSO/N. Marriner)

Ⓓ **10 380** (5/92)
Breezes from the Orient, Vol.2
Reyer: Sélam; *R. Strauss:* Salome (exc); *Bizet:* Pêcheurs de Perles (exc). (G. Ottenthal, B. Lazzaretti, W. Glashof, Berlin St Hedwig's Cath Ch, Berlin RSO/G.M. Guida, R. Servile/H.M. Schneidt)

Ⓓ **10 416** (10/92)
Jochen Kowalski sings Opera Arias
Hasse: Artaserse (exc); *Gluck:* Orphée (exc); *Handel:* Rinaldo (exc); *Mozart:* Ascanio in Alba (exc); *Gluck:* Telemaco (exc); *Donizetti:* Linda di Chamounix (exc); *Rossini:* Tancredi (exc). (J. Kowalski, Berlin RSO/H. Fricke)

Ⓓ **10 420** (8/94)
Handel—Overtures
Handel: Alcina (exc); Ariodante (exc); Berenice (exc); Solomon (exc); Agrippina (exc); Rodrigo (exc). (ASMF/K. Sillito)

Ⓓ **10 429**
Bernstein/Gershwin—HR-Brass
Gershwin: Strike up the Band I (exc); Porgy and Bess (exc); Damsel in Distress (exc); Girl Crazy (exc); Lady, be Good! (exc); *Bernstein:* West Side Story (exc). (HR-Brass/J. Whigham)

Ⓓ **10 448** (3/94)
Zemlinsky—Orchestral Works and Songs
Zemlinsky: Symphonische Gesänge, Op.20; König Kandaules (exc); Ballettstücke. (F. Grundheber, Hamburg PO/G. Albrecht)

Ⓓ **10 459** (10/95)
Music from Charlottenburg Castle
Corelli: String Sonatas (exc); Trio Sonatas, Op. 2 (exc); *Ariosti:* Cantatas (exc); *Torelli:* Trio Sonatas, Op. 1 (exc); Concerti musicali, Op. 6 (exc); *Bononcini:* Polifemo (exc); Cefalo (exc); *Steffani:* Scherzo Guardati. (A. Monoyios, Berlin Barock Compagney)

Ⓓ **10 461**
Falla—Orchestral Works
Falla: Sombrero de tres picos (exc); Homenajes; Vida breve (exc). (Württemberg St Orch/G. Navarro)

Ⓓ **10 466**
American Classics - Volume 2
Barber: Medea's Meditation, Op. 23a; *Bernstein:* Fancy Free; West Side Story (exc); *Copland:* Salón México; *Gershwin:* Porgy and Bess (exc). (Stuttgart RSO/N. Marriner)

Ⓓ **10 470**
Monteverdi—Arie e Duetti
Monteverdi: Sancta Maria; Ego flos campi; O bone Jesu, o piissime Jesu; Selva morale e spirituale (exc); Venite, venite, siccientes; Fuge, fuge, anima mea; Madrigals, Bk.7 (exc); Madrigals, Bk.8 (exc); Scherzi musicali (1632) (exc); Scherzi musicali (1607) (exc); Ballo delle ingrate; Incoronazione di Poppea (exc); Incoronazione di Poppea (exc). (M. van der Sluis, A. Köhler, Lautten Compagney)

Ⓓ **10 481**
R.Strauss—Opera Concert
R. Strauss: Arabella (exc); Ariadne auf Naxos (exc); Capriccio (exc); Rosenkavalier (exc). (P. Coburn, M. Crider, R. Klepper, M. Borst, B. Skovhus, F. Hawlata, Bavarian Rad Chor, Munich RSO/M. Honeck)

Ⓓ **10 492**
Mozart—Don Giovanni - Harmoniemusik
Mozart: Don Giovanni (exc). (Linos Ens)

Ⓓ **10 493**
Mozart—Le Nozze di Figaro—Harmoniemusik
Mozart: Nozze di Figaro (exc); Entführung (exc). (Linos Ens)

Ⓓ **10 494**
Mozart—Wind Band Music
Mozart: Zauberflöte (exc); Così fan tutte (exc). (Linos Ens)

Ⓓ **10 530**
Salieri—Concertos
Salieri: Triple Concerto in D; Flute and Oboe Concerto; Scuola de' gelosi (exc). (J. Bálint, L. Lencsés, B. Bánfalvi, Budapest Stgs, K. Botvay (vc/dir)/K. Botvay)

Ⓓ **10 547** (6/95)
Handel—Arias
Handel: Admeto (exc); Orlando (exc); Rodelinda (exc); Alcina (exc); Rinaldo (exc); Giulio Cesare (exc); Radamisto (exc); Flavio (exc). (A. Köhler, Halle Op House Handel Fest Orch/H. Arman)

Ⓓ **10 704**
Young Voices of the Opera-Michele Pertusi
Rossini: Italiana in Algeri (exc); *Donizetti:* Lucia di Lammermoor (exc); *Verdi:* Attila (exc); Don Carlo (exc); Macbeth (exc); *Gomes:* Salvator Rosa (exc); *Gounod:* Faust (exc); *Bellini:* Puritani (exc). (M. Pertusi, C. Alvarez, Bulgarian Nat Chor, Sofia PO/E. Tabakov)

Ⓓ **10 705**
Theo Mackeben—Film Music
Mackeben: Patrioten (exc); Anita und der Teufel (exc); Frauen sind keine Engel (exc); Es war eine rauschende Ballnacht (exc); Bal paré (exc); Tanz auf dem Vulkan (exc); Heimat (exc); Heimat (exc); Bel Ami (exc); Mädchen in Weiss (exc); Herz der Königin (exc); Goldene Käfig (exc). (Cologne RSO/E. Smola/H. Geese)

Ⓓ **10 706**
Young Voices of the Opera-Alexandrina Pendatchanska
Gounod: Roméo et Juliette (exc); Faust (exc); *Massenet:* Hérodiade (exc); *Rossini:* Semiramide (exc); *Bellini:* Sonnambula (exc); *Verdi:* Traviata (exc); *Tchaikovsky:* Eugene Onegin (exc). (A. Pendachanska, Sofia SO/M. Angelov)

Ⓓ **10 809** (10/91)
Mozart—Overtures, Dances & Marches
Mozart: Zauberflöte (exc); Nozze di Figaro (exc); Ascanio

in Alba (exc); Idomeneo (exc); Schauspieldirektor (exc); Così fan tutte (exc); Entführung (exc); Finta giardiniera (exc); Lucio Silla (exc); Clemenza di Tito (exc); Don Giovanni (exc); March, K62; March, K189; March, K214; March, K215; Idomeneo (exc); March, K237; March, K248; March, K249; Nozze di Figaro (exc); Marches, K335; Marches, K408; March, K445; Minuets, K461; Contredanses, K462; Minuets, K463; German Dances, K509; Contredanse, K534; Contredanse, K535; Contredanse, K587; German Dances, K600; Contredanses, K603; German Dances, K605. (Staatskapelle Dresden/H. Vonk, Salzburg Mozarteum Orch/H. Graf)

ⓓ **10 810**
Mozart—Opera Highlights
Mozart: Zauberflöte (exc); Zauberflöte (exc); Zauberflöte (exc); Zauberflöte (exc); Zauberflöte (exc); Idomeneo (exc); Idomeneo (exc); Idomeneo (exc); Idomeneo (exc); Nozze di Figaro (exc); Nozze di Figaro (exc); Nozze di Figaro (exc); Nozze di Figaro (exc); Nozze di Figaro (exc); Nozze di Figaro (exc); Nozze di Figaro (exc); Mitridate (exc); Mitridate (exc); Finta giardiniera (exc); Don Giovanni (exc); Don Giovanni (exc); Don Giovanni (exc); Don Giovanni (exc); Don Giovanni (exc); Entführung (exc); Entführung (exc); Così fan tutte (exc); Così fan tutte (exc); Clemenza di Tito (exc). (Staatskapelle Dresden/H. Vonk, H. Prey, Bratislava PO/K. Wöss, Bulgarian Svetoslav Obretenov Ch, Sofia PO/G. Robev, S. Jo, Berlin RSO/R. Paternostro, J. Protschka, Munich RO/K. Eichhorn, G. Sabbatini, NHK Chbr Sols, S. Sass, Hungarian St Op Orch/E. Lukács, M. Pertusi, S. Ghazarian, Berlin St Op Chor, Berlin Staatskapelle/O. Suitner, R. Bruson, C. Bartoli, D. Lojarro, G. Ottenthal, G. Pasino, M. Knapp, M. Chingari, C. Otelli, J. Kowalski, CPE Bach Orch/Hartmut Haenchen, Berlin RIAS Chbr Ch/H.M. Schneidt, A. Tomowa-Sintow, Bulgarian RSO/V. Stefanov)

ⓓ **60 008-2** (1/90)
Gluck—Orfeo
Gluck: Orfeo ed Euridice (Cpte). (J. Kowalski, D. Schellenberger, C. Fliegner, Berlin Rad Chor, CPE Bach Orch/Hans Haenchen)

ⓓ **60 010-2** (5/90)
Schreker—(Der) Schatzgräber
Schreker: Schatzgräber (Cpte). (J. Protschka, G. Schnaut, H. Stamm, P. Haage, H. Helm, H. Kruse, C. Schultz, P. Galliard, U. Malmberg, F.F. Nentwig, U. Krekow, D. Weller, Hamburg St Op Chor, Hamburg St Op Orch/G. Albrecht)

ⓓ **60 013** (1/93)
Weill—Der Kuhhandel
Weill: Kuhhandel (exc). (L. Peacock, E. Büchner, C. Schotenröhr, W. Raffeiner, U. Holdorf, O. Hillebrandt, D. Niemirowicz, I. Most, F. Mayer, R. Zimmermann, R. Röttger, F. Gerihsen, H. Heidbüchel, J. Wagner, Cologne Rad Chor, Cologne RSO/J. Latham-König)

ⓓ **60 014-2**
Giordano: Andrea Chenier
Giordano: Andrea Chénier (Cpte). (F. Bonisolli, M. Gulegina, R. Bruson, H. Zednik, E. Dundekova, G. Pasino, M. Pertusi, H. Helm, C. Otelli, P. Lefebvre, G. Linos, S. Rinaldi-Miliani, Hungarian Rad Chor, Frankfurt RSO/M. Viotti)

ⓓ **60 015-1** (9/90)
Weill—Happy End
Weill: Happy End (Cpte). (W. Raffeiner, S. Kimbrough, G. Ramm, K. Ploog, Cologne Pro Musica, König Ens/J. Latham-König)

ⓓ **60 016-2** (1/92)
Zemlinsky—Der Kreidekreis
Zemlinsky: Kreidekreis (Cpte). (R. Behle, G. Schreckenbach, R. Hermann, S. Lorenz, R. Goldberg, U. Peter, H. Helm, G. Ottenthal, K. Borris, G. Saks, C. Lindsley, Berlin RSO/S. Soltesz)

ⓓ **60 017-2** (3/91)
Lortzing: Undine
Lortzing: Undine (Cpte). (M. Krause, J. Protschka, C. Hampe, J. Janssen, K. Häger, I. Most, H. Kruse, A. Schmidt, G. Wewel, D. Schortemeier, Cologne Rad Chor, Cologne RSO/K. Eichhorn)

ⓓ **60 019-2** (5/91)
Zemlinsky: Es war einmal
Zemlinsky: Es war einmal (Cpte). (E. Johansson, K. Westi, P-A. Wahlgren, A. Haugland, O. Hedegaard, G. Paevatalu, C. Christiansen, S. Lillesøe, Danish Nat Rad Chor, Danish Nat RSO/H. Graf)

ⓓ **60 020-1** (4/92)
Weill—Operas
Weill: Down in the Valley (Cpte); Jasager (Cpte). (I. Davidson, M. Acito, D. Collup, J. Mabry, D.P. Lang, T. Schmeisser, H. Helling, U. Schütte, T. Bräutigam, T. Fischer, M. Knöppel, Fredonia Chbr Sngrs, Dortmund Univ Chbr Ch, Buffalo College Wind Plyrs, Westphalia CO/W. Gundlach)

ⓓ **60 024-2** (12/91)
Schreker—Der Ferne Klang
Schreker: Ferne Klang (Cpte). (G. Schnaut, T. Moser, S. Nimsgern, H. Helm, V. von Halem, B. Scherler, J.W. Prein, R. Hermann, G. Saks, R. Wörle, C. Otelli, J. Juon, Berlin RIAS Chbr Ch, Berlin Rad Chor, Berlin RSO/G. Albrecht)

ⓓ **60 027-2** (6/93)
Gluck—Paride ed Elena
Gluck: Paride ed Elena (Cpte). (R. Alexander, C. McFadden, D. Frey, K. Ganninger, Stagione Voc Ens, Stagione/M. Schneider)

ⓓ **60 028** (12/93)
Weill—The Seven Deadly Sins; Mahagonny
Weill: Sieben Todsünden (Cpte); Mahagonny-Gesänge (Cpte). (D. Bierett, D. Ellenbeck, K. Markus, C. Feller, M. Smith, T. Schmidt, G. Ramm, H. Hiestermann, P.N. Kante, W. Raffeiner, H. Franzen, König Ens/J. Latham-König, Cologne RSO/L. Zagrosek)

ⓓ **60 029** (1/94)
Kreutzer—A Night in Granada
Kreutzer: Nachtlager in Granada (Cpte). (H. Prey, R. Klepper, M. Pabst, W.M. Friedrich, C. Hauptmann, M. Blasius, Cologne Rad Chor, Cologne RSO/H. Froschauer)

ⓓ **60 038** (11/94)
Busoni—Arlecchino
Busoni: Arlecchino (Cpte). (R. Wörle, M. Bellamy, R. Pape, S. Lorenz, P. Lika, Berlin RSO/G. Albrecht)

ⓓ **60 039** (11/93)
Busoni—Turandot
Busoni: Turandot (Cpte). (L. Plech, J. Protschka, R. Pape, G. Schreckenbach, F. Molsberger, C. Lindsley, R. Wörle, J.W. Prein, G. Schwarz, Berlin RIAS Chbr Ch, Berlin RSO/G. Albrecht)

ⓓ **60 043-2**
Hasse—Piramo e Tisbe
Hasse: Piramo e Tisbe (Cpte). (B. Schlick, A. Monoyios, W. Jochens, Stagione/M. Schneider)

ⓓ **60 049-2** (12/94)
Spohr—Faust
Spohr: Faust (Cpte). (B. Skovhus, F. Hawlata, H. Martinpelto, A. Reiter, R. Orrego, U. Wand, R. Swensen, B. Wohlfarth, C. Späth, M. Borst, Stuttgart Rad Chor, Kaiserslautern Rad Orch/K. Arp)

ⓓ **60 052** (11/95)
Manfred Gurlitt—Wozzeck
Gurlitt: Wozzeck (Cpte). (R. Hermann, C. Lindsley, A. Scharinger, J. Gottschick, R. Wörle, E. Wottrich, C. Berggold, R. Ginzel, R. Schudel, G. Schreckenbach, Berlin RIAS Chbr Ch, Berlin Rad Children's Ch, Berlin Deutsches SO/G. Albrecht)

ⓓ **60 062-2** (6/95)
Shostakovich—The Gamblers
Shostakovich: Gamblers (Cpte). (V. Bogachev, A. Babikin, S. Suleymanov, A. Naumenko, A. Arkhipov, N. Nizinenko, M. Krutikov, V. Verestnikov, A. Maslennikov, NW German PO/M. Yurovsky)

OO **70 213**
Handel and Mozart Arias for Countertenor
Handel: Rinaldo (exc); Giulio Cesare (exc); Serse (exc); Giustino (exc); Alcina (exc); Rodelinda (exc); *Mozart:* Mitridate (exc); Ombra felice, K255. (J. Kowalski, CPE Bach Orch/Hartmut Haenchen)

OO **70 416**
Jochen Kowalski sings Opera Arias
Hasse: Artaserse (exc); *Gluck:* Orphée (exc); *Handel:* Rinaldo (exc); *Mozart:* Ascanio in Alba (exc); *Gluck:* Telemaco (exc); *Donizetti:* Linda di Chamounix (exc); *Rossini:* Tancredi (exc). (J. Kowalski, Berlin RSO/H. Fricke)

O **80 213**
Handel and Mozart Arias for Countertenor
Handel: Rinaldo (exc); Giulio Cesare (exc); Serse (exc); Giustino (exc); Alcina (exc); Rodelinda (exc); *Mozart:* Mitridate (exc); Ombra felice, K255. (J. Kowalski, CPE Bach Orch/Hartmut Haenchen)

O **80 416**
Jochen Kowalski sings Opera Arias
Hasse: Artaserse (exc); *Gluck:* Orphée (exc); *Handel:* Rinaldo (exc); *Mozart:* Ascanio in Alba (exc); *Gluck:* Telemaco (exc); *Donizetti:* Linda di Chamounix (exc); *Rossini:* Tancredi (exc). (J. Kowalski, Berlin RSO/H. Fricke)

Caprice

ⓓ **CAP21428** (4/93)
Virtuoso Arias - Soffel
Pergolesi: Stabat Mater (exc); *Mozart:* Clemenza di Tito (exc); *Rossini:* Tancredi (exc); Donna del Lago (exc); Siège de Corinthe (exc); Maometto II (exc); Italiana in Algeri (exc); *Donizetti:* Favorita (exc); *Flotow:* Martha (exc); *Meyerbeer:* Huguenots (exc); *Bizet:* Carmen (exc); *Ravel:* Shéhérazade (exc). (D. Soffel, Swedish CO/M. Liljefors)

ⓓ **CAP22028**
Börtz—Backanterna
Börtz: Bacchae (Cpte). (S. Lindenstrand, L. Andersson-Palme, S. Wahlund, P. Mattei, A. Soldh, B. Lindholm, P. Hoffman, C. Staern, E. Andreassen, A-M. Mühle, K. Hammarström, A. Tomson, E. Österberg, C. Morling, A. Fleetwood, L. Hoel, H. Ströberg, I. Tobiasson, C.M. Dellow, P. Mattsson, P. Stormare, Stockholm Royal Op Chor, Stockholm Royal Orch/K. Ingebretsen)

ⓓ **CAP22029** (9/93)
Lidholm—A Dream Play
Lidholm: Dream Play (Cpte). (H. Martinpelto, H. Hagegård, I. Tobiasson, S. Wahlund, C. Appelgren, L. Kullenbo, A. Helleland, A. Bergström, S. Sandlund, H. Westberg, R. Cederlöf, N. Stemme, C. Unander-Scharin, Stockholm Royal Ch, Stockholm Royal Orch/K. Ingebretsen)

ⓓ **CAP22030** (7/94)
J.C.F.Haeffner—Electra
Haeffner: Electra (Cpte). (H. Martinpelto, P. Mattei, H. Hinz, M. Samuelson, K. Hedlund, S. Tysklind, A. Häggstam, C. Högman, L. Wedin, S-E. Alexandersson, Stockholm Rad Chor, Drottningholm Baroque Ens/T. Schuback)

ⓓ **CAP22032**
Berwald X 2—Historic Recordings, Vol.4
F. Berwald: Symphony 3; Symphony 1; Estrella de Soria (exc); Estrella de Soria (exc); Symphony 3; Symphony 1; Estrella de Soria (exc). (Gothenburg SO, Stockholm PO, Swedish RSO/T. Mann/S. Broman)

Cascavelle

ⓓ **VEL1006** (12/92)
Henze—Boulevard Solitude
Henze: Boulevard Solitude (Cpte). (E. Vassilieva, J. Pruett, C-J. Falkman, J-M. Salzmann, B. Brewer, D. Ottevaere, Children's Chor, Lausanne Op Chor, Rencontres Musicales Orch/I. Anguelov)

ⓓ **VEL1015**
Festive Brass
Phalèse: Danserye; *Mouret:* Symphonies de fanfares (exc); *Lully:* Chaconne; Passacaille; Sicilienne; *Attaingnant:* Dance collection (1530) (exc); *M-A. Charpentier:* Te Deum, H146 (exc); *Cherubini:* Marches (exc); *Rameau:* Dardanus (exc); *Dukas:* Péri (exc); *Gounod:* Faust (exc); *A. Philidor:* Grande fanfares. (/A. Besançon, Suisse Romande Brass Ens.)

ⓓ **VEL2001** (11/92)
Martin—Orchestral Works
Martin: Petite Symphonie Concertante; Sturm (exc); Cello Concerto; Flute Ballade. (D. Fischer-Dieskau, P. Fournier, A. Pépin, SRO/E. Ansermet/F. Martin)

ⓓ **VEL2006** (11/92)
Martin—Vocal Works
Martin: Mystère de la Nativité; Pilate. (E. Ameling, A. Heynis, L. Devos, H. Cuénod, E. Tappy, P. Mollet, D. Olsen, A. Vessières, C. Clavensy, J-C. Benoit, E. Zareska, A. Chedel, Lausanne Pro Arte Ch, Jeunes de l'Eglise Ch, Geneva Motet Ch, SRO/E. Ansermet)

ⓓ **VEL2010** (1/93)
Memories of the Suisse Romande - Suzanne Danco
Britten: Illuminations; *Falla:* Canciones populares españolas; *Smetana:* Bartered Bride (exc); *Chabrier:* Sulamite; *Debussy:* Pelléas et Mélisande (exc); Enfant prodigue (exc). (S. Danco, SRO/E. Ansermet/I. Karr, Piantoni Cercle Choral, A. Vessières, P. Mollet)

Catalyst

ⓓ **09026 61825-2** (1/94)
Glass—Organ Works
Glass: Dance II; Dance IV; Mad Rush; Contrary Motion; Satyagraha (exc). (D. Joyce)

ⓓ **09026 62638-2**
Robert Moran—The Dracula Diary
Moran: Dracula Diary (Cpte). (L. Knoop, J. Maddalena, R. Very, J. S. Sikon, J. Grove, M. Chioldi, Houston Op Studio/W. Holmquist)

Ⓓ **09026 62669-2** (4/95) ▭ **09026 62669-4** (4/95)
MacMillan—Visitatio sepulchri; Busqueda
MacMillan: Visitatio Sepulchri (Cpte); Búsqueda (Cpte). (O. Blackburn, C. Bunning, T. Dives, R. O. Forbes, A. Oke, S. Richardson, R. Bryson, J. Stevenson, Ruth Anderson, C. Spink, A. Bentley, Scottish CO/I. Bolton/J. MacMillan)

Cavalier

Ⓓ **CAVCD003**
Russian Orchestral Works
Borodin: Prince Igor (exc); *Tchaikovsky:* Sleeping Beauty (exc); Romeo and Juliet. (Philh, Ljubljana RSO/L. Siegel/A. Nanut)

Ⓓ **CAVCD017**
Classical Concert, Vol.1
Suppé: Leichte Kavallerie (exc); Schöne Galathee (exc); Banditenstreiche (exc); Dichter und Bauer (exc); *Gluck:* Iphigénie en Aulide (exc); *Debussy:* Après-midi; *Sibelius:* Valse triste; *Mendelssohn:* Midsummer Night's Dream (exc); *Khachaturian:* Gayaneh (exc). (German Fest Orch/A. Scholz)

Ⓓ **CAVCD018**
Classical Concert, Vol.2
Auber: Muette de Portici (exc); *Mascagni:* Cavalleria Rusticana (exc); *Bizet:* Carmen Suites; *Fučík:* Marinarella; Florentiner, Op.214. (German Fest Orch/A. Scholz)

CBC Records

Ⓓ **MVCD1047**
Vivier—Kopernicus
Vivier: Kopernikus (Cpte). (Y. Parent, P. Vaillancourt, M-D. Parent, J. Fleury, D. Doane, M. Ducharme, Y. Saint-Amant, N. Forget, F. Martel, G. Plante, A. Moisan, L. Bouchard, A. Trudel, M. Bélanger/L. Vaillancourt)

Ⓓ **MVCD1053** (5/93)
Schubert—Lieder
Schubert: Seligkeit, D433; Frühlingsglaube, D686; Lied im Grünen, D917; Lachen und Weinen, D777; Jüngling an der Quelle, D300; Auf dem Wasser zu singen, D774; Junge Nonne, D828; Verschworenen (exc); Claudine von Villa Bella (exc); Einsame, D800; Nacht und Träume, D827; Mutter Erde, D788; Hirt auf dem Felsen, D965; Fischerweise, D881; Heidenröslein, D257; An Silvia, D891; Liebhaber in allen Gestalten, D558; An die Musik, D547. (E. Wiens, J. Valdepeñas, R. Jansen)

Ⓓ **PSCD2001**
Lois Marshall sings Oratorio & Operatic Arias
Handel: Solomon (exc); Solomon (exc); Acis and Galatea (exc); *Haydn:* Creation (exc); Seasons (exc); *Mozart:* Entführung (exc); Don Giovanni (exc); Clemenza di Tito (exc). (L. Marshall, LSO, RPO/Anthony Bernard/T. Beecham/E. Pedrazzoli)

Ⓓ **PSCD2002** (12/92)
Maureen Forrester sings Handel Arias
Handel: Serse (exc); Rodelinda (exc); Ottone (exc); Giulio Cesare (exc); Jephtha (exc); Jephtha (exc); Theodora (exc); Samson (exc); Hercules (exc). (M. Forrester, Vienna RSO/B. Priestman, Vienna St Op Orch/R. Zeller, ECO/J. Somary, Zagreb Sols/A. Janigro)

Ⓓ **SMCD5103**
The Hannaford Street Silver Band
Ballantine: Hannaford Street March; *Walton:* Crown Imperial; *Holst:* Moorside Suite; *Vaughan Williams:* English Folk Song Suite; Prelude on Welsh Hymns; *G. Langford:* Fantasy on British Sea Songs; *Calvert:* Canadian Folk Song Suite; *J. Scott Irvine:* Hannaford Overture; *H. Clarke:* Side Partners; *Lavallée:* Indian Question (exc). (Hannaford St Silver Band/S. Chenette)

Ⓓ **SMCD5110** (1/93)
Handel—Floridante (Excerpts)
Handel: Floridante (exc). (N. Argenta, I. Attrot, C. Robbin, L. Maguire, M. Braun, Tafelmusik, A. Curtis (hpd/dir))

Ⓓ **SMCD5111**
Gershwin—Orchestral Works
Gershwin: Rhapsody in Blue; Second Rhapsody; Porgy and Bess Suite. (W. Tritt, Hamilton PO/B. Brott)

Ⓓ **SMCD5125** (12/94)
Glitter and Be Gay—Coloratura Soprano Arias
Bernstein: Candide (1988) (exc); *Delibes:* Lakmé (exc); *J. Strauss II:* Fledermaus (exc); *Offenbach:* Contes d'Hoffmann (exc); *R. Strauss:* Ariadne auf Naxos (exc); *Gluck:* Orfeo ed Euridice (exc); *Mozart:* Zaïde (exc); Entführung (exc); Vorrei spiegarvi, K418. (T. Dahl, Calgary PO/M. Bernardi)

Ⓓ **SMCD5126**
A Night in Venice & Other Operetta Excerpts
J. Strauss II: Nacht in Venedig (exc); *Heuberger:* Opernball (exc); *Kálmán:* Gräfin Mariza (exc); Csárdásfürstin (exc); *Lavallée:* Widow (exc); *Lehár:* Land des Lächelns (exc); *J. Strauss II:* Lagunen-Walzer; Annina, Op. 415; Nacht in Venedig Quadrille, Op. 416. (J. Kolomyjec, M. DuBois, Kitchener-Waterloo SO/R. Armenian)

Ⓓ **SMCD5127**
Great Baritone Arias
Bizet: Pêcheurs de perles (exc); *Donizetti:* Don Pasquale (exc); *Gounod:* Faust (exc); *Massenet:* Hérodiade (exc); *Mozart:* Così fan tutte (exc); Don Giovanni (exc); Nozze di Figaro (exc); *A. Thomas:* Hamlet (exc); *Verdi:* Ballo in maschera (exc); Don Carlo (exc); Falstaff (exc); Traviata (exc). (G. Laperrière, Three Rivers SO/G. Bellemare)

Ⓓ **SMCD5134**
Delius—Intermezzi & Pieces for Small Orchestra
Delius: Irmelin Prelude; Koanga (exc); Village Romeo and Juliet (exc); Fennimore and Gerda Intermezzo; Violin Concerto; First cuckoo; Summer Night on the River; Sleigh ride. (P. Djokic, Nova Scotia SO/G. Tintner)

Ⓓ **SMCD5139** (6/95)
A Gilbert & Sullivan Gala
Sullivan: Gondoliers (exc); HMS Pinafore (exc); Iolanthe (exc); Mikado (exc); Pirates of Penzance (exc); Trial by Jury (exc); Yeomen of the Guard (exc). (T. Dahl, M. Forrester, T. Chiles, R. Suart, D. Grant, D. Morphy, Winnipeg Sngrs, Winnipeg G & S Soc, Winnipeg SO/B. Tovey)

Ⓓ **SMCD5142** (11/95)
Ben Heppner sings Richard Strauss
R. Strauss: Guntram (exc); Feuersnot (exc); Frau ohne Schatten (exc); Intermezzo Interludes (exc); Liebe der Danae (exc); Daphne (exc); Schweigsame Frau (exc); Rosenkavalier (exc). (B. Heppner, Toronto SO/A. Davis)

CBS

Ⓓ **CD37228** (6/87)
Pavarotti sings Verdi
Verdi: Simon Boccanegra (exc); Ernani (exc); Attila (exc); Due Foscari (exc); Vespri siciliani (exc); Aida (exc); Opera fragment - Io la vidi. (L. Pavarotti, G. Morresi, A. Giacomotti, A. Savastano, La Scala Orch/C. Abbado)

Ⓓ **CD37852** (10/85)
Puccini—La Rondine
Puccini: Rondine (Cpte). (K. Te Kanawa, P. Domingo, M. Nicolesco, D. Rendall, L. Nucci, L. Watson, G. Knight, L. Finnie, E. Gale, O. Broome, M. Midgley, M. Thomas, U. Connors, B. Ogston, V. Midgley, L. Benson, D. Beavan, A. Byers, W. Evans, Ambrosian Op. Chor, LSO/L. Maazel)

Ⓓ **CD38450** (8/88)
Donizetti—Il campanello di notte
Donizetti: Campanello di notte (Cpte). (A. Baltsa, E. Dara, C. Gaifa, B. Casoni, A. Romero, Vienna St Op Chor, Vienna SO/G. Bertini)

Ⓓ **CD38875** (9/86)
Glass—Einstein on the Beach
Glass: Einstein on the Beach (Cpte). (L. Childs, S. Johnson, P. Mann, S. Sutton, P. Zukofsky, Philip Glass Ens/M. Riesman)

Ⓓ **CD39133** (7/85)
Bravura - Violin Showpieces
Falla: Suite populaire espagnole; Vida breve (exc); *Kreisler:* Liebesleid; Liebesfreud; Tambourin chinois; Pugnani tempo di menuetto; *Mozart:* Serenade, K250 (exc); *Schumann:* Romanzen, Op. 94 (exc); *Rachmaninov:* Songs, Op. 34 (exc); *Wieniawski:* Capriccio-Valse, Op. 7; *Sarasate:* Introduction and Tarantella, Op. 43. (C-L. Lin, S. Rivers)

Ⓓ **CD39160** (10/85)
Puccini—Turandot
Puccini: Turandot (Cpte). (E. Marton, J. Carreras, K. Ricciarelli, R. Kerns, H. Wildhaber, H. Zednik, J.P. Bogart, W. Kmentt, K. Rydl, Vienna Boys' Ch, Vienna St Op Chor, Vienna St Op Orch/L. Maazel)

Ⓓ **CD39208**
A Portrait of Kiri te Kanawa
Puccini: Tosca (exc); Gianni Schicchi (exc); *Verdi:* Traviata (exc); *Humperdinck:* Hänsel und Gretel (exc); *Mozart:* Don Giovanni (exc); *R.Strauss:* Lieder, Op. 27 (exc); *Schubert:* Gretchen am Spinnrade, D118; *Schumann:* Myrthen, Op. 25 (exc); *Fauré:* Songs, Op.7 (exc); *Walton:* Old Sir Faulk; Daphne; Through gilded trellises. (K. Te Kanawa, LPO, Cologne Gürzenich Orch, Paris Op Orch, LSO, R. Amner/J. Pritchard/L. Maazel/A. Davis)

Ⓓ **CD39672** (9/86)
Glass: Satyagraha
Glass: Satyagraha (Cpte). (D. Perry, C. Cummings, R. Liss, R. McFarland, S. Reeve, S. Woods, NYC Op Chor, NYC Op Orch/C. Keene)

Ⓓ **CD42168**
Puccini—Turandot: excs
Puccini: Turandot (exc). (E. Marton, W. Kmentt, J.P. Bogart, J. Carreras, K. Ricciarelli, R. Kerns, H. Wildhaber, H. Zednik, K. Rydl, Vienna Boys' Ch, Vienna St Op Chor, Vienna St Op Orch/L. Maazel)

Ⓓ **CD42369** (11/87)
Giordano—Andrea Chenier
Giordano: Andrea Chénier (Cpte). (J. Carreras, E. Marton, G. Zancanaro, T. Pane, T. Takács, K. Takács, F. Federici, G. Vághelyi, T. Bátor, J. Tóth, K. Sárkány, I. Rozsos, J. Moldvay, E. Farkas, J. Gregor, Hungarian Rad & TV Chor, Hungarian St Orch/G. Patanè)

Ⓓ **CD42457** (2/88)
Glass—Akhnaten
Glass: Akhnaten (Cpte). (P. Esswood, M. Vargas, M. Liebermann, T. Hannula, H. Holzapfel, C. Hauptmann, D. Warrilow, Stuttgart Op Chor, Stuttgart Op Orch/D.R. Davies)

Ⓓ **CD42564** (9/88)
R. Strauss—Der Rosenkavalier
R. Strauss: Rosenkavalier (Cpte). (C. Ludwig, G. Jones, W. Berry, L. Popp, E. Gutstein, P. Domingo, M. Lilowa, M. Dickie, E. Loose, L. Dutoit, L. Pantscheff, H. Lackner, H. Prögihöf, E. Aichberger, K. Terkal, E. Mühlberger, H. Saidula, J. Herndl, M. Guggia, F. Setzer, R. Resch, K. Bernhard, L. Hoppe, H. Gneuer, F. Riedl, A. Maly, K. Neugebauer, M. Heigl, Vienna St Op Chor, VPO/L. Bernstein)

Ⓓ **CD45693** (4/90)
Portrait—Ezio Pinza
Mozart: Don Giovanni (exc); Mentre ti lascio, K513; Nozze di Figaro (exc); Zauberflöte (exc); Entführung (exc); Don Giovanni (exc); *Puccini:* Bohème (exc); *Rossini:* Barbiere di Siviglia (exc); *Mussorgsky:* Boris Godunov (exc); *Verdi:* Simon Boccanegra (exc); *Halévy:* Juive (exc). (E. Pinza, NY Met Op Chor, NY Met Op Orch/B. Walter/F. Cleva/E. Cooper)

Ⓓ **CD45694** (7/90)
Lily Pons—Opera & Song Recital
Delibes: Lakmé (exc); *Verdi:* Rigoletto (exc); *Bellini:* Puritani (exc); *Rossini:* Barbiere di Siviglia (exc); *A. Thomas:* Mignon (exc); *Meyerbeer:* Dinorah (exc); *Delibes:* Filles de Cadiz; *Fauré:* Songs, Op.7 (exc); *Ponce:* Estrellita; *Bachelet:* Chère nuit; *J. Strauss II:* Blauen Donau, Op. 314; *Rachmaninov:* Songs, Op. 4 (exc). (L. Pons, orch/P. Cimara, Columbia SO/A. Kostelanetz/M. Abravanel)

Ⓓ **CD45701** (2/90)
Bruno Walter conducts Wagner Overtures
Wagner: Meistersinger (exc); Lohengrin (exc); Fliegende Holländer (exc); Siegfried (exc); Tannhäuser (exc). (Columbia SO/B. Walter, Occidental Coll Concert Ch)

Ⓓ **CD45886** (4/91)
Weill: Happy End & Seven Deadly Sins
Weill: Sieben Todsünden (Cpte); Happy End (Cpte). (L. Lenya, male qt, orch, chor/W. Brückner-Rüggeberg)

Ⓓ **CD46465** (9/91)
Elgar—Orchestral Music
Elgar: Pomp and Circumstance Marches; Falstaff; Cockaigne; Imperial March; Crown of India (Cpte); Enigma Variations; Serenade. (LPO, ECO/D. Barenboim)

Ⓓ **CD46466**
Wagner: Orchestral Music
Wagner: Meistersinger (exc); Tannhäuser (exc); Fliegende Holländer (exc); Lohengrin (exc); Rienzi (exc); Faust Overture; Rheingold (exc); Walküre (exc); Siegfried (exc); Götterdämmerung (exc); Tristan und Isolde (exc). (Cleveland Orch/G. Szell)

Ⓓ **CD47682**
Songs and Waltzes from Vienna
J. Strauss II: Fledermaus (exc); Zigeunerbaron (exc); Wiener Blut; Kaiser, Op. 437; Blauen Donau, Op. 314; *E. Arnold:* Da draussen in der Wachau; *Dostal:* Heut' macht die Welt; *Leopoldi:* Wien, sterbene; *Benatzky:* Ich muss wieder einmal in Grinzing sein; *Stolz:* Im Prater blüh'n wieder die Bäume; *Mendelssohn:* Lieder, Op. 34 (exc); *Sieczyński:* Wien, du Stadt meiner Träume; *Traditional:* C'est mon ami; *Anon:* Maman, dites-moi; Mère Michel. (NYPO/B. Walter, Lotte Lehmann, P. Ulanowsky)

Ⓓ **CD76890** (5/88)
Puccini—Le villi
Puccini: Villi (Cpte). (L. Nucci, R. Scotto, P. Domingo, T. Gobbi, Ambrosian Op Chor, National PO/L. Maazel)

Ⓓ **CD77341** (8/88)
Weill—Aufstieg und Fall der Stadt Mahagonny
Weill: Mahagonny (Cpte). (L. Lenya, H. Sauerbaum, H. Günter, G. Litz, P. Markwort, F. Göllnitz, S. Roth, G. Mund,

F. Göllnitz, NW German Rad Chor, NW German RO/W. Brückner-Rüggeberg)

Ⓓ **CD79213** (10/89)
Puccini—Edgar
Puccini: Edgar (Cpte). (R. Scotto, C. Bergonzi, G. Killebrew, V. Sardinero, M. Munkittrick, NY Schola Cantorum, NY City Op Children's Chor, NY Op Orch/E. Queler)

Ⓓ **CD79217** (11/88)
Humperdinck—Hänsel und Gretel
Humperdinck: Hänsel und Gretel (Cpte). (F. von Stade, I. Cotrubas, C. Ludwig, S. Nimsgern, K. Te Kanawa, R. Welting, E. Söderström, Cologne Op Children's Ch, Cologne Gürzenich Orch/J. Pritchard)

Ⓓ **CD79229** (9/89)
Korngold—Violanta
Korngold: Violanta (Cpte). (E. Marton, S. Jerusalem, W. Berry, H. Laubenthal, G. Stoklassa, R. Hesse, M. Schmidt, H. Weber, P. Hansen, K. Hautermann, R. Freyer, Bavarian Rad Chor, Munich RO/M. Janowski)

Ⓓ **CD79300** (2/90)
Massenet—Le cid
Massenet: Cid (Cpte). (C. Ingram, T. Hodges, A. Voketaitis, G. Bumbry, E. Bergquist, J. Gardner, P. Domingo, P. Plishka, P. Lightfoot, J. Adams, Byrne Camp Chorale, NY Op Orch/E. Queler)

Ⓓ **CD79310** (3/90)
Cilea—Adriana Lecouvreur
Cilea: Adriana Lecouvreur (Cpte). (R. Scotto, P. Domingo, S. Milnes, E. Obraztsova, G. Luccardi, F. Andreolli, L. Watson, A. Murray, P. Crook, P. Hudson, Ambrosian Op Chor, Philh/James Levine)

Ⓓ **CD79312** (11/88)
Puccini: Il Trittico
Puccini: Tabarro (Cpte); Suor Angelica (Cpte); Gianni Schicchi (Cpte). (I. Wixell, R. Scotto, P. Domingo, M. Sénéchal, D. Wicks, G. Knight, R. Scotto, M. Horne, I. Cotrubas, T. Gobbi, I. Cotrubas, P. Domingo, A. di Stasio, F. Andreolli, S. Fortunato, A. Domingo, A. Mariotti, G. Luccardi, C. del Bosco, S. Malagù, Ambrosian Op Chor, Desborough School Ch, New Philh, LSO/L. Maazel, P. Payne, G. Knight, A. Howard, D. Cryer, M. Cable, E. Bainbridge, S. Minty, G. Jennings, U. Connors, A. Gunson, D. Jones)

Ⓓ **CD79323** (9/89)
Massenet—Cendrillon
Massenet: Cendrillon (Cpte). (F. von Stade, N. Gedda, J. Berbié, J. Bastin, R. Welting, T. Cahill, E. Bainbridge, C. Meloni, P. Crook, C. du Plessis, J. Noble, Ambrosian Op Chor, Philh/J. Rudel)

Ⓓ **CD79328** (12/89)
Verdi—Aroldo
Verdi: Aroldo (Cpte). (M. Caballé, G. Cecchele, L. Lebherz, J. Pons, V. Manno, P. Rogers, M. Busching, NY Oratorio Soc, Westchester Ch Soc, NY Op Orch/E. Queler)

Ⓓ **CD79400** (10/89)
Meyerbeer—Le prophète
Meyerbeer: Prophète (Cpte). (M. Horne, J. McCracken, R. Scotto, J. Bastin, J. Hines, J. Dupouy, C. du Plessis, Ambrosian Op Chor, Haberdashers' Aske's Sch Ch, RPO/H. Lewis)

Ⓓ **MK37298** (5/85) ▭ **40-37298**
Puccini and Verdi Arias
Puccini: Villi (exc); Tosca (exc); Rondine (exc); Bohème (exc); Manon Lescaut (exc); Gianni Schicchi (exc); Madama Butterfly (exc); *Verdi:* Don Carlo (exc); Trovatore (exc); Traviata (exc). (K. Te Kanawa, LPO/J. Pritchard)

▭ **40-44529** (3/89)
Weill—Die sieben Todsünden; Kleine Dreigroschenmusik
Weill: Sieben Todsünden (Cpte); Kleine Dreigroschenmusik. (J. Migenes, R. Tear, S. Kale, A. Opie, R. Kennedy, LSO/M. Tilson Thomas)

▭ **40-45531** (1/90)
Bernstein—Music from 'West Side Story'
Bernstein: West Side Story Symphonic Dances; West Side Story (exc). (K. Labèque, M. Labèque, J-P. Drouet, S. Gualda, T. Gurtu)

CdM Russian Season

Ⓓ **LDC288 005/6** ▭ **KC488 005**
Bass Arias from Russian Opera
Glinka: Life for the Tsar (exc); *Dargomïzhsky:* Rusalka (exc); *Tchaikovsky:* Eugene Onegin (exc); *Mussorgsky:* Boris Godunov (exc); *Borodin:* Prince Igor (exc); *Rimsky-Korsakov:* Songs, Op.49 (exc); *Glinka:* Ruslan and Lyudmila (exc); *Mussorgsky:* Boris Godunov (exc); Khovanshchina (exc); *Rubinstein:* Demon (exc); *Borodin:* Prince Igor (exc); *Tchaikovsky:* Iolanta (exc); *Rimsky-Korsakov:* Sadko (exc); Songs, Op.49 (exc). (P. Gluboky, A. Safiulin, Soviet Cinema Orch/E. Khachaturian)

Ⓓ **LDC288 009** ▭ **KC488 009**
The Canterville Ghost
Knaifel: Canterville Ghost (exc). (S. Suleymanov, T. Monogarova, A. Levental, Moscow Forum Th Orch/M. Yurovsky)

Ⓓ **LDC288 022**
Popular Scenes from Russian Operas
Tchaikovsky: Eugene Onegin (exc); *Rubinstein:* Demon (exc); *Mussorgsky:* Boris Godunov (exc); Khovanshchina (exc); *Rimsky-Korsakov:* Mlada (exc); Tsar's Bride (exc); *Borodin:* Prince Igor (exc); *Glinka:* Life for the Tsar (exc). (Bolshoi Th Chor, Bolshoi Th Orch/A. Chistiakov)

Ⓓ **LDC288 029/30** (7/92)
Karetnikov—Till Eulenspiegel
Karetnikov: Till Eulenspiegel (Cpte). (B. Kudriavtsev, E. Mazo, A. Martynov, L. Mkrtchian, A. Pruzhansky, A. Mochalov, P. Gluboky, Chor, Soviet Cinema Orch/E. Khachaturian/V. Polianski)

Ⓓ **LDC288 035/6**
Serov—Judith
Serov: Judith (Cpte). (I. Udulova, E. Zaremba, M. Krutikov, N. Vassiliev, A. Babikin, V. Kudriashov, S. Suleymanov, P. Gluboky, M. Mikhailov, I. Zhurina, M. Shutova, L. Kuznetsov, Russian Academic Chbr Chor, Male Chbr Ch, Bolshoi Th Orch/A. Chistiakov)

Ⓓ **LDC288 045**
Fried—The Diary of Anne Frank
G. Fried: Diary of Anne Frank (Cpte). (E. Ben-Zvi, Bolshoi Th Orch/A. Chistiakov)

Ⓓ **LDC288 046**
Rimsky-Korsakov—Kashchey the Immortal
Rimsky-Korsakov: Kashchey (Cpte). (A. Arkhipov, I. Jourina, N. Terentieva, V. Verestnikov, V. Matorin, Yurlov Russian Ch, Bolshoi Th Orch/A. Chistiakov)

Ⓓ **LDC288 053**
Overtures & Orchestral Scenes from Russian Opera
Borodin: Prince Igor (exc); *Rimsky-Korsakov:* Invisible City of Kitezh (exc); Tale of Tsar Saltan (exc); Mlada (exc); *Glinka:* Life for the Tsar (exc); *Mussorgsky:* Khovanshchina (exc); *Tchaikovsky:* Mazeppa (exc); *Taneyev:* Oresteia (exc). (Bolshoi Th Orch/A. Chistiakov)

Ⓓ **LDC288 056/7** (8/93)
Rimsky-Korsakov—The Tsar's Bride
Rimsky-Korsakov: Tsar's Bride (Cpte). (P. Gluboky, E. Kudriavchenko, V. Verestnikov, N. Nizinenko, A. Mishenkin, N. Terentieva, V. Kudriashov, I. Udalova, E. Okolycheva, T. Pechuria, V. Pashinsky, N. Larionova, Y. Markelov, Sveshnikov Russian Academy Ch, Bolshoi Th Orch/A. Chistiakov)

Ⓓ **LDC288 060** (9/93)
Contemporary Listening—Kasparov
Kasparov: Landscape; Nevermore (exc); Credo; Cantus firmus; Postlude; Variations (1990); Silencium. (Moscow Contemp Music Ens/A. Vinogradov)

Ⓓ **LDC288 079** (10/94)
Rachmaninov—Aleko
Rachmaninov: Aleko (Cpte). (V. Matorin, N. Erassova, V. Pochapsky, V. Taraschenko, G. Borisova, Russian St Ch, Orch/A. Chistiakov)

Ⓓ **LDC288 080** (10/94)
Rachmaninov—The Miserly Knight
Rachmaninov: Miserly knight (Cpte). (M. Krutikov, V. Kudriashov, A. Arkhipov, V. Verestnikov, P. Gluboky, Bolshoi Th Orch/A. Chistiakov)

Ⓓ **LDC288 081**
Rachmaninov—Francesca da Rimini
Rachmaninov: Francesca da Rimini (Cpte). (M. Lapina, V. Taraschenko, V. Matorin, N. Rechetniak, N. Vasiliev, Russian St Ch, Bolshoi Th Orch/A. Chistiakov)

Centaur

Ⓓ **CRC2084**
Music from Cranberry Isles
Telemann: Musique de table (exc); *Gluck:* Orfeo ed Euridice (exc); *Vivaldi:* Cello Sonata, RV42 (exc); Concerto, RV101; *Schaffrath:* Bassoon Sonata in G minor (exc); *Handel:* German Airs (exc); Berenice (exc); Violin Sonatas (exc); *A. Scarlatti:* Pirro e Demetrio (exc); *Bach:* Chorales, BWV651-668 (exc). (S.S. Frank, J. Baker, S.L. Bloom, W. Winstead, P. Wolfe, B. Karp, P. Sykes)

Ⓓ **CRC2164** (3/94)
Ferruccio Tagliavini—Early Operatic Recordings
Donizetti: Elisir d'amore (exc); *Verdi:* Rigoletto (exc); *Puccini:* Bohème (exc); *Mascagni:* Amico Fritz (exc); *Cilea:* Arlesiana (exc); *Verdi:* Falstaff (exc); *Wolf-Ferrari:* Quattro rusteghi (exc); *Bellini:* Sonnambula (exc); *Verdi:* Lombardi (exc); *Puccini:* Tosca (exc); *Rossini:* Barbiere di Siviglia (exc); *Puccini:* Tosca (exc); *Massenet:* Manon (exc); *A. Thomas:* Mignon (exc); *Puccini:* Bohème (exc). (Ferruccio Tagliavini, M. Olivero, P. Tassinari, M. Huder, E. Mascherini, EIAR Orch/U. Tansini)

Chandos

Ⓓ **CHAN0521** (11/91)
Purcell—Dido and Aeneas
Purcell: Dido (Cpte). (E. Kirkby, D. Thomas, J. Nelson, J. Noorman, J. Rees, E. Van Evera, R. Bevan, T. Bonner, Taverner Ch, Taverner Plyrs/A. Parrott)

Ⓓ **CHAN0540** (12/93)
J.C.Bach—Orchestral Works
J. C. Bach: Grand Overtures, Op. 18 (exc); Adriano in Siria (exc); Symphonies, Op. 6 (exc); Sinfonia concertante, T289/4. (AAM, S. Standage (vn/dir))

Ⓓ **CHAN0558** (11/94)
Purcell—Dioclesian and Timon of Athens Masques
Purcell: Timon of Athens, Z632 (exc); Dioclesian, Z627 (exc). (C. Pierard, I. Davies, C. de la Hoyde, J. Bowman, J. M. Ainsley, I. Bostridge, M. George, M. Brook, N. Berg, Collegium Musicum 90/R. Hickox)

Ⓓ **CHAN0568** (7/95)
Purcell—Dioclesian (Part II)
Purcell: Dioclesian, Z627 (Cpte). (C. Pierard, J. Bowman, J. M. Ainsley, M. Padmore, M. George, Collegium Musicum 90 Chor, Collegium Musicum 90/R. Hickox)

Ⓓ **CHAN0571**
A Purcell Miscellany
Purcell: If music be the food of love, Z379/3; Lord, what is man?, Z192; Fairy Queen, Z629 (exc); Musick's Hand-Maid, Part 2 (exc); Choice Collection of Lessons (exc); Suite, Z770; Staircase Overture; Overture, Z772; Overture, Z771; Overture, Z770; Timon of Athens, Z632 (exc); Abdelazer, Z570 (exc); Trumpet Sonata 2; Choice Collection of Lessons (exc); Dioclesian Suite (exc). (C. Bott, M. Bennett, Purcell Qt, R. Woolley)

Ⓓ **CHAN0586**
Purcell—Dido and Aeneas
Purcell: Dido (Cpte). (M. Ewing, K.M. Daymond, R. Evans, S. Burgess, M. Plazas, P.H. Stephen, P. Rozario, J. MacDougall, J. Bowman, Collegium Musicum 90 Chor, Collegium Musicum 90/R. Hickox)

Ⓓ **CHAN4501** (11/92) ▭ **BBTD4501** (11/92)
The World's Most Beautiful Melodies
Dvořák: Gipsy Melodies (exc); *Gounod:* Ave Maria; *Brahms:* Volks-Kinderlieder (exc); *Purcell-Cockram:* Passing by; *Puccini:* Madama Butterfly (exc); *Tchaikovsky:* Songs, Op. 6 (exc); *Dvořák:* Rusalka (exc); *Puccini:* Turandot (exc); *Delibes:* Filles de Cadiz; *Traditional:* My love is like a red, red rose; *Schubert:* Du bist die Ruh', D776; *Debussy:* Préludes (exc); *Puccini:* Gianni Schicchi (exc); *Mozart:* Nozze di Figaro (exc); *Sullivan:* Lost chord. (P. McCann, I. Robertson, Black Dyke Mills Band/P. Parkes)

Ⓓ **CHAN4505** (7/93) ▭ **BBTD4505**
Black Dyke plays Rossini
Rossini: Scala di seta (exc); Barbiere di Siviglia (exc); Barbiere di Siviglia (exc); Cenerentola (exc); Tancredi (exc); Guillaume Tell (exc); Boutique Fantasque (exc). (P. McCann, J. Clough, Black Dyke Mills Band/P. Parkes/T. Walmsley)

Ⓓ **CHAN4507** (9/93) ▭ **BBTD4507** (9/93)
A Tribute to Elgar, Delius and Vaughan Williams
Handel: Overture in D minor; *Elgar:* Wand of Youth Suite 1 (exc); Wand of Youth Suite 2 (exc); Bavarian Dances; *Delius:* Marche-caprice; *Holst:* Perfect Fool (exc). (Black Dyke Mills Band/P. Parkes)

Ⓓ **CHAN4513** (11/93) ▭ **BBTD4513**
British Bandsman Centenary Concert
Steadman-Allen: Centenary Fanfare (1987); Beacons; *J. Ord Hume:* BB & CF; *Sullivan:* Yeomen of the Guard (exc); *P. Graham:* Brilliante; *Paganini:* Moto perpetuo, Op. 11; *Grieg:* Elegiac melodies (exc); *Ball:* Journey into Freedom; *Broadbent:* British Bandsman; *Howarth:* Legends; *Rimsky-Korsakov:* Tale of Tsar Saltan (exc); *Sullivan:* Pineapple Poll (exc); *Elgar:* Pomp and Circumstance Marches (exc); *Sullivan:* Lost chord. (W. Lang, M. Murphy, J. Shepherd, P. McCann, R. Childs, N. Childs, Besses o' the Barn Band, Black Dyke Mills Band, Yorkshire Imperial Band/H. Mortimer/R. Newsome/P. Parkes/James Scott)

Ⓓ **CHAN4514** (9/93) ▭ **BBTD4514** (9/93)
Black Dyke Mills Band play Overtures
Verdi: Forza del destino (exc); *Suppé:* Schöne Galathee (exc); Leichte Kavallerie (exc); *Nicolai:* Lustigen Weiber von Windsor (exc); *Rossini:* Italiana in Algeri (exc);

Donizetti: Fille du régiment (exc); *Weber:* Oberon (exc); *Auber:* Domino noir (exc). (Black Dyke Mills Band/P. Parkes/D. Hurst)

CHAN4528 (1/94) **BBTD4528** (1/94)
The Lion and the Eagle
Sullivan: Yeomen of the Guard (exc); *French:* Phil the Fluter's Ball (exc); *Various:* National Anthems (exc); *Holst:* Suite 2 (exc); *G. Langford:* Scottish Lament; Stephen Foster Fantasy; *Elgar:* Pomp and Circumstance Marches (exc); *Sousa:* Stars and Stripes Forever; *Ball:* Rhapsody on Negro Spirituals I; *Sharpe:* Music of George Gershwin. (Black Dyke Mills Band/R. Newsome)

CHAN6511 **MBTD6511**
Russian Masterpieces
Shostakovich: Festive Overture; *Prokofiev:* Romeo and Juliet Suites (exc); Scythian Suite (exc); Love for 3 Oranges Suite (exc); *Khachaturian:* Gayaneh (exc); *Rimsky-Korsakov:* Mlada (exc); Tale of Tsar Saltan (exc); Dubinushka; Scheherazade (exc); *Glazunov:* Seasons (exc); *Stravinsky:* Firebird (exc); *Tchaikovsky:* Festival Coronation March. (SNO, LSO/N. Järvi)

CHAN6518
Organ Classics
Bach: Toccata and Fugue, BWV565; Cantata 147 (exc); *Boëllmann:* Suite gothique (exc); *Clarke:* Suite in D (exc); *Mendelssohn:* Midsummer Night's Dream (exc); *Wagner:* Lohengrin (exc); *Karg-Elert:* Choral-Improvisationen, Op. 65 (exc); *Purcell:* Choice Collection of Lessons (exc); *W. Davies:* Solemn Melody; *Widor:* Symphony 5 (exc); *Bach:* Toccata, Adagio and Fugue, BWV564; *Liszt:* Prelude and Fugue, S260. (M. Austin)

CHAN6523 **MBTD6523**
Elgar—Orchestral works
Elgar: Symphony 2; Crown of India (Cpte). (SNO/A. Gibson)

CHAN6530
Brass Favourites
Fučík: Entry of the Gladiators; *Grieg:* Elegiac Melodies (exc); *Brahms:* Hungarian Dances (exc); *Traditional:* Believe me, if all those endearing young charms; *Sainte Jacome:* Fairies of the Waters; *Matt:* Fame and Glory; *Rossini:* Guillaume Tell (exc); *MacDowell:* Woodland Sketches (exc); *J. Strauss II:* Unter Donner und Blitz; *J.M. Black:* When the Saints; *Sullivan:* Gondoliers (exc); *Gounod:* Faust (exc); *Rossini:* Soirées musicales (exc); *Godard:* Jocelyn (exc); *Coates:* London Suite (exc); *G. Langford:* Famous British Marches. (Fairey Band/K. Dennison)

CHAN6535 (10/91) **MBTD6535** (10/91)
Stravinsky—Symphonies of Wind Instruments
Stravinsky: Symphonies of wind instruments; Pieces (1914); Bal'mont Poems; Little Songs (exc); Songs (1953-54) (exc); Mavra (exc); Japanese lyrics; Ragtime; Studies, Op. 7 (exc); Cinq doigts (exc); Rite of Spring (exc). (Nash Ens/S. Rattle, Chilingirian Qt, J. Manning/Robert Russell Bennett, R. Lumsden, A. Shasby, R. McMahon)

CHAN6539 (10/91) **MBTD6539** (10/91)
Classic Brass
J. Strauss II: Fledermaus (exc); *Schubert:* Marches militaires, D733 (exc); *Gregson:* Plantagenets; *Knipper:* Cossack Patrol; *Newsome:* Concorde; *Ball:* Rhapsody on Negro Spirituals 2; *Chabrier:* Joyeuse Marche; *Donizetti:* Fille du régiment (exc); *Offenbach:* Contes d'Hoffmann (exc); *Chabrier:* España. (P. McCann, Black Dyke Mills Band/G. Brand/R. Newsome)

CHAN6544 (2/92)
Elgar—Orchestral Favourites
Elgar: Chanson de Matin; Chanson de Nuit; Sérénade lyrique; Salut d'amour; Dream Children; Contrasts; Soliloquy; Caractacus (exc); Falstaff (exc); Bavarian Dances; Sursum corda; Sospiri; Beau Brummel (exc); Starlight Express (exc); Spanish Lady (exc); Adieu. (Bournemouth Sinfonietta/N. del Mar/G. Hurst, L. Goossens)

CHAN6545 (11/92)
Vaughan Williams—Orchestral Works
Vaughan Williams: Flos campi; Viola Suite; Hymn-Tune Preludes; Poisoned Kiss (exc); Running set. (F. Riddle, Bournemouth Sinfonietta Ch, Bournemouth Sinfonietta/N. del Mar/G. Hurst)

CHAN6548
Schumann—Overtures
Schumann: Manfred (exc); Julius Cäsar; Genoveva (exc); Overture, Scherzo and Finale. (LSO/N. Järvi)

CHAN6551
Renato Bruson at the Wigmore Hall
J. Martini: Plaisir d'amour; *Gluck:* Paride ed Elena (exc); *Piccinni:* Faux Lord (exc); *Donizetti:* Lu tradeimiento; Conocchia; Me voglio fa'na casa; *Tosti:* Ultima canzone; *Di Capua:* I' te vurria vasà; *Verdi:* Romanze (1838) (exc); Romanze (1845) (exc); Seduzione. (R. Bruson, C. Sheppard)

CHAN6560 **MBTD6560**
Jubilate - Music for the Kings & Queens of England
Gibbons: Hosanna to the Son of David; *Traditional:* Greensleeves (Alas! my love); *Blow:* Let Thy hand be strengthened; *Weelkes:* O Lord, grant the King a long life; *Purcell:* Tempest, Z631 (exc); *Locke:* Musick for His Majesty's Cornetts and Sackbutts; *Tallis:* O sacrum convivium; *Henry VIII:* Pastyme with good companye; *Byrd:* O Lord, make Thy servant; *Purcell:* Birthday Ode, Z332 (exc); March and Canzona, Z860 (exc); *Prince Albert:* Jubilate; *S. S. Wesley:* Thou wilt keep him; *G. Langford:* Fanfare and National Anthem. (St Peter ad Vincula Ch, M. Goossens, PJBE, Hurwitz Chbr Ens, A. Davis, A. Davis/J.T. Williams)

CHAN6571/2
Around the World with the Besses
Sullivan: Yeomen of the Guard (exc); *Traditional:* Annie Laurie; David of the White Rock; *Newsome:* In Dublin's Fair City; *G. Langford:* Famous British Marches; Australian Fantasy; *Code:* Zanette; *Grainger:* Colonial Song (wind); *Hanmer:* Down Under; *Stieberitz:* Kamerad, weisst du noch?; Grüne Korps; Reiterfreuden; Fackeltanz; Gruss aus Danzig; An der Rawka; Es Sind die Allen; *Lithgow:* Invercargill; Southstralia; Royal Australian Navy; Southlanders; National Guard; Westralia. (P. Read, G. McEvoy, Besses o' the Barn Band/R. Newsome/A. Evans)

CHAN6581
Summertime
Sor: Romanesca; *Satie:* Gymnopédies (exc); Gnossiennes (exc); *Mertz:* Bardenklänge (exc); *Villa-Lobos:* Distribuição de flores; *Gershwin:* Porgy and Bess (exc); *Ibert:* Entr'acte (1937); *Bach:* Toccata, Adagio and Fugue, BWV564 (exc); *Coste:* Regrets, Op. 36; *Sor:* Marche funèbre pour harpolyre; *Vaňhal:* Variations, Op. 42. (J. Anderson, J. Anderson, S. Wynberg)

CHAN6587
Berlioz—Ballet Music
Berlioz: Béatrice et Bénédict (exc); Troyens (exc); Enfance du Christ (exc); Roméo et Juliette (exc); Tristia (exc). (NSW Cons Op School, Sydney SO/R. Pickler)

CHAN6593 (11/93)
Wagner—Twilight of the Gods: Act3 Scenes 2/3
Wagner: Götterdämmerung (exc). (R. Hunter, A. Remedios, C. Grant, N. Bailey, M. Curphey, Sadler's Wells Op Chor, Sadler's Wells Op Orch/R. Goodall)

CHAN6597 (4/94)
Mozart—Don Giovanni for Wind Ensemble
Mozart: Don Giovanni (exc). (Athena Ens)

CHAN6598
Russian Dances
Glazunov: Scènes de ballet; Raymonda (exc); *Khachaturian:* Gayaneh (exc); Masquerade (exc); Spartacus (exc); *Prokofiev:* Pushkin Waltzes; Romeo and Juliet Suites (exc); Stone Flower (exc); *Rimsky-Korsakov:* Mlada (exc); Snow Maiden (exc); *Shostakovich:* Taiti trot; *Tchaikovsky:* Nutcracker (exc); Sleeping Beauty (exc). (SNO/N. Järvi)

CHAN6600
Bizet—Orchestral works
Bizet: Carmen Suites; Arlésienne Suites. (Ulster Orch/Y. P. Tortelier)

CHAN6608
Violin Favourites
Schubert: Rondo, D438; *Dvořák:* Romance, Op. 11; *Fauré:* Berceuse, Op. 16; *Kreisler:* Pugnani Praeludium and Allegro; Schön Rosmarin; *Massenet:* Thaïs (exc); *Elgar:* Salut d'amour; *Saint-Saëns:* Introduction and Rondo capriccioso; *Tortelier:* Your Grey-Blue Eyes. (Y.P. Tortelier (vn/dir), Renaissance Sngrs, Ulster Orch)

CHAN7000/1 (5/95)
Shostakovich—Orchestral Works
Shostakovich: Ballet Suite 1; Ballet Suite 2; Ballet Suite 3; Ballet Suite 4; Ballet Suite 5; Festive Overture; Katerina Izmaylova (exc). (SNO/N. Järvi)

CHAN7023/4
Rossini—The Barber of Seville
Rossini: Barbiere di Siviglia (Cpte). (A. Opie, D. Jones, B. Ford, A. Shore, P. Rose, J. Rhys-Davies, P. Snipp, C. Ross, ENO Chor, ENO Orch/G. Bellini)

CHAN8301 (7/83) **CBTD1008**
The Special Sound of Chandos
Holst: Planets (exc); *Tchaikovsky:* Hamlet (exc); *Weber:* Clarinet Concerto 1 (exc); *Purcell:* Dido (exc); *Harty:* Irish Symphony (exc); *Arnold:* Tam O'Shanter; *J. Strauss II:* Egyptischer Marsch, Op. 335; *Handel:* Solomon (exc); *Stravinsky:* Pulcinella Suite (exc); *Schurmann:* Studies of Francis Bacon (exc). (SNO/A. Gibson, J. Kelly, LSO/G. Simon, J. Hilton, CBSO/N. Järvi, Taverner Plyrs/A. Parrott, Ulster Orch/B. Thomson, LJSO/J. Rothstein, Cantilena/A. Shepherd, ECO, BBC SO/G. Schurmann)

CHAN8310/1 (7/84)
Tchaikovsky—Orchestral Works
Tchaikovsky: Romeo and Juliet; Serenade for N. Rubinstein; Festival Overture; Mazeppa (exc); Hamlet (Cpte). (J. Kelly, D. Hammond-Stroud, LSO/G. Simon)

CHAN8316 (8/84)
Berlioz: Overtures
Berlioz: King Lear; Rob Roy; Carnaval romain; Corsaire; Béatrice et Bénédict (exc). (SNO/A. Gibson)

CHAN8327/9 **DBTD3004** (12/84)
Rimsky-Korsakov—Suites
Rimsky-Korsakov: May Night (exc); Snow Maiden (exc); Christmas Eve (exc); Mlada (exc); Invisible city of Kitezh (exc); Golden Cockerel Suite (exc); Tale of Tsar Saltan (exc). (SNO/N. Järvi)

CHAN8362 (6/85) **LBTD013** (6/85)
Treasures of Operetta
Ziehrer: Schätzmeister (exc); *J. Strauss II:* Casanova (exc); *Kálmán:* Csárdásfürstin (exc); *O. Straus:* Tapfere Soldat (exc); *Tauber:* Old Chelsea (exc); *Messager:* Véronique (exc); *Herbert:* Naughty Marietta (exc); *Lehár:* Lustige Witwe (exc); Giuditta (exc); *Zeller:* Obersteiger (exc); *Monckton:* Arcadians (exc). (M. Hill Smith, P. Morrison, Chandos Concert Orch/S. Barry)

CHAN8363 (1/86)
Britten—Cello Symphony; Death in Venice Suite
Britten: Cello Symphony; Death in Venice Suite (Cpte). (R. Wallfisch, ECO/S. Bedford)

CHAN8364
R. Strauss—Closing Scenes from Capriccio & Daphne
R. Strauss: Capriccio (exc); Daphne (exc). (C. Farley, RTBF New SO/J. Serebrier)

CHAN8379 (9/85)
Scottish Overtures
Mendelssohn: Hebrides; *Berlioz:* Waverley; *Arnold:* Tam O'Shanter; *Verdi:* Macbeth (exc); *MacCunn:* Land of the mountain and the flood. (SNO/A. Gibson)

CHAN8412 (8/86) **ABTD1149** (8/86)
Smetana—Orchestral Works
Smetana: Bartered Bride (exc); String Quartet 1. (LSO/G. Simon)

CHAN8429 (6/87)
Elgar—Orchestral Works
Elgar: Pomp and Circumstance Marches; Cockaigne; Crown of India (Cpte). (SNO/A. Gibson)

CHAN8432 (8/87)
Elgar/Vaughan Williams—Orchestral Works
Elgar: Sursum corda; Sospiri; Beau Brummel (exc); Starlight Express (exc); Spanish Lady (exc); Adieu; *Vaughan Williams:* Poisoned Kiss (exc); Hymn-Tune Preludes; Running set; Sea songs. (Bournemouth Sinfonietta/G. Hurst)

CHAN8457 (10/86)
Falla—El amor brujo; Nights in the gardens of Spain
Falla: Amor Brujo (Cpte); Nights in the Gardens of Spain; Vida breve (exc). (Sarah Walker, M. Fingerhut, LSO/G. Simon)

CHAN8500 (3/87) **ABTD1210** (3/87)
Russian Music for Violin and Piano
Tchaikovsky: Sérénade mélancolique; Valse-scherzo, Op. 34; Souvenir d'un lieu cher, Op. 42; *Glazunov:* Raymonda (exc); *Prokofiev:* Melodies, Op. 35b; *Rachmaninov:* Pieces, Op. 6 (exc); *Stravinsky:* Mavra (exc); Russian Dance (exc). (L. Mordkovitch, M. Gusak-Grin)

CHAN8561 (7/88) **LBTD019** (7/88)
Treasures of Operetta, Vol. 2
Jacobi: Sybil (exc); *Posford:* Balalaika (exc); *Monckton:* Quaker Girl (exc); *Millöcker:* Arme Jonathan (exc); *Ziehrer:* Schätzmeister (exc); *German:* Merrie England (exc); *Ziehrer:* Fremdenführer (exc); *Lehár:* Lustige Witwe (exc); *Benatzky:* Im weissen Rössl (exc); *Lehár:* Paganini (exc); *Messager:* Monsieur Beaucaire (exc); *J. Strauss II:* Casanova (exc). (M. Hill Smith, P. Morrison, Ambrosian Sngrs, Chandos Concert Orch/S. Barry)

CHAN8587 (7/88) **ABTD1279** (7/88)
Shostakovich: Orchestral Works
Shostakovich: Symphony 9; Festive Overture; Katerina Izmaylova (exc); Taiti trot. (SNO/N. Järvi)

Ⓒ **CHAN8595** (12/88) ▭ **ABTD1290** (12/88)
Brahms—Symphony No 4; Schumann—Genoveva Overture
Brahms: Symphony 4; *Schumann:* Genoveva (exc). (LSO/N. Järvi)

Ⓒ **CHAN8729** (9/89) ▭ **ABTD1369** (9/89)
Prokofiev—Ballet & Opera Suites
Prokofiev: Tale of the Buffoon (exc); Pas d'Acier; Love for 3 Oranges Suite. (SNO/N. Järvi)

Ⓒ **CHAN8758** (2/90)
R. Strauss—Opera Excerpts
R. Strauss: Rosenkavalier (exc); Salome (exc); Capriccio (exc). (F. Lott, SNO/N. Järvi)

Ⓒ **CHAN8759** (2/90) ▭ **LBTD023** (2/90)
Treasures of Operetta III
Ziehrer: Drei Wünsche (exc); *Messager:* Monsieur Beaucaire (exc); *O. Straus:* Walzertraum (exc); *Tauber:* Singende Traum (exc); *Lehár:* Land des Lächelns (exc); *Fraser-Simson:* Maid of the Mountains (exc); *Herbert:* Fortune Teller (exc); *Eysler:* Bruder Straubinger (exc); *Stuart:* Florodora (exc); *Lehár:* Friederike (exc); *Sidney Jones:* Geisha (exc); *Ganne:* Saltimbanques (exc). (M. Hill Smith, P. Morrison, Chandos Sngrs, Chandos Concert Orch/S. Barry)

Ⓒ **CHAN8766** (1/90) ▭ **ABTD1404** (1/90)
Hindemith & Weber: Orchestral Works
Hindemith: Symphonic Metamorphosis; *Weber:* Euryanthe (exc); Freischütz (exc); Oberon (exc); Beherrscher der Geister; Turandot (exc). (Philh/N. Järvi)

Ⓒ **CHAN8772** (7/90) ▭ **ABTD1410** (7/90)
Walton—Symphony No 2; Troilus and Cressida Suite
Walton: Symphony 2; Troilus and Cressida Suite. (LPO/B. Thomson)

Ⓒ **CHAN8834** (12/90) ▭ **ABTD1457** (12/90)
R. Strauss: Orchestral and Vocal Works
R. Strauss: Macbeth; Rosenkavalier (exc); Lieder, Op. 44 (exc). (L. Finnie, E. Paling, SNO/N. Järvi)

Ⓒ **CHAN8840** (10/90)
La flûte enchantée
Jolivet: Flute Concerto; *Chaminade:* Flute Concertino, Op.107; *Martin:* Flute Ballade; *Godard:* Suite, Op. 116; *Saint-Saëns:* Ascanio (exc); *Ibert:* Flute Concerto. (S. Milan, M. Dussek, CLS/R. Hickox)

Ⓒ **CHAN8865** (2/91) ▭ **ABTD1480** (2/91)
Rossini: Opera Arias
Rossini: Italiana in Algeri (exc); Donna del Lago (exc); Signor Bruschino (exc); Adelaide di Borgogna (exc); Otello (exc); Barbiere di Siviglia (exc); Bianca e Falliero (exc); Cenerentola (exc). (D. Jones, C. Smith, K. Steffan, H. Nicholl, G. Finley, S. Birchall, Richard Hickox Sngrs, CLS/R. Hickox)

Ⓒ **CHAN8877**
Kodály—Orchestral Works
Kodály: Galánta Dances; Peacock Variations; Háry János Suite. (Chicago SO/N. Järvi)

Ⓒ **CHAN8911/2** (3/91) ▭ **DBTD2026** (3/91)
Nielsen—Saul and David
Nielsen: Saul and David (Cpte). (A. Haugland, P. Lindroos, T. Kiberg, K. Westi, A. Gjevang, C. Christiansen, J. Klint, Danish Nat Rad Chor, Danish Nat RSO/N. Järvi)

Ⓒ **CHAN8920/2** (5/92)
Mozart—Don Giovanni
Mozart: Don Giovanni (Cpte). (R. Bruson, S. Ghazarian, G. Ottenthal, P. Pace, G. Sabbatini, N. Ghiuselev, S. Rinaldi-Miliani, F. de Grandis, Cologne Rad Chor, Cologne RSO/N. Järvi)

Ⓒ **CHAN8930** (2/92) ▭ **ABTD1528** (2/92)
Wagner—Arias
Wagner: Tannhäuser (exc); Lohengrin (exc); Götterdämmerung (exc); Tristan und Isolde (exc). (G. Jones, Cologne RSO/R. Paternostro)

Ⓒ **CHAN8978** (10/91)
Marilyn Hill Smith sings Kálmán & Lehár
Lehár: Giuditta (exc); Wo die Lerche singt (exc); Land des Lächelns (exc); Zigeunerliebe (exc); Paganini (exc); Zarewitsch (exc); Eva (exc); Schön ist die Welt (exc); Frasquita (exc); *Kálmán:* Veilchen vom Montmartre (exc); Herzogin von Chicago (exc); Zirkusprinzessin (exc); Kaiserin Josephine (exc); Hollandweibchen (exc); Faschingsfee (exc). (M. Hill Smith, Chandos Concert Orch/S. Barry)

Ⓒ **CHAN8987** (3/92)
Rachmaninov—Monna Vanna, Act 1; Piano Concerto No. 4
Rachmaninov: Monna Vanna (exc); Piano Concerto 4. (S. Milnes, S. McCoy, B. Walker, N. Karousatos, J. Thorsteinsson, Icelandic Op Chor, W. Black, Iceland SO/I. Buketoff)

Ⓒ **CHAN9036** (8/92)
Madetoja—Orchestral Works
Madetoja: Symphony 3; Ostrobothnians Suite; Comedy Overture, Op. 53; Okon Fuoko Suite 1. (Iceland SO/P. Sakari)

Ⓒ **CHAN9060** (10/92)
Hindemith—Orchestral Works
Hindemith: Symphony in E flat; Nobilissima Visione; Neues vom Tage (exc). (BBC PO/Y. P. Tortelier)

Ⓒ **CHAN9066** (4/93)
Weber—Overtures
Weber: Peter Schmoll (exc); Turandot (exc); Abu Hassan (exc); Preciosa (exc); Euryanthe (exc); Oberon (exc); Freischütz (exc); Silvana (exc); Beherrscher der Geister; Jubel-Ouverture. (Philh/N. Järvi)

Ⓒ **CHAN9080** (11/92)
Janáček—Orchestral Works
Janáček: Taras Bulba; Cunning Little Vixen (exc); Jealousy; Fiddler's Child. (Czech PO/J. Bělohlávek)

Ⓒ **CHAN9081**
Rachmaninov—Orchestral Works
Rachmaninov: Symphonic Dances; Aleko (exc); Caprice bohémien. (Philh/N. Järvi)

Ⓒ **CHAN9096** (3/93)
Prokofiev—Orchestral Works
Prokofiev: War and Peace Suite; Summer Night, Op. 123; Russian Overture. (Philh/N. Järvi)

Ⓒ **CHAN9110** (5/93) ▭ **LBTD031** (5/93)
Edwardian Echoes
Ancliffe: Nights of Gladness; *Baynes:* Destiny; *Bucalossi:* Grasshopper's Dance; *Caryll:* Pink Lady (exc); *Herman Finck:* In the Shadows; *Fletcher:* Parisian Sketches; *German:* Merrie England (exc); Nell Gwyn; *Haydn Wood:* Paris Suite (exc); *M. Phillips:* Rebel Maid (exc); *Monckton:* Arcadians (exc); Our Miss Gibbs (exc); Runaway Girl (exc). (M. Hill Smith, Southern Fest Orch/R. White)

Ⓒ **CHAN9131** (5/93)
Enescu/Shostakovich/Strauss—Chamber Works
Enescu: String Octet; *R. Strauss:* Capriccio (exc); *Shostakovich:* Pieces, Op.11. (ASMF Chbr Ens)

Ⓒ **CHAN9143/5** (6/93)
Heise—King and Marshal
Heise: Drot og Marsk (Cpte). (P. Elming, B. Norup, E. Johansson, K. Westi, C. Christiansen, A. Haugland, O. Hedegaard, I. Nielsen, R. Johansen, Danish Nat Rad Ch, Danish Nat RSO/M. Schønwandt)

Ⓒ **CHAN9149** (9/93)
Rimsky-Korsakov/Glinka—Vocal Works
Rimsky-Korsakov: Mozart and Salieri (Cpte); Songs, Op.42 (exc); Songs, Op.3 (exc); *Glinka:* I recall a wonderful moment; Farewell to St Petersburg (exc); Wedding Song; I am here; How sweet it is to be with you; Fire of longing; Say not that it grieves the heart; Farewell to St Petersburg (exc); Declaration; Doubt. (V. Bogachev, N. Storozhev, Montreal I Musici/Y. Turovsky, V. Bogachev, N. Storozhev)

Ⓒ **CHAN9190** (7/94)
Tchaikovsky—Orchestral Works
Tchaikovsky: Symphony 2; Serenade for N. Rubinstein; Mazeppa (exc); Festival Overture. (LSO/G. Simon)

Ⓒ **CHAN9210** (3/94)
Twentieth-Century American Music
Copland: Fanfare for the Common Man; *Gershwin:* Rhapsody in Blue; *Bernstein:* Prelude, Fugue and Riffs; West Side Story (exc); *Stravinsky:* Ebony Concerto. (H. de Boer, L. Lortie, Netherlands Wind Ens/R. Dufallo)

Ⓒ **CHAN9216**
Academy Classics
Debussy: Suite bergamasque (exc); *Dvor7ák:* Humoresques, Op. 101 (exc); *Elgar:* Salut d'amour; *Gershwin:* Porgy and Bess (exc); *Grieg:* Elegiac Melodies; Lyric Pieces, Op. 65 (exc); *Grainger:* Mock Morris; *Mozart:* Musikalischer Spass (exc); Divertimento, K334 (exc); *Pachelbel:* Canon and Gigue (exc); *Rachmaninov:* Songs, Op. 34 (exc); *Ravel:* Pavane pour une infante défunte; *Tchaikovsky:* Souvenir de Florence (exc); *Walton:* Henry V Suite (exc). (ASMF Chbr Ens)

Ⓒ **CHAN9227** (8/94) ▭ **ABTD1604** (8/94)
Encore!
Bolzoni: Minuetto; *Darzins:* Valse mélancolique; *Chabrier:* Roi malgré lui (exc); *Debussy:* Suite bergamasque (exc); *Dvořák:* Humoresques, Op. 101 (exc); *Ellington:* Solitude; *Gershwin:* Promenade; *Glinka:* Kamarinskaya; Valse-fantaisie; *Medins:* Symphonic Suite 1 (exc); *Mussorgsky:* Gopak; *Schumann:* Gesänge, Op. 107 (exc); *Shostakovich:* Gadfly Suite (exc); *Sibelius:* Andante festivo; *Sousa:* Stars and Stripes forever. (Detroit SO/N. Järvi)

Ⓒ **CHAN9245** (1/94)
Walton—The Bear
Walton: Bear (Cpte). (D. Jones, A. Opie, J. Shirley-Quirk, Northern Sinfonia/R. Hickox)

Ⓒ **CHAN9254/5** (3/94)
Britten—The Rape of Lucretia
Britten: Rape of Lucretia (Cpte). (J. Rigby, N. Robson, C. Pierard, D. Maxwell, A. Miles, A. Opie, P. Rozario, A. Gunson, CLS/R. Hickox)

Ⓒ **CHAN9299** (10/94)
Tippett—Orchestral Works
Tippett: Symphony 2; New Year Suite. (Bournemouth SO/R. Hickox)

Ⓒ **CHAN9304**
Lullabies
Delius: Norwegian Songs (1889-90) (exc); *Braga:* Nigue-nigue-ninhas; *Bizet:* Berceuse; *Mussorgsky:* Eremushka's lullaby; *Schumann:* Jugend Lieder, Op. 79 (exc); *Grieg:* Songs, Op. 15 (exc); *Menotti:* Consul (exc); *Glinka:* Farewell to St Petersburg (exc); *Haydn:* All through the night; *Cimara:* Fiocca la neve; *Wagner:* Mélodies (exc); *Longás Torres:* Canciones españolas (exc); *Tchaikovsky:* Songs, Op. 16 (exc); *Wolf:* Songs for a woman's voice (exc); *Rachmaninov:* Songs, Op. 26 (exc); *Brahms:* Lieder, Op. 49 (exc); *Milhaud:* Chants hébraïques (exc); *Weber:* Wiegenlied, J96; *Fauré:* Songs, Op. 23 (exc); *Dvořák:* Songs, B142 (exc); *Alfano:* Liriche (exc); *Grechaninov:* Lullaby, Op. 1/5; *Schubert:* Wiegenlied, D498. (N. Pelle, Montreal I Musici/Y. Turovsky)

Ⓒ **CHAN9336/8** (4/95)
Mussorgsky—Songs
Mussorgsky: Where art thou, little star?; Hour of Jollity; Sadly rustled the leaves; Prayer; Tell me why; Old man's song; King Saul; Lullaby; Dear one, why are thine eyes?; Feast; What are words of love to you?; Ragamuffin; Pride; He-Goat; Song of the flea; Darling Savishna; Classicist; Eremushka's lullaby; From my tears; Hebrew song; Garden by the Don; Orphan; Gathering mushrooms; Evening song; Sunless; Nursery; Songs and Dances of Death; Child's song; Sphinx; Softly the spirit flew; It scatters and breaks; Seminarist; Wanderer; Is spinning man's work?; Vision; From my tears; Not like thunder; I have many palaces and gardens; But if I could meet thee again; Wild wind blows; Night; Kalistratushka; Outcast; Salammbô (exc); Meines Herzen Sehnsucht; Gopak; You drunken sot; Magpie; Forgotten; On the Dnieper. (A. Haugland, P. Rosenbaum)

Ⓒ **CHAN9354**
R Strauss/Wagner—Orchestral and Vocal Works
Wagner: Siegfried Idyll; Wesendonk Lieder; Wesendonk Lieder (exc); *R. Strauss:* Duet Concertino; Ariadne auf Naxos (exc). (J. van Nes, L. Hatfield, R. Plane, S. Reay, Northern Sinfonia/R. Hickox)

Ⓒ **CHAN9355** (9/95)
Delius—Orchestral Works
Delius: Dance Rhapsody 1; Dance Rhapsody 2; North Country Sketches; In a Summer Garden; Village Romeo and Juliet (exc). (Bournemouth SO/R. Hickox)

Ⓒ **CHAN9364**
Elegy
Rachmaninov: Morceaux de fantaisie, Op. 3 (exc); Songs, Op. 21 (exc); Songs, Op. 38 (exc); *Glière:* Romance; *Prokofiev:* Love for 3 Oranges (exc); War and Peace Suite (exc); *Borodin:* Petite Suite (exc); *Khachaturian:* Spartacus Suite 2 (exc); *Shostakovich:* Preludes, Op. 34 (exc); *Rubinstein:* Soirées, Op. 44 (exc); *Rakov:* Canzonetta; *Grechaninov:* Meditation; *Stravinsky:* Petrushka (exc); *Shebalin:* Suite (exc); *Rebikov:* Christmas tree (exc); *Tchaikovsky:* Souvenirs de Hapsal, Op. 2 (exc); *Glinka:* Do not tempt me needlessly. (Bekova Sisters)

Ⓒ **CHAN9370/1** (5/95)
Walton—Troilus and Cressida
Walton: Troilus and Cressida (Cpte). (A. Davies, J. Howarth, N. Robson, Y. Howard, J. Thornton, C. Bayley, D. Owen-Lewis, A. Opie, P. Bodenham, K. Mills, B. Budd, S. Dowson, B. Cookson, Op North Chor, English Northern Philh/R. Hickox)

Ⓒ **CHAN9386**
Borodin—Orchestral Works
Borodin: Symphony 2; Petite Suite; Prince Igor (exc). (Stockholm PO/G. Rozhdestvensky)

Ⓒ **CHAN9392** (11/95)
Vaughan Williams—Riders to the Sea etc.
Vaughan Williams: Riders to the Sea (Cpte); Household Music; Flos campi. (I. Attrot, L. Dawson, L. Finnie, K. M.

Daymond, P. H. Stephen, P. Dukes, Northern Sinfonia Chor, Northern Sinfonia/R. Hickox)

Channel Classics

Ⓒ **CCS5193** (8/93)
Krása—Brundibár
Krása: Brundibár (Cpte); *Domažlický:* Czech Songs. (P. Krištofová, V. Ondračka, G. Přibilová, T. Staněk, M. Alexandridis, K. Tichá, D. Horáčková, J. Kratěnová, B. Drofová, J. Flegl, J. Mráček, Z. Jiroušek, O. Smola, P. Mišejka, Disman Rad Children's Ch, Disman Rad Children's Orch/J. Karas)

Ⓒ **CCS5593** (12/93)
Mendelssohn—Hochzeit des Camacho
Mendelssohn: Hochzeit des Camacho (Cpte). (R. Hofman, A. Ulbrich, S. Weir, H. Rhys-Evans, N. van der Meel, W. Wild, U. Malmberg, U. Cold, Aachen Youth Ch, Modus Novus Ch, Anima Eterna/J. van Immerseel)

Ⓒ **CG9103** (7/93)
Guitar Duets
Dowland: Ballad settings (exc); *Sor:* Divertissement, Op.34; *Granados:* Goyescas (exc); *Kleynjans:* Climats; *Bach:* Trio Sonatas, BWV525-530 (exc); Wohltemperierte Klavier (exc); *Albéniz:* España, Op.165 (exc); Cantos de España (exc); Mallorca; *Falla:* Vida breve (exc); Sombrero de tres picos Suites (exc). (T. Kropat, T. Krumeich)

Le Chant du Monde

Ⓒ **LDC278 1035/6**
Rimsky-Korsakov—The Tsar's Bride
Rimsky-Korsakov: Tsar's Bride (Cpte). (E. Nesterenko, G. Vishnevskaya, V. Valaitis, B. Morozov, V. Atlantov, I. Arkhipova, A. Sokolov, E. Andreeva, G. Borisova, V. Borisenko, V. Malchenko, N. Lebedeva, K. Baskov, Bolshoi Th Chor, Bolshoi Th Orch/F. Mansorov)

Ⓒ **LDC278 1037/8**
The Tale of Tsar Saltan
Rimsky-Korsakov: Tale of Tsar Saltan (Cpte). (I. Petrov, E. Smolenskaya, L. Nikitina, E. Shumilova, E. Verbitskaya, V. Ivanovsky, G. Oleinichenko, P. Chekin, A. Ivanov, Bolshoi Th Chor, Bolshoi Th Orch/V. Nebolsin)

Ⓒ **LDC278 1054/5**
Auber—Manon Lescaut
Auber: Manon Lescaut (Cpte). (E. Vidal, A. Gabriel, A. Cognet, R. Massis, B. Lafon, A. Laiter, C. Estourelle, G. Dubernet, D. Longuet, M-T. Orain, French Music Th Chor, Picardy Regional Orch/P. Fournillier)

Ⓒ **LDC278 1068** (8/92)
Chabrier—Une Education Manquée/Mélodies
Chabrier: Éducation manquée (Cpte); Roi malgré lui (exc); Chanson pour Jeanne; Île heureuse; Gwendoline (exc); Ballade des gros dindons; Pastorale des cochons roses. (C. Castelli, C. Collart, X. Depraz, Orch/C. Bruck, C. Castelli, H. Boschi)

Ⓒ **LDC278 1083/5** (4/93)
Saint-Saëns—Henry VIII
Saint-Saëns: Henry VIII (Cpte). (P. Rouillon, M. Command, L. Vignon, A. Gabriel, P. Bohée, A. Laiter, G. Serkoyan, J-M. Loisel, Rouen Théâtre des Arts Chor, French Lyrique Orch/A. Guingal)

Ⓒ **LDC278 769**
Gluck—Iphigénie en Tauride
Gluck: Iphigénie en Tauride (Cpte). (R. Crespin, G. Chauvet, R. Massard, M. Benegas, V. de Narké, Buenos Aires Colón Th Chor, Buenos Aires Colón Th Orch/G. Sébastian)

Ⓒ **LDC278 911/2**
Massenet—Two Operas
Massenet: Jongleur de Notre Dame (Cpte); Navarraise (Cpte). (A. Vanzo, R. Massard, A. Bastin, J. Dupouy, C. Meloni, P. Thau, Y. Bisson, ORTF Chor, French Rad Maîtrise, ORTF PO/P. Dervaux, A. Vanzo, G. Moizan, J. Mars, L. Lovano, J. Peyron, M. Vigneron, French Rad Lyric Chor, French Rad Lyric Orch/J-C. Hartemann)

Ⓒ **LDC278 994**
Martinů—Two Operas
Martinů: Comedy on the Bridge (Cpte); Alexandre Bis (Cpte). (N. Sautereau, B. Demigny, J. Berbié, J. Mars, J. Giraudeau, J. Peyron, G. Friedmann, L. Lovano, French Rad Lyric Orch/M. Rosenthal, C. Collart, A. Doniat, G. Friedmann, M. Vigneron, B. Kal/J. Doussard)

Ⓒ **LDC278 995/6**
Martinů—Julietta
Martinů: Julietta (Cpte). (A. Esposito, J. Giraudeau, J. Peyron, B. Demigny, P. Germain, L. Lovano, S. Michel, B. Kal, I. Kolassi, Chorale Madrigal, French Rad Lyric Orch/C. Bruck)

Chesky

Ⓒ **Chesky CD108**
Light Classics, Volume II
Puccini: Tosca (exc); *Mussorgsky:* Khovanshchina (exc); *Offenbach:* Orphée aux enfers (exc); *Verdi:* Aida (exc); *Binge:* Elizabethan Serenade; *Dvořák:* In Nature's Realm; *Kabalevsky:* Colas Breugnon (exc); *Smetana:* Má vlast (exc). (D. Sellar, Phil Pops Orch, London Prom, London Pops Orch, RPO, National PO/C. Gerhardt)

Ⓒ **Chesky CD17**
Beethoven—Symphonies Nos 2 and 5
Beethoven: Leonore (exc); Symphony 2; Symphony 5. (RPO/R. Leibowitz)

Ⓒ **Chesky CD19**
Brahms—Symphony No 1
Wagner: Tannhäuser (exc); *Brahms:* Symphony 1. (Beecham Choral Soc, RPO, LSO/J. Horenstein)

Ⓒ **Chesky CD31**
Dvorak—New World Symphony
Wagner: Fliegende Holländer (exc); Siegfried Idyll; *Dvořák:* Symphony 9. (RPO/J. Horenstein)

Ⓒ **Chesky CD32** (10/90)
Earl Wild plays his transcriptions of Gershwin
Gershwin: Porgy and Bess (exc); *Wild:* Gershwin Variations; Virtuoso Etudes. (E. Wild)

Ⓒ **Chesky CD35**
Orchestral Works
R. Strauss: Rosenkavalier (exc); *Ravel:* Boléro (exc); *Tchaikovsky:* Romeo and Juliet (exc). (RCA SO, RPO, National PO/C. Gerhardt)

Ⓒ **Chesky CD36**
Brahms/R.Strauss—Orchestral works
R. Strauss: Salome (exc); *Brahms:* Piano Concerto 2 (exc). (G. Bachauer, RPO, LSO/A. Dorati)

Ⓒ **Chesky CD56**
A Gershwin Concert
Gershwin: Piano Concerto; Rhapsody in Blue; *Enescu:* Romanian Rhapsodies, Op. 11 (exc); *Prokofiev:* Love for 3 Oranges Suite. (R. Lewenthal, RCA Victor SO, RPO, Metropolitan SO/O. Danon)

Ⓒ **Chesky CD57**
A Portrait Of France
Debussy: Après-midi; Petite Suite (exc); *Gounod:* Marche funèbre d'une marionette; Faust (exc); *Offenbach:* Orphée aux enfers (exc); *Pierné:* March of the Little Lead Soldiers; *Ravel:* Boléro; La Valse; *Saint-Saëns:* Danse macabre. (Paris Cons, London Fest Orch/R. Leibowitz)

Ⓒ **Chesky CD61**
Rene Leibowitz—An Evening of Opera
Auber: Diamants de la couronne (exc); *Bizet:* Carmen Suites (exc); *Borodin:* Prince Igor (exc); *Dukas:* Apprenti sorcier; *Mozart:* Nozze di Figaro (exc); *Offenbach:* Contes d'Hoffmann (exc); *Puccini:* Manon Lescaut (exc). (Paris Cons/R. Leibowitz)

Ⓒ **Chesky CD62**
Alexander Gibson—A Concert Tour
Chopin: Sylphides (exc); *Dvořák:* Carnival; *Grieg:* Peer Gynt (exc); Norwegian Dances, Op. 35 (exc); *Sibelius:* Finlandia; Legends (exc); *J. Strauss, II:* Tritsch-Tratsch; *Suppé:* Dichter und Bauer (exc); *Wagner:* Lohengrin (exc); *Weber:* Invitation to the Dance. (London Fest Orch, New SO/A. Gibson)

Ⓒ **Chesky CD70**
J.Strauss II-Overtures, Waltzes and Polkas
J. Strauss II: Fledermaus (exc); Perpetuum mobile; Kaiser, Op. 437; Tritsch-tratsch; G'schichten aus dem Wienerwald, Op. 325; Künstlerleben, Op. 316; Zigeunerbaron (exc); Annen-Polka, Op. 117; Wein, Weib und Gesang. (Vienna St Op Orch/J. Horenstein)

Ⓒ **Chesky CD96**
The German Album
Wagner: Tannhäuser (exc); *Liszt:* Mephisto Waltz 2, S111; *Schumann:* Symphony 3; Manfred (exc). (RPO, International SO/R. Leibowitz)

Cirrus

Ⓒ **CICD1001**
Orchestral Favourites.
Ravel: Boléro; *Rimsky-Korsakov:* Sadko (exc); *Shostakovich:* Gadfly Suite (exc); *Prokofiev:* Romeo and Juliet Suites (exc). (LSO/Y.P. Tortelier)

Ⓒ **CICD1005** (12/87)
Wagner: Orchestral Works
Wagner: Meistersinger (exc); Tannhäuser (exc); Götterdämmerung (exc); Tristan und Isolde (exc). (LSO/W. Morris)

Claremont

Ⓒ **CDGSE78-50-26** (7/89)
Wagner: Tristan und Isolde excerpts
Wagner: Tristan und Isolde (exc); Tristan und Isolde (exc); Tristan und Isolde (exc). (L. Melchior, W. Widdop, F. Leider, G. Ljungberg, G. Guszalewicz, I. Andrésen, H. Fry, C. Victor, E. Habich, M. Noe, K. McKenna, SO, LSO/A. Coates/L. Blech/L. Collingwood, Berlin St Op Orch)

Ⓒ **CDGSE78-50-33** (7/90)
Lauritz Melchior & Albert Coates
Wagner: Tannhäuser (exc); Siegfried (exc); Siegfried (exc); Siegfried (exc); Siegfried (exc); Siegfried (exc); Götterdämmerung (exc). (L. Melchior, A. Reiss, N. Gruhn, R. Bockelmann, LSO, orch/A. Coates)

Ⓒ **CDGSE78-50-35/6** (11/91)
Wagner—Historical recordings
Wagner: Walküre (exc); Rheingold (exc); Rheingold (exc). (W. Widdop, H. Fry, F. Schorr, G. Ljungberg, L. Trenton, F. Austral, F. Leider, E. Suddaby, N. Walker, A. Fear, K. McKenna, LSO/A. Coates, SO/L. Collingwood, Berlin St Op Orch/L. Blech)

Ⓒ **CDGSE78-50-37/8** (11/91)
Wagner—Historic recordings
Wagner: Götterdämmerung (exc). (W. Widdop, R. Laubenthal, A. Fear, D. Zádor, F. Collier, I. Andrésen, E. List, F. Austral, G. Ljungberg, M. Offers, G. Palmer, E. Arden, N. Eadie, T. de Garmo, L. Kindermann, E. Marherr-Wagner, Berlin St Op Chor, LSO/A. Coates, SO, Berlin St Op Orch/L. Collingwood/L. Blech)

Ⓒ **CDGSE78-50-46** (11/92)
Walter Widdop (1892-1949)
Wagner: Lohengrin (exc); Tristan und Isolde (exc); Walküre (exc); Götterdämmerung (exc); *Bach:* Mass in B minor, BWV232 (exc); *Handel:* Jephtha (exc); *Gounod:* Faust (exc); *Manson:* Songs of Love and Youth (exc); *Wallace:* Maritana (exc); *Handel:* Judas Maccabaeus (exc). (W. Widdop, G. Ljungberg, C. Victor, F. Austral, E. Schumann, LSO/L. Collingwood/A. Coates, Orch/J. Harrison, anon/J. Barbirolli)

Ⓒ **CDGSE78-50-47** (3/93)
The Harrison Sisters—An English Musical Heritage
Dvořák: Gipsy Melodies (exc); *Elgar:* Salut d'amour; *Delius:* Violin Sonata 1; Cello Sonata; *Smetana:* From the homeland (exc); *Brahms:* Cello Sonata 1; *Wagner:* Meistersinger (exc); *Elgar:* Cello Concerto (exc); *van Biene:* Broken melody; *Popper:* Characterstücke, Op. 3 (exc). (May Harrison, Margaret Harrison, B. Harrison, Princess Victoria, A. Bax, R. Paul, Margaret Harrison, G. Moore, H. Craxton, C. Salzedo, orch)

Ⓒ **CDGSE78-50-50** (9/93)
Richard Crooks sings Ballads & Sacred Songs
O. Straus: Walzertraum (exc); *Lincke:* Frau Luna (exc); *Foster:* Ah! may the red rose; Come, where my love lies dreaming; *Traditional:* All through the night; *Coates:* Birdsongs at Eventide; *M. Phillips:* Open your window to the morn; *S. Adams:* Nirvana; *Liddle:* How lovely are Thy dwellings; *S. Adams:* Star of Bethlehem; Holy City; *Stainer:* Crucifixion (exc); *Hardelot:* Because; *Geehl:* For you alone; *Landenburg:* Too late tomorrow; *Macmurrough:* Macushla; *Herbert:* Naughty Marietta (exc); *Sanderson:* Until; *Silésu:* Little love, a little kiss. (R. Crooks, orch/J. Barbirolli, F. la Forge, M. Andrews, J. Crawford, H. Dawson, F. Schauwecker)

Ⓒ **CDGSE78-50-52** (5/94)
Three Tenors
Puccini: Bohème (exc); *Mascagni:* Cavalleria rusticana (exc); *Massenet:* Élégie; *Verdi:* Rigoletto (exc); *Leoncavallo:* Pagliacci (exc); *Flotow:* Martha (exc); *Donizetti:* Elisir d'amore (exc); *Mozart:* Don Giovanni (exc); *Massenet:* Manon (exc); *Wagner:* Meistersinger (exc); *Puccini:* Tosca (exc); *Wagner:* Lohengrin (exc); *Borodin:* Prince Igor (exc); *Gounod:* Reine de Saba (exc); *Woodforde-Finden:* Request; *Clutsam:* I know of two bright eyes; *R. Strauss:* Lieder, Op.29 (exc). (E. Caruso, R. Crooks, W. Widdop, orch/C. Nicholls/W. Pelletier/N. Shilkret/Rosario Bourdon, Berlin St Op Orch/C. Schmalstich/L. Collingwood/M. Sargent, P. Kahn, J. Lee, BNOC Orch/A. Buesst, A. Galli-Curci, F. Perini, G. De Luca, M. Elman/W.B. Rogers)

Ⓒ **CDGSE78-50-54** (2/95)
Coates conducts Wagner, Weber & Mendelssohn
Wagner: Tannhäuser (exc); Tannhäuser (exc); Tannhäuser (exc); Tannhäuser (exc); Tannhäuser (exc); Tannhäuser (exc); *Weber:* Freischütz (exc); *Mendelssohn:* Elijah (exc). (B. Jones, W. Widdop, L. Melchior, F. Schorr, E. Halland, J. Uys, Cape Town Melodic Ch, chor, New SO, LSO, SO, Cape Town SO/A. Coates)

Ⓓ **CDGSE78-50-58**
Richard Crooks (1900-1972)
Foster: Beautiful Dreamer; Old Folks at Home; My old Kentucky home; Come, where my love lies dreaming; Oh! Susanna; Old black Joe; Jeanie with the light brown hair; Massa's in de cold, cold ground; Ah! may the red rose; Camptown races; *Mendelssohn:* Paulus (exc); *Handel:* Judas Maccabaeus (exc); *Massenet:* Élégie; *Franck:* Panis Angelicus; *Knapp:* Open the Gates of the Temple; *Godard:* Jocelyn (exc); *Balfe:* Killarney; *Wagner:* Lohengrin (exc). (R. Crooks, Balladeers, R. Colicchio, F. La Forge, orch)

Clarinet Classics

Ⓓ **CC0006** (3/94)
Clarinet Virtuosi of the Past—Hermstedt
Mozart: Clemenza di Tito (exc); *Müller:* Clarinet Quartet 2; *Paer:* Sargino (exc); *Spohr:* Lieder, Op. 103 (Cpte); Faust (exc); Alruna Variations. (E. Ritchie, V. Soames, A. Colman, M. Souter, A. Blayden, J. Purvis)

Classics for Pleasure

Ⓓ **CD-CFPD4450** ▭ **TC-CFPD4450** (12/85)
Verdi—La traviata
Verdi: Traviata (Cpte). (V. de los Angeles, C. del Monte, M. Sereni, S. Chissari, S. Bertona, S. Tedesco, V. Polotto, S. Maionica, B. Giaiotti, R. Ercolani, Rome Op Chor, Rome Op Orch/T. Serafin)

Ⓓ **CD-CFPD4454** ▭ **TC-CFPD4454** (8/86)
Bizet—Carmen
Bizet: Carmen (Cpte). (G. Bumbry, J. Vickers, M. Freni, K. Paskalis, E. Lublin, V. Cortez, M. Trempont, A. Voli, C. Meloni, B. Gontcharenko, R. Outin, L. Frémont, Petits Chanteurs à la Croix de Bois, Paris Op Chor, Paris Op Orch/R. Frühbeck de Burgos)

Ⓓ **CD-CFPD4700** ▭ **TC-CFPD4700** (3/87)
Verdi—Rigoletto
Verdi: Rigoletto (Cpte). (C. MacNeil, R. Grist, N. Gedda, A. Ferrin, A. di Stasio, R. Raimondi, L. Leoni, F. Ricciardi, B. di Bella, M. Fiorentini, A. Giacomotti, Rome Op Chor, Rome Op Orch/F. Molinari-Pradelli)

Ⓓ **CD-CFPD4708** ▭ **TC-CFPD4708**
Puccini—La bohème
Puccini: Bohème (Cpte). (R. Scotto, Alfredo Kraus, C. Neblett, S. Milnes, M. Manuguerra, P. Plishka, I. Tajo, R. Capecchi, P. Crook, M. Lewis, J. Noble, Trinity Boys' Ch, Ambrosian Op Chor, National PO/James Levine)

Ⓓ **CD-CFPD4721** (10/91) ▭ **TC-CFPD4721** (10/91)
Bizet—Les Pêcheurs de Perles
Bizet: Pêcheurs de Perles (Cpte). (I. Cotrubas, A. Vanzo (ten), G. Sarabia, R. Soyer, Paris Op Chor, Paris Op Orch/G. Prêtre)

Ⓓ **CD-CFPD4724** (9/91) ▭ **TC-CFPD4724** (9/91)
Mozart—Le nozze di Figaro
Mozart: Nozze di Figaro (Cpte). (S. Bruscantini, G. Sciutti, F. Calabrese, S. Jurinac, R. Stevens, M. Sinclair, I. Wallace, H. Cuénod, D. McCoshan, G. Griffiths, J. Sinclair, Glyndebourne Fest Chor, Glyndebourne Fest Orch/V. Gui)

Ⓓ **CD-CFPD4730** (4/94) ▭ **TC-CFPD4730** (4/93)
Gilbert & Sullivan—The Mikado; Iolanthe (highlights)
Sullivan: Mikado (Cpte); Iolanthe (exc). (J. Holmes, J. Wakefield, C. Revill, D. Dowling, J.H. Nash, M. Studholme, P. Kern, D. Nash, J. Allister, Sadlers Wells Op Chor, Sadlers Wells Op Orch/A. Faris, E. Shilling, D. Dowling, S. Bevan, Leon Greene, E. Harwood, J. Moyle, H. Begg, P. Kern, E. Robson, C. Morey)

Ⓓ **CD-CFPD4733** (5/94) ▭ **TC-CFPD4733** (5/94)
Donizetti—L'Elisir d'amore
Donizetti: Elisir d'amore (Cpte). (R. Carteri, L. Alva, R. Panerai, G. Taddei, A. Vercelli, La Scala Chor, La Scala Orch/T. Serafin)

Ⓓ **CD-CFPD4736** ▭ **TC-CFPD4736**
Verdi—Otello
Verdi: Otello (Cpte). (C. Craig, R. Plowright, N. Howlett, B. Bottone, S. Kale, S. Squires, S. Rea, M. Rivers, G. Traynor, ENO Chor, ENO Orch/M. Elder)

Ⓓ **CD-CFPSD4751**
Berlioz—Orchestral Works
Berlioz: Symphonie fantastique; Corsaire; Carnaval romain; Béatrice et Bénédict (exc); Benvenuto Cellini (exc); King Lear; Enfance du Christ (exc); Damnation de Faust (exc). (Hallé Ch, Hallé/J. Loughran/M. Handford)

Ⓓ **CD-CFPSD4778**
Gay—The Beggar's Opera
Gay: Beggar's Opera (Cpte). (E. Morison, Z. Walker, J. Cameron, J. Neville, M. Sinclair, R. Roberts, I. Wallace, E. Porter, O. Brannigan, P. Rogers, C. Shacklock, D. Heard, A. Young, R. Hardy, A. Pollak, J. Jacobs, Pro Arte Chor, PAO/M. Sargent)

Ⓓ **CD-CFPSD4793**
J. Strauss II—Die Fledermaus
J. Strauss II: Fledermaus (Cpte). (G. Scheyrer, W. Lipp, K. Terkal, A. Dermota, E. Waechter, C. Ludwig, W. Berry, E. Majkut, L. Martini, E. Kunz, Philh Chor, Philh/O. Ackermann)

Ⓓ **CD-CFPSD4796**
German—Merrie England
German: Merrie England (Cpte). (M. Sinclair, W. McAlpine, P. Glossop, J. Bronhill, P. Kern, H. Glynne, Rita Williams Sngrs, M. Collins Orch/M. Collins)

Ⓓ **CD-CFPSD4799**
Verdi—La traviata (in English)
Verdi: Traviata (Cpte). (V. Masterson, J. Brecknock, C. du Plessis, D. Jones, S. Squires, G. Pogson, J. Gibbs, D. Dowling, R. Earle, ENO Chor, ENO Orch/C. Mackerras)

Ⓓ **CD-CFP4238** ▭ **TC-CFP40238**
Gilbert and Sullivan
Sullivan: Mikado (exc); Yeomen of the Guard (exc); Iolanthe (exc); Gondoliers (exc); Pirates of Penzance (exc); HMS Pinafore (exc). (Richard Lewis, E. Morison, M. Thomas, G. Evans, M. Sinclair, George Baker, I. Wallace, A. Young, E. Graham, J. Cameron, O. Brannigan, Glyndebourne Fest Chor, PAO/M. Sargent)

Ⓓ **CD-CFP4277**
These you have Loved
Bach: Cantata 147 (exc); *Handel:* Concerti grossi, op 6 (exc); *Grieg:* Peer Gynt (exc); *Puccini:* Tosca (exc); *Bizet:* Carmen (exc); *Chopin:* Fantaisie-impromptu; *Liszt:* Liebesträume, S541 (exc); *Chopin:* Polonaises (exc); *Zeller:* Obersteiger (exc); *Brahms:* Symphony 3 (exc); *Verdi:* Trovatore (exc); *Tchaikovsky:* Eugene Onegin (exc); *Mozart:* Horn Concerti (exc); *Elgar:* Salut d'amour; *Puccini:* Turandot (exc); *Rachmaninov:* Paganini Rhapsody (exc); *Handel:* Messiah (exc). (King's College Ch, ASMF/D. Willcocks, Y. Menuhin (vn/dir), Bath Fest Orch, Hallé/J. Barbirolli, M. Callas, Paris Cons/G. Prêtre, J. Ogdon, E. Schwarzkopf, Philh/O. Ackermann, LSO/A. Boult, Rome Op Chor, Rome Op Orch/T. Schippers, RPO/T. Beecham, B. Tuckwell/N. Marriner/L. Collingwood, F. Corelli/F. Molinari-Pradelli, A. Anievas, New PO/M. Atzmon, Ambrosian Sngrs, ECO/C. Mackerras)

Ⓓ **CD-CFP4304** (2/89) ▭ **TC-CFP40304** (2/89)
Delius: Orchestral Works
Delius: Fennimore and Gerda Intermezzo; First cuckoo; Summer Night on the River; Song before Sunrise; Sleigh Ride; Irmelin Prelude; Village Romeo and Juliet (exc); Koanga (exc). (LPO/V. Handley)

Ⓓ **CD-CFP4485** ▭ **TC-CFP4485**
Lehár—The Merry Widow: highlights
Lehár: Lustige Witwe (exc). (J. Bronhill, D. Dowling, H. Glynne, M. Lowe, T. Round, W. McAlpine, J. Kentish, R. Herincx, J. Larsen, William Booth, Sadler's Wells Op Chor, Sadler's Wells Op Orch/W. Reid)

Ⓓ **CD-CFP4499** ▭ **TC-CFP4499**
Strauss—Champagne and Laughter
J. Strauss II: Blauen Donau, Op. 314; Casanova (exc); Kaiser, Op. 437; Fledermaus (exc); Radetzky March; *J. Strauss II:* Tritsch-Tratsch; Unter Donner und Blitz; Perpetuum Mobile; Champagner, Op. 211. (Hallé/J. Barbirolli, E. Schwarzkopf, chor, Philh/O. Ackermann, Philh Promenade Orch/H. Krips, B. Fassbaender, N. Gedda, R. Holm, A. Rothenberger, W. Berry, D. Fischer-Dieskau, Vienna St Op Chor, Vienna SO/W. Boskovsky)

Ⓓ **CD-CFP4515** ▭ **TC-CFP4515**
Meditation
Chopin: Nocturnes (exc); *Massenet:* Thaïs (exc); *Mendelssohn:* Midsummer Night's Dream (exc); *Borodin:* String Quartet 2 (exc); *Albinoni:* Adagio; *Gluck:* Orfeo ed Euridice (exc); *Fauré:* Pavane; *Gounod:* Mors et Vita (exc). (RLPO/C. Groves)

Ⓓ **CD-CFP4523**
Prokofiev—Orchestral Works
Prokofiev: Symphony 1; Symphony 7; Love for 3 Oranges Suite (exc). (Philh/N. Malko)

Ⓓ **CD-CFP4529**
Gilbert & Sullivan: Overtures
Sullivan: Mikado (exc); Sorcerer (exc); Gondoliers (exc); Patience (exc); Iolanthe (exc); Pirates of Penzance (exc); Ruddigore (exc); HMS Pinafore (exc); Cox and Box (exc); Princess Ida (exc); Yeomen of the Guard (exc). (PAO/M. Sargent)

Ⓓ **CD-CFP4543**
Encores you love
Copland: Fanfare for the Common Man; *Khachaturian:* Spartacus Suite 2 (exc); *Gounod:* Mors et Vita (exc); *MacCunn:* Land of the mountain and the flood; *Satie:* Gymnopédies (exc); *Massenet:* Thaïs (exc); *Traditional:* Suo Gan; *Barber:* Adagio for Strings. (Hallé/M. Handford)

Ⓓ **CD-CFP4557** (11/89) ▭ **TC-CFP4557** (11/89)
Baroque Favourites
Pachelbel: Canon and Gigue (exc); *Purcell:* Chaconne, Z730; *Vivaldi:* Concerti grossi, op 3 (exc); *Corelli:* Concerti grossi, op 6 (exc); *Gluck:* Orfeo ed Euridice (exc); *Monteverdi:* Madrigals, Bk 8 (exc); *Handel:* Concerti grossi, op 6 (exc). (ASMF/N. Marriner, Y. Menuhin (vn/dir), R. Masters, E. Goren, S. Humphreys, Bath Fest CO, Derek Simpson, Bath Fest Orch, G. English, H. Cuénod, Bath Fest Ens, R. Leppard (hpd/dir)/Y. Menuhin)

Ⓓ **CD-CFP4569** (8/90) ▭ **TC-CFP4569** (8/90)
Puccini: Arias
Puccini: Bohème (exc); Bohème (exc); Manon Lescaut (exc); Manon Lescaut (exc); Manon Lescaut (exc); Tosca (exc); Tosca (exc); Tosca (exc); Madama Butterfly (exc); Madama Butterfly (exc); Fanciulla del West (exc); Turandot (exc); Turandot (exc); Turandot (exc); Suor Angelica (exc); Gianni Schicchi (exc). (N. Gedda, ROHO/G. Patanè, R. Scotto, National PO/James Levine, C. Craig, Orch, M. Collins, M. Caballé, B. Marti, LSO/C. Mackerras, A. Stella/A. Erede, F. Corelli/F. Ferraris, M. Freni/L. Magiera, ROH Chor/L. Gardelli, G. Campora, Rome Op Orch/G. Santini, A. Shuard/E. Downes, F. Cavalli, RPO/A. Fistoulari)

Ⓓ **CD-CFP4575** ▭ **TC-CFP4575**
Verdi Arias
Verdi: Aida (exc); Aida (exc); Aida (exc); Rigoletto (exc); Rigoletto (exc); Traviata (exc); Traviata (exc); Traviata (exc); Nabucco (exc); Trovatore (exc); Ballo in maschera (exc); Forza del Destino (exc); Forza del Destino (exc); Don Carlo (exc); Otello (exc). (P. Domingo, New Philh/R. Muti, A. Moffo, Philh/Colin Davis, C. Craig, Orch/M. Collins, B. Sills, N. Gedda, John Alldis Ch, RPO/A. Ceccato, R. Bruson, La Scala Chor, La Scala Orch/L. von Matačić, ROHO/G. Patanè, B. Casoni, Ambrosian Op Chor/L. Gardelli, F. Cavalli/A. Fistoulari, E. Obraztsova/R. Stapleton, M. Caballé/A. Guadagno, A. Shuard/E. Downes)

Ⓓ **CD-CFP4577** (2/91)
A Viennese Evening
J. Strauss II: Zigeunerbaron (exc); Rosen aus dem Süden; *E. Strauss:* Alpenrose; *J. Strauss II:* Champagner, Op. 211; Pesther Csárdás; Perpetuum Mobile; Fledermaus (exc); Morgenblätter, Op. 279; *E. Strauss:* Unter der Enns; *J. Strauss II:* Explosionen, Op. 43; Im Krapfenwald'l, Op. 336; *J. strauss I:* Radetzky March. (Hallé/B. Tovey)

Ⓓ **CD-CFP4582** ▭ **TC-CFP4582**
Flowers in Music
Tchaikovsky: Nutcracker (exc); *Delibes:* Lakmé (exc); *J. Strauss II:* Rosen aus dem Süden; *Sullivan:* Gondoliers (exc); Ruddigore (exc); Mikado (exc); *J. Strauss II:* Wo die Zitronen blüh'n; *Debussy:* Estampes (exc); *Schubert:* Heidenröslein, D257; *Gounod:* Faust (exc); *Bizet:* Carmen (exc); *Delius:* Village Romeo and Juliet (exc); *Puccini:* Madama Butterfly (exc); *Tchaikovsky:* Sleeping Beauty (exc). (LSO/A. Previn, M. Mesplé, D. Millet, Paris Opéra-Comique Orch/A. Lombard, VJSO/W. Boskovsky, Glyndebourne Fest Chor, PAO/M. Sargent, P. Bowden, Richard Lewis, G. Evans, Y. Egorov, J. Baker, G. Parsons, M. Command, Paris Op Orch/G. Prêtre, N. Gedda, RPO/M. Davies, R. Scotto, A. di Stasio, Rome Op Orch/J. Barbirolli)

Ⓓ **CD-CFP4600** ▭ **TC-CFP4600**
Puccini—Madam Butterfly (highlights)
Puccini: Madama Butterfly (exc). (M. Collier, A. Robson, C. Craig, G. Griffiths, Sadler's Wells Op Orch/B. Balkwill)

Ⓓ **CD-CFP4601** ▭ **TC-CFP4601**
Musicals - Volume 2
Gershwin: Porgy and Bess Suite; *Rodgers:* Oklahoma (exc); *Bernstein:* West Side Story Symphonic Dances; *Rodgers:* King and I (exc). (RLPO/Carl Davis)

Ⓓ **CD-CFP4602** ▭ **TC-CFP4602**
Favourite Opera
Bizet: Carmen (exc); Carmen (exc); Pêcheurs de perles (exc); *Mozart:* Don Giovanni (exc); Don Giovanni (exc); Zauberflöte (exc); *Puccini:* Manon Lescaut (exc); Turandot (exc); Tosca (exc); Bohème (exc); *Verdi:* Nabucco (exc); Rigoletto (exc); Traviata (exc); Trovatore (exc); *Mascagni:* Amico Fritz (exc); *Offenbach:* Contes d'Hoffmann (exc); *Rossini:* Barbiere di Siviglia (exc); *Gounod:* Faust (exc). (H. Donath, E. Schwarzkopf, M. Callas, N. Sautereau, J. Sutherland, M. Freni, V. de los Angeles, E. Obraztsova, J. Collard, J. Berbié, L. Pavarotti, N. Gedda, P. Domingo, C. Craig, C. del Monte, R. Soyer, W. Berry, T. Gobbi, E. Blanc, R. Massard, M. Sereni, Rome Op Chor, Ambrosian Op Chor, R. Duclos Ch, Paris Op Chor, La Scala Chor, La Scala Orch, orch, Rome Op Orch, New Philh, Paris Opéra-Comique Orch, Philh, ROHO, ECO, Paris Cons, Bavarian

St Op Orch/D. Barenboim/G. Patanè/G. Gavazzeni/D. Barenboim/A. Cluytens/W. Sawallisch/A. Galliera/L. von Matačić/T. Serafin/M. Collins/G. Prêtre/P. Dervaux/C.M. Giulini/B. Bartoletti/G. Santini/T. Schippers, Paris Op Orch)

Ⓓ **CD-CFP4606** ▭ **TC-CFP4606**
Favourite Movie Classics
Wagner: Walküre (exc); *Barber:* Adagio for Strings; *Mozart:* Così fan tutte (exc); *J. Strauss II:* Blauen Donau, Op. 314; *Dvořák:* Rusalka (exc); *Ponchielli:* Gioconda (exc); *Mozart:* Clarinet Concerto, K622 (exc); *Rossini:* Barbiere di Siviglia (exc); *Puccini:* Gianni Schicchi (exc); *Mahler:* Symphony 5 (exc); *Boccherini:* String Quintets, G271-6 (exc); *Addinsell:* Warsaw Concerto. (M. Caballé, L. Popp, J. Aler, A. Marriner, D. Adni, LPO, Philadelphia, VJSO, Munich RO, Sinfonia of London, LMP, Philh, LSO, New Philh, ASMF, Bournemouth SO/A. Boult/E. Ormandy/B. Haitink/W. Boskovsky/S. Soltesz/R. Irving/J. Glover/C.M. Giulini/C. Mackerras/J. Barbirolli/N. Marriner/K. Alwyn)

Ⓓ **CD-CFP4607** ▭ **TC-CFP4607**
Favourite Strauss
J. Strauss II: Blauen Donau, Op. 314; Champagner, Op. 211; G'schichten aus dem Wienerwald, Op. 325; Auf der Jagd, Op. 373; Nacht in Venedig (exc); Wiener Blut; Neue Pizzicato-Polka, Op. 449; Künstlerleben, Op. 316; Kaiser, Op. 437; *E. Strauss:* Bahn frei; *J. Strauss I:* Seufzer-Galopp; Radetzky March. (VJSO/W. Boskovsky)

Ⓓ **CD-CFP4608** ▭ **TC-CFP4608**
Favourite Classics 1
Vivaldi: Concerti, Op. 8 (exc); *Bach:* Cantata 147 (exc); *Clarke:* Suite in D (exc); *Handel:* Messiah (exc); *Rossini:* Scala di seta (exc); *Mendelssohn:* Midsummer Night's Dream (exc); *Sibelius:* Karelia Suite (exc); *Puccini:* Madama Butterfly (exc); *Tchaikovsky:* Serenade, Op. 48 (exc); *Grieg:* Peer Gynt (exc); *Verdi:* Aida (exc); *Elgar:* Enigma Variations (exc); *Prokofiev:* Lt. Kijé Suite (exc); *Vaughan Williams:* Greensleeves Fantasia; *Walton:* Façade Suites (exc); *Canteloube:* Chants d'Auvergne (exc); *Chabrier:* España. (M. Caballé, V. de los Angeles, P. Domingo, Y. Menuhin, M. André, J. Parker-Smith, Ambrosian Sngrs, Beecham Choral Soc, Camerata Lysy, ASMF, ECO, Polish CO, LSO, Hallé, LPO, RPO, New Philh, Sinfonia of London, Lamoureux Orch, Philh, A. Lysy/N. Marriner/C. Mackerras/J. Maksymiuk/A. Previn/J. Barbirolli/N. del Mar/T. Beecham/R. Muti/A. Boult/K. Tennstedt/O.A. Hughes/J-P. Jacquillat/H. von Karajan)

Ⓓ **CD-CFP4609** ▭ **TC-CFP4609**
Favourite Gilbert & Sullivan
Sullivan: Pirates of Penzance (exc); HMS Pinafore (exc); Mikado (exc); Iolanthe (exc); Patience (exc); Yeomen of the Guard (exc). (E. Morison, J. Sinclair, M. Thomas, M. Sinclair, Richard Lewis, A. Young, J. Milligan, George Baker, J. Cameron, G. Evans, J. Shaw, O. Brannigan, I. Wallace, Glyndebourne Fest Chor, PAO/M. Sargent)

Ⓓ **CD-CFP4612** ▭ **TC-CFP4612**
Favourite Mozart
Mozart: Symphony 40 (exc); Nozze di Figaro (exc); Piano Concerto 23 (exc); German Dances, K605 (exc); Violin Concerto, K211 (exc); Così fan tutte (exc); Piano Sonata, K331 (exc); Horn Concerti (exc); Musikalischer Spass (exc); Zauberflöte (exc); Serenade, K525 (exc); Don Giovanni (exc); Entführung (exc); Symphony 38 (exc); Mass, K427 (exc). (E. Mathis, M. Marshall, E. Gruberová, A. Baltsa, C. Desderi, J. Van Dam, G. Frick, Y. Menuhin (vn/dir), A. Civil, A. Fischer, R. Buchbinder, South German Madrigal Ch, ECO, LPO, Philh, ASMF, Bath Fest Orch, VPO, RPO, BRSO, South-West German CO/D. Barenboim/B. Haitink/A. Boult/N. Marriner/R. Muti/R. Kempe/G. Cantelli/Colin Davis/J. Krips/J. Tate/W. Gönnenwein)

Ⓓ **CD-CFP4613** ▭ **TC-CFP4613**
Favourite TV Classics
Orff: Carmina burana (exc); *Vivaldi:* Concerti, Op. 8 (exc); *Beethoven:* Bagatelles (exc); *Albinoni:* Adagio; *Handel:* Water Music (exc); *Mozart:* Horn Concerti (exc); *Delibes:* Lakmé (exc); *Rimsky-Korsakov:* Tale of Tsar Saltan (exc); *Grieg:* Peer Gynt (exc); *Rossini:* Barbiere di Siviglia (exc); *Dukas:* Apprenti sorcier (exc); *Dvořák:* Symphony 9 (exc); *Verdi:* Nabucco (exc); *Satie:* Gymnopédies (exc); *Delibes:* Sylvia (exc); *Bach:* Suites, BWV1066-9 (exc); *Smetana:* Má Vlast (exc); *Puccini:* Turandot (exc). (M. Mesplé, D. Millet, N. Gedda, T. Gobbi, I. Brown, K. Jakowicz, A. Civil, M. Lympany, Ambrosian Op Chor, Philh Chor, ASMF, CBSO, Hallé, LPO, New Philh, Oslo PO, Paris Opéra-Comique Orch, Philh, Polish CO, Prague CO, ROHO, RPO, Staatskapelle Dresden/A. Lombard/A. Galliera/C. Mackerras/G. Patanè/J. Maksymiuk/L. Frémaux/M. Jansons/N. Marriner/O.A. Hughes/P. Berglund/R. Kempe/R. Muti/T. Beecham/Z. Macal)

Ⓓ **CD-CFP4616**
Ave Maria
Gounod: Ave Maria; *Handel:* Messiah (exc); Berenice (exc); Serse (exc); *Schubert:* Ave Maria, D839; *Liszt:* Ave Maria, S659; *Bizet:* Agnus Dei; *Pachelbel:* Canon and Gigue (exc); *Bruckner:* Ave Maria (1861); *Kreutzer:* Schäfers Sonntagslied (exc); *T. Giordani:* Caro mio ben; *Weber:* Pieces, J81-6 (exc); *Kienzl:* Evangelimann (exc); *Verdi:* Otello (exc). (A. Rothenberger, Tolz Boys' Ch, Graunke SO/G. Schmidt-Gaden, Ambrosian Sngrs, ECO/C. Mackerras, ASMF/N. Marriner, F. Wunderlich, Bavarian St Op Orch/H. Müller-Kray, K. Hochreither, R. Schock, Bielefeld Childrens' Ch, NW German PO/W. Schüchter, Toulouse CO/L. Auriacombe, New Philh Chor/W. Pitz, G. Frick, Bavarian St Op Chor/W. Mattes, Berlin Symphonia, R. van Husen, M. Höffgen, N. Gedda, Munich St. Wolfgang Children's Ch, Bavarian St Orch/R. Heger, E. Grümmer, Berlin Deutsche Op Orch/R. Kraus)

Ⓓ **CD-CFP4635**
Music of the Four Countries
Smyth: Wreckers (exc); *Harty:* With the wild geese; *MacCunn:* Land of the mountain and the flood; *German:* Welsh Rhapsody. (SNO/A. Gibson)

Ⓓ **CD-CFP4656** ▭ **TC-CFP4656**
Herbert von Karajan conducts Opera
Beethoven: Fidelio (exc); *Verdi:* Trovatore (exc); Don Carlo (exc); Aida (exc); Otello (exc); Falstaff (exc); *Wagner:* Lohengrin (exc); Meistersinger (exc); Tristan und Isolde (exc); *R. Strauss:* Rosenkavalier (exc). (H. Dernesch, J. Vickers, H. Donath, H. Laubenthal, P. Cappuccilli, A. Baltsa, E. Gruberová, J. Carreras, M. Freni, T. Gobbi, A. Tomowa-Sintow, K. Ridderbusch, S. Nimsgern, E. Schwarzkopf, C. Ludwig, T. Stich-Randall, Berlin Deutsche Op Chor, Leipzig Rad Chor, Dresden St Op Chor, BPO, VPO, Philh, Staatskapelle Dresden/H. von Karajan, E. Waechter)

Ⓓ **CD-CFP4658** ▭ **TC-CFP4658**
Everlasting Love
Mozart: Piano Concerto 21 (exc); *Verdi:* Traviata (exc); *Liszt:* Liebesträume, S541 (exc); *Elgar:* Salut d'amour; *Wieniawski:* Légende, Op. 17; *Mascagni:* Cavalleria rusticana (exc); *Mozart:* Horn Concerti (exc); *Rachmaninov:* Paganini Rhapsody (exc); *Holst:* Planets (exc); *Rodrigo:* Concierto de Aranjuez (exc); *Bizet:* Carmen Suites (exc); *Bruch:* Violin Concerto 1 (exc); *Wagner:* Tristan und Isolde (exc). (S. Hough, J. Ogdon, T. Little, P. Lane, C. Briggs, C. Ousset, A. Diaz, Y. Menuhin, Hallé, RPO, RLPO, CBSO, Spanish Nat Orch, Stuttgart RSO, LSO, VPO/B. Thomson/A. Ceccato/L. Collingwood/M. Handford/S. Kovacevich/S. Rattle/J. Loughran/R. Frühbeck de Burgos/N. Marriner/A. Boult/R. Kempe)

Ⓓ **CD-CFP4659** ▭ **TC-CFP4659**
Everlasting Happiness
Boccherini: String Quintets, G271-6 (exc); *Beethoven:* Symphony 8 (exc); *Bach:* Cantata 208 (exc); *Grieg:* Peer Gynt (exc); *Dvořák:* Humoresques, Op. 101 (exc); *Tchaikovsky:* Andante cantabile, Op. 11; *Pachelbel:* Canon and Gigue (exc); *Fauré:* Dolly (exc); *Berlioz:* Damnation de Faust (exc); *Debussy:* Petite Suite (exc); *Bizet:* Carmen (exc); *Elgar:* Wand of Youth Suite 1 (exc); *Rossini:* Sonate a quattro (exc); *Mozart:* Divertimento, K334 (exc); *Beethoven:* Symphony 6 (exc). (M. Lympany, ASMF, Philadelphia, RPO, Hallé, FRNO, RLPO, Polish CO, Stockholm CO/N. Marriner/R. Muti/T. Beecham/M. Handford/J. Martinon/V. Handley/J. Maksymiuk/F. Welser-Möst)

Ⓓ **CD-CFP4660** ▭ **TC-CFP4660**
Everlasting Peace
Bach: Suites, BWV1066-9 (exc); *Albinoni:* Adagio; *Gluck:* Orfeo ed Euridice (exc); *Schumann:* Kinderszenen (exc); *Beethoven:* Piano Sonata 8 (exc); *Mahler:* Symphony 5 (exc); *Chopin:* Nocturnes (exc); *Elgar:* Enigma Variations (exc); *Fauré:* Pavane; *Handel:* Messiah (exc); *Mozart:* Flute and Harp Concerto, K299 (exc); *Saint-Saëns:* Carnaval des animaux (exc); *Humperdinck:* Hänsel und Gretel (exc). (M. Lympany, L. Pennario, J. Ogdon, J. Snowden, C. Thomas, A. Shepherd, P. Katin, P. Fowke, Hallé, ASMF, Hollywood Bowl SO, RLPO, LPO, FRNO, ECO/O.A. Hughes/N. Marriner/M. Rózsa/C. Mackerras/V. Handley/T. Beecham/A. Litton/C. Dragon)

Ⓓ **CD-CFP4661** ▭ **TC-CFP4661**
Everlasting Tranquillity
Massenet: Thaïs (exc); *Beethoven:* Piano Sonata 14 (exc); *Chopin:* Sylphides (exc); *Elgar:* Serenade (exc); *Satie:* Gymnopédies (exc); *Vaughan Williams:* Greensleeves Fantasia; *Puccini:* Madama Butterfly (exc); *Delibes:* Coppélia (exc); *Traditional:* Suo Gan; *Debussy:* Suite bergamasque (exc); *Mozart:* Clarinet Concerto, K622 (exc); *Godard:* Jocelyn (exc); *Minkus:* Bayadère (exc); *Mendelssohn:* Midsummer Night's Dream (exc). (A. Marriner, M. Lympany, D. Adni, Rome Op Chor, Sydney SO, Stuttgart RSO, Hallé, Philh, LPO, Rome Op Orch, Paris Op Orch, LMP/M. Handford/R. Irving/V. Handley/O.A. Hughes/J. Barbirolli/J-B. Mari/J. Glover/N. Marriner/J. Lanchbery/A. Litton)

Ⓓ **CD-CFP4670** ▭ **TC-CFP4670**
Wagner—Götterdämmerung (highlights)
Wagner: Götterdämmerung (exc). (R. Hunter, A. Remedios, LPO/C. Mackerras)

Ⓓ **CD-CFP9000** (11/87)
Orchestral Favourites
Tchaikovsky: 1812; *Borodin:* Prince Igor (exc); *Glinka:* Ruslan and Lyudmila (exc); *Tchaikovsky:* Marche slave; *Wagner:* Lohengrin (exc); *Mussorgsky:* Night on the Bare Mountain. (LPO/C. Mackerras/W. Susskind/A. Davison)

Ⓓ **CD-CFP9008** (11/87)
Wagner Orchestral Works
Wagner: Walküre (exc); Götterdämmerung (exc); Lohengrin (exc); Meistersinger (exc). (LPO/K.A. Rickenbacher)

Ⓓ **CD-CFP9013** ▭ **TC-CFP4498**
Duets from Famous Operas
Mozart: Don Giovanni (exc); *Rossini:* Barbiere di Siviglia (exc); *Verdi:* Trovatore (exc); *Mussorgsky:* Boris Godunov (exc); *Giordano:* Andrea Chénier (exc); *Bizet:* Pêcheurs de perles (exc); *Puccini:* Madama Butterfly (exc); Tosca (exc); Bohème (exc). (G. Sciutti, E. Waechter, M. Callas, T. Gobbi, G. Tucci, F. Corelli, E. Lear, D. Uzunov, A. Stella, P. Pedani, N. Gedda, E. Blanc, V. de los Angeles, J. Björling, C. Bergonzi, M. Freni, M. Sereni, Rome Op Chor, Sofia National Op Chor, Philh, Rome Op Orch, Paris Cons, Paris Opéra-Comique Orch/C.M. Giulini/A. Galliera/T. Schippers/A. Cluytens/G. Santini/P. Dervaux/G. Prêtre)

Claves

Ⓓ **CD50-0705**
Purcell—Songs
Purcell: If music be the food of love, Z379/1; Ah! how pleasant, Z353; Libertine, Z600 (exc); Sweet, be no longer sad, Z418; Rule a Wife and Have a Wife, Z587 (exc); I saw that you were grown so high, Z387; Fool's Preferment, Z571 (exc); Aureng-Zebe, Z573 (exc); More love or more disdain, Z397; Sylvia, now your scorn give over, Z420; Turn then thine eyes, Z425; Oedipus, Z583 (exc); Pausanias, Z585 (exc); Mock Marriage, Z605 (exc); King Arthur, Z628 (exc); Evening hymn, Z193; Queen's Epicedium, Z383; Lord, what is man?, Z192. (P. Huttenlocher, J.E. Dähler)

Ⓓ **CD50-8305**
Ernst Haefliger sings Mozart Arias
Mozart: Così fan tutte (exc); Don Giovanni (exc); Misero, o sogno, K431; Entführung (exc); Zauberflöte (exc); Clemenza di Tito (exc); Idomeneo (exc); Per pietà, non ricercate, K420. (E. Haefliger, ECO/J.E. Dähler)

Ⓓ **CD50-8503**
Philip Jones Brass Ensemble Lollipops
G. Langford: London Miniatures; *Rimsky-Korsakov:* Tale of Tsar Saltan (exc); *Traditional:* Song of the Seahorse; *Arban:* Tyrolean Variations; *Koetsier:* Kleiner Zirkusmarsch, Op. 79; *Grieg:* Norwegian Dances, Op. 35 (exc); *Joplin:* Bethena; *Parker:* Londoner in New York. (J. Fletcher, PJBE, F. Lloyd)

Ⓓ **CD50-8804** (4/89)
Rossini—Guilliame Tell arrangements for wind
Rossini: Guillaume Tell (exc). (Consortium Classicum)

Ⓓ **CD50-8904/5** (10/89)
Rossini—Il Signor Bruschino
Rossini: Signor Bruschino (Cpte). (B. Praticò, N. de Carolis, P. Orciani, L. Canonici, P. Spagnoli, K. Lytting, F. Massa, Turin PO/M. Viotti)

Ⓓ **CD50-9023**
Maria Bayo—Arie Antiche
Pasquini: Bella bocca; *Zannetti:* Avvezzati, mio core; *Cavalli:* Son ancor pargoletta; *Alessandro Melani:* Vezzosa Aurora; *Strozzi:* Cantate, Op. 2 (exc); Spesso per entro al petto; *Frescobaldi:* Arie musicali Bk 1 (exc); *Caccini:* Nuove musiche (1614) (exc); *Stradella:* Così amor mi fai languir; *Busatti:* Pupillette; *Buzzoleni:* Si che morte; *Gagliano:* Mie speranze; *Carissimi:* Fuggite, fuggite; *A. Scarlatti:* Cara e dolce; Pirro e Demetrio (exc); *Carissimi:* Non posso vivere; *Astorga:* In questo core; *Perti:* Sperar io non dovrei; *Busatti:* Dite ch'io canti; *A. Scarlatti:* Speranza mi tradisce; Pompeo (exc); Pensieri, oh Dio. (M. Bayo, U. Duetschler)

Ⓓ **CD50-9120**
Mozart—Opera and Concert Arias
Mozart: Finta semplice (exc); Bacio di mano, K541; Per questa bella mano, K612; Nozze di Figaro (exc); Don Giovanni (exc); Così fan tutte (exc). (N. De Carolis, Venice and Padua CO/B. Giuranna)

Ⓓ **CD50-9201** (2/93)
Schoeck—Orchestral Works
Schoeck: Violin Concerto; Penthesilea (exc). (B. Boller, Swiss YSO/A. Delfs)

Ⓓ **CD50-9202** (11/92)
Donizetti/Rossini—Tenor Arias
Donizetti: Linda di Chamounix (exc); Duca d'Alba (exc); Elisir d'Amore (exc); Anna Bolena (exc); Don Pasquale (exc); Lucia di Lammermoor (exc); *Rossini:* Barbiere di Siviglia (exc); Italiana in Algeri (exc); Occasione fa il ladro (exc); Donna del lago (exc). (R. Vargas, ECO/M. Viotti)

Ⓓ **CD50-9208/9** (5/93)
Rossini—L'occasione fa il ladro
Rossini: Occasione fa il ladro (Cpte). (M. Bayo, N. de Carolis, I. Zennaro, F. Provvisionato, F. Previati, F. Massa, ECO/M. Viotti)

Ⓓ **CD50-9211** (5/93)
Rossini—L'inganno felice
Rossini: Inganno felice (Cpte). (N. de Carolis, A. Felle, I. Zennaro, F. Previati, D. Serraiocco, ECO/M. Viotti)

Ⓓ **CD50-9303**
Guitar Recital—Emanuele Segre
Giuliani: Rossiniana No. 1, Op. 119; Giulianate, Op. 148; *Rossini:* Semiramide (exc); *Paganini:* Guitar Sonata, MS87; Guitar Sonatas, MS84 (exc); Guitar Sonata, MS3. (E. Segre)

The Cleveland Orchestra

Ⓓ **TCO93-75**
The Cleveland Orchestra-75th Anniversary CD Edition
Rachmaninov: Symphony 2; *Debussy:* Pelléas et Mélisande (exc); *Rimsky-Korsakov:* Scheherazade; *Shostakovich:* Symphony 1; *Sibelius:* Symphony 3; Symphony 2; *Wagner:* Siegfried Idyll; *Mozart:* Requiem; *Schumann:* Introduction and Allegro, Op. 92; *R. Strauss:* Bourgeois gentilhomme Suite (exc); *Ravel:* Tombeau; *Prokofiev:* Symphony 1; *Mahler:* Lied von der Erde; *Prokofiev:* Scythian Suite; *Stravinsky:* Chant du Rossignol; *Messiaen:* Oiseaux exotiques; *Ravel:* Daphnis et Chloé Suites (exc); *Druckman:* Windows; *Tchaikovsky:* Manfred Symphony; *Schubert:* Symphony 10 (exc); *Mahler:* Rückert Lieder; *Weill:* Sieben Todsünden (Cpte); *Beethoven:* Grosse Fuge; *Ruggles:* Sun-treader; *Brahms:* Piano Quartet 1. (A. Silja, J. Raskin, J. Baker, F. Kopleff, E. Haefliger, Richard Lewis, D. George, V. Vogel, T. Paul, J. van Dam, J. Gottschick, F-J. Kapellmann, R. Serkin, Cleveland Orch Chor, Cleveland Orch/N. Sokoloff/E. Leinsdorf/A. Rodzinski/G. Szell/P. Boulez/L. Maazel/C. von Dohnányi)

Cloud Nine Records

Ⓓ **ACN6002** (10/89)
Gershwin: Piano Works
Gershwin: Shall we dance? (exc); Lady, Be Good! (exc); Strike up the Band I (exc); Oh, Kay! (exc); Rosalie (exc); Funny Face (exc); Treasure Girl (exc); Girl Crazy (exc); Pardon My English (exc); Show Girl (exc); Damsel in distress (exc); Porgy and Bess (exc); Shocking Miss Pilgrim (exc); Goldwyn Follies (exc); Tra-la-la; By Strauss. (E. Parkin)

Club 99

Ⓓ **CL99-007** (1/94)
Maria Nemeth/Tiana Lemnitz
Korngold: Tote Stadt (exc); *Verdi:* Trovatore (exc); Aida (exc); *Puccini:* Tosca (exc); *Verdi:* Ballo in maschera (exc); *Mozart:* Entführung (exc); *Wagner:* Fliegende Holländer (exc); *Weber:* Oberon (exc); *Wagner:* Wesendonk Lieder; *Schubert:* Am Grabe Anselmos, D504. (M. Németh, T. Lemnitz, M. Raucheisen, orch)

Ⓓ **CL99-014** (12/90)
Dino Borgioli (1891-1960)
Bellini: Puritani (exc); Sonnambula (exc); *Giordano:* Fedora (exc); *Boito:* Mefistofele (exc); *A. Thomas:* Mignon (exc); *Bizet:* Pêcheurs de Perles (exc); *Donizetti:* Don Pasquale (exc); *Bellini:* Puritani (exc); *Donizetti:* Don Pasquale (exc); *Bizet:* Pêcheurs de Perles (exc); *Donizetti:* Favorita (exc); Elisir d'amore (exc); *Mascagni:* Amico Fritz (exc); *Rossini:* Barbiere di Siviglia (exc); *Puccini:* Bohème (exc); *Donizetti:* Don Pasquale (exc); *R. Strauss:* Lieder, Op. 27 (exc); *Donaudy:* O del mio amato ben; *Hageman:* Do not go, my love. (D. Borgioli, E. Surinach, B. Franci, R. Pampanini, G. Vanelli, A. Brosa, orch, I. Newton)

Ⓓ **CL99-020** (1/94)
Maria Ivogün & Lotte Schöne—Opera Recital
Puccini: Turandot (exc); *Mozart:* Zauberflöte (exc); Così fan tutte (exc); *Nicolai:* Lustigen Weiber von Windsor (exc); *Massenet:* Manon (exc); *Cornelius:* Barbier von Bagdad (exc); *Bellini:* Sonnambula (exc); *J. Strauss II:* Blauen Donau, Op. 314; *Handel:* Allegro, il penseroso ed il moderato (exc); *J. Strauss II:* Fledermaus (exc); *Verdi:* Traviata (exc); *Mozart:* Rè pastore (exc); Entführung (exc); Zauberflöte (exc); *Verdi:* Rigoletto (exc); *Rossini:* Barbiere di Siviglia (exc). (M. Ivogün, L. Schöne, Berlin St Op Orch/F. Zweig/L. Blech/E. Orthmann, K. Erb, orch)

Ⓓ **CL99-022** (5/91)
Germaine Lubin (1891-1979)
Wagner: Tannhäuser (exc); Lohengrin (exc); Siegfried (exc); Walküre (exc); *Schubert:* Erlkönig, D328; *Schumann:* Lieder und Gesänge, Op. 51 (exc); Myrthen, Op. 25 (exc); *Reyer:* Sigurd (exc); *Chopin:* Etudes (exc); *Bach:* Cantata 68 (exc); *Puccini:* Tosca (exc); *Wagner:* Tristan und Isolde (exc). (G. Lubin, orch/H. Defosse, E.I. Kahn, J. Krieger)

Ⓓ **CL99-025** (11/91)
Giovanni Zenatello (1876-1949)
Giordano: Andrea Chénier (exc); *Bizet:* Carmen (exc); *Leoncavallo:* Pagliacci (exc); *Puccini:* Tosca (exc); *Verdi:* Ballo in maschera (exc); *Bizet:* Carmen (exc); *Puccini:* Manon Lescaut (exc); *Verdi:* Otello (exc); Otello (exc); *Giordano:* Andrea Chénier (exc); *Leoncavallo:* Pagliacci (exc); *Verdi:* Aida (exc). (G. Zenatello, M. Gay, A. Granforte, Apollo Chor, M. Rappold, orch, La Scala Orch/Rosario Bourdon/C. Sabajno, G. Marion, A. Boemi)

Ⓓ **CL99-031** (7/90)
Dmitri Smirnov—Opera & Song Recital
Puccini: Tosca (exc); Manon Lescaut (exc); Tabarro (exc); Bohème (exc); *Rossini:* Barbiere di Siviglia (exc); *Boito:* Mefistofele (exc); *Bizet:* Pêcheurs de perles (exc); *Massenet:* Manon (exc); Manon (exc); Manon (exc); *Donizetti:* Elisir d'amore (exc); *Verdi:* Rigoletto (exc); Traviata (exc); *Mascagni:* Cavalleria Rusticana (exc); *Leoncavallo:* Mattinata. (D. Smirnov, orch)

Ⓓ **CL99-034** (1/94)
Marcel Journet (1867-1933)
Massenet: Thaïs (exc); *A. Thomas:* Hamlet (exc); *Luce:* Vos yeux; Fin du rêve; *Wagner:* Walküre (exc); *G. Charpentier:* Louise (exc); *Bizet:* Jolie fille de Perth (exc); *Gounod:* Faust (exc). (M. Journet, M. Cozette, F. Heldy, M. Berthon, C. Vezzani, SO/H. Busser, anon/Rosario Bourdon/P. Coppola)

Ⓓ **CL99-042** (12/91)
Frieda Hempel (1885-1955) & Hermann Jadlowker (1877-1953)
Puccini: Bohème (exc); *Gounod:* Roméo et Juliette (exc); *Meyerbeer:* Huguenots (exc); *Donizetti:* Fille du Régiment (exc); *Bizet:* Carmen (exc); *Verdi:* Traviata (exc); *Donizetti:* Lucia di Lammermoor (exc); *T. Giordani:* Caro mio ben; *Carissimi:* Vittoria! vittoria!; *Schubert:* Schwanengesang, D957 (exc); Winterreise (exc); *Caccini:* Nuove musiche (1602) (exc); *Lotti:* Arminio (exc). (F. Hempel, H. Jadlowker, orch, anon)

Ⓓ **CL99-052** (1/94)
Rosa Raisa (1893-1963)
Bellini: Norma (exc); *Verdi:* Trovatore (exc); *Meyerbeer:* Africaine (exc); *Ponchielli:* Gioconda (exc); *Boito:* Mefistofele (exc); *Verdi:* Trovatore (exc); *Giordano:* Andrea Chénier (exc); *Puccini:* Tosca (exc); *Mascagni:* Cavalleria rusticana (exc); *Ponchielli:* Gioconda (exc); *Mascagni:* Cavalleria rusticana (exc); *Verdi:* Trovatore (exc); Aida (exc); Aida (exc); Ernani (exc); Vespri siciliani (exc); *Anon:* Eili, eili. (R. Raisa, A. Tokatyan, G. Rimini, G. Crimi, orch)

Ⓓ **CL99-060** (7/90)
Enrico Caruso—Opera & Song Recital
Verdi: Aida (exc); Trovatore (exc); *Puccini:* Bohème (exc); Bohème (exc); *P. M. Costa:* Sei morta nella vita mia; *Donizetti:* Dom Sébastien (exc); *Verdi:* Rigoletto (exc); *Bizet:* Carmen (exc); *Flotow:* Martha (exc); *Verdi:* Trovatore (exc); Aida (exc); *Boito:* Mefistofele (exc); *Alvarez:* Partida; *Donizetti:* Elisir d'amore (exc); *De Curtis:* Canta pe'me. (E. Caruso, F. Alda, G. Farrar, L. Tetrazzini, J. Jacoby, P. Amato, L. Homer, orch/W.B. Rogers, G. Scognamiglio, anon, V. Bellezza, S. Cottone)

Ⓓ **CL99-074** (9/90)
Conchita Supervia (1895-1936)
Bizet: Carmen (exc); *Saint-Saëns:* Samson et Dalila (exc); *Grieg:* Peer Gynt (exc); *A. Thomas:* Mignon (exc); *Puccini:* Bohème (exc); *Gounod:* Faust (exc); *R. Strauss:* Rosenkavalier (exc); *Humperdinck:* Hänsel und Gretel (exc); *Mozart:* Nozze di Figaro (exc). (C. Supervia, V. Bettoni, I.M. Ferraris, orch/A. Albergoni/G. Cloëz/A. Capdevila)

Ⓓ **CL99-089** (1/94)
Adamo Didur (1874-1946)
Tchaikovsky: Queen of Spades (exc); *Meyerbeer:* Huguenots (exc); *Boito:* Mefistofele (exc); Mefistofele (exc); *Meyerbeer:* Robert le Diable (exc); *Mugnone:* Vita brettone (exc); *Donizetti:* Elisir d'amore (exc); *Verdi:* Aida (exc); *Halévy:* Juive (exc); *Flotow:* Martha (exc); *Leoni:* Oracolo (exc); *Offenbach:* Contes d'Hoffmann (exc); *Gomes:* Salvator Rosa (exc); *A. Thomas:* Mignon (exc); *Gounod:* Faust (exc); *Traditional:* Folksongs of Little Russia; *Tosti:* Si tu le voulais; *Moniuszko:* O mother; *Noskowski:* Our mountaineers. (A. Didur, T. Leliwa, anon, orch)

Ⓓ **CL99-101** (1/94)
Vanni Marcoux (1877-1962)
Février: Monna Vanna (exc); *Massenet:* Don Quichotte (exc); Don Quichotte (exc); Cléopâtre (exc); Panurge (exc); *Berlioz:* Damnation de Faust (exc); *A. Thomas:* Hamlet (exc); *G. Charpentier:* Louise (exc); *Laparra:* Habanera (exc); *Mozart:* Don Giovanni (exc); *Mussorgsky:* Boris Godunov (exc); Boris Godunov (exc); *Schubert:* Forelle, D550; Winterreise (exc); *Hahn:* Je me metz; Offrande. (Vanni-Marcoux, O. Ricquier, M. Cozette, orch, anon, anon)

Ⓓ **CL99-109** (7/91)
Johanna Gadski (1871-1932)
Mascagni: Cavalleria rusticana (exc); *Mozart:* Zauberflöte (exc); Nozze di Figaro (exc); *Verdi:* Ballo in maschera (exc); Trovatore (exc); Aida (exc); Aida (exc); *R. Strauss:* Salome (exc); *Thuille:* Lobetanz (exc); *Wagner:* Lohengrin (exc); Tannhäuser (exc); Tristan und Isolde (exc); Fliegende Holländer (exc); Walküre (exc); Walküre (exc); Siegfried (exc); Götterdämmerung (exc); *Schubert:* Du bist die Ruh', D776; Erlkönig, D328; Gretchen am Spinnrade, D118. (J. Gadski, orch, anon)

Ⓓ **CL99-509/10** (9/90)
Hina Spani (1896-1969)
Granados: Tonadillas (exc); *Nin:* Cantos de España (exc); *Obradors:* Coplas de curro dulce; *López Buchardo:* Canción del carretero; *Ugarte:* Dia del fiesta; *Brahms:* Volkskinderlieder (exc); Lieder, Op. 72 (exc); *Parisotti:* Se tu m'ami; *Paradis:* Quel ruscelletto; *Tirindelli:* O primavera; *Verdi:* Trovatore (exc); *Wagner:* Lohengrin (exc); *Catalani:* Wally (exc); *Gounod:* Faust (exc); *Caccini:* Nuove musiche (1602) (exc); *Ciampi:* Tre cicisbei ridicoli (exc); *A. Scarlatti:* Donna ancora è fedele (exc); *Puccini:* Madama Butterfly (exc); *Massenet:* Manon (exc); *Puccini:* Tosca (exc); *Dvořák:* Gipsy melodies (exc); *Wagner:* Lohengrin (exc); *Verdi:* Ballo in maschera (exc); *Leoncavallo:* Pagliacci (exc); *Puccini:* Bohème (exc); *Verdi:* Trovatore (exc); *Puccini:* Manon Lescaut (exc); *Verdi:* Otello (exc); *Puccini:* Manon Lescaut (exc); Madama Butterfly (exc); *Mascagni:* Cavalleria rusticana (exc); *Puccini:* Tosca (exc). (H. Spani, P. Masini, A. Granforte, G. Zenatello, La Scala Orch, orch/C. Sabajno/G. Nastrucci)

Ⓓ **CL99-587/8** (1/91)
Eugenia Burzio (1872-1922)
Cilea: Adriana Lecouvreur (exc); *Mascagni:* Cavalleria rusticana (exc); *Verdi:* Forza del destino (exc); *Ponchielli:* Gioconda (exc); *Verdi:* Aida (exc); Trovatore (exc); *Boito:* Mefistofele (exc); *Verdi:* Forza del destino (exc); *Puccini:* Fanciulla del West (exc); *E. Romano:* Zulma (exc); *Bellini:* Norma (exc); *Meyerbeer:* Africaine (exc); *Gounod:* Ave Maria; *Boito:* Mefistofele (exc); *Verdi:* Forza del destino (exc); Otello (exc); Otello (exc); *Cilea:* Adriana Lecouvreur (exc); *Pacini:* Saffo (exc); *Verdi:* Ballo in maschera (exc); *Donizetti:* Favorita (exc); *Ponchielli:* Gioconda (exc); *Mascagni:* Cavalleria rusticana (exc). (E. Burzio, G. Acerbi, A. Magini-Coletti, G. De Luca, orch)

Collets

▭ **CML2004**
Russian Orchestral Favourites
Glinka: Ruslan and Lyudmila (exc); *Borodin:* In the Steppes of Central Asia; *Rimsky-Korsakov:* Capriccio espagnol; *Glazunov:* Méditation, Op. 32; *Tchaikovsky:* Marche slave; *Mussorgsky:* Night on the bare mountain; *Scriabin:* Symphonic Poem. (USSR RSO/V. Fedoseyev, L. Kogan, USSR Academy SO/E. Svetlanov/B. Demchenko)

▭ **CML2020**
Russian Fairy Tales
Liadov: Baba-Yaga, Op. 56; Kikimora, Op. 63; Enchanted Lake, Op. 62; *Rimsky-Korsakov:* Golden Cockerel Suite (exc); Skazka. (Leningrad PO/E. Mravinsky, USSR Academy SO/E. Svetlanov)

▭ **CML2026**
Arensky—Orchestral Works
Arensky: Symphony 1; Symphony 2; Dream on the Volga (exc). (USSR SO/E. Svetlanov)

▭ **CML2037**
Tchaikovsky—Eugene Onegin (highlights)
Tchaikovsky: Eugene Onegin (exc). (Y. Mazurok, T. Milashkina, V. Atlantov, Bolshoi Th Chor, Bolshoi Th Orch/M. Ermler)

Collins Classics

① **Coll1008-2**
Romantic works for flute and harp
Naderman: Nocturne, Tyrolienne and Rondoletto; *Tournier:* Au matin; *Bizet:* Carmen (exc); *Debussy:* Arabesques (exc); Suite bergamasque (exc); Syrinx; *Fauré:* Fantaisie; *Demillac:* Petite suite médiévale; *Kreisler:* Schön Rosmarin; *Elgar:* Chanson de matin; *Bizet:* Arlésienne Suites (exc); *Chopin:* Rossini Variations. (J. Stinton, A. Brewer)

① **Coll1019-2** (2/90)
Britten—Orchestral Works
Britten: Gloriana Suite; Sea Interludes, Op. 33a; Passacaglia, Op. 33b; Sinfonia da Requiem. (LSO/S. Bedford)

① **Coll1102-2** (2/91)
Britten & Saxton: Orchestral Works
Britten: Paul Bunyan (exc); Piano Concerto; *Saxton:* Resurrection of Christ. (J. MacGregor, ECO/S. Bedford)

① **Coll1207-2** (10/91)
Wagner—Orchestral Works
Wagner: Parsifal (exc); Tristan und Isolde (exc); Walküre (exc); Siegfried (exc); Götterdämmerung (exc). (Philh/Y. Simonov)

① **Coll1247-2** (12/91)
An Evening with Victoria De Los Angeles
A. Scarlatti: Pirro e Demetrio (exc); *Paisiello:* Zingari in fiera (exc); *Parisotti:* Se tu m'ami; *Pergolesi:* Serva Padrona (exc); *Brahms:* Lieder, Op. 63 (exc); Lieder, Op. 86 (exc); Lieder, Op. 47 (exc); Lieder, Op. 49 (exc); Lieder, Op. 48 (exc); Lieder, Op. 105 (exc); Lieder, Op. 84 (exc); *Traditional:* Noi de la Mare; Josep i Maria; Rossinyol; Mariner; *Granados:* Tonadillas (exc); *Obradors:* Vito; Molondrón; Aquel Sombrero; *Francisco de la Torre:* Pámpano Verde; *Valverde:* Clavelitos; *Traditional:* Blow the wind southerly; *Bizet:* Carmen (exc). (V. de los Angeles, G. Parsons)

① **Coll1288-2** (1/92)
American Music for Brass
Copland: Fanfare for the Common Man; Salón México; Ceremonial Fanfare; *Bernstein:* West Side Story (exc); Prelude, Fugue and Riffs; *Cowell:* Fanfare to the Forces of the Latin American Allies; *Barber:* Mutations from Bach; *Ives:* America Variations. (LSO Brass Ens/E. Crees)

① **Coll1294-2**
Wagner—Overtures and Preludes
Wagner: Rienzi (exc); Fliegende Holländer (exc); Tannhäuser (exc); Meistersinger (exc); Lohengrin (exc). (Philh/Y. Simonov)

① **Coll1336-2** (9/92)
Delius—Orchestral Works
Delius: Brigg Fair; In a Summer Garden; Koanga (exc); First cuckoo; Song before Sunrise; Summer Evening; Summer Night on the River; Village Romeo and Juliet (exc). (LSO/B. Wordsworth)

① **Coll1348-2** (9/92)
Holst/Rimsky-Korsakov—Orchestral Works
Holst: Planets; *Rimsky-Korsakov:* Mlada (exc). (The Sixteen, Philh/E. Svetlanov)

① **Coll1350-2** (7/92)
Saxton—Caritas
Saxton: Caritas (Cpte). (E. Davies, J. Best, C. Ventris, L. Hibberd, R. Bryson, D. Gwynne, P. Wilson, G. Bell, B. Budd, B. Cookson, L. Ormiston, English Northern Philh/D. Masson)

① **Coll1415-2** (1/95)
Maxwell Davies—The Lighthouse
Maxwell Davies: Lighthouse (Cpte). (N. Mackie, C. Keyte, I. Comboy, BBC PO/P. Maxwell Davies)

① **Coll1444-2**
Maximum Max—Music of Maxwell Davies
Maxwell Davies: Sunday Morning; Sir Charles his Pavan; Ojai Festival; Farewell to Stromness; Yesnaby Ground; Lighthouse (exc); Caroline Mathilde Suite (exc); O magnum mysterium (exc); Boyfriend Suite (exc); Black Pentecost (exc); Lullaby for Lucy; Strathclyde Concerto 4 (exc); Orkney Wedding. (BBC PO/P. Maxwell Davies, P. Maxwell Davies, N. Mackie, C. Keyte, I. Comboy, P. Forbes, C. Trevor, The Sixteen/H. Christophers, Aquarius/N. Cleobury, D. Jones, D. Wilson-Johnson, L. Morrison, Scottish CO, RPO)

① **Coll1461-2** (7/95)
Weir—Blond Eckbert
Weir: Blond Eckbert (Cpte). (N. Jones, A-M. Owens, C. Ventris, N. Folwell, ENO Chor, ENO Orch/S. Edwards)

① **Coll3008-2**
Favourite Trumpet Concertos
Haydn: Trumpet Concerto; *Hummel:* Trumpet Concerto; *Harut'unyan:* Trumpet Concerto; *Clarke:* Suite in D (exc); *Purcell:* Indian Queen, Z630 (exc). (M. Murphy, Consort of London/R. Haydon Clark)

① **Coll3025-2**
Puccini & Verdi Heroines
Puccini: Gianni Schicchi (exc); Tosca (exc); Bohème (exc); Manon Lescaut (exc); Madama Butterfly (exc); Turandot (exc); *Verdi:* Don Carlo (exc); Ernani (exc); Ballo in maschera (exc); Forza del destino (exc); Otello (exc). (S. Murphy, WNO Orch, J. Smith)

① **Coll7013-2** (4/92)
Purcell—The Fairy Queen
Purcell: Fairy Queen, Z629 (Cpte). (G. Fisher, L. Anderson, A. Murray, M. Chance, J.M. Ainsley, I. Partridge, R. Suart, M. George, The Sixteen, The Sixteen Orch/H. Christophers)

① **Coll7030-2** (6/94)
Britten—The Turn of the Screw
Britten: Turn of the Screw (Cpte). (P. Langridge, F. Lott, S. Pay, E. Hulse, P. Cannan, N. Secunde, Aldeburgh Fest Ens/S. Bedford)

① **Coll7034-2** (8/95)
Maxwell Davies—Resurrection
Maxwell Davies: Resurrection (Cpte). (D. Jones, C. Robson, M. Hill, N. Jenkins, H. Herford, G. Finley, J. Best, BBC PO/P. Maxwell Davies)

① **Coll7036-2** (4/95)
M.Berkeley—Baa Baa Black Sheep-A Jungle Tale
M. Berkeley: Baa Baa Black Sheep (Cpte). (M. Lorimer, W. Dazeley, A. Taylor-Morley, G. Mosley, E. Hulse, H. Newman, F. Kimm, P. Sheffield, M. Holland, C. Bayley, P. McCann, B. Cookson, Op North Chor, English Northern Philh/P. Daniel)

Colonnade

① **VAN201**
Carnival of Venice
Pierné: Canzonetta; *Jeanjean:* Carnival of Venice; *Lully:* Gavotte; *Glière:* Pieces, Op. 35 (exc); *Milhaud:* Duo Concertante; *Lovreglio:* Fantasia, Op.45; *Massenet:* Thaïs (exc); *Ravel:* Pièce en forme de Habanera; *Fauré:* Sicilienne; *Poulenc:* Clarinet Sonata; *Finzi:* Bagatelles (exc); *Cahuzac:* Cantilène; *Messager:* Solo de Concours. (M. Langdon-Davies, M. Tanner)

Colosseum

① **COL34 9004** (12/91)
Manfred Schenk sings Wagner
Wagner: Fliegende Holländer (exc); Meistersinger (exc); Tannhäuser (exc); Tristan und Isolde (exc); Walküre (exc). (M. Schenk, Nuremberg SO/K. Seibel)

① **COL34 9007**
Mendelssohn: Overtures, Vol.1
Mendelssohn: Hochzeit des Camacho (exc); Trumpet Ov; Midsummer Night's Dream (exc); Meeresstille; Heimkehr aus der Fremde (exc); Hebrides. (Nuremberg SO/K. Seibel)

Concert Artists

① **CACD9004** ▭ **FED4-TC-9004**
Zumbro plays Granados & Falla
Falla: Amor brujo (exc); *Granados:* Goyescas; Goyescas (exc); Pelele; Crepúsculo. (N. Zumbro)

Concord Concerto

① **CCD42012** ▭ **CC2012**
Arrangements for Two Guitars
Bernstein: West Side Story Symphonic Dances; *Gershwin:* Porgy and Bess (exc); Rhapsody in Blue; Preludes (exc); Show Girl (exc). (C. Barbaosa-Lima, S. Isbin)

Condon Collection

① **690.07.004**
Saint-Saëns - Piano Rolls
Saint-Saëns: Samson Improvisations; Samson et Dalila (exc); Allegro appassionato, Op.70; Déluge (exc); Carnaval des Animaux (exc); Etudes, Op.52 (exc); Danse macabre; Etudes, Op.111 (exc); *Chopin:* Impromptus (exc); *Saint-Saëns:* Valse mignonne; Mazurka 1; Valse nonchalante, Op. 110; Mazurka 3; Rapsodie d'Auvergne. (C. Saint-Saëns, M. Ilgenfritz, A. Tollefsen, K. Nirinska, E. d'Albert, G. Schnitzer)

① **690.07.007**
Artur Rubinstein - Piano Rolls
Chopin: Barcarolle; Nocturnes (exc); Preludes (exc); Polonaises (exc); *Rimsky-Korsakov:* Golden Cockerel (exc); *Debussy:* Isle joyeuse; *Brahms:* Piano Pieces, Op.76 (exc); Rhapsodies, Op.79 (exc); *Debussy:* Plus que lente; *Prokofiev:* Pieces, Op.4 (exc); *Falla:* Amor brujo (exc); *Albéniz:* Iberia (exc); Iberia (exc). (A. Rubinstein)

① **690.07.013**
Wilhelm Backhaus—Piano Rolls
Delibes: Source (exc); *Liszt:* Midsummer Night's Dream—paraphrase, S410; *Wagner:* Meistersinger (exc); *Liszt:* Tannhäuser—paraphrase, S445/1; *Beethoven:* Piano Sonata 8 (exc); *Liszt:* Concert Studies, S144 (exc); *Pick-Mangiagalli:* Olaf's Dance; *Chopin:* Piano Concerto 1 (exc); *Kreisler:* Liebesleid; *R. Strauss:* Lieder, Op.17 (exc); *Mozart:* Don Giovanni (exc); *Liszt:* Widmung, S566; *Brahms:* Paganini Variations (exc). (W. Backhaus)

Conifer

① **CDCF250/1** (11/94)
Smyth—The Wreckers
Smyth: Wreckers (Cpte). (P. Sidhom, D. Wilson-Johnson, B. Bannatyne-Scott, A. Roden, A. Sand, J. Lavender, A-M. Owens, J. Howarth, Huddersfield Choral Soc, BBC PO/O. de la Martinez)

① **CDCF903** (11/93) ▭ **MCFC903** (11/93)
By Arrangement—Tetra Guitar Quartet
Bernstein: West Side Story (exc); *Weill:* Dreigroschenoper (exc); *Prokofiev:* Lt Kijé Suite (exc); *Bock:* Fiddler on the Roof (exc); *Walton:* Façade Suites (exc). (Tetra)

① **CDCF905** (10/94)
Karen Jones—The Flute Album
Fauré: Songs, Op. 7 (exc); Morceau de concours; *Dutilleux:* Sonatine; *Villa-Lobos:* Assobio a jato; *Godard:* Suite, Op. 116; *Fürstenau:* Adagio and Variations, Op. 133; *Debussy:* Prélude à l'après-midi d'un faune; *Saint-Saëns:* Romance, Op. 36; Ascanio (exc); *Doppler:* Casilda fantaisie; *Borne:* Carmen Fantasy. (K. Jones, A. Brewer, S. J. Pendlebury, C. Edwards)

① **CDHD149** ▭ **MCHD149**
Gigli Favourites
Bizet: Pêcheurs de perles (exc); *Donizetti:* Elisir d'amore (exc); *Flotow:* Martha (exc); *Meyerbeer:* Africaine (exc); *Verdi:* Forza del destino (exc); *Leoncavallo:* Pagliacci (exc); *Mascagni:* Cavalleria Rusticana (exc); *Puccini:* Bohème (exc); Manon Lescaut (exc); Tosca (exc); *Toselli:* Serenade; *Drigo:* Arlekinda (exc); *Gastaldon:* Musica proibita; *Denza:* Funiculì-funiculà; *Cottrau:* Addio a Napoli; *Crescenzo:* Quanno 'a femmena vo'. (B. Gigli, orch, G. De Luca, NY Met Op Chor, NY Met Op Orch/G. Setti)

① **CDHD170**
Gigli—Centenary Tribute
Donizetti: Favorita (exc); *Gounod:* Roméo et Juliette (exc); *Giordano:* Andrea Chénier (exc); *Mascagni:* Iris (exc); *Donizetti:* Elisir d'amore (exc); Lucia di Lammermoor (exc); *Verdi:* Traviata (exc); *Bizet:* Pêcheurs de perles (exc); *Boito:* Mefistofele (exc); *Ponchielli:* Gioconda (exc); Gioconda (exc); *Di Capua:* Maria, marì!; *Denza:* Se; *De Curtis:* Carmela. (B. Gigli, orch, L. Bori/Rosario Bourdon/J. Pasternack, NY Met Op Orch/G. Setti, G. De Luca/N. Shilkret)

① **CDHD201** (3/94) ▭ **MCHD201** (3/94)
Galli-Curci in Opera and Song
Rossini: Semiramide (exc); *Bellini:* Sonnambula (exc); Sonnambula (exc); Sonnambula (exc); *Donizetti:* Lucia di Lammermoor (exc); Lucia di Lammermoor (exc); Lucia di Lammermoor (exc); *Verdi:* Trovatore (exc); Traviata (exc); *Rimsky-Korsakov:* Golden Cockerel (exc); *A. Scarlatti:* Solitudini amene (exc); *Donizetti:* Don Pasquale (exc); *Verdi:* Rigoletto (exc); Rigoletto (exc); *Bishop:* Lo, here the gentle lark; Echo Song; *Yradier:* Paloma. (A. Galli-Curci, T. Schipa, G. De Luca, orch/Rosario Bourdon, NY Met Op Orch/G. Setti, H. Samuels)

① **CDHD214** (9/94) ▭ **MCHD214** (9/94)
Jussi Björling - Arias, Lieder and Songs
Flotow: Martha (exc); *Verdi:* Rigoletto (exc); Rigoletto (exc); Trovatore (exc); *Gounod:* Faust (exc); *Meyerbeer:* Africaine (exc); *Verdi:* Aida (exc); *Bizet:* Carmen (exc); *Ponchielli:* Gioconda (exc); *Massenet:* Manon (exc); *Puccini:* Tosca (exc); Tosca (exc); Fanciulla del West (exc); *Rossini:* Stabat mater (exc); *Verdi:* Requiem (exc); *R. Strauss:* Lieder, Op.27 (exc); *Beethoven:* Adelaide, Op.46; *Schrader:* Summer night; *Traditional:* Ack Värmerland, du sköma; *Millöcker:* Bettelstudent (exc). (J. Björling, H. Schymberg, H. Ebert, orch/N. Grevillius)

① **CDHD226** ▭ **MCHD226**
Chaliapin—Bass of the Century
Rossini: Barbiere di Siviglia (exc); *Dargomïzhsky:* Rusalka

(exc); *Glinka:* Ruslan and Lyudmila (exc); *Gounod:* Faust (exc); *Mussorgsky:* Boris Godunov (exc); Boris Godunov (exc); *Glinka:* Night Review; *Koenemann:* When the King went forth to war; Song of the Volga Boatmen; *Mussorgsky:* Song of the Flea; *Traditional:* Down the Peterskaya Road; *Massenet:* Élégie; *Traditional:* Dark Eyes; Sten'ka Razin; Twelve Robbers; *Archangelsky:* Creed; *Grechaninov:* Liturgy, Op. 79 (exc). (F. Chaliapin, orch/E. Goossens, LSO/M. Steinmann, M. Cozette, Paris Op Chor, Paris Op Orch/H. Busser, M. Carosio, ROH Chor/V. Bellezza/L. Collingwood/A. Coates, Balalaika Orch, C. Sharpe, I. Newton, Aristov Ch/A.A. Scriabin, J. Bazilevsky, Paris Russian Met Church Ch/N. Afonsky, anon)

Ⓓ **CDHD227** ▭ **MCHD227**
Gigli in Opera and Song
Handel: Serse (exc); *Donizetti:* Lucia di Lammermoor (exc); *Verdi:* Lombardi (exc); Attila (exc); Rigoletto (exc); Rigoletto (exc); *Gounod:* Faust (exc); *Mascagni:* Cavalleria Rusticana (exc); *Massenet:* Manon (exc); *Leoncavallo:* Pagliacci (exc); *Puccini:* Manon Lescaut (exc); Manon Lescaut (exc); Bohème (exc); Tosca (exc); *Rossini:* Stabat mater (exc); *Tosti:* Serenata; *De Curtis:* Non ti scordar di me. (B. Gigli, A. Galli-Curci, L. Homer, A. Bada, G. De Luca, E. Pinza, E. Rethberg, I. Pacetti, orch/E. Goossens/J. Barbirolli, G. Noto, NY Met Op Orch, NY Met Op Chor/G. Setti/Rosario Bourdon, La Scala Orch/F. Ghione/C. Sabajno/U. Berrettoni/D. Olivieri, Berlin St Op Orch/A. Melichar)

Ⓓ **CDHD235**
The Puccini Album
Puccini: Manon Lescaut (exc); Manon Lescaut (exc); Bohème (exc); Bohème (exc); Bohème (exc); Bohème (exc); Bohème (exc); Bohème (exc); Bohème (exc); Bohème (exc); Tosca (exc); Tosca (exc); Tosca (exc); Madama Butterfly (exc); Madama Butterfly (exc); Madama Butterfly (exc); Fanciulla del West (exc); Gianni Schicchi (exc); Turandot (exc); Turandot (exc). (L. Bori, M. Caniglia, M. Farneti, J. Hammond, C. Muzio, M. Sheridan, H. Spani, E. Turner, F. Ansseau, J. Björling, A. Cortis, B. Gigli, J. Hislop, G. Lauri-Volpi, A. Pertile, T. Schipa, A. Valente, L. Borgonovo, A. Granforte, E. Pinza, Hallé, La Scala Orch, orch/J. Barbirolli/Rosario Bourdon/G. W. Byng/P. Coppola/F. Ghione/W. Goehr/N. Grevillius/L. Heward/L. Molajoli/G. Nastrucci/J. Pasternack/S. Robinson/C. Sabajno)

Ⓓ **75605 55004-2**
Rossini—Overtures
Rossini: Cenerentola (exc); Barbiere di Siviglia (exc); Italiana in Algeri (exc); Scala di Seta (exc); Guillaume Tell (exc); Gazza Ladra (exc); Tancredi (exc). (ROHO/C. Rizzi)

Continuum

Ⓓ **CCD1025**
Delius & Dyson—Music for Cello & Piano
Delius: Cello Sonata; Romance (1896); Koanga (exc); Hassan (exc); Summer Night on the River; *Dyson:* Prelude, Fantasy and Chaconne; Rustic Songs (exc); Canterbury Pilgrims (exc). (A. Shulman, I. Brown)

Ⓓ **CCD1054**
Delius—Complete partsongs
Delius: German Partsongs (exc); Her ute skal gildet staa; Irmelin (exc); Danish Songs (exc); Village Romeo and Juliet (exc); Appalachia (exc); On Craig Dhu; Wanderer's Song; Midsummer Song; Children's Songs; To be sung of a summer night; Hassan (exc); Splendour falls. (J. Nolan, S. Douse, A. Ball, M. Brafield, Elysian Sngrs/M. Greenall)

CPI Records

Ⓓ **CPI329402**
Tchaikovsky—Symphony No 5;Glinka—Ruslan and Ludmilla -Overture
Glinka: Ruslan and Lyudmila (exc); *Tchaikovsky:* Symphony 5; *Elgar:* Enigma Variations (exc). (New England Conservatory Youth PO/B. Zander)

CPO

Ⓓ **CPO999 003-2**
Siegfried Wagner—Complete Overtures, Volume 1
S. Wagner: Herzog Wildfang (exc); Friedensengel (exc); Schmied von Marienburg (exc); Heilige Lind (exc). (Rhineland-Pfalz State PO/W. A. Albert)

Ⓓ **CPO999 007-2**
Hindemith—Orchestral Works, Volume 4
Hindemith: Neues vom Tage (exc); Symphony in B flat (1951); Symphony in E flat. (Melbourne SO/W.A. Albert)

Ⓓ **CPO999 032-2**
Moniuszko—Halka
Moniuszko: Halka (Cpte). (B. Zagórzanka, W. Ochman, J. Ostapiuk, R. Racewicz, A. Hiolski, M. Woiciechowski, Wielki Th Chor, Wielki Th Orch/R. Satanowski)

Ⓓ **CPO999 044-2** (12/90)
Viardot-Garcia—Songs
Viardot-Garcia: Madrid; Sérénade; Havanaise; Bonjour mon coeur; Grands oiseaux blancs; Petite chevière; Chêne et le roseau; Chanson de la pluie; Enfant et la mère; Désespoir; Adieu les beaux jours; Scène d'Hermione; Seize ans; Danse; Oiselet; Aime-moi; *Jommelli:* Calandrina; *Gluck:* Orphée (exc). (K. Ott/C. Keller)

Ⓓ **CPO999 076-2**
Goetz—Orchestral Works
Goetz: Symphony, Op. 9; Violin Concerto, Op. 22; Widerspenstigen Zähmung (exc). (G. Schneider, Hanover Rad PO/W.A. Albert)

Ⓓ **CPO999 082-2**
Krenek—Der Sprung über den Schatten
Krenek: Sprüng über den Schatten (Cpte). (T. Brüning, L. Kemeny, S. Maclean, D. Amos, J. Pflieger, U. Neuweiler, J. Dürmüller, Bielefeld City Th Chor, Bielefeld PO/D. de Villiers)

Ⓓ **CPO999 093-2**
Spohr—Overtures
Spohr: Macbeth overture, Op.75; Prüfung overture, Op.15; Alruna overture, Op.21; Faust overture, Op.60; Jessonda (exc); Berggeist (exc); Pietro von Abano (exc); Alchymist (exc). (Berlin RSO/C. Fröhlich)

Ⓓ **CPO999 104-2**
Mozart—Lo Sposo Deluso/L'Oca del Cairo
Mozart: Sposo Deluso (Cpte); Oca del Cairo (Cpte); Chi sà, K582; Dite almeno, K479. (L. Schoon, R. Van der Paal, I. Micu, B. Loonen, H. Bekaert, H. Bekaert, R. Van der Paal, B. Loonen, I. Micu, L. Schoon, R. Bischoff, G. Anthoni, Transparant Chbr Op Ens, Transparant Chbr Op Orch/H. Rotman)

Ⓓ **CPO999 110-2** (11/93)
Keiser—Masagniello furioso
Keiser: Masagniello furioso (Cpte). (M. Schopper, B. Schlick, D. Röschmann, D. Cordier, W. Jochens, H. van der Kamp, H. Meens, J. Dreyer, W. Mikus, Bremen Voc Ens, Fiori Musicali/T. Albert)

Ⓓ **CPO999 113-2** (8/93)
Moniuszko—Overtures
Moniuszko: Halka (exc); Countess (exc); Verbum Nobile (exc); Fairy Tale; Jawnuta (exc); Raftsman (exc); Paria (exc). (Bydgoszcz PSO/R. Satanowski)

Ⓓ **CPO999 129-2** (11/95)
J. C. Bach—Opera Overtures, Vol. 1
J. C. Bach: Favourite Overtures (exc); Catone in Utica (exc); Birthday Cantata (exc); Overture, T277/4; Giulia Overture. (Hanover Band/A. Halstead)

Ⓓ **CPO999 160-2**
Trojahn—Enrico
Trojahn: Enrico (Cpte). (R. Salter, T. Schmidt, F. Lucey, L. Magnusson, H. G. Nöcker, J. Zinkler, E. Lorenz, P. Umstadt, T. Mohr, R. Trebes, N. Hillebrand, Stuttgart RSO/D. R. Davies)

Ⓓ **CPO999 185-2**
Rihm—The Conquest of Mexico
Rihm: Eroberung von Mexico (Cpte). (R. Salter, R. Behle, C. Fugiss, S. Otto, P. Kollek, H. J. Frey, G. Becker, Hamburg St Op Chor, Hamburg PO/I. Metzmacher)

Ⓓ **CPO999 210-2** (9/94)
Telemann—Don Quichotte
Telemann: Don Quichotte (Cpte). (R. Nolte, M. Schopper, S. Stapf, M. Bach, H. Hallaschka, A. Köhler, K-H. Brandt, Bremen Voc Ens, Stagione/M. Schneider)

Ⓓ **CPO999 247-2** (8/94)
Spohr—Faust
Spohr: Faust (Cpte). (M. Vier, E. von Jordis, D. Jennings, I. Bric, M. Eichwalder, D. Walker, U. Neuweiler, H. Kegler, W. Pugh, C. Taha, D. Abbott, M. Kowollik, Bielefeld Op Chor, Bielefeld PO/G. Moull)

Ⓓ **CPO999 258-2** (6/95)
Biber—Arminio
Biber: Arminio (Cpte). (B. Schlick, G. Schwarz, G. Türk, X. Meijer, G. Kenda, B. Landauer, M. Forster, H. Oswald, O. Rastbichler, I. Troupova, R. Schwarzer, F. Mehltretter, Salzburg Hofmusik/W. Brunner)

Ⓓ **CPO999 300-2**
Siegfried Wagner—Overtures, Vol. 2
S. Wagner: Bärenhäuter (exc); An allem ist Hütchen schuld (exc); Flüchlein, das jeder mitbekam (exc). (Rhineland-Pfalz State PO/W. A. Albert)

Ⓓ **CPO999 303-2** (8/95)
Schillings—Mona Lisa
Schillings: Mona Lisa (Cpte). (B. Bilandzija, K. Wallprecht, A. Bonnema, M. Gasztecki, K. Russ, U. Köberle, J. Sabrowski, B. Gebhardt, E. Reimer, A. Lawrence, G. Kosbahn, Kiel Op Chor, Kiel PO/K. Seibel)

Ⓓ **CPO999 328-2** (10/95)
Delius—Romeo und Julia auf dem Dorfe
Delius: Village Romeo and Juliet (Cpte). (D. Midhoe, A. Kovács, A. Görner, K. Russ, A. Sikira, E-C. Reimer, K. Wallprecht, L. Kappaun, K-P. Hallacker, I. Schwarz, C. Forsén, A. Vogt, M. Koht, C. Vincent, I. Uhlemann, R. Klöpper, H-J. Förter-Barth, H. Hoffmann, B. Bilandzija, H. Fischer, U. Köberle, B. Gebhardt, D. Henschel, J. Sabrowski, M. Fleitmann, Kiel Op Chor, Kiel PO/K. Seibel)

Cramer Music

Ⓓ **CRACD 1**
Wedding Album
Wagner: Lohengrin (exc); *Clarke:* Suite in D (exc); *Mendelssohn:* Organ Sonatas (exc); *Handel:* Fireworks Music (exc); *Karg-Elert:* Choral-Improvisationen, Op. 65 (exc); *Fauré:* Songs, Op. 7 (exc); *Verdi:* Aida (exc); *C.S. Lang:* Tuba tune; *Gounod:* Ave Maria; *Purcell:* Choice Collection of Lessons (exc); *Elgar:* Organ Sonata 2 (exc); *M-A. Charpentier:* Te Deum, H146 (exc); *Schubert:* Ave Maria, D839; *Handel:* Occasional Oratorio (exc); *Vierne:* Symphony 3 (exc); *Bach:* Cantata 147 (exc); *Guilmant:* Grand Choeur in D; *Parry:* Chorale Preludes (1912) (exc); *Stanley:* Organ Voluntaries, Book 2 (exc); *Widor:* Symphony 5 (exc); *Handel:* Water Music (exc); *Widor:* Symphony 1 (exc); *Pachelbel:* Canon and Gigue; *Mendelssohn:* Midsummer Night's Dream (exc). (A. Marsden-Thomas)

CRD

Ⓓ **CRD3402** (9/92) ▭ **CRDC4102** (3/83)
Symphonic Marches for Concert Brass
Verdi: Aida (exc); *Mozart:* Zauberflöte (exc); *Tchaikovsky:* Symphony 6 (exc); *Puccini:* Turandot (exc); *Grieg:* Sigurd Jorsalfar, Op. 56 (exc); *J. Strauss I:* Radetzky March; *Berlioz:* Symphonie fantastique (exc); *Mussorgsky:* Capture of Kars. (Locke Brass Consort/J. Stobart)

Ⓓ **CRD3468** (10/91) ▭ **CRDC4168** (10/91)
Mozart—Works for Flute Quartet
Mozart: Flute Quartets; Zauberflöte (exc). (N. Hadden, C. Mackintosh, J. Schlapp, S. Comberti)

Cybelia

Ⓓ **CY833/6** (12/88)
Messiaen—Saint François d'Assise
Messiaen: Saint François d'Assise (Cpte). (C. Eda-Pierre, J. Van Dam, K. Riegel, M. Philippe, G. Gautier, M. Sénéchal, J-P. Courtis, Paris Op Chor, Paris Op Orch/S. Ozawa)

Ⓓ **CY853**
Ancelin—Filius Hominus
Ancelin: Filius Hominis (Cpte). (R. Gilfry, M. Shearer, J. Topart, P. Lefebvre, Branco Krsmanovitch Chor, Lille Nat Orch/J-C. Casadesus)

Ⓓ **CY879**
Probst—Maximilien Kolbe
Probst: Maximilien Kolbe (Cpte). (A. Snarski, V. Sanso, P. Gérimon, P. Danais, Childrens' Ch, Male Chor, Inst Ens/O. Holt)

Da Capo

Ⓓ **8 224031/2**
Nørgård—Siddharta; For a Change
Nørgård: Siddhartha (Cpte); For a Change. (S. F. Andersen, A. Haugland, E. Guillaume, E. Harbo, K. Janken, C. Christiansen, P. Elming, T. Kiberg, A. Frellesvig, M. Nyhus, G. Mortensen, Danish Nat Rad Ch, Danish Nat Rad Childrens' Ch, Danish Nat RSO/J. Latham-König)

Danacord

Ⓓ **DACOCD306**
Mikael Beier plays popular music for Flute and Harp
Nielsen: Suite for flute, viola and harp (exc); *Ravel:* Pièce en forme de habanera; *Debussy:* Fille aux cheveux de lin; *Fauré:* Sicilienne; *Massenet:* Thaïs (exc); *Bizet:* Arlésienne Suites (exc); Carmen (exc); *Saint-Saëns:* Carnaval des animaux (exc); *Anon:* Greensleeve to a Ground; *Donizetti:*

Flute and Harp Sonata; *Spohr:* Sonata, Op. 114; *Paradis:* Sicilienne. (M. Beier, M. Eriksson)

① **DACOCD311/2** (8/88)
Lauritz Melchior Anthology - Vol.1
Verdi: Traviata (exc); Trovatore (exc); *Nessler:* Trompeter von Säckingen (exc); *L. Friedman:* Meet me tonight in dreamland; *Kjerulf:* My heart and my lyre; *Heise:* Eagle ascends; Though the tide turns; *Gade:* Oft when I ride; *Bechgaard:* Sailor's Farewell; Sailor's Farewell; *J. P. E. Hartmann:* Little Christine (exc); *Heise:* My lord and king; Fair is the gentle spring; Eagle ascends; *Hassler:* Entrust all your doings; *Berggreen:* Welcome again; *Weyse:* Blessed Day; *Anon:* Praise the Lord; *Berggreen:* Just think one day; *Anon:* Praise to Thee; *Weyse:* Ever dauntless; *Mortensen:* Dimlit fogs of night; *Wennerberg:* Gluntarne (exc); *Lange-Müller:* Florence, city of flowers; *Allen:* Sun smiles so kind; *Andersen:* Now all chasms are bursting; So many birds are flying; *Puccini:* Tosca (exc); *Wagner:* Walküre (exc); Lohengrin (exc); *J. P. E. Hartmann:* Little Christine (exc); *Kjellerup:* Beloved mine; *Heise:* When that I was; *Andersen:* Waves of Kongea; *Rygaard:* Flag; Denmark; *Bonnén:* When peace came over the land; *Hovalt:* Christiansborg. (L. Melchior, H. Hansen, A. Neumann, Anon, Brass Ens, Anon, Orch, Anon)

① **DACOCD313/4** (8/88)
Lauritz Melchior Anthology - Vol. 2
Wagner: Rienzi (exc); Lohengrin (exc); Tannhäuser (exc); Tannhäuser (exc); Walküre (exc); Walküre (exc); Walküre (exc); Siegfried (exc); Siegfried (exc); Parsifal (exc); Parsifal (exc); Wesendonk Lieder (exc); Meistersinger (exc); *Verdi:* Aida (exc); *Meyerbeer:* Africaine (exc); *Weingartner:* Liebesfeier, Op. 16/2; *Trunk:* Mir träumte von einer Königskind; Als ob ein Toter im Grab; In meiner Heimat; Erster Strahl; *R. Strauss:* Lieder, Op. 27 (exc); *Sjöberg:* Tonerna; *Klenau:* To my bride; *Hageman:* Do not go, my love. (L. Melchior, E. Bettendorf, F. Leider, M. Ober, orch/F. Weissmann/P. Breisach)

① **DACOCD315/6** (8/88)
Lauritz Melchior Anthology - Vol. 3
Wagner: Walküre (exc); Meistersinger (exc); Rienzi (exc); Lohengrin (exc); Tannhäuser (exc); Tannhäuser (exc); Tristan und Isolde (exc); Tristan und Isolde (exc); Walküre (exc); Walküre (exc); Walküre (exc); Walküre (exc); Walküre (exc); Götterdämmerung (exc); Götterdämmerung (exc); Meistersinger (exc); Meistersinger (exc); Meistersinger (exc); Meistersinger (exc); *Meyerbeer:* Africaine (exc); *Leoncavallo:* Pagliacci (exc); *Verdi:* Otello (exc). (L. Melchior, F. Leider, G. Guszalewicz, F. Schorr, L. Topas, R. Watzke, O. Helgers, E. Schumann, G. Parr, B. Williams, Orch, LSO, Berlin St Op Orch, New SO/J. Barbirolli/L. Blech/A. Coates/R. Heger/L. Collingwood)

① **DACOCD317/8**
Lauritz Melchior Anthology - Vol.4
Wagner: Walküre (exc); Walküre (exc). (L. Melchior, Lotte Lehmann, E. List, VPO/B. Walter, H. Hotter, M. Fuchs, M. Klose, Berlin St Op Orch/B. Seidler-Winkler, E. Flesch, A. Jerger)

① **DACOCD319/21**
The Lauritz Melchior Anthology - Vol.5
Wagner: Walküre (exc); Siegfried (exc); Siegfried (exc); Siegfried (exc); Siegfried (exc); Siegfried (exc); Siegfried (exc); Siegfried (exc); Siegfried (exc). (L. Melchior, H. Tessmer, F. Schorr, A. Reiss, E. Habich, LSO/R. Heger/A. Coates, E. Schipper, M. Olczewska, R. Bockelmann, F. Easton, Vienna St Op Orch, ROHO/K. Alwin, D. Larsen, M. Wedel, Danish RSO/T. Jensen, N. Gruhn, L. Melchior)

① **DACOCD322/4**
Lauritz Melchior Anthology - Vol.6
Wagner: Lohengrin (Cpte). (L. Melchior, H. Traubel, A. Varnay, H. Janssen, D. Ernster, F. Guerrera, NY Met Op Chor, NY Met Op Orch/F. Stiedry)

① **DACOCD348**
Danish Songs
Weyse: Sleeping-Draught (exc); Ludlam's Cave (exc); Adventure in Rosenborg Gardens (exc); Night is so calm; *Heise:* Fleeting wish; By the wide marsh; Agnete's cradle song; *Lange-Müller:* Folksongs, Op. 18 (exc); Songs, Op. 14 (exc); Songs, Op. 11 (exc); Autumn; *Wellejus:* To you; New Spring; Pair of ducks; Short song; Nocturne; I will return; Midsummer Song; Rose; I will light a star. (A.B. Garde, H. Wellejus)

① **DACOCD357/9**
Nielsen Collection, Volume 3 - Operas
Nielsen: Maskarade (Cpte); Saul and David (Cpte). (H. Byrding, I. Steffensen, T. Thygesen, E. Nørby, M. Jacobsen, P. Wiedemann, R. Guldbaek, E.M. Edlers, G. Leicht, N.J. Bondo, F. Andersson, O. Svendsen, R. Guldbaek, N. Møller, I. Frey, O. Wolstad, M. Wedel, Danish Rad Chor, Danish RSO/L. Grøndahl/T. Jensen)

① **DACOCD378** (3/92)
Mette Hanskov plays music for Double Bass
Glière: Intermezzo and Tarantelle, Op. 9 (exc); *Granados:* Danzas españolas (exc); Goyescas (exc); *Bottesini:* Elegie in D; *Traditional:* Forest Idyll; Old Rocking Chair; Jeder Bauern Bubi; Rumlekvadrillen; *Kuchynska:* Canzonetta; *Černý:* Mazurka; *J. Keller:* Pastorale; *Bottesini:* Double Bass Concerto 2. (M. Hanskov, T. Lønskov, N.E. Aggesen)

① **DACOCD410** (12/94)
Langaard—Complete Symphonies, Vol.7
Langgaard: Antikrist (exc); Symphony 13; Symphony 16. (Rubinstein PO/I. Stupel)

① **DACOCD433**
Cartas de Amor
Granados: Valses poéticos; *Sor:* Fantasia, Op. 63; *Oberleitner:* Steyer'sche Ländler; *Wagner:* Tannhäuser (exc); *Horetzky:* Polonaise Nationale; *Ratzkowski:* Toast, butter and jam. (Ratzkowski/Thomsen Gtr Duo)

Danica

① **DCD8143**
Hanne Stavad - Song Recital
Brahms: Lieder, Op. 43 (exc); Lieder, Op. 91; *Heise:* Gudrun's Sorrow; *Lutosławski:* Iłłakowicz Poems; *Nielsen:* Songs, FS12 (exc); Songs and Verses, FS14 (exc); *Nørgård:* Divine Circus (exc); *Schubert:* Tod und das Mädchen, D531; Ganymed, D544; Lachen und Weinen, D777; Seligkeit, D433; Wandrers Nachtlied II, D768. (H. Stavad, P. Westenholz, M. Zeuthen)

Dante

① **LYS001**
La Colorature des Coloratures - Volume 1
Mozart: Entführung (exc); Zauberflöte (exc); *Rossini:* Barbiere di Siviglia (exc); *Donizetti:* Lucia di Lammermoor (exc); Zingara; *Adam:* Toréador (exc); *Verdi:* Ernani (exc); Rigoletto (exc); Vespri Siciliani (exc); *Meyerbeer:* Dinorah (exc); *Rimsky-Korsakov:* Sadko (exc); Tsar's Bride (exc); Golden Cockerel (exc); *Wagner:* Tristan und Isolde (exc). (M. Korjus, Berlin St Op Orch, Berlin RSO, orch/F. Schönbaumsfeld/J. Müller/E. Nick/B. Seidler-Winkler/Anon)

① **LYS003/4** (3/93)
Charles Panzéra - Song Recital
Fauré: Songs, Op.4 (exc); Songs, Op.4 (exc); *Gounod:* Soir; *Fauré:* Songs, Op.18 (exc); Songs, Op.23 (exc); Songs, Op.7 (exc); Songs, Op.39 (exc); Songs, Op.43 (exc); Songs, Op.46 (exc); Songs, Op.51 (exc); Songs, Op.51 (exc); Songs, Op.58 (exc); Songs, Op.58 (exc); Bonne Chanson, Op.61; Songs, Op.83 (exc); Songs, Op.76 (exc); Horizon chimérique; Songs, Op.4 (exc); *Duparc:* Chanson triste; Soupir; Invitation au voyage; Vague et la cloche; Phidylé; Élégie; Extase; Manoir de Rosemonde; Sérénade florentine; Testament; Lamento; Vie antérieure; Invitation au voyage; Vague et la cloche; Phidylé; *Chausson:* Poème de l'amour et de la mer (exc); *Caplet:* Vieux coffret (exc); *Debussy:* Ballades de François Villon (exc); Pelléas et Mélisande (exc); *Berlioz:* Damnation de Faust (exc); *Schubert:* Schwanengesang, D957 (exc). (C. Panzéra, M. Panzéra-Baillot, Pasdeloup Orch, SO/P. Coppola, Y. Brothier, St Gervais Chor)

① **LYS013/5** (8/95)
Tchaikovsky—The Queen of Spades
Tchaikovsky: Queen of Spades (Cpte); Queen of Spades (exc); Queen of Spades (exc). (N. Khanayev, X. Derzhinskaya, F. Petrova, A. Baturin, P. Selivanov, N. Obukhova, S. Ostroumov, Y. Manchavin, M. Novoyenin, K. Terekin, L. Stavrovskaya, N. Chubienko, Bolshoi Th Chor, Bolshoi Th Orch/S. Samosud, N. Khanayev, A. Baturin, P. Nortsov, K. Terekin, B. Zlatogorova, X. Derzhinskaya, S. Ostroumov, Y. Manchavin, M. Novoyenin, M. Maksakova, V. Barsova, V. Politkovsky, G. Nelepp)

① **LYS10/1** (1/94)
Tchaikovsky—Eugene Onegin
Tchaikovsky: Eugene Onegin (Cpte). (P. Nortsov, G. Zhukovskaya, S. Lemeshev, B. Zlatogorova, A. Pirogov, M. Butienina, K. Antarova, I. Kovalenko, A. Yakhontov, Y. Manchavin, Bolshoi Th Chor, Bolshoi Th Orch/V. Nebolsin)

① **LYS2**
Erna Sack—A German Nightingale
Denza: Funiculì-Funiculà; *Pestalozzi:* Ciribiribin; *Scotto:* Vieni, vieni; *Arditi:* Parla Waltz; *Buzzi-Peccia:* Morenito; *Czernik:* Chi sa?; *J. Strauss II:* Tänzerin Fanny Elssler (exc); Fledermaus (exc); *Klischnegg:* Kätzchen (exc); *Lincke:* Lysistrata (exc); *Melichar:* Nanon (exc); *Millöcker:* Dubarry (exc); *Lehár:* Gold und Silber; *J. Strauss II:* Frühlingsstimmen, Op. 410. (E. Sack, Berlin Staatskapelle)

Dabringhaus und Grimm

① **L3267** (3/88)
Weber—Der Freischütz arr for Winds
Weber: Freischütz (exc). (Consortium Classicum)

① **MDG611 0547-2**
Rachmaninov—Piano Transcriptions; Piano Sonata No 2
Rachmaninov: Piano Sonata 2; Songs, Op. 34 (exc); Daisies; Lilacs; Polka de W R; *Bach:* Solo Violin Partitas and Sonatas (exc); *Rimsky-Korsakov:* Tale of Tsar Saltan (exc); *Mussorgsky:* Gopak; *Tchaikovsky:* Songs, Op. 16 (exc); *Bizet:* Arlésienne Suites (exc); *Schubert:* Schöne Müllerin (exc); *Mendelssohn:* Midsummer Night's Dream (exc); *Kreisler:* Liebesleid; Liebesfreud. (F. Höricke)

Datum

① **DAT12320**
Mussorgsky—Khovanshchina
Mussorgsky: Khovanshchina (Cpte). (M. Petri, A. Berdini, M. Picchi, G. Malaspina, B. Christoff, I. Companeez, H. Handt, J. Mancini, D. Lopatto, A. Mineo, G. Canello, Rome RAI Chor, Rome RAI Orch/A. Rodzinski)

Decca

OO **400 049-5DH**
Rossini: Overtures
Rossini: Guillaume Tell (exc); Signor Bruschino (exc); Viaggio a Reims (exc); Scala di Seta (exc); Gazza Ladra (exc); Turco in Italia (exc); Italiana in Algeri (exc). (National PO/R. Chailly)

▭ **400 053-4DH** (7/75)
World's Best Loved Tenor Arias
Leoncavallo: Pagliacci (exc); *Flotow:* Martha (exc); *Bizet:* Carmen (exc); *Puccini:* Bohème (exc); Tosca (exc); Turandot (exc); *Verdi:* Rigoletto (exc); Aida (exc); Trovatore (exc); *Gounod:* Faust (exc). (L. Pavarotti, John Alldis Ch, Vienna Volksoper Orch, New Philh, BPO, LSO, RPO, LPO, Vienna Op. Orch/L. Magiera/R. Bonynge/H. von Karajan/Z. Mehta/N. Rescigno)

① **400 057-2DH** (3/83)
Verdi—La Traviata - excerpts
Verdi: Traviata (exc). (J. Sutherland, L. Pavarotti, M. Manuguerra, D. Jones, M. Lambriks, A. Oliver, J. Summers, J. Tomlinson, G. Tadeo, London Op. Chor, National PO/R. Bonynge)

① **410 117-2DH2** (2/85)
Giordano—Andrea Chenier
Giordano: Andrea Chénier (Cpte). (L. Pavarotti, M. Caballé, L. Nucci, P. de Palma, A. Varnay, K. Kuhlmann, T. Krause, H. Cuénod, N. Howlett, G. Morresi, R. Hamer, F. Andreolli, C. Ludwig, G. Tadeo, WNO Chor, National PO/R. Chailly)

① **410 137-2DH** (11/83)
Wagner: Excerpts from The Ring
Wagner: Walküre (exc); Rheingold (exc); Siegfried (exc); Götterdämmerung (exc). (VPO/G. Solti)

OO **410 137-5DH**
Wagner: Excerpts from The Ring
Wagner: Walküre (exc); Rheingold (exc); Siegfried (exc); Götterdämmerung (exc). (VPO/G. Solti)

① **410 150-2DH3** (4/84)
Mozart—Le Nozze di Figaro
Mozart: Nozze di Figaro (Cpte). (S. Ramey, L. Popp, T. Allen, K. Te Kanawa, F. von Stade, J. Berbié, K. Moll, R. Tear, P. Langridge, G. Tadeo, Y. Kenny, London Op Chor, LPO/G. Solti)

① **410 175-2DH3** (12/85)
Boito—Mefistofele
Boito: Mefistofele (Cpte). (N. Ghiaurov, L. Pavarotti, M. Freni, M. Caballé, N. Condò, P. de Palma, D. Jones, R. Leggate, Trinity Boys' Ch, National PO/O. de Fabritiis)

① **410 193-2DH3** (11/85)
Donizetti—Lucia di Lammermoor
Donizetti: Lucia di Lammermoor (Cpte). (J. Sutherland, L. Pavarotti, S. Milnes, N. Ghiaurov, H. Tourangeau, R. Davies, P.F. Poli, ROH Chor, ROHO/R. Bonynge)

① **410 210-2DH2** (9/85)
Verdi—Un ballo in maschera
Verdi: Ballo in maschera (Cpte). (M. Price, L. Pavarotti, R. Bruson, K. Battle, C. Ludwig, R. Lloyd, M. King, P. Weber, A. Oliver, P. Hall, London Op Chor, RCM Jnr Chor, National PO/G. Solti)

① **410 227-2DH2** (3/85)
Beethoven—Fidelio
Beethoven: Fidelio (Cpte). (H. Dernesch, P. Hofmann, T. Adam, H. Sotin, S. Ghazarian, D. Kuebler, G. Howell, R.

Johnson, P. Kraus, Chicago Sym Chor, Chicago SO/G. Solti)

Ⓓ **411 618-2DH2** (3/87)
Verdi—Otello
Verdi: Otello (Cpte). (M. del Monaco, R. Tebaldi, A. Protti, N. Romanato, A. Cesarini, A.R. Satre, F. Corena, T. Krause, L. Arbace, Vienna Children's Ch, Vienna St Op Chor, VPO/H. von Karajan)

Ⓓ **411 622-2DM2** (12/89)
Donizetti—Lucia di Lammermoor
Donizetti: Lucia di Lammermoor (Cpte). (J. Sutherland, R. Cioni, R. Merrill, C. Siepi, A.R. Satre, K. Macdonald, R. Pelizzoni, Santa Cecilia Academy Chor, Santa Cecilia Academy Orch/J. Pritchard)

Ⓓ **411 626-2DM3** (9/89)
Mozart—Don Giovanni
Mozart: Don Giovanni (Cpte). (C. Siepi, S. Danco, L. della Casa, H. Gueden, A. Dermota, F. Corena, W. Berry, K. Böhme, Vienna St Op Chor, VPO/J. Krips)

Ⓓ **411 644-2DH2** (2/85)
Stravinsky—Rake's Progress
Stravinsky: Rake's Progress (Cpte). (P. Langridge, C. Pope, S. Ramey, Sarah Walker, J. Dobson, A. Varnay, S. Dean, M. Best, London Sinfonietta Chor, London Sinfonietta/R. Chailly)

Ⓓ **411 665-2DM3** (2/91)
Puccini: Il trittico
Puccini: Tabarro (Cpte); Suor Angelica (Cpte); Gianni Schicchi (Cpte). (R. Merrill, R. Tebaldi, M. del Monaco, R. Ercolani, S. Maionica, L. Danieli, R. Tebaldi, G. Simionato, L. Danieli, M.T. Pace, A. di Stasio, D. Carral, J. Valtriani, G. Tavolaccini, F. Corena, R. Tebaldi, A. Lazzari, L. Danieli, R. Ercolani, D. Carral, A. di Ninno, G. Foiani, P. Washington, S. Maionica, M.T. Pace, MMF Chor, MMF Orch/L. Gardelli)

Ⓓ **411 805-2DH3** (4/88)
Mozart—Idomeneo
Mozart: Idomeneo (Cpte). (L. Pavarotti, A. Baltsa, L. Popp, E. Gruberová, L. Nucci, Timothy Jenkins, N. Storozhev, Vienna St Op Concert Ch, VPO/J. Pritchard)

Ⓓ **411 862-2DH3** (11/88)
Mussorgsky—Boris Godunov (arr Rimsky-Korsakov)
Mussorgsky: Boris Godunov (Cpte). (N. Ghiaurov, L. Spiess, G. Vishnevskaya, M. Talvela, A. Diakov, A. Maslennikov, M. Paunov, Z. Kélémen, O. Miljakovic, N. Dobrianova, B. Cvejic, M. Lilowa, A. Maslennikov, S. Markov, S.R. Frese, P. Karolidis, Vienna Boys' Ch, Sofia Rad Chor, Vienna St Op Chor, VPO/H. von Karajan)

Ⓓ **411 871-2DM2** (8/91)
Puccini—Tosca
Puccini: Tosca (Cpte). (R. Tebaldi, M. del Monaco, G. London, S. Maionica, P. de Palma, F. Corena, G. Morese, E. Palerini, Santa Cecilia Academy Chor, Santa Cecilia Academy Orch/F. Molinari-Pradelli)

Ⓓ **411 877-2DM2** (2/89)
Verdi—(La) Traviata
Verdi: Traviata (Cpte). (J. Sutherland, C. Bergonzi, R. Merrill, M.T. Pace, D. Carral, P. de Palma, P. Pedani, S. Maionica, G. Foiani, A. Mercuriali, M. Frosini, MMF Chor, MMF Orch/J. Pritchard)

Ⓓ **414 036-2DH2** (1/89)
Puccini—Tosca
Puccini: Tosca (Cpte). (M. Freni, L. Pavarotti, S. Milnes, R. Van Allan, M. Sénéchal, I. Tajo, P. Hudson, J. Tomlinson, W. Baratti, Wandsworth Sch Boys' Ch, London Op Chor, National PO/N. Rescigno)

Ⓓ **414 087-2DM3** (1/89)
Verdi—Aida
Verdi: Aida (Cpte). (R. Tebaldi, G. Simionato, C. Bergonzi, C. MacNeil, A. Van Mill, F. Corena, P. de Palma, E. Ratti, Vienna Singverein, VPO/H. von Karajan)

Ⓓ **414 100-2DM15** (3/89)
Wagner: Der Ring des Nibelungen
Wagner: Rheingold (Cpte); Walküre (Cpte); Siegfried (Cpte); Götterdämmerung (Cpte). (G. London, K. Flagstad, C. Watson, E. Waechter, W. Kmentt, S. Svanholm, J. Madeira, G. Neidlinger, P. Kuen, W. Kreppel, K. Böhme, O. Balsborg, H. Plümacher, I. Malaniuk, J. King, R. Crespin, G. Frick, H. Hotter, B. Nilsson, C. Ludwig, V. Schlosser, B. Lindholm, B. Fassbaender, H. Watts, H. Dernesch, V. Little, M. Tyler, C. Hellmann, W. Windgassen, H. Hotter, G. Stolze, M. Höffgen, J. Sutherland, G. Frick, C. Watson, D. Fischer-Dieskau, C. Ludwig, L. Popp, G. Jones, M. Guy, H. Watts, G. Hoffman, A. Välkki, Vienna St Op Chor, VPO/G. Solti)

Ⓓ **414 101-2DH3** (10/84)
Wagner (Das) Rheingold
Wagner: Rheingold (Cpte). (G. London, K. Flagstad, S. Svanholm, P. Kuen, G. Neidlinger, C. Watson, W. Kmentt, E. Waechter, J. Madeira, W. Kreppel, K. Böhme, O. Balsborg, H. Plümacher, I. Malaniuk, VPO/G. Solti)

Ⓓ **414 105-2DH4** (4/85)
Wagner—(Die) Walküre
Wagner: Walküre (Cpte). (J. King, R. Crespin, B. Nilsson, H. Hotter, C. Ludwig, G. Frick, V. Schlosser, B. Lindholm, H. Dernesch, B. Fassbaender, C. Hellmann, V. Little, M. Tyler, H. Watts, VPO/G. Solti)

Ⓓ **414 110-2DH4** (12/84)
Wagner—Siegfried
Wagner: Siegfried (Cpte). (W. Windgassen, H. Hotter, B. Nilsson, G. Stolze, G. Neidlinger, M. Höffgen, K. Böhme, J. Sutherland, VPO/G. Solti)

Ⓓ **414 115-2DH4** (5/85)
Wagner—Götterdämmerung
Wagner: Götterdämmerung (Cpte). (B. Nilsson, W. Windgassen, G. Frick, G. Neidlinger, D. Fischer-Dieskau, C. Watson, C. Ludwig, L. Popp, G. Jones, M. Guy, H. Watts, G. Hoffman, A. Välkki, Vienna St Op Chor, VPO/G. Solti)

Ⓓ **414 145-2LM2** (1/90) ⊟ **414 145-4DY2**
Sullivan—Iolanthe
Sullivan: Iolanthe (Cpte). (Y. Newman, A. Styler, G. Knight, M. Sansom, J. Reed, D. Adams, T. Round, K. Sandford, J. Toye, P. Wales, D. Bradshaw, D'Oyly Carte Op Chor, Grenadier Guards Band, New SO/I. Godfrey)

Ⓓ **414 264-2DH2** (1/85)
Schoenberg—Moses und Aron
Schoenberg: Moses und Aron (Cpte). (F. Mazura, P. Langridge, A. Haugland, B. Bonney, M. Zakai, D. Harper, T. Dymit, H. Wittges, K. Link, J. Braham, B. Pearson, C. Anderson, K. Zajac, R. Cohn, P. Grizzell, S. Schweikert, E. Gottlieb, K. Brunssen, Roald Henderson, B. Nystrom, W. Kirkwood, Glen Ellyn Children's Chor, Chicago Sym Chor, Chicago SO/G. Solti)

Ⓓ **414 269-2DH2** (7/85)
Verdi—Rigoletto
Verdi: Rigoletto (Cpte). (S. Milnes, J. Sutherland, L. Pavarotti, M. Talvela, H. Tourangeau, C. Grant, G. Knight, R. Cassinelli, C. du Plessis, K. Te Kanawa, J. Gibbs, J. Clément, Ambrosian Op Chor, LSO/R. Bonynge)

Ⓓ **414 274-2DH2** (5/85)
Puccini—Turandot
Puccini: Turandot (Cpte). (J. Sutherland, L. Pavarotti, M. Caballé, T. Krause, P.F. Poli, P. de Palma, N. Ghiaurov, P. Pears, S. Markov, Wandsworth Sch Boys' Ch, John Alldis Ch, LPO/Z. Mehta)

Ⓓ **414 283-2LM2** (1/90) ⊟ **414 283-4DY2** (12/84)
Sullivan—HMS Pinafore
Sullivan: HMS Pinafore (Cpte). (J. Reed, J. Skitch, T. Round, J. Hindmarsh, D. Adams, G. Cook, E. Wilson Hyde, J. Wright, G. Knight, D'Oyly Carte Op Chor, New SO/I. Godfrey)

⊟ **414 286-4DY2** (12/84)
Sullivan—The Pirates of Penzance
Sullivan: Pirates of Penzance (Cpte). (D. Adams, P. Potter, J. Reed, V. Masterson, G. Cook, O. Brannigan, C. Palmer, P. Wales, J. Allister, S. Maisey, D'Oyly Carte Op Chor, RPO/I. Godfrey)

⊟ **414 341-4DY2** (7/85)
Sullivan—The Mikado
Sullivan: Mikado (Cpte). (D. Adams, T. Round, P. Pratt, K. Sandford, A. Styler, J. Hindmarsh, B. Dixon, J. Toye, A. Drummond-Grant, O. Grundy, D'Oyly Carte Op Chor, New SO/I. Godfrey)

Ⓓ **414 349-2DH3** (7/85)
Ponchielli—La Gioconda
Ponchielli: Gioconda (Cpte). (M. Caballé, L. Pavarotti, S. Milnes, A. Hodgson, N. Ghiaurov, A. Baltsa, J. Del Carlo, R. Romani, N. Jenkins, S. Varcoe, London Op Chor, Finchley Children's Music Group, National PO/B. Bartoletti)

Ⓓ **414 362-2DM2**
Mozart—Die Zauberflöte
Mozart: Zauberflöte (Cpte). (H. Gueden, W. Lipp, L. Simoneau, W. Berry, K. Böhme, P. Schoeffler, A. Jaresch, E. Loose, J. Hellwig, C. Ludwig, H. Rössl-Majdan, D. Siebert, R. Boesch, E. Boerner, J. Gostic, L. Pantscheff, E. Majkut, H. Pröglhöf, Vienna St Op Chor, VPO/K. Böhm)

Ⓓ **414 408-2DH** (2/86)
Suppé Overtures
Suppé: Leichte Kavallerie (exc); Fatinitza (exc); Morgen, ein Mittag, ein Abend in Wien (exc); Banditenstreiche (exc); Schöne Galathee (exc); Dichter und Bauer (exc); Pique Dame (exc). (Montreal SO/C. Dutoit)

Ⓓ **414 414-2DH2** (7/85)
R. Strauss—Salome
R. Strauss: Salome (Cpte). (B. Nilsson, E. Waechter, G. Stolze, G. Hoffman, W. Kmentt, J. Veasey, T. Krause, N. Douglas, Z. Koznowski, H. Holecek, T. Kirschbichler, L. Maikl, VPO/G. Solti)

Ⓓ **414 461-2DH2** (6/86)
Donizetti—(L') elisir d'amore
Donizetti: Elisir d'amore (Cpte). (J. Sutherland, L. Pavarotti, D. Cossa, S. Malas, M. Casula, Ambrosian Sngrs, ECO/R. Bonynge)

Ⓓ **414 476-2DH3** (4/88)
Bellini—Norma
Bellini: Norma (Cpte). (J. Sutherland, M. Caballé, L. Pavarotti, S. Ramey, K. Begley, D. Montague, WNO Chor, WNO Orch/R. Bonynge)

Ⓓ **414 483-2DH2** (12/85)
Janáček—Jenufa
Janáček: Jenufa (Cpte). (E. Söderström, W. Ochman, E. Randová, P. Dvorský, L. Popp, M. Mrázová, V. Zítek, D. Jedlička, I. Mixová, V. Soukupová, J. Pokorná, J. Jonášová, Vienna St Op Chor, VPO/C. MacKerras)

Ⓓ **414 489-2DH3** (9/85)
Bizet—Carmen
Bizet: Carmen (Cpte). (T. Troyanos, P. Domingo, K. Te Kanawa, J. Van Dam, N. Burrowes, J. Berbié, M. Roux, M. Sénéchal, T. Allen, P. Thau, J. Loreau, G. Berbié, John Alldis Ch, Haberdashers' Aske's Sch Ch, LPO/G. Solti)

Ⓓ **414 520-2DH2** (11/86)
Donizetti—La fille du régiment
Donizetti: Fille du régiment (Cpte). (J. Sutherland, L. Pavarotti, S. Malas, M. Sinclair, E. Coates, J. Bruyère, E. Garrett, Alan Jones II, ROH Chor, ROHO/R. Bonynge)

Ⓓ **414 559-2DH3** (2/86)
Gershwin—Porgy and Bess
Gershwin: Porgy and Bess (Cpte). (W. White, L. Mitchell, B. Hendricks, F. Quivar, F. Clemmons, B. Conrad, M. Boatwright, Arthur Thompson, J.V. Pickens, S. Hagan, William Brown, C. Deane, A. Ford, I. Jones, J. Buck, R. Snook, R. Nealley, A. Leatherman, D. Zucca, J. Jones, Cleveland Orch Children's Chor, Cleveland Orch Chor, Cleveland Orch/L. Maazel)

Ⓓ **414 577-2DH3** (4/86)
Britten—Peter Grimes
Britten: Peter Grimes (Cpte). (P. Pears, C. Watson, J. Pease, J. Watson, R. Nilsson, O. Brannigan, L. Elms, G. Evans, J. Lanigan, D. Kelly, M. Studholme, I. Kells, ROH Chor, ROHO/B. Britten)

Ⓓ **414 581-2DH3** (2/86)
Wagner—Tannhäuser
Wagner: Tannhäuser (Cpte). (R. Kollo, H. Dernesch, V. Braun, C. Ludwig, H. Sotin, W. Hollweg, M. Jungwirth, K. Equiluz, N. Bailey, Vienna Boys' Ch, Vienna St Op Chor, VPO/G. Solti)

Ⓓ **414 590-2DH2** (1/89)
Macagni—Cavalleria Rusticana; Leoncavallo—(I) Pagliacci
Mascagni: Cavalleria Rusticana (Cpte); *Leoncavallo:* Pagliacci (Cpte). (J. Varady, L. Pavarotti, P. Cappuccilli, C. Gonzales, I. Bormida, London Voices, National PO/G. Gavazzeni, L. Pavarotti, M. Freni, I. Wixell, L. Saccomani, V. Bello/G. Patanè)

Ⓓ **414 597-2DH2** (11/86)
Puccini—Tosca
Puccini: Tosca (Cpte). (K. Te Kanawa, G. Aragall, L. Nucci, M. King, P. de Palma, S. Malas, P. Hudson, N. Folwell, I. Martinez, ROH Children's Chor, WNO Chor, National PO/G. Solti)

Ⓓ **414 663-2LM** (10/90)
Britten: The Burning Fiery Furnace
Britten: Burning Fiery Furnace (Cpte). (P. Pears, B. Drake, J. Shirley-Quirk, R. Tear, S. Dean, P. Leeming, EOG Chor, EOG Orch/B. Britten)

Ⓓ **417 011-2DH2** (7/86)
Pavarotti's Greatest Hits
Verdi: Rigoletto (exc); *Franck:* Panis angelicus; *Bellini:* Vanne, o rosa fortunata; *Gounod:* Faust (exc); *Verdi:* Requiem (exc); Aida (exc); *Schubert:* Ave Maria, D839; *Leoncavallo:* Pagliacci (exc); *Ponchielli:* Gioconda (exc); *Donizetti:* Elisir d'amore (exc); *Puccini:* Tosca (exc); *Denza:* Funiculì-Funiculà; *Puccini:* Turandot (exc); *Donizetti:* Fille du régiment (exc); *Puccini:* Bohème (exc); *R. Strauss:* Rosenkavalier (exc); *Leoncavallo:* Mattinata; *Rossini:* Soirées musicales (exc); *De Curtis:* Torna a Surriento; *Donizetti:* Favorita (exc); *Bizet:* Carmen (exc); *Bellini:* Puritani (exc); *Verdi:* Trovatore (exc). (L. Pavarotti, LSO/R. Bonynge, National PO/K.H. Adler, Bologna Teatro Comunale Orch, Vienna Volksoper Orch/L. Magiera,

VPO/G. Solti/G. Patanè, New Philh, ECO/N. Rescigno/A. Guadagno, LPO/Z. Mehta, E. Garrett, ROH Chor, ROHO, BPO/H. von Karajan, Philh/P. Gamba/G. Chiaramello, J. Sutherland, N. Ghiaurov, G. Luccardi)

Ⓓ **417 129-2DH2** (11/86)
Janáček—The Cunning Little Vixen
Janáček: Cunning Little Vixen (Cpte); Cunning Little Vixen Suite. (L. Popp, E. Randová, L. Márová, G. Jahn, I. Mixová, R. Novák, E. Zikmundová, D. Jedlička, V. Krejčík, B. Blachut, V. Zítek, Bratislava Children's Ch, Vienna St Op Chor, VPO/C. MacKerras)

Ⓓ **417 137-2DH2** (3/87)
Verdi—Il Trovatore
Verdi: Trovatore (Cpte). (L. Pavarotti, J. Sutherland, I. Wixell, M. Horne, N. Ghiaurov, N. Burrowes, G. Clark, P. Knapp, W. Evans, London Op Chor, National PO/R. Bonynge)

Ⓓ **417 143-2DH4** (9/86)
Wagner—Parsifal
Wagner: Parsifal (Cpte). (R. Kollo, D. Fischer-Dieskau, G. Frick, C. Ludwig, Z. Kélémen, H. Hotter, R. Tear, H. Lackner, R. Hansmann, M. Schiml, H. Zednik, E. Aichberger, L. Popp, A. Hargan, A. Howells, K. Te Kanawa, G. Knight, M. Lilowa, B. Finnilä, Vienna Boys' Ch, Vienna St Op Chor, VPO/G. Solti)

Ⓓ **417 154-2DH4** (2/87)
Rossini—Guglielmo Tell
Rossini: Guillaume Tell (Cpte). (S. Milnes, M. Freni, L. Pavarotti, N. Ghiaurov, J. Tomlinson, D. Jones, E. Connell, F. Mazzoli, C.A. Suarez, P. de Palma, R. Van Allan, Ambrosian Op Chor, National PO/R. Chailly)

Ⓓ **417 164-2DM2** (5/92)
Rossini—Il barbiere di Siviglia
Rossini: Barbiere di Siviglia (Cpte). (M. Ausensi, T. Berganza, U. Benelli, F. Corena, N. Ghiaurov, S. Malagù, D. Mantovani, Naples Scarlatti Chor, Naples Scarlatti Orch/S. Varviso)

Ⓓ **417 168-2DM2** (3/90)
Verdi—Falstaff
Verdi: Falstaff (Cpte). (G. Evans, R. Merrill, I. Ligabue, M. Freni, Alfredo Kraus, G. Simionato, R. Elias, J. Lanigan, P. de Palma, G. Foiani, RCA Italiana Op Chor, RCA Italiana Op Orch/G. Solti)

Ⓓ **417 185-2DMO2**
Mozart—Così fan tutte
Mozart: Così fan tutte (Cpte). (L. della Casa, C. Ludwig, E. Loose, A. Dermota, E. Kunz, P. Schoeffler, Vienna St Op Chor, VPO/K. Böhm)

▣ **417 254-4DY2**
Gilbert & Sullivan—The Gondoliers
Sullivan: Gondoliers (Cpte). (T. Round, A. Styler, M. Sansom, J. Wright, J. Reed, G. Knight, J. Toye, J. Skitch, K. Sandford, J. Roach, M. Wakeham, J. Riordan, G. Cook, D. Bradshaw, C. Jones, D. Gill, D'Oyly Carte Op Chor, New SO/I. Godfrey)

Ⓓ **417 289-2DH** (9/87)
Con amore
Kreisler: Gitana; Liebesleid; Pugnani Praeludium and Allegro; Liebesfreud; *Poldini:* Marionnettes (exc); *Wieniawski:* Scherzo-tarantelle, Op. 16; Etudes-Caprices, Op. 18 (exc); *Elgar:* Salut d'amour; Capricieuse; *Tchaikovsky:* Morceaux, Op. 51 (exc); *Nováček:* Concert caprices, Op. 5 (exc); *Debussy:* Beau soir; *Chopin:* Nocturnes (exc); *Gossec:* Rosine (exc); *Chaminade:* Sérénade espagnole; *Saint-Saëns:* Etudes, Op. 52 (exc); *Brahms:* Hungarian Dances (exc). (K-W. Chung, P. Moll)

Ⓓ **417 315-2DM3** (2/90)
Mozart—Le Nozze di Figaro
Mozart: Nozze di Figaro (Cpte). (C. Siepi, H. Gueden, A. Poell, L. della Casa, S. Danco, H. Rössl-Majdan, F. Corena, M. Dickie, H. Meyer-Welfing, H. Pröglhöf, A. Felbermayer, Vienna St Op Chor, VPO/E. Kleiber)

▣ **417 331-4DA**
Verdi—(La) Traviata
Verdi: Traviata (exc). (J. Sutherland, C. Bergonzi, D. Carral, R. Merrill, P. Pedani, M.T. Pace, P. de Palma, G. Foiani, S. Maionica, MMF Chor, MMF Orch/J. Pritchard)

Ⓓ **417 345-2DH2** (12/86)
R. Strauss—Elektra
R. Strauss: Elektra (Cpte). (B. Nilsson, R. Resnik, M. Collier, G. Stolze, T. Krause, T. Franc, M. Sjöstedt, M. Lilowa, G. Unger, L. Heppe, P. Tinsley, H. Watts, M. Lehane, Y. Minton, J. Cook, F. Weathers, VPO/G. Solti)

Ⓓ **417 348-2DH2** (2/89)
Berg—Wozzeck;Schoenberg—Erwartung
Berg: Wozzeck (Cpte); *Schoenberg:* Erwartung (Cpte). (E. Waechter, A. Silja, H. Winkler, H. Laubenthal, H. Zednik, A. Malta, G. Jahn, A. Silja, Vienna St Op Chor, VPO/C. von Dohnányi)

Ⓓ **417 358-2LM2** (1/90) ▣ **417 358-4DY2**
Sullivan—Yeoman of the Guard; Trial by Jury
Sullivan: Yeomen of the Guard (Cpte); Trial by Jury (Cpte). (A. Raffell, P. Potter, D. Adams, D. Palmer, J. Reed, K. Sandford, D. Palmer, T. Lawlor, E. Harwood, A. Hood, G. Knight, M. Eales, A. Hood, T. Round, J. Reed, K. Sandford, D. Adams, A. Raffell, D'Oyly Carte Op Chor, RPO/M. Sargent, ROHO/I. Godfrey)

Ⓓ **417 363-2DH2** (11/86)
Offenbach—(Les) Contes d'Hoffman
Offenbach: Contes d'Hoffmann (Cpte). (P. Domingo, J. Sutherland, H. Tourangeau, G. Bacquier, J. Charon, A. Neury, P. Plishka, M. Lilowa, H. Cuénod, R. Jacques, Suisse Romande Rad Ch, SRO/R. Bonynge)

Ⓓ **417 395-2DH**
Le nozze di Figaro: Highlights
Mozart: Nozze di Figaro (exc). (K. Te Kanawa, L. Popp, F. von Stade, S. Ramey, T. Allen, K. Moll, LPO/G. Solti)

ʘʘ **417 395-5DH**
Le nozze di Figaro: Highlights
Mozart: Nozze di Figaro (exc). (K. Te Kanawa, L. Popp, F. von Stade, S. Ramey, T. Allen, K. Moll, LPO/G. Solti)

Ⓓ **417 402-2DH2** (4/87)
Mozart—Die Entführung aus dem Serail
Mozart: Entführung (Cpte). (E. Gruberová, K. Battle, G. Winbergh, H. Zednik, M. Talvela, W. Quadflieg, Vienna St Op Concert Ch, VPO/G. Solti)

Ⓓ **417 407-2DH2** (1/87)
Verdi—Nabucco
Verdi: Nabucco (Cpte). (T. Gobbi, E. Suliotis, B. Prevedi, D. Carral, C. Cava, G. Foiani, W. Kräutler, A. d'Auria, Vienna St Op Chor, Vienna St Op Orch/L. Gardelli)

Ⓓ **417 410-2DM2** (8/89)
Gluck—Orfeo ed Euridice
Gluck: Orfeo ed Euridice (Cpte). (M. Horne, P. Lorengar, H. Donath, ROH Chor, ROHO/G. Solti)

Ⓓ **417 413-2DH2** (8/87)
Tchaikovsky—Eugene Onegin
Tchaikovsky: Eugene Onegin (Cpte). (B. Weikl, T. Kubiak, S. Burrows, J. Hamari, N. Ghiaurov, A. Reynolds, E. Hartle, M. Sénéchal, R. Van Allan, W. Mason, John Alldis Ch, ROHO/G. Solti)

Ⓓ **417 416-2DH3** (9/87)
Verdi—Aida
Verdi: Aida (Cpte). (L. Price, R. Gorr, J. Vickers, R. Merrill, G. Tozzi, P. Clabassi, F. Ricciardi, M. Sighele, Rome Op Chor, Rome Op Orch/G. Solti)

Ⓓ **417 420-2DH2** (10/88)
Verdi—Luisa Miller
Verdi: Luisa Miller (Cpte). (M. Caballé, L. Pavarotti, S. Milnes, B. Giaiotti, A. Reynolds, R. Van Allan, A. Céline, F. Pavarotti, London Op Chor, National PO/P. Maag)

Ⓓ **417 424-2DH2** (4/87)
Bellini—La Sonnambula
Bellini: Sonnambula (Cpte). (J. Sutherland, L. Pavarotti, N. Ghiaurov, I. Buchanan, D. Jones, J. Tomlinson, P. de Palma, London Op Chor, National PO/R. Bonynge)

Ⓓ **417 439-2DH3** (5/90)
Verdi—Aida
Verdi: Aida (Cpte). (M. Chiara, G. Dimitrova, L. Pavarotti, L. Nucci, P. Burchuladze, L. Roni, E. Gavazzi, M. Renée, La Scala Chor, La Scala Orch/L. Maazel)

Ⓓ **417 493-2DH3** (3/87)
R. Strauss—(Der) Rosenkavalier
R. Strauss: Rosenkavalier (Cpte). (R. Crespin, Y. Minton, M. Jungwirth, H. Donath, O. Wiener, L. Pavarotti, A. Howells, M. Dickie, E. Loose, R. Schwaiger, A. Jerger, H. Lackner, H. Prikopa, K. Equiluz, A. Dermota, A. Auger, R. Yachmi-Caucig, I. Mayr, K. Terkal, H. Pipal, A. Tomaschek, A. Maly, L. Heppe, A. Tomaschek, F. Setzer, F. Strack, N. Simkowsky, J. Reautschnigg, Vienna St Op Chor, VPO/G. Solti)

Ⓓ **417 497-2DH4** (7/87)
Wagner—(Der) Meistersinger
Wagner: Meistersinger (Cpte). (N. Bailey, R. Kollo, H. Bode, K. Moll, B. Weikl, A. Dallapozza, J. Hamari, G. Nienstedt, Adalbert Kraus, M. Egel, M. Schomberg, W. Appel, M. Sénéchal, H. Berger-Tuna, K. Rydl, R. Hartmann, W. Klumlikboldt, Gumpoldskirchner Spatzen, Vienna St Op Chor, VPO/G. Solti)

Ⓓ **417 577-2DH3** (6/87)
Puccini—Madama Butterfly
Puccini: Madama Butterfly (Cpte). (M. Freni, L. Pavarotti, R. Kerns, C. Ludwig, M. Sénéchal, G. Stendoro, E. Schary, M. Rintzler, H. Helm, S.R. Frese, Vienna St Op Chor, VPO/H. von Karajan)

Ⓓ **417 588-2DH3** (4/89)
Bellini—(I) Puritani
Bellini: Puritani (Cpte). (J. Sutherland, L. Pavarotti, P. Cappuccilli, N. Ghiaurov, A. Caminada, G. Luccardi, R. Cazzaniga, ROH Chor, LSO/R. Bonynge)

Ⓓ **417 645-2DH** (11/87)
Kiri - Portrait
Canteloube: Chants d'Auvergne (exc); *Gay:* Beggar's Opera (exc); *Handel:* Messiah (exc); *Brahms:* Deutsches Requiem, Op. 45 (exc); *Mozart:* Vado ma dove?, K583; Nozze di Figaro (exc); *Puccini:* Tosca (exc); *Bizet:* Carmen (exc); *Villa-Lobos:* Bachianas Brasileiras 5. (K. Te Kanawa, ECO/J. Tate, National PO/R. Bonynge, Chicago SO/G. Solti, Vienna CO/G. Fischer, LPO, L. Harrell, Inst. Ens, Chicago Sym Chor)

Ⓓ **417 686-2DC** (1/89)
Puccini—Operatic Arias
Puccini: Madama Butterfly (exc); Tosca (exc); Tosca (exc); Turandot (exc); Turandot (exc); Bohème (exc); Bohème (exc); Bohème (exc); Fanciulla del West (exc); Gianni Schicchi (exc); Manon Lescaut (exc). (F. Weathers, Vienna Op. Orch/A. Quadri, G. di Stefano, Santa Cecilia Academy Orch/F. Patanè, A. Cerquetti, MMF Orch/G. Gavazzeni, R. Tebaldi, New Philh/O. de Fabritiis, B. Prevedi, ROHO/E. Downes, C. Bergonzi/T. Serafin, M. Chiara, Vienna Volksoper Orch/N. Santi, V. Zeani, J. Björling/A. Erede)

Ⓓ **417 747-2DM**
Johann Strauss Favourites
J. Strauss II: Fledermaus (exc); Perpetuum mobile; Accelerationen, Op. 234; Unter Donner und Blitz; Morgenblätter, Op. 279; Persischer Marsch; Explosionen, Op. 43; Wiener Blut; Pizzicato Polka; Egyptischer Marsch, Op. 335; Künstlerleben, Op. 316; Tritsch-Tratsch; Radetzky March. (VPO/W. Boskovsky)

Ⓓ **417 763-2DM**
Verdi—Aida - excerpts
Verdi: Aida (exc). (R. Tebaldi, C. Bergonzi, G. Simionato, C. MacNeil, A. Van Mill, F. Corena, P. de Palma, Vienna Singverein, VPO/H. von Karajan)

Ⓓ **417 771-2DM** (4/89)
de Falla: Orchestral & Stage Works
Falla: Nights in the Gardens of Spain; Sombrero de tres picos (Cpte); Vida breve (exc). (A. de Larrocha, T. Berganza, SRO/S. Comissiona/E. Ansermet)

Ⓓ **417 778-2DM** (5/89)
English Orchestral Music
Vaughan Williams: Greensleeves Fantasia; English Folk Song Suite; *Elgar:* Serenade; *Butterworth:* Banks of Green Willow; *Warlock:* Capriol Suite; *Delius:* First cuckoo; Village Romeo and Juliet (exc). (ASMF/N. Marriner)

Ⓓ **417 780-2DM**
Joan Sutherland's Greatest Hits
Handel: Samson (exc); *Arditi:* Bacio; *Lehár:* Lustige Witwe (exc); *J. Strauss II:* Casanova (exc); *Donizetti:* Fille du régiment (exc); *Delibes:* Lakmé (exc); *Bellini:* Norma (exc); *Gounod:* Faust (exc); *Donizetti:* Lucia di Lammermoor (exc). (J. Sutherland, C. Siepi, R. Merrill, R. Pelizzoni, Ambrosian Light Op Chor, Santa Cecilia Academy Chor, London Sym Chor, ROH Chor, ROHO, LSO, New Philh, Santa Cecilia Academy Orch/F. Molinari-Pradelli/R. Bonynge/J. Pritchard)

Ⓓ **417 781-2DM**
Eighteenth Century Miniatures
Pachelbel: Canon and Gigue (exc); Canon and Gigue (exc); *Albinoni:* Adagio; *Bach:* Cantata 147 (exc); Cantata 208 (exc); Suites, BWV1066-9 (exc); Fantasia and Fugue, BWV542 (exc); *Boccherini:* String Quintets, G271-6 (exc); *Hoffstetter:* String Quartets, Op. 3 (exc); *Handel:* Concerti grossi, op 6 (exc); Solomon (exc); Berenice (exc). (Stuttgart CO, U. Bremsteller/K. Münchinger)

Ⓓ **417 786-2DM** (10/89)
Spanish Orchestral Works
Falla: Amor brujo (Cpte); *Granados:* Goyescas (exc); *Albéniz:* Suite española 1. (N. Mistral, New Philh/R. Frühbeck de Burgos)

Ⓓ **417 796-2DM**
Luciano Pavarotti—'Mattinata'
Caldara: Alma del core; *Pergolesi:* Tre giorni son che Nina; *Bellini:* Vaga luna; *T. Giordani:* Caro mio ben; *Rossini:* Soirées musicales (exc); *Gluck:* Orfeo ed Euridice (exc); *Tosti:* Alba separa; Ultima canzone; *Donizetti:* Barcaiolo; *Leoncavallo:* Mattinata; *Beethoven:* In questa tomba oscura, WoO133; *Tosti:* Aprile; Chanson de l'adieu; *Durante:* Danza, danza, fanciulla. (L. Pavarotti, Philh/P. Gamba, National PO/A. Tonini)

417 828-2DM2 (7/89)
Rossini—Italiana in Algeri
Rossini: Italiana in Algeri (Cpte). (T. Berganza, L. Alva, R. Panerai, F. Corena, G. Tavolaccini, M.T. Pace, P. Montarsolo, MMF Chor, MMF Orch/S. Varviso)

417 839-2DH (6/88)
Bizet—L'Arlésienne & Carmen Suites
Bizet: Arlésienne Suites; Carmen Suites. (Montreal SO/C. Dutoit)

417 839-5DH
Bizet—L'Arlésienne & Carmen Suites
Bizet: Arlésienne Suites; Carmen Suites. (Montreal SO/C. Dutoit)

421 046-2DH2 (12/87)
J. Strauss—(Der) Fledermaus
J. Strauss II: Fledermaus (Cpte). (H. Gueden, E. Köth, W. Kmentt, G. Zampieri, W. Berry, R. Resnik, E. Waechter, P. Klein, H. Schubert, E. Kunz, R. Tebaldi, F. Corena, B. Nilsson, M. del Monaco, T. Berganza, J. Sutherland, J. Björling, L. Price, G. Simionato, E. Bastianini, L. Welitsch, Vienna St Op Chor, VPO/H. von Karajan)

421 049-2DH2 (11/87)
Puccini—La bohème
Puccini: Bohème (Cpte). (M. Freni, L. Pavarotti, E. Harwood, R. Panerai, G. Maffeo, N. Ghiaurov, M. Sénéchal, M. Sénéchal, G. Pietsch, H-D. Appelt, H-D. Pohl, Schöneberg Boys' Ch, Berlin Deutsche Op Chor, BPO/H. von Karajan)

421 053-2DH4 (10/87)
Wagner—Lohengrin
Wagner: Lohengrin (Cpte). (P. Domingo, J. Norman, E. Randová, S. Nimsgern, H. Sotin, D. Fischer-Dieskau, Vienna St Op Concert Ch, VPO/G. Solti)

421 125-2DH3 (7/88)
Mozart—(Le) Nozze di Figaro
Mozart: Nozze di Figaro (Cpte). (J. Van Dam, I. Cotrubas, T. Krause, A. Tomowa-Sintow, F. von Stade, J. Berbié, J. Bastin, H. Zednik, K. Equiluz, Z. Kélémen, C. Barbaux, Vienna St Op Chor, VPO/H. von Karajan)

421 240-2DM3 (12/91)
Gounod—Faust
Gounod: Faust (Cpte). (F. Corelli, J. Sutherland, N. Ghiaurov, R. Massard, M. Elkins, M. Sinclair, R. Myers, Ambrosian Op Chor, LSO/R. Bonynge)

421 245-2DH ▭ **421 245-4DH**
Puccini—La Bohème excerpts
Puccini: Bohème (exc). (M. Freni, L. Pavarotti, R. Panerai, E. Harwood, N. Ghiaurov, G. Maffeo, M. Sénéchal, Berlin Deutsche Op Chor, BPO/H. von Karajan)

421 247-2DH ▭ **421 247-4DH**
Puccini—Madama Butterfly excerpts
Puccini: Madama Butterfly (exc). (M. Freni, L. Pavarotti, C. Ludwig, R. Kerns, M. Sénéchal, Vienna St Op Chor, VPO/H. von Karajan)

421 303-2DA ▭ **421 303-4DA**
Rigoletto: Scenes and Arias
Verdi: Rigoletto (exc). (S. Milnes, J. Sutherland, L. Pavarotti, M. Talvela, H. Tourangeau, G. Knight, J. Gibbs, C. du Plessis, R. Cassinelli, J. Clément, Ambrosian Op Chor, LSO/R. Bonynge)

421 306-2DA
Marilyn Horne sings Rossini
Rossini: Siège de Corinthe (exc); Donna del lago (exc); Otello (exc); Tancredi (exc). (M. Horne, Ambrosian Op Chor, RPO, SRO/H. Lewis)

421 310-2DA ▭ **421 310-4DA**
Il Trovatore—highlights
Verdi: Trovatore (exc). (L. Pavarotti, I. Wixell, J. Sutherland, M. Horne, N. Ghiaurov, G. Clark, N. Burrowes, P. Knapp, London Op Chor, National PO/R. Bonynge)

421 313-2DA
Wagner: Der Ring des Nibelungen - Great Scenes
Wagner: Rheingold (exc); Walküre (exc); Siegfried (exc); Götterdämmerung (exc). (B. Nilsson, W. Windgassen, H. Hotter, G. London, G. Stolze, G. Frick, E. Waechter, W. Kmentt, K. Flagstad, S. Svanholm, O. Balsborg, H. Plümacher, I. Malaniuk, V. Schlosser, B. Lindholm, B. Fassbaender, H. Watts, H. Dernesch, V. Little, M. Tyler, C. Hellmann, VPO/G. Solti)

421 325-2DA
La traviata—highlights
Verdi: Traviata (exc). (J. Sutherland, C. Bergonzi, R. Merrill, M.T. Pace, D. Carral, P. de Palma, P. Pedani, S. Maionica, G. Foiani, MMF Chor, MMF Orch/J. Pritchard)

421 426-2DH2 (9/88)
Puccini—Manon Lescaut
Puccini: Manon Lescaut (Cpte). (K. Te Kanawa, J. Carreras, P. Coni, I. Tajo, W. Matteuzzi, M. Zimmermann, L. Freschi, P. de Palma, G. Tadeo, C. Gaifa, N. de Carolis, Bologna Teatro Comunale Chor, Bologna Teatro Comunale Orch/R. Chailly)

421 497-2DM2 (3/90)
Donizetti—Lucrezia Borgia
Donizetti: Lucrezia Borgia (Cpte). (J. Sutherland, G. Aragall, I. Wixell, M. Horne, G. Clark, P. de Palma, L. Visser, J. Bröcheler, G. Ewer, R. Van Allan, N. Zaccaria, D. Wilson-Johnson, P. Taylor, London Op Chor, National PO/R. Bonynge)

421 527-2DH (6/89)
Fête à la française
Chabrier: Joyeuse marche; España; *Dukas:* Apprenti sorcier; *Satie:* Gymnopédies (exc); *Saint-Saëns:* Samson et Dalila (exc); *Bizet:* Jeux d'enfants; *A. Thomas:* Raymond (exc); *Ibert:* Divertissement. (Montreal SO/C. Dutoit)

421 611-2DH
Puccini—Tosca - excerpts
Puccini: Tosca (exc). (K. Te Kanawa, G. Aragall, L. Nucci, M. King, S. Malas, P. de Palma, P. Hudson, N. Folwell, WNO Chor, ROH Children's Chor, National PO/G. Solti)

421 670-2DM2 (1/89)
Puccini—Tosca
Puccini: Tosca (Cpte). (L. Price, G. di Stefano, G. Taddei, C. Cava, P. de Palma, F. Corena, L. Monreale, A. Mariotti, H. Weiss, Vienna St Op Chor, VPO/H. von Karajan)

421 818-2DH2 (11/90)
Ballet Gala
Minkus: Grand pas; *Pugni:* Pas de quatre; *Offenbach:* Papillon (exc); *Minkus:* Don Quixote (exc); *Drigo:* Corsaire (exc); *Auber:* Grand Pas Classique; *C. Lambert:* Rendez-vous; *Pugni:* Esmerelda (exc); *Tommasini:* Good-Humoured Ladies (exc); *A. Thomas:* Françoise de Rimini (exc). (English Concert Orch/R. Bonynge)

421 849-2LH2 (6/89)
Britten—Albert Herring
Britten: Albert Herring (Cpte). (P. Pears, S. Fisher, J. Peters, J. Noble, O. Brannigan, E. Evans, A. Cantelo, S. Rex, J. Ward, C. Wilson, S. Amit, A. Pashley, S. Terry, ECO/B. Britten)

421 852-2DH2 (10/89)
Janáček: Operatic & Chamber Works
Janáček: Káťa Kabanová (Cpte); Capriccio; Concertino. (E. Söderström, P. Dvorský, N. Kniplová, D. Jedlička, V. Krejčík, Z. Švehla, L. Márová, J. Souček, J. Pavlová, G. Jahn, Vienna St Op Chor, VPO/C. Mackerras, P. Crossley, London Sinfonietta/D. Atherton)

421 858-2LM (9/89)
Britten—Curlew River
Britten: Curlew River (Cpte). (P. Pears, J. Shirley-Quirk, H. Blackburn, B. Drake, B. Webb, EOG Chor, EOG Orch/B. Britten)

421 865-2DA
Wagner—Opera Choruses
Wagner: Lohengrin (exc); Tannhäuser (exc); Fliegende Holländer (exc); Meistersinger (exc); Parsifal (exc). (Vienna St Op Chor, VPO, Chicago Sym Chor, Chicago SO/G. Solti)

421 866-2DA
Offenbach - Les Contes d'Hoffmann
Offenbach: Contes d'Hoffmann (exc). (P. Domingo, J. Sutherland, G. Bacquier, H. Cuénod, H. Tourangeau, Suisse Romande Rad Ch, Lausanne Pro Arte Ch, Du Brassus Ch, SRO/R. Bonynge)

421 867-2DA ▭ **421 867-4DA**
Verdi: Nabucco excerpts
Verdi: Nabucco (exc). (T. Gobbi, B. Prevedi, C. Cava, E. Suliotis, D. Carral, A. d'Auria, G. Foiani, W. Kräutler, Vienna St Op Chor, Vienna St Op Orch/L. Gardelli)

421 870-2DA ▭ **421 870-4DA**
Mascagni—Cavalleria Rusticana; Leoncavallo—(I) Pagliacci
Mascagni: Cavalleria Rusticana (exc); *Leoncavallo:* Pagliacci (exc). (J. Varady, L. Pavarotti, I. Bormida, P. Cappuccilli, C. Gonzales, M. Freni, L. Saccomani, I. Wixell, V. Bello, London Op Chor, Finchley Children's Music Group, National PO/G. Gavazzeni/G. Patanè)

421 873-2DA ▭ **421 873-4DA**
Puccini—Madama Butterfly -highlights
Puccini: Madama Butterfly (exc). (R. Tebaldi, F. Cossotto, C. Bergonzi, E. Sordello, Santa Cecilia Academy Chor, Santa Cecilia Academy Orch/T. Serafin)

421 881-2DA
The Age of Bel Canto - Sutherland
Piccinni: Cecchina (exc); *Handel:* Samson (exc); *Bononcini:* Astarto (exc); *Shield:* Rosina (exc); *Mozart:* Zauberflöte (exc); *Boïeldieu:* Angéla (exc); *Rossini:* Semiramide (exc); *Weber:* Freischütz (exc); *Donizetti:* Don Pasquale (exc); *Verdi:* Attila (exc); *Bellini:* Straniera (exc); *Bononcini:* Griselda (exc); *C.H. Graun:* Montezuma (exc). (J. Sutherland, M. Horne, R. Conrad, New SO, LSO, LPO/R. Bonynge, London Sym Chor)

421 885-2DA ▭ **421 885-4DA**
Donizetti—Lucia di Lammermoor - Highlights
Donizetti: Lucia di Lammermoor (exc). (J. Sutherland, L. Pavarotti, S. Milnes, N. Ghiaurov, H. Tourangeau, R. Davies, P.F. Poli, ROH Chor, ROHO/R. Bonynge)

421 886-2DA
Bellini—Norma - Highlights
Bellini: Norma (exc). (J. Sutherland, M. Horne, John Alexander, R. Cross, London Sym Chor, LSO/R. Bonynge)

421 888-2DA ▭ **421 888-4DA**
Puccini—Tosca - Scenes and Arias
Puccini: Tosca (exc). (M. Freni, L. Pavarotti, S. Milnes, R. Van Allan, M. Sénéchal, I. Tajo, P. Hudson, J. Tomlinson, W. Baratti, Wandsworth Sch Boys' Ch, London Op Chor, National PO/N. Rescigno)

421 891-2DA
Marilyn Horne sings Rossini, Bellini & Donizetti
Rossini: Barbiere di Siviglia (exc); *Bellini:* Capuleti (exc); *Rossini:* Semiramide (exc); Italiana in Algeri (exc); *Donizetti:* Lucrezia Borgia (exc); *Rossini:* Semiramide (exc); Italiana in ALgeri (exc); Cenerentola (exc); *Donizetti:* Fille du régiment (exc). (M. Horne, Geneva Op Chor, SRO, LSO, ROHO/H. Lewis/R. Bonynge)

421 896-2DA
Puccini—Great Operatic Duets
Puccini: Madama Butterfly (exc); Tosca (exc); Manon Lescaut (exc); Bohème (exc); Bohème (exc); Turandot (exc). (M. Freni, K. Te Kanawa, J. Sutherland, L. Pavarotti, G. Aragall, J. Carreras, R. Panerai, National PO, VPO, BPO, LPO, Bologna Teatro Comunale Orch/H. von Karajan/G. Solti/R. Chailly/Z. Mehta)

421 898-2DM
J. Strauss II—Die Fledermaus Highlights
J. Strauss II: Fledermaus (exc). (G. Janowitz, R. Holm, S. Lukan, W. Kmentt, W. Windgassen, E. Waechter, H. Holecek, E. Kunz, E. Kuchar, Vienna St Op Chor, VPO/K. Böhm)

421 899-2DA (4/93)
Teresa Berganza - Mozart Arias
Mozart: Nozze di Figaro (exc); Clemenza di Tito (exc); Così fan tutte (exc); Ch'io mi scordi di te, K505; Così fan tutte (exc); Clemenza di Tito (exc); Ombra felice, K255; Misero me, K77; Al desio, K577. (T. Berganza, G. Parsons, LSO/J. Pritchard, LPO/G. Solti, Vienna St Op Orch/I. Kertész, Vienna CO/G. Fischer)

425 034-2DM
Kodály—Orchestral Works
Kodály: Háry János Suite; Galánta Dances; Peacock Variations; Marosszék Dances. (Philh Hungarica/A. Dorati)

425 037-2DM
Pavarotti in Concert
Bononcini: Griselda (exc); *Handel:* Atalanta (exc); *A. Scarlatti:* Pompeo (exc); *Bellini:* Ma rendi pur contento; Dolente imagine; Malinconia, ninfa gentile; Bella Nice, che d'amore; Vanne, o rosa fortunata; *Tosti:* Serenata; Luna d'estate; Malià; Non t'amo più; *Respighi:* Nevicata; Pioggia; Nebbie; *Rossini:* Soirées musicales (exc). (L. Pavarotti, Bologna Teatro Comunale Orch/R. Bonynge)

425 048-2DX ▭ **425 048-4DX**
Joan Sutherland - Home Sweet Home
Benedict: Gypsy and the Bird; *Arditi:* Parla Waltz; *Ricci:* Crispino e la comare (exc); *Tosti:* Ideale; *Arditi:* Bacio; *Tosti:* Serenata; *Leoncavallo:* Mattinata; *Massenet:* Chérubin (exc); *Friml:* Rose Marie (exc); *Fraser-Simson:* Maid of the Mountains (exc); *German:* Tom Jones (exc); *Bishop:* Lo! here the gentle lark; *Flotow:* Martha (exc); *Wallace:* Maritana (exc); *Balfe:* Bohemian Girl (exc); *Bishop:* Home sweet home. (J. Sutherland, A. Murray, R. Bonynge, T. Bonifacio, Ambrosian Light Op Chor, LSO, New Philh/R. Bonynge)

425 169-2DM3 (3/91)
Mozart: Don Giovanni
Mozart: Don Giovanni (Cpte). (B. Weikl, M. Price, S. Sass, L. Popp, S. Burrows, G. Bacquier, A. Sramek, K. Moll, London Op Chor, LPO/G. Solti)

Ⓓ **425 177-2LM2** (1/90)
Sullivan—The Gondoliers
Sullivan: Gondoliers (Cpte). (T. Round, A. Styler, M. Sansom, J. Wright, J. Reed, G. Knight, J. Toye, J. Skitch, K. Sandford, J. Roach, M. Wakeham, J. Riordan, G. Cook, D. Bradshaw, C. Jones, D. Gill, D'Oyly Carte Op Chor, New SO/I. Godfrey)

Ⓓ **425 204-2DNL** (3/89)
Ute Lemper sings Kurt Weill
Weill: Silbersee (exc); Dreigroschenoper (exc); Berliner Requiem (exc); Nannas Lied; Mahagonny (exc); Je ne t'aime pas; One touch of Venus (exc). (U. Lemper, Berlin Rad Ens/J. Mauceri, W. Meyer, K. Rautenberg)

Ⓓ **425 407-2DM2**
Giordano—Andrea Chénier
Giordano: Andrea Chénier (Cpte). (M. del Monaco, R. Tebaldi, E. Bastianini, M. Caruso, M.T. Mandalari, F. Cossotto, S. Maionica, D. Mantovani, V. Polotto, D. Caselli, A. Mercuriali, M. Cazzato, A. Guidi, F. Corena, Santa Cecilia Academy Chor, Santa Cecilia Academy Orch/G. Gavazzeni)

Ⓓ **425 410-2DM2** (9/90)
Donizetti—Maria Stuarda
Donizetti: Maria Stuarda (Cpte). (J. Sutherland, H. Tourangeau, L. Pavarotti, R. Soyer, J. Morris, M. Elkins, Bologna Teatro Comunale Chor, Bologna Teatro Comunale Orch/R. Bonynge)

Ⓓ **425 417-2DM2** (2/90)
Catalani—(La) Wally
Catalani: Wally (Cpte). (R. Tebaldi, M. del Monaco, P. Cappuccilli, J. Diaz, L. Marimpietri, S. Malagù, A. Mariotti, Turin Lyric Chor, Monte Carlo Nat Op Orch/F. Cleva)

Ⓓ **425 430-2DH** (9/89) ▭ **425 430-4DH** (9/89)
Cecilia Bartoli sings Rossini Arias
Rossini: Italiana in Algeri (exc); Donna del lago (exc); Tancredi (exc); Otello (exc); Stabat mater (exc); Pietra del paragone (exc); Cenerentola (exc). (C. Bartoli, A. Schoenberg Ch, Vienna Volksoper Orch/G. Patanè)

Ⓓ **425 475-2DM2** (1/90)
Delibes—Sylvia; Massenet—(Le) Cid
Delibes: Sylvia (Cpte); *Massenet:* Cid (exc). (New Philh, National PO/R. Bonynge)

Ⓓ **425 481-2DM3** (2/90)
Rossini—Semiramide
Rossini: Semiramide (Cpte). (J. Sutherland, M. Horne, J. Rouleau, J. Serge, P. Clark, S. Malas, M. Langdon, L. Fyson, Ambrosian Op Chor, LSO/R. Bonynge)

Ⓓ **425 485-2DM2** (12/89)
Delibes—Lakmé
Delibes: Lakmé (Cpte). (J. Sutherland, A. Vanzo, G. Bacquier, J. Berbié, C. Calès, G. Annear, J. Clément, M. Sinclair, E. Belcourt, Monte Carlo Op Chor, Monte Carlo Op Orch/R. Bonynge)

Ⓓ **425 488-2DM3**
Bellini—Norma
Bellini: Norma (Cpte). (J. Sutherland, M. Horne, John Alexander, R. Cross, J. Ward, Y. Minton, London Sym Chor, LSO/R. Bonynge)

Ⓓ **425 493-2DM2** (1/90)
Joan Sutherland: The Art of the Prima Donna
Arne: Artaxerxes (exc); *Handel:* Samson (exc); *Bellini:* Norma (exc); Puritani (exc); Sonnambula (exc); *Rossini:* Semiramide (exc); *Gounod:* Faust (exc); Roméo et Juliette (exc); *Verdi:* Otello (exc); Traviata (exc); Rigoletto (exc); *Mozart:* Entführung (exc); *A. Thomas:* Hamlet (exc); *Delibes:* Lakmé (exc); *Meyerbeer:* Huguenots (exc). (J. Sutherland, ROH Chor, ROHO/F. Molinari-Pradelli)

Ⓓ **425 520-2DH3** (9/89)
Rossini—Il barbiere di Siviglia
Rossini: Barbiere di Siviglia (Cpte). (L. Nucci, C. Bartoli, W. Matteuzzi, E. Fissore, P. Burchuladze, G. Banditelli, M. Pertusi, Bologna Teatro Comunale Chor, Bologna Teatro Comunale Orch/G. Patanè)

Ⓓ **425 531-2DM2** (3/90)
Puccini—Madama Butterfly
Puccini: Madama Butterfly (Cpte). (R. Tebaldi, C. Bergonzi, E. Sordello, F. Cossotto, A. Mercuriali, M. Cazzato, L. Nerozzi, P. Washington, O. Nanni, V. Carbonari, Santa Cecilia Academy Chor, Santa Cecilia Academy Orch/T. Serafin)

Ⓓ **425 534-2DM2** (2/90)
Puccini—(La) Bohème
Puccini: Bohème (Cpte). (R. Tebaldi, C. Bergonzi, G. d'Angelo, E. Bastianini, R. Cesari, C. Siepi, F. Corena, P. de Palma, A. d'Orazi, Santa Cecilia Academy Chor, Santa Cecilia Academy Orch/T. Serafin)

Ⓓ **425 628-2DH2** (12/89)
Verdi—Simon Boccanegra
Verdi: Simon Boccanegra (Cpte). (L. Nucci, K. Te Kanawa, G. Aragall, P. Burchuladze, P. Coni, C. Colombara, E. Gavazzi, A. Zoroberto, La Scala Chor, La Scala Orch/G. Solti)

Ⓓ **425 651-2DM3** (8/90)
Massenet—Esclarmonde
Massenet: Esclarmonde (Cpte). (J. Sutherland, G. Aragall, H. Tourangeau, R. Davies, L. Quilico, R. Lloyd, I. Caley, G. Clark, C. Grant, Finchley Children's Music Group, John Alldis Ch, National PO/R. Bonynge)

Ⓓ **425 681-2DM2** (7/90) ▭ **425 681-4DM2** (7/90)
Tutto Pavarotti
Dalla: Caruso; *Di Capua:* O sole mio; *Cardillo:* Core 'ngrato; *Tosti:* 'A vucchella; *V. Valente:* Passione; *Bixio:* Mamma; *Adam:* Minuit, Chrétiens (exc); *Bizet:* Agnus Dei; *Rossini:* Stabat mater (exc); *Verdi:* Aida (exc); *Donizetti:* Elisir d'amore (exc); Don Pasquale (exc); *Verdi:* Luisa Miller (exc); Traviata (exc); Trovatore (exc); Rigoletto (exc); Ballo in maschera (exc); *Ponchielli:* Gioconda (exc); *Flotow:* Martha (exc); *Bizet:* Carmen (exc); *Massenet:* Werther (exc); *Meyerbeer:* Africaine (exc); *Boito:* Mefistofele (exc); *Leoncavallo:* Pagliacci (exc); *Giordano:* Fedora (exc); *Puccini:* Fanciulla del West (exc); Manon Lescaut (exc); *Mascagni:* Cavalleria Rusticana (exc); *Puccini:* Tosca (exc); Bohème (exc); Turandot (exc). (L. Pavarotti, National PO/G. Chiaramello, Bologna Teatro Comunale Orch/A. Guadagno/H. Mancini/K.H. Adler, LSO/I. Kertész, Vienna Volksoper Orch/L. Magiera, ECO/R. Bonynge, Ambrosian Sngrs, New Philh, Vienna Op Orch/E. Downes, G. Flossmann, P. Baillie, Vienna Op Chor/N. Rescigno, K. Battle, R. Lloyd, M. King, London Op Chor/G. Solti/O. de Fabritiis, J. Varady, I. Bormida/G. Gavazzeni, BPO/H. von Karajan, John Alldis Ch, LPO/Z. Mehta, orch)

Ⓓ **425 713-2LM** (9/90)
Britten—Prodigal Son
Britten: Prodigal Son (Cpte). (P. Pears, J. Shirley-Quirk, B. Drake, R. Tear, EOG Chor, EOG Orch/B. Britten)

Ⓓ **425 720-2DM** (12/90)
Purcell—Dido and Aeneas
Purcell: Dido (Cpte). (J. Baker, R. Herincx, P. Clark, M. Sinclair, E. Poulter, R. James, C. Wilson, D. Dorow, J. Mitchinson, St Anthony Sngrs, ECO/A. Lewis)

Ⓓ **425 815-2DH2** (9/90)
Cilea—Adriana Lecouvreur
Cilea: Adriana Lecouvreur (Cpte). (J. Sutherland, C. Bergonzi, L. Nucci, C. Ciurca, F.E. d'Artegna, M. Sénéchal, F. Ginzer, D. Stuart-Roberts, P. Bronder, B. Terfel, C. Cue, WNO Chor, WNO Orch/R. Bonynge)

Ⓓ **425 847-2DWO** ▭ **425 847-4DWO**
Your hunded best tunes vol. 1
Handel: Solomon (exc); *Schubert:* Ave Maria, D839; *Bach:* Cantata 147 (exc); *Pachelbel:* Canon and Gigue (exc); *Malotte:* Lord's Prayer; *Mozart:* Serenade, K525 (exc); *Mendelssohn:* Violin Concerto, Op.64 (exc); *Puccini:* Madama Butterfly (exc); *Tchaikovsky:* Nutcracker Suite (exc); *Grieg:* Piano Concerto (exc); *Verdi:* Nabucco (exc); *Elgar:* Pomp and Circumstance Marches (exc). (ASMF/N. Marriner, J. Sutherland, Ambrosian Sngrs/R. Bonynge, St John's College Ch/G. Guest, Stuttgart CO/K. Münchinger, S. Burrows/W. Morris, R. Ricci, LSO/P. Gamba, R. Tebaldi, Santa Cecilia Academy Orch/T. Serafin, VPO/H. von Karajan, R. Lupu/A. Previn, Vienna St Op Chor, Vienna Op Orch/L. Gardelli, LPO/G. Solti, New PO)

Ⓓ **425 848-2DWO** ▭ **425 848-4DWO**
Your hundred best tunes vol 2
Offenbach: Orphée aux enfers (exc); *J. Strauss II:* Casanova (exc); *Bach:* Cantata 208 (exc); *Beethoven:* Bagatelles (exc); *Sullivan:* Lost Chord; *Grétry:* Zémire et Azor (exc); *Verdi:* Rigoletto (exc); *Mascagni:* Cavalleria Rusticana (exc); *Clarke:* Suite in D (exc); *Handel:* Messiah (exc); *Parry:* Jerusalem; *Verdi:* Traviata (exc); *Beethoven:* Piano Concerto 5 (exc); *Vaughan Williams:* Greensleeves Fantasia. (SRO/E. Ansermet, J. Sutherland, Ambrosian Light Op Chor, New PO/R. Bonynge, Stuttgart CO/K. Münchinger, Vladimir Ashkenazy, S. Burrows, Ambrosian Sngrs/W. Morris, Richard Hickox Orch/R. Hickox, L. Pavarotti, LSO, National PO/G. Gavazzeni, PJBE, K. Te Kanawa, Chicago SO/G. Solti, Canterbury Cath Ch/A. Wicks, ASMF/N. Marriner)

Ⓓ **425 849-2DWO** ▭ **425 849-4DWO**
Your hundred best tunes vol 3
Grieg: Peer Gynt (exc); *Roberton:* All in the April Evening; *Verdi:* Aida (exc); *Massenet:* Thaïs (exc); *S. Adams:* Holy City; *Mendelssohn:* Elijah (exc); *Stainer:* Crucifixion (exc); *Rachmaninov:* Piano Concerto 2 (exc); *Godard:* Jocelyn (exc); *Dvořák:* Symphony 9 (exc); *Bizet:* Pêcheurs de Perles (exc). (VPO/H. von Karajan, Treorchy Male Ch, Santa Cecilia Academy Chor, Santa Cecilia Academy Orch/C. Franci, N. Kennedy, National PO/R. Bonynge, S. Burrows, Ambrosian Sngrs/W. Morris, K. Ferrier, Boyd Neel Orch/B. Neel, St John's College Ch/G. Guest, Vladimir Ashkenazy, LSO/A. Previn, K. McKellar, Orch/P. Knight/I. Kertész, L. Pavarotti, N. Ghiaurov/R. Stapleton)

Ⓓ **425 850-2DWO** ▭ **425 850-4DWO**
Your Hundred Best Tunes, Vol.4
Mendelssohn: Hebrides; *Puccini:* Bohème (exc); *Rodrigo:* Concierto de Aranjuez (exc); *Balfe:* Bohemian Girl (exc); *Hoffstetter:* String Quartets, Op. 3 (exc); *Sullivan:* Gondoliers (exc); *Ketèlbey:* Sanctuary of the Heart; *Gounod:* Ave Maria; *J. Seymour Irvine:* Lord's my Shepherd; *Traditional:* Blow the Wind Southerly; Londonderry Air; *Sibelius:* Karelia Suite (exc); *Debussy:* Suite bergamasque (exc); *Beethoven:* Symphony 9 (exc). (VPO/C. von Dohnányi, L. Pavarotti, BPO/H. von Karajan, C. Bonell, Montreal SO/C. Dutoit, J. Sutherland, LSO/R. Bonynge, Stuttgart CO/K. Münchinger, T. Round, D'Oyly Carte Op Chor, D'Oyly Carte Op Orch, New SO/I. Godfrey, RPO/E. Rogers, L. Price, Huddersfield Choral Soc/W. Morris, K. Ferrier, PJBE, Philh/Vladimir Ashkenazy, P. Rogé, P. Lorengar, Y. Minton, S. Burrows, M. Talvela, Chicago Sym Chor, Chicago SO/G. Solti)

Ⓓ **425 851-2DWO** ▭ **425 851-4DWO**
Your hundred best tunes vol 5
Mozart: Nozze di Figaro (exc); *Handel:* Serse (exc); *Mozart:* Ave verum corpus, K618; *Gounod:* Mors et Vita (exc); *Handel:* Tolomeo (exc); *Beethoven:* Romances (exc); *Canteloube:* Chants d'Auvergne (exc); *Rimsky-Korsakov:* Scheherazade (exc); *Tchaikovsky:* Piano Concerto 1 (exc); *Brahms:* Lieder, Op. 49 (exc); *Monk:* Abide with me; *Mozart:* Horn Concerti (exc); *Handel:* Messiah (exc). (LPO/G. Solti, LSO/G. Szell, St John's College Ch/G. Guest, Richard Hickox Orch/R. Hickox, K. McKellar, ROHO/A. Boult/W. Boskovsky, Vienna Mozart Ens, K. Te Kanawa, ECO/J. Tate/L. Stokowski, Vladimir Ashkenazy/L. Maazel, R. Tebaldi, New PO/A. Guadagno, King's College Ch/S. Cleobury, B. Tuckwell/P. Maag, ASMF Chor, ASMF/N. Marriner)

Ⓓ **425 852-2DWO** ▭ **425 852-4DWO**
Your hundred best tunes vol 6
Rossini: Gazza ladra (exc); *Zeller:* Obersteiger (exc); *Mozart:* Piano Concerto 21 (exc); *E. Nevin:* Rosary; *Bach:* Toccata and Fugue, BWV565; *Handel:* Coronation Anthems (exc); *J. Strauss II:* Blauen Donau, Op. 314. (National PO/R. Chailly, H. Gueden, Vienna Operetta Chor, Vienna St Op Orch/R. Stolz, R. Lupu, ECO/U. Segal, S. Burrows, J. Constable, P. Hurford, King's College Ch/D. Willcocks, VPO/W. Boskovsky)

Ⓓ **425 853-2DWO** ▭ **425 853-4DWO**
Your hundred best tunes vol 7
Suppé: Dichter und Bauer (exc); *Dvořák:* Rusalka (exc); *Wagner:* Lohengrin (exc); *Schubert:* Deutsche messe (exc); *Handel:* Water Music Suite (exc); *Dvořák:* Symphony 9 (exc); *Sibelius:* Finlandia; *Liszt:* Liebesträume, S541 (exc); *Tchaikovsky:* Songs, Op. 6 (exc); *Allegri:* Miserere mei (exc); *Mozart:* Clarinet Concerto, K622 (exc); *Tchaikovsky:* 1812 (exc). (VPO/G. Solti, P. Lorengar, Santa Cecilia Academy Orch/G. Patanè/H. Stein, St Paul's Cath Ch, C. Dearnley, LSO/G. Szell, S. Burrows, Ambrosian Sngrs/W. Morris, Philh/Vladimir Ashkenazy, J. Bolet, N. Ghiaurov, Z. Ghiaurov, King's College Ch/D. Willcocks, G. de Peyer/P. Maag, Los Angeles PO/Z. Mehta)

Ⓓ **425 854-2DWO** ▭ **425 854-4DWO**
Youtr Hundred Best Tunes, Vol. 8
Schubert: Rosamunde (exc); *Saint-Saëns:* Samson et Dalila (exc); *Beethoven:* Piano Sonata 14 (exc); *Mendelssohn:* Hear my prayer; *Albinoni:* Adagio; *Franck:* Panis angelicus; *Beethoven:* Symphony 6 (exc); *Tchaikovsky:* Romeo and Juliet (exc); *Bruch:* Violin Concerto 1 (exc); *Traditional:* Battle Hymn of the Republic. (VPO/K. Münchinger, M. Horne, Vienna Op Orch/H. Lewis, Vladimir Ashkenazy, A. Roberts, St John's College Ch, P. White/G. Guest, Richard Hickox Orch/R. Hickox, L. Pavarotti, Wandsworth Sch Boys' Ch, National PO/K. H. Adler, Chicago SO/G. Solti/H. von Karajan, K-W. Chung, RPO/R. Kempe, R. Merrill, London Fest Chor, London Fest Orch/S. Black)

Ⓓ **425 864-2DH2** (1/90)
Verdi—Rigoletto
Verdi: Rigoletto (Cpte). (L. Nucci, J. Anderson, L. Pavarotti, N. Ghiaurov, S. Verrett, N. de Carolis, V. Mosca, P. de Palma, R. Scaltriti, A.C. Antonacci, C. de Bortoli, M. Laurenza, Bologna Teatro Comunale Chor, Bologna Teatro Comunale Orch/R. Chailly)

Ⓓ **425 950-2DM3** (5/90)
R. Strauss—Rosenkavalier
R. Strauss: Rosenkavalier (Cpte). (M. Reining, S. Jurinac, L. Weber, H. Gueden, A. Poell, A. Dermota, H. Rössl-Majdan, P. Klein, J. Hellwig, B. Seidl, F. Bierbach, W.

Berry, H. Pröglhöf, A. Jaresch, E. Majkut, W. Loibner, E. Hochstätter, M. Trupp, A. Buchbauer, L. Fleck, F. Maier, O. Vajda, W. Daucha, R. Stumper, F. Erbner, F. Settmacher, Vienna St Op Chor, VPO/E. Kleiber)

Ⓓ **425 959-2DM** (4/90)
Lisa della Casa sings R. Strauss
R. Strauss: Vier letzte Lieder; Arabella (exc); Arabella (exc); Ariadne auf Naxos (exc); Capriccio (exc). (L. della Casa, H. Gueden, P. Schoeffler, A. Poell, F. Bierbach, VPO/K. Böhm/R. Moralt/H. Hollreiser)

Ⓓ **425 964-2DM** (6/90)
Rachmaninov from Ampico Piano Rolls
Rachmaninov: Morceaux de fantaisie, Op.3; Morceaux de salon, Op.10 (exc); Preludes (exc); Etudes-tableaux, Op.39 (exc); Lilacs; Polka de W. R.; *Mussorgsky:* Gopak; *Schubert:* Schöne Müllerin (exc); *Rimsky-Korsakov:* Tale of Tsar Saltan (exc); *Various:* National Anthems (exc); *Kreisler:* Liebesleid; Liebesfreud. (S. Rachmaninov)

Ⓓ **425 985-2DM**
Mascagni—Cavalleria Rusticana
Mascagni: Cavalleria Rusticana (Cpte). (R. Tebaldi, J. Björling, E. Bastianini, L. Dani, R. Corsi, MMF Chor, MMF Orch/A. Erede)

Ⓓ **430 038-2DM3** (10/90)
Donizetti: La favorita
Donizetti: Favorita (Cpte). (F. Cossotto, L. Pavarotti, G. Bacquier, N. Ghiaurov, I. Cotrubas, P. de Palma, Bologna Teatro Comunale Chor, Bologna Teatro Comunale Orch/R. Bonynge)

Ⓓ **430 042-2DM3**
Ponchielli—La Gioconda
Ponchielli: Gioconda (Cpte). (R. Tebaldi, C. Bergonzi, R. Merrill, O. Dominguez, N. Ghiuselev, M. Horne, S. Maionica, P. De Palma, Santa Cecilia Academy Chor, Santa Cecilia Academy Orch/L. Gardelli)

Ⓓ **430 066-2DH2** (5/91)
Gay: The Beggar's Opera
Gay: Beggar's Opera (Cpte). (K. Te Kanawa, J. Morris, J. Sutherland, S. Dean, A. Marks, A. Lansbury, R. Resnik, A. Rolfe Johnson, G. Clark, A. Murray, A. Wilkens, J. Gibbs, W. Mitchell, M. Hordern, London Voices, National PO/R. Bonynge)

Ⓓ **430 075-2DH** (3/90)
Weill—(Das) Dreigroschenoper
Weill: Dreigroschenoper (Cpte). (R. Kollo, U. Lemper, Milva, M. Adorf, H. Dernesch, W. Reichmann, S. Tremper, R. Boysen, Berlin RIAS Chbr Ch, Berlin RIAS Sinfonietta/J. Mauceri)

Ⓓ **430 091-2DWO** (6/91) ▭ **430 091-4DWO** (6/91)
The World of the Organ
Widor: Symphony 5 (exc); *Bach:* Schübler Chorales, BWV645-650 (exc); *Mozart:* Fantasia, K608; *Walton:* Crown Imperial; *Clarke:* Suite in D (exc); *Handel:* Saul (exc); *Purcell:* Choice Collection of Lessons (exc); *Elgar:* Imperial March; *Vierne:* Symphony 1 (exc); *Wagner:* Tannhäuser (exc); *Guilmant:* March, Op. 15; *Schumann:* Pedal Studies, Op. 56 (exc); *Karg-Elert:* Choral-Improvisationen, Op. 65 (exc). (S. Preston)

Ⓓ **430 095-2DWO** (6/91) ▭ **430 095-4DWO** (6/91)
The World of Gilbert & Sullivan, Vol.1
Sullivan: HMS Pinafore (exc); Mikado (exc); Yeomen of the Guard (exc); Pirates of Penzance (exc); Iolanthe (exc); Gondoliers (exc). (J. Reed, J. Skitch, J. Wright, G. Knight, J. Hindmarsh, D'Oyly Carte Op Chor, New SO/I. Godfrey, C. Wright, V. Masterson, P.A. Jones, P. Wales, RPO/R. Nash, E. Harwood/M. Sargent, O. Brannigan, J. Allister, D. Adams, T. Round, A. Styler, J. Toye)

Ⓓ **430 096-2DWO** (6/91) ▭ **430 096-4DWO** (6/91)
The World of Kathleen Ferrier
Traditional: Blow the wind southerly; Keel row; *Anon:* My bonny lad; *Bridge:* Go not happy day; *Britten:* Folk Songs (exc); *Traditional:* Kitty my love; *Handel:* Rodelinda (exc); Serse (exc); *Gluck:* Orfeo ed Euridice (exc); *Mendelssohn:* Elijah (exc); *Bach:* St Matthew Passion, BWV244 (exc); *Schubert:* Gretchen am Spinnrade, D118; Junge Nonne, D828; An die Musik, D547; Musensohn, D764; *Brahms:* Lieder, Op. 94 (exc); Lieder, Op. 47 (exc); *Mahler:* Rückert Lieder (exc). (K. Ferrier, P. Spurr, F. Stone, LSO/M. Sargent, Boyd Neel Orch/B. Neel, National SO, VPO/B. Walter)

Ⓓ **430 168-2DH** (4/91)
Ute Lemper sings Kurt Weill
Weill: Sieben Todsünden (Cpte); Mahagonny-Gesänge (Cpte). (U. Lemper, H. Wildhaber, P. Haage, T. Mohr, M. Jungwirth, S. Tremper, Berlin RIAS Sinfonietta/J. Mauceri)

Ⓓ **430 226-2DH** (4/91)
Verdi—Choruses
Verdi: Nabucco (exc); Lombardi (exc); Macbeth (exc); Masnadieri (exc); Trovatore (exc); Traviata (exc); Ballo in maschera (exc); Don Carlo (exc); Aida (exc); Otello (exc); Requiem (exc). (Chicago Sym Chor, Chicago SO/G. Solti)

OO **430 226-5DH**
Verdi—Choruses
Verdi: Nabucco (exc); Lombardi (exc); Macbeth (exc); Masnadieri (exc); Trovatore (exc); Traviata (exc); Ballo in maschera (exc); Don Carlo (exc); Aida (exc); Otello (exc); Requiem (exc). (Chicago Sym Chor, Chicago SO/G. Solti)

Ⓓ **430 250-2DM2** (8/91)
Verdi—La Traviata
Verdi: Traviata (Cpte). (R. Tebaldi, G. Poggi, A. Protti, A. Vercelli, R. Cavallari, P. de Palma, A. Sacchetti, D. Caselli, I. Sardi, M. Bianchi, L. Mancini, Santa Cecilia Academy Chor, Santa Cecilia Academy Orch/F. Molinari-Pradelli)

Ⓓ **430 253-2DM2** (8/91)
Puccini—Manon Lescaut
Puccini: Manon Lescaut (Cpte). (R. Tebaldi, M. del Monaco, M. Borriello, F. Corena, P. de Palma, L. Ribacchi, A. Sacchetti, A. Zagonara, A. Mercuriali, D. Caselli, Santa Cecilia Academy Chor, Santa Cecilia Academy Orch/F. Molinari-Pradelli)

Ⓓ **430 256-2DM2** (8/91)
Cilea—Adriana Lecouvreur
Cilea: Adriana Lecouvreur (Cpte). (R. Tebaldi, M. del Monaco, G. Fioravanti, G. Simionato, S. Maionica, F. Ricciardi, D. Carral, F. Cadoni, A. Mercuriali, G. Foiani, Santa Cecilia Academy Chor, Santa Cecilia Academy Orch/F. Capuana)

Ⓓ **430 261-2DM** (2/92) ▭ **430 261-4DM** (2/92)
Handel—Orchestral Works
Handel: Concerti grossi, Op. 3; Alcina (exc); Ariodante (exc). (ASMF/N. Marriner)

Ⓓ **430 370-2DH** (9/92)
R. Strauss—Works for Horn
R. Strauss: Horn Concerto 1; Horn Concerto 2; Andante, Av86a; Capriccio (exc); Alphorn; Introduction, Theme and Variations. (B. Tuckwell, M. McLaughlin, RPO/Vladimir Ashkenazy, Vladimir Ashkenazy)

Ⓓ **430 372-2DH2** (10/91)
Janáček—Operatic and Orchestral Works
Janáček: Makropulos Affair (Cpte); Lachian Dances. (E. Söderström, P. Dvorský, V. Krejčík, A. Czaková, V. Zítek, Z. Švehla, D. Jedlička, J. Joran, I. Mixová, B. Blachut, B. Vítková, Vienna St Op Chor, VPO/C. Mackerras, LPO/F. Huybrechts)

Ⓓ **430 375-2DH2** (10/91)
Janáček—Operatic and Orchestral Works
Janáček: From the House of the Dead (Cpte); Mládí; Nursery rhymes (Cpte). (D. Jedlička, J. Janská, J. Zahradníček, V. Krejčík, R. Novák, A. Švorc, B. Blachut, I. Žídek, J. Souček, E. Zikmundová, Z. Soušek, V. Zítek, Z. Švehla, Vienna St Op Chor, VPO/C. Mackerras, London Sinfonietta Chor, London Sinfonietta/D. Atherton)

Ⓓ **430 381-2DM2** (1/92)
R.Strauss—Die Aegyptische Helena
R. Strauss: Aegyptische Helena (Cpte). (G. Jones, M. Kastu, D. Bryant, B. Hendricks, W. White, C. Rayam, B. Lane, G. Kirkland, P. Dell, M. Cimarella, K. Grimshaw, K. Jewell Chorale, Detroit SO/A. Dorati)

Ⓓ **430 384-2DM2** (5/92)
R. Strauss—Ariadne auf Naxos
R. Strauss: Ariadne auf Naxos (Cpte). (L. Price, T. Troyanos, E. Gruberová, R. Kollo, W. Berry, B. McDaniel, M. Jungwirth, G. Unger, K. Equiluz, D. Cook, E. Hartle, N. Burrowes, H. Zednik, E. Kunz, A. Sramek, P. Weber, G. Tichy, LPO/G. Solti)

Ⓓ **430 387-2DM2** (5/92)
R. Strauss—Arabella
R. Strauss: Arabella (Cpte). (L. della Casa, H. Gueden, G. London, O. Edelmann, I. Malaniuk, A. Dermota, W. Kmentt, E. Waechter, H. Pröglhöf, M. Coertse, Vienna St Op Chor, VPO/G. Solti)

Ⓓ **430 391-2DM3** (5/92)
Wagner—Die Walküre
Wagner: Walküre (Cpte). (J. Vickers, G. Brouwenstijn, B. Nilsson, G. London, R. Gorr, D. Ward, M. Collier, Judith Pierce, J. Malyon, M. Elkins, J. Veasey, N. Berry, M. Guy, J. Edwards, LSO/E. Leinsdorf)

Ⓓ **430 433-2DH** (10/90) ▭ **430 433-4DH** (10/90)
Carreras, Domingo and Pavarotti in Concert
Cilea: Arlesiana (exc); *Cardillo:* Core 'ngrato; *Lara:* Granada; *Giordano:* Andrea Chénier (exc); *Meyerbeer:* Africaine (exc); *Lehár:* Land des Lächelns (exc); *Puccini:* Tosca (exc); Turandot (exc); Turandot (exc); *Crescenzo:* Rondine al nido; *De Curtis:* Torna a Surriento; *Sorozábal:* Tabernera del puerto (exc); *Bernstein:* West Side Story (exc); *Mendoza y Cortez:* Cielito lindo; *A. Lloyd Webber:* Cats (exc); *Louiguy:* Vie en rose; *Leoncavallo:* Mattinata; *Lacalle:* Amapola; *Di Capua:* O sole mio; *Filiberto:* Caminito; *Annibale:* 'O paese d' 'o sole. (J. Carreras, P. Domingo, L. Pavarotti, MMF Orch, Rome Op Orch/Z. Mehta)

OO **430 433-5DH**
Carreras, Domingo and Pavarotti in Concert
Cilea: Arlesiana (exc); *Cardillo:* Core 'ngrato; *Lara:* Granada; *Giordano:* Andrea Chénier (exc); *Meyerbeer:* Africaine (exc); *Lehár:* Land des Lächelns (exc); *Puccini:* Tosca (exc); Turandot (exc); Turandot (exc); *Crescenzo:* Rondine al nido; *De Curtis:* Torna a Surriento; *Sorozábal:* Tabernera del puerto (exc); *Bernstein:* West Side Story (exc); *Mendoza y Cortez:* Cielito lindo; *A. Lloyd Webber:* Cats (exc); *Louiguy:* Vie en rose; *Leoncavallo:* Mattinata; *Lacalle:* Amapola; *Di Capua:* O sole mio; *Filiberto:* Caminito; *Annibale:* 'O paese d' 'o sole. (J. Carreras, P. Domingo, L. Pavarotti, MMF Orch, Rome Op Orch/Z. Mehta)

Ⓓ **430 448-2DM** (5/91)
The Solti Collection—Wagner Overtures
Wagner: Fliegende Holländer (exc); Tannhäuser (exc); Meistersinger (exc); Tristan und Isolde (exc). (Chicago SO/G. Solti)

Ⓓ **430 470-2DH** ▭ **430 470-4DH**
Essential Pavarotti II
Verdi: Rigoletto (exc); *Puccini:* Tosca (exc); *Verdi:* Traviata (exc); *Giordano:* Fedora (exc); *Meyerbeer:* Africaine (exc); *Puccini:* Fanciulla del West (exc); Manon Lescaut (exc); *Massenet:* Werther (exc); *Verdi:* Aida (exc); *Puccini:* Bohème (exc); *Tosti:* Marechiare; *Schubert:* Ave Maria, D839; *Tosti:* Serenata; *Franck:* Panis angelicus; *Mancini:* In un palco della scala; *T. Giordani:* Caro mio ben; *Bixio:* Mamma; *Puccini:* Turandot (exc). (L. Pavarotti, LSO/R. Bonynge, National PO/N. Rescigno, J. Sutherland, London Op Chor/O. de Fabritiis, La Scala Orch, M. Freni, BPO/H. von Karajan/G. Chiaramello/K.H. Adler, Bologna Teatro Comunale Orch, Wandsworth Sch Boys' Ch, orch/H. Mancini, Philh/P. Gamba, RPO)

Ⓓ **430 481-2DX2** (8/91)
Renata Tebaldi sings Opera Arias
Puccini: Madama Butterfly (exc); Bohème (exc); Tosca (exc); *Boito:* Mefistofele (exc); *Verdi:* Aida (exc); Otello (exc); Trovatore (exc); Forza del destino (exc); *Rossini:* Guillaume Tell (exc); *Cilea:* Adriana Lecouvreur (exc); *Refice:* Cecilia (exc); *Puccini:* Gianni Schicchi (exc); Suor Angelica (exc); *Giordano:* Andrea Chénier (exc); *Catalani:* Wally (exc); *Verdi:* Don Carlo (exc); Ballo in maschera (exc); Giovanna d'Arco (exc); *Puccini:* Turandot (exc); *Ponchielli:* Gioconda (exc); *Puccini:* Rondine (exc); *Mascagni:* Cavalleria Rusticana (exc); *Cilea:* Arlesiana (exc). (R. Tebaldi, Santa Cecilia Academy Orch/T. Serafin, C. Bergonzi/F. Molinari-Pradelli, VPO/H. von Karajan, A.R. Satre, A. Cesarini, Geneva Grand Th Orch/A. Erede, MMF Orch/L. Gardelli/G. Gavazzeni, Monte Carlo Nat Op Orch/F. Cleva, New Philh/O. de Fabritiis)

Ⓓ **430 491-2DH2** ▭ **430 491-4DH**
Verdi—La Traviata
Verdi: Traviata (Cpte). (J. Sutherland, L. Pavarotti, M. Manuguerra, D. Jones, M. Lambriks, A. Oliver, J. Summers, J. Tomlinson, G. Tadeo, W. Elvin, D. Wilson-Johnson, London Op Chor, National PO/R. Bonynge)

Ⓓ **430 498-2DWO** (6/91) ▭ **430 498-4DWO** (6/91)
The World of Mozart
Mozart: Serenade, K525 (exc); Piano Concerto 21 (exc); Nozze di Figaro (exc); Symphony 40 (exc); Piano Sonata, K331 (exc); Così fan tutte (exc); Clarinet Concerto, K622 (exc); Ave verum corpus, K618; Maurerische Trauermusik, K477; Requiem (exc); Symphony 25 (exc); Musikalischer Spass (exc). (ASMF/N. Marriner, Vladimir Ashkenazy (pf/dir), Philh, K. Te Kanawa, LPO/G. Solti, COE, A. Schiff, L. Popp, B. Fassbaender, T. Krause, Vienna Op Orch/I. Kertész, G. de Peyer, LSO/P. Maag, St John's College Ch, P. White/G. Guest, ASMF Chor, Vienna Mozart Ens/W. Boskovsky)

Ⓓ **430 500-2DWO** (10/91) ▭ **430 500-4DWO** (10/91)
World of Handel
Handel: Solomon (exc); Rodelinda (exc); Judas Maccabaeus (exc); Water Music - Suite (exc); Semele (exc); Berenice (exc); Samson (exc); Israel in Egypt (exc); Organ Concertos (exc); Coronation Anthems (exc); Messiah (exc). (ASMF/N. Marriner, Handel Op Chor, RPO/C. Farncombe, LSO/G. Szell, K. McKellar, ROHO/A. Boult, J. Sutherland/F. Molinari-Pradelli, G. Malcolm, King's College Ch, ECO/D. Willcocks, A. Reynolds, M. Horne, Vienna Cantata Orch/H. Lewis, ASMF Chor)

Ⓓ **430 502-2DH2** (3/91)
Debussy—Pelléas et Mélisande
Debussy: Pelléas et Mélisande (Cpte). (D. Henry, C. Alliot-Lugaz, G. Cachemaille, P. Thau, C. Carlson, F. Golfier, P. Ens, Montreal Sym Chor, Montreal SO/C. Dutoit)

Ⓓ **430 513-2DH** (12/91) ⊟ **430 513-4DH**
Mozart—Arias
Mozart: Nozze di Figaro (exc); Chi sà, K582; Così fan tutte (exc); Alma grande e nobil core, K578; Don Giovanni (exc); Clemenza di Tito (exc); Ch'io mi scordi di te, K505. (C. Bartoli, A. Schiff, Vienna CO/G. Fischer)

Ⓓ **430 549-2DM4**
Meyerbeer—Les Huguenots
Meyerbeer: Huguenots (Cpte). (J. Sutherland, M. Arroyo, H. Tourangeau, G. Bacquier, D. Cossa, J. Ward, J. Gibbs, J. Noble, J. Wakefield, G. Thomas, A. Vrenios, N. Ghiuselev, C. Grant, J. Coster, K. Te Kanawa, J. Clément, A. Auger, M. Lehane, A. Opie, Ambrosian Op Chor, New PO/R. Bonynge)

Ⓓ **430 636-2DM2** (4/92)
Massenet—Don Quichotte
Massenet: Don Quichotte (Cpte); Scènes alsaciennes. (N. Ghiaurov, G. Bacquier, R. Crespin, M. Command, A. Dutertre, P. Garazzi, J-M. Frémeau, J. Loreau, Suisse Romande Rad Chor, SRO/K. Kord, National PO/R. Bonynge)

Ⓓ **430 694-2DHO2** (7/95)
Verdi—Il trovatore
Verdi: Trovatore (Cpte). (L. Pavarotti, A. Banaudi, L. Nucci, S. Verrett, F. E. d'Artegna, B. Frittoli, P. de Palma, R. Scaltriti, E. Facini, MMF Chor, MMF Orch/Z. Mehta)

Ⓓ **430 712-2DM** (8/91)
American Orchestral Works
Grofé: Grand Canyon Suite; *Gershwin:* Porgy and Bess Suite. (Detroit SO/A. Dorati)

Ⓓ **430 716-2DM** (8/91) ⊟ **430 716-4DM** (8/91)
Pavarotti—Gala Concert at the Albert Hall
Puccini: Tosca (exc); Turandot (exc); *De Curtis:* Torna a Surriento; *Verdi:* Macbeth (exc); Giorno di Regno (exc); Lombardi (exc); Luisa Miller (exc); *Donizetti:* Lucia di Lammermoor (exc); *Cilea:* Arlesiana (exc); *Berlioz:* Troyens (exc). (L. Pavarotti, RPO/K.H. Adler)

Ⓓ **430 718-2DM** (8/91)
French Ballet Music
Gounod: Faust (exc); *Offenbach:* Gaîté Parisienne (Cpte). (Montreal SO/C. Dutoit)

Ⓓ **430 721-2DM** (12/91)
Beethoven—Orchestral Works
Beethoven: Symphony 6; Egmont (exc); Leonore (exc). (Philh/Vladimir Ashkenazy)

Ⓓ **430 724-2DM** (12/91)
Great Operatic Duets
Verdi: Traviata (exc); *Puccini:* Tosca (exc); *Ponchielli:* Gioconda (exc); *Bellini:* Norma (exc); *Verdi:* Ballo in maschera (exc); *Puccini:* Manon Lescaut (exc); *Verdi:* Otello (exc). (J. Sutherland, L. Pavarotti, K. Te Kanawa, G. Aragall, M. Caballé, A. Baltsa, S. Milnes, M. Price, J. Carreras, London Op Chor, National PO, Bologna Teatro Comunale Orch, NYC Op Orch/R. Bonynge/G. Solti/B. Bartoletti/R. Chailly)

Ⓓ **430 773-2DC4** (4/92)
Schubert—Complete Symphonies, etc
Schubert: Symphony 1; Symphony 2; Symphony 3; Symphony 4; Symphony 5; Symphony 6; Symphony 8; Symphony 9; Overture, D591; Teufels Lustschloss (exc); Fierrabras (exc). (VPO/I. Kertész)

Ⓓ **430 792-2DC6** (4/92)
Beethoven—Complete Symphonies, etc
Beethoven: Symphony 1; Symphony 2; Symphony 3; Symphony 4; Symphony 5; Symphony 6; Symphony 7; Symphony 8; Symphony 9; Egmont (exc); Coriolan; Leonore (exc). (P. Lorengar, Y. Minton, S. Burrows, M. Talvela, Chicago Sym Chor, Chicago SO/G. Solti)

Ⓓ **433 033-2DM2** (3/92)
Giordano & Zandonai—Operas
Giordano: Fedora (Cpte); *Zandonai:* Francesca da Rimini (exc). (M. Olivero, M. del Monaco, T. Gobbi, S. Maionica, L. Cappellino, R. Cassinelli, P. Binder, K. Te Kanawa, L. Monreale, V. Carbonari, A. Cesarini, L. Monreale, A. Bokatti, S. Caspari, P. Rogers, P. de Palma, M. Olivero, M. del Monaco, V. Carbonari, A. Gasparini, A. Cesarini/N. Rescigno, Monte Carlo Op Chor, Monte Carlo Nat Op Orch/L. Gardelli)

Ⓓ **433 036-2DM2** (10/92)
Donizetti/Cimarosa—Operas
Donizetti: Don Pasquale (Cpte); *Cimarosa:* Maestro di cappella (Cpte). (F. Corena, G. Sciutti, J. Oncina, T. Krause, A. Mercuriali, F. Corena, Vienna St Op Chor, Vienna St Op Orch, ROHO/I. Kertész/A. Quadri)

Ⓓ **433 064-2DWO**
Your Hundred Best Opera Tunes Volume I
Puccini: Turandot (exc); *Bizet:* Carmen (exc); *Verdi:* Trovatore (exc); *Puccini:* Bohème (exc); *Giordano:* Fedora (exc); *Gounod:* Faust (exc); *Verdi:* Rigoletto (exc); *Puccini:* Madama Butterfly (exc); *Gounod:* Faust (exc); *Mozart:* Nozze di Figaro (exc); *Rossini:* Barbiere di Siviglia (exc); *Bizet:* Carmen (exc); *Donizetti:* Lucia di Lammermoor (exc); *G. Charpentier:* Louise (exc); *Tchaikovsky:* Eugene Onegin (exc). (L. Pavarotti, John Alldis Ch, LPO/Z. Mehta, M. Horne, Vienna Op Orch/H. Lewis, J. Sutherland, London Op Chor, National PO/R. Bonynge, M. Freni, BPO/H. von Karajan, J. Björling, MMF Orch/A. Erede, R. Massard, M. Elkins, M. Sinclair, LSO, ROH Chor, ROHO, R. Tebaldi, C. Bergonzi, Santa Cecilia Academy Orch/T. Serafin, B. Fassbaender, Vienna Haydn Orch/I. Kertész, S. Milnes/S. Varviso, K. Te Kanawa/G. Solti, N. Ghiaurov, R. Davies, H. Tourangeau, F. Corelli, Ambrosian Op Chor)

Ⓓ **433 065-2DWO** ⊟ **433 065-4DWO**
Your Hundred Best Opera Tunes Volume II
Puccini: Gianni Schicchi (exc); *Verdi:* Nabucco (exc); *Handel:* Rodelinda (exc); *Donizetti:* Elisir d'amore (exc); *Delibes:* Lakmé (exc); *Puccini:* Tosca (exc); *Mascagni:* Cavalleria Rusticana (exc); Cavalleria Rusticana (exc); *Wagner:* Meistersinger (exc); Tannhäuser (exc); *Dvořák:* Rusalka (exc); *Donizetti:* Favorita (exc); *Gluck:* Orfeo ed Euridice (exc); *Verdi:* Rigoletto (exc). (R. Tebaldi, MMF Orch/L. Gardelli, Vienna St Op Chor, Vienna Op Orch, M. Horne, Vienna Cantata Orch/H. Lewis, G. di Stefano/F. Molinari-Pradelli, J. Sutherland, ROHO, F. Corelli, Santa Cecilia Academy Orch/L. Maazel, J. Varady, London Op Chor, National PO/G. Gavazzeni, J. King/D. Bernet, V. Braun, H. Dernesch, VPO/G. Solti/G. Patanè/T. Serafin, L. Pavarotti/E. Downes, T. Berganza/A. Gibson, A. Mariotti, H. Tourangeau, S. Milnes, M. Talvela, LSO/R. Bonynge, P. Lorengar)

Ⓓ **433 066-2DWO** ⊟ **433 066-4DWO**
Your Hundred Best Opera Tunes III
Puccini: Bohème (exc); *Delibes:* Lakmé (exc); *Mozart:* Nozze di Figaro (exc); Così fan tutte (exc); *Gounod:* Faust (exc); *Bizet:* Pêcheurs de perles (exc); *Catalani:* Wally (exc); *Verdi:* Luisa Miller (exc); *Leoncavallo:* Pagliacci (exc); *Massenet:* Werther (exc); *Bellini:* Puritani (exc); *Leoncavallo:* Pagliacci (exc); *Puccini:* Tosca (exc); Tosca (exc); *Verdi:* Traviata (exc); *Ponchielli:* Gioconda (exc). (L. Pavarotti, BPO/H. von Karajan, J. Sutherland, J. Berbié, Monte Carlo Nat Op Orch/R. Bonynge, T. Krause, Vienna Haydn Orch/I. Kertész, L. Popp, B. Fassbaender, ROHO/F. Molinari-Pradelli, L. de Luca, J. Borthayre, Paris Cons/A. Erede, R. Tebaldi/F. Cleva, C. Bergonzi, Santa Cecilia Academy Orch/G. Gavazzeni, J. McCracken, Ragazza del Colosseo Chor, Santa Cecilia Academy Chor/L. Gardelli, G. di Stefano, Zurich Tonhalle Orch/F. Patanè, I. Wixell, National PO/G. Patanè, K. Te Kanawa/G. Solti, J. Björling, MMF Orch, G. Taddei, P. de Palma, Vienna St Op Chor, VPO/H. von Karajan)

Ⓓ **433 067-2DWO** ⊟ **433 067-4DWO**
Your Hundred Best Opera Tunes IV
Wagner: Walküre (exc); Tannhäuser (exc); *Gluck:* Orfeo ed Euridice (exc); *Mozart:* Don Giovanni (exc); *Verdi:* Trovatore (exc); Aida (exc); *Bizet:* Carmen (exc); Carmen (exc); *Puccini:* Madama Butterfly (exc); *Saint-Saëns:* Samson et Dalila (exc); *Gounod:* Faust (exc); *Verdi:* Don Carlo (exc); *Puccini:* Turandot (exc); *Cilea:* Adriana Lecouvreur (exc); *Offenbach:* Contes d'Hoffmann (exc); *Verdi:* Ballo in maschera (exc). (V. Schlosser, B. Lindholm, B. Fassbaender, H. Watts, H. Dernesch, V. Little, M. Tyler, C. Hellmann, VPO/G. Solti, T. Krause, Vienna Op Orch/A. Quadri, T. Berganza, ROHO/A. Gibson, L. Popp, John Alldis Ch, Vienna Haydn Orch/I. Kertész, C. Bergonzi, Santa Cecilia Academy Orch/G. Gavazzeni, L. Price, Rome Op Orch, P. Domingo, LPO, Vienna St Op Orch/H. von Karajan, M. Horne/H. Lewis, N. Ghiaurov, LSO/E. Downes, G. Bumbry, ROHO, M. Chiara, Vienna Volksoper Orch/N. Santi, M. del Monaco, R. Tebaldi/F. Capuana, J. Sutherland, H. Tourangeau, Suisse Romande Rad Ch, Lausanne Pro Arte Ch, SRO/R. Bonynge, R. Tebaldi, New Philh/O. de Fabritiis, J. Van Dam, T. Troyanos, N. Burrowes, J. Berbié, T. Allen, P. Thau)

Ⓓ **433 068-2DWO** ⊟ **433 068-4DWO**
Your Hundred Best Opera Tunes V
Verdi: Rigoletto (exc); *Rossini:* Barbiere di Siviglia (exc); *Mozart:* Don Giovanni (exc); *Verdi:* Trovatore (exc); Trovatore (exc); *Puccini:* Bohème (exc); *Mozart:* Nozze di Figaro (exc); Zauberflöte (exc); *Bellini:* Norma (exc); *Leoncavallo:* Pagliacci (exc); *Mozart:* Don Giovanni (exc); *Bizet:* Carmen (exc); *Meyerbeer:* Africaine (exc); *Ponchielli:* Gioconda (exc); *Verdi:* Forza del destino (exc); *Wagner:* Tristan und Isolde (exc); Walküre (exc). (L. Pavarotti, LSO/R. Bonynge, T. Berganza/A. Gibson, G. Bacquier, ECO, London Op Chor, National PO, E. Harwood, M. Freni, R. Panerai, M. Sénéchal, BPO/H. von Karajan, K. Te Kanawa, LPO/G. Solti, T. Krause, Vienna Haydn Orch/I. Kertész, J. Sutherland, London Sym Chor, G. Simionato, Geneva Grand Th Orch/A. Erede, M. del Monaco, Santa Cecilia Academy Orch/F. Molinari-Pradelli, John Alldis Ch/Z. Mehta, R. Resnik, E. Bastianini, SRO/T. Schippers, C. Bergonzi/G. Gavazzeni, E. Suliotis, Rome Orch/S. Varviso, B. Nilsson, VPO/H. Knappertsbusch, H. Hotter)

Ⓓ **433 069-2DWO** ⊟ **433 069-4DWO**
Your Hundred Best Opera Tunes VI
Puccini: Madama Butterfly (exc); *Verdi:* Aida (exc); Traviata (exc); Rigoletto (exc); *Puccini:* Rondine (exc); *Donizetti:* Favorita (exc); *Puccini:* Fanciulla del West (exc); Turandot (exc); *Verdi:* Trovatore (exc); *Puccini:* Manon Lescaut (exc); *Verdi:* Vespri Siciliani (exc); *Gounod:* Faust (exc); *Giordano:* Andrea Chénier (exc); *Verdi:* Otello (exc); *Cilea:* Arlesiana (exc); *Verdi:* Aida (exc); Traviata (exc); *Mascagni:* Cavalleria Rusticana (exc); *Verdi:* Trovatore (exc). (M. Freni, VPO/H. von Karajan, L. Pavarotti, Vienna Volksoper Orch/L. Magiera, MMF Orch/J. Pritchard, J. Sutherland, C. Bergonzi, MMF Chor, LSO/R. Bonynge, R. Tebaldi, New Philh/O. de Fabritiis, F. Cossotto, Bologna Teatro Comunale Orch, J. Björling/A. Erede, F. Weathers, Vienna Op Orch/A. Quadri, London Op Chor, National PO, Santa Cecilia Academy Orch/G. Gavazzeni, M. Chiara, ROHO/N. Santi, N. Ghiaurov, London Sym Chor/E. Downes, M. del Monaco, Santa Cecilia Academy Chor/C. Franci, A. Cerquetti, D. Fischer-Dieskau, Berlin Deutsche Op Orch/L. Maazel, Geneva Grand Th Orch)

Ⓓ **433 162-2DH**
Verdi—Aida highlights
Verdi: Aida (exc). (M. Chiara, G. Dimitrova, L. Pavarotti, L. Nucci, P. Burchuladze, L. Roni, E. Gavazzi, La Scala Chor, La Scala Orch/L. Maazel)

ꝏ **433 162-5DH**
Verdi—Aida highlights
Verdi: Aida (exc). (M. Chiara, G. Dimitrova, L. Pavarotti, L. Nucci, P. Burchuladze, L. Roni, E. Gavazzi, La Scala Chor, La Scala Orch/L. Maazel)

Ⓓ **433 163-2DM2** (5/92)
Purcell—The Fairy Queen
Purcell: Fairy Queen, Z629 (Cpte). (J. Vyvyan, M. Wells, N. Burrowes, A. Hodgson, J. Bowman, C. Brett, P. Pears, I. Partridge, O. Brannigan, J. Shirley-Quirk, Ambrosian Op Chor, ECO/B. Britten)

Ⓓ **433 166-2DM2** (5/92)
Purcell—Stage Works
Purcell: Indian Queen, Z630 (exc); King Arthur, Z628 (Cpte). (C. Keyte, A. Cantelo, Wilfred Brown, I. Partridge, R. Tear, St Anthony Sngrs, ECO/C. Mackerras, E. Morison, H. Harper, M. Thomas, J. Whitworth, D. Galliver, Wilfred Brown, J. Cameron, H. Alan, T. Anthony, Philomusica of London/A. Lewis)

Ⓓ **433 210-2DH2** (10/91)
Mozart—Die Zauberflöte
Mozart: Zauberflöte (Cpte). (R. Ziesak, S. Jo, U. Heilmann, M. Kraus, K. Moll, A. Schmidt, H. Zednik, Lotte Leitner, A. Pieczonka, A. Kuettenbaum, J. van Nes, M.E. Cencic, M. Rausch, M. Leitner, W. Schmidt, H. Franzen, C. Bieber, H.J. Porcher, Vienna Boys' Ch, Vienna St Op Concert Ch, VPO/G. Solti)

Ⓓ **433 220-2DWO** (5/92) ⊟ **433 220-4DWO** (5/92)
The World of the Violin
Massenet: Thaïs (exc); *Elgar:* Salut d'amour; Capricieuse; *Saint-Saëns:* Introduction and Rondo capriccioso; *Prince Albert:* Melody for the Violin; *Wieniawski:* Scherzo-tarantelle, Op. 16; *Sarasate:* Danzas españolas (exc); *Beethoven:* Romances (exc); *Kreisler:* Liebesfreud; Liebesleid; Schön Rosmarin; *Falla:* Vida breve (exc); *Paganini:* Caprices, Op. 1 (exc); *Vecsey:* Vent; *Sarasate:* Zigeunerweisen. (N. Kennedy, National PO/R. Bonynge, K-W. Chung, P. Moll, RPO/C. Dutoit, I. Brown, J. Partridge, A. Campoli, D. Ibbott, W. Boskovsky (vn/dir), Vienna Mozart Ens, R. Holmes, J. Walker, R. Ricci, E. Lush, LSO/P. Gamba)

Ⓓ **433 221-2DWO** ⊟ **433 221-4DWO**
The World of Verdi
Verdi: Nabucco (exc); Rigoletto (exc); Rigoletto (exc); Rigoletto (exc); Vespri siciliani (exc); Aida (exc); Aida (exc); Forza del destino (exc); Traviata (exc); Traviata (exc); Luisa Miller (exc); Otello (exc); Trovatore (exc); Trovatore (exc); Trovatore (exc). (Ambrosian Sngrs, LSO/C. Abbado, J. Sutherland, R. Cassinelli, J. Gibbs, C. du Plessis, Ambrosian Op Chor/R. Bonynge, H. Tourangeau, S. Milnes, M. Chiara, ROHO/N. Santi, J. Vickers, Rome Op Chor/G. Solti, G. Jones, Vienna Op Orch/A. Quadri, MMF Orch/J. Pritchard, C. Bergonzi, MMF Chor, Santa Cecilia Academy Orch/G. Gavazzeni, G. Evans, SRO/B. Balkwill, London Op Chor, National PO, M. Horne, P. Knapp, L. Pavarotti, G. Clark, Rome Op Orch)

433 223-2DWO **433 223-4DWO**
The World of Operetta
Lehár: Land des Lächelns (exc); Paganini (exc); Frasquita (exc); Friederike (exc); *Romberg:* Student Prince (exc); *Sieczyński:* Wien, du Stadt meiner Träume; *Romberg:* Student Prince (exc); Desert Song (exc); *Friml:* Rose Marie (exc); *German:* Tom Jones (exc); *Lehár:* Lustige Witwe (exc); Lustige Witwe (exc); *O. Straus:* Tapfere Soldat (exc); *Millöcker:* Dubarry (exc); *Lehár:* Paganini (exc). (J. Sutherland, S. Burrows, W. Krenn, Ambrosian Light Op Chor, New Philh, National PO/R. Bonynge/R. Stapleton)

433 316-2DH (9/92)
Verismo Arias - Mirella Freni
Cilea: Arlesiana (exc); Adriana Lecouvreur (exc); *Giordano:* Andrea Chénier (exc); *Catalani:* Wally (exc); Loreley (exc); *Alfano:* Risurrezione (exc); *Zandonai:* Francesca da Rimini (exc); *Puccini:* Gianni Schicchi (exc); *Mascagni:* Cavalleria Rusticana (exc); Lodoletta (exc); Iris (exc). (M. Freni, Venice La Fenice Orch/R. Abbado)

433 323-2DH **433 323-4DH**
The Essential Mozart
Mozart: Serenade, K525 (exc); Nozze di Figaro (exc); Piano Concerto 21 (exc); Piano Sonata, K331 (exc); Symphony 40 (exc); Horn Concerti (exc); Requiem (exc); Contredanses, K609 (exc); German Dances, K605 (exc); Clarinet Concerto, K622 (exc); Piano Sonata K545 (exc); Divertimento, K334 (exc); Symphony 29 (exc); Vespers, K321 (exc); Musikalischer Spass (exc). (Vienna Mozart Ens/W. Boskovsky, LPO/G. Solti, R. Lupu, ECO/U. Segal, A. Schiff, COE, B. Tuckwell (hn/dir), Vienna St Op Chor, VPO/I. Kertész, A. Prinz/K. Münchinger, ASMF/N. Marriner, F. Palmer, St Johns College Ch, Wren Orch/G. Guest)

433 400-2DM2 (6/93)
Ravel & Debussy—Stage Works
Ravel: Enfant et les Sortilèges (Cpte); *Debussy:* Martyre de St Sébastien (Cpte); *Ravel:* Heure espagnole (Cpte). (F. Wend, M-L. de Montmollin, G. Touraine, A. Migliette, S. Danco, J. Bise, G. Bobillier, L. Lovano, P. Mollet, H. Cuénod, Geneva Motet Ch, SRO/E. Ansermet, S. Danco, N. Waugh, M-L. de Montmollin, Peilz Chor Union, S. Danco, P. Derenne, M. Hamel, H. Rehfuss, A. Vessières)

433 437-2DA (12/93) **433 437-4DA**
Pavarotti—King of the High Cs
Bellini: Puritani (exc); *Donizetti:* Fille du Régiment (exc); Favorita (exc); *Puccini:* Bohème (exc); *Rossini:* Guillaume Tell (exc); *R. Strauss:* Rosenkavalier (exc); *Verdi:* Trovatore (exc). (A. Auger, G. Flossmann, L. Pavarotti, P. Baillie, R. Bunger, H. Lackner, E. Garrett, ROH Chor, Vienna Op Chor, ROHO, Vienna Op Orch, BPO, VPO/R. Bonynge/E. Downes/N. Rescigno/H. von Karajan/G. Solti)

433 438-2DA **433 438-4DA**
Puccini: Turandot—excs
Puccini: Turandot (exc). (J. Sutherland, L. Pavarotti, M. Caballé, T. Krause, P.F. Poli, P. de Palma, N. Ghiaurov, P. Pears, John Alldis Ch, Wandsworth Sch Boys' Ch, LPO/Z. Mehta)

433 439-2DA (12/93) **433 439-4DA**
Great Love Duets
Puccini: Bohème (exc); Madama Butterfly (exc); Manon Lescaut (exc); Tosca (exc); *Verdi:* Otello (exc); Traviata (exc). (J. Sutherland, R. Tebaldi, M. Freni, M. Price, C. Ludwig, L. Pavarotti, F. Corelli, C. Cossutta, R. Panerai, G. Maffeo, N. Ghiaurov, R. van Allan, National PO, VPO, BPO, SRO/R. Bonynge/G. Solti/H. von Karajan/A. Guadagno/N. Rescigno)

433 440-2DA **433 440-4DA**
Golden Opera
Delibes: Lakmé (exc); *Bizet:* Carmen (exc); *Rossini:* Barbiere di Siviglia (exc); *Catalani:* Wally (exc); *Verdi:* Nabucco (exc); Traviata (exc); Aida (exc); Rigoletto (exc); *Puccini:* Madama Butterfly (exc); Tosca (exc); Gianni Schicchi (exc); *Offenbach:* Contes d'Hoffmann (exc); *Saint-Saëns:* Samson et Dalila (exc); *Gounod:* Faust (exc); *Mozart:* Così fan tutte (exc). (J. Sutherland, J. Berbié, Monte Carlo Nat Op Orch/R. Bonynge, M. Horne, Vienna Op Orch/H. Lewis, S. Milnes, LPO/S. Varviso, L. Popp, B. Fassbaender, T. Krause, Vienna Haydn Orch/I. Kertész, R. Tebaldi/F. Cleva, Vienna St Op Chor, C. Bergonzi, MMF Chor, MMF Orch/J. Pritchard, L. Pavarotti, Vienna Volksoper Orch/L. Magiera, LSO, H. Tourangeau, M. Talvela, R. Crespin, ROHO/E. Downes, F. Corelli, A. Mariotti, Santa Cecilia Academy Orch/L. Maazel/L. Gardelli, Suisse Romande Rad Ch, Lausanne Pro Arte Ch, SRO, N. Ghiaurov, Ambrosian Op Chor/N. Rescigno)

433 441-2DA **433 441-4DA**
Mozart—Die Zauberflöte: excs
Mozart: Zauberflöte (exc). (S. Burrows, P. Lorengar, C. Deutekom, M. Talvela, H. Prey, G. Stolze, R. Holm, H. van Bork, Y. Minton, H. Plümacher, Vienna St Op Chor, VPO/G. Solti)

433 442-2DA
Verdi—Famous Arias
Verdi: Aida (exc); Aida (exc); Aida (exc); Ballo in maschera (exc); Luisa Miller (exc); Otello (exc); Traviata (exc); Rigoletto (exc); Rigoletto (exc); Trovatore (exc). (L. Pavarotti, LSO/R. Bonynge, J. Sutherland, ROH Chor, ROHO/F. Molinari-Pradelli, R. Tebaldi, New Philh/O. de Fabritiis, D. Fischer-Dieskau, Berlin Deutsche Op Orch/L. Maazel, R. Crespin/E. Downes, J. Vickers, Rome Op Orch/G. Solti, L. Price, A. Cerquetti, MMF Orch/G. Gavazzeni, C. Bergonzi, Santa Cecilia Academy Orch, G. Simionato, Geneva Grand Th Orch/A. Erede, M. del Monaco, MMF Chor)

433 443-2DA **433 443-4DA**
Great Opera Choruses
Verdi: Nabucco (exc); Trovatore (exc); Aida (exc); Macbeth (exc); Otello (exc); *Leoncavallo:* Pagliacci (exc); *Puccini:* Madama Butterfly (exc); *Gounod:* Faust (exc); *Beethoven:* Fidelio (exc); *Wagner:* Tannhäuser (exc); *Mussorgsky:* Boris Godunov (exc). (Vienna St Op Chor, London Op Chor, Santa Cecilia Academy Chor, Ambrosian Op Chor, Chicago Sym Chor, VPO, National PO, Santa Cecilia Academy Orch, LPO, LSO, Chicago SO/L. Gardelli/R. Bonynge/C. Franci/H. von Karajan/G. Solti, M. del Monaco, T. Krause, A. Protti, A. Cesarini, J. McCracken, R. Massard, M. Elkins, M. Sinclair, R. Johnson, P. Kraus, V. Braun, H. Dernesch, N. Ghiaurov, A. Maslennikov)

433 444-2DA **433 444-4DA**
Verdi—Aida: excs
Verdi: Aida (exc). (L. Price, R. Gorr, J. Vickers, R. Merrill, G. Tozzi, P. Clabassi, F. Ricciardi, Rome Op Chor, Rome Op Orch/G. Solti)

433 468-2DM (6/92)
Ferrier Edition - Volume 1
Gluck: Orfeo ed Euridice (exc). (K. Ferrier, A. Ayars, Z. Vlachopoulos, Glyndebourne Fest Chor, Southern PO/F. Stiedry)

433 470-2DM (6/92) **433 470-4DM** (6/92)
Ferrier Edition - Volume 3
Gluck: Orfeo ed Euridice (exc); *Handel:* Rodelinda (exc); *Bach:* St Matthew Passion, BWV244 (exc); Cantata 11 (exc); *Handel:* Serse (exc); *Mendelssohn:* Elijah (exc); *Pergolesi:* Stabat mater. (J. Taylor, K. Ferrier, Nottingham Oriana Ch, LSO, National SO, Jacques Orch, Boyd Neel Orch/M. Sargent/R. Jacques/B. Neel/Roy Henderson)

433 473-2DM (6/92)
Ferrier Edition - Volume 6
Stanford: Irish Idyll, Op. 77 (exc); Songs, Op. 140 (exc); *Parry:* English Lyrics, Set 6 (exc); *Vaughan Williams:* House of Life (exc); *Bridge:* Go not, happy day; *Warlock:* Sleep; Pretty Ring Time; *Britten:* Folk Songs (exc); *Traditional:* Kitty, my love; *Purcell:* Bess of Bedlam, Z370; Fairy Queen, Z629 (exc); *Handel:* Atalanta (exc); Admeto (exc); *Wolf:* Mörike Lieder (exc); *Jensen:* Altar; *Bach:* Sacred Songs, BWV489-507 (exc); Sacred Songs, BWV439-488 (exc); Anna Magdalena Notenbuch (1725) (exc). (K. Ferrier, F. Stone, P. Spurr, M. Silver, J. Newmark)

433 519-2DH (1/92)
Works for Violin and Orchestra
Saint-Saëns: Introduction and Rondo capriccioso; *Massenet:* Thaïs (exc); *Sarasate:* Zigeunerweisen; *Chausson:* Poème; *Ravel:* Tzigane; *Ysaÿe:* Caprice d'après l'Étude. (J. Bell, RPO/A. Litton)

OO **433 519-5DH**
Works for Violin and Orchestra
Saint-Saëns: Introduction and Rondo capriccioso; *Massenet:* Thaïs (exc); *Sarasate:* Zigeunerweisen; *Chausson:* Poème; *Ravel:* Tzigane; *Ysaÿe:* Caprice d'après l'Étude. (J. Bell, RPO/A. Litton)

433 604-2DSP (1/92)
Brahms—Violin Concerto & Massenet—Méditation
Brahms: Violin Concerto; *Massenet:* Thaïs (exc). (B. Belkin, LSO/I. Fischer, N. Kennedy, National PO/R. Bonynge)

433 606-2DSP
Rossini—Overtures
Rossini: Gazza ladra (exc); Scala di seta (exc); Barbiere di Siviglia (exc); Semiramide (exc); Guillaume Tell (exc). (LSO/P. Gamba)

433 612-2DSP (1/92)
Prokofiev—Popular Orchestral Works
Prokofiev: Peter and the Wolf; Symphony 1; Lt. Kijé Suite; Love for 3 Oranges Suite (exc). (R. Richardson, LSO/M. Sargent, Paris Cons/A. Boult, LPO/W. Weller)

433 618-2DSP (1/92) **433 618-4DSP** (1/92)
Sullivan—The Mikado (excerpts)
Sullivan: Mikado (exc). (J. Ayldon, C. Wright, J. Reed, K. Sandford, M. Rayner, J. Broad, V. Masterson, P.A. Jones, P. Wales, L. Holland, D'Oyly Carte Op Chor, RPO/R. Nash)

433 620-2DSP
Holst—Orchestral Works
Holst: Perfect Fool (exc); Planets. (LPO/A. Boult, Los Angeles Master Chorale, Los Angeles PO/Z. Mehta)

433 623-2DSP **433 623-4DSP**
Famous Tenor Arias
Verdi: Aida (exc); Luisa Miller (exc); *Meyerbeer:* Africaine (exc); *Verdi:* Ballo in Maschera (exc); *Massenet:* Werther (exc); *Bizet:* Carmen (exc); *Gounod:* Faust (exc); *Puccini:* Tosca (exc); *Giordano:* Andrea Chénier (exc); *Verdi:* Forza del destino (exc); *Giordano:* Fedora (exc); *Mascagni:* Cavalleria rusticana (exc); *Puccini:* Fanciulla del West (exc); Turandot (exc). (C. Bergonzi, Santa Cecilia Academy Orch/G. Gavazzeni, G. di Stefano, Zurich Tonhalle Orch/F. Patanè, B. Prevedi, ROHO/E. Downes)

433 624-2DSP
Great Soprano Arias
Puccini: Madama Butterfly (exc); Gianni Schicchi (exc); *Catalani:* Wally (exc); *Verdi:* Rigoletto (exc); Vespri Siciliani (exc); Aida (exc); *Gounod:* Faust (exc); *Verdi:* Otello (exc); *Ponchielli:* Gioconda (exc); *Puccini:* Bohème (exc); Tosca (exc). (R. Crespin, ROHO/E. Downes, R. Tebaldi, MMF Orch/L. Gardelli, M. Chiara, National PO/K.H. Adler, J. Sutherland, ROH Chor/F. Molinari-Pradelli/N. Santi, G. Jones, F. Weathers, Vienna Op Orch/A. Quadri, E. Suliotis, Rome Orch/S. Varviso, Vienna Volksoper Orch, Santa Cecilia Academy Orch)

433 625-2DSP (4/92) **433 625-4DSP** (4/92)
Stokowski conducts Famous Russian Works
Tchaikovsky: Marche Slave; *Borodin:* Prince Igor (exc); *Mussorgsky:* Night on the bare mountain; *Rimsky-Korsakov:* Capriccio espagnol; *Tchaikovsky:* 1812. (LSO, Royal Phil Chor, WNO Chor, RPO, New Philh, Grenadier Guards Band/L. Stokowski)

433 626-2DSP (1/92) **433 626-4DSP** (1/92)
Bizet—Carmen (highlights)
Bizet: Carmen (exc). (R. Resnik, M. del Monaco, G. Spanellys, Y. Minton, T. Krause, J. Prudent, A. Hallett, J. Sutherland, Geneva Grand Th Chor, SRO/T. Schippers)

433 631-2DSP **433 631-4DSP**
Baroque Favourites
Pachelbel: Canon and Gigue (exc); *Albinoni:* Adagio; *Corelli:* Concerti Grossi, Op. 6 (exc); *Bach:* Suites, BWV1066-9 (exc); *Handel:* Solomon (exc); Oboe Concertos (exc); Water Music (exc); *Bach:* Christmas Oratorio, BWV248 (exc); *Mozart:* Divertimento, K334 (exc); *Gluck:* Paride ed Elena (exc). (J-P. Rampal, Stuttgart CO/K. Münchinger, L. Koch)

433 636-2DSP **433 636-4DSP**
Puccini—Famous Arias
Puccini: Madama Butterfly (exc); Tosca (exc); Tosca (exc); Turandot (exc); Turandot (exc); Bohème (exc); Bohème (exc); Bohème (exc); Fanciulla del West (exc); Gianni Schicchi (exc); Manon Lescaut (exc). (F. Weathers, Vienna Op Orch/A. Quadri, G. di Stefano, Santa Cecilia Academy Orch/F. Patanè, A. Cerquetti, MMF Orch/G. Gavazzeni, R. Tebaldi, New Philh/O. de Fabritiis, B. Prevedi, ROHO/E. Downes, C. Bergonzi/T. Serafin, M. Chiara, Vienna Volksoper Orch/N. Santi, V. Zeani, J. Björling/A. Erede)

433 639-2DSP **433 639-4DSP**
Wagner—Orchestral Works
Wagner: Götterdämmerung (exc); Rheingold (exc); Siegfried (exc); Walküre (exc); Meistersinger (exc). (LSO/L. Stokowski)

433 667-2DH
Mozart—Die Zauberflöte : Highlights
Mozart: Zauberflöte (exc). (R. Ziesak, S. Jo, U. Heilmann, M. Kraus, K. Moll, H. Zednik, Lotte Leitner, A. Pieczonka, A. Kuettenbaum, J. van Nes, W. Schmidt, H. Franzen, Vienna Boys' Ch, Vienna St Op Concert Ch, VPO/G. Solti)

OO **433 667-5DH**
Mozart—Die Zauberflöte : Highlights
Mozart: Zauberflöte (exc). (R. Ziesak, S. Jo, U. Heilmann, M. Kraus, K. Moll, H. Zednik, Lotte Leitner, A. Pieczonka, A. Kuettenbaum, J. van Nes, W. Schmidt, H. Franzen, Vienna Boys' Ch, Vienna St Op Concert Ch, VPO/G. Solti)

433 669-2DH2 (11/91)
Verdi—Otello
Verdi: Otello (Cpte). (L. Pavarotti, K. Te Kanawa, L. Nucci, A. Rolfe Johnson, J. Keyes, E. Ardam, D. Kavrakos, A.

Opie, R. Cohn, NY Met Op Children's Ch, Chicago Sym Chor, Chicago SO/G. Solti)

① **433 706-2DMO3** (2/93)
Bellini—Beatrice di Tenda; Operatic Arias
Bellini: Beatrice di Tenda (Cpte); Norma (exc); Puritani (exc); Sonnambula (exc). (J. Sutherland, L. Pavarotti, C. Opthof, J. Veasey, J. Ward, J. Sutherland, M. Elkins, P. Duval, N. Monti, R. Capecchi, R. Cross, E. Flagello, F. Corena, London Sym Chor, MMF Chor, Ambrosian Op Chor, LSO, MMF Orch/R. Bonynge)

① **433 710-2DH** (12/91) ⊡ **433 710-4DH** (12/91)
O Holy Night
Adam: Minuit, Chrétiens (exc); *Niedermeyer:* Pietà, Signore; *Franck:* Panis angelicus; *Mercadante:* Sette ultime parole (exc); *Schubert:* Ave Maria, D839; *Yon:* Gesù, bambino; *Gluck:* Orfeo ed Euridice (exc); *Rossini:* Stabat Mater (exc); *Verdi:* Requiem (exc); *Gounod:* Ave Maria; *Schubert/Melichar:* Mille cherubini in coro; *Bizet:* Agnus Dei; *Berlioz:* Grande messe des morts (exc); *Traditional:* O come, all ye faithful. (L. Pavarotti, National PO/K.H. Adler, Philh/P. Gamba, LSO/I. Kertész, VPO/G. Solti, Wandsworth Sch Boys' Ch, London Voices)

① **433 723-2DMO3**
Handel—Alcina; Giulio Cesare—excs
Handel: Alcina (Cpte); Giulio Cesare (exc). (J. Sutherland, T. Berganza, M. Sinclair, L. Alva, G. Sciutti, M. Freni, E. Flagello, J. Sutherland, M. Elkins, M. Horne, M. Sinclair, R. Conrad, LSO, New SO/R. Bonynge)

① **433 761-2DMO2** (8/93)
Puccini—Turandot
Puccini: Turandot (Cpte). (I. Borkh, M. del Monaco, R. Tebaldi, F. Corena, Mario Carlin, R. Ercolani, N. Zaccaria, G. Fanelli, E. Giordano, Santa Cecilia Academy Chor, Santa Cecilia Academy Orch/A. Erede)

① **433 770-2DMO2** (9/93)
Ponchielli—La Gioconda
Ponchielli: Gioconda (Cpte). (A. Cerquetti, M. del Monaco, E. Bastianini, F. Sacchi, C. Siepi, G. Simionato, G. Giorgetti, A. Cesarini, MMF Chor, MMF Orch/G. Gavazzeni)

① **433 822-2DH** ⊡ **433 822-4DH**
Essential Opera
Bizet: Carmen (exc); *Puccini:* Tosca (exc); *Verdi:* Trovatore (exc); *Puccini:* Bohème (exc); *Mozart:* Nozze di Figaro (exc); *Verdi:* Rigoletto (exc); Nabucco (exc); *Bizet:* Carmen (exc); *Catalani:* Wally (exc); *Rossini:* Barbiere di Siviglia (exc); *Verdi:* Aida (exc); *Puccini:* Gianni Schicchi (exc); Turandot (exc); *Offenbach:* Contes d'Hoffmann (exc); *Puccini:* Madama Butterfly (exc); *Mozart:* Don Giovanni (exc); *Puccini:* Manon Lescaut (exc); *Mascagni:* Cavalleria rusticana (exc). (LPO/G. Solti, K. Te Kanawa, National PO, Chicago Sym Chor, Chicago SO, L. Pavarotti, BPO/H. von Karajan, F. von Stade, J. Sutherland, H. Tourangeau, S. Milnes, LSO/R. Bonynge, P. Domingo, R. Tebaldi, Monte Carlo Nat Op Orch/F. Cleva, L. Nucci, Bologna Teatro Comunale Orch/G. Patanè, La Scala Chor, La Scala Orch/L. Maazel, MMF Orch/L. Gardelli/Z. Mehta, SRO, M. Freni, VPO, B. Weikl, J. Carreras/G. Gavazzeni, M. Caballé, N. Ghiaurov, T. Krause, John Alldis Ch, Suisse Romande Rad Chor, Lausanne Pro Arte Ch/R. Chailly)

① **433 851-2DMO2** (2/93)
Massenet—Le Roi de Lahore
Massenet: Roi de Lahore (Cpte). (L. Lima, J. Sutherland, S. Milnes, N. Ghiaurov, J. Morris, H. Tourangeau, London Voices, National PO/R. Bonynge)

① **433 854-2DMO2** (7/93)
Verdi—I Masnadieri
Verdi: Masnadieri (Cpte). (J. Sutherland, F. Bonisolli, M. Manuguerra, S. Ramey, A. Davies, S. Alaimo, J. Harris, WNO Chor, WNO Orch/R. Bonynge)

433 857-2DMO3 (5/93)
A. Thomas—Hamlet
A. Thomas: Hamlet (Cpte). (S. Milnes, J. Sutherland, G. Winbergh, B. Conrad, J. Morris, J. Tomlinson, K. Lewis, A.H. Morgan, P. Gelling, P. Garazzi, J. Rouleau, WNO Chor, WNO Orch/R. Bonynge)

433 865-2DWO ⊡ **433 865-4DWO**
The World of Puccini
Puccini: Bohème (exc); Gianni Schicchi (exc); Fanciulla del West (exc); Suor Angelica (exc); Rondine (exc); Tosca (exc); Tosca (exc); Tosca (exc); Madama Butterfly (exc); Manon Lescaut (exc); Turandot (exc); Turandot (exc); Turandot (exc). (M. Freni, L. Mitchell, J. Sutherland, M. Chiara, E. Harwood, V. Zeani, R. Tebaldi, F. Cossotto, L. Pavarotti, M. Sénéchal, B. Prevedi, J. McCracken, C. Bergonzi, G. di Stefano, G. Maffeo, R. Panerai, N. Ghiaurov, Santa Cecilia Academy Chor, BPO, National PO, ROHO, Santa Cecilia Academy Orch, New Philh, Vienna Volksoper Orch/H. von Karajan/K.H. Adler/E. Downes/F. Patanè/R. Bonynge/L. Gardelli/N. Santi/T. Serafin)

① **433 868-2DWO** (2/93) ⊡ **433 868-4DWO** (2/93)
The World of Gilbert & Sullivan - Volume 2
Sullivan: HMS Pinafore (exc); Mikado (exc); Patience (exc); Iolanthe (exc); Gondoliers (exc); Ruddigore (exc); Sorcerer (exc); Yeomen of the Guard (exc); Princess Ida (exc); Pirates of Penzance (exc). (J. Hindmarsh, J. Wright, P.A. Jones, V. Masterson, P. Wales, J. Toye, M. Sansom, A. Hood, E. Harwood, G. Knight, L. Holland, C. Palmer, J. Allister, T. Round, C. Wright, P. Potter, J. Skitch, D. Adams, J. Reed, K. Sandford, M. Rayner, A. Styler, T. Lawlor, A. Raffell, G. Cook, D'Oyly Carte Op Chor, New SO, RPO, ROHO/I. Godfrey/R. Nash/M. Sargent)

⊡ **433 870-4DWO**
Classical Favourites
Handel: Solomon (exc); *Pachelbel:* Canon and Gigue (exc); *Bach:* Suites, BWV1066-9 (exc); *Handel:* Water Music (exc); *Grieg:* Peer Gynt (exc); *Brahms:* Hungarian Dances (exc); *Mozart:* Piano Concerto 21; *Tchaikovsky:* Serenade, Op. 48 (exc); *Offenbach:* Contes d'Hoffmann (exc); *J. Strauss II:* Pizzicato Polka; *Smetana:* Má Vlast (exc); *Vaughan Williams:* Greensleeves Fantasia; *Delius:* Koanga (exc); *Elgar:* Enigma Variations (exc); Pomp and Circumstance Marches (exc). (ASMF/N. Marriner, Richard Hickox Orch/R. Hickox, RPO/W. Weller, Vladimir Ashkenazy (pf/dir), Philh, SRO/R. Bonynge, VPO/W. Boskovsky, Israel PO, Chicago SO/G. Solti, LPO)

① **433 908-2DM2** (9/92)
Falla—Orchestral Music
Falla: Amor Brujo (Cpte); Vida breve (exc); Sombrero de tres picos (Cpte); Nights in the Gardens of Spain; Retablo de maese Pedro (Cpte); Psyché; Harpsichord Concerto. (P. Lorengar, J. Smith, J. Smith, K. Te Kanawa, T. Berganza, M. de Gabarain, M. Horne, N. Jenkins, A. Oliver, P. Knapp, A. de Larrocha, R. Vignoles, Martin Katz, F. Lavilla, J. Constable, Ambrosian Sngrs, LPO/R. Frühbeck de Burgos/J. López-Cobos, London Sinfonietta/S. Rattle, SRO/E. Ansermet)

① **436 075-2DH** (2/92)
Rossini Heroines
Rossini: Zelmira (exc); Nozze di Teti e di Peleo (exc); Maometto II (exc); Donna del Lago (exc); Elisabetta (exc); Semiramide (exc). (C. Bartoli, Venice La Fenice Chor, Venice La Fenice Orch/I. Martin)

OO **436 075-5DH**
Rossini Heroines
Rossini: Zelmira (exc); Nozze di Teti e di Peleo (exc); Maometto II (exc); Donna del Lago (exc); Elisabetta (exc); Semiramide (exc). (C. Bartoli, Venice La Fenice Chor, Venice La Fenice Orch/I. Martin)

① **436 097-2DH**
Verdi—Rigoletto - Highlights
Verdi: Rigoletto (exc). (L. Pavarotti, L. Nucci, J. Anderson, N. Ghiaurov, S. Verrett, Bologna Teatro Comunale Chor, Bologna Teatro Comunale Orch/R. Chailly)

OO **436 097-5DH**
Verdi—Rigoletto - Highlights
Verdi: Rigoletto (exc). (L. Pavarotti, L. Nucci, J. Anderson, N. Ghiaurov, S. Verrett, Bologna Teatro Comunale Chor, Bologna Teatro Comunale Orch/R. Chailly)

① **436 133-2DWO**
World of Rossini
Rossini: Scala di seta (exc); Barbiere di Siviglia (exc); Barbiere di Siviglia (exc); Soirées musicales (exc); Tancredi (exc); Gazza ladra (exc); Semiramide (exc); Stabat Mater (exc); Cenerentola (exc); Guillaume Tell (exc). (National PO/R. Chailly, L. Nucci, Bologna Teatro Comunale Orch/G. Patanè, C. Bartoli, L. Pavarotti/R. Bonynge, M. Horne, SRO/H. Lewis, J. Sutherland, LSO/I. Kertész, A. Schoenberg Ch, Vienna Volksoper Orch)

① **436 145-2DSP** ⊡ **436 145-4DSP**
Gilbert & Sullivan: HMS Pinafore—excs
Sullivan: HMS Pinafore (exc). (J. Reed, J. Skitch, T. Round, D. Adams, G. Cook, E. Wilson Hyde, J. Hindmarsh, J. Wright, G. Knight, D'Oyly Carte Op. Chor, New SO/I. Godfrey)

① **436 148-2DSP** ⊡ **436 148-4DSP**
Gilbert & Sullivan—Pirates of Penzance - highlights
Sullivan: Pirates of Penzance (exc). (D. Adams, P. Potter, J. Reed, V. Masterson, G. Cook, C. Palmer, P. Wales, J. Allister, S. Maisey, D'Oyly Carte Op Chor, RPO/I. Godfrey)

① **436 202-2DM** (9/94)
Italian Songs
A. Scarlatti: Pompeo (exc); *Bellini:* Malinconia, ninfa gentile; *Cimara:* Stornello; *Donizetti:* Soirées d'automne (exc); *Gluck:* Paride ed Elena (exc); *Mascagni:* Serenata; Tua stella; *Mercadante:* Sposa del marinaro; *Paradis:* M'ha presa alla sua ragna; *Parisotti:* Se tu m'ami; *Ponchielli:* Noi leggevamo insieme; *Puccini:* È l'uccellino; *Ricci:* Carrettiere del Vomero; *Rossini:* Soirées musicales (exc); *Tosti:* Sogno; *Zandonai:* Assiuolo. (R. Tebaldi, R. Bonynge)

① **436 216-2DMO2**
Cavalli/Leppard—La Calisto
Cavalli: Calisto (Cpte). (I. Cotrubas, U. Trama, P. Gottlieb, J. Bowman, J. Baker, H. Cuénod, J. Hughes, F. Davià, O. Brannigan, T. Kubiak, M. Biggar, E. Hartle, T. Cahill, I. Brodie, Glyndebourne Fest Chor, LPO/R. Leppard)

① **436 227-2DM2**
Handel—Acis and Galatea; Baroque Arias
Handel: Acis and Galatea (Cpte); Alcina (exc); *Bononcini:* Griselda (exc); *Piccinni:* Cecchina (exc); *Paisiello:* Amor contrastato (exc); *Arne:* Love in a village (exc); Artaxerxes (exc); *Shield:* Rosina (exc). (J. Sutherland, P. Pears, D. Galliver, O. Brannigan, St Anthony Sngrs, Philomusica of London/A. Boult/Granville Jones/A. Lewis)

① **436 243-2DH3** (5/92)
R. Strauss—Die Frau ohne Schatten
R. Strauss: Frau ohne Schatten (Cpte). (J. Varady, P. Domingo, H. Behrens, J. Van Dam, R. Runkel, A. Dohmen, S. Jo, R. Gambill, E. Ardam, E. Lind, G. Hornik, H. Franzen, W. Gahmlich, Vienna Boys' Ch, Vienna St Op Chor, VPO/G. Solti)

① **436 261-2DHO3** (8/94)
Puccini—Il Trittico
Puccini: Tabarro (Cpte); Suor Angelica (Cpte); Gianni Schicchi (Cpte). (J. Pons, M. Freni, G. Giacomini, P. de Palma, F. de Grandis, G. Scalchi, R. Cassinelli, B. Frittoli, R. Emili, M. Freni, E. Suliotis, G. Scalchi, E. Podles, N. Curiel, B. Frittoli, V. Esposito, O. Romanko, D. Beronesi, L. Cherici, S. Macculi, L. Nucci, M. Freni, R. Alagna, E. Podles, R. Cassinelli, B. Frittoli, B. Guerrini, G. Giorgetti, E. Fissore, O. Mori, N. Curiel, C. Cue, A. Mariotti, D. Jenis, D. Serraiocco, Prato Voci Bianche Chor, MMF Chor, MMF Orch/B. Bartoletti)

① **436 267-2DH** (12/92) ⊡ **436 267-4DH** (12/92)
Arie Antiche—Bartoli
A. Scarlatti: Honestà negli amore (exc); Donna ancora è fedele (exc); Pompeo (exc); Spesso vibra; *T. Giordani:* Caro mio ben; *Lotti:* Arminio (exc); *Cesti:* Orontea (exc); *Paisiello:* Amor contrastato (exc); Nina (exc); *Anon:* O leggiadri occhi belli; *A. Marcello:* Qual fiamma che m'accende; *Caldara:* Selve amiche; Sebben, crudele; *Caccini:* Nuove Musiche (1602) (exc); Nuove Musiche (1614) (exc); *Parisotti:* Se tu m'ami; *Paisiello:* Zingari in fiera (exc); *Cavalli:* Giasone (exc); *Vivaldi:* Sposa son disprezzata; *Carissimi:* Vittoria! vittoria!. (C. Bartoli, G. Fischer)

① **436 284-2DH**
A Song of Thanksgiving
Handel: Messiah (exc); *Mozart:* Vespers, K339 (exc); *Gluck:* Orfeo ed Euridice (exc); *Vaughan Williams:* Song of Thanksgiving; *Puccini:* Madama Butterfly (exc); *Handel:* Coronation Anthems (exc); *Mendelssohn:* Elijah (exc); *Schubert:* Ave Maria, D839; *Canteloube:* Chants d'Auvergne (exc); *Mozart:* Ave verum corpus, K618; *Copland:* Old American Songs 1 (exc); *C. Hall:* Jenny Rebecca; *Bernstein:* West Side Story (exc). (F. von Stade, M.D. Hanks, Salt Lake Children's Ch, Mormon Tabernacle Ch, Utah SO/J. Silverstein)

① **436 300-2DX** ⊡ **436 300-4DX**
Opera Gala Sampler
Wagner: Walküre (exc); *Puccini:* Bohème (exc); *Bizet:* Carmen (exc); *Donizetti:* Lucia di Lammermoor (exc); *Puccini:* Tosca (exc); *Rossini:* Tancredi (exc); *Verdi:* Nabucco (exc); *Mozart:* Nozze di Figaro (exc); *Puccini:* Tosca (exc); *Offenbach:* Contes d'Hoffmann (exc); *Puccini:* Turandot (exc); *Giordano:* Fedora (exc); *Verdi:* Nabucco (exc); *Wagner:* Tannhäuser (exc); *Bellini:* Norma (exc); *Puccini:* Manon Lescaut (exc); *Donizetti:* Lucia di Lammermoor (exc); *Puccini:* Madama Butterfly (exc). (K. Te Kanawa, J. Sutherland, M. Freni, M. Caballé, E. Suliotis, R. Tebaldi, V. Schlosser, B. Lindholm, H. Dernesch, V. Little, M. Tyler, H. Tourangeau, M. Horne, T. Berganza, B. Fassbaender, H. Watts, C. Hellmann, L. Pavarotti, R. Davies, F. Corelli, P. Domingo, J. Björling, C. Bergonzi, S. Milnes, P. di Proenza, V. Braun, N. Ghiaurov, Vienna St Op Chor, ROH Chor, Lausanne Pro Arte Ch, VPO, ROHO, SRO, BPO, LPO, Santa Cecilia Academy Orch, LSO, National PO, MMF Orch, Vienna Op Orch, Paris Cons/G. Solti/R. Bonynge/H. von Karajan/H. Lewis/L. Maazel/L. Gardelli/J. Pritchard/N. Rescigno/Z. Mehta/A. Erede/T. Serafin/G. Gavazzeni/N. Santi)

① **436 301-2DA** (10/93)
Renata Tebaldi & Franco Corelli—Arias & Duets
Puccini: Manon Lescaut (exc); Bohème (exc); Tosca (exc); *Cilea:* Adriana Lecouvreur (exc); *Ponchielli:* Gioconda (exc); *Verdi:* Aida (exc); Aida (exc); *Zandonai:* Francesca

da Rimini (exc). (R. Tebaldi, F. Corelli, A. Mariotti, R. Cambiata, Leman Chor, SRO, New Philh, Santa Cecilia Academy Orch/A. Guadagno/R. Bonynge/L. Maazel)

Ⓒ **436 303-2DA** (10/93)
Duets from Norma & Semiramide
Bellini: Norma (exc); *Rossini:* Semiramide (exc). (J. Sutherland, M. Horne, John Alexander, L. Fyson, LSO/R. Bonynge)

Ⓒ **436 305-2DA** (10/93) ▭ **436 305-4DA** (10/93)
Delibes—Lakmé (highlights)
Delibes: Lakmé (exc). (J. Sutherland, A. Vanzo, G. Bacquier, J. Berbié, C. Calès, G. Annear, J. Clément, M. Sinclair, E. Belcourt, Monte Carlo Op Chor, Monte Carlo Op Orch/R. Bonynge)

Ⓒ **436 310-2DA** ▭ **436 310-4DA**
Bizet—Carmen - Highlights
Bizet: Carmen (exc). (T. Troyanos, P. Domingo, J. van Dam, K. Te Kanawa, John Alldis Ch, LPO/G. Solti)

Ⓒ **436 311-2DA**
Mozart—Le Nozze di Figaro-Highlights
Mozart: Nozze di Figaro (exc). (J. Van Dam, I. Cotrubas, T. Krause, A. Tomowa-Sintow, F. von Stade, J. Berbié, J. Bastin, H. Zednik, K. Equiluz, Z. Kélémen, C. Barbaux, Vienna St Op Chor, VPO/H. von Karajan)

Ⓒ **436 312-2DA** ▭ **436 312-4DA**
Puccini—La Bohème-Highlights
Puccini: Bohème (exc). (R. Tebaldi, C. Bergonzi, G. d'Angelo, E. Bastianini, R. Cesari, C. Siepi, F. Corena, P. de Palma, A. d'Orazi, Santa Cecilia Academy Chor, Santa Cecilia Academy Orch/T. Serafin)

Ⓒ **436 313-2DA** ▭ **436 313-4DA**
Sutherland/Pavarotti—Operatic Duets
Donizetti: Lucia di Lammermoor (exc); *Verdi:* Rigoletto (exc); *Donizetti:* Elisir d'amore (exc); Maria Stuarda (exc); Fille du régiment (exc); *Bellini:* Puritani (exc). (J. Sutherland, G. Knight, L. Pavarotti, R. Cassinelli, J. Gibbs, ROHO, LSO, ECO, Bologna Teatro Comunale Orch/R. Bonynge)

Ⓒ **436 314-2DA** ▭ **436 314-4DA**
Great Tenor Arias
Flotow: Martha (exc); *Cilea:* Arlesiana (exc); *Giordano:* Andrea Chénier (exc); *Meyerbeer:* Africaine (exc); *Verdi:* Forza del destino (exc); Trovatore (exc); *Massenet:* Manon (exc); *Donizetti:* Favorita (exc); *Verdi:* Ballo in maschera (exc); *Giordano:* Fedora (exc); *Massenet:* Werther (exc); *Giordano:* Andrea Chénier (exc); *Cilea:* Adriana Lecouvreur (exc); *Leoncavallo:* Pagliacci (exc). (L. Pavarotti, New Philh/R. Bonynge, J. Björling, MMF Orch/A. Erede, M. del Monaco, Santa Cecilia Academy Orch/G. Gavazzeni, C. Bergonzi, J. McCracken, Vienna Op Orch/D. Bernet, B. Prevedi, ROHO/E. Downes, G. di Stefano, Zurich Tonhalle Orch/G. Patanè, New SO)

Ⓒ **436 315-2DA** ▭ **436 315-4DA**
Great Operatic Duets
Delibes: Lakmé (exc); *Offenbach:* Contes d'Hoffmann (exc); *Donizetti:* Lucia di Lammermoor (exc); *Puccini:* Madama Butterfly (exc); *Bellini:* Norma (exc); *Verdi:* Don Carlo (exc); *Berlioz:* Béatrice et Benédict (exc); *Verdi:* Forza del destino (exc). (J. Sutherland, J. Berbié, Monte Carlo Nat Op Orch/R. Bonynge, H. Tourangeau, Suisse Romande Rad Ch, Lausanne Pro Arte Ch, SRO, L. Pavarotti, ROHO, M. Freni, C. Ludwig, VPO/H. von Karajan, M. Horne, LSO, C. Bergonzi, D. Fischer-Dieskau, T. Franc, ROH Chor/G. Solti, A. Cantelo, H. Watts/Colin Davis, M. del Monaco, E. Bastianini, Santa Cecilia Academy Orch/F. Molinari-Pradelli)

Ⓒ **436 316-2DA** ▭ **436 316-4DA**
Golden Operetta
J. Strauss II: Fledermaus (exc); Fledermaus (exc); *Lehár:* Land des Lächelns (exc); *Zeller:* Obersteiger (exc); *Lehár:* Giuditta (exc); Lustige Witwe (exc); Lustige Witwe (exc); Schön ist die Welt (exc); Graf von Luxemburg (exc); *J. Strauss II:* Wiener Blut (exc); Nacht in Venedig (exc); Zigeunerbaron (exc); Casanova (exc); *Lecocq:* Coeur et la main (exc); *Offenbach:* Périchole (exc); Grande-Duchesse de Gérolstein (exc). (H. Gueden, Vienna St Op Orch/R. Stolz, J. Björling, Inst Ens, Vienna Operetta Chor, W. Kmentt/R. Moralt, J. Sutherland, Ambrosian Light Op Chor, New Philh/R. Bonynge, W. Krenn, Vienna Volksoper Orch/A. Paulik, R. Holm, G. Janowitz, VPO/K. Böhm, SRO, R. Crespin/A. Lombard, P. Lorengar/W. Weller)

Ⓒ **436 317-2DA** ▭ **436 317-4DA**
Puccini—Famous Arias
Puccini: Madama Butterfly (exc); Bohème (exc); Fanciulla del West (exc); Manon Lescaut (exc); Turandot (exc); Suor Angelica (exc); Fanciulla del West (exc); Tosca (exc); Rondine (exc); Gianni Schicchi (exc). (M. Freni, E. Harwood, M. Chiara, M. Caballé, J. Sutherland, R. Tebaldi, B. Nilsson, L. Pavarotti, M. Sénéchal, P. F. Poli, P. de Palma, F. Corelli, R. Panerai, T. Krause, S. Milnes, N. Ghiaurov, A. Mariotti, John Alldis Ch, VPO, National PO, Vienna Volksoper Orch, LPO, Santa Cecilia Academy Orch, New Philh, MMF Orch, BPO/H. von Karajan/O. de Fabritiis/N. Santi/Z. Mehta/S. Varviso/L. Maazel/L. Gardelli)

ꝏ **436 320-5DH**
Pavarotti in Hyde Park
Verdi: Luisa Miller (exc); Nabucco (exc); Lombardi (exc); Vespri Siciliani (exc); *Meyerbeer:* Africaine (exc); *Mascagni:* Cavalleria Rusticana (exc); *Massenet:* Werther (exc); *Leoncavallo:* Pagliacci (exc); *Wagner:* Lohengrin (exc); *Puccini:* Tosca (exc); Manon Lescaut (exc); Turandot (exc); *Bizet:* Carmen (exc); *Bixio:* Mamma; Mia canzone al vento; *De Curtis:* Non ti scordar di me; Torna a Surriento; *Di Capua:* 'O sole mio. (L. Pavarotti, A. Griminelli, Philh Chor, Philh/L. Magiera, C. Swann)

Ⓒ **436 402-2DWO** (6/93) ▭ **436 402-4DWO** (6/93)
The World of Wedding Music
Wagner: Lohengrin (exc); *Goss:* Praise, my soul; *Gounod:* Ave Maria; *Clarke:* Suite in D (exc); *J. Seymour Irvine:* Lord's my Shepherd; *Bach:* Suites, BWV1066-9 (exc); *Mozart:* Exsultate jubilate, K165 (exc); *Karg-Elert:* Choral-Improvisationen, Op. 65 (exc); *Filitz:* Lead us, heavenly Father; *Mozart:* Vespers, K339 (exc); *Purcell:* Choice Collection of Lessons (exc); *W. Davies:* God be in my head; *Brahms:* Chorale Preludes, Op. 122 (exc); *Stainer:* Love divine; *Schubert:* Ave Maria, D839; *Widor:* Symphony 5 (exc); *Bach:* Cantata 147 (exc); *Handel:* Samson (exc); *Mendelssohn:* Midsummer Night's Dream (exc). (K. Te Kanawa, L. Price, F. Palmer, J. Sutherland, S. Cleobury, R. Farnes, S. Preston, P. Hurford, B. Runnett, P. White, King's College Ch, Huddersfield Choral Soc, St John's College Ch, Utah SO, VPO, Wren Orch, ROHO/S. Cleobury/J. Rudel/W. Morris/H. von Karajan/G. Guest/F. Molinari-Pradelli)

Ⓒ **436 406-2DWO** ▭ **436 406-4DWO**
The World of Tchaikovsky
Tchaikovsky: Romeo and Juliet (exc); Swan Lake (exc); Serenade, Op. 48 (exc); Piano Concerto 1 (exc); Eugene Onegin (exc); Marche slave; Nutcracker Suite (exc); Symphony 6 (exc); Sleeping Beauty (exc); 1812 (exc). (S. Burrows, B. Weikl, Vladimir Ashkenazy, John Alldis Ch, VPO, LSO, ASMF, ROHO, Los Angeles PO, Philh/H. von Karajan/L. Maazel/N. Marriner/G. Solti/Z. Mehta/Vladimir Ashkenazy)

Ⓒ **436 417-2DH** (7/93) ▭ **436 417-4DH** (7/93)
Ute Lemper sings Kurt Weill, Vol.2
Weill: Happy End (exc); Marie Galante (exc); Lady in the Dark (exc); Youkali. (U. Lemper, J. Cohen, London Voices, Berlin RIAS Sinfonietta/J. Mauceri)

Ⓒ **436 418-2DHO2** (4/94)
Wagner—Der fliegende Holländer
Wagner: Fliegende Holländer (Cpte). (R. Hale, H. Behrens, K. Rydl, J. Protschka, I. Vermillion, U. Heilmann, Vienna St Op Concert Ch, VPO/C. von Dohnányi)

Ⓒ **436 461-2DM** (10/93)
Ten Top Sopranos
Puccini: Bohème (exc); *Mozart:* Nozze di Figaro (exc); *Verdi:* Ballo in maschera (exc); *Wagner:* Lohengrin (exc); *R. Strauss:* Elektra (exc); *Puccini:* Madama Butterfly (exc); *Verdi:* Aida (exc); *Catalani:* Wally (exc); *Ponchielli:* Gioconda (exc); *Donizetti:* Lucia di Lammermoor (exc). (M. Freni, K. Te Kanawa, K. Battle, J. Norman, B. Nilsson, L. Price, R. Tebaldi, M. Caballé, J. Sutherland, R. Crespin, L. Pavarotti, H. Sotin, Vienna St Op Concert Ch, Paris Op Chor, BPO, LPO, National PO, VPO, ROHO, Rome Op Orch, Monte Carlo Op Orch, Paris Cons/H. von Karajan/G. Solti/E. Downes/F. Cleva/B. Bartoletti/N. Santi)

Ⓒ **436 462-2DM** (10/93)
Ten Top Mezzos
Rossini: Barbiere di Siviglia (exc); *Mozart:* Nozze di Figaro (exc); *Saint-Saëns:* Samson et Dalila (exc); *Purcell:* Dido (exc); *Mozart:* Idomeneo (exc); *Wagner:* Götterdämmerung (exc); *Donizetti:* Favorita (exc); *Verdi:* Don Carlo (exc); *Gluck:* Paride ed Elena (exc); *Rossini:* Cenerentola (exc). (C. Bartoli, F. von Stade, R. Resnik, J. Baker, A. Baltsa, C. Ludwig, F. Cossotto, G. Bumbry, T. Berganza, M. Horne, St Anthony Sngrs, Bologna Teatro Comunale Orch, LPO, ROHO, ECO, VPO/G. Patanè/G. Solti/E. Downes/A. Lewis/J. Pritchard/R. Bonynge/A. Gibson/H. Lewis)

Ⓒ **436 463-2DM** (10/93) ▭ **436 463-4DM** (10/93)
Ten Top Tenors
Puccini: Bohème (exc); *Verdi:* Trovatore (exc); Traviata (exc); Simon Boccanegra (exc); *Puccini:* Tosca (exc); *Verdi:* Luisa Miller (exc); *Meyerbeer:* Africaine (exc); *Puccini:* Manon Lescaut (exc); *Verdi:* Aida (exc); *Wagner:* Walküre (exc); *Giordano:* Fedora (exc); *Leoncavallo:* Pagliacci (exc); *Ponchielli:* Gioconda (exc); *Cilea:* Arlesiana (exc); *Massenet:* Werther (exc); *Puccini:* Turandot (exc); *Bizet:* Carmen (exc); *Offenbach:* Contes d'Hoffmann (exc). (L. Pavarotti, G. Aragall, F. Corelli, C. Bergonzi, J. Carreras, W. Matteuzzi, J. Vickers, M. del Monaco, J. Björling, G. di Stefano, P. Domingo, P. Coni, London Op Chor, Bologna Teatro Comunale Chor, Suisse Romande Rad Chor, Lausanne Pro Arte Ch, New SO, BPO, National PO, Berlin Deutsche Op Orch, La Scala Orch, Santa Cecilia Academy Orch, Bologna Teatro Comunale Orch, Rome Op Orch, LSO, MMF Orch, Zurich Tonhalle Orch, LPO, SRO/F. Molinari-Pradelli/H. von Karajan/R. Bonynge/L. Maazel/G. Solti/G. Gavazzeni/R. Chailly/E. Leinsdorf/A. Erede/F. Patanè)

Ⓒ **436 464-2DM** (10/93)
Ten Top Baritones & Basses
Rossini: Barbiere di Siviglia (exc); *Mozart:* Nozze di Figaro (exc); Zauberflöte (exc); *Donizetti:* Elisir d'amore (exc); *Verdi:* Nabucco (exc); Traviata (exc); Don Carlo (exc); Forza del destino (exc); Otello (exc); *Mussorgsky:* Boris Godunov (exc). (O. Miljakovic, G. Aragall, W. Kräutler, I. Caley, L. Nucci, T. Gobbi, D. Fischer-Dieskau, E. Bastianini, E. Coda, S. Milnes, S. Ramey, M. Talvela, F. Corena, P. Burchuladze, N. Ghiaurov, Vienna St Op Chor, MMF Chor, Vienna St Op Concert Ch, Sofia Rad Chor, Bologna Teatro Comunale Orch, LPO, VPO, MMF Orch, Vienna Op Orch, Berlin Deutsche Op Orch, English Concert Orch, Santa Cecilia Academy Orch/G. Patanè/G. Solti/F. Molinari-Pradelli/L. Gardelli/L. Maazel/E. Downes/S. Varviso/H. von Karajan)

Ⓒ **436 472-2DM**
Great Opera Arias
Puccini: Tosca (exc); Manon Lescaut (exc); *Mozart:* Nozze di Figaro (exc); *Rossini:* Barbiere di Siviglia (exc); *Verdi:* Ernani (exc); *Massenet:* Werther (exc); *Beethoven:* Fidelio (exc); *Boito:* Mefistofele (exc); Mefistofele (exc); *Puccini:* Manon Lescaut (exc); *Giordano:* Andrea Chénier (exc); *Rossini:* Donna del lago (exc); *Puccini:* Bohème (exc); *Verdi:* Masnadieri (exc). (K. Te Kanawa, S. Dunn, H. Behrens, M. Freni, J. Sutherland, M. Caballé, F. von Stade, M. Horne, G. Aragall, L. Pavarotti, J. Carreras, L. Nucci, N. Ghiaurov, National PO, Bologna Teatro Comunale Orch, LPO, Chicago SO, NYC Op Orch/G. Solti/R. Chailly/G. Patanè/O. de Fabritiis/R. Bonynge)

Ⓒ **436 475-2DM**
Dance of the Hours: ballet music from the opera
Ponchielli: Gioconda (exc); *Saint-Saëns:* Samson et Dalila (exc); *Gounod:* Faust (exc); *Verdi:* Aida (exc); Otello (exc); Vespri siciliani (exc). (National PO, Montreal SO, Bologna Teatro Comunale Orch/B. Bartoletti/C. Dutoit/R. Chailly)

Ⓒ **436 627-2DHO2** (7/93)
Beethoven—Fidelio
Beethoven: Fidelio (Cpte). (G. Schnaut, J. Protschka, H. Welker, K. Rydl, R. Ziesak, U. Heilmann, T. Krause, F. Struckmann, Vienna St Op Concert Ch, VPO/C. von Dohnányi)

Ⓒ **436 631-2DH2** (4/93)
Krenek—Jonny spielt auf
Krenek: Jonny spielt auf (Cpte). (K. St. Hill, H. Kruse, A. Marc, M. Kraus, M. Posselt, D. Scholz, M. Petzold, M. Weichert, E. Noack, Leipzig Op Chor, Chinchilla, Leipzig Gewandhaus/L. Zagrosek)

Ⓒ **436 636-2DH3** (4/93)
Korngold—Das Wunder der Heliane
Korngold: Wunder der Heliane (Cpte). (A. Tomowa-Sintow, H. Welker, J.D. de Haan, R. Runkel, R. Pape, N. Gedda, M. Petzold, Berlin Rad Chor, Berlin RSO/J. Mauceri)

Ⓒ **436 656-2DH** (4/94)
Organ Transcriptions - Thomas Trotter
Elgar: Pomp and Circumstance Marches (exc); Chanson de matin; *Gounod:* Marche funèbre d'une marionette; *Mendelssohn:* Midsummer Night's Dream (exc); *Rossini:* Guillaume Tell (exc); *Suppé:* Dichter und Bauer (exc); *Tchaikovsky:* Nutcracker Suite (exc); *Wagner:* Tannhäuser (exc); Walküre (exc). (T. Trotter)

Ⓒ **436 902-2DHO2** (11/93)
Rossini—La Cenerentola
Rossini: Cenerentola (Cpte). (C. Bartoli, W. Matteuzzi, A. Corbelli, E. Dara, F. Costa, G. Banditelli, M. Pertusi, Bologna Teatro Comunale Chor, Bologna Teatro Comunale Orch/R. Chailly)

Ⓒ **436 990-2DWO** (6/93) ▭ **436 990-4DWO** (6/93)
The World of Benjamin Britten
Britten: Young Persons Guide; Spring Symphony (exc); Noyes Fludde (exc); Serenade (exc); Billy Budd (exc); Ceremony of Carols (exc); Hymn to the Virgin; War Requiem (exc); Peter Grimes (exc); Folk Songs (exc); Simple Symphony. (LSO/B. Britten, J. Vyvyan, N. Procter, P. Pears, ROH Chor, ROHO, T. Anthony, O. Brannigan, D. Pinto, D. Angadi, S. Alexander, C. Clack, M-T. Pinto, E. O'Donovan, E Suffolk Children's Orch, ECO/N. del Mar, B. Tuckwell, P. Glossop, D. Bowman, G. Dempsey, Ambrosian Op Chor, St John's College Ch/G. Guest, M.

Robles, G. Vishnevskaya, Bach Ch, LSC, Highgate Sch Ch, B. Britten)

Ⓓ **440 042-2DMO2** (5/94)
Verdi—Un ballo in maschera
Verdi: Ballo in maschera (Cpte). (R. Tebaldi, L. Pavarotti, S. Milnes, H. Donath, R. Resnik, L. Monreale, N. Christov, J. van Dam, P. F. Poli, M. Alessandrini, Santa Cecilia Academy Chor, Santa Cecilia Academy Orch/B. Bartoletti)

Ⓓ **440 045-2DMO2** (5/94)
Verdi—Otello
Verdi: Otello (Cpte). (C. Cossutta, M. Price, G. Bacquier, P. Dvorský, K. Equiluz, J. Berbié, K. Moll, S. Dean, H. Helm, Vienna Boys' Ch, Vienna St Op Chor, VPO/G. Solti)

Ⓓ **440 048-2DMO2** (7/94)
Verdi—Macbeth
Verdi: Macbeth (Cpte). (D. Fischer-Dieskau, E. Suliotis, N. Ghiaurov, L. Pavarotti, R. Cassinelli, R. Myers, J. Noble, D. Reed, L. Fyson, H. Lawrence, Ambrosian Op Chor, LPO/L. Gardelli)

Ⓓ **440 051-2DMO2** (4/94)
Puccini—Tosca
Puccini: Tosca (Cpte). (B. Nilsson, F. Corelli, D. Fischer-Dieskau, S. Maionica, P. de Palma, A. Mariotti, D. Mantovani, L. Arbace, P. Veronelli, Santa Cecilia Academy Chor, Santa Cecilia Academy Orch/L. Maazel)

Ⓓ **440 054-2DMO2** (4/94)
Boito—Mefistofele
Boito: Mefistofele (Cpte). (C. Siepi, M. del Monaco, R. Tebaldi, F. Cavalli, L. Danieli, P. de Palma, Santa Cecilia Academy Chor, Santa Cecilia Academy Orch/T. Serafin)

Ⓓ **440 057-2DMO4** (10/94)
Wagner—Die Meistersinger von Nürnberg
Wagner: Meistersinger (Cpte). (P. Schoeffler, G. Treptow, H. Gueden, O. Edelmann, K. Dönch, A. Dermota, E. Schürhoff, A. Poell, H. Meyer-Welfing, W. Felden, E. Majkut, W. Wernigk, H. Gallos, H. Pröglhöf, F. Bierbach, L. Pantscheff, Vienna St Op Chor, VPO/H. Knappertsbusch)

Ⓓ **440 062-2DM**
Wagner—Overtures
Wagner: Tannhäuser (exc); Fliegende Holländer (exc); Walküre (exc); Parsifal (exc); Siegfried (exc); Rienzi (exc). (F. Lechleitner, VPO/H. Knappertsbusch)

Ⓓ **440 066-2DM**
Ampico Piano Roll Recordings (1919-1929)
Bach: Partitas, BWV825-30 (exc); *Beethoven:* Ruinen von Athen (exc); *Gluck:* Orfeo ed Euridice (exc); *Mendelssohn:* Songs without words (exc); *Henselt:* Etudes, Op. 2 (exc); *Liszt:* Müllerlieder, S565 (exc); *Schubert:* Impromptus (exc); *Chopin:* Scherzos (exc); Nocturnes (exc); Waltzes (exc); *Liszt:* Chants polonais, S480; *Bizet:* Arlésienne Suites (exc); *Paderewski:* Humoresques de concert, Op. 14 (exc); *Rubinstein:* Barcarolle, Op. 50/3; *Tchaikovsky:* Seasons (exc); Morceaux, Op. 40 (exc). (S. Rachmaninov)

Ⓓ **440 069-2DWO** ▭ **440 069-4DWO**
The World of Wagner
Wagner: Meistersinger (exc); Tannhäuser (exc); Götterdämmerung (exc); Tristan und Isolde (exc); Fliegende Holländer (exc); Walküre (exc); Siegfried (exc); Lohengrin (exc). (V. Schlosser, B. Lindholm, B. Fassbaender, H. Watts, H. Dernesch, V. Little, M. Tyler, C. Hellmann, B. Nilsson, W. Windgassen, V. Braun, G. Frick, Vienna St Op Chor, Vienna St Op Concert Ch, VPO, Chicago SO/G. Solti)

Ⓓ **440 200-2DHO2** (11/93)
Puccini—Manon Lescaut
Puccini: Manon Lescaut (Cpte). (M. Freni, L. Pavarotti, D. Croft, G. Taddei, R. Vargas, C. Bartoli, F. Davià, A. Laciura, P. Groves, J. Courtney, NY Met Op Chor, NY Met Op Orch/James Levine)

Ⓓ **440 280-2DH** ▭ **440 280-4DH**
Kiri on Broadway
F. Loewe: My Fair Lady (exc); *Weill:* One Touch of Venus (exc); *Rodgers:* Too Many Girls (exc); Carousel (exc); *Porter:* Kiss me Kate (exc); *Bernstein:* West Side Story (exc); *Rodgers:* Sound of Music (exc). (K. Te Kanawa, J. Carreras, London Voices, Mormon Tabernacle Ch, LSO, Nelson Riddle Orch, Utah SO, orch/J. Mauceri/N. Riddle/J. Rudel/L. Bernstein)

440 289-2DH ▭ **440 289-4DH**
Rossini—Il barbiere di Siviglia - excerpts
Rossini: Barbiere di Siviglia (exc). (C. Bartoli, G. Banditelli, W. Matteuzzi, L. Nucci, E. Fissore, P. Burchuladze, Bologna Teatro Comunale Chor, Bologna Teatro Comunale Orch/G. Patanè)

Ⓓ **440 318-2DWO** (4/94) ▭ **440 318-4DWO** (4/94)
World of British Classics, Volume II
Holst: Planets; Perfect Fool (exc); Egdon Heath. (LP Ch, LPO/G. Solti/A. Boult)

Ⓓ **440 323-2DWO** (4/94) ▭ **440 323-4DWO** (4/94)
World of British Classics, Volume V
Delius: First cuckoo; Summer Night on the River; Air and Dance; Koanga (exc); Village Romeo and Juliet (exc); Hassan (exc); Fennimore and Gerda Intermezzo; Song before Sunrise; Sea Drift. (ASMF/N. Marriner, J. Shirley-Quirk, LSC, RPO/R. Hickox)

Ⓓ **440 331-2DH** (1/94)
Prokofiev—Orchestral Works
Prokofiev: Violin Concerto 1; Violin Concerto 2; Love for 3 Oranges Suite. (J. Bell, Montreal SO/C. Dutoit)

ꝏ **440 331-5DH**
Prokofiev—Orchestral Works
Prokofiev: Violin Concerto 1; Violin Concerto 2; Love for 3 Oranges Suite. (J. Bell, Montreal SO/C. Dutoit)

Ⓓ **440 333-2DH** (10/95)
Ravel—Vocal Works
Ravel: Enfant et les sortilèges (Cpte); Shéhérazade; Shéhérazade. (C. Alliot-Lugaz, C. Dubosc, M-F. Lefort, O. Beaupré, C. Carlson, G. Gautier, D. Henry, L. Sarrazin, Montreal SO/C. Dutoit)

Ⓓ **440 400-2DM**
Luciano Pavarotti
Giordano: Fedora (exc); *Boito:* Mefistofele (exc); *Cilea:* Adriana Lecouvreur (exc); *Mascagni:* Iris (exc); *Meyerbeer:* Africaine (exc); *Massenet:* Werther (exc); *Giordano:* Andrea Chénier (exc); *Puccini:* Fanciulla del West (exc); Manon Lescaut (exc). (L. Pavarotti, N. Howlett, National PO/O. de Fabritiis/R. Chailly)

Ⓓ **440 401-2DM**
Kiri Te Kanawa — Mozart Arias
Mozart: Nozze di Figaro (exc); Schauspieldirektor (exc); Ah, lo previdi, K272; Vado, ma dove?, K583; Oh, temerario Arbace!, K79; Chi sà, K582; Idomeneo (exc); Bella mia fiamma, K528; Nehmt meinen Dank, K383. (K. Te Kanawa, LPO/G. Solti, VPO/J. Pritchard, Vienna CO/G. Fischer)

Ⓓ **440 402-2DM**
Leontyne Price
Mozart: Don Giovanni (exc); *Verdi:* Aida (exc); *Puccini:* Tosca (exc); *R. Strauss:* Ariadne auf Naxos (exc); *Verdi:* Requiem (exc); *Schubert:* Ave Maria, D839; *Mozart:* Exsultate jubilate, K165 (exc); *Traditional:* Sweet little Jesus boy (exc); *Gershwin:* Porgy and Bess (exc). (L. Price, Vienna Singverein, Rome Op Orch, LPO, VPO, orch/H. von Karajan/G. Solti/E. Leinsdorf/F. Reiner)

Ⓓ **440 403-2DM**
Giuseppe di Stefano
Giordano: Andrea Chénier (exc); Andrea Chénier (exc); *Puccini:* Tosca (exc); Turandot (exc); *Massenet:* Werther (exc); Manon (exc); *Bizet:* Carmen (exc); Pêcheurs de perles (exc); *Gounod:* Faust (exc); *Donizetti:* Elisir d'amore (exc); *Ponchielli:* Gioconda (exc); *Verdi:* Forza del destino (exc); *Boito:* Mefistofele (exc). (G. di Stefano, C. Siepi, Santa Cecilia Academy Chor, Santa Cecilia Academy Orch, Zurich Tonhalle Orch, MMF Orch/F. Patanè/F. Molinari-Pradelli/T. Serafin/F. Previtali)

Ⓓ **440 404-2DM**
Joan Sutherland
Bellini: Norma (exc); Puritani (exc); *Donizetti:* Lucia di Lammermoor (exc); Linda di Chamounix (exc); *Verdi:* Attila (exc); Ernani (exc); Vespri Siciliani (exc). (J. Sutherland, N. Sautereau, Paris Op Chor, ROH Chor, ROHO, London Sym Chor, LSO, Paris Cons/F. Molinari-Pradelli/R. Bonynge/N. Santi)

Ⓓ **440 405-2DM**
Elena Souliotis
Donizetti: Anna Bolena (exc); *Mascagni:* Cavalleria Rusticana (exc); *Ponchielli:* Gioconda (exc); *Verdi:* Nabucco (exc); Macbeth (exc); Luisa Miller (exc); Ballo in maschera (exc); Ballo in maschera (exc); Forza del destino (exc). (E. Suliotis, A. di Stasio, G. Foiani, Vienna St Op Concert Ch, Vienna Op Orch, Rome Op Orch, Rome Orch/L. Gardelli/O. de Fabritiis/S. Varviso)

Ⓓ **440 406-2DM**
Giulietta Simionato
Rossini: Barbiere di Siviglia (exc); *Verdi:* Don Carlo (exc); Trovatore (exc); Ballo in maschera (exc); Forza del destino (exc); *Bellini:* Norma (exc); Capuleti (exc); *Rossini:* Cenerentola (exc); *Saint-Saëns:* Samson et Dalila (exc); *A. Thomas:* Mignon (exc); *Massenet:* Werther (exc); *Bizet:* Carmen (exc); *Donizetti:* Favorita (exc). (G. Simionato, M. del Monaco, C. Bergonzi, A. Balbi, Santa Cecilia Academy Chor, MMF Chor, Santa Cecilia Academy Orch, MMF Orch, SRO/F. Previtali/F. Ghione/A. Erede/G. Solti/F. Molinari-Pradelli/A. Paoletti)

Ⓓ **440 407-2DM**
Mario del Monaco
Verdi: Aida (exc); Forza del Destino (exc); Ernani (exc); Ballo in maschera (exc); Trovatore (exc); Otello (exc); *Ponchielli:* Gioconda (exc); *Puccini:* Tosca (exc); Madama Butterfly (exc); Turandot (exc); Fanciulla del West (exc); *Giordano:* Fedora (exc); Andrea Chénier (exc); *Meyerbeer:* Africaine (exc); *Leoncavallo:* Pagliacci (exc); *Di Capua:* O sole mio; *De Curtis:* Torna a Surriento; *Lara:* Granada. (R. Tebaldi, M. del Monaco, A. Cesarini, P. de Palma, C. MacNeil, F. Corena, MMF Chor, Santa Cecilia Academy Chor, Santa Cecilia Academy Orch, New SO, SRO, MMF Orch, orch/A. Erede/F. Molinari-Pradelli/G. Gavazzeni/E. Nicelli/F. Capuana)

Ⓓ **440 408-2DM**
Renata Tebaldi
Puccini: Madama Butterfly (exc); Bohème (exc); Turandot (exc); Tosca (exc); Gianni Schicchi (exc); Suor Angelica (exc); Fanciulla del West (exc); Manon Lescaut (exc); *Verdi:* Aida (exc); Otello (exc); Forza del destino (exc); *Cilea:* Adriana Lecouvreur (exc); *Giordano:* Andrea Chénier (exc); *Boito:* Mefistofele (exc); *Catalani:* Wally (exc). (R. Tebaldi, L. Ribacchi, C. Bergonzi, M. del Monaco, C. MacNeil, Santa Cecilia Academy Chor, Santa Cecilia Academy Orch, VPO, MMF Orch, Monte Carlo Nat Op Orch/T. Serafin/A. Erede/F. Molinari-Pradelli/H. von Karajan/L. Gardelli/F. Capuana/G. Gavazzeni/F. Cleva)

Ⓓ **440 409-2DM**
Dietrich Fischer-Dieskau
Mozart: Nozze di Figaro (exc); Mentre ti lascio, K513; *Haydn:* Acide e Galatea (exc); *Verdi:* Macbeth (exc); Traviata (exc); Don Carlo (exc); *Puccini:* Tosca (exc); *Mahler:* Lied von der Erde (exc); *Schumann:* Szenen aus Goethes Faust (exc); *Wagner:* Götterdämmerung (exc); Parsifal (exc). (D. Fischer-Dieskau, C. Ludwig, Vienna Mozart Orch/R. Peters, LPO/L. Gardelli, Berlin Deutsche Op Orch/L. Maazel, ROHO/G. Solti, Santa Cecilia Academy Chor, Santa Cecilia Academy Orch, Vienna St Op Chor, VPO/L. Bernstein, ECO/B. Britten)

Ⓓ **440 410-2DM**
Plácido Domingo
Bizet: Carmen (exc); *Wagner:* Lohengrin (exc); *R. Strauss:* Frau ohne Schatten (exc); *Offenbach:* Contes d'Hoffmann (exc); *Meyerbeer:* Africaine (exc). (P. Domingo, T. Troyanos, John Alldis Ch, LPO/G. Solti, J. Norman, E. Randová, H. Sotin, Vienna St Op Chor, VPO, P. di Proenza, Suisse Romande Rad Chor, Pro Arte Ch, Brassus Chorale, SRO/R. Bonynge, MMF Orch, Rome Op Orch/Z. Mehta)

Ⓓ **440 411-2DM**
Anita Cerquetti
Verdi: Aida (exc); Vespri siciliani (exc); *Bellini:* Norma (exc); *Spontini:* Agnes von Hohenstaufen (exc); *Verdi:* Nabucco (exc); Ernani (exc); *Puccini:* Tosca (exc); *Verdi:* Forza del destino (exc); *Ponchielli:* Gioconda (exc). (A. Cerquetti, G. Simionato, M. del Monaco, E. Bastianini, MMF Chor, MMF Orch/G. Gavazzeni)

Ⓓ **440 412-2DM**
Mirella Freni
Puccini: Bohème (exc); Tosca (exc); Madama Butterfly (exc); *Rossini:* Guillaume Tell (exc); *Verdi:* Falstaff (exc); *Leoncavallo:* Pagliacci (exc); *Boito:* Mefistofele (exc); *Bellini:* Bianca e Fernando (exc); *Pratella:* Ninnananna di Modigliana; Ninnananna romagnola. (M. Freni, R. Scotto, C. Ludwig, L. Pavarotti, RCA Italiana Op Chor, Bologna Teatro Comunale Chor, BPO, National PO, RCA Italiana Op Orch, VPO, Bologna Teatro Comunale Orch/H. von Karajan/R. Chailly/G. Solti/G. Patanè/N. Rescigno/O de Fabritiis/L. Magiera)

Ⓓ **440 414-2DM**
Arleen Auger
Mozart: Nozze di Figaro (exc); Don Giovanni (exc); Mass, K427 (exc); *Haydn:* Berenice che fai?; Son pietosa, son bonina; Arianna a Naxos; Solo e pensoso; Miseri noi. (A. Auger, Drottningholm Court Th Orch/A. Östman, AAM, Handel & Haydn Soc Orch/C. Hogwood)

Ⓓ **440 415-2DM**
Marilyn Horne
Handel: Semele (exc); Rodelinda (exc); *Mozart:* Clemenza di Tito (exc); *Gluck:* Alceste (1776) (exc); *Arditi:* Leggero invisibile; *Bizet:* Carmen (exc); *Saint-Saëns:* Samson et Dalila (exc); *Gounod:* Sapho (exc); *Rossini:* Italiana in Algeri (exc); Donna del lago (exc). (M. Horne, New SO/R. Bonynge, Vienna Cantata Orch/H. Lewis, ROHO, SRO, LSO, W. Blankenship, Vienna Op Orch, Geneva Op Chor, NYC Op Orch)

Ⓓ **440 416-2DM**
Régine Crespin
Gluck: Iphigénie en Tauride (exc); *Berlioz:* Damnation de Faust (exc); *Gounod:* Sapho (exc); *Bizet:* Carmen (exc); Carmen (exc); *Offenbach:* Grande-Duchesse de Gérolstein (exc); Belle Hélène (exc); Périchole (exc); *Hahn:* Ciboulette (exc); *Christiné:* Phi-Phi (exc); *Messager:* Amour masqué (exc); *O. Straus:* Drei Walzer (exc). (R. Crespin, Geneva Grand Th Chor, SRO, Vienna Volksoper Orch/A. Lombard/G. Sébastian)

Ⓓ **440 417-2DM**
Carlo Bergonzi
Verdi: Aida (exc); Luisa Miller (exc); Forza del destino (exc); Trovatore (exc); Ballo in maschera (exc); Ballo in maschera (exc); Don Carlo (exc); Traviata (exc); *Ponchielli:* Gioconda (exc); *Meyerbeer:* Africaine (exc); *Giordano:* Andrea Chénier (exc); *Cilea:* Adriana Lecouvreur (exc); *Puccini:* Tosca (exc); Manon Lescaut (exc); Bohème (exc). (D. Carral, S. Stahlman, C. Bergonzi, F. Corena, L. Arbace, Santa Cecilia Academy Chor, Santa Cecilia Academy Orch, ROHO/G. Gavazzeni/G. Solti/T. Serafin/L. Gardelli/J. Pritchard)

Ⓓ **440 418-2DM**
Cesare Siepi
Mozart: Nozze di Figaro (exc); Don Giovanni (exc); *Verdi:* Don Carlo (exc); Nabucco (exc); Ernani (exc); Simon Boccanegra (exc); *Gomes:* Salvator Rosa (exc); *Meyerbeer:* Huguenots (exc); Robert le Diable (exc); *Halévy:* Juive (exc); *Ponchielli:* Gioconda (exc); *Boito:* Mefistofele (exc). (C. Siepi, VPO, Santa Cecilia Academy Orch, MMF Orch/E. Kleiber/J. Krips/A. Erede/G. Gavazzeni/T. Serafin)

Ⓓ **440 419-2DM**
Gérard Souzay
Rameau: Indes galantes (exc); *Gounod:* Philémon et Baucis (exc); Roméo et Juliette (exc); *Berlioz:* Damnation de Faust (exc); *Bizet:* Pêcheurs de perles (exc); Jolie fille de Perth (exc); *Massenet:* Jongleur de Notre Dame (exc); *Offenbach:* Contes d'Hoffmann (exc); *Chabrier:* Roi malgré lui (exc); *Gounod:* Chanson de printemps; Ce que je suis sans toi; Mélodies (1855) (exc); Ma belle amie est morte; Viens! Les gazons sont verts!; Deux pigeons. (G. Souzay, J. Bonneau, New SO/P. Bonneau)

Ⓓ **440 606-2DF2**
Wagner—Orchestral Favourites
Wagner: Rienzi (exc); Fliegende Holländer (exc); Tristan und Isolde (exc); Tannhäuser (exc); Lohengrin (exc); Siegfried Idyll; Meistersinger (exc); Parsifal (exc); Götterdämmerung (exc). (Vienna Singverein, Vienna St Op Chor, VPO/G. Solti)

Ⓓ **440 679-2DH** (9/94)
Carnaval!
Adam: Pantins de Violette (exc); Si j'étais roi (exc); *Balfe:* Puits d'amour (exc); *Boïeldieu:* Fête du village voisin (exc); *F. David:* Perle du Brésil (exc); *Delibes:* Roi l'a dit (exc); *Grétry:* Fausses apparences (exc); *Hérold:* Pré aux clercs (exc); *Massenet:* Don César de Bazan (exc); *Massé:* Reine Topaze (exc); *Messager:* Madame Chrysanthème (exc); *Offenbach:* Mari à la porte (exc); *A. Thomas:* Songe d'une nuit d'été (exc). (S. Jo, ECO/R. Bonynge)

Ⓓ **440 843-2DH**
Verdi—Otello Highlights
Verdi: Otello (exc). (K. Te Kanawa, E. Ardam, L. Pavarotti, A. Rolfe Johnson, L. Nucci, Chicago Sym Chor, Chicago SO/G. Solti)

Ⓓ **440 850-2DHO2** (3/94)
B.Goldschmidt—Der gewaltige Hahnrei
B. Goldschmidt: Gewaltige Hahnrei (Cpte); Mediterranean Songs (Cpte). (R. Alexander, R. Wörle, M. Kraus, C. Otelli, H. Lawrence, M. Petzold, E. Wottrich, M. Posselt, C. Berggold, F-J. Kapellmann, Berlin Rad Chor, Berlin Deutsches SO, J. M. Ainsley, Leipzig Gewandhaus/L. Zagrosek)

Ⓓ **440 854-2DH** (12/94)
Ullmann—Der Kaiser von Atlantis
Ullmann: Kaiser von Atlantis (Cpte); Abendphantasie; Frühling; Wo bist du. (M. Kraus, F. Mazura, M. Petzold, C. Oelze, W. Berry, H. Lippert, I. Vermillion, Leipzig Gewandhaus/L. Zagrosek, J. Alder)

Ⓓ **440 947-2DH** ⊟ **440 947-4DH**
Essential Opera II
Wagner: Walküre (exc); *Bizet:* Carmen (exc); *Mozart:* Don Giovanni (exc); Nozze di Figaro (exc); Nozze di Figaro (exc); Così fan tutte (exc); Zauberflöte (exc); *Puccini:* Madama Butterfly (exc); Turandot (exc); Tosca (exc); Bohème (exc); *Verdi:* Traviata (exc); Rigoletto (exc); *Leoncavallo:* Pagliacci (exc); *Rossini:* Barbiere di Siviglia (exc); *Bizet:* Pêcheurs de perles (exc); *Cilea:* Arlesiana (exc); *Delibes:* Lakmé (exc); *Gounod:* Faust (exc). (M. Caballé, M. Freni, L. Popp, J. Sutherland, K. Te Kanawa, C. Bartoli, J. Berbié, B. Fassbaender, T. Troyanos, G. Cross, J. Carreras, P. Domingo, L. Pavarotti, M. Kraus, T. Krause, G. Maffeo, G. Quilico, R. Panerai, N. Ghiaurov, S. Ramey, John Alldis Ch, Ambrosian Op Chor, London Op Chor, Vienna St Op Chor, BPO, Bologna Teatro Comunale Orch, LPO, LSO, MMF Orch, Monte Carlo Nat Op Orch, Montreal SO, National PO, Rome Op Orch, Vienna Haydn Orch, VPO/R. Bonynge/C. Dutoit/I. Kertész/Z. Mehta/G. Patanè/H. von Karajan/G. Solti)

Ⓓ **443 000-2DF2** (5/94)
Verdi—La Traviata
Verdi: Traviata (Cpte). (P. Lorengar, G. Aragall, D. Fischer-Dieskau, S. Malagù, M. Fiorentino, P. F. Poli, V. Carbonari, S. Maionica, G. Foiani, A. Losa, Berlin Deutsche Op Chor, Berlin Deutsche Op Orch/L. Maazel)

Ⓓ **443 006-2DF2**
Kodály—Orchestral Works
Kodály: Háry János Suite; Galánta Dances; Peacock Variations; Marosszék Dances; Theatre Overture; Concerto for Orchestra; Summer Evening; Symphony in C. (Philh Hungarica/A. Dorati)

Ⓓ **443 015-2DF2**
Smetana/Dvořák—Orchestral Works
Smetana: Má vlast; Bartered Bride (exc); Hakon Jarl; *Dvořák:* Prague Waltzes; Nocturne; Czech Suite, B93. (Israel PO/W. Weller/I. Kertész, Detroit SO/A. Dorati)

Ⓓ **443 018-2DF2** (5/94)
Pavarotti/Freni/Ricciarelli—Live
Verdi: Traviata (exc); Aida (exc); Macbeth (exc); Forza del destino (exc); Lombardi (exc); Corsaro (exc); Falstaff (exc); Otello (exc); Ballo in maschera (exc); *Puccini:* Turandot (exc); Turandot (exc); *Verdi:* Traviata (exc); *Massenet:* Werther (exc); *Verdi:* Vespri Siciliani (exc); *Ponchielli:* Gioconda (exc); *Donizetti:* Elisir d'amore (exc); Fille du régiment (exc); *Meyerbeer:* Africaine (exc); *Boito:* Mefistofele (exc); *Mascagni:* Amico Fritz (exc); *Verdi:* Traviata (exc); *Puccini:* Tosca (exc); *Donizetti:* Elisir d'amore (exc); *Verdi:* Aida (exc). (M. Freni, K. Ricciarelli, L. Pavarotti, Verona Arena Orch, Ater Orch, Parma Teatro Regio Orch/A. Gatto/L. Magiera/B. Martinotti/G. Patanè)

Ⓓ **443 204-2DH11(1)**
Puccini—Operas
Puccini: Tosca (Cpte). (M. Freni, L. Pavarotti, S. Milnes, R. Van Allan, M. Sénéchal, I. Tajo, P. Hudson, J. Tomlinson, W. Baratti, Wandsworth Sch Boys' Ch, London Op Chor, National PO/N. Rescigno)

Ⓓ **443 204-2DH11(2)**
Puccini—Five Great Operas
Puccini: Bohème (Cpte). (M. Freni, L. Pavarotti, E. Harwood, R. Panerai, G. Maffeo, N. Ghiaurov, M. Sénéchal, G. Pietsch, H-D. Appelt, H-D. Pohl, Schöneberg Boys' Ch, Berlin Deutsche Op Chor, BPO/H. von Karajan)

Ⓓ **443 204-2DH11(3)**
Puccini—Five Great Operas
Puccini: Turandot (Cpte). (J. Sutherland, L. Pavarotti, M. Caballé, T. Krause, P.F. Poli, P. de Palma, N. Ghiaurov, P. Pears, S. Markov, Wandsworth Sch Boys' Ch, John Alldis Ch, LPO/Z. Mehta)

Ⓓ **443 204-2DH11(5)**
Puccini—Five Great Operas
Puccini: Manon Lescaut (Cpte). (M. Freni, L. Pavarotti, D. Croft, G. Taddei, R. Vargas, C. Bartoli, F. Davià, A. Laciura, P. Groves, J. Courtney, NY Met Op Chor, NY Met Op Orch/James Levine)

Ⓓ **443 331-2LRX** ⊟ **443 331-4LRX**
Music for Relaxation, Vol 6 - The Morning After
Grieg: Peer Gynt (exc); *Bach:* Schübler Chorales, BWV645-650; *Delius:* Florida Suite (exc); *Segovia:* Neblina (exc); *Nielsen:* Aladdin Suite (exc); *J. Strauss II:* Morgenblätter, Op. 279; *Traditional:* Early one Morning; *Ravel:* Daphnis et Chloé Suites (exc); *Haydn:* Symphony 6 (exc); *Elgar:* Chanson de matin; *Bruch:* Scottish Fantasy; *Canteloube:* Chants d'Auvergne (exc); *Ponchielli:* Gioconda (exc). (VPO/H. von Karajan, P. Hurford, WNO Orch/C. MacKerras, E. Fernández, San Francisco SO/H. Blomstedt/W. Boskovsky, ASMF/N. Marriner, LSC, LSO/L. Stokowski, E. Ramor, Z. Thirring, Philh Hungarica/A. Dorati, LPO/A. Boult, K-W. Chung, RPO/R. Kempe, K. Te Kanawa, ECO/J. Tate, National PO/B. Bartoletti)

Ⓓ **443 334-2LRX** ⊟ **443 334-4LRX**
Music for Relaxation, Vol 9 - A Touch of Romance
Tchaikovsky: Romeo and Juliet (exc); *Kreisler:* Liebesfreud; Liebesleid; *Delius:* Village Romeo and Juliet (exc); *Liszt:* Liebesträume, S541 (exc); *Berlioz:* Damnation de Faust (exc); Roméo et Juliette (exc); *Prokofiev:* Romeo and Juliet (exc); *Elgar:* Salut d'amour; *Duparc:* Extase; *Canteloube:* Chants d'Auvergne (exc); *Khachaturian:* Spartacus (exc); *Beethoven:* Bagatelles (exc); *Saint-Saëns:* Samson et Dalila (exc). (K. te Kanawa, F. von Stade, M. Horne, E. Gruenberg, K-W. Chung, J. Bolet, P. Moll, Vladimir Ashkenazy, VPO/H. von Karajan/A. Khachaturian/L. Maazel, Philh/E. Howarth, ASMF/N. Marriner, Chicago SO/G. Solti, SRO/E. Ansermet, LSO/L. Stokowski, ECO/J. Tate, Vienna Op Orch/H. Lewis)

Ⓓ **443 335-2LRX** ⊟ **443 335-4LRX**
Music for Relaxation, Vol 10 - The Night Before
Offenbach: Contes d'Hoffmann (exc); *Mozart:* Serenade, K239 (exc); *Dvořák:* Serenade, Op. 22 (exc); *Chopin:* Nocturnes (exc); *Suk:* Serenade, Op. 6 (exc); *Berlioz:* Béatrice et Bénédict (exc); *Chopin:* Preludes (exc); Mazurkas (exc); *Hoffstetter:* String Quartets, Op. 3 (exc); *Beach:* Sketches, Op. 15 (exc); *Handel:* Concerti grossi, Op. 6 (exc); *Tárrega:* Recuerdos de la Alhambra; *Humperdinck:* Hänsel und Gretel (exc); *Brahms:* Serenade 2 (exc); *Dvořák:* Czech Suite, B93 (exc); *Salzedo:* Chanson dans la nuit; *Canteloube:* Chants d'Auvergne (exc). (J. Sutherland, A. Cantelo, K. Te Kanawa, L. Popp, H. Tourangeau, H. Watts, B. Fassbaender, Vladimir Ashkenazy, M. Robles, A. Feinberg, E. Fernández, Suisse Romande Rad Chor, Lausanne Pro Arte Ch, SRO, ASMF, LPO, Los Angeles CO, Stuttgart CO, VPO, LSO, Detroit SO, ECO/R. Bonynge/N. Marriner/C. Hogwood/K. Münchinger/G. Solti/I. Kertész/A. Dorati/J. Tate/Colin Davis)

Ⓓ **443 377-2DM**
Ten Top Sopranos 2
Delibes: Lakmé (exc); *Canteloube:* Chants d'Auvergne (exc); *Giordano:* Andrea Chénier (exc); *Verdi:* Otello (exc); *Mozart:* Entführung (exc); *Bach:* St Matthew Passion, BWV244 (exc); *Mozart:* Zaïde (exc); *Puccini:* Madama Butterfly (exc); *Schubert:* Ave Maria, D839; *Mozart:* Zauberflöte (exc). (J. Sutherland, M. Caballé, M. Caballé, R. Tebaldi, K. Battle, E. Ameling, L. Popp, M. Freni, L. Price, S. Jo, A. R. Satre, C. Ludwig, L. Pavarotti, ROHO, ECO, National PO, VPO, Stuttgart CO, Vienna Haydn Orch/F. Molinari-Pradelli/J. Tate/R. Chailly/H. von Karajan/G. Solti/K. Münchinger/I. Kertész)

Ⓓ **443 378-2DM**
Ten Top Mezzos 2
Rossini: Italiana in Algeri (exc); *Cherubini:* Medea (exc); *Bach:* Cantata 170 (exc); *Gluck:* Orfeo ed Euridice (exc); *Bizet:* Carmen (exc); *Rossini:* Donna del lago (exc); *Berlioz:* Damnation de Faust (exc); *Verdi:* Trovatore (exc); *Ponchielli:* Gioconda (exc); *Schoenberg:* Gurrelieder (exc). (C. Bartoli, F. Cossotto, J. Baker, T. Berganza, T. Troyanos, M. Horne, G. Simionato, F. von Stade, A. Baltsa, B. Fassbaender, M. del Monaco, A. Balbi, A. Schoenberg Ch, John Alldis Ch, Ambrosian Op Chor, MMF Chor, Vienna Volksoper Orch, Santa Cecilia Academy Orch, ASMF, ROHO, LPO, RPO, Geneva Grand Th Orch, Chicago SO, National PO, Berlin RSO/G. Patanè/L. Gardelli/N. Marriner/A. Gibson/G. Solti/H. Lewis/A. Erede/B. Bartoletti/R. Chailly)

Ⓓ **443 379-2DM**
Ten Top Tenors 2
Rossini: Guillaume Tell (exc); *Verdi:* Forza del destino (exc); *Giordano:* Andrea Chénier (exc); *Verdi:* Otello (exc); *Wagner:* Lohengrin (exc); *Gounod:* Faust (exc); *Bach:* St Matthew Passion, BWV244 (exc); *Wagner:* Meistersinger (exc); *Lehár:* Land des Lächelns (exc); *Lara:* Granada. (L. Pavarotti, C. Bergonzi, G. di Stefano, M. del Monaco, P. de Palma, P. Domingo, F. Corelli, F. Wunderlich, R. Kollo, J. Björling, J. Carreras, N. Bailey, Vienna Op Chor, Santa Cecilia Academy Chor, Stuttgart Hymnus Boys' Ch, Vienna St Op Chor, Vienna Op Orch, Santa Cecilia Academy Orch, VPO, LSO, Stuttgart CO, orch, MMF Orch, Rome Op Orch/N. Rescigno/G. Gavazzeni/F. Patanè/A. Erede/G. Solti/R. Bonynge/K. Münchinger/Z. Mehta)

Ⓓ **443 380-2DM**
Ten Top Baritones & Basses 2
Leoncavallo: Pagliacci (exc); *Mozart:* Don Giovanni (exc); *Verdi:* Macbeth (exc); *Schumann:* Szenen aus Goethes Faust (exc); *Donizetti:* Duca d'Alba (exc); *Wagner:* Tannhäuser (exc); Fliegende Holländer (exc); *Verdi:* Don Carlos (exc); *Rimsky-Korsakov:* Sadko (exc); *Bellini:* Puritani (exc). (R. Merrill, G. Evans, D. Fischer-Dieskau, L. Nucci, T. Krause, S. Ramey, G. London, S. Milnes, N. Ghiaurov, P. Cappuccilli, R. Cazzaniga, VPO, New SO, SRO, Bologna Teatro Comunale Orch, ECO, Vienna Op Orch, LPO, LSO/H. Knappertsbusch/E. Downes/B. Balkwill/R. Chailly/B. Britten/G-F. Masini/A. Quadri/S. Varviso/R. Bonynge)

Ⓓ **443 389-2DWO** ⊟ **443 389-4DWO**
The World of Gershwin
Gershwin: Cuban Overture; Girl Crazy (exc); Funny Face (exc); Rhapsody in Blue; Oh, Kay! (exc); American in Paris; Porgy and Bess. (I. Davis, Cleveland Orch/L. Maazel, Boston Pops/A. Fiedler, orch/F. Chacksfield)

Ⓓ **443 393-2DWO** ⊟ **443 393-4DWO**
The World of Henry Purcell
Purcell: Abdelazer, Z570 (exc); Birthday Ode, Z323 (exc); Bess of Bedlam, Z370; Tempest, Z631 (exc); Oedipus,

Z583 (exc); Fairy Queen, Z629 (exc); King Arthur, Z628 (exc); King Arthur, Z628 (exc); Choice Collection of Lessons (exc); I was glad, Z19; March and Canzona, Z860; Funeral Sentences (exc); Pausanias, Z585 (exc); Chaconne, Z730; Fairy Queen, Z629; Dido (exc). (H. Harper, K. Ferrier, H. Watts, A. Deller, J. Whitworth, P. Esswood, I. Partridge, H. Alan, T. Anthony, S. Dean, D. Dupré, J. Ryan, P. Spurr, T. Dart, P. Hurford, John Scott, S. Cleobury, St. John's College Ch, M. Laird Brass Ens, Symphoniae Sacrae, AAM, Oiseau-Lyre Orch Ens, Philomusica of London, ECO/C. Hogwood/A. Lewis/B. Britten/G. Guest, J. Vyvyan, St Anthony Sngrs, J. Bowman, B. Britten)

◉ **443 444-2DH** (1/95)
Hungarian Connections
Bartók: Hungarian Sketches; Romanian folkdances, Sz68; *Kodály:* Háry János Suite; *Liszt:* Faust Episodes, S110 (exc); Hungarian Rhapsodies, S359 (exc); *Leó Weiner:* Prinz Csonger Suite (exc). (L. Kaptain, Chicago SO/G. Solti)

◉ **443 452-2DH** (11/94) ▭ **443 452-4DH** (11/94)
Mozart Portraits—Bartoli
Mozart: Così fan tutte (exc); Nozze di Figaro (exc); Don Giovanni (exc); Davidde penitente, K469 (exc); Exsultate, jubilate, K165. (C. Bartoli, Vienna CO/G. Fischer)

◉ **443 464-2DF2** (9/95)
Rimsky-Korsakov—Scheherazade, etc
Rimsky-Korsakov: Scheherazade; May Night (exc); Tale of Tsar Saltan (exc); Tale of Tsar Saltan (exc); Russian Easter Festival Ov; Christmas Eve (exc); Sadko; Dubinushka; Snow Maiden (exc). (Geneva Motet Ch, SRO/E. Ansermet)

◉ **443 488-2DF2** (10/95)
Kodály—Háry János; Psalmus Hungaricus etc
Kodály: Háry János (Cpte); Peacock Variations; Peacock; Psalmus Hungaricus. (E. Komlóssy, L. Palócz, G. Melis, Z. Bende, O. Szönyi, Margit László, P. Ustinov, L. Kozma, Edinburgh Fest Chor, Brighton Fest Chor, Wandsworth Sch Boys' Ch, LSC, LSO/I. Kertész)

◉ **443 530-2LF2** (7/95)
Mozart—Die Entführung aus dem Serail
Mozart: Entführung (Cpte); Zauberflöte (exc); Così fan tutte (exc); Nozze di Figaro (exc); Don Giovanni (exc); Schauspieldirektor (exc). (W. Lipp, E. Loose, W. Ludwig, P. Klein, E. Koréh, H. Woester, Vienna St Op Chor, VPO, LSO/J. Krips)

◉ **443 536-2LF2**
Rossini—Le barbiere di Siviglia
Rossini: Barbiere di Siviglia (Cpte). (E. Bastianini, G. Simionato, A. Misciano, F. Corena, C. Siepi, R. Cavallari, A. La Porta, G. Zampieri, MMF Chor, MMF Orch/A. Erede)

◉ **443 539-2LF2** (6/95)
Gounod—Romeo et Juliette
Gounod: Roméo et Juliette (Cpte). (R. Jobin, J. Micheau, O. Ricquier, H. Rehfuss, C. Cambon, L. Rialland, P. Mollet, A. Philippe, C. Collart, C. Roquetty, Paris Op Chor, Paris Op Orch/A. Erede)

◉ **443 542-2LF2** (7/95)
Donizetti—L'Elisir d'amore
Donizetti: Elisir d'amore (Cpte). (H. Gueden, G. di Stefano, R. Capecchi, F. Corena, L. Mandelli, MMF Chor, MMF Orch/F. Molinari-Pradelli)

◉ **443 571-2DCS** (4/95)
Bartók—Duke Bluebeard's Castle
Bartók: Duke Bluebeard's castle (Cpte). (W. Berry, C. Ludwig, LSO/I. Kertész)

◉ **443 581-2DCS2** (5/95)
An Introduction to Der Ring des Nibelungen
Wagner: Ring des Nibelungen Introduction. (D. Cooke, Sols, VPO/G. Solti)

◉ **443 585-2DF2** ▭ **433 585-4DWO2**
Your Hundred Best Tunes - Top 20
Bach: Cantata 147 (exc); *Beethoven:* Piano Concerto 5 (exc); Symphony 6 (exc); Symphony 9 (exc); *Bizet:* Pêcheurs de perles (exc); *Bruch:* Violin Concerto 1 (exc); *Elgar:* Enigma Variations (exc); *Handel:* Messiah (exc); Solomon (exc); *Mascagni:* Cavalleria Rusticana (exc); *Massenet:* Thaïs (exc); *Mozart:* Clarinet Concerto, K622 (exc); Piano Concerto 21 (exc); Ave verum corpus, K618; *Pachelbel:* Canon and Gigue (exc); *Rachmaninov:* Piano Concerto 2 (exc); *Shostakovich:* Gadfly (exc); *Sibelius:* Finlandia; *Verdi:* Aida (exc); Nabucco (exc). (P. Lorengar, Y. Minton, S. Burrows, L. Pavarotti, M. Talvela, N. Ghiaurov, N. Kennedy, K-W. Chung, G. de Peyer, Vladimir Ashkenazy, R. Lupu, P. White, Santa Cecilia Academy Chor, St John's College Ch, ASMF Chor, Chicago Sym Chor, Vienna St Op Chor, Santa Cecilia Academy Orch, ASMF, Chicago SO, National SO, LSO, Hallé, Stuttgart CO, ECO, Philh, Vienna Op Orch, RPO/C. Franci/G. Solti/G. Guest/R. Bonynge/P. Maag/O. A. Hughes/K. Münchinger/N. Marriner/A. Previn/G. Gavazzeni/U. Segal/Vladimir Ashkenazy/L. Gardelli/R. Kempe/R. Stapleton)

◉ **443 672-2DMO2** (8/95)
Weber—Der Freischütz
Weber: Freischütz (Cpte). (H. Behrens, R. Kollo, H. Donath, P. Meven, W. Brendel, K. Moll, R. Grumbach, R. Boysen, H. Sapell, Bavarian Rad Chor, BRSO/R. Kubelík)

◉ **443 675-2DMO2**
R Strauss—Ariadne auf Naxos
R. Strauss: Ariadne auf Naxos (Cpte). (Leonie Rysanek, S. Jurinac, R. Peters, J. Peerce, W. Berry, G. Adam, M. Dickie, K. Equiluz, M. Coertse, H. Rössl-Majdan, L. Maikl, K. Preger, L. Pantscheff, H. Pröglhöf, VPO/E. Leinsdorf)

◉ **443 682-2DMO4** (5/95)
Wagner—Tristan und Isolde
Wagner: Tristan und Isolde (Cpte). (J. Mitchinson, L. E. Gray, A. Wilkens, G. Howell, P. Joll, N. Folwell, A. Davies, G. Moses, J. Harris, WNO Chor, WNO Orch/R. Goodall)

◉ **443 690-2DHO2** (11/95)
Wagner—Das Rheingold
Wagner: Rheingold (Cpte). (R. Hale, H. Schwarz, K. Begley, P. Schreier, F-J. Kapellmann, N. Gustafson, T. Sunnegårdh, E. W. Schulte, E. Zaremba, J-H. Rootering, W. Fink, G. Fontana, I. Komlósi, M. Hintermeier, Cleveland Orch/C. von Dohnányi)

◉ **443 693-2DH4** (12/94)
Berlioz—Les Troyens
Berlioz: Troyens (Cpte). (F. Pollet, G. Lakes, D. Voigt, G. Quilico, H. Perraguin, J-P. Courtis, M. Philippe, C. Dubosc, J-L. Maurette, R. Schirrer, C. Carlson, J. M. Ainsley, M. Belleau, G. Cross, M. Beauchemin, Montreal Sym Chor, Montreal SO/C. Dutoit)

◉ **443 756-2DF2**
The Essential Beethoven
Beethoven: Egmont (exc); Piano Sonata 14; Fidelio (exc); Bagatelles (exc); Symphony 5; Piano Concerto 5; Romances (exc); Symphony 9 (exc). (P. Lorengar, Y. Minton, S. Burrows, M. Talvela, W. Boskovsky, Vladimir Ashkenazy, Chicago Sym Chor, Chicago SO, Vienna Mozart Ens/G. Solti)

◉ **443 762-2DF2**
The Essential Mozart
Mozart: Nozze di Figaro (exc); Nozze di Figaro (exc); Serenade, K525; Piano Concerto 21; Ave verum corpus, K618; Horn Concerti (exc); Symphony 40; Vespers, K339 (exc); Clarinet Concerto, K622; Don Giovanni (exc); Piano Sonata, K331 (exc); Divertimento, K334 (exc); Exsultate, jubilate, K165 (exc). (L. Price, T. Berganza, F. Palmer, G. Bacquier, G. de Peyer, B. Tuckwell, R. Lupu, A. Schiff, St John's College Ch, Vienna Haydn Orch, LSO, ASMF, ECO, COE, Wren Orch, VPO, Vienna Mozart Ens/R. Bonynge/W. Boskovsky/G. Guest/H. von Karajan/I. Kertész/P. Maag/N. Marriner/J. Pritchard/U. Segal/G. Solti)

◉ **443 765-2DF2**
The Essential Dvořák
Dvořák: Slavonic Dances (exc); Humoresques, Op. 101 (exc); Rusalka (exc); Cello Concerto; Carnival; Serenade, Op. 22 (exc); Gipsy Melodies (exc); Scherzo capriccioso; Symphony 9. (P. Lorengar, J. Sutherland, L. Harrell, J. Cooper, VPO, Santa Cecilia Academy Orch, Philh, LSO, ASMF, New Philh/F. Reiner/G. Patanè/Vladimir Ashkenazy/I. Kertész/N. Marriner/R. Bonynge/A. Dorati)

◉ **443 850-2DF2** (9/95)
Rossini—Overtures
Rossini: Guillaume Tell (exc); Signor Bruschino (exc); Viaggio a Reims (exc); Scala di seta (exc); Gazza ladra (exc); Turco in Italia (exc); Italiana in ALgeri (exc); Barbiere di Siviglia (exc); Torvaldo e Dorliska (exc); Cambiale di matrimonio (exc); Otello (exc); Semiramide (exc); Siège de Corinthe (exc); Tancredi (exc). (National PO/R. Chailly)

◉ **443 853-2DF2**
Verdi—Rigoletto
Verdi: Rigoletto (Cpte). (C. MacNeil, J. Sutherland, R. Cioni, C. Siepi, S. Malagù, F. Corena, A. di Stasio, A. Mercuriali, G. Morresi, L. Valle, G. Corti, M. Fiori, Santa Cecilia Academy Chor, Santa Cecilia Academy Orch/N. Sanzogno)

◉ **443 871-2DF2** (7/95)
Bizet—Carmen
Bizet: Carmen (Cpte). (R. Resnik, M. del Monaco, J. Sutherland, T. Krause, G. Spanellys, Y. Minton, J. Prudent, A. Hallett, C. Calès, R. Geay, Geneva Grand Th Chor, SRO/T. Schippers)

◉ **443 928-2DM**
Montserrat Caballé sings Opera Arias
Verdi: Luisa Miller (exc); *Bellini:* Norma (exc); *Boito:* Mefistofele (exc); *Puccini:* Turandot (exc); *Giordano:* Andrea Chénier (exc); *Ponchielli:* Gioconda (exc). (M. Caballé, A. Baltsa, L. Pavarotti, S. Milnes, B. Giaiotti, G. Morresi, London Op Chor, John Alldis Ch, National PO, WNO Orch, LPO/P. Maag/R. Bonynge/O. de Fabritiis/Z. Mehta/R. Chailly/B. Bartoletti)

◉ **443 930-2DM** (10/95)
Jussi Björling sings Opera Arias
Ponchielli: Gioconda (exc); *Puccini:* Fanciulla del West (exc); *Giordano:* Fedora (exc); *Cilea:* Arlesiana (exc); *Verdi:* Ballo in maschera (exc); *Puccini:* Manon Lescaut (exc); *Verdi:* Requiem (exc); *Mascagni:* Cavalleria rusticana (exc); *Lehár:* Land des Lächelns (exc). (J. Björling, R. Tebaldi, L. Dani, R. Corsi, MMF Chor, MMF Orch/A. Erede, VPO/F. Reiner, Inst Ens)

◉ **443 931-2DM**
Pilar Lorengar sings Opera Arias
Puccini: Bohème (exc); Rondine (exc); Madama Butterfly (exc); Turandot (exc); Gianni Schicchi (exc); *Dvořák:* Rusalka (exc); *G. Charpentier:* Louise (exc); *Bizet:* Carmen (exc); Pêcheurs de Perles (exc); *Massenet:* Manon (exc); *Mozart:* Nozze di Figaro (exc); *Beethoven:* Fidelio (exc); *Weber:* Freischütz (exc); *Wagner:* Tannhäuser (exc); *Korngold:* Tote Stadt (exc). (P. Lorengar, Santa Cecilia Academy Orch/G. Patanè, Vienna St Op Orch/W. Weller)

◉ **444 108-2DA**
Ballet Music from Opera
Rossini: Guillaume Tell (exc); *Donizetti:* Favorita (exc); *Gounod:* Reine de Saba (exc); *Massenet:* Roi de Lahore (exc); *Berlioz:* Troyens (exc); *Saint-Saëns:* Henry VIII (exc); *Massenet:* Ariane (exc); *Gounod:* Faust (exc). (F. Corelli, N. Ghiaurov, LSO, National PO/R. Bonynge)

◉ **444 110-2DA**
Massenet/ Meyerbeer/ Delibes/ Thomas—Ballet Music
Massenet: Cid (exc); *Meyerbeer:* Patineurs; *A. Thomas:* Hamlet (exc); *Delibes:* Naïla (exc). (National PO, LSO/R. Bonynge)

◉ **444 111-2DA**
Adam—Le Diable à quatre; Ballet Music & Entr'actes
Adam: Diable à quatre (Cpte); *Massenet:* Navarraise (exc); *Bizet:* Don Procopio (exc); *Gounod:* Tribut de Zamora (exc); *Massenet:* Érinnyes (exc); Don César de Bazan (exc). (LSO/R. Bonynge)

◉ **444 154-2DM**
Puccini—Orchestral Works
Puccini: Preludio sinfonico; Capriccio sinfonico; Villi (exc); Edgar (exc); Minuets; Manon Lescaut (exc); Crisantemi. (Berlin RSO/R. Chailly)

◉ **444 178-2DHO2** (4/95)
R. Strauss—Salome
R. Strauss: Salome (Cpte). (C. Malfitano, B. Terfel, K. Riegel, H. Schwarz, K. Begley, R. Stene, P. Rose, M. Gantner, F. Olsen, G. Paucker, W. Zeh, R. Braga, VPO/C. von Dohnányi)

◉ **444 183-2DH**
Rossini—La Cenerentola - Highlights
Rossini: Cenerentola (exc). (C. Bartoli, W. Matteuzzi, A. Corbelli, E. Dara, F. Costa, G. Banditelli, M. Pertusi, Bologna Teatro Comunale Chor, Bologna Teatro Comunale Orch/R. Chailly)

◉ **444 388-2DWO** ▭ **444 388-4DWO**
The World of Baroque Favourites
Pachelbel: Canon and Gigue (exc); *Bach:* Suites, BWV1066-9 (exc); *Handel:* Water Music (exc); *Albinoni:* Adagio; *Handel:* Solomon (exc); *Vivaldi:* Concerti, Op. 8 (exc); *Handel:* Berenice (exc); *bach:* Cantata 208 (exc); *Vivaldi:* Concerto, RV93; *Bach:* Cantata 147 (exc); *Purcell:* Chaconne, Z730; *Bach:* Suites, BWV1066-9 (exc). (M. Haselböck, E. Fernández, Stuttgart CO/K. Münchinger, ASMF/N. Marriner, ECO/G. Malcolm/B. Britten)

◉ **444 389-2DWO** (9/95) ▭ **444 389-4DWO**
The World of Borodin
Borodin: Prince Igor (exc); String Quartet 2 (exc); Prince Igor (exc); Scherzo in A flat; In the Steppes of Central Asia; For the shores; Symphony 2. (N. Ghiaurov, Z. Ghiaurov, Vladimir Ashkenazy, Borodin Qt, London Sym Chor, LSO, SRO/G. Solti/E. Downes/E. Ansermet/J. Martinon)

◉ **444 390-2DWO** (11/95) ▭ **444 390-4DWO** (11/95)
The World of The Harpsichord
Bach: Italian Concerto, BWV971; Chromatic Fantasia and Fugue, BWV903; Toccatas, BWV910-16 (exc); French Suites, BWV812-17 (exc); *Paradis:* Keyboard Sonatas (exc); *Daquin:* Premier livre de pièces de clavecin (exc); *Rimsky-Korsakov:* Tale of Tsar Saltan (exc); *Rameau:* Pièces de clavecin (exc); *Couperin:* Livre de clavecin III

(exc); *Templeton:* Bach goes to town; *Malcolm:* Bach before the mast. (G. Malcolm)

Ⓒ **444 442-2DHO3** (6/95)
Schreker—Die Gezeichneten
Schreker: Gezeichneten (Cpte). (A. Muff, M. Pederson, L. Polgár, E. Connell, H. Kruse, R. Wörle, E. Wottrich, O. Widmer, M. Görne, K. Sigmundsson, P. Salomaa, M. Posselt, C. Berggold, M. Petzold, H. Lippert, R. Beyer, M. Rüping, J. Becker, G. Schwarz, K. Borris, I. Nguyen-Huu, R. Schudel, R. Ginzel, J. Gottschick, F. Molsberger, P. Menzel, M. Köhler, J. Metzger, H. Czerny, Berlin Rad Chor, Berlin Deutsches SO/L. Zagrosek)

Ⓒ **444 450-2DH** (2/95) ▭ **444 450-4DH** (2/95)
Pavarotti in Central Park
Verdi: Vespri siciliani (exc); Luisa Miller (exc); *Donizetti:* Lucia di Lammermoor (exc); *Cilea:* Arlesiana (exc); *Leoncavallo:* Mattinata; *Mascagni:* Serenata; *Bixio:* Mia canzone al vento; *Ellington:* It don't mean a thing; *Traditional:* I can go to God; *Di Lazzaro:* Chitarra romana; *Sibella:* Girometta; *Denza:* Occhi di fata; *Borne:* Carmen Fantasy; *Crescenzo:* Rondine al nido; *De Curtis:* Non ti scordar di me; *Massenet:* Werther (exc); *Puccini:* Tosca (exc); *Di Capua:* 'O sole mio; *Puccini:* Turandot (exc). (L. Pavarotti, A. Griminelli, Harlem Boys Ch, NYPO/W. J. Turnbull/L. Magiera)

Ⓒ **444 458-2DH**
Solti—Carnegie Hall Project
Wagner: Meistersinger (exc); *Brahms:* Haydn Variations; *Shostakovich:* Symphony 9; *R. Strauss:* Don Juan; *Smetana:* Bartered Bride (exc). (Solti Orchestral Project/G. Solti)

Ⓒ **444 460-2DH** ▭ **444 460-4DH**
Pavarotti and Friends II
Di Lazzaro: Chitarra romana; *Mancini:* Breakfast at Tiffany's (exc); *A. Lloyd Webber:* Phantom of the Opera (exc); *Leoncavallo:* Mattinata; *Mario:* Santa Lucia luntana; *Vollenweider:* Night Fire Dance; *Donizetti:* Lucia di Lammermoor (exc); *Kamen:* Please Forgive Me; Who Wants to Live Forever; Three Musketeers (exc); *Morante:* Notte è piscatore; *Dvořák:* Rusalka (exc); *Di Capua:* 'O sole mio; *Pavarotti:* Ave Maria; *Verdi:* Traviata (exc). (L. Pavarotti, N. Gustafson, A. Bocelli, Giorgia, B. Adams, A. Vollenweider, B. Adams Band, A. Vollenweider Band, Bologna Teatro Comunale Orch/L. Magiera/M. Kamen)

Ⓒ **444 529-2DMO2** (9/95)
Cavalli—L'Ormindo
Cavalli: Ormindo (Cpte). (J. Wakefield, P-C. Runge, I. Garcisanz, H. van Bork, J. Allister, H. Cuénod, A. Howells, J. Berbié, F. Davià, R. Van Allan, LPO/R. Leppard)

Ⓒ **444 543-2DF2**
Essential Handel
Handel: Solomon (exc); Semele (exc); Water Music (exc); Rodelinda (exc); Organ Concertos (exc); Keyboard Suites Set II (exc); Berenice (exc); Jephtha (exc); Judas Maccabaeus (exc); Serse (exc); Coronation Anthems (exc); Fireworks Music; Samson (exc); Organ Concertos (exc); Samson (exc); Concerti grossi, Op. 3 (exc); Ode for St Cecilia's Day (exc); Rinaldo (exc); Rodelinda (exc); Messiah (exc). (E. Ameling, M. Horne, K. Ferrier, P. Pears, A. Rolfe Johnson, K. McKellar, G. Howell, M. Robles, C. Hogwood, T. Dart, Handel Op Chor, East Anglian Chs, ASMF Chor, King's College Ch, ASMF, ROHO, Concertgebouw, Handel Op Orch, LSO, ECO, LPO, Vienna Cantata Orch/N. Marriner/A. Boult/R. Leppard/J. Rifkin/C. Farncombe/G. Szell/D. Willcocks/I. Brown/F. Molinari-Pradelli/B. Britten/R. Bonynge/H. Lewis, B. Greevy, P. Hurford, J. Sutherland)

Ⓒ **444 549-2DF2**
Essential Holst
Holst: Planets; Perfect Fool (exc); Egdon Heath; St Paul's Suite; Moorside Suite; Rig Veda - Group 3; Motets, H159-60; Ave Maria; This have I done; Hymn of Jesus. (LPO/G. Solti/A. Boult, St Paul CO/C. Hogwood, Grimethorpe Colliery Band/E. Howarth, Purcell Sngrs, O. Ellis/I. Holst, BBC Sym Chor, BBC SO)

Ⓒ **444 552-2DF2**
Essential Saint-Saëns
Saint-Saëns: Symphony 3; Violin Concerto 3; Samson et Dalila (exc); Samson et Dalila (exc); Danse macabre; Introduction and Rondo capriccioso; Carnaval des animaux; Havanaise; Piano Concerto 2. (A. Priest, Los Angeles PO/Z. Mehta, J. Bell, Montreal SO/C. Dutoit, M. Horne, Vienna Op Orch/H. Lewis, Philh, K-W. Chung, RPO, P. Rogé, C. Ortiz, London Sinfonietta)

Ⓒ **444 555-2DF2**
Essential Puccini
Puccini: Bohème (exc); Gianni Schicchi (exc); Fanciulla del West (exc); Suor Angelica (exc); Madama Butterfly (exc); Preludio sinfonico; Manon Lescaut (exc); Tosca (exc); Rondine (exc); Turandot (exc). (R. Tebaldi, G. d'Angelo, M. Chiara, K. Te Kanawa, M. Freni, J. Sutherland, M. Caballé, F. Cossotto, C. Bergonzi, J. Björling, J. Carreras, L. Pavarotti, M. Sénéchal, P.F. Poli, P. de Palma, R. Cesari, E. Bastianini, S. Milnes, T. Krause, C. Siepi, F. Corena, I. Tajo, N. Ghiaurov, Santa Cecilia Academy Chor, London Op Chor, Wandsworth Sch Boys Ch, John Alldis Ch, Santa Cecilia Academy Orch, MMF Orch, Vienna Op Orch, Berlin RSO, Bologna Teatro Comunale Orch, National PO, New PO, LPO/T. Serafin/L. Gardelli/A. Erede/N. Santi/R. Chailly/N. Rescigno/O. de Fabritiis/Z. Mehta)

Ⓒ **444 630-2DHO2**
Schulhoff—Plameny (The Flames)
Schulhoff: Plameny (Cpte). (K. Westi, J. Eaglen, I. Vermillion, J.W. Prein, G. Wolf, C. Lindsley, C. Höhn, R. Schudel, E. Dressen, C. Berggold, K. Borris, Berlin RIAS Chbr Ch, Berlin Deutsches SO/J. Mauceri)

Ⓒ **448 042-2DC9**
Karajan - The Great Decca Recordings, 1959-1963
Brahms: Symphony 1; *Haydn:* Symphony 103; Symphony 104; *Brahms:* Tragic Overture; Symphony 3; *Mozart:* Symphony 40; Symphony 41; *Tchaikovsky:* Romeo and Juliet; *Beethoven:* Symphony 7; *Dvořák:* Symphony 8; *Tchaikovsky:* Swan Lake Suite; Nutcracker Suite; Sleeping Beauty (exc); *Adam:* Giselle (Cpte); *Grieg:* Peer Gynt (exc); *Holst:* Planets; *J. Strauss II:* Fledermaus (exc); Annen-Polka, Op. 117; *Jos Strauss:* Delirien; *J. Strauss II:* Zigeunerbaron (exc); Auf der Jagd, Op. 373; G'schichten aus dem Wienerwald, Op. 325; *R. Strauss:* Till Eulenspiegel; Salome (exc); Don Quixote; Tod und Verklärung; Also sprach Zarathustra. (Vienna St Op Chor, VPO/H. von Karajan)

Ⓒ **448 119-2DHO2** (8/95)
Verdi—La Traviata
Verdi: Traviata (Cpte). (A. Gheorghiu, F. Lopardo, L. Nucci, L-M. Jones, G. Knight, R. Leggate, R. Van Allan, R. Earle, M. Beesley, N. Griffiths, B. Secombe, R. Gibson, ROH Chor, ROHO/G. Solti)

Ⓒ **448 300-2DH** ▭ **448 300-4DH**
Cecilia Bartoli—A Portrait
Mozart: Clemenza di Tito (exc); Così fan tutte (exc); Nozze di Figaro (exc); Don Giovanni (exc); Ch'io mi scordi di te, K505; *Parisotti:* Se tu m'ami; *T. Giordani:* Caro mio ben; *Caccini:* Nuove musiche (1602) (exc); *Schubert:* Pastorella al Prato, D528; Didone abbandonata, D510; *Rossini:* Beltà crudele; Semiramide (exc); Maometto II (exc); Cenerentola (exc). (C. Bartoli, L. Schatzberger, AAM/C. Hogwood, A. Schiff, Vienna CO/G. Fischer, G. Fischer, C. Spencer, Venice La Fenice Orch/I. Marin, Bologna Teatro Comunale Chor, Bologna Teatro Comunale Orch/R. Chailly)

Dell'Arte

Ⓒ **CDDA9020** (1/90)
Toscanini conducts music by his contemporaries
Brahms: Handel Variations; *Roger-Ducasse:* Sarabande; *Sibelius:* Legends (exc); *R. Harris:* Symphony 3; *Paganini:* Moto perpetuo, Op.11; *Kabalevsky:* Colas Breugnon (exc). (Chor, NBC SO/A. Toscanini)

Ⓒ **CDDA9021** (6/90)
Toscanini conducts French Works
Debussy: Marche écossaise; *Meyerbeer:* Dinorah (exc); *Roussel:* Festin de l'araignée ballet; *Franck:* Symphony. (NBC SO/A. Toscanini)

Delos

Ⓒ **DE1003**
A Distant Mirror & Shakespeare's Music
Aleyn: Gloria; *Traditional:* Angelus ad Virginem; *Anon:* Estampie (14th cent); I have so longe keepe shepe; En l'amoureux vergier; Orsus vous dormez trop!; Witches Dance I; Witches Dance II; Willow Song; *R. Cooke:* Stella Celi; *Matheus de Sancto Johanne:* Are post libamina; *Bittering:* Nesciens mater; *Pycard:* Gloria; *Machaut:* Gais et Jolis; Rose, liz; *Grimace:* A l'arme, a l'arme; *Vaillant:* Par maintes foys; *Anthonello de Caserta:* Notes pour moi; *Borlet:* Ma tredol rossignol; *Andrieu:* Armes, Amours; *Morley:* Ayres (1600) (exc); *Purcell:* Fairy Queen, Z629 (exc); Tempest, Z631 (exc); *Humfrey:* Willow Song; *Arne:* Love's Labours Lost (exc); As You Like It (exc); Tempest (exc). (Folger Consort)

Ⓒ **DE1007**
Saxophone Colors
Bach: Flute Sonatas, BWV1030-5 (exc); *Debussy:* Première rapsodie; *Villa-Lobos:* Fantasia (1948); *Gershwin:* Porgy and Bess (exc); *Heiden:* Saxophone Sonata; *Feld:* Elegy (1981); *Orrego-Salas:* Quattro Liriche (1967). (E. Rousseau/H. Graf)

Ⓒ **DE1030** (9/94)
W.Schuman—The Mighty Casey; A Question of Taste
Schuman: Mighty Casey (Cpte); Question of Taste (Cpte). (S. Robinson, F. Pomponi, C. Thorpe, D. Corman, R. Cusick, D. Dreyer, C. Conde, A. Parks, J. Russell, K. Chester, S. Rosenbaum, A. Norton, E. Grohowski, T. P. Groves, E. Bishop, D. Corman, S. Wilde, C. Scimone, Juilliard Op Center, Juilliard Orch/G. Schwarz)

Ⓒ **DE3026** (11/86)
A. Auger - Bach and Handel arias
Handel: Messiah (exc); Giulio Cesare (exc); Atalanta (exc); Alexander's Feast (exc); Rinaldo (exc); Samson (exc); *Bach:* Cantata 209 (exc); Anna Magdalena Notenbuch (1725) (exc); Cantata 202 (exc); St Matthew Passion, BWV244 (exc). (A. Auger, Mostly Mozart Orch/G. Schwarz)

Ⓒ **DE3029**
Love Songs
Copland: Pastorale; *Obradors:* Canciones clásicas españolas (exc); *Ovalle:* Azulão; *R.Strauss:* Lieder, Op. 17 (exc); *Marx:* Selige Nacht; *Poulenc:* Fiançailles pour rire (exc); *Cimara:* Stornello; *Quilter:* Songs, Op. 25 (exc); *O. Straus:* Drei Walzer (exc); *Quilter:* Songs, Op. 3 (exc); *Schumann:* Myrthen, Op. 25 (exc); *R.Strauss:* Lieder, Op. 36 (exc); *Mahler:* Rückert Lieder (exc); *Turina:* Poema en forma de canciones (exc); *Lippé:* How do I love thee?; *Coward:* Conversation Piece (exc); *Gounod:* Sérénade; *Schubert:* Claudine von Villa Bella (exc); *Bridge:* Love went a-riding; *Foster:* Why, no-one to love; *Donaudy:* O del mio amato ben; *Britten:* Folk Songs (exc); *Copland:* Dickinson Poems (exc); *F. Loewe:* Camelot (exc). (A. Auger, D. Baldwin)

Ⓒ **DE3040** (3/87)
Wagner—Orchestral Excerpts from the Operas
Wagner: Tannhäuser (exc); Rheingold (exc); Götterdämmerung (exc); Meistersinger (exc). (Seattle SO/G. Schwarz)

Ⓒ **DE3052** (9/90)
R. Strauss: Orchestral Works
R. Strauss: Also sprach Zarathustra; Salome (exc); Intermezzo Interludes (exc). (Seattle SO/G. Schwarz)

Ⓒ **DE3053**
Wagner: Opera Overtures and Preludes
Wagner: Fliegende Holländer (exc); Lohengrin (exc); Parsifal (exc). (Seattle SO/G. Schwarz)

Ⓒ **DE3105** (7/92)
Hanson—Choral and Orchestral Works
Hanson: Symphony 4; Serenade, Op. 35; Lament for Beowulf; Pastorale, Op. 38; Merry Mount (exc). (Seattle SO, Seattle Sym Chorale, NY Chbr SO/G. Schwarz)

Ⓒ **DE3108** (6/92) ▭ **CS3108** (6/92)
Alessandra Marc—Opera Recital
Verdi: Forza del destino (exc); Aida (exc); *Catalani:* Wally (exc); *Cilea:* Adriana Lecouvreur (exc); *Puccini:* Tosca (exc); Turandot (exc); *G. Charpentier:* Louise (exc); *Wagner:* Tannhäuser (exc). (A. Marc, NZ SO/H. Wallberg)

Ⓒ **DE3109** (10/92)
R.Strauss—Orchestral Works
R. Strauss: Rosenkavalier (exc); Burleske; Frau ohne Schatten Fantasy. (C. Rosenberger, Seattle SO/G. Schwarz)

Ⓒ **DE3120** (4/94)
Wagner—Orchestral and Vocal Works
Wagner: Siegfried (exc); Lohengrin (exc); Tristan und Isolde (exc); Walküre (exc); Faust Overture. (A. Marc, Seattle SO/G. Schwarz)

Denon

Ⓒ **CO-1741** (5/88)
Mozart: Operatic Arias
Mozart: Finta giardiniera (exc); Nozze di Figaro (exc); Don Giovanni (exc); Così fan tutte (exc); Zauberflöte (exc). (H. Prey, Salzburg Mozarteum Orch/B. Weil)

Ⓒ **CO-73335** (10/89)
Celebrated Baroque Pieces
Handel: Water Music (exc); *Pachelbel:* Canon and Gigue (exc); *Bonporti:* Concerti a quattro, op 11 (exc); *Geminiani:* Concerti grossi (Corelli op 5) (exc); *Handel:* Serse (exc); *Vivaldi:* Concerto, RV151; *Albinoni:* Adagio; *Handel:* Concerti grossi, op 6 (exc); *Bach:* Suites, BWV1066-9 (exc); *Vivaldi:* Concerto, RV395 (exc); *Bach:* 2-Violin Concerto (exc); Cantata 147 (exc); *Galuppi:* Harpsichord Concerto. (Solisti Italiani)

Ⓒ **CO-75118** (12/93)
Violin Show Pieces
Elgar: Capricieuse; Salut d'amour; *Rimsky-Korsakov:* Tale of Tsar Saltan (exc); *Rachmaninov:* Songs, Op.34 (exc); *Szymanowski:* Myths, Op.30 (exc); *Bernstein:* West Side Story (exc); *Khachaturian:* Masquerade (exc); *Suk:* Pieces, Op.17 (exc); *Fauré:* Berceuse, Op.16; *Massenet:* Thaïs

(exc); *Sarasate:* Introduction and Tarantella, Op.43. (Chee-Yun, A. Eguchi)

Ⓓ **CO-75372**
Mozart—Overtures
Mozart: Nozze di Figaro (exc); Idomeneo (exc); Don Giovanni (exc); Entführung (exc); Così fan tutte (exc); Clemenza di Tito (exc); Zauberflöte (exc); Schauspieldirektor (exc); Thamos, K345 (exc). (Sinfonia Varsovia/E. Krivine)

Ⓓ **CO-77715** (6/92)
Tchaikovsky/Wagner—Orchestral Works
Tchaikovsky: Symphony 6; *Wagner:* Tristan und Isolde (exc). (Frankfurt RSO/E. Inbal)

Ⓓ **CO-77949** (8/92)
J. Strauss II—Operetta Highlights
J. Strauss II: Zigeunerbaron (exc); Tausend und eine Nacht (exc); Brautschau, Op. 417; Schatz; Kriegsabenteuer, Op. 415; Wahrsagerin; Tik-Tak; Du und Du, Op. 367; Fledermaus Polka, Op. 362; Im Sturmschritt, Op. 348; Tausend und eine Nacht; Indigo-Marsch, Op. 349; Glücklich ist, Op. 368; Auf freiem Fusse, Op. 345; Aus der Heimath, Op. 347; Bajadere, Op. 351. (Vienna Op Ball Orch/U. Theimer)

Ⓓ **CO-78902** (12/94)
Berlioz—Symphonie fantastique, Op 14 etc
Berlioz: Symphonie fantastique; Troyens (exc). (Lyon Nat Orch/E. Krivine)

Ⓓ **CO-78926**
Evening Tunes in Prague
Fibich: At twilight; *Blodek:* In the Well (exc); *Martinů:* Spalíček (exc); *Tchaikovsky:* Suite 4 (exc); Andante cantabile, Op. 11; *Sibelius:* Valse triste; *Dvořák:* Humoresques, Op. 101 (exc); Nocturne; *Nedbal:* Valse triste; *Borodin:* String Quartet 2 (exc); *Janáček:* Idyll. (Prague CO/B. Novotný)

Ⓓ **CO-78932** (10/95)
Bartók—Duke Bluebeard's castle
Bartók: Duke Bluebeard's castle (Cpte). (F. Struckmann, K. Szendrényi, Frankfurt RSO/E. Inbal)

Ⓓ **CO-79250** (12/92)
18th Century English Theatre Music
Purcell: Married Beau, Z603 (exc); Gordian Knot Unty'd, Z597 (exc); *Handel:* Pastor Fido (exc). (Cologne Stravaganza)

Ⓓ **CO-79785**
Donizetti—10 Opera Arias
Donizetti: Roberto Devereux (exc); Lucia di Lammermoor (exc); Elisir d'amore (exc); Duca d'alba (exc); Favorita (exc); Linda di Chamounix (exc); Don Pasquale (exc); Maria di Rohan (exc); Dom Sébastien (exc). (A. Cupido, Danish Rad Chbr Ch, Danish Rad Concert Orch/M. Elquist)

Ⓓ **C37-7301**
Duo Recital
Debussy: Petite Suite (exc); Suite bergamasque (exc); *Bizet:* Carmen (exc); *Gossec:* Rosine (exc); *Bach:* Suites, BWV1066-9 (exc); *Ibert:* Pièce; Entr'acte (1937); *Liszt:* Paganini Studies, S140 (exc); *Bazzini:* Ronde des lutins; *Gounod:* Ave Maria; *Donizetti:* Flute and Harp Sonata; *Chopin:* Rossini Variations; *Handel:* Serse (exc). (M. Larrieu, S. Mildonian)

Deutsche Grammophon

Ⓓ **400 044-2GH** (3/83)
Offenbach: Overtures
Offenbach: Barbe-Bleue (exc); Belle Hélène (exc); Contes d'Hoffmann (exc); Grande-Duchesse de Gérolstein (exc); Orphée aux enfers (exc); Vert-vert (exc). (BPO/H. von Karajan)

Ⓓ **410 025-2GH** (8/83)
Bernstein and Gershwin
Gershwin: Rhapsody in Blue; Preludes (exc); *Bernstein:* West Side Story Symphonic Dances. (L. Bernstein, Los Angeles PO/L. Bernstein, L. Bernstein (pf/dir))

Ⓓ **410 088-2GH3** (12/83)
Bizet—Carmen
Bizet: Carmen (Cpte). (A. Baltsa, J. Carreras, K. Ricciarelli, J. Van Dam, C. Barbaux, J. Berbié, G. Quilico, H. Zednik, M. Melbye, A. Malta, Schöneberg Boys' Ch, Paris Op. Chor, BPO/H. von Karajan)

Ⓓ **410 092-2GH3** (12/82)
Verdi—Aida
Verdi: Aida (Cpte). (K. Ricciarelli, E. Obraztsova, P. Domingo, L. Nucci, N. Ghiaurov, R. Raimondi, P. de Palma, L.V. Terrani, La Scala Chor, La Scala Orch/C. Abbado)

Ⓓ **410 503-2GH2** (12/83)
Verdi—Falstaff
Verdi: Falstaff (Cpte). (R. Bruson, L. Nucci, K. Ricciarelli, B. Hendricks, D. Gonzalez, L.V. Terrani, B. Boozer, M. Sells, F. Egerton, W. Wilderman, Los Angeles Master Chorale, Los Angeles PO/C.M. Giulini)

Ⓓ **410 512-2GH2** (5/84)
Verdi—Nabucco
Verdi: Nabucco (Cpte). (P. Cappuccilli, G. Dimitrova, P. Domingo, L.V. Terrani, E. Nesterenko, K. Rydl, V. Horn, L. Popp, Berlin Deutsche Op Chor, Berlin Deutsche Op Orch/G. Sinopoli)

Ⓓ **410 645-2GH**
Puccini—Turandot (highlights)
Puccini: Turandot (exc). (K. Ricciarelli, P. de Palma, R. Raimondi, P. Domingo, B. Hendricks, G. Hornik, H. Zednik, F. Araiza, Vienna St Op Chor, Vienna Boys' Ch, VPO/H. von Karajan)

Ⓓ **410 967-2GH3** (1/85)
Mozart—Die Zauberflöte
Mozart: Zauberflöte (Cpte). (E. Mathis, K. Ott, F. Araiza, G. Hornik, J. Van Dam, C. Nicolai, H. Kruse, J. Perry, A. Tomowa-Sintow, A. Baltsa, H. Schwarz, W. Bünten, C. Schulz, T. Pfülb, V. Horn, V. von Halem, H. Hopfner, L. Valenta, Berlin Deutsche Op Chor, BPO/H. von Karajan)

Ⓓ **413 145-2GW2** (12/91)
Beethoven—Orchestral Works
Beethoven: Violin Concerto; Leonore (exc); Piano Concerto 5; Fidelio (exc); Leonore (exc). (W. Schneiderhan, BPO/E. Jochum, C. Eschenbach, Boston SO/S. Ozawa, Staatskapelle Dresden/K. Böhm)

Ⓓ **413 297-2GX2** (11/91)
Saint-Saëns—Samson et Dalila
Saint-Saëns: Samson et Dalila (Cpte). (P. Domingo, E. Obraztsova, R. Bruson, P. Thau, R. Lloyd, G. Friedmann, C. Zaharia, M. Huber, Paris Orch Chor, Paris Orch/D. Barenboim)

Ⓓ **413 309-2GH** ▭ **413 309-4GH**
Baroque Favourites
Albinoni: Adagio; *Vivaldi:* Concerti, Op. 10 (exc); *Bach:* Suites, BWV1066-9 (exc); *Pachelbel:* Canon and Gigue; *Gluck:* Orfeo ed Euridice (exc); *Mozart:* Serenade, K239. (BPO/H. von Karajan)

Ⓓ **413 315-2GH4** (11/86)
Wagner—Tristan und Isolde
Wagner: Tristan und Isolde (Cpte). (R. Kollo, M. Price, B. Fassbaender, K. Moll, D. Fischer-Dieskau, W. Götz, A. Dermota, Wolfgang Hellmich, E. Büchner, Leipzig Rad Chor, Staatskapelle Dresden/C. Kleiber)

Ⓓ **413 321-2GH**
Verdi—Nabucco (highlights)
Verdi: Nabucco (exc). (P. Cappuccilli, P. Domingo, E. Nesterenko, G. Dimitrova, L.V. Terrani, K. Rydl, V. Horn, Berlin Deutsche Op Chor, Berlin Deutsche Op Orch/G. Sinopoli)

Ⓓ **413 322-2GH** (2/85) ▭ **413 322-4GH** (10/84)
Bizet—Carmen (highlights)
Bizet: Carmen (exc). (A. Baltsa, J. Carreras, K. Ricciarelli, J. Van Dam, C. Barbaux, J. Berbié, G. Quilico, H. Zednik, M. Melbye, A. Malta, Paris Op. Chor, BPO/H. von Karajan)

Ⓓ **413 347-2GH4** (10/84)
Wagner—Parsifal
Wagner: Parsifal (Cpte). (P. Hofmann, J. Van Dam, K. Moll, D. Vejzovic, S. Nimsgern, V. von Halem, C.H. Ahnsjö, K. Rydl, M. Lambriks, A. Gjevang, H. Hopfner, G. Tichy, B. Hendricks, J. Perry, D. Soffel, I. Nielsen, A. Michael, R. Yachmi-Caucig, H. Schwarz, Berlin Deutsche Op Chor, BPO/H. von Karajan)

Ⓓ **413 432-2GW2** (12/91) ▭ **413 432-4GW2**
J. Strauss II—Overtures, Polkas & Waltzes
J. Strauss II: Fledermaus (exc); Kaiser, Op. 437; Tritsch-Tratsch; Zigeunerbaron (exc); Auf der Jagd, Op. 373; G'schichten aus dem Wienerwald, Op. 325; Eljen a Magyar!, Op. 332; Unter Donner und Blitz; Blauen Donau, Op. 314; Pizzicato Polka; Rosen aus dem Süden; Wiener Blut; Egyptischer Marsch, Op. 335; Annen-Polka, Op. 117; Perpetuum Mobile; Morgenblätter, Op. 279. (Berlin RSO/F. Fricsay, VPO/K. Böhm, BPO/H. von Karajan)

Ⓓ **413 451-2GH**
Be My Love
Lara: Granada; *Cardillo:* Core 'ngrato; *Lehár:* Land des Lächelns (exc); *Leoncavallo:* Mattinata; *Lecuona:* Siboney; *Freire:* Ay, Ay, Ay; *Brodszky:* Toast of New Orleans (exc); *Grever:* Muñequita Linda; Jurame; *Simons:* Marta; *De Curtis:* Non ti scordar di me; *Hardelot:* Because; *Loges:* Ich schenk dir eine neue Welt; *Lacalle:* Amapola. (P. Domingo, LSO/M. Peeters/K-H. Loges)

Ⓓ **413 490-2GH** (11/84)
Elgar: Orchestral Works
Elgar: Enigma Variations; Pomp and Circumstance Marches (exc); Crown of India (exc). (BBC SO/L. Bernstein)

Ⓓ **413 815-2GH2** (3/85)
Puccini—Tosca
Puccini: Tosca (Cpte). (K. Ricciarelli, J. Carreras, R. Raimondi, G. Hornik, H. Zednik, F. Corena, V. von Halem, W. Bünten, Berlin Deutsche Op Chor, BPO/H. von Karajan)

Ⓓ **413 851-2GW2** (12/91)
Modern American Favourites
Gershwin: Rhapsody in Blue; American in Paris; *Bernstein:* West Side Story Symphonic Dances; *Gershwin:* Piano Concerto; *Russo:* Blues Pieces, Op.50. (S. Stöckigt, Leipzig Gewandhaus/K. Masur, San Francisco SO/S. Ozawa, R. Szidon, LPO/E. Downes, Siegel-Schwall Band)

Ⓓ **413 893-2GH2** (3/85)
Puccini—Manon Lescaut
Puccini: Manon Lescaut (Cpte). (M. Freni, P. Domingo, R. Bruson, K. Rydl, R. Gambill, B. Fassbaender, G. Macpherson, J. Fryatt, H. Thomas, M. Curtis, J. Tomlinson, ROH Chor., Philh/G. Sinopoli)

Ⓓ **415 132-2GH2** (3/86)
Verdi—La traviata
Verdi: Traviata (Cpte). (I. Cotrubas, P. Domingo, S. Milnes, S. Malagù, H. Jungwirth, W. Gullino, B. Grella, A. Giacomotti, G. Foiani, W. Gullino, P. Winter, P. Friess, Bavarian St Op Chor, Bavarian St Orch/C. Kleiber)

Ⓓ **415 141-2GH3** (7/85)
Wagner—Das Rheingold
Wagner: Rheingold (Cpte). (D. Fischer-Dieskau, J. Veasey, G. Stolze, E. Wohlfahrt, Z. Kélémen, S. Mangelsdorff, D. Grobe, R. Kerns, O. Dominguez, M. Talvela, K. Ridderbusch, H. Donath, E. Moser, A. Reynolds, BPO/H. von Karajan)

Ⓓ **415 145-2GH4** (7/85)
Wagner—Die Walküre
Wagner: Walküre (Cpte). (J. Vickers, G. Janowitz, R. Crespin, T. Stewart, J. Veasey, M. Talvela, L. Rebmann, D. Mastilovic, C. Ordassy, I. Steger, H. Jenckel, B. Ericson, C. Ahlin, L. Brockhaus, BPO/H. von Karajan)

Ⓓ **415 150-2GH4** (7/85)
Wagner—Siegfried
Wagner: Siegfried (Cpte). (Jess Thomas, T. Stewart, H. Dernesch, G. Stolze, Z. Kélémen, O. Dominguez, K. Ridderbusch, C. Gayer, BPO/H. von Karajan)

Ⓓ **415 155-2GH4** (7/85)
Wagner—Götterdämmerung
Wagner: Götterdämmerung (Cpte). (H. Dernesch, H. Brilioth, K. Ridderbusch, Z. Kélémen, T. Stewart, G. Janowitz, C. Ludwig, L. Rebmann, E. Moser, A. Reynolds, L. Chookasian, C. Ligendza, Berlin Deutsche Op Chor, BPO/H. von Karajan)

Ⓓ **415 253-2GH2** (4/85)
Bernstein—West Side Story, etc
Bernstein: West Side Story (Cpte); On the Waterfront Suite. (K. Te Kanawa, N. Bernstein, J. Carreras, A. Bernstein, T. Troyanos, M. Horne, K. Ollmann, L. Edeiken, S. Zambalis, A. Réaux, D. Livingstone, M. Nelson, S. Bogardus, P. Thom, T. Lester, R. Harrell, Broadway Chor, Broadway Orch/L. Bernstein, Israel PO)

▭ **415 253-4GH2** (7/85)
Bernstein—West Side Story
Bernstein: West Side Story (Cpte). (K. Te Kanawa, N. Bernstein, J. Carreras, A. Bernstein, T. Troyanos, M. Horne, K. Ollmann, L. Edeiken, S. Zambalis, A. Réaux, D. Livingstone, M. Nelson, S. Bogardus, P. Thom, T. Lester, R. Harrell, Broadway Chor, Broadway Orch/L. Bernstein)

Ⓓ **415 276-2GH** (8/85)
Beethoven—Orchestral Works
Beethoven: Triple Concerto; Egmont (exc); Fidelio (exc); Coriolan. (A-S. Mutter, Y-Y. Ma, M. Zeltser, BPO/H. von Karajan)

Ⓓ **415 278-2GH4** (10/85)
Wagner—Die Meistersinger
Wagner: Meistersinger (Cpte). (D. Fischer-Dieskau, P. Domingo, C. Ligendza, P. Lagger, R. Hermann, H. Laubenthal, C. Ludwig, G. Feldhoff, P. Maus, R. Bañuelas, L. Driscoll, K-E. Mercker, M. Vantin, K. Lang, I. Sardi, M. Nikolič, V. von Halem, Berlin Deutsche Op Chor, Berlin Deutsche Op Orch/E. Jochum)

Ⓓ **415 283-2GH** (10/85)
Opera Choruses
Mozart: Zauberflöte (exc); *Beethoven:* Fidelio (exc);

Weber: Freischütz (exc); *Wagner:* Tannhäuser (exc); *Verdi:* Nabucco (exc); Lombardi (exc); Macbeth (exc); Trovatore (exc); Aida (exc). (Berlin Deutsche Op Chor, Berlin Deutsche Op Orch/G. Sinopoli)

415 283-5GH
Opera Choruses
Mozart: Zauberflöte (exc); *Beethoven:* Fidelio (exc); *Weber:* Freischütz (exc); *Wagner:* Tannhäuser (exc); *Verdi:* Nabucco (exc); Lombardi (exc); Macbeth (exc); Trovatore (exc); Aida (exc). (Berlin Deutsche Op Chor, Berlin Deutsche Op Orch/G. Sinopoli)

415 284-2GH (8/85)
R. Strauss—Der Rosenkavalier (highlights)
R. Strauss: Rosenkavalier (exc). (A. Tomowa-Sintow, K. Moll, A. Baltsa, G. Hornik, J. Perry, H. Müller-Molinari, V. Cole, Vienna St Op Chor, VPO/H. von Karajan)

415 285-2GH (10/85)
Verdi—Il Trovatore (highlights)
Verdi: Trovatore (exc). (R. Plowright, A. di Stasio, B. Fassbaender, P. Domingo, W. Gullino, G. Zancanaro, E. Nesterenko, Santa Cecilia Academy Chor, Santa Cecilia Academy Orch/C.M. Giulini)

415 286-2GH (9/85)
Verdi—Aida (highlights)
Verdi: Aida (exc). (K. Ricciarelli, E. Obraztsova, P. Domingo, L. Nucci, N. Ghiaurov, R. Raimondi, La Scala Chor, La Scala Orch/C. Abbado)

415 287-2GH (1/86)
Mozart—Die Zauberflöte (highlights)
Mozart: Zauberflöte (exc). (E. Mathis, F. Araiza, K. Ott, J. Van Dam, G. Hornik, J. Perry, H. Kruse, A. Tomowa-Sintow, A. Baltsa, H. Schwarz, Berlin Deutsche Op Chor, BPO/H. von Karajan)

415 288-2GH2 (11/85)
Verdi—Rigoletto
Verdi: Rigoletto (Cpte). (P. Cappuccilli, I. Cotrubas, P. Domingo, N. Ghiaurov, E. Obraztsova, K. Moll, H. Schwarz, W. Gullino, L. de Corato, O. Fredricks, D. Sagemüller, A. Michael, Vienna St Op Chor, VPO/C.M. Giulini)

415 316-2GH4 (12/85)
Verdi—Don Carlos
Verdi: Don Carlos (Cpte). (P. Domingo, K. Ricciarelli, L.V. Terrani, L. Nucci, R. Raimondi, N. Ghiaurov, N. Storozhev, A. Murray, T. Raffalli, A. Savastano, A. Auger, La Scala Chor, La Scala Orch/C. Abbado)

415 366-2GH (7/86)
Placido Domingo Recital
Verdi: Aida (exc); Rigoletto (exc); Luisa Miller (exc); Ballo in maschera (exc); Traviata (exc); *Bizet:* Carmen (exc); *Donizetti:* Elisir d'amore (exc); *Offenbach:* Contes d'Hoffmann (exc); *Puccini:* Turandot (exc); *Flotow:* Martha (exc). (P. Domingo, La Scala Orch/C. Abbado, VPO/C.M. Giulini, ROHO/L. Maazel, Bavarian St Orch/C. Kleiber, Los Angeles PO, SRO/R. Bonynge/H. von Karajan)

415 432-2GH2 (11/86)
Weber—Der Freischütz
Weber: Freischütz (Cpte). (G. Janowitz, P. Schreier, E. Mathis, T. Adam, B. Weikl, F. Crass, S. Vogel, G. Paul, G. Lieb, Leipzig Rad Chor, Staatskapelle Dresden/C. Kleiber)

415 489-2GH3 (11/86)
Berg—Lulu
Berg: Lulu (Cpte). (T. Stratas, F. Mazura, K. Riegel, Y. Minton, R. Tear, T. Blankenheim, G. Nienstedt, H. Pampuch, J. Bastin, H. Schwarz, J. Manning, U. Boese, A. Ringart, C. Meloni, P-Y. Le Maigat, Paris Op. Orch/P. Boulez)

415 498-2GH2 (1/86)
Rossini—Il viaggio a Reims
Rossini: Viaggio a Reims (Cpte). (C. Gasdia, K. Ricciarelli, L. Cuberli, L.V. Terrani, E. Gimenez, F. Araiza, S. Ramey, R. Raimondi, E. Dara, G. Surian, L. Nucci, Prague Phil Chor, COE/C. Abbado)

415 524-2GH (3/86)
Lehár—The Merry Widow (highlights)
Lehár: Lustige Witwe (exc). (E. Harwood, T. Stratas, R. Kollo, W. Hollweg, Z. Kélémen, D. Grobe, W. Krenn, Berlin Deutsche Op Chor, BPO/H. von Karajan)

415 688-2GH3 (9/86)
Verdi—Macbeth
Verdi: Macbeth (Cpte). (P. Cappuccilli, S. Verrett, N. Ghiaurov, P. Domingo, A. Savastano, C. Zardo, G. Foiani, S. Fontana, A. Mariotti, S. Malagù, La Scala Chor, La Scala Orch/C. Abbado)

415 692-2GH2 (9/86)
Verdi—Simon Boccanegra
Verdi: Simon Boccanegra (Cpte). (P. Cappuccilli, M. Freni, J. Carreras, N. Ghiaurov, J. Van Dam, G. Foiani, A. Savastano, La Scala Chor, La Scala Orch/C. Abbado)

415 695-2GH2 (10/86)
Rossini—Il barbiere di Siviglia
Rossini: Barbiere di Siviglia (Cpte). (H. Prey, T. Berganza, L. Alva, E. Dara, P. Montarsolo, S. Malagù, R. Cesari, Ambrosian Op Chor, LSO/C. Abbado)

415 840-2GGA
Mendelssohn & Weber—Orchestral Works
Mendelssohn: Midsummer Night's Dream (exc); *Weber:* Oberon (exc); Freischütz (exc). (E. Mathis, U. Boese, Bavarian Rad Chor, BRSO/R. Kubelík)

415 847-2GGA (4/87)
Saint-Saëns—Orchestral Works
Saint-Saëns: Symphony 3; Samson et Dalila (exc); Déluge (exc); Danse macabre. (G. Litaize, Chicago SO, Paris Orch/D. Barenboim)

415 851-2GGA
Popular Orchestral Works
Smetana: Má Vlast (exc); *Dvořák:* Slavonic Dances (exc); *Brahms:* Hungarian Dances (exc); *Borodin:* Prince Igor (exc); *Liszt:* Préludes. (Chicago SO/D. Barenboim)

415 853-2GGA (4/88)
R. Strauss: Orchestral Works
R. Strauss: Also sprach Zarathustra; Till Eulenspiegel; Salome (exc). (M. Schwalbé, BPO/H. von Karajan)

415 855-2GGA (4/88)
Tchaikovsky: Orchestral works
Tchaikovsky: 1812; Serenade, Op. 48; Eugene Onegin (exc). (Don Cossack Ch, BPO/H. von Karajan)

415 963-2GH **415 963-4GH**
Bernstein—West Side Story (highlights)
Bernstein: West Side Story (exc). (K. Te Kanawa, J. Carreras, T. Troyanos, K. Ollmann, M. Horne, Broadway Chor, Broadway Orch/L. Bernstein)

415 963-5GH
Bernstein—West Side Story (highlights)
Bernstein: West Side Story (exc). (K. Te Kanawa, J. Carreras, T. Troyanos, K. Ollmann, M. Horne, Broadway Chor, Broadway Orch/L. Bernstein)

415 981-2GH
Verdi—Don Carlos (highlights)
Verdi: Don Carlos (exc). (R. Raimondi, P. Domingo, L. Nucci, N. Ghiaurov, N. Storozhev, K. Ricciarelli, L.V. Terrani, A. Murray, La Scala Chor, La Scala Orch/C. Abbado)

419 038-2GX2 (12/91)
Weber—Oberon
Weber: Oberon (Cpte). (D. Grobe, B. Nilsson, P. Domingo, H. Prey, J. Hamari, M. Schiml, A. Auger, Bavarian Rad Chor, BRSO/R. Kubelík)

419 049-2GGA (4/87)
Beethoven—Symphony No 3. Leonore Overture
Beethoven: Symphony 3; Leonore (exc). (BPO/H. von Karajan)

419 051-2GGA (8/87) **419 051-4GGA** (1/87)
Beethoven: Orchestral Works
Beethoven: Symphony 5; Symphony 8; Fidelio (exc). (BPO/H. von Karajan)

419 063-2GGA (4/87) **419 063-4GGA**
Rimsky-Korsakov—Scheherazade & Borodin—Polovtsian Dances
Rimsky-Korsakov: Scheherazade; *Borodin:* Prince Igor (exc). (BPO/H. von Karajan)

419 070-2GGA (6/88)
Weber: Orchestral Works
Weber: Beherrscher der Geister; Invitation to the Dance; Abu Hassan (exc); Euryanthe (exc); Freischütz (exc); Oberon (exc); Peter Schmoll (exc). (BPO/H. von Karajan)

419 091-4GW
Placido Domingo sings Favourite Arias, Songs and Tangos
Verdi: Rigoletto (exc); Aida (exc); Trovatore (exc); Traviata (exc); Ernani (exc); Macbeth (exc); *Donizetti:* Elisir d'amore (exc); Lucia di Lammermoor (exc); *Leoncavallo:* Mattinata; *Bizet:* Carmen (exc); Pêcheurs de perles (exc); *Lara:* Granada; *Meyerbeer:* Africaine (exc); *De Curtis:* Non ti scordar di me; *Filiberto:* Caminito; *Lehár:* Land des Lächelns (exc); *Puccini:* Fanciulla del West (exc); *Grever:* Muñequita Linda; *Cardillo:* Core 'ngrato; *Gardel:* Mi Buenos Aires Querido. (P. Domingo, P. Cappuccilli, N. Ghiaurov, VPO/C.M. Giulini, Los Angeles PO, LSO/M. Peeters/C. Abbado/K-H. Loges, Orch/R. Pansera, R. Wagner Chorale, Bavarian St Orch/C. Kleiber, ROHO/Z. Mehta, La Scala Orch)

419 169-2GH (10/86)
Wagner—Orchestral Works
Wagner: Siegfried Idyll; Meistersinger (exc); Fliegende Holländer (exc); Lohengrin (exc). (NYPO/G. Sinopoli)

419 176-2GH (12/86)
Tchaikovsky: Orchestral works
Tchaikovsky: Symphony 1; Eugene Onegin (exc). (BPO/H. von Karajan)

419 179-2GH3 (10/86)
Mozart—Don Giovanni
Mozart: Don Giovanni (Cpte). (S. Ramey, A. Tomowa-Sintow, A. Baltsa, K. Battle, G. Winbergh, F. Furlanetto, A. Malta, P. Burchuladze, Berlin Deutsche Op Chor, BPO/H. von Karajan)

419 203-2GH3 (5/87)
Verdi: La forza del destino
Verdi: Forza del destino (Cpte). (R. Plowright, J. Carreras, R. Bruson, P. Burchuladze, A. Baltsa, J. Pons, J. Tomlinson, M. Curtis, J. Rigby, R. Van Allan, P. Salomaa, Ambrosian Op Chor, Philh/G. Sinopoli)

419 225-2GH2 (5/87)
R. Strauss: Ariadne auf Naxos
R. Strauss: Ariadne auf Naxos (Cpte). (A. Tomowa-Sintow, A. Baltsa, K. Battle, G. Lakes, H. Prey, U. Malmberg, K. Rydl, H. Sojer, J. Protschka, B. Bonney, H. Müller-Molinari, D. Upshaw, H. Zednik, O. Schenk, VPO/James Levine)

419 237-2GH (12/88)
Schubert: Lieder
Schubert: Claudine von Villa Bella (exc); Liebhaber in allen Gestalten, D558; An die Laute, D905; Geheimes, D719; Seligkeit, D433; Alinde, D904; Suleika I, D720; Nacht und Träume, D827; Nähe des Geliebten, D162; Ständchen, D889; Lachen und Weinen, D777; Gott im Frühling, D448; Refrainlieder, D866 (exc); Rastlose Liebe, D138; Junge Nonne, D828; Lied der Delphine, D857/1; Hirt auf dem Felsen, D965. (K. Battle, James Levine, K. Leister)

419 257-2GH3 (10/87)
'Cav' and 'Pag', etc
Mascagni: Cavalleria Rusticana (Cpte); *Leoncavallo:* Pagliacci (Cpte); *Verdi:* Traviata (exc); *Puccini:* Manon Lescaut (exc); *Schmidt:* Notre Dame (exc); *Massenet:* Thaïs (exc); *Giordano:* Fedora (exc); *Cilea:* Adriana Lecouvreur (exc); *Puccini:* Suor Angelica (exc); *Wolf-Ferrari:* Gioielli della Madonna (exc); *Mascagni:* Amico Fritz (exc). (J. Carlyle, C. Bergonzi, G. Taddei, U. Benelli, R. Panerai, F. Cossotto, A. Martino, C. Bergonzi, G. Guelfi, M.G. Allegri, La Scala Chor, La Scala Orch, BPO/H. von Karajan)

419 424-2GB
Mozart—Die Zauberflöte - excerpts
Mozart: Zauberflöte (exc). (F. Crass, F. Wunderlich, R. Peters, E. Lear, H. Hillebrecht, C. Ahlin, S. Wagner, D. Fischer-Dieskau, L. Otto, F. Lenz, R. Schwaiger, A. Fahberg, R. Kostia, Berlin RIAS Chor, BPO/K. Böhm)

419 436-2GH2 (6/87)
Beethoven—Fidelio
Beethoven: Fidelio (Cpte). (G. Janowitz, R. Kollo, H. Sotin, M. Jungwirth, L. Popp, A. Dallapozza, D. Fischer-Dieskau, K. Terkal, A. Sramek, Vienna St Op Chor, VPO/L. Bernstein)

419 622-2GH (10/87)
Verdi: Overtures & Preludes
Verdi: Nabucco (exc); Ernani (exc); Masnadieri (exc); Macbeth (exc); Corsaro (exc); Battaglia di Legnano (exc); Luisa Miller (exc); Rigoletto (exc); Traviata (exc); Vespri siciliani (exc); Ballo in maschera (exc); Forza del destino (exc); Aida (exc). (BPO/H. von Karajan)

419 636-2GH3 (2/88)
Bizet—Carmen
Bizet: Carmen (Cpte). (T. Berganza, P. Domingo, I. Cotrubas, S. Milnes, Y. Kenny, A. Nafé, G. Sandison, G. Pogson, S. Harling, R. Lloyd, Watson Coll Boys' Chor, Ambrosian Sngrs, LSO/C. Abbado)

419 640-2GH2 (11/87)
Puccini—La Fanciulla del West
Puccini: Fanciulla del West (Cpte). (C. Neblett, P. Domingo, S. Milnes, F. Egerton, R. Lloyd, G. Howell, P. Hudson, A. Wilkens, J. Summers, J. Dobson, M. Rivers, T. McDonnell, P. Crook, R. Leggate, W. Elvin, M. King, E. Garrett, H. Owen, ROH Chor, ROHO/Z. Mehta)

419 869-2GGA (5/88)
Rossini: Overtures
Rossini: Barbiere di Siviglia (exc); Cenerentola (exc); Gazza ladra (exc); Italiana in Algeri (exc); Signor Bruschino (exc); Siège de Corinthe (exc). (LSO/C. Abbado)

Ⓓ **423 113-2GH**
Puccini—Tosca - excerpts
Puccini: Tosca (exc). (K. Ricciarelli, J. Carreras, R. Raimondi, G. Hornik, H. Zednik, F. Corena, V. von Halem, Berlin Deutsche Op Chor, BPO/H. von Karajan)

Ⓓ **423 114-2GH**
Verdi—Rigoletto
Verdi: Rigoletto (exc). (P. Domingo, P. Cappuccilli, I. Cotrubas, N. Ghiaurov, E. Obraztsova, H. Schwarz, K. Moll, Vienna St Op Chor, VPO/C.M. Giulini)

Ⓓ **423 115-2GH**
Mozart—(Le) Nozze di Figaro - excerpts
Mozart: Nozze di Figaro (exc). (D. Fischer-Dieskau, G. Janowitz, E. Mathis, H. Prey, T. Troyanos, P. Lagger, B. Vogel, Berlin Deutsche Op Chor, Berlin Deutsche Op Orch/K. Böhm)

Ⓓ **423 144-2GH2** (5/88)
Verdi—Luisa Miller
Verdi: Luisa Miller (Cpte). (K. Ricciarelli, P. Domingo, R. Bruson, G. Howell, E. Obraztsova, W. Ganzarolli, A. Michael, L. de Corato, ROH Chor, ROHO/L. Maazel)

Ⓓ **423 148-2GH**
Verdi—La forza del destino (highlights)
Verdi: Forza del destino (exc). (R. Plowright, R. Bruson, J. Carreras, A. Baltsa, P. Burchuladze, J. Rigby, R. Van Allan, M. Curtis, P. Salomaa, Ambrosian Op Chor, Philh/G. Sinopoli)

Ⓓ **423 389-2GH4** (11/88)
Wagner—Die Walküre
Wagner: Walküre (Cpte). (G. Lakes, J. Norman, H. Behrens, J. Morris, C. Ludwig, K. Moll, M. Napier, L. Kelm, M. Mims, R. Runkel, A. Wilkens, D. Kesling, M. Parsons, R. Engert-Ely, NY Met Op Orch/James Levine)

Ⓓ **423 472-2GGA** (12/88)
Bizet—L'Arlesienne; Carmen Suites
Bizet: Arlésienne Suites; Carmen Suites (exc). (LSO/C. Abbado)

Ⓓ **423 481-2GX6** (3/89)
Beethoven: Complete Symphonies
Beethoven: Symphony 1; Symphony 2; Symphony 3; Symphony 4; Symphony 5; Symphony 6; Symphony 7; Symphony 8; Symphony 9; Prometheus (exc); Egmont (exc); Coriolan; Fidelio (exc); Leonore (exc); König Stefan (exc). (G. Jones, H. Schwarz, R. Kollo, K. Moll, Vienna St Op Chor, VPO/L. Bernstein)

Ⓓ **423 567-2GH3** (12/88)
Puccini—Madame Butterfly
Puccini: Madama Butterfly (Cpte). (M. Freni, J. Carreras, J. Pons, T. Berganza, A. Laciura, M. Curtis, M. Rørholm, K. Rydl, P. Salomaa, H. Komatsu, Ambrosian Op Chor, Philh/G. Sinopoli)

Ⓓ **423 584-2GH**
Rossini—Barber of Seville Highlights
Rossini: Barbiere di Siviglia (exc). (L. Alva, E. Dara, T. Berganza, H. Prey, P. Montarsolo, S. Malagù, Ambrosian Op Chor, LSO/C. Abbado)

Ⓓ **423 587-2GH2** (2/89)
Berg—Wozzeck
Berg: Wozzeck (Cpte). (F. Grundheber, H. Behrens, W. Raffeiner, P. Langridge, H. Zednik, A. Haugland, A. Gonda, Vienna Boys' Ch, Vienna St Op Chor, VPO/C. Abbado)

Ⓓ **423 601-2GH2** (8/88)
Puccini—La Bohème
Puccini: Bohème (Cpte). (A. Réaux, J. Hadley, B. Daniels, T. Hampson, J. Busterud, P. Plishka, J. McKee, G. Beni, D. Bernardini, P. Kreider, Children's Ch, Santa Cecilia Academy Chor, Santa Cecilia Academy Orch/L. Bernstein)

Ⓓ **423 613-2GH** (8/88)
Wagner—Opera excerpts
Wagner: Tannhäuser (exc); Siegfried Idyll; Tristan und Isolde (exc). (J. Norman, VPO/H. von Karajan)

Ⓓ **423 662-2GH** (7/88)
New Year's Day Concert, Vienna, 1988
Rezniček: Donna Diana (exc); *Jos Strauss:* Brennende Liebe; Auf Ferienreisen; Im Fluge; *J. Strauss II:* Fledermaus (exc); Neue Pizzicato-Polka, Op. 449; Freut euch des Lebens, Op. 340; Ballo in maschera Quadrille, Op. 272; *J.Strauss II:* Tritsch-Tratsch; *J. Strauss II:* Leichtes Blut, Op. 319; *J.Strauss II:* Seid umschlungen, Millionen; Perpetuum mobile; *J. Strauss II:* Banditen-Galopp, Op. 378; *J.Strauss II:* Blauen Donau, Op. 314; *J.Strauss I:* Radetzky March. (Vienna Boys' Ch, VPO/C. Abbado)

Ⓓ **423 719-2GH** (3/89)
Ravel—L'heure espagnole
Ravel: Heure espagnole (Cpte). (J. Berbié, M. Sénéchal, J. Giraudeau, G. Bacquier, J. Van Dam, FRNO/L. Maazel)

Ⓓ **423 850-2GH3** (9/84)
R. Strauss—Der Rosenkavalier
R. Strauss: Rosenkavalier (Cpte). (A. Tomowa-Sintow, A. Baltsa, K. Moll, J. Perry, G. Hornik, V. Cole, H. Müller-Molinari, H. Zednik, W. Lipp, G. Sima, C. Feller, V. von Halem, K. Equiluz, F. Kasemann, K. Terkal, B. Poschner-Klebel, W. Winsauer, M. Hintermeier, H. Nitsche, A. Tomaschek, J. Reinprecht, W. Scheider, G. Panzenböck, I. Koblitz, W. Holzherr, W. Zeh, H. Lichtenberger, J. Reautschnigg, Vienna St Op Concert Ch, VPO/H. von Karajan)

Ⓓ **423 855-2GH2** (6/84)
Puccini—Turandot
Puccini: Turandot (Cpte). (K. Ricciarelli, P. Domingo, B. Hendricks, G. Hornik, H. Zednik, F. Araiza, R. Raimondi, P. de Palma, S. Nimsgern, Vienna St Op Chor, Vienna Boys' Ch, VPO/H. von Karajan)

Ⓓ **423 858-2GH2** (2/85)
Verdi—Il Trovatore
Verdi: Trovatore (Cpte). (P. Domingo, R. Plowright, G. Zancanaro, B. Fassbaender, E. Nesterenko, A. di Stasio, W. Gullino, A. Giacomotti, A. Verrecchia, Santa Cecilia Academy Chor, Santa Cecilia Academy Orch/C.M. Giulini)

Ⓓ **423 861-2GH2**
Rossini—La Cenerentola
Rossini: Cenerentola (Cpte). (T. Berganza, L. Alva, R. Capecchi, P. Montarsolo, M. Guglielmi, L. Zannini, U. Trama, Scottish Op Chor, LSO/C. Abbado)

Ⓓ **423 959-2GH2** (3/89)
Tchaikovsky—Eugene Onegin
Tchaikovsky: Eugene Onegin (Cpte). (T. Allen, M. Freni, N. Shicoff, A.S. von Otter, P. Burchuladze, R. Lang, R. Engert-Ely, M. Sénéchal, J. Hartfiel, Leipzig Rad Chor, Staatskapelle Dresden/James Levine)

Ⓓ **427 194-2GR**
Beethoven—Symphony No 3 & Overtures
Beethoven: Symphony 3; Fidelio (exc); Leonore (exc). (VPO, Staatskapelle Dresden/K. Böhm)

Ⓓ **427 256-2GGA2**
Beethoven—Overtures
Beethoven: Prometheus (exc); König Stefan (exc); Ruinen von Athen (exc); Egmont (exc); Coriolan; Namensfeier; Fidelio (exc); Leonore (exc); Consecration of the House Ov. (BPO/H. von Karajan)

Ⓓ **427 306-2GH6** (9/89)
Beethoven: Complete Symphonies
Beethoven: Symphony 1; Symphony 2; Symphony 3; Symphony 4; Symphony 5; Symphony 6; Symphony 7; Symphony 8; Symphony 9; Coriolan; Leonore (exc); Egmont (exc); Meeresstille. (G. Beňačková, M. Lipovšek, G. Winbergh, H. Prey, Vienna St Op Concert Ch, VPO/C. Abbado)

Ⓓ **427 331-2GH2** (10/89)
Rossini—The Italian Girl in Algiers
Rossini: Italiana in Algeri (Cpte). (A. Baltsa, F. Lopardo, E. Dara, R. Raimondi, P. Pace, A. Gonda, A. Corbelli, Vienna St Op Chor, VPO/C. Abbado)

Ⓓ **427 340-2GH** (8/89)
Smetana—Ma Vlast; Bartered Bride Excerpts
Smetana: Má Vlast (exc); Bartered Bride (exc). (VPO/James Levine)

Ⓓ **427 341-2GH2** (10/90)
Schubert: Fierabras
Schubert: Fierrabras (Cpte). (J. Protschka, K. Mattila, R. Holl, T. Hampson, R. Gambill, L. Polgár, C. Studer, B. Balleys, H. Welker, A. Schoenberg Ch, COE/C. Abbado)

Ⓓ **427 413-2GC3** (8/89)
Busoni—Doktor Faust
Busoni: Doktor Faust (Cpte). (D. Fischer-Dieskau, W. Cochran, A. de Ridder, H. Hillebrecht, K.C. Kohn, F. Grundheber, M. Schmidt, M. Rintzler, H. Sotin, Bavarian Rad Chor, BRSO/F. Leitner)

Ⓓ **427 417-2GC3** (7/89)
Pfitzner—Palestrina
Pfitzner: Palestrina (Cpte). (N. Gedda, K. Ridderbusch, B. Weikl, H. Steinbach, D. Fischer-Dieskau, V. von Halem, J. van Kesteren, P. Meven, H. Prey, F. Lenz, Adalbert Kraus, F. Mazura, H. Donath, B. Fassbaender, G. Nienstedt, R. Freyer, Tolz Boys' Ch, Bavarian Rad Chor, BRSO/R. Kubelík)

Ⓓ **427 440-2GX3** (9/91)
Bizet—Carmen
Bizet: Carmen (Cpte). (M. Horne, J. McCracken, A. Maliponte, T. Krause, C. Boky, M. Baldwin, R. Christopher, A. Velis, R. Gibbs, D. Gramm, NY Met Op Children's Ch, Manhattan Op Chor, NY Met Op Orch/L. Bernstein)

Ⓓ **427 625-2GH3** (9/89)
Wagner—Tannhäuser
Wagner: Tannhäuser (Cpte). (P. Domingo, C. Studer, A. Schmidt, A. Baltsa, M. Salminen, W. Pell, K. Rydl, C. Biber, O. Hillebrandt, B. Bonney, ROH Chor, Philh/G. Sinopoli)

Ⓓ **427 635-2GH2** (11/89)
Verdi—Un ballo in maschera
Verdi: Ballo in maschera (Cpte). (J. Barstow, P. Domingo, L. Nucci, S. Jo, F. Quivar, K. Rydl, G. Simic, J-L. Chaignaud, W. Witte, A. Tomaschek, Vienna St Op Chor, VPO/H. von Karajan)

Ⓓ **427 682-2GH2** (3/90)
Offenbach—Les Contes d'Hoffmann
Offenbach: Contes d'Hoffmann (Cpte). (P. Domingo, E. Gruberová, C. Eder, A. Schmidt, G. Bacquier, J. Diaz, J. Morris, G. Friedmann, R. Van Allan, H. Stamm, C. Ludwig, R. Gambill, P. Crook, M. Sénéchal, K. Rydl, R. Leggate, U. Malmberg, French Rad Chor, FNO/S. Ozawa)

Ⓓ **427 708-2GX3**
The Best of Domingo
Verdi: Aida (exc); Rigoletto (exc); Luisa Miller (exc); Ballo in maschera (exc); Traviata (exc); *Bizet:* Carmen (exc); *Donizetti:* Elisir d'amore (exc); *Offenbach:* Contes d'Hoffmann (exc); *Puccini:* Turandot (exc); *Flotow:* Martha (exc); *Lara:* Granada; *Cardillo:* Core 'ngrato; *Lehár:* Land des Lächelns (exc); *Leoncavallo:* Mattinata; *Lecuona:* Siboney; *Freire:* Ay, Ay, Ay; *Brodszky:* Toast of New Orleans (exc); *Grever:* Jurame; Muñequita Linda; *Simons:* Marta; *De Curtis:* Non ti scordar di me; *Hardelot:* Because; *Loges:* Ich schenk dir eine neue Welt; *Lacalle:* Amapola; *Gardel:* Volver; Mi Buenos Aires querido; Día que me quieras; Cuesta abajo; *Filiberto:* Caminito; *Cobián:* Nostalgias; *O. Fresedo:* Vida mía; *Mores:* Uno; *Troilo:* María; *J. A. Caruso:* Alma de Bohemio. (P. Domingo, La Scala Orch/C. Abbado, VPO/C.M. Giulini, ROHO/L. Maazel, Bavarian St Orch/C. Kleiber, Los Angeles PO, SRO/R. Bonynge/H. von Karajan, LSO/M. Peeters/K-H. Loges, orch/R. Pansera)

Ⓓ **429 089-2GSE6**
Beethoven: Symphonies, etc
Beethoven: Symphony 1; Symphony 2; Symphony 3; Symphony 4; Symphony 5; Symphony 6; Symphony 7; Symphony 8; Symphony 9; Fidelio (exc); Leonore (exc); Egmont (exc); Coriolan; Ruinen von Athen (exc); Prometheus (exc). (A. Tomowa-Sintow, A. Baltsa, P. Schreier, J. Van Dam, Vienna Singverein, BPO/H. von Karajan)

Ⓓ **429 164-2GR** (5/90)
Rossini & Verdi: Overtures & Preludes
Rossini: Barbiere di Siviglia (exc); Italiana in Algeri (exc); Gazza ladra (exc); Scala di seta (exc); *Verdi:* Nabucco (exc); Traviata (exc); Vespri Siciliani (exc); Ballo in maschera (exc); Forza del destino (exc); Aida (exc). (BPO/H. von Karajan)

Ⓓ **429 168-2GR** (4/90) ▣ **429 168-4GR** (4/90)
Wagner: Excerpts from Der Ring
Wagner: Rheingold (exc); Walküre (exc); Siegfried (exc); Götterdämmerung (exc). (D. Grobe, D. Fischer-Dieskau, J. Veasey, G. Stolze, H. Donath, E. Moser, A. Reynolds, J. Vickers, T. Stewart, Jess Thomas, H. Dernesch, H. Brilioth, BPO/H. von Karajan)

Ⓓ **429 169-2GR** (4/90)
Wagner—Choruses
Wagner: Fliegende Holländer (exc); Lohengrin (exc); Tannhäuser (exc); Meistersinger (exc); Götterdämmerung (exc); Parsifal (exc). (E. Schärtel, J. Greindl, Bayreuth Fest Chor, Bayreuth Fest Orch/W. Pitz)

Ⓓ **429 385-2GH4** (8/91)
Wagner—Götterdämmerung
Wagner: Götterdämmerung (Cpte). (H. Behrens, R. Goldberg, M. Salminen, E. Wlaschiha, B. Weikl, C. Studer, H. Schwarz, H-K. Hong, D. Kesling, M. Parsons, H. Dernesch, T. Troyanos, A. Gruber, NY Met Op Chor, NY Met Op Orch/James Levine)

Ⓓ **429 407-2GH4** (3/92)
Wagner—Siegfried
Wagner: Siegfried (Cpte). (R. Goldberg, J. Morris, H. Behrens, H. Zednik, E. Wlaschiha, B. Svendén, K. Moll, K. Battle, NY Met Op Orch/James Levine)

Ⓓ **429 494-2GDC** (6/90) ▭ **429 494-4GDC** (6/90)
Intermezzo
Mascagni: Cavalleria Rusticana (exc); *Cilea:* Adriana Lecouvreur (exc); *Puccini:* Manon Lescaut (exc); *Leoncavallo:* Pagliacci (exc); *Massenet:* Thaïs (exc); *Wolf-Ferrari:* Gioielli della Madonna (exc); *Verdi:* Traviata (exc); *Schmidt:* Notre Dame (exc); *Mussorgsky:* Khovanshchina (exc); *Puccini:* Suor Angelica (exc); *Giordano:* Fedora (exc); *Mascagni:* Amico Fritz (exc); *Offenbach:* Contes d'Hoffmann (exc); *Ponchielli:* Gioconda (exc). (Gothenburg SO/N. Järvi)

Ⓓ **429 562-2GX2**
The Best of the New Year's Concerts in Vienna
J. Strauss II: Fledermaus (exc); Tritsch-Tratsch; *Jos Strauss:* Sphärenklänge; Ohne Sorgen; *J. Strauss II:* G'schichten aus dem Wienerwald, Op. 325; *Jos Strauss:* Frauenherz; *J. Strauss II:* Pizzicato Polka; Rosen aus dem Süden; *Jos Strauss:* Libelle; Transaktionen; *J. Strauss II:* Vergnügungszug; Accelerationen, Op. 234; Perpetuum mobile; *Jos Strauss:* Aquarellen; *J. Strauss II:* Unter Donner und Blitz; Kaiser, Op. 437; Waldmeister (exc); Morgenblätter, Op. 279; *Jos Strauss:* Tanzende Muse; Delirien; *J. Strauss II:* Eljen a Magyar!, Op. 332; Blauen Donau, Op. 314; Radetzky March. (VPO/L. Maazel)

Ⓓ **429 724-2GH2** (7/92)
Berlioz—Requiem, etc
Berlioz: Grande Messe des Morts (Cpte); Corsaire; Benvenuto Cellini (exc); Carnaval Romain. (L. Pavarotti, Ernst Senff Chor, BPO/James Levine)

Ⓓ **429 734-2GH2** (8/91) ▭ **429 734-4GH2** (8/91)
Bernstein—Candide
Bernstein: Candide (1988) (Cpte). (J. Hadley, J. Anderson, A. Green, C. Ludwig, N. Gedda, D. Jones, K. Ollmann, N. Jenkins, R. Suart, J. Treleaven, L. Benson, C. Bayley, LSC, LSO/L. Bernstein)

Ⓓ **429 744-2GH2** (2/91)
Donizetti: L'elisir d'amore
Donizetti: Elisir d'amore (Cpte). (K. Battle, L. Pavarotti, L. Nucci, E. Dara, D. Upshaw, NY Met Op Chor, NY Met Op Orch/James Levine)

Ⓓ **429 758-2GH3** (11/90)
Mussorgsky—Khovanshchina
Mussorgsky: Khovanshchina (Cpte). (A. Haugland, V. Atlantov, V. Popov, A. Kocherga, P. Burchuladze, M. Lipovšek, B. Poschner-Klebel, H. Zednik, J. Borowska, W. Gahmlich, Vienna Boys' Ch, Slovak Phil Chor, Vienna St Op Chor, Vienna St Op Orch/C. Abbado)

Ⓓ **429 762-2GH2**
Beethoven: Overtures
Beethoven: Prometheus (exc); König Stefan (exc); Ruinen von Athen (exc); Consecration of the House Ov; Namensfeier; Coriolan; Egmont (exc); Fidelio (exc); Leonore (exc). (VPO/C. Abbado)

Ⓓ **429 788-2GH**
Offenbach: Les contes d'Hoffmann highlights
Offenbach: Contes d'Hoffmann (exc). (P. Domingo, E. Gruberová, C. Eder, G. Bacquier, J. Diaz, J. Morris, French Rad Chor, FNO/S. Ozawa)

Ⓓ **429 789-2GH**
Wagner: Tannhäuser highlights
Wagner: Tannhäuser (exc). (P. Domingo, C. Studer, A. Baltsa, M. Salminen, A. Schmidt, W. Pell, K. Rydl, C. Biber, O. Hillebrandt, B. Bonney, ROH Chor, Philh/G. Sinopoli)

▭ **429 825-4GMM** (8/90)
Mozart—Die Zauberflöte (highlights)
Mozart: Zauberflöte (exc). (E. Lear, R. Peters, F. Wunderlich, D. Fischer-Dieskau, F. Crass, F. Lenz, L. Otto, H. Hillebrecht, C. Ahlin, S. Wagner, A. Fahberg, R. Schwaiger, R. Kostia, Berlin RIAS Chbr Ch, BPO/K. Böhm)

Ⓓ **429 864-2GX3** (12/90)
Mozart: Idomeneo
Mozart: Idomeneo (Cpte). (W. Ochman, P. Schreier, E. Mathis, J. Varady, H. Winkler, E. Büchner, S. Vogel, Leipzig Rad Chor, Staatskapelle Dresden/K. Böhm)

Ⓓ **429 868-2GX2** (12/90)
Mozart: Die Entführung aus dem Serail
Mozart: Entführung (Cpte). (A. Auger, R. Grist, P. Schreier, H. Neukirch, K. Moll, O. Mellies, Leipzig Rad Chor, Staatskapelle Dresden/K. Böhm)

Ⓓ **429 869-2GX3** (12/90)
Mozart: Le nozze di Figaro
Mozart: Nozze di Figaro (Cpte). (H. Prey, E. Mathis, D. Fischer-Dieskau, G. Janowitz, T. Troyanos, P. Johnson, P. Lagger, E. Wohlfahrt, M. Vantin, K. Hirte, B. Vogel, Berlin Deutsche Op Chor, Berlin Deutsche Op Orch/K. Böhm)

Ⓓ **429 870-2GX3** (12/90)
Mozart: Don Giovanni
Mozart: Don Giovanni (Cpte). (D. Fischer-Dieskau, B. Nilsson, M. Arroyo, R. Grist, P. Schreier, E. Flagello, A. Mariotti, M. Talvela, Czech Sngrs Chor, Prague Nat Th Orch/K. Böhm)

Ⓓ **429 874-2GX2** (12/90)
Mozart: Così fan tutte
Mozart: Così fan tutte (Cpte). (G. Janowitz, B. Fassbaender, R. Grist, P. Schreier, H. Prey, R. Panerai, Vienna St Op Chor, VPO/K. Böhm)

Ⓓ **429 877-2GX3** (12/90)
Mozart: Die Zauberflöte & Der Schauspieldirektor
Mozart: Zauberflöte (Cpte); Schauspieldirektor (Cpte). (E. Lear, R. Peters, F. Wunderlich, D. Fischer-Dieskau, F. Crass, H. Hotter, F. Lenz, L. Otto, H. Hillebrecht, C. Ahlin, S. Wagner, R. Schwaiger, A. Fahberg, R. Kostia, J. King, M. Talvela, H. Hilten, M. Vantin, M. Röhrl, Berlin RIAS Chbr Ch, BPO, R. Grist, A. Auger, P. Schreier, K. Moll, Staatskapelle Dresden/K. Böhm)

Ⓓ **429 878-2GX2** (12/90)
Mozart: La clemenza di Tito
Mozart: Clemenza di Tito (Cpte). (P. Schreier, J. Varady, T. Berganza, M. Schiml, E. Mathis, T. Adam, Leipzig Rad Chor, Staatskapelle Dresden/K. Böhm)

Ⓓ **429 984-2GH** (3/91)
Russian Orchestral Works
Tchaikovsky: 1812; Marche slave; *Borodin:* In the Steppes of Central Asia; Prince Igor (exc); *Rimsky-Korsakov:* Russian Easter Festival Ov; Capriccio Espagnol. (Gothenburg Sym Chor, Gothenburg Sym Brass, T. Sporsén, Gothenburg SO/N. Järvi)

ꝏ **429 984-5GH**
Russian Orchestral Works
Tchaikovsky: 1812; Marche slave; *Borodin:* In the Steppes of Central Asia; Prince Igor (exc); *Rimsky-Korsakov:* Russian Easter Festival Ov; Capriccio Espagnol. (Gothenburg Sym Chor, Gothenburg Sym Brass, T. Sporsén, Gothenburg SO/N. Järvi)

Ⓓ **431 103-2GB** (5/93)
Great Voices—Montserrat Caballé
Gounod: Faust (exc); *Meyerbeer:* Huguenots (exc); *G. Charpentier:* Louise (exc); *Bizet:* Carmen (exc); *Gounod:* Roméo et Juliette (exc); *R. Strauss:* Salome (exc); *Puccini:* Manon Lescaut (exc). (M. Caballé, P. Domingo, New Philh/R. Giovaninetti, FNO/L. Bernstein, NY Met Op Orch/James Levine)

Ⓓ **431 104-2GB** (5/93)
Great Voices - Plácido Domingo
Bizet: Carmen (exc); *Puccini:* Manon Lescaut (exc); Fanciulla del West (exc); *Verdi:* Traviata (exc); Macbeth (exc); *Wagner:* Meistersinger (exc); *Cardillo:* Core 'ngrato; *Lara:* Granada; *Leoncavallo:* Mattinata; *Freire:* Ay, ay, ay; *De Curtis:* Non ti scordar di me. (P. Domingo, T. Berganza, M. Caballé, I. Cotrubas, D. Fischer-Dieskau, P. Lagger, C. Ligendza, Ambrosian Sngrs, Bavarian St Op Chor, Berlin Deutsche Op Chor, LSO, NY Met Op Orch, ROHO, Bavarian St Orch, La Scala Orch, Berlin Deutsche Op Orch/C. Abbado/James Levine/Z. Mehta/C. Kleiber/E. Jochum/K-H. Loges/M. Peeters)

Ⓓ **431 110-2GB** (5/93)
Great Voices - Fritz Wunderlich
Mozart: Zauberflöte (exc); Entführung (exc); *Verdi:* Traviata (exc); *Tchaikovsky:* Eugene Onegin (exc); *Lortzing:* Zar und Zimmermann (exc); Waffenschmied (exc); *Rossini:* Barbiere di Siviglia (exc); *Verdi:* Rigoletto (exc); Don Carlos (exc); *Puccini:* Bohème (exc); Tosca (exc); *Schubert:* Heidenröslein, D257; *Beethoven:* Zärtliche Liebe, WoO123; *Denza:* Funiculì-Funiculà; *May:* Lied geht um die Welt (exc). (F. Wunderlich, BPO/K. Böhm, Bavarian St Orch/E. Jochum, H. Gueden, Bavarian Rad Chor, BRSO/B. Bartoletti, Bavarian St Op Orch/O. Gerdes, I. Hallstein, Bamberg SO/H. Gierster, H. Prey, E. Köth, Munich RO/H. Moltkau/K. Eichhorn/H. Stein, South-West German RSO/E. Smola, H. Giesen, R. Lamy Sngrs, Graunke SO/H. Carste)

Ⓓ **431 160-2GR** (8/91)
Bizet & Offenbach—Orchestral Works
Bizet: Carmen Suites (exc); Arlésienne Suites; *Offenbach:* Contes d'Hoffmann (exc); Orphée aux Enfers (exc). (BPO/H. von Karajan)

Ⓓ **431 469-2GGA** (8/91)
Works for Violin and Piano
Franck: Violin Sonata; *Szymanowski:* Myths, Op.30; King Roger (exc); Kurpian Song. (K. Danczowska, K. Zimerman)

Ⓓ **431 544-2GH** (7/91)
Meditation
Traditional: Catalan Folk-song; *Brahms:* Lieder, Op. 49 (exc); *Chopin:* Preludes (exc); *Falla:* Canciones populares españolas (exc); *Fauré:* Songs, Op. 7 (exc); *Gluck:* Orfeo ed Euridice (exc); *Gounod:* Ave Maria; *Handel:* Violin Sonatas (exc); *Kreisler:* Liebesleid; *Lully:* Gavotte; *Massenet:* Élégie; *Mendelssohn:* Song without words, Op.109; *Rachmaninov:* Songs, Op.34 (exc); *Ravel:* Vocalise; *Saint-Saëns:* Carnaval des Animaux (exc); *Schubert:* Ave Maria, D839; *Schumann:* Kinderszenen (exc); *Tchaikovsky:* Morceaux, Op.19 (exc). (M. Maisky, P. Gililov)

ꝏ **431 544-5GH**
Meditation
Traditional: Catalan Folk-song; *Brahms:* Lieder, Op. 49 (exc); *Chopin:* Preludes (exc); *Falla:* Canciones populares españolas (exc); *Fauré:* Songs, Op. 7 (exc); *Gluck:* Orfeo ed Euridice (exc); *Gounod:* Ave Maria; *Handel:* Violin Sonatas (exc); *Kreisler:* Liebesleid; *Lully:* Gavotte; *Massenet:* Élégie; *Mendelssohn:* Song without words, Op.109; *Rachmaninov:* Songs, Op.34 (exc); *Ravel:* Vocalise; *Saint-Saëns:* Carnaval des Animaux (exc); *Schubert:* Ave Maria, D839; *Schumann:* Kinderszenen (exc); *Tchaikovsky:* Morceaux, Op.19 (exc). (M. Maisky, P. Gililov)

Ⓓ **431 601-2GCE10**
Tchaikovsky Compact Edition
Tchaikovsky: Symphony 6; Symphony 5; Romeo and Juliet; Symphony 4; Symphony 2; Symphony 3; Serenade, Op.48; Symphony 1; Rococo Variations; Swan Lake (exc); 1812; Marche slave; Francesca da Rimini; Piano Concerto 1; Violin Concerto; Sleeping Beauty (exc); Nutcracker Suite; Capriccio italien; Eugene Onegin (exc). (Los Angeles PO/C.M. Giulini, Boston SO, San Francisco SO/S. Ozawa, VPO, New Philh/C. Abbado, BPO/H. von Karajan, M. Rostropovich, Chicago SO/D. Barenboim, M. Argerich, RPO, G. Kremer/C. Dutoit/L. Maazel/M. Rostropovich, M. Freni, A.S. von Otter, T. Allen, N. Shicoff, P. Burchuladze, J. Hartfiel, Leipzig Rad Chor, Staatskapelle Dresden/James Levine)

Ⓓ **431 619-2GH3** (9/91)
Mozart—Le nozze di Figaro
Mozart: Nozze di Figaro (Cpte). (F. Furlanetto, D. Upshaw, T. Hampson, K. Te Kanawa, A.S. von Otter, T. Troyanos, P. Plishka, A. Laciura, M. Forrest, R. Capecchi, H. Grant-Murphy, NY Met Op Chor, NY Met Op Orch/James Levine)

Ⓓ **431 628-2GH** (4/91)
Vienna New Year's Concert, 1991
J. Strauss II: Waldmeister (exc); *Jos Strauss:* Tanzende Muse; *Lanner:* Werber, Op.103; *J. Strauss I:* Seufzer-Galopp; *Mozart:* Contredanses, K609 (exc); German Dances, K605 (exc); *Jos Strauss:* Aquarellen; *J. Strauss II:* Freikugeln, Op. 326; Stürmisch in Lieb' und Tanz; Blauen Donau, Op. 314; Kaiser, Op. 437; Furioso-Polka, Op. 260; Radetzky March; *E. Strauss:* Carmen; *Schubert:* Galop and Ecossaises, D735 (exc). (VPO/C. Abbado)

Ⓓ **431 653-2GH** (5/91) ▭ **431 653-4GH** (5/91)
Rossini—Overtures
Rossini: Barbiere di Siviglia (exc); Semiramide (exc); Italiana in Algeri (exc); Guillaume Tell (exc); Cenerentola (exc); Scala di seta (exc); Gazza ladra (exc). (COE/C. Abbado)

Ⓓ **431 669-2GH2** (7/91)
Prokofiev—The Fiery Angel
Prokofiev: Fiery Angel (Cpte). (N. Secunde, S. Lorenz, H. Zednik, P. Salomaa, K. Moll, G. Zachrisson, B. Terfel, R. Lang, R. Engert-Ely, C.G. Holmgren, Ohlin Voc Ens, Gothenburg Pro Musica Chbr Ch, Gothenburg SO/N. Järvi)

Ⓓ **431 741-2GC2** (12/91)
Hindemith—Cardillac & Mathis der Maler excs
Hindemith: Cardillac (Cpte); Mathis der Maler (exc). (D. Fischer-Dieskau, L. Kirschstein, D. Grobe, K.C. Kohn, E. Katz, E. Söderström, W. Nett, Cologne Rad Chor, Cologne RSO/J. Keilberth, D. Fischer-Dieskau, P. Lorengar, D. Grobe, Berlin RSO/L. Ludwig)

Ⓓ **431 751-2GC** (2/92)
Stravinsky—Songs
Stravinsky: Pastorale; Verlaine Poems; Balmont Poems; Japanese Lyrics; Little Songs; Pribaoutki; Cat's Cradle Songs; Songs (1953-54); Stories for Children (exc); Mavra (exc); Shakespeare Songs; In Memoriam D. Thomas; Elegy for JFK; Wolf Songs. (P. Bryn-Julson, A. Murray, R. Tear, J. Shirley-Quirk, Paris InterContemporain Ens/P. Boulez)

Ⓓ **431 775-2GH2** (7/92)
Puccini—Tosca
Puccini: Tosca (Cpte). (M. Freni, P. Domingo, S. Ramey,

B. Terfel, A. Laciura, A. Veccia, R. Lukas, B. Secombe, L. Tiernan, ROH Chor, Philh/G. Sinopoli)

Ⓓ **431 778-2GH** (11/91)
Bizet—Orchestral Works
Bizet: Carmen Suites (exc); Arlésienne Suites; Jeux d'enfants. (Paris Bastille Orch/Myung-Whun Chung)

Ⓓ **431 810-2GH2** (9/91)
R. Strauss—Salome
R. Strauss: Salome (Cpte). (C. Studer, B. Terfel, H. Hiestermann, Leonie Rysanek, C. Bieber, M. Rørholm, F. Molsberger, R. Lukas, W. Murray, B. Rundgren, K. Lang, Berlin Deutsche Op Orch/G. Sinopoli)

Ⓓ **431 875-2GDO**
Rita Streich sings Mozart Arias
Mozart: Entführung (exc); Zauberflöte (exc); Rè Pastore (exc); Alcandro, lo confesso, K294; Ah se in ciel, K538; Vado, ma dove?, K583; Popoli di Tessaglia, K316; Vorrei spiegarvi, K418; No, no, che non sei capace, K419; Mia speranza adorata!, K416; Nehmt meinen Dank, K383. (R. Streich, Berlin RIAS Orch/F. Fricsay, Salzburg Mozarteum Camerata Academica/B. Paumgartner, BRSO/C. Mackerras)

Ⓓ **435 091-2GCE10**
DG Beethoven Edition
Beethoven: Symphony 3; Symphony 5; Symphony 7; Symphony 6; Fidelio (exc); Prometheus (exc); Egmont (exc); Symphony 9; Coriolan; Piano Concerto 1; Triple Concerto; Piano Concerto 3; Piano Sonata 17; Piano Sonata 8; Piano Concerto 4; Piano Concerto 5; Violin Concerto; Romances; Piano Sonata 14; Piano Sonata 21; Piano Sonata 23; Violin Sonata 5; Violin Sonata 9. (Los Angeles PO/C.M. Giulini, VPO/C. Abbado/L. Bernstein, G. Janowitz, H. Rössl-Majdan, W. Kmentt, W. Berry, Vienna Singverein, BPO/H. von Karajan, C. Eschenbach, M. Zeltser, A-S. Mutter, Y-Y. Ma, W. Kempff/F. Leitner, M. Pollini/K. Böhm, P. Zukerman, Chicago SO, LPO/D. Barenboim, D. Barenboim, Y. Menuhin)

Ⓓ **435 145-2GX5(1)**
Fritz Wunderlich—Opera Arias, Lieder, etc (part 1)
Mozart: Zauberflöte (exc); Entführung (exc); *Verdi:* Traviata (exc); *Tchaikovsky:* Eugene Onegin (exc); *Lortzing:* Zar und Zimmermann (exc); Waffenschmied (exc); *Rossini:* Barbiere di Siviglia (exc); *Verdi:* Rigoletto (exc); Don Carlos (exc); *Puccini:* Bohème (exc); Tosca (exc); *Handel:* Serse (exc); Giulio Cesare (exc); *Gluck:* Iphigénie en Tauride (exc); *Bellini:* Sonnambula (exc); *Maillart:* Dragons de Villars (exc); *Kreutzer:* Nachtlager in Granada (exc); *Bizet:* Pêcheurs de Perles (exc); *Schubert:* Schöne Müllerin (Cpte); Forelle, D550; Frühlingsglaube, D686; Heidenröslein, D257; *Schumann:* Dichterliebe, Op. 48 (Cpte); *Beethoven:* Zärtliche Liebe, WoO123; Adelaide, Op.46; Resignation, WoO149; Kuss, Op.128; *Schubert:* An Silvia, D891; Lied eines Schiffers an die Dioskuren, D360; Liebhaber in allen Gestalten, D558; Einsame, D800; Im Abendrot, D799; Schwanengesang, D957 (exc); An die Laute, D905; Musensohn, D764; An die Musik, D547; *Lara:* Granada; *Di Capua:* O sole mio; *Leoncavallo:* Mattinata; *Denza:* Funiculì-Funiculà; *De Curtis:* Vergiss mein nicht; *Stolz:* Ob blond, ob braun, ich liebe alle Frau'n; *Spoliansky:* Heute nacht oder nie; *May:* Lied geht um die Welt (exc). (F. Wunderlich, H. Gueden, I. Hallstein, H. Prey, E. Köth, C. Ludwig, H. Giesen, Bavarian Rad Chor, Vienna St Op Chor, BPO, Bavarian St Op Orch, BRSO, Bamberg SO, Munich RO, South-West German RSO, Vienna Volksoper Orch, Spilar Schrammeln/K. Böhm/E. Jochum/B. Bartoletti/O. Gerdes/H. Gierster/H. Moltkau/K. Eichhorn/H. Stein/E. Smola/R. Kubelík/F. Leitner/R. Stolz/F.J. Breuer, Graunke SO, R. Lamy Sngrs, Munich PO)

Ⓓ **435 145-2GX5(2)**
Fritz Wunderlich—Opera Arias, Lieder, etc, (part 2)
Schmidseder: Ich hab' die schönen Maderln; *Stolz:* Wien wird schön erst bei Nacht; *Sieczyński:* Wien, du Stadt meiner Träume; *Eysler:* Ich kenn' ein kleines Wegerl; *J. Strauss II:* Tänzerin Fanny Elssler (exc); *Benatzky:* Ich weiss auf der Wieden; Ich muss wieder einmal in Grinzing sein; *Stolz:* Im Prater blüh'n wieder die Bäume. (F. Wunderlich, Vienna St Op Chor, Vienna Volksoper Orch, Spilar Schrammeln/R. Stolz)

Ⓓ **435 211-2GX15** (4/92)
Wagner—Der Ring des Nibelungen
Wagner: Rheingold (Cpte); Walküre (Cpte); Siegfried (Cpte); Götterdämmerung (Cpte). (D. Fischer-Dieskau, J. Veasey, G. Stolze, E. Wohlfahrt, Z. Kélémen, S. Mangelsdorff, D. Grobe, R. Kerns, O. Dominguez, M. Talvela, K. Ridderbusch, H. Donath, E. Moser, A. Reynolds, J. Vickers, G. Janowitz, R. Crespin, T. Stewart, M. Talvela, L. Rebmann, D. Mastilovic, C. Ordassy, I. Steger, H. Jenckel, B. Ericson, C. Ahlin, L. Brockhaus, Jess Thomas, T. Stewart, H. Dernesch, C. Gayer, H. Brilioth, K. Ridderbusch, T. Stewart, G. Janowitz, C. Ludwig, L. Rebmann, L. Chookasian, C. Ligendza, G. Stolze, Berlin Deutsche Op Chor, BPO/H. von Karajan)

Ⓓ **435 309-2GH2** (4/93)
Donizetti—Lucia di Lammermoor
Donizetti: Lucia di Lammermoor (Cpte). (C. Studer, P. Domingo, J. Pons, S. Ramey, J. Larmore, F. de la Mora, A. Laciura, Ambrosian Op Chor, LSO/I. Marin)

Ⓓ **435 321-2GWP12** (2/92)
150 Years - Vienna Philharmonic
Haydn: Symphony 102; *Ravel:* Piano Concerto; *Schoenberg:* Pelleas und Melisande; *R. Strauss:* Tod und Verklärung; *Brahms:* Symphony 2; *Beethoven:* Grosse Fuge; Leonore (exc); Symphony 9; *Bruckner:* Symphony 9; *Schubert:* Symphony 8; *Beethoven:* Symphony 5; *Schubert:* Symphony 9; *Schmidt:* Husarenlied Variations; *Beethoven:* Missa Solemnis; *Stravinsky:* Pulcinella Suite; *Dukas:* Apprenti sorcier; *Bruckner:* Symphony 5; *R. Strauss:* Sinfonia Domestica; Till Eulenspiegel; *Wagner:* Meistersinger (exc); *Mozart:* Symphony 38; *Mahler:* Symphony 4. (VPO, L. Bernstein (pf/dir)/L. Bernstein/K. Böhm/W. Furtwängler, I. Seefried, R. Anday, A. Dermota, P. Schoeffler, Vienna Singakademie Chor/H. von Karajan/O. Klemperer/H. Knappertsbusch, T. Eipperle, L. Willer, J. Patzak, G. Hann, Vienna St Op Chor/C. Krauss/C. Schuricht/R. Strauss, H. Gueden/B. Walter)

Ⓓ **435 324-2GWP** (2/92)
VPO under Wilhelm Furtwängler
Brahms: Symphony 2; *Beethoven:* Grosse Fuge; Leonore (exc). (VPO/W. Furtwängler)

Ⓓ **435 333-2GWP** (2/92)
VPO under Richard Strauss
R. Strauss: Sinfonia Domestica; Till Eulenspiegel; *Wagner:* Meistersinger (exc). (VPO/R. Strauss)

Ⓓ **435 335-2GWP2** (2/92)
VPO plays Johann & Josef Strauss
J. Strauss II: Du und Du, Op. 367; Annen-Polka, Op. 117; Blauen Donau, Op. 314; Kaiser, Op. 437; Leichtes Blut, Op. 319; Perpetuum Mobile; Vergnügungszug; *Jos Strauss:* Sphärenklänge; *J. Strauss II:* Kaiser, Op. 437; Frühlingsstimmen, Op. 410; Pizzicato Polka; *Jos Strauss:* Dorfschwalben aus Österreich; *J. Strauss I:* Radetzky March; *J. Strauss II:* Waldmeister (exc); Accelerationen, Op. 234; G'schichten aus dem Wienerwald, Op. 325; Auf der Jagd, Op. 373; Rosen aus dem Süden; Wein, Weib und Gesang; Fledermaus (exc); Ballo in maschera Quadrille, Op. 272; Tritsch-Tratsch; Kaiser, Op. 437. (VPO/E. Kleiber/C. Krauss/G. Szell/B. Walter/H. Knappertsbusch/K. Böhm/H. von Karajan/W. Furtwängler/W. Boskovsky/J. Krips/L. Maazel/C. Abbado/Z. Mehta)

Ⓓ **435 344-2GH2** (3/92)
Debussy—Pelléas et Mélisande
Debussy: Pelléas et Mélisande (Cpte). (F. Le Roux, M. Ewing, J. Van Dam, J-P. Courtis, C. Ludwig, P. Pace, R. Mazzola, Vienna St Op Chor, VPO/C. Abbado)

Ⓓ **435 440-2GH** (7/92)
Kathleen Battle at Carnegie Hall
Handel: Serse (exc); Giulio Cesare (exc); *Mozart:* Als Luise die Briefe, K520; Ridente la calma, K152; *Liszt:* S'il est un charmant gazon, S284; Comment, disaient-ils, S276; Enfant, si j'étais roi, S283; Oh! quand je dors, S282; *R. Strauss:* Lieder, Op.68 (exc); *Rachmaninov:* Songs, Op.34 (exc); Songs, Op.21 (exc); Songs, Op.4 (exc); *Gershwin:* Porgy and Bess (exc); *Traditional:* Good News; *G. Charpentier:* Louise (exc); *J. Strauss II:* Fledermaus (exc); *Traditional:* Over my Head I hear Music; He's got the whole world in His hands; Swing low, sweet chariot. (K. Battle, M. Garrett)

Ⓓ **435 487-2GH** ▭ **435 487-4GH**
Bernstein—Candide (highlights)
Bernstein: Candide (1988) (exc). (J. Hadley, J. Anderson, C. Ludwig, A. Green, N. Gedda, D. Jones, K. Ollmann, LSC, LSO/L. Bernstein)

ꝏ 435 487-5GH
Bernstein—Candide (highlights)
Bernstein: Candide (1988) (exc). (J. Hadley, J. Anderson, C. Ludwig, A. Green, N. Gedda, D. Jones, K. Ollmann, LSC, LSO/L. Bernstein)

Ⓓ **435 488-2GH**
Mozart—Le nozze di Figaro (highlights)
Mozart: Nozze di Figaro (exc). (T. Hampson, K. Te Kanawa, D. Upshaw, F. Furlanetto, A.S. von Otter, P. Plishka, T. Troyanos, NY Met Op Chor, NY Met Op Orch/James Levine)

Ⓓ **435 489-2GH**
Wagner—Götterdämmerung (highlights)
Wagner: Götterdämmerung (exc). (H. Behrens, R. Goldberg, M. Salminen, NY Met Op Chor, NY Met Op Orch/James Levine)

Ⓓ **435 594-2GGA** (9/92)
Rachmaninov—Orchestral Works
Rachmaninov: Symphony 1; Rock, Op.7; Aleko (exc); Vocalise. (BPO/L. Maazel)

Ⓓ **435 617-2GH** (5/92) ▭ **435 617-4GH** (5/92)
Beethoven in Berlin—New Year's Eve Concert
Beethoven: Egmont (exc); Ah! perfido, Op. 65; Leonore (exc); Choral Fantasia. (C. Studer, B. Ganz, E. Kissin, Berlin RIAS Chbr Ch, BPO/C. Abbado)

Ⓓ **435 705-2GX3** (1/93)
Berg—Operas
Berg: Wozzeck (Cpte); Lulu (Cpte). (D. Fischer-Dieskau, E. Lear, H. Melchert, F. Wunderlich, G. Stolze, K.C. Kohn, A. Oelke, Berlin Deutsche Op Chor, Berlin Deutsche Op Orch/K. Böhm, E. Lear, D. Fischer-Dieskau, D. Grobe, P. Johnson, L. Driscoll, J. Greindl, G. Feldhoff, K-E. Mercker, L. Clam, A. Oelke, B. Scherler, W.W. Dicks)

Ⓓ **435 709-2GX2** (8/92)
Joplin—Treemonisha
Joplin: Treemonisha (Cpte). (C. Balthrop, B. Allen, C. Rayam, W. White, B. Harney, C. Johnson, K. Hicks, D. Duckens, D. Ransom, R. Bazemore, E. Pierson, Houston Grand Op Chor, Houston Grand Op Orch/G. Schuller)

Ⓓ **435 712-2GX2** (8/92)
Lehár—The Merry Widow. Suppé—Overtures
Lehár: Lustige Witwe (Cpte); *Suppé:* Morgen, ein Mittag, ein Abend in Wien (exc); Leichte Kavallerie (exc); Pique Dame (exc); Schöne Galathee (exc); Banditenstreiche (exc); Dichter und Bauer (exc). (E. Harwood, R. Kollo, Z. Kélémen, W. Hollweg, T. Stratas, W. Krenn, D. Grobe, Berlin Deutsche Op Chor, BPO/H. von Karajan)

Ⓓ **435 718-2GX3** (9/92)
Wagner—Parsifal
Wagner: Parsifal (Cpte). (J. King, T. Stewart, F. Crass, G. Jones, D. McIntyre, K. Ridderbusch, H. Esser, B. Rundgren, E. Schwarzenberg, S. Wagner, D. Slembeck, H. Zednik, H. Bode, M. Kyriaki, I. Paustian, D. Siebert, W. Fine, Bayreuth Fest Chor, Bayreuth Fest Orch/P. Boulez)

Ⓓ **435 741-2GDO2** (5/93)
Mozart—Die Zauberflöte
Mozart: Zauberflöte (Cpte). (M. Stader, R. Streich, E. Haefliger, D. Fischer-Dieskau, J. Greindl, K. Borg, M. Vantin, L. Otto, M. Schech, L. Losch, M. Klose, M. Guilleaume, M. Reith, D. Eustrati, H. Vandenburg, Berlin RIAS Chbr Ch, Berlin RIAS Orch/F. Fricsay)

Ⓓ **435 748-2GDO2**
Arias and Waltzes - Rita Streich
Mozart: Nozze di Figaro (exc); *Donizetti:* Lucia di Lammermoor (exc); *Rimsky-Korsakov:* Golden Cockerel (exc); *J. Strauss II:* G'schichten aus dem Wienerwald, Op. 325; *Nicolai:* Lustigen Weiber von Windsor (exc); *Dvořák:* Rusalka (exc); *Puccini:* Gianni Schicchi (exc); Turandot (exc); *Rimsky-Korsakov:* Sadko (exc); *Suppé:* Boccaccio (exc); *J. Strauss II:* Frühlingsstimmen, Op. 410; *Saint-Saëns:* Parysatis (exc); *J. Strauss II:* Fledermaus (exc); *Bellini:* Capuleti (exc); *Donizetti:* Linda di Chamounix (exc); *Verdi:* Falstaff (exc); Romanze (1845) (exc); *Arditi:* Parla Waltz; *Meyerbeer:* Dinorah (exc); *Bizet:* Pêcheurs de Perles (exc); *Offenbach:* Contes d'Hoffmann (exc); *Godard:* Jocelyn (exc); *Massenet:* Manon (exc); *Delibes:* Lakmé (exc). (R. Streich, Berlin RIAS Chbr Ch, Berlin RSO/K. Gaebel/R. Kraus, Berlin Deutsche Op Chor, Berlin Deutsche Op Orch/R. Peters)

Ⓓ **435 757-2GH2** (9/92)
Borodin—Orchestral Works
Borodin: Symphony 1; Symphony 2; Symphony 3; Prince Igor (exc); String Quartet 2 (exc); In the Steppes of Central Asia; Petite Suite. (Gothenburg Sym Chor, Gothenburg SO/N. Järvi)

Ⓓ **435 763-2GH2** (12/92)
Rossini—Il barbiere di Siviglia
Rossini: Barbiere di Siviglia (Cpte). (P. Domingo, K. Battle, F. Lopardo, L. Gallo, R. Raimondi, G. Sima, C. Chausson, Venice La Fenice Chor, COE/C. Abbado)

Ⓓ **435 776-2GH2** (9/92)
Penella—El Gato Montés
Penella: Gato Montés (Cpte). (J. Pons, P. Domingo, V. Villarroel, T. Berganza, C. Chausson, M. Perelstein, A. Barrio, C. Alvarez, P. Farrés, M.L. Galindo, C. Bergasa, Angeles Blancas, R. Muñiz, Madrid Zarzuela Chor, Madrid SO/M. Roa)

Ⓓ **435 797-2GH2** (11/92)
Verdi—La traviata
Verdi: Traviata (Cpte). (C. Studer, L. Pavarotti, J. Pons, W. White, S. Kelly, A. Laciura, B. Pola, J. Wells, J. Robbins, J. Hanriot, M. Sendrowitz, R. Crolius, NY Met Op Chor, NY Met Op Orch/James Levine)

⦶ **435 851-2GH** (10/92)
Falla—La vida breve
Falla: Vida breve (Cpte). (T. Berganza, P.P. Iñigo, A. Nafé, J. Carreras, J. Pons, M. Mairena, R. Contreras, M. Cid, Ambrosian Op Chor, LSO/G. Navarro)

⦶ **435 865-2GH** (12/93)
Rossini—Il Signor Bruschino
Rossini: Signor Bruschino (Cpte). (S. Ramey, C. Desderi, K. Battle, F. Lopardo, M. Pertusi, J. Larmore, O. Arévalo, ECO/I. Marin)

⦶ **435 866-2GH** (12/93)
Kathleen Battle sings Italian Opera Arias
Bellini: Capuleti (exc); *Rossini:* Tancredi (exc); *Donizetti:* Don Pasquale (exc); Linda di Chamounix (exc); *Bellini:* Sonnambula (exc); *Rossini:* Viaggio a Reims (exc). (K. Battle, R. Croft, R. Stene, M.S. Doss, Ambrosian Op Chor, LPO/B. Campanella)

OO **435 866-5CH**
Kathleen Battle sings Italian Opera Arias
Bellini: Capuleti (exc); *Rossini:* Tancredi (exc); *Donizetti:* Don Pasquale (exc); Linda di Chamounix (exc); *Bellini:* Sonnambula (exc); *Rossini:* Viaggio a Reims (exc). (K. Battle, R. Croft, R. Stene, M.S. Doss, Ambrosian Op Chor, LPO/B. Campanella)

⦶ **435 874-2GH** (10/93)
Wagner—Overtures and Preludes
Wagner: Rienzi (exc); Tannhäuser (exc); Meistersinger (exc); Lohengrin (exc); Fliegende Holländer (exc). (NY Met Op Orch/James Levine)

OO **435 874-5GH**
Wagner—Overtures and Preludes
Wagner: Rienzi (exc); Tannhäuser (exc); Meistersinger (exc); Lohengrin (exc); Fliegende Holländer (exc). (NY Met Op Orch/James Levine)

⦶ **435 880-2GH**
Donizetti—L'elisir d'amore (highlights)
Donizetti: Elisir d'amore (exc). (K. Battle, L. Pavarotti, L. Nucci, E. Dara, D. Upshaw, NY Met Op Chor, NY Met Op Orch/James Levine)

⦶ **437 341-2GDO3** (5/93)
Mozart—Don Giovanni
Mozart: Don Giovanni (Cpte). (D. Fischer-Dieskau, S. Jurinac, M. Stader, I. Seefried, E. Haefliger, K.C. Kohn, I. Sardi, W. Kreppel, Berlin RIAS Chbr Ch, Berlin RSO/F. Fricsay)

⦶ **437 345-2GDO2** (5/93)
Beethoven—Fidelio
Beethoven: Fidelio (Cpte); Leonore (exc). (Leonie Rysanek, E. Haefliger, D. Fischer-Dieskau, G. Frick, I. Seefried, F. Lenz, K. Engen, Bavarian St Op Chor, Bavarian St Orch, BPO/F. Fricsay)

⦶ **437 395-2GX2**
Schumann—Complete Symphonies, etc
Schumann: Symphony 1; Symphony 2; Symphony 3; Symphony 4; Genoveva (exc); Manfred (exc). (BPO/R. Kubelík)

⦶ **437 404-2GX2** (10/94)
Famous Ballet Works
Offenbach: Gaîté Parisienne (exc); *Gounod:* Faust (exc); *Tchaikovsky:* Sleeping Beauty (exc); *Delibes:* Coppélia (exc); *Chopin:* Sylphides (Cpte); *Ravel:* Boléro. (BPO/H. von Karajan)

⦶ **437 501-2GH4** (11/94)
Wagner—Parsifal
Wagner: Parsifal (Cpte). (P. Domingo, J. Morris, K. Moll, J. Norman, E. Wlaschiha, J-H. Rootering, A. Glassman, J. Robbins, H.G. Murphy, J. Bunnell, P. Groves, A. Laciura, K. Erickson, K. Uecker, J. Guyer, W. White, H. Katagiri, NY Met Op Chor, NY Met Op Orch/James Levine)

⦶ **437 511-2GH2** (12/93)
Shostakovich—Lady Macbeth of the Mtsensk District
Shostakovich: Lady Macbeth of Mtsensk (Cpte). (M. Ewing, S. Larin, A. Haugland, P. Langridge, H. Zednik, Kristine Ciesinski, I. Levinsky, R. Tesarowicz, A. Kocherga, E. Zaremba, K. Moll, G. Gritziuk, C. Alvarez, G. Petitot, J-P. Mazaloubaud, A. Woodrow, J-C. Costa, J. Savignol, J. Ochagavia, P. Duminy, M. Agnetti, J. Tilli, M.J. Wray, Paris Opéra-Bastille Chor, Paris Opéra-Bastille Orch/Myung-Whun Chung)

⦶ **437 523-2GH** (6/93)
Grieg—Dramatic Works with Orchestra
Grieg: Land Sighting, Op.31; Olav Trygvason; Peer Gynt Suites. (R. Stene, A. Gjevang, H. Hagegård, Gothenburg Sym Chor, Gothenburg SO/N. Järvi)

⦶ **437 544-2GH** (12/93) ▭ **437 544-4GH** (12/93)
Carmen-Fantasie
Sarasate: Zigeunerweisen; *Wieniawski:* Légende, Op.17; *Tartini:* Devil's Trill Sonata; *Ravel:* Tzigane; *Massenet:* Thaïs (exc); *Sarasate:* Carmen Fantasy; *Fauré:* Berceuse, Op.16. (A-S. Mutter, VPO/James Levine)

OO **437 544-5GH**
Carmen-Fantasie
Sarasate: Zigeunerweisen; *Wieniawski:* Légende, Op.17; *Tartini:* Devil's Trill Sonata; *Ravel:* Tzigane; *Massenet:* Thaïs (exc); *Sarasate:* Carmen Fantasy; *Fauré:* Berceuse, Op.16. (A-S. Mutter, VPO/James Levine)

⦶ **437 547-2GH**
Puccini—Tosca (highlights)
Puccini: Tosca (exc). (M. Freni, P. Domingo, S. Ramey, B. Terfel, A. Laciura, A. Veccia, R. Lukas, L. Tiernan, B. Secombe, Philh/G. Sinopoli)

⦶ **437 671-2GDO3** (10/94)
Mozart—Le nozze di Figaro
Mozart: Nozze di Figaro (Cpte). (R. Capecchi, I. Seefried, D. Fischer-Dieskau, M. Stader, H. Töpper, L. Benningsen, I. Sardi, P. Kuen, F. Lenz, G. Wieter, R. Schwaiger, Berlin RIAS Chbr Ch, Berlin RSO/F. Fricsay)

⦶ **437 677-2GDO2** (9/93)
Irmgard Seefried - Opera Recital
Mozart: Rè Pastore (exc); Idomeneo (exc); Così fan tutte (exc); *Bizet:* Carmen (exc); *Handel:* Giulio Cesare (exc); *Mozart:* Nozze di Figaro (exc); Don Giovanni (exc); *Beethoven:* Fidelio (exc); *Respighi:* Tramonto; *Mozart:* Così fan tutte (exc); *Weber:* Freischütz (exc); *A. Thomas:* Mignon (exc); *Lortzing:* Wildschütz (exc); *R. Strauss:* Rosenkavalier (exc). (I. Seefried, Vienna SO, Berlin RSO, BPO, Bavarian St Orch, BRSO, Lucerne Fest Strings, Lamoureux Orch, Bamberg SO, Staatskapelle Dresden/F. Leitner/K. Böhm/F. Fricsay/E. Jochum/R. Baumgartner/J. Fournet/C. Stepp, M. Schech, E. Haefliger, N. Merriman, D. Fischer-Dieskau, I. Sardi, R. Streich, I. Steingruber, K. Böhme, Dresden St Op Chor)

⦶ **437 680-2GDO2** (10/94)
Rita Streich - Lieder Recital
Mozart: An Chloe, K524; Kleine Spinnerin, K531; Lied der Trennung, K519; Veilchen, K476; Zauberer, K472; Sehnsucht nach dem Frühling, K596; Moto di gioia, K579; Oiseaux, si tous les ans, K307; Dans un bois solitaire, K308; Kinderspiel, K598; Sei du mein Trost, K391; Verschweigung, K518; Warnung, K433; *Schubert:* Forelle, D550; Auf dem Wasser zu singen, D774; Seligkeit, D433; *Wolf:* Wohin mit der Freud?; Wiegenlied (1878); Kleine; Nachtgruss, UP92; *R. Strauss:* Lieder, Op.69 (exc); *Milhaud:* Chansons de Ronsard; *Traditional:* 's Schätzli; Canto delle risaiole; Au clair de la lune; Z' Lauterbach han; *Schubert:* Heidenröslein, D257; Claudine von Villa Bella (exc); So lasst mich scheinen, D877/3; Nähe des Geliebten, D162; Liebhaber in allen Gestalten, D558; Hirt auf dem Felsen, D965; An den Mond, D193; Vögel, D691; Lied im Grünen, D917; *Schumann:* Myrthen, Op.25 (exc); Liederkreis, Op.39 (exc); Jugend Lieder, Op.79 (exc); Lieder und Gesänge, Op.77 (exc); *Brahms:* Lieder, Op.106 (exc); Lieder, Op.107 (exc); Lieder, Op.84 (exc); Lieder, Op.49 (exc); *Wolf:* Eichendorff Lieder (exc); Goethe Lieder (exc); Mörike Lieder (exc). (R. Streich, E. Werba, G. Weissenborn, H. Geusser)

⦶ **437 696-2GX3** (8/93)
Cimarosa—Il Matrimonio segreto
Cimarosa: Matrimonio segreto (Cpte). (A. Auger, J. Varady, D. Fischer-Dieskau, J. Hamari, R. Davies, A. Rinaldi, ECO/D. Barenboim)

⦶ **437 700-2GX3** (8/93)
R.Strauss—Arabella
R. Strauss: Arabella (Cpte). (L. della Casa, A. Rothenberger, D. Fischer-Dieskau, K.C. Kohn, I. Malaniuk, E.M. Rogner, G. Paskuda, F. Uhl, C. Hoppe, H. Günter, C. Reich, W. Matthes, Bavarian St Op Chor, Bavarian St Orch/J. Keilberth)

⦶ **437 704-2GX2** (9/91)
Verdi—Rigoletto
Verdi: Rigoletto (Cpte). (D. Fischer-Dieskau, R. Scotto, C. Bergonzi, I. Vinco, F. Cossotto, L. Testi, M. Fiorentini, P. de Palma, V. Carbonari, C. Alda, A. Giacomotti, G. Morresi, La Scala Chor, La Scala Orch/R. Kubelík)

⦶ **437 710-2GX2** (8/93)
Wagner—Der fliegende Holländer
Wagner: Fliegende Holländer (Cpte). (T. Stewart, G. Jones, K. Ridderbusch, H. Esser, S. Wagner, H. Ek, Bayreuth Fest Chor, Bayreuth Fest Orch/K. Böhm)

⦶ **437 721-2GC3** (8/93)
Orff—Antigonae
Orff: Antigonae (Cpte). (I. Borkh, C. Hellmann, C. Alexander, G. Stolze, F. Uhl, E. Haefliger, K. Borg, H. Plümacher, K. Engen, Bavarian Rad Chor, BRSO/F. Leitner)

⦶ **437 726-2GH**
Verdi—La traviata (highlights)
Verdi: Traviata (exc). (C. Studer, L. Pavarotti, J. Pons, NY Met Op Chor, NY Met Op Orch/James Levine)

OO **437 726-5GH**
Verdi—La traviata (highlights)
Verdi: Traviata (exc). (C. Studer, L. Pavarotti, J. Pons, NY Met Op Chor, NY Met Op Orch/James Levine)

⦶ **437 730-2GX3** (9/91)
Verdi—Don Carlos
Verdi: Don Carlo (Cpte). (F. Labò, A. Stella, F. Cossotto, E. Bastianini, B. Christoff, I. Vinco, A. Maddalena, A. Cattelani, F. Piva, P. de Palma, G. Matteini, La Scala Chor, La Scala Orch/G. Santini)

⦶ **437 782-2GH**
Classical Hits
Hoffstetter: String Quartets, Op.3 (exc); *Gluck:* Orfeo ed Euridice (exc); *M. Haydn:* Notturno, MH185 (exc); *Boccherini:* String Quintets, G271-6 (exc); *Mozart:* Serenade, K525 (exc); *Beethoven:* Prometheus (exc); *Mendelssohn:* Midsummer Night's Dream (exc); *Schubert:* Rosamunde (exc). (Orpheus CO)

OO **437 782-5GH**
Classical Hits
Hoffstetter: String Quartets, Op.3 (exc); *Gluck:* Orfeo ed Euridice (exc); *M. Haydn:* Notturno, MH185 (exc); *Boccherini:* String Quintets, G271-6 (exc); *Mozart:* Serenade, K525 (exc); *Beethoven:* Prometheus (exc); *Mendelssohn:* Midsummer Night's Dream (exc); *Schubert:* Rosamunde (exc). (Orpheus CO)

⦶ **437 783-2GH** (12/93)
Haydn—Orchestral Works
Haydn: Symphony 60; Symphony 91; Armida (exc). (Orpheus CO)

⦶ **437 787-2GH**
Honey and Rue-Kathleen Battle
Barber: Knoxville; *Gershwin:* Porgy and Bess (exc); *Previn:* Honey and Rue. (K. Battle, St Luke's Orch/A. Previn)

⦶ **437 790-2GH** (11/93)
R. Strauss—Orchestral Works
R. Strauss: Rosenkavalier (exc); Intermezzo Interludes (exc); Capriccio (exc); Salome (exc). (VPO/A. Previn)

⦶ **437 797-2GH3** (2/94)
Rossini—Semiramide
Rossini: Semiramide (Cpte). (C. Studer, J. Larmore, S. Ramey, F. Lopardo, J. Faulkner, J-H. Rootering, R. Tesarowicz, O. Arévalo, Ambrosian Op Chor, LSO/I. Marin)

⦶ **437 808-2GH3** (11/94)
Wagner—Lohengrin
Wagner: Lohengrin (Cpte). (S. Jerusalem, C. Studer, W. Meier, H. Welker, K. Moll, A. Schmidt, Vienna St Op Concert Ch, VPO/C. Abbado)

⦶ **437 825-2GH**
Wagner—Der Ring des Nibelungen - Highlights
Wagner: Rheingold (exc); Walküre (exc); Siegfried (exc); Götterdämmerung (exc). (H. Behrens, J. Norman, K. Battle, H-K. Hong, M. Napier, L. Kelm, M. Mims, C. Ludwig, D. Kesling, A. Wilkens, R. Engert-Ely, M. Parsons, R. Runkel, R. Goldberg, M. Baker, S. Jerusalem, J. Morris, E. Wlaschiha, M. Salminen, NY Met Op Orch/James Levine)

⦶ **437 841-2GH**
Rossini—Il barbiere di Siviglia (highlights)
Rossini: Barbiere di Siviglia (exc). (K. Battle, P. Domingo, F. Lopardo, L. Gallo, R. Raimondi, COE/C. Abbado)

⦶ **437 842-2GH6**
Grieg—Complete Music with Orchestra
Grieg: Piano Concerto; In Autumn; Symphonic Dances; Holberg Suite; Elegiac Melodies; Melodies, Op.53; Nordic Melodies, Op.63; Lyric Pieces; Lyric Suite, Op.54; Peer Gynt (Cpte); Sigurd Jorsalfar (Cpte); Funeral March; Norwegian Dances, Op.35; Symphony; Land Sighting, Op.31; Olav Trygvason; Old Norwegian Romance; Songs, Op.21 (exc); Songs, Op.39 (exc); Songs, Op.25 (exc); Songs, Op.33 (exc); Norway, Op.58 (exc); Mountain Thrall, Op.32; Southern Convent, Op.20; Bergljot, Op.42. (B. Bonney, M. Eklöf, A. Gjevang, H. Hagegård, C.G. Holmgren, U. Malmberg, K.M. Sandve, R. Stene, L. Zilberstein, Ohlin Voc Ens, Pro Musica Chbr Ch, Gothenburg Sym Chor, R. Tellefsen, Gothenburg SO/N. Järvi)

⦶ **437 928-2GX2** (4/95)
Beethoven—Symphonies & Overtures
Beethoven: Symphony 6; Symphony 7; Symphony 8;

Fidelio (exc); Leonore (exc). (VPO, Staatskapelle Dresden/K. Böhm)

Ⓓ **439 005-2GHS**
Beethoven—Orchestral Works
Beethoven: Symphony 8; Coriolan; Fidelio (exc); Leonore (exc). (BPO/H. von Karajan)

OO **439 005-5GHS**
Beethoven—Orchestral Works
Beethoven: Symphony 8; Coriolan; Fidelio (exc); Leonore (exc). (BPO/H. von Karajan)

Ⓓ **439 101-2GX2** (11/93)
Gluck—Orfeo ed Euridice
Gluck: Orfeo ed Euridice (Cpte). (G. Simionato, S. Jurinac, G. Sciutti, Vienna St Op Chor, VPO/H. von Karajan)

Ⓓ **439 104-2GDO**
Schubert—Symphony No 8; J.Strauss II—Waltzes
Schubert: Symphony 8; *J. Strauss I:* Radetzky March; *J. Strauss II:* Zigeunerbaron (exc); Kaiser, Op. 437; Annen-Polka, Op. 117; Perpetuum mobile; Blauen Donau, Op. 314; *Jos Strauss:* Delirien. (VPO/H. von Karajan)

Ⓓ **439 108-2GGA**
Bach/Gluck/Handel—Keyboard Works & trans by Wilhelm Kempff
Bach: English Suites, BWV806-811 (exc); Capriccio, BWV992; Chorales, BWV651-668 (exc); Es ist gewisslich an der Zeit, BWV307; Flute Sonatas, BWV1030-5 (exc); Herzlich tut mich verlangen, BWV727; Cantata 147 (exc); In dulci jubilo, BWV751; Cantata 29 (exc); *Handel:* Keyboard Suites Set II (exc); *Bach:* Cantata 140 (exc); Harpsichord Concerto, BWV1056 (exc); Orgel-Büchlein, BWV599-644 (exc); *Gluck:* Orfeo ed Euridice (exc). (W. Kempff)

Ⓓ **439 147-2GMA** ⊟ **439 147-4GMA**
Mad about Baroque
Handel: Solomon (exc); *Pachelbel:* Canon and Gigue (exc); *Mouret:* Symphonies de Fanfares (exc); *Bach:* Cantata 147 (exc); *Handel:* Water Music (exc); Serse (exc); *Purcell:* Birthday Ode, Z323 (exc); *Vivaldi:* Concerti, Op.8 (exc); *Handel:* Messiah (exc); *Albinoni:* Adagio; *Handel:* Fireworks Music (exc); *Vivaldi:* Concerto, RV93 (exc); *Corelli:* Concerti Grossi, Op.6 (exc); *Handel:* Oboe Concertos (exc); Concerti Grossi, Op.6 (exc); *Daquin:* Premier livre de pièces de clavecin (exc); *Bach:* Brandenburg Concertos (exc). (R. Wolfgang, S. Standage, D. Reichenberg, T. Pinnock, English Concert/T. Pinnock, Berne Camerata/T. Füri, G. Söllscher, Orpheus CO, H. Läubin, W. Läubin, B. Läubin, S. Preston, N. Schmitt, English Concert Ch)

Ⓓ **439 150-2GMA** ⊟ **439 150-4GMA**
Mad about Mozart
Mozart: Nozze di Figaro (exc); Piano Concerto 21 (exc); Serenade, K525 (exc); Requiem (exc); Symphony 40 (exc); Exsultate, jubilate, K165 (exc); Don Giovanni (exc); Nozze di Figaro (exc); Zauberflöte (exc); Clarinet Quintet, K581 (exc); Serenade, K361 (exc); Symphony 41 (exc). (A. Auger, W. Schulz, H. Schellenberger, E. Brunner, R. Serkin, Hagen Qt, NY Met Op Orch, Orpheus CO, LSO, BRSO, VPO/James Levine/C. Abbado/L. Bernstein, Bavarian Rad Chor)

Ⓓ **439 151-2GMA** ⊟ **439 151-4GMA**
Mad about Puccini
Puccini: Turandot (exc); Gianni Schicchi (exc); Bohème (exc); Bohème (exc); Tosca (exc); Madama Butterfly (exc); Manon Lescaut (exc). (P. Domingo, M. Freni, B. Daniels, A. Réaux, J. Hadley, T. Hampson, J. Busterud, G. Beni, P. Plishka, S. Ramey, J. Carreras, J. Pons, A. Laciura, K. Ricciarelli, Vienna St Op Chor, Ambrosian Op Chor, VPO, Venice La Fenice Orch, Santa Cecilia Academy Orch, Philh/H. von Karajan/R. Abbado/L. Bernstein/G. Sinopoli)

Ⓓ **439 152-2GMA** ⊟ **439 152-4GMA**
Mad about Romance
Mascagni: Cavalleria Rusticana (exc); *Rachmaninov:* Vocalise; *Ravel:* Pavane; *Vaughan Williams:* Greensleeves Fantasia; *Fauré:* Pavane; *Ravel:* Piano Concerto (exc); *Borodin:* String Quartet 2 (exc); *Grieg:* Elegiac Melodies (exc); Lyric Suite, Op.54 (exc); *Puccini:* Crisantemi; *Fauré:* Songs, Op.7 (exc); *Giordano:* Fedora (exc); *Grieg:* Holberg Suite (exc); *Offenbach:* Contes d'Hoffmann (exc). (J. Eskin, Orpheus CO, Gothenburg SO/N. Järvi, BPO/L. Maazel, Philh/C.M. Giulini, Tanglewood Fest Chor, Boston SO/S. Ozawa, M. Argerich, LSO/C. Abbado)

⊟ **439 153-4GMA**
Mad about Sopranos
Puccini: Tosca (exc); *Verdi:* Traviata (exc); *Mozart:* Nozze di Figaro (exc); *Offenbach:* Contes d'Hoffmann (exc); *Mozart:* Don Giovanni (exc); *Wagner:* Walküre (exc); *Verdi:* Aida (exc); *Mozart:* Nozze di Figaro (exc); Così fan tutte (exc); Zauberflöte (exc); Zauberflöte (exc); *Puccini:* Turandot (exc); Madama Butterfly (exc); Manon Lescaut (exc); Turandot (exc); *Mozart:* Don Giovanni (exc); *R. Strauss:* Rosenkavalier (exc); *Wagner:* Götterdämmerung (exc). (M. Freni, T. Berganza, C. Studer, L. Pavarotti, K. Te Kanawa, E. Gruberová, French Rad Chor, K. Battle, J. Norman, K. Ricciarelli, D. Upshaw, M. McLaughlin, K. Ott, E. Mathis, B. Hendricks, A. Tomowa-Sintow, A. Baltsa, J. Perry, H. Behrens, Philh, NY Met Op Orch, VPO, FNO, BPO, La Scala Orch/G. Sinopoli/James Levine/S. Ozawa/H. von Karajan/C. Abbado)

Ⓓ **439 200-2GH6**
Beethoven—Symphonies and Overtures
Beethoven: Symphony 1; Symphony 2; Symphony 3; Symphony 4; Symphony 5; Symphony 6; Symphony 7; Symphony 8; Symphony 9; Egmont (exc); Coriolan; Fidelio (exc); Leonore (exc). (J. Perry, A. Baltsa, V. Cole, J. Van Dam, Vienna Singverein, BPO/H. von Karajan)

Ⓓ **439 251-2GY**
The Leonard Bernstein Album
Bernstein: West Side Story Symphonic Dances (exc); West Side Story (exc); Meditations (exc); Quiet Place (exc); Candide (1988) (exc); Symphony 2 (exc); On the town (exc); Serenade (exc); West Side Story (exc). (Los Angeles PO/L. Bernstein, orch, chor, Israel PO, Austrian RSO, J. Anderson, J. Hadley, C. Ludwig, LSO, London Voices, T. Hampson, F. von Stade, T. Daly, D. Garrison, K. Ollmann/M. Tilson Thomas, G. Kremer, J. Norman, J. Carreras, K. Te Kanawa, T. Troyanos, L. Edeiken, M. Rostropovich, L. Foss, W. White)

OO **439 251-5GY**
The Leonard Bernstein Album
Bernstein: West Side Story Symphonic Dances (exc); West Side Story (exc); Meditations (exc); Quiet Place (exc); Candide (1988) (exc); Symphony 2 (exc); On the town (exc); Serenade (exc); West Side Story (exc). (Los Angeles PO/L. Bernstein, orch, chor, Israel PO, Austrian RSO, J. Anderson, J. Hadley, C. Ludwig, LSO, London Voices, T. Hampson, F. von Stade, T. Daly, D. Garrison, K. Ollmann/M. Tilson Thomas, G. Kremer, J. Norman, J. Carreras, K. Te Kanawa, T. Troyanos, L. Edeiken, M. Rostropovich, L. Foss, W. White)

Ⓓ **439 346-2GX2** (5/94)
Prussian and Austrian Marches
Beethoven: March in F, WoO18; *Scholz:* Torgau March; *Suppé:* O du mein Österreich; *Lindemann:* Unter dem Grillenbanner; *Moltke:* Grossen Kurfürsten Reitermarsch; *Walch:* Pariser Einzugsmarsch; *J.F. Wagner II:* Unter dem Doppeladler; *Mühlberger:* Mir sein die Kaiserjäger; *Fučík:* Florentiner, Op.214; *Anon:* Marsch der Finnländischen Reiterei; *Piefke:* Königgrätz Marsch; *Fučík:* Regimentskinder; *Schrammel:* Wien bleibt Wien; *R. Henrion:* Kreuzritter-Fanfare; *Anon:* Petersburg March; *R. Henrion:* Fehrbelliner Reitermarsch; *M. Haydn:* Pappenheim March; *Ertl:* Hoch- und Deutschmeister; *Komzák II:* Vindobona; *Frederick the Great:* Hohenfriedberg; *Komzák II:* Erzherzog Albrecht-Marsch; *J.F. Wagner II:* Tiroler Holzhackerbuab'n; *Piefke:* Preussens Gloria; *M. Haydn:* Coburg March; *Seiffert:* Kärntner Liedermarsch; *Wagnes:* Bosniaken kommen; *Radeck:* Fridericus-Rex; *Teike:* Alte Kameraden; *J. Strauss II:* Zigeunerbaron (exc); *Sonntag:* Nibelungen-Marsch; *J. Strauss I:* Radetzky March. (Berlin Phil Wind Qnt, BPO/H. von Karajan)

Ⓓ **439 415-2GCL**
Rossini—Overtures
Rossini: Gazza ladra (exc); Scala di seta (exc); Semiramide (exc); Barbiere di Siviglia (exc); Italiana in Algeri (exc); Guillaume Tell (exc). (BPO/H. von Karajan)

Ⓓ **439 421-2GCL** ⊟ **439 421-4GCL**
Verdi—La traviata (highlights)
Verdi: Traviata (exc). (I. Cotrubas, P. Domingo, S. Milnes, S. Malagù, H. Jungwirth, W. Gullino, B. Grella, A. Giacomotti, G. Foiani, Bavarian St Op Chor, Bavarian St Orch/C. Kleiber)

Ⓓ **439 423-2GCL** (3/94)
Wagner—Der Ring des Nibelungen (highlights)
Wagner: Rheingold (exc); Walküre (exc); Siegfried (exc); Götterdämmerung (exc). (D. Fischer-Dieskau, T. Stewart, G. Janowitz, H. Dernesch, Jess Thomas, C. Gayer, J. Veasey, Z. Kélémen, G. Stolze, K. Ridderbusch, D. Grobe, BPO/H. von Karajan)

Ⓓ **439 425-2GCL** ⊟ **439 425-4GCL**
Music from America - Gershwin and Bernstein
Gershwin: Rhapsody in Blue; American in Paris; *Bernstein:* Candide Overture; West Side Story Symphonic Dances. (S. Stöckigt, Leipzig Gewandhaus/K. Masur, San Francisco SO/S. Ozawa, Boston Pops/A. Fiedler)

Ⓓ **439 439-2GCL**
J. Strauss II—Waltzes and Polkas
J. Strauss II: Fledermaus (exc); Frühlingsstimmen, Op. 410; Egyptischer Marsch, Op. 335; Freikugeln, Op. 326; Kaiser, Op. 437; Pizzicato Polka; Unter Donner und Blitz; Rosen aus dem Süden; Indigo und die Vierzig Räuber (exc); Eljen a Magyar!, Op. 332; Zigeunerbaron (exc); Blauen Donau, Op.314. (VPO/L. Maazel)

Ⓓ **439 440-2GCL**
Weber—Der Freischütz (highlights)
Weber: Freischütz (exc). (G. Janowitz, E. Mathis, P. Schreier, T. Adam, G. Leib, G. Paul, Leipzig Rad Chor, Staatskapelle Dresden/C. Kleiber)

Ⓓ **439 445-2GCL** ⊟ **439 445-4GCL**
Wagner—Overtures and Preludes
Wagner: Fliegende Holländer (exc); Lohengrin (exc); Meistersinger (exc); Parsifal (exc); Tannhäuser (exc). (Bayreuth Fest Orch/K. Böhm, BPO/R. Kubelík, BRSO/E. Jochum, Berlin Deutsche Op Orch/O. Gerdes)

Ⓓ **439 449-2GCL** ⊟ **439 449-4GCL**
Mozart—Le nozze di Figaro - Highlights
Mozart: Nozze di Figaro (exc). (D. Fischer-Dieskau, G. Janowitz, E. Mathis, H. Prey, T. Troyanos, P. Lagger, B. Vogel, Berlin Deutsche Op Chor, Berlin Deutsche Op Orch/K. Böhm)

Ⓓ **439 451-2GCL**
Smetana—Orchestral Works
Smetana: Má Vlast (exc); Bartered Bride (exc). (Boston SO/R. Kubelík, BPO/H. von Karajan)

Ⓓ **439 461-2GCL** ⊟ **439 461-4GCL**
Puccini—Tosca (highlights)
Puccini: Tosca (exc). (K. Ricciarelli, J. Carreras, R. Raimondi, G. Hornik, H. Zednik, F. Corena, V. von Halem, Schöneberg Boys' Ch, Berlin Deutsche Op Chor, BPO/H. von Karajan)

Ⓓ **439 467-2GCL** (4/95) ⊟ **439 467-4GCL** (4/95)
R. Strauss—Vocal and Orchestral Works
R. Strauss: Vier letzte Lieder; Capriccio (exc); Tod und Verklärung. (G. Janowitz, BPO/H. von Karajan, BRSO, Staatskapelle Dresden/K. Böhm)

Ⓓ **439 469-2GCL**
Wagner—Tristan und Isolde (highlights)
Wagner: Tristan und Isolde (exc). (W. Windgassen, B. Nilsson, E. Waechter, C. Ludwig, P. Schreier, Bayreuth Fest Chor, Bayreuth Fest Orch/K. Böhm)

Ⓓ **439 474-2GCL** ⊟ **439 474-4GCL**
Purcell—Opera & Choral Works
Purcell: Dido (exc); Fairy Queen, Z629 (exc); Te Deum and Jubilate, Z232. (T. Troyanos, S. Armstrong, B. McDaniel, P. Johnson, Margaret Baker, M. Lensky, Hamburg Monteverdi Ch, Hamburg NDR CO/C. Mackerras, E. Harrhy, J. Nelson, E. Priday, J. Smith, T. Penrose, S. Varcoe, D. Thomas, Monteverdi Ch, EBS/J.E. Gardiner, Oxford Christ Church Cath Ch, English Concert/S. Preston)

Ⓓ **439 482-2GCL** ⊟ **439 482-4GCL**
Verdi—Aida (highlights)
Verdi: Aida (exc). (K. Ricciarelli, P. Domingo, R. Raimondi, E. Obraztsova, L. Nucci, N. Ghiaurov, P. de Palma, La Scala Chor, La Scala Orch/C. Abbado)

Ⓓ **439 496-2GCL** ⊟ **439 496-4GCL**
Bizet—Carmen (highlights)
Bizet: Carmen (exc). (T. Berganza, P. Domingo, S. Milnes, I. Cotrubas, Y. Kenny, A. Nafé, R. Lloyd, Watson Coll Boys' Chor, Ambrosian Sngrs, LSO/C. Abbado)

Ⓓ **439 672-2GX2** (11/94)
Bach/Gluck—Piano Works & Transcriptions
Bach: Chorales, BWV651-668 (exc); Es ist gewisslich an der Zeit, BWV307; Flute Sonatas, BWV1030-5 (exc); Herzlich tut mich verlangen, BWV727; Cantata 147 (exc); In dulci jubilo, BWV751; Cantata 29 (exc); Cantata 140 (exc); Harpsichord Concerto, BWV1056 (exc); Orgel-Büchlein, BWV599-644 (exc); *Gluck:* Orfeo ed Euridice (exc); *Bach:* English Suites, BWV806-811 (exc); French Suites, BWV812-17 (exc); Wohltemperierte Klavier (exc); Capriccio, BWV992; Toccatas, BWV910-16 (exc). (W. Kempff)

Ⓓ **439 687-2GX2**
Wagner—Overtures and Preludes
Wagner: Rienzi (exc); Fliegende Holländer (exc); Tannhäuser (exc); Lohengrin (exc); Lohengrin (exc); Meistersinger (exc); Meistersinger (exc); Walküre (exc); Tristan und Isolde (exc); Tristan und Isolde (exc); Siegfried Idyll; Götterdämmerung (exc); Parsifal (exc). (VPO, Bayreuth Fest Orch, Berlin Deutsche Op Orch, BPO, BRSO/K. Böhm/O. Gerdes/R. Kubelík/E. Jochum/H. von Karajan)

Ⓓ **439 708-2GX2** (7/95)
Mozart—Die Entführung aus dem Serail
Mozart: Entführung (Cpte). (E. Köth, L. Schädle, F. Wunderlich, F. Lenz, K. Böhme, R. Boysen, Bavarian St Op Chor, BRSO/E. Jochum)

Ⓓ **439 711-2GX2** (2/95)
Gluck—Orphée et Eurydice
Gluck: Orfeo ed Euridice (Cpte). (D. Fischer-Dieskau, M. Stader, R. Streich, Berlin RIAS Chbr Ch, Berlin Motet Ch, Berlin RSO/F. Fricsay)

Ⓓ **439 717-2GX2** (12/94)
Weber—Der Freischütz
Weber: Freischütz (Cpte). (I. Seefried, Richard Holm, R. Streich, K. Böhme, E. Waechter, W. Kreppel, A. Peter, E. Ginsberg, P. Kuen, Bavarian Rad Chor, BRSO/E. Jochum)

Ⓓ **439 720-2GX2**
Verdi—La traviata
Verdi: Traviata (Cpte). (R. Scotto, G. Raimondi, E. Bastianini, G. Tavolaccini, A. Bonato, F. Ricciardi, G. Morresi, V. Carbonari, S. Maionica, A. Mercuriali, La Scala Chor, La Scala Orch/A. Votto)

Ⓓ **439 768-2GH** (5/94) ▭ **439 768-4GH** (5/94)
Wagner—Gala - New Year's Eve Concert 1993
Wagner: Tannhäuser (exc); Lohengrin (exc); Meistersinger (exc); Walküre (exc). (C. Studer, W. Meier, S. Jerusalem, B. Terfel, BPO/C. Abbado)

Ⓓ **439 805-2GH2** (12/94)
Verdi—Otello
Verdi: Otello (Cpte). (P. Domingo, C. Studer, S. Leiferkus, R. Vargas, M. Schade, D. Graves, I. d'Arcangelo, G. Prestia, P. Duminy, Hauts-de-Seine Maîtrise, Paris Opéra-Bastille Chor, Paris Opéra-Bastille Orch/Myung-Whun Chung)

Ⓓ **439 865-2GH** (7/94)
Cheryl Studer sings Strauss and Wagner
R. Strauss: Vier letzte Lieder; *Wagner:* Wesendonk Lieder; Tristan und Isolde (exc). (C. Studer, Staatskapelle Dresden/G. Sinopoli)

Ⓓ **439 892-2GH** (12/94) ▭ **439 892-4GH**
Russian Overtures
Glinka: Ruslan and Lyudmila (exc); *Borodin:* Prince Igor (exc); *Shostakovich:* Festive Overture; *Prokofiev:* Semyon Kotko (exc); *Kabalevsky:* Colas Breugnon (exc); *Rimsky-Korsakov:* Tsar's Bride (exc); *Mussorgsky:* Khovanshchina (exc); *Tchaikovsky:* Overture in F; *Glazunov:* Ouverture Solennelle. (Russian Nat Orch/M. Pletnev)

Ⓓ **439 894-2GH** (12/94) ▭ **439 894-4GH** (12/94)
Speak Low - Songs by Kurt Weill
Weill: Sieben Todsünden (Cpte); Lady in the dark (exc); Propaganda Songs (exc); Nannas Lied; Happy End (exc); Je ne t'aime pas; Abschiedsbrief; One touch of Venus (exc). (A.S. von Otter, B. Forsberg, N German RSO/J.E. Gardiner)

Ⓓ **439 906-2GH3** (11/94)
Tchaikovsky—Mazeppa
Tchaikovsky: Mazeppa (Cpte). (S. Leiferkus, G. Gorchakova, A. Kocherga, L. Dyadkova, S. Larin, M. Pederson, R. Margison, H. Zednik, Stockholm Royal Op Chor, Gothenburg SO/N. Järvi)

Ⓓ **439 911-2GH** (2/95) ▭ **439 911-4GH** (2/95)
Lehár—Die lustige Witwe
Lehár: Lustige Witwe (Cpte). (C. Studer, B. Skovhus, B. Terfel, R. Trost, B. Bonney, U. Peper, K-M. Fredriksson, H. Zednik, R. Savage, L. Alcantara, P. Salmon, C. Backes, J. Clarkson, A. Kazimierczuk, Wiener Tschuschenkapelle, VPO/J. E. Gardiner)

Ⓓ **439 932-2GH** (10/95)
Haydn—Symphonies, etc
Haydn: Symphony 98; Symphony 100; Mondo della luna (exc). (COE/C. Abbado)

Ⓓ **439 972-2GGA2** (1/95)
Verdi—Overtures & Preludes
Verdi: Oberto (exc); Giorno di regno (exc); Nabucco (exc); Ernani (exc); Giovanna d'Arco (exc); Alzira (exc); Attila (exc); Masnadieri (exc); Macbeth (exc); Corsaro (exc); Battaglia di Legnano (exc); Luisa Miller (exc); Rigoletto (exc); Traviata (exc); Vespri siciliani (exc); Aroldo (exc); Ballo in maschera (exc); Forza del destino (exc); Aida (exc). (BPO/H. von Karajan)

Ⓓ **445 238-2GH** (2/95) ▭ **445 238-4GH** (2/95)
Mussorgsky—Orchestral and Choral Works
Mussorgsky: St John's Night; Destruction of Sennacherib; Salammbô (exc); Oedipus in Athens (exc); Joshua; Pictures. (E. Zaremba, Prague Phil Chor, BPO/C. Abbado)

Ⓓ **445 248-2GC2** (9/94)
Henze—Der junge Lord
Henze: Junge Lord (Cpte). (B. McDaniel, L. Driscoll, V. Little, M. Röhrl, I. Sardi, E. Krukowski, H. Krebs, P. Johnson, R. Hesse, L. Otto, E. Mathis, B. Jasper, M. Türke, D. Grobe, G. Treptow, F. Hoppe, Schöneberg Boys' Ch, Berlin Deutsche Op Chor, Berlin Deutsche Op Orch/C. von Dohnányi)

Ⓓ **445 251-2GC** (10/94)
Holliger—Vocal Works
Holliger: Siebengesang; Magische Tänzer (Cpte). (H. Holliger, Stuttgart Schola Cantorum, Basle SO/F. Travis, E. Gilhofer, H. Riediker, D. Dorow, P. Langridge, Basle Th Ch/H. Zender)

Ⓓ **445 282-2GH** ▭ **445 282-4GH**
Adagio Karajan
Mahler: Symphony 5 (exc); *Pachelbel:* Canon and Gigue (exc); *Massenet:* Thaïs (exc); *Brahms:* Symphony 3 (exc); *Vivaldi:* Sinfonia, RV169 (exc); *Grieg:* Peer Gynt Suites (exc); *Mozart:* Divertimento, K287 (exc); *Albinoni:* Adagio; *Beethoven:* Symphony 7 (exc); *Bach:* Suites, BWV1066-9 (exc); *Sibelius:* Valse triste. (BPO/H. Von Karajan)

Ⓓ **445 295-2GH2**
Wagner—Das Rheingold
Wagner: Rheingold (Cpte). (J. Morris, C. Ludwig, S. Jerusalem, H. Zednik, E. Wlaschiha, N. Gustafson, M. Baker, S. Lorenz, B. Svendén, K. Moll, J-H. Rootering, H-K. Hong, D. Kesling, M. Parsons, NY Met Op Orch/James Levine)

Ⓓ **445 319-2GX2** (11/94)
R. Strauss—Salome
R. Strauss: Salome (Cpte). (G. Jones, D. Fischer-Dieskau, R. Cassilly, M. Dunn, W. Ochman, U. Boese, H. Sotin, H. Wilhelm, K. Moll, C. Schultz, F. Grundheber, W. Hartmann, Hamburg St Op Orch/K. Böhm)

Ⓓ **445 322-2GX2** (11/94)
R. Strauss—Daphne
R. Strauss: Daphne (Cpte). (H. Gueden, J. King, P. Schoeffler, F. Wunderlich, V. Little, H. Braun, K. Equiluz, H. Pröglhöf, R. Streich, E. Mechera, Vienna St Op Chor, Vienna SO/K. Böhm)

Ⓓ **445 325-2GX3** (11/94)
R. Strauss—Die Frau ohne Schatten
R. Strauss: Frau ohne Schatten (Cpte). (Leonie Rysanek, J. King, B. Nilsson, W. Berry, R. Hesse, P. Wimberger, Lotte Rysanek, E. Aichberger, G. Jahn, H. Helm, L. Alvary, M. Dickie, Vienna St Op Chor, Vienna St Op Orch/K. Böhm)

Ⓓ **445 329-2GX2** (11/94)
R. Strauss—Elektra
R. Strauss: Elektra (Cpte). (I. Borkh, J. Madeira, M. Schech, F. Uhl, D. Fischer-Dieskau, F. Teschler, R. Reinecke, H. Ambros, G. Unger, S. Vogel, I. Steingruber, C. Ahlin, M. Sjöstedt, S. Wagner, J. Hellwig, G. Schreyer, Dresden St Op Chor, Staatskapelle Dresden/K. Böhm)

Ⓓ **445 332-2GX2** (11/94)
R. Strauss—Ariadne auf Naxos
R. Strauss: Ariadne auf Naxos (Cpte). (L. della Casa, I. Seefried, H. Gueden, R. Schock, P. Schoeffler, A. Poell, O. Czerwenka, M. Dickie, A. Jaresch, R. Streich, H. Rössl-Majdan, L. Otto, P. Klein, A. Neugebauer, VPO/K. Böhm)

Ⓓ **445 335-2GX2** (11/94)
R. Strauss—Die schweigsame Frau
R. Strauss: Schweigsame Frau (Cpte). (H. Hotter, G. von Milinkovic, H. Prey, F. Wunderlich, H. Gueden, P. Alarie, H. Plümacher, J. Knapp, K. Dönch, A. Pernerstorfer, Vienna St Op Chor, VPO/K. Böhm)

Ⓓ **445 338-2GX3** (11/94)
R. Strauss—Der Rosenkavalier
R. Strauss: Rosenkavalier (Cpte). (C. Ludwig, T. Troyanos, T. Adam, E. Mathis, O. Wiener, A. de Ridder, C. Ahlin, G. Unger, K. Lövaas, L. Pantscheff, K. Hirte, A. Pfeifle, S.R. Frese, R. Licha, Vienna St Op Chor, VPO/K. Böhm)

Ⓓ **445 342-2GX3** (11/94)
R. Strauss—Arabella
R. Strauss: Arabella (Cpte). (M. Reining, L. della Casa, H. Hotter, G. Hann, R. Anday, H. Handl, H. Taubmann, J. Patzak, J. Witt, A. Poell, R. Michaelis, F. Szkokan, Vienna St Op Chor, VPO/K. Böhm)

Ⓓ **445 347-2GX2** (11/94)
R. Strauss—Capriccio
R. Strauss: Capriccio (Cpte). (G. Janowitz, D. Fischer-Dieskau, P. Schreier, H. Prey, K. Ridderbusch, T. Troyanos, D. Thaw, A. Auger, A. de Ridder, K.C. Kohn, BRSO/K. Böhm)

Ⓓ **445 354-2GX14** (10/94)
Wagner—Der Ring des Nibelungen
Wagner: Rheingold (Cpte); Walküre (Cpte); Siegfried (Cpte); Götterdämmerung (Cpte). (J. Morris, C. Ludwig, S. Jerusalem, H. Zednik, E. Wlaschiha, M.A. Häggander, M. Baker, S. Lorenz, B. Svendén, K. Moll, J-H. Rootering, H-K. Hong, D. Kesling, M. Parsons, G. Lakes, J. Norman, H. Behrens, K. Moll, M. Napier, L. Kelm, M. Mims, R. Runkel, A. Wilkens, D. Kesling, M. Parsons, R. Engert-Ely, R. Goldberg, K. Moll, K. Battle, M. Salminen, B. Weikl, C. Studer, H. Schwarz, H. Dernesch, T. Troyanos, A. Gruber, NY Met Op Chor, NY Met Op Orch/James Levine)

Ⓓ **445 400-2GDO10** (11/94)
Ferenc Fricsay - A Portrait
Beethoven: Symphony 9; *Bartók:* Violin Concerto 2; Dance Suite; Cantata profana; *R. Strauss:* Don Juan; Duet Concertino; Burleske; Till Eulenspiegel; *Liebermann:* Furioso; *Blacher:* Paganini Variations; *Egk:* French Suite; *Einem:* Piano Concerto; *Stravinsky:* Rite of Spring (Cpte); Petrushka (Cpte); Movements; *Rossini:* Barbiere di Siviglia (exc); Tancredi (exc); Signor Bruschino (exc); Gazza Ladra (exc); Semiramide (exc); *Verdi:* Nabucco (exc); Traviata (exc); Forza del Destino (exc); Aida (exc); Vespri siciliani (exc); *Brahms:* Symphony 2; Haydn Variations; Alto Rhapsody, Op. 53; *Mozart:* Requiem; Adagio and Fugue, K546; *Tchaikovsky:* Symphony 6; Violin Concerto; *Kodály:* Marosszék Dances; Symphony in C; Psalmus Hungaricus; *Smetana:* Má Vlast (exc). (I. Seefried, M. Forrester, E. Haefliger, D. Fischer-Dieskau, Berlin St Hedwig's Cath Ch, BPO/F. Fricsay, H. Krebs, T. Varga, Berlin RIAS Chbr Ch, Berlin RIAS Orch, H. Geusser, W. Fugmann, M. Weber, G. Herzog, Berlin RSO, VPO, E. Grümmer, G. Pitzinger, H. Hotter, Y. Menuhin)

Ⓓ **445 406-2GDO** (11/94)
Rossini/Verdi—Overtures and Preludes
Rossini: Barbiere di Siviglia (exc); Tancredi (exc); Signor Bruschino (exc); Gazza ladra (exc); Semiramide (exc); *Verdi:* Nabucco (exc); Traviata (exc); Forza del destino (exc); Aida (exc); Vespri siciliani (exc). (Berlin RIAS Orch/F. Fricsay)

Ⓓ **445 412-2GDO2** (7/95)
Mozart—Die Entführung aus dem Serail
Mozart: Entführung (Cpte); Exsultate, jubilate, K165. (M. Stader, R. Streich, E. Haefliger, M. Vantin, J. Greindl, W. Franck, Berlin RIAS Chbr Ch, Berlin RIAS Orch, Berlin RSO/F. Fricsay)

Ⓓ **445 448-2GX2**
Beethoven—Fidelio
Beethoven: Fidelio (Cpte). (G. Jones, J. King, T. Adam, F. Crass, E. Mathis, P. Schreier, M. Talvela, E. Büchner, G. Leib, Leipzig Rad Chor, Dresden St Op Chor, Staatskapelle Dresden/K. Böhm)

Ⓓ **445 451-2GX2**
Verdi—Il Trovatore
Verdi: Trovatore (Cpte). (C. Bergonzi, A. Stella, E. Bastianini, F. Cossotto, I. Vinco, A. Bonato, F. Ricciardi, G. Morresi, A. Mercuriali, La Scala Chor, La Scala Orch/T. Serafin)

Ⓓ **445 461-2GMH**
Beethoven—Fidelio - Highlights
Beethoven: Fidelio (exc). (D. Fischer-Dieskau, H. Sotin, R. Kollo, G. Janowitz, M. Jungwirth, L. Popp, A. Dallapozza, K. Terkal, A. Sramek, Vienna St Op Chor, VPO/L. Bernstein)

Ⓓ **445 463-2GMH**
Mozart—Don Giovanni - Highlights
Mozart: Don Giovanni (exc). (S. Milnes, J. Macurdy, A. Tomowa-Sintow, P. Schreier, T. Zylis-Gara, W. Berry, D. Duesing, E. Mathis, Vienna St Op Chor, VPO/K. Böhm)

Ⓓ **445 464-2GMH**
Mozart—Die Zauberflöte - Highlights
Mozart: Zauberflöte (exc). (F. Crass, R. Peters, E. Lear, F. Wunderlich, D. Fischer-Dieskau, L. Otto, F. Lenz, Berlin RIAS Chbr Ch, BPO/K. Böhm)

Ⓓ **445 465-2GMH**
Puccini—La Fanciulla del West - Highlights
Puccini: Fanciulla del West (exc). (C. Neblett, P. Domingo, S. Milnes, F. Egerton, J. Summers, J. Dobson, M. Rivers, T. McDonnell, P. Crook, R. Leggate, W. Elvin, M. King, A. Wilkens, G. Howell, ROH Chor, ROHO/Z. Mehta)

Ⓓ **445 466-2GMH**
Puccini—Manon Lescaut - Highlights
Puccini: Manon Lescaut (exc). (M. Freni, R. Bruson, P. Domingo, K. Rydl, R. Gambill, G. MacPherson, M. Curtis, J. Tomlinson, ROH Chor, Philh/G. Sinopoli)

Ⓓ **445 467-2GMH**
Tchaikovsky—Eugene Onegin - Highlights
Tchaikovsky: Eugene Onegin (exc). (T. Allen, M. Freni, N. Shicoff, A.S. von Otter, P. Burchuladze, R. Lang, R. Engert-Ely, J. Hartfiel, Leipzig Rad Chor, Staatskapelle Dresden/James Levine)

Ⓓ **445 470-2GMH**
Wagner—Die Meistersinger - Highlights
Wagner: Meistersinger (exc). (C. Ligendza, C. Ludwig, P. Domingo, H. Laubenthal, D. Fischer-Dieskau, R. Hermann, Berlin Deutsche Op Chor, Berlin Deutsche Op Orch/E. Jochum)

Ⓓ **445 524-2GMA**
Battle in Salzburg
Purcell: Fairy Queen, Z629 (exc); Oedipus, Z583 (exc); Pausanias, Z585 (exc); *Handel:* Joshua (exc); *Mendelssohn:* Lieder, Op.47 (exc); Lieder, Op.19a (exc); *R. Strauss:* Lieder, Op.29 (exc); Lieder, Op.68 (exc); *Mozart:* Ridente la calma, K152; Veilchen, K476; Moto di gioia, K579; *Fauré:* Songs, Op.58 (exc); Songs, Op.39 (exc); En prière; Songs, Op.23 (exc); *Traditional:* Honor, Honor; His name so sweet; Witness; He's got the whole world in His hands. (K. Battle, James Levine)

Ⓓ **445 525-2GMA** ▭ **445 525-4GMA**
Domingo Favourites
Donizetti: Elisir d'amore (exc); Lucia di Lammermoor (exc); *Verdi:* Ernani (exc); Trovatore (exc); Aida (exc); Nabucco (exc); Don Carlos (exc); *Halévy:* Juive (exc); *Meyerbeer:* Africaine (exc); *Bizet:* Pêcheurs de perles (exc); Carmen (exc); *Puccini:* Tosca (exc); Manon Lescaut (exc); Turandot (exc). (P. Domingo, M. Freni, R. Bruson, A. Veccia, R. Wagner Chorale, Berlin Deutsche Op Chor, Vienna St Op Chor, Los Angeles PO, Berlin Deutsche Op Orch, La Scala Orch, Philh, VPO/C.M. Giulini/C. Abbado/G. Sinopoli/H. von Karajan)

Ⓓ **445 552-2GMA** ▭ **445 552-4GMA**
Battle and Domingo
Verdi: Forza del destino (exc); Traviata (exc); *Donizetti:* Don Pasquale (exc); Lucia di Lammermoor (exc); Elisir d'amore (exc); *Rossini:* Italiana in Algeri (exc); *Gounod:* Roméo et Juliette (exc); *Mozart:* Don Giovanni (exc); *Lehár:* Lustige Witwe (exc). (K. Battle, P. Domingo, NY Met Op Orch/James Levine)

Ⓓ **445 822-2GH** (5/95)
Une flûte à l'opéra
Verdi: Traviata (exc); *Godard:* Jocelyn (exc); *Rossini:* Guillaume Tell (exc); *Massenet:* Thaïs (exc); *Verdi:* Ballo in maschera (exc); *Massé:* Noces de Jeannette (exc); *Bizet:* Carmen (exc). (P. Gallois, London Fest Orch/R. Pople)

Ⓓ **445 867-2GH**
Verdi—Otello-Highlights
Verdi: Otello (exc). (P. Domingo, C. Studer, S. Leiferkus, R. Vargas, M. Schade, D. Graves, I. d'Arcangelo, G. Prestia, P. Duminy, Hauts-de-Seine Maîtrise, Paris Opéra-Bastille Chor, Paris Opéra-Bastille Orch/Myung-Whun Chung)

Ⓓ **445 868-2GH**
Wagner—Parsifal-Highlights
Wagner: Parsifal (exc). (P. Domingo, J. Morris, K. Moll, J. Norman, J-H. Rootering, A. Glassman, J. Robbins, H. G. Murphy, J. Bunnell, P. Groves, A. Laciura, J. Guyer, W. White, NY Met Op Chor, NY Met Op Orch/James Levine)

Ⓓ **445 869-2GH**
Wagner—Lohengrin - Highlights
Wagner: Lohengrin (exc). (S. Jerusalem, C. Studer, W. Meier, H. Welker, K. Moll, Vienna St Op Concert Ch, VPO/C. Abbado)

Ⓓ **445 903-2GH3** (10/95)
Mozart—Le Nozze di Figaro
Mozart: Nozze di Figaro (Cpte). (L. Gallo, S. McNair, B. Skovhus, C. Studer, C. Bartoli, A. C. Antonacci, I. d'Arcangelo, C. Allemano, P. Jelosits, I. Gáti, A. Rost, Vienna St Op Chor, VPO/C. Abbado)

Ⓓ **447 069-2GH**
Verdi/Puccini/Muzio—Works for String Quartet
Puccini: Crisantemi; *Verdi:* String Quartet; Luisa Miller (exc). (Hagen Qt)

Ⓓ **447 349-2GDB2**
Homage to Pierre Fournier
Dvořák: Cello Concerto; Rondo, B171; *Bloch:* Schelomo; *Bruch:* Kol Nidrei; *Schubert:* Arpeggione Sonata, D821; *Francoeur:* Cello Sonata in E; *Haydn:* Duos, HobVI (exc); *Weber:* Violin Sonatas, J99-104 (exc); *Chopin:* Nocturnes (exc); *Rimsky-Korsakov:* Golden Cockerel (exc); Tale of Tsar Saltan (exc); *Schumann:* Adagio and Allegro, Op. 70; *Gounod:* Ave Maria; *Brahms:* Lieder, Op. 86 (exc); *Popper:* Dance of the Elves (exc); *Saint-Saëns:* Carnaval des animaux (exc); *Paganini:* Moses in Egypt Variations (exc). (P. Fournier, J. Fonda, L. Crowson, BPO, Lamoureux Orch/G. Szell/A. Wallenstein/J. Martinon)

Ⓓ **447 352-2GDB2**
A Portrait of Gundula Janowitz
Mozart: Ah, lo previdi, K272; A questo seno, K374; Alma grande e nobil core, K578; Vado, ma dove?, K583; Bella mia fiamma, K528; Misera! dove son, K369; *Wagner:* Tannhäuser (exc); Lohengrin (exc); Rienzi (exc); *Weber:* Freischütz (exc); Oberon (exc); *Schubert:* Suleika I, D720; Suleika II, D717; Du bist die Ruh', D776; Schwestergruss, D762; Forelle, D550; Jäger, ruhe von der Jagd, D838; Raste Krieger!, D837; Ave Maria, D839. (G. Janowitz, I. Gage, Vienna SO/W. Boettcher, Berlin Deutsche Op Orch/F. Leitner)

Ⓓ **447 361-2GDB2**
French Orchestral Music
Berlioz: Carnaval romain; Damnation de Faust (exc); *Bizet:* Carmen Suites (exc); Arlésienne (exc); *Dukas:* Apprenti sorcier; *Honegger:* Piano Concertino; *Dukas:* Péri (Cpte); *Roussel:* Bacchus et Ariane Suites (exc); *Satie:* Parade (Cpte); *Milhaud:* Carnaval d'Aix. (M. Weber, C. Helffer, Bamberg SO, Lamoureux Orch, BPO, Berlin RIAS Orch, Monte Carlo Op Orch/F. Fricsay/I. Markevitch/F. Leitner/L. Frémaux)

Ⓓ **447 364-2GDB2**
Great Opera Overtures
Rossini: Barbiere di Siviglia (exc); Gazza ladra (exc); *Bellini:* Norma (exc); *Verdi:* Nabucco (exc); Traviata (exc); Vespri siciliani (exc); Forza del destino (exc); Aida (exc); *Bizet:* Carmen (exc); *Mascagni:* Cavalleria Rusticana (exc); *J. Strauss II:* Fledermaus (exc); *Gluck:* Orfeo ed Euridice (exc); *Mozart:* Entführung (exc); Zauberflöte (exc); Nozze di Figaro (exc); *Beethoven:* Fidelio (exc); *Weber:* Freischütz (exc); *Wagner:* Fliegende Holländer (exc); Tannhäuser (exc); Meistersinger (exc); *Tchaikovsky:* Eugene Onegin (exc). (BPO, Monte Carlo Nat Op Orch, La Scala Orch, Bavarian St Orch, Munich Bach Orch, Bavarian St Op Orch, Berlin Deutsche Op Orch, Bavarian Nat Orch, Bamberg SO, Lamoureux Orch, Staatskapelle Dresden/H. von Karajan/L. Frémaux/C. Kleiber/K. Richter/E. Jochum/K. Böhm/H. Löwlein/I. Markevitch/R. Kubelík/James Levine/F. Fricsay)

Ⓓ **447 370-2GDB2**
J. Strauss II—Die Fledermaus
J. Strauss II: Fledermaus (Cpte). (A. Schlemm, R. Streich, P. Anders, H. Krebs, H. Brauer, A. Müller, H. Wocke, E. Heyer, S. Menz, F. Hoppe, Berlin RIAS Chbr Ch, Berlin RIAS Orch/F. Fricsay)

Ⓓ **447 406-2GOR** (7/95)
Berlioz—Symphonie fantastique etc
Berlioz: Symphonie fantastique; *Cherubini:* Anacréon (exc); *Auber:* Muette de Portici (exc). (Lamoureux Orch/I. Markevitch)

Ⓓ **447 441-2GOR**
R. Strauss—Tone Poems
R. Strauss: Also sprach Zarathustra; Don Juan; Till Eulenspiegel; Salome (exc). (BPO/H. von Karajan)

Ⓓ **447 655-2GX2** (9/95)
Verdi—Don Carlo
Verdi: Don Carlo (Cpte). (E. Fernandi, S. Jurinac, G. Simionato, E. Bastianini, C. Siepi, M. Stefanoni, N. Zaccaria, N. Balatsch, C. Schmidt, N. Foster, A. Rothenberger, Vienna St Op Chor, VPO/H. von Karajan)

Ⓓ **447 659-2GX2** (9/95)
Verdi—Il trovatore
Verdi: Trovatore (Cpte). (F. Corelli, L. Price, E. Bastianini, G. Simionato, N. Zaccaria, L. Dutoit, S. R. Frese, R. Zimmer, K. Equiluz, Salzburg Fest Chbr Ch, Vienna St Op Chor, VPO/H. von Karajan)

Ⓓ **447 662-2GX3** (9/95)
Mozart—Idomeneo
Mozart: Idomeneo (Cpte). (W. Kmentt, E. Haefliger, P. Lorengar, E. Grümmer, R. Capecchi, E. Waechter, G. Littasy, Vienna St Op Chor, VPO/F. Fricsay)

Deutsche Harmonia Mundi

Ⓓ **GD77009** (7/90)
Rameau—Hippolye et Aricie Suite
Rameau: Hippolyte et Aricie (exc). (Petite Bande/S. Kuijken)

Ⓓ **GD77059** (2/91)
Lully—Bourgeois Gentilhomme; Campra—L'Europa galante
Lully: Bourgeois Gentilhomme; *Campra:* Europe galante. (R. Yakar, M. Kweksilber, D. Jungmann, R. Jacobs, K. Heider, M. Lecocq, N. Lohmann, S. Nimsgern, D. Schortemeier, F. Müller-Heuser, M. Friesenhausen, Tolz Boys' Ch, Petite Bande/G. Leonhardt)

Ⓓ **GD77109** (2/91)
Handel: Partenope
Handel: Partenope (Cpte). (K. Laki, R. Jacobs, J.Y. Skinner, S. Varcoe, H. Müller-Molinari, M. Hill, Petite Bande/S. Kuijken)

Ⓓ **GD77110** (2/91)
Handel: Alessandro
Handel: Alessandro (Cpte). (R. Jacobs, S. Boulin, I. Poulenard, J. Nirouët, S. Varcoe, G. de Mey, R. Bollen, Petite Bande/S. Kuijken)

Ⓓ **GD77144** (6/91)
Rameau—Zoroastre
Rameau: Zoroastre (Cpte). (J. Elwes, G. de Reyghere, M. van der Sluis, A. Mellon, G. Reinhart, J. Bona, M. Verschaeve, F. Fauché, P. Cantor, Ghent Collegium Vocale, Petite Bande/S. Kuijken)

Ⓓ **GD77174**
Gluck—Le Cinesi
Gluck: Cinesi (Cpte). (I. Poulenard, A.S. von Otter, G. Banditelli, G. de Mey, SCB/R. Jacobs)

Ⓓ **GD77233**
English Harpsichord Music
Blow: Praeludium in G; Ground in G; Lessons; *Croft:* Suite 3; *Purcell:* Indian Queen, Z630 (exc); *Croft:* Suite in A. (B. Tracey)

Ⓓ **RD77184** (9/92)
Pergolesi—La Serva Padrona
Pergolesi: Serva Padrona. (M. Bonifaccio, S. Nimsgern, Collegium Aureum, F. Maier (vn/dir))

Ⓓ **RD77192** (1/93)
Handel—Rodelinda
Handel: Rodelinda (Cpte). (B. Schlick, C. Schubert, D. Cordier, K. Wessel, C. Prégardien, G. Schwarz, Stagione/M. Schneider)

Ⓓ **RD77231** (3/92)
Purcell—Instrumental Music
Purcell: Chaconne, Z730; Fairy Queen, Z629 (exc); Dido (exc); King Arthur, Z628 (exc); Abdelazer, Z570 (exc). (Freiburg Baroque Orch/T. Hengelbrock)

Ⓓ **RD77252** (9/92)
Purcell—Airs and Instrumental Music
Purcell: Choice Collection of Lessons (exc); If music be the food of love, Z379/1; Fantasia, Z731; Fairy Queen, Z629 (exc); St Cecilia's Day Ode, Z328 (exc); Hornpipes (exc); Overture, Z772; Lord, what is man?, Z192; Chaconne, Z730; Oedipus, Z583 (exc); Lovely Albina, Z394; Viola da gamba Fantasies, Z735-43; Grounds (exc); Pavans, Z748-51 (exc); Evening Hymn, Z193. (H. Crook, Capriccio Stravagante, S. Sempé (hpd/dir), S. Sempé)

Ⓓ **05472 77269-2** (8/93)
Rameau—Suites from Operas
Rameau: Dardanus (exc); Indes galantes (exc). (Collegium Aureum/R. Peters/G. Leonhardt)

Ⓓ **05472 77284-2** (4/94)
Telemann—Pimpinone
Telemann: Pimpinone (Cpte). (M. Schopper, M. Bach, Stagione/M. Schneider)

Ⓓ **05472 77289-2** (4/94)
Bach/Vivaldi—Orchestral Works
Bach: Suites, BWV1066-9 (exc); Cantata 42 (exc); 3-Violin Concerto, BWV1064; *Vivaldi:* Concerto, RV158; Olimpiade (exc); Concerti Grossi, Op. 3 (exc). (Freiburg Baroque Orch/T. Hengelbrock)

Ⓓ **05472 77295-2** (10/94)
Handel/Purcell—Works
Purcell: Dioclesian Suite (exc); Dioclesian, Z627 (exc); If music be the food of love, Z379/1; O! how happy's he, Z403; Lost is my quiet for ever, Z502; *Handel:* Concerti grossi, Op. 6 (exc); Amarilli vezzosa. (N. Argenta, M. Chance, Freiburg Baroque Orch/G. von der Goltz)

Ⓓ **05472 77316-2**
Haydn—L'infedeltà delusa.
Haydn: Infedeltà delusa (Cpte). (N. Argenta, L. Lootens, M. Schäfer, C. Prégardien, S. Varcoe, Petite Bande/S. Kuijken)

Ⓓ **05472 77318-2**
Delight in Disorder—English Consort of Two Parts, 1640-1680
Playford: English Dancing Master, Part One (exc); English Dancing Master, Appendix (exc); Unidentified Marches and Tunes (exc); *W. Lawes:* Why soe pall; *H. Lawes:* Bid me to live; *N. Matteis I:* Trumpet Passages; Chaconne, Plaint, Ecchi; *Locke:* Unidentified Fantazie Suite in A minor; *Various:* Court Masques; *Purcell:* Unidentified Toccata in A minor; Fairy Queen, Z629 (exc); Grounds (exc); *Anon:* Black Joak. (P. Memelsdorff, A. Staier)

Discover International

Ⓓ **DICD920107/8** (1/94)
Puccini—La Bohème
Puccini: Bohème (Cpte). (M. Gauci, G. Aragall, M. Krause, V. Sardinero, C. Bergasa, M. Rosca, J. Joris, F. De Moor, W. Brans, Brussels BRT Phil Chor, Brussels BRT PO/A. Rahbari)

Ⓓ **DICD920114**
Beethoven—Egmont-Incidental Music, Op 84; Leonora Overture, No 3
Beethoven: Egmont; Leonore (exc). (M. Gauci, D. Schortemeier, Brussels BRT PO/A. Rahbari, LPO)

Ⓓ **DICD920119** (7/94)
Puccini—Gianni Schicchi
Puccini: Gianni Schicchi (Cpte). (E. Tumagian, M. Gauci, Y. Ramiro, M. Perelstein, F. Careccia, D. Verdoodt, O. Van De Voorde, F. Van Eetveldt, M. Rosca, M. Meersman, R. Fabry, J. Joris, Brussels BRT PO/A. Rahbari)

Ⓓ **DICD920120** (7/94)
Puccini—Suor Angelica
Puccini: Suor Angelica (Cpte). (M. Gauci, L. Van Deyck, M. Karadjian, R. Fabry, D. Grossberger, B. Degelin, D. Verdoodt, M. Vliegen, J. Greggoor Chor, Brussels BRT PO/A. Rahbari)

Ⓓ **DICD920141**
French Music for Flute and Harp
Boieldieu: Flute and Harp Sonata; *Bizet:* Carmen Suites (exc); *Damase:* Flute and Harp Sonata (exc); *Françaix:* Piccoli duetti; *Ravel:* Pavane pour une infante défunte. (S. Kudo, R. Talitman)

Ⓓ **DICD920149**
The Magic of the Strauss Dynasty
J. Strauss II: Prinz Methusalem (exc); Vom Donaustrande, Op. 356; Wiener bonbons; Zigeunerbaron (exc); Im Krapfenwald'l, Op. 336; Tritsch-Tratsch; Wiener Blut; Neue Pizzicato-Polka, Op. 449; Leichtes Blut, Op. 319; G'schichten aus dem Wienerwald, Op. 325; Unter Donner und Blitz; Fortuna-Galopp, Op. 69; Radetzky March; *E. Strauss:* Bahn frei; *Jos Strauss:* Feuerfest!. (Vienna Strauss Festival Orch/P. Guth)

Ⓓ **DICD920201**
Mozart—Orchestral Works
Mozart: Don Giovanni (exc); Symphony 38; Concertone, K190. (J. Suk, O. Vlček, J. Kolar, M. Kaňka, Prague Virtuosi/O. Vlček)

Ⓓ **DICD920204**
Mozart—Concert Arias
Mozart: Ah, lo previdi, K272; Ah, se in ciel, K538; Rè pastore (exc); Bella mia fiamma, K528; Alcandro, lo confesso, K294; Voi avete un cor fedele, K217. (V. Girard, Prague Virtuosi/O. Vlček)

Ⓓ **DICD920209** (4/95)
Puccini—Il Tabarro
Puccini: Tabarro (Cpte). (E. Tumagian, M. Slatinaru, N. Martinucci, A. Leonel, M. Rosca, L. van Deyck, J. Gregoor Ch, Brussels BRT Phil Chor, Brussels BRT PO/A. Rahbari)

Ⓓ **DICD920225/6** (2/95)
Verdi—Simon Boccanegra
Verdi: Simon Boccanegra (Cpte). (E. Tumagian, M. Gauci, G. Aragall, P. Mikuláš, V. Sardinero, V. de Kanel, G. Tomckowiack, M. Pieck, Brussels BRT Phil Chor, Brussels BRT PO/A. Rahbari)

Ⓓ **DICD920289**
Haydn—Symphonies Nos 44 and 45;Sinfonia-Acide e Galatea
Haydn: Symphony 44; Symphony 45; Acide e Galatea (exc). (Sinfonia/D. Vermeulen)

Disques Montaigne

Ⓓ **MUN2011** (11/88)
Berlioz—Symphonie fantastique; Overtures
Berlioz: Symphonie fantastique; Corsaire; Benvenuto Cellini (exc). (FNO/C. Munch)

Ⓓ **TCE8710** (8/88)
Debussy—Pelléas et Mélisande; Nocturnes
Debussy: Pelléas et Mélisande (Cpte); Nocturnes. (J. Jansen, M. Grancher, M. Roux, A. Vessières, S. Michel, F. Ogéas, M. Vigneron, FRN Chor, FNO/D-E. Inghelbrecht)

Ⓓ **TCE8740**
Pieree Monteux conducts...
Beethoven: Symphony 2; *Stravinsky:* Petrushka (Cpte); *Rimsky-Korsakov:* Golden Cockerel Suite (exc); *Prokofiev:* Symphony 1; *Tchaikovsky:* Symphony 5. (FNO/P. Monteux)

Ⓓ **TCE8750** (5/88)
Milhaud—Christophe Colomb
Milhaud: Christophe Colomb (Cpte). (R. Massard, J. Micheau, X. Depraz, X. Depraz, J. Marchat, J. Davy, J. Davy, L. Lovano, L. Lovano, L. Lovano, J. Giraudeau, J. Giraudeau, J. Peyron, P. Germain, J. Chalude, French Rad Chor, French Rad Lyric Orch/M. Rosenthal)

Ⓓ **TCE8760**
Stravinsky: Stage Works
Stravinsky: Oedipus Rex (Cpte); Scènes de ballet (exc); Nightingale (Cpte). (L. Simoneau, E. Zareska, B. Cottret, G. Serkoyan, M. Hamel, G. Abdoun, J. Cocteau, J. Micheau, J. Giraudeau, G. Moizan, M. Roux, L. Lovano, B. Cottret, C. Gayraud, French Rad and TV Chor, FNO/I. Stravinsky/A. Cluytens)

Ⓓ **782014** (9/93)
Maderna—Hyperion
Maderna: Hyperion (Cpte). (P. Walmsley-Clark, B. Ganz, J. Zoon, Jeunes Sols Voc Ens, Asko Ens/P. Eötvös)

Divertimento

Ⓓ **DIV31011**
Various Orchestral Works
Offenbach: Orphée aux enfers (exc); Contes d'Hoffmann (exc); *J. Strauss II:* Künstlerleben, Op. 316; Blumenfest, Op. 111; G'schichten aus dem Wienerwald, Op. 325; Leichtes Blut, Op. 319; Damenspende; Sperl-Polka. (K. Swoboda, Vienna Ravel Orch/J-P. Rouchon)

Ⓓ **DIV31013**
Mozart/Salieri—Arias for Countertenors
Mozart: Exsultate, jubilate K165; Idomeneo (exc); Ascanio in Alba (exc); Clemenza di Tito (exc); *Salieri:* Fremat Thyrannus; Axur (exc); Armida (exc); Annibale in Capua (exc). (A. Raunig, Vienna Amadeus Ens/W. Kobera)

Divine Art

Ⓓ **2-4102** ▭ **4-4102**
The Classic and Romantic Horn
Beethoven: Horn Sonata; *Saint-Saëns:* Romance, Op. 67; *Hindemith:* Horn Sonata; *T. Johns:* Holland Park; *Gershwin:* Oh, Kay! (exc); *Van Heusen:* Joker is Wild (exc); *Weill:* Knickerbocker Holiday (exc). (T. Johns, J. Lynch, B. Kellock)

Divox

Ⓓ **CDX29104-2**
The Unforgettables
Kreisler: Marche miniature viennoise; Caprice viennois; *Toselli:* Serenade; *Pergolesi:* Tre giorni son che Nina; *Raff:* Pieces, Op. 85 (exc); *Brahms:* Hungarian Dances (exc); *Rachmaninov:* Songs, Op. 34 (exc); *Haydn:* Keyboard Trio 25 (exc); *Traditional:* Londonderry Air; *G. Braga:* Melodies (exc); *Dvořák:* Slavonic Dances (exc); *Kreisler:* Old refrain; *Mussorgsky:* Fair at Sorochintsï (exc). (Andreas Trio)

Dorian

Ⓓ **DOR90209**
Baroque Inventions
D. Scarlatti: Keyboard Sonatas (exc); *Bach:* French Suites, BWV812-17 (exc); *Handel:* Rodelinda (exc); Chaconne in G, HWV435. (J. Gray, R. Pearl)

Doyen

Ⓓ **DOYCD004** (8/92) ▭ **DOYMC004**
Rule Brittania
Fučík: Entry of the Gladiators; *Bizet:* Carmen (exc); *Shostakovich:* Flea (exc); *Bach:* Harpsichord Concerto, BWV1056 (exc); *Goffin:* Rhapsody in Brass; *Rossini:* Boutique fantasque (exc); *Traditional:* Old Chalet; *Respighi:* Pines of Rome; *Kabalevsky:* Comedians (exc); *Puccini:* Turandot (exc); *Traditional:* Steal away to Jesus; *L. Pearson:* Fantasy Variations; *Botsford:* Black and White Rag; *Sparke:* Partita. (Britannia Building Soc Band/H. Snell)

Ⓓ **DOYCD005** (9/92) ▭ **DOYMC005** (9/92)
Flower of Scotland
W. Rimmer: Australasian; *Sparke:* Capriccio; *Ball:* Softly sounds the little bell; Star Lake; *R. Williamson:* Flower of Scotland; *R. Heath:* Frolic for Trombones; *Rodgers:* Carousel (exc); *Borodin:* Prince Igor (exc); *Crüger:* Nun danket alle Gott; *Gershwin:* Strike Up the Band I (exc); *D. Rose:* Holiday for Strings; *Foster:* Beautiful Dreamer; *P. Graham:* Prelude to a New Age; *Hazell:* Mr Jums; *Friedmann:* Slavonic Rhapsody 2. (G. Lindsay, A. Murphy, B. Deans, M. Stenhouse, D. Platt, Glasgow CWS Band/H. Snell/R. Tennant)

Ⓓ **DOYCD013** (12/92) ▭ **DOYMC013** (12/92)
A Night at the Opera
Wagner: Tannhäuser (exc); *J. Strauss II:* Fledermaus (exc); *Saint-Saëns:* Samson et Dalila (exc); *Verdi:* Traviata (exc); Forza del Destino (exc); *Wagner:* Walküre (exc). (Grimethorpe Colliery Band/E. Howarth)

Dutton Laboratories

Ⓓ **CDAX8006** (3/94)
The Delius Collection
Delius: Brigg Fair; In a Summer Garden; First cuckoo; Summer Night on the River; Village Romeo and Juliet (exc); Dance; Preludes; Piano Pieces (exc); *Grainger:* Brigg Fair. (N. Stone, E. Howard Jones, Oriana Madrigal Soc/C. Kennedy Scott, LSO, New SO/G. Toye)

Ⓓ **CDAX8008** (9/94)
Sir Henry Wood conducts Proms Favourites
Coates: London Suite; London Bridge; *Grainger:* Molly on the Shore, BFMS1; Mock Morris; Handel in the Strand; *Wagner:* Walküre (exc); *Berlioz:* Carnaval Romain; *Gounod:* Marche funèbre d'une marionette; *Elgar:* Pomp and Circumstance Marches (exc); *Henry Wood:* Sea-Song Fantasia; *Järnefelt:* Praeludium. (Queen's Hall Orch, British SO, LPO, LSO, SO/Henry Wood)

Ⓓ **CDAX8009** (11/94)
Stokowski conducts a Russian Spectacular
Mussorgsky: Night on the Bare Mountain; Boris Godunov (exc); Pictures (exc); Khovanshchina (exc); *Borodin:* Prince Igor (exc). (Philadelphia/L. Stokowski)

Ⓓ **CDAX8010** (2/95)
Hallé Orchestra Wartime Recordings
Borodin: Prince Igor (exc); Symphony 2; *Liadov:* Kikimora, Op. 63; *Shostakovich:* Piano Concerto 1; *Tchaikovsky:* Sleeping Beauty (exc). (E. Joyce, A. Lockwood, Hallé/C. Lambert/L. Heward/A. Boult/M. Sargent)

Ⓓ **CDK1200** (5/95)
This is Full Frequency Range Recording
Bizet: Arlésienne Suites (exc); *Berlioz:* Damnation de Faust (exc); *Glière:* Red Poppy Suite (exc); *Tchaikovsky:* Marche slave; *Wagner:* Götterdämmerung (exc); *Saint-Saëns:* Danse macabre; *Tchaikovsky:* Oprichnik (exc); *Wolf-Ferrari:* Gioielli della Madonna (exc); *Delius:* Irmelin Prelude; *Chabrier:* España. (National SO/Sidney Beer/A. Fistoulari/B. Neel/V. Olof)

Ⓓ **CDLXT2505**
Thomas Jensen conducts Nielsen, Vol.2
Nielsen: Flute Concerto; Clarinet Concerto; Maskarade (exc). (H. Gilbert-Jespersen, I. Erikson, Danish St RSO/T. Jensen/M. Wöldike)

Ⓓ **CDLX7001** (7/93)
Beecham conducts Favourite Overtures, Volume 1
Rossini: Scala di seta (exc); Guillaume Tell (exc); Gazza ladra (exc); Semiramide (exc); *Mendelssohn:* Hebrides; Ruy Blas; *Suppé:* Morgen, ein Mittag, ein Abend in Wien (exc); *Nicolai:* Lustigen Weiber von Windsor (exc). (LPO/T. Beecham)

Ⓓ **CDLX7003** (6/94)
Vintage Beecham
Handel: Solomon (exc); *Dvořák:* Legends (exc); *Offenbach:* Contes d'Hoffmann (exc); *Bizet:* Carmen Suites (exc); *Delius:* Koanga (exc); *Mendelssohn:* Midsummer Night's Dream (exc); Midsummer Night's Dream (exc); *J. Strauss II:* Frühlingsstimmen, Op. 410; *Borodin:* Prince Igor (exc); Prince Igor (exc). (Leeds Fest Chor, LPO/T. Beecham)

Ⓓ **CDLX7007** (6/94)
Beecham conducts Wagner
Wagner: Meistersinger (exc); Meistersinger (exc); Fliegende Holländer (exc); Tannhäuser (exc); Lohengrin (exc); Götterdämmerung (exc). (T. Lemnitz, T. Ralf, H. Janssen, L. Weber, ROH Chor, LPO/T. Beecham)

Ⓓ **CDLX7008** (8/94)
Bruno Walter conducts the LSO
Beethoven: Coriolan; *Haydn:* Symphony 86; *Schumann:* Symphony 4; *Smetana:* Bartered Bride (exc); *Corelli:* Concerti Grossi, Op.6 (exc). (LSO/B. Walter)

Ⓓ **CDLX7009** (10/94)
Beecham conducts Favourite Overtures, Volume 2
Mozart: Nozze di Figaro (exc); Don Giovanni (exc); Zauberflöte (exc); *Weber:* Oberon (exc); Freischütz (exc); *Brahms:* Tragic Overture; *Wagner:* Faust Overture; *Berlioz:* Carnaval Romain; *Rossini:* Scala di seta (exc). (LPO, BPO/T. Beecham)

Ⓓ **CDLX7011** (10/94)
Beecham conducts Delius
Delius: Appalachia; Koanga (exc); Hassan (exc); Hassan (exc); First Cuckoo; Summer Night on the River; Norwegian Songs (1889-90) (exc); Norwegian Songs (1888) (exc). (D. Labbette, J. van der Gucht, T. Beecham, BBC Chor, London Select Ch, ROH Chor, LPO, RPS Orch/T. Beecham)

Ⓓ **CDLX7012** (2/95)
The Incomparable Heddle Nash
Puccini: Bohème (exc); *Mozart:* Così fan tutte (exc); Così fan tutte (exc); Don Giovanni (exc); *Rossini:* Barbiere di Siviglia (exc); *Verdi:* Rigoletto (exc); Rigoletto (exc); *Bizet:* Jolie fille de Perth (exc); *J. Strauss II:* Fledermaus (exc). (I. Souez, D. Labbette, S. Andreva, H. Nash, J. Brownlee, D. Noble, R. Alva, R. Easton, LPO/T. Beecham, Glyndebourne Fest Orch/F. Busch, orch/C. Raybould)

Ⓓ **CDLX7013** (7/95)
The Unforgettable Isobel Baillie
Handel: Samson (exc); *Bach:* Cantata 68 (exc); Cantata 201 (exc); *Mozart:* Finta giardiniera (exc); *Handel:* Rodelinda (exc); *Haydn:* Creation (exc); *Handel:* Messiah (exc); Messiah (exc); *Mendelssohn:* Elijah (exc); *Handel:* Theodora (exc); Joshua (exc); *Mozart:* Nozze di Figaro (exc); *Offenbach:* Contes d'Hoffmann (exc); *Schubert:* Hirt auf dem Felsen, D965; An die Musik, D547; *Arne:* Tempest (exc). (I. Baillie, C. Draper, G. Ison, G. Moore, Hallé, CBO, Liverpool PO, orch/W. Braithwaite/B. Cameron/L. Heward/M. Sargent/C. Prentice/S. Robinson)

Ⓓ **CDLX7016** (9/95)
The Art of Sir Hamilton Harty
Bax: Overture to a Picaresque Comedy; *Berlioz:* Roméo et Juliette (exc); Tristia (exc); *Sibelius:* Valse triste; *Smetana:* Bartered Bride (exc); *Schubert:* Marches militaires, D733 (exc); *Handel:* Fireworks Music Suite; Water Music Suite. (LPO/H. Harty)

Ⓓ **CDSJB1001** (3/95)
Barbirolli in New York - 1938 Wagner Concert
Wagner: Rienzi (exc); Tannhäuser (exc); Tristan und ISolde (exc); Meistersinger (exc); Siegfried Idyll. (NYPO/J. Barbirolli)

Ⓓ **2CDAX2001** (5/94)
Beecham conducts Gounod's Faust
Gounod: Faust (Cpte); Faust (exc). (H. Nash, M. Licette, R. Easton, H. Williams, D. Vane, M. Brunskill, R. Carr, BBC Ch, SO, LPO/T. Beecham/C. Raybould)

EBS

Ⓓ **EBS6023**
Contrasts - Music for Trombone & Piano
Galliard: Bassoon Sonatas (exc); *Castérède:* Trombone Sonatine; *Bach:* Suites, BWV1066-9 (exc); *Nestico:* Reflective Mood; *Martin:* Trombone Ballade; *Bozza:* Ballade; *Telemann:* Fantaisies, TWV40: 2-13 (exc); *E. Crespo:* Improvisation 1; *Mozart:* Zauberflöte (exc). (S. Clark, A. Romm)

Ⓓ **EBS6038**
The American Horn Quartet
K. Turner: Horn Quartet 3; *W. Perkins:* 4-Horn Concerto; *Hindemith:* 4-Horn Sonata; *Bernstein:* West Side Story (exc). (American Hn Qt)

Ⓓ **EBS6071**
Bruch—Orchestral Works
Bruch: Loreley (exc); Suite, Op. 79b; Romance, Op. 85; Symphony 1. (R. Moog, Rhenish PO/W. Balzer)

ECM New Series

Ⓓ **437 439-2**
Meredith Monk—Facing North and other works
M. Monk: Facing North; Vessel; Recent Ruins (exc). (M. Monk, M. Monk, R. Een)

Ⓓ **437 773-2** (10/93)
Meredith Monk—Atlas
M. Monk: Atlas (Cpte). (C. Arávalo, T. Bogdan, J. Brenner, S-Z. Chen, A. Easter, R. Een, D. Emerson, E. Eyre, K. Geissinger, C. Gonzalez, D. Hanchard, W. Hill, S. Kalm, M. Monk, R. Osborne, W. Pauley, R. Wong, Orch/W. Hankin)

Edel

Ⓓ **EDL2562-2** ⊙ **EDL2562-1** ▭ **EDL2562-4**
Carreras, Domingo, Pavarotti Greatest Hits
Giordano: Fedora (exc); *Padilla:* Valencia; *Leoncavallo:* Pagliacci (exc); *Lara:* Solamente una vez; *Verdi:* Luisa Miller (exc); *Puccini:* Manon Lescaut (exc); *Verdi:* Rigoletto (exc); *Lacalle:* Amapola; *Bixio:* Mamma; *Puccini:* Fanciulla del West (exc); *Leoncavallo:* Mattinata; *Giménez:* Boda de Luis Alonso (exc); *Serrano:* Alma da Dios (exc); *Puccini:* Bohème (exc); *Cardillo:* Core 'ngrato; *Puccini:* Turandot (exc); *Di Capua:* 'O sole mio. (J. Carreras, P. Domingo, L. Pavarotti, Orch)

Electrecord

Ⓓ **ELCD104**
Caudella—Orchestral works
Caudella: Symphonic Pieces, Op. 28; Fantasy-Capriccio, Op. 25; Fantasy 5; Dochia, Op. 47; Violin Concerto, Op. 61; Petru Rareş (exc). (Iaşi Moldova PO/I. Baciu/G. Vintilă, Sibiu PO/P. Sbârcea, F. Diaconescu, D. Podlovski)

Ⓓ **ELCD109**
Timisoara Memorial
Mozart: Requiem (exc); Zauberflöte (exc); *Wagner:* Meistersinger (exc); *Verdi:* Rigoletto (exc); Simon Boccanegra (exc); *Drăgoi:* Rustic Divertimento; *Boboc:* Divertimento; *Georgescu:* Exorcisms. (R. Miloia, C. Airizer, I. Mogoş, Timişoara Banatul Phil Chor, Timişoara Banatul PO, Timişoara Romanian Op Orch/N. Boboc/M. Beleavcenco/I. Iancu/R. Georgescu)

Nonesuch

Ⓓ **7559-79281-2** (3/93)
J. Adams—The Death of Klinghoffer
J. Adams: Death of Klinghoffer (Cpte). (S. Sylvan, S. Friedman, J. Maddalena, T. Hammons, T.J. Young, E. Perry, S. Nadler, London Op Chor, Lyon Op Orch/K. Nagano)

Ⓓ **7559-79286-2** (1/94)
Glass—Hydrogen Jukebox
Glass: Hydrogen Jukebox (Cpte). (M. Goldray, C. Wincene, A. Sterman, F. Cassara, J. Pugliese, R. Peck, E. Futral, M.A. Eaton, M.A. Hart, R. Fracker, G. Purnhagen, N. Watson, A. Ginsberg, P. Glass/M. Goldray)

Ⓓ **7559-79289-2**
Ashley—Improvement
Ashley: Improvement (Cpte). (J. Humbert, T. Buckner, J. La Barbara, S. Ashley, A. Klein, A.X. Neuburg, R. Ashley, Chor, T. Erbe, T. Hamilton)

Ⓓ **7559-79323-2** (1/94)
Glass—Einstein on the Beach
Glass: Einstein on the Beach (Cpte). (L. Childs, G. Dolbashian, J. McGruder, S. Sutton, G. Fulkerson, chor, Philip Glass Ens/M. Riesman)

Ⓓ **7559-79330-2** (11/94)
Patinkin—Experiment
Hupfeld: As Time Goes By; *Kern:* You Were Never Lovelier (exc); *Menken:* Little Shop of Horrors (stage) (exc); *Sondheim:* Company (exc); Merrily We Roll Along (exc); Follies (exc); So Many People; *Bernstein:* West Side Story (exc); *Waller:* Ain't Misbehavin' (exc); *Chapin:* Taxi; *C-M. Schönberg:* Misérables (exc); *Warren:* Billy Rose's Diamond Horseshoe (exc); *Rodgers:* Babes in Arms (exc); *Berlin:* Always; *B. Lane:* Finian's Rainbow (exc); *Porter:* Nymph Errant (exc). (M. Patinkin, Orch/E. Stern)

Ⓓ **7559-79345-2** (12/94) ▭ **7559-79345-4**
I Wish It So - Dawn Upshaw
Bernstein: Candide (1988) (exc); Madwoman of Central Park West (exc); West Side Story (exc); *Blitzstein:* Juno (exc); No for an Answer (exc); Reuben, Reuben (exc); *Sondheim:* Anyone can Whistle (exc); Saturday Night (exc); Girls of Summer (exc); Merrily We Roll Along (exc); Evening Primrose (exc); *Weill:* One Touch of Venus (exc); Lady in the Dark (exc); Lost in the Stars (exc). (D. Upshaw, orch/E. Stern, E. Stern, L. Stifelman)

Ⓓ **7559-79347-2**
Glass—La Belle et la Bête
Glass: Belle et la Bête (Cpte). (J. Felty, G. Purnhagen, J. Kuether, A. M. Martinez, H. Neill, Z. Zhou, Philip Glass Ens/M. Riesman)

EMI

Ⓓ **CDC2 53045-2** ▭ **EL2 53045-4**
Heavy Classix
Wagner: Walküre (exc); *Khachaturian:* Gayaneh (exc); *Berlioz:* Symphonie fantastique (exc); *Mussorgsky:* Pictures (exc); *Tchaikovsky:* 1812 (exc); Symphony 6 (exc); *Chabrier:* España; *Borodin:* Prince Igor (exc); *Berlioz:* Damnation de Faust (exc); *Holst:* Planets (exc); *Prokofiev:* Romeo and Juliet Suites (exc); *Elgar:* Pomp and Circumstance Marches (exc); *Wagner:* Lohengrin (exc); *Stravinsky:* Firebird (exc); *Mahler:* Symphony 1 (exc). (BPO/K. Tennstedt, RPO/Y. Temirkanov, Philadelphia/R. Muti, Oslo PO/M. Jansons, Toulouse Capitole Orch/M. Plasson, Chicago SO/S. Ozawa, CBSO/L. Frémaux, LSO/A. Previn, Dresden PO/H. Kegel/S. Rattle)

Ⓓ **CDC5 55016-2**
Maria Callas - La Divina 2
Gluck: Alceste (1776) (exc); *Bizet:* Carmen (exc); *Verdi:* Ernani (exc); *Puccini:* Manon Lescaut (exc); *Verdi:* Aida (exc); *Gluck:* Orphée (exc); *Verdi:* Vespri Siciliani (exc); *G. Charpentier:* Louise (exc); *Puccini:* Bohème (exc); *A. Thomas:* Mignon (exc); *Verdi:* Traviata (exc); Don Carlo (exc); *Saint-Saëns:* Samson et Dalila (exc); *Bellini:* Sonnambula (exc); *Cilea:* Adriana Lecouvreur (exc); *Donizetti:* Lucia di Lammermoor (exc). (M. Callas, N. Sautereau, J. Berbié, R. Duclos Ch, FRNO, Paris Op Orch, Philh, Paris Cons, Lisbon San Carlos Nat Th Orch, La Scala Orch/G. Prêtre/N. Rescigno/T. Serafin/F. Ghione, Philh Chor)

Ⓓ **CDC5 55017-2** (6/94)
Domingo Opera Classics
Verdi: Aida (exc); *Mozart:* Così fan tutte (exc); *Verdi:* Ballo in maschera (exc); *Puccini:* Manon Lescaut (exc); *Verdi:* Don Carlo (exc); *Handel:* Giulio Cesare (exc); *Boito:* Mefistofele (exc); *Mozart:* Don Giovanni (exc); *Meyerbeer:* Africaine (exc); *Puccini:* Fanciulla del West (exc); *Verdi:* Forza del Destino (exc); *Puccini:* Tosca (exc); *Mascagni:* Nerone (exc); *Gounod:* Faust (exc); *Puccini:* Tosca (exc); *Verdi:* Otello (exc). (P. Domingo, R. Grist, M. Caballé, ROH Chor, Ambrosian Op Chor, New Philh, Munich RO, ROHO, National PO, LSO, La Scala Orch, Paris Op Orch, Philh/R. Muti/E. Kohn/B. Bartoletti/C.M. Giulini/J. Rudel/J. Barker/G. Prêtre/James Levine)

Ⓓ **CDC5 55018-2** (4/94)
Domingo sings and conducts Tchaikovsky
Tchaikovsky: Romeo and Juliet; Songs, Op. 6 (exc); Capriccio italien; Eugene Onegin (exc); 1812. (P. Domingo, O. Harnoy, Philh/P. Domingo/R. Behr)

Ⓓ **CDC5 55090-2** (10/94) ▭ **EL5 55090-4** (10/94)
Amanda Roocroft—Recital
Handel: Samson (exc); Giulio Cesare (exc); *Mozart:* Così fan tutte (exc); Idomeneo (exc); *Puccini:* Rondine (exc); Gianni Schicchi (exc); Manon Lescaut (exc); *Verdi:* Otello (exc); *Dvořák:* Rusalka (exc); *G. Charpentier:* Louise (exc); *Duparc:* Chanson triste; *R. Strauss:* Lieder, Op.27 (exc); Lieder, Op.39 (exc). (A. Roocroft, LPO/F. Welser-Möst)

Ⓓ **CDC5 55095-2**
Prima Diva
Rossini: Barbiere di Siviglia (exc); *Bellini:* Norma (exc); *R. Strauss:* Vier letzte Lieder (exc); *Lehár:* Lustige Witwe (exc); *Canteloube:* Chants d'Auvergne (exc); *Puccini:* Madama Butterfly (exc); *Mozart:* Don Giovanni (exc); *Verdi:* Forza del destino (exc); *Puccini:* Gianni Schicchi (exc); *Cilea:* Adriana Lecouvreur (exc); *Gershwin:* Porgy and Bess (exc); *A. Lloyd Webber:* Requiem (exc); *Mozart:* Zauberflöte (exc); *Offenbach:* Belle Hélène (exc); *Handel:* Alcina (exc); *Mozart:* Così fan tutte (exc); *J. Strauss II:* Fledermaus (exc). (M. Callas, E. Schwarzkopf, V. de los Angeles, J. Sutherland, M. Caballé, K. Te Kanawa, B. Hendricks, J. Norman, K. Battle, C. Studer, La Scala Chor, Philh Chor, NY Choral Artists, E. Ericson Chbr Ch, Philh, La Scala Orch, Berlin RSO, Lamoureux Orch, Rome Op Orch, RPO, LSO, New Princess Th Orch, Swedish RSO, ECO, Toulouse Capitole Orch, ASMF, VPO, ROHO/A. Galliera/T. Serafin/G. Szell/L. von Matačić/J-P. Jacquillat/G. Santini/C.M. Giulini/A. Guadagno/C. Mackerras/Myung-Whun Chung/J. McGlinn/E. Ericson/J. Tate/M. Plasson/N. Marriner/R. Muti/J. Barker)

Ⓓ **CDC5 55108-2** (2/95)
R. Strauss/Mozart—Chamber Works
Mozart: String Quintet, K406; *R. Strauss:* Capriccio (exc); Metamorphosen. (A. Posch, Vienna Stg Sextet)

Ⓓ **CDC5 55141-2**
Lehár—Die lustige Witwe
Lehár: Lustige Witwe (Cpte). (F. Lott, T. Hampson, R. Poulton, J. Aler, E. Szmytka, R. Schasching, K. Azesberger, Glyndebourne Fest Chor, LPO/F. Welser-Möst)

Ⓓ **CDC5 55151-2** (6/95)
Operetta Duets
Friml: Rose Marie (exc); *Romberg:* Desert Song (exc); New Moon (exc); Student Prince (exc); *Hahn:* Ciboulette (exc); *Messager:* Véronique (exc); *Yvain:* Ta bouche (exc); *Christiné:* Phi-Phi (exc); *Offenbach:* Barbe-bleue (exc); *Millöcker:* Gasparone (exc); *Heuberger:* Opernball (exc); *J. Strauss II:* Zigeunerbaron (exc); Wiener Blut (exc); *Lehár:* Land des Lächelns (exc); Lustige Witwe (exc). (B. Hendricks, G. Quilico, Lyon Op Orch/L. Foster)

Ⓓ **CDC5 55212-2** (4/95)
Schoenberg—Orchestral Works
Schoenberg: Chamber Symphony 1; Erwartung (Cpte); Variations, Op.31. (P. Bryn-Julson, Birmingham Contemp Mus Group, CBSO/S. Rattle)

Ⓓ **CDC5 55216-2** ▭ **EL555216-4**
Maria Callas - La Divina 3
Giordano: Andrea Chénier (exc); *Spontini:* Vestale (exc); *Massenet:* Manon (exc); *Puccini:* Manon Lescaut (exc); *Bizet:* Carmen (exc); *Rossini:* Barbiere di Siviglia (exc); *Delibes:* Lakmé (exc); *Verdi:* Aida (exc); *Puccini:* Bohème (exc); Turandot (exc); *Leoncavallo:* Pagliacci (exc); *Verdi:*

Trovatore (exc); *Puccini:* Madama Butterfly (exc); *Meyerbeer:* Dinorah (exc). (M. Callas, G. di Stefano, N. Gedda, T. Gobbi, Philh, La Scala Orch, Paris Cons, Paris Op Orch/T. Serafin/G. Prêtre/A. Galliera/A. Votto/H. von Karajan)

Ⓓ **CDC5 55225-2** (5/95)
Pfitzner plays and conducts Pfitzner
Pfitzner: Christ-Elflein (exc); Palestrina (exc); Duo, Op.43; Lieder, Op.7 (exc); Lieder, Op.9 (exc); Lieder, Op.10 (exc); Lieder, Op.19 (exc); Lieder, Op.22 (exc); Lieder, Op.26 (exc); Lieder, Op.29 (exc); Lieder, Op.32 (exc); Lieder, Op.40 (exc). (G. Hüsch, M. Strub, L. Hoelscher, H. Pfitzner, Berlin St Op Orch/H. Pfitzner)

Ⓓ **CDC5 55233-2** (9/95)
German Opera Arias
Korngold: Tote Stadt (exc); *Lortzing:* Zar und Zimmermann (exc); Wildschütz (exc); *Marschner:* Hans Heiling (exc); Vampyr (exc); *Weber:* Euryanthe (exc); *Spohr:* Faust (exc); *Kreutzer:* Nachtlager in Granada (exc); *Schreker:* Ferne Klang (exc); *Humperdinck:* Königskinder (exc); *Wagner:* Tannhäuser (exc); Walküre (exc). (T. Hampson, Pestalozzi Children's Ch, Munich RO/F. Luisi)

Ⓓ **CDC5 55250-2**
Farinelli and his Time
E. Duni: Demofoonte (exc); *Giacomelli:* Merope (exc); *Metastasio:* Partenza; *Farinelli:* Partenza; *Handel:* Ariodante (exc); *Broschi:* Artaserse (exc); *Hasse:* Artaserse (exc); *Ariosti:* Artaserse (exc); *Hasse:* Orfeo (exc); *Handel:* Serse (exc); *Pergolesi:* Adriano in Siria (exc). (A. Christofellis, Seicentonovecento Ens/F. Colusso)

Ⓓ **CDC5 55259-2**
The Age of the Castrato
Bononcini: Griselda (exc); *E. Duni:* Dolce compagna; Sperai vicino il lido; *Hasse:* Artaserse (exc); *Porpora:* Solfeggi; *Broschi:* Merope (exc); *Hasse:* Orfeo (exc); *E. Duni:* Demofoonte (exc); *Leo:* Catone in Utica (exc). (A. Christofellis, Inst Ens)

Ⓓ **CDC5 55350-2**
Cheryl Studer - A Portrait
R. Strauss: Frau ohne Schatten (exc); Elektra (exc); *Wagner:* Walküre (exc); Meistersinger (exc); Tristan und Isolde (exc); *Gounod:* Faust (exc); *Mozart:* Don Giovanni (exc); *Bellini:* Sonnambula (exc); *Verdi:* Vespri siciliani (exc); Attila (exc); Requiem (exc). (C. Studer, C. Sieden, U. Vinzing, A. Muff, E. Marton, R. Goldberg, S. Ramey, BRSO/W. Sawallisch/B. Haitink, Bavarian St Orch/J. Tate, Toulouse Capitole Orch/M. Plasson, VPO, La Scala Chor, La Scala Orch, Munich RO/G. Ferro/R. Muti, Bavarian Rad Chor)

Ⓓ **CDC5 55396-2** ▭ **EL5 55396-4**
Amanda Roocroft - Mozart and his Contemporaries
Mozart: Così fan tutte (exc); Don Giovanni (exc); Idomeneo (exc); Alma grande e nobil core, K578; Basta vincesti, K486a; *Cimarosa:* Artemisia (exc); Sacrificio d'Abramo (exc); *Haydn:* Berenice che fai. (A. Roocroft, ASMF/N. Marriner)

Ⓓ **CDC5 55475-2**
Itzhak Perlman - À la carte
Massenet: Thaïs (exc); *Glazunov:* Mazurka-Oberek; *Rachmaninov:* Vocalise; *Sarasate:* Zigeunerweisen; *Rimsky-Korsakov:* Russian Fantasia; *Glazunov:* Meditation, Op.32; *Tchaikovsky:* Souvenir d'un lieu cher, Op.42 (exc); *Wieniawski:* Légende, Op.17; *Kreisler:* Old Refrain; *Sarasate:* Introduction and Tarantella, Op.43; *Kreisler:* Schön Rosmarin. (I. Perlman, Abbey Road Ens/L. Foster)

Ⓓ **CDC5 55479-2** (11/95)
Wagner—Orchestral Works
Wagner: Rienzi (exc); Tristan und Isolde (exc); Meistersinger (exc); Siegfried Idyll; Parsifal (exc); Lohengrin (exc). (J. Eaglen, LCP/R. Norrington)

Ⓓ **CDC5 55540-2** ▭ **EL5 55540-4**
Roberto Alagna sings Operatic Arias
Donizetti: Lucia di Lammermoor (exc); *Massenet:* Werther (exc); *Cilea:* Arlesiana (exc); *Rossini:* Guillaume Tell (exc); *Verdi:* Rigoletto (exc); *Bizet:* Carmen (exc); *Boito:* Mefistofele (exc); *Rabaud:* Mârouf (exc); *Flotow:* Martha (exc); *Gounod:* Polyeucte (exc); *Donizetti:* Don Pasquale (exc); *Gounod:* Roméo et Juliette (exc); *Puccini:* Bohème (exc). (R. Alagna, LPO/R. Armstrong)

Ⓓ **CDC7 47008-2** (2/84)
Mozart—Die Zauberflöte (highlights)
Mozart: Zauberflöte (exc). (R. Bracht, S. Jerusalem, N. Bailey, W. Kmentt, E. Kunz, A. von Mattoni, E. Gruberová, L. Popp, M. Richardson, D. Soffel, O. Wenkel, W. Brendel, B. Lindner, H. Zednik, P. Hofmann, A. Haugland, Bavarian Rad Chor, BRSO/B. Haitink)

Ⓓ **CDC7 47014-2** (4/84)
Mozart: Opera Overtures
Mozart: Nozze di Figaro (exc); Zauberflöte (exc); Clemenza di Tito (exc); Lucio Silla (exc); Entführung (exc); Don Giovanni (exc); Idomeneo (exc); Così fan tutte (exc); Schauspieldirektor (exc). (ASMF/N. Marriner)

Ⓓ **CDC7 47019-2** (8/84)
Mozart—Opera Arias
Mozart: Rè pastore (exc); Nozze di Figaro (exc); Entführung (exc); Idomeneo (exc); Don Giovanni (exc); Così fan tutte (exc); Clemenza di Tito (exc). (L. Popp, Munich RO/L. Slatkin)

Ⓓ **CDC7 47020-2** (8/84)
Lehár: Waltzes
Lehár: Gold und Silber; Ballsirenen; Luxembourg; Ziguenerliebe; Wo die Lerche singt; Eva; Giuditta (exc). (VJSO/W. Boskovsky)

Ⓓ **CDC7 47122-2** (6/85)
Mozart: Concert and Operatic Arias
Mozart: Misera! dove son, K369; Idomeneo (exc); Ah, lo previdi, K272; Lucio Silla (exc); Idomeneo (exc); Zauberflöte (exc); Nozze di Figaro (exc). (B. Hendricks, J-L. Garcia, L. Pearson, ECO/J. Tate)

Ⓓ **CDC7 47274-2**
Verdi: Opera Choruses
Verdi: Nabucco (exc); Lombardi (exc); Macbeth (exc); Macbeth (exc); Trovatore (exc); Vespri Siciliani (exc); Forza del destino (exc); Aida (exc). (Ambrosian Op. Chor, ROH Chor, New Philh, Philh/R. Muti)

Ⓓ **CDC7 47282-2** (11/86)
Maria Callas - Operatic Recital
Cilea: Adriana Lecouvreur (exc); *Giordano:* Andrea Chénier (exc); *Catalani:* Wally (exc); *Boito:* Mefistofele (exc); *Rossini:* Barbiere di Siviglia (exc); *Meyerbeer:* Dinorah (exc); *Delibes:* Lakmé (exc); *Verdi:* Vespri siciliani (exc); *Cherubini:* Medea (exc); *Spontini:* Vestale (exc). (M. Callas, Philh/T. Serafin, La Scala Orch)

Ⓓ **CDC7 47283-2** (6/86)
Maria Callas - Mad Scenes & Bel Canto Arias
Donizetti: Anna Bolena (exc); *A. Thomas:* Hamlet (exc); *Bellini:* Pirata (exc); *Donizetti:* Fille du régiment (exc); Lucrezia Borgia (exc); Elisir d'amore (exc); *Bellini:* Pirata (exc). (M. Callas, M. Sinclair, J. Lanigan, D. Robertson, J. Rouleau, Philh Chor, Philh/N. Rescigno, A. Young/A. Tonini, Paris Cons)

Ⓓ **CDC7 47284-2** (1/86)
Elisabeth Schwarzkopf sings Operetta
Heuberger: Opernball (exc); *J. Strauss II:* Casanova (exc); *Lehár:* Zarewitsch (exc); Graf von Luxemburg (exc); Giuditta (exc); *Zeller:* Vogelhändler (exc); Obersteiger (exc); *Suppé:* Boccaccio (exc); *Millöcker:* Dubarry (exc); *Sieczyński:* Wien, du Stadt meiner Träume. (E. Schwarzkopf, chor, Philh/O. Ackermann)

Ⓓ **CDC7 47355-2** (12/86)
Mozart—Concert Arias
Mozart: Vorrei spiegarvi, K418; Exsultate, jubilate, K165; Rè pastore (exc); Basta vincesti, K486a; Idomeneo (exc); Misera! dove son, K369; Moto di gioia, K579. (K. Battle, RPO/A. Previn, B. Griffiths, D. Harris)

Ⓓ **CDC7 47398-2** (2/87)
Placido Domingo: Vienna, City of My Dreams
Lehár: Paganini (exc); Lustige Witwe (exc); Land des Lächelns (exc); *Zeller:* Vogelhändler (exc); *Kálmán:* Gräfin Mariza (exc); *Fall:* Rose von Stambul (exc); Fidele Bauer (exc); *Sieczyński:* Wien, du Stadt meiner Träume; *O. Straus:* Walzertraum (exc); *J. Strauss II:* Nacht in Venedig (exc). (P. Domingo, ECO/J. Rudel, Ambrosian Sngrs)

Ⓓ **CDC7 47454-2** (10/87)
Kiri sings Gershwin
Gershwin: Scandals 1924 (exc); Primrose (exc); Damsel in Distress (exc); Goldwyn Follies (exc); Oh, Kay! (exc); Girl Crazy (exc); Porgy and Bess (exc); Strike Up The Band I (exc); Strike Up The Band II (exc); Strike Up The Band I (exc); By Strauss. (K. Te Kanawa, NY Choral Artists, Foursome, New Princess Th Orch/J. McGlinn)

Ⓓ **CDC7 47467-2**
My Favourite Kreisler
Kreisler: Caprice viennois; Schön Rosmarin; Romance, Op. 4; Liebesfreud; Pugnani Tempo di Menuetto; Liebesleid; Cartier Chasse; Martini Preghiera; *Dvořák:* Slavonic Dances (exc); Gipsy melodies (exc); *Paganini:* Moto perpetuo, Op. 11; *Tartini:* Violin Sonatas (1732) (exc); *Rachmaninov:* Songs, Op. 38 (exc); *Gluck:* Orphée (exc); *Gaertner:* Aus Wien; *Chopin:* Mazurkas (exc). (I. Perlman, S. Sanders)

Ⓓ **CDC7 47544-2** (6/87)
French music for violin and orchestra
Chausson: Poème; *Fauré:* Berceuse, Op. 16; *Lalo:* Symphonie espagnole (exc); *Massenet:* Thaïs (exc); *Saint-Saëns:* Déluge (exc); *Berlioz:* Rêverie et caprice; *Ravel:* Tzigane. (A. Dumay, Monte Carlo PO, A. Dumay)

Ⓓ **CDC7 47717-2** (9/87)
Borodin/Rimsky-Korsakov—Orchestral Works
Borodin: Prince Igor (exc); *Rimsky-Korsakov:* Scheherazade. (Beecham Choral Soc, RPO/T. Beecham)

Ⓓ **CDC7 47730-2** (9/87)
Maria Callas sings Verdi Arias, Vol.1
Verdi: Macbeth (exc); Nabucco (exc); Ernani (exc); Don Carlo (exc); Vespri Siciliani (exc); Lombardi (exc); Ballo in maschera (exc); Aida (exc). (M. Callas, Philh, Paris Cons/N. Rescigno)

Ⓓ **CDC7 47841-2** (10/87)
Puccini: Opera Recital
Puccini: Turandot (exc); Madama Butterfly (exc); Manon Lescaut (exc); Gianni Schicchi (exc); Tosca (exc); Bohème (exc); Villi (exc); Rondine (exc). (M. Caballé, LSO/C. Mackerras)

Ⓓ **CDC7 47943-2** (9/87)
Maria Callas sings Verdi Arias, Vol.2
Verdi: Corsaro (exc); Trovatore (exc); Ballo in maschera (exc); Attila (exc); Otello (exc); Aroldo (exc); Don Carlo (exc). (M. Callas, Paris Op Orch, Paris Cons/N. Rescigno)

Ⓓ **CDC7 47966-2** (12/87)
Puccini and Bellini Arias
Puccini: Manon Lescaut (exc); Madama Butterfly (exc); Bohème (exc); Suor Angelica (exc); Gianni Schicchi (exc); Turandot (exc); *Bellini:* Sonnambula (exc). (M. Callas, Philh, La Scala Orch/T. Serafin)

Ⓓ **CDC7 49005-2**
Maria Callas - Operatic Arias
Massenet: Werther (exc); *Gounod:* Faust (exc); *Rossini:* Cenerentola (exc); Guillaume Tell (exc); Semiramide (exc); *Mozart:* Don Giovanni (exc); Nozze di Figaro (exc); *Weber:* Oberon (exc). (M. Callas, Paris Cons/G. Prêtre/N. Rescigno)

Ⓓ **CDC7 49059-2** (2/88)
Callas à Paris
Gluck: Orphée (exc); Alceste (1776) (exc); Iphigénie en Tauride (exc); *Bizet:* Carmen (exc); Pêcheurs de Perles (exc); *Saint-Saëns:* Samson et Dalila (exc); *Gounod:* Roméo et Juliette (exc); *A. Thomas:* Mignon (exc); *Massenet:* Cid (exc); Manon (exc); *G. Charpentier:* Louise (exc); *Berlioz:* Damnation de Faust (exc). (M. Callas, FRNO, Paris Cons/G. Prêtre)

Ⓓ **CDC7 49067-2** (12/88)
Opera Arias and Duets
Verdi: Rigoletto (exc); Traviata (exc); *Gounod:* Faust (exc); *Rossini:* Semiramide (exc); *Delibes:* Lakmé (exc); *Donizetti:* Elisir d'amore (exc); Lucia di Lammermoor (exc); Fille du Régiment (exc). (J. Anderson, Alfredo Kraus, Paris Op Orch/M. Veltri)

Ⓓ **CDC7 49148-2** (1/89)
Romanzas de Zarzuelas
Guerrero y Torres: Gavilanes (exc); *F. Alonso:* Coplas de Ronda (exc); *Sorozábal:* Del manojo de rosas (exc); *Moreno Torroba:* Luisa Fernanda (exc); *Sorozábal:* Tabernera del puerto (exc); *Bretón:* Dolores (exc); *Moreno Torroba:* Maravilla (exc); *Soutullo:* Del Soto del Parral (exc); *Guerrero y Torres:* Rosa del azafrán (exc); *Serrano:* Canción del olvidó (exc); *Chapí:* Bruja (exc); *Guerrero y Torres:* Huésped del Sevillano (exc); *F. Alonso:* Parranda (exc). (P. Domingo, Madrid Zarzuela Chor, Madrid Rondalla Lírica, Madrid SO/M. Moreno-Buendia)

Ⓓ **CDC7 49155-2** (2/89)
Rossini: Overtures
Rossini: Barbiere di Siviglia (exc); Scala di seta (exc); Semiramide (exc); Guillaume Tell (exc); Cenerentola (exc); Gazza ladra (exc); Cambiale di matrimonio (exc). (ASMF/N. Marriner)

Ⓓ **CDC7 49179-2** (7/90)
Handel—Arias
Handel: Acis and Galatea (exc); Giulio Cesare (exc); Joshua (exc); Allegro, il penseroso ed il moderato (exc); Messiah (exc); Solomon (exc); Alcina (exc). (K. Battle, ASMF/N. Marriner)

Ⓓ **CDC7 49219-2** (1/89)
Operas Arias for Trumpet
Mozart: Zauberflöte (exc); Entführung (exc); *Bellini:* Norma (exc); Puritani (exc); *Delibes:* Lakmé (exc); *Donizetti:* Elisir d'amore (exc); Don Pasquale (exc); *Verdi:* Rigoletto (exc); *Ponchielli:* Gioconda (exc); *Rossini:* Semiramide (exc); *Offenbach:* Contes d'Hoffmann (exc); *Puccini:* Bohème (exc); *Bizet:* Carmen (exc). (M. André, Toulouse Capitole Chor, Toulouse Capitole Orch/M. Plasson)

CDC7 49319-2 (4/89)
Lucia Popp sings Slavonic Opera Arias
Dvořák: Armida (exc); Rusalka (exc); *Janáček:* Jenufa (exc); *Smetana:* Bartered Bride (exc); Dalibor (exc); *Prokofiev:* War and Peace (exc); *Tchaikovsky:* Queen of Spades (exc); Eugene Onegin (exc). (L. Popp, Munich RO/S. Soltesz)

CDC7 49428-2
Maria Callas - The Unknown Recordings
Wagner: Tristan und Isolde (exc); *Verdi:* Don Carlo (exc); *Bellini:* Pirata (exc); *Rossini:* Cenerentola (exc); Guillaume Tell (exc); Semiramide (exc); *Verdi:* Lombardi (exc); Vespri Siciliani (exc); Attila (exc). (M. Callas, Athens Fest Orch, Concertgebouw, Philh, Paris Op Orch/A. Votto/N. Rescigno/A. Tonini)

CDC7 49490-2
Beethoven—Orchestral Works
Beethoven: Symphony 3; Consecration of the House Ov; Fidelio (exc). (Philadelphia/R. Muti)

CDC7 49502-2
Maria Callas—The Voice of the Century
Bellini: Norma (exc); Sonnambula (exc); *Rossini:* Barbiere di Siviglia (exc); *Verdi:* Traviata (exc); Rigoletto (exc); *Puccini:* Tosca (exc); Madama Butterfly (exc); *Catalani:* Wally (exc); *Puccini:* Turandot (exc); *Bizet:* Carmen (exc); *Massenet:* Werther (exc). (M. Callas, Alfredo Kraus, R. Ercolani, C. Forti, W. Dickie, La Scala Chor, La Scala Orch, Philh, Lisbon San Carlos Nat Th Orch, Paris Cons, Paris Op Orch/T. Serafin/A. Votto/H. von Karajan/A. Galliera/F. Ghione/G. Prêtre)

CDC7 49503-2 (12/89)
Leoncavallo—Pagliacci
Leoncavallo: Pagliacci (Cpte). (J. Björling, V. de los Angeles, L. Warren, R. Merrill, P. Franke, Columbus Boychoir, R. Shaw Chorale, RCA Victor Orch/R. Cellini)

CDC7 49652-2 (9/88)
Chabrier—Orchestral Works
Chabrier: Joyeuse marche; España; Suite pastorale; Roi malgré lui (exc); Prélude pastorale; Bourrée fantasque; Pièces pittoresques (exc). (Toulouse Capitole Orch/M. Plasson)

CDC7 49700-2 (6/88)
Lucia Popp sings Viennese Operetta
Lehár: Lustige Witwe (exc); Giuditta (exc); Land des Lächelns (exc); Friederike (exc); *Suppé:* Boccaccio (exc); *Millöcker:* Dubarry (exc); *Zeller:* Obersteiger (exc); *Lincke:* Frau Luna (exc); *J. Strauss II:* Tänzerin Fanny Elssler (exc); Casanova (exc); *Stolz:* Favorit (exc); Frühjahrsparade (exc); *Dostal:* Ungarische Hochzeit (exc). (L. Popp, Ambrosian Op. Chor, ASMF/N. Marriner)

CDC7 49759-2 (11/88)
Wagner: Opera Scenes and Arias
Wagner: Tristan und Isolde (exc); Tannhäuser (exc); Fliegende Holländer (exc); Götterdämmerung (exc). (J. Norman, Ambrosian Op Chor, LPO/K. Tennstedt)

CDC7 49797-2 (1/90)
Mussorgsky—Orchestral Works
Mussorgsky: Pictures; Night on the Bare Mountain; Khovanshchina (exc). (Oslo PO/M. Jansons)

CDC7 49811-2 (9/89)
Covent Garden Gala Concert
Meyerbeer: Africaine (exc); *Puccini:* Bohème (exc); Fanciulla del West (exc); *Verdi:* Macbeth (exc); Aida (exc); Otello (exc); Otello (exc); Traviata (exc); *J. Strauss II:* Fledermaus (exc); *Moreno Torroba:* Chulapona (exc); *Soutullo:* Ultimo Romantico (exc). (C. Studer, E. Randová, P. Domingo, T. Allen, ROHO/J. Barker)

CDC7 49819-2
Christmas Salon
Németi: Weihnachts-Kinderlieder; *Handel:* Serse (exc); *Humperdinck:* Hänsel und Gretel (exc); *Schmalstich:* Peterchens Mondfahrt (exc); *Gounod:* Ave Maria; *Kahnt:* Stille Nacht; *Rhode:* Weihnachten; *Heykens:* Ave Maria; *Lindemann:* Weihnachtsmann kommt. (Cölln Salon Orch)

CDC7 49849-2 (12/89)
Famous Opera Choruses
Beethoven: Fidelio (exc); *Berlioz:* Troyens (exc); *Bizet:* Carmen (exc); *Donizetti:* Lucia di Lammermoor (exc); *Giordano:* Andrea Chénier (exc); *Mascagni:* Cavalleria Rusticana (exc); *Verdi:* Aida (exc); Nabucco (exc); Otello (exc); Trovatore (exc); *Wagner:* Lohengrin (exc); *Weber:* Freischütz (exc). (J.M. Ainsley, A. Miles, H. Field, Haberdashers' Aske's Sch Ch, ROH Chor, ROHO/B. Haitink)

CDC7 49863-2 (2/90)
French Opera Arias
G. Charpentier: Louise (exc); *Debussy:* Enfant prodigue (exc); *Berlioz:* Damnation de Faust (exc); *Offenbach:* Contes d'Hoffmann (exc); *Gluck:* Iphigénie en Tauride (exc); *Massenet:* Manon (exc); Cid (exc); Hérodiade (exc); *Bizet:* Pêcheurs de perles (exc); *Verdi:* Don Carlos (exc). (K. Te Kanawa, ROHO/J. Tate)

CDC7 49993-2 (9/90)
Janáček—Fate
Janáček: Fate (Cpte). (H. Field, P. Langridge, K. Harries, P. Bronder, S. Kale, C. Teare, E. Gaskell, D. Hood, Mary Davies, G. Keeble, B. Mora, M. Holland, C. Bell, R. Moseley-Morgan, G. Rhys-Davies, P. Lloyd-Evans, R. Mason, T. German, F. Manning, C. Edwards, S. Linay, Y. Jones, M. Preston-Roberts, WNO Chor, WNO Orch/C. Mackerras)

CDC7 54004-2 (2/91)
Chabrier: Vocal & Orchestral Works
Chabrier: Gwendoline (exc); Gwendoline (exc); Ode à la musique; Habanera; Valses romantiques; Larghetto; Sulamite. (B. Hendricks, S. Mentzer, P. del Vescovo, Toulouse Mid-Pyrénées Chor, Toulouse Capitole Orch/M. Plasson)

CDC7 54016-2
Tenorissimo!
Leoncavallo: Pagliacci (exc); *Ponchielli:* Gioconda (exc); *Donizetti:* Elisir d'amore (exc); *Rossini:* Guillaume Tell (exc); *Puccini:* Bohème (exc); *Bellini:* Puritani (exc); *Verdi:* Otello (exc); *Giordano:* Andrea Chénier (exc); *Bizet:* Carmen (exc); *Puccini:* Tosca (exc); *Massenet:* Manon (exc); *Bizet:* Pêcheurs de perles (exc); *Verdi:* Trovatore (exc); *Puccini:* Turandot (exc); *Gounod:* Roméo et Juliette (exc); *Massenet:* Werther (exc); *Verdi:* Requiem (exc); Aida (exc). (E. Caruso, S. Cottone, B. Gigli, orch/C. Sabajno, T. Schipa, G. Thill/E. Bigot, J. Björling/N. Grevillius, G. di Stefano, M. Callas, N. Rossi-Lemeni, C. Forti, La Scala Chor, La Scala Orch/T. Serafin, M. del Monaco, Milan SO/A. Quadri, F. Corelli, Rome Op Orch/G. Santini, J. Vickers, Paris Op Orch/R. Frühbeck de Burgos, C. Bergonzi, Paris Cons/G. Prêtre, N. Gedda, FRNO, A. Vanzo, F. Bonisolli, Berlin Deutsche Op Chor, BPO/H. von Karajan, J. Carreras, Rhine Op Chor, Strasbourg PO/A. Lombard, Alfredo Kraus, Toulouse Capitole Orch/M. Plasson, N. Shicoff, L. Pavarotti/R. Muti, P. Domingo, New Philh)

CDC7 54053-2 (11/90)
Roman Heroes
Mascagni: Nerone (exc); *Handel:* Giulio Cesare (exc); *Bellini:* Norma (exc); *Berlioz:* Benvenuto Cellini (exc); *Verdi:* Attila (exc); *Handel:* Ezio (exc); *Spontini:* Vestale (exc); *Wagner:* Rienzi (exc); *Puccini:* Tosca (exc). (P. Domingo, Ambrosian Op Chor, National PO/E. Kohn, P. Domingo jnr)

CDC7 54056-2 (10/90)
Suppé—Overtures
Suppé: Leichte Kavallerie (exc); Tantalusqualen (exc); Morgen, ein Mittag, ein Abend in Wien (exc); Wiener Jubel (exc); Dichter und Bauer (exc); Irrfahrt um's Glück (exc); Frau Meisterin (exc); Pique Dame (exc). (ASMF/N. Marriner)

CDC7 54057-2
J. Strauss II—Vocal Arrangements
J. Strauss II: Tritsch-Tratsch; Kaiser, Op. 437; Rosen aus dem Süden; Nacht in Venedig (exc); Demolirer-Polka, Op. 269; Fledermaus (exc); Vergnügungszug; G'schichten aus dem Wienerwald, Op. 325; Wiener Blut; Neue Pizzicato-Polka, Op. 449; Indigo und die vierzig Räuber (exc); Perpetuum mobile; Blauen Donau, Op. 314. (Kings Sngrs, S. Meyer, M. Barrueco, G. Hörtnagel)

CDC7 54062-2 (11/90)
Kiri Te Kanawa—Italian Opera Arias
Puccini: Turandot (exc); Suor Angelica (exc); *Cilea:* Adriana Lecouvreur (exc); *Giordano:* Andrea Chénier (exc); *Leoncavallo:* Pagliacci (exc); *Boito:* Mefistofele (exc); *Verdi:* Trovatore (exc); Traviata (exc); Forza del destino (exc). (K. Te Kanawa, LSO/Myung-Whun Chung)

CDC7 54089-2 (12/91)
J. Strauss II—Waltzes & Overtures
J. Strauss II: Künstlerleben, Op. 316; Rosen aus dem Süden; Zigeunerbaron (exc); G'schichten aus dem Wienerwald, Op. 325; Kaiser, Op. 437; Fledermaus (exc); Blauen Donau, Op. 314. (LPO/F. Welser-Möst)

CDC7 54091-2 (4/91)
Rossini—Overtures
Rossini: Scala di seta (exc); Signor Bruschino (exc); Italiana in Algeri (exc); Barbiere di Siviglia (exc); Gazza ladra (exc); Semiramide (exc); Guillaume Tell (exc). (LCP/R. Norrington)

CDC7 54108-2 (2/91)
Tchaikovsky—Violin Works
Tchaikovsky: Violin Concerto; *Tartini:* Devil's Trill Sonata; *Kreisler:* Liebesleid; *Prokofiev:* Love for 3 Oranges Suite (exc); *Bloch:* Baal Shem (exc); *Wieniawski:* Etudes-Caprices, Op.18 (exc); *Tchaikovsky:* String Quartet 1 (exc); *Bazzini:* Ronde des lutins. (I. Perlman, Israel PO/Z. Mehta, J.G. Guggenheim)

CDC7 54237-2 (2/92)
Berlioz—Orchestral Works
Berlioz: Harold in Italy; Benvenuto Cellini (exc); Waverley. (G. Caussé, Toulouse Capitole Orch/M. Plasson)

CDC7 54266-2 (3/92)
Domingo and Perlman—Together
Toselli: Serenade; *Ponce:* Estrellita; *Massenet:* Élégie; *Kálmán:* Csárdásfürstin (exc); *Kreisler:* Old Refrain; *Rachmaninov:* Songs, Op. 4 (exc); *Offenbach:* Contes d'Hoffmann (exc); *Tosti:* Ideale; *Traditional:* Danny Boy; *Handel:* Serse (exc); *Romberg:* Student Prince (exc); *Godard:* Jocelyn (exc); *Tchaikovsky:* Songs, Op. 6 (exc); *R. Strauss:* Lieder, Op. 27 (exc). (P. Domingo, I. Perlman, NY Studio Orch/J. Tunick)

CDC7 54312-2
Sprezzatura
Monteverdi: Madrigals, Bk.7 (exc); *Caccini:* Nuove musiche (1602) (exc); *Anon:* Sinfonia; *Lambardi:* Aria di Cupido; *Anon:* Gagliarda; *Gesualdo:* Canzon francese; Gagliarda del Principe di Venosa; *Rore:* Anchor che col partire; *Kapsperger:* Chitarrone Book IV (exc); *Landi:* Mort d'Orfeo (exc); *G. Strozzi:* Sonata per basso solo; *Vitali:* Toccata; Capritio sopra otto figure; *Handel:* Qual fior che all'alba ride; Clori, mia bella Clori; *Vivaldi:* Trio, RV82. (Tragicomedia)

CDC7 54321-2
Mozart—Le nozze di Figaro (highlights)
Mozart: Nozze di Figaro (exc). (T. Allen, K. Battle, J. Hynninen, M. Price, A. Murray, K. Rydl, M. Nicolesco, A. Ramirez, E. Gavazzi, P. Pace, F. De Grandis, Vienna St Op Concert Ch, VPO/R. Muti)

CDC7 54322-2
Offenbach—Les contes d'Hoffmann (highlights)
Offenbach: Contes d'Hoffmann (exc). (N. Shicoff, A. Murray, L. Serra, R. Plowright, J. Norman, J. Van Dam, R. Tear, J. Taillon, M. Vanaud, D. Duesing, T. Dran, Brussels Nat Op Chor, Brussels Nat Op Orch/S. Cambreling)

CDC7 54323-2
Mozart—Don Giovanni (highlights)
Mozart: Don Giovanni (exc). (W. Shimell, S. Ramey, C. Studer, C. Vaness, F. Lopardo, S. Mentzer, N. de Carolis, VPO/R. Muti)

CDC7 54324-2
Puccini—Tosca (highlights)
Puccini: Tosca (exc). (R. Scotto, P. Domingo, R. Bruson, A. Velis, R. Capecchi, P. Hudson, I. Perlman, Ambrosian Op Chor, St Clement Danes Sch Ch, Philh/James Levine)

CDC7 54325-2 **EL754325-4**
Gershwin—Porgy and Bess (highlights)
Gershwin: Porgy and Bess (exc). (W. White, C. Haymon, D. Evans, C. Clarey, H. Blackwell, B. Hubbard, M. Simpson, Gregg Baker, B. Coleman, J. Worthy, M. Wallace, M. Brathwaite, A. Paige, P. Ingram, W. Marshall, Glyndebourne Fest Chor, LPO/S. Rattle)

CDC7 54326-2
Verdi—La forza del destino (highlights)
Verdi: Forza del destino (exc). (M. Freni, P. Domingo, G. Zancanaro, D. Zajick, P. Plishka, S. Bruscantini, S. Sammaritano, La Scala Chor, La Scala Orch/R. Muti)

CDC7 54327-2
Humperdinck—Hänsel und Gretel (highlights)
Humperdinck: Hänsel und Gretel (exc). (A.S. von Otter, B. Bonney, M. Lipovšek, H. Schwarz, A. Schmidt, B. Hendricks, Tolz Boys' Ch, BRSO/J. Tate)

CDC7 54328-2
Wagner—Die Walküre (highlights)
Wagner: Walküre (exc). (E. Marton, C. Studer, J. Morris, R. Goldberg, M. Salminen, W. Meier, A. Soldh, R. Falcon, U. Walther, U. Kunz, S. Herman, M. Hintermeier, C. Watkinson, M. Lilowa, BRSO/B. Haitink)

CDC7 54329-2 (3/92)
Domingo sings Mozart Arias
Mozart: Finta Giardiniera (exc); Idomeneo (exc); Don Giovanni (exc); Don Giovanni (exc); Entführung (exc); Clemenza di Tito (exc); Davidde penitente, K469 (exc); Zauberflöte (exc); Nozze di Figaro (exc); Così fan tutte (exc); Così fan tutte (exc). (P. Domingo, C. Vaness, Munich RO/E. Kohn)

CDC7 54330-2 (1/93)
Arrangements for Trumpet and Organ
Bach: Cantata 75 (exc); *Purcell:* Fairy Queen, Z629 (exc); *Stanley:* Sonata in D minor; *Handel:* Oboe Concertos (exc); *Bach:* Cantata 22 (exc); *Corelli:* Oboe Concerto; *Loeillet de Gant:* Recorder Sonatas, Op.3 (exc);

Boismortier: Sonatas, Op.91 (exc); *Bach:* Chorales, BWV651-668 (exc). (M. André, H. Bilgram)

Ⓓ **CDC7 54352-2** (1/93)
Sarah Chang - Debut
Sarasate: Carmen Fantasy; *Elgar:* Salut d'amour; *Khachaturian:* Gayaneh (exc); *Elgar:* Capricieuse; *Kreisler:* Pugnani Tempo di Menuetto; *Paganini:* Caprices, Op. 1 (exc); *Chopin:* Nocturnes (exc); *Shostakovich:* Preludes, Op. 34 (exc); *Gershwin:* Porgy and Bess (exc); *Liszt:* Consolations, S172 (exc); *Tchaikovsky:* Souvenir d'un lieu cher, Op. 42 (exc); *Prokofiev:* Love for 3 Oranges Suite (exc). (S. Chang, S. Rivers)

Ⓓ **CDC7 54358-2**
Gounod—Faust (highlights)
Gounod: Faust (exc). (R. Leech, J. Van Dam, C. Studer, T. Hampson, Toulouse Capitole Chor, Toulouse Capitole Orch/M. Plasson)

Ⓓ **CDC7 54411-2** (7/92)
On Wings of Song
Purcell: Birthday Ode, Z323 (exc); Indian Queen, Z630 (exc); Lost is my quiet for ever, Z502; King Arthur, Z628 (exc); What can we poor females do?, Z518; *Mendelssohn:* Wasserfahrt; Duets, Op.63 (exc); Lieder, Op.34 (exc); Lieder, Op.19a (exc); Abendlied; *Rossini:* Soirées musicales (exc); Péchés de vieillesse I (exc); Soirées musicales (exc); Duetto buffo di due gatti; *Gounod:* Siesta; *Delibes:* Trois oiseaux; *Massenet:* Rêvons, c'est l'heure; Joie!; *Paladilhe:* Au bord de l'eau; *Aubert:* Cache-cache; *Balfe:* Trust her not; *Sullivan:* Coming home; *Quilter:* Shakespeare Songs, Op. 23 (exc); *Britten:* Ballads (1937). (F. Lott, A. Murray, G. Johnson)

Ⓓ **CDC7 54437-2** (2/93)
Callas Rarities
Beethoven: Ah! perfido, Op.65; *Mozart:* Don Giovanni (exc); Entführung (exc); *Weber:* Oberon (exc); *Rossini:* Armida (exc); *Donizetti:* Lucrezia Borgia (exc); *Verdi:* Don Carlo (exc); Vespri Siciliani (exc); Trovatore (exc); Lombardi (exc); Aida (exc). (M. Callas, F. Corelli, Paris Cons, MMF Orch, Rome RAI Orch, Philh, Paris Op Orch/N. Rescigno/T. Serafin/A. Simonetto/A. Tonini/G. Prêtre)

Ⓓ **CDC7 54438-2** (9/92)
Cherubini—Overtures
Cherubini: Elisa (exc); Medea (exc); Hôtellerie portugaise (exc); Deux journées (exc); Anacréon (exc); Faniska (exc); Abencérages (exc); Concert Overture. (ASMF/N. Marriner)

Ⓓ **CDC7 54484-2**
Verdi—Opera Choruses
Verdi: Nabucco (exc); Ernani (exc); Lombardi (exc); Attila (exc); Trovatore (exc); Rigoletto (exc); Forza del destino (exc); Macbeth (exc); Requiem (exc). (M. Freni, D. Zajick, La Scala Chor, La Scala Orch/R. Muti)

Ⓓ **CDC7 54490-2**
Donizetti—Don Pasquale (highlights)
Donizetti: Don Pasquale (exc). (M. Freni, G. Winbergh, L. Nucci, S. Bruscantini, Philh/R. Muti)

Ⓓ **CDC7 54492-2**
Mozart—Die Zauberflöte (highlights)
Mozart: Zauberflöte (exc). (D. Upshaw, A. Schmidt, B. Hoch, A. Rolfe Johnson, LCP/R. Norrington)

Ⓓ **CDC7 54493-2**
R. Strauss—Der Rosenkavalier (highlights)
R. Strauss: Rosenkavalier (exc). (K. Te Kanawa, A.S. von Otter, B. Hendricks, K. Rydl, F. Grundheber, C. Powell, R. Leech, A. Sramek, Dresden St Op Chor, Staatskapelle Dresden/B. Haitink)

Ⓓ **CDC7 54494-2**
R. Strauss—Die Frau ohne Schatten (highlights)
R. Strauss: Frau ohne Schatten (exc). (R. Kollo, C. Studer, A. Muff, U. Vinzing, H. Schwarz, BRSO/W. Sawallisch)

Ⓓ **CDC7 54495-2**
Verdi—Rigoletto (highlights)
Verdi: Rigoletto (exc). (G. Zancanaro, D. Dessì, V. La Scola, P. Burchuladze, La Scala Chor, La Scala Orch/R. Muti)

Ⓓ **CDC7 54524-2**
The José Carreras Album
Mascagni: Cavalleria rusticana (exc); *Bizet:* Carmen (exc); *Puccini:* Turandot (exc); *Gounod:* Faust (exc); Roméo et Juliette (exc); *Lalo:* Roi d'Ys (exc); *Halévy:* Juive (exc); *Offenbach:* Périchole (exc); *Leoncavallo:* Pagliacci (exc); *Verdi:* Don Carlo (exc); Macbeth (exc); Aida (exc). (J. Carreras, J. Hamari, A. Varnay, M. Freni, P. Plishka, P. Cappuccilli, A. Baltsa, R. Raimondi, Ambrosian Op Chor, Rhine Op Chor, Philh, ROHO, Strasbourg PO, Toulouse Capitole Orch, BPO, New Philh, VPO/R. Muti/J. Delacôte/A. Lombard/M. Plasson/H. von Karajan)

Ⓓ **CDC7 54581-2** (4/93)
R.Strauss—Orchestral Music from Operas
R. Strauss: Intermezzo Interludes (exc); *R.Strauss:* Capriccio (exc); *R. Strauss:* Schweigsame Frau (exc); *R.Strauss:* Guntram (exc); Frau ohne Schatten (exc). (Rotterdam PO/J. Tate)

Ⓓ **CDC7 54583-2** (12/92)
Wagner—Overtures and Orchestral Works
Wagner: Meistersinger (exc); Tristan und Isolde (exc); Tannhäuser (exc); Götterdämmerung (exc); Walküre (exc); Lohengrin (exc); Rienzi (exc). (Oslo PO/M. Jansons)

Ⓓ **CDC7 54585-2** (3/93)
Wolf-Ferrari—Overtures & Intermezzi
Wolf-Ferrari: Segreto di Susanna (exc); Quattro rusteghi (exc); Dama boba (exc); Campiello (exc); Amore medico (exc); Gioielli della Madonna (exc). (ASMF/N. Marriner)

Ⓓ **CDC7 54586-2** (8/93)
Broadway Showstoppers
Bernstein: Pennsylvania Avenue (exc); *Gershwin:* Capitol Revue (exc); *Kern:* O Lady, Lady (exc); Sunny (exc); Sweet Adeline (exc); Very Warm for May (exc); *A. Schwartz:* Band Wagon (exc); Between the Devil (exc); *Weill:* Knickerbocker Holiday (exc); *Youmans:* No, No, Nanette (exc). (K. Criswell, R. Luker, J. Kaye, L. Richardson, T. Miller, J. Lehman, G. Dvorsky, B. Barrett, C. Groenendaal, K. Colson, D. Gaines, Ambrosian Sngrs, London Sinfonietta/J. McGlinn)

Ⓓ **CDC7 54610-2** (4/93)
R.Strauss conducts Strauss
R. Strauss: Alpensinfonie; Rosenkavalier film. (Bavarian St Orch, Tivoli Augmented Orch/R. Strauss)

Ⓓ **CDC7 54626-2** (8/93)
Operetta Arias
Lehár: Giuditta (exc); Lustige Witwe (exc); Friederike (exc); *Stolz:* Favorit (exc); *Zeller:* Vogelhändler (exc); *J. Strauss II:* Fledermaus (exc); *Messager:* Madame Chrysanthème (exc); Amour masqué (exc); *Offenbach:* Vie parisienne (exc); Voyage dans la lune (exc); *Sullivan:* Pirates of Penzance; Mikado (exc); *Romberg:* New Moon (exc); *F. Loewe:* My Fair Lady (exc); *Herbert:* Naughty Marietta (exc). (B. Hendricks, C. Henry, S. Minty, L. Richardson, Ambrosian Sngrs, Philh/L. Foster, H. Bean, G. Quilico)

Ⓓ **CDC7 54643-2** (12/94)
Rossini—Bicentenary Gala Concert
Rossini: Siège de Corinthe (exc); Donna del lago (exc); Cenerentola (exc); Stabat mater (exc); Guillaume Tell (exc); Petite Messe Solennelle (exc); Barbiere di Siviglia (exc); Zelmira (exc); Viaggio a Reims (exc). (M. Fortuna, D. Voigt, M. Horne, K. Kuhlmann, M. Lerner, F. von Stade, R. Blake, C. Estep, C. Merritt, T. Hampson, J. Opalach, H. Runey, G. Hogan, S. Ramey, NY Concert Chorale, St Luke's Orch/R. Norrington)

Ⓓ **CDC7 54702-2** ▭ **EL754702-4**
Maria Callas - La Divina
Puccini: Madama Butterfly (exc); *Bizet:* Carmen (exc); *Catalani:* Wally (exc); *Rossini:* Barbiere di Siviglia (exc); *Bellini:* Norma (exc); *Saint-Saëns:* Samson et Dalila (exc); *Verdi:* Rigoletto (exc); Traviata (exc); *Gounod:* Roméo et Juliette (exc); *Puccini:* Bohème (exc); *Mozart:* Don Giovanni (exc); *Mascagni:* Cavalleria Rusticana (exc); *Ponchielli:* Gioconda (exc); *Puccini:* Gianni Schicchi (exc); Turandot (exc); Tosca (exc). (M. Callas, E. Ticozzi, Alfredo Kraus, La Scala Chor, La Scala Orch, Philh, FRNO, Paris Cons, Lisbon San Carlos Nat Th Orch/T. Serafin/G. Prêtre/F. Ghione/N. Rescigno/A. Votto)

Ⓓ **CDC7 54776-2** (5/93)
René Kollo sings Wagner and Strauss
Wagner: Wesendonk Lieder; Tristan und Isolde (exc); *R. Strauss:* Lieder, Op.33 (exc); *Wagner:* Walküre (exc); *R. Strauss:* Vier letzte Lieder (exc). (R. Kollo, I. Haubold, Berlin Deutsche Op Orch/C. Thielemann)

Ⓓ **CDC7 54778-2**
Tchaikovsky—The Dance Album
Tchaikovsky: Swan Lake (exc); Symphony 3 (exc); Serenade, Op.48 (exc); Piano Trio, Op.50 (exc); Eugene Onegin (exc); Sleeping Beauty (exc); Symphony 5 (exc); Nutcracker (exc). (Chung Trio, LSO/A. Previn/J. Barbirolli, Philh/R. Muti/J. Lanchbery, RPO/T. Beecham, Ambrosian Sngrs)

Ⓓ **CDC7 54785-2**
Harry Enfield's Guide to Opera
Verdi: Traviata (exc); Rigoletto (exc); Nabucco (exc); *Puccini:* Gianni Schicchi (exc); Turandot (exc); Bohème (exc); Madama Butterfly (exc); Tosca (exc); *Mozart:* Don Giovanni (exc); Nozze di Figaro (exc); Nozze di Figaro (exc); *Bizet:* Carmen (exc); Pêcheurs de perles (exc). (C. Baker, J. Rodgers, Anne Dawson, L. Kitchen, J. Cairns, C. Powell, D.M. Anderson, E. Barham, K. Latham, D. Maxwell, S. Dowson, B. Budd, A. Michaels-Moore, Op North Chor, English Northern Philh/P. Daniel)

Ⓓ **CDC7 54838-2** (1/94)
Franz Lehár
Lehár: Lustige Witwe (exc); Zigeunerliebe (exc); Eva (exc); Paganini (exc); Zarewitsch (exc); Friederike (exc); Land des Lächelns (exc); Schön ist die Welt (exc); Giuditta (exc). (E. Réthy, M. Reining, V. Schwarz, J. Novotná, R. Tauber, VPO, Vienna SO, Berlin Staatskapelle/F. Lehár)

Ⓓ **CDC7 54851-2** (1/94)
Gershwin—Blue Monday, etc
Gershwin: Blue Monday (Cpte); Piano Concerto; *Levant:* Caprice. (A. Burton, G. Hopkins, W. Sharp, A. Woodley, J.J. Offenbach, L. Stifelman, Concordia/M. Alsop)

Ⓓ **CDEMTVD59** ⊙ **EMTVD59**
Classic Experience 3
Dvořák: Symphony 9 (exc); *Smetana:* Má Vlast (exc); *Rossini:* Barbiere di Siviglia (exc); *Verdi:* Traviata (exc); *J. Strauss II:* Fledermaus (exc); *Mendelssohn:* Symphony 4 (exc); *Tchaikovsky:* Nutcracker Suite (exc); *Chopin:* Waltzes (exc); *Mozart:* Symphony 40 (exc); *Elgar:* Chanson de Matin; *Rodrigo:* Concierto de Aranjuez (exc); *Elgar:* Symphony 1 (exc); *Villa-Lobos:* Bachianas Brasileiras 5 (exc); *Bizet:* Pêcheurs de Perles (exc); *Debussy:* Suite Bergamasque (exc); *Leoncavallo:* Pagliacci (exc); *Verdi:* Nabucco (exc); *Bach:* Cantata 208 (exc); *Beethoven:* Piano Concerto 5 (exc); *Mendelssohn:* Hebrides (exc); *Rimsky-Korsakov:* Scheherazade (exc); *Prokofiev:* Peter and the Wolf (exc); *Bizet:* Arlésienne Suites (exc); *Luigini:* Ballet égyptien (exc); *Rimsky-Korsakov:* Tale of Tsar Saltan (exc); *Ponchielli:* Gioconda (exc); *Khachaturian:* Gayaneh (exc); *Dukas:* Apprenti Sorcier (exc); *Stravinsky:* Rite of Spring (exc); *Chabrier:* España; *Tchaikovsky:* Capriccio italien (exc); *Beethoven:* Symphony 9 (exc). (Alfredo Kraus, R. Scotto, D. Alexeev, A. Romero, B. Hendricks, E. Blanc, N. Gedda, D. Adni, J. Carreras, Emil Gilels, J. Morris, Ambrosian Op Chor, Westminster Ch, Oslo PO, Staatskapelle Dresden, Philh, Munich RO, BPO, RPO, ASMF, LPO, Paris Opéra-Comique Orch, Cleveland Orch, LSO, Philadelphia, Sinfonia of London/M. Jansons/P. Berglund/R. Muti/P. Domingo/K. Tennstedt/A. Previn/N. Marriner/A. Boult/E. Bátiz/P. Dervaux/G. Szell/S. Edwards/H. von Karajan/A. Fistoulari/R. Irving/A. Khachaturian/P. Kletzki)

Ⓓ **CDGO2039**
Music for a Country Cottage
Coates: Merrymakers; *C. Williams:* Starlings; *Collins:* Vanity Fair; *Tomlinson:* Little Serenade; English folk-dances Suite 1; *Melachrino:* Woodland Revel; *Delius:* Village Romeo and Juliet (exc); *Bastow:* Galloping Major; *Gardiner:* Shepherd Fennell's Dance; *Binge:* Watermill; Sailing by; *Farnon:* A la claire fontaine; *A. Langford:* Waltz for Strings; *Hanmer:* Pastorale; *Coleridge Taylor:* Petite Suite de Concert (exc); *Bayco:* Elizabethan Masque; *C.A. Gibbs:* Fancy Dress (exc). (PAO, orch, LSO, Light Music Soc Orch, New Century Orch, Philh/G. Vinter/C. Williams/G. Weldon/J. Barbirolli/G. Melachrino/S. Torch/V. Dunn/Johnny Scott)

Ⓓ **CDH5 65072-2** (6/94)
Glyndebourne Recorded - 1934-1994
Mozart: Nozze di Figaro (exc); Così fan tutte (exc); Don Giovanni (exc); *Gay:* Beggar's Opera (exc); *Mozart:* Così fan tutte (exc); Idomeneo (exc); *Rossini:* Cenerentola (exc); *Mozart:* Nozze di Figaro (exc); *Rossini:* Comte Ory (exc); *Mozart:* Idomeneo (exc); *Rossini:* Barbiere di Siviglia (exc); *Monteverdi:* Incoronazione di Poppea (exc); *Mozart:* Entführung (exc); Don Giovanni (exc); Così fan tutte (exc); Nozze di Figaro (exc); *Gershwin:* Porgy and Bess (exc). (A. Mildmay, A. Rautawaara, H. Nash, W. Domgraf-Fassbaender, J. Brownlee, L. Helletsgruber, K. von Pataky, Roy Henderson, I. Souez, S. Baccaloni, C. Willis, E. Kunz, B. Thebom, Richard Lewis, J. Oncina, M. de Gabarain, I. Wallace, S. Bruscantini, M. Sinclair, D. McCoshan, F. Calabrese, C. Canne-Meijer, S. Barabas, S. Jurinac, L. Simoneau, V. de los Angeles, L. Alva, M. László, M. Price, T. Allen, E. Gale, D. Ziegler, C. Desderi, C. Vaness, G. Rolandi, W. White, C. Haymon, G. Sciutti, M. Redgrave, Glyndebourne Fest Chor, Glyndebourne Fest Orch, RPO, LPO, orch/F. Busch/M. Mudie/V. Gui/J. Pritchard/B. Haitink/S. Rattle)

Ⓓ **CDH5 65201-2** (2/95)
Leonie Rysanek - Operatic Recital
Wagner: Fliegende Holländer (exc); *R. Strauss:* Arabella (exc); Rosenkavalier (exc); *Albert:* Tiefland (exc); *Verdi:* Forza del destino (exc); Aida (exc). (Leonie Rysanek, E. Grümmer, E. Köth, S. Wagner, R. Schock, S. Björling, ROH Chor, Berlin Deutsche Op Chor, Philh, BPO, Berlin SO/W. Schüchter)

Ⓓ **CDH5 65352-2**
Nicolai Gedda Lieder Recital
Handel: Atalanta (exc); *Schubert:* Liebe hat gelogen, D751; Schiffer, D536; Nacht und Träume, D827; Rastlose

Liebe, D138; *R. Strauss:* Lieder, Op.27 (exc); Lieder, Op.10 (exc); Lieder, Op.15 (exc); Lieder, Op.32 (exc); *Duparc:* Invitation au voyage; Manoir de Rosemonde; Phidylé; Chanson triste; *Poulenc:* Airs chantés (exc); *Miaskovsky:* Moon and the cloud; *Khachaturian:* Nina's Song; *Rachmaninov:* Songs, Op.26 (exc); Songs, Op.21 (exc); Aleko (exc); *Nápravník:* Dubrovsky (exc); *Massenet:* Werther (exc); *Malawski:* Russian Song. (N. Gedda, E. Werba)

Ⓓ **CDH5 65500-2**
Boris Christoff - Italian Opera Arias
Mozart: Don Giovanni (exc); *Gluck:* Iphigénie en Aulide (exc); *Bellini:* Norma (exc); Sonnambula (exc); *Verdi:* Vespri siciliani (exc); Nabucco (exc); Ernani (exc); Simon Boccanegra (exc); Don Carlo (exc); Forza del destino (exc); *Boito:* Mefistofele (exc); Mefistofele (exc). (B. Christoff, Rome Op Chor, Philh/W. Schüchter/A. Fistoulari/H. von Karajan/I. Dobroven/N. Malko, Rome Op Orch/V. Gui)

Ⓓ **CDH5 65501-2**
Alfred Deller - HMV Recordings, 1949-54
Ciconia: O rosa bella; *Bedyngham:* O rosa bella; *Dowland:* Second Booke of Songs (exc); In darknesse let mee dwell; Second Booke of Songs (exc); Second Booke of Songs (exc); *Campion:* Ayres (1601) (exc); *Rosseter:* What then is love but mourning?; *Morley:* Ayres (1600) (exc); *J. Wilson:* Take, o take those lips away; *R. Johnson II:* Where the bee sucks; Full fathom five; *Anon:* Willow song; Peg-a-Ramsay; Caleno custure me; *Traditional:* Greensleeves (Alas, my love!); *Purcell:* Fairy Queen, Z629 (exc); Pausanias, Z585 (exc); Oedipus, Z583 (exc); If music be the food of love, Z379/1; King Richard II, Z581 (exc); Old Bachelor, Z607 (exc); Fairy Queen, Z629 (exc); Evening Hymn, Z193. (A. Deller, A. Wenzinger, M. Majer, G. Flügel, D. Dupré, D. Dupré, W. Bergmann, B. Lam, T. Weil, stg orch, G. Jones)

Ⓓ **CDH7 61001-2** (4/88)
R. Strauss—Lieder & Arias
R. Strauss: Vier letzte Lieder; Capriccio (exc); Arabella (exc). (E. Schwarzkopf, J. Metternich, A. Felbermayer, Philh/O. Ackermann/L. von Matačić)

Ⓓ **CDH7 61003-2** (6/88)
Kathleen Ferrier sings Opera and Songs
Mahler: Kindertotenlieder; *Gluck:* Orfeo ed Euridice (exc); *Purcell:* Birthday Ode, Z323 (exc); Indian Queen, Z630 (exc); *Handel:* Ottone (exc); *Greene:* Praise the Lord (exc); O God of my righteousness (exc); *Mendelssohn:* Duets, Op. 63 (exc); *Purcell:* King Arthur, Z628 (exc). (K. Ferrier, I. Baillie, Netherlands Op Chor, Netherlands Op Orch, G. Moore, VPO/B. Walter/C. Bruck)

Ⓓ **CDH7 61006-2**
Purcell—Dido and Aeneas
Purcell: Dido (Cpte). (K. Flagstad, T. Hemsley, E. Schwarzkopf, A. Mandikian, E. McNab, S. Rex, A. Pollak, D. Lloyd, Mermaid Sngrs, Mermaid Orch/Geraint Jones)

Ⓓ **CDH7 61009-2** (6/88)
Chaliapin sings Russian Opera Arias
Mussorgsky: Boris Godunov (exc); Boris Godunov (exc); Boris Godunov (exc); *Glinka:* Life for the Tsar (exc); Ruslan and Lyudmila (exc); Ruslan and Lyudmila (exc); *Dargomïzhsky:* Rusalka (exc); *Rubinstein:* Demon (exc); *Borodin:* Prince Igor (exc); *Rimsky-Korsakov:* Sadko (exc); *Rachmaninov:* Aleko (exc). (F. Chaliapin, G. Pozemkovsky, Paris Russian Op Chor, ROH Chor, Paris Russian Op Orch, LSO, ROHO, orch, anon/M. Steinmann/A. Coates/L. Collingwood/V. Bellezza, chor/E. Goossens)

Ⓓ **CDH7 61020-2** (10/88)
Wagner: Die Walküre, Act I
Wagner: Walküre (exc). (Lotte Lehmann, L. Melchior, E. List, VPO/B. Walter)

Ⓓ **CDH7 61046-2** (5/89)
Enrico Caruso: Opera Arias and Songs - 1902-1904
Franchetti: Germania (exc); *Verdi:* Rigoletto (exc); Aida (exc); *Massenet:* Manon (exc); *Donizetti:* Elisir d'amore (exc); *Boito:* Mefistofele (exc); *Puccini:* Tosca (exc); *Mascagni:* Iris (exc); *Leoncavallo:* Mattinata; *Giordano:* Fedora (exc); *Ponchielli:* Gioconda (exc); *Denza:* Non t'amo più; *Tosti:* Mia canzone; *Cilea:* Adriana Lecouvreur (exc); *Zardo:* Luna fedel; *Trimarchi:* Bacio ancora; *Meyerbeer:* Huguenots (exc); *Pini-Corsi:* Tu non mi vuoi più ben; *Bizet:* Pêcheurs de Perles (exc); *Leoncavallo:* Pagliacci (exc); *Mascagni:* Cavalleria rusticana (exc). (E. Caruso, anon, S. Cottone, F. Cilea, R. Leoncavallo, U. Giordano)

Ⓓ **CDH7 61051-2** (9/88)
Beniamino Gigli - Operatic Arias
Gounod: Faust (exc); *Bizet:* Carmen (exc); Pêcheurs de perles (exc); *Massenet:* Manon (exc); *Handel:* Serse (exc); *Donizetti:* Elisir d'amore (exc); Lucia di Lammermoor (exc); *Verdi:* Rigoletto (exc); Rigoletto (exc); Aida (exc); *Leoncavallo:* Pagliacci (exc); *Mascagni:* Cavalleria Rusticana (exc); *Puccini:* Bohème (exc); Bohème (exc); Tosca (exc); *Giordano:* Andrea Chénier (exc); Andrea Chénier (exc); *Pietri:* Maristella (exc). (B. Gigli, A. Galli-Curci, L. Homer, G. De Luca, E. Pinza, A. Bada, M. Caniglia, orch, La Scala Orch, NY Met Op Orch/E. Goossens/F. Ghione/J. Barbirolli/G. Setti/W. Goehr/C. Sabajno/O. de Fabritiis/U. Berrettoni)

Ⓓ **CDH7 61052-2** (5/90)
Beniamino Gigli—Arias and Duets (1932-1949)
Mascagni: Cavalleria Rusticana (exc); *Rossini:* Stabat mater (exc); *Leoncavallo:* Pagliacci (exc); *Puccini:* Tosca (exc); *Verdi:* Trovatore (exc); *Giordano:* Fedora (exc); *Puccini:* Turandot (exc); *Verdi:* Forza del destino (exc); *Halévy:* Juive (exc); *Lalo:* Roi d'Ys (exc); *Giordano:* Andrea Chénier (exc); *Massenet:* Manon (exc); Werther (exc); *Mascagni:* Cavalleria Rusticana (exc); *Verdi:* Trovatore (exc); *Cilea:* Arlesiana (exc); *Mascagni:* Lodoletta (exc); Amico Fritz (exc). (B. Gigli, D. Giannini, La Scala Orch/C. Sabajno, I. Pacetti/F. Ghione, G. Tomei, Rome Op Orch/O. de Fabritiis, C. Elmo, orch/U. Berrettoni, Anon/P. Mascagni, ROHO/R. Zamboni, chor, Philh/S. Robinson)

Ⓓ **CDH7 61053-2** (10/88)
Jussi Björling sings Operatic Arias
Donizetti: Elisir d'amore (exc); *Verdi:* Trovatore (exc); Ballo in maschera (exc); Aida (exc); *Leoncavallo:* Pagliacci (exc); *Puccini:* Bohème (exc); Bohème (exc); Tosca (exc); Fanciulla del West (exc); Turandot (exc); *Giordano:* Fedora (exc); *Cilea:* Arlesiana (exc); *Meyerbeer:* Africaine (exc); *Gounod:* Faust (exc); *Massenet:* Manon (exc); *Flotow:* Martha (exc); *Rossini:* Stabat Mater (exc). (J. Björling, A-L. Björling, Stockholm Royal Op Orch, Stockholm Concert Soc Orch, orch/N. Grevillius)

Ⓓ **CDH7 63030-2** (8/89)
Kirsten Flagstad - Wagner Opera Arias
Wagner: Tannhäuser (exc); Siegfried (exc); Götterdämmerung (exc); Tristan und Isolde (exc); Tristan und Isolde (exc); Wesendonk Lieder. (K. Flagstad, S. Svanholm, E. Höngen, Philh/I. Dobroven/G. Sébastian/W. Furtwängler, G. Moore)

Ⓓ **CDH7 63199-2** (1/90)
Sena Jurinac—Opera and Song Recital
Mozart: Così fan tutte (exc); Idomeneo (exc); *Smetana:* Bartered Bride (exc); Kiss (exc); *Tchaikovsky:* Maid of Orleans (exc); Queen of Spades (exc); *R. Strauss:* Vier letzte Lieder. (S. Jurinac, B. Thebom, Glyndebourne Fest Orch/F. Busch, Philh/W. Braithwaite/L. Collingwood, Stockholm PO)

Ⓓ **CDH7 63200-2** (4/90)
Tito Schipa—Recital
Gluck: Orfeo ed Euridice (exc); *A. Scarlatti:* Sento nel core; Donna ancora è fedele (exc); Pirro e Demetrio (exc); *Bellini:* Sonnambula (exc); *Donizetti:* Elisir d'amore (exc); Lucia di Lammermoor (exc); Don Pasquale (exc); *Verdi:* Rigoletto (exc); *Ponchielli:* Gioconda (exc); *Verdi:* Falstaff (exc); *Massenet:* Manon (exc); Werther (exc); Werther (exc); *Mascagni:* Cavalleria Rusticana (exc); Amico Fritz (exc); *Puccini:* Bohème (exc); Tosca (exc). (T. Schipa, orch, La Scala Orch, M. Favero/C. Sabajno/D. Olivieri/M. Cordone, T. Dal Monte, La Scala Chor/F. Ghione/G. Antonicelli)

Ⓓ **CDH7 63201-2** (7/90)
Elisabeth Schwarzkopf—Early Recordings
Bach: Cantata 51; Cantata 208 (exc); Cantata 68 (exc); *Handel:* Allegro, il penseroso ed il moderato (exc); *Mozart:* Exsultate, jubilate, K165; *Beethoven:* Ah perfido, Op.65; Fidelio (exc). (E. Schwarzkopf, Philh, VPO/P. Gellhorn/W. Susskind/H. von Karajan/J. Krips, Inst Ens)

Ⓓ **CDH7 63495-2** (8/90)
Victoria de los Angeles—Early Recordings
Verdi: Ernani (exc); Otello (exc); *Puccini:* Bohème (exc); *Boito:* Mefistofele (exc); *Rossini:* Cenerentola (exc); *Mascagni:* Cavalleria Rusticana (exc); *Catalani:* Wally (exc); *Mozart:* Nozze di Figaro (exc); *Wagner:* Tannhäuser (exc); Lohengrin (exc); *Massenet:* Manon (exc); *Gounod:* Faust (exc). (V. de los Angeles, G. Borelli, Rome Op Orch/G. Morelli, Philh/W. Susskind/A. Fistoulari)

Ⓓ **CDH7 63708-2**
Mozart—Opera Arias
Mozart: Nozze di Figaro (exc); Don Giovanni (exc); Idomeneo (exc); Entführung (exc); Entführung (exc); Zauberflöte (exc). (E. Schwarzkopf, Philh, VPO/J. Pritchard/W. Braithwaite/J. Krips/H. von Karajan)

Ⓓ **CDH7 64028-2** (4/92)
Victoria de los Angeles sings Spanish Songs
Falla: Vida breve (exc); *Granados:* Goyescas (exc); *Turina:* Canto a Sevilla; Saeta; Poema en forma de canciones (exc); *Falla:* Canciones populares españolas. (V. de los Angeles, Philh/S. Robinson/A. Fistoulari/W. Susskind, LSO, G. Moore)

Ⓓ **CDH7 64029-2** (3/92)
Richard Tauber - Opera Recital
Mozart: Don Giovanni (exc); Don Giovanni (exc); Zauberflöte (exc); *Méhul:* Joseph (exc); *Offenbach:* Contes d'Hoffmann (exc); *A. Thomas:* Mignon (exc); *Tchaikovsky:* Eugene Onegin (exc); *Smetana:* Bartered Bride (exc); *Wagner:* Meistersinger (exc); *Puccini:* Madama Butterfly (exc); Turandot (exc); *Korngold:* Tote Stadt (exc). (R. Tauber, orch/W. Goehr/H. Geehl, chor, Berlin Staatskapelle/E. Hauke/K. Besl, Berlin St Op Orch/G. Szell, E. Rethberg, Lotte Lehmann)

Ⓓ **CDH7 64252-2** (6/93)
Christoff sings Russian Arias & Songs
Mussorgsky: Boris Godunov (exc); Boris Godunov (exc); Boris Godunov (exc); Khovanshchina (exc); Song of the Flea; *Borodin:* Prince Igor (exc); *Rimsky-Korsakov:* Sadko (exc); Invisible City of Kitezh (exc); *Tchaikovsky:* Eugene Onegin (exc); *Traditional:* Song of the Volga Boatmen; Siberian Prisoner's Song; *Mussorgsky:* Songs and Dances of Death (exc); Softly the spirit flew. (B. Christoff, G. Moore, ROH Chor, Philh/I. Dobroven/N. Malko/H. von Karajan/W. Schüchter)

Ⓓ **CDH7 64255-2** (5/92)
Wagner—Die Walküre, Act 2
Wagner: Walküre (exc). (L. Melchior, Lotte Lehmann, M. Fuchs, E. Flesch, H. Hotter, A. Jerger, M. Klose, E. List, VPO/B. Walter, Berlin St Op Orch/B. Seidler-Winkler)

Ⓓ **CDH7 64701-2** (12/93)
Kreisler plays Kreisler
Kreisler: Caprice viennois; Tambourin chinois; Schön Rosmarin; Gitana; Liebesleid; Liebesfreud; Polichinelle; Beethoven Rondino; Couperin Précieuse; Chanson Louis XIII; Dittersdorf Scherzo; *Bach:* Solo Violin Partitas and Sonatas (exc); *Traditional:* Londonderry Air; *Schubert:* Rosamunde (exc); *Brandl:* Liebe Augustin (exc); *Poldini:* Marionnettes (exc); *Tchaikovsky:* String Quartet 1 (exc); *Dvořák:* Humoresques, Op.101 (exc); *Glazunov:* Spanish Serenade, Op.20/2; *Weber:* Violin Sonatas, J99-104 (exc); *Heuberger:* Opernball (exc); *Rimsky-Korsakov:* Sadko (exc); *C. Scott:* Pieces, Op.47 (exc); *Falla:* Vida breve (exc). (F. Kreisler, F. Rupp, M. Raucheisen, Kreisler Qt)

Ⓓ **CDH7 64704-2** (10/93)
Wagner—Die Walküre (Act 3)
Wagner: Walküre (exc). (A. Varnay, S. Björling, Leonie Rysanek, B. Friedland, L. Thomamüller, E. Wild, R. Siewert, E. Lausch, H. Töpper, I. Malaniuk, H. Ludwig, Bayreuth Fest Orch/H. von Karajan)

Ⓓ **CDH7 64707-2** (10/93)
Jussi Björling, Vol.2
Verdi: Rigoletto (exc); Rigoletto (exc); Rigoletto (exc); Trovatore (exc); *Bizet:* Pêcheurs de Perles (exc); *Offenbach:* Belle Hélène (exc); *Gounod:* Roméo et Juliette (exc); *Bizet:* Carmen (exc); *Massenet:* Manon (exc); *Verdi:* Requiem (exc); *Ponchielli:* Gioconda (exc); *Mascagni:* Cavalleria Rusticana (exc); Cavalleria Rusticana (exc); *Borodin:* Prince Igor (exc); *Puccini:* Manon Lescaut (exc); Bohème (exc); *Giordano:* Andrea Chénier (exc); *Rachmaninov:* Songs, Op.4 (exc); Songs, Op.21 (exc); *Leoncavallo:* Mattinata; *Tosti:* Ideale; *Beethoven:* Adelaide, Op.46; *R. Strauss:* Lieder, Op.27 (exc). (J. Björling, H. Schymberg, A-L. Björling, H. Ebert, orch, Stockholm Royal Op Orch, Stockholm Concert Soc Orch/N. Grevillius)

Ⓓ **CDH7 69520-2** (11/88)
Lehár—Die lustige Witwe
Lehár: Lustige Witwe (Cpte). (E. Schwarzkopf, E. Kunz, A. Niessner, N. Gedda, E. Loose, J. Schmidinger, O. Kraus, BBC Chor, Philh/O. Ackermann)

Ⓓ **CDH7 69530-2** (11/88)
J. Strauss II—Eine Nacht in Venedig
J. Strauss II: Nacht in Venedig (Cpte). (E. Schwarzkopf, N. Gedda, E. Loose, E. Kunz, K. Dönch, P. Klein, H. Ludwig, H. Ludwig, Chor, Philh/O. Ackermann)

Ⓓ **CDH7 69787-2** (12/89)
Richard Tauber sings Operetta Arias
J. Strauss II: Fledermaus (exc); Fledermaus (exc); Zigeunerbaron (exc); Zigeunerbaron (exc); *Lehár:* Lustige Witwe (exc); Lustige Witwe (exc); Zigeunerliebe (exc); Paganini (exc); Friederike (exc); Land des Lächelns (exc); *Kálmán:* Zirkusprinzessin (exc); Gräfin Mariza (exc); *Heuberger:* Opernball (exc); *Sieczyński:* Wien, du Stadt meiner Träume; *O. Straus:* Walzertraum (exc); *Zeller:* Vogelhändler (exc); *Stolz:* Lied ist aus (exc). (R. Tauber, V. Schwarz, Lotte Lehmann, K. Branzell, G. Merrem-Nikisch, W. Staegemann, C. Vantoni, Chor, Orch, Berlin Staatskapelle, Odeon Künstlerorchester, Berlin Künstlertheater Orch/F. Weissmann/E. Hauke/E. Korngold/F. Lehár/F. Schönbaumsfeld)

Ⓓ **CDH7 69789-2** (10/89)
Melchior sings Wagner
Wagner: Rienzi (exc); Tannhäuser (exc); Tannhäuser (exc); Lohengrin (exc); Walküre (exc); Walküre (exc); Siegfried (exc); Siegfried (exc); Siegfried (exc); Götterdämmerung (exc); Tristan und Isolde (exc); Meistersinger (exc); Meistersinger (exc). (L. Melchior, A. Reiss, N. Gruhn, LSO, Berlin St Op Orch/J. Barbirolli/A. Coates/R. Heger/L. Collingwood/L. Blech)

Ⓓ **CDH7 69791-2** (9/89)
Dame Eva Turner sings Opera Arias and Songs
E. Turner: Introductory talk; *Verdi:* Trovatore (exc); Aida (exc); Aida (exc); Aida (exc); *Ponchielli:* Gioconda (exc); Gioconda (exc); *Puccini:* Tosca (exc); Madama Butterfly (exc); Turandot (exc); *Mascagni:* Cavalleria rusticana (exc); *Wagner:* Lohengrin (exc); Tannhäuser (exc); *Grieg:* Melodies of the Heart, Op. 5 (exc); *Tosti:* Addio; *Ronald:* Summertime (exc); *Del Riego:* Homing; *Hardelot:* Because; Sometimes in my dreams. (E. Turner, E. Turner, E. Rubadi, F. Ciniselli, L. Paci, B. Carmassi, orch, anon/T. Beecham/L. Molajoli/S. Robinson/J. Batten, La Scala Chor, La Scala Orch, anon)

Ⓓ **CDH7 69793-2** (3/89)
Elisabeth Schwarzkopf & Irmgard Seefried sing Duets
Humperdinck: Hänsel und Gretel (exc); *R.Strauss:* Rosenkavalier (exc); *Monteverdi:* Madrigals, Bk.7 (exc); Madrigals, Bk 8 (exc); Madrigals, Bk.1 (exc); Madrigals, Bk.8 (exc); *Carissimi:* E pur vuole; Lungi omai deh spiega; Il mio core è un mar; A piè d'un verde alloro; *Dvořák:* Moravian Duets, B60 (Cpte); Moravian Duets, B62 (exc). (E. Schwarzkopf, I. Seefried, G. Moore, Philh/J. Krips, VPO/H. von Karajan)

Ⓓ **CDM5 65067-2** (7/94)
Delius—Orchestral Miniatures
Delius: Summer Evening; Sleigh Ride; Fennimore and Gerda Intermezzo; First cuckoo; Summer night on the river; Song before sunrise; Koanga (exc); Irmelin Prelude; Hassan (exc); Air and Dance. (Northern Sinfonia/R. Hickox)

Ⓓ **CDM5 65073-2** (6/94)
Berwald—Orchestral Works
F. Berwald: Queen of Golconda (exc); Piano Concerto; Bayadères; Violin Concerto, Op.2; Serious and joyful fancies. (A. Tellefsen, M. Migdal, RPO/U. Björlin)

Ⓓ **CDM5 65111-2** (7/95)
Britten—The Little Sweep; Rejoice in the Lamb
Britten: Little Sweep (Cpte); Rejoice in the Lamb. (R. Lloyd, R. Tear, S. Monck, H. Begg, C. Benson, C. Fordham, C. Wearing, M. Wells, D. Glick, C. Huehns, K. Willis, Finchley Children's Music Group, King's College Ch, Medici Qt, J. Constable, F. Grier, T. Fry/P. Ledger, S. Channing, J. Bowman, R. Morton, M. Creed, J. Lancelot, D. Corkhill)

Ⓓ **CDM5 65127-2**
Holst—At the Boar's Head; The Wandering Scholar
Holst: At the Boar's Head (Cpte); Wandering Scholar (Cpte). (P. Langridge, J. Tomlinson, E. Ross, F. Palmer, D. Wilson-Johnson, P. Hall, R. Suart, M. George, Liverpool Phil Ch, RLPO/D. Atherton, M. Rippon, N. Burrowes, M. Langdon, R. Tear, ECO/S. Bedford)

Ⓓ **CDM5 65150-2**
Massenet/Charpentier—Orchestral Works
Massenet: Cid (exc); Vierge (exc); Scènes pittoresques; *G. Charpentier:* Impressions d'Italie. (CBSO/L. Frémaux, Paris Opéra-Comique Orch/P. Dervaux)

Ⓓ **CDM5 65155-2**
Chabrier—Une Education manquée; Mélodies
Chabrier: Éducation manquée (Cpte); Ballade des gros dindons; Cigales; Pastorale des cochons roses; Villanelle des petits canards. (L. Berton, J. Berbié, J-C. Benoit, Paris Cons/J-C. Hartemann, J-C. Benoit, H. Puig-Roget)

Ⓓ **CDM5 65156-2** (10/94)
Poulenc—La Voix humaine
Poulenc: Voix Humaine (Cpte); *Cocteau:* Bel indifférent. (D. Duval, E. Piaf, Paris Opéra-Comique Orch/G. Prêtre, Inst Ens)

Ⓓ **CDM5 65204-2**
Orchestral Masterworks
Ravel: Boléro; *Tchaikovsky:* Capriccio Italien; *Mussorgsky:* Night on the Bare Mountain; *Glinka:* Kamarinskaya; *Borodin:* Prince Igor (exc); *Ravel:* La Valse. (Pittsburgh SO/W. Steinberg)

Ⓓ **CDM5 65208-2**
Wagner—Orchestral Works from the Operas
Wagner: Meistersinger (exc); Parsifal (exc); Tannhäuser (exc); Siegfried Idyll; Tristan und Isolde (exc). (Pittsburgh SO/W. Steinberg, Los Angeles PO, Concert Arts SO/E. Leinsdorf)

Ⓓ **CDM5 65253-2** (3/95)
Cziffra Edition, Volume 4
Daquin: Premier livre de pièces de clavecin (exc); *Lully:* Gavotte en rondeau; *Rameau:* Pièces de clavecin (exc); Dardanus (exc); *Couperin:* Livre de clavecin I (exc); Livre de clavecin II (exc); Livre de clavecin III (exc); Livre de clavecin IV (exc); *Ravel:* Tombeau de Couperin (exc); Sonatine; Jeux d'eau. (G. Cziffra)

Ⓓ **CDM5 65255-2** (3/95)
Cziffra Edition, Volume 6
Bach: Schübler Chorales, BWV645-650 (exc); Orgel-Büchlein, BWV599-644 (exc); *D. Scarlatti:* Keyboard Sonatas (exc); *Couperin:* Livre de clavecin II (exc); *Lully:* Gavotte; *Rameau:* Dardanus (exc); *Mozart:* Piano Sonata, K331 (exc); *Mendelssohn:* Midsummer Night's Dream (exc); *Bizet:* Arlésienne (exc); *Franck:* Prélude, Choral et Fugue; *Debussy:* Plus que lente; *Dohnányi:* Concert Etudes, Op. 28 (exc); *Khachaturian:* Gayaneh (exc). (G. Cziffra)

Ⓓ **CDM5 65269-2** (9/95)
Ravel—L'Heure espagnole
Ravel: Heure espagnole (Cpte). (D. Duval, J. Giraudeau, R. Hérent, J. Vieuille, C. Clavensy, Paris Opéra-Comique Orch/A. Cluytens)

Ⓓ **CDM5 65341-2**
Purcell—Theatre Music
Purcell: Fairy Queen, Z629 (exc); Indian Queen, Z630 (exc); King Arthur, Z628 (exc); Bonduca, Z574 (exc); Old Bachelor, Z607 (exc); Abdelazer, Z570 (exc); Pausanias, Z585 (exc); Married Beau, Z603 (exc); Distressed Innocence, Z577 (exc); Amphitryon, Z572 (exc); Double Dealer, Z592 (exc); Dido (exc). (J. Carlyle, V. de los Angeles, H. Harper, P. Johnson, Ambrosian Sngrs, Bath Fest Orch/Y. Menuhin, ECO/J. Barbirolli)

Ⓓ **CDM5 65424-2**
Rimsky-Korsakov/Prokofiev—Orchestral Works
Rimsky-Korsakov: Scheherazade; Golden Cockerel Suite (exc); *Prokofiev:* Love for 3 Oranges (exc). (Concert Arts SO/E. Leinsdorf, Pittsburgh SO/W. Steinberg)

Ⓓ **CDM5 65426-2**
The Art of Virgil Fox
Luther: Ein feste Burg; *Wagner:* Tannhäuser (exc); *Tchaikovsky:* Songs, Op.6 (exc); *Traditional:* All through the night; *Massenet:* Thaïs (exc); *Liszt:* Liebesträume, S541 (exc); *Debussy:* Suite bergamasque (exc); *Kreisler:* Old refrain; *Macdowell:* Woodland Sketches (exc); *Tchaikovsky:* String Quartet 1 (exc); *Mascagni:* Cavalleria rusticana (exc); *Grieg:* Lyric Pieces, Op.43 (exc); *Traditional:* Londonderry Air; *Saint-Saëns:* Carnaval des animaux (exc); *Dvořák:* Gipsy Melodies (exc); *Grieg:* Melodies of the heart, Op.5 (exc); *Sullivan:* Lost Chord. (V. Fox)

Ⓓ **CDM5 65430-2**
The Orchestra Sings
Verdi: Traviata (exc); *Rossini:* Barbiere di Siviglia (exc); *Puccini:* Bohème (exc); *Gounod:* Faust (exc); *Flotow:* Martha (exc); *Leoncavallo:* Pagliacci (exc); *Puccini:* Madama Butterfly (exc); *Verdi:* Rigoletto (exc); *Puccini:* Madama Butterfly (exc); *Rimsky-Korsakov:* Sadko (exc); *Wagner:* Tannhäuser (exc); *Saint-Saëns:* Samson et Dalila (exc); *Puccini:* Bohème (exc); *Wagner:* Tannhäuser (exc); *Bizet:* Carmen (exc). (Capitol SO, Hollywood Bowl SO/C. Dragon/Alfred Newman)

Ⓓ **CDM5 65565-2**
Poulenc—Les Mamelles de Tirésias; Le Bal masqué
Poulenc: Mamelles de Tirésias (Cpte); Bal masqué. (D. Duval, M. Legouhy, J. Giraudeau, E. Rousseau, R. Jeantet, J. Thirache, F. Leprin, S. Rallier, J. Hivert, G. Jullia, Paris Opéra-Comique Chor, Paris Opéra-Comique Orch/A. Cluytens, J-C. Benoit, M. Charpentier, Paris Cons/G. Prêtre)

Ⓓ **CDM5 65575-2**
Montserrat Caballé
Puccini: Madama Butterfly (exc); Tosca (exc); *Rossini:* Guillaume Tell (exc); *Bellini:* Pirata (exc); Puritani (exc); *Verdi:* Giovanna d'Arco (exc); Macbeth (exc); *Boito:* Mefistofele (exc); *Verdi:* Don Carlo (exc); Aida (exc); *Puccini:* Manon Lescaut (exc); Bohème (exc); *Mascagni:* Cavalleria rusticana (exc); *Puccini:* Turandot (exc); Turandot (exc); Rondine (exc). (M. Caballé, J. Hamari, Alfredo Kraus, A. Ferrin, S. Elenkov, E. Bainbridge, T. Allen, S. Milnes, R. Raimondi, A. Varnay, J. Carreras, Ambrosian Op Chor, Rhine Op Chor, LSO, RPO, Rome RAI Orch, Philh, ROHO, New Philh, Strasbourg PO/C. Mackerras/L. Gardelli/G. Gavazzeni/R. Muti/James Levine/A. Guadagno/J. Rudel/C.M. Giulini/B. Bartoletti/A. Lombard)

Ⓓ **CDM5 65576-2**
Jessye Norman
Wagner: Tannhäuser (exc); *Offenbach:* Contes d'Hoffmann (exc); Belle Hélène (exc); *Berlioz:* Roméo et Juliette (exc); *Wagner:* Fliegende Holländer (exc); Tristan und Isolde (exc). (J. Norman, A. Murray, N. Shicoff, D. Duesing, J. Aler, LPO/K. Tennstedt, Brussels Théâtre de la Monnaie Chor, Brussels Théâtre de la Monnaie Orch/S. Cambreling, Toulouse Capitole Orch/M. Plasson, Westminster Ch, Philadelphia/R. Muti, Ambrosian Op Chor)

Ⓓ **CDM5 65577-2**
Elisabeth Schwarzkopf
Mozart: Nozze di Figaro (exc); *Beethoven:* Fidelio (exc); *Mozart:* Nozze di Figaro (exc); Don Giovanni (exc); Così fan tutte (exc); *Weber:* Freischütz (exc); *Wagner:* Lohengrin (exc); *Smetana:* Bartered Bride (exc); *R. Strauss:* Rosenkavalier (exc); Ariadne auf Naxos (exc); Arabella (exc); *Heuberger:* Opernball (exc); *J. Strauss II:* Fledermaus (exc). (E. Schwarzkopf, J. Metternich, Philh/J. Pritchard/A. Galliera/C.M. Giulini/K. Böhm/W. Susskind/H. Schmidt/H. von Karajan/L. von Matačić/O. Ackermann)

Ⓓ **CDM5 65578-2**
Kiri Te Kanawa
G. Charpentier: Louise (exc); *Massenet:* Manon (exc); Hérodiade (exc); *Berlioz:* Damnation de Faust (exc); *Gluck:* Iphigénie en Tauride (exc); *Puccini:* Suor Angelica (exc); *Leoncavallo:* Pagliacci (exc); *Giordano:* Andrea Chénier (exc); *Cilea:* Adriana Lecouvreur (exc); *R. Strauss:* Rosenkavalier (exc); *Tchaikovsky:* Eugene Onegin (exc). (K. Te Kanawa, ROHO/J. Tate, LSO/Myung-Whun Chung, Staatskapelle Dresden/B. Haitink, WNO Orch/C. Mackerras)

Ⓓ **CDM5 65579-2**
Victoria de los Angeles
Rossini: Barbiere di Siviglia (exc); *Gounod:* Faust (exc); *Verdi:* Traviata (exc); Otello (exc); *Puccini:* Bohème (exc); Madama Butterfly (exc); Suor Angelica (exc); Gianni Schicchi (exc); *Mascagni:* Cavalleria rusticana (exc); *Leoncavallo:* Pagliacci (exc); *Catalani:* Wally (exc); *Massenet:* Manon (exc); *Bizet:* Carmen (exc); *Giménez:* Tempranica (exc); *Caballero:* Gigantes y Cabezudos (exc); *Barbieri:* Barberillo de Lavapiès (exc). (V. de los Angeles, C. del Monte, J. Björling, C. Vozza, French Rad Chor, RPO, Paris Op Orch, Rome Op Orch, RCA Victor Orch, Paris Opéra-Comique Orch, FRNO, Spanish Nat Orch/V. Gui/A. Cluytens/T. Serafin/G. Morelli/T. Beecham/G. Santini/R. Cellini/P. Monteux/R. Frühbeck de Burgos)

Ⓓ **CDM5 65585-2**
Walton—Film Music
Walton: Henry V Suite; Battle of Britain (exc); Troilus and Cressida (exc); As You Like It (exc); History of the English Speaking Peoples (exc). (LP Ch, LPO/Carl Davis)

Ⓓ **CDM5 65664-2**
Purcell—Dido and Aeneas
Purcell: Dido (Cpte). (V. de los Angeles, P. Glossop, H. Harper, P. Johnson, E. Robson, R. Tear, Ambrosian Sngrs, ECO/J. Barbirolli)

Ⓓ **CDM7 63075-2**
Bizet—Carmen (highlights)
Bizet: Carmen (exc). (M. Callas, N. Gedda, A. Guiot, R. Massard, N. Sautereau, J. Berbié, C. Calès, J. Mars, R Duclos Ch, J. Pesneaud Children's Ch, Paris Op. Orch/G. Prêtre)

Ⓓ **CDM7 63076-2**
Rossini—Il Barbiere di Siviglia (highlights)
Rossini: Barbiere di Siviglia (exc). (M. Callas, L. Alva, T. Gobbi, F. Ollendorff, N. Zaccaria, G. Carturan, chor, Philh/A. Galliera)

Ⓓ **CDM7 63077-2**
Beethoven—Fidelio (highlights)
Beethoven: Fidelio (exc). (H. Dernesch, J. Vickers, K. Ridderbusch, Z. Kélémen, J. van Dam, H. Donath, H. Laubenthal, W. Hollweg, S.R. Frese, Berlin Deutsche Op Chor, BPO/H. von Karajan)

Ⓓ **CDM7 63087-2**
Puccini—Tosca (highlights)
Puccini: Tosca (exc). (M. Callas, C. Bergonzi, T. Gobbi, R. Ercolani, G. Tadeo, U. Trama, Paris Op Chor, Paris Cons/G. Prêtre)

Ⓓ **CDM7 63088-2**
Verdi—La traviata (highlights)
Verdi: Traviata (exc). (R. Scotto, Alfredo Kraus, R. Bruson, Sarah Walker, C. Buchan, S. Mariategui, H. Newman, R. Van Allan, R. Kennedy, Ambrosian Op. Chor, Royal Marines Band, Philh/R. Muti)

Ⓓ **CDM7 63089-2**
Verdi—Don Carlo—Highlights
Verdi: Don Carlo (exc). (P. Domingo, M. Caballé, S. Verrett, R. Raimondi, S. Milnes, G. Foiani, D. Wallis, Ambrosian Op Chor, ROHO/C.M. Giulini)

Ⓓ **CDM7 63090-2**
Gounod—Faust (highlights)
Gounod: Faust (exc). (P. Domingo, M. Freni, N. Ghiaurov, T. Allen, M. Command, M. Vento, Paris Op. Chor, Paris Op. Orch/G. Prêtre)

Ⓓ **CDM7 63091-2** (7/89)
Bellini—Norma (highlights)
Bellini: Norma (exc). (M. Callas, F. Corelli, C. Ludwig, N. Zaccaria, La Scala Chor, La Scala Orch/T. Serafin)

Ⓓ **CDM7 63092-2**
Verdi—Nabucco (highlights)
Verdi: Nabucco (exc). (M. Manuguerra, V. Luchetti, N. Ghiaurov, R. Scotto, E. Obraztsova, R. Lloyd, K. Collins, A. Edwards, Ambrosian Op Chor, Philh/R. Muti)

Ⓓ **CDM7 63103-2**
Placido Domingo sings Opera Arias
Verdi: Aida (exc); Giovanna d'Arco (exc); Ballo in maschera (exc); Don Carlo (exc); *Gounod:* Faust (exc); *Boito:* Mefistofele (exc); *Puccini:* Manon Lescaut (exc); Tosca (exc). (P. Domingo, S. Milnes, S. Estes, M. Freni, R. Capecchi, R. Scotto, Ambrosian Op Chor, New Philh, ROHO, LSO, Philh, Paris Op Orch/James Levine/C.M. Giulini/G. Prêtre/J. Rudel/B. Bartoletti/R. Muti)

Ⓓ **CDM7 63104-2** (10/89)
Alfredo Krauss - Opera Recital
Mozart: Così fan tutte (exc); *Bellini:* Puritani (exc); *Donizetti:* Lucia di Lammermoor (exc); Fille du Régiment (exc); *Verdi:* Rigoletto (exc); Traviata (exc); *Puccini:* Bohème (exc); *Gounod:* Roméo et Juliette (exc); *Bizet:* Jolie fille de Perth (exc); *Massenet:* Werther (exc); Manon (exc). (Alfredo Kraus, M. Caballé, A. Ferrin, S. Elenkov, J-N. Bèguelin, Philh/K. Böhm/J. Rudel/R. Muti, Ambrosian Op Chor, RPO/N. Rescigno, Paris Op Chor, Paris Op Orch/B. Campanella, National PO/James Levine, Toulouse Capitole Orch/M. Plasson, French Rad New PO/G. Prêtre, LPO)

Ⓓ **CDM7 63105-2**
Giuseppe di Stefano sings Opera Arias & Songs
A. Thomas: Mignon (exc); *Bizet:* Pêcheurs de perles (exc); *Massenet:* Manon (exc); *Verdi:* Traviata (exc); Forza del destino (exc); *Puccini:* Tosca (exc); Fanciulla del West (exc); Gianni Schicchi (exc); Turandot (exc); *Cilea:* Arlesiana (exc); *Traditional:* A la Barcillunsia; Cantu a Timùni. (G. di Stefano, orch, LSO, La Scala Orch, Milan SO/A. Erede/A. Votto/A. Tonini, R. Carteri)

Ⓓ **CDM7 63109-2** (10/89)
Tito Gobbi - Opera Aria Recital
Cilea: Arlesiana (exc); *Leoncavallo:* Zazà (exc); *Verdi:* Don Carlo (exc); Otello (exc); Forza del destino (exc); *Mozart:* Nozze di Figaro (exc); *Verdi:* Ballo in maschera (exc); *Donizetti:* Elisir d'amore (exc); *Verdi:* Nabucco (exc); Macbeth (exc); *Giordano:* Andrea Chénier (exc); *Wolf-Ferrari:* Gioielli della madonna (exc); *Puccini:* Fanciulla del West (exc); *Rossini:* Guillaume Tell (exc); *Donizetti:* Elisir d'amore (exc); *Verdi:* Simon Boccanegra (exc); *Cilea:* Adriana Lecouvreur (exc); *Giordano:* Fedora (exc); *Verdi:* Falstaff (exc); Otello (exc). (T. Gobbi, La Scala Orch, RPO, Philh, LSO, Rome Op Orch/U. Berrettoni/A. Erede/J. Robertson/W. Braithwaite/G. Santini/O. de Fabritiis, N. Monti)

Ⓓ **CDM7 63110-2** (10/89)
Mirella Freni: Opera Recital
Mozart: Nozze di Figaro (exc); *Bellini:* Puritani (exc); *Verdi:* Traviata (exc); *Bizet:* Carmen (exc); Pêcheurs de Perles (exc); *Massenet:* Manon (exc); *G. Charpentier:* Louise (exc); *Puccini:* Gianni Schicchi (exc); Rondine (exc); Tosca (exc); Manon Lescaut (exc); Turandot (exc); Madama Butterfly (exc); Suor Angelica (exc); *Cilea:* Adriana Lecouvreur (exc). (M. Freni, Rome Op Orch/F. Ferraris, La Scala Orch/A. Votto, Orch/L. Magiera)

Ⓓ **CDM7 63111-2**
José Carreras sings Opera & Operetta Arias
Verdi: Don Carlo (exc); Aida (exc); *Mascagni:* Cavalleria Rusticana (exc); *Leoncavallo:* Pagliacci (exc); *Puccini:* Turandot (exc); *Offenbach:* Périchole (exc). (J. Carreras, P. Cappuccilli, M. Freni, A. Baltsa, A. Varnay, T. Berganza, Berlin Deutsche Op Chor, Vienna St Op Chor, Ambrosian Op Chor, Rhine Op Chor, BPO, VPO, Philh, Strasbourg PO, Toulouse Capitole Orch/R. Muti/H. von Karajan/A. Lombard/M. Plasson)

Ⓓ **CDM7 63113-2** (11/89)
Rossini—Overtures
Rossini: Barbiere di Siviglia (exc); Semiramide (exc); Scala di seta (exc); Gazza ladra (exc); Italiana in Algeri (exc); Guillaume Tell (exc). (Philh/H. von Karajan)

Ⓓ **CDM7 63160-2** (1/90)
Dukas: Orchestral works
Dukas: Symphony; Ariane et Barbe-bleue (exc); Apprenti sorcier; Péri (Cpte). (FRNO, Paris Op Orch, Philh/J. Martinon/P. Dervaux/I. Markevitch)

Ⓓ **CDM7 63182-2** (2/90)
The Incomparable Callas
Bellini: Norma (exc); *Donizetti:* Lucia di Lammermoor (exc); *Verdi:* Ernani (exc); Aida (exc); *Ponchielli:* Gioconda (exc); *Puccini:* Tosca (exc); *Bizet:* Carmen (exc); *Saint-Saëns:* Samson et Dalila (exc); *Gluck:* Orphée (exc); *Gounod:* Roméo et Juliette (exc); *Massenet:* Cid (exc); *A. Thomas:* Mignon (exc). (M. Callas, La Scala Orch/T. Serafin, M. Elkins, Philh/N. Rescigno, Paris Cons/A. Votto, N. Sautereau, J. Berbié, Paris Op Orch/G. Prêtre, FRNO)

Ⓓ **CDM7 63350-2** (5/90)
R. Strauss—Orchestral Works
R. Strauss: Don Juan; Tod und verklärung; Salome (exc); Metamorphosen. (Philh/O. Klemperer)

Ⓓ **CDM7 63379-2** (7/90)
Beecham conducts French Orchestral Works
Bizet: Carmen Suites (exc); *Fauré:* Pavane; Dolly; *Debussy:* Après-midi; *Saint-Saëns:* Rouet d'Omphale; *Delibes:* Roi s'amuse (exc). (FRNO, RPO/T. Beecham)

Ⓓ **CDM7 63401-2** (9/92)
French Favourites
Chabrier: Gwendoline (exc); *Gounod:* Faust (exc); *Massenet:* Cendrillon (exc); *Bizet:* Roma (exc); *Grétry:* Zémire et Azor (exc); *Bizet:* Patrie; *Massenet:* Vierge (exc); *Chabrier:* España. (RPO, FRNO, LPO/T. Beecham)

Ⓓ **CDM7 63409-2**
Mozart—Le nozze di Figaro - highlights
Mozart: Nozze di Figaro (exc). (G. Taddei, A. Moffo, E. Waechter, E. Schwarzkopf, F. Cossotto, I. Vinco, D. Gatta, R. Ercolani, E. Fusco, P. Cappuccilli, Philh/C.M. Giulini)

Ⓓ **CDM7 63410-2**
Puccini—Turandot (highlights)
Puccini: Turandot (exc). (M. Caballé, J. Carreras, M. Freni, P. Plishka, V. Sardinero, R. Corazza, R. Cassinelli, M. Sénéchal, Rhine Op Chor, Strasbourg PO/A. Lombard)

Ⓓ **CDM7 63411-2**
Puccini—Madama Butterfly (highlights)
Puccini: Madama Butterfly (exc). (R. Scotto, C. Bergonzi, A. di Stasio, R. Panerai, S. Padoan, Rome Op Chor, Rome Op Orch/J. Barbirolli)

Ⓓ **CDM7 63412-2**
Beecham Lollipops
Tchaikovsky: Eugene Onegin (exc); *Sibelius:* Valse triste; *Berlioz:* Damnation de Faust (exc); *Dvořák:* Legends (exc); *Debussy:* Enfant prodigue (exc); *Chabrier:* Joyeuse marche; *Gounod:* Roméo et Juliette (exc); *P.A. Vidal:* Zino-Zina (exc); *Grieg:* Symphonic Dances (exc); *Berlioz:* Marche Troyenne; *Delius:* Summer Evening; *Saint-Saëns:* Samson et Dalila (exc); *Mozart:* Thamos, K345 (exc); Divertimento, K131 (exc); March, K249. (RPO/T. Beecham)

Ⓓ **CDM7 63447-2** ⊟ **EG763447-4**
Delibes—Lakmé (highlights)
Delibes: Lakmé (exc). (M. Mesplé, D. Millet, C. Burles, R. Soyer, J-C. Benoit, Paris Opéra-Comique Chor, Paris Opéra-Comique Orch/A. Lombard)

Ⓓ **CDM7 63449-2**
Wagner—Der fliegende Holländer (excerpts)
Wagner: Fliegende Holländer (exc). (J. van Dam, K. Moll, D. Vejzovic, P. Hofmann, T. Moser, K. Borris, Vienna St Op Chor, BPO/H. von Karajan)

Ⓓ **CDM7 63450-2**
Verdi—Aida (highlights)
Verdi: Aida (exc). (M. Caballé, P. Domingo, F. Cossotto, N. Ghiaurov, P. Cappuccilli, L. Roni, ROH Chor, New Philh/R. Muti)

Ⓓ **CDM7 63451-2**
Mozart—Magic Flute (highlights)
Mozart: Zauberflöte (exc). (N. Gedda, G. Janowitz, W. Berry, R-M. Pütz, G. Frick, L. Popp, G. Unger, E. Schwarzkopf, C. Ludwig, M. Höffgen, A. Giebel, A. Reynolds, J. Veasey, Philh Chor, Philh/O. Klemperer)

Ⓓ **CDM7 63452-2**
R. Strauss—Der Rosenkavalier (highlights)
R. Strauss: Rosenkavalier (exc). (E. Schwarzkopf, O. Edelmann, C. Ludwig, T. Stich-Randall, E. Waechter, K. Meyer, Philh Chor, Philh/H. von Karajan)

Ⓓ **CDM7 63453-2**
Wagner—Lohengrin (excerpts)
Wagner: Lohengrin (exc). (R. Kollo, A. Tomowa-Sintow, S. Nimsgern, D. Vejzovic, K. Ridderbusch, R. Kerns, Berlin Deutsche Op Chor, BPO/H. von Karajan)

Ⓓ **CDM7 63454-2**
Verdi—Otello: excerpts
Verdi: Otello (exc). (J. Vickers, M. Freni, P. Glossop, A. Bottion, M. Sénéchal, M. Machi, S. Malagù, Berlin Deutsche Op Chor, BPO/H. von Karajan)

Ⓓ **CDM7 63611-2**
Klemperer conducts Beethoven Overtures
Beethoven: Fidelio (exc); Leonore (exc); König Stefan (exc); Consecration of the House Ov; Coriolan. (Philh/O. Klemperer)

Ⓓ **CDM7 63617-2** (11/90)
Wagner—Orchestral Works, Vol. 1
Wagner: Rienzi (exc); Tannhäuser (exc); Lohengrin (exc); Tristan und Isolde (exc). (Philh/O. Klemperer)

Ⓓ **CDM7 63618-2** (11/90)
Wagner—Orchestral Works, Vol.2
Wagner: Meistersinger (exc); Rheingold (exc); Walküre (exc); Siegfried (exc); Götterdämmerung (exc); Götterdämmerung (exc); Parsifal (exc). (Philh/O. Klemperer)

Ⓓ **CDM7 63619-2**
Mozart-Overtures; Serenade, K477 & Masonic Funeral Music
Mozart: Nozze di Figaro (exc); Don Giovanni (exc); Così fan tutte (exc); Clemenza di Tito (exc); Maurerische Trauermusik, K477; Serenade, K525; Entführung (exc); Zauberflöte (exc). (Philh, New Philh/O. Klemperer)

Ⓓ **CDM7 63654-2** (12/90)
Schwarzkopf Encores
Bach: Anna Magdalena Notenbuch (1725) (exc); *Gluck:* Rencontre imprévue (exc); *Beethoven:* Lieder, Op. 83 (exc); *Loewe:* Kleiner Haushalt, Op.71; *Wagner:* Wesendonk Lieder (exc); *Brahms:* Lieder, Op. 106 (exc); Deutsche Volkslieder (exc); Deutsche Volkslieder (exc); *Mahler:* Lieder und Gesänge (exc); Rückert Lieder (exc); Knaben Wunderhorn (exc); *Tchaikovsky:* Songs, Op. 38 (exc); *Wolf-Ferrari:* Canzoniere (exc); *J. Martini:* Plaisir d'amour; *Hahn:* Si mes vers; *Debussy:* Mandoline; *Quilter:* Arnold Book of Old Songs (exc); *Arne:* Love's Labours Lost (exc); Tempest (exc); *Traditional:* 's Schätzli; O du liebs Ängeli; Maria auf dem Berge; Danny Boy; *J. Strauss II:* Frühlingsstimmen, Op. 410 (exc). (E. Schwarzkopf, G. Moore, G. Parsons, VPO/J. Krips)

Ⓓ **CDM7 63657-2** (12/90)
Schwarzkopf sings Opera Arias
Mozart: Nozze di Figaro (exc); Così fan tutte (exc); Don Giovanni (exc); *Verdi:* Requiem (exc); *Humperdinck:* Hänsel und Gretel (exc); *Lehár:* Lustige Witwe (exc); *J. Strauss II:* Fledermaus (exc); *Puccini:* Turandot (exc); *R. Strauss:* Ariadne auf Naxos (exc); Rosenkavalier (exc); Capriccio (exc). (E. Schwarzkopf, VPO, Philh, La Scala Chor, La Scala Orch, E. Grümmer, K. Schmitt-Walter/H. von Karajan/W. Furtwängler/V. de Sabata/O. Ackermann/T. Serafin/W. Sawallisch)

Ⓓ **CDM7 63855-2** (4/92)
Beethoven—Orchestral Works
Beethoven: Symphony 3; Leonore (exc). (Philh/O. Klemperer)

Ⓓ **CDM7 63932-2**
Puccini—La bohème (highlights)
Puccini: Bohème (exc). (N. Gedda, M. Freni, M. Sereni, M. Adami, M. Basiola II, F. Mazzoli, P. Montarsolo, Rome Op Chor, Rome Op Orch/T. Schippers)

Ⓓ **CDM7 63933-2** ⊟ **EG763933-4**
Cav & Pag (highlights)
Mascagni: Cavalleria rusticana (exc); *Leoncavallo:* Pagliacci (exc). (M. Caballé, J. Carreras, M. Manuguerra, J. Hamari, A. Varnay, R. Scotto, K. Nurmela, T. Allen, U. Benelli, Southend Boys' Ch, Ambrosian Op Chor, Philh/R. Muti)

Ⓓ **CDM7 63934-2**
Donizetti—Lucia di Lammermoor (highlights)
Donizetti: Lucia di Lammermoor (exc). (M. Callas, Ferruccio Tagliavini, P. Cappuccilli, B. Ladysz, L. del Ferro, M. Elkins, R. Casellato, Philh Chor, Philh/T. Serafin)

Ⓓ **CDM7 63935-2**
Saint-Saëns—Samson et Dalila (highlights)
Saint-Saëns: Samson et Dalila (exc). (J. Vickers, R. Gorr, E. Blanc, R. Corazza, J. Potier, J-P. Hurteau, R. Duclos Ch, Paris Op Orch/G. Prêtre)

Ⓓ **CDM7 63936-2**
Massenet—Werther-Highlights
Massenet: Werther (exc). (T. Troyanos, Alfredo Kraus, C. Barbaux, M. Manuguerra, L. Richardson, M. Lewis, LPO/M. Plasson)

ⓓ **CDM7 69546-2** (10/88)
Lucia Popp
Handel: Rodelinda (exc); Serse (exc); Ottone (exc); Giulio Cesare (exc); Joshua (exc); *Mozart:* Exsultate, jubilate, K165; Vespers, K339 (exc); Vespers, K321 (exc). (L. Popp, ECO/G. Fischer, L. Pearson, Ambrosian Sngrs)

ⓓ **CDM7 69548-2** (1/89)
Georges Thill sings French Opera Arias
Gluck: Alceste (1776) (exc); *Berlioz:* Damnation de Faust (exc); Troyens (exc); *Gounod:* Roméo et Juliette (exc); Roméo et Juliette (exc); *Massenet:* Cid (exc); *Gounod:* Faust (exc); *Bizet:* Carmen (exc); *Rossini:* Guillaume Tell (exc); *Massenet:* Werther (exc); Werther (exc); *Saint-Saëns:* Samson et Dalila (exc). (G. Thill, G. Féraldy, Orch/E. Bigot/F. Heurteur/P. Gaubert/J. Szyfer/M. Frigara)

ⓓ **CDM7 69549-2** (10/88)
Ruggero Raimondi: Italian Opera Arias
Rossini: Barbiere di Siviglia (exc); *Verdi:* Macbeth (exc); Trovatore (exc); Forza del destino (exc); Don Carlo (exc); Don Carlo (exc); Aida (exc). (R. Raimondi, M. Arroyo, N. Ghiaurov, J. Carreras, Berlin Deutsche Op Chor, Ambrosian Op Chor, Vienna St Op Chor, LSO, New Philh, BPO, RPO, VPO/James Levine/R. Muti/H. von Karajan/L. Gardelli/C.M. Giulini, ROHO)

ⓓ **CDM7 69572-2** (1/90)
Weber: Overtures
Weber: Euryanthe (exc); Beherrscher der Geister; Abu Hassan (exc); Jubel-ouverture; Freischütz (exc); Preciosa (exc); Oberon (exc). (Philh/W. Sawallisch)

ⓓ **CDM7 69596-2**
The Movies go to the Opera
Puccini: Madama Butterfly (exc); Turandot (exc); *Delibes:* Lakmé (exc); *Puccini:* Bohème (exc); *Rossini:* Barbiere di Siviglia (exc); *Wagner:* Walküre (exc); *Verdi:* Forza del destino (exc); *Catalani:* Wally (exc); *Bizet:* Pêcheurs de perles (exc); *Puccini:* Manon Lescaut (exc); Gianni Schicchi (exc); Rondine (exc); *Mascagni:* Cavalleria rusticana (exc). (R. Scotto, J. Carreras, M. Mesplé, D. Millet, M. Adani, M. Freni, M. Callas, N. Gedda, E. Blanc, M. Caballé, C. del Monte, V. de los Angeles, Rome Op Orch, Rhine Op Chor, Strasbourg PO, Paris Opéra-Comique Orch, Philh, LPO, New Philh, LSO/J. Barbirolli/A. Lombard/T. Schippers/A. Galliera/A. Boult/C.M. Giulini/T. Serafin/P. Dervaux/B. Bartoletti/G. Santini/C. Mackerras/R. Muti)

ⓓ **CDM7 69853-2** (12/88)
Baroque Classics
Handel: Solomon (exc); Organ Concertos (exc); *Purcell:* Fantasia, Z731; Indian Queen, Z630 (exc); Abdelazer, Z570 (exc); Gordian Knot Unty'd, Z597 (exc); *Pachelbel:* Canon and Gigue; *Bach:* Cantata 29 (exc); Cantata 156 (exc); Cantata 31 (exc); Christmas Oratorio, BWV248 (exc); Cantata 106 (exc); Cantata 147 (exc); Cantata 174 (exc). (Taverner Plyrs, Taverner Consort, A. Lawrence-King/A. Parrott)

ⓓ **CDP7 98844-2** ⊙ **GO2034**
Josef Locke—Hear My Song
Luckesch: Hör mein Lied, Violetta; *Westendorf:* I'll take you home again, Kathleen; *Holzman:* Blaze away; *Temple:* Count your blessings; *Lehár:* Friederike (exc); Land des Lächelns (exc); *Romberg:* Student Prince; *Bixio:* Parlami d'amore, Mariù; *Rapée:* Charmaine; *Androzzo:* If I can help somebody; *Mantovani:* Cara mia; *De Curtis:* Torna a Surriento; *Hamblen:* It is no secret; *J. Thornton:* When you were sweet sixteen; *Farrelly:* Rose of Slievenamon; *J. Kennedy:* You'll never forget about Ireland; *Cormack:* Eileen O'Grady; *Murray:* I'll walk beside you; *O'Keefe:* At the end of the day; *Tauber:* Old Chelsea (exc); *H. Kennedy:* How can you buy Killarney; *Carr:* When you talk about Old Ireland; *D. Murphy:* If I were a blackbird; *J. Patterson:* Garden where the praties grow; *Benatzky:* Im weissen Rössl (exc). (J. Locke, E. Broadbent, Anon, orch, Melachrino Orch/E. Robinson/P. Green/N. Paramor/R. Martin/F. Chacksfield/J. Campbell/G. Scott-Wood/Geraldo)

ⓓ **CDS5 55004-2** (4/94)
Tchaikovsky—Eugene Onegin (in English)
Tchaikovsky: Eugene Onegin (Cpte). (T. Hampson, K. Te Kanawa, N. Rosenshein, P. Bardon, J. Connell, L. Finnie, E. Bainbridge, N. Gedda, R. Van Allan, WNO Chor, WNO Orch/C. Mackerras)

ⓓ **CDS5 55104-2** (7/94)
Braunfels—Verkündigung
Braunfels: Verkündigung (Cpte). (S. Nimsgern, C. Rüggeberg, A. Trauboth, C. Shirasaka-Teratani, J. Bröcheler, C. Bladin, C. Brüggemann, A. Kajiyama, S. Sevenich, B. Dommer, R-D. Krüll, Cologne Sym Chor, Cologne SO/D.R. Davies)

ⓓ **CDS5 55142-2** (8/94)
Wagner—Die Meistersinger von Nürnberg
Wagner: Meistersinger (Cpte). (B. Weikl, B. Heppner, C. Studer, K. Moll, S. Lorenz, D. van der Walt, C. Kallisch, H-J. Ketelsen, M. Schade, H. Wilbrink, U. Ress, H. Sapell, R. Wagenführer, R. Büse, G. Götzen, F. Kunder, R. Pape, Bavarian St Op Chor, Bavarian St Orch/W. Sawallisch)

ⓓ **CDS5 55152-2** (9/94)
Lehár—Die lustige Witwe
Lehár: Lustige Witwe (Cpte). (F. Lott, T. Hampson, R. Poulton, J. Aler, E. Szmytka, R. Schasching, K. Azesberger, D. Bogarde, Glyndebourne Fest Chor, LPO/F. Welser-Möst)

ⓓ **CDS5 55170-2**
Beethoven—Fidelio
Beethoven: Fidelio (Cpte). (C. Ludwig, J. Vickers, W. Berry, G. Frick, I. Hallstein, G. Unger, F. Crass, K. Wehofschitz, R. Wolansky, Philh Chor, Philh/O. Klemperer)

ⓓ **CDS5 55173-2**
Mozart—Die Zauberflöte
Mozart: Zauberflöte (Cpte). (G. Janowitz, L. Popp, N. Gedda, W. Berry, G. Frick, F. Crass, G. Unger, R-M. Pütz, E. Schwarzkopf, C. Ludwig, M. Höffgen, A. Giebel, A. Reynolds, J. Veasey, K. Liebl, Philh Chor, Philh/O. Klemperer)

ⓓ **CDS5 55176-2**
R. Strauss—Ariadne auf Naxos
R. Strauss: Ariadne auf Naxos (Cpte). (E. Schwarzkopf, I. Seefried, R. Streich, R. Schock, K. Dönch, H. Prey, F. Ollendorff, H. Krebs, G. Unger, L. Otto, G. Hoffman, A. Felbermayer, H. Cuénod, A. Neugebauer, Philh/H. von Karajan)

ⓓ **CDS5 55179-2**
Wagner—Der fliegende Holländer
Wagner: Fliegende Holländer (Cpte). (T. Adam, A. Silja, M. Talvela, E. Kozub, A. Burmeister, G. Unger, BBC Chor, New Philh/O. Klemperer)

ⓓ **CDS5 55209-2**
Nono—Prometeo
Nono: Prometeo (Cpte). (I. Ade-Jesemann, M. Bair-Ivenz, P. Hall, Freiburg Sols Ch, Modern Ens/I. Metzmacher)

ⓓ **CDS5 55234-2** (2/95)
Purcell—The Fairy Queen
Purcell: Fairy Queen, Z629 (Cpte). (L. Hunt, C. Pierard, S. Bickley, H. Crook, M. Padmore, D. Wilson-Johnson, R. Wistreich, London Schütz Ch, LCP/R. Norrington)

ⓓ **CDS5 55237-2** (7/95)
Hindemith—Mathis der Maler
Hindemith: Mathis der Maler (Cpte). (D. Fischer-Dieskau, J. King, G. Feldhoff, M. Schmidt, P. Meven, W. Cochran, A. Malta, D. Grobe, R. Wagemann, U. Koszut, T. Schmidt, Bavarian Rad Chor, BRSO/R. Kubelík)

ⓓ **CDS5 55471-2** (10/95)
Bellini—Norma
Bellini: Norma (Cpte). (J. Eaglen, E. Mei, V. La Scola, D. Kavrakos, E. Gavazzi, C. Remigio, MMF Chor, MMF Orch/R. Muti)

ⓓ **CDS5 55489-2** (10/95)
Mozart—La clemenza di Tito
Mozart: Clemenza di Tito (Cpte). (G. Winbergh, C. Vaness, D. Ziegler, M. Senn, C. Barbaux, L. Polgár, Vienna St Op Chor, VPO/R. Muti)

ⓓ **CDS7 47037-8** (12/84)
Mozart—Don Giovanni
Mozart: Don Giovanni (Cpte). (T. Allen, C. Vaness, M. Ewing, E. Gale, K. Lewis, R. Van Allan, J. Rawnsley, D. Kavrakos, Glyndebourne Fest Chor, LPO/B. Haitink)

ⓓ **CDS7 47068-2** (8/88)
Donizetti—Don Pasquale
Donizetti: Don Pasquale (Cpte). (S. Bruscantini, M. Freni, G. Winbergh, L. Nucci, G. Fabbris, Ambrosian Op Chor, Philh/R. Muti)

ⓓ **CDS7 47083-8** (1/84)
Verdi—Ernani
Verdi: Ernani (Cpte). (P. Domingo, M. Freni, R. Bruson, N. Ghiaurov, J. Michieli, G. Manganotti, A. Giacomotti, La Scala Chor, La Scala Orch/R. Muti)

ⓓ **CDS7 47157-8** (9/86)
Offenbach—Belle Hélène
Offenbach: Belle Hélène (Cpte). (J. Norman, J. Aler, C. Burles, G. Bacquier, J-P. Lafont, C. Alliot-Lugaz, J. Loreau, R. Trentin, G. Desroches, N. Carreras, A. Levallier, Toulouse Capitole Chor, Toulouse Capitole Orch/M. Plasson)

ⓓ **CDS7 47175-8** (9/85)
Puccini—Tosca
Puccini: Tosca (Cpte). (M. Callas, G. di Stefano, T. Gobbi, F. Calabrese, A. Mercuriali, M. Luise, D. Caselli, A. Cordova, La Scala Chor, La Scala Orch/V. de Sabata)

ⓓ **CDS7 47178-8** (4/86)
Lehár—Die lustige Witwe
Lehár: Lustige Witwe (Cpte). (E. Schwarzkopf, E. Waechter, J. Knapp, N. Gedda, H. Steffek, H. Strohbauer, K. Equiluz, F. Böheim, Philh Chor, Philh/L. von Matačić)

ⓓ **CDS7 47235-8** (6/87)
Puccini—La bohème
Puccini: Bohème (Cpte). (V. de los Angeles, J. Björling, L. Amara, R. Merrill, J. Reardon, G. Tozzi, F. Corena, W. Nahr, G. del Monte, T. Powell, Columbus Boychoir, RCA Victor Chor, RCA Victor SO/T. Beecham)

ⓓ **CDS7 47260-8** (12/87)
Mozart—Don Giovanni
Mozart: Don Giovanni (Cpte). (E. Waechter, J. Sutherland, E. Schwarzkopf, G. Sciutti, L. Alva, G. Taddei, P. Cappuccilli, G. Frick, Philh Chor, Philh/C.M. Giulini)

ⓓ **CDS7 47271-8** (1/87)
Verdi—Aida
Verdi: Aida (Cpte). (M. Caballé, F. Cossotto, P. Domingo, P. Cappuccilli, N. Ghiaurov, L. Roni, N. Martinucci, E. Casas, ROH Chor, New Philh/R. Muti)

ⓓ **CDS7 47296-8** (2/86)
Wagner—Tannhäuser
Wagner: Tannhäuser (Cpte). (K. König, L. Popp, B. Weikl, W. Meier, K. Moll, S. Jerusalem, W. Groenroos, D. Litaker, R. Scholze, G. Sima, Bavarian Rad Chor, BRSO/B. Haitink)

ⓓ **CDS7 47304-8** (3/86)
Bellini—Norma
Bellini: Norma (Cpte). (M. Callas, E. Stignani, M. Filippeschi, N. Rossi-Lemeni, P. Caroli, R. Cavallari, La Scala Chor, La Scala Orch/T. Serafin)

ⓓ **CDS7 47308-8** (4/89)
Bellini—I Puritani
Bellini: Puritani (Cpte). (M. Callas, G. di Stefano, R. Panerai, N. Rossi-Lemeni, A. Mercuriali, C. Forti, A. Cattelani, La Scala Chor, La Scala Orch/T. Serafin)

ⓓ **CDS7 47322-8** (5/86)
Wagner—Tristan und Isolde
Wagner: Tristan und Isolde (Cpte). (L. Suthaus, K. Flagstad, B. Thebom, J. Greindl, D. Fischer-Dieskau, E. Evans, R. Schock, R. Davies, ROH Chor, Philh/W. Furtwängler)

ⓓ **CDS7 47362-8** (3/87)
Offenbach—La Périchole
Offenbach: Périchole (Cpte). (T. Berganza, J. Carreras, G. Bacquier, M. Sénéchal, M. Trempont, P. Delange, M. Command, S. Nigoghossian, H. Brambilla, H. Amiel, Toulouse Capitole Chor, Toulouse Capitole Orch/M. Plasson)

ⓓ **CDS7 47365-8** (3/87)
Gounod—Roméo et Juliette
Gounod: Roméo et Juliette (Cpte). (Alfredo Kraus, C. Malfitano, J. Van Dam, G. Quilico, A. Murray, G. Bacquier, J. Taillon, C. Burles, K. Ollmann, J-M. Frémeau, Midi-Pyrenees Regional Ch, Toulouse Capitole Chor, Toulouse Capitole Orch/M. Plasson)

ⓓ **CDS7 47378-8** (9/86)
Bellini—La Sonnambula
Bellini: Sonnambula (Cpte). (M. Callas, N. Monti, N. Zaccaria, E. Ratti, F. Cossotto, G. Morresi, F. Ricciardi, La Scala Chor, La Scala Orch/A. Votto)

ⓓ **CDS7 47393-8** (9/86)
Puccini—Manon Lescaut
Puccini: Manon Lescaut (Cpte). (M. Callas, G. di Stefano, G. Fioravanti, F. Calabrese, D. Formichini, F. Cossotto, C. Forti, V. Tatone, G. Morresi, F. Ricciardi, F. Ventriglia, La Scala Chor, La Scala Orch/T. Serafin)

ⓓ **CDS7 47440-8** (1/87)
Donizetti—Lucia di Lammermoor
Donizetti: Lucia di Lammermoor (Cpte). (M. Callas, Ferruccio Tagliavini, P. Cappuccilli, B. Ladysz, M. Elkins, L. del Ferro, R. Casellato, Philh Chor, Philh/T. Serafin)

ⓓ **CDS7 47450-8** (12/86)
Verdi—Otello
Verdi: Otello (Cpte). (P. Domingo, K. Ricciarelli, J. Diaz, E. Di Cesare, C. Zaharia, P. Malakova, J. Macurdy, E. Tumagian, G. Pigliucci, La Scala Chor, La Scala Orch/L. Maazel)

Ⓓ **CDS7 47469-8** (2/87)
Verdi—Rigoletto
Verdi: Rigoletto (Cpte). (T. Gobbi, M. Callas, G. di Stefano, N. Zaccaria, A. Lazzarini, P. Clabassi, G. Gerbino, R. Ercolani, W. Dickie, E. Galassi, C. Forti, L. Mandelli, V. Tatozzi, La Scala Chor, La Scala Orch/T. Serafin)

Ⓓ **CDS7 47475-8** (11/87)
Puccini—La bohème
Puccini: Bohème (Cpte). (M. Callas, G. di Stefano, A. Moffo, R. Panerai, M. Spatafora, N. Zaccaria, C. Badioli, F. Ricciardi, C. Forti, E. Coda, La Scala Chor, La Scala Orch/A. Votto)

Ⓓ **CDS7 47480-8** (5/87)
J. Strauss II—Die Fledermaus
J. Strauss II: Fledermaus (Cpte). (L. Popp, E. Lind, P. Seiffert, P. Domingo, W. Brendel, A. Baltsa, K. Rydl, H. Zednik, U. Steinsky, H. Lohner, Bavarian Rad Chor, Munich RO/P. Domingo)

Ⓓ **CDS7 47485-8** (5/87)
Verdi—La forza del destino
Verdi: Forza del destino (Cpte). (M. Freni, P. Domingo, G. Zancanaro, P. Plishka, D. Zajick, S. Bruscantini, G. Surian, E. Gavazzi, F. Garbi, S. Sammaritano, La Scala Chor, La Scala Orch/R. Muti)

Ⓓ **CDS7 47493-8** (4/87)
Gounod—Faust
Gounod: Faust (Cpte). (P. Domingo, M. Freni, N. Ghiaurov, T. Allen, M. Command, J. Taillon, M. Vento, Paris Op Chor, Paris Op Orch/G. Prêtre)

Ⓓ **CDS7 47498-8** (9/87)
Verdi—Un ballo in Maschera
Verdi: Ballo in maschera (Cpte). (M. Callas, G. di Stefano, T. Gobbi, E. Ratti, F. Barbieri, S. Maionica, N. Zaccaria, E. Giordano, R. Ercolani, La Scala Chor, La Scala Orch/A. Votto)

Ⓓ **CDS7 47538-8** (11/87)
Verdi—La traviata
Verdi: Traviata (Cpte). (R. Scotto, Alfredo Kraus, R. Bruson, Sarah Walker, C. Buchan, S. Mariategui, H. Newman, R. Van Allan, R. Kennedy, M-R. Cosotti, C. Keyte, Ambrosian Op. Chor, Royal Marines Band, Philh/R. Muti)

Ⓓ **CDS7 47559-8** (2/88)
Bizet—La Jolie Fille de Perth
Bizet: Jolie fille de Perth (Cpte). (J. Anderson, Alfredo Kraus, G. Quilico, J. Van Dam, G. Bacquier, M. Zimmermann, French Rad Chor, French Rad New PO/G. Prêtre)

Ⓓ **CDS7 47581-8** (10/87)
Verdi—La Forza del Destino
Verdi: Forza del destino (Cpte). (M. Callas, R. Tucker, C. Tagliabue, N. Rossi-Lemeni, E. Nicolai, R. Capecchi, P. Clabassi, G. del Signore, R. Cavallari, D. Caselli, La Scala Chor, La Scala Orch/T. Serafin)

Ⓓ **CDS7 47634-8** (6/87)
Rossini—Il Barbiere di Siviglia
Rossini: Barbiere di Siviglia (Cpte). (T. Gobbi, M. Callas, L. Alva, F. Ollendorff, N. Zaccaria, G. Carturan, Mario Carlin, chor, Philh/A. Galliera)

Ⓓ **CDS7 47701-8** (7/87)
Verdi—Don Carlos
Verdi: Don Carlo (Cpte). (P. Domingo, M. Caballé, S. Verrett, S. Milnes, R. Raimondi, G. Foiani, S. Estes, D. Wallis, R. Davies, J. Noble, M-R. del Campo, Ambrosian Op Chor, ROHO/C.M. Giulini)

Ⓓ **CDS7 47727-8** (7/87)
Mozart—Così fan tutte
Mozart: Così fan tutte (Cpte). (C. Vaness, D. Ziegler, L. Watson, J. Aler, D. Duesing, C. Desderi, Glyndebourne Fest Chor, LPO/B. Haitink)

Ⓓ **CDS7 47827-8** (3/88)
Mozart—Die Zauberflöte
Mozart: Zauberflöte (Cpte). (K. Moll, E. Moser, A. Rothenberger, P. Schreier, W. Berry, O. Miljakovic, T. Adam, W. Brokmeier, W. Badorek, G. Wewel, W. Badorek, G. Wewel, L. Kirschstein, I. Gramatzki, B. Fassbaender, W. Gampert, P. Hinterreiter, A. Stein, Bavarian St Op Chor, Bavarian St Op Orch/W. Sawallisch)

Ⓓ **CDS7 47891-8** (9/88)
Roussel—Padmavati
Roussel: Padmâvatî (Cpte). (M. Horne, N. Gedda, J. Van Dam, J. Berbié, C. Burles, M. Vento, L. Dale, Orféon Donostiarra, Toulouse Capitole Orch/M. Plasson)

Ⓓ **CDS7 47895-8** (7/88)
Saint-Saëns—Samson et Delila
Saint-Saëns: Samson et Dalila (Cpte). (J. Vickers, R. Gorr, E. Blanc, A. Diakov, A. Diakov, R. Corazza, J. Potier, J-P. Hurteau, R. Duclos Ch, Paris Op Orch/G. Prêtre)

Ⓓ **CDS7 47905-8** (8/87)
Mascagni—L'Amico Fritz
Mascagni: Amico Fritz (Cpte). (M. Freni, L. Pavarotti, L. Didier Gambardella, V. Sardinero, B. di Bella, L. Pontiggia, M. Major, ROH Chor, ROHO/G. Gavazzeni)

Ⓓ **CDS7 47951-8** (3/88)
Mozart—Die Zauberflöte
Mozart: Zauberflöte (Cpte). (L. Popp, E. Gruberová, S. Jerusalem, W. Brendel, R. Bracht, N. Bailey, H. Zednik, B. Lindner, M. Richardson, D. Soffel, O. Wenkel, P. Hofmann, A. Haugland, W. Kmentt, E. Kunz, A. von Mattoni, Tolz Boys' Ch, Bavarian Rad Chor, BRSO/B. Haitink)

Ⓓ **CDS7 47959-8** (10/87)
Puccini—Madama Butterfly
Puccini: Madama Butterfly (Cpte). (M. Callas, N. Gedda, M. Borriello, L. Danieli, R. Ercolani, Mario Carlin, L. Villa, P. Clabassi, E. Campi, La Scala Chor, La Scala Orch/H. von Karajan)

Ⓓ **CDS7 47971-8** (11/87)
Puccini—Turandot
Puccini: Turandot (Cpte). (M. Callas, E. Fernandi, E. Schwarzkopf, M. Borriello, R. Ercolani, P. de Palma, N. Zaccaria, G. Nessi, G. Mauri, La Scala Chor, La Scala Orch/T. Serafin)

Ⓓ **CDS7 47981-8** (10/87)
Cav & Pag
Mascagni: Cavalleria Rusticana (Cpte); *Leoncavallo:* Pagliacci (Cpte). (M. Callas, G. di Stefano, R. Panerai, A.M. Canali, E. Ticozzi, G. di Stefano, M. Callas, T. Gobbi, R. Panerai, N. Monti, La Scala Chor, La Scala Orch/T. Serafin)

Ⓓ **CDS7 49014-8** (11/87)
R. Strauss—Capriccio
R. Strauss: Capriccio (Cpte). (E. Schwarzkopf, E. Waechter, N. Gedda, D. Fischer-Dieskau, H. Hotter, C. Ludwig, R. Christ, A. Moffo, D. Troy, K. Schmitt-Walter, Philh/W. Sawallisch)

Ⓓ **CDS7 49017-8** (2/88)
Wagner—Lohengrin
Wagner: Lohengrin (Cpte). (Jess Thomas, E. Grümmer, C. Ludwig, D. Fischer-Dieskau, G. Frick, O. Wiener, Vienna St Op Chor, VPO/R. Kempe)

Ⓓ **CDS7 49030-8** (11/87)
Verdi—Aida
Verdi: Aida (Cpte). (M. Callas, F. Barbieri, R. Tucker, T. Gobbi, G. Modesti, N. Zaccaria, F. Ricciardi, E. Galassi, La Scala Chor, La Scala Orch/T. Serafin)

Ⓓ **CDS7 49187-8** (11/87)
Verdi—La Traviata
Verdi: Traviata (Cpte). (M. Callas, Alfredo Kraus, M. Sereni, L. Zannini, M.C. de Castro, P. de Palma, A. Malta, V. Susca, A. Maddalena, M. Leitao, Lisbon San Carlos Nat Th Chor, Lisbon San Carlos Nat Th Orch/F. Ghione)

Ⓓ **CDS7 49240-2** (6/88)
Bizet—Carmen
Bizet: Carmen (Cpte). (V. de los Angeles, N. Gedda, J. Micheau, E. Blanc, D. Monteil, M. Croisier, M. Linval, J-C. Benoit, M. Hamel, B. Plantey, X. Depraz, Petits Chanteurs de Versailles, French Rad Maîtrise, French Rad Chor, FRNO/T. Beecham)

Ⓓ **CDS7 49309-2** (1/89)
R. Strauss—Daphne
R. Strauss: Daphne (Cpte). (L. Popp, R. Goldberg, K. Moll, P. Schreier, O. Wenkel, L. Baumann, A. Senger, W. Vater, M. Hölle, D. Wirtz, U-M. Flake, Bavarian Rad Chor, BRSO/B. Haitink)

Ⓓ **CDS7 49331-2** (7/88)
Poulenc—Les Dialogues des Carmelites
Poulenc: Dialogues des Carmélites (Cpte). (D. Duval, R. Crespin, D. Scharley, L. Berton, R. Gorr, X. Depraz, P. Finel, J. Fourrier, G. Desmoutiers, L. Rialland, R. Bianco, J. Mars, R. Romagnoni, C. Paul, M. Forel, M. Conti, Paris Op Chor, Paris Op Orch/P. Dervaux)

Ⓓ **CDS7 49337-2** (1/89)
R. Strauss—Intermezzo
R. Strauss: Intermezzo (Cpte). (L. Popp, P. Brammer, D. Fischer-Dieskau, G. Fuchs, A. Dallapozza, K. Hirte, G. Greindl-Rosner, M. Finke, R. Grumbach, J.W. Wilsing, K. Moll, E. Woska, E. Rüggeberg, E. Rüggeberg, K. Hautermann, BRSO/W. Sawallisch)

Ⓓ **CDS7 49344-2** (12/87)
Rossini—Il Turco in Italia
Rossini: Turco in Italia (Cpte). (N. Rossi-Lemeni, M. Callas, F. Calabrese, N. Gedda, J. Gardino, P. de Palma, M. Stabile, La Scala Chor, La Scala Orch/G. Gavazzeni)

Ⓓ **CDS7 49347-2** (12/87)
Verdi—Il Trovatore
Verdi: Trovatore (Cpte). (G. di Stefano, M. Callas, R. Panerai, F. Barbieri, N. Zaccaria, L. Villa, R. Ercolani, G. Mauri, R. Ercolani, La Scala Chor, La Scala Orch/H. von Karajan)

Ⓓ **CDS7 49350-2** (2/88)
Debussy—Pelléas et Mélisande
Debussy: Pelléas et Mélisande (Cpte). (R. Stilwell, F. von Stade, J. Van Dam, R. Raimondi, N. Denize, C. Barbaux, P. Thomas, Berlin Deutsche Op Chor, BPO/H. von Karajan)

Ⓓ **CDS7 49354-2** (1/88)
R. Strauss—Der Rosenkavalier
R. Strauss: Rosenkavalier (Cpte). (E. Schwarzkopf, C. Ludwig, O. Edelmann, T. Stich-Randall, E. Waechter, N. Gedda, K. Meyer, P. Kuen, L. Welitsch, A. Felbermayer, H. Pröglhöf, F. Bierbach, E. Majkut, G. Unger, K. Friedrich, Loughton High School for Girls' Ch, Bancroft School Boys' Ch, Philh Chor, Philh/H. von Karajan)

Ⓓ **CDS7 49361-2** (10/89)
Offenbach: Operettas
Offenbach: Pomme d'api (Cpte); M. Choufleuri (Cpte); Mesdames de la Halle (Cpte). (J-P. Lafont, L. Pezzino, M. Mesplé, J-P. Lafont, M. Mesplé, C. Burles, M. Trempont, M. Hamel, E. Greger, M. Hamel, J-P. Lafont, M. Trempont, M. Pouradier-Duteil, O. Dumaine, M. Quillevéré, C. Burles, J-M. Frémeau, L. Pezzino, M. Mesplé, J. Laforge Choral Ens, Monte Carlo PO, M. Rosenthal)

Ⓓ **CDS7 49364-2** (1/89)
Puccini—Tosca
Puccini: Tosca (Cpte). (R. Scotto, P. Domingo, R. Bruson, J. Cheek, A. Velis, R. Capecchi, P. Hudson, I. Perlman, D. Martinez, Ambrosian Op Chor, St Clement Danes Sch Ch, Philh/James Levine)

Ⓓ **CDS7 49430-2** (7/88)
Delibes—Lakmé
Delibes: Lakmé (Cpte). (M. Mesplé, C. Burles, R. Soyer, D. Millet, J-C. Benoit, B. Antoine, M. Linval, A. Disney, J. Peyron, Paris Opéra-Comique Chor, Paris Opéra-Comique Orch/A. Lombard)

Ⓓ **CDS7 49487-2** (1/89)
Beethoven: Complete Symphonies
Beethoven: Symphony 1; Symphony 2; Symphony 3; Symphony 4; Symphony 5; Symphony 6; Symphony 7; Symphony 8; Symphony 9; Fidelio (exc); Leonore (exc); Consecration of the House Ov. (C. Studer, D. Ziegler, P. Seiffert, J. Morris, Westminster Ch, Philadelphia/R. Muti)

Ⓓ **CDS7 49518-2** (2/88)
Ponchielli—La Gioconda
Ponchielli: Gioconda (Cpte). (M. Callas, P.M. Ferraro, P. Cappuccilli, I. Companeez, I. Vinco, F. Cossotto, L. Monreale, R. Ercolani, C. Forti, La Scala Chor, La Scala Orch/A. Votto)

Ⓓ **CDS7 49534-2** (12/88)
Wagner—Die Walküre
Wagner: Walküre (Cpte). (R. Goldberg, C. Studer, E. Marton, J. Morris, W. Meier, M. Salminen, A. Soldh, R. Falcon, S. Herman, U. Walther, M. Lilowa, M. Hintermeier, C. Watkinson, U. Kunz, BRSO/B. Haitink)

Ⓓ **CDS7 49568-2** (6/89)
Gershwin—Porgy and Bess
Gershwin: Porgy and Bess (Cpte). (W. White, C. Haymon, H. Blackwell, C. Clarey, D. Evans, M. Simpson, Gregg Baker, B. Hubbard, B. Coleman, J. Worthy, Curtis Watson, M. Wallace, M. Brathwaite, A. Paige, W. Johnson, P. Ingram, L. Thompson, Colenton Freeman, C. Johnson, A. Tilvern, B.J. Mitchell, T. Maynard, R. Travis, W. Marshall, Glyndebourne Fest Chor, LPO/S. Rattle)

Ⓓ **CDS7 49605-2** (11/89)
Verdi—Rigoletto
Verdi: Rigoletto (Cpte). (G. Zancanaro, D. Dessì, V. La Scola, P. Burchuladze, M. Senn, G. Surian, F. Franci, E. Gavazzi, L. Gallo, N. Curiel, M. Pertusi, V. Esposito, E. Panariello, La Scala Chor, La Scala Orch/R. Muti)

Ⓓ **CDS7 49610-2** (11/88)
Massenet—Manon
Massenet: Manon (Cpte). (I. Cotrubas, Alfredo Kraus, G. Quilico, J. Van Dam, J-M. Fremeau, C. Burles, G. Raphanel, C. Alliot-Lugaz, M. Mahé, J. Loreau, Toulouse Capitole Chor, Toulouse Capitole Orch/M. Plasson)

Ⓓ **CDS7 49641-2** (12/88)
Offenbach—Les Contes d'Hoffmann
Offenbach: Contes d'Hoffmann (Cpte). (N. Shicoff, L. Serra, J. Norman, R. Plowright, D. Bryant, A. Murray, J. van Dam, A. Oliver, D. Duesing, K. Rydl, J. Taillon, R. Tear, A. Murray, K. Rydl, Brussels Nat Op Chor, Brussels Nat Op Orch/S. Cambreling)

Così fan tutte (exc); *Beethoven:* Symphony 6 (exc); *Schubert:* Symphony 8 (exc); *Mendelssohn:* Symphony 4 (exc); *Beethoven:* Symphony 9 (exc); *Wagner:* Tristan und Isolde (exc); Meistersinger (exc); *Brahms:* Symphony 4 (exc); *Bruckner:* Symphony 4 (exc); *Mahler:* Symphony 2 (exc); Symphony 9 (exc); *R. Strauss:* Tod und Verklärung (exc). (E. Schwarzkopf, E. Höngen, H. Hopf, O. Edelmann, Bayreuth Fest Chor, New Philh, VPO, Glyndebourne Fest Orch, Philh, Bayreuth Fest Orch, BPO, LSO, Staatskapelle Dresden/O. Klemperer/W. Furtwängler/F. Busch/R. Kempe/F. Weingartner/B. Walter)

CHS5 65192-2 (12/94)
Mussorgsky—Boris Godunov
Mussorgsky: Boris Godunov (Cpte). (B. Christoff, N. Gedda, E. Zareska, A. Bielecki, K. Borg, L. Lebedeva, L. Romanova, W. Pasternak, R. Bonte, E. Bousquet, Paris Russian Chor, FRNO/I. Dobroven)

CHS5 65356-2
Mozart—Die Zauberflöte
Mozart: Zauberflöte (Cpte). (I. Seefried, W. Lipp, A. Dermota, E. Kunz, J. Greindl, P. Schoeffler, P. Klein, E. Oravez, C. Goltz, M. Kenney, S. Wagner, H. Steffek, Luise Leitner, F. Meusburger, H. Beirer, F. Bierbach, F. Liewehr, F. Höbling, Vienna St Op Chor, VPO/W. Furtwängler)

CHS5 65506-2 (9/95)
Victor de Sabata conducts
Verdi: Requiem (Cpte); Traviata (exc); Vespri siciliani (exc); *Wolf-Ferrari:* Quattro rusteghi (exc); Segreto di Susanna (exc); *Respighi:* Fountains of Rome; *Rossini:* Guillaume Tell (exc). (E. Schwarzkopf, O. Dominguez, G. di Stefano, C. Siepi, La Scala Chor, La Scala Orch, Santa Cecilia Academy Orch/V. de Sabata)

CHS5 65513-2
Furtwängler conducts Brahms & Beethoven
Brahms: Symphony 1; Symphony 2; Symphony 3; Symphony 4; Haydn Variations; Hungarian Dances (exc); *Beethoven:* Coriolan; Leonore (exc). (VPO, BPO/W. Furtwängler)

CHS5 65517-2
Wagner—Lohengrin
Wagner: Lohengrin (Cpte). (R. Schock, M. Cunitz, M. Klose, J. Metternich, G. Frick, H. Günter, NW German Rad Chor, Cologne Rad Chor, Hamburg RSO/W. Schüchter)

CHS5 65590-2
CBSO 75th Anniversary Set
Mozart: Serenade, K525; Exsultate jubilate, K165 (exc); *Handel:* Joshua (exc); *Grainger:* Irish Tune from County Derry; *Puccini:* Madama Butterfly (exc); *Sibelius:* Rakastava; *Dvořák:* Carnival; *Järnefelt:* Praeludium; Berceuse; *Handel:* Messiah (exc); *Moszkowski:* Danzas españolas; *Dohnányi:* Schleier der Pierrette (exc); *Glinka:* Ruslan and Lyudmila (exc); *Walton:* Wise Virgins; *Fauré:* Cantique de Jean Racine; *Rachmaninov:* Vocalise; *Brahms:* Piano Quartet 1. (G. Catley, J. Hammond, Webster Booth, CBSO Chor, CBO, CBSO/L. Heward/G. Weldon/L. Frémaux/S. Rattle)

CHS5 65751-2
Verdi—Otello
Verdi: Otello (Cpte). (R. Vinay, D. Martinis, P. Schoeffler, A. Dermota, A. Jaresch, S. Wagner, J. Greindl, G. Monthy, F. Bierbach, Vienna St Op Chor, VPO/W. Furtwängler)

CHS7 61030-2 (3/89)
Mozart—Don Giovanni
Mozart: Don Giovanni (Cpte). (J. Brownlee, I. Souez, L. Helletsgruber, A. Mildmay, K. von Pataky, S. Baccaloni, Roy Henderson, D. Franklin, Glyndebourne Fest Chor, Glyndebourne Fest Orch/F. Busch)

CHS7 61034-2 (3/90)
Mozart—Die Zauberflöte
Mozart: Zauberflöte (Cpte). (T. Lemnitz, E. Berger, H. Roswaenge, G. Hüsch, W. Strienz, W. Grossmann, H. Tessmer, I. Beilke, H. Scheppan, E. Marherr-Wagner, R. Berglund, C. Spletter, E. Fabbry, Favres Solisten Vereinigung, BPO/T. Beecham)

CHS7 61038-2 (8/88)
Debussy—Pelléas et Mélisande, etc
Debussy: Pelléas et Mélisande (Cpte); Fêtes galantes I (Cpte); Fêtes galantes II (Cpte); Chansons de Bilitis (Cpte); Promenoir des deux amants (Cpte); Proses lyriques (exc); Ballades de François Villon (exc); Pelléas et Mélisande (exc); Ariettes oubliées (exc). (J. Jansen, I. Joachim, H. Etcheverry, P. Cabanel, G. Cernay, L.B. Sedira, A. Narçon, E. Rousseau, M. Teyte, M. Garden, A. Cortot, C. Debussy, Y. Gouverné Ch, SO/R. Desormière)

CHS7 63025-2 (8/89)
Mussorgsky—Songs
Mussorgsky: Sadly rustled the leaves; Where art thou, little star; Hour of Jollity; Tell me why; I have many palaces and gardens; What are words of love to you?; King Saul; Old man's song; But if I could meet thee again; Wild wind blows; Night; Kalistratushka; Salammbô (exc); Prayer; Outcast; Lullaby; Dear one, why are thine eyes?; From my tears; Gopak; Darling Savishna; Seminarist; Hebrew song; Magpie; Gathering mushrooms; Feast; Ragamuffin; He-Goat; Garden by the Don; Classicist; Orphan; Child's song; Nursery; Eremushka's lullaby; Peepshow; Evening song; Forgotten; Sunless; Songs and Dances of Death; Epitaph; Sphinx; Not like thunder; Softly the spirit flew; Is spinning man's work; It scatters and breaks; Vision; Pride; Wanderer; On the Dnieper; Song of the flea. (B. Christoff, A. Labinsky, G. Moore, FRNO/G. Tzipine)

CHS7 63045-2 (7/89)
Wagner—Die Walküre
Wagner: Walküre (Cpte). (L. Suthaus, Leonie Rysanek, M. Mödl, F. Frantz, M. Klose, G. Frick, G. Schreyer, E. Köth, J. Hellwig, D. Schmedes, D. Hermann, H. Töpper, J. Blatter, R. Siewert, VPO/W. Furtwängler)

CHS7 63195-2 (3/90)
Massenet—Werther
Massenet: Werther (Cpte). (G. Thill, N. Vallin, M. Roque, G. Féraldy, A. Narçon, H. Niel, L. Guénot, Cantoria Children's Ch, Paris Opéra-Comique Chor, Paris Opéra-Comique Orch/E. Cohen)

CHS7 63331-2 (5/90)
Verdi—Aida
Verdi: Aida (Cpte). (M. Caniglia, E. Stignani, B. Gigli, G. Bechi, T. Pasero, I. Tajo, A. Zagonara, M. Huder, Rome Op Chor, Rome Op Orch/T. Serafin)

CHS7 63500-2 (9/90)
Wagner—Die Meistersinger
Wagner: Meistersinger (Cpte). (O. Edelmann, H. Hopf, E. Schwarzkopf, F. Dalberg, E. Kunz, G. Unger, I. Malaniuk, H. Pflanzl, E. Majkut, H. Berg, J. Janko, K. Mikorey, G. Stolze, H. Tandler, H. Borst, A. Van Mill, W. Faulhaber, Bayreuth Fest Chor, Bayreuth Fest Orch/H. von Karajan)

CHS7 63538-2 (3/90)
Horowitz—The HMV Recordings, 1930-51
Bach: Nun freut euch, BWV734; *D. Scarlatti:* Keyboard Sonatas (exc); Keyboard Sonatas (exc); *Haydn:* Keyboard Sonata 62; *Chopin:* Etudes (exc); Etudes (exc); Etudes (exc); Impromptus (exc); Nocturnes (exc); Mazurkas (exc); Mazurkas (exc); Mazurkas (exc); Scherzos (exc); *Debussy:* Etudes (exc); *Poulenc:* Pastourelle (exc); Pièces (1928) (exc); *Beethoven:* Variations, WoO80; *Schumann:* Arabeske; Toccata; Fantasiestücke, Op. 12 (exc); Presto passionato; *Liszt:* Harmonies poétiques, S173 (exc); Piano Sonata, S178; *Rachmaninov:* Piano Concerto 3; Preludes (exc); *Rimsky-Korsakov:* Tale of Tsar Saltan (exc); *Stravinsky:* Petrushka (exc); *Prokofiev:* Toccata, Op. 11; *Stravinsky:* Petrushka (exc). (V. Horowitz, LSO/A. Coates)

CHS7 63715-2 (3/91)
Mozart: Die Entführung, etc
Mozart: Entführung (Cpte); Clemenza di Tito (exc); Zauberflöte (exc); Entführung (exc); Idomeneo (exc); Misero! o sogno, K431. (L. Marshall, I. Hollweg, L. Simoneau, G. Unger, G. Frick, H. Laubenthal, Beecham Choral Soc, RPO/T. Beecham, L. Simoneau, Paris Champs-Élysées Orch/A. Jouve)

CHS7 63802-2(1) (9/92)
Tetrazzini—The London Records (pt 1)
Verdi: Rigoletto (exc); *A. Thomas:* Mignon (exc); *Delibes:* Lakmé (exc); *Meyerbeer:* Dinorah (exc); *Donizetti:* Lucia di Lammermoor (exc); *Mozart:* Nozze di Figaro (exc); *Rossini:* Barbiere di Siviglia (exc); *Verdi:* Traviata (exc); *Mozart:* Don Giovanni (exc); *Gounod:* Roméo et Juliette (exc); *J. Strauss II:* Frühlingsstimmen, Op. 410; *Verdi:* Ballo in maschera (exc); *Donizetti:* Lucia di Lammermoor (exc); *Benedict:* Carnival of Venice Variations; *Bellini:* Sonnambula (exc); *Bizet:* Pêcheurs de perles (exc); *Tosti:* Aprile; Serenata; *Gounod:* Mireille (exc); *Chapí:* Hijas del Zebedeo (exc); *Donizetti:* Linda di Chamounix (exc); *Verdi:* Vespri Siciliani (exc); *Rossini:* Semiramide (exc); *Grieg:* Peer Gynt (exc); *F. David:* Perle du Brésil (exc); *Bizet:* Carmen (exc); *Verdi:* Traviata (exc); *Delibes:* Lakmé (exc); *Mozart:* Don Giovanni (exc); *Verdi:* Aida (exc); *Donizetti:* Linda di Chamounix (exc); *A. Thomas:* Hamlet (exc); Mignon (exc); *Proch:* Air and Variations. (L. Tetrazzini, orch/P. Pitt, P. Pitt, chor)

CHS7 63802-2(2) (9/92)
Tetrazzini—The London Records (pt 2)
Bellini: Sonnambula (exc); *Verdi:* Traviata (exc); *Meyerbeer:* Huguenots (exc); *Bellini:* Puritani (exc); *Venzano:* O che assorta; *Bishop:* Home, sweet home; *Ricci:* Crispino e la comare (exc); *Meyerbeer:* Etoile du Nord (exc); *A. Thomas:* Mignon (exc); *Mozart:* Zauberflöte (exc); *Lotti:* Arminio (exc); *Verdi:* Forza del destino (exc); *A. Tate:* Somewhere a voice is calling; *Veracini:* Rosalinda (exc); *Gounod:* Faust (exc); *G. Braga:* Melodies (exc); *Pergolesi:* Tre giorni son che Nina; *Lemaire:* Vous dansez, Marquise; *Lama:* Piccolo amore; Cara piccina; *V. Valente:* Nuttata napulitana; *Hoschna:* Madame Sherry (exc); *De Curtis:* So 'nnammurato 'e te!; *Lama:* 'O mare canta!; *Drigo:* Arlekinda (exc); *Lama:* Come le rose. (L. Tetrazzini, A. Baggiore, T. Amici, inst ens, orch/P. Pitt, P. Pitt)

CHS7 63860-2 (7/91)
Mozart: Don Giovanni
Mozart: Don Giovanni (Cpte). (C. Siepi, E. Grümmer, E. Schwarzkopf, E. Berger, A. Dermota, O. Edelmann, W. Berry, D. Ernster, Vienna St Op Chor, VPO/W. Furtwängler)

CHS7 63864-2 (9/91)
Mozart—Così fan tutte
Mozart: Così fan tutte (Cpte). (I. Souez, L. Helletsgruber, I. Eisinger, H. Nash, W. Domgraf-Fassbaender, J. Brownlee, Glyndebourne Fest Chor, Glyndebourne Fest Orch/F. Busch)

CHS7 64037-2 (1/92)
Wagner—Tristan und Isolde
Wagner: Tristan und Isolde (Cpte). (L. Melchior, K. Flagstad, M. Klose, S. Kalter, S. Nilsson, E. List, H. Janssen, B. Hitchin, F. Sale, O. Dua, L. Horsman, Parry Jones, R. Devereux, ROH Chor, LPO/F. Reiner/T. Beecham)

CHS7 64041-2 (11/91)
Rossini—L'Italiana in Algeri
Rossini: Italiana in Algeri (Cpte). (G. Simionato, C. Valletti, M. Cortis, M. Petri, G. Sciutti, M. Masini, E. Campi, La Scala Chor, La Scala Orch/C.M. Giulini)

CHS7 64487-2 (4/93)
R. Strauss—Der Rosenkavalier & Lieder
R. Strauss: Rosenkavalier (exc); Lieder, Op.27 (exc); Lieder, Op.17 (exc); Lieder, Op.41 (exc); Lieder, Op.48 (exc); Lieder, Op.21 (exc); Lieder, Op.36 (exc); Lieder, Op.69 (exc); Lieder, Op.17 (exc); Lieder, Op.29 (exc); Lieder, Op.48 (exc); Lieder, Op.15 (exc); Lieder, Op.43 (exc); Lieder, Op.56 (exc); Lieder, Op.56 (exc); Lieder, Op.27 (exc); Lieder, Op.29 (exc); Lieder, Op.17 (exc). (Lotte Lehmann, M. Olczewska, R. Mayr, E. Schumann, V. Madin, B. Paalen, H. Gallos, A. Michalsky, K. Ettl, W. Wernigk, Vienna St Op Chor, VPO/R. Heger, Vienna St Op Orch/K. Alwin, orch/L. Collingwood/F. Weissmann, I. Newton, K. Alwin, L. Rosenek, anon, anon, Berlin St Op Orch)

CHS7 64496-2 (5/93)
Beethoven—Fidelio
Beethoven: Fidelio (Cpte). (M. Mödl, W. Windgassen, O. Edelmann, G. Frick, S. Jurinac, R. Schock, A. Poell, A. Hendriks, F. Bierbach, Vienna St Op Chor, VPO/W. Furtwängler)

CHS7 64673-2
Joseph Schmidt - Complete EMI Recordings Volume 1
Meyerbeer: Africaine (exc); *Flotow:* Martha (exc); Alessandro Stradella (exc); *Kienzl:* Evangelimann (exc); *Korngold:* Tote Stadt (exc); *Adam:* Postillon de Lonjumeau (exc); *Massenet:* Manon (exc); Cid (exc); *Tchaikovsky:* Eugene Onegin (exc); *Schubert:* Schwanengesang, D957 (exc); Schöne Müllerin (exc); *Morey:* Vallière (exc); *Götze:* Page des Königs (exc); *J. Strauss II:* Tausend und eine Nacht (exc); Zigeunerbaron (exc); Simplizius (exc); *Lehár:* Zigeunerliebe (exc); *Benatzky:* Wenn du treulos bist; *Tauber:* Singende Traum (exc); *Spoliansky:* Lied einer Nacht (exc); *Niederberger:* Buon notte, schöne Signorina; *Donizetti:* Elisir d'amore (exc); *Verdi:* Rigoletto (exc); Trovatore (exc); Trovatore (exc); *Leoncavallo:* Pagliacci (exc); *Puccini:* Bohème (exc); Tosca (exc); Tosca (exc); Fanciulla del West (exc); Turandot (exc); *Serrano:* Trust de los Tenorios (exc); *Leoncavallo:* Mattinata; *Labriola:* Voga, voga; *Biscardi:* Ariatella; *Denza:* Funiculì-funiculà; *Buzzi-Peccia:* Lolita; *Di Capua:* O sole mio. (G. Ljungberg, J. Schmidt, F. Günther, M. Saal, chor, orch, Berlin St. Op. Orch, Berlin SO, Berlin City Op Orch, Berlin Staatskapelle/F. Günther/C. Schmalstich/F. Weissmann/L. Blech/E. Kaiser/R. Tauber/W. Goehr/O. Dobrindt/F. Brunner)

CHS7 64676-2
Joseph Schmidt - Complete EMI Recordings Volume 2
May: Lied geht um die Welt (exc); Wenn du Jung bist (exc); Wenn du Jung bist (exc); Stern fällt vom Himmel (exc); Stern fällt vom Himmel (exc); Heut' ist der schönste Tag (exc); Heut' ist der schönste Tag (exc); *Niederberger:* In deinen Augen; *Van Aaken:* Nur dir will ich gehören; *Ernst:* Liebe kleine Frau; *Altmann:* Wenn der alte Brunnen rauscht; Laute mit verblasstem Band; *Niederberger:* Warum gehst du vorbei an mir; *Lewinnek:* Einmal glaub't ich an deine Liebe; *J. Strauss II:* Wiener Bonbons; *Dellinger:* Don César (exc); *Gambardella:* O marenariello; *Schootemeyer:* I love Holland; *May:* Lied geht um die Welt (exc); Stern fällt vom Himmel (exc); Stern fällt vom Himmel (exc); Lied geht um die Welt (exc); *Rossini:* Soirées musicales (exc); *Yradier:* Paloma; *Di Capua:* Maria, Marì;

Anon: Tiritomba; *Crescenzo:* Tarantella sincera; *Tagliaferri:* Piscatore 'e pusilleco; Nun mi sceta; *Cottrau:* Santa Lucia; *Tosti:* Penso; *Tagliaferri:* Mandulinata a Napule; *Tosti:* Addio. (J. Schmidt, chor, orch/O. Dobrindt/F. Günther/F. Löhner/E. Kaiser/W. Goehr, F. Brunner Salon Orch)

CHS7 64860-2(1) (4/94)
La Scala Edition - Vol.1, 1878-1914 (pt 1)
Verdi: Vespri Siciliani (exc); *Bellini:* Sonnambula (exc); *Verdi:* Don Carlo (exc); *Ponchielli:* Gioconda (exc); *Verdi:* Traviata (exc); Otello (exc); Otello (exc); Otello (exc); *Halévy:* Juive (exc); Juive (exc); *Donizetti:* Favorita (exc); *Verdi:* Otello (exc); *Wagner:* Lohengrin (exc); *Verdi:* Ernani (exc); *Rossini:* Barbiere di Siviglia (exc); *Mascagni:* Cavalleria Rusticana (exc); *Bellini:* Norma (exc); *Verdi:* Otello (exc); Falstaff (exc); *Donizetti:* Lucrezia Borgia (exc); *Puccini:* Manon Lescaut (exc); *Leoncavallo:* Medici (exc); *Mascagni:* Guglielmo Ratcliff (exc); *Saint-Saëns:* Samson et Dalila (exc); *Giordano:* Andrea Chénier (exc); *Bellini:* Puritani (exc); *Mascagni:* Iris (exc); *Massenet:* Roi de Lahore (exc); *Wagner:* Lohengrin (exc); *Tchaikovsky:* Eugene Onegin (exc); *Puccini:* Bohème (exc); Bohème (exc). (La Scala Orch/A. Toscanini, A. Patti, A. Barili, G. Kaschmann, S. Cottone, F. Marconi, G. Bellincioni, F. Tamagno, anon, V. Maurel, L. Escalais, F. Navarini, M. Battistini, orch/C. Sabajno, G. Oxilia, F. Viñas, F. Valero, T. Arkel, G.B. De Negri, E. Teodorini, E. Garbin, G. Pacini, A. Parsi-Pettinella, M. Sammarco, A. Bonci, F. De Lucia, G. Borgatti, E. Giraldoni, E. Caruso, E. Carelli)

CHS7 64860-2(2) (4/94)
La Scala Edition - Vol.1, 1878-1914 (pt 2)
Puccini: Bohème (exc); *Boito:* Mefistofele (exc); *De Lara:* Méssaline (exc); *Boito:* Mefistofele (exc); *Donizetti:* Linda di Chamounix (exc); *Franchetti:* Germania (exc); Germania (exc); Germania (exc); *Berlioz:* Damnation de Faust (exc); *Giordano:* Siberia (exc); Siberia (exc); Siberia (exc); *Verdi:* Rigoletto (exc); Aida (exc); *Donizetti:* Don Pasquale (exc); Don Pasquale (exc); *Tchaikovsky:* Queen of Spades (exc); *Verdi:* Traviata (exc); *Franchetti:* Figlia di Iorio (exc); *Ponchielli:* Gioconda (exc); Gioconda (exc); Gioconda (exc); *Mascagni:* Cavalleria Rusticana (exc); *Spontini:* Vestale (exc); *Saint-Saëns:* Samson et Dalila (exc); *Mascagni:* Isabeau (exc); *Puccini:* Fanciulla del West (exc); *Bellini:* Norma (exc); *Verdi:* Nabucco (exc); *Wagner:* Tristan und Isolde (exc); *Verdi:* Rigoletto (exc); Rigoletto (exc); Rigoletto (exc). (O. Luppi, orch/E. Vitale, F. Chaliapin, La Scala Orch/C. Sabajno, F. Tamagno, anon, G. Mansueto, G. De Tura, chor, E. Bruno, E. Caruso, S. Cottone, A. Pinto, M. Sammarco, A. Magini-Coletti, G. Zenatello, R. Delle Ponti, R. Storchio, G. De Luca, T. Ruffo, G. Finzi-Magrini, C. Boninsegna, A. Pini-Corsi, E. Badini, L. Sobinov, A. Didur, R. Stracciari, E. Giraldoni, E. Petri, P. Amato, R. Grassi, E. Burzio, G. Anselmi, E. Mazzoleni, A. Paoli, B. De Muro, T. Poli-Randaccio, G. Russ, V. Guerrini, C. Galeffi, E. Ferrari-Fontana, H. Lázaro, G. Pareto)

CHS7 64864-2(1) (4/94)
La Scala Edition - Vol.2, 1915-46 (pt 1)
Rossini: Barbiere di Siviglia (exc); Barbiere di Siviglia (exc); Mosè in Egitto (exc); *Donizetti:* Don Pasquale (exc); *Boito:* Mefistofele (exc); *Donizetti:* Lucia di Lammermoor (exc); *Bellini:* Sonnambula (exc); *Verdi:* Rigoletto (exc); *Boito:* Nerone (exc); Nerone (exc); *Giordano:* Andrea Chénier (exc); *Humperdinck:* Hänsel und Gretel (exc); *Verdi:* Aida (exc); *Ponchielli:* Gioconda (exc); *Verdi:* Trovatore (exc); Trovatore (exc); *Puccini:* Madama Butterfly (exc); Turandot (exc); Turandot (exc); *Verdi:* Don Carlo (exc); *Donizetti:* Fille du Régiment (exc); *Verdi:* Trovatore (exc); Trovatore (exc); Traviata (exc); *Spontini:* Vestale (exc); *Donizetti:* Elisir d'amore (exc); Elisir d'amore (exc). (R. Stracciari, E. De Hidalgo, N. De Angelis, D. Borgioli, B. Gigli, E. Pinza, T. dal Monte, M. Fleta, M. Journet, A. Pertile, C. Supervia, I.M. Ferraris, G. Arangi-Lombardi, G. Cobelli, C. Muzio, B. Franci, G. Masini, R. Pampanini, M. Zamboni, A. Baracchi, E. Venturini, G. Nessi, T. Pasero, I. Minghini-Cattaneo, G. Dalla Rizza, S. Baccaloni, T. Schipa, La Scala Chor, La Scala Orch, chor, orch/G. Polacco/C. Sabajno/A. Albergoni/L. Molajoli/G. Santini/E. Panizza/A. Guarnieri)

CHS7 64864-2(2) (4/94)
La Scala Edition - Vol.2, 1915-46 (pt 2)
Rossini: Guillaume Tell (exc); *Verdi:* Rigoletto (exc); *Puccini:* Madama Butterfly (exc); *Giordano:* Andrea Chénier (exc); *Verdi:* Nabucco (exc); Trovatore (exc); *Ponchielli:* Gioconda (exc); *Massenet:* Werther (exc); *Puccini:* Manon Lescaut (exc); *Verdi:* Otello (exc); *Puccini:* Turandot (exc); Suor Angelica (exc); *Boito:* Mefistofele (exc); *Wolf-Ferrari:* Campiello (exc); *Mascagni:* Amico Fritz (exc); *Puccini:* Bohème (exc); *Verdi:* Macbeth (exc); *Puccini:* Bohème (exc); *Verdi:* Rigoletto (exc); Ballo in maschera (exc); *Giordano:* Fedora (exc); *Verdi:* Otello (exc); *Bellini:* Puritani (exc); *Verdi:* Falstaff (exc); Traviata (exc). (H. Spani, L. Pagliughi, G. Masini, B. Gigli, E. Stignani, G. Cigna, T. Schipa, A. Ziliani, F. Merli, G. Lauri-Volpi, A. Oltrabella, P. Tassinari, M. Favero, G. Lugo, A. Sved, L. Albanese, A. Poli, G. Malipiero, G. Bechi, T. Gobbi, M. Caniglia, M. Carosio, M. Stabile, G. Nessi, L. Donaggio, La Scala Chor, La Scala Orch, Rome Op Orch, orch, Philh/C. Sabajno/V. Veneziani/L. Ricci/L. Molajoli/F. Ghione/M. Cordone/G. Antonicelli/G. Marinuzzi/U. Berrettoni/T. Serafin/A. Erede/D. Olivieri/A. Toscanini)

CHS7 64901-2 (12/93)
Beethoven—Fidelio
Beethoven: Fidelio (Cpte). (K. Flagstad, J. Patzak, P. Schoeffler, J. Greindl, E. Schwarzkopf, A. Dermota, H. Braun, H. Gallos, L. Pantscheff, Vienna St Op Chor, VPO/W. Furtwängler)

CHS7 64929-2
Jascha Heifetz
Vivaldi: Sonatas, Op.2 (exc); *Beethoven:* Violin Sonata 9; *Paganini:* Caprices, Op.1 (exc); *Franck:* Violin Sonata; *Clérambault:* Largo in C minor; *Bazzini:* Ronde des lutins; *R. Strauss:* Stimmungsbilder (exc); *Wieniawski:* Polonaise, Op.4; *Glazunov:* Méditation, Op.32; *Wieniawski:* Scherzo-Tarantelle, Op.16; *Debussy:* Enfant Prodigue (exc); *Albéniz:* Suite española 1 (exc); *Elgar:* Capricieuse; *Moszkowski:* Pieces, Op.45 (exc); *Falla:* Vida breve (exc); *C. Scott:* Tallahassee Suite (exc); Danse nègre; *Dohnányi:* Ruralia Hungarica (exc); *Korngold:* Much Ado About Nothing Suite (exc); *Milhaud:* Saudades do Brasil (exc); *Castelnuovo-Tedesco:* Alt Wien (exc); *Poulenc:* Mouvements perpétuels (exc); *Szymanowski:* King Roger (exc); *Dinicu:* Hora staccato. (J. Heifetz, A. Sándor, B. Moiseiwitsch, A. Rubinstein, E. Bay)

CHS7 64935-2 (4/94)
Wagner—Opera Excerpts
Wagner: Tannhäuser (exc); Lohengrin (exc); Walküre (exc); Götterdämmerung (exc); Götterdämmerung (exc); Fliegende Holländer (exc); Tristan und Isolde (exc); Meistersinger (exc); Parsifal (exc). (K. Flagstad, VPO, Philh, BPO/W. Furtwängler)

CHS7 69523-2 (11/88)
Lehár—Land of Smiles
Lehár: Land des Lächelns (Cpte). (E. Schwarzkopf, E. Kunz, N. Gedda, E. Loose, O. Kraus, BBC Chor, Philh/O. Ackermann)

CHS7 69631-2 (1/89)
Mozart—Die Zauberflöte
Mozart: Zauberflöte (Cpte). (I. Seefried, W. Lipp, A. Dermota, E. Kunz, L. Weber, G. London, P. Klein, E. Loose, S. Jurinac, F. Riegler, E. Schürhoff, H. Steinmassl, E. Dörpinghans, A. Stückl, E. Majkut, L. Pantscheff, H. Pröglhöf, Vienna Singverein, VPO/H. von Karajan)

CHS7 69635-2 (12/88)
Mozart—Così fan tutte
Mozart: Così fan tutte (Cpte). (E. Schwarzkopf, N. Merriman, L. Otto, L. Simoneau, R. Panerai, S. Bruscantini, Chor, Philh/H. von Karajan)

CHS7 69741-2(1) (4/92)
Record of Singing, Vol.4—Anglo-American School (pt 1)
Hook: Hours of Love; *Bizet:* Jolie fille de Perth (exc); *Puccini:* Rondine (exc); *Handel:* Atalanta (exc); *Villa-Lobos:* Serestas (exc); *G. Charpentier:* Louise (exc); *Hahn:* Études latines (exc); *Mozart:* Zauberflöte (exc); *Korngold:* Tote Stadt (exc); *Wagner:* Tannhäuser (exc); Lohengrin (exc); *Gluck:* Alceste (1776) (exc); *Saint-Saëns:* Samson et Dalila (exc); *Bizet:* Carmen (exc); *Wolf:* Mörike Lieder (exc); *Elgar:* Sea Pictures (exc); *Bach:* Mass in B minor, BWV232 (exc). (M. Ritchie, Philh/L. Collingwood, G. Catley, LSO/S. Robinson, D. Kirsten, RCA Victor Orch/J-P. Morel, F. Quartararo, E. Houston, P. Miguel, E. Steber/W. Susskind, M. Teyte, G. Moore, D. Maynor, Boston SO/S. Koussevitzky, J. Hammond, A. Varnay/G. Sébastian, H. Traubel, NYPSO/A. Rodzinski, R. Bampton, Victor SO/W. Pelletier, B. Thebom/W. Braithwaite, J. Tourel, F. Nielsen, G. Ripley/G. Weldon, K. Ferrier, Vienna SO/H. von Karajan)

CHS7 69741-2(2) (4/92)
Record of Singing, Vol.4—Anglo-American School (pt 2)
Monro: My lovely Celia; *Boughton:* Immortal Hour (exc); *Britten:* Folk Songs (exc); *Herbert:* Naughty Marietta (exc); *Mozart:* Don Giovanni (exc); *Vaughan Williams:* Hugh the Drover (exc); *Ponchielli:* Gioconda (exc); *Purcell:* King Richard II, Z581 (exc); *Peel:* In Summertime on Bredon; *Villa-Lobos:* Miniatures (exc); *Nin:* Villancicos (exc); *Wolf:* Goethe Lieder (exc); *Leoncavallo:* Pagliacci (exc); *Massenet:* Hérodiade (exc); *Handel:* Judas Maccabaeus (exc); *Mussorgsky:* Boris Godunov (exc); *Handel:* Scipione (exc). (D. Lloyd, Webster Booth, J. Cockerill, P. Pears, B. Britten, J. Peerce/A. Fistoulari, W. Midgley, ROHO/R. Goodall, J. Johnston/J. Robertson, R. Tucker, NY Met Op Orch/E. Cooper, A. Deller, B. Lam, T. Weil, R. Irwin, F. Fuller, H. Villa-Lobos, I. Gorin, A. Baller, M. Harrell, L. Warren, RCA Orch/R. Cellini, R. Merrill, N. Walker, orch, G. London, V. Pleasants, O. Natzke, H. Robinson Cleaver, Philh/L. Collingwood/J-P. Morel, G. Moore)

CHS7 69741-2(3) (4/92)
Record of Singing, Vol.4—French School
Dell' Acqua: Chanson Provençale; *Séverac:* Ma poupée chérie; *Mozart:* Dans un bois solitaire, K308; *Hahn:* Rossignol des lilas; *Fauré:* En prière; *Rimsky-Korsakov:* Songs, Op. 2 (exc); *Respighi:* Stornellatrice; *Anon:* Amor amaro; *Ravel:* Mélodies populaires grecques (exc); *Godard:* Vivandière (exc); *Saint-Saëns:* Samson et Dalila (exc); *Berlioz:* Troyens (exc); *Lipatti:* Sensation; Amoureuse; Pas; Capital de la douleur; *Massenet:* Werther (exc); *Duparc:* Invitation au voyage; *Gounod:* Mélodies (1855) (exc); *Bassani:* Posate, dormite; *Lalo:* Roi d'ys (exc). (M. Robin, orch/G. Briez, M. Angelici, M. Fauré, I. Joachim, L. Bergmann, G. Boué, A. Collard, G. Guillamat, V. Perlemuter, R. Doria, T. Janopoulo, V. de los Angeles, G. Moore, S. Danco, E. Bellinzona, I. Kolassi, S. Michel, Paris Opéra-Comique Orch/L. Fourestier, H. Bouvier, Paris Op Orch, R. Gorr, Philh/L. Collingwood, H. Cuénod, M. Lipatti, R. Jobin/A. Cluytens, P. Bernac, F. Poulenc, C. Maurane, L. Bienvenu, G. Souzay, J. Bonneau, S. Juyol)

CHS7 69741-2(4) (4/92)
Record of Singing, Vol.4—German School
Schubert: Schweizerlied, D559; Claudine von Villa Bella (exc); *Mozart:* Zauberflöte (exc); Nehmt meinen Dank, K383; *Beethoven:* Fidelio (exc); *Brahms:* Liebeslieder Walzer, Op. 52 (exc); *Wolf:* Mörike Lieder (exc); *Lehár:* Eva (exc); *Reger:* Schlichte Weisen, Op.76 (exc); *Tchaikovsky:* Queen of Spades (exc); *Verdi:* Aida (exc); *Puccini:* Tosca (exc); *R. Strauss:* Arabella (exc); *Menotti:* Consul (exc); *R. Strauss:* Lieder, Op. 27 (exc); *Wolf:* Goethe Lieder (exc); *Mozart:* Don Giovanni (exc); *R. Strauss:* Capriccio (exc); *Mozart:* Zauberflöte (exc); *Schubert:* Schöne Müllerin (exc); *Weber:* Freischütz (exc); *Lortzing:* Undine (exc); *Schumann:* Liederkreis, Op.39 (exc); *Schubert:* Jüngling an der Quelle, D300; *Mozart:* Zauberflöte (exc); Così fan tutte (exc); *Beethoven:* Fidelio (exc); *Brahms:* Lieder, Op. 86 (exc); *Wagner:* Tannhäuser (exc); *Schubert:* Fahrt zum Hades, D526; *Mozart:* Zauberflöte (exc); *Pfitzner:* Lieder, Op.2 (exc); *Weber:* Freischütz (exc). (E. Schumann, G. Moore, E. Köth, Berlin St Op Orch/A. Rother, M. Stader, orch/H. Erisman, E. Schwarzkopf, Philh/A. Galliera, I. Seefried, H. von Nordberg, F. Wührer, M. Reining, VPO/F. Lehár, E. Grümmer, H. Diez, S. Jurinac/L. Collingwood, L. Welitsch/J. Krips, G. Brouwenstijn, Hilversum RO/P. Van Kempen, Leonie Rysanek/W. Schüchter, I. Borkh, H. Konetzni, E. Höngen, H. Zipper, H. Meyer-Welfing/R. Moralt, A. Dermota/K. Böhm, W. Ludwig/O. Ackermann, J. Patzak, M. Raucheisen, P. Anders, Berlin Deutsche Op Orch, R. Schock, D. Fischer-Dieskau, K. Schmitt-Walter, A. Stauch, E. Kunz, M. Rothmüller/J. Robertson, P. Schoeffler, Vienna St Op Chor, Vienna St Op Orch, H. Hotter, L. Weber/I. Dobroven, T. Herrmann, G. Frick, Berlin Deutsche Op Chor, Berlin SO, F. Beckmann, J. Herrmann, B. Seidler-Winkler/B. Seidler-Winkler)

CHS7 69741-2(5) (4/92)
Record of Singing, Vol.4—Scandinavian School
Purcell: Dido (exc); *Sibelius:* Songs, Op.37 (exc); *Dowland:* Second Booke of Songs (exc); *Cilea:* Adriana Lecouvreur (exc); *Bizet:* Pêcheurs de perles (exc); *Gounod:* Roméo et Juliette (exc); *Offenbach:* Contes d'Hoffmann (exc); *Wolf:* Goethe Lieder (exc); *Wagner:* Tannhäuser (exc); *Gounod:* Mors et vita (exc); *Debussy:* Chansons de Bilitis (exc). (K. Flagstad, Philh/W. Braithwaite, L. Lail, S-G. Andrén, A. Schiøtz, J.G. Schmidt, S. Islandi, Tivoli Concert Orch/S. Felumb, N. Gedda/A. Galliera, J. Björling, Stockholm Royal Op Orch/N. Grevillius, H. Hasslo, orch, B. Sönnerstedt, F. Jensen, J. Berglund/L. Blech, K. Borg, Exclusive Orch, G. Leppée, L. Demant)

CHS7 69741-2(6) (4/92)
Record of Singing, Vol.4—Russian & Slavonic Schools
Mussorgsky: Night; Khovanshchina (exc); *Offenbach:* Périchole (exc); *Tchaikovsky:* Songs, Op.6 (exc); *Mussorgsky:* Fair at Sorochintsï (exc); *Rimsky-Korsakov:* Snow Maiden (exc); *Verstovsky:* Askold's Grave (exc); *Nápravník:* Dubrovsky (exc); *Smetana:* Dalibor (exc); *Rimsky-Korsakov:* Sadko (exc); *Tchaikovsky:* Mazeppa (exc); *Verdi:* Nabucco (exc); *Borodin:* Sleeping Princess; *Tchaikovsky:* Songs, Op.47 (exc); *Rubinstein:* Persian Songs, Op.34 (exc); *Kodály:* Sadly rustle the leaves. (M. Predit, G. Moore, Z. Dolukhanova, orch, C. Novikova, N. Obukhova, M. Sakharov, G. Vinogradov, Bolshoi Th Orch/S. Samosud, I. Zhadan/A. Orlov, G. Nelepp, Moscow All-Union Rad Ch, Moscow All-Union RSO/V. Smirnov, I. Kozlovsky, B. Blachut, Prague Op Orch, J. Charvát, P. Lisitsian/N. Golovanov, A. Ivanov, B. Christoff, Rome Op Orch/V. Gui, M. Reizen, A. Coates, B. Gmyrya, L. Ostrin, E. Koréh, H. von Nordberg)

CHS7 69741-2(7) (4/92)
Record of Singing, Vol.4—Italian School
Donizetti: Elisir d'amore (exc); *Verdi:* Trovatore (exc); *A. Thomas:* Mignon (exc); *Falvo:* Dicitencello vuie; *Boito:* Mefistofele (exc); *Massenet:* Werther (exc); *Verdi:* Otello

(exc); *Donizetti:* Favorita (exc); *Giordano:* Andrea Chénier (exc); *Tosti:* 'A Vucchella; *Puccini:* Tosca (exc); *Verdi:* Don Carlo (exc); *Bellini:* Sonnambula (exc); *Glinka:* Life for the Tsar (exc); *Mussorgsky:* Boris Godunov (exc); *Massenet:* Werther (exc); *Verdi:* Trovatore (exc); *Donizetti:* Favorita (exc); *Bizet:* Pêcheurs de perles (exc); *Puccini:* Turandot (exc); *Bellini:* Capuleti (exc); *A. Scarlatti:* Su venite e consiglio; *Respighi:* Nebbie; *Bellini:* Fervido desiderio; *Puccini:* Manon Lescaut (exc); *Verdi:* Don Carlo (exc); Trovatore (exc); *Rossini:* Armida (exc); *Puccini:* Bohème (exc). (Ferruccio Tagliavini, RCA Victor Orch/A. Dorati, B. Gigli, C. Elmo, orch/U. Berrettoni, G. di Stefano, La Scala Orch/E. Tieri, L. Infantino, RPO/A. Erede, G. Malipiero, G. Prandelli, Milan SO/A. Quadri, M. del Monaco, P. Silveri, LSO/W. Goehr, T. Gobbi, Rome Op Orch/O. de Fabritiis, G. Valdengo, Kingsway SO, G. Malaspina, ROH Chor, ROHO/M. Mudie, G. Bechi, R. Arié/J. Krips, N. Rossi-Lemeni, Philh/T. Benintende-Neglia, T. Pasero, G. Simionato, F. Barbieri, M. Caruso, E. Stignani, Rome Academy Orch/V. Bellezza, A. Noni, E. Arizmendi/J.E. Martini, M. Carosio/A. Fistoulari, M. László, L. Cortese, A. Anzellotti, G. Favaretto, G. Gatti, G. Moore, R. Tebaldi, SRO, M. Grandi, Z. Milanov/F. Weissmann, M. Callas, Rome RAI Orch/A. Simonetto, S. Scuderi)

Ⓓ **CMS5 65061-2(2)** (4/94)
The Fabulous Victoria de los Angeles (pt 2)
Toldrá: Canciones Gallegas (exc); *Turina:* Tríptico, Op.45 (exc); *Rodrigo:* Villancicos (exc); *Falla:* Psyché; Soneto a Córdoba; *Sacrati:* Proserpina (exc); *A. Scarlatti:* Pirro e Demetrio (exc); *Handel:* Joshua (exc); *Schubert:* Tod und das Mädchen, D531; Schöne Müllerin (exc); An die Musik, D547; *Brahms:* Lieder, Op.59 (exc); Lieder, Op.84 (exc); *Fauré:* Songs, Op.27 (exc); Songs, Op.46 (exc); *Purcell:* Indian Queen, Z630 (exc); Lost is my quiet for ever, Z502; *Haydn:* Schlaf in deiner engen Kammer; *J.C. Bach:* Canzonette (exc); *Beethoven:* Irish Songs, WoO154 (exc); Irish Songs, WoO152 (exc); Welsh Songs, WoO155 (exc); *Schubert:* Nur wer die Sehnsucht kennt, D877/4; *Berlioz:* Trébuchet; *Dvořák:* Moravian Duets, B69 (exc); *Tchaikovsky:* Duets, Op.46 (exc); *Saint-Saëns:* Pastorale; *Fauré:* Pleurs d'or, Op.72; *Brahms:* Lieder, Op.94 (exc); *Mozart:* Partenza, K436. (V. de los Angeles, G. Soriano, A. Challan, French Stg Trio, J-C. Gérard, E. Schwarzkopf, D. Fischer-Dieskau, G. Moore)

Ⓓ **CMS5 65119-2** (10/95)
Delius—Orchestral Works
Delius: Brigg Fair; Appalachia; In a Summer Garden; Hassan (exc); Song before Sunrise; Koanga (exc); First Cuckoo; Summer Night on the River; Late Swallows; Village Romeo and Juliet (exc); Irmelin Prelude; Song of Summer; Fennimore and Gerda Intermezzo. (R. Tear, A. Jenkins, Ambrosian Sngrs, Hallé, LSO/J. Barbirolli)

Ⓓ **CMS5 65212-2** (10/94)
Wagner—Les introuvables du Ring
Wagner: Rheingold (exc); Walküre (exc); Walküre (exc); Walküre (exc); Walküre (exc); Siegfried (exc); Götterdämmerung (exc); Götterdämmerung (exc); Götterdämmerung (exc); Götterdämmerung (exc); Götterdämmerung (exc). (L. Otto, M. Muszely, K. Flagstad, H. Dernesch, B. Nilsson, S. Wagner, J. Blatter, R. Siewert, H. Melchert, R. Schock, S. Svanholm, W. Cochran, B. Kusche, J. Metternich, D. Fischer-Dieskau, F. Frantz, H. Hotter, H. Sotin, G. Frick, Berlin Deutsche Op Chor, Berlin Deutsche Op Orch/F. Konwitschny, Berlin Staatskapelle/R. Kempe, Philh/K. Böhm/L. Ludwig/G. Sébastian/W. Sawallisch/W. Furtwängler/H. Weigert, New Philh/O. Klemperer, BRSO/R. Kubelík)

Ⓓ **CMS5 65224-2** (10/94)
Vaughan Williams—Hugh the Drover
Vaughan Williams: Hugh the Drover (Cpte). (R. Tear, S. Armstrong, R. Lloyd, M. Rippon, H. Watts, J. Fryatt, H. Newman, T. Sharpe, L. Fyson, O. Broome, S. Burgess, D. Johnston, L. Richardson, S. Minty, N. Jenkins, B. Ogston, D. Read, S. Davies, St Paul's Cath Ch, Ambrosian Op Chor, RPO/C. Groves)

Ⓓ **CMS5 65256-2** (9/95)
Gounod—Faust
Gounod: Faust (Cpte). (N. Gedda, V. de los Angeles, B. Christoff, J. Borthayre, M. Angelici, S. Michel, R. Jeantet, Paris Op Chor, Paris Op Orch/A. Cluytens)

Ⓓ **CMS5 65260-2** (9/95)
Offenbach—Les Contes d'Hoffmann
Offenbach: Contes d'Hoffmann (Cpte). (R. Jobin, R. Doria, V. Bovy, G. Boué, F. Revoil, R. Faure, L. Musy, A. Pernet, C. Soix, R. Bourdin, R. Lapelletrie, C. Cambon, A. Philippe, S. Borghese, Bourvil, A. Vessières, R. Amade, C. Maurane, H. Delahaye, Paris Opéra-Comique Chor, Paris Opéra-Comique Orch/A. Cluytens)

Ⓓ **CMS5 65263-2** (9/95)
Saint-Saëns—Samson et Dalila
Saint-Saëns: Samson et Dalila (Cpte). (J. Luccioni, H. Bouvier, P. Cabanel, C. Cambon, Paris Op Chor, Paris Op Orch/L. Fourestier)

Ⓓ **CMS5 65266-2** (9/95)
Bizet—Les pêcheurs de perles
Bizet: Pêcheurs de Perles (Cpte). (M. Angelici, H. Legay (ten), M. Dens, L. Noguera, Paris Opéra-Comique Chor, Paris Opéra-Comique Orch/A. Cluytens)

Ⓓ **CMS5 65284-2**
Cornelius—Der Barbier von Bagdad & Busoni—Arlecchino
Cornelius: Barbier von Bagdad (Cpte); *Busoni:* Arlecchino (Cpte). (O. Czerwenka, E. Schwarzkopf, N. Gedda, H. Prey, G. Unger, G. Hoffman, E. Waechter, A. Jaresch, R. Christ, chor, Philh/E. Leinsdorf, K. Gester, E. Malbin, I. Wallace, G. Evans, F. Ollendorff, M. Dickie, Glyndebourne Fest Orch/J. Pritchard)

Ⓓ **CMS5 65287-2** (7/95)
Giordano—Andrea Chénier
Giordano: Andrea Chénier (Cpte). (F. Corelli, A. Stella, M. Sereni, P. De Palma, L. Moneta, S. Malagù, G. Modesti, D. Mantovani, P. Pedani, A. di Stasio, P. Montarsolo, Rome Op Chor, Rome Op Orch/G. Santini)

Ⓓ **CMS5 65290-2**
Gounod—Roméo et Juliette
Gounod: Roméo et Juliette (Cpte). (F. Corelli, M. Freni, X. Depraz, H. Gui, E. Lublin, C. Calès, M. Vilma, R. Cardona, Y. Bisson, C. Grigoriou, M. Auzeville, P. Thau, Paris Op Chor, Paris Op Orch/A. Lombard)

Ⓓ **CMS5 65293-2** (12/94)
Puccini—Turandot
Puccini: Turandot (Cpte). (M. Caballé, J. Carreras, M. Freni, V. Sardinero, R. Corazza, R. Cassinelli, P. Plishka, M. Sénéchal, E. Tumagian, Strasbourg Cath Maîtrise, Rhine Op Chor, Strasbourg PO/A. Lombard)

Ⓓ **CMS5 65296-2**
Verdi—Otello
Verdi: Otello (Cpte). (J. McCracken, G. Jones, D. Fischer-Dieskau, P. De Palma, F. Andreolli, A. di Stasio, A. Giacomotti, L. Monreale, G. Thomas, Upton Hse School Boys' Ch, Hammersmith School Girls' Ch, Ambrosian Op Chor, New Philh/J. Barbirolli)

Ⓓ **CMS5 65299-2** (2/95)
Charpentier—Louise
G. Charpentier: Louise (Cpte). (B. Sills, N. Gedda, J. Van Dam, M. Dunn, M. Hill, E. Lublin, Maîtrise de la Résurrection, Paris Op Chor, Paris Op Orch/J. Rudel)

Ⓓ **CMS5 65318-2** (9/95)
Bizet—Carmen
Bizet: Carmen (Cpte). (S. Michel, R. Jobin, M. Angelici, M. Dens, G. Chellet, R. Notti, J. Vieuille, F. Leprin, J. Thirache, X. Smati, Paris Opéra-Comique Chor, Paris Opéra-Comique Orch/A. Cluytens)

Ⓓ **CMS5 65363-2** (2/95)
Millöcker—Gasparone
Millöcker: Gasparone (Cpte). (A. Rothenberger, G. Wewel, W. Brokmeier, H. Prey, G.W. Dieberitz, M. Finke, G. Fuchs, Bavarian St Op Chor, Munich RO/H. Wallberg)

Ⓓ **CMS5 65372-2** (2/95)
Lehár—Das Land des Lächelns
Lehár: Land des Lächelns (Cpte). (A. Rothenberger, H. Friedauer, N. Gedda, R. Holm, J. Moeller, Bavarian Rad Chor, Graunke SO/W. Mattes)

Ⓓ **CMS5 65375-2**
Lehár—Der Graf von Luxemburg
Lehár: Graf von Luxemburg (Cpte). (N. Gedda, K. Böhme, G. Litz, W. Brokmeier, L. Popp, R. Holm, H.G. Grimm, W. Anheisser, H. Günther, Bavarian St Op Chor, Graunke SO/W. Mattes)

Ⓓ **CMS5 65378-2** (2/95)
Lehár—Giuditta
Lehár: Giuditta (Cpte). (E. Moser, N. Gedda, K. Hirte, L. Baumann, J. Jung, T. Wiedenhofer, J. von Pawels, G. Wewel, B. Lindner, M. Finke, F. Lenz, Munich Concert Chor, Munich RO/W. Boskovsky)

Ⓓ **CMS5 65387-2** (2/95)
Millöcker—Der Bettelstudent
Millöcker: Bettelstudent (Cpte). (G. Litz, R. Streich, R. Holm, H. Prey, G. Unger, N. Gedda, K.H. Bennert, Bavarian Rad Chor, Graunke SO/F. Allers)

Ⓓ **CMS5 65476-2**
Janáček—Jenufa
Janáček: Jenufa (Cpte). (L. Domanínská, V. Přibyl, N. Kniplová, I. Žídek, M. Boháčová, M. Mrázová, J. Jindrák, Z. Kroupa, J. Procházková, E. Hlobilová, B. Effenberková, A. Rousková, Prague Nat Th Chor, Prague Nat Th Orch/B. Gregor)

Ⓓ **CMS5 65479-2**
Massenet—Thaïs
Massenet: Thaïs (Cpte). (B. Sills, S. Milnes, N. Gedda, R. Van Allan, A-M. Connors, A. Murray, P. Kern, N. Burrowes, B. Etheridge, John Alldis Ch, New Philh/L. Maazel)

Ⓓ **CMS5 65550-2** (7/95)
Walton—Troilus and Cressida
Walton: Troilus and Cressida (Cpte). (R. Cassilly, J. Baker, G. English, E. Bainbridge, M. Rivers, R. Van Allan, R. Lloyd, B. Luxon, G. Macpherson, G. Sullivan, H. Thomas, Alan Jones II, D. McCoshan, ROH Chor, ROHO/L. Foster)

Ⓓ **CMS5 65621-2**
Fischer-Dieskau - The Opera Singer
Lortzing: Zar und Zimmermann (exc); Wildschütz (exc); Undine (exc); *Nicolai:* Lustigen Weiber von Windsor (exc); *Puccini:* Bohème (exc); *Wagner:* Tannhäuser (exc); Parsifal (exc); *Pfitzner:* Arme Heinrich (exc); *Verdi:* Trovatore (exc); Rigoletto (exc); Vespri siciliani (exc); Don Carlo (exc); Ballo in maschera (exc); Falstaff (exc); Don Carlo (exc); *Gounod:* Faust (exc); *Schubert:* Zwillingsbrüder (exc); *Mendelssohn:* Beiden Pädagogen (exc); Heimkehr aus der Fremde (exc); *Handel:* Rinaldo (exc); *Hindemith:* Mathis der Maler (exc). (D. Fischer-Dieskau, R. Streich, G. Frick, R. Schock, N. Gedda, Berlin Deutsche Op Chor, Bavarian Rad Chor, BPO, Berlin SO, Philh, BRSO, Berlin RSO, Bavarian St Op Orch, Munich RO/W. Schüchter/R. Kubelík/W. Sawallisch/A. Erede/G. Patanè/H. Wallberg, J-P. Rampal, R. Veyron-Lacroix, J. Neilz)

Ⓓ **CMS5 65655-2**
Boito—Mefistofele
Boito: Mefistofele (Cpte). (B. Christoff, G. Prandelli, O. Moscucci, A. Pini, P. de Palma, Rome Op Chor, Rome Op Orch/V. Gui)

Ⓓ **CMS5 65658-2**
Donizetti—L'elisir d'amore
Donizetti: Elisir d'amore (Cpte). (R. Carteri, L. Alva, R. Panerai, G. Taddei, A. Vercelli, La Scala Chor, La Scala Orch/T. Serafin)

Ⓓ **CMS5 65661-2**
Humperdinck—Hänsel und Gretel
Humperdinck: Hänsel und Gretel (Cpte). (I. Seefried, A. Rothenberger, G. Hoffman, W. Berry, L. Maikl, E. Höngen, Vienna Boys' Ch, VPO/A. Cluytens)

Ⓓ **CMS5 65665-2**
Wagner—Parsifal
Wagner: Parsifal (Cpte). (W. Ellsworth, P. Joll, D. McIntyre, W. Meier, N. Folwell, D. Gwynne, T. German, W. Mackie, Mary Davies, M. Morgan, J. Harris, N. Ackerman, E. Ritchie, C. Teare, R. Cullis, E. Collier, C. Bell, K. Harries, WNO Chor, WNO Orch/R. Goodall)

Ⓓ **CMS5 65716-2**
Rostropovich as Accompanist
Mussorgsky: Sunless; Where art thou, little star?; Gopak; Lullaby; Darling Savishna; Orphan; Eremushka's Lullaby; Songs and Dances of Death; *Rimsky-Korsakov:* Sadko (exc); Tsar's Bride (exc); *Tchaikovsky:* Snow Maiden (exc); *Rimsky-Korsakov:* Songs, Op.40 (exc); Songs, Op.2 (exc); Songs, Op.39 (exc); Songs, Op.42 (exc); In Spring, Op.43 (exc); To the Poet, Op.45 (exc); Songs, Op.56 (exc); *Tchaikovsky:* Songs, Op.47 (exc); Songs, Op.6 (exc); Songs, Op.28 (exc); Songs, Op.73 (exc); Songs, Op.16 (exc); Songs, Op.38 (exc); *Prokofiev:* Russian Folksongs, Op. 104 (exc); *Shostakovich:* Suite of Romances, Op.127; Satires. (G. Vishnevskaya, U. Hoelscher, M. Rostropovich, V. Devetzi, M. Rostropovich, LPO/M. Rostropovich)

Ⓓ **CMS7 63000-2** (7/89)
Bellini—Norma
Bellini: Norma (Cpte). (M. Callas, C. Ludwig, F. Corelli, N. Zaccaria, P. de Palma, E. Vincenzi, La Scala Chor, La Scala Orch/T. Serafin)

Ⓓ **CMS7 63214-2** (10/90)
Wagner: Tannhäuser
Wagner: Tannhäuser (Cpte). (H. Hopf, E. Grümmer, D. Fischer-Dieskau, M. Schech, G. Frick, F. Wunderlich, R. Gonszar, G. Unger, R. Süss, L. Otto, Berlin St Op Chor, Berlin St Op Orch/F. Konwitschny)

Ⓓ **CMS7 63222-2** (12/89)
Offenbach—Les contes d'Hoffamnn
Offenbach: Contes d'Hoffmann (Cpte). (N. Gedda, G. d'Angelo, E. Schwarzkopf, V. de los Angeles, J-C. Benoit, N. Ghiuselev, G. London, E. Blanc, M. Sénéchal, J-P. Laffage, R. Geay, C. Gayraud, J. Collard, R. Duclos Ch, Paris Cons/A. Cluytens)

Ⓓ **CMS7 63226-2** (11/89)
Verdi—Giovanna d'Arco
Verdi: Giovanna d'Arco (Cpte). (M. Caballé, P. Domingo,

S. Milnes, K. Erwen, R. Lloyd, Ambrosian Op Chor, LSO/James Levine)

Ⓓ **CMS7 63229-2** (1/90)
Verdi—Aida
Verdi: Aida (Cpte). (B. Nilsson, G. Bumbry, F. Corelli, M. Sereni, B. Giaiotti, F. Mazzoli, P. de Palma, M. Fiorentini, Rome Op Chor, Rome Op Orch/Z. Mehta)

Ⓓ **CMS7 63244-2** (2/90)
The Art of Maria Callas
Bellini: Norma (exc); Pirata (exc); Sonnambula (exc); Puritani (exc); *Cherubini:* Medea (exc); *Donizetti:* Anna Bolena (exc); Lucia di Lammermoor (exc); *Gluck:* Iphigénie en Tauride (exc); *Mascagni:* Cavalleria Rusticana (exc); *Ponchielli:* Gioconda (exc); *Puccini:* Madama Butterfly (exc); Tosca (exc); *Rossini:* Barbiere di Siviglia (exc); Turco in Italia (exc); *Spontini:* Vestale (exc); *Verdi:* Ballo in maschera (exc); Macbeth (exc); Traviata (exc); Trovatore (exc); Vespri Siciliani (exc). (M. Callas, M. Filippeschi, N. Rossi-Lemeni, La Scala Chor, La Scala Orch/T. Serafin, Philh/N. Rescigno/A. Votto, R. Panerai, M. Sinclair, J. Lanigan, D. Robertson, J. Rouleau, G. Sarri, R. Arié, MMF Chor, MMF Orch, Paris Cons/G. Prêtre, A.M. Canali, C. Forti, N. Gedda/H. von Karajan/V. de Sabata, E. Ticozzi, G. di Stefano, F. Calabrese/G. Gavazzeni, Alfredo Kraus, P. de Palma, Lisbon San Carlos Nat Th Chor, Lisbon San Carlos Nat Th Orch/F. Ghione)

Ⓓ **CMS7 63263-2** (12/89)
Mozart—Die Entführung aus dem Serail
Mozart: Entführung (Cpte). (A. Rothenberger, L. Popp, N. Gedda, G. Unger, G. Frick, L. Rudolf, Vienna St Op Chor, VPO/J. Krips)

Ⓓ **CMS7 63266-2** (1/90)
Mozart—Le nozze di Figaro
Mozart: Nozze di Figaro (Cpte). (G. Taddei, A. Moffo, E. Waechter, E. Schwarzkopf, F. Cossotto, D. Gatta, I. Vinco, R. Ercolani, P. Cappuccilli, E. Fusco, Philh Chor, Philh/C.M. Giulini)

Ⓓ **CMS7 63386-2** (6/90)
Borodin—Prince Igor & Complete Solo Songs
Borodin: Prince Igor (Cpte); Those folk; Song of the dark forest; From my tears; Sea princess; Pretty girl no longer loves me; Magic Garden; Arabian melody; Fishermaiden; Listen to my song; Sleeping princess; Pride; Sea; Why art thou so early, dawn?; My songs are poisoned; False note; For the shores. (C. Chekerliski, J. Wiener, T. Todorov, B. Christoff, R. Penkova, L. Mihailov, A. Milkovsky, K. Dulguerov, B. Christoff, M. Tortelier, A. Tcherepnin, J. Reiss, Lamoureux Orch/G. Tzipine, Sofia National Op Chor, Sofia National Op Orch/J. Semkow)

Ⓓ **CMS7 63513-2** (9/90)
Verdi—Simon Boccanegra
Verdi: Simon Boccanegra (Cpte). (T. Gobbi, V. de los Angeles, G. Campora, B. Christoff, W. Monachesi, P. Dari, P. Caroli, S. Bertona, Rome Op Chor, Rome Op Orch/G. Santini)

Ⓓ **CMS7 63595-2** (3/91)
Wagner—Siegfried
Wagner: Siegfried (Cpte). (A. Remedios, N. Bailey, R. Hunter, G. Dempsey, D. Hammond-Stroud, A. Collins, C. Grant, M. London, Sadler's Wells Op Orch/R. Goodall)

Ⓓ **CMS7 63625-2** (2/91)
Cherubini: Medea, etc
Cherubini: Medea (Cpte); *Beethoven:* Ah! perfido, Op.65. (M. Callas, M. Picchi, R. Scotto, G. Modesti, M. Pirazzini, L. Marimpietri, E. Galassi, A. Giacomotti, La Scala Chor, La Scala Orch/T. Serafin, M. Callas, Paris Cons/N. Rescigno)

Ⓓ **CMS7 63628-2** (2/91)
Verdi: La traviata
Verdi: Traviata (Cpte). (M. Callas, G. di Stefano, E. Bastianini, S. Zanolli, L. Mandelli, G. Zampieri, A. la Porta, A. Zerbini, S. Maionica, F. Ricciardi, La Scala Chor, La Scala Orch/C.M. Giulini)

Ⓓ **CMS7 63631-2** (2/91)
Donizetti: Lucia di Lammermoor
Donizetti: Lucia di Lammermoor (Cpte). (M. Callas, G. di Stefano, R. Panerai, N. Zaccaria, L. Villa, G. Zampieri, Mario Carlin, La Scala Chor, Berlin RIAS Orch/H. von Karajan)

Ⓓ **CMS7 63634-2** (3/91) ▭ **TC-CFPD4446** (8/85)
Puccini: Madama Butterfly
Puccini: Madama Butterfly (Cpte). (V. de los Angeles, J. Björling, M. Sereni, M. Pirazzini, P. de Palma, A. la Porta, S. Bertona, P. Montarsolo, B. Giaiotti, A. Sacchetti, P. Caroli, Rome Op. Chor, Rome Op. Orch/G. Santini)

Ⓓ **CMS7 63637-2** (3/91)
Gluck: Orfeo ed Euridice
Gluck: Orfeo ed Euridice (Cpte). (A. Baltsa, M. Marshall, E. Gruberová, Ambrosian Op Chor, Philh/R. Muti)

Ⓓ **CMS7 63640-2**
Verdi—Il Trovatore
Verdi: Trovatore (Cpte). (F. Corelli, G. Tucci, R. Merrill, G. Simionato, F. Mazzoli, L. Moneta, A. Mercuriali, M. Rinaudo, Rome Op Chor, Rome Op Orch/T. Schippers)

Ⓓ **CMS7 63646-2** (5/91)
Mozart: Le Nozze di Figaro
Mozart: Nozze di Figaro (Cpte). (G. Evans, J. Blegen, D. Fischer-Dieskau, H. Harper, T. Berganza, B. Finnilä, W. McCue, J. Fryatt, J. Robertson, M. Donnelly, E. Gale, John Alldis Ch, ECO/D. Barenboim)

Ⓓ **CMS7 63650-2** (3/91)
Cav and Pag
Mascagni: Cavalleria rusticana (Cpte); *Leoncavallo:* Pagliacci (Cpte). (J. Carreras, R. Scotto, K. Nurmela, T. Allen, U. Benelli, M. Caballé, J. Carreras, M. Manuguerra, J. Hamari, A. Varnay, Southend Boys' Ch, Ambrosian Op Chor, Philh/R. Muti)

Ⓓ **CMS7 63712-2** (3/91)
Orff—Operas
Orff: Kluge (Cpte); Mond (Cpte). (M. Cordes, G. Frick, E. Schwarzkopf, G. Wieter, R. Christ, B. Kusche, P. Kuen, H. Prey, G. Neidlinger, R. Christ, K. Schmitt-Walter, H. Graml, P. Kuen, P. Lagger, A. Peter, H. Hotter, Childrens' Chor, Philh/W. Sawallisch)

Ⓓ **CMS7 63835-2** (10/91)
Bruckner, Wagner & Hindemith—Orchestral Works
Bruckner: Symphony 8; *Wagner:* Walküre (exc); *Hindemith:* Nobilissima Visione. (N. Bailey, New Philh, Philh/O. Klemperer)

Ⓓ **CMS7 63841-2** (9/91)
Mozart—Don Giovanni
Mozart: Don Giovanni (Cpte). (N. Ghiaurov, C. Watson, C. Ludwig, M. Freni, N. Gedda, W. Berry, P. Montarsolo, F. Crass, New Philh Chor, New Philh/O. Klemperer)

Ⓓ **CMS7 63845-2** (9/91)
Mozart—Così fan tutte
Mozart: Così fan tutte (Cpte). (M. Price, Y. Minton, L. Popp, L. Alva, G. Evans, H. Sotin, John Alldis Ch, New Philh/O. Klemperer)

Ⓓ **CMS7 63849-2** (9/91)
Mozart—Le nozze di Figaro
Mozart: Nozze di Figaro (Cpte). (G. Evans, R. Grist, G. Bacquier, E. Söderström, T. Berganza, A. Burmeister, M. Langdon, W. Hollweg, W. Brokmeier, C. Grant, M. Price, John Alldis Ch, New Philh/O. Klemperer)

Ⓓ **CMS7 63918-2** (7/91)
Wagner—The Valkyrie
Wagner: Walküre (Cpte). (A. Remedios, M. Curphey, R. Hunter, N. Bailey, A. Howard, C. Grant, K. Clarke, Anne Evans, A. Conoley, E. Connell, A. Collins, Sarah Walker, S. Squires, H. Attfield, ENO Orch/R. Goodall)

Ⓓ **CMS7 63967-2** (3/92)
Mascagni/Leoncavallo—Cav & Pag
Mascagni: Cavalleria Rusticana (Cpte); *Leoncavallo:* Pagliacci (Cpte). (V. de los Angeles, F. Corelli, M. Sereni, A. Lazzarini, C. Vozza, F. Corelli, L. Amara, T. Gobbi, M. Zanasi, M. Spina, Rome Op Chor, Rome Op Orch/G. Santini, La Scala Chor, La Scala Orch/L. von Matačić)

Ⓓ **CMS7 63970-2** (4/92)
Puccini—La Fanciulla del West
Puccini: Fanciulla del West (Cpte). (B. Nilsson, J. Gibin, A. Mongelli, R. Ercolani, A. Cassinelli, N. Zaccaria, C. Forti, G. Carturan, E. Sordello, F. Andreolli, G. Costariol, D. Mantovani, D. Formichini, A. Costantino, L. Monreale, G. Morresi, A. Mercuriali, La Scala Chor, La Scala Orch/L. von Matačić)

Ⓓ **CMS7 63973-2** (5/92)
Massenet—Werther
Massenet: Werther (Cpte). (N. Gedda, V. de los Angeles, R. Soyer, M. Mesplé, J-C. Benoit, A. Mallabrera, C. Grigoriou, French Rad Maîtrise, Paris Orch/G. Prêtre)

Ⓓ **CMS7 63980-2** (2/92)
Wagner—Rienzi
Wagner: Rienzi (Cpte). (R. Kollo, S. Wennberg, N. Hillebrand, J. Martin, T. Adam, S. Vogel, P. Schreier, G. Leib, I. Springer, Leipzig Rad Chor, Dresden St Op Chor, Staatskapelle Dresden/H. Hollreiser)

Ⓓ **CMS7 63990-2**
Mozart—Idomeneo
Mozart: Idomeneo (Cpte). (N. Gedda, A. Dallapozza, A. Rothenberger, E. Moser, P. Schreier, E. Büchner, T. Adam, Leipzig Rad Chor, Staatskapelle Dresden/H. Schmidt-Isserstedt)

Ⓓ **CMS7 64008-2(1)** (1/92)
Wagner Singing on Record (pt 1)
Wagner: Fliegende Holländer (exc); Fliegende Holländer (exc); Fliegende Holländer (exc); Fliegende Holländer (exc); Fliegende Holländer (exc); Meistersinger (exc); Meistersinger (exc); Meistersinger (exc); Meistersinger (exc); Meistersinger (exc); Meistersinger (exc); Tannhäuser (exc); Tannhäuser (exc); Tannhäuser (exc); Tannhäuser (exc); Tannhäuser (exc); Lohengrin (exc); Lohengrin (exc); Lohengrin (exc); Lohengrin (exc); Lohengrin (exc); Lohengrin (exc); Lohengrin (exc); Lohengrin (exc). (H. Hermann Nissen, A. Endrèze, M. Fuchs, F. Beckmann, E. Rethberg, B. Nilsson, H. Hotter, F. Schorr, G. Thill, G. Martinelli, R. Bockelmann, L. Melchior, E. Schumann, G. Parr, B. Williams, T. Ralf, T. Lemnitz, M. Müller, M. Lorenz, M. Reining, H. Janssen, G. Hüsch, K. Flagstad, A. Pertile, M. Singher, M. Lawrence, H. Spani, Lotte Lehmann, M. Klose, M. Wittrisch, H. Roswaenge, Berlin St Op Orch, SO, Philh, LSO, orch, ROH Chor, LPO, Bayreuth Fest Orch, VPO, La Scala Orch/B. Seidler-Winkler/C. Schmalstich/L. Blech/S. Meyrowitz/L. Ludwig/A. Coates/J. Barbirolli/E. Bigot/T. Beecham/Rosario Bourdon/K. Elmendorff/R. Moralt/H.U. Müller/F. Zweig/J. Schüler/F. Zaun/P. Coppola/C. Sabajno/I. Dobroven/F. Weissmann, La Scala Chor)

Ⓓ **CMS7 64008-2(2)** (1/92)
Wagner Singing on Record (pt 2)
Wagner: Tristan und Isolde (exc); Tristan und Isolde (exc); Tristan und Isolde (exc); Tristan und Isolde (exc); Tristan und Isolde (exc); Tristan und Isolde (exc); Tristan und Isolde (exc); Parsifal (exc); Parsifal (exc); Rheingold (exc); Walküre (exc); Walküre (exc); Walküre (exc); Walküre (exc); Walküre (exc); Siegfried (exc); Siegfried (exc); Siegfried (exc); Siegfried (exc); Götterdämmerung (exc); Götterdämmerung (exc); Götterdämmerung (exc); Götterdämmerung (exc). (F. Leider, N. Larsen-Todsen, A. Helm, L. Melchior, M. Seinemeyer, G. Lubin, A. Kipnis, F. Wolff, F. Schorr, M. Lorenz, M. Lawrence, M. Journet, R. Bockelmann, H. Hermann Nissen, M. Olczewska, E. Schipper, R. Laubenthal, F. Austral, W. Widdop, E. List, L. Weber, H. Janssen, ROH Chor, Berlin Staatskapelle Chor, Berlin St Op Orch, Bayreuth Fest Orch, LSO, Paris Cons, Berlin Staatskapelle, Pasdeloup Orch, SO, Vienna St Op Orch, orch, LPO/L. Blech/A. Coates/F. Weissmann/E. Viebig/K. Elmendorff/S. Wagner/J. Barbirolli/P. Gaubert/P. Coppola/C. Schmalstich/B. Seidler-Winkler/K. Alwin/H. Defosse/E. Mörike/T. Beecham, E. Marherr-Wagner/R. Heger)

Ⓓ **CMS7 64074-2(2)** (9/92)
Christa Ludwig—Recital (pt 2)
Ravel: Chansons madécasses; *Saint-Saëns:* Flûte invisible; *Rachmaninov:* Songs, Op.4 (exc); *Rossini:* Péchés de vieillesse I (exc); *Wagner:* Wesendonk Lieder; *Handel:* Giulio Cesare (exc); *Bach:* St John Passion, BWV245 (exc); *Wagner:* Tristan und Isolde (exc). (C. Ludwig, G. Moore, G. Parsons, D. Whittaker, A. Fleming, Philh/O. Klemperer, Berlin SO/H. Stein/K. Forster)

Ⓓ **CMS7 64110-2** (4/92)
Wagner—The Rhinegold
Wagner: Rheingold (Cpte). (N. Bailey, K. Pring, E. Belcourt, G. Dempsey, D. Hammond-Stroud, L. McDonall, R. Ferguson, N. Welsby, A. Collins, R. Lloyd, C. Grant, V. Masterson, S. Squires, H. Attfield, ENO Orch/R. Goodall)

Ⓓ **CMS7 64123-2**
The Art of Michael Rabin (1936-1972)
Paganini: Violin Concerto 1; *Wieniawski:* Violin Concerto 2; Violin Concerto 1; *Paganini:* Violin Concerto 1; *Tchaikovsky:* Violin Concerto; *Mendelssohn:* Violin Concerto, Op.64; *Bruch:* Scottish Fantasy; *Glazunov:* Violin Concerto; *Paganini:* Caprices, Op.1; *Bach:* Solo Violin Partitas and Sonatas (exc); *Ysaÿe:* Violin Sonatas, Op.27 (exc); *Wieniawski:* Etudes-Caprices, Op.18 (exc); *Debussy:* Plus que lente; *Ravel:* Pièce en forme de habanera; Tzigane; *Massenet:* Thaïs (exc); *Kreisler:* Caprice viennois; *Saint-Saëns:* Introduction and Rondo capriccioso; Havanaise; Introduction and Rondo capriccioso; *Sarasate:* Danzas españolas (exc); Zigeunerweisen; *Dinicu:* Hora staccato; *Paganini:* Moto perpetuo, Op.11; *Elgar:* Capricieuse; *Brandl:* Liebe Augustin (exc); *Rimsky-Korsakov:* Tale of Tsar Saltan (exc); *Chopin:* Nocturnes (exc); *Mompou:* Scènes d'enfants (exc); *Scriabin:* Etudes, Op.8 (exc); *Engel:* Sea-Shell; *Prokofiev:* Love for 3 Oranges Suite (exc); *Suk:* Pieces, Op.17 (exc). (M. Rabin, Philh/E. Goossens/A. Boult/L. von Matačić/A. Galliera, L. Pommers, Hollywood Bowl SO/F. Slatkin)

Ⓓ **CMS7 64154-2** (2/93)
Wagner—Die Meistersinger
Wagner: Meistersinger (Cpte). (F. Frantz, R. Schock, E. Grümmer, G. Frick, B. Kusche, G. Unger, M. Höffgen, G.

Neidlinger, H. Wilhelm, W. Stoll, M. Schmidt, L. Clam, Herold Kraus, R. Koffmane, A. Metternich, H. Pick, H. Prey, Berlin St Hedwig's Cath Ch, Berlin Deutsche Op Chor, Berlin St Op Chor, BPO/R. Kempe)

Ⓓ **CMS7 64159-2** (11/92)
R. Strauss—Ariadne auf Naxos
R. Strauss: Ariadne auf Naxos (Cpte). (G. Janowitz, T. Zylis-Gara, S. Geszty, J. King, T. Adam, H. Prey, S. Vogel, H.J. Rotzsch, P. Schreier, E. Wüstmann, A. Burmeister, A. Stolte, E-A. Winds, Staatskapelle Dresden/R. Kempe)

Ⓓ **CMS7 64162-2** (5/92) ⊟ **TC-CFPD4704** (9/87)
Rossini—Il barbiere di Siviglia
Rossini: Barbiere di Siviglia (Cpte). (S. Bruscantini, V. de los Angeles, L. Alva, I. Wallace, C. Cava, L. Sarti, D. Robertson, Glyndebourne Fest Chor, RPO/V. Gui)

Ⓓ **CMS7 64165-2** (6/93)
Puccini—Trittico
Puccini: Tabarro (Cpte); Suor Angelica (Cpte); Gianni Schicchi (Cpte). (T. Gobbi, M. Mas, G. Prandelli, P. de Palma, P. Clabassi, M. Pirazzini, V. de los Angeles, F. Barbieri, M. Doro, C. Vozza, L. Marimpietri, S. Chissari, A. Marcangeli, T. Cantarini, S. Bertona, M. Huder, T. Gobbi, V. de los Angeles, C. del Monte, A.M. Canali, A. Zagonara, L. Marimpietri, C. Cornoldi, S. Meletti, P. Montarsolo, F. Valentini, G. Raymondi, Rome Op Chor, Rome Op Orch/V. Bellezza/T. Serafin/G. Santini)

Ⓓ **CMS7 64169-2** (2/93)
Bellini—Il pirata
Bellini: Pirata (Cpte). (P. Cappuccilli, M. Caballé, B. Marti, G. Baratti, R. Raimondi, F. Raffanelli, Rome RAI Chor, Rome RAI Orch/G. Gavazzeni)

Ⓓ **CMS7 64180-2** (5/92)
Rossini—Le Comte Ory
Rossini: Comte Ory (Cpte). (J. Oncina, S. Barabas, I. Wallace, C. Canne-Meijer, M. Roux, M. Sinclair, J. Sinclair, D. Troy, Glyndebourne Fest Chor, Glyndebourne Fest Orch/V. Gui)

Ⓓ **CMS7 64183-2** (5/92)
Rossini—La Cenerentola
Rossini: Cenerentola (Cpte). (M. de Gabarain, J. Oncina, S. Bruscantini, I. Wallace, A. Noni, F. Cadoni, H. Alan, Glyndebourne Fest Chor, Glyndebourne Fest Orch/V. Gui/B. Balkwill)

Ⓓ **CMS7 64212-2**
Vaughan Williams—The Pilgrim's Progress
Vaughan Williams: Pilgrim's Progress (Cpte). (J. Noble, R. Herincx, J. Carol Case, W. Evans, C. Keyte, G. Shaw, B. Dickerson, S. Armstrong, M. Hayward Segal, G. Jennings, I. Partridge, J. Shirley-Quirk, T. Sharpe, R. Lloyd, N. Burrowes, A. Hodgson, J. Ward, R. Angas, J. Elwes, D. Wallis, W. Eathorne, G. English, LP Ch, LPO/A. Boult)

Ⓓ **CMS7 64244-2** (11/92)
Wagner—The Twilight of the Gods
Wagner: Götterdämmerung (Cpte). (R. Hunter, A. Remedios, A. Haugland, D. Hammond-Stroud, N. Welsby, M. Curphey, K. Pring, V. Masterson, S. Squires, H. Attfield, A. Collins, G. Knight, Anne Evans, ENO Chor, ENO Orch/R. Goodall)

Ⓓ **CMS7 64309-2**
Kálmán—Best-loved Melodies
Kálmán: Gräfin Mariza (exc); Csárdásfürstin (exc); Veilchen vom Montmartre (exc); Zirkusprinzessin (exc); Gräfin Mariza (exc); Kaiserin Josephine (exc); Zigeunerprimas (exc); Dorfkinder. (A. Rothenberger, E. Moser, P. Domingo, N. Gedda, F. Wunderlich, A. Dallapozza, ECO, Graunke SO, Bavarian St Orch, Vienna SO/J. Rudel/W. Mattes/H. Moltkau/C. Wildmann/R. Stolz, Ambrosian Sngrs, W. Brokmeier, W. Anheisser, Bavarian St Op Chor, O. Miljakovic, K. Böhme, B. Kusche)

Ⓓ **CMS7 64335-2** (4/93)
Rossini—L'assedio di Corinto
Rossini: Siège de Corinthe (Cpte). (B. Sills, S. Verrett, J. Diaz, H. Theyard, G. Howell, R. Lloyd, D. Wallis, G. Scano, Ambrosian Op Chor, LSO/T. Schippers)

Ⓓ **CMS7 64339-2** (2/93)
Verdi—Macbeth
Verdi: Macbeth (Cpte). (S. Milnes, F. Cossotto, R. Raimondi, J. Carreras, G. Bernardi, C. del Bosco, L. Fyson, N. Taylor, J. Noble, M. Borgato, Ambrosian Op Chor, New Philh/R. Muti)

Ⓓ **CMS7 64346-2** (12/92)
R. Strauss—Orchestral Works, Vol.2
R. Strauss: Violin Concerto; Sinfonia Domestica; Also sprach Zarathustra; Tod und Verklärung; Rosenkavalier (exc); Salome (exc); Bourgeois Gentilhomme Suite; Schlagobers (exc); Josephslegende (exc). (U. Hoelscher, Staatskapelle Dresden/R. Kempe)

Ⓓ **CMS7 64372-2**
Mozart—Don Giovanni
Mozart: Don Giovanni (Cpte). (A. Campo, T. Stich-Randall, S. Danco, A. Moffo, N. Gedda, M. Cortis, A. Vessières, R. Arié, Aix-en-Provence Fest Chor, Paris Cons/H. Rosbaud)

Ⓓ **CMS7 64376-2**
Mozart—Le nozze di Figaro
Mozart: Nozze di Figaro (Cpte). (R. Panerai, R. Streich, H. Rehfuss, T. Stich-Randall, P. Lorengar, C. Gayraud, M. Cortis, H. Cuénod, G. Friedmann, A. Vessières, M. Ignal, Aix-en-Provence Fest Chor, Paris Cons/H. Rosbaud)

Ⓓ **CMS7 64382-2** (12/92)
Gounod—Mireille
Gounod: Mireille (Cpte). (J. Vivalda, N. Gedda, C. Gayraud, M. Dens, M. Ignal, A. Vessières, C. Jacquin, M. Cortis, R. Tropin, Aix-en-Provence Fest Chor, Paris Cons/A. Cluytens)

Ⓓ **CMS7 64386-2** (11/92)
Delius—A Village Romeo and Juliet, etc
Delius: Village Romeo and Juliet (Cpte); Sea Drift. (D. Dowling, F. Sharp, M. Ritchie, R. Soames, L. Dyer, G. Clinton, D. Bond, M. Avis, G. Garside, L. Strauss-Smith, D. Munro, Marion Davies, P. Hattey, G. Clinton, Chor, RPO/T. Beecham)

Ⓓ **CMS7 64394-2**
Gilbert & Sullivan—The Gondoliers
Sullivan: Gondoliers (Cpte). (Richard Lewis, J. Cameron, E. Morison, M. Thomas, G. Evans, M. Sinclair, E. Graham, A. Young, O. Brannigan, H. Watts, J. Milligan, S. Hitchens, L. Renton, Glyndebourne Fest Chor, PAO/M. Sargent)

Ⓓ **CMS7 64397-2**
Gilbert & Sullivan—HMS Pinafore/Trial by Jury
Sullivan: HMS Pinafore (Cpte); Trial by Jury (Cpte). (George Baker, J. Cameron, Richard Lewis, E. Morison, O. Brannigan, J. Milligan, M. Thomas, M. Sinclair, E. Morison, Richard Lewis, George Baker, J. Cameron, O. Brannigan, B. Turgeon, Glyndebourne Fest Chor, PAO/M. Sargent)

Ⓓ **CMS7 64400-2**
Sullivan—Iolanthe & Di Ballo
Sullivan: Iolanthe (Cpte); Di Ballo. (M. Thomas, J. Cameron, M. Sinclair, E. Morison, George Baker, I. Wallace, A. Young, O. Brannigan, A. Cantelo, H. Harper, Glyndebourne Fest Chor, PAO/M. Sargent, RLPO/C. Groves)

Ⓓ **CMS7 64403-2**
Gilbert & Sullivan—The Mikado
Sullivan: Mikado (Cpte). (O. Brannigan, Richard Lewis, G. Evans, I. Wallace, J. Cameron, E. Morison, M. Thomas, J. Sinclair, M. Sinclair, Glyndebourne Fest Chor, PAO/M. Sargent)

Ⓓ **CMS7 64406-2**
Sullivan—Patience & Irish Symphony
Sullivan: Patience (Cpte); Irish Symphony. (E. Morison, George Baker, J. Cameron, M. Thomas, H. Harper, E. Harwood, M. Sinclair, J. Shaw, T. Anthony, A. Young, Glyndebourne Fest Chor, PAO/M. Sargent, RLPO/C. Groves)

Ⓓ **CMS7 64409-2**
Sullivan—Pirates of Penzance & Orch. Works
Sullivan: Pirates of Penzance (Cpte); In Memoriam; Sorcerer (exc); Cox and Box (exc); Princess Ida (exc). (J. Milligan, Richard Lewis, George Baker, E. Morison, J. Cameron, O. Brannigan, M. Sinclair, M. Thomas, H. Harper, Glyndebourne Fest Chor, PAO/M. Sargent, CBSO/V. Dunn)

Ⓓ **CMS7 64412-2**
Gilbert & Sullivan—Ruddigore/Shakespeare Music
Sullivan: Ruddigore (Cpte); Tempest (exc); Merchant of Venice (exc). (E. Morison, George Baker, M. Sinclair, E. Harwood, P. Bowden, H. Blackburn, Richard Lewis, O. Brannigan, J. Rouleau, Glyndebourne Fest Chor, PAO/M. Sargent, CBSO/V. Dunn)

Ⓓ **CMS7 64415-2**
Gilbert & Sullivan—Yeomen of the Guard
Sullivan: Yeomen of the Guard (Cpte). (D. Dowling, Richard Lewis, J. Carol Case, A. Young, G. Evans, O. Brannigan, E. Morison, M. Thomas, M. Sinclair, D. Hume, J. Carol Case, Glyndebourne Fest Chor, PAO/M. Sargent)

Ⓓ **CMS7 64467-2**
Classical Music of Spain, Vol.2
Falla: Vida breve (exc); Nights in the Gardens of Spain (exc); Canciones populares españolas (exc); *Albéniz:* Suite española 1 (exc); Iberia (exc); *Falla:* Homenaje Debussy; Amor brujo (exc); *Granados:* Danzas españolas (exc); Goyescas (exc); *Moreno Torroba:* Sonatina in A (exc); *Albéniz:* Suite española 1 (exc); *Rodrigo:* Fantasía (exc); *Albéniz:* Iberia (exc); *Turina:* Poema en forma de canciones (exc); *Granados:* Danzas españolas (exc); Allegro de concierto; *Turina:* Danzas fantásticas (exc). (V. de los Angeles, G. Moore, G. Soriano, A. de Larrocha, E. Bitetti, Spanish Nat Orch, Paris Cons, Philh, LPO/R. Frühbeck de Burgos/A. R. Marbà/W. Susskind/E. Bátiz)

Ⓓ **CMS7 64530-2** (10/93)
Rachmaninov—Orchestral Works
Rachmaninov: Symphony 1; Symphony 2; Symphony 3; Isle of the Dead; Symphonic Dances; Vocalise; Aleko (exc). (LSO/A. Previn)

Ⓓ **CMS7 64622-2** (3/93)
Donizetti—Lucia di Lammermoor
Donizetti: Lucia di Lammermoor (Cpte). (E. Gruberová, Alfredo Kraus, R. Bruson, R. Lloyd, K. Kuhlmann, B. Bottone, B. Lazzaretti, Ambrosian Op Chor, RPO/N. Rescigno)

Ⓓ **CMS7 64642-2** (4/93)
Verdi—Don Carlo (4 act version)
Verdi: Don Carlo (Cpte). (M. Filippeschi, A. Stella, E. Nicolai, T. Gobbi, B. Christoff, G. Neri, P. Clabassi, L. di Lelio, P. Caroli, O. Moscucci, Rome Op Chor, Rome Op Orch/G. Santini)

Ⓓ **CMS7 64646-2** (6/93)
Verdi—La forza del destino
Verdi: Forza del destino (Cpte). (M. Arroyo, C. Bergonzi, P. Cappuccilli, R. Raimondi, B. Casoni, G. Evans, A. Zerbini, F. Andreolli, M. Cova, V. Carbonari, D. Hammond-Stroud, Ambrosian Op Chor, RPO/L. Gardelli)

Ⓓ **CMS7 64650-2** (7/93)
Wagner—Fliegende Holländer
Wagner: Fliegende Holländer (Cpte). (J. van Dam, D. Vejzovic, K. Moll, P. Hofmann, K. Borris, T. Moser, Vienna St Op Chor, BPO/H. von Karajan)

Ⓓ **CMS7 64727-2** (2/94)
Britten—Opera excerpts and Folksongs
Britten: Rape of Lucretia (exc); Peter Grimes (exc); Folk Songs (exc); Folk Songs (exc); Folk Songs (exc). (N. Evans, P. Pears, J. Cross, F. Sharp, N. Lumsden, D. Dowling, M. Ritchie, F. Nielsen, EOGCO/R. Goodall, S. Wyss, B. Britten, P. Pears, J. Cross, T. Culbert, BBC Th Chor, ROHO)

Ⓓ **CMS7 64846-2** (2/95)
Bellini—I Capuleti e i Montecchi
Bellini: Capuleti (Cpte). (E. Gruberová, A. Baltsa, D. Raffanti, G. Howell, J. Tomlinson, ROH Chor, ROHO/R. Muti)

Ⓓ **CMS7 64852-2**
Puccini—Manon Lescaut
Puccini: Manon Lescaut (Cpte). (M. Caballé, P. Domingo, V. Sardinero, N. Mangin, R. Tear, D. Wallis, R. Van Allan, B. Dickerson, R. Lloyd, I. Partridge, G. Howell, Ambrosian Op Chor, New Philh/B. Bartoletti)

Ⓓ **CMS7 64938-2** (1/94)
Bellini—Il Pirata
Bellini: Pirata (Cpte); Pirata (exc). (C. Ego, M. Callas, P.M. Ferraro, G. Peterson, Chester Watson, R. Sarfaty, American Op Soc Chor, American Op Soc Orch/N. Rescigno, Concertgebouw, M. Callas)

Ⓓ **CMS7 64941-2** (1/94)
Donizetti—Anna Bolena
Donizetti: Anna Bolena (Cpte). (M. Callas, N. Rossi-Lemeni, G. Simionato, G. Raimondi, P. Clabassi, G. Carturan, L. Rumbo, La Scala Chor, La Scala Orch/G. Gavazzeni)

Ⓓ **CMS7 64944-2** (1/94)
Verdi—Macbeth
Verdi: Macbeth (Cpte). (E. Mascherini, M. Callas, I. Tajo, G. Penno, L. Della Pergola, D. Caselli, A. Barbesi, I. Vinco, M. Tommasini, A. Vercelli, La Scala Chor, La Scala Orch/V. de Sabata)

Ⓓ **CMS7 64947-2** (4/94)
Monteverdi—L'Orfeo
Monteverdi: Orfeo (Cpte). (N. Rogers, P. Kwella, E. Kirkby, J. Smith, H. Afonso, C. Denley, G. Laurens, M. Bolognesi, R. Covey-Crump, J. Potter, S. Varcoe, D. Thomas, T. Edwards, G. Shaw, Chiaroscuro, London Cornett and Sackbutt Ens/T. Caudle, London Baroque/C. Medlam)

Ⓓ **CMS7 69290-2** (4/88)
Beethoven—Fidelio
Beethoven: Fidelio (Cpte). (H. Dernesch, J. Vickers, Z. Kélémen, K. Ridderbusch, H. Donath, H. Laubenthal, J. Van Dam, W. Hollweg, S.R. Frese, Berlin Deutsche Op Chor, BPO/H. von Karajan)

Ⓓ **CMS7 69293-2** (4/88)
Humperdinck—Hänsel und Gretel
Humperdinck: Hänsel und Gretel (Cpte). (E. Grümmer, E.

Schwarzkopf, M. von Ilosvay, J. Metternich, A. Felbermayer, E. Schürhoff, Loughton High School for Girls Ch, Bancroft's School Chor, Philh/H. von Karajan)

CMS7 69300-2 (4/88)
Verdi—Aida
Verdi: Aida (Cpte). (M. Freni, A. Baltsa, J. Carreras, P. Cappuccilli, R. Raimondi, J. Van Dam, T. Moser, K. Ricciarelli, Vienna St Op Chor, VPO/H. von Karajan)

CMS7 69304-2 (4/88)
Verdi—Don Carlos
Verdi: Don Carlo (Cpte). (J. Carreras, M. Freni, A. Baltsa, P. Cappuccilli, N. Ghiaurov, R. Raimondi, J. Van Dam, E. Gruberová, H. Nitsche, C. Meletti, B. Hendricks, Berlin Deutsche Op Chor, BPO/H. von Karajan)

CMS7 69308-2 (4/88)
Verdi—Otello
Verdi: Otello (Cpte). (J. Vickers, M. Freni, P. Glossop, A. Bottion, M. Sénéchal, S. Malagù, J. Van Dam, M. Macchi, H. Helm, Berlin Deutsche Op Chor, BPO/H. von Karajan)

CMS7 69311-2 (9/95)
Verdi—Il Trovatore
Verdi: Trovatore (Cpte). (F. Bonisolli, L. Price, P. Cappuccilli, E. Obraztsova, R. Raimondi, M. Venuti, H. Nitsche, M. Egel, Berlin Deutsche Op Chor, BPO/H. von Karajan)

CMS7 69314-2 (8/88)
Wagner—Lohengrin
Wagner: Lohengrin (Cpte). (R. Kollo, A. Tomowa-Sintow, D. Vejzovic, S. Nimsgern, K. Ridderbusch, R. Kerns, Berlin Deutsche Op Chor, BPO/H. von Karajan)

CMS7 69319-2 (7/88)
Wagner—Tristan und Isolde
Wagner: Tristan und Isolde (Cpte). (J. Vickers, H. Dernesch, C. Ludwig, K. Ridderbusch, W. Berry, B. Weikl, P. Schreier, M. Vantin, P. Schreier, Berlin Deutsche Op Chor, BPO/H. von Karajan)

CMS7 69327-2
Puccini—Turandot
Puccini: Turandot (Cpte). (B. Nilsson, F. Corelli, R. Scotto, G. Mazzini, F. Ricciardi, P. de Palma, B. Giaiotti, A. Mercuriali, G. Morresi, Rome Op Chor, Rome Op Orch/F. Molinari-Pradelli)

CMS7 69330-2 (11/88)
Mozart—Così fan tutte
Mozart: Così fan tutte (Cpte). (E. Schwarzkopf, C. Ludwig, H. Steffek, Alfredo Kraus, G. Taddei, W. Berry, Philh Chor, Philh/K. Böhm)

CMS7 69339-2 (5/89)
Flotow—Martha
Flotow: Martha (Cpte). (A. Rothenberger, B. Fassbaender, N. Gedda, H. Prey, D. Weller, H.G. Knoblich, Bavarian St Op Chor, Bavarian St Orch/R. Heger)

CMS7 69342-2 (9/89)
Weber—Der Freischütz
Weber: Freischütz (Cpte). (E. Grümmer, R. Schock, L. Otto, K.C. Kohn, H. Prey, G. Frick, E. Wiemann, F. Hoppe, W.W. Dicks, Berlin Deutsche Op Chor, BPO/J. Keilberth)

CMS7 69348-2 (7/89)
Nicolai—Die Lustige Weiber von Windsor
Nicolai: Lustigen Weiber von Windsor (Cpte). (R-M. Pütz, G. Litz, E. Mathis, G. Frick, E. Gutstein, K. Engen, F. Wunderlich, F. Lenz, C. Hoppe, Bavarian St Op Chor, Bavarian St Orch/R. Heger)

CMS7 69357-2 (7/89)
Zeller—Der Vogelhändler
Zeller: Vogelhändler (Cpte). (A. Rothenberger, G. Litz, W. Berry, G. Unger, J. Förster, K. Dönch, A. Dallapozza, R. Holm, W. Anheisser, Vienna St Op Chor, Vienna SO/W. Boskovsky)

CMS7 69573-2 (4/89)
Massenet—Werther
Massenet: Werther (Cpte). (Alfredo Kraus, T. Troyanos, M. Manuguerra, C. Barbaux, J. Bastin, P. Langridge, J-P. Lafont, L. Richardson, M. Lewis, Covent Garden Sngrs, LPO/M. PLasson)

CMS7 69576-2 (11/88)
Verdi—Un ballo in maschera
Verdi: Ballo in maschera (Cpte). (M. Arroyo, P. Domingo, P. Cappuccilli, R. Grist, F. Cossotto, G. Howell, R. Van Allan, G. Giorgetti, K. Collins, D. Barrett, Haberdashers' Aske's Sch Girls' Ch, ROH Chor, Medici Qt, New Philh/R. Muti)

CMS7 69639-2
Mozart—Le nozze di Figaro
Mozart: Nozze di Figaro (Cpte). (E. Kunz, I. Seefried, G. London, E. Schwarzkopf, S. Jurinac, E. Höngen, M. Rus, E. Majkut, W. Felden, R. Schwaiger, Vienna St Op Chor, VPO/H. von Karajan)

CMS7 69654-2 (5/89)
Puccini—Madama Butterfly
Puccini: Madama Butterfly (Cpte). (R. Scotto, C. Bergonzi, R. Panerai, A. di Stasio, P. de Palma, G. Morresi, S. Padoan, P. Montarsolo, M. Rinaudo, Rome Op Chor, Rome Op Orch/J. Barbirolli)

CMS7 69657-2 (4/92)
Puccini—La bohème
Puccini: Bohème (Cpte). (M. Freni, N. Gedda, M. Adani, M. Sereni, M. Basiola II, F. Mazzoli, C. Badioli, P. Montarsolo, V. Pandano, M. Rinaudo, Rome Op Chor, Rome Op Orch/T. Schippers)

CMS7 69704-2 (4/89)
Bizet—Operatic Works
Bizet: Pêcheurs de perles (Cpte); Ivan IV (exc). (J. Micheau, N. Gedda (ten), E. Blanc, J. Mars, Paris Opéra-Comique Chor, Paris Opéra-Comique Orch/P. Dervaux, J. Micheau, H. Legay, M. Sénéchal, M. Roux, P. Savignol, L. Noguera, FRN Chor, FRNO/G. Tzipine)

CMS7 69760-2 (5/89)
Handel—Julius Caeser
Handel: Giulio Cesare (Cpte). (J. Baker, V. Masterson, Sarah Walker, D. Jones, J. Bowman, J. Tomlinson, C. Booth-Jones, D. James, ENO Chor, ENO Orch/C. Mackerras)

CMS7 69936-2 (8/89)
Humperdinck—Königskinder
Humperdinck: Königskinder (Cpte). (A. Dallapozza, H. Donath, H. Prey, H. Schwarz, K. Ridderbusch, G. Unger, B. Lindner, G. Wewel, H. Ankersen, F. Lenz, O. Wenkel, T. Nicolai, Tolz Boys' Ch, Bavarian Rad Chor, Munich RO/H. Wallberg)

CMS7 69951-2 (3/89)
Rossini—William Tell
Rossini: Guillaume Tell (Cpte). (G. Bacquier, M. Caballé, N. Gedda, K. Kováts, G. Howell, M. Mesplé, J. Taillon, L. Hendrikx, C. Burles, R. Cassinelli, N. Christov, Ambrosian Op Chor, RPO/L. Gardelli)

CMS7 69974-2 (8/89)
Puccini—Tosca
Puccini: Tosca (Cpte). (M. Callas, C. Bergonzi, T. Gobbi, L. Monreale, R. Ercolani, G. Tadeo, U. Trama, D. Sellar, Paris Op Chor, Paris Cons/G. Prêtre)

CMS7 69980-2 (10/89)
Donizetti—Lucia di Lammermoor
Donizetti: Lucia di Lammermoor (Cpte). (M. Callas, G. di Stefano, T. Gobbi, R. Arié, A.M. Canali, V. Natali, G. Sarri, MMF Chor, MMF Orch/T. Serafin)

CMS7 69983-2 (7/89)
Gounod—Faust
Gounod: Faust (Cpte). (N. Gedda, V. de los Angeles, B. Christoff, E. Blanc, L. Berton, R. Gorr, V. Autran, Paris Op Chor, Paris Op Orch/A. Cluytens)

CZS4 83177-2(2) (6/95)
Itzhak Perlman Edition (pt 2)
Prokofiev: Violin Concerto 1; *Castelnuovo-Tedesco:* Violin Concerto 2; *Khachaturian:* Violin Concerto; *Shostakovich:* Violin Concerto 1; *Bartók:* Violin Concerto 2; *Conus:* Violin Concerto; *Sinding:* Suite, Op.10; *Brahms:* Violin Sonata 1; Violin Sonata 2; Violin Sonata 3; *Paganini:* Caprices, Op.1; *Tchaikovsky:* Piano Trio, Op.50; Souvenir d'un lieu cher, Op.42 (exc); Sérénade mélancolique; String Quartet 1 (exc); Souvenirs de Hapsal, Op.2 (exc); Souvenir d'un lieu cher, Op.42 (exc); *Rachmaninov:* Songs, Op.21 (exc); Songs, Op.38 (exc); Songs, Op.34 (exc); *Stravinsky:* Chanson russe; Divertimento; Suite italienne (violin); Duo Concertant; *Kreisler:* Caprice viennois; *Dvořák:* Gipsy Melodies (exc); *Kreisler:* Pugnani Tempo di Menuetto; *Dvořák:* Slavonic Dances (exc); *Gluck:* Orfeo ed Euridice (exc); *Granados:* Danzas españolas (exc); *Chopin:* Mazurkas (exc); *Kreisler:* Francoeur Siciliano and Rigaudon; *Chaminade:* Sérénade espagnole; *Lehár:* Frasquita (exc); *Kreisler:* Toy Soldier; Syncopation; *Grainger:* Molly on the Shore; *Kreisler:* Martini Andantino; *Dvořák:* Slavonic Dances (exc); *Kreisler:* Schön Rosmarin; Liebesleid; Scherzo-Caprice, Op.6; *Albéniz:* España, Op.165 (exc); *Kreisler:* Tambourin chinois. (I. Perlman, Vladimir Ashkenazy, L. Harrell, B. Canino, S. Sanders, BBC SO, Israel PO, LSO, Pittsburgh SO, Philadelphia/G. Rozhdestvensky/Z. Mehta/A. Previn/E. Ormandy)

CZS5 68098-2
Rimsky-Korsakov—Orchestral Works
Rimsky-Korsakov: Scheherazade; Russian Easter Festival Ov; Capriccio espagnol; Tale of Tsar Saltan (exc); Tale of Tsar Saltan (exc); Golden Cockerel Suite (exc); Snow Maiden (exc); Dubinushka; May Night (exc). (Philh, Paris Cons/A. Cluytens/P. Kletzki/E. Kurtz/C. Silvestri/L. von Matačić/C. Mackerras)

CZS5 68110-2
R. Strauss—Orchestral Works
R. Strauss: Also sprach Zarathustra; Till Eulenspiegel; Don Juan; Heldenleben; Salome (exc); Rosenkavalier (exc). (Staatskapelle Dresden/R. Kempe)

CZS5 68113-2
Vive Offenbach!
Offenbach: Périchole (exc); Périchole (exc); Barbe-bleue (exc); M. Choufleuri (exc); Orphée aux enfers (exc); Belle Hélène (exc); Belle Hélène (exc); Grande-Duchesse de Gérolstein (exc); Grande-Duchesse de Gérolstein (exc); Grande-Duchesse de Gérolstein (exc); Vie parisienne (exc); Mesdames de la halle (exc); Pomme d'Api (exc); Fille du Tambour-Major (exc); Brigands (exc); Contes d'Hoffmann (exc); Contes d'Hoffmann (exc); Contes d'Hoffmann (exc). (G. Bacquier, T. Berganza, S. Lafaye, R. Amade, L. Noguera, J. Rhodes, M. Mesplé, C. Burles, M. Sénéchal, M. Péna, J. Berbié, M. Command, M. Trempont, D. Millet, M. Hamel, P. Guigue, J-C. Benoit, B. Sinclair, L. Masson, J. Norman, J. Aler, E. Lublin, Y. Printemps, R. Crespin, C. Château, J-P. Lafont, L. Pezzino, L. Chatel, G. Raphanel, C. Alliot-Lugaz, T. Raffalli, J-L. Viala, M. Robin, E. Schwarzkopf, J. Collard, Bourvil, A. Philippe, V. de los Angeles, N. Gedda, R. Duclos Ch, Toulouse Capitole Chor, Lyon Op Chor, H. Büsser, Toulouse Capitole Orch, Lamoureux Orch, Monte Carlo PO, Paris Cons, Lyon Op Orch, Paris Op Orch, Paris Opéra-Comique Orch, Bordeaux Aquitaine Orch/I. Markevitch/R. Benzi/M. Rosenthal/J-P. Marty/F. Nuvolone/J.E. Gardiner/P. Dervaux/A. Cluytens/M. Plasson)

CZS5 68229-2 (11/94)
Constantin Silvestri—A profile
Rimsky-Korsakov: May Night (exc); *Ravel:* Rapsodie espagnole; *Elgar:* In the South; *Dvořák:* Symphony 8; *Glinka:* Ruslan and Lyudmila (exc); *Borodin:* Prince Igor (exc); Prince Igor (exc); *Tchaikovsky:* Symphony 5. (Philh, VPO, Bournemouth SO, LPO, Paris Cons/C. Silvestri)

CZS5 68286-2
Hahn—Ciboulette & Mozart (highlights)
Hahn: Ciboulette (exc); Mozart (Cpte). (A. Grandjean, W. Clément, M. Hamel, F. Ogéas, J-C. Benoit, P. Carton, M. Escande, A. Rozanne, M. Arene, H. Hennetier, T. Sourseva, S. Simon-Gérard, R. Moncade, G. Dumond, Paris Champs-Élysées Chor, Paris Champs-Élysées Orch/P. Bonneau, French Concert Orch/A. Jouve)

CZS5 68292-2
Operetta Arias and Duets
Chabrier: Étoile (exc); *Lecocq:* Petit Duc (exc); *Pierre Petit:* Maréchale sans Gêne (exc); *Auber:* Domino noir (exc); *Lecocq:* Coeur et la main (exc); *Messager:* Petite fonctionnaire (exc); *Pierné:* Fragonard (exc); *Messager:* Véronique (exc); *Audran:* Gillette de Narbonne (exc); *Ganne:* Saltimbanques (exc); *Offenbach:* Madame Favart (exc); *Messager:* Véronique (exc); *Lehár:* Lustige Witwe (exc); Graf von Luxemburg (exc); *Lecocq:* Fille de Madame Angot (exc); *Audran:* Mascotte (exc); *Massé:* Noces de Jeannette (exc); *Planquette:* Cloches de Corneville (exc); *Lecocq:* Fille de Madame Angot (exc); *Audran:* Mascotte (exc); *Messager:* Monsieur Beaucaire (exc); *Adam:* Si j'étais roi (exc); *Lehár:* Paganini (exc); *Friml:* Rose Marie (exc); *Youmans:* Carioca (exc); *Romberg:* Nina Rosa (exc); Gipsy Song (exc); *Yvain:* Au soleil du Mexique (exc); *Sylviano:* Fox mélodie; *Mandru:* Valse berceuse; *Christiné:* Temps des merveilleuses (exc); *Stolz:* Je rêve d'un simple amour; *Künneke:* C'est vous. (F. Révoil, S. Laydeker, A. Baugé, N. Vallin, orch/R. Desormière/M. Cariven/R. Blareau/E. Beruilly/G. Andolfi)

CZS5 68295-2
Messager/Lecocq—Operetta Highlights
Messager: Basoche (exc); Fortunio (exc); *Lecocq:* Petit duc (exc). (L. Berton, N. Broissin, N. Renaux, F. Betti, H. Legay, M. Sénéchal, R. Hérent, G. Godin, M. Dens, J-C. Benoit, P. Germain, W. Clément, Raymond St Paul Chor, Colonne Concerts Orch, Lamoureux Concerts Orch/J. Pernoo/J. Gressier)

CZS5 68485-2
Les Introuvables de János Starker
Bach: Solo Cello Suites; *Kodály:* Cello Sonata, Op.8; *Boccherini:* Cello Concerto, G482; *Bach:* Suites, BWV1066-9 (exc); *Kreisler:* Boccherini Allegretto; *Saint-Saëns:* Allegro appassionato; *Debussy:* Préludes (exc); *Chopin:* Nocturnes (exc); *Popper:* Hungarian Rhapsody, Op.68; *Bach:* Harpsichord Concerto, BWV1056 (exc); *Schubert:* Allegretto grazioso; Moments musicaux, D780 (exc); *Mussorgsky:* Fair at Sorochintsï (exc); *Schumann:* Kinderszenen (exc); *Debussy:* Petite Suite (exc); *A. Tcherepnin:* Ode; *Paganini:* Caprices, Op.1 (exc); *Haydn:* Cello Concerto in D; *Schumann:* Cello Concerto; *Saint-Saëns:* Cello Concerto 1; *Dvořák:* Cello Concerto; *Dohnányi:* Konzertstück, Op.12; *Fauré:* Elégie; *Milhaud:*

Cello Concerto 1; *Prokofiev:* Cello Concerto, Op.58. (J. Starker, G. Moore, Philh/C.M. Giulini/W. Susskind)

Ⓓ **CZS5 68550-2**
Russian Music
Glinka: Ruslan and Lyudmila (exc); *Borodin:* In the Steppes of Central Asia; Prince Igor (exc); *Balakirev:* Russian Ov II; *Tchaikovsky:* Hamlet; Tempest; Romeo and Juliet; Francesca da Rimini; *Mussorgsky:* Night on the Bare Mountain; Khovanshchina (exc); Fair at Sorochintsï (exc); *Liadov:* Russian Folksongs, Op.58. (Philh/C. Silvestri/A. Cluytens/L. von Matačić/I. Markevitch/C.M. Giulini/H. von Karajan/C. Mackerras/N. Malko)

Ⓓ **CZS5 68559-2**
Italian Opera Choruses
Verdi: Nabucco (exc); Macbeth (exc); Rigoletto (exc); Giovanna d'Arco (exc); Trovatore (exc); Ernani (exc); Traviata (exc); Aida (exc); Don Carlo (exc); Forza del destino (exc); Otello (exc); *Rossini:* Mosè in Egitto (exc); Siège de Corinthe (exc); Guillaume Tell (exc); *Bellini:* Puritani (exc); Pirata (exc); *Donizetti:* Don Pasquale (exc); Lucia di Lammermoor (exc); *Mascagni:* Cavalleria rusticana (exc); *Leoncavallo:* Pagliacci (exc); *Boito:* Mefistofele (exc); *Puccini:* Turandot (exc); Madama Butterfly (exc). (Ambrosian Op Chor, La Scala Chor, Berlin Deutsche Op Chor, ROH Chor, Rome RAI Chor, Strasbourg Cath Maîtrise, Rhine Op Chor, Philh, New Philh, La Scala Orch, LSO, BPO, RPO, ROHO, Rome RAI Orch, Strasbourg PO/R. Muti/James Levine/H. von Karajan/L. Gardelli/T. Schippers/G. Gavazzeni/N. Rescigno/J. Rudel/A. Lombard, P. Tinsley, E. Shelley, D. Hughes, R. Lloyd)

Ⓓ **CZS5 68616-2**
Wagner—Orchestral Works from Operas
Wagner: Walküre (exc); Götterdämmerung (exc); Rheingold (exc); Siegfried (exc); Tannhäuser (exc); Rienzi (exc); Lohengrin (exc); Meistersinger (exc). (BPO/K. Tennstedt)

Ⓓ **CZS7 62539-2**
Wagner—Overtures & Preludes
Wagner: Tannhäuser (exc); Tannhäuser (exc); Fliegende Holländer (exc); Tristan und Isolde (exc); Tristan und Isolde (exc); Meistersinger (exc); Lohengrin (exc); Parsifal (exc); Rheingold (exc); Walküre (exc); Siegfried (exc); Götterdämmerung (exc). (New Philh, LPO, LSO/A. Boult)

Ⓓ **CZS7 62751-2** (1/90)
The Strausses of Vienna
J. Strauss I: Radetzky March; Seufzer-Galopp; *J. Strauss II:* Blauen Donau, Op. 314; Champagner, Op. 211; Wein, Weib und Gesang; G'schichten aus dem Wienerwald, Op. 325; Auf der Jagd, Op. 373; Kaiser, Op. 437; Rosen aus dem Süden; Blindekuh (exc); Immer heiterer, Op. 235; Im Krapfenwald'l, Op. 336; Wiener Blut; Neue Pizzicato-Polka, Op. 449; Wo die Zitronen blüh'n; Eljen a Magyar!, Op. 332; Künstlerleben, Op. 316; Nacht in Venedig (exc); Neu-Wien, Op. 342; *Jos Strauss:* Plappermäulchen; Künstlergruss; Allerlei; Perlen der Liebe; *E. Strauss:* Ohne Aufenthalt, Op. 112; Bahn frei; Ohne Bremse. (VJSO/W. Boskovsky)

Ⓓ **CZS7 62877-2**
Les inspirations insolites d'Erik Satie
Satie: Aventures de Mercure; Socrate; Messe des Pauvres; Gymnopédies (exc); Geneviève de Brabant; Pantins dansent; Piège de Méduse; Choses vues à droite et à gauche. (D. Millet, A. Guiot, A. Esposito, M. Mesplé, Paris Orch/P. Dervaux, R. Duclos Ch, G. Litaize, Paris Cons/L. Auriacombe, J-C. Benoit, P. Bertin, Paris Op Chor, Lamoureux Orch/A. Ciccolini, H. Deschamps, J-M. Falcucci, M. Laurence, Y.P. Tortelier, A. Ciccolini, A. Ciccolini (pf/dir))

Ⓓ **CZS7 62993-2**
Fritz Wunderlich—Great German Tenor
Mozart: Don Giovanni (exc); Don Giovanni (exc); Entführung (exc); *Handel:* Serse (exc); *Boïeldieu:* Dame blanche (exc); *Donizetti:* Elisir d'amore (exc); *Lortzing:* Wildschütz (exc); Wildschütz (exc); *Cornelius:* Barbier von Bagdad (exc); *Flotow:* Martha (exc); *Nicolai:* Lustigen Weiber von Windsor (exc); *Massenet:* Manon (exc); *A. Thomas:* Mignon (exc); Mignon (exc); *Smetana:* Bartered Bride (exc); Bartered Bride (exc); *Tchaikovsky:* Eugene Onegin (exc); Eugene Onegin (exc); Queen of Spades (exc); *Kienzl:* Evangelimann (exc); *Verdi:* Rigoletto (exc); *Puccini:* Bohème (exc); Bohème (exc); Madama Butterfly (exc); Madama Butterfly (exc); *J. Strauss II:* Nacht in Venedig (exc); Nacht in Venedig (exc); Nacht in Venedig (exc); *Millöcker:* Bettelstudent (exc); *Lehár:* Giuditta (exc); Zarewitsch (exc); Land des Lächelns (exc); *Kálmán:* Gräfin Mariza (exc); *Fall:* Fidele Bauer (exc); Rose von Stambul (exc); Rose von Stambul (exc); *Neuendorff:* Rattenfänger; *Heins:* Zwei dunkle Augen. (F. Wunderlich, E. Grümmer, A. Rothenberger, G. Litz, G. Frick, E. Mathis, P. Lorengar, H. Prey, M. Muszely, M. Cordes, S. Wagner, L. Otto, R. Schock, L. Schmidt, Munich St Wolfgang Children's Ch, Günther Arndt Ch, Berlin SO, Bavarian St Orch, Bamberg SO, Graunke SO/H. Stein/H. Zanotelli/B. Klobučar/H. Müller-Kray/R. Heger/R. Kempe/M. von Zallinger/F. Walter/W. Schmidt-Boelcke/H. Moltkau/C. Michalski, Berlin FFB Orch/W. Eisbrenner)

Ⓓ **CZS7 67123-2** (2/91)
Wagner: Der Ring des Nibelungen
Wagner: Rheingold (Cpte); Walküre (Cpte); Siegfried (Cpte); Götterdämmerung (Cpte). (F. Frantz, I. Malaniuk, W. Windgassen, G. Neidlinger, J. Patzak, J. Greindl, G. Frick, A. Poell, L. Fehenberger, E. Grümmer, R. Siewert, S. Jurinac, M. Gabory, H. Rössl-Majdan, W. Windgassen, H. Konetzni, M. Mödl, E. Cavelti, G. Frick, J. Hellwig, M. Gabory, G. Scheyrer, D. Schmedes, O. Bennings, I. Malaniuk, E. Cavelti, H. Rössl-Majdan, L. Suthaus, A. Pernerstorfer, F. Frantz, J. Greindl, R. Streich, M. Klose, J. Greindl, M. Klose, A. Poell, S. Jurinac, H. Rössl-Majdan, Rome RAI Chor, Rome RAI Orch/W. Furtwängler)

Ⓓ **CZS7 67425-2**
Baroque Passion
M-A. Charpentier: Te Deum, H146 (exc); *Lully:* Folies d'Espagne; *Delalande:* Sinfonies pour les soupers du Roi; *Rameau:* Fêtes d'Hébé (exc); *Gluck:* Orfeo ed Euridice (exc); *Albinoni:* Adagio; *Pachelbel:* Canon and Gigue (exc); *Corelli:* Concerti grossi, Op.6 (exc); *Vivaldi:* Concerto, RV537; Concerto, RV425; Concerti, Op.8 (exc); *A. Marcello:* Oboe Concerto in D minor; *Boccherini:* String Quintets, G271-6 (exc); *Purcell:* King Arthur, Z628 (exc); Abdelazer, Z570 (exc); *Handel:* Messiah (exc); Water Music (exc); Serse (exc); *Bach:* Suites, BWV1066-9 (exc); Cantata 147 (exc); Flute Sonatas, BWV1030-5 (exc); 2-Violin Concerto; *Telemann:* Recorder Overture-Suite (exc); 2-Oboe & Trumpet Concerto 2 (exc). (ASMF/P. Ledger, Piguet Ob Ens, B. Soustrot, T. Caens, G. Touvron, J-P. Leroy, Paris Orch Ens/J-P. Wallez, ECO/R. Leppard/N. Marriner, X. Darasse, Toulouse CO/L. Auriacombe, A. Calvayrac, A. Bernes, A. Saint-Clivier, G. Armand, M. Bourgue, Bath Fest Orch/Y. Menuhin/C. Mackerras, M. Debost, L. Rogg, Y. Menuhin (vn/dir), C. Ferras, E. Shaffer, Philh, P. Pierlot, J-P. Taurignan)

Ⓓ **CZS7 67440-2**
The Best of Rossini
Rossini: Barbiere di Siviglia (exc); Barbiere di Siviglia (exc); Barbiere di Siviglia (exc); Barbiere di Siviglia (exc); Cenerentola (exc); Cenerentola (exc); Gazza ladra (exc); Gazza ladra (exc); Semiramide (exc); Semiramide (exc); Guillaume Tell (exc); Guillaume Tell (exc); Scala di seta (exc); Petite Messe Solennelle (exc); Stabat Mater (exc); Péchés de vieillesse I (exc); Péchés de vieillesse VI (exc); Péchés de vieillesse XI (exc); Péchés de vieillesse II (exc); Duetto buffo di due gatti; Soirées musicales (exc). (T. Gobbi, E. Gruberová, S. Ramey, M. Callas, M. Mesplé, J. Anderson, M. Caballé, N. Gedda, P. Lorengar, A. Ciccolini, C. Berberian, B. Canino, J. Berbié, J. Reiss, Philh/C.M. Giulini/A. Galliera, Munich RO/G. Kuhn/J. Delacôte, Paris Cons/N. Rescigno/R. Muti, Paris Op Orch/G-F. Masini/M. Veltri, RPO/L. Gardelli, Ambrosian Op Chor, K. Labèque, M. Labèque/S. Cleobury, Berlin St Hedwig's Cath Ch, Berlin SO/K. Forster, Stockholm Chbr Ch/E. Ericson, K. Hindart, LSO/F. Pourcel, ASMF/N. Marriner)

Ⓓ **CZS7 67474-2** (7/92)
Viva España!
Chabrier: España; *Albéniz:* Iberia (exc); *Ravel:* Rapsodie espagnole; *Turina:* Danzas fantásticas; *Rodrigo:* Concierto de Aranjuez; *Falla:* Vida breve (exc); Amor brujo (Cpte); Nights in the Gardens of Spain; Sombrero de tres picos (exc). (Paris Cons/P. Dervaux/R. Frühbeck de Burgos/A. Cluytens, Spanish Nat Orch, A. Diaz, G. Soriano, Philh/A. Vandernoot/C.M. Giulini, O. Dominguez)

Ⓓ **CZS7 67515-2** (5/93)
Offenbach—Operetta highlights
Offenbach: Vie parisienne (exc); Belle Hélène (exc); Orphée aux enfers (exc). (M. Roux, M. Hamel, W. Clément, L. Dachary, N. Renaux, L. Berton, D. Dassy, C. Devos, Duvaleix, B. Demigny, G. Rey, A. Doniat, C. Collart, A. Grandjean, H. Prudon, F. Betti, Raymond St Paul Chor, Lamoureux Orch/J. Gressier)

Ⓓ **CZS7 67546-2**
Entry of the Gladiators—Famous Marches
Beethoven: Ruinen von Athen (exc); March in C, WoO20; *Mendelssohn:* Midsummer Night's Dream (exc); *Wagner:* Kaisermarsch; *Tchaikovsky:* Marche slave; *Elgar:* Caractacus (exc); *Berlioz:* Symphonie fantastique (exc); *Tchaikovsky:* Symphony 6 (exc); *Respighi:* Pines of Rome (exc); *Verdi:* Aida (exc); *Anon:* Parade March in E flat; *Grawert:* Hohenfriedberger March; *Sousa:* Stars and Stripes Forever; *Elgar:* Imperial March; *Prokofiev:* Love for 3 Oranges Suite (exc); *Elgar:* Pomp and Circumstance Marches (exc); *Tchaikovsky:* Nutcracker Suite (exc); *R. Henrion:* Fehrbelliner Reitermarsch; *Meyerbeer:* Coronation March; *Piefke:* Preussens Gloria; *Fučík:* Entry of the Gladiators; *Sousa:* Gladiator; *J. Strauss I:* Radetzky March. (St Luke's Orch/D.R. Davies, Berlin RSO/C. Richter, Rotterdam PO/J. Tate, BPO/S. Ozawa, RLPO/C. Groves, Toulouse Capitole Orch/M. Plasson, Philadelphia/R. Muti, ROHO/B. Haitink, Kaisereiche Wind Ens, Nonpareil Wind Band/T. Foley, Bavarian St Orch/W. Sawallisch, Dresden PO/H. Kegel, Philh/J. Lanchbery, Berlin Police Orch, Prague Fest Orch/P. Urbanek, Hallé/B. Tovey)

Ⓓ **CZS7 67700-2**
The Tchaikovsky Box
Tchaikovsky: Andante cantabile, Op.11; Serenade, Op.48; Symphony 4; Capriccio Italien; 1812; Symphony 5; Songs, Op.6 (exc); Marche Slave; Romeo and Juliet; Symphony 6; Piano Concerto 1; Violin Concerto; Eugene Onegin (exc); Swan Lake (exc); Sleeping Beauty (exc); Nutcracker (exc). (B. Christoff, I. Perlman, A. Gavrilov, ASMF/N. Marriner, LSO/J. Barbirolli/A. Previn, Philh/R. Muti/S. Ozawa, Oslo PO/M. Jansons, BPO/Vladimir Ashkenazy, RPO/T. Beecham, A. Labinsky, Philadelphia/E. Ormandy)

Ⓓ **CZS7 67726-2** (9/93)
Paul Kletzki—A Profile
Glinka: Jota Aragonesa; *Rimsky-Korsakov:* Tale of Tsar Saltan (exc); *Tchaikovsky:* Andante cantabile, Op.11; *Sibelius:* Symphony 2; *Schubert:* Rosamunde (exc); *Mahler:* Symphony 4; Symphony 5 (exc). (E. Loose, Philh, RPO/P. Kletzki)

Ⓓ **CZS7 67729-2** (9/93)
Efrem Kurtz - A profile
Rimsky-Korsakov: Snow Maiden (exc); Golden Cockerel Suite (exc); *Liadov:* Kikimora, Op.63; *Shostakovich:* Symphony 1; *Khachaturian:* Masquerade (exc); *Glinka:* Life for the Tsar (exc); *Rimsky-Korsakov:* Dubinushka; *Liadov:* Baba-Yaga, Op.56; Enchanted Lake, Op.62; Musical Snuff-box, Op.32; *Kabalevsky:* Comedians; *Prokofiev:* Symphony 1. (Philh, RPO/E. Kurtz)

Ⓓ **CZS7 67813-2**
Opera Arias and Duets
Gounod: Roméo et Juliette (exc); *Delibes:* Lakmé (exc); *A. Thomas:* Hamlet (exc); Mignon (exc); *Massenet:* Manon (exc); *Bizet:* Pêcheurs de perles (exc); *Offenbach:* Contes d'Hoffmann (exc); *Donizetti:* Lucia di Lammermoor (exc); *Verdi:* Rigoletto (exc); *Rossini:* Gazza ladra (exc); *Bellini:* Capuleti (exc); Sonnambula (exc); *Rossini:* Barbiere di Siviglia (exc); *Lalo:* Roi d'Ys (exc); *Massenet:* Manon (exc); *Bizet:* Pêcheurs de perles (exc); *Meyerbeer:* Huguenots (exc); *Gounod:* Roméo et Juliette (exc); Mireille (exc); *Gluck:* Orphée (exc). (M. Mesplé, N. Gedda, Paris Op Orch/J-P. Marty/G-F. Masini/P. Dervaux)

Ⓓ **CZS7 67869-2**
J. Strauss II—Operetta Highlights
J. Strauss II: Fledermaus (exc); Zigeunerbaron (exc); Walzer aus Wien (exc). (J. Brumaire, L. Berton, P. Fleta, R. Corazza, J-C. Benoit, J. Pruvost, M. Roux, A. Forli, J. Micheau, J. Danjou, C. Gayraud, G. Chauvet, M. Lecocq, R. Duclos Ch, Société des Concerts du Conservatoire Orch/F. Pourcel, Pasdeloup Ass Orch/A. Lombard, M. Robin, M. Dens, V. Barthelemy, M. Sénéchal, H. Boulangeot, D. Marty, H. Hennetier, J. Levasseur, J. Cauchard, D. Monteil, Raymond St Paul Ch, Raymond St Paul Orch/J. Gressier)

Ⓓ **CZS7 67872-2**
Lehár—Operettas (highlights in French)
Lehár: Lustige Witwe (exc); Paganini (exc); Land des Lächelns (exc). (J. Vivalda, M. Dens, M. Linval, R. Amade, P. Germain, J. Pruvost, J-C. Benoit, A. Forli, N. Sautereau, G. Godin, C. Devos, L. Noguera, L. Berton, C. Collart, R. Duclos Ch, Raymond St Paul Chor, Paris Cons, Orch/F. Pourcel/M. Cariven)

Ⓓ **CZS7 67875-2**
Moulin Rouge
Auric: Moulin Rouge (exc); *O. Straus:* Drei Walzer (exc). (J. Micheau, M. Altéry, Raymond St Paul Chor, SO/P. Bonneau, Orch, Paris Grand Orch/J. Metehen)

ОО **DCC7 47014-5**
Mozart: Opera Overtures
Mozart: Nozze di Figaro (exc); Zauberflöte (exc); Clemenza di Tito (exc); Lucio Silla (exc); Entführung (exc); Don Giovanni (exc); Idomeneo (exc); Così fan tutte (exc); Schauspieldirektor (exc). (ASMF/N. Marriner)

ОО **DCC7 54089-5**
J. Strauss II—Waltzes & Overtures
J. Strauss II: Künstlerleben, Op. 316; Rosen aus dem Süden; Zigeunerbaron (exc); G'schichten aus dem Wienerwald, Op. 325; Kaiser, Op. 437; Fledermaus (exc); Blauen Donau, Op. 314. (LPO/F. Welser-Möst)

ОО **DCC7 54091-5**
Rossini—Overtures
Rossini: Scala di seta (exc); Signor Bruschino (exc); Italiana in Algeri (exc); Barbiere di Siviglia (exc); Gazza ladra (exc); Semiramide (exc); Guillaume Tell (exc). (LCP/R. Norrington)

EG749768-2 (5/90)
Cabaret Songs—Michael Finstein
Cohan: Over there; *Berlin:* Oh! How I hate; *Gottlieb:* Would you rather be a Colonel; *R. Lloyd:* Good morning, Mr Zip-Zip-Zip; *Baskette:* Good-bye, Broadway; *Novello:* Keep the Home fires burning; *Darewski:* Sister Susie's sewing; *Jerome:* Just a baby's prayer at twilight; *J. Judge:* It's a long way to Tipperary; *Haydn Wood:* Roses of Picardy; *Donaldson:* How 'ya gonna keep; *Cohan:* I want to hear a Yankee Doodle Tune; *Katscher:* When day is done; *Lehár:* Land des Lächelns (exc); *Sieczyński:* Wien, du Stadt meiner Träume; *Schoenberg:* Cabaret Songs (exc); *Weill:* Reiterlied; Im Volkston; Schöne Kind; *Stolz:* Zwei Herzen in Dreivierteltakt (exc). (M. Feinstein, A. Guzelimian)

EG763078-4 (10/89)
Mozart—Don Giovanni (highlights)
Mozart: Don Giovanni (exc). (E. Waechter, J. Sutherland, E. Schwarzkopf, L. Alva, G. Sciutti, G. Taddei, P. Cappuccilli, Philh Chor, Philh/C.M. Giulini)

MDC7 47014-8
Mozart: Opera Overtures
Mozart: Nozze di Figaro (exc); Zauberflöte (exc); Clemenza di Tito (exc); Lucio Silla (exc); Entführung (exc); Don Giovanni (exc); Idomeneo (exc); Così fan tutte (exc); Schauspieldirektor (exc). (ASMF/N. Marriner)

MDC7 54089-8
J. Strauss II—Waltzes & Overtures
J. Strauss II: Künstlerleben, Op. 316; Rosen aus dem Süden; Zigeunerbaron (exc); G'schichten aus dem Wienerwald, Op. 325; Kaiser, Op. 437; Fledermaus (exc); Blauen Donau, Op. 314. (LPO/F. Welser-Möst)

MDC7 54091-8
Rossini—Overtures
Rossini: Scala di seta (exc); Signor Bruschino (exc); Italiana in Algeri (exc); Barbiere di Siviglia (exc); Gazza ladra (exc); Semiramide (exc); Guillaume Tell (exc). (LCP/R. Norrington)

ZDMB5 65427-2
Stokowski's United Artists Recordings
Respighi: Pines of Rome; *Khachaturian:* Symphony 2; *Shostakovich:* Symphony 1; Preludes, Op.34 (exc); Lady Macbeth of Mtsensk (exc); *Bloch:* Schelomo; *Frescobaldi:* Secondo libro di toccate (exc); *Palestrina:* Motets, Bk 2 (1581) (exc); *Cesti:* Tu mancavi a tormentarmi; *G. Gabrieli:* Symphoniae sacrae (1597) (exc). (G. Neikrug, Sym of the Air/L. Stokowski)

ZDMF7 64830-2 (5/94)
The Art of Nathan Milstein
Glazunov: Violin Concerto; *Prokofiev:* Violin Concerto 2; *Saint-Saëns:* Violin Concerto 3; *Tchaikovsky:* Violin Concerto; *Brahms:* Violin Concerto; *Beethoven:* Violin Concerto; *Dvořák:* Violin Concerto; *Vivaldi:* Concerti Grossi, Op.3 (exc); Sonatas, Op.2 (exc); *Handel:* Violin Sonatas (exc); Flute Sonatas (exc); *T.A. Vitali:* Ciacona; *Corelli:* Sonatas, Op.5 (exc); *Tartini:* Devil's Trill Sonata; *Bach:* Suites, BWV1066-9 (exc); *Mozart:* Violin Sonata, K296; Violin Sonata, K304; *Beethoven:* Violin Sonata 5; *Prokofiev:* Violin Sonata 2; *Rachmaninov:* Vocalise; *Mussorgsky:* Fair at Sorochintsï (exc); *Glazunov:* Meditation, Op.32; *Tchaikovsky:* Valse-Scherzo, Op.34; Souvenir d'un lieu cher, Op.42 (exc); *Rimsky-Korsakov:* Russian Fantasia; Tale of Tsar Saltan (exc); *Brahms:* Hungarian Dances (exc); *Massenet:* Thaïs (exc); *Gluck:* Orfeo ed Euridice (exc); *Chopin:* Nocturnes (exc); *Falla:* Canciones populares españolas (exc); *Wieniawski:* Scherzo-Tarantelle, Op.16; *Debussy:* Préludes (exc); *Sarasate:* Introduction and Tarantella, Op.43; *Kreisler:* Pugnani Praeludium and Allegro. (N. Milstein, Pittsburgh SO/W. Steinberg, New Philh/R. Frühbeck de Burgos, Philh/A. Fistoulari/E. Leinsdorf, E. Morini, H. Shapiro, CO, L. Pommers, A. Balsam, R. Firkušný, orch/R. Irving, N. Milstein (vn/dir))

EMI Eminence

CD-EMX2123 (2/90) **TC-EMX2123** (2/88)
Maria Callas sings Operatic Arias
Rossini: Barbiere di Siviglia (exc); *Verdi:* Macbeth (exc); Don Carlo (exc); *Puccini:* Tosca (exc); *Gluck:* Alceste (1776) (exc); *Bizet:* Carmen (exc); *Saint-Saëns:* Samson et Dalila (exc); *Massenet:* Manon (exc); *G. Charpentier:* Louise (exc). (M. Callas, N. Gedda, R. Duclos Ch, Philh, Paris Cons, FRNO, Paris Op Orch/A. Galliera/N. Rescigno/G. Prêtre)

CD-EMX2175
Music of Gershwin
Gershwin: Rhapsody in Blue; American in Paris; Porgy and Bess Suite; Preludes. (L. Pennario, Hollywood Bowl SO/L. Slatkin)

CD-EMX2187 (1/92)
Tchaikovsky—Symphony No. 5, etc
Tchaikovsky: Symphony 5; Eugene Onegin (exc). (E. Hannan, LPO/S. Edwards)

CD-EMX2198 (3/93)
A Delius Festival
Delius: Songs of Farewell; Late Swallows; Song before Sunrise; To be sung of a Summer Night; Village Romeo and Juliet (exc); Cynara; Margot la Rouge (exc); Wanderer's Song; Koanga (exc). (R. Tear, J. Shirley-Quirk, RCS, Baccholian Sngrs, King's College Ch, Hallé, RLPO, RPO, Philh/M. Sargent/J. Barbirolli/P. Ledger/M. Davies/C. Groves/G. Weldon)

CD-EMX2211 **TC-EMX2211**
Mozart—Così fan tutte (highlights)
Mozart: Così fan tutte (exc). (E. Schwarzkopf, N. Merriman, L. Otto, L. Simoneau, R. Panerai, S. Bruscantini, Philh/H. von Karajan)

CD-EMX2215
Gounod—Faust (highlights)
Gounod: Faust (exc). (N. Gedda, V.de los Angeles, R. Gorr, L. Berton, B. Christoff, E. Blanc, V. Autran, Paris Op Chor, Paris Op Orch/A. Cluytens)

CD-EMX2220 **TC-EMX2220**
Mozart—Die Zauberflöte (highlights)
Mozart: Zauberflöte (exc). (I. Seefried, W. Lipp, A. Dermota, E. Kunz, L. Weber, G. London, S. Jurinac, F. Riegler, E. Schürhoff, E. Loose, P. Klein, Vienna Singverein, VPO/H. Von Karajan)

CD-EMX2227 (12/94) **TC-EMX2227** (12/94)
Holst—Orchestral Works
Holst: St Paul's Suite; Fugal Concerto; Brook Green Suite; Somerset Rhapsody; Perfect Fool (exc). (J. Snowden, D. Theodore, ECO/Y. Menuhin)

CD-EMX2228 **TC-EMX2228**
Wagner—Die Meistersinger von Nürnberg—excs
Wagner: Meistersinger (exc). (F. Frantz, G. Frick, H. Wilhelm, W. Stoll, B. Kusche, G. Neidlinger, M. Schmidt, L. Clam, Herold Kraus, R. Koffmane, A. Metternich, H. Pick, R. Schock, G. Unger, E. Grümmer, M. Höffgen, H. Prey, Berlin St Hedwig's Cath Ch, Berlin Deutsche Op Chor, Berlin St Op Chor, BPO/R. Kempe)

CD-EMX2231 (3/95)
Britten—Orchestral Works
Britten: Gloriana Suite; Sea Interludes, Op. 33a; Pas de Six Suite. (RLPO/T. Yuasa)

CD-EMX2234
French and Italian Operatic Arias
Delibes: Lakmé (exc); *Meyerbeer:* Huguenots (exc); *Gounod:* Roméo et Juliette (exc); *A. Thomas:* Hamlet (exc); *Donizetti:* Lucia di Lammermoor (exc); *Rossini:* Semiramide (exc); Barbiere di Siviglia (exc). (E. Gruberová, Munich RO/G. Kuhn)

CD-EMX2241
Ravel—L'enfant et les sortilèges.
Ravel: Enfant et les sortilèges (Cpte). (S.D. Wyner, J. Taillon, J. Bastin, J. Berbié, P. Huttenlocher, P. Langridge, A. Auger, L. Finnie, L. Richardson, Ambrosian Sngrs, LSO/A. Previn)

CD-EMX9519 **TC-EMX2099**
Great Sopranos of Our Time
Verdi: Aida (exc); *Donizetti:* Lucia di Lammermoor (exc); *Bizet:* Pêcheurs de perles (exc); *Rossini:* Barbiere di Siviglia (exc); *Puccini:* Bohème (exc); *Delibes:* Lakmé (exc); *Mozart:* Così fan tutte (exc); *Puccini:* Madama Butterfly (exc); *Mozart:* Don Giovanni (exc). (M. Caballé, M. Callas, I. Cotrubas, V. de los Angeles, M. Freni, E. Gruberová, E. Schwarzkopf, R. Scotto, J. Sutherland, Rome Op Orch/J. Barbirolli, Philh/K. Böhm/C.M. Giulini, Munich RO/G. Kuhn, Glyndebourne Fest Orch/V. Gui/T. Schippers/T. Serafin, Paris Op Orch/G. Prêtre, New Philh/R. Muti)

EMI Laser

CDZ100 **LZ100**
Best Loved Classics 1
Bach: Toccata and Fugue, BWV565; *Handel:* Water Music (exc); *Mozart:* Don Giovanni (exc); *Haydn:* Trumpet Concerto (exc); *Schubert:* Forelle, D550; *Mendelssohn:* Midsummer Night's Dream (exc); *Rossini:* Guillaume Tell (exc); *Bizet:* Carmen (exc); *Chopin:* Fantaisie-impromptu; *Tchaikovsky:* Nutcracker (exc); *Saint-Saëns:* Samson et Dalila (exc); *Mahler:* Symphony 5 (exc); *Liszt:* Hungarian Rhapsodies, S359 (exc). (L. Rogg, Linde Consort/H-M. Linde, T. Allen, LPO/B. Haitink, M. André, Philh/R. Muti, J. Baker, G. Parsons, LSO/A. Previn, R. Massard, R. Duclos Ch, Paris Op Orch/G. Prêtre, A. Lucchesini, M. Callas, FRNO/K. Tennstedt/W. Boskovsky)

CDZ101 **LZ101**
Best Loved Classics 2
Handel: Solomon (exc); *Mozart:* Horn Concerti (exc); *Rossini:* Barbiere di Siviglia (exc); *Liszt:* Paganini Studies, S140 (exc); *Mendelssohn:* Violin Concerto, Op.64 (exc); *J. Strauss II:* Casanova (exc); *Sibelius:* Karelia Suite (exc); *Wagner:* Walküre (exc); *Khachaturian:* Spartacus Suite 2 (exc); *Falla:* Amor Brujo (exc); *Verdi:* Nabucco (exc); *Borodin:* Prince Igor (exc). (ASMF/N. Marriner, R. Vlatkovič, ECO/J. Tate, T. Gobbi, Philh/A. Galliera, A. Lucchesini, Y. Menuhin, LSO/R. Frühbeck de Burgos, L. Popp, Ambrosian Op Chor, Hallé/J. Barbirolli, BPO/K. Tennstedt, RPO/Y. Temirkanov/C.M. Giulini, ROH Chor, ROHO/L. Gardelli/H. von Karajan)

CDZ102 **LZ102**
Best Loved Classics 3
Vivaldi: Concerti, Op.8 (exc); *Bach:* Cantata 208 (exc); *Handel:* Messiah (exc); *Mozart:* Symphony 40 (exc); *Chopin:* Waltzes (exc); *Mendelssohn:* Hebrides; *Offenbach:* Contes d'Hoffmann (exc); *Lehár:* Gold und Silber; *Verdi:* Traviata (exc); *Puccini:* Tosca (exc); *Vaughan Williams:* Greensleeves Fantasia; *Ravel:* Pavane; *Mascagni:* Cavalleria Rusticana (exc). (Y. Menuhin, Camerata Lysy/A. Lysy, ASMF/N. Marriner, E. Harwood, ECO/C. Mackerras/J. Tate, D. Alexeev, BPO/H. von Karajan, Stuttgart RSO, VJSO/W. Boskovsky, Philh/R. Muti, P. Domingo/James Levine, Sinfonia of London/J. Barbirolli, LSO/A. Previn, P. Tinsley, ROH Chor, ROHO/L. Gardelli)

CDZ103 **LZ103**
Best Loved Classics 4
Orff: Carmina Burana (exc); *Bach:* Suites, BWV1066-9 (exc); *Mozart:* Serenade, K525 (exc); *Handel:* Messiah (exc); *Mendelssohn:* Symphony 4 (exc); *Chopin:* Polonaises (exc); *Rimsky-Korsakov:* Tale of Tsar Saltan (exc); *Ketèlbey:* In a Persian Market; *Verdi:* Traviata (exc); *Bizet:* Arlésienne Suites (exc); *J. Strauss II:* Blauen Donau, Op. 314; *Leoncavallo:* Pagliacci (exc); *Elgar:* Enigma Variations (exc); *Tchaikovsky:* Capriccio Italien. (Philh Chor, Philh/R. Muti, ASMF/N. Marriner, Ambrosian Sngrs, ECO/C. Mackerras, BPO/K. Tennstedt, A. Lucchesini/J. Lanchbery, Alfredo Kraus, R. Scotto, FNO/S. Ozawa, VJSO/W. Boskovsky, F. Corelli, La Scala Orch/L. von Matačić, LSO/A. Boult)

CDZ104 **LZ104**
Best Loved Classics 5
Clarke: Suite in D (exc); *Bach:* Cantata 147 (exc); *Mozart:* Nozze di Figaro (exc); *Albinoni:* Adagio; *Weber:* Invitation to the Dance; *Chopin:* Nocturnes (exc); *Verdi:* Aida (exc); *Ponchielli:* Gioconda (exc); *Grieg:* Peer Gynt (exc); *Sibelius:* Karelia Suite (exc); *Puccini:* Madama Butterfly (exc); *Walton:* Façade Suites (exc); *Debussy:* Après-midi; *Wagner:* Lohengrin (exc). (M. André, J. Parker-Smith, ASMF/N. Marriner, T. Allen, Scottish CO/R. Armstrong, I. Brown, Philh/H. von Karajan, R. Buchbinder, New Philh/R. Muti, RPO/T. Beecham, Hallé/J. Barbirolli, M. Caballé, LSO/C. Mackerras/O.A. Hughes/A. Previn, BPO/K. Tennstedt, P. Domingo)

CDZ105
Best Loved Classics 6
Pachelbel: Canon and Gigue (exc); *Beethoven:* Symphony 7 (exc); *Boccherini:* String Quintets, G271-6 (exc); *Mozart:* Zauberflöte (exc); *Schubert:* Rosamunde (exc); *Chopin:* Waltzes (exc); *Mendelssohn:* Midsummer Night's Dream (exc); *Bizet:* Carmen (exc); *J. Strauss II:* G'schichten aus dem Wienerwald, Op. 325; *Tchaikovsky:* Swan Lake Suite (exc); *Barber:* Adagio for strings; *Puccini:* Gianni Schicchi (exc); *Grieg:* Piano Concerto (exc). (ASMF/N. Marriner, Staatskapelle Dresden/J. Tate, T. Allen, Scottish CO/R. Armstrong, R. Buchbinder, LSO/A. Previn, M. Callas, FRNO/G. Prêtre, VJSO/W. Boskovsky, Philadelphia/R. Muti/E. Ormandy, M. Caballé/C. Mackerras, S. Richter, Monte Carlo Op Orch/L. von Matačić)

CDZ112 **LZ112**
Music for Weddings
Wagner: Lohengrin (exc); *Clarke:* Suite in D (exc); *Gounod:* Ave Maria; *Karg-Elert:* Choral-Improvisationen, Op. 65 (exc); *Boëllmann:* Suite gothique (exc); *Bach:* Cantata 147 (exc); *Albinoni:* Adagio; *Franck:* Panis angelicus; *Mendelssohn:* Midsummer Night's Dream (exc); *Bach:* Suites, BWV1066-9 (exc); *Schubert:* Ave Maria, D839; *Bach:* In dulci jubilo, BWV729; *Handel:* Serse (exc); *J. Seymour Irvine:* Lord's my shepherd; *Liszt:* Liebesträume, S541 (exc); *Widor:* Symphony 5 (exc). (J. Baker, F. Corelli, L. Goossens, M. André, G. Moore, G. Ohlsson, F. Bayco, J. Parker-Smith, P. Ledger, G. Thalben-Ball (org/dir), N. Rawsthorne, Temple Church Ch, Chor, Orch/R. Mingardo)

CDZ114 (1/89) **LZ114**
Best of Baroque
Albinoni: Adagio; *Bach:* Suites, BWV1066-9 (exc); *Gluck:* Orfeo ed Euridice (exc); *Handel:* Messiah (exc); Berenice

(exc); *Bach:* 2-Violin Concerto; *Handel:* Solomon (exc); *Pachelbel:* Canon and Gigue (exc); *Handel:* Serse (exc); Water Music Suite. (RLPO/C. Groves, Scottish CO/K. Montgomery, Y. Menuhin (vn/dir), C. Ferras, Y. Menuhin (vn/dir), C. Ferras, Festival CO, ASMF/N. Marriner, R. Kilbey Stgs/R. Kilbey, RPO/G. Weldon)

Ⓓ **CDZ115**
Greensleeves
Vaughan Williams: Greensleeves Fantasia; *Delius:* Village Romeo and Juliet (exc); *Vaughan Williams:* Lark ascending; *Butterworth:* Shropshire Lad; Banks of Green Willow; *Elgar:* Serenade; *Delius:* First cuckoo; *Vaughan Williams:* English Folk Song Suite. (Sinfonia of London/J. Barbirolli, LSO, H. Bean, New Philh/A. Boult, English Sinfonia/N. Dilkes, LPO, Hallé)

Ⓓ **CDZ7 67015-2** (7/91)
Mozart—Opera Arias
Mozart: Nozze di Figaro (exc); Nozze di Figaro (exc); Nozze di Figaro (exc); Entführung (exc); Entführung (exc); Don Giovanni (exc); Don Giovanni (exc); Don Giovanni (exc); Così fan tutte (exc); Così fan tutte (exc); Così fan tutte (exc); Zauberflöte (exc); Zauberflöte (exc); Zauberflöte (exc). (C. Desderi, LPO/B. Haitink, M. Price, VPO/R. Muti, F. Cossotto, Philh/C.M. Giulini, A. Moffo, A. Rothenberger/J. Krips, I. Hollweg, RPO/T. Beecham, G. Frick, R. Soyer, H. Donath, ECO/D. Barenboim, T. Allen, N. Gedda, New Philh/O. Klemperer, M. Ewing, M. Marshall, A. Baltsa, J. Van Dam, C. Vaness, F. Araiza, G. Taddei/K. Böhm, W. Berry, Bavarian St Op Orch/W. Sawallisch, S. Jerusalem, BRSO, L. Popp)

Ⓓ **CDZ7 67253-2**
Funeral Music
Purcell: March and Canzona, Z860 (exc); *Ravel:* Pavane; *Grieg:* Peer Gynt (exc); *Chopin:* Piano Sonata 2 (exc); *Mahler:* Symphony 1 (exc); *Wagner:* Götterdämmerung (exc); *Mozart:* Maurerische Trauermusik, K477; *Handel:* Saul (exc); *Purcell:* Dido (exc); *Schubert:* String Quartet, D810 (exc); *Walton:* Henry V Suite (exc); *Sibelius:* Valse triste. (Taverner Plyrs/A. Parrott, Paris Cons/A. Cluytens, Hallé/J. Barbirolli, RAF Central Band, LPO/K. Tennstedt/A. Boult, ASMF/N. Marriner, V. de los Angeles, ECO/J. Tate/Carl Davis/R.E.C. Davies)

Entr'acte

Ⓓ **ESCD6502**
Erich Wolfgang Korngold: Songs and Arias
Korngold: Tote Stadt (exc); Much Ado about Nothing (exc); Elizabeth and Essex (exc); Sea Hawk (exc); Silent Serenade (exc); Kathrin (exc); Ring des Polykrates (exc); Einfache Lieder, Op. 9 (exc). (P.J. Baker, G. Calusdian)

EPM Classical Collector

Ⓓ **150 012** (11/90)
Massenet—Manon
Massenet: Manon (Cpte); Manon (exc). (G. Féraldy, J. Rogatchewsky, G. Villier, L. Guénot, A. Gaudin, J. Vieuille, E. de Creus, A. Vavon, Mlle Rambert, Mlle Ravery, A. Bernadet, M. Fenoyer, P. Payen, M. Julliot, Paris Opéra-Comique Chor, Paris Opéra-Comique Orch/E. Cohen, G. Féraldy, orch)

Ⓓ **150 052** (5/91)
Germaine Lubin—Opera & Song Recital
Weber: Freischütz (exc); *Wagner:* Lohengrin (exc); Tannhäuser (exc); Tristan und Isolde (exc); Walküre (exc); Siegfried (exc); Götterdämmerung (exc); *Schubert:* Erlkönig, D328; *Schumann:* Myrthen, Op. 25 (exc); *Debussy:* Promenoir des deux amants (exc); *Wolf:* Spanisches Liederbuch (exc); Mörike Lieder (exc); *Schumann:* Lieder und Gesänge, Op. 51 (exc); *Chopin:* Etudes (exc); *Durante:* Vergin, tutto amor. (G. Lubin, orch, anon/H. Defosse, J. Krieger, E.I. Kahn, R. Verdière)

Ⓓ **150 122** (9/93)
Milhaud—Historic Recordings 1928-1948
Milhaud: Choéphores (exc); Printemps I; Poèmes juifs (exc); *Satie:* Mélodies (1916); *Milhaud:* Homme et son désir; Soirées de Pétrograd (exc); Boeuf sur le toit; Poèmes de Jean Cocteau; Saudades do Brasil (exc); Euménides (exc); Création du Monde; Salade (exc); Chants hébraïques; Enlèvement d'Europe; Abandon d'Ariane; Déliverance de Thésée; Songes; Piano Concerto 1; Saudades do Brasil (exc); Automne (exc); Amours de Ronsard (exc); Concertino de printemps; Suite provençale; Fête de la musique; Scaramouche. (D. Milhaud, J. Bathori, Desormière Ens/D. Milhaud, R. Bénédetti, J. Wiener, M. Singher, J. Planel, G. Petit, A. Valencin, M. Brega, J. Hazart, Pro Musica Ens, Paris SO, M. Long, FRNO, orch, R. Mahé, E. Schenneberg, C. Rouquetty, P. Froumenty, Y. Astruc/R. Desormière, E. Fels, R. Gourgues, J. Claverie, M. Meyer, E. Chastenet/L. de Vocht, Antwerp Caecilia Chorale, Antwerp Concerts Orch, C. Croiza)

Erato

Ⓓ **0630-10699-2** (11/95)
Puccini—La Bohème
Puccini: Bohème (Cpte). (K. Te Kanawa, R. Leech, N. Gustafson, A. Titus, R. Scandiuzzi, C. Chausson, A. Ewing, B. Banks, L. Fyson, Ambrosian Sngrs, St Clement Danes Sch Ch, LSO/K. Nagano)

Ⓓ **2292-45003-2** (6/90)
Gluck—Iphigénie en Aulide
Gluck: Iphigénie en Aulide (Cpte). (L. Dawson, J. Van Dam, A.S. von Otter, J. Aler, B. Delétré, G. Cachemaille, R. Schirrer, G. Laurens, A. Monoyios, I. Eschenbrenner, Monteverdi Ch, Lyon Op Orch/J.E. Gardiner)

Ⓓ **2292-45028-2** (9/90)
Rameau—Platée
Rameau: Platée (Cpte). (G. Ragon, J. Smith, G. de Mey, V. le Texier, G. Laurens, B. Delétré, V. Gens, M. Verschaeve, F. Herr Voc Ens, Musiciens du Louvre/M. Minkowski)

Ⓓ **2292-45147-2** (4/87)
Vivaldi—Orlando Furioso
Vivaldi: Orlando Furioso (Cpte). (M. Horne, V. de los Angeles, L.V. Terrani, C. Gonzales, L. Kozma, S. Bruscantini, N. Zaccaria, Amici della Polifonia Chor, Solisti Veneti/C. Scimone)

Ⓓ **2292-45162-2**
M A Charpentier—David et Jonathas
M-A. Charpentier: David et Jonathas (Cpte). (P. Esswood, C. Alliot-Lugaz, P. Huttenlocher, R. Soyer, A. David, P. Marinov, A. David, R. Jacobs, F. Le Roux, Lyon Enfants de la Cigale Ch, Lyon Lycée Musical Ch, Lyon Op Chor, English Bach Fest Baroque Orch/M. Corboz)

Ⓓ **2292-45186-2**
Marilyn Horne sings Handel Opera Arias
Handel: Rinaldo (exc); Serse (exc); Partenope (exc); Agrippina (exc); Orlando (exc). (M. Horne, Solisti Veneti/C. Scimone)

Ⓓ **2292-45207-2** (9/85)
Bizet—Carmen
Bizet: Carmen (Cpte). (J. Migenes, P. Domingo, F. Esham, R. Raimondi, L. Watson, S. Daniel, J-P. Lafont, G. Garino, F. Le Roux, J.P. Bogart, J. Guiomar, A. di Leo, French Rad Chor, FNO/L. Maazel)

Ⓓ **2292-45209-2** (12/84) ▭ **2292-45209-4**
Bizet—Carmen (Excerpts)
Bizet: Carmen (exc). (J. Migenes, P. Domingo, R. Raimondi, F. Esham, S. Daniel, L. Watson, J.P. Bogart, F. Le Roux, French Rad. Chor, FNO/L. Maazel)

OO 2292-45209-5
Bizet—Carmen (Excerpts)
Bizet: Carmen (exc). (J. Migenes, P. Domingo, R. Raimondi, F. Esham, S. Daniel, L. Watson, J.P. Bogart, F. Le Roux, French Rad. Chor, FNO/L. Maazel)

Ⓓ **2292-45263-2** (11/91)
Purcell—Dido and Aeneas
Purcell: Dido (Cpte). (T. Troyanos, R. Stilwell, F. Palmer, P. Kern, E. Gale, A. Hodgson, L. Maxwell, P. Langridge, ECO Chor, ECO/R. Leppard)

Ⓓ **2292-45311-2** (5/88)
Puccini—La bohème
Puccini: Bohème (Cpte). (B. Hendricks, J. Carreras, A.M. Blasi, G. Quilico, R. Cowan, F.E. d'Artegna, F. Davià, M. Sénéchal, FRN Chor, FNR Maîtrise, FNO/J. Conlon)

Ⓓ **2292-45331-2** (4/92)
Prokofiev—War and Peace
Prokofiev: War and Peace (Cpte). (L. Miller, G. Vishnevskaya, Katherine Ciesinski, M. Paunova, D. Petkov, W. Ochman, S. Toczyska, N. Gedda, V. de Kanel, M. Smith, N. Ghiuselev, E. Tumagian, French Rad Chor, FNO/M. Rostropovich)

Ⓓ **2292-45404-2** (1/92)
Rossini—L'Italiana in Algeri
Rossini: Italiana in Algeri (Cpte). (M. Horne, E. Palacio, D. Trimarchi, S. Ramey, K. Battle, C. Foti, N. Zaccaria, Prague Phil Chor, Solisti Veneti/C. Scimone)

Ⓓ **2292-45405-2** (4/92)
Fauré—Pénélope
Fauré: Pénélope (Cpte). (J. Norman, A. Vanzo, P. Huttenlocher, J. Van Dam, J. Taillon, C. Alliot-Lugaz, C. Barbaux, D. Borst, M. Command, N. Lerer, P. Guigue, G. Friedmann, F. Le Roux, J. Laforge Choral Ens, Monte Carlo PO/C. Dutoit)

Ⓓ **2292-45407-2** (10/91)
Chausson—King Arthur
Chausson: Roi Arthus (Cpte). (G. Quilico, T. Zylis-Gara, G. Winbergh, R. Massis, G. Friedmann, F. Loup, G. Cachemaille, T. Dran, R. Schirrer, A. Laiter, French Rad Chor, French Rad New PO/A. Jordan)

Ⓓ **2292-45408-2**
Handel—Tamerlano
Handel: Tamerlano (Cpte). (D.L. Ragin, N. Robson, N. Argenta, M. Chance, J. Findlay, R. Schirrer, EBS/J.E. Gardiner)

Ⓓ **2292-45418-2** (6/90)
Mussorgsky—Boris Godunov
Mussorgsky: Boris Godunov (Cpte). (R. Raimondi, V. Polozov, G. Vishnevskaya, P. Plishka, R. Tesarowicz, K. Riegel, M. Raitzin, N. Storozhev, M.A. Fish, C. Dubosc, M. Zakai, N. Gedda, L. Miller, Chevy Chase Sch Ch, Washington Oratorio Soc, Washington Chor Arts Soc, Washington NSO/M. Rostropovich)

Ⓓ **2292-45419-2** (6/90)
Rossini—Zelmira
Rossini: Zelmira (Cpte). (C. Gasdia, B. Fink, W. Matteuzzi, C. Merritt, J. Garcia, B. Senator, V. Midgley, L. Fyson, Ambrosian Sngrs, Solisti Veneti/C. Scimone)

Ⓓ **2292-45475-2** (10/90)
Mozart: Così fan tutte
Mozart: Così fan tutte (Cpte). (L. Cuberli, C. Bartoli, J. Rodgers, K. Streit, F. Furlanetto, J. Tomlinson, Berlin RIAS Chbr Ch, BPO/D. Barenboim)

Ⓓ **2292-45487-2** (11/90)
Donizetti—Don Pasquale
Donizetti: Don Pasquale (Cpte). (G. Bacquier, B. Hendricks, L. Canonici, G. Quilico, R. Schirrer, Lyon Op Chor, Lyon Op Orch/G. Ferro)

Ⓓ **2292-45490-2** (9/91)
Handel—Amadigi di Gaula
Handel: Amadigi di Gaula (Cpte). (N. Stutzmann, J. Smith, E. Harrhy, B. Fink, P. Bertin, Musiciens du Louvre/M. Minkowski)

Ⓓ **2292-45501-2** (5/91)
Mozart: Le nozze di Figaro
Mozart: Nozze di Figaro (Cpte). (J. Tomlinson, J. Rodgers, A. Schmidt, L. Cuberli, C. Bartoli, P. Pancella, G. von Kannen, G. Clark, R. Brunner, P. Rose, H. Leidland, Berlin RIAS Chbr Ch, BPO/D. Barenboim)

Ⓓ **2292-45516-2** (10/91)
Gluck—La rencontre imprévue
Gluck: Rencontre imprévue (Cpte). (L. Dawson, C. Le Coz, C. Dubosc, S. Marin-Degor, G. de Mey, J-L. Viala, G. Flechter, J-P. Lafont, G. Cachemaille, F. Dudziak, Lyon Op Orch/J.E. Gardiner)

Ⓓ **2292-45522-2** (4/92)
Marais—Alcyone
Marais: Alcyone (Cpte). (J. Smith, G. Ragon, P. Huttenlocher, V. le Texier, S. Boulin, B. Delétré, J-P. Fouchécourt, V. Gens, Musiciens du Louvre/M. Minkowski)

Ⓓ **2292-45556-2**
Purcell—The Indian Queen
Purcell: Indian Queen, Z630 (Cpte). (S. Varcoe, J. Smith, M. Hill, J. Elwes, R. Hardy, G. Fisher, A. Stafford, D. Thomas, D. Harris, Monteverdi Ch, EBS/J.E. Gardiner)

Ⓓ **2292-45588-2** (3/92)
Mozart—Don Giovanni
Mozart: Don Giovanni (Cpte). (F. Furlanetto, L. Cuberli, W. Meier, J. Rodgers, U. Heilmann, J. Tomlinson, M. Pertusi, M. Salminen, Berlin RIAS Chbr Ch, BPO/D. Barenboim)

Ⓓ **2292-45596-2** (8/91)
Mussorgsky—Pictures, etc
Mussorgsky: Pictures; Khovanshchina (exc). (Rotterdam PO/J. Conlon)

Ⓓ **2292-45627-2** (7/92)
Stravinsky—The Nightingale
Stravinsky: Nightingale (Cpte). (P. Bryn-Julson, I. Caley, F. Palmer, J. Tomlinson, N. Howlett, M. George, E. Laurence, BBC Sngrs, BBC SO/P. Boulez)

Ⓓ **2292-45662-2** (9/92)
Wagner—Parsifal
Wagner: Parsifal (Cpte). (R. Goldberg, W. Schöne, R. Lloyd, Y. Minton, A. Haugland, H. Tschammer, P. Frey, G. Cachemaille, T. Herz, H. Schaer, C. Bladin, M. Roider, B-M. Aruhn, E. Saurova, G. Oertel, J. Chamonin, Prague Phil Chor, Monte Carlo Op Orch/A. Jordan)

Ⓓ **2292-45683-2**
Mozart—Così fan tutte
Mozart: Così fan tutte (Cpte). (K. Te Kanawa, F. von Stade, T. Stratas, D. Rendall, P. Huttenlocher, J. Bastin, Rhine Op Chor, Strasbourg PO/A. Lombard)

Ⓓ **2292-45684-2** (12/91)
Debussy—Pelléas et Mélisande
Debussy: Pelléas et Mélisande (Cpte). (E. Tappy, R. Yakar, P. Huttenlocher, F. Loup, J. Taillon, C. Alliot-Lugaz, M. Brodard, Monte Carlo Op Chor, Monte Carlo Nat Op Orch/A. Jordan)

Ⓓ **2292-45685-2** (4/92)
Gounod—Faust
Gounod: Faust (Cpte). (G. Aragall, M. Caballé, P. Plishka, P. Huttenlocher, A. Terzian, J. Taillon, J. Brun, Rhine Op Chor, Strasbourg PO/A. Lombard)

Ⓓ **2292-45686-2** (5/92)
Offenbach—La Périchole
Offenbach: Périchole (Cpte). (R. Crespin, A. Vanzo, J. Bastin, G. Friedmann, J. Trigeau, A. Besançon, P. Guigue, R. Roberts, E. Saurova, G. Baudoz, I. Meister, Rhine Op Chor, Strasbourg PO/A. Lombard)

Ⓓ **2292-45715-2** (10/92)
Mondonville—Titon et L'Aurore
Mondonville: Titon et l'Aurore (Cpte). (J-P. Fouchécourt, C. Napoli, P. Huttenlocher, J. Smith, A. Monoyios, F. Herr Voc Ens, Musiciens du Louvre/M. Minkowski)

Ⓓ **2292-45757-2** (6/92)
Popular Russian Orchestral Works
Glinka: Ruslan and Lyudmila (exc); *Glazunov:* Raymonda (exc); *Mussorgsky:* Khovanshchina (exc); *Tchaikovsky:* Francesca da Rimini. (Leningrad PO/E. Mravinsky)

Ⓓ **2292-45762-2** (6/92)
Orchestral Music from Wagner's Operas
Wagner: Lohengrin (exc); Götterdämmerung (exc); Tristan und Isolde (exc); Tannhäuser (exc); Walküre (exc). (Leningrad PO/E. Mravinsky)

Ⓓ **2292-45763-2** (6/92)
Mravinsky conducts... (including free CD interview & rehearsal)
Beethoven: Symphony 1; Symphony 3; Symphony 5; Symphony 7; Symphony 6; *Mozart:* Symphony 33; Symphony 39; *Shostakovich:* Symphony 5; Symphony 10; Symphony 12; *Tchaikovsky:* Symphony 5; Symphony 6; *Glinka:* Ruslan and Lyudmila (exc); *Glazunov:* Raymonda (exc); *Mussorgsky:* Khovanshchina (exc); *Tchaikovsky:* Francesca da Rimini; *Wagner:* Lohengrin (exc); Götterdämmerung (exc); Tristan und Isolde (exc); Walküre (exc). (Leningrad PO/E. Mravinsky)

Ⓓ **2292-45773-2** (6/92)
Berlioz—Béatrice et Bénédict
Berlioz: Béatrice et Bénédict (Cpte). (S. Graham, J-L. Viala, S. McNair, C. Robbin, G. Cachemaille, G. Bacquier, V. le Texier, P. Magnant, Lyon Op Chor, Lyon Op Orch/J. Nelson)

Ⓓ **2292-45786-2**
Der Ring des Nibelungen - Excerpts
Wagner: Götterdämmerung (exc); Siegfried (exc); Walküre (exc). (D. Polaski, Chicago SO/D. Barenboim)

Ⓓ **2292-45790-2**
Rossini—Ermione
Rossini: Ermione (Cpte). (C. Gasdia, M. Zimmermann, E. Palacio, C. Merritt, W. Matteuzzi, S. Alaimo, M. Bolognesi, E. Tandura, Prague Phil Chor, Monte Carlo PO/C. Scimone)

Ⓓ **2292-45792-2**
Chabrier—Le Roi Malgré Lui
Chabrier: Roi malgré lui (Cpte). (B. Hendricks, I. Garcisanz, G. Quilico, P. Jeffes, J-P. Lafont, C. de Moor, A. Battedou, M. Shopland, A. Munier, M. Sieyes, M. Walker, P. Bohée, P. Vilet, French Rad Chor, French Rad New PO/C. Dutoit)

Ⓓ **2292-45797-2** ▭ **2292-45797-4**
The Ultimate Opera Collection
Verdi: Aida (exc); *Bizet:* Carmen (exc); *Puccini:* Bohème (exc); *Handel:* Serse (exc); *Mozart:* Così fan tutte (exc); *Gounod:* Faust (exc); *Gluck:* Orfeo ed Euridice (exc); *Leoncavallo:* Pagliacci (exc); *Donizetti:* Elisir d'Amore (exc); *Handel:* Rinaldo (exc); *Puccini:* Turandot (exc); *Mozart:* Zauberflöte (exc). (P. Domingo, Berlin Deutsche Op Chor/N. Santi, J. Migenes, French Rad Chor, FNO/L. Maazel, J. Carreras/J. Conlon, M. Horne, Solisti Veneti/C. Scimone, K. Te Kanawa, F. von Stade, Strasbourg PO/A. Lombard, G. Aragall, Rhine Op Chor, J. Baker, Glyndebourne Fest Chor, LPO/R. Leppard, J. Bastin, M. Caballé, R. Raimondi, B. Hendricks, L. Canonici, Lyon Op Chor, Lyon Op Orch/P. Verrot, S. Jo, Suisse Romande Chbr Ch, Lausanne Pro Arte Ch, Paris Orch Ens/A. Jordan)

Ⓓ **2292-45801-2**
Wedding Music
Bach: Toccata and Fugue, BWV565; Cantata 147 (exc); *Handel:* Messiah (exc); *Albinoni:* Adagio; *Clarke:* Suite in D (exc); *Mendelssohn:* Midsummer Night's Dream (exc); *Gounod:* Ave Maria; *Fauré:* Messe basse; *Franck:* Panis angelicus; *Wagner:* Lohengrin (exc). (M-C. Alain, ECO Chor, ECO/R. Leppard, M. André, Württemberg CO/J. Faerber, J.E. Hansen, C. Maurane, A. Steyer, Paris Audite Nova Vocal Ens/J. Sourisse)

Ⓓ **2292-45806-2** (3/93)
Handel—Teseo
Handel: Teseo (Cpte). (E. James, J. Gooding, D. Jones, D.L. Ragin, C. Napoli, J. Gall, F. Bazola-Minori, Musiciens du Louvre/M. Minkowski)

Ⓓ **2292-45823-2** (12/92)
Mouret—Les Amours de Ragonde
Mouret: Amours de Ragonde (Cpte). (M. Verschaeve, J-P. Fouchécourt, S. Marin-Degor, J-L. Bindi, N. Rime, G. Ragon, J-L. Serre, Musiciens du Louvre/M. Minkowski)

Ⓓ **2292-45859-2** (2/93)
Massenet—Orchestral Works
Massenet: Scènes alsaciennes; Scènes pittoresques; Don Quichotte (exc). (Monte Carlo Op Orch/J.E. Gardiner)

Ⓓ **2292-45860-2**
Famous Romances and Adagios
Barber: Adagio for Strings; *Khachaturian:* Spartacus (exc); *Schmidt:* Notre Dame (exc); *Grieg:* Peer Gynt (exc); *Sibelius:* Valse Triste; *Mascagni:* Amico Fritz (exc); *Rachmaninov:* Vocalise; *Satie:* Gymnopédies (exc). (Monte Carlo PO/L. Foster)

Ⓓ **2292-45864-2** (5/93)
Gluck—Orfeo ed Euridice
Gluck: Orfeo ed Euridice (Cpte). (J. Baker, E. Speiser, E. Gale, Glyndebourne Fest Chor, LPO/R. Leppard)

Ⓓ **2292-45919-2**
Purcell—Excerpts from King Arthur
Purcell: King Arthur, Z628 (exc). (J. Smith, G. Fisher, E. Priday, A. Stafford, P. Elliott, S. Varcoe, Monteverdi Ch, EBS/J.E. Gardiner)

Ⓓ **2292-45925-2** (6/93)
Berlioz—Orchestral Works
Berlioz: Symphonie fantastique; Benvenuto Cellini (exc); Carnaval Romain. (Strasbourg PO/A. Lombard)

Ⓓ **2292-45964-2**
Tchaikovsky—Ballet Suites II
Tchaikovsky: Nutcracker Suite; Capriccio Italien; Eugene Onegin (exc). (Bolshoi SO/A. Lazarev)

Ⓓ **2292-45973-2** (5/86)
Tchaikovsky—Yolanta
Tchaikovsky: Iolanta (Cpte). (G. Vishnevskaya, N. Gedda, W. Groenroos, D. Petkov, T. Krause, V. Cortez, J. Anderson, T. Gedda, C. Gaetano, F. Dumont, France Groupe Vocal, Paris Orch/M. Rostropovich)

Ⓓ **2292-45983-2**
Messager—Fortunio
Messager: Fortunio (Cpte). (T. Dran, C. Alliot-Lugaz, G. Cachemaille, F. Dudziak, M. Trempont, P. Rocca, R. Schirrer, M. Fockenoy, N. Rivenq, B. Desnoues, S. Stewart, Lyon Op Chor, Lyon Op Orch/J.E. Gardiner)

Ⓓ **2292-45984-2**
Monteverdi—Ballet Music
Monteverdi: Tirsi e Clori; Orfeo (exc); De la bellezza; Ballo delle ingrate; Volgendo il ciel. (P. Kwella, A. Rolfe Johnson, L. Dale, A. Woodrow, Monteverdi Ch, EBS/J.E. Gardiner)

Ⓓ **2292-45998-2**
Strauss—Waltzes & Polkas
J. Strauss II: Fledermaus (exc); Pizzicato Polka; Kaiser, Op. 437; Unter Donner und Blitz; Blauen Donau, Op. 314; Annen-Polka, Op. 117; G'schichten aus dem Wienerwald, Op. 325; Tritsch-Tratsch; Egyptischer Marsch, Op. 335; Radetzky March. (Chicago SO/D. Barenboim)

Ⓓ **4509-91701-2** (6/93)
Donizetti—L'Elisir d'amore
Donizetti: Elisir d'amore (Cpte). (M. Devia, R. Alagna, P. Spagnoli, B. Praticò, F. Provvisionato, Tallis Chbr Ch, ECO/M. Viotti)

Ⓓ **4509-91715-2** ▭ **4509-91715-4**
The Ultimate Opera Collection 2
Bizet: Carmen (exc); *Gounod:* Faust (exc); *Mozart:* Don Giovanni (exc); *Saint-Saëns:* Samson et Dalila (exc); *Ponchielli:* Gioconda (exc); *Mozart:* Nozze di Figaro (exc); *Verdi:* Rigoletto (exc); *Donizetti:* Don Pasquale (exc); *Mozart:* Così fan tutte (exc); *Puccini:* Bohème (exc); *Rossini:* Italiana in Algeri (exc); *Handel:* Samson (exc); *Giordano:* Fedora (exc); *Bizet:* Carmen (exc); *Mozart:* Finta semplice (exc); *Wagner:* Tannhäuser (exc); Tannhäuser (exc). (P. Domingo, French Rad Chor, FNO/L. Maazel, M. Caballé, Rhine Op Chor, Strasbourg PO/A. Lombard, T. Hampson, Concertgebouw/N. Harnoncourt, M. Horne, Monte Carlo PO/L. Foster, Berlin Deutsche Op Orch/N. Santi, C. Bartoli, Berlin RIAS Chor, BPO/D. Barenboim, L. Canonici, Lyon Op Chor, Lyon Op Orch/P. Verrot, B. Hendricks/G. Ferro, K. Te Kanawa, J. Carreras, G. Quilico/J. Conlon, Prague Phil Chor, Solisti Veneti/C. Scimone, F. Lott, ECO/R. Leppard, J. Migenes, D. Upshaw, Ambrosian Sngrs, Philh/M. Janowski, VCM)

Ⓓ **4509-91717-2** (12/93)
Rimsky-Korsakov—Orchestral Works
Rimsky-Korsakov: Scheherazade; Tale of Tsar Saltan (exc). (Chicago SO/D. Barenboim)

Ⓓ **4509-91723-2** (5/94)
Russian Opera Choruses
Rimsky-Korsakov: Snow Maiden (exc); Mlada (exc); Tsar's Bride (exc); Christmas Eve (exc); Invisible city of Kitezh (exc); *Glinka:* Life for the Tsar (exc); *Mussorgsky:* Boris Godunov (exc); *Borodin:* Prince Igor (exc). (Bolshoi Th Chor, Bolshoi SO/A. Lazarev)

Ⓓ **4509-91737-2** (8/94)
Lully—Phaëton
Lully: Phaëton (Cpte). (H. Crook, R. Yakar, J. Smith, V. Gens, G. Thervel, J-P. Fouchécourt, P. Huttenlocher, L. Naouri, V. Pochon, J. Varnier, F. Couderc, Sagittarius Ens, Musiciens du Louvre/M. Minkowski)

Ⓓ **4509-92866-2**
Wagner—Famous Overtures
Wagner: Meistersinger (exc); Götterdämmerung (exc); Parsifal (exc); Parsifal (exc); Tristan und Isolde (exc). (Basle SO, Monte Carlo PO/A. Jordan, Bamberg SO/T. Guschlbauer)

Ⓓ **4509-92870-2** (12/93)
Mussorgsky—Pictures at an Exhibition; Khovanshchina - excerpt
Mussorgsky: Pictures; Khovanshchina (exc). (Rotterdam PO/J. Conlon)

Ⓓ **4509-92875-2** (1/94) ▭ **4509-92875-4** (1/94)
Vienna - Operetta Arias
Heuberger: Opernball (exc); *Kálmán:* Gräfin Mariza (exc); *Lehár:* Frasquita (exc); Lustige Witwe (exc); Paganini (exc); Schön ist die Welt (exc); Zarewitsch (exc); *O. Straus:* Tapfere Soldat (exc); *J. Strauss II:* Fledermaus (exc); Wiener Blut (exc); *Stolz:* Favorit (exc); Venus im Seide (exc). (J. Migenes, Vienna Volksoper Orch/L. Schifrin)

Ⓓ **4509-93209-2**
Debussy—Transcriptions for Piano - Four hands & Piano Duet
Debussy: Prélude à l'après-midi d'un faune; *Schumann:* Pedal Studies, Op. 56; *Saint-Saëns:* Introduction and Rondo capriccioso; Alceste caprice; *Tchaikovsky:* Swan Lake; *Wagner:* Fliegende Holländer (exc). (J-F. Heisser, G. Pludermacher)

Ⓓ **4509-94358-2** ▭ **4509-94358-4**
Stressbusters
Elgar: Serenade; *Fauré:* Elégie; *Rodrigo:* Concierto de Aranjuez; *Dvořák:* Serenade, Op. 22; *Beethoven:* Piano Sonata 8 (exc); *Mozart:* Flute and Harp Concerto, K299 (exc); Piano Concerto 21 (exc); *Bach:* 2-Violin Concerto; *Verdi:* Traviata (exc); *Anon:* Holy Week (exc); *Chopin:* Piano Concerto 2. (BBC SO/A. Davis, P. Tortelier, J. Hubeau, T. Santos, Monte Carlo Nat Op Orch/C. Scimone, Lausanne CO/A. Jordan, M-J. Pires, J-P. Rampal, L. Laskine, J-F. Paillard CO/J-F. Paillard, Lisbon Gulbenkian Orch/T. Guschlbauer, G. Jarry, P. Amoyal, LSO/C. Rizzi, Paris Gregorian Ch/F. Polgar)

Ⓓ **4509-94808-2** (8/94)
Rimsky-Korsakov—Orchestral Works
Rimsky-Korsakov: Capriccio Espagnol; Russian Easter Festival Ov; Tsar's Bride (exc); May Night (exc); Golden Cockerel Suite (exc). (Bolshoi SO/A. Lazarev)

Ⓓ **4509-94821-2**
Mozart—Così fan tutte - Highlights
Mozart: Così fan tutte (exc). (L. Cuberli, C. Bartoli, J. Rodgers, K. Streit, F. Furlanetto, J. Tomlinson, Berlin RIAS Chbr Ch, BPO/D. Barenboim)

Ⓓ **4509-94822-2**
Mozart—Le nozze di Figaro - Highlights
Mozart: Nozze di Figaro (exc). (J. Tomlinson, J. Rodgers, A. Schmidt, L. Cuberli, C. Bartoli, P. Pancella, G. von Kannen, G. Clark, R. Brunner, P. Rose, H. Leidland, Berlin RIAS Chbr Ch, BPO/D. Barenboim)

Ⓓ **4509-94823-2**
Mozart—Don Giovanni- Highlights
Mozart: Don Giovanni (exc). (F. Furlanetto, M. Salminen, L. Cuberli, U. Heilmann, W. Meier, J. Tomlinson, M.Pertusi, J. Rodgers, Berlin RIAS Chbr Ch, Berlin CO/D. Barenboim)

Ⓓ **4509-95311-2** (5/95)
Rameau—Castor et Pollux
Rameau: Castor et Pollux (Cpte). (P. Jeffes, P. Huttenlocher, J. Smith, C. Buchan, L. Wallington, B. Parsons, J. Rees, G. Fisher, J. Hancorn, H. Herford, English Bach Fest Chor, English Bach Fest Baroque Orch/C. Farncombe)

Ⓓ **4509-95312-2** (5/95)
Rameau—Dardanus
Rameau: Dardanus (Cpte). (C. Eda-Pierre, F. von Stade, G. Gautier, M. Devlin, R. Soyer, J. Van Dam, V. Dietschy, H. Garetti, A. Dutertre, M. Marandon, J-P. Courtis, Paris Op Chor, Paris Op Orch/R. Leppard)

Ⓓ **4509-95789-2** (2/95) ⊟ **4509-95789-4** (2/95)
Zarzuelas-The Passion of Spain
Guerrero y Torres: Huésped del Sevillano (exc); *Soriano:* Guitarrico (exc); *Penella:* Gato Montés (exc); *Vives:* Bohemios (exc); *Serrano:* Dolorosa (exc); *Luna:* Sangre de Reyes (exc); *Barbieri:* Barberillo de Lavapiès (exc); *Giménez:* Barbero de Sevilla (exc); *Vert:* Leyenda del beso (exc); *Calleja:* Emigrantes (exc); *Sorozábal:* Tabernera del Puerto (exc); *Caballero:* Dúo de la Africana (exc); *Serrano:* Trust de los Tenorios (exc). (J. Carreras, I. Rey, ECO/E. Ricci)

Ⓓ **4509-96370-2**
Chabrier—España
Chabrier: Joyeuse Marche; Suite Pastorale; Bourrée Fantasque; España; Gwendoline (exc); Roi malgré lui (exc). (FNO/A. Jordan)

Ⓓ **4509-96371-2** (7/95)
Gardiner—The Purcell Collection
Purcell: King Arthur, Z628 (Cpte); Indian Queen, Z630 (Cpte); Birthday Ode, Z323; Funeral Sentences; St Cecilia's Day Ode, Z328; Tempest, Z631 (Cpte); Timon of Athens, Z632 (Cpte); Dioclesian, Z627 (exc). (J. Smith, G. Fisher, E. Priday, G. Ross, A. Stafford, P. Elliott, S. Varcoe, Monteverdi Ch, EBS/J.E.Gardiner, M. Hill, J. Elwes, R. Hardy, D. Thomas, D. Harris, F. Lott, C. Brett, J. Williams, T. Allen, Monteverdi Orch, Equale Brass, B. Gordon, C. Hall, R. Earle, L. Dawson, R. Covey-Crump, M. George)

Ⓓ **4509-96374-2** (7/95)
Albinoni—Il nascimento dell'aurora
Albinoni: Nascimento dell'Aurora (Cpte). (J. Anderson, M. Zimmermann, S. Klare, S. Browne, Y. Yamaj, Solisti Veneti/C. Scimone)

Ⓓ **4509-96394-2** (11/95)
Fenelon—Le Chevalier Imaginaire
Fénelon: Chevalier Imaginaire (Cpte). (L. Villanueva, A. Tomicich, M. Armitstead, M. Davies, P. Doghan, L. Masson, Paris InterContemporain Ens/P. Eötvös)

Ⓓ **4509-96529-2** ⊟ **4509-96529-4**
Ultimate Ballet
Khachaturian: Gayaneh (exc); Masquerade (exc); Spartacus (exc); *Debussy:* Après-midi; *Mendelssohn:* Midsummer Night's Dream (exc); *Prokofiev:* Romeo and Juliet Suites (exc); *Tchaikovsky:* Eugene Onegin (exc); Nutcracker Suite (exc); Sleeping Beauty (exc); Swan Lake Suite (exc). (Bolshoi SO, SRO, Suisse Romande Chbr Ch/A. Lazarev/A. Jordan)

Ⓓ **4509-96551-2** (7/95)
Purcell—The Indian Queen
Purcell: Indian Queen, Z630 (Cpte). (R. Hardy, M. Hill, J. Elwes, A. Stafford, D. Thomas, S. Varcoe, G. Fisher, D. Harris, J. Smith, Monteverdi Ch, EBS/J.E. Gardiner)

Ⓓ **4509-96552-2** (7/95)
Purcell—King Arthur
Purcell: King Arthur, Z628 (Cpte). (J. Smith, G. Fisher, E. Priday, G. Ross, A. Stafford, P. Elliott, S. Varcoe, Monteverdi Ch, EBS/J.E. Gardiner)

Ⓓ **4509-96555-2** (7/95)
Purcell—The Tempest
Purcell: Tempest, Z631 (Cpte). (D. Thomas, R. Earle, C. Hall, R. Hardy, J. Smith, S. Varcoe, J. Elwes, Monteverdi Ch, Monteverdi Orch/J.E. Gardiner)

Ⓓ **4509-96556-2** (7/95)
Purcell—Timon of Athens; Dioclesian
Purcell: Timon of Athens, Z632 (Cpte); Dioclesian, Z627 (exc). (L. Dawson, G. Fisher, R. Covey-Crump, P. Elliott, M. George, S. Varcoe, Monteverdi Ch, EBS/J.E. Gardiner)

Ⓓ **4509-96558-2** (6/95)
Charpentier—Médée
M-A. Charpentier: Médée (Cpte). (L. Hunt, B. Delétré, M. Zanetti, M. Padmore, J-M. Salzmann, N. Rime, Arts Florissants Chor, Arts Florissants Orch/W. Christie)

Ⓓ **4509-96958-2**
Monteverdi—L'Orfeo
Monteverdi: Orfeo (Cpte). (G. Quilico, A. Michael, C. Watkinson, S. Whittingham, F. Voutsinos, E. Tappy, C. Alliot-Lugaz, D. Borst, F. Le Roux, G. de Mey, H. Ledroit, Chapelle Royale Ch, Lyon Op Orch/M. Corboz)

Ⓓ **4509-96971-2**
Marcel Landowski—Edition
Landowski: Piano Concerto 2; Ondes martenot Concerto; Trumpet Concerto; Symphony 1; Symphony 3; Symphony 4; Symphony 2; Fantôme de l'opéra (exc); Enfant appelle; Prison; Vieille Maison; Messe de l'Aurore; Cahier pour quatre jours; Fou. (A. d'Arco, ORTF Nat Orch/J. Martinon, J. Loriod, Contemporary Music CO/J. Bondon, M. André, Strasbourg PO/A. Lombard, FNO/G. Prêtre, D. Wilson-Johnson, M. Bouquet, Loire PO/M. Soustrot, G. Vishnevskaya, M. Rostropovich (vc/dir), Lille Nat Orch/M. Landowski, D. Sanges, C. Dubosc, J-P. Lafont, M. Sénéchal, R. Ercolani, C. Davesnes, C. Genelle, Y. Le Goff, Nantes Op Chor, I. Caley, A. Michael, M. Brodard, Colonne Orch Ch, Colonne Orch/P. Cao, A. Mitterhofer, C. Carlson, J. Van Dam, P. Huttenlocher, R. Corazza, Rhine Op Chor)

Ⓓ **4509-97239-2** (6/95)
Virtuoso Arias
Rossini: Barbiere di Siviglia (exc); *Bellini:* Sonnambula (exc); *Delibes:* Lakmé (exc); *Verdi:* Rigoletto (exc); *Meyerbeer:* Dinorah (exc); *Donizetti:* Lucia di Lammermoor (exc); *R. Strauss:* Ariadne auf Naxos (exc); *Bernstein:* Candide (1956) (exc); *Yoon:* Barley Field; *Mozart:* Zauberflöte (exc). (S. Jo, Monte Carlo PO/P. Olmi, Paris Orch Ens/A. Jordan)

Ⓓ **4509-98477-2** (6/95)
Purcell—Dido and Aeneas
Purcell: Dido (Cpte). (V. Gens, N. Berg, S. Marin-Degor, C. Brua, S. Daneman, G. Mechaly, J-P. Fouchécourt, Arts Florissants Voc Ens, Arts Florissants Instr Ens/W. Christie)

Ⓓ **4509-98481-2**
Violin Encores
Gershwin: Preludes; *Gluck:* Orfeo ed Euridice (exc); *Khachaturian:* Gayaneh (exc); *Kroll:* Banjo and Fiddle; *Massenet:* Thaïs (exc); *Paganini:* Sonatas, Op. 3 (exc); *Prokofiev:* Peter and the Wolf; *Rachmaninov:* Vocalise; *Schubert:* Ave Maria, D839; Erlkönig, D328; German Dance, D618; *Vieuxtemps:* Morceaux de salon, Op. 32 (exc); *Wieniawski:* Légende, Op. 17. (A. Markov, D. Cogan)

Ⓓ **4509-98497-2**
Recital—Janet Baker
Mozart: Vado, ma dove?, K583; Chi sà, K582; Ch'io mi scordi di te, K505; Exsultate jubilate, K165; Clemenza di Tito (exc); Nozze di Figaro (exc). (J. Baker, Scottish CO/R. Leppard)

Ⓓ **4509-98498-2**
Recital—Teresa Berganza
Haydn: Moglie quando è buona; Ah crudel! poiché lo brami; Che vive amante; Ein' Magd, ein' Dienerin; Miseri noi!; Sono Alcina; Il meglio mio carattere; Son pietosa, son bonina. (T. Berganza, Scottish CO/R. Leppard)

Ⓓ **4509-98499-2**
Recital—Montserrat Caballé
R. Strauss: Vier letzte Lieder; *Wagner:* Tannhäuser (exc); Tristan und Isolde (exc); *Gounod:* Faust (exc). (M. Caballé, Strasbourg PO/A. Lombard)

Ⓓ **4509-98501-2**
Recital—Marilyn Horne
Auber: Zerline (exc); *Saint-Saëns:* Samson et Dalila (exc); *Offenbach:* Grande-Duchesse de Gérolstein (exc); *Gounod:* Sapho (exc); *Godard:* Vivandière (exc); *Massenet:* Hérodiade (exc); *Donizetti:* Favorita (exc); *Cherubini:* Medea (exc). (M. Horne, Monte Carlo PO/L. Foster)

Ⓓ **4509-98502-2**
Recital-Françoise Pollet
Gounod: Reine de Saba (exc); Cinq mars (exc); *Rossini:* Guillaume Tell (exc); *Halévy:* Juive (exc); *Berlioz:* Troyens (exc); *Saint-Saëns:* Henry VIII (exc); *Reyer:* Sigurd (exc); *Massenet:* Cid (exc); *Verdi:* Don Carlos (exc); *Massenet:* Sapho (exc). (F. Pollet, Montpellier PO/C. Diederich)

Ⓓ **4509-98503-2**
Recital—Ruggero Raimondi
Bizet: Carmen (exc); *Berlioz:* Damnation de Faust (exc); *Mussorgsky:* Boris Godunov (exc); *Mozart:* Don Giovanni (exc); *Verdi:* Otello (exc); *Massenet:* Don Quichotte (exc); *Tosti:* Mia canzone; Ancora!; Non t'amo più. (R. Raimondi, Paris Op Orch/E. Tchakarov, Solisti Veneti/C. Scimone)

Ⓓ **4509-98504-2**
Recital—Frederica Von Stade
Monteverdi: Ohimè ch'io cado; Scherzi musicali (1632) (exc); Incoronazione di Poppea (exc); *Cavalli:* Didone (exc); Xerse (exc); Egisto (exc); Orimonte (exc); Scipione Affricano (exc); Calisto (exc); *Mozart:* Così fan tutte (exc). (F. Von Stade, Scottish CO/R. Leppard, Strasbourg PO/A. Lombard)

Ⓓ **4509-98507-2** (6/95)
Purcell—The Fairy Queen
Purcell: Fairy Queen, Z629. (C. Bott, Jeffrey Thomas, M. Schopper, Amsterdam Baroque Ch, Amsterdam Baroque Orch/T. Koopman)

Ⓓ **4509-98508-2** (10/95)
Debussy—Rodrigue et Chimène
Debussy: Rodrigue et Chimène (Cpte). (L. Dale, D. Brown, H. Jossoud, G. Ragon, J-P. Fouchécourt, J. van Dam, J. Bastin, V. le Texier, J-L. Meunier, J. Delescluse, Lyon Op Chor, Lyon Op Orch/K. Nagano)

Ⓓ **4509-98531-2**
Monteverdi—Orfeo
Monteverdi: Orfeo (Cpte). (E. Tappy, M. Schwartz, W. Staempfli, L. Sarti, Y. Perrin, M. Conrad, F. Loup, J. Bise, J. Staempfli, T. Altmeyer, V. Girod, P. Huttenlocher, O. Dufour, Lausanne Voc Ens, Lausanne Instr Ens/M. Corboz)

Ⓓ **4509-98532-2** (11/95)
Rameau—Naïs
Rameau: Naïs (Cpte). (L. Russell, I Caley, I. Caddy, J. Tomlinson, R. Jackson, B. Parsons, A. Ransome, A. Mackay, J. Smith, English Bach Fest Chor, English Bach Fest Orch/N. McGegan)

Ⓓ **4509-98535-2** (6/95)
Purcell—King Arthur
Purcell: King Arthur, Z628 (Cpte). (V. Gens, C. McFadden, S. Piau, S. Waters, M. Padmore, I. Paton, J. Best, P. Salomaa, F. Bazola-Minori, Arts Florissants Chor, Arts Florissants Orch/W. Christie)

Ⓓ **4509-98955-2**
Boulez conducts Stravinsky
Stravinsky: Pulcinella Suite (exc); Chant du Rossignol; Nightingale (Cpte); Russian Peasant Songs; Pieces (1914); Madrid; Etudes; Histoire du Soldat; Concertino. (A. Murray, A. Rolfe Johnson, S. Estes, Paris InterContemporain Ens, P. Fontanarosa, P. Gallois, B. Grenat, Y. Couëffe, FNO/P. Boulez, P. Bryn-Julson, I. Caley, F. Palmer, J. Tomlinson, N. Howlett, M. George, E. Laurence, BBC Sngrs, BBC SO, M. Cantin, J-N. Melleret, A. Gantiez, S. Duschesne, French Rad Chor, InterContemporain Qt, R. Lawson, R. Planchon, P. Chéreau, A. Vitez, L. Beauregard, D. Pateau, L. Hadady, A. Damiens, J-M. Lamothe, J. Wetherill, C. Vasse, J-J. Gaudon, B. Sluchin, J. Naulais, S. Gazeau, P. Strauch)

Ⓓ **4509-99607-2**
Gluck—Operas; Schubert—Symphonies Nos 8 & 9
Gluck: Iphigénie en Aulide (Cpte); Rencontre imprévue (Cpte); *Schubert:* Symphony 8; Symphony 9; *Gluck:* Don Juan (Cpte). (L. Dawson, J. Van Dam, A. S. von Otter, J. Aler, B. Delétré, G. Cachemaille, R. Schirrer, G. Laurens, A. Monoyios, I. Eschenbrenner, Monteverdi Ch, L. Dawson, C. Le Coz, C. Dubosc, S. Marin-Degor, G. de Mey, J-L. Viala, G. Flechter, J-P. Lafont, G. Cachemaille, F. Dudziak, EBS, Lyon Op Orch/J. E. Gardiner)

Ⓓ **4509-99713-2**
Baroque Works
Campra: Messe de Requiem; *Carissimi:* Jonas; Jephte; Judicium Extremum; *Monteverdi:* Tirsi e Clori; Orfeo (exc); De la bellezza; Ballo delle ingrate; Volgendo il ciel; *D. Scarlatti:* Stabat mater; *Cavalli:* Salve Regina; *Gesualdo:* Sacrarum cantionum (5vv) (exc); *Clemens non Papa:* O Maria vernans rosa; *Purcell:* Jehova quam multi sunt, Z135; *Locke:* How doth the city sit solitary; *Purcell:* My beloved spake, Z28; O God, Thou hast cast us out, Z36; *Blow:* Salvator Mundi; *Purcell:* Hear my prayer, O Lord, Z15; *Humfrey:* O Lord my God. (G. Fisher, E. Priday, J. Nelson, D. Harris, R. Holton, S. H. Jones, P. Kwella, A. Stafford, C. Brett, C. Robson, M. Davies, W. Evans, M. Hill, J-C. Orliac, M. Tucker, N. Robson, A. Rolfe Johnson, L. Dale, A. Woodrow, S. Varcoe, S. Roberts, J. Tomlinson, O. Grundy, R. Earle, D. Thomas, His Majesties Sagbutts and Cornetts, Monteverdi Ch, EBS/J. E. Gardiner)

Eri-Elysium Recordings

Ⓓ **GRK702**
Beethoven edited Mahler
Beethoven: Symphony 3; Coriolan; Leonore (exc). (B. Martinů PO/P. Tiboris)

Ermitage

Ⓓ **ERM151**
Katia Ricciarelli in Recital
Bellini: Capuleti (exc); *Donizetti:* Anna Bolena (exc); Lucrezia Borgia (exc); *Verdi:* Corsaro (exc); Forza del destino (exc); *Puccini:* Tosca (exc); Madama Butterfly (exc); *Catalani:* Wally (exc); *Cilea:* Adriana Lecouvreur (exc). (K. Ricciarelli, Svizzera Italiana Orch/B. Amaducci)

Etcetera

Ⓓ **KTC1007** ▭ **XTC1007** (8/83)
Carolyn Watkinson recital
Bizet: Chanson d'avril; Pêcheurs de Perles (exc); Adieux de l'hôtesse; *Brahms:* Lieder, Op. 7 (exc); Lieder, Op. 85 (exc); Lieder, Op. 107 (exc); Lieder, Op. 43 (exc); *Dvořák:* Songs, B124; *Berg:* Songs, Op. 2; *Ives:* Walking; Grantchester; Tom sails away; Cage; Side show; *Traditional:* Water of Tyne. (C. Watkinson, T. Crone)

Ⓓ **KTC1013**
Purcell: Songs
Purcell: Oedipus, Z583 (exc); King Arthur, Z628 (exc); Dioclesian, Z627 (exc); Indian Queen, Z630 (exc); Rule a Wife and Have a Wife, Z587 (exc); Rival Sisters, Z609 (exc); Fatal hour comes on apace, Z421; Love's power in my heart, Z395; More love or more disdain, Z397; Who can behold Florella's charms, Z441; Pausanias, Z585 (exc); Queen's Epicedium, Z383; Morning Hymn, Z198; Evening hymn, Z193; Sleep, Adam, sleep, Z195; Lord, what is man?, Z192. (A. Dalton, F. Borstlap, A. Uittenbosch)

Ⓓ **KTC1037** (2/87) ▭ **XTC1037**
Bernstein: Songs
Bernstein: I hate music; Bonne cuisine (exc); Two Love Songs; So pretty; Piccola Serenata; Silhouette; Mass (exc); Pennsylvania Avenue (exc); Candide (1982) (exc); Peter Pan (exc). (R. Alexander, T. Crone)

Ⓓ **KTC1041** (5/90)
Nelly Miricioiu—Recital
Duparc: Invitation au voyage; Soupir; Chanson triste; *Granados:* Tonadillas (exc); *Respighi:* Notturno; Pioggia; Ma come potrei; Ultima ebbrezza; Invito alla danza; *Proch:* Air and Variations; *Puccini:* Rondine (exc); Tosca (exc); *Catalani:* Wally (exc). (N. Miricioiu, D. Harper)

Ⓓ **KTC1064** (3/89)
Baroque Opera Arias
Purcell: Dido (exc); *Handel:* Serse (exc); Rodelinda (exc); Ariodante (exc); Rinaldo (exc); Hercules (exc); *Gluck:* Orfeo ed Euridice (exc). (C. Watkinson, Amsterdam Bach Sols/J.W. de Vriend)

Ⓓ **KTC1125**
Showpieces for Violin & Orchestra
Chausson: Poème; *Fauré:* Berceuse, Op. 16; *Wieniawski:* Faust Fantaisie; *Massenet:* Thaïs (exc); *Sarasate:* Carmen Fantasy. (P. Graffin, RPO/Y. Menuhin)

Ⓓ **KTC1145** (6/93)
Barber—Scenes and Arias
Barber: Andromache's Farewell, Op. 39; Antony and Cleopatra (exc); Songs, Op. 10 (exc); Songs, Op. 13 (exc); Vanessa (exc); Knoxville. (R. Alexander, Netherlands PO/E. de Waart)

Ⓓ **KTC2002** (10/86) ▭ **XTC2002**
Renata Scotto: Aria and song recital
A. Scarlatti: Cara e dolce; Bellezza, che s'ama; *Rossini:* Soirées musicales (exc); *Liszt:* Petrarch Sonnets, S270; *Verdi:* Preghiera del poeta; Brigidino; Pietà, Signor; Stornello; *Puccini:* Storiella d'amore; Edgar (exc); *Respighi:* Soupir; Au milieu du jardin; *Mascagni:* Zanetto (exc); Nerone (exc); M'ama, non m'ama; *Puccini:* Tosca (exc). (R. Scotto, I. Davis)

Ⓓ **KTC2014** (12/89)
Birtwistle—Punch and Judy
Birtwistle: Punch and Judy (Cpte). (S. Roberts, J. DeGaetani, P. Bryn-Julson, P. Langridge, D. Wilson-Johnson, J. Tomlinson, London Sinfonietta/D. Atherton)

Ⓓ **KTC2019**
200 years of Russian Music for Organ
Glinka: Fugues; *Odoyevsky:* Lullaby; *Taneyev:* Choral Variations; *Cui:* Organ Preludes; *L. Homilius:* Prelude in G; *Lyapunov:* Prelude pastorale; *N. Tcherepnin:* Cherubimic Hymn; *Nikolayev:* Fugue in E flat minor; *Glière:* Christmas Song Fugue; *Glazunov:* Fantasy, Op. 110; Prelude and Fugue, Op. 98; Prelude and Fugue, Op. 93; *Shostakovich:* Lady Macbeth of Mtsensk (exc); *Gedike:* Preludes and Fugues, Op. 34 (exc); *Nirenburg:* English Fantasia; Russian Fantasia; *Gubaidulina:* Light and Dark; *Schnittke:* Organ Pieces (1981). (A. Fiseisky)

▭ **XTC1041**
Nelly Miricioiu at Wigmore Hall
Mozart: Vado ma dove?, K583; *Duparc:* Invitation au voyage; Soupir; Chanson triste; *Granados:* Tonadillas (exc); *Respighi:* Notturno; Pioggia; Ma come potrei; Ultima ebbrezza; Invito alla danza; *Proch:* Air and Variations; *Puccini:* Rondine (exc); Tosca (exc); *Catalani:* Wally (exc). (N. Miricioiu, D. Harper)

Eurodisc

Ⓓ **GD69003**
Wagner—Der Ring des Nibelungen
Wagner: Rheingold (Cpte); Walküre (Cpte); Siegfried (Cpte); Götterdämmerung (Cpte). (T. Adam, Y. Minton, P. Schreier, C. Vogel, S. Nimsgern, M. Napier, E. Büchner, K-H. Stryczek, O. Wenkel, R. Bracht, M. Salminen, L. Popp, U. Priew, H. Schwarz, S. Jerusalem, J. Norman, J. Altmeyer, K. Moll, E-M. Bundschuh, R. Falcon, C. Studer, O. Wenkel, U. Priew, C. Borchers, K. Kuhlmann, A. Gjevang, R. Kollo, T. Adam, N. Sharp, M. Salminen, H.G. Nöcker, N. Sharp, A. Gjevang, D. Evangelatos, R. Falcon, Leipzig Rad Chor, Dresden St Op Chor, Staatskapelle Dresden/M. Janowski, P. Schreier)

Ⓓ **GD69005** (10/84)
Wagner—Die Walküre
Wagner: Walküre (Cpte). (S. Jerusalem, J. Norman, J. Altmeyer, T. Adam, Y. Minton, K. Moll, E-M. Bundschuh, R. Falcon, C. Studer, O. Wenkel, U. Priew, C. Borchers, K. Kuhlmann, A. Gjevang, Staatskapelle Dresden/M. Janowski)

Ⓓ **GD69006** (10/84)
Wagner—Siegfried
Wagner: Siegfried (Cpte). (R. Kollo, T. Adam, J. Altmeyer, P. Schreier, S. Nimsgern, O. Wenkel, M. Salminen, N. Sharp, Staatskapelle Dresden/M. Janowski)

Ⓓ **GD69007** (10/84)
Wagner—Götterdämmerung
Wagner: Götterdämmerung (Cpte). (J. Altmeyer, R. Kollo, M. Salminen, S. Nimsgern, H.G. Nöcker, N. Sharp, O. Wenkel, L. Popp, U. Priew, H. Schwarz, A. Gjevang, D. Evangelatos, R. Falcon, Leipzig Rad Chor, Dresden St Op Chor, Staatskapelle Dresden/M. Janowski)

Ⓓ **GD69008** (4/90)
Wagner—Die Meistersinger
Wagner: Meistersinger (Cpte). (O. Wiener, Jess Thomas, C. Watson, H. Hotter, B. Kusche, F. Lenz, L. Benningsen, J. Metternich, D. Thaw, C. Hoppe, W. Carnuth, F. Klarwein, K. Ostertag, A. Keil, G. Wieter, M. Proebstl, H.B. Ernst, Bavarian St Op Chor, Bavarian St Op Orch/J. Keilberth)

Ⓓ **GD69018** ▭ **GK69018**
Fritz Wunderlich—Recital
Handel: Serse (exc); *Mozart:* Zauberflöte (exc); *T. Giordani:* Caro mio ben; *Lortzing:* Undine (exc); *Liszt:* Es muss ein Wunderbares sein, S314; *Tchaikovsky:* Songs, Op. 6 (exc); *J. Strauss II:* Zigeunerbaron (exc); Nacht in Venedig (exc); Nacht in Venedig (exc); *Zeller:* Vogelhändler (exc); *Lehár:* Zarewitsch (exc); Schön ist die Welt (exc); Giuditta (exc); Friederike (exc); *Kálmán:* Zirkusprinzessin (exc); *Clewing:* Singende Traum (exc); *Roland:* Ferien vom Ich (exc); *de Curtis:* Vergiss mein nicht; *di Capua:* O sole mio; *Lara:* Granada. (F. Wunderlich, R. Lamy Sngrs, Berlin RIAS Chor, Berlin SO, Hamburg St Op Orch, Munich RO, Berlin FFB Orch/G. Becker/A. Rother/W. Schmidt-Boelcke/A. Melichar)

Ⓓ **GD69019**
Hermann Prey—Recital
Gounod: Faust (exc); *Offenbach:* Contes d'Hoffmann (exc); *Lortzing:* Beiden Schützen (exc); Zar und Zimmermann (exc); Hans Sachs (exc); *Wagner:* Meistersinger (exc); *Kreutzer:* Nachtlager in Granada (exc); *Nessler:* Trompeter von Säckingen (exc); *J. Martini:* Plaisir d'amour; *Toselli:* Serenade; *Jarre:* Doctor Zhivago (exc); *Lennon & McCartney:* Yesterday; *C. François:* My way. (H. Prey, Berlin SO, Berlin Deutsche Op Orch, Munich Bavaria Orch, orch/H-M. Rabenstein/H. Hollreiser/W. Schmidt-Boelcke)

Ⓓ **GD69021** (2/91)
Lehár: Operetta Highlights
Lehár: Schön ist die Welt (exc); Friederike (exc). (R. Schock, S. Geszty, M. Schramm, Berlin SO/W. Schmidt-Boelcke)

Ⓓ **GD69022** (2/91)
Oscar Straus: Operetta excerpts
O. Straus: Walzertraum (exc); Musik kommt; Ronde (exc); Rund um die Liebe (exc); Tapfere Soldat (exc); Letzte Walzer (exc). (R. Schock, W. Lipp, L. Schmidt, F. Gruber, M. Schramm, B. Kusche, Günther Arndt Ch, Berlin SO/R. Stolz)

Ⓓ **GD69023** (2/91)
Fall & Millöcker: Operetta highlights
Fall: Rose von Stambul (exc); *Millöcker:* Dubarry (exc). (E. Köth, R. Schock, H. Wilhelm, Günther Arndt Ch, Berlin SO/F. Fox)

Ⓓ **GD69024** (2/91)
Abraham—Operetta excerpts
Abraham: Viktoria und ihr Husar (exc); Blume von Hawaii (exc). (R. Schock, M. Schramm, L. Ebnet, F. Gruber, Günther Arndt Ch, Berlin SO/W. Schmidt-Boelcke)

Ⓓ **GD69025** (2/91)
Künnecke—Der Vetter aus Dingsda (highlights)
Künneke: Vetter aus Dingsda (exc). (R. Holm, U. Schirrmacher, E. Krukowski, B. Mira, K-E. Mercker, R. Schock, C. Nicolai, Berlin SO/W. Schmidt-Boelcke)

Ⓓ **GD69026** (2/91)
Zeller: Der Vogelhändler highlights
Zeller: Vogelhändler (exc). (E. Köth, R. Holm, R. Schock, K-E. Mercker, K. Herford, R. Glawitsch, E. Pauly, Günther Arndt Ch, Berlin SO/F. Fox)

Ⓓ **GD69027** (2/91)
Jessel: Schwarzwaldmädel highlights
Jessel: Schwarzwaldmädel (exc). (M. Schramm, A. Herrfurth, L. Schädle, U. Schirrmacher, R. Schock, K-E. Mercker, F. Ollendorff, W. Reichert, Berlin RIAS Chbr Ch, Berlin SO/W. Schmidt-Boelcke)

Ⓓ **GD69028** (2/91)
Benatzky: Im weissen Rössl (highlights)
Benatzky: Im weissen Rössl (exc). (E. Köth, I. Hallstein, R. Schock, P. Alexander, W. Hufnagel, chor, SO/J. Fehring)

Ⓓ **GD69029** (2/91)
Fred Raymond: Maske in Blau highlights
Raymond: Maske in Blau (exc). (M. Schramm, M. Rökk, R. Schock, K-E. Mercker, Berlin Deutsche Op Chor, Berlin SO/W. Schmidt-Boelcke)

Ⓓ **GD69043** (4/90)
Puccini: Il Trittico
Puccini: Tabarro (Cpte); Suor Angelica (Cpte); Gianni Schicchi (Cpte). (S. Nimsgern, I. Tokody, G. Lamberti, T. Pane, G. Auer, W. Baniewicz, L. Popp, M. Lipovšek, M. Schiml, D. Jennings, B. Calm, M.G. Ferroni, M. Georg, V. Errante, E. van Lier, K. Hautermann, M. Schmitt, A. Schiller, R. Panerai, H. Donath, P. Seiffert, W. Baniewicz, T. Pane, V. Errante, C. Kunz, G. Auer, F. Federici, R. Riener, M. Georg, Bavarian Rad Chor, Munich RO/G. Patanè)

Ⓓ **GD69069** (3/91)
Orff—Die Kluge; Der Mond
Orff: Kluge (Cpte); Mond (Cpte). (T. Stewart, G. Frick, L. Popp, R. Kogel, M. Schmidt, C. Nicolai, F. Gruber, H. Friedrich, K. Böhme, J. van Kesteren, H. Friedrich, R. Kogel, F. Gruber, B. Kusche, R. Grumbach, F. Crass, H. Buchta, R. Kiermeyer Children's Ch, Bavarian Rad Chor, Munich RO/K. Eichhorn)

Ⓓ **GD69113**
Anna Moffo Recital
Donizetti: Linda di Chamounix (exc); *Gounod:* Roméo et Juliette (exc); *Verdi:* Lombardi (exc); Traviata (exc); *Leoncavallo:* Pagliacci (exc); *G. Charpentier:* Louise (exc); *Puccini:* Tosca (exc); Suor Angelica (exc); Madama Butterfly (exc); *Lehár:* Zarewitsch (exc); Lustige Witwe (exc); *J. Strauss II:* Fledermaus (exc); *Stolz:* Favorit (exc); *N. Brown:* Kissing Bandit (exc). (A. Moffo, Munich RO/K. Eichhorn, H. Galatis Orch/H. Galatis, Berlin SO/W. Eisbrenner)

Ⓓ **GD69294**
Humperdinck—Hansel & Gretel
Humperdinck: Hänsel und Gretel (Cpte). (A. Moffo, H. Donath, D. Fischer-Dieskau, C. Berthold, A. Auger, L. Popp, C. Ludwig, Tolz Boys' Ch, Munich RSO/K. Eichhorn)

Ⓓ **GD69295**
Salon Music
Offenbach: Orphée aux enfers (exc); *Liszt:* Liebesträume, S541 (exc); *Brahms:* Hungarian Dances (exc); *Wagner:* Albumblatt; *F. Ries:* Capricciosa; *Puccini:* Bohème (exc); *Saint-Saëns:* Carnaval des animaux (exc); *Waldteufel:* Estudiantina; *Massenet:* Thaïs (exc). (Cölln Salon Orch)

Ⓓ **GD69296**
Paris Salon Music
A. Thomas: Mignon (exc); *Delibes:* Sylvia (exc); *Wieniawski:* Légende, Op. 17; *Offenbach:* Contes d'Hoffmann (exc); *Liszt:* Grand galop chromatique, S219; *Gounod:* Faust (exc); *Delibes:* Source (exc); *Ganne:* Extase; *Gillet:* Babillage; *Ganne:* Marche Lorraine. (Cölln Salon Orch)

Ⓒ **GD69297**
Vienna Salon Music
Suppé: Morgen, ein Mittag, ein Abend in Wien (exc); *Kreisler:* Schön Rosmarin; *J. Strauss II:* Im Krapfenwald'l, Op. 336; *E. Strauss:* Bahn frei; *J. Strauss II:* Mephistos Höllenrufe, Op. 101; Champagner Galopp; *Lehár:* Gold und Silber; *Kreisler:* Syncopation; *Lanner:* Werber, Op. 103; *J. Strauss II:* Auf der Jagd, Op. 373; Pizzicato Polka; *Schrammel:* Wien bleibt Wien. (Cölln Salon Orch)

Ⓒ **GD69298**
Music from Opera and Operetta
Mascagni: Cavalleria rusticana (exc); *Puccini:* Turandot (exc); *Pasculli:* Gran concerto; *Mozart:* Nozze di Figaro (exc); *Korngold:* Tote Stadt (exc); *Lehár:* Giuditta (exc); *Pasculli:* Oboe concerto; *Bock:* Fiddler on the Roof (exc). (T. Indermühle, Salonisti)

Ⓒ **GD69299**
Serenata
Toselli: Serenade; *Sibelius:* Suite mignonne; Valse triste; *Ravel:* Heure espagnole (exc); *Enescu:* Romanian Rhapsodies, Op. 11 (exc); *Debussy:* Préludes (exc); Plus que lente; *Yoshitomo:* East Asian Suite; *Godard:* Impressions de campagne (exc). (Salonisti)

Ⓒ **GD69322**
Bizet—Orchestral Works
Bizet: Symphony; Carmen Suites. (Bamberg SO/G. Prêtre)

Ⓒ **RD69037**
Suppé—Overtures
Suppé: Leichte Kavallerie (exc); Pique Dame (exc); Morgen, ein Mittag, ein Abend in Wien (exc); Banditenstreiche (exc); Schöne Galathee (exc); Dichter und Bauer (exc). (RPO/G. Kuhn)

Ⓒ **RD69073** (9/90)
Catalani—La Wally
Catalani: Wally (Cpte). (E. Marton, F.E. d'Artegna, A. Titus, F. Araiza, J. Kaufman, B. Calm, M. Pertusi, Bavarian Rad Chor, Munich RO/P. Steinberg)

Ⓒ **VD69256**
Mozart—Opera Arias
Mozart: Zauberflöte (exc); Zauberflöte (exc); Zauberflöte (exc); Zauberflöte (exc); Don Giovanni (exc); Don Giovanni; Don Giovanni (exc); Don Giovanni (exc); Entführung (exc); Entführung (exc); Così fan tutte (exc); Così fan tutte (exc); Nozze di Figaro (exc); Idomeneo (exc). (F. Wunderlich, M. Talvela, I. Cotrubas, E. Köth, A. Titus, L. Price, P. de Palma, P. Domingo, J. Varady, F. Araiza, E. Gruberová, P. Schreier, S. Milnes, L. Popp, orch)

Ⓒ **258 357**
Lehár—Zarewitsch excerpts
Lehár: Zarewitsch (exc). (R. Schock, P. von Felinau, R. Holm, K-E. Mercker, H. Wisniewska, K. Lang, Berlin Deutsche Op Chor, Berlin SO/R. Stolz)

Ⓒ **258 369**
J. Strauss II—Die Fledermauss excerpts
J. Strauss II: Fledermaus (exc). (R. Schock, W. Lipp, W. Berry, E. Steiner, C. Curzi, C. Nicolai, R. Holm, I. Dressel, Vienna St Op Chor, Vienna SO/R. Stolz)

Ⓒ **258 370** (4/88)
J. Strauss II—Wiener Blut Highlights
J. Strauss II: Wiener Blut (exc). (B. Kusche, R. Schock, H. Gueden, F. Liewehr, M. Schramm, E. Kunz, W. Lipp, F. Gruber, Vienna St Op Chor, Vienna SO/R. Stolz)

Ⓒ **258 373** (4/88)
Lehár—Das Land des Lächelns excerpts
Lehár: Land des Lächelns (exc). (M. Schramm, F. Gruber, R. Schock, L. Schmidt, Günther Arndt Ch, Berlin SO/R. Stolz)

Ⓒ **258 376**
Suppé—Boccacio & Schöne Galathee excerpts
Suppé: Boccaccio (exc); Schöne Galathee (exc). (R. Holm, U. Schirrmacher, A. Oelke, R. Glawitsch, R. Schock, E. Marlo, P. Manuel, E. Krukowski, Günther Arndt Ch, Berlin SO/F. Fox, A. Moffo, R. Kollo, R. Wagemann, F. Gruber, Bavarian Rad Chor, Munich RO/K. Eichhorn)

Ⓒ **258 665**
Music of Vienna, Vol.10
Jos. Strauss: Frohsinn; Feuerfest!; Aus der Ferne; *J. Strauss II:* Pizzicato Polka; *Jos. Strauss:* Frauenwürde; Jokey; Heiterer Muth; *E. Strauss:* Bahn frei; *Labitzky:* Schönbrunner; *Gungl:* Träume auf dem Ozean; *Fahrbach I:* Im Kahlenbergerdörfel; *Suppé:* Fatinitza (exc); *Kéler:* Am schönen Rhein; *Komzák II:* Barataria; Volksliedchen und Märchen; Erzherzog Albrecht-Marsch; Bäd'ner Mad'ln; *Rosas:* Sobre las olas. (Berlin SO, Vienna SO/R. Stolz)

Ⓒ **258 667**
Music of Vienna, Vol.12
Ziehrer: Herreinspaziert!, Op. 518; Fächer, Op.525; *Heuberger:* Opernball (exc); *O. Straus:* Walzertraum (exc); *Lehár:* Gold und Silber; *Fučík:* Entry of the Gladiators; *Fall:* Rose von Stambul (exc); *Translateur:* Wiener Praterleben; *Komzák III:* Münchner Kindl, Op.286; *Kálmán:* Dorfkinder; *Stolz:* Wiener Café. (Berlin SO, Vienna SO/R. Stolz)

Ⓒ **352 878** (2/89)
Flotow—Martha
Flotow: Martha (Cpte). (L. Popp, D. Soffel, S. Jerusalem, K. Ridderbusch, S. Nimsgern, P. Lika, Bavarian Rad Chor, Munich RO/H. Wallberg)

Ⓒ **352 884**
Donizetti—Don Pasquale
Donizetti: Don Pasquale (Cpte). (E. Nesterenko, L. Popp, F. Araiza, B. Weikl, P. Lika, Bavarian Rad Chor, Munich RSO/H. Wallberg)

Ⓒ **352 887**
Smetana—The Bartered Bride
Smetana: Bartered Bride (Cpte). (T. Stratas, R. Kollo, H. Zednik, W. Berry, J.W. Wilsing, G. Wewezow, A. Malta, M. Bence, J. Perry, K. Dönch, T. Nicolai, Bavarian Rad Chor, Munich RSO/J. Krombholc)

Ⓒ **353 266**
Debussy—Pelléas et Mélisande
Debussy: Pelléas et Mélisande (Cpte). (C. Dormoy, M. Command, G. Bacquier, R. Soyer, J. Taillon, M. Pouradier-Duteil, X. Tamalet, Bourgogne Chor, Lyon Op Orch/S. Baudo)

Europa Musica

Ⓒ **GD69004** (10/84)
Wagner—Rheingold
Wagner: Rheingold (Cpte). (T. Adam, Y. Minton, P. Schreier, C. Vogel, S. Nimsgern, M. Napier, E. Büchner, K-H. Stryczek, O. Wenkel, R. Bracht, M. Salminen, L. Popp, U. Priew, H. Schwarz, Staatskapelle Dresden/M. Janowski)

Ⓒ **350211** (12/91)
Rossini—Armida
Rossini: Armida (Cpte). (C. Gasdia, W. Matteuzzi, B. Ford, C. Merritt, C.H. Workman, F. Furlanetto, Ambrosian Op Chor, Solisti Veneti/C. Scimone)

Ⓒ **350213**
Schubert—Overtures
Schubert: Overture, D590; Overture, D591; Overture, D4; Freunde von Salamanka (exc); Overture, D470; Zwillingsbrüder (exc); Alfonso und Estrella (exc); Fierrabras (exc). (Tuscany Rad & TV Orch/D. Renzetti)

Ⓒ **350214**
Verdi—Sinfonie & Cori
Verdi: Vespri siciliani (exc); Trovatore (exc); Nabucco (exc); Forza del destino (exc); Lombardi (exc); Macbeth (exc); Ernani (exc); Aida (exc). (Forum Op Chor, Forum PO/G. Bellini)

Ⓒ **350221**
Cherubini—Orchestral Works
Cherubini: Symphony in D; Medea (exc); Ifigenia in Aulide (exc); Crescendo (exc). (Tuscany Rad & TV Orch/D. Renzetti)

Ⓒ **350262**
Pergolesi—Sinfonie
Pergolesi: Olimpiade (exc); Frate 'nnamorato (exc); Salustia (exc); Piccola sinfonia; Flaminio (exc); Simphonia in F; Adriano in Siria (exc); Simphonia in B flat; Prigionier superbo (exc). (Santa Cecilia Orch da Camera/A. Vlad)

The Everest Collection

Ⓒ **EVC9004** (4/95)
R. Strauss/Canning—Orchestral Works
R. Strauss: Don Juan; Till Eulenspiegel; Salome (exc); *Canning:* Hymn Tune Fantasy. (NY Stadium SO, Houston SO/L. Stokowski)

Eye of the Storm

Ⓒ **EOS5001** (6/95)
Wagner—Overtures and Preludes
Wagner: Rienzi (exc); Tannhäuser (exc); Lohengrin (exc); Tristan und Isolde (exc); Meistersinger (exc); Parsifal (exc). (NQHO/B. Wordsworth)

Fidelio Classics

Ⓒ **9201** (9/93)
Wagner—The Ring - An orchestral adventure
Wagner: Götterdämmerung (exc); Rheingold (exc); Siegfried (exc); Walküre (exc). (Netherlands Rad PO/E. de Waart)

Finlandia

Ⓒ **4509-95583-2**
Virtuoso Trumpet
Khachaturian: Gayaneh (exc); *Brahms:* Waltzes, Op. 39 (exc); *Gounod:* Roméo et Juliette (exc); *Ropartz:* Andante and Allegro; *Bozza:* Lied; *J. Strauss II:* Frühlingsstimmen, Op. 410; *Rachmaninov:* Songs, Op. 34 (exc); *Méndez:* Scherzo; *Tchaikovsky:* Morceaux, Op. 51 (exc); Album for the young (exc); *Mozart:* Zauberflöte (exc); *Shchedrin:* Imitating Albéniz; *Rossini:* Barbiere di Siviglia (exc); *A. Lloyd Webber:* Castle Hedingham; *Rougnon:* Solo; *Balakirev:* Songs (1858-64) (exc). (J. Harjanne, J. Harjanne, J. Lagerspetz)

Ⓒ **4509-95605-2**
Contrabasso con amroe
J.C. Bach: Unidentified Concerto; *Abel:* Sonata in C; *Bruch:* Kol Nidrei; *Granados:* Goyescas (exc); *Albéniz:* España, Op. 165 (exc); *Cassadó:* Requiebros; *Bottesini:* Tarantella; *Sperger:* Double Bass Sonata; *Tabakov:* Motives. (J. Katrama, M. Rahkonen)

Ⓒ **4509-95606-2** (12/94)
Kim Borg - Songs and Arias
Mozart: Zauberflöte (exc); *Rossini:* Barbiere di Siviglia (exc); *Verdi:* Don Carlo (exc); *Borodin:* Prince Igor (exc); *Tchaikovsky:* Eugene Onegin (exc); *Mussorgsky:* Khovanshchina (exc); Boris Godunov (exc); *Sibelius:* Songs, Op. 13 (exc); Songs, Op. 17 (exc); Songs, Op. 36 (exc); Songs, Op. 61 (exc); Row, row, duck; Finlandia; *Kilpinen:* Reflections, Opp. 33-4 (exc); *Mussorgsky:* Songs and Dances of Death; Where art thou, little star; Garden by the Don; Song of the Flea; *Schubert:* König in Thule, D367; Prometheus, D674; Erlkönig, D328; Wer sich der Einsamkeit ergibt, D478; Wer nie sein Brot mit Tränen ass, D480; An die Türen, D479; *Schumann:* Romanzen und Balladen, Op. 49 (exc); *Brahms:* Ernste Gesänge, Op. 121; *Wolf:* Mörike Lieder (exc); Michelangelo Gedichte (Cpte); *Loewe:* Balladen, Op. 20 (exc); Kleiner Haushalt, Op. 71. (K. Borg, E. Werba, M. Raucheisen, Munich PO, Bamberg SO, Berlin RSO/A. Rother/H. Stein)

Ⓒ **4509-96867-2** (4/95)
Madetoja—Orchestral Works
Madetoja: Ostrobothnians Suite; Symphony 3; Okon Fuoko Suite 1. (Finnish RSO/J-P. Saraste)

Ⓒ **4509-97894-2**
Contrabasso con Sentimento
Massenet: Thaïs (exc); *Kreisler:* Liebesfreud; Liebesleid; Schön Rosmarin; *Rachmaninov:* Songs, Op. 34 (exc); *Falla:* Canciones populares españolas; *Albinoni:* Adagio; *Tchaikovsky:* Nocturne, op. 19/4; *Ravel:* Pièce en forme de habanera; *Bottesini:* Romanza drammatica; Bellini Fantasia. (J. Katrama, M. Rahkonen)

FNAC Music

Ⓒ **592196** (10/93)
Rameau—Pygmalion
Rameau: Pygmalion (Cpte); Temple de la gloire (exc). (J-P. Fouchécourt, G. de Reyghere, N. Fournié, S. Piau, Concert Spirituel Orch/H. Niquet)

Ⓒ **592245** (6/94)
Handel—Scipione
Handel: Scipione (Cpte). (D. L. Ragin, S. Piau, D. Lamprecht, O. Lallouette, V. Tabery, G. Flechter, Talens Lyriques/C. Rousset)

Ⓒ **592326** (4/95)
Jommelli—Armida abbandonata
Jommelli: Armida abbandonata (Cpte). (E. Malas-Godlewska, C. Brua, G. Ragon, V. Gens, L. Polverelli, P. Petibon, C. Perrin, Talens Lyriques/C. Rousset)

Fonè

Ⓒ **88F17-37**
Mascagni—Il piccolo Marat
Mascagni: Piccolo Marat (Cpte). (U. Borsò, N. Rossi-Lemeni, V. Zeani, C. Betner, R. Rota, A. Poli, M. Frosini, R. Spagli, A. Frati, E. Vessari, C.M. Sperti, Livorno Teatro La Gran Guardia Chor, Livorno Teatro La Gran Guardia Orch/O. de Fabritiis)

Ⓒ **93F10**
Mascagni—L'amico Fritz
Mascagni: Amico Fritz (Cpte). (S. Pacetti, P. Ballo, P. Romanò, A. Ariostini, C. Bosi, F. Militano, A. Rossi, Cooperativa Artisti Associati Chor, Tuscan Accademia Strumentale Orch/A. Pinzauti)

① **93F13**
Mascagni—I Rantzau
Mascagni: Rantzau (Cpte). (B. Anderson, G. Boldrini, D. Colaianni, O. Garaventa, C. Bosi, R. Lantieri, F. Bertoli, Livorno Cel-Teatro Chor, Livorno Cel-Teatro Orch/B. Rigacci)

① **94F04**
Homage to Fritz Kreisler, Volume 1
Kreisler: Pugnani Praeludium and Allegro; Porpora Menuet; Leclair Tambourin; Beethoven Rondino; Boccherini Allegretto; Gitana; Liebesfreud; Tambourin chinois; Cavatina; Schön Rosmarin; Liebesleid; *Gluck:* Orfeo ed Euridice (exc); *Rimsky-Korsakov:* Sadko (exc); *Chopin:* Mazurkas (exc); *Schubert:* Impromptus (exc); *Dvořák:* Gipsy Melodies (exc); *Brahms:* Hungarian Dances (exc); *Rimsky-Korsakov:* Golden Cockerel (exc); *Albéniz:* España, Op. 165 (exc). (S. Accardo, L. Manzini)

Fonitcetra

① **CDAR2022**
Verdi—I due Foscari
Verdi: Due Foscari (Cpte). (G. Guelfi, C. Bergonzi, M. Vitale, P. Lombardo, M. Bersieri, L. Pellegrino, A. Bertocci, G. Barbieri, Milan RAI Chor, Milan RAI SO/C.M. Giulini)

① **CDAR2023**
Mascagni—Iris
Mascagni: Iris (Cpte). (M. Olivero, S. Puma, S. Meletti, G. Neri, A. Oliva, S. De Tommaso, Mario Carlin, Turin RAI Chor, Turin RAI Orch/A. Questa)

① **CDAR2025**
Massenet—Don Quichotte
Massenet: Don Quichotte (Cpte). (B. Christoff, C. Badioli, T. Berganza, O. Rovero, P. Malgarini, A. Nobile, T. Frascati, C. Bagno, Milan RAI Chor, Milan RAI SO/A. Simonetto)

① **CDC64** (4/95)
Rossini—Adelaide di Borgogna
Rossini: Adelaide di Borgogna (Cpte). (M. Devia, M. Dupuy, A. Caforio, A. Bertolo, E. Tandura, M. Farruggia, G. Fallisi, New Cambridge Chor, M. Franca Fest Orch/A. Zedda)

① **CDC81**
Donizetti—L'Ajo nell'imbarazzo
Donizetti: Ajo nell'imbarazzo (Cpte). (A. Corbelli, P. Barbacini, L. Serra, V. Gobbi, E. Dara, A. Haengel, D. Menicucci, Turin Teatro Regio Orch/B. Campanella)

① **CDMR5003**
Martini & Rossi Festival, Volume 3
Rossini: Guillaume Tell (exc); *Mascagni:* Iris (exc); *Rossini:* Barbiere di Siviglia (exc); *Giordano:* Andrea Chénier (exc); *Bellini:* Sonnambula (exc); *Verdi:* Forza del destino (exc); *Puccini:* Madama Butterfly (exc); *Bellini:* Puritani (exc); *Wagner:* Tannhäuser (exc). (M. Carosio, G. di Stefano, Turin RAI Orch/O. de Fabritiis)

① **CDMR5014**
Martini & Rossi Festival, Volume 14
Bizet: Pêcheurs de perles (exc); Carmen (exc); *Gounod:* Faust (exc); *Cilea:* Adriana Lecouvreur (exc); *Spontini:* Agnes von Hohenstaufen (exc); *Verdi:* Ernani (exc); Aida (exc); Forza del destino (exc). (R. Carteri, A. Cerquetti, F. Corelli, Milan RAI SO/O. de Fabritiis/A. Basile)

① **CDMR5023**
Martini & Rossi Festival, Volume 23
A. Thomas: Mignon (exc); *Puccini:* Gianni Schicchi (exc); *Massenet:* Werther (exc); Manon (exc); *Puccini:* Tosca (exc); Manon Lescaut (exc); *Meyerbeer:* Africaine (exc); *Verdi:* Aida (exc); *Rossini:* Guillaume Tell (exc). (R. Tebaldi, G. Prandelli, Rome RAI Orch/A. Basile, Milan RAI SO/N. Sanzogno)

① **CDO104**
Maria Callas
Bellini: Norma (exc); Puritani (exc); *Mozart:* Entführung; *Ponchielli:* Gioconda (exc); *Spontini:* Vestale (exc); *Verdi:* Traviata (exc); *Wagner:* Tristan und Isolde (exc). (M. Callas, Turin RAI Orch, San Remo RAI Orch, Milan RAI SO/A. Basile/A. Simonetto/G. Santini/A. Votto)

① **CDO28**
Puccini—Turandot
Puccini: Turandot (Cpte). (G. Cigna, F. Merli, M. Olivero, A. Poli, G. del Signore, A. Zagonara, L. Neroni, A. Giannotti, G. Bravura, Turin EIAR Chor, Turin EIAR Orch/F. Ghione)

① **CDO29**
Verdi—Aida
Verdi: Aida (Cpte). (M. Curtis Verna, M. Pirazzini, F. Corelli, G. Guelfi, G. Neri, A. Zerbini, A. Cesarini, Turin Rad Chor, Turin RSO/A. Questa)

① **CDO9** (2/95)
Verdi—La Traviata
Verdi: Traviata (Cpte). (M. Callas, F. Albanese, U. Savarese, E.M. Gandolfo, I. Marietti, M. Caruso, A. Albertini, M. Zorgniotti, T. Soley, Chor, Turin RAI Orch/G. Santini)

① **RFCD2002**
Rossini—Il Signor Bruschino
Rossini: Signor Bruschino (Cpte). (E. Dara, A. Rinaldi, M. Devia, D. Gonzalez, A. Antoniozzi, N. Curiel, E. Favano, M. Farruggia, Turin RAI Orch/D. Renzetti)

① **RFCD2003**
Rossini—La scala di seta
Rossini: Scala di seta (Cpte). (R. Coviello, L. Serra, W. Matteuzzi, N. de Carolis, C. Bartoli, O. di Credico, Bologna Teatro Comunale Orch/G. Ferro)

① **RFCD2005**
Donizetti—Elisabetta,al castello di Kenilworth
Donizetti: Elisabetta (Cpte). (M. Devia, J. Kundlák, D. Mazzola, B. Anderson, C. Striuli, C. Foti, Milan RAI Chor, Milan RAI SO/J. Latham-König)

① **RFCD2008** (9/94)
Rossini—Bianca e Falliero
Rossini: Bianca e Falliero (Cpte). (K. Ricciarelli, M. Horne, C. Merritt, G. Surian, P. Orciani, A. Riva, E. Gavazzi, D. D'Auria, Prague Phil Chor, London Sinf Op Orch/D. Renzetti)

① **RFCD2014**
Wolf-Ferrari—Il Campiello
Wolf-Ferrari: Campiello (Cpte). (D. Mazzucato, U. Benelli, G. Devinu, M-R. Cosotti, M. Bolgan, C. de Mola, M. Comencini, I. d'Arcangelo, M. Biscotti, C. Striuli, G. Principini, Trieste Teatro Verdi Chor, Trieste Teatro Verdi Orch/N. Bareza)

① **RFCD2015**
Donizetti—La Favorite
Donizetti: Favorita (Cpte). (G. Scalchi, L. Canonici, R. Massis, G. Surian, M. Laurenza, E. Gavazzi, Milan RAI Chor, Milan RAI SO/D. Renzetti)

① **RFCD2018**
Rossini—Semiramide
Rossini: Semiramide (Cpte). (I. Tamar, G. Scalchi, M. Pertusi, G. Kunde, M. Valenti, I. d'Arcangelo, S. Zadvorny, L. Petroni, Prague Phil Chor, Bologna Teatro Comunale Orch/A. Zedda)

Forlane

① **FF009** (11/94)
Weber—Clarinet Concertos Nos 1 and 2; Oberon Overture
Weber: Clarinet Concerto 1; Clarinet Concerto 2; Oberon (exc). (S. Dangain, Luxembourg Rad & TV SO/L. de Froment)

① **FF020**
Wagner/Liszt—Orchestral Works
Wagner: Siegfried Idyll; Tannhäuser (exc); Meistersinger (exc); Walküre (exc); *Liszt:* Préludes. (Luxembourg RSO/L. de Froment)

① **FF027**
Italian Dances and Overtures
Bizet: Carmen Suites (exc); *Berlioz:* Carnaval romain; *Auber:* Muette de Portici (exc); *Rossini:* Guillaume Tell (exc); Barbiere di Siviglia (exc); *Boccherini:* String Quintets, G271-6 (exc). (Luxembourg Rad & TV SO/L. de Froment/P. Cao, French Inst Ens)

① **FF028**
Musiques de Ballet
Borodin: In the Steppes of Central Asia; *Tchaikovsky:* Nutcracker Suite; Romeo and Juliet (exc); *Bizet:* Carmen Suites (exc); Arlésienne (exc); *Delibes:* Sylvia (exc); *Berlioz:* Damnation de Faust (exc); *Gounod:* Faust (exc). (Luxembourg Rad & TV SO/L. de Froment)

① **FF029**
The Most Beautiful Promenade Concert
Mozart: Serenade, K525 (exc); *Schubert:* Ave Maria, D839; *Bach:* Cantata 147 (exc); Suites, BWV1066-9 (exc); Musikalisches Opfer, BWV1079 (exc); *Albinoni:* Adagio; *Pachelbel:* Canon and Gigue (exc); *Khachaturian:* Gayaneh (exc); *Grieg:* Peer Gynt Suites (exc); *J. Strauss II:* Blauen Donau, Op. 314; G'schichten aus dem Wienerwald, Op. 325; *Rimsky-Korsakov:* Tale of Tsar Saltan (exc); Sadko (exc); *Beethoven:* Symphony 9 (exc). (Luxembourg Rad & TV SO/L. de Froment)

① **FF038**
Cello for Happy Days
Granados: Danzas españolas (exc); Goyescas (exc); *Fauré:* Songs, Op. 7 (exc); Papillon; Sicilienne; *Senaillé:* Premier livre de sonates (exc); *Rubinstein:* Melodies, Op. 3 (exc); *Rachmaninov:* Vocalise; *Falla:* Amor brujo (exc); *Saint-Saëns:* Carnaval des animaux (exc); *Popper:* Tarantella, Op. 33; *Kreisler:* Liebesleid; *Ravel:* Pièce en forme de habanera; *Rimsky-Korsakov:* Tale of Tsar Saltan (exc). (A. Lamasse, D. Hovora)

① **FF042**
Gems of Baroque Music
Hummel: Trumpet Concerto; *Vivaldi:* Concerti, Op. 10 (exc); *Handel:* Water Music Suite; Concerti grossi, Op. 3 (exc); *Rameau:* Indes galantes (exc). (G. Millière, D. Roux, Luxembourg Rad & TV SO/P. Cao/L. de Froment)

① **FF044**
French Overtures and Ballet Music
Gounod: Faust (exc); *Berlioz:* Damnation de Faust (exc); *Lalo:* Roi d'Ys (exc); *Delibes:* Roi l'a dit (exc); Source (exc); Lakmé (exc). (Luxembourg Rad & TV SO/L. de Froment)

① **FF045** (11/94)
Grieg/Lalo—Orchestral Works
Grieg: Peer Gynt Suites; Lyric Suite, Op. 54 (exc); *Lalo:* Roi d'Ys (exc). (Mexico City PO/F. Lozano, Luxembourg Rad & TV SO/L. de Froment)

① **FF046**
Fantasia
Elgar: Pomp and Circumstance Marches (exc); *Khachaturian:* Gayaneh (exc); *J. Strauss II:* Fledermaus (exc); *Gluck:* Orfeo ed Euridice (exc); *Liszt:* Préludes; *Dukas:* Apprenti sorcier; *Wagner:* Walküre (exc). (Luxembourg Rad & TV SO/P. Cao/L. de Froment)

① **FF047**
Falla/Ravel—Orchestral Works
Falla: Sombrero de tres picos Suites (exc); Amor Brujo (exc); Vida breve (exc); Nights in the Gardens of Spain; *Ravel:* Alborada del gracioso. (J.F. Osorio, Mexico City PO/F. Lozano, Luxembourg Rad & TV SO/L. de Froment)

① **FF049**
Smetana—Orchestral Works
Smetana: Má vlast (exc); Bartered Bride (exc). (Luxembourg RSO/L. Hager)

① **FF051**
Les Immortels
Pachelbel: Canon and Gigue (exc); *Beethoven:* Piano Sonata 8 (exc); *Handel:* Serse (exc); *Mozart:* Ave verum corpus, K618; Serenade, K525 (exc); *Bach:* Cantata 147 (exc); Suites, BWV1066-9 (exc); Harpsichord Concerto, BWV1056 (exc); *Albinoni:* Adagio; *Vivaldi:* Concerti, Op. 8 (exc); *M. Haydn:* Notturno, MH185 (exc); *Gluck:* Orfeo ed Euridice (exc). (Munich Pro Arte Orch/K. Redel)

① **FF058**
An Evening in Moscow
Tchaikovsky: Sleeping Beauty (exc); Nutcracker Suite (exc); Swan Lake (exc); *Glinka:* Ruslan and Lyudmila (exc); *Borodin:* Prince Igor (exc); *Mussorgsky:* Khovanshchina (exc); *Khachaturian:* Gayaneh (exc); *Rimsky-Korsakov:* Golden Cockerel (exc). (Rhineland-Pfalz State PO/K. Redel)

① **FF060**
Famous Russian Operatic Choruses
Borodin: Prince Igor (exc); *Tchaikovsky:* Eugene Onegin (exc); Queen of Spades (exc); *Rimsky-Korsakov:* Tale of Tsar Saltan (exc); Sadko (exc); *Glinka:* Life for the Tsar (exc); *Mussorgsky:* Boris Godunov (exc). (N. Ghiaurov, Bulgarian Nat Ch, Sofia PO/R. Raichev/E. Tchakarov)

① **UCD10902**
The Art of Montserrat Caballé, Vol. 1
Donizetti: Ah, Rammenta; Me voglio fa'na case; Amore e morte; Zingara; Lagrima; *Bellini:* Vaga luna; Ma rendi pur contento; Malinconia, ninfa gentile; Abbandono; Allegro marinaro; *Vivaldi:* Ottone in vilia (exc); Ercole sul Termodonte (exc); Atenaide (exc); Bajazet (exc); Griselda (exc); *Paisiello:* Amor contrastato (exc); *B. Marcello:* Quella fiamma; *Parisotti:* Se tu m'ami; *T. Giordani:* Caro mio ben. (M. Caballé, M. Zanetti)

① **UCD16567** (2/89)
Haydn: Orchestral Works
Haydn: Horn Concerto 1; Horn Concerto 2; Vera Costanza (exc); Fedeltà premiata (exc); Speziale (exc). (D. Bourgue, Versailles Camerata/A. du Closel)

① **UCD16568**
Berlioz—Harold in Italy
Berlioz: Harold in Italy; Benvenuto Cellini (exc). (B. Pasquier, Montpellier PO/C. Diederich)

① **UCD16572** (9/89)
Weber—Abu Hassan; Kampf und Sieg
Weber: Abu Hassan (Cpte); Kampf und Sieg, J190 (exc). (E. Schwarzkopf, E. Witte, M. Bohnen, chor, Berlin RSO/L. Ludwig, Leipzig Rad Chor, Leipzig RSO/H. Kegel)

Ⓓ **UCD16578/9** (6/89)
Massenet—Amadis
Massenet: Amadis (Cpte). (H. Perraguin, D. Streiff, D. Henry, A. Garcin, N. Chabrier, P. Descombes, Hauts-de-Seine Maîtrise, Paris Op Chor, Paris Op Orch/P. Fournillier)

Ⓓ **UCD16584**
Mozart Orchestral Works
Mozart: Flute and Harp concerto, K299; Zauberflöte (exc); Flute Concerto, K313; Symphony 32. (B. Fromanger, C. Michel, Nice PO/K. Redel)

Ⓓ **UCD16651**
Boris Christoff - Recital
Monteverdi: Incoronazione di Poppea; *Rameau:* Dardanus (exc); *Gluck:* Iphigénie en Aulide (exc); *Mozart:* Cosi dunque tradisci, K432; *Beethoven:* Fidelio (exc); *Verdi:* Macbeth (exc). (N. Stanchiev, B. Christoff, Bulgarian Nat Chor, Bulgarian RSO/E. Gracis)

Ⓓ **UCD16652/3** (10/92)
Tomasi—Don Juan & Triomphe de Jeanne
Tomasi: Don Juan de Mañara (Cpte); Triomphe de Jeanne. (R. Jobin, M. Angelici, A. Vessières, J. Brumaire, B. Demigny, P. Cabanel, J. Peyron, H. Vermeil, French Rad Chor, R. Gorr, J. Doucet, M. Lupovici, French Rad Maîtrise, French Rad and TV Chor, FNO/H. Tomasi)

Ⓓ **UCD16681** (8/93)
The Great Italian Arias
Leoncavallo: Pagliacci (exc); *Puccini:* Bohème (exc); *Rossini:* Guillaume Tell (exc); Barbiere di Siviglia (exc); *Donizetti:* Lucrezia Borgia (exc); *Boito:* Mefistofele (exc); *Verdi:* Nabucco (exc); Attila (exc); Don Carlo (exc); Rigoletto (exc); *Giordano:* Andrea Chénier (exc); *Puccini:* È l'uccellino. (J. Van Dam, C. Musquer, Loire PO/M. Soustrot)

Ⓓ **UCD16727** (8/95)
L'Incomparable Georges Thill
Massenet: Hérodiade (exc); *Verdi:* Aida (exc); *Halévy:* Juive (exc); *Gluck:* Alceste (1776) (exc); *Massenet:* Cid (exc); *Meyerbeer:* Huguenots (exc); *Leoncavallo:* Pagliacci (exc); *Wagner:* Lohengrin (exc); *Verdi:* Traviata (exc); *Rossini:* Guillaume Tell (exc); *Méhul:* Joseph (exc); *Massenet:* Sapho (exc); *Gounod:* Roméo et Juliette (exc); *Messager:* Fortunio (exc); *Bruneau:* Attaque du moulin (exc). (G. Thill, orch/F. Heurteur/E. Bigot/P. Gaubert/P. Chagnon/A. Bruneau)

Ⓓ **UCD16738** (8/95)
Great Handel Arias
Handel: Alcina (exc); Ariodante (exc); Giulio Cesare (exc); Serse (exc). (A. Murray, OAE/C. Mackerras)

Ⓓ **UCD16741**
Bulgarian Voices, Vol. 1
Bizet: Carmen (exc); *Gounod:* Faust (exc); *Massenet:* Manon (exc); Werther (exc); *Saint-Saëns:* Samson et Dalila (exc); *Bizet:* Jolie fille de Perth (exc); *Rameau:* Dardanus (exc). (R. Kabaivanska, L. Vassileva, A. Milcheva, N. Nikolov, N. Ghiuselev, N. Ghiaurov, B. Christoff, Bulgarian RSO/V. Stefanov/I. Marinov/R. Raichev/E. Gracis)

Ⓓ **UCD16742**
Bulgarian Voices, Vol. 2
Catalani: Wally (exc); *Puccini:* Madama Butterfly (exc); *Giordano:* Andrea Chénier (exc); *Ponchielli:* Gioconda (exc); *Verdi:* Traviata (exc); *Cilea:* Adriana Lecouvreur (exc); *Verdi:* Forza del destino (exc); *Leoncavallo:* Pagliacci (exc); *Verdi:* Aida (exc); *Mascagni:* Cavalleria rusticana (exc); *Verdi:* Nabucco (exc); Otello (exc); Vespri siciliani (exc). (R. Kabaivanska, A. Tomowa-Sintow, G. Dimitrova, J. Wiener-Chenisheva, M. Nikolova, Sofia PO, Bulgarian Nat Op Orch, Bulgarian RSO/R. Raichev/V. Stefanov/S. Pennaci/I. Marinov)

Ⓓ **UCD16743**
Bulgarian Voices, Vol. 3
Borodin: Prince Igor (exc); *Tchaikovsky:* Eugene Onegin (exc); *Glinka:* Life for the Tsar (exc); *Mussorgsky:* Khovanshchina (exc); *Rachmaninov:* Aleko (exc); *Mussorgsky:* Boris Godunov (exc). (B. Karnobatlova, A. Milcheva, P. Kurchumov, N. Ghiaurov, D. Petkov, N. Ghiuselev, Bulgarian RSO, Plovdiv PO, Sofia PO/V. Stefanov/R. Raichev/E. Tchakarov)

Ⓓ **UCD19022**
The unforgettable André Baugé
Rossini: Barbiere di Siviglia (exc); *Planquette:* Cloches de Corneville (exc); Rip Van Winkle (exc); *Audran:* Mascotte (exc); *Messager:* Monsieur Beaucaire (exc); *Lecocq:* Fille de Madame Angot (exc); *Adam:* Si j'étais roi (exc); *Levadé:* Vieilles de chez-nous; *Chaminade:* Anneau d'argent; *O. Straus:* Walzertraum (exc); *Lehár:* Lustige Witwe (exc); Paganini (exc); *J. Strauss II:* Walzer aus Wien (exc); *Romberg:* Nina Rosa (exc); *Friml:* Rose Marie (exc); *Yvain:* Au soleil du Mexique (exc); *Christiné:* Temps des merveilleuses (exc); *Mandru:* Valse berceuse; *G. Martini:* Plaisir d'amour. (N. Vallin, A. Baugé, orch)

Ⓓ **UCD19053**
L'Incomparable Tino Rossi
Toselli: Serenade; *Bizet:* Pêcheurs de perles (exc); *F. Bazini:* Romance de Maître Pathélin; *Gounod:* Où voulez-vous aller?; *Godard:* Jocelyn (exc); *Tosti:* Si tu le voulais; Ideale; *Lalo:* Roi d'Ys (exc); *Massenet:* Manon (exc); *Richepin:* Paradis du rêve; *Haydn Wood:* Roses of Picardy; *Scotto:* Marinella (exc); *Trénet:* Sérénade portugaise; *Cardillo:* Core 'ngrato; *Denza:* Si vous l'aviez compris; *Christiné:* Reviens. (T. Rossi, chor, orch/M. Cariven/P. Chagnon)

The Fourties

Ⓓ **FT1507/8**
Verdi—Il trovatore
Verdi: Trovatore (Cpte). (J. Björling, N. Greco, F. Valentino, B. Castagna, N. Moscona, M. Stellman, L. Oliviero, A. Kent, NY Met Op Chor, NY Met Op Orch/F. Calusio)

Ⓓ **FT1511/2**
Donizetti—Lucia di Lammermoor
Donizetti: Lucia di Lammermoor (Cpte). (L. Pons, F. Jagel, J. Brownlee, E. Pinza, T. Votipka, NY Met Op Chor, NY Met Op Orch/G. Papi)

Foyer

Ⓓ **15-CF2011** (6/88)
Wagner—Der Ring de Nibelungen
Wagner: Rheingold (Cpte); Walküre (Cpte); Siegfried (Cpte); Götterdämmerung (Cpte). (H. Hotter, I. Malaniuk, E. Witte, P. Kuen, G. Neidlinger, B. Falcon, G. Stolze, H. Uhde, M. von Ilosvay, L. Weber, J. Greindl, E. Zimmermann, H. Plümacher, G. Litz, R. Vinay, R. Resnik, A. Varnay, J. Greindl, B. Friedland, L. Thomamüller, B. Falcon, L. Sorrell, E. Schubert, G. Litz, S. Plate, M. von Ilosvay, W. Windgassen, H. Hotter, R. Streich, J. Greindl, H. Uhde, N. Hinsch-Gröndahl, I. Malaniuk, M. von Ilosvay, R. Resnik, Bayreuth Fest Chor, Bayreuth Fest Orch/C. Krauss)

Ⓓ **2-CF2016**
Gounod—Philémon et Baucis
Gounod: Philémon et Baucis (Cpte). (A. Misciano, R. Scotto, R. Panerai, P. Montarsolo, J. Torriani, Milan RAI Chor, Milan RAI SO/N. Sanzogno)

Ⓓ **2-CF2030**
Rossini—Armida
Rossini: Armida (Cpte). (C. Deutekom, O. Garaventa, E. Gimenez, P. Bottazzo, B. Trotta, A. Maddalena, G. Antonini, Venice La Fenice Chor, Venice La Fenice Orch/C. Franci)

Ⓓ **2-CF2032**
Mozart—Ascanio in Alba/Coronation Mass
Mozart: Ascanio in Alba (Cpte); Mass, K317. (G. Jahn, E. Gabry, W. Krenn, S. Mangelsdorff, R. van Vrooman, Salzburg Fest Chbr Ch, Salzburg Mozarteum Orch/L. Hager, A. Giebel, H. Rössl-Majdan, H. Handt, P. Mollet, Turin RAI Chor, Turin RAI Orch/M. Rossi)

Ⓓ **2-CF2033**
Puccini—Manon Lescaut
Puccini: Manon Lescaut (Cpte). (M. Olivero, P. Domingo, G. Fioravanti, A. Mariotti, E. Lorenzi, R. Pallini, F. Federici, F. Ricciardi, G. Casarini, O. Begali, C. del Bosco, Verona Arena Chor, Verona Arena Orch/N. Santi)

Ⓓ **2-CF2045**
Donizetti—Linda di Chamounix
Donizetti: Linda di Chamounix (Cpte). (M. Rinaldi, Alfredo Kraus, E. Dara, R. Bruson, E. Zilio, C. Cava, M.G. Allegri, A. Ceroni, La Scala Chor, La Scala Orch/G. Gavazzeni)

Ⓓ **2-CF2048**
Donizetti—Caterina Cornaro
Donizetti: Caterina Cornaro (Cpte). (M. Caballé, J. Carreras, L. Saccomani, E. Serra, M. Mazzieri, N. Williams, A. Edwards, LSC, LSO/C.F. Cillario)

Ⓓ **2-CF2054**
Donizetti—La favorita
Donizetti: Favorita (Cpte). (F. Cossotto, Alfredo Kraus, S. Bruscantini, R. Raimondi, M. Zotti, A. Pedroni, NHK Italian Op Chor, NHK SO/O. de Fabritiis)

Ⓓ **2-CF2066**
Mozart—Così fan tutte
Mozart: Così fan tutte (Cpte). (G. Janowitz, B. Fassbaender, R. Grist, P. Schreier, H. Prey, D. Fischer-Dieskau, Vienna St Op Chor, VPO/K. Böhm)

Ⓓ **2-CF2092**
Verdi—Don Carlo
Verdi: Don Carlo (Cpte). (F. Corelli, M. Caballé, G. Bumbry, S. Milnes, C. Siepi, J. Macurdy, P. Plishka, F. von Stade, L. Goeke, R. MacWherter, L. Amara, NY Met Op Chor, NY Met Op Orch/F. Molinari-Pradelli)

Ⓓ **2-CF2093**
Donizetti—Maria Stuarda
Donizetti: Maria Stuarda (Cpte). (M. Caballé, M.V. Menendez, J. Carreras, M. Mazzieri, E. Serra, R. Bezinian, Paris ORTF Lyric Chor, Paris ORTF Lyric Orch/N. Santi)

Ⓓ **3-CF2007** (6/88)
Wagner—Das Rheingold
Wagner: Rheingold (Cpte). (H. Hotter, I. Malaniuk, E. Witte, P. Kuen, G. Neidlinger, B. Falcon, G. Stolze, H. Uhde, M. von Ilosvay, L. Weber, J. Greindl, E. Zimmermann, H. Plümacher, G. Litz, Bayreuth Fest Orch/C. Krauss)

Ⓓ **3-CF2035**
Meyerbeer—Le Prophète
Meyerbeer: Prophète (Cpte). (M. Horne, N. Gedda, M. Rinaldi, A. Giacomotti, R. Amis el Hage, F. Peter, B. Carmeli, Turin RAI Chor, Turin RAI Orch/H. Lewis)

Ⓓ **4-CF2008** (6/88)
Wagner—Die Walküre
Wagner: Walküre (Cpte). (R. Vinay, R. Resnik, A. Varnay, H. Hotter, I. Malaniuk, J. Greindl, B. Friedland, L. Thomamüller, B. Falcon, L. Sorrell, E. Schubert, G. Litz, S. Plate, M. von Ilosvay, Bayreuth Fest Orch/C. Krauss)

Ⓓ **4-CF2009** (6/88)
Wagner—Siegfried
Wagner: Siegfried (Cpte). (W. Windgassen, H. Hotter, A. Varnay, P. Kuen, G. Neidlinger, M. von Ilosvay, J. Greindl, R. Streich, Bayreuth Fest Orch/C. Krauss)

Ⓓ **4-CF2010** (6/88)
Wagner—Götterdämmerung
Wagner: Götterdämmerung (Cpte). (A. Varnay, W. Windgassen, J. Greindl, G. Neidlinger, H. Uhde, N. Hinsch-Gröndahl, I. Malaniuk, E. Zimmermann, H. Plümacher, G. Litz, M. von Ilosvay, R. Resnik, Bayreuth Fest Chor, Bayreuth Fest Orch/C. Krauss)

FSM

Ⓓ **FCD91114**
Virtuoso Chamber Music with Guitar
Giuliani: Marches (1814); *Boccherini:* Guitar Quintets, G445-453 (exc); *Danzi:* Duo, Op. 64; *Dotzauer:* Potpourri, Op. 21; *Gluck:* Iphigénie en Aulide (exc); *Hünten:* Waltzes (exc); *Diabelli:* Beethoven Pot-pourri (1817). (R. Greiss, C. Ragaz, M. Ostertag, B.B. Bagger, G. Bach)

Gallo

Ⓓ **CD-674**
Fidelio Ensemble play Bizet, Gounod & D'Indy
Gounod: Petite Symphonie; *Indy:* Chansons et Danses, Op. 50; *Bizet:* Jeux d'enfants; Carmen Suites (exc). (Fidelio Ens)

Ⓓ **CD-676**
Stanislas Ensemble - 20th Cent Chamber Works
Eisler: Septet 1; Septet 2; *Weill:* Dreigroschenoper (exc); *Schoenberg:* Eiserne Brigade; Weihnachtsmusik. (Stanislas Ens)

Ⓓ **CD-816**
Mozart—Concert Arias
Mozart: Schauspieldirektor (exc); Nozze di Figaro (exc); Don Giovanni (exc); Alcandro, lo confesso, K512; Così dunque tradisci, K432; Mentre ti lascio, K513; Bacio di mano, K541; Rivolgete a lui lo sguardo, K584; Io ti lascio, KAnh245. (G. Bacquier, Collegium Academicum Orch/R. Dunand)

Gamut Classics

Ⓓ **GAMCD535** (11/93)
Barber—Choral Music
Barber: Reincarnation, Op. 16; Virgin Martyrs, Op. 8/1; Stopwatch; Agnus Dei, Op. 11; Antony and Cleopatra (exc); Twelfth Night; Hermit Songs, Op. 29 (exc); Songs, Op. 13 (exc); Let down the bars, O Death, Op. 8/2; To be sung on the water; Vanessa (exc). (Cambridge Univ Chbr Ch/T. Brown)

Ⓓ **GAMD506** (4/92)
An Anthology Of English Song
Purcell: Oedipus, Z583 (exc); *Elgar:* Is she not passing fair?; *Ireland:* Sea Fever; *Vaughan Williams:* Linden Lea; House of Life (exc); Songs of Travel (exc); *Hageman:* Do not go, my love; *Leslie:* Annabelle Lee; *Woodforde-Finden:* Indian Love Lyrics (exc); *Quilter:* Songs, Op. 3 (exc); *C. A.*

Gibbs: Cherry Tree; *M.V. White:* To Mary; *Gwynn Williams:* My little Welsh home; *Bond:* Perfect Day; *Parry:* English Lyrics, Set 2 (exc); *Handel:* Tolomeo (exc); *Coates:* Birdsongs at Eventide; *Traditional:* Blow the wind southerly. (V. Masterson, Sarah Walker, S. Burrows, P. Jeffes, T. Allen, R. Herincx, J. Constable)

Georgian Recordings

GR002
Country House Musick
Arne: Love's Labours Lost (exc); As You Like It (exc); Tempest (exc); *Handel:* Fireworks Music (exc); Fantasia in C; Tolomeo (exc); *Haydn:* Canzonettas I (exc); *J. C. Bach:* Unidentified Flute Sonata; *Hook:* Lass of Richmond Hill. (M. Ashton, Concert Royal, J. Treherne)

Gega

GD113/5
Mussorgsky—Khovanschina
Mussorgsky: Khovanshchina (Cpte). (S. Elenkov, Z. Gadjev, L. Bodurov, S. Popov, N. Ghiuselev, S. Mineva, Angel Petkov, S. Marinova, E. Ugrinov, R. Doikov, N. Vasilev, D. Stanchev, P. Bakardjiev, W. Vrachovski, Sofia National Op Chor, Sofia National Op Orch/R. Raichev)

Glossa

GCD920201 (11/94)
Music in the time of Velázquez
Sanz: Spanish Guitar Instruction II (exc); Spanish Guitar Instruction I (exc); *Martín y Coll:* Folías; Canarios; *Hidalgo:* Templo de Palas (exc); Los celos hacen estrellas (exc); Ay, que me río de Amor; Estatua de Prometeo (exc); Cuydado pastor; *Marín:* Ojos que me desdenais; Song Collection (1690) (exc); *Selma y Salaverde:* Primo libro de Canzoni (exc); Susanna passeggiata; *Ruiz de Ribayaz:* Luz y norte musical para caminar (exc); *Guerau:* Poema harmónico (exc); *Durón:* Salir (exc). (Romanesca)

Gramavision

R2-79470 (4/93)
Davis—The Life and Times of Malcolm X
A. Davis: X (Cpte). (E. Perry, T.J. Young, P. Baskerville, H. Harris, H. Perry, C. Aaronson, T.D. Price, R. Bazemore, J. Daniecki, R. Edwards, R. Byrne, Episteme, St. Luke's Orch/W.H. Curry)

Grammofono 2000

AB78512
Wagner—Die Walküre (Act 3)
Wagner: Walküre (exc). (K. Flagstad, R. Bockelmann, M. Müller, M. Craven, E. Stenning, T. Bardsley, L. Seymour, E. Arden, E. Coates, G. Garside, G. Ripley, LPO/W. Furtwängler)

Grande Musique d'Espagne

GME221
Falla—Orchestral Works
Falla: Retablo de maese Pedro (Cpte); Harpsichord Concerto (exc); Amor Brujo (Cpte). (T. Tourné, P. Lavirgen, R. Cesari, I. Rivadeneyra, Madrid Concerts Orch/P. de Freitas Branco/J. Arámbarri, G. Gálvez, R. Lopez del Cid, J. Vaya, A. Menendez, L. Anton, R. Vivo/J.M. Franco Gil)

GME225
Arriaga—String and Orchestral Works
Arriaga: Esclavos felices (exc); Symphony in D (exc); Overture, Op. 1 (exc); String Quartet 2 (exc). (Spanish Nat Rad Qt, Madrid Concerts Orch/J. Arámbarri)

Grasmere Music

GRCD41
Avondale - The Sun Life Band
Verner: Avondale; *F. Loewe:* My Fair Lady (exc); *Dukas:* Apprenti Sorcier; *Arban:* Tyrolean Variations; *Auber:* Muette de Portici (exc); *Richardson:* Tom marches on; *P. Graham:* Prisms; *H. Clarke:* From the shores of the mighty Pacific; *Godard:* Jocelyn (exc); *Smetana:* Bartered Bride (exc). (P. Richards, S. Walkley, L. Baglin, Sun Life Band/R. Newsome/B. Hurdley)

Guild

GMCD7102
Coronation Music from St Paul's
Bliss: Jubilante Fanfares (exc); *Parry:* I was glad; *Vaughan Williams:* O taste and see; Mass in G minor (exc); *Goss:* Praise my soul; *Purcell:* King Arthur, Z628 (exc); *Stanford:* Services, Op. 10 (exc); *Anon:* Psalm 121; *Dearnley:* Dominus regit me; Let thy hand be strengthened; *Britten:* Te Deum in C; *Vaughan Williams:* Old Hundredth; *S. S. Wesley:* Thou wilt keep him; *Various:* National Anthems (exc). (St Paul's Cath Ch, Kneller Hall Trumpeters, M. Blatchly, C. Dearnley, Barry Rose/C. Dearnley/Barry Rose/T. Sharpe)

Happy Days

CDHD253/4 **MCHD253/4**
Vintage Gilbert and Sullivan
Sullivan: HMS Pinafore (Cpte); Mikado (Cpte). (H. Lytton, George Baker, C. Goulding, E. Griffin, D. Fancourt, S. Granville, N. Briercliffe, B. Lewis, S. Robertson, D. Fancourt, D. Oldham, M. Green, S. Granville, L. Rands, B. Bennett, M. Eyre, E. Nickell-Lean, Jo Curtis, D'Oyly Carte Op Chor, SO/M. Sargent)

Harmonia Mundi

HMA190 1039
Popular 17th Century English Tunes
Playford: English Dancing Master, Part one (exc); English Dancing Master, Part Two (exc); English Dancing Master, Appendix (exc); *Farnaby:* St Paul's Wharf; Tower Hill; *Coprario:* Tower Hill; *Susato:* Danserye (exc); *Anon:* Caleno custure me; Packington's Pound; Fortune my Foe; Greensleeves; Folia de la Spagna; Chi Passa; *Traditional:* All in a Garden Green; *Anon:* Light O'Love; Come live with me; *Traditional:* Clean Contrary Way; Gilderoy; Gilliecrankie; Miller of the Dee; *Arne:* Love in a Village (exc). (Broadside Band/J. Barlow)

HMA190 1083 (12/87) **HMA43 1083**
M-A. Charpentier—Les Arts Florissants
M-A. Charpentier: Arts Florissants (Cpte). (J. Feldman, A. Mellon, G. Reinhart, C. Dussaut, G. Laurens, D. Visse, P. Cantor, Arts Florissants Voc Ens, Arts Florissants Instr Ens/W. Christie)

HMA190 1095 **HMA43 1095**
M-A. Charpentier—Actéon; Comtesse d'Escarbagnas
M-A. Charpentier: Actéon (Cpte); Comtesse d'Escarbagnas Ov, H494. (D. Visse, A. Mellon, G. Laurens, J. Feldman, F. Paut, D. Visse, M. Laplénie, P. Cantor, Arts Florissants Voc Ens, Arts Florissants Instr Ens/W. Christie)

HMA190 1183 (5/87)
Works for Lute and Voice
Caccini: Nuove musiche (1602) (exc); *Bottrigari:* So ben mi c'ha bon tempo; Mi parto; *Ferrari:* M'amo tanto costei; Averto ò cor; *Melli:* Capriccio chromatico; *Purcell:* Oedipus, Z583 (exc); Pausanias, Z585 (exc); *Anon:* Miserere my maker; *R. Johnson II:* Care-charming sleep; *Monteverdi:* Incoronazione di Poppea (exc); *Steffani:* Qui l'auretta; *Weiss:* Prelude and Fugue in D minor; *Schein:* O Scheiden, o bitter Scheiden; *Hammerschmidt:* Kunst des Küssens; *Krieger:* An die Einsamkeit; *Gräfe:* Aria di Giovannini (exc); *Mozart:* Abendempfindung, K523. (R. Jacobs, K. Junghänel)

HMA190 1244
Charpentier—Theatre Music; Sonatas
M-A. Charpentier: Sonate a 8, H548; Suite a 4, H545; Andromède, H504; Circé, H496. (London Baroque/C. Medlam)

HMA190 1276 (9/88)
Blow—Venus and Adonis
Blow: Venus and Adonis (Cpte). (N. Argenta, L. Dawson, S. Varcoe, E. van Evera, J.M. Ainsley, C. Daniels, Gordon Jones, R. Covey-Crump, Chor, London Baroque/C. Medlam)

HMA190 200 **HMA43 200**
Purcell—King Arthur excerpts
Purcell: King Arthur, Z628 (exc). (Deller Consort, King's Musick/A. Deller)

HMA190 214
Purcell—Theatre Music and Sacred Songs
Purcell: Olinda in the shades unseen, Z404; Dioclesian Suite (exc); Timon of Athens, Z632 (exc); Indian Queen, Z630 (exc); How pleasant is this flowery plain, Z543; Old Bachelor, Z607 (exc); Birthday Ode, Z323 (exc); Fairy Queen, Z629 (exc); There ne'er was so wretched a lover, Z513; Oedipus, Z583 (exc); St Cecilia's Day Ode, Z334; Pavan, Z752; Awake, ye dead, Z182; Earth trembled, Z197; Dioclesian, Z627 (exc). (Deller Consort, A. Deller (alto/dir))

HMA190 764 (12/87)
Berio—Laborintus II
Berio: Laborintus II. (C. Legrand, J. Baucomont, C. Meunier, E. Sanguineti, Chorale Expérimentale, Musique Vivante Ens/L. Berio)

HMC40 1175/8
Cavalli—Xerse
Cavalli: Xerse (Cpte). (R. Jacobs, J. Nelson, J. Gall, I. Poulenard, J. Feldman, J. Elwes, G. de Mey, R. Wistreich, J. Nirouët, D. Visse, A. Mellon, F. Fauché, Ens/R. Jacobs)

HMC40 1282/4 (7/89)
Cavalli—Giasone
Cavalli: Giasone (Cpte). (M. Chance, H. van der Kamp, M. Schopper, C. Dubosc, B. Delétré, A. Mellon, G. Banditelli, D. Visse, G. de Mey, G. Fagotto, Concerto Vocale, R. Jacobs)

HMC40 1289/90 (12/88)
Charpentier—David et Jonathas
M-A. Charpentier: David et Jonathas (Cpte). (G. Lesne, M. Zanetti, J-F. Gardeil, B. Delétré, J-P. Fouchécourt, D. Visse, R. Bischoff, Arts Florissants Voc Ens, Arts Florissants Instr Ens/W. Christie)

HMC40 466
Rossini—Overtures
Rossini: Barbiere di Siviglia (exc); Guillaume Tell (exc); Gazza ladra (exc); Cenerentola (exc); Italiana in Algeri (exc); Cambiale di matrimonio (exc); Scala di Seta (exc); Semiramide (exc). (Plovdiv PO/R. Raychev)

HMC40 5210/2 (11/88)
Gluck—Echo and Narcissus
Gluck: Echo et Narcisse (Cpte). (S. Boulin, K. Streit, D. Massell, P. Galliard, G. Hoffstedt, C. Högman, H. Krogen, E.M. Tersson, Hamburg St Op Chor, Concerto Cologne/R. Jacobs)

HMC90 1100/2
Cesti—Orontea
Cesti: Orontea (Cpte). (A. Bierbaum, C. Cadelo, H. Müller-Molinari, G. Reinhart, G. de Mey, R. Jacobs, G. Sarti, D. James, I. Poulenard, J. Feldman, Baroque Instr Ens/R. Jacobs)

HMC90 1129 **HMC40 1129**
Monteverdi and Ferrari vocal works
Monteverdi: Scherzi musicali (1632) (exc); Madrigals, Bk.7 (exc); L'Arianna (exc); Madrigals, Bk.8 (exc); *Ferrari:* Queste pungenti spine; *Monteverdi:* Incoronazione di Poppea (exc). (Concerto Vocale)

HMC90 1139/41 (3/85)
M-A. Charpentier—Medée
M-A. Charpentier: Médée (Cpte). (J. Feldman, J. Bona, A. Mellon, G. Ragon, P. Cantor, S. Boulin, Arts Florissants Chor, Arts Florissants Orch/W. Christie)

HMC90 1249
Lully—Excerpts from Atys
Lully: Atys (exc). (B. Delétré, J-P. Fouchécourt, G. Ragon, A. Mellon, G. de Mey, J. Bona, F. Semellaz, G. Laurens, N. Rime, J-F. Gardeil, M. Laplénie, I. Desrochers, V. Gens, Arts Florissants Chor, Arts Florissants Orch/W. Christie)

HMC90 1257/9 (7/87) **HMC40 1257/9**
Lully—Atys
Lully: Atys (Cpte). (B. Delétré, M. Zanetti, J-P. Fouchécourt, G. Ragon, A. Steyer, A. Mellon, G. de Mey, J. Bona, F. Semellaz, G. Laurens, N. Rime, J-F. Gardeil, M. Laplénie, S. Maciejewski, I. Desrochers, V. Gens, Arts Florissants Chor, Arts Florissants Orch/W. Christie)

HMC90 1308/9 (1/90) **HMC40 1308/9** (1/90)
Purcell—The Fairy Queen
Purcell: Fairy Queen, Z629 (Cpte). (N. Argenta, L. Dawson, I. Desrochers, W. van Gent, V. Gens, S. Piau, N. Rime, C. Daniels, J-P. Fouchécourt, M. le Brocq, C. le Paludier, B. Loonen, F. Piolino, T. Randle, F. Bazola-Minori, J. Corréas, G. Banks-Martin, B. Delétré, T. Lander, R. Taylor, Arts Florissants Chor, Arts Florissants Orch/W. Christie)

HMC90 1312/3 (7/90) **HMC40 1312/3** (7/90)
Handel—Flavio
Handel: Flavio (Cpte). (J. Gall, D.L. Ragin, L. Lootens, B. Fink, C. Högman, G. Fagotto, U. Messthaler, Ens 415/R. Jacobs)

HMC90 1330/2 (4/91) **HMC40 1330/2** (4/91)
Monteverdi—L'incoronazione di Poppea
Monteverdi: Incoronazione di Poppea (Cpte). (D. Borst, G. Laurens, J. Larmore, A. Köhler, M. Schopper, L. Lootens, M.C. Kiehr, H.M. Ørbaek, C. Homberger, G. de Mey, A. Lebeda, R. Jakobi, M. Bovet, G. Türk, C. Högman, Concerto Vocale/R. Jacobs)

HMC90 1367/9 (2/92) **HMC40 1367/9** (2/92)
Rameau—Les indes galantes
Rameau: Indes galantes (Cpte). (C. McFadden, J. Corréas, I. Poulenard, N. Rivenq, M. Ruggeri, H. Crook, B. Delétré, J-P. Fouchécourt, S. Piau, N. Rime, Arts Florissants Chor, Arts Florissants Orch/W. Christie)

Ⓓ **HMC90 1385/7** (4/92) ▭ **HMC40 1385/7**
Handel—Giulio Cesare
Handel: Giulio Cesare (Cpte). (J. Larmore, B. Schlick, B. Fink, M. Rørholm, D.L. Ragin, F. Zanasi, O. Lallouette, D. Visse, Cologne Concerto/R. Jacobs)

Ⓓ **HMC90 1396/8** (9/92) ▭ **HMC40 1396/8** (9/92)
Campra—Idoménée
Campra: Idoménée (Cpte). (B. Delétré, S. Piau, M. Zanetti, J-P. Fouchécourt, M. Boyer, J. Corréas, R. Dugay, J-C. Sarragosse, M. Saint-Palais, A. Pichard, A. Mopin, Arts Florissants Chor, Arts Florissants Orch/W. Christie)

Ⓓ **HMC90 1420** (12/93)
Weill—The Seven Deadly Sins; Songs
Weill: Sieben Todsünden (Cpte); Complainte de la Seine; Youkali; Nannas Lied; Wie lange noch; Es regnet; Berlin im Licht. (B. Fassbaender, K-H. Brandt, H. Sojer, H. Komatsu, I. Urbas, C. Garben, Hanover Rad PO/C. Garben)

Ⓓ **HMC90 1424/5** (1/93)
Montéclair—Jephté
Montéclair: Jephté (Cpte). (J. Bona, S. Daneman, C. Brua, N. Rivenq, M. Padmore, B. Loonen, J-C. Saragosse, S. Pitour, S. Colas, M. Saint-Palais, F. Bazola-Minori, P. Foucher, A. Pichard, Arts Florissants Chor, Arts Florissants Orch/W. Christie)

Ⓓ **HMC90 1435/7** (7/93)
Rameau—Castor et Pollux
Rameau: Castor et Pollux (Cpte). (H. Crook, J. Corréas, A. Mellon, V. Gens, R. Schirrer, S. Piau, M. Padmore, C. Brua, S. Daneman, A. Brand, J-C. Sarragosse, Arts Florissants Chor, Arts Florissants Orch/W. Christie)

Ⓓ **HMC90 1456/7** (8/93)
Lully—Armide
Lully: Armide. (G. Laurens, H. Crook, V. Gens, N. Rime, B. Delétré, G. Ragon, J. Hancock, L. Coadou, Collegium Vocale, Chapelle Royale Ch, Chapelle Royale Orch/P. Herreweghe)

Ⓓ **HMC90 1458**
Handel—Giulio Cesare - excerpts
Handel: Giulio Cesare (exc). (J. Larmore, B. Fink, M. Rørholm, B. Schlick, D.L. Ragin, F. Zanasi, Cologne Concerto/R. Jacobs)

Ⓓ **HMC90 1501**
Rameau—Castor & Pollux - Highlights
Rameau: Castor et Pollux (exc). (H. Crook, J. Corréas, A. Mellon, V. Gens, S. Piau, M. Padmore, C. Brua, S. Daneman, A. Brand, J-C. Sarragosse, Arts Florissants Chor, Arts Florissants Orch/W. Christie)

Ⓓ **HMC90 1506**
Campra—Idoménée - Highlights
Campra: Idoménée (exc). (B. Delétré, S. Piau, M. Zanetti, J-P. Fouchécourt, M. Boyer, J. Corréas, R. Dugay, A. Pichard, A. Mopin, Arts Florissants Chor, Arts Florissants Orch/W. Christie)

Ⓓ **HMC90 1515/7** (9/95)
Cavalli—La Calisto
Cavalli: Calisto (Cpte). (M. Bayo, M. Lippi, S. Keenlyside, G. Pushee, A. Mantovani, S. Theodoridou, G. Ragon, B. Banks, D. Visse, D. Pittsinger, J. Vindevogel, Concerto Vocale/R. Jacobs)

Ⓓ **HMC90 1520** (7/95)
Falla/García Lorca—Vocal Works
Lorca: Canciones españolas antiguas; *Falla:* Corregidor y la molinera. (G. Ortega, Teatre lliure CO/J. Pons)

Ⓓ **HMC90 1552** (8/95)
The Three Countertenors
Di Capua: 'O sole mio; *Bizet:* Carmen (exc); *Massenet:* Cid (exc); *Bernstein:* West Side Story (exc); *Saint-Saëns:* Samson et Dalila (exc); *Scholl:* White as Lilies; *Offenbach:* Périchole (exc); *C. François:* My Way; *Donizetti:* Elisir d'Amore (exc). (P. Bertin, A. Scholl, D. Visse, F. Couturier, K.E. Schröder, Camargue PO/Reinhardt Wagner)

Ⓓ **HMC90 1553/4**
Monteverdi—Orfeo
Monteverdi: Orfeo (Cpte). (L. Dale, E. Ben-Nun, J. Larmore, A. Scholl, P. Gérimon, B. Fink, H. Peeters, N. Rivenq, Concerto Vocale/R. Jacobs)

Ⓓ **HMC90 243** (8/87) ▭ **HMA43 243**
Purcell—The Indian Queen
Purcell: Indian Queen, Z630 (Cpte). (M. Bevan, H. Sheppard, M. Deller, P. Elliott, A. Deller, Deller Ch, King's Musick/A. Deller)

Ⓓ **HMC90 249** ▭ **HMC40 249**
Purcell: Music for a while
Purcell: Bonduca, Z574 (exc); Don Quixote, Z578 (exc); Fairy Queen, Z629 (exc); Indian Queen, Z630 (exc); King Arthur, Z628 (exc); King Richard II, Z581 (exc); Dioclesian, Z627 (exc); Pausanias, Z585 (exc); Oedipus, Z583 (exc); Not all my torments, Z400; Evening Hymn, Z193. (A. Deller, W. Kuijken, W. Christie, R. Skeaping)

Ⓓ **HMC90 252/3** ▭ **HMC40 252/3**
Purcell—King Arthur & Timon of Athens
Purcell: King Arthur, Z628 (Cpte); Timon of Athens, Z632 (Cpte). (H. Sheppard, J. Knibbs, R. Hardy, A. Deller, M. Deller, P. Elliott, L. Nixon, M. Bevan, N. Beavan, Deller Ch, King's Musick/A. Deller)

Ⓓ **HMC90 5173** (7/86) ▭ **HMC40 5173** (7/86)
Purcell—Dido & Aeneas
Purcell: Dido (Cpte). (G. Laurens, P. Cantor, J. Feldman, D. Visse, A. Mellon, B. Borden, E. Lestrigant, M. Laplénie, Arts Florissants Voc Ens, Arts Florissants Instr Ens/W. Christie)

Ⓓ **HMC90 5183** (4/88)
Handel: Arias for Senesino
Handel: Giulio Cesare (exc); Rodelinda (exc); Tolomeo (exc); Riccardo Primi (exc); Orlando (exc); Flavio (exc). (D. Minter, Philh Baroque Orch/N. McGegan)

Ⓓ **HMC90 5215** (6/93)
Dusapin—Medeamaterial
Dusapin: Medeamaterial (Cpte). (H. Leidland, Chor, Collegium Vocale, Chapelle Royale Orch/P. Herreweghe)

Ⓓ **HMP390 1293**
Berlioz—Choral Works
Berlioz: Ballet des ombres; Tristia (exc); Roméo et Juliette (exc); Lélio (exc); Sara la baigneuse; Mélodies, Op. 2 (exc); Enfance du Christ (exc); Prière du matin; Veni creator; Mélodies, Op. 2 (exc); Trébuchet; Mélodies, Op. 2 (exc); Béatrice et Bénédict (exc). (B. Brewer, J-P. Courtis, Lyon Nat Ch, N. Lee, L. Mallié, Inst Ens/B. Tetu)

Ⓓ **HMP390 257/8**
Purcell—The Fairy Queen
Purcell: Fairy Queen, Z629 (Cpte). (Deller Consort, Stour Music Fest Chor, Stour Music Fest CO, A. Deller (alto/dir))

Ⓓ **HMP390 466**
Rossini—Overtures
Rossini: Barbiere di Siviglia (exc); Cambiale di matrimonio (exc); Cenerentola (exc); Gazza Ladra (exc); Guillaume Tell (exc); Italiana in Algeri (exc); Scala di Seta (exc); Semiramide (exc). (Plovdiv PO/R. Raychev)

Ⓓ **HMP390 802**
Great Baroque Masters: Charpentier
M-A. Charpentier: Alma Redemptoris, H21; Ave Regina, H22; In nativitatem Domini canticum, H416 (exc); Tenebrae Lessons du mercredi saint (exc); O Deus, O Salvator noster, H372; Te Deum, H146 (exc); David et Jonathas (exc); Médée (exc); Malade Imaginaire (exc); Comtesse d'Escarbagnas, Ov, H494. (Arts Florissants Voc Ens, Arts Florissants Instr Ens/W. Christie, Paris Chapelle Royale Chor, Paris Chapelle Royale Orch/P. Herreweghe, Concerto Vocale)

Ⓓ **HMP390 804**
Great Baroque Masters: Handel
Handel: Tanti strali al sen; Keyboard Suites, Set I (exc); Water Music (exc); Nisi Dominus; Susanna (exc); Giulio Cesare (exc); Orlando (exc); Flavio (exc). (J. Nelson, R. Jacobs, Concerto Vocale, K. Gilbert, Philh Baroque Orch/N. McGegan, Deller Consort, King's Musick/M. Deller, L. Hunt, D. Minter, D. Thomas, D.L. Ragin, Ens 415/R. Jacobs)

Ⓓ **HMP390 805**
Great Baroque Masters—Lully
Anglebert: Lully Transcriptions (exc); *Lully:* Atys (exc); Dies Irae; Omnes gentes; Dixit Dominus. (D. Brown, M. Zanetti, A. Steyer, M. Boyer, G. Laurens, G. Lesne, J-P. Fouchécourt, G. Ragon, H. Crook, H. Lamy, M. Laplénie, B. Delétré, P. Kooy, F. Fauché, K. Gilbert, Paris Chapelle Royale Chor, Paris Chapelle Royale Orch/P. Herreweghe, Arts Florissants Chor, Arts Florissants Orch/W. Christie)

Ⓓ **HMP390 806**
Great Baroque Masters: Monteverdi
Monteverdi: Vespers (exc); Vespers (exc); Fuge, fuge, anima mea; Selva morale e spirituale (exc); Ballo delle ingrate (exc); Madrigals, Bk 8 (exc); Scherzi musicali (1632) (exc); Madrigals, Bk.5 (exc); Incoronazione di Poppea (exc). (Collegium Vocale, Chapelle Royale Orch/P. Herreweghe, Arts Florissants Voc Ens, Arts Florissants Instr Ens/W. Christie, Concerto Vocale/R. Jacobs)

Ⓓ **HMP390 807**
Great Baroque Masters—Purcell
Purcell: Fairy Queen, Z629 (exc); King Arthur, Z628 (exc); Dido (exc); Sonatas, Z790-801 (exc); Chaconne, Z730; Oedipus, Z583 (exc); King Arthur, Z628 (exc); O Solitude, Z406; St Cecilia's Day Ode, Z339; Birthday Ode, Z331. (N. Argenta, R. Hardy, G. Laurens, A. Deller, J-P. Fouchécourt, M. Bevan, B. Delétré, W. Kuijken, W. Christie, R. Elliott, J. Ryan, Deller Consort, King's Musick/A. Deller, London Baroque, Arts Florissants Chor, Arts Florissants Orch/W. Christie)

▭ **HMU40 1358/60** (3/92)
Rossi—Orfeo
Rossi: Orfeo (Cpte). (A. Mellon, M. Zanetti, D. Favat, S. Piau, N. Isherwood, C. Pelon, N. Rime, J-P. Fouchécourt, J. Corréas, M. Boyer, C. Eloir, B. Delétré, B. Thivel, J-M. Salzmann, D. Michel-Dansac, B. Malleret, Arts Florissants Voc Ens, Arts Florissants Instr Ens/W. Christie)

Ⓓ **HMU90 7016** (8/90)
Handel: Arias for Montagnana
Handel: Ezio (exc); Sosarme (exc); Esther (exc); Acis and Galatea (exc); Tolomeo (exc); Orlando (exc); Athalia (exc); Deborah (exc). (D. Thomas, Philh Baroque Orch/N. McGegan)

Ⓓ **HMU90 7022** (7/92)
Spanish Songs & Theatre Music
Hidalgo: Celos aun del aire matan (exc); *Falconieri:* Primo libro di canzone (exc); *Hidalgo:* Crédito; *Selma y Salaverde:* Canzon prima a due; *Hidalgo:* En los floridos páramos; Ay amor; Templo de Palas (exc); *Selma y Salaverde:* Canzon terza; Canzon prima; *Hidalgo:* Los celos hacen estrellas (exc); *Selma y Salaverde:* Canzon ottavo. (Newberry Consort/M. Springfels)

Ⓓ **HMU90 7035** (1/93)
Sweeter than Roses - Purcell Songs
Purcell: O Solitude, Z406; St Cecilia's Day Ode, Z328 (exc); Rival Sisters, Z609 (exc); Indian Queen, Z630 (exc); If music be the food of love, Z379/3; Not all my torments, Z400; Bess of Bedlam, Z370; Oedipus, Z583 (exc); Pausanias, Z585 (exc); Birthday Ode, Z321 (exc); Lord what is man?, Z192; Sleep, Adam, sleep, Z195; Evening Hymn, Z193; Fatal hour comes on apace, Z421; St Cecilia's Day Ode, Z339 (exc); Welcome Song, Z324 (exc); Fairy Queen, Z629 (exc). (D. Minter, P. O'Dette, M. Meyerson, M. Meyerson, M. Springfels)

Ⓓ **HMU90 7036** (12/91)
Handel—Arias for Cuzzoni
Handel: Rodelinda (exc); Riccardo Primi (exc); Giulio Cesare (exc); Scipione (exc); Ottone (exc); Tamerlano (exc); Alessandro (exc); Flavio (exc). (L. Saffer, Philh Baroque Orch/N. McGegan)

Ⓓ **HMU90 7056** (3/93)
Handel—Arias for Durastanti
Handel: Agrippina (exc); Radamisto (exc); Muzio Scevola (exc); Ottone (exc); Giulio Cesare (exc); Arianna (exc). (L. Hunt, Philh Baroque Orch/N. McGegan)

Ⓓ **HMU90 7063/5** (3/93)
Handel—Agrippina
Handel: Agrippina (Cpte). (S. Bradshaw, W. Hill, L. Saffer, N. Isherwood, D. Minter, M. Dean, R. Popken, B. Szilágyi, G. Banditelli, Capella Savaria/N. McGegan)

Ⓓ **HMU90 7073/5** (3/93)
Handel—Ottone
Handel: Ottone (Cpte). (D. Minter, L. Saffer, M. Dean, J. Gondek, R. Popken, P. Spence, Freiburg Baroque Orch/N. McGegan)

Ⓓ **HMU90 7110** (4/95)
Purcell—Dido and Aeneas, etc
Purcell: Dido (Cpte); Gordian Knot Unty'd, Z597 (exc). (L. Hunt, M. Dean, L. Saffer, E. Rabiner, D. Deam, C. Brandes, R. Rainero, P. Elliott, Cambridge Clare College Ch, Philh Baroque Orch/N. McGegan)

Ⓓ **HMU90 7111/3** (6/94)
Handel—Radamisto
Handel: Radamisto (Cpte). (R. Popken, J. Gondek, L. Saffer, D. Hanchard, M. Frimmer, M. Dean, N. Cavallier, Freiburg Baroque Orch, N. McGegan (hpd/dir))

Ⓓ **HMU90 7121** (7/95)
Rameau—Orchestral Suites
Rameau: Naïs (exc); Temple de la Gloire (exc). (Philh Baroque Orch/N. McGegan)

Ⓓ **HMU90 7122** (4/95)
Lully/Philidor—Stage Works
A. Philidor: Mariage de la Grosse Cathos; *Lully:* Bourgeois gentilhomme; Cadmus; Nopces de Village. (London Ob Band, M-A. Petit/P. Goodwin)

Ⓓ **HMU90 7130/2**
Handel—Giustino
Handel: Giustino (Cpte). (M. Chance, D. Röschmann, D. Kotoski, J. Gondek, D. Ely, J. Lane, M. Padmore, D. Minter, Halle Cantamus Chbr Ch, Freiburg Baroque Orch/N. McGegan)

ⓘ **HMU90 7149**
Handel—Arias
Handel: Clori, Tirsi e Fileno (exc); Theodora (exc); Ottone (exc); Arianna (exc); Susanna (exc); Messiah (exc); Radamisto (exc); Agrippina (exc). (L. Hunt, Philh Baroque Orch/N. McGegan)

ⓘ **HMU90 7167**
Purcell & Blow—Songs & Intrumental Music
Purcell: Pavans, Z748-51 (exc); Sonatas, Z790-801 (exc); Sonatas, Z802-11 (exc); Yorkshire Feast Song, Z333 (exc); Lord, what is man?, Z192; Cupid, the slyest rogue alive, Z367; O Solitude, Z406; Amidst the shades, Z355; When first Amintas sued for a kiss, Z430; Blessed Virgin's Expostulation, Z196; Fly swift, ye hours, Z369; Bonduca, Z574 (exc); Mock Marriage, Z605 (exc); Tempest, Z631 (exc); *Blow:* It grieves me; Self-banished; Welcome, every guest. (C. Brandes, Arcadian Academy, N. McGegan (hpd/dir))

ⓘ **HMX290 1528/33(1)** (7/95)
A Purcell Companion (pt 1)
Purcell: Dido (Cpte); Funeral Sentences (exc); March and Canzona, Z860; Te Deum and Jubilate, Z232 (exc); Bell Anthem, Z49; Remember not, Lord, our offences, Z50; Blow up the Trumpet in Sion, Z10; Hear my prayer, O Lord, Z15; My heart is inditing, Z30; O Lord God of hosts, Z37; Fantasia, Z731; Sonatas, Z802-11 (exc); Pavan, Z752; Chaconne, Z730; Pavans, Z748-51; Sonatas, Z790-801 (exc); Overture, Z771; Welcome Song, Z336 (exc); Overture, Z772; Overture, Z770. (G. Laurens, P. Cantor, J. Feldman, D. Visse, A. Mellon, B. Borden, E. Lestrigant, M. Laplénie, Arts Florissants Voc Ens, Arts Florissants Instr Ens/W. Christie, T. Bonner, P. Kwella, K. Wessel, P. Agnew, W. Kendall, P. Kooy, Collegium Vocale/P. Herreweghe, London Baroque)

ⓘ **HMX290 1528/33(2)** (7/95)
A Purcell Companion (pt 2)
Purcell: King Arthur, Z628 (exc); Bonduca, Z574 (exc); Don Quixote, Z578 (exc); Fairy Queen, Z629 (exc); Indian Queen, Z630 (exc); King Arthur, Z628 (exc); King Richard II, Z581 (exc); Dioclesian, Z627 (exc); Pausanias, Z585 (exc); Oedipus, Z583 (exc); Not all my torments, Z400; Evening Hymn, Z193; Organ Voluntaries, Z717-20; Verse, Z716; Choice Collection of Lessons (exc); Grounds (exc); Voluntary on the Old 100th, Z721; Trumpet Voluntary; *Blow:* Organ Voluntaries; *Locke:* Voluntaries; *Purcell:* O Solitude, Z406; If music be the food of love, Z379/1. (H. Sheppard, J. Knibbs, R. Hardy, A. Deller, M. Deller, P. Elliott, L. Nixon, M. Bevan, N. Beavan, Deller Ch, King's Musick/A. Deller, A. Deller, W. Kuijken, W. Christie, R. Skeaping, J. Butt)

Hat-Hut

ⓘ **ARTCD6060**
Herbert Distel—La Stazione
Distel: Stazione (Cpte). (A. Schwarz, M. Meysenbug, F. Paternina, T. Fontana, V. Manzoni)

Herald

ⓘ **HAVPCD181** ▭ **HAVPC181**
The Age of Elegance
Handel: Radamisto (exc); Chaconne in G, HWV435; Keyboard Suites Set II (exc); *Haydn:* Keyboard Sonata 15; Keyboard Sonata 9; Keyboard Sonata 7. (A. Noble)

Hispavox

ⓘ **CDZ7 67328-2** (10/92)
Zarzuelas
Chapí: Revoltosa (Cpte); *Bretón:* Verbena de la Paloma (Cpte). (T. Tourné, M. R. Gabriel, A.M. Higueras, R. Cesari, M. Hernandez, R. Diez, S. Garcia, A. Viñes, T. Tourné, D. Ripolles, E. Garcia, R. Cesari, A.P. Bayod, A. Armentia, M. del Carmen Andres, M. del Pilar Alonso, J. Bermejo, A. Fernandez, J. Portillo, J.R. Henche, J.L. Cancela, Madrid Coros Cantores, Madrid Concerts Orch/P. Sorozábal/F. Moreno Torroba)

ⓘ **CDZ7 67329-2** (10/92)
Moreno Torroba—Luisa Fernanda
Moreno Torroba: Luisa Fernanda (Cpte). (T. Tourné, E. Alsina, R. Cesari, P. Lavirgen, J. Bermejo, A. Fernandez, P. Tamayo, J.R. Henche, A. Curros, S. Videras, V. Larrea, R. Campos, Hispavox Lyric Chor, Madrid Concerts Orch/F. Moreno Torroba)

ⓘ **CDZ7 67330-2** (10/92)
Sorozábal—Katiuska
Sorozábal: Katiuska (Cpte). (P. Lorengar, Alfredo Kraus, R. Cesari, M. Gas, E. Serrano, S.P. Carpio, A.M. Fernandez, F. Maroto, J. Marin, Madrid Coros Cantores, Madrid Concerts Orch/P. Sorozábal)

ⓘ **CDZ7 67453-2** (10/92)
Usandizaga—Las Golondrinas
Usandizaga: Golondrinas (Cpte). (J. Cubeiro, I. Rivas, V. Sardinero, R. Alonso, Madrid Coros Cantores, Spanish Lyric Orch/F. Moreno Torroba)

ⓘ **CDZ7 67454-2** (10/92)
Barbieri—El Barberillo de Lavapies
Barbieri: Barberillo de Lavapiès (Cpte). (M.C. Ramirez, D. Perez, L. Sagi-Vela, F. Saura, R. Alonso, L. Frutos, Madrid Coros Cantores, Spanish Lyric Orch/F. Moreno Torroba)

ⓘ **CZS7 67322-2** (10/92)
Vives—Zarzuelas
Vives: Doña Francisquita (Cpte); Bohemios (Cpte). (T. Tourné, M. R. Gabriel, P. Lavirgen, S. Garcia, J. Catania, C. Gimines, L. Frutos, A.M. Higueras, P. Lavirgen, S. Garcia, P. Farrés, M. del Carmen Ramirez, M. Oran, M. Aragon, L. Frutos, E. Fuentes, Madrid Coros Cantores, Madrid Concerts Orch/P. Sorozábal)

Hungaroton

ⓘ **HCD12850/1** (1/90)
Respighi—Belfagor
Respighi: Belfagor (Cpte). (L. Miller, S. Sass, G. Lamberti, L. Polgár, K. Takács, M. Kalmár, M. Zempléni, P.L. Bárány, Z. Komarniczky, M. Lukin, J. Tóth, Hungarian Rad & TV Chor, Hungarian St Orch/L. Gardelli)

ⓘ **HCD31197/8** (7/93)
Respighi—Semirama
Respighi: Semirama (Cpte). (E. Marton, V. Kincses, L. Bartolini, L. Miller, L. Polgár, T. Clementis, Hungarian Rad & TV Chor, Hungarian St Orch/L. Gardelli)

ⓘ **HCD31304/6** (1/93)
Handel—Floridante
Handel: Floridante (Cpte). (D. Minter, M. Zádori, I. Gáti, J. Moldvay, A. Markert, K. Farkas, Capella Savaria/N. McGegan)

ⓘ **HCD31307/8** (6/91)
Mascagni—Lodoletta
Mascagni: Lodoletta (Cpte). (M. Spacagna, A. Ulbrich, Z. Bazsinka, J. Sánta, P. Kelen, K. Szilágyi, M. Kálmándi, L. Polgár, A. Laczó, J. Mukk, Hungarian St Op Children's Chor, Hungarian Rad & TV Chor, Hungarian St Orch/C. Rosekrans)

Hyperion

ⓘ **CDA66056** (6/88)
Purcell: Songs and Dialogues
Purcell: In all our Cynthia's shining sphere, Z496; Dioclesian, Z627 (exc); Old Bachelor, Z607 (exc); Amphitryon, Z572 (exc); Go, tell Amynta, gentle swain, Z489; Why, my Daphne, why complaining, Z525; What can we poor females do, Z518; Hence, fond deceiver, Z492; In some kind dream, Z497; What a sad fate is mine, Z428; Lost is my quiet for ever, Z502; Stript of their green our groves appear, Z444; King Arthur, Z628 (exc). (E. Kirkby, D. Thomas, A. Rooley)

ⓘ **CDA66070** (12/89)
Purcell: Songs
Purcell: If music be the food of love, Z379/2; If music be the food of love, Z379/3; O! fair Cederia, Z402; Aureng-Zebe, Z573 (exc); Wedding Ode, Z325 (exc); Fly swift, ye hours, Z369; Double Dealer, Z592 (exc); Not all my torments, Z400; King Arthur, Z628 (exc); Love thou can'st hear, Z396; Dioclesian, Z627 (exc); Pausanias, Z585 (exc); Sophonisba, Z590 (exc); Ah! cruel nymph, Z352; Oedipus, Z583 (exc). (P. Esswood, J. Sonnleitner, C. Medlam)

ⓘ **CDA66090** (12/86)
Rare piano encores
Rossini: Péchés de vieillesse X (exc); *Mozart:* Don Giovanni (exc); *Gershwin:* Promenade; *Reger:* Schlichte Weisen, Op. 76 (exc); *Grainger:* Blithe bells; *Wagner:* Albumblatt; *Gaertner:* Viennese Dances (exc); *Rachmaninov:* Songs, Op. 8 (exc); *Bizet:* Carmen (exc); *Rubinstein:* Valse caprice; *Grieg:* Melodies of the Heart, Op. 5 (exc); *Bruckner:* Erinnerung; *Liszt:* Valses oubliées, S215 (exc); Soirées de Vienne, S427 (exc); Valse à capriccio, S401. (L. Howard)

ⓘ **CDA66099** (2/88)
Holst—Savitri; Songs
Holst: Sávitri (Cpte); Songs, H174. (F. Palmer, P. Langridge, S. Varcoe, Richard Hickox Sngrs, CLS/R. Hickox, P. Kwella)

ⓘ **CDA66101/2** (8/87)
Boughton—The Immortal Hour
Boughton: Immortal Hour (Cpte). (R. Kennedy, P. Taylor, Anne Dawson, D. Wilson-Johnson, V. Hill, R. Bryson, P. Taylor, R. Bryson, M. Davies (ten), G. Mitchell Ch, ECO/A. Melville)

ⓘ **CDA66108** (11/88)
Purcell's London: English Consort Music
G. Keller: Trumpet Sonatas (exc); *N. Matteis I:* Divisions on a Ground in D minor (exc); *Baltzar:* Pavan and Galliard in C (exc); *Blow:* Chaconne in G (exc); *J. Eccles:* Judgment of Paris (exc); *Anon:* Sonata in D (exc); *Croft:* Twin Rivals Suite (exc); *Purcell:* Choice Collection of Lessons (exc). (Parley of Instr/R. Goodman/P. Holman)

ⓘ **CDA66216** (11/87)
The Grand Organ
Wagner: Meistersinger (exc); *Liszt:* Consolations, S172 (exc); *Mendelssohn:* Midsummer Night's Dream (exc); Athalie (exc); *Weber:* Jubel-Ouverture; *Saint-Saëns:* Carnaval des animaux (exc); Danse Macabre; *Prokofiev:* Toccata, Op.11. (T. Trotter)

ⓘ **CDA66255** (1/89)
Italian Baroque Trumpet Music
Stradella: Trumpet Sonata; *Albrici:* 2-Trumpet Sonata; *Fantini:* Trumpet tutor (1638) (exc); *C. Pallavicino:* Diocletiano (exc); *N. Matteis I:* 3-Trumpet Concerto; *F. Mancini:* Gl'Amanti Generosi (exc); *Franceschini:* 2-Trumpet Sonata in D; *Cazzati:* Trumpet Sonatas, Op.35 (exc); *Viviani:* Capricci, Op.4 (exc); *Corelli:* Trumpet Sonata in D; *Bononcini:* Sinfonias, Op.3 (exc). (S. Keavy, C. Steele-Perkins, Parley of Instr)

ⓘ **CDA66288** (7/89)
'Mr Henry Purcell's Most Admirable Composure's'
Purcell: We sing to him, Z199; Dioclesian, Z627 (exc); How long, great God, Z189; Not all my torments, Z400; Oedipus, Z583 (exc); King Arthur, Z628 (exc); Knotting Song, Z371; Fairy Queen, Z629 (exc); Welcome Song, Z344 (exc); Tyrannic Love, Z613 (exc); Rival Sisters, Z609 (exc); Fatal hour comes on apace, Z421; If music be the food of love, Z379/1; St Cecilia's Day Ode, Z339 (exc); Evening hymn, Z193 (exc). (J. Bowman, King's Consort/R. King)

ⓘ **CDA66483** (12/91) ▭ **KA66483** (12/91)
Handel—Heroic Arias
Handel: Amadigi di Gaula (exc); Rinaldo (exc); Serse (exc); Giulio Cesare (exc); Giustino (exc); Ariodante (exc); Ottone (exc); Alcina (exc). (J. Bowman, King's Consort/R. King)

ⓘ **CDA66486** (3/92)
Rachmaninov—Piano Transcriptions
Rimsky-Korsakov: Tale of Tsar Saltan (exc); *Kreisler:* Liebesleid; Liebesfreud; *Bizet:* Arlésienne Suites (exc); *Schubert:* Schöne Müllerin (exc); *Mussorgsky:* Fair at Sorochintsï (exc); *Bach:* Solo violin partitas and sonatas (exc); *Rachmaninov:* Daisies; Lilacs; Polka de W. R.; Songs, Op.34 (exc); *Mendelssohn:* Midsummer Night's Dream (exc); *Tchaikovsky:* Songs, Op.16 (exc). (H. Shelley)

ⓘ **CDA66569** (8/92)
Vaughan Williams—Choral Works
Vaughan Williams: Song of Thanksgiving; Choral Hymns; Magnificat; Shepherds of the Delectable Mountains; Old Hundredth. (J. Gielgud, L. Dawson, L. Kitchen, C. Wyn-Rogers, J.M. Ainsley, J. Bowen, Adrian Thompson, A. Opie, B. Terfel, J. Best, John Scott, R. Judd, London Oratory Jnr Ch, Corydon Sngrs, CLS/M. Best)

ⓘ **CDA66591/2** (1/92)
Gay—The Beggar's Opera
Gay: Beggar's Opera (Cpte). (B. Mills, Adrian Thompson, Anne Dawson, R. Jackson, C. Daniels, Sarah Walker, Sarah Walker, I. Honeyman, R. Bryson, C. Wyn-Rogers, B. Hoskins, I. Caddy, Broadside Band/J. Barlow)

ⓘ **CDA66600**
Rondeaux Royaux - Baroque Pops
M-A. Charpentier: Te Deum, H146 (exc); *Bach:* Suites, BWV1066-9 (exc); *Pachelbel:* Canon and Gigue; *Handel:* Solomon (exc); Sonata a 5 (exc); Concerti a due cori (exc); Water music (exc); *Boyce:* Symphonies (exc); *Locke:* Tempest (exc); *Purcell:* Fairy Queen, Z629 (exc); Abdelazer, Z570 (exc); *Clarke:* Suite in D (exc); *Gallo:* Trio Sonatas (exc); *Corelli:* Concerti grossi, Op.6 (exc); *Albinoni:* Concerti, Op.9 (exc); *Vivaldi:* Concerto, RV540 (exc); *Rameau:* Dardanus (exc); Indes Galantes (exc); *Fux:* Rondeau a 7; *Georg Muffat:* Concerto grosso in G (exc); *Telemann:* Recorder and Flute Concerto (exc); Trumpet Concerto (exc); *Bach:* Cantata 21 (exc); Easter Oratorio, BWV249 (exc). (Brandenburg Consort/R. Goodman)

ⓘ **CDA66605** (10/92)
Organ Fireworks, Vol.4
D. Johnson: Trumpet tune in A; *Lemare:* Toccata di Concerto, Op.59; *Buck:* Star-Spangled Banner Variations, Op.23; *Guilmant:* Judas Maccabaeus paraphrase; *Whitlock:* Pieces for organ (exc); *D. Bourgeois:* Howells Variations, Op. 87; *Vierne:* Pièces en stile libre (exc); *Batiste:* Grand offertoire in D; *Shostakovich:* Lady Macbeth

of Mtsensk (exc); *Bonnet:* Pièces nouvelles, Op.7 (exc); *Widor:* Symphony 6 (exc); *Lefébure-Wély:* Sortie in E flat. (C. Herrick)

Ⓓ **CDA66608** (5/93)
Dibdin—Three Operas
Dibdin: Ephesian Matron (Cpte); Brickdust Man (Cpte); Grenadier (Cpte). (B. Mills, J. Streeton, M. Padmore, A. Knight, Y. Barclay, K. West, S. Bisatt, K. West, A. Mayor, Opera Restor'd/P. Holman)

Ⓓ **CDA66667** (6/94)
Four and Twenty Fiddlers
Locke: Curtain Tune in C; Curtain Tune in D; Suite of Brawles; Suite in G minor; Tempest (exc); *Banister:* Musick att the Bath; *Grabu:* Valentinian (exc); Albion and Albanius (exc); *Purcell:* Staircase Overture; Chaconne, Z730. (Parley of Instr/P. Holman)

Ⓓ **CDA66690** (4/94)
Rutland Boughton—Bethlehem
Boughton: Bethlehem (Cpte). (H. Field, R. Bryan, R. Bryson, R. Evans, J. Bowen, A. Peacock, A. Opie, J. MacDougall, R. Van Allan, C. Seaton, C. Campbell, I. Boughton, G. Matheson-Bruce, Holst Sngrs, New London Children's Ch, CLS/A. Melville)

Ⓓ **CDA66704** (3/95)
Bruckner/R. Strauss—Chamber Works
Bruckner: String Quintet; Intermezzo and Trio; *R. Strauss:* Capriccio (exc). (Raphael Ens)

Ⓓ **CDA66745** (5/95) ▭ **KA66745**
Vivaldi—Opera Arias and Sinfonias
Vivaldi: Griselda (exc); Tito Manlio (exc); Ottone in Villa (exc); Atenaide (exc); Bajazet (exc); Incoronazione di Dario (exc); Catone in Utica (exc). (E. Kirkby, L. Mazzarri, Brandenburg Consort/R. Goodman)

Ⓓ **CDA66749** (4/95)
Tippett—Songs and Purcell Realisations
Purcell: If music be the food of love, Z379/2; Fairy Queen, Z629 (exc); Fatal hour comes on apace, Z421; Bess of Bedlam, Z370; Pausanias, Z585 (exc); *Tippett:* Music; Songs for Ariel; Songs for Achilles; Boyhood's End; Heart's Assurance. (M. Hill, C. Ogden, A. Ball)

Ⓓ **CDA66751/3** (7/93)
Handel—Ottone
Handel: Ottone (Cpte). (J. Bowman, C. McFadden, M. George, J. Smith, D. Visse, C. Denley, King's Consort/R. King)

Ⓓ **CDA66759**
Lampe—Pyramus and Thisbe
Lampe: Cuckoo Concerto; Pyramus and Thisbe (Cpte). (M. Padmore, S. Bisatt, M. Sanderson, A. Treharne, A. Knight, P. Milne, A. McMahon, J. Edwards, P. Hyde, C. Baldy, R. Brown, Opera Restor'd/P. Holman)

Ⓓ **CDA66764** (5/95)
Alexander Mackenzie—Orchestral Music
Mackenzie: Cricket on the Hearth (exc); Twelfth Night, Op. 40; Benedictus; Scottish Rhapsody 2; Coriolanus Suite. (BBC Scottish SO/M. Brabbins)

Ⓓ **CDA66800** (11/95)
Arriaga/Voříšek—Symphonies
Arriaga: Symphony in D; Esclavos felices (exc); *Voříšek:* Symphony, Op. 24. (Scottish CO/C. Mackerras)

Ⓓ **CDA66803** (8/95)
Chabrier—Briséïs, ou Les amants de Corinthe
Chabrier: Briséïs (Cpte). (J. Rodgers, M. Padmore, S. Keenlyside, M. George, K. Harries, Scottish Op Chor, BBC Scottish SO/J. Y. Ossonce)

Ⓓ **CDA66901/2** (10/94)
Vaughan Williams—Hugh the Drover
Vaughan Williams: Hugh the Drover (Cpte). (B. Bottone, R. Evans, R. Van Allan, A. Opie, Sarah Walker, N. Jenkins, R. Poulton, K. M. Daymond, H. Nicoll, A. Hutton, J. Gooding, W. Evans, J. Saunders, A. Coote, L. Atkinson, P. Robinson, J. Pearce, P. Im Thurn, New London Children's Ch, Corydon Sngrs, Corydon Orch/M. Best)

Ⓓ **CDA67001/3** (10/95)
Purcell—Complete Ayres for the Theatre
Purcell: Dioclesian Suite (1697); King Arthur Suite (1697); Fairy Queen Suite (1697); Indian Queen Suite; Married Beau, Z603 (exc); Old Bachelor, Z607 (exc); Amphitryon, Z572 (exc); Double Dealer, Z592 (exc); Distressed Innocence, Z577; Gordian Knot Unty'd, Z597; Abdelazer, Z570 (exc); Bonduca, Z574 (exc); Virtuous Wife, Z611; Sonata While the Sun Rises, Z629/27; Overture, Z631/1; Sir Anthony Love, Z588 (exc); Timon of Athens, Z632 (exc); Indian Queen, Z630 (exc). (Parley of Instr, Parley of Instr Baroque Orch)

Ⓓ **CDA67061/2** (11/95)
Britten—Purcell Realizations
Purcell: Knotting Song, Z371; King Arthur, Z628 (exc); If music be the food of love, Z379/3; Turn then thine eyes, Z425; Oedipus, Z583 (exc); Pious Celinda, Z410; Fool's Preferment, Z571 (exc); On the brow of Richmond Hill, Z405; Bess of Bedlam, Z370; If music be the food of love, Z379/1; Rule a Wife and Have a Wife, Z587 (exc); Not all my torments, Z400; Mock Marriage, Z605 (exc); Pausanias, Z585 (exc); O Solitude, Z406; Indian Queen, Z630 (exc); I take no pleasure, Z388; Fairy Queen, Z629 (exc); Rival Sisters, Z609 (exc); Oroonoko, Z584 (exc); Birthday Ode, Z323 (exc); I spy Celia, Z499; Lost is my quiet for ever, Z502; What can we poor females do, Z518; Maid's Last Prayer, Z601 (exc); Queen's Epicedium, Z383; Blessed Virgin's Expostulation, Z196; In guilty night, Z134; Lord, what is man?, Z192; We sing to him, Z199; Evening Hymn, Z193; Job's Curse, Z191; Morning Hymn, Z198; In the black dismal dungeon of despair, Z190; Dulcibella, Z485; When Myra sings, Z521; Don Quixote, Z578 (exc); *Weldon:* O Lord, rebuke me not (exc). (F. Lott, S. Gritton, Sarah Walker, J. Bowman, J. M. Ainsley, I. Bostridge, A. Rolfe Johnson, R. Jackson, S. Keenlyside, G. Johnson)

Ⓓ **CDH88030** ▭ **KH88030**
Favourite Classics
Bach: Suites, BWV1066-9 (exc); *Gluck:* Orfeo ed Euridice (exc); *Tchaikovsky:* Andante cantabile, Op.11; *Elgar:* Salut d'amour; *Handel:* Solomon (exc); *Fauré:* Shylock Suite (exc); *Boccherini:* String Quintets, G271-6 (exc); *Tchaikovsky:* Nocturne, Op. 19/4; *Pachelbel:* Canon and Gigue; *Borodin:* String Quartet 2 (exc); *Gounod:* Ave maria; *Massenet:* Vierge (exc); *Mozart:* Andante, K315; *Dvořák:* Nocturne; *Clarke:* Suite in D (exc). (London Fest Orch/R. Pople)

Ⓓ **CDJ33009** (1/91) ▭ **KJ33009** (1/91)
Schubert: Complete Lieder, Vol.9
Schubert: Misero pargoletto, D42; Didone abbandonata, D510; Vierjährige Posten (exc); Claudine von Villa Bella (exc); Verschworenen (exc); Rosamunde (exc); Blanka, D631; Daphne am Bach, D411; Lambertine, D301; Thekla, D595; Lied der Delphine, D857/1; Canzonen, D688; Pastorella al Prato, D528; Sänger am Felsen, D482; Gute Hirt, D449; Lilla an die Morgenröte, D273; Hirt auf dem Felsen, D965. (A. Auger, T. King, G. Johnson)

Ⓓ **CDS44041/8** (3/94)
Rachmaninov—Complete Piano Music
Rachmaninov: Morceaux de fantaisie, Op.3; Preludes (exc); Prelude (1891); Prelude (1917); Morceaux de salon, Op.10; Moments musicaux, Op.16; Piano Sonata 2; Morceau de fantaisie (1899); Song Without Words (?1887); Pièce (1917); Fughetta (1899); Fragments (1917); Oriental Sketch (1917); Nocturnes (1887/8); Pièces (?1887); Etudes-tableaux, Op.33; Etudes-tableaux, Op.39; Piano Sonata 1; Piano Sonata 2; Chopin Variations, Op.22; Corelli Variations; Morceaux de fantaisie, Op.3 (exc); *Mendelssohn:* Midsummer Night's Dream (exc); *Rimsky-Korsakov:* Tale of Tsar Saltan (exc); *Kreisler:* Liebesleid; Liebesfreud; *Bizet:* Arlésienne Suites (exc); *Schubert:* Schöne Müllerin (exc); *Mussorgsky:* Fair at Sorochintsï (exc); *Bach:* Solo Violin Partitas and Sonatas (exc); *Rachmaninov:* Daisies; Lilacs; Polka de W.R.; Songs, Op.34 (exc); *Mendelssohn:* Midsummer Night's Dream (exc); *Tchaikovsky:* Songs, Op.16 (exc). (H. Shelley)

Ⓓ **KING 1**
Music of the King's Consort
Handel: Birthday Ode for Queen Anne (exc); Fireworks Music (exc); Joshua (exc); Acis and Galatea (exc); Amadigi di Gaula (exc); *Albinoni:* Concerti, Op.9 (exc); *G. Gabrieli:* Symphoniae sacrae II (exc); *Purcell:* Wedding Ode, Z325 (exc); St Cecilia's Day Ode, Z328 (exc); Birthday Ode, Z332 (exc); Birthday Ode, Z323 (exc); *Dowland:* First Book of Songs (exc); *Telemann:* Musique de Table (exc); Oboe Concerto 4 (exc); *Vivaldi:* Concerto, RV560 (exc); *Bach:* Cantata 170 (exc); Violin and Oboe Concerto, BWV1060 (exc); *Pergolesi:* Stabat mater (exc); *Mozart:* Church Sonatas (exc); *Schütz:* Christmas Story, SWV435 (exc). (King's Consort/R. King)

Ⓓ **KING2**
Essential Purcell
Purcell: Birthday Ode, Z338; Welcome Song, Z324 (exc); O! fair Cederia, Z402; Hear my prayer, O Lord, Z15; Dido (exc); Let mine eyes, Z24; Wedding Ode, Z325 (exc); If music be the food of love, Z379/1; Bell Anthem, Z49; Hosanna to the highest, Z187; Funeral Sentences (exc); King Arthur, Z628 (exc); St Cecilia's Day Ode, Z334 (exc); Birthday Ode, Z323 (exc); She loves, Z413; Welcome Song, Z343 (exc); Remember not, Lord, our offences, Z50; Evening hymn, Z193; Te Deum and Jubilate, Z232 (exc); St Cecilia's Day Ode, Z328 (exc). (B. Bonney, G. Fisher, S. Gritton, E. O'Dwyer, N. Witcomb, J. Bowman, M. Chance, J. M. Ainsley, R. Covey-Crump, C. Daniels, M. Padmore, M. George, New College Ch, King's Consort Ch, King's Consort/R. King)

IMG Records

Ⓓ **IMGCD1603**
Prokofiev—Orchestral Works
Prokofiev: Love for 3 Oranges Suite; Symphony 1; Lt Kijé Suite (exc). (LPO/E. Bátiz)

Ⓓ **IMGCD1610**
Borodin/Stravinsky—Orchestral Works
Borodin: Prince Igor (exc); *Stravinsky:* Petrushka (Cpte); Circus Polka; Fireworks. (Mexico St SO/E. Bátiz, RPO)

Ⓓ **IMGCD1611**
Wagner/Mussorgsky/Beethoven—Orchestral Works
Wagner: Lohengrin (exc); Walküre (exc); Tristan und Isolde (exc); Meistersinger (exc); *Mussorgsky:* Khovanshchina (exc); Night on the Bare Mountain; *Beethoven:* Prometheus (exc); Coriolan; Egmont (exc). (Sydney SO/J. Serebrier)

Ⓓ **IMGCD1617**
Tchaikovsky—Gala 2
Tchaikovsky: Sleeping Beauty (exc); Eugene Onegin (exc); Swan Lake (exc); Nutcracker (exc); Festival Coronation March; Jurists' March; Marche slave; Souvenir d'un lieu cher, Op. 42 (exc); Elegy; Andante cantabile, Op. 11. (Brno St PO, RPO/J. Serebrier)

Ⓓ **IMGCD1801** (10/93) ▭ **IMGMC1801** (10/93)
Bernstein—West Side Story
Bernstein: West Side Story (Cpte). (B. Bonney, M. Ball, L. Williams, C. Howard, M. Carewe, L. Gibson, J. O'Grady, D. Chessor, L. Benson, A. Busher, J. Graeme, M. Pearn, Royal Phil Chor, RPO/B. Wordsworth)

IMP

Ⓓ **BOXD9**
Essential Mozart—Symphonies and Overtures
Mozart: Symphony 31; Symphony 38; Symphony 29; Symphony 32; Symphony 33; Symphony 27; Symphony 28; Symphony 34; Sinfonia concertante, K297b; Nozze di Figaro (exc); Finta giardiniera (exc); Symphony 25. (English Sinfonia/C. Groves, C. O'Neal, K. Puddy, B. Sewell, M. Baines)

Ⓓ **DPCD1015** ▭ **CIMPCD1015**
Karaoke Opera
Bizet: Carmen (exc); Pêcheurs de Perles (exc); *Saint-Saëns:* Samson et Dalila (exc); *Offenbach:* Contes d'Hoffmann (exc); *Rossini:* Barbiere di Siviglia (exc); *Verdi:* Traviata (exc); Rigoletto (exc); *Mozart:* Don Giovanni (exc); *Leoncavallo:* Pagliacci (exc); *Puccini:* Madama Butterfly (exc); Bohème (exc); Gianni Schicchi (exc); Turandot (exc). (S. McCulloch, A-M. Owens, J. Oakman, S. Page, Prague Phil Chor, Czech PO/J. Bigg)

Ⓓ **DPCD998**
Opera Stars in Concert
Verdi: Vespri siciliani (exc); *Bellini:* Puritani (exc); *Verdi:* Traviata (exc); *Offenbach:* Contes d'Hoffmann (exc); *Puccini:* Tosca (exc); *Rossini:* Semiramide (exc); *Donizetti:* Lucrezia Borgia (exc); *Verdi:* Don Carlo (exc); *Gounod:* Faust (exc); *Bizet:* Carmen Suites (exc); *Donizetti:* Elisir d'amore (exc); *Verdi:* Rigoletto (exc); Ballo in maschera (exc); *Puccini:* Gianni Schicchi (exc); *Rossini:* Barbiere di Siviglia (exc); *Cilea:* Arlesiana (exc); *Bizet:* Carmen (exc). (K. Ricciarelli, L.V. Terrani, Alfredo Kraus, P. Coni, R. Raimondi, Madrid SO/G.P. Sanzogno)

Ⓓ **DUET 10CD**
Popular Ballet Music
Chopin: Sylphides; *Adam:* Giselle (exc); *Delibes:* Coppélia (exc); Sylvia (exc); *Bizet:* Arlésienne Suites; *Saint-Saëns:* Samson et Dalila (exc). (Philadelphia/E. Ormandy)

Ⓓ **DUET 15CD**
Mozart: Favourites
Mozart: Nozze di Figaro (exc); Symphony 40; Serenade, K525; Zauberflöte (exc); Piano Concerto 21 (exc); Piano Concerto 20. (Cleveland Orch, Philadelphia, Columbia SO, R. Casadesus, R. Serkin/G. Szell/E. Ormandy/B. Walter)

Ⓓ **DUET 4CD**
Rimsky-Korsakov: Orchestral Works
Rimsky-Korsakov: Golden Cockerel Suite (exc); Capriccio Espagnol; Christmas Eve (exc); Snow Maiden (exc); Scheherazade. (Philadelphia/E. Ormandy)

Ⓓ **DUET 8CD**
Tchaikovsky: Orchestral Works
Tchaikovsky: Capriccio Italien; Eugene Onegin (exc); Serenade, Op.48; Romeo and Juliet; 1812. (Mormon Tabernacle Ch, Philadelphia/E. Ormandy)

GLRS102
The Magnificent Gigli
Ponchielli: Gioconda (exc); *Donizetti:* Elisir d'amore (exc); Lucia di Lammermoor (exc); *Flotow:* Martha (exc); *Meyerbeer:* Africaine (exc); *Puccini:* Manon Lescaut (exc); Bohème (exc); Bohème (exc); *Boito:* Mefistofele (exc); *Bizet:* Pêcheurs de Perles (exc); *Gounod:* Faust (exc); *Niedermeyer:* Pietà, Signore; *Grieg:* Songs, Op.48 (exc); *Drigo:* Arlekinda (exc); *Mascagni:* Cavalleria Rusticana (exc). (B. Gigli, E. Pinza, G. De Luca, orch, NY Met Op Chor, NY Met Op Orch/G. Setti/E. Goossens, La Scala Orch/C. Sabajno, Berlin St Op Orch/B. Seidler-Winkler)

GLRS103 (9/94)
The Magnificent Björling
Verdi: Rigoletto (exc); *Puccini:* Tosca (exc); *Verdi:* Aida (exc); *Puccini:* Bohème (exc); *Verdi:* Trovatore (exc); *Meyerbeer:* Africaine (exc); *Puccini:* Fanciulla del West (exc); Tosca (exc); *Flotow:* Martha (exc); *Massenet:* Manon (exc); *Bizet:* Carmen (exc); *Gounod:* Faust (exc); *Di Capua:* O sole mio; *Tosti:* Ideale; *J. Strauss II:* Zigeunerbaron (exc); *Millöcker:* Bettelstudent (exc); *Offenbach:* Belle Hélène (exc); *Verdi:* Requiem (exc); *Rossini:* Stabat Mater (exc). (J. Björling, H. Schymberg, orch/N. Grevillius)

GLRS105
The Magnificent Flagstad
Wagner: Walküre (exc); Walküre (exc); Tristan und Isolde (exc); Tannhäuser (exc); Lohengrin (exc); Lohengrin (exc); *Beethoven:* Fidelio (exc); Ah! perfido, Op.65; *Weber:* Oberon (exc). (K. Flagstad, Philadelphia/E. Ormandy, orch/H. Lange)

GLRS106
Kreisler plays Kreisler
Kreisler: Liebesleid; Liebesfreud; Caprice viennois; Gypsy caprice; Schön Rosmarin; Tambourin chinois; Shepherd's madrigal; *Massenet:* Thaïs (exc); *Dvořák:* Humoresques, Op.101 (exc); *Lehár:* Frasquita (exc); *Dvořák:* Slavonic Dances (exc); *Foster:* Old Folks at Home; *Tchaikovsky:* String Quartet 1 (exc); *Albéniz:* España, Op.165 (exc); *Rimsky-Korsakov:* Golden Cockerel (exc); *Kreisler:* Beethoven Rondino; *C. Scott:* Pieces, Op.47 (exc); *Drdla:* Souvenir. (F. Kreisler, C. Lamson, F. Rupp)

MCD15 (10/90) **MCC15** (10/90)
Opera Spectacular
Bizet: Carmen (exc); Pêcheurs de Perles (exc); *Gounod:* Faust (exc); *Delibes:* Lakmé (exc); *Leoncavallo:* Pagliacci (exc); *Puccini:* Gianni Schicchi (exc); Madama Butterfly (exc); Tosca (exc); Turandot (exc); *Rossini:* Barbiere di Siviglia (exc); *Verdi:* Nabucco (exc); Rigoletto (exc); Trovatore (exc); *Wagner:* Walküre (exc). (V. Masterson, C. Powell, E. Barham, A. Michaels-Moore, ROH Chor, RPO/R. Stapleton)

MCD42
Three Sopranos
Bellini: Norma (exc); *Leoncavallo:* Pagliacci (exc); *Puccini:* Villi (exc); *Saint-Saëns:* Samson et Dalila (exc); *Puccini:* Bohème (exc); *Verdi:* Ballo in maschera (exc); *Offenbach:* Contes d'Hoffmann (exc); *Puccini:* Gianni Schicchi (exc); *Gastaldon:* Musica proibita; *Tosti:* A vucchella; *Bizet:* Carmen (exc); *J. Strauss II:* Fledermaus (exc); *Verdi:* Aida (exc). (R. Scotto, I. Cotrubas, E. Obraztsova, Czech SO/A. Krieger)

MCD43
Domingo Live from Miami
Meyerbeer: Africaine (exc); *Donizetti:* Lucia di Lammermoor (exc); Don Pasquale (exc); Elisir d'amore (exc); *Puccini:* Manon Lescaut (exc); Tosca (exc); Gianni Schicchi (exc); *Sorozábal:* Del Manojo de Rosas (exc); *Moreno Torroba:* Luisa Fernanda (exc); *Giménez:* Boda de Luis Alonso (exc); *Penella:* Gato Montés (exc). (P. Domingo, A. Panagulias, Miami SO/E. Kohn)

MCD45 (11/92)
Spanish Royal Gala
Chueca: Bateo (exc); Gran Via (exc); *Moreno Torroba:* Luisa Fernanda (exc); *Barbieri:* Barberillo de Lavapiès (exc); *Chapí:* Puñado de Rosas (exc); *Giménez:* Tempranica (exc); *Soutullo:* Ultimo Romantico (exc); *Vives:* Doña Francisquita (exc); *Serrano:* Claveles (exc); *Sorozábal:* Tabernera del Puerto (exc); *Bretón:* Dolores (exc); *Guerrero (y Torres):* Huésped del Sevillano (exc); Gavilanes (exc). (G. Sanchez, T. Verdera, P. Perez Inigo, P. Domingo, chor, Madrid SO/E. G. Asensio)

MCD64
Tchaikovsky—Soprano Arias
Tchaikovsky: Cherevichki (exc); Queen of Spades (exc); Iolanta (exc); Maid of Orleans (exc); Eugene Onegin (exc); Oprichnik (exc); Enchantress (exc); Maid of Orleans (exc); Mazeppa (exc). (C. Farley, Melbourne SO, Sicilian SO/J. Serebrier)

MCD75 (8/94)
Copland/Gershwin—Orchestral Works
Copland: Rodeo (exc); Billy the Kid Suite; *Gershwin:* Porgy and Bess Suite. (Bournemouth SO/J. Farrer)

MCD76
Nettle and Markham in America
Bernstein: West Side Story (exc); *R. R. Bennett:* Four-Piece Suite; *Grainger:* Porgy and Bess Fantasy. (D. Nettle, Richard Markham)

MCD81
Mendelssohn—Orchestral Works
Mendelssohn: Symphony 1; Hochzeit des Camacho (exc); Hebrides; Meeresstille; Athalie (exc); Trumpet Ov. (Philh/F. d'Avalos)

MCD82 (1/95)
Russian Masterpieces
Rimsky-Korsakov: Tale of Tsar Saltan (exc); *Mussorgsky:* Pictures; *Balakirev:* Islamey; Overture on Russian Themes; *Rachmaninov:* Isle of the Dead. (Philh/D.V. Yu)

MCD88
Mendelssohn—Symphonies and Overtures
Mendelssohn: Symphony 3; Symphony 4; Ruy Blas; Heimkehr aus der Fremde (exc). (Philh/F. D'Avalos)

ORCD11006 **ORZC11006**
Classical Masterpieces
Rossini: Guillaume Tell (exc); *Rimsky-Korsakov:* Scheherazade (exc); *Sibelius:* Karelia Suite (exc); *Vaughan Williams:* Greensleeves Fantasia; *Holst:* Planets (exc); *Ravel:* Daphnis et Chloe1 Suites (exc); *R. Strauss:* Don Juan. (RPO, LSO, New Finnish SO, Scottish CO/M. Reed/J. Mauceri/J. Engstrom/W. Boettcher/R. Hickox/Vladimir Ashkenazy/Y. Butt)

ORCD11009 **ORZC11009**
The Magnificent Organ
Bach: Toccata and Fugue, BWV565; *Daquin:* Nouveau livre de noëls (exc); *Clarke:* Suite in D (exc); *Handel:* Berenice (exc); Water Music (exc); *W. Davies:* Solemn Melody; *Lemare:* Andantino; *Traditional:* Londonderry Air; *Sullivan:* Lost Chord; *Boëllmann:* Suite Gothique; *Widor:* Symphony 5 (exc). (Barry Rose, C. Dearnley, F. Jackson)

ORCD11010 **ORZC11010**
Baroque Beauties
Handel: Solomon (exc); *Daquin:* Premier livre de pièces de clavecin (exc); *Handel:* Serse (exc); Water Music (exc); *Bach:* Suites, BWV1066-9 (exc); Cantata 208 (exc); *Pachelbel:* Canon and Gigue (exc); *Bach:* Brandenburg Concertos (exc); *Purcell:* Oedipus, Z583 (exc); *Albinoni:* Adagio. (E. Ritchie, J. Bowman, J. Purvis, J. Ogdon, B. Lucas, R. Aldwinckle, Scottish CO/J. Laredo, King's Consort/R. King, CLS/R. Hickox, ECO/P. Ledger)

ORCD11015 **ORZC11015**
Magic of Vienna
M. Rosenthal: Strauss Fantasia; *J. Strauss II:* Blauen Donau, Op.314; Rosen aus dem Süden; Fledermaus (exc); Wiener Blut; Unter Donner und Blitz; Champagner, Op.211; Radetzky March. (J. Weber, RPO/M. Reed, LSO, London Concert Orch/J. Georgiadis)

PCDS012 **PCDSC012**
Instruments of the Orchestra - Master Sampler
Britten: Young Person's Guide (exc); *Mozart:* Serenade, K525 (exc); *Gershwin:* American in Paris (exc); *Holst:* Planets (exc); *Mozart:* Sinfonia concertante, K297b (exc); *Vaughan Williams:* Greensleeves Fantasia; *Bizet:* Carmen (exc); *Massenet:* Thaïs (exc); *Fauré:* Requiem (exc); *Albinoni:* Adagio; *Rachmaninov:* Paganini Rhapsody (exc); *Copland:* Fanfare for the Common Man; *Mussorgsky:* Pictures (exc); *Elgar:* Pomp and Circumstance Marches (exc). (RPO/E. Bátiz, Serenata of London, LSO/R. Williams/R. Hickox, English Sinfonia/C. Groves, Scottish CO/W. Boettcher/R. Frühbeck de Burgos, LSC, J. Laredo, S. Costa/C. Seaman/Carl Davis/B. Tuckwell)

PCDS013 **PCDSC013**
Instruments of the Orchestra - Strings
Britten: Young Person's Guide (exc); *Vaughan Williams:* Greensleeves Fantasia; *Mendelssohn:* Violin Concerto, Op. 64 (exc); *Borodin:* String Quartet 2 (exc); *Elgar:* Cello Concerto (exc); *Mozart:* Flute and Harp Concerto, K299 (exc); *J. Strauss II:* G'schichten aus dem Wienerwald, Op. 325 (exc); Pizzicato Polka; *Rodrigo:* Concierto de Aranjuez (exc); *Walton:* Henry V Suite (exc); *Saint-Saëns:* Carnaval des animaux (exc); *Mozart:* Serenade, K525 (exc); *Barber:* Adagio for Strings; *Massenet:* Thaïs (exc). (RPO/E. Bátiz, Scottish CO/W. Boettcher, Vienna Pops Orch/L. Villinger, J. Laredo (vn/dir), Zagreb Sols/T. Ninič, P. Tortelier/C. Groves, Philippa Davies, R. Masters, CLS/R. Hickox, LSO/J. Georgiadis, M. Conn, St John's Smith Square Orch/J. Lubbock/A. Previn/B. Wordsworth, Serenata of London, ECCO/E. Aadland)

PCDS014 **PCDSC014**
Instruments of the Orchestra - Woodwind
Britten: Young Person's Guide (exc); *Mozart:* Sinfonia concertante, K297b (exc); *Debussy:* Après-midi (exc); *Mussorgsky:* Pictures (exc); *Dvořák:* Symphony 9 (exc); *Telemann:* Essercizii Musici (exc); *Bach:* Suites, BWV1066-9 (exc); *Mozart:* Clarinet Quintet, K581 (exc); *Sibelius:* Legends (exc); *Mozart:* Oboe Quartet, K370 (exc); *Sousa:* Stars and Stripes Forever; *Delius:* First cuckoo; *Vivaldi:* Concerto, RV409 (exc); *Bizet:* Carmen (exc); *Vivaldi:* Concerti, Op. 10 (exc). (RPO/E. Bátiz, C. O'Neal, K. Puddy, B. Sewell, M. Baines, English Sinfonia/C. Groves, LSO/R. Frühbeck de Burgos/R. Williams/B. Tuckwell, B. Kol, A. Brodo, D. Shemer, J. Dower, London Bach Orch, Gabrieli Qt/C. Mackerras, D. Boyd/M. Reed, C. Gonella, G. Sollima, ECCO/E. Aadland, J. Hall, London Divertimenti/P. Barritt)

PCDS016 **PCDSC016**
Instruments of the Orchestra - Percussion
Britten: Young Person's Guide (exc); *Holst:* Planets (exc); *Walton:* Henry V Suite (exc); *J. Strauss II:* Unter Donner und Blitz; *Shostakovich:* Symphony 5 (exc); *Gershwin:* American in Paris (exc); *Walton:* Belshazzar's Feast (exc); *Orff:* Carmina Burana (exc); *Bizet:* Carmen Suites (exc); *Ravel:* Boléro (exc). (RPO/E. Bátiz, LSO/R. Hickox/A. Previn/J. Georgiadis, Hallé/S. Skrowaczewski/R. Williams, B. Luxon, Brighton Fest Chor, London Collegium Musicum, P. Walmsley-Clark, Southend Boys' Ch, LSC/R. Frühbeck de Burgos)

PCDS018 **PCDSC018**
Instruments of the Orchestra - The Orchestra
Britten: Young Person's Guide (exc); *Suppé:* Leichte Kavallerie (exc); *Khachaturian:* Gayaneh (exc); *Beethoven:* Symphony 5 (exc); *Bizet:* Carmen Suites (exc); *Mozart:* Symphony 40 (exc); *Walton:* Henry V Suite (exc); *Saint-Saëns:* Carnaval des animaux (exc); *Handel:* Water Music (exc); *Brahms:* Haydn Variations; *Falla:* Amor Brujo (exc); *Tchaikovsky:* Capriccio Italien; *Elgar:* Pomp and Circumstance Marches (exc). (RPO/E. Bátiz/M. Reed, LSO/Y. Ahronovitch/W. Morris/R. Frühbeck de Burgos, St John's Smith Square Orch/J. Lubbock/A. Previn/B. Wordsworth, CLS/R. Hickox, Hallé/S. Skrowaczewski/K. Koizumi/B. Tuckwell)

PCDS10 **PCDSC10**
Discover the Classics—Power and Glory
Bach: Toccata and Fugue, BWV565; *Elgar:* Pomp and Circumstance Marches (exc); *Holst:* Planets (exc); *Beethoven:* Piano Concerto 5 (exc); *Chopin:* Etudes (exc); *Handel:* Messiah (exc); *Verdi:* Aida (exc); *Gounod:* Faust (exc); *Tchaikovsky:* Storm; 1812 (exc); *Beethoven:* Symphony 9 (exc). (D. Hill, LSO, B. Tuckwell/R. Hickox, C. Ortiz, CLS, Scottish Phil Sngrs, Scottish CO/G. Malcolm, LSC/G. Rozhdestvensky/Y. Ahronovitch, A. Hargan, D. Jones, D. Rendall, G. Howell/W. Morris)

PCDS11
English Sinfonia - 30th Anniversary
Mozart: Symphony 25 (exc); *Elgar:* Chanson de Matin; *Schubert:* Zwillingsbrüder (exc); *Haydn:* Symphony 92 (exc); *Schubert:* Symphony 5 (exc); *Mozart:* Symphony 28 (exc); *Schubert:* Rosamunde (exc); *Mozart:* Symphony 29 (exc); *Warlock:* Capriol Suite (exc); *Haydn:* Symphony 104 (exc); *Fauré:* Masques et Bergamasques (exc); *Mozart:* Nozze di Figaro (exc); *Schubert:* Symphony 3 (exc). (English Sinfonia/C. Groves)

PCDS15 **PCDSC15**
Instruments of the Orchestra - Brass
Britten: Young Person's Guide (exc); *Copland:* Fanfare for the Common Man; *Haydn:* Trumpet Concerto (exc); *Bizet:* Carmen Suites (exc); *Mussorgsky:* Pictures (exc); *Wagner:* Walküre (exc); *Elgar:* Enigma Variations (exc); *Vivaldi:* Concerto, RV539 (exc); *Tchaikovsky:* Symphony 5 (exc); *Clarke:* Suite in D (exc); *Orff:* Carmina Burana (exc); *Mozart:* Horn Concerti (exc); *Beethoven:* Symphony 3 (exc); *Verdi:* Aida (exc). (RPO/E. Bátiz/Carl Davis, C. Steele-Perkins, ECO/A. Halstead, LSO/R. Frühbeck de Burgos/R. Williams/B. Tuckwell, F. Lloyd, H. Johnstone, Scottish CO/J. Laredo/K. Koizumi, G. Ashton, L. Pearson, Southend Boys' Ch, LSC/R. Hickox, R. Watkins, CLS/W. Morris)

PCDS19 **PCDSC19**
Music of the World - This Sceptred Isle
Elgar: Pomp and Circumstance Marches (exc); *Delius:* First cuckoo; *Britten:* Folk Songs (exc); *Holst:* Planets (exc); *Vaughan Williams:* Tallis Fantasia; *Handel:* Coronation Anthems (exc); *Grainger:* Handel in the Strand; *Sullivan:* Orpheus with his Lute; *Elgar:* Salut d'Amour; Enigma Variations; *Clarke:* Suite in D (exc); *Purcell:* Dido (exc); *A. Lloyd Webber:* Requiem (exc); *Britten:* Frank Bridge Variations (exc); *Vaughan Williams:* English Folk Song Suite; *Holst:* St Paul's Suite; *Walton:* Henry V Suite (exc); *Vaughan Williams:* Old Hundredth. (LSO/B. Tuckwell, English Sinfonia/C. Groves, P. Esswood, J.

Ridgway/R. Hickox, Scottish CO/W. Boettcher, Regent Chbr Ch, CLS/G. Cole, D. Nettle, Richard Markham, E. Ritchie, J. Purvis, W. Bouton, L. Hall, G. Ashton, L. Pearson, King's Consort, R. King (treb/dir), G. Fisher, G. Moralee, F. Wight, Rosebery Chor, Rosebery CO/J.Farrer, R. Canter/J. Judd, RPO/A. Previn, Westminster Abbey Ch, London Brass/M. Neary)

PCDS20 **PCDSC20**
Music of the World—Germany—Rhine Magic
Bach: Toccata and Fugue, BWV565; *Beethoven:* Symphony 7 (exc); *Bach:* Brandenburg Concertos (exc); *Joachim:* Violin Concerto, Op. 11 (exc); *Brahms:* Academic Festival Overture (exc); *Pachelbel:* Canon and Gigue (exc); *Mendelssohn:* Hebrides; *Schumann:* Piano Concerto (exc); *R. Strauss:* Don Juan (exc); *Orff:* Carmina Burana (exc); *Beethoven:* Symphony 9 (exc); *Wagner:* Lohengrin (exc). (D. Hill, LSO/W. Morris, ECO/P. Ledger, E. Oliveira, LPO/L. Botstein, BBC PO/E. Downes, Scottish CO/J. Laredo, Berne SO/P. Maag, C. Ortiz, RPO/L. Foster/Y. Butt, LSC/R. Hickox, G. Howell/B. Tuckwell)

PCDS21 **PCDSC21**
Music of the World—Danube Dreams
J. Strauss II: Blauen Donau, Op. 314; *Schubert:* An Silvia, D891; Forelle, D550; Trout Quintet, D667; *Mozart:* Horn Concerti (exc); *J. Strauss I:* Radetzky March; *Lehár:* Lustige Witwe (exc); *J. Strauss II:* Tritsch-Tratsch; *Haydn:* Trumpet Concerto; *Suppé:* Leichte Kavallerie (exc); *Weber:* Freischütz (exc); *Mahler:* Symphony 5 (exc); *Mozart:* Symphony 41. (RPO/M. Reed, F. Lott, G. Johnson, Nash Ens, R. Watkins, CLS/R. Hickox, LSO/J.Georgiadis, R. Scotto, Eslovaca Philharmonica Orch/K. Leitner, C. Steele-Perkins, ECO/A. Halstead, BBC PO/E. Downes, ROH Male Chor/R. Stapleton/W. Morris, St John's Smith Square Orch/O. Gilmour)

PCDS22 **PCDSC22**
Music of the World—La Douce France
Berlioz: Symphonie Fantastique (exc); *Debussy:* Suite bergamasque (exc); *Ravel:* String Quartet (exc); *Adam:* Giselle (exc); *Saint-Saëns:* Symphony 3 (exc); *Massenet:* Thaïs (exc); *Fauré:* Requiem (exc); *Daquin:* Premier livre de pièces de clavecin (exc); *Debussy:* Après-midi; *Bizet:* Arlésienne Suites (exc); *Canteloube:* Chants d'Auvergne (exc); *Widor:* Symphony 5 (exc); *Gounod:* Faust (exc); *Offenbach:* Orphée aux enfers (exc). (RPO/A Previn, M. Tirimo, New World Qt, Bolshoi Th Orch/A. Zhuraitis, D. Chorzempa, Berne SO/P. Maag, M. Hasson, I. Brown, Westminster Cath Ch, CLS/D. Hill, R. Aldwinckle, LSO/R. Frühbeck de Burgos, P. Edmund-Davies, P. Rozario, Philh/J. Pritchard, M. Neary, LSC/R. Hickox/M. Reed)

PCDS23 **PCDSC23**
Music of the World—Italy & Spain—The Latin Quarter
Vivaldi: Concerti, Op. 8 (exc); *Tárrega:* Recuerdos de la Alhambra; *Rossini:* Barbiere di Siviglia (exc); *Leoncavallo:* Pagliacci (exc); *Mascagni:* Cavalleria Rusticana (exc); *Albéniz:* Suite española 1 (exc); *Bizet:* Carmen (exc); *D. Scarlatti:* Keyboard Sonatas (exc); *Rodrigo:* Concierto de Aranjuez (exc); *Falla:* Amor brujo (exc); *Verdi:* Nabucco (exc); *Puccini:* Madama Butterfly (exc); *Falla:* Sombrero de tres picos Suites (exc). (M. Kayath, J. Oakman, C. Powell, R. Aldwinckle, M. Conn, S. McCulloch, Scottish CO, COE, Czech SO, RPO, St. John's Smith Square Orch, LSC, LSO, J. Laredo (vn/dir)/J. Judd/J. Bigg/M. Reed/R. Stapleton/J. Lubbock/R. Frühbeck de Burgos/R. Hickox)

PCDS24 **PCDSC24**
Music of the World—Scandinavia & Eastern Europe—Forests & Fjords
Grieg: Peer Gynt (exc); *Sibelius:* Symphony 2 (exc); *Svendsen:* Romance, Op. 26; *Dvořák:* Slavonic Dances (exc); *Smetana:* Má Vlast (exc); *Kodály:* Háry János Suite (exc); *Chopin:* Etudes (exc); *Dvořák:* Symphony 9 (exc); *Liszt:* Consolations, S172 (exc); *Bartók:* Concerto for Orchestra (exc); *Janáček:* Sinfonietta (exc); *Grieg:* Piano Concerto (exc). (RPO/P. Dreier, LSO/C. Mackerras, R. Sushanskaya, English Stg Orch/W. Boughton, J. Ogdon, B. Lucas, Philh/F. d'Avalos, Hungarian Nat PO/T. Ferenc, C. Ortiz/B. Tuckwell, I. Llewelyn-Jones, J.L. Prats/E. Bátiz)

PCDS25 **PCDSC25**
Music of the World—Russia—Across the Steppes
Glinka: Ruslan and Lyudmila (exc); *Prokofiev:* Romeo and Juliet (exc); *Rachmaninov:* Paganini Rhapsody; *Khachaturian:* Spartacus Suite 2 (exc); *Tchaikovsky:* Piano Trio, Op. 50 (exc); *Borodin:* Prince Igor (exc); *Mussorgsky:* Pictures (exc); Pictures (exc); *Rimsky-Korsakov:* Scheherazade (exc); *Stravinsky:* Rite of Spring (exc); *Tchaikovsky:* Symphony 6 (exc). (LSO/Y. Ahronovitch, Bolshoi Th Orch/A. Zhuraitis, S. Costa, RPO/C. Seaman/B. Tovey, Solomon Trio, G. Saba/R. Williams/J. Mauceri, Boston PO/B. Zander/G. Rozhdestvensky)

PCDS26 **PCDSC26**
Music of the World—From the New World
Gershwin: Rhapsody in Blue; *Barber:* Violin Concerto; *Gershwin:* Gershwin Songbook (exc); *Copland:* Billy the Kid (exc); *Gershwin:* Porgy and Bess (exc); *Copland:* Rodeo (exc); *Barber:* Adagio for Strings; *Bernstein:* Chichester Psalms (exc); *Sousa:* Stars and Stripes Forever; *Moncayo García:* Huapango. (RPO, A. Litton (pf/dir), A.A. Meyers/C. Seaman, Richard Rodney Bennett, Bournemouth SO/J. Farrer, D. Newman, Minería SO/H. de la Fuente, Zagreb Sols/R. Hickox/M. Reed, Xalapa SO)

PCDS4 **PCDSC4**
Discover the Classics—Master Disc
Wagner: Walküre (exc); *Mussorgsky:* Night on the bare mountain; *Dvořák:* Symphony 9 (exc); *Tchaikovsky:* Romeo and Juliet (exc); *Saint-Saëns:* Carnaval des animaux (exc); *Beethoven:* Piano Sonata 14 (exc); *Schubert:* Ave Maria, D839; *Gounod:* Faust (exc); *Vivaldi:* Concerti, Op. 8 (exc); *Beethoven:* Symphony 6 (exc); *Elgar:* Enigma Variations (exc); *Ravel:* Pavane; *Mozart:* Zauberflöte (exc); *Tchaikovsky:* 1812 (exc); *Elgar:* Pomp and Circumstance Marches (exc). (LSO, B. Tuckwell/Y. Ahronovitch/B. Wordsworth, J. Ogdon, F. Lott, G. Johnson, LSC/R. Hickox, Scottish CO, J. Laredo (vn/dir)/W. Morris, English Sinfonia/C. Groves, B. Hoch, Hong Kong PO/K. Schermerhorn)

PCDS6 **PCDSC6**
Discover the Classics—Myths and Legends
Wagner: Fliegende Holländer (exc); *Holst:* Planets (exc); *Dukas:* Apprenti sorcier (exc); *Mussorgsky:* Pictures (exc); *Ravel:* Pavane; *Debussy:* Après-midi; *Offenbach:* Contes d'Hoffmann (exc); *Tchaikovsky:* Sleeping Beauty (exc); *Mozart:* Zauberflöte (exc); *Handel:* Solomon (exc); *Beethoven:* Prometheus (exc). (LSO, B. Tuckwell, London Voices/R. Hickox, NYO/C. Seaman/R. Williams, English Sinfonia/C. Groves/R. Frühbeck de Burgos, G. Saba, B. Hoch, Hong Kong PO/K. Schermerhorn, Scottish CO/J. Laredo, COE/J. Judd)

PCDS8 **PCDSC8**
Discover the Classics—Heroes and Heroines
Glinka: Ruslan and Lyudmila (exc); *Beethoven:* Symphony 3 (exc); *Mendelssohn:* Fair Melusina; *Beethoven:* Egmont (exc); *Wagner:* Walküre (exc); Lohengrin (exc); *Handel:* Joshua (exc); *Bizet:* Carmen Suites (exc); *Elgar:* Enigma Variations (exc); *Rimsky-Korsakov:* Scheherazade (exc); *J. Strauss I:* Radetzky March; *Tchaikovsky:* Marche slave. (LSO/Y. Ahronovitch/W. Morris, Berne SO/P. Maag, B. Tuckwell, J. Bowman, Kings Consort/R. King/R. Frühbeck de Burgos/J. Mauceri/J. Georgiadis)

PCD1023
Favourite Overtures
Berlioz: Corsaire; *Borodin:* Prince Igor (exc); *Mendelssohn:* Fair Melusina; *Wagner:* Meistersinger (exc); *Brahms:* Academic Festival Overture; *Suppé:* Leichte Kavallerie (exc). (BBC PO/E. Downes)

PCD1043
Opera Favourites
Bizet: Carmen (exc); Pêcheurs de Perles (exc); *Saint-Saëns:* Samson et Dalila (exc); *Offenbach:* Contes d'Hoffmann (exc); *Rossini:* Barbiere di Siviglia (exc); *Verdi:* Traviata (exc); Rigoletto (exc); *Mozart:* Don Giovanni (exc); *Puccini:* Madama Butterfly (exc); Bohème (exc); Gianni Schicchi (exc); Turandot (exc). (S. McCulloch, A-M. Owens, J. Oakman, S. Page, Prague Phil Chor, Czech PO/J. Bigg)

PCD1051 (12/93)
Rachmaninov—Piano Transcriptions
Rachmaninov: Preludes (exc); Daisies; Lilacs; Romance; Polka de W. R.; Aleko Dances; Songs, Op.34 (exc); Polka Italienne; *Rimsky-Korsakov:* Tale of Tsar Saltan (exc); *Bach:* Solo Violin Partitas and Sonatas (exc); *Kreisler:* Liebesleid; Liebesfreud; *Liszt:* Hungarian Rhapsodies, S244 (exc); *Tchaikovsky:* Songs, Op.16 (exc); *Mendelssohn:* Midsummer Night's Dream (exc). (J. Weber, B. Michel)

PCD1055
Tchaikovsky—Glorious Melodies, Volume 1
Tchaikovsky: Romeo and Juliet; Piano Concerto 1 (exc); Eugene Onegin (exc); Piano Trio, Op. 50 (exc); Serenade, Op. 48 (exc); Symphony 6 (exc). (J. Lill, C. Farley, RPO, LSO, Melbourne SO, Solomon Trio, Zagreb Sols/K. Koizumi/J. Judd/J. Serebrier/G. Rozhdestvensky)

PCD1057
Crazy for Gershwin
Gershwin: Porgy and Bess (exc); Rhapsody in Blue; *Hayman:* Gershwin Medley; *Gershwin:* Girl Crazy (exc). (D. Newman, A. Woodley, Oklahoma City Ambassadors Ch, D. Syme, Minería SO/H. de la Fuente, Xalapa SO/J. Brooks/Joel Levine, New Philh)

PCD1075
Opera Intermezzi; Bizet—Carmen Suites Nos 1 & 2
Bizet: Carmen Suites; *Ponchielli:* Gioconda (exc); *Mascagni:* Cavalleria Rusticana (exc); *Puccini:* Manon Lescaut (exc); *Offenbach:* Contes d'Hoffmann (exc); *Leoncavallo:* Pagliacci (exc); *Massenet:* Thaïs (exc); *Puccini:* Suor Angelica (exc); *Verdi:* Traviata (exc). (D. Nolan, Philh/I. Westrip)

PCD1086
Jonathan Woods plays Harpsichord
Soler: Fandango; Keyboard Sonatas I (exc); Keyboard Sonatas II (exc); *Boccherini:* String Quintets, G271-6 (exc); *Anon:* My Lady Carey's Dompe; Coranto; Scottish Gigue; *Gluck:* Armide (exc); *Philips:* Galliard; *Couperin:* Livre de clavecin IV (exc); *Farnaby:* Tower Hill; *Purcell:* Dido (exc); Grounds (exc); Musick's Hand-maid, Part 2 (exc); *D. Scarlatti:* Keyboard Sonatas (exc); *Mozart:* Piano Sonata, K331 (exc); *Exaudet:* Gavotte; *Anglés:* Aria; *Kerll:* Batalla Imperial. (J. Woods)

PCD1091
Jeux à deux
Gossec: Tambourin; *Satie:* Gymnopédies (exc); *Couperin:* Livre de clavecin III (exc); *Gluck:* Orfeo ed Euridice (exc); *Debussy:* Children's Corner (exc); *Fauré:* Sicilienne; *Ibert:* Entr'acte (1937); *Debussy:* Suite bergamasque (exc); *Gaubert:* Esquisses (1914) (exc); *Lully:* Gavotte; *Gaubert:* Madrigal; *Ravel:* Pièce en forme de habanera; *Fauré:* Berceuse, Op. 16. (R. Aitken, E. Goodman)

PCD1104
Baroque Encores
Handel: Solomon (exc); Water Music (exc); *Albinoni:* Adagio; *Corelli:* Concerti grossi, Op. 6 (exc); *Torelli:* Sinfonia, G23; *Bach:* Suites, BWV1066-9 (exc); *Vivaldi:* Concerti, Op. 8 (exc); *Purcell:* Fairy Queen, Z629 (exc). (Oxford City Orch/M. Papadopoulos)

PCD1105
Weber—Overtures
Weber: Abu Hassan (exc); Euryanthe (exc); Freischütz (exc); Oberon (exc); Preciosa (exc); Peter Schmoll (exc); Jubel-Ouverture; Beherrscher der Geister. (Hallé/S. Skrowaczewski)

PCD1109
Overtures and Arias from Opera
Rossini: Gazza ladra (exc); *Leoncavallo:* Pagliacci (exc); *Verdi:* Traviata (exc); Otello (exc); Don Carlo (exc); Don Carlo (exc); *Wagner:* Tannhäuser (exc). (S. Milnes, F. Becerra, Xalapa SO, Minería SO/H. de la Fuente)

PCD2001
Favourite String Works
Albinoni: Adagio; *Handel:* Solomon (exc); *Bach:* Suites, BWV1066-9 (exc); *Handel:* Berenice; *Pachelbel:* Canon and Gigue (exc); *Purcell:* Chaconne, Z730; Abdelazer, Z570 (exc); *Bach:* Violin Concerto, BWV1041 (exc). (Scottish CO/J. Laredo)

PCD2002
Organ Spectacular
Bach: Toccata and Fugue, BWV565; *Franck:* Chorales (exc); *Meyerbeer:* Prophète (exc); *Guilmant:* March, Op. 15; *Saint-Saëns:* Fantaisie in E flat; *Brahms:* Chorale Preludes, Op. 122 (exc); *Liszt:* Prelude and Fugue, S260; *Vierne:* Pièces en stile libre (exc). (D. Hill)

PCD2003
Mendelssohn—Symphony No. 4; Overtures
Mendelssohn: Symphony 1; Hebrides; Fair Melusina; Heimkehr aus der Fremde (exc). (Berne SO/P. Maag)

PCD2028
Falla—Ballet and Opera
Falla: Amor brujo (Cpte); Vida breve (exc); Sombrero de tres picos (exc). (N.F. Herrera, M.L. Salinas, Mexico St SO/E. Bátiz)

PCD2045
Favourite Overtures
Berlioz: Corsaire; *Borodin:* Prince Igor (exc); *Mendelssohn:* Fair Melusina; *Wagner:* Meistersinger (exc); *Brahms:* Academic Festival Overture; *Suppé:* Leichte Kavallerie (exc). (BBC PO/E. Downes)

PCD802
String Masterpieces
Albinoni: Adagio; *Bach:* Suites, BWV1066-9 (exc); Violin Concerto, BWV1041 (exc); *Handel:* Berenice (exc); Solomon (exc); *Pachelbel:* Canon and Gigue (exc); *Purcell:* Abdelazer, Z570 (exc); Chaconne, Z730. (Scottish CO, J. Laredo (vn/dir))

PCD804
Russian Spectacular
Khachaturian: Gayaneh (exc); Spartacus Suite 2 (exc); Masquerade (exc); *Prokofiev:* Lt Kijé Suite (exc); Love for 3 Oranges Suite (exc); *Borodin:* Prince Igor (exc); *Glinka:* Ruslan and Lyudmila (exc); *Mussorgsky:* Night on the bare mountain; *Shostakovich:* Gadfly Suite (exc). (LSO/Y. Ahronovitch)

Ⓓ **PCD805** (8/85)
Music of the Masters
Beethoven: Prometheus (exc); *Mozart:* Divertimenti, K136-8 (exc); *Rossini:* Barbiere di Siviglia (exc); *Fauré:* Pavane; *Wagner:* Siegfried Idyll. (COE/J. Judd)

Ⓓ **PCD823** (9/86)
Organ Spectacular
Bach: Toccata and Fugue, BWV565; *Franck:* Chorales (exc); *Meyerbeer:* Prophète (exc); *Guilmant:* March, Op. 15; *Saint-Saëns:* Fantaisie in E flat; *Brahms:* Chorale Preludes, Op. 122 (exc); *Liszt:* Prelude and Fugue, S260; *Vierne:* Suite 3 (exc). (D. Hill)

Ⓓ **PCD824** (6/86)
Mendelssohn—Orchestral Works
Mendelssohn: Symphony 4; Hebrides; Fair Melusina; Heimkehr aus der Fremde (exc). (Berne SO/P. Maag)

Ⓓ **PCD827** (11/86)
The Art of the Coloratura
Handel: Allegro, il penseroso ed il moderato (exc); *Mozart:* Zauberflöte (exc); Vorrei spiegarvi, K418; *Arne:* Artaxerxes (exc); *Benedict:* Wren; *Proch:* Air and Variations; *Milhaud:* Chansons de Ronsard; *Alabiev:* Nightingale; *Glière:* Soprano Concerto. (B. Hoch, Hong Kong PO/K. Schermerhorn)

Ⓓ **PCD858** (10/87)
Piano Transcriptions
Liszt: Faust—paraphrase, S407; *Grainger:* Rosenkavalier ramble; *R.Strauss:* Lieder, Op. 17 (exc); *Wagner:* Tristan und Isolde (exc); *Ravel:* La Valse; *Offenbach:* Contes d'Hoffmann (exc); *Grainger:* Waltz of the Flowers—paraphrase; *Gershwin:* Strike Up The Band I (exc); Goldwyn Follies (exc). (G. Saba)

Ⓓ **PCD881** (4/88)
Monteverdi—Solos and Duets
Monteverdi: Madrigals, Bk.7 (exc); Ritorno d'Ulisse in Patria (exc); Cantate Domino II; Sancta Maria; Exulta, filia Sion; O bone Jesu, o piissime Jesu; Selva morale e spirituale (exc). (E. Kirkby, E. Tubb, Consort of Musicke/A. Rooley)

Ⓓ **PCD894** (8/88)
Great Baroque Arias, Part I
Handel: Ode for St Cecilia's Day (exc); Serse (exc); Semele (exc); Acis and Galatea (exc); Joshua (exc); Jephtha (exc); Alexander's Feast (exc); Samson (exc); *Bach:* Cantata 208 (exc); *Weldon:* Tempest (exc); *Purcell:* Dido (exc); *Vivaldi:* Orlando Furioso (exc). (G. Fisher, J. Bowman, J.M. Ainsley, M. George, King's Consort/R. King)

Ⓓ **PCD902** (4/89)
An Evening in Vienna
J. Strauss II: Fledermaus (exc); Frühlingsstimmen, Op. 410; Annen-Polka, Op. 117; Rosen aus dem Süden; Wein, Weib und Gesang; Auf der Jagd, Op. 373; Explosionen, Op. 43; Windsor-Klänge; *Jos Strauss:* Feuerfest!; *Ziehrer:* Busserl, Op. 389. (LSO, J. Georgiadis)

Ⓓ **PCD905** (1/89)
Bizet—Orchestral Works
Bizet: Arlésienne Suites; Carmen Suites (exc). (LSO/R. Frühbeck de Burgos)

Ⓓ **PCD908** (4/89)
Great Opera Choruses
Bizet: Carmen (exc); *Verdi:* Trovatore (exc); Nabucco (exc); Macbeth (exc); *Gounod:* Faust (exc); *Verdi:* Aida (exc); *Borodin:* Prince Igor (exc). (Southend Boys' Ch, LSC, LSO/R. Hickox)

Ⓓ **PCD924** (11/89) ▭ **CIMPC924** (11/89)
Spanish Spectacular
Rimsky-Korsakov: Capriccio espagnol; *Albéniz:* Suite española 1 (exc); *Falla:* Amor brujo (exc); *Ravel:* Alborada del gracioso; *Granados:* Goyescas (exc); *Falla:* Sombrero de tres picos Suites (exc). (LSO/R. Frühbeck de Burgos)

Ⓓ **PCD939** (11/90) ▭ **CIMPC939** (11/90)
Mozart: Orchestral Works
Mozart: Sinfonia concertante, K297b; Symphony 25; Nozze di Figaro (exc); Finta Giardiniera (exc). (C. O'Neal, K. Puddy, B. Sewell, M. Baines, English Sinfonia/C. Groves)

Ⓓ **PCD967** (5/92)
Schubert—Orchestral Works
Schubert: Symphony 3; Symphony 4; Overture, D591; Overture, D4; Verschworenen (exc). (English Sinfonia/C. Groves)

Ⓓ **PCD968** (3/93) ▭ **CIMPC968** (3/93)
Schubert—Orchestral Works
Schubert: Symphony 2; Symphony 6; Zwillingsbrüder (exc). (English Sinfonia/C. Groves)

Ⓓ **PWKS4230**
Mario Lanza in Concert
Donizetti: Elisir d'amore (exc); *Giordano:* Andrea Chénier (exc); *Puccini:* Bohème (exc); Madama Butterfly (exc); Tosca (exc); *Verdi:* Rigoletto (exc); Traviata (exc); *Toselli:* Serenade; *Cardillo:* Core 'ngrato; *Brodszky:* Because You're Mine (exc); *Friml:* Firefly (exc); *Romberg:* New Moon (exc); *Moya:* Song of songs; *Aaronson:* Loveliest night of the year; *Grieg:* Melodies of the Heart, Op. 5 (exc); *Gounod:* Ave Maria; *Youmans:* Great Day (exc); Great Day (exc); *De Curtis:* Torna a Surriento; *Nutile:* Mamma mia, che vo' sapè; *Jurmann:* Cosi Cosà; *N. Brown:* Going Hollywood (exc); *Brooks:* Kiss; *Bixio:* Parlami d'amore Mariù. (F. Yeend, M. Lanza, Hollywood Bowl SO/E. Ormandy, orch/R. Sinatra/C. Callinicos/I. Aaronson)

Ⓓ **PWK1157**
Gilbert & Sullivan Spectacular
Sullivan: Gondoliers (exc); Pirates of Penzance (exc); HMS Pinafore (exc); Mikado (exc). (M. Studholme, J. Allister, E. Bohan, I. Wallace, English Chorale, London Concert Orch/M. Dods)

Ⓓ **TCD1014**
An Invitation to the Classics
Vivaldi: Concerti, Op.8 (exc); *Grieg:* Peer Gynt (exc); *J. Strauss II:* Blauen Donau, Op. 314; *Tchaikovsky:* Piano concerto 1 (exc); *Debussy:* Suite bergamasque (exc); *Handel:* Water Music (exc); *Schumann:* Kinderszenen (exc); *Bizet:* Carmen suites (exc); *Beethoven:* Piano Sonata 14 (exc); *Haydn:* Trumpet Concerto (exc); *Chopin:* Waltzes (exc); *Khachaturian:* Spartacus Suite 2 (exc); *Handel:* Messiah (exc); *Ravel:* Boléro; *Mozart:* Piano concerto 21 (exc); *Brahms:* Waltzes, Op. 39 (exc); *J. Strauss II:* Annen-Polka, Op. 117; *Tchaikovsky:* Nutcracker (exc); *Mozart:* Symphony 40 (exc); *Beethoven:* Symphony 3 (exc); *Liszt:* Liebesträume, S541 (exc); *Mozart:* Nozze di Figaro (exc); *Tchaikovsky:* Sleeping Beauty (exc); *Beethoven:* Piano sonata 8 (exc); *J. Strauss I:* Radetzky March; *Beethoven:* Bagatelles (exc); *Mozart:* Clarinet concerto, K622 (exc); *Saint-Saëns:* Carnaval des animaux (exc); *Clarke:* Suite in D (exc); *Mendelssohn:* Songs without words (exc); *Bach:* Suites, BWV1066-9 (exc); *J. Strauss II:* Wiener Blut; *Mozart:* Piano Sonata K331 (exc); *Tchaikovsky:* Swan Lake Suite (exc); *Rimsky-Korsakov:* Scheherazade (exc); *Bach:* Cantata 208 (exc); *Khachaturian:* Gayaneh (exc); *Suppé:* Leichte Kavallerie (exc); *Vivaldi:* Concerto, RV93 (exc); *Beethoven:* Symphony 5 (exc); *Pachelbel:* Canon and Gigue (exc); *Mozart:* Serenade K525 (exc); *J. Strauss II:* Tritsch-Tratsch; *Elgar:* Pomp and Circumstance Marches (exc). (Scottish CO, J. Laredo (vn/dir), RPO/P. Dreier, LSO/J. Georgiadis, J. Lill/J. Judd, M. Tirimo, CLS/R. Hickox, C. Ortiz/R. Frühbeck de Burgos, J. Ogdon, C. Steele-Perkins, ECO/A. Halstead/Y. Ahronovitch, Scottish Phil Sngrs/R. Williams, H. Shelley (pf/dir), A. Servadei, St. John's Smith Square Orch/J. Lubbock/W. Morris, I. Llewelyn-Jones, English Sinfonia/C. Groves, D. Campbell/B. Wordsworth, G. Ashton, L. Pearson, Philippa Davies, T. Owen, J. Georgiadis/J. Mauceri, G. Fisher, King's Consort, R. King (org/dir)/M. Reed, ECCO/E. Aadland, Serenata of London/B. Tuckwell/G. Malcolm)

Ⓓ **TCD1070**
Invitation to the Opera
Mozart: Nozze di Figaro (exc); *Verdi:* Traviata (exc); *Rossini:* Barbiere di Siviglia (exc); *Wagner:* Meistersinger (exc); *Borodin:* Prince Igor (exc); *J. Strauss II:* Fledermaus (exc); *Wagner:* Tannhäuser (exc); *Bizet:* Carmen (exc); *Mozart:* Zauberflöte (exc); *Bizet:* Pêcheurs de Perles (exc); *Tchaikovsky:* Eugene Onegin (exc); *Verdi:* Aida (exc); *Saint-Saëns:* Samson et Dalila (exc); *Verdi:* Traviata (exc); *Rossini:* Barbiere di Siviglia (exc); *Puccini:* Bohème (exc); *Offenbach:* Contes d'Hoffmann (exc); *Puccini:* Tosca (exc); *Delibes:* Lakmé (exc); *Leoncavallo:* Pagliacci (exc); *Puccini:* Gianni Schicchi (exc); Turandot (exc); *Wagner:* Lohengrin (exc); *Mozart:* Zauberflöte (exc); *Verdi:* Nabucco (exc); *Gounod:* Faust (exc); *Mascagni:* Cavalleria rusticana (exc); *Weber:* Freischütz (exc); *Verdi:* Trovatore (exc); *Wagner:* Tannhäuser (exc); *Verdi:* Aida (exc); *Borodin:* Prince Igor (exc). (B. Hoch, C. Farley, S. McCulloch, V. Masterson, A.-M. Owens, C. Powell, G. Gudbjörnsson, A. Davies, J. Oakman, E. Barham, A. Michaels-Moore, J. Howard, ROH Chor, LSC, London Choral Soc, Prague Phil Chor, LSO, COE, BBC PO, RPO, Hong Kong PO, Melbourne SO, Czech SO, English Sinfonia/C. Groves/V. Tausky/J. Judd/B. Tuckwell/E. Downes/J. Georgiadis, J. Barstow/B. Tuckwell/R. Stapleton/K. Schermerhorn/M. Reed/J. Serebrier/J. Bigg/R. Hickox)

Ⓓ **TCD1073**
The Best of Richard Hickox
Orff: Carmina burana; *Holst:* Planets; *Bizet:* Carmen (exc); *Verdi:* Trovatore (exc); Nabucco (exc); Macbeth (exc); Aida (exc); *Gounod:* Faust (exc); *Borodin:* Prince Igor (exc). (P. Walmsley-Clark, J. Graham-Hall, D. Maxwell, Southend Boys' Ch, LSC, London Voices, LSO/R. Hickox)

INA Mémoire Vive

Ⓓ **262004**
Alfred Deller—Renaissance and Baroque songs
Dowland: Second Booke of Songs (exc); Third and Last Booke of Songs (exc); *R. Johnson II:* Care-charming sleep; *Palestrina:* Io son ferito; *Monteverdi:* Currite populi; Salve Regina a 1; *Grandi:* Motets (1610) (exc); *Bach:* Anna Magdalena Notenbuch (1725) (exc); *Purcell:* If music be the food of love, Z379/1; Dioclesian, Z627 (exc); Bonduca, Z574 (exc); Birthday Ode, Z321 (exc); St Cecilia's Day Ode, Z339 (exc); Oedipus, Z583 (exc); O Solitude, Z406. (A. Deller, H. Lester, R. Spencer, D. Dupré)

Intercord

Ⓓ **INT830 899**
Virtuoso Orchestral Music
Mozart: Nozze di Figaro (exc); *Rossini:* Scala di Seta (exc); Italiana in Algeri (exc); *Weber:* Oberon (exc); *Glinka:* Ruslan and Lyudmila (exc); *Smetana:* Bartered Bride (exc); *Genzmer:* Prologue (1959); Prologue (1991). (Polish Chmbr PO/W. Rajski)

Ⓓ **INT860 908**
Wagner/Mahler—Orchestral Works
Wagner: Tristan und Isolde (exc); *Mahler:* Symphony 10 (exc). (South-West German RSO/M. Gielen)

Ⓓ **INT860 912**
Beethoven—Orchestral Works
Beethoven: Violin Concerto; Leonore (exc); Consecration of the House Ov. (C. Tetzlaff, South-West German RSO/M. Gielen)

International Record Collectors

Ⓓ **IRCC-CD800** (9/92)
Souvenirs from Meyerbeer Operas
Meyerbeer: Huguenots (exc); Huguenots (exc); Huguenots (exc); Huguenots (exc); Huguenots (exc); Robert le Diable (exc); Robert le Diable (exc); Robert le Diable (exc); Robert le Diable (exc); Prophète (exc); Prophète (exc); Prophète (exc); Prophète (exc); Prophète (exc); Dinorah (exc); Dinorah (exc); Dinorah (exc); Dinorah (exc). (E. Norena, A. Parsi-Pettinella, L. Landouzy, A. Affre, M. Lafargue, A. Gresse, J-F. Delmas, chor, B.A. de Montalant, E. Clément, M. Journet, N. de Angelis, F. Viñas, S. Cahier, M. Kurt, M. Matzenauer, O. Metzger, L. Homer, G. Huguet, F. Hempel, M. Ancona, L. Fugère, orch, anon)

Ⓓ **IRCC-CD802** (8/92)
Souvenirs of Rare French Opera
Donizetti: Lucia di Lammermoor (exc); *De Lara:* Méssaline (exc); Méssaline (exc); *Reyer:* Sigurd (exc); Sigurd (exc); Sigurd (exc); *Leroux:* Reine Fiammette (exc); *V.A. Duvernoy:* Hellé (exc); *Février:* Gismonda (exc); *Massenet:* Ariane (exc); *Saint-Saëns:* Barbares (exc); *Gounod:* Polyeucte (exc); Tribut de Zamora (exc); Reine de Saba (exc); *Février:* Monna Vanna (exc); *Bruneau:* Virginie (exc); *Nougès:* Aigle (exc); *T. Dubois:* Aben-Hamet (exc); *Massenet:* Roma (exc); Roma (exc); *Bourgault-Ducoudray:* Thamara (exc); *Bruneau:* Attaque du moulin (exc). (L. Korsoff, A. Scotti, A. Ghasne, M. Renaud, R. Caron, L. Escalais, M. Carré, M. Namara, L. Muratore, C. Rousselière, Z. de Lussan, M. Rappold, F. Ansseau, G. Féraldy, H. Albers, M. Imbert, L. Dupré, L. Beyle, A. Affre, A. Talexis, X. Leroux, anon, orch/P. Coppola)

Ⓓ **IRCC-CD805**
Geraldine Farrar - 60th Anniversary Issue
Schumann: Myrthen, Op.25 (exc); *Massenet:* Poème d'amour (exc); *Humperdinck:* Königskinder (exc); *Gounod:* Roméo et Juliette (exc); Faust (exc); *Boito:* Mefistofele (exc); *Mozart:* Exsultate, jubilate, K165 (exc); *Verdi:* Traviata (exc); *Horn:* Cherry Ripe; *Bemberg:* Chant vénitien; *R. Strauss:* Lieder, Op.17 (exc); *Mozart:* Nozze di Figaro (exc); *Gluck:* Rencontre imprévue (exc); *Heuberger:* Opernball (exc); *Lehár:* Frasquita (exc); *Wolf-Ferrari:* Donne curiose (exc); Donne curiose (exc); *Leoncavallo:* Roland von Berlin (exc); *Mattei:* Dear heart; *Schubert:* Gretchen am Spinnrade, D118 (exc); *Gounod:* Faust (exc); *Berlioz:* Damnation de Faust (exc); *Boito:* Mefistofele (exc); *Wagner:* Tannhäuser (exc). (G. Farrar, H. Jadlowker, K. Jörn, F. Lapitino, C. Gotthelf, orch, anon)

Ⓓ **IRCC-CD808** (6/94)
Souvenirs of 19th Century Italian Opera
Apolloni: Ebreo (exc); *Petrella:* Jone (exc); *Ruggi:* Due Ciabattini (exc); *Petrella:* Contessa d'Amalfi (exc); *Faccio:* Amleto (exc); *Usiglio:* Educande di Sorrento (exc); *Marchetti:* Ruy Blas (exc); Ruy Blas (exc); Ruy Blas (exc); Ruy Blas (exc); *Campana:* Esmeralda (exc); *Gomes:* Guarany (exc); Guarany (exc); Guarany (exc); Guarany (exc); *Ponchielli:* Promessi Sposi (exc); Lina (exc); *Bottesini:* Ero e Leandro (exc). (A. DiGiorgio, A. Scampini, G. De Luca, F. Corradetti, A. Santini, C. Owen, E. Petri, E.

Bucalo, T. Desana, C. Boninsegna, L. Colazza, L. del Lungo, E. Caronna, E. Foggi, B. Sayão, E. Mazzoleni, G. Zenatello, A. Amadi, P. Amato, E. Vannuccini, M. Carosio, A. Pinto, anon, orch)

Ⓓ **IRCC-CD810**
American Singers, Volume 1
Meyerbeer: Robert le Diable (exc); *Leoncavallo:* Pagliacci (exc); *Herbert:* Natoma (exc); *Flotow:* Martha (exc); *Cilea:* Adriana Lecouvreur (exc); *Flotow:* Martha (exc); *Walthew:* May Day; *Bizet:* Carmen (exc); *Mussorgsky:* Boris Godunov (exc); *Lehmann:* In a Persian Garden (exc); *Verdi:* Aida (exc); Aida (exc); Aida (exc); *Rossini:* Stabat mater (exc); *J. Strauss II:* Fledermaus (exc); *Herbert:* Naughty Marietta (exc); *Stern:* Printemps; *Wagner:* Parsifal (exc); *Massenet:* Thaïs (exc); *Balfe:* Bohemian Girl (exc); *Homer:* Uncle Rome. (C. White, L. Homer, P. Althouse, L.I. Marsh, C. Whitehill, M. Ober, anon, orch)

Interphon Classics

Ⓓ **409 005-2**
Mozart Edition, Vol.5
Mozart: Flute and Harp Concerto, K299; Horn Concerti (exc); Andante, K616; Zauberflöte (exc). (Mozart Fest Orch/A. Lizzio, J. Falout, Camerata Labacensis/K. Redel, P. Schmalfuss, LPO/C. Rainer)

Ⓓ **409 015-2**
Mozart Edition, Vol.15
Mozart: Serenade, K525; Divertimenti, K136-8; Così fan tutte (exc). (Camerata Academica/A. von Pitamic, Slovak PO/L. Pešek, London Fest Orch/K. Redel)

Intuition Records

Ⓓ **INT3113-2**
Zapateado - Suzy Whang
Kroll: Banjo and Fiddle; *Gershwin:* Porgy and Bess (exc); *Saint-Saëns:* Introduction and Rondo capriccioso; *Sarasate:* Carmen fantasy (exc); Danzas españolas (exc); *Khachaturian:* Gayaneh (exc); *Sarasate:* Zigeunerweisen; *Elgar:* Salut d'amour; *Tchaikovsky:* Souvenir d'un lieu cher, Op. 42; *Debussy:* Suite bergamasque (exc). (S. Whang, K. Hashimoto)

Italian Opera Rarities

Ⓓ **LO7701/3**
Donizetti—Fausta
Donizetti: Fausta (Cpte). (R. Kabaivanska, R. Bruson, G. Giacomini, G. Dalle Molle, L. Roni, A. Vespasiani, T. Pane, Rome Op Chor, Rome Op Orch/D. Oren)

Ⓓ **LO7704/5**
Boito—Nerone
Boito: Nerone (Cpte). (B. Prevedi, A. Ferrin, A. Cassis, I. Ligabue, R. Baldani, A. Zerbini, G. Corradi, A. Di Stasio, C. Vozza, Turin RAI Chor, Turin RAI Orch/G. Gavazzeni)

Ⓓ **LO7706/7**
Donizetti—Maria di Rudenz
Donizetti: Maria di Rudenz (Cpte). (K. Ricciarelli, S. Baleani, L. Nucci, A. Cupido, G. Surian, S. Eupani, Venice La Fenice Chor, Venice La Fenice Orch/E. Inbal)

Ⓓ **LO7708/9**
Ponchielli—I Lituani
Ponchielli: Lituani (Cpte). (O. Garaventa, Y. Hayashi, A. Cassis, C. De Bortoli, A. Riva, S. Ghione, Turin RAI Chor, Turin RAI Orch/G. Gavazzeni)

Ⓓ **LO7716/8** (10/94)
Donizetti—Les Martyrs
Donizetti: Martyrs (Cpte). (L. Gencer, O. Garaventa, F. Furlanetto, R. Bruson, F. Signor, O. di Credico, M. Guggia, Venice La Fenice Chor, Venice La Fenice Orch/G. Gelmetti)

Jecklin

Ⓓ **JD506-2** (11/87)
Flute Concertos
Cimarosa: 2-Flute Concerto; *Gluck:* Flute Concerto; Orfeo ed Euridice (exc); *Pokorny:* Flute Concerto. (P-L. Graf, G. Guéneux, Zurich Camerata/R. Tschupp)

Jewish Music Productions

▭ **BB 001** (9/85)
Alman & Shostakovich—Jewish legends in music
Alman: King Ahaz (exc); *Shostakovich:* Jewish Folk Poetry, Op. 79. (H. Lawrence, C. Rosen, L. Berkman, A. Saunders)

▭ **BB 002**
Michelow and Williamson in Recital
Lavry: Love song; *Ravel:* Mélodies hébraïques; Chants populaires (exc); *Ben Haim:* Star fell down; Songs without words; *Hadda:* Exchanges of love; *Williamson:* Red Sea (exc); Now is the singing day. (S. Michelow, M. Williamson)

Kiwi-Pacific Records

Ⓓ **CDSLD-82**
Southern Voices—NZ International Opera Singers
Bach: Cantata 82 (exc); *Balfe:* Bohemian Girl (exc); *Britten:* Curlew River (exc); *Delibes:* Lakmé (exc); *Donizetti:* Lucia di Lammermoor (exc); *Handel:* Giulio Cesare (exc); *Lehár:* Paganini (exc); *Mozart:* Don Giovanni (exc); Entführung (exc); Zauberflöte (exc); *Prokofiev:* Alexander Nevsky (exc); *Puccini:* Gianni Schicchi (exc); Madama Butterfly (exc); *Schumann:* Szenen aus Goethes Faust (exc); *Sullivan:* Iolanthe (exc); *Tchaikovsky:* Eugene Onegin (exc); *Verdi:* Ballo in maschera (exc); Vespri siciliani (exc); *Wagner:* Meistersinger (exc). (F. Alda, R. Buckman, M. Major, K. Te Kanawa, H. Begg, P. Payne, P. Baillie, A. Austin, R. Greager, P. Power, K. Lewis, J. Carreras, D. Dowling, B. Drake, B. Mora, D. McIntyre, R. Macann, O. Natzke, I. Te Wiata, N. Mangin, Sadler's Wells Op Chor, ROH Chor, orch, Sadler's Wells Op Orch, ROHO, EOG Orch, NZ SO, Australian Op & Ballet Orch, BBC SO, ECO, Chelsea Op Group Orch, Ireland National SO, LPO, Melbourne SO/E. Goossens/A. Faris/K. Rankl/Colin Davis/D. Willcocks/R. Bonynge/B. Haitink/M. Sargent/B. Britten/V. Tunnard/J. Pritchard/M. Shostakovich/C. Roller/J. Matheson/M. Gielen/B. Law/W. Southgate, A. Ross)

Ⓓ **CDTRL075**
Malvina Major—Opera Recital
Mozart: Entführung (exc); Don Giovanni (exc); *Rossini:* Elisabetta (exc); Barbiere di Siviglia (exc); *Bizet:* Carmen (exc); *Verdi:* Otello (exc); *Puccini:* Suor Angelica (exc). (M. Major, NZ SO/J. Matheson/P. Gamba, P. Hornblow, M. Findley)

Klavier Records

Ⓓ **CTD88104**
Holdridge conducts Holdridge
Holdridge: Scenes of Summer; Lazarus and His Beloved Suite; Violin Concerto 2; Andante; Ballet Fantasy; Grand Waltz; *Albinoni:* Adagio. (G. Dicterow, LSO, Los Angeles Str Orch/L. Holdridge)

Ⓓ **KCD11040**
Offenbach—Overtures
Offenbach: Orphée aux enfers (exc); Grande-Duchesse de Gérolstein (exc); Belle Hélène (exc); Barbe-Bleue (exc); Vie Parisienne (exc); *Berlioz:* Carnaval romain; Benvenuto Cellini (exc). (CBSO/L. Frémaux)

Ⓓ **KCD11060**
American Variations
Gould: American Salute; *Ticheli:* Amazing Grace; *H. Clarke:* Carnival of Venice; *Ives:* America Variations; *E. Picchi:* Fantaisie Original; *Romberg:* Student Prince (exc); *Rob Bennett:* Old American Dances; *Goldman:* Scherzo; *Bellstedt:* Napoli; *Reeves:* Yankee Doodle; *W. Rogers:* Volunteer; *F. Simon:* March of the Majorettes. (B. Bowman, Cincinnati Wind Sym/E. Corporon)

Koch International Classics

Ⓓ **321 214**
Wiener Sängerknaben - Kein Schöner Land
Traditional: Kein schöner Land; Guten Abend; Mond ist aufgegangen; *Reger:* Schlichte Weisen, Op. 76 (exc); *Traditional:* Zwa Sterndal am Himmel; Hört, ihr Herr'n; *Humperdinck:* Hänsel und Gretel (exc); *Orff:* Andachtsjodler; *Isaac:* Isbruck, ich muss dich lassen; *Anon:* Wachtlied und Kärntner Abendjodler; *Schubert:* Nacht, D983c; Nachthelle, D892; *Mendelssohn:* Midsummer Night's Dream (exc); *Brahms:* Volks-Kinderlieder (exc); Lieder, Op. 49 (exc); *Schubert:* Wiegenlied, D498; *Flies:* Wiegenlied. (Vienna Boys' Ch, U. Harrer, H. Deutsch)

Ⓓ **321 759**
Ziehrer—Militärmusik Steiermark
Ziehrer: Freiherr von Schönfeld, Op. 442; Fremdenführer (exc); Verliebte Eskadron (exc); Boshaft, Op. 424; Zauber der Montur, Op. 493; Hoch und Nieder, Op. 372; Nachtschwärmer, Op. 466; Landstreicher (exc); Hunderttausend Eljen, Op. 51. (Steiermark Military Band/R. Bodingbauer)

Ⓓ **322 559**
Postmusik Innsbruck play Ziehrer and Lortzing
Somma: Traum eines österreichischen Reservisten; *Lortzing:* Waffenschmied (exc). (Innsbruck Postmusik/F. Pedarnig)

Ⓓ **34026-2** ▭ **24026-4**
Gilbert & Sullivan—The Pirates of Penzance Highlights
Sullivan: Pirates of Penzance (exc). (M. Rivers, Gareth Jones, P. Creasey, E. Roberts, S. Masterton-Smith, P. Birchall, P. Cameron, J. Arthur, S. Gorton, D'Oyly Carte Op Chor, D'Oyly Carte Op Orch/J. Pryce-Jones)

Ⓓ **34027-2** ▭ **24027-4**
Gilbert & Sullivan—The Mikado Highlights
Sullivan: Mikado (exc). (L. Garrett, S. Bullock, F. Palmer, J. Rigby, B. Bottone, E. Idle, M. Richardson, R. Angas, R. Van Allan, ENO Chor, ENO Orch/Peter Robinson)

Ⓓ **34028-2** ▭ **24028-4**
Gilbert & Sullivan—Iolanthe Highlights
Sullivan: Iolanthe (exc). (R. Stuart, L. Richard, P. Creasey, J. Rath, Philip Blake Jones, J. Pert, R. Hanley, Y. Patrick, M. Mitchell, L. Owen, E. Woollett, D'Oyly Carte Op Chor, D'Oyly Carte Op Orch/J. Pryce-Jones)

Ⓓ **34029-2** ▭ **24029-4**
Gilbert & Sullivan—HMS Pinafore Highlights
Sullivan: HMS Pinafore (exc). (N. Grace, L. Ormiston, E. Ritchie, G. Sandison, C. Gillett, T. Lawlor, J. Roebuck, P. Parfitt, P. Thomson, New Sadler's Wells Op Chor, New Sadler's Wells Op Orch/S. Phipps)

Ⓓ **34036-2** ▭ **24036-4**
A Pageant of Opera
Mysliveček: Bellerofonte (exc); *Smetana:* Brandenburgers in Bohemia (exc); *Fibich:* Bride of Messina (exc); *Martinů:* Ariane (exc); Greek Passion (exc); *Dvořák:* Rusalka (exc); *Martinů:* Julietta (exc); *Smetana:* Bartered Bride (exc); *Martinů:* Spaliček (exc); *Janáček:* Jenufa (exc); *Hába:* Mother (exc); *Martinů:* Miracles of Mary (exc); *Janáček:* Cunning Little Vixen (exc); *Dvořák:* Kate and the Devil (exc); *Janáček:* Káťa Kabanová (exc); *Dvořák:* Dimitrij (exc); *Janáček:* From the House of the Dead (exc); *Smetana:* Libuše (exc). (V. Urbanová, M. Hajóssyová, G. Beňačková, R. Cullis, H. Field, J. Marková, D. Tikalová, V. Soukupová, I. Mixová, M. Čadikovičová, A. Barová, I. Žídek, B. Vich, P. Dvorský, J. Mitchinson, A. Davies, V. Krejčík, B. Blachut, L.M. Vodička, V. Zítek, K. Kalaš, J. Horáček, J. Horáček, J. Tomlinson, K. Berman, Kantiléna Children's Chor, Kühn Chor, Prague Rad Chor, Czech Phil Chor, Prague Nat Th Chor, Brno Janáček Op Orch, Prague CO, Prague Nat Th Orch, Czech PO, Brno St PO, Prague SO/Z. Peskó/J.H. Tichý/F. Jílek/V. Neumann/C. Mackerras/J. Krombholc/Z. Košler/J. Jirouš/J. Bělohlávek/J. Pinkas/G. Albrecht)

Ⓓ **37005-2** (9/90)
Menotti/Barber—Orchestral Works
Barber: Souvenirs Suite; *Menotti:* Amahl and the Night Visitors (exc); Sebastian Suite. (NZ SO/A. Schenck)

Ⓓ **37006-2** (2/91)
Weill: Die Dreigroschenoper
Weill: Dreigroschenoper (Cpte). (A. Shoumanova, M. Jung, H. Becht, A. Herrmann, S. Myszak, E. Demerdjiev, N. Afeyan, W. Kmentt, Bulgarian TV & Rad Mixed Chor, Bulgarian TV & Rad SO/V.C. Symonette)

Ⓓ **37011-2** (1/91)
Legendary Conductors
Haydn: Symphony 88; *Mozart:* Symphony 39; *Gluck:* Alceste (1776) (exc); *Beethoven:* Leonore (exc). (VPO/C. Krauss, Berlin St Op Orch/E. Kleiber, Concertgebouw/W. Mengelberg/B. Walter)

Ⓓ **37028-2** (7/91)
Gershwin—Songs & Duets
Gershwin: Rosalie (exc); Damsel in distress (exc); Hi-Ho!; Treasure Girl (exc); Strike up the band I (exc); Funny Face (exc); Our Nell (exc); Strike up the band II (exc); Primrose (exc); Till Then; Pardon my English (exc); Show Girl (exc); Lady, be good! (exc); Porgy and Bess (exc); Of thee I sing (exc). (J. Kaye, W. Sharp, S. Blier)

Ⓓ **37048-2**
Wallace—Kabbalah
S. Wallace: Kabbalah (Cpte). (K. Holvik, E. Means, R. Wong, A. Montano, P. Warrick-Smith, E. Bowers, J. Godfrey, H. Munday, M. Sokol, R. Osborne, I. Crawford, T. Christensen, A. Sterman, C. Paisner, T. Gilson, B. Ruyle/M. Barrett)

Ⓓ **37050-2** (10/91)
Blitzstein—Songs
Blitzstein: Reuben, Reuben (exc); Cradle will Rock (exc); No for an Answer (exc); Airborne Symphony (exc); Regina (exc); This is the Garden (exc); Juno (exc); From Marion's Book (exc); Jimmie's Got a Goil; Stay in my Arms; Goloopchik (exc); Zipperfly; Magic Barrel (exc). (K. Holvik, W. Sharp, S. Blier)

Ⓓ **37053-2** (11/91)
The Young Otto Klemperer
Weill: Kleine Dreigroschenmusik (exc); *R. Strauss:* Till

Eulenspiegel; Salome (exc); *Brahms:* Symphony 1. (Berlin St Op Orch/O. Klemperer)

Ⓓ **37054-2**
Horenstein and the Berlin Philharmonic
Mozart: Nozze di Figaro (exc); Clemenza di Tito (exc); *Bach:* Chorales, BWV651-668 (exc); Orgel-Büchlein, BWV599-644 (exc); *Haydn:* Symphony 94; *Schubert:* Symphony 5. (BPO/J. Horenstein)

Ⓓ **37059-2** (4/92)
Furtwängler—The Early Recordings
Bach: Brandenburg Concertos (exc); Suites, BWV1066-9 (exc); *Mozart:* Nozze di Figaro (exc); Entführung (exc); Serenade, K525; *Schubert:* Rosamunde (exc); *Beethoven:* Egmont (exc); Symphony 5; *Weber:* Freischütz (exc); *Rossini:* Gazza ladra (exc); Barbiere di Siviglia (exc). (BPO/W. Furtwängler)

Ⓓ **37073-2** (4/92)
Furtwängler—Early Recordings 1926-1937
Weber: Freischütz (exc); Invitation to the Dance; *Mendelssohn:* Midsummer Night's Dream (exc); Hebrides; *Berlioz:* Damnation de Faust (exc); *Wagner:* Lohengrin (exc); Tristan und Isolde (exc); Götterdämmerung (exc); *Brahms:* Hungarian Dances (exc); *J. Strauss II:* Fledermaus (exc); *R. Strauss:* Till Eulenspiegel. (BPO/W. Furtwängler)

Ⓓ **37087-2** (6/92)
Songs of Kurt Weill
Weill: Berliner Requiem (exc); Silbersee (exc); Dreigroschenoper (exc); Love Life (exc); Berlin im Licht; Mahagonny (exc); Lady in the Dark (exc); Happy End (exc); Marie Galante (exc); Je ne t'aime pas; Street Scene (exc); One touch of Venus (exc); Firebrand of Florence (exc); Nannas Lied; Youkali; Knickerbocker Holiday (exc). (A. Réaux, R. Kapilow)

Ⓓ **37092-2** (4/92)
Copland—Orchestral Works
Copland: Tender Land Suite; Latin-American sketches; Red Pony Suite. (Phoenix SO/J. Sedares)

Ⓓ **37104-2**
Cage/Monk—Pianos and Voices
Cage: Pieces (1935 rev 1974); Room (1943); Wonderful widow of eighteen springs; Nowth upon Nacht; *M. Monk:* Specimen Days (exc); Paris; Education of the Girlchild (exc); Games (exc); Double Fiesta; *Cage:* Ophelia (1946); In a Landscape (1948); Etudes australes Bks I-IV; Tossed as it is Untroubled—Meditation (1943); Root of an Unfocus (1944); Primitive (1942). (A. de Mare, A. de Mare)

Ⓓ **37111-2** (1/92)
R. Strauss—Friedenstag
R. Strauss: Friedenstag (Cpte). (R. Roloff, A. Marc, W. Wilderman, G. Shirley, M. Wittges, P. van Derick, P. Schmidt, R. Broitman, S. Lusmann, T. Cook, R. Cassilly, J. Wood, K. Williams, NY Gay Men's Chor, Collegiate Chorale, Collegiate Orch/R. Bass)

Ⓓ **37119-2**
Richard Strauss Conducts
Gluck: Iphigénie en Aulide (exc); *Mozart:* Zauberflöte (exc); Symphony 40; *Weber:* Euryanthe (exc); *Cornelius:* Barbier von Bagdad (exc); *Wagner:* Fliegende Holländer (exc); Tristan und Isolde (exc). (BPO, Berlin St Op Orch/R. Strauss)

Ⓓ **37124-2** (5/93)
Virgil Thomson—Lord Byron
V. Thomson: Lord Byron (Cpte). (M. Lord, R. Zeller, D. Fortunato, R. Johnson, J. Ommerlé, G. Mercer, A. Csengery, T. Woodman, S. Owen, L. Jonason, D. Vanderlinde, M. Dry, Monadnock Fest Chor, Monadnock Fest Orch/J. Bolle)

Ⓓ **37126-2** (11/92)
Victor de Sabata conducts the BPO
Verdi: Aida (exc); *Wagner:* Tristan und Isolde (exc); *Kodály:* Galánta Dances; *Respighi:* Roman Festivals. (BPO/V. de Sabata)

Ⓓ **37129-2** (5/93)
Clemens Kraus Conducts
Brahms: Symphony 3; *R. Strauss:* Bourgeois Gentilhomme Suite; Salome (exc). (VPO/C. Krauss)

Ⓓ **37132-2** (1/93)
Richard Strauss Conducts
R. Strauss: Rosenkavalier film; Alpensinfonie. (Bavarian St Orch, Tivoli Augmented Orch/R. Strauss)

Ⓓ **37137-2**
The Art of Harold Samuel
Bach: English Suites, BWV806-811 (exc); Partitas, BWV825-30 (exc); Partitas, BWV825-30 (exc); Chromatic Fantasia and Fugue, BWV903; Wohltemperierte Klavier (exc); Wohltemperierte Klavier (exc); Wohltemperierte Klavier (exc); Fantasia, BWV906; *C.P.E. Bach:* Kenner III (exc); Kenner I (exc); *J.C. Bach:* Keyboard Sonatas, Op.5 (exc); *Clementi:* Keyboard Sonatas, Op.12 (exc); *Schubert:* Moments musicaux, D780 (exc); Waltzes, D779 (exc); Waltzes, D365 (exc); *Gluck:* Iphigénie en Aulide (exc); *Brahms:* Piano Pieces, Op.117 (exc); *Bach:* Violin Sonatas, BWV1014-19 (exc); Brandenburg Concertos (exc). (H. Samuel, I. Menges, NBC SO/F. Black)

Ⓓ **37700-2** (12/92)
Albert Coates Conducts, Vol.1 - Russian Favourites
Glinka: Ruslan and Lyudmila (exc); Kamarinskaya; *Borodin:* In the Steppes of Central Asia; Prince Igor (exc); *Liadov:* Russian Folksongs, Op.58; *Mussorgsky:* Fair at Sorochintsï (exc); *Tchaikovsky:* Marche Slave; *Rimsky-Korsakov:* May Night (exc); Dubinushka; Maid of Pskov (exc); Mlada (exc); Snow Maiden (exc); *Stravinsky:* Firebird (exc). (LSO/A. Coates)

Ⓓ **37704-2** (4/93)
Albert Coates conducts the LSO, Vol.2
Liszt: Hungarian Rhapsodies, S359 (exc); *Weber:* Oberon (exc); *Wagner:* Rheingold (exc); Walküre (exc); Götterdämmerung (exc); *Humperdinck:* Hänsel und Gretel (exc); *Dvořák:* Carnival; *R. Strauss:* Don Juan; *Bach:* Fantasia and Fugue, BWV537; *R. Strauss:* Tod und Verklärung; *Respighi:* Fountains of Rome; *Holst:* Planets (exc); *Ravel:* La Valse. (LSO/A. Coates)

Ⓓ **399 223**
Operetta Highlights 1
Lehár: Graf von Luxemburg (exc); *O. Straus:* Walzertraum (exc). (H. Brauner, R. Holm, E. Liebesberg, D. Hermann, R. Christ, H. Prikopa, Vienna Volksoper Chor, Vienna Volksoper Orch/F. Bauer-Theussl)

Ⓓ **399 225**
Operetta Highlights 3
Abraham: Blume von Hawaii; Viktoria und ihr Husar (exc); *Benatzky:* Im weissen Rössl (exc). (H. Brauner, K. Equiluz, H. Winter, A. Niessner, Vienna Volksoper Chor, Vienna Volksoper Orch/J.L. Gruber, F. Loor, K. Terkal/F. Bauer-Theussl)

Ⓓ **399 226**
Operetta Highlights 4
Kálmán: Csárdásfürstin (exc); *Lehár:* Paganini (exc). (Lotte Rysanek, E. Liebesberg, R. Christ, H. Prikopa, E. Mechera, K. Equiluz, Vienna Volksoper Chor, Vienna Volksoper Orch/F. Bauer-Theussl)

Koch Schwann

Ⓓ **310037**
Alexander von Zemlinsky conducts
Mozart: Don Giovanni (exc); Così fan tutte (exc); Entführung (exc); *Beethoven:* Fidelio (exc); *Rossini:* Gazza ladra (exc); *Flotow:* Alessandro Stradella (exc); *Maillart:* Dragons de Villars (exc); *Smetana:* Má Vlast (exc); *Weinberger:* Schwanda the Bagpiper (exc). (Berlin St Op Orch/A. von Zemlinsky, Berlin Charlottenburg Op Orch, BPO)

Ⓓ **310061** (9/90)
Rossini—Barbiere di Siviglia - excerpts
Rossini: Barbiere di Siviglia (exc). (Munich Rococo Sols)

Ⓓ **310110**
Banda Classica - Harmoniemusik
A. Wranitzky: Hunting marches (exc); *Mozart:* Clemenza di Tito (exc); *W.F.E. Bach:* Marches; *Weber:* Adagio and Rondo, J115; *Salieri:* Armonia per un tempio della notte; *Kreutzer:* Waltzes (exc); *Beethoven:* Fidelio (exc); *Cherubini:* March in F; *Weber:* March, J307; *Lefébure-Wély:* Sortie; *Joplin:* Bethena; Rose Bud March; Pleasant Moments; Magnetic Rag; Ragtime Dance; *Milhaud:* Scaramouche. (Banda Classica/C. Siegmann)

Ⓓ **310115**
Classics To Broadway
Mozart: Zauberflöte (exc); *Schubert:* Marches Militaires, D733 (exc); *Brahms:* Hungarian Dances (exc); *J. Strauss II:* Fledermaus (exc); *Falla:* Amor Brujo (exc); *Saint-Saëns:* Carnaval des animaux (exc); *Gershwin:* Porgy and Bess Suite; *Berlin:* Piano Medley. (A. Paratore, J. Paratore)

Ⓓ **310212**
Innsbrucker Salonquintett
Lehár: Jetzt geht's los, Op. 1; *Kálmán:* Gräfin Mariza (exc); Csárdásfürstin (exc); Herbstmanöver (exc); Hollandweibchen (exc); Faschingsfee (exc); Herzogin von Chicago (exc); Bajadere (exc); Zigeunerprimas (exc); Zirkusprinzessin (exc); *Ziehrer:* Herreinspaziert!, Op. 518; *Jahn:* Dogana Serenade; *Loubé:* Wunschkonzert aus Wien; *Knümann:* Ungarisch; *Jahn:* Veldidena. (Innsbruck Salon Qnt)

Ⓓ **310302** (7/92)
Franchetti—Cristoforo Colombo
Franchetti: Cristoforo Colombo (Cpte). (R. Bruson, R. Scandiuzzi, R. Ragatzu, M. Berti, G. Pasino, V. Ombuena, A. Ulbrich, E. Turco, P. Lefebvre, F. Previati, D. Jenis, Hungarian Rad Chor, Frankfurt RSO/M. Viotti)

Ⓓ **310322** (10/92)
Massenet—Cléopâtre
Massenet: Cléopâtre (Cpte). (K. Harries, D. Henry, J-L. Maurette, D. Streiff, M. Olmeda, M. Hacquard, C. Massoz, P. Georges, Massenet Fest Chor, Saint-Etienne Nouvel Orch/P. Fournillier)

Ⓓ **310402**
Guitar Music from the Age of Viennese Classicism
Giuliani: Variazioni Concertanti; *Carulli:* Nocturne Concertante; *Coste:* Grande Duo; *Mertz:* Am Grabe der Geliebten; Barcarole; Unruhe; *Rossini:* Barbiere di Siviglia (exc). (Tedesco Duo)

Ⓓ **310882** (4/94)
Hasse—Piramo e Tisbe
Hasse: Piramo e Tisbe (Cpte). (B. Schlick, S. Gari, M. Lecocq, Capella Clementina/H. Müller-Brühl)

Ⓓ **311155**
Johann Strauss II—Waltzes, Polkas and Overtures
J. Strauss II: Blauen Donau, Op. 314; Unter Donner und Blitz; Rosen aus dem Süden; Eljen a Magyar!, Op. 332; Annen-Polka, Op. 117; Auf der Jagd, Op. 373; Kaiser, Op. 437; Fledermaus (exc); Zigeunerbaron (exc). (Mazovian PO/P. Kantschieder)

Ⓓ **311162**
World Famous Conductors from Silesia
Wagner: Siegfried Idyll; *Beethoven:* Leonore (exc); *Haydn:* Symphony 104; Symphony 92; *Gluck:* Iphigénie en Aulide (exc); *Moszkowski:* Suite, Op. 39 (exc); *Saint-Saëns:* Henry VIII (exc); *Fauré:* Pavane; *Flotow:* Martha (exc); *Suppé:* Schöne Galathee (exc); *Grieg:* Holberg Suite. (Berlin St Op Orch/O. Klemperer, VPO/H. Weisbach, LSO, NY Nat SO/W. Damrosch, Vienna St Op Orch/L. Reichwein, Berlin RIAS Orch/H. Sandberg)

Ⓓ **311392** (5/93)
Milhaud—Little Symphonies and Little Operas
Milhaud: Chamber Symphony 1; Chamber Symphony 2; Chamber Symphony 3; Chamber Symphony 4; Chamber Symphony 5; Chamber Symphony 6; Enlèvement d'Europe; Abandon d'Ariane; Déliverance de Thésée. (Capella Cracoviensis/K.A. Rickenbacher)

Ⓓ **312642**
Unicef Gala 1991
Leoncavallo: Pagliacci (exc); *Mozart:* Nozze di Figaro (exc); Zauberflöte (exc); *Puccini:* Gianni Schicchi (exc); Turandot (exc); *Meyerbeer:* Huguenots (exc); *Handel:* Serse (exc); *Verdi:* Simon Boccanegra (exc); *Rossini:* Barbiere di Siviglia (exc); *Giordano:* Andrea Chénier (exc); *Okamura:* We don't give up our dreams; *Gershwin:* Porgy and Bess (exc); *Kern:* Show Boat (exc); *Traditional:* Didn't my Lord deliver Daniel; Ride on, King Jesus; My Fatherland. (B. Glenn, H. Kashiwagi, Deng, R. Oostwoud, E.B. Holmes, P. Kang, Japanese Int Children's Chor, S. Harrison, A. Juffinger, K. Murata, S. Katz)

Ⓓ **312682**
Opera Gala with Young Artists - Volume II
Mozart: Clemenza di Tito (exc); Così fan tutte (exc); Don Giovanni (exc); Entführung (exc); *Rossini:* Barbiere di Siviglia (exc); *A. Thomas:* Hamlet (exc); *Puccini:* Bohème (exc); *Gounod:* Roméo et Juliette (exc); *Verdi:* Don Carlo (exc); *Wagner:* Lohengrin (exc); Meistersinger (exc); Rheingold (exc); *R. Strauss:* Rosenkavalier (exc). (L. Aikin, V. Esposito, B. Frittoli, C. Taha, A. Ulbrich, R. Morloc, V. Ombuena, J. Sacher, A. Scholz, A. Anisimov, Berlin RSO/J. Märkl)

Ⓓ **312692**
Massenet—Esclarmonde
Massenet: Esclarmonde (Cpte). (D. Mazzola, J. Sempere, H. Perraguin, G. Gabelle, C. Treguier, J-P. Courtis, Massenet Fest Chor, Budapest Liszt SO/P. Fournillier)

Ⓓ **312702** (12/94)
Massenet—Grisélidis
Massenet: Grisélidis (Cpte). (M. Command, C. Larcher, B. Desnoues, J-P. Courtis, J-L. Viala, D. Henry, C. Treguier, M. Sieyes, Lyon Nat Ch, Lyon Op Chor, Budapest F. Liszt SO/P. Fournillier)

Ⓓ **312722**
J. Strauss II—Eine Nacht in Venedig
J. Strauss II: Nacht in Venedig (Cpte). (E. Réthy, K. Friedrich, R. Boesch, K. Preger, A. Jerger, H. Mayer-Gänsbacher, M. Schober, Bregenz Fest Chor, Vienna SO/A. Paulik)

Ⓓ **312732**
Lehár—Der Zarewitsch (excs)
Lehár: Zarewitsch (exc); *Traditional:* Song of the Volga boatmen; I gaze at the sky. (G. di Stefano, D. Koller, D. Hanak, H. Holecek, Orig Volga Cossacks Chor, Vienna

Operetta Chor, Vienna Operetta Orch, Balalaika Sols/E-G. Scherzer)

Ⓓ **312942**
Beethoven—Fidelio
Beethoven: Fidelio (Cpte). (J. Rutishauser, J. Stępień, D. Washington, J. Ostapiuk, M. Didusch, E. Holland, A. Dymovski, Warsaw Nat Op Chor, Masurian PO/P. Kantschieder)

Ⓓ **313112** (7/94)
Gounod—Sapho
Gounod: Sapho (Cpte). (M. Command, S. Coste, C. Papis, E. Faury, L. Sarrazin, P. Georges, S. Martinez, Saint-Etienne Lyric Chor, Saint-Etienne Nouvel Orch/P. Fournillier)

Ⓓ **313242**
Beethoven—Symphony No 3
Beethoven: Symphony 3; Leonore (exc). (Masurian PO/P. Kantschieder)

Ⓓ **313482** (1/94)
Wagner—Parsifal
Wagner: Parsifal (Cpte). (R. Kollo, T. Adam, U. Cold, G. Schröter, R. Bunger, F. Teschler, H. Gebhardt, H.C. Polster, E. Breul, G. Pohl, H-J. Wachsmuth, R. Werner, H. Ambros, H. Terner, I. Ludwig-Jahns, I. Springer, Leipzig Rad Chor, Berlin Rad Chor, Leipzig St Thomas Church Ch, Leipzig RSO/H. Kegel)

Ⓓ **313772**
Franck—Pieces for two pianos and piano for four hands
Franck: God Save the King Duet; Lucille de Grétry Duet; Hulda (exc). (D. Blumenthal, J. Bogart)

Ⓓ **314002**
Early songs by famous composers
Haydn: Lieder für das Clavier I (exc); *Mozart:* An die Freude, K53; *Beethoven:* An die Hoffnung, Op. 32; *Weber:* Wiegenlied, J96; *Schubert:* Gretchen am Spinnrade, D118; *Mendelssohn:* Lieder, Op. 8 (exc); *Schumann:* Myrthen, Op. 25 (exc); *Liszt:* Es muss ein Wunderbares sein, S314; *Brahms:* Lieder, Op. 3 (exc); *Wolf:* Über Nacht; *Mahler:* Lieder und Gesänge (exc); *R. Strauss:* Weihnachtslied; *Pfitzner:* Lieder, Op. 2 (exc); *Reger:* Tränen im Auge, Op. 8/2; *Schoenberg:* Lieder, Op. 2 (exc); *Webern:* Lieder (1901-04) (exc); *Marx:* Lied eines Mädchens; *Hauer:* Hölderlin-Lieder, Op. 6 (exc); *Berg:* Schliesse mir die augen beide (exc); *Krenek:* Lieder, Op. 19 (exc); *Blacher:* Romeo und Julia (exc); *Einem:* Bitte an den Hund; *Orff:* Blond ist mein Haar. (R. Klepper, E. Werba)

Ⓓ **314006** (10/91)
Henze—Die Bassariden
Henze: Bassariden (Cpte). (K. Riegel, A. Schmidt, M. Burt, R. Tear, W. Murray, K. Armstrong, C. Lindsley, O. Wenkel, Berlin Rad Chbr Ch, South German Rad Chor, Berlin RSO/G. Albrecht)

Ⓓ **314010** (12/87)
Wolf—Der Corregidor
Wolf: Corregidor (Cpte). (W. Hollweg, H. Donath, D. Fischer-Dieskau, D. Soffel, K. Moll, V. von Halem, H. Berger-Tuna, P. Maus, G. Schreckenbach, Berlin RIAS Chbr Ch, Berlin RSO/G. Albrecht)

Ⓓ **314012** (12/85)
Zemlinsky: Florentinische Tragidie
Zemlinsky: Florentinische Tragödie. (D. Soffel, K. Riegel, G. Sarabia, Berlin RSO/G. Albrecht)

Ⓓ **314013** (4/86)
Zemlinsky—Geburtstag der Infantin
Zemlinsky: Geburtstag der Infantin (exc). (I. Nielsen, K. Riegel, B. Haldas, D. Weller, C. Studer, O. Fredricks, M. Hirsti, Berlin RSO/G. Albrecht)

Ⓓ **314014**
Szymanowski—Krol Roger
Szymanowski: King Roger (Cpte). (F. Skulski, B. Zagórzanka, Z. Nikodem, S. Kowalski, J. Ostapiuk, R. Racewicz, Warsaw Wiekl Th Chor, Warsaw Wiekl Th Orch/R. Satanowski)

Ⓓ **314018**
Virtuoso Operatic Arias for Soprano and Clarinet
Nicolai: Variazioni concertanti, Op. 26; *Spohr:* Faust (exc); *Schubert:* Verschworenen (exc); *Vogler:* Erwin und Elmire (exc); *F.J. Škroup:* Libussa's Wedding (exc); *Poissl:* Athalia (exc); *Crusell:* Lilla Slafinnen (exc); *Mozart:* Clemenza di Tito (exc). (I. Siebert, D. Klöcker, South-West German RSO/K. Donath)

Ⓓ **314025** (11/89)
Schoeck—Massimilla Doni
Schoeck: Massimilla Doni (Cpte). (E. Mathis, J. Protschka, H. Winkler, H. Stamm, R. Hermann, D. van der Walt, C. Lindsley, A. Küttenbaum, U. Ress, Cologne Rad Chor, Cologne RSO/G. Albrecht)

Ⓓ **314042** (9/91)
Mendelssohn—Die Hochzeit des Camacho
Mendelssohn: Hochzeit des Camacho (Cpte). (R. Schudel, C. Swanson, C. Bieber, W. Mok, V. Horn, R. Lukas, J. Becker, W. Murray, F. Molsberger, Berlin RIAS Chbr Ch, BRSO/B. Klee)

Ⓓ **314052**
Opera Gala
Beethoven: Leonore (exc); *Rossini:* Barbiere di Siviglia (exc); *Mozart:* Nozze di Figaro (exc); Nozze di Figaro (exc); Nozze di Figaro (exc); Nozze di Figaro (exc); Don Giovanni (exc); *Donizetti:* Favorita (exc); Fille du Régiment (exc); *Rossini:* Italiana in Algeri (exc); *Verdi:* Ernani (exc); Ballo in Maschera (exc); Simon Boccanegra (exc); Traviata (exc); *Bellini:* Puritani (exc); Puritani (exc); *Rossini:* Viaggio a Reims (exc). (C. Gonzales, R. Ragatzu, O. Romanko, M. Bacelli, S. Pasqualini, E. Ferretti, R. Wörle, M. Biscotti, G. Saks, A. Silvestrelli, Ernst-Senff Chbr Chor, Berlin RSO/R. Buckley)

Ⓓ **314061**
Norbert Schultze—Schwarzer Peter
Schultze: Schwarzer Peter (Cpte). (T. Altmeyer, H.G. Knoblich, B. McDaniel, G. Vespermann, O. Höpfner, H. Kruse, G. van Jüten, M. Mödl, F. Müller-Heuser, B. Mira, C. Genest, W. Schneider, J. Schoenenberg, K-R. Liecke, A. Goerke, Heiner Kruse, J. Meinertzhagen, E. Hallhuber, Siegland Cantata Ch, Cologne Children's Ch, Cologne RSO/N. Schultze)

Ⓓ **314069** (1/92)
Zemlinsky—Kleider Machen Leute
Zemlinsky: Kleider machen Leute (Cpte). (H. Winkler, E. Mathis, W. Slabbert, H. Franzen, S. Kaluza, V. Vogel, U. Hunziker, B. Jensson, U.S. Eggimann, R. Hartmann, P. Keller, R. Rohner, J. Will, R. Scholze, R. Lenhart, K. Justus, S. Salminen, C. Otelli, U. Peter, Zurich Op Hse Chor, Zurich Op Orch/R. Weikert)

Ⓓ **314073**
Canzone Sacre
Bizet: Agnus Dei; *A. Scarlatti:* O di Betlemme altera; *Niedermeyer:* Pietà, Signore; *Herbeck:* Pueri concinite; *Franck:* Panis angelicus; *Gounod:* Ave Maria; *Handel:* Serse (exc); *Schubert:* Ave Maria, D839; *Paisiello:* Motetto in Pastorale; *G. Martini:* O sacrum convivium; *B. Marcello:* Estro poetico-armonico (exc); *T. Giordani:* Caro mio ben; *Bruckner:* Ave Maria (1882). (G. Sabbatini, A. Juffinger)

Ⓓ **314074** (6/92)
Verdi—Otello
Verdi: Otello (Cpte). (C. Murgu, M. Gulegina, R. Bruson, M. Saltarin, H. Yoshida, G. Pasino, M. Pertusi, G. de Angelis, Tokyo Little Sngrs, Fujiwara Op Chor, Tokyo PO/G Kuhn)

Ⓓ **314088** (5/92)
Mozart—Don Giovanni
Mozart: Don Giovanni (Cpte). (A. Dohmen, F. Pedaci, I. Galgani, B. Lucarini, M. Berti, E. Turco, A. Cauli, A. Silvestrelli, Marchigiano V. Bellini Lyric Chor, Marchigiano PO/G. Kuhn)

Ⓓ **314372** (8/95)
Schulhoff—Orchestral Works
Schulhoff: Plameny (exc); Symphony 1; Suite. (Brno St PO/I. Yinon)

Ⓓ **314502** (6/94)
Vienna State Opera—Live Recordings (sampler)
Bizet: Carmen (exc); *Wagner:* Walküre (exc); *R. Strauss:* Rosenkavalier (exc); *Verdi:* Don Carlo (exc); *Wagner:* Meistersinger (exc); *Mozart:* Nozze di Figaro (exc); *Wagner:* Lohengrin (exc); Fliegende Holländer (exc); *Borodin:* Prince Igor (exc); *Schmidt:* Notre Dame (exc); *Verdi:* Aida (exc); *Mozart:* Zauberflöte (exc); *Wagner:* Walküre (exc); *Verdi:* Ballo in maschera (exc); *Wagner:* Götterdämmerung (exc); *R. Strauss:* Frau ohne Schatten (exc); *Mascagni:* Cavalleria Rusticana (exc); *Wagner:* Rienzi (exc); *R. Strauss:* Rosenkavalier (exc). (S. Svanholm, V. Ursuleac, T. Mazaroff, P. Pierotic, P. Schoeffler, M. Klose, M. Müller, H. Hotter, H. Braun, A. Jerger, M. Lorenz, M. Reining, W. Grossmann, A. Konetzni, M. Ahlersmeyer, H. Konetzni, H. Roswaenge, M. Jeritza, F. Völker, E. Hadrabová, M. Gerhard, Vienna St Op Chor, Vienna St Op Orch/K. Böhm/W. Furtwängler/H. Knappertsbusch/C. Krauss/J. Krips/W. Loibner/L. Ludwig/R. Moralt/H. Reichenberger/H. Tietjen/B. Walter)

Ⓓ **314512** (7/94)
Vienna State Opera Live, Vol.1
R. Strauss: Rosenkavalier (exc); *Tchaikovsky:* Eugene Onegin (exc); *Verdi:* Otello (exc); *Rossini:* Barbiere di Siviglia (exc); *Benedict:* Carnival of Venice Variations; *Bellini:* Sonnambula (exc); *Verdi:* Aida (exc); *Wagner:* Tannhäuser (exc); Meistersinger (exc); Parsifal (exc); *Albert:* Tiefland (exc); *Gounod:* Faust (exc); *Wagner:* Götterdämmerung (exc); Götterdämmerung (exc); Meistersinger (exc); Lohengrin (exc); Lohengrin (exc); *Lehár:* Giuditta (exc); Giuditta (exc). (V. Ursuleac, R. Mayr, E. Hadrabová, M. Gerhart, H. Gallos, B. Paalen, K. von Pataky, C. Kullman, T. dal Monte, L. Montesanto, A. Sinnone, G. Lauri-Volpi, G. Rünger, J. Kalenberg, R. Bockelmann, K. Thorborg, J. Pölzer, R. Pauly, E. Pinza, L. Melchior, A. Konetzni, J. von Manowarda, K. Flagstad, T. Ralf, L. Helletsgruber, L. Hofmann, E. Schipper, M. Hussa, R. Tauber, J. Novotná, Vienna St Op Chor, Vienna St Op Orch/C. Krauss/H. Reichenberger/V. de Sabata/G. del Campo/R. Heger/F. Weingartner/K. Alwin/H. Knappertsbusch/J. Krips/F. Lehár)

Ⓓ **314522** (8/94)
Vienna State Opera Live, Vol.2
Wagner: Parsifal (exc); Meistersinger (exc). (H. Grahl, H. Alsen, A. Konetzni, H. Wiedemann, R. Bockelmann, J. von Manowarda, J. Katona, E. Bürger, E. Fuchs, G. Hann, G. Heckel, K. Mikorey, J. Brombacher, W. Markgraf, A. von Diehl, H. Krenn, E. Laholm, E. Zimmermann, T. Lemnitz, R. Berglund, Vienna St Op Chor, Nuremberg Op Chor, Vienna St Op Orch/H. Knappertsbusch/W. Furtwängler)

Ⓓ **314532** (11/94)
Vienna State Opera Live, Vol.3
R. Strauss: Salome (exc); Salome (exc); *Mozart:* Idomeneo (exc); *Weber:* Freischütz (exc); *Wagner:* Meistersinger (exc); Siegfried (exc); Götterdämmerung (exc). (J. Witt, E. Schürhoff, E. Schulz, P. Schoeffler, A. Dermota, D. With, H. Alsen, H. Schweiger, C. Bissuti, K. Ettl, H. Hotter, J. Sattler, M. Bugarinovic, J. Sabel, E. Réthy, E. Böttcher, A. Konetzni, E. Kunz, M. Rus, F. Völker, E. Rethberg, J. von Manowarda, J. Prohaska, C. Reich, J. Kalenberg, H. Wiedemann, M. Lorenz, R. Anday, W. Wernigk, L. Helletsgruber, H. Trundt, E. Schipper, M. Angerer, Vienna St Op Chor, Vienna St Op Orch/R. Strauss/J. Krips)

Ⓓ **314542** (12/94)
Vienna State Opera Live, Vol.4
Verdi: Aida (exc); Don Carlo (exc); *Leoncavallo:* Pagliacci (exc); *Gounod:* Faust (exc); *Wagner:* Tannhäuser (exc); Fliegende Holländer (exc); *Puccini:* Tosca (exc); Turandot (exc); *Leoncavallo:* Pagliacci (exc); *Saint-Saëns:* Samson et Dalila (exc); *Verdi:* Aida (exc). (J. Björling, M. Németh, K. Thorborg, A. Sved, L. Hofmann, T. Mazaroff, P. Pierotic, M. Reining, P. Tutsek, C. Bissuti, H. Alsen, M. Bokor, F. Ginrod, A. Kipnis, E. Réthy, A. Jerger, K. Norbert, J. Kalenberg, B. Paalen, S. Björling, K. Ettl, G. Monthy, A. Michalsky, R. Anday, R. Maison, K. von Pataky, N. Zec, Vienna St Op Chor, Vienna St Op Orch/V. de Sabata/B. Walter/K. Alwin/J. Krips/W. Furtwängler/R. Heger/L. Reichwein/R. Moralt/W. Loibner/H. Reichenberger)

Ⓓ **314552** (11/94)
Vienna State Opera Live, Vol.5
R. Strauss: Aegyptische Helena (exc); Frau ohne Schatten (exc); Daphne (exc). (V. Ursuleac, F. Völker, M. Bokor, H. Roswaenge, A. Jerger, T. Ralf, H. Konetzni, E. Höngen, H. Alsen, E. Loose, W. Wenkoff, E. Boettcher, M. Frutschnigg, J. Herrmann, E. Schulz, G. Monthy, M. Rus, W. Wernigk, A. Poell, T. Neralič, R. Neumann, M. Reining, A. Dermota, A. Rauch, Vienna St Op Chor, Vienna St Op Orch/C. Krauss/K. Böhm/R. Moralt)

Ⓓ **314562** (1/95)
Vienna State Opera Live, Vol.6
Wagner: Tristan und Isolde (exc); Parsifal (exc); Parsifal (exc); Götterdämmerung (exc); *Verdi:* Aida (exc); *Wagner:* Walküre (exc); Siegfried (exc); Meistersinger (exc). (M. Lorenz, V. Ursuleac, A. Jerger, E. Zimmermann, B. Paalen, N. Zec, H. Gallos, H. Duhan, H. Wiedemann, V. Madin, A. Arnold, Wolken, W. Wernigk, A. Muzzarelli, H. Reich, K. Ettl, A. Konetzni, M. Klose, P. Schoeffler, S. Roth, H. Braun, Adolf Vogel, J. von Manowarda, D. Ilitsch, E. Nikolaidi, M. Ahlersmeyer, H. Alsen, L. Hofmann, J. Kalenberg, Vienna St Op Chor, Vienna St Op Orch/W. Furtwängler/L. Reichwein/H. Knappertsbusch/L. Ludwig/C. Krauss)

Ⓓ **314572** (2/95)
Vienna State Opera Live, Vol.7
Bizet: Carmen (exc); *Pfitzner:* Palestrina (exc); *Schmidt:* Notre Dame (exc); *Verdi:* Aida (exc); *Smetana:* Bartered Bride (exc). (T. Mazaroff, E. Réthy, E. Brems, A. Arnold, P. Pierotic, G. Monthy, D. Komarek, O. Levko-Antosch, M. Bokor, J. Witt, A. Jerger, E. Szánthó, H. Alsen, K. Ettl, F. Destal, G. Maikl, W. Wernigk, A. Gregorig, K. Friedrich, E. Schulz, M. Németh, K. Thorborg, A. Sved, A. Dermota, E. Kaufmann, E. Nikolaidi, A. Pernerstorfer, Vienna St Op Chor, Vienna St Op Orch/B. Walter/R. Moralt)

Ⓓ **314582** (4/95)
Vienna State Opera Live, Vol.8
Verdi: Ballo in maschera (exc); Aida (exc); Falstaff (exc). (M. Lorenz, M. Ahlersmeyer, H. Konetzni, E. Nikolaidi, A. Noni, S. Roth, M. Rus, F. Worff, S. Svanholm, D. Ilitsch, H. Hotter, J. von Manowarda, G. Hann, K. Kronenberg, E. Réthy, A. Kern, A. Dermota, J. Witt, M. Bugarinovic, W. Wernigk, Vienna St Op Chor, Vienna St Op Orch/K. Böhm/V. Gui/C. Krauss)

Ⓓ **314592** (8/95)
Vienna State Opera Live, Vol.9
Wagner: Rheingold (exc); Walküre (exc); Siegfried (exc); Götterdämmerung (exc). (J. Prohaska, N. Zec, H. Alsen, A. Konetzni, L. Hofmann, F. Völker, H. Konetzni, R. Merker, K. Thorborg, L. Helletsgruber, E. Flesch, M. Bokor, D. With, A. Michalsky, F. Stroinigg, B. Paalen, E. Weichert, R. Schubert, G. Kappel, E. Zimmermann, J. Kalenberg, E. Schipper, W. Achsel, R. Anday, J. von Manowarda, G. Rünger, E. Szánthó, Vienna St Op Orch/J. Krips/B. Walter/R. Heger)

Ⓓ **314602** (3/95)
Vienna State Opera Live, Vol.10
Mozart: Nozze di Figaro (exc); *Wagner:* Meistersinger (exc); *Bizet:* Carmen (exc); *Puccini:* Turandot (exc); *Verdi:* Don Carlo (exc); *Nicolai:* Lustigen Weiber von Windsor (exc); *Wagner:* Meistersinger (exc); Tannhäuser (exc); Siegfried (exc); Götterdämmerung (exc); *Verdi:* Falstaff (exc); *Puccini:* Gianni Schicchi (exc). (L. Hofmann, H. Alsen, G. Maikl, G. Monthy, H. Wiedemann, V. Madin, A. Arnold, E. Fritsch, R. Tomek, J. Kiepura, E. Réthy, M. Németh, A. Kipnis, N. Ardelli, H. Konetzni, E. Nikolaidi, L. Helletsgruber, M. Reining, M. Ahlersmeyer, K. Bollhammer, E. Majkut, M. Cebotari, M. Rohs, A. Jerger, V. Ursuleac, F. Völker, E. Zimmermann, E. Szánthó, A. Muzzarelli, H. Reich, K. Ettl, J. Kalenberg, R. Sallaba, V. Mansinger, K. Thorborg, M. Lorenz, W. Wernigk, M. Bugarinovic, D. With, D. Komarek, A. Dermota, O. Levko-Antosch, N. Zec, E. Godin, M. Schober, O. Drapal, F. Worff, W. Achsel, F. Skokan, F. Schramm, Vienna St Op Chor, Vienna St Op Orch/K. Böhm/C. Krauss/K. Alwin/H. Reichenberger/B. Walter/F. Weingartner/H. Knappertsbusch/W. Furtwängler/W. Loibner)

Ⓓ **314612** (5/95)
Vienna State Opera Live, Vol.11
Wagner: Tristan und Isolde (exc). (M. Lorenz, A. Konetzni, M. Klose, H. Alsen, P. Schoeffler, G. Monthy, H. Gallos, K. Ettl, W. Franter, Vienna St Op Chor, Vienna St Op Orch/W. Furtwängler)

Ⓓ **314622** (11/95)
Vienna State Opera Live, Vol.12
R. Strauss: Rosenkavalier (exc); *Wagner:* Tannhäuser (exc); Meistersinger (exc); *Gounod:* Faust (exc); *R. Strauss:* Salome (exc); *Wagner:* Walküre (exc); *Giordano:* Andrea Chénier (exc); *Mascagni:* Cavalleria rusticana (exc); *Leoncavallo:* Pagliacci (exc). (Lotte Lehmann, E. Hadrabová, V. Madin, E. Schumann, A. Michalsky, R. Tomek, B. Sterneck, B. Paalen, W. Wernigk, J. Kalenberg, R. Mayr, F. Schorr, G. Maikl, F. Markhoff, K. Ettl, L. Hofmann, K. Thorborg, E. Laholm, H. Wiedemann, H. Roswaenge, J. Berglund, L. Helletsgruber, A. Sved, G. Graarud, M. Jeritza, E. Schipper, J. von Manowarda, Wolken, F. Völker, M. Bokor, R. Anday, D. With, E. Szánthó, Vienna St Op Chor, Vienna St Op Orch/H. Knappertsbusch/R. Heger/F. Weingartner/J. Krips/H. Reichenberger/C. Krauss)

Ⓓ **314632** (6/95)
Vienna State Opera Live, Vol.13
Mozart: Nozze di Figaro (exc); *Puccini:* Fanciulla del West (exc); *Leoncavallo:* Pagliacci (exc); *Mascagni:* Cavalleria Rusticana (exc); *Salmhofer:* Iwan Tarassenko (exc); *Schmidt:* Notre Dame (exc); *Wagner:* Parsifal (exc); *Weber:* Freischütz (exc); *Wagner:* Fliegende Holländer (exc); Tannhäuser (exc); *Verdi:* Aida (exc). (A. Jerger, M. Reining, P. Schoeffler, M. Perras, D. With, O. Levko-Antosch, K. Ettl, W. Wernigk, H. Gallos, V. Madin, D. Komarek, A. Piccaver, G. Monthy, E. Schumann, E. Schipper, A. Konetzni, T. Mazaroff, K. Kolowratnik, R. Tomek, F. Szkokan, J. Sawka, H. Alsen, N. Zec, F. Destal, E. Nikolaidi, E. Rutgers, J. Pölzer, A. Muzzarelli, W. Rode, J. von Manowarda, W. Schirp, B. Gigli, M. Németh, R. Anday, A. Sved, A. Kipnis, Vienna St Op Chor, Vienna St Op Orch/W. Loibner/H. Duhan/K. Alwin/H. Knappertsbusch/R. Moralt/L. Reichwein)

Ⓓ **314642** (8/95)
Vienna State Opera Live, Vol.14
Wagner: Rheingold (exc); Walküre (exc); Götterdämmerung (exc); Meistersinger (exc); Parsifal (exc). (J. von Manowarda, B. Paalen, V. Ursuleac, G. Graarud, V. Madin, J. Kalenberg, E. Zimmermann, H. Wiedemann, F. Markhoff, L. Helletsgruber, D. With, E. Szánthó, F. Schorr, M. Jeritza, F. Hüni-Mihacsek, F. Völker, R. Mayr, E. Hadrabová, M. Bokor, R. Anday, A. Michalsky, H. Trundt, E. Schipper, R. Bockelmann, N. Zec, G. Maikl, H. Duhan, A. Arnold, Wolken, R. Tomek, A. Muzzarelli, H. Reich, K. Ettl, G. Rünger, Vienna St Op Chor, Vienna St Op Orch/C. Krauss)

Ⓓ **314652** (10/95)
Vienna State Opera Live, Vol.15
R. Strauss: Arabella (exc); Friedenstag (Cpte); Ariadne auf Naxos (exc). (V. Ursuleac, M. Bokor, A. Jerger, A. Kern, G. Rünger, R. Mayr, H. Hotter, H. Alsen, J. Witt, H. Wiedemann, C. Bissuti, N. Zec, A. Dermota, H. Gallos, G. Monthy, K. Kamann, W. Franter, V. Madin, M. Bugarinovic, A. Konetzni, S. Svanholm, E. Schulz, A. Pichler, A. Muzzarelli, F. Jelinek, H. Baier, D. Komarek, E. Nikolaidi, E. Rutgers, A. Poell, W. Wernigk, Alfred Vogel, R. Sallaba, Vienna St Op Chor, Vienna St Op Orch/C. Krauss/R. Moralt, V. Ursuleac)

Ⓓ **314662** (9/95)
Vienna State Opera Live, Vol.16
Wagner: Rienzi (exc); Lohengrin (exc); Walküre (exc); Walküre (exc); Walküre (exc); Götterdämmerung (exc); *Leoncavallo:* Pagliacci (exc); *R. Strauss:* Frau ohne Schatten (exc); Elektra (exc); *Wagner:* Götterdämmerung (exc); Götterdämmerung (exc); *Verdi:* Don Carlo (exc); Otello (exc). (F. Völker, R. Anday, H. Gallos, K. Ettl, Z. Zika, J. von Manowarda, E. Schipper, G. Rünger, V. Ursuleac, R. Mayr, H. Konetzni, J. Pölzer, A. Konetzni, E. Szánthó, W. Achsel, K. Hammes, A. Jerger, Vienna St Op Chor, Vienna St Op Orch/J. Krips/F. Ruhlmann/C. Krauss/H. Knappertsbusch/K. Alwin)

Ⓓ **314672**
Vienna State Opera Live, Vol.17
Mozart: Zauberflöte (exc); *Weber:* Freischütz (exc); *Wagner:* Lohengrin (exc); *R. Strauss:* Elektra (exc); *Wagner:* Götterdämmerung (exc); Tannhäuser (exc); *Wolf-Ferrari:* Gioielli della Madonna (exc); *R. Strauss:* Rosenkavalier (exc); Rosenkavalier (exc). (E. Berger, M. Reining, J. von Manowarda, C. Bissuti, T. Lemnitz, E. Rutgers, M. Bohnen, F. Völker, V. Soetber, W. Franter, P. Kötter, M. Teschemacher, H. Alsen, A. Konetzni, R. Pauly, E. Schipper, S. Svanholm, D. Söderqvist, E. Schürhoff, P. Tutsek, H. Konetzni, M. Lorenz, A. Schellenberg, G. Maikl, V. Madin, H. Gallos, K. Ettl, N. Ardelli, M. Bokor, A. Jerger, B. Sterneck, E. Schumann, E. Flesch, B. Paalen, A. Michalsky, Vienna St Op Chor, Vienna St Op Orch/H. Knappertsbusch)

Ⓓ **314682**
Vienna State Opera Live, Vol.18
Wagner: Meistersinger (exc); Lohengrin (exc). (J. Herrmann, K. Böhme, R. Sallaba, G. Monthy, E. Kunz, F. Krenn, E. Toriff, H. Gallos, W. Wernigk, H. Schweiger, R. Neumann, F. Worff, T. Ralf, P. Klein, M. Reining, M. Rohs, K. Ettl, J. von Manowarda, F. Völker, M. Müller, J. Prohaska, M. Klose, W. Grossmann, Berlin St Op Chor, Vienna St Op Chor, Vienna St Op Orch/K. Böhm/H. Tietjen)

Ⓓ **314692**
Vienna State Opera Live, Vol.19
Gluck: Iphigénie en Aulide (exc); *Wagner:* Tannhäuser (exc); Walküre (exc); Walküre (exc); Götterdämmerung (exc); Meistersinger (exc); Walküre (exc); *Weber:* Freischütz (exc); *Wagner:* Fliegende Holländer (exc); *Smetana:* Dalibor (exc); Dalibor (exc). (P. Schoeffler, K. Böhme, R. Sallaba, G. Monthy, E. Kunz, F. Krenn, E. Toriff, H. Gallos, W. Wernigk, H. Schweiger, R. Neumann, K. Ettl, S. Svanholm, P. Klein, M. Reining, M. Rohs, H. Braun, H. Konetzni, S. Roth, A. Poell, P. Tutsek, J. Pölzer, H. Alsen, E. Rutgers, E. Schürhoff, M. Bugarinovic, M. Lorenz, F. Normann, M. Rus, J. Berglund, M. Németh, A. Jerger, T. Mazaroff, W. Franter, E. Réthy, Vienna St Op Chor, Vienna St Op Orch/L. Ludwig/L. Reichwein/H. Knappertsbusch/K. Böhm/Wolfgang Martin)

Ⓓ **314702**
Vienna State Opera Live, Vol.20
Wagner: Walküre (exc); Meistersinger (exc); Tannhäuser (exc); Tannhäuser (exc). (K. Kamann, H. Alsen, G. Maikl, G. Monthy, H. Wiedemann, F. Krenn, A. Arnold, E. Fritsch, R. Tomek, Walter Hellmich, H. Reich, K. Ettl, M. Lorenz, E. Zimmermann, M. Reining, E. Szánthó, F. Völker, M. Müller, W. Grossmann, A. Konetzni, A. Jerger, L. Helletsgruber, E. Hadrabová, D. Komarek, R. Anday, A. Michalsky, D. With, B. Paalen, A. Báthy, Vienna St Op Chor, Vienna St Op Orch/W. Furtwängler)

Ⓓ **314712**
Vienna State Opera Live, Vol.21
Mozart: Così fan tutte (exc); *R. Strauss:* Capriccio (exc); *Pfitzner:* Palestrina (exc); *Orff:* Carmina burana (exc); *Borodin:* Prince Igor (exc); *Egk:* Columbus (exc); Joan von Zarissa (exc). (J. Patzak, K. Kronenberg, P. Schoeffler, M. Cebotari, A. Jerger, A. Dermota, E. Kunz, M. Rohs, W. Wenkoff, A. Noni, T. Neralič, J. Witt, H. Hotter, E. Schürhoff, E. Boettcher, E. Rutgers, M. Schober, H. Gallos, W. Wernigk, F. Worff, A. Poell, S. Roth, Alfred Vogel, H. Alsen, E. Réthy, A. Pichler, A. Michalsky, D. Söderqvist, H. Braun, E. Nikolaidi, D. Ilitsch, F. Jelinek, F. Normann, W. Franter, Vienna St Op Chor, Vienna St Op Orch, Bavarian St Op Orch/C. Krauss/K. Böhm/R. Moralt/L. Ludwig/W. Egk)

Ⓓ **314722**
Vienna State Opera Live, Vol.22
Leoncavallo: Pagliacci (exc); *Wagner:* Fliegende Holländer (exc); Parsifal (exc); Götterdämmerung (exc); Walküre (exc); Siegfried (exc); *Mozart:* Nozze di Figaro (exc). (H. Braun, D. Söderqvist, I. Beilke, L. Timm, G. Sommerschuh, M. Bugarinovic, R. Fischer, J. Sattler, W. Wernigk, J. Witt, E. Kunz, H. Hotter, G. Neidlinger, F. Normann, J. von Manowarda, Vienna St Op Chor, Vienna St Op Orch/A. Paulik/R. Moralt/H. Knappertsbusch/L. Reichwein/C. Krauss)

Ⓓ **314732**
Vienna State Opera Live, Vol.23
R. Strauss: Ariadne auf Naxos (Cpte); *Wagner:* Meistersinger (exc). (M. Reining, I. Seefried, A. Noni, M. Lorenz, P. Schoeffler, E. Kunz, M. Rus, P. Klein, R. Sallaba, E. Loose, M. Frutschnigg, E. Rutgers, J. Witt, A. Muzzarelli, H. Schweiger, F. Jelinek, H. Baier, J. Herrmann, E. Kunz, M. Lorenz, P. Klein, M. Reining, M. Rohs, Vienna St Op Chor, Vienna St Op Orch/K. Böhm)

Ⓓ **314742**
Vienna State Opera Live, Vol.24
Wagner: Rheingold (exc); Walküre (exc); Siegfried (exc); Siegfried (exc); Siegfried (exc); Götterdämmerung (exc); Götterdämmerung (exc). (H. Konetzni, D. Söderqvist, H. Braun, D. Ilitsch, E. Schulz, O. Levko-Antosch, A. Kern, E. Schumann, A. Konetzni, W. Achsel, L. Helletsgruber, A. Michalsky, E. Szánthó, D. With, E. Schürhoff, E. Nikolaidi, M. Bugarinovic, M. Frutschnigg, B. Paalen, R. Anday, S. Svanholm, E. Zimmermann, J. Kalenberg, M. Lorenz, F. Destal, J. Prohaska, E. Schipper, H. Hotter, P. Schoeffler, L. Hofmann, N. Zec, A. Kipnis, Vienna St Op Chor, Vienna St Op Orch/H. Knappertsbusch)

Ⓓ **315762**
Mozart—La Clemenza di Tito - arranged for Flute Quartet
Mozart: Clemenza di Tito (Cpte). (P. Bernold, BWV Trio)

Ⓓ **315922** (11/95)
Puccini—La Bohème
Puccini: Bohème (Cpte). (K. Ricciarelli, F. Araiza, L. Broglia, S. Antonucci, A. Noli, P. Burchuladze, A. Mariotti, C. Giombi, A. Casertano, A. Piccinni, Limberg Cath Children's Ch, Verona Arena Chor, Verona Arena Orch/A. Guadagno)

Kontrapunkt

Ⓓ **32009/11**
Kuhlau—Lulu
Kuhlau: Lulu (Cpte). (R. Saarman, A. Frellesvig, T. Kiberg, U. Cold, E. Harbo, K. von Binzer, H. Jakobsen, B. Øland, H. Rummel, B. Friboe, H. Ørvad, L. Lind, Danish Rad Chor, Danish RSO/M. Schønwandt)

Ⓓ **32036/7** (6/90)
Mussorgsky—Boris Godunov (abridged)
Mussorgsky: Boris Godunov (exc). (A. Haugland, S.F. Andersen, H. Zednik, E. Harbo, A. Møller, S. Lillesøe, M. Myhus, G. Paevatalu, DR Rad Ch, DR RSO/D. Kitaienko)

Ⓓ **32044**
Cantos de España—Jacob Christensen and Michaela Fukačová
Granados: Danzas españolas (exc); *Albéniz:* España, Op. 165 (exc); *Fauré:* Sicilienne; Berceuse, Op. 16; Songs, Op. 7 (exc); *Ravel:* Pièce en forme de habanera; *Falla:* Canciones populares españolas (exc); *Albéniz:* Cantos de España (exc); *Nin:* Suite espagnole; *Granados:* Goyescas (exc); *Falla:* Vida breve (exc). (J. Christensen, M. Fukačová)

Ⓓ **32117**
Rimsky-Korsakov—Opera Suites, Vol.
Rimsky-Korsakov: Tale of Tsar Saltan (exc); Invisible City of Kitezh (exc); Snow Maiden (exc). (Odense SO/E. Serov)

Ⓓ **32153/4**
Kodály—Symphonic Works
Kodály: Marosszék Dances; Galánta Dances; Peacock Variations; Háry János Suite; Summer Evening; Symphony in C. (Helsinki PO/J. Fürst)

Ⓓ **32157**
Nielsen—Orchestral Works
Nielsen: Symphony 1; Helios; Saul and David (exc). (Odense SO/E. Serov)

Ⓓ **32178** (11/94)
Nielsen—Orchestral Works
Nielsen: Symphony 2; Snefrid; Amor and the Poet (exc). (Odense SO/E. Serov)

Ⓓ **32203** (11/95)
Nielsen—Orchestral Works
Nielsen: Symphony 3; String Quartet Movements, FS3c (exc); Maskarade. (E.H. Thaysen, L.T. Bertelsen, Odense SO/E. Serov)

K617

Ⓓ **K617051**
Essyad—Le Collier des Ruses
Essyad: Collier des Ruses (Cpte). (C. Bonnet, F. Gonzalez, V. Reinbold, Ens/P. Nahon)

Largo

Ⓓ **Largo 5105**
Elegia: Works for Double-bass and Piano
Fauré: Songs, Op.7 (exc); *Saint-Saëns:* Carnaval des animaux (exc); *Paganini:* Moses in Egypt Variations; *Koussevitzky:* Chanson triste, Op. 2; Valse miniature, Op. 1/2; *Glière:* Intermezzo and Tarantelle, Op. 9; Prelude and Scherzo, Op. 32 (exc); *Bottesini:* Elegie in D; *Gounod:* Ave Maria; *Vivaldi:* Largo; Siciliano; *Mozart:* Zauberflöte (exc). (Y. Kawahara, R. Hoffmann)

Ⓓ **Largo 5114**
Weill—Berlin im licht
Weill: Berlin im Licht; Klops-Lied; Slow fox and algi-song; Frauentanz (Cpte); Frauentanz (exc); Gustav XII; Konjunktur (exc); Marie Galante (exc); Johnny Johnson (exc); Stille Stadt. (R. Hardy, H.K. Gruber, Modern Ens, U. Wiget)

Larrikin

Ⓓ **CDLRH221** (3/89)
Dame Nellie Melba - Opera and Song Recital
Puccini: Bohème (exc); *Verdi:* Rigoletto (exc); Traviata (exc); Traviata (exc); *Mozart:* Nozze di Figaro (exc); *Gounod:* Faust (exc); *Donizetti:* Lucia di Lammermoor (exc); *Traditional:* Comin' thro' the rye; *Claribel:* Come back to Erin; *Foster:* Old folks at home; *Bishop:* Home, sweet home; *Traditional:* Believe me, if all those endearing young charms; Ye banks and braes; *Bishop:* Lo, here the gentle lark; *Duparc:* Chanson triste; *M.V. White:* John Anderson, my Jo; *Traditional:* Annie Laurie; *Dvořák:* Gipsy Melodies (exc); *Traditional:* Auld Lang Syne; *Wetzger:* By the Brook; *Melba:* Farewell Speech. (N. Melba, E. Caruso, J. Brownlee, orch/W.B. Rogers, H. Craxton/L. Ronald, G. Lapierre, N. Melba, Coldstream Guards Band/M. Rogan, N. Melba, J. Lemmoné, N. Melba)

LaserLight

Ⓓ **14 012** ▭ **78 012**
Mussorgsky—Orchestral Works
Mussorgsky: Pictures; Night on the bare Mountain; Khovanshchina (exc). (Berlin RSO, Budapest PO, Plovdiv PO/G. Levine, J. Sándor/R. Raichev)

Ⓓ **14 212**
Lehár—Die lustige Witwe
Lehár: Lustige Witwe (exc). (S. Németh, M. Tiboldi, M. Vásári, G. Leblanc, L. Kokas, L. Csere, L. Hadics, Budapest Operetta Chor, Budapest Operetta Orch/L. Makláry)

Ⓓ **15 504** ▭ **79 504**
Sabre Dance
Khachaturian: Gayaneh (exc); *Ponchielli:* Gioconda (exc); *Rossini:* Barbiere di Siviglia (exc); *Tchaikovsky:* Eugene Onegin (exc); *Rimsky-Korsakov:* Tale of Tsar Saltan (exc); *Berlioz:* Damnation de Faust (exc); *Grieg:* Peer Gynt (exc); *Delibes:* Coppélia (exc); *Offenbach:* Orphée aux enfers (exc); *Dvořák:* Slavonic Dances (exc); *Smetana:* Bartered Bride (exc). (Hungarian St. Orch/A. Fischer, Budapest PO/A. Kórodi, Staatskapelle Dresden/H. Vonk, Vienna SO/Y. Ahronovitch, Berlin RSO/H. Fricke, Cologne RSO/P. Steinberg, RTL SO/L. Hager)

Ⓓ **15 506** (10/90) ▭ **79 506** (10/90)
Rossini: Overtures
Rossini: Barbiere di Siviglia (exc); Italiana in Algeri (exc); Scala di Seta (exc); Tancredi (exc); Semiramide (exc); Siège de Corinthe (exc); Gazza Ladra (exc). (Plovdiv PO/R. Raychev)

Ⓓ **15 510** ▭ **79 510**
Great Classical Marches
Elgar: Pomp and Circumstance Marches (exc); *Tchaikovsky:* Marche slave; *Berlioz:* Damnation de Faust (exc); *Beethoven:* Fidelio (exc); *Spontini:* Borussia; *Meyerbeer:* Prophète (exc); *Spontini:* Pas de Guerriers; *Saro/Brüll:* Bombardon-Marsch; *Liszt:* Rákóczy March; *Chabrier:* Joyeuse marche; *Liszt:* Festmarsch, S115. (Dresden PO/H. Kegel, Hungarian St. Orch/A. Fischer, Budapest SO/T. Pál, Berlin RSO/C. Richter/G. Németh, Plovdiv PO/R. Raychev)

Ⓓ **15 511** (5/90) ▭ **79 511** (5/90)
Mozart: Symphonies and Overtures
Mozart: Symphony 41; Symphony 40; Zauberflöte (exc). (LPO, J. Sándor, Hungarian CO/V. Tátrai)

Ⓓ **15 513** ▭ **79 513**
Dream Melodies
Massenet: Thaïs (exc); *Dvořák:* Serenade, Op. 22 (exc); *Beethoven:* Romances (exc); *Gluck:* Orfeo ed Euridice (exc); *Svendsen:* Romance, Op. 26; *Schumann:* Kinderszenen (exc); *Grieg:* Elegiac Melodies (exc); *Ponchielli:* Gioconda (exc). (Budapest PO/A. Kórodi, F Liszt CO, M. Szenthelyi, Hungarian St. Orch/G. Győriványi-Ráth, Budapest Stgs, Dresden PO/H. Kegel)

Ⓓ **15 514** ▭ **79 514**
Most Famous Overtures
Glinka: Ruslan and Lyudmila (exc); *Wagner:* Tannhäuser (exc); *Nicolai:* Lustigen Weiber von Windsor (exc); *Wagner:* Meistersinger (exc); *Smetana:* Bartered Bride (exc); *Rossini:* Guillaume Tell (exc). (New PO, J. Sándor, LSO, Philh/L. Siegel, Vienna SO/Y. Ahronovitch, Budapest SO)

Ⓓ **15 519** ▭ **79 519**
Verdi Overtures
Verdi: Forza del Destino (exc); Traviata (exc); Nabucco (exc); Rigoletto (exc); Ballo in maschera (exc); Otello (exc); Vespri Siciliani (exc); Battaglia di Legnano (exc); Aida (exc); Macbeth (exc); Aroldo (exc). (Sofia SO/V. Stefanov)

Ⓓ **15 520** (10/90) ▭ **79 520** (10/90)
Rossini: Overtures
Rossini: Cambiale di matrimonio (exc); Cenerentola (exc); Matilde di Shabran (exc); Viaggio a Reims (exc); Guillaume Tell (exc); Boutique fantasque (exc). (Plovdiv PO/R. Raychev)

Ⓓ **15 521** ▭ **79 521**
Wagner Overtures and Preludes
Wagner: Meistersinger (exc); Tristan und Isolde (exc); Fliegende Holländer (exc); Lohengrin (exc); Parsifal (exc); Tannhäuser (exc). (Vienna SO/Y. Ahronovitch, Budapest SO/G. Lehel)

Ⓓ **15 523** (10/90) ▭ **79 523** (10/90)
Beethoven: Orchestral Works
Beethoven: Piano Concerto 5; Coriolan; Leonore (exc). (A. Dikov, Sofia PO/E. Tabakov, Dresden PO/H. Kegel)

Ⓓ **15 602** ▭ **79 602**
Spanish Guitar Music
Rodrigo: Concierto de Aranjuez; *Sor:* Guitar Sonata, Op. 25; *Granados:* Danzas españolas (exc); *Albéniz:* Suite española 1 (exc); *Falla:* Homenaje Debussy; Vida breve (exc). (Z. Tokos, Budapest Stgs, B. Bánfalvi, M. Rost, J. Rost)

Ⓓ **15 606** (11/90) ▭ **79 606** (11/90)
Gershwin: Orchestral Works
Gershwin: American in Paris; Rhapsody in Blue; Porgy and Bess (exc). (J. Jandó, Budapest PO, J. Sándor, Budapest Stgs)

Ⓓ **15 610** ▭ **79 610**
Tchaikovsky - Favourite Waltzes
Tchaikovsky: Eugene Onegin (exc); Nutcracker (exc); Swan Lake (exc); Sleeping Beauty (exc); Nutcracker (exc); Serenade, Op. 48 (exc); Symphony 5 (exc). (Staatskapelle Dresden/H. Vonk, BRSO, Berlin CO/P. Wohlert, Prague Fest Orch/P. Urbanek)

Ⓓ **15 611** (11/90) ▭ **79 611** (11/90)
Suppé—Overtures
Suppé: Leichte Kavallerie (exc); O du mein Österreich; Fatinitza (exc); Pique Dame (exc); Dichter und Bauer (exc); Banditenstreiche (exc); Schöne Galathee (exc); Flotten Burschen (exc); Morgen, ein Mittag, ein Abend in Wien (exc). (Hungarian St Op Orch, J. Sandor)

Ⓓ **15 612** ▭ **79 612**
Wagner - Magic Fire Music
Wagner: Tannhäuser (exc); Walküre (exc); Götterdämmerung (exc); Götterdämmerung (exc); Rheingold (exc); Meistersinger (exc); Lohengrin (exc). (Budapest SO/G. Lehel, Vienna SO/Y. Ahronovitch, Sofia Rad SO/V. Kazandjiev)

Ⓓ **15 614** (10/90) ▭ **79 614** (10/90)
Bizet: Orchestral Works
Bizet: Arlésienne Suites; Carmen Suites (exc). (Budapest PO/J. Sándor)

Ⓓ **15 616** (5/90) ▭ **79 616**
French Ballet Music
Delibes: Sylvia (exc); Coppélia (exc); *Gounod:* Faust (exc). (Berlin RSO/H. Fricke, Budapest PO, J. Sándor)

Ⓓ **15 619** ▭ **79 619**
Johann Strauss II—Famous Overtures
J. Strauss II: Zigeunerbaron (exc); Fledermaus (exc); Wiener Blut (exc); Nacht in Venedig (exc); Cagliostro in Wien (exc); Aschenbrödel (exc); Radetzky March. (VJSO/J. Francek)

Ⓓ **15 621** ▭ **79 621**
Famous Marches and Dances
Prokofiev: Love for 3 Oranges Suite (exc); *Rimsky-Korsakov:* Snow Maiden (exc); *Grieg:* Sigurd Jorsalfar (exc); *Rossini:* Guillaume Tell (exc); *Offenbach:* Contes d'Hoffmann (exc); *F. Erkel:* Hunyadi László (exc); *Berlioz:* Harold in Italy (exc); *Rimsky-Korsakov:* Mlada (exc); *Mussorgsky:* Khovanshchina (exc); Fair at Sorochintsï (exc); *Ponchielli:* Gioconda (exc). (Budapest PO, J. Sándor, Plovdiv PO/R. Raychev/A. Kórodi)

Ⓓ **15 622** ▭ **79 622**
Famous Classical Overtures
Beethoven: Fidelio (exc); *Schubert:* Rosamunde (exc); *Mozart:* Zauberflöte (exc); Don Giovanni (exc); Cosi fan tutte (exc); *Beethoven:* Egmont (exc); *Rossini:* Barbiere di Siviglia (exc); *Beethoven:* Leonore (exc). (Budapest SO/T. Pál, Budapest PO/J. Kovács, J. Sándor, Staatskapelle Dresden/H. Vonk, LSO/A. Scholz, Dresden PO/H. Kegel)

Ⓓ **15 625** ▭ **79 625**
Meditation
Massenet: Thaïs (exc); *Mozart:* Piano Concerto 21 (exc); *Delibes:* Coppélia (exc); *Schubert:* String Quintet (exc); *Bach:* Suites, BWV1066-9 (exc); *Mozart:* Clarinet Concerto, K622 (exc); *Schubert:* Symphony 8 (exc); *Albinoni:* Concerti, Op. 9 (exc); *Gluck:* Orfeo ed Euridice (exc). (Budapest PO/A. Kórodi, I. Székely, F. Liszt CO/J. Rolla, Berlin RSO/H. Fricke, Bartók Qt, M. Perényi, Leipzig New Bach Collegium Musicum/M. Pommer, B. Kovács/J. Kovács, L. Güttler, C. Kircheis, H. Rucker, Dresden PO/H. Kegel)

Laudis

Ⓓ **LCD3 4002** (6/88)
Wagner—Rheingold
Wagner: Rheingold (Cpte). (H. Hotter, H. Uhde, G. Stolze, E. Witte, G. Neidlinger, P. Kuen, L. Weber, J. Greindl, I. Malaniuk, B. Falcon, M. von Ilosvay, E. Zimmermann, H. Plümacher, G. Litz, Bayreuth Fest Orch/C. Krauss)

Ⓓ **LCD4 4003** (6/88)
Wagner—Walküre
Wagner: Walküre (Cpte). (R. Vinay, R. Resnik, A. Varnay, H. Hotter, J. Greindl, I. Malaniuk, B. Friedland, B. Falcon, L. Sorrell, M. von Ilosvay, L. Thomamüller, G. Litz, S. Plate, E. Schubert, Bayreuth Fest Orch/C. Krauss)

Ⓓ **LCD4 4004** (6/88)
Wagner—Siegfried
Wagner: Siegfried (Cpte). (W. Windgassen, P. Kuen, H. Hotter, G. Neidlinger, A. Varnay, M. von Ilosvay, J. Greindl, R. Streich, Bayreuth Fest Orch/C. Krauss)

Ⓓ **LCD4 4005** (6/88)
Wagner—Götterdämmerung
Wagner: Götterdämmerung (Cpte). (A. Varnay, W. Windgassen, J. Greindl, G. Neidlinger, H. Uhde, N. Hinsch-Gröndahl, I. Malaniuk, E. Zimmermann, H. Plümacher, G. Litz, M. von Ilosvay, R. Resnik, Bayreuth Fest Chor, Bayreuth Fest Orch/C. Krauss)

LDR

Ⓓ **LDRCD1006** ▭ **LDRZC1006**
Well-Tempered Trumpet
Handel: Water Music (exc); *Puccini:* Bohème (exc); *Bach:* Now vengeance hath been taken; Alleluja; Thanks to God; Cantata 147 (exc); Suites, BWV1066-9 (exc); *L. Pearson:* English Heritage. (C. Steele-Perkins, L. Pearson)

Léman Classics

Ⓓ **LC42801**
Oboe Alone
Wagner: Tristan und Isolde (exc); *Telemann:* Fantaisies, TWV40: 2-13 (exc); *Tomasi:* Evocations; *Reade:* Aspects of a Landscape; *Holliger:* Studie über Mehrklänge; *Berio:* Sequenza VII; *M. Berkeley:* Snake. (N. Daniel, N. Daniel)

Libra

Ⓓ **LRCD156** (5/90) ▭ **LRS156** (5/90)
Georgian Harpsichord Music
Handel: Tolomeo (exc); *Chilcot:* Harpsichord Suites (exc); *Pasquali:* Lesson 4; *Paradis:* Keyboard Sonatas (exc); *Arne:* Keyboard sonatas (exc); *J.C. Bach:* Keyboard sonatas, op 5 (exc); *Haydn:* Keyboard Sonata in C; *Earl of Kelly:* Favourite Minuets. (G. Gifford)

Lindenberg

Ⓓ **LBCD23**
Mozart/Haydn/Beethoven—Organ Works
Mozart: Adagio and Allegro, K594; Variations, K24; Variations, K25; Andante, K616; Ach Gott von Himmel,

K620b; Zauberflöte (exc); Fantasia, K608; *Haydn:* Flute-clock Pieces, HobXIX (exc); *Beethoven:* Mechanical clock pieces, WoO33 (exc). (C. Ingelse)

Linn Records

Ⓓ **CKD005** ⊙ **CKH005**
Udite Amanti—17th Century Italian Love Songs
Monteverdi: Madrigals, Bk.7 (exc); *Caccini:* Nuove musiche (1602) (exc); *Peri:* Euridice (exc); *India:* Le musiche IV (1621) (exc); Le musiche I (1609) (exc); Le musiche V (1623) (exc); *Carissimi:* Lamento in morte di Maria Stuarda; *Rossi:* Quando spiega la notte; *Merula:* Hor ch'è tempo di dormire; *Landi:* Sant'Alessio (exc); *Strozzi:* Udite, udite Amanti. (J. Feldman, N. North)

Ⓓ **CKD008** ⊙ **CKH008** ▭ **CKC008**
Scotland's Music
Anon: Saints' Days (exc); Saints' Days (exc); *Traditional:* Pi li li liu; Airs by Fingal; Deirdre's Lament; *Anon:* Sanctus Ierarchia; Kyrie trope; Hac in anni janua; *Traditional:* Gowans are Gay; *Anon:* Ex te lux oritur; *Traditional:* Pleugh Song; *Anon:* Salve festa Dies; *R. Johnston:* Dicant nunc judei; *Carver:* O bone Jesu; *Anon:* Support your servand; Galliarda la Royne; *Lauder:* Golden Pavan; *Anon:* Come my children dear; *Traditional:* Why should I be so sad; *Clerk:* Dic mihi saeve puer; *Oswald:* Sonata on Scot's Tunes; *Earl of Kelly:* Maid of the Mill Overture; *J. Thomson:* Bagatelle; Lieder (exc); *MacCunn:* I will think of thee my love; Jeanie Deans (exc); In the glen; *MacKenzie:* Benedictus; *McGuire:* Calgacus. (Chant Ch/J. O'Donnell, Cappella Nova/A. Tavener, M. McMaster, B. Shaljean, SCB, Kings Sngrs, Hilliard Ens, Scottish Early Music Consort, N. Morrison, J. Kitchen, Baltimore Consort, R. Leith, J. Toll, S. LeBlanc, C. Medlam, I. Seifert, R. Gwilt, BBC SO/C. Bell, J. Keaney, P. MacMahon, L. Glover, K. Sturrock/A. Hazeldene/T. Yuasa)

Ⓓ **CKD035** (9/95)
Purcell—The Indian Queen
Purcell: Indian Queen, Z630 (Cpte). (T. Bonner, C. Bott, R. Covey-Crump, P. Harvey, Purcell Simfony Voices, Purcell Simfony)

London

Ⓓ **417 355-2LM2**
Sullivan—Cox and Box; Ruddigore
Sullivan: Ruddigore (Cpte); Cox and Box (Cpte). (J. Hindmarsh, J. Reed, G. Knight, M. Sansom, J. Allister, S. Riley, T. Round, K. Sandford, D. Adams, A. Styler, J. Riordan, D. Adams, D'Oyly Carte Op Chor, ROHO, New SO/I. Godfrey)

Ⓓ **421 390-2LM** (8/89)
Delius: Orchestral Works
Delius: Song before sunrise; First cuckoo; Summer Night on the River; Air and Dance; Village Romeo and Juliet (exc); Hassan (exc); Fennimore and Gerda Intermezzo; Koanga (exc). (ASMF/N. Marriner)

Ⓓ **425 190-2LM2** (1/90)
Sullivan—Mikado
Sullivan: Mikado (Cpte). (J. Ayldon, C. Wright, J. Reed, K. Sandford, M. Rayner, V. Masterson, P.A. Jones, P. Wales, L. Holland, J. Broad, D'Oyly Carte Op Chor, RPO/R. Nash)

Ⓓ **425 193-2LM2** (1/90)
Sullivan—Patience
Sullivan: Patience (Cpte). (M. Sansom, J. Reed, K. Sandford, Y. Newman, J. Toye, B. Lloyd-Jones, G. Knight, D. Adams, J. Cartier, P. Potter, D'Oyly Carte Op Chor, New SO/I. Godfrey)

Ⓓ **425 196-2LM2** (1/90)
Sullivan—The Pirates of Penzance
Sullivan: Pirates of Penzance (Cpte). (D. Adams, P. Potter, J. Reed, V. Masterson, G. Cook, O. Brannigan, C. Palmer, P. Wales, J. Allister, S. Maisey, D'Oyly Carte Op Chor, RPO/I. Godfrey)

Ⓓ **425 659-2LM** (12/90)
Britten: Orchestral Works
Britten: Young Person's Guide; Peter Grimes (exc); Matinées musicales; Soirées musicales. (LSO, ROHO, National PO/B. Britten/R. Bonynge)

Ⓓ **425 663-2LH2** (5/90)
Britten—Midsummer Night's Dream
Britten: Midsummer Night's Dream (Cpte). (A. Deller, E. Harwood, P. Pears, T. Hemsley, J. Veasey, H. Harper, J. Shirley-Quirk, H. Watts, O. Brannigan, N. Lumsden, K. Macdonald, D. Kelly, R. Tear, K. Raggett, R. Dakin, J. Prior, I. Wodehouse, G. Clark, S. Terry, Downside School Boys' Ch, Emanuel School Boys' Ch, LSO/B. Britten)

Ⓓ **425 666-2LH2** (5/90)
Britten—Rape of Lucretia; Phaedra
Britten: Rape of Lucretia (Cpte); Phaedra. (J. Baker, P. Pears, H. Harper, B. Luxon, J. Shirley-Quirk, B. Drake, J. Hill, E. Bainbridge, ECO/B. Britten, J. Baker/S. Bedford)

Ⓓ **425 669-2LH2** (5/90)
Britten—Death in Venice
Britten: Death in Venice (Cpte). (P. Pears, J. Shirley-Quirk, J. Shirley-Quirk, J. Shirley-Quirk, J. Shirley-Quirk, J. Bowman, K. Bowen, P. Leeming, N. Williams, P. MacKay, I. Saunders, EOG Chor, ECO/S. Bedford)

Ⓓ **425 672-2LH2** (5/90)
Britten—Turn of the Screw
Britten: Turn of the Screw (Cpte). (P. Pears, J. Vyvyan, D. Hemmings, O. Dyer, J. Cross, A. Mandikian, EOG Orch/B. Britten)

Ⓓ **433 200-2LHO2** (11/93)
Britten—Owen Wingrave, etc.
Britten: Owen Wingrave (Cpte); Hölderlin Fragments; Poet's Echo. (B. Luxon, J. Shirley-Quirk, N. Douglas, S. Fisher, H. Harper, J. Vyvyan, J. Baker, P. Pears, Wandsworth Sch Boys' Ch, ECO/B. Britten, G. Vishnevskaya, M. Rostropovich, B. Britten, P. Pears)

Ⓓ **436 393-2LM** (11/93)
Britten—The Little Sweep, etc
Britten: Little Sweep (Cpte); Gemini Variations; Children's Crusade. (D. Hemmings, J. Vyvyan, N. Evans, A. Cantelo, T. Anthony, P. Pears, M. Ingram, Marilyn Baker, R. Fairhurst, L. Vaughan, G. Soskin, Alleyn's Sch Ch, EOG Orch/B. Britten, G. Jeney, Z. Jeney, Wandsworth Sch Boys' Ch, chbr ens/R. Burgess)

Ⓓ **436 397-2LM** (11/93)
Britten—Noye's Fludde. The Golden Vanity
Britten: Noye's Fludde (Cpte); Golden Vanity. (Wandsworth Sch Boys' Ch, B. Britten/R. Burgess, O. Brannigan, S. Rex, D. Pinto, D. Angadi, S. Alexander, T. Anthony, C. Clack, M-T. Pinto, E. O'Donovan, Chor, E. Suffolk Children's Orch, EOG Orch/N. del Mar)

Ⓓ **436 781-2LM**
Wiener Tanzgala 1
J. Strauss II: Fledermaus (exc); Ritter Pásmán (exc); Zigeunerbaron (exc); Graduation Ball (Cpte); *Lehár:* Gold und Silber; *Weber:* Invitation to the Dance. (VPO/W. Boskovsky)

Ⓓ **436 785-2LM**
Wiener Tanzgala 5
J. Strauss II: Waldmeister (exc); Cagliostro in Wien (exc); Prinz Methusalem (exc); Indigo und die vierzig Räuber (exc); Spitzentuch der Königin (exc); Carneval in Rom (exc); *Rezniček:* Donna Diana (exc); *Suppé:* Schöne Galathee (exc); *Heuberger:* Opernball (exc); *Nicolai:* Lustigen Weiber von Windsor (exc). (VPO/W. Boskovsky)

Ⓓ **436 807-2LM2**
Sullivan—The Sorcerer. The Zoo
Sullivan: Sorcerer (Cpte); Zoo (exc). (D. Adams, D. Palmer, A. Styler, S. Riley, J. Reed, C. Palmer, V. Masterson, J. Allister, A. Hood, M. Reid, K. Sandford, J. Ayldon, J. Goss, J. Metcalfe, G. Shovelton, D'Oyly Carte Op Chor, RPO/I. Godfrey/R. Nash)

Ⓓ **436 810-2LM2**
Gilbert & Sullivan—Princess Ida; Pineapple Poll
Sullivan: Princess Ida (Cpte); Pineapple Poll (Cpte). (K. Sandford, P. Potter, D. Palmer, J. Skitch, J. Reed, D. Adams, A. Raffell, G. Cook, E. Harwood, C. Palmer, A. Hood, V. Masterson, D'Oyly Carte Op Chor, RPO/M. Sargent, Philh/C. MacKerras)

Ⓓ **436 813-2LM2**
Sullivan—The Grand Duke. Overture Di Ballo. Henry VIII
Sullivan: Grand Duke (Cpte); Di Ballo; Henry VIII (exc). (J. Reed, M. Reid, K. Sandford, M. Rayner, J. Ayldon, J. Ellison, J. Conroy-Ward, B. Lilley, L. Holland, J. Goss, J. Metcalfe, P. Leonard, A. Eggleston, B. Lloyd-Jones, G. Prendergast, D'Oyly Carte Op Chor, RPO/R. Nash, Philh/C. Mackerras)

Ⓓ **436 816-2LM2**
Sullivan—Utopia Ltd. Macbeth & Marmion Ovs etc
Sullivan: Utopia Ltd (Cpte); Macbeth (exc); Victoria and Merrie England Suite 1; Marmion; Imperial March. (K. Sandford, J. Reed, J. Ayldon, J. Ellison, M. Buchan, J. Conroy-Ward, M. Reid, J. Broad, M. Rayner, C. Wright, D. Porter, P. Field, J. Goss, J. Merri, L. Holland, R. Griffiths, D'Oyly Carte Op Chor, RPO/R. Nash)

Ⓓ **436 896-2LA** (6/95)
Lehár—Operetta Highlights
Lehár: Zarewitsch (exc); Graf von Luxemburg (exc). (H. Gueden, W. Kmentt, Vienna Volksoper Chor, Vienna Volksoper Orch/M. Schönherr)

Ⓓ **436 897-2DM**
Lehár Gala
Lehár: Lustige Witwe (exc); Schön ist die Welt (exc); Land des Lächelns (exc); Paganini (exc); Zarewitsch (exc); Friederike (exc); Graf von Luxemburg (exc); Eva (exc); Zigeunerliebe (exc). (R. Holm, P. Lorengar, W. Krenn, Vienna Volksoper Orch/A. Paulik, Vienna Op Orch/W. Weller)

Ⓓ **436 898-2DM**
Operetta Gala
J. Strauss II: Zigeunerbaron (exc); Nacht in Venedig (exc); *Millöcker:* Bettelstudent (exc); *Suppé:* Boccaccio (exc); *Kálmán:* Zirkusprinzessin (exc); *Dostal:* Clivia (exc); *Künneke:* Vetter aus Dingsda (exc); *Kattnigg:* Bel Ami (exc); *Dostal:* Ungarische Hochzeit (exc); *Kattnigg:* Mädels vom Rhein (exc); *Czernik:* Chi sa?; *J. Strauss II:* Zigeunerbaron (exc); *Zeller:* Vogelhändler (exc); *Kálmán:* Csárdásfürstin (exc). (R. Holm, P. Lorengar, W. Krenn, Vienna Volksoper Orch/A. Paulik, Vienna Op Chor, Vienna Op Orch/W. Weller)

Ⓓ **436 899-2LA** (6/95)
Lehár—Die Lustige Witwe - Highlights
Lehár: Lustige Witwe (exc). (H. Gueden, E. Loose, P. Grunden, W. Kmentt, P. Klein, K. Equiluz, K. Dönch, H. Duhan, M. Rus, L. Pantscheff, Vienna St Op Chor, Vienna St Op Orch/R. Stolz)

Ⓓ **436 900-2LA** (6/95)
Lehár—Giuditta Highlights
Lehár: Giuditta (exc). (H. Gueden, E. Loose, W. Kmentt, M. Dickie, E. Majkut, K. Equiluz, K. Dönch, H. Duhan, W. Berry, H. Pröglhöf, Vienna St Op Chor, Vienna St Op Orch/R. Moralt)

Ⓓ **440 081-2LRX**
Music for Relaxation, Vol 1 - Nocturne
Debussy: Suite bergamasque (exc); *Chopin:* Nocturnes (exc); *Grieg:* Lyric Suite, Op. 54 (exc); *Elgar:* Dream Children; *Beethoven:* Piano Sonata 14 (exc); *Massenet:* Navarraise (exc); *Borodin:* String Quartet 2 (exc); *Chopin:* Nocturnes (exc); *Korngold:* Much Ado About Nothing Suite (exc); *Massenet:* Vierge (exc); *Grieg:* Lyric Pieces, Op. 54 (exc); *Mendelssohn:* Midsummer Night's Dream (exc); *Fauré:* Pavane. (LPO/B. Herrmann, J. Cooper, LSO/S. Black, New SO/R. Agoult, R. Lupu/R. Bonynge, RPO, I. Vered, J. Sakonov (vn/dir), London Fest Orch, A. de Larrocha, New Philh/R. Frühbeck de Burgos)

Ⓓ **440 230-2LF2**
Puccini—Madama Butterfly
Puccini: Madama Butterfly (Cpte). (R. Tebaldi, G. Campora, G. Inghilleri, N. Rankin, P. de Palma, M. Luise, G. Diozzi, F. Corena, M. Calvino, L. Pizzeri, Santa Cecilia Academy Chor, Santa Cecilia Academy Orch/A. Erede)

Ⓓ **440 233-2LF2**
Puccini—La Bohème
Puccini: Bohème (Cpte). (R. Tebaldi, G. Prandelli, H. Gueden, G. Inghilleri, F. Corena, R. Arié, M. Luise, I. Santafe, Santa Cecilia Academy Chor, Santa Cecilia Academy Orch/A. Erede)

Ⓓ **440 236-2LF2**
Puccini—Tosca
Puccini: Tosca (Cpte). (R. Tebaldi, G. Campora, E. Mascherini, D. Caselli, P. de Palma, F. Corena, A. Sacchetti, G. F. Volante, Santa Cecilia Academy Chor, Santa Cecilia Academy Orch/A. Erede)

Ⓓ **440 239-2LF2**
Verdi—Aida
Verdi: Aida (Cpte). (R. Tebaldi, E. Stignani, M. del Monaco, A. Protti, D. Caselli, F. Corena, P. de Palma, Santa Cecilia Academy Chor, Santa Cecilia Academy Orch/A. Erede)

Ⓓ **440 242-2LF2** (7/94)
Verdi—Rigoletto
Verdi: Rigoletto (Cpte). (A. Protti, H. Gueden, M. del Monaco, C. Siepi, G. Simionato, F. Corena, L. Ribacchi, P. de Palma, M. L. Castelli, D. Caselli, L. Rossi, P. Poldi, Santa Cecilia Academy Chor, Santa Cecilia Academy Orch/A. Erede)

Ⓓ **440 245-2LF2** (5/94)
Verdi—Otello
Verdi: Otello (Cpte). (M. del Monaco, R. Tebaldi, A. Protti, P. de Palma, A. Mercuriali, L. Ribacchi, F. Corena, P. L. Latinucci, D. Caselli, Santa Cecilia Academy Chor, Santa Cecilia Academy Orch/A. Erede)

Ⓓ **440 490-2LM5(1)**
Kirsten Flagstad Edition
Wagner: Wesendonk Lieder; *Mahler:* Kindertotenlieder; Lieder eines fahrenden Gesellen; *Sibelius:* Songs, Op. 17 (exc); Songs, Op. 37 (exc); Songs, Op. 38 (exc); Songs, Op. 36 (exc); Arioso, Op. 3; Songs, Op. 13 (exc); Twelfth Night, Op. 60 (exc); *Grieg:* Songs, Op. 18 (exc); Songs,

Op. 60 (exc); Songs, Op. 59 (exc); Songs, Op. 21 (exc); *Alnaes:* Hundred violins; Yearnings of Spring; About love; February morning; *Lie:* Key; Letter; *Grieg:* Garborg Songs (1895); Songs, Op. 70 (exc); Songs, Op. 39 (exc); Songs, Op. 69 (exc); Songs, Op. 18 (exc); Songs, Op. 21 (exc); Songs, Op. 26 (exc); Songs, Op. 25 (exc); Songs, Op. 48 (exc); Songs, Op. 60 (exc); Melodies of the Heart, Op. 5 (exc); *Wagner:* Walküre (exc); Walküre (exc); Lohengrin (exc); Parsifal (exc); Götterdämmerung (exc). (K. Flagstad, S. Svanholm, E. McArthur, VPO, Oslo PO, Norwegian St RO, LSO/A. Boult/H. Knappertsbusch/G. Solti/Ø. Fjeldstad)

Ⓓ **440 495-2LM**
Kirsten Flagstad Edition, Vol. 5
Wagner: Walküre (exc); Walküre (exc); Lohengrin (exc); Parsifal (exc); Götterdämmerung (exc). (K. Flagstad, VPO/H. Knappertsbusch/G. Solti, Oslo PO, Norwegian Rad Orch/Ø. Fjeldstad)

Ⓓ **443 381-2LM**
Hallelujah! - Great Choral Classics
Handel: Messiah (exc); *Mozart:* Ave verum corpus, K618; *Mendelssohn:* Elijah (exc); *Puccini:* Madama Butterfly (exc); *Handel:* Coronation Anthems (exc); *Franck:* Psalm 150; *Verdi:* Nabucco (exc); *Beethoven:* Christus am Oelberge, Op. 85 (exc); *Anon:* Come, come, ye saints; *Traditional:* Shaker Chants and Spirituals (exc); Deep River; *Anon:* Battle Hymn of the Republic. (S. Cook, Mormon Tabernacle Ch, J. Longhurst, R. Cundick, Utah SO/J. Silverstein/J. Rudel/J. Ottley)

Ⓓ **825 126-2**
Amadeus - Original Soundtrack
Pergolesi: Stabat Mater (exc); *Traditional:* Bubak and Hungaricus; *Mozart:* Symphony 25 (exc); Serenade, K361 (exc); Entführung (exc); 2-Piano Concerto, K365 (exc); Mass, K427 (exc); Sinfonia concertante, K364 (exc); Piano Concerto 22 (exc); Nozze di Figaro (exc); Don Giovanni (exc); Zaïde (exc); Requiem (exc); Piano Concerto 20 (exc); Symphony 29 (exc). (Westminster Abbey Ch, Ens, Ambrosian Op. Chor, I. Cooper, A. Queffélec, F. Lott, Academy Chor, L. Chilingirian, C. Erdélyi, I. Moravec, S. Ramey, R. Stilwell, I. Buchanan, W. White, A. Howells, D. Rees, P. Payne, A. Oliver, R. Leggate, J. Tomlinson, ASMF/N. Marriner)

Ⓓ **827 267-2**
More Amadeus - Original Soundtrack
Mozart: Zauberflöte (exc); Zauberflöte (exc); Maurerische Trauermusik, K477; Piano Concerto 20 (exc); Serenade, K525 (exc); Flute and Harp Concerto, K299 (exc); German Dances, K509 (exc); Entführung (exc); Ich möchte wohl der Kaiser sein, K539; *Salieri:* Axur (exc); *T. Giordani:* Caro mio ben. (ASMF/N. Marriner, L. Kennedy, C. Zacharias, W. Bennett, O. Ellis, Ambrosian Op Chor, M. Esposito, Anon)

Lyric

Ⓓ **LCD146** (6/90)
Frida Leider sings Wagner
Wagner: Tristan und Isolde (exc); Tristan und Isolde (exc); Tristan und Isolde (exc); Götterdämmerung (exc); Götterdämmerung (exc); Götterdämmerung (exc). (F. Leider, E. Marherr-Wagner, L. Melchior, F. Soot, K. Thorborg, L. Weber, H. Janssen, M. Nedzadel, orch, LPO, Berlin St Op Orch, LSO/L. Blech/A. Coates/J. Barbirolli/T. Beecham, ROH Chor)

Ⓓ **LCD173** (2/94)
Verdi—Il trovatore, etc
Verdi: Trovatore (Cpte); Forza del destino (exc). (J. Björling, G. Cigna, M. Basiola I, G. Wettergren, C. Zambelli, M. Huder, O. Dua, L. Horsman, G. Zammit, ROH Chor, LPO/V. Gui, G. Cigna, G. Vaghi, E. Ghirardini, Rome RAI Chor, Rome RAI Orch/O. de Fabritiis)

Ⓓ **LCD181**
Leoncavallo—Pagliacci
Leoncavallo: Pagliacci (Cpte). (M. del Monaco, R. Noli, A. Poli, O. Borgonova, P. de Palma, Naples San Carlo Op Chor, Naples San Carlo Op Orch/V. Bellezza)

Ⓓ **SRO805** (11/90)
Gina Cigna—Opera Recital
Gounod: Faust (exc); *Verdi:* Forza del destino (exc); *Ponchielli:* Gioconda (exc); *Giordano:* Andrea Chénier (exc); *Cilea:* Adriana Lecouvreur (exc); *Bellini:* Norma (exc); *Verdi:* Ballo in maschera (exc); *Catalani:* Wally (exc); *Puccini:* Fanciulla del West (exc); Turandot (exc); *Verdi:* Aida (exc); Otello (exc). (G. Cigna, C. Elmo, A. Pertile, F. Merli, orch/L. Molajoli, Turin EIAR Orch/U. Tansini/F. Ghione, La Scala Orch/A. Erede)

Ⓓ **SRO819** (9/91)
Rossini—Il barbiere di Siviglia (abridged)
Rossini: Barbiere di Siviglia (exc). (F. de Lucia, F. Novelli, M. Resemba, G. Schottler, S. Valentino, A. di Tommaso, N. Sabatano, Naples San Carlo Op Chor, Naples San Carlo Op Orch/S. Sassano)

Ⓓ **SRO830** (2/92)
Smetana—The Bartered Bride, etc
Smetana: Bartered Bride (Cpte); *Weber:* Freischütz (exc); *Bizet:* Carmen (exc); *Wagner:* Lohengrin (exc); *J. Strauss II:* Rosen aus dem Süden; *O. Straus:* Land without Music (exc); Tapfere Soldat (exc); *Tauber:* Old Chelsea (exc); *Romberg:* Desert Song (exc); *German:* Merrie England (exc); *Tosti:* Addio. (H. Konetzni, R. Tauber, H. Tessmer, F. Krenn, M. Rothmüller, M. Jarred, A. Matters, S. Kalter, S. Andreva, G. Hinze, G. Clifford, ROH Chor, LPO/T. Beecham, R. Tauber, orch/N. Treep, P. Kahn)

Ⓓ **SRO839** (10/93)
Alfano—Risurrazione
Alfano: Risurrezione (Cpte); *Puccini:* Turandot (exc). (M. Olivero, G. Gismondo, A. Boyer, A. Di Stasio, N. Condò, V. Magrini, P. Pace, M. Stefanoni, Turin RAI Chor, Turin RAI Orch/E. Boncompagni, L. Kelm, J.F. West, chor, orch/C. Keene)

Lyrita

Ⓓ **SRCD209** (6/93)
Holst—Orchestral Works
Holst: Winter Idyll; Cotswold Symphony (exc); Song of the Night; Indra; Invocation; Sita (exc); Morning of the Year (exc); Lure. (L. McAslan, A. Baillie, LPO, LSO/D. Atherton)

Ⓓ **SRCD2217**
Tippett—The Midsummer Marriage
Tippett: Midsummer Marriage (Cpte). (A. Remedios, J. Carlyle, R. Herincx, E. Harwood, S. Burrows, H. Watts, S. Dean, E. Bainbridge, D. Whelan, A. Daniels, ROH Chor, ROHO/Colin Davis)

Ⓓ **SRCD2218** (3/93)
Alwyn—Miss Julie
Alwyn: Miss Julie (Cpte). (J. Gomez, B. Luxon, D. Jones, J. Mitchinson, Philh/V. Tausky)

Manchester Camerata

Ⓓ **MCL20**
Camerata Celebration 1972-1992
Mozart: Nozze di Figaro (exc); *Vivaldi:* Concerto, RV537; *Senaillé:* Premier livre de Sonates (exc); *Weber:* Clarinet Concertino; *Stravinsky:* Suites (exc); *Bartók:* Divertimento; *Haydn:* Symphony 83 (exc). (Manchester Camerata/C. Rizzi)

Mandala

Ⓓ **MAN4805**
Light Music: The French Touch
Bizet: Symphony; *Pierné:* Ramuntcho (exc); Konzertstück; *Chabrier:* Bourrée fantasque. (L. Laskine, Paris Cons/J-B. Mari)

Ⓓ **MAN4806**
Music for Guitar and Cello
Baumann: Duo, Op. 62; *Granados:* Goyescas (exc); *Villa-Lobos:* Bachianas Brasileiras 5 (exc); *Biberian:* Bagatelles; *Falla:* Canciones populares españolas (exc); *Gnattali:* Duo Sonata; *Obrovska:* Bartók Hommage; *Constant:* Elégie Slave; *Brouwer:* Reinhardt Variations; *Walton:* Bagatelles; *L. Berkeley:* Sonatina, Op. 52/1; *Dyens:* Sausade 3. (C. Heurtefeux, R. Flachot)

Marco Polo

Ⓓ **DCCD9001** (1/93)
Nørgård—Gilgamesh
Nørgård: Gilgamesh (Cpte); Voyage into the Golden Screen. (B. Haugan, H. Lannerbäck, B-M. Aruhn, J. Hviid, R. Eckhoff, M. Baekkelund, B. Eriksson, S. Grippe, A. Bartler, R. Leanderson, chor, Swedish RSO/T. Vetö, Danish RSO/O. Knussen)

Ⓓ **8 220323**
R. Strauss: Rarely heard orchestral works
R. Strauss: Symphony in D minor; Interludio; Rosenkavalier film (exc). (Hong Kong PO/K. Schermerhorn)

Ⓓ **8 223122**
Spohr—Orchestral Works
Spohr: Symphony 4; Faust (exc); Jessonda (exc). (Budapest SO/A. Walter)

Ⓓ **8 223162** (7/89)
Pfitzner: Orchestral Works
Pfitzner: Piano Concerto; Christ-Elflein (exc); Herz (exc). (W. Harden, Bratislava RSO/H. Beissel)

Ⓓ **8 223270/1** (8/90)
Schreker—Der Ferne Klang
Schreker: Ferne Klang (Cpte). (E. Grigorescu, T. Harper, A. Haller, H. Fiehl, R. Bunse, E. Pilarl, P. Friess, W. Hahn, P.N. Kante, R. Leisenheimer, W. Pickersgill, Hagen Op Chor, Hagen PO/M. Halász)

Ⓓ **8 223272**
Dvořák—Opera Overtures
Dvořák: King and Charcoal Burner (exc); Jacobin (exc); Rusalka (exc); Kate and the Devil (exc); Dimitrij (exc); Armida (exc). (Košice St PO/R. Stankovsky)

Ⓓ **8 223306/7** (11/91)
Marschner—Hans Heiling
Marschner: Hans Heiling (Cpte). (T. Mohr, M. Hajóssyová, E. Seniglová, M. Eklöf, K. Markus, L. Neshyba, Slovak Phil Chor, Slovak PO/E. Körner)

Ⓓ **8 223318**
Erkel—Opera Transcriptions
F. Erkel: Bátori Mária (exc); Hunyadi László (exc); Hungarian March; Bánk Bán (exc); Sarolta (exc); Dózsa György (exc); *S. Erkel:* Brankovics (exc). (I. Kassai)

Ⓓ **8 223320**
Rubinstein—Orchestral Works
Rubinstein: Symphony 5; Faust, Op. 68; Dmitry Donskoy (exc). (Bucharest George Enescu PO/H. Andreescu)

Ⓓ **8 223324** (4/92)
Von Schillings—Orchestral Works
Schillings: Violin Concerto; Moloch (exc); King Oedipus. (E. Rozsa, Košice St PO/A. Walter)

Ⓓ **8 223328/30** (12/91)
Schreker—Die Gezeichneten
Schreker: Gezeichneten (Cpte). (C. van Tassel, S. Cowan, W. Oosterkamp, M. Schmiege, W. Cochran, H. Meens, F. Lang, E.D. Smid, M. Dirks, E. Godding, C. van Tassel, E. Bollongino, Dutch Rad Phil Chor, Dutch Rad PO/E. de Waart)

Ⓓ **8 223339/40**
Szymanowski—King Roger; Prince Potemkin - excerpt
Szymanowski: King Roger (Cpte); Prince Potemkin. (A. Hiolski, B. Zagórzanka, H. Grychnik, W. Ochman, L. Mróz, A. Malewicz-Madey, Cracow Phil Boys' Chor, Katowice St Phil Chor, Katowice St Phil Orch/K. Stryja, Katowice RSO/A. Wit)

Ⓓ **8 223342** (9/95)
Marschner—Overtures
Marschner: Kaiser Adolph von Nassau (exc); Falkners Braut (exc); Prinz Friedrich von Homburg (exc); Lukretia (exc); Bäbu (exc); Goldschmeid von Ulm (exc); Templer und die Jüdin (exc); Grande Ouverture solenne. (Košice St PO/A. Walter)

Ⓓ **8 223354** (1/92)
Massenet—Orchestral Suites
Massenet: Suite 1; Esclarmonde Suite; Cendrillon Suite. (Hong Kong PO/K. Jean)

Ⓓ **8 223369**
Humperdinck—Orchestral Works
Humperdinck: Dornröschen (exc); Kaufmann von Venedig (exc); Maurische Rhapsodie; Marketenderin (exc). (Bratislava RSO, M. Fischer-Dieskau)

Ⓓ **8 223381** (1/94)
Salieri—Overtures
Salieri: Angiolina (exc); Armida (exc); Axur (exc); Cesare in Farmacusa (exc); Danaides (exc); Don Chisciotte (exc); Eraclito e Democrito (exc); Grotta di Trofonio (exc); Moro (exc); Ricco d'un giorno (exc); Secchia rapita (exc); Talismano (Vienna) (exc). (Bratislava RSO/M. Dittrich)

Ⓓ **8 223397** (9/93)
Malipiero—Orchestral Works
Malipiero: Sette Invenzioni; Quattro Invenzioni; Finto Arlecchino (exc); Vivaldiana. (Veneto PO/P. Maag)

Ⓓ **8 223400**
Cui—Orchestral Works
Cui: Suite 2; Suite 4; Filibustier (exc). (Bratislava RSO/R. Stankovsky)

Ⓓ **8 223403** (9/92)
Virtuoso Cello Encores
Cassadó: Dance of the Green Devil; *Popper:* Russian Song Fantasy; Serenade, Op.54/2; *Bach:* Suites, BWV1066-9 (exc); *Schubert:* Schwanengesang, D957 (exc); *F. Schubert II:* Bagatelles, Op.13 (exc); *Granados:* Goyescas (exc); *Shostakovich:* Gadfly Suite (exc); *Ravel:* Sites auriculaires (exc); *Debussy:* Préludes (exc); *Senaillé:* Premier livre de Sonates (exc); *Vieuxtemps:* Etudes, Op.48 (exc); *Barchet:* Images de Menton (exc); *Offenbach:* Danse bohémienne, Op.28; *Rachmaninov:* Songs, Op.34 (exc); *Gershwin:* Short Story. (M. Kliegel, R. Havenith)

Ⓓ **8 223419** (6/93)
Edward German—Orchestral Works
German: Nell Gwyn Overture; Nell Gwyn (exc); Gipsy Suite; Henry VIII (exc); Conqueror (exc); Romeo and Juliet (exc); Tom Jones (exc); Merrie England Dances (exc). (Bratislava RSO/A. Leaper)

Ⓓ **8 223446** (11/93)
Holbrooke—Orchestral Works
Holbrooke: Ulalume; Bronwen (exc); Bells (exc); Raven; Byron. (Slovak Phil Chor, Bratislava RSO/A. Leaper)

Ⓓ **8 223452** (5/93)
Kempff—Piano Works
Bach: Chorales, BWV651-668 (exc); Nun freut euch, BWV734; Flute Sonatas, BWV1030-5 (exc); Es ist gewisslich an der Zeit, BWV307; Herzlich tut mich verlangen, BWV727; Cantata 147 (exc); In dulci jubilo, BWV751; Cantata 29 (exc); Schübler Chorales, BWV645-650 (exc); Harpsichord Concerto, BWV1056 (exc); Orgel-Büchlein, BWV599-644 (exc); *Handel:* Lessons (exc); *Gluck:* Orfeo ed Euridice (exc); *Kempff:* Italian Suite, Op. 68; Piano Sonata, Op. 47; Pastorale variée. (I. Biret)

Ⓓ **8 223460** (6/93)
Sullivan—Ballet Music
Sullivan: Ile enchantée (Cpte); Thespis (exc). (RTE Concert Orch/A. Penny)

Ⓓ **8 223461** (6/93)
Sullivan—Incidental Music
Sullivan: Merchant of Venice (exc); Henry VIII (exc); Sapphire Necklace (exc); In Memoriam. (E. Lawler, RTE Concert Orch/A. Penny)

Ⓓ **8 223498**
Bruneau—Orchestral Highlights
Bruneau: Messidor (exc); Naïs Micoulin (exc); Attaque du moulin (exc). (Rhine State PO/J. Lockhart)

Ⓓ **8 223503** (1/95)
Rabaud—Orchestral Works
Rabaud: Mârouf (exc); Procession Nocturne, Op. 6; Suite anglaise 2; Églogue, Op. 7; Suite anglaise 3; Divertissement, Op. 2. (Rhineland-Pfalz State PO/L. Segerstam)

Ⓓ **8 223592/3** (4/94)
Weber—Peter Schmoll und seine Nachbarn
Weber: Peter Schmoll (Cpte). (R. Busching, J. Schmidt, A. Pfeffer, S. Basa, H. J. Porcher, H-J. Schöpflin, Hagen PO/G. Markson)

Ⓓ **8 223596**
O. Strauss—His Most Popular Works
O. Straus: Rund um die Liebe (exc); Walzertraum (exc); Alt-Wiener Reigen, Op. 45; Tapfere Soldat (exc); Didi (exc); Prinzessin von Tragant (exc); Ballnacht; Madame de ... (exc); Ronde (exc). (V. Kincses, Budapest Strauss SO/A. Walter)

Ⓓ **8 223627/8** (11/94)
Pfitzner—Das Herz
Pfitzner: Herz (Cpte). (A. Wenhold, V. Horn, R. Cunningham, B. Johanning, K. Quandt, R. Dressler, L. Chioreanu, I. Melle, R. Atanasova, L. Hübel, I. Christoph, N. Barowski, Thüringian Landestheater Chor, Thüringian SO/R. Reuter)

Ⓓ **8 223638**
Raff—Orchestral Works
Raff: Symphony 6; Jubel-Overture, Op. 103; Dame Kobold (exc); Festmarsch, Op. 159. (Košice St PO/U. Schneider)

Ⓓ **8 223647**
Suppé—Overtures, Vol. 1
Suppé: Dichter und Bauer (exc); Irrfahrt um's Glück (exc); Juanita (exc); Carnaval (exc); Boccaccio (exc); Frau Meisterin (exc); Banditenstreiche (exc); Wanderers Ziel (exc); Pique Dame (exc). (Košice St PO/A. Walter)

Ⓓ **8 223648** (6/95)
Suppé—Overtures, Volume 2
Suppé: Schöne Galathee (exc); Isabella (exc); Modell (exc); Tantalusqualen (exc); Krämer und sein Kommis (exc); Paragraph 3 (exc); Boccaccio (exc); Fatinitza (exc); Juanita (exc). (Košice St PO/A. Walter)

Ⓓ **8 223675**
Glière—Orchestral Works
Glière: Bronze Horseman Suite; Shakh-Senem (exc); Gyul'sara (exc); Heroic March. (St Petersburg State SO/A. Anichanov)

Ⓓ **8 223683**
Suppé—Overtures, Volume 3
Suppé: Leichte Kavallerie (exc); Tricoche und Cacolet (exc); Boccaccio (exc); Afrikareise (exc); Fatinitza (exc); Humorous Variations; Heimkehr von der Hochzeit (exc); Herzenseintracht; Franz Schubert (exc); Triumph Overture. (Košice St PO/A. Walter)

Ⓓ **8 223706/7** (10/95)
Azio Corghi—Divara-Wasser und Blut
Corghi: Divara (Cpte). (S. von der Burg, C. Krieg, H. Hildmann, M. Holm, H. Fitz, R. Schwarts, E. L. Thingboe, S. McLeod, G. Wunderer, D. Midboe, M. Baba, G. Kiefer, M. Coles, B. Trottmann, Münster City Th Chor, Münster SO/W. Humburg)

Ⓓ **8 223713/4** (6/95)
Siegfried Wagner—Der Bärenhäuter
S. Wagner: Bärenhäuter (Cpte). (V. Horn, H. Kiichli, K. Lukic, T. Koon, B. Johanning, L. Hübel, A. Feilhaber, K. Quandt, N. Barowski, R. Hartmann, A. Wenhold, A. Waller, Thüringian Landestheater Chor, Thüringian SO/K. Bach)

Ⓓ **8 223721**
Holbrooke—Orchestral Works
Holbrooke: Children of Don (exc); Birds of Rhiannon; Dylan (exc). (Ukraine National SO/A. Penny)

Ⓓ **8 223774**
Ropartz—Choral Works
Ropartz: Psalm 136; Dimanche; Nocturne; Vêpres sonnent; Miracle de Saint Nicolas. (C. Papis, D. Henry, V. le Texier, I. Brissot, E. LeBrun, C. Lajarrige, Ile de France Regional Ch, Nancy SO/M. Piquemal)

Ⓓ **8 223777/8** (11/95)
S. Wagner—Schwarzschwanenreich
S. Wagner: Schwarzschwanenreich (Cpte). (B. Johanning, W. Raffeiner, K. Quandt, A. Wenhold, J. M. Schmitz, R. Hartmann, L. Chioreanu, K. Lukic, Thüringian Landestheater Chor, Thüringian SO/K. Bach)

Marquis

Ⓓ **ERAD137**
Danzas y Canciones
Morel: Danza brasiliera; Romance Criollo; Danza in E minor; *Bustamente:* Misionera; *Lauro:* Valses Venezolanos (1963) (exc); Valses Venezolanos (1968) (exc); *Falla:* Amor brujo (exc); *Pipó:* Canción y Danza 1; *Brouwer:* Estudios Sencillos (exc); Decamerón negro (exc); *Traditional:* Greensleeves (Alas! my love); *Sainz de la Maza:* Habanera; Campanas del Alba; *Falla:* Vida breve (exc). (R. Gauk)

Mastersound

Ⓓ **DFCDI-012**
Art of Ofra Harnoy
Franck: Violin Sonata; *Ben Haim:* Songs without words (exc); *Sarasate:* Danzas españolas (exc); *Gershwin:* Porgy and Bess (exc); *Tchaikovsky:* Nocturne, Op. 19/4; *Popper:* Dance of the Elves; *Chopin:* Nocturnes (exc). (O. Harnoy, W. Aide, H. Bowkun)

Ⓓ **DFCDI-111** (4/92)
The Art of the Coloratura
J. Strauss II: Blauen Donau, Op. 314; *Benedict:* Wren; *Alabiev:* Nightingale; *Dell' Acqua:* Villanelle; *Delibes:* Filles de Cadiz; *Proch:* Air and Variations; *Offenbach:* Contes d'Hoffmann (exc); *Delibes:* Lakmé (exc); *Verdi:* Rigoletto (exc); *Donizetti:* Lucia di Lammermoor (exc); *Rossini:* Barbiere di Siviglia (exc); Barbiere di Siviglia (exc); *Rimsky-Korsakov:* Golden Cockerel (exc); Sadko (exc); *Kern:* I dream too much (exc); *Olivieri:* J'attendrai; *Various:* National Anthems (exc). (L. Pons, G. De Luca, orch/A. Kostelanetz, F. La Forge/G. Cloëz/Rosario Bourdon/J. Barbirolli/W. Pelletier)

Max Sound

▭ **MSCB3** (12/85)
English Nat Opera North Chorus recital
Handel: Coronation Anthems (exc); *Bruckner:* Ave Maria (1861); Tota pulchra es; Christus factus est; *Bizet:* Carmen (exc); *Brahms:* Zigeunerlieder, Op. 103 (exc); *Seiber:* Hungarian Folksongs (exc); *Traditional:* Deep river; Joshua fit de battle of Jericho. (ENON Chor, S. Westrop, S. Westrop/J. Pryce-Jones)

Kevin Mayhew Ltd

Ⓓ **KMCD1007** ▭ **KMK1007**
Great Organ Transcriptions-David Briggs
Bach: Suites, BWV1066-9 (exc); Flute Sonatas, BWV1030-5 (exc); Cantata 29 (exc); *Debussy:* Après-midi; *Elgar:* Pomp and Circumstance Marches (exc); Dream of Gerontius (exc); *Prokofiev:* Love for 3 oranges (exc); *Rachmaninov:* Vocalise; *Rimsky-Korsakov:* Tale of Tsar Saltan (exc); *Susato:* Danserye; *Tchaikovsky:* Nutcracker (exc). (D. Briggs)

Mediterraneo

Ⓓ **MED92102**
Airs, Dances and Prayers
Sarasate: Zigeunerweisen; *Massenet:* Thaïs (exc); *Bloch:* Baal Shem (exc); *Verdi:* Lombardi (exc); *Bach:* Solo Violin Partitas and Sonatas (exc); *Paganini:* Cantabile, Op. 17; *Wieniawski:* Polonaise, Op. 4. (R. Marchesi, R. Guglielmo)

Mel Recordings

Ⓓ **MELCD022-2**
Soirée at Snape
Weill: Knickerbocker Holiday (exc); Johnny Johnson (exc); Lady in the Dark (exc); Street Scene (exc); *Bernstein:* Peter Pan (exc); Wonderful Town (exc); *Sondheim:* Anyone can whistle (exc); *Gershwin:* Porgy and Bess (exc); *Kern:* Show Boat (exc); *Berlin:* Follow the Fleet (exc); *Gershwin:* Girl Crazy (exc); *W. Marshall:* Improvisation on Gershwin themes; *Traditional:* Joshua fit de battle of Jericho; Steal away to Jesus; Sometimes I feel like a motherless child; Deep River; I got a robe. (M. Marshall, W. Marshall)

Melodiya

Ⓓ **74321 17090-2** (12/94)
Tchaikovsky—Eugene Onegin
Tchaikovsky: Eugene Onegin (Cpte). (E. Belov, G. Vishnevskaya, S. Lemeshev, L. Avdeyeva, I. Petrov, V. Petrova, E. Verbitskaya, A. Sokolov, I. Mikhailov, G. Pankov, Bolshoi Th Chor, Bolshoi Th Orch/B. Khaikin)

Ⓓ **74321 17091-2** (10/94)
Tchaikovsky—The Queen of Spades
Tchaikovsky: Queen of Spades (Cpte). (V. Atlantov, T. Milashkina, V. Levko, V. Valaitis, A. Fedoseyev, G. Borisova, A. Sokolov, V. Yaroslavtsev, V. Vlasov, K. Baskov, Y. Dementiev, N. Grigorieva, N. Lebedeva, Bolshoi Th Chor, Bolshoi Th Orch/M. Ermler)

Ⓓ **74321 25189-2**
Yevgeny Mravinsky Edition - Vols 1-10
Weber: Oberon (exc); *Schubert:* Symphony 8; *Brahms:* Symphony 3; *Mozart:* Nozze di Figaro (exc); Symphony 39; *Sibelius:* Legends (exc); Symphony 7; *Stravinsky:* Agon (Cpte); *Shostakovich:* Symphony 15; *Bruckner:* Symphony 9; *Tchaikovsky:* Nutcracker (exc); *Prokofiev:* Romeo and Juliet (exc); *Hindemith:* Harmonie der Welt; *Honegger:* Symphony 3; *Beethoven:* Symphony 4; *Tchaikovsky:* Symphony 5; *Debussy:* Après-midi; *Bartók:* Music for strings, percussion and celesta; *Stravinsky:* Apollon musagète (Cpte); *Shostakovich:* Symphony 6; Symphony 10; *Wagner:* Meistersinger (exc); Lohengrin (exc); Lohengrin (exc); Tannhäuser (exc); Tristan und Isolde (exc); Götterdämmerung (exc); Walküre (exc). (Leningrad PO/E. Mravinsky)

Ⓓ **74321 25190-2**
Mravinsky Edition, Vol 1
Weber: Oberon (exc); *Schubert:* Symphony 8; *Brahms:* Symphony 2. (Leningrad PO/E. Mravinsky)

Ⓓ **74321 25191-2**
Mravinsky Edition, Vol 2
Mozart: Nozze di Figaro (exc); Symphony 39; *Sibelius:* Legends (exc); Symphony 7. (Leningrad PO/E. Mravinsky)

Ⓓ **74321 25199-2**
Mravinsky Edition, Vol 10
Wagner: Meistersinger (exc); Lohengrin (exc); Lohengrin (exc); Tannhäuser (exc); Tristan und Isolde (exc); Götterdämmerung (exc); Walküre (exc). (Leningrad PO/E. Mravinsky)

Melodram

Ⓓ **MEL26516**
Christa Ludwig: Recital
Verdi: Don Carlo (exc); Aida (exc). (C. Ludwig, G. Jones, P. Domingo, K. Paskalis, N. Ghiaurov, H. Hotter, Leonie Rysanek, Vienna St Op Chor, Vienna St Op Orch/B. Klobučar, L. Amara, R. Tucker, E. Flagello, E. Karlsrud, R. MacWherter, NY Met Op Chor, NY Met Op Orch/F. Cleva)

Memoir Records

Ⓓ **CDMOIR404** (7/91) ▭ **CMOIR404**
Ezio Pinza—Recital
Verdi: Ernani (exc); *Mussorgsky:* Boris Godunov (exc); *Mozart:* Nozze di Figaro (exc); Don Giovanni (exc); Zauberflöte (exc); *Gounod:* Faust (exc); Faust (exc); *A. Thomas:* Caïd (exc); *Handel:* Serse (exc); *Puccini:* Bohème (exc); *Bellini:* Norma (exc); *Verdi:* Simon Boccanegra (exc);

Vespri Siciliani (exc); Requiem (exc); Don Carlo (exc); *Tosti:* Chanson de l'adieu; *Paisiello:* Amor contrastato (exc); *Mussorgsky:* Song of the Flea. (E. Pinza, NY Met Op Chor, NY Met Op Orch, orch/Rosario Bourdon/E. Panizza/B. Reibold/B. Walter/H. Barlow/W. Pelletier/G. Setti/D. Voorhees)

CDMOIR405 **CMOIR405**
Great Tenors
Puccini: Manon Lescaut (exc); Tosca (exc); *Meyerbeer:* Africaine (exc); *Verdi:* Luisa Miller (exc); *Donizetti:* Elisir d'amore (exc); *Leoncavallo:* Mattinata; *Verdi:* Rigoletto (exc); Otello (exc); *Wagner:* Lohengrin (exc); Walküre (exc); Rienzi (exc); *Offenbach:* Contes d'Hoffmann (exc); Contes d'Hoffmann (exc); *Adam:* Postillon de Lonjumeau (exc); *Gounod:* Faust (exc); *Berlioz:* Troyens (exc). (B. Gigli, J. Björling, G. Lauri-Volpi, A. Pertile, T. Schipa, J. Schmidt, I. Kozlovsky, G. Martinelli, F. Völker, L. Melchior, M. Lorenz, R. Tauber, M. Wittrisch, H. Roswaenge, H. Nash, G. Thill, chor, Berlin St Op Chor, orch, La Scala Orch, Berlin St Op Orch, NY Met Op Orch, Bayreuth Fest Orch, Philadelphia, SO/J. Pasternack/N. Grevillius/F. Ghione/C. Sabajno/S. Meyerowitz/W. Pelletier/H. Tietjen/E. Ormandy/C. Schmalstich/E. Orthmann/B. Seidler-Winkler/C. Raybould/E. Bigot)

CDMOIR406 **CMOIR406**
Mozart—Historical Recordings
Mozart: Nozze di Figaro (exc); Nozze di Figaro (exc); Nozze di Figaro (exc); Nozze di Figaro (exc); Zauberflöte (exc); Zauberflöte (exc); Zauberflöte (exc); Zauberflöte (exc); Zauberflöte (exc); Zauberflöte (exc); Don Giovanni (exc); Don Giovanni (exc); Don Giovanni (exc); Don Giovanni (exc); Don Giovanni (exc); Don Giovanni (exc); Così fan tutte (exc). (L. Helletsgruber, Lotte Lehmann, W. Domgraf-Fassbaender, T. dal Monte, G. Hüsch, P. Anders, T. Lemnitz, H. Nash, A. Kipnis, L. Schöne, E. Pinza, P. Munsel, F. Leider, J. Patzak, E. Schumann, R. Tauber, I. Souez, Glyndebourne Fest Orch, Berlin St Op Orch, orch, BPO/F. Busch/M. Gurlitt/T. Beecham/H. Schmidt-Isserstedt/C. Schmalstich/A. Goodman/F. Zweig/J. Barbirolli/L. Blech/G.W. Byng/Rosario Bourdon/W. Goehr)

CDMOIR408 (2/92)
Great Sopranos
Wagner: Tannhäuser (exc); Parsifal (exc); *Weber:* Oberon (exc); *Beethoven:* Fidelio (exc); *Mozart:* Zauberflöte (exc); Nozze di Figaro (exc); *Offenbach:* Périchole (exc); *Massenet:* Manon (exc); *Donizetti:* Fille du Régiment (exc); *Spontini:* Vestale (exc); *Puccini:* Madama Butterfly (exc); Turandot (exc); *Catalani:* Wally (exc). (Lotte Lehmann, F. Leider, M. Teschemacher, K. Flagstad, T. Lemnitz, E. Schumann, M. Teyte, N. Vallin, T. dal Monte, R. Ponselle, M. Seinemeyer, L. Schöne, H. Spani, Berlin St Op Orch, LSO, Stuttgart Op Orch, Philadelphia, BPO, orch, La Scala Orch/F. Weissmann/J. Barbirolli/G. Görlich/E. Ormandy/T. Beecham/G.W. Byng/F. Ruhlmann/J. Pasternack/Rosario Bourdon/F. Zweig/C. Sabajno)

CDMOIR409 (9/92)
Three Tenors—Björling, Gigli & Tauber
Meyerbeer: Africaine (exc); *Puccini:* Tosca (exc); Tosca (exc); *Millöcker:* Bettelstudent (exc); *Rossini:* Soirées musicales (exc); *Tosti:* Ideale; *Grieg:* Melodies of the Heart, Op. 5 (exc); *De Curtis:* Torna a Surriento; *Yradier:* Paloma; *Traditional:* Kommt a Vogerl geflogen; *Gounod:* Faust (exc); *Ponchielli:* Gioconda (exc); *Flotow:* Martha (exc); *Leoncavallo:* Mattinata; *Sieczyński:* Wien, du Stadt meiner Träume; *Traditional:* Ack Värmerland, du sköna; *Geehl:* For you alone; *De Curtis:* Senza nisciuno; *Di Capua:* O sole mio; *Puccini:* Turandot (exc). (J. Björling, R. Tauber, B. Gigli, orch/N. Grevillius, La Scala Orch/F. Ghione/W. Goehr, Stockholm Royal Op Orch/D. Olivieri, M. Spoliansky/I. Lewis, Dajos Bela Orch)

CDMOIR411 (1/93) **CMOIR411** (1/93)
Sacred Songs and Arias
Bizet: Agnus Dei; *Verdi:* Requiem (exc); Requiem (exc); *Rossini:* Stabat Mater (exc); Stabat Mater (exc); *Franck:* Panis angelicus; *Handel:* Serse (exc); *Faure:* Crucifix; *Gounod:* Ave Maria; *Bach:* Cantata 147 (exc); *Mendelssohn:* Elias (exc); *Mozart:* Exsultate, jubilate, K165 (exc); *Handel:* Messiah (exc); *Haydn:* Creation (exc); *Traditional:* Swing low, sweet chariot; *Grechaninov:* Liturgy, Op. 79 (exc). (G. Thill, J. Björling, E. Pinza, E. Caruso, F. Austral, B. Gigli, T. Schipa, M. Journet, J. McCormack, F. Schorr, E. Schumann, P. Dawson, I. Baillie, P. Robeson, F. Chaliapin, ROH Chor, Berlin St Op Chor, Paris Russian Met Church Ch, orch, La Scala Orch, ROHO, Berlin St Op Orch, G. Moore, LSO, Hallé, R. Clapham/Anthony Bernard/N. Grevillius/C. Sabajno/J. Barbirolli/B. Seidler-Winkler/Rosario Bourdon/W.B. Rogers/A. Melichar/L. Collingwood/L. Heward/N. Afonsky/G.W. Byng)

CDMOIR412
Great Voices of the Century Sing Puccini
Puccini: Bohème (exc); Bohème (exc); Bohème (exc); Bohème (exc); Bohème (exc); Bohème (exc); Fanciulla del West (exc); Madama Butterfly (exc); Madama Butterfly (exc); Madama Butterfly (exc); Madama Butterfly (exc); Tosca (exc); Tosca (exc); Tosca (exc); Tosca (exc); Gianni Schicchi (exc); Turandot (exc); Turandot (exc); Turandot (exc). (R. Pampanini, M. Favero, L. Schöne, C. Muzio, M. Seinemeyer, Lotte Lehmann, H. Spani, J. Hammond, E. Turner, M. Fleta, A. Ziliani, B. Gigli, J. Björling, G. Lauri-Volpi, A. Valente, A. Cortis, G. De Luca, L. Borgonovo, L. Tibbett, G. Tomei, Berlin St Op Chor, NY Met Op Chor, orch, La Scala Orch, Berlin St Op Orch, Rome Op Orch, NY Met Op Orch, Hallé/L. Molajoli/L. Blech/Rosario Bourdon/N. Grevillius/F. Weissmann/F. Ghione/C. Sabajno/O. de Fabritiis/G. Setti/L. Heward/M. di Veroli)

CDMOIR413
The Very Best of Gilbert & Sullivan
Sullivan: Mikado (exc); Yeomen of the Guard (exc); HMS Pinafore (exc); Pirates of Penzance (exc); Iolanthe (exc); Trial by Jury (exc); Gondoliers (exc). (D. Oldham, R. Flynn, B. Bennett, M. Eyre, E. Nickell-Lean, M. Green, S. Granville, N. Briercliffe, B. Lewis, George Baker, H. Lytton, E. Griffin, L. Sheffield, D. Fancourt, A. Davies, W. Lawson, D'Oyly Carte Op Chor, SO/I. Godfrey/M. Sargent/H. Norris)

CDMOIR417 (6/93)
Great Voices of the Century—Beniamino Gigli
Puccini: Bohème (exc); *Giordano:* Andrea Chénier (exc); *Mascagni:* Cavalleria Rusticana (exc); *Boito:* Mefistofele (exc); *Verdi:* Rigoletto (exc); Forza del destino (exc); *Donizetti:* Elisir d'amore (exc); *Bizet:* Pêcheurs de perles (exc); Pêcheurs de perles (exc); *Meyerbeer:* Africaine (exc); *Flotow:* Martha (exc); *Toselli:* Serenade; *Bixio:* Canzone dell'amore; *De Curtis:* Carmela; *Denza:* Occhi di fata; *Di Chiara:* Spagnola; *Cottrau:* Addio a Napoli. (B. Gigli, D. Giannini, G. De Luca, orch, La Scala Orch/E. Goossens/J. Pasternack/C. Sabajno/F. Ghione/Rosario Bourdon/J. Barbirolli/D. Olivieri/W. Goehr/L. Collingwood)

CDMOIR418 (5/93)
Great Voices of the Century—John McCormack
Donizetti: Elisir d'amore (exc); *Handel:* Semele (exc); Atalanta (exc); *Mozart:* Don Giovanni (exc); Ridente la calma, K152; *Bizet:* Pêcheurs de perles (exc); *Verdi:* Traviata (exc); *Rachmaninov:* Songs, Op.26 (exc); *Wolf:* Goethe Lieder (exc); Spanisches Liederbuch (exc); *Foster:* Jeanie with the light brown hair; *J. Patterson:* Garden where the Praties Grow; *Macmurrough:* Macushla; *Traditional:* Foggy, foggy dew; Star of the County Down; *Crouch:* Kathleen Mavourneen; *A. Sanders:* Little Town; *E. Ball:* Barry of Ballymore (exc); *Dufferin:* Terence's farewell to Kathleen; *Traditional:* Off to Philadelphia; *C. Marshall:* I hear you calling me. (J. McCormack, L. Bori, E. Schneider, G. Moore, S. Clay, orch, F. Kreisler/J. Pasternack/W.B. Rogers)

CDMOIR419 **CMOIR419**
Vienna Nights - Golden Age of Operetta
J. Strauss II: Fledermaus (exc); Zigeunerbaron (exc); Fledermaus (exc); Fledermaus (exc); Nacht in Venedig (exc); Frühlingsstimmen, Op. 410; Nacht in Venedig (exc); Nacht in Venedig (exc); Zigeunerbaron (exc); *Zeller:* Obersteiger (exc); Vogelhändler (exc); *Lehár:* Paganini (exc); Lustige Witwe (exc); Lustige Witwe (exc); Lustige Witwe (exc); Giuditta (exc); Land des Lächelns (exc); Graf von Luxemburg (exc); *Millöcker:* Bettelstudent (exc); Dubarry (exc); *Künneke:* Vetter aus Dingsda (exc); *Sieczyński:* Wien, du Stadt meiner Träume. (G. Alpar, E. Bettendorf, M. Korjus, Lotte Lehmann, A. Rautawaara, E. Rethberg, E. Schumann, H. Schymberg, L. Schöne, P. Anders, J. Björling, H.E. Groh, J. Patzak, R. Tauber, G. Thill, M. Wittrisch, K. Schmitt-Walter, P. Ulanowsky, Berlin Deutsche Op Orch, Berlin St Op Orch, orch/K. Alwin/L. Blech/Rosario Bourdon/G. Bret/L. Collingwood/O. Dobrindt/N. Grevillius/E. Korngold/W. Lutze/A. Melichar/P. Hühn/L. Rüth/C. Schmalstich/N. Schultze/T. Mackeben)

CDMOIR422 (6/94)
Great Voices in Tchaikovsky
Tchaikovsky: Queen of Spades (exc); Queen of Spades (exc); Queen of Spades (exc); Queen of Spades (exc); Queen of Spades (exc); Maid of Orleans (exc); Iolanta (exc); Iolanta (exc); Iolanta (exc); Eugene Onegin (exc); Eugene Onegin (exc); Eugene Onegin (exc); Eugene Onegin (exc); Eugene Onegin (exc); Songs, Op.6 (exc); Songs, Op.47 (exc); Songs, Op.38 (exc); Songs, Op.47 (exc); Songs, Op.60 (exc); Songs, Op.38 (exc). (J. Rogatchewsky, H. Schlusnus, M. Michailova, K. Tugarinova, X. Belmas, A. Didur, M. Jeritza, L. Lipkowska, V. Kastorsky, M. Maksakov, L. Sobinov, Lotte Lehmann, D. Smirnov, J. Patzak, G. Baklanoff, N. Koshetz, L. Tibbett, F. Chaliapin, E. Caruso, anon, A. Kitschin, G. Scognamiglio, orch, Berlin St Op Orch/A. Melichar/A. Kitschin/Wolfgang Martin, Inst Ens/N. Shilkret)

CDMOIR425 (12/94)
Three Tenors, Volume 2
Verdi: Aida (exc); *Puccini:* Manon Lescaut (exc); *Wagner:* Meistersinger (exc); *Offenbach:* Belle Hélène (exc); *M. Sandoval:* Eres tú; *Moszkowski:* Serenata, Op.15/1; *Lehár:* Frasquita (exc); *Donaudy:* O bei nidi d'amore; *Friml:* Vagabond King (exc); *Puccini:* Bohème (exc); *Leoncavallo:* Pagliacci (exc); *Donizetti:* Elisir d'amore (exc); *Lortzing:* Undine (exc); *Bizet:* Carmen (exc); *Giordano:* Andrea Chénier (exc); *Offenbach:* Contes d'Hoffmann (exc); *Alfvén:* Songs, Op.28 (exc); *R. Strauss:* Lieder, Op.17 (exc); *Lehár:* Land des Lächelns (exc); Friederike (exc); *Di Capua:* Maria Marì; *Cottrau:* Santa Lucia. (J. Björling, B. Gigli, R. Tauber, orch, Stockholm Royal Op Orch, La Scala Orch, Berlin Staatskapelle, Berlin Künstlertheater Orch/N. Grevillius/J. Pasternack/E. Hauke/Rosario Bourdon/F. Ghione/O. de Fabritiis, H. Ebert/F. Weissmann/N. Shilkret/J. Barbirolli)

CDMOIR428 (7/95)
Rosa Ponselle and Giovanni Martinelli sing Verdi
Verdi: Aida (exc); Aida (exc); Aida (exc); Aida (exc); Aida (exc); Trovatore (exc); Trovatore (exc); Trovatore (exc); Trovatore (exc); Ernani (exc); Ernani (exc); Forza del destino (exc); Forza del destino (exc); Forza del destino (exc). (R. Ponselle, E. Baker, G. Martinelli, R. Stracciari, E. Pinza, NY Met Op Chor, NY Met Op Orch, orch/Rosario Bourdon/G. Setti/J. Pasternack/W.B. Rogers/R. Romani)

CDMOIR429
Charles Kullman - Serenade
Marvell: World is mine tonight; *Herbert:* Fortune Teller (exc); *Toselli:* Serenade; *Di Capua:* 'O sole mio; *Herbert:* Naughty Marietta (exc); *Grieg:* Melodies of the Heart, Op.5 (exc); *Baddeley:* By the Dark Lagoon; *C. Böhm:* Lieder, Op.326 (exc); *Gounod:* Faust (exc); *Bizet:* Carmen (exc); *Schubert:* Schwanengesang, D957 (exc); *Fibich:* Moods, Op.41, Part 2 (exc); *Mahler:* Rückert Lieder (exc); *Schubert:* Ave Maria, D839; *Ravini:* Serenade; *Handel:* Serse (exc); *Drdla:* Souvenir; *Ross:* Mon coeur est pour toi; *Künneke:* Vetter aus Dingsda (exc); *Penn:* Smilin' through; *Sullivan:* Lost Chord; *G.A. Russell:* Vale. (C. Kullman, orch/W. Goehr/O. Dobrindt/F. Hartley/J. Batten/M. Sargent)

Memories

DR3101/3
Piccinni—La Cecchina
Piccinni: Cecchina (Cpte). (M.A. Peters, G. Morino, B. Praticò, A. Ruffini, G. Morigi, P. Spagnoli, S. Mingardo, M.C. Zanni, PAO/B. Campanella)

DR3104/5
Donizetti—L'Elisir d'amore
Donizetti: Elisir d'amore (Cpte). (A. Scarabelli, C. Merritt, A. Romero, S. Bruscantini, B. Briscik, Parma Teatro Regio Chor, Toscanini SO/H. Soudant)

DR3109
Vinci—Opera Arias
Vinci: Semiramide riconosciuta (exc); Didone abbandonata (exc); Caduta de' Decemvri (exc); Cecato fauzo (exc); Festa di Bacco (exc); Catone in Utica (exc). (M.A. Peters, Italian International Orch/M. Carraro)

HR4152/3
Rossini: Armida
Rossini: Armida (Cpte). (C. Deutekom, O. Garaventa, E. Gimenez, P. Bottazzo, B. Trotta, A. Maddalena, G. Antonini, Venice La Fenice Chor, Venice La Fenice Orch/C. Franci)

HR4156/7
Mozart: Mitridate, re di Ponto
Mozart: Mitridate (Cpte). (S. Kolk, M. Zara, E. Gabry, B. Fassbaender, I. Cotrubas, P. Baillie, R. Didusch, Salzburg Mozarteum Orch/L. Hager)

HR4186/7
Bellini—Il Pirata
Bellini: Pirata (Cpte). (P. Cappuccilli, M. Caballé, F. Labò, G. Baratti, U. Trama, F. Raffanelli, MMF Chor, MMF Orch/F. Capuana)

HR4191/2
Cesare Valletti—Public Performances
Mozart: Don Giovanni (exc); Betulia Liberata (exc); *Rossini:* Barbiere di Siviglia (exc); Italiana in Algeri (exc); *Donizetti:* Lucia di Lammermoor (exc); *Bellini:* Sonnambula (exc); Sonnambula (exc); *Verdi:* Traviata (exc); *Massenet:* Manon (exc); Werther (exc). (C. Valletti, VPO/H. von Karajan, Turin RAI Orch/M. Rossi, Orch/A. Basile, La Scala Orch/L. Bernstein, ROHO/N. Rescigno)

HR4204/5
Franco Corelli—Opera Arias
Meyerbeer: Huguenots (exc); *Verdi:* Ernani (exc); Battaglia di Legnano (exc); Trovatore (exc); *Bizet:* Carmen (exc);

Donizetti: Poliuto (exc); *Massenet:* Werther (exc); *Puccini:* Turandot (exc); Tosca (exc); *Cilea:* Adriana Lecouvreur (exc); *Giordano:* Andrea Chénier (exc). (F. Corelli, La Scala Orch/G. Gavazzeni, NY Met Op Orch/T. Schippers, VPO/H. von Karajan, Milan RAI SO/O. de Fabritiis/A. Votto/M. Rossi/K.H. Adler, Naples San Carlo Op Orch, Vienna St. Op Orch/L. von Matačić)

Ⓓ **HR4213/5**
Meyerbeer: L'Africana
Meyerbeer: Africaine (Cpte). (J. Norman, V. Luchetti, G. Guelfi, M. Sighele, A. Ferrin, G. Casarini, D. Formichini, G. Matteini, G. del Vivo, M. Rinaudo, MMF Chor, MMF Orch/R. Muti)

Ⓓ **HR4216/7**
Bellini—Norma
Bellini: Norma (Cpte). (J. Sutherland, M. Horne, C. Bergonzi, C. Siepi, R. MacWherter, C. Ordassy, NY Met Op Chor, NY Met Op Orch/R. Bonynge)

Ⓓ **HR4220/1**
Great Voices-Tito Schipa
Handel: Serse (exc); *Gluck:* Orfeo ed Euridice (exc); *Mozart:* Don Giovanni (exc); *Rossini:* Barbiere di Siviglia (exc); *Donizetti:* Elisir d'amore (exc); Lucia di Lammermoor (exc); Favorita (exc); Don Pasquale (exc); *Bellini:* Sonnambula (exc); *A. Thomas:* Mignon (exc); *Flotow:* Martha (exc); *Verdi:* Luisa Miller (exc); Rigoletto (exc); Traviata (exc); *Gounod:* Faust (exc); *Ponchielli:* Gioconda (exc); *Massenet:* Manon (exc); Werther (exc); Werther (exc); *Puccini:* Bohème (exc); Tosca (exc); *Mascagni:* Cavalleria Rusticana (exc); Amico Fritz (exc); *Cilea:* Arlesiana (exc); *Giordano:* Andrea Chénier (exc); Marcella (exc). (T. Schipa, T. dal Monte, N. Garelli, A. Galli-Curci, M. Favero, orch/Anon, E. Badini)

Ⓓ **HR4223/4**
Nicolai Ghiaurov
Mozart: Don Giovanni (exc); Don Giovanni (exc); Don Giovanni (exc); *Rossini:* Mosè in Egitto (exc); Mosè in Egitto (exc); *Verdi:* Nabucco (exc); Requiem (exc); Don Carlo (exc); Don Carlo (exc); Don Carlo (exc); *Mussorgsky:* Boris Godunov (exc); *Gounod:* Faust (exc). (N. Ghiaurov, M. Freni, T. Zylis-Gara, G. Evans, V. von Halem, G. Lane, G. Corradi, P. Cappuccilli, D. Petkov, S. Artale, G. Raimondi, Rome RAI Chor, La Scala Chor, chor, VPO, Rome RAI Orch, La Scala Orch/H. von Karajan/W. Sawallisch/G. Gavazzeni/C. Abbado/T. Schippers/G. Prêtre)

Ⓓ **HR4225/7**
Mozart—Don Giovanni
Mozart: Don Giovanni (Cpte). (E. Pinza, R. Bampton, J. Novotná, B. Sayão, C. Kullman, A. Kipnis, M. Harrell, N. Cordon, NY Met Op Chor, NY Met Op Orch/B. Walter)

Ⓓ **HR4233/4**
Alfredo Kraus—Public Performances
Mozart: Don Giovanni (exc); *Cherubini:* Ali-Baba (exc); *Rossini:* Barbiere di Siviglia (exc); *Donizetti:* Favorita (exc); Favorita (exc); *Bellini:* Puritani (exc); *Verdi:* Rigoletto (exc); Traviata (exc); *Bizet:* Pêcheurs de Perles (exc); *Massenet:* Werther (exc); *Cilea:* Arlesiana (exc). (Alfredo Kraus, VPO/H. von Karajan, La Scala Orch/N. Sanzogno, Naples San Carlo Op Orch, Milan RAI SO/A. Basile, Buenos Aires Colón Th Orch/B. Bartoletti, Trieste Teatro Verdi Orch/F. Molinari-Pradelli, Lisbon San Carlos Nat Th Orch/F. Ghione/A. La Rosa Parodi)

Ⓓ **HR4235/6**
Great Voices-Renata Tebaldi
Verdi: Giovanna d'Arco (exc); Traviata (exc); Forza del Destino (exc); Otello (exc); *Catalani:* Wally (exc); *Puccini:* Manon Lescaut (exc); Bohème (exc); Tosca (exc); Madama Butterfly (exc); Fanciulla del West (exc); *Giordano:* Andrea Chénier (exc). (R. Tebaldi, G. di Stefano, R. Tucker, G. Guelfi, F. Corelli, Milan RAI Chor, Milan RAI SO, MMF Orch, Florence Teatro Comunale Orch, NY Met Op Orch, Rome RAI Orch, Vienna St Op Orch/A. Simonetto/T. Serafin/D. Mitropoulos/F. Stiedry/A. Basile/A. Paoletti/L. von Matačić)

Ⓓ **HR4239/40**
Opera Arias—Leyla Gencer
Bellini: Norma (exc); *Cherubini:* Medea (exc); *Donizetti:* Anna Bolena (exc); Belisario (exc); Maria Stuarda (exc); *Verdi:* Ballo in maschera (exc); Don Carlo (exc); Forza del destino (exc); Macbeth (exc); Trovatore (exc). (L. Gencer, Venice La Fenice Orch/C. Franci, La Scala Orch/G. Gavazzeni, MMF Orch/F. Molinari-Pradelli, Milan RAI SO/F. Previtali, Bologna Teatro Comunale Orch/O. de Fabritiis/A. Votto, Rome Op Orch)

Ⓓ **HR4271**
Jessye Norman—Florence Recital, 1971
Purcell: Dido (exc); *Wagner:* Wesendonk Lieder; *Mahler:* Rückert Lieder (exc); *Ravel:* Sainte; Mélodies hébraïques; *Traditional:* Sometimes I feel like a motherless child; My Lord, what a morning; Oh what a beautiful City; There is a balm in Gilead; Ev'ry time I feel de Spirit; *Wolf:* Mörike Lieder (exc); *Debussy:* Beau soir. (J. Norman, I. Gage)

Ⓓ **HR4273/4**
Great Voices—Pietro Cappuccilli
Bellini: Pirata (exc); *Catalani:* Loreley (exc); *Donizetti:* Roberto Devereux (exc); *Rossini:* Barbiere di Siviglia (exc); *Verdi:* Don Carlo (exc); Rigoletto (exc); Simon Boccanegra (exc); Trovatore (exc). (P. Cappuccilli, Naples San Carlo Op Chor, Naples San Carlo Op Orch, Alfredo Kraus/N. Sanzogno/M. Rossi, L. Gencer, A.M. Rota, M. Caballé, MMF Chor, MMF Orch/F. Capuana, Turin RAI Orch, I. Vinco, La Scala Chor, La Scala Orch/G. Gavazzeni, G. Tucci, B. Prevedi, U. Carosi, N. Ghiaurov, Rome RAI Chor, Rome RAI Orch/T. Schippers, M. Freni, G. Foiani, F. Schiavi, G. Raimondi/C. Abbado)

Ⓓ **HR4275/6**
Birgit Nilsson—Public Performances 1954-1969
Wagner: Lohengrin (exc); Tristan und Isolde (exc); Walküre (exc); *Puccini:* Tosca (exc); Turandot (exc); *Schubert:* Dem Unendlichen, D291; Junge Nonne, D828; Auflösung, D807; *R. Strauss:* Lieder, Op.41 (exc); Lieder, Op.22 (exc); Lieder, Op.48 (exc); Lieder, Op.10 (exc). (B. Nilsson, W. Windgassen, A. Varnay, H. Uhde, J. Vickers, P. Domingo, F. Corelli, Bayreuth Fest Chor, Bayreuth Fest Orch/E. Jochum/K. Böhm, NY Met Op Orch/H. von Karajan, NY Met Op Chor/G. Schick, La Scala Chor, La Scala Orch/G. Gavazzeni, anon)

Ⓓ **HR4277/8**
Mirella Freni—Public Performances 1963-1970
A. Scarlatti: Griselda (exc); *Mozart:* Don Giovanni (exc); *Donizetti:* Fille du Régiment (exc); *Bellini:* Puritani (exc); *Verdi:* Otello (exc); *Gounod:* Faust (exc); *Massenet:* Manon (exc); *Puccini:* Bohème (exc). (M. Freni, N. Ghiaurov, L. Pavarotti, A. di Stasio, W. Ganzarolli, B. Giaiotti, S. Bruscantini, S. Malagù, G. Raimondi, VPO, La Scala Chor, La Scala Orch, Rome RAI Chor, Rome RAI Orch, Naples Scarlatti Chor, Naples Scarlatti Orch/N. Sanzogno/H. von Karajan/R. Muti/G. Prêtre/P. Maag)

Ⓓ **HR4279/80**
Montserrat Caballè—Opera Arias
Spontini: Agnes von Hohenstaufen (exc); *Rossini:* Donna del Lago (exc); *Donizetti:* Lucrezia Borgia (exc); *Bellini:* Pirata (exc); *Verdi:* Ernani (exc); Luisa Miller (exc); Trovatore (exc); Ballo in maschera (exc); Otello (exc); *Puccini:* Madama Butterfly (exc). (M. Caballé, Rome RAI Chor, Rome RAI Orch/R. Muti, Turin RAI Orch/P. Bellugi, La Scala Orch/E. Gracis, MMF Chor, MMF Orch/F. Capuana, Milan RAI Chor, Milan RAI SO/G. Gavazzeni, NY Met Op Chor, NY Met Op Orch/T. Schippers/B. Bartoletti/Z. Mehta, Madrid Zarzuela Orch/G. Rivoli)

Ⓓ **HR4281/2**
Wagner—Der Fliegende Holländer
Wagner: Fliegende Holländer (Cpte). (F. Crass, Leonie Rysanek, K. Ridderbusch, C. Heater, A.M. Bessel, La Scala Chor, La Scala Orch/W. Sawallisch)

Ⓓ **HR4287/8**
Donizetti—Lucia Di Lammermoor
Donizetti: Lucia di Lammermoor (Cpte). (R. Scotto, G. Raimondi, G. Guelfi, A. Ferrin, F. Raffanelli, B. Prior, P. de Palma, La Scala Chor, La Scala Orch/C. Abbado)

Ⓓ **HR4291/2**
Great Voices - Renata Scotto
Donizetti: Lucia di Lammermoor (exc); Elisir d'amore (exc); *Bellini:* Straniera (exc); *Verdi:* Lombardi (exc); Traviata (exc); Requiem (exc). (R. Scotto, La Scala Chor, La Scala Orch/C. Abbado, MMF Chor, MMF Orch/G. Gavazzeni, Palermo Teatro Massimo Chor, Palermo Teatro Massimo Orch/N. Sanzogno, Rome Op Orch, ROH Chor, ROHO/C.F. Cillario, Milan RAI Chor, Rome RAI Chor, Rome RAI Orch)

Ⓓ **HR4293/4**
The very best of Maria Callas
Bellini: Norma (exc); Pirata (exc); Puritani (exc); Sonnambula (exc); *Donizetti:* Lucia di Lammermoor (exc); *Puccini:* Bohème (exc); Tosca (exc); *Rossini:* Armida (exc); Barbiere di Siviglia (exc); Cenerentola (exc); Semiramide (exc); *Verdi:* Don Carlo (exc); Ernani (exc); Forza del destino (exc); Macbeth (exc); Nabucco (exc); Traviata (exc); Trovatore (exc). (M. Callas, Paris Op Chor, Paris Op Orch/G. Sébastian, Rome RAI Orch/A. Simonetto, FRNO/G. Prêtre, Berlin RSO/H. von Karajan, N German RSO/N. Rescigno, La Scala Orch/L. Bernstein, Milan RAI SO, Turin RAI Orch/G. Santini, Athens Fest Orch/A. Votto, BBC SO/M. Sargent, NY Met Op Orch/D. Mitropoulos, F. Albanese)

Ⓓ **HR4300/1**
Great Voices—Sesto Bruscantini
A. Scarlatti: Griselda (exc); *Cimarosa:* Chi dell'altrui (exc); *Mozart:* Don Giovanni (exc); *Cherubini:* Lodoïska (exc); *Rossini:* Barbiere di Siviglia (exc); Italiana in Algeri (exc); Turco in Italia (exc); *Donizetti:* Elisir d'amore (exc); Favorita (exc); *Bellini:* Puritani (exc). (S. Bruscantini, N. Ghiaurov, D. Petkov, L. Alva, T. Berganza, M. Petri, V. Meucci, G. Sciutti, R. Mattioli, C. Merritt, A. Scarabelli, F. Cossotto, A. Pedroni, Alfredo Kraus, B. Giaiotti, Naples Scarlatti Chor, Rome RAI Chor, Turin RAI Chor, Milan RAI Chor, Parma Teatro Regio Chor, Naples Scarlatti Orch, Rome RAI Orch, Turin RAI Orch, Milan RAI SO, Toscanini SO, NHK SO/N. Sanzogno/R. Muti/C.M. Giulini/O. de Fabritiis/H. Soudant)

Ⓓ **HR4337/8**
Verdi: I Lombardi
Verdi: Lombardi (Cpte). (R. Scotto, L. Pavarotti, R. Raimondi, U. Grilli, M. Rinaudo, A. Colella, S. Mezzetti, F. Iacopucci, A. di Stasio, Rome Op Chor, Rome Op Orch/G. Gavazzeni)

Ⓓ **HR4362/4**
Mozart: Don Giovanni
Mozart: Don Giovanni (Cpte). (N. Ghiaurov, G. Janowitz, T. Zylis-Gara, M. Freni, Alfredo Kraus, G. Evans, R. Panerai, V. von Halem, Vienna St Op Chor, VPO/H. von Karajan)

Ⓓ **HR4370/1**
Verdi—Ernani
Verdi: Ernani (Cpte). (F. Corelli, L. Price, M. Sereni, C. Siepi, C. Ordassy, C. Anthony, C. Russel, NY Met Op Chor, NY Met Op Orch/T. Schippers)

Ⓓ **HR4372/3**
Great Voices Giuseppe Di Stefano
Rossini: Barbiere di Siviglia (exc); *Donizetti:* Lucia di Lammermoor (exc); *Bellini:* Puritani (exc); *Verdi:* Luisa Miller (exc); Rigoletto (exc); Traviata (exc); Forza del destino (exc); *A. Thomas:* Mignon (exc); *Puccini:* Bohème (exc); Tosca (exc); Madama Butterfly (exc); Turandot (exc). (G. di Stefano, Mexico Palacio Chor, Mexico Palacio Orch/R. Cellini, La Scala Chor, Berlin RIAS Orch/H. von Karajan/G. Picco, Palermo Teatro Massimo Orch/N. Sanzogno/U. Mugnai, M. Callas, La Scala Orch/C.M. Giulini, A. Protti/A. Votto/E. Tieri, R. Tebaldi, F. Alonso, Rome RAI Orch)

Ⓓ **HR4374/5**
Verdi—Un Ballo in maschera
Verdi: Ballo in maschera (Cpte). (Leonie Rysanek, C. Bergonzi, R. Merrill, A. Rothenberger, J. Madeira, L. Vichey, B. Giaiotti, C. Marsh, A. Velis, R. Nagy, NY Met Op Chor, NY Met Op Orch/N. Santi)

Ⓓ **HR4376/7**
Tito Gobbi—Opera Arias
Mozart: Don Giovanni (exc); *Verdi:* Don Carlo (exc); Otello (exc); *Leoncavallo:* Pagliacci (exc); *Puccini:* Tosca (exc); Fanciulla del West (exc). (T. Gobbi, Vienna St Op Chor, Vienna St Op Orch/W. Furtwängler, Chicago Lyric Op Chor, Chicago Lyric Op Orch/A. Votto, NHK Sym Chor, NHK SO/A. Erede, Milan RAI SO/A. Simonetto, ROH Chor, ROHO/C.F. Cillario, La Scala Orch)

Ⓓ **HR4380/1**
Strauss—Elektra
R. Strauss: Elektra (Cpte). (I. Borkh, J. Madeira, L. della Casa, M. Lorenz, K. Böhme, A. Pernerstorfer, A. Felbermayer, K. Loraine, E. Majkut, G. Littasy, A. Gerber-Candy, K. Meyer, S. Draksler, S. Wagner, M. Horne, L. Otto, Vienna St Op Chor, VPO/D. Mitropoulos)

Ⓓ **HR4382/3**
Gluck—Orphée et Eurydice
Gluck: Orfeo ed Euridice (Cpte). (G. Simionato, S. Jurinac, G. Sciutti, Vienna St Op Chor, VPO/H. von Karajan)

Ⓓ **HR4386/7**
Great Voices - Giulietta Simionato
Gluck: Orfeo ed Euridice (exc); *Rossini:* Italiana in Algeri (exc); Tancredi (exc); Cenerentola (exc); *Meyerbeer:* Huguenots (exc); *Donizetti:* Anna Bolena (exc); *Verdi:* Trovatore (exc); Aida (exc). (G. Simionato, N. Ghiaurov, F. Corelli, P. Clabassi, E. Bastianini, N. Zaccaria, La Scala Chor, Milan RAI Chor, Vienna St Op Chor, VPO, Milan RAI SO, La Scala Orch/H. von Karajan/N. Sanzogno/G. Gavazzeni/L. von Matačić)

Ⓓ **HR4392/3**
Great Voices - Marilyn Horne
Handel: Rinaldo (exc); *Meyerbeer:* Prophète (exc); *Rossini:* Italiana in Algeri (exc); Siège de Corinthe (exc); Otello (exc); Donna del Lago (exc); *Donizetti:* Anna Bolena (exc); *Bellini:* Norma (exc); *Berlioz:* Troyens (exc). (M. Horne, N. Gedda, P. de Palma, C. Cava, J. Sutherland, Turin RAI Chor, Rome RAI Chor, Venice La Fenice Orch, Turin RAI Orch, La Scala Orch, orch, NY Met Op Orch, Rome RAI Orch/J. Fisher/H. Lewis/C. Franci/T. Schippers/R. Bonynge/G. Prêtre)

Ⓓ **HR4396/7**
Great Voices—Leontyne Price
Mozart: Don Giovanni (exc); *Verdi:* Ernani (exc); Trovatore (exc); Aida (exc); Requiem (exc); *Puccini:* Turandot (exc). (L. Price, VPO, Vienna St Op Chor/H. von Karajan, NY Met Op Orch/T. Schippers/L. von Matačić, La Scala Chor, La Scala Orch/F. Molinari-Pradelli, C. Valletti, L. Dutoit, E. Bastianini, F. Corelli, G. Simionato, D. Usunow, F. Cossotto, G. di Stefano, N. Zaccaria, NY Met Op Chor, Vienna St Op Orch)

Ⓓ **HR4400/1**
Great Voices - Ettore Bastianini
Donizetti: Poliuto (exc); *Verdi:* Ernani (exc); Trovatore (exc); Traviata (exc); Forza del destino (exc); Aida (exc); *Giordano:* Andrea Chénier (exc); *Cilea:* Adriana Lecouvreur (exc). (E. Bastianini, M. Callas, M. del Monaco, A. Cerquetti, A. Cesarini, I. Vinco, A. Stella, F. Corelli, L. Price, R. Tebaldi, M. Olivero, La Scala Chor, MMF Chor, NY Met Op Chor, Vienna St Op Chor, Naples San Carlo Op Chor, La Scala Orch, MMF Orch, NY Met Op Orch, VPO, Vienna St Op Orch, Naples San Carlo Op Orch/A. Votto/D. Mitropoulos/G. Gavazzeni/C.M. Giulini/N. Santi/L. von Matačić/M. Rossi)

Ⓓ **HR4404/5**
Verdi—La Traviata
Verdi: Traviata (Cpte). (R. Scotto, L. Pavarotti, P. Glossop, N. Berry, N. Roberts, J. Dobson, D. Wicks, R. Best, D. Kelly, R. Vaughn, K. Reddish, ROH Chor, ROHO/C.F. Cillario)

Ⓓ **HR4406/7**
Verdi—Otello
Verdi: Otello (Cpte). (M. del Monaco, G. Tucci, T. Gobbi, M. Caruso, G. De Juliis, A. di Stasio, P. Clabassi, T. Okamura, NHK Sym Chor, NHK SO/A. Erede)

Ⓓ **HR4408/9(1)** (11/92)
Singers in Genoa, Vol.1 (disc 1)
Massenet: Roi de Lahore (exc); *Verdi:* Otello (exc); *Rossini:* Guillaume Tell (exc); *Verdi:* Otello (exc); Simon Boccanegra (exc); Otello (exc); *Brediceanu:* Vai, mindruto; *Mascagni:* Cavalleria Rusticana (exc); *A. Thomas:* Hamlet (exc); *Meyerbeer:* Africaine (exc); *Puccini:* Manon Lescaut (exc); *Gounod:* Roméo et Juliette (exc); *Verdi:* Ernani (exc); *Halévy:* Juive (exc); *Donizetti:* Don Pasquale (exc); *Cilea:* Adriana Lecouvreur (exc); *Verdi:* Falstaff (exc); *Donizetti:* Lucia di Lammermoor (exc); *Verdi:* Luisa Miller (exc); *Donizetti:* Lucrezia Borgia (exc); *Bellini:* Puritani (exc); *Donizetti:* Favorita (exc); *Berlioz:* Damnation de Faust (exc); *Bizet:* Pêcheurs de Perles (exc); *Leoncavallo:* Bohème (exc); *Cilea:* Adriana Lecouvreur (exc); *Verdi:* Traviata (exc); Rigoletto (exc); *Mascagni:* Iris (exc); *Boito:* Mefistofele (exc). (A. Cotogni, A. Aramburo, F. Signorini, G.B. de Negri, V. Arimondi, F. Tamagno, H. Darclée, F. Valero, R. Blanchart, F. Viñas, C. Ferrani, R. Pinkert, G. Kaschmann, F. Navarini, A. Pini-Corsi, E. Corsi, E. Garbin, A. Stehle, V. Maurel, N. Melba, F. Giraud, I. de Frate, A. Bonci, O. Luppi, G. De Luca, E. Caruso, R. Storchio, A. Pandolfini, E. Ventura, T. Ruffo, M. Farneti, T. Arkel, anon, orch)

Ⓓ **HR4408/9(2)** (11/92)
Singers in Genoa, Vol.1 (disc 2)
Mascagni: Cavalleria Rusticana (exc); *Rossini:* Barbiere di Siviglia (exc); Barbiere di Siviglia (exc); *Wagner:* Walküre (exc); *Puccini:* Manon Lescaut (exc); *Giordano:* Fedora (exc); *Rossini:* Barbiere di Siviglia (exc); *Bellini:* Norma (exc); *Donizetti:* Favorita (exc); Lucia di Lammermoor (exc); *Verdi:* Trovatore (exc); *Wagner:* Meistersinger (exc); *Bellini:* Norma (exc); *Giordano:* Andrea Chénier (exc); *Marchetti:* Ruy Blas (exc); *Puccini:* Manon Lescaut (exc); *Wagner:* Walküre (exc); *Puccini:* Fanciulla del West (exc); Tosca (exc); Fanciulla del West (exc); *Verdi:* Otello (exc); Otello (exc); Rigoletto (exc); Rigoletto (exc); *Giordano:* Marcella (exc); *Verdi:* Ballo in maschera (exc). (G. Bellincioni, R. Stracciari, V. Bettoni, G. Borgatti, L. Cavalieri, E. Carelli, M. Barrientos, M. de Macchi, G. Bellantoni, J. Palet, G. Pacini, A. Pinto, G. Russ, V. Guerrini, E. Giraldoni, T. Parvis, P. Schiavazzi, C. Formichi, I. Calleja, L. Montesanto, G. Martinelli, A. Paoli, N. Zerola, H. Lázaro, D. Viglione-Borghese, E. Perea, G. Danise, anon, orch, La Scala Orch/L. Molajoli, E. Ventura)

Ⓓ **HR4500/1**
Verdi—Falstaff
Verdi: Falstaff (Cpte). (M. Stabile, P. Silveri, R. Tebaldi, A. Noni, C. Valletti, C. Elmo, A.M. Canali, M. Caruso, G. Nessi, S. Maionica, La Scala Chor, La Scala Orch/V. de Sabata)

Ⓓ **HR4576**
Leoncavallo—I Pagliacci
Leoncavallo: Pagliacci (Cpte). (R. Tucker, M. Sighele, K. Nurmela, W. Alberti, E. Lorenzi, MMF Chor, MMF Orch/R. Muti)

Mercury

Ⓓ **432 005-2MM**
Orchestral Works
Kodály: Galánta Dances; Marosszék Dances; Háry János Suite; *Bartók:* Hungarian Sketches; Romanian folkdances, Sz68. (Philh Hungarica, Minneapolis SO/A. Dorati)

Ⓓ **432 753-2MM**
Prokofiev—Orchestral Works
Prokofiev: Symphony 5; Scythian Suite; Love for 3 Oranges Suite. (LSO, Minneapolis SO/A. Dorati)

Ⓓ **434 303-2MM**
Chabrier/Roussel—Orchestral Works
Chabrier: España; Suite pastorale; Joyeuse marche; Bourrée fantasque; Roi malgré lui (exc); Gwendoline (exc); *Roussel:* Suite, Op.33. (Detroit SO/P. Paray)

Ⓓ **434 305-2MM**
Tchaikovsky—Orchestral Works
Tchaikovsky: Symphony 5; Marche slave; Eugene Onegin (exc). (LSO, Minneapolis SO/A. Dorati)

Ⓓ **434 308-2MM**
Borodin/Rimsky-Korsakov—Suites
Rimsky-Korsakov: Golden Cockerel Suite (exc); Capriccio Espagnol; Russian Easter Festival Ov; *Borodin:* Prince Igor (exc). (LSO/A. Dorati)

Ⓓ **434 309-2MM**
Suppé/Auber—Overtures
Suppé: Schöne Galathee (exc); Pique Dame (exc); Leichte Kavallerie (exc); Dichter und Bauer (exc); Morgen, ein Mittag, ein Abend in Wien (exc); Boccaccio (exc); *Auber:* Cheval de Bronze (exc); Fra Diavolo (exc); Muette de Portici (exc). (Detroit SO/P. Paray)

Ⓓ **434 321-2MM** (8/93)
Bizet/Thomas—Orchestral Works
Bizet: Patrie; Carmen Suites (exc); Arlésienne Suites; *A. Thomas:* Mignon (exc); Raymond (exc). (Detroit SO/P. Paray)

Ⓓ **434 322-2MM**
Works for Wind Ensemble
Sullivan: Pineapple Poll (exc); *Rossini:* Boutique Fantasque; *Gounod:* Faust (exc); *Wagner:* Lohengrin (exc); Rheingold (exc). (Eastman Wind Ens/F. Fennell)

Ⓓ **434 325-2MM** (7/93)
Bartok/Berg—Bluebeard/Wozzeck
Bartók: Duke Bluebeard's castle (Cpte); *Berg:* Wozzeck (exc). (M. Székely, O. Szőnyi, H. Pilarczyk, LSO/A. Dorati)

Ⓓ **434 332-2MM** (11/93)
French Marches & Overtures
Meyerbeer: Coronation march; *Gounod:* Marche funèbre d'une marionette; *Saint-Saëns:* Suite algérienne (exc); Marche héroïque, Op.34; *Various:* National Anthems (exc); *Adam:* Si j'étais roi (exc); *Boïeldieu:* Dame blanche (exc); *Offenbach:* Belle Hélène (exc); Orphée aux enfers (exc); Contes d'Hoffmann (exc); *Rossini:* Guillaume Tell (exc). (Detroit SO/P. Paray)

Ⓓ **434 342-2MM**
Wagner—Preludes and Overtures
Wagner: Meistersinger (exc); Parsifal (exc); Lohengrin (exc); Lohengrin (exc); Tannhäuser (exc); Tristan und Isolde (exc). (LSO/A. Dorati)

Ⓓ **434 345-2MM**
Rossini/Verdi—Overtures
Verdi: Forza del destino (exc); Nabucco (exc); Vespri siciliani (exc); Traviata (exc); *Rossini:* Gazza ladra (exc); Scala di seta (exc); Cenerentola (exc); Barbiere di Siviglia (exc); Italiana in Algeri (exc); Signor Bruschino (exc). (LSO, Minneapolis SO/A. Dorati)

Ⓓ **434 348-2MM**
Antal Dorati conducts Richard Strauss
R. Strauss: Don Juan; Tod und Verklärung; Till Eulenspiegel; Rosenkavalier (exc). (Minneapolis SO/A. Dorati)

Ⓓ **434 351-2MM**
Szeryng plays Kreisler
Kreisler: Caprice Viennois; Schön Rosmarin; Liebesleid; Liebesfreud; Scherzo-caprice, Op. 6; Pugnani Tempo di Menuetto; Pugnani Praeludium and Allegro; Chanson Louis XIII; Tambourin chinois; Porpora Menuet; Old Refrain; Beethoven Rondino; Boccherini Allegretto; *Leclair:* Violin Sonatas, Op. 9 (exc); *Gluck:* Orfeo ed Euridice (exc); *Locatelli:* Caprices, Op. 3 (exc). (H. Szeryng, C. Reiner)

Ⓓ **434 352-2MM**
Kaleidoscope
Smetana: Bartered Bride (exc); *Nicolai:* Lustigen Weiber von Windsor (exc); *J. Strauss I:* Radetzky March; *Weber:* Abu Hassan (exc); Invitation to the Dance; *Meyerbeer:* Prophète (exc); *Brahms:* Hungarian Dances (exc); *A. Thomas:* Mignon (exc); *Tchaikovsky:* Mazeppa (exc); *Suppé:* Banditenstreiche (exc); *Offenbach:* Orphée aux enfers (exc); *Glinka:* Jota aragonesa. (LSO/C. Mackerras)

Meridian

Ⓓ **CDE84162** ▭ **KE77162**
Vocal Music for Choir
Mendelssohn: Duets, Op. 63 (exc); *Brahms:* Lieder, Op. 49 (exc); Lieder, Op. 84 (exc); Lieder und Romanzen, Op. 44 (exc); *Mozart:* Ridente la calma, K152; An Chloe, K524; *Mendelssohn:* Lieder, Op. 34 (exc); *Schubert:* Musensohn, D764; Gott in der Natur, D757; *Brahms:* Deutsche Volkslieder (exc); Lieder und Romanzen, Op. 44 (exc); *Mendelssohn:* Duets, Op. 77 (exc); *Schubert:* An Silvia, D891; Psalm 23, D706; *Mozart:* Zauberflöte (exc); *Mendelssohn:* Midsummer Night's Dream (exc); *Schubert:* Nacht und Träume, D827. (Winchester Quiristers, R. Bottone/Julian Smith)

Ⓓ **CDE84195** (10/90) ▭ **KE77195** (10/90)
Vivaldi: Orchestral and Vocal Works
Vivaldi: Concerti, op 8 (exc); In furore giustissimae, RV626; Incoronazione di Dario (exc); Griselda (exc); Fida ninfa (exc). (Elizabeth Wallfisch, K. Eckersley, Fiori Musicali, P. Rapson)

Ⓓ **CDE84196** ▭ **KE77196**
Rossini—Songs
Rossini: Péchés de vieillesse I (exc); Soirées musicales (exc); Mi lagnerò tacendo (exc); Tancredi (exc); Barbiere di Siviglia (exc); Gazza ladra (exc); Péchés de vieillesse X (exc); Péchés de vieillesse III (exc); Nouvelles compositions (exc); Péchés de vieillesse II (exc); Soirées musicales (exc). (Combattimento)

Ⓓ **CDE84241**
Music for Flute & Harp
Anon: Greensleeves; *Vivaldi:* Trio Sonata, RV82; *Boismortier:* Sonatas, Op.91 (exc); *Gluck:* Orfeo ed Euridice (exc); *Mozart:* Violin Sonata, K14; *Krumpholtz:* Flute and Harp Sonata in F; *Rossini:* Andante in F (wind); *Chopin:* Rossini Variations; *Berlioz:* Enfance du Christ (exc). (C. Conway, J. Hughes, D. Watkins)

Ⓓ **CDE84264**
The Palm Court
E. Martin: Evensong; *Waldteufel:* Amour et printemps; *Dvořák:* Gipsy melodies (exc); *Brahms:* Hungarian Dances (exc); *Glazunov:* Meditation, Op.32; *Dvořák:* Slavonic Dances (exc); *Tchaikovsky:* Sleeping Beauty (exc); *Sullivan:* Mikado (exc); *Heuberger:* Opernball (exc); *Valdez:* Sérénade du Tzigane; *Yoshitomo:* Geisha and butterfly; *Eilenberg:* Sérénade des mandolines; *Meyer-Helmund:* Evening in St Petersburg; *Gershwin:* Capitol Revue (exc). (London Salon Ens)

Ⓓ **DUOCD89009** (12/91) ▭ **KD89009** (12/91)
The Romantic Englishman
Spofforth: Hail! smiling morn; *Walmisley:* Music, all powerful; *Webbe I:* Discord, dire sister; *Horsley:* Come, gentle zephyr; *Goss:* List! for the breeze; *Beale:* Come, let us join the roundelay; *Battishill:* Sylvia blushes when I woo her; *T. Philips:* Crows in the cornfield; *Hatton:* When ev'ning's twilight; *Bishop:* By the simplicity of Venus' doves; *Parry:* Partsongs (1904-12); *Stainer:* Cupid look about thee; *Benedict:* Lily of Killarney (exc); *Pearsall:* There is a paradise on earth; *Sterndale Bennett:* Come live with us; *Molloy:* Tomorrow will be Friday; *Sullivan:* Long day closes. (Hilliard Ens, L-L. Kiesel)

Mezhdunarodnaya Kniga

Ⓓ **MK417030**
Fine Night with Alexander Shirinsky
A. Marcello: Oboe Concerto in D minor (exc); *Wagner:* Albumblatt; *Brahms:* Hungarian Dances (exc); FAE Sonata; *Dvořák:* Slavonic Dances (exc); *Granados:* Danzas españolas (exc); *Sarasate:* Caprice basque; *Debussy:* Beau soir; *Kreisler:* Caprice viennois; *Prokofiev:* Love for 3 Oranges Suite (exc); *Shostakovich:* Preludes, Op. 34 (exc); *Shchedrin:* Humoresque; Imitating Albéniz. (A. Shirinsky, N. Rozova)

Ⓓ **MK417047**
Erik Kurmangaliev - Recital
Glinka: Ruslan and Lyudmila (exc); Life for the Tsar (exc); *Tchaikovsky:* Moscow Cantata (exc); *Rimsky-Korsakov:* Snow Maiden (exc); *Gluck:* Orfeo ed Euridice (exc); *Handel:* Admeto (exc). (E. Kurmangaliev, Moscow Maly SO/V. Ponkin)

MGB

Ⓓ **CD6112** (10/94)
Schoeck—Venus
Schoeck: Venus (Cpte). (F. Lang, L. Popp, J. O'Neal, H. Fassbender, B. Skovhus, Z. Alföldi, Heidelberg Chbr Ch, Basle Boys' Ch, Swiss Workshop PO/M. Venzago)

Mode Records

Ⓓ **Mode38/9**
Cage—Europeras 3 & 4
Cage: Europera 3; Europera 4. (Long Beach Op, A. Culver (dir))

Motette

Ⓓ **CD20171**
Romantic Organ Music
Reger: Chorale Fantasias, Op. 52 (exc); Pieces, Op. 59 (exc); *Karg-Elert:* Choral-Improvisationen, Op. 65 (exc); Sinfonische Choräle, Op. 87 (exc); *Wagner:* Lohengrin (exc). (H. Bönisch, P. Bönisch, H. Herrmann)

Mozart Edition

Ⓓ **MECD1002** (5/91)
Operetta Melodies
J. Strauss II: Zigeunerbaron (exc); *Suppé:* Pique Dame (exc); *Zeller:* Vogelhändler (exc); *Millöcker:* Gasparone (exc); *Offenbach:* Belle Hélène (exc); *Suppé:* Boccaccio (exc); *J. Strauss II:* Ritter Pasman; *Millöcker:* Bettelstudent (exc); Dubarry (exc); *Heuberger:* Opernball (exc); *Offenbach:* Orphée aux enfers (exc); *Millöcker:* Verwunschene Schloss (exc); *J. Strauss II:* Nacht in Venedig (exc). (Raphaele Concert Orch/E. Rondell/P. Walden)

Multisonic

Ⓓ **310151-2**
Mozart/Smetana/Wagner—Vocal and Orchestral Works
Smetana: Libuše (exc); Libuše (exc); *Mozart:* Zauberflöte (exc); Symphony 38; *Wagner:* Tristan und Isolde (exc). (L. Dvořáková, Prague RSO, Czech PO/V. Talich)

Ⓓ **310154-2** (6/94)
Janáček—Šárka
Janáček: Šárka (Cpte). (A. Nováková, A. Jurečka, F. Kunc, J. Válka, Brno Rad Chor, Brno RSO/B. Bakala)

Ⓓ **310185-2** (9/94)
Smetana—The Bartered Bride
Smetana: Bartered Bride (Cpte). (L. Červinková, B. Blachut, R. Vonásek, K. Kalaš, L. Mráz, V. Krilová, J. Heriban, J. Palivcová, J. Pechová, B. Vich, J. Soumar, Prague Rad Chor, Prague RSO/K. Ančerl)

Music & Arts

Ⓓ **ATRA-3008**
Toscanini's Farewell Concert
Wagner: Lohengrin (exc); Siegfried (exc); Götterdämmerung (exc); Tannhäuser (exc); Meistersinger (exc). (NBC SO/A. Toscanini)

Ⓓ **MACD-263**
Flagstad sings Wagner—1955 New York Farewell Concert
Wagner: Walküre (exc); Tristan und Isolde (exc); Götterdämmerung (exc); Wesendonk Lieder. (K. Flagstad, NBC SO/E. McArthur)

Ⓓ **MACD-619** (5/91)
Beethoven: Fidelio
Beethoven: Fidelio (Cpte). (K. Flagstad, R. Maison, F. Schorr, E. List, M. Farell, K. Laufkötter, A. Gabor, NY Met Op Chor, NY Met Op Orch/A. Bodanzky)

Ⓓ **MACD-631**
Sir Thomas Beecham/RPO Concerts—1954-59
Mozart: Symphony 35; *Tchaikovsky:* Nutcracker Suite; *Wagner:* Meistersinger (exc); Tannhäuser (exc). (RPO/T. Beecham)

Ⓓ **MACD-645** (9/91)
Verdi—Otello
Verdi: Otello (Cpte). (G. Martinelli, E. Rethberg, L. Tibbett, N. Massue, T. Votipka, N. Moscona, G. Cehanovsky, NY Met Op Chor, NY Met Op Orch/E. Panizza)

Ⓓ **MACD-647** (7/91)
Wagner—Tristan und Isolde
Wagner: Tristan und Isolde (Cpte). (L. Melchior, K. Flagstad, K. Thorborg, E. List, J. Huehn, G. Cehanovsky, D. Beattie, A. Marlowe, NY Met Op Chor, NY Met Op Orch/E. Leinsdorf)

Ⓓ **MACD-689**
Casals Festival at Prades, Volume II
Bach: Viola da Gamba Sonatas, BWV1027-9 (exc); *Brahms:* Piano Trio 1; Clarinet Trio; *Schumann:* Piano Trio 2; *Mozart:* Piano Quartet, K493; *Bach:* Wohltemperierte Klavier (exc); *Beethoven:* Violin Sonata 1; *Mozart:* Oboe Quartet, K370; Idomeneo (exc); *Brahms:* Piano Trio 2; *Schumann:* Piano Trio 1. (V. de los Angeles, M. Tabuteau, D. Oppenheim, Y. Menuhin, A. Grumiaux, A. Pernel, J. Szigeti, M. Thomas, K. Tuttle, P. Casals, P. Tortelier, R. von Tobel, W. Kapell, London Musicum Collegium/P. Casals)

Ⓓ **MACD-696** (7/92)
Wagner—Siegfried
Wagner: Siegfried (Cpte). (L. Melchior, F. Schorr, K. Flagstad, K. Laufkötter, E. Habich, K. Thorborg, E. List, S. Andreva, NY Met Op Orch/A. Bodanzky)

Ⓓ **MACD-730**
Bruckner—Symphony No. 9 etc
Bruckner: Symphony 9; *Wagner:* Tristan und Isolde (exc). (BPO/W. Furtwängler)

Ⓓ **MACD-767** (4/94)
Honegger conducts Honegger
Honegger: Tempête; Pastorale d'été; Symphonic Movements (exc); Aventures du roi Pausole (exc); Chant de Nigamon; Symphony 3. (SO, Odeon Grand Orch/A. Honegger, Pasdeloup Orch/Rhené-Baton)

Ⓓ **MACD-771**
Stokowski in Rare and Unusual Repertoire
Kodály: Háry János Suite; Budavári Te Deum; *Falla:* Nights in the Gardens of Spain. (Budapest RSO, American Youth Performs Chor, American Youth Performs Orch, W. Kapell, PSO/L. Stokowski)

Ⓓ **MACD-772** (3/94)
The Art of Egon Petri
Chopin: Preludes (exc); *Busoni:* Indianisches Tagebuch; Elegien (exc); Perpetuum Mobile; Fantasia Contrappuntistica; *Medtner:* Fairy Tales, Op.20; Forgotten Melodies, Op.38 (exc); *Schumann:* Fantasiestücke, Op.12; *Mozart:* Piano Concerto 9 (exc); *Bach:* Prelude, Fugue and Allegro, BWV998; Cantata 208 (exc); Chorales, BWV651-668 (exc); Applicatio, BWV841-843; *Liszt:* Forelle, S564; *Chopin:* Nocturnes (exc); *Haydn:* Variations, HobXVII:6; *Gluck:* Orfeo ed Euridice (exc); Alceste (1776) (exc); *Beethoven:* Piano Sonata 27; *Schubert:* Divertissement, D823 (exc); *Chopin:* Nocturnes (exc); Piano Sonata 3; *Beethoven:* Piano Sonata 30; Piano Sonata 31; Piano Sonata 32; *Liszt:* Venezia e Napoli, S162; *Chopin:* Polonaises (exc). (E. Petri, C. Bussotti)

Ⓓ **MACD-780** (7/94)
The Mengelberg Legacy
Tchaikovsky: Symphony 5; *Dvořák:* Violin Concerto; *Beethoven:* Symphony 3; *Debussy:* Fantaisie; *Brahms:* Symphony 3; Violin Concerto; *Schubert:* Arpeggione Sonata, D821; *Bruch:* Violin Concerto 1; *Wagner:* Tannhäuser (exc); *Beethoven:* Egmont (exc). (M. Neuss, H. Krebbers, G. Bustabo, G. Cassadó, W. Gieseking, Concertgebouw/W. Mengelberg)

Ⓓ **MACD-784**
Horenstein in Paris - November 1956
Beethoven: Egmont (exc); *Haydn:* Symphony 100; *Mahler:* Kindertotenlieder; *Gluck:* Alceste (1776) (exc); *Prokofiev:* Symphony 5; *Nielsen:* Symphony 6. (M. Anderson, American SO, FNO, Hallé/J. Horenstein)

Ⓓ **MACD-793**
Furtwängler conducts Beethoven
Beethoven: Symphony 7; Symphony 8; Leonore (exc). (Stockholm PO/W. Furtwängler)

Ⓓ **MACD-797**
Overture! Opera Overtures of late 18th and early 19th Centuries
Beethoven: Fidelio (exc); *Mozart:* Entführung (exc); *Rossini:* Barbiere di Siviglia (exc); Guillaume Tell (exc); Semiramide (exc); *Weber:* Freischütz (exc). (NY Harmonie Ens/S. Richman)

Ⓓ **MACD-826**
Furtwängler conducts World War II Concerts
Weber: Freischütz (exc); *Schubert:* Symphony 9; *Beethoven:* Coriolan. (BPO/W. Furtwängler)

Ⓓ **MACD-867**
Kipnis as Boris
Mussorgsky: Boris Godunov (exc); Boris Godunov (exc). (A. Kipnis, I. Petina, A. De Paolis, N. Moscona, NY Met Op Chor, NY Met Op Orch/G. Szell, NYPO/F. Reiner)

Ⓓ **MACD-876**
Wagner—Der Fliegende Holländer
Wagner: Fliegende Holländer (Cpte). (H. Uhde, A. Varnay, L. Weber, W. Windgassen, E. Schärtel, J. Traxel, Bayreuth Fest Chor, Bayreuth Fest Orch/H. Knappertsbusch)

Music Collection International

Ⓓ **MCCD086** ▭ **MCTC086**
The Essential Caruso
Giordano: Fedora (exc); *Trimarchi:* Bacio ancora; *Donizetti:* Elisir d'amore (exc); *Meyerbeer:* Huguenots (exc); *Puccini:* Bohème (exc); *Verdi:* Forza del destino (exc); *Leoncavallo:* Pagliacci (exc); *Verdi:* Rigoletto (exc); *Puccini:* Madama Butterfly (exc); *Goldmark:* Königin von Saba (exc); *Cardillo:* Core 'ngrato; *Verdi:* Aida (exc); *Puccini:* Bohème (exc); Manon Lescaut (exc); *Mascagni:* Cavalleria Rusticana (exc); *Rossini:* Stabat Mater (exc); *Verdi:* Requiem (exc); *Tosti:* Luna d'estate; *Cottrau:* Santa Lucia; *Verdi:* Rigoletto (exc); *Tosti:* Alba separa; *Cohan:* Over there. (E. Caruso, anon, A. Scotti, orch, A. Galli-Curci, F. Perini, G. de Luca, G. Farrar/W.B. Rogers, U. Giordano/J. Pasternack)

Ⓓ **MCCD090** ▭ **MCTC090**
Carreras & Friends sing Opera Arias & Songs
Bernstein: Candide (1988) (exc); *Leoncavallo:* Mattinata; *Bizet:* Carmen (exc); *Puccini:* Gianni Schicchi (exc); *Gounod:* Faust (exc); *Mascagni:* Cavalleria Rusticana (exc); *Massenet:* Cid (exc); Werther (exc); *Catalani:* Wally (exc); *Theodorakis:* Train leaves at eight; *Tosti:* Ultima canzone; *Massenet:* Thaïs (exc); *Rossini:* Italiana in Algeri (exc); *Bernstein:* West Side Story (exc); *Lara:* Granada; *Verdi:* Traviata (exc); *Massenet:* Thaïs (exc). (J. Carreras, A. Baltsa, K. Ricciarelli, R. Raimondi, A. Smith, Orch/Anon Cond)

Ⓓ **MCCD099**
Opera's Greatest Arias
Bizet: Carmen (exc); *Cilea:* Arlesiana (exc); *Di Capua:* O sole mio; *Donizetti:* Elisir d'amore (exc); Favorita (exc); *Gounod:* Roméo et Juliette (exc); *Mascagni:* Cavalleria Rusticana (exc); *Massenet:* Werther (exc); *Meyerbeer:* Africaine (exc); *Puccini:* Bohème (exc); Fanciulla del West (exc); Manon Lescaut (exc); Tosca (exc); Turandot (exc); *Verdi:* Aida (exc); Forza del destino (exc); Luisa Miller (exc); Macbeth (exc); Rigoletto (exc); Rigoletto (exc). (C. Bergonzi, P. Ballo, A. Cupido, P. Dvorský, G. Pastine, V. Scuderi, J. Sempere, A. Solovianenko, G. Tieppo, N. Todisco, F. Bonisolli, S. Fisichella, E. Ivanov, M. Malagnini, Verona Arena Orch/A. Guadagno)

Ⓓ **OQ0008**
Tchaikovsky & Gounod—Ballet music
Tchaikovsky: Nutcracker (exc); *Gounod:* Faust (exc); *Delibes:* Coppélia (exc). (Adelaide SO/J. Serebrier)

Ⓓ **OQ0009**
Wagner—Orchestral music from operas
Wagner: Tannhäuser (exc); Tristan und Isolde (exc); Meistersinger (exc); Rienzi (exc). (LPO, Mexico St SO/E. Bátiz)

Ⓓ **OQ0011**
A Baroque Collection
Pachelbel: Canon and Gigue (exc); *Gluck:* Orfeo ed Euridice (exc); *Bach:* Suites, BWV1066-9 (exc); *Boccherini:* String Quintets, G271-6 (exc); *Albinoni:* Adagio; *Handel:* Water Music (exc); Serse (exc); *A. Marcello:* Oboe Concerto in D minor. (J-M. Quenon, Adelaide SO, RTBF SO/J. Serebrier)

Music Masters (USA)

Ⓓ **67078-2**
Stravinsky The Composer - Volume 1
Stravinsky: Symphony in 3 movements; Fanfare (1964); Fanfare (1953); Apollo (exc); Requiem canticles; Symphony of Psalms; Rite of Spring (Cpte); Oedipus rex (exc). (J. Humphrey, W. White, J. Ostendorf, J. Cheek, J. Garrison, P. Newman, C. Gekker, C. Albach, S. Radcliff, NY Choral Artists, St Luke's Orch/R. Craft)

Ⓓ **67100-2** (11/93)
Weill—Lost in the Stars
Weill: Lost in the Stars (Cpte). (G. Hopkins, A. Woodley, R. Pindell, C. Clarey, C. Woods, J. Howard, R. Vogt, NY Concert Chorale, St Luke's Orch/J. Rudel)

Ⓓ **67110-2** (9/94)
Stravinsky—The Composer, Volume V
Stravinsky: Suites; Etudes, Op. 7; Norwegian Moods; Concerto for two solo pianos; Ode (1943); Rag-time; Piano-Rag Music; Renard (Cpte). (T. Baker, D. Martin, D. Evitts, W. Pauley, M. Wait, T. Schultz, St Luke's Orch/R. Craft)

Ⓓ **67118-2**
Mozart—Harmoniemusik
Mozart: Nozze di Figaro (exc); Don Giovanni (exc); Zauberflöte (exc); Così fan tutte (exc); Entführung (exc); Clemenza di Tito (exc); *Beethoven:* Fidelio (exc). (Amadeus Ens/J. Rudel)

Ⓓ **67131-2** (3/95)
Stravinsky—The Rake's Progress
Stravinsky: Rake's Progress (Cpte). (J. Garrison, J. West, J. Cheek, W. White, M. Lowery, S. Love, A. Woodley, J. Johnson, Gregg Smith Sngrs, St Luke's Orch/R. Craft)

Music Memoria

Ⓓ **MM30221** ▭ **MM040079**
18 French Divas
Massenet: Hérodiade (exc); *Gounod:* Au rossignol; *Auber:* Diamants de la Couronne (exc); *G. Charpentier:* Louise (exc); *A. Thomas:* Mignon (exc); *Wagner:* Tannhäuser (exc); *Fauré:* Requiem (exc); *Rossini:* Barbiere di Siviglia (exc); *Gluck:* Alceste (1776) (exc); *Bruneau:* Virginie (exc); *Berlioz:* Troyens (exc); *Saint-Saëns:* Cloche; *Gounod:* Cinq Mars (exc); *F. David:* Lalla-Roukh (exc); *Mozart:* Entführung (exc); *Massenet:* Marie-Magdeleine (exc); *Auber:* Domino Noir (exc); *Donizetti:* Fille du Régiment (exc). (E. Calvé, M. de Reszké, L. Korsoff, Y. Gall, N. Vallin, G. Lubin, J. Laval, G. Ritter-Ciampi, S. Balguérie, G. Féraldy, G. Frozier-Marrot, G. Cernay, C. Tirard, S. Petit-Renaux, L. Pons, G. Martinelli, F. Révoil, R. Doria, orch, anon/A. Wolff)

Ⓓ **MM30231** (10/90) ▭ **MM40086**
Don Pasquale & Tito Schipa Recital
Donizetti: Don Pasquale (Cpte); Elisir d'amore (exc); Elisir d'amore (exc); Lucia di Lammermoor (exc); *Bellini:* Sonnambula (exc); Sonnambula (exc); *Verdi:* Rigoletto (exc); *Leoncavallo:* Pagliacci (exc); *Cilea:* Arlesiana (exc); *Mascagni:* Ave Maria; *Rimsky-Korsakov:* Songs, Op. 2 (exc). (E. Badini, A. Saraceni, T. Schipa, A. Poli, G. Callegari, La Scala Chor, La Scala Orch/C. Sabajno, T. Schipa, A. Galli-Curci, T. dal Monte, orch/Rosario Bourdon/F. Ghione)

Ⓓ **MM30276**
Rossini—Barbiere di Siviglia, etc
Rossini: Barbiere di Siviglia (Cpte); *Tosti:* Ideale; *Denza:* Occhi di fata; *Tosti:* Aprile; *Tanara:* Nina; *Bizet:* Agnus Dei; *Catalani:* Wally (exc); *Verdi:* Nabucco (exc); *Leoncavallo:* Zazà (exc); *Meyerbeer:* Africaine (exc). (R. Stracciari, M. Capsir, D. Borgioli, S. Baccaloni, V. Bettoni, C. Ferrani, A. Bordonali, La Scala Chor, La Scala Orch/L. Molajoli, R. Stracciari, orch)

Ⓓ **MM30283** ▭ **MM40105**
Great Wagnerian Singers, Vol.1
Wagner: Fliegende Holländer (exc); Fliegende Holländer (exc); Rienzi (exc); Rienzi (exc); Lohengrin (exc); Lohengrin (exc); Lohengrin (exc); Lohengrin (exc); Tannhäuser (exc); Tannhäuser (exc); Tannhäuser (exc); Tannhäuser (exc); Tannhäuser (exc); Tannhäuser (exc); Tristan und Isolde (exc); Tristan und Isolde (exc); Tristan und Isolde (exc); Tristan und Isolde (exc); Meistersinger (exc); Meistersinger (exc); Meistersinger (exc); Meistersinger (exc); Meistersinger (exc); Meistersinger (exc). (E. Rethberg, F. Völker, M. Journet, Lotte Lehmann, M. Müller, R. Bockelmann, G. Hüsch, M. Lorenz, F. Leider, E. Marherr-Wagner, L. Melchior, K. Flagstad, A. Kipnis, H. Roswaenge, F. Schorr, E. Schumann, B. Williams, G. Parr, Berlin St Op Orch, Bayreuth Fest Orch, Bayreuth Fest Chor, SO, LSO, orch/J. Prüwer/A. Melichar/H. Weigert/F. Weissmann/H. Tietjen/K. Elmendorff/H.U. Müller/H. Schmidt-Isserstedt/L. Blech/A. Coates/R. Heger/H. Lange/C. Schmalstich/J. Barbirolli/F. Zweig)

Ⓓ **MM30285** ▭ **MM40107**
Great Wagnerian Singers, Vol.2
Wagner: Rheingold (exc); Rheingold (exc); Walküre (exc); Walküre (exc); Siegfried (exc); Siegfried (exc); Siegfried (exc); Götterdämmerung (exc); Götterdämmerung (exc); Parsifal (exc); Parsifal (exc); Parsifal (exc); *R. Strauss:* Arabella (exc). (R. Bockelmann, F. Schorr, W. Henke, G. Gusalewicz, F. Völker, M. Müller, F. Leider, M. Lorenz, L. Melchior, N. Gruhn, F. Easton, A. Kipnis, F. Wolff, Lotte Lehmann, Bayreuth Fest Chor, orch, Berlin St Op Orch, Bayreuth Fest Orch, LSO, ROHO, Philadelphia, Berlin Staatskapelle/L. Blech/H. Tietjen/A. Coates/R. Heger/S. Wagner/F. Weissmann/J. Barbirolli/E. Ormandy/R. Jäger, K. Heidersbach)

Ⓓ **MM30321** (10/91)
Jacques Thibaud—Violin Recital
Bach: Brandenburg Concertos (exc); *Debussy:* Violin Sonata; Préludes (exc); *Fauré:* Berceuse, Op.16; *Mozart:* Serenade, K250 (exc); *Albéniz:* España, Op.165 (exc); *Desplanes:* Intrada; *Saint-Saëns:* Havanaise; Déluge (exc); *Granados:* Danzas españolas (exc); *Falla:* Vida breve (exc). (J. Thibaud, A. Cortot, T. Janopoulo, G. de Lausnay, Paris Ecole Normale CO, A. Cortot (pf/dir))

Ⓓ **MM30323**
Verdi: Rigoletto
Verdi: Rigoletto (Cpte). (R. Massard, R. Doria, A. Vanzo, A. Legros, D. Scharley, J-P. Laffage, A. Adam, C. Rouquetty, M. Forel, M. Dupré, J. Scellier, chor, orch/J. Etcheverry)

Ⓓ **MM30325** (2/92)
Gluck—Orphée (abridged)
Gluck: Orphée (exc). (A. Raveau, G. Féraldy, J. Delille, Vlassof Chor, Vlassof Orch/H. Tomasi)

Ⓓ **MM30352** (7/91)
Caruso—Italian Opera Arias
Verdi: Rigoletto (exc); Rigoletto (exc); Rigoletto (exc); Traviata (exc); Aida (exc); Aida (exc); Trovatore (exc); Trovatore (exc); Ballo in maschera (exc); Macbeth (exc); Forza del destino (exc); *Donizetti:* Favorita (exc); Lucia di Lammermoor (exc); *Puccini:* Tosca (exc); Bohème (exc); *Gomes:* Schiavo (exc); *Mascagni:* Cavalleria rusticana (exc); *Rossini:* Petite messe solennelle (exc). (E. Caruso, A. Gluck, J. Gadski, A. Galli-Curci, F. Perini, G. De Luca, L. Homer, M. Egener, A. Bada, M. Journet, orch, NY Met Op Chor, NY Met Op Orch)

Ⓓ **MM30373** (12/91)
Gounod—Mélodies
Gounod: Mélodies (1855) (exc); Au rossignol; Reine de Saba (exc); Vierge d'Athénes; Cinq Mars (exc); Dites, la jeune belle; Vallon; Soir; Viens! les gazons sont verts!; A la brise; Quanti mai; Chanson de printemps; Mignon; Absent; Sérénade; Philémon et Baucis (exc). (R. Doria, J. Boguet)

Ⓓ **MM30376** (4/92)
Excerpts from Puccini's Tosca
Puccini: Tosca (exc). (N. Vallin, E. di Mazzei, A. Endrèze, Paris Opéra-Comique Chor, Paris Opéra-Comique Orch/G. Cloëz)

Ⓓ **MM30377**
18 Tenors d'Expression Française
Verdi: Trovatore (exc); *Reyer:* Sigurd (exc); *Grétry:* Fausses apparences (exc); *Auber:* Muette de Portici (exc); *Verdi:* Traviata (exc); Aida (exc); *Chaminade:* Ronde d'amour (exc); *Verdi:* Otello (exc); *Massenet:* Jongleur de Notre Dame (exc); Grisélidis (exc); Werther (exc); Werther (exc); *Méhul:* Joseph (exc); *Bizet:* Pêcheurs de perles (exc); *Saint-Saëns:* Mélodies persanes, Op. 26 (exc); *Massenet:* Hérodiade (exc); *Halévy:* Juive (exc); *Gounod:* Faust (exc). (L. Escalais, E. Scaramberg, L. Campagnola, E. Marcelin, L. Muratore, P. Franz, E. Rambaud, C. Vezzani, C. Friant, M. Villabella, J. Rogatchewsky, G. Thill, G. Micheletti, J. Luccioni, D. Devriès, R. Maison, R. Verdière, F. Ansseau, P. Deldi, orch, anon, M. Journet, Paris Op Orch/P. Coppola, SO)

Ⓓ **MM30428**
Pablo Casals - Recital
Granados: Goyescas (exc); *Saint-Saëns:* Carnaval des Animaux (exc); *Bach:* Toccata, Adagio and Fugue, BWV564 (exc); *Wagner:* Meistersinger (exc); Tannhäuser (exc); *Chopin:* Nocturnes (exc); Preludes (exc); *Fauré:* Songs, Op.7 (exc); *Godard:* Jocelyn (exc); *Schubert:* Moments Musicaux, D780 (exc); *Rubinstein:* Melodies, Op.3 (exc); *Dvořák:* Cello Concerto. (P. Casals, N. Mednikoff, Czech PO/G. Szell)

Ⓓ **MM30446**
Lily Pons - Recital
Delibes: Lakmé (exc); *Rossini:* Barbiere di Siviglia (exc); *Longás Torres:* Rossignol et l'Empereur; *A. Thomas:* Mignon (exc); *Meyerbeer:* Dinorah (exc); *Rimsky-Korsakov:* Golden Cockerel (exc); *Grétry:* Zémire et Azor (exc); *Mozart:* Entführung (exc); *Verdi:* Rigoletto (exc); Rigoletto (exc); *Donizetti:* Lucia di Lammermoor (exc); *Rossini:* Barbiere di Siviglia (exc); *Parisotti:* Se tu m'ami; *Bach:* Cantata 201; *Paradis:* Quel ruscelletto; *Saint-Saëns:* Parysatis (exc); *Gounod:* Mireille (exc). (L. Pons, G. De Luca, Orch/Rosario Bourdon/A. Kostelanetz, Renaissance Qt, H. Bove/W. Pelletier/G. Cloëz, Anon)

Ⓓ **MM30451** (11/92)
Mascagni—Cavalleria Rusticana, etc
Mascagni: Cavalleria rusticana (exc); *Rossini:* Guillaume Tell (exc); *Gounod:* Faust (exc); *Donizetti:* Favorita (exc); *Wagner:* Tannhäuser (exc); *Verdi:* Otello (exc); *Massenet:* Roi de Lahore (exc); Hérodiade (exc); *De Lara:* Méssaline (exc). (G. Cernay, G. Micheletti, A. Endrèze, A. Hena, M. Arty, chor, orch/G. Cloëz/F. Ruhlmann/H. Defosse)

Musica Oscura

Ⓓ **070971**
The Scyence of Luytinge
A. Holborne: Countess of Pembroke's Funeral; Countess of Pembroke's Paradise; Sighs Galliard; Funeral Galliard; *M. Galilei:* Lute Bk I (exc); *W. Lawes:* Golden Grove; Royall Consort 1; *Locke:* Cupid and Death (exc); *Blow:* Musick's Hand-maid, pt 2 (exc). (A. Rooley)

Ⓓ **070973** (10/95)
Purcell—Don Quixote—The Musical
Purcell: Don Quixote: The Musical (Cpte). (P. Scofield, R. Hudd, E. Kirkby, E. Tubb, D. Thomas, Consort of Musicke, City Waites, Purcell Simfony/A. Rooley)

Ⓓ **070974**
King of the Low Seas
Caccini: Nuove Musiche (1614) (exc); Rapimento di Cefalo (exc); *Puliaschi:* Musiche varie (exc). (D. Thomas, A. Rooley)

Ⓓ **070979** (10/95)
Sound the Trumpets from Shore to Shore
Purcell: Bonduca, Z574 (exc); Birthday Ode, Z323 (exc); Dioclesian, Z627 (exc); What a sad fate is mine, Z428; *D. Purcell:* Pilgrim (exc); 2-Trumpet Sonata; *Finger:* Oboe and Violin Sonata; *Leveridge:* Black and gloomy as the grave; *Topham:* Sonatas, Op. 3 (exc); *Blow:* Lovely Selina; *Weldon:* Judgment of Paris (exc); *Barrett:* 2-Trumpet and Oboe Sonata; *J. Eccles:* Ah, how lovely; Judgment of Paris (exc). (E. Kirkby, E. Tubb, English Tpt Virtuosi, A. Hoskins (tpt/dir), M. Hoskins (tpt/dir), A. Rooley)

Musica Sveciae

Ⓓ **MSCD407**
Swedish music—Gustavian Composers
Uttini: Aline (exc); Thetis and Peleus (exc); *Kraus:* Symphony in E flat; *Naumann:* Amphion (exc); Coro and Alonzo (exc); *Vogler:* Symphony in C. (Stockholm Nat Museum CO/C. Génetay, B. Rosengren)

Ⓓ **MSCD412**
Music from the Age of Liberty
Agrell: Sinfonias, Op. 1 (exc); *Höpken:* Catone in Utica (exc); *Johnsen:* Sinfonia in F II; *Zellbell I:* Sinfonia in C; *Wesström:* Sinfonia in D; *Brant:* Sinfonia in D minor. (Swedish Nat Museum CO/C. Génetay)

Ⓓ **MSCD612**
Lyrical Songs and Ballads for Mixed Choir
Peterson-Berger: Ran (exc); Summer Evening; Six Songs (exc); Poems from Arne (exc); Album, Op. 11 (exc); Ten Songs (exc); Spring Song III; *Stenhammar:* Spring Night, Op. 30/2; Choral Songs (Cpte); *Alfvén:* Blockheads; In our meadow; Retribution; Roses and Violets; Miller's Daughter; My birthday; Now listen, young Dora; Song of Dalarna; Anders was a jolly lad; Evening; May; Papillon; Midsummer Tune. (Uppsala Univ Chmbr Ch/S. Parkman)

Ⓓ **MSCD617**
Swedish Ballads
Söderman: King Heimer and Aslög; *Peterson-Berger:* Swedish folk ballads (exc); Böljeby waltz; Arnljot (exc); *Stenhammar:* Florez and Blanzeflor; Stockholm poems; *Rangström:* From King Erik's ballads. (I. Wixell, Stockholm PO/J. Arnell)

Musidisc

Ⓓ **20135-2** (3/92)
Messager—Passionement. Les p'tites Michu (excerpts)
Messager: Passionêment (Cpte); P'tites Michu (exc). (L. Dachary, C. Harbell, C. Collart, A. Doniat, D. Tirmont, G. Friedmann, Hieronimus, R. Lenoty, ORTF Lyric Orch/J-P. Kreder, C. Collart, C. Harbell, C. Maurane, C. Devos, French Rad Lyric Orch/R. Ellis)

Ⓓ **20136-2** (3/92)
Lecocq—Operettas
Lecocq: Jour et la Nuit (Cpte); Rose Mousse (Cpte). (L. Berton, L. Dachary, F. Betti, C. Manfredini, M. Siderer, G. Aurel, H. Bedex, G. Rey, M. Hamel, G. Moryn, P. Roi, French Rad Lyric Orch/R. Ellis, L. Dachary, J. Maréchal, A. Doniat, J. Peyron, R. Lenoty, G. Parat, R. Vallier, ORTF Lyric Orch/J-C. Hartemann)

Ⓓ **20138-2** (3/92)
Offenbach—Operettas
Offenbach: Madame l'Archiduc (Cpte); Chanson de Fortunio (Cpte). (L. Dachary, J. Levasseur, R. Bredy, D. Tirmont, P. Miguel, R. Amade, G. Rey, A. Doniat, R. Lenoty, J. Pruvost, M. Martin, M. Fauchey, M. Vigneron, L. Lovano, L. Dachary, M. Hamel, R. Amade, F. Betti, A. Doniat, R. Destain, J. Pruvost, P. Saugey, ORTF Lyric Chorale, ORTF Lyric Orch/J-C. Hartemann)

Ⓓ **20151-2** (3/92)
Ganne—Operettas
Ganne: Hans (Cpte); Saltimbanques (exc). (M. Dens, N. Broissin, J. Peyron, A. Balbon, G. Parat, R. Lenoty, M. Sansonnetti, G. Rey, Génio, P. Roi, M. Enot, R. Liot, J. Levasseur, J. Mollien, A. Caurat, M. Rossignol, French Rad Chor, French Rad Lyric Orch/J. Gressier, J. Micheau, R. Massard, G. Moizan, R. Amade, M. Roux, chor, orch/P. Dervaux)

Ⓓ **20152-2** (3/92)
Boieldieu—Les voitures versées
Boïeldieu: Voitures Versées (Cpte). (C. Collart, L. Dachary, D. Boursin, H. Hennetier, C. Petit, A. Doniat, B. Demigny, A. Mallabrera, J. Peyron, French Rad Lyric Orch/J. Brebion)

Ⓓ **20160-2** (3/92)
Planquette—Rip van Winkle
Planquette: Rip van Winkle (Cpte). (C. Daguerressar, L. Dachary, J. Pruvost, F. Betti, L. Lovano, R. Lenoty, J. Peyron, C. Collart, J. Pierre, P. Oriadey, J. Giovannetti, French Rad Lyric Chor, French Rad Lyric Orch/M. Cariven)

Ⓓ **20167-2** (3/92)
Adam—Le Toréador
Adam: Toréador (Cpte). (M. Mesplé, R. Amade, C. Clavensy, ORTF Lyric Orch/E. Bigot)

Ⓓ **20179-2** (3/92)
Terrasse—Operettas
Terrasse: Travaux d'Hercule (Cpte); Fiancée du Scaphandrier (Cpte). (G. Rey, L. Dachary, D. Tirmont, C. Harbell, R. Lenoty, B. Alvi, L. Lovano, M. Fauchey, Lestelly, C. Daguerressar, M. Siderer, H. Hennetier, G. Parat, French Rad Lyric Chor, French Rad Lyric Orch/M. Cariven, L. Dachary, C. Jacquin, G. Friedmann, J. Tharande, M. Hamel, ORTF Lyric Orch/J. Doussard)

Ⓓ **20234-2** (11/93)
Gounod—Philémon et Baucis
Gounod: Philémon et Baucis (Cpte). (J-C. Orliac, A-M. Rodde, P. Néquecaur, F. Giband, French Rad Lyric Orch/H. Gallois)

Ⓓ **20238-2** (11/93)
Messager—Coups de Roulis
Messager: Coups de Roulis (Cpte). (L. Dachary, C. Collart, G. Rey, D. Tirmont, A. Doniat, J. Pruvost, P. Saugey, M. Fauchey, R. Lenoty, C. Daguerressar, Génio, J. Hoffmann, ORTF Lyric Chorale, ORTF Lyric Orch/M. Cariven)

Ⓓ **20239-2** (11/93)
Delibes—Opéras-Comiques
Delibes: Roi l'a dit (Cpte); Omelette à la Follembuche (exc); Serpent à plumes (exc). (J. Micheau, M. Sénéchal, A. Martineau, G. Wion, R. Lenoty, G. Aurel, G. Donnarieix, A. Lequenne, G. Parat, M. Le Breton, P. Saugey, J. Scellier, J. Peyron, M. Hamel, French Rad Lyric Chor, French Rad Lyric Orch/A. Girard, L. Dachary, C. Jacquin, J. Mollien, R. Lenoty, M. Pieri, C. Harbell, M. Stiot, J. Peyron, B. Plantey, ORTF Lyric Orch/J. Brebion)

Ⓓ **20240-2** (11/93)
Audran—Miss Helyett. La Poupée
Audran: Miss Helyett (Cpte); Poupée (exc). (L. Dachary, C. Collart, G. Ristori, L. Arseguet, A. Doniat, D. Tirmont, M. Hamel, R. Lenoty, G. Rey, ORTF Lyric Chorale, ORTF Lyric Orch/M. Cariven, H. Hennetier, J. Peyron, R. Massard, Duvaleix, R. Lenoty, Génio, G. Ristori, P. Roi, J. Pruvost, French Rad Lyric Chor, French Rad Lyric Orch)

Ⓓ **20241-2** (11/93)
Messager—Monsieur Beaucaire
Messager: Monsieur Beaucaire (Cpte). (W. Clément, L. Dachary, N. Broissin, R. Lenoty, L. Lovano, H. Bedex, J. Pruvost, G. Foix, M. Enot, A. Balbon, G. Moryn, French Rad Lyric Chor, French Rad Lyric Orch/J. Gressier)

Ⓓ **202552** (4/94)
Bazin—Le Voyage en Chine; Maître Pathelin
Bazin: Voyage en Chine (Cpte); Maître Pathelin (Cpte). (C. Collart, M. Sénéchal, L. Dachary, A. Balbon, A. Martineau, G. Rey, R. Lenoty, Duvaleix, C. Harbell, M. Stiot, L. Felder, B. Plantey, G. Friedmann, M. Jarry, J. Peyron, M. Hamel, French Rad Lyric Chor, French Rad Lyric Orch/M. Cariven/J. Brebion)

Ⓓ **202572** (4/94)
Messager—La Basoche
Messager: Basoche (Cpte). (N. Sautereau, C. Maurane, I. Jaumillot, L. Noguera, L. Lovano, A. Doniat, J. Scellier, Génio, G. Parat, A. Martineau, J. Villisech, P. Saugey, French Rad Lyric Chor, French Rad Lyric Orch/T. Aubin)

Ⓓ **20300-2**
Adam—Si J'étais roi
Adam: Si j'étais roi (Cpte). (A. Mallabrera, L. Berton, R. Bianco, H. Médus, B. Alvi, A. Gabriel, P. Héral, Orch, Chor/R. Blareau)

Ⓓ **20427-2**
Massenet—Hérodiade - excerpts
Massenet: Hérodiade (exc). (D. Scharley, M. Le Bris, G. Chauvet, R. Massard, A. Legros, Paris ORTF Lyric Orch/J. Etcheverry)

Myto

Ⓓ **1MCD921.55**
Ivan Kozlovsky Recital
Leoncavallo: Pagliacci (exc); *Moniuszko:* Halka (exc); *Puccini:* Bohème (exc); Madama Butterfly (exc); *Verdi:* Rigoletto (exc); Traviata (exc); *Wagner:* Lohengrin (exc). (I. Kozlovsky, E. Shumskaya, I. Burlak, P. Selivanov, USSR SO/Anon)

Ⓓ **1MCD943104**
R. Strauss—Capriccio (highlights) & Lieder
R. Strauss: Capriccio (exc); Lieder, Op.15 (exc); Lieder, Op.17 (exc); Lieder, Op.43 (exc); Lieder, Op.56 (exc); Lieder, Op.36 (exc); Lieder, Op.26 (exc). (V. Ursuleac, F. Klarwein, H. Hotter, K. Kronenberg, G. Hann, G. Wieter, C. Krauss, Bavarian St Op Orch/C. Krauss)

Ⓓ **2MCD90317** (2/94)
Verdi—Un Ballo in maschera
Verdi: Ballo in maschera (Cpte); Trovatore (exc); Requiem (exc). (Z. Milanov, J. Björling, A. Sved, S. Andreva, B. Castagna, N. Cordon, N. Moscona, A. Kent, J. Carter, L. Oliviero, NY Met Op Chor, NY Met Op Orch/E. Panizza, J. Björling, N. Greco, B. Castagna, L. Oliviero/F. Calusio, orch/N. Grevillius)

Ⓓ **2MCD943103**
Lortzing—Zar und Zimmermann
Lortzing: Zar und Zimmermann (Cpte); Zar und Zimmermann (exc); Wildschütz (exc). (G. Hann, H. Buchta, M. Gripekoven, B. Müller, W. Strienz, E. Mayer, H. Hölzlin, H. Schmid-Berikoven, Stuttgart Rad Chor, Stuttgart RO/B. Zimmermann, G. Hann, chor, Berlin RSO/H. Steinkopf)

Ⓓ **3MCD93381** (3/94)
Wagner—Die Walküre, etc
Wagner: Walküre (Cpte); Lohengrin (exc); Tannhäuser (exc). (L. Suthaus, M. Müller, P. Buchner, J. Herrmann, M. Klose, J. Greindl, I. Grunow, F. Fleig, C. Breske, F. Schmalz, E. Hufnagel, H. Grohmann, E. Hagemann, C. Schäblen, Berlin City Op Orch/F. Fricsay, L. Suthaus, orch)

National Trust

Ⓓ **NTCD006**
Voice and Harp Recital
Anon: Have you seen but a white lily grow?; *R. Johnson II:* As I walked forth; *Arne:* Love's Labours Lost (exc); As You Like It (exc); *Croft:* Suite 3 (exc); *Purcell:* Oedipus, Z583 (exc); *Parisotti:* Se tu m'ami; *Gluck:* Paride ed Elena (exc); *Durante:* Danza, danza, fanciulla; *Schubert:* An die Musik, D547; Heidenröslein, D257; Seligkeit, D433; *Meyer:* Air de Sara; Air par M Mereau; Du déserteur; *Watkins:* Petite Suite; *Chausson:* Mélodies, Op. 2 (exc); *Cannon:* Chansons de femme (exc); *Traditional:* She moved through the fair; Scarborough Fair; Barbara Allen; *Anon:* Sumer is icumen in. (C. de Rothschild, D. Watkins)

Naxos

Ⓓ **8 550051** (7/91)
Borodin & Mussorgsky—Orchestral Works
Mussorgsky: Pictures; Night on the Bare Mountain; *Borodin:* In the Steppes of Central Asia; Prince Igor (exc). (Slovak PO/D. Nazareth)

Ⓓ **8 550061** (10/90)
Bizet—Concert Suites
Bizet: Arlésienne Suites; Carmen Suites (exc). (Slovak PO/A. Bramall)

Ⓓ **8 550072**
Beethoven—Overtures
Beethoven: Egmont (exc); Fidelio (exc); Leonore (exc); Coriolan; Consecration of the House Ov; Ruinen von Athen (exc); Prometheus (exc). (Slovak PO/S. Gunzenhauser)

Ⓓ **8 550080**
The Best of French Ballet
Delibes: Coppélia (exc); Sylvia (exc); Source (exc); Roi s'amuse; Kassya (exc). (Bratislava RSO/O. Lenárd)

Ⓓ **8 550081**
Invitation to the Dance
Weber: Invitation to the Dance; *Adam:* Giselle (exc); *Gounod:* Faust (exc); *Ponchielli:* Gioconda (exc); *Delibes:* Lakmé (exc). (Bratislava RSO/O. Lenárd)

Ⓓ **8 550098** (10/90)
Rimsky-Korsakov—Orchestral Works
Rimsky-Korsakov: Scheherazade; Sadko; Golden Cockerel Suite (exc). (Bratislava RSO/O. Lenárd)

Ⓓ **8 550231** (1/91)
Berlioz: Orchestral Works
Berlioz: Carnaval Romain; King Lear; Benvenuto Cellini (exc); Corsaire; Damnation de Faust (exc); Roméo et Juliette (exc). (Polish St PO/K. Jean)

Ⓓ **8 550236**
Rossini—Overtures
Rossini: Barbiere di Siviglia (exc); Cenerentola (exc); Semiramide (exc); Guillaume Tell (exc); Gazza ladra (exc); Scala di seta (exc); Italiana in Algeri (exc); Signor Bruschino (exc). (Zagreb PO/M. Halász)

Ⓓ **8 550241** (4/91)
Verdi—Opera Choruses
Verdi: Nabucco (exc); Don Carlo (exc); Traviata (exc); Battaglia di Legnano (exc); Trovatore (exc); Ernani (exc); Otello (exc); Macbeth (exc); Forza del Destino (exc); Aida (exc). (Slovak Phil Chor, Bratislava RSO/O. Dohnányi)

Ⓓ **8 550306**
Violin Miniatures
Kreisler: Schön Rosmarin; *Boccherini:* String Quintets, G271-6 (exc); *Rachmaninov:* Paganini Rhapsody (exc); *Kreisler:* Beethoven Rondino; *Fibich:* Moods, Op. 41, Part 1 (exc); *Elgar:* Salut d'amour; *Kreisler:* Liebesleid; Liebesfreud; *Granados:* Danzas españolas (exc); *Debussy:* Suite bergamasque (exc); *Brahms:* Hungarian Dances (exc); *Schubert:* Moments musicaux, D780 (exc); *Massenet:* Thaïs (exc); *Dvořák:* Humoresques, Op. 101 (exc); *Tchaikovsky:* Souvenirs de Hapsal, Op. 2 (exc); *Dvořák:* Slavonic Dances (exc); *Tchaikovsky:* Morceaux, Op. 40 (exc); *Kreisler:* Caprice viennois. (T. Nishizaki, J. Jandó)

Ⓓ **8 550342** (2/91)
R. Strauss: Orchestral Works
R. Strauss: Aus Italien; Liebe der Danae (exc); Rosenkavalier (exc). (Slovak PO/Z. Košler)

Ⓓ **8 550343** (5/92)
Italian and French Opera Arias
Verdi: Rigoletto (exc); Aida (exc); *Bizet:* Carmen (exc); *Gounod:* Faust (exc); *Massenet:* Werther (exc); *Puccini:* Villi (exc); Tosca (exc); Turandot (exc); Manon Lescaut (exc); Madama Butterfly (exc); *Lara:* Granada; *De Curtis:* Torna a Surriento; *Di Capua:* O sole mio. (P. Dvorský, Bratislava RSO/O. Lenárd)

Ⓓ **8 550381** (9/91)
Prokofiev—Orchestral Suites
Prokofiev: Lt. Kijé Suite; Love for 3 Oranges Suite (exc); Romeo and Juliet Suites (exc); Cinderella Suite 1. (Košice St PO/A. Mogrelia)

Ⓓ **8 550383** (12/91)
Mozart—Tenor Arias
Mozart: Zauberflöte (exc); Entführung (exc); Don Giovanni (exc); Così fan tutte (exc); Clemenza di Tito (exc). (J. Dickie, Capella Istropolitana/J. Wildner)

Ⓓ **8 550435** (12/91)
Mozart—Arias and Duets
Mozart: Entführung (exc); Nozze di Figaro (exc); Don Giovanni (exc); Zauberflöte (exc); Così fan tutte (exc). (A. Martin, D. Robin, Capella Istropolitana/J. Wildner, Vienna Mozart Orch/K. Leitner)

Ⓓ **8 550468**
Famous Operetta Overtures
J. Strauss II: Fledermaus (exc); Zigeunerbaron (exc); Nacht in Venedig (exc); *Suppé:* Morgen, ein Mittag, ein Abend in Wien (exc); Schöne Galathee (exc); Leichte Kavallerie (exc); *Offenbach:* Belle Hélène (exc); Orphée aux enfers (exc). (Košice St PO/A. Walter)

Ⓓ **8 550486** (9/92)
Rimsky-Korsakov—Orchestral Works
Rimsky-Korsakov: Snow Maiden (exc); Golden Cockerel Suite (exc); Mlada (exc). (Bratislava RSO/D. Johanos)

Ⓓ **8 550497**
Thomas Harper—Opera Recital
Leoncavallo: Pagliacci (exc); *Verdi:* Ballo in maschera (exc); Aida (exc); Don Carlo (exc); Rigoletto (exc); Macbeth (exc); Trovatore (exc); *Puccini:* Tosca (exc); Fanciulla del West (exc); Bohème (exc); Manon Lescaut (exc); Turandot (exc); *Giordano:* Andrea Chénier (exc); *Ponchielli:* Gioconda (exc). (T. Harper, Slovak Phil Chor, Bratislava RSO/M. Halász)

Ⓓ **8 550501**
Orchestral Spectacular
Chabrier: España; *Rimsky-Korsakov:* Capriccio espagnol; *Mussorgsky:* Night on the Bare Mountain; *Borodin:* Prince Igor (exc); *Ravel:* Boléro. (RPO/A. Leaper)

Ⓓ **8 550600** (10/93)
Dvořák—Overtures
Dvořák: Vanda (exc); In Nature's Realm; Carnival; Othello; My Home. (BBC PO/S. Gunzenhauser)

Ⓒ **8 550605** (2/93)
Favourite Soprano Arias
Bellini: Puritani (exc); Capuleti (exc); Sonnambula (exc); *Donizetti:* Linda di Chamounix (exc); Lucia di Lammermoor (exc); *Puccini:* Turandot (exc); Gianni Schicchi (exc); Rondine (exc); *Verdi:* Rigoletto (exc). (L. Orgonášová, Bratislava RSO/W. Humburg)

Ⓒ **8 550606** (11/92)
Soprano Arias from Italian Operas
Verdi: Don Carlo (exc); Otello (exc); Forza del destino (exc); *Catalani:* Wally (exc); *Puccini:* Manon Lescaut (exc); Tosca (exc); Suor Angelica (exc); Gianni Schicchi (exc); Turandot (exc); Villi (exc); Bohème (exc). (M. Gauci, Belgian Rad & TV Orch/A. Rahbari)

Ⓒ **8 550608**
Schumann—Overtures
Schumann: Overture, scherzo and finale; Genoveva (exc); Braut von Messina; Julius Cäsar; Hermann und Dorothea; Szenen aus Goethes Faust (exc); Manfred (exc). (Polish Nat RSO/J. Wildner)

Ⓒ **8 550660/1** (7/94)
Purcell—The Fairy Queen
Purcell: Fairy Queen, Z629 (Cpte). (Scholars Baroque Ens)

Ⓒ **8 550684** (12/94)
Duets and Arias from Italian Operas
Donizetti: Elisir d'amore (exc); *Leoncavallo:* Pagliacci (exc); *Mascagni:* Cavalleria Rusticana (exc); *Ponchielli:* Gioconda (exc); *Verdi:* Don Carlo (exc); Forza del destino (exc); Rigoletto (exc). (A. di Mauro, G. Aragall, E. Tumagian, Bratislava RSO/A. Rahbari)

Ⓒ **8 550700**
Handel—Recorder Sonatas
Handel: Recorder Sonatas (exc); Trio Sonata, HWV405; Scipione (exc); Musical Clock Pieces, HWV587-604 (exc). (L. Czidra, Z. Harsányi, Z. Harsányi, Z. Pertis, P. Kelemen)

Ⓒ **8 550726** (6/94)
Rimsky-Korsakov—Scheherazade; Tsar Saltan
Rimsky-Korsakov: Scheherazade; Tale of Tsar Saltan (exc). (Philh/E. Bátiz)

Ⓒ **8 550741** (12/94)
Romantic Music for Flute and Harp
Bizet: Carmen (exc); *Massenet:* Thaïs (exc); *Durand:* Waltz in E flat; *Bizet:* Arlésienne Suites (exc); *Debussy:* Petite Suite (exc); *Ravel:* Rapsodie espagnole (exc); *Durand:* Chaconne, Op. 62; *Gluck:* Orfeo ed Euridice (exc); *Mozart:* Andante, K315; *Chopin:* Rossini Variations; *Schuëcker:* Mazurka, Op. 12; *Rimsky-Korsakov:* Sadko (exc); *Tchaikovsky:* Morceaux, Op. 51 (exc); *J. Strauss II:* Tritsch-Tratsch. (J. Bálint, N. Mercz)

Ⓒ **8 550785** (1/95)
Le Grand Tango
Tagell: Flamenco; *Cassadó:* Cello Suite; *Falla:* Vida breve (exc); Amor brujo (exc); *Rachmaninov:* Cello Pieces, Op. 2 (exc); *Popper:* Suite, Op. 50 (exc); Stücke, Op. 11 (exc); Gavotte 2; Menuetto, Op. 65/2; Tarantella, Op. 33; *Tchaikovsky:* Morceaux, Op. 51 (exc); *Piazzolla:* Grand Tango. (M. Kliegel, B. Glemser)

Ⓒ **8 550928** (2/95)
Weber—Orchestral Works
Weber: Symphony 1; Symphony 2; Turandot; Silvana (exc); Drei Pintos (exc). (Queensland PO/J. Georgiadis)

Ⓒ **8 550958** (5/95)
Brahms—Transciptions for piano
Brahms: Theme and Variations; *Gluck:* Iphigénie en Aulide (exc); *Brahms:* Sarabandes; Gigues; Gavottes; Kleine Klavierstück (c1860); Canon in F minor; Rákóczy March; Schubert Ländler; Schubert Impromptu; *Schumann:* Piano Quintet, Op. 44 (exc). (I. Biret)

Ⓒ **8 550999**
Berlioz—Overtures
Berlioz: Benvenuto Cellini (exc); Waverley; Béatrice et Bénédict (exc); King Lear; Carnaval romain; Rob Roy; Corsaire. (San Diego SO/Y. Talmi)

Ⓒ **8 553001** (10/95)
Delius—Orchestral Works
Delius: Paris; Brigg Fair; Eventyr; Irmelin Prelude; Koanga (exc). (NZ SO/M. Fredman)

Ⓒ **8 553018**
Verdi—Overtures, Volume 1
Verdi: Aroldo (exc); Corsaro (exc); Luisa Miller (exc); Traviata (exc); Alzira (exc); Ballo in maschera (exc); Oberto (exc); Aida (exc); Attila (exc); Vespri Siciliani (exc). (Hungarian St Op Orch/P.G. Morandi)

Ⓒ **8 553027**
Bizet—Orchestral Works
Bizet: Jeux d'enfants; Symphony; Jolie Fille de Perth Suite (exc). (NZ SO/D. Johanos)

Ⓒ **8 553030** (2/95)
Opera Duets
Rossini: Guillaume Tell (exc); *Bizet:* Pêcheurs de Perles (exc); *Donizetti:* Lucia di Lammermoor (exc); *Verdi:* Vespri Siciliani (exc); Forza del destino (exc); Otello (exc). (J. Lotrič, I. Morozov, Slovak RSO/J. Wildner, Slovak Op Chor)

Ⓒ **8 553089**
Verdi—Overtures, Volume 2
Verdi: Ernani (exc); Giorno di regno (exc); Don Carlos (exc); Giovanna d'Arco (exc); Rigoletto (exc); Nabucco (exc); Masnadieri (exc); Macbeth (exc); Battaglia di Legnano (exc); Due Foscari (exc); Forza del destino (exc). (Hungarian St Op Orch/P.G. Morandi)

Ⓒ **8 553124** (9/95)
Massenet—Hérodiade Orchestral Suites Nos 1-3
Massenet: Hérodiade (exc); Suite 1; Scènes hongroises; Scènes dramatiques. (NZ SO/J-Y. Ossonce)

Ⓒ **8 553171**
J. Strauss II—Die Fledermaus - Highlights
J. Strauss II: Fledermaus (exc). (G. Fontana, J. Hopferwieser, J. Dickie, B. Karwautz, R. Yachmi-Caucig, A. Martin, A. Werner, E. Wessner, A. Calix, Bratislava City Chor, Bratislava RSO/J. Wildner)

Ⓒ **8 553195** (11/95)
Berlioz—Orchestral Works
Berlioz: Roméo et Juliette (exc); Troyens (exc). (San Diego Master Chorale, San Diego SO/Y. Talmi)

Ⓒ **8 660001/2** (10/91)
Puccini—Tosca
Puccini: Tosca (Cpte). (N. Miricioiu, G. Lamberti, S. Carroli, A. Piccinni, M. Dvorský, J. Špaček, J. Durco, S. Benacka, Slovak Phil Chor, Bratislava RSO/A. Rahbari)

Ⓒ **8 660003/4** (4/91)
Puccini: La bohème
Puccini: Bohème (Cpte). (L. Orgonášová, J. Welch, C. Gonzales, F. Previati, B. Senator, I. Urbas, R. Novák, J. Sulzenko, L. Hallon, S. Benacka, Bratislava Children's Ch, Slovak Phil Chor, Bratislava RSO/W. Humburg)

Ⓒ **8 660008/10** (3/91)
Mozart: Così fan tutte
Mozart: Così fan tutte (Cpte). (J. Borowska, R. Yachmi-Caucig, P. Coles, J. Dickie, A. Martin, P. Mikuláš, Slovak Phil Chor, Capella Istropolitana/J. Wildner)

Ⓒ **8 660011/2**
Verdi—La Traviata
Verdi: Traviata (Cpte). (M. Krause, Y. Ramiro, G. Tichy, R. Braga, I. Neshybová, P. Oswald, P. Maurery, L. Neshyba, J. Špaček, P. Šubert, Slovak Phil Chor, Bratislava RSO/A. Rahbari)

Ⓒ **8 660013/4** (3/92)
Verdi—Rigoletto
Verdi: Rigoletto (Cpte). (E. Tumagian, A. Ferrarini, Y. Ramiro, J. Špaček, L. Neshyba, J. Saparová, A. Michalková, J. Abel, P. Šubert, I. Neshybová, R. Szücs, Slovak Phil Chor, Bratislava RSO/A. Rahbari)

Ⓒ **8 660015/6** (5/92)
Puccini—Madama Butterfly
Puccini: Madama Butterfly (Cpte). (M. Gauci, Y. Ramiro, G. Tichy, N. Boschkowá, J. Abel, R. Szücs, A. Michalková, J. Špaček, V. Kubovčík, Slovak Phil Chor, Bratislava RSO/A. Rahbari)

Ⓒ **8 660017/8** (1/94)
J.Strauss II—Die Fledermaus
J. Strauss II: Fledermaus (Cpte). (G. Fontana, B. Karwautz, J. Dickie, J. Hopferwieser, A. Martin, R. Yachmi-Caucig, A. Werner, E. Wessner, H. Krämmer, A. Calix, A.E. Hollander, Bratislava City Chor, Bratislava RSO/J. Wildner)

Ⓒ **8 660019/20** (12/92)
Puccini—Manon Lescaut
Puccini: Manon Lescaut (Cpte). (M. Gauci, K. Kaludov, V. Sardinero, M. Rosca, D. George, L. Van Deyck, H. Lauwers, L. Van Gijsegem, J. Gregoor Ch, Brussels BRT Phil Chor, Brussels BRT PO/A. Rahbari)

Ⓒ **8 660021** (4/93)
Leoncavallo—I Pagliacci
Leoncavallo: Pagliacci (Cpte). (N. Martinucci, M. Gauci, E. Tumagian, B. Skovhus, M. Dvorský, Slovak Phil Chor, Bratislava RSO/A. Rahbari)

Ⓒ **8 660022** (3/93)
Mascagni—Cavalleria Rusticana
Mascagni: Cavalleria Rusticana (Cpte). (S. Evstatieva, G. Aragall, E. Tumagian, A. di Mauro, A. Michalková, Slovak Phil Chor, Bratislava RSO/A. Rahbari)

Ⓒ **8 660025/6** (9/93)
Wagner—Der Fliegende Holländer
Wagner: Fliegende Holländer (Cpte). (A. Muff, I. Haubold, E. Knodt, P. Seiffert, M. Schiml, J. Hering, Austrian RSO/P. Steinberg)

Ⓒ **8 660027/9** (3/94)
Rossini—Il barbiere di Siviglia
Rossini: Barbiere di Siviglia (Cpte). (R. Servile, S. Ganassi, R. Vargas, A. Romero, F. de Grandis, I. Kertesi, K. Sárkány, Hungarian Rad Chor, Failoni CO/W. Humburg)

Ⓒ **8 660030/1** (7/94)
Mozart—Die Zauberflöte
Mozart: Zauberflöte (Cpte). (E. Norberg-Schulz, H. Kwon, H. Lippert, G. Tichy, K. Rydl, R. Holzer, W. Gahmlich, Lotte Leitner, J. Faulkner, W. Winsauer, A. Gonda, R. Pap, M. Richter, M. Uray, P. Jelosits, P. Köves, Hungarian Fest Chor, Budapest Failoni Orch/M. Halász)

Ⓒ **8 660033/4** (10/95)
Verdi—Aida
Verdi: Aida (Cpte). (M. Dragoni, B. Dever, K. Johannsson, M. Rucker, F.E. D'Artegna, R. Ferrari, A. Marceno, M. Trini, RTE Phil Ch, RTE Chbr Ch, Culwick Choral Soc, Bray Choral Soc, Dublin County Ch, Dun Laoghaire Choral Soc, Cantabile Sngrs, Goethe Institut Ch, Musica Sacra Sngrs, Phoenix Sngrs, Irish Army Band, Ireland National SO/R. Saccani)

Ⓒ **8 660037/8** (11/95)
Rossini—Tancredi
Rossini: Tancredi (Cpte). (E. Podles, S. Jo, S. Olsen, P. Spagnoli, A. M. di Micco, L. Lendi, L. Baert, F. Coryn, E. Demeyere, Capella Brugensis, Collegium Instr Brugense/A. Zedda)

Ⓒ **8 660040/1**
Mozart—Ascanio in Alba
Mozart: Ascanio in Alba (Cpte). (M. Chance, J. Feldman, H. Milner, L. Windsor, R. Mannion, Paris Sorbonne Uni Ch, Concerto Armonico/J. Grimbert)

New World

Ⓒ **NW288/9-2** (7/90)
The Mother of us All
V. Thomson: Mother of us all (Cpte). (M. Dunn, J. Atherton, P. Booth, B. Godfrey, W. Lewis, L. Maxwell, H. Vanni, D. Perry, A. Putnam, J. McKee, G. Ives, Santa Fé Op Chor, Santa Fé Op Orch/R. Leppard)

Ⓒ **NW322/4-2**
Barber—Antony and Cleopatra
Barber: Antony and Cleopatra (Cpte). (J. Wells, E. Hinds, R. Grayson, K. Cowdrick, J. Bunnell, E. Halfvarson, M. Cleveland, C. Damsel, S. Cole, D. Hickox, D. Hamilton, K. Weaver, Westminster Ch, Spoleto Fest Orch/C. Badea)

Ⓒ **NW340/1-2** (10/86) ▭ **NWMC340/1** (10/86)
Bernstein—Candide: 1982 version
Bernstein: Candide (1982) (Cpte). (D. Eisler, E. Mills, J. Langston, S. Reeve, M. Clement, J. Castle, J. Billings, J. Harrold, NYC Op Chor, NYC Op Orch/J. Mauceri)

Ⓒ **80221-2** (4/94)
I Wants to be a Actor Lady
Operti: Black Crook (exc); *Cohan:* Little Johnny Jones (exc); *Rice:* Evangeline (exc); Conrad the Corsair (exc); *Von Tilzer:* I wants to be a Actor Lady; *Luders:* Prince of Pilsen (exc); *Kern:* How'd you like to spoon with me; *Irwin:* Bully Song; *Englander:* Passing Show (exc); *W. Morse:* Wang (exc); *Gaunt:* Trip to Chinatown (exc); *De Koven:* Robin Hood (exc); *Emmet:* Lullaby; *Herbert:* Babes in Toyland (exc). (Cincinnati Uni Sngrs, Cincinnati Uni Th Orch/E. Rivers)

Ⓒ **80313-2**
Copland/Glass/Ornstein/Wernick—Chamber Works
Copland: Flute Duo; *Glass:* Einstein on the Beach (exc); *Ornstein:* Violin Sonata, Op. 31; *Wernick:* Cadenzas and Variations II. (G. Fulkerson, A. Feinberg, R. Shannon)

Newport Classic

Ⓒ **NCD60117** (1/92)
Telemann—Pimpione
Telemann: Pimpinone (Cpte). (J. Ostendorf, J. Baird, St Luke's Baroque Orch/R. Palmer)

Ⓒ **NCD60125** (5/92)
Handel—Siroe
Handel: Siroe, Rè di Persia (Cpte). (D. Fortunato, J. Baird,

J. Ostendorf, A. Matthews, S. Rickards, F. Urrey, Brewer CO/R. Palmer)

NPD85514
The Treble Boys - Wonder Solos & Duets
Couperin: Victoria Christo resurgenti; *Vaughan Williams:* Pilgrim's Progress Songs (exc); *Dering:* Cantica sacra (1662) (exc); *Piccolo:* Wonder; *B. Marcello:* Give ear unto me; *Copland:* Old American Songs 2 (exc); *Dering:* Duo Seraphim; *Fauré:* Requiem (exc); *Handel:* Wash me throughly; *Traditional:* I sing of a maiden; *Purcell:* Lost is my quiet for ever, Z502; *Handel:* Messiah (exc); *Campion:* Ayres, Bk 1 (exc); *Britten:* Corpus Christi; *Lindley:* Ave Maria; *Dering:* Cantiones sacrae (exc); *Humperdinck:* Hänsel und Gretel (exc). (S. Van Dyck, T. Huffman, A. Camus, T. Whittemore, T. Whittemore, A. Piccolo, A. Piccolo)

NPD85540 (3/93)
Handel/Bononcini—Muzio Scevola
Handel: Muzio Scevola (Cpte); *Bononcini:* Muzio Scevola (exc); Mutio Scevola (exc). (J. Ostendorf, D. Fortunato, J. Baird, E. Mills, J. Lane, A. Matthews, F. Urrey, Brewer CO/R. Palmer)

NPD85551
Eugene Fodor—Virtuoso Violin
Sarasate: Danzas españolas (exc); *Kreisler:* Caprice viennois; *Paganini:* Caprices, Op. 1 (exc); *Tchaikovsky:* Souvenir d'un lieu cher, Op. 42 (exc); *F. Valle:* Prelude XV; *Wieniawski:* Polonaise, Op. 4; *Chopin:* Nocturnes (exc); *Prokofiev:* Love for 3 Oranges Suite (exc); *Bazzini:* Ronde des lutins. (E. Fodor, D. Saunders)

NPD85568
Handel—Arias
Handel: Ariodante (exc); Joseph and his Brethren (exc); Rinaldo (exc); Siroe, Rè di Persia (exc); Siroe, Rè di Persia (exc); Parnasso in festa (exc); Muzio Scevola (exc); Muzio Scevola (exc); Ottone (exc); Joshua (exc); Joshua (exc); Semele (exc). (J. Baird, Brewer CO/R. Palmer)

NPD85575 (12/94)
Handel—Sosarme
Handel: Sosarme (Cpte). (D. Fortunato, J. Aler, J. Baird, D. Minter, N. Watson, J. Lane, R. Pellerin, Taghkanic Chorale, Amor Artis Orch/J. Somary)

NPD85594 (10/95)
Rorem—A Childhood Miracle; Three Sisters who are not Sisters
Rorem: Childhood Miracle (Cpte); Three Sisters Who Are Not Sisters (Cpte). (D. Dunn, M. Couture, M. Tsingopoulos, P. Castaldi, M. Cidoni, P. Greene, A. Matthews, F. Urrey, C. Flamm, M. Tsingopoulos, M. Singer, J. van Buskirk, Magic Circle CO/R. Evans Harrell)

NPD85595
Haydn—La canterina
Haydn: Canterina (Cpte); Symphony 1; *L. Hofmann:* Flute Concerto in D. (B. Harris, J. Garrison, D. Fortunato, J. Guyer, E. Newbold, Palmer CO/R. Palmer)

NPD85605
Rorem—Miss Julie
Rorem: Miss Julie (Cpte). (T. Fried, P. Torre, H. Sarris, D. Blackburn, M. Mulligan, Laurelyn Watson, J. Ernster, MSM Op Chor, MSM Op Orch/D. Gilbert)

Nightingale Classics

NC070560-2 (2/93)
Bellini—Beatrice di Tenda
Bellini: Beatrice di Tenda (Cpte). (E. Gruberová, D. Bernardini, I. Morozov, V. Kasarova, B. Robinšak, D. Sumegi, Vienna Jeunesse Ch, Austrian RSO/P. Steinberg)

NC070561-2 (9/94)
Donizetti—Linda di Chamounix
Donizetti: Linda di Chamounix (Cpte). (E. Gruberová, D. Bernardini, A. Melander, E. Kim, M. Groop, S. Palatchi, U. Precht, K. Hedlund, Mikaeli Chbr Ch, Swedish RSO/F. Haider)

NC070562-2 (12/94)
Bellini—I Puritani
Bellini: Puritani (Cpte). (E. Gruberová, J. Lavender, E. Kim, F.E. D'Artegna, K. Lytting, D. Siegele, C. Tuand, Bavarian Rad Chor, Munich RO/F. Luisi)

NC070563-2 (5/95)
Donizetti—Roberto Devereux
Donizetti: Roberto Devereux (Cpte). (D. Bernardini, E. Gruberová, D. Ziegler, E. Kim, B. Boutet, M. Kazbek, F. Richert, Rhine Op Chor, Strasbourg PO/F. Haider)

NC090560-2
The Anniversary Concert - Gruberova
Saint-Saëns: Parysatis (exc); *Alabiev:* Nightingale; *Fauré:* Berceuse, Op. 16; Dolly (exc); *Gounod:* Mireille (exc); *Auber:* Manon Lescaut (exc); *Meyerbeer:* Dinorah (exc); *Elgar:* Wand of Youth Suite 1 (exc); *Delibes:* Lakmé (exc); *R. Strauss:* Intermezzo Interludes (exc); *Dell' Acqua:* Villanelle; *Benedict:* Gypsy and the Bird; *Bernstein:* Candide (1988) (exc). (E. Gruberová, Tokyo PO/F. Haider)

Nimbus

NC5008
Elgar: Music for Strings
Elgar: Introduction and Allegro; Elegy; Sospiri; Serenade; Chanson de matin; Chanson de nuit; Spanish Lady (exc). (English Stg Orch/W. Boughton)

NI5017
John Wallace: Man - the measure of all things
Monteverdi: Orfeo (exc); *Torelli:* Sinfonia, G4; *Albinoni:* Sonata a 6; Concerto a 6; Sonata di Concerto a 7; *Vivaldi:* Concerto RV537; *Franceschini:* 2-Trumpet Sonata in D; *Purcell:* Trumpet Sonata 1; *Bononcini:* Sinfonias, Op. 3 (exc); *Alberti:* Sinfonia Teatrale a 4. (J. Wallace, John Miller, D. Mason, W. Stokes, G. Hunt, D. Presly, C. Pendrill, M. Alexander, R. Waller, Philh/C. Warren-Green, R. Premru)

NI5066 **NC5066**
Sullivan—Overtures
Sullivan: Yeomen of the Guard (exc); Princess Ida (exc); Pirates of Penzance (exc); HMS Pinafore (exc); Sorcerer (exc); Ruddigore (exc); Gondoliers (exc); Patience (exc); Iolanthe (exc); Di Ballo. (Scottish CO/A. Faris)

NI5076
Ravel & R. Strauss—Works for string ensemble
Ravel: String Quartet; *R. Strauss:* Capriccio (exc). (Medici Qt)

NI5078
Rossini—Opera Overtures
Rossini: Guillaume Tell (exc); Italiana in Algeri (exc); Signor Bruschino (exc); Cenerentola (exc); Tancredi (exc); Barbiere di Siviglia (exc); Scala di Seta (exc); Semiramide (exc). (Scottish CO/J.Laredo)

NI5102
Alfredo Kraus sings Arie Antiche
A.Scarlatti: Pompeo (exc); Flavio (exc); *T. Giordani:* Caro mio ben; *A. Scarlatti:* Clearco in Negroponte (exc); *Pergolesi:* Tre giorni son che Nina; *Handel:* Serse (exc); *Parisotti:* Se tu m'ami; *Tenaglia:* Begl'occhi, merce; *Gluck:* Orfeo ed Euridice (exc); *Hasse:* Ritornerai fra poco; *A.Scarlatti:* Pirro e Demetrio (exc); *Gluck:* Paride ed Elena (exc); *Rosa:* Vado ben spesso; *Niedermeyer:* Pietà, Signore. (Alfredo Kraus, J. Tordesillas)

NI5106 (8/88) **NC5106**
Rossini—Opera Arias
Rossini: Tancredi (exc); Pietra del paragone (exc); Barbiere di Siviglia (exc); Signor Bruschino (exc); Occasione fa il ladro (exc); Italiana in Algeri (exc); Cenerentola (exc). (R. Giménez, D. Goodall, Scottish Phil Sngrs, Scottish CO/M. Veltri)

NI5117 **NC5117**
Holst—Orchestral Works
Holst: Planets; Perfect Fool (exc). (Philh/W. Boughton)

NI5120 **NC5120**
Popular Operatic Overtures
J. Strauss II: Fledermaus (exc); *Suppé:* Dichter und Bauer (exc); *Smetana:* Bartered Bride (exc); *Weber:* Freischütz (exc); *Hérold:* Zampa (exc); *Verdi:* Forza del destino (exc); *Glinka:* Ruslan and Lyudmila (exc). (Philh/W. Boughton)

NI5123
Baroque Arias for Soprano and Trumpet
Handel: Rinaldo (exc); *A. Scarlatti:* Prigioniero fortunato (exc); Su le sponde del Tebro; *Albinoni:* Statira (exc); *Von Reutter:* Quoniam; *Predieri:* Zenobia (exc); *Bach:* Cantata 51; *Handel:* Amadigi di Gaula (exc); Samson (exc). (H. Field, J. Wallace, John Miller, Philh/S. Wright)

NI5154 (6/89) **NC5154**
Weber: Orchestral Works
Weber: Invitation to the Dance; Beherrscher der Geister; Oberon (exc); Euryanthe (exc); Freischütz (exc); Abu Hassan (exc); Peter Schmoll (exc). (Hanover Band/R. Goodman)

NI5184/5 (7/89)
Méhul: Orchestral Works
Méhul: Symphony 1; Symphony 2; Symphony 3; Symphony 4; Chasse de jeune Henri (exc); Trésor supposé (exc). (Lisbon Gulbenkian Orch/M. Swierczewski)

NI5194 (7/90)
Kodály—Háry János Suite; Tchaikovsky—Symphony No 5
Tchaikovsky: Symphony 5; *Kodály:* Háry János Suite. (LSO/R. Frühbeck de Burgos)

NI5214
Mirages - Songs by Fauré, Gounod & Ravel
Fauré: Mirages; Songs, Op.7 (exc); *Gounod:* Mélodies (1855) (exc); Au rossignol; Ô ma belle rebelle; Mélodies (1855) (exc); Medjé; Boire à l'ombre; Philémon et Baucis (exc); *Ravel:* Chants populaires; Don Quichotte à Dulcinée; *Anon:* Parabole du mauvais riche. (S. Gehrman, N. Walker)

NI5217 (4/90)
Tippett conducts Tippett
Tippett: Midsummer Marriage (exc); Suite for Prince Charles; Praeludium. (A. Hodgson, Op. North Chor, English Northern Philh/M. Tippett, R. Cullis, M. Curtis, M. McDonald, M. Best)

NI5224 (5/90) **NC5224** (5/90)
Bellini & Donizetti: Arias
Bellini: Puritani (exc); Sonnambula (exc); *Donizetti:* Favorita (exc); Fille du régiment (exc); Elisir d'amore (exc); Don Pasquale (exc); Lucia di Lammermoor (exc). (R. Giménez, S.C. Dyson, F. Carroll, Scottish Phil Sngrs, Scottish CO/M. Veltri)

NI5235 (9/90)
R. Strauss: Orchestral Works
R. Strauss: Don Juan; Till Eulenspiegel; Tod und Verklärung; Rosenkavalier (exc). (BBC Welsh SO/T. Otaka)

NI5284 **NC5284**
Kodaly—Orchestral works
Kodály: Háry János Suite; Galánta Dances; Peacock Variations. (Hungarian St Orch/A. Fischer)

NI5295
Britten—Orchestral Works
Britten: Young Person's Guide; Sea Interludes, Op. 33a; Gloriana Suite (exc); Suite on English Folk Tunes. (English SO/W. Boughton)

NI5300
Mozart Arias—Raúl Giménez
Mozart: Finta giardiniera (exc); Rè pastore (exc); Don Giovanni (exc); Così fan tutte (exc); Zauberflöte (exc); Clemenza di Tito (exc); Misero, o sogno, K431 (exc). (R. Giménez, ROHO/B. Wordsworth)

NI5341 (1/94)
Haydn—Orchestral Works
Haydn: Symphony 89; Symphony 91; Vera costanza (exc). (Austro-Hungarian Haydn Orch/A. Fischer)

NI5387 **NC5387**
Kelly's Classic Challenge II
Weber: Marcia Vivace; *Glinka:* Ruslan and Lyudmila (exc); *Rachmaninov:* Symphony 2 (exc); *Chopin:* Berceuse; *Bach:* Violin and Oboe Concerto, BWV1060 (exc); *Beethoven:* Symphony 7 (exc); *Britten:* Sea Interludes, Op. 33a (exc); *Mozart:* Clarinet Concerto, K622 (exc); *Mendelssohn:* String Symphony 4 (exc); *Shostakovich:* Piano concerto 2 (exc); *Grainger:* Irish Tune from County Derry; *Barber:* Adagio for strings. (Wallace Collection, Philh, BBC Welsh SO, V. Perlemuter, O.Shumsky, R. Miller, Hanover Band/R. Goodman/W. Boughton/T. Otaka, C. Lawson, English Stg Orch, Martin Jones, Scottish CO)

NI5424 (10/95)
Nicolae Bretan—Golem; Arald
Bretan: Golem (Cpte); Arald (Cpte). (A. Agache, T. Daróczi, S. Şandru, D. Zancu, Chor, Moldova PO/C. Mandeal, D. Zancu, A. Agache, I. Voineag, S. Şandru)

NI5450/3
Spirit of England II
Holst: Planets; Perfect Fool (exc); *Elgar:* Enigma Variations; Wand of Youth Suite 2; *Parry:* English Suite; *Finzi:* Eclogue; *Bridge:* There is a willow; *Delius:* Florida Suite; *Vaughan Williams:* Wasps (exc); *Ireland:* Downland Suite (exc); *Walton:* Henry V (exc); *L. Berkeley:* Serenade, Op. 12; *Britten:* Sea Interludes, Op. 33a; Young Person's Guide. (Martin Jones, Philh, English SO, English Stg Orch/W. Boughton)

NI7010
Meditations at Sunset
Finzi: Eclogue; *J. C. Bach:* Grand Overtures, Op. 18 (exc); *Prokofiev:* Romeo and Juliet Suites (exc); *Respighi:* Ancient Airs and Dances (exc); *Kodály:* Háry János (exc); *Haydn:* Symphony 13 (exc); *Elgar:* Serenade (exc); *Boyce:* Symphonies (exc); *Bartók:* Violin Concerto 1 (exc); *Grieg:* Holberg Suite (exc). (G. Hetzel, Martin Jones, English Stg Orch, BBC Welsh SO, Hungarian St SO, Austro-Hungarian Haydn Orch/W. Boughton/T. Otaka/A. Fischer)

Ⓓ **NI7801** (10/89) ▭ **NC7801**
Great Singers, Vol.1
Bellini: Norma (exc); Puritani (exc); Puritani (exc); Sonnambula (exc); *Bizet:* Carmen (exc); *Donizetti:* Lucrezia Borgia (exc); *Leoncavallo:* Pagliacci (exc); *Mascagni:* Amico Fritz (exc); *Mozart:* Don Giovanni (exc); Zauberflöte (exc); *Puccini:* Bohème (exc); Turandot (exc); *Rossini:* Barbiere di Siviglia (exc); *Refice:* Ombra di Nube; *Saint-Saëns:* Samson et Dalila (exc); *Verdi:* Ballo in maschera (exc). (M. Favero, T. Schipa, La Scala Orch/G. Antonicelli, A. Galli-Curci, orch/G. Polacco, C. Muzio/L. Refice, R. Ponselle, NY Met Op Chor, NY Met Op Orch/G. Setti, L. Tetrazzini, E. Turner/S. Robinson, E. Schumann-Heink, C. Supervia/G. Cloëz, M. Anderson/L. Collingwood, E. Caruso, B. Gigli/E. Goossens, G. Lauri-Volpi, J. McCormack/W.B. Rogers, R. Tauber, Vienna St Op Orch/K. Alwin, R. Stracciari, L. Tibbett/Rosario Bourdon)

Ⓓ **NI7802** (10/89) ▭ **NC7802**
Divas 1906-1935
Beethoven: Fidelio (exc); *Boito:* Mefistofele (exc); *Borodin:* Prince Igor (exc); *Donaudy:* O del mio amato ben; *Gounod:* Roméo et Juliette (exc); *Massenet:* Don César de Bazan (exc); Manon (exc); *Mozart:* Zauberflöte (exc); *Puccini:* Bohème (exc); Madama Butterfly (exc); *Rimsky-Korsakov:* Sadko (exc); *Rossini:* Barbiere di Siviglia (exc); *A. Thomas:* Mignon (exc); *Verdi:* Aida (exc); Ballo in maschera (exc); Rigoletto (exc); Trovatore (exc); *Yradier:* Calasera. (L. Tetrazzini, N. Melba, A. Patti, F. Hempel, A. Galli-Curci, R. Ponselle, Lotte Lehmann, E. Turner, N. Koshetz, E. Norena, M. Németh, C. Muzio, orch, A. Barili, R. Romani/M. Gurlitt/T. Beecham/L. Molajoli/W.B. Rogers)

Ⓓ **NI7803** (10/89) ▭ **NC7803**
Enrico Caruso—Opera Recital
Donizetti: Dom Sébastien (exc); Duca d'Alba (exc); Elisir d'amore (exc); *Goldmark:* Königin von Saba (exc); *Gomes:* Schiavo (exc); *Halévy:* Juive (exc); *Leoncavallo:* Pagliacci (exc); Pagliacci (exc); *Massenet:* Manon (exc); Manon (exc); *Meyerbeer:* Africaine (exc); *Puccini:* Manon Lescaut (exc); Tosca (exc); *Verdi:* Aida (exc); Ballo in maschera (exc); Ballo in maschera (exc); Forza del destino (exc); Rigoletto (exc); Rigoletto (exc); Trovatore (exc). (E. Caruso, orch, anon, NY Met Op Chor/J. Pasternack)

Ⓓ **NI7804** (10/89) ▭ **NC7804**
Giovanni Martinelli—Opera Recital
Giordano: Andrea Chénier (exc); Andrea Chénier (exc); Fedora (exc); *Leoncavallo:* Pagliacci (exc); Pagliacci (exc); *Mascagni:* Cavalleria Rusticana (exc); Cavalleria Rusticana (exc); Iris (exc); *Rossini:* Guillaume Tell (exc); *Tchaikovsky:* Eugene Onegin (exc); *Verdi:* Aida (exc); Ernani (exc); Forza del destino (exc); Forza del destino (exc); Forza del destino (exc); Traviata (exc); Trovatore (exc). (G. Martinelli, F. Lapitino, orch/W.B. Rogers/J. Pasternack/Rosario Bourdon, G. De Luca, R. Ponselle, E. Pinza, NY Met Op Chor, NY Met Op Orch/G. Setti/N. Shilkret, G. Anthony, chor)

Ⓓ **NI7805** (10/89) ▭ **NC7805**
Rosa Ponselle—Opera & Song Recital
Arensky: On wings of dream; *Bellini:* Norma (exc); Norma (exc); *Di Capua:* Maria, marì; *De Curtis:* Carmela; *Bond:* Perfect day; *Ponchielli:* Gioconda (exc); *Rimsky-Korsakov:* Songs, Op. 2 (exc); *Spontini:* Vestale (exc); *Verdi:* Aida (exc); Aida (exc); Ernani (exc); Forza del destino (exc); Otello (exc). (R. Ponselle, orch/Rosario Bourdon, G. Martinelli, E. Pinza, NY Met Op Chor, NY Met Op Orch/G. Setti, M. Telva, M. Elman, R. Romani/J. Pasternack)

Ⓓ **NI7806** (5/90) ▭ **NC7806**
Galli-Curci—Opera & Song Recital
Gounod: Roméo et Juliette (exc); *Auber:* Manon Lescaut (exc); *Rossini:* Barbiere di Siviglia (exc); *Meyerbeer:* Dinorah (exc); *Bellini:* Puritani (exc); *Verdi:* Traviata (exc); Traviata (exc); Traviata (exc); *A. Thomas:* Mignon (exc); *Donizetti:* Don Pasquale (exc); *Bellini:* Sonnambula (exc); Sonnambula (exc); *dell' Acqua:* Villanelle; *Donizetti:* Linda di Chamounix (exc); *Verdi:* Rigoletto (exc); *Donizetti:* Lucia di Lammermoor (exc); Lucia di Lammermoor (exc); *Bishop:* Pretty Mocking Bird. (A. Galli-Curci, orch/J. Pasternack/Rosario Bourdon, T. Schipa, G. De Luca)

Ⓓ **NI7807** (5/90) ▭ **NC7807**
Beniamino Gigli—Vol. 1: 1918-24
Ponchielli: Gioconda (exc); *Boito:* Mefistofele (exc); *Puccini:* Tosca (exc); Tosca (exc); *Donizetti:* Favorita (exc); *Gounod:* Faust (exc); *Mascagni:* Iris (exc); *Lalo:* Roi d'Ys (exc); *Leoncavallo:* Pagliacci (exc); *Giordano:* Andrea Chénier (exc); *Meyerbeer:* Africaine (exc); *Catalani:* Loreley (exc); *Flotow:* Martha (exc); *Cannio:* O surdato 'nnammurato; *De Curtis:* Tu sola; *Saint-Saëns:* Carnaval des animaux (exc); *Drigo:* Arlekinda (exc); *Buzzi-Peccia:* Povero Pulcinella; *Denza:* Funiculì-Funiculà. (B. Gigli, orch/C. Sabajno/J. Pasternack/Rosario Bourdon)

Ⓓ **NI7808** (10/90) ▭ **NC7808** (10/90)
Luisa Tetrazzini—Opera & Song Recital
Donizetti: Lucia di Lammermoor (exc); *Rossini:* Barbiere di Siviglia (exc); *Bellini:* Sonnambula (exc); *Donizetti:* Lucia di Lammermoor (exc); *Eckert:* Eco; *A. Thomas:* Mignon (exc); *Verdi:* Rigoletto (exc); Ballo in maschera (exc); *Delibes:* Lakmé (exc); *Proch:* Air and Variations; *Verdi:* Trovatore (exc); *Brahms:* Lieder, Op. 84 (exc); *Venzano:* O che assorta; *Verdi:* Traviata (exc); *Veracini:* Rosalinda (exc); *Pergolesi:* Tre giorni son che Nina; *Verdi:* Vespri siciliani (exc); Rigoletto (exc). (L. Tetrazzini, J. Jacoby, E. Caruso, P. Amato, orch)

Ⓓ **NI7809** (12/90) ▭ **NC7809** (12/90)
Caruso in Song
Crescenzo: Tarantella sincera; *Geehl:* For you alone; *Hardelot:* Because; *Rossini:* Soirées musicales (exc); *Szulc:* Hantise d'amour; *Ciociano:* Cielo turchino; *Pennino:* Pecchè; *Cottrau:* Santa Lucia; *Di Capua:* O sole mio; *Alvarez:* Partida; *Niedermeyer:* Pietà, Signore; *Billi:* Campane a sera; *Alvarez:* A Granada; *Cohan:* Over there; *Fucito:* Sultano a Tte; *Califona:* Vieni sul mar; *Pergolesi:* Tre giorni son che Nina; *Handel:* Serse (exc); *Rossini:* Petite messe solennelle (exc). (E. Caruso, orch/W.B. Rogers/J. Pasternack)

Ⓓ **NI7810** (11/90) ▭ **NC7810**
Titta Ruffo—Opera Recital
A. Thomas: Hamlet (exc); *Verdi:* Traviata (exc); *Ponchielli:* Gioconda (exc); Gioconda (exc); *Leoncavallo:* Pagliacci (exc); Zazà (exc); *Ferradini:* Non penso a lei; *Donizetti:* Favorita (exc); *Massenet:* Thaïs (exc); *Verdi:* Otello (exc); Otello (exc); Otello (exc); Nabucco (exc); *Meyerbeer:* Africaine (exc); *Verdi:* Ballo in maschera (exc); *Puccini:* Tosca (exc); *Rossini:* Barbiere di Siviglia (exc); *Verdi:* Rigoletto (exc); Falstaff (exc); *Ponchielli:* Gioconda (exc). (T. Ruffo, orch/C. Sabajno/W.B. Rogers/J. Pasternack, E. Caruso, B. Gigli/Rosario Bourdon)

Ⓓ **NI7811** (2/91) ▭ **NC7811** (2/91)
Ernestine Schumann-Heink—Opera & Song Recital
Donizetti: Lucrezia Borgia (exc); *Arditi:* Leggero invisibile; *Becker:* Frühlingszeit; *Meyerbeer:* Prophète (exc); Prophète (exc); *Wagner:* Rheingold (exc); *Millöcker:* I und mei Bua; *Wagner:* Rienzi (exc); *Handel:* Rinaldo (exc); *Schubert:* Erlkönig, D328; *Wagner:* Wesendonk Lieder (exc); *H. Reimann:* Spinnerliedchen; *Molloy:* Kerry Dance; *Brahms:* Lieder, Op. 49 (exc); *C. Böhm:* Lieder, Op. 326 (exc); *Traditional:* Du, du liegst mir im Herzen; *Lieurance:* By the Waters of Minnetonka; *Wagner:* Rheingold (exc); Götterdämmerung (exc). (E. Schumann-Heink, orch, H. Witherspoon, J. Hofmann/Rosario Bourdon)

Ⓓ **NI7814** (4/91) ▭ **NC7814** (4/91)
Claudia Muzio—Opera Arias & Songs
Mascagni: Cavalleria rusticana (exc); *Puccini:* Bohème (exc); Bohème (exc); Tosca (exc); *Verdi:* Forza del destino (exc); Otello (exc); Trovatore (exc); Traviata (exc); *Giordano:* Andrea Chénier (exc); *Boito:* Mefistofele (exc); *Cilea:* Adriana Lecouvreur (exc); Arlesiana (exc); *Bellini:* Sonnambula (exc); *Buzzi-Peccia:* Colombetta; *Parisotti:* Se tu m'ami; *Delibes:* Filles de Cadiz; Bonjour, Suzon; *Refice:* Ombra di nube; *Reger:* Schlichte Weisen, Op.76 (exc). (C. Muzio, orch/L. Molajoli/L. Refice, F. Merli)

Ⓓ **NI7817** ▭ **NC7817**
Beniamino Gigli—Vol.2
Donizetti: Elisir d'amore (exc); Elisir d'amore (exc); *Puccini:* Manon Lescaut (exc); *Verdi:* Forza del destino (exc); *Donizetti:* Lucia di Lammermoor (exc); *Verdi:* Traviata (exc); *A. Thomas:* Mignon (exc); *Bizet:* Pêcheurs de perles (exc); Pêcheurs de perles (exc); *Ponchielli:* Gioconda (exc); *Massenet:* Manon (exc); *Puccini:* Bohème (exc); *Gounod:* Faust (exc); *Rimsky-Korsakov:* Sadko (exc); *Puccini:* Tosca (exc); *Verdi:* Rigoletto (exc); *Gluck:* Paride ed Elena (exc); *Cilea:* Arlesiana (exc); *Caccini:* Nuove musiche (1602) (exc). (B. Gigli, G. De Luca, orch/Rosario Bourdon, NY Met Op Orch/G. Setti/E. Goossens/J. Pasternack/J. Barbirolli/N. Shilkret, La Scala Orch/F. Ghione/D. Olivieri, Berlin St Op Orch/B. Seidler-Winkler/L. Collingwood)

Ⓓ **NI7827/8**
Mozart—Die Zauberflöte
Mozart: Zauberflöte (Cpte). (T. Lemnitz, E. Berger, H. Roswaenge, G. Hüsch, W. Strienz, W. Grossmann, H. Tessmer, I. Beilke, H. Scheppan, E. Marherr-Wagner, R. Berglund, C. Spletter, E. Fabbry, Favres Solisten Vereinigung, BPO/T. Beecham)

Ⓓ **NI7829**
Charpentier—Louise
G. Charpentier: Louise (exc). (N. Vallin, G. Thill, A. Pernet, A. Lecouvreur, C. Gaudel, Rougel Chor, orch/E. Bigot)

Ⓓ **NI7830** (12/92) ▭ **NC7830** (12/92)
Richard Tauber in Opera
R. Strauss: Rosenkavalier (exc); *Wagner:* Walküre (exc); *Kienzl:* Evangelimann (exc); *Smetana:* Bartered Bride (exc); *Puccini:* Tosca (exc); Tosca (exc); *Verdi:* Trovatore (exc); *Mozart:* Don Giovanni (exc); Zauberflöte (exc); *Tchaikovsky:* Eugene Onegin (exc); *Bizet:* Carmen (exc); *Puccini:* Bohème (exc); *Korngold:* Tote Stadt (exc); *Puccini:* Madama Butterfly (exc); Turandot (exc); *Wagner:* Meistersinger (exc); *Lortzing:* Undine (exc); *Offenbach:* Contes d'Hoffmann (exc). (R. Tauber, E. Bettendorf, Lotte Lehmann, Berlin St Op Chor, Berlin Schauspielhaus Orch, Berlin Staatskapelle, Berlin St Op Orch, orch/K. Besl/G. Szell/H. Weigert/E. Hauke, chor)

Ⓓ **NI7831** (10/92) ▭ **NC7831** (10/92)
Mattia Battistini (1856-1928)
Tchaikovsky: Eugene Onegin (exc); *Verdi:* Ballo in maschera (exc); Ernani (exc); *Flotow:* Martha (exc); *Donizetti:* Favorita (exc); Dom Sébastien (exc); *Hérold:* Zampa (exc); *Berlioz:* Damnation de Faust (exc); *Massenet:* Werther (exc); *A. Thomas:* Hamlet (exc); *Nouguès:* Quo vadis? (exc); *Verdi:* Traviata (exc); *Donizetti:* Linda di Chamounix (exc); *Verdi:* Macbeth (exc); *Donizetti:* Favorita (exc); *Verdi:* Don Carlo (exc). (M. Battistini, E. Corsi, L. Colazza, A. Sillich, M. Mokrzycka, La Scala Chor, anon, C. Sabajno, orch/C. Sabajno)

Ⓓ **NI7832** (8/92) ▭ **NC7832** (8/92)
Maria Ivogün (1891-1987)
Bishop: Lo, here the gentle lark; *Handel:* Allegro, il penseroso ed il moderato (exc); *Donizetti:* Don Pasquale (exc); Lucia di Lammermoor (exc); *Rossini:* Barbiere di Siviglia (exc); *Verdi:* Traviata (exc); *Chopin:* Nocturnes (exc); *Meyerbeer:* Huguenots (exc); *Nicolai:* Lustigen Weiber von Windsor (exc); *Schubert:* Ständchen, D889; Winterreise (exc); *J. Strauss II:* Frühlingsstimmen, Op. 410; G'schichten aus dem Wienerwald, Op. 325; *Kreisler:* Liebesfreud; *Traditional:* O du liebs ängeli; Z' Lauterbach han; 's Schätzli; Maria auf dem Berge; *J. Strauss II:* Blauen Donau, Op. 314; Fledermaus (exc). (M. Ivogün, M. Raucheisen, orch, Berlin St Op Orch/L. Blech)

Ⓓ **NI7833** (12/92) ▭ **NC7833** (12/92)
Schöne & Tauber in Operetta
Lehár: Paganini (exc); *Suppé:* Schöne Galathee (exc); *Berté:* Dreimäderlhaus (exc); *J. Strauss II:* Fledermaus (exc); Lustige Krieg (exc); Indigo und die Vierzig Räuber (exc); Cagliostro in Wien (exc); *Kálmán:* Gräfin Mariza (exc); *Millöcker:* Arme Jonathan (exc); *Zeller:* Vogelhändler (exc); Obersteiger (exc); *Nessler:* Trompeter von Säckingen (exc); *Lehár:* Zigeunerliebe (exc); Land des Lächelns (exc); Lustige Witwe (exc); *Kálmán:* Zirkusprinzessin (exc); *J. Strauss II:* G'schichten aus dem Wienerwald, Op. 325. (L. Schöne, R. Tauber, Berlin St Op Orch, Vienna Th an der Wien Orch, Berlin Schauspielhaus Orch, Berlin Künstlertheater Orch, Berlin Staatskapelle, Odeon Künstlerorchester, orch/H. Weigert/A. Paulik/E. Hauke/F. Lehár/E. Korngold)

Ⓓ **NI7834** ▭ **NC7834**
Caruso in Ensemble
Verdi: Forza del destino (exc); Rigoletto (exc); Aida (exc); *Puccini:* Bohème (exc); Madama Butterfly (exc); *Donizetti:* Lucia di Lammermoor (exc); *Flotow:* Martha (exc); Martha (exc); *Verdi:* Forza del destino (exc); Trovatore (exc); Trovatore (exc); Lombardi (exc); Ballo in maschera (exc). (E. Caruso, A. Scotti, M. Sembrich, G. Severina, J. Gadski, G. Farrar, G. Ciaparelli-Viafora, F. Daddi, M. Journet, F. Alda, J. Jacoby, P. Amato, L. Homer, F. Hempel, L. Rothier, A. de Segurola, M. Duchêne, NY Met Op Chor, orch/W.B. Rogers/G. Scognamiglio)

Ⓓ **NI7835**
Jussi Björling—The first ten years
Verdi: Trovatore (exc); *Puccini:* Tosca (exc); *Borodin:* Prince Igor (exc); *Verdi:* Rigoletto (exc); Rigoletto (exc); *Leoncavallo:* Pagliacci (exc); *Mascagni:* Cavalleria Rusticana (exc); *Atterberg:* Fanal (exc); *Puccini:* Fanciulla del West (exc); *Rimsky-Korsakov:* Sadko (exc); *Laparra:* Illustre Fregona (exc); *Traditional:* Ack Värmerland, du sköna; Allt under himmelens fäste; *Verdi:* Trovatore (exc); Aida (exc); *Meyerbeer:* Africaine (exc); *Ponchielli:* Gioconda (exc); *Puccini:* Bohème (exc); *Massenet:* Manon (exc); *Rossini:* Stabat mater (exc); *Verdi:* Requiem (exc). (J. Björling, orch/N. Grevillius)

Ⓓ **NI7836/7** (3/93)
Conchita Supervia (1895-1936)
Rossini: Italiana in Algeri (exc); Barbiere di Siviglia (exc); Barbiere di Siviglia (exc); Cenerentola (exc); *Gounod:* Faust (exc); *A. Thomas:* Mignon (exc); *Saint-Saëns:* Samson et Dalila (exc); *Delibes:* Bonjour, Suzon; Églogue; *Falla:* Canciones populares españolas; *Baldomir:* Meus Amores; *Serrano:* Alegría del Batallón (exc); Mal de Amores (exc); *Yradier:* Paloma; *Valverde:* Clavelitos; *Bizet:* Carmen (exc). (C. Supervia, A. Vavon, A. Bernadet, G. Micheletti, C. Scattola, G. Manuritta, CO, orch/A. Albergoni/G. Cloëz/A. Capdevila/M. Romero, F. Marshall/P. Godes)

Ⓓ **NI7840/1** (7/93)
The Era of Adelina Patti
Verdi: Falstaff (exc); Don Carlos (exc); *Tosti:* Dopo; *Rameau:* Pièces de clavecin (exc); *Gluck:* Rencontre imprévue (exc); *Yradier:* Calasera; *Meyerbeer:* Prophète (exc); *Bizet:* Carmen (exc); *Massenet:* Hérodiade (exc); Manon (exc); Hérodiade (exc); *A. Thomas:* Hamlet (exc); *Adam:* Chalet (exc); *Wagner:* Lohengrin (exc); Meistersinger (exc); *F. Erkel:* Hunyadi László (exc); *Donizetti:* Favorita (exc); *Mozart:* Don Giovanni (exc); Don Giovanni (exc); Nozze di Figaro (exc); *Flotow:* Martha (exc); *Bellini:* Puritani (exc); *Donizetti:* Lucrezia Borgia (exc); *Bellini:* Sonnambula (exc); *Rossini:* Barbiere di Siviglia (exc); *Mozart:* Don Giovanni (exc); *Verdi:* Ernani (exc); *Donizetti:* Lucia di Lammermoor (exc); *Verdi:* Otello (exc); *Mozart:* Nozze di Figaro (exc); *Gounod:* Soir; *R. Strauss:* Lieder, Op.17 (exc); *Gomes:* Guarany (exc); *Hatton:* Simon the cellarer; *Hook:* 'Twas within a mile; *Bishop:* Home, sweet home. (V. Maurel, P. Plançon, E. Eames, L. Fugère, A. Patti, F. Viñas, E. Calvé, M. Renaud, F. de Lucia, F. Tamagno, N. Melba, F. Litvinne, W. Hesch, L. Nordica, M. Ancona, E. de Reszke, M. Sembrich, F. Marconi, M. Battistini, Lilli Lehmann, C. Santley, anon, L. Ronald, J. Huguet, A. Pini-Corsi, orch, A. Barili)

Ⓓ **NI7842** (10/93)
Jussi Björling, Vol.2
Beethoven: Adelaide, Op.46; *Schubert:* An Silvia, D891; Schwanengesang, D957 (exc); An die Leier, D737; *R. Strauss:* Lieder, Op.27 (exc); *Sibelius:* Songs, Op.36 (exc); *Alfvén:* Songs, Op.28 (exc); *Eklöf:* Morning; *Sjöberg:* Tonerna; *Tosti:* Ideale; *Puccini:* Tosca (exc); Tosca (exc); Fanciulla del West (exc); Bohème (exc); *Verdi:* Rigoletto (exc); Rigoletto (exc); *Flotow:* Martha (exc); *Gounod:* Faust (exc); *Bizet:* Carmen (exc); *Offenbach:* Belle Hélène (exc); *J. Strauss II:* Zigeunerbaron (exc); *Millöcker:* Bettelstudent (exc). (J. Björling, H. Schymberg, H. Ebert, orch/N. Grevillius)

Ⓓ **NI7843/4**
Mascagni/Leoncavallo—Cav & Pag
Leoncavallo: Pagliacci (Cpte); *Mascagni:* Cavalleria Rusticana (Cpte). (B. Gigli, I. Pacetti, M. Basiola I, L. Paci, G. Nessi, L.B. Rasa, B. Gigli, G. Bechi, M. Marcucci, G. Simionato, La Scala Chor, La Scala Orch/F. Ghione/P. Mascagni)

Ⓓ **NI7845** (7/93)
Giacomo Lauri-Volpi (1892-1979)
Bellini: Puritani (exc); *Boito:* Mefistofele (exc); *Massenet:* Werther (exc); *Puccini:* Tosca (exc); *Mascagni:* Cavalleria Rusticana (exc); *Leoncavallo:* Pagliacci (exc); *Puccini:* Bohème (exc); *Verdi:* Trovatore (exc); *Bellini:* Puritani (exc); Norma (exc); *Meyerbeer:* Huguenots (exc); *Gomes:* Schiavo (exc); *Offenbach:* Contes d'Hoffmann (exc); *Bizet:* Carmen (exc); *Gounod:* Faust (exc); *Meyerbeer:* Africaine (exc); *Giordano:* Andrea Chénier (exc); *Puccini:* Madama Butterfly (exc); Manon Lescaut (exc); Fanciulla del West (exc); Turandot (exc). (G. Lauri-Volpi, L. Borgonovo, NY Met Op Chor, NY Met Op Orch/G. Setti, La Scala Orch/F. Ghione, orch/Rosario Bourdon, SO/M. Cordone)

Ⓓ **NI7846** (10/93)
Rosa Ponselle, Vol.2
Puccini: Madama Butterfly (exc); Tosca (exc); *Verdi:* Forza del destino (exc); Trovatore (exc); *Mascagni:* Cavalleria Rusticana (exc); *Tosti:* Addio; *Herbert:* Mademoiselle Modiste (exc); *Rimsky-Korsakov:* Sadko (exc); *Puccini:* Manon Lescaut (exc); *Halévy:* Juive (exc); *Wagner:* Lohengrin (exc); *Verdi:* Aida (exc); Aida (exc); *Massenet:* Élégie; *Gounod:* Ave Maria; *Charles:* When I have sung my songs. (R. Ponselle, G. Martinelli, E. Baker, chor, orch, R. Romani/R. Romani/Rosario Bourdon)

Ⓓ **NI7847** (7/93)
Kirsten Flagstad (1895-1962)
Wagner: Walküre (exc); Walküre (exc); Tannhäuser (exc); Lohengrin (exc); Lohengrin (exc); *Weber:* Oberon (exc); *Beethoven:* Fidelio (exc); Ah! perfido, Op.65; *Wagner:* Tristan und Isolde (exc); Götterdämmerung (exc). (K. Flagstad, orch/H. Lange, Philadelphia/E. Ormandy, San Francisco Op Orch/E. McArthur)

Ⓓ **NI7848** (10/93)
Great Singers at the Berlin State Opera
Mozart: Entführung (exc); *Beethoven:* Fidelio (exc); *Donizetti:* Don Pasquale (exc); *Wagner:* Rienzi (exc); Fliegende Holländer (exc); Tannhäuser (exc); Tannhäuser (exc); Tristan und Isolde (exc); Meistersinger (exc); *Verdi:* Trovatore (exc); Traviata (exc); *Humperdinck:* Hänsel und Gretel (exc); *Puccini:* Bohème (exc); Turandot (exc); *R. Strauss:* Rosenkavalier (exc); Rosenkavalier (exc). (M. Perras, E. Berger, H. Gottlieb, M. Wittrisch, W. Domgraf-Fassbaender, G. Sinimberghi, F. Völker, F. Schorr, T. Lemnitz, L. Melchior, F. Leider, E. Marherr-Wagner, M. Lorenz, H. Schlusnus, H. Roswaenge, G. Hüsch, M. Cebotari, L. Schöne, E. Ruziczka, A. Kipnis, Berlin St Op Orch, Berlin Staatskapelle, orch, LSO/B. Seidler-Winkler/F. Zweig/A. Melichar/L. Blech/A. Coates/C. Schmalstich/J. Schüler/H.U. Müller/E. Orthmann/C. Krauss)

Ⓓ **NI7849** (3/94)
Frieda Hempel (1885-1955)
Verdi: Rigoletto (exc); *Donizetti:* Lucia di Lammermoor (exc); *Rossini:* Barbiere di Siviglia (exc); *Mozart:* Nozze di Figaro (exc); Zauberflöte (exc); Zauberflöte (exc); *Adam:* Toréador (exc); *Meyerbeer:* Huguenots (exc); *Gounod:* Mireille (exc); *Meyerbeer:* Robert le Diable (exc); *Offenbach:* Contes d'Hoffmann (exc); *Verdi:* Traviata (exc); Ernani (exc); Ballo in maschera (exc); Rigoletto (exc); *J. Strauss II:* Wein, Weib und Gesang; *Lortzing:* Wildschütz (exc); *Mangold:* Zweigesang. (F. Hempel, P. Amato, orch, B. Seidler-Winkler)

Ⓓ **NI7850** (3/94)
Antonio Cortis (1891-1952)
Verdi: Rigoletto (exc); Trovatore (exc); *Bizet:* Carmen (exc); *Gounod:* Faust (exc); *Massenet:* Manon (exc); Werther (exc); *Mascagni:* Cavalleria Rusticana (exc); Iris (exc); *Puccini:* Tosca (exc); Turandot (exc); Bohème (exc); Bohème (exc); *Donizetti:* Favorita (exc); *Giordano:* Cena delle Beffe (exc); *Vives:* Doña Francisquita (exc); *Gaztambide:* Vieja (exc); *Serrano:* Alegría del Batallón (exc); *Cortis:* Calabazas; Tropezón. (A. Cortis, La Scala Orch/C. Sabajno, orch)

Ⓓ **NI7851** (12/93)
Legendary Voices
Bellini: Sonnambula (exc); *Gomes:* Schiavo (exc); *Puccini:* Tosca (exc); *Herbert:* Mademoiselle Modiste (exc); *A. Thomas:* Mignon (exc); *Verdi:* Rigoletto (exc); Aida (exc); *Mascagni:* Cavalleria Rusticana (exc); *Verdi:* Ernani (exc); *Mozart:* Zauberflöte (exc); *Schubert:* Erlkönig, D328; *Schumann:* Myrthen, Op.25 (exc); *Wagner:* Walküre (exc); Tristan und Isolde (exc); *Ponchielli:* Gioconda (exc); *Millöcker:* Bettelstudent (exc); *Cilea:* Arlesiana (exc); *Tchaikovsky:* Eugene Onegin (exc). (L. Tetrazzini, E. Caruso, R. Ponselle, T. Schipa, G. De Luca, E. Turner, A. Piccaver, E. Pinza, A. Kipnis, Lotte Lehmann, K. Flagstad, J. Björling, T. Gobbi, F. Wunderlich, orch/R. Romani, NY Met Op Chor, NY Met Op Orch/G. Setti, G. Anthony/T. Beecham/M. Gurlitt/Rosario Bourdon, Berlin St Op Orch/E. Orthmann, G. Moore, Odeon CO, VPO/B. Walter/H. Lange/N. Grevillius, La Scala Orch/U. Berrettoni, Bavarian St Orch/M. von Zallinger)

Ⓓ **NI7852** (8/94)
Galli-Curci, Vol.2
Delibes: Lakmé (exc); *Donizetti:* Lucia di Lammermoor (exc); Lucia di Lammermoor (exc); *Verdi:* Rigoletto (exc); *F. David:* Perle du Brésil (exc); *Bizet:* Pêcheurs de Perles (exc); *Proch:* Air and Variations; *Verdi:* Trovatore (exc); Trovatore (exc); *Rimsky-Korsakov:* Golden Cockerel (exc); Sadko (exc); *A. Thomas:* Hamlet (exc); *Donizetti:* Lucia di Lammermoor (exc); *Verdi:* Rigoletto (exc); Traviata (exc); *Gounod:* Philémon et Baucis (exc). (A. Galli-Curci, B. Gigli, L. Homer, E. Pinza, A. Bada, G. De Luca, T. Schipa, orch, NY Met Op Orch/G. Setti)

Ⓓ **NI7853** (7/94)
Lauri-Volpi sings Verdi
Verdi: Luisa Miller (exc); Rigoletto (exc); Forza del destino (exc); Aida (exc); Aida (exc); Aida (exc); Aida (exc); Otello (exc). (G. Lauri-Volpi, L. Manfrini, I. Minghini-Cattaneo, E. Rethberg, G. De Luca, M. Caniglia, M. Basiola I, La Scala Chor, Rome Op Orch/R. Arduini, La Scala Orch/F. Ghione, G. Bechi/C. Sabajno, Berlin St Op Orch/F. Zweig, orch/Rosario Bourdon/G. Marinuzzi)

Ⓓ **NI7856** (9/94)
Legendary Tenors
Verdi: Otello (exc); *Tchaikovsky:* Eugene Onegin (exc); *Verdi:* Luisa Miller (exc); *Massenet:* Manon (exc); *Goldmark:* Königin von Saba (exc); *Verdi:* Otello (exc); *Rimsky-Korsakov:* May Night (exc); *Tosti:* Ideale; *Mascagni:* Cavalleria rusticana (exc); *Leoncavallo:* Zazà (exc); *A. Thomas:* Mignon (exc); *Flotow:* Martha (exc); *Wagner:* Walküre (exc); *Mozart:* Don Giovanni (exc); *Boïeldieu:* Dame blanche (exc); *Massenet:* Manon (exc); *Leoncavallo:* Pagliacci (exc); *Giordano:* Andrea Chénier (exc); *Puccini:* Turandot (exc); *Massenet:* Werther (exc). (F. Tamagno, D. Smirnov, A. Bonci, E. Clément, L. Slezak, E. Caruso, L. Sobinov, G. Lauri-Volpi, A. Pertile, G. Martinelli, J. Patzak, H. Roswaenge, L. Melchior, R. Tauber, D. Devriès, G. Thill, B. Gigli, R. Zanelli, J. Björling, T. Schipa, anon, F. La Forge, orch, LSO, La Scala Orch/J. Barbirolli/W. Goehr/G. Cloëz/E. Bigot/C. Sabajno/N. Grevillius/M. Cordone)

Ⓓ **NI7857** (10/94)
Farrar in Italian Opera
Mozart: Nozze di Figaro (exc); Don Giovanni (exc); *Wolf-Ferrari:* Donne curiose (exc); Segreto di Susanna (exc); *Puccini:* Bohème (exc); Bohème (exc); Bohème (exc); Bohème (exc); Tosca (exc); Tosca (exc); Madama Butterfly (exc); Madama Butterfly (exc); Madama Butterfly (exc); Madama Butterfly (exc); Madama Butterfly (exc). (G. Farrar, E. Caruso, A. Scotti, G. Ciaparelli-Viafora, J. Jacoby, orch)

Ⓓ **NI7859** (10/94)
Caruso, Farrar & Journet in French Opera
Gounod: Philémon et Baucis (exc); *Massenet:* Manon (exc); *A. Thomas:* Mignon (exc); *Massenet:* Jongleur de Notre Dame (exc); *Bizet:* Pêcheurs de perles (exc); Pêcheurs de perles (exc); *Gounod:* Faust (exc); Faust (exc); Faust (exc); Faust (exc); Faust (exc); Faust (exc); Faust (exc); Faust (exc); Faust (exc); Faust (exc); Faust (exc). (G. Farrar, E. Caruso, M. Journet, orch/W.B. Rogers, M. Ancona, A. Scotti)

Ⓓ **NI7860** (1/95)
Emma Eames & Pol Plançon
Meyerbeer: Robert le Diable (exc); Etoile du Nord (exc); Dinorah (exc); *Bizet:* Carmen (exc); *Gounod:* Faust (exc); Faust (exc); Roméo et Juliette (exc); Roméo et Juliette (exc); *Berlioz:* Damnation de Faust (exc); Damnation de Faust (exc); *A. Thomas:* Caïd (exc); *Mozart:* Nozze di Figaro (exc); Nozze di Figaro (exc); Don Giovanni (exc); Zauberflöte (exc); Zauberflöte (exc); *Wagner:* Lohengrin (exc); *Schubert:* Gretchen am Spinnrade, D118; *Rossini:* Stabat mater (exc); *Bellini:* Sonnambula (exc). (E. Eames, P. Plançon, E. de Gogorza, M. Sembrich, L. Homer, anon, orch)

Ⓓ **NI7862/3** (3/95)
Puccini—La Bohème
Puccini: Bohème (Cpte). (L. Albanese, B. Gigli, T. Menotti, A. Poli, A. Baracchi, D. Baronti, C. Scattola, N. Palai, La Scala Chor, La Scala Orch/U. Berrettoni)

Ⓓ **NI7864**
More Legendary Voices
C. Marshall: I hear you calling me; *Handel:* Semele (exc); *Leoncavallo:* Pagliacci (exc); *Korngold:* Tote Stadt (exc); *Giordano:* Andrea Chénier (exc); *Bizet:* Pêcheurs de perles (exc); *Lehár:* Paganini (exc); *Mozart:* Don Giovanni (exc); Nozze di Figaro (exc); *Zeller:* Vogelhändler (exc); *Massenet:* Don Quichotte (exc); *Mozart:* Nozze di Figaro (exc); *Saint-Saëns:* Samson et Dalila (exc); *Boito:* Mefistofele (exc); *Wagner:* Meistersinger (exc); *Traditional:* Blow the wind southerly; *Bellini:* Puritani (exc). (J. McCormack, T. Ruffo, M. Jeritza, B. Gigli, R. Tauber, E. Schumann, F. Chaliapin, C. Supervia, C. Muzio, L. Melchior, K. Ferrier, M. Callas, O. Kline, Berlin St Op Orch, Philadelphia, orch/H. Weigert/C. Sabajno/W. Goehr/L. Collingwood/A. Albergoni/G. Cloëz/E. Ormandy/Rosario Bourdon/J. Pasternack/L. Molajoli)

Ⓓ **NI7865** (3/95)
Great Singers at the Mariinsky Theatre
Moniuszko: Halka (exc); *Ponchielli:* Gioconda (exc); *Verdi:* Traviata (exc); Traviata (exc); *Tchaikovsky:* Eugene Onegin (exc); Queen of Spades (exc); Queen of Spades (exc); Queen of Spades (exc); *Glinka:* Life for the Tsar (exc); *Rimsky-Korsakov:* Snow Maiden (exc); *Rubinstein:* Demon (exc); *Serov:* Judith (exc); *Mozart:* Zauberflöte (exc); *Auber:* Fra Diavolo (exc); *Meyerbeer:* Huguenots (exc); *Gounod:* Mireille (exc); *Massenet:* Thaïs (exc); *A. Thomas:* Hamlet (exc); *Delibes:* Lakmé (exc); Lakmé (exc); *Verdi:* Requiem (exc); *Boito:* Mefistofele (exc). (A. Nezhdanova, M. Kovalenko, E. Bronskaya, L. Lipkowska, O. Boronat, E. Katulskaya, E. Popello-Davidova, E. Zbrueva, A. Labinsky, D. Yuzhin, D. Smirnov, E. Vitting, L. Sobinov, M. Karakash, V. Kastorsky, L. Sibiriakov, orch)

Ⓓ **NI7866** (7/95)
Caruso in Opera, Volume 2
Flotow: Martha (exc); *Verdi:* Rigoletto (exc); Trovatore (exc); Trovatore (exc); *Donizetti:* Don Pasquale (exc); Favorita (exc); *Mascagni:* Cavalleria rusticana (exc); *Puccini:* Bohème (exc); Bohème (exc); Tosca (exc); *Meyerbeer:* Huguenots (exc); *Bizet:* Carmen (exc); *Leoncavallo:* Bohème (exc); *Tchaikovsky:* Eugene Onegin (exc); *Giordano:* Andrea Chénier (exc); Andrea Chénier (exc); *Gounod:* Reine de Saba (exc); *Verdi:* Macbeth (exc); *Rubinstein:* Nero (exc); *Meyerbeer:* Africaine (exc); *Puccini:* Bohème (exc). (E. Caruso, N. Melba, orch, anon)

Ⓓ **NI7867** (10/95)
Legendary Baritones
Massenet: Jongleur de Notre Dame (exc); *Tosti:* Au temps du grand roi; *Verdi:* Falstaff (exc); Traviata (exc); Ballo in maschera (exc); *Massenet:* Roi de Lahore (exc); *Verdi:* Otello (exc); *Puccini:* Tosca (exc); *Verdi:* Ernani (exc); Falstaff (exc); Due Foscari (exc); *Wagner:* Tannhäuser (exc); *Marschner:* Hans Heiling (exc); *Leoncavallo:* Zazà (exc); *Verdi:* Rigoletto (exc); *Giordano:* Andrea Chénier (exc); *Rossini:* Barbiere di Siviglia (exc); *Lortzing:* Wildschütz (exc); *Verdi:* Attila (exc). (L. Fugère, V. Maurel, A. Magini-Coletti, M. Battistini, M. Ancona, M. Renaud, E. Giraldoni, R. Stracciari, G. De Luca, T. Ruffo, P. Amato, J. Schwarz, H. Schlusnus, R. Zanelli, C. Galeffi, J.C. Thomas, L. Tibbett, G. Hüsch, I. Gorin, E. Petri, orch, Victor SO, Berlin St Op Orch/F. Tours/N. Shilkret/F. Weissmann/B. Reibold)

Ⓓ **NI7870**
Tito Schipa in Song
A. Scarlatti: Donna ancora è fedele (exc); Pirro e Demetrio (exc); Sento nel core; *Pergolesi:* Tre giorni son che Nina; *Handel:* Serse (exc); *Gluck:* Orfeo ed Euridice (exc); *Donaudy:* O del mio amato ben; *Liszt:* O Lieb, so lang du lieben kannst, S298; *Sibella:* Farfalletta; Girometta; *Padilla:* Princesita; *Calleja:* Emigrantes (exc); *Alvarez:* Partida; *Serrano:* Alma da Dios (exc); *Oteo:* Mi viejo amor; *Ponce:* A la orilla de un palmar; *Palacios:* A Granada; *Freire:* Ay, ay, ay; *Michelena:* A la luz de la luna; *Guaracha:* Rumberos; *Falla:* Canciones populares españolas (exc); *Longás Torres:* En effeuillant la Marguerite; *Rimsky-Korsakov:* Songs, Op.2 (exc). (T. Schipa, E. de Gogorza, J. Echántz, orch/D. Olivieri, La Scala Orch/C. Sabajno/Rosario Bourdon/A. Semprini/J. Pasternack)

Ⓓ **NI7872**
Geraldine Farrar in French Opera
Massenet: Manon (exc); *A. Thomas:* Mignon (exc); Mignon (exc); *Gounod:* Roméo et Juliette (exc); Roméo et Juliette (exc); *Massenet:* Thaïs (exc); *Offenbach:* Contes d'Hoffmann (exc); *Bizet:* Carmen (exc); Carmen (exc); Carmen (exc); Carmen (exc); Carmen (exc). (G. Farrar, E. Clément, G. Martinelli, A. Scotti, P. Amato, orch, La Scala Orch/W.B. Rogers/A. Toscanini)

NMC

Ⓓ **NMCD011** (10/93)
Lutyens—Vocal and Chamber Works
Lutyens: Chamber Concerto 1; Valley of Hatsu-se; Tempi, Op. 42; Isis and Osiris (exc); Triolet I; Triolet II; Requiescat. (J. Manning, Jane's Minstrels/R. Montgomery)

Notes

Ⓓ **PGP21001** (5/93)
Rossini—L'inganno felice
Rossini: Inganno felice (Cpte). (E. Cundari, F. Jacopucci, P. Montarsolo, G. Tadeo, Sergio Pezzetti, Naples RAI Orch/C. Franci)

Novalis

Ⓓ **150 014-2** (5/88)
Mozart—Gala Concert
Mozart: Così fan tutte (exc); Mentre ti lascio, K513; Bacio di mano, K541; Zauberflöte (exc); Nozze di Figaro (exc); Don Giovanni (exc). (J. Van Dam, Paris Orch Ens/J-P. Wallez)

Ⓓ **150 041-2**
Mozart—Overtures
Mozart: Don Giovanni (exc); Clemenza di Tito (exc); Mitridate (exc); Idomeneo (exc); Lucio Silla (exc); Bastien und Bastienne (exc); Finta semplice (exc); Schauspieldirektor (exc); Nozze di Figaro (exc); Così fan tutte (exc); Zauberflöte (exc); Betulia liberata (exc). (ECO/L. Hager)

Ⓓ **150 044-2**
Classical Masterpieces
Weber: Invitation to the Dance; *Mozart:* Serenade, K525; *Schubert:* Rosamunde (exc); *Gluck:* Orfeo ed Euridice (exc). (ECO/J. Judd)

Ⓓ **150 079-2**
Borodin—Orchestral Works
Borodin: Prince Igor (exc); In the Steppes of Central Asia; Symphony 2. (Moscow RSO/V. Fedoseyev)

Ⓓ **150 084-2**
Mozart—Don Giovanni
Mozart: Don Giovanni (Cpte). (A. Dohmen, M. Pick-Hieronimi, S. Isokoski, B. Balleys, S. MacAllister, P. Spagnoli, A. Kohn, Ludwigshafen Th Chor, Vienna Academy Orch/M. Haselböck)

Ⓓ **150 108-2**
Handel—Orchestral Works from Operas and Oratorios
Handel: Concerto, HWV335b; Concerti grossi, Op. 3 (exc); Rinaldo (exc); Solomon (exc); Ariodante (exc); Alcina (exc); Messiah (exc); Serse (exc); Acis and Galatea (exc); Saul (exc); Giulio Cesare (exc); Concerto, HWV335a; Scipione (exc). (ECO/C. Mackerras)

Novelbond

◑ **Novelbond1**
The Scarlet Letter—Sketches from the Opera
Joseph James: Scarlet Letter (exc). (V. Tierney, D.M. Anderson, Philh/A. Greenwood)

Novello

Ⓓ **NVLCD109** (3/90)
Weir—Mini-Operas
Weir: Consolations of Scholarship; Missa del Cid; King Harald's Saga. (J. Manning, L. Hirst, N. Herrett, Lontano/O. de la Martinez, Combattimento/D. Mason)

Nuova Era

Ⓓ **6715/6** (5/89)
Donizetti—Don Pasquale
Donizetti: Don Pasquale (Cpte). (E. Dara, L. Serra, A. Bertolo, A. Corbelli, G. Pasella, Turin Teatro Regio Chor, Turin Teatro Regio Orch/B. Campanella)

Ⓓ **6726**
Italian Overtures
Cimarosa: Due baroni di Rocca Azzurra (exc); Due supposti conti (exc); Italiana in Londra (exc); *Paisiello:* Zingari in fiera (exc); Nina (exc); Barbiere di Siviglia (exc); *Rossini:* Cambiale di matrimonio (exc); Scala di Seta (exc). (Haydn Philh/E. Rojatti)

Ⓓ **6732/3** (10/91)
Donizetti—Maria di Rohan
Donizetti: Maria di Rohan (Cpte). (M. Nicolesco, G. Morino, P. Coni, F. Franci, V. Alaimo, G. Colafelice, Slovak Phil Chor, Italian International Op Orch/M. de Bernart)

Ⓓ **6752/3** (10/91)
Donizetti—Gianni di Parigi
Donizetti: Gianni di Parigi (Cpte). (L. Serra, A. Romero, G. Morino, E. Zilio, E. Fissore, S. Manga, Milan RAI Chor, Milan RAI SO/C.F. Cillario)

Ⓓ **6764/5**
Bellini—La Sonnambula
Bellini: Sonnambula (Cpte). (M. Devia, L. Canonici, A. Verducci, E. Battaglia, L. Musella, G. Riva, V. Gattozzi, Como City Chor, Piacenza SO/M. Viotti)

Ⓓ **6766**
Donizetti—Excerpts from Don Pasquale
Donizetti: Don Pasquale (exc). (E. Dara, L. Serra, A. Corbelli, A. Bertolo, Turin Teatro Regio Chor, Turin Teatro Regio Orch/B. Campanella)

Ⓓ **6776/7** (10/89)
Donizetti—Poliuto
Donizetti: Poliuto (Cpte). (N. Martinucci, E. Connell, R. Bruson, F. Federici, A. dell'Innocenti, B. Lazzaretti, G. Mazzini, Rome Op Chor, Rome Op Chor/J. Latham-König)

Ⓓ **6778/9**
Donizetti—Imelda de' Lambertazzi
Donizetti: Imelda (Cpte). (F. Sovilla, D. d'Auria, F. Tenzi, A. Martin, G. Sarti, Lugano Rad & TV Ch, Lugano Rad & TV Orch/M. Andreae)

Ⓓ **6786/7** (11/89)
Puccini—Turandot
Puccini: Turandot (Cpte). (G. Dimitrova, N. Martinucci, C. Gasdia, G. Ceccarini, T. Pane, P. de Palma, R. Scandiuzzi, A. Casertano, A. Giacomotti, Genoa Teatro Comunale Chor, Genoa Teatro Comunale Orch/D. Oren)

Ⓓ **6794/6**
Donizetti—Lucia di Lammermoor
Donizetti: Lucia di Lammermoor (Cpte). (D. Mazzola, G. Morino, S. Carroli, M. Rinaudo, E. Ruta, S. Paolillo, M. Ferrara, Naples San Carlo Op Chor, Naples San Carlo Op Orch/M. de Bernart)

Ⓓ **6813/4** (4/90)
Handel—Rinaldo
Handel: Rinaldo (Cpte). (M. Horne, C. Gasdia, E. Palacio, C. Weidinger, N. de Carolis, C. Colombara, C. Calvi, C. Tosetta, Venice La Fenice Orch/J. Fisher)

Ⓓ **6820**
Luciana Serra—Opera Recital
Donizetti: Don Pasquale (exc); Fille du Régiment (exc); *Rossini:* Barbiere di Siviglia (exc); *Donizetti:* Gianni di Parigi (exc). (L. Serra, W. Matteuzzi, R. Blake, Turin Teatro Regio Orch, Milan RAI SO, Bologna Teatro Comunale Orch/B. Campanella/C.F. Cillario)

Ⓓ **6823/4** (10/91)
Donizetti—La Favorita
Donizetti: Favorita (Cpte). (A. Tabiadon, G. Morino, P. Coni, A. Verducci, A. Ruffini, M. Farruggia, Slovak Phil Chor, Italian International Orch/F. Luisi)

Ⓓ **6842/4** (10/91)
Bellini—I Puritani
Bellini: Puritani (Cpte). (M. Devia, W. Matteuzzi, C. Robertson, P. Washington, E. Jankovic, F. Federici, Catania Teatro Massimo Bellini Chor, Catania Teatro Massimo Bellini Orch/R. Bonynge)

Ⓓ **6851** (10/90)
Giuseppe Morino—King of Bel Canto
Mozart: Così fan tutte (exc); *Meyerbeer:* Huguenots (exc); *Donizetti:* Elisir d'amore (exc); Fille du régiment (exc); Duca d'Alba (exc); *Bellini:* Pirata (exc); Puritani (exc); *Gounod:* Faust (exc); Roméo et Juliette (exc); *Lalo:* Roi d'Ys (exc); *Bizet:* Pêcheurs de perles (exc); *Massenet:* Manon (exc). (G. Morino, Warmia Nat PO/B. Amaducci)

Ⓓ **6852/4** (12/90)
Salieri—Axur, re d'Ormus
Salieri: Axur (Cpte). (A. Martin, C. Rayam, E. Mei, E. Nova, A. Vespasiani, M. Valentini, M. Porcelli, M. Cecchetti, S. Turchetta, G.B. Palmieri, Guido d'Arezzo Ch, Russian PO, R. Clemencic (hpd/dir))

Ⓓ **6863/5**
Handel—Julius Caesar
Handel: Giulio Cesare (Cpte). (M. Dupuy, P. Orciani, R. Pierotti, J. Ligi, S. Anselmi, P. Spagnoli, G. De Matteis, S. Mingardo, Bassano Pro Arte Orch/M. Panni)

Ⓓ **6871**
Puccini—Excerpts from Turandot
Puccini: Turandot (exc). (G. Dimitrova, N. Martinucci, C. Gasdia, R. Scandiuzzi, Genoa Teatro Comunale Chor, Genoa Teatro Comunale Orch/D. Oren)

Ⓓ **6872/3** (9/91)
Nina, o sia La Pazza per Amore
Paisiello: Nina (Cpte). (M. Bolgan, D. Bernardini, F. Musinu, F. Pediconi, G. Surian, C. Bosi, B. Cegile, Catania Teatro Massimo Bellini Chor, Catania Teatro Massimo Bellini Orch/R. Bonynge)

Ⓓ **6887**
Bellini—Excerpts from La Sonnambula
Bellini: Sonnambula (exc). (M. Devia, L. Canonici, A. Verducci, Como City Chor, Piacenza SO/M. Viotti)

Ⓓ **6888/9**
Salieri: La Locandiera
Salieri: Locandiera (Cpte). (A. Ruffini, G. Sarti, O. di Credico, P. Guarnera, L. Petroni, P. Leolini, Toscanini SO/F. Luisi)

Ⓓ **6892**
William Matteuzzi sings Opera Arias
Bellini: Puritani (exc); *Donizetti:* Fille du régiment (exc); *Rossini:* Italiana in Algeri (exc); *Various:* Ape musicale (exc). (M. Devia, A. Scarabelli, L. Serra, W. Matteuzzi, C. Robertson, P. Washington, G. Musinu, Bologna Teatro Comunale Chor, Bologna Teatro Comunale Orch, Teatro La Fenice Chor, Teatro La Fenice Orch, Catania Teatro Massimo Bellini Chor, Catania Teatro Massimo Bellini Orch/B. Campanella/V. Parisi/R. Bonynge)

Ⓓ **6905**
Donizetti—Great Love Duets
Donizetti: Lucia di Lammermoor (exc); Fille du régiment (exc); Favorita (exc); Elisir d'amore (exc); Imelda (exc); Don Pasquale (exc). (D. Mazzola, G. Morino, Naples San Carlo Op Chor, Naples San Carlo Op Orch/M. de Bernart, L. Serra, W. Matteuzzi, Bologna Teatro Comunale Chor, Bologna Teatro Comunale Orch/B. Campanella, A. Tabiadon, P. Coni, Bratislava Phil Ch, Italian International Orch/F. Luisi, A. Scarabelli, C. Merritt, Parma Teatro Regio Chor, Toscanini SO/H. Soudant, F. Sovilla, A. Martin, Lugano Rad & TV Ch, Lugano Rad & TV Orch/M. Andreae, A. Bertolo, Turin Teatro Regio Chor, Turin Teatro Regio Orch)

Ⓓ **6917/9**
Leoncavallo: La bohème
Leoncavallo: Bohème (Cpte). (L. Mazzaria, J. Summers, M. Malagnini, M. Senn, B. Praticò, P. Spagnoli, S. Pagliuca, R. Emili, C. de Mola, Turin Fenice Chor, Turin Fenice Orch/J. Latham-König)

Ⓓ **6928/9**
Carvalho—Testoride Argonauta
Carvalho: Testoride Argonauta (Cpte). (E. von Magnus, C. Rayam, L. Meeuwsen, D. Hennecke, L. Åkerlund, Clemencic Consort Baroque Orch/R. Clemenčić)

Ⓓ **6930/1**
Fux—Dafne in Lauro
Fux: Dafne in Lauro (Cpte). (M. van der Sluis, L. Åkerlund, G. Lesne, S. Piccollo, M. Klietmann, Cappella Voc Ens, Clemencic Consort/R. Clemenčić)

Ⓓ **6932/3**
Vivaldi—L'Olimpiade
Vivaldi: Olimpiade (Cpte). (A.W. Schultze, L. Meeuwsen, E. von Magnus, M. van der Sluis, G. Lesne, A. Christofellis, W. Oberholtzer, Cappella Voc Ens, Clemencic Consort/R. Clemenčić)

① **6934/5**
Keiser—Croesus
Keiser: Croesus (Cpte). (M. Klietmann, S. Mizugushi, P. Grigorova, M. van der Sluis, A. Martin, M. Tucker, L. Åkerlund, J. Benet, U. Targler, P. Mildenhall, Cappella Voc Ens, Clemencic Consort/R. Clemenčić)

① **6944/5** (10/91)
Bizet—The Pearl Fishers
Bizet: Pêcheurs de Perles (Cpte). (A. Ruffini, G. Morino (ten), B. Praticò, E. Abumradi, Slovak Phil Chor, Italian International Orch/C. Piantini)

① **6971/3**
Mercadante—Il bravo
Mercadante: Bravo (Cpte). (D. di Domenico, A. Tabiadon, J. Perry, S. Bertocchi, S. Antonucci, L. de Lisi, A. Riva, G. de Matteis, M.C. Zanni, Bratislava Phil Ch, Italian International Orch/B. Aprea)

① **6982/3** (7/91)
Bellini—Zaira
Bellini: Zaira (Cpte). (K. Ricciarelli, S. Alaimo, R. Vargas, A. Papadjiakou, S. Silbano, R. de Candia, L. Roni, G.B. Palmieri, Catania Teatro Massimo Bellini Chor, Catania Teatro Massimo Bellini Orch/P. Olmi)

① **6994/5** (4/92)
Paisiello—Don Chisciotte
Paisiello: Don Chisciotte (Cpte). (P. Barbacini, R. Franceschetto, M.A. Peters, E. Zilio, M. Bolognesi, B. Praticò, B. Lucarini, F. Arnone, Ann Rossi, Rome Op Orch/P.G. Morandi)

① **7020/1** (3/92)
Bellini—I Capuleti ed i Montecchi
Bellini: Capuleti (Cpte). (K. Ricciarelli, D. Montague, D. Raffanti, M. Lippi, A. Salvadori, Venice La Fenice Chor, Venice La Fenice Orch/B. Campanella)

① **7043** (2/93)
Paisiello—La Serva Padrona
Paisiello: Serva Padrona (Cpte). (A.V. Banks, G.L. Ricci, Milan CO/P. Vaglieri)

① **7076/7** (2/94)
Bellini—Bianca e Fernando
Bellini: Bianca e Fernando (Cpte). (Y.O. Shin, G. Kunde, A. Tomicich, H. Fu, A. Caforio, S. Nigoghossian, W. Coppola, E. Manhart, Bellini Th Chor, Bellini Th Orch/A. Licata)

① **7132/3** (5/93)
Rossini—La pietra del paragone
Rossini: Pietra del paragone (Cpte). (P. Barbacini, H. Müller-Molinari, A. Trovarelli, M.C. Nocentini, R. Scaltriti, V. di Matteo, P. Rumetz, A. Svab, Modena Teatro Comunale Chor, Camerata Musicale Orch/C. Desderi)

① **7140/2** (5/93)
Rossini—Le siège de Corinthe
Rossini: Siège de Corinthe (Cpte). (L. Serra, M. Lippi, M. Comencini, D. Raffanti, A. Gaforio, V. Martino, F. Facini, F. Provvisionato, Prague Phil Chor, Genoa Carlo Felice Th Chor, Genoa Carlo Felice Th Orch/P. Olmi)

① **7154/5** (2/94)
Bellini—Adelson e Salvini
Bellini: Adelson e Salvini (Cpte). (F. Previati, B. Williams, A. Nafé, A. Tomicich, L. Rizzi, E. Jankovic, R. Coviello, G. Tosi, Bellini Th Chor, Bellini Th Orch/A. Licata)

① **7179/80**
Mercadante—Il Giuramento
Mercadante: Giuramento (Cpte). (G. de Liso, G. Morino, M. Olmeda, M. Barrard, E. Procuronoff, P. Aubert, Nantes Op Chor, Loire PO/G. Carella)

Ode

① **CDMANU1317** (11/92)
Wagner—Opera Excerpts
Wagner: Fliegende Holländer (exc); Parsifal (exc); Tannhäuser (exc); Meistersinger (exc). (A. Marc, C. Doig, D. McIntyre, NZ SO/H. Wallberg)

① **CDODE1062**
Mina Foley - Mina Foley
Verdi: Traviata (exc); Rigoletto (exc); *Donizetti:* Linda di Chamounix (exc); *Bellini:* Norma (exc); *G. Charpentier:* Louise (exc); *Chaminade:* Été; *Benedict:* Gypsy and the Bird; *J. Strauss II:* Casanova (exc); *Bishop:* Lo, here the gentle lark; *Verdi:* Forza del destino (exc); *Mozart:* Zauberflöte (exc); *Rimsky-Korsakov:* Songs, Op. 2 (exc); *Delibes:* Lakmé (exc); *Verdi:* Ernani (exc). (M. Foley, Orch)

① **CDODE1365** (12/92)
Oscar Natzke - A Legend in His Time
Handel: Samson (exc); *Mozart:* Zauberflöte (exc); Zauberflöte (exc); Don Giovanni (exc); *Rossini:* Barbiere di Siviglia (exc); *Mussorgsky:* Song of the Flea; *Ketèlbey:* Sanctuary of the heart; In a Monastery Garden; *W.H. Weiss:* Village Blacksmith; *Beethoven:* Lieder, Op.48 (exc); Zärtliche Liebe, WoO123; *Schumann:* Romanzen und Balladen, Op.49 (exc); *Tchaikovsky:* Songs, Op.47 (exc); *Malashkin:* Oh could I but express in song; *Lehmann:* In a Persian Garden (exc); *Hewitt:* Out where the big ships go; *Traditional:* Shenandoah; Blow the man down; Hullaballo balay; Drunken Sailor; Rio Grande; Billy boy; *L. Fischer:* Kritikaster (exc); *M. Phillips:* Wimmen oh wimmen. (O. Natzke, H. Greenslade, chor, orch/H. Geehl/W. Braithwaite)

L'Oiseau-Lyre

① **410 553-2OH** (12/83)
18th Century Orchestral Works
Pachelbel: Canon and Gigue; *Vivaldi:* Concerti Grossi, Op. 3 (exc); Concerto, RV537; *Gluck:* Orfeo ed Euridice (exc); *Handel:* Solomon (exc); Berenice (exc); Water Music (exc). (J. Holloway, M. Huggett, C. Mackintosh, E. Wilcock, S. Preston, M. Laird, I. Wilson, AAM/C. Hogwood)

① **417 123-2OH** (9/86)
Purcell: Songs and Airs
Purcell: Fairy Queen, Z629 (exc); Birthday Ode, Z321 (exc); If music be the food of love, Z379/3; Not all my torments, Z400; Olinda in the shades unseen, Z404; Urge me no more, Z426; Bess of Bedlam, Z370; Lovely Albina, Z394; Pausanias, Z585 (exc); Tempest, Z631 (exc); When first Amintas sued for a kiss, Z430; Timon of Athens, Z632 (exc); Evening Hymn, Z193. (E. Kirkby, C. Hogwood, A. Rooley, R. Campbell, C. Mackintosh)

① **421 333-2OH3** (12/88)
Mozart—Le nozze di Figaro; Some Variant Versions
Mozart: Nozze di Figaro (Cpte). (P. Salomaa, B. Bonney, H. Hagegård, A. Auger, A. Nafé, D. Jones, C. Feller, E. Gimenez, F. Egerton, E. Florimo, N. Argenta, Drottningholm Court Th Chor, Drottningholm Court Th Orch/A. Östman)

① **425 835-2OH** (4/91)
Mozart—Concert and Opera Arias
Mozart: Rè pastore (exc); Voi avete un cor fedele, K217; Ah, lo previdi, K272; Zaïde (exc); Nehmt meinen Dank, K383; Ch'io mi scordi di te, K505. (E. Kirkby, AAM/C. Hogwood, S. Lubin)

① **425 943-2OH3** (12/90)
Mozart—Don Giovanni
Mozart: Don Giovanni (Cpte). (H. Hagegård, A. Auger, D. Jones, B. Bonney, N. van der Meel, G. Cachemaille, B. Terfel, K. Sigmundsson, Drottningholm Court Th Orch, Drottningholm Court Th Orch/A. Östman)

① **430 845-2OH3** (8/91)
Handel—Orlando
Handel: Orlando (Cpte). (J. Bowman, A. Auger, C. Robbin, E. Kirkby, D. Thomas, AAM/C. Hogwood)

① **433 545-2OH2** (2/93)
Monteverdi—L'Orfeo
Monteverdi: Orfeo (Cpte). (J.M. Ainsley, J. Gooding, C. Bott, T. Bonner, C. Robson, A. King, R. Evans, M. George, S. Grant, New London Consort/P. Pickett)

① **436 132-2OH** (7/93)
Emma Kirkby sings Mrs Arne
Arne: Comus (exc); Rosamond (exc); Tempest (exc); *Lampe:* Britannia (exc); Dione (exc); *Handel:* Ariodante (exc); Alcina (exc); Alexander's Feast (exc); Allegro, il penseroso ed il moderato (exc); Saul (exc); Overture, HWV Anh13; Hornpipe, HWV356; March, HWV345. (E. Kirkby, AAM/C. Hogwood)

① **436 992-2OHO** (7/94)
Purcell—Dido and Aeneas
Purcell: Dido (Cpte). (C. Bott, J. M. Ainsley, E. Kirkby, D. Thomas, E. Priday, S. Stowe, J. Baird, D. Lochmann, M. Chance, AAM Chor, AAM/C. Hogwood)

OO **436 992-5OHO**
Purcell—Dido and Aeneas
Purcell: Dido (Cpte). (C. Bott, J. M. Ainsley, E. Kirkby, D. Thomas, E. Priday, S. Stowe, J. Baird, D. Lochmann, M. Chance, AAM Chor, AAM/C. Hogwood)

① **440 085-2OHO2** (2/94)
Mozart—Die Zauberflöte
Mozart: Zauberflöte (Cpte). (B. Bonney, S. Jo, K. Streit, G. Cachemaille, K. Sigmundsson, H. Hagegård, M. Petzold, L. Watson, R. Ziesak, P. Hansen, I. Vermillion, D. Naseband, K. Suzuki, S. Schnorr, R. Wörle, P. Salomaa, H. Lippert, O. Widmer, Drottningholm Court Th Chor, Drottningholm Court Th Orch/A. Östman)

① **440 220-2OH** (7/94)
Blow—Venus and Adonis
Blow: Venus and Adonis (Cpte). (C. Bott, M. George, L. Crabtree, J. Gooding, A. King, S. Grant, C. Robson, P. Agnew, Westminster Abbey Sch Chor, New London Consort/P. Pickett)

① **443 191-2OM**
Mozart—Le nozze di Figaro - Highlights
Mozart: Nozze di Figaro (exc). (P. Salomaa, B. Bonney, H. Hagegård, A. Auger, A. Nafé, D. Jones, C. Feller, E. Gimenez, F. Egerton, E. Florimo, N. Argenta, Drottningholm Court Th Chor, Drottningholm Court Th Orch/A. Östman)

① **443 201-2OM**
Popular Baroque Works
Pachelbel: Canon and Gigue; *Handel:* Water Music (exc); *Vivaldi:* Concerti, Op. 10 (exc); *Bach:* Christmas Oratorio, BWV248 (exc); *Corelli:* Concerti Grossi, Op. 6 (exc); *Bach:* Suites, BWV1066-9 (exc); *A. Marcello:* Oboe Concerto in D minor; *Handel:* Berenice (exc); *Bach:* 4-Harpsichord Concerto. (S. Preston, C. Shanks, C. Tilney, C. Rousset, D. Moroney, AAM, C. Hogwood (hpd/dir))

① **443 267-2OX2**
Christopher Hogwood - A Profile
Arne: Overtures in 8 parts (exc); *Telemann:* Flute, Oboe d'amore & Viola d'amore Concerto; *Rebel:* Élémens (exc); *Handel:* Water Music (exc); *Bach:* French Suites, BWV812-17 (exc); Brandenburg Concertos (exc); *Vivaldi:* Concerto, RV414; Concerti, Op. 8 (exc); *Boyce:* Symphonies (exc); *Gluck:* Orfeo ed Euridice (exc); *Mozart:* Ave verum corpus, K618; Flute and Harp Concerto, K299; *Haydn:* Symphony 107; *Beethoven:* Egmont (exc). (S. Preston, L. Beznosiuk, C. Shanks, C. Mackintosh, M. Huggett, C. Coin, F. Kelly, C. Hogwood, Winchester Cath Ch, Winchester Quiristers, AAM/C. Hogwood)

① **444 131-2OHO2** (3/95)
Mozart—La Clemenza di Tito
Mozart: Clemenza di Tito (Cpte). (U. Heilmann, D. Jones, C. Bartoli, D. Montague, B. Bonney, G. Cachemaille, AAM Chor, AAM/C. Hogwood)

① **444 620-2OH**
The Glory of Purcell
Purcell: Double Dealer, Z592 (exc); Birthday Ode, Z323; Old Bachelor, Z607 (exc); Birthday Ode, Z321 (exc); Oedipus, Z583 (exc); Amphitryon, Z572 (exc); King Arthur, Z628 (exc); Bonduca, Z574 (exc); Fairy Queen, Z629 (exc); Sonatas, Z802-11 (exc); Dido (exc); Abdelazer, Z570 (exc); Bess of Bedlam, Z370; Married Beau, Z603 (exc); Bell Anthem, Z49 (exc); Hear, my prayer, O God, Z14. (E. Kirkby, C. Bott, A. Deller, J. Whitworth, J. Bowman, C. Robson, M. Hill, W. Kendall, S. Roberts, C. Keyte, C. Mackintosh, M. Huggett, R. Campbell, C. Coin, A. Rooley, P. Chateauneuf, C. Hogwood, AAM Chor, Winchester Cath Ch, St Anthony Sngrs, Taverner Ch, AAM, Oiseau-Lyre Orch Ens, Brandenburg Consort, C. Hogwood (hpd/dir)/A. Lewis/D. Hill)

Olympia

① **OCD115** (12/87)
Tchaikovsky—Eugene Onegin
Tchaikovsky: Eugene Onegin (Cpte). (Y. Mazurok, T. Milashkina, V. Atlantov, T. Sinyavskaya, E. Nesterenko, T. Tugarinova, L. Avdeyeva, L. Kuznetsov, V. Yaroslavtsev, A. Yapridze, Bolshoi Th. Chor, Bolshoi Th. Orch/M. Ermler)

① **OCD121**
Russian Favourites
Glinka: Ruslan and Lyudmila (exc); *Borodin:* In the Steppes of Central Asia; *Rimsky-Korsakov:* Capriccio Espagnol; *Scriabin:* Symphonic Poem; *Mussorgsky:* Night on the bare mountain; *Glazunov:* Méditation, Op. 32; *Tchaikovsky:* Marche Slave. (USSR RSO, USSR Academy SO/V. Fedoseyev/B. Demchenko/E. Svetlanov, L. Kogan)

① **OCD145** (9/93)
Russian Operas
Rimsky-Korsakov: Mozart and Salieri (Cpte); *Mussorgsky:* Marriage (Cpte). (A. Fedin, E. Nesterenko, S. Girshenko, V. Chasovennaya, V. Khrulev, A. Podbolotov, L. Kolmakova, V. Ribasenko, USSR Ministry of Culture SO/G. Rozhdestvensky, Bolshoi Th Orch/M. Ermler)

① **OCD273**
Nikolai Petrov plays Encores
Weber: Piano Sonata 1 (exc); *Bach:* Cantata 147 (exc); *Couperin:* Livre de clavecin III (exc); *Schumann:* Romanzen, Op. 28 (exc); Paganini Studies, Op. 3 (exc); *Debussy:* Préludes (exc); *Saint-Saëns:* Carnaval des animaux (exc); *Mendelssohn:* Fantaisies, Op. 16 (exc); *Ravel:* Jeux d'eau; *Rachmaninov:* Songs, Op. 34 (exc); *Ravel:* Enfant et les sortilèges (exc); *Previn:* Invisible Drummer (exc); *Schulhoff:* Jazz Etudes (exc); *Shchedrin:* Collage Toccata; *Poulenc:* Mouvements perpétuels; *Ginastera:* Danzas Argentinas (exc); *Kapustin:* Intermezzo. (N. Petrov)

Ⓒ **OCD291** (5/93)
Kabalevsky—Colas Breugnon
Kabalevsky: Colas Breugnon (Cpte). (L. Boldin, N. Isakova, V. Kayevchenko, E. Masimenko, G. Dudarev, N. Gutorovich, A. Mishchevski, A. Shitkova, L. Yeliseev, M. Syromyatnikov, V. Zamberg, Moscow Stanislavsky Th Chor, Moscow Stanislavsky Th Orch/G. Zhemchuzhin)

Ⓒ **OCD370**
Berle Sanford Rosenberg Live From Budapest
Donizetti: Favorita (exc); Dom Sébastien (exc); *Puccini:* Bohème (exc); *Leoncavallo:* Bohème (exc); *Rossini:* Guillaume Tell (exc); *Donizetti:* Fille du Régiment (exc); *Borodin:* Prince Igor (exc); *Tchaikovsky:* Eugene Onegin (exc); *Meyerbeer:* Africaine (exc); *Puccini:* Villi (exc); *Gounod:* Faust (exc); *Massenet:* Cid (exc). (B.S. Rosenberg, Budapest Concert Orch/J. Acs)

Ⓒ **OCD382**
18th Century Polish Miniatures
Radziwiłł: Divertimento; Serenada; *Zywny:* Polonaise; *Pekiel:* Polish Dances; *Holland:* Agatha (exc); *Kurpiński:* Cavatina; *Janiewicz:* Divertimento; *Hasse:* King of Poland's March; King of Poland's Dance; *Dobrzyński:* Andante, Op. 42; *Ogiński:* Polonaise. (Warsaw CO/M. Sewen)

Ⓒ **OCD386** (8/93)
Moniuszko—Overtures
Moniuszko: Paria (exc); Countess (exc); Verbum nobile (exc); Halka (exc); Raftsman (exc); Fairy Tale; Concert Polonaise. (Katowice RSO/G. Fitelberg/J. Krenz, Warsaw Nat PO/W. Rowicki)

Ⓒ **OCD485**
M Haydn—Symphonies, Volume 4
M. Haydn: Divertimento, MH68; Symphony, MH474; Andromeda e Perseo (exc). (Oradea PO/R. Rimbu)

Ⓒ **OCD5002**
The Mravinsky Legacy—Volumes 1-6
Wagner: Tannhäuser (exc); *Bruckner:* Symphony 9; *Wagner:* Tristan und Isolde (exc); *Mussorgsky:* Khovanshchina (exc); *Liadov:* Baba-Yaga, Op. 56; *Tchaikovsky:* Symphony 5; *Wagner:* Götterdämmerung (exc); *R. Strauss:* Alpensinfonie; *Mozart:* Nozze di Figaro (exc); *Bartók:* Music for Strings, Percussion and Celesta; *Sibelius:* Legends (exc); Symphony 7; *Wagner:* Lohengrin (exc); *Stravinsky:* Agon; *Shostakovich:* Symphony 15; *Beethoven:* Symphony 4; *Salmanov:* Symphony 4. (Leningrad PO/E. Mravinsky)

Ⓒ **OCD5008**
400 years of Dutch Music
Schuyt: Padovane et Gagliarda (exc); *Sweelinck:* Pseaumes des David III (exc); Du fonds de ma pensée; *Mercker:* Padouane und Galliard (exc); *Hacquart:* Harmonia parnassia (exc); Cantiones sacrae (exc); *Rosier:* Sonatas (exc); *Blankenburg:* Apologie des femmes; *De Fesch:* Concerts, Op.3a (exc); *Wassenaer:* Concerti armonici (exc); *Hellendaal:* Concertos, Op. 3 (exc); *J.N. Lentz:* Harpsichord Concerto 2; *C. E. Graf:* Symphonies, Op.14 (exc); *Meder:* Sinfonies, Op.3 (exc); *Fodor:* Symphony 4; *Wilms:* Symphony, Op.23; *Bree:* Allegro; *Verhulst:* Symphony, Op.46; *Verhey:* Flute Concerto, Op.43; *Zweers:* Symphony 3; *Wagenaar:* Cyrano de bergerac; *Vermeulen:* Symphony 3; *Ruyneman:* Hiëroglyphen; *Pijper:* Piano Concerto; *H. Andriessen:* Kuhnau Variations; *Vermeulen:* Symphony 4; *Baaren:* Septet; *Horst:* Choros II; *Ketting:* Due canzoni; *T. de Leeuw:* Mouvements rétrogrades; *Escher:* Univers de Rimbaud; *Janssen:* Malic Moulds; *Loevendie:* Turkish Folk Poems; *Laman:* Fleurs du Mal; *H. Andriessen:* Symphony 4; Ricercare; *Diepenbrock:* Lydische Nacht; *Van Gilse:* Thijl (exc); *Badings:* Symphonic prologue. (T. Willemstijn, D. Dorow, J. van Nes, C. Patriasz, M. ten Houte de Lange, J. Giraudeau, H. van der Kamp, M. van Egmond, J. de Wit, K. Verheul, F. Minderaa, A. Rozeboom, K. White, V. Zarzo, J. Walta, P. Stotijn, R. Brautigam, G. Janssen, Netherlands Chbr Ch, Amsterdam Cantori, Budapest Ifúsági Ch, Hague PO/T. Koopman, T. Koopman (hpd/dir)/N. Harnoncourt/E. Bour/A. Dorati/F. Leitner/H. Vonk/A. Medveczky/L. Vis/E. Spanjaard/A. Lombard/R. van Driesten)

Ⓒ **OCD507**
400 Years of Dutch Music, Volume 8
H. Andriessen: Symphony 4; Ricercare; *Diepenbrock:* Lydische Nacht; *Van Gilse:* Thijl (exc); *Badings:* Symphonic prologue. (Hague PO/E. Spanjaard)

Ondine

Ⓒ **ODE714-2** (11/92)
Madetoja—Juha
Madetoja: Juha (Cpte). (J. Hynninen, M. Lokka, E. Erkkilä, A. Välkki, M. Haverinen, T. Valtasaari, M. Wirkkala, M. Metsomäki, K. Haartti, K. Airinen, K. Olli, Finnish Rad Youth Ch, Finnish RSO/J. Jalas)

Ⓒ **ODE731-2** (4/90)
Jorma Hynninen sings Opera Arias
Leoncavallo: Pagliacci (exc); *Verdi:* Traviata (exc); Trovatore (exc); Ballo in maschera (exc); Forza del destino (exc); Rigoletto (exc); Don Carlo (exc); *Tchaikovsky:* Eugene Onegin (exc); Queen of Spades (exc); *Mozart:* Nozze di Figaro (exc); Don Giovanni (exc). (J. Hynninen, Estonian SO/E. Klas)

Ⓒ **ODE749-2**
Kortekangas—Grand Hotel & Memoria
Kortekangas: Grand Hotel; Memoria. (E-L. Saarinen, S. Tiilikainen, K. Laurikainen, Avanti CO, Finnish Chbr Ch, Tapiola Chbr Ch/O. Pohjola/E-O. Söderström, O. Kortekangas, J. Liimatainen, T. Ferchen/E. Pohjola)

Ⓒ **ODE750-2**
E.Rautavaara—Vincent
Rautavaara: Vincent (Cpte). (J. Hynninen, M. Heinikari, M. Putkonen, E-L. Saarinen, S. Rautavaara, Finnish Nat Op Chor, Finnish Nat Op Orch/F. Manchurov)

Ⓒ **ODE768-2** (9/92)
Dilbèr sings Coloratura Arias
Bellini: Puritani (exc); Sonnambula (exc); *Verdi:* Rigoletto (exc); *Meyerbeer:* Dinorah (exc); *Delibes:* Lakmé (exc); *Donizetti:* Lucia di Lammermoor (exc); *R. Strauss:* Ariadne auf Naxos (exc); *J. Strauss II:* Frühlingsstimmen, Op. 410. (Dilbèr, Estonia Op Orch/E. Klas)

Ⓒ **ODE776-2** (4/93)
Tubin—Barbara von Tisenhusen
Tubin: Barbara von Tisenhusen (Cpte). (H. Raamat, T. Sild, M. Jôgeva, U. Kreen, I. Kuusk, V. Puura, A. Kollo, H. Miilberg, M. Palm, Estonia Op Chor, Estonia Op Orch/P. Lilje)

Ⓒ **ODE780-2** (8/92)
Sallinen—Kullervo
Sallinen: Kullervo (Cpte). (J. Hynninen, E-L. Saarinen, M. Salminen, J. Silvasti, S. Vihavainen, A-L. Jakobson, P. Mäkelä, J. Kotilainen, P. Etelävuori, M. Putkonen, M. Heinikari, E. Ruuttunen, V-M. Loiri, Finnish Nat Op Chor, Finnish Nat Op Orch/U. Söderblom)

Ⓒ **ODE794-2D** (5/93)
Bergman—The Singing Tree
Bergman: Singing Tree (Cpte). (P. Lindroos, C. Hellekant, K. Hannula, P. Salomaa, S. Tiilikainen, M. Wallén, A-L. Jakobson, M. Harju, T-M. Tuomela, E-K. Vilke, T. Nyman, P. Lindroos, Dominante Ch, Tapiola Chbr Ch, Finnish Nat Op Orch/U. Söderblom)

Opal

Ⓒ **OPALCDS9843** (4/90)
Karl Muck conducts Wagner
Wagner: Siegfried Idyll; Parsifal (exc); Parsifal (exc); Parsifal (exc). (G. Pistor, C. Bronsgeest, L. Hofmann, Bayreuth Fest Chor, Berlin St Op Chor, Berlin St Op Orch, Bayreuth Fest Orch/K. Muck)

Ⓒ **OPALCD9839** (4/89)
Pupils of Theodore Leschetizky
Schubert: Impromptus (exc); *Liszt:* Hungarian Rhapsodies, S244 (exc); *Weber:* Piano Sonata 1 (exc); *Leschetizky:* Arabesque in A flat; *D. Scarlatti:* Keyboard Sonatas (exc); *Gluck:* Orfeo ed Euridice (exc); *Beethoven:* Piano Sonata 3 (exc); *J. Strauss II:* Kuss-Walzer, Op. 400; *Arensky:* Suite, Op.15 (exc); *Schütt:* Impromptu-Rococo; *Chopin:* Nocturnes (exc); *Liszt:* Chants polonais, S480 (exc); *Chopin:* Nocturnes (exc); Nocturnes (exc); *Rameau:* Pièces de clavecin (exc); *Leschetizky:* Toccata; *Chopin:* Nocturnes (exc). (E. Leginska, B. Moiseiwitsch, M. Hambourg, O. Gabrilowitsch, H. Bauer, I. Paderewski, I. Friedman, F. la Forge, M. Novello, T. Leschetizky)

Ⓒ **OPALCD9846** (2/92)
Francesco Tamagno—Complete Recordings
Verdi: Otello (exc); Trovatore (exc); *Giordano:* Andrea Chénier (exc); *Meyerbeer:* Prophète (exc); *Massenet:* Hérodiade (exc); *Rossini:* Guillaume Tell (exc); *Saint-Saëns:* Samson et Dalila (exc). (F. Tamagno, Anon)

⊙ **OPAL837/8**
Wagner—Parsifal - highlights
Wagner: Parsifal (exc); Parsifal (exc). (/K. Muck, G. Pistor, C. Bronsgeest, L. Hofmann, Bayreuth Fest Chor, Berlin St Op Chor, Bayreuth Fest Orch, Berlin St Op Orch)

Opera in Arabic

Ⓒ **SADEK1001**
Mozart—Così fan tutte
Mozart: Così fan tutte (Cpte). (R. El Hefni, A. El Sharqawi, A. Radi, H. Kami, R. Zaidan, R. Al Wakeel, Silesian Chbr Music Chor, Polish Nat RO/Y. El Sisi)

Ⓒ **SADEK1002**
Mozart—Le Nozze di Figaro
Mozart: Nozze di Figaro (Cpte). (R. Zaidan, N. Allouba, R. Al Wakeel, N. Erian, A. Radi, A. El Sharqawi, C. Rathl, S. Bedair, Silesian Chbr Music Chor, Polish Nat RO/Y. El Sisi)

Ⓒ **SADEK1003**
Mozart—Don Giovanni
Mozart: Don Giovanni (Cpte). (R. Al Wakeel, N. Allouba, N. Erian, T.S. El Din, S. Bedair, R. Zaidan, C. Rathl, Silesian Chbr Music Chor, Polish Nat RO/Y. El Sisi)

Opera Rara

Ⓒ **ORCH103** (10/90)
Italian Opera—1810-20
Pucitta: Vestale (exc); *Generali:* Adelina (exc); *Rossini:* Ah! per pietà t'arresta; *Mosca:* Bestie in uomini (exc); *Manfroce:* Ecuba (exc); *Mayr:* Rosa bianca (exc); *García:* Califfo di Bagdad (exc); *Pacini:* Annetta e Lucindo (exc); *Mayr:* Medea (exc); Elena (exc); *Pavesi:* Agatina (exc); *Mayr:* Cora (exc); *Coccia:* Clotilde (exc); *Weber:* Non paventar mia vita; *Rossini:* Torvaldo e Dorliska (exc); *Morlacchi:* Barbiere di Siviglia (exc); *Winter:* Maometto II (exc); *Meyerbeer:* Romilda (exc); *Pacini:* Adelaide (exc); *Donizetti:* Enrico (exc); *Rossini:* Ricciardo e Zoriade (exc); *Meyerbeer:* Semiramide (exc); Emma (exc); *Mercadante:* Apoteosi d'Ercole (exc); *Mayr:* Alfredo il Grande (exc); *Donizetti:* Falegname di Livonia (exc); *Carafa:* Gabriella (exc). (A. Bolton, M. Bovino, E. Harrhy, M. Hill Smith, Y. Kenny, B. Mills, S. Bickley, D. Jones, A. Mason, D. Montague, M. Moreno, P. Walker, P. Doghan, K. John, R. Leggate, C. Merritt, H. Nichol, P. Nilon, J. Best, P. Guy-Bromley, J. Cashmore, G. Dolton, C. du Plessis, R. Smythe, G. Mitchell Ch, Philh/D. Parry, S. Drake)

Ⓒ **ORCH104** (8/95)
A Hundred Years of Italian Opera: 1820-1830
Balducci: Tazia (exc); *Bellini:* Adelson e Salvini (exc); Zaira (exc); *Carafa:* Nozze di Lammermoor (exc); *Coccia:* Maria Stuart (exc); Rosmonda (exc); *C. Conti:* Giovanna Shore (exc); *Cordella:* Sposo di provincia (exc); *Donizetti:* Alfredo il Grande (exc); Chiara e Serafina (exc); Nozze in villa (exc); Paria (exc); Zingara (exc); *L. Ricci:* Diavolo condannato (exc); *Mayr:* Fedra (exc); *Mercadante:* Amleto (exc); Gabriella di Vergy (exc); Nitocri (exc); Testa di bronzo (exc); *Meyerbeer:* Esule di Granata (exc); Margherita d'Anjou (exc); *Pacini:* Contestabile di Chesner (exc); *Rossini:* Ugo re d'Italia (exc); Zelmira (exc). (C. Daniels, L. Davies, N. Focile, E. Harrhy, M. Hill Smith, Y. Kenny, L. Kitchen, S. McCulloch, B. Mills, J. Rhys-Davies, T. Goble, D. Jones, F. Kimm, A. Mason, D. Montague, P. Spence, P. Walker, B. Ford, B. McBride, P. Nilon, I. Sharpe, I. Thompson, D. Ashman, K. M. Daymond, G. Dolton, I. Platt, J. Rawnsley, R. Smythe, J. Viera, C. Bayley, M. Glanville, A. Miles, A. Thorburn, G. Mitchell Ch, Philh, RPO/D. Parry)

Ⓒ **ORC001** (12/90)
Donizetti: Ugo, Conte di Parigi
Donizetti: Ugo, Conte di Parigi (Cpte). (M. Arthur, D. Jones, E. Harrhy, J. Price, Y. Kenny, C. du Plessis, G. Mitchell Ch, New Philh/A. Francis)

Ⓒ **ORC002** (4/93)
Offenbach—Christopher Columbus
Offenbach: Christopher Columbus (Cpte). (M. Arthur, J. Roberts, J. Peters, L. Gray, M. Hill Smith, C. du Plessis, A. Opie, Anna Dawson, A. Bregonzi, C. Harré, J. Duxbury, R. Ashe, C. Kite, K. Smales, A. Dixey, G. Mitchell Ch, LMP/A. Francis)

Ⓒ **ORC003** (9/94)
Donizetti—Gabriella di Vergy
Donizetti: Gabriella di Vergy (Cpte); Gabriella di Vergy (1826) (exc); Gabriella di Vergy (1826) (exc); Gabriella di Vergy (1826) (exc). (L. Andrew, C. du Plessis, M. Arthur, J. Tomlinson, J. Davies, J. Winfield, E. Harrhy, D. Jones, G. Mitchell Ch, RPO/A. Francis)

Ⓒ **ORC004** (9/94)
Donizetti—Ne m'oubliez pas; Arias
Donizetti: Ne m'oubliez pas (Cpte); Imelda (exc); Dom Sébastien (exc); Gianni di Parigi (exc); Roberto Devereux (exc); Diluvio universale (exc). (M. Elkins, A. Oliver, C. du Plessis, M. Elkins, G. Mitchell Ch, Philh/J. Judd)

Ⓒ **ORC005** (4/94)
Meyerbeer—Dinorah
Meyerbeer: Dinorah (Cpte). (D. Cook, C. du Plessis, A. Oliver, D. Jones, M. Hill Smith, R. Earle, I. Caley, G. Mitchell Ch, Philh/J. Judd)

Ⓒ **ORC006** (2/93)
Donizetti—Maria Padilla
Donizetti: Maria Padilla (Cpte). (L. McDonall, D. Jones, G.

Clark, C. du Plessis, R. Earle, I. Caley, R. Kennedy, J. Davies, G. Mitchell Ch, LSO/A. Francis)

① **ORC007** (8/94)
Offenbach—Robinson Crusoe
Offenbach: Robinson Crusoé (Cpte). (J. Brecknock, Y. Kenny, R. Kennedy, E. Hartle, M. Hill Smith, A. Oliver, S. Browne, A. Opie, W. Parfitt, G. Mitchell Ch, RPO/A. Francis)

① **ORC008** (5/92) ⊙ **OR008** (6/88)
Donizetti—Emilia di Liverpool
Donizetti: Emilia di Liverpool (Cpte); Eremitaggio di Liverpool (Cpte). (Y. Kenny, A. Mason, B. Mills, S. Bruscantini, G. Dolton, C. Merritt, C. Thornton-Holmes, G. Mitchell Ch, Philh/D. Parry, G. Dolton, Y. Kenny, C. Merritt, S. Bruscantini, B. Mills, A. Mason, C. Thornton-Holmes, G. Mitchell Ch, Philh/D. Parry)

① **ORC009** (7/89) ⊙ **OR009** (7/89)
Donizetti—Assedio di Calais
Donizetti: Assedio di Calais (Cpte). (C. du Plessis, D. Jones, R. Smythe, E. Harrhy, J. Treleaven, N. Bailey, N. Focile, G. Mitchell Ch, Philh/D. Parry)

① **ORC010** (9/92)
Meyerbeer—Il Crociato in Egitto
Meyerbeer: Crociato in Egitto (Cpte). (I. Platt, B. Ford, D. Montague, Y. Kenny, D. Jones, L. Kitchen, U. Benelli, G. Mitchell Ch, RPO/D. Parry)

① **ORC011** (11/94)
Mayr—Medea in Corinto
Mayr: Medea (Cpte). (J. Eaglen, Y. Kenny, B. Ford, R. Giménez, A. Miles, A. Mason, P. Nilon, N. Archer, G. Mitchell Ch, Philh/D. Parry)

① **ORC12**
Mercadante—Orazi e Curiazi
Mercadante: Orazi e Curiazi (Cpte). (N. Miricioiu, A. Michaels-Moore, M. Jerome, A. Miles, J. Rhys-Davies, P. Nilon, G. Mitchell Ch, Philh/D. Parry)

⊙ **ORH102**
A Hundred Years of Italian Opera
Mayr: Adelasia ed Aleramo (exc); Alfredo il Grande (exc); Elena (exc); Finte Rivali (exc); Fedra (exc); Cora (exc); Ginevra di Scozia (exc); Rosa bianca (exc). (N. Christie, S. Dugdale, E. Harrhy, M. Hill Smith, Y. Kenny, D. Jones, D. Montague, M. Moreno, P. Walker, P. Doghan, K. John, R. Leggate, R. Smythe, Philh/D. Parry)

① **ORR201**
19th Century Heroines-Yvonne Kenny
Nicolini: Baccanali di Roma (exc); *Meyerbeer:* Crociato in Egitto (exc); *Donizetti:* Alahor in Granata (exc); *Coccia:* Rosmonda (exc); *Portugal:* Morte di Semiramide (exc); *Carafa:* Gabriella (exc). (Y. Kenny, I. Platt, L. Kitchen, U. Benelli, D. Jones, R. Smythe, J. Meek, C. McKerracher, D. Montague, P. Doghan, G. Mitchell Ch, Philh, RPO/D. Parry)

Opus

① **9156 0931/2** (5/90)
Puccini—(La) Bohème
Puccini: Bohème (Cpte). (V. Kincses, P. Dvorský, S. Haljáková, I. Konsulov, B. Póka, D. Niemirowicz, S. Benňačka, S. Janči, V. Schrenkel, Bratislava Children's Ch, Bratislava Nat Op Chor, Bratislava RSO/O. Lenárd)

① **9156 1824** (10/89)
Dvorský sings Operatic Arias
Puccini: Tosca (exc); Madama Butterfly (exc); Bohème (exc); *Massenet:* Werther (exc); *Cilea:* Arlesiana (exc); *Gounod:* Faust (exc); *Donizetti:* Favorita (exc); *Verdi:* Rigoletto (exc); *Mascagni:* Cavalleria Rusticana (exc). (P. Dvorský, V. Kincses, S. Haljáková, I. Konsulov, M. Hajóssyová, S. Kopčák, M. Nitranová, Bratislava RSO, Czech RSO/O. Lenárd)

① **9352 1719**
Works by Patzelt and Speer
Patzelt: Castor et Pollux (Cpte); *Speer:* Musicalisch Türckischer (exc). (K. Zajíčková-Vyskočilová, J. Saparová, P. Oswald, P. Mikuláš, V. Stracenská, M. Beňačková, Musica aeterna/P. Baxa, P. Oswald)

① **9356 1928/9** (10/89)
Bellini—(La) Sonnambula
Bellini: Sonnambula (Cpte). (J. Valásková, J. Kundlák, P. Mikuláš, E. Antoličová, J. Saparová, J. Galla, V. Schrenkel, Slovak Phil Chor, Bratislava RSO/O. Lenárd)

① **9356 2047**
Romantic Operatic Duets
Bellini: Capuleti (exc); Norma (exc); *Donizetti:* Anna Bolena (exc). (O. Stapp, I. Kirilová, Košice St PO/P. Vronský)

Opus 111

① **OPS30-113/5** (11/94)
Handel—Poro, Re dell'Indie
Handel: Poro (Cpte). (G. Banditelli, R. Bertini, B. Fink, G. Lesne, S. Naglia, R. Abbondanza, Europa Galante/F. Biondi)

① **OPS30-64**
Classics of the Americas, Vol.6
Gershwin: Rhapsody in blue; Preludes; Cuban Overture; Porgy and Bess (exc). (G. Rabol, Jazzogène Big Band/J-L. Fillon)

① **OPS30-90/1** (4/94)
Traetta—Buovo d'Antona
Traetta: Buovo d'Antona (Cpte). (H. Crook, C. Trogu-Röhrich, R. Balconi, D. del Monaco, F. R. Ermolli, G. Fagotto, G. Zambon, Teatro la Fenice Orch/A. Curtis)

Orfeo

① **C005822H** (10/89)
Egk—Peer Gynt
Egk: Peer Gynt (Cpte). (R. Hermann, N. Sharp, C. Wulkopf, J. Perry, H. Hopfner, H. Hopf, K. Lövaas, H. Weber, P. Hansen, P. Lika, W. Wild, F. Lenz, Bavarian Rad Chor, Munich RO/H. Wallberg)

① **C009821A**
Famous Bass Arias
Mozart: Entführung (exc); Don Giovanni (exc); *Beethoven:* Fidelio (exc); *Lortzing:* Zar und Zimmermann (exc); Waffenschmied (exc); *Weber:* Freischütz (exc); *Wagner:* Fliegende Holländer (exc); Meistersinger (exc); *Cornelius:* Barbier von Bagdad (exc). (K. Moll, Munich RO/K. Eichhorn)

① **C023822H** (8/88)
Leoncavallo—La bohème
Leoncavallo: Bohème (Cpte). (L. Popp, B. Weikl, F. Bonisolli, A. Milcheva, A. Titus, R. Grumbach, A. Malta, N. Orth, S. Lis, J.W. Wilsing, F. Lenz, Bavarian Rad Chor, Munich RO/H. Wallberg)

① **C027823F** (6/87)
Gluck—Alceste
Gluck: Alceste (1776) (Cpte). (J. Norman, N. Gedda, T. Krause, R. Gambill, P. Lika, S. Nimsgern, B. Weikl, R. Bracht, K. Rydl, Bavarian Rad Chor, BRSO/S. Baudo)

① **C027901A**
Gluck—Alceste Excerpts
Gluck: Alceste (1776) (exc). (J. Norman, N. Gedda, S. Nimsgern, T. Krause, R. Gambill, Bavarian Rad Chor, BRSO/S. Baudo)

① **C028821A**
Famous Operatic Duets
Verdi: Otello (exc); Don Carlo (exc); Vespri Siciliani (exc); Forza del destino (exc); *Puccini:* Bohème (exc); *Ponchielli:* Gioconda (exc); *Bizet:* Pêcheurs de perles (exc). (C. Bergonzi, D. Fischer-Dieskau, BRSO/J. López-Cobos)

① **C048831A**
Kreisler: Famous Transcriptions for Violin and Piano
Kreisler: Beethoven Rondino; *Tartini:* Devil's Trill Sonata; *Mozart:* Serenade, K250 (exc); *Wieniawski:* Etudes-Caprices, Op. 18 (exc); *Brahms:* Hungarian Dances (exc); *Tchaikovsky:* Souvenirs de Hapsal, Op. 2 (exc); *Dvořák:* Slavonic Dances (exc); *C. Scott:* Pieces, Op. 47 (exc); *Albéniz:* España, Op. 165 (exc); *Falla:* Vida breve (exc). (D. Sitkovetsky, B. Canino)

① **C052832H** (12/87)
Gluck—Iphigénie en Tauride
Gluck: Iphigénie en Tauride (Cpte). (P. Lorengar, F. Bonisolli, W. Groenroos, A.J. Smith, S. Klare, A. Nowski, D. Fischer-Dieskau, Bavarian Rad Chor, BRSO/L. Gardelli)

① **C055832I** (5/91)
Mozart—Zaide
Mozart: Zaïde (Cpte). (J. Blegen, W. Hollweg, W. Schöne, T. Moser, R. Holl, W. Bellon, Salzburg Mozarteum Orch/L. Hager)

① **C057832A**
Verdi—Alzira
Verdi: Alzira (Cpte). (J-H. Rootering, R. Bruson, D. George, F. Araiza, D. Bonilla, I. Cotrubas, S. Lis, A. Ionita, Bavarian Rad Chor, Munich RO/L. Gardelli)

① **C062833F**
Wagner—Die Feen
Wagner: Feen (Cpte). (L.E. Gray, K. Lövaas, K. Laki, John Alexander, J. Anderson, R. Hermann, K. Moll, J-H. Rootering, C. Studer, R. Bracht, Bavarian Rad Chor, BRSO/W. Sawallisch)

① **C063841A**
Mozart—Don Giovanni arr for Wind Ensemble
Mozart: Don Giovanni (exc). (Mozart Wind Ens)

① **C071831A**
Stravinsky—Oedipus Rex
Stravinsky: Oedipus rex (Cpte). (T. Moser, J. Norman, S. Nimsgern, R. Bracht, A. Ionita, M. Piccoli, Bavarian Rad Male Chor, BRSO/Colin Davis)

① **C072831A**
The Art of the Coloratura
Arditi: Bacio; *Glière:* Soprano Concerto; *Rachmaninov:* Songs, Op.4 (exc); *Proch:* Air and Variations; *J. Strauss II:* Frühlingsstimmen, Op. 410; *Alabiev:* Nightingale; *Adam:* Toréador (exc); *Dell' Acqua:* Villanelle; *Delibes:* Filles de Cadiz. (E. Gruberová, Stuttgart RSO/K. Eichhorn)

① **C077831A**
Bernd Weikl sings Operetta
Millöcker: Gasparone (exc); *O. Straus:* Walzertraum (exc); *Eysler:* Bruder Straubinger (exc); *Kálmán:* Gräfin Mariza (exc); *Zeller:* Vogelhändler (exc); *Lincke:* Im Reiche des Indra (exc); *Stolz:* Wien wird schön erst bei Nacht; *Lehár:* Eva (exc); *Berté:* Dreimäderlhaus (exc); *Kreutzer:* Verschwender (exc); *J. Strauss II:* Nacht in Venedig (exc); Zigeunerbaron (exc); Tänzerin Fanny Elssler (exc); *Abraham:* Viktoria und ihr Husar (exc); *Lehár:* Graf von Luxemburg (exc). (B. Weikl, Austrian RSO/K. Eichhorn)

① **C081841A** (11/86)
Grace Bumbry: Famous Opera Arias
Verdi: Forza del destino (exc); Trovatore (exc); *Cilea:* Adriana Lecouvreur (exc); *Catalani:* Wally (exc); *Massenet:* Cid (exc); *Ponchielli:* Gioconda (exc); *G. Charpentier:* Louise (exc); *Cherubini:* Medea (exc); *Gounod:* Sapho (exc); *Gluck:* Alceste (1776) (exc). (G. Bumbry, Stuttgart RSO/S. Soltesz)

① **C085843F** (8/89)
Mozart—La finta semplice
Mozart: Finta semplice (Cpte). (H. Donath, A. Rolfe Johnson, T. Berganza, R. Holl, J-R. Ihloff, T. Moser, R. Lloyd, Salzburg Mozarteum Orch/L. Hager)

① **C092841A**
Mozart—The Magic Flute arr for Wind Ens
Mozart: Zauberflöte (exc). (Munich Wind Ens)

① **C096841A** (11/86)
Famous Opera Arias
Handel: Giulio Cesare (exc); *Gluck:* Orfeo ed Euridice (exc); *Mozart:* Clemenza di Tito (exc); *Bellini:* Capuleti (exc); *Tchaikovsky:* Maid of Orleans (exc); *Bizet:* Carmen (exc); *Saint-Saëns:* Samson et Dalila (exc); *Massenet:* Werther (exc); *Wagner:* Götterdämmerung (exc). (B. Fassbaender, Stuttgart RSO/H. Graf)

① **C101841A** (11/86)
Famous Operatic Arias
Mozart: Lucio Silla (exc); *R. Strauss:* Ariadne auf Naxos (exc); *Bellini:* Sonnambula (exc); *Cherubini:* Medea (exc); *A. Thomas:* Mignon (exc). (E. Gruberová, Munich RO/L. Gardelli)

① **C102842H** (1/90)
Einem—Dantons Tod
Einem: Dantons Tod (Cpte). (T. Adam, W. Hollweg, W. Gahmlich, H. Hiestermann, K. Laki, H. Berger-Tuna, K. Rydl, F. Wyzner, C. Doig, K. Terkal, A. Muff, I. Mayr, G. Sima, M. Lipovšek, Austrian Rad Chor, Austrian RSO/L. Zagrosek)

① **C105842H** (6/87)
Verdi—Oberto
Verdi: Oberto (Cpte). (R. Baldani, G. Dimitrova, A. Browner, C. Bergonzi, R. Panerai, Bavarian Rad Chor, Munich RO/L. Gardelli)

① **C106841A** (11/86)
Famous Opera Arias
Mozart: Così fan tutte (exc); *Weber:* Freischütz (exc); *Wagner:* Tannhäuser (exc); *R. Strauss:* Ariadne auf Naxos (exc); Daphne (exc); *Puccini:* Manon Lescaut (exc); Turandot (exc); *Giordano:* Andrea Chénier (exc); *Verdi:* Ballo in maschera (exc); Ernani (exc). (A. Tomowa-Sintow, Munich RO/P. Sommer)

① **C119841A** (11/86)
Lucia Aliberti: Famous Opera Arias
Donizetti: Lucia di Lammermoor (exc); Linda di Chamounix (exc); Lucrezia Borgia (exc); Don Pasquale (exc); *Bellini:* Sonnambula (exc); Puritani (exc); Pirata (exc). (L. Aliberti, Munich RO/L. Gardelli)

① **C124862H** (5/92)
Suder—Kleider machen Leute
Suder: Kleider machen Leute (Cpte). (K. König, Morris Morgan, P. Coburn, W. Probst, W. Plate, S. Klare, J-H.

Rootering, K. Geber, B. Nachbaur, B. Lindner, D. Pauli, Bavarian Rad Chor, Bamberg SO/U. Mund)

Ⓓ **C126901A** (5/91)
Salonmusik
J. Gilbert: Puppchen (exc); *Ketèlbey:* In a Persian Market; *Lincke:* Geburtstagsstädchen; *Schmalstich:* Sehnsucht; *Fetrás:* Mondnacht auf der Alster; *Lehár:* Blaue Mazur (exc); *E. Strauss:* Helenen-Quadrille; *Gounod:* Sérénade; *J. Strauss II:* Wein, Weib und Gesang; *Tchaikovsky:* Swan Lake Suite (exc); *Leoncavallo:* Mattinata; *Fučík:* Florentiner, Op. 214. (Berlin Ens)

Ⓓ **C131851A**
Virtuoso cello arrangements
Offenbach: Harmonies des bois; Larmes de Jacqueline; Harmonie du soir; Deux âmes au ciel; *Françaix:* Rondino staccato; Sérénade; Mouvement perpétuel; Berceuse; *Popper:* Tarantella, Op. 33; *F. Schubert II:* Bagatelles, Op. 13 (exc); *Fauré:* Songs, Op. 7 (exc); *Paganini:* Moses in Egypt Variations; *Wagner:* Tannhäuser (exc); *Sarasate:* Danzas españolas (exc). (W. Thomas, Munich CO/H. Stadlmair)

Ⓓ **C135872H** (3/88)
Gluck—La Corona & La Danza
Gluck: Corona (Cpte); Danza (Cpte). (A. Słowakiewicz, H. Górzyńska, L. Juranek, B. Nowicka, E. Ignatowicz, K. Myrlak, Bavarian Rad Chor, Warsaw Chbr Op Orch/T. Bugaj)

Ⓓ **C137862H** (11/87)
Spontini—Olympia
Spontini: Olimpie (Cpte). (J. Varady, S. Toczyska, Ferruccio Tagliavini, D. Fischer-Dieskau, G. Fortune, J. Becker, Berlin RIAS Chbr Ch, Berlin Deutsche Op Chor, Berlin RSO/G. Albrecht)

Ⓓ **C161871A**
Famous Overtures
Wagner: Meistersinger (exc); *Verdi:* Forza del destino (exc); *Mozart:* Zauberflöte (exc); *Beethoven:* Leonore (exc); *Brahms:* Tragic Overture. (Bavarian St Orch/W. Sawallisch)

Ⓓ **C162871A** (9/88)
Zimmermann—Weisse Rose
U. Zimmermann: Weisse Rose (Cpte). (G. Fontana, L-M. Harder, Inst. Ens/U. Zimmermann)

Ⓓ **C168881A**
Pfitzner: Overtures and Entr'actes
Pfitzner: Palestrina (exc); Käthchen von Heilbronn (exc); Rose vom Liebesgarten (exc). (BRSO/W. Sawallisch)

Ⓓ **C174881A** (4/89)
Bizet—Djamileh
Bizet: Djamileh (Cpte). (L. Popp, F. Bonisolli, J-P. Lafont, J. Pineau, Bavarian Rad Chor, Munich RO/L. Gardelli)

Ⓓ **C178891A** (1/90)
Gluck—I Cinesi
Gluck: Cinesi (Cpte). (K. Erickson, A. Milcheva, M. Schiml, T. Moser, Munich RO/L. Gardelli)

Ⓓ **C179891A** (6/90)
Marjana Lipovšek sings Famous Opera Arias
Gluck: Orfeo ed Euridice (exc); *Handel:* Serse (exc); *Mozart:* Clemenza di Tito (exc); Così fan tutte (exc); *Verdi:* Don Carlo (exc); Trovatore (exc); *Bizet:* Carmen (exc); *Massenet:* Werther (exc); *Saint-Saëns:* Samson et Dalila (exc). (M. Lipovšek, Munich RO/G. Patanè)

Ⓓ **C180891A** (9/90)
Popular Czech Music
Smetana: Bartered bride (exc); Our lasses, T49; March, B58; *Fibich:* At twilight (exc); *Dvořák:* Polonaise, B100; Festival march; Kate and the Devil (exc); *Blodek:* In the well (exc); *Janáček:* Lachian Dances (exc); *Nedbal:* Valse triste; Polenblut (exc); *Suk:* Filled with longing; *Kovařovic:* Miners' Polka; *Martinů:* Bouquet (exc). (Czech PO/V. Neumann)

Ⓓ **C186951**
Verdi—Heroines, Vol. 1
Verdi: Nabucco (exc); Trovatore (exc); Traviata (exc); Ballo in maschera (exc); Forza del destino (exc). (J. Varady, L. Odinius, Bavarian St Orch/D. Fischer-Dieskau)

Ⓓ **C189891A**
Music for Two Guitars
Rodrigo: Concierto de Aranjuez; *Falla:* Vida breve (exc); *Albéniz:* Cantos de España (exc); Suite española 1 (exc); *Lauro:* Valses venezolanos (1968) (exc); *Granados:* Valses poéticos; *Piazzolla:* Tango Suite. (W. Feybli, D. Erni)

Ⓓ **C214902H** (4/91)
Gazzaniga: Don Giovanni
Gazzaniga: Don Giovanni (Cpte). (J. Aler, E. Steinsky, P. Coburn, M. Kinzel, G. von Kannen, R. Swensen, J. Kaufman, J-L. Chaignaud, A. Scharinger, A. Rosner, Bavarian Rad Chor, Munich RO/S. Soltesz)

Ⓓ **C223911A**
Fagotto Concertante
Mozart: Bassoon Concerto, K191; *M. Haydn:* Symphony, MH133 (exc); *Villa-Lobos:* Ciranda das sete notas; *Françaix:* Bassoon Divertissement; *Gershwin:* Porgy and Bess Suite. (M. Turkovic, Stuttgart CO/M. Sieghart)

Ⓓ **C236901A**
Music of the Strauss Family
J. Strauss II: Fledermaus (exc); Auf der Jagd, Op. 373; Blauen Donau, Op. 314; Frühlingsstimmen, Op. 410; Annen-Polka, Op. 117; G'schichten aus dem Wienerwald, Op. 325; Kaiser, Op. 437; Radetzky March; *Jos Strauss:* Jokey; Auf Ferienreisen; Plappermäulchen; Feuerfest!. (Vienna SO/W. Sawallisch)

Ⓓ **C237901A**
Wagner—Orchestral and Vocal works
Wagner: Wesendonk Lieder; Liebesverbot (exc); Götterdämmerung (exc). (M. Lipovšek, Vienna SO/G. Prêtre)

Ⓓ **C240912H** (11/91)
Spohr—Jessonda
Spohr: Jessonda (Cpte). (J. Varady, R. Behle, K. Moll, T. Moser, D. Fischer-Dieskau, P. Haage, P. Galliard, C. Meyer-Esche, Hamburg St Op Chor, Hamburg PO/G. Albrecht)

Ⓓ **C242912H** (12/92)
Gluck—La rencontre imprévue
Gluck: Rencontre imprévue (Cpte). (J. Kaufman, I. Vermillion, A. Stumphius, A-M. Rodde, R. Gambill, C.H. Ahnsjö, U. Ress, M. Walker, J-H. Rootering, P. Orecchia, Munich RO/L. Hager)

Ⓓ **C243913F** (10/92)
Mozart—Così fan tutte
Mozart: Così fan tutte (Cpte). (A.C. Antonacci, M. Bacelli, L. Cherici, R. Decker, A. Dohmen, S. Bruscantini, Marchigiano V. Bellini Lyric Chor, Marchigiano PO/G. Kuhn)

Ⓓ **C247911A**
Works for Brass Ensemble
Mozart: Nozze di Figaro (exc); *Ponchielli:* Gioconda (exc); *Verdi:* Traviata (exc); *Puccini:* Bohème (exc); *Liszt:* Hungarian Rhapsodies, S244 (exc); *Gershwin:* Porgy and Bess (exc); *Bernstein:* West Side Story (exc); *Roblee:* In a big band mood; Dixie Dancing. (Munich Brass)

Ⓓ **C256922H** (7/93)
Spontini—La Vestale
Spontini: Vestale (Cpte). (R. Plowright, F. Araiza, P. Lefebre, G. Pasino, A. Cauli, F. de Grandis, Bavarian Rad Chor, Munich RSO/G. Kuhn)

Ⓓ **C261921A**
Maria Dragoni sings Famous Opera Arias
B. Marcello: Didone (exc); *Jommelli:* Didone Abbandonata (exc); *Mozart:* Don Giovanni (exc); Entführung (exc); *Puccini:* Madama Butterfly (exc); Tosca (exc); *Rossini:* Semiramide (exc); *Verdi:* Don Carlo (exc); Traviata (exc); Trovatore (exc). (M. Dragoni, Munich RSO/G. Kuhn)

Ⓓ **C262932H** (9/95)
Haydn—L'Anima del Filosofo (Orfeo ed Euridice)
Haydn: Anima del filosofo (Cpte). (R. Swensen, H. Donath, S. Greenberg, T. Quasthoff, P. Hansen, A. Suzuki, Bavarian Rad Chor, Munich RO/L. Hager)

Ⓓ **C288921A**
Beethoven—Egmont-Incidental Music, Op 84.
Beethoven: Egmont (Cpte); Leonore (exc). (R. Ziesak, U. Tukur, Hamburg PO/G. Albrecht)

Ⓓ **C289932H** (1/94)
Schumann—Genoveva
Schumann: Genoveva (Cpte). (J. Faulkner, K. Lewis, H. Stamm, A. Titus, R. Behle, C. Schultz, J. Tilli, Hamburg St Op Chor, Hamburg PO/G. Albrecht)

Ⓓ **C291931A**
Soirée dansante
J. Strauss I: Fortuna-Galopp, Op. 69; *J. Strauss II:* Cagliostro in Wien (exc); Tritsch-Tratsch; Morgenblätter, Op. 279; Persischer Marsch; Accelerationen, Op. 234; Wiener Blut; *Jos Strauss:* Emanzipierte; Sphärenklänge; Lock-Polka; *E. Strauss:* Auf und davon!. (Vienna SO Strauss Ens/J. Wildner)

Ⓓ **C312941A**
Wagner—Cantatas and Overtures
Wagner: Neujahrs-Kantate; Nicolai Volkshymne; Faust Overture; Descendons, descendons; Tag erscheint; An Webers Grabe; Rienzi (exc). (F. Wagner, Bamberg Sym Chor, Bamberg SO/K. A. Rickenbacher)

Ⓓ **C323941A** (5/95)
Puccini—Famous Opera Arias
Puccini: Rondine (exc); Bohème (exc); Gianni Schicchi (exc); Manon Lescaut (exc); Suor Angelica (exc); Tosca (exc); Madama Butterfly (exc); Turandot (exc). (J. Varady, Berlin RSO/M. Viotti)

Ⓓ **C335931A**
Salzburg Festival highlights (1956-85)
Mozart: Nozze di Figaro (exc); Nozze di Figaro (exc); *R. Strauss:* Arabella (exc); *Verdi:* Macbeth (exc); *Mozart:* Così fan tutte (exc); *Messiaen:* Saint François d'Assise (exc). (E. Schwarzkopf, I. Seefried, L. della Casa, G. Bumbry, P. Schreier, E. Kunz, H. Prey, D. Fischer-Dieskau, O. Edelmann, VPO, Austrian RSO/K. Böhm/J. Keilberth/W. Sawallisch/L. Zagrosek)

Ⓓ **C342932I** (9/94)
R. Strauss—Salome
R. Strauss: Salome (Cpte). (I. Borkh, H. Hotter, M. Lorenz, I. Barth, L. Fehenberger, K. Sabo, M. Proebstl, A. Peter, A. Keil, F. Friedrich, C. Hoppe, G. Ebeling, Bavarian St Orch/J. Keilberth)

Ⓓ **C343932I** (9/94)
Egk—Die Verlobung in San Domingo
Egk: Verlobung in San Domingo (Cpte). (E. Lear, M. Bence, H.G. Nöcker, H. Nasseri, F. Wunderlich, M. Yahia, Richard Holm, K.C. Kohn, Bavarian St Orch/W. Egk)

Ⓓ **C344932I**
Verdi—La Traviata
Verdi: Traviata (Cpte). (T. Stratas, F. Wunderlich, H. Prey, M.L. Gilles, B. Fassbaender, F. Lenz, J. Knapp, H.B. Ernst, G. Missenhardt, H. Weber, Bavarian St Op Chor, Bavarian St Orch/G. Patanè)

Ⓓ **C351943D** (3/95)
Handel—Giulio Cesare
Handel: Giulio Cesare (Cpte). (W. Berry, L. Popp, C. Ludwig, F. Wunderlich, K.C. Kohn, H.G. Nöcker, H.B. Ernst, M. Proebstl, Stuttgart Rad Chor, Munich PO/F. Leitner)

Ⓓ **C354942I** (2/95)
Janáček—The Excursions of Mr Brouček.
Janáček: Excursions of Mr Brouček (Cpte). (L. Fehenberger, F. Wunderlich, K. Böhme, W. Lipp, K. Engen, A. Fahberg, L. Benningsen, P. Kuen, K. Ostertag, Bavarian St Orch, Bavarian St Op Chor/J. Keilberth)

Ⓓ **C355943D** (5/95)
Wagner—Tristan und Isolde
Wagner: Tristan und Isolde (Cpte). (G. Treptow, H. Braun, M. Klose, F. Frantz, P. Schoeffler, A. Peter, P. Kuen, F.R. Bender, Bavarian St Op Chor, Bavarian St Orch/H. Knappertsbusch)

Ⓓ **C356944L**
Wagner—Götterdämmerung
Wagner: Götterdämmerung (Cpte). (B. Nilsson, B. Aldenhoff, G. Frick, O. Kraus, H. Uhde, Leonie Rysanek, I. Malaniuk, G. Sommerschuh, E. Lindermeier, R. Michaelis, I. Barth, H. Töpper, M. Schech, Bavarian St Op Chor, Bavarian St Orch/H. Knappertsbusch)

Ⓓ **C357942I** (2/95)
Mozart—Così fan tutte
Mozart: Così fan tutte (Cpte). (I. Seefried, D. Hermann, L. Otto, A. Dermota, E. Kunz, P. Schoeffler, Vienna St Op Chor, VPO/K. Böhm)

Ⓓ **C363941B** (6/95)
Lucia Popp - Lieder Recital
Prokofiev: Russian Folksongs, Op. 104 (exc); *Kodály:* Hungarian Folk Music (exc); *Dvořák:* In Folk Tone, B146; *Mahler:* Lieder und Gesänge (exc); *Brahms:* Deutsche Volkslieder (exc); Lieder, Op.14 (exc); Lieder, Op.7 (exc); *Mozart:* Oiseaux, si tous les ans, K307; *Rachmaninov:* Songs, Op.21 (exc); *Puccini:* Gianni Schicchi (exc); *Dvořák:* Rusalka (exc); *Lehár:* Lustige Witwe (exc). (L. Popp, G. Parsons)

Ⓓ **C364941B** (3/95)
Schoek—Penthesilea
Schoeck: Penthesilea (Cpte). (H. Dernesch, J. Marsh, M. Gessendorf, M. Lipovšek, G. Sima, T. Adam, H. Hiestermann, P. Weber, Austrian Rad Chor, Austrian RSO/G. Albrecht)

Ⓓ **C365941A**
Christa Ludwig - Salzburg Festival highlights
R. Strauss: Ariadne auf Naxos (exc); *Mozart:* Nozze di Figaro (exc); Così fan tutte (exc); *Gluck:* Iphigénie en Aulide (exc); *R. Strauss:* Ariadne auf Naxos (exc); *Beethoven:* Fidelio (exc); *R. Strauss:* Rosenkavalier (exc); Frau ohne Schatten (exc). (C. Ludwig, P. Schoeffler, I. Seefried, R. Panerai, J. King, E. Mathis, F. Crass, T. Troyanos, W. Berry, VPO/K. Böhm)

Ⓓ **C391952I**
Gluck—Orfeo ed Euridice
Gluck: Orfeo ed Euridice (Cpte). (D. Fischer-Dieskau, E. Söderström, R-M. Pütz, Cologne Rad Chor, Cappella Coloniensis/F. Leitner)

Ⓓ **C392952I**
Mozart—Die Entführung aus dem Serail
Mozart: Entführung (Cpte). (A. Rothenberger, R. Grist, F. Wunderlich, G. Unger, F. Corena, M. Heltau, Vienna St Op Chor, VPO/Z. Mehta)

Ⓓ **C393952I**
Von Einem—Der Prozess
Einem: Prozess (Cpte). (M. Lorenz, P. Klein, E. Koréh, E. Majkut, P. Batic, A. Poell, L. Szemere, L. Hofmann, O. Czerwenka, W. Berry, A. Pernerstorfer, L. della Casa, Luise Leitner, Vienna St Op Chor, VPO/K. Böhm)

Ⓓ **C394101B**
Great Mozart Singers Series, Vol. 1
Mozart: Nozze di Figaro (exc); Nozze di Figaro (exc); Nozze di Figaro (exc); Don Giovanni (exc); Don Giovanni (exc); Don Giovanni (exc); Don Giovanni (exc); Entführung (exc); Zauberflöte (exc); Don Giovanni (exc); Nozze di Figaro (exc); Nozze di Figaro (exc); Nozze di Figaro (exc). (R. Mayr, M. Gerhart, H. Duhan, E. Schumann, R. Tauber, M. Perras, H. Roswaenge, J. Novotná, W. Domgraf-Fassbaender, A. Kipnis, E. Pinza, M. Bokor, L. Helletsgruber, E. Rethberg, M. Cebotari, H. Hotter, H. Braun, I. Beilke, E. Kunz, G. Sommerschuh, R. Fischer, J. Witt, G. Neidlinger, orch, VPO, Philh/A. Toscanini/B. Walter/K. Alwin/J. Krips/C. Krauss/G.W. Byng/W. Goehr)

Ⓓ **C394201B**
Great Mozart Singers Series, Vol. 2
Mozart: Zauberflöte (exc); Zauberflöte (exc); Nozze di Figaro (exc); Don Giovanni (exc); Entführung (exc); Zauberflöte (exc); Così fan tutte (exc); Così fan tutte (exc); Nozze di Figaro (exc); Zauberflöte (exc); Don Giovanni (exc). (W. Lipp, E. Kunz, H. Gueden, I. Seefried, P. Schoeffler, E. Schwarzkopf, C. Siepi, A. Dermota, E. Köth, R. Schock, E. Grümmer, C. Ludwig, D. Fischer-Dieskau, L. della Casa, W. Berry, L. Simoneau, K. Dönch, E. Waechter, VPO/W. Furtwängler/G. Szell/G. Solti/K. Böhm/H. von Karajan)

Ⓓ **C394301B**
Great Mozart Singers Series, Vol. 3
Mozart: Entführung (exc); Nozze di Figaro (exc); Nozze di Figaro (exc); Don Giovanni (exc); Così fan tutte (exc); Così fan tutte (exc); Idomeneo (exc); Idomeneo (exc); Don Giovanni (exc); Zauberflöte (exc); Così fan tutte (exc). (F. Wunderlich, S. Jurinac, E. Lear, G. Sciutti, W. Berry, M. Freni, N. Ghiaurov, A. Rothenberger, G. Janowitz, B. Fassbaender, H. Donath, P. Schreier, J. Varady, E. Mathis, E. Gruberová, I. Cotrubas, C. Boesch, E. Tappy, M. Talvela, M. Marshall, A. Baltsa, K. Battle, F. Araiza, J. Morris, J. Van Dam, VPO/I. Kertész/H. Wallberg/K. Böhm/H. von Karajan/S. Ozawa/James Levine/R. Muti)

Ⓓ **C394401B**
Great Mozart Singers Series, Vol. 4
Mozart: Per pietà, non ricercate, K420; Nehmt meinen Dank, K383; Misera! dove son, K369; Così dunque tradisci, K432; Rè pastore (exc); Voi avete un cor fedele, K217; Bacio di mano, K541; Vorrei spiegarvi, K418; No, no, che non sei capace, K419; Misero, o sogno, K431; Basta, vincesti, K486a; Mentre ti lascio, K513. (L. Simoneau, E. Köth, E. Mathis, G. Tozzi, H. Gueden, G. Sciutti, G. Evans, R. Grist, I. Hallstein, P. Schreier, I. Cotrubas, J. Van Dam, Camerata Academica/B. Paumgartner)

Ⓓ **C394501B**
Great Mozart Singers Series, Vol. 5
Mozart: Alcandro, lo confesso, K512; Exsultate, jubilate, K165; Ombra felice, K255; Vado, ma dove?, K583; Bella mia fiamma, K528; Alma grande e nobil core, K578; Si mostra la sorte, K209; A questo seno, K374; Per pietà, non ricercate, K420; Idomeneo (exc). (K. Moll, A. Auger, B. Fassbaender, H. Donath, J. Varady, L. Popp, F. Araiza, A. Murray, G. Winbergh, M. Marshall, Salzburg Mozarteum Orch/W. Weller/L. Hager/G. Wimberger/T. Guschlbauer/R. Weikert)

Ⓓ **C395951B**
Dvořák—Violin Concerto; Symphony No. 9
Dvořák: Violin Concerto; Symphony 9; *Smetana:* Bartered Bride (exc). (J. Suk, Czech PO/K. Ančerl)

Ⓓ **C407952I**
Orff—Antigonae
Orff: Antigonae (Cpte). (C. Goltz, I. Barth, H. Uhde, P. Kuen, K. Ostertag, E. Haefliger, K. Böhme, M. Schech, B. Kusche, Bavarian St Op Chor, Bavarian St Orch/G. Solti)

Ottavo

Ⓓ **OTRC48710**
Spanish Dances
Falla: Vida breve (exc); Sombrero de tres picos Suites (exc); *Albéniz:* España, Op. 165 (exc); Suite española 1 (exc); Cantos de España (exc); *Rodrigo:* Tonadilla; *Granados:* Danzas españolas (exc). (R. de Haan, E. Westerhof)

Ⓓ **OTRC79239**
Segovia Guitar Quartet - Carmen
Bizet: Carmen Suites; Arlésienne Suites (exc). (Segovia Gtr Qt)

Partridge

Ⓓ **Part1118-2**
Arion Ensemble Recital
Purcell: Fairy Queen, Z629 (exc); *Rossini:* Sonate a quattro (exc); *Dvořák:* Waltzes; *Grieg:* Nordic Melodies, Op. 63. (Arion Ens/A. Lascae)

Ⓓ **Part1132-2**
Schubert—Lieder
Schubert: Hirt auf dem Felsen, D965; Verschworenen (exc); Offertory, D136 (exc); König in Thule, D367; Gretchen am Spinnrade, D118; Gretchen's Bitte, D564; Impromptus (exc); An mein Klavier, D342; Seligkeit, D433; Schwestergruss, D762; Einsame, D800; Junge Nonne, D828. (D. Aalbers, F. van den Brink, S. Hoogland)

Paula

Ⓓ **PACD56** (12/90)
Nielsen: Songs
Nielsen: Songs, FS12; Songs, FS18 (exc); Strophic Songs, FS42 (exc); Ballad of the Bear, FS109; Springtime in Funen (exc); Maskarade (exc); Tove (exc); Danish Songs (exc); Songs and Verses, FS14 (exc); Songbook, FS125 (exc); Little Danish Songs, FS114 (exc); Merchant's Committee Cantata (exc); Hymns and sacred songs (exc). (J. Klint, R. Bevan)

Pavane

Ⓓ **ADW7158** (5/93)
Rossini—Il Signor Bruschino
Rossini: Signor Bruschino (Cpte). (J. Mahler, J. Wolański, A. Słowakiewicz, K. Myrlak, D. Niemirowicz, H. Górzyńska, K. Moleda, B. Jaszkowski, Warsaw Chbr Op Orch/J. Kaspszyk)

Ⓓ **ADW7236/7** (11/91)
Mozart—Apollo et Hyacinthus
Mozart: Apollo et Hyacinthus (Cpte). (C. Günther, S. Pratschske, M. Schäfer, C. Fliegner, P. Cieslewicz, Nice Baroque Ens/G. Schmidt-Gaden)

Ⓓ **ADW7277**
Prokofiev/Ravel/Schumann—Piano Works
Schumann: Arabeske; *Ravel:* Gaspard de la Nuit; *Prokofiev:* Piano Sonata 8; March and Scherzo (exc); *Gluck:* Orfeo ed Euridice (exc). (E. Moguilevsky)

Ⓓ **ADW7289**
Mozart—Opera Arias; Exsultate, jubilate
Mozart: Zauberflöte (exc); Entführung (exc); Così fan tutte (exc); Exsultate jubilate, K165. (A. Winska, Warsaw PO/W. Michniewski)

Pearl

Ⓓ **EVC1(1)** (12/90)
The Caruso Edition, Vol.1 (pt 1)
Franchetti: Germania (exc); *Verdi:* Rigoletto (exc); Aida (exc); *Massenet:* Manon (exc); *Donizetti:* Elisir d'amore (exc); *Boito:* Mefistofele (exc); *Puccini:* Tosca (exc); *Mascagni:* Iris (exc); *Giordano:* Fedora (exc); *Ponchielli:* Gioconda (exc); *Leoncavallo:* Pagliacci (exc); *Mascagni:* Cavalleria rusticana (exc); *Denza:* Non t'amo più; *Tosti:* Mia canzone; *Cilea:* Adriana Lecouvreur (exc); *Zardo:* Luna fedel; *Trimarchi:* Bacio ancora; *Zardo:* Luna fedel; *Donizetti:* Elisir d'amore (exc); *Puccini:* Tosca (exc); *Franchetti:* Germania (exc); *Verdi:* Rigoletto (exc); *Mascagni:* Cavalleria rusticana (exc); *Pini-Corsi:* Tu non mi vuoi più ben; *Puccini:* Tosca (exc); *Meyerbeer:* Huguenots (exc); *Verdi:* Rigoletto (exc); *Donizetti:* Elisir d'amore (exc); *Verdi:* Aida (exc); *Puccini:* Tosca (exc); *Mascagni:* Cavalleria rusticana (exc); *Leoncavallo:* Pagliacci (exc); *Massenet:* Manon (exc); *Leoncavallo:* Mattinata; *Bizet:* Pêcheurs de perles (exc); *Donizetti:* Don Pasquale (exc); *Bizet:* Carmen (exc); *Meyerbeer:* Huguenots (exc); *Ponchielli:* Gioconda (exc); *Mascagni:* Cavalleria rusticana (exc). (E. Caruso, anon, S. Cottone, U. Giordano, F. Cilea, R. Leoncavallo)

Ⓓ **EVC1(2)** (12/90)
The Caruso Edition, Vol.1 (pt 2)
Flotow: Martha (exc); *Puccini:* Bohème (exc); *Gounod:* Faust (exc); *Verdi:* Trovatore (exc); *Donizetti:* Favorita (exc); *Verdi:* Forza del destino (exc); Aida (exc); *Barthélemy:* Triste ritorno; *Tosti:* Ideale; *Meyerbeer:* Africaine (exc); *Verdi:* Rigoletto (exc); *Puccini:* Bohème (exc); *Giordano:* Andrea Chénier (exc); *Leoncavallo:* Pagliacci (exc); *Puccini:* Bohème (exc); *Bizet:* Pêcheurs de perles (exc); *Donizetti:* Dom Sébastien (exc); *Barthélemy:* Adorables tourments; *Donizetti:* Lucia di Lammermoor (exc); *Verdi:* Rigoletto (exc); *Puccini:* Bohème (exc); Madama Butterfly (exc). (E. Caruso, A. Scotti, B. Abott, L. Homer, N. Melba, M. Ancona, M. Sembrich, G. Severina, F. Daddi, M. Journet, G. Farrar, G. Ciaparelli-Viafora, orch/W.B. Rogers)

Ⓓ **EVC2** (3/91)
The Caruso Edition, Vol.2—1908-12
Buzzi-Peccia: Lolita; *Verdi:* Rigoletto (exc); Trovatore (exc); Aida (exc); *Tosti:* Pour un baiser; *Nutile:* Mamma mia, che vo' sapè; *Verdi:* Forza del destino (exc); Aida (exc); Trovatore (exc); *Puccini:* Tosca (exc); *Goldmark:* Königin von Saba (exc); *Bizet:* Carmen (exc); Carmen (exc); *Meyerbeer:* Huguenots (exc); *Verdi:* Trovatore (exc); Trovatore (exc); Aida (exc); Otello (exc); *Flotow:* Martha (exc); *Gounod:* Faust (exc); Faust (exc); Faust (exc); Faust (exc); *Franchetti:* Germania (exc); *Puccini:* Madama Butterfly (exc); *Ponchielli:* Gioconda (exc); *Leoncavallo:* Pagliacci (exc); *Mascagni:* Cavalleria rusticana (exc); *Tosti:* Addio; *Geehl:* For you alone; *Verdi:* Ballo in maschera (exc); Forza del destino (exc); Aida (exc); *Leoncavallo:* Bohème (exc); *Donizetti:* Elisir d'amore (exc); *Massenet:* Manon (exc); *Gomes:* Schiavo (exc); *A. Mascheroni:* Eternamente; *Cardillo:* Core 'ngrato; *De Curtis:* Canta pe'me; *C. G. Gardner:* Love is mine; *Flotow:* Martha (exc). (E. Caruso, L. Homer, J. Gadski, F. Alda, M. Journet, G. Farrar, G. Gilibert, A. Scotti, P. Amato, J. Jacoby, NY Met Op Chor, orch)

Ⓓ **EVC3(1)** (10/91)
The Caruso Edition, Vol.3 (pt 1)
Faure: Crucifix; *Verdi:* Lombardi (exc); *Crescenzo:* Tarantella sincera; *Donizetti:* Lucia di Lammermoor (exc); *Rossini:* Soirées musicales (exc); *Verdi:* Rigoletto (exc); *Caruso:* Dreams of Long Ago; *Sullivan:* Lost Chord; *Hardelot:* Because; *Granier:* Hosanna; *Massenet:* Manon (exc); *Puccini:* Bohème (exc); *Verdi:* Don Carlo (exc); Trovatore (exc); *Tchaikovsky:* Songs, Op. 38 (exc); *Verdi:* Rigoletto (exc); *Bizet:* Agnus Dei; *Puccini:* Manon Lescaut (exc); *Kahn:* Ave Maria; *Massenet:* Élégie; *Leoncavallo:* Lasciati amar; *Crescenzo:* Guardanno 'a luna; *O'Hara:* Your eyes have told me; *Cottrau:* Fenesta che lucive; *Rossini:* Stabat Mater (exc); *Faure:* Rameaux; *Mascagni:* Cavalleria rusticana (exc); *Verdi:* Otello (exc); *Tchaikovsky:* Songs, Op. 38 (exc); *Ricciardi:* Amor mio; *V. Valente:* Manella mia; *C. G. Gardner:* Trusting Eyes; *Ronald:* Sérénade espagnole; *Tosti:* Parted!; *Verdi:* Ballo in maschera (exc); *Alvarez:* Partida; *Chapí:* Milagro de la Virgen (exc); *Verdi:* Traviata (exc); *Gomes:* Guarany (exc); *Szulc:* Hantise d'amour; *Bizet:* Carmen (exc). (E. Caruso, M. Journet, F. Alda, L. Tetrazzini, J. Jacoby, A. Bada, P. Amato, G. Farrar, A. Scotti, E. Schumann-Heink, T. Ruffo, F. Hempel, L. Rothier, A. de Segurola, M. Duchêne, A. Gluck, E. Destinn, NY Met Op Chor, NY Met Op Orch, orch/W.B. Rogers, G. Scognamiglio/G. Scognamiglio, M. Elman, P. Kahn)

Ⓓ **EVC3(2)** (10/91)
The Caruso Edition, Vol.3 (pt 2)
Tosti: Mia Canzone; *Ciociano:* Cielo turchino; *Pennino:* Pecchè; *Verdi:* Requiem (exc); *Donizetti:* Duca d'Alba (exc); *Denza:* Si vous l'aviez compris; *Leoncavallo:* Sérénade française; *Franck:* Procession; *Massenet:* Cid (exc); *Tosti:* Luna d'estate; *Di Capua:* 'O sole mio; *Gounod:* Reine de Saba (exc); *Rotoli:* Mia sposa sarà la mia bandiera; *Verdi:* Macbeth (exc); *Puccini:* Bohème (exc); *Adam:* Minuit, chrétiens (exc). (E. Caruso, M. Elman, orch/W.B. Rogers, G. Scognamiglio)

Ⓓ **EVC4(1)** (10/91)
The Caruso Edition, Vol.4 (pt 1)
Faure: Sancta Maria; *Caruso:* Tiempo antico; *Cottrau:* Santa Lucia; *Tchaikovsky:* Songs, Op.6 (exc); Eugene Onegin (exc); *Godard:* Chanson de juin; *Giordano:* Andrea Chénier (exc); *Saint-Saëns:* Samson et Dalila (exc); *Bizet:* Pêcheurs de perles (exc); *Verdi:* Rigoletto (exc); Rigoletto (exc); *Donizetti:* Lucia di Lammermoor (exc); *Flotow:* Martha (exc); *Gastaldon:* Musica proibita; *Crescenzo:* Uocchie celeste; *Tosti:* Alba separa; *Rubinstein:* Nero (exc); *Anton y Michelena:* A la luz de la luna; *P.M. Costa:* Sei morta nella vita mia; *Alvarez:* Partida; *Verdi:* Forza del destino (exc); *Cohan:* Over there; *Niedermeyer:* Pietà, Signore; *Alvarez:* A Granada; *Billi:* Campane a sera; *Olivieri:* Inno di Garibaldi. (E. Caruso, A. Galli-Curci, F. Perini, G. De Luca, M. Egener, A. Bada, M. Journet, E. de

Gogorza, F. Lapitino, orch/W.B. Rogers, NY Met Op Chor/J. Pasternack, V. Bellezza)

Ⓓ **EVC4(2)** (10/91)
The Caruso Edition, Vol.4 (pt 2)
Arona: Campana di San Giusto; *Planquette:* Régiment de Sambre et Meuse; *Fucito:* Sultano a Tte; *Saint-Saëns:* Samson et Dalila (exc); *Donizetti:* Elisir d'amore (exc); *Tosti:* 'A Vucchella; *Califona:* Vieni sul mar; *De Curtis:* Tu ca nun chiagne; *Cottrau:* Addio a Napoli; *Pergolesi:* Tre giorni son che Nina; *Crescenzo:* Première caresse; *De Curtis:* Senza nisciuno; *Gomes:* Salvator Rosa (exc); *Bracco:* Serenata; *Fucito:* Scordame; *Secchi:* Love me or not; *Handel:* Serse (exc); *Posadas:* Noche feliz; *Halévy:* Juive (exc); *Gioè:* I' m'arricordo 'e Napule; *Donaudy:* Vaghissima sembianza; *Meyerbeer:* Africaine (exc); *Lully:* Amadis (exc); *Bartlett:* Dream; *Rossini:* Petite messe solennelle (exc). (E. Caruso, L. Homer, M. Journet, G. De Luca, orch/J. Pasternack)

Ⓓ **GEMMCDS9001/3(1)** (6/93)
Singers of Imperial Russia, Vol.2 (pt 1)
Glinka: Ruslan and Lyudmila (exc); *Borodin:* Prince Igor (exc); *Tchaikovsky:* Queen of Spades (exc); Songs, Op.63 (exc); *Glinka:* Fire of longing; *Nápravník:* Dubrovsky (exc); *Tchaikovsky:* Eugene Onegin (exc); Eugene Onegin (exc); *Meyerbeer:* Robert le Diable (exc); *Rubinstein:* Voyevode; *Schumann:* Romanzen und Balladen, Op.49 (exc); *Glinka:* Life for the Tsar (exc); *Serov:* Judith (exc); *Lishin:* She laughed; *Rimsky-Korsakov:* Tsar's bride (exc); *Wagner:* Walküre (exc); *Rimsky-Korsakov:* Sadko (exc); *Borodin:* Prince Igor (exc); *Rubinstein:* Asra; *Denza:* Vieni a me; Occhi di fata; *Rubinstein:* Demon (exc); *Glinka:* Ruslan and Lyudmila (exc); *Auber:* Fra Diavolo (exc); *Verdi:* Rigoletto (exc); *Leoncavallo:* Pagliacci (exc); *Moniuszko:* Halka (exc); *Meyerbeer:* Prophète (exc); Huguenots (exc); *Tchaikovsky:* Eugene Onegin (exc); *Verdi:* Trovatore (exc); *Plotnikov:* With the sweet scent of lilacs; *Borodin:* Prince Igor (exc); *Rimsky-Korsakov:* May Night (exc); *Verdi:* Aida (exc); *Ponchielli:* Gioconda (exc). (V. Kastorsky, A. Labinsky, D. Bukhtoyarov, V. Sharonov, G. Morskoi, O. Kamionsky, P. Orlov, D. Yuzhin, A. Zaniboni, orch, anon/B. Seidler-Winkler, chor)

Ⓓ **GEMMCDS9001/3(2)** (6/93)
Singers of Imperial Russia, Vol.2 (pt 2)
Verdi: Aida (exc); *Serov:* Judith (exc); *Bellini:* Norma (exc); *Tchaikovsky:* Enchantress (exc); *Puccini:* Madama Butterfly (exc); *Wagner:* Fliegende Holländer (exc); *Tchaikovsky:* Oprichnik (exc); Queen of Spades (exc); Queen of Spades (exc); *Delibes:* Lakmé (exc); *Rimsky-Korsakov:* Sadko (exc); Tsar's Bride (exc); *Delibes:* Lakmé (exc); *Massenet:* Élégie; *Slonov:* Word of farewell; *A.J. Romberg:* Black clouds; *Meyerbeer:* Temptation; *Villamov:* Pray; *Tchaikovsky:* Eugene Onegin (exc); *Halévy:* Juive (exc); *Tchaikovsky:* Iolanta (exc); *Rossini:* Barbiere di Siviglia (exc); *Tchaikovsky:* Cherevichki (exc); *A.D. Davidov:* Leave me!; *Bleichman:* My lips are silent; *Dargomïzhsky:* Rusalka (exc); *Borodin:* Prince Igor (exc); *Meyerbeer:* Robert le Diable (exc); *Boito:* Mefistofele (exc); *Halévy:* Juive (exc); *Meyerbeer:* Huguenots (exc); *Glinka:* Life for the Tsar (exc); *Gounod:* Faust (exc); Faust (exc). (N. Ermolenko-Yuzhina, D. Yuzhin, A. Panina, M. Michailova, L. Sibiriakov, Moscow Imperial Op Chor, M.T. Manasevich, orch, anon)

Ⓓ **GEMMCDS9004/6(1)** (6/93)
Singers of Imperial Russia, Vol.3 (pt 1)
Niewiadomski: Sophia; *Zeleński:* Black skirt; *Verdi:* Traviata (exc); *Gall:* I love men; *Puccini:* Bohème (exc); *Nevhauser:* For good night; *Zarzycki:* Sad song; *Moniuszko:* Halka (exc); *Komorowski:* Guelder-rose; *Puccini:* Tosca (exc); *Halévy:* Juive (exc); *Rachmaninov:* Songs, Op.8 (exc); *Rubinstein:* Persian Songs, Op.34 (exc); *Rimsky-Korsakov:* By the sea, Op.46 (exc); Songs, Op.8 (exc); Sadko (exc); *Glinka:* Ruslan and Lyudmila (exc); Life for the Tsar (exc); *Verdi:* Traviata (exc); *Samuel-Rousseau:* Tarass Boulba (exc); *Rimsky-Korsakov:* Snow Maiden (exc); *Rossini:* Barbiere di Siviglia (exc); *Rimsky-Korsakov:* Tsar's Bride (exc); *Tchaikovsky:* Eugene Onegin (exc); Eugene Onegin (exc); Eugene Onegin (exc); *Nápravník:* Dubrovsky (exc); *Glinka:* Ruslan and Lyudmila (exc); *Dargomïzhsky:* Rusalka (exc); *Borodin:* Prince Igor (exc). (I. Bohuss, J. Korolewicz-Wayda, A. El-Tour, N. Zabela-Vrubel, M. Kuznetsova, L. Lipkowska, D. Smirnov, anon, orch/O.I. Arkadiev/J. Harrison)

Ⓓ **GEMMCDS9004/6(2)** (6/93)
Singers of Imperial Russia, Vol.3 (pt 2)
Grechaninov: Dobrinya Nikitich (exc); *Tchaikovsky:* Queen of Spades (exc); *Rimsky-Korsakov:* Snow Maiden (exc); *Mussorgsky:* Boris Godunov (exc); Fair at Sorochintsï (exc); *Kashevarov:* Tranquillity; *Grechaninov:* She was yours; *Rachmaninov:* Songs, Op.26 (exc); *Grechaninov:* Lullaby, Op.1/5; I wish I were with you; *Rimsky-Korsakov:* Songs, Op. 2 (exc); *Amani:* Cool summer evening; *Glinka:* Life for the Tsar (exc); *Rimsky-Korsakov:* Snow Maiden (exc); *Arensky:* Dream on the Volga (exc); *Gounod:* Faust (exc); *Sokolovsky:* By the blue sea; *Glinka:* Ruslan and Lyudmila (exc); *Schubert:* Erlkönig, D328; *Tchaikovsky:* Queen of Spades (exc); *Glinka:* Doubt; *Dargomïzhsky:* Rusalka (exc); *Borodin:* Prince Igor (exc); *Rubinstein:* Nero (exc); *Bizet:* Carmen (exc); *Glinka:* Life for the Tsar (exc); *Bemberg:* Chant hindou. (D. Smirnov, K.E. Kaidanov, E. Zbrueva, E. Witting, orch/P. Pitt/J. Harrison, anon, R.O. Von Beke, chor, anon)

Ⓓ **GEMMCDS9007/9(1)** (6/93)
Singers of Imperial Russia, Vol.4 (pt 1)
Tchaikovsky: Queen of Spades (exc); *Halévy:* Juive (exc); *Tosti:* Segreto; *Rubinstein:* Donkey and the Nightingale; *Meyerbeer:* Africaine (exc); *Tchaikovsky:* Songs, Op.60 (exc); *Verdi:* Aida (exc); *Bizet:* Pêcheurs de Perles (exc); *Mascagni:* Cavalleria Rusticana (exc); *A.D. Davidov:* Leave me!; *Nápravník:* Dubrovsky (exc); *Tchaikovsky:* Queen of Spades (exc); *Bizet:* Carmen (exc); *Dimitriev:* In the wild north; *Grechaninov:* She was yours; *Bleichman:* Far off; *Rubinstein:* Demon (exc); *Dargomïzhsky:* Rusalka (exc); *Tchaikovsky:* Eugene Onegin (exc); *Glinka:* Ruslan and Lyudmila (exc); *Bleichman:* Princesse lointaine (exc); *Tchaikovsky:* Cherevichki (exc); *A.D. Davidov:* What happiness!; *Gounod:* Faust (exc); *Verdi:* Traviata (exc); Traviata (exc); *Bizet:* Pêcheurs de perles (exc); *Grechaninov:* Dobrinya Nikitich (exc); *Gounod:* Roméo et Juliette (exc); *F. David:* Perle du Brésil (exc); *Nápravník:* Harold (exc); *Glinka:* Ruslan and Lyudmila (exc); *Gounod:* Sérénade; *Rimsky-Korsakov:* Sadko (exc); *Glinka:* Life for the Tsar (exc); *Bizet:* Pêcheurs de perles (exc); *Cui:* Bolero. (A. Davidov, E. Zbrueva, M. Michailova, V. Kastorsky, A. Bogdanovich, A. Nezhdanova, anon, chor, U. Masetti, anon, orch)

Ⓓ **GEMMCDS9007/9(2)** (6/93)
Singers of Imperial Russia, Vol.4 (pt 2)
Rimsky-Korsakov: Snow Maiden (exc); *Meyerbeer:* Huguenots (exc); *Gounod:* Mireille (exc); *Auber:* Fra Diavolo (exc); *Rimsky-Korsakov:* Golden Cockerel (exc); Tsar's Bride (exc); *Rossini:* Barbiere di Siviglia (exc); *Tosti:* Serenata; *Verdi:* Vespri siciliani (exc); *Rachmaninov:* Songs, Op.21 (exc); *Rimsky-Korsakov:* Songs, Op.2 (exc); *Glinka:* Life for the Tsar (exc); *Dimitriev:* Night; *Mussorgsky:* Boris Godunov (exc); *Glinka:* Life for the Tsar (exc); *Cui:* Oh, if Mother Volga; *Traditional:* Convict's song; *Verstovsky:* Askold's Grave (exc); *Bellini:* Sonnambula (exc); *Glinka:* Night Review; *Rubinstein:* Demon (exc); *Vil'boa:* Seafarers; *Glinka:* Elegy; *Cui:* Aeolian Harps; *Rubinstein:* Kalashnikov the Merchant (exc); *Moniuszko:* Halka (exc); *Tchaikovsky:* Enchantress (exc); Songs, Op.6 (exc); Queen of Spades (exc); *Rimsky-Korsakov:* In spring, Op.43 (exc); *Rubinstein:* Demon (exc); *Verstovsky:* Askold's Grave (exc); *A. Simon:* Song of love triumphant (exc); *Tchaikovsky:* Eugene Onegin (exc); *Cui:* Feast in time of plague (exc); Prisoner in the Caucasus (exc). (A. Nezhdanova, L. Sibiriakov, M. Michailova, G. Nikitina, A. Labinsky, E. Witting, A. Aleksandrovich, N. Shevelev, orch, anon, chor)

Ⓓ **GEMMCDS9050/2(1)** (5/94)
Music from the New York Stage, Vol. 1 (part 1)
Mason: Nearer, My God, to Thee; *Kiallmark:* Old Oaken Bucket; *Kerker:* Castles in the Air (exc); *Various:* Ship Ahoy (exc); *De Koven:* Robin Hood (exc); Robin Hood (exc); *Scanlan:* Mavourneen (exc); *Various:* 1492 (exc); *Olcott:* Irish Artist (exc); *Various:* Grand Vizier (exc); *Irwin:* Bully Song; *Sidney Jones:* Artist's Model (exc); Geisha (exc); *Stanford:* Shamus O'Brien (exc); *Olcott:* Sweet Inniscarra (exc); *Herbert:* Serenade (exc); *Kerker:* Belle of New York (exc); *Irwin:* Frog Song; *Stromberg:* Pousse Café (exc); *Kerker:* Yankee Doodle Dandy (exc); *Caryll:* Runaway Girl (exc); *Stromberg:* Hurly Burly (exc); *Herbert:* Fortune Teller (exc); Fortune Teller (exc); *Sloane:* Kate Kip, Buyer (exc); *Olcott:* Romance of Athlone (exc); *Englander:* Rounders (exc); *Stromberg:* Whirl-i-Gig (exc); *Various:* Rogers Brothers in Central Park (exc); *Stuart:* Florodora (exc); *Cole:* Maiden With the Dreamy Eyes; *Caryll:* Toreador (exc); *B. Williams:* Sons of Ham (exc); *Talbot:* Chinese Honeymoon (exc); *Witmark:* Chaperons (exc); *J. W. Johnson:* Under the Bamboo Tree; *Stromberg:* Twirly-Whirly (exc); *A. H. Wilson:* Prince of Tatters (exc); *J. Edwards:* When Johnny Comes Marching Home (exc); *Rubens:* Three Little Maids (exc); *Cohan:* Mother Goose (exc); *G. Edwards:* In Zanzibar; *J. Schwartz:* Piff! Paff! Pouf (exc). (H. C. Barnabee, K. Barry, M. Cahill, G. Cameron, G. Carroll, E. Carus, G. M. Cohan, E. Cowles, M. Crichton, J. B. Davis, M. Farkoa, E. M. Favor, L. Fields, H. Fredricks, G. Frothingham, L. Gunning, D. Hopper, G. P. Huntley, M. Irwin, E. Jackson, R. Jose, W. H. MacDonald, A. Nielsen, C. Olcott, Old Homestead Double Qt, J. O'Mara, E. May, J. T. Powers, Gus Rogers, M. Rogers, L. Russell, T. Q. Seabrooke, W. H. Thompson, J. Weber, Bert Williams, A. H. Wilson, Broadway Cast)

Ⓓ **GEMMCDS9053/5** (5/94)
Music from the New York Stage, Vol. 2: 1908—1913
B. Williams: I'm Tired of Eating in the Restaurants; *Cohan:* Fifty Miles from Boston (exc); *Hoschna:* Three Twins (exc); *M. Klein:* Pied Piper (exc); *Various:* Mr Hamlet of Broadway (exc); *Flynn:* Yip-I-Addy-I-Ay; *Various:* Midnight Sons (exc); *Sutton:* I Don't Care; *Butterfield:* When You and I Were Young, Maggie; *Snyder:* Oh, How that German Could Love; *Norworth:* Jolly Bachelors (exc); *Hubbell:* Jolly Bachelors (exc); *Snyder:* That Beautiful Rag; *Pryor:* Travel, Travel, Little Star; *B. Williams:* Moriah; *Various:* Ragged Robin (exc); Yankee Girl (exc); *J. Edwards:* Molly May (exc); *Various:* Summer Widowers (exc); Ziegfeld Follies of 1910 (exc); *A. Philipp:* Alma, Where Do You Live (exc); *Reinhardt:* Spring Maid (exc); *Janis:* Slim Princess (exc); *C. King:* Slim Princess (exc); *E. Ball:* Barry of Ballymore (exc); *Various:* Belle Paree (exc); Belle Paree (exc); *Norworth:* Little Miss Fix-It (exc); *Berlin:* Woodman, Spare that Tree; *M. Klein:* Around the World; *Lehár:* Gypsy Love (exc); *Various:* Vera Violetta (exc); *Tully:* Bird of Paradise (exc); *E. Ball:* Macushla (exc); *Various:* Whirl of Society (exc); Passing Show of 1912 (exc); Ziegfeld Follies of 1912 (exc); *Friml:* Firefly (exc); *E. Ball:* Isle O' Dreams (exc). (A. Albro, N. Bayes, I. Berlin, E. Brice, G. Cameron, C. Campbell, G. M. Cohan, C. Crawford, M. Ellis, I. Franklin, Hawaiian Qnt, C. Hayden, E. Janis, A. Jolson, S. Kellogg, C. King, G. LaRue, C. McDonald, T. McNaughton, S. Mayhew, Montgomery & Stone, J. Norworth, W. Oakland, C. Olcott, M. Raymond, B. Ring, H. Santrey, T. Shattuck, M. Sylva, E. Tanguay, B. Taylor, Bert Williams, Orig Broadway Cast)

Ⓓ **GEMMCDS9056/8** (5/94)
Music from the New York Stage, Vol. 3: 1913-17
Golden: You Can't Play Every Instrument in the Band; *Various:* Honeymoon Express (exc); Ziegfeld Follies of 1913 (exc); *Kern:* Look in Her Eyes; *Herbert:* Sweethearts (exc); *De Koven:* Rob Roy (exc); *Various:* Girl on the Film (exc); *Berlin:* Follow the Crowd; *Various:* Shameen Dhu (exc); *A. Philipp:* Midnight Girl (exc); *S. Hein:* When You're All Dressed Up and No Place to Go; *Various:* Ziegfeld Follies of 1914 (exc); *Darewski:* Sister Susie's sewing; *Various:* Dancing Around (exc); *Van Alstyne:* Pretty Baby; *Caryll:* Chin-Chin (exc); *Cuvillier:* Lilac Domino (exc); *Berlin:* Watch Your Step (exc); *Rubens:* Tonight's the Night (exc); *E. Ball:* Trilby (exc); *Various:* Ziegfeld Follies of 1915 (exc); *Herbert:* Princess Pat (exc); *Sousa:* New York Hippodrome March; *Hubbell:* Ladder of Roses; *Lehár:* Alone at Last (exc); *Friml:* Katinka (exc); *Golden:* Sybil (exc); *Jolson:* Robinson Crusoe, Jr (exc); *Various:* Heart O' Th' Heather (exc); *Kern:* My Castle in the Air; *Various:* Betty (exc); *E. Carroll:* So Long, Letty (exc); *Various:* Century Girl (exc); Follow Me (exc); *Kern:* Have a Heart (exc); *Berlin:* Dance and Grow Thin; *Felix:* Pom-Pom (exc); *B. Grant:* Step This Way (exc). (S. Ash, R. Atwell, I. Berlin, E. Brice, J. Cawthorn, J. Collins, M. Farrell, G. Grossmith, M. Hajos, L. Henson, R. Hitchcock, A. Jolson, C. King, H. Lewis, B. Linn, C. McDonald, G. MacFarlane, M. Naudain, C. Olcott, E. Painter, F. Pollock, M. Romaine, Six Brown Brothers, Sousa's Band, J. C. Thomas, B. B. Van, Van & Schenck, Bert Williams, N. M. Wills, Orig Broadway Cast)

Ⓓ **GEMMCDS9059/61** (5/94)
Music from the New York Stage, Vol. 4: 1917-20
Kern: Oh Boy! (exc); Oh Boy! (exc); *Herbert:* Eileen (exc); *Various:* Passing Show of 1917 (exc); Hitchy-Koo (exc); Ziegfeld Follies of 1917 (exc); *Romberg:* Maytime (exc); *Various:* Doing Our Bit (exc); *Valverde:* Land of Joy (exc); *Various:* Odds and Ends of 1917 (exc); *Von Tilzer:* If You Only Knew; *Various:* Ziegfeld Midnight Frolic (exc); Cohan Revue of 1918 (exc); *Jolson:* Sinbad (exc); *Snyder:* How'd You Like to be My Daddy?; *H. Carroll:* Oh, Look! (exc); *Various:* Why Worry? (exc); Why Worry? (exc); *Bayes:* Ladies First (exc); *Balfe:* Bohemian Girl (exc); *Kern:* She's a Good Fellow (exc); *Various:* Monte Christo, Jr (exc); Ziegfeld Follies of 1919 (exc); *Berlin:* Ziegfeld Follies of 1919 (exc); *Various:* Greenwich Village Follies of 1919 (exc); Oh, What a Girl! (exc); *Jacobi:* Apple Blossoms (exc); *Tierney:* Irene (exc); *Various:* My Lady Friends (exc). (S. Ash, Avon Comedy Four, N. Bayes, F. Brice, E. Cantor, E. Day, Duncan Sisters, G. Evans, Farber Sisters, H. Fox, I. Franklin, A. Jolson, LaCalle's Spanish Orch, H. Lewis, T. Lewis & His Orch, J. Norworth, T. Powers, H. Scott, J. Steel, V. Stiles, J. C. Thomas, Van & Schenck, E. Walker, F. Watson, Watson Sisters, S. Welsh, A. Wheaton, F. White, Bert Williams, Orig Broadway Cast/V. Herbert)

Ⓓ **GEMMCDS9073(1)** (5/94)
Giovanni Zenatello, Vol.1 (pt 1)
Giordano: Andrea Chénier (exc); *Puccini:* Manon Lescaut (exc); *Gounod:* Faust (exc); *Berlioz:* Damnation de Faust (exc); *Verdi:* Traviata (exc); *Wagner:* Meistersinger (exc); *Giordano:* Siberia (exc); Siberia (exc); *Leoncavallo:* Pagliacci (exc); *Giordano:* Andrea Chénier (exc); *Verdi:* Ballo in maschera (exc); Aida (exc); *Boito:* Mefistofele (exc); *Donizetti:* Lucia di Lammermoor (exc); *Boito:* Mefistofele (exc); *Verdi:* Aida (exc); Traviata (exc); Trovatore (exc); Ballo in maschera (exc); *Franchetti:* Figlia di Iorio (exc); *Bizet:* Carmen (exc); *Ponchielli:* Gioconda (exc); *Verdi:* Otello (exc); *Leoncavallo:* Pagliacci (exc); *Ponchielli:* Gioconda (exc); *Puccini:* Manon Lescaut (exc);

Denza: Vieni a me; Verdi: Ballo in maschera (exc); Otello (exc); Giordano: Andrea Chénier (exc); Saint-Saëns: Samson et Dalila (exc); Verdi: Traviata (exc); Bizet: Carmen (exc); Ponchielli: Gioconda (exc); Boito: Mefistofele (exc); Puccini: Bohème (exc). (G. Zenatello, R. Storchio, N. Frascani, A. Parsi-Pettinella, A. Didur, M. Barrientos, E. Burzio, E. Giraldoni, E. Cervi-Caroli, P. Amato, E. Petri, chor, anon, R. Delle Ponti, orch)

Ⓘ **GEMMCDS9073(2)** (5/94)
Giovanni Zenatello, Vol.1 (pt 2)
Gounod: Faust (exc); *Mascagni:* Cavalleria rusticana (exc); *Puccini:* Tosca (exc); *Verdi:* Ballo in maschera (exc); *Leoncavallo:* Pagliacci (exc); *Verdi:* Aida (exc); Otello (exc); *Leoncavallo:* Pagliacci (exc); *Verdi:* Forza del destino (exc); *Puccini:* Manon Lescaut (exc); *Verdi:* Trovatore (exc); *Rotoli:* Mia sposa sarà la mia bandiera; *Puccini:* Bohème (exc); *Verdi:* Otello (exc); Ballo in maschera (exc); *Franchetti:* Germania (exc); *Leoncavallo:* Mattinata; *Giordano:* Andrea Chénier (exc); *Meyerbeer:* Huguenots (exc); *Wagner:* Meistersinger (exc); *Montanari:* Serenatella; *Cosentino:* Mattinata; *Puccini:* Bohème (exc); Fanciulla del West (exc); *Cilea:* Adriana Lecouvreur (exc); *Puccini:* Madama Butterfly (exc); *Marchetti:* Ruy Blas (exc); *Puccini:* Tosca (exc); *Rosa:* Star vicino; *Schubert:* Du bist die Ruh', D776; *Wagner:* Meistersinger (exc); *Giordano:* Siberia (exc); *Leoncavallo:* Pagliacci (exc); Bohème (exc); *Verdi:* Trovatore (exc); Aida (exc); Aida (exc). (G. Zenatello, P. Amato, M. Sammarco, L. Pasini-Vitale, E. Mazzoleni, L. Cannetti, E. Bruno, chor, anon, orch)

Ⓘ **GEMMCDS9074(1)** (5/94)
Giovanni Zenatello, Vol.2 (pt 1)
Verdi: Traviata (exc); *Gomes:* Guarany (exc); *Ponchielli:* Gioconda (exc); *Bellini:* Norma (exc); *Puccini:* Tosca (exc); *Verdi:* Aida (exc); *Mascagni:* Cavalleria rusticana (exc); *Puccini:* Fanciulla del West (exc); *Verdi:* Trovatore (exc); Otello (exc); *Gomes:* Guarany (exc); *Puccini:* Tosca (exc); Manon Lescaut (exc); Bohème (exc); *Donizetti:* Lucia di Lammermoor (exc); *Puccini:* Tosca (exc); *Verdi:* Otello (exc); Trovatore (exc); Aida (exc); *Mascagni:* Cavalleria rusticana (exc); *Verdi:* Trovatore (exc); *Gounod:* Faust (exc); *Mascagni:* Cavalleria rusticana (exc); *Ponchielli:* Gioconda (exc); *Verdi:* Aida (exc); Trovatore (exc); Aida (exc); *Mascagni:* Cavalleria rusticana (exc); *Verdi:* Aida (exc); *Leoncavallo:* Pagliacci (exc); *Verdi:* Traviata (exc); *Bizet:* Carmen (exc); *Giordano:* Andrea Chénier (exc). (G. Zenatello, E. Mazzoleni, E. Bruno, M. Pereira, M. Gay, A. Nielsen, E. Destinn, J. Mardones, chor, anon, orch)

Ⓘ **GEMMCDS9074(2)** (5/94)
Giovanni Zenatello, Vol.2 (pt 2)
Verdi: Otello (exc); *Gounod:* Faust (exc); *Puccini:* Bohème (exc); *Gounod:* Faust (exc); *Verdi:* Requiem (exc); Trovatore (exc); Aida (exc); *Leoncavallo:* Pagliacci (exc); *Donizetti:* Lucia di Lammermoor (exc); *Verdi:* Ballo in maschera (exc); Otello (exc); Otello (exc); Otello (exc); *Giordano:* Andrea Chénier (exc); *Puccini:* Tosca (exc); *Bizet:* Carmen (exc); *Puccini:* Manon Lescaut (exc); *Leoncavallo:* Pagliacci (exc); *Verdi:* Ballo in maschera (exc); *Bizet:* Carmen (exc). (G. Zenatello, A. Verlet, M. Rappold, M. Matzenauer, A. Middleton, T. Chalmers, E. Baroni, A. Granforte, H. Spani, G. Noto, L. Cilla, E. Cotreil, M. Sampieri, M. Gay, G. Marion, A. Boemi, chor, La Scala Chor, Apollo Chor, orch, La Scala Orch/C. Sabajno/V. Bellezza/B. Reibold/Rosario Bourdon)

Ⓘ **GEMMCDS9076**
Stokowski conducts Wagner, Volume III
Wagner: Rheingold (exc); Walküre (exc); Walküre (exc); Siegfried (exc); Götterdämmerung (exc); Götterdämmerung (exc). (A. Davis, F. Jagel, L. Tibbett, Philadelphia/L. Stokowski)

Ⓘ **GEMMCDS9095(1)** (4/95)
Povla Frijsh (pt 1)
Gluck: Semiramide riconosciuta (exc); *Fosse:* Retour du printemps; *Schumann:* Minnespiel, Op.101 (exc); Lieder, Op.104 (exc); Liederkreis, op.39 (exc); Lieder und Gesänge, Op.96 (exc); *Schubert:* Du liebst mich nicht, D756; Schwanengesang, D957 (exc); Schmetterling, D633; Gruppe aus dem Tartarus, D583; *Mozart:* Sehnsucht nach dem Frühling, K596; *Fauré:* Songs, Op.18 (exc); Songs, Op.23 (exc); Songs, Op.18 (exc); *Duparc:* Manoir de Rosemonde; *Chausson:* Mélodies, Op.36 (exc); *Debussy:* Fleur des blés; Voici que le printemps; *Hahn:* Infidélité; *Roussel:* Mélodies, Op.50 (exc); *Février:* Intruse; *Poulenc:* Poèmes Apollinaire (1931) (exc); *Ravel:* Histoires naturelles (exc); *Milhaud:* Poèmes juifs (exc); *G. Dupont:* Mandoline; *Thompson:* Velvet shoes; *Naginski:* Pasture; *R. Clarke:* Shy one; *Dvořák:* Gipsy Melodies (exc). (P. Frijsh, C. Dougherty)

Ⓘ **GEMMCDS9095(2)** (4/95)
Povla Frijsh (pt 2)
Grieg: Songs, Op.25 (exc); *Sinding:* Songs, Op.18 (exc); *A. Grøndahl:* Songs, Op.13 (exc); *Torelli:* Tu lo sai; *Schubert:* Claudine von Villa Bella (exc); *Staub:* Heure sicilienne; *Křička:* Albatros; *Cui:* Songs, Op.57 (exc); *Grieg:* Melodies of the Heart, Op.5 (exc); *Jordan:* Lullaby; *Grieg:* Songs, Op.48 (exc); Songs, Op.25 (exc); *Tchaikovsky:* Songs, Op.38 (exc); *Koechlin:* Rondels, Op.8 (exc); *Georges:* Pluie; *Fauré:* Songs, Op.2 (exc); *Schubert:* Gott im Frühling, D448; *A. Grøndahl:* Linden; *Henriques:* Maiden, do not sleep; *Chausson:* Temps des Lilas; *Grieg:* Melodies of the Heart, Op.5 (exc); *Schubert:* Erlkönig, D328; *Torelli:* Tu lo sai; *Grieg:* Melodies of the Heart, Op.5 (exc); Songs, Op.48 (exc). (P. Frijsh, C. Dougherty, D. Bucktrout, E. Nielsen, P. James Orch/P. James, WNYC Concert Orch/H. Newmann)

Ⓘ **GEMMCDS9111(1)**
Singers of Imperial Russia, Vol.5 (pt 1)
Meyerbeer: Huguenots (exc); *Nápravník:* Don Juan (exc); *Abaza:* Misty morning; *Boito:* Mefistofele (exc); *Verdi:* Don Carlo (exc); *Ehrlich:* At the gates of Eden; *De Bové:* These days are past; *Traditional:* Prisoner's Song; *Dobrovolsky:* Ermak; *Stolypin:* Two Giants; *Glazunov:* Bacchic song; *Traditional:* Not the autumn drizzle; *Dobrovolsky:* Anchor; *Schubert:* Schwanengesang, D957 (exc); *Gounod:* Faust (exc); *Serov:* Judith (exc); *Rossini:* Stabat mater (exc); *Verdi:* Requiem (exc); *Meyerbeer:* Huguenots (exc); *Dargomïzhsky:* Rose, little rose; *Tchaikovsky:* Queen of Spades (exc); *Mendelssohn:* Duets, Op.63 (exc); *Rubinstein:* Little bird sang and sang; *Grodzski:* Snow-white seagull's cry; *Traditional:* Stormy breezes; *Chopin:* Waltzes (exc); *Donizetti:* Lucia di Lammermoor (exc); *F. David:* Perle du Brésil (exc); *Dluski:* Oh, sing to me; *Nápravník:* Harold (exc); *Weber:* Freischütz (exc). (L. Sibiriakov, M. Michailova, E. Vitting, E. Katulskaya, E. Bronskaya, K. Tugarinova, chor, anon, orch/B. Seidler-Winkler/G.I. Wahrlich)

Ⓘ **GEMMCDS9111(2)**
Singers of Imperial Russia, Vol.5 (pt 2)
Glinka: Life for the Tsar (exc); Life for the Tsar (exc); Life for the Tsar (exc); *Dargomïzhsky:* Rusalka (exc); Rusalka (exc); Rusalka (exc); *Tchaikovsky:* Eugene Onegin (exc); Eugene Onegin (exc); Eugene Onegin (exc); Oprichnik (exc); Queen of Spades (exc); *Nápravník:* Don Juan (exc); *Verdi:* Traviata (exc); *Borodin:* Prince Igor (exc); *Rimsky-Korsakov:* Sadko (exc); *Mussorgsky:* Boris Godunov (exc); *A. Thomas:* Mignon (exc); *Cui:* Prisoner in the Caucasus (exc); *Rachmaninov:* Songs, Op.26 (exc); *Traditional:* Blow, foul weather; *Rimsky-Korsakov:* May Night (exc); May Night (exc); *Traditional:* In the blue sky; *Zubov:* Let us ride; *Glinka:* Life for the Tsar (exc); Cherry-tree blossoms; *Tchaikovsky:* Queen of Spades (exc); Eugene Onegin (exc); *Nápravník:* Don Juan (exc); *Rimsky-Korsakov:* Sadko (exc); *Bizet:* Carmen (exc); *Tosti:* On the earth; *Glazunov:* Masquerade (exc). (M. Michailova, G. Nikitina, A. Labinsky, L. Sibiriakov, A. Makarova, N. Bolshakov, E. Zbrueva, M. Maksakov, S. Preobrazhensky, A. Bogdanovich, I. Gryzunov, I. Damaev, E. Katulskaya, N. Severesky, D. Zakharova, M. Karakash, E. Vitting, M. Davydova, E. Popova, A. Labinsky, anon, orch)

Ⓘ **GEMMCDS9121**
Wagner—Die Meistersinger, Act 3, etc
Wagner: Meistersinger (exc); Tannhäuser (exc); Tannhäuser (exc); Walküre (exc); Siegfried (exc); Siegfried (exc); Fliegende Holländer (exc); Lohengrin (exc). (H. Hermann Nissen, T. Ralf, M. Teschemacher, S. Nilsson, E. Fuchs, M. Kremer, H. Jung, Dresden St Op Chor, Saxon St Orch/K. Böhm, G. Hüsch, G. Ljungberg, W. Widdop, A. Reiss, L. Melchior, F. Schorr, Berlin St Op Orch, orch, LSO, Philadelphia/F. Weissmann/H.U. Müller/A. Coates/E. Ormandy)

Ⓘ **GEMMCDS9137** (4/95)
Wagner—Der Ring des Nibelungen
Wagner: Rheingold (exc); Walküre (exc); Siegfried (exc); Götterdämmerung (exc); Siegfried (exc); Götterdämmerung (exc); Rheingold (exc); Rheingold (exc); Walküre (exc); Walküre (exc); Walküre (exc); Walküre (exc); Siegfried (exc); Siegfried (exc); Siegfried (exc); Siegfried (exc); Götterdämmerung (exc); Götterdämmerung (exc); Götterdämmerung (exc). (F. Leider, L. Trenton, E. Suddaby, G. Ljungberg, F. Austral, N. Gruhn, F. Easton, N. Eadie, E. Arden, T. de Garmo, L. Kindermann, N. Walker, G. Guszalewicz, E. Leisner, E. Marherr-Wagner, M. Olczewska, R. Laubenthal, W. Widdop, K. McKenna, W. Henke, L. Melchior, H. Tessmer, A. Reiss, G. Palmer, M. Offers, H. Fry, F. Schorr, R. Bockelmann, A. Fear, E. Habich, E. Schipper, F. Collier, I. Andrésen, D. Zádor, E. List, chor, LSO, Berlin St Op Orch, Vienna St Op Orch, orch, Berlin St Op Chor/L. Collingwood/L. Blech/K. Muck/A. Coates/J. Barbirolli/R. Heger/K. Alwin)

Ⓘ **GEMMCDS9159(1)**
De Luca Edition, Vol.1 (pt 1)
Cilea: Adriana Lecouvreur (exc); *T. Giordani:* Caro mio ben; *Massenet:* Roi de Lahore (exc); *Donizetti:* Favorita (exc); *Verdi:* Ballo in maschera (exc); *A. Thomas:* Hamlet (exc); *Meyerbeer:* Dinorah (exc); *Mozart:* Don Giovanni (exc); *Donizetti:* Don Pasquale (exc); Favorita (exc); *Giordano:* Siberia (exc); Siberia (exc); Siberia (exc); *Berlioz:* Damnation de Faust (exc); *Leoncavallo:* Zazà (exc); *Denza:* Occhi di fata; *Donizetti:* Don Pasquale (exc); *Verdi:* Rigoletto (exc); *Tchaikovsky:* Queen of Spades (exc); *De Leva:* Pastorale; *Verdi:* Trovatore (exc); Ballo in maschera (exc); *Rossini:* Barbiere di Siviglia (exc); *Verdi:* Ernani (exc); *Donizetti:* Favorita (exc); *Mozart:* Don Giovanni (exc); *Meyerbeer:* Dinorah (exc); *Massenet:* Roi de Lahore (exc); Hérodiade (exc); *Morlacchi:* Brilla la luna. (G. De Luca, E. Ceresoli, R. Storchio, G. Pini-Corsi, O. Gennari, V. Pozzi-Camolla, F. Corradetti, F. Cilea, R. delle Ponti, anon)

Ⓘ **GEMMCDS9159(2)**
De Luca Edition, Vol.1 (pt 2)
De Luca: Dolce Madonna; *A. Thomas:* Hamlet (exc); *Rotoli:* Mia sposa sarà la mia bandiera; *Ponchielli:* Gioconda (exc); *Verdi:* Traviata (exc); *Donizetti:* Linda di Chamounix (exc); *Mozart:* Nozze di Figaro (exc); *Rossini:* Guillaume Tell (exc); *Tosti:* Ideale; *Ruggi:* Due Ciabattini (exc); *De Leva:* E voi passate nel vial; *Fasolo:* Lungi è amor; *Leoncavallo:* Zazà (exc); *Franchetti:* Germania (exc); *Wagner:* Tannhäuser (exc); *Donizetti:* Don Pasquale (exc); *Ponchielli:* Gioconda (exc); *Verdi:* Traviata (exc); *Donizetti:* Lucia di Lammermoor (exc); Elisir d'amore (exc); *Rossini:* Guillaume Tell (exc); *Verdi:* Rigoletto (exc); Rigoletto (exc); Rigoletto (exc); *Ponchielli:* Gioconda (exc); *Verdi:* Aida (exc). (G. De Luca, A. Gonzaga, F. Corradetti, E. Burzio, A. Galli-Curci, M. Egener, E. Caruso, A. Bada, M. Journet, G. Martinelli, J. Mardones, F. Perini, L. Homer, B. Gigli, L. Pons, E. Rethberg, G. Lauri-Volpi, anon, orch/J. Pasternack/N. Shilkret/G. Setti/W. Pelletier/Rosario Bourdon)

Ⓘ **GEMMCDS9160(1)**
De Luca Edition, Vol.2 (pt 1)
Verdi: Ernani (exc); Ballo in maschera (exc); *Rossini:* Barbiere di Siviglia (exc); *Verdi:* Trovatore (exc); *Mozart:* Nozze di Figaro (exc); *Buzzi-Peccia:* Serenata gelata; *Capolongo:* Nuttata è sentimento; *De Leva:* Pastorale; *Verdi:* Traviata (exc); *Handel:* Rinaldo (exc); *Grechaninov:* Lullaby, Op.1/5; *A. H. Edwards:* God bless you, my dear; *Sibella:* Ultima rosa; *Donizetti:* Favorita (exc); *Verdi:* Rigoletto (exc); Forza del destino (exc); *Gounod:* Faust (exc); *Cardillo:* Oi luna; *Debussy:* Beau soir; *Fatuo:* Mattinata; *Massenet:* Hérodiade (exc); *Leoncavallo:* Zazà (exc); *Verdi:* Don Carlo (exc); *Donizetti:* Don Pasquale (exc); *Bellini:* Puritani (exc); *Romilli:* Marietta; *Rossini:* Guillaume Tell (exc); *Romilli:* Rosa; *Tosti:* Voi dormite, Signora. (G. De Luca, A. Galli-Curci, E. Caruso, G. Farrar, G. Martinelli, L. Bori, J. Mardones, orch)

Ⓘ **GEMMCDS9160(2)**
De Luca Edition, Vol.2 (pt 2)
Diaz: Benvenuto Cellini (exc); *Meyerbeer:* Dinorah (exc); *Denza:* Occhi di fata; *De Leva:* Canta il mare; *Fatuo:* Siviglia; *Cimara:* Stornello; *Verdi:* Rigoletto (exc); Rigoletto (exc); Rigoletto (exc); *Donizetti:* Lucia di Lammermoor (exc); *Puccini:* Bohème (exc); *Verdi:* Forza del destino (exc); Forza del destino (exc); *Bizet:* Pêcheurs de perles (exc); *Ponchielli:* Gioconda (exc); Gioconda (exc); *Verdi:* Ernani (exc); Don Carlo (exc); Traviata (exc); Traviata (exc); *Gounod:* Faust (exc); *Wolf-Ferrari:* Gioielli della madonna (exc); *Verdi:* Trovatore (exc); Trovatore (exc); *Rossini:* Barbiere di Siviglia (exc). (G. De Luca, A. Galli-Curci, G. Anthony, A. Tedesco, L. Homer, B. Gigli, A. Bada, E. Pinza, G. Martinelli, L. Pons, NY Met Op Chor, orch, NY Met Op Orch/G. Setti)

Ⓘ **GEMMCDS9176**
Gigli - Arias, Duets & Songs, 1926-1937
Massenet: Manon (exc); *Gounod:* Faust (exc); *Bizet:* Pêcheurs de perles (exc); *Puccini:* Bohème (exc); *Verdi:* Forza del destino (exc); Rigoletto (exc); *Puccini:* Tosca (exc); *De Curtis:* Lucia, luci; 'A canzone 'e Napule; *Cottrau:* Santa Lucia; *Di Capua:* 'O sole mio; *De Curtis:* Addio bel sogno; *Bixio:* Canzone dell'amore; *Rossini:* Stabat mater (exc); *Handel:* Serse (exc); *Donizetti:* Elisir d'amore (exc); *Giordano:* Andrea Chénier (exc); *Mascagni:* Cavalleria Rusticana (exc); Cavalleria Rusticana (exc); *Leoncavallo:* Pagliacci (exc); Pagliacci (exc); Mattinata; *De Curtis:* Torna a Surriento; Non ti scordar di me; *Melichar:* Serenata veneziana; *De Curtis:* Soltanto tu, Maria; *Melichar:* Anima mia; *Gounod:* Ave Maria; *Bizet:* Agnus Dei; *Franck:* Panis Angelicus; *Schumann:* Myrthen, Op.25 (exc); *Becce:* Tu sei la mia vita; *Curci:* Notte in Venezia; *Blanc:* Giovinezza; *Puccini:* Inno a Roma; *Bizet:* Carmen (exc); *Cilea:* Arlesiana (exc); *Verdi:* Aida (exc); *Puccini:* Bohème (exc); *Grieg:* Songs, Op.48 (exc). (B. Gigli, T. Ruffo, D. Giannini, I. Pacetti, M. Caniglia, Berlin Solisten Vereinigung, chor, La Scala Chor, La Scala Orch, Berlin St Op Orch, orch/J. Barbirolli/E. Goossens/Rosario Bourdon/F. Ghione/C. Sabajno/D. Olivieri/A. Melichar/B. Seidler-Winkler/G. Antonicelli/W. Goehr)

Ⓓ **GEMMCDS9180**
Verdi—Rigoletto, etc
Verdi: Rigoletto (Cpte); *Serrano:* Alma da Dios (exc); *Martin y Guerrero:* Gavilanes (exc); *Payán:* O Señorita; *T. Evans:* Lady of Spain; *Lehár:* Frasquita (exc); *Kaper:* Just one of my dreams; *Donizetti:* Lucia di Lammermoor (exc); *Bizet:* Pêcheurs de perles (exc); *Benedict:* Carnival of Venice Variations. (L. Piazza, L. Pagliughi, T. Folgar, S. Baccaloni, V. De Cristoff, A. Baracchi, L. Brambilla, G. Nessi, G. Menni, La Scala Chor, La Scala Orch/C. Sabajno, T. Folgar, chor, orch, pf trio, L. Pagliughi, J. Amadio, N. Nelson)

Ⓓ **GEMMCDS9365** (3/90)
R. Strauss: Der Rosenkavalier (abridged), etc
R. Strauss: Rosenkavalier (exc); Aegyptische Helena (exc); Aegyptische Helena (exc); Lieder, Op.19 (exc); Lieder, Op.27 (exc). (Lotte Lehmann, M. Olczewska, R. Mayr, E. Schumann, V. Madin, B. Paalen, H. Gallos, A. Michalsky, K. Ettl, Vienna St Op Chor, VPO/R. Heger, R. Pauly, Berlin St Op Orch/F. Busch, R. Hutt, R. Strauss)

Ⓓ **GEMMCDS9369** (3/91)
Mozart: Don Giovanni
Mozart: Don Giovanni (Cpte). (J. Brownlee, I. Souez, L. Helletsgruber, A. Mildmay, K. von Pataky, S. Baccaloni, Roy Henderson, D. Franklin, Glyndebourne Fest Chor, Glyndebourne Fest Orch/F. Busch)

Ⓓ **GEMMCDS9371** (3/90)
Mozart—(Die) Zauberflöte
Mozart: Zauberflöte (Cpte). (T. Lemnitz, E. Berger, H. Roswaenge, G. Hüsch, W. Strienz, W. Grossmann, H. Tessmer, I. Beilke, H. Scheppan, E. Marherr-Wagner, R. Berglund, C. Spletter, E. Fabbry, Favres Solisten Vereinigung, BPO/T. Beecham)

Ⓓ **GEMMCDS9373** (3/90)
Toscanini & the NYPSO—1926-36
Beethoven: Symphony 5; Symphony 7; *Brahms:* Haydn Variations; *Dukas:* Apprenti sorcier; *Gluck:* Orfeo ed Euridice (exc); *Haydn:* Symphony 101; *Mendelssohn:* Midsummer Night's Dream (exc); Midsummer Night's Dream (exc); *Mozart:* Symphony 35; *Rossini:* Semiramide (exc); Italiana in Algeri (exc); *Verdi:* Traviata (exc); *Wagner:* Götterdämmerung (exc); Lohengrin (exc); Siegfried Idyll; *Rossini:* Barbiere di Siviglia (exc). (NYPSO/A. Toscanini)

Ⓓ **GEMMCDS9375**
Mozart: Le nozze di Figaro
Mozart: Nozze di Figaro (Cpte). (W. Domgraf-Fassbaender, A. Mildmay, Roy Henderson, A. Rautawaara, L. Helletsgruber, C. Willis, N. Allin, I. Tajo, H. Nash, M. Jones, F. Dunlop, W. Radford, Glyndebourne Fest Chor, Glyndebourne Fest Orch/F. Busch)

Ⓓ **GEMMCDS9402**
Verdi: Aida
Verdi: Aida (Cpte). (D. Giannini, I. Minghini-Cattaneo, A. Pertile, G. Inghilleri, L. Manfrini, G. Masini, G. Nessi, La Scala Chor, La Scala Orch/C. Sabajno)

Ⓓ **GEMMCDS9406** (3/91)
Mozart: Così fan tutte
Mozart: Così fan tutte (Cpte). (I. Souez, L. Helletsgruber, I. Eisinger, H. Nash, W. Domgraf-Fassbaender, J. Brownlee, Glyndebourne Fest Chor, Glyndebourne Fest Orch/F. Busch)

Ⓓ **GEMMCDS9422**
Bellini: Norma
Bellini: Norma (Cpte). (G. Cigna, E. Stignani, G. Breviario, T. Pasero, E. Renzi, A. Perris, Turin EIAR Chor, Turin EIAR Orch/V. Gui)

Ⓓ **GEMMCDS9452** (3/91)
The Emperor Tibbett
Gruenberg: Emperor Jones (exc); *D. Taylor:* King's Henchman (exc); *Verdi:* Rigoletto (exc); Ballo in maschera (exc); Falstaff (exc); Trovatore (exc); Simon Boccanegra (exc); Otello (exc); *Puccini:* Tosca (exc); Tosca (exc); Tabarro (exc); *Leoncavallo:* Pagliacci (exc); *Giordano:* Andrea Chénier (exc); *Massenet:* Hérodiade (exc); *Gounod:* Faust (exc); *Wagner:* Tannhäuser (exc); *Lehár:* Rogue Song (exc). (L. Tibbett, E. Rethberg, G. Martinelli, L. Warren, E. Pinza, A. de Paolis, chor, orch/G. Setti/A. Smallens/N. Shilkret/E. Panizza/Rosario Bourdon, NY Met Op Chor, NY Met Op Orch)

Ⓓ **GEMMCDS9910**
Wagner—Flying Dutchman/Götterdämmerung (excs)
Wagner: Fliegende Holländer (Cpte); Götterdämmerung (exc). (F. Destal, M. Lawrence, A. Kipnis, R. Maison, I. Petina, H. Fleischer, Buenos Aires Colón Th Chor, Buenos Aires Colón Th Orch/F. Busch/E. Kleiber)

Ⓓ **GEMMCDS9922** (4/92)
New York Philharmonic - 150th Anniversary
Sullivan: Mikado (exc); *Beethoven:* Symphony 5 (exc); *Mengelberg:* Praeludium; *Schelling:* Victory Ball; *Wagner:* Fliegende Holländer (exc); Walküre (exc); *J. Strauss II:* Künstlerleben, Op. 316; G'schichten aus dem Wienerwald, Op. 325; *Tchaikovsky:* Marche Slave; *Beethoven:* Symphony 5; *Brahms:* Haydn Variations; *Verdi:* Traviata (exc); *R. Strauss:* Don Quixote; *Wagner:* Parsifal (exc); *Debussy:* Nocturnes (exc); Images (exc); *Purcell:* Suite for Strings; *Respighi:* Fountains of Rome. (NYPO, NYPSO/J. Stransky/W. Mengelberg/A. Toscanini/T. Beecham/F. Reiner/J. Barbirolli, A. Wallenstein, R. Pollain)

Ⓓ **GEMMCDS9923(1)** (7/92)
Covent Garden on Record, Vol.1 (pt 1)
Bellini: Sonnambula (exc); *Mozart:* Don Giovanni (exc); *Gounod:* Faust (exc); *Massenet:* Roi de Lahore (exc); *Bellini:* Sonnambula (exc); Puritani (exc); *Verdi:* Traviata (exc); *Ponchielli:* Gioconda (exc); *Mozart:* Don Giovanni (exc); *Rossini:* Barbiere di Siviglia (exc); *Verdi:* Rigoletto (exc); *Donizetti:* Lucrezia Borgia (exc); *Gounod:* Roméo et Juliette (exc); *A. Thomas:* Hamlet (exc); *Flotow:* Martha (exc); *Verdi:* Otello (exc); *Wagner:* Rheingold (exc); *Gounod:* Philémon et Baucis (exc); *Mascagni:* Cavalleria rusticana (exc); Cavalleria rusticana (exc); *Bizet:* Carmen (exc); Carmen (exc); *Gounod:* Faust (exc); *Donizetti:* Favorita (exc); *Rossini:* Barbiere di Siviglia (exc); *Verdi:* Traviata (exc); *Mascagni:* Cavalleria rusticana (exc); *Leoncavallo:* Pagliacci (exc); *Wagner:* Lohengrin (exc); *Verdi:* Falstaff (exc); Otello (exc). (A. Patti, V. Maurel, P. Gailhard, J. Lassalle, M. Sembrich, M. Battistini, F. Marconi, F. d'Andrade, S. Arnoldson, N. Melba, F. Navarini, R. Pinkert, E. de Reszke, E. Eames, E. Schumann-Heink, H. Witherspoon, P. Plançon, F. de Lucia, E. Calvé, A. Alvarez, A. Pini-Corsi, G. Bellincioni, M. Ancona, F. Viñas, M. Delna, anon, orch/C. Sabajno, S. Cottone/L. Ronald, A. Barili, C. Sabajno)

Ⓓ **GEMMCDS9923(2)** (7/92)
Covent Garden on Record, Vol.1 (pt 2)
Verdi: Otello (exc); *Meyerbeer:* Prophète (exc); *Verdi:* Trovatore (exc); *Leoncavallo:* Pagliacci (exc); *Donizetti:* Favorita (exc); *Meyerbeer:* Huguenots (exc); *Gounod:* Roméo et Juliette (exc); *Mozart:* Don Giovanni (exc); *A. Thomas:* Hamlet (exc); *Verdi:* Aida (exc); Aida (exc); *Puccini:* Bohème (exc); *Mozart:* Don Giovanni (exc); Don Giovanni (exc); *Beethoven:* Fidelio (exc); *Rossini:* Barbiere di Siviglia (exc); *Puccini:* Bohème (exc); *Verdi:* Rigoletto (exc); *Gounod:* Faust (exc); *Verdi:* Rigoletto (exc); *Mascagni:* Cavalleria Rusticana (exc); *Verdi:* Rigoletto (exc); *Mascagni:* Cavalleria Rusticana (exc); *Wagner:* Tristan und Isolde (exc); Walküre (exc); *Rossini:* Barbiere di Siviglia (exc); Barbiere di Siviglia (exc); *Gounod:* Roméo et Juliette (exc); *Wagner:* Rheingold (exc); *Verdi:* Aida (exc). (F. Tamagno, F. de Lucia, M. Ancona, M. Journet, E. Scaramberg, G. Bréjean-Silver, M. Renaud, F. Litvinne, J. Gadski, L. Homer, Lilli Lehmann, A. Scotti, A. Bonci, G. Anselmi, F. Valero, E. Caruso, O. Fremstad, A. Van Rooy, T. Ruffo, P. Plançon, T. Bertram, G. Russ, anon, orch, chor, B. Seidler-Winkler)

Ⓓ **GEMMCDS9924(1)** (7/92)
Covent Garden on Record, Vol.2 (pt 1)
Verdi: Aida (exc); Aida (exc); *Wagner:* Lohengrin (exc); *Puccini:* Bohème (exc); *Bizet:* Carmen (exc); *Massenet:* Hérodiade (exc); *Puccini:* Tosca (exc); *Verdi:* Ballo in maschera (exc); *Cilea:* Adriana Lecouvreur (exc); *Verdi:* Rigoletto (exc); *Gounod:* Faust (exc); *Puccini:* Manon Lescaut (exc); *Verdi:* Rigoletto (exc); Ballo in maschera (exc); *Meyerbeer:* Huguenots (exc); *Puccini:* Madama Butterfly (exc); *Gluck:* Orfeo ed Euridice (exc); *Giordano:* Andrea Chénier (exc); *Puccini:* Manon Lescaut (exc); *Verdi:* Traviata (exc); Trovatore (exc); Rigoletto (exc); Aida (exc); *Mozart:* Don Giovanni (exc); *Gounod:* Faust (exc); *Giordano:* Andrea Chénier (exc); *Puccini:* Bohème (exc); *Wagner:* Meistersinger (exc). (F. Viñas, E. Destinn, N. Melba, E. Caruso, C. Dalmores, E. Calvé, G. Anselmi, C. Boninsegna, M. Sammarco, V. Arimondi, P. Amato, S. Kurz, L. Kirkby-Lunn, G. Zenatello, R. Stracciari, M. Battistini, C. Whitehill, anon, orch, NY Met Op Chor, E. Corsi/B. Seidler-Winkler/C. Sabajno/G. Setti/P. Pitt)

Ⓓ **GEMMCDS9924(2)** (7/92)
Covent Garden on Record, Vol.2 (pt 2)
Bizet: Carmen (exc); *Wagner:* Fliegende Holländer (exc); *Donizetti:* Lucia di Lammermoor (exc); *Wagner:* Tannhäuser (exc); *Ponchielli:* Gioconda (exc); *Mozart:* Don Giovanni (exc); *Verdi:* Rigoletto (exc); *Franchetti:* Germania (exc); *Verdi:* Traviata (exc); Rigoletto (exc); *Mozart:* Don Giovanni (exc); *Bizet:* Pêcheurs de Perles (exc); *Meyerbeer:* Huguenots (exc); *Giordano:* Fedora (exc); *Puccini:* Tosca (exc); *Verdi:* Otello (exc); *Saint-Saëns:* Samson et Dalila (exc); *Wagner:* Götterdämmerung (exc); *Puccini:* Bohème (exc); *Debussy:* Pelléas et Mélisande (exc); *Verdi:* Aida (exc); *Puccini:* Tosca (exc); *Wagner:* Walküre (exc); *Puccini:* Bohème (exc); *Delibes:* Lakmé (exc); *Verdi:* Otello (exc); *Wagner:* Walküre (exc); Walküre (exc). (M. Gay, E. Destinn, M. Journet, K. Fleischer-Edel, G. De Luca, J. McCormack, M. Sammarco, L. Tetrazzini, O. Luppi, A. Bonci, J. Nivette, E. Garbin, A. Scotti, G. Zenatello, L. Kirkby-Lunn, A. Talexis, G. Russ, M. Saltzmann-Stevens, M. Kousnietzoff, Vanni-Marcoux, L. Slezak, W. Hyde, S. Sedlmair, G. Anselmi, M. Kurt, P. Cornelius, orch, anon/B. Seidler-Winkler/P. Pitt/P. Coppola/G.W. Byng)

Ⓓ **GEMMCDS9925(1)** (7/92)
Covent Garden on Record—Vol.3 (pt 1)
Mozart: Don Giovanni (exc); *Gounod:* Faust (exc); *Verdi:* Rigoletto (exc); *Meyerbeer:* Huguenots (exc); *G. Charpentier:* Louise (exc); *Verdi:* Rigoletto (exc); *Puccini:* Manon Lescaut (exc); *R. Strauss:* Rosenkavalier (exc); *Wagner:* Walküre (exc); *Puccini:* Bohème (exc); *Verdi:* Falstaff (exc); *Boito:* Mefistofele (exc); *Saint-Saëns:* Samson et Dalila (exc); *Verdi:* Aida (exc); *Mozart:* Zauberflöte (exc); *Puccini:* Madama Butterfly (exc); Madama Butterfly (exc); *Donizetti:* Don Pasquale (exc); *Gluck:* Orfeo ed Euridice (exc); *Verdi:* Trovatore (exc); *Mozart:* Zauberflöte (exc); *Verdi:* Aida (exc); *Saint-Saëns:* Samson et Dalila (exc); *Leoncavallo:* Pagliacci (exc); *Wagner:* Götterdämmerung (exc); *Puccini:* Bohème (exc). (G. De Luca, L. Sibiriakov, L. Edvina, L. Lipkowska, G. Martinelli, M. Siems, M. Kurt, J. Urlus, C. Muzio, A. Scotti, A. Didur, P. Franz, M. Licette, J. Hislop, D. Gilly, G. dalla Rizza, G. Pareto, C. Butt, E. Turner, N. Allin, F. Austral, M. Fleta, E. Thornton, D. Noble, W. Widdop, chor, orch, Sadlers Wells Op Orch, LSO, anon/P. Pitt/Henry Wood/T. Beecham/C. Sabajno/W. Braithwaite/A. Coates)

Ⓓ **GEMMCDS9925(2)** (7/92)
Covent Garden on Record—Vol.3 (pt 2)
R. Strauss: Ariadne auf Naxos (exc); *Wagner:* Walküre (exc); Walküre (exc); Walküre (exc); Walküre (exc); *Verdi:* Rigoletto (exc); *R. Strauss:* Ariadne auf Naxos (exc); Rosenkavalier (exc); *Verdi:* Aida (exc); Aida (exc); *Puccini:* Madama Butterfly (exc); *Giordano:* Andrea Chénier (exc); *Donizetti:* Lucia di Lammermoor (exc); *Rossini:* Barbiere di Siviglia (exc); *Puccini:* Tosca (exc); *Wagner:* Fliegende Holländer (exc); *Mozart:* Nozze di Figaro (exc); Nozze di Figaro (exc); *Boito:* Mefistofele (exc); *Verdi:* Otello (exc); *Puccini:* Bohème (exc); *Verdi:* Otello (exc). (Lotte Lehmann, L. Melchior, G. Ljungberg, F. Leider, F. Schorr, A. Piccaver, M. Ivogün, R. Mayr, A. Andrassy, E. Rethberg, B. Franci, M. Sheridan, A. Pertile, G. Lauri-Volpi, T. dal Monte, D. Borgioli, M. Jeritza, E. Schumann, F. Chaliapin, N. Melba, J. Brownlee, G. Zenatello, Berlin St Op Orch, orch, La Scala Orch/F. Weissmann/L. Blech/L. Collingwood/B. Walter/C. Sabajno/F. Ghione/Rosario Bourdon/V. Bellezza)

Ⓓ **GEMMCDS9926(1)** (7/92)
Covent Garden on Record—Vol.4 (pt 1)
Verdi: Otello (exc); *Massenet:* Manon (exc); *Verdi:* Falstaff (exc); *Mozart:* Entführung (exc); *Verdi:* Trovatore (exc); Trovatore (exc); *Puccini:* Turandot (exc); *Gluck:* Armide (exc); *Wagner:* Tannhäuser (exc); Tannhäuser (exc); *Puccini:* Bohème (exc); *Saint-Saëns:* Samson et Dalila (exc); *Verdi:* Otello (exc); Otello (exc); Aida (exc); *Gounod:* Faust (exc); Faust (exc); *Mussorgsky:* Boris Godunov (exc); *Wagner:* Meistersinger (exc); *Puccini:* Manon Lescaut (exc); *Wagner:* Walküre (exc); *Mozart:* Don Giovanni (exc); *Ponchielli:* Gioconda (exc); *Puccini:* Tosca (exc). (G. Zenatello, L. Cilla, E. Cotreil, M. Sampieri, F. Heldy, F. Ansseau, M. Stabile, M. Ivogün, A. Pertile, F. Leider, L. Schöne, H. Janssen, L. Melchior, D. Borgioli, G. Thill, G. Inghilleri, O. Dua, R. Zanelli, I. Minghini-Cattaneo, J. Hislop, F. Chaliapin, A. Kipnis, R. Pampanini, W. Widdop, H. Nash, R. Ponselle, C. Melis, chor, La Scala Chor, orch, Berlin St Op Orch, Bayreuth Fest Orch, LSO, La Scala Orch/V. Bellezza/P. Coppola/F. Zweig/K. Elmendorff/J. Barbirolli/A. Coates/P. Gaubert/C. Sabajno/E. Goossens/E. Orthmann)

Ⓓ **GEMMCDS9926(2)** (7/92)
Covent Garden on Record—Vol.4 (pt 2)
J. Strauss II: Fledermaus (exc); Fledermaus (exc); *Bellini:* Norma (exc); *Giordano:* Andrea Chénier (exc); *Mozart:* Zauberflöte (exc); *Verdi:* Forza del destino (exc); *Puccini:* Turandot (exc); Turandot (exc); Bohème (exc); *Wagner:* Meistersinger (exc); *Rossini:* Cenerentola (exc); *Puccini:* Bohème (exc); Bohème (exc); *Verdi:* Aida (exc); *Wagner:* Tristan und Isolde (exc); *Verdi:* Otello (exc); *Mozart:* Zauberflöte (exc); *Wagner:* Lohengrin (exc); *Beethoven:* Fidelio (exc); *Verdi:* Rigoletto (exc); *Mozart:* Don Giovanni (exc); *Verdi:* Traviata (exc). (Lotte Lehmann, E. Schumann, E. Pinza, B. Gigli, I. Andrésen, R. Ponselle, M. Németh, A. Cortis, J. Cross, R. Bockelmann, C. Supervia, G. Moore, D. Labbette, H. Nash, E. Rethberg, G. Lauri-Volpi, K. Flagstad, L. Tibbett, G. Martinelli, N. Massue, R. Tauber, T. Lemnitz, T. Ralf, H. Roswaenge, L. Pagliughi, M. Caniglia, J. Brownlee, S. Andreva, R. Alva, R. Easton, NY Met Op Chor, ROH Chor, orch, NY Met Op Orch, La Scala Orch, Berlin St Op Orch, Vienna St Op Orch, Berlin Staatskapelle/F. Weissmann/K. Alwin/G. Setti/U.

Berrettoni/F. Zweig/Rosario Bourdon/C. Sabajno/C. Schmalstich/A. Albergoni/T. Beecham/H. Lange/W. Pelletier/L. Blech/B. Seidler-Winkler/B. Walter, LPO/P. Cimara)

Ⓓ **GEMMCDS9941**
Wagner—Tannhaüser
Wagner: Tannhäuser (Cpte). (S. Pilinszky, M. Müller, H. Janssen, R. Jost-Arden, I. Andrésen, G. Belti-Pilinszky, G. von Tschurtschenthaler, J. Sattler, C. Stralendorf, E. Berger, Bayreuth Fest Chor, Bayreuth Fest Orch/K. Elmendorff)

Ⓓ **GEMMCDS9961**
Sullivan—Operettas
Sullivan: Gondoliers (Cpte); Trial by Jury (Cpte). (D. Oldham, George Baker, W. Lawson, A. Davies, H. Lytton, B. Lewis, M. Bennett, A. Hosking, L. Sheffield, G. Gowrie, R. Walker, H. Aitken, R. Stear, S. Gordon, B. Elburn, D. Hemingway, W. Lawson, D. Oldham, L. Sheffield, A. Hosking, George Baker, D'Oyly Carte Op Chor, orch/H. Norris)

Ⓓ **GEMMCDS9964**
Rosa Ponselle - Columbia Acoustics
Bellini: Norma (exc); *Verdi:* Ernani (exc); Vespri Siciliani (exc); Trovatore (exc); Trovatore (exc); Trovatore (exc); Forza del destino (exc); Forza del destino (exc); Aida (exc); Aida (exc); Aida (exc); Otello (exc); *Mascagni:* Cavalleria Rusticana (exc); *Leoncavallo:* Pagliacci (exc); *Di Capua:* Maria, Mari; O sole mio; *Tosti:* Addio; *Rimsky-Korsakov:* Sadko (exc); *Offenbach:* Contes d'Hoffmann (exc); *J. Strauss II:* Blauen Donau, Op.314; *Rossini:* Guillaume Tell (exc); *Halévy:* Juive (exc); *Meyerbeer:* Africaine (exc); *Wagner:* Lohengrin (exc); *Ponchielli:* Gioconda (exc); *Puccini:* Manon Lescaut (exc); Bohème (exc); Tosca (exc); Madama Butterfly (exc); Manon Lescaut (exc); *Löhr:* Rose of my Heart; Where my caravan has rested; *Traditional:* Comin' thro' the rye; *Starr:* Little Alabama coon; *Foster:* Old folks at home; *Bishop:* Home, sweet home; *Herbert:* Mademoiselle Modiste (exc); *Novello:* Keep the home fires burning; *Vanderpool:* Values; *Mana-Zucca:* Rachem; *Wallace:* Maritana (exc). (R. Ponselle, C. Hackett, C. Ponselle, R. Stracciari, orch)

Ⓓ **GEMMCDS9987** (9/93)
Gounod—Faust
Gounod: Faust (Cpte). (C. Vezzani, M. Berthon, M. Journet, L. Musy, M. Coiffier, J. Montfort, M. Cozette, chor, orch/H. Busser)

Ⓓ **GEMMCDS9997/9(1)** (6/93)
Singers of Imperial Russia, Vol.1 (pt 1)
Meyerbeer: Huguenots (exc); Prophète (exc); *Wagner:* Siegfried (exc); *Mussorgsky:* Songs and Dances of Death (exc); *Tchaikovsky:* Songs, Op.63 (exc); *Vilboa:* Seafarers; *Tosti:* Penso!; *Rubinstein:* Nacht; *Puccini:* Tosca (exc); *Tchaikovsky:* Queen of Spades (exc); *Nápravník:* Harold (exc); *A.D. Davidov:* Night, love and the moon; *Bizet:* Carmen (exc); *Tchaikovsky:* Oprichnik (exc); *Cui:* I remember the evening; *Vrangel:* In my soul winter reigns; *Auber:* Fra Diavolo (exc); *Tchaikovsky:* Queen of Spades (exc); *Nápravník:* Dubrovsky (exc); *Rubinstein:* We three; Demon (exc); Asra; *Ippolitov-Ivanov:* In the long grey twilight; *Rossini:* Barbiere di Siviglia (exc); *Tchaikovsky:* Songs, Op.38 (exc); *Dargomïzhsky:* Rusalka (exc); *Cui:* Angelo (exc); *Moniuszko:* Halka (exc); *Tchaikovsky:* Eugene Onegin (exc); *Borodin:* Prince Igor (exc); *Verdi:* Rigoletto (exc); *Rimsky-Korsakov:* Snow Maiden (exc); *Ivanov:* Zabava Putyatishna (exc); *Rimsky-Korsakov:* May Night (exc); *Gounod:* Où voulez-vous aller?; *Grechaninov:* Dobrinya Nikitich (exc); *Nikolayev:* I cannot banish grief; *Tchaikovsky:* Songs, Op.60 (exc). (I. Ershov, V. Sharonov, M. Mei-Figner, N. Figner, I. Tartakov, L. Sobinov, anon)

Ⓓ **GEMMCDS9997/9(2)** (6/93)
Singers of Imperial Russia, Vol.1 (pt 2)
Gounod: Faust (exc); *Flotow:* Martha (exc); *Nikolayev:* Rest; *Wagner:* Lohengrin (exc); *Massenet:* Werther (exc); Manon (exc); *Bizet:* Pêcheurs de perles (exc); *A. Thomas:* Mignon (exc); *Rimsky-Korsakov:* Snow Maiden (exc); *Arensky:* Raphael (exc); *Meyerbeer:* Huguenots (exc); *Tosti:* Si tu le voulais; *Gall:* Hidden love; *Meyerbeer:* Robert le Diable (exc); *Boito:* Mefistofele (exc); *Verdi:* Don Carlo (exc); *Moniuszko:* O, mother; *Gounod:* Faust (exc); *Verdi:* Ernani (exc); *Moniuszko:* Quack's prophecy; Haunted Manor (exc); O, mother; Quack's prophecy; *Noskowski:* Our mountaineers; *Hertz:* Old King; *Gall:* Hidden love; *Moniuszko:* Verbum Nobile (exc); Old age; *Maszynski:* Bagpiper's Song; *Moniuszko:* Phantoms (exc); Halka (exc); *Gall:* Enchanted princess; *Moniuszko:* Rokiczana (exc); Sail! young raftsmen; *Boito:* Mefistofele (exc); *Halévy:* Juive (exc); *Meyerbeer:* Robert le Diable (exc); *Gounod:* Faust (exc); *Boito:* Mefistofele (exc); *Meyerbeer:* Huguenots (exc). (L. Sobinov, A. Didur, anon, orch, D.G. Kornilov, S. Cottone)

Ⓓ **GEMMCD9016**
Mattia Battistini, Vol.3
Gluck: Paride ed Elena (exc); *Berlioz:* Damnation de Faust (exc); *Gounod:* Faust (exc); Faust (exc); *A. Thomas:* Hamlet (exc); *Massenet:* Hérodiade (exc); Thaïs (exc); *Mozart:* Don Giovanni (exc); *Bellini:* Puritani (exc); *Donizetti:* Favorita (exc); Favorita (exc); *Rossini:* Barbiere di Siviglia (exc); *Verdi:* Trovatore (exc); Forza del destino (exc); Don Carlo (exc); *Ponchielli:* Gioconda (exc); *Rubinstein:* Demon (exc); *Gounod:* Soir. (M. Battistini, E. Barbieri, A. Janni, E. Corsi, J. de Witt, anon, orch)

Ⓓ **GEMMCD9024**
German—Orchestral and Vocal Music
German: Nell Gwyn Overture; Romeo and Juliet (exc); Glorious Devon; Henry VIII (exc); Gipsy Suite; Tom Jones (exc); Merrie England (exc); Theme and Diversions; Rolling down to Rio; Symphonic Suite (exc); Tempter (exc); March Rhapsody. (Webster Booth, P. Dawson, Plaza Th Orch, Hastings Municipal Orch, orch, SO, New SO, LSO/F. Tours/B. Cameron/E. German/M. Sargent/C. Greenwood)

Ⓓ **GEMMCD9043**
Jussi Björling - Songs and Arias, Volume 3
de Curtis: Torna a Surriento; Carmela; *Toselli:* Serenade; *Leoncavallo:* Mattinata; *Di Capua:* O sole mio; *Tosti:* Ideale; *Borodin:* Prince Igor (exc); *Laparra:* Illustre fregona (exc); *Atterberg:* Fanal (exc); *Verdi:* Rigoletto (exc); Rigoletto (exc); Trovatore (exc); Trovatore (exc); *Puccini:* Tosca (exc); Tosca (exc); Bohème (exc); Fanciulla del West (exc); *Ponchielli:* Gioconda (exc); *Flotow:* Martha (exc); *Meyerbeer:* Africaine (exc); *Gounod:* Roméo et Juliette (exc); *Massenet:* Manon (exc); *Gounod:* Faust (exc); *Rossini:* Stabat mater (exc); *Verdi:* Requiem (exc). (J. Björling, orch, Stockholm Royal Op Orch/N. Grevillius)

Ⓓ **GEMMCD9049**
Flagstad and Melchior sing Wagner
Wagner: Fliegende Holländer (exc); Tannhäuser (exc); Tannhäuser (exc); Lohengrin (exc); Wesendonk Lieder (exc); Tristan und Isolde (exc); Meistersinger (exc); Walküre (exc); Walküre (exc); Siegfried (exc); Parsifal (exc). (K. Flagstad, L. Melchior, Philadelphia/E. Ormandy, Victor SO/E. McArthur, orch/H. Lange, chor)

Ⓓ **GEMMCD9065** (7/94)
Beecham conducts French Works
Berlioz: Damnation de Faust (exc); *Franck:* Symphony; *Debussy:* Après-midi; *Offenbach:* Contes d'Hoffmann (exc). (LPO/T. Beecham)

Ⓓ **GEMMCD9081**
Sir Thomas Beecham and the LPO, Volume 3
Mozart: Don Giovanni (exc); Mass, K427 (exc); Piano Concerto 12; *Schubert:* Symphony 5. (D. Labbette, L. Kentner, Leeds Fest Chor, LPO/T. Beecham)

Ⓓ **GEMMCD9082**
Meta Seinemeyer
Weber: Freischütz (exc); *Verdi:* Ballo in maschera (exc); Aida (exc); Otello (exc); Otello (exc); *Puccini:* Bohème (exc); *Giordano:* Andrea Chénier (exc); Andrea Chénier (exc); *Liszt:* O lieb, so lang du lieben kannst, S298; *Rubinstein:* Nacht; Dew is sparkling, Op.72/1; *Weingartner:* Liebesfeier, Op.16/2. (M. Seinemeyer, T. Pattiera, orch/F. Weissmann)

Ⓓ **GEMMCD9084**
Sir Thomas Beecham and the LPO, Volume 4
Respighi: Rossiniana (exc); *Rossini:* Gazza ladra (exc); Scala di seta (exc); Semiramide (exc); Guillaume Tell (exc); *Mendelssohn:* Ruy Blas; Midsummer Night's Dream (exc). (LPO/T. Beecham)

Ⓓ **GEMMCD9088**
Titta Ruffo (1877-1953)
Gounod: Faust (exc); *Flotow:* Martha (exc); *Verdi:* Rigoletto (exc); Rigoletto (exc); Rigoletto (exc); Rigoletto (exc); *Mozart:* Don Giovanni (exc); *Verdi:* Otello (exc); Otello (exc); Falstaff (exc); *A. Thomas:* Hamlet (exc); *Massenet:* Thaïs (exc); *Bizet:* Carmen (exc); *Leoncavallo:* Pagliacci (exc); Chatterton (exc); *Paladilhe:* Patrie (exc); *Schumann:* Romanzen und Balladen, Op.49 (exc). (T. Ruffo, M. Galvany, E. Caruso, chor, orch/W.B. Rogers/C. Sabajno/J. Pasternack)

Ⓓ **GEMMCD9091**
Dino Borgioli
Cesti: Orontea (exc); *Rossini:* Barbiere di Siviglia (exc); *Bellini:* Sonnambula (exc); Sonnambula (exc); *Donizetti:* Elisir d'amore (exc); Favorita (exc); Don Pasquale (exc); *Verdi:* Traviata (exc); *Gounod:* Faust (exc); Faust (exc); *Bizet:* Carmen (exc); Pêcheurs de Perles (exc); *Mascagni:* Amico Fritz (exc); *Sadero:* Barcarola; *Hageman:* Do not go, my love. (D. Borgioli, M. Gentile, G. Pedroni, I. Mannarini, A. Rettore, E. Surinach, M. Zamboni, R. Pampanini, I. Newton, anon, La Scala Chor, orch/L. Molajoli)

Ⓓ **GEMMCD9093**
The Artistry of Richard Crooks, Volume 1
Handel: Floridante (exc); *Arne:* Comus (exc); *Haydn:* Lieder für das Clavier II (exc); *Handel:* Partenope (exc); *Franz:* Lieder, Op.14 (exc); *Pessard:* Adieu du matin; *Grieg:* Songs, Op.48 (exc); *Schubert:* Schwanengesang, D957 (exc); *Grieg:* Melodies of the Heart, Op.5 (exc); *Traditional:* Have you seen the whyte lilie grow?; *Franz:* Lieder, Op.10 (exc); *Purcell-Cockram:* Passing by; *Verdi:* Aida (exc); *Bizet:* Carmen (exc); *Puccini:* Tosca (exc); *Sullivan:* Lost Chord; *MacMurrough:* Macushla; *Coates:* Birdsongs at eventide; *Foster:* Oh, Susanna; Jeanie with the light brown hair; *Romberg:* Desert Song (exc); *Friml:* Vagabond King (exc); *Foster:* Beautiful dreamer; *E. Nevin:* Rosary; *Friml:* Amour toujours; *Romberg:* Student Prince (exc); *Herbert:* Naughty Marietta (exc). (R. Crooks, F. Schauwecker, Berlin St Op Orch/C. Schmalstich, orch, inst ens, F. La Forge, chor/J. Barbirolli, H. Dawkes, A. Matthews)

Ⓓ **GEMMCD9094**
Beecham & the LPO, Vol.5
Wagner: Meistersinger (exc); *Grieg:* Peer Gynt Suites (exc); *Weber:* Oberon (exc); *Dvořák:* Slavonic Rhapsodies (exc); Legends (exc); *Wagner:* Fliegende Holländer (exc); Lohengrin (exc); *Suppé:* Morgen, ein Mittag, ein Abend in Wien (exc); *Mozart:* Nozze di Figaro (exc). (LPO/T. Beecham)

Ⓓ **GEMMCD9104**
Pasquale Amato (1878-1942)
Rossini: Barbiere di Siviglia (exc); *Bellini:* Puritani (exc); *Donizetti:* Favorita (exc); *Verdi:* Due Foscari (exc); Rigoletto (exc); Ballo in maschera (exc); Forza del destino (exc); Aida (exc); *Gounod:* Faust (exc); *Bizet:* Carmen (exc); *Meyerbeer:* Africaine (exc); *Ponchielli:* Gioconda (exc); *Verdi:* Otello (exc); Otello (exc); *Puccini:* Tosca (exc); *Leoncavallo:* Pagliacci (exc). (P. Amato, M. Journet, M. Matzenauer, E. Caruso, J. Gadski, A. Bada, NY Met Op Chor, chor, orch/G. Setti/W.B. Rogers)

Ⓓ **GEMMCD9106**
Dmitri Smirnov
Meyerbeer: Huguenots (exc); *Bizet:* Pêcheurs de perles (exc); Carmen (exc); *Massenet:* Manon (exc); *Verdi:* Rigoletto (exc); *Puccini:* Tabarro (exc); *Glinka:* Ruslan and Lyudmila (exc); *Dargomïzhsky:* Rusalka (exc); *Tchaikovsky:* Eugene Onegin (exc); *Mussorgsky:* Boris Godunov (exc); Boris Godunov (exc); Fair at Sorochintsï (exc); *Borodin:* Prince Igor (exc); *Rimsky-Korsakov:* May Night (exc); Sadko (exc); *Tchaikovsky:* Queen of Spades (exc); *Leoncavallo:* Mattinata. (D. Smirnov, K.E. Kaidanov, M. Davydova, anon, orch/J. Harrison)

Ⓓ **GEMMCD9112**
Walter Widdop
Bach: St Matthew Passion, BWV244 (exc); *Handel:* Messiah (exc); Acis and Galatea (exc); Jephtha (exc); Judas Maccabaeus (exc); *Gounod:* Faust (exc); Reine de Saba (exc); *Borodin:* Prince Igor (exc); *Tchaikovsky:* Eugene Onegin (exc); *A.G. Thomas:* Esmeralda (exc); *Balfe:* Come into the garden, Maud; *Dibdin:* Tom Bowling; *Braham:* Death of Nelson. (W. Widdop, Phil Ch, anon, orch/C. Kennedy Scott/J. Barbirolli/L. Collingwood/J. Harrison/M. Sargent)

Ⓓ **GEMMCD9117**
Graziella Pareto
Bellini: Sonnambula (exc); *Verdi:* Rigoletto (exc); *Donizetti:* Lucia di Lammermoor (exc); *Verdi:* Rigoletto (exc); Rigoletto (exc); Traviata (exc); Traviata (exc); *Bizet:* Pêcheurs de perles (exc); *Donizetti:* Don Pasquale (exc); *Verdi:* Traviata (exc); *Mozart:* Nozze di Figaro (exc); *Sibella:* O bimba, bimbetta; *Bellini:* Sonnambula (exc); *Longás Torres:* Dolor de amar; *Traditional:* Pastoreta; Heren riera; Caçador; *Guetary:* Mi Niña; *Ponce:* Estrellita. (G. Pareto, L. Bergamini, M. Dragoni, G. Manuritta, F. Longás Torres, chor, orch/P. Pitt/C. Sabajno)

Ⓓ **GEMMCD9122**
20 Great Basses sing Great Arias
Gounod: Faust (exc); *Handel:* Acis and Galatea (exc); *Mozart:* Don Giovanni (exc); *Rimsky-Korsakov:* Sadko (exc); *Borodin:* Prince Igor (exc); *Rimsky-Korsakov:* May Night (exc); *Mendelssohn:* Heimkehr aus der Fremde (exc); *R. Strauss:* Rosenkavalier (exc); *Mozart:* Zauberflöte (exc); *Tchaikovsky:* Eugene Onegin (exc); *Meyerbeer:* Huguenots (exc); *Verdi:* Don Carlo (exc); *Mozart:* Zauberflöte (exc); *Rossini:* Barbiere di Siviglia (exc); *Wagner:* Götterdämmerung (exc); *Flotow:* Martha (exc); *Wagner:* Lohengrin (exc); *A. Thomas:* Caïd (exc); *Verdi:* Vespri siciliani (exc); *Mussorgsky:* Boris Godunov (exc); *Puccini:* Bohème (exc); *Handel:* Messiah (exc). (P. Plançon, M. McEachern, S. Baccaloni, M. Reizen, A. Pirogov, S. Krasovsky, P. Dawson, R. Mayr, W. Strienz, A. Kipnis, J. Mardones, E. Pinza, P. Knüpfer, F. Chaliapin, E. List, M. Journet, I. Andrésen, R. Radford, Vanni-Marcoux, H. Williams, chor, Berlin St Op Orch, Vienna St Op Chor,

orch, Glyndebourne Fest Orch, B. Paalen, BPO/F. Busch/F. Zweig/G.W. Byng/P. Coppola/T. Beecham/E. Goossens/R. Heger/Rosario Bourdon, VPO/E. Mörike)

Ⓓ **GEMMCD9125**
20 Great Violinists plays 20 Masterpieces
Kreisler: Liebesfreud; *Chopin:* Nocturnes (exc); *Bruch:* Kol Nidrei; *Bach:* Solo Violin Partitas and Sonatas (exc); *Gluck:* Orfeo ed Euridice (exc); *Brahms:* Hungarian Dances (exc); *Corelli:* Sonatas, Op.5 (exc); *Drdla:* Souvenir; *Ambrosio:* Serenade, Op.4; *Wieniawski:* Souvenir de Moscou, Op.6; *Handel:* Violin Sonatas (exc); *Paganini:* Caprices, Op.1 (exc); *Reger:* Solo Violin Sonatas, Op.91 (exc); *Suk:* Pieces, Op.17 (exc); *Kreisler:* Tartini's Corelli Variations; *Scriabin:* Nocturnes, Op.5 (exc); *Ravel:* Tzigane; *Bach:* Solo Violin Partitas and Sonatas (exc); *Wieniawski:* Mazurkas, Op.19 (exc); *Sarasate:* Zigeunerweisen (exc). (F. Kreisler, M. Elman, B. Huberman, N. Milstein, G. Neveu, L. Auer, A. Busch, F. Drdla, G. Enescu, J. Kubelík, C. Flesch, J. Heifetz, G. Kulenkampff, R. Ricci, A. Campoli, D. Oistrakh, Z. Francescatti, J. Joachim, E. Ysaÿe, P. de Sarasate, C. Lamson, M. van Gool, S. Schultze, E. Kris, A. Sándor, C. Fürstner, C. DeCreus, B. Seidler-Winkler, anon, E.C. Harris, F. Dyck, A. Giakov, M. Fauré)

Ⓓ **GEMMCD9128**
Pablo Casals - Bow and Baton
Vivaldi: Concerti grossi, Op.3 (exc); *Bach:* Sacred Songs, BWV439-488 (exc); Solo Violin Partitas and Sonatas (exc); Suites, BWV1066-9 (exc); *Tartini:* Cello Concerto in D (exc); *Giuseppe Valentini:* Violin Sonatas, Op.8 (exc); *Laserna:* Tonadilla; *Haydn:* Sonatas, HobVI:1-6 (exc); *Boccherini:* Cello Sonata, G4; *Beethoven:* Menuet, WoO10/2; *Mendelssohn:* Song without words, Op.109; *Schumann:* Kinderszenen (exc); *Dvořák:* Gipsy Melodies (exc); *Rimsky-Korsakov:* Tale of Tsar Saltan (exc); *Cassadó:* Requiebros; *Beethoven:* Coriolan; *Brahms:* Haydn Variations. (P. Casals, Blas-Net, O. Schulhof, LSO/P. Casals)

Ⓓ **GEMMCD9129**
Great Tenors, Vol.2
Mozart: Entführung (exc); *Rossini:* Barbiere di Siviglia (exc); *Giordano:* Andrea Chénier (exc); *Bizet:* Pêcheurs de Perles (exc); *Wagner:* Lohengrin (exc); *Mascagni:* Cavalleria Rusticana (exc); *Rimsky-Korsakov:* Sadko (exc); *Tchaikovsky:* Eugene Onegin (exc); Eugene Onegin (exc); *Bellini:* Puritani (exc); *Bizet:* Carmen (exc); *Giordano:* Fedora (exc); *Handel:* Judas Maccabaeus (exc); *Ponchielli:* Gioconda (exc); *Donizetti:* Favorita (exc); *Verdi:* Traviata (exc); Rigoletto (exc); *Giordano:* Andrea Chénier (exc); *Lehár:* Land des Lächelns (exc); *Traditional:* Star of the County Down. (H. Roswaenge, T. Schipa, J. Björling, E. Clément, M. Journet, L. Slezak, E. Caruso, I. Kozlovsky, L. Sobinov, D. Smirnov, G. Lauri-Volpi, F. Ansseau, F. Heldy, G. Martinelli, W. Widdop, B. Gigli, M. Fleta, M. Wittrisch, M. Teschemacher, J. Hislop, A. Pertile, R. Tauber, J. McCormack, orch/N. Grevillius/M. Gurlitt/P. Coppola/F. Zweig, La Scala Orch/C. Sabajno, E. Schneider/Rosario Bourdon, chor, L. Schöne, Berlin St Op Orch)

Ⓓ **GEMMCD9130**
Great Sopranos, Vol.2
Cilea: Adriana Lecouvreur (exc); *Millöcker:* Dubarry (exc); *Mozart:* Nozze di Figaro (exc); Nozze di Figaro (exc); *Ponchielli:* Gioconda (exc); *Bach:* Cantata 68 (exc); *Mascagni:* Cavalleria Rusticana (exc); *Mozart:* Don Giovanni (exc); *Verdi:* Aida (exc); *Massenet:* Manon (exc); *Offenbach:* Contes d'Hoffmann (exc); *Mozart:* Nozze di Figaro (exc); *Bizet:* Carmen (exc); *Mozart:* Nozze di Figaro (exc); *Wagner:* Lohengrin (exc); *Bizet:* Carmen (exc); *A. Thomas:* Mignon (exc); *Puccini:* Bohème (exc); *Bishop:* Should he upbraid; *A. Thomas:* Mignon (exc). (C. Muzio, G. Moore, A. Galli-Curci, N. Melba, M. Jeritza, I. Baillie, C. Boninsegna, A. Patti, E. Turner, G. Farrar, A. Gluck, L. Homer, M. Sembrich, C. Supervia, E. Bettendorf, K. Flagstad, M. Garden, E. Destinn, L. Bori, D. Labbette, M. Licette, L. Ronald, CBO, orch/N. Shilkret/B. Cameron/G. Cloëz/E. Ormandy/P. Pitt)

Ⓓ **GEMMCD9131** (2/95)
Bruno Walter live
Bruckner: Symphony 4; *Weber:* Oberon (exc); *Smetana:* Bartered Bride (exc). (NBC SO/B. Walter)

Ⓓ **GEMMCD9143**
Claudia Muzio, Volume 2
Puccini: Manon Lescaut (exc); Tosca (exc); *Verdi:* Trovatore (exc); *Leoncavallo:* Pagliacci (exc); *Ponchielli:* Gioconda (exc); *Verdi:* Otello (exc); *Giordano:* Canzone guerresca; *A. Thomas:* Mignon (exc); *Puccini:* Madama Butterfly (exc); *Verdi:* Aida (exc); *Wolf-Ferrari:* Segreto di Susanna (exc); *Verdi:* Aida (exc); *Rossini:* Guillaume Tell (exc); *Verdi:* Trovatore (exc); *G. Charpentier:* Louise (exc); *Massenet:* Manon (exc); *Verdi:* Ballo in maschera (exc); *Delibes:* Bonjour, Suzon!; *Puccini:* Suor Angelica (exc); Gianni Schicchi (exc); Bohème (exc); Bohème (exc); *Parisotti:* Se tu m'ami. (C. Muzio, orch)

Ⓓ **GEMMCD9145**
Richard Tauber - Operatic Arias
Mozart: Don Giovanni (exc); Entführung (exc); Zauberflöte (exc); *Wagner:* Walküre (exc); *Tchaikovsky:* Eugene Onegin (exc); *Nessler:* Trompeter von Säckingen (exc); *Flotow:* Martha (exc); Martha (exc); *Verdi:* Traviata (exc); Traviata (exc); *Leoncavallo:* Pagliacci (exc); *Puccini:* Tosca (exc); Turandot (exc); *Albert:* Tiefland (exc); *Zeller:* Vogelhändler (exc); *J. Strauss II:* Zigeunerbaron (exc); Zigeunerbaron (exc). (R. Tauber, B. Ziegler, C. Vanconti, orch/W. Goehr, Berlin Schauspielhaus Orch/E. Hauke)

Ⓓ **GEMMCD9146**
Florence Austral
Handel: Allegro, il penseroso ed il moderato (exc); *Mozart:* Nozze di Figaro (exc); *Haydn:* Creation (exc); *Mendelssohn:* Elijah (exc); *Chopin:* Polish Songs (exc); *Wagner:* Tristan und Isolde (exc); Götterdämmerung (exc); Walküre (exc); *Gounod:* Faust (exc). (F. Austral, T. Davies, W. Widdop, F. Chaliapin, P. Kahn, orch, LSO/A. Coates)

Ⓓ **GEMMCD9156**
Busoni and his Circle, Volume 2
Debussy: Pour le piano (exc); *Busoni:* Sonatina 4; Sonatina 4 (exc); *Sibelius:* Lyric Pieces, Op.41; *Mussorgsky:* Seamstress; *Rimsky-Korsakov:* Tale of Tsar Saltan (exc); *Stravinsky:* Petrushka; *Mozart:* Gigue, K574; *Bach:* Solo Violin Partitas and Sonatas (exc); *Medtner:* Forgotten Melodies, Op.38 (exc); *Chopin:* Etudes (exc); *Liszt:* Concert Studies, S144 (exc). (M. von Zadora, E. Weiss, L. Sirota, E. Petri, C. Zecchi)

Ⓓ **GEMMCD9161** (8/95)
Edmond Clément (1867-1928)
Meyerbeer: Robert le diable (exc); *Lalo:* Roi d'ys (exc); *Delibes:* Lakmé (exc); *Massenet:* Manon (exc); Werther (exc); *Godard:* Jocelyn (exc); *Gounod:* Roméo et Juliette (exc); *Boito:* Mefistofele (exc); *Mascagni:* Cavalleria rusticana (exc); *E. Bernard:* Ca fait peur; *Weckerlin:* Romances et Chansons (exc); *Pessard:* Adieu du matin; *J. Martini:* Plaisir d'amour; *Bemberg:* Neige; *Lully:* Au clair de la lune; *Massenet:* Poème d'avril (exc); *Weckerlin:* Romances et Chansons (exc); *T. Dubois:* Jeunes fillettes; *Debussy:* Romance; *Koechlin:* Si tu le veux; *Tiersot:* En passant par la Lorraine; *Traditional:* Filles de la Rochelle; *Bizet:* Pêcheurs de perles (exc). (E. Clément, M. Journet, G. Farrar, F. la Forge, anon, orch/Rosario Bourdon)

Ⓓ **GEMMCD9168**
Alessandro Bonci
Puccini: Bohème (exc); *Flotow:* Martha (exc); *Donizetti:* Elisir d'amore (exc); *Massenet:* Manon (exc); *Ponchielli:* Gioconda (exc); *Gounod:* Faust (exc); *Donizetti:* Favorita (exc); *Meyerbeer:* Africaine (exc); *Verdi:* Rigoletto (exc); *Giordano:* Fedora (exc); *Puccini:* Fanciulla del West (exc); Manon Lescaut (exc); *Verdi:* Luisa Miller (exc); *Donizetti:* Elisir d'amore (exc); *Puccini:* Tosca (exc); *Verdi:* Ballo in maschera (exc); *A. Thomas:* Mignon (exc); *Leoncavallo:* Pagliacci (exc). (A. Bonci, orch)

Ⓓ **GEMMCD9169**
Gluck—Orphée
Gluck: Orphée (exc); Orphée (exc). (A. Raveau, G. Féraldy, J. Delille, Vlassof Chor, Paris SO/H. Tomasi)

Ⓓ **GEMMCD9172**
Emmy Destinn (1878-1930)
Mozart: Zauberflöte (exc); *Schubert:* Schöne Müllerin (exc); Schwanengesang, D957 (exc); *Weber:* Freischütz (exc); Freischütz (exc); *Wagner:* Fliegende Holländer (exc); Lohengrin (exc); *Liszt:* Oh, quand je dors, S282; *Verdi:* Trovatore (exc); Aida (exc); Aida (exc); *A. Thomas:* Mignon (exc); Mignon (exc); *Smetana:* Bartered Bride (exc); Dalibor (exc); Kiss (exc); *Ponchielli:* Gioconda (exc); *Tchaikovsky:* Queen of Spades (exc); *Dvořák:* Rusalka (exc); *Puccini:* Madama Butterfly (exc). (E. Destinn, anon, orch/B. Seidler-Winkler/W.B. Rogers/F. Kark)

Ⓓ **GEMMCD9175** (11/95)
Heddle Nash - Serenade
Bizet: Carmen (exc); *Gounod:* Faust (exc); *Bizet:* Pêcheurs de perles (exc); Jolie fille de Perth (exc); *Mascagni:* Cavalleria rusticana (exc); *Verdi:* Rigoletto (exc); Trovatore (exc); *Puccini:* Bohème (exc); *Rossini:* Soirées musicales (exc); *J. Strauss II:* Fledermaus (exc); *Lehár:* Friederike (exc); *R. Strauss:* Lieder, Op.17 (exc); *Delius:* English Songs (exc); *MacMurrough:* Macushla; *J. R. Thomas:* Eileen Allanna; *Traditional:* Annie Laurie; *Ascher:* Alice, where art thou?. (H. Nash, M. Parry, J. Griffiths, M. Licette, M. Brunskill, D. Noble, Liverpool PO/M. Sargent, orch, BNOC Chor, BNOC Orch/A. Buesst, G. Moore, Male Qt, anon/J. Batten, chor/C. Raybould)

Ⓓ **GEMMCD9178**
Riccardo Stracciari
Gounod: Faust (exc); *Verdi:* Traviata (exc); Trovatore (exc); Ballo in maschera (exc); Ernani (exc); Rigoletto (exc); *Rossini:* Barbiere di Siviglia (exc); *Verdi:* Forza del destino (exc); *A. Thomas:* Hamlet (exc); *Giordano:* Andrea Chénier (exc); *Leoncavallo:* Zazà (exc); *Catalani:* Wally (exc); *Berlioz:* Damnation de Faust (exc); *Donizetti:* Favorita (exc); *Meyerbeer:* Dinorah (exc); *Rossini:* Barbiere di Siviglia (exc); *Verdi:* Rigoletto (exc); Otello (exc); *Mozart:* Don Giovanni (exc); *De Curtis:* Nostalgia; Sto penzanno 'a Maria. (R. Stracciari, M. Barrientos, C. Hackett, N. Fusati, A. Rettore, orch/G. Polacco)

Ⓓ **GEMMCD9179**
The Art of Serge Koussevitzky
Vivaldi: Concerti grossi, Op.3 (exc); *Corelli:* Suite for Strings (Pinelli); *H. Casadesus:* Concerto in D; *Handel:* Concerti grossi, Op.6 (exc); Semele (exc); *Mozart:* Zauberflöte (exc); *Schubert:* Rosamunde (exc); *Liszt:* Mephisto Waltz 2, S111; *Traditional:* Fair Harvard; *Grieg:* Elegiac Melodies (exc). (D. Maynor, Harvard Glee Club, Radcliffe Choral Soc, Boston SO/S. Koussevitzky)

Ⓓ **GEMMCD9221** (9/92)
Luisa Tetrazzini—Vol.1
Verdi: Rigoletto (exc); *A. Thomas:* Mignon (exc); *Delibes:* Lakmé (exc); *Meyerbeer:* Dinorah (exc); *Donizetti:* Lucia di Lammermoor (exc); *Mozart:* Nozze di Figaro (exc); *Rossini:* Barbiere di Siviglia (exc); *Verdi:* Traviata (exc); *Mozart:* Don Giovanni (exc); *Gounod:* Roméo et Juliette (exc); *J. Strauss II:* Frühlingsstimmen, Op. 410; *Verdi:* Ballo in maschera (exc); *Donizetti:* Lucia di Lammermoor (exc); *Benedict:* Carnival of Venice Variations; *Bellini:* Sonnambula (exc); *Bizet:* Pêcheurs de Perles (exc); *Tosti:* Aprile. (L. Tetrazzini, orch/P. Pitt, P. Pitt)

Ⓓ **GEMMCD9222** (9/92)
Luisa Tetrazzini—Vol.2
Tosti: Serenata; *Bizet:* Pêcheurs de Perles (exc); *Gounod:* Mireille (exc); *Chapí:* Hijas del Zebedeo (exc); *Donizetti:* Linda di Chamounix (exc); *Verdi:* Vespri siciliani (exc); *Rossini:* Semiramide (exc); *Grieg:* Peer Gynt (exc); *F. David:* Perle du Brésil (exc); *Bizet:* Carmen (exc); *Verdi:* Traviata (exc); *Delibes:* Lakmé (exc); *Mozart:* Don Giovanni (exc); *Verdi:* Aida (exc); *Donizetti:* Linda di Chamounix (exc); *A. Thomas:* Hamlet (exc); Mignon (exc); *Proch:* Air and Variations. (L. Tetrazzini, orch/P. Pitt, P. Pitt, chor)

Ⓓ **GEMMCD9223** (9/92)
Luisa Tetrazzini—Vol.3
Bellini: Sonnambula (exc); *Meyerbeer:* Huguenots (exc); *Bellini:* Puritani (exc); *Bishop:* Home, sweet home; *Venzano:* O che assorta; *Verdi:* Traviata (exc); *Ricci:* Crispino e la Comare (exc); *Meyerbeer:* Etoile du Nord (exc); *Veracini:* Rosalinda (exc); *Gounod:* Faust (exc); *G. Braga:* Melodies (exc); *Chapí:* Hijas del Zebedeo (exc); *T. Moore:* Irish Melodies (exc); *Verdi:* Ballo in maschera (exc); *Bellini:* Sonnambula (exc); *Verdi:* Traviata (exc); *Benedict:* Carnival of Venice Variations; *Donizetti:* Lucia di Lammermoor (exc). (L. Tetrazzini, orch, inst ens)

Ⓓ **GEMMCD9224** (9/92)
Luisa Tetrazzini—Vol.4
Eckert: Eco; *Rossini:* Barbiere di Siviglia (exc); *F. David:* Perle du Brésil (exc); *A. Thomas:* Mignon (exc); *Verdi:* Rigoletto (exc); *Delibes:* Lakmé (exc); *Bellini:* Sonnambula (exc); *Proch:* Air and Variations; *Donizetti:* Lucia di Lammermoor (exc); *Verdi:* Rigoletto (exc); *Cowen:* Swallows; *Gilbert:* Bonnie Sweet Bessie; *Veracini:* Rosalinda (exc); *Verdi:* Trovatore (exc); *De Koven:* Rhapsody and Serenata inutile; *Venzano:* O che assorta; *Meyerbeer:* Dinorah (exc). (L. Tetrazzini, E. Caruso, P. Amato, M. Journet, orch, A. Bada, J. Jacoby)

Ⓓ **GEMMCD9225** (9/92)
Luisa Tetrazzini—Vol.5
Pergolesi: Tre giorni son che Nina; *Donizetti:* Linda di Chamounix (exc); *Bizet:* Carmen (exc); *Grieg:* Peer Gynt (exc); *Verdi:* Forza del destino (exc); Vespri siciliani (exc); *Mozart:* Zauberflöte (exc); *Drigo:* Arlekinda (exc); *Lama:* Come le rose; *Hoschna:* Madame Sherry (exc); *Lemaire:* Vous dansez, Marquise; *V. Valente:* Nuttata napulitana; *De Curtis:* So 'nnammurato 'e te; *Lama:* Napule che canta; *Bovio:* Cara piccina; *Lama:* Piccolo amore; *Donizetti:* Lucia di Lammermoor (exc); *Verdi:* Rigoletto (exc); *Rossini:* Barbiere di Siviglia (exc); *Gounod:* Roméo et Juliette (exc); *Bellini:* Sonnambula (exc). (L. Tetrazzini, A. Baggiore, orch, anon)

Ⓓ **GEMMCD9306** (2/89)
Ezio Pinza—Opera Recital
Verdi: Aida (exc); Ernani (exc); Don Carlo (exc); Vespri siciliani (exc); Requiem (exc); *Mozart:* Don Giovanni (exc); Zauberflöte (exc); *Meyerbeer:* Robert le Diable (exc); *A. Thomas:* Caïd (exc); *Gounod:* Faust (exc); *Bellini:* Norma (exc); *Donizetti:* Favorita (exc); *Boito:* Mefistofele (exc); Mefistofele (exc); *Donizetti:* Lucia di Lammermoor (exc); *Halévy:* Juive (exc); Juive (exc); *Bellini:* Puritani (exc); *Verdi:* Trovatore (exc); Simon Boccanegra (exc). (E. Pinza, G. Martinelli, NY Met Op Chor, Chor, Cibelli, NY Met Op Orch/G. Setti/Rosario Bourdon, orch/C. Sabajno)

Ⓓ **GEMMCD9308** (2/89)
Amelita Galli-Curci - Aria and Song Recital
Bellini: Sonnambula (exc); Puritani (exc); *Donizetti:* Linda di Chamounix (exc); Don Pasquale (exc); *Verdi:* Rigoletto (exc); Traviata (exc); *Mozart:* Nozze di Figaro (exc); *Auber:* Manon Lescaut (exc); *F. David:* Perle du Brésil (exc); *Meyerbeer:* Etoile du nord (exc); *Bizet:* Pêcheurs de perles (exc); *Delibes:* Filles de Cadiz; *Massenet:* Manon (exc); *Chopin:* Messagero amoroso; *Rimsky-Korsakov:* Sadko (exc); *Valverde:* Clavelitos. (A. Galli-Curci, orch)

Ⓓ **GEMMCD9309** (5/89)
Enrico Caruso - Opera and Song Recital
Verdi: Rigoletto (exc); Trovatore (exc); Trovatore (exc); Trovatore (exc); Ballo in maschera (exc); Forza del destino (exc); Aida (exc); Otello (exc); Otello (exc); *Meyerbeer:* Africaine (exc); *Puccini:* Bohème (exc); Bohème (exc); Bohème (exc); Tosca (exc); Tosca (exc); *Leoncavallo:* Pagliacci (exc); Pagliacci (exc); Bohème (exc); *Tosti:* Parted!; 'A Vucchella; *Di Capua:* O sole mio. (E. Caruso, F. Alda, E. Schumann-Heink, T. Ruffo, N. Melba, A. Scotti, orch, anon)

Ⓓ **GEMMCD9310** (3/89)
Franz Lehár conducts Richard Tauber
Lehár: Lustige Witwe (exc); Land des Lächelns (exc); Rastelbinder (exc); Wilde Rosen; Zigeunerliebe (exc); Zigeunerliebe (exc); Giuditta (exc); Fürst der Berge (exc); Friederike (exc). (R. Tauber/F. Lehár, orch, Berlin St Op Orch/D. Bela, J. Novotná, C. Vanconti, G. Eweler, H.H. Bollman, Berlin SO, V. Schwarz, VPO, Vienna St Op Orch/E. Hauke)

Ⓓ **GEMMCD9312** (4/90)
Adelina Patti
Mozart: Nozze di Figaro (exc); *Lotti:* Arminio (exc); *Foster:* Old folks at home; *Mozart:* Don Giovanni (exc); *Gounod:* Faust (exc); *Arditi:* Bacio; *T. Moore:* Irish Melodies (exc); *Gounod:* Ave Maria; *Keppel:* Robin Adair; *Bishop:* Home, sweet home; *Rothchild:* Si vous n'avez rien; *Traditional:* Comin' thro' the rye; Banks of Allan Water; *Patti:* On parting; *Hook:* 'Twas within a mile; *Patti:* New Year Message; *Crouch:* Kathleen Mavourneen; *Tosti:* Serenata; *Bellini:* Norma (exc); *A. Thomas:* Mignon (exc); *Bellini:* Sonnambula (exc); *Yradier:* Calasera. (A. Patti, A. Patti, L. Ronald, A. Barili)

Ⓓ **GEMMCD9314** (12/89)
Feodor Chaliapin - Aria and Song Recital
Glinka: Ruslan and Lyudmila (exc); *Serov:* Power of Evil (exc); *Mussorgsky:* Boris Godunov (exc); Boris Godunov (exc); Boris Godunov (exc); Boris Godunov (exc); Song of the flea; *Archangelsky:* Creed; *Mozart:* Don Giovanni (exc); *Rossini:* Barbiere di Siviglia (exc); *Bellini:* Sonnambula (exc); *Boito:* Mefistofele (exc); *Gounod:* Faust (exc); *Massenet:* Don Quichotte (exc). (F. Chaliapin, Paris Russian Op Chor, Russian Metropolitan Church Ch, M. Cozette, Paris Op Chor, O. Kline, LSO, Balalaika Orch, orch, Paris Op Orch/M. Steinmann/O. Tchernoyarov/G.W. Byng/Rosario Bourdon/L. Collingwood/N. Afonsky/J. Barbirolli/E. Goossens/H. Büsser)

Ⓓ **GEMMCD9315** (9/89)
Kreisler/McCormack Duets
G. Braga: Melodies (exc); *Leroux:* Nil; *Godard:* Jocelyn (exc); *Schubert:* Ave Maria, D839; *Gounod:* Ave Maria; *Schubert:* Schwanengesang, D957 (exc); *Mascagni:* Ave Maria; *Moszkowski:* Klavierstücke, Op. 15 (exc); *De Curtis:* Carmela; *Meyer-Helmund:* Fensterin, Op.73/2; *C. Böhm:* Lieder, Op. 326 (exc); *Raff:* Serenade, Op.1; *Offenbach:* Contes d'Hoffmann (exc); *Kramer:* Last Hour, Op.34/6; *J.W. Johnson:* Since you went away; *Rachmaninov:* Songs, Op.4 (exc); Songs, Op.26 (exc); *R. Strauss:* Lieder, Op.27 (exc); *Larchet:* Padriac the Fiddler; *Traditional:* I saw from the beach. (J. McCormack, F. Kreisler, V. O'Brien, L. Schwab, E. Schneider, Victor Orch/W.B. Rogers)

Ⓓ **GEMMCD9316** (9/88)
Beniamino Gigli
Ponchielli: Gioconda (exc); *Puccini:* Manon Lescaut (exc); Bohème (exc); Tosca (exc); *Toselli:* Serenade; *Mario:* Santa Lucia luntana; *Bizet:* Pêcheurs de perles (exc); *Meyerbeer:* Africaine (exc); *Verdi:* Traviata (exc); Rigoletto (exc); *A. Thomas:* Mignon (exc); *Boito:* Mefistofele (exc); *Cottrau:* Addio a Napoli; *Donaudy:* O bei nidi d'amore; *Di Capua:* Maria, mari; *Crescenzo:* Quanno a femmena vo'. (B. Gigli, G. De Luca, A. Galli-Curci, L. Homer, orch, NY Met Op Orch/Rosario Bourdon/G. Setti/J. Pasternack/N. Shilkret)

Ⓓ **GEMMCD9317** (1/89)
Rosa Ponselle sings Italian Opera
Verdi: Traviata (Cpte); *Bellini:* Norma (exc). (R. Ponselle, F. Jagel, L. Tibbett, E. Vettori, H. Wakefield, A. Bada, A. Gandolfi, M. Picco, P. Ananian, NY Met Op Chor, NY Met Op Orch/E. Panizza, M. Telva/G. Setti, R. Ponselle)

Ⓓ **GEMMCD9319** (8/89)
Heddle Nash sings Opera Arias & Songs
Handel: Jephtha (exc); *Mozart:* Zauberflöte (exc); Don Giovanni (exc); *Rossini:* Barbiere di Siviglia (exc); *Donizetti:* Elisir d'amore (exc); *Meyerbeer:* Africaine (exc); *Gounod:* Faust (exc); *A. Thomas:* Mignon (exc); *Verdi:* Rigoletto (exc); Rigoletto (exc); *Leoncavallo:* Pagliacci (exc); *Puccini:* Bohème (exc); *Balfe:* Bohemian Girl (exc); *Wallace:* Maritana (exc); *Sullivan:* Gondoliers (exc); *Carey:* Sally in our alley. (H. Nash, M. Licette, D. Noble, orch, BNOC Orch/E. Goossens)

Ⓓ **GEMMCD9322** (2/89)
Tito Schipa sings Opera Arias and Songs
Handel: Serse (exc); *Rossini:* Barbiere di Siviglia (exc); *Donizetti:* Elisir d'amore (exc); Elisir d'amore (exc); *Verdi:* Traviata (exc); Rigoletto (exc); *Flotow:* Martha (exc); *Delibes:* Lakmé (exc); *A. Thomas:* Mignon (exc); *Massenet:* Werther (exc); *Leoncavallo:* Pagliacci (exc); *Liszt:* O lieb, so lang du lieben kannst, S298; *Padilla:* Valencia; Princesita; *Arona:* Campana di San Giusto; *J. Martini:* Plaisir d'amour; *Barthélemy:* Chi se nne scorda occhiu!. (T. Schipa, orch, La Scala Orch/C. Sabajno, A. Galli-Curci/Rosario Bourdon)

Ⓓ **GEMMCD9324** (1/90)
Fritz Kreisler plays Encores
Mendelssohn: Songs without words (exc); *Tchaikovsky:* Morceaux, Op. 10 (exc); *Dvořák:* Gipsy Melodies (exc); *Massenet:* Thaïs (exc); *Bizet:* Arlésienne Suites (exc); *Kreisler:* Dittersdorf Scherzo; Liebesfreud; Liebesleid; Beethoven Rondino; Caprice viennois; Tambourin chinois; *Lehár:* Frasquita (exc); Giuditta (exc); *Godowsky:* Impressions (exc); *Falla:* Vida breve (exc); *Debussy:* Petite Suite (exc); *Dvořák:* Slavonic Dances (exc); Violin Sonatina (exc); *Albéniz:* España, Op.165 (exc); Recuerdos de Viaje (exc). (F. Kreisler, A. Sándor, C. Lamson, H. Kreisler, M. Raucheisen, H. Squire)

Ⓓ **GEMMCD9327** (7/89)
The Vocal Prime of Richard Tauber
Mozart: Zauberflöte (exc); Don Giovanni (exc); *Lortzing:* Undine (exc); *J. Strauss II:* Fledermaus (exc); *Albert:* Tiefland (exc); *Wagner:* Meistersinger (exc); *Offenbach:* Contes d'Hoffmann (exc); *Rossini:* Barbiere di Siviglia (exc); *Verdi:* Rigoletto (exc); Trovatore (exc); Forza del destino (exc); *Bizet:* Carmen (exc); *Puccini:* Madama Butterfly (exc); *Grieg:* Songs, Op.33 (exc); *Tosti:* Chanson de l'adieu; *Liszt:* Es muss ein Wunderbares sein, S314. (R. Tauber, V. Schwarz, B. Ziegler, orch/E. Hauke)

Ⓓ **GEMMCD9331** (11/89)
Frida Leider sings Wagner
Wagner: Götterdämmerung (exc); Götterdämmerung (exc); Tristan und Isolde (exc); Tristan und Isolde (exc); Parsifal (exc). (F. Leider, A. von Stosch, E. Marherr-Wagner, L. Melchior, H. Janssen, W. Schirp, ROH Chor, ROHO/W. Furtwängler, Berlin St Op Orch/L. Blech, LSO/J. Barbirolli)

Ⓓ **GEMMCD9347** (4/90)
Ferruccio Busoni & Egon Petri
Chopin: Etudes (exc); Etudes (exc); Preludes (exc); Nocturnes (exc); *Bach:* Wohltemperierte Klavier (exc); Nun freut euch, BWV734; *Beethoven:* Ecossaises, WoO83 (exc); *Liszt:* Hungarian Rhapsodies, S244 (exc); *Busoni:* Sonatina 6; Indianisches Tagebuch; Bach Fantasia; Elegien (exc); Sonatina 3; *Mozart:* Don Giovanni (exc); *Liszt:* Rhapsodie espagnole, S254. (F. Busoni, E. Petri, Minneapolis SO/D. Mitropoulos)

Ⓓ **GEMMCD9364**
Beethoven—Concertos
Pergolesi: Tre giorni son che Nina; *Mozart:* Don Giovanni (exc); *Bellini:* Sonnambula (exc); Sonnambula (exc); *Donizetti:* Lucia di Lammermoor (exc); Don Pasquale (exc); Favorita (exc); *Verdi:* Rigoletto (exc); Rigoletto (exc); Rigoletto (exc); *Puccini:* Bohème (exc); *A. Thomas:* Mignon (exc); *Massenet:* Manon (exc); Werther (exc); *Donaudy:* O del mio amato ben; *P.M. Costa:* Napulitanata; *Huarte:* Madrigal español; *Tosti:* 'A Vucchella; *Nutile:* Mamma mia, che vo' sapè; *Cottrau:* Santa Lucia; *Califona:* Vieni sul mar. (T. Schipa, T. dal Monte, A. Galli-Curci, L. Bori, orch)

Ⓓ **GEMMCD9367** (5/90)
Gigli—Arias and Duets
Bizet: Pêcheurs de Perles (exc); *Buzzi-Peccia:* Torna amore; *De Curtis:* Carmela; Voce 'e notte; *Denza:* Se; *Donizetti:* Elisir d'amore (exc); Elisir d'amore (exc); Lucia di Lammermoor (exc); Lucia di Lammermoor (exc); Lucia di Lammermoor (exc); Lucia di Lammermoor (exc); *Nutile:* Mamma mia, che vo' sapè; *Ponchielli:* Gioconda (exc); Gioconda (exc); *Rimsky-Korsakov:* Sadko (exc); *Seismit-Doda:* Notte lunare; *Verdi:* Lombardi (exc). (B. Gigli, M. Talley, orch, H. Heller, A. Galli-Curci, L. Homer, A. Bada, G. De Luca, E. Pinza, NY Met Op Orch/G. Setti, NY Met Op Chor/Rosario Bourdon, E. Rethberg, T. Ruffo/N. Shilkret/B. Reibold, Vitaphone Orch)

Ⓓ **GEMMCD9383** (3/90)
Julius Patzak—Opera & Operetta Recital
Donizetti: Elisir d'amore (exc); *Verdi:* Ballo in maschera (exc); Traviata (exc); Trovatore (exc); *Puccini:* Fanciulla del West (exc); Bohème (exc); *A. Thomas:* Mignon (exc); *Massenet:* Manon (exc); Manon (exc); Werther (exc); *Tchaikovsky:* Eugene Onegin (exc); *Offenbach:* Contes d'Hoffmann (exc); Goldschmied von Toledo (exc); *Flotow:* Martha (exc); *Nicolai:* Lustigen Weiber von Windsor (exc); *Smetana:* Bartered Bride (exc); *Suppé:* Boccaccio (exc); *J. Strauss II:* Lustige Krieg (exc); Nacht in Venedig (exc); *Millöcker:* Bettelstudent (exc); Gasparone (exc); *Traditional:* Ich hab' amal a Räuscherl g'habt. (J. Patzak, G. Rünger, Berlin St Op Orch, orch, Vienna Schrammel Qt/M. Gurlitt/H. Weigert/J. Prüwer/A. Melichar, Berlin St Op Chor, F. Völker)

Ⓓ **GEMMCD9384**
Songs of the Sea—Peter Dawson
McCall: Boots; *Stanford:* Songs of the Sea; *A. Arlen:* Rivetter; *N. Gay:* Fleet's not in port very long; *Traditional:* Mountains o' Mourne; *Reeve:* I am a friar of orders grey; *Audran:* Poupée; *Hatton:* Simon the cellarer; *W.G. James:* Australian Bush Songs (exc); *Hedgcock:* On the road to Mandalay; *Berlin:* Follow the Fleet (exc); *Whiting:* Saddle your blues; *German:* Rolling down to Rio; *Stuart:* Bandolero; *Pinsutti:* Bedouin Love Song; *Löhr:* Chorus, gentlemen; *Lamb:* Volunteer organist. (P. Dawson, orch, chor, G. Moore, Anon, Anon)

Ⓓ **GEMMCD9394** (5/90)
Helge Roswaenge—Operatic Recital
Boïeldieu: Dame blanche (exc); *Mozart:* Così fan tutte (exc); Don Giovanni (exc); *Puccini:* Madama Butterfly (exc); Bohème (exc); Bohème (exc); Tosca (exc); *Weber:* Freischütz (exc); *Bizet:* Carmen (exc); *Verdi:* Forza del destino (exc); *Beethoven:* Fidelio (exc); *Verdi:* Trovatore (exc). (H. Roswaenge, H. von Debička, G. Hüsch, M. Perras, Berlin St Op Orch/F. Weissmann/M. Gurlitt/B. Seidler-Winkler)

Ⓓ **GEMMCD9398** (9/91)
Friedrich Schorr
Haydn: Jahreszeiten (exc); *Mozart:* Zauberflöte (exc); *Weber:* Euryanthe (exc); *Beethoven:* Fidelio (exc); *Mendelssohn:* Elias (exc); Elias (exc); *Wagner:* Tannhäuser (exc); Tannhäuser (exc); Tannhäuser (exc); Meistersinger (exc); *Schubert:* Schwanengesang, D957 (exc); *Wolf:* Goethe Lieder (exc); Sechs Gedichte (exc); *R. Strauss:* Lieder, Op.29 (exc). (F. Schorr, New SO, Berlin St Op Orch, LSO/A. Coates/L. Blech/J. Barbirolli/R. Heger, anon, E. Bettendorf, orch)

Ⓓ **GEMMCD9409**
Lotte Lehmenn—Vol.1
Puccini: Tosca (exc); Tosca (exc); Madama Butterfly (exc); Madama Butterfly (exc); Turandot (exc); Bohème (exc); *J. Strauss II:* Fledermaus (exc); Fledermaus (exc); Zigeunerbaron (exc); *Godard:* Jocelyn (exc); *Jensen:* O lass dich halten; Murmelndes Lüftchen; *Eulenberg:* Monatrose; Wilde Rose; Weisse und rote Rose; Rankende Rose; Seerose; *H. Werner:* Heidenröslein. (Lotte Lehmann, R. Tauber, K. Branzell, W. Staegemann, H. Lange, J. Kiepura, Berlin St Op Chor, chor, D. Bela, M. Spoliansky, Berlin St Op Orch, Berlin City Op Orch/M. Gurlitt/F. Weissmann/F. Zweig)

Ⓓ **GEMMCD9410**
Lotte Lehmann—Vol.2
Offenbach: Contes d'Hoffmann (exc); *Wagner:* Walküre (exc); Tristan und Isolde (exc); *Albert:* Toten Augen (exc); *R. Strauss:* Rosenkavalier (exc); Ariadne auf Naxos (exc); Arabella (exc); *Giordano:* Andrea Chénier (exc); *Wagner:* Wesendonk Lieder (exc); *R. Strauss:* Lieder, Op.17 (exc); Lieder, Op.29 (exc); Lieder, Op.27 (exc); Lieder, Op.56 (exc); *Lehár:* Eva (exc); *Meyer-Helmund:* Zauberlied (exc); *Ketèlbey:* Sanctuary of the Heart. (Lotte Lehmann, K. Heidersbach, Berlin St Op Orch, D. Bela, H. Weigert, Berlin City Op Orch/F. Zweig/H. Weigert/F. Weissmann/Dr Römer/R. Jäger/M. Gurlitt, Berlin St Op Chor)

Ⓓ **GEMMCD9411**
Tom Burke—A Centenary Tribute
Verdi: Rigoletto (exc); Aida (exc); *Puccini:* Bohème (exc); Tosca (exc); Tosca (exc); Turandot (exc); *Leoncavallo:* Pagliacci (exc); *Massenet:* Manon (exc); *Traditional:* Stormalong; *Crouch:* Kathleen Mavourneen; *Balfe:* Killarney; *Joseph Robinson:* Snowy-breasted pearl; *G.A. Barker:* Irish emigrant; *Traditional:* Minstrel boy; *Handel:* Serse (exc); *A. G. Thomas:* Esmeralda (exc); *Tosti:* My dreams; *Toselli:* Serenade; *Alfred Cellier:* Dorothy (exc); *Balfe:* Excelsior; *Di Capua:* O sole mio. (T. Burke, orch, Anon, F. Richardson, chor, pf trio)

Ⓓ **GEMMCD9419** (3/92)
Herbert Ernst Groh—Opera Recital
Mozart: Entführung (exc); Zauberflöte (exc); *Wagner:* Fliegende Holländer (exc); Meistersinger (exc); *Verdi:* Forza del destino (exc); *Leoncavallo:* Pagliacci (exc); *Bizet:* Pêcheurs de Perles (exc); *A. Thomas:* Mignon (exc); *Offenbach:* Contes d'Hoffmann (exc); *Adam:* Postillon de Lonjumeau (exc); *Nicolai:* Lustigen Weiber von Windsor (exc); *Cornelius:* Barbier von Bagdad (exc); Barbier von Bagdad (exc); *Nessler:* Trompeter von Säckingen (exc); *Zeller:* Vogelhändler (exc); *J. Strauss II:* Zigeunerbaron (exc); Nacht in Venedig (exc); *Heuberger:* Opernball (exc); *Zeller:* Vogelhändler (exc); *Fall:* Rose von Stambul (exc). (H.E. Groh, G. Hüsch, E. Bettendorf, orch/F. Weissmann/O. Dobrindt)

Ⓓ **GEMMCD9442**
Feuermann—The Columbia Records, Vol.1
Haydn: Cello Concerto in D; *Beethoven:* Mozart Variations, WoO46; *Schubert:* Arpeggione Sonata, D821; *Chopin:* Nocturnes (exc); Waltzes (exc); *Sgambati:* Serenata napoletana, Op.24/2; *Gluck:* Orfeo ed Euridice (exc). (E. Feuermann, SO/M. Sargent, T. van der Pas, anon, G. Moore)

Ⓓ **GEMMCD9443** (10/91)
Feuermann—The Columbia Records, Vol.2
Brahms: Cello Sonata 1; *Beethoven:* Serenade, Op.8; *Reger:* Suites, Op.131c (exc); *Mendelssohn:* Songs without Words (exc); *Schumann:* Kinderszenen (exc); *Gounod:* Ave Maria; *Drigo:* Arlekinda (exc); *Cui:* Kaleydoskop (exc); *Rimsky-Korsakov:* Sadko (exc). (E. Feuermann, T. van der Pas, S. Goldberg, P. Hindemith, W. Rebner, M. Taube, G. Moore)

Ⓓ **GEMMCD9445**
Elisabeth Schumann—Vol.2
Bach: St Matthew Passion, BWV244 (exc); Cantata 159 (exc); Anna Magdalena Notenbuch (1725) (exc); *Mozart:* Nozze di Figaro (exc); Nozze di Figaro (exc); Zauberflöte (exc); Don Giovanni (exc); *Smetana:* Kiss (exc); *Schubert:* Ave Maria, D839; *Schumann:* Jugend Lieder, Op. 79 (exc); Myrthen, Op. 25 (exc); Lieder und Gesänge, Op. 77 (exc); Romanzen und Balladen, Op. 53 (exc); Gedichte, Op. 36 (exc); Gedichte, Op. 37 (exc); Gesänge, Op. 89 (exc); Liederkreis, Op.39 (exc); *Liszt:* Oh, quand je dors, S282; *Wagner:* Mélodies (exc); *Grieg:* Peer Gynt (exc); *J. Strauss II:* Fledermaus (exc). (E. Schumann, orch/K. Alwin/L. Rosenek/W. Goehr, K. Alwin, G. Reeves)

Ⓓ **GEMMCD9448** (2/91)
Stokowski conducts Wagner
Wagner: Tannhäuser (exc); Tannhäuser (exc); Parsifal (exc); Parsifal (exc). (Philadelphia/L. Stokowski)

Ⓓ **GEMMCD9450**
Amelita Galli-Curci—Vol.2
Proch: Air and Variations; *A. Scarlatti:* Io vi miro ancor; *A. Thomas:* Hamlet (exc); *Gounod:* Philémon et Baucis (exc); *Adam:* Toréador (exc); *Rossini:* Semiramide (exc); Barbiere di Siviglia (exc); *Bellini:* Puritani (exc); *Verdi:* Traviata (exc); Trovatore (exc); Trovatore (exc); *Grieg:* Peer Gynt (exc); *Benedict:* Capinera; *T. Giordani:* Caro mio ben; *T. Moore:* Irish Melodies (exc); *Bishop:* Echo Song; Lo, here the gentle lark; Home, sweet home. (A. Galli-Curci, T. Schipa, orch)

Ⓓ **GEMMCD9451** (10/91)
Alexander Kipnis
Gounod: Faust (exc); *Mozart:* Nozze di Figaro (exc); *Wagner:* Tristan und Isolde (exc); *Brahms:* Lieder, Op. 32 (exc); *Verdi:* Don Carlo (exc); *Meyerbeer:* Huguenots (exc); *Halévy:* Juive (exc); *Wagner:* Walküre (exc); Meistersinger (exc); *Gounod:* Faust (exc); *Mozart:* Zauberflöte (exc); Nozze di Figaro (exc); *Traditional:* Kalinka; Soldier's Song; *Verdi:* Simon Boccanegra (exc); *Wolf:* Vier Gedichte (exc); *Brahms:* Lieder, Op. 43 (exc); Lieder, Op. 58 (exc). (A. Kipnis, E. Ruziczka, anon, G. Moore, orch, Berlin Charlottenburg Op Orch, Berlin St Op Orch/J. Heidenreich/L. Blech/E. Orthmann)

Ⓓ **GEMMCD9455**
Malcolm McEachern—Song Recital
Handel: Acis and Galatea (exc); Israel in Egypt (exc); Samson (exc); Judas Maccabaeus (exc); Alexander's Feast (exc); *Mendelssohn:* Elijah (exc); Heimkehr aus der Fremde (exc); *Verdi:* Vespri Siciliani (exc); Nabucco (exc); *Gounod:* Faust (exc); *Jude:* Mighty deep; *Speaks:* On the road to Mandalay; *W. G. James:* Australian Bush Songs (exc); *Balfe:* Excelsior!; *Sergeant:* Blow, blow, thou winter wind; *Damrosch:* Danny Deever; *Koenemann:* Song of the Volga Boatmen; *Traditional:* Hundred Pipers; Drinking; *Offenbach:* Geneviève de Brabant (exc). (M. McEachern, orch, H. Williams, Aeolian Orch, B.C. Hilliam, S. Chapple, F. Titterton, chor)

Ⓓ **GEMMCD9458**
Lucrezia Bori—Opera & Song Recital
Mozart: Don Giovanni (exc); *A. Thomas:* Mignon (exc); *Gounod:* Roméo et Juliette (exc); Roméo et Juliette (exc); *Delibes:* Lakmé (exc); *Bizet:* Carmen (exc); *Donizetti:* Don Pasquale (exc); *Verdi:* Traviata (exc); *Puccini:* Bohème (exc); Bohème (exc); Bohème (exc); *Rimsky-Korsakov:* Snow Maiden (exc); *Arditi:* Bacio; *Granados:* Tonadillas (exc); *Traditional:* Seguidilla; *Valverde:* Cruz de Mayo. (L. Bori, B. Gigli, M. Fleta, G. De Luca, T. Schipa, orch)

Ⓓ **GEMMCD9468**
Vaughan Williams
Vaughan Williams: Wasps (exc); Old King Cole (exc); Hugh the Drover (exc). (Aeolian Orch/R. Vaughan Williams, Mary Lewis, C. Willis, N. Walker, T. Davies, F. Collier, P. Dawson, W. Anderson, chor, orch/M. Sargent)

Ⓓ **GEMMCD9473** (9/91)
Heddle Nash—Vol.2
Puccini: Bohème (exc); Bohème (exc); *Gounod:* Faust (exc); *Massenet:* Manon (exc); *Offenbach:* Belle Hélène (exc); *Millöcker:* Dubarry (exc); *Bishop:* My pretty Jane; *M.V. White:* To Mary; *Lehár:* Friederike (exc). (H. Nash, M. Licette, R. Easton, BBC Chor, SO/T. Beecham, J. Brownlee, D. Labbette, S. Andreva, LPO, orch, G. Moore, anon, R. Alva)

Ⓓ **GEMMCD9474**
Mengelberg conducts the NYPSO
Handel: Alcina (exc); *Bach:* Suites, BWV1066-9 (exc); *J.C. Bach:* Grand Overtures, Op. 18 (exc); *Mozart:* Zauberflöte (exc); *Beethoven:* Egmont (exc); *Mendelssohn:* Athalie (exc); *Meyerbeer:* Prophète (exc); *Wagner:* Siegfried (exc); *Humperdinck:* Hänsel und Gretel (exc); *Saint-Saëns:* Rouet d'Omphale. (NYPSO/W. Mengelberg)

Ⓓ **GEMMCD9485**
Harty conducts Berlioz
Berlioz: Béatrice et Bénédict (exc); Roméo et Juliette (exc); Roméo et Juliette (exc); Carnaval Romain; Troyens (exc); Marche Troyenne; Corsaire; Tristia (exc); Damnation de Faust (exc). (Hallé, LPO, LSO/H. Harty)

Ⓓ **GEMMCD9497** (9/91)
Pol Plançon
Gounod: Faust (exc); Philémon et Baucis (exc); *Bellini:* Sonnambula (exc); *Adam:* Minuit, Chrétiens (exc); *A. Thomas:* Caïd (exc); *Gounod:* Roméo et Juliette (exc); *Godard:* Embarquez-vous?; *Mozart:* Zauberflöte (exc); *Massenet:* Si tu veux, Mignonne; *Haydn:* Jahreszeiten (exc); *Gounod:* Jésus de Nazareth; *Flégier:* Cor; *Gounod:* Faust (exc); *Faure:* Rameaux; *Schumann:* Romanzen und Balladen, Op. 49 (exc); *Verdi:* Don Carlos (exc); *Berlioz:* Damnation de Faust (exc); *Flotow:* Martha (exc); *A. Thomas:* Caïd (exc); *Meyerbeer:* Etoile du nord (exc); *A. Thomas:* Mignon (exc); *Rossini:* Stabat mater (exc). (P. Plançon, anon, orch)

Ⓓ **GEMMCD9912**
Vanni Marcoux—Recital
Février: Monna Vanna (exc); *Massenet:* Jongleur de Notre Dame (exc); Cléopâtre (exc); Don Quichotte (exc); Panurge (exc); *Laparra:* Habanera (exc); *A. Thomas:* Hamlet (exc); *Verdi:* Don Carlos (exc); *Mussorgsky:* Boris Godunov (exc); *Debussy:* Pelléas et Mélisande (exc); *Berlioz:* Damnation de Faust (exc); *Schumann:* Myrthen, Op.25 (exc); *Duparc:* Manoir de Rosemonde; *Fauré:* Songs, Op.23 (exc); *J. Martini:* Plaisir d'amour. (Vanni-Marcoux, O. Ricquier, M. Cozette, P. Coppola, orch/P. Coppola)

Ⓓ **GEMMCD9928** (9/92)
The Young Claudio Arrau
Liszt: Années de pèlerinage 3 (exc); *Schumann:* Carnaval; *Debussy:* Estampes (exc); Tarantelle styrienne; *Chopin:* Ballades (exc); Etudes (exc); Etudes (exc); Waltzes (exc); Scherzos (exc); *Bizet:* Carmen (exc). (C. Arrau)

Ⓓ **GEMMCD9934**
Dame Isobel Baillie
Purcell: Blessed Virgin's Expostulation, Z196; *Bach:* Cantata 201 (exc); Cantata 68 (exc); *Handel:* Rodelinda (exc); Joshua (exc); Theodora (exc); Samson (exc); *Mozart:* Finta giardiniera (exc); Nozze di Figaro (exc); *Schubert:* Hirt auf dem Felsen, D965; Gretchen am Spinnrade, D118; An die Musik, D547; *Mendelssohn:* Lieder, Op. 34 (exc); Hear my prayer; *Offenbach:* Contes d'Hoffmann (exc); *Arditi:* Bacio. (I. Baillie, N. Walker, C. Draper, E. Hall, A. Pini, A. Goldsborough, G. Ison, C. Raybould, G. Moore, CBO, orch/B. Cameron/C. Prentice/S. Robinson, ens, Anon)

Ⓓ **GEMMCD9936** (10/92)
Mattia Battistini, Vol.1
Leoncavallo: Pagliacci (exc); *Mozart:* Don Giovanni (exc); *Hérold:* Zampa (exc); *Verdi:* Forza del destino (exc); Traviata (exc); Traviata (exc); Rigoletto (exc); Ballo in maschera (exc); *Wagner:* Tannhäuser (exc); *Flotow:* Martha (exc); *Nouguès:* Quo vadis (exc); *Massenet:* Werther (exc); *Tosti:* Ancora; *Alvarez:* Mantilla; *Carissimi:* Vittoria! Vittoria!. (M. Battistini, M. Mokrzycka, anon, orch/C. Sabajno, C. Sabajno)

Ⓓ **GEMMCD9937**
Antonio Scotti
Bellini: Sonnambula (exc); *Donizetti:* Don Pasquale (exc); Don Pasquale (exc); Elisir d'amore (exc); *Mozart:* Don Giovanni (exc); Don Giovanni (exc); Don Giovanni (exc); Nozze di Figaro (exc); *Massenet:* Roi de Lahore (exc); *Verdi:* Rigoletto (exc); *Gounod:* Faust (exc); *Verdi:* Don Carlo (exc); Ballo in maschera (exc); Otello (exc); Falstaff (exc); *Puccini:* Tosca (exc); *Offenbach:* Contes d'Hoffmann (exc); *Paladilhe:* Mandolinata; *Di Capua:* Maria, Mari; *Traditional:* Scetate. (A. Scotti, M. Sembrich, G. Farrar, anon, orch)

Ⓓ **GEMMCD9939** (10/92)
Josef Hassid & Ida Haendel - 1940-42 Recordings
Tchaikovsky: Souvenir d'un lieu cher, Op.42 (exc); *Elgar:* Capricieuse; *Dvořák:* Humoresques, Op.101 (exc); *Massenet:* Thaïs (exc); *Sarasate:* Danzas españolas (exc); *Kreisler:* Caprice viennois; *Achron:* Hebrew Melody; *Schubert:* Violin Sonata, D408; Rosamunde (exc); *Falla:* Vida breve (exc); *Albéniz:* España, Op.165 (exc); *Sarasate:* Zigeunerweisen; *Ravel:* Tzigane. (J. Hassid, I. Haendel, G. Moore, A. Kotowska, I. Newton, N. Mewton-Wood)

Ⓓ **GEMMCD9943** (3/93)
The Art of Paderewski, Vol.2
Couperin: Livre de clavecin III (exc); Livre de clavecin I (exc); *Liszt:* Lieder, S558 (exc); Hungarian Rhapsodies, S244 (exc); Concert Studies, S144 (exc); Études d'exécution, S139 (exc); *Stojowski:* Chant d'amour; By the brookside; *Schelling:* Nocturne; *Wagner:* Tristan und Isolde (exc); *Liszt:* Tristan und Isolde—paraphrase, S447; Fliegende Holländer—paraphrase, S440. (I. Paderewski)

Ⓓ **GEMMCD9944**
Friedrich Schorr sings Wagner
Wagner: Meistersinger (exc); Meistersinger (exc); Meistersinger (exc); Meistersinger (exc); Meistersinger (exc); Meistersinger (exc); Meistersinger (exc); Fliegende Holländer (exc). (F. Schorr, G. Ljungberg, R. Laubenthal, E. Rethberg, E. Schumann, L. Melchior, B. Williams, G. Parr, Berlin St Op Orch/L. Blech, LSO/L. Collingwood/A. Coates, orch/J. Barbirolli)

Ⓓ **GEMMCD9945**
Bruno Walter conducts Haydn, Schubert & J.Strauss II
Haydn: Symphony 92; Symphony 96; *Schubert:* Symphony 8; *J. Strauss II:* Fledermaus (exc). (VPO, Paris Cons/B. Walter)

Ⓓ **GEMMCD9947**
Georges Thill
Bach: Cantata 65 (exc); *Wagner:* Lohengrin (exc); Lohengrin (exc); *Rimsky-Korsakov:* Sadko (exc); *Verdi:* Traviata (exc); *Puccini:* Bohème (exc); *Bizet:* Carmen (exc); *Massenet:* Hérodiade (exc); *Berlioz:* Damnation de Faust (exc); *Gounod:* Roméo et Juliette (exc); *Massenet:* Werther (exc); *Fauré:* Songs, Op.43 (exc); En prière; Songs, Op.7 (exc); Songs, Op.3 (exc); Songs, Op.46 (exc); Poèmes d'un jour; *Gounod:* Medjé; *Traditional:* Rêve passe. (G. Thill, orch/G. Bret/F. Heurteur/E. Bigot/P. Gaubert, M. Fauré, chor, Garde Républicaine SO)

Ⓓ **GEMMCD9948**
Ninon Vallin in Opera and Song
Lalo: Roi d'Ys (exc); *Bizet:* Pêcheurs de perles (exc); Carmen (exc); Carmen (exc); *Massenet:* Hérodiade (exc); *G. Charpentier:* Louise (exc); *Debussy:* Enfant prodigue (exc); *Messager:* Fortunio (exc); *Balakirev:* Songs (1858-64) (exc); *Chabrier:* Île heureuse; *Fauré:* Songs, Op.23 (exc); *Duparc:* Phidylé; *Bemberg:* Chant hindou; *Debussy:* Ariettes oubliées (exc). (N. Vallin, M. Sibille, C. Friant, M. Villabella, P. Darck, M. Fauré, M. Long, A. de Pierlas, anon, orch/G. Cloëz/Anon/F. Ruhlmann, Anon)

Ⓓ **GEMMCD9956** (1/93)
Joseph Hislop (1884-1977)
Gounod: Faust (exc); *Donizetti:* Lucia di Lammermoor (exc); *Verdi:* Rigoletto (exc); Rigoletto (exc); Forza del destino (exc); *Wagner:* Lohengrin (exc); Meistersinger (exc); *Massenet:* Werther (exc); *Puccini:* Bohème (exc); Bohème (exc); Madama Butterfly (exc); *Mascagni:* Cavalleria Rusticana (exc); *Lehár:* Friederike (exc); *Coates:* I heard you singing; *Traditional:* Songs of the North II (exc); Eriksay Love-lilt. (J. Hislop, L. Schöne, A. Granforte, W. Parnis, D. Gilly, M. Hayward, P. Kahn, orch/P. Coppola/J. Barbirolli/J. Heuvel/G.W. Byng/J. Harrison)

Ⓓ **GEMMCD9993** (8/93)
Arthur Friedheim—complete recordings, etc
Weber: Piano Sonata 1 (exc); *Beethoven:* Piano Sonata 14 (exc); *Chopin:* Piano Sonata 2 (exc); Scherzos (exc); *Liszt:*

Paganini Studies, S140 (exc); Hungarian Rhapsodies, S244 (exc); Hungarian Rhapsodies, S244 (exc); Études d'exécution, S139 (exc); Concert Studies, S144 (exc); *Gounod:* Faust (exc); *Rachmaninov:* Suite 2 (exc); *Liszt:* Hungarian Rhapsodies, S244 (exc); *Beethoven:* Piano Sonata 8 (exc); *Chopin:* Berceuse; Impromptus (exc); Waltzes (exc); Etudes (exc); *Liszt:* Hungarian Rhapsodies, S244 (exc); *Beethoven:* Ruinen von Athen (exc). (A. Friedheim, A. Siloti, E. von Sauer)

Ⓒ **IF2000(1)**
Ignaz Friedman—Solo Recordings (discs 1-3)
D. Scarlatti: Keyboard Sonatas (exc); *Mozart:* Piano Sonata, K331 (exc); *Gluck:* Alceste (1776) (exc); *Anon:* Judgement of Paris (exc); *Hummel:* Rondo, Op. 11; *Paderewski:* Humoresques de concert, Op. 14 (exc); *Friedman:* Talk about Paderewski; *Beethoven:* Piano Sonata 14; *Weber:* Invitation to the Dance, J260; *Schubert:* Marches militaires, D733 (exc); *Liszt:* Lieder, S558 (exc); Lieder, S558 (exc); *Schubert:* Alt Wien; *Chopin:* Preludes (exc); Preludes (exc); Etudes (exc); Etudes (exc); Etudes (exc); Ballades (exc); Mazurkas (exc); Mazurkas (exc); Ballades (exc); Mazurkas (exc); Mazurkas (exc); Mazurkas (exc); Mazurkas (exc); Mazurkas (exc); Impromptus (exc); Polonaises (exc); Polonaises (exc); Berceuse; Waltzes (exc); Waltzes (exc); Piano Sonata 2 (exc); Nocturnes (exc); *Friedman:* Talk about Chopin; *Mendelssohn:* Songs without Words (exc); Fantaisies, Op.16 (exc); *Liszt:* Hungarian Rhapsodies, s244 (exc). (I. Friedman, I. Friedman)

Ⓒ **SHECD9582** ⊙ **SHE582** (10/85)
Bridge—The Christmas Rose
Bridge: Christmas Rose (Cpte). (W. Eathorne, E. James, M. Davies, H. Herford, D. Wilson-Johnson, Chelsea Op Group Chor, Chelsea Op Group Orch/H. Williams)

Ⓒ **SHECD9590** ⊙ **SHE590** (7/86)
Valerie Masterson—Recital
Arne: Judgment of Paris (exc); As You Like It (exc); Artaxerxes (exc); *Handel:* Nel dolce dell'oblio; *Bishop:* Lo, here the gentle lark; *Gounod:* Mélodies (1855) (exc); Absent; Sérénade; *Bizet:* Vielle chanson; Pastel; Tarantelle; *Satie:* Diva de l'empire. (V. Masterson, R. Vignoles, R. Adeney)

Ⓒ **SHECD9613**
Jane Austen Songs
Dibdin: Joys of the Country; Soldier's Adieu; Lucky Escape; *Harington:* How Sweet in the Woodlands; *Billington:* William; *T. Giordani:* Queen Mary's Lamentation; *S. Storace:* Captivity; *Haydn:* Canzonettas I (exc); *T. Shaw:* Stranger (exc); *Shield:* Robin Hood (exc); *Webbe I:* Mansion of Peace; *E.S. Biggs:* Hindustani Girl's Lament; *T. Moore:* Irish Melodies (exc); *Hook:* Christmas Box, Op.86 (exc). (P. Wright, J. Gillaspie)

Philips

Ⓒ **411 148-2PH** (3/84)
Mozart: Opera Arias
Mozart: Zaïde (exc); Finta Giardiniera (exc); Clemenza di Tito (exc); Così fan tutte (exc); Rè pastore (exc); Lucio Silla (exc); Idomeneo (exc); Zauberflöte (exc). (K. Te Kanawa, LSO/Colin Davis)

Ⓒ **411 448-2PH** (11/84)
Tchaikovsky Orchestral Works
Tchaikovsky: Romeo and Juliet; 1812; Eugene Onegin (exc); Oprichnik (exc). (Tanglewood Fest Chor, Boston SO, ROHO/Colin Davis)

Ⓒ **411 484-2PH** (2/86)
Leoncavallo—I Pagliacci
Leoncavallo: Pagliacci (Cpte). (P. Domingo, T. Stratas, J. Pons, A. Rinaldi, F. Andreolli, La Scala Chor, La Scala Orch/G. Prêtre)

Ⓒ **412 133-2PH3** (2/85)
Verdi—Macbeth
Verdi: Macbeth (Cpte). (R. Bruson, M. Zampieri, R. Lloyd, N. Shicoff, C.H. Ahnsjö, P. Salomaa, M. Nikolič, A. Schmidt, L. Aliberti, Berlin Deutsche Op Chor, Berlin Deutsche Op Orch/G. Sinopoli)

Ⓒ **412 148-2PH3** (9/85)
Rossini—Maometto II
Rossini: Maometto II (Cpte). (J. Anderson, M. Zimmermann, E. Palacio, S. Ramey, L. Dale, Ambrosian Op. Chor, Philh/C. Scimone)

Ⓒ **412 231-2PH** (3/85)
Travels with my Cello
Rimsky-Korsakov: Tale of Tsar Saltan (exc); *Lehár:* Lustige Witwe (exc); *Debussy:* Children's Corner (exc); *Schumann:* Kinderszenen (exc); *Albéniz:* Recuerdos de viaje (exc); *Saint-Saëns:* Carnaval des animaux (exc); *Gounod:* Ave Maria; *W. Lloyd Webber:* Andante affettuoso; *J. Strauss II:* Pizzicato Polka; *Albinoni:* Adagio; *Grainger:* Irish Tune from County Derry; *Khachaturian:* Gayaneh (exc). (J. Lloyd Webber, ECO/N. Cleobury)

Ⓒ **412 475-2PH2** (7/85)
Wagner—Das Rheingold
Wagner: Rheingold (Cpte). (T. Adam, A. Burmeister, W. Windgassen, E. Wohlfahrt, G. Neidlinger, A. Silja, H. Esser, G. Nienstedt, V. Soukupová, M. Talvela, K. Böhme, D. Siebert, H. Dernesch, R. Hesse, Bayreuth Fest Orch/K. Böhm)

Ⓒ **412 478-2PH4** (2/85)
Wagner—Die Walküre
Wagner: Walküre (Cpte). (J. King, Leonie Rysanek, B. Nilsson, T. Adam, A. Burmeister, G. Nienstedt, D. Mastilovic, L. Synek, H. Dernesch, G. Hopf, Š. Červená, E. Schärtel, S. Wagner, Bayreuth Fest Orch/K. Böhm)

Ⓒ **412 483-2PH4** (8/85)
Wagner—Siegfried
Wagner: Siegfried (Cpte). (W. Windgassen, T. Adam, B. Nilsson, E. Wohlfahrt, G. Neidlinger, V. Soukupová, K. Böhme, E. Köth, Bayreuth Fest Orch/K. Böhm)

Ⓒ **412 488-2PH4** (5/85)
Wagner—Götterdämmerung
Wagner: Götterdämmerung (Cpte). (B. Nilsson, W. Windgassen, J. Greindl, G. Neidlinger, T. Stewart, L. Dvořáková, M. Mödl, D. Siebert, H. Dernesch, S. Wagner, M. Höffgen, A. Burmeister, A. Silja, Bayreuth Fest Chor, Bayreuth Fest Orch/K. Böhm)

Ⓒ **412 548-2PH2** (12/85)
Rossini—Petite messe solennelle
Rossini: Petite messe solennelle; Mosè in Egitto (exc). (K. Ricciarelli, M. Zimmermann, J. Carreras, S. Ramey, Ambrosian Sngrs, C. Sheppard, P. Berkowitz, R. Nunn, Ambrosian Op. Chor, Philh/C. Scimone)

Ⓒ **412 592-2PH2** (1/86)
Verdi—Rigoletto
Verdi: Rigoletto (Cpte). (R. Bruson, E. Gruberová, N. Shicoff, R. Lloyd, B. Fassbaender, K. Rydl, J. Rigby, W. Matteuzzi, A. Gabba, M.G. Pittavini, G. Moses, Santa Cecilia Academy Chor, Santa Cecilia Academy Orch/G. Sinopoli)

Ⓒ **412 655-2PH** (8/85)
Wagner—Arias & Lieder
Wagner: Tristan und Isolde (exc); Wesendonk Lieder. (J. Norman, LSO/Colin Davis)

Ⓒ **412 714-2PH2** (6/86)
Donizetti—The Elixir of Love
Donizetti: Elisir d'amore (Cpte). (K. Ricciarelli, J. Carreras, L. Nucci, D. Trimarchi, S. Rigacci, Turin RAI Chor, Turin RAI Orch/C. Scimone)

Ⓒ **412 885-2PH2** (4/86) ⊟ **412 885-4PX2**
Puccini—Tosca
Puccini: Tosca (Cpte). (M. Caballé, J. Carreras, I. Wixell, S. Ramey, P. de Palma, D. Trimarchi, W. Elvin, A. Murray, ROH Chor, ROHO/Colin Davis)

Ⓒ **416 137-2PH** (2/86)
Mascagni—Cavalleria Rusticana
Mascagni: Cavalleria Rusticana (Cpte). (E. Obraztsova, P. Domingo, R. Bruson, A. Gall, F. Barbieri, La Scala Chor, La Scala Orch/G. Prêtre)

Ⓒ **416 148-2PH2** (6/86)
Gluck—Iphigénie en Tauride
Gluck: Iphigénie en Tauride (Cpte). (D. Montague, J. Aler, T. Allen, N. Argenta, S. Boulton, C. Alliot-Lugaz, R. Massis, Monteverdi Ch, Lyon Op Orch/J.E. Gardiner)

Ⓒ **416 299-2PH** (7/86)
Purcell—Dido and Aeneas
Purcell: Dido (Cpte). (J. Norman, T. Allen, M. McLaughlin, P. Kern, E. Gale, H. Walker, D. Jones, D.L. Ragin, P. Power, Chor, ECO/R. Leppard)

Ⓒ **416 370-2PH3** (7/86)
Mozart—Le Nozze di Figaro
Mozart: Nozze di Figaro (Cpte). (J. Van Dam, B. Hendricks, R. Raimondi, L. Popp, A. Baltsa, F. Palmer, R. Lloyd, A. Baldin, N. Jenkins, D. Maxwell, C. Pope, Ambrosian Op Chor, ASMF/N. Marriner)

Ⓒ **416 390-2PH4** (6/86)
Wagner—Parsifal
Wagner: Parsifal (Cpte). (Jess Thomas, G. London, H. Hotter, I. Dalis, G. Neidlinger, M. Talvela, N. Møller, G. Nienstedt, Š. Červená, U. Boese, G. Stolze, G. Paskuda, G. Janowitz, A. Silja, E-M. Gardelli, D. Siebert, R. Bartos, Š. Červená, Bayreuth Fest Chor, Bayreuth Fest Orch/H. Knappertsbusch)

Ⓒ **416 431-2PH** (12/86)
Works by Berlioz
Berlioz: Harold in Italy; Tristia; Troyens (exc). (N. Imai, John Alldis Ch, LSO/Colin Davis)

Ⓒ **416 432-2PH4** (12/86)
Berlioz—The Trojans
Berlioz: Troyens (Cpte). (J. Veasey, J. Vickers, B. Lindholm, P. Glossop, H. Begg, R. Soyer, A. Raffell, A. Howells, I. Partridge, P. Thau, E. Bainbridge, R. Davies, R. Herincx, D. Wicks, D. Lennox, Wandsworth Sch Boys' Ch, ROH Chor, ROHO/Colin Davis)

Ⓒ **416 460-2PH** (1/87)
Barbara Hendricks sings Gershwin
Gershwin: Strike Up The Band I (exc); Shall we dance? (exc); Goldwyn Follies (exc); Girl Crazy (exc); Damsel in Distress (exc); Porgy and Bess (exc); Blue Monday (exc). (B. Hendricks, K. Labèque, M. Labèque)

Ⓒ **416 492-2PH2** (5/87) ⊟ **416 492-4PX2**
Puccini—La bohème
Puccini: Bohème (Cpte). (K. Ricciarelli, J. Carreras, A. Putnam, I. Wixell, H. Hagegård, R. Lloyd, G. de Angelis, W. Elvin, F. Egerton, R. Hazell, D. Whelan, ROH Chor, ROHO/Colin Davis)

Ⓒ **416 633-2PH3** (4/87)
Mozart—Così fan tutte
Mozart: Così fan tutte (Cpte). (M. Caballé, J. Baker, I. Cotrubas, N. Gedda, W. Ganzarolli, R. Van Allan, ROH Chor, ROHO/Colin Davis)

Ⓒ **416 654-2PH2** (2/87)
Massenet—Werther
Massenet: Werther (Cpte). (J. Carreras, F. von Stade, T. Allen, I. Buchanan, R. Lloyd, P. Crook, M. King, L. Humphries, D. Bell, ROHO/Colin Davis)

Ⓒ **416 698-2PH** (3/87)
Encore! Travels with my cello, Vol. 2
Gershwin: Porgy and Bess (exc); *Taube:* Nocturne; *Mozart:* Piano Sonata, K331 (exc); *Debussy:* Suite bergamasque (exc); *Traditional:* Skye Boat Song; *Bizet:* Carmen (exc); *Vangelis:* Après-midi; *Narita:* Song of the seashore; *Lennon & McCartney:* When I'm 64; *Bernstein:* West Side Story (exc); *Bach:* Cantata 147 (exc); *Rimsky-Korsakov:* Sadko (exc); *Lehár:* Land des Lächelns (exc). (J. Lloyd Webber, S-B. Taube, Vangelis, RPO/N. Cleobury)

Ⓒ **416 870-2PH**
Mozart—Le Nozze di Figaro excerpts
Mozart: Nozze di Figaro (exc). (R. Raimondi, L. Popp, B. Hendricks, J. Van Dam, A. Baltsa, F. Palmer, A. Baldin, N. Jenkins, R. Lloyd, D. Maxwell, C. Pope, Ambrosian Op Chor, ASMF/N. Marriner)

Ⓒ **416 952-2PH2** (9/87)
Berlioz—Beatrice & Benedict
Berlioz: Béatrice et Bénédict (Cpte). (J. Baker, R. Tear, C. Eda-Pierre, H. Watts, T. Allen, J. Bastin, R. Lloyd, R. Van Allan, John Alldis Ch, LSO/Colin Davis)

Ⓒ **416 955-2PH3** (1/89)
Berlioz—Benvenuto Cellini
Berlioz: Benvenuto Cellini (Cpte). (N. Gedda, J. Bastin, R. Massard, R. Soyer, D. Blackwell, R. Lloyd, R. Herincx, C. Eda-Pierre, H. Cuénod, J. Berbié, ROH Chor, BBC SO/Colin Davis)

Ⓒ **416 973-2PM** ⊟ **416 973-4PM**
Jose Carreras sings Musicals
Bernstein: West Side Story (exc); *Brodszky:* Because you're mine (exc); *Hupfeld:* As time goes by; *Fain:* Love is a many splendoured thing; *Steiner:* Gone with the Wind (exc); *A. Lloyd Webber:* Cats (exc); *Bargoni:* Concerto d'autumno; *Hardelot:* Because; *Lara:* Solamente una vez; *Lecuona:* Siboney; *Di Capua:* O sole mio; *Lara:* Granada; *Bixio:* Parlami d'amore, Mariù; *Cardillo:* Core 'ngrato; *Lehár:* Land des Lächelns (exc); *Brodszky:* Toast of New Orleans (exc). (J. Carreras, orch/R. Farnon, ECO/E. G. Asensio/E. Müller/R. Benzi)

Ⓒ **420 084-2PH**
Frederica von Stade sings Haydn, Mozart & Rossini Arias
Haydn: Fedeltà premiata (exc); Mondo della luna (exc); *Mozart:* Nozze di Figaro (exc); Clemenza di Tito (exc); Don Giovanni (exc); *Rossini:* Barbiere di Siviglia (exc); Otello (exc); Cenerentola (exc). (F. von Stade, Lausanne CO, Rotterdam PO/A. Dorati/E. de Waart)

Ⓒ **420 109-2PM2** (12/92)
Rossini—Mosè in Egitto
Rossini: Mosè in Egitto (Cpte). (R. Raimondi, J. Anderson, Z. Gal, S. Browne, S. Fisichella, E. Palacio, K. Lewis, S. Nimsgern, Ambrosian Op Chor, Philh/C. Scimone)

① **420 164-2PH3** (5/87)
Gound—Faust
Gounod: Faust (Cpte). (F. Araiza, K. Te Kanawa, E. Nesterenko, A. Schmidt, P. Coburn, M. Lipovšek, G. Cachemaille, Bavarian Rad Chor, BRSO/Colin Davis)

① **420 190-2PH3** (11/89)
Halévy—Juive
Halévy: Juive (Cpte). (J. Carreras, J. Varady, J. Anderson, F. Furlanetto, D. Gonzalez, R. Massis, R. Schirrer, Ambrosian Op Chor, Philh/A. de Almeida)

① **420 240-2PH** (11/87)
Rameau—Arbaris & Dardanus Suites
Rameau: Abaris (exc); Dardanus (exc). (Eighteenth Century Orch/F. Brüggen)

① **420 468-2PH3** (11/88)
Rossini—La Cenerentola
Rossini: Cenerentola (Cpte). (A. Baltsa, F. Araiza, S. Alaimo, R. Raimondi, C. Malone, F. Palmer, J. del Carlo, Ambrosian Op Chor, ASMF/N. Marriner)

① **420 886-2PSL**
Wagner: Opera Preludes and Siegfried Idyll
Wagner: Meistersinger (exc); Parsifal (exc); Lohengrin (exc); Tristan und Isolde (exc); Siegfried Idyll. (Concertgebouw/B. Haitink)

① **420 950-2PH** (10/88)
Kiri te Kanawa sings Mozart arias
Mozart: Entführung (exc); Mitridate (exc); Don Giovanni (exc); Ch'io mi scordi di te, K505; Misera, dove son, K369. (K. Te Kanawa, M. Uchida, ECO/J. Tate)

① **422 048-2PH** (8/88)
Jessye Norman—Song Recital
Ochs: Dank sei dir, Herr; *Handel:* Rinaldo (exc); *Schumann:* Myrthen, Op. 25 (exc); Liederkreis, Op.39 (exc); *Schubert:* Musensohn, D764; Auf dem See, D543; Meeres Stille, D216; Ave Maria, D839; An die Natur, D372; Rastlose Liebe, D138; Gretchen am Spinnrade, D118; Liebe hat gelogen, D751; Tod und das Mädchen, D531; Erlkönig, D328; *Brahms:* Lieder, Op. 63 (exc); *R.Strauss:* Wir beide wollen springen; *Traditional:* He's got the whole world in His hands; Great day. (J. Norman, G. Parsons)

① **422 084-2PH2** (11/88)
R. Strauss—Ariadne auf Naxos
R. Strauss: Ariadne auf Naxos (Cpte). (J. Norman, J. Varady, E. Gruberová, P. Frey, D. Fischer-Dieskau, O. Bär, G. Wolf, A. Conrad, M. Finke, E. Lind, M. Rørholm, J. Kaufman, M. Finke, R. Asmus, Leipzig Gewandhaus/K. Masur)

① **422 235-2PH** (6/89)
Jessye Norman—European Tour, 1987
Haydn: Arianna a Naxos; *Handel:* Rinaldo (exc); *Ochs:* Dank sei dir, Herr; *Mahler:* Knaben Wunderhorn (exc); Lieder und Gesänge (exc); *Berg:* Liebe; Schliesse mir die Augen beide; Early Songs (exc); Mignon; *R. Strauss:* Lieder, Op. 32 (exc); Lieder, Op. 17 (exc); Lieder, Op. 48 (exc); Wir beide wollen springen; *Traditional:* Great Day; He's got the whole world in his hands; *Ravel:* Vocalise. (J. Norman, G. Parsons)

▭ **422 269-4PMI**
Best of Mozart
Mozart: Nozze di Figaro (exc); Piano Sonata, K331 (exc); Serenade, K525 (exc); Clarinet Concerto, K622 (exc); Piano Concerto 23 (exc); Violin Concerto, K218 (exc); Horn Concerti (exc); Symphony 40 (exc); Piano Concerto 21 (exc); Violin Concerto, K219 (exc); Flute Concerto, K313 (exc). (A. Brendel, S. Kovacevich, J. Brymer, A. Civil, H. Szeryng, C. Monteux, BBC SO/Colin Davis, I Musici, ASMF/N. Marriner, New Philh/A. Gibson, LSO)

① **422 366-2PH3** (8/89)
Bizet—Carmen
Bizet: Carmen (Cpte). (J. Norman, N. Shicoff, M. Freni, S. Estes, G. Raphanel, J. Rigby, F. Le Roux, G. Garino, N. Rivenq, J-P. Courtis, French Rad Maîtrise, French Rad Chor, FNO/S. Ozawa)

① **422 374-2PH3** (11/92)
Offenbach—Les contes d'Hoffmann
Offenbach: Contes d'Hoffmann (Cpte). (F. Araiza, E. Lind, C. Studer, J. Norman, A.S. von Otter, S. Ramey, R. Cassinelli, J-L. Chaignaud, B. Martinovich, F. Palmer, G. Gautier, R. Tomaszewski, P. Menzel, J. Hartfiel, Leipzig Rad Chor, Staatskapelle Dresden/J. Tate)

① **422 381-2PH3** (11/90)
Mozart: Così fan tutte
Mozart: Così fan tutte (Cpte). (K. Mattila, A.S. von Otter, E. Szmytka, F. Araiza, T. Allen, J. Van Dam, Ambrosian Op Chor, ASMF/N. Marriner)

① **422 387-2PH** (5/89)
Dvořák—Orchestral Works
Dvořák: Cello Concerto; Rusalka (exc); Carnival. (J. Lloyd Webber, Czech PO/V. Neumann)

① **422 391-2PH4** (12/89)
Rossini—William Tell
Rossini: Guillaume Tell (Cpte). (G. Zancanaro, C. Studer, C. Merritt, G. Surian, F. de Grandis, A. Felle, L. d'Intino, L. Rono, V. Terranova, E. Gavazzi, A. Noli, La Scala Chor, La Scala Orch/R. Muti)

① **422 401-2PH** (4/92)
Jessye Norman - Lucky To Be Me
Rodgers: Love me Tonight (exc); Boys from Syracuse (exc); *Legrand:* Parapluies de Cherbourg (exc); Yentl (exc); *Weill:* Knickerbocker Holiday (exc); Lady in the dark (exc); One touch of Venus (exc); *Gershwin:* Girl Crazy (exc); *Bernstein:* On the Town (exc); *F. Loewe:* My Fair Lady (exc); *Joel:* Just the way you are. (J. Norman, J.T. Williams)

① **422 406-2PH2** (10/89)
Rossini—Le Comte Ory
Rossini: Comte Ory (Cpte). (J. Aler, S. Jo, G. Cachemaille, D. Montague, G. Quilico, R. Pierotti, M. Castets, F. Dudziak, N. Rivenq, Lyon Op Chor, Lyon Op Orch/J.E. Gardiner)

① **422 420-2PM2** (11/89)
Verdi—I Lombardi
Verdi: Lombardi (Cpte). (C. Deutekom, P. Domingo, R. Raimondi, J. lo Monaco, S. Dean, C. Grant, M. Aparici, K. Erwen, D. Malvisi, Ambrosian Sngrs, RPO/L. Gardelli)

① **422 423-2PM2** (11/89)
Verdi—I Masnadieri
Verdi: Masnadieri (Cpte). (R. Raimondi, C. Bergonzi, P. Cappuccilli, M. Caballé, J. Sandor, M. Mazzieri, W. Elvin, Ambrosian Sngrs, New Philh/L. Gardelli)

① **422 426-2PM2** (12/89)
Verdi—I due Foscari
Verdi: Due Foscari (Cpte). (P. Cappuccilli, J. Carreras, K. Ricciarelli, S. Ramey, V. Bello, E. Connell, M. Antoniak, F. Handlos, Austrian Rad Chor, Austrian RSO/L. Gardelli)

① **422 432-2PM2** (3/90)
Verdi—Stiffelio
Verdi: Stiffelio (Cpte). (J. Carreras, S. Sass, M. Manuguerra, W. Ganzarolli, E. di Cesare, M. Venuti, T. Moser, Austrian Rad Chor, Austrian RSO/L. Gardelli)

① **422 435-2PM2** (11/89)
Verdi—La battaglia di Legnano
Verdi: Battaglia di Legnano (Cpte). (K. Ricciarelli, J. Carreras, M. Manuguerra, N. Ghiuselev, H. Lichtenberger, D. Kavrakos, J. Summers, F. Handlos, A. Murray, Austrian Rad Chor, Austrian RSO/L. Gardelli)

① **422 523-2PME8(2)**
The Complete Mozart Edition Vol 23 (pt 2)
Mozart: Se tutti i mali miei, K83; Cara la dolce fiamma, K293e; Alcandro, lo confesso, K294; Se al labbro mio non credi, K295; Liebe himmlisches Gefühl, K119; In te spero, K440; Müsst ich auch, K434; Warnung, K433; Ah!, spiegarti, o Dio, K178; Schon lacht der holde Frühling, K580; Finta semplice (exc); Mitridate (exc); Finta semplice (exc); Lucio Silla (exc); Idomeneo (exc); Spiegarti non poss'io, K489; Welch ängstliches Beben, K389; Nozze di Figaro (exc); Al desio, K577; Moto di gioia, K579; Per queste tue manine, K540b; Rivolgete a lui lo sguardo, K584; Sineds' Bardengesang, KAnh25; Del gran regno, K434; Bandel, K441; Dite almeno, K479; Mandina amabile, K480; Libertà a Nice, K532; Beim Auszug in das Feld, K552; Caro mio, KAnh5; Nun liebes Weibchen, K625. (J. Kaufmann, Munich RSO/J-P. Weigle, H-P. Blochwitz, E. Lind, Dresden PO, S. Burrows, ASMF/Colin Davis, C. Eda-Pierre, E. Szmytka/N. Marriner, E. Wiens, G. Gudbjörnsson, I. Vermillion, P. Schreier (ten/dir), P. Schreier, Staatskapelle Dresden/K. Böhm, R. Tear, B. Terfel, A. Scharinger, R. Pape, R. Jansen, R. Lloyd, E. Mathis)

① **422 525-2PME2**
The Complete Mozart Edition Vol 25
Mozart: Thamos, K345 (Cpte); Idomeneo (exc); Petits riens; Ballet intermezzo, K299c; Pantalon und Colombine. (K. Eichstaedt, G. Pohl, E. Büchner, H.C. Polster, T. Adam, Berlin Rad Chor, Berlin Staatskapelle/B. Klee, Netherlands CO/D. Zinman, ASMF/N. Marriner)

① **422 526-2PME2** (11/91)
The Complete Mozart Edition Vol 26
Mozart: Apollo et Hyacinthus (Cpte). (C. Wulkopf, E. Mathis, A. Rolfe Johnson, A. Auger, H. Schwarz, Salzburg Chbr Ch, Salzburg Mozarteum Orch/L. Hager)

① **422 527-2PME** (5/92)
The Complete Mozart Edition Vol 27
Mozart: Bastien und Bastienne (Cpte); Zufriedenheit, K349; Komm, liebe Zither, K351. (G. Nigl, D. Orieschnig, D. Busch, Vienna SO/U.C. Harrer, D. Orieschnig, W. Würdinger)

① **422 528-2PME2** (11/91)
The Complete Mozart Edition Vol 28
Mozart: Finta semplice (Cpte). (B. Hendricks, S. Lorenz, D. Johnson, A. Murray, E. Lind, H-P. Blochwitz, A. Schmidt, CPE Bach Orch/P. Schreier)

① **422 529-2PME3** (2/92)
The Complete Mozart Edition Vol 29
Mozart: Mitridate (Cpte). (W. Hollweg, A. Auger, E. Gruberová, A. Baltsa, I. Cotrubas, D. Kuebler, C. Weidinger, Salzburg Mozarteum Orch/L. Hager)

① **422 530-2PME3** (1/92)
The Complete Mozart Edition Vol 30
Mozart: Ascanio in Alba (Cpte). (A. Baltsa, E. Mathis, P. Schreier, L. Sukis, A. Auger, Salzburg Chbr Ch, Salzburg Mozarteum Orch/L. Hager)

① **422 531-2PME2** (1/92)
The Complete Mozart Edition Vol 31
Mozart: Sogno di Scipione (Cpte). (P. Schreier, L. Popp, E. Gruberová, C.H. Ahnsjö, T. Moser, E. Mathis, Salzburg Chbr Ch, Salzburg Mozarteum Orch/L. Hager)

① **422 532-2PME3** (2/92)
The Complete Mozart Edition Vol 32
Mozart: Lucio Silla (Cpte). (P. Schreier, A. Auger, J. Varady, E. Mathis, H. Donath, W. Krenn, Salzburg Rad Chor, Salzburg Mozarteum Chor, Salzburg Mozarteum Orch/L. Hager)

① **422 533-2PME3** (5/92)
The Complete Mozart Edition Vol 33
Mozart: Finta Giardiniera (Cpte). (J. Conwell, E. di Cesare, T. Moser, L. Sukis, B. Fassbaender, J-R. Ihloff, B. McDaniel, Salzburg Mozarteum Orch/L. Hager)

① **422 534-2PME3** (5/92)
The Complete Mozart Edition Vol 34
Mozart: Finta Giardiniera (Cpte). (H. Donath, G. Unger, W. Hollweg, J. Norman, T. Troyanos, I. Cotrubas, H. Prey, N German Rad Chor, N German RSO/H. Schmidt-Isserstedt)

① **422 536-2PME2** (4/92)
The Complete Mozart Edition Vol 36
Mozart: Zaïde (Cpte); Schauspieldirektor (Cpte). (E. Mathis, P. Schreier, I. Wixell, W. Hollweg, R. Süss, A. Ude, Berlin Staatskapelle/B. Klee, R. Welting, I. Cotrubas, A. Rolfe Johnson, C. Grant, LSO/Colin Davis)

① **422 537-2PME3** (12/91)
The Complete Mozart Edition Vol 37
Mozart: Idomeneo (Cpte). (F. Araiza, S. Mentzer, B. Hendricks, R. Alexander, U. Heilmann, W. Hollweg, H. Peeters, Bavarian Rad Chor, BRSO/Colin Davis)

① **422 538-2PME2** (4/92)
The Complete Mozart Edition Vol 38
Mozart: Entführung (Cpte). (C. Eda-Pierre, N. Burrowes, S. Burrows, R. Tear, R. Lloyd, C. Jürgens, John Alldis Ch, ASMF/Colin Davis)

① **422 539-2PME** (5/92)
The Complete Mozart Edition Vol 39
Mozart: Sposo deluso (Cpte); Oca del Cairo (Cpte). (F. Palmer, I. Cotrubas, R. Tear, A. Rolfe Johnson, C. Grant, LSO/Colin Davis, D. Fischer-Dieskau, E. Wiens, P. Schreier, D. Johnson, P. Coburn, A. Scharinger, I. Nielsen, CPE Bach Orch/P. Schreier)

① **422 540-2PME3** (1/92)
The Complete Mozart Edition Vol 40
Mozart: Nozze di Figaro (Cpte). (W. Ganzarolli, M. Freni, I. Wixell, J. Norman, Y. Minton, M. Casula, C. Grant, R. Tear, D. Lennox, P. Hudson, L. Watson, BBC Chor, BBC SO/Colin Davis)

① **422 541-2PME3** (1/92) ▭ **422 541-4PX2**
The Complete Mozart Edition Vol 41
Mozart: Don Giovanni (Cpte). (I. Wixell, M. Arroyo, K. Te Kanawa, M. Freni, S. Burrows, W. Ganzarolli, R. Van Allan, L. Roni, ROH Chor, ROHO/Colin Davis)

① **422 542-2PME3** (1/92) ▭ **422 542-4PX2**
The Complete Mozart Edition Vol 42
Mozart: Così fan tutte (Cpte). (M. Caballé, J. Baker, I. Cotrubas, N. Gedda, W. Ganzarolli, R. Van Allan, ROH Chor, ROHO/Colin Davis)

① **422 543-2PME3** (4/92)
The Complete Mozart Edition Vol 43
Mozart: Zauberflöte (Cpte). (M. Price, L. Serra, P. Schreier, M. Melbye, K. Moll, T. Adam, R. Tear, M. Venuti, M.

McLaughlin, A. Murray, H. Schwarz, F. Höher, M. Diedrich, F. Klos, R. Goldberg, H. Reeh, A. Ude, Leipzig Rad Chor, Staatskapelle Dresden/Colin Davis)

Ⓓ **422 544-2PME2** (4/92)
The Complete Mozart Edition Vol 44
Mozart: Clemenza di Tito (Cpte). (S. Burrows, J. Baker, Y. Minton, F. von Stade, L. Popp, R. Lloyd, ROH Chor, ROHO/Colin Davis)

Ⓓ **422 545-2PME3** (12/91)
The Complete Mozart Edition Vol.45
Mozart: Londoner Notenskizzenbuch; Don Giovanni (exc); Entführung (exc); Rondo, K371; Piano and Wind Quintet, K452a; Contredanse, K535b; Contredanse, K565a; Tantum ergo, K197; Tantum ergo, K142; Modulierendes Präludium; Idomeneo (exc); March, Kdeest; Musical Dice Game. (ASMF/N. Marriner, Netherlands Wind Ens, T. Brown, K. Sillito, M. Uchida, N. Black, T. King, J. Farrell, R. O'Neill, Leipzig Rad Chor, Leipzig RSO, P. Schreier, M. Frimmer, E. Smith, B. Hendricks, S. Mentzer, A. Röhn, BRSO/Colin Davis)

Ⓓ **422 574-2PH2** (4/89)
R. Strauss—Eleketra
R. Strauss: Elektra (Cpte). (H. Behrens, C. Ludwig, N. Secunde, R. Ulfung, J. Hynninen, B. Matthews, E. Rawlins, D. Labelle, B. Cresswell, M. Napier, J. Khara, W. Hillhouse, D. Kesling, C. Haymon, Tanglewood Fest Chor, Boston SO/S. Ozawa)

Ⓓ **422 979-2PCC**
Romantic Music for Two Guitars
Albéniz: España, Op. 165 (exc); Danza; *Carulli:* Serenade, Op. 96/3; *Paganini:* Sonata concertata in A; *Granados:* Goyescas (exc); Danzas españolas (exc); *Sor:* Divertissement, Op. 34. (I. Presti, A. Lagoya)

Ⓓ **426 040-2PH** ▭ **426 040-4PH**
Carmen—Highlights
Bizet: Carmen (exc). (J. Norman, M. Freni, N. Shicoff, S. Estes, G. Raphanel, J. Rigby, G. Garino, F. Le Roux, French Rad Chor, FNO/S. Ozawa)

ꝏ **426 040-5PH**
Carmen—Highlights
Bizet: Carmen (exc). (J. Norman, M. Freni, N. Shicoff, S. Estes, G. Raphanel, J. Rigby, G. Garino, F. Le Roux, French Rad Chor, FNO/S. Ozawa)

Ⓓ **426 057-2PH** ▭ **426 057-4PH**
Glorious Pipes
Bach: Cantata 147 (exc); *Zamfir:* Pastel roumain; *Franck:* Panis angelicus; *Schubert:* Ave Maria, D839; *Zamfir:* Impression romantique; *Couperin:* Livre de clavecin II (exc); *Gounod:* Ave Maria; *Handel:* Serse (exc); *Purcell:* Choice Collection of Lessons (exc); *Mozart:* Ave verum corpus, K618; *Zamfir:* Impression sur un bambou; Danse de la forêt. (G. Zamfir, D. Bish)

ꝏ **426 057-5PH**
Glorious Pipes
Bach: Cantata 147 (exc); *Zamfir:* Pastel roumain; *Franck:* Panis angelicus; *Schubert:* Ave Maria, D839; *Zamfir:* Impression romantique; *Couperin:* Livre de clavecin II (exc); *Gounod:* Ave Maria; *Handel:* Serse (exc); *Purcell:* Choice Collection of Lessons (exc); *Mozart:* Ave verum corpus, K618; *Zamfir:* Impression sur un bambou; Danse de la forêt. (G. Zamfir, D. Bish)

Ⓓ **426 115-2PM2** (3/90)
Verdi—Attilla
Verdi: Attila (Cpte). (R. Raimondi, C. Deutekom, S. Milnes, C. Bergonzi, R. Cassinelli, J. Bastin, Finchley Children's Music Group, Ambrosian Sngrs, RPO/L. Gardelli)

Ⓓ **426 118-2PM2** (3/90)
Verdi—Il Corsaro
Verdi: Corsaro (Cpte). (J. Carreras, J. Norman, M. Caballé, G-P. Mastromei, J. Noble, C. Grant, A. Oliver, Ambrosian Sngrs, New Philh/L. Gardelli)

Ⓓ **426 233-2PH2** (4/90)
Donizetti—Maria Stuarda
Donizetti: Maria Stuarda (Cpte). (E. Gruberová, A. Baltsa, F. Araiza, F.E. d'Artegna, S. Alaimo, I. Vermillion, Bavarian Rad Chor, Munich RO/G. Patanè)

Ⓓ **426 243-2PH2** (1/91)
Saint-Saëns: Samson et Dalila
Saint-Saëns: Samson et Dalila (Cpte). (J. Carreras, A. Baltsa, J. Summers, S. Estes, P. Burchuladze, R. Swensen, D.G. Smith, U. Malmberg, Bavarian Rad Chor, BRSO/Colin Davis)

Ⓓ **426 261-2PH** (9/93)
Schoenberg—Vocal Works
Schoenberg: Erwartung (Cpte); Cabaret Songs. (J. Norman, NY Met Op Orch/James Levine)

ꝏ **426 261-5PH**
Schoenberg—Vocal Works
Schoenberg: Erwartung (Cpte); Cabaret Songs. (J. Norman, NY Met Op Orch/James Levine)

ꝏ **426 271-5PH**
Wagner: Overtures & Preludes
Wagner: Fliegende Holländer (exc); Lohengrin (exc); Meistersinger (exc); Tannhäuser (exc); Tristan und Isolde (exc). (BPO/S. Ozawa)

Ⓓ **426 276-2PH2** (11/90) ▭ **426 276-4PH2** (11/90)
Mozart—Die Zauberflöte
Mozart: Zauberflöte (Cpte). (K. Te Kanawa, C. Studer, F. Araiza, O. Bär, S. Ramey, A. Baldin, E. Lind, Y. Kenny, I. Vermillion, A. Collins, C. Fliegner, M. Baur, C. Günther, E. Barham, H. Peeters, E. Barham, H. Peeters, Ambrosian Op Chor, ASMF/N. Marriner)

Ⓓ **426 307-2PH** (12/91)
Vienna Boys' Choir - Recital
Handel: Rinaldo (exc); Samson (exc); *Mozart:* Exsultate jubilate, K165; Ave verum corpus, K618; Vespers, K321 (exc); Sub tuum praesidium, K198; *Schubert:* Hirt auf dem Felsen, D965; *Herbeck:* Pueri concinite; *J. Strauss II:* Frühlingsstimmen, Op. 410. (Vienna Boys' Ch/U.C. Harrer)

Ⓓ **426 308-2PH2** (1/91)
Beethoven—Fidelio
Beethoven: Fidelio (Cpte). (J. Norman, R. Goldberg, E. Wlaschiha, K. Moll, P. Coburn, H-P. Blochwitz, A. Schmidt, Dresden St Op Chor, Staatskapelle Dresden/B. Haitink)

Ⓓ **426 450-2PBQ**
Handel—Arias
Handel: Ariodante (exc); Lucrezia (exc); Rodelinda (exc); Serse (exc); Hercules (exc); Joshua (exc); Atalanta (exc). (J. Baker, ECO/R. Leppard)

Ⓓ **426 560-2PM2** (1/91)
Verdi: Un ballo in maschera
Verdi: Ballo in maschera (Cpte). (M. Caballé, J. Carreras, I. Wixell, S. Ghazarian, P. Payne, R. Lloyd, G. Howell, J. Summers, R. Leggate, W. Elvin, ROH Chor, ROHO/Colin Davis)

Ⓓ **426 563-2PM2** (1/91)
Donizetti—Lucia di Lammermoor
Donizetti: Lucia di Lammermoor (Cpte). (M. Caballé, J. Carreras, V. Sardinero, S. Ramey, A. Murray, C.H. Ahnsjö, V. Bello, Ambrosian Op Chor, New Philh/J. López-Cobos)

Ⓓ **426 640-2PSL** (11/90)
Prokofiev—Orchestral Works
Prokofiev: Love for 3 Oranges Suite; Lt. Kijé Suite; Symphony 1. (LSO/N. Marriner)

Ⓓ **426 714-2PH** (4/91)
Rameau & Purcell: Orchestral Works
Purcell: Fantasia, Z731; Chaconne, Z730; *Rameau:* Castor et Pollux (exc); *Purcell:* Viola da gamba fantasia, Z745. (Eighteenth Century Orch/F. Brüggen)

Ⓓ **426 740-2PH** (7/90)
Dmitri Hvorostovsky sings Tchaikovsky & Verdi Arias
Tchaikovsky: Eugene Onegin (exc); Queen of Spades (exc); Enchantress (exc); Iolanta (exc); Mazeppa (exc); *Verdi:* Traviata (exc); Macbeth (exc); Luisa Miller (exc); Trovatore (exc); Don Carlo (exc). (D. Hvorostovsky, Rotterdam PO/V. Gergiev)

Ⓓ **432 105-2PH** (12/91) ▭ **432 105-4PH** (12/91)
Mascagni—Cavalliera Rusticana
Mascagni: Cavalleria Rusticana (Cpte). (J. Norman, G. Giacomini, D. Hvorostovsky, M. Senn, R. Laghezza, Paris Orch Chor, Paris Orch/S. Bychkov)

Ⓓ **432 114-2PH** (3/94)
Purcell—Dido and Aeneas, etc
Purcell: St Cecilia's Day Ode, Z339; Dido (Cpte). (R. Holton, N. Jenkin, M. Chance, P. Tindall, G. Mosley, C. Watkinson, T. Shaw, E. Priday, D. Deam, S. Beesley, J. Kenny, Monteverdi Ch, EBS/J. E Gardiner)

Ⓓ **432 129-2PH3** (1/92)
Mozart—Don Giovanni
Mozart: Don Giovanni (Cpte). (T. Allen, S. Sweet, K. Mattila, M. McLaughlin, F. Araiza, S. Alaimo, C. Otelli, R. Lloyd, Ambrosian Op Chor, ASMF/N. Marriner)

Ⓓ **432 147-2PH3** (6/92)
Mussorgsky—Khovanshchina
Mussorgsky: Khovanshchina (Cpte). (B. Minzhilkiev, V. Galusin, A. Steblianko, V. Alexeev, N. Okhotnikov, O. Borodina, E. Tselovalnik, K. Pluzhnikov, J. Prokina, N. Gassiev, V. Gerelo, Leningrad Kirov Th Chor, Leningrad Kirov Th Orch/V. Gergiev)

Ⓓ **432 153-2PH2** (10/94)
R. Strauss—Salome
R. Strauss: Salome (Cpte). (J. Norman, J. Morris, W. Raffeiner, K. Witt, R. Leech, A. Markert, F. Schiller, H. Peeters, J. Commichau, R. Tomaszewski, M. Henneberg, Staatskapelle Dresden/S. Ozawa)

Ⓓ **432 157-2PH2** (9/91)
J. Strauss II—Die Fledermaus
J. Strauss II: Fledermaus (Cpte); Unter Donner und Blitz. (K. Te Kanawa, E. Gruberová, W. Brendel, R. Leech, O. Bär, B. Fassbaender, T. Krause, A. Wendler, K. Göttling, O. Schenk, Vienna St Op Chor, VPO/A. Previn)

Ⓓ **432 416-2PH3** (6/93)
Haydn—L'incontro improvviso/Arias
Haydn: Incontro Improvviso (Cpte); Ah tu non senti; Se tu mi sprezzi; Acide e Galatea (exc); Circe (exc). (C.H. Ahnsjö, L. Zoghby, M. Marshall, D. Jones, D. Trimarchi, B. Luxon, J. Prescott, J. Hooper, N. Scarpinati, C.H. Ahnsjö, A. Baldin, M. Devlin, Lausanne CO/A. Dorati)

Ⓓ **432 434-2PH3** (6/93)
Haydn—Orlando Paladino
Haydn: Orlando Paladino (Cpte). (A. Auger, E. Ameling, G. Killebrew, G. Shirley, C.H. Ahnsjö, B. Luxon, D. Trimarchi, M. Mazzieri, G. Carelli, Lausanne CO/A. Dorati)

Ⓓ **432 438-2PH2** (6/93)
Haydn—Armida
Haydn: Armida (Cpte). (J. Norman, C.H. Ahnsjö, N. Burrowes, S. Ramey, R. Leggate, A. Rolfe Johnson, Lausanne CO/A. Dorati)

Ⓓ **432 453-2PM2** (12/92)
Rossini—Elisabetta, Regina d'Inghilterra
Rossini: Elisabetta (Cpte). (M. Caballé, J. Carreras, V. Masterson, R. Creffield, U. Benelli, N. Jenkins, Ambrosian Sngrs, LSO/G-F. Masini)

Ⓓ **432 456-2PM2** (12/92)
Rossini—Otello
Rossini: Otello (Cpte). (J. Carreras, F. von Stade, G. Pastine, S. Fisichella, N. Condò, S. Ramey, K. Lewis, A. Leoz, Ambrosian Op Chor, Philh/J. López-Cobos)

Ⓓ **432 486-2PM3**
Verdi—31 Tenor Arias
Verdi: Oberto (exc); Giorno di regno (exc); Lombardi (exc); Ernani (exc); Due Foscari (exc); Giovanna d'Arco (exc); Alzira (exc); Attila (exc); Macbeth (exc); Masnadieri (exc); Corsaro (exc); Battaglia di Legnano (exc); Rigoletto (exc); Luisa Miller (exc); Trovatore (exc); Vespri siciliani (exc); Simon Boccanegra (exc); Aroldo (exc); Ballo in maschera (exc); Forza del destino (exc); Don Carlo (exc); Aida (exc); Otello (exc); Falstaff (exc). (C. Bergonzi, Ambrosian Sngrs, New Philh/N. Santi, RPO/L. Gardelli)

Ⓓ **432 512-2PSL**
Mozart—Overtures
Mozart: Zauberflöte (exc); Don Giovanni (exc); Così fan tutte (exc); Nozze di Figaro (exc); Idomeneo (exc); Entführung (exc); Clemenza di Tito (exc); Schauspieldirektor (exc); Lucio Silla (exc). (LPO/B. Haitink)

Ⓓ **432 571-2PH**
Essential Canadian Brass
R. Strauss: Also sprach Zarathustra (exc); *Vivaldi:* Concerto, RV537; *G. Gabrieli:* Canzoni et Sonate (1615) (exc); *Mozart:* Piano Sonata, K331 (exc); Serenade, K361; *Bach:* Fugue, BWV578; Toccata and Fugue, BWV565; Wohltemperierte Klavier (exc); *Handy:* Beale Street Blues; *Rossini:* Barbiere di Siviglia (exc); *Rimsky-Korsakov:* Tale of Tsar Saltan (exc); *Traditional:* Virgen de la Macarena; *LaRocca:* Tiger Rag; *Traditional:* Amazing Grace; *Weill:* Dreigroschenoper (exc); *Pachelbel:* Canon and Gigue (exc); *R. Henderson:* Saints' Halleluja. (Canadian Brass)

ꝏ **432 571-5PH**
Essential Canadian Brass
R. Strauss: Also sprach Zarathustra (exc); *Vivaldi:* Concerto, RV537; *G. Gabrieli:* Canzoni et Sonate (1615) (exc); *Mozart:* Piano Sonata, K331 (exc); Serenade, K361; *Bach:* Fugue, BWV578; Toccata and Fugue, BWV565; Wohltemperierte Klavier (exc); *Handy:* Beale Street Blues; *Rossini:* Barbiere di Siviglia (exc); *Rimsky-Korsakov:* Tale of Tsar Saltan (exc); *Traditional:* Virgen de la Macarena; *LaRocca:* Tiger Rag; *Traditional:* Amazing Grace; *Weill:* Dreigroschenoper (exc); *Pachelbel:* Canon and Gigue (exc); *R. Henderson:* Saints' Halleluja. (Canadian Brass)

Ⓓ **432 578-2PM2** (11/91)
Britten—Peter Grimes
Britten: Peter Grimes (Cpte). (J. Vickers, H. Harper, J. Summers, E. Bainbridge, J. Dobson, F. Robinson, P. Payne, T. Allen, J. Lanigan, R. Van Allan, T. Cahill, A. Pashley, ROH Chor, ROHO/Colin Davis)

432 618-4PM
Mozart—Die Zauberflöte Highlights
Mozart: Zauberflöte (exc). (L. Serra, M. Price, K. Moll, P. Schreier, M. Melbye, Leipzig Rad Chor, Staatskapelle Dresden/Colin Davis)

432 692-2PH **432 692-4PH**
The Essential José Carreras
Puccini: Bohème (exc); *Leoncavallo:* Pagliacci (exc); *Puccini:* Manon Lescaut (exc); *Donizetti:* Elisir d'amore (exc); *Verdi:* Trovatore (exc); *Puccini:* Tosca (exc); Turandot (exc); *Annibale:* 'O paese d' 'o sole; *Ramirez:* Misa Criolla (exc); *Lara:* Granada; *Bernstein:* West Side Story (exc); *Di Capua:* O sole mio; *Cardillo:* Core 'ngrato; *Tosti:* A vucchella; *Leoncavallo:* Mattinata; *Verdi:* Luisa Miller (exc); *Franck:* Panis Angelicus; *Donizetti:* Lucia di Lammermoor (exc). (J. Carreras, ROHO/Colin Davis, LSO/J. López-Cobos, Turin RAI Orch/C. Scimone, K. Ricciarelli, ROH Chor, Laredo Choral Salvé, Bilbao Choral Soc, Inst Ens/J.L. Ocejo, ECO/R. Benzi, Orch/R. Farnon/E. Müller/E.G. Asensio, RPO, Vienna SO/U.C. Harrer, S. Ramey, New Philh, Ambrosian Op Chor)

434 016-2PM3 (10/92)
Rossini—Overtures
Rossini: Guillaume Tell (exc); Maometto II (exc); Semiramide (exc); Siège de Corinthe (exc); Ricciardo e Zoriade (exc); Cenerentola (exc); Otello (exc); Gazza Ladra (exc); Armida (exc); Cambiale di matrimonio (exc); Viaggio a Reims (exc); Scala di Seta (exc); Barbiere di Siviglia (exc); Ermione (exc); Tancredi (exc); Italiana in Algeri (exc); Torvaldo e Dorliska (exc); Signor Bruschino (exc); Bianca e Falliero (exc); Turco in Italia (exc); Demetrio e Polibio (exc); Inganno felice (exc); Eduardo e Cristina (exc); Edipo a Colono (exc); Sinfonia di Bologna (exc); Sinfonia al Conventello (exc). (Ambrosian Sngrs, ASMF/N. Marriner)

434 093-2PH2 (2/94)
Gluck—Orfeo ed Euridice
Gluck: Orfeo ed Euridice (Cpte). (D.L. Ragin, S. McNair, C. Sieden, Monteverdi Ch, EBS/J.E. Gardiner)

434 097-2PH3 (6/93)
Prokofiev—War & Peace
Prokofiev: War and Peace (Cpte). (A. Gergalov, Y. Prokina, S. Volkova, L. Kanunnikova, S. Alexashkin, G. Gregorian, O. Borodina, Y. Marusin, A. Morozov, M. Kit, N. Okhotnikov, V. Gerelo, Kirov Th Chor, Kirov Th Orch/V. Gergiev)

434 102-2PH (9/94)
The Heroic Bel Canto Tenor
Donizetti: Caterina Cornaro (exc); Dom Sébastien (exc); Duca d'Alba (exc); Poliuto (exc); *Rossini:* Papal Cantata (exc); Otello (exc); Ermione (exc); Elisabetta (exc). (C. Merritt, Munich RSO/J. Fiore)

434 109-2PH
Wagner for Brass
Wagner: Walküre (exc); Götterdämmerung (exc); Tannhäuser (exc); Meistersinger (exc); Lohengrin (exc); Rienzi (exc); Wesendonk Lieder (exc). (Canadian Brass, BPO, Bayreuth Fest Orch/E. de Waart)

434 128-2PH2 (12/92)
Rossini—Il Turco in Italia
Rossini: Turco in Italia (Cpte). (S. Alaimo, S. Jo, E. Fissore, R. Giménez, S. Mentzer, P. Bronder, A. Corbelli, Ambrosian Op Chor, ASMF/N. Marriner)

434 131-2PH (4/93)
Leoncavallo—I Pagliacci
Leoncavallo: Pagliacci (Cpte). (L. Pavarotti, D. Dessì, J. Pons, P. Coni, E. Gavazzi, Westminster Symphonic Ch, Philadelphia Boys' Ch, Philadelphia/R. Muti)

OO **434 131-5PH**
Leoncavallo—I Pagliacci
Leoncavallo: Pagliacci (Cpte). (L. Pavarotti, D. Dessì, J. Pons, P. Coni, E. Gavazzi, Westminster Symphonic Ch, Philadelphia Boys' Ch, Philadelphia/R. Muti)

434 152-2PM
Jose Carreras - Classics
Leoncavallo: Pagliacci (exc); *Lehár:* Land des Lächelns (exc); *Gounod:* Ave Maria; *Puccini:* Turandot (exc); Bohème (exc); *Donizetti:* Lucia di Lammermoor (exc); *Bernstein:* West Side Story (exc); *Mercadante:* Giuramento (exc); *Ponchielli:* Gioconda (exc); *Mascagni:* Amico Fritz (exc); *Cilea:* Arlesiana (exc); *Donizetti:* Elisir d'amore (exc); *Puccini:* Tosca (exc); *Rossini:* Guillaume Tell (exc). (J. Carreras, LSO, ECO, Vienna SO, ROHO, New Philh, RPO, LPO, R. Farnon Orch/J. López-Cobos/R. Benzi/U.C. Harrer/Colin Davis/R. Farnon)

434 173-2PM (1/93)
Arie Amorose
T. Giordani: Caro mio ben; *Caccini:* Nuove musiche (1602) (exc); Ragion sempre addita; *Sarri:* Sen core l'agnelletta; *Cesti:* Orontea (exc); *Lotti:* Arminio (exc); *A. Scarlatti:* Spesso vibra; Honestà negli amore (exc); Sento nel core; *Caldara:* Come raggio di sol; Selve amiche; Sebben crudele; *Bononcini:* Del più a me non v'ascondete; *Durante:* Danza, danza, fanciulla; *Pergolesi:* Frate 'nnamorato (exc); *J. Martini:* Plaisir d'amour; *Piccinni:* Faux Lord (exc); *Paisiello:* Amor contrastato (exc). (J. Baker, ASMF/N. Marriner)

434 420-2PM32(1)
Richard Wagner Edition (Pt.1)
Wagner: Fliegende Holländer (Cpte); Götterdämmerung (Cpte); Lohengrin (Cpte); Meistersinger (Cpte); Parsifal (Cpte). (S. Estes, L. Balslev, M. Salminen, R. Schunk, A. Schlemm, G. Clark, G. Jones, M. Jung, F. Hübner, H. Becht, F. Mazura, J. Altmeyer, G. Killebrew, N. Sharp, I. Gramatzki, M. Schiml, P. Frey, C. Studer, G. Schnaut, E. Wlaschiha, M. Schenk, E.W. Schulte, K. Ridderbusch, J. Cox, H. Bode, H. Sotin, K. Hirte, F. Stricker, A. Reynolds, G. Nienstedt, H. Steinbach, P. Hofmann, S. Estes, H. Sotin, W. Meier, F. Mazura, M. Salminen, Bayreuth Fest Chor, Bayreuth Fest Orch/W. Nelsson/P. Boulez/P. Schneider/S. Varviso/James Levine)

434 420-2PM32(2)
Richard Wagner Edition (pt 2)
Wagner: Rheingold (Cpte); Siegfried (Cpte); Tannhäuser (Cpte); Tristan und Isolde (Cpte); Walküre (Cpte). (D. McIntyre, H. Schwarz, H. Zednik, H. Pampuch, H. Becht, C. Reppel, S. Jerusalem, M. Egel, O. Wenkel, M. Jung, D. McIntyre, G. Jones, H. Zednik, H. Becht, O. Wenkel, F. Hübner, N. Sharp, W. Windgassen, A. Silja, E. Waechter, G. Bumbry, J. Greindl, G. Stolze, F. Crass, G. Paskuda, G. Nienstedt, E-M. Gardelli, W. Windgassen, B. Nilsson, C. Ludwig, M. Talvela, E. Waechter, C. Heater, P. Hofmann, J. Altmeyer, G. Jones, D. McIntyre, H. Schwarz, M. Salminen, C. Reppel, K. Clarke, K. Middleton, Bayreuth Fest Chor, Bayreuth Fest Orch/P. Boulez/W. Sawallisch/K. Böhm, G. Schnaut, M. Schiml, I. Gramatzki, G. Killebrew, E. Glauser)

434 421-2PH2 (10/92)
Wagner Edition—Das Rheingold
Wagner: Rheingold (Cpte). (D. McIntyre, H. Schwarz, H. Zednik, H. Pampuch, H. Becht, C. Reppel, S. Jerusalem, M. Egel, O. Wenkel, M. Salminen, F. Hübner, N. Sharp, I. Gramatzki, M. Schiml, Bayreuth Fest Orch/P. Boulez)

434 422-2PH3 (10/92)
Wagner Edition—Die Walküre
Wagner: Walküre (Cpte). (P. Hofmann, J. Altmeyer, G. Jones, D. McIntyre, H. Schwarz, M. Salminen, C. Reppel, K. Clarke, K. Middleton, G. Schnaut, E. Glauser, M. Schiml, I. Gramatzki, G. Killebrew, Bayreuth Fest Orch/P. Boulez)

434 423-2PH3 (10/92)
Wagner Edition—Siegfried
Wagner: Siegfried (Cpte). (M. Jung, D. McIntyre, G. Jones, H. Zednik, H. Becht, O. Wenkel, F. Hübner, N. Sharp, Bayreuth Fest Orch/P. Boulez)

434 424-2PH4 (10/92)
Wagner Edition—Götterdämmerung
Wagner: Götterdämmerung (Cpte). (G. Jones, M. Jung, F. Hübner, H. Becht, F. Mazura, J. Altmeyer, G. Killebrew, N. Sharp, I. Gramatzki, M. Schiml, O. Wenkel, G. Schnaut, K. Clarke, Bayreuth Fest Chor, Bayreuth Fest Orch/P. Boulez)

434 425-2PH3 (10/92)
Wagner Edition—Tristan und Isolde
Wagner: Tristan und Isolde (Cpte). (W. Windgassen, B. Nilsson, C. Ludwig, M. Talvela, E. Waechter, C. Heater, E. Wohlfahrt, G. Nienstedt, P. Schreier, Bayreuth Fest Chor, Bayreuth Fest Orch/K. Böhm)

434 595-2PH2 (9/93)
Puccini—Tosca
Puccini: Tosca (Cpte). (C. Vaness, G. Giacomini, G. Zancanaro, D. Serraiocco, P. de Palma, A. Mariotti, O. Mori, C. Austin, J. Smith, Philadelphia Boys' Ch, Westminster Symphonic Ch, Philadelphia/R. Muti)

434 599-2PH2 (10/92)
Wagner Edition—Der Fleigende Holländer
Wagner: Fliegende Holländer (Cpte). (S. Estes, L. Balslev, M. Salminen, R. Schunk, A. Schlemm, G. Clark, Bayreuth Fest Chor, Bayreuth Fest Orch/W. Nelsson)

434 602-2PH4 (10/92)
Wagner Edition—Lohengrin
Wagner: Lohengrin (Cpte). (P. Frey, C. Studer, G. Schnaut, E. Wlaschiha, M. Schenk, E.W. Schulte, Bayreuth Fest Chor, Bayreuth Fest Orch/P. Schneider)

434 607-2PH3 (10/92)
Wagner Edition—Tannhäuser
Wagner: Tannhäuser (Cpte). (W. Windgassen, A. Silja, E. Waechter, G. Bumbry, J. Greindl, G. Stolze, F. Crass, G. Paskuda, G. Nienstedt, E-M. Gardelli, Bayreuth Fest Chor, Bayreuth Fest Orch/W. Sawallisch)

434 611-2PH4 (10/92)
Wagner Edition—Die Meistersinger
Wagner: Meistersinger (Cpte). (K. Ridderbusch, J. Cox, H. Bode, H. Sotin, K. Hirte, F. Stricker, A. Reynolds, G. Nienstedt, H. Steinbach, J. Dene, R. Licha, W. Appel, N. Orth, H. Feldhoff, H. Bauer, N. Hillebrand, B. Weikl, Bayreuth Fest Chor, Bayreuth Fest Orch/S. Varviso)

434 616-2PH4 (10/92)
Wagner Edition—Parsifal
Wagner: Parsifal (Cpte). (P. Hofmann, S. Estes, H. Sotin, W. Meier, F. Mazura, M. Salminen, M. Pabst, M. Hölle, R. Engert-Ely, S. Fues, H. Pampuch, P. Maus, D. Sasson, S. Roberts, M. Schmitt, A. Browner, H. Leidland, M. Neubauer, Bayreuth Fest Chor, Bayreuth Fest Orch/James Levine)

434 725-2PM **434 725-4PM**
Kiri Te Kanawa - Classics
Mozart: Entführung (exc); *Handel:* Samson (exc); *Gounod:* St Cecilia Mass (exc); *Mozart:* Idomeneo (exc); Don Giovanni (exc); *Schubert:* Ave Maria, D839; *Mozart:* Vespers, K339 (exc); Zauberflöte (exc); *Gounod:* Faust (exc); *Mozart:* Exsultate jubilate, K165; *J. Strauss II:* Fledermaus (exc). (K. Te Kanawa, St Paul's Cath Ch, ECO, LSO, BRSO, VPO/J. Tate/Barry Rose/Colin Davis/A. Previn)

434 726-2PM **434 726-4PH**
Vienna Boys' Choir - Portrait
Mozart: Mass, K317 (exc); Inter natos mulierum, K72 (exc); Sub tuum praesidium, K198; vespers, K321 (exc); Mass, K220 (exc); *Handel:* Messiah (exc); Rinaldo (exc); *Schubert:* Deutsche messe (exc); *Caldara:* Missa Laetare (exc); *Haydn:* Mass 5 (exc); Mass 7 (exc); *Traditional:* Quanno nascete ninno; Hark! the herald angels sing. (Vienna Boys' Ch, Chorus Viennensis, Vienna SO, Capella Caldara, Vienna Volksoper Orch/U.C. Harrer)

434 727-2PM **434 727-4PM**
Pepe Romero - Guitar Solos
Anon: Jeux interdits; *Albéniz:* Suite española 1 (exc); Recuerdos de Viaje (exc); Mallorca; España, Op.165 (exc); *Granados:* Danzas españolas (exc); Goyescas (exc); *Romero:* Malagueña; Preludes (exc); *Tárrega:* Pavana; Capricho árabe; *Sor:* Mozart Variations, Op.9. (P. Romero, Celín Romero)

434 782-2PM2 (10/93)
Bizet—Les Pêcheurs de Perles
Bizet: Pêcheurs de Perles (Cpte). (P. Alarie, L. Simoneau (ten), R. Bianco, X. Depraz, E. Brasseur Ch, Lamoureux Concerts Orch/J. Fournet)

434 784-2PM2 (5/93)
Gluck—Orphée et Eurydice
Gluck: Orphée (Cpte). (L. Simoneau, S. Danco, P. Alarie, R. Blanchard Voc Ens, Lamoureux Orch/H. Rosbaud)

434 912-2PH (9/94) **434 912-4PH** (9/94)
Bel Canto Arias
Rossini: Barbiere di Siviglia (exc); Guillaume Tell (exc); *Donizetti:* Favorita (exc); Duca d'Alba (exc); Poliuto (exc); Elisir d'amore (exc); Don Pasquale (exc); Dom Sébastien (exc); Lucia di Lammermoor (exc); *Bellini:* Pirata (exc); Puritani (exc). (D. Hvorostovsky, Philh/I. Marin)

434 916-2PH (6/93)
Gilbert & Sullivan—Overtures
Sullivan: HMS Pinafore (exc); Yeomen of the Guard (exc); Iolanthe (exc); Di ballo; Mikado (exc); Pirates of Penzance (exc); Macbeth (exc); Gondoliers (exc); Patience (exc). (ASMF/N. Marriner)

OO **434 916-5PH**
Gilbert & Sullivan—Overtures
Sullivan: HMS Pinafore (exc); Yeomen of the Guard (exc); Iolanthe (exc); Di ballo; Mikado (exc); Pirates of Penzance (exc); Macbeth (exc); Gondoliers (exc); Patience (exc). (ASMF/N. Marriner)

434 926-2PH (6/93)
The Pleasure of Love
J. Martini: Plaisir d'amour; *Caldara:* Come raggio di sol; Sebben crudele; *A. Scarlatti:* Pompeo (exc); *Handel:* Serse (exc); Rinaldo (exc); *Mercadante:* Cardellino; *Durante:* Danza, danza fanciulla; *Niedermeyer:* Pietà, Signore; *Perti:* Sperar io non dovrei; *T. Giordani:* Caro mio ben; *Stradella:* Così Amor mi fai languir; *Gluck:* Paride ed Elena (exc); *Bononcini:* Griselda (exc); *Donizetti:* Te voglio bene assaje. (J. Carreras, ECO/V. Sutej)

OO **434 926-5PH**
The Pleasure of Love
J. Martini: Plaisir d'amour; *Caldara:* Come raggio di sol; Sebben crudele; *A. Scarlatti:* Pompeo (exc); *Handel:* Serse

(exc); Rinaldo (exc); *Mercadante:* Cardellino; *Durante:* Danza, danza fanciulla; *Niedermeyer:* Pietà, Signore; *Perti:* Sperar io non dovrei; *T. Giordani:* Caro mio ben; *Stradella:* Così Amor mi fai languir; *Gluck:* Paride ed Elena (exc); *Bononcini:* Griselda (exc); *Donizetti:* Te voglio bene assaje. (J. Carreras, ECO/V. Sutej)

Ⓓ **434 986-2PM**
Duetti Amorosi
Verdi: Corsaro (exc); *Rossini:* Elisabetta (exc); *Donizetti:* Lucia di Lammermoor (exc); *Verdi:* Ballo in Maschera (exc); *Puccini:* Tosca (exc). (M. Caballé, J. Carreras, V. Masterson, I. Wixell, S. Ghazarian, R. Lloyd, G. Howell, W. Elvin, P. de Palma, New Philh, LSO, ROH Chor, ROHO/L. Gardelli/G-F. Masini/J. López-Cobos/Colin Davis)

Ⓓ **434 992-2PH** (8/94) ▭ **434 992-4PH** (8/94)
The Sorceress—Original Soundtrack
Handel: Rinaldo (exc); Alcina (exc); Giulio Cesare (exc); Ariodante (exc); Agrippina (exc); Admeto (exc); Giustino (exc). (K. te Kanawa, AAM/C. Hogwood)

Ⓓ **438 013-2PH2** (10/93)
Humperdinck—Hänsel und Gretel
Humperdinck: Hänsel und Gretel (Cpte). (A. Murray, E. Gruberová, G. Jones, F. Grundheber, B. Bonney, C. Oelze, C. Ludwig, Staatskapelle Dresden/Colin Davis)

Ⓓ **438 138-2PH2** (11/93)
Sullivan—Yeomen of the Guard
Sullivan: Yeomen of the Guard (Cpte). (R. Lloyd, K. Streit, S. Dean, N. Mackie, T. Allen, B. Terfel, S. McNair, J. Rigby, A. Collins, J. Howarth, A. Michaels-Moore, ASMF Chor, ASMF/N. Marriner)

Ⓓ **438 141-2PH3** (10/93)
Tchaikovsky—Queen of Spades
Tchaikovsky: Queen of Spades (Cpte). (G. Grigorian, M. Gulegina, I. Arkhipova, N. Putilin, V. Chernov, O. Borodina, V. Solodovnikov, S. Alexashkin, E. Boitsov, N. Gassiev, G. Bezebenkov, L. Filatova, T. Filimonova, Kirov Th Chor, Kirov Th Orch/V. Gergiev)

Ⓓ **438 166-2PH** ▭ **438 166-4PH**
Best of the Classical Bits
Handel: Solomon (exc); *Mozart:* Serenade, K525 (exc); *Rachmaninov:* Paganini Rhapsody (exc); *Rossini:* Guillaume Tell (exc); *Grieg:* Peer Gynt (exc); *Gershwin:* Rhapsody in Blue (exc); *Tchaikovsky:* Romeo and Juliet (exc); *Vivaldi:* Concerti, Op. 8 (exc); *J. Strauss II:* Blauen Donau, Op. 314; *Pachelbel:* Canon and Gigue (exc); *Albinoni:* Adagio; *Tchaikovsky:* Nutcracker Suite (exc); *Sibelius:* Karelia Suite (exc); *Elgar:* Enigma Variations (exc); *Ravel:* Boléro (exc); *Orff:* Carmina Burana (exc); *Bach:* Suites, BWV1066-9 (exc). (ASMF, Concertgebouw, ECO, Monte Carlo Op Orch, I Musici, Vienna SO, Staatskapelle Dresden, BPO, Shin-yu Kai Ch/N. Marriner/N. Järvi/R. Leppard, W. Haas/E. De Waart, P. Carmirelli/W. Sawallisch, H. Szeryng, M. T. Garatti/S. Ozawa, B. Davidovich)

Ⓓ **438 235-2PH2** (12/93)
Tchaikovsky—Eugene Onegin
Tchaikovsky: Eugene Onegin (Cpte). (D. Hvorostovsky, N. Focile, N. Shicoff, O. Borodina, A. Anisimov, Sarah Walker, I. Arkhipova, F. Egerton, H. Hennequin, S. Zadvorny, St Petersburg Chbr Ch, Paris Orch/S. Bychkov)

Ⓓ **438 238-2PH2** (12/93)
Verdi—La Traviata
Verdi: Traviata (Cpte). (K. Te Kanawa, Alfredo Kraus, D. Hvorostovsky, S. Mazzoni, O. Borodina, B. Banks, R. Scaltriti, G. Gatti, D. Di Stefano, M. La Guardia, A. Calamai, MMF Chor, MMF Orch/Z. Mehta)

Ⓓ **438 241-2PH4**
Wagner—Tristan und Isolde
Wagner: Tristan und Isolde (Cpte). (P. Hofmann, H. Behrens, Y. Minton, H. Sotin, B. Weikl, H. Steinbach, H. Zednik, R. Grumbach, T. Moser, Bavarian Rad Chor, BRSO/L. Bernstein)

Ⓓ **438 309-2PM** ▭ **438 309-4PM**
A Romantic Organ Extravaganza
Wagner: Tannhäuser (exc); Walküre (exc); Meistersinger (exc); *Rheinberger:* Organ Sonata 11 (exc); *Gigout:* Ten Organ Pieces (exc); *Vierne:* Pièces en stile libre (exc); *Boëllmann:* Suite gothique. (D. Chorzempa)

Ⓓ **438 359-2PM2** (8/93)
Puccini—Tosca
Puccini: Tosca (Cpte). (M. Caballé, J. Carreras, I. Wixell, S. Ramey, P. de Palma, D. Trimarchi, W. Elvin, A. Murray, ROH Chor, ROHO/Colin Davis)

Ⓓ **438 493-2PH** (3/93) ▭ **438 493-4PH** (3/93)
New Year's Concert 1993
J. Strauss I: Sperl-Galop; Radetzky March; *J. Strauss II:* Publicisten; Diplomaten-Polka, Op. 448; Veilchen-Polka; Indigo und die vierzig Räuber (exc); Klipp Klapp Galop, Op. 466; Egyptischer Marsch, Op. 335; Pizzicato Polka; Perpetuum mobile; Auf der Jagd, Op. 373; Blauen Donau, Op. 314; *Jos Strauss:* Transaktionen; *Lanner:* Steyrische-Tänze, Op. 165; Hans-Jörgel, Op. 194. (VPO/R. Muti)

Ⓓ **438 494-2PH**
Mozart—Don Giovanni Highlights
Mozart: Don Giovanni (exc). (T. Allen, S. Sweet, K. Mattila, M. McLaughlin, F. Araiza, S. Alaimo, C. Otelli, R. Lloyd, ASMF/N. Marriner)

Ⓓ **438 495-2PH**
Mozart—Die Zauberflöte Highlights
Mozart: Zauberflöte (exc). (K. Te Kanawa, C. Studer, F. Araiza, O. Bär, S. Ramey, A. Baldin, E. Lind, Y. Kenny, I. Vermillion, A. Collins, Ambrosian Op Chor, ASMF/N. Marriner)

Ⓓ **438 496-2PH**
Beethoven—Fidelio Highlights
Beethoven: Fidelio (exc). (J. Norman, R. Goldberg, E. Wlaschiha, K. Moll, P. Coburn, H-P. Blochwitz, A. Schmidt, Dresden St Op Chor, Staatskapelle Dresden/B. Haitink)

Ⓓ **438 497-2PH**
Weber—Der Freischütz Highlights
Weber: Freischütz (exc). (K. Mattila, F. Araiza, E. Lind, E. Wlaschiha, S. Lorenz, K. Moll, T. Thomaschke, W. Quadflieg, A. Scheibner, Leipzig Rad Chor, Staatskapelle Dresden/Colin Davis)

Ⓓ **438 498-2PH**
Rossini—Il barbiere di Siviglia Highlights
Rossini: Barbiere di Siviglia (exc). (A. Baltsa, S. Burgess, F. Araiza, T. Allen, D. Trimarchi, R. Lloyd, ASMF/N. Marriner)

Ⓓ **438 499-2PH**
Rossini—William Tell Highlights
Rossini: Guillaume Tell (exc). (G. Zancanaro, C. Studer, C. Merritt, F. de Grandis, L. Rono, La Scala Chor, La Scala orch/R. Muti)

Ⓓ **438 500-2PH**
Wagner—Lohengrin Highlights
Wagner: Lohengrin (exc). (P. Frey, C. Studer, G. Schnaut, E. Wlaschiha, M. Schenk, Bayreuth Fest Chor, Bayreuth Fest Orch/P. Schneider)

Ⓓ **438 501-2PH**
Wagner—Tristan und Isolde Highlights
Wagner: Tristan und Isolde (exc). (P. Hofmann, H. Behrens, Y. Minton, B. Weikl, Bavarian Rad Chor, BRSO/L. Bernstein)

Ⓓ **438 502-2PH**
Offenbach—Tales of Hoffmann Highlights
Offenbach: Contes d'Hoffmann (exc). (F. Araiza, E. Lind, C. Studer, J. Norman, A.S. von Otter, S. Ramey, R. Cassinelli, F. Palmer, G. Gautier, R. Tomaszewski, P. Menzel, Leipzig Rad Chor, Staatskapelle Dresden/J. Tate)

Ⓓ **438 503-2PH**
J. Strauss II—Die Fledermaus Highlights
J. Strauss II: Fledermaus (exc); Unter Donner und Blitz. (K. Te Kanawa, E. Gruberová, W. Brendel, R. Leech, O. Bär, B. Fassbaender, T. Krause, K. Göttling/A. Previn, Vienna St Op Chor, VPO/A. Previn)

Ⓓ **438 504-2PH**
Saint-Saëns—Samson et Dalila Highlights
Saint-Saëns: Samson et Dalila (exc). (A. Baltsa, J. Carreras, J. Summers, S. Estes, P. Burchuladze, R. Swensen, D.G. Smith, U. Malmberg, Bavarian Rad Chor, BRSO/Colin Davis)

Ⓓ **438 663-2PH** (1/94)
American Classics
Gershwin: American in Paris; *Ellington:* Harlem; *Bernstein:* West Side Story Symphonic Dances; *J. Adams:* Chairman Dances. (Hollywood Bowl Orch/J. Mauceri)

Ⓓ **438 664-2PM2** (5/94)
R. Strauss—Salome
R. Strauss: Salome (Cpte). (W. Wegner, J. Metternich, L. Szemere, G. von Milinkovic, W. Kmentt, D. Hermann, O. Czerwenka, W. Berry, Adolf Vogel, H. Pröglhöf, D. Frass, Vienna SO/R. Moralt)

Ⓓ **438 667-2PM2** (4/94)
Schoenberg—Moses und Aron
Schoenberg: Moses und Aron (Cpte). (G. Reich, L. Devos, W. Mann, E. Csapó, E. Obrowsky, R. Lucas, R. Salter, L. Illavský, Vienna Boys' Ch, Austrian Rad Chor, Austrian RSO/M. Gielen)

Ⓓ **438 670-2PM3** (10/94)
Mozart—Le nozze di Figaro
Mozart: Nozze di Figaro (Cpte). (W. Berry, R. Streich, P. Schoeffler, S. Jurinac, C. Ludwig, I. Malaniuk, O. Czerwenka, E. Majkut, M. Dickie, K. Dönch, R. Schwaiger, Vienna St Op Chor, Vienna SO/K. Böhm)

Ⓓ **438 674-2PM3** (10/94)
Mozart—Don Giovanni
Mozart: Don Giovanni (Cpte). (G. London, H. Zadek, S. Jurinac, G. Sciutti, L. Simoneau, W. Berry, E. Waechter, L. Weber, Vienna Chbr Ch, Vienna SO/R. Moralt)

Ⓓ **438 678-2PM3** (10/94)
Mozart—Così fan tutte
Mozart: Così fan tutte (Cpte). (T. Stich-Randall, I. Malaniuk, G. Sciutti, W. Kmentt, W. Berry, D. Ernster, Vienna St Op Chor, Vienna SO/R. Moralt)

Ⓓ **438 685-2PH** (6/94) ▭ **438 685-4PH** (6/94)
The Great Waltz
Tiomkin: Great Waltz (exc); *R. R. Bennett:* Murder on the Orient Express (exc); *R. Strauss:* Rosenkavalier (exc); *Herrmann:* Snows of Kilimanjaro (exc); *F. Loewe:* Gigi (exc); *Prokofiev:* Cinderella (exc); *Sondheim:* Little Night Music (exc); *Bernstein:* Candide (1956) (exc); *Rózsa:* Madame Bovary (exc); *Waxman:* Hotel Berlin (exc); *Steiner:* Jezebel (exc); *Korngold:* Prince and the Pauper (exc); *Ravel:* La Valse. (Hollywood Bowl SO/J. Mauceri)

Ⓓ **438 706-2PM2** (5/94)
Beethoven—Overtures; Minuets; Dances
Beethoven: Coriolan; Egmont (exc); König Stefan (exc); Prometheus (exc); Fidelio (exc); Leonore (exc); Consecration of the House Ov; Namensfeier; Ruinen von Athen (exc); Menuets, WoO7; German Dances, WoO8; Contredanses, WoO14. (Leipzig Gewandhaus/K. Masur, ASMF/N. Marriner)

Ⓓ **438 763-2PM2**
Chopin/Delibes/Gounod—Ballet Music
Delibes: Coppélia (Cpte); *Chopin:* Sylphides (Cpte); *Gounod:* Faust (exc). (Rotterdam PO/D. Zinman)

Ⓓ **438 867-2PH** ▭ **438 867-4PH**
Songs of the Earth
Ravel: Daphnis et Chloé Suites (exc); *Grieg:* Peer Gynt (exc); *Nielsen:* Helios; *Debussy:* Après-midi; *Waxman:* Dusk; *Wagner:* Tristan und Isolde (exc); *Schoenberg:* Gurrelieder (exc). (B. Dukov, Hollywood Bowl SO/J. Mauceri)

Ⓓ **438 872-2PH** (5/94) ▭ **438 872-4PH** (5/94)
Songs and Dances of Death
Rimsky-Korsakov: Sadko (exc); Kashchey (exc); Snow Maiden (exc); Tsar's Bride (exc); *Borodin:* Prince Igor (exc); *Rubinstein:* Demon (exc); Nero (exc); *Rachmaninov:* Aleko (exc); *Mussorgsky:* Songs and Dances of Death. (D. Hvorostovsky, Kirov Th Orch/V. Gergiev)

Ⓓ **438 921-2PB10** (2/94)
Splendour of the Baroque
Bach: Brandenburg Concertos; Violin Concerto, BWV1042; Triple Concerto, BWV1044; *Vivaldi:* Concerti Grossi, Op. 3 (exc); Concerti, Op. 8 (exc); Concerto, RV445; Concerto, RV484; Concerto, RV577; Concerto, RV558; *Torelli:* Concerti Grossi, Op. 8 (exc); *Bononcini:* Sinfonias, Op. 3 (exc); *Telemann:* Viola Concerto in G; Trumpet Concerto in D; *Albinoni:* Adagio; Concerti, Op. 9 (exc); Concerti, Op. 9 (exc); Concerti, Op. 10 (exc); *Manfredini:* Concerti Grossi, Op. 3 (exc); *Bonporti:* Concerti a Quattro, Op. 11 (exc); *Corelli:* Concerti Grossi, Op. 6 (exc); *Pachelbel:* Canon and Gigue (exc); *A. Scarlatti:* Giardino di rose; *Locatelli:* Concertos, Op. 3 (exc); Concerti Grossi, Op. 1 (exc); *De Fesch:* Concerts, Op. 3a (exc); *Handel:* Water Music; Concerti Grossi, Op. 6 (exc); *Boyce:* Cambridge Installation Ode (exc); *Capuzzi:* Violone Concerto; *Leo:* Cello Concertos (exc); *Leclair:* Concertos, Op. 7 (exc); *Gaviniès:* Violin Concertos, Op. 4 (exc); *Pergolesi:* Olimpiade (exc); *Quantz:* Flute Concerto in G; *Zelenka:* Concerto a 8 in G; *Geminiani:* Concerti Grossi (Corelli, Op. 5) (exc); *Jacchini:* Trattenimenti, Op. 5 (exc). (I Musici, New Philh/R. Leppard, ECO, C. Bernard, Rouen CO/A. Beaucamp, Staatskapelle Dresden/V. Negri, J-P. Rampal, Antiqua Musica Orch/J. Roussel, German Bach Sols/H. Winschermann, D. Smithers, ASMF/N. Marriner)

Ⓓ **438 938-2PH** (9/94) ▭ **438 938-4PH** (9/94)
España!
Falla: Vida breve (exc); Amor brujo (exc); *Lecuona:* Malagueņa; *Albéniz:* Suite española 1; Pavana capricho; Iberia (exc); Navarra; *Infante:* Danses Andalouses. (K. Labèque, M. Labèque)

Ⓓ **438 940-2PH**
Opera Fantasy
Rossini: Guillaume Tell (exc); Viaggio a Reims (exc); *Verdi:* Traviata (exc); *Mozart:* Così fan tutte (exc); Don Giovanni (exc); *Bellini:* Norma (exc); Sonnambula (exc); *Cui:* Suite Miniature 1; *Puccini:* Tosca (exc); *Tchaikovsky:* Queen of Spades (exc); *Moscheles:* Concertante in F. (J. Zoon, H. de Vries, London Studio SO)

① **438 953-2PM2** (11/94)
Alarie/Simoneau - Arias & Duets
Mozart: Idomeneo (exc); Idomeneo (exc); Don Giovanni (exc); Così fan tutte (exc); Clemenza di Tito (exc); *Verdi:* Traviata (exc); *Gounod:* Roméo et Juliette (exc); Mireille (exc); *A. Thomas:* Mignon (exc); *Bizet:* Pêcheurs de Perles (exc); *Offenbach:* Contes d'Hoffmann (exc); *Bizet:* Carmen (exc); *Delibes:* Lakmé (exc); Lakmé (exc). (P. Alarie, M. Moralès, L. Simoneau, Vienna SO/B. Paumgartner, Lamoureux Orch/P. Dervaux/A. Jouve)

① **438 960-2PM3**
Maurice Gendron
Schubert: Arpeggione Sonata, D821; *Beethoven:* Mozart Variations, Op. 66; Mozart Variations, WoO46; Handel Variations, WoO45; *Debussy:* Cello Sonata; *Françaix:* Berceuse; Rondino staccato; Nocturne; Mouvement perpétuel; Sérénade; *Fauré:* Cello Sonata 2; *Messiaen:* Quatuor (exc); *Popper:* Serenade, Op. 54/2; *Handel:* Serse (exc); *Saint-Saëns:* Carnaval des animaux (exc); *Schumann:* Kinderszenen (exc); *Rimsky-Korsakov:* Tale of Tsar Saltan (exc); *Paganini:* Moses in Egypt Variations; *Moszkowski:* Pieces, Op. 45 (exc); *Kreisler:* Liebesleid; *Falla:* Vida breve (exc); *Bach:* Orgel-Büchlein, BWV599-644 (exc); *Chopin:* Introduction and polonaise brillant, Op. 3; *Fitzenhagen:* Moto perpetuo; *Granados:* Danzas españolas (exc); *Dvořák:* Humoresques, Op. 101 (exc). (M. Gendron, J. Françaix, P. Gallion)

① **442 011-2PH** (4/94) ▭ **442 011-4PH** (4/94)
Russian Orchestral Works
Glinka: Ruslan and Lyudmila (exc); *Khachaturian:* Gayaneh (exc); Spartacus (exc); *Borodin:* Prince Igor (exc); *Liadov:* Baba-Yaga, Op. 56; Kikimora, Op. 63; *Tchaikovsky:* 1812. (Dutch Royal Marine Band, Kirov Th Chor, Kirov Th Orch/V. Gergiev)

① **442 079-2PB2** (7/94)
Schumann—Complete Symphonies, etc
Schumann: Symphony 1; Symphony 2; Symphony 3; Symphony 4; Genoveva (exc); Manfred (exc). (Concertgebouw/B. Haitink)

① **442 082-2PM3** (9/94)
Charpentier—Louise
G. Charpentier: Louise (Cpte). (B. Monmart, A. Laroze, L. Musy, S. Michel, L. Rialland, P. Giannotti/J. Fournet, Paris Opéra-Comique Chor, Paris Opéra-Comique Orch/J. Fournet)

① **442 086-2PM3** (12/94)
R. Strauss—Der Rosenkavalier
R. Strauss: Rosenkavalier (Cpte). (E. Lear, F. von Stade, J. Bastin, R. Welting, D. Hammond-Stroud, J. Carreras, S. van Sante, J. Atherton, N. Morpurgo, R. van Haarlem, H. Smit, W. Goedhardt, M. Coppens, A. van Limpt, A. Bello, M. Dieleman, T. van der Putten, F. Fiselier, P. Bindels, A. Kooijmans, W. Huisman, R. Vedder, Netherlands Op Chor, Rotterdam PO/E. de Waart)

① **442 090-2PM2** (10/94)
Donizetti—Don Pasquale
Donizetti: Don Pasquale (Cpte). (R. Capecchi, B. Rizzoli, P. Munteanu, G. Valdengo, C. Adorni, Naples San Carlo Op Chor, Naples San Carlo Op Orch/F. Molinari-Pradelli)

① **442 093-2PM2** (9/94)
Donizetti—Linda di Chamounix
Donizetti: Linda di Chamounix (Cpte). (A. Stella, C. Valletti, R. Capecchi, G. Taddei, F. Barbieri, G. Modesti, R. Corsi, P. de Palma, Naples San Carlo Op Chor, Naples San Carlo Op Orch/T. Serafin)

① **442 096-2PM3** (12/94)
Handel—Ariodante
Handel: Ariodante (Cpte). (J. Baker, E. Mathis, N. Burrowes, J. Bowman, D. Rendall, S. Ramey, A. Oliver, London Voices, ECO/R. Leppard)

① **442 100-2PM2** (3/95)
Rossini—Mosè
Rossini: Mosè (Cpte). (N. Rossi-Lemeni, A. Lazzari, G. Taddei, M. Filippeschi, P. de Palma, P. Clabassi, L. Danieli, C. Mancini, B. Rizzoli, F. Mazzoli, Naples San Carlo Op Chor, Naples San Carlo Op Orch/T. Serafin)

① **442 103-2PM2** (9/94)
Wagner—Der fliegende Holländer
Wagner: Fliegende Holländer (Cpte). (F. Crass, A. Silja, J. Greindl, F. Uhl, R. Fischer, G. Paskuda, Bayreuth Fest Chor, Bayreuth Fest Orch/W. Sawallisch)

① **442 106-2PM2**
Puccini—La Bohème; Gianni Schicchi
Puccini: Bohème (Cpte); Gianni Schicchi (Cpte). (A. Stella, G. Poggi, B. Rizzoli, R. Capecchi, G. Mazzini, G. Modesti, M. Luise, G. Onesti, P. de Palma, G. Gaudioso, A. Terrosi, R. Capecchi, B. Rizzoli, A. Lazzari, V. Palombini, P. de Palma, O. Rovero, N. Tarallo, P. Clabassi, G. Modesti, A. La Porta, M. Minetto, F. Mazzoli, G. Onesti, G. Gaudioso, Naples San Carlo Op Chor, Naples San Carlo Op Orch/F. Molinari-Pradelli)

① **442 128-2PH** (12/94) ▭ **442 128-4PH** (12/94)
Bizet—Orchestral Suites
Bizet: Arlésienne Suites; Carmen Suites. (Paris Orch/S. Bychkov)

① **442 138-2PH3** (1/95)
Rimsky-Korsakov—Sadko
Rimsky-Korsakov: Sadko (Cpte). (V. Galusin, V. Tsidipova, S. Alexashkin, M. Tarassova, L. Dyadkova, B. Minzhilkiev, G. Grigorian, A. Gergalov, V. Ognovenko, N. Gassiev, N. Putilin, Y. Boitsov, G. Bezebenkov, Kirov Th Chor, Kirov Th Orch/V. Gergiev)

① **442 260-2PM2** (10/94)
Puccini—La Bohème
Puccini: Bohème (Cpte). (K. Ricciarelli, J. Carreras, A. Putnam, I. Wixell, H. Hagegård, R. Lloyd, G. de Angelis, W. Elvin, F. Egerton, R. Hazell, D. Whelan, ROH Chor, ROHO/Colin Davis)

① **442 272-2PM2** (10/94)
The Best of Bizet
Bizet: Carmen Suites (exc); Arlésienne Suites; Chanson d'avril; Pêcheurs de perles (exc); Jeux d'enfants; Symphony; Carmen (exc); Variations chromatiques; Agnus Dei; Jolie Fille de Perth Suite. (J. Rhodes, L. Simoneau, A. Lance, J. Carreras, G. Souzay, R. Bianco, D. Baldwin, M-F. Bucquet, Vienna Boys' Ch, Lamoureux Concerts Orch, LSO, Paris Op Orch, Vienna SO/A. Dorati/J. Fournet/R. Benzi/U. C. Harrer)

① **442 278-2PM2**
Prokofiev—Favourite Orchestral Works
Prokofiev: Love for 3 Oranges Suite; Romeo and Juliet Suites (exc); Symphony 1; Lt Kijé Suite; Peter and the Wolf; Scythian Suite. (A. McCowen, LSO/N. Marriner, Rotterdam PO/E. de Waart, Concertgebouw/B. Haitink, Los Angeles PO/A. Previn)

① **442 281-2PM2**
R. Strauss—Five Great Tone Poems
R. Strauss: Don Juan; Heldenleben; Till Eulenspiegel; Also sprach Zarathustra; Tod und Verklärung; Rosenkavalier (exc). (Concertgebouw/B. Haitink/E. Jochum)

① **442 313-2PM6**
Sir Neville Marriner—A Birthday Celebration
Bach: Brandenburg Concertos; Violin Concerto, BWV1042; Violin Concerto, BWV1041; 2-Violin Concerto; Suites, BWV1066-9 (exc); *Mendelssohn:* Midsummer Night's Dream (Cpte); *Mozart:* Clarinet Concerto, K622; Symphony 25; Symphony 26; Symphony 27; Symphony 29; *Handel:* Solomon (exc); Water Music; *Tchaikovsky:* Nutcracker Suite; *Rossini:* Guillaume Tell (exc); *Rodrigo:* Concierto de Aranjuez (exc); *Ravel:* Boléro; *Elgar:* Pomp and Circumstance Marches (exc); *Beethoven:* Wellingtons Sieg. (H. Szeryng, M. Hasson, A. Auger, A. Murray, J. Brymer, P. Romero, Ambrosian Sngrs, Philh, Staatskapelle Dresden, Concertgebouw, ASMF/N. Marriner)

① **442 383-2PH**
Gluck—Orphée et Eurydice-Highlights
Gluck: Orfeo ed Euridice (exc). (S. McNair, D. L. Ragin, C. Sieden, Monteverdi Ch, EBS/J. E. Gardiner)

① **442 384-2PH**
Tchaikovsky—Eugene Onegin - Highlights
Tchaikovsky: Eugene Onegin (exc). (Sarah Walker, N. Focile, O. Borodina, I. Arkhipova, D. Hvorostovsky, N. Shicoff, A. Anisimov, St Petersburg Chbr Ch, Paris Orch/S. Bychkov)

① **442 403-2PM**
Offenbach—Ballet Music
Offenbach: Gaîté Parisienne (Cpte); Voyage dans la lune (exc); Orphée aux enfers (exc). (Pittsburgh SO/A. Previn, Philh/A. de Almeida)

① **442 410-2PM** (9/94)
Queen of the Night—Cheryl Studer sings Mozart
Mozart: Entführung (exc); Zauberflöte (exc); Idomeneo (exc); Nozze di Figaro (exc); Don Giovanni (exc); Clemenza di Tito (exc); Così fan tutte (exc). (C. Studer, ASMF/N. Marriner)

① **442 435-2PH**
Humperdinck—Hänsel und Gretel - Highlights
Humperdinck: Hänsel und Gretel (exc). (F. Grundheber, G. Jones, A. Murray, E. Gruberová, C. Ludwig, B. Bonney, C. Oelze, Dresden St Op Chor, Staatskapelle Dresden/Colin Davis)

① **442 436-2PH**
Sullivan—The Yeomen of the Guard - Highlights
Sullivan: Yeomen of the Guard (exc). (S. McNair, J. Howarth, J. Rigby, A. Collins, K. Streit, T. Allen, B. Terfel, R. Lloyd, S. Dean, ASMF Chor, ASMF/N. Marriner)

① **442 437-2PH**
Prokofiev—War and Peace - Highlights
Prokofiev: War and Peace (exc). (A. Gergalov, Y. Prokina, S. Alexashkin, G. Grigorian, Y. Marusin, I. Bogacheva, S. Volkova, N. Okhotnikov, V. Gerelo, Kirov Th Chor, Kirov Th Orch/V. Gergiev)

① **442 438-2PH**
Puccini—Tosca - Highlights
Puccini: Tosca (exc). (C. Vaness, G. Giacomini, P. de Palma, G. Zancanaro, C. Austin, O. Mori, A. Mariotti, Philadelphia Boys' Ch, Westminster Symphonic Ch, Philadelphia/R. Muti)

① **442 439-2PH**
Tchaikovsky—The Queen of Spades - Highlights
Tchaikovsky: Queen of Spades (exc). (M. Gulegina, T. Filimonova, I. Arkhipova, O. Borodina, G. Grigorian, V. Solodovnikov, E. Boitsov, N. Putilin, V. Chernov, S. Alexashkin, G. Bezebenkov, Kirov Th Chor, Kirov Th Orch/V. Gergiev)

① **442 440-2PH**
Verdi—La Traviata - Highlights
Verdi: Traviata (exc). (K. Te Kanawa, S. Mazzoni, O. Borodina, Alfredo Kraus, B. Banks, D. Hvorostovsky, R. Scaltriti, G. Gatti, D. Di Stefano, MMF Chor, MMF Orch/Z. Mehta)

① **442 482-2PH**
Cavalleria Rusticana & I Pagliacci - Highlights
Mascagni: Cavalleria rusticana (exc); *Leoncavallo:* Pagliacci (exc). (P. Domingo, E. Obraztsova, R. Bruson, A. Gall, F. Barbieri, T. Stratas, J. Pons, A. Rinaldi, F. Andreolli, La Scala Chor, La Scala Orch/G. Prêtre)

① **442 537-2PH3** (4/95)
Borodin—Prince Igor
Borodin: Prince Igor (Cpte). (M. Kit, G. Gorchakova, G. Grigorian, V. Ognovenko, B. Minzhilkiev, O. Borodina, N. Gassiev, G. Selezniev, K. Pluzhnikov, E. Perlasova, T. Novikova, Kirov Th Chor, Kirov Th Orch/V. Gergiev)

① **442 550-2PM2**
Verdi—Complete Ballet Music &c
Verdi: Lombardi (exc); Trovatore (exc); Otello (exc); Don Carlos (exc); Vespri Siciliani (exc); Macbeth (exc); *Ponchielli:* Gioconda (exc); *Wagner:* Tannhäuser (exc). (Monte Carlo Op Orch, LSO/A. de Almeida, Staatskapelle Dresden/S. Varviso, Concertgebouw/E. de Waart)

① **442 600-2PH** ▭ **442 600-4PH**
The Great Carreras
Verdi: Trovatore (exc); *Puccini:* Bohème (exc); *Gounod:* Ave maria; *Puccini:* Tosca (exc); Tosca (exc); *Franck:* Panis angelicus; *Puccini:* Manon Lescaut (exc); *Leoncavallo:* Bohème (exc); *Rossini:* Otello (exc); *Puccini:* Turandot (exc); *R. Strauss:* Rosenkavalier (exc); *Donizetti:* Elisir d'amore (exc); *Verdi:* Battaglia di Legnano (exc); Battaglia di Legnano (exc); Ballo in maschera (exc); *Leoncavallo:* Pagliacci (exc); *Di Capua:* 'O sole mio (exc); *Rossini:* Soirées musicales (exc). (J. Carreras, K. Ricciarelli, F. von Stade, R. Leggate, D. Trimarchi, M. G. Gormley, ROH Chor, ROHO/Colin Davis, Vienna SO/U. C. Harrer, RPO/R. Benzi, Philh/J. López-Cobos, Rotterdam PO/E. de Waart, Turin RAI Orch/C. Scimone, Vienna RSO/L. Gardelli, ECO/E. Müller/E. G. Asensio)

① **442 602-2PM** ▭ **442 602-4PM**
3 x 3 Tenors
Mozart: Don Giovanni (exc); *Gluck:* Orphée (exc); *Verdi:* Rigoletto (exc); *Berlioz:* Troyens (exc); *Verdi:* Lombardi (exc); Aida (exc); Ballo in maschera (exc); *Donizetti:* Lucia di Lammermoor (exc); *Lehár:* Land des Lächelns (exc); *Britten:* Peter Grimes (exc); *Mascagni:* Cavalleria rusticana (exc); *Puccini:* Bohème (exc); *Verdi:* Traviata (exc); *Leoncavallo:* Pagliacci (exc). (L. Simoneau, R. Tucker, J. Vickers, P. Domingo, C. Bergonzi, J. Carreras, F. Araiza, Alfredo Kraus, L. Pavarotti, M. Aparici, H. Harper, J. Summers, E. Obraztsova, F. Barbieri, Vienna SO/R. Moralt, Lamoureux Orch/H. Rosbaud, Naples San Carlo Op Orch/F. Molinari-Pradelli, ROH Chor, ROHO/Colin Davis, RPO/L. Gardelli, New Philh/N. Santi/J. López-Cobos, ECO/R. Benzi/A. Zedda, La Scala Chor, La Scala Orch/G. Prêtre, MMF Orch/Z. Mehta, Philadelphia/R. Muti)

① **442 640-2PM** (7/95)
Wagner—Die Walküre, Act 1
Wagner: Walküre (exc). (J. King, Leonie Rysanek, G. Nienstedt, Bayreuth Fest Orch/K. Böhm)

① **442 775-2PH** (7/95) ▭ **442 775-4PH** (7/95)
Russian Spectacular
Mussorgsky: Boris Godunov (exc); *Tchaikovsky:* Marche slave; Capriccio italien; Eugene Onegin (exc); *Liadov:* Enchanted Lake, Op. 62. (Kirov Th Chor, Kirov Th Orch/V. Gergiev)

Ⓓ **442 781-2PH** ▭ **442 781-4PH**
Spanish Guitar Favourites
Giménez: Boda de Luis Alonso (exc); Mundo comedia es (exc); *Boccherini:* Guitar Quintets, G445-453 (exc); *Romero:* Fantasía cubana; Malagueñas; *Falla:* Amor Brujo (exc); *Sor:* Divertissement, Op. 34; *M. Praetorius:* Terpsichore (exc); *Tárrega:* Capricho árabe; *Turina:* Oración del torero; *Moreno Torroba:* Estampas. (P. Romero, Celedonio Romero, Celín Romero, Celino Romero, A. Romero, W. Hellweg)

Ⓓ **442 785-2PH** (8/95) ▭ **442 785-4PH** (8/95)
The Incomparable Alfredo Kraus
Offenbach: Contes d'Hoffmann (exc); *Cilea:* Arlesiana (exc); *Donizetti:* Lucrezia Borgia (exc); Fille du régiment (exc); Dom Sébastien (exc); Favorita (exc); *Gounod:* Faust (exc); *Lalo:* Roi d'Ys (exc); *Meyerbeer:* Crociato in Egitto (exc); *Delibes:* Lakmé (exc); *R. Strauss:* Rosenkavalier (exc). (Alfredo Kraus, P. Gyton, WNO Chor, WNO Orch/C. Rizzi)

Ⓓ **446 057-2PB14** (10/94)
Wagner—The Ring Cycle - Bayreuth Festival 1967
Wagner: Rheingold (Cpte); Walküre (Cpte); Siegfried (Cpte); Götterdämmerung (Cpte). (T. Adam, A. Burmeister, W. Windgassen, E. Wohlfahrt, G. Neidlinger, A. Silja, H. Esser, G. Nienstedt, V. Soukupová, M. Talvela, K. Böhme, D. Siebert, H. Dernesch, R. Hesse, J. King, Leonie Rysanek, B. Nilsson, A. Burmeister, G. Nienstedt, D. Mastilovic, L. Synek, H. Dernesch, G. Hopf, Š. Červená, E. Schärtel, S. Wagner, W. Windgassen, T. Adam, E. Köth, J. Greindl, T. Stewart, L. Dvořáková, M. Mödl, S. Wagner, M. Höffgen, A. Burmeister, A. Silja, Bayreuth Fest Chor, Bayreuth Fest Orch/K. Böhm)

Ⓓ **446 067-2PH6**
Beethoven—Complete Symphonies
Beethoven: Symphony 1; Symphony 2; Symphony 3; Symphony 4; Symphony 5; Symphony 6; Symphony 7; Symphony 8; Symphony 9; Egmont (exc); Leonore (exc). (S. Sweet, J. Rappé, P. Frey, F. Grundheber, Dresden St Op Chor, Staatskapelle Dresden/Colin Davis)

Ⓓ **446 081-2PH** (9/95)
The Echoing Air—The Music of Henry Purcell
Purcell: Staircase Overture; Hogwood Suite; Chaconne, Z730; If music be the food of love, Z379/3; Libertine, Z600 (exc); Blessed Virgin's Expostulation, Z196; Bonduca, Z574 (exc); O Solitude, Z406; Fairy Queen, Z629 (exc); Pausanias, Z585 (exc); King Arthur, Z628 (exc); She that would gain a faithful lover, Z414; Cupid, the slyest rogue alive, Z367; Indian Queen, Z630 (exc); Oedipus, Z583 (exc); Fatal hour comes on apace, Z421. (S. McNair, C. Steele-Perkins, S. Standage, AAM/C. Hogwood)

Ⓓ **446 151-2PM2**
Verdi—Il Trovatore
Verdi: Trovatore (Cpte). (J. Carreras, K. Ricciarelli, Y. Mazurok, S. Toczyska, R. Lloyd, P. Cannan, R. Leggate, R. Earle, J. Treleaven, ROH Chor, ROHO/Colin Davis)

Ⓓ **446 196-2PM**
Rossini—Overtures
Rossini: Barbiere di Siviglia (exc); Guillaume Tell (exc); Cenerentola (exc); Italiana in Algeri (exc); Scala di seta (exc); Gazza ladra (exc); Semiramide (exc); Signor Bruschino (exc); Turco in Italia (exc). (ASMF/N. Marriner)

Ⓓ **446 198-2PM**
Bizet—Orchestral Works
Bizet: Arlésienne Suites (exc); Carmen Suites (exc); Jeux d'enfants. (LSO/N. Marriner, Concertgebouw/B. Haitink)

Ⓓ **446 331-2PH2** (9/95)
Tippett—The Knot Garden; A Child of Our Time
Tippett: Knot Garden (Cpte); Child of Our Time. (R. Herincx, Y. Minton, J. Gomez, J. Barstow, T. Carey, R. Tear, T. Hemsley, ROHO, J. Norman, J. Baker, R. Cassilly, J. Shirley-Quirk, BBC Sngrs, BBC Choral Soc, BBC SO/Colin Davis)

Ⓓ **446 337-2PM3**
Wagner—Lohengrin
Wagner: Lohengrin (Cpte). (Jess Thomas, A. Silja, A. Varnay, R. Vinay, F. Crass, T. Krause, Bayreuth Fest Chor, Bayreuth Fest Orch/W. Sawallisch)

Ⓓ **446 403-2PH**
Journey to the Stars - A Sci-Fi Fantasy Adventure
Blomdahl: Aniara (exc); *Herrmann:* Day the Earth Stood Still (exc); *Goldsmith:* Star Trek V (exc); *Barron:* Forbidden Planet (exc); *Waxman:* Bride of Frankenstein (exc); *Corigliano:* Altered States (exc); *R. Strauss:* Also sprach Zarathustra (exc); *Ligeti:* Atmosphères; *A. North:* 2001 (exc); *J. T. Williams:* Witches of Eastwick (exc); *Elfman:* Edward Scissorhands (exc); *Bliss:* Things to come (exc); *J. T. Williams:* Star Wars (exc). (Hollywood Bowl Orch/J. Mauceri)

Ⓓ **446 448-2PH2** (4/84)
Rossini—Il Barbiere di Siviglia
Rossini: Barbiere di Siviglia (Cpte). (T. Allen, A. Baltsa, F. Araiza, D. Trimarchi, R. Lloyd, S. Burgess, M. Best, Ambrosian Op Chor, ASMF/N. Marriner)

Ⓓ **446 613-2PM**
Wagner—Das Rheingold - Highlights
Wagner: Rheingold (exc). (D. McIntyre, H. Schwarz, H. Zednik, H. Pampuch, H. Becht, C. Reppel, S. Jerusalem, M. Egel, O. Wenkel, Bayreuth Fest Orch/P. Boulez)

Ⓓ **446 614-2PM**
Wagner—Die Walküre - Highlights
Wagner: Walküre (exc). (P. Hofmann, J. Altmeyer, G. Jones, D. McIntyre, H. Schwarz, M. Salminen, C. Reppel, K. Clarke, K. Middleton, G. Schnaut, M. Schiml, I. Gramatzki, G. Killebrew, E. Glauser, Bayreuth Fest Orch/P. Boulez)

Ⓓ **446 615-2PM**
Wagner—Siegfried - Highlights
Wagner: Siegfried (exc). (M. Jung, G. Jones, H. Zednik, N. Sharp, Bayreuth Fest Orch/P. Boulez)

Ⓓ **446 616-2PM**
Wagner—Götterdämmerung - Highlights
Wagner: Götterdämmerung (exc). (G. Jones, M. Jung, F. Hübner, H. Becht, F. Mazura, J. Altmeyer, Bayreuth Fest Orch/P. Boulez)

Ⓓ **446 617-2PM**
Wagner—Tristan und Isolde - Highlights
Wagner: Tristan und Isolde (exc). (W. Windgassen, B. Nilsson, C. Ludwig, M. Talvela, E. Waechter, C. Heater, Bayreuth Fest Chor, Bayreuth Fest Orch/K. Böhm)

Ⓓ **446 618-2PM**
Der Fliegende Holländer - Highlights
Wagner: Fliegende Holländer (exc). (S. Estes, L. Balslev, M. Salminen, R. Schunk, A. Schlemm, G. Clark, Bayreuth Fest Chor, Bayreuth Fest Orch/W. Nelsson)

Ⓓ **446 619-2PM**
Wagner—Lohengrin - Highlights
Wagner: Lohengrin (exc). (P. Frey, C. Studer, G. Schnaut, E. Wlaschiha, M. Schenk, E.W. Schulte, Bayreuth Fest Chor, Bayreuth Fest Orch/P. Schneider)

Ⓓ **446 620-2PM**
Wagner—Tannhäuser - Highlights
Wagner: Tannhäuser (exc). (W. Windgassen, A. Silja, E. Waechter, G. Bumbry, J. Greindl, G. Stolze, F. Crass, G. Paskuda, G. Nienstedt, E-M. Gardelli, Bayreuth Fest Chor, Bayreuth Fest Orch/W. Sawallisch)

Ⓓ **446 621-2PM**
Wagner—Die Meistersinger von Nürnberg - Highlights
Wagner: Meistersinger (exc). (K. Ridderbusch, J. Cox, H. Bode, H. Sotin, K. Hirte, F. Stricker, A. Reynolds, G. Nienstedt, H. Steinbach, Bayreuth Fest Chor, Bayreuth Fest Orch/S. Varviso)

Pierre Verany

Ⓓ **PV730005**
The Most Beautiful Operatic Arias
Mozart: Zauberflöte (exc); Così fan tutte (exc); Don Giovanni (exc). (M. Bourgue Wind Ens)

Ⓓ **PV730022**
Bizet—Symphony No 1; Offenbach—Overtures
Bizet: Symphony; Jolie Fille de Perth Suite; *Offenbach:* Vie Parisienne (exc); Voyage dans la lune (exc); Périchole (exc); Fille du Tambour-major (exc). (Loire PO/M. Soustrot)

Ⓓ **PV730023**
Ballets from the Great Operas
Bizet: Carmen (exc); *Borodin:* Prince Igor (exc); *Mussorgsky:* Khovanshchina (exc); *Verdi:* Macbeth (exc); *Ponchielli:* Gioconda (exc); *Gounod:* Faust (exc); *Tchaikovsky:* Eugene Onegin (exc). (Slovak PO/K. Redel)

Ⓓ **PV730050**
Overtures
Bellini: Norma (exc); *Donizetti:* Don Pasquale (exc); Roberto Devereux (exc); *Rossini:* Semiramide (exc); Guillaume Tell (exc); *Verdi:* Traviata (exc); Nabucco (exc); Forza del Destino (exc). (South-West German RSO/K. Arp)

Ⓓ **PV786104**
Great French Overtures
Hérold: Zampa (exc); *Auber:* Muette de Portici (exc); *Adam:* Poupée de Nuremberg (exc); Si j'étais roi (exc); *Méhul:* Chasse de jeune Henri (exc); *Boïeldieu:* Calife de Bagdad (exc); *Cherubini:* Medea (exc); *Grétry:* Magnifique (exc). (Munich RO/K. Redel)

Ⓓ **PV786111**
Campra—Tancrède (highlights)
Campra: Tancrède (exc). (C. Dussaut, J. Bona, A. Arapian, Provence Instr Ens, Provence Vocal Ens/C. Zaffini)

Ⓓ **PV787033**
Mozart—Opera Excerpts (arr Wind)
Mozart: Zauberflöte (exc); Così fan tutte (exc); Don Giovanni (exc). (M. Bourgue Wind Ens)

Ⓓ **PV788093/4** (8/89)
Debussy—Pelléas et Mélisande
Debussy: Pelléas et Mélisande (Cpte). (M. Walker, E. Manchet, V. Le Texier, P. Meven, C. Yahr, Anon, P. Le Hémonet, Nice Op Chor, Nice PO/J. Carewe)

Ⓓ **PV792051** (6/94)
Chausson/Fauré—Orchestral Works
Chausson: Symphony, Op. 20; *Fauré:* Pelléas et Mélisande Suite; Pénélope (exc). (Loire PO/M. Soustrot)

Ⓓ **PV794092** (2/95)
Vivaldi—Dorilla in Tempe
Vivaldi: Dorilla in Tempe (Cpte). (M. C. Kiehr, J. Elwes, P. Cantor, J. Nirouët, C. Caroli, L. Florentin, Nice Op Chor, Nice Baroque Ens/G. Bezzina)

Pilz

Ⓓ **441002-2**
Original Bolshoi Theatre Orchestra
Adam: Giselle (Cpte); *Tchaikovsky:* Swan Lake (exc); *Minkus:* Bayadère (exc); Paquita (exc); *Tchaikovsky:* Sleeping Beauty (exc); *Minkus:* Don Quixote (Cpte); *Hérold:* Fille mal Gardée (exc); *Adam:* Corsaire (exc); *Gounod:* Faust (exc). (Bolshoi Th Orch/G. Zhemchuzhin)

Ⓓ **442118-2**
Wagner—Operas in Historical Recordings
Wagner: Tannhäuser (Cpte); Fliegende Holländer (Cpte); Lohengrin (Cpte). (A. Seider, M. Schech, K. Paul, M. Bäumer, O. von Rohr, F. Klarwein, B. Kusche, K. Ostertag, R. Wünzer, R. Streich, H. Hotter, V. Ursuleac, G. Hann, K. Ostertag, L. Willer, F. Klarwein, G. Vincent, M. Schech, A. Boehm, M. Klose, K. Böhme, W. Wolff, Bavarian St Op Chor, Bavarian St Op Orch/R. Heger/C. Krauss/R. Kempe)

Plant Life

Ⓓ **PLCD076**
Principia Musica
Purcell: Chaconne, Z730; *Locke:* Tempest (exc); *N. Matteis I:* 2-trumpet Concerto; *Quarles:* Lesson in F minor; *C. Simpson:* Division in E minor; *Blow:* Venus and Adonis (exc); *Purcell:* Trumpet Sonata 2. (S. Keavy, J. Impett, J. Hellyer Jones, Cambridge Baroque Camerata/J. Hellyer Jones, M. Richards, I. Gammie)

Point Music

Ⓓ **432 967-2PTH**
John Moran—The Manson Family
J. Moran: Manson Family (Cpte). (R. Sortomme, I. Pop, T. Roche, P. Snell, J. Moran, C. Lane, B. McGrath, R. Greenawalt, Ens)

Ⓓ **434 873-2PTH** (6/93)
Jon Gibson—In Good Company
Gibson: Waltz; Song 3; Extensions II; *J. Adams:* Nixon in China (exc); *Reich:* Reed Phase; *Jennings:* Terry's G Dorian Blues; *Glass:* Einstein on the Beach (exc); *Riley:* Tread on the Trail. (J. Gibson, M. Goldray, M. Riesman, L.M. Young, B. Ruyle, J. Snyder)

Polskie Nagrania

Ⓓ **PNCD020** (6/90)
Penderecki: Orchestral Works
Penderecki: Cello concerto 2; Viola concerto; Dream of Jacob; Paradise Lost. (I. Monighetti, S. Kamasa, Polish Nat RO/A. Wit)

Ⓓ **PNCD087**
Famous Operetta Arias
J. Strauss II: Zigeunerbaron (exc); Fledermaus (exc); Nacht in Venedig (exc); *Millöcker:* Bettelstudent (exc); *Zeller:* Vogelhändler (exc); Obersteiger (exc); *Lehár:* Friederike (exc); Land des Lächelns (exc); Paganini (exc); Lustige Witwe (exc); Giuditta (exc); *Künneke:* Vetter aus Dingsda (exc); *Kálmán:* Gräfin Mariza (exc). (R. Karczykowski, Polish Nat RSO/R. Bibl)

Ⓓ **PNCD132**
Polish Religious Music
Anon: Gaude Mater Polonia; Mother of God; O dawn, always bright; *Gomółka:* Blessed are those; *Moniuszko:* Halka (exc); Ostra Brama Litany 4 (exc); *Rybicki:* Ave

Maria, Op. 15/1; *Świder:* What do you want from us; *Maklakiewicz:* Polish Mass; *Traditional:* Angel said unto the Shepherds; Let's all go to the stable; Lying in the manger; Stille Nacht; O look, brethren; Dear Shepherds; Triumphs of the Heavenly King; When Christ is born; Lord is born. (Warsaw Cath Ch, Warsaw CO/M. Sewen/A. Filaber, W. Szwejkowski, J. Kaufman)

Polyphonic

Ⓓ **QPRL049D** (8/92) ▭ **CPRL049D** (8/92)
Boosey & Hawkes National Brass Band Gala Concert 1991
Arne: Rule Britannia; *H. Clarke:* Showers of Gold; *Geldard:* Tribute to Ted Heath; *Bizet:* Pêcheurs de perles (exc); *Vinter:* Triumphant Rhapsody; *Simpson:* Energy; *Delius:* Village Romeo and Juliet (exc); *Frackenpohl:* Pop Suite (exc); *Traditional:* David of the White Rock; *Tchaikovsky:* 1812. (R. Webster, R. Childs, N. Childs, British Tuba Qt, Britannia Building Soc Band, Desford Colliery Caterpillar Band, CWS, IMI Yorkshire Imperial Band/G. Brand/J. Watson)

Ⓓ **QPRL053D** (9/93) ▭ **CPRL053D** (9/93)
Slavonic Brass
Smetana: Bartered Bride (exc); *Borodin:* Prince Igor (exc); *Liszt:* Préludes; *Dvořák:* Slavonic Dances (exc); *Tchaikovsky:* Symphony 6 (exc); *Dvořák:* Symphony 9 (exc); *Rimsky-Korsakov:* Capriccio espagnol; *Dvořák:* Rusalka (exc); *Ippolitov-Ivanov:* Caucasian Sketches (exc); *Tchaikovsky:* Symphony 4 (exc); *Mussorgsky:* Pictures (exc). (Black Dyke Mills Band/J. Watson)

Praga

Ⓓ **PR250 003**
Shostakovich—Orchestral Works
Shostakovich: Nose Suite; Symphony 15. (L. Löbl, J. Jindrák, B. Avksentiev, Czech PO/G. Rozhdestvensky/E. Serov)

Ⓓ **PR250 022/3** (6/93)
Smetana—The Two Widows
Smetana: Two Widows (Cpte). (J. Jonášová, M. Machotková, M. Švejda, D. Jedlička, A. Hampel, D. Šounová-Brouková, Prague Rad Chor, Prague RSO/J. Krombholc)

Ⓓ **PR250 035**
Rimsky-Korsakov—Orchestral Works
Rimsky-Korsakov: Scheherazade; Invisible city of Kitezh. (Prague SO, Prague RSO/V. Smetáček)

Ⓓ **PR254 005**
Edition Live Karel Ančerl
Mozart: Don Giovanni (exc); Ergo interest, K143 (exc); Vespers, K339 (exc); Mass, K317 (exc); Rè pastore (exc); Violin Concerto, K211; Symphony 31. (I. Seefried, W. Schneiderhan, J. Suk, Prague Phil Chor, Czech PO/K. Ančerl)

Ⓓ **PR254 045**
Dvořák—Orchestral Works
Dvořák: Armida (exc); Heirs of the White Mountain; Symphony 6. (Prague Rad Sym Chor, Prague SO/M. Konvalinka/T. Koutník/V. Smetáček)

Preiser

Ⓓ **89001** (2/90)
Toti dal Monte (1898-1975)
Bellini: Sonnambula (exc); *Donizetti:* Lucia di Lammermoor (exc); Fille du Régiment (exc); Fille du Régiment (exc); Linda di Chamounix (exc); *A. Thomas:* Mignon (exc); *Bizet:* Pêcheurs de Perles (exc); Pêcheurs de Perles (exc); *Verdi:* Falstaff (exc); *Bishop:* Lo, here the gentle lark; *Traditional:* Carnevale di Venezia. (T. dal Monte, La Scala Orch, Orch/C. Sabajno/J. Pasternack/G. Santini/G. Nastrucci/Rosario Bourdon, La Scala Chor)

Ⓓ **89002** (2/90)
Miguel Fleta (1893-1938)
Bellini: Puritani (exc); *Donizetti:* Favorita (exc); *Verdi:* Rigoletto (exc); *Meyerbeer:* Africaine (exc); *Verdi:* Aida (exc); Aida (exc); *Bizet:* Carmen (exc); Carmen (exc); Pêcheurs de perles (exc); *Leoncavallo:* Pagliacci (exc); *Puccini:* Bohème (exc); Tosca (exc); Tosca (exc); *Mascagni:* Amico Fritz (exc); *Zandonai:* Giulietta e Romeo (exc). (M. Fleta, F. Austral, E. Thornton, L. Bori, orch)

Ⓓ **89003** (2/90)
Riccardo Stracciari (1875-1955)
Rossini: Barbiere di Siviglia (exc); *Donizetti:* Lucia di Lammermoor (exc); *Verdi:* Nabucco (exc); *Wagner:* Tannhäuser (exc); *Berlioz:* Damnation de Faust (exc); *Meyerbeer:* Dinorah (exc); Africaine (exc); *Massenet:* Roi de Lahore (exc); *Ponchielli:* Gioconda (exc); *Verdi:* Otello (exc); *Leoncavallo:* Pagliacci (exc); *Puccini:* Tosca (exc); *Di Capua:* O sole mio. (R. Stracciari, orch)

Ⓓ **89004** (2/90)
Frida Leider (1888-1975) - I
Gluck: Armide (exc); *Mozart:* Don Giovanni (exc); *Beethoven:* Fidelio (exc); *Wagner:* Siegfried (exc); Tristan und Isolde (exc); Tristan und Isolde (exc); Parsifal (exc); Wesendonk Lieder (exc); Wesendonk Lieder (exc). (F. Leider, orch, Berlin St Op Orch, LSO/J. Barbirolli/L. Blech/A. Coates, R. Laubenthal, L. Melchior)

Ⓓ **89005** (2/90)
Franz Völker (1899-1965) - I
Wagner: Rienzi (exc); Rienzi (exc); Fliegende Holländer (exc); Lohengrin (exc); Lohengrin (exc); Meistersinger (exc); Meistersinger (exc); *Halévy:* Juive (exc); *Meyerbeer:* Africaine (exc); *Verdi:* Trovatore (exc); Aida (exc); Otello (exc); *Leoncavallo:* Pagliacci (exc). (F. Völker, Berlin St Op Orch/A. Melichar/H. Weigert/J. Prüwer/M. Gurlitt/J. Heidenreich)

Ⓓ **89006** (9/90)
Heinrich Schlusnus (1888-1952) - I
Marschner: Hans Heiling (exc); *Lortzing:* Zar und Zimmermann (exc); *Wagner:* Tannhäuser (exc); *Verdi:* Trovatore (exc); Traviata (exc); Rigoletto (exc); Ballo in maschera (exc); Vespri siciliani (exc); Simon Boccanegra (exc); *Bizet:* Carmen (exc); *Borodin:* Prince Igor (exc); *Tchaikovsky:* Eugene Onegin (exc); Queen of Spades (exc); *Leoncavallo:* Pagliacci (exc). (H. Schlusnus, Berlin St Op Orch/L. Blech/J. Schüler/G. Steeger/A. Melichar)

Ⓓ **89007** (9/90)
Aureliano Pertile (1885-1952) - I
Donizetti: Lucia di Lammermoor (exc); Favorita (exc); Favorita (exc); *Rossini:* Guillaume Tell (exc); *Verdi:* Luisa Miller (exc); Trovatore (exc); Trovatore (exc); Forza del destino (exc); Otello (exc); *Bizet:* Carmen (exc); *Ponchielli:* Gioconda (exc); *Puccini:* Manon Lescaut (exc); Manon Lescaut (exc). (A. Pertile, A. Rozsa, B. Franci, E. Lattuada, G. Nessi, A. Buades, La Scala Orch/C. Sabajno/G. Nastrucci/L. Molajoli)

Ⓓ **89008** (6/90)
Irene Minghini-Cattaneo (1892-1944)
Bellini: Norma (exc); *Donizetti:* Favorita (exc); *Verdi:* Trovatore (exc); Ballo in maschera (exc); Aida (exc); *Ponchielli:* Gioconda (exc); *Bizet:* Carmen (exc); *Saint-Saëns:* Samson et Dalila (exc). (I. Minghini-Cattaneo, L. Cecil, A. Pertile, A. Gelli, D. de Martis, A. Granforte, La Scala Orch/C. Sabajno, orch/J. Barbirolli)

Ⓓ **89009** (2/90)
Gino Bechi (b. 1913)
Verdi: Rigoletto (exc); Rigoletto (exc); Rigoletto (exc); Trovatore (exc); Ballo in maschera (exc); Forza del destino (exc); Otello (exc); Don Carlo (exc); Falstaff (exc); *Leoncavallo:* Pagliacci (exc); *Catalani:* Wally (exc). (G. Bechi, T. Pasero, G. Bernelli, G. Lauri-Volpi, Rome Op Orch, La Scala Orch, Orch, Santa Cecilia Academy Orch, Milan SO/L. Ricci/U. Berrettoni/R. Arduini/A. Votto/V. Bellezza/A. Quadri)

Ⓓ **89010** (6/90)
Tancredi Pasero (1893-1983) - I
Rossini: Barbiere di Siviglia (exc); *Bellini:* Sonnambula (exc); Norma (exc); *Verdi:* Ernani (exc); Trovatore (exc); Don Carlo (exc); Forza del destino (exc); *Meyerbeer:* Huguenots (exc); *Gounod:* Faust (exc); Faust (exc); Faust (exc); *A. Thomas:* Mignon (exc); *Ponchielli:* Gioconda (exc); *Boito:* Mefistofele (exc). (T. Pasero, B. Scacciati, F. Merli, G. Cigna, P. Civil, G. Zinetti, orch/L. Molajoli)

Ⓓ **89011** (5/90)
Marjorie Lawrence (1909-1979)
Reyer: Sigurd (exc); *Wagner:* Lohengrin (exc); Lohengrin (exc); Walküre (exc); Walküre (exc); Götterdämmerung (exc); *R. Strauss:* Salome (exc). (M. Lawrence, M. Singher, Y. Brothier, J. Claverie, Pasdeloup Orch/P. Coppola)

Ⓓ **89012** (9/90)
Giacomo Lauri-Volpi (1894-1979)
Bellini: Norma (exc); Puritani (exc); *Verdi:* Rigoletto (exc); Aida (exc); *Gounod:* Faust (exc); *Bizet:* Carmen (exc); *Offenbach:* Contes d'Hoffmann (exc); *Ponchielli:* Gioconda (exc); *Gomes:* Schiavo (exc); *Meyerbeer:* Africaine (exc); *Giordano:* Andrea Chénier (exc); *Puccini:* Manon Lescaut (exc); Madama Butterfly (exc); Tosca (exc). (G. Lauri-Volpi, E. Rethberg, G. De Luca, L. Borgonovo, orch/Rosario Bourdon, NY Met Op Chor, NY Met Op Orch/G. Setti, La Scala Orch/F. Ghione)

Ⓓ **89013** (10/90)
Giannina Arangi-Lombardi (1890-1951)
Donizetti: Lucrezia Borgia (exc); *Verdi:* Lombardi (exc); Ernani (exc); Trovatore (exc); Ballo in maschera (exc); Aida (exc); *Ponchielli:* Gioconda (exc); Gioconda (exc); *Mascagni:* Cavalleria rusticana (exc); *Puccini:* Bohème (exc); Tosca (exc). (G. Arangi-Lombardi, E. Molinari, G. Zinetti, La Scala Orch/L. Molajoli, Milan SO)

Ⓓ **89014** (1/91)
Ebe Stignani (1903-1974)
Gluck: Alceste (1776) (exc); Orfeo ed Euridice (exc); *Rossini:* Semiramide (exc); *Bellini:* Norma (exc); *Donizetti:* Favorita (exc); Linda di Chamounix (exc); *Verdi:* Trovatore (exc); Don Carlo (exc); Ballo in maschera (exc); Forza del destino (exc); *Mascagni:* Amico Fritz (exc); *A. Thomas:* Mignon (exc); *Saint-Saëns:* Samson et Dalila (exc). (E. Stignani, G. Cigna, EIAR Orch/U. Tansini/V. Gui/A. la Rosa Parodi/G. Marinuzzi)

Ⓓ **89015** (11/90)
Carlo Tagliabue (1898-1978)
Rossini: Barbiere di Siviglia (exc); *Bellini:* Puritani (exc); *Wagner:* Tannhäuser (exc); *Verdi:* Ernani (exc); Rigoletto (exc); Trovatore (exc); Ballo in maschera (exc); Forza del destino (exc); Otello (exc); *Bizet:* Carmen (exc); Pêcheurs de perles (exc); *Leoncavallo:* Pagliacci (exc). (C. Tagliabue, orch, Turin EIAR Orch, La Scala Orch/U. Berrettoni/G. Marinuzzi/A. la Rosa Parodi/U. Tansini)

Ⓓ **89016** (11/90)
Gina Cigna (b. 1900)
Bellini: Norma (exc); *Verdi:* Ballo in maschera (exc); Forza del destino (exc); *Gounod:* Faust (exc); Faust (exc); *Boito:* Mefistofele (exc); *Catalani:* Wally (exc); *Ponchielli:* Gioconda (exc); *Cilea:* Adriana Lecouvreur (exc); Adriana Lecouvreur (exc); *Puccini:* Fanciulla del West (exc). (G. Cigna, P. Civil, T. Pasero, I. Mannarini, C. Elmo, orch/L. Molajoli, EIAR Orch/U. Tansini)

Ⓓ **89018** (5/90)
Helge Rosvaenge (1897-1972)
Auber: Fra Diavolo (exc); *Adam:* Postillon de Lonjumeau (exc); *Weber:* Oberon (exc); *Beethoven:* Fidelio (exc); *Bizet:* Carmen (exc); *Verdi:* Trovatore (exc); Aida (exc); *Leoncavallo:* Pagliacci (exc); *Puccini:* Tosca (exc); *Glinka:* Life for the Tsar (exc); *R. Strauss:* Rosenkavalier (exc); *Wille:* Königsballade (exc). (H. Roswaenge, Berlin St Op Orch/B. Seidler-Winkler, VPO/R. Moralt)

Ⓓ **89019** (12/90)
Alexander Kipnis (1891-1978)
Mozart: Entführung (exc); Nozze di Figaro (exc); Don Giovanni (exc); Zauberflöte (exc); *Rossini:* Barbiere di Siviglia (exc); *Weber:* Freischütz (exc); *Flotow:* Martha (exc); *Lortzing:* Wildschütz (exc); *Nicolai:* Lustigen Weiber von Windsor (exc); *Gounod:* Faust (exc); *Verdi:* Simon Boccanegra (exc); Don Carlo (exc); *Wagner:* Meistersinger (exc); *R. Strauss:* Rosenkavalier (exc); *Traditional:* Kalinka; Soldier's Song. (A. Kipnis, E. Ruziczka, chor, Berlin St Op Orch/C. Schmalstich/E. Orthmann)

Ⓓ **89020** (2/91)
Leo Slezak (1873-1946)
Weber: Euryanthe (exc); *Auber:* Muette de Portici (exc); *Rossini:* Guillaume Tell (exc); *Halévy:* Juive (exc); Juive (exc); *Meyerbeer:* Huguenots (exc); Huguenots (exc); Prophète (exc); *Wagner:* Lohengrin (exc); *Verdi:* Ernani (exc); Rigoletto (exc); Trovatore (exc); Ballo in maschera (exc); *Gounod:* Roméo et Juliette (exc); *Goldmark:* Königin von Saba (exc); Königin von Saba (exc). (L. Slezak, L. Demuth, W. Hesch, E. Bland, orch)

Ⓓ **89021**
Marcel Journet (1867-1933)
Rossini: Barbiere di Siviglia (exc); *Wagner:* Tannhäuser (exc); Lohengrin (exc); *Berlioz:* Damnation de Faust (exc); *Gounod:* Faust (exc); Faust (exc); Faust (exc); *Bizet:* Jolie fille de Perth (exc); Carmen (exc); *Massenet:* Thaïs (exc); Thaïs (exc); Jongleur de Notre Dame (exc); *G. Charpentier:* Louise (exc); *Luce:* O Salutaris; *Letorey:* Ceux qui pieusement sont morts. (M. Journet, F. Ansseau, M. Cozette, orch/Rosario Bourdon/P. Coppola/H. Busser, inst ens)

Ⓓ **89022** (1/91)
Fernand Ansseau (1890-1972)
Berlioz: Damnation de Faust (exc); *Wagner:* Lohengrin (exc); *Meyerbeer:* Africaine (exc); *Gounod:* Roméo et Juliette (exc); *Bizet:* Carmen (exc); Carmen (exc); *Février:* Monna Vanna (exc); *Massenet:* Werther (exc); *Leoncavallo:* Pagliacci (exc); *Puccini:* Tosca (exc). (F. Ansseau, F. Heldy, orch/P. Coppola)

Ⓓ **89023** (9/90)
Conchita Supervia (1895-1936)
Mozart: Nozze di Figaro (exc); *Rossini:* Barbiere di Siviglia (exc); Barbiere di Siviglia (exc); Cenerentola (exc); *Bizet:* Carmen (exc); Carmen (exc); *Saint-Saëns:* Samson et Dalila (exc); *Humperdinck:* Hänsel und Gretel (exc); *R. Strauss:* Rosenkavalier (exc). (C. Supervia, G. Manuritta, A. Apolloni, I. Mannarini, G. Nessi, A. Baracchi, I.M. Ferraris, orch/A. Albergoni)

Ⓓ **89024**
Marcel Wittrisch (1901-1955)
Rossini: Barbiere di Siviglia (exc); *Meyerbeer:* Huguenots (exc); *Verdi:* Ernani (exc); Trovatore (exc); Traviata (exc);

Cornelius: Barbier von Bagdad (exc); *Bizet:* Pêcheurs de Perles (exc); Carmen (exc); *Offenbach:* Contes d'Hoffmann (exc); *Delibes:* Lakmé (exc); *Mascagni:* Cavalleria Rusticana (exc); Cavalleria Rusticana (exc); *Leoncavallo:* Pagliacci (exc); *Puccini:* Bohème (exc). (M. Wittrisch, M. Teschemacher, W. Strienz, M. Klose, G. Hüsch, M. Korjus, Berlin St Op Orch/C. Schmalstich/E. Orthmann/F. Zweig/H.U. Müller/L. Blech/B. Seidler-Winkler/K. Bendix)

Ⓒ **89025** (10/90)
Tiana Lemnitz (b. 1897)
Mozart: Nozze di Figaro (exc); Zauberflöte (exc); *Weber:* Freischütz (exc); Freischütz (exc); *Wagner:* Tannhäuser (exc); Lohengrin (exc); *Verdi:* Aida (exc); Otello (exc). (T. Lemnitz, BPO, Berlin St Op Orch/B. Seidler-Winkler/T. Beecham/J. Schüler/F.A. Schmidt/L. Blech)

Ⓒ **89026** (1/91)
Francesco Merli (1887-1976) - I
Verdi: Forza del destino (exc); Forza del destino (exc); Aida (exc); Aida (exc); Aida (exc); Otello (exc); *Wagner:* Lohengrin (exc); *Meyerbeer:* Africaine (exc); *Mascagni:* Cavalleria Rusticana (exc); *Ponchielli:* Gioconda (exc); *Giordano:* Andrea Chénier (exc); *Leoncavallo:* Pagliacci (exc). (F. Merli, G. Vanelli, G. Arangi-Lombardi, orch/L. Molajoli)

Ⓒ **89027** (2/91)
Sigrid Onegin (1889-1943)
Gluck: Orfeo ed Euridice (exc); *Donizetti:* Lucrezia Borgia (exc); Favorita (exc); *Meyerbeer:* Huguenots (exc); Prophète (exc); Prophète (exc); *Verdi:* Don Carlo (exc); *Bizet:* Carmen (exc); *Saint-Saëns:* Samson et Dalila (exc); *Brahms:* Alto Rhapsody, Op. 53. (S. Onegin, Berlin Doctors' Ch, Berlin St Op Orch, orch/Rosario Bourdon/L. Blech/K. Singer)

Ⓒ **89028** (10/90)
Ivar Andresen (1896-1940)
Mozart: Zauberflöte (exc); *Halévy:* Juive (exc); *Meyerbeer:* Huguenots (exc); *Verdi:* Macbeth (exc); Forza del destino (exc); *Wagner:* Lohengrin (exc); Tannhäuser (exc); Tannhäuser (exc); Meistersinger (exc); Götterdämmerung (exc); Parsifal (exc). (I. Andrésen, E. Habich, Berlin St Op Orch/F. Zweig/F. Weissmann/L. Blech, chor, orch)

Ⓒ **89029** (11/90)
Meta Seinemeyer (1895-1929)
Verdi: Ballo in maschera (exc); Don Carlo (exc); Aida (exc); Otello (exc); *Giordano:* Andrea Chénier (exc); *Puccini:* Manon Lescaut (exc); Bohème (exc); Bohème (exc); Madama Butterfly (exc); *Rimsky-Korsakov:* Tsar's Bride (exc); *Rubinstein:* Nacht. (M. Seinemeyer, T. Pattiera, H. Jung, Berlin St Op Orch/F. Weissmann)

Ⓒ **89030**
Feodor Chaliapin (1873-1938)
Rossini: Barbiere di Siviglia (exc); *Bellini:* Norma (exc); Sonnambula (exc); *Donizetti:* Lucrezia Borgia (exc); *Meyerbeer:* Robert le Diable (exc); *Verdi:* Ernani (exc); Don Carlo (exc); *Boito:* Mefistofele (exc); *Gounod:* Faust (exc); Faust (exc); Faust (exc); *Delibes:* Lakmé (exc); *Glinka:* Ruslan and Lyudmila (exc); *Rubinstein:* Demon (exc); Demon (exc). (F. Chaliapin, La Scala Orch/C. Sabajno, M. Michailova, M. Kovalenko, Moscow Imperial Op Orch/M.I. Semenov, orch/I.P. Arkadiev)

Ⓒ **89031** (6/91)
Elisabeth Schumann (1885-1952)
Mozart: Nozze di Figaro (exc); Don Giovanni (exc); Rè pastore (exc); Exsultate, jubilate, K165 (exc); *Bach:* St Matthew Passion, BWV244 (exc); Cantata 159 (exc); *Handel:* Joshua (exc); *R. Strauss:* Lieder, Op. 27 (exc); Lieder, Op. 43 (exc); *Marx:* Lieder und Gesänge (exc); *Flies:* Wiegenlied; *Mozart:* Warnung, K433; *Mahler:* Knaben Wunderhorn (exc); *Schumann:* Jugend Lieder, Op. 79 (exc); Lieder und Gesänge, Op. 77 (exc); Myrthen, Op. 25 (exc). (E. Schumann, orch, Vienna St Op Orch/G.W. Byng/K. Alwin/L. Collingwood, G. Reeves)

Ⓒ **89032**
Lauritz Melchior (1890-1973) - I
Wagner: Rienzi (exc); Tannhäuser (exc); Tannhäuser (exc); Meistersinger (exc); Wesendonk Lieder (exc); Walküre (exc); Siegfried (exc); *Verdi:* Aida (exc); *Weingartner:* Liebesfeier, Op. 16/2. (L. Melchior, E. Bettendorf, F. Leider, M. Arndt-Ober, orch)

Ⓒ **89033**
Joseph Schwarz (1880-1926)
Rossini: Guillaume Tell (exc); *Verdi:* Rigoletto (exc); Rigoletto (exc); Trovatore (exc); Trovatore (exc); Traviata (exc); Ballo in maschera (exc); Otello (exc); *Meyerbeer:* Africaine (exc); *Offenbach:* Contes d'Hoffmann (exc); *Liszt:* Oh! quand je dors, S282; *Lewandowski:* Kol nidre. (J Schwarz, C. Dux, orch)

Ⓒ **89034** (2/92)
Giuseppe Lugo (1900-1980)
Verdi: Luisa Miller (exc); *Bizet:* Pêcheurs de Perles (exc); *Massenet:* Hérodiade (exc); Manon (exc); Werther (exc); *Mascagni:* Cavalleria rusticana (exc); *Leoncavallo:* Pagliacci (exc); *Puccini:* Bohème (exc); Bohème (exc); Tosca (exc); Tosca (exc); *Leoncavallo:* Mattinata; *Di Capua:* O sole mio; *Bixio:* Mia canzone al vento; Cuore diglielo anche tu. (G. Lugo, orch/A. Wolff/E. Cohen, F. Weiss/D. Olivieri)

Ⓒ **89035** (12/91)
Erna Berger (1900-1990) - I
Mozart: Nozze di Figaro (exc); Don Giovanni (exc); *Rossini:* Barbiere di Siviglia (exc); *Verdi:* Rigoletto (exc); Traviata (exc); *Nicolai:* Lustigen Weiber von Windsor (exc); *Auber:* Fra Diavolo (exc); *Bizet:* Pêcheurs de perles (exc); *J. Strauss II:* Fledermaus (exc); *Puccini:* Bohème (exc); Madama Butterfly (exc); *Grieg:* Peer Gynt (exc); *R. Strauss:* Rosenkavalier (exc); *Weber:* Non paventar mia vita. (E. Berger, V. Ursuleac, H. Schlusnus, C. Müller, Berlin St Op Orch, Berlin City Op Orch/C. Krauss/F. Zweig/C. Schmalstich/L. Blech/W. Schütze/A. Melichar/J. Schüler/W.F. Reuss, T. Lemnitz)

Ⓒ **89036** (1/92)
Giuseppe de Luca (1876-1950) - I
Mozart: Nozze di Figaro (exc); *Rossini:* Barbiere di Siviglia (exc); Guillaume Tell (exc); *Bellini:* Puritani (exc); *Donizetti:* Favorita (exc); Don Pasquale (exc); *Verdi:* Trovatore (exc); Ballo in maschera (exc); Rigoletto (exc); Don Carlo (exc); *Gounod:* Faust (exc); *Meyerbeer:* Dinorah (exc); *Diaz:* Benvenuto Cellini (exc); *Massenet:* Hérodiade (exc). (G. De Luca, L. Bori, A. Galli-Curci, orch)

Ⓒ **89037** (12/92)
Hina Spani (1896-1969)
Verdi: Ballo in maschera (exc); Trovatore (exc); Trovatore (exc); *Wagner:* Lohengrin (exc); Lohengrin (exc); *Gounod:* Faust (exc); *Massenet:* Manon (exc); *Leoncavallo:* Pagliacci (exc); *Puccini:* Manon Lescaut (exc); Bohème (exc); Tosca (exc); Madama Butterfly (exc); *Catalani:* Wally (exc); *López Buchardo:* Canción del carretero; *Ugarte:* Dia del fiesta. (H. Spani, A. Granforte, La Scala Orch/C. Sabajno, Inst Ens/G. Nastrucci)

Ⓒ **89038** (11/91)
Giovanni Zenatello (1876-1949)
Verdi: Ballo in maschera (exc); Otello (exc); Otello (exc); *Giordano:* Andrea Chénier (exc); *Leoncavallo:* Pagliacci (exc); *Puccini:* Manon Lescaut (exc); Tosca (exc); *Bizet:* Carmen (exc); Carmen (exc). (G. Zenatello, G. Marion, A. Boemi, H. Spani, A. Granforte, M. Gay, Apollo Chor, orch, La Scala Orch/Rosario Bourdon/C. Sabajno)

Ⓒ **89039** (8/92)
Karin Branzell (1891-1974)
Gluck: Orfeo ed Euridice (exc); *Donizetti:* Favorita (exc); *Verdi:* Trovatore (exc); Trovatore (exc); Ballo in maschera (exc); *Meyerbeer:* Prophète (exc); Prophète (exc); *A. Thomas:* Mignon (exc); *Gounod:* Faust (exc); *Bizet:* Carmen (exc); *Saint-Saëns:* Samson et Dalila (exc); Samson et Dalila (exc); *Ponchielli:* Gioconda (exc); *Wagner:* Rheingold (exc); *Kienzl:* Evangelimann (exc). (K. Branzell, orch)

Ⓒ **89040** (2/92)
Carlo Galeffi (1884-1961)
Rossini: Barbiere di Siviglia (exc); *Gounod:* Faust (exc); *Verdi:* Ernani (exc); Trovatore (exc); Trovatore (exc); Rigoletto (exc); Rigoletto (exc); Rigoletto (exc); Rigoletto (exc); Ballo in maschera (exc); Aida (exc); Aida (exc); *Mascagni:* Guglielmo Ratcliff (exc); *Leoncavallo:* Pagliacci (exc); *Giordano:* Andrea Chénier (exc). (C. Galeffi, G. Arangi-Lombardi, E. Dominici, M. Gentile, L.B. Rasa, La Scala Orch/L. Molajoli)

Ⓒ **89041** (3/91)
Eidé Norena (1884-1968)
Handel: Atalanta (exc); *Haydn:* Schöpfung (exc); *Mozart:* Zauberflöte (exc); *Rossini:* Guillaume Tell (exc); *Meyerbeer:* Huguenots (exc); *Verdi:* Rigoletto (exc); *A. Thomas:* Hamlet (exc); Hamlet (exc); *Bizet:* Carmen (exc); *Verdi:* Otello (exc); *Puccini:* Turandot (exc). (E. Norena, orch/J. Messner/P. Coppola/H. Defosse/G. Cloëz/F. Ruhlmann)

Ⓒ **89042** (7/92)
Nazzareno de Angelis (1881-1962)
Rossini: Mosè in Egitto (exc); Barbiere di Siviglia (exc); *Weber:* Freischütz (exc); *Meyerbeer:* Robert le Diable (exc); *Halévy:* Juive (exc); *Verdi:* Nabucco (exc); Don Carlo (exc); *Wagner:* Walküre (exc); *Gounod:* Faust (exc); Faust (exc); *Boito:* Mefistofele (exc); Mefistofele (exc). (N. de Angelis, E. Cheni, I. Mannarini, E. Venturini, G. Cigna, orch/L. Molajoli)

Ⓒ **89043** (10/91)
Antonio Cortis (1891-1952)
Verdi: Rigoletto (exc); Trovatore (exc); *Meyerbeer:* Africaine (exc); *Gounod:* Faust (exc); *Bizet:* Carmen (exc); Carmen (exc); *Massenet:* Manon (exc); Werther (exc); *Mascagni:* Cavalleria rusticana (exc); Iris (exc); *Giordano:* Andrea Chénier (exc); *Puccini:* Bohème (exc); Tosca (exc); Turandot (exc). (A. Cortis, A. Rozsa, La Scala Orch/C. Sabajno)

Ⓒ **89044** (4/93)
Dusolina Giannini (1902-1986)
Bellini: Norma (exc); *Verdi:* Forza del destino (exc); Forza del destino (exc); Aida (exc); Otello (exc); *Bizet:* Carmen (exc); *Puccini:* Manon Lescaut (exc); Madama Butterfly (exc); *Di Capua:* 'O sole mio; *V. Valente:* Manella mia; *Traditional:* Luisé; Ohie Meneche. (D. Giannini, La Scala Orch/C. Sabajno, Berlin St Op Orch/C. Schmalstich, orch/J. Barbirolli/G.W. Byng)

Ⓒ **89045** (2/92)
Mattia Battistini (1856-1928)
Mozart: Don Giovanni (exc); *Flotow:* Martha (exc); *Donizetti:* Favorita (exc); Dom Sébastien (exc); *Hérold:* Zampa (exc); *Berlioz:* Damnation de Faust (exc); *Verdi:* Ernani (exc); Ballo in maschera (exc); Traviata (exc); *A. Thomas:* Hamlet (exc); *Cocchi:* Per la patria. (M. Battistini, E. Corsi, A. Sillich, L. Colazza, orch)

Ⓒ **89046** (5/92)
Rosette Anday (1903-1977)
Donizetti: Favorita (exc); *Verdi:* Trovatore (exc); *Wagner:* Götterdämmerung (exc); *Saint-Saëns:* Samson et Dalila (exc); Samson et Dalila (exc); *Bizet:* Carmen (exc); *Bach:* St Matthew Passion, BWV244 (exc); *Ochs:* Dank sei dir, Herr; *Mendelssohn:* Elias (exc); *Hummel:* Hallelujah; *Gluck:* Orphée (exc); *Verdi:* Trovatore (exc); *Wagner:* Tristan und Isolde (exc); *Kienzl:* Evangelimann (exc). (R. Anday, Vienna St Op Orch/K. Alwin, Berlin St Op Orch/J. Prüwer, LSO/R. Heger, orch, H. Dawson)

Ⓒ **89047** (10/92)
Xenia Belmas (1890-1981)
Meyerbeer: Huguenots (exc); *Verdi:* Ernani (exc); Aida (exc); *A. Thomas:* Mignon (exc); *Rimsky-Korsakov:* Snow Maiden (exc); *Tchaikovsky:* Queen of Spades (exc); *Mascagni:* Cavalleria rusticana (exc); Cavalleria rusticana (exc); *Leoncavallo:* Pagliacci (exc); *Puccini:* Bohème (exc). (X. Belmas, W. Domgraf-Fassbaender, orch/A. Kitschin)

Ⓒ **89048** (12/91)
Apollo Granforte (1886-1975) - I
Rossini: Barbiere di Siviglia (exc); *Wagner:* Tannhäuser (exc); *Verdi:* Trovatore (exc); Rigoletto (exc); Rigoletto (exc); Rigoletto (exc); Rigoletto (exc); Rigoletto (exc); Rigoletto (exc); Traviata (exc); Otello (exc); *Leoncavallo:* Pagliacci (exc); Zazà (exc). (A. Granforte, F. Zaccarini, A. Saraceni, I. Mannarini, G. Menni, N. Palai, Ottavi, N. Sanchioni/G-F. Masini, A. Rozsa, P. Girardi, La Scala Orch/C. Sabajno/G. Nastrucci)

Ⓒ **89049** (11/92)
Margarete Teschemacher (1903-1959)
Mozart: Nozze di Figaro (exc); *Weber:* Oberon (exc); Freischütz (exc); *Lortzing:* Waffenschmied (exc); *Wagner:* Wesendonk Lieder (exc); Lohengrin (exc); *Verdi:* Don Carlo (exc); *R. Strauss:* Arabella (exc); Daphne (exc). (M. Teschemacher, I. Beilke, M. Wittrisch, Berlin St Op Orch/B. Seidler-Winkler/F. Zaun, Berlin City Op Orch/H.U. Müller, Saxon St Orch/K. Böhm)

Ⓒ **89050** (3/92)
Ezio Pinza (1892-1957)
Mozart: Don Giovanni (exc); *Bellini:* Norma (exc); Norma (exc); *Donizetti:* Favorita (exc); *Verdi:* Ernani (exc); Vespri siciliani (exc); Don Carlo (exc); Trovatore (exc); Requiem (exc); *Meyerbeer:* Robert le Diable (exc); *Halévy:* Juive (exc); *A. Thomas:* Caïd (exc); Mignon (exc); *Gounod:* Faust (exc); *Puccini:* Bohème (exc); *Tosti:* Ultima canzone. (E. Pinza, orch/Rosario Bourdon, NY Met Op Chor, NY Met Op Orch/G. Setti)

Ⓒ **89051** (7/94)
Elisabeth Rethberg (1894-1976)
Mozart: Nozze di Figaro (exc); Zauberflöte (exc); Ridente la calma, K152; *Meyerbeer:* Africaine (exc); *Bizet:* Carmen (exc); Carmen (exc); Pastorale; *Smetana:* Bartered Bride (exc); *J. Strauss II:* Zigeunerbaron (exc); *Puccini:* Madama Butterfly (exc); *R. Strauss:* Lieder, Op.48 (exc); Lieder, Op.17 (exc); *Patáky:* Einsame; *Giordano:* Andrea Chénier (exc); *Puccini:* Bohème (exc); Tosca (exc); Madama Butterfly (exc). (E. Rethberg, R. Tauber, anon, orch)

Ⓒ **89052**
Friederich Schorr (1889-1953)
Mozart: Don Giovanni (exc); Zauberflöte (exc); *Beethoven:* Fidelio (exc); *Weber:* Euryanthe (exc); *Meyerbeer:* Huguenots (exc); *Wagner:* Fliegende Holländer (exc); Fliegende Holländer (exc); Tannhäuser (exc);

Meistersinger (exc); Meistersinger (exc); Walküre (exc). (F. Schorr, E. Bettendorf, O. Helgers, M. Kurt, orch, chor)

Ⓒ **89053**
Max Lorenz (1901-1975)
Wagner: Rienzi (exc); Fliegende Holländer (exc); Tannhäuser (exc); Tannhäuser (exc); Lohengrin (exc); Lohengrin (exc); Meistersinger (exc); Meistersinger (exc); *Halévy:* Juive (exc); *Bizet:* Carmen (exc); *Meyerbeer:* Africaine (exc); *Verdi:* Forza del destino (exc); Aida (exc); Aida (exc); *Leoncavallo:* Pagliacci (exc). (K. Heidersbach, E. Gentner-Fischer, M. Lorenz, Berlin St Op Orch/C. Schmalstich)

Ⓒ **89054** (10/93)
Miliza Korjus (1912-1980)
Mozart: Zauberflöte (exc); *Adam:* Toréador (exc); *Donizetti:* Zingara (exc); Lucia di Lammermoor (exc); *Verdi:* Ernani (exc); Rigoletto (exc); Vespri Siciliani (exc); *Gounod:* Mireille (exc); *Meyerbeer:* Dinorah (exc); *Offenbach:* Contes d'Hoffmann (exc); *Delibes:* Lakmé (exc); *Rimsky-Korsakov:* Tsar's Bride (exc); Sadko (exc); Golden Cockerel (exc); *Proch:* Air and Variations. (M. Korjus, Berlin RO/J. Müller, Berlin St Op Orch/B. Seidler-Winkler/E. Nick/F. Schönbaumsfeld)

Ⓒ **89055** (11/94)
Cesare Formichi (1883-1949)
Verdi: Rigoletto (exc); Rigoletto (exc); Rigoletto (exc); Traviata (exc); Otello (exc); *Wagner:* Walküre (exc); *Saint-Saëns:* Samson et Dalila (exc); *Massenet:* Jongleur de Notre Dame (exc); Thaïs (exc); Thaïs (exc); *Giordano:* Andrea Chénier (exc); *Puccini:* Tosca (exc); Tosca (exc); *Hahn:* D'une prison; *Fontenailles:* Obstination; *Brogi:* Volontario; Fior di Campo. (C. Formichi, I.M. Ferraris, G. Holst, orch/A. Ketèlbey/H. Harty)

Ⓒ **89057** (11/93)
Charles Kullmann (1903-1982)
Wagner: Lohengrin (exc); Meistersinger (exc); *Verdi:* Forza del destino (exc); Aida (exc); *Gounod:* Faust (exc); *Offenbach:* Contes d'Hoffmann (exc); *Tchaikovsky:* Eugene Onegin (exc); *Borodin:* Prince Igor (exc); *Smetana:* Bartered Bride (exc); *R. Strauss:* Rosenkavalier (exc); *Puccini:* Turandot (exc); *J. Strauss II:* Zigeunerbaron (exc); Nacht in Venedig (exc); Indigo und die vierzig Räuber (exc); *Meyer-Helmund:* Zauberlied (exc). (C. Kullman, W. Grossmann, E. Fuchs, E. Berger, orch/W. Goehr/E. Hauke, Berlin St Op Orch/E. Orthmann/O. Dobrindt/C. Schmalstich, Berlin City Op Orch/A. von Zemlinsky/F. Zweig)

Ⓒ **89059** (12/92)
Mark Reizen (1895-1992) - I
Glinka: Life for the Tsar (exc); Ruslan and Lyudmila (exc); Ruslan and Lyudmila (exc); *Dargomizhsky:* Rusalka (exc); *Mussorgsky:* Boris Godunov (exc); Khovanshchina (exc); *Rubinstein:* Demon (exc); *Borodin:* Prince Igor (exc); *Tchaikovsky:* Eugene Onegin (exc); *Rimsky-Korsakov:* Sadko (exc); *Rachmaninov:* Aleko (exc). (M. Reizen, Bolshoi Th Orch/V. Nebolsin/A. Melik-Pashayev/S. Samosud/N. Golovanov)

Ⓒ **89060** (8/93)
Alfred Piccaver (1884-1958)
Donizetti: Favorita (exc); Dom Sébastien (exc); *Verdi:* Rigoletto (exc); *Weber:* Silvana (exc); *Cornelius:* Barbier von Bagdad (exc); *A. Thomas:* Mignon (exc); *Gounod:* Roméo et Juliette (exc); *Offenbach:* Contes d'Hoffmann (exc); *Massenet:* Werther (exc); *Tchaikovsky:* Eugene Onegin (exc); *Puccini:* Manon Lescaut (exc); Bohème (exc); Tosca (exc); Fanciulla del West (exc). (A. Piccaver, orch)

Ⓒ **89061** (8/93)
Pavel Lisitian (born 1911)
Verdi: Trovatore (exc); Ballo in maschera (exc); Traviata (exc); *Gounod:* Faust (exc); *Leoncavallo:* Pagliacci (exc); Zazà (exc); *Rubinstein:* Nero (exc); *Tchaikovsky:* Eugene Onegin (exc); Mazeppa (exc); Enchantress (exc); Queen of Spades (exc); *Rimsky-Korsakov:* Sadko (exc); *Chukhadjian:* Arshak II (exc). (P. Lisitsian, E. Shumskaya, Bolshoi Th Orch/V. Piradov/O. Bron/A. Orlov/V. Nebolsin/S. Samosud/A. Melik-Pashayev/N. Golovanov)

Ⓒ **89062** (3/93)
Giovanni Martinelli (1885-1969)
Verdi: Rigoletto (exc); Trovatore (exc); Forza del destino (exc); Aida (exc); Aida (exc); *Giordano:* Andrea Chénier (exc); Andrea Chénier (exc); Fedora (exc); *Mascagni:* Cavalleria Rusticana (exc); Cavalleria Rusticana (exc); *Leoncavallo:* Pagliacci (exc); Pagliacci (exc); Zazà (exc); *Puccini:* Bohème (exc); Tosca (exc). (G. Martinelli, G. Anthony, G. De Luca, E. Pinza, NY Met Op Chor, NY Met Op Orch/G. Setti, orch/J. Pasternack/Rosario Bourdon)

Ⓒ **89063** (8/93)
Rosetta Pampanini (1896-1973)
Gounod: Faust (exc); *Catalani:* Wally (exc); *Giordano:* Andrea Chénier (exc); *Puccini:* Manon Lescaut (exc); Bohème (exc); Madama Butterfly (exc); Madama Butterfly (exc); Turandot (exc); *Mascagni:* Amico Fritz (exc); *Zandonai:* Giuliano (exc); *Pietri:* Maristella (exc); *Wagner:* Lohengrin (exc); *Verdi:* Aida (exc); *Mascagni:* Iris (exc); *Puccini:* Manon Lescaut (exc). (R. Pampanini, F. Ciniselli, D. Borgioli, orch, EIAR Orch/A. Albergoni/E. Panizza/L. Molajoli/U. Tansini)

Ⓒ **89064**
Pasquale Amato (1878-1942)
Rossini: Barbiere di Siviglia (exc); *Donizetti:* Favorita (exc); *Verdi:* Due Foscari (exc); Rigoletto (exc); Rigoletto (exc); Traviata (exc); Traviata (exc); Ballo in maschera (exc); Otello (exc); Otello (exc); *Meyerbeer:* Dinorah (exc); Africaine (exc); *Puccini:* Tosca (exc); *Franchetti:* Germania (exc); *De Curtis:* Torna a Surriento; *De Christofaro:* Vola, vola!; Chiarastella. (P. Amato, M. Matzenauer, F. Hempel, A. Bada, orch/W.B. Rogers, NY Met Op Chor, NY Met Op Orch/G. Setti, chor, anon, anon)

Ⓒ **89065** (9/94)
Maria Reining (1903-1991)
Mozart: Nozze di Figaro (exc); *Wagner:* Tannhäuser (exc); Tannhäuser (exc); *Giordano:* Andrea Chénier (exc); *Puccini:* Manon Lescaut (exc); Bohème (exc); Madama Butterfly (exc); *Albert:* Toten Augen (exc); *R. Strauss:* Lieder, Op.41 (exc); Lieder, Op.27 (exc); Lieder, Op.37 (exc); *Lehár:* Eva (exc); Friederike (exc). (M. Reining, M. Lorenz, Prussian St Orch/H.U. Müller, VPO/R. Moralt/F. Lehár, Berlin RSO/A. Rother, Vienna St Op Orch)

Ⓒ **89066**
Zara Dolukhanova
Handel: Arianna (exc); Flavio (exc); *Rossini:* Semiramide (exc); Semiramide (exc); *Meyerbeer:* Huguenots (exc); *Gounod:* Faust (exc); *Massenet:* Werther (exc); *Verdi:* Don Carlo (exc); *Mussorgsky:* Khovanshchina (exc); *Tchaikovsky:* Snow Maiden (exc); *Rimsky-Korsakov:* Sadko (exc); Kashchey (exc). (G. Sakharova, Z. Dolukhanova, USSR Rad Orch, Moscow CO/A. Kovalyov/R. Barshai/A. Gauk/O. Bron)

Ⓒ **89067**
Andrei Ivanov (1900-1970)
Rossini: Guillaume Tell (exc); *Wagner:* Tannhäuser (exc); *Verdi:* Rigoletto (exc); *A. Thomas:* Hamlet (exc); *Bizet:* Carmen (exc); *Rubinstein:* Demon (exc); Demon (exc); Nero (exc); *Offenbach:* Contes d'Hoffmann (exc); *Tchaikovsky:* Eugene Onegin (exc); Mazeppa (exc); *Borodin:* Prince Igor (exc); *Rachmaninov:* Aleko (exc); *Rimsky-Korsakov:* Tsar's Bride (exc). (A. Ivanov, I. Maslennikova, E. Kruglikova, Bolshoi Th Orch/S. Samosud/A. Orlov/K. Kondrashin/A. Melik-Pashayev)

Ⓒ **89068**
Lauritz Melchior (1890-1973) - II
Wagner: Lohengrin (exc); Lohengrin (exc); Tannhäuser (exc); Walküre (exc); Siegfried (exc); Parsifal (exc); Parsifal (exc); *Trunk:* Mir träumte von einer Königskind; Als ob ein Toter im Grab; In meiner Heimat; Erster Strahl; *Sjöberg:* Tonerna; *R. Strauss:* Lieder, Op.27 (exc). (L. Melchior, E. Bettendorf, G. Guszalewicz, Berlin St Op Orch/F. Weissmann/L. Blech/P. Breisach, orch)

Ⓒ **89069**
Josef von Manowarda (1890-1942)
Gounod: Faust (exc); *Wagner:* Meistersinger (exc); Meistersinger (exc); Rheingold (exc); Walküre (exc); Siegfried (exc); *Schubert:* Schiffer, D536; Wandrers Nachtlied I, D224; Schwanengesang, D957 (exc); *Loewe:* Balladen, Op.68 (exc); Spirito Santo, Op.143; Legends, Op.75 (exc); Lieder, Op.145 (exc); Gesänge, Op.123 (exc); *Wolf:* Mörike Lieder (exc); *Brahms:* Lieder, Op.105 (exc); Lieder, Op.96 (exc). (J. von Manowarda, L. Hafgren, M. Olczewska, F. Soot, W. Henke, orch, F. Rupp, A. Sándor)

Ⓒ **89070** (8/94)
Franz Völker (1899-1965) - II
Mozart: Zauberflöte (exc); *Weber:* Freischütz (exc); *Beethoven:* Fidelio (exc); *Halévy:* Juive (exc); *Wagner:* Rienzi (exc); Fliegende Holländer (exc); Tannhäuser (exc); Walküre (exc); *Verdi:* Otello (exc); *Leoncavallo:* Pagliacci (exc); *Smetana:* Dalibor (exc); *Albert:* Tiefland (exc). (F. Völker, I. Langhammer, Berlin Staatskapelle/F.A. Schmidt/G. Steeger/A. Melichar/J. Schüler, chor)

Ⓒ **89071** (3/94)
Gerhard Hüsch (1901-1984) - II
Mozart: Nozze di Figaro (exc); Così fan tutte (exc); *Gumbert:* An des Rheines grünen Ufern; *Lortzing:* Undine (exc); Zar und Zimmermann (exc); *Nicolai:* Lustigen Weiber von Windsor (exc); *Wagner:* Tannhäuser (exc); *Humperdinck:* Hänsel und Gretel (exc); Königskinder (exc); *Verdi:* Trovatore (exc); Ballo in maschera (exc); *Gounod:* Faust (exc); *A. Thomas:* Mignon (exc); *Giordano:* Andrea Chénier (exc); *Puccini:* Tosca (exc). (G. Hüsch, Berlin St Op Orch/H.U. Müller, Berlin City Op Orch/A. von Zemlinsky, E. Fuchs, W. Strienz)

Ⓒ **89072** (10/94)
Aureliano Pertile (1885-1952) - II
Donizetti: Elisir d'amore (exc); Lucia di Lammermoor (exc); *Bellini:* Puritani (exc); *Flotow:* Martha (exc); *Wagner:* Lohengrin (exc); Lohengrin (exc); *Leoncavallo:* Pagliacci (exc); *Giordano:* Andrea Chénier (exc); Andrea Chénier (exc); Andrea Chénier (exc); *Puccini:* Manon Lescaut (exc); Manon Lescaut (exc); Manon Lescaut (exc); Bohème (exc); *Cilea:* Adriana Lecouvreur (exc). (A. Pertile, I.A. Tellini, M.L. Fanelli, M. Sheridan, A. Granforte, La Scala Orch/C. Sabajno/G. Nastrucci)

Ⓒ **89073** (10/94)
Giuseppe de Luca (1876-1950) - II
Verdi: Ernani (exc); Rigoletto (exc); Rigoletto (exc); Trovatore (exc); Trovatore (exc); Traviata (exc); Traviata (exc); Forza del destino (exc); Don Carlo (exc); Aida (exc); *Gounod:* Faust (exc); *Bizet:* Pêcheurs de perles (exc); *Ponchielli:* Gioconda (exc); Gioconda (exc); *Puccini:* Bohème (exc); *Wolf-Ferrari:* Gioielli della Madonna (exc). (G. De Luca, G. Anthony, A. Tedesco, A. Galli-Curci, B. Gigli, E. Rethberg, NY Met Op Chor, NY Met Op Orch/G. Setti, orch/Rosario Bourdon)

Ⓒ **89074** (4/95)
Tancredi Pasero (1893-1983) - II
Mozart: Nozze di Figaro (exc); Don Giovanni (exc); Zauberflöte (exc); *Rossini:* Barbiere di Siviglia (exc); Semiramide (exc); *Bellini:* Sonnambula (exc); Sonnambula (exc); *Verdi:* Nabucco (exc); Luisa Miller (exc); Rigoletto (exc); Simon Boccanegra (exc); Requiem (exc); *Mussorgsky:* Boris Godunov (exc); *Gounod:* Faust (exc); *Boito:* Mefistofele (exc); *Porrino:* Orazi (exc); *Beethoven:* In questa tomba oscura, WoO133; *Niedermeyer:* Pietà Signore. (T. Pasero, G. Bernelli, G. Bechi, orch, La Scala Orch, EIAR Orch, Rome Teatro Reale Orch, SO/A. Sabino/U. Tansini/L. Ricci/D. Marzollo)

Ⓒ **89076**
Josef Herrmann (1903-1955)
Marschner: Hans Heiling (exc); *Weber:* Freischütz (exc); Peter Schmoll (exc); *Beethoven:* Fidelio (exc); *Wagner:* Fliegende Holländer (exc); Fliegende Holländer (exc); Meistersinger (exc); Meistersinger (exc); Rheingold (exc); Walküre (exc); *Verdi:* Otello (exc); Otello (exc); *Leoncavallo:* Pagliacci (exc). (J. Herrmann, K. Böhme, W. Treffner, H. Tessmer, M. Düren, Berlin St Op Orch/B. Seidler-Winkler, VPO/R. Moralt, Saxon St Orch/K. Böhm, Leipzig RSO/R. Merten, orch)

Ⓒ **89077** (10/94)
Torsten Ralf (1901-1954)
Wagner: Lohengrin (exc); Meistersinger (exc); Walküre (exc); *Bizet:* Carmen (exc); *Verdi:* Otello (exc); Otello (exc); Otello (exc); *Puccini:* Fanciulla del West (exc); *Albert:* Tiefland (exc); *R. Strauss:* Daphne (exc); Frau ohne Schatten (exc). (T. Ralf, T. Lemnitz, F. Beckmann, J. Herrmann, Berlin St Op Orch, Saxon St Orch/B. Seidler-Winkler/H.U. Müller/K. Böhm)

Ⓒ **89078**
Alexander Pirogov (1899-1964)
Meyerbeer: Huguenots (exc); *Boito:* Mefistofele (exc); *Gounod:* Faust (exc); *Glinka:* Ruslan and Lyudmila (exc); *Dargomizhsky:* Rusalka (exc); *Mussorgsky:* Boris Godunov (exc); Boris Godunov (exc); Khovanshchina (exc); *Borodin:* Prince Igor (exc); *Rimsky-Korsakov:* Tsar's Bride (exc); Sadko (exc); Tale of Tsar Saltan (exc); Songs, Op.49 (exc); *Rachmaninov:* Aleko (exc); Francesca da Rimini (exc). (A. Pirogov, I. Kozlovsky, Bolshoi Th Orch/S. Samosud/V. Nebolsin/A. Melik-Pashayev/N. Golovanov)

Ⓒ **89079** (4/94)
Maria Jeritza (1887-1982)
Weber: Freischütz (exc); *Wagner:* Fliegende Holländer (exc); Lohengrin (exc); Walküre (exc); Wesendonk Lieder (exc); Tristan und Isolde (exc); *Tchaikovsky:* Maid of Orleans (exc); *Massenet:* Hérodiade (exc); Thaïs (exc); Cid (exc); *Delibes:* O mer, ouvre-toi; *Ponchielli:* Gioconda (exc); *Mascagni:* Cavalleria Rusticana (exc); *Giordano:* Fedora (exc); *Puccini:* Tosca (exc); *Goldmark:* Heimchen am Herd (exc); *Korngold:* Tote Stadt (exc). (M. Jeritza, orch)

Ⓒ **89080** (2/95)
Mark Reizen (1895-1992) - II
Dargomizhsky: Rusalka (exc); *Gounod:* Faust (exc); *Rossini:* Barbiere di Siviglia (exc); *Verdi:* Vespri Siciliani (exc); Don Carlo (exc); Simon Boccanegra (exc); *Wagner:* Walküre (exc); *Mussorgsky:* Boris Godunov (exc). (M. Reizen, G. Nelepp, B. Zlatogorova, Bolshoi Th Orch/V. Nebolsin/S. Samosud/N. Golovanov)

Ⓒ **89081**
Georgi Nelepp (1904-1957)
Verstovsky: Askold's Grave (exc); *Glinka:* Ruslan and Lyudmila (exc); *Moniuszko:* Halka (exc); *Smetana:* Bartered Bride (exc); *Wagner:* Meistersinger (exc); *Verdi:*

Aida (exc); *Bizet:* Carmen (exc); *Tchaikovsky:* Enchantress (exc); Queen of Spades (exc); *Puccini:* Madama Butterfly (exc). (G. Nelepp, I. Petrov, V. Barsova, E. Shumilova, G. Korotkov, Bolshoi Th Orch, USSR RSO, orch/K. Kondrashin/N. Golovanov/A. Melik-Pashayev/V. Nebolsin/S. Samosud)

Ⓓ **89082** (7/95)
Margarete Klose (1902-1968)
Gluck: Orfeo ed Euridice (exc); Alceste (1776) (exc); Paride ed Elena (exc); *Verdi:* Trovatore (exc); Trovatore (exc); Ballo in maschera (exc); Don Carlo (exc); Aida (exc); *Wagner:* Walküre (exc); *Bizet:* Carmen (exc); Carmen (exc); *Saint-Saëns:* Samson et Dalila (exc). (M. Klose, M. Wittrisch, M. Perras, W. Grossmann, T. Gerson, S. Fischer, Berlin St Op Orch/B. Seidler-Winkler/F. Zweig/F.A. Schmidt, Berlin Deutsche Op Orch/G. Steeger)

Ⓓ **89083**
Emanuel List (1890-1967)
Mozart: Zauberflöte (exc); *Weber:* Freischütz (exc); *Lortzing:* Waffenschmied (exc); *Nicolai:* Lustigen Weiber von Windsor (exc); *Wagner:* Lohengrin (exc); Götterdämmerung (exc); *Gounod:* Faust (exc); Faust (exc); *R. Strauss:* Rosenkavalier (exc); *Kremser:* Andreas Hofer; *L. Fischer:* Kritikaster (exc); *Reissiger:* Schlesische Zecher und der Teufel; *Binder:* Wenn ich einmal der Herrgott wär'!; *Peters:* Strömt herbei ihr Völkerscharen; *Ziehrer:* Fremdenführer (exc); *Traditional:* Kol nidrei. (E. List, M. Seinemeyer, E. Schürhoff, O. Schulhof, Berlin St Op Orch, Lower Austria Orch, orch, anon/F. Weissmann/E. Mörike/O. Dobrindt/W. Loibner, Berlin St Op Chor)

Ⓓ **89084** (4/95)
Kerstin Thorborg (1896-1970)
Gluck: Orfeo ed Euridice (exc); *Bizet:* Carmen (exc); *Saint-Saëns:* Samson et Dalila (exc); *Wagner:* Lohengrin (exc); Rheingold (exc); Walküre (exc); Götterdämmerung (exc); Tristan und Isolde (exc); Parsifal (exc); *Schubert:* Allmacht, D852; Ständchen D889; *Brahms:* Lieder, Op.94 (exc); *Wolf:* Mörike Lieder (exc); Goethe Lieder (exc). (K. Thorborg, E. Rethberg, J. Huehn, L. Rosenek, Berlin St Op Orch/F. Weissmann, NY Met Op Orch/E. Leinsdorf, RCA SO/K. Riedel)

Ⓓ **89086**
Lauritz Melchior (1890-1973) - III
Wagner: Rienzi (exc); Tannhäuser (exc); Tannhäuser (exc); Tristan und Isolde (exc); Walküre (exc); Walküre (exc); Siegfried (exc); Götterdämmerung (exc); *Meyerbeer:* Africaine (exc); *Leoncavallo:* Pagliacci (exc); *Verdi:* Otello (exc). (L. Melchior, A. Reiss, O. Helgers, LSO/J. Barbirolli/A. Coates/R. Heger, Berlin St Op Orch/L. Blech, New SO)

Ⓓ **89088** (7/95)
Walther Ludwig (1902-1981)
Mozart: Così fan tutte (exc); Entführung (exc); Entführung (exc); Don Giovanni (exc); Zauberflöte (exc); *Nicolai:* Lustigen Weiber von Windsor (exc); *Flotow:* Alessandro Stradella (exc); *A. Thomas:* Mignon (exc); *Bizet:* Carmen (exc); *Puccini:* Madama Butterfly (exc); *Kienzl:* Kuhreigen (exc); Evangelimann (exc); *Graener:* Friedemann Bach (exc); Lieder, Op.71 (exc). (W. Ludwig, M. Perras, G. Hüsch, F. Leitner, Berlin St Op Orch, Berlin City Op Orch, orch/B. Seidler-Winkler/F. Zaun/G. Steeger/H. von Benda/W. Ladwig)

Ⓓ **89090**
Hans Hermann Nissen (1893-1980)
Marschner: Hans Heiling (exc); *Gounod:* Faust (exc); *Meyerbeer:* Africaine (exc); *Wagner:* Fliegende Holländer (exc); Meistersinger (exc); Meistersinger (exc); Walküre (exc); Parsifal (exc); *Loewe:* Odins Meeresritt, Op.118; Gedichte, Op.61 (exc); *Schumann:* Romanzen und Balladen, Op.45 (exc); *Wolf:* Eichendorff Lieder (exc); Mörike Lieder (exc); *Pfitzner:* Lieder, Op.9 (exc). (H. Hermann Nissen, B. Seidler-Winkler, Berlin SO/F. Zweig)

Ⓓ **89091**
Francesco Merli (1887-1976) - II
Bellini: Norma (exc); *Verdi:* Lombardi (exc); Forza del destino (exc); *Marchetti:* Ruy Blas (exc); *Gomes:* Guarany (exc); *Verdi:* Otello (exc); Otello (exc); *Catalani:* Loreley (exc); *Zandonai:* Giuliano (exc); *Wolf-Ferrari:* Sly (exc). (F. Merli, B. Scacciati, N. de Angelis, G. Vanelli, C. Muzio, orch/L. Molajoli)

Ⓓ **89092**
Erna Berger (1900-1990) - II
Mozart: Zauberflöte (exc); Zauberflöte (exc); *Donizetti:* Don Pasquale (exc); Fille du Régiment (exc); *Flotow:* Martha (exc); *Verdi:* Rigoletto (exc); Rigoletto (exc); Rigoletto (exc); Rigoletto (exc); Traviata (exc); Traviata (exc); *Puccini:* Bohème (exc); *R. Strauss:* Ariadne auf Naxos (exc); *Oboussier:* Zeit, Verkünderin der besten Freuden; Weine du nicht; Dein süsses Bild, Edone; *Flies:* Wiegenlied; *Brahms:* Lieder, Op.49 (exc). (E. Berger, G. Sinimberghi, J. Patzak, W. Domgraf-Fassbaender, W. Grossmann, W. Beck, M. Wittrisch, M. Klose, H. Altmann, H-W. Schleif, E. Harich-Schneider, BPO/B. Seidler-Winkler/T. Beecham, Berlin St Op Orch/E. Baltzer/L. Blech/Wolfgang Martin, Berlin City Op Orch/F. Zweig/H. Schmidt-Isserstedt, Berlin RO/C. Krauss)

Ⓓ **89094**
Maria Ivogün (1891-1987)
Mozart: Entführung (exc); Entführung (exc); Zauberflöte (exc); *Rossini:* Barbiere di Siviglia (exc); *Donizetti:* Lucia di Lammermoor (exc); Don Pasquale (exc); *Meyerbeer:* Huguenots (exc); *Nicolai:* Lustigen Weiber von Windsor (exc); *Cornelius:* Barbier von Bagdad (exc); *Verdi:* Rigoletto (exc); Traviata (exc); Traviata (exc); *Bizet:* Carmen (exc); *Puccini:* Bohème (exc); Bohème (exc). (M. Ivogün, K. Erb, orch)

Ⓓ **89095**
Karl Erb (1877-1958)
Mozart: Zauberflöte (exc); *Haydn:* Schöpfung (exc); *Beethoven:* Fidelio (exc); *Weber:* Euryanthe (exc); *Nicolai:* Lustigen Weiber von Windsor (exc); *Mendelssohn:* Paulus (exc); *Wagner:* Tannhäuser (exc); Lohengrin (exc); Rheingold (exc); *Gounod:* Faust (exc); *A. Thomas:* Mignon (exc); *Goldmark:* Königin von Saba (exc); *Wagner:* Fliegende Holländer (exc); *Verdi:* Falstaff (exc); *Weingartner:* Dame Kobold (exc); *Schubert:* Auf der Riesenkoppe, D611; Ganymed, D544. (K. Erb, orch, anon)

Ⓓ **89096**
Alexander Svéd (1906-1979)
Berlioz: Damnation de Faust (exc); *Rossini:* Guillaume Tell (exc); *Verdi:* Macbeth (exc); Rigoletto (exc); Trovatore (exc); Ballo in maschera (exc); Otello (exc); *Puccini:* Tosca (exc); *Wagner:* Tannhäuser (exc); Meistersinger (exc); *Schubert:* Wanderer, D489; An die Musik, D547; *Schumann:* Myrthen, Op.25 (exc); Dichterliebe, Op.48 (exc); *Bizet:* Agnus Dei. (A. Sved, V. Ursuleac, A. Beltrami, orch/D. Olivieri, Berlin St Op Orch/C. Krauss, Radio Italiana SO/A. Simonetto)

Ⓓ **89097**
Helene Wildbrunn (1882-1972)
Gluck: Alceste (1776) (exc); *Mozart:* Don Giovanni (exc); *Beethoven:* Fidelio (exc); *Weber:* Oberon (exc); *Verdi:* Ballo in maschera (exc); *Wagner:* Tristan und Isolde (exc); Walküre (exc); Siegfried (exc); Götterdämmerung (exc); *Ponchielli:* Gioconda (exc); *Mascagni:* Cavalleria rusticana (exc); *Puccini:* Tosca (exc). (H. Wildbrunn, orch)

Ⓓ **89098**
Frida Leider (1888-1975) - II
Wagner: Tristan und Isolde (exc); Walküre (exc); Walküre (exc); Götterdämmerung (exc); *Schubert:* Erlkönig, D328; Auf dem Wasser zu singen, D774; *Schumann:* Myrthen, Op.25 (exc); Jugend Lieder, Op.79 (exc); Gedichte, Op.90 (exc); Myrthen, Op.25 (exc); *Schubert:* Winterreise (exc); *Wolf:* Alte Weisen (exc); Goethe Lieder (exc). (F. Leider, E. Marherr-Wagner, F. Schorr, G. Ljungberg, Berlin St Op Orch/L. Blech, M. Raucheisen)

Ⓓ **89099**
Paul Franz (1876-1950)
Meyerbeer: Huguenots (exc); *Wagner:* Lohengrin (exc); Lohengrin (exc); Tannhäuser (exc); Walküre (exc); Siegfried (exc); Parsifal (exc); *Verdi:* Aida (exc); *Gounod:* Roméo et Juliette (exc); Roméo et Juliette (exc); *Bizet:* Carmen (exc); *Saint-Saëns:* Samson et Dalila (exc); *Reyer:* Sigurd (exc); Sigurd (exc); *Massenet:* Hérodiade (exc). (P. Franz, orch)

Ⓓ **89102**
Ludwig Hofmann (1895-1963)
Mozart: Zauberflöte (exc); *Flotow:* Martha (exc); *Lortzing:* Waffenschmied (exc); Undine (exc); Zar und Zimmermann (exc); *Pabst:* Lied an die Flasche; *Nicolai:* Lustigen Weiber von Windsor (exc); *L. Fischer:* Kritikaster (exc); *Wagner:* Lohengrin (exc); Meistersinger (exc); *Gounod:* Faust (exc); *Offenbach:* Contes d'Hoffmann (exc); *Cornelius:* Verratene Liebe; *Schumann:* Gedichte, Op.35 (exc); *Fürst:* Wagen rollt; *Krenek:* Jonny spielt auf (exc). (L. Hofmann, A. Peters, M. Salvatini, J. Prüwer, Berlin Staatskapelle, Berlin St Op Orch, Berlin City Op Orch, orch/J. Prüwer/F.A. Schmidt/M. Gurlitt)

Ⓓ **89105**
Apollo Granforte (1886-1975) - II
Rossini: Barbiere di Siviglia (exc); *Donizetti:* Dom Sébastien (exc); *Verdi:* Rigoletto (exc); *Ponchielli:* Gioconda (exc); *Verdi:* Otello (exc); *Yradier:* Paloma; *Gutierrez:* Alma Llanera; *Verdi:* Ballo in maschera (exc); Otello (exc); *Mario:* Leggenda di Piave; *Blanc:* Giovinezza; *Gounod:* Faust (exc); *Giordano:* Andrea Chénier (exc); *Leoncavallo:* Pagliacci (exc); *Verdi:* Aida (exc); *Ihne:* Inno al Duce; *Puccini:* Inno a Roma. (A. Granforte, H. Monti, orch/G.W. Byng, La Scala Orch/C. Sabajno)

Ⓓ **89110**
Heinrich Schlusnus (1888-1952) - II
Mozart: Don Giovanni (exc); Zauberflöte (exc); *Abt:* Wenn man beim Wein; *Rossini:* Barbiere di Siviglia (exc); Guillaume Tell (exc); *Verdi:* Rigoletto (exc); Traviata (exc); Trovatore (exc); Don Carlo (exc); Forza del destino (exc); Otello (exc); Otello (exc); Otello (exc); *Meyerbeer:* Africaine (exc); Africaine (exc); *Bizet:* Pêcheurs de perles (exc); *Offenbach:* Contes d'Hoffmann (exc); *Tchaikovsky:* Eugene Onegin (exc); *Puccini:* Bohème (exc). (H. Schlusnus, S. Kurz, R. Hutt, orch)

Ⓓ **89201** (2/92)
Helge Roswaenge (1897-1972) - I
Puccini: Bohème (exc); Tosca (exc); *Verdi:* Trovatore (exc); Traviata (exc); *Bizet:* Carmen (exc); *Mascagni:* Cavalleria Rusticana (exc); *Mozart:* Così fan tutte (exc); Don Giovanni (exc); *Adam:* Postillon de Lonjumeau (exc); *Boïeldieu:* Dame blanche (exc); *Flotow:* Martha (exc); *Verdi:* Trovatore (exc); *Puccini:* Bohème (exc); *Verdi:* Rigoletto (exc); Aida (exc); *Gounod:* Faust (exc); *Bizet:* Carmen (exc); *Verdi:* Rigoletto (exc); Aida (exc); *Massenet:* Manon (exc); *Puccini:* Bohème (exc); Madama Butterfly (exc). (H. Roswaenge, H. von Debička, E. Leisner, R. Watzke, F. Hüni-Mihacsek, T. de Garmo, T. Scheidl, orch)

Ⓓ **89203**
Leo Slezak (1873-1946)
Schubert: Schwanengesang, D957 (exc); Musensohn, D764; Schöne Müllerin (exc); Winterreise (exc); Du bist die Ruh', D776; Jüngling an der Quelle, D300; Litanei, D343; Im Abendrot, D799; Nacht und Träume, D827; An die Musik, D547; *Schumann:* Liederkreis, Op.39 (exc); Myrthen, Op.25 (exc); *Brahms:* Lieder, Op.106 (exc); Lieder, Op.86 (exc); *Wolf:* Eichendorff Lieder (exc); Mörike Lieder (exc); *R. Strauss:* Lieder, Op.10 (exc); Lieder, Op.48 (exc); Lieder, Op.32 (exc); Lieder, Op.29 (exc); Lieder, Op.27 (exc); Lieder, Op.17 (exc); *Loewe:* Tom der Reimer, Op.135a; *Hildach:* Lenz; *Wagner:* Lohengrin (exc); Tannhäuser (exc); Meistersinger (exc); *Halévy:* Juive (exc); *Leoncavallo:* Pagliacci (exc); *Verdi:* Otello (exc). (L. Slezak, T. Scheidl, H. Schacker, M. Raucheisen, Berlin St Op Orch/M. Gurlitt)

Ⓓ **89209** (4/95)
Helge Roswaenge (1897-1972) - II
Meyerbeer: Huguenots (exc); *Verdi:* Rigoletto (exc); Traviata (exc); Vespri Siciliani (exc); Vespri Siciliani (exc); Aida (exc); Otello (exc); *Wagner:* Meistersinger (exc); Meistersinger (exc); *Flotow:* Martha (exc); *A. Thomas:* Mignon (exc); *Meyerbeer:* Africaine (exc); *Bizet:* Carmen (exc); *Offenbach:* Contes d'Hoffmann (exc); *Massenet:* Manon (exc); *Puccini:* Madama Butterfly (exc); Turandot (exc); *Mozart:* Entführung (exc); *Weber:* Freischütz (exc); Oberon (exc); *Cornelius:* Barbier von Bagdad (exc); *Auber:* Fra Diavolo (exc); *Adam:* Postillon de Lonjumeau (exc); *Verdi:* Rigoletto (exc); Ballo in maschera (exc); Ballo in maschera (exc); Traviata (exc); Traviata (exc); Forza del destino (exc); *Puccini:* Tosca (exc); *Künneke:* Grosse Sünderin (exc); Grosse Sünderin (exc). (H. Roswaenge, P. Yoder, L. Kindermann, H. Reinmar, H. Schlusnus, M. Kuttner, H. von Debička, I. Roswaenge, M. Korjus, M. Perras, T. Lemnitz, Berlin St Op Orch/F.A. Schmidt/S. Meyrowitz/A. Melichar/H. Weigert, BPO/E. Orthmann/B. Seidler-Winkler/E. Künneke, orch)

Ⓓ **89210**
The Art of Emmi Leisner
Handel: Serse (exc); *Traditional:* O Jesulein süss; *Mendelssohn:* Paulus (exc); Elias (exc); *Gluck:* Orfeo ed Euridice (exc); *Verdi:* Trovatore (exc); Trovatore (exc); Don Carlo (exc); *Wagner:* Tristan und Isolde (exc); *Bizet:* Carmen (exc); *Saint-Saëns:* Samson et Dalila (exc); *Verdi:* Don Carlo (exc); *Bruch:* Odysseus (exc); Achilleus (exc); *Schubert:* Ave Maria, D839; *Bach:* Christmas Oratorio, BWV248 (exc); Cantata 53; *Handel:* Rodelinda (exc); Giulio Cesare (exc); *Beethoven:* Scottish Songs, Op.108 (exc); *Dvořák:* Biblical Songs (exc); *Brahms:* Ernste Gesänge, Op.121 (Cpte). (E. Leisner, R. Hutt, anon, inst ens, orch)

Ⓓ **89211**
Helge Roswaenge (1897-1972) - III
Mozart: Zauberflöte (exc); *Beethoven:* Fidelio (exc); *Wagner:* Lohengrin (exc); *Cornelius:* Barbier von Bagdad (exc); *Gounod:* Faust (exc); Faust (exc); *Bizet:* Carmen (exc); *Massenet:* Manon (exc); *Verdi:* Trovatore (exc); Forza del destino (exc); *Puccini:* Bohème (exc); Bohème (exc); *R. Strauss:* Rosenkavalier (exc); *Wille:* Königsballade (exc); *Glinka:* Life for the Tsar (exc); *Mussorgsky:* Boris Godunov (exc); *Tchaikovsky:* Eugene Onegin (exc); Enchantress (exc); *Verdi:* Trovatore (exc); Aida (exc); Aida (exc); *Leoncavallo:* Pagliacci (exc); Pagliacci (exc); *Puccini:* Tosca (exc); *Lehár:* Giuditta (exc). (H. Roswaenge, M. Teschemacher, W. Strienz, G. Hüsch, M. Cebotari, F. Beckmann, T. Lemnitz, Berlin St Op Orch,

VPO, BPO, Berlin RSO, Berlin Volksoper Orch/T. Beecham/B. Seidler-Winkler/R. Moralt/H. Steinkopf/E. Baltzer)

Ⓒ **89212**
Heinrich Schlusnus (1888-1952)
A. Thomas: Hamlet (exc); *Verdi:* Rigoletto (exc); Trovatore (exc); Traviata (exc); Forza del destino (exc); Otello (exc); *Giordano:* Andrea Chénier (exc); *Rossini:* Barbiere di Siviglia (exc); *Verdi:* Ballo in maschera (exc); Vespri siciliani (exc); Simon Boccanegra (exc); *Bizet:* Carmen (exc); *Borodin:* Prince Igor (exc); *Tchaikovsky:* Queen of Spades (exc); Eugene Onegin (exc); *Gumbert:* An des Rheines grünen Ufern; *Mozart:* Don Giovanni (exc); Don Giovanni (exc); *Marschner:* Hans Heiling (exc); *Wagner:* Tannhäuser (exc); Tannhäuser (exc); *Nessler:* Trompeter von Säckingen (exc); *Rossini:* Barbiere di Siviglia (exc); *Verdi:* Ballo in maschera (exc); *Leoncavallo:* Pagliacci (exc); *Gounod:* Faust (exc); *Offenbach:* Contes d'Hoffmann (exc); *Lortzing:* Zar und Zimmermann (exc); *Verdi:* Trovatore (exc); Traviata (exc); Forza del destino (exc); Rigoletto (exc); Vespri siciliani (exc); Don Carlo (exc). (H. Schlusnus, E. Berger, Berlin St Op Orch/J. Heidenreich/J. Prüwer/M. Gurlitt/H. Weigert/A. Melichar/L. Blech/C. Krauss/J. Schüler/G. Steeger/A. Rother)

Ⓒ **89214**
Friedrich Schorr sings Wagner
Wagner: Fliegende Holländer (exc); Tannhäuser (exc); Tannhäuser (exc); Rheingold (exc); Walküre (exc); Götterdämmerung (exc); Meistersinger (exc); Meistersinger (exc); Meistersinger (exc); Meistersinger (exc); Meistersinger (exc). (F. Schorr, Berlin St Op Orch/L. Blech, LSO/A. Coates/L. Collingwood/J. Barbirolli/Rosario Bourdon)

Ⓒ **89217**
Alfred Piccaver—The Complete Electric Recordings 1928-1930
Beethoven: Fidelio (exc); *Wagner:* Lohengrin (exc); Lohengrin (exc); Meistersinger (exc); *Flotow:* Martha (exc); *Verdi:* Trovatore (exc); Forza del destino (exc); Aida (exc); Requiem (exc); *Gounod:* Faust (exc); *Meyerbeer:* Africaine (exc); *Ponchielli:* Gioconda (exc); *Massenet:* Manon (exc); Manon (exc); Werther (exc); *Mascagni:* Cavalleria Rusticana (exc); Cavalleria Rusticana (exc); Cavalleria Rusticana (exc); *Leoncavallo:* Pagliacci (exc); *Giordano:* Andrea Chénier (exc); Fedora (exc); *Puccini:* Bohème (exc); Bohème (exc); Tosca (exc); Tosca (exc); Madama Butterfly (exc); Fanciulla del West (exc); Turandot (exc); Turandot (exc); *Leoncavallo:* Mattinata; *Tosti:* Pour un baiser; *Tirindelli:* Di te; *Tosti:* Addio; Ideale; *De Curtis:* Torna a Surriento; *E. Nevin:* Rosary; *Woodforde-Finden:* Indian Love Lyrics (exc); *Geehl:* For you alone. (A. Piccaver, M. Angerer, T. Scheidl, J. Prüwer, anon, Berlin St Op Orch/J. Prüwer/M. Gurlitt)

Ⓒ **89301** (5/91)
The Art of Frida Leider
Mozart: Nozze di Figaro (exc); *Beethoven:* Fidelio (exc); Ah! perfido, Op.65; *Weber:* Oberon (exc); *Wagner:* Rienzi (exc); Tannhäuser (exc); Tristan und Isolde (exc); Wesendonk Lieder (exc); *Verdi:* Aida (exc); Aida (exc); *Puccini:* Tosca (exc); *Mozart:* Nozze di Figaro (exc); Don Giovanni (exc); *Verdi:* Trovatore (exc); Trovatore (exc); Trovatore (exc); Trovatore (exc); Ballo in maschera (exc); Don Carlo (exc); Aida (exc); *Wagner:* Walküre (exc); *Puccini:* Tosca (exc); *R. Strauss:* Ariadne auf Naxos (exc); *Wagner:* Fliegende Holländer (exc); Fliegende Holländer (exc); Tannhäuser (exc); Tristan und Isolde (exc); Walküre (exc); Walküre (exc); Siegfried (exc); Siegfried (exc); Götterdämmerung (exc); Parsifal (exc); Wesendonk Lieder (exc). (F. Leider, R. Hutt, H. Schlusnus, O. Helgers, M. Abendroth, C. Günther, L. Melchior, F. Soot, orch)

Ⓒ **89302** (6/92)
The Young Lotte Lehmann
Weber: Freischütz (exc); Freischütz (exc); Freischütz (exc); *Wagner:* Tannhäuser (exc); Lohengrin (exc); Lohengrin (exc); *Gounod:* Faust (exc); *Wagner:* Meistersinger (exc); Meistersinger (exc); Walküre (exc); Walküre (exc); *Albert:* Toten Augen (exc); *R. Strauss:* Lieder, Op.27 (exc); *Mozart:* Nozze di Figaro (exc); *Weber:* Oberon (exc); *Lortzing:* Undine (exc); *Halévy:* Juive (exc); *Bizet:* Carmen (exc); *Offenbach:* Contes d'Hoffmann (exc); *Goetz:* Widerspenstigen Zähmung (exc); *Tchaikovsky:* Eugene Onegin (exc); *Verdi:* Otello (exc); *Massenet:* Manon (exc); *R. Strauss:* Rosenkavalier (exc); *Korngold:* Tote Stadt (exc); *Mozart:* Nozze di Figaro (exc); Nozze di Figaro (exc); Don Giovanni (exc); Zauberflöte (exc); *Nicolai:* Lustigen Weiber von Windsor (exc); *A. Thomas:* Mignon (exc); Mignon (exc); *Massenet:* Manon (exc); *Puccini:* Bohème (exc); Madama Butterfly (exc); Suor Angelica (exc); Manon Lescaut (exc); Tosca (exc); *Hildach:* Spielmann. (Lotte Lehmann, R. Hutt, M. Bohnen, H. Schlusnus, orch, Berlin St Op Orch/G. Szell/K. Besl/H. Weigert)

Ⓒ **89303(1)** (2/93)
Titta Ruffo Edition (pt 1)
Mozart: Don Giovanni (exc); *Leoncavallo:* Zazà (exc); *Verdi:* Ballo in maschera (exc); *Ferradini:* Non penso a lei; *Capolongo:* Suonno è fantasia; *Brogi:* Visione veneziana; *Massenet:* Thaïs (exc); *Titta:* E suonan le campane; *Mozart:* Don Giovanni (exc); *Soriano:* Guitarrico (exc); *Meyerbeer:* Dinorah (exc); *Verdi:* Otello (exc); *Franchetti:* Cristoforo Colombo (exc); *Verdi:* Nabucco (exc); *Titta:* Oh che m'importa?; *Schumann:* Romanzen und Balladen, Op.49 (exc); *Gounod:* Faust (exc); *Puccini:* Tosca (exc); *Verdi:* Forza del Destino (exc); *Meyerbeer:* Africaine (exc); *Verdi:* Ballo in maschera (exc); *Mozart:* Don Giovanni (exc); *Rossini:* Barbiere di Siviglia (exc); *Verdi:* Rigoletto (exc); *Meyerbeer:* Africaine (exc); *Verdi:* Otello (exc); *A. Thomas:* Hamlet (exc); *P.M. Costa:* Sei morta nella vita mia; Munasterio; *Trémisot:* Novembre; *Paladilhe:* Patrie (exc). (T. Ruffo, E. Caruso, orch)

Ⓒ **89303(2)** (2/93)
Titta Ruffo Edition (pt 2)
Giordano: Andrea Chénier (exc); *Massenet:* Roi de Lahore (exc); *Verdi:* Ernani (exc); *Franchetti:* Cristoforo Colombo (exc); *Seismit-Doda:* Querida; *Verdi:* Falstaff (exc); *Padilla:* Relicario; *Rubinstein:* Demon (exc); *Flotow:* Martha (exc); *Verdi:* Falstaff (exc); *De Tejada:* Perjura!; *Berlioz:* Damnation de Faust (exc); *Gounod:* Faust (exc); *Delibes:* Lakmé (exc); *Goublier:* Credo du Paysan; *Buzzi-Peccia:* Lolita; *Cottrau:* Santa Lucia; *Tosti:* Marechiare; *Schipa-Hua:* Cubanita; *Rotoli:* Mia sposa sarà la mia bandiera; *Tosti:* Chitarrata abruzzese; *Verdi:* Forza del destino (exc); *Ponchielli:* Gioconda (exc); *Puccini:* Bohème (exc); *Capolongo:* Suonno è fantasia; *Brogi:* Visione veneziana; *Billi:* Tizianello (exc); *Pugnacci:* Gitano Re; *P. M. Costa:* Sei morta nella vita mia; *Giordano:* Andrea Chénier (exc); *Meyerbeer:* Africaine (exc); *De Curtis:* Torna a Surriento. (T. Ruffo, B. Gigli, orch)

Ⓒ **89995**
Famous Italian Baritones
Donizetti: Favorita (exc); Dom Sébastien (exc); *Verdi:* Ballo in maschera (exc); Otello (exc); Ernani (exc); *Rossini:* Barbiere di Siviglia (exc); *Gounod:* Faust (exc); *A. Thomas:* Hamlet (exc); *Verdi:* Rigoletto (exc); Due Foscari (exc); Nabucco (exc); Due Foscari (exc); Otello (exc); Traviata (exc); *Leoncavallo:* Zazà (exc); *Puccini:* Tosca (exc); *Verdi:* Falstaff (exc); *Rossini:* Guillaume Tell (exc); *Leoncavallo:* Pagliacci (exc); *Verdi:* Trovatore (exc); *Catalani:* Wally (exc); *Cilea:* Arlesiana (exc); *Massenet:* Hérodiade (exc). (A. Magini-Coletti, M. Battistini, M. Ancona, A. Scotti, M. Sammarco, R. Stracciari, G. De Luca, T. Ruffo, D. Viglione-Borghese, P. Amato, C. Galeffi, E. Molinari, C. Formichi, G. Danise, A. Granforte, L. Montesanto, M. Stabile, B. Franci, M. Basiola I, C. Tagliabue, G. Bechi, T. Gobbi, G. Taddei, orch, La Scala Orch/F. Ghione/C. Sabajno/U. Berrettoni)

Ⓒ **89996** (6/95)
Kyra Vayne (b.1916)
Borodin: Prince Igor (exc); *Verdi:* Ernani (exc); *Gluck:* Paride ed Elena (exc); *Boito:* Mefistofele (exc); *Tchaikovsky:* Queen of Spades (exc); *Spontini:* Vestale (exc); *Puccini:* Tosca (exc); *Verdi:* Forza del destino (exc); *Schubert:* Im Frühling, D882; *Tchaikovsky:* Songs, Op.54 (exc); To forget; Songs, Op.6 (exc); *Mussorgsky:* Lullaby; But if I could meet thee again; Garden by the Don; *Glière:* Lark; *Grechaninov:* Epicedium; *Rachmaninov:* Songs, Op.21 (exc); Songs, Op.4 (exc); Songs, Op.14 (exc). (K. Vayne, anon, orch, C. Tilney)

Ⓒ **89998**
Antonio Paoli (1871-1946)
Meyerbeer: Prophète (exc); Huguenots (exc); Robert le Diable (exc); *Verdi:* Rigoletto (exc); Rigoletto (exc); Trovatore (exc); Aida (exc); Aida (exc); Otello (exc); Otello (exc); Otello (exc); Otello (exc); *Massenet:* Cid (exc); *Saint-Saëns:* Samson et Dalila (exc); *Leoncavallo:* Pagliacci (exc); *Giordano:* Andrea Chénier (exc); *Samara:* Mademoiselle de belle Isle (exc). (A. Paoli, A. de Segurola, V. de Goetzen, G. Sala, F. Chiesa, anon, orch)

Ⓒ **90015** (4/91)
Wagner—Die Walküre, Act 1
Wagner: Walküre (exc). (M. Lorenz, M. Teschemacher, K. Böhme, Saxon St Orch/K. Elmendorff)

Ⓒ **90020**
Giuseppe Taddei sings Arias and Neapolitan Songs
Bellini: Puritani (exc); *Donizetti:* Favorita (exc); *Verdi:* Ballo in maschera (exc); Don Carlo (exc); Vespri Siciliani (exc); *Giordano:* Andrea Chénier (exc); *Cilea:* Adriana Lecouvreur (exc); Arlesiana (exc); *Mario:* Santa Lucia luntana; *Falvo:* Dicitencello vuie; *De Curtis:* Voce 'e notte; Senza nisciuno; *Tosti:* Marechiare; *Tagliaferri:* Napule canta; *V. Valente:* Passione; *Di Capua:* I' te vurria vasà; *Pennino:* Pecchè?; *Lama:* Silenzio cantatore. (G. Taddei, Naples San Carlo Op Orch/U. Rapalo, orch/G. Stellari)

Ⓒ **90022**
Anton Dermota
Mozart: Entführung (exc); Così fan tutte (exc); Zauberflöte (exc); Per pietà non ricercate, K420; *Beethoven:* Fidelio (exc); *Weber:* Freischütz (exc); *Donizetti:* Elisir d'amore (exc); *Tchaikovsky:* Eugene Onegin (exc); *Puccini:* Tosca (exc). (A. Dermota, Berlin St Op Orch, Ljubljana RSO/A. Rother/S. Hubad)

Ⓒ **90034** (12/90)
Maria Cebotari (1910-49)
Mozart: Nozze di Figaro (exc); Don Giovanni (exc); *Nicolai:* Lustigen Weiber von Windsor (exc); *J. Strauss II:* Zigeunerbaron (exc); *Gounod:* Faust (exc); *Puccini:* Bohème (exc); Madama Butterfly (exc); *R. Strauss:* Ariadne auf Naxos (exc). (M. Cebotari, M. Wittrisch, Philh, VPO, Berlin St Op Orch/J. Krips/H. von Karajan/F. Prohaska/F. Zweig)

Ⓒ **90035** (11/90)
Mozart—Le Nozze di Figaro
Mozart: Nozze di Figaro (Cpte). (P. Schoeffler, M. Cebotari, M. Ahlersmeyer, M. Teschemacher, A. Kolniak, E. Waldenau, K. Böhme, K. Wessely, H. Buchta, H.H. Fiedler, H. Franck, Stuttgart Rad Chor, Stuttgart RO/K. Böhm)

Ⓒ **90043** (6/92)
Wagner—Lohengrin, etc
Wagner: Lohengrin (Cpte); Fliegende Holländer (exc). (F. Völker, M. Müller, M. Klose, J. Prohaska, L. Hofmann, W. Grossmann, Berlin St Op Chor, Berlin St Op Orch/R. Heger, M. Müller, J. Prohaska, J. Greindl, Berlin RSO/A. Rother)

Ⓒ **90074**
Puccini—Gianni Schicchi
Puccini: Gianni Schicchi (Cpte). (G. Taddei, G. Rapisardi, G. Savio, A. Dubbini, G. del Signore, R. Ferrari, P.L. Latinucci, F. Corena, A. Albertini, L. Avogadro, F. Calabrese, Turin RAI Orch/A. Simonetto)

Ⓒ **90078** (1/95)
Hilde Konetzni
Mozart: Don Giovanni (exc); *Wagner:* Tannhäuser (exc); *Beethoven:* Fidelio (exc); *Weber:* Freischütz (exc); *Puccini:* Tosca (exc); Madama Butterfly (exc); *Smetana:* Bartered Bride (exc); *R. Strauss:* Rosenkavalier (exc); Lieder, Op.69 (exc); Lieder, Op.88 (exc); Lieder, Op.21 (exc). (H. Konetzni, Vienna SO, Berlin Deutsche Op Orch, Berlin St Op Orch, VPO, R. Strauss/H. Swarowsky/H. Schmidt-Isserstedt/H. von Karajan, M-L. Schilp)

Ⓒ **90083** (9/92)
Maria Reining
Mozart: Nozze di Figaro (exc); *Wagner:* Lohengrin (exc); Tannhäuser (exc); Meistersinger (exc); *R. Strauss:* Rosenkavalier (exc); Lieder, Op. 41 (exc); *J. Strauss II:* Fledermaus (exc); *Suppé:* Boccaccio (exc); *Lehár:* Zarewitsch (exc); Paganini (exc). (M. Reining, P. Schoeffler, VPO/J. Krips, Berlin Deutsche Op Orch/W. Lutze, Zurich Tonhalle Orch/H. Knappertsbusch, R. Strauss)

Ⓒ **90096**
Helge Roswaenge sings Verdi & Puccini
Verdi: Trovatore (exc); Ballo in maschera (exc); Ballo in maschera (exc); Vespri siciliani (exc); Aida (exc); *Puccini:* Madama Butterfly (exc); Turandot (exc); Tosca (exc). (H. Roswaenge, H. Scheppan, H. Schlusnus, M. Cebotari, H. Ranczak, H. Wrana, Berlin RSO/A. Rother/H. Steinkopf)

Ⓒ **90103**
Helge Roswaenge Recital (1959)
Mozart: Così fan tutte (exc); *Beethoven:* Fidelio (exc); *Weber:* Oberon (exc); *R. Strauss:* Rosenkavalier (exc); Lieder, Op.10 (exc); *Mascagni:* Cavalleria Rusticana (exc); *Puccini:* Fanciulla del West (exc); Tosca (exc); *Verdi:* Forza del Destino (exc); Trovatore (exc); *Bizet:* Carmen (exc); *Leoncavallo:* Pagliacci (exc). (H. Roswaenge, G. Behm, M. Abendroth, W. Stoll, H. Braun, Philh Hungarica/Z. Rozsnyai, Berlin St Op Orch/H. Löwlein)

Ⓒ **90112** (11/92)
Clemens Krauss conducts the VPO
Haydn: Symphony 88; *J. Strauss II:* Perpetuum mobile; Annen-Polka, Op. 117; Morgenblätter, Op. 279; Fledermaus (exc); Zigeunerbaron (exc); Leichtes Blut, Op. 319; Tausend und eine Nacht; *Ziehrer:* Weana Mad'ln, Op.388; *Jos Strauss:* Sphärenklänge; *J. Strauss II:* Liebeslieder, Op. 114. (VPO/C. Krauss)

Ⓒ **90116**
Knappertsbuch conducts the Vienna Philharmonic
Wagner: Rienzi (exc); Tannhäuser (exc); Götterdämmerung (exc); *Verdi:* Aida (exc); *Ziehrer:* Weana Mad'ln, Op. 388; *J. Strauss II:* Leichtes Blut, Op. 319; Pizzicato Polka. (M. Lorenz, VPO/H. Knappertsbusch)

90136
Martha Mödl sings
Verdi: Don Carlo (exc); Macbeth (exc); *Bizet:* Carmen (exc); Carmen (exc); *Wagner:* Tristan und Isolde (exc); Götterdämmerung (exc). (M. Mödl, Berlin City Op Orch/H. Löwlein/A. Rother)

90139
Vienna Philharmonic on the way to New Year's Concerts
J. Strauss II: Du und Du, Op. 367; Perpetuum mobile; Annen-Polka, Op. 117; Morgenblätter, Op. 279; Fledermaus (exc); Frühlingsstimmen, Op. 410; Tritsch-Tratsch; Blauen Donau, Op. 314; Kaiser, Op. 437; Pizzicato Polka; Leichtes Blut, Op. 319; *Ziehrer:* Weana Mad'ln, Op.388. (VPO/E. Kleiber/C. Krauss/G. Szell/B. Walter/H. Knappertsbusch)

90150 (1/94)
Lehár conducts Lehár
Lehár: Lustige Witwe Overture (exc); Eva (exc); Paganini (exc); Giuditta (exc); Musikalische Memoiren; Friederike (exc); Schön ist die Welt (exc); Zarewitsch (exc); Zigeunerliebe (exc); Wien, du bist das Herz der Welt; Giuditta (exc). (E. Réthy, M. Reining, R. Tauber, VPO, Vienna SO/F. Lehár, J. Novotná)

90151 (11/93)
Wagner—Die Walküre - Act I, etc
Wagner: Walküre (exc); Tristan und Isolde (exc). (M. Reining, F. Krauss, J. von Manowarda, Stuttgart RSO/C. Leonhardt, J. Sattler, Vienna SO/H. Weisbach)

90157 (8/94)
Beethoven/Wagner—Orchestral Works
Beethoven: Symphony 6; Leonore (exc); *Wagner:* Siegfried dyll. (VPO/B. Walter)

90164 (1/94)
Wagner—Götterdämmerung
Vagner: Götterdämmerung (Cpte). (M. Fuchs, S. Svanholm, F. Dalberg, R. Burg, E. Koch, E. Fischer, C. Kallab, H. Scheppan, I. Langhammer, M. Booth, H. Pachnow, C. Siewart, Bayreuth Fest Chor, Bayreuth Fest Orch/K. Elmendorff)

90168 (5/94)
Wagner—Die Meistersinger, Act 2, etc
Vagner: Meistersinger (exc); Fliegende Holländer (exc); Lohengrin (exc); Walküre (exc). (G. Hann, H. Noort, T. Kempf, W. Schirp, E. Kunz, K. Wessely, M-L. Schilp, H. Heinz Nissen, A. Fügel, L. Windisch, H. Florian, W. Ulbricht, E. Schneider, E. Heyer, W. Lang, A. Will, Berlin Rad Chor, Berlin RO/A. Rother, Berlin Deutsche Op Orch/H. Steinkopf)

90174 (2/94)
Wagner—Die Meistersinger von Nürnberg
Vagner: Meistersinger (Cpte). (P. Schoeffler, L. Suthaus, H. Scheppan, F. Dalberg, E. Kunz, E. Witte, C. Kallab, F. Krenn, B. Arnold, H. Fehn, G. Witting, G. Rödin, K. Krollmann, H. Gosebruch, F. Sauer, A. Dome, E. Pina, Bayreuth Fest Chor, Bayreuth Fest Orch/H. Abendroth)

90175 (5/94)
Verdi—Macbeth (complete) & Don Carlos (excerpts)
'erdi: Macbeth (Cpte); Don Carlo (exc). (M. Ahlersmeyer, . Höngen, H. Alsen, J. Witt, W. Franter, V. Madin, K. Ettl, . Boettcher, Vienna St Op Chor, Vienna St Op Orch/K. öhm, H. Konetzni, E. Höngen, G. Oeggl, A. Pernerstorfer, . Welitsch/E. Baltzer)

90189
Knappertsbusch in London and Switzerland
rahms: Symphony 2; *Wagner:* Lohengrin (exc); Lohengrin xc); Rienzi (exc); Meistersinger (exc). (Zurich Tonhalle rch, LPO, SRO/H. Knappertsbusch)

90190 (1/95)
Paul Schoeffler—Recital
lozart: Nozze di Figaro (exc); Don Giovanni (exc); auberflöte (exc); *Wagner:* Meistersinger (exc); eistersinger (exc); Meistersinger (exc); Walküre (exc); *erdi:* Otello (exc); *Schumann:* Liederkreis, Op.39 (exc); *rahms:* Lieder, Op.86 (exc); Lieder, Op.32 (exc); Lieder, p.43 (exc). (P. Schoeffler, M. Reining, E. Lush, LPO, urich Tonhalle Orch, LSO, National SO/K. Rankl/H. nappertsbusch/C. Krauss)

90195 (8/94)
Beethoven—Fidelio
eethoven: Fidelio (Cpte); *Weber:* Oberon (exc). (H. onetzni, T. Ralf, P. Schoeffler, H. Alsen, I. Seefried, P. ein, T. Neralič, H. Gallos, H. Schweiger, Vienna St Op hor, Vienna St Op Orch/K. Böhm, H. Konetzni, Vienna O/L. Ludwig)

90200
Hans Hotter in Early Recordings
arschner: Hans Heiling (exc); *Wagner:* Fliegende olländer (exc); Meistersinger (exc); Meistersinger (exc); Walküre (exc); *Verdi:* Aida (exc); Otello (exc); Falstaff (exc); *Bizet:* Carmen (exc); *Leoncavallo:* Pagliacci (exc). (H. Hotter, Berlin Deutsche Op Orch, Bavarian St Orch, Berlin Staatskapelle, Leipzig RSO/A. Rother/H. Hollreiser/R. Heger/H. Weisbach, H. Scheppan)

Ⓓ **90203**
Mozart—Le nozze di Figaro (sung in German)
Mozart: Nozze di Figaro (Cpte). (E. Kunz, I. Beilke, H. Hotter, H. Braun, G. Sommerschuh, R. Fischer, G. Neidlinger, J. Witt, W. Wernigk, F. Normann, L. Timm, Vienna St Op Chor, VPO/C. Krauss)

Ⓓ **90205** (8/95)
Strauss conducts Strauss, Vol.1
R. Strauss: Don Quixote; Heldenleben; Alpensinfonie; Japanische Festmusik; Rosenkavalier (exc). (O. Uhl, P. Haass, Bavarian St Orch/R. Strauss)

Ⓓ **90207**
Wagner—Die Walküre (Acts 2 & 3)
Wagner: Walküre (exc). (F. Krauss, M. Reining, E. Schlüter, R. Bockelmann, H. Jung, J. von Manowarda, I. Roster, T. Eipperle, P. Kapper, C. Carlsson, M. Kuhn-Liebel, M. Strack, E. Waldenau, P. Baumann, Stuttgart RSO/C. Leonhardt)

Ⓓ **90209**
Humperdinck—Hänsel und Gretel;Weber—Abu Hassan
Humperdinck: Hänsel und Gretel (Cpte); *Weber:* Abu Hassan (Cpte). (M-L. Schilp, E. Berger, E. Waldenau, H. Heinz Nissen, H. Erdmann, G. Walker, M. Arndt-Ober, E. Witte, E. Schwarzkopf, M. Bohnen, Berlin Deutsche Op Chor, chor, Berlin RSO/A. Rother/L. Ludwig)

Ⓓ **90213**
Max Lorenz sings Wagner
Wagner: Rienzi (exc); Tannhäuser (exc); Tannhäuser (exc); Tristan und Isolde (exc); Walküre (exc); Siegfried (exc); Meistersinger (exc). (M. Lorenz, H. Scheppan, M. Klose, M. Reining, K. Schmitt-Walter, G. Rödin, W. Hiller, Berlin St Op Orch, VPO, Berlin RSO/J. Schüler/R. Heger/B. Seidler-Winkler/R. Moralt/A. Rother)

Ⓓ **90217** (11/94)
R. Strauss—Ariadne auf Naxos
R. Strauss: Ariadne auf Naxos (Cpte). (M. Reining, I. Seefried, A. Noni, M. Lorenz, P. Schoeffler, E. Kunz, M. Rus, P. Klein, R. Sallaba, E. Loose, M. Frutschnigg, E. Rutgers, J. Witt, A. Muzzarelli, H. Schweiger, F. Jelinek, H. Baier, Vienna St Op Orch/K. Böhm)

Ⓓ **90222** (8/95)
Maria Cebotari sings Richard Strauss
R. Strauss: Salome (exc); Feuersnot (exc); Rosenkavalier (exc); Daphne (exc); Taillefer. (M. Cebotari, P. Buchner, T. Lemnitz, W. Ludwig, K. Schmitt-Walter, H. Hotter, R. Lamy Sngrs, Berlin RSO/A. Rother)

Ⓓ **90223**
Wagner—Rienzi (excerpts)
Wagner: Rienzi (exc); Rienzi (exc). (M. Lorenz, H. Scheppan, R. von der Linde, M. Klose, J. Prohaska, G. Rödin, W. Hiller, Berlin St Op Chor, Berlin St Op Orch/J. Schüler, Berlin RSO/A. Rother)

Ⓓ **90227**
Hilde Gueden - As The World Knew Her
Mozart: Rè pastore (exc); Idomeneo (exc); Nozze di Figaro (exc); Nozze di Figaro (exc); Zauberflöte (exc); Exsultate, jubilate, K165; *Verdi:* Rigoletto (exc); Traviata (exc); Falstaff (exc); *Puccini:* Gianni Schicchi (exc); Turandot (exc); *Lehár:* Giuditta (exc). (H. Gueden, VPO, Santa Cecilia Academy Orch, Vienna St Op Orch/A. Erede/C. Krauss/W. Loibner)

Ⓓ **90230**
Verdi—Otello
Verdi: Otello (Cpte); Otello (exc). (T. Ralf, H. Konetzni, P. Schoeffler, J. Witt, P. Klein, E. Nikolaidi, T. Neralič, V. Madin, R. Neumann, M. Lorenz, Vienna St Op Chor, Vienna St Op Orch/K. Böhm)

Ⓓ **90232**
Wagner—Der Fliegende Holländer
Wagner: Fliegende Holländer (Cpte); Meistersinger (exc); Meistersinger (exc). (J. Berglund, M. Müller, L. Hofmann, F. Völker, L. Asmus, E. Zimmermann, Bayreuth Fest CHor, Bayreuth Fest Orch/R. Kraus, L. Hofmann, Berlin St Op Orch/F.A. Schmidt, J. Berglund, Stockholm Royal Orch/N. Grevillius)

Ⓓ **90234** (6/95)
Wagner—Die Meistersinger von Nürnberg
Wagner: Meistersinger (Cpte). (P. Schoeffler, A. Seider, I. Seefried, H. Alsen, E. Kunz, P. Klein, E. Schürhoff, F. Krenn, A. Dermota, V. Madin, G. Maikl, J. Witt, W. Wernigk, A. Muzzarelli, A. Jerger, M. Rus, Vienna St Op Chor, VPO/K. Böhm)

Ⓓ **90237** (11/95)
R Strauss—Daphne
R. Strauss: Daphne (Cpte); An den Baum Daphne; Daphne (exc). (M. Reining, K. Friedrich, H. Alsen, A. Dermota, M. Frutschnigg, G. Monthy, R. Sallaba, H. Schweiger, H. Baier, E. Loose, M. Schober, Vienna St Op Chor, VPO/K. Böhm/W. Hagen-Groll, M. Teschemacher, T. Ralf, Dresden St Op Orch)

Ⓓ **90243** (9/95)
Wagner—Tristan und Isolde
Wagner: Tristan und Isolde (Cpte). (M. Lorenz, P. Buchner, M. Klose, L. Hofmann, J. Prohaska, E. Fuchs, E. Zimmermann, F. Fleischer, B. Arnold, Berlin St Op Chor, Berlin Staatskapelle/R. Heger)

Ⓓ **90249**
Mozart in tempore belli
Mozart: Entführung (exc); Don Giovanni (exc); Zauberflöte (exc). (I. Seefried, E. Loose, E. Rutgers, H. Konetzni, E. Höngen, E. Nikolaidi, A. Dermota, P. Klein, J. Witt, E. Kunz, P. Schoeffler, H. Alsen, Vienna St Op Chor, VPO/R. Moralt/K. Böhm)

Ⓓ **90250**
Wagner—Der fliegende Holländer
Wagner: Fliegende Holländer (Cpte). (H. Hotter, V. Ursuleac, G. Hann, K. Ostertag, L. Willer, F. Klarwein, Bavarian St Op Chor, Bavarian St Op Orch/C. Krauss)

Ⓓ **90251**
Beethoven—Symphony No.3, etc
Beethoven: Symphony 3; Leonore (exc). (VPO/W. Furtwängler)

Ⓓ **90254**
Mozart—Die Zauberflöte
Mozart: Zauberflöte (Cpte). (T. Eipperle, L. Piltti, W. Ludwig, K. Schmitt-Walter, J. von Manowarda, G. Hann, H. Buchta, L. Preisig, M. Martensen, E. Pfeil, Y. Hochreiter, Regensburg Cath Ch, E. Kristjansson, A. Welitsch, M. Osswald, Stuttgart Rad Chor, Stuttgart RO/J. Keilberth)

Ⓓ **93144**
Lehár—Das Land des Lächelns - excerpts
Lehár: Land des Lächelns (exc). (G. di Stefano, D. Koller, V. Goodall, H. Holecek, Vienna Volksoper Orch/H. Lambrecht)

President Records

Ⓓ **PCOM1109**
Le Maître de Musique—Original Soundtrack
Verdi: Rigoletto (exc); *Mozart:* Alcandro, lo confesso, K294; *D. Miller:* Waltz; *Mahler:* Symphony 4 (exc); Lied von der Erde (exc); *Mozart:* Don Giovanni (exc); *Wolf:* Michelangelo Gedichte (exc); *Schumann:* Myrthen, Op. 25 (exc); Gedichte, Op. 35 (exc); *Bellini:* Bianca e Fernando (exc); Bianca e Fernando (exc); *Verdi:* Traviata (exc); *Mahler:* Rückert Lieder (exc); *Schubert:* An die Musik, D547 (exc). (J. van Dam, RTBF SO/R. Zollman, D. Bryant, G. Daniel, P. Declerck, U. Gorniak, A. Leonardo/D. Miller, J. Pruett/A. Vandernoot, J-C. Vanden, J. Bakker, K. Kusaka, D. Miller)

Ⓓ **PCOM1120**
Duo Kassner-Quer—Tambor de granaderos
Chapí: El tambor de granaderos (exc); *Chueca:* Paraguas (exc); *Mozart:* Adagio, K540; Ergo interest, K143; *Penella:* Don Gil de Alcalá (exc); *Pérez-Quer:* How you awaken; *Prokofiev:* Tales of an old grandmother; *Schubert:* Impromptus (exc); *Traditional:* Bende su dunyaya; Matchkanin Yolu; Zeybek. (G. Pérez-Quer, D. Kassner)

Priory

Ⓓ **PRCD338**
The Symphonic Organ, Volume 1
Wagner: Tannhäuser (exc); *Grieg:* Peer Gynt Suites (exc); *Goldmark:* Rustic Wedding (exc); *Kodály:* Epigrams (exc); *Elgar:* Serenade (exc); *Humperdinck:* Hänsel und Gretel (exc); *Gounod:* Marche funèbre d'une marionette; *Khachaturian:* Gayaneh (exc); *Dvořák:* Carnival. (T. Murray)

Ⓓ **PRCD370** (11/92)
Great European Organs, No 26
Stanford: Fantasia and Toccata, Op. 57; *Reger:* Preludes and Fugues, Op. 56 (exc); *Shostakovich:* Lady Macbeth of Mtsensk (exc); *Schmidt:* Chaconne (1925); *Ravanello:* Theme and Variations. (K. John)

Ⓓ **PRCD479**
The Symphonic Organ, Volume 2
Elgar: Pomp and Circumstance Marches (exc); Salut d'amour; Caractacus (exc); *Tchaikovsky:* Nutcracker Suite (exc); Violin Concerto (exc); Symphony 6 (exc); *Walton:* Orb and Sceptre; Henry V Suite (exc); *Wagner:* Meistersinger (exc); Walküre (exc). (A. Partington)

Pro Arte

Ⓓ **CDD585**
The French Connection
Gossec: Tambourin; *Ravel:* Rapsodie espagnole (exc); *Fauré:* Songs, Op. 7 (exc); Pavane; Morceau de Concours (1898); Berceuse, Op. 16; *Donjon:* Offertoire; *Saint-Saëns:* Carnaval des animaux (exc); *Satie:* Gymnopédies (exc); *Gaubert:* Madrigal; *Massenet:* Thaïs (exc); *Debussy:* Children's Corner (exc); *Caplet:* Rêverie et petite valse (exc); *Bizet:* Jeux d'enfants (exc). (L. Nashman, J. Arpin)

Ⓓ **CDD597**
Pirates of Penzance (1929)
Sullivan: Pirates of Penzance (Cpte). (George Baker, P. Dawson, S. Robertson, D. Oldham, L. Sheffield, E. Griffin, N. Briercliffe, N. Walker, D. Gill, D'Oyly Carte Op Chor, SO/M. Sargent)

Ⓓ **CDD598**
H.M.S. Pinafore (1930)
Sullivan: HMS Pinafore (Cpte). (H. Lytton, B. Lewis, E. Griffin, George Baker, C. Goulding, D. Fancourt, N. Briercliffe, S. Granville, S. Robertson, D'Oyly Carte Op Chor, Orch/M. Sargent)

Ⓓ **CDS539**
Tchaikovsky Spectaculars
Tchaikovsky: Mazeppa (exc); Festival Coronation March; Romeo and Juliet; Marche slave; 1812. (Dallas SO/E. Mata)

Ⓓ **CDS580**
Tempest - The Classic Storms
Britten: Sea Interludes, Op. 33a (exc); *Berlioz:* Troyens (exc); *Rossini:* Barbiere di Siviglia (exc); *Beethoven:* Symphony 6 (exc); *J. Strauss II:* Unter Donner und Blitz; *R. Strauss:* Don Quixote (exc); *Sibelius:* Tempest Suites (exc); *Rimsky-Korsakov:* Scheherazade (exc). (Helsinki PO/S. Comissiona)

Ⓓ **CDS584**
Tchaikovsky—Waltzes
Tchaikovsky: Swan Lake (exc); Nutcracker (exc); Sleeping Beauty (exc); Serenade, Op.48 (exc); Symphony 5 (exc); Eugene Onegin (exc). (Houston SO/S. Comissiona)

Proprius

Ⓓ **PRCD9008** (10/91) ⊙ **PROP9911** (10/91)
Anne Sofie Von Otter — Recital
Handel: Hercules (exc); Giulio Cesare (exc); *Monteverdi:* Scherzi musicali (1607) (exc); Lamento d'Arianna a 1; *Roman:* Swedish Mass (exc); *Telemann:* Kanarienvogel Kantate (exc); *Handel:* Semele (exc). (A.S. von Otter, Drottningholm Baroque Ens/A. Öhrwall)

Quintana

▭ **QUI40 3008**
Transcriptions of Mozart for Wind Ensemble
Mozart: Clemenza di Tito (exc); Entführung (exc); Così fan tutte (exc); Zauberflöte (exc); Nozze di Figaro (exc); Don Giovanni (exc). (Budapest Wind Ens/K. Berkes)

Radio Nacional de Espana

Ⓓ **650004**
Opera Stars in Concert
Verdi: Vespri Siciliani (exc); *Bellini:* Puritani (exc); *Verdi:* Traviata (exc); *Offenbach:* Contes d'Hoffmann (exc); *Puccini:* Tosca (exc); *Rossini:* Semiramide (exc); *Donizetti:* Lucrezia Borgia (exc); *Verdi:* Don Carlo (exc); *Gounod:* Faust (exc); *Bizet:* Carmen suites (exc); *Donizetti:* Lucrezia Borgia (exc); Elisir d'amore (exc); *Verdi:* Rigoletto (exc); Ballo in maschera (exc); *Puccini:* Gianni Schicchi (exc); *Rossini:* Barbiere di Siviglia (exc); *Cilea:* Arlesiana (exc); *Bizet:* Carmen (exc). (R. Raimondi, P. Coni, Alfredo Kraus, K. Ricciarelli, L.V. Terrani/G.P. Sanzogno, Madrid SO)

RCA Victor

Ⓓ **GD60048** ▭ **GK60048**
Mario Lanza sings Songs from The Student Prince & The Desert Song
Brodszky: Student Prince; *Romberg:* Student Prince (exc); Desert Song (exc). (E. Doubleday, J. Raskin, M. Lanza, R. Murcell, D. Arthur, chor, orch/C. Callinicos)

Ⓓ **GD60049** ▭ **GK60049**
'The Great Caruso' and other Caruso favourites
Verdi: Rigoletto (exc); *Puccini:* Tosca (exc); *Donizetti:* Elisir d'amore (exc); *Ponchielli:* Gioconda (exc); *Leoncavallo:* Pagliacci (exc); *Califona:* Vieni sul mar; *De Curtis:* Senza nisciuno; *Gastaldon:* Musica proibita; *Donaudy:* Vaghissima sembianza; *Bracco:* Serenata; *Buzzi-Peccia:* Lolita; *Tosti:* Luna d'estate; Alba separa; Pour un baiser; Mia canzone; Ideale; *Cottrau:* Santa Lucia. (M. Lanza, RCA Victor Orch/C. Callinicos, orch/P. Baron)

Ⓓ **GD60172**
Verdi—Rigoletto
Verdi: Rigoletto (Cpte). (R. Merrill, R. Peters, J. Björling, G. Tozzi, A.M. Rota, V. Tatozzi, S. Celli, T. Frascati, A. la Porta, L. Grandi, L. Monreale, S. Chissari, A. Mineo, Rome Op Chor, Rome Op Orch/J. Perlea)

Ⓓ **GD60176** (1/90)
Prokofiev: Vocal & Orchestral Works
Prokofiev: Alexander Nevsky; Lt. Kijé Suite; *Glinka:* Ruslan and Lyudmila (exc). (R. Elias, Chicago Sym Chor, Chicago SO/F. Reiner)

Ⓓ **GD60188** ▭ **GK60188**
Rossini: Il barbiere di Siviglia highlights
Rossini: Barbiere di Siviglia (exc). (R. Merrill, R. Peters, C. Valletti, G. Tozzi, F. Corena, M. Roggero, NY Met Op Chor, NY Met Op Orch/E. Leinsdorf)

Ⓓ **GD60189** ▭ **GK60189**
Puccini: La Bohème highlights
Puccini: Bohème (exc). (A. Moffo, R. Tucker, M. Costa, R. Merrill, G. Tozzi, P. Maero, Rome Op Chor, Rome Op Orch/E. Leinsdorf)

Ⓓ **GD60190** ▭ **GK60190**
Bizet: Carmen highlights
Bizet: Carmen (exc). (L. Price, F. Corelli, R. Merrill, M. Freni, M. Linval, G. Macaux, Vienna St Op Chor, VPO/H. von Karajan)

Ⓓ **GD60192** ▭ **GK60192**
Puccini: Tosca highlights
Puccini: Tosca (exc). (Z. Milanov, J. Björling, L. Warren, Rome Op Chor, Rome Op Orch/E. Leinsdorf)

Ⓓ **GD60203** ▭ **GK60203**
Verdi: Rigoletto highlights
Verdi: Rigoletto (exc). (R. Merrill, A. Moffo, Alfredo Kraus, R. Elias, E. Flagello, RCA Italiana Op Chor, RCA Italiana Op Orch/G. Solti)

Ⓓ **GD60205**
Opera Choruses
Verdi: Aida (exc); *Gounod:* Faust (exc); *Verdi:* Nabucco (exc); *Berlioz:* Damnation de Faust (exc); *Bizet:* Carmen (exc); *Verdi:* Trovatore (exc); Rigoletto (exc); Traviata (exc); *Wagner:* Lohengrin (exc); *J. Strauss II:* Fledermaus (exc); *A. Thomas:* Mignon (exc); *Mascagni:* Cavalleria Rusticana (exc); *Puccini:* Madama Butterfly (exc). (John Alldis Ch, LSO/E. Leinsdorf, R. Shaw Chorale, RCA Victor Orch/R. Cellini, Harvard Glee Club, Radcliffe Choral Soc, Boston SO/C. Munch, L. Price, M. Linval, G. Macaux, Vienna St Op Chor, VPO/H. von Karajan, D. Krebill, T. Jamerson, H. Enns, RCA Italiana Op Chor, RCA Italiana Op Orch/G. Solti/G. Prêtre, Rome Op Chor, Rome Op Orch, D. Poleri, M. Singher, Vienna Boys' Ch/Robert Shaw)

Ⓓ **GD60251**
Verdi: Falstaff
Verdi: Falstaff (Cpte). (G. Valdengo, F. Guarrera, H. Nelli, T. Stich-Randall, A. Madasi, C. Elmo, N. Merriman, G. Carelli, J.C. Rossi, N. Scott, R. Shaw Chorale, NBC SO/A. Toscanini)

Ⓓ **GD60255**
Beethoven: Orchestral Works
Beethoven: Symphony 5; Symphony 8; Leonore (exc). (NBC SO/A. Toscanini)

Ⓓ **GD60264** (12/91)
Wagner—Opera excerpts
Wagner: Walküre (exc); Walküre (exc); Siegfried Idyll; Tristan und Isolde (exc). (H. Traubel, L. Melchior, NBC SO/A. Toscanini)

Ⓓ **GD60267** (11/92)
Toscanini Collection, Vol.45
Beethoven: Leonore (exc); Consecration of the House Ov; Coriolan; Egmont (exc); Prometheus (exc); Leonore (exc); String Quartet 16 (exc). (NBC SO/A. Toscanini)

Ⓓ **GD60273** (10/92)
Toscanini Collection - Beethoven
Beethoven: Fidelio (Cpte). (R. Bampton, J. Peerce, H. Janssen, S. Belarsky, E. Steber, J. Laderoute, N. Moscona, Chor, NBC SO/A. Toscanini)

Ⓓ **GD60274**
Berlioz—Roméo et Juliette/Bizet—Suites
Berlioz: Roméo et Juliette (Cpte); *Bizet:* Arlésienne Suites (exc); Carmen (exc). (G. Swarthout, J. Garris, N. Moscona, chor, NBC SO/A. Toscanini)

Ⓓ **GD60276** (6/91)
Toscanini conducts Boito & Verdi
Boito: Mefistofele (exc); *Verdi:* Rigoletto (exc); Lombardi (exc). (N. Moscona, Z. Milanov, N. Merriman, J. Peerce, L. Warren, Columbus Boychoir, R. Shaw Chorale, V. della Chiesa, NBC SO/A. Toscanini)

Ⓓ **GD60278**
Cherubini/Cimarosa—Orchestral Works
Cherubini: Symphony in D; Ali-Baba (exc); Anacréon (exc); Medea (exc); *Cimarosa:* Matrimonio segreto (exc); Matrimonio per raggiro (exc). (NBC SO/A. Toscanini)

Ⓓ **GD60279** (1/91)
Toscanini Collection, Vol.24
Dvořák: Symphony 9; *Kodály:* Háry János Suite; *Smetana:* Má Vlast (exc). (NBC SO/A. Toscanini)

Ⓓ **GD60280**
Toscanini Collection
Gluck: Iphigénie en Aulide (exc); Orfeo ed Euridice (exc); Orfeo ed Euridice (exc); *Beethoven:* Fidelio (exc). (N. Merriman, B. Gibson, R. Bampton, R. Shaw Chorale, NBC SO/A. Toscanini)

Ⓓ **GD60286**
Toscanini Collection - Mozart
Mozart: Nozze di Figaro (exc); Symphony 35; Bassoon Concerto, K191; Divertimento, K287. (L. Sharrow, NBC SO/A. Toscanini)

Ⓓ **GD60288** (9/91)
Puccini—La Bohème
Puccini: Bohème (Cpte). (L. Albanese, J. Peerce, A. McKnight, F. Valentino, G. Cehanovsky, N. Moscona, S. Baccaloni, Chor, NBC SO/A. Toscanini)

Ⓓ **GD60289** (11/92)
Toscanini Collection - Rossini Overtures
Rossini: Italiana in Algeri (exc); Signor Bruschino (exc); Barbiere di Siviglia (exc); Cenerentola (exc); Gazza ladra (exc); Siège de Corinthe (exc); Semiramide (exc); Guillaume Tell (exc). (NBC SO/A. Toscanini)

Ⓓ **GD60292**
Schumann/Weber—Orchestral Works
Schumann: Symphony 3; Manfred (exc); *Weber:* Euryanthe (exc); Freischütz (exc); Oberon (exc). (NBC SO/A. Toscanini)

Ⓓ **GD60296** (11/92)
Toscanini Collection, Vol.31
R. Strauss: Don Juan; Till Eulenspiegel; Salome (exc); *Wagner:* Götterdämmerung (exc); Siegfried Idyll. (NBC SO/A. Toscanini)

Ⓓ **GD60299**
Verdi: Requiem, etc
Verdi: Requiem (Cpte); Pezzi sacri (exc); Nabucco (exc); Luisa Miller (exc); Inno delle Nazioni. (H. Nelli, F. Barbieri, G. di Stefano, C. Siepi, R. Shaw Chorale, Westminster Ch, J. Peerce, NBC SO/A. Toscanini)

Ⓓ **GD60300**
Verdi: Aida
Verdi: Aida (Cpte). (H. Nelli, E. Gustavson, R. Tucker, G. Valdengo, N. Scott, D. Harbour, V. Assandri, T. Stich-Randall, R. Shaw Chorale, NBC SO/A. Toscanini)

Ⓓ **GD60301** (7/91)
Verdi—Un ballo in maschera
Verdi: Ballo in maschera (Cpte). (H. Nelli, J. Peerce, R. Merrill, V. Haskins, C. Turner, N. Moscona, N. Scott, G. Cehanovsky, J.C. Rossi, R. Shaw Chorale, NBC SO/A. Toscanini)

Ⓓ **GD60302** (3/92)
Verdi—Otello
Verdi: Otello (Cpte). (R. Vinay, H. Nelli, G. Valdengo, V. Assandri, L. Chabay, N. Merriman, N. Moscona, A. Newman, Chor, NBC SO/A. Toscanini)

Ⓓ **GD60303** (4/92)
Verdi—La Traviata
Verdi: Traviata (Cpte). (L. Albanese, J. Peerce, R. Merrill, M. Stellman, J. Moreland, J. Garris, G. Cehanovsky, P. Dennis, A. Newman, Chor, NBC SO/A. Toscanini)

Ⓓ **GD60304**
Toscanini Collection - Wagner
Wagner: Siegfried (exc); Götterdämmerung (exc); Götterdämmerung (exc); Götterdämmerung (exc). (H. Traubel, L. Melchior, NBC SO/A. Toscanini)

Ⓓ **GD60305** (11/92)
Toscanini Collection - Wagner
Wagner: Lohengrin (exc); Meistersinger (exc); Meistersinger (exc); Parsifal (exc); Faust Overture. (NBC SO/A. Toscanini)

Ⓓ **GD60306**
Wagner—Orchestral Works
Wagner: Tannhäuser (exc); Lohengrin (exc); Tristan und Isolde (exc); Walküre (exc); Götterdämmerung (exc); Götterdämmerung (exc). (NBC SO/A. Toscanini)

Ⓓ **GD60308** (1/91)
Toscanini Collection, Vol.40
Waldteufel: Patineurs; *L. Mozart:* Cassation in G; *J. Strauss II:* Tritsch-tratsch; Blauen Donau, Op. 314; *Suppé:* Dichter und Bauer (exc); *Ponchielli:* Gioconda (exc); *Paganini:* Moto perpetuo, Op. 11; *Bach:* Suites, BWV1066-9 (exc); *Weber:* Invitation to the Dance; *Glinka:* Jota aragonesa. (NBC SO/A. Toscanini)

Ⓓ **GD60310**
Various Overtures and Preludes
Hérold: Zampa (exc); *Humperdinck:* Hänsel und Gretel (exc); *Kabalevsky:* Colas Breugnon (exc); *Mozart:* Zauberflöte (exc); *Rossini:* Guillaume Tell (exc); *Smetana:* Bartered Bride (exc); *A. Thomas:* Mignon (exc); *Verdi:* Forza del destino (exc); *Weber:* Freischütz (exc). (NBC SO/A. Toscanini)

Ⓓ **GD60315** (11/92)
Toscanini Collection, Vol.71
Beethoven: Symphony 1 (exc); Symphony 5 (exc); *Berlioz:* Damnation de Faust (exc); *Bizet:* Arlésienne Suites (exc); Carmen Suites (exc); *Donizetti:* Don Pasquale (exc); *Respighi:* Ancient Airs and Dances (exc); *Massenet:* Scènes pittoresques (exc); *Mendelssohn:* Midsummer Night's Dream (exc); *Mozart:* Symphony 39 (exc); *Pizzetti:* Pisanelle (exc); *Wolf-Ferrari:* Segreto di Susanna (exc). (La Scala Orch/A. Toscanini)

Ⓓ **GD60318** (11/92)
Toscanini Collection, Vol.66
Gluck: Orfeo ed Euridice (exc); *Rossini:* Barbiere di Siviglia (exc); Italiana in Algeri (exc); Semiramide (exc); *Verdi:* Traviata (exc); *Wagner:* Götterdämmerung (exc); Lohengrin (exc). (NYPSO, NYPO/A. Toscanini)

Ⓓ **GD60322** (11/92)
Toscanini Collection, Vol.39
Ravel: Daphnis et Chloé Suites (exc); *Franck:* Psyché (exc); *Dukas:* Apprenti Sorcier; *Saint-Saëns:* Danse Macabre; *Berlioz:* Carnaval Romain; Roméo et Juliette (exc); Damnation de Faust (exc); *A. Thomas:* Mignon (exc). (NBC SO/A. Toscanini)

Ⓓ **GD60324** (5/90)
Beethoven—Complete Symphonies
Beethoven: Symphony 1; Symphony 2; Symphony 3; Symphony 4; Symphony 5; Symphony 6; Symphony 7; Symphony 8; Symphony 9; Leonore (exc). (E. Farrell, N. Merriman, J. Peerce, N. Scott, R. Shaw Chorale, NBC SO/A. Toscanini)

Ⓓ **GD60326** (5/90)
Verdi—Operas & Choral Works
Verdi: Aida (Cpte); Falstaff (Cpte); Pezzi sacri (exc); Requiem (Cpte); Nabucco (exc); Luisa Miller (exc); Inno delle Nazioni. (H. Nelli, E. Gustavson, R. Tucker, G. Valdengo, N. Scott, D. Harbour, V. Assandri, T. Stich-Randall, R. Shaw Chorale, G. Valdengo, F. Guarrera, H. Nelli, T. Stich-Randall, A. Madasi, C. Elmo, N. Merriman, G. Carelli, J.C. Rossi, N. Scott, H. Nelli, F. Barbieri, G. di Stefano, C. Siepi, Westminster Ch, J. Peerce, NBC SO/A. Toscanini)

Ⓓ **GD60387** (9/90)
Rossini—Overtures
Rossini: Guillaume Tell (exc); Scala di seta (exc); Signor Bruschino (exc); Barbiere di Siviglia (exc); Gazza ladra (exc); Cenerentola (exc). (Chicago SO/F. Reiner)

Ⓓ **GD60398** (8/90)
Leontyne Price sings Strauss arias
R. Strauss: Frau ohne Schatten (exc); Rosenkavalier (exc); Guntram (exc); Ariadne auf Naxos (exc); Salome (exc); Aegyptische Helena (exc). (L. Price, New Philh, Boston SO/E. Leinsdorf, LSO/F. Cleva)

Ⓓ **GD60459** (9/90)
Puccini: La Rondine
Puccini: Rondine (Cpte). (A. Moffo, D. Barioni, G. Sciutti, P. de Palma, M. Sereni, S. Brigham-Dimiziani, V. de Notaristefani, F. Mattiucci, M. Basiola II, F. Iacopucci, R. El Hage, RCA Italiana Op Chor, RCA Italiana Op Orch/F. Molinari-Pradelli)

GD60495(1) (7/91)
The Complete Caruso Collection (pt 1)
Franchetti: Germania (exc); *Verdi:* Rigoletto (exc); Aida (exc); *Massenet:* Manon (exc); *Donizetti:* Elisir d'amore (exc); *Boito:* Mefistofele (exc); *Puccini:* Tosca (exc); *Mascagni:* Iris (exc); *Giordano:* Fedora (exc); *Ponchielli:* Gioconda (exc); *Leoncavallo:* Pagliacci (exc); *Mascagni:* Cavalleria rusticana (exc); *Denza:* Non t'amo più; *Tosti:* Mia canzone; *Cilea:* Adriana Lecouvreur (exc); *Zardo:* Luna fedel; *Trimarchi:* Bacio ancora; *Zardo:* Luna fedel; *Donizetti:* Elisir d'amore (exc); *Puccini:* Tosca (exc); *Franchetti:* Germania (exc); *Verdi:* Rigoletto (exc); *Mascagni:* Cavalleria rusticana (exc); *Pini-Corsi:* Tu non mi vuoi più ben; *Puccini:* Tosca (exc); *Meyerbeer:* Huguenots (exc); *Verdi:* Rigoletto (exc); *Donizetti:* Elisir d'amore (exc); *Verdi:* Aida (exc); *Puccini:* Tosca (exc); *Mascagni:* Cavalleria rusticana (exc); *Leoncavallo:* Pagliacci (exc); *Massenet:* Manon (exc); *Leoncavallo:* Mattinata; *Bizet:* Pêcheurs de perles (exc); *Donizetti:* Don Pasquale (exc); *Bizet:* Carmen (exc); *Meyerbeer:* Huguenots (exc); *Ponchielli:* Gioconda (exc); *Mascagni:* Cavalleria rusticana (exc). (E. Caruso, anon, S. Cottone, U. Giordano, F. Cilea, R. Leoncavallo)

Ⓓ **GD60495(2)** (7/91)
The Complete Caruso Collection (pt 2)
Flotow: Martha (exc); *Puccini:* Bohème (exc); *Gounod:* Faust (exc); *Verdi:* Trovatore (exc); *Donizetti:* Favorita (exc); *Verdi:* Forza del destino (exc); Aida (exc); *Barthélemy:* Triste ritorno; *Tosti:* Ideale; *Meyerbeer:* Africaine (exc); *Verdi:* Rigoletto (exc); *Puccini:* Bohème (exc); *Giordano:* Andrea Chénier (exc); *Leoncavallo:* Pagliacci (exc); *Puccini:* Bohème (exc); *Bizet:* Pêcheurs de perles (exc); *Donizetti:* Dom Sébastien (exc); *Barthélemy:* Adorables tourments; *Donizetti:* Lucia di Lammermoor (exc); *Verdi:* Rigoletto (exc); *Puccini:* Bohème (exc); Madama Butterfly (exc); *Buzzi-Peccia:* Lolita; *Verdi:* Rigoletto (exc). (E. Caruso, A. Scotti, B. Abott, L. Homer, N. Melba, M. Ancona, M. Sembrich, G. Severina, F. Daddi, M. Journet, G. Farrar, G. Ciaparelli-Viafora, orch/W.B. Rogers)

Ⓓ **GD60495(3)** (7/91)
The Complete Caruso Collection (pt 3)
Verdi: Trovatore (exc); Trovatore (exc); Aida (exc); *Tosti:* Pour un baiser; *Puccini:* Tosca (exc); *Nutile:* Mamma mia, che vo' sapè; *Verdi:* Forza del destino (exc); Aida (exc); *Goldmark:* Königin von Saba (exc); *Bizet:* Carmen (exc); *Meyerbeer:* Huguenots (exc); *Verdi:* Trovatore (exc); Trovatore (exc); *Flotow:* Martha (exc); *Gounod:* Faust (exc); *Franchetti:* Germania (exc); *Ponchielli:* Gioconda (exc); *Puccini:* Madama Butterfly (exc); *Geehl:* For you alone; *Verdi:* Otello (exc); *Mascagni:* Cavalleria Rusticana (exc); *Leoncavallo:* Pagliacci (exc); *Tosti:* Addio; *Verdi:* Trovatore (exc). (E. Caruso, A. Scotti, L. Homer, M. Journet, G. Farrar, J. Gadski, F. Alda, G. Lejeune-Gilibert, NY Met Op Chor, orch/W.B. Rogers, F. Lapitino)

Ⓓ **GD60495(4)** (7/91)
The Complete Caruso Collection (pt 4)
Verdi: Aida (exc); Ballo in maschera (exc); *Leoncavallo:* Bohème (exc); *A. Mascheroni:* Eternamente; *Cardillo:* Core 'ngrato; *Gomes:* Schiavo (exc); *De Curtis:* Canta pe'me; *Donizetti:* Elisir d'amore (exc); *Verdi:* Forza del destino (exc); *C. G. Gardner:* Love is mine; *Verdi:* Aida (exc); Ballo in maschera (exc); *Massenet:* Manon (exc); *Faure:* Crucifix; *Verdi:* Lombardi (exc); *Flotow:* Martha (exc); *Crescenzo:* Tarantella sincera; *Donizetti:* Lucia di Lammermoor (exc); *Rossini:* Soirées musicales (exc); *Verdi:* Rigoletto (exc); *Caruso:* Dreams of Long Ago; *Sullivan:* Lost Chord; *Hardelot:* Because; *Granier:* Hosanna; *Massenet:* Manon (exc); *Puccini:* Bohème (exc); *Verdi:* Don Carlo (exc); Trovatore (exc); *Tchaikovsky:* Songs, Op. 38 (exc); *Verdi:* Rigoletto (exc); *Bizet:* Agnus Dei; *Puccini:* Manon Lescaut (exc); *Kahn:* Ave Maria; *Massenet:* Élégie; *Leoncavallo:* Lasciati amar; *Crescenzo:* Guardanno 'a luna; *O'Hara:* Your eyes have told me; *Cottrau:* Fenesta che lucive; *Rossini:* Stabat Mater (exc); *Faure:* Rameaux; *Mascagni:* Cavalleria rusticana (exc). (E. Caruso, L. Homer, P. Amato, M. Journet, F. Alda, J. Jacoby, L. Tetrazzini, A. Bada, G. Farrar, A. Scotti, E. Schumann-Heink, G. Scognamiglio, M. Elman, P. Kahn, orch/G. Scognamiglio/W.B. Rogers, NY Met Op Chor)

Ⓓ **GD60495(5)** (7/91)
The Complete Caruso Collection (pt 5)
Verdi: Otello (exc); *Tchaikovsky:* Songs, Op. 38 (exc); *Ricciardi:* Amor mio; *V. Valente:* Manella mia; *C.G. Gardner:* Trusting eyes; *Ronald:* Sérénade espagnole; *Tosti:* Parted!; *Verdi:* Ballo in maschera (exc); *Alvarez:* Partida; *Chapí:* Milagro de la Virgen (exc); *Verdi:* Traviata (exc); *Gomes:* Guarany (exc); *Szulc:* Hantise d'amour; *Bizet:* Carmen (exc); *Tosti:* Mia canzone; *Ciociano:* Cielo turchino; *Pennino:* Pecchè?; *Verdi:* Requiem (exc); *Donizetti:* Duca d'Alba (exc); *Denza:* Si vous l'aviez compris; *Leoncavallo:* Sérénade française; *Franck:* Procession; *Massenet:* Cid (exc); *Tosti:* Luna d'estate; *Di Capua:* 'O sole mio; *Gounod:* Reine de Saba (exc); *Rotoli:* Mia sposa sarà la mia bandiera; *Verdi:* Macbeth (exc); *Puccini:* Bohème (exc); *Adam:* Minuit, Chrétiens (exc); *Faure:* Sancta Maria; *Caruso:* Tiempo antico; *Cottrau:* Santa Lucia; *Tchaikovsky:* Songs, Op. 6 (exc); Eugene Onegin (exc); *Godard:* Chanson de juin; *Giordano:* Andrea Chénier (exc); *Saint-Saëns:* Samson et Dalila (exc); *Bizet:* Pêcheurs de perles (exc). (E. Caruso, T. Ruffo, F. Hempel, L. Rothier, A. de Segurola, M. Duchêne, A. Gluck, E. Destinn, F. Alda, NY Met Op Chor, NY Met Op Orch, orch/W.B. Rogers/G. Scognamiglio, G. Scognamiglio, F. Lapitino, M. Elman/J. Pasternack)

Ⓓ **GD60495(6)** (7/91)
The Complete Caruso Collection (pt 6)
Verdi: Rigoletto (exc); Rigoletto (exc); *Donizetti:* Lucia di Lammermoor (exc); *Flotow:* Martha (exc); *Gastaldon:* Musica proibita; *Crescenzo:* Uocchie celeste; *Tosti:* Alba separa; *Rubinstein:* Nero (exc); *Anton y Michelena:* A la luz de la luna; *P.M. Costa:* Sei morta nella vita mia; *Alvarez:* Partida; *Verdi:* Forza del destino (exc); *Cohan:* Over there; *Niedermeyer:* Pietà, Signore; *Alvarez:* A Granada; *Billi:* Campane a sera; *Olivieri:* Inno di Garibaldi; *Arona:* Campana di San Giusto; *Planquette:* Régiment de Sambre et Meuse; *Fucito:* Sultano a Tte; *Saint-Saëns:* Samson et Dalila (exc); *Donizetti:* Elisir d'amore (exc); *Tosti:* 'A Vucchella; *Califona:* Vieni sul mar; *De Curtis:* Tu ca nun chiagne; *Cottrau:* Addio a Napoli; *Pergolesi:* Tre giorni son che Nina; *Crescenzo:* Première caresse; *De Curtis:* Senza nisciuno; *Gomes:* Salvator Rosa (exc); *Bracco:* Serenata; *Fucito:* Scordame; *Secchi:* Love me or not; *Handel:* Serse (exc); *Posadas:* Noche feliz; *Halévy:* Juive (exc); *Gioè:* I' m'arricordo 'e Napule; *Donaudy:* Vaghissima sembianza; *Meyerbeer:* Africaine (exc); *Lully:* Amadis (exc); *Bartlett:* Dream; *Rossini:* Petite messe solennelle (exc). (E. Caruso, A. Galli-Curci, F. Perini, G. De Luca, M. Egener, A. Bada, M. Journet, E. de Gogorza, L. Homer, orch, V. Bellezza/J. Pasternack)

Ⓓ **GD60516**
Mario Lanza—For the first time
Leoncavallo: Pagliacci (exc); *Verdi:* Otello (exc); Aida (exc); Aida (exc); *Puccini:* Bohème (exc); *Taccani:* Come prima; *Stoll:* Tarantella; *Di Capua:* O sole mio; *Stoll:* Neapolitan Dance; *Bette:* Hofbrauhaus Song; *Asso:* O mon amour; *Stoll:* Mazurka; Pineapple pickers; *Grieg:* Melodies of the Heart, Op. 5 (exc); *Schubert:* Ave Maria, D839; *Kaper:* I know, I know, I know; *Nutile:* Mamma mia, che vo' sapè; *Kern:* Girl from Utah (exc); *Cardillo:* Core 'ngrato. (M. Lanza, orch/C. Savina, J. Rediske Band/G. Stoll, Rome Op Orch/C. Callinicos, RCA Victor Orch/R. Sinatra, chor)

Ⓓ **GD60522** (9/92)
Alexander Kipnis—Opera & Song Recital
Mussorgsky: Boris Godunov (exc); Song of the flea; *Borodin:* Prince Igor (exc); *Rimsky-Korsakov:* Sadko (exc); *Tchaikovsky:* Eugene Onegin (exc); *Dargomïzhsky:* Rusalka (exc); *Grechaninov:* Lullaby, Op.1/5; My native land; *Rachmaninov:* Songs, Op.4 (exc); *Stravinsky:* Stories for Children (exc). (A. Kipnis, C. Dougherty, A. Leskaya, I. Tamarin, Victor Chorale, Victor SO/N. Berezowski)

Ⓓ **GD60573** (10/91)
Puccini: Manon Lescaut
Puccini: Manon Lescaut (Cpte). (L. Albanese, J. Björling, R. Merrill, F. Calabrese, Mario Carlin, A.M. Rota, E. Campi, Rome Op Chor, Rome Op Orch/J. Perlea)

Ⓓ **GD60682**
Brahms—Symphony No.2/Tragic Overture
Brahms: Symphony 2; Tragic Overture; *Schumann:* Genoveva (exc). (Boston SO/C. Munch)

Ⓓ **GD60686**
Wagner—Opera Excerpts
Wagner: Tannhäuser (exc); Walküre (exc); Götterdämmerung (exc); Tristan und Isolde (exc). (E. Farrell, Boston SO/C. Munch)

Ⓓ **GD60700**
Fiedler's Favourite Marches
Verdi: Aida (exc); *Herbert:* Babes in Toyland (exc); *Sousa:* Semper fidelis; Stars and Stripes forever; *Tchaikovsky:* Suite 1 (exc); *Berlioz:* Damnation de Faust (exc); *Ippolitov-Ivanov:* Caucasian Sketches (exc); *Beethoven:* Ruinen von Athen (exc); *Alford:* Colonel Bogey; *J. Strauss I:* Radetzky March; *Elgar:* Pomp and Circumstance Marches (exc); *Saint-Saëns:* Suite algérienne (exc); *Rimsky-Korsakov:* Mlada (exc); *Hanssen:* Valdres March; *Bagley:* National Emblem; *Gould:* American Salute; *Traditional:* Yankee Doodle; *Morse:* Up the Street; *Planquette:* Sambre-et-Meuse; *Gershwin:* Strike up the Band II (exc); *Emmett:* Dixie. (Boston Pops/A. Fiedler)

Ⓓ **GD60720** ▭ **GK60720**
Mario Lanza—Be my love
Brodszky: Toast of New Orleans (exc); *Romberg:* Student Prince (exc); *N. Brown:* Going Hollywood (exc); *Romberg:* New Moon (exc); *Rodgers:* Spring is here (exc); *Youmans:* Great Day (exc); *Fain:* Right This Way (exc); *Traditional:* Londonderry air; *Olcott:* Romance of Athlone (exc); *Forrest/Wright:* Kismet (exc); *Hardelot:* Because; *Friml:* Vagabond King (exc); *Denza:* Funiculì-funiculà; *De Curtis:* Torna a Surriento; *Di Capua:* Maria, marì; O sole mio; *Anon:* Neapolitan Love Song; *Rascel:* Arrivederci, Roma; *Herbert:* Naughty Marietta (exc); *Kern:* Sally (exc); *Alstyne:* Memories; *Kern:* Music in the Air (exc); *Schubert:* Ave Maria, D839; *Rodgers:* Carousel (exc). (M. Lanza, orch/R. Sinatra/I. Aaronson, J. Alexander Ch, chor/E. Morricone/C. Savina/H. René/C. Callinicos)

Ⓓ **GD60818** (5/92)
Great Operatic Duets
Rossini: Semiramide (exc); *Donizetti:* Anna Bolena (exc); *Bellini:* Norma (exc); *Offenbach:* Contes d'Hoffmann (exc); *Verdi:* Aida (exc); *Puccini:* Madama Butterfly (exc); *Ponchielli:* Gioconda (exc). (M. Caballé, S. Verrett, Ambrosian Op Chor, New Philh/A. Guadagno)

Ⓓ **GD60865**
Leoncavallo—Pagliacci/Puccini—Tabarro
Leoncavallo: Pagliacci (Cpte); *Puccini:* Tabarro (Cpte). (P. Domingo, M. Caballé, S. Milnes, B. McDaniel, L. Goeke, John Alldis Ch, LSO/N. Santi, S. Milnes, L. Price, P. Domingo, P. de Palma, R. El Hage, O. Dominguez, New Philh/E. Leinsdorf)

Ⓓ **GD60866** ▭ **GK60866**
The Placido Domingo Album
Mozart: Don Giovanni (exc); *Flotow:* Martha (exc); *Gounod:* Faust (exc); Roméo et Juliette (exc); *Bizet:* Carmen (exc); *Wagner:* Lohengrin (exc); *Donizetti:* Elisir d'amore (exc); *Puccini:* Bohème (exc); Tosca (exc); Tosca (exc); Turandot (exc); *Leoncavallo:* Pagliacci (exc); *Giordano:* Andrea Chénier (exc); *Mascagni:* Cavalleria rusticana (exc); *Tchaikovsky:* Eugene Onegin (exc); *Verdi:* Trovatore (exc); Traviata (exc); Rigoletto (exc); Rigoletto (exc); Rigoletto (exc); Luisa Miller (exc); Simon Boccanegra (exc); Ballo in maschera (exc); Vespri siciliani (exc); Aida (exc); Don Carlo (exc); Otello (exc); Otello (exc); Forza del destino (exc). (P. Domingo, P. Plishka, G. Psaros, John Alldis Ch, L. Price, S. Milnes, K. Ricciarelli, RPO, LSO, New Philh, LPO, National PO, Santa Cecilia Academy Orch/E. Downes/N. Santi/S. Milnes/G. Solti/Z. Mehta/James Levine/E. Leinsdorf/A. Guadagno/G. Gavazzeni)

Ⓓ **GD60874** (5/93)
R. Strauss—Scenes from Elektra & Salome
R. Strauss: Elektra (exc); Salome (exc); Salome (exc). (I. Borkh, P. Schoeffler, F. Yeend, Chicago Lyric Op Chor, Chicago SO/F. Reiner)

Ⓓ **GD60889(1)**
The Mario Lanza Collection
Brodszky: Toast of New Orleans (exc); Because you're mine (exc); Student Prince (exc); *Romberg:* Student Prince (exc); *Aaronson:* Loveliest night of the year; *Verdi:* Rigoletto (exc); *Hardelot:* Because; *Geehl:* For you alone; *Rodgers:* Carousel (exc); *Lehár:* Land des Lächelns (exc); *Schertzinger:* One Night of Love (exc); *Van Alstyne:* Sing a Jingle (exc); *Rodgers:* Spring is here (exc); *Callinicos:* You are my love; *Kauderer:* Call me fool; *Kern:* Very Warm for May (exc); *Beelby:* My Song, My Love; *Noble:* Say it with Music (exc); *Romberg:* Maytime (exc); *Lara:* Granada; *Buzzi-Peccia:* Lolita; *Drigo:* Arlekinda (exc); *N. Brown:* Going Hollywood (exc); *Rózsa:* Quo Vadis (exc); *T. Evans:* Lady of Spain; *Taylor:* Lord don't play favourites (exc); *Malotte:* Lord's Prayer; *Levin:* And here you are; *Moya:* Song of Songs; *A. Tate:* Somewhere a voice is calling; *Fiorito:* I never knew; *Pestalozzi:* Ciribiribin; *Brodszky:* Rich, Young and Pretty (exc); *Di Capua:* 'O sole mio; *Rodgers:* South Pacific (exc); *J. Green:* Raintree Country (exc); *B. Merrill:* If you were mine; *Reed:* Behold!; *De Paul:* Li'l Abner (exc); *Verdi:* Traviata (exc); *Kalmanoff:* Night to Remember. (E. Doubleday, E. Malbin, M. Lanza, J. Alexander Ch, orch, RCA Victor Orch/R. Sinatra/C. Callinicos/H. René/C. Savina, C. Callinicos)

Ⓓ **GD60889(2)**
The Mario Lanza Collection
Romberg: New Moon (exc); Desert Song (exc); *Verdi:* Aida (exc); *Bizet:* Carmen (exc); *Verdi:* Rigoletto (exc); *Leoncavallo:* Pagliacci (exc); *Mascagni:* Cavalleria Rusticana (exc); *Liebert:* Come dance with me; *Rascel:* Arrivederci Roma; *Raye:* Do you wonder. (M. Lanza, orch, RCA Victor Orch/C. Callinicos, C. Callinicos, E. Malbin, J. Alexander Ch)

Ⓓ **GD60923** (3/93)
Legendary Performers - Paderewski
Beethoven: Piano Sonata 14; *Chopin:* Etudes (exc); Etudes (exc); Piano Sonata 2 (exc); *Schumann:* Nachtstücke (exc); *Liszt:* Paganini Studies, S140 (exc); *Chopin:* Nocturnes (exc); *Wagner:* Tristan und Isolde (exc); *Chopin:* Polonaises (exc); *Liszt:* Hungarian Rhapsodies, S244 (exc); *Rachmaninov:* Preludes (exc); *J. Strauss II:* Man lebt nur einmal, Op. 167; *Paderewski:* Humoresques de Concert, Op.14 (exc). (I. Paderewski)

Ⓓ **GD60924**
James Galway - Man with the Golden Flute
Dinicu: Hora Staccato; *Drigo:* Arlekinda (exc); *Paganini:* Moto perpetuo, Op.11; *Bach:* Suites, BWV1066-9 (exc); *Miyagi:* Haru no umi; *Godard:* Suite, Op.116 (exc); *Rimsky-Korsakov:* Tale of Tsar Saltan (exc); *Saint-Saëns:* Ascanio (exc); *Chopin:* Waltzes (exc); *Gluck:* Orfeo ed Euridice (exc); *Doppler:* Fantaisie, Op. 26. (J. Galway, National PO/C. Gerhardt)

Ⓓ **GD60941** (11/92)
Rarities - Montserrat Caballé
Rossini: Donna del Lago (exc); Otello (exc); Stabat mater (exc); Armida (exc); Tancredi (exc); Siège de Corinthe (exc); *Donizetti:* Belisario (exc); Parisina d'Este (exc); Torquato Tasso (exc); Gemma di Vergy (exc); *Verdi:* Giorno di regno (exc); Lombardi (exc); Due Foscari (exc); Alzira (exc); Attila (exc); Corsaro (exc); Aroldo (exc). (M. Caballé, M. Elkins, C. Vozza, M. Sunara, E. Mauro, L. Kozma, T. McDonnell, RCA Italiana Op Chor, Ambrosian Op Chor, RCA Italiana Op Orch, LSO/C.F. Cillario/A. Guadagno)

Ⓓ **GD61175**
The Glory of the Human Voice-Florence Foster Jenkins
Mozart: Zauberflöte (exc); *Liadov:* Musical snuff-box, Op. 32; *McMoon:* Like a bird; *Delibes:* Lakmé (exc); *McMoon:* Serenata mexicano; *F. David:* Perle du Brésil (exc); *Pavlovich:* Biassy; *J. Strauss II:* Fledermaus (exc); *Gounod:* Faust (exc). (F. Foster-Jenkins, C. McMoon, Jenny Williams, T. Burns)

Ⓓ **GD81969** (11/88)
Verdi—Otello
Verdi: Otello (Cpte). (J. Vickers, Leonie Rysanek, T. Gobbi, F. Andreolli, Mario Carlin, M. Pirazzini, F. Mazzoli, F. Calabrese, R. Kerns, Rome Op Chor, Rome Op Orch/T. Serafin)

Ⓓ **GD82046** (9/89)
Giordano—Andrea Chenier
Giordano: Andrea Chénier (Cpte). (P. Domingo, R. Scotto, S. Milnes, M. Sénéchal, J. Kraft, M. Ewing, A. Monk, T. Sharpe, S. Harling, I. Bushkin, M. King, P. de Palma, N. Beavan, G. Killebrew, E. Dara, John Alldis Ch, National PO/James Levine)

Ⓓ **GD82951** (3/86)
Verdi—Otello
Verdi: Otello (Cpte). (P. Domingo, R. Scotto, S. Milnes, F. Little, P. Crook, J. Kraft, P. Plishka, M. King, Ambrosian Op Chor, National PO/James Levine)

Ⓓ **GD83969**
Puccini—La bohème
Puccini: Bohème (Cpte). (A. Moffo, R. Tucker, M. Costa, R. Merrill, P. Maero, G. Tozzi, F. Corena, G. Onesti, A. Zagonara, F. Tosin, Rome Op Chor, Rome Op Orch/E. Leinsdorf)

Ⓓ **GD84145** (9/88)
Puccini—Madama Butterfly
Puccini: Madama Butterfly (Cpte). (A. Moffo, C. Valletti, R. Cesari, R. Elias, Mario Carlin, N. Catalani, M.T. Pace, F. Corena, L. Monreale, Rome Op Chor, Rome Op Orch/E. Leinsdorf)

Ⓓ **GD84265**
Con Amore
Puccini: Bohème (exc); *Mascagni:* Cavalleria Rusticana (exc); *Bizet:* Carmen (exc); *Verdi:* Trovatore (exc); Aida (exc); *Leoncavallo:* Pagliacci (exc); *Puccini:* Tosca (exc); *Donizetti:* Elisir d'amore (exc); *Verdi:* Rigoletto (exc); Rigoletto (exc). (P. Domingo, G. Psaros, L. Price, R. Davies, John Alldis Ch, LSO, New Philh, LPO/E. Leinsdorf/N. Santi/Z. Mehta/G. Solti/S. Milnes)

Ⓓ **GD84514** (1/89)
Puccini—Tosca
Puccini: Tosca (Cpte). (Z. Milanov, J. Björling, L. Warren, L. Monreale, Mario Carlin, F. Corena, N. Catalani, V. Preziosa, G. Bianchini, Rome Op Chor, Rome Op Orch/E. Leinsdorf)

Ⓓ **GD84516** (9/88)
Verdi—Macbeth
Verdi: Macbeth (Cpte). (L. Warren, Leonie Rysanek, J. Hines, C. Bergonzi, W. Olvis, G. Pechner, H. Sternberg, O. Hawkins, C. Ordassy, NY Met Op Chor, NY Met Op Orch/E. Leinsdorf)

Ⓓ **GD84586** (10/89)
Mozart—Die Zauberflöte
Mozart: Zauberflöte (Cpte). (I. Cotrubas, Z. Donat, E. Tappy, C. Boesch, M. Talvela, J. Van Dam, H. Hiestermann, E. Kales, R. Yakar, T. Schmidt, I. Mayr, M. Huber, T. Paulsen, C. Baumgartner, K. Terkal, H. Von Bömches, P. Weber, H. Nitsche, Vienna St Op Chor, VPO/James Levine)

Ⓓ **GD85234** (4/89) ▭ **GK85234** (4/89)
Gershwin—Porgy and Bess Highlights
Gershwin: Porgy and Bess (exc). (L. Price, W. Warfield, J.W. Bubbles, R. Henson, B. Webb, M. Burton, Alonzo Jones, B. Hall, RCA Victor Chor, RCA Victor Orch/S. Henderson)

Ⓓ **GD86182**
Handel—Julius Caesar
Handel: Giulio Cesare (Cpte). (N. Treigle, B. Sills, M. Forrester, B. Wolff, S. Malas, D. Cossa, W. Beck, M. Devlin, NY Met Op Chor, NY Met Op Orch/J. Rudel)

Ⓓ **GD86199** (10/88)
Bizet: Carmen
Bizet: Carmen (Cpte). (L. Price, F. Corelli, M. Freni, R. Merrill, M. Linval, G. Macaux, J-C. Benoit, M. Besançon, B. Demigny, F. Schooten, Vienna Boys' Ch, Vienna St Op Chor, VPO/H. von Karajan)

Ⓓ **GD86502** (7/88)
Bellini—Norma
Bellini: Norma (Cpte). (M. Caballé, F. Cossotto, P. Domingo, R. Raimondi, K. Collins, E. Bainbridge, Ambrosian Op. Chor, LPO/C.F. Cillario)

Ⓓ **GD86503** (8/88)
Verdi—Ernani
Verdi: Ernani (Cpte). (C. Bergonzi, L. Price, M. Sereni, E. Flagello, J. Hamari, F. Iacopucci, H. Mueller, RCA Italiana Op Chor, RCA Italiana Op Orch/T. Schippers)

Ⓓ **GD86504** (9/88)
Donizetti—Lucia di Lammermoor
Donizetti: Lucia di Lammermoor (Cpte). (A. Moffo, C. Bergonzi, M. Sereni, E. Flagello, C. Vozza, P. Duval, V. Pandano, RCA Italiana Op Chor, RCA Italiana Op Orch/G. Prêtre)

Ⓓ **GD86505** (9/88)
Rossini—Il Barbiere di Siviglia
Rossini: Barbiere di Siviglia (Cpte). (R. Merrill, R. Peters, C. Valletti, F. Corena, G. Tozzi, M. Roggero, C. Marsh, NY Met Op Chor, NY Met Op Orch/E. Leinsdorf)

Ⓓ **GD86506** (9/88)
Verdi: Rigoletto
Verdi: Rigoletto (Cpte). (R. Merrill, A. Moffo, Alfredo Kraus, E. Flagello, R. Elias, D. Ward, A. di Stasio, P. de Palma, R. Kerns, C. Vozza, M. Rinaudo, T. Toscano, E. Titta, RCA Italiana Op Chor, RCA Italiana Op Orch/G. Solti)

Ⓓ **GD86510** (8/88)
Mascagni—Cavalleria Rusticana
Mascagni: Cavalleria Rusticana (Cpte). (Z. Milanov, J. Björling, R. Merrill, C. Smith, M. Roggero, R. Shaw Chorale, RCA Orch/R. Cellini)

Ⓓ **GD86534** (12/87)
Verdi Arias and Duets
Verdi: Giovanna d'Arco (exc); Masnadieri (exc); Jérusalem (exc); Corsaro (exc); Trovatore (exc); Vespri Siciliani (exc); Ballo in maschera (exc); Don Carlo (exc); Otello (exc). (K. Ricciarelli, P. Domingo, R. Truffelli, Rome Polyphonic Chor, Rome PO, Santa Cecilia Academy Orch/G. Gavazzeni)

Ⓓ **GD86642** (9/90)
Donizetti—Lucrezia Borgia
Donizetti: Lucrezia Borgia (Cpte). (M. Caballé, Alfredo Kraus, E. Flagello, S. Verrett, F. Ricciardi, F. Iacopucci, F. Romano, F. Mazzoli, G. Baratti, V.M. Brunetti, R. El Hage, C. Sforza, F. Ruta, A. Mineo, RCA Italiana Op Chor, RCA Italiana Op Orch/J. Perlea)

Ⓓ **GD86643** (8/88)
Verdi—Il Trovatore
Verdi: Trovatore (Cpte). (J. Björling, Z. Milanov, L. Warren, F. Barbieri, N. Moscona, M. Roggero, P. Franke, G. Cehanovsky, N. Sprinzena, R. Shaw Chorale, RCA Victor Orch/R. Cellini)

Ⓓ **GD86644** (9/90)
R. Strauss—Salome
R. Strauss: Salome (Cpte). (M. Caballé, S. Milnes, Richard Lewis, R. Resnik, J. King, J. Hamari, M. Rippon, G. Griffiths, N. Howlett, D. Kelly, D. Wicks, E. Bainbridge, LSO/E. Leinsdorf)

Ⓓ **GD86645** (11/88)
Verdi—Un ballo in maschera
Verdi: Ballo in maschera (Cpte). (L. Price, C. Bergonzi, R. Merrill, R. Grist, S. Verrett, E. Flagello, F. Mazzoli, M. Basiola II, P. de Palma, F. Iacopucci, RCA Italiana Op Chor, RCA Italiana Op Orch/E. Leinsdorf)

Ⓓ **GD86646** (10/88)
Verdi—Luisa Miller
Verdi: Luisa Miller (Cpte). (A. Moffo, C. Bergonzi, C. MacNeil, G. Tozzi, S. Verrett, E. Flagello, G. Carturan, P. de Palma, RCA Italiana Op Chor, RCA Italiana Op Orch/F. Cleva)

Ⓓ **GD86652** (8/88)
Verdi—Aida
Verdi: Aida (Cpte). (Z. Milanov, F. Barbieri, J. Björling, L. Warren, B. Christoff, P. Clabassi, Mario Carlin, B. Rizzoli, Rome Op Chor, Rome Op Orch/J. Perlea)

Ⓓ **GD86677** (9/88)
Mozart—Così fan tutte
Mozart: Così fan tutte (Cpte). (L. Price, T. Troyanos, J. Raskin, G. Shirley, S. Milnes, E. Flagello, Ambrosian Op Chor, New Philh/E. Leinsdorf)

Ⓓ **GD86802**
Copland—Suites
Copland: Appalachian Spring Suite; Tender Land Suite; Billy the Kid Suite. (Boston SO, Philadelphia/A. Copland/E. Ormandy)

Ⓓ **GD86805** (3/89)
Orchestral Works
Berlioz: Béatrice et Bénédict (exc); *Franck:* Symphony; *Indy:* Symphonie, Op. 25. (N. Henriot-Schweitzer, Boston SO, Chicago SO/P. Monteux/C. Munch)

Ⓓ **GD87766** (5/90)
Rachmaninov plays Rachmaninov
Rachmaninov: Preludes (exc); Preludes (exc); Etudes-tableaux, Op.33 (exc); Etudes-tableaux, Op.39 (exc); Daisies; Oriental Sketch (1917); Morceaux de fantaisie, Op.3 (exc); Morceaux de fantaisie, Op.3 (exc); Morceaux de salon, Op.10 (exc); Lilacs; Moments musicaux, Op.16 (exc); Polka de W. R.; *Bach:* Solo Violin Partitas and Sonatas (exc); *Mendelssohn:* Midsummer Night's Dream (exc); *Kreisler:* Liebesfreud; *Schubert:* Schöne Müllerin (exc); *Mussorgsky:* Fair at Sorochintsï (exc); *Tchaikovsky:* Songs, Op. 16 (exc); *Rimsky-Korsakov:* Tale of Tsar Saltan (exc). (S. Rachmaninov)

Ⓓ **GD87767** (11/89)
Korngold—Die Tote Stadt
Korngold: Tote Stadt (Cpte). (R. Kollo, C. Neblett, B. Luxon, R. Wageman, H. Prey, G. Fuchs, P. Clark, A. de Ridder, W. Brokmeier, Tolz Boys' Ch, Bavarian Rad Chor, Munich RO/E. Leinsdorf)

Ⓓ **GD87799** (2/89) ▭ **GK87799**
The Pearl Fishers Duet plus Duets and Scenes
Bizet: Pêcheurs de Perles (exc); *Puccini:* Tosca (exc); *Verdi:* Don Carlo (exc); *Puccini:* Manon Lescaut (exc); Bohème (exc); *Verdi:* Forza del Destino (exc); Aida (exc); *Puccini:* Turandot (exc); *Verdi:* Otello (exc). (J. Björling, R. Merrill, Z. Milanov, L. Albanese, R. Tebaldi, E. Markow, G. Tozzi, M. Sereni, P. de Palma, T. Frascati, RCA Victor SO, Rome Op Orch, Rome Op Chor/R. Cellini/E. Leinsdorf/J. Perlea)

Ⓓ **GD87808** (3/90)
Lawrence Tibbett sings Opera Arias
Leoncavallo: Pagliacci (exc); *Rossini:* Barbiere di Siviglia (exc); *Verdi:* Ballo in Maschera (exc); Simon Boccanegra (exc); Falstaff (exc); *Puccini:* Tosca (exc); *Bizet:* Carmen (exc); *Gounod:* Faust (exc); *Wagner:* Walküre (exc); *Gruenberg:* Emperor Jones (exc); *Hanson:* Merry Mount (exc); *Gershwin:* Porgy and Bess (exc). (L. Tibbett, Orch, NY Met Op Orch, NY Met Op Chor, Philadelphia/Rosario Bourdon/N. Shilkret/W. Pelletier/G. Setti/L. Stokowski/A. Smallens, L.M. Belleri, F. Cingolani, R. Bampton)

Ⓓ **GD87810** (1/90)
Rosa Ponselle - Opera & Song Recital
Verdi: Ernani (exc); Otello (exc); Forza del destino (exc); Forza del destino (exc); Aida (exc); Aida (exc); *Meyerbeer:* Africaine (exc); *Spontini:* Vestale (exc); *Ponchielli:* Gioconda (exc); *Bellini:* Norma (exc); *Gounod:* Ave Maria; *Fontenailles:* À l'aimé; *Rimsky-Korsakov:* Songs, Op. 2 (exc); *Charles:* When I have sung my songs; *Sadero:* Amuri, amuri; *Traditional:* Carmen-Carmela. (R. Ponselle, G. Martinelli, E. Pinza, NY Met Op Chor, NY Met Op Orch, orch/G. Setti/Rosario Bourdon, R. Romani, I. Chichagov, R. Ponselle)

Ⓓ **GD87811** (10/90) ▭ **GK87811** (10/90)
Beniamino Gigli—Operatic Arias
Giordano: Andrea Chénier (exc); *Donizetti:* Favorita (exc); Elisir d'amore (exc); Elisir d'amore (exc); Lucia di Lammermoor (exc); *Gounod:* Faust (exc); Roméo et Juliette (exc); *Lalo:* Roi d'Ys (exc); *Puccini:* Tosca (exc); *Ponchielli:* Gioconda (exc); Gioconda (exc); *Bizet:* Pêcheurs de perles (exc); *Verdi:* Attila (exc); Lombardi (exc); *Gomes:* Schiavo (exc); Guarany (exc). (B. Gigli, E. Rethberg, E. Pinza, L. Bori, T. Ruffo, NY Met Op Chor, NY Met Op Orch, orch/G. Setti/J. Pasternack/Rosario Bourdon/E. Sivieri)

Ⓓ **GD87896** (1/91)
Gluck—Orfeo ed Euridice
Gluck: Orfeo ed Euridice (Cpte). (S. Verrett, A. Moffo, J. Raskin, Rome Polyphonic Chor, Virtuosi di Roma/R. Fasano)

Ⓓ **GD87899** (7/90)
Barber—Vanessa
Barber: Vanessa (Cpte). (E. Steber, R. Elias, R. Resnik, N. Gedda, G. Tozzi, G. Cehanovsky, R. Nagy, NY Met Op Chor, NY Met Op Orch/D. Mitropoulos)

Ⓓ **GD87911** (1/90)
Marian Anderson - Opera, Oratorio & Song Recital
Bach: St Matthew Passion, BWV244 (exc); *Handel:* Messiah (exc); *Schubert:* Ave Maria, D839; Schwanengesang, D957 (exc); Schöne Müllerin (exc); Tod und das Mädchen, D531; *Schumann:* Gedichte, Op. 35 (exc); Myrthen, Op. 25 (exc); *Brahms:* Lieder, Op. 105 (exc); Alto Rhapsody, Op. 53; *R. Strauss:* Lieder, Op. 27 (exc); *Rachmaninov:* Songs, Op. 4 (exc); *Verdi:* Ballo in maschera (exc); *Traditional:* Go down, Moses; Crucifixion/Hear the lamb's crying; My Lord, what a morning. (M. Anderson, Victor Sinfonietta/Robert Shaw, Philadelphia/E. Ormandy, NY Met Op Chor, NY Met Op Orch/D. Mitropoulos, J. Peerce, Orch/Mr Prince, Victor SO/C. O'Connell, K. Vehanen, F. Rupp, W. Primrose, San Francisco Municipal Chor, San Francisco SO/P. Monteux)

Ⓓ **GD87915** (10/90)
Wagner: Arias and Duets
Wagner: Tristan und Isolde (exc); Lohengrin (exc); Walküre (exc); Walküre (exc); Parsifal (exc); Götterdämmerung (exc); Götterdämmerung (exc). (K. Flagstad, L. Melchior, G. Dilworth, San Francisco Op Orch, Philadelphia, RCA Victor SO, orch/E. MacArthur/E. Ormandy/H. Lange)

Ⓓ **GD87969** (12/89)
Tito Schipa - Opera & Song Recital
Massenet: Werther (exc); *Cilea:* Arlesiana (exc); *Rossini:* Barbiere di Siviglia (exc); *Massenet:* Manon (exc); *Donizetti:* Elisir d'amore (exc); *Leoncavallo:* Pagliacci (exc); *Verdi:* Rigoletto (exc); *Mozart:* Don Giovanni (exc); *Handel:* Serse (exc); *Verdi:* Traviata (exc); *Bellini:* Sonnambula (exc); *Donizetti:* Lucia di Lammermoor (exc); *Freire:* Ay, Ay, Ay; *Padilla:* Princesita; *Lacalle:* Amapola; *Tosti:* Marechiare; 'A Vucchella; *Paladilhe:* Suzanne (exc); *Marvasi:* Chi se nne scorda cchiu; *Schipa:* Pianefforte 'e notte. (T. Schipa, A. Galli-Curci, orch/Rosario Bourdon/J. Pasternack/Mr Prince/M. Campanino, J. Huarte)

Ⓓ **GD87971** (12/88)
Verdi—The Force of Destiny
Verdi: Forza del destino (Cpte). (L. Price, R. Tucker, R. Merrill, G. Tozzi, S. Verrett, E. Flagello, G. Foiani, P. de Palma, C. Vozza, R. Bottcher, M. Rinaudo, RCA Italiana Op Chor, RCA Italiana Op Orch/T. Schippers)

Ⓓ **GD87981** (5/89)
Bizet—Carmen
Bizet: Carmen (Cpte). (R. Stevens, J. Peerce, L. Albanese, R. Merrill, P. Lenchner, M. Roggero, G. Cehanovsky, A. de Paolis, H. Thompson, O. Hawkins, NY Lycée Français Children's Ch, R. Shaw Chorale, RCA Victor Orch/F. Reiner)

▭ **GK85277**
Legendary Performers - Björling
Verdi: Aida (exc); *Puccini:* Manon Lescaut (exc); *Verdi:* Rigoletto (exc); *Mascagni:* Cavalleria Rusticana (exc); *Borodin:* Prince Igor (exc); *Giordano:* Andrea Chénier (exc); *Flotow:* Martha (exc); *Donizetti:* Elisir d'amore (exc); *Tchaikovsky:* Eugene Onegin (exc); *Puccini:* Turandot (exc); Tosca (exc). (J. Björling, Rome Op. Orch/J. Perlea, RCA Orch/R. Cellini, Stockholm Royal Op Orch/N. Grevillius, R. Tebaldi, G. Tozzi/E. Leinsdorf, F. Corena)

Ⓓ **RD60032** (11/89)
Mozart: Orchestral Works
Mozart: Symphony 36; Symphony 40; Nozze di Figaro (exc). (BPO)

Ⓓ **RD60119** (4/90)
Nineteenth Century Orchestral Works
Smetana: Má Vlast (exc); *Liszt:* Préludes; *Sibelius:* Finlandia; *Glinka:* Ruslan and Lyudmila (exc); *Tchaikovsky:* 1812. (Berlin SO/C.P. Flor)

Ⓓ **RD60195** (3/92)
Mussorgsky—Orchestral & Vocal Works
Mussorgsky: Khovanshchina (exc); Songs and Dances of Death; Pictures. (S. Leiferkus, RPO/Y. Temirkanov)

Ⓓ **RD60242** ▭ **RK60242**
Evelyn Glennie - Rhythm Song
Musser: Etude in C; *Inns:* Robbin' Harry; *Smadbeck:* Rhythm song; *G. Stout:* Mexican Dance 1; Mexican Dance 2; *Glennie:* Little Prayer; *Abe:* Michi; *Fauré:* Berceuse, Op.16; *Rimsky-Korsakov:* Tale of Tsar Saltan (exc); *Monti:* Csárdás; *Joplin:* Maple leaf Rag; *Chopin:* Etudes (exc); *Saint-Saëns:* Introduction and Rondo Capriccioso. (E. Glennie, National PO/B. Wordsworth)

Ⓓ **RD60440** (9/91)
Mozart—Le nozze di Figaro
Mozart: Nozze di Figaro (Cpte). (A. Titus, H. Donath, F. Furlanetto, J. Varady, M. Schmiege, C. Kallisch, S. Nimsgern, H. Zednik, C.H. Ahnsjö, G. Auer, I. Kertesi, Bavarian Rad Chor, BRSO/Colin Davis)

Ⓓ **RD60697**
Ofra Harnoy—Salut D'Amour
Popper: Hungarian Rhapsody, Op.68; *Fauré:* Songs, Op.7 (exc); *Rimsky-Korsakov:* Tale of Tsar Saltan (exc); *Liszt:* Elegie, S131; *Bloch:* From Jewish Life (exc); *Coulthard:* Villanelle; *Granados:* Danzas españolas (exc); *Piatti:* Caprices, Op.25 (exc); *Elgar:* Salut d'amour; *Foss:* Capriccio; *Fauré:* Elégie; *Falla:* Amor brujo (exc); *Saint-Saëns:* Carnaval des Animaux (exc); *Sarasate:* Danzas españolas (exc); *Tchaikovsky:* Morceaux, Op. 51 (exc); *Debussy:* Préludes (exc); *Gershwin:* Porgy and Bess (exc). (O. Harnoy, M. Dussek, C. Wilson, H. Bowkun)

Ⓓ **RD60739**
Tchaikovsky Gala in Leningrad
Tchaikovsky: Eugene Onegin (exc); Maid of Orleans (exc); Songs, Op. 65 (exc); Sérénade mélancolique; Valse-scherzo, Op. 34; Rococo Variations; 1812. (J. Norman, I. Perlman, Y-Y. Ma, E. Shenderovich, Leningrad PO, Leningrad Military Orch/Y. Temirkanov)

Ⓓ **RD60755** (10/91)
Beethoven—Orchestral Works
Beethoven: Symphony 3; Leonore (exc). (N German RSO/G. Wand)

Ⓓ **RD60758** (10/92)
Tchaikovsky—Cello Works
Tchaikovsky: Rococo Variations; Eugene Onegin (exc); Morceaux, Op. 51 (exc); Andante cantabile, Op.11; Sérénade mélancolique; Pezzo capriccioso; Nocturne, Op.19/4; Seasons (exc). (O. Harnoy, LPO/C. Mackerras)

Ⓓ **RD60827** (1/92)
Modern Pictures - Günter Wand
Stravinsky: Dumbarton Oaks; *Webern:* Pieces, Op. 10; *Martin:* Petite Symphonie Concertante; *Fortner:* Bluthochzeit (exc). (N German RSO/G. Wand)

Ⓓ **RD60861**
It ain't necessarily so & other violin miniatures
Gershwin: Porgy and Bess (exc); *Ravel:* Valses nobles et sentimentales (exc); Pièce en forme de habanera; *Falla:* Suite populaire espagnole (exc); *Bartók:* Romanian Folkdances, Sz56; *Bloch:* Baal Shem (exc); *Debussy:* Petite suite (exc); Plus que lente; Préludes (exc); *Stravinsky:* Suite italienne (violin) (exc); *Prokofiev:* Melodies, Op.35b (exc); *Shostakovich:* Preludes, Op.34 (exc); *Schnittke:* Praeludium. (V. Spivakov, S. Bezrodny, S. Rozhdestvensky)

Ⓓ **RD61191**
Gala Lirica
Giménez: Torre del oro (exc); *Verdi:* Macbeth (exc); Rigoletto (exc); Rigoletto (exc); Forza del destino (exc); Traviata (exc); *Serrano:* Alma da Dios (exc); *Bizet:* Carmen (exc); *Donizetti:* Fille du régiment (exc); *Puccini:* Tosca (exc); *Massenet:* Cid (exc); *Rossini:* Tancredi (exc); *Catalani:* Wally (exc); *Sorozábal:* Tabernera del puerto (exc); *Barbieri:* Barberillo de Lavapiès (exc). (P. Domingo, P. Lavirgen, T. Berganza, Alfredo Kraus, J. Pons, G. Aragall, M. Caballé, P. Lorengar, J. Carreras, Seville SO/E. Colomer/L.A. Garcia-Navarro/E. Garcia-Asensio/P. Domingo)

Ⓓ **RD70729** (9/87)
Verdi—Simon Boccanegra
Verdi: Simon Boccanegra (Cpte). (P. Cappuccilli, K. Ricciarelli, P. Domingo, R. Raimondi, G-P. Mastromei, M. Mazzieri, P. de Palma, O. Jachetti, RCA Chor, RCA Orch/G. Gavazzeni)

Ⓓ **RD80105** (11/86)
Puccini—Tosca
Puccini: Tosca (Cpte). (L. Price, P. Domingo, S. Milnes, C. Grant, F. Egerton, P. Plishka, J. Gibbs, M. Rippon, D. Pearl, Wandsworth Sch Boys' Ch, John Alldis Ch, New Philh/Z. Mehta)

Ⓓ **RD80370** (9/88)
Verdi—Sicillian Vespers
Verdi: Vespri Siciliani (Cpte). (M. Arroyo, P. Domingo, S. Milnes, R. Raimondi, M. Ewing, T. Sharpe, R. Van Allan, L. Goeke, K. Collins, J. Morris, A. Byers, John Alldis Ch, New Philh/James Levine)

Ⓓ **RD80371** (9/86)
Puccini—La Bohème
Puccini: Bohème (Cpte). (M. Caballé, P. Domingo, J. Blegen, S. Milnes, V. Sardinero, R. Raimondi, N. Mangin, N. Castel, A. Byers, F. Whiteley, W. Mason, Wandsworth Sch Boys' Ch, John Alldis Ch, LPO/G. Solti)

Ⓓ **RD81864** (10/87)
Verdi—The Force of Destiny
Verdi: Forza del destino (Cpte). (L. Price, P. Domingo, S. Milnes, B. Giaiotti, F. Cossotto, G. Bacquier, K. Moll, M. Sénéchal, G. Knight, M. King, W. Elvin, John Alldis Ch, LSO/James Levine)

Ⓓ **RD82109** (9/86)
Gershwin—Porgy and Bess
Gershwin: Porgy and Bess (Cpte). (D.R. Albert, C. Dale, B. Lane, W. Shakesnider, L. Marshall, C. Brice, Andrew Smith, A.B. Smalls, Houston Grand Op Chor, Houston Grand Op Orch/J. DeMain)

Ⓓ **RD83091**
Mascagni—Cavalleria Rusticana
Mascagni: Cavalleria Rusticana (Cpte). (R. Scotto, P. Domingo, P. Elvira, I. Jones, J. Kraft, Ambrosian Op. Chor, National PO/James Levine)

Ⓓ **RD84680** (2/86)
Porgy and Bess—Highlights
Gershwin: Porgy and Bess (exc). (D.R. Albert, C. Dale, Andrew Smith, W. Shakesnider, B. Lane, C. Brice, A.B. Smalls, L. Marshall, Houston Grand Op. Chor, Houston Grand Op Orch/J. DeMain)

Ⓓ **RD85666** (10/87)
Works for Piano and Orchestra
Saint-Saëns: Piano Concerto 2; *Falla:* Nights in the Gardens of Spain; *Franck:* Symphonic Variations; *Prokofiev:* Love for 3 Oranges Suite (exc); *Falla:* Amor Brujo (exc). (A. Rubinstein, Philadelphia/E. Ormandy, Sym of the Air/A. Wallenstein)

Ⓓ **RD85932** (9/87)
Puccini—Turandot
Puccini: Turandot (Cpte). (B. Nilsson, J. Björling, R. Tebaldi, M. Sereni, P. de Palma, T. Frascati, G. Tozzi, A. de Paolis, L. Monreale, A. Zagonara, Rome Op Chor, Rome Op Orch/E. Leinsdorf)

Ⓓ **RD86160** (3/88)
Puccini—Madama Butterfly
Puccini: Madama Butterfly (Cpte). (L. Price, R. Tucker, P. Maero, R. Elias, P. de Palma, R. Kerns, A. di Stasio, V. Carbonari, A. la Porta, M. Rinaudo, RCA Italiana Op Chor, RCA Italiana Op Orch/E. Leinsdorf)

Ⓓ **RD86180** (9/88)
Verdi—La Traviata
Verdi: Traviata (Cpte). (M. Caballé, C. Bergonzi, S. Milnes, D. Krebill, N. Stokes, F. Iacopucci, G. Boucher, T. Jamerson, H. Enns, C. Sforza, F. Ruta, F. Tasin, RCA Italiana Op Chor, RCA Italiana Op Orch/G. Prêtre)

Ⓓ **RD86194** (8/88)
Verdi—Il Trovatore
Verdi: Trovatore (Cpte). (P. Domingo, L. Price, S. Milnes, F. Cossotto, B. Giaiotti, E. Bainbridge, R. Davies, S. Riley, N. Taylor, Ambrosian Op Chor, New Philh/Z. Mehta)

Ⓓ **RD86198** (8/88)
Verdi—Aida
Verdi: Aida (Cpte). (L. Price, G. Bumbry, P. Domingo, S. Milnes, R. Raimondi, H. Sotin, B. Brewer, J. Mathis, John Alldis Ch, LSO/E. Leinsdorf)

Ⓓ **RD86218**
Mario Lanza—The Legendary Tenor
Brodszky: Toast of New Orleans (exc); *Hardelot:* Because; *Forrest/Wright:* Kismet (exc); *Traditional:* Funiculi, funicula; *Aaronson:* Loveliest night of the year; *Verdi:* Aida (exc); *Brooks:* Kiss; *Brodszky:* Serenade; *De Curtis:* Torna a Surriento; *Romberg:* Desert Song (exc); *Rascel:* Arrivederci Roma; *Friml:* Vagabond King (exc); *Leoncavallo:* Pagliacci (exc); *Lara:* Granada; *Brodszky:* Because you're mine (exc); *Tosti:* Marechiare; *Cottrau:* Santa Lucia; *Leoncavallo:* Mattinata; *Di Capua:* O sole mio. (M. Lanza, orch/R. Sinatra/C. Callinicos/I. Aaronson/R. Heindorf/P. Baron, C. Callinicos, J. Gimpel, J. Raskin, J. Alexander Ch/F. Ferrara, RCA Victor Orch)

Ⓓ **RD87016**
Leontyne Price sings Verdi Arias
Verdi: Aida (exc); Macbeth (exc); Traviata (exc); Ernani (exc); Otello (exc); Ballo in maschera (exc); Trovatore (exc); Forza del destino (exc). (L. Price, Rome Op Orch, RCA Italiana Op Orch/O. de Fabritiis/F. Molinari-Pradelli/T. Schippers/E. Leinsdorf/A. Basile)

Ⓓ **RD87716** (6/89)
Classic Marches
Berlioz: Damnation de Faust (exc); *Beethoven:* Ruinen von Athen (exc); *Meyerbeer:* Prophète (exc); *Mendelssohn:* Midsummer Night's Dream (exc); *Ippolitov-Ivanov:* Caucasian Sketches (exc); *J. Strauss I:* Radetzky March; *Pierné:* Cydalise et le chèvre-pied (exc); *Tchaikovsky:* Nutcracker (exc); *Elgar:* Pomp and Circumstance Marches (exc); *Verdi:* Aida (exc); *Gounod:* Marche funèbre d'une marionette; *Prokofiev:* Love for 3 Oranges Suite (exc); *Sibelius:* Karelia Suite (exc); *J. T. Williams:* Empire Strikes Back (exc); *Herbert:* Babes in Toyland (exc); *Ganz:* St Louis Symphony; *Sousa:* Stars and Stripes Forever. (St Louis SO/L. Slatkin)

Ⓓ **RD87905** (1/89)
Mendelssohn—Overtures
Mendelssohn: Midsummer Night's Dream (exc); Hochzeit des Camacho (exc); Meeresstille; Ruy Blas; Athalie (exc); Hebrides. (Bamberg SO/C.P. Flor)

▭ **RK61044** (11/92)
Eternal Caballé
Cano: Hijo de la luna; *Traditional:* Ojos verdes; Paraules d'Amor; El dia que naci yo; En Aranjuez con tu amor; *Donizetti:* Lucrezia Borgia (exc); Anna Bolena (exc); Maria Stuarda (exc); Roberto Devereux (exc); *Massenet:* Cid (exc); *Bizet:* Carmen (exc); *Saint-Saëns:* Samson et Dalila (exc); *Puccini:* Gianni Schicchi (exc); *Cilea:* Adriana Lecouvreur (exc); *Verdi:* Rigoletto (exc); Vespri Siciliani (exc); Trovatore (exc); Traviata (exc); *Bellini:* Norma (exc); *Rossini:* Siège de Corinthe (exc); *G. Charpentier:* Louise (exc); *Serrano:* Canción del Olvidó (exc); *Luna:* Niño judío (exc); *A. Lloyd Webber:* Phantom of the Opera (exc). (M. Caballé, Ambrosian Op Chor, RCA Italiana Op Chor, Chor, ECO, Philh, Barcelona SO, LPO, RCA Italiana Op Orch, Orch/J.M. Cano/J. Collado/N. Rescigno/G-F. Masini/C.F. Cillario/G. Prêtre/E.M. Marco/M. Yates, R. Miralles (pf/dir))

Ⓓ **VD60484** ▭ **VK60484**
Mozart: Orchestral Works
Mozart: Piano Concerto 20; Piano Concerto 21; Don Giovanni (exc). (G. Anda (pf/dir), Vienna SO, Chicago SO/F. Reiner)

Ⓓ **VD60487**
Rimsky-Korsakov: Orchestral Works
Rimsky-Korsakov: Scheherazade; Tale of Tsar Saltan (exc); Russian Easter Festival Ov. (LSO/A. Previn, Chicago SO/L. Stokowski)

Ⓓ **VD60493**
Wagner: Orchestral Works
Wagner: Meistersinger (exc); Tannhäuser (exc); Tristan und Isolde (exc). (Philadelphia/E. Ormandy)

Ⓓ **VD60535** ▭ **VK60535**
Borodin—Orchestral Works
Borodin: Symphony 2; In the Steppes of Central Asia; Prince Igor (exc). (John Alldis Ch, National PO/L. Tjeknavorian)

Ⓓ **09026 60593-2** (12/92)
Massenet—Chérubin
Massenet: Chérubin (Cpte). (F. von Stade, S. Ramey, J. Anderson, D. Upshaw, J-M. Ivaldi, H. Garetti, M. Trempont, B. Balleys, M. Sénéchal, C.H. Ahnsjö, A. Arapian, R. Scholze, Bavarian St Op Chor, Munich RSO/P. Steinberg)

Ⓓ **09026 60597-2** (11/92)
Puccini—La Fanciulla del West
Puccini: Fanciulla del West (Cpte). (E. Marton, D. O'Neill, A. Fondary, W. Planté, J-H. Rootering, B. Montgomery, F. Hawlata, H. Berger-Tuna, C. Wulkopf, J-M. Ivaldi, R. Swensen, D. Serraiocco, M. Cooke, J. Vacik, H. Weber, L. Baumann, R. Scholze, R. Kandblinder, Bavarian Rad Chor, Munich RSO/L. Slatkin)

Ⓓ **09026 60705-2** (10/92)
Verdi—Falstaff
Verdi: Falstaff (Cpte). (R. Panerai, A. Titus, S. Sweet, J. Kaufmann, F. Lopardo, M. Horne, S. Quittmeyer, P. de Palma, U. Ress, F.E. d'Artegna, Bavarian Rad Chor, BRSO/Colin Davis)

OO **09026 60739-5**
Tchaikovsky Gala in Leningrad
Tchaikovsky: Eugene Onegin (exc); Maid of Orleans (exc); Songs, Op. 65 (exc); Sérénade mélancolique; Valse-scherzo, Op. 34; Rococo Variations; 1812. (J. Norman, I. Perlman, Y-Y. Ma, E. Shenderovich, Leningrad PO, Leningrad Military Orch/Y. Temirkanov)

OO **09026 60755-5**
Beethoven—Orchestral Works
Beethoven: Symphony 3; Leonore (exc). (N German RSO/G. Wand)

OO **09026 60758-5**
Tchaikovsky—Cello Works
Tchaikovsky: Rococo Variations; Eugene Onegin (exc); Morceaux, Op. 51 (exc); Andante cantabile, Op.11; Sérénade mélancolique; Pezzo capriccioso; Nocturne, Op.19/4; Seasons (exc). (O. Harnoy, LPO/C. Mackerras)

Ⓓ **09026 60898-2** (12/93)
Puccini—Turandot
Puccini: Turandot (Cpte). (E. Marton, B. Heppner, M. Price, B. de Simone, R. Swensen, U. Ress, J-H. Rootering, C.H. Ahnsjö, O. Mori, Augsburg Cath Boys' Ch, Bavarian Rad Chor, Munich RO/R. Abbado)

Ⓓ **09026 60930-2** (12/92)
R. Strauss—Orchestral Works
R. Strauss: Also sprach Zarathustra; Bourgeois gentilhomme Suite; Rosenkavalier (exc). (Chicago SO/F. Reiner)

Ⓓ **09026 60962-2** (12/92)
Beethoven—Orchestral Works
Beethoven: Symphony 3; Coriolan; Leonore (exc). (Chicago SO/F. Reiner)

Ⓓ **09026 60992-2** (11/92)
Tchaikovsky—The Queen of Spades
Tchaikovsky: Queen of Spades (Cpte). (V. Atlantov, M. Freni, M. Forrester, S. Leiferkus, D. Hvorostovsky, Katherine Ciesinski, E. Gavazzi, J. Rodescu, D. Petersen, R. Clement, J. Chaminé, J. Taylor, D. Labelle, American Boychoir, Tanglewood Fest Chor, Boston SO/S. Ozawa)

Ⓓ **09026 61163-2** (3/93)
The Romantic Tenor
Lehár: Land des Lächelns (exc); Giuditta (exc); Zarewitsch (exc); *Rossini:* Soirées musicales (exc); *Bernstein:* West Side Story (exc); *Grever:* Jurame; *Chopin:* Etudes (exc); *Ponce:* Estrellita; *Leoncavallo:* Mattinata; *Lennon & McCartney:* Yesterday; *Di Capua:* O sole mio; *Tauber:* Singende Traum (exc); *Lara:* Granada; *J. Martini:* Plaisir d'amour; *De Curtis:* Non ti scordar di me. (F. Araiza, Munich RSO/R. Weikert)

OO **09026 61191-5**
Gala Lirica
Giménez: Torre del oro (exc); *Verdi:* Macbeth (exc); Rigoletto (exc); Rigoletto (exc); Forza del destino (exc); Traviata (exc); *Serrano:* Alma da Dios (exc); *Bizet:* Carmen (exc); *Donizetti:* Fille du régiment (exc); *Puccini:* Tosca (exc); *Massenet:* Cid (exc); *Rossini:* Tancredi (exc); *Catalani:* Wally (exc); *Sorozábal:* Tabernera del puerto (exc); *Barbieri:* Barberillo de Lavapiès (exc). (P. Domingo, P. Lavirgen, T. Berganza, Alfredo Kraus, J. Pons, G. Aragall, M. Caballé, P. Lorengar, J. Carreras, Seville SO/E. Colomer/L.A. Garcia-Navarro/E. Garcia-Asensio/P. Domingo)

Ⓓ **09026 61203-2** (11/92)
Berlioz—Symphonie fantastique
Berlioz: Symphonie fantastique; Béatrice et Bénédict (exc); Corsaire. (RPO/Y. Temirkanov)

▭ **09026 61204-4** (11/92)
From the Official Barcelona Games Ceremony
Various: Barcelona Games Medley; *Massenet:* Cid (exc); Hérodiade (exc); *Bellini:* Norma (exc); *Verdi:* Macbeth (exc); Ballo in maschera (exc); Otello (exc); *Leoncavallo:* Pagliacci (exc); *Rossini:* Italiana in Algeri (exc); *Donizetti:* Favorita (exc); *Ponchielli:* Gioconda (exc); *A. Thomas:* Mignon (exc); *Offenbach:* Contes d'Hoffmann (exc). (M. Caballé, T. Berganza, P. Domingo, J. Carreras, J. Pons, G. Aragall, Barcelona SO/G. Navarro)

OO **09026 61204-5**
From the Official Barcelona Games Ceremony
Various: Barcelona Games Medley; *Massenet:* Cid (exc); Hérodiade (exc); *Bellini:* Norma (exc); *Verdi:* Macbeth (exc); Ballo in maschera (exc); Otello (exc); *Leoncavallo:* Pagliacci (exc); *Rossini:* Italiana in Algeri (exc); *Donizetti:* Favorita (exc); *Ponchielli:* Gioconda (exc); *A. Thomas:* Mignon (exc); *Offenbach:* Contes d'Hoffmann (exc). (M. Caballé, T. Berganza, P. Domingo, J. Carreras, J. Pons, G. Aragall, Barcelona SO/G. Navarro)

Ⓓ **09026 61205-2** (3/93)
Handel—Opera Arias
Handel: Orlando (exc); Aci, Galatea e Polifemo (exc); Rinaldo (exc); Giulio Cesare (exc); Floridante (exc); Radamisto (exc); Partenope (exc). (N. Stutzmann, Hanover Band/R. Goodman)

Ⓓ **09026 61207-2** ▭ **09026 61207-4**
Handel—Orchestral Works
Handel: Water Music (exc); Fireworks Music; Concerti grossi, Op. 6 (exc); Serse (exc). (RCA Victor SO/L. Stokowski, Schneider CO/A. Schneider, Boston Pops/A. Fiedler)

Ⓓ **09026 61209-2** ▭ **09026 61209-4**
Mussorgsky—Pictures at an Exhibition
Mussorgsky: Pictures; Night on the Bare Mountain; *Rimsky-Korsakov:* Golden Cockerel (exc); *Prokofiev:* Symphony 1; *Ippolitov-Ivanov:* Caucasian Sketches (exc). (Philadelphia/E. Ormandy)

Ⓓ **09026 61211-2**
Music of France
Debussy: Après-midi; *Saint-Saëns:* Danse macabre; *Fauré:* Pelléas et Mélisande Suite (exc); *Offenbach:* Orphée aux enfers (exc); *Debussy:* Clair de lune; *Meyerbeer:* Prophète (exc); *Ravel:* Pavane; *Dukas:*

Apprenti sorcier; *Various:* National Anthems (exc). (Philadelphia/E. Ormandy)

Ⓓ **09026 61212-2** ▭ **09026 61212-4**
Beethoven—Overtures
Beethoven: Egmont (exc); Ruinen von Athen (exc); Prometheus (exc); Coriolan; Fidelio (exc); Leonore (exc). (Bamberg SO/E. Jochum)

Ⓓ **09026 61214-2**
German Opera Arias
Nicolai: Lustigen Weiber von Windsor (exc); *Flotow:* Martha (exc); *Mozart:* Clemenza di Tito (exc); Don Giovanni (exc); *Beethoven:* Fidelio (exc); *Weber:* Freischütz (exc); *Wagner:* Fliegende Holländer (exc); Meistersinger (exc); Rienzi (exc); *R. Strauss:* Rosenkavalier (exc); *Cornelius:* Barbier von Bagdad (exc); *Goldmark:* Königin von Saba (exc). (P. Seiffert, Munich RO/J. Kout)

Ⓓ **09026 61236-2** (12/92)
Leontyne Price - Prima Donna Collection
Purcell: Dido (exc); *Mozart:* Nozze di Figaro (exc); *Verdi:* Traviata (exc); Otello (exc); *Meyerbeer:* Africaine (exc); *Massenet:* Manon (exc); *Cilea:* Adriana Lecouvreur (exc); *G. Charpentier:* Louise (exc); *Puccini:* Turandot (exc); *Korngold:* Tote Stadt (exc); *Barber:* Vanessa (exc); *Handel:* Atalanta (exc); *Mozart:* Don Giovanni (exc); *Weber:* Freischütz (exc); *Wagner:* Tannhäuser (exc); *Verdi:* Macbeth (exc); Macbeth (exc); *Boito:* Mefistofele (exc); *Dvořák:* Rusalka (exc); *Debussy:* Enfant prodigue (exc); *Giordano:* Andrea Chénier (exc); *Zandonai:* Francesca da Rimini (exc); *Puccini:* Suor Angelica (exc); *Menotti:* Amelia al ballo (exc); *Gluck:* Alceste (1776) (exc); *Mozart:* Don Giovanni (exc); *Verdi:* Lombardi (exc); Simon Boccanegra (exc); *Flotow:* Martha (exc); *Offenbach:* Périchole (exc); *Wagner:* Walküre (exc); *J. Strauss II:* Fledermaus (exc); *Bizet:* Carmen (exc); *Mascagni:* Cavalleria Rusticana (exc); *Massenet:* Thaïs (exc); *Puccini:* Gianni Schicchi (exc); *Poulenc:* Dialogues des Carmélites (exc); *Handel:* Semele (exc); *Mozart:* Idomeneo (exc); *Berlioz:* Damnation de Faust (exc); *Weber:* Oberon (exc); *Bellini:* Norma (exc); *Verdi:* Rigoletto (exc); *Wagner:* Tristan und Isolde (exc); *Leoncavallo:* Pagliacci (exc); *Cilea:* Adriana Lecouvreur (exc); *Britten:* Gloriana (exc). (L. Price, C. Vozza, E. Bainbridge, D. Barioni, P. de Palma, R. El Hage, B. Martinovich, Ambrosian Op Chor, RCA Italiana Op Orch, New Philh, LSO, Philh/F. Molinari-Pradelli/N. Santi/E. Downes/H. Lewis)

Ⓓ **09026 61242-2**
Caruso Sings Verdi
Verdi: Rigoletto (exc); Rigoletto (exc); Rigoletto (exc); Ballo in maschera (exc); Ballo in maschera (exc); Otello (exc); Otello (exc); Requiem (exc); Traviata (exc); Trovatore (exc); Trovatore (exc); Trovatore (exc); Forza del destino (exc); Forza del destino (exc); Lombardi (exc); Macbeth (exc); Aida (exc); Aida (exc); Don Carlo (exc). (E. Caruso, L. Tetrazzini, J. Jacoby, P. Amato, F. Hempel, L. Rothier, A. de Segurola, T. Ruffo, A. Gluck, E. Schumann-Heink, A. Scotti, F. Alda, M. Journet, J. Gadski, NY Met Op Chor, orch/W.B. Rogers/G. Scognamiglio)

Ⓓ **09026 61243-2**
Caruso sings Verismo Arias
Puccini: Bohème (exc); Bohème (exc); Bohème (exc); Bohème (exc); *Ponchielli:* Gioconda (exc); *Mascagni:* Cavalleria rusticana (exc); Cavalleria rusticana (exc); Cavalleria rusticana (exc); *Puccini:* Tosca (exc); *Leoncavallo:* Bohème (exc); *Puccini:* Madama Butterfly (exc); Madama Butterfly (exc); *Franchetti:* Germania (exc); *Giordano:* Andrea Chénier (exc); Andrea Chénier (exc); *Puccini:* Manon Lescaut (exc); *Leoncavallo:* Pagliacci (exc); Pagliacci (exc). (E. Caruso, N. Melba, G. Farrar, G. Ciaparelli-Viafora, A. Scotti, F. Lapitino, orch/W.B. Rogers/J. Pasternack, anon)

Ⓓ **09026 61244-2**
Caruso sings French Opera Arias
Gounod: Faust (exc); Faust (exc); *Massenet:* Cid (exc); *Bizet:* Carmen (exc); *Saint-Saëns:* Samson et Dalila (exc); Samson et Dalila (exc); *Bizet:* Pêcheurs de perles (exc); *Massenet:* Manon (exc); Manon (exc); *Halévy:* Juive (exc). (E. Caruso, M. Journet, G. Farrar, G. Lejeune-Gilibert, A. Scotti, L. Homer, F. Lapitino, NY Met Op Chor, orch/W.B. Rogers/J. Pasternack)

Ⓓ **09026 61245-2** (9/93)
Ezio Pinza - Recital
Tosti: Ultima canzone; *Puccini:* Bohème (exc); *A. Thomas:* Caïd (exc); *Mozart:* Zauberflöte (exc); *Gounod:* Faust (exc); *Bellini:* Norma (exc); *Verdi:* Ernani (exc); Requiem (exc); *Mozart:* Don Giovanni (exc); *Verdi:* Trovatore (exc); *Monteverdi:* L'Arianna (exc); *Handel:* Floridante (exc); *Legrenzi:* Eteocle e Polinice (exc); *A. Scarlatti:* Flavio (exc); *Monteverdi:* Incoronazione di Poppea (exc); *Cavalli:* Donzelle fuggite; *Torelli:* Tu lo sai; *Paisiello:* Amor contrastato (exc); *T. Giordani:* Caro mio ben; *Falconieri:* O bellissimi capelli; *Sarti:* Armida e Rinaldo (exc); *Bononcini:* Trionfo di Camilla (exc); *Verdi:* Simon Boccanegra (exc); *Rossini:* Barbiere di Siviglia (exc); *Mussorgsky:* Boris Godunov (exc); *Weill:* Knickerbocker Holiday (exc). (E. Pinza, NY Met Op Chor, NY Met Op Orch, orch/Rosario Bourdon/G. Setti, F. Kitzinger, RCA Victor Orch, R. Shaw Chorale/E. Leinsdorf, Twentieth Cent Fox Chor, Twentieth Cent Fox SO/Alfred Newman, Johnny Green Orch/J. Green)

Ⓓ **09026 61249-2** (1/94)
Marches in Hi-Fi
Verdi: Aida (exc); *Herbert:* Babes in Toyland (exc); *Sousa:* Semper fidelis; Stars and Stripes Forever; *Tchaikovsky:* Suite 1 (exc); *Traditional:* Yankee Doodle; *Morse:* Up the Street; *Berlioz:* Damnation de Faust (exc); *Rodgers:* King and I (exc); *Ippolitov-Ivanov:* Caucasian Sketches (exc); *Planquette:* Sambre-et-Meuse; *Beethoven:* Ruinen von Athen (exc); *Alford:* Colonel Bogey; *Emmett:* Dixie; *Gould:* American Salute; *Gershwin:* Strike up the Band II (exc); *Mendelssohn:* Athalie (exc); *Sibelius:* Karelia Suite (exc); *Rózsa:* Ben-Hur (exc). (Boston Pops/A. Fiedler)

Ⓓ **09026 61265-2(1)** (3/93)
Rachmaninov—The Complete Recordings (pt 1)
Rachmaninov: Piano Concerto 2; Piano Concerto 3; Piano Concerto 1; Piano Concerto 4; Paganini Rhapsody; Isle of the Dead; Vocalise; Symphony 3; *Beethoven:* Violin Sonata 8; *Schubert:* Sonata, D574; *Grieg:* Violin Sonata 3; *Bach:* Partitas, BWV825-30 (exc); *Handel:* Keyboard Suites Set I (exc); *Mozart:* Piano Sonata, K331 (exc); *Beethoven:* Variations, WoO80; *Liszt:* Chants polonais, S480 (exc); Müllerlieder, S565 (exc); Schwanengesang, S560 (exc); Polonaises, S223 (exc); *Mendelssohn:* Songs without Words (exc); *Schubert:* Impromptus (exc); *Liszt:* Concert Studies, S145 (exc); *Gluck:* Orfeo ed Euridice (exc); *Mendelssohn:* Studies, Op.104b (exc); *Schumann:* Spanisches Liederspiel, Op.74 (exc); *Paderewski:* Humoresques de Concert, Op.14 (exc); *Kreisler:* Liebesfreud. (S. Rachmaninov, Philadelphia/L. Stokowski/E. Ormandy, F. Kreisler/S. Rachmaninov)

Ⓓ **09026 61265-2(2)** (3/93)
Rachmaninov—The Complete Recordings (pt 2)
Chopin: Piano Sonata 2; *Schumann:* Carnaval; *Chopin:* Nocturnes (exc); Waltzes (exc); Ballades (exc); Mazurkas (exc); Waltzes (exc); *Bach:* Solo Violin Partitas and Sonatas (exc); *Mendelssohn:* Midsummer Night's Dream (exc); *Kreisler:* Liebesfreud; *Schubert:* Schöne Müllerin (exc); *Rachmaninov:* Polka de W.R; Etudes-tableaux, Op.39 (exc); Preludes (exc); *Mussorgsky:* Fair at Sorochintsï (exc); *Tchaikovsky:* Songs, Op.16 (exc); *Rimsky-Korsakov:* Tale of Tsar Saltan (exc); *Beethoven:* Ruinen von Athen (exc); *Borodin:* Scherzo in A flat; *Tchaikovsky:* Seasons (exc); *Scriabin:* Preludes, Op.11 (exc); *J. Strauss II:* Man lebt nur einmal, Op. 167; *Traditional:* Powder and Paint; *Rachmaninov:* Polka italienne; Piano Concerto 2; Preludes (exc); Etudes-tableaux, Op.33 (exc); Daisies; Oriental Sketch (1917); Morceaux de Fantaisie, Op.3 (exc); Morceaux de Fantaisie, Op.3 (exc); Morceaux de Salon, Op.10 (exc); Lilacs; Moments Musicaux, Op.16 (exc). (S. Rachmaninov, N. Plevitskaya, N. Rachmaninov, Philadelphia/L. Stokowski)

Ⓓ **09026 61275-2** (2/94)
Strings! The Definitive Collection
Pachelbel: Canon and Gigue; *Bach:* Suites, BWV1066-9 (exc); *Vivaldi:* Concerto, RV151; *Hoffstetter:* String Quartets, Op. 3 (exc); *Elgar:* Salut d'amour; *Purcell:* Chaconne, Z730; *Marais:* La gamme (exc); *Barber:* Adagio for Strings; *Handel:* Serse (exc); *Boccherini:* String Quintets, G271-6 (exc); *Albinoni:* Adagio; *Handel:* Concerti Grossi, Op. 6 (exc). (Guildhall Str Ens, R. Salter (vn/dir))

Ⓓ **09026 61354-2** (6/93)
Mussorgsky—Orchestral & Choral Works
Mussorgsky: Khovanshchina (exc); Joshua; Salammbô (exc); Scherzo in B flat; Destruction of Sennacherib; St John's Night; Oedipus in Athens (exc); Capture of Kars. (Z. Gal, LSC, LSO/C. Abbado)

Ⓓ **09026 61356-2** ▭ **09026 61356-4**
Domingo Sings Caruso
Leoncavallo: Bohème (exc); Pagliacci (exc); *Donizetti:* Elisir d'Amore (exc); *Massenet:* Manon (exc); Cid (exc); *Cilea:* Arlesiana (exc); *Flotow:* Martha (exc); *Puccini:* Fanciulla del West (exc); Bohème (exc); *Verdi:* Rigoletto (exc); Aida (exc); *Meyerbeer:* Africaine (exc); *Gounod:* Faust (exc); *Halévy:* Juive (exc); *Mascagni:* Cavalleria rusticana (exc). (P. Domingo, G. Psaros, John Alldis Ch, LSO/N. Santi/E. Leinsdorf, LPO/G. Solti, RPO/E. Downes)

Ⓓ **09026 61357-2** (6/93)
Leontyne Price Sings Mozart
Mozart: Ch'io mi scordi di te, K505; Nozze di Figaro (exc); Idomeneo (exc); Zauberflöte (exc); Rè pastore (exc); Bella mia fiamma, K528; Idomeneo (exc); Nozze di Figaro (exc); Don Giovanni (exc); Don Giovanni (exc). (L. Price, V. Aveling, P. de Palma, New Philh/P.H. Adler/N. Santi, RCA Italiana Op Orch/F. Molinari-Pradelli, LSO/E. Downes)

Ⓓ **09026 61389-2** (9/94)
Serenata Andaluza—Alicia de Larrocha
Falla: Pièces espagnoles; Fantasía bética; Vida breve (exc); Serenata andaluza; Retablo de maese Pedro (exc); *Montsalvatge:* Divagación; Divertimentos; Si, à Mompou; Berceuse; Sonatine pour Yvette. (A. de Larrocha)

Ⓓ **09026 61400-2** (11/93)
Berlioz/Saint-Saëns—Orchestral Works
Berlioz: Carnaval romain; Béatrice et Bénédict (exc); Corsaire; Troyens (exc); Benvenuto Cellini (exc); Roméo et Juliette (exc); *Saint-Saëns:* Rouet d'Omphale. (Boston SO/C. Munch)

Ⓓ **09026 61411-2**
Lily Pons Recital
Donizetti: Lucia di Lammermoor (exc); *Verdi:* Rigoletto (exc); Rigoletto (exc); *Rossini:* Barbiere di Siviglia (exc); *Delibes:* Lakmé (exc); *Rimsky-Korsakov:* Golden Cockerel (exc); *Meyerbeer:* Dinorah (exc); *Handel:* Floridante (exc); *Debussy:* Ariettes oubliées (exc); Ariettes oubliées (exc); Mandoline; *Fauré:* Songs, Op.39 (exc); *Bishop:* Echo song; Pretty mocking bird; *Benedict:* Capinera; *Jacobson:* Chanson de Marie Antoinette; *La Forge:* Cupid captive. (L. Pons, G. De Luca, orch/Rosario Bourdon/W. Pelletier/J. Barbirolli/A. Kostelanetz, Renaissance Qnt, F. La Forge)

Ⓓ **09026 61412-2** (9/93)
Nellie Melba - Recital
Verdi: Rigoletto (exc); *A. Thomas:* Hamlet (exc); *Gounod:* Faust (exc); *Verdi:* Traviata (exc); *Puccini:* Bohème (exc); *Verdi:* Otello (exc); *Mozart:* Rè Pastore (exc); *G. Charpentier:* Louise (exc); *Lalo:* Roi d'Ys (exc); *Massenet:* Don César de Bazan (exc); *Arditi:* Se saran rose; *Hahn:* Si mes vers; D'une prison; *Debussy:* Fêtes galantes I (exc); Âme évaporée; Mandoline; *Bemberg:* Anges pleurent; Chant vénitien; *Traditional:* Ye banks and braes; *M.V. White:* John Anderson, my Jo; *Traditional:* Comin' thro' the rye; *Dvořák:* Gipsy Melodies (exc). (N. Melba, orch/W.B. Rogers, G. Lapierre, N. Melba, A. Sassoli, F. St Leger, J. Kubelík)

Ⓓ **09026 61420-2** ▭ **09026 61420-4**
Mario Lanza - Don't Forget Me
Verdi: Rigoletto (exc); Rigoletto (exc); Forza del destino (exc); *Mascagni:* Cavalleria Rusticana (exc); *Meyerbeer:* Africaine (exc); *Denza:* Funiculì-Funiculà; *Cardillo:* Core 'ngrato; *Rossini:* Soirées musicales (exc); *Alstyne:* Your eyes have told me so; *Coward:* Private Lives (exc); *Cottrau:* Santa Lucia; *Rapée:* Diane; *Mario:* Santa Lucia luntana; *Friml:* Firefly (exc); *Bixio:* Parlami d'amore Mariù; *Romberg:* Student Prince (exc); *De Curtis:* Canta pe'me; Tu, ca nun chiagne!; Non ti scordar di me; *Cioffi:* 'Na sera e' maggio; *Kern:* Show Boat (exc); *Rodgers:* Carousel (exc); *T. Evans:* If. (M. Lanza, orch/R. Sinatra/C. Callinicos)

Ⓓ **09026 61429-2** (1/94)
Offenbach in America
Offenbach: Belle Hélène (exc); Contes d'Hoffmann (exc); Geneviève de Brabant (exc); Périchole (exc); Grande-Duchesse de Gérolstein (exc); Belles américaines; Musette, Op. 24; Orphée aux enfers (exc); *Ibert:* Divertissement. (Boston Pops/A. Fiedler)

Ⓓ **09026 61440-2** ▭ **09026 61440-4**
Opera's Greatest Moments
Verdi: Traviata (exc); *Puccini:* Gianni Schicchi (exc); *Rossini:* Barbiere di Siviglia (exc); *Bizet:* Pêcheurs de Perles (exc); *Puccini:* Bohème (exc); *Tchaikovsky:* Queen of Spades (exc); *Catalani:* Wally (exc); *Donizetti:* Elisir d'amore (exc); *Wagner:* Walküre (exc); *Verdi:* Forza del Destino (exc); *Leoncavallo:* Pagliacci (exc); *Mozart:* Nozze di Figaro (exc); *Verdi:* Rigoletto (exc); *Puccini:* Madama Butterfly (exc); *Mozart:* Zauberflöte (exc); *Verdi:* Aida (exc); *Bizet:* Carmen (exc); *Puccini:* Turandot (exc). (A. Moffo, H. Donath, M. Caballé, E. Marton, J. Norman, L. Price, J. Varady, I. Cotrubas, T. Berganza, R. Tucker, J. Björling, P. Domingo, Alfredo Kraus, M. Lanza, B. Heppner, R. Merrill, D. Hvorostovsky, Rome Op Chor, Cordoba Grand Th Chor, Rome Op Orch, Munich RSO, NY Met Op Orch, RCA Victor SO, LPO, Boston SO, Staatskapelle Dresden, RCA Italiana Op Orch, BRSO, VPO, Seville SO/F. Previtali/G. Patanè/E. Leinsdorf/R. Cellini/G. Solti/S. Ozawa/P. Steinberg/N. Santi/M. Janowski/T. Schippers/Colin Davis/James Levine/C. Callinicos/L. A. Garcia-Navarro/R. Abbado, LSO)

Ⓓ **09026 61450-2** (11/93) ▭ **09026 61450-4** (11/93)
Together - Julian Bream & John Williams
W. Lawes: Suite in D; *Carulli:* Duo, Op.34; *Sor:* Divertissement, Op.34; *Albéniz:* Cantos de España (exc); *Granados:* Goyescas (exc); *Falla:* Vida breve (exc); *Ravel:* Pavane pour une infante défunte; *Fauré:* Dolly; *Granados:* Danzas españolas (exc). (J. Bream, J. Williams)

Ⓓ **09026 61457-2**
Shirley Verrett in Opera
Gluck: Orphée (exc); *Donizetti:* Anna Bolena (exc); Favorita (exc); *Berlioz:* Roméo et Juliette (exc); Damnation de Faust (exc); *Gounod:* Sapho (exc); *Massenet:* Werther (exc); *Saint-Saëns:* Samson et Dalila (exc); *Verdi:* Forza del destino (exc); Ballo in maschera (exc). (S. Verrett, C. Bergonzi, R. El Hage, RCA Italiana Op Chor, RCA Italiana Op Orch/G. Prêtre/T. Schippers/E. Leinsdorf)

Ⓓ **09026 61497-2**
Hi-Fi Fiedler
Rimsky-Korsakov: Golden Cockerel Suite (exc); *Rossini:* Guillaume Tell (exc); *Tchaikovsky:* Marche slave (exc); *Chabrier:* España; *Liszt:* Hungarian Rhapsodies, S359 (exc); Rákóczy march. (Boston Pops/A. Fiedler)

Ⓓ **09026 61503-2** (3/94)
Stokowski Favourites
Liszt: Hungarian Rhapsodies, S244 (exc); *Enescu:* Romanian Rhapsodies, Op. 11 (exc); *Smetana:* Má Vlast (exc); Bartered Bride (exc); *Wagner:* Tannhäuser (exc); Tristan und Isolde (exc). (Chor, RCA Victor SO, Sym of the Air/L. Stokowski)

Ⓓ **09026 61505-2**
Copland/Gould - Composers Conduct
Copland: Appalachian Spring Suite; Tender Land Suite; *Gould:* Fall River Legend (exc); Latin-American Symphonette (exc). (Boston SO/A. Copland, Morton Gould Orch/M. Gould)

Ⓓ **09026 61509-2** (6/93)
A Salute to American Music
S. Ward: America the Beautiful; *Menotti:* Amelia al ballo (exc); *Weill:* Street Scene (exc); Knickerbocker Holiday (exc); *V. Thomson:* Blake Songs (exc); *Griffes:* Fiona Macleod Poems (exc); *Foster:* Ah! May the red rose (exc); *Bernstein:* Chichester Psalms (exc); West Side Story (exc); Candide (1988) (exc); *Copland:* Old American Songs 2 (exc); *Bolcom:* Tyger; *Gershwin:* Porgy and Bess (exc); *M.D. Levy:* Mourning Becomes Electra (exc); *Barber:* Vanessa (exc); Antony and Cleopatra (exc); *Floyd:* Susannah (exc); *Berlin:* God bless America. (L. Price, M. O'Flynn, R. Fleming, K. Holvik, D. Woods, C. Vaness, P. Pancella, T. Troyanos, F. von Stade, M. Horne, J. Hadley, P. Groves, Daniel Smith, J. Mattsey, S. Milnes, R. Merrill, S. Ramey, Collegiate Chorale, NY Met Op Orch/J. Conlon)

Ⓓ **09026 61580-2(1)** (4/94)
RCA/Met 110 Singers, 100 Years (pt 1)
Donizetti: Lucia di Lammermoor (exc); *Puccini:* Tosca (exc); *Berlioz:* Damnation de Faust (exc); *Bizet:* Carmen (exc); *A. Thomas:* Hamlet (exc); *Meyerbeer:* Africaine (exc); Prophète (exc); *Donizetti:* Elisir d'amore (exc); *Wagner:* Fliegende Holländer (exc); *Puccini:* Bohème (exc); *Ponchielli:* Gioconda (exc); *Halévy:* Juive (exc). (M. Sembrich, orch, D. Lyons, E. Eames, P. Plançon, E. Calvé, N. Melba, G. Campanari, anon, E. Schumann-Heink, A. Scotti, J. Gadski, M. Journet, L. Homer, E. Caruso/J. Pasternack)

Ⓓ **09026 61580-2(2)** (4/94)
RCA/Met 100 Singers, 100 Years (pt 2)
Wolf-Ferrari: Donne Curiose (exc); *Tchaikovsky:* Queen of Spades (exc); *Verdi:* Ballo in Maschera (exc); *Giordano:* Cena delle Beffe (exc); *Leoncavallo:* Pagliacci (exc); *Wagner:* Parsifal (exc); *Verdi:* Traviata (exc); Rigoletto (exc); *Mascagni:* Amico Fritz (exc); *Tchaikovsky:* Eugene Onegin (exc); *Mussorgsky:* Boris Godunov (exc); *Verdi:* Traviata (exc). (G. Farrar, H. Jadlowker, orch, E. Destinn/W.B. Rogers, P. Amato, F. Alda/Rosario Bourdon, A. Gluck, C. Whitehill/T. Levy, J. McCormack, L. Tetrazzini, M. Fleta, L. Bori, G. Martinelli/J. Pasternack, P. Althouse, M. Ober, G. De Luca, NY Met Op Orch/G. Setti, C. Linton)

Ⓓ **09026 61580-2(3)** (4/94)
RCA/Met 100 Singers, 100 Years (pt 3)
Verdi: Forza del destino (exc); *Meyerbeer:* Africaine (exc); Dinorah (exc); *Korngold:* Tote Stadt (exc); *Rossini:* Barbiere di Siviglia (exc); *Wagner:* Meistersinger (exc); *Bellini:* Norma (exc); *D. Taylor:* King's Henchman (exc); *Donizetti:* Lucia di Lammermoor (exc); *Wagner:* Tannhäuser (exc); *Mozart:* Don Giovanni (exc); *Puccini:* Fanciulla del West (exc). (R. Ponselle, orch/Rosario Bourdon, B. Gigli, A. Galli-Curci, Folkmann, M. Jeritza/J. Pasternack, F. Lapitino, T. Ruffo, E. Johnson, F. Schorr, E. Rethberg, G. Lauri-Volpi, L. Tibbett, NY Met Op Orch, NY Met Op Chor/G. Setti, T. Dal Monte, L. Melchior, RCA SO/E. McArthur, E. Pinza, Cibelli)

Ⓓ **09026 61580-2(4)** (4/94)
RCA/Met 100 Singers, 100 Years (pt 4)
G. Charpentier: Louise (exc); *Gounod:* Roméo et Juliette (exc); *Rimsky-Korsakov:* Golden Cockerel (exc); *Donizetti:* Elisir d'amore (exc); *Gluck:* Alceste (1776) (exc); *Massenet:* Manon (exc); *Hageman:* Caponsacchi (exc); *Wagner:* Tristan und Isolde (exc); *Bizet:* Carmen (exc); *Wagner:* Walküre (exc); *Mozart:* Nozze di Figaro (exc); *Wagner:* Lohengrin (exc). (G. Moore, RCA SO/W. Pelletier, G. Swarthout, L. Pons/A. Kostelanetz, T. Schipa, orch/Rosario Bourdon, R. Bampton, R. Crooks, H. Jepson/A. Smallens, K. Flagstad, H. Lange, B. Castagna, K. Thorborg/K. Riedel, B. Sayão, H. Traubel/B. Reibold)

Ⓓ **09026 61580-2(5)** (4/94)
RCA/Met 100 Singers, 100 Years (pt 5)
Giordano: Andrea Chénier (exc); *Puccini:* Manon Lescaut (exc); *R. Strauss:* Rosenkavalier (exc); *Gounod:* Faust (exc); *Mussorgsky:* Boris Godunov (exc); *Offenbach:* Contes d'Hoffmann (exc); *Puccini:* Madama Butterfly (exc); *Barber:* Vanessa (exc); *Donizetti:* Lucia di Lammermoor (exc). (Z. Milanov, RCA SO/A. Basile, J. Björling, E. Campi, Rome Op Orch, Rome Op Chor/J. Perlea, R. Stevens, E. Berger/F. Reiner, L. Warren/W. Pelletier, A. Kipnis/N. Berezowski, J. Novotná/F. Weissmann, L. Albanese/V. Trucco, E. Steber, R. Elias, R. Resnik, N. Gedda, G. Tozzi, G. Cehanovsky, NY Met Op Orch/D. Mitropoulos, J. Peerce/E. Leinsdorf)

Ⓓ **09026 61580-2(6)** (4/94)
RCA/Met 100 Singers, 100 Years (pt 6)
A. Thomas: Mignon (exc); *Verdi:* Aida (exc); *Puccini:* Manon Lescaut (exc); *Verdi:* Don Carlo (exc); Otello (exc); *Wagner:* Meistersinger (exc); *Verdi:* Macbeth (exc); *Puccini:* Bohème (exc); *Bellini:* Sonnambula (exc); *Rossini:* Barbiere di Siviglia (exc); *Verdi:* Ballo in maschera (exc); Otello (exc). (P. Munsel, RCA SO/S. Levin, R. Tucker/A. Toscanini, NBC SO, D. Kirsten/J-P. Morel, R. Merrill/R. Cellini, R. Vinay, G. Valdengo, S. Svanholm/F. Weissmann, J. Hines, NY Met Op Orch/E. Leinsdorf, G. di Stefano, R. Peters, C. Valletti, M. Anderson/D. Mitropoulos, T. Gobbi, Rome Op Orch/T. Serafin)

Ⓓ **09026 61580-2(7)** (4/94)
RCA/Met 100 Singers, 100 Years (pt 7)
Verdi: Macbeth (exc); Macbeth (exc); Traviata (exc); *Puccini:* Turandot (exc); *Leoncavallo:* Pagliacci (exc); *Barber:* Antony and Cleopatra (exc); *Bizet:* Carmen (exc); *Wagner:* Lohengrin (exc); *Verdi:* Aida (exc). (C. Bergonzi, NY Met Op Orch/E. Leinsdorf, Leonie Rysanek, G. Pechner, C. Ordassy, A. Moffo, Rome Op Orch/F. Previtali, B. Nilsson, J. Björling, J. Vickers/T. Serafin, L. Price, New Philh/T. Schippers, F. Corelli, VPO/H. von Karajan, S. Kónya, Boston SO, G. Bumbry, P. Domingo, LSO)

Ⓓ **09026 61580-2(8)** (4/94)
RCA/Met 100 Singers, 100 Years (pt 8)
Bizet: Carmen (exc); *Verdi:* Otello (exc); *M.D. Levy:* Mourning Becomes Electra (exc); *Puccini:* Bohème (exc); *Verdi:* Rigoletto (exc); Trovatore (exc); *Donizetti:* Favorita (exc); *Cilea:* Adriana Lecouvreur (exc); *Mozart:* Zauberflöte (exc); *Rossini:* Italiana in Algeri (exc); *Mozart:* Così fan tutte (exc); *Verdi:* Otello (exc). (M. Freni, VPO/H. von Karajan, R. Scotto, National PO/James Levine, S. Milnes, New Philh/A. Guadagno, M. Caballé, LPO/G. Solti, Alfredo Kraus, RCA Italiana Op Orch, F. Cossotto/Z. Mehta, S. Verrett/G. Prêtre, P. Domingo/N. Santi, M. Talvela, M. Horne, Solisti Veneti/C. Scimone, K. Te Kanawa, Strasbourg PO/A. Lombard, K. Ricciarelli, Rome PO/G. Gavazzeni)

Ⓓ **09026 61583-2(5)** (8/93)
Julian Bream Edition (pt 5)
Dowland: Almains (exc); Galliards (exc); Ballad Settings (exc); Pavans (exc); Jigs, Corantos, Toys, etc (exc); Fantasies (exc); *Britten:* Chinese Songs; Folk Songs (exc); Gloriana (exc); *Walton:* Anon in Love; *Seiber:* French Folk Songs; *Fricker:* O Mistress Mine; *Britten:* Nocturnal; *Morley:* Ayres (1600) (exc); *Rosseter:* What then is love but mourning; If she forsake me; When Laura smiles; *Ford:* Come, Phyllis; Musicke of Sundrie Kindes I (exc); *Dowland:* Second Booke of Songs (exc); First Book of Songs (exc); Pilgrimes solace (exc); Third and Last Booke of Songs (exc); First Book of Songs (exc); Second Booke of Songs (exc); Third and Last Booke of Songs (exc); In darknesse let mee dwell; *Bach:* Suite, BWV996; Partita in C minor, BWV997; Trio Sonatas, BWV525-530 (exc); *Villa-Lobos:* Guitar Concerto; Preludes; Etudes; *Rodrigo:* Concierto de Aranjuez; *L. Berkeley:* Guitar concerto; *Brouwer:* Concerto elegiaco; *Narváez:* Seys libros del delphin (exc). (P. Pears, J. Bream, J. Bream, G. Malcolm, LSO/A. Previn, Monteverdi Orch/J.E. Gardiner, RCA Victor CO/L. Brouwer)

Ⓓ **09026 61601-2** (9/94)
J. Bream Edition, Vol.18: Music for Voice & Gtr
Britten: Chinese Songs; Folk Songs (exc); Gloriana (exc); *Walton:* Anon in Love; *Seiber:* French Folk Songs; *Fricker:* O Mistress Mine; *Britten:* Nocturnal. (P. Pears, J. Bream)

Ⓓ **09026 61634-2**
Verdi & Puccini Duets
Verdi: Otello (exc); Ballo in maschera (exc); Aida (exc); *Puccini:* Manon Lescaut (exc); Madama Butterfly (exc); Tosca (exc). (L. Price, E. Bainbridge, G. Bumbry, P. Domingo, John Alldis Ch, LSO, New Philh/N. Santi/E. Leinsdorf/Z. Mehta)

Ⓓ **09026 61635-2** (5/95)
Margaret Price sings Mozart
Mozart: Clemenza di Tito (exc); Nozze di Figaro (exc); Entführung (exc); Rè Pastore (exc); Don Giovanni (exc); Idomeneo (exc); Kleine deutsche Kantate, K619; Vado, ma dove?, K583; Vorrei spiegarvi, K418; Ch'io mi scordi di te, K490; Al desio, K577; Bella mia fiamma, K528; Ch'io mi scordi di te, K505; Nehmt meinen Dank, K383; *Mussorgsky:* Nursery; *Liszt:* Petrarch Sonnets, S270. (M. Price, ECO, LPO/J. Lockhart, J. Lockhart)

Ⓓ **09026 61674-2** (1/94)
Borodin—Orchestral Works
Borodin: Prince Igor (exc); Prince Igor (exc); Symphony 1; Symphony 3. (Russian St SO/E. Svetlanov)

Ⓓ **09026 61700-2** (2/94)
Works for Violin & Orchestra
Mendelssohn: Violin Concerto, Op. 64; *Vaughan Williams:* Lark Ascending; *Dvořák:* Romance, Op.11; *Massenet:* Thaïs (exc). (A.A. Meyers, Philh/A. Litton)

Ⓓ **09026 61778-2(02)** (11/94)
The Heifetz Collection, Vol.2 - 1925-34
Achron: Hebrew Melody; *Albéniz:* Suite española 1; *Bach:* English Suites, BWV806-811 (exc); Solo Violin Partitas and Sonatas (exc); *Castelnuovo-Tedesco:* Sea murmurs, Op. 24a; Alt Wien (exc); *Clérambault:* Largo in C minor; *Couperin:* Livre de Clavecin III (exc); *Debussy:* Préludes (exc); Plus que lente; Enfant prodigue (exc); *Dohnányi:* Ruralia hungarica (exc); *Drigo:* Airs de ballet (exc); *Elgar:* Capricieuse; *Falla:* Canciones populares españolas (exc); *Glazunov:* Violin Concerto; *Godowsky:* Triakontameron (exc); *Grieg:* Lyric Pieces, Op. 71 (exc); Stimmungen, Op. 73 (exc); Violin Sonata 3 (exc); *Hummel:* Rondo, Op. 11; *Korngold:* Much Ado About Nothing Suite (exc); *Mendelssohn:* Lieder, Op. 34 (exc); *Milhaud:* Saudades do Brasil (exc); *Moszkowski:* Pieces, Op. 45 (exc); *Mozart:* Violin Concerto, K219; *Paganini:* Caprices, Op. 1 (exc); *Ponce:* Estrellita; *Ravel:* Tzigane; *Rimsky-Korsakov:* Tale of Tsar Saltan (exc); *Sarasate:* Danzas españolas (exc); *Schubert:* Ave Maria, D839; Impromptus (exc); Piano Sonata, D850 (exc); *R. Strauss:* Stimmungsbilder (exc); Violin Sonata; *Vivaldi:* Sonatas, Op. 2 (exc); *Wieniawski:* Scherzo-tarantelle, Op. 16. (J. Heifetz, I. Achron, A. Sándor, LPO/J. Barbirolli)

Ⓓ **09026 61778-2(03)** (11/94)
The Heifetz Collection, Vol. 3
Bach: Solo Violin Partitas and Sonatas (exc); *Bazzini:* Ronde des lutins; *Dinicu:* Hora staccato; *Falla:* Vida breve (exc); *Glazunov:* Méditation, Op. 32; *Grieg:* Violin Sonata 2; *Paganini:* Caprices, Op. 1 (exc); *Poulenc:* Mouvements perpétuels (exc); *C. Scott:* Tallahassee Suite; *Szymanowski:* King Roger (exc); *Vieuxtemps:* Violin Concerto 4; *Wieniawski:* Violin Concerto 2; Polonaise, Op. 4. (J. Heifetz, E. Bay, A. Sándor, LPO/J. Barbirolli)

Ⓓ **09026 61778-2(06)** (11/94)
The Heifetz Collection, Vol. 6
Arensky: Violin Concerto (exc); *Bach:* 2-Violin Concerto; English Suites, BWV806-811 (exc); *Bax:* Mediterranean; *Beethoven:* German Dances, WoO8 (exc); *Bruch:* Scottish Fantasy; *Castelnuovo-Tedesco:* Sea murmurs, Op. 24a; Tango, Op. 24b; *Chopin:* Nocturnes (exc); *Debussy:* Ariettes oubliées (exc); Chansons de Bilitis (exc); Préludes (exc); *Falla:* Canciones populares españolas (exc); Amor Brujo (exc); *Halffter:* Danzas (exc); *Korngold:* Much Ado About Nothing Suite (exc); Much Ado About Nothing Suite (exc); *Medtner:* Fairy tales, Op. 20 (exc); *Mendelssohn:* Piano Trio 1 (exc); Songs without words (exc); *Milhaud:* Saudades do brasil (exc); *Mozart:* Divertimento, K334 (exc); *Nin:* Cantos de España (exc); *Poldowski:* Tango; *Ravel:* Valses nobles et sentimentales (exc); *Rimsky-Korsakov:* Tale of Tsar Saltan (exc); *Sarasate:* Danzas españolas (exc); *Schubert:* Piano Sonata, D850 (exc); *Tansman:* Pieces (exc); *Vieuxtemps:* Violin Concerto 5. (J. Heifetz, E. Bay, RCA Victor CO/F. Waxman, RCA Victor SO/W. Steinberg, LSO/M. Sargent)

Ⓓ **09026 61778-2(19)** (11/94)
The Heifetz Collection, Vol. 19
Aguirre: Huella, Op. 49; *Benjamin:* Jamaican Rumba; *Rob Bennett:* Hexapoda; *Traditional:* White Christmas; *Brahms:* Hungarian Dances (exc); *C. Burleigh:* Pictures, Op. 30 (exc); Small Concert Pieces, Op. 21 (exc); *Chopin:* Nocturnes (exc); *Debussy:* Beau soir; Suite bergamasque (exc); Children's Corner (exc); *Dvořák:* Humoresques, Op. 101 (exc); *Dyer:* Outlandish Suite (exc); *Foster:* Jeanie with the light brown hair; Old folks at home; *S. Gardner:* Pieces, Op. 5 (exc); *Gershwin:* Porgy and Bess (exc); Preludes; *Gluck:* Orfeo ed Euridice (exc); *Godard:* Jocelyn (exc); *Godowsky:* Impressions (exc); *Grasse:* Wellenspiel; *Herbert:* A la valse; *Krein:* Dance 4; *Löhr:* Where my caravan has rested; *Prokofiev:* Love for 3 Oranges Suite

(exc); Romeo and Juliet Pieces (exc); *Ravel:* Pièce en forme de habanera; *Rimsky-Korsakov:* Golden Cockerel (exc); *Rossini:* Barbiere di Siviglia (exc); *Saint-Saëns:* Carnaval des animaux (exc); *Schumann:* Waldszenen (exc); *Shostakovich:* Preludes, Op. 34 (exc); *Tchaikovsky:* Souvenir d'un lieu cher, Op. 42 (exc); *Traditional:* Deep River; Gweedore Brae; *F. Valle:* Prelude XV; *Weill:* Dreigroschenoper (exc); *C. C. White:* Levee Dance, Op. 27/2. (J. Heifetz, B. Crosby, E. Bay, M. Kaye, orch/S. Camarata/V. Young)

09026 61778-2(35) (11/94)
The Heifetz Collection, Vol. 35
Rob Bennett: Song Sonata; *Gershwin:* Porgy and Bess (exc); *Mendelssohn:* Octet, Op. 20; *Rachmaninov:* Songs, Op. 38 (exc); *Shostakovich:* Fantastic dances (exc); *Shulman:* American Folksongs Suite (exc); *Stravinsky:* Berceuse; *Toch:* Divertimenti, Op. 37 (exc); *Heifetz:* Heifetz on Music. (J. Heifetz, I. Baker, A. Belnick, J. Stepansky, W. Primrose, V. Majewski, G. Piatigorsky, G. Rejto, B. Smith, E. Bay)

09026 61778-2(40) (11/94)
The Heifetz Collection, Vol. 40
Achron: Hebrew Melody; *Debussy:* Plus que lente; *Dinicu:* Hora Staccato; *Drigo:* Airs de Ballet (exc); *Gershwin:* Porgy and Bess (exc); Preludes; *Godowsky:* Triakontameron (exc); *Khachaturian:* Gayaneh (exc); *Korngold:* Much Ado About Nothing Suite (exc); *Kroll:* Banjo and Fiddle; *Mendelssohn:* Lieder, Op. 34 (exc); *Ponce:* Estrellita; *Poulenc:* Presto; *Prokofiev:* Love for 3 Oranges Suite (exc); *Rachmaninov:* Songs, Op. 38 (exc); Cello Pieces, Op. 2 (exc); Songs, Op. 34 (exc); *Sarasate:* Danzas españolas (exc); *Schubert:* Ave Maria, D839; *Wieniawski:* Scherzo-tarantelle, Op. 16. (J. Heifetz, E. Bay, B. Smith)

09026 61790-2 (12/93)
Concerto! Stoltzman plays Copland etc.
Copland: Clarinet Concerto; *G. Jenkins:* Goodbye; *Bernstein:* West Side Story (exc); Clarinet Sonata; *Gershwin:* Shall We Dance (exc); Porgy and Bess (exc); Short Story; Preludes. (R. Stoltzman, LSO/M. Tilson Thomas/E. Stern)

09026 61792-2 (8/94)
Reiner conducts Wagner & Humperdinck
Wagner: Meistersinger (exc); Götterdämmerung (exc); Lohengrin (exc); Tannhäuser (exc); *Humperdinck:* Hänsel und Gretel (exc). (Chicago SO, RCA Victor Orch/F. Reiner)

09026 61806-2 (12/93)
Puccini—Tosca
Puccini: Tosca (Cpte). (R. Kabaivanska, L. Pavarotti, I. Wixell, F. Federici, M. Bolognesi, A. Mariotti, U. Carosi, G. Zecchillo, V. Gricolo, Rome Op Chor, Rome Op Orch/D. Oren)

09026 61863-2 (8/94)
Saint-Saëns/Falla/Franck—Piano Works
Saint-Saëns: Piano Concerto 2; *Falla:* Nights in the Gardens of Spain; *Franck:* Symphonic Variations; *Prokofiev:* Love for 3 Oranges Suite (exc); *Falla:* Amor Brujo (exc). (A. Rubinstein, Philadelphia/E. Ormandy, Sym of the Air/A. Wallenstein)

09026 61867-2
Christmas Treasures
Tchaikovsky: Nutcracker (exc); *Traditional:* Angels we have heard on high; First Nowell; *Mozart:* German Dances, K605 (exc); *Adam:* Minuit, Chrétiens (exc); *Traditional:* Deck the hall; O come, all ye faithful; Santa Claus is coming to town; *Schubert:* Ave Maria, D839; *Traditional:* Carol of the Bells; I saw three ships; Hark! the herald angels sing; *Humperdinck:* Hänsel und Gretel (exc); *L. Anderson:* Sleigh Ride; *Traditional:* Guardian Angels; God rest you, merry gentlemen; White Christmas; Ride on, King Jesus; Stille Nacht; O little town of Bethlehem; *Handel:* Messiah (exc). (L. Price, R. Elias, M. Anderson, M. Lanza, G. Tozzi, R. Shaw Chorale, Chor, Luboff Ch, Chicago SO, Boston Pops, Orch, New SO/F. Reiner/Robert Shaw/L. Engel/A. Fiedler/P. Baron/Robert Russell Bennett/L. Stokowski/L. de Paur)

09026 61884-2 **09026 61884-4**
Mario Lanza—Live in London
Cilea: Arlesiana (exc); *Monteverdi:* L'Arianna (exc); *A. Scarlatti:* Honestà negli amore (exc); *Niedermeyer:* Pietà, Signore; *Giannini:* Tell me, o blue, blue sky; *Behrend:* Bonjour, ma belle; *Charles:* House on the Hill; *Puccini:* Tosca (exc); *Nutile:* Mamma mia, che vo' sapè; *Tosti:* 'A vucchella; Marechiare; *Romberg:* New Moon (exc); *Herbert:* Naughty Marietta (exc); *Brodszky:* Because you're mine (exc); *V. Young:* Seven Hills of Rome (exc); *Verdi:* Rigoletto (exc). (M. Lanza, C. Callinicos)

09026 61885-2 (5/94) **09026 61885-4** (5/94)
Here's A Howdy Do—A Gilbert & Sullivan Festival
Sullivan: HMS Pinafore (exc); Mikado (exc); Gondoliers (exc); Ruddigore (exc); Pirates of Penzance (exc). (King's Sngrs)

09026 61886-2 **09026 61886-4**
Operas Greatest Love Songs
Bizet: Carmen (exc); *Mozart:* Nozze di Figaro (exc); *Flotow:* Martha (exc); *Puccini:* Madama Butterfly (exc); *Verdi:* Aida (exc); Traviata (exc); *Puccini:* Tosca (exc); Bohème (exc); *Massenet:* Chérubin (exc); *Mozart:* Zauberflöte (exc); *Puccini:* Turandot (exc); Tosca (exc); *Verdi:* Rigoletto (exc); *Gounod:* Roméo et Juliette (exc); *Wagner:* Tristan und Isolde (exc). (F. Corelli, J. Varady, P. Domingo, A. Moffo, J. Björling, M. Caballé, L. Pavarotti, R. Tucker, D. Upshaw, E. Tappy, M. Price, L. Price, VPO, BRSO, LSO, Rome Op Orch, RCA Italiana Op Orch, Munich RSO, New Philh, Philh/H. von Karajan/Colin Davis/N. Santi/E. Leinsdorf/J. Perlea/G. Prêtre/D. Oren/P. Steinberg/James Levine/R. Abbado/G. Solti/H. Lewis)

09026 61893-2 (9/94)
Pierre Monteux Edition
Beethoven: Ruinen von Athen (exc); Symphony 4; *Bach:* Passacaglia and Fugue, BWV582; *Beethoven:* Symphony 8; *Berlioz:* Symphonie fantastique; Benvenuto Cellini (exc); Troyens (exc); Damnation de Faust (exc); *Brahms:* Symphony 2; Schicksalslied, Op. 54; *Mahler:* Kindertotenlieder; *Chausson:* Symphony, Op. 20; Poème de l'amour et de la mer; *Chabrier:* Roi malgré lui (exc); *Debussy:* Images; Images oubliées (exc); Nocturnes; *Liszt:* Préludes; *Scriabin:* Poème de l'extase; *Saint-Saëns:* Havanaise; *Debussy:* La Mer; *Delibes:* Coppélia (exc); Sylvia (exc); *Gounod:* Faust (exc); *Franck:* Symphony; Pièces (1878) (exc); *Indy:* Istar, Op. 42; Symphonie, Op. 25; Fervaal (exc); Symphony 2; *Ravel:* Daphnis et Chloé Suites (exc); Valses nobles et sentimentales; Alborada del gracioso; La valse; *Lalo:* Roi d'Ys (exc); *Ibert:* Escales; *Rimsky-Korsakov:* Scheherazade; Sadko; Symphony 2; *R. Strauss:* Heldenleben; Tod und Verklärung; *Stravinsky:* Petrushka (Cpte); Rite of Spring (Cpte); *Tchaikovsky:* Symphony 4; Symphony 5; Symphony 6. (G. Swarthout, M. Anderson, L. Kogan, M. Shapiro, Berkshire Fest Chor, Stanford Univ Chor, San Francisco SO, Chicago SO, Boston SO, RCA Victor SO/P. Monteux)

09026 61924-2 (12/94)
Donizetti—Don Pasquale
Donizetti: Don Pasquale (Cpte). (R. Bruson, E. Mei, F. Lopardo, T. Allen, A. Giacomotti, Bavarian Rad Chor, Munich RO/R. Abbado)

09026 61958-2 (8/94)
Russian Showpieces
Mussorgsky: Pictures; *Tchaikovsky:* Suite 1 (exc); *Mussorgsky:* Night on the Bare Mountain; *Borodin:* Prince Igor (exc); *Tchaikovsky:* Marche slave; *Kabalevsky:* Colas Breugnon (exc); *Glinka:* Ruslan and Lyudmila (exc). (Chicago SO/F. Reiner)

09026 61983-2 (8/94)
Leontyne Price sings Barber
Barber: Hermit Songs, Op. 29; Songs, Op. 10 (exc); Songs, Op. 2 (exc); Songs, Op. 13 (exc); Nuvoletta, Op. 25; Knoxville; Antony and Cleopatra (exc). (L. Price, S. Barber, New Philh/T. Schippers)

09026 62504-2 (11/95)
Great Tenor Arias - Ben Heppner
Leoncavallo: Bohème (exc); *Verdi:* Luisa Miller (exc); Forza del destino (exc); Aida (exc); Trovatore (exc); *Puccini:* Manon Lescaut (exc); Turandot (exc); Fanciulla del West (exc); *Bizet:* Carmen (exc); *Meyerbeer:* Africaine (exc); *Massenet:* Hérodiade (exc); Cid (exc); *Giordano:* Andrea Chénier (exc). (B. Heppner, Bavarian Rad Chor, Munich RO/R. Abbado)

09026 62538-2 (1/95)
Weber—Der Freischütz
Weber: Freischütz (Cpte). (S. Sweet, P. Seiffert, R. Ziesak, K. Rydl, A. Schmidt, M. Hölle, A. Scharinger, P. Matić, R. Trekel, Berlin Rad Chor, Berlin RO/M. Janowski)

09026 62540-2 (7/95)
Cathy Berberian sings Berio & Weill
Berio: Recital I; Folk Songs; *Weill:* Dreigroschenoper (exc); Marie Galante (exc); Happy End (exc). (C. Berberian, London Sinfonietta, Juilliard Ens/L. Berio)

09026 62541-2 (10/95)
Pavarotti - The Early Years, Vol.1
Bellini: Puritani (exc); *Donizetti:* Elisir d'amore (exc); Fille du régiment (exc); *Massenet:* Manon (exc); *Puccini:* Bohème (exc); Bohème (exc); *Rossini:* Stabat mater (exc). (M. Freni, L. Pavarotti, G. Morresi, La Scala Chor, Rome SO, Catania Teatro Massimo Bellini Orch, La Scala Orch, Modena Teatro Comunale Orch, Santa Cecilia Academy Orch/N. Bonavolontà/N. Sanzogno/A. Quadri/P. Maag/C. M. Giulini/L. Magiera)

09026 62546-2 (4/95)
Salut d'amour
Elgar: Salut d'amour; *Rentaro:* Kojyo No Tsuki; *Falla:* Suite populaire espagnole; *Debussy:* Plus que lente; Préludes (exc); *Kreisler:* Scherzo-caprice, Op. 6; Liebesleid; Liebesfreud; *Rachmaninov:* Songs, Op. 34 (exc); *Paradies:* Sicilienne; *F. Valle:* Prelude XV; *Kosaku:* Aka-Tonbo; *Gershwin:* Porgy and Bess (exc); *Ravel:* Pièce en forme de Habanera. (A. A. Meyers, S. Rivers)

09026 62547-2 (1/95)
Divas in Song—Marilyn Horne's 60th Birthday
Britten: On This Island, Op. 11 (exc); *Schubert:* Musensohn, D764; *Rachmaninov:* Songs, Op. 34 (exc); *Mahler:* Knaben Wunderhorn (exc); *Granados:* Goyescas (exc); *R. Strauss:* Lieder, Op. 10 (exc); Lieder, Op. 17 (exc); *Brahms:* Lieder, Op. 43 (exc); *Schoenberg:* Cabaret Songs (exc); *J. Strauss II:* Frühlingsstimmen, Op. 410; *Foster:* If you've only got a moustache; *Turina:* Poema en forma de canciones (exc); *Lehár:* Lustige Witwe (exc); Land des Lächelns (exc); *Kander:* Sullivan Ballou Letter; *J. Martini:* Plaisir d'amour; *Rodgers:* Oklahoma! (exc); *Kern:* Show Boat (exc); *Bolcom:* Cabaret Songs (exc); *Copland:* Old American Songs 2 (exc). (M. Horne, M. Caballé, H. Donath, R. Fleming, R. A. Swenson, F. von Stade, O. Bjarnason, S. Ramey, W. Jones, Martin Katz, M. Burgueras, K. Donath, J. Levine)

09026 62550-2
Ten Tenors in Love
Puccini: Tosca (exc); *Mozart:* Zauberflöte (exc); *Flotow:* Martha (exc); *Testa:* Il corragio di dire ti amo; *De Curtis:* Non ti scordar di me; *Verdi:* Traviata (exc); *Crescenzo:* Première caresse; *Grieg:* Melodies of the Heart, Op. 5 (exc); *Donizetti:* Elisir d'amore (exc); *Brodszky:* Toast of New Orleans (exc); *Verdi:* Aida (exc); Trovatore (exc); *Lehár:* Giuditta (exc); *Bizet:* Carmen (exc); *Donizetti:* Favorita (exc); *Puccini:* Bohème (exc); *Lehár:* Land des Lächelns (exc); *Puccini:* Turandot (exc). (L. Pavarotti, F. Wunderlich, E. Caruso, P. Domingo, M. Lanza, R. Tucker, J. Peerce, J. Björling, F. Araiza, B. Heppner, Rome Op Chor, Rome Op Orch, Hamburg St Op Orch, orch, LSO, Berlin SO, RCA Victor Orch, Barcelona SO, RCA Orch, Munich RO/D. Oren/A. Rother/J. Pasternack/E. Morricone/C. Callinicos/F. Previtali/W. Bass/N. Santi/R. Sinatra/J. Perlea/A. Basile/A. Melichar/F. Reiner/G. Navarro/R. Cellini/R. Weikert/R. Abbado)

09026 62587-2 (8/95)
Dvořák/Smetana/Weinberger—Orchestral Works
Dvořák: Symphony 9; Carnival; *Smetana:* Bartered Bride (exc); *Weinberger:* Schwanda the Bagpiper (exc). (Chicago SO/F. Reiner)

09026 62595-2
Opera Duets
Verdi: Forza del destino (exc); *Bizet:* Pêcheurs de perles (exc); *Puccini:* Bohème (exc); *Zandonai:* Francesca da Rimini (exc); *Ponchielli:* Gioconda (exc); *Verdi:* Vespri siciliani (exc); *Puccini:* Madama Butterfly (exc); *Verdi:* Otello (exc). (K. Ricciarelli, P. Domingo, S. Milnes, LSO/A. Guadagno, Santa Cecilia Academy Orch/G. Gavazzeni)

09026 62596-2
Prima Donna Collection - Higlights
Purcell: Dido (exc); *Gluck:* Alceste (1776) (exc); *Verdi:* Rigoletto (exc); *G. Charpentier:* Louise (exc); *Verdi:* Simon Boccanegra (exc); *Bizet:* Carmen (exc); *Wagner:* Tristan und Isolde (exc); *Puccini:* Suor Angelica (exc); *Massenet:* Manon (exc); *Giordano:* Andrea Chénier (exc); *Dvořák:* Rusalka (exc); *Korngold:* Tote Stadt (exc); *Barber:* Vanessa (exc). (L. Price, RCA Italiana Op Orch/F. Molinari-Pradelli, LSO/E. Downes, Philh/H. Lewis, New Philh/N. Santi)

09026 62646-2 (11/95)
Wagner—Lohengrin
Wagner: Lohengrin (Cpte). (B. Heppner, S. Sweet, E. Marton, S. Leiferkus, J-H. Rootering, B. Terfel, Bavarian Rad Chor, BRSO/Colin Davis)

09026 62647-2
Marilyn Horne - The Men in My Life
Van Heusen: Going My Way (exc); *Gershwin:* Lady, Be Good! (exc); Delicious (exc); Goldwyn Follies (exc); *Berlin:* Call Me Madam (exc); *Styne:* Bells are Ringing (exc); Gypsy (exc); *Porter:* Du Barry Was a Lady (exc); Rosalie (exc); Anything Goes (exc); *Kern:* Very Warm for May (exc); *Rodgers:* South Pacific (exc); Pal Joey (exc); *B. Merrill:* I Get Embarrassed; *A. Lloyd Webber:* Phantom of the Opera (exc); *Sondheim:* Company (exc); *Bernstein:* West Side Story (exc). (M. Horne, J. Hadley, T. Hampson, S. Ramey, S. Malas, American Th Orch/P. Gemignani)

09026 62674-2
Fortissimo!
R. Strauss: Also sprach Zarathustra (exc); *Vaughan Williams:* Symphony 1 (exc); *Wagner:* Walküre (exc);

Mussorgsky: Night on the Bare Mountain; *Prokofiev:* Romeo and Juliet Suites (exc); *Puccini:* Turandot (exc); *Tchaikovsky:* Nutcracker (exc); *Copland:* Fanfare for the Common Man; *Elgar:* Pomp and Circumstance Marches (exc); *Hancock:* Introit for a Feast Day; *Mussorgsky:* Pictures (exc); *Orff:* Carmina Burana (exc); *Stravinsky:* Rite of Spring (exc); *Rossini:* Guillaume Tell (exc); *R. Strauss:* Festliches Präludium; *Tchaikovsky:* 1812. (E. Marton, G. Hancock, Philh Chor, Bavarian Rad Chor, Bamberg SO, Philh, Staatskapelle Dresden, Dallas SO, Munich RO, St. Louis SO, Musica Sacra, RPO, Leningrad PO, Leningrad Military Orch/H. Stein/L. Slatkin/M. Janowski/E. Mata/C. P. Flor/R. Abbado/R. Westenburg/Y. Temirkanov/G. Patanè)

Ⓒ **09026 62681-2**
Mr Jerry Hadley—Golden Days
Friml: Vagabond King (exc); Firefly (exc); *Herbert:* Naughty Marietta (exc); Red Mill (exc); Princess Pat (exc); Only Girl (exc); Fortune Teller (exc); Angel Face (exc); Indian Summer; *Romberg:* New Moon (exc); Desert Song (exc); Student Prince (exc); Student Prince (exc); Night is Young (exc); I love to go swimmin'. (J. Hadley, M. Lanza, T. Randall, Harvard Glee Club, American Th Orch/P. Gemignani)

Ⓒ **09026 62684-2** (10/95)
Rimsky-Korsakov—Symphony No 3, etc
Rimsky-Korsakov: Symphony 3; Sadko; Mlada (exc); Maid of Pskov (exc); Tale of Tsar Saltan (exc); Tsar's Bride (exc). (Russian St SO/E. Svetlanov)

Ⓒ **09026 62689-2**
The Voices of Living Stereo, Volume 1
Gluck: Orfeo ed Euridice (exc); *Puccini:* Tosca (exc); Madama Butterfly (exc); *Donizetti:* Lucia di Lammermoor (exc); *Barber:* Vanessa (exc); *Rossini:* Barbiere di Siviglia (exc); *Verdi:* Macbeth (exc); *Puccini:* Turandot (exc); *Verdi:* Trovatore (exc); Otello (exc); *Puccini:* Bohème (exc); *Bizet:* Carmen (exc). (Z. Milanov, A. Moffo, R. Peters, E. Steber, Leonie Rysanek, R. Tebaldi, B. Nilsson, L. Price, L. Londi, R. Stevens, R. Elias, R. Resnik, Mario Carlin, J. Peerce, N. Gedda, C. Bergonzi, J. Björling, J. Vickers, R. Tucker, F. Corelli, R. Merrill, L. Warren, T. Gobbi, G. Tozzi, Rome Op Chor, Rome Op Orch, NY Met Op Orch, VPO/P. Monteux/E. Leinsdorf/T. Serafin/D. Mitropoulos/H. von Karajan/A. Basile)

Ⓒ **09026 62699-2** ▭ **09026 62699-4**
Opera's Greatest Duets
Verdi: Otello (exc); Trovatore (exc); Forza del Destino (exc); Don Carlo (exc); Traviata (exc); Otello (exc); *Bizet:* Pêcheurs de Perles (exc); *Mozart:* Don Giovanni (exc); *Puccini:* Madama Butterfly (exc); Bohème (exc); Bohème (exc); *Offenbach:* Contes d'Hoffmann (exc); *Gershwin:* Porgy and Bess (exc); *Bellini:* Norma (exc). (L. Price, P. Domingo, S. Milnes, R. Elias, R. Tucker, E. Mathis, A. Titus, M. Horne, M. Freni, L. Pavarotti, M. Caballé, S. Verrett, W. Warfield, C. Bergonzi, New Philh, LSO, Rome Op Orch, BRSO, NY Met Op Orch, Bologna Teatro Comunale Orch, RCA Victor SO, RCA Italiana Op Orch/N. Santi/A. Guadagno/A. Basile/R. Kubelík/James Levine/L. Magiera/S. Henderson/G. Prêtre)

Ⓒ **09026 62710-2** (4/95)
Rachmaninov—Orchestral Works
Rachmaninov: Paganini Rhapsody; Symphonic Dances; Aleko (exc). (D. Alexeev, St Petersburg PO/Y. Temirkanov)

Ⓒ **09026 62712-2** (11/95)
Weber—Symphonies, etc
Weber: Symphony 1; Symphony 2; Freischütz (exc). (Philh/C. P. Flor)

Ⓒ **09026 68014-2** (10/95)
Pavarotti - The Early Years, Vol.2
Bellini: Capuleti (exc); Puritani (exc); *Donizetti:* Lucia di Lammermoor (exc); *Puccini:* Turandot (exc); *Verdi:* Luisa Miller (exc); Rigoletto (exc); Traviata (exc); Lombardi (exc). (M. Freni, S. Mazzetti, L. Pavarotti, B. Giaiotti, G. Ferrin, A. Giacomotti, chor, La Scala Chor, Grudgionz Fest Chor, Rome SO, Turin SO, Modena Teatro Comunale Orch, Rome Op Orch, La Scala Orch, Grudgionz Fest Orch/N. Bonavolontà/R. Muti/F. Molinari-Pradelli/M. Rossi/L. Magiera/G. Gavazzeni/C. Abbado/G-F. Masini)

Ⓒ **09026 68130-2**
Mario Lanza at his Best
Denza: Funiculì-Funiculà; *Falvo:* Dicitencello vuie; *Di Capua:* Maria, marì; *De Curtis:* Voce 'e notte!; Canta pe'me; *Cannio:* 'O surdato 'nnammurato; *Gambardella:* Comme facette mammeta; *Mario:* Santa Lucia luntana; *Cottrau:* Fenesta che lucive; *De Curtis:* Tu, ca nun chiagne!; *Cioffi:* 'Na sera 'e maggio; *N. Valente:* Passione; *Friml:* Vagabond King (exc). (M. Lanza, J. Raskin, Chor, Orch/F. Ferrara/C. Callinicos)

Ⓒ **09026 68132-2**
Pops Caviar—Russian Orchestral Fireworks
Borodin: In the Steppes of Central Asia; Prince Igor (exc); *Rimsky-Korsakov:* Russian Easter Festival Ov; Tale of Tsar Saltan (exc); *Khachaturian:* Gayaneh (exc); Masquerade (exc); *Tchaikovsky:* Eugene Onegin (exc); Sleeping Beauty (exc). (Boston Pops/A. Fiedler)

Ⓒ **09026 68139-2**
Rossini—Overtures
Rossini: Scala di seta (exc); Italiana in Algeri (exc); Barbiere di Siviglia (exc); Gazza ladra (exc); Semiramide (exc); Siège de Corinthe (exc); Guillaume Tell (exc). (Hanover Band/R. Goodman)

Ⓒ **09026 68185-2**
Encore!
L. Anderson: Fiddle-faddle; Syncopated clock; *Gershwin:* Promenade; *Falla:* Vida breve (exc); *Elgar:* Salut d'amour; *Boccherini:* String Quintets, G271-6 (exc); *Tchaikovsky:* Serenade, Op. 48 (exc); *Albéniz:* Suite española 1 (exc); *Rossini:* Sonate a quattro (exc); *Bach:* Motets (exc); *Corelli:* Suite for Strings (Arbos) (exc); *Vivaldi:* Concerti, Op. 8 (exc); *Schubert:* Minuets and Trios, D89 (exc); *Mozart:* Symphony 24; *Kreisler:* Marche miniature viennoise; *Prokofiev:* Love for 3 Oranges (exc); *Shostakovich:* Golden Age (exc); *Bartók:* Romanian Folkdances, Sz68 (exc); *Bock:* Fiddler on the Roof (exc); *Poltoratzsky:* Souvenir; *Sieczyński:* Wien, du Stadt meiner Träume. (Moscow Virtuosi/V. Spivakov)

Ⓒ **09026 68225-2** (10/95)
R. Strauss—Orchestral Works
R. Strauss: Also sprach Zarathustra; Rosenkavalier (exc); Don Juan. (BRSO/L. Maazel)

Ⓒ **74321 18574-2** ▭ **74321 18574-4**
Mario Lanza - The Ultimate Collection
Verdi: Rigoletto (exc); *Rimsky-Korsakov:* Sadko (exc); *Leoncavallo:* Pagliacci (exc); *Puccini:* Tosca (exc); *Brodszky:* Student Prince (exc); *Romberg:* Student Prince (exc); *Rodgers:* Carousel (exc); *Friml:* Firefly (exc); *Brodszky:* Toast of New Orleans (exc); Because you're mine (exc); *Taccani:* Come prima; *Rascel:* Arrivederci Roma; *Cottrau:* Santa Lucia; *Lara:* Granada; *Gounod:* Ave Maria; *Padilla:* Valencia; *Aaronson:* Loveliest Night of the Year; *Di Capua:* 'O sole mio; *Hardelot:* Because; *Denza:* Funiculì-Funiculà. (M. Lanza, E. Shapiro, chor, J. Alexander Ch, orch/R. Sinatra/C. Callinicos/H. René/F. Ferraro/G. Stoll/C. Savina)

Ⓒ **74321 24209-2**
Italian Opera Choruses
Bellini: Norma (exc); *Giordano:* Andrea Chénier (exc); *Leoncavallo:* Pagliacci (exc); *Mascagni:* Cavalleria Rusticana (exc); *Puccini:* Madama Butterfly (exc); Turandot (exc); *Verdi:* Aida (exc); Ernani (exc); Forza del destino (exc); Macbeth (exc); Nabucco (exc); Otello (exc); Rigoletto (exc); Traviata (exc); Trovatore (exc). (John Alldis Ch, Ambrosian Op Chor, RCA Italiana Op Chor, NY Met Op Chor, R. Shaw Chorale, Augsburg Cath Boys' Ch, Munich Rad Chor, LSO, National PO, RCA Italiana Op Orch, New Philh, NY Met Op Orch, LPO, orch, Munich RO/E. Leinsdorf/James Levine/G. Solti/Z. Mehta/N. Santi/T. Schippers/C. F. Cillario/Robert Shaw/R. Abbado)

Ⓒ **74321 24218-2**
Gershwin—Porgy & Bess Highlights
Gershwin: Porgy and Bess (exc); *Bernstein:* West Side Story Symphonic Dances. (L. Price, B. Webb, B. Hall, M. Stewart, M. Burton, J.W. Bubbles, R. Henson, W. Warfield, M. Boatwright, Alonzo Jones, RCA Victor Chor, RCA Victor Orch/S. Henderson/Robert Russell Bennett)

Ⓒ **74321 24284-2** ▭ **74321 24284-4**
Opera's Greatest Heroines
Puccini: Madama Butterfly (exc); *Mozart:* Nozze di Figaro (exc); *Verdi:* Ballo in maschera (exc); *Rossini:* Barbiere di Siviglia (exc); *Delibes:* Lakmé (exc); *Verdi:* Aida (exc); *Bach:* St Matthew Passion, BWV244 (exc); *Verdi:* Rigoletto (exc); *Grieg:* Peer Gynt (exc); *Gounod:* Faust (exc); *Puccini:* Bohème (exc); *R. Strauss:* Lieder, Op. 27 (exc); *Gounod:* Ave Maria; *Verdi:* Traviata (exc); *Brahms:* Alto Rhapsody, Op. 53; *Bizet:* Carmen (exc); *Puccini:* Gianni Schicchi (exc); *Rachmaninov:* Songs, Op. 34 (exc); *Puccini:* Tosca (exc); *Mozart:* Nozze di Figaro (exc); *Verdi:* Vespri Siciliani (exc); *Massenet:* Werther (exc); *G. Martini:* Plaisir d'amour; *Bellini:* Norma (exc); *Canteloube:* Chants d'Auvergne (exc); *Rossini:* Otello (exc); *Donizetti:* Anna Bolena (exc); *Debussy:* Ariettes oubliées (exc); *Verdi:* Forza del destino (exc). (L. Albanese, M. Caballé, A. Galli-Curci, N. Melba, A. Moffo, L. Pons, R. Ponselle, L. Price, M. Price, K. Ricciarelli, E. Steber, M. Horne, F. von Stade, S. Verrett, C. Vozza, M. Anderson, Martin Katz, F. Rupp, NY Met Op Chor, RCA Italiana Op Chor, San Francisco Sym Chor, orch, American SO, ECO, New Philh, NY Met Op Orch, RCA Italiana Op Orch, RCA Victor Orch, Rome PO, San Francisco SO, Victor Sinfonietta, VPO/Rosario Bourdon/C. F. Cillario/E. Downes/G. Gavazzeni/H. von Karajan/E. Leinsdorf/J. Lockhart/D. Mitropoulos/P. Monteux/J-P. Morel/J. Pasternack/W. Pelletier/G. Prêtre/W. B. Rogers/T. Schippers/Robert Shaw/L. Stokowski/F. Weissmann)

Ⓒ **74321 24790-2**
Carl Orff 100 Years Edition
Orff: Carmina Burana; Kluge (Cpte); Mond (Cpte); Christmas Play (Cpte); Easter Play (Cpte); Astutuli (Cpte). (T. Stewart, G. Frick, L. Popp, R. Kogel, M. Schmidt, C. Nicolai, F. Gruber, H. Friedrich, K. Böhme, J. van Kesteren, H. Friedrich, R. Kogel, F. Gruber, B. Kusche, R. Grumbach, H. Buchta, F. Crass, H. Prey, C. Orff, R. Kiermeyer Children's Ch, Tolz Boys' Ch, Bavarian Rad Chor, Munich RO/K. Eichhorn)

Ⓒ **74321 25278-2**
Beethoven—Fidelio
Beethoven: Fidelio (Cpte). (J. Altmeyer, S. Jerusalem, S. Nimsgern, P. Meven, C. Nossek, R. Wohlers, T. Adam, K. König, F-P. Späthe, Leipzig Rad Chor, Berlin Rad Men's Chor, Leipzig Gewandhaus/K. Masur)

Ⓒ **74321 25279-2**
Bizet—Carmen
Bizet: Carmen (Cpte). (A. Moffo, F. Corelli, H. Donath, P. Cappuccilli, A. Auger, J. Berbié, J-C. Benoit, K-E. Mercker, B. McDaniel, J. Van Dam, Schoenberg Boys' Ch, Berlin Deutsche Op Chor, Berlin Deutsche Op Orch/L. Maazel)

Ⓒ **74321 25280-2**
Donizetti—L'Elisir d'amore
Donizetti: Elisir d'amore (Cpte). (L. Popp, P. Dvorský, B. Weikl, E. Nesterenko, E. Hobarth, Bavarian Rad Chor, Munich RO/H. Wallberg)

Ⓒ **74321 25281-2**
Humperdinck—Hänsel und Gretel
Humperdinck: Hänsel und Gretel (Cpte). (A. Moffo, H. Donath, D. Fischer-Dieskau, C. Berthold, A. Auger, L. Popp, C. Ludwig, Tolz Boys' Ch, Munich RO/K. Eichhorn)

Ⓒ **74321 25282-2**
Leoncavallo—I Pagliacci; Mascagni—Cavalleria rusticana
Leoncavallo: Pagliacci (Cpte); *Mascagni:* Cavalleria Rusticana (Cpte). (V. Atlantov, L. Popp, B. Weikl, W. Brendel, A. Ionita, M. Arroyo, F. Bonisolli, B. Weikl, L. Budai, J. Falk, Tolz Boys' Ch, Bavarian Rad Chor, Munich RO/L. Gardelli)

Ⓒ **74321 25283-2** (10/95)
Mozart—Die Entführung aus dem Serail
Mozart: Entführung (Cpte). (E. Gruberová, G. Ebel, F. Araiza, N. Orth, R. Bracht, H. Leipnitz, Bavarian Rad Chor, Munich RO/H. Wallberg)

Ⓒ **74321 25284-2**
Mozart—Don Giovanni
Mozart: Don Giovanni (Cpte). (A. Titus, J. Varady, A. Auger, E. Mathis, T. Moser, R. Panerai, R. Scholze, J-H. Rootering, Bavarian Rad Chor, BRSO/R. Kubelík)

Ⓒ **74321 25285-2** (6/95)
Puccini—Gianni Schicchi
Puccini: Gianni Schicchi (Cpte). (R. Panerai, H. Donath, P. Seiffert, W. Baniewicz, T. Pane, V. Errante, C. Kunz, G. Auer, F. Federici, R. Riener, M. Georg, Bavarian Rad Chor, Munich RO/G. Patanè)

Ⓒ **74321 25286-2** (10/95)
Verdi—Rigoletto
Verdi: Rigoletto (Cpte). (B. Weikl, L. Popp, G. Aragall, J-H. Rootering, K. Takács, A. Malta, H. Jungwirth, A. Ionita, R. Riener, R. Freyer, G. Auer, K. Hautermann, Bavarian Rad Chor, Munich RO/L. Gardelli)

Ⓒ **74321 25287-2** (6/95)
Weber—Der Freischütz
Weber: Freischütz (Cpte). (C. Watson, R. Schock, L. Schädle, G. Frick, C. Nicolai, K. Böhme, F. Ollendorff, K. Meisel, K. Lang, Berlin Deutsche Op Chor, Berlin Deutsche Op Orch/L. von Matačić)

Ⓒ **74321 25817-2** ▭ **74321 25817-4**
Café Classics - Operatic
Verdi: Traviata; *Puccini:* Bohème (exc); *Bellini:* Norma (exc); *Verdi:* Forza del destino (exc); *Wagner:* Tristan und Isolde (exc); *Delibes:* Lakmé (exc); *Puccini:* Madama Butterfly (exc); *Verdi:* Traviata (exc); *Offenbach:* Contes d'Hoffmann (exc); *Bizet:* Pêcheurs de perles (exc); *Verdi:* Aida (exc); *Leoncavallo:* Pagliacci (exc); *Verdi:* Rigoletto (exc); *Puccini:* Gianni Schicchi (exc); *Purcell:* Dido (exc); *Puccini:* Turandot (exc). (A. Moffo, M. Caballé, L. Price, M. Mesplé, H. Donath, D. Millet, S. Verrett, R. Tucker, P. Domingo, J. Björling, M. Lanza, Alfredo Kraus, B. Heppner, R. Merrill, Rome Op Chor, Rome Op Orch, LPO, Philh, Paris Opéra-Comique Orch, RCA Italiana Op Orch, New Philh, RCA Victor Orch, LSO, Munich RO/F. Previtali/G. Solti/C. F. Cillario/T. Schippers/H. Lewis/A. Lombard/E.

Leinsdorf/G. Prêtre/A. Guadagno/R. Cellini/C. Callinicos/N. Santi/G. Patanè/F. Molinari-Pradelli/R. Abbado)

Ⓓ **74321 25819-2** ⊟ **74321 25819-4**
Café Classics - Strings
Bach: Suites, BWV1066-9 (exc); *Elgar:* Salut d'amour; *Pachelbel:* Canon and Gigue (exc); *Barber:* Adagio for strings; *Handel:* Serse (exc); *Bach:* Cantata 147 (exc); *Albinoni:* Adagio; *Vivaldi:* Concerti, Op. 8 (exc); *Boccherini:* String Quintets, G271-6 (exc); *Bach:* 2-Violin Concerto (exc); *Britten:* Simple Symphony (exc); *Marais:* La gamme (exc); *Ravel:* String Quartet (exc); *Purcell:* Chaconne, Z730. (J-L. Garcia, V. Spivakov (vn/dir), A. Futer, Guarneri Qt, Guildhall Str Ens, J-F. Paillard CO, ECO, Moscow Virtuosi/J-F. Paillard/L. Slatkin, R. Salter (vn/dir))

Ⓓ **74321 25821-2** ⊟ **74321 25821-4**
Café Classics—Music of Spain
Albéniz: Suite española 1; *Granados:* Danzas españolas; *Rodrigo:* Concierto de Aranjuez; *Lalo:* Symphonie espagnole (exc); *Bizet:* Carmen (exc); *Tárrega:* Recuerdos de la Alhambra (exc); *Falla:* Nights in the Gardens of Spain; *Granados:* Goyescas (exc); *Falla:* Amor brujo (exc); *Rimsky-Korsakov:* Capriccio espagnol (exc). (T. Berganza, I. Perlman, J. Bream, J. Williams, A. Rubinstein, COE, Seville SO, LSO, St Louis SO, RCA Victor SO/J. E. Gardiner/G. Navarro/A. Previn/V. Golschmann/K. Kondrashin)

Ⓓ **74321 29237-2**
Mozart—Overtures
Mozart: Don Giovanni (exc); Così fan tutte (exc); Nozze di Figaro (exc); Zauberflöte (exc); Entführung (exc); Schauspieldirektor (exc); Sposo deluso (exc); Mitridate (exc); Finta semplice (exc); Clemenza di Tito (exc); Idomeneo (exc); Lucio Silla (exc). (Basle SO/M. Atzmon)

Ⓓ **74321 29251-2**
Janáček—Orchestral Works
Janáček: Sinfonietta; Cunning Little Vixen Suite; Taras Bulba. (USSR RSO, Bolshoi Th Brass Ens, Leningrad PO, USSR Ministry of Culture SO/G. Rozhdestvensky)

Record Collector

Ⓓ **TRC3** (4/95)
The Art of Aristodemo Giorgini
Meyerbeer: Africaine (exc); *Puccini:* Tosca (exc); *Mascagni:* Stornelli marini; *Giordano:* Fedora (exc); *Bellini:* Puritani (exc); Puritani (exc); Sonnambula (exc); *Bizet:* Pêcheurs de perles (exc); Pêcheurs de perles (exc); *Verdi:* Luisa Miller (exc); *Cilea:* Adriana Lecouvreur (exc); *Massenet:* Werther (exc); *Rossini:* Barbiere di Siviglia (exc); *Donizetti:* Don Pasquale (exc); Lucia di Lammermoor (exc); *Leoncavallo:* Pagliacci (exc); *Boito:* Mefistofele (exc); *Puccini:* Bohème (exc); Tosca (exc); Fanciulla del West (exc); *De Curtis:* Tu parte. (A. Giorgini, F. Federici, anon, orch)

Regent

Ⓓ **REGCD104** (10/89) ⊟ **REGC104** (10/89)
The Bel Canto Bassoon
Saint-Saëns: Bassoon Sonata; *Donizetti:* Elisir d'amore (exc); *Tamplini:* Donizetti's Don Pasquale Fantasia; *Rachmaninov:* Songs, Op. 34 (exc); *Rimsky-Korsakov:* Tale of Tsar Saltan (exc); *Cokken:* William Tell Fantasia; *Elgar:* Romance, Op. 62; *Orselli:* Traviata Reminiscienze; *Kreisler:* Liebesleid; *Orselli:* Ballo in Maschera Fantasia; *Ibert:* Carignane; *Berr:* Una voce poco fa Fantasia. (K. Walker, J. Drake)

Relief

Ⓓ **CR1861**
Beethoven—Symphonies Nos 1 & 4; Fidelio—Ov
Beethoven: Symphony 1; Symphony 4; Fidelio (exc). (NBC SO/A. Toscanini)

Ⓓ **CR1891**
Beethoven—Symphony No 3; Leonore Overtures Nos 1 & 2
Beethoven: Symphony 3; Leonore (exc). (NBC SO/A. Toscanini)

Ⓓ **CR921036**
Joseph Schmidt—Opera and Operetta Arias
Verdi: Rigoletto (exc); Rigoletto (exc); Traviata (exc); Trovatore (exc); Ballo in maschera (exc); *Donizetti:* Elisir d'amore (exc); *Puccini:* Tosca (exc); *Mascagni:* Cavalleria Rusticana (exc); *Halévy:* Juive (exc); *Mozart:* Zauberflöte (exc); *Smetana:* Bartered Bride (exc); *Lehár:* Land des Lächelns (exc); *Stolz:* Favorit (exc). (I. Eisinger, J. Schmidt, M. Bohnen, BPO, Berlin City Op Orch/S. Meyrowitz)

REM Editions

Ⓓ **REM11036**
Chailley—Songs
Chailley: A ma femme; Pèlerin d'Assise; Poèmes sur la mort; Chansons légères; Bonheur est dans le pré; Menuisier du Roi; Quand il neige; Madrigaux Galants; Berceuse de la Mésange; Noëls Polonais; Thyl de Flandre (exc). (M. Piquemal, A. Steyer, É. Norska, M. Renault-Rousseau, K. Bronk-Zdunowska)

Ⓓ **REM310990**
Harpsichord Works
Lully: Mascarade (exc); Courante in G minor; Naissance de Vénus (exc); Gigue in G minor; Armide (exc); *Anglebert:* Harpsichord Works (exc); *Caix d'Hervelois:* Suite in F; *Rameau:* Pygmalion (exc). (O. Baumont)

Ⓓ **REM311120**
Orchestre du Conservatiore du Quebec -Concert 1989
Wagner: Tannhäuser (exc); *P. Mercure:* Kaléidoscope; *Franck:* Chasseur maudit; *R. Strauss:* Rosenkavalier (exc). (Quebec Cons Orch/F-P. Decker)

Ⓓ **REM311151**
Schubert—Lieder
Schubert: Suleika I, D720; Jüngling an der Quelle, D300; Am See, D746; Nachtviolen, D752; Hirt auf dem Felsen, D965; Seligkeit, D433; Fischerweise, D881; An die Nachtigall, D196; Ganymed, D544; Im Frühling, D882; Claudine von Villa Bella (exc); Lied im Grünen, D917; Auf dem Wasser zu singen, D774; Nähe des Geliebten, D162; Auf dem Strom, D943. (M. Musacchio, M. Dedieu-Vidal)

Ricercar

Ⓓ **RIC063033**
Gretry—Extracts from Le Jugement de Midas
Grétry: Jugement de Midas (exc). (M. van der Sluis, F. Vanhecke, S. Gari, J. Elwes, J. Bastin, M. Verschaeve, Paris Chapelle Royale Chor, Petite Bande, G. Leonhardt)

Ⓓ **RIC100084/5**
Grétry—La Caravane du Caire
Grétry: Caravane du Caire (Cpte). (J. Bastin, G. Ragon, P. Huttenlocher, G. de Mey, V. Le Texier, I. Poulenard, G. de Reyghere, C. Napoli, M-N. De Callataÿ, E. Crommen, M-P. Fayt, J. Dur, C. Massoz, Namur Chbr Ch, Ricercar Acad/M. Minkowski)

Ⓓ **RIC126114**
Rossini—Overtures (arr Wind Ens)
Rossini: Barbiere di Siviglia (exc); Matilde di Shabran (exc); Semiramide (exc); Guillaume Tell (exc); Tancredi (exc); Italiana in Algeri (exc); Rendez-vous de chasse. (Ricercar Acad/M. Ponseele)

Ⓓ **RIC93001**
Compendium of Baroque Musical Instruments
Pohle: Sonata à 8; *Schmelzer:* Sonata a 7 flauti; *Hammerschmidt:* Sonata super Nun Lob Mein Seel den Herren; *Scheidt:* Canzon super O Nachbar Roland; *Correa de Arauxo:* Libro de Tientos y Discursos (exc); *Selma y Salaverde:* Primo libro de canzoni (exc); *Ruiz de Ribayaz:* Luz y norte musical para caminar (exc); *Frescobaldi:* Primo libro di Toccate (exc); Canzoni with Titles (exc); *Landi:* Mort d'Orfeo (exc); *Trabaci:* Toccata Seconda and Ligature; *Turini:* 2-Recorder Sonata prima; *Bartolotti:* Passacaglie; *Frescobaldi:* Secondo Libro di Toccate (exc); *Jenkins:* Almain and Two Thumps; *Krausen:* Baryton Partitas (exc); *Greeting:* Pleasant Companion (exc); *Farnaby:* Fantasia, MBXXIV/6; *J. Philidor:* Marche de timbales; *Dampierre:* Hunting-horn fanfares (exc); *Raison:* Second livre d'orgue (exc); *Marais:* Pièces de viole II/2 (exc); *D. Gaultier:* Rhétorique des Dieux (exc); *Visée:* Silvains de M. Couperin; *Couperin:* Nouveaux Concerts (exc); *Chédeville:* Virtuose; *Löwe von Eisenach:* Capriccio primo; *Weckmann:* Tod ist verschlungen; *Bruhns:* O werter heil'ger Geist; Prelude and Fugue in E minor I; *J.J. Walther:* Scherzi (exc); *M. Keller:* Pastorella; *Kosteletztki:* Schene neue Aufzug; *Bach:* Cantata 1 (exc); Cantata 76 (exc); *Pachelbel:* Canon and Gigue; *Handel:* Flute Sonatas (exc); *Bach:* Schübler Chorales, BWV645-650 (exc); *Vivaldi:* Concerto, RV97; Allegro Transcription; *Fontanelli:* Mandolin Suonata; *Geminiani:* Cello Sonatas, Op. 5 (exc); *C.H. Graun:* Flauto terzetto Concerto; *Telemann:* Getreue Music-Meister (exc); *C.P.E. Bach:* Trio Sonata, H588; *Graupner:* 3-Chalumeaux Suite; *Handel:* 2-Clarinets and Horn Ov, HWV424; *E.P. Chédeville:* Suite de Noëls; *Mozart:* Minuet, K1d; Minuet, K1f; Londoner Notenskizzenbuch (exc); *W.F. Bach:* Keyboard Sonata, F2; *Tůma:* Regis supermi nuntia; *Grétry:* Caravane du Caire (exc). (Ricercar Consort)

Ⓓ **RIS084067**
Lekeu—Symphonic Works
Lekeu: Barberine (exc); Etude symphonique 1; Etude symphonique 2; Fantaisie on Angevin Airs; Adagio. (Liège PO/P. Bartholomée)

Ⓓ **RIS090072/4** (2/92)
Mozart—Lucio Silla
Mozart: Lucio Silla (Cpte). (A. Rolfe Johnson, L. Cuberli, A. Murray, B-M. Aruhn, C. Barbaux, A. Van Baasbank, Brussels Théâtre de la Monnaie Chor, Brussels Théâtre de la Monnaie Orch/S. Cambreling)

Ⓓ **RIS093070/1** (1/92)
Verdi—Simon Boccanegra
Verdi: Simon Boccanegra (Cpte). (J. Van Dam, N. Gustafson, A. Cupido, D. Pittsinger, W. Stone, C. Krause, A. Gregoire, Brussels Théâtre de la Monnaie Chor, Brussels Théâtre de la Monnaie Orch/S. Cambreling)

Ⓓ **RIS099083** (10/92)
Lekeu—Vocal Works
Lekeu: Andromède; Burgraves. (D. Bryant, Z. Vandersteene, P. Huttenlocher, J. Bastin, Namur Sym Chor, Liège PO/P. Bartholomée)

Romantic Robot

Ⓓ **RR1941** (8/92)
Terezín - The Music 1941-44
G. Klein: Piano Sonata; Trio; *Ullmann:* String Quartet 3; Piano Sonata 6; Abendphantasie; Immer Inmitten; Jiddische Lieder; Little Cakewalk; *Krása:* Tanec; Brundibár; *P. Haas:* Chinese Poetry Songs. (E. Berendsen, K. Průša, Bambini di Praga, V. Nishri, E. Leichner, J. Pokorný, D. Bloch, Czech Stg Trio, Martinů Qt, Prague FISYO/M. Klemens)

Ⓓ **RR1973** (6/93)
An American in Prague
Copland: Inscape; Billy the Kid Suite; *Ives:* Unanswered Question; *Stravinsky:* Ode (1943); *Martinů:* Half-time; *Schuman:* New England Triptych; *Bernstein:* Candide (1956) (exc). (Czech PO/A. Copland)

Romophone

Ⓓ **81001-2** (11/93)
Emma Eames (1865-1952)
C. Böhm: Lieder, Op.326 (exc); *Gounod:* Faust (exc); Ave Maria; *Hahn:* Incrédule; *Beach:* Browning Songs, Op. 44 (exc); *Tosti:* Addio; *Puccini:* Tosca (exc); *Massenet:* Élégie; *Schubert:* An Silvia, D891; *Gounod:* Roméo et Juliette (exc); *Various:* National Anthems (exc); *Emmett:* Dixie; *Hollman:* Chanson d'amour; *Massenet:* Élégie; *Gounod:* Ave Maria; *Mozart:* Don Giovanni (exc); Zauberflöte (exc); *Faure:* Crucifix; *Verdi:* Otello (exc); *Bizet:* Carmen (exc); *Mascagni:* Cavalleria Rusticana (exc); *Gounod:* Roméo et Juliette (exc); Faust (exc); *C. Böhm:* Lieder, Op.326 (exc); *Gounod:* Faust (exc); *Mozart:* Nozze di Figaro (exc); *Puccini:* Tosca (exc); *H. Parker:* Love in May; *E. Nevin:* I once had a sweet little doll; *Koechlin:* Si tu le veux; *Massenet:* Chérubin (exc); *Henschel:* Spring; *Beach:* Browning Songs, Op. 44 (exc); *Bemberg:* Chanson de baisers; *Delibes:* Lakmé (exc); *Wagner:* Lohengrin (exc); *Mozart:* Nozze di Figaro (exc); *Verdi:* Trovatore (exc); *Tosti:* Dopo; *Messager:* Véronique (exc); *Schubert:* Gretchen am Spinnrade, D118. (E. Eames, J. Hollman, E. de Gogorza, C. Dalmores, P. Plançon, M. Sembrich, L. Homer, H. Gilles, anon, orch, anon)

Ⓓ **81002-2** (11/93)
Emmy Destinn (1878-1930)
A. Thomas: Mignon (exc); *Puccini:* Madama Butterfly (exc); *Verdi:* Aida (exc); *Ponchielli:* Gioconda (exc); *Wagner:* Tannhäuser (exc); *Gomes:* Guarany (exc); *Puccini:* Tosca (exc); *Traditional:* Wedding; Goodnight; My Homeland; *Schubert:* Wiegenlied, D498; *Mozart:* Zauberflöte (exc); *Dvořák:* Rusalka (exc); *Kovařovic:* Nazarene (exc); *Tchaikovsky:* Queen of Spades (exc); Queen of Spades (exc); *Verdi:* Trovatore (exc); Trovatore (exc); *Tosti:* Ultima canzone; *Gounod:* Ave Maria; *Flies:* Wiegenlied; *Gounod:* Sérénade; *Stange:* Bekehrte; *Liszt:* Oh! quand je dors, S282; *Jindřich:* My sweetheart; *Destinn:* Wooing; Maiden's song; *Traditional:* O Mountains; *Jindřich:* Ostroh Castle; *Destinn:* Last tears; *Hess:* Home; *Štěpán:* On my way; *Destinn:* Romance; *Smetana:* Kiss (exc); *Verdi:* Ballo in maschera (exc); *Dvořák:* In Folk Tone, B146 (exc). (E. Destinn, E. Caruso, D. Gilly, M. Duchêne, G. Martinelli, orch/W.B. Rogers/J. Pasternack)

Ⓓ **81003-2** (3/94)
Galli-Curci—Acoustic Recordings, Vol.1
Alvarez: Partida; *Verdi:* Rigoletto (exc); Rigoletto (exc); *Donizetti:* Lucia di Lammermoor (exc); *Gounod:* Roméo et Juliette (exc); *Bishop:* Home, sweet home; *Donizetti:* Lucia di Lammermoor (exc); *Auber:* Manon Lescaut (exc); *Grieg:* Peer Gynt (exc); *Delibes:* Lakmé (exc); *Buzzi-Peccia:* Little birdies; *T. Giordani:* Caro mio ben; *Rossini:* Barbiere di Siviglia (exc); *Meyerbeer:* Dinorah (exc); *Bellini:* Sonnambula (exc); *Flotow:* Martha (exc); *Mozart:* Nozze di

Figaro (exc); *Seppilli:* Little Dorry; *Proch:* Air and Variations; *F. David:* Perle du Brésil (exc); *Bellini:* Puritani (exc); *Massenet:* Crépuscule; *Benedict:* Capinera; *Verdi:* Rigoletto (exc); Traviata (exc); Traviata (exc); *Chopin:* Waltzes (exc); *Samuels:* When Chloris sleeps; *Bishop:* Lo, here the gentle lark; *Delibes:* Filles de Cadiz; *A. Thomas:* Mignon (exc); *Donizetti:* Don Pasquale (exc); *Bellini:* Sonnambula (exc); Sonnambula (exc); *Verdi:* Traviata (exc); *Dell' Acqua:* Villanelle; *Valverde:* Clavelitos. (A. Galli-Curci, E. Caruso, F. Perini, G. De Luca, M. Egener, M. Journet, A. Bada, orch/J. Pasternack)

Ⓓ **81004-2** (8/94)
Galli-Curci—Acoustic Recordings, Vol.2
Bellini: Puritani (exc); *J.F. Cooke:* Ol' Car'lina; *Bishop:* Echo Song; *Rimsky-Korsakov:* Golden Cockerel (exc); *Adam:* Toréador (exc); *Bizet:* Pêcheurs de Perles (exc); *Flotow:* Martha (exc); *Foster:* Old Folks at Home; *Puccini:* Madama Butterfly (exc); *Meyerbeer:* Etoile du Nord (exc); *Donizetti:* Lucia di Lammermoor (exc); *Rimsky-Korsakov:* Sadko (exc); *Donizetti:* Linda di Chamounix (exc); *Molloy:* Love's Old Sweet Song; *Bellini:* Sonnambula (exc); Puritani (exc); *Verdi:* Rigoletto (exc); *Dykes:* Lead kindly light; *Danks:* Silver threads among the gold; *Herbert:* Orange Blossoms (exc); Mademoiselle Modiste (exc); *Verdi:* Trovatore (exc); *Massenet:* Don César de Bazan (exc); Manon (exc); *Meyerbeer:* Dinorah (exc); *Pierné:* Sérénade; *Strickland:* Mah Lindy Lou; *G.A. Russell:* Say a little prayer for me; *Bishop:* Pretty mocking bird; *Traditional:* No te vayas te lo pido; *Rossini:* Semiramide (exc); *Bellini:* Sonnambula (exc); *Delibes:* Coppélia (exc); *Verdi:* Trovatore (exc); Traviata (exc); Rigoletto (exc); *Donizetti:* Lucia di Lammermoor (exc); Don Pasquale (exc); *Conrad:* Memory Lane; *Ponce:* Estrellita. (A. Galli-Curci, T. Schipa, orch/J. Pasternack/Rosario Bourdon)

Ⓓ **81005-2** (1/94)
Claudia Muzio (1889-1936)
Puccini: Bohème (exc); *Verdi:* Traviata (exc); Trovatore (exc); *Tchaikovsky:* Eugene Onegin (exc); *Gomes:* Salvator Rosa (exc); *Giordano:* Andrea Chénier (exc); *Sodero:* Crisantemi; *Bachelet:* Chère nuit; *Catalani:* Wally (exc); *Leoncavallo:* Pagliacci (exc); *Puccini:* Bohème (exc); *Leoncavallo:* Zazà (exc); *Chopin:* Aspiration; *A. Mascheroni:* Eternamente; *Cilea:* Adriana Lecouvreur (exc); *Catalani:* Loreley (exc); *Boito:* Mefistofele (exc); *Giordano:* Madame Sans-Gêne (exc); *Bellini:* Bianca e Fernando (exc); *Verdi:* Forza del destino (exc); *Massenet:* Hérodiade (exc); *Anon:* Odorano le rose; *Meyerbeer:* Africaine (exc); *Handel:* Rinaldo (exc); *Verdi:* Lombardi (exc); *Rossini:* Separazione; *Mascagni:* Amico Fritz (exc); *Gluck:* Paride ed Elena (exc); *Buzzi-Peccia:* Mal d'amore; *Monahan:* Shepherd's love; *Verdi:* Vespri siciliani (exc); *Guagni-Benvenuti:* Guardami!; *Bizet:* Carmen (exc); *Offenbach:* Contes d'Hoffmann (exc); *Herbert:* Orange Blossoms (exc); *Parisotti:* Se tu m'ami. (C. Muzio, G. Tommasini, M. Laurenti, A. Spalding, R. Gaylor, anon, orch)

Ⓓ **81006-2** (11/94)
Rosa Ponselle (1897-1981)
Verdi: Aida (exc); Ernani (exc); Forza del destino (exc); Otello (exc); Aida (exc); *C. Scott:* Lullaby; *Brahms:* Lieder, Op.49 (exc); *Shelley:* Love's sorrow; *Tosti:* Addio; *Monro:* My lovely Celia; *G.B. De Curtis:* Carmé; *Di Capua:* Maria, Marì; *Tosti:* Serenata; *Ponchielli:* Gioconda (exc); *Meyerbeer:* Africaine (exc); *Hewitt:* Little old garden; *J.A. Bland:* Carry me back; *Foster:* My old Kentucky home; *Bishop:* Home, sweet home; *Bond:* Perfect day; *Foster:* Old folks at home; *G. Dupont:* Rosita; *E. Nevin:* Rosary; *Di Chiara:* Spagnola; *Silberta:* Beloved. (R. Ponselle, G. Martinelli, orch/J. Pasternack/Rosario Bourdon, F. Lapitino, Male Qt)

Ⓓ **81007-2** (11/94)
Rosa Ponselle—Victor Recordings 1926-1929
Verdi: Aida (exc); *Spontini:* Vestale (exc); *Tosti:* 'A vucchella; Luna d'estate; *Massenet:* Élégie; *Gounod:* Ave Maria; *Schubert:* Schwanengesang, D957 (exc); *Verdi:* Aida (exc); *Rimsky-Korsakov:* Songs, Op.2 (exc); *Tosti:* Serenata; Addio; *Kahn:* Ave Maria; *Verdi:* Ernani (exc); Forza del destino (exc); *Dvořák:* Gipsy Melodies (exc); *Rubinstein:* Since first I met thee; *Verdi:* Forza del destino (exc); Trovatore (exc); Forza del destino (exc); *Bellini:* Norma (exc); Norma (exc). (R. Ponselle, G. Martinelli, E. Baker, C. Ponselle, E. Pinza, M. Telva, chor, NY Met Op Chor, F. Lapitino, orch/Rosario Bourdon/G. Setti)

Ⓓ **81008-2** (8/94)
Mary Garden (1874-1967)
G. Charpentier: Louise (exc); *Cadman:* At dawning; *Traditional:* Annie Laurie; *Hahn:* Swing; My Ships; *Alfano:* Risurrezione (exc); *J.H. Rogers:* At parting; *A. Tate:* Somewhere a voice is calling; *A. Hume:* Afton Water; *G. Charpentier:* Louise (exc); *A.F. Harrison:* In the Gloaming; *Debussy:* Beau soir; *Szulc:* Clair de lune; *Grechaninov:* Over the Steppe; *Bizet:* Carmen (exc); *Traditional:* Jock O'Hazeldean. (M. Garden, J. Dansereau, A. Russell, orch/Rosario Bourdon/N. Shilkret)

Ⓓ **81009-2** (8/94)
Edith Mason—Complete Recordings 1924-1928
Puccini: Madama Butterfly (exc); *Gounod:* Faust (exc); *Cadman:* American Indian Songs, Op.45 (exc); *Strickland:* Dreamin' Time; *Flotow:* Martha (exc); *Tosti:* Addio; *Puccini:* Madama Butterfly (exc); *Gounod:* Faust (exc); *Flotow:* Martha (exc); *Tosti:* Addio; Serenata; *Del Riego:* O dry those tears; *Cadman:* American Indian Songs, Op.45 (exc); *Woodforde-Finden:* Indian Love Lyrics (exc); *Strickland:* Dreamin' Time; *Mendelssohn:* Hear my prayer (exc); *Tosti:* Serenata; *G. Charpentier:* Louise (exc); *E. Nevin:* Mighty lak' a rose; *Cadman:* American Indian Songs, Op.45 (exc); *J.A. Bland:* Carry me back; *Foster:* My old Kentucky home. (E. Mason, Male Trio, Inst Ens, orch/F. Black)

Ⓓ **81010-2** (1/95)
Claudia Muzio—Complete Pathé Recordings, 1917-8
Puccini: Manon Lescaut (exc); Tosca (exc); *Verdi:* Trovatore (exc); *Leoncavallo:* Pagliacci (exc); *Ponchielli:* Gioconda (exc); *Verdi:* Otello (exc); *Olivieri:* Inno di Garibaldi; *Giordano:* Canzone guerresca; *A. Thomas:* Mignon (exc); *Puccini:* Madama Butterfly (exc); *Verdi:* Aida (exc); *Puccini:* Bohème (exc); *Giordano:* Madame Sans-Gêne (exc); *Boito:* Mefistofele (exc); *Catalani:* Wally (exc); *Verdi:* Forza del destino (exc); *Wolf-Ferrari:* Segreto di Susanna (exc); *Verdi:* Aida (exc); *Puccini:* Madama Butterfly (exc); *Verdi:* Traviata (exc); *Mascagni:* Cavalleria Rusticana (exc); *Rossini:* Guillaume Tell (exc); *G. Braga:* Melodies (exc); *Offenbach:* Contes d'Hoffmann (exc); *Verdi:* Trovatore (exc); *G. Charpentier:* Louise (exc); *Bizet:* Carmen (exc); *Massenet:* Manon (exc); *Verdi:* Ballo in maschera (exc); *Delibes:* Bonjour! Suzon; *Sanderson:* Until; *Puccini:* Suor Angelica (exc); Gianni Schicchi (exc); *Verdi:* Vespri Siciliani (exc); Ernani (exc); *Puccini:* Bohème (exc); *Roxas:* O ben tornato, amore; *Buzzi-Peccia:* Baciami!; *H.T. Burleigh:* Jean; *A. Mascheroni:* Eternamente; *Donaudy:* O del mio amato ben; *Traditional:* Torna, amore; Mon jardin. (C. Muzio, K. Howard, orch, A. Spalding)

Ⓓ **81011-2(1)** (5/95)
Dame Nellie Melba (pt 1)
Verdi: Rigoletto (exc); *Puccini:* Bohème (exc); Bohème (exc); Tosca (exc); *Gounod:* Faust (exc); *Verdi:* Traviata (exc); *Tosti:* Addio; Serenata; *Blangini:* Per valli, per boschi; *Bemberg:* Ange est venu; *Hahn:* Si mes vers; *Mozart:* Nozze di Figaro (exc); *A. Thomas:* Hamlet (exc); *Arditi:* Se saran rose; *Donizetti:* Lucia di Lammermoor (exc); *Bishop:* Lo! here the gentle lark; *Handel:* Allegro, il penseroso ed il moderato (exc); *Tosti:* Mattinata; *Debussy:* En sourdine; *Ronald:* Cycle of life (exc); In Sunshine and Shadow (exc); *Hahn:* D'une prison; *Traditional:* Believe me, if all those endearing young charms; *Verdi:* Otello (exc); *Puccini:* Bohème (exc); *Ronald:* Summertime (exc); *Traditional:* Ye banks and braes; *Puccini:* Bohème (exc). (N. Melba, E. Caruso, A. Sassoli, C. Gilibert, orch/W.B. Rogers, N. Melba, anon)

Ⓓ **81011-2(2)** (5/95)
Dame Nellie Melba (pt 2)
Verdi: Traviata (exc); *Bishop:* Lo! here the gentle lark; *Mozart:* Nozze di Figaro (exc); *Arditi:* Se saran rose; *Gounod:* Faust (exc); *Handel:* Allegro, il penseroso ed il moderato (exc); *Donizetti:* Lucia di Lammermoor (exc); *Massenet:* Don César de Bazan (exc); *A. Thomas:* Hamlet (exc); *Lalo:* Roi d'Ys (exc); *Puccini:* Tosca (exc); *Verdi:* Otello (exc); *Tosti:* Addio; *Ronald:* Summertime (exc); *Wetzger:* By the brook; *Mozart:* Rè pastore (exc); *Gounod:* Ave Maria; *Lehmann:* Magdalen at Michael's gate; *Debussy:* Âme évaporée; Mandoline; *G. Charpentier:* Louise (exc); Louise (exc); *Foster:* Old folks at home; *M.V. White:* John Anderson, my Jo; *Traditional:* Comin' thro' the rye; *Bemberg:* Anges pleurent; Chant vénitien; *Traditional:* Annie Laurie; *Dvořák:* Gipsy melodies (exc); Gipsy melodies (exc); *Debussy:* Romance. (N. Melba, G. Lapierre, F. St Leger, orch/W.B. Rogers, J. Lemmoné, N. Melba, J. Kubelík)

Ⓓ **81012-2** (2/95)
Elisabeth Rethberg— Brunswick Recordings 1924-1929
Verdi: Aida (exc); *Puccini:* Bohème (exc); Tosca (exc); Madama Butterfly (exc); *Giordano:* Andrea Chénier (exc); *Flies:* Wiegenlied; *Schubert:* Schwanengesang, D957 (exc); Ave Maria, D839; *Mendelssohn:* Lieder, Op.34 (exc); *Loewe:* Canzonette; *Grieg:* Melodies of the Heart, Op.5 (exc); Peer Gynt (exc); *Tchaikovsky:* Songs, Op.6 (exc); *Gounod:* Au printemps; *Massenet:* Élégie; *G. Braga:* Melodies (exc); *Korschat:* Verlassen; *Hildach:* Spielmann; *Schubert:* Ave Maria, D839; *Schumann:* Myrthen, Op.25 (exc); *Taubert:* Es steht ein Baum; *Jensen:* Murmelndes Lüftchen; *Rubinstein:* Du bist wie eine Blume; *Lassen:* Es war ein Traum; *Handel:* Sosarme (exc); Serse (exc); *Mozart:* Nozze di Figaro (exc); Zauberflöte (exc); *Weber:* Freischütz (exc); *Wagner:* Lohengrin (exc); Lohengrin (exc); Tannhäuser (exc); Tannhäuser (exc); *Verdi:* Aida (exc); Otello (exc); *Massenet:* Élégie; *G. Braga:* Melodies (exc); *Griffes:* Auf geheimen Waldespfade; *Densmore:* Spring Fancy; *Cadman:* Moonlight Song, Op.42/2; *Bishop:* Home, sweet home; *Traditional:* Believe me, if all those endearing young charms; Snowy-breasted pearl; Londonderry Air. (E. Rethberg, M. Rosen, F. Fradkin, D. Lieberfeld, F. Persson, anon, anon, stg qt, orch)

Ⓓ **81014-2** (10/95)
Elisabeth Rethberg (1894-1976)
Wagner: Tannhäuser (exc); Lohengrin (exc); *Verdi:* Aida (exc); Aida (exc); *Mozart:* Rè pastore (exc); Don Giovanni (exc); *Gounod:* Faust (exc); *Verdi:* Ballo in maschera (exc); Ballo in maschera (exc); Otello (exc); Lombardi (exc); Attila (exc); *Wagner:* Meistersinger (exc); Fliegende Holländer (exc); *Suppé:* Boccaccio (exc); *J. Strauss II:* Fledermaus (exc); *Mozart:* Nozze di Figaro (exc); *J. Strauss II:* Zigeunerbaron (exc); *Bizet:* Carmen (exc); *Meyerbeer:* Africaine (exc); *Puccini:* Madama Butterfly (exc); *Mascagni:* Cavalleria rusticana (exc); *Wolf:* Italienisches Liederbuch (exc); Spanisches Liederbuch (exc); *Mendelssohn:* Lieder, Op.34 (exc); *Brahms:* Lieder, Op.84 (exc); *Wagner:* Tannhäuser (exc). (E. Rethberg, G. Lauri-Volpi, G. De Luca, B. Gigli, E. Pinza, F. Schorr, C. Van Bos, K. Ruhrseitz, Berlin SO/F. Zweig/F. Weissmann, Victor SO/Rosario Bourdon)

Ⓓ **81016-2**
Lucrezia Bori (1887-1960)
Leoncavallo: Pagliacci (exc); *Verdi:* Traviata (exc); *Rossini:* Soirées musicales (exc); *Puccini:* Bohème (exc); *Valverde:* Nina Pancha (exc); *Pagans:* Malagueña; *Yradier:* Paloma; *C. Marshall:* I hear you calling me; *Verdi:* Rigoletto (exc); *Valverde:* Clavelitos; *Mascagni:* Iris (exc); *Offenbach:* Contes d'Hoffmann (exc); *Chapí:* Revoltosa (exc); Puñado de Rosas (exc); *Mozart:* Nozze di Figaro (exc); *Sibella:* Villanella; *Donizetti:* Don Pasquale (exc); *Mozart:* Don Giovanni (exc); *Wolf-Ferrari:* Segreto di Susanna (exc); *Mozart:* Così fan tutte (exc); *T. Moore:* Irish Melodies (exc); *Puccini:* Bohème (exc); *Rimsky-Korsakov:* Snow Maiden (exc); *Gounod:* Roméo et Juliette (exc); Roméo et Juliette (exc); *Puccini:* Bohème (exc); *Mascagni:* Amico Fritz (exc); *Arditi:* Bacio; *Massenet:* Manon (exc); *Granados:* Tonadillas (exc); *Pestalozzi:* Ciribiribin; *Delibes:* Lakmé (exc); *Mascagni:* Amico Fritz (exc); *Bizet:* Carmen (exc); *Varney:* Amour mouillé (exc); *Delfino:* Milonguita; *Novello:* Little Damozel; *Puccini:* Bohème (exc); Bohème (exc). (L. Bori, J. McCormack, J. Jacoby, R. Werrenrath, A. de Segurola, G. de Luca, B. Gigli, M. Fleta, T. Schipa, Victor Orch/W.B. Rogers/J. Pasternack/Rosario Bourdon/N. Shilkret)

Ⓓ **81019-2**
Elisabeth Schumann
Mozart: Exsultate jubilate, K165 (exc); Rè pastore (exc); Nozze di Figaro (exc); Nozze di Figaro (exc); Don Giovanni (exc); *J. Strauss II:* Fledermaus (exc); Fledermaus (exc); *Zeller:* Vogelhändler (exc); Vogelhändler (exc); Obersteiger (exc); *Ziehrer:* Landstreicher (exc); Fremdenführer (exc); *Berté:* Dreimäderlhaus (exc); *Heuberger:* Opernball (exc); *Kreisler:* Sissy (exc); *Jos Strauss:* Sphärenklänge; *Benatzky:* Ich muss wieder einmal in Grinzing sein; *Sieczyński:* Wien, du Stadt meiner Träume. (E. Schumann, orch, Vienna St Op Orch/G.W. Byng/L. Collingwood/K. Alwin/W. Goehr/L. Rosenek)

Ⓓ **82001-2** (12/94)
Pol Plançon—Complete Victor Recordings
Bellini: Sonnambula (exc); *Adam:* Minuit, Chrétiens (exc); *Faure:* Rameaux; *A. Thomas:* Caïd (exc); *Berlioz:* Damnation de Faust (exc); *Gounod:* Roméo et Juliette (exc); *Rossini:* Stabat Mater (exc); *Gounod:* Faust (exc); *Niedermeyer:* Lac; *Schumann:* Romanzen und Balladen, Op.49 (exc); *Adam:* Chalet (exc); *Gounod:* Faust (exc); *Godard:* Embarquez-vous; *Gounod:* Philémon et Baucis (exc); *Mozart:* Zauberflöte (exc); *Gounod:* Vallon; *Massenet:* Si tu veux, Mignonne; *Haydn:* Jahreszeiten (exc); *Gounod:* Jésus de Nazareth; *Ferrari:* Lazzarone; *Georges:* Filibustier; *Bemberg:* Soupir; *Flégier:* Cor; *Meyerbeer:* Dinorah (exc); *Faure:* Credo; *Gounod:* Faust (exc); *Berlioz:* Damnation de Faust (exc); *Adam:* Minuit, Chrétiens (exc); *Gounod:* Faust (exc); *A. Thomas:* Caïd (exc); *Faure:* Rameaux; *Schumann:* Romanzen und Balladen, Op.49 (exc); *Gounod:* Faust (exc); *Verdi:* Don Carlos (exc); *Berlioz:* Damnation de Faust (exc); *Flotow:* Martha (exc); *Meyerbeer:* Etoile du Nord (exc); Robert le Diable (exc); *A. Thomas:* Mignon (exc); *Rossini:* Stabat Mater (exc). (P. Plançon, E. Eames, C. Dalmores, anon, orch)

Ⓓ **82002-2** (8/95)
Edmond Clément (1867-1928)
Rossini: Barbiere di Siviglia (exc); *Gounod:* Roméo et Juliette (exc); *Massenet:* Manon (exc); *Boïeldieu:* Dame Blanche (exc); *Massenet:* Manon (exc); *Weckerlin:* Romances et Chansons (exc); *Pessard:* Adieu du matin; *Arcadet:* Chanson lorraine; *Massenet:* Poème d'Avril (exc);

Bemberg: Neige; Ça fait peur aux oiseaux; *Lalo:* Roi d'ys (exc); *Godard:* Jocelyn (exc); *Massenet:* Werther (exc); *Faure:* Rameaux; *Meyerbeer:* Robert le Diable (exc); *Bizet:* Pêcheurs de perles (exc); *Gounod:* Roméo et Juliette (exc); *Godard:* Danté et Béatrice (exc); *Boito:* Mefistofele (exc); *Schumann:* Duette, Op.34 (exc); *Lully:* Au clair de la lune. (E. Clément, M. Journet, G. Farrar, anon, F. La Forge, orch/Rosario Bourdon)

Rose Collection

Ⓓ **3201**
Ravel/Bizet—Orchestral Works
Ravel: Boléro; *Bizet:* Carmen Suites (exc); Arlésienne Suites (exc). (Ljubljana RSO/A. Nanut, Paris RSO/L. Bertrand)

Ⓓ **3212**
Wagner—Great Overtures
Wagner: Tannhäuser (exc); Lohengrin (exc); Meistersinger (exc); Fliegende Holländer (exc); Rienzi (exc); Faust Overture. (LPO/A. Scholz, London Fest Orch/J. Armstrong)

Ⓓ **3229**
Popular Orchestral Works
Suppé: Leichte Kavallerie (exc); Schöne Galathee (exc); Dichter und Bauer (exc); *Mozart:* Così fan tutte (exc); *Rossini:* Guillaume Tell (exc); *Adam:* Si j'étais roi (exc); *Nicolai:* Lustigen Weiber von Windsor (exc); *J. Strauss II:* Fledermaus (exc). (Paris RSO/L. Bertrand, Philh/A. Scholz)

Royal Northern College of Music

Ⓓ **RNCMPP1**
Vaughan Williams—The Pilgrim's Progress
Vaughan Williams: Pilgrim's Progress (Cpte). (R. Whitehouse, W. Griffiths, J. Neale, G. Wili, M. Wharfedale, P. Westhead, S. Chaundy, M. Murphy, C. Bradshaw, A. Kettlewell, J. Lloyd-Roberts, D. Moore, M. Snell, H. Waddington, M. Pope, R. Peel, J. Marsden, A. Morris, D. Vaughan-Lewis, H. Matthews, R. Simonetti, A. Rasmussen, S. Wallace, A. Fraser, G. Taylor, K. Caun, E. Pollard, T. Jackson, K. Wilkinson, S. Parr, L. Rushton, E. Môn, A. Coote, RNCM Op Chor, RNCM Op Orch/I. Kennaway)

Royal Opera House Records

Ⓓ **75605 55013-2** ▭ **75605 55013-4**
The Puccini Experience
Puccini: Villi (exc); Edgar (exc); Manon Lescaut (exc); Manon Lescaut (exc); Bohème (exc); Tosca (exc); Tosca (exc); Madama Butterfly (exc); Fanciulla del West (exc); Rondine (exc); Tabarro (exc); Suor Angelica (exc); Gianni Schicchi (exc); Turandot (exc). (A. Gheorghiu, N. Rautio, J. Botha, F. Egerton, R. Leggate, A. Michaels-Moore, E. Garrett, M. Druiett, ROH Chor, ROHO/E. Downes)

RPO

Ⓓ **CDRPD9001** ▭ **ZCRPD9001**
Classical Spectacular
Rossini: Guillaume Tell (exc); *Sousa:* Stars and Stripes Forever; *Verdi:* Nabucco (exc); *Elgar:* Pomp and Circumstance Marches (exc); *Ravel:* Boléro; *J. Strauss II:* Blauen Donau, Op. 314; *Borodin:* Prince Igor (exc); *Tchaikovsky:* 1812; *Rossini:* Barbiere di Siviglia (exc); *Sousa:* Liberty Bell; *Grieg:* Peer Gynt (exc); *Bizet:* Pêcheurs de Perles (exc); *J. Strauss I:* Radetzky March; *Bizet:* Carmen Suites (exc); *Suppé:* Leichte Kavallerie (exc); *Khachaturian:* Gayaneh (exc); *Sibelius:* Finlandia; *Offenbach:* Orphée aux enfers (exc); *Vaughan Williams:* Greensleeves Fantasia; *Mascagni:* Cavalleria Rusticana (exc); *Verdi:* Aida (exc). (G. Gudbjörnsson, J. Howard, London Choral Soc, Scots Guards Band, Welsh Guards Band, RPO/M. Reed, Musketeers of the Sealed Knot)

Ⓓ **CDRPD9006** ▭ **ZCRPD9006**
Opera Spectacular 1 & 2
Bizet: Carmen (exc); Carmen (exc); Pêcheurs de perles (exc); *Delibes:* Lakmé (exc); *Gounod:* Faust (exc); *Leoncavallo:* Pagliacci (exc); *Puccini:* Gianni Schicchi (exc); Madama Butterfly (exc); Tosca (exc); Turandot (exc); *Rossini:* Barbiere di Siviglia (exc); *Verdi:* Nabucco (exc); Rigoletto (exc); Trovatore (exc); *Wagner:* Walküre (exc); *Dvořák:* Rusalka (exc); *Giordano:* Andrea Chénier (exc); *Mascagni:* Cavalleria Rusticana (exc); *Mozart:* Zauberflöte (exc); *Puccini:* Bohème (exc); Tosca (exc); *Verdi:* Aida (exc); Traviata (exc); *Wagner:* Tannhäuser (exc); Fliegende Holländer (exc); Lohengrin (exc); *Weber:* Freischütz (exc). (V. Masterson, J. Barstow, C. Powell, E. Barham, A. Davies, A. Michaels-Moore, ROH Chor, RPO/R. Stapleton)

Ⓓ **CDRPO5006** ▭ **ZCRPO5006**
Orchestral Lollipops
Rossini: Barbiere di Siviglia (exc); *Bach:* Suites, BWV1066-9 (exc); *Mendelssohn:* Midsummer Night's Dream (exc); *Chabrier:* Joyeuse marche; *Verdi:* Aida (exc); *Smetana:* Bartered Bride (exc); *Berlioz:* Damnation de Faust (exc); *Mozart:* Serenade, K525 (exc); *Schubert:* Rosamunde (exc); *Tchaikovsky:* Serenade, Op. 48 (exc); *Grieg:* Elegiac Melodies (exc); *Massenet:* Thaïs (exc); *Wagner:* Meistersinger (exc). (J. Bryant, J. Georgiadis, RPO/E. Bátiz)

Ⓓ **CDRPO5009**
Classical Spectacular I
Rossini: Guillaume Tell (exc); *Sousa:* Stars and stripes forever; *Verdi:* Nabucco (exc); *Elgar:* Pomp and Circumstance Marches (exc); *Ravel:* Boléro; *J. Strauss II:* Blauen Donau, Op. 314; *Borodin:* Prince Igor (exc); *Tchaikovsky:* 1812. (RPO, London Choral Soc, Scots Guards Band, Welsh Guards Band/M. Reed)

Ⓓ **CDRPO5010**
Classical Spectacular 2
Rossini: Barbiere di Siviglia (exc); *Sousa:* Liberty Bell; *Grieg:* Peer Gynt (exc); *Bizet:* Pêcheurs de perles (exc); *J. Strauss I:* Radetzky March; *Bizet:* Carmen Suites (exc); *Khachaturian:* Gayaneh (exc); *Suppé:* Leichte Kavallerie (exc); *Sibelius:* Finlandia. (G. Gudbjörnsson, J. Howard, London Choral Soc, Scots Guards Band, Welsh Guards Band, RPO/M. Reed)

Ⓓ **CDRPO7009** ▭ **ZCRPO7009**
Opera Spectacular II
Wagner: Lohengrin (exc); *Dvořák:* Rusalka (exc); *Wagner:* Fliegende Holländer (exc); *Giordano:* Andrea Chénier (exc); *Wagner:* Tannhäuser (exc); *Puccini:* Tosca (exc); *Verdi:* Traviata (exc); *Mozart:* Zauberflöte (exc); *Verdi:* Aida (exc); *Weber:* Freischütz (exc); *Puccini:* Bohème (exc); *Mascagni:* Cavalleria rusticana (exc). (J. Barstow, A. Davies, ROH Chor, RPO/R. Stapleton)

Ⓓ **CDRPO7010** ▭ **ZCRPO7010**
Ballet Spectacular
Tchaikovsky: Swan Lake Suite; Sleeping Beauty (exc); Nutcracker Suite (exc); Nutcracker (exc); *Massenet:* Cid (exc); *Falla:* Amor Brujo (exc); *Hérold:* Fille mal gardée (exc); *Khachaturian:* Spartacus (exc). (RPO/B. Tovey)

Ⓓ **CDRPO7014** (5/90) ▭ **ZCRPO7014** (5/90)
Ashkenazy Live in Moscow
Mussorgsky: Khovanshchina (exc); *Beethoven:* Piano Concerto 3; *Ravel:* Daphnis et Chloé Suites (exc); *Tchaikovsky:* Nutcracker Suite (exc). (RPO, Vladimir Ashkenazy (pf/dir)/Vladimir Ashkenazy)

Ⓓ **CDRPO7018** ▭ **ZCRPO7018**
Leeds Castle Classics
Sibelius: Finlandia; *Verdi:* Nabucco (exc); *Tchaikovsky:* 1812; *Elgar:* Land of Hope and Glory; *Parry:* Jerusalem; *Handel:* Messiah (exc); *Copland:* Fanfare for the Common Man; *J. Strauss II:* Blauen Donau, Op. 314; Unter Donner und Blitz; *Sousa:* Stars and Stripes Forever. (Brighton Fest Chor, Royal Artillery Band, RPO/Carl Davis)

Ⓓ **CDRPO7019**
The Sword and The Grail
Wagner: Lohengrin (exc); Rheingold (exc); Walküre (exc); Siegfried (exc); Götterdämmerung (exc); Tannhäuser (exc); Parsifal (exc); Rienzi (exc). (W. Lewis, RPO/G. Ötvös)

Ⓓ **CDRPO7025** ▭ **ZCRPO7025**
Classical Spectacular 3
Wagner: Lohengrin (exc); *Elgar:* Enigma Variations (exc); *J. Strauss II:* Unter Donner und Blitz; *Offenbach:* Contes d'Hoffmann (exc); *Waldteufel:* Patineurs; *Handel:* Messiah (exc); *Dvořák:* Symphony 9 (exc); *Grieg:* Peer Gynt (exc); *Arne:* Rule Britannia; *Parry:* Jerusalem; *Elgar:* Pomp and Circumstance Marches (exc). (J. Mooney, London Choral Soc, RPO/A. Inglis)

RSR

Ⓓ **RSRD1002** (9/93)
Black Dyke Mills Band, Vol.2 - Sovereign Heritage
Berlioz: Corsaire; Benvenuto Cellini (exc); *Lucas:* Chorale and Variations; *Howells:* Pageantry; *Yorke:* Shipbuilders; *Farnon:* Vie de Matelot; *Beaver:* Sovereign Heritage. (Black Dyke Mills Band/G. Brand/R. Newsome/P. Parkes)

Russian Disc

Ⓓ **RDCD10903**
Weber/Schubert/Tchaikovsky—Orchestral Works
Weber: Euryanthe (exc); *Schubert:* Symphony 8; *Tchaikovsky:* Symphony 4. (USSR SO/E. Mravinsky)

Ⓓ **RDCD10905**
The Mravinsky Collection
Tchaikovsky: Nutcracker Suite; Symphony 5; *Brahms:* Symphony 3; *Mussorgsky:* Khovanshchina (exc). (Leningrad PO/E. Mravinsky)

Ⓓ **RDCD10907**
The Mravinsky Collection—Brahms/Sibelius/Weber
Weber: Oberon (exc); *Sibelius:* Legends (exc); *Brahms:* Symphony 4. (Leningrad PO/E. Mravinsky)

Ⓓ **RDCD11166** (3/94)
Wagner—Orchestral excerpts from Operas
Wagner: Tannhäuser (exc); Tristan und Isolde (exc); Lohengrin (exc); Meistersinger (exc); Siegfried (exc); Götterdämmerung (exc); Walküre (exc). (Leningrad PO/E. Mravinsky)

Ⓓ **RDCD11341**
Prokofiev/Stravinsky—Songs and Arias
Prokofiev: Alexander Nevsky (exc); On guard of peace (exc); Songs without words, Op. 35 (exc); Romances, Op. 73; Russian Folksongs, Op. 104 (exc); Ugly Duckling; Children's Songs, Op. 68 (exc); Songs, Op. 66b (exc); *Stravinsky:* Songs, Op. 6 (exc); Mavra (exc). (Z. Dolukhanova, All-Union Rad Orch/S. Samosud, B. Kozel, N. Svetlanova, V. Khvostin)

Ⓓ **RDCD11356** (10/94)
Rubinstein—Symphony No 2;Feramors - Ballet Music
Rubinstein: Symphony 2; Feramors. (Moscow St SO/I. Golovshin)

Ⓓ **RDCD11372**
Tchaikovsky—Romances; Rachmaninov—Aleko Aria
Tchaikovsky: Songs, Op. 47 (exc); Songs, Op. 60 (exc); I should like in a single word; Songs, Op. 57 (exc); Songs, Op. 63 (exc); Songs, Op. 6 (exc); Songs, Op. 73 (exc); Songs, Op. 38 (exc); Songs, Op. 28 (exc); Songs, Op. 16 (exc); *Rachmaninov:* Songs, Op. 14 (exc); Songs, Op. 8 (exc); Songs, Op. 14 (exc); Aleko (exc); *Sviridov:* Romances (exc). (E. Nesterenko, E. Shenderovich)

Ⓓ **RDCD15023**
Zara Dolukhanova sings
Tchaikovsky: Moscow cantata (exc); Maid of Orleans (exc); *Prokofiev:* Alexander Nevsky (exc); *Mussorgsky:* Khovanshchina (exc); *Rimsky-Korsakov:* Kashchey (exc); *Meyerbeer:* Huguenots (exc); *Saint-Saëns:* Samson et Dalila (exc); *Verdi:* Ave Maria; Don Carlo (exc); *Rossini:* Semiramide (exc); *Mozart:* Nozze di Figaro (exc); *Rossini:* Barbiere di Siviglia (exc). (Z. Dolukhanova, Moscow PO/G. Stolarov)

Saga Classics

Ⓓ **SCD9023**
Melodies for Flute and Harp
Chopin: Rossini Variations; *Inghelbrecht:* Scaphé; Dryades; *Vivaldi:* Concerti, Op. 8 (exc); *Fauré:* Sicilienne; Fantaisie; *Bizet:* Arlésienne Suites (exc); *Telemann:* Solos (1734) (exc); *Jongen:* Danse lente; *Bernstein:* West Side Story (exc); *Rossini:* Andante in F (harp); *Gossec:* Gavotte; *Paradies:* Sicilienne; *H. Andriessen:* Interlude; *Molnar:* Japanese Phantasy. (L. Schouten, R. Ederveen)

Sain

Ⓓ **SCDC2002** ▭ **C2002**
Elen AP Robert - Soprano
Gounod: Faust (exc); *Haydn:* Schöpfung (exc); *Mozart:* Veilchen, K476; *Mendelssohn:* Lieder, Op. 86 (exc); *Schubert:* Forelle, D550; *Brahms:* Lieder, Op. 84 (exc); *Traditional:* Bailero; *Iwan:* Why snow is white; *Grace Williams:* Early morning; *Elwyn-Edwards:* Land of Magic; *Hughes-Jones:* Summer evening. (E. Ap Robert, A. Bryn Parri)

Ⓓ **SCDC2070** (11/95)
Susan Bullock
Dvořák: Rusalka (exc); *Traditional:* Suo Gan; *Bernstein:* West Side Story (exc); *Puccini:* Madama Butterfly (exc); *E. T. Davies:* Ynys y Plant; *Bizet:* Carmen (exc); *Britten:* Folk Songs (exc); *Sondheim:* Follies (exc); *Traditional:* Bugeilio'r Gwenith Gwyn; *Mozart:* Nozze di Figaro (exc); *Glyn:* Gwynt yr haf. (S. Bullock, A. Davies, A. Bryn Parri)

Ⓓ **SCDC2076** ▭ **C2076**
David Lloyd-Early Recordings, 1940-1941
Penn: Smilin' through; *Mozart:* Zauberflöte (exc); Don Giovanni (exc); *Traditional:* All through the night; Men of Harlech; *Parry:* Jerusalem; England; *Joseph Parry:* Jesu, lover of my soul; *James James:* Land of my fathers; *Sanderson:* Until; *Toselli:* Serenade; *Puccini:* Bohème (exc); *Brahe:* Bless this house; *Speaks:* Sylvia; *Traditional:* David of the White Rock; Stars in heaven are bright; Over the stone; *J. Hughes:* Cwm Rhondda. (J. Hammond, D.

Lloyd, G. Moore, R. Douglas, Chor, Sadler's Wells Orch, Welsh Guards Band, CBO/T. S. Chandler/L. Heward)

Ⓓ **SCDC2085** (11/95)
Arthur Davies
Puccini: Madama Butterfly (exc); *R. S. Hughes:* Arafa Don; *Verdi:* Traviata (exc); *Hardelot:* Because; *William Davies:* O! Na byddai'n haf o hyd; *Lehár:* Land des Lächelns (exc); *Bizet:* Carmen (exc); *I. Lewis:* Bugail Aberdyfi; *Giordano:* Fedora (exc); *J. Henry:* Galwad y Tywysog; *Puccini:* Bohème (exc); *Elwyn-Edwards:* Mae hiraeth yn y môr; *Gounod:* Roméo et Juliette (exc); *Glyn:* Gwynt yr haf. (A. Davies, S. Bullock, A. Bryn Parri)

Ⓓ **SCD4058**
Louise Jones—Violin Recital
Mozart: Violin Sonata, K304; *Traditional:* David of the White Rock; Fair Lisa; *Vitali:* Ciacona; *Gluck:* Orfeo ed Euridice (exc); *Kreisler:* Pugnani Praeludium and Allegro; *Fauré:* Songs, Op.7 (exc); *Beethoven:* Violin Sonata 5. (L. Jones, K. Sturrock)

Salabert Actuels

Ⓓ **SCD8906** (9/90)
Xenakis—Oresteia
Xenakis: Orestia (Cpte). (S. Sakkas, S. Gualda, Strasbourg Univ Music Dept Chor, Colmar Women's Voices, Anjou Voc Ens, Basse-Normandie Ens/D. Debart)

Ⓓ **SCD9101** (9/93)
Maderna—Satyricon
Maderna: Satyricon (Cpte). (P. Sperry, A. Tomicich, L. Oliveri, M. Vargas, Divertimento Ens/S. Gorli)

Saydisc

Ⓓ **CD-SDL386** (11/91) ⊟ **CSDL386** (11/91)
Baroque Guitar Quartets
Handel: Concerti grossi, Op. 3 (exc); *Bach:* Passacaglia and Fugue, BWV582; *Corelli:* Trio Sonatas, Op. 2 (exc); Trio Sonatas, Op. 3 (exc); *Purcell:* Fairy Queen, Z629 (exc); *Vivaldi:* Concerto, RV532. (English Gtr Qt)

Ⓓ **CD-SDL399** ⊟ **CSDL399**
Spanish Guitar Quartets
Albéniz: Suite española 1 (exc); *Traditional:* Mexican Songs; *Soler:* Organ Concertos (exc); *Falla:* Vida breve (exc); *Milán:* El Maestro: Pavanas (exc); *Granados:* Danzas españolas (exc). (English Gtr Qt)

Ⓓ **CD-SDL400** (6/93) ⊟ **CSDL400** (6/93)
English National Songs
Traditional: Greensleeves (Alas! my love); When the king enjoys; Northern Lass; Vicar of Bray; Nancy Dawson; A-hunting we will go; Drink to me only; Begone dull care; Early one morning; *W. Lawes:* Gather ye rosebuds a 1; *Purcell:* King Arthur, Z628 (exc); *Carey:* Sally in our alley; *Leveridge:* Roast Beef of Old England; *Arne:* Rule Britannia; Love in a Village (exc); British Grenadiers; *Various:* National Anthems (exc); *Mr. Collins:* Chapter of Kings; *Hook:* Lass of Richmond Hill; *Dibdin:* Tom Bowling; *Bishop:* Home, sweet home. (L. Skeaping, J. Potter, Broadside Band/J. Barlow)

Scalen'Disc

Ⓓ **ARI155**
Fauré—Prométhée
Fauré: Prométhée (Cpte). (F. Soulié, E. Berger, J. Castellat, R. Esso, V. Millot, L. Vignon, Guy Fletcher, O. Lallouette, R. Velazquez, Ariège-Pyrénées Voc Ens, Equinoxe, Midi-Pyrénées Regional Orch/D. Dondeyne)

Seaview Music

Ⓓ **CD007365**
The Classic Buskers-Omnibusk
Offenbach: Orphée aux enfers (exc); *Rossini:* Barbiere di Siviglia (exc); *Handel:* Theme and Variations in G minor; *Chopin:* Waltzes (exc); *Verdi:* Nabucco (exc); *Bizet:* Arlésienne Suites (exc); *Handel:* Solomon (exc); *Elgar:* Chanson de Matin; *Haydn:* Trumpet Concerto; *Mendelssohn:* Violin Concerto, Op. 64 (exc); *Saint-Saëns:* Samson et Dalila (exc); *Hubay:* Scènes de la Csárda (exc); *Verdi:* Rigoletto (exc); *Vivaldi:* Concerto, RV445 (exc); *Mozart:* Così fan tutte (exc); *Satie:* Gnossiennes (exc); *J. Strauss II:* Unter Donner und Blitz (exc); *Handel:* Messiah (exc); *Mendelssohn:* Midsummer Night's Dream (exc); *Sousa:* Stars and Stripes Forever; *Traditional:* Mocairita; *M.S. Murray:* Beethoven Finales. (Classic Buskers)

Ⓓ **CD007366**
The Ocarina is no Trombone
Beethoven: Symphony 1 (exc); *Anon:* Tarantella; *Sor:* Romanesca; *Offenbach:* Orphée aux enfers (exc); *Sullivan:* HMS Pinafore (exc); Mikado (exc); Yeomen of the Guard (exc); *Anon:* My Lady Carey's Dompe; Division to a Ground; Chinese Flute Piece; *Arnie:* Tulips from Amsterdam; *Arban:* Carnaval de Venise; *Traditional:* Mindra Mea; Trece Lelea; Hora Oltenilor; *Verdi:* Rigoletto (exc); *Traditional:* Hanabe No Uta; Japanese Lullaby; *Schubert:* Trout Quintet, D667; *Satie:* Gymnopédies (exc); *Traditional:* Sicilian Folk Dances; *Wagner:* Lohengrin (exc); *Brewer:* Lark's Festival. (Classic Buskers, Chuckerbutty Ocarina Qt)

Sheffield Lab

Ⓓ **CD-7/8** (8/87)
Prokofiev & Wagner: Orchestral Works
Wagner: Walküre (exc); Tristan und Isolde (exc); Götterdämmerung (exc); Siegfried (exc); *Prokofiev:* Romeo and Juliet (exc). (Los Angeles PO/E. Leinsdorf)

Ⓓ **CD25** (2/88) ⊙ **TLP25** ⊟ **CAS25** (2/88)
The Moscow Sessions - I
Tchaikovsky: Symphony 5; *Glinka:* Ruslan and Lyudmila (exc); *Mussorgsky:* Khovanshchina (exc). (Moscow PO/L. Leighton Smith)

Ⓓ **10043-2-G**
Leinsdorf Sessions, Volume 1
Prokofiev: Romeo and Juliet (exc); *Debussy:* Après-midi; *Wagner:* Siegfried (exc). (Los Angeles PO/E. Leinsdorf)

Ⓓ **10052-2-G**
Leinsdorf Sessions, Volume 2
Stravinsky: Firebird Suite (1911); Firebird Suite (1919) (exc); *Wagner:* Tristan und Isolde (exc); Walküre (exc); Götterdämmerung (exc). (Los Angeles PO/E. Leinsdorf)

Silva Screen

Ⓓ **FILMCD127** (10/93)
Vampire Circus—The Essential Vampire Theme Collection
Delibes: Lakmé (exc); *Whitaker:* Vampire Circus (exc); *Gerald Fried:* Return of Dracula (exc); *Fiedel:* Fright Night (exc); *Cirino:* Transylvania Twist (exc); *J. Elias:* Vamp (exc); *Licht:* Children of the Night (exc); *B. May:* Thirst (exc); *Holdridge:* Transylvania 6-5000 (exc); *Mollin:* Forever Knight (exc); *Eidelman:* To Die For (exc); *McKenzie:* Son of Darkness (exc); *Cobert:* Dracula (exc); *Richard Stone:* Sundown (exc). (L. Garrett, L. Christian, Philh/A. Greenwood/N. Richardson, OST/G. Fried/B. Fiedel/C. Cirino/J. Elias/D. Licht/B. May/L. Holdridge/F. Mollin/C. Eidelman/M. McKenzie/R. Cobert/R. Stone)

Ⓓ **SILKD6004** (4/95) ⊟ **SILKC6004** (4/95)
Simple Gifts—Lesley Garrett
Handel: Messiah (exc); *Delibes:* Filles de Cadiz; *Rimsky-Korsakov:* Sadko (exc); *Boyce:* Solomon (exc); *Massenet:* Manon (exc); *Cilea:* Adriana Lecouvreur (exc); *Gounod:* Roméo et Juliette (exc); *Grieg:* Peer Gynt (exc); *Puccini:* Madama Butterfly (exc); *Sullivan:* Mikado (exc); *Tchaikovsky:* Songs, Op. 6 (exc); *Canteloube:* Chants d'Auvergne (exc); *Bach:* Cantata 202 (exc); *Lehár:* Giuditta (exc); *Traditional:* Shaker Chants and Spirituals (exc). (L. Garrett, RPO/P. Robinson)

Ⓓ **SILKD6005** ⊟ **SILKC6005**
Tito-Tito Beltrán
Puccini: Bohème (exc); *Giordano:* Fedora (exc); *Donizetti:* Elisir d'amore (exc); *Verdi:* Traviata (exc); *Bizet:* Pêcheurs de perles (exc); *Mozart:* Zauberflöte (exc); *R. Strauss:* Rosenkavalier (exc); *Rossini:* Barbiere di Siviglia (exc); *Gounod:* Faust (exc); *Donizetti:* Don Pasquale (exc); *Rossini:* Soirées musicales (exc). (T. Beltrán, RPO/R. Stapleton)

4SILVATC105 **SILVACD105(SILV)**
Flower Duet from Lakme - Lesley Garrett
Delibes: Lakmé (exc); Lakmé (exc); *Burgon:* Nunc Dimittis. (L. Garrett, Philh/A. Greenwood/G. Burgon, N. Raine)

Ⓓ **SONGCD903** (11/91) ⊟ **SONGC903** (11/91)
Diva! A Soprano at the Movies
Catalani: Wally (exc); *Delibes:* Lakmé (exc); *Mozart:* Nozze di Figaro (exc); *Gounod:* Faust (exc); *Puccini:* Bohème (exc); *Dvořák:* Rusalka (exc); *Puccini:* Gianni Schicchi (exc); *Canteloube:* Chants d'Auvergne (exc); *Rossini:* Barbiere di Siviglia (exc); *Hammerstein:* Carmen Jones (exc); *Offenbach:* Contes d'Hoffmann (exc); *Forrest/Wright:* Kismet (exc). (L. Garrett, Philh/A. Greenwood)

Ⓓ **SONGCD907** ⊟ **SONGC907**
Lesley Garrett—Prima Donna
Handel: Samson (exc); *Orff:* Carmina burana (exc); *Massenet:* Manon (exc); *Puccini:* Bohème (exc); Rondine (exc); *J. Strauss II:* Fledermaus (exc); *Canteloube:* Chants d'Auvergne (exc); *Handel:* Rinaldo (exc); *Weill:* Street Scene (exc); *Flotow:* Martha (exc); *Rossini:* Cenerentola (exc); *Gershwin:* Porgy and Bess (exc); *Burgon:* Nunc dimittis; *Herbert:* Enchantress (exc). (L. Garrett, Philh/I. Bolton/G. Burgon)

Simax

Ⓓ **PSC1821(1)**
Kirsten Flagstad, Vol.1 (pt 1)
Traditional: Aa Ola Ola, min eigen Onge; *Thrane:* Aagots Fjeldsang; *Grieg:* Songs, Op.33 (exc); *Rosenfeldt:* Ingalill; *Bishop:* Home, sweet home; *A. Grøndahl:* Endnu et streif kun af sol; Eventide; *Grieg:* Peer Gynt (exc); *O. Bull:* Saeterjentens Søndag; *Sinding:* Songs, Op.22 (exc); *Lie:* Snow; *Alnaes:* Happiness; *O. Bull:* Saeterjentens Søndag; *Grieg:* Peer Gynt (exc); Songs, Op.39 (exc); Songs, Op.15 (exc); *Alnaes:* Sidste reis; *Palenz:* A.B.C.-Viser; *Thommesen:* Lille-Barnet; *Nordraak:* Ingrid Sletten; *Wagner:* Tannhäuser (exc); Tristan und Isolde (exc); Walküre (exc); Lohengrin (exc). (K. Flagstad, M. Flagstad, E. Alnaes, orch/H. Lange)

Ⓓ **PSC1821(2)**
Kirsten Flagstad, Vol.1 (pt 2)
R. Strauss: Lieder, Op.10 (exc); *Beethoven:* Lieder, Op.48 (exc); Zärtliche Liebe, WoO123; *Grieg:* Songs, Op.25 (exc); Songs, Op.60 (exc); Melodies of the heart, Op.5 (exc); Songs, Op.48 (exc); Songs, Op.70 (exc); Songs, Op.69 (exc); *Alnaes:* Happiness; *Grieg:* Songs, Op.26 (exc); *Schubert:* Im Abendrot, D799; *Franz:* Lieder, Op.17 (exc); *Brahms:* Lieder, Op.63 (exc); *Schubert:* Lachen und Weinen, D777; Forelle, D550; *Grieg:* Songs, Op.26 (exc); Songs, Op.60 (exc); *Hurum:* Pale nights; *R. Strauss:* Lieder, Op.17 (exc); Lieder, Op.27 (exc); *Wagner:* Walküre (exc); Lohengrin (exc); *Beethoven:* Fidelio (exc); *Weber:* Oberon (exc); *Beethoven:* Ah, perfido, Op.65; *Wagner:* Tristan und Isolde (exc); Götterdämmerung (exc); Parsifal (exc). (K. Flagstad, L. Melchior, E. McArthur, Philadelphia/E. Ormandy, San Francisco SO, RCA Victor SO/E. McArthur)

Ⓓ **PSC3121** (12/94)
Braein—Anne Pedersdotter
Braein: Anne Pedersdotter (Cpte). (K. Ekeberg, S. Carlsen, V. Hanssen, K. M. Sandve, R. Eriksen, S. A. Thorsen, T. Stensvold, C. Ehrstedt, G. Oskarsson, A. Helleland, I. M. Brekke, T. Gilje, R. Nygård, Norwegian Nat Op Chor, Norwegian Nat Op Orch/P. Å. Andersson)

Sine Qua Non

Ⓓ **39820212** (1/94)
Puccini—La Fanciulla del West
Puccini: Fanciulla del West (Cpte). (G. Jones, C. Murgu, C. Otelli, V. Ombuena, F. E. D'Artegna, M. Pertusi, E. Turco, G. Pasino, G. de Angelis, P. Lefebvre, O. Mori, M. Taghadossi, C. Bosi, F. Montagud, A. Stragapede, D. Serraiocco, F. Memeo, Hungarian Rad Chor, Frankfurt RSO/M. Viotti)

Ⓓ **39820222**
Deng - Tenor
Puccini: Turandot (exc); Bohème (exc); Tosca (exc); Madama Butterfly (exc); Manon Lescaut (exc); *Ponchielli:* Gioconda (exc); *Leoncavallo:* Pagliacci (exc); *Giordano:* Andrea Chénier (exc); Fedora (exc); *Verdi:* Luisa Miller (exc); Ballo in maschera (exc); Aida (exc); Trovatore (exc). (Deng, Württemberg PO/R. Paternostro)

Ⓓ **39820242**
Verdi—Macbeth
Verdi: Macbeth (Cpte). (R. Bruson, G. Jones, R. Scandiuzzi, A. Cupido, M. Tashiro, G. de Angelis, T. Kohama, Fujiwara Op Chor, Tokyo PO/G. Kuhn)

Sir Thomas Beecham Trust

Ⓓ **BEECHAM3** (11/90)
Delius—Vocal & Orchestral Works
Delius: Sea Drift; Summer Night on the River; In a Summer Garden; Brigg Fair; First cuckoo; Village Romeo and Juliet (exc); Koanga (exc). (J. Brownlee, London Select Ch, LPO, RPS Orch, SO/T. Beecham)

Sonpact

Ⓓ **SPT93007** (9/94)
Boieldieu—La Calife de Bagdad
Boieldieu: Calife de Bagdad (Cpte). (L. Dale, L. Mayo, J. Michelini, C. Cheriez, H. Rhys-Evans, Camerata de Provence Chor, Camerata de Provence Orch/A. de Almeida)

Sony Classical

Ⓓ **MDK47176** ⊟ **MDT47176**
Favourite Arias by the World's Favourite Tenors
Cilea: Adriana Lecouvreur (exc); *Donizetti:* Elisir d'amore (exc); Lucia di Lammermoor (exc); *Giordano:* Andrea Chénier (exc); Fedora (exc); *Leoncavallo:* Pagliacci (exc); *Mascagni:* Iris (exc); *Massenet:* Cid (exc); *Puccini:* Bohème (exc); Gianni Schicchi (exc); Madama Butterfly (exc);

Tosca (exc); Turandot (exc); Turandot (exc); *R. Strauss:* Rosenkavalier (exc); *Verdi:* Luisa Miller (exc); Rigoletto (exc); Traviata (exc). (J. Carreras, P. Domingo, L. Pavarotti, I. Wixell, Toscanini SO, ROHO, NYPO, Hungarian St Orch, LSO, NY Op Orch, VPO, Munich RO, Philh, Vienna St Op Orch/E. Buckley/J. Pritchard/Z. Mehta/M. Tilson Thomas/L. Maazel/G. Patanè/E. Queler/L. Bernstein/James Levine)

Ⓓ **MK39210**
Zarzuela Arias and Duets
Soutullo: Leyenda del Beso (exc); *Serrano:* Dolorosa (exc); Trust de los Tenorios (exc); *Bretón:* Dolores (exc); *Luna:* Niño judío (exc); *Moreno Torroba:* Luisa Fernanda (exc); *Giménez:* Boda de Luis Alonso (exc); *Caballero:* Dúo de la Africana (exc). (P. Lorengar, P. Domingo, Austrian RSO/G. Navarro)

Ⓓ **MK42137** (9/87)
Carnaval—Wynton Marsalis
Arban: Carnaval de Venise; Fantasie brillante; *H. Clarke:* Débutante; Sounds from the Hudson; *Traditional:* Believe me, if all those endearing young charms; *J. Levy:* Grand Russian Fantasia; *Paganini:* Moto perpetuo, Op. 11; *T. Moore:* Irish Melodies (exc); *Rimsky-Korsakov:* Tale of Tsar Saltan (exc); *Bellstedt:* Napoli (exc); *Traditional:* Sometimes I feel like a motherless child. (W. Marsalis, Eastman Wind Ens/D. Hunsberger)

Ⓓ **MPK52569** (5/93)
Joseph Szigeti Recital
Corelli: Sonatas, Op.5 (exc); *Beethoven:* Violin Sonata 6; *Ravel:* Violin Sonata (1923-27); *Hindemith:* Sonata (1935); *Debussy:* Suite bergamasque (exc); *Lalo:* Roi d'Ys (exc); *Tchaikovsky:* Morceaux, Op. 51 (exc). (J. Szigeti, A. Farkas, M. Horszowski, C. Bussotti, A. Foldes, H. Kaufman)

Ⓓ **M2K35181** (6/87)
Puccini—Madama Butterfly
Puccini: Madama Butterfly (Cpte). (R. Scotto, P. Domingo, I. Wixell, G. Knight, F. Andreolli, J. Summers, A. Murray, M. King, C. Keyte, A. Byers, Ambrosian Op Chor, Philh/L. Maazel)

Ⓓ **M2K42181**
Giordano—Fedora
Giordano: Fedora (Cpte). (E. Marton, J. Carreras, J. Martin, V. Kincses, J. Gregor, I. Rozsos, K. Kováts, J. Bokor, J. Németh, A. Fülöp, P. Kovács, I. Baski, S. Blazsó, I. Rohmann, T. Csányi, Hungarian Rad & TV Chor, Hungarian Radio & TV Orch/G. Patanè)

Ⓓ **M3K35192** (11/87)
Mozart—Don Giovanni
Mozart: Don Giovanni (Cpte). (R. Raimondi, E. Moser, K. Te Kanawa, T. Berganza, K. Riegel, J. Van Dam, M. King, J. Macurdy, Paris Op Chor, Paris Op Orch/L. Maazel)

Ⓓ **SBK39436**
Mozart—Greatest Hits
Mozart: Piano Concerto 21 (exc); Nozze di Figaro (exc); Piano Sonata, K545 (exc); Divertimento, K334 (exc); Piano Sonata, K331 (exc); Serenade, K525; Don Giovanni (exc); Variations, K265. (R. Casadesus, G. Gould, P. Entremont, A. Previn, Cleveland Orch, Philadelphia/G. Szell/L. Lane/E. Ormandy)

Ⓓ **SBK39438**
Wagner—Greatest Hits
Wagner: Meistersinger (exc); Lohengrin (exc); Lohengrin (exc); Walküre (exc); Tristan und Isolde (exc); Tannhäuser (exc); Tannhäuser (exc). (Mormon Tabernacle Ch, Cleveland Orch, Philadelphia, NYPO/G. Szell/E. Ormandy/L. Bernstein)

Ⓓ **SBK39446**
Prokofiev—Greatest Hits
Prokofiev: Symphony 1; Love for 3 Oranges Suite (exc); Lt. Kijé Suite; Peter and the Wolf (exc). (NYPO, Philadelphia/L. Bernstein/E. Ormandy)

Ⓓ **SBK39448**
Bernstein—Greatest Hits
Bernstein: On the Town; On the Waterfront Suite (exc); West Side Story Symphonic Dances (exc); West Side Story (exc). (NYPO/L. Bernstein/A. Kostelanetz)

Ⓓ **SBK39454**
Gershwin—Greatest Hits
Gershwin: Rhapsody in Blue; Preludes; Piano Concerto; American in Paris; Porgy and Bess Suite. (L. Bernstein (pf/dir), O. Levant, A. Previn, Columbia SO, orch, Philadelphia/A. Kostelanetz/E. Ormandy)

Ⓓ **SBK46533** ▭ **SBT46533**
Beethoven—Symphony No. 9. Fidelio Ov
Beethoven: Symphony 9; Fidelio (exc). (A. Addison, J. Hobson, Richard Lewis, Donald Bell, Cleveland Orch Chor, Cleveland Orch/G. Szell)

Ⓓ **SBK46548** ▭ **SBT46548**
Opera Arias
Donizetti: Elisir d'amore (exc); *Bellini:* Norma (exc); *Verdi:* Otello (exc); *Puccini:* Madama Butterfly (exc); *Mozart:* Nozze di Figaro (exc); *Verdi:* Rigoletto (exc); *Puccini:* Bohème (exc); Gianni Schicchi (exc); Tosca (exc); Bohème (exc); *Mozart:* Don Giovanni (exc). (P. Domingo, ROH Chor, ROHO/J. Pritchard, R. Scotto, National PO/James Levine/G. Gavazzeni, Philh/L. Maazel, I. Cotrubas, New Philh, K. Te Kanawa, LPO, Paris Op Orch, I. Wixell)

Ⓓ **SBK47655**
Saint-Saëns—Popular orchestral works
Saint-Saëns: Symphony 3; Samson et Dalila (exc); Suite algérienne (exc); Danse macabre; Carnaval des animaux. (E. Power Biggs, Philadelphia/E. Ormandy, P. Entremont (pf/dir), G. Casadesus, Inst Ens)

Ⓓ **SBK47657**
Tchaikovsky—Symphony No. 6, etc
Tchaikovsky: Symphony 6; Capriccio italien; Eugene Onegin (exc). (Philadelphia/E. Ormandy)

Ⓓ **SBK48159**
Bizet—Orchestral Suites
Bizet: Arlésienne Suites; Carmen Suites (exc). (Philadelphia/E. Ormandy)

Ⓓ **SBK48162**
Popular Orchestral Works
Kodály: Háry János Suite; *Mussorgsky:* Pictures; *Prokofiev:* Lt Kijé Suite. (Cleveland Orch/G. Szell)

Ⓓ **SBK48175** (11/92)
George Szell conducts Wagner
Wagner: Rheingold (exc); Walküre (exc); Siegfried (exc); Götterdämmerung (exc); Meistersinger (exc); Tristan und Isolde (exc). (Cleveland Orch/G. Szell)

Ⓓ **SBK48265**
Elgar—Orchestral Works
Elgar: Enigma Variations; Pomp and Circumstance Marches; Crown of India (Cpte). (LPO/D. Barenboim)

Ⓓ **SBK48279** (6/93) ▭ **SBT48279** (6/93)
Offenbach/Rachmaninov/Smetana—Orchestral Works
Smetana: Bartered Bride (exc); *Offenbach:* Gaîté Parisienne (exc); *Rachmaninov:* Symphonic Dances. (Cleveland Orch/G. Szell, Philadelphia/E. Ormandy)

Ⓓ **SBK48285**
Handel—Orchestral Works
Handel: Water Music (exc); Fireworks Music; Ariodante (exc). (Grande Ecurie/J-C. Malgoire)

Ⓓ **SBK53255** (8/94) ▭ **SBT53255** (8/94)
Berlioz—Orchestral Works
Berlioz: Harold in Italy; Damnation de Faust (exc); Marche troyenne; Troyens (exc). (J. de Pasquale, Philadelphia/E. Ormandy/C. Munch, Paris Orch/D. Barenboim)

Ⓓ **SBK53261** (7/94) ▭ **SBT53261**
Prokofiev/Shostakovich—Orchestral Works
Shostakovich: Symphony 5; Age of Gold Suite (exc); *Prokofiev:* Love for 3 Oranges Suite. (Philadelphia/E. Ormandy)

Ⓓ **SBK53511** ▭ **SBT53511**
R. Strauss—Essential Classics
R. Strauss: Tod und Verklärung; Sinfonia Domestica; Salome (exc). (Cleveland Orch/G. Szell, Philadelphia/E. Ormandy)

Ⓓ **SB2K64391**
Leonard Bernstein - Man of Music
Bernstein: Candide Overture; On the Town (exc); West Side Story (exc); Fancy Free (exc); Symphony 1 (exc); Symphony 2 (exc); Symphony 3 (exc); Chichester Psalms (exc); Mass (exc); Dybbuk (exc); Prelude, Fugue and Riffs; *Copland:* Fanfare for the Common Man; *Mozart:* Piano Concerto 25 (exc); *Mahler:* Symphony 5 (exc); *Barber:* Adagio for Strings; *Shostakovich:* Symphony 5 (exc); *Ives:* Central Park in the dark; *Stravinsky:* Rite of Spring (exc); *Haydn:* Schöpfung (exc); *Beethoven:* König Stefan (exc); *Vaughan Williams:* Greensleeves Fantasia; *Sibelius:* Finlandia. (J. Tourel, J. Bogart, J. Reardon, A. Titus, B. Wand, G. Chakaris, B. Goodman, Camerata Sngrs, chor, orch, NYPO, NY City Ballet Orch, Columbia Jazz Combo, Israel PO/L. Bernstein, L. Bernstein (pf/dir)/J. Green)

Ⓓ **SB5K48396**
Beethoven— Symphonies and Overtures
Beethoven: Symphony 1; Symphony 2; Symphony 3; Symphony 4; Symphony 5; Symphony 6; Symphony 7; Symphony 8; Symphony 9; Egmont (exc); König Stefan (exc); Fidelio (exc). (A. Addison, J. Hobson, Richard Lewis, D. Bell, Cleveland Orch Chor, Cleveland Orch/G. Szell)

Ⓓ **SFK47279**
Passport to Spain
Bizet: Carmen (exc); *Albéniz:* Cantos de España (exc); *Falla:* Amor brujo (exc); *Granados:* Danzas españolas (exc); *Falla:* Vida breve (exc); *Chabrier:* España; *Granados:* Goyescas (exc); *Falla:* Sombrero de tres picos Suites (exc); Sombrero de tres picos Suites (exc); *Traditional:* Cant del ocells; *Ravel:* Boléro; *Calero:* Macarenas. (L. Munroe, National PO, A. Kostelanetz Orch, Philadelphia, NYPO/L. Stokowski/A. Kostelanetz/E. Ormandy/L. Bernstein/S. Henderson)

Ⓓ **SK33452**
Classical Barbra
Debussy: Beau soir; *Canteloube:* Chants d'Auvergne (exc); *Wolf:* Eichendorff Lieder (exc); *Fauré:* Pavane; Songs, Op.7 (exc); *Orff:* Carmina Burana (exc); *Handel:* Rinaldo (exc); *Ochs:* Dank sei Dir, Herr; *Schumann:* Liederkreis, Op. 39 (exc); *Ogermann:* I loved you. (B. Streisand, Columbia SO/C. Ogerman, C. Ogerman)

Ⓓ **SK44995**
Maureen McGovern sings Gershwin
Gershwin: Preludes (exc); Damsel in distress (exc); Porgy and Bess (exc); Strike up the Band II (exc); Strike up the Band I (exc); Shall we dance? (exc); Scandals 1924 (exc); Rosalie (exc); Primrose (exc); Goldwyn Follies (exc); Girl Crazy (exc); Lady, be Good (exc); Oh, Kay! (exc); Funny Face (exc); Of thee I sing (exc); By Strauss; Corner of Heaven with you. (M. McGovern, J. Harris, Jazz Ens)

Ⓓ **SK45808** (4/90)
New Year's Day Concert 1990
J. Strauss II: Zigeunerbaron (exc); Emancipitre, Op. 282; Donauweibchen, Op. 427; Wiener blut; Im Sturmschritt, Op. 348; G'schichten aus dem Wienerwald, Op. 325; Tritsch-Tratsch; Explosionen, Op. 43; Blauen Donau, Op. 314; *Jos Strauss:* Sport; Sympathie; Eingesendet; *J. Strauss I:* Indianer-Galopp; Radetzky March. (G. Glasl, VPO/Z. Mehta)

Ⓓ **SK45816** (7/90)
Humoresque—Favourite Violin Encores
Rimsky-Korsakov: Tale of Tsar Saltan (exc); *Tchaikovsky:* Songs, Op. 6 (exc); *Gershwin:* Porgy and Bess (exc); *Kreisler:* Liebesleid; *Brahms:* Hungarian Dances (exc); *Borodin:* String Quartet 2 (exc); *Rubinstein:* Soirées, Op. 44 (exc); *Chopin:* Nocturnes (exc); *Debussy:* Suite bergamasque (exc); *Benjamin:* Jamaican Rumba; *Traditional:* Greensleeves (Alas! My love); *Mendelssohn:* Lieder, Op. 34 (exc); *Foster:* Jeanie with the light brown hair; *Satie:* Gymnopédies (exc); *Schubert:* Schwanengesang, D957 (exc); *Debussy:* Préludes (exc); *Rachmaninov:* Songs, Op. 34 (exc); *Dvořák:* Humoresques, op 101 (exc); *Schubert:* Ave Maria, D839; *Copland:* Rodeo (exc). (I. Stern, Columbia SO/F. Brieff, M. Katims)

Ⓓ **SK45855** (1/91)
Mozart: Bastien und Bastienne
Mozart: Bastien und Bastienne (Cpte); Moto di gioia, K579; Nozze di Figaro (exc); Misero! o sogno, K431; Mentre ti lascio, K513. (V. Cole, E. Gruberová, L. Polgár, F. Liszt CO/R. Leppard, V. Cole, E. Gruberová, L. Polgár)

Ⓓ **SK45938** (2/91)
Carlos Kleiber conducts Johann Strauss
J. Strauss II: Accelerationen, Op. 234; Bauern-Polka, Op. 276; Fledermaus (exc); Künstlerleben, Op. 316; Eljen a Magyar!, Op. 332; Im Krapfenwald'l, Op. 336; Frühlingsstimmen, Op. 410; Ritter Pasman; Blauen Donau, Op. 314; Pizzicato Polka; *Jos Strauss:* Libelle; Moulinet; Plappermäulchen; Jokey; *J. Strauss I:* Radetzky March. (VPO/C. Kleiber)

Ⓓ **SK45965** (1/92)
Esa-Pekka Salonen conducts Stravinsky
Stravinsky: Pulcinella (Cpte); Ragtime; Renard; Octet. (Y. Kenny, J. Aler, J. Tomlinson, N. Robson, D. Wilson-Johnson, London Sinfonietta/E-P. Salonen)

Ⓓ **SK46672** (8/92) ▭ **ST46672** (8/92)
Baroque Duets
Handel: Samson (exc); Birthday Ode for Queen Anne (exc); O come chiare e bella (exc); *A. Scarlatti:* Su le sponde del Tebro; Si suoni la tromba; Con voce festiva; Rompe sprezza con un sospir; Mio tesoro, per te moro; *Bach:* Cantata 51 (exc); Cantata 21 (exc); *Predieri:* Zenobia (exc); *Stradella:* Barcheggio Sinfonia 1. (K. Battle, W. Marsalis, St Luke's Orch/J. Nelson)

Ⓓ **SK46693** (1/92)
Gazzaniga—Don Giovanni
Gazzaniga: Don Giovanni (Cpte). (D. Johnson, E. Szmytka, L. Serra, E. Schmid, J. Tilli, C. Allemano, E. Szmytka, F. Furlanetto, A. Scharinger, H. Wildhaber, Stuttgart Chbr Ch, Tafelmusik/B. Weil)

Ⓓ **SK46695** (5/92)
Mozart—Overtures, etc
Mozart: Idomeneo (exc); Entführung (exc); Schauspieldirektor (exc); Nozze di Figaro (exc); Don Giovanni (exc); Così fan tutte (exc); Clemenza di Tito (exc); Zauberflöte (exc); Serenade, K525. (Tafelmusik/B. Weil)

Ⓓ **SK47178** (4/92)
Wagner—Tannhäuser without Words
Wagner: Tannhäuser (exc). (Pittsburgh Mendelssohn Ch, Pittsburgh SO/L. Maazel)

Ⓓ **SK47187** (9/92)
A Vienna Souvenir
Lanner: D'ersten Gedanken, Op. 1; Schmetterlinge, Op. 65; Dampf, Op. 94; Bestürmung von Constantine, Op. 127; *J. Strauss I:* Chinese Galop, Op. 20; Vier Temperamente, Op. 59; *J. Strauss II:* Rasch in der Tat; Fledermaus (exc); *Lanner:* Amalien, Op. 14; *Schubert:* Grazer Galopp, D925. (Vienna Ens)

Ⓓ **SK47192** (3/92)
Ferruccio Furlanetto sings Mozart
Mozart: Nozze di Figaro (exc); Zauberflöte (exc); Don Giovanni (exc); Così fan tutte (exc). (F. Furlanetto, Vienna SO/I. Marin)

Ⓓ **SK48017**
Bernstein—Candide:Original Broadway Cast
Bernstein: Candide (1956) (exc). (B. Cook, R. Rounseville, M. Adrian, W. Olvis, I. Pettina, G. Blackwell, T. Pyle, N. Roland, W. Chapman, R. Mesrobian, M. Beck Th Chor, M. Beck Th Orch/S. Krachmalnick)

Ⓓ **SK48045** (7/93)
Flute Concertos
C. Stamitz: Flute Concerto in G; *Richter:* Flute Concerto in E minor; *J. Stamitz:* Flute Concerto in G; *L. Hofmann:* Flute Concerto in D; *Gluck:* Orfeo ed Euridice (exc). (Barthold Kuijken, Tafelmusik/J. Lamon)

Ⓓ **SK48094** ▣ **ST48094**
Favourite Puccini Arias
Puccini: Gianni Schicchi (exc); Rondine (exc); Bohème (exc); Madama Butterfly (exc); Villi (exc); Madama Butterfly (exc); Manon Lescaut (exc); Suor Angelica (exc); Bohème (exc); Tosca (exc); Turandot (exc); Turandot (exc). (K. Te Kanawa, R. Scotto, E. Marton, P. Domingo, J. Carreras, Vienna St Op Chor, LPO, LSO, Philh, New Philh, Vienna St Op Orch, Hungarian St Orch, Munich RO/J. Pritchard/L. Maazel/G. Gavazzeni/M. Tilson Thomas/G. Patanè, G. Knight, Ambrosian Op Chor)

Ⓓ **SK48201** ▣ **ST48201**
The Sondheim Songbook
Bernstein: West Side Story (exc); *Styne:* Gypsy (exc); *Rodgers:* Do I Hear a Waltz? (exc); *M. Rodgers:* Mad Show (exc); *Sondheim:* Anyone Can Whistle (exc); Company (exc); Little Night Music (exc). (Orig Broadway Cast)

Ⓓ **SK48211** (8/93) ▣ **ST48211** (8/93)
Bernstein—West Side Story: film soundtrack
Bernstein: West Side Story (Cpte). (M. Nixon, J. Bryant, R. Tamblyn, Orig Film Cast/J. Green)

Ⓓ **SK48224**
John Williams—The Green Album
Berlin: God bless America; *P.M. Williams:* Theme for Earth Day; *Traditional:* Shenandoah; *Guthrie:* This is your Land; *Simon:* America; *Traditional:* Deep river; *Grofé:* Grand Canyon Suite (exc); *Copland:* Appalachian Spring (exc); *Bernstein:* Candide (1988) (exc); *Nash:* Last Whale (exc); *Tiomkin:* Alamo (exc); *Copland:* Tender Land (exc); *Halley:* Appalachian Morning; *S. Ward:* America the Beautiful. (Tanglewood Fest Chor, Boston Pops/J.T. Williams)

Ⓓ **SK48232** ▣ **ST48232**
Joy to the World
Traditional: Christmas Festival; Visit from St Nicholas (Reisman); White Christmas; *Herbert:* Babes in Toyland (exc); *J. T. Williams:* Home Alone (exc); *Traditional:* Christmas Bouquet; *Jessel:* Parade of the Wooden Soldiers; *Traditional:* Christmas Night Medley; We wish you a merry Christmas; *L. Anderson:* Sleigh Ride; *Traditional:* Merry Little Sing-Along. (R. Williams, Tanglewood Fest Chor, Boston Pops/J. T. Williams)

Ⓓ **SK48235** (12/92) ▣ **ST48235** (12/92)
A Carnegie Hall Christmas Concert
Traditional: Twelve Days of Christmas; Mary's Boy Child; Gesù bambino; *Mozart:* Exsultate Jubilate, K165 (exc); *Rodgers:* Sound of Music (exc); *Traditional:* Winter Wonderland; We three Kings; I wonder as I wander; Mary had a baby; Who was Mary?; Sister Mary had but one child; Go tell it on the Mountain; Christmas Song; Have yourself a merry little Christmas; Stille Nacht; Joy to the world; *Humperdinck:* Hänsel und Gretel (exc); *M. Praetorius:* Es ist ein Ros'; *Traditional:* Maria Wiegenlied; I saw three ships; First Nowell; Away in a manger; Deck the hall; Holly and the Ivy; Angels we have heard on high; *Adam:* Minuit, Chrétiens (exc). (K. Battle, F. von Stade, W. Marsalis, Chor, Orch/A. Previn, Jazz Ens)

Ⓓ **SK48381** ▣ **ST48381**
Encore - Katia & Marielle Labeque
A.Berio: Polka; *Bach:* Cantata 147 (exc); *Gershwin:* Preludes; *Stravinsky:* Tango; *Berio:* Wasserklavier; *Brahms:* Waltzes, Op. 39 (exc); *A. Berio:* Maria Isabella; *Tchaikovsky:* Seasons (exc); *Gershwin:* Shall we dance? (exc); *Bernstein:* West Side Story (exc); *Joplin:* Bethena; Entertainer; *A. Berio:* Primavera; *Jaell-Trautmann:* Valses (exc); *Stravinsky:* Three easy pieces (exc); *Bartók:* Mikrokosmos (exc); *Schumann:* Klavierstücke, Op. 85 (exc). (K. Labèque, M. Labèque)

Ⓓ **SK52489** (6/94)
Verdi—Ballet Music from the Operas
Verdi: Vespri Siciliani (exc); Macbeth (exc); Don Carlos (exc); Otello (exc); Aida (exc). (NY Met Op Orch/James Levine)

Ⓓ **SK52491**
Popular American Music
Grofé: Grand Canyon Suite; *Herbert:* Hero and Leander; Babes in Toyland (exc); Eileen (exc); Fortune Teller (exc); It happened in Nordland (exc); Mademoiselle Modiste (exc); Naughty Marietta (exc); Only Girl (exc); Red Mill (exc). (Pittsburgh SO/L. Maazel)

Ⓓ **SK52498**
Highlights on Period Instruments
Vivaldi: Concerto, RV418; Concerti Grossi, Op. 3 (exc); *Handel:* Concerti grossi, Op. 3 (exc); *Geminiani:* Concerti Grossi, Op. 2 (exc); *Mozart:* Serenade, K250 (exc); Serenade, K525; Entführung (exc); Zauberflöte (exc). (A. Bylsma, Tafelmusik, J. Lamon (vn/dir)/B. Weil)

Ⓓ **SK52565** (7/93)
New Year's Eve Concert 1992
R. Strauss: Don Juan; Burleske; Till Eulenspiegel; Rosenkavalier (exc). (R. Fleming, K. Battle, F. von Stade, A. Schmidt, M. Argerich, BPO/C. Abbado)

Ⓓ **SK52568** (6/93) ▣ **ST52568** (6/93)
Midori—Encore!
Kreisler: Pugnani Praeludium and Allegro; Marche miniature viennoise; Syncopation; *Sarasate:* Danzas españolas (exc); Introduction and Tarantella, Op. 43; *Paganini:* Cantabile, Op. 17; *Cui:* Kaleydoskop (exc); *Bacewicz:* Oberek 2; *Elgar:* Salut d'amour; Chanson de matin; *Shostakovich:* Preludes, Op. 34 (exc); *Dvořák:* Slavonic Dances (exc); *Prokofiev:* Love for 3 Oranges Suite (exc); *Tchaikovsky:* Souvenir d'un lieu cher, Op. 42 (exc); *Szymanowski:* Myths, Op. 30 (exc); *Gluck:* Orfeo ed Euridice (exc); *Fauré:* Berceuse, Op. 16; *Scriabin:* Etudes, Op. 8 (exc); *Bartók:* Romanian Folkdances, Sz56; *Ysaÿe:* Rêve d'enfant, Op. 14. (Midori, R. McDonald)

Ⓓ **SK53276** (4/94)
Nielsen—Orchestral Works
Nielsen: Clarinet Concerto; Flute Concerto; Rhapsody Overture; Saul and David (exc); Springtime in Funen. (A. Bäverstam, L. Ekdahl, A. Thors, K. M. Sandve, P. Høyer, P. Flemström, H. Rosengren, Swedish Boys' Ch, Swedish Rad Ch, Swedish RSO/E-P. Salonen)

Ⓓ **SK53288** (1/94)
Offenbach—Overtures
Offenbach: Fille du tambour-major (exc); Orphée aux enfers (exc); Belle Hélène (exc); Barbe-Bleue (exc); Grande-Duchesse de Gérolstein (exc); Monsieur et Madame Denis (exc); Vie parisienne (exc); Vert-vert (exc). (Vienna SO/B. Weil)

Ⓓ **SK53539**
There is Nothin' Like a Dame—Broadway's Broads
Styne: Gentlemen Prefer Blondes (exc); *Rodgers:* Babes In Arms (exc); *Porter:* Kiss Me, Kate (exc); *Kern:* Roberta (exc); *F. Loewe:* My Fair Lady (exc); *Styne:* Gypsy (exc); *Bernstein:* Candide (1956) (exc); Wonderful Town (exc); *Cy Coleman:* Sweet Charity (exc); *J. Herman:* Mame (exc); *Sondheim:* Company (exc); Little Night Music (exc); *J. Herman:* Dear World (exc); *Youmans:* No, No Nanette (exc). (Orig Broadway Cast, Broadway Cast)

Ⓓ **SK53541**
There's No Business Like Showbusiness—Broadway Showstoppers
Porter: Kiss Me, Kate (exc); *Kander:* Cabaret (stage) (exc); *Kern:* Show Boat (exc); *Cy Coleman:* Barnum (exc); *Styne:* Gypsy (exc); *Bernstein:* Wonderful Town (exc); *Styne:* Hallelujah, Baby (exc); *Cy Coleman:* Sweet Charity (exc); *J. Herman:* Mame (exc); *Kander:* 70, Girls, 70 (exc); *F. Loewe:* My Fair Lady (exc); *Bernstein:* West Side Story (exc); *De Paul:* Lil' Abner (exc); *Strouse:* Annie (exc); *Yeston:* Nine (exc); *Hamlisch:* Chorus Line (exc); *Berlin:* Annie Get Your Gun (exc). (Orig Broadway Cast, Broadway Cast, Orig London Cast, Orig Film Cast)

Ⓓ **SK53542**
Embraceable You—Broadway In Love
Rodgers: Boys from Syracuse (exc); *B. Lane:* Finian's Rainbow (exc); *Styne:* Gentlemen Prefer Blondes (exc); *Rodgers:* On Your Toes (exc); *F. Loewe:* Brigadoon (exc); *Rodgers:* Pal Joey (exc); *Styne:* Bells Are Ringing (exc); *Kern:* Show Boat (exc); *Bernstein:* West Side Story (exc); *Porter:* Anything Goes (exc); *Rodgers:* Oklahoma! (exc); King and I (exc); *Youmans:* No, No Nanette (exc); *Strouse:* All American (exc); *Kander:* Cabaret (stage) (exc); *Cy Coleman:* Barnum (exc). (Orig Broadway Cast, Broadway Cast)

Ⓓ **SK53549**
Woody Allen Classics
Weill: Kleine Dreigroschenmusik (exc); *Schubert:* String Quartet, D887 (exc); *Satie:* Gymnopédies (exc); *Bach:* Viola da gamba Sonatas, BWV1027-9 (exc); Harpsichord Concerto, BWV1056 (exc); *Puccini:* Manon Lescaut (exc); *Mendelssohn:* Midsummer Night's Dream (exc); Symphony 3 (exc); *Gershwin:* Rhapsody in Blue; *Prokofiev:* Lt. Kijé Suite (exc); Alexander Nevsky (exc); Love for 3 Oranges Suite (exc). (R. Scotto, Y-Y. Ma, K. Cooper, I. Kipnis, G. Graffman, Juilliard Qt, Westminster Ch, LSO, RPO, London Stgs, Cleveland Orch, BRSO, NYPO, Los Angeles PO/M. Tilson Thomas/P. Entremont/N. Marriner/G. Gavazzeni/G. Szell/A. Davis/Z. Mehta/T. Schippers)

Ⓓ **SK53968**
Opera Duets
Massenet: Werther (exc); *Mascagni:* Cavalleria Rusticana (exc); *Bellini:* Norma (exc); *Bizet:* Carmen (exc); *Verdi:* Trovatore (exc); Traviata (exc). (A. Baltsa, J. Carreras, J. Howard, Tallis Chbr Ch, LSO/P. Domingo)

Ⓓ **SK53978** (1/95)
Prometheus
Beethoven: Prometheus (exc); *Liszt:* Prometheus; *Scriabin:* Prometheus; *Nono:* Prometeo Suite (exc). (I. Ade-Jesemann, M. Bair-Ivenz, S. Otto, P. Hall, U. Krumbiegel, M. Schadock, M. Argerich, M. Hasel, M. Preis, C. Gössling, Berlin Singakademie, Freiburg Sols Ch, BPO/C. Abbado)

Ⓓ **SK58973**
Wagneriana—Wagner Transcriptions
Wagner: Tannhäuser Overture; Albumblatt; Walküre (exc); Walküre (exc); Walküre (exc); Götterdämmerung (exc); Tristan und Isolde Vorspiel; *Raff:* Meistersinger Reminiscenzen (exc). (C. Katsaris)

Ⓓ **SK64133** (1/94) ▣ **ST64133** (1/94)
The Essential Philip Glass
Glass: Lightning; Changing Opinion; Façades; Gentleman's Honor; Satyagraha (exc); Akhnaten (exc); Einstein on the Beach (exc); Dance 8; Metamorphosis Four; Closing. (Philip Glass Ens, J. Pendarvis, B. Fowler, P. Dunkel, D. Perry, P. Esswood, M. Riesman, P. Glass, NYC Op Orch, NYC Op Chor, Stuttgart St Orch, Stuttgart St Orch, Stuttgart State Chor)

Ⓓ **SK64600**
Bobby McFerrin-Paper Music
Mozart: Nozze di Figaro (exc); *Boccherini:* String Quintets, G271-6 (exc); *Fauré:* Pavane; *Stravinsky:* Pulcinella Suite (exc); *Vivaldi:* Concerto, RV531; *Mendelssohn:* Midsummer Night's Dream (exc); *Bach:* Violin Concerto, BWV1041 (exc); *Mozart:* Serenade, K525; *Tchaikovsky:* Andante cantabile, Op. 11 (exc). (St Paul CO, B. McFerrin (sngr/dir)/B. McFerrin)

Ⓓ **SMK39030**
Placido Domingo sings Great Love Scenes
Puccini: Madama Butterfly (exc); *Cilea:* Adriana Lecouvreur (exc); *Puccini:* Rondine (exc); *Massenet:* Manon (exc); *G. Charpentier:* Louise (exc); *Gounod:* Roméo et Juliette (exc). (P. Domingo, R. Scotto, K. Te Kanawa, I. Cotrubas, Philh, LSO, National PO, New Philh/L. Maazel/James Levine/K. H. Adler/G. Prêtre)

Ⓓ **SMK47518** (11/92)
Beethoven—Orchestral Works
Beethoven: Symphony 9; Fidelio (exc). (M. Arroyo, R. Sarfaty, N. di Virgilio, N. Scott, Juilliard Chor, NYPO/L. Bernstein)

Ⓓ **SMK47521** (11/92)
Beethoven—Orchestral Works
Beethoven: Violin Concerto; Consecration of the House Ov; Leonore (exc). (I. Stern, NYPO/L. Bernstein)

Ⓓ **SMK47525** (11/92)
Berlioz—Orchestral Works
Berlioz: Symphonie fantastique; Benvenuto Cellini (exc); Damnation de Faust (exc); Carnaval romain. (NYPO/L. Bernstein)

Ⓓ **SMK47529** (11/92)
Bernstein conducts Bernstein
Bernstein: West Side Story Symphonic Dances; Candide Overture; *Gershwin:* Rhapsody in Blue; American in Paris. (NYPO, L. Bernstein (pf/dir)/L. Bernstein)

Ⓓ **SMK47531** (11/92)
Bizet—Orchestral Suites
Bizet: Carmen Suites (exc); Arlésienne Suites. (NYPO/L. Bernstein)

Ⓓ **SMK47532** (11/92)
Bizet/Offenbach/Suppé—Orchestral Works
Bizet: Symphony; *Offenbach:* Gaîté Parisienne (exc); Orphée aux enfers (exc); *Suppé:* Schöne Galathee (exc). (NYPO/L. Bernstein)

Ⓓ **SMK47600** (9/93)
Ballet Music from Famous Operas
Borodin: Prince Igor (exc); *Gounod:* Faust (exc); *Ponchielli:* Gioconda (exc); *Rimsky-Korsakov:* Snow Maiden (exc); *Saint-Saëns:* Samson et Dalila (exc); *Verdi:* Aida (exc); Aida (exc). (NYPO/L. Bernstein)

Ⓓ **SMK47601** (9/93)
Opera Overtures
Mozart: Nozze di Figaro (exc); *Nicolai:* Lustigen Weiber von Windsor (exc); *Rezniček:* Donna Diana (exc); *J. Strauss II:* Fledermaus (exc); *A. Thomas:* Mignon (exc); *Weber:* Freischütz (exc); Euryanthe (exc); Oberon (exc); *Smetana:* Bartered Bride (exc). (NYPO/L. Bernstein)

Ⓓ **SMK47606**
Rossini/Suppé—Overtures
Rossini: Guillaume Tell (exc); Italiana in Algeri (exc); Gazza ladra (exc); Barbiere di Siviglia (exc); Semiramide (exc); Scala di seta (exc); *Suppé:* Leichte Kavallerie (exc); Dichter und Bauer (exc). (NYPO/L. Bernstein)

Ⓓ **SMK47607**
Russian Orchestral Pieces
Glinka: Ruslan and Lyudmila (exc); *Borodin:* In the Steppes of Central Asia; *Glière:* Red Poppy Suite (exc); *Ippolitov-Ivanov:* Caucasian Sketches (exc); *Mussorgsky:* Khovanshchina (exc); *Prokofiev:* Lt. Kijé Suite (exc); Scythian Suite; Love for 3 Oranges Suite (exc); *Shostakovich:* Age of Gold Suite (exc). (NYPO/L. Bernstein)

Ⓓ **SMK47609** (9/93)
Schubert/Schumann—Orchestral Works
Schubert: Symphony 5; Teufels Lustschloss (exc); *Schumann:* Cello Concerto; Genoveva (exc). (L. Rose, NYPO/L. Bernstein)

Ⓓ **SMK47625** (9/94)
R. Strauss—Orchestral Works
R. Strauss: Don Quixote; Festliches Präludium; Salome (exc). (W. Lincer, L. Munroe, E. Power Biggs, NYPO/L. Bernstein)

Ⓓ **SMK47636**
Tchaikovsky—Ballet Music
Tchaikovsky: Nutcracker Suite; Swan Lake (exc); Sleeping Beauty (exc); Eugene Onegin (exc). (NYPO/L. Bernstein)

Ⓓ **SMK47643**
Wagner—Opera Orchestral Music
Wagner: Fliegende Holländer (exc); Rienzi (exc); Lohengrin (exc); Lohengrin (exc); Meistersinger (exc); Walküre (exc); Walküre (exc); Tannhäuser (exc). (NYPO/L. Bernstein)

Ⓓ **SMK47644**
Wagner—Orchestral and Vocal Works
Wagner: Tannhäuser (exc); Götterdämmerung (exc); Wesendonk Lieder; Tristan und Isolde (exc). (E. Farrell, NYPO/L. Bernstein)

Ⓓ **SMK48155** ⊡ **SMT48155**
Carreras and Caballe sing Souvenirs
Donizetti: Amor marinaro; *Rodgers:* South Pacific (exc); *Rossini:* Turco in Italia (exc); *Bellini:* Ricordanza; *Giordano:* Andrea Chénier (exc); *Verdi:* Aroldo (exc); *Schubert:* Ave Maria, D839; *Wagner:* Tristan und Isolde (exc); Tannhäuser (exc); *Puccini:* Turandot (exc); Tosca (exc); *Donizetti:* Gemma di Vergy (exc); Poliuto (exc); *Ribas:* Per tu amor; *Brahms:* Lieder, Op. 49 (exc). (M. Caballé, J. Carreras, LSO/J. Tunick, National PO/R. Chailly, Hungarian St Op Orch/G. Patanè, NY Op Orch/E. Queler, Vienna St Op Orch, NYPO/Z. Mehta/M. Tilson Thomas, Martin Katz/L. Maazel, Barcelona Liceo SO/J. Casas, Vienna SO/O. Caetani)

Ⓓ **SMK48464** (12/93)
Boulez conducts Schoenberg - Volume 2
Schoenberg: Glückliche Hand; Variations, Op. 31; Verklärte Nacht. (S. Nimsgern, BBC Sngrs, BBC SO, NYPO/P. Boulez)

Ⓓ **SMK48466** (12/93)
Boulez conducts Schoenberg—Volume 3
Schoenberg: Erwartung (Cpte); Pierrot lunaire; Lied der Waldtaube. (J. Martin, J. Norman, Y. Minton, D. Barenboim, M. Debost, A. Pay, P. Zukerman, L. Harrell, Paris InterContemporain Ens, BBC SO/P. Boulez)

Ⓓ **SMK52650**
Glenn Gould conducts and plays Wagner
Wagner: Siegfried Idyll; Meistersinger (exc); Götterdämmerung (exc); Siegfried Idyll. (G. Gould, Toronto SO/G. Gould)

Ⓓ **SMK53500**
Mozart—Die Entführung aus dem Serail - Highlights
Mozart: Entführung (exc). (C. Studer, E. Szmytka, K. Streit, R. Gambill, G. Missenhardt, Vienna St Op Concert Ch, Vienna SO/B. Weil)

Ⓓ **SMK53501**
Rossini—Il barbiere di Siviglia - Highlights
Rossini: Barbiere di Siviglia (exc). (M. Horne, R. Pierotti, P. Barbacini, L. Nucci, E. Dara, S. Ramey, S. Sammaritano, La Scala Chor, La Scala Orch/R. Chailly)

Ⓓ **SMK53502**
Rossini—La Cenerentola - Highlights
Rossini: Cenerentola (exc). (L. V. Terrani, E. Ravaglia, M. Schmiege, F. Araiza, D. Trimarchi, E. Dara, A. Corbelli, W German Rad Chor, Cappella Coloniensis/G. Ferro)

Ⓓ **SMK53503**
Rossini—La gazza ladra - Highlights
Rossini: Gazza ladra (exc). (K. Ricciarelli, L. d'Intino, B. Manca di Nissa, W. Matteuzzi, R. Coviello, S. Ramey, F. Furlanetto, Prague Phil Chor, Turin RSO/G. Gelmetti)

Ⓓ **SMK53504**
Rossini—L'italiana in Algeri - Highlilghts
Rossini: Italiana in Algeri (exc). (L. V. Terrani, J. M. Bima, L. Rizzi, F. Araiza, A. Corbelli, E. Dara, W. Ganzarolli, W German Rad Chor, Cappella Coloniensis/G. Ferro)

Ⓓ **SMK53505**
Rossini—Il turco in Italia - Highlights
Rossini: Turco in Italia (exc). (M. Caballé, J. Berbié, E. Palacio, P. Barbacini, E. Dara, L. Nucci, S. Ramey, Ambrosian Op Chor, National PO/R. Chailly)

Ⓓ **SMK53506**
Verdi—Aida - Highlights
Verdi: Aida (exc). (A. Millo, D. Zajick, P. Domingo, J. Morris, S. Ramey, T. Cook, C. Anthony, NY Met Op Chor, NY Met Op Orch/James Levine)

Ⓓ **SMK53507**
Verdi—Don Carlo - Highlights
Verdi: Don Carlo (exc). (A. Millo, D. Zajick, J. Bunnell, M. Sylvester, J. H. Murray, V. Chernov, F. Furlanetto, P. Plishka, NY Met Op Chor, NY Met Op Orch/James Levine)

Ⓓ **SMK53508**
Verdi—Luisa Miller - Highlights
Verdi: Luisa Miller (exc). (A. Millo, P. Domingo, V. Chernov, J-H. Rootering, F. Quivar, P. Plishka, W. White, NY Met Op Chor, NY Met Op Orch/James Levine)

Ⓓ **SMK53550**
Puccini—Tosca - Highlights
Puccini: Tosca (exc). (E. Marton, J. Carreras, J. Pons, F. Gerdesits, I. Tajo, J. Németh, J. Gregor, B. Héja, Hungarian Rad & TV Chor, Hungarian St Orch/M. Tilson Thomas)

Ⓓ **SMK58934** (11/94)
Delius—Orchestral Works
Delius: Over the Hills and Far Away; North Country Sketches; Eventyr; Koanga (exc). (BBC Chor, RPO/T. Beecham)

Ⓓ **SMK58936**
A Musical Heritage
Boyce: Symphonies (exc); *Vaughan Williams:* Greensleeves Fantasia; *Delius:* Hassan (exc); *Purcell:* Chaconne, Z730; *Elgar:* Chanson de nuit; Chanson de matin; *Purcell:* Dido (exc); *Warlock:* Capriol Suite; *Handel:* Solomon (exc); *Purcell:* Old Bachelor, Z607 (exc); Gordian Knot Unty'd, Z597 (exc). (ECO, J-L. Garcia (vn/dir)/R. Leppard)

Ⓓ **SMK64108** (7/95)
Wagner—Orchestral Music
Wagner: Meistersinger (exc); Tannhäuser (exc); Faust Overture; Tristan und Isolde (exc); Siegfried Idyll. (NYPO/P. Boulez)

Ⓓ **SMK64243**
Prokofiev—Orchestral & Piano Works
Prokofiev: Piano Concerto 1; Piano Concerto 2; Romeo and Juliet Pieces; Love for 3 Oranges Suite (exc). (V. Feltsman, LSO/M. Tilson Thomas, FNO/L. Maazel)

Ⓓ **SMK64467** (8/95)
J. Strauss II/Brahms/Smetana—Orchestral Works
J. Strauss II: Blauen Donau, Op. 314; G'schichten aus dem Wienerwald, Op. 325; Kaiser, Op. 437; Wiener Blut; Zigeunerbaron (exc); Fledermaus (exc); *Brahms:* Hungarian Dances (exc); *Smetana:* Má vlast (exc). (Columbia SO, NYPO/B. Walter)

Ⓓ **SMK66171** (10/94)
The Beggar's Opera—1968 London Cast
Gay: Beggar's Opera (Cpte). (J. Waters, P. Gilmore, F. Cuka, J. Carter, J. Cossins, H. Hazell, P. Kenton, D. Calder, A. Richards, R. Durden, London Cast/N. Rhoden)

Ⓓ **SMK66573**
Encores
Bach: Solo Cello Suites (exc); Pastorale, BWV590; Concertos, BWV592-7 (exc); *Handel:* Serse (exc); *Saint-Saëns:* Carnaval des animaux (exc); *Popper:* Vito, Op. 54/5 (exc); *Campagnoli:* Romanza; *Schumann:* Kinderszenen (exc); *Boccherini:* Cello Sonata, G4 (exc); *Traditional:* Cant del Ocells; *Haydn:* Keyboard Sonata 9 (exc); *Falla:* Canciones populares españolas. (P. Casals, C. A. Barker, E. Istomin, Prades Fest Orch, orch)

Ⓓ **SMK66927**
Beethoven—Symphonies Nos 1 and 2;Overture-Leonore
Beethoven: Symphony 1; Symphony 2; Leonore (exc). (ECO/M. Tilson Thomas, BRSO/Colin Davis)

Ⓓ **SMK66938**
R.Strauss—Orchestral Works
R. Strauss: Don Quixote; Don Juan; Liebe der Danae (exc). (Y-Y. Ma, B. Fine, Boston SO/S. Ozawa, Cleveland Orch/L. Maazel, Toronto SO/A. Davis)

Ⓓ **SMK66940**
Baroque Music
M-A. Charpentier: Te Deum, H146 (exc); *Pachelbel:* Canon and Gigue; *Bach:* ORgel-Büchlein, BWV599-644 (exc); *Handel:* Solomon (exc); *Bach:* Cantata 156 (exc); *Gluck:* Orfeo ed Euridice (exc); *Handel:* Keyboard Suites, Set II (exc); *Bach:* Suites, BWV1066-9 (exc); *A. Marcello:* Oboe Concerto in D minor (exc); *Handel:* Berenice (exc); *Bach:* Cantata 78 (exc); *Vivaldi:* Concerti Grossi, Op. 3 (exc); *Purcell:* Abdelazer, Z570 (exc); Old Bachelor, Z607 (exc). (ECO/R. Leppard)

Ⓓ **SM2K35902** (10/95)
Bellini—Norma
Bellini: Norma (Cpte). (R. Scotto, T. Troyanos, G. Giacomini, P. Plishka, P. Crook, A. Murray, Ambrosian Op Chor, National PO/James Levine)

Ⓓ **SM2K46299**
Stravinsky—The Rake's Progress
Stravinsky: Rake's Progress (Cpte). (A. Young, J. Raskin, J. Reardon, R. Sarfaty, K. Miller, J. Manning, D. Garrard, P. Tracey, Sadler's Wells Op Chor, RPO/I. Stravinsky)

Ⓓ **SM2K48456** (12/93)
Schoenberg—Moses und Aaron. Chamber Symphony No 2
Schoenberg: Moses und Aron (Cpte); Chamber Symphony 2. (G. Reich, R. Cassilly, R. Angas, F. Palmer, G. Knight, J. Winfield, R. Hermann, J. Noble, J. Manning, G. Knight, H. Watts, P. Langridge, M. Rippon, D. Wicks, BBC Sngrs, Orpheus Boys' Ch, Paris InterContemporain Ens, BBC SO/P. Boulez)

Ⓓ **SM2K64456**
Wagner—Orchestral Music
Wagner: Siegfried Idyll; Meistersinger (exc); Fliegende Holländer (exc); Lohengrin (exc); Parsifal (exc); Tannhäuser (exc). (Occidental Coll Concert Ch, Columbia SO/B. Walter)

Ⓓ **SM2K66616** (2/95)
Offenbach—Orpheus in the Underworld
Offenbach: Orphée aux enfers (Cpte). (D. Fieldsend, M. Hegarty, B. Patterson, R. Suart, F. McCafferty, J. Pert, Gareth Jones, S. Wyn Gibson, R. Arthars, J. Pullen, C. Donohue, D. Cavendish, P. Baxter, R. Woodall, D'Oyly Carte Op Chor, D'Oyly Carte Op Orch/J.O. Edwards)

Ⓓ **SM22K46290(3)** (7/91)
Stravinsky—The Complete Edition (pt 3)
Stravinsky: Japanese Lyrics; Jeu de cartes; Little Songs; Mass; Mavra (Cpte); Monumentum pro Gesualdo; Movements; Noces (Cpte); Norwegian Moods; Octet; Ode (1943); Oedipus Rex (Cpte); Orpheus (Cpte); Owl and pussycat; Pastorale; Pater noster; Perséphone (Cpte); Petrushka (Cpte); Petrushka (exc); Piano-Rag Music. (E. Lear, Columbia SO/R. Craft, Cleveland Orch/I. Stravinsky, C. Berberian, A. Baxter, A. Albert, Gregg Smith Sngrs, Columbia Sym Wnd & Brass, S. Belinck, M. Simmons, P. Rideout, S. Kolk, CBC SO, C. Rosen, M. Allen, R. Sarfaty,

L. Driscoll, R. Oliver, S. Barber, A. Copland, L. Foss, R. Sessions, American Concert Ch, Columbia Perc Ens, J. Westbrook, G. Shirley, S. Verrett, D. Gramm, Chester Watson, J. Reardon, L. Driscoll, Washington Op Soc Chor, Washington Op Soc Orch, Chicago SO, R. Craft, Toronto Fest Sngrs, V. Zorina, M. Molese, Ithaca Coll Concert Ch, Texas Boys' Ch, I. Stravinsky, Columbia Chbr Ens)

① **SM22K46290(4)** (7/91)
Stravinsky—The Complete Edition (pt 4)
Stravinsky: Bal'mont Poems; Verlaine Poems; Praeludium; Pribaoutki; Pulcinella (Cpte); Pulcinella Suite; Rag-Time; Rake's Progress (Cpte); Renard; Requiem Canticles; Rite of Spring (Cpte); Nightingale (Cpte); Russian Peasant Songs; Scènes de ballet; Scherzo à la russe; Scherzo fantastique; Septet; Serenade in A; Sermon, Narrative and Prayer. (E. Lear, Columbia SO/I. Stravinsky, D. Gramm, Columbia Jazz Ens, C. Berberian, I. Jordan, G. Shirley, Columbia Chbr Ens, A. Young, J. Raskin, J. Reardon, R. Sarfaty, K. Miller, J. Manning, D. Garrard, P. Tracey, Sadler's Wells Op Chor, RPO, L. Driscoll, W. Murphy, T. Koves, L. Anderson, E. Bonazzi, C. Bressler, Ithaca Coll Concert Ch/R. Craft, R. Grist, L. Driscoll, M. Picassi, K. Smith, D. Gramm, H. Beattie, E. Bonazzi, Washington Op Soc Chor, Washington Op Soc Orch, Gregg Smith Sngrs, G. Smith, CBC SO/I. Stravinsky, S. Verrett, J. Horton)

① **SM3K46291** (8/92)
Stravinsky—Ballets, Vol.1
Stravinsky: Firebird (Cpte); Scherzo à la russe; Scherzo fantastique; Fireworks; Rite of Spring (Cpte); Petrushka (Cpte); Noces; Renard; Histoire du soldat Suite. (M. Allen, R. Sarfaty, L. Driscoll, G. Shirley, W. Murphy, D. Gramm, R. Oliver, T. Koves, S. Barber, A. Copland, L. Foss, R. Sessions, Columbia Perc Ens, Columbia Chbr Ens, Columbia SO, CBC SO/I. Stravinsky)

① **SM3K47154** (5/92)
Bernstein—Theatre Works Volume 1
Bernstein: On the Town (Cpte); On the Town; Candide Overture; West Side Story Symphonic Dances; On the Waterfront Suite; Fancy Free (Cpte); Trouble in Tahiti (Cpte); Facsimile. (B. Comden, A. Green, N. Walker, J. Reardon, C. Alexander, G. Gaynes, R. Striboneen, chor, orch, NYPO, J. Patrick, A. Butler, M. Clark, M. Brown, Columbia Wind Ens/L. Bernstein)

① **SM3K47211**
Mozart Legendary Interpretations—Opera and Concert Arias
Mozart: Requiem; Rè pastore (exc); Nozze di Figaro (exc); Zauberflöte (exc); Entführung (exc); Exsultate, jubilate, K165 (exc); Schauspieldirektor (exc); Entführung (exc); Nozze di Figaro (exc); Zauberflöte (exc); Don Giovanni (exc); Così fan tutte (exc); Don Giovanni (exc); Entführung (exc); Zauberflöte (exc); Mentre ti lascio, K513; Nozze di Figaro (exc); Nozze di Figaro (exc); Mentre ti lascio, K513; Per questa bella mano, K612; Rivolgete a lui lo sguardo, K584. (I. Seefried, J. Tourel, L. Simoneau, W. Warfield, Westminster Ch, NYPO/B. Walter, L. Pons, orch, E. Steber, Columbia SO, E. Pinza, NY Met Op Orch, G. London)

① **SM3K47265** (4/92)
Debussy—Pelléas et Mélisande
Debussy: Pelléas et Mélisande (Cpte). (G. Shirley, E. Söderström, D. McIntyre, D. Ward, Y. Minton, A. Britten, D. Wicks, ROH Chor, ROHO/P. Boulez)

① **SM3K64103** (3/95)
Berlioz—Orchestral and Vocal Works
Berlioz: Lélio; Béatrice et Bénédict (exc); Troyens (exc); Nuits d'été; Mort de Cléopâtre; Symphonie fantastique; Benvenuto Cellini (exc); Carnaval romain. (J-L. Barrault, Y. Minton, J. Mitchinson, S. Burrows, J. Shirley-Quirk, LSC, BBC SO, LSO, NYPO/P. Boulez)

① **SM3K64263** (11/94)
Mozart—Don Giovanni
Mozart: Don Giovanni (Cpte). (C. Siepi, E. Grümmer, L. della Casa, R. Streich, L. Simoneau, F. Corena, W. Berry, G. Frick, Vienna St. Op. Chor, VPO/D. Mitropoulos)

① **SM3K64539**
Bellini—Beatrice di Tenda
Bellini: Beatrice di Tenda (Cpte). (M. Nicolesco, V. La Scola, P. Cappuccilli, S. Toczyska, I. Zennaro, Prague Phil Chor, Monte Carlo Nat Op Orch/A. Zedda)

◙ **SM33452**
Classical Barbra
Debussy: Beau soir; *Canteloube:* Chants d'Auvergne (exc); *Wolf:* Eichendorff Lieder (exc); *Fauré:* Pavane; Songs, Op.7 (exc); *Orff:* Carmina Burana (exc); *Handel:* Rinaldo (exc); *Ochs:* Dank sei Dir, Herr; *Schumann:* Liederkreis, Op. 39 (exc); *Ogermann:* I loved you. (B. Streisand, Columbia SO/C. Ogerman, C. Ogerman)

◙ **SM42137**
Carnaval—Wynton Marsalis
Arban: Carnaval de Venise; Fantasie brillante; *H. Clarke:* Débutante; Sounds from the Hudson; *Traditional:* Believe me, if all those endearing young charms; *J. Levy:* Grand Russian Fantasia; *Paganini:* Moto perpetuo, Op. 11; *T. Moore:* Irish Melodies (exc); *Rimsky-Korsakov:* Tale of Tsar Saltan (exc); *Bellstedt:* Napoli (exc); *Traditional:* Sometimes I feel like a motherless child. (W. Marsalis, Eastman Wind Ens/D. Hunsberger)

◙ **SM48155**
Carreras and Caballe sing Souvenirs
Donizetti: Amor marinaro; *Rodgers:* South Pacific (exc); *Rossini:* Turco in Italia (exc); *Bellini:* Ricordanza; *Giordano:* Andrea Chénier (exc); *Verdi:* Aroldo (exc); *Schubert:* Ave Maria, D839; *Wagner:* Tristan und Isolde (exc); Tannhäuser (exc); *Puccini:* Turandot (exc); Tosca (exc); *Donizetti:* Gemma di Vergy (exc); Poliuto (exc); *Ribas:* Per tu amor; *Brahms:* Lieder, Op. 49 (exc). (M. Caballé, J. Carreras, LSO/J. Tunick, National PO/R. Chailly, Hungarian St Op Orch/G. Patanè, NY Op Orch/E. Queler, Vienna St Op Orch, NYPO/Z. Mehta/M. Tilson Thomas, Martin Katz/L. Maazel, Barcelona Liceo SO/J. Casas, Vienna SO/O. Caetani)

① **SX10K66246**
The Bruno Walter Edition, Volume I
Mahler: Symphony 1; Symphony 2; Lieder eines fahrenden Gesellen; Symphony 4; Lieder eines fahrenden Gesellen; Symphony 6; Symphony 9; Lied von der Erde; *Wagner:* Siegfried Idyll; Meistersinger (exc); Fliegende Holländer (exc); Lohengrin (exc); Parsifal (exc); Tannhäuser (exc); *Beethoven:* Violin Concerto; *Mendelssohn:* Violin Concerto, Op. 64. (D. Halban, E. Cundari, M. Miller, N. Merriman, M. Forrester, E. Haefliger, J. Szigeti, N. Milstein, B. Walter, Westminster Ch, Occidental Coll Concert Ch, Columbia SO, NYPO/B. Walter)

① **SX2K48040** (8/92)
Gluck—Orfeo ed Euridice
Gluck: Orfeo ed Euridice (Cpte). (M. Chance, N. Argenta, S. Beckerbauer, Stuttgart Chbr Ch, Tafelmusik/F. Bernius)

① **SX3K53385**
New Year's Concerts 1989 and 1992
J. Strauss II: Accelerationen, Op. 234; Bauern-Polka, Op. 276; Bei uns z'Haus, Op. 361; Fledermaus (exc); Künstlerleben, Op. 316; Eljen a Magyar!, Op. 332; Im Krapfenwald'l, Op. 336; Frühlingsstimmen, Op. 410; Ritter Pasman; Blauen Donau, Op. 314; Pizzicato Polka; *Jos Strauss:* Libelle; Moulinet; Plappermäulchen; Jokey; *J. Strauss I:* Radetzky March; *Nicolai:* Lustigen Weiber von Windsor (exc); *J. Strauss I:* Radetzky March; *J. Strauss II:* Stadt und Land; Vergnügungszug; Zigeunerbaron (exc); Tausend und eine Nacht; Neue Pizzicato-Polka, Op. 449; Persischer Marsch; Tritsch-Tratsch; Unter Donner und Blitz; Blauen Donau, Op. 314; *Jos Strauss:* Sphärenklänge; Dorfschwalben aus Österreich. (VPO/C. Kleiber)

① **S2K37859** (9/89)
Rossini— Il Turco in Italia
Rossini: Turco in Italia (Cpte). (S. Ramey, M. Caballé, E. Dara, E. Palacio, J. Berbié, P. Barbacini, L. Nucci, Ambrosian Op Chor, National PO/R. Chailly)

① **S2K39311** (8/88)
Rossini—La Donna del Lago
Rossini: Donna del Lago (Cpte). (K. Ricciarelli, L.V. Terrani, D. Gonzalez, D. Raffanti, S. Ramey, C. Valdenassi, O. di Credico, A. d'Uva, Prague Philharmonic Ch, COE/M. Pollini)

① **S2K44983** (4/91)
Boito: Mefistofele
Boito: Mefistofele (Cpte). (S. Ramey, P. Domingo, E. Marton, T. Takács, S. Tedesco, E. Farkas, A. Pataki, Hungaroton Op Chor, Nyiregyházi Boys' Ch, Hungarian St Orch/G. Patanè)

① **S2K45539** (3/91)
Tchaikovsky: Eugene Onegin
Tchaikovsky: Eugene Onegin (Cpte). (Y. Mazurok, A. Tomowa-Sintow, N. Gedda, R. Troeva-Mircheva, N. Ghiuselev, S. Popangelova, M. Lilowa, M. Lecocq, S. Georgiev, D. Stanchev, Sofia National Op Chor, Sofia Fest Orch/E. Tchakarov)

① **S2K45847** (10/90)
Puccini: Tosca
Puccini: Tosca (Cpte). (E. Marton, J. Carreras, J. Pons, I. Gáti, F. Gerdesits, I. Tajo, J. Német, J. Gregor, B. Héja, Hungarian Rad & TV Chor, Hungarian St Orch/M. Tilson Thomas)

① **S2K46433** (6/91)
Rossini: La cenerentola
Rossini: Cenerentola (Cpte). (L.V. Terrani, F. Araiza, D. Trimarchi, E. Dara, E. Ravaglia, M. Schmiege, A. Corbelli, W German Rad Chor, Cappella Coloniensis/G. Ferro)

① **S2K47189** (6/92)
Puccini—La Fanciulla del West
Puccini: Fanciulla del West (Cpte). (M. Zampieri, P. Domingo, J. Pons, S. Bertocchi, L. Roni, M. Chingari, A. Bramante, N. Verri, A. Salvadori, E. Gavazzi, G. Savoiardo, O. Mori, F. Memeo, A. Bottion, E. Panariello, P. Spagnoli, C. Giombi, U. Scalavino, La Scala Chor, La Scala Orch/L. Maazel)

① **S2K47290** (10/91)
Cherubini—Lodoïska
Cherubini: Lodoïska (Cpte). (M. Devia, F. Pedaci, B. Lombardo, T. Moser, A. Corbelli, W. Shimell, M. Luperi, D. Serraiocco, P. Spina, E. Panariello, E. Capuano, R. Cazzaniga, A. Bramante, La Scala Chor, La Scala Orch/R. Muti)

① **S2K48053** (5/92)
Mozart—Die Entführung aus dem Serail
Mozart: Entführung (Cpte). (C. Studer, E. Szmytka, K. Streit, R. Gambill, G. Missenhardt, M. Heltau, Vienna St Op Chor, Vienna SO/B. Weil)

① **S2K48070** (6/94)
Verdi—Il Trovatore
Verdi: Trovatore (Cpte). (P. Domingo, A. Millo, V. Chernov, D. Zajick, J. Morris, S. Kelly, A. Laciura, G. Bater, T. Willson, NY Met Op Chor, NY Met Op Orch/James Levine)

① **S2K48073** (9/92)
Verdi—Luisa Miller
Verdi: Luisa Miller (Cpte). (A. Millo, P. Domingo, V. Chernov, J-H. Rootering, F. Quivar, P. Plishka, W. White, J. Bills, NY Met Op Chor, NY Met Op Orch/James Levine)

① **S2K48474** (7/93)
Puccini—Manon Lescaut
Puccini: Manon Lescaut (Cpte). (N. Rautio, P. Dvorský, G. Quilico, L. Roni, M. Berti, C. N. Bandera, A. Bramante, M. Bolognesi, S. Sammaritano, E. Cossutta, E. Panariello, La Scala Chor, La Scala Orch/L. Maazel)

① **S2K52486** (10/93)
Verdi—La Traviata
Verdi: Traviata (Cpte). (T. Fabbricini, R. Alagna, P. Coni, N. Curiel, A. Trevisan, E. Cossutta, O. Mori, E. Capuano, F. Musinu, E. Gavazzi, E. Panariello, S. Sammaritano, La Scala Chor, La Scala Orch/R. Muti)

① **S2K52492** (10/93)
Gluck—Iphigénie en Tauride
Gluck: Iphigénie en Tauride (Cpte). (C. Vaness, G. Winbergh, T. Allen, A. Zoroberto, M. Remor, S. Brunet, G. Surian, A. Veccia, E. Turco, S. Krasteva, La Scala Chor, La Scala Orch/R. Muti)

① **S2K53336** (12/93)
Rossini—Il Viaggio a Reims
Rossini: Viaggio a Reims (Cpte). (S. McNair, C. Studer, L. Serra, L.V. Terrani, R. Giménez, W. Matteuzzi, S. Ramey, R. Raimondi, E. Dara, G. Surian, L. Gallo, Berlin Rad Chor, BPO/C. Abbado)

① **S2K58961** (11/94)
Verdi—Falstaff
Verdi: Falstaff (Cpte). (J. Pons, R. Frontali, D. Dessì, M. O'Flynn, R. Vargas, B. Manca di Nissa, D. Ziegler, E. Gavazzi, P. Barbacini, L. Roni, La Scala Chor, La Scala Orch/R. Muti)

① **S2K64573**
J. Strauss II—Die Fledermaus
J. Strauss II: Fledermaus (Cpte). (R. Arthars, A. Grummet, D. Fieldsend, K. Mahsoori, G. Sandison, D. Hawksley, L. Black, H. Ludlow, W. Schoemann, P. Barnhill, D'Oyly Carte Op Chor, D'Oyly Carte Op Orch/J. O. Edwards)

① **S2K66314**
Verdi—Rigoletto
Verdi: Rigoletto (Cpte). (R. Bruson, A. Rost, R. Alagna, D. Kavrakos, M. Pentcheva, G. Giuseppini, A. Trevisan, E. Gavazzi, S. Sammaritano, N. Zanini, A. de Gobbi, M. Laurenza, E. Panariello, La Scala Chor, La Scala Orch/R. Muti)

① **S2K66563** (4/95)
Vives—Dona Francisquita
Vives: Doña Francisquita (Cpte). (A. Arteta, P. Domingo, L. Mirabal, E. del Portal, M. Perelstein, C. Alvarez, C. Chausson, Cordoba Grand Th Chor, Seville SO/M. Roa)

Ⓓ **S2K66836** (7/95)
Goldschmidt—Beatrice Cenci, etc
B. Goldschmidt: Beatrice Cenci (Cpte); Clouds; Rosenzweig; Nebelweben; Time. (S. Estes, D. Jones, R. Alexander, F. Kimm, P. Rose, E. Wottrich, S. Lorenz, R. Beyer, S. Stoll, J. D. de Haan, I. Bostridge, Berlin Rad Chor, Berlin Deutsches SO/L. Zagrosek, I. Vermillion, B. Goldschmidt)

Ⓓ **S2K66850**
Schreker—Irrelohe
Schreker: Irrelohe (Cpte). (M. Pabst, L. DeVol, G. Simic, E. Randová, M. Pederson, H. Zednik, N. Belamaric, S. Holecek, H. Wildhaber, Vienna Singverein, Vienna SO/P. Gülke)

Ⓓ **S3K37862** (9/88)
Rossini—Il Barbiere di Siviglia
Rossini: Barbiere di Siviglia (Cpte). (L. Nucci, M. Horne, P. Barbacini, E. Dara, S. Ramey, R. Pierotti, S. Alaimo, La Scala Chor, La Scala Orch/R. Chailly)

Ⓓ **S3K39073** (8/88)
Rossini—Tancredi
Rossini: Tancredi (Cpte). (M. Horne, L. Cuberli, E. Palacio, N. Zaccaria, B. Manca di Nissa, P. Schuman, Venice La Fenice Chor, Venice La Fenice Orch/R. Weikert)

Ⓓ **S3K44878** (6/90) ▭ **S3T44878** (6/90)
Borodin—Prince Igor
Borodin: Prince Igor (Cpte). (B. Martinovich, S. Evstatieva, K. Kaludov, N. Ghiuselev, N. Ghiaurov, A. Milcheva, M. Popov, S. Georgiev, Anton Petkov, Sofia National Op Chor, Sofia Fest Orch/E. Tchakarov)

Ⓓ **S3K45720** (12/90)
Tchaikovsky—The Queen of Spades
Tchaikovsky: Queen of Spades (Cpte). (W. Ochman, S. Evstatieva, P. Dilova, I. Konsulov, Y. Mazurok, Angel Petkov, P. Petrov, M. Popov, S. Georgiev, S. Toczyska, W. Katsarova, R. Bareva, E. Stoyanova, Gouslarche Boys' Ch, Svetoslav Obretenov Nat Chor, Sofia Fest Orch/E. Tchakarov)

Ⓓ **S3K45763** (4/92)
Mussorgsky—Boris Godunov (original version)
Mussorgsky: Boris Godunov (Cpte). (N. Ghiaurov, M. Svetlev, S. Mineva, N. Ghiuselev, D. Petkov, J. Franck, Angel Petkov, B. Martinovich, R. Troeva-Mircheva, L. Hadjieva, S. Popangelova, P. Dilova, M. Popov, Bodra Smyana Children's Ch, Sofia National Op Chor, Sofia Fest Orch/E. Tchakarov)

Ⓓ **S3K45831** (10/90)
Mussorgsky: Khovanshchina
Mussorgsky: Khovanshchina (Cpte). (N. Ghiaurov, Z. Gadjev, K. Kaludov, S. Popov, N. Ghiuselev, A. Milcheva, M.P. Popova, Angel Petkov, M. Dimchewska, D. Stanchev, S. Georgiev, R. Doikov, A. Selimski, Sofia National Op Chor, Sofia National Op Orch/E. Tchakarov)

Ⓓ **S3K45850** (10/90)
Rossini: La gazza ladra
Rossini: Gazza ladra (Cpte). (K. Ricciarelli, W. Matteuzzi, S. Ramey, B. Manca di Nissa, L. d'Intino, F. Furlanetto, R. Coviello, O. di Credico, P. Lefebre, F. Musinu, M. Lippi, Prague Phil Chor, Turin RSO/G. Gelmetti)

Ⓓ **S3K45973** (5/91)
Verdi—Aida
Verdi: Aida (Cpte). (A. Millo, D. Zajick, P. Domingo, J. Morris, S. Ramey, T. Cook, C. Anthony, H-K. Hong, NY Met Op Chor, NY Met Op Orch/James Levine)

Ⓓ **S3K46429** (6/91)
Charpentier—Louise
G. Charpentier: Louise (Cpte). (I. Cotrubas, P. Domingo, G. Bacquier, J. Berbié, M. Sénéchal, L. Guitton, E. Manchet, L. Reid, J. Jarvis, S. Minty, A. Butler, M. Midgley, L. Richardson, P. Clark, G. Jennings, P. Bartlett, M. Cable, M. Dickinson, D. Murray, J. Noble, L. Fyson, P. Bamber, W. Mason, V. Midgley, J. Lewington, P. Halstead, O. Broome, P. Bedford, N. Jenkins, E. Fleet, M. Brown, C. Parker, J. Brown, M. Clark, U. Connors, A. MacGregor, I. Thompson, Ambrosian Op Chor, New Philh/G. Prêtre)

Ⓓ **S3K46487** (9/91)
Glinka—A Life for the Tsar
Glinka: Life for the Tsar (Cpte). (B. Martinovich, A. Pendachanska, C. Merritt, S. Toczyska, S. Georgiev, M. Popov, K. Videv, Sofia National Op Chor, Sofia Fest Orch/E. Tchakarov)

Ⓓ **S3K52500** (4/93)
Verdi—Don Carlo
Verdi: Don Carlo (Cpte). (M. Sylvester, A. Millo, D. Zajick, V. Chernov, F. Furlanetto, S. Ramey, P. Plishka, J. Bunnell, D. Croft, J. H. Murray, K. Battle, NY Met Op Chor, NY Met Op Orch/James Levine)

Ⓓ **S3K53286** (6/94)
Mozart—Le Nozze di Figaro
Mozart: Nozze di Figaro (Cpte). (M. Pertusi, M. McLaughlin, L. Gallo, K. Mattila, M. Bacelli, N. Curiel, A. Nosotti, U. Benelli, G. Sica, G. Tadeo, MMF Chor, MMF Orch/Z. Mehta)

Ⓓ **S3K58968** (3/95)
Rossini—Armida
Rossini: Armida (Cpte). (R. Fleming, D. Kaasch, G. Kunde, I. d'Arcangelo, J. Francis, C. Bosi, I. Zennaro, B. Fowler, S. Zadvorny, Bologna Teatro Comunale Chor, Bologna Teatro Comunale Orch/D. Gatti)

Ⓓ **S3K58977** (5/94)
Mussorgsky—Boris Godunov
Mussorgsky: Boris Godunov (Cpte). (A. Kocherga, S. Larin, M. Lipovšek, S. Ramey, G. Nikolsky, P. Langridge, H. Wildhaber, S. Leiferkus, L. Nichiteanu, V. Valente, Y. Gorokhovskaya, E. Zaremba, A. Fedin, A. Shagidullin, M. Krutikov, W. Drabowicz, Slovak Phil Chor, Berlin Rad Chor, Tolz Boys' Ch, BPO/C. Abbado)

Ⓓ **S3K66357**
Spontini—La Vestale
Spontini: Vestale (Cpte). (K. Huffstodt, A. M. Moore, J. P. Raftery, D. Graves, D. Kavrakos, A. Bramante, S. Sammaritano, La Scala Chor, La Scala Orch/R. Muti)

Ⓓ **S4K45989** (1/91)
Nielsen: Symphonies, Concertos, etc
Nielsen: Symphony 1; Symphony 2; Symphony 3; Symphony 4; Symphony 5; Symphony 6; Maskarade (exc); Flute Concerto; Clarinet Concerto; Helios; Pan and Syrinx; Rhapsody Overture. (J. Baker, S. Drucker, NYPO/L. Bernstein, R. Guldbaek, N. Møller, Royal Danish Orch, Philadelphia/E. Ormandy)

Ⓓ **474364-2**
Suzanne Murphy: There is an Isle
Traditional: There is an Isle; Galway Bay; *Anon:* Stuttering Lovers; *E. F. Lambert:* She is far from the land; *Traditional:* Danny Boy; *Anon:* Spanish Lady; *Traditional:* She moved through the fair; *Crouch:* Kathleen Mavourneen; *Balfe:* Bohemian Girl (exc); *Traditional:* Last rose of summer; Silent O Moyle; Ard ti Cuain; *M. Herbert:* Lake Isle of Innisfree; *Wallace:* Maritana (exc); *Traditional:* Castle of Dromore; I will walk with my love; I have a bonnet trimmed with blue; *Dunhill:* Cloths of Heaven; *D. Allen:* Limerick You're a Lady. (S. Murphy, WNO Orch/Julian Smith)

Stradivarius

Ⓓ **STR10022**
La nuova musica, Vol.5
Ravel: Valses nobles et sentimentales; *Hindemith:* Concerto for Orchestra; *Castiglioni:* sequenze; *Schoenberg:* Moses und Aron (exc). (Rome RAI Orch, Hamburg RO, Hamburg Rad Ch/H. Rosbaud)

Ⓓ **STR10061**
Maderna—Satyricon; Ages
Maderna: Satyricon (Cpte); Ages. (W. Neill, D. Brown, P. Sperry, M. Kraak, P. Holden, T. Haenen, A. Haenen, E. Lioni, Hilversum RO, Milan RAI Chor, Milan RAI SO/B. Maderna)

Suite

Ⓓ **CDS1-5001**
Maria Callas - La divina
Bellini: Puritani (exc); *Wagner:* Tristan und Isolde (exc); *Verdi:* Nabucco (exc); *Ponchielli:* Gioconda (exc); *Verdi:* Trovatore (exc); *Mozart:* Entführung (exc); *Rossini:* Armida (exc); *Meyerbeer:* Dinorah (exc). (M. Callas, Turin RAI Orch, Milan RAI SO, La Scala Orch/A. Basile/O. de Fabritiis/A. Votto/A. Simonetto)

Supraphon

Ⓓ **CO-1746/8** (10/88)
Fibich—Šárka
Fibich: Šárka (Cpte). (V. Zítek, V. Přibyl, J. Klán, E. Děpoltová, E. Randová, J. Janská, B. Effenberková, J. Pavlová, A. Barová, V. Bakalová, D. Suryová, Brno Janáček Op Chor, Brno St PO/J. Štych)

Ⓓ **C37-7303** (11/85)
Janáček: Operatic Orchestral Suites
Janáček: Cunning Little Vixen (exc); Fate (exc); From the House of the Dead (exc). (Czech PO/F. Jílek)

Ⓓ **SU0013-2**
Dvořák—Rusalka
Dvořák: Rusalka (Cpte). (M. Šubrtová, E. Haken, M. Ovčačíková, I. Žídek, A. Míková, J. Wysoczanská, E. Hlobilová, V. Krilová, I. Mixová, V. Bednář, Prague Nat Th Chor, Prague Nat Th Orch/Z. Chalabala)

Ⓓ **SU0045-2**
Janáček—Osud
Janáček: Fate (Cpte). (V. Přibyl, M. Hajóssyová, J. Palivcová, V. Krejčík, J. Holešovský, J. Pokorná, J. Krátká, D. Suryová, Z. Kareninová, R. Novák, F. Caban, J. Olejníček, M. Steinerová, M. Polášková, J. Souček, A. Jurečka, J. Doubek, B. Kurfürst, A. Barová, J. Janská, J. Hladíková, J. Škrobánek, M. Jílková, Brno Janáček Op Chor, Brno Janáček Op Orch/F. Jílek)

Ⓓ **SU0077-2**
Smetana—Dalibor
Smetana: Dalibor (Cpte). (L.M. Vodička, I. Kusnjer, E. Urbanová, V. Kříž, J. Kalendocsky, M. Kopp, J. Marková, Bohuslav Maršík, Prague Nat Th Chor, Prague Nat Th Orch/Z. Košler)

Ⓓ **SU0200-2**
Smetana—Libuše
Smetana: Libuše (Cpte). (E. Urbanová, V. Kříž, L. Vele, J. Markvart, M. Podskalský, P. Červinka, H. Kaupová, M. Volková, Prague Nat Th Chor, Prague Nat Th Orch/O. Dohnányi)

Ⓓ **10 2751-2** (4/93)
Janáček—Jenufa
Janáček: Jenufa (Cpte). (G. Beňačková, V. Přibyl, N. Kniplová, V. Krejčík, J. Pokorná, A. Barová, K. Berman, V. Halíř, K. Belanová, D. Suryová, C. Strádalová, J. Janská, Brno Janáček Op Chor, Brno Janáček Op Orch/F. Jílek)

Ⓓ **10 2941-2** (9/94)
Janáček—From the House of the Dead
Janáček: From the House of the Dead (Cpte). (R. Novák, M. Jirglová, V. Přibyl, J. Stříška, K. Berman, J. Horáček, B. Blachut, I. Žídek, J. Jindrák, K. Průša, A. Míková, M. Karpíšek, J. Souček, V. Kočí, M. Švejda, Czech Phil Chor, Czech PO/V. Neumann)

Ⓓ **10 3471-2** (4/93)
Janáček—The Cunning Little Vixen
Janáček: Cunning Little Vixen (Cpte). (M. Hajóssyová, G. Beňačková, I. Mixová, L. Domanínská, B. Effenberková, K. Průša, H. Buldrová, M. Mrázová, R. Novák, M. Frydlewicz, K. Hanuš, D. Tikalová, J. Souček, Kühn Children's Chor, Czech Phil Chor, Czech PO/V. Neumann)

Ⓓ **10 3511-2** (10/91)
Smetana—The Bartered Bride
Smetana: Bartered Bride (Cpte). (G. Beňačková, P. Dvorský, M. Kopp, R. Novák, J. Jindrák, M. Mrázová, J. Horáček, M. Veselá, J. Jonášová, A. Hampel, K. Hanuš, Czech Phil Chor, Czech PO/Z. Košler)

Ⓓ **10 3611-2** (3/91)
Martinů—The Greek Passion
Martinů: Greek Passion (Cpte). (J. Mitchinson, H. Field, J. Tomlinson, P. Joll, G. Moses, A. Davies, R. Cullis, C. Savory, J. Lawton, J. Harris, D. Gwynne, J. Jonášová, M. Geliot, Kühn Children's Chor, Czech Phil Chor, Brno St PO/C. Mackerras)

Ⓓ **10 3641-2**
Dvořák—Rusalka
Dvořák: Rusalka (Cpte). (G. Beňačková, R. Novák, V. Soukupová, W. Ochman, D. Drobková, J. Jonášová, D. Šounová-Brouková, A. Barová, J. Marková, R. Tuček, Prague Phil Chor, Czech PO/V. Neumann)

Ⓓ **10 4395-2** (12/92)
Martinu—Ariane
Martinů: Ariane (Cpte). (C. Lindsley, N. Phillips, V. Doležal, R. Novák, M. Kopp, L. Vele, Czech PO/V. Neumann)

Ⓓ **10 8016-2** (11/93)
Janáček—Káta Kabanová
Janáček: Káťa Kabanová (Cpte). (D. Tikalová, B. Blachut, L. Komancová, Z. Kroupa, B. Vích, V. Kočí, I. Mixová, R. Jedlička, E. Hlobilová, M. Lemariová, Prague Nat Th Chor, Prague Nat Th Orch/J. Krombholc)

Ⓓ **10 8176-2** (6/93)
Martinů—Julietta
Martinů: Julietta (Cpte). (M. Tauberová, I. Žídek, A. Zlesák, Z. Otava, V. Bednář, I. Mixová, V. Jedenáctík, J. Procházková, L. Hanzalíková, J. Horáček, K. Kalaš, M. Čadikovičová, S. Jelínková, V. Soukupová, J. Jindrák, J. Veverka, Z. Švehla, M. Lemariová, K. Berman, D. Jedlička, J. Stříška, B. Lalák, Prague Nat Th Chor, Prague Nat Th Orch/J. Krombholc)

Ⓓ **10 8258-2** (1/94)
Hába—The Mother
Hába: Mother (Cpte). (V. Urbanová, O. Spisar, M. Lemariová, M. Sandtnerová, J. Polívková, L. Havlák, M. Borský, V. Jedenáctík, E. Zikmundová, P. Kočí, J. Janoušek, Prague Nat Th Chor, Prague Nat Th Orch/J. Jirouš)

Ⓓ **10 8351-2** (5/95)
Janáček—The Makropulos Case
Janáček: Makropulos Affair (Cpte). (L. Prylová, I. Žídek, R. Vonásek, H. Tattermuschová, P. Kočí, V. Kočí, K. Berman, J. Joran, J. Procházková, M. Karpíšek, M. Musilová, Prague Nat Th Chor, Prague Nat Th Orch/B. Gregor)

Ⓓ **11 0006-2** (3/92)
Mysliveček—Il Bellerofonte
Mysliveček: Bellerofonte (Cpte). (C. Lindsley, G. May, D. Ahlstedt, R. Giménez, K. Laki, S. Margita, Czech Phil Chor, Prague CO/Z. Peskó)

Ⓓ **11 0345-2**
Edith Gruberová - Operatic Recital
Verdi: Vespri siciliani (exc); Traviata (exc); Ernani (exc); *Bellini:* Puritani (exc); *Donizetti:* Lucia di Lammermoor (exc); Roberto Devereux (exc); Maria Stuarda (exc). (E. Gruberová, J. Marková, V. Walterová, L.M. Vodička, P. Horáček, Smetana Th Chor, Czech PO/F. Haider)

Ⓓ **11 0377-2**
Smetana Festival
Smetana: Má vlast (exc); Bartered Bride (exc); Triumph Symphony (exc); Libuše (exc). (Prague SO/J. Bělohlávek)

Ⓓ **11 0388-2** (10/91)
Berlioz—Overtures
Berlioz: Benvenuto Cellini (exc); Rob Roy; King Lear; Corsaire. (Brno St PO/P. Vronský)

Ⓓ **11 0572-2**
Popular Classics
R. Strauss: Till Eulenspiegel; *Liszt:* Préludes; *Berlioz:* Carnaval Romain; *Beethoven:* Leonore (exc); *Weber:* Invitation to the Dance, J260. (Czech PO/K. Ančerl)

Ⓓ **11 0624-2**
Bohemian & Czech orchestral music
Fučík: Florentiner, Op. 214; *Dvořák:* Humoresques, Op. 101 (exc); *Nedbal:* Valse triste; *Dvořák:* Rusalka (exc); *Fibich:* Moods, Op. 41, Part 1 (exc); *Smetana:* Bartered Bride (exc); Kiss (exc); *Martinů:* Bouquet (exc); *Janáček:* Lachian Dances (exc); *V. Novák:* Slovak Suite (exc); *Suk:* Towards a New Life. (Czech PO/V. Neumann)

⊟ **11 0640-4**
Famous Opera Overtures
Gluck: Iphigénie en Aulide (exc); *Mozart:* Zauberflöte (exc); *Glinka:* Ruslan and Lyudmila (exc); *Weber:* Freischütz (exc); *Rossini:* Guillaume Tell (exc); *Verdi:* Forza del destino (exc); *Wagner:* Lohengrin (exc); Lohengrin (exc). (Czech PO/K. Ančerl/Z. Chalabala/B. Liška)

Ⓓ **11 0724-2**
Famous Operetta Overtures
Suppé: Dichter und Bauer (exc); Leichte Kavallerie (exc); *Offenbach:* Orphée aux Enfers (exc); Belle Hélène (exc); *J. Strauss II:* Fledermaus (exc). (Czech PO/V. Neumann)

Ⓓ **11 1107-2**
Rimsky-Korsakov—Suites from the Operas
Rimsky-Korsakov: Invisible City of Kitezh (exc); Golden Cockerel Suite (exc); Symphony 2. (Prague SO/V. Smetáček, BRNO St PO/J. Bělohlávek)

Ⓓ **11 1115-2**
Smetana—Orchestral Works
Smetana: Bartered Bride (exc); Louisen-Polka, B12; Georginen-Polka, B13; Aus dem Studentenleben, B30/110; Venkovanka, T123; Bettina Polka, B114; Our lasses, T49. (Brno St PO/F. Jílek, Prague Nat Th Chor, Prague Nat Th Orch/Z. Chalabala, Czech PO/K. Sejna)

Ⓓ **11 1116-2**
Berlioz & d'Indy—Orchestral Works
Berlioz: Corsaire; Benvenuto Cellini (exc); *Indy:* Wallenstein, Op. 12 (exc); Istar, Op. 42. (Prague SO/Z. Fekete)

Ⓓ **11 1118-2**
Beethoven—Overtures
Beethoven: Egmont (exc); König Stefan (exc); Ruinen von Athen (exc); Leonore (exc); Coriolan; Ah! perfido, Op. 65. (E. Děpoltová, Czech PO/F. Vajnar)

Ⓓ **11 1166-2**
Mozart—Overtures
Mozart: Schuldigkeit des ersten Gebots, K35 (exc); Apollo et Hyacinthus (exc); Bastien und Bastienne (exc); Finta semplice (exc); Mitridate (exc); Ascanio in Alba (exc); Sogno di Scipione (exc); Lucio Silla (exc); Finta giardiniera (exc); Rè pastore (exc); Idomeneo (exc); Entführung (exc); Schauspieldirektor (exc); Nozze di Figaro (exc); Don Giovanni (exc); Così fan tutte (exc); Zauberflöte (exc); Clemenza di Tito (exc); Idomeneo (exc). (Prague CO/O. Vlček/B. Novotný)

Ⓓ **11 1259-2** (3/93)
Dvořák—Dimitrij
Dvořák: Dimitrij (Cpte). (L.M. Vodička, D. Drobková, M. Hajóssyová, L. Aghova, P. Mikuláš, I. Kusnjer, L. Vele, Czech Phil Chor, Prague Rad Chor, Czech PO/G. Albrecht)

Ⓓ **11 1269-2**
Debussy/Sibelius—Pelleas and Melisande
Debussy: Pelléas et Mélisande (exc); *Sibelius:* Pelleas and Melisande. (Czech PO/S. Baudo)

Ⓓ **11 1276-2** (4/94)
Smetana—Libuše
Smetana: Libuše (Cpte). (G. Beňačková, V. Zítek, A. Švorc, L.M. Vodička, K. Průša, R. Tuček, E. Děpoltová, V. Soukupová, Prague Nat Th Chor, Prague Nat Th Orch/Z. Košler)

Ⓓ **11 1287-2**
Gala Concert from Prague
Smetana: Bartered bride (exc); March, B58; Our lasses, T49; *Fibich:* At twilight (exc); *Dvořák:* Polonaise, B100; Kate and the Devil (exc); Festival March; *Blodek:* In the well (exc); *Janáček:* Lachian Dances (exc); *Nedbal:* Valse triste; Polenblut (exc); *Suk:* Filled with longing; *Kovařovic:* Miners' Polka; *Martinů:* Bouquet (exc). (Czech PO/V. Neumann)

Ⓓ **11 1337-2** (5/94)
Emmy Destinn (1878-1930)
Mozart: Nozze di Figaro (exc); Zauberflöte (exc); *Weber:* Freischütz (exc); *Wagner:* Fliegende Holländer (exc); Tannhäuser (exc); Lohengrin (exc); *Gounod:* Faust (exc); *Bizet:* Carmen (exc); *A. Thomas:* Mignon (exc); *Smetana:* Bartered Bride (exc); Dalibor (exc); *Tchaikovsky:* Queen of Spades (exc); *Verdi:* Trovatore (exc); Aida (exc); *Ponchielli:* Gioconda (exc); *Leoncavallo:* Pagliacci (exc); *Mascagni:* Cavalleria Rusticana (exc); *Puccini:* Tosca (exc); Madama Butterfly (exc); *R. Strauss:* Salome (exc). (E. Destinn, orch/B. Seidler-Winkler/W.B. Rogers/F. Kark/A. Pilz)

Ⓓ **11 1491-2** (4/93)
Jarmila Novotna sings Czech Songs and Arias
Kovařovic: Dogs' Heads (exc); *Smetana:* Kiss (exc); *Dvořák:* Rusalka (exc); Humoresques, Op.101 (exc); *Fibich:* At twilight (exc); *Masaryk:* Songs of Lidice; *Traditional:* I saw my country die; I saw my country die; Song of the Slavs; *Stelibský:* In the skies over Prague; *Traditional:* May the Lord love us; *Smetana:* Choruses, T119 (exc); *Dvořák:* Gipsy Melodies (exc); *Smetana:* Bartered Bride (exc); Kiss (exc); *Dvořák:* Rusalka (exc). (J. Novotná, orch, A. Sándor/A. von Zemlinsky, J. Masaryk, chor/W. Pelletier, J. Stelibský/R. Blum, chbr ens, RCA Victor Orch/F. Weissmann/A. Wallenstein, G. King)

Ⓓ **11 1492-2** (12/94)
Fibich—The Bride of Messina
Fibich: Bride of Messina (Cpte). (L. Márová, V. Zítek, I. Žídek, G. Beňačková, K. Hanuš, J. Horáček, M. Švejda, N. Šormová, Prague Rad Chor, Prague Nat Th Chor, Prague Nat Th Orch/F. Jílek)

Ⓓ **11 1800-2** (9/94)
Dvořák—Kate and the Devil
Dvořák: Kate and the Devil (Cpte). (A. Barová, R. Novák, M. Ježil, D. Suryová, J. Horáček, J. Hladík, A. Šťáva, B. Šulcová, N. Romanová, P. Kamas, O. Polášek, Brno Janáček Op Chor, Brno Janáček Op Orch/J. Pinkas)

Ⓓ **11 1802-2** (1/94)
Martinů—The Miracle of Our Lady
Martinů: Miracles of Mary (Cpte). (A. Barová, J. Marková, V. Zítek, D. Jedlička, E. Děpoltová, A. Kratochvílová, M. Mrázová, J. Jindrák, Bohumil Maršík, V. Kocián, I. Kusnjer, J. Vavruška, B. Vítková, K. Průša, Prague Children's Ch, Prague Rad Chor, Prague SO/J. Bělohlávek)

Ⓓ **11 1804-2** (5/94)
Smetana—The Brandenburgers in Bohemia
Smetana: Brandenburgers in Bohemia (Cpte). (K. Kalaš, J. Joran, I. Žídek, Z. Otava, A. Votava, B. Vich, M. Šubrtová, M. Fidlerová, V. Soukupová, E. Haken, J. Jindrák, Prague Nat Th Chor, Prague Nat Th Orch/J.H. Tichý)

Ⓓ **11 1810-2**
Dvořák/Janáček—Orchestral music
Dvořák: Symphony 9; *Janáček:* Cunning Little Vixen Suite. (Prague SO/P. Altrichter)

Ⓓ **11 1823-2**
Fibich—Orchestral Works
Fibich: Comenius; Záboj, Slavoj and Luděk; Toman, Op.49; Fall of Arkona (exc). (Prague SO/V. Válek)

Ⓓ **11 1837-2**
Menuhin conducting Czech Music
Dvořák: Serenade, Op. 22; *Martinů:* Concertino 2 (1933); *Saint-Saëns:* Muse et le poète; *Smetana:* Bartered Bride (exc). (E. Michell, L. Gorokhov, S. Mulligan, Brno St PO/Y. Menuhin)

Ⓓ **11 1846-2**
Emmy Destinn Opera Gala
Verdi: Forza del destino (exc); Trovatore (exc); Ballo in maschera (exc); *Leoncavallo:* Pagliacci (exc); *Mascagni:* Cavalleria Rusticana (exc); *Wagner:* Lohengrin (exc); Tristan und Isolde (exc); *Dvořák:* Rusalka (exc). (E. Randová, Brno St PO/O. Lenárd)

Ⓓ **11 1851-2**
Famous Opera Arias
Verdi: Ballo in maschera (exc); Trovatore (exc); Forza del destino (exc); Aida (exc); Don Carlo (exc); *Puccini:* Tosca (exc); *Bellini:* Norma (exc); *Mozart:* Don Giovanni (exc). (E. Urbanová, J. Svobodová, Prague SO/J. Bělohlávek)

Ⓓ **11 1865-2**
Alois Hába—Centenary
Hába: String Quartet 11; String Quartet 12; String Quartet 15; String Quartet 16; Bassoon Quartet; Trombone Suite; Fantazie, Op. 40; Cello Suite, Op. 81a; Saxophone Suite, Op. 99; Suite, Op. 24; Suite, Op. 100; Piano Suite, Op. 88; Piano Sonata, Op. 62; Cimbalom Suite; Symfonická fantazie; New land (exc); Way of life. (Novák Qt, F. Herman, J. Seidl, M. Masier, L. Vaněk, Z. Pulec, R. Suk, B. Bydžovský, K. Kučera, Czech Nonet, J. Chovanec, S. Rascher, M. Etlík, V. Koula, J. Horák, E. Kovárnová, Film SO/Š. Koníček, K. Zlatníková)

Ⓓ **11 1878-2** (3/95)
The Unknown Janáček
Janáček: I'm waiting for you!; War Song 1; War Song 2; Fanfare in A; Fanfare in D minor; Festival Chorus; Along an overgrown path (exc); Jealousy; Jenufa (exc); Taras Bulba (exc); Excursions of Mr Brouček (exc); Living Corpse; March of the Blue Boys; I'm waiting for you!. (A. Bárta, Prague Phil Chor, J. Holeňa, L. Kozderka, K. Kohout, K. Kučera, M. Brázda, M. Gajdošová, L. Zavadilík, A. Formáček, D. Kellerová, J. Bělor, R. Firkušný, I. Ardašev, J. Pavlová, Y. Tannenbergerova, Brno St PO/L. Svárovský, M. Kopp, A. Barová, J. Janská, V. Doležal, M. Ungrová, J. Jiskrová, P. Šumpík, E. Podařilová, F. Kantor, M. Opršal)

Ⓓ **11 1905-2** (1/94)
Czech Orchestral Works
Janáček: Taras Bulba; Cunning Little Vixen (exc); *V. Novák:* Slovak Suite. (Czech PO/V. Talich)

Ⓓ **11 1935-2**
Mozart—Orchestral Works
Mozart: Zauberflöte (exc); Piano Concerto 23; Bassoon Concerto, K191; Horn Concerti (exc). (M. Štefek, K. Bidlo, H. Czerny-Stefańska, Czech PO/K. Ančerl)

Ⓓ **11 2118-2**
Czech Festive Music
Various: National Anthems (exc); *Janáček:* Sinfonietta (exc); *Smetana:* Libuše (exc); Má Vlast (exc); *Dvořák:* Slavonic Dances (exc); *Suk:* Towards a New Life. (Czech PO/L. Pešek/J. Bělohlávek/V. Neumann, Prague Nat Th Orch/Z. Košler, Prague SO/P. Altrichter, Brno St PO/F. Jílek)

Ⓓ **11 2122-2** (10/94)
Smetana—The Two Widows
Smetana: Two Widows (Cpte). (N. Šormová, M. Machotková, J. Zahradníček, J. Horáček, Z. Švehla, D. Šounová-Brouková, Prague Nat Th Chor, Prague Nat Th Orch/F. Jílek)

Ⓓ **11 2136-2(1)** (12/94)
Emmy Destinn—Complete Edition, Discs 1 & 2
Bizet: Carmen (exc); Carmen (exc); *A. Thomas:* Mignon (exc); *Grieg:* Songs, Op.60 (exc); *Leoncavallo:* Roland von Berlin (exc); *Traditional:* Už mou milou; *Verdi:* Aida (exc); *Traditional:* Měla jsem chlapce; *A. Thomas:* Mignon (exc); *Mendelssohn:* Hohelied; *Schubert:* Schwanengesang, D957 (exc); *Smetana:* Bartered Bride (exc); *Schubert:* Schöne Müllerin (exc); *Wagner:* Tannhäuser (exc); *Mozart:* Nozze di Figaro (exc); *Wagner:* Fliegende Holländer (exc); Lohengrin (exc); *A. Thomas:* Mignon (exc); *Wagner:* Tannhäuser (exc); Lohengrin (exc); *Bizet:* Carmen (exc); *Wagner:* Fliegende Holländer (exc); Lohengrin (exc); *Bizet:* Carmen (exc); *Smetana:* Evening Songs (exc); *Traditional:* Pršívalo, jen se lilo; Andulko šafářova; Marjánko, Marjánko; Když jsem přišel včera večer k ní; *R. Strauss:* Salome (exc); *A. Thomas:* Mignon (exc); *Mascagni:* Cavalleria Rusticana (exc); *Verdi:* Aida (exc); *Puccini:* Madama Butterfly (exc); *Wagner:* Tannhäuser (exc); *Smetana:* Dalibor (exc); *Kovařovic:* Dogs' Heads (exc). (E. Destinn, E. Kraus, anon, R. Leoncavallo, orch/F. Kark/B. Seidler-Winkler, F. Kark)

Ⓓ **11 2136-2(2)** (12/94)
Emmy Destinn—Complete Edition, Discs 3 & 4
Meyerbeer: Huguenots (exc); *Puccini:* Madama Butterfly (exc); *Wagner:* Tannhäuser (exc); *Leoncavallo:* Pagliacci

(exc); *Mascagni:* Cavalleria rusticana (exc); *Verdi:* Aida (exc); *Mozart:* Nozze di Figaro (exc); *Smetana:* Bartered Bride (exc); Kiss (exc); *Gounod:* Ave Maria; *Meyerbeer:* Huguenots (exc); *Hummel:* Hallelujah; *Mozart:* Zauberflöte (exc); *Mascagni:* Cavalleria rusticana (exc); *Bizet:* Carmen (exc); *Weber:* Freischütz (exc); *Mozart:* Nozze di Figaro (exc); *Meyerbeer:* Robert le Diable (exc); Africaine (exc); *Wagner:* Lohengrin (exc); *Gounod:* Faust (exc); *Mozart:* Zauberflöte (exc); *Verdi:* Trovatore (exc); *Puccini:* Madama Butterfly (exc); *Gounod:* Ave Maria; *Puccini:* Tosca (exc); *Wagner:* Tannhäuser (exc); *Smetana:* Dalibor (exc); *Tchaikovsky:* Queen of Spades (exc); *Smetana:* Bartered Bride (exc); *Jindřich:* Jen kdybych věděl; Je teskno dnes. (E. Destinn, K. Jörn, O. Mařák, anon, orch, Odeon Orch/A. Pilz/F. Karl/B. Seidler-Winkler)

Ⓓ **11 2136-2(3)** (12/94)
Emmy Destinn—Complete Edition, Discs 5 to 8
Gounod: Faust (Cpte); *Wagner:* Lohengrin (exc); *Bizet:* Carmen (Cpte). (K. Jörn, E. Destinn, P. Knüpfer, D. Zádor, M. Götze, I. von Scheele-Müller, A. Neudahm, R. Berger, E. Destinn, E. Destinn, O. Metzger, K. Jörn, M. Nast, H. Bachmann, M. Dietrich, G. Parbs, J. Lieban, R. Krasa, F. Dahn, Berlin Court Op Chor, orch, Odeon Orch/B. Seidler-Winkler/A. Pilz)

Ⓓ **11 2136-2(4)** (12/94)
Emmy Destinn—Complete Edition, Discs 9 & 10
Wagner: Tannhäuser (exc); *Weber:* Freischütz (exc); *Wagner:* Tristan und Isolde (exc); *Puccini:* Madama Butterfly (exc); Tosca (exc); *Ponchielli:* Gioconda (exc); *Verdi:* Aida (exc); *Rossini:* Soirées musicales (exc); *Wagner:* Lohengrin (exc); *A. Thomas:* Mignon (exc); *Saint-Saëns:* Samson et Dalila (exc); *Hummel:* Hallelujah; *Wagner:* Fliegende Holländer (exc); *Verdi:* Aida (exc); *Halévy:* Juive (exc); *Wagner:* Tristan und Isolde (exc); *Gounod:* Ave Maria; *Mascagni:* Cavalleria Rusticana (exc); *Ponchielli:* Gioconda (exc); *Puccini:* Madama Butterfly (exc); Tosca (exc); Tosca (exc); *Mascagni:* Cavalleria Rusticana (exc); *Verdi:* Aida (exc); *Weber:* Freischütz (exc). (E. Destinn, L. Kirkby-Lunn, J. McCormack, D. Gilly, orch/P. Pitt)

Ⓓ **11 2136-2(5)** (12/94)
Emmy Destinn—Complete Edition, Discs 11 & 12
Puccini: Bohème (exc); *Leoncavallo:* Pagliacci (exc); *Verdi:* Aida (exc); Trovatore (exc); Forza del destino (exc); *A. Thomas:* Mignon (exc); *Puccini:* Madama Butterfly (exc); *Verdi:* Aida (exc); *Ponchielli:* Gioconda (exc); *Wagner:* Tannhäuser (exc); *Gomes:* Guarany (exc); *Puccini:* Tosca (exc); *Traditional:* Wedding; Goodnight; My Homeland; *Schubert:* Wiegenlied, D498; *Mozart:* Zauberflöte (exc); *Dvořák:* Rusalka (exc); *Kovařovic:* Nazarene (exc); *Tchaikovsky:* Queen of Spades (exc); *Verdi:* Trovatore (exc); *Tosti:* Ultima canzone; *Verdi:* Trovatore (exc); *Gounod:* Ave Maria; *Flies:* Wiegenlied; *Gounod:* Sérénade; *Stange:* Bekehrte; *Liszt:* Oh quand je dors, S282; *Jindřich:* My sweetheart; *Destinn:* Wooing; Maiden's song; *Jindřich:* O Mountains; Ostroh Castle; *Destinn:* Last tears; *Hess:* Home; *Štěpán:* On my way; *Destinn:* Romance; *Smetana:* Kiss (exc); *Verdi:* Ballo in maschera (exc); *Dvořák:* In Folk Tone, B146 (exc). (E. Destinn, G. Zenatello, E. Caruso, D. Gilly, M. Duchêne, F. Lapitino, R. Bourdon, W.B. Rogers, C. Barone, chor, orch/W.B Rogers/J. Pasternack, G. Martinelli)

11 2140-2
Martinů—Comedy on the Bridge; Alexandre bis
Martinů: Comedy on the Bridge (Cpte); Alexandre Bis (Cpte). (J. Krátká, R. Tuček, A. Barová, R. Novák, V. Krejčík, J. Hladík, J. Dufek, B. Kurfürst, Brno Janáček Op Orch/F. Jílek, D. Šounová-Brouková, R. Tuček, V. Krejčík, R. Novák, A. Barová)

11 2153-2 (2/95)
Janáček—Excursions of Mr Brouček
Janáček: Excursions of Mr Brouček (Cpte). (V. Přibyl, M. Švejda, Bohumil Maršík, J. Jonášová, R. Novák, J. Marková, L. Márová, V. Krejčík, J. Souček, J. Olejníček, R. Tuček, K. Hanuš, Czech Phil Chor, Czech PO/F. Jílek)

11 2180-2 (9/95)
Smetana—The Kiss
Smetana: Kiss (Cpte). (E. Haken, E. Děpoltová, L.M Vodička, V. Zítek, L. Márová, K. Hanuš, B. Effenberková, Z. Jankovský, Brno Janáček Op Chor, Brno Janáček Op Orch/F. Vajnar)

11 2185-2
Smetana—Dalibor
Smetana: Dalibor (Cpte). (V. Přibyl, J. Jindrák, N. Kniplová, A. Švorc, J. Horáček, Z. Švehla, H. Svobodová-Janků, D. Jedlička, Prague Nat Th Chor, Prague Nat Th Orch/J. Krombholc)

11 2190-2 (12/94)
Dvořák—The Jacobin
Dvořák: Jacobin (Cpte). (V. Zítek, V. Přibyl, D. Šounová-Brouková, K. Průša, R. Tuček, M. Machotková, K. Berman, B. Blachut, I. Mixová, Kantiléna Children's Chor, Kühn Chor, Brno St PO/J. Pinkas)

Ⓓ **11 2201-2** (11/95)
Smetana—The Devil's Wall
Smetana: Devil's Wall (Cpte). (V. Bednář, I. Mixová, I. Židek, M. Šubrtová, A. Votava, L. Domanínská, K. Berman, L. Mráz, Prague Nat Th Chor, Prague Nat Th Orch/Z. Chalabala)

Ⓓ **11 2250-2**
Dvořák—The Jacobin (highlights)
Dvořák: Jacobin (exc). (V. Zítek, V. Přibyl, D. Šounová-Brouková, K. Průša, R. Tuček, M. Machotková, K. Berman, B. Blachut, I. Mixová, Kantiléna Children's Chor, Kühn Chor, Brno St PO/J. Pinkas)

Ⓓ **11 2252-2**
Dvořák—Rusalka (highlights)
Dvořák: Rusalka (exc). (G. Beňačková, R. Novák, V. Soukupová, W. Ochman, D. Drobková, J. Jonášová, D. Šounová-Brouková, A. Barová, Prague Phil Chor, Czech PO/V. Neumann)

⦿ **1116 3311/3** (5/85)
Foerster—Eva
Foerster: Eva (Cpte). (E. Děpoltová, L.M. Vodička, A. Barová, J. Souček, L. Márová, K. Petr, Prague Rad Chor, Prague RSO/F. Vajnar)

⦿ **1116 3314G** (5/85)
Martinů—Comedy on the Bridge
Martinů: Comedy on the Bridge (Cpte). (J. Krátká, R. Tuček, R. Novák, A. Barová, V. Krejčík, J. Hladík, J. Dufek, B. Kurfürst, Brno Janáček Chbr Op Orch/F. Jílek)

Symposium

Ⓓ **SYMCD1042** (2/89)
Otto Klemperer and the Kroll Years
Beethoven: Coriolan; *Wagner:* Siegfried Idyll; *Ravel:* Alborada del gracioso; *Debussy:* Nocturnes (exc); *Auber:* Fra Diavolo (exc); *Offenbach:* Belle Hélène (exc); *Weill:* Kleine Dreigroschenmusik. (Berlin St Op Orch/O. Klemperer)

Ⓓ **SYMCD1043**
Furtwängler Conducts
Weber: Freischütz (exc); *Bach:* Brandenburg Concertos (exc); *Mozart:* Nozze di Figaro (exc); *Schubert:* Rosamunde (exc); *Rossini:* Barbiere di Siviglia (exc); *Beethoven:* Egmont (exc); *Wagner:* Götterdämmerung (exc); *Brahms:* Hungarian Dances (exc). (BPO/W. Furtwängler)

Ⓓ **SYMCD1065** (12/89)
The Harold Wayne Collection, Vol.1
Meyerbeer: Robert le Diable (exc); *Verdi:* Simon Boccanegra (exc); *Ponchielli:* Gioconda (exc); *Rossini:* Italiana in Algeri (exc); *Bellini:* Capuleti (exc); *Vaccai:* Giulietta e Romeo (exc); *Donizetti:* Lucrezia Borgia (exc); *Rossini:* Semiramide (exc); *Meyerbeer:* Prophète (exc); *Rossini:* Barbiere di Siviglia (exc); *Verdi:* Otello (exc); *Rubinstein:* Asra; *Bellini:* Norma (exc); *Verdi:* Don Carlo (exc); Ernani (exc); *A. Thomas:* Hamlet (exc); *Leoncavallo:* Medici (exc); *Verdi:* Otello (exc); *Bellini:* Puritani (exc); *Malibran:* Prendi, per me sei libero; *Donizetti:* Lucia di Lammermoor (exc); *Verdi:* Luisa Miller (exc); *Donizetti:* Favorita (exc); *Verdi:* Ernani (exc). (G. Gravina, G. Fabbri, G.B. de Negri, G. Kaschmann, F. Toresella, L. Signoretti, anon, S. Cottone)

Ⓓ **SYMCD1069** (10/90)
The Harold Wayne Collection, Vol.2
Tchaikovsky: Eugene Onegin (exc); *Meyerbeer:* Africaine (exc); *Verdi:* Requiem (exc); Rigoletto (exc); *Boito:* Mefistofele (exc); *Rubinstein:* Nero (exc); *Gounod:* Roméo et Juliette (exc); *Flotow:* Martha (exc); *Donizetti:* Lucrezia Borgia (exc); Lucrezia Borgia (exc); *Gomes:* Guarany (exc); *Rubinstein:* Nero (exc); *Verdi:* Rigoletto (exc); *Boito:* Mefistofele (exc); *Marchetti:* Ruy Blas (exc); *Meyerbeer:* Africaine (exc); *Donizetti:* Lucia di Lammermoor (exc); *Verdi:* Forza del destino (exc); *Donizetti:* Favorita (exc); *Bellini:* Puritani (exc); *Masini:* Mulattieri. (F. Marconi, B. Mililotti, M. Galvany, N. della Torre, A. Cotogni, S. Cottone, C. Sabajno, anon, orch)

Ⓓ **SYMCD1073** (6/90)
The Harold Wayne Collection, Vol.3
Ponchielli: Gioconda (exc); *Paloni:* Non guardarmi così; *Mascagni:* Bella cantiam l'amore; *Sidney Jones:* Geisha (exc); *Denza:* In questa sera; *Godard:* Chanson de Florian; *Cilea:* Adriana Lecouvreur (exc); *Mozart:* Nozze di Figaro (exc); *Scuderi:* Dormi pure; *Mascagni:* Cavalleria rusticana (exc); *Franchetti:* Cristoforo Colombo (exc); *Rubinstein:* Demon (exc); *Wagner:* Tannhäuser (exc); *Verdi:* Don Carlo (exc); *Massenet:* Hérodiade (exc); *Verdi:* Aida (exc); *Giordano:* Andrea Chénier (exc); *Gounod:* Faust (exc); *Berlioz:* Damnation de Faust (exc); *Verdi:* Traviata (exc); *Wagner:* Meistersinger (exc); *Giordano:* Fedora (exc); *Boito:* Mefistofele (exc); *Mascagni:* Cavalleria rusticana (exc); *Verdi:* Traviata (exc); *Giordano:* Andrea Chénier (exc). (F. Marconi, A. Pandolfini, F. Valero, E. Giraldoni, G. Zenatello, G. Bellincioni, F. Giraud, S. Cottone, anon, C. Sabajno, P. Mascagni, B. Mililotti)

Ⓓ **SYMCD1077** (5/91)
The Harold Wayne Collection, Vol.4
Wagner: Tannhäuser (exc); Meistersinger (exc); *Tosti:* Oblio; Ancora; *Bizet:* Carmen (exc); *Verdi:* Luisa Miller (exc); *Bizet:* Carmen (exc); *Donizetti:* Lucrezia Borgia (exc); *Ponchielli:* Gioconda (exc); *Arditi:* Parla Waltz; *Westerhout:* Ovunque tu; *Anon:* Serenata; *L. Giordigiani:* Ogni Sabato; *Tosti:* Ideale; *Massenet:* Manon (exc); *Gounod:* Mireille (exc); *Leoncavallo:* Pagliacci (exc); *Puccini:* Bohème (exc); Manon Lescaut (exc); *Boito:* Mefistofele (exc); *Parisotti:* Se tu m'ami; *Wagner:* Lohengrin (exc); *Gounod:* Faust (exc); Faust (exc); *Donizetti:* Lucrezia Borgia (exc). (F. Giraud, E. Teodorini, A. Garulli, E. Bendazzi-Garulli, C. Ferrani, G. Rossi, E. Ceresoli, G. Apostolu, anon, orch)

Ⓓ **SYMCD1078** (7/90)
Willem Mengelberg conducts
Gluck: Alceste (1776) (exc); *Beethoven:* Leonore (exc); Egmont (exc); *Schubert:* Rosamunde (exc); *Weber:* Oberon (exc); *Berlioz:* Carnaval Romain; *Wagner:* Lohengrin (exc); *Mahler:* Symphony 5 (exc); *Tchaikovsky:* Marche Slave. (Concertgebouw, NYPO, NYPSO/W. Mengelberg)

Ⓓ **SYMCD1081** (7/91)
The Harold Wayne Collection, Vol.5
Meyerbeer: Prophète (exc); *Wagner:* Meistersinger (exc); *Smetana:* Dalibor (exc); *Wagner:* Tannhäuser (exc); *Verdi:* Trovatore (exc); *Wagner:* Lohengrin (exc); Rheingold (exc); Rheingold (exc); Rheingold (exc); Walküre (exc); Siegfried (exc); Siegfried (exc); Tannhäuser (exc); Walküre (exc); Götterdämmerung (exc); Tannhäuser (exc); Tannhäuser (exc); Fliegende Holländer (exc); Lohengrin (exc); Lohengrin (exc); Tristan und Isolde (exc); *Verdi:* Aida (exc). (H. Winkelmann, O. Briesemeister, H. Breuer, T. Bertram, A. von Bary, E. Feuge, C. Whitehill, S. Sedlmair, L. Slezak, E. Schmedes, anon)

Ⓓ **SYMCD1085**
The Harold Wayne Collection, Vol.6
Boieldieu: Dame blanche (exc); *A. Thomas:* Mignon (exc); *Verdi:* Rigoletto (exc); Traviata (exc); *Mozart:* Così fan tutte (exc); *Rossini:* Barbiere di Siviglia (exc); *Verdi:* Trovatore (exc); *Rossini:* Semiramide (exc); *A. Thomas:* Mignon (exc); *Rossini:* Barbiere di Siviglia (exc); *Weber:* Oberon (exc); *Massenet:* Cid (exc); *Donizetti:* Lucrezia Borgia (exc); *Meyerbeer:* Prophète (exc); *A. Thomas:* Mignon (exc); *Brahms:* Lieder, Op.86 (exc); *Schubert:* Schwanengesang, D957 (exc); *Beethoven:* Zärtliche Liebe, WoO123; *Grieg:* Melodies of the Heart, Op.5 (exc); *Wagner:* Tannhäuser (exc); *Loewe:* Balladen, Op.56 (exc); *Mascagni:* M'ama, non m'ama; *Anon:* Unsere Quelle. (H. Buff-Giessen, I. Abendroth, A. Bahr-Mildenburg, A. Schläger, M. Brandt, G. Walter, S. Sedlmair, K. Scheidemantel, L. Beeth, anon)

Ⓓ **SYMCD1089** (9/91)
Historic Baritones of the French School
Donizetti: Favorita (exc); *Adam:* Minuit, chrétiens (exc); *Gounod:* Roméo et Juliette (exc); Faust (exc); *Meyerbeer:* Africaine (exc); *Saint-Saëns:* Ascanio (exc); *Massenet:* Roi de Lahore (exc); Si tu veux, mignonne; Pensée d'automne; *Berlioz:* Damnation de Faust (exc); *Massé:* Paul et Virginie (exc); *Mozart:* Don Giovanni (exc); *Fontenailles:* Deux coeurs; *Paladilhe:* Mandolinata; *De Lara:* Rondel de l'adieu; *Chabrier:* Roi malgré lui (exc); *Grétry:* Richard Coeur-de-Lion (exc); *Adam:* Si j'étais Roi (exc); *Paer:* Maître de chapelle (exc); *Messager:* Basoche (exc); *Massenet:* Jongleur de Notre Dame (exc); *Isouard:* Joconde (exc); *Halévy:* Charles VI (exc); *Gounod:* Soir; *Reyer:* Sigurd (exc); *Poise:* Joli Gilles (exc); *De Lara:* Méssaline (exc); *Périer:* Dors, mon enfant. (J.B. Faure, L. Melchissédec, J. Lassalle, V. Maurel, L. Fugère, G. Soulacroix, M-N. Bouvet, J. Noté, M. Renaud, A. Ghasne, J. Périer, anon, orch)

Ⓓ **SYMCD1093** (10/92)
The Harold Wayne Collection, Vol.7
Verdi: Falstaff (exc); *Traditional:* Drink to me only; *Schubert:* Ständchen, D889; *Traditional:* My love Nell; *Wagner:* Tannhäuser (exc); *Debussy:* Pelléas et Mélisande (exc); *Mozart:* Nozze di Figaro (exc); *Sullivan:* Thou'rt passing hence; *Handel:* Theodora (exc); Serse (exc); *Bishop:* Home, sweet home; *Traditional:* Robin Adair; *Stanford:* Shamus O'Brien (exc); *Meyer-Helmund:* Ich hätte nicht daran gedacht; *Massenet:* Manon (exc); *Meyer-Helmund:* Morgen send'ich dir die Veilchen; *Offenbach:* Contes d'Hoffmann (exc); *Wagner:* Lohengrin (exc); *Tosti:* Ninon; *Traditional:* Maman, dites-moi; *Flotow:* Martha (exc); *Tchaikovsky:* Maid of Orleans (exc); *Hawley:*

Sweetest flower that blows; *Marchesi:* Folletta. (D. Bispham, M. Garden, C. Santley, E. Albani, J. O'Mara, F. Saville, O. Ouroussov, E. Palliser, anon, C. Debussy, Henry Wood)

Ⓓ **SYMCD1096/7** (11/91)
Sir Thomas Beecham, Bart conducts Beecham SO & LPO
Dvořák: Symphony 5; *Gounod:* Faust (exc); *Brahms:* Hungarian Dances (exc); *Tchaikovsky:* Nutcracker (exc); *Schubert:* Marches militaires, D733 (exc); *Massenet:* Thaïs (exc); *Mendelssohn:* Midsummer Night's Dream (exc); *Wagner:* Tannhäuser (exc); *J. Strauss II:* Fledermaus (exc); *Rossini:* Guillaume Tell (exc); *Missa:* Muguette (exc); *Mascagni:* Cavalleria Rusticana (exc); *Mendelssohn:* Songs without Words (exc); *Weber:* Oberon (exc); *Mozart:* Nozze di Figaro (exc); *Massenet:* Manon (exc); *R. Strauss:* Rosenkavalier (exc); *Tchaikovsky:* Symphony 6 (exc); *Stravinsky:* Firebird Suite (1911) (exc); *Rossini:* Barbiere di Siviglia (exc); *Gounod:* Roméo et Juliette (exc); *Lully:* Amants magnifiques (exc); *Debussy:* Petite Suite (exc); *Beethoven:* Symphony 7 (exc). (LPO, SO/T. Beecham)

Ⓓ **SYMCD1100** (3/93)
Harold Wayne Collection, Vol.8
Gounod: Philémon et Baucis (exc); *Faure:* Rameaux; *A. Thomas:* Caïd (exc); *Meyerbeer:* Huguenots (exc); *Gounod:* Roméo et Juliette (exc); *Godard:* Embarquez-vous; *Wagner:* Walküre (exc); Meistersinger (exc); Tannhäuser (exc); Rheingold (exc); *Traditional:* Mühlrad; *De Lara:* Méssaline (exc); *Mozart:* Don Giovanni (exc); *Rotoli:* Serenata; *Gounod:* Faust (exc); *Tosti:* Invano; *Bizet:* Carmen (exc); *Verdi:* Falstaff (exc); *Gounod:* Faust (exc); *Stern:* Coquette; *Gounod:* Roméo et Juliette (exc); *Bishop:* Home, sweet home; *P.A. Vidal:* Printemps nouveau; *Bizet:* Carmen (exc); *Traditional:* Magali; *Mascagni:* Cavalleria rusticana (exc); *Wagner:* Tannhäuser (exc); *Holmès:* Chemin du ciel. (P. Plançon, A. Van Rooy, A. Scotti, S. Adams, E. Calvé, M. Renaud, anon)

Ⓓ **SYMCD1101** (10/92)
The Harold Wayne Collection, Vol.9
Gounod: Chanson de printemps; *Gluck:* Iphigénie en Tauride (exc); *Massenet:* Marquise; *Hahn:* Heure exquise; *De Lara:* Rondel de l'adieu; *C. Erlanger:* Fédia; *Verdi:* Otello (exc); *Fauré:* Songs, Op. 23 (exc); Songs, Op. 23 (exc); *Saint-Saëns:* Samson et Dalila (exc); Samson et Dalila (exc); *Nápravník:* Harold (exc); *Wagner:* Tristan und Isolde (exc); Tristan und Isolde (exc); Walküre (exc); Walküre (exc); *Schumann:* Dichterliebe, Op.48 (exc); Dichterliebe, Op.48 (exc); *Gounod:* Sapho (exc); Faust (exc); *Massenet:* Cid (exc). (V. Maurel, F. Litvinne, anon, A. Cortot)

Ⓓ **SYMCD1103**
Renée Doria—Opera Recital
Rossini: Comte Ory (exc); *Hérold:* Pré aux Clercs (exc); *Meyerbeer:* Huguenots (exc); *F. David:* Perle du Brésil (exc); *Meyerbeer:* Dinorah (exc); *Gounod:* Mireille (exc); *Massenet:* Thaïs (exc); *Saint-Saëns:* Parysatis (exc); *Rimsky-Korsakov:* Golden Cockerel (exc). (R. Doria, M. Sénéchal, A. Migliette, anon, chor, orch, Paris Sols Orch/J. Etcheverry, Pasdeloup Ass Orch/J. Allain/J-C. Hartemann/P. Stoll)

Ⓓ **SYMCD1105** (7/93)
The Harold Wayne Collection, Vol.10
Koenemann: When the king went forth to war; *Slonov:* Arise, red sun; *Tchaikovsky:* Songs, Op.60 (exc); *Traditional:* Night; *Glinka:* Life for the Tsar (exc); *Tchaikovsky:* Songs, Op.65 (exc); *Rimsky-Korsakov:* Sadko (exc); *Gounod:* Roméo et Juliette (exc); *Tchaikovsky:* Eugene Onegin (exc); *Wagner:* Walküre (exc); *Grechaninov:* Over the Steppe; *Verdi:* Traviata (exc); *Glinka:* Ruslan and Lyudmila (exc); *Meyerbeer:* Huguenots (exc); *Rubinstein:* Demon (exc); *Verstovsky:* Askold's Grave (exc); *Gounod:* Faust (exc); Faust (exc); *Donizetti:* Zingara (exc); *Verdi:* Traviata (exc); *Bizet:* Pastorale; *Glinka:* Ruslan and Lyudmila (exc); Life for the Tsar (exc); *Rimsky-Korsakov:* Snow Maiden (exc); *Mascagni:* M'ama, non m'ama. (F. Chaliapin, I. Alchevsky, V. Sharonov, M. Kuznetsova, A. Labinsky, E. Orel, anon)

Ⓓ **SYMCD1109** (6/93)
Great Violinists, Vol.5 - Adolf Busch
Corelli: Sonatas, Op.5 (exc); *Bach:* Solo Violin Partitas and Sonatas (exc); Solo Violin Partitas and Sonatas (exc); *Tartini:* Violin Sonatas (1745) (exc); *Gossec:* Rosine (exc); *Hoffstetter:* String Quartets, Op.3 (exc); *Mozart:* String Quartet, K575 (exc); *Schubert:* String Quartet, D887 (exc); *Verdi:* String Quartet (exc); *Brahms:* Hungarian Dances (exc); Hungarian Dances (exc); *Kreisler:* Pugnani Praeludium and Allegro; Dittersdorf Scherzo; *Bach:* Solo Violin Partitas and Sonatas (exc); Violin Sonatas, BWV1020-25 (exc); *Brahms:* Violin Concerto (exc). (A. Busch, B. Seidler-Winkler, Busch Qt, anon, NBC SO/F. Black, R. Serkin)

Ⓓ **SYMCD1111** (8/93)
The Harold Wayne Collection, Vol.11
E. Mascheroni: Lorenza (exc); *Mascagni:* Cavalleria rusticana (exc); *Puccini:* Bohème (exc); *Giordano:* Fedora (exc); *Massenet:* Manon (exc); *Mascagni:* Iris (exc); *Giordano:* Andrea Chénier (exc); *Tosti:* Dopo; *Puccini:* Tosca (exc); Tosca (exc); *Cilea:* Adriana Lecouvreur (exc); *Massenet:* Roi de Lahore (exc); *Donizetti:* Favorita (exc); *Verdi:* Ballo in maschera (exc); *A. Thomas:* Hamlet (exc); *Mozart:* Don Giovanni (exc); *Donizetti:* Favorita (exc); Don Pasquale (exc); *Franchetti:* Germania (exc); *Mascagni:* Cavalleria rusticana (exc); *Bottesini:* Ero e Leandro (exc); *Ponchielli:* Gioconda (exc); *Puccini:* Tosca (exc). (E. Carelli, G. De Luca, A. Pinto, E. Ventura, M. Sammarco, E. Ceresoli, F. Cilea, anon, E. Mascheroni, S. Cottone)

Ⓓ **SYMCD1113** (12/93)
The Harold Wayne Collection, Vol.13
Verdi: Trovatore (exc); *Meyerbeer:* Dinorah (exc); *Verdi:* Ballo in maschera (exc); *Saint-Saëns:* Samson et Dalila (exc); *A. Thomas:* Mignon (exc); *Mozart:* Don Giovanni (exc); *Puccini:* Bohème (exc); *Verdi:* Aida (exc); Forza del destino (exc); *Parisotti:* Se tu m'ami; *Ponchielli:* Gioconda (exc); *Verdi:* Rigoletto (exc); *Gounod:* Faust (exc); *Ponchielli:* Gioconda (exc); *Verdi:* Aida (exc); *Wagner:* Rheingold (exc). (E. Scaramberg, A. Stehle, R. Stracciari, G. Bréjean-Silver, I. Calleja, M. Camporelli, F. Corradetti, N. de Angelis, E. Feinhals, E. Mazzoleni, G. Pacini, A. Parsi-Pettinella, L. Pasini-Vitale, E. Garbin, L. Longobardi, G. Lukacewska, O. Luppi, A. Magini-Coletti, R. Pinkert, G. Russ, M. Sammarco, G. Armanini, M. Barrientos, A. Bonci, La Scala Chor, anon, orch)

Ⓓ **SYMCD1117**
Alfred Orda—Opera Recital
Handel: Berenice (exc); *Donizetti:* Dom Sébastien (exc); *Verdi:* Rigoletto (exc); *Moniuszko:* Verbum Nobile (exc); *Marchetti:* Ruy Blas (exc); *Ponchielli:* Lituani (exc); *Massenet:* Roi de Lahore (exc); *Ponchielli:* Figliuol Prodigo (exc); *Massenet:* Hérodiade (exc); *Tchaikovsky:* Mazeppa (exc); *Zeleński:* Konrad Wallenrod (exc); *Verdi:* Otello (exc); *Gomes:* Schiavo (exc); *Leoncavallo:* Pagliacci (exc); *Rimsky-Korsakov:* Sadko (exc). (A. Orda, Polish RSO/S. Rachoń/H. Debich/K. Missona)

Ⓓ **SYMCD1123**
Sullivan—Sesquicentenial Commemorative Issue
Sullivan: Orpheus with his lute; Prodigal Son (exc); Sailor's grave; Mary Morison; Thou'rt passing hence; Sorcerer (exc); Henry VIII (exc); I would I were a king; Pirates of Penzance (exc); Pirates of Penzance (exc); Martyr of Antioch (exc); Iolanthe (exc); Iolanthe (exc); Mikado (exc); Golden Legend (exc); Golden Legend (exc); Yeomen of the Guard (exc); Gondoliers (exc); Gondoliers (exc); Gondoliers (exc); Ivanhoe (exc); Ivanhoe (exc); Ivanhoe (exc); Rose of Persia (exc); Rose of Persia (exc). (D. Labbette, E. Williams, B. Davies, J. Harrison, C. Santley, W. Passmore, A. Black, R. Radford, R. Temple, I. Jay, E. Lloyd, H. Lytton, L. Henri, H. Dearth, H. Williams, C. Tubb, E. Thornton, E. Jones-Hudson, V. Essex, J. Coates, C. Herwin, D. Bispham, P. Dawson, E. Evans, W. Glynne, C.H. Workman, anon, orch, inst ens)

Ⓓ **SYMCD1125** (6/93)
Lucien Fugère—Opera & Song Recital
Messager: Basoche (exc); *Massenet:* Jongleur de Notre Dame (exc); *Flotow:* Ombre (exc); *Mozart:* Zauberflöte (exc); Don Giovanni (exc); *Chabrier:* Roi malgré lui (exc); *Meyerbeer:* Dinorah (exc); *Halévy:* Val d'Andorre (exc); *G. Charpentier:* Louise (exc); *Massé:* Saisons (exc); *Gounod:* Médecin malgré lui (exc); *Gluck:* Rencontre imprévue (exc); *Paer:* Maître de Chapelle (exc); *Chaminade:* Ronde d'amour; *P. Henrion:* Vieux ruban; *Levadé:* Vieilles de chez-nous; *Chaminade:* Anneau d'argent; *Widor:* Mélodies, Op. 43 (exc); *Couperin:* Livre de clavecin IV (exc). (L. Fugère, orch, anon)

Ⓓ **SYMCD1126** (12/93)
The Harold Wayne Collection, Vol.14
Granier: Hosanna; *Verdi:* Otello (exc); *Rossini:* Guillaume Tell (exc); *Massenet:* Mage (exc); *Halévy:* Juive (exc); *Flégier:* Stances; *Saint-Saëns:* Samson et Dalila (exc); *Meyerbeer:* Huguenots (exc); *Rossini:* Guillaume Tell (exc); *Meyerbeer:* Africaine (exc); Prophète (exc); Robert le Diable (exc); *Reyer:* Sigurd (exc); *Verdi:* Lombardi (exc); *Rupès:* Pastorale Languedoçienne; *Verdi:* Aida (exc); Jérusalem (exc); *Massenet:* Cid (exc); *Granier:* Pierre l'ermite (exc); *Verdi:* Otello (exc). (L. Escalais, O. Luppi, A. Magini-Coletti, A. Talexis, A. Algos, F. Corradetti, G. Masotti, G. Sala, anon)

Ⓓ **SYMCD1128** (12/94)
The Harold Wayne Collection, Vol.15
Verdi: Trovatore (exc); Otello (exc); *Gounod:* Polyeucte (exc); *Massenet:* Hérodiade (exc); *Boito:* Mefistofele (exc); *Mascagni:* Cavalleria Rusticana (exc); *Wagner:* Lohengrin (exc); *Verdi:* Aida (exc); *Meyerbeer:* Africaine (exc); *Saint-Saëns:* Samson et Dalila (exc); *Donizetti:* Favorita (exc); *Verdi:* Trovatore (exc); *Bizet:* Carmen (exc); *Meyerbeer:* Africaine (exc); *Massenet:* Cid (exc); *Verdi:* Otello (exc); *Tosti:* Marechiare; *Mozart:* Don Giovanni (exc); *De Lara:* Rondel de l'adieu; *Paladilhe:* Mandolinata; *Tosti:* Ninon; *Verdi:* Falstaff (exc); *Hardelot:* Year ago; *Tosti:* Au temps du grand roi. (L. Escalais, F. Litvinne, V. Maurel, anon, orch)

Ⓓ **SYMCD1130** (4/93)
Joseph Holbrooke—Historic Recordings
Holbrooke: Children of Don (exc); Children of Don (exc); Dylan (exc); Dylan (exc); Bronwen (exc); Piano Quartet 1 (exc); Enchanter (exc); Piano Pieces, Op. 101 (exc); Piano Pieces, Op. 105 (exc); Symphony 3 (exc). (D. Vane, J. Coates, N. Walker, J. Holbrooke, Phil Qt, orch, SO/C. Powell/A. Hammond/C. Raybould/J. Holbrooke)

Ⓓ **SYMCD1136** (8/93)
Opera in Chicago, Vol.1
Mendelssohn: Hear my prayer (exc); *Flotow:* Martha (exc); *Gounod:* Faust (exc); *Puccini:* Madama Butterfly (exc); Madama Butterfly (exc); *Cadman:* American Indian Songs, Op.45 (exc); *Del Riego:* O dry those tears; *Cadman:* American Indian Songs, Op.45 (exc); *Woodforde-Finden:* Indian Love Lyrics (exc); *Strickland:* Dreamin' time; *Tosti:* Serenata; Addio; *Debussy:* Ariettes oubliées (exc); *Verdi:* Traviata (exc); *Massenet:* Jongleur de Notre Dame (exc); Hérodiade (exc); *G. Charpentier:* Louise (exc); *Massenet:* Thaïs (exc); *Alfano:* Risurrezione (exc); *G. Charpentier:* Louise (exc); *Grechaninov:* Over the Steppe; *Bizet:* Carmen (exc); *Traditional:* John Anderson, my Jo. (E. Mason, M. Garden, orch, C. Debussy, J. Dansereau)

Ⓓ **SYMCD1138** (12/93)
The Harold Wayne Collection, Vol.16
Verdi: Trovatore (exc); Trovatore (exc); Trovatore (exc); Trovatore (exc); Trovatore (exc); Traviata (exc); Traviata (exc); Traviata (exc); Ballo in maschera (exc); Ballo in maschera (exc); Ballo in maschera (exc); Ballo in maschera (exc); Forza del destino (exc); Aida (exc); Aida (exc). (G. Zenatello, A. Parsi-Pettinella, P. Amato, E. Bruno, E. Mazzoleni, L. Cannetti, E. Burzio, N. Frascani, anon, orch, chor)

Ⓓ **SYMCD1148** (12/93)
The Harold Wayne Collection, Vol.17
Verdi: Aida (exc); Aida (exc); Aida (exc); Aida (exc); Otello (exc); Otello (exc); Otello (exc); Otello (exc); Otello (exc); Otello (exc); *Marchetti:* Ruy Blas (exc); *Ponchielli:* Gioconda (exc); Gioconda (exc); Gioconda (exc). (G. Zenatello, E. Mazzoleni, E. Bruno, L. Pasini-Vitale, P. Amato, anon, orch)

Ⓓ **SYMCD1149** (1/95)
Fernando De Lucia
Rossini: Barbiere di Siviglia (exc); Barbiere di Siviglia (exc); Barbiere di Siviglia (exc); Barbiere di Siviglia (exc); *Bellini:* Sonnambula (exc); Sonnambula (exc); *Donizetti:* Elisir d'amore (exc); Favorita (exc); *Verdi:* Luisa Miller (exc); Rigoletto (exc); Rigoletto (exc); Traviata (exc); Traviata (exc); Traviata (exc); *Gounod:* Faust (exc); Faust (exc); *Bizet:* Carmen (exc); Carmen (exc); *Mascagni:* Cavalleria rusticana (exc); *Massenet:* Werther (exc); *Puccini:* Tosca (exc); *Giordano:* Fedora (exc). (F. de Lucia, A. Pini-Corsi, M. Galvany, J. Huguet, E. Badini, C. Boninsegna, anon, orch)

Ⓓ **SYMCD1158** (5/94)
The Harold Wayne Collection, Vol.18
Puccini: Manon Lescaut (exc); Manon Lescaut (exc); Bohème (exc); Bohème (exc); Bohème (exc); Tosca (exc); Tosca (exc); Madama Butterfly (exc); Fanciulla del West (exc); *Mascagni:* Cavalleria Rusticana (exc); Cavalleria Rusticana (exc); *Leoncavallo:* Pagliacci (exc); Pagliacci (exc); Pagliacci (exc); Pagliacci (exc); Pagliacci (exc). (G. Zenatello, M. Sammarco, L. Cannetti, E. Mazzoleni, anon, orch)

Ⓓ **SYMCD1168** (5/94)
The Harold Wayne Collection, Vol.19
Rosa: Star vicino; *Donizetti:* Lucia di Lammermoor (exc); *Bellini:* Norma (exc); *Boito:* Mefistofele (exc); Mefistofele (exc); Mefistofele (exc); *Franchetti:* Germania (exc); Figlia di Iorio (exc); *Giordano:* Andrea Chénier (exc); Andrea Chénier (exc); Andrea Chénier (exc); *Wagner:* Meistersinger (exc); Meistersinger (exc); *Meyerbeer:* Huguenots (exc); *Gounod:* Faust (exc); Faust (exc); *Saint-Saëns:* Samson et Dalila (exc); *Bizet:* Carmen (exc); Carmen (exc); *Gomes:* Guarany (exc); *Denza:* Vieni a me; *Rotoli:* Mia sposa sarà la mia bandiera. (G. Zenatello, M. Barrientos, E. Mazzoleni, A. Didur, E. Giraldoni, E. Cervi-Caroli, A. Nielsen, anon, orch)

Ⓓ **SYMCD1170** (7/95)
The Harold Wayne Collection, Vol.20
Donizetti: Don Pasquale (exc); Duca d'Alba (exc); *Verdi:* Luisa Miller (exc); Traviata (exc); *Bizet:* Pêcheurs de Perles (exc); *A. Thomas:* Mignon (exc); *Massenet:* Manon (exc); *Mascagni:* Cavalleria Rusticana (exc); *Massenet:*

Werther (exc); *Leoncavallo:* Pagliacci (exc); *Giordano:* Fedora (exc); *Mascagni:* Iris (exc); *Paderewski:* Manru (exc); *D. Scarlatti:* Consolati e spera; *Handel:* Serse (exc); *Mendelssohn:* Lieder, Op.8 (exc); *R. Strauss:* Lieder, Op.27 (exc); Lieder, Op.10 (exc); *Mugnone:* Mattinata; Spes ultima Dea; *Alagna:* Canzuna Siciliana; *Tosti:* Non t'amo più; Vorrei morire. (G. Anselmi, Bettinelli, L. Mugnone, anon)

) **SYMCD1172** (12/94)
The Harold Wayne Collection, Vol.21
Schumann: Romanzen und Balladen, Op.49 (exc); *Meyerbeer:* Huguenots (exc); *Paladilhe:* Patrie (exc); *Yradier:* Paloma; *Meyerbeer:* Africaine (exc); *Gounod:* Soir; Prière; *V.A. Duvernoy:* Hellé (exc); *Reyer:* Sigurd (exc); *Schumann:* Dichterliebe, Op.48 (exc); *Wagner:* Walküre (exc); *Massenet:* Werther (exc); *Schumann:* Myrthen, Op.25 (exc); *Nicolai:* Blümchen; *Schumann:* Liederkreis, Op.39 (exc); *A. Thomas:* Mignon (exc); *E. Bourgeois:* Véritable Manola; *Bizet:* Carmen (exc); *Berlioz:* Damnation de Faust (exc); *Wagner:* Walküre (exc); *Godard:* Jocelyn (exc); *Gounod:* Au Rossignol; *G. Braga:* Melodies (exc); *Massenet:* Hérodiade (exc); *Tosti:* T'amo ancora; *Massenet:* Âme des fleurs; *De Lara:* Champs de pavots; *Gounod:* Faust (exc); *Verdi:* Traviata (exc). (J-F. Delmas, P. Gailhard, R. Caron, E. Van Dyck, L. David, V. Capoul, M. de Reszke, A. Adini, P. Aramis, G. Bréjean-Silver, J. de Reszke, anon, orch)

SYMCD1173
The Harold Wayne Collection, Vol.22
Verdi: Rigoletto (exc); *Bizet:* Pêcheurs de perles (exc); *Reyer:* Sigurd (exc); *Wagner:* Walküre (exc); *Massenet:* Werther (exc); *Meyerbeer:* Huguenots (exc); Africaine (exc); *Massenet:* Manon (exc); *Gounod:* Roméo et Juliette (exc); *Massenet:* Manon (exc); Manon (exc); *Gounod:* Roméo et Juliette (exc); *Puccini:* Bohème (exc); *Gounod:* Reine de Saba (exc); *Bizet:* Carmen (exc); *Wagner:* Lohengrin (exc); *Massenet:* Werther (exc); Werther (exc); *Verdi:* Rigoletto (exc); *Mascagni:* Cavalleria rusticana (exc); *Reyer:* Sigurd (exc); *Giordano:* Fedora (exc); *Mascagni:* Cavalleria rusticana (exc); *Wagner:* Lohengrin (exc). (G. Bréjean-Silver, P. Cornubert, E. Scaramberg, F. Litvinne, anon, orch)

SYMCD1175
Ave Maria
Gounod: Ave Maria; *P. S. Palmer:* Gate of the Year; *Widor:* Ave Maria; *Bruckner:* Ave Maria (1882); *Cherubini:* Ave Maria; *Bizet:* Agnus Dei; *Verdi:* Ave Maria; Otello (exc); *E. Mascheroni:* Ave Maria; *E. Martin:* Evensong; *Bruch:* Feuerkreuz (exc); *A. Coates:* Ave Maria; *Turina:* Ave Maria; *P. Kahn:* Ave Maria; *Liddle:* How lovely are thy dwellings; *Reger:* Schlichte Weisen, Op. 76 (exc); *Franck:* Ave Maria; *Ashford:* My task; *Mascagni:* Ave Maria; *Rossini:* Péchés de vieillesse I (exc); *Head:* Ave Maria; *Stolz:* Ave Maria. (M. Hayward Segal, P. Dudakoff, M. Keogh, K. Bowyer)

SYMCD1176/7
Ponchielli—La Gioconda
Ponchielli: Gioconda (Cpte). (Z. Milanov, G. Martinelli, C. Morelli, A. Kaskas, N. Moscona, B. Castagna, W. Engelman, G. Paltrinieri, NY Met Op Chor, NY Met Op Orch/E. Panizza)

SYMCD1178/9
Wagner—Tannhäuser
Wagner: Tannhäuser (exc). (E. Laholm, K. Flagstad, H. Janssen, R. Pauly, E. List, J. Carter, M. Harrell, M. Gellman, NY Met Op Chor, NY Met Op Orch/E. Reinsdorf)

ahra

FURT1004/7 (3/95)
Furtwängler conducts the Berlin Philharmonic
Beethoven: Symphony 9; Coriolan; Symphony 6; *Wagner:* Tristan und Isolde (exc); *Brahms:* Piano Concerto 2; Symphony 1 (exc); *Bruckner:* Symphony 6 (exc); Symphony 7 (exc). (T. Briem, E. Höngen, P. Anders, R. Watzke, A. Aeschbacher, Bruno Kittel Ch, BPO/W. Furtwängler)

elarc

CD80039
Stravinsky—The Firebird. Borodin—Music from Prince Igor
Borodin: Prince Igor (exc); *Stravinsky:* Firebird Suite (1919) (exc). (Atlanta Sym Chor, Atlanta SO/Robert Shaw)

CD80041 (12/83)
Tchaikovsky: Orchestral Works
Tchaikovsky: 1812; Capriccio Italien; Mazeppa (exc). (Cincinnati SO/E. Kunzel)

CD80048 (10/84)
Bizet—Carmen Suite. Grieg—Peer Gynt Suite
Bizet: Carmen Suites (exc); *Grieg:* Peer Gynt (exc). (St. Louis SO/L. Slatkin)

CD80072 (12/83)
Russian Orchestral Works
Rimsky-Korsakov: Russian Easter Festival Ov.; *Glinka:* Ruslan and Lyudmila (exc); *Borodin:* In the Steppes of Central Asia; *Glière:* Red Poppy Suite (exc); *Tchaikovsky:* Marche slave. (St. Louis SO/L. Slatkin)

CD80107 (5/85)
Tchaikovsky—Symphony 5. Rimsky-Korsakov—Tsar Saltan March
Tchaikovsky: Symphony 5; *Rimsky-Korsakov:* Tale of Tsar Saltan (exc). (RPO/A. Previn)

CD80109 (9/85)
Berlioz: Requiem, etc
Berlioz: Grande messe des morts (Cpte); *Verdi:* Pezzi sacri (exc); *Boito:* Mefistofele (exc). (J. Aler, Atlanta Sym Chor, Atlanta SO/Robert Shaw, J. Cheek, Morehouse-Spelman Chor, Callanwolde Young Sngrs)

CD80115 (9/86)
Orchestral Spectaculars
Rimsky-Korsakov: Mlada (exc); Snow Maiden (exc); *Dukas:* Apprenti sorcier; *Weinberger:* Schwanda the Bagpiper (exc); *Saint-Saëns:* Samson et Dalila (exc); *Liszt:* Préludes. (Cincinnati Pops/E. Kunzel)

CD80117 (10/87)
Copland—Orchestral Works
Copland: John Henry; Lincoln Portrait; Tender Land (exc); Old American Songs 1; Jubilee Variation; Ceremonial Fanfare; Outdoor Ov. (K. Hepburn, S. Milnes, Cincinnati Pops/E. Kunzel)

CD80126 (10/87)
Works by Britten and Prokofiev
Britten: Young Person's Guide; Gloriana Suite (exc); *Prokofiev:* Peter and the Wolf. (RPO/A. Previn, A. Previn)

CD80130 (10/87)
Tchaikovsky—Symphony No. 6; Eugen Onegin Polonaise
Tchaikovsky: Symphony 6; Eugene Onegin (exc). (Cleveland Orch/C. von Dohnányi)

CD80145 (11/87)
Beethoven—Pastoral Symphony; Leonore Overture No. 3
Beethoven: Symphony 6; Leonore (exc). (Cleveland Orch/C. von Dohnányi)

CD80149 (11/87)
Falla—Theatre Music
Falla: Sombrero de tres picos (Cpte); Homenajes; Vida breve (exc). (F. Quivar, M. May Fest Chor, Cincinnati SO/J. López-Cobos)

CD80152 (3/88)
Verdi: Requiem & Opera Choruses
Verdi: Requiem (Cpte); Don Carlo (exc); Macbeth (exc); Otello (exc); Nabucco (exc); Aida (exc). (S. Dunn, D. Curry, J. Hadley, P. Plishka, Atlanta Sym Chor, Atlanta SO/Robert Shaw)

CD80154 (10/88)
Wagner: The 'Ring' without Words
Wagner: Rheingold (exc); Walküre (exc); Siegfried (exc); Götterdämmerung (exc). (BPO/L. Maazel)

CD80164 (12/88)
Berlioz—Orchestral Works
Berlioz: Benvenuto Cellini (exc); Roméo et Juliette (exc); Damnation de Faust (exc); Corsaire; Troyens (exc); Marche Troyenne; *Various:* National Anthems (exc). (S. McNair, R. Leech, St David's Baltimore Ch, Baltimore Sym Chor, Baltimore SO/D. Zinman)

CD80170 (10/89)
Symphonic Spectacular
Shostakovich: Festive Overture; *Wagner:* Walküre (exc); *Falla:* Amor brujo (exc); *Bizet:* Arlésienne Suites (exc); *Järnefelt:* Praeludium; *Chabrier:* España; *Tchaikovsky:* Marche slave; *Halvorsen:* Entry March of the Boyars; *Enescu:* Romanian Rhapsodies, Op. 11 (exc); *Khachaturian:* Gayaneh (exc). (Cincinnati Pops/E. Kunzel)

CD80224 (11/90)
Bizet—Orchestral Works
Bizet: Symphony; Carmen Suites (exc); Arlésienne Suites (exc). (Cincinnati SO/J. López-Cobos)

CD80258 (7/91)
Wagner—Die Walküre, Act 1
Wagner: Walküre (exc). (K. König, S. Dunn, P. Meven, Pittsburgh SO/L. Maazel)

CD80260
Pops Plays Puccini
Puccini: Gianni Schicchi (exc); Tosca (exc); Turandot (exc); Madama Butterfly (exc); Manon Lescaut (exc); Bohème (exc). (Cincinnati Pops/E. Kunzel)

CD80284 (5/92) **CS30284** (5/92)
Gilbert & Sullivan—The Mikado
Sullivan: Mikado (Cpte). (D. Adams, A. Rolfe Johnson, R. Suart, R. Van Allan, N. Folwell, M. McLaughlin, A. Howells, J. Watson, F. Palmer, WNO Chor, WNO Orch/C. Mackerras)

CD80294 (11/92) **CS30294** (11/92)
Gaîté Parisienne
Offenbach: Gaîté Parisienne (Cpte); Geneviève de Brabant (exc); Belles américaines; *Ibert:* Divertissement. (Cincinnati Pops/E. Kunzel)

CD80296 (4/92)
Mussorgsky—Orchestral Works
Mussorgsky: Pictures; Night on the bare mountain; Khovanshchina (exc). (Atlanta SO/Y. Levi)

CD80302 (12/91)
Mozart—Die Zauberflöte
Mozart: Zauberflöte (Cpte). (B. Hendricks, J. Anderson, J. Hadley, T. Allen, R. Lloyd, G. Hornik, H. Wildhaber, U. Steinsky, P.M. Schnitzer, G. Sima, J. Bernheimer, D. Ison, N. Watts, J. Dawson, P. Svensson, A. Miles, Scottish Chbr Chor, Scottish CO/C. Mackerras)

CD80303 **CS30303**
Empire Brass on Broadway
A. Lloyd Webber: Phantom of the Opera (exc); Cats (exc); Evita (exc); *J. Herman:* Hello, Dolly! (exc); *M. Leigh:* Man of La Mancha (exc); *Bernstein:* West Side Story (exc); *Strouse:* Annie (exc); Bye Bye Birdie (exc); *M. Willson:* Music Man (exc); *F. Loesser:* Guys and Dolls (exc); *C-M. Schönberg:* Misérables (exc); *Rodgers:* Sound of Music (exc); South Pacific (exc); *Porter:* Gay Divorce (exc); *Cy Coleman:* Sweet Charity (exc). (Empire Brass Qnt)

CD80305 (1/94) **CS30305** (1/94)
Classical Brass II - On the Edge
Khachaturian: Gayaneh (exc); *Saint-Saëns:* Samson et Dalila (exc); *Bizet:* Arlésienne Suites (exc); Carmen (exc); *Shostakovich:* Festive Overture; *Ippolitov-Ivanov:* Caucasian Sketches (exc); *Fauré:* Requiem (exc); *Enescu:* Romanian Rhapsodies, Op. 11 (exc); *Prokofiev:* Love for 3 Oranges (exc); *Janáček:* Sinfonietta (exc); *Glière:* Red Poppy (exc); *Stravinsky:* Firebird (exc); *Bernstein:* Candide (1988) (exc); *Copland:* Rodeo (exc); *Offenbach:* Orphée aux enfers (exc). (Empire Brass)

CD80317
Falla—La Vida Breve
Falla: Vida breve (Cpte). (A. Nafé, A. Ordóñez, K. Notare, C. Keen, M. Wadsworth, M. Cid, W. McGraw, G. Moreno, M. May Fest Chor, Cincinnati SO/J. López-Cobos)

CD80334 (11/94)
Rossini—Overtures
Rossini: Guillaume Tell (exc); Gazza ladra (exc); Italiana in Algeri (exc); Semiramide (exc); Tancredi (exc); Barbiere di Siviglia (exc); Scala di seta (exc). (Atlanta SO/Y. Levi)

CD80345
Mozart—Die Zauberflöte
Mozart: Zauberflöte (exc). (B. Hendricks, J. Hadley, T. Allen, R. Lloyd, J. Anderson, U. Steinsky, G. Hornik, P. Svensson, H. Wildhaber, P.M. Schnitzer, G. Sima, J. Bernheimer, D. Ison, N. Watts, J. Dawson, A. Miles, Scottish Chbr Chor, Scottish CO/C. Mackerras)

CD80353 (11/93) **CS30353** (11/93)
Sullivan—The Pirates of Penzance
Sullivan: Pirates of Penzance (Cpte). (D. Adams, J.M. Ainsley, R. Suart, R. Evans, N. Folwell, R. van Allan, G. Knight, J. Williams, J. Gossage, WNO Chor, WNO Orch/C. Mackerras)

CD80360 (4/94)
Mozart—Così fan tutte
Mozart: Così fan tutte (Cpte). (F. Lott, M. McLaughlin, N. Focile, J. Hadley, A. Corbelli, G. Cachemaille, Edinburgh Fest Chor, Scottish CO/C. Mackerras)

CD80364 **CS30364**
Verdi without Words
Verdi: Aida (exc); Otello (exc); Trovatore (exc); Traviata (exc); Rigoletto (exc); Falstaff (exc); Nabucco (exc). (Cincinnati Pops/E. Kunzel)

CD80371
R. Strauss—Der Rosenkavalier Suite, etc
R. Strauss: Salome; Rosenkavalier (exc); Burleske; Festliches Präludium. (J. Kahane, M. Chertok, Cincinnati SO/J. López-Cobos)

⌽ **CD80374** (1/95)
Sullivan—HMS Pinafore
Sullivan: HMS Pinafore (Cpte). (R. Suart, F. Palmer, R. Evans, T. Allen, M. Schade, D. Adams, V. Seymour, R. Van Allan, J. King, P. Lloyd-Evans, WNO Chor, WNO Orch/C. Mackerras)

⌽ **CD80378**
Russian Sketches
Glinka: Ruslan and Lyudmila (exc); *Ippolitov-Ivanov:* Caucasian Sketches; *Rimsky-Korsakov:* Russian Easter Festival Ov; *Tchaikovsky:* Francesca da Rimini; Eugene Onegin (exc). (Baltimore SO/D. Zinman)

⌽ **CD80379**
Wagner—Overtures in Surround Sound
Wagner: Meistersinger (exc); Rienzi (exc); Faust Overture; Fliegende Holländer (exc); Tristan und Isolde (exc); Tannhäuser (exc). (Cincinnati SO/J. López-Cobos)

⌽ **CD80388** (8/95)
Mozart—Le Nozze di Figaro
Mozart: Nozze di Figaro (Cpte). (A. Miles, N. Focile, A. Corbelli, C. Vaness, S. Mentzer, S. Murphy, A. Antoniozzi, R. Davies, R. Evans, Scottish Chbr Chor, Scottish CO/C. Mackerras)

⌽ **CD80391**
Autumn Songs
R. Strauss: Stimmungsbilder (exc); *Schumann:* Romanzen, Op.28 (exc); *Debussy:* Préludes (exc); Children's Corner (exc); *Bach:* Wohltemperierte Klavier (exc); *Chopin:* Nocturnes (exc); *Schumann:* Fantasiestücke, Op.12 (exc); *Mozart:* Piano Sonata, K545 (exc); *Grieg:* Piano Sonata, Op. 7 (exc); *Rubinstein:* Melodies, Op.3 (exc); *Tchaikovsky:* Seasons (exc); *Mendelssohn:* Songs without Words (exc); *Daquin:* Premier livre de pièces de clavecin (exc); *Chopin:* Waltzes (exc); *Rimsky-Korsakov:* Tale of Tsar Saltan (exc); *Durand:* Waltz in E flat; *Rachmaninov:* Preludes (exc); *Liszt:* Consolations, S172 (exc); *Gershwin:* Preludes (exc). (J. O'Conor)

⌽ **CD80399**
Mozart—Così fan tutte—Highlights
Mozart: Così fan tutte (exc). (F. Lott, M. McLaughlin, N. Focile, J. Hadley, A. Corbelli, G. Cachemaille, Edinburgh Fest Chor, Scottish CO/C. Mackerras)

⌽ **CD80401**
The Very Best of Erich Kunzel
C. Palmer: Round-Up; *Various:* 2001 (exc); *Goldsmith:* Star Trek (exc); *Prima:* Sing, sing, sing; *Steiner:* Gone with the wind (exc); *A. North:* Unchained (exc); *Puccini:* Turandot (exc); *Bach:* Fugue, BWV578; *J. T. Williams:* Star Wars (exc); *Elfman:* Batman (exc); *Grofé:* Grand Canyon Suite (exc); *Barry:* From Russia With Love (exc); *J. T. Williams:* Olympic Fanfare (1984); *A. Lloyd Webber:* Phantom of the Opera (exc); *Rota:* Godfather (exc); *Mancini:* Pink Panther (exc); *Puccini:* Gianni Schicchi (exc); *E. Strauss:* Ohne Aufenthalt, Op. 112; *Traditional:* Honor, honor; Do Lord; *Fiedel:* Terminator (exc). (F. Laine, R. Leech, Central St Uni Chor, Cincinnati Pops/E. Kunzel)

⌽ **CD80407**
Divine Sopranos
Haydn: Creation (exc); *Rachmaninov:* Songs, Op. 34 (exc); *Fauré:* Requiem (exc); *Berlioz:* Nuits d'été (exc); *Brahms:* Deutsches Requiem, Op. 45 (exc); *Orff:* Carmina Burana (exc); *Vivaldi:* Gloria, RV589 (exc); *Handel:* Messiah (exc); *R. Strauss:* Vier letzte Lieder (exc); *Mozart:* Zauberflöte (exc); *Catalani:* Wally (exc); *Rodgers:* Sound of Music (exc); *Sullivan:* Mikado (exc); *Mahler:* Symphony 2 (exc). (D. Upshaw, S. McNair, J. Blegen, E. Ameling, A. Auger, P. Jensen, B. Hendricks, D. Soviero, F. von Stade, M. McLaughlin, K. Battle, Atlanta Sym Chbr Chor, Atlanta SO/Robert Shaw, Baltimore SO/D. Zinman, VPO/A. Previn, Scottish CO/C. Mackerras, Cincinnati Pops/E. Kunzel, WNO Chor, WNO Orch, St Louis Sym Chor, St Louis SO/L. Slatkin)

⌽ **CD80411**
The Artistry of Fernando de la Mora
Gounod: Roméo et Juliette (exc); Faust (exc); *Verdi:* Traviata (exc); Rigoletto (exc); *Puccini:* Bohème (exc); Tosca (exc); *Cilea:* Arlesiana (exc); *Bizet:* Carmen (exc); Pêcheurs de Perles (exc); *Donizetti:* Fille du régiment (exc); *Ponchielli:* Gioconda (exc); *Massenet:* Werther (exc); *Giordano:* Fedora (exc). (F. de la Mora, WNO Orch/C. Mackerras)

⌽ **CD82005** (2/94)
Wagner—Orchestral Music from Operas
Wagner: Meistersinger (exc); Götterdämmerung (exc); Rienzi (exc); Fliegende Holländer (exc). (Minnesota Orch/N. Marriner)

⌽ **ECHOCD2**
Absolute Heaven
Boito: Mefistofele (exc); *Poulenc:* Mass in G (exc); *Mozart:* Mass, K427 (exc); *Beethoven:* Christus am Oelberge, Op. 85 (exc); *Rachmaninov:* Vespers, Op. 37 (exc); *Duruflé:* Requiem (exc); *Dvořák:* Te Deum (exc); *Vivaldi:* Gloria, RV589 (exc); *Bach:* Magnificat, BWV243 (exc); *Fauré:* Requiem (exc); *Verdi:* Requiem (exc); *Mascagni:* Cavalleria Rusticana (exc); *Schubert:* Mass, D167 (exc); *Berlioz:* Grande messe des morts (exc); *Mahler:* Symphony 8 (exc). (D. Carter, E. Wiens, J. Blegen, S. Dunn, C. Brewer, D. Upshaw, H. Grant, D. Gordon, M. Sylvester, W. Stone, J. Cheek, Morehouse-Spelman Chor, Morehouse-Spelman Chor, R. Shaw Fest Sngrs, Atlanta Sym Chor, Atlanta Sym Chbr Chor, Ohio State Univ Chorale, Ohio State Univ Sym Ch, S Florida Univ Chor, Tampa Bay Master Chorale, Atlanta Boy Ch, Atlanta SO/Robert Shaw)

Teldec

⌽ **0630-11470-2**
The Best of Barbara Bonney
Schubert: Ave Maria, D839; Nur wer die Sehnsucht kennt, D877/4; *Mozart:* Exsultate jubilate, K165; Don Giovanni (exc); Nozze di Figaro (exc); Zauberflöte (exc); *Schubert:* Kennst du das Land, D321; *Mozart:* Veilchen, K476; *Wolf:* Italienisches Liederbuch (exc); *Mendelssohn:* Lieder, Op. 34 (exc); Symphony 2 (exc); *Fauré:* Requiem (exc); *Bach:* Cantata 199 (exc); *Haydn:* Stabat Mater (exc); *J. Strauss II:* Fledermaus (exc). (B. Bonney, E. Wiens, E. von Magnus, C. Boesch, G. Parsons, Leipzig Rad Chor, Leipzig Gewandhaus, Philh, VCM, Concertgebouw, Zurich Op Orch/K. Masur/M. Legrand/N. Harnoncourt)

⌽ **2292-42494-2** (7/85)
Monteverdi—Orfeo
Monteverdi: Orfeo (Cpte). (L. Kozma, R. Hansmann, C. Berberian, E. Katanosaka, N. Simkowsky, J. Villisech, M. van Egmond, G. Theuring, N. Rogers, K. Equiluz, VCM/N. Harnoncourt)

⌽ **2292-42496-2**
Monteverdi—Il ritorno d'Ulisse in Patria
Monteverdi: Ritorno d'Ulisse in Patria (Cpte). (S.O. Eliasson, L. Anderko, N. Simkowsky, R. Hansmann, M. Baker-Genovesi, N. Lerer, K. Hansen, W. Wyatt, K. Equiluz, P. Esswood, N. Rogers, M. van Egmond, M. Dickie, A-M. Mühle, Junge Kantorei, VCM/N. Harnoncourt)

⌽ **2292-42510-2**
Rameau—Castor et Pollux
Rameau: Castor et Pollux (Cpte). (Z. Vandersteene, G. Souzay, J. Scovotti, M. Schéle, R. Leanderson, N. Lerer, J. Villisech, H. Reiter, S-E. Alexandersson, Stockholm Chbr Ch, VCM/N. Harnoncourt)

⌽ **2292-42547-2**
Monteverdi—L'Incoronazione di Poppea
Monteverdi: Incoronazione di Poppea (Cpte). (H. Donath, E. Söderström, C. Berberian, P. Esswood, G. Luccardi, R. Hansmann, J. Gartner, M. Minetto, C. Gaifa, P. Langridge, E. Fissore, Anon, Margaret Baker, VCM/N. Harnoncourt)

⌽ **2292-42600-2** (3/86)
Mozart—Idomeneo
Mozart: Idomeneo (Cpte). (W. Hollweg, T. Schmidt, R. Yakar, F. Palmer, K. Equiluz, R. Tear, S. Estes, Zurich Op Hse Chor, Zurich Op Hse Mozart Orch/N. Harnoncourt)

⌽ **2292-42643-2** (5/88)
Mozart—Die Entführung aus dem Serail
Mozart: Entführung (Cpte). (Y. Kenny, L. Watson, P. Schreier, W. Gamlich, M. Salminen, W. Reichmann, Zurich Op. Hse Chor, Zurich Op Hse Mozart Orch/N. Harnoncourt)

⌽ **2292-42716-2** (7/89)
Mozart—The Magic Flute
Mozart: Zauberflöte (Cpte). (B. Bonney, E. Gruberová, H-P. Blochwitz, A. Scharinger, M. Salminen, T. Hampson, P. Keller, E. Schmid, P. Coburn, D. Ziegler, M. Lipovšek, S. Gienger, M. Baur, A. Fischer, T. Moser, A. Suhonen, A. Maly, W. Kmentt, Vienna Singverein, G. Jesserer, Zurich Op Hse Chor, Zurich Op Orch/N. Harnoncourt)

⌽ **2292-44184-2** (3/90)
Mozart—Don Giovanni
Mozart: Don Giovanni (Cpte). (T. Hampson, E. Gruberová, R. Alexander, B. Bonney, H-P. Blochwitz, L. Polgár, A. Scharinger, R. Holl, Netherlands Op Chor, Concertgebouw/N. Harnoncourt)

⌽ **2292-44928-2** (3/91)
Mozart: Lucio Silla
Mozart: Lucio Silla (Cpte). (P. Schreier, E. Gruberová, C. Bartoli, Y. Kenny, D. Upshaw, A. Schoenberg Ch, VCM/N. Harnoncourt)

⌽ **2292-46015-2** (4/92)
Brodsky Unlimited - Encores
Copland: Rodeo (exc); *Elgar:* Chanson de matin; *D. Brubeck:* Strange Meadow Lark; Raggy Waltz; *Debussy:* Children's Corner (exc); Préludes (exc); *Falla:* Amor Brujo (exc); Vida breve (exc); *Gershwin:* Porgy and Bess (exc); *Traditional:* Nanatsu-no-ko; *Shostakovich:* Preludes, Op. 34 (exc); *Prokofiev:* Symphony 1 (exc); Music for Children (exc); *Ravel:* Ma mère l'oye (exc); *M. Thomas:* Cabo de Gata. (Brodsky Qt)

⊙ **2292-46336-1** ▭ **2292-46336-4** (12/91)
Meeting Venus—soundtrack
Wagner: Tannhäuser (exc); *Schumann:* Myrthen, Op. 25 (exc). (K. Te Kanawa, R. Kollo, H. Hagegård, W. Meier, Ambrosian Sngrs, Philh/M. Janowski, R. Vignoles)

OO **2292-46336-5**
Meeting Venus—soundtrack
Wagner: Tannhäuser (exc); *Schumann:* Myrthen, Op. 25 (exc). (K. Te Kanawa, R. Kollo, H. Hagegård, W. Meier, Ambrosian Sngrs, Philh/M. Janowski, R. Vignoles)

⌽ **4509-90055-2**
Sensual Classics
Rachmaninov: Piano Concerto 2 (exc); *Bizet:* Carmen (exc); *Vivaldi:* Concerto, RV425 (exc); *Borodin:* String Quartet 2 (exc); *Beethoven:* Piano Sonata 14 (exc); *Albinoni:* Concerti, Op. 9 (exc); *Khachaturian:* Spartacus Suite 2 (exc); *Ravel:* Daphnis et Chloé Suites (exc); *Mahler:* Symphony 5 (exc); *Saint-Saëns:* Carnaval des animaux (exc); *Rachmaninov:* Symphony 2 (exc); *Chopin:* Preludes (exc); *Stravinsky:* Berceuse; *Schumann:* Kinderszenen (exc); *Ravel:* Boléro; *Bach:* Suites, BWV1066-9 (exc). (A. Sultanov, LSO/M. Shostakovich, FNO/L. Maazel, U. Orlandi, Solisti Veneti/C. Scimone, Brodsky Qt, R. Buchbinder, J. Chambon, Saarland Rad CO/K. Ristenpart, Monte Carlo PO/L. Foster, Cleveland Orch/C. von Dohnányi, NYPO/Z. Mehta, G. Pekinel, S. Pekinel, French Rad PO/M. Janowski, Philh/K. Sanderling, S. Grützmann/E. Inbal, C. Katsaris, F. Liszt CO)

⌽ **4509-90799-2** (10/93)
Rossi—Le Canterine Romane
Rossi: Disperate speranza a 3; Piango, prego a 3; Infelice pensier a 2; Luigi Passacaille; Palazzo incantato (exc); Occhi belli a 2; Sarabanda; Balletto; Noi siam tre donzellette a 3; Ai sospiri a 2; Arie di passacaglia; Speranza al tuo pallore a 2; Poi che mancò speranza; Fan battaglia a 3. (Tragicomedia)

⌽ **4509-90845-2** (1/94)
Delius—Orchestral Works
Delius: Brigg Fair; In a Summer Garden; Paris; First cuckoo; Summer Night on the River; Village Romeo and Juliet (exc). (BBC SO/A. Davis)

⌽ **4509-90851-2** (11/93)
Verdi—Rigoletto
Verdi: Rigoletto (Cpte). (A. Agache, L. Vaduva, R. Leech, S. Ramey, J. Larmore, A. Miles, P. Bardon, B. Banks, P. Sidhom, R. Evans, G. Moses, P. Bradbury, F. Visentin, WNO Chor, WNO Orch/C. Rizzi)

⌽ **4509-90857-2** (5/94)
Mozart—La Clemenza di Tito
Mozart: Clemenza di Tito (Cpte). (P. Langridge, L. Popp, A. Murray, D. Ziegler, R. Ziesak, L. Polgár, Zurich Op Hse Chor, Zurich Op Orch/N. Harnoncourt)

⌽ **4509-90861-2** (10/94)
Mozart—Le Nozze di Figaro
Mozart: Nozze di Figaro (Cpte). (A. Scharinger, B. Bonney, T. Hampson, C. Margiono, P. Lang, A. Murray, K. Moll, P. Langridge, C. Späth, K. Langan, I. Rey, Netherlands Op Chor, Concertgebouw/N. Harnoncourt)

⌽ **4509-90865-2**
So in Love - Samuel Ramey on Broadway
Gershwin: Porgy and Bess (exc); *B. Lane:* On a clear Day (exc); *F. Loewe:* Camelot (exc); *B. Lane:* Finian's Rainbow (exc); *F. Loewe:* Gigi (exc); *Weill:* Lost in the Stars (exc); *Porter:* Kiss me Kate (exc); *Sondheim:* Sweeney Todd (exc); *Porter:* Gay Divorce (exc); *Bernstein:* On the Town (exc); *Strouse:* All American (exc); *M. Leigh:* Man Of La Mancha (exc); *A. Lloyd Webber:* Phantom of the Opera (exc); *F. loesser:* Most Happy Fella (exc); *F. Loewe:* My Fair Lady (exc); *Kern:* Show Boat (exc). (S. Ramey, London Studio SO/E. Stratta, M. Renzi)

⌽ **4509-90872-2** (7/94)
Gounod—Faust
Gounod: Faust (Cpte). (J. Hadley, C. Gasdia, S. Ramey, A. Agache, S. Mentzer, B. Fassbaender, P. Fourcade, WNO Chor, WNO Orch/C. Rizzi)

⌽ **4509-91181-2**
Lettera Amorosa
Monteverdi: Madrigals, Bk 7 (exc); *Kapsperger:* Lute Book

Lara: Granada; *De Curtis:* Non ti scordar di me; Tu, ca nun chiagne!; *Leoncavallo:* Pagliacci (exc); *Puccini:* Turandot (exc); *Verdi:* Rigoletto (exc); Traviata (exc); *Schifrin:* Tribute to Hollywood; Around the World. (J. Carreras, P. Domingo, L. Pavarotti, Los Angeles Music Center Op Chor, Los Angeles PO/Z. Mehta)

4509-96200-5
The Three Tenors 1994
Massenet: Cid (exc); *Moreno Torroba:* Maravilla (exc); *Massenet:* Werther (exc); *Rodgers:* Spring is Here (exc); *Lara:* Granada; *De Curtis:* Non ti scordar di me; Tu, ca nun chiagne!; *Leoncavallo:* Pagliacci (exc); *Puccini:* Turandot (exc); *Verdi:* Rigoletto (exc); Traviata (exc); *Schifrin:* Tribute to Hollywood; Around the World. (J. Carreras, P. Domingo, L. Pavarotti, Los Angeles Music Center Op Chor, Los Angeles PO/Z. Mehta)

4509-96200-8
The Three Tenors 1994
Massenet: Cid (exc); *Moreno Torroba:* Maravilla (exc); *Massenet:* Werther (exc); *Rodgers:* Spring is Here (exc); *Lara:* Granada; *De Curtis:* Non ti scordar di me; Tu, ca nun chiagne!; *Leoncavallo:* Pagliacci (exc); *Puccini:* Turandot (exc); *Verdi:* Rigoletto (exc); Traviata (exc); *Schifrin:* Tribute to Hollywood; Around the World. (J. Carreras, P. Domingo, L. Pavarotti, Los Angeles Music Center Op Chor, Los Angeles PO/Z. Mehta)

4509-96231-2 **4509-96231-4**
Gardening Classics
Bach: Cantata 211 (exc); *Beethoven:* Violin Sonata 5 (exc); *Cilea:* Adriana Lecouvreur (exc); *Copland:* Rodeo (exc); *Delius:* Village Romeo and Juliet (exc); First cuckoo; *Gershwin:* Porgy and Bess (exc); *Mendelssohn:* Lieder, Op. 34 (exc); *Respighi:* Birds (exc); *Rimsky-Korsakov:* Tale of Tsar Saltan (exc); *Schumann:* Myrthen, Op. 25 (exc); *Tárrega:* Recuerdos de la Alhambra; *Tchaikovsky:* Nutcracker (exc); *Vaughan Williams:* Lark ascending; *Vivaldi:* Concerti, Op. 8 (exc). (Solisti Veneti/C. Scimone, M. Vengerov, I. Golan, P. Domingo, Berlin Deutsche Op Orch/N. Santi, BBC SO/A. Davis, Bolshoi SO/A. Lazarev, R. Alexander, NYPO/Z. Mehta, S. Nakarjakov, A. Markovich, B. Bonney, G. Parsons, COE, M. Blankestijn (vn/dir), K. Te Kanawa, R. Vignoles, T. Little, W. Lendle, Brodsky Qt, R. Hansmann, VCM/N. Harnoncourt)

4509-96800-2
Jennifer Larmore—Where Shall I Fly?
Mozart: Clemenza di Tito (exc); Così fan tutte (exc); Finta giardiniera (exc); Finta semplice (exc); Mitridate (exc); Nozze di Figaro (exc); *Handel:* Ariodante (exc); Rinaldo (exc); Serse (exc); Semele (exc); Hercules (exc). (J. Larmore, Lausanne CO/J. López-Cobos)

4509-97304-2 (10/95)
Nono—Intolleranza 1960
Nono: Intolleranza 1960 (Cpte). (D. Rampy, U. Koszut, K. Harries, J. van der Schaaf, W. Probst, J. Dieken, C. Hoening, C. Otto, H. Wenning, Stuttgart Op Chor, Stuttgart Op Orch/B. Kontarsky)

4509-97444-2
Gershwin—Orchestral Works
Gershwin: American in Paris; Cuban Overture; Porgy and Bess (exc). (R. Alexander, Gregg Baker, NY Choral Artists, NYPO/Z. Mehta)

4509-97463-2
A Portrait of Thomas Hampson-Arias and Songs
Bach: Cantata 194 (exc); *Handel:* Apollo e Dafne (exc); *Mozart:* Nozze di Figaro (exc); *Puccini:* Bohème (exc); *Bizet:* Pêcheurs de Perles (exc); *Mendelssohn:* Erste Walpurgisnacht (exc); *Fauré:* Requiem (exc); *Loewe:* Balladen, Op. 2 (exc); *Mendelssohn:* Lieder, Op. 84 (exc); *Schumann:* Lieder, Op. 40 (exc); *Brahms:* Lieder, Op. 49 (exc); *Mahler:* Lieder eines fahrenden Gesellen (exc); Knaben Wunderhorn (exc); Lieder und Gesänge (exc); *MacDowell:* Lieder, Op. 12 (exc); *Griffes:* Meeres Stille; *Ives:* Du bist wie eine Blume; *Zemlinsky:* Bucklichte Männlein; *Copland:* Old American Songs 1 (exc). (T. Hampson, J. Hadley, G. Parsons, D. Lutz, A. Guzelimian, VCM, Concertgebouw, WNO Orch, COE, Philh, St Paul CO/N. Harnoncourt/C. Rizzi/M. Legrand/L. Berio/A. Wolff)

4509-97505-2
Mozart—Famous Opera Choruses
Mozart: Idomeneo (exc); Entführung (exc); Nozze di Figaro (exc); Zauberflöte (exc); Così fan tutte (exc); Clemenza di Tito (exc); Thamos, K345 (exc); Lucio Silla (exc). (M. Salminen, Zurich Op Hse Chor, Zurich Op Hse Mozart Orch, Netherlands Op Chor, Concertgebouw, Collegium Vocale, Netherlands Chbr Ch, A. Schoenberg Ch, VCM/N. Harnoncourt, Zurich Op Orch)

4509-97507-2
Mozart—Famous Opera Arias
Mozart: Don Giovanni (exc); Nozze di Figaro (exc); Zauberflöte (exc); Così fan tutte (exc); Entführung (exc); Idomeneo (exc); Clemenza di Tito (exc); Lucio Silla (exc). (E. Gruberová, B. Bonney, C. Margiono, Y. Kenny, L. Popp, P. Lang, C. Bartoli, A. Murray, H-P. Blochwitz, D. van der Walt, W. Hollweg, P. Langridge, T. Hampson, A. Scharinger, Concertgebouw, Zurich Op Orch, Zurich Op Hse Mozart Orch, VCM/N. Harnoncourt)

4509-97508-2
Verdi—Rigoletto - Highlights
Verdi: Rigoletto (exc). (A. Agache, R. Leech, L. Vaduva, J. Larmore, S. Ramey, WNO Chor, WNO Orch/C. Rizzi)

4509-97684-2
Purcell—The Fairy Queen
Purcell: Fairy Queen, Z629 (Cpte). (B. Bonney, E. von Magnus, S. McNair, M. Chance, L. Dale, R. Hall, A. Michaels-Moore, A. Schoenberg Ch, VCM/N. Harnoncourt)

4509-97868-2 (2/95) **4509-97868-4** (2/95)
The Last Night of the Proms 1994
Bach: Toccata and Fugue, BWV565; *Walton:* Belshazzar's Feast; *Miki:* Marimba spiritual; *Massenet:* Thaïs (exc); *Elgar:* Pomp and Circumstance Marches (exc); *Henry Wood:* Sea-Song Fantasia; *Arne:* Rule Britannia; *Parry:* Jerusalem. (B. Terfel, E. Glennie, BBC Sngrs, BBC Sym Chor, BBC SO/A. Davis)

4509-97906-2
Wagner-Das Rheingold-Highlights
Wagner: Rheingold (exc). (E. Johansson, H. Leidland, L. Finnie, B. Svendén, A. Küttenbaum, J. Turner, G. Clark, H. Pampuch, K. Schreibmayer, G. von Kannen, B. Brinkmann, P. Kang, J. Tomlinson, M. Hölle, Bayreuth Fest Orch/D. Barenboim)

4509-97907-2
Wagner—Die Walküre-Highlights
Wagner: Walküre (exc). (N. Secunde, Anne Evans, E. Johansson, E-M. Bundschuh, R. Floeren, L. Finnie, S. Close, H. Dijkstra, B. Svendén, H. Katagiri, P. Elming, J. Tomlinson, M. Hölle, Bayreuth Fest Orch/D. Barenboim)

4509-97908-2
Wagner—Siegfried-Highlights
Wagner: Siegfried (exc). (Anne Evans, H. Leidland, B. Svendén, S. Jerusalem, G. Clark, G. von Kannen, P. Kang, J. Tomlinson, Bayreuth Fest Orch/D. Barenboim)

4509-97909-2
Wagner—Götterdämmerung-Highlights
Wagner: Götterdämmerung (exc). (Anne Evans, E-M. Bundschuh, H. Leidland, W. Meier, A. Küttenbaum, J. Turner, B. Svendén, L. Finnie, U. Priew, S. Jerusalem, P. Kang, G. von Kannen, B. Brinkmann, Bayreuth Fest Chor, Bayreuth Fest Orch/D. Barenboim)

4509-98645-2
Handel—Apollo e Dafne; Giulio Cesare - excerpts
Handel: Apollo e Dafne; Giulio Cesare (exc). (R. Alexander, T. Hampson, VCM/N. Harnoncourt)

4509-98824-2
Thomas Hampson Collection,Vol III-Operatic Scenes
Puccini: Bohème (exc); *Bizet:* Pêcheurs de Perles (exc); *Donizetti:* Elisir d'amore (exc); *Verdi:* Vespri Siciliani (exc); Don Carlos (exc); *Mozart:* Così fan tutte (exc); Don Giovanni (exc); Nozze di Figaro (exc); Don Giovanni (exc). (T. Hampson, J. Hadley, WNO Orch/C. Rizzi, L. Polgár, R. Holl, Netherlands Op Chor, C. Margiono, D. Ziegler, B. Bonney, Concertgebouw/N. Harnoncourt)

9031-71381-2 (11/91)
Mozart—Così fan Tutte
Mozart: Così fan tutte (Cpte). (C. Margiono, D. Ziegler, A. Steiger, D. van der Walt, G. Cachemaille, T. Hampson, Netherlands Op Chor, Concertgebouw/N. Harnoncourt)

9031-72306-2 (11/92)
Donizetti—Lucia di Lammermoor
Donizetti: Lucia di Lammermoor (Cpte). (E. Gruberová, N. Shicoff, A. Agache, A. Miles, D. Montague, B. Lombardo, F. Piccoli, Ambrosian Sngrs, LSO/R. Bonynge)

9031-72309-2 (3/93)
Mozart—La finta giardiniera
Mozart: Finta Giardiniera (Cpte). (E. Gruberová, T. Moser, U. Heilmann, C. Margiono, M. Bacelli, D. Upshaw, A. Scharinger, VCM/N. Harnoncourt)

9031-73242-2
Rossini—Arias
Rossini: Viaggio a Reims (exc); Stabat Mater (exc); Cenerentola (exc); Alla voce della gloria; Semiramide (exc); Italiana in Algeri (exc). (S. Ramey, WNO Chor, WNO Orch/G. Ferro)

9031-73283-2 (11/93)
Hampson and Hadley
Puccini: Bohème (exc); *Donizetti:* Belisario (exc); Elisir d'amore (exc); Lucia di Lammermoor (exc); *Verdi:* Vespri siciliani (exc); Don Carlos (exc); *Bizet:* Pêcheurs de perles (exc); *Meyerbeer:* Dinorah (exc); *J. Strauss II:* Fledermaus (exc). (J. Hadley, T. Hampson, WNO Orch/C. Rizzi)

9031-74448-2 (10/91)
Wagner—Parsifal
Wagner: Parsifal (Cpte). (S. Jerusalem, J. Van Dam, M. Hölle, W. Meier, G. von Kannen, J. Tomlinson, K. Schreibmayer, C. Hauptmann, M. Rørholm, A. Küttenbaum, H. Pampuch, P. Maus, E. Wiens, C. Hauman, D. Bechly, H. Leidland, P. Coburn, S. Burgess, W. Meier, Berlin St Op Chor, BPO/D. Barenboim)

9031-74785-2
Schubert/Mozart—Orchestral Works
Schubert: Symphony 8; Rosamunde (exc); *Mozart:* Lucio Silla (exc). (Vienna SO, Concertgebouw/N. Harnoncourt)

9031-74786-2 (12/92)
Johann Strauss II—Orchestral Works
J. Strauss II: Zigeunerbaron (exc); Kreuzfidel, Op.301; Leichtes Blut, Op. 319; G'schichten aus dem Wienerwald, Op. 325; Egyptischer Marsch, Op. 335; Wiener Bonbons; Pizzicato Polka; Unter Donner und Blitz; Blauen Donau, Op. 314; Fledermaus (exc). (Concertgebouw/N. Harnoncourt)

9031-74789-2
Canon and Gigue—Popular Classics
Albinoni: Adagio; *Bach:* Suites, BWV1066-9 (exc); *Boccherini:* String Quintets, G271-6 (exc); *Pachelbel:* Canon and Gigue; *Handel:* Serse (exc); *Haydn:* Divertimento, HobII/11; *Gluck:* Orfeo ed Euridice (exc); *Hoffstetter:* String Quartets, Op. 3 (exc); *M. Haydn:* Horn Concerto, MH53. (D. Clevenger, F Liszt CO, J. Rolla (vn/dir))

9031-74885-2 (11/93)
Rossini—Il barbiere di Siviglia
Rossini: Barbiere di Siviglia (Cpte). (H. Hagegård, J. Larmore, R. Giménez, A. Corbelli, S. Ramey, B. Frittoli, U. Malmberg, Geneva Grand Th Chor, Lausanne CO/J. López-Cobos)

9031-76047-2 (8/93)
Wagner—Parsifal
Wagner: Parsifal (Cpte). (W. Windgassen, G. London, L. Weber, M. Mödl, H. Uhde, A. Van Mill, W. Fritz, W. Faulhaber, H. Ludwig, E. Wild, G. Baldauf, G. Stolze, H. Schünemann, E. Zimmermann, P. Brivkalne, M. Lacorn, R. Siewert, Bayreuth Fest Chor, Bayreuth Fest Orch/H. Knappertsbusch)

9031-76348-2 (2/93)
Verdi—La Traviata
Verdi: Traviata (Cpte). (E. Gruberová, N. Shicoff, G. Zancanaro, P. Spence, M. Bacelli, K. Begley, P. Sidhom, D. Barrell, A. Miles, P. Bronder, N. Folwell, F. Visentin, Ambrosian Sngrs, LSO/C. Rizzi)

9031-76435-2
Furtwängler conducts Orchestral Works
Bruckner: Symphony 7 (exc); *Gluck:* Alceste (1776) (exc); *Beethoven:* String Quartet 13 (exc). (BPO/W. Furtwängler)

9031-76437-2
Verdi—Falstaff & Otello excerpts
Verdi: Falstaff (exc); Otello (exc). (G. Cigna, V. Palombini, A. Pertile, G. Nessi, M. Stabile, A. Poli, L. Donaggio, La Scala Chor, La Scala Orch/A. Erede)

9031-76442-2 (8/93)
Wagner—Excerpts from the 1936 Bayreuth Festival
Wagner: Lohengrin (exc); Walküre (exc); Siegfried (exc). (M. Müller, M. Klose, F. Völker, M. Lorenz, E. Zimmermann, J. Prohaska, J. von Manowarda, Bayreuth Fest Chor, Bayreuth Fest Orch/H. Tietjen)

9031-76444-2
Jochum conducts Beethoven & Wagner
Beethoven: Symphony 3; *Wagner:* Tannhäuser (exc). (BPO/E. Jochum)

9031-76455-2
Mozart—Così fan Tutte (Highlights)
Mozart: Così fan tutte (exc). (C. Margiono, D. Ziegler, G. Cachemaille, D. van der Walt, A. Steiger, T. Hampson, Netherlands Op Chor, Concertgebouw/N. Harnoncourt)

9031-76456-2 (5/93)
Tchaikovsky—Orchestral Works
Tchaikovsky: Romeo and Juliet; Francesca da Rimini; Mazeppa (exc); Festival Coronation March. (Leipzig Gewandhaus/K. Masur)

9031-77705-2 (5/93)
Works for Trumpet & Piano
Gershwin: Rhapsody in Blue; *Arensky:* Concert Waltz; *Arban:* Carnaval de Venise; *Ravel:* Pavane; *Bernstein:* Rondo for Lifey; *Glazunov:* Album leaf; *Fibich:* At twilight

(exc); *Rimsky-Korsakov:* Tale of Tsar Saltan (exc); *Dinicu:* Hora staccato; *Glière:* Waltz, Op. 48/2; *Rueff:* Trumpet Sonatina; *Stolte:* Burleske; *J.P.E. Hartmann:* Arbucklenian Polka. (S. Nakarjakov, A. Markovich)

TER Classics

CDTEO1001 **ZCTEO1001**
Golden Operetta Highlights: Bitter Sweet
Coward: Bitter Sweet (exc). (V. Masterson, R. Ashe, M. Smith, D. Maxwell, New Sadlers Wells Op Chor, New Sadlers Wells Op Orch/M. Reed)

CDTEO1003 **ZCTEO1003**
Golden Operetta Highlights: Merry Widow
Lehár: Lustige Witwe (exc). (E. Harrhy, H. Kucharek, J. Moyle, A. Oke, G. Winslade, P. Parfitt, M. Curtis, New Sadler's Wells Op Chor, New Sadler's Wells Op Orch/B. Wordsworth)

CDTEO1004 **ZCTEO1004**
Golden Operetta Highlights: Count of Luxembourg
Lehár: Graf von Luxemburg (exc). (M. Hill Smith, N. Jenkins, V. Tierney, H. Nicoll, L. Richard, New Sadler's Wells Op Chor, New Sadler's Wells Op Orch/B. Wordsworth)

CDTEO1005 **ZCTEO1005**
Golden Operetta Highlights: Student Prince
Romberg: Student Prince (exc). (D. Rendall, M. Hill Smith, N. Bailey, D. Montague, J. Howard, R. Ashe, N. Jenkins, D. Maxwell, B. Bottone, S. Page, Ambrosian Chor, Philh/J.O. Edwards)

CDTEO1006 **ZCTEO1006**
Golden Operetta Highlights: Candide
Bernstein: Candide (1988) (exc). (N. Grace, M. Beudert, M. Hill Smith, A. Howard, M. Tinkler, B. Bottone, Scottish Op Chor, Scottish Op Orch/J. Brown)

CDTEO1007 **ZCTEO1007**
Golden Operetta Highlights: Countess Maritza
Kálmán: Gräfin Mariza (exc). (M. Hill Smith, R. Remedios, L. Barber, T. Davies, L. Livingstone, J. Moyle, New Sadlers Wells Op Chor, New Sadlers Wells Op Orch/B. Wordsworth)

CDTEO1008 **ZCTEO1008**
Golden Operetta Highlights: Orpheus in the Underworld
Offenbach: Orphée aux enfers (exc). (B. Bottone, S. Burgess, S. Kale, L. Watson, ENO Chor, ENO Orch/M. Elder)

CDTER1050 **ZCTER1050** (1/84)
Lehár—Count of Luxembourg (excerpts)
Lehár: Graf von Luxemburg (exc). (M. Hill Smith, N. Jenkins, V. Tierney, H. Nicoll, L. Richard, New Sadler's Wells Op. Chor, New Sadler's Wells Op. Orch/B. Wordsworth)

CDTER1051 **ZCTER1051** (1/84)
Kálmán—Countess Maritza (highlights)
Kálmán: Gräfin Mariza (exc). (M. Hill Smith, R. Remedios, L. Barber, L. Livingstone, T. Davies, J. Moyle, New Sadler's Wells Op Chor, New Sadler's Wells Op Orch/B. Wordsworth)

CDTER1111 (12/86) **ZCTER1111** (12/86)
Lehar—The Merry Widow
Lehár: Lustige Witwe (exc). (E. Harrhy, H. Kucharek, J. Moyle, A. Oke, G. Winslade, P. Parfitt, M. Curtis, New Sadler's Wells Op. Chor, New Sadler's Wells Op. Orch/B. Wordsworth)

CDTER1121 (3/87) **ZCTER1121** (3/87)
Gilbert & Sullivan—The Mikado (Highlights)
Sullivan: Mikado (exc). (R. Angas, B. Bottone, E. Idle, R. Van Allan, M. Richardson, L. Garrett, J. Rigby, S. Bullock, F. Palmer, ENO Chor, ENO Orch/Peter Robinson)

CDTER1124 (7/88) **ZCTER1124** (7/88)
Menotti—Amahl and the Night Visitors
Menotti: Amahl and the Night Visitors (Cpte). (J. Rainbird, L. Haywood, J. Dobson, D. Maxwell, Curtis Watson, C. Painter, ROH Chor, ROHO, D. Syrus)

CDTER1125 **ZCTER1125**
Menotti—The Boy Who Grew Too Fast
Menotti: Boy who grew too fast (Cpte). (G. Godfrey, J. Howarth, M. Morelle, P. Crook, E. Garrett, E. Bainbridge, D. Wallder, A. Machell, T. Duffy, A. Plant, ROHO, D. Syrus)

CDTER1134 **ZCTER1134**
Offenbach—Orpheus in the Underworld
Offenbach: Orphée aux enfers (exc). (R. Angas, S. Squires, B. Bottone, C. Pope, E. Robinson, F. Kimm, S. Masterton-Smith, I. Morris, S. Burgess, S. Kale, L. Watson, E. Belcourt, E. Byles, G. Adams, ENO Chor, ENO Orch/M. Elder)

CDTER1156 (8/88) **ZCTER1156** (8/88)
Bernstein—Candide
Bernstein: Candide (1988) (exc). (N. Grace, M. Beudert, M. Hill Smith, A. Howard, M. Tinkler, G. Miles, B. Bottone, Scottish Op Chor, SNO/J. Brown)

CDTER2 1128 **ZCTED 1128** (9/87)
Gilbert & Sullivan—Ruddigore
Sullivan: Ruddigore (Cpte). (M. Hill Smith, G. Sandison, J. Davies, A. Hann, L. Ormiston, J. Ayldon, D. Hillman, H. Innocent, T. Lawlor, New Sadler's Wells Op Chor, New Sadler's Wells Op Orch/S. Phipps)

CDTER2 1150 (5/88) **ZCTED 1150** (5/88)
Sullivan—HMS Pinafore
Sullivan: HMS Pinafore (Cpte). (N. Grace, G. Sandison, C. Gillett, E. Ritchie, T. Lawlor, P. Parfitt, P. Thomson, J. Roebuck, L. Ormiston, New Sadler's Wells Op Chor, New Sadler's Wells Op Orch/S. Phipps)

CDTER2 1160 (11/89) **ZCTED 1160** (11/89)
Noël Coward—Bitter Sweet
Coward: Bitter Sweet (Cpte). (V. Masterson, M. Smith, R. Ashe, D. Maxwell, New Sadlers Wells Op Chor, New Sadlers Wells Op Orch/M. Reed)

CDTER2 1172 (3/91) **ZCTED 1172** (3/91)
Romberg—The Student Prince
Romberg: Student Prince (Cpte). (D. Rendall, M. Hill Smith, N. Bailey, D. Montague, J. Howard, R. Ashe, N. Jenkins, D. Maxwell, B. Bottone, Leon Greene, S. Page, A. Mutis, N. Colicos, S. Green, B. Rankin, R. Hart, R. Lock, M. Friedman, Ambrosian Chor, Philh/J.O. Edwards)

CDTER2 1177 (9/90) **ZCTED 1177** (9/90)
Gilbert & Sullivan—Pirates of Penzance
Sullivan: Pirates of Penzance (Cpte). (M. Rivers, P. Creasey, E. Roberts, M. Hill Smith, Gareth Jones, S. Masterton-Smith, S. Gorton, P. Birchall, P. Cameron, D'Oyly Carte Op Chor, D'Oyly Carte Op Orch/J. Pryce-Jones)

CDTER2 1178 (9/90) **ZCTED 1178** (9/90)
Sullivan—The Mikado
Sullivan: Mikado (Cpte). (M. Ducarel, B. Bottone, E. Roberts, M. Rivers, Gareth Jones, D. Rees, T. Ker, Y. Patrick, S. Gorton, D'Oyly Carte Op Chor, D'Oyly Carte Op Orch/J. Pryce-Jones)

CDTER2 1185 **ZCTER2 1185**
Weill—Street Scene
Weill: Street Scene (Cpte). (Kristine Ciesinski, R. Van Allan, J. Kelly, B. Bottone, F. Doria, J. Douglas, C. Daniels, Timothy Jenkins, M. Dickinson, A. Hickey, ENO Chor, ENO Orch/Carl Davis)

CDTER2 1187 (5/92) **ZCTED 1187** (5/92)
Gilbert & Sullivan—The Gondoliers
Sullivan: Gondoliers (Cpte); Di Ballo. (D. Fieldsend, A. Oke, L.E. Ross, R. Hanley, R. Suart, J. Pert, E. Woollett, P. Creasey, J. Rath, C. Kelly, T. Morgan, D. Cavendish, T. Barrett, G. Vaughan, Y. Patrick, P. Baxter, E. Elliott, D'Oyly Carte Op Chor, D'Oyly Carte Op Orch/J. Pryce-Jones)

CDTER2 1188 (5/92) **ZCTED 1188** (5/92)
Gilbert & Sullivan—Iolanthe
Sullivan: Iolanthe (Cpte); Thespis (exc). (R. Suart, L. Richard, P. Creasey, J. Rath, Philip Blake Jones, E. Woollett, J. Pert, R. Hanley, Y. Patrick, M. Mitchell, L. Owen, D'Oyly Carte Op Chor, D'Oyly Carte Op Orch/J. Pryce-Jones)

CDTER2 1195 (5/93) **ZCTED 1195** (5/93)
Sullivan—The Yeomen of the Guard
Sullivan: Yeomen of the Guard (Cpte); Yeomen of the Guard (exc). (D. Maxwell, D. Fieldsend, T. Sharpe, J. Jenson, F. Gray, G. Montaine, L.E. Ross, J. Roebuck, J. Pert, C. Lesley-Green, D'Oyly Carte Op Chor, D'Oyly Carte Op Orch/J.O. Edwards)

CDTER2 1197 (2/94) **ZCTER2 1197** (2/94)
Bernstein—West Side Story
Bernstein: West Side Story (Cpte). (T. Olafimihan, P. Manuel, C. O'Connor, S. Burgess, N. Warnford, J. Paton, E. Stephenson, N. Carty, K. Daniels, M. Michaels, A. Sarple, A. Edmeads, G. Stevens, N. Ferranti, Chor, National SO/J.O. Edwards)

CDVIR8307 (1/89) **ZCVIR8307** (1/89)
Josephine Barstow sings Verdi Arias
Verdi: Forza del destino (exc); Otello (exc); Macbeth (exc); Aida (exc); Don Carlo (exc). (J. Barstow, ENO Orch/M. Elder, S. Burgess, J. Connell)

CDVIR8314 (10/91) **ZCVIR8314** (10/91)
Is it really me?
H. Schmidt: 110 in the Shade (exc); *Romberg:* Desert Song (exc); *F. Loewe:* My Fair Lady (exc); *Novello:* Dancing Years (exc); *Lehár:* Zigeunerliebe (exc); *Grainer:* Robert and Elizabeth (exc); *Coward:* Conversation Piece (exc); *F. Loesser:* Most Happy Fella (exc); *Bernstein:* Candide (1956) (exc); *Kálmán:* Csárdásfürstin (exc); *Rodgers:* Oklahoma! (exc); *Lehár:* Graf von Luxemburg (exc); *Kálmán:* Gräfin Mariza (exc); *Romberg:* Student Prince (exc). (M. Hill Smith, Philh, National SO/J.O. Edwards, Scottish Op Orch/J. Brown, New Sadler's Wells Op Chor, New Sadler's Wells Op Orch/B. Wordsworth)

CDVIR8315
Carousel Waltz
Rodgers: Carousel (exc); Cinderella (exc); King and I (exc); *Lehár:* Lustige Witwe (exc); *F. Loewe:* My Fair Lady (exc); Gigi (exc); *Coward:* Bitter Sweet (exc); *Strouse:* I and Albert (exc); *Romberg:* Student Prince (exc); *Sondheim:* Little Night Music (exc); *Sullivan:* Thespis (exc); *Forrest/Wright:* Song of Norway (exc); *Bernstein:* Candide (1956) (exc); *Novello:* Dancing Years (exc). (Philh, National SO/J.O. Edwards, D'Oyly Carte Op Orch/J. Pryce-Jones, Scottish Op Orch, New Sadler's Wells Op Orch/M. Reed, Orch/G. Hossack)

CDVIR8316 (5/93) **ZCVIR8316** (5/93)
Sullivan—Overtures
Sullivan: HMS Pinafore (exc); Pirates of Penzance (exc); Patience (exc); Iolanthe (exc); Princess Ida (exc); Mikado (exc); Gondoliers (exc); Yeomen of the Guard (exc); Ruddigore (exc); Di Ballo. (New Sadler's Wells Op Orch, D'Oyly Carte Op Orch/J. Pryce-Jones/S. Phipps/J.O. Edwards)

CDVIR8317 (5/94) **ZCVIR8317** (5/94)
If I Loved You - Love Duets from the Musicals
A. Lloyd Webber: Phantom of the Opera (exc); *F. Loewe:* Brigadoon (exc); *Berlin:* Annie Get Your Gun (exc); *M. Willson:* Music Man (exc); *F. Loesser:* Guys and Dolls (exc); *Bernstein:* West Side Story (exc); *Kern:* Show Boat (exc); *Friml:* Rose Marie (exc); *Rodgers:* Oklahoma (exc); King and I (exc); King and I (exc); Carousel (exc); South Pacific (exc). (V. Masterson, T. Allen, Philh/J.O. Edwards)

Tessitura

049-2
R. Strauss/Wagner—Opera Scenes
R. Strauss: Elektra (exc); Rosenkavalier (exc); Ariadne auf Naxos (exc); Frau ohne Schatten (exc); *Wagner:* Götterdämmerung (exc). (C. Ludwig, W. Berry, U. Schirrmacher, A. Bernard, Y. Nagano, S. Wagner, Berlin Deutsche Op Chor, Berlin Deutsche Op Orch/H. Hollreiser)

Testament

SBT1003 (9/91)
The Young Menuhin—Encores, Vol.1
F. Ries: Capricciosa; *Paganini:* Violin Concerto 2 (exc); *Nováček:* Concert caprices, Op.5 (exc); *Rimsky-Korsakov:* Tsar's Bride (exc); *Ravel:* Tzigane; *Paganini:* Caprices, Op.1 (exc); *Falla:* Vida breve (exc); *Rimsky-Korsakov:* Tale of Tsar Saltan (exc); *Bazzini:* Ronde des lutins; *Paganini:* Moto perpetuo, Op.11; *Wieniawski:* Souvenir de Moscou, Op.6; *Kreisler:* Tambourin chinois; *Debussy:* Préludes (exc); *Sarasate:* Danzas españolas (exc); *Brahms:* Hungarian Dances (exc); *Paganini:* Caprices, Op.1 (exc); *Dvořák:* Slavonic Dances (exc); *Brahms:* Hungarian Dances (exc). (Y. Menuhin, L. Persinger, H. Giesen, A. Balsam, M. Gazelle, F. Webster)

SBT1005 (10/92)
Ten Top Tenors
Leoncavallo: Pagliacci (exc); *Cardillo:* Core 'ngrato; *Adam:* Postillon de Lonjumeau (exc); *Auber:* Fra Diavolo (exc); *Gounod:* Faust (exc); *Puccini:* Tosca (exc); *Korngold:* Tote Stadt (exc); *J. Strauss II:* Zigeunerbaron (exc); *Bizet:* Carmen (exc); *Massenet:* Werther (exc); *Donizetti:* Elisir d'amore (exc); *Rachmaninov:* Songs, Op.26 (exc); *Ponchielli:* Gioconda (exc); *Verdi:* Rigoletto (exc); *Wagner:* Lohengrin (exc); Meistersinger (exc); *Verdi:* Trovatore (exc); *Mario:* Leggenda di Piave; *Donizetti:* Favorita (exc); *Tosti:* 'A Vucchella. (E. Caruso, H. Roswaenge, B. Gigli, R. Tauber, G. Thill, J. McCormack, J. Björling, L. Melchior, G. Martinelli, T. Schipa, orch/W.B. Rogers, Berlin St Op Chor, Berlin St Op Orch/B. Seidler-Winkler/E. Goossens, La Scala Orch/F. Ghione/G. Szell, Vienna Th Orch/A. Paulik/P. Gaubert/F. Heurteur, F. Kreisler, E. Schneider/N. Grevillius, Philadelphia/E. Ormandy, LSO/L. Collingwood/Rosario Bourdon)

SBT1008 (12/92)
Viva Rossini
Rossini: Barbiere di Siviglia (exc); Barbiere di Siviglia (exc); Barbiere di Siviglia (exc); Barbiere di Siviglia (exc); Barbiere di Siviglia (exc); Barbiere di Siviglia (exc); Barbiere di Siviglia (exc); Cenerentola (exc); Cenerentola (exc); Guillaume Tell (exc); Guillaume Tell (exc); Guillaume Tell (exc); Guillaume Tell (exc); Guillaume Tell (exc); Mosè in Egitto (exc); Semiramide (exc); Semiramide (exc); Stabat Mater (exc); Stabat Mater (exc). (T. Ruffo, D.

Borgioli, J. McCormack, M. Sammarco, L. Tetrazzini, A. Didur, M. Barrientos, R. Stracciari, G. Huguet, F. de Lucia, A. Pini-Corsi, A. Rossi, C. Supervia, L. Pagliughi, G. Martinelli, G. De Luca, J. Mardones, A. Sved, A. d'Arkor, F. Tamagno, E. Pinza, A.M. Turchetti, E. Stignani, C. Boninsegna, E. Caruso, F. Austral, orch, anon, anon, chor, ROH Chor/J. Barbirolli/A. Albergoni)

Ⓓ **SBT1010** (10/92)
Ginette Neveu & Josef Hassid
Kreisler: W.F.Bach Grave; *Suk:* Pieces, Op.17 (exc); *Chopin:* Nocturnes (exc); *Gluck:* Orfeo ed Euridice (exc); *Paradies:* Sicilienne; *Kreisler:* Tartini's Corelli Variations; *Elgar:* Capricieuse; *Tchaikovsky:* Souvenir d'un lieu cher, Op.42 (exc); *Massenet:* Thaïs (exc); *Dvořák:* Humoresques, Op.101 (exc); *Sarasate:* Danzas españolas (exc); *Achron:* Hebrew Melody; *Kreisler:* Caprice viennois; *Elgar:* Capricieuse. (G. Neveu, J. Hassid, B. Seidler-Winkler, G. Beck, G. Moore, I. Newton)

Ⓓ **SBT1012** (2/93)
Cantelli conducts Wagner & Brahms
Brahms: Symphony 1; *Wagner:* Siegfried Idyll; Siegfried (exc). (D. Brain, Philh/G. Cantelli)

Ⓓ **SBT1013** (12/92)
Dame Joan Hammond—A Celebration
Puccini: Gianni Schicchi (exc); Tosca (exc); Bohème (exc); Madama Butterfly (exc); Manon Lescaut (exc); *Massenet:* Thaïs (exc); *Offenbach:* Contes d'Hoffmann (exc); *Saint-Saëns:* Etienne Marcel (exc); *Cilea:* Adriana Lecouvreur (exc); *Giordano:* Andrea Chénier (exc); *Catalani:* Wally (exc); *Verdi:* Don Carlo (exc); Aida (exc); *Tchaikovsky:* Eugene Onegin (exc); *Dvořák:* Rusalka (exc). (J. Hammond, Hallé/L. Heward, CBO, Philh/L. Collingwood/S. Robinson/V. Tausky/W. Susskind/G. Curiel, RLPO/C. Lambert)

Ⓓ **SBT1014** (5/93)
Delius—Orchestral Works
Delius: First cuckoo; Violin Concerto; Hassan (exc); Koanga (exc); Piano Concerto; Caprice and Elegy; Légende. (A. Sammons, H. Holst, B. Harrison, B. Moiseiwitsch, G. Moore, RLPO/M. Sargent, Hallé, Philh/C. Lambert, CO/E. Fenby)

Ⓓ **SBT1015** (4/93)
Toscanini—Unpublished HMV Recordings, 1935/38
Brahms: Symphony 2; *Mendelssohn:* Midsummer Night's Dream (exc); *Rossini:* Semiramide (exc). (BBC SO/A. Toscanini)

Ⓓ **SBT1017** (7/93)
Orchestral Works - Cantelli
Dukas: Apprenti Sorcier; *Ravel:* Pavane; *Falla:* Sombrero de tres picos Suites (exc); *Ravel:* Daphnis et Chloé Suites (exc); *Rossini:* Siège de Corinthe (exc); *Casella:* Paganiniana, Op.65. (Philh, Santa Cecilia Academy Orch/G. Cantelli)

Ⓓ **SBT1018** (7/93)
Kirsten Flagstad
Ochs: Dank sei dir, Herr; *Handel:* Serse (exc); Messiah (exc); *Bach:* St Matthew Passion, BWV244 (exc); *Purcell:* Dido (exc); *Gluck:* Orfeo ed Euridice (exc); *Wagner:* Walküre (exc); Tristan und Isolde (exc). (K. Flagstad, C. Shacklock, S. Svanholm, Philh/W. Braithwaite/A. Fistoulari/W. Susskind/K. Böhm)

Ⓓ **SBT1019** (8/93)
Tito Gobbi - Opera Arias & Songs
Mozart: Don Giovanni (exc); *Verdi:* Don Carlo (exc); *Puccini:* Fanciulla del West (exc); *Rossini:* Barbiere di Siviglia (exc); *Leoncavallo:* Pagliacci (exc); *Verdi:* Otello (exc); *Mozart:* Nozze di Figaro (exc); *Verdi:* Traviata (exc); Rigoletto (exc); Macbeth (exc); *N. Valente:* Torna!; *Tosti:* 'A Vucchella; *Denza:* Occhi di fata; *Falvo:* Dicitencello vuie; *Pigarelli:* Montanara; *Sadero:* Gondoliera Veneziana; *Cottrau:* Santa Lucia; *Di Capua:* 'O sole mio; *Tosti:* Marechiare; *Anon:* Fenesta che lucive. (T. Gobbi, La Scala Orch/U. Berrettoni, RPO/A. Erede, Philh/J. Robertson/W. Susskind, LSO/W. Braithwaite, Orch/A. La Rosa Parodi/P. Green, Inst Ens)

Ⓓ **SBT1026** (4/94)
Irmgard Seefried
Mozart: Vado, ma dove?, K583; Chi sà, K582; Zaïde (exc); Kleine Spinnerin, K531; Kinderspiel, K598; Sehnsucht nach dem Frühling, K596; An Chloe, K524; Warnung, K433; Zauberer, K472; Ridente la calma, K152; Als Luise die Briefe, K520; Veilchen, K476; Dans un bois solitaire, K308; Traumbild, K530; Zufriedenheit, K349; Abendempfindung, K523; *Flies:* Wiegenlied; *Brahms:* Lieder, Op.49 (exc); *Schubert:* Wiegenlied, D498; Nacht und Träume, D827; Heidenröslein, D257; Auf dem Wasser zu singen, D774; Du bist die Ruh, D776; *Wolf:* Mörike Lieder (exc); Mörike Lieder (exc); Songs for a Woman's Voice (exc). (I. Seefried, G. Moore, H. von Nordberg, W. Schmidt, LMP/H. Blech)

Ⓓ **SBT1034** (11/94)
Guido Cantelli conducts Rossini, Mendelssohn & Beethoven
Beethoven: Symphony 5 (exc); *Mendelssohn:* Symphony 4; *Rossini:* Gazza ladra (exc). (Philh/G. Cantelli)

Ⓓ **SBT1035**
Rudolf Kempe conducts Wagner
Wagner: Fliegende Holländer (exc); Tannhäuser (exc); Meistersinger (exc); Götterdämmerung (exc). (G. Unger, Berlin St Hedwig's Cath Ch, Berlin Deutsche Op Chor, Berlin St Op Chor, BPO/R. Kempe)

Ⓓ **SBT1036** (11/94)
Lisa Della Casa sings Richard Strauss
R. Strauss: Ariadne auf Naxos (exc); Lieder, Op.27 (exc); Lieder, Op.69 (exc); Lieder, Op.49 (exc); Lieder, Op.36 (exc); Lieder, Op.17 (exc); Lieder, Op.39 (exc). (L. Della Casa, L. Otto, N. Puttar, L. Kirschstein, R. Schock, S. Peschko, BPO/A. Erede)

Ⓓ **SBT1039**
Mario Del Monaco—The HMV Milan Recordings
Verdi: Aida (exc); Otello (exc); Otello (exc); *Leoncavallo:* Bohème (exc); Pagliacci (exc); Pagliacci (exc); *Puccini:* Manon Lescaut (exc); Turandot (exc); *Mascagni:* Amico Fritz (exc); Cavalleria Rusticana (exc); Cavalleria Rusticana (exc); *Giordano:* Andrea Chénier (exc); Andrea Chénier (exc); Andrea Chénier (exc); *Cilea:* Adriana Lecouvreur (exc); *Meyerbeer:* Africaine (exc); *Flotow:* Martha (exc); *Bizet:* Carmen (exc); *Massenet:* Werther (exc); *Wagner:* Lohengrin (exc). (M. del Monaco, Milan SO/A. Quadri/T. Benintende-Neglia)

Ⓓ **SBT1040** (6/94)
Mozart—Così fan tutte (excerpts)
Mozart: Così fan tutte (exc); Così fan tutte (exc). (S. Jurinac, B. Thebom, A. Noni, Richard Lewis, E. Kunz, M. Borriello, Glyndebourne Fest Orch/F. Busch, Philh/W. Susskind)

Ⓓ **SBT1044** (2/95)
Ravel—L'enfant et les sortilèges
Ravel: Enfant et les sortilèges (Cpte). (N. Sautereau, D. Scharley, S. Michel, O. Turba-Rabier, C. Verneuil, A. Vessières, Y. le Marc'Hadour, J. Peyron, M. Angelici, M. Legouhy, M. Prigent, French Rad Maîtrise, FRN Chor, FRNO/E. Bour)

Ⓓ **SBT1058** (4/95)
James Johnston - Opera Arias and Songs
Verdi: Aida (exc); Trovatore (exc); Simon Boccanegra (exc); *Gounod:* Faust (exc); *Bizet:* Carmen (exc); *Wagner:* Meistersinger (exc); *Puccini:* Bohème (exc); Madama Butterfly (exc); *Leoncavallo:* Pagliacci (exc); *Mascagni:* Cavalleria Rusticana (exc); Cavalleria Rusticana (exc); *Vaughan Williams:* Hugh the Drover (exc); *German:* Merrie England (exc); *Leoncavallo:* Mattinata; *Traditional:* Dark-eyed sailor; Bonny labouring boy; Star of the County Down; Ireland, mother Ireland. (J. Johnston, J. Gartside, A. Shuard, O. Price, Philh, orch, ROHO, W. Reynold Orch/M. Mudie/L. Collingwood/J. Robertson/E. Robinson/F. Collinson)

Ⓓ **SBT1059** (9/95)
Erich Kunz (b. 1909)
Mozart: Nozze di Figaro (exc); Don Giovanni (exc); Don Giovanni (exc); Zauberflöte (exc); *Lortzing:* Waffenschmied (exc); Zar und Zimmermann (exc); Wildschütz (exc); *Zeller:* Vogelhändler (exc); *J. Strauss II:* Lustige Krieg (exc); Nacht in Venedig (exc); Nacht in Venedig (exc); Zigeunerbaron (exc); *E. Arnold:* Wenn der Herrgott net will; *Pick:* Wiener Fiakerlied; *Zillner:* Es steht ein alter Nussbaum; *E. Arnold:* Da draussen in der Wachau; *Krakauer:* Du guater Himmelvater; *L. Gruber:* Mei Muaterl war a Weanerin; *Kratzl:* Glück is' a Vogerl; *Fellner:* Ewiges Wien. (E. Kunz, I. Seefried, VPO/H. von Karajan/O. Ackermann/R. Moralt, Vienna Volksoper Orch/A. Paulik, Kemmeter-Faltl Schrammel Ens, Philh)

Ⓓ **SBT1060**
Igor Markevitch
Bartók: Dance Suite; *Ravel:* La Valse; *Satie:* Parade (Cpte); *Busoni:* Tanzwalzer, Op.53; *Liadov:* Kikimora, Op.63; *Chabrier:* Roi malgré lui (exc); *Liszt:* Mephisto Waltz 2, S111. (Philh/I. Markevitch)

Ⓓ **SBT1062**
Nicolai Malko
Borodin: Prince Igor (exc); Prince Igor (exc); Symphony 3; *Rimsky-Korsakov:* Maid of Pskov (exc); *Liadov:* Russian Folksongs, Op.58; *Glazunov:* Vendredis (exc). (Philh/N. Malko)

Ⓓ **SBT3051** (6/95)
Debussy—Pelléas et Mélisande
Debussy: Pelléas et Mélisande (Cpte). (J. Jansen, V. de los Angeles, G. Souzay, P. Froumenty, J. Collard, F. Ogéas, J. Vieuille, Raymond St Paul Chor, FRNO/A. Cluytens)

Thorofon

Ⓓ **CTH2044**
Music Between the World Wars
Schoenberg: Begleitungsmusik, Op. 34; *Hindemith:* Neues vom Tage (exc); Slow Piece and Rondo; *Blacher:* Concertante Musik; *Egk:* Wiener Strophenlied; *Toch:* Geographical Fugue; *Pepping:* Deutsche Choralmesse; *Juon:* Sonata 3. (Berlin RSO/G. Bertini, Cologne RSO/O. Maga, O. Sala/L. Maazel, I. Hallstein, Munich RO/L. Hager, Aachen Youth Ch/F. Wey, H. Schütz Ch/W. Matkowitz, H. Maile, H. Göbel)

Timbre Records

Ⓓ **DMHCD1**
Kammerspiel
Haydn: Keyboard Trio 25; *Mendelssohn:* Piano Trio 1; *Gershwin:* Porgy and Bess Suite. (Kammerspiel)

Timpani

Ⓓ **1C1021**
Le Flem—Orchestral Works
LeFlem: Magicienne de la Mer Suite; *Le Flem:* Fantaisie; *LeFlem:* Symphony 1. (M-C. Girod, Britanny Orch/C. Schnitzler)

Tring International

Ⓓ **TRP002** (7/94) ▭ **MCTRP002**
Bizet—Carmen Suites. Grieg—Peer Gynt Suites
Bizet: Carmen Suites; *Grieg:* Peer Gynt Suites. (RPO/M. Ermler)

Ⓓ **TRP004** ▭ **MCTRP004**
Mozart—Symphonies Nos 40 & 41. Nozze di Figaro Ov
Mozart: Symphony 40; Symphony 41; Nozze di Figaro (exc). (RPO/J. Glover)

Ⓓ **TRP008** ▭ **MCTRP008**
Wagner—Orchestral Works
Wagner: Walküre (exc); Rienzi (exc); Lohengrin (exc); Fliegende Holländer (exc); Tannhäuser (exc); Siegfried Idyll. (RPO/V. Handley)

Ⓓ **TRP015** ▭ **MCTRP015**
Tchaikovsky—Orchestral Works
Tchaikovsky: Romeo and Juliet; Capriccio Italien; Eugene Onegin (exc); 1812. (RPO/Y. Simonov)

Ⓓ **TRP021**
Haydn—Orchestral Works
Haydn: Symphony 94; Symphony 100; Fedeltà premiata (exc). (RPO/S. Sanderling)

Ⓓ **TRP026** (6/95)
Beethoven—Symphony No. 3 and Fidelio Overture
Beethoven: Symphony 3; Fidelio (exc). (RPO/G. Herbig)

Ⓓ **TRP030**
19th Century Orchestral Music
Glinka: Ruslan and Lyudmila (exc); *Ponchielli:* Gioconda (exc); *Verdi:* Traviata (exc); *A. Thomas:* Mignon (exc); *Weber:* Invitation to the Dance; *Liszt:* Faust Episodes, S110 (exc); *Berlioz:* Damnation de Faust (exc). (RPO/Y. Simonov)

Ⓓ **TRP036** (9/95)
Delius—Orchestral Works
Delius: Brigg Fair; Koanga (exc); Hassan (exc); Song before sunrise; First Cuckoo; Village Romeo and Juliet (exc); Irmelin Prelude; Over the hills and far away. (RPO/C. Seaman)

Ⓓ **TRP038**
Mozart—Symphonies Nos 36 and 39
Mozart: Zauberflöte (exc); Symphony 36; Symphony 39. (RPO/J. Lockhart)

Ⓓ **TRP044**
Operatic Overtures and Intermezzi
Verdi: Forza del destino (exc); Ballo in maschera (exc); Luisa Miller (exc); Aida (exc); Giovanna d'Arco (exc); Vespri siciliani (exc); *Giordano:* Fedora (exc); *Puccini:* Suor Angelica (exc); Manon Lescaut (exc); *Mascagni:* Cavalleria rusticana (exc); *Leoncavallo:* Pagliacci (exc). (RPO/A. Licata)

Trittico

Ⓓ **TCvan27102** ▭ **TCvan45-27102**
My Favourite Things
Castelnuovo-Tedesco: Figaro; *Kreisler:* Liebesleid; Liebesfreud; Schön Rosmarin; *Paganini:* Violin Concerto 2 (exc); *Bach:* Suites, BWV1066-9 (exc); *Traditional:* Frère

Jacques; *Lennon & McCartney:* Yellow Submarine; *Elgar:* Salut d'amour; *Tchaikovsky:* Nutcracker Suite (exc); *Brahms:* Lieder, Op. 49 (exc); *LeGrand:* Parapluies de Cherbourg (exc); *Gershwin:* Porgy and Bess (exc); *Rodgers:* Sound of Music (exc); *Bettis:* One moment in time; *Kreisler:* Tambourin chinois; *Sze-Du:* Chinese Folk Tune; *Mancini:* Pink Panther (exc). (Vanessa-Mae, New Belgian CO/N. Cleobury)

Unicorn-Kanchana

Ⓓ **DKPCD9052** (3/88) ▭ **DKPC9052**
Works by Peter Maxwell Davies
Maxwell Davies: Miss Donnithorne's Maggot; Eight Songs for a Mad King. (M. Thomas, J. Eastman, Fires of London/P. Maxwell Davies)

Ⓓ **DKPCD9055** (6/88) ▭ **DKPC9055** (6/88)
Cabaret Classics
Weill: Marie Galante (exc); *Zemlinsky:* Lieder, Op.27 (exc); *Schoenberg:* Cabaret Songs (exc); *Satie:* Diva de l'Empire; Allons-y Chochotte; *Weill:* Lady in the Dark (exc); Street Scene (exc); Knickerbocker Holiday (exc). (J. Gomez, J. Constable)

Ⓓ **DKPCD9070** (12/88)
A Celebration of Scotland
Maxwell Davies: Orkney Wedding; Kinloche his Fantassie; Seven Songs Home; Yesnaby Ground; Two Fiddlers (exc); Jimmack the Postie; Farewell to Stromness; Lullaby for Lucy; Renaissance Scottish Dances. (G. McIlwham, St Mary's Edinburgh Ch, Scottish CO/P. Maxwell Davies, P. Maxwell Davies)

Ⓓ **DKPCD9073/4** (12/88)
Nielsen—Maskarade
Nielsen: Maskarade (Cpte). (I. Hansen, G. Plesner, T. Landy, M. Schmidt Johansen, C. Sørensen, G. Bastian, E. Brodersen, T. Hyldgaard, J. Klint, O.V. Hansen, A. Haugland, Danish Rad Chor, Danish RSO/J. Frandsen)

Ⓓ **DKPCD9100** (3/91)
Maxwell Davies—The Martyrdom of St Magnus
Maxwell Davies: Martyrdom of St Magnus (Cpte). (T. Dives, C. Gillett, P. Thomson, R. Morris, K. Thomas, Scottish Chbr Op Ens/M. Rafferty)

Ⓓ **DKPCD9132** (5/93)
Kuhlau—Theatre Music
Kuhlau: Elf's hill, Op. 100 (exc); Lulu (exc); Triplet brothers from Damascus (exc); Robber's castle (exc); William Shakespeare (exc). (Odense SO/O. Maga/E. Serov)

Ⓓ **DKPCD9138** (9/93)
Britten/Cole Porter—Blues & Cabaret Songs
Britten: Cabaret Songs; When you're feeling; On this Island, Op.11 (exc); Johnson over Jordan (exc); Paul Bunyan (exc); On the Frontier (exc); This Way to the Tomb (exc); *Porter:* Paris (exc); Gay Divorce (exc); Leave it to me (exc); Miss Otis Regrets; Nymph Errant (exc). (J. Gomez, Martin Jones, Ens)

▭ **DKPC9036** (1/87)
Music inspired by Hans Christian Andersen
Enna: Match Girl (exc); *Weyse:* Festen påa Kenilworth (exc); *Schierbeck:* In Denmark I was born; *J. P. E. Hartmann:* Raven (exc); *L. Glass:* Hill of the Elves Suite; *Høffding:* Det er ganske vist. (Odense SO/O. Schmidt)

▭ **DKPC9044** (6/85)
Knussen—Where the Wild Things are
Knussen: Where the Wild Things are (Cpte). (R. Hardy, M. King, H. Hetherington, S. Richardson, S. Rhys-Williams, A. Gallacher, London Sinfonietta/O. Knussen)

Ⓓ **UKCD2050/2** (8/93)
Herrmann—Wuthering Heights
Herrmann: Wuthering Heights (Cpte). (M. Beaton, D. Bell, J. Kitchiner, P. Bowden, J. Ward, E. Bainbridge, M. Rippon, D. Kelly, M. Snashall, Elizabethan Sngrs, PAO/B. Herrmann)

Ⓓ **UKCD2056** ▭ **UKC364**
Grieg—Stage Works
Grieg: Olav Trygvason; Land Sighting, Op. 31; Peer Gynt (exc). (T. Carlsen, V. Hanssen, A. Hansli, Oslo Phil Chor, LSO/P. Dreier)

Ⓓ **UKCD2073** (8/95)
The Delius Collection, Volume 3
Delius: Koanga (exc); Idyll; Songs of Sunset; Village Romeo and Juliet (exc). (F. Lott, Sarah Walker, T. Allen, Ambrosian Sngrs, RPO/E. Fenby/N. del Mar)

United Recordings

Ⓓ **88040-2**
Judith Weir—Three Operas
Weir: Consolations of Scholarship; Missa del Cid; King Harald's Saga. (L. Hirst, Lontano/O. de la Martinez, N. Herrett, Combattimento/D. Mason, J. Manning)

Vanguard Classics

Ⓓ **08.2003.72** (9/93)
Purcell—Celebrated Songs,Sacred Airs and Concert Pieces
Purcell: Oedipus, Z583 (exc); If music be the food of love, Z379/1; Not all my torments, Z400; King Arthur, Z628 (exc); Pausanias, Z585 (exc); Fatal hour comes on apace, Z421; Birthday Ode, Z321 (exc); Indian Queen, Z630 (exc); Bonduca, Z574 (exc); Dioclesian, Z627 (exc); Don Quixote, Z578 (exc); I love and I must, Z382; Don Quixote, Z578 (exc); Fairy Queen, Z629 (exc); Blessed Virgin's Expostulation, Z196; Close thine eyes, Z184; Fantasia, Z731; Sonatas, Z802-11 (exc); Pavan, Z752; Sonata, Z780; Viola da gamba Fantasia, Z745; Hornpipes (exc); Choice Collection of Lessons (exc); Musick's Hand-maid, Part 2 (exc). (A. Cantelo, A. Deller, M. Bevan, N. Marriner, P. Gibbs, G. Jones, D. Dupré, G. Malcolm, W. Bergmann, Baroque Plyrs)

Ⓓ **08.2030.71** (4/94)
Monteverdi—Il Ballo delle ingrate;Lamento d'Arianna
Monteverdi: Ballo delle ingrate; L'Arianna (exc). (A. Cantelo, H. Sheppard, S. Le Sage, E. McLoughlin, M. Worthley, P. Todd, A. Deller (alto/dir), D. Ward, M. Bevan, J. Bream, D. Dupré, D. Vaughan, Deller Consort, Ambrosian Sngrs, London Chbr Plyrs)

Ⓓ **08.2032.71** (4/94)
Purcell—Dido and Aeneas
Purcell: Dido (Cpte). (M. Thomas, M. Bevan, H. Sheppard, H. Watts, E. Dales, R. Tear, Oriana Concert Ch, Oriana Concert Orch, H. Lester/A. Deller)

Ⓓ **08.4016.71** (8/92)
Music of Samuel Barber
Barber: Essay for Orchestra 2; Music for a scene from Shelley; Stopwatch; Virgin Martyrs, Op. 8/1 (exc); Hand of Bridge; Serenade, Op. 1; Adagio for Strings. (Sym of the Air/V. Golschmann, R. DeCormier Chorale, Washington Cath Ch/P. Callaway, P. Neway, E. Alberts, W. Lewis, P. Maero, Zagreb Sols/A. Janigro)

Ⓓ **08.4040.72** (12/92)
Gluck—Orfeo ed Euridice
Gluck: Orfeo ed Euridice (Cpte). (M. Forrester, T. Stich-Randall, H. Steffek, Vienna Academy Ch, Vienna St Op Orch/C. Mackerras)

Ⓓ **08.5069.71** (1/95)
Bach—Cantatas; Handel—Airs
Bach: Cantata 54; Cantata 170; Mass in B minor, BWV232 (exc); *Handel:* Orlando (exc); Jephtha (exc); Theodora (exc). (A. Deller, Leonhardt Baroque Ens, G. Leonhardt (org/dir), Handel Fest Orch/A. Lewis)

Ⓓ **08.8029.71**
Mischa Elman - Favourite Encores
Massenet: Thaïs (exc); *Arensky:* Violin Pieces, Op. 30 (exc); *Schumann:* Kinderszenen (exc); *Cui:* Kaleydoskop (exc); *Drigo:* Airs de ballet (exc); *Sarasate:* Zigeunerweisen; *Schubert:* Ave Maria, D839; *Dvořák:* Humoresques, Op. 101; *Gossec:* Gavotte; *Chopin:* Nocturnes (exc); *Schumann:* Waldszenen (exc); *Beethoven:* Menuet, WoO10/2; *Fauré:* Berceuse, Op. 16; *Smetana:* From the homeland (exc); *Debussy:* Plus que lente; *Gluck:* Paride ed Elena (exc); *Benjamin:* From San Domingo; *Kroll:* Juanita. (M. Elman, J. Seiger)

Ⓓ **08.9081.72**
Russian Opera Arias & Songs
Tchaikovsky: Eugene Onegin (exc); *Rimsky-Korsakov:* Sadko (exc); Snow Maiden (exc); *Tchaikovsky:* Queen of Spades (exc); *Glinka:* Life for the Tsar (exc); *Borodin:* Prince Igor (exc); *Glinka:* Doubt; *Dargomizhsky:* I am sad; Darling girl; *Rimsky-Korsakov:* I still love him; *Rachmaninov:* Songs, Op.14 (exc); *Glazunov:* Songs, Op.27 (exc); *Tchaikovsky:* Songs, Op.47 (exc); To forget; *Rubinstein:* Nacht; *Glière:* Songs, Op.18 (exc); *Rimsky-Korsakov:* Songs, Op.3 (exc); In Spring, Op.43 (exc); *Tchaikovsky:* Songs, Op.73 (exc); *Rachmaninov:* Songs, Op.4 (exc); *Mussorgsky:* Songs and Dances of Death; Nursery; He-Goat; Gopak. (N. Davrath, E. Werba, Vienna St Op Orch/V. Golschmann)

Victoria

Ⓓ **VCD19008**
Wien, Wien, nur du allein
Jos. Strauss: Ohne Sorgen; *Sieczyński:* Wien, du Stadt meiner Träume; *Kálmán:* Csárdásfürstin (exc); *Benatzky:* Ich bin gut aufgelegt; *Jos. Strauss:* Moulinet; *Stolz:* In Wien gibt's manch winziges Gasserl; *Benatzky:* Ich muss wieder einmal in Grinzing sein; Im Salzkammergut; *Jos. Strauss:* Frauenherz; *Lehár:* Lustige Witwe (exc); *L. Gruber:* Mei Muaterl war a Weanerin; *Roll:* Lannermusik; *Stolz:* Im Prater blüh'n wieder die Bäume; Wien wird schön erst bei Nacht; *Lehár:* Giuditta (exc). (E.C. Lund, S.C. Lund, Vienna Op Ball Orch/U. Theimer)

Ⓓ **VCD19037**
Brynjar Hoff - Encores for Oboe
Bach: Easter Oratorio, BWV249 (exc); *Pergolesi:* Frate 'nnamorato (exc); *Cui:* Kaleydoskop (exc); *Holford:* Dance for a Gnome; Goblin; *Saint-Saëns:* Carnaval des animaux (exc); *Auric:* Impromptu (1946); *Mendelssohn:* Lieder, Op. 34 (exc); *Handel:* Rondo; *Halvorsen:* Norwegian Folk Songs; *Rachmaninov:* Songs, Op. 34 (exc); *Gluck:* Orfeo ed Euridice (exc); *Rameau:* Fêtes d'Hébé (exc); *Grieg:* Symphonic Dances (exc); *Ravel:* Pièce en forme de Habanera; *Schumann:* Myrthen, Op. 25 (exc); *Templeton:* Scherzo caprice; *Ochs:* Dank sei dir, Herr; *Purcell:* Hornpipes (exc); *Tchaikovsky:* Songs, Op. 6 (exc); *Debussy:* Préludes (exc). (B. Hoff, R. Levin)

Video Artists International

Ⓓ **VAIA 1010-2**
Dittersdorf—Arcifanfano, King of Fools
Dittersdorf: Arcifanfano (Cpte). (E. Steber, A. Russell, P. Brooks, J. McCollum, H. Rehfuss, David Smith, J. Sopher, Clarion Music Soc/N. Jenkins)

Ⓓ **VAIA1004** (1/93)
Wagner—Tristan und Isolde
Wagner: Tristan und Isolde (Cpte). (L. Melchior, K. Flagstad, S. Kalter, E. List, H. Janssen, F. Sale, O. Dua, L. Horsman, R. Devereux, ROH Chor, LPO/F. Reiner)

Ⓓ **VAIA1006**
Berlioz—Les troyens
Berlioz: Troyens (Cpte). (R. Resnik, R. Cassilly, E. Steber, M. Singher, R. Sarfaty, J. Dennison, K. Smith, F. Wyatt, W. Lewis, Chester Watson, G. Peterson, American Op Soc Chor, American Op Soc Orch/R. Lawrence)

Ⓓ **VAIA1009**
Ilona Tokody. Portrait of the Artist
Bellini: Norma (exc); *Puccini:* Madama Butterfly (exc); *Alfano:* Risurrezione (exc); *Boito:* Mefistofele (exc); *Puccini:* Bohème (exc); *Leoncavallo:* Zazà (exc); *Mascagni:* Cavalleria Rusticana (exc); *Catalani:* Wally (exc); *Puccini:* Gianni Schicchi (exc); *Kodály:* Transylvanian Spinning-Room (exc); *Massenet:* Élégie; *Goldfaden:* Shulamis (exc); *Tosti:* Non t'amo più!; Ideale; *Grever:* Jurame. (J. Carreras, J. Simándy, I. Tokody, orch/Anon)

Ⓓ **VAIA1012**
Eleanor Sterber sings R. Strauss
R. Strauss: Frau ohne Schatten (exc); Vier letzte Lieder; *Beethoven:* Ah! perfido, Op.65. (E. Steber, S. Svanholm, O. Wiener, C. Goltz, I. Steingruber, Orch/K. Böhm/James Levine)

Ⓓ **VAIA1016**
Jon Vickers - Italian Opera Arias
Cilea: Arlesiana (exc); *Flotow:* Martha (exc); *Giordano:* Andrea Chénier (exc); *Leoncavallo:* Pagliacci (exc); *Ponchielli:* Gioconda (exc); *Puccini:* Tosca (exc); *Verdi:* Don Carlo (exc); Otello (exc); Trovatore (exc). (J. Vickers, Rome Op Orch/T. Serafin)

Ⓓ **VAIA1017** (8/93)
Leonard Warren—Early Recordings
Leoncavallo: Pagliacci (exc); *Verdi:* Traviata (exc); Rigoletto (exc); Aida (exc); *Bizet:* Carmen (exc). (L. Warren, E. Steber, A. Tokatyan, J. Dickenson, L. Alvary, L. Browning, R. Bampton, chor, orch/W. Pelletier, A. Carron, L. Summers, N. Cordon)

Ⓓ **VAIA1026**
Berlioz—Les Troyens - Highlights
Berlioz: Troyens (exc). (M. del Monaco, N. Rankin, G. Simionato, La Scala Orch/R. Kubelik)

Ⓓ **VAIA1034**
Britten—Billy Budd
Britten: Billy Budd (Cpte). (T. Uppman, P. Pears, F. Dalberg, H. Alan, G. Evans, M. Langdon, A. Marlowe, B. Drake, I. Te Wiata, W. McAlpine, D. Tree, Ronald Lewis, R. Davies, H. Littlejohn, E. Jones, J. Cameron, A. Hobson, ROH Chor, ROHO/B. Britten)

Ⓓ **VAIA1036**
The Complete Josef Hofmann - Volume 3
Chopin: Waltzes (exc); Waltzes (exc); Polonaises (exc); Impromptus (exc); Fantaisie-Impromptu; Berceuse; *Liszt:* Chants Polonais, S480 (exc); Liebesträume, S541 (exc); Concert Studies, S145 (exc); Venezia e Napoli, S162 (exc); *Schubert:* Marches Militaires, D733 (exc); *Liszt:* Lieder, S558 (exc); *Gluck:* Alceste (1776) (exc); *Beethoven:* Piano Sonata 14 (exc); *Schumann:* Fantasiestücke, Op.12 (exc); *Grieg:* Lyric Pieces, Op.43 (exc); *Mendelssohn:* Songs without Words (exc); Andante and Rondo Capriccioso, Op.14; Songs without Words

(exc); Songs without Words (exc); *Moszkowski:* Jongleuse, Op.52/4; Caprice espagnole, Op.37; *Paderewski:* Humoresques de Concert, Op.14 (exc); *Rubinstein:* Valse Caprice; Pieces, Op.93 (exc); *Hofmann:* Sanctuary; *Rachmaninov:* Preludes (exc); Preludes (exc); *H. Parker:* Valse Gracile; *F.C. Dillon:* Birds at Dawn, Op.20/2; *Sternberg:* Etude, Op.120; *Chopin:* Polonaises (exc); *Mendelssohn:* Songs without Words (exc); *Schubert:* Marches Militaires, D733 (exc); *Liszt:* Lieder, S558 (exc); *Chopin:* Nocturnes (exc); Waltzes (exc); *Rachmaninov:* Preludes (exc). (J. Hofmann)

Ⓒ **VAIA1046**
Spanish Orchestral Favorites
Falla: Sombrero de tres picos Suites (exc); *Granados:* Danzas españolas (exc); *Arbós:* Noche de Arabia; *Bretón:* Dolores (exc); *Turina:* Danzas fantásticas (exc); *Granados:* Goyescas (exc); *Turina:* Procesión del Rocio; *Albéniz:* Iberia (exc). (Madrid SO/E.F. Arbós)

Ⓒ **VAIA1047**
The Complete Josef Hofmann, Volume 4
D. Scarlatti: Keyboard Sonatas (exc); *Gluck:* Alceste (1776) (exc); *Beethoven:* Ruinen von Athen (exc); *Rubinstein:* Melodies, Op.3 (exc); *Hofmann:* Mignonettes (exc); *Rachmaninov:* Preludes (exc); *Wagner:* Walküre (exc); *Chopin:* Scherzos (exc); Nocturnes (exc); Waltzes (exc); Polonaises (exc); *Liszt:* Chants Polonais, S480 (exc); Concert Studies, S145 (exc); Paganini Studies, S140 (exc); Hungarian Rhapsodies, S244 (exc); Hungarian Rhapsodies, S244 (exc). (J. Hofmann)

Ⓒ **VAIA1059**
Walter—Early Electrical Recordings (1925-1931)
Schumann: Symphony 4; *Wagner:* Lohengrin (exc); Parsifal (exc); Fliegende Holländer (exc); Götterdämmerung (exc); Götterdämmerung (exc). (Paris Mozart Fest Orch, RPS Orch, British SO/B. Walter)

Ⓒ **VAIA1071**
Mafalda Favero (1903-1981)
Mascagni: Amico Fritz (exc); Amico Fritz (exc); Amico Fritz (exc); Lodoletta (exc); *Leoncavallo:* Pagliacci (exc); *Puccini:* Manon Lescaut (exc); Bohème (exc); Bohème (exc); Bohème (exc); Madama Butterfly (exc); Madama Butterfly (exc); Turandot (exc); Turandot (exc); *Wagner:* Lohengrin (exc); *Mozart:* Don Giovanni (exc); *Flotow:* Martha (exc); *Verdi:* Otello (exc); *Bottacchiari:* Ombra (exc). (M. Favero, T. Schipa, A. Ziliani, orch, La Scala Orch/A. Sabino/F. Ghione/G. Antonicelli, I. Ruotolo)

Ⓒ **VAIA1072** (11/95)
Eleanor Steber Collection, Volume 1
Debussy: Enfant prodigue (exc); *Verdi:* Ernani (exc); Traviata (exc); *Leoncavallo:* Pagliacci (exc); *Rossini:* Barbiere di Siviglia (exc); *A. Thomas:* Mignon (exc); *Massenet:* Hérodiade (exc); *Flotow:* Martha (exc); *Puccini:* Bohème (exc); Turandot (exc); Gianni Schicchi (exc); *Traditional:* Danny Boy; *J.A. Bland:* Carry me back; *Rossini:* Stabat Mater (exc). (E. Steber, A. Tokatyan, G. Cehanovsky, L. Warren, anon, orch/W. Pelletier/E. Goossens/H. Barlow)

Ⓒ **VAIA1073** (9/95)
Ravel—L'Heure espagnole
Ravel: Heure espagnole (Cpte). (J. Krieger, L. Arnoult, R. Gilles, J. Aubert, H. Dufranne, SO/G. Truc)

Ⓒ **VAIA1076** (4/95)
Puccini—Tosca
Puccini: Tosca (Cpte). (C. Melis, P. Pauli, A. Granforte, G. Azzimonti, N. Palai, A. Gelli, G. Bottini, La Scala Chor, La Scala Orch/C. Sabajno)

Ⓒ **VAIA1078** (3/95)
Puccini—La Bohème
Puccini: Bohème (Cpte). (R. Torri, A. Giorgini, T. Vitulli, E. Badini, A. Baracchi, L. Manfrini, S. Baccaloni, G. Nessi, La Scala Chor, La Scala Orch/C. Sabajno)

Ⓒ **VAIA1082**
Cav and Pag
Mascagni: Cavalleria rusticana (Cpte); *Leoncavallo:* Pagliacci (Cpte). (D. Sanzio, G. Breviario, P. Biasini, M. Pantaleoni, O. de Franco, A. Valente, A. Saraceni, A. Granforte, L. Basi, N. Palai, La Scala Chor, La Scala Orch/C. Sabajno)

Ⓒ **VAIA1083**
Verdi—Aida
Verdi: Aida (Cpte). (G. Arangi-Lombardi, M. Capuana, A. Lindi, A. Borgioli, T. Pasero, S. Baccaloni, G. Nessi, La Scala Chor, Milan SO/L. Molajoli)

Ⓒ **VAIA1084**
Rose Bampton sings Verdi and Wagner
Verdi: Aida (exc); *Wagner:* Lohengrin (exc); Tannhäuser (exc); Tristan und Isolde (exc). (R. Bampton, L. Summers, A. Carron, L. Warren, N. Cordon, chor, orch/W. Pelletier/W. Steinberg)

Ⓒ **VAIA1093**
Debussy—Pelléas et Mélisande (excerpts)
Debussy: Pelléas et Mélisande (exc); Pelléas et Mélisande (exc). (M. Nespoulous, C. Croiza, Y. Brothier, A. Maguenat, C. Panzéra, H. Dufranne, A. Narçon, Vanni-Marcoux, orch/G. Truc/P. Coppola)

Ⓒ **VAIA1097**
Verdi—Rigoletto
Verdi: Rigoletto (Cpte). (L. Piazza, L. Pagliughi, T. Folgar, S. Baccaloni, V. de Cristoff, A. Baracchi, L. Brambilla, G. Nessi, G. Menni, La Scala Chor, La Scala Orch/C. Sabajno)

Ⓒ **VAIA1098**
Verdi—Falstaff
Verdi: Falstaff (Cpte). (G. Rimini, E. Ghirardini, P. Tassinari, I.A. Tellini, R. d'Alessio, A. Buades, R. Monticone, E. Venturini, G. Nessi, S. Baccaloni, La Scala Chor, Milan SO/L. Molajoli)

Ⓒ **VAIA1108**
Verdi—La Traviata
Verdi: Traviata (Cpte). (A. Rozsa, A. Ziliani, L. Borgonovo, O. de Franco, G. Callegari, A. Lenzi, A. Gelli, La Scala Chor, La Scala Orch/C. Sabajno)

Virgin Classics

Ⓒ **CUV5 61122-2** (11/94)
Britten—Noye's Fludde; Serenade
Britten: Noye's Fludde (Cpte); Serenade. (D. Maxwell, L. Ormiston, A. Gallifant, T. Lamb, N. Berry, R. Pasco, C. Johnson, P. Hewetson, J. Brown, M. Hill, F. Lloyd, CLS/R. Hickox)

Ⓒ **CUV5 61128-2** (11/94)
Humperdinck—Fairy-tale Music
Humperdinck: Hänsel und Gretel (exc); Blaue Vogel (exc); Königskinder Overture; Königskinder (exc); Dornröschen (exc). (Bamberg SO/K.A. Rickenbacher)

Ⓒ **CUV5 61135-2**
Mussorgsky—Orchestral Works
Mussorgsky: Pictures; Night on the bare Mountain; *Borodin:* Prince Igor (exc). (RLPO/C. Mackerras)

Ⓒ **CUV5 61139-2** (11/94)
Rossini—Arias
Rossini: Siège de Corinthe (exc); Tancredi (exc); Bianca e Falliero (exc); Elisabetta (exc); Otello (exc); Guillaume Tell (exc); Semiramide (exc). (K. Ricciarelli, Lyon Op Chor, Lyon Op Orch/G. Ferro)

Ⓒ **CUV5 61194-2**
Gershwin/Bernstein—Orchestral Works
Gershwin: Rhapsody in Blue; American in Paris; *Bernstein:* West Side Story Symphonic Dances; On the Town. (G. Ohlsson, Minnesota Orch/E. de Waart)

Ⓒ **CUV5 61201-2**
Hindemith—Orchestral Works
Hindemith: Symphonic Metamorphosis; Mathis der Maler; Neues vom Tage (exc). (Bamberg SO/K.A. Rickenbacher)

Ⓒ **CUV5 61257-2**
Holst—The Planets, etc
Holst: Planets; Perfect Fool (exc). (Liverpool Phil Ch, RLPO/C. Mackerras)

Ⓒ **VCD5 45039-2** (10/94)
Floyd—Susannah
Floyd: Susannah (Cpte). (C. Studer, J. Hadley, S. Ramey, K. Chester, M. Druiett, S. Cole, S. Kale, D. Pittsinger, A. Howells, D. Jones, J. Glennon, E. Laurence, Lyon Op Chor, Lyon Op Orch/K. Nagano)

Ⓒ **VCD7 59054-2** (1/92)
R. Strauss—Salomé
R. Strauss: Salomé (Cpte). (K. Huffstodt, J. Van Dam, J. Dupouy, H. Jossoud, J-L. Viala, H. Perraguin, J. Bastin, A. Gabriel, V. le Texier, F. Dumont, Y. Bisson, C. Goldsack, Lyon Op Orch/K. Nagano)

Ⓒ **VCD7 59227-2** (9/92)
Poulenc—The Carmelites
Poulenc: Dialogues des Carmélites (Cpte). (C. Dubosc, R. Yakar, R. Gorr, B. Fournier, M. Dupuy, J. Van Dam, J-L. Viala, M. Sénéchal, F. le Roux, Lyon Op Chor, Lyon Op Orch/K. Nagano)

Ⓒ **VCD7 59249-2** (8/88) ▭ **VCD7 59249-4** (8/88)
Britten—Paul Bunyan
Britten: Paul Bunyan (Cpte). (P. Wagner, J. Lawless, D. Dressen, E.C. Nelson, C. Ware, V. Sutton, M. Fristad, J. Bohn, P. Jorgenson, T. Dahl, T. Shaffer, L. Weller, J. McKee, J. Westbrock, M. Jette, S. Herber, J. Hardy, Plymouth Music Series Chor, Plymouth Music Series Orch/P. Brunelle)

Ⓒ **VCD7 59253-2** (8/90) ▭ **VCD7 59253-4** (8/90)
Copland—The Tender Land
Copland: Tender Land (Cpte). (E. Comeaux, J. Hardy, M. Jette, L. Lehr, D. Dressen, J. Bohn, V. Sutton, A. Smuda, M. Fristad, S. Herber, Plymouth Music Series Chor, Plymouth Music Series Orch/P. Brunelle)

Ⓒ **VCD7 59305-2** (8/93)
Britten—A Midsummer Night's Dream
Britten: Midsummer Night's Dream (Cpte). (J. Bowman, L. Watson, J. Graham-Hall, H. Herford, D. Jones, J. Gomez, N. Bailey, P. Walker, D. Maxwell, R. Bryson, Adrian Thompson, A. Gallacher, R. Horn, R. Suart, S. Hart, G. Pierre, A. Mead, N. Watson, D. Fletcher, Trinity Boys' Ch, CLS/R. Hickox)

Ⓒ **VCD7 59313-2** (11/93)
Busoni—Operas
Busoni: Arlecchino (Cpte); Turandot (Cpte). (E. T. Richter, S. Mentzer, T. Mohr, W. Holzmair, P. Huttenlocher, S. Dahlberg, M. Gessendorf, S. Dahlberg, F-J. Selig, G. Sima, F. Struckmann, A-M. Rodde, M. Schäfer, M. Kraus, W. Holzmair, Lyon Op Chor, Lyon Op Orch/K. Nagano)

Ⓒ **VCD7 59566-2** (12/89) ▭ **VCD7 59566-4** (12/89)
Prokofiev—The Love for Three Oranges
Prokofiev: Love for 3 Oranges (Cpte). (G. Bacquier, J-L. Viala, H. Perraguin, V. Le Texier, G. Gautier, D. Henry, G. Reinhart, M. Lagrange, C. Caroli, B. Fournier, C. Dubosc, J. Bastin, B. Uria-Monzon, Lyon Op Chor, Lyon Op Orch/K. Nagano)

Ⓒ **VCK7 59077-2** (6/92)
Stravinsky—Ballet Music
Stravinsky: Rite of Spring (Cpte); Perséphone (Cpte). (A. Rolfe Johnson, A. Fournet, Tiffin Boys' Ch, LP Ch, LPO/K. Nagano)

Ⓒ **VC5 45051-2** (4/95)
Grieg—Choral Works
Grieg: Bergljot, Op.42; Olav Trygvason; Funeral March. (L. Fjeldstad, S. Kringelborn, R. Stene, P. Vollestad, Trondheim Sym Chor, Trondheim SO/O.K. Ruud)

Ⓒ **VC5 45093-2**
Britten—The Company of Heaven; Paul Bunyan - excerpts
Britten: Company of Heaven; Paul Bunyan (exc). (C. Pope, D. Dressen, P. Barkworth, S. Allen, C. Herrick, P. Forbes, B. Mills, A. Murgatroyd, Angus Smith, LP Ch, ECO/P. Brunelle)

Ⓒ **VC5 45116-2**
The Pocket Purcell
Purcell: Indian Queen, Z630 (exc); Abdelazer, Z570 (exc); Gordian Knot Unty'd, Z597 (exc); If music be the food of love, Z379/1; Fantasia, Z731; Close thine eyes, Z184; Grounds (exc); Bell Anthem, Z49; Organ Voluntaries, Z717-20 (exc); Funeral Sentences (exc); Viola da gamba Fantasies, Z735-43 (exc); Of all the instruments, Z263; Fairy Queen, Z629 (exc). (Taverner Consort, Taverner Ch, Taverner Plyrs/A. Parrott)

Ⓒ **VC7 59022-2** (8/91)
Smyth—Vocal and Orchestral Works
Smyth: Boatswain's Mate (exc); Mass; March of the Women. (E. Harrhy, J. Hardy, D. Dressen, J. Bohn, Plymouth Music Series Chor, Plymouth Music Series Orch/P. Brunelle)

Ⓒ **VC7 59048-2** (2/92)
Tippett—The Ice Break
Tippett: Ice Break (Cpte). (H. Harper, D. Wilson-Johnson, S. Sylvan, C. Page, C. Clarey, T. Randle, B. Bottone, D. Maxwell, C. Robson, Sarah Walker, London Sinfonietta Chor, London Sinfonietta/D. Atherton)

Ⓒ **VC7 59076-2** (6/92)
Janáček—Orchestral Music
Janáček: From the House of the Dead (exc); Sinfonietta; Taras Bulba; Violin Concerto. (C. Tetzlaff, Philh/L. Pešek)

Ⓒ **VC7 59285-2** (11/94)
Favourite Czech Orchestral Works
Dvořák: Hussite; Romance, Op. 11; Silent Woods; *Fučík:* Lustige Dorfschmiede; Alte Brummbär; Entry of the Gladiators; *Nedbal:* Valse triste; *Smetana:* Bartered Bride (exc); Má vlast (exc). (M. Stewart, T. Walden, A. Pendlebury, RLPO/L. Pešek)

Ⓒ **VC7 59324-2** (6/94)
Purcell—O Solitude - Songs and Airs
Purcell: O solitude, Z406; Not all my torments, Z400; Stript of their green our groves appear, Z444; Blessed Virgin's Expostulation, Z196; If music be the food of love, Z379/1; Fatal hour comes on apace, Z421; Queen's Epicedium, Z383; Cupid, the slyest rogue alive, Z367; Bess of Bedlam, Z370; Evening Hymn, Z193; O solitude, Z406; Tyrannic Love, Z613 (exc); Fairy Queen, Z629 (exc); Pausanias, Z585 (exc); Tempest, Z631 (exc); Don Quixote, Z578

(exc); Sophonisba, Z590 (exc); Indian Queen, Z630 (exc); Dioclesian, Z627 (exc); King Arthur, Z628 (exc). (N. Argenta, N. North, R. Boothby, P. Nicholson)

Ⓓ **VC7 59617-2**
A capella Mozart
Mozart: Zauberflöte (exc); Symphony 40; Ave verum corpus, K618; String Quartet, K387 (exc); Così fan tutte (exc); Serenade, K525 (exc); Horn Concerti (exc); Don Giovanni (exc); Gigue, K574; Piano Concerto 21 (exc); Requiem (exc); Piano Sonata, K331 (exc); Fantasia, K608. (Swingle Sngrs)

Ⓓ **VC7 59618-2** (4/91)
Nielsen—Orchestral Works
Nielsen: Symphony 4; Symphony 5; Maskarade (exc). (BBC SO/A. Davis)

Ⓓ **VC7 59668-2** (7/88)
French Impressions
Debussy: Petite Suite (exc); Après-midi; *Fauré:* Pavane; Elégie; *Pierné:* March of the Little Lead Soldiers; *Massenet:* Thaïs (exc); Vierge (exc); *Satie:* Gymnopédies (exc); *Saint-Saëns:* Carnaval des animaux (exc); *Tortelier:* Alla Maud. (M. Tortelier, J-L. Garcia, P. Tortelier (vc/dir), M. Reeves, ECO/P. Tortelier)

Ⓓ **VJ5 61109-2**
French Connections
Debussy: Petite Suite (exc); *Fauré:* Pavane; *Pierné:* March of the Little Lead Soldiers; *Massenet:* Thaïs (exc); *Satie:* Gymnopédies (exc); *Fauré:* Elégie; *Saint-Saëns:* Carnaval des Animaux (exc); *Debussy:* Après-midi; *Massenet:* Vierge (exc); *Tortelier:* Alla Maud. (J-L. Garcia, P. Tortelier, M. Tortelier, P. Tortelier (vc/dir), M. Reeves, ECO/P. Tortelier)

Ⓓ **VJ7 59644-2** (12/91) ▭ **VJ7 59644-4** (12/91)
Handel—Favourite Arias
Handel: Serse (exc); Acis and Galatea (exc); Esther (exc); Athalia (exc); Judas Maccabaeus (exc); Samson (exc); Messiah (exc); Joshua (exc); Rinaldo (exc); Semele (exc); Ode for St Cecilia's Day (exc); Amadigi di Gaula (exc); Solomon (exc); Choice of Hercules (exc). (R. White, City of London Baroque Sinfonia/I. Bolton)

Ⓓ **VJ7 59654-2** (12/91) ▭ **VJ7 59654-4** (12/91)
Fanfare for the Common Man
Carl Davis: Philharmonic Fanfare; *J. Strauss II:* Fledermaus (exc); Fledermaus Polka, Op. 362; Tik-Tak; Fledermaus Csárdás; Du und Du, Op. 367; *Brahms:* String Sextet 2 (exc); *Copland:* Fanfare for the Common Man; *Delius:* Village Romeo and Juliet (exc). (LPO/Carl Davis)

▭ **VJ7 59689-4**
Wagner—Orchestral Works
Wagner: Siegfried Idyll; Meistersinger (exc); Lohengrin (exc); Tristan und Isolde (exc); Tannhäuser (exc). (French Rad PO/M. Janowski)

Ⓓ **VMT7 59699-2**
Tchaikovsky—Symphonies, Vol.1
Tchaikovsky: Symphony 1; Symphony 2; Symphony 3; Symphony 4; Capriccio italien; Eugene Onegin (exc); Serenade, Op.48. (Bournemouth SO/A. Litton)

Vox

Ⓓ **CDX2 5501**
Novaes/Klemperer
Beethoven: Piano Concerto 4; *Chopin:* Piano Concerto 2; *Schumann:* Piano Concerto; *Bach:* Prelude and Fugue, BWV535 (exc); *Gluck:* Orfeo ed Euridice (exc); *Saint-Saëns:* Alceste Caprice; *Brahms:* Piano Pieces, Op. 76 (exc); Piano Pieces, Op. 117 (exc); Waltzes, Op. 39 (exc); *Beethoven:* Ruinen von Athen (exc). (G. Novaes, Vienna SO/O. Klemperer)

Ⓓ **115451-2** (8/93)
Handel—Imeneo
Handel: Imeneo (Cpte). (J. Ostendorf, J. Baird, D. Fortunato, B. Hoch, J. Opalach, Brewer Chbr Chor, Brewer CO/R. Palmer)

Wergo

Ⓓ **WER60054-50** (7/89)
Magnificathy—the many voices of Cathy Berberian
Monteverdi: Madrigals, Bk 7 (exc); *Debussy:* Chansons de Bilitis; *Cage:* Flower; Wonderful widow of eighteen springs; *Bussotti:* Passion selon Sade (exc); *Weill:* Happy End (exc); *Lennon & McCartney:* Ticket to ride; *Gershwin:* Porgy and Bess (exc); *Berberian:* Stripsody. (C. Berberian, B. Canino, B. Canino)

Ⓓ **WER60106-50** (2/89)
Hindemith—Vocal Works
Hindemith: Sancta Susanna (Cpte); Gesänge, Op. 9. (J. Martin, H. Donath, G. Schnaut, G. Schreckenbach, Berlin RIAS Chbr Ch, Berlin RSO/G. Albrecht)

Ⓓ **WER60132-50** (2/89)
Hindemith—Mörder; Dämon
Hindemith: Mörder, Hoffnung der Frauen (Cpte); Dämon (Cpte). (F. Grundheber, G. Schnaut, W. Gahmlich, V. von Halem, B-O. Magnusson, L. Peacock, G. Schreckenbach, B. Haldas, Berlin RIAS Chbr Ch, Berlin RSO/G. Albrecht)

Ⓓ **WER60146-50** (7/89)
Hindemith—Nusch-Nuschi
Hindemith: Nusch-Nuschi (Cpte). (H. Stamm, M. Schumacher, V. von Halem, J. Becker, D. Knutson, W. Gahmlich, P. Maus, A. Ramirez, V. Schweizer, C. Lindsley, G. Schreckenbach, G. Sieber, G. Resick, G. Pohl, W. Marschall, M. Kleber, Berlin RSO/G. Albrecht)

Ⓓ **WER60148/9-50** (7/89)
Hindemith—Cardillac
Hindemith: Cardillac (Cpte). (S. Nimsgern, V. Schweizer, R. Schunk, H. Stamm, J. Protschka, G. Schnaut, A. Schmidt, Berlin Rad Chbr Ch, Berlin RSO/G. Albrecht)

Ⓓ **WER6170-2** (12/91)
Ligeti—Le Grand Macabre
Ligeti: Grand Macabre (Cpte). (E. Davies, E. Davies, P. Walmsley-Clark, O. Fredricks, K. Smith, C. Puhlmann-Richter, P. Haage, D. Weller, U. Krekow, J. Leutgeb, E. Salzer, L. Modos, H. Prikopa, E.L. Strachwitz, Gumpoldskirchner Spatzen, Austrian Rad Chor, A. Schoenberg Ch, Austrian RSO/E. Howarth)

Ⓓ **WER6173-2** (6/91)
T.W.Adorno—Chamber & Choral Works
Adorno: Pieces, Op.2; Short Orchestral Pieces; Däubler Gedichte; Schatz des Indianer-Joe; Kinderjahr. (Buchberger Qt, Frankfurt Op Orch/G. Bertini, Frankfurt Chbr Ch/H.M. Beuerle, M. Kiener, H. Neiser)

Ⓓ **WER6174-2**
Orff—Kleines Konzert
Orff: Kleines Konzert; Carmina Burana (exc); Mond (exc); Kluge (exc). (Mainz Wind Ens/K.R. Schöll)

Ⓓ **WER6192-2**
Hindemith—Neues vom Tage
Hindemith: Neues vom Tage (Cpte). (E. Werres, C. Nicolai, R. Pries, H. Hiestermann, M. Borst, O.G. de Gracia, A. Sandner, C. Antunes, W. Geuer, T. Donecker, C. Scheeben, D. Gillessen, H. Feckler, S. Bitter, Cologne Pro Musica, Cologne RSO/J. Latham-König)

Ⓓ **WER6204-2** (12/92)
Henze—The English Cat
Henze: English Cat (Cpte). (R. Berkeley-Steele, M. Coles, A. Watt, I. Platt, J. Pike, L. Kennedy, G. Nilsson, D. Bennett, C. Court, J. Bremar, R. Hallawell, G. Davenport, Parnassus Orch/M. Stenz)

Ⓓ **WER6255-2** (9/94)
Hindemith—Mathis der Maler
Hindemith: Mathis der Maler (Cpte). (R. Hermann, J. Protschka, V. von Halem, H. Winkler, H. Stamm, H. Kruse, U. Hielscher, U. Ress, S. Hass, G. Rossmanith, M. Schmiege, N German Rad Chor, Cologne Rad Chor, Cologne RSO/G. Albrecht)

Ⓓ **WER6259-2** (11/95)
K A Hartmann—Simplicius Simplicissimus
K. A. Hartmann: Simplicius Simplicissimus (Cpte). (H. Donath, E. Büchner, K. König, B. Brinkmann, R. Scholze, H. Berger-Tuna, W. Euba, Munich Concert Ch, BRSO/H. Fricke)

Word

Ⓓ **FCD7404**
Best of Mozart
Mozart: Zauberflöte (exc); Symphony 41 (exc); Symphony 39 (exc); Clarinet Concerto, K622 (exc); Clarinet Quintet, K581 (exc); Symphony 38 (exc); Oboe Concerto, K314 (exc); Nozze di Figaro (exc). (LPO, Mozart Fest Orch, J. Ostra, A. Gigliotti, Philarte Qt, C. Del Fonte, Camerata Academica/Anon)

Ⓓ **FCD7406**
Best of Tchaikovsky
Tchaikovsky: Mazeppa (exc); Symphony 6; Symphony 5 (exc); Nutcracker (exc); Capriccio italien; 1812. (Dallas SO/Anon, Ljubljana RSO, Berlin Fest Orch, New Philh)

Ⓓ **FCD7409**
World's Greatest Overtures
J. Strauss II: Fledermaus (exc); *Suppé:* Dichter und Bauer (exc); *Brahms:* Academic Festival Overture; *Beethoven:* Egmont (exc); *Wagner:* Fliegende Holländer (exc); *Tchaikovsky:* 1812. (Minnesota Orch, Utah SO, London Prom/Anon)

Ⓓ **FCD7410**
World's Greatest Choruses
Handel: Messiah (exc); *Wagner:* Lohengrin (exc); *Mozart:* Mass, K317 (exc); *Palestrina:* Missa Brevis (exc); *Mahler:* Symphony 4 (exc); *Schubert:* Deutsche Messe; *Bizet:* Agnus Dei; *Verdi:* Nabucco (exc); *Beethoven:* Symphony 9 (exc). (Bavarian Fest Orch, Bavarian Fest Chor, Ljubljana Rad Orch, Ljubljana Rad Chor, Salzburg Camerata Academica, Austrian Broadcast Ch, E. Andor, Zagreb Rad & TV SO, Mozarteum Ch, Württemberg St Orch, London Fest Orch, London Fest Ch/Anon)

Ⓓ **FCD7411**
World's Greatest Waltzes
J. Strauss II: Kaiser, Op. 437; *Tchaikovsky:* Swan Lake (exc); *J. Strauss II:* Zigeunerbaron (exc); *Tchaikovsky:* Symphony 5 (exc); *J. Strauss II:* Wein, Weib und Gesang; *Tchaikovsky:* Serenade, Op. 48 (exc); *J. Strauss II:* Künstlerleben, Op. 316; *Tchaikovsky:* Nutcracker (exc); *J. Strauss II:* Frühlingsstimmen, Op. 410. (Royal Prom Orch, Houston SO, Bamberg SO, London Fest Orch/Anon)

Video and LaserDisc index

Abbey Music

95542 (9/92)
Symphony for the Spire
Saint-Saëns: Symphony 3 (exc); *Popper:* Hungarian Rhapsody, Op. 68; *Puccini:* Tosca (exc); *Verdi:* Luisa Miller (exc); *Brodszky:* Toast of New Orleans (exc); *Doyle:* Henry V (exc); *R. Strauss:* Vier letzte Lieder (exc); Lieder, Op. 27 (exc); *Handel:* Fireworks Music (exc); *Parry:* Jerusalem. (O. Harnoy, C. Heston, P. Domingo, K. Branagh, P. Doyle, J. Norman, ECO/R. Armstrong)

Archiv Produktion

072 436-1AH2 (2/94) **072 436-3AH2** (2/94)
Mozart—Così fan tutte
Mozart: Così fan tutte (Cpte). (A. Roocroft, R. Mannion, E. James, R. Trost, R. Gilfry, C. Nicolai, Monteverdi Ch, EBS/J. E. Gardiner, P. Mumford)

072 439-1AH2 (3/95) **072 439-3AH** (3/95)
Mozart—Le nozze di Figaro
Mozart: Nozze di Figaro (Cpte). (B. Terfel, A. Hagley, R. Gilfry, H. Martinpelto, P.H. Stephen, S. McCulloch, C. Feller, F. Egerton, J. Clarkson, C. Backes, Monteverdi Ch, EBS/J.E. Gardiner, J-L. Thamin)

Artificial Eye

ARTOP1
Hans Jürgen Syberberg's production of Parsifal
Wagner: Parsifal (Cpte). (R. Goldberg, W. Schöne, R. Lloyd, Y. Minton, A. Haugland, H. Tschammer, Prague Phil Chor, Monte Carlo PO/A. Jordan, H.J. Syberberg)

ART014 (2/92)
Joseph Losey's film of Don Giovanni
Mozart: Don Giovanni (Cpte). (R. Raimondi, E. Moser, K. Te Kanawa, T. Berganza, K. Riegel, J. Van Dam, M. King, J. Macurdy, Paris Op Chor, Paris Op Orch/L. Maazel)

Castle Vision

CASH5051
Puccini Favourites from Covent Garden and the Arena di Verona
Puccini: Madama Butterfly (exc); Tosca (exc); Fanciulla del West (exc); Bohème (exc); Manon Lescaut (exc); Turandot (exc). (R. Kabaivanska, Verona Arena Orch/M. Arena, G. Aragall, I. Wixell, E. Marton/D. Oren, P. Domingo, ROHO/N. Santi, N. Shicoff, I. Cotrubas, M. Zschau, T. Allen/L. Gardelli, K. Te Kanawa/G. Sinopoli, G. Dimitrova, N. Martinucci, Verona Arena Chor)

CASH5052
Verdi Operatic Favourites
Verdi: Aida (exc); Ernani (exc); Nabucco (exc); Lombardi (exc); Otello (exc); Falstaff (exc). (M. Chiara, N. Martinucci, F. Cossotto, G. Scandola, Verona Arena Chor, Verona Arena Orch/A. Guadagno, M. Freni, La Scala Orch/R. Muti, G. Dimitrova, O. Garaventa, B. Baglioni/M. Arena, J. Carreras, La Scala Chor, P. Cappuccilli, V. Atlantov, K. Te Kanawa/Z. Peskó, R. Bruson, B. Boozer, J. Dobson, F. Egerton, D. Gonzalez, B. Hendricks, L. Nucci, K. Ricciarelli, L.V. Terrani, W. Wilderman, ROH Chor, ROHO/C.M. Giulini/G. Gavazzeni)

CVI2001
Royal Opera House production of Falstaff, 1983
Verdi: Falstaff (Cpte). (R. Bruson, L. Nucci, K. Ricciarelli, B. Hendricks, D. Gonzalez, L.V. Terrani, B. Boozer, J. Dobson, F. Egerton, W. Wilderman, ROH Chor, ROHO/C.M. Giulini, R. Eyre)

CVI2002
La Scala production of Andrea Chénier, 1985
Giordano: Andrea Chénier (Cpte). (J. Carreras, E. Marton, P. Cappuccilli, La Scala Chor, La Scala Orch/R. Chailly, L. Puggelli)

CVI2003
Nabucco from the Arena di Verona, 1981
Verdi: Nabucco (Cpte). (R. Bruson, G. Dimitrova, O. Garaventa, B. Baglioni, D. Petkov, F.E. d'Artegna, A. Ceroni, G. di Rocco, Verona Arena Chor, Verona Arena Orch/M. Arena, R. Giacchieri)

CVI2004
Turandot from the Arena di Verona, 1983
Puccini: Turandot (Cpte). (G. Dimitrova, N. Martinucci, C. Gasdia, G. Polidori, P.F. Poli, A. Bevacqua, I. Vinco, G. Corradi, O. Mori, Verona Arena Chor, Verona Arena Orch/M. Arena, G. Montaldo)

CVI2005
Il Trovatore from the Arena di Verona, 1985
Verdi: Trovatore (Cpte). (F. Bonisolli, R. Plowright, G. Zancanaro, F. Cossotto, Verona Arena Chor, Verona Arena Orch/R. Giovaninetti, G.P. Griffi)

CVI2006
Tosca from the Arena di Verona, 1984
Puccini: Tosca (Cpte). (E. Marton, G. Aragall, I. Wixell, Verona Arena Chor, Verona Arena Orch/D. Oren, S. Bussotti)

CVI2007
Madama Butterfly from the Arena di Verona, 1983
Puccini: Madama Butterfly (Cpte). (R. Kabaivanska, N. Antinori, L. Saccomani, E. Jankovic, M. Ferrara, G. Zecchillo, M. Zotti, G. Brunelli, Verona Arena Chor, Verona Arena Orch/M. Arena, G. Chazalettes)

CVI2008
Glyndebourne Festival Opera 1981
Britten: Midsummer Night's Dream (Cpte). (J. Bowman, I. Cotrubas, R. Davies, D. Duesing, C. Buchan, F. Lott, L. Visser, C. Powell, C. Appelgren, R. Bryson, P. Power, A. Gallacher, Adrian Thompson, D. Bell, M. Warr, S. Jones, J. Whiting, S. King, D. Nash, Glyndebourne Fest Chor, LPO/B. Haitink, P. Hall)

CVI2013
Aida from the Arena di Verona, 1981
Verdi: Aida (Cpte). (M. Chiara, F. Cossotto, N. Martinucci, G. Scandola, C. Zardo, A. Zanazzo, G. Corradi, Verona Arena Ballet, Verona Arena Chor, Verona Arena Orch/A. Guadagno, G. Sbragia)

CVI2014
Royal Opera House Production of La Bohème, 1982
Puccini: Bohème (Cpte). (I. Cotrubas, N. Shicoff, M. Zschau, T. Allen, J. Rawnsley, G. Howell, B. Donlan, J. Gibbs, ROH Chor, ROHO/L. Gardelli, J. Copley)

CVI2015
Royal Opera House Production of Peter Grimes
Britten: Peter Grimes (Cpte). (J. Vickers, H. Harper, N. Bailey, E. Bainbridge, J. Dobson, F. Robinson, P. Payne, P. Gelling, J. Lanigan, J. Tomlinson, M. Hill Smith, A. Pashley, ROH Chor, ROHO/Colin Davis, E. Moshinsky)

CVI2016
Glyndebourne Festival Opera, 1981
Rossini: Barbiere di Siviglia (Cpte). (J. Rawnsley, M. Ewing, M-R. Cosotti, C. Desderi, F. Furlanetto, C. McCord, R. Dean, Glyndebourne Fest Chor, LPO/S. Cambreling, J. Cox)

CVI2017
Royal Opera House Production of Der Rosenkavalier, 1984
R. Strauss: Rosenkavalier (Cpte). (K. Te Kanawa, A. Baltsa, A. Haugland, B. Bonney, J. Summers, Y. Ramiro, C. Buchan, R. Tear, S. Maisey, J. Gibbs, R. Earle, K. Begley, J. Dobson, P. Crook, ROH Chor, ROHO/G. Solti, J. Schlesinger)

CVI2018
Glyndebourne Festival Opera, 1985
Bizet: Carmen (Cpte). (M. Ewing, B. McCauley, M. McLaughlin, D. Holloway, E. Collier, J. Rigby, G. Sandison, P. Evangelides, M. Walker, X. Depraz, F. Davià, Glyndebourne Fest Chor, LPO/B. Haitink, P. Hall)

CVI2019
Glyndebourne Festival Opera, 1983
Mozart: Idomeneo (Cpte). (P. Langridge, J. Hadley, Y. Kenny, C. Vaness, T. Hemsley, A. Roden, R. Kennedy, Glyndebourne Fest Chor, LPO/B. Haitink, T. Nunn)

CVI2020
Royal Opera House 1978
Puccini: Fanciulla del West (Cpte). (C. Neblett, P. Domingo, S. Carroli, F. Egerton, R. Lloyd, G. Howell, P. Hudson, A. Wilkens, J. Summers, J. Dobson, M. Rivers, T. McDonnell, P. Crook, R. Leggate, W. Elvin, M. King, E. Garrett, H. Owen, ROH Chor, ROHO/N. Santi, P. Faggioni)

CVI2021
A year in the life of Placido Domingo
Puccini: Manon Lescaut (exc); Fanciulla del West (exc); Tosca (exc); *Verdi:* Ernani (exc); Traviata (exc); Otello (exc); *Bizet:* Carmen (exc); *Offenbach:* Contes d'Hoffmann (exc); *J. Strauss II:* Fledermaus (exc). (P. Domingo)

CVI2023
Royal Opera House Production of Die Fledermaus, 1983-1984
J. Strauss II: Fledermaus (Cpte). (K. Te Kanawa, H. Heichele, H. Prey, D. O'Neill, B. Luxon, D. Soffel, J. Meinrad, ROH Chor, ROHO/P. Domingo, L. Lindtberg)

CVI2024
Glyndebourne Festival Opera, 1983
R. Strauss: Intermezzo (Cpte). (F. Lott, R. Ashford, J. Pringle, E. Gale, I. Caley, R. Bryson, R. Woodland, G. Winslade, I. Caddy, B. Donlan, A. Gallacher, Y. Howard, D. Brook, M. Jagusz, C. Pierard, Glyndebourne Fest Chor, LPO/G. Kuhn, J. Cox)

CVI2025
Otello—Verona Production 1982
Verdi: Otello (Cpte). (V. Atlantov, K. Te Kanawa, P. Cappuccilli, A. Bevacqua, A. Schiavon, F. Raffanelli, G. Casarini, O. Mori, Verona Arena Chor, Verona Arena Orch/Z. Peskó, G. De Bosio)

CVI2026
Royal Opera House Production of Samson & Dalila, 1981
Saint-Saëns: Samson et Dalila (Cpte). (J. Vickers, S. Verrett, J. Summers, J. Tomlinson, G. Howell, J. Dobson, M. Davies, M. Best, ROH Chor, ROHO/Colin Davis, E. Moshinsky)

CVI2027
La Scala production of I Lombardi, 1984
Verdi: Lombardi (Cpte). (G. Dimitrova, J. Carreras, S. Carroli, C. Bini, La Scala Chor, La Scala Orch/G. Gavazzeni, G. Lavia)

CVI2028
Royal Opera House Production of Manon Lescaut, 1983
Puccini: Manon Lescaut (Cpte). (K. Te Kanawa, P.

Domingo, T. Allen, F. Robinson, R. Leggate, A. Cooper, G. Macpherson, J. Fryatt, M. Curtis, R. Earle, ROH Chor, ROHO/G. Sinopoli, G. Friedrich)

CVI2029
La Scala production of Nabucco, 1987
Verdi: Nabucco (Cpte). (R. Bruson, G. Dimitrova, B. Beccaria, R. Pierotti, P. Burchuladze, La Scala Chor, La Scala Orch/R. Muti, R. de Simone)

CVI2030
Full Circle—Janet Baker's final year in opera
Handel: Alceste (exc); *Donizetti:* Maria Stuarda (exc); *Gluck:* Orfeo ed Euridice (exc); *Elgar:* Dream of Gerontius (exc). (J. Baker)

CVI2033
Royal Opera House Production of Don Carlo, 1985
Verdi: Don Carlo (Cpte). (L. Lima, I. Cotrubas, B. Baglioni, G. Zancanaro, R. Lloyd, J. Rouleau, M. Best, L. Biagioni, ROH Chor, ROHO/B. Haitink, L. Visconti)

CVI2034
I Vespri Siciliani—Bologna Teatro Comunale Production 1986
Verdi: Vespri Siciliani (Cpte). (S. Dunn, V. Luchetti, L. Nucci, B. Giaiotti, Bologna Teatro Comunale Chor, Bologna Teatro Comunale Orch/R. Chailly, L. Ronconi)

CVI2035
Glyndebourne Festival Opera, 1982
Gluck: Orfeo ed Euridice (Cpte). (J. Baker, E. Speiser, E. Gale, Glyndebourne Fest Chor, LPO/R. Leppard, P. Hall)

CVI2036
Glyndebourne Festival Opera, 1984
R. Strauss: Arabella (Cpte). (A. Putnam, G. Rolandi, J. Bröcheler, A. Korn, R. Sarfaty, G. Bradley, K. Lewis, G. Winslade, J. Munro, G. Moses, E. Hartle, J. Hall, Glyndebourne Fest Chor, LPO/B. Haitink, J. Cox)

CVI2037
Eugene Onegin—Chicago Lyric Opera Production 1985
Tchaikovsky: Eugene Onegin (Cpte). (W. Brendel, M. Freni, P. Dvorský, Sandra Walker, N. Ghiaurov, J. Craft, G. Bean, J. Fryatt, Chicago City Ballet, Chicago Lyric Op Chor, Chicago Lyric Op Orch/B. Bartoletti, P.L. Samaritani)

CVI2038
English National Opera 1982
Donizetti: Maria Stuarda (Cpte). (J. Baker, R. Plowright, D. Rendall, J. Tomlinson, A. Opie, A. Bostock, ENO Chor, ENO Orch/C. Mackerras, J. Copley)

CVI2039
Der Freischütz—Württemberg State Opera Production 1981
Weber: Freischütz (Cpte). (C. Ligendza, T. Krämer, R. Viljakainen, W. Probst, Württemberg St Op Chor, Württemberg St Op Orch/D.R. Davies, A. Freyer)

CVI2040
Glyndebourne Festival Opera, 1984
Monteverdi: Incoronazione di Poppea (Cpte). (M. Ewing, D. Bailey, C. Clarey, D. Duesing, R. Lloyd, H. Walker, P. Kern, E. Gale, A-M. Owens, K. Lewis, R. Bryson, J. Miller, L. Kitchen, P. Evangelides, L. Garrett, Glyndebourne Fest Chor, LPO/R. Leppard, P. Hall)

CVI2041
Boris Godunov—Bolshoi Opera Production 1987
Mussorgsky: Boris Godunov (Cpte). (E. Nesterenko, V. Piavko, T. Sinyavskaya, Bolshoi Th Chor, Bolshoi Th Orch/A. Lazarev, I. Morozova)

CVI2045
Royal Opera House 1981
Offenbach: Contes d'Hoffmann (Cpte). (P. Domingo, L. Serra, A. Baltsa, I. Cotrubas, C. Powell, R. Lloyd, G. Evans, S. Nimsgern, N. Ghiuselev, R. Tear, P. Gelling, G. Howell, P. Cannan, P. Crook, F. Egerton, B. Dickerson, E. Garrett, R. Leggate, J. Rawnsley, D. Bergsma, ROH Chor, ROHO/G. Prêtre, J. Schlesinger)

CVI2047
La Scala production of Ernani, 1982
Verdi: Ernani (Cpte). (P. Domingo, M. Freni, R. Bruson, N. Ghiaurov, La Scala Chor, La Scala Orch/R. Muti, L. Ronconi)

CVI2048
Glyndebourne Festival Opera, 1984-5
Knussen: Where the Wild Things are (Cpte); Higglety Pigglety Pop! (Cpte). (K. Beardsley, M. King, H. Hetherington, J. Munro, S. Rhys-Williams, A. Gallacher, C. Buchan, D. Rees, A. Gallacher, N. Jenkins, R. Hardy, S. Richardson, London Sinfonietta/O. Knussen, F. Corsaro)

CVI2050
Glyndebourne Festival Opera 1982
Prokofiev: Love for 3 Oranges (Cpte). (W. White, R. Davies, N. Condò, J. Pringle, U. Benelli, P-C. Runge, D. Hammond-Stroud, R. Van Allan, N. Morpurgo, Y. Lea, S. Moore, C. Alliot-Lugaz, R. Bryson, F. Kimm, H. Hetherington, Glyndebourne Fest Chor, LPO/B. Haitink, F. Corsaro)

CVI2051
Glyndebourne Festival Opera, 1985
Britten: Albert Herring (Cpte). (J. Graham-Hall, P. Johnson, F. Palmer, D. Hammond-Stroud, R. Van Allan, A. Oliver, E. Gale, P. Kern, A. Opie, J. Rigby, M. Bovino, B. Lord, R. Peachey, LPO/B. Haitink, P. Hall)

CVI2053
Glyndebourne Festival Opera, 1983
Rossini: Cenerentola (Cpte). (K. Kuhlmann, L. Dale, A. Rinaldi, C. Desderi, M. Taddei, L. Zannini, R. Kennedy, Glyndebourne Fest Chor, LPO/D. Renzetti, J. Cox)

CVI2055
Attila from the Arena di Verona Opera Festival, 1985
Verdi: Attila (Cpte). (E. Nesterenko, M. Chiara, S. Carroli, V. Luchetti, Verona Arena Chor, Verona Arena Orch/N. Santi, G. Montaldo)

CVI2057
Il Trittico live from La Scala, 1983
Puccini: Tabarro (Cpte); Suor Angelica (Cpte); Gianni Schicchi (Cpte). (P. Cappuccilli, S. Sass, N. Martinucci, R. Plowright, D. Vejzovic, J. Pons, C. Gasdia, Y. Marusin, La Scala Chor, La Scala Orch/G. Gavazzeni, S. Bussotti)

CVI2058
Royal Opera House Production of Andrea Chenier, 1985
Giordano: Andrea Chénier (Cpte). (P. Domingo, A. Tomowa-Sintow, G. Zancanaro, J. Dobson, P. Johnson, C. Buchan, J. Summers, ROH Chor, ROHO/J. Rudel, M. Hampe)

CVI2060
I due Foscari—La Scala Production 1988
Verdi: Due Foscari (Cpte). (R. Bruson, A. Cupido, L. Roark-Strummer, L. Roni, R. Cazzaniga, M. Tagliasacchi, A. Bottion, A. Bramante, La Scala Chor, La Scala Orch/G. Gavazzeni, P. L. Pizzi)

CVI2061 (5/90)
Don Giovanni at La Scala, 1987
Mozart: Don Giovanni (Cpte). (T. Allen, E. Gruberová, A. Murray, S. Mentzer, F. Araiza, C. Desderi, N. de Carolis, S. Kopčák, La Scala Chor, La Scala Orch/R. Muti, G. Strehler)

CVI2062 (5/90)
Riccardo Muti conducts Così fan tutte at La Scala
Mozart: Così fan tutte (Cpte). (D. Dessì, D. Ziegler, A. Scarabelli, J. Kundlák, A. Corbelli, C. Desderi, La Scala Chor, La Scala Orch/R. Muti, M. Hampe)

CVI2063
La Scala production of William Tell, 1989 (Acts 1 and 2)
Rossini: Guillaume Tell (exc). (G. Zancanaro, C. Studer, C. Merritt, G. Surian, A. Felle, L. d'Intino, La Scala Chor, La Scala Orch/R. Muti, G. Bertola)

CVI2064
La Scala production of William Tell, 1989 (Acts 3 and 4)
Rossini: Guillaume Tell (exc). (G. Zancanaro, C. Studer, C. Merritt, G. Surian, A. Felle, L. d'Intino, La Scala Chor, La Scala Orch/R. Muti, G. Bertola)

CVI2065
Highlights from the Royal Opera House, Covent Garden
Offenbach: Contes d'Hoffmann (exc); *Puccini:* Bohème (exc); Manon Lescaut (exc); *R. Strauss:* Rosenkavalier (exc); *Verdi:* Don Carlo (exc); Falstaff (exc). (L. Serra, A. Baltsa, C. Powell, P. Domingo, R. Tear/G. Prêtre, I. Cotrubas, M. Zschau, N. Shicoff, T. Allen, J. Rawnsley, G. Howell/L. Gardelli, K. Te Kanawa/G. Sinopoli, B. Bonney, A. Howells/G. Solti, L. Lima, G. Zancanaro, R. Lloyd/B. Haitink, K. Ricciarelli, B. Hendricks, D. Gonzalez, R. Bruson/C.M. Giulini, ROHO)

CVI2067
Opera Highlights from La Scala
Verdi: Ernani (exc); *Giordano:* Andrea Chénier (exc); *Verdi:* Nabucco (exc); Lombardi (exc). (P. Domingo, M. Freni, R. Bruson, N. Ghiaurov, La Scala Chor, La Scala Orch/R. Muti, J. Carreras, E. Marton, P. Cappuccilli/R. Chailly, P. Burchuladze, G. Dimitrova, S. Carroli/G. Gavazzeni)

CVI2068
Opera Highlights from Verona 1
Puccini: Tosca (exc); *Verdi:* Otello (exc); Trovatore (exc); *Puccini:* Turandot (exc). (E. Marton, G. Aragall, I. Wixell, Verona Arena Orch/D. Oren, V. Atlantov, K. Te Kanawa, P. Cappuccilli/Z. Peskó, R. Plowright, F. Bonisolli/R. Giovaninetti, N. Martinucci, C. Gasdia, I. Vinco, G. Dimitrova, Verona Arena Chor/M. Arena)

CVI2070
Great Puccini Love Scenes from Covent Garden, La Scala and Verona
Puccini: Madama Butterfly (exc); Fanciulla del West (exc); Manon Lescaut (exc); Tabarro (exc); Tosca (exc); Bohème (exc). (R. Kabaivanska, N. Antinori, P. Domingo, C. Neblett, K. Te Kanawa, T. Allen, M. Curtis, S. Sass, N. Martinucci, P. Cappuccilli, E. Marton, G. Aragall, I. Cotrubas, N. Shicoff, M. Zschau, J. Rawnsley, G. Howell, Verona Arena Orch, ROHO, La Scala Orch/M. Arena/N. Santi/G. Sinopoli/G. Gavazzeni/D. Oren/L. Gardelli)

CVI2071
Highlights from Glyndebourne
Rossini: Barbiere di Siviglia (exc); *Gluck:* Orfeo ed Euridice (exc); *Bizet:* Carmen (exc); *Mozart:* Idomeneo (exc); *Rossini:* Cenerentola (exc); *Monteverdi:* Incoronazione di Poppea (exc). (M. Ewing, J. Rawnsley, LPO/S. Cambreling, J. Baker/R. Leppard, B. McCauley/B. Haitink, P. Langridge, Y. Kenny, J. Hadley, C. Vaness, K. Kuhlmann, L. Dale/D. Renzetti, D. Bailey, Glyndebourne Fest Chor)

CVI2228
La Scala production of I Vespri Siciliani 1990
Verdi: Vespri Siciliani (Cpte). (C. Studer, C. Merritt, G. Zancanaro, F. Furlanetto, G. Banditelli, E. Capuano, F. Musinu, E. Gavazzi, P. Barbacini, M. Chingari, F. Poggi, La Scala Chor, La Scala Orch/R. Muti)

Covent Garden Pioneer

CVI1718 (9/93)
Verdi—Otello
Verdi: Otello (Cpte). (P. Domingo, K. Te Kanawa, S. Leiferkus, R. Leggate, R. Remedios, C. Powell, M. Beesley, R. Earle, C. Lackner, ROH Chor, ROHO/G. Solti, E. Moshinsky)

CVI1719 (9/93)
Verdi—Stiffelio
Verdi: Stiffelio (Cpte). (J. Carreras, C. Malfitano, G. Yurisch, G. Howell, R. Leggate, A. Paxton, L. Atkinson, ROH Chor, ROHO/E. Downes, E. Moshinsky)

CVI1720 (10/93)
R. Strauss—Salomé
R. Strauss: Salome (Cpte). (M. Ewing, M. Devlin, K. Riegel, G. Knight, R. Leggate, ROHO/E. Downes, P. Hall)

Decca

071 101-3DH
Solti plays Berlioz and Wagner
Wagner: Fliegende Holländer (exc); Tannhäuser (exc); Tristan und Isolde (exc); *Berlioz:* Roméo et Juliette (exc). (Chicago SO/G. Solti)

071 103-1DH **071 103-3DH**
Monteverdi—L'Orfeo
Monteverdi: Orfeo (Cpte). (P. Huttenlocher, D. Turban, T. Schmidt, G. Linos, S. Calabro, H. Franzen, W. Gröschel, R. Hermann, P. Keller, F. Araiza, R. Hartmann, C. Boesch, Zurich Op Monteverdi Ens/N. Harnoncourt, J-P. Ponnelle)

071 119-1DH (2/92) **071 119-3DH** (2/92)
Pavarotti and Levine in Recital at the Met
Mozart: Così fan tutte (exc); *Rossini:* Soirées musicales (exc); *Bellini:* Dolente imagine; Malinconia, ninfa gentile; Vanne, o rosa fortunata; Bella Nice, che d'amore; Ma rendi pur contento; *Verdi:* Lombardi (exc); *Massenet:* Werther (exc); *Respighi:* Nevicata; Pioggia; Nebbie; *Flotow:* Martha (exc); *Mascagni:* Serenata; *Sibella:* Girometta; *Denza:* Occhi di fata; *Puccini:* Tosca (exc); Turandot (exc); *Bellini:* Vaga luna; *Tosti:* Marechiare. (L. Pavarotti, James Levine, B. Large)

071 121-1DH **071 121-3DH**
Fiesta - Evelyn Glennie in Rio
Bizet: Carmen Suites; *Rosauro:* Marimba Concerto. (E. Glennie, LSO/B. Wordsworth, R. Greenberg)

071 123-1DH **071 123-3DH**
Carreras, Domingo and Pavarotti in Concert
Cilea: Arlesiana (exc); *Cardillo:* Core 'ngrato; *Lara:* Granada; *Giordano:* Andrea Chénier (exc); *Meyerbeer:* Africaine (exc); *Lehár:* Land des Lächelns (exc); *Puccini:* Tosca (exc); Turandot (exc); Turandot (exc); *Crescenzo:* Rondine al nido; *De Curtis:* Torna a Surriento; *Sorozábal:* Tabernera del puerto (exc); *Bernstein:* West Side Story (exc); *Mendoza y Cortez:* Cielito lindo; *A. Lloyd Webber:* Cats (exc); *Louiguy:* Vie en rose; *Leoncavallo:* Mattinata; *Lacalle:* Amapola; *Di Capua:* O sole mio; *Filiberto:* Caminito; *Annibale:* O paese d' 'o sole. (J. Carreras, P. Domingo, L. Pavarotti, MMF Orch, Rome Op Orch/Z. Mehta)

071 124-1DH (2/92) **071 124-3DH** (2/92)
Tchaikovsky—Eugene Onegin
Tchaikovsky: Eugene Onegin (Cpte). (B. Weikl, T. Kubiak, S. Burrows, J. Hamari, N. Ghiaurov, A. Reynolds, E. Hartle, M. Sénéchal, R. Van Allan, W. Mason, John Alldis Ch, ROHO/G. Solti, P. Weigl)

071 134-1DH **071 134-3DH**
Delius—A Village Romeo and Juliet
Delius: Village Romeo and Juliet (Cpte). (B. Mora, S. Dean, S. Linay, A. Davies, H. Field, T. Hampson, E. Dobie, K. Barber, P.A. Caya, V. Pirillo, R.L. Demers, J. Antoniou, M. Venuti, S. Lombana, A. Mellis, D. McShane, A. Schoenberg Ch, Austrian RSO/C. Mackerras, P. Weigl)

071 135-1DH (11/92)
La Stupenda - A Portrait of Dame Joan Sutherland
Meyerbeer: Huguenots (exc); *Donizetti:* Lucia di Lammermoor (exc); Fille du Régiment (exc); Lucrezia Borgia (exc); *J. Strauss II:* Fledermaus (exc); *Delibes:* Lakmé (exc); *Offenbach:* Contes d'Hoffmann (exc); *Handel:* Alcina (exc); *Bellini:* Puritani (exc); Norma (exc); *Rossini:* Semiramide (exc); Barbiere di Siviglia (exc); *Offenbach:* Périchole (exc); *A. Thomas:* Mignon (exc); *Poulenc:* Dialogues des Carmélites (exc); *Verdi:* Trovatore (exc); *Cilea:* Adriana Lecouvreur (exc). (J. Sutherland, Orch/Anon, D. Bailey)

071 140-1DH **071 140-3DH**
Pavarotti—30th Anniversary Gala Concert
Puccini: Tosca (exc); *Mozart:* Don Giovanni (exc); *Donizetti:* Elisir d'amore (exc); *Puccini:* Bohème (exc); *Donizetti:* Favorita (exc); Lucia di Lammermoor (exc); *Cilea:* Arlesiana (exc); *Verdi:* Forza del Destino (exc); Trovatore (exc); Traviata (exc). (L. Pavarotti, R. Kabaivanska, G. Furlanetto, P. Pace, E. Dara, G. Sabbatini, P. Cappuccilli, P. Coni, S. Verrett, J. Anderson, Bologna Teatro Comunale Orch/L. Magiera, C. Swann)

071 141-1DH (11/92) **071 141-3DH** (11/92)
Cecilia Bartoli - A Portrait
Parisotti: Se tu m'ami; *Vivaldi:* Sposa son disprezzata; *Mozart:* Così fan tutte (exc); Clemenza di Tito (exc); *Rossini:* Péchés de vieillesse I (exc); Beltà crudele; Pastorella; Péchés de vieillesse III (exc); Canzonetta spagnuola; Donna del Lago (exc); Barbiere di Siviglia (exc); *Mozart:* Nozze di Figaro (exc). (C. Bartoli, G. Fischer, D. Thomas)

071 142-1DH **071 142-3DH**
Essential Opera
Bizet: Carmen (exc); *Rossini:* Barbiere di Siviglia (exc); *Puccini:* Madama Butterfly (exc); *Bizet:* Carmen (exc); *Verdi:* Aida (exc); *Puccini:* Turandot (exc); *Mozart:* Nozze di Figaro (exc); *Puccini:* Bohème (exc); *Mascagni:* Cavalleria Rusticana (exc); *Puccini:* Tosca (exc); Turandot (exc); *Verdi:* Rigoletto (exc). (NY Met Op Orch/James Levine, L. Nucci/R. Weikert, M. Freni, VPO/H. von Karajan, P. Domingo, NY Met Op Ballet, NY Met Op Chor, L. Pavarotti, MMF Orch, Rome Op Orch/Z. Mehta, M. Ewing/K. Böhm, G. Raimondi, La Scala Orch/G. Prêtre, R. Kabaivanska, New PO/B. Bartoletti, J. Sutherland, I. Jones/R. Bonynge, L. Mitchell, P. Plishka, B. Schexnayder, A. Glassman, A. Laciura)

071 143-1DH (5/93) **071 143-3DH** (5/93)
Menotti/Poulenc—Operas
Poulenc: Voix Humaine (Cpte); *Menotti:* Telephone (Cpte). (C. Farley, C. Farley, R. Smythe, Scottish CO/J. Serebrier, M. Newman)

071 145-1DH (6/93) **071 145-3DH** (6/93)
Falla—Nights in the Gardens/Peter's Puppet Show
Falla: Retablo de maese Pedro (Cpte); Nights in the Gardens of Spain. (X. Cabero, J. Cabero, J. Diaz, Opera Atelier, A. de Larrocha, Montreal SO/C. Dutoit, L. Weinstein)

071 149-1DH **071 149-3DH**
The Essential Sutherland
Donizetti: Don Pasquale (exc); *Bellini:* Norma (exc); *Donizetti:* Fille du Régiment (exc); *Verdi:* Trovatore (exc); Traviata (exc); *Lehár:* Lustige Witwe (exc); *Poulenc:* Dialogues des Carmélites (exc); *Cilea:* Adriana Lecouvreur (exc); *Meyerbeer:* Huguenots (exc); *Delibes:* Lakmé (exc); *Rossini:* Semiramide (exc); *Donizetti:* Lucrezia Borgia (exc); *J. Strauss II:* Fledermaus (exc); *Verdi:* Traviata (exc); *Donizetti:* Lucia di Lammermoor (exc); *Bishop:* Home, sweet home. (J. Sutherland, C. Grant, G. Yurisch, H. Begg, C. Johnston, R. Stevens, P. Price, A. Austin, J. Shaw, H. Tourangeau, M. Horne, G. Ewer, R. Allman, R. Gard, M. Brynnel, L. Pavarotti, M. Donnelly, Sydney Eliz Orch, Sydney Eliz PO, Australian Op & Ballet Orch, ROHO/R. Bonynge)

071 150-1DH (11/91) **071 150-3DH** (11/91)
Pavarotti in Hyde Park
Verdi: Luisa Miller (exc); Nabucco (exc); Lombardi (exc); Vespri Siciliani (exc); *Meyerbeer:* Africaine (exc); *Mascagni:* Cavalleria Rusticana (exc); *Massenet:* Werther (exc); *Leoncavallo:* Pagliacci (exc); *Wagner:* Lohengrin (exc); *Puccini:* Tosca (exc); Manon Lescaut (exc); Turandot (exc); *Bizet:* Carmen (exc); *Bixio:* Mamma; Mia canzone al vento; *De Curtis:* Non ti scordar di me; Torna a Surriento; *Di Capua:* 'O sole mio. (L. Pavarotti, A. Griminelli, Philh Chor, Philh/L. Magiera, C. Swann)

071 400-1DH2 (11/88) **071 400-3DH**
Vienna State Opera production of Elektra
R. Strauss: Elektra (Cpte). (Leonie Rysanek, A. Varnay, C. Ligendza, H. Beirer, D. Fischer-Dieskau, J. Greindl, C. Reppel, O. Varla, C. Doig, K. Böhme, C. Lorand, K. Borris, A. Gall, R. Yachmi-Caucig, M. Nikolova, M. Vance, Vienna St Op Chor, VPO/K. Böhm, G. Friedrich)

071 401-1DH2 (10/88) **071 401-3DH**
Verdi's Rigoletto filmed on location in Mantua
Verdi: Rigoletto (Cpte). (I. Wixell, E. Gruberová, L. Pavarotti, F. Furlanetto, V. Vergara, I. Wixell, F. Barbieri, R. Corazza, B. Weikl, K. Kuhlmann, R. Bracht, Vienna St Op Chor, VPO/R. Chailly, J-P. Ponnelle)

071 402-1DH2 (10/88) **071 402-3DH**
Puccini's Tosca filmed on location in Rome
Puccini: Tosca (Cpte). (R. Kabaivanska, P. Domingo, S. Milnes, G. Luccardi, M. Ferrara, A. Mariotti, B. Grella, D. Medici, P. Domingo jnr, Ambrosian Sngrs, New Philh/B. Bartoletti, G. de Bosio)

071 403-3DH (9/93)
Verdi—Falstaff
Verdi: Falstaff (Cpte). (G. Bacquier, R. Stilwell, K. Armstrong, J-R. Ihloff, M-R. Cosotti, M. Szirmay, S. Lindenstrand, J. Lanigan, P. Maus, U. Cold, Schöneberg Boys' Ch, Berlin Deutsche Op Chor, Vienna St Op Chor, VPO/G. Solti, G. Friedrich)

071 404-3DH (5/90)
Puccini—Madama Butterfly
Puccini: Madama Butterfly (Cpte). (M. Freni, P. Domingo, R. Kerns, C. Ludwig, M. Sénéchal, G. Stendoro, E. Schary, M. Rintzler, Vienna St Op Chor, VPO/H. von Karajan, J-P. Ponnelle)

071 405-1DH2 **071 405-3DH**
Solti conducts Arabella in Vienna, 1977
R. Strauss: Arabella (Cpte). (G. Janowitz, S. Ghazarian, B. Weikl, H. Kraemmer, M. Lilowa, E. Gruberová, R. Kollo, G. Fransson, H. Helm, K. Rydl, M. Mödl, VPO/G. Solti, O. Schenk)

071 406-1DH2 **071 406-3DH**
Jean-Pierre Ponnelle's production of Poppea
Monteverdi: Incoronazione di Poppea (Cpte). (R. Yakar, E. Tappy, T. Schmidt, P. Esswood, M. Salminen, H. Gardow, R. Lenhart, J. Perry, M. Minetto, A. Oliver, P. Huttenlocher, K. Brettschneider, P. Keller, S. Calabro, Zurich Op Monteverdi Ens/N. Harnoncourt, J-P. Ponnelle)

071 407-1DH2 (11/92) **071 407-3DH** (11/92)
Vicenza production of Mitridate, 1986
Mozart: Mitridate (Cpte). (G. Winbergh, Y. Kenny, A. Murray, A. Gjevang, J. Rodgers, P. Straka, M. Roncato, VCM/N. Harnoncourt, J-P. Ponnelle)

071 408-1DH3 (8/93) **071 408-3DH2** (8/93)
Peter Sellars's prodution of Guilio Cesare
Handel: Giulio Cesare (Cpte). (J. Gall, S. Larson, M. Westbrook-Geha, L. Hunt, D. Minter, J. Maddalena, H. Hildebrand, C. Cobb, Staatskapelle Dresden/C. Smith, P. Sellars)

071 409-1DH2 (4/94) **071 409-3DH2** (4/94)
Mussorgsky—Boris Godunov
Mussorgsky: Boris Godunov (Cpte). (R. Lloyd, A. Steblianko, O. Borodina, A. Morozov, V. Ognovenko, Y. Boitsov, I. Yan, S. Leiferkus, L. Dyadkova, O. Kondina, E. Perlasova, L. Filatova, V. Solodovnikov, M. Kit, Y. Fedotov, G. Karasyov, Kirov Th Chor, Kirov Th Orch/V. Gergiev, A. Tarkovsky)

071 411-1DH2
Peter Sellars' production of Don Giovanni
Mozart: Don Giovanni (Cpte). (E. Perry, D. Labelle, L. Hunt, A.L. Zhu, Carroll Freeman, H. Perry, E. James, J. Patterson, A. Schoenberg Ch, VPO/C. Smith, P. Sellars)

071 412-1DH2 **071 412-3DH**
Mozart—Le nozze di Figaro
Mozart: Nozze di Figaro (Cpte). (S. Sylvan, J. Ommerlé, J. Maddalena, J. West, S. Larson, S.E. Kuzma, D. Evitts, F. Kelley, W. Cotton, H. Hildebrand, L. Torgove, A. Schoenberg Ch, Vienna SO/C. Smith, P. Sellars)

071 421-1DH2 (7/93) **071 421-3DH2** (7/93)
Borodin—Prince Igor
Borodin: Prince Igor (Cpte). (S. Leiferkus, A. Tomowa-Sintow, A. Steblianko, N. Ghiuselev, P. Burchuladze, E. Zaremba, R. Leggate, E. Garrett, F. Egerton, Royal Ballet, ROH Chor, ROHO/B. Haitink, H. Burton)

071 422-1DH2 (5/93) **071 422-3DH** (5/93)
Verdi—Macbeth
Verdi: Macbeth (Cpte). (L. Nucci, S. Verrett, S. Ramey, V. Luchetti, A. Barasorda, S. Fontana, G. Casarini, G. Morresi, G. Sarti, A.C. Antonacci, Bologna Teatro Comunale Chor, Bologna Teatro Comunale Orch/R. Chailly, C. D'Anna)

071 423-1DH2 (5/93) **071 423-3DH** (5/93)
Verdi—Simon Boccanegra
Verdi: Simon Boccanegra (Cpte). (A. Agache, K. Te Kanawa, M. Sylvester, R. Scandiuzzi, A. Opie, M. Beesley, R. Gibson, E. Sikora, ROH Chor, ROHO/G. Solti, B. Large)

071 425-1DH2 (4/94) **071 425-3DH2** (4/94)
R. Strauss—Die Frau ohne Schatten
R. Strauss: Frau ohne Schatten (Cpte). (C. Studer, T. Moser, E. Marton, R. Hale, M. Lipovšek, B. Terfel, A. Rost, H. Lippert, E. Norberg-Schulz, E. Ardam, M. Hemm, H. Franzen, W. Gahmlich, Vienna St Op Chor, Salzburg Children's Ch, VPO/G. Solti, G. Friedrich)

071 426-1DH2 (6/95) **071 426-3DH** (6/95)
R. Strauss—Capriccio
R. Strauss: Capriccio (Cpte). (K. te Kanawa, H. Hagegård, D. Kuebler, S. Keenlyside, V. Braun, T. Troyanos, M. Sénéchal, D. Travis, San Francisco Op Orch/D. Runnicles)

071 428-3DH
Britten—Peter Grimes
Britten: Peter Grimes (Cpte). (P. Langridge, J. Cairns, A. Opie, A. Howard, A. Woodrow, A. Greenan, S. Gorton, R. Poulton, E. Byles, M. Richardson, M. Bovino, S. Pring, ENO Chor, ENO Orch/D. Atherton, T. Albery, B. Gavin)

071 431-3DH (9/95)
Verdi—La Traviata
Verdi: Traviata (Cpte). (A. Gheorghiu, F. Lopardo, L. Nucci, L-M. Jones, G. Knight, R. Leggate, R. Van Allan, R. Earle, M. Beesley, N. Griffiths, B. Secombe, R. Gibson, ROH Chor, ROHO/G. Solti, R. Eyre)

084 474-3 (12/90)
The Essential Kiri
Mozart: Nozze di Figaro (exc); Zauberflöte (exc); *Bizet:* Carmen Suites (exc); *Gounod:* Faust (exc); *G. Charpentier:* Louise (exc); *Verdi:* Forza del Destino (exc); *Puccini:* Tosca (exc); Rondine (exc); *F. Loewe:* My Fair Lady (exc). (K. Te Kanawa, J. Irons, W. Mitchell, London Voices, LSO/J. Mauceri)

Deutsche Grammophon

070 443-1GH2 (4/95) **072 443-3GH2** (4/95)
R. Strauss—Der Rosenkavalier
R. Strauss: Rosenkavalier (Cpte). (F. Lott, A.S. von Otter, K. Moll, B. Bonney, G. Hornik, K. Ikaia-Purdy, A. Gonda, H. Zednik, O. Miljakovic, Lotte Leitner, W. Bankl, P. Wimberger, W. Kmentt, F. Kasemann, P. Jelosits, Vienna St Op Chor, Vienna St Op Orch/C. Kleiber, O. Schenk)

072 105-1GH2 (10/88) **072 105-3GH**
La Bohème at La Scala, 1967
Puccini: Bohème (Cpte). (M. Freni, G. Raimondi, A. Martino, R. Panerai, G. Maffeo, I. Vinco, C. Badioli, La Scala Chor, La Scala Orch/H. von Karajan, F. Zeffirelli)

072 109-1GH **072 109-3GH**
R. Strauss—Salome
R. Strauss: Salome (Cpte). (T. Stratas, B. Weikl, H. Beirer, A. Varnay, W. Ochman, H. Schwarz, VPO/K. Böhm)

072 110-1GH (11/89)
Hommage a Sevilla—Placido Domingo in scenes from various operas
Mozart: Don Giovanni (exc); *Rossini:* Barbiere di Siviglia (exc); *Bizet:* Carmen (exc); *Verdi:* Forza del Destino (exc); *Beethoven:* Fidelio (exc); *Penella:* Gato Montés (exc). (P. Domingo, V. Vergara, VPO/James Levine, J-P. Ponnelle, V. Alonso)

072 124-3GH
Beethoven in Berlin - New Year's Concert
Beethoven: Egmont (exc); Ah! perfido, Op.65; Leonore (exc); Choral Fantasia. (C. Studer, B. Ganz, E. Kissin, Berlin RIAS Chbr Ch, BPO/C. Abbado)

072 139-3GH (10/95)
Janáček—From the House of the Dead
Janáček: From the House of the Dead (Cpte). (N. Ghiaurov, E. Szmytka, B. McCauley, B. Nikolov, R. Novák, H. Peeters, J. Veverka, P. Langridge, P. Kamas, R. Haan, C. Young, A. Oliver, H. Zednik, M. Pederson, M. Kopp, A. Rost, Vienna St Op Chor, VPO/C. Abbado, K.M. Grüber)

072 146-3GH
New Year's Concert in Vienna 1989
J. Strauss II: Accelerationen, Op. 234; Bauern-Polka, Op.

276; Bei uns z'Haus, Op. 361; Fledermaus (exc); Künstlerleben, Op. 316; Eljen a Magyar!, Op. 332; Im Krapfenwald'l, Op. 336; Frühlingsstimmen, Op. 410; Ritter Pasman; Blauen Donau, Op. 314; *Jos Strauss:* Libelle; Moulinet; Plappermäulchen; *J. Strauss II:* Pizzicato Polka; Radetzky March. (VPO/C. Kleiber, B. Large)

072 175-1GH **072 175-3GH**
New Year's Concert in Vienna 1991
Rossini: Gazza ladra (exc); *Jos Strauss:* Tanzende Muse; *Schubert:* Galop and Ecossaises, D735 (exc); *Lanner:* Werber, Op.103; *J. Strauss I:* Seufzer-Galopp; *J. Strauss II:* Waldmeister (exc); *Mozart:* Contredanses, K609 (exc); German Dances, K605 (exc); *Jos Strauss:* Aquarellen; *J. Strauss II:* Freikugeln, Op. 326; *E. Strauss:* Carmen; *J. Strauss II:* Kaiser, Op. 437; Piefke und Pufke; *J. Strauss II:* Furioso-Polka, Op. 260; Stürmisch in Lieb' und Tanz; Blauen Donau, Op. 314; Radetzky March. (VPO/C. Abbado)

072 187-1GH **072 187-3GH**
Hommage a Sevilla
Mozart: Don Giovanni (exc); *Rossini:* Barbiere di Siviglia (exc); *Bizet:* Carmen (exc); *Verdi:* Forza del Destino (exc); *Beethoven:* Fidelio (exc); *Penella:* Gato Montés (exc). (P. Domingo, V. Vergara, V. Alonso, VPO/James Levine, J-P. Ponnelle, H. Hohlfeld)

072 189-3GH
Kathleen Battle at the Metropolitan Museum
Gershwin: Porgy and Bess (exc); *Handel:* Serse (exc); Joshua (exc); *Mozart:* Veilchen, K476; Moto di gioia, K579; Ridente la calma, K152; *R. Strauss:* Lieder, Op.17 (exc); *Liszt:* Oh! quand je dors, S282; *Purcell:* Pausanias, Z585 (exc); *Puccini:* Gianni Schicchi (exc); *J. Strauss II:* Fledermaus (exc); *Handel:* Giulio Cesare (exc); *Traditional:* He's got the whole world in His hands; *Obradors:* Canciones clásicas españolas (exc); *Traditional:* Swing low sweet chariot. (K. Battle, W. Jones, H. Burton)

072 196-3GH
Karajan—The Best on Video
Beethoven: Symphony 6 (exc); Symphony 5 (exc); *Rachmaninov:* Piano Concerto 2 (exc); *Wagner:* Tannhäuser (exc); *Verdi:* Forza del Destino (exc). (A. Weissenberg, BPO/H. von Karajan)

072 400-1GH2 (9/91) **072 400-3GH**
Die Fledermaus at the Munich National Theatre
J. Strauss II: Fledermaus (Cpte). (P. Coburn, J. Perry, E. Waechter, J. Hopferwieser, W. Brendel, B. Fassbaender, B. Kusche, F. Gruber, I. Steinbeisser, F. Muxeneder, I. Ungar, Bavarian St Op Ballet, Bavarian St Op Chor, Bavarian St Op Orch/C. Kleiber, O. Schenk)

072 401-3GH
Otello from Berlin, 1974
Verdi: Otello (Cpte). (J. Vickers, M. Freni, P. Glossop, A. Bottion, M. Sénéchal, S. Malagù, J. Van Dam, M. Macchi, Berlin Deutsche Op Chor, BPO/H. von Karajan)

072 402-3GH
La Cenerentola at La Scala, 1981
Rossini: Cenerentola (Cpte). (F. von Stade, F. Araiza, C. Desderi, P. Montarsolo, M. Guglielmi, L. Zannini, P. Plishka, La Scala Chor, La Scala Orch/C. Abbado, J-P. Ponnelle)

072 403-1GH2 **072 403-3GH**
Böhm conducts Figaro at Vienna
Mozart: Nozze di Figaro (Cpte). (H. Prey, M. Freni, D. Fischer-Dieskau, K. Te Kanawa, M. Ewing, H. Begg, P. Montarsolo, J. van Kesteren, W. Caron, H. Kraemmer, J. Perry, VPO/K. Böhm, J-P. Ponnelle)

072 404-1GH2 **072 404-3GH**
Abbado conducts The Barber of Seville at La Scala
Rossini: Barbiere di Siviglia (Cpte). (H. Prey, T. Berganza, L. Alva, E. Dara, P. Montarsolo, S. Malagù, R. Cesari, L. Roni, La Scala Chor, La Scala Orch/C. Abbado, J-P. Ponnelle)

072 405-1GH2 (9/91) **072 405-3GH**
Munich National Theatre 1979—Rosenkavalier
R. Strauss: Rosenkavalier (Cpte). (G. Jones, B. Fassbaender, M. Jungwirth, L. Popp, B. Kusche, F. Araiza, G. Wewezow, D. Thaw, A. Waas, S. Sonnenschein, H. Wilbrink, A. Peter, G. Paskuda, F. Lenz, N. Orth, O. Kobayashi, Bavarian St Op Chor, Bavarian St Op Orch/C. Kleiber, O. Schenk)

072 408-1GH **072 408-3GH**
Mozart—Die Entführung aus dem Serail
Mozart: Entführung (Cpte). (E. Gruberová, R. Grist, F. Araiza, N. Orth, M. Talvela, T. Holtzmann, Bavarian St Op Chor, Bavarian St Orch/K. Böhm, A. Everding)

072 409-1GH2 **072 409-3GH**
Bizet—Carmen
Bizet: Carmen (Cpte). (A. Baltsa, J. Carreras, L. Mitchell, S. Ramey, M. Merritt, D. Kesling, B. Hubbard, A. Laciura, V. Hartman, A. Berberian, N. Castel, NY Met Op Ballet, NY Met Op Chor, NY Met Op Orch/James Levine, B. Large)

072 410-1GH2 **072 410-3GH**
Turandot at the Metropolitan Opera, 1987
Puccini: Turandot (Cpte). (E. Marton, P. Domingo, L. Mitchell, B. Schexnayder, A. Glassman, A. Laciura, P. Plishka, H. Cuénod, Arthur Thompson, NY Met Op Ballet, NY Met Op Chor, NY Met Op Orch/James Levine, F. Zeffirelli)

072 411-3GH (10/91)
Ariadne auf Naxos at the Metropolitan Opera, 1988
R. Strauss: Ariadne auf Naxos (Cpte). (J. Norman, T. Troyanos, K. Battle, J. King, F.F. Nentwig, S. Dickson, A. Korn, A. Laciura, A. Glassman, B. Bonney, G. Bean, D. Upshaw, J. Franck, N. Castel, NY Met Op Orch/James Levine, B. Large)

072 413-1GH2 (2/92) **072 413-3GH**
Verdi—Il Trovatore
Verdi: Trovatore (Cpte). (L. Pavarotti, E. Marton, S. Milnes, D. Zajick, J. Wells, L. di Franco, M. Baker, R. Morrison, J. Bills, NY Met Op Chor, NY Met Op Orch/James Levine, F. Melano)

072 414-3GH
Rossini—Il Barbiere di Siviglia
Rossini: Barbiere di Siviglia (Cpte). (L. Nucci, K. Battle, R. Blake, E. Dara, F. Furlanetto, L. di Franco, D. Hamilton, NY Met Op Chor, NY Met Op Orch/R. Weikert)

072 416-1GH2 **072 416-3GH**
Metropolitan Opera Production of Aida, 1989
Verdi: Aida (Cpte). (A. Millo, D. Zajick, P. Domingo, S. Milnes, P. Burchuladze, D. Kavrakos, M. Baker, M.J. Wray, NY Met Op Ballet, NY Met Op Chor, NY Met Op Orch/James Levine, B. Large)

072 418-1GH2 (5/92) **072 418-3GH** (5/92)
Levine conducts Das Rheingold
Wagner: Rheingold (Cpte). (J. Morris, C. Ludwig, S. Jerusalem, H. Zednik, E. Wlaschiha, M.A. Häggander, M. Baker, A. Held, B. Svendén, J-H. Rootering, M. Salminen, K. Erickson, D. Kesling, M. Parsons, NY Met Op Orch/James Levine, O. Schenk, B. Large)

072 419-1GH3 (5/92) **072 419-3GH2** (5/92)
Levine conducts Die Walküre
Wagner: Walküre (Cpte). (G. Lakes, J. Norman, H. Behrens, J. Morris, C. Ludwig, K. Moll, P. Sellers, K. Ikonomu, M. Thigpen, J. Castle, J. Bower, D. Kesling, W. Hillhouse, S. Kelly, NY Met Op Orch/James Levine, O. Schenk, B. Large)

072 420-1GH3 (5/92) **072 420-3GH2** (5/92)
Levine conducts Siegfried
Wagner: Siegfried (Cpte). (S. Jerusalem, J. Morris, H. Behrens, H. Zednik, E. Wlaschiha, B. Svendén, M. Salminen, D. Upshaw, NY Met Op Orch/James Levine, O. Schenk, B. Large)

072 421-1GH3 (5/92) **072 421-3GH2** (5/92)
Levine conducts Götterdämmerung
Wagner: Götterdämmerung (Cpte). (H. Behrens, S. Jerusalem, M. Salminen, E. Wlaschiha, A. Raffell, H. Lisowska, C. Ludwig, K. Erickson, D. Kesling, M. Parsons, G. Bean, J. Castle, A. Gruber, NY Met Op Chor, NY Met Op Orch/James Levine, O. Schenk, B. Large)

072 422-3GH7 (5/92)
Levine conducts Wagner's Ring
Wagner: Rheingold (Cpte); Walküre (Cpte); Siegfried (Cpte); Götterdämmerung (Cpte). (J. Morris, C. Ludwig, S. Jerusalem, H. Zednik, E. Wlaschiha, M.A. Häggander, M. Baker, A. Held, B. Svendén, J-H. Rootering, M. Salminen, K. Erickson, D. Kesling, M. Parsons, G. Lakes, J. Norman, H. Behrens, K. Moll, P. Sellers, K. Ikonomu, M. Thigpen, J. Castle, J. Bower, D. Kesling, W. Hillhouse, S. Kelly, S. Jerusalem, J. Morris, D. Upshaw, M. Salminen, A. Raffell, H. Lisowska, C. Ludwig, G. Bean, J. Castle, A. Gruber, NY Met Op Chor, NY Met Op Orch/James Levine, O. Schenk, B. Large)

072 423-3GH (11/91)
Bernstein—Candide
Bernstein: Candide (1988) (Cpte). (J. Hadley, J. Anderson, A. Green, C. Ludwig, N. Gedda, D. Jones, K. Ollmann, N. Jenkins, R. Suart, J. Treleaven, L. Benson, C. Bayley, LSC, LSO/L. Bernstein, H. Burton)

072 424-1GH2 (4/93) **072 424-3GH** (4/93)
Mozart—The Magic Flute
Mozart: Zauberflöte (Cpte). (K. Battle, L. Serra, F. Araiza, M. Hemm, K. Moll, A. Schmidt, H. Zednik, B. Kilduff, J. Gondek, M. Lerner, J. Christin, T. Huffman, B. Schott, P-C. Brevig, M. Baker, M. Devlin, J. Courtney, B. Fitch, NY Met Op Chor, NY Met Op Orch/James Levine, G. Mostart, B. Large)

072 426-1GH2 (7/92) **072 426-3GH** (7/92)
Puccini—Tosca
Puccini: Tosca (Cpte). (H. Behrens, P. Domingo, C. MacNeil, J. Courtney, A. Laciura, I. Tajo, R. Christopher, R. Vernon, M. Fogerty, NY Met Op Chor, NY Met Op Orch/G. Sinopoli, F. Zeffirelli)

072 428-1GH2 **072 428-3GH**
The Metropolitan Opera Gala
Verdi: Rigoletto (exc); Otello (exc); *J. Strauss II:* Fledermaus (exc). (L. Pavarotti, L. Nucci, C. Studer, N. Ghiaurov, B. Svendén, P. Domingo, M. Freni, J. Diaz, U. Heilmann, S. Kelly, P. Plishka, C. Anthony, D. Croft, H. Prey, B. Daniels, G. Hornik, A.S. von Otter, B. Kilduff, G. Millo, A. Dobriansky, J. Anderson, K. Battle, F. Furlanetto, T. Hampson, A. Millo, S. Milnes, S. Ramey, F. von Stade, NY Met Op Chor, NY Met Op Orch/James Levine, B. Large)

072 430-1GH2 (8/93) **072 430-3GH** (8/93)
Corigliano—The Ghosts of Versailles
Corigliano: Ghosts of Versailles (Cpte). (T. Stratas, P. Kazaras, R. Fleming, N. Rosenshein, T. Dahl, R. Drews, S. Zambalis, G. Quilico, J. Christin, H. Hagegård, M. Horne, J. Courtney, G. Clark, NY Met Op Ballet, NY Met Op Chor, NY Met Op Orch/James Levine, C. Graham)

072 431-1GH2 (6/94) **072 431-3GH** (6/94)
Debussy—Pelléas et Mélisande
Debussy: Pelléas et Mélisande (Cpte). (N. Archer, A. Hagley, D. Maxwell, K. Cox, P. Walker, S. Burkey, P. Massocchi, WNO Chor, WNO Orch/P. Boulez, P. Stein)

072 432-1GH2 (7/93) **072 432-3GH**
Donizetti—L'Elisir d'amore
Donizetti: Elisir d'amore (Cpte). (K. Battle, L. Pavarotti, J. Pons, E. Dara, K. Uecker, NY Met Op Chor, NY Met Op Orch/James Levine, B. Large)

072 433-1GH2 (4/94) **072 433-3GH** (4/94)
Puccini—La Fanciulla del West
Puccini: Fanciulla del West (Cpte). (B. Daniels, P. Domingo, S. Milnes, A. Laciura, J. Robbins, Y. Yannissis, H.J. Tian, S. Kelly, K. Josephson, C. Anthony, J. Courtney, R. Vernon, B. Fitch, M. Forest, K. Short, D. Croft, V. Hartman, Michael Best, NY Met Op Chor, NY Met Op Orch/L. Slatkin, G. del Monaco, B. Large)

072 434-1GH2 (10/95) **072 434-3GH** (10/95)
Verdi—Falstaff
Verdi: Falstaff (Cpte). (P. Plishka, B. Pola, M. Freni, B. Bonney, F. Lopardo, M. Horne, S. Graham, P. de Palma, A. Laciura, J. Courtney, NY Met Op Chor, NY Met Op Orch/James Levine, F. Zeffirelli)

072 435-1GH2 (11/94) **072 435-3GH2** (11/94)
Wagner—Parsifal
Wagner: Parsifal (Cpte). (S. Jerusalem, B. Weikl, K. Moll, W. Meier, F. Mazura, J-H. Rootering, P. Groves, J. Wells, H.G. Murphy, J. Bunnell, J.H. Murray, B. Fitch, K. Erickson, K. Uecker, G. Geyer, W. White, G. Bean, NY Met Op Chor, NY Met Op Orch/James Levine)

072 440-3GH (7/95)
Mozart—Don Giovanni
Mozart: Don Giovanni (Cpte). (C. Siepi, E. Grümmer, L. della Casa, E. Berger, A. Dermota, O. Edelmann, W. Berry, D. Ernster, Vienna St Op Chor, VPO/W. Furtwängler, H. Graf)

072 442-3GH (11/94)
R. Strauss—Ariadne auf Naxos
R. Strauss: Ariadne auf Naxos (Cpte). (G. Janowitz, T. Schmidt, E. Gruberová, R. Kollo, W. Berry, B. McDaniel, M. Jungwirth, H. Zednik, K. Equiluz, H. de Groote, A. Gall, O. Miljakovic, E. Kunz, A. Sramek, P. Weber, G. Tichy, VPO/K. Böhm, F. Sanjust)

EMI

LDA9 91242-1 (10/91) **MVC9 91242-3** (10/91)
Kiri Te Kanawa—Live Mozart Recital
Mozart: Clemenza di Tito (exc); Vado, ma dove?, K583; Chi sà, K582; Exsultate, jubilate, K165; Nozze di Figaro (exc); Zauberflöte (exc); Nehmt meinen Dank, K383; Don Giovanni (exc). (K. Te Kanawa, WNO Orch/C. Mackerras, J.M. Williams, H. Owen)

LDB4 91283-1 (3/95) **MVD4 91283-3** (3/95)
Maria Callas at Covent Garden
Verdi: Don Carlo (exc); *Bizet:* Carmen (exc); *Puccini:* Tosca (exc). (M. Callas, R. Cioni, T. Gobbi, R. Bowman, D. Wicks, ROH Chor, ROHO/G. Prêtre/C.F. Cillario, F. Zeffirelli)

LDB49 1131-4 **MVD49 1131-3**
Gershwin—Porgy and Bess
Gershwin: Porgy and Bess (Cpte). (W. White, C. Haymon, H. Blackwell, C. Clarey, D. Evans, M. Simpson, Gregg

Baker, B. Hubbard, B. Coleman, J. Worthy, Curtis Watson, M. Wallace, M. Brathwaite, A. Paige, W. Johnson, P. Ingram, L. Thompson, Colenton Freeman, C. Johnson, A. Tilvern, B.J. Mitchell, T. Maynard, R. Travis, W. Marshall, Glyndebourne Fest Chor, LPO/S. Rattle, T. Nunn)

LDB491007-1 (6/93) **MVD491007-3** (6/93)
Rossini Bicentennial Birthday Gala
Rossini: Gazza ladra (exc); Donna del lago (exc); Stabat mater (exc); Cenerentola (exc); Zelmira (exc); Bianca e Falliero (exc); Guillaume Tell (exc); Barbiere di Siviglia (exc); Petite messe solennelle (exc); Italiana in Algeri (exc); Zelmira (exc); Siège de Corinthe (exc); Viaggio a Reims (exc). (M. Fortuna, D. Voigt, M. Horne, K. Kuhlmann, M. Lerner, F. von Stade, R. Blake, C. Estep, C. Merritt, T. Hampson, J. Opalach, H. Runey, G. Hogan, S. Ramey, NY Concert Chorale, St Luke's Orch/R. Norrington, K. Browning)

LDB9 91234-1 **MVD9 91234-3**
Tennstedt conducts Wagner in Tokyo
Wagner: Tannhäuser (exc); Rienzi (exc); Götterdammerung (exc); Meistersinger (exc); Walküre (exc). (LPO/K. Tennstedt)

LDB9 91243-1 **MVD9 91243-3**
Itzak Perlman Live in Russia
Bazzini: Ronde des lutins; *Bloch:* Baal Shem (exc); *Kreisler:* Liebesleid; *Prokofiev:* Love for 3 Oranges Suite (exc); *Tartini:* Devil's Trill Sonata; *Tchaikovsky:* String Quartet 1 (exc); Violin Concerto; *Wieniawski:* Etudes-caprices, Op. 18 (exc). (I. Perlman, J.G. Guggenheim, Israel PO/Z. Mehta, R. Dalrymple)

LDB9 91258-1 (11/91) **MVC9 91258-3** (11/91)
Maria Callas at the Paris Opera December 1958
Verdi: Forza del Destino (exc); *Bellini:* Norma (exc); *Verdi:* Trovatore (exc); *Rossini:* Barbiere di Siviglia (exc); *Puccini:* Tosca (exc). (M. Callas, J. Mars, A. Lance, T. Gobbi, L. Rialland, J-P. Hurteau, Paris Op Chor, Paris Op Orch/G. Sébastian, R. Benamou)

LDC99 1311-1 (3/93) **MVD99 1311-3** (3/93)
Wagner—Der fliegende Holländer
Wagner: Fliegende Holländer (Cpte). (R. Hale, J. Varady, J. Rhyänen, P. Seiffert, A. Schlemm, U. Ress, Bavarian St Op Chor, Bavarian St Orch/W. Sawallisch)

LDD4 91134-1 **MVB4 91134-3**
Verdi—Don Carlo
Verdi: Don Carlo (Cpte). (L. Pavarotti, D. Dessì, L. d'Intino, P. Coni, S. Ramey, A. Anisimov, A. Silvestrelli, M. Laurenza, O. Zanetti, M. Bolognesi, N. Focile, La Scala Chor, La Scala Orch/R. Muti, F. Zeffirelli)

LDD9 91276-1 (5/92) **MVB9 91276-3** (5/92)
Sawallisch conducts Das Rheingold
Wagner: Rheingold (Cpte). (R. Hale, M. Lipovšek, R. Tear, H. Pampuch, E. Wlaschiha, N. Gustafson, J. Hopferwieser, F. Cerny, H. Schwarz, J-H. Rootering, K. Moll, J. Kaufman, A.M. Blasi, B. Calm, Bavarian St Orch/W. Sawallisch)

LDE9 91279-1 (5/92) **MVB9 91279-3** (5/92)
Sawallisch conducts Die Walküre
Wagner: Walküre (Cpte). (R. Schunk, J. Varady, H. Behrens, R. Hale, M. Lipovšek, K. Moll, A. Trauboth, N. Gustafson, M. Seibel, C. Wulkopf, G. Wewezow, C. Borchers, B. Calm, A. Pellekoorne, Bavarian St Orch/W. Sawallisch)

LDE9 91283-1 (5/92) **MVD9 91283-3** (5/92)
Sawallisch conducts Siegfried
Wagner: Siegfried (Cpte). (R. Kollo, R. Hale, H. Behrens, H. Pampuch, E. Wlaschiha, H. Schwarz, K. Moll, J. Kaufman, Bavarian St Orch/W. Sawallisch)

LDF9 91287-1 (5/92) **MVD9 91287-3** (5/92)
Sawallisch conducts Götterdämmerung
Wagner: Götterdämmerung (Cpte). (H. Behrens, R. Kollo, M. Salminen, E. Wlaschiha, H.G. Nöcker, L. Balslev, W. Meier, J. Kaufman, A.M. Blasi, B. Calm, M. Lipovšek, I. Karrasch, P. Thorn, Bavarian St Op Chor, Bavarian St Orch/W. Sawallisch)

LDX9 91275-1 (5/92) **MVX9 91275-3** (5/92)
Sawallisch conducts Wagner's Ring
Wagner: Rheingold (Cpte); Walküre (Cpte); Siegfried (Cpte); Götterdämmerung (Cpte). (R. Hale, H. Behrens, R. Kollo, R. Schunk, J. Varady, E. Wlaschiha, H. Pampuch, M. Lipovšek, R. Tear, K. Moll, H. Schwarz, K. Moll, M. Salminen, H.G. Nöcker, L. Balslev, W. Meier, J-H. Rootering, F. Cerny, J. Hopferwieser, N. Gustafson, J. Kaufman, A.M. Blasi, B. Calm, A. Trauboth, N. Gustafson, C. Wulkopf, A. Pellekoorne, M. Seibel, C. Borchers, B. Calm, G. Wewezow, J. Kaufman, M. Lipovšek, I. Karrasch, P. Thorn, R. Hale, Bavarian St Op Chor, Bavarian St Orch/W. Sawallisch)

MVP99 1042 2 (6/87)
The Academy of St Martin in the Fields at Longleat
Grieg: Holberg Suite (exc); *Handel:* Berenice (exc); *Pachelbel:* Canon and Gigue (exc); *Mozart:* Divertimenti, K136-8 (exc); *Borodin:* String Quartet 2 (exc); *Rossini:* Sonate a quattro (exc); *Bach:* Suites, BWV1066-9 (exc); *Handel:* Solomon (exc); Messiah (exc); *Bach:* Cantata 147 (exc); Cantata 208 (exc); *Gluck:* Orfeo ed Euridice (exc). (ASMF/N. Marriner, D. Heather)

IMP

SLL7013
Glyndebourne Festival Opera, 1973
Mozart: Nozze di Figaro (Cpte). (K. Skram, I. Cotrubas, B. Luxon, K. Te Kanawa, F. von Stade, N. Condò, M. Rintzler, J. Fryatt, B. Dickerson, T. Lawlor, E. Gale, Glyndebourne Fest Chor, LPO/J. Pritchard, P. Hall)

SLL7014
Glyndebourne Festival Opera, 1976
Verdi: Falstaff (Cpte). (D. Gramm, B. Luxon, K. Griffel, E. Gale, M-R. Cosotti, N. Condò, R. Penkova, J. Fryatt, B. Dickerson, U. Trama, Glyndebourne Fest Chor, LPO/J. Pritchard, J-P. Ponnelle)

SLL7015
Glyndebourne Festival Opera, 1978
Mozart: Zauberflöte (Cpte). (F. Lott, M. Sandoz, L. Goeke, B. Luxon, T. Thomaschke, W. White, J. Fryatt, E. Conquet, T. Cahill, P. Parker, F. Kimm, K. Flowers, L. John, E. Stokes, N. McKinnon, J. Rath, R. Berkeley-Steele, Glyndebourne Fest Chor, LPO/B. Haitink, J. Cox)

SLL7016
Glyndebourne Festival Opera, 1980
Mozart: Entführung (Cpte). (V. Masterson, L. Watson, R. Davies, J. Hoback, W. White, J. Bissmeier, Glyndebourne Fest Chor, LPO/G. Kuhn, P. Wood)

SLL7017
Glyndebourne Festival Opera, 1972
Verdi: Macbeth (Cpte). (K. Paskalis, J. Barstow, J. Morris, K. Erwen, I. Caley, B. Donlan, I. Caddy, J. Tomlinson, R. Woodland, Glyndebourne Fest Chor, LPO/J. Pritchard, M. Hadjimischev)

SL1056 (7/90)
Verdi—Rigoletto
Verdi: Rigoletto (Cpte). (T. Gobbi, L. Pagliughi, M. Filippeschi, G. Neri, A.M. Canali, M. Giorda, R. Bruni, V. Gottardi, G. Varni, Rome Op Chor, Rome Op Orch/T. Serafin, C. Gallone)

SL1058 (7/90)
Leoncavallo—Pagliacci
Leoncavallo: Pagliacci (Cpte). (G. Masini, O. Fineschi, T. Gobbi, G. Sinimberghi, Rome Op Chor, Rome Op Orch/G. Morelli, M. Costa)

SL2001
Glyndebourne Festival Opera, 1977
Mozart: Don Giovanni (Cpte). (B. Luxon, H. Branisteanu, R. Yakar, E. Gale, L. Goeke, S. Dean, J. Rawnsley, P. Thau, Glyndebourne Fest Chor, LPO/B. Haitink, P. Hall)

SL2002
Glyndebourne Festival Opera, 1975
Mozart: Così fan tutte (Cpte). (H. Döse, S. Lindenstrand, D. Perriers, A. Austin, T. Allen, F. Petri, Glyndebourne Fest Chor, LPO/J. Pritchard, A. Slack)

SL2003
Glyndebourne Festival Opera, 1974
Mozart: Idomeneo (Cpte). (Richard Lewis, L. Goeke, B. Betley-Sieradzka, J. Barstow, A. Oliver, J. Fryatt, D. Wicks, Glyndebourne Fest Chor, LPO/J. Pritchard, J. Cox)

SL2004
Glyndebourne Festival Opera, 1980
Beethoven: Fidelio (Cpte). (E. Söderström, A. de Ridder, R. Allman, C. Appelgren, E. Gale, I. Caley, M. Langdon, D. Johnston, R. Bryson, Glyndebourne Fest Chor, LPO/B. Haitink, P. Hall)

SL2006 (7/90)
Glyndebourne Festival Opera, 1987
Verdi: Traviata (Cpte). (M. McLaughlin, W. MacNeil, B. Ellis, J. Turner, E. Hartle, D. Hillman, G. Sandison, C. Thornton-Holmes, J. Hall, M. Harrison, C. Kerry, Glyndebourne Fest Chor, LPO/B. Haitink, P. Hall)

SL2007 (7/90)
Donizetti—Don Pasquale
Donizetti: Don Pasquale (Cpte). (G. Evans, L. Watson, R. Davies, R. Smythe, J. Dobson, WNO Chor, Welsh Philh/R. Armstrong, B. Coleman)

SL2008
Glyndebourne Festival Opera, 1977
Stravinsky: Rake's Progress (Cpte). (L. Goeke, F. Lott, S. Ramey, R. Elias, J. Fryatt, N. Willis, R. Van Allan, T. Lawlor, Glyndebourne Fest Chor, LPO/B. Haitink, J. Cox)

MCEG Virgin Vision

VVD1089 (4/93)
Mefistofele from the San Francisco Opera
Boito: Mefistofele (Cpte). (S. Ramey, D. O'Neill, G. Beňačková, J. Christin, D. Harper, E. Manhart, D. Wunsch, San Francisco Op Chor, San Francisco Op Orch/M. Arena, R. Carsen)

VVD1090
Orlando Furioso from the San Francisco Opera
Vivaldi: Orlando Furioso (Cpte). (M. Horne, S. Patterson, K. Kuhlmann, Sandra Walker, W. Matteuzzi, J. Gall, K. Langan, San Francisco Op Chor, San Francisco Op Orch/R. Behr, P.L. Pizzi)

VVD341 (5/90)
Madama Butterfly at La Scala, 1986
Puccini: Madama Butterfly (Cpte). (Y. Hayashi, P. Dvorský, G. Zancanaro, H-N. Kim, E. Gavazzi, A.C. Antonacci, S. Fontana, La Scala Chor, La Scala Orch/L. Maazel, K. Asari)

VVD342 (5/90)
Don Giovanni at the Drottingholm Court Theatre 1987
Mozart: Don Giovanni (Cpte). (H. Hagegård, H. Döse, B. Nordin, A. Soldh, G. Winbergh, E. Saedén, T. Wallström, B. Rundgren, Drottningholm Baroque Ens, Drottningholm Court Th Chor/A. Östman, G. Järvefelt)

VVD343
John Cranko's ballet of Onegin
Tchaikovsky: Eugene Onegin (exc). (Canada Nat Ballet)

VVD344 (5/90)
English National Opera production of Britten's Gloriana
Britten: Gloriana (Cpte). (Sarah Walker, A. Rolfe Johnson, J. Rigby, N. Howlett, E. Vaughan, A. Opie, R. Van Allan, M. Donnelly, ENO Chor, ENO Orch/M. Elder, C. Graham)

VVD378
Aida from La Scala, 1985
Verdi: Aida (Cpte). (M. Chiara, G. Dimitrova, L. Pavarotti, J. Pons, N. Ghiaurov, P. Burchuladze, E. Gavazzi, F. Garbi, La Scala Chor, La Scala Orch/L. Maazel, L. Ronconi)

VVD383
Julius Caesar from the ENO
Handel: Giulio Cesare (Cpte). (J. Baker, V. Masterson, Sarah Walker, D. Jones, J. Bowman, J. Tomlinson, J. Kitchiner, T.E. Williams, ENO Chor, ENO Orch/C. Mackerras, J. Copley)

VVD384
Macbeth from the Deutsche Oper, Berlin
Verdi: Macbeth (Cpte). (R. Bruson, M. Zampieri, J. Morris, D. O'Neill, D. Griffith, Berlin Deutsche Op Chor, Berlin Deutsche Op Orch/G. Sinopoli, B. Large)

VVD390
Ronald Hynd's ballet of The Merry Widow
Lehár: Lustige Witwe (exc). (Canada Nat Ballet)

VVD392
Rusalka from English National Opera
Dvořák: Rusalka (Cpte). (E. Hannan, R. Macann, A. Howard, J. Treleaven, P. Cannan, C. Pope, E. Hulse, L. McLeod, F. Kimm, E. Byles, ENO Chor, ENO Orch/M. Elder, D. Pountney)

VVD393
Samson et Dalila from the San Francisco Opera
Saint-Saëns: Samson et Dalila (Cpte). (P. Domingo, S. Verrett, W. Brendel, A. Voketaitis, K. Langan, R. Tate, San Francisco Op Chor, San Francisco Op Orch/J. Rudel, N. Joel)

VVD475
Così fan tutte from The Drottningholm Palace Theatre
Mozart: Così fan tutte (Cpte). (A.C. Biel, M. Höglind, U. Severin, L. Tibell, M. Lindén, E. Florimo, Drottningholm Court Th Chor, Drottningholm Court Th Orch/A. Östman, T. Olofsson)

VVD545
Billy Budd from the ENO
Britten: Billy Budd (Cpte). (T. Allen, P. Langridge, R. Van Allan, N. Howlett, P. Guy-Bromley, C. Bayley, E. Byles, M. Richardson, J. Connell, B. Banks, H. Milner, M. Rivers, A. Cunningham, C. Ross, R. Reaville, C. Booth-Jones, R. Reaville, ENO Chor, ENO Orch/D. Atherton, T. Albery)

VVD603
La Bohème from the San Francisco Opera
Puccini: Bohème (Cpte). (M. Freni, L. Pavarotti, S. Pacetti, G. Quilico, S. Dickson, N. Ghiaurov, I. Tajo, San Francisco Op Chor, San Francisco Op Orch/T. Severini, F. Zambello)

VVD616
La Finta Giardiniera from Drottningholm
Mozart: Finta Giardiniera (Cpte). (B-M. Aruhn, S. Kale, R. Croft, E. Pilat, A. Skoglund, A.C. Biel, P. Salomaa, Drottningholm Court Th Chor, Drottningholm Court Th Orch/A. Östman, G. Järvefelt)

VVD617
English National Opera production of The Rape of Lucretia
Britten: Rape of Lucretia (Cpte). (J. Rigby, A. Rolfe Johnson, K. Harries, R. Smythe, R. Van Allan, A. Opie, C. Pope, A-M. Owens, ENO Orch/L. Friend)

VVD663 (7/90)
Mozart—Die Zauberflöte
Mozart: Zauberflöte (Cpte). (A.C. Biel, B.L. Frandsen, S. Dahlberg, M. Samuelson, L. Polgár, P. Salomaa, M. Khyle, B. Larsson, A. Soldh, L. Sallay, I. Blom, E. Berg, A-C. Larsson, A. Tomson, T. Annmo, O. Sköld, T. Lilleqvist, Drottningholm Court Th Chor, Drottningholm Court Th Orch/A. Östman, T. Olofsson)

VVD664
Tippett—King Priam
Tippett: King Priam (Cpte). (R. Macann, J. Price, O. Ebrahim, Sarah Walker, H. Haskin, A. Mason, N. Jenkins, J. Hancorn, E. Hartle, R. Suart, M. Curtis, C. Gillett, Kent Op Chor, Kent Op Orch/R. Norrington, N. Hynter)

VVD665 (7/90)
Rossini—La Cenerentola
Rossini: Cenerentola (Cpte). (A. Murray, F. Araiza, G. Quilico, W. Berry, A. Denning, D. Evangelatos, W. Schöne, Vienna St Op Chor, VPO/R. Chailly, M. Hampe)

VVD673
San Francisco Opera
Meyerbeer: Africaine (Cpte). (S. Verrett, P. Domingo, R.A. Swenson, J. Diaz, M. Devlin, P. Skinner, J. Rouleau, K. Anderson, P. Spence, M. Delavan, San Francisco Op Chor, San Francisco Op Orch/M. Arena, B. Large)

VVD726
Vienna State Opera 1986
Ponchielli: Gioconda (Cpte). (E. Marton, P. Domingo, M. Manuguerra, M. Lilowa, K. Rydl, L. Shemchuk, A. Sramek, J. Pita, G. Simic, A. Burgstaller, Vienna St Op Chor, Vienna St Op Orch/A. Fischer, H. Käch)

VVD779
Sydney Opera House 1986
Donizetti: Lucia di Lammermoor (Cpte). (J. Sutherland, R. Greager, M. Donnelly, C. Grant, P. Price, S. Baigildin, R. Donald, Australian Op Chor, Sydney Eliz Orch/R. Bonynge, J. Copley)

VVD780
Sydney Opera House Gala Concert
Handel: Radamisto (exc); Semele (exc); Alcina (exc); *Rossini:* Donna del lago (exc); Cambiale di matrimonio (exc); Semiramide (exc); *Delibes:* Lakmé (exc); *Hérold:* Zampa (exc); *Offenbach:* Contes d'Hoffmann (exc); *Saint-Saëns:* Samson et Dalila (exc); *Auber:* Fra Diavolo (exc); *Meyerbeer:* Huguenots (exc); *Donizetti:* Don Pasquale (exc); *Bellini:* Norma (exc); *Benedict:* Gypsy and the Bird; *Foster:* Beautiful dreamer. (J. Sutherland, M. Horne, Sydney Eliz Orch/R. Bonynge, J. Widdicombe)

VVD781
Sydney Opera House 1985
J. Strauss II: Fledermaus (Cpte). (J. Sutherland, M. Brynnel, H. Begg, A. Austin, M. Lewis, G. Wilcock, A-M. McDonald, R. Gard, G. Yurisch, G. Ewer, Australian Op Chor, Sydney Eliz Orch/R. Bonynge, A. Besch)

VVD805 (12/90)
1989 Lyon production of The Love for Three Oranges
Prokofiev: Love for 3 Oranges (Cpte). (G. Bacquier, J-L. Viala, H. Perraguin, V. Le Texier, G. Gautier, D. Henry, G. Reinhart, M. Lagrange, C. Caroli, B. Fournier, C. Dubosc, J. Bastin, B. Uria-Monzon, Lyon Op Chor, Lyon Op Orch/K. Nagano, L. Erlo)

VVD828
Live from Sydney Opera House, 1988
Lehár: Lustige Witwe (Cpte). (J. Sutherland, G. Wilcock, A-M. McDonald, R. Stevens, A. Austin, N. Kirkby, C. Dawes, D. Brennan, C. Clack, J. Germain, I. Cassimatis, D. Soloman, R. Raisbeck, G. Ewer, Australian Op Chor, Sydney Eliz PO/R. Bonynge, V. Lumsden)

VVD841
Vienna State Opera 1990
Wagner: Lohengrin (Cpte). (P. Domingo, C. Studer, D. Vejzovic, H. Welker, R. Lloyd, G. Tichy, Vienna St Op Chor, Vienna St Op Orch/C. Abbado, B. Large)

VVD847
Glyndebourne Touring Opera, 1990
Britten: Death in Venice (Cpte). (R. Tear, A. Opie, M. Chance, G. Finley, C. Ventris, Glyndebourne Fest Chor, London Sinfonietta/Graeme Jenkins, S. Lawless)

VVD848
Die Entführung aus dem Serail from Drottningholm
Mozart: Entführung (Cpte). (A. Winska, E. Hellstrom, R. Croft, B-O. Morgan, T. Szule, E. Schaffer, Drottningholm Court Th Chor, Drottningholm Court Th Orch/A. Östman, H. Clemen)

VVD928
Glyndebourne Festival Opera, 1989
Janáček: Jenufa (Cpte). (R. Alexander, P. Langridge, A. Silja, M. Baker, A. Hagley, M. Davies, R. Poulton, G. Sandison, L. Ormiston, H. Cannell, D. Cowley, S. Pring, L. Davies, Glyndebourne Fest Chor, LPO/A. Davis, N. Lehnhoff)

VVD929
Glyndebourne Festival Opera, 1988
Janáček: Káťa Kabanová (Cpte). (N. Gustafson, B. McCauley, F. Palmer, D. Adams, R. Davies, J. Graham-Hall, L. Winter, R. Poulton, C. Bunning, L. Ormiston, Glyndebourne Fest Chor, LPO/A. Davis, N. Lehnhoff)

VVD946
Mozart—Idomeneo
Mozart: Idomeneo (Cpte). (S. Kale, D. Kuebler, A.C. Biel, A. Soldh, J-E. Jacobsson, L. Tibell, O. Sköld, Drottningholm Court Th Chor, Drottningholm Court Th Orch/A. Östman, M. Hampe)

VVD950
Nuria Espert's Covent Garden production of Carmen
Bizet: Carmen (Cpte). (M. Ewing, L. Lima, L. Vaduva, G. Quilico, J. Howarth, J. Rigby, B. Caproni, F. Egerton, C. Booth-Jones, R. Earle, ROH Chor, ROHO/Z. Mehta, B. Gavin)

VVD951
Adolf Dresen's Covent Garden production of Fidelio
Beethoven: Fidelio (Cpte). (G. Beňačková, J. Protschka, M. Pederson, R. Lloyd, M. McLaughlin, N. Archer, H. Tschammer, L. Atkinson, M. Beesley, ROH Chor, ROHO/C. von Dohnányi, D. Bailey)

VVD952
Covent Garden production of Die Fledermaus
J. Strauss II: Fledermaus (Cpte). (N. Gustafson, J. Howarth, L. Otey, B. Bottone, A. Michaels-Moore, J. Kowalski, E. Garrett, J. Dobson, G. Groves, J. Sessions, J. Sutherland, L. Pavarotti, M. Horne, ROH Chor, ROHO/R. Bonynge, H. Burton)

VVD986
Covent Garden production of Orfeo ed Euridice
Gluck: Orfeo ed Euridice (Cpte). (J. Kowalski, G. Webster, J. Budd, ROH Chor, ROHO/Hartmut Haenchen, H. Kupfer)

Philips

070 103-1PH **070 103-3PH**
Cavalleria Rusticana filmed at La Scala and Vizzini, Sicily
Mascagni: Cavalleria Rusticana (Cpte). (E. Obraztsova, P. Domingo, R. Bruson, A. Goll, F. Barbieri, La Scala Chor, La Scala Orch/G. Prêtre, F. Zeffirelli)

070 104-1PHI **070 104-3PH** (7/90)
Franco Zeffirelli's film of I Pagliacci
Leoncavallo: Pagliacci (Cpte). (P. Domingo, T. Stratas, J. Pons, A. Rinaldi, F. Andreolli, La Scala Orch, La Scala Chor/G. Prêtre, F. Zeffirelli)

070 118-3PH
Jessye Norman sings Carmen
Bizet: Carmen (exc). (J. Norman, N. Shicoff, S. Estes, FNO/S. Ozawa)

070 152-3PH
New Year's Concert 1992
Nicolai: Lustigen Weiber von Windsor (exc); *J. Strauss II:* Stadt und Land; *Jos Strauss:* Dorfschwalben aus Österreich; Feuerfest; *J. Strauss II:* Vergnügungszug; Zigeunerbaron (exc), Tausend und eine Nacht, Neue Pizzicato-Polka, Op. 449; Persischer Marsch; Tritsch-Tratsch; *Jos Strauss:* Sphärenklänge; *J. Strauss II:* Unter Donner und Blitz; *Jos Strauss:* Jokey; *J. Strauss II:* Blauen Donau, Op. 314; Radetzky March. (VPO/C. Kleiber, B. Large)

070 155-1PH **070 155-3PH**
The Sorceress—Original Soundtrack
Handel: Rinaldo (exc); Alcina (exc); Giulio Cesare (exc); Ariodante (exc); Agrippina (exc); Admeto (exc); Giustino (exc). (K. te Kanawa, AAM/C. Hogwood)

070 166-1PH **070 166-3PH**
Essential Ballet - Stars of Russian Dance
Tchaikovsky: Eugene Onegin (exc); *Minkus:* Paquita (exc); *Tchaikovsky:* Swan Lake (exc); Nutcracker (exc); Sleeping Beauty (exc); *Adam:* Corsaire (exc); Giselle (exc); *Stravinsky:* Firebird; *Saint-Saëns:* Carnaval des animaux (exc); *Minkus:* Don Quixote (exc); *Dvořák:* String Quartet 9 (exc); *Gavrilin:* Aniuta; *Drigo:* Diana and Actaeon (exc). (Kirov Th Orch/V. Gergiev/V. Fedotov, Moscow RSO/A. Sotnikov)

070 400-3PHE
Britten—The Turn of the Screw
Britten: Turn of the Screw (Cpte). (P. Langridge, R. Tear, H. Donath, M. Ginn, L. Watson, A. June, H. Harper, V. Müller, ROHO/Colin Davis, P. Weigl)

070 401-1PHE2 (5/92) **070 401-3PHE** (5/92)
Wagner—Das Rheingold
Wagner: Rheingold (Cpte). (D. McIntyre, H. Schwarz, H. Zednik, H. Pampuch, H. Becht, C. Reppel, S. Jerusalem, M. Egel, O. Wenkel, M. Salminen, F. Hübner, N. Sharp, I. Gramatzki, M. Schiml, Bayreuth Fest Orch/P. Boulez, P. Chéreau)

070 402-1PHE3 (5/92) **070 402-3PHE2** (5/92)
Wagner—Die Walküre
Wagner: Walküre (Cpte). (P. Hofmann, J. Altmeyer, G. Jones, D. McIntyre, H. Schwarz, M. Salminen, C. Reppel, K. Middleton, K. Clarke, G. Schnaut, M. Schiml, I. Gramatzki, G. Killebrew, E. Glauser, Bayreuth Fest Orch/P. Boulez, P. Chéreau)

070 403-1PHE3 (5/92) **070 403-3PHE2** (5/92)
Wagner—Siegfried
Wagner: Siegfried (Cpte). (M. Jung, D. McIntyre, G. Jones, H. Zednik, H. Becht, O. Wenkel, F. Hübner, N. Sharp, Bayreuth Fest Orch/P. Boulez, P. Chéreau)

070 404-1PHE3 (5/92) **070 404-3PHE2** (5/92)
Wagner—Götterdämmerung
Wagner: Götterdämmerung (Cpte). (G. Jones, M. Jung, F. Hübner, H. Becht, F. Mazura, J. Altmeyer, G. Killebrew, N. Sharp, I. Gramatzki, M. Schiml, O. Wenkel, G. Schnaut, K. Clarke, Bayreuth Fest Chor, Bayreuth Fest Orch/P. Boulez, P. Chéreau)

070 405-1PHG2 (9/91) **070 405-3PH** (7/90)
Bavarian State Opera production of The Magic Flute, 1983
Mozart: Zauberflöte (Cpte). (L. Popp, E. Gruberová, F. Araiza, W. Brendel, K. Moll, J-H. Rootering, N. Orth, G. Sieber, P. Coburn, D. Evangelatos, C. Wulkopf, C. Rossdeutscher, C. Immler, S. Bandemehr, H. Winkler, K. Helm, K. Böhme, F. Klarwein, G. Auer, D. Thaw, Bavarian St Op Chor, Bavarian St Op Orch/W. Sawallisch, P. Windgassen)

070 406-1PHE2 (11/91) **070 406-3PH** (11/91)
The Flying Dutchman from the Bayreuth Festival, 1985
Wagner: Fliegende Holländer (Cpte). (S. Estes, L. Balslev, M. Salminen, R. Schunk, A. Schlemm, G. Clark, Bayreuth Fest Chor, Bayreuth Fest Orch/W. Nelsson, H. Kupfer)

070 408-1PHE2
Jonathan Miller's production of The Beggar's Opera
Gay: Beggar's Opera (Cpte). (C. Hall, R. Daltrey, R. Ashe, P. Bayliss, S. Johns, P. Routledge, G. Brown, G. Tibbs, A. Pedley, I. Blair, E. Sharling, K. Stott, B. Hoskins, G. Crowden, EBS/J.E. Gardiner, J. Miller)

070 409-1PHE3
Bayreuth Festival Production of Tristan and Isolda, 1983
Wagner: Tristan und Isolde (Cpte). (R. Kollo, J. Meier, H. Schwarz, M. Salminen, H. Becht, R. Schunk, H. Pampuch, M. Egel, Bayreuth Fest Chor, Bayreuth Fest Orch/D. Barenboim, J-P. Ponnelle)

070 410-1PHG3
Bayreuth Production of Parsifal, 1981
Wagner: Parsifal (Cpte). (S. Jerusalem, B. Weikl, H. Sotin, E. Randová, L. Roar, M. Salminen, T. Krämer, H.K. Ecker, M. Schiml, H. Schwarz, H. Pampuch, M. Egel, N. Sharp, C. Richardson, M.A. Häggander, M. Neubauer, Bayreuth Fest Chor, Bayreuth Fest Orch/H. Stein, W. Wagner, B. Large)

070 411-1PHG2 (9/91) **070 411-3PHG2**
Lohengrin from the Bayreuth Festival
Wagner: Lohengrin (Cpte). (P. Hofmann, K. Armstrong, E. Connell, L. Roar, S. Vogel, B. Weikl, Bayreuth Fest Chor, Bayreuth Fest Orch/W. Nelsson, G. Friedrich)

070 412-1PH2 **070 412-3PH2**
Bayreuth Festival production of Tannhäuser, 1978
Wagner: Tannhäuser (Cpte). (S. Wenkoff, G. Jones, B. Weikl, H. Sotin, R. Schunk, F. Mazura, J. Pickering, H. Feldhoff, K. Brettschneider, L. Charles, K. Haigen, Bayreuth Fest Chor, Bayreuth Fest Orch/Colin Davis, G. Friedrich)

070 413-1PH3 (3/92) **070 413-3PH2**
Wagner—Die Meistersinger - Bayreuth, 1984
Wagner: Meistersinger (Cpte). (B. Weikl, S. Jerusalem, M.A. Häggander, M. Schenk, H. Prey, G. Clark, M. Schiml, J. Vermeersch, A. Molnár, M. Egel, U. Holdorf, P. Maus, H. Pampuch, S. Sólyom-Nagy, H.K. Ecker, D. Schweikart, M. Hölle, Bayreuth Fest Chor, Bayreuth Fest Orch/H. Stein, W. Wagner, B. Large)

070 416-1PHE2
Drottningholm production of Cosi Fan Tutte
Mozart: Così fan tutte (Cpte). (A.C. Biel, M. Höglind, U. Severin, L. Tibell, M. Lindén, E. Florimo, Drottningholm Court Th Chor, Drottningholm Court Th Orch/A. Östman, W. Decker)

070 418-1PHE2
Drottingholm Production of La Finta Giadiniera
Mozart: Finta Giardiniera (Cpte). (B-M. Aruhn, S. Kale, R. Croft, E. Pilat, A. Skoglund, A.C. Biel, P. Salomaa, Drottningholm Court Th Chor, Drottningholm Court Th Orch/A. Östman, G. Järvefelt)

070 419-1PHE2 (9/93)
Drottningholm production of Don Giovanni
Mozart: Don Giovanni (Cpte). (H. Hagegård, H. Döse, B. Nordin, A. Soldh, G. Winbergh, E. Saedén, T. Wallström, B. Rundgren, Drottningholm Court Th Chor, Drottningholm Court Th Orch/A. Östman, G. Järvefelt)

070 421-1PHG2
Mozart—Le Nozze di Figaro
Mozart: Nozze di Figaro (Cpte). (M. Samuelson, G. Resick, P-A. Wahlgren, S. Lindenstrand, A. C. Biel, K. Mang-Habashi, E. Saedén, T. Lilleqvist, B. Leinmark, K-R. Lindgren, B. Larsson, Drottningholm Court Th Chor, Drottningholm Court Th Orch/A. Östman, G. Järvefelt, T. Olofsson)

070 422-1PHG2
Mozart—Die Zauberflöte
Mozart: Zauberflöte (Cpte). (A.C. Biel, B.L. Frandsen, S. Dahlberg, M. Samuelson, L. Polgár, P. Salomaa, M. Khyle, B. Larsson, A. Soldh, L. Sallay, I. Blom, E. Berg, A-C. Larsson, A. Tomson, T. Annmo, O. Sköld, T. Lilleqvist, Drottningholm Court Th Chor, Drottningholm Court Th Orch/A. Östman, G. Järvefelt, T. Olofsson)

070 429-3
Animated Film of The Magic Flute
Mozart: Zauberflöte (Cpte). (M. Price, L. Serra, P. Schreier, M. Melbye, K. Moll, T. Adam, R. Tear, M. Venuti, M. McLaughlin, A. Murray, H. Schwarz, F. Höher, M. Diedrich, F. Klos, R. Goldberg, H. Reeh, A. Ude, Leipzig Rad Chor, Staatskapelle Dresden/Colin Davis)

070 433-1PHG2 **070 433-3PH2**
Mussorgsky—Khovanshchina
Mussorgsky: Khovanshchina (Cpte). (B. Minzhilkiev, Y. Marusin, K. Pluzhnikov, V. Trofimov, N. Okhotnikov, O. Borodina, E. Tselovalnik, T. Kravtsova, V. Lebed, M. Chernozhukov, N. Gassiev, V. Gerelo, Y. Fedotov, A. Khramtsov, Kirov Ballet, Kirov Th Chor, Kirov Th Orch/V. Gergiev, B. Large)

070 434-1PH2 (6/94) **070 434-3PH** (6/94)
Tchaikovsky—The Queen of Spades
Tchaikovsky: Queen of Spades (Cpte). (G. Grigorian, M. Gulegina, L. Filatova, S. Leiferkus, A. Gergalov, O. Borodina, V. Solodovnikov, S. Alexashkin, E. Boitsov, N. Gassiev, G. Bezebenkov, E. Perlasova, T. Filimonova, Kirov Th Chor, Kirov Th Orch/V. Gergiev, Y. Temirkanov)

070 435-1PH2 **070 435-3PH2**
Wagner—Tannhäuser
Wagner: Tannhäuser (Cpte). (R. Versalle, C. Studer, W. Brendel, R. Engert-Ely, H. Sotin, W. Pell, S. Vogel, C. Bieber, S. Sólyom-Nagy, J. Robinson, Bayreuth Fest Chor, Bayreuth Fest Orch/G. Sinopoli, W. Wagner, B. Large)

070 436-1PH2 **070 436-3PH2**
Wagner—Lohengrin
Wagner: Lohengrin (Cpte). (P. Frey, C. Studer, G. Schnaut, E. Wlaschiha, M. Schenk, E.W. Schulte, Bayreuth Fest Chor, Bayreuth Fest Orch/P. Schneider, W. Herzog, B. Large)

070 439-1PHG2 (7/95) **070 439-3PH** (7/95)
Rimsky-Korsakov—Sadko
Rimsky-Korsakov: Sadko (Cpte). (V. Galusin, V. Tsidipova, S. Alexashkin, M. Tarassova, L. Dyadkova, B. Minzhilkiev, G. Grigorian, A. Gergalov, V. Ognovenko, N. Gassiev, N. Putilin, Y. Boitsov, G. Bezebenkov, Kirov Ballet, Kirov Th Chor, Kirov Th Orch/V. Gergiev, B. Large)

Pickwick

RPT2032
Canadian Opera Company
Janáček: Makropulos Affair (Cpte). (S. Sundine, G. Clark, R. Margison, K. Brett, C. Opthof, B. Boutet, R. Orth, S. Horst, G. Rideout, G. Prata, Canadian Op Chor, Canadian Op Orch/B. Klobučar, L. Mansouri)

Pioneer

CVI1771 (10/95)
Gounod—Roméo et Juliette
Gounod: Roméo et Juliette (Cpte). (R. Alagna, L. Vaduva, R. Lloyd, F. Le Roux, A. M. Panzarella, P. Sidhom, Sarah Walker, P. C. Clarke, ROH Chor, ROHO/C. Mackerras, B. Large)

PLMCB00221 (4/93)
Vienna State Opera production of Elektra
R. Strauss: Elektra (Cpte). (E. Marton, B. Fassbaender, C. Studer, J. King, F. Grundheber, G. Simic, W. Winsauer, N. Sasaki, W. Gahmlich, C. Otelli, G. Lechner, M. Lilowa, G. Sima, M. Hintermeier, B. Poschner-Klebel, J. Borowska, Vienna St Op Chor, Vienna St Op Orch/C. Abbado, B. Large)

PLMCB00271
Robert Helpman's Ballet of The Merry Widow
Lehár: Lustige Witwe (Cpte). (Canada Nat Ballet, Canada Nat Ballet Orch/E. Florio, N. Campbell)

PLMCB00281 (5/93)
San Francisco production of La Bohème
Puccini: Bohème (Cpte). (M. Freni, L. Pavarotti, S. Pacetti, G. Quilico, S. Dickson, N. Ghiaurov, I. Tajo, D. Harper, M. Coles, San Francisco Op Chor, San Francisco Op Orch/T. Severini, B. Large)

PLMCB00421
Vienna State Opera production of Wozzeck
Berg: Wozzeck (Cpte). (F. Grundheber, H. Behrens, W. Raffeiner, P. Langridge, H. Zednik, A. Haugland, A. Gonda, Vienna St Op Chor, Vienna St Op Orch/C. Abbado, B. Large)

PLMCB00501
Tchaikovsky—Symphony No 2.Eugene Onegin (Highlights)
Tchaikovsky: Symphony 2; Eugene Onegin (exc). (L. Shernikh, A. Nenadovsky, Moscow RSO/V. Fedoseyev, R. Greenberg)

PLMCB00551
A Concert of Russian Music
Glinka: Ruslan and Lyudmila (exc); *Tchaikovsky:* Violin Concerto; *Shostakovich:* Symphony 5. (V. Mullova, LSO/M. Shostakovich, H. Chappell)

PLMCB00621
Gluck—Orphée et Eurydice
Gluck: Orfeo ed Euridice (Cpte). (J. Kowalski, G. Webster, J. Budd, ROH Chor, ROHO/Hartmut Haenchen, H. Kupfer)

PLMCB00791 (9/93)
R.Strauss—Salome
R. Strauss: Salome (Cpte). (M. Ewing, M. Devlin, K. Riegel, G. Knight, R. Leggate, ROHO/E. Downes, P. Hall)

PLMCB00861
Verdi—Stiffelio
Verdi: Stiffelio (Cpte). (J. Carreras, C. Malfitano, G. Yurisch, G. Howell, R. Leggate, A. Paxton, L. Atkinson, ROH Chor, ROHO/E. Downes, E. Moshinsky)

PLMCB00931 (6/95)
Offenbach—Les Contes D'Hoffmann
Offenbach: Contes d'Hoffmann (Cpte). (D. Galvez-Vallejo, N. Dessay, I. Vernet, B. Hendricks, B. Balleys, J. Van Dam, G. Bacquier, H. Jossoud, J. Verzier, L. Malidor, Lyon Op Chor, Lyon Op Orch/K. Nagano)

PLMCC00261
Puccini—Madama Butterfly
Puccini: Madama Butterfly (Cpte). (Y. Hayashi, P. Dvorský, G. Zancanaro, H-N. Kim, E. Gavazzi, A. Testa, A.C. Antonacci, S. Fontana, C. Giombi, La Scala Chor, La Scala Orch/L. Maazel, D. Bailey)

PLMCC00291 (3/93)
Glyndebourne production of La Traviata
Verdi: Traviata (Cpte). (M. McLaughlin, W. MacNeil, B. Ellis, J. Turner, E. Hartle, D. Hillman, G. Sandison, C. Thornton-Holmes, J. Hall, C. Kerry, Glyndebourne Fest Chor, LPO/B. Haitink, P. Hall)

PLMCC00301
Covent Garden production of Fidelio
Beethoven: Fidelio (Cpte). (G. Beňačková, J. Protschka, M. Pederson, R. Lloyd, M. McLaughlin, N. Archer, H. Tschammer, L. Atkinson, M. Beesley, ROH Chor, ROHO/C. von Dohnányi, D. Bailey)

PLMCC00631 (4/93)
Mussorgsky—Khovanschina
Mussorgsky: Khovanshchina (Cpte). (N. Ghiaurov, V. Atlantov, Y. Marusin, A. Kocherga, P. Burchuladze, L. Shemchuk, B. Poschner-Klebel, H. Zednik, J. Borowska, W. Gahmlich, T. Breese, Slovak Phil Chor, Vienna Boys' Ch, Vienna St Op Chor, Vienna St Op Orch/C. Abbado, A. Kirchner)

PLMCC00641 (4/93)
Australian Opera production of Lucia di Lammermoor
Donizetti: Lucia di Lammermoor (Cpte). (J. Sutherland, R. Greager, M. Donnelly, C. Grant, P. Price, S. Baigildin, R. Donald, Australian Op Chor, Sydney Eliz Orch/R. Bonynge, J. Copley)

PLMCC00691 (4/93)
Boito—Mefistofele
Boito: Mefistofele (Cpte). (S. Ramey, D. O'Neill, G. Beňačková, J. Christin, D. Harper, E. Manhart, D. Wunsch, San Francisco Op Chor, San Francisco Op Orch/M. Arena, R. Carsen)

PLMCC00701 (6/93)
Offenbach—Les Brigands
Offenbach: Brigands (Cpte). (M. Trempont, V. Chevalier, C. Alliot-Lugaz, R. Cassinelli, G. Fletcher, J-L. Meunier, A. Garcin, M. Barscha, A. Normand, J-L. Viala, J-L. Maurette, G. Gautier, B. Pisani, R. Schirrer, J. Loreau, Lyon Op Chor, Lyon Op Orch/C. Gibault, L. Erlo, A. Maratrat)

PLMCC00711 (9/93)
Verdi—Luisa Miller
Verdi: Luisa Miller (Cpte). (J. Anderson, T. Ichihara, E. Tumagian, P. Plishka, S. Anselmi, R. Tesarowicz, B. Desnoues, M. Pastor, Montpellier Op Chor, Lyon Op Chor, Lyon Op Orch/M. Arena, C. Viller)

PLMCC00841
Glyndebourne Festival Opera, 1992
Tchaikovsky: Queen of Spades (Cpte). (Y. Marusin, N. Gustafson, F. Palmer, S. Leiferkus, D. Kharitonov, M-A. Todorovitch, G. Matheson-Bruce, A. Slater, R. Burt, G. Pogson, C. Thornton-Holmes, E. Hartle, R. Tovey, Glyndebourne Fest Chor, LPO/A. Davis, G. Vick)

PLMCC00851
Verdi—Otello
Verdi: Otello (Cpte). (P. Domingo, K. Te Kanawa, S. Leiferkus, R. Leggate, R. Remedios, C. Powell, M. Beesley, R. Earle, C. Lackner, ROH Chor, ROHO/G. Solti, E. Moshinsky)

PLMCC00941 (7/95)
Mozart—Mitridate, rè di Ponto
Mozart: Mitridate (Cpte). (B. Ford, L. Orgonášová, A. Murray, J. Kowalski, L. Watson, J. Lavender, J. Fugelle, ROHO/P. Daniel)

PLMCD00091
Covent Garden production of Carmen
Bizet: Carmen (Cpte). (M. Ewing, L. Lima, L. Vaduva, G. Quilico, J. Howarth, J. Rigby, B. Caproni, F. Egerton, C. Booth-Jones, R. Earle, ROH Chor, ROHO/Z. Mehta, B. Gavin)

PLMCD00151 (3/93)
Salzburg Festival production of La Cenerentola
Rossini: Cenerentola (Cpte). (A. Murray, F. Araiza, G. Quilico, W. Berry, A. Denning, D. Evangelatos, W. Schöne, Vienna St Op Chor, VPO/R. Chailly, M. Hampe, C. Viller)

PLMCD00181
Australian Opera Production of Les Huguenots
Meyerbeer: Huguenots (Cpte). (J. Sutherland, A. Thane, S. Johnston, J. Wegner, J. Pringle, L. Gaffney, D. Lemke, K. Henderson, D. Collins-White, N. Kirkby, A. Austin, C. Grant, S. Baigildin, K. Harms, N. Wilkie, J. Cole, K.E. Brown, M. McKay, J. Bermingham, D. Hibbard, S. Bennett, G. Scott, Australian Op Dance Ens, Australian Op Chor, Australian Op & Ballet Orch/R. Bonynge, V. Lumsden)

PLMCD00601 (3/93)
San Francisco production of L'Africaine
Meyerbeer: Africaine (Cpte). (S. Verrett, P. Domingo, J. Diaz, R.A. Swenson, M. Devlin, P. Skinner, P. Spence, J. Rouleau, M. Delavan, San Francisco Op Chor, San Francisco Op Ballet, San Francisco Op Orch/M. Arena, B. Large)

PLMCD00721 (9/93)
Johann Strauss—Die Fledermaus
J. Strauss II: Fledermaus (Cpte). (N. Gustafson, J.

Howarth, L. Otey, B. Bottone, A. Michaels-Moore, J. Kowalski, E. Garrett, J. Dobson, G. Groves, J. Sessions, J. Sutherland, L. Pavarotti, M. Horne, ROH Chor, ROHO/R. Bonynge, H. Burton)

PLMCD00771 (6/95)
Handel—Giulio Cesare
Handel: Giulio Cesare (Cpte). (J. Baker, V. Masterson, Sarah Walker, D. Jones, J. Bowman, J. Tomlinson, J. Kitchiner, T.E. Williams, B. Casey, ENO Chor, ENO Orch/C. MacKerras)

RCA Victor

09026 62706-3 (7/95)
Heifetz in Performance
Mozart: Serenade, K250 (exc); *Prokofiev:* Love for 3 Oranges (exc); *Debussy:* Préludes (exc); *Rachmaninov:* Songs, Op. 38 (exc); *Gershwin:* Porgy and Bess (exc); *Bach:* Solo Violin Partitas and Sonatas (exc); *Bruch:* Scottish Fantasy. (J. Heifetz, B. Smith, FNO/Anon)

780 346 (9/91) **790 346** (5/90)
Toscanini conducts Aida from NBC Studio 8-H, 1949
Verdi: Aida (Cpte). (H. Nelli, E. Gustavson, R. Tucker, G. Valdengo, N. Scott, D. Harbour, V. Assandri, T. Stich-Randall, R. Shaw Chorale, NBC SO/A. Toscanini)

780 355 (9/91) **790 355** (12/90)
Toscanini—Carnegie Hall Concert, 3/11/51
Brahms: Symphony 1; *Weber:* Euryanthe (exc). (NBC SO/A. Toscanini, D. Rodgers)

790 351
Toscanini conducts Wagner from NBC Studio 8-H, 1948
Wagner: Lohengrin (exc); Tannhäuser (exc); Siegfried (exc); Götterdämmerung (exc); Walküre (exc). (NBC SO/A. Toscanini, H. Keith)

790 353 (12/90)
Toscanini—Carnegie Hall Concert, 15/03/52
Franck: Rédemption (exc); *Sibelius:* En Saga; *Debussy:* Nocturnes (exc); *Rossini:* Guillaume Tell (exc). (NBC SO/A. Toscanini)

Sony Classical

SHV498602
Das Konzert—November 1989
Beethoven: Piano Concerto 1; *Mozart:* Piano Sonata, K330 (exc); *Beethoven:* Symphony 7; *Mozart:* Così fan tutte (exc). (D. Barenboim, D. Barenboim (pf/dir), BPO/D. Barenboim)

SLV45985
Karajan - His Video Legacy. New Year's Concert 1987
J. Strauss II: Zigeunerbaron (exc); Annen-Polka, Op. 117; Fledermaus (exc); Vergnügungszug; Pizzicato Polka; Kaiser, Op. 437; Perpetuum mobile; Unter Donner und Blitz; Frühlingsstimmen, Op. 410; Blauen Donau, Op. 314; *Jos Strauss:* Sphärenklänge; Delirien; Ohne Sorgen; *J. Strauss I:* Beliebte Annen, Op. 137; Radetzky March. (K. Battle, VPO/H. von Karajan, H. Burton)

SLV46383 (4/93) **SHV46383** (4/93)
Salzburg production of Don Giovanni, 1987
Mozart: Don Giovanni (Cpte). (S. Ramey, A. Tomowa-Sintow, J. Varady, K. Battle, G. Winbergh, F. Furlanetto, A. Malta, P. Burchuladze, Vienna St Op Chor, VPO/H. von Karajan, U. Märkle)

SLV46401 **SHV46401**
New Year's Eve Concert 1983
Rossini: Guillaume Tell (exc); *Smetana:* Má Vlast; *Sibelius:* Valse triste; *Jos Strauss:* Delirien; *J. Strauss II:* Zigeunerbaron (exc). (BPO/H. von Karajan, U. Märkle)

SLV46402 **SHV46402**
New Year's Eve Concert 1985
Weber: Freischütz (exc); *Leoncavallo:* Pagliacci (exc); *Puccini:* Manon Lescaut (exc); *Liszt:* Hungarian Rhapsodies, S359 (exc); *Ravel:* Boléro. (BPO/H. von Karajan, H. Burton)

SLV46405 **SHV46405**
Music for Europe
Mozart: Don Giovanni (exc); Ch'io mi scordi di te, K505; Symphony 29; Symphohy 35. (C. Studer, B. Canino, BPO/C. Abbado)

SLV48361 **SHV48361**
A Carnegie Hall Christmas
Traditional: Twelve Days of Christmas; Mary's Boy Child; Gesù bambino; *Mozart:* Exsultate Jubilate, K165 (exc); *Rodgers:* Sound of Music (exc); *Traditional:* Winter Wonderland; We three Kings; I wonder as I wander; Mary had a baby; Who was Mary?; Sister Mary had but one child; Go tell it on the Mountain; Christmas Song; Have yourself a merry little Christmas; Stille Nacht; Joy to the World; *Humperdinck:* Hänsel und Gretel (exc); *M. Praetorius:* Es ist ein Ros'; *Traditional:* Maria Wiegenlied; I saw three ships; First Nowell; Away in a Manger; Deck the hall; Holly and the ivy; Angels we have heard on high; *Adam:* Minuit, Chrétiens (exc). (K. Battle, F. von Stade, W. Marsalis, Chor, St Luke's Orch/A. Previn, Jazz Ens)

SLV48362 **SHV48362**
Concert for the Planet Earth
Gomes: Schiavo (exc); *Serrano:* Trust de los tenorios (exc); *Sorozábal:* Tabernera del puerto (exc); *Meyerbeer:* Africaine (exc); *Bonfa:* Black Orpheus (exc); *Jobim:* Dindi; Eu sei que vou te amar; *Marsalis:* 1, 2, 3, 4; Death of Jazz; Oh, but on the third day; *Paganini:* Violin Concerto 1; *Puccini:* Tosca (exc); *Saint-Saëns:* Samson et Dalila (exc); *Gardel:* Día que me quieras; *Bernstein:* Candide (1982) (exc); *Bizet:* Carmen (exc); *Donizetti:* Favorita (exc); *Mascagni:* Iris (exc); *Barroso Neto:* Aquarela do Brasil. (P. Domingo, D. Graves, S. Chang, Wynton Marsalis Septet, G. Costa, A.C. Jobim, W. Marsalis, Rio de Janeiro Municipal Th Chor, Rio de Janeiro Municipal Th Orch/J. DeMain)

SLV48433 **SHV48433**
Glenn Gould's Greatest Hits
Bach: Goldberg Variations (exc); *Walton:* Façade (exc); *Scriabin:* Pieces, Op.49 (exc); *Bach:* Violin Sonatas, BWV1014-19 (exc); *Mahler:* Symphony 2 (exc); *Beethoven:* Bagatelles (exc); Cello Sonata 3 (exc); *R. Strauss:* Elektra (exc); *Bach:* Wohltemperierte Klavier (exc); *G. Gould:* So You Want to Write a Fugue?. (G. Gould, G. Gould/G. Gould, E. Benson-Guy, M. Forrester, P. Rideout, P. Rideout, G. Wry, E. Murdoch, Y. Menuhin, L. Rose, Canadian Qt, Orch/B. Brott)

SLV53488 **SHV53488**
Dvořák in Prague - A Celebration
Dvořák: Carnival; Romance, Op. 11; Silent woods; Humoresques, Op. 101 (exc); Symphony 9 (exc); Rusalka (exc); Psalm 149; Humoresques, Op. 101 (exc); Gipsy Melodies (exc); Piano Trio 4 (exc); Slavonic Dances (exc); Slavonic Dances (exc). (F. Von Stade, I. Perlman, Y-Y. Ma, R. Firkušný, Prague Phil Chor, Boston SO/S. Ozawa, B. Large)

S2LV46406 (2/94) **SHV46406** (2/94)
Mozart—Le Nozze di Figaro
Mozart: Nozze di Figaro (Cpte). (L. Gallo, M. McLaughlin, R. Raimondi, C. Studer, G. Sima, M. Lilowa, R. Mazzola, H. Zednik, F. Kasemann, I. Gáti, Y. Tannenbergerova, Vienna St Op Chor, Vienna St Op Orch/C. Abbado, J. Miller)

S2LV48312 (8/93) **S2HV48312** (8/93)
Verdi—Don Carlo
Verdi: Don Carlo (Cpte). (J. Carreras, F.I. D'Amico, A. Baltsa, P. Cappuccilli, F. Furlanetto, M. Salminen, F. de Grandis, A. Bandelli, H. Nitsche, V. Horn, Bulgarian Nat Chor, Vienna St Op Chor, Salzburg Chbr Ch, BPO/H. von Karajan, U. Märkle)

S2LV48313 (6/94) **S2HV48313** (6/94)
R. Strauss—Der Rosenkavalier
R. Strauss: Rosenkavalier (Cpte). (A. Tomowa-Sintow, A. Baltsa, K. Moll, J. Perry, G. Hornik, V. Cole, H. Müller-Molinari, H. Zednik, W. Lipp, G. Sima, A. Sramek, K. Rydl, J. van Kesteren, F. Kasemann, K. Terkal, G. Ottenthal, G. de Gyldenfeldt, C. Slania, H. Nitsche, A. Tomaschek, J. Reinprecht, W. Scheider, G. Panzenböck, I. Koblitz, W. Holzherr, W. Zeh, H. Lichtenberger, M. Heigl, Vienna St Op Concert Ch, VPO/H. von Karajan, H. von Karajan)

S2LV48353 (10/93) **SHV48353** (10/93)
Verdi—La Traviata
Verdi: Traviata (Cpte). (T. Fabbricini, R. Alagna, P. Coni, N. Curiel, A. Trevisan, E. Cossutta, O. Mori, E. Capuano, F. Musinu, E. Gavazzi, E. Panariello, S. Sammaritano, La Scala Chor, La Scala Orch/R. Muti)

S2LV48422 (9/93) **SHV48422** (9/93)
Verdi—Falstaff - 1982 Salzburg Festival
Verdi: Falstaff (Cpte). (G. Taddei, R. Panerai, R. Kabaivanska, J. Perry, C. Ludwig, T. Schmidt, P. de Palma, H. Zednik, F. Davià, Salzburg Ballet Sch, Vienna St Op Ballet, Vienna St Op Chor, VPO/H. von Karajan, H. von Karajan)

S6LV48400(2) **S12HV48400(2)**
Glenn Gould Collection (Part 2)
Prokofiev: Visions fugitives (exc); Piano Sonata 7; *Scriabin:* Preludes, Op.33 (exc); Pieces, Op.45 (exc); *Shostakovich:* Piano Quintet, Op.57; *Bach:* Art of Fugue (exc); *Beethoven:* Variations, Op.34; *Hindemith:* Marienleben (exc); *Webern:* Variations, Op.27; *Beethoven:* Cello Sonata 3; *R. Strauss:* Lieder, Op.27 (exc); *Mozart:* Piano Sonata, K333; *R. Strauss:* Burleske; *Schubert:* Symphony 5 (exc); *R. Strauss:* Elektra (exc); Vier letzte lieder (exc); *Schoenberg:* Pierrot lunaire (exc); *Ravel:* La Valse (exc); *Debussy:* Première rapsodie; *R. Strauss:* Violin Sonata (exc); *Beethoven:* Piano Sonata 17; *Scriabin:* Pieces, Op.49 (exc); *R. Strauss:* Lieder, Op.67 (exc); *Bach:* Goldberg Variations (exc); *Casella:* Ricercari, Op.52 (exc); *Bach:* Wohltemperierte Klavier (exc); *Beethoven:* Piano Concerto 5; *Bach:* Wohltemperierte Klavier (exc). (G. Gould, G. Gould, G. Gould/G. Gould, R. Roslak, E. Benson-Guy, L. Marshall, M. Forrester, P. Rideout, P. Rideout, R. Oberlin, G. Wry, E. Murdoch, J. Baker, J. Campbell, Y. Menuhin, O. Shumsky, L. Rose, Canadian Qt, Symphonia Qt, Ottawa SO/T. Mayer, Toronto SO/V. Golschmann/K. Ančerl, Orch/B. Brott/P. Scherman)

Teldec

4509-90212-6 (10/93) **4509-92698-3** (10/93)
Puccini—Tosca
Puccini: Tosca (Cpte). (C. Malfitano, P. Domingo, R. Raimondi, G. Prestia, M. Buffoli, G. Gatti, S. Sammaritano, F. Federici, S. Scatarzi, Rome RAI Chor, Rome RAI Orch/Z. Mehta)

4509-91122-6 (10/93) **4509-91122-3** (10/93)
Wagner—Das Rheingold
Wagner: Rheingold (Cpte). (J. Tomlinson, L. Finnie, G. Clark, H. Pampuch, G. von Kannen, E. Johansson, K. Schreibmayer, B. Brinkmann, B. Svendén, M. Hölle, P. Kang, H. Leidland, A. Küttenbaum, J. Turner, Bayreuth Fest Orch/D. Barenboim, H. Kupfer, H.H. Hohlfeld)

4509-91123-6 (10/93) **4509-91123-3** (10/93)
Wagner—Die Walküre
Wagner: Walküre (Cpte). (P. Elming, N. Secunde, Anne Evans, J. Tomlinson, L. Finnie, M. Hölle, E. Johansson, E-M. Bundschuh, R. Floeren, S. Close, H. Dijkstra, B. Svendén, H. Katagiri, Bayreuth Fest Orch/D. Barenboim, H. Kupfer, H.H. Hohlfeld)

4509-92051-6 **4509-92051-3** (6/94)
Glinka—A Life for the Tsar
Glinka: Life for the Tsar (Cpte). (E. Nesterenko, M. Mescheriakova, A. Lomonosov, E. Zaremba, B. Bezhko, Bolshoi Th Chor, Bolshoi SO/A. Lazarev, N. Kuznetsov)

4509-92052-6 **4509-92052-3** (8/94)
Rimsky-Korsakov—Mlada
Rimsky-Korsakov: Mlada (Cpte). (N. Ananiashvili, O. Kulko, M. Gavrilova, G. Nikolsky, G. Borisova, M. Maslov, L. Nam, O. Velichko, V. Kudriashov, T. Pechuria, Y. Statnik, K. Nikitin, Y. Malkhassiants, Bolshoi Ballet, Bolshoi Th Chor, Bolshoi SO/A. Lazarev, B. Pokrovsky)

4509-92170-6 **4509-92170-3**
Rossini—L'occasione fa il ladro
Rossini: Occasione fa il ladro (Cpte). (S. Patterson, N. de Carolis, R. Gambill, M. Bacelli, A. Corbelli, S. Kale, Stuttgart RSO/G. Gelmetti)

4509-94191-6
Tchaikovsky—The Maid of Orleans
Tchaikovsky: Maid of Orleans (Cpte). (N. Rautio, O. Kulko, M. Gavrilova, M. Krutikov, V. Redkin, G. Nikolsky, A. Mishenkin, M. Mikhailov, A. Babikin, Z. Smolyaninova, Bolshoi Th Chor, Bolshoi SO/A. Lazarev, B. Pokrovsky)

4509-94193-6 **4509-94193-3**
Wagner—Siegfried
Wagner: Siegfried (Cpte). (S. Jerusalem, J. Tomlinson, Anne Evans, G. Clark, G. von Kannen, B. Svendén, P. Kang, H. Leidland, Bayreuth Fest Orch/D. Barenboim, H. Kupfer)

4509-95038-6 (4/95) **4509-95038-3** (4/95)
The Art of Conducting—Great Conductors of the Past
Beethoven: Symphony 5 (exc); Symphony 5 (exc); Symphony 5 (exc); Symphony 5 (exc); *Shostakovich:* Symphony 5 (exc); *Bruckner:* Symphony 7 (exc); *Gounod:* Faust (exc); *R. Strauss:* Till Eulenspiegel; *Weber:* Freischütz (exc); *Wagner:* Tannhäuser (exc); *Mozart:* Symphony 40; *Brahms:* Symphony 2; *Beethoven:* Egmont (exc); Symphony 9; *Wagner:* Meistersinger (exc); *Schubert:* Symphony 8; *Brahms:* Symphony 4; *Verdi:* Forza del destino (exc); Traviata (exc); *Respighi:* Pines of Rome; *Purcell:* Dido (exc); *Tchaikovsky:* Symphony 5; *Bach:* Toccata and Fugue, BWV565; *Beethoven:* Egmont (exc); *Tchaikovsky:* Violin Concerto; *Beethoven:* Symphony 7; *Brahms:* Academic Festival Overture; *Beethoven:* Symphony 5; Symphony 5; *Debussy:* La Mer; *Shostakovich:* Symphony 5; *Mahler:* Symphony 4; *Beethoven:* Symphony 9. (/A. Toscanini, NBC SO/H. von Karajan, BPO/O. Klemperer, Stuttgart PO/G. Szell, Chicago SO/L. Bernstein, LSO/J. Barbirolli, Hallé/T. Beecham, RPO/R. Strauss, VPO/F. Weingartner, Paris SO/F. Busch, Staatskapelle Dresden/B. Walter, Vancouver Fest Orch, Philh, New Philh/L. Stokowski, BBC SO, NYPO/S. Koussevitzky, Boston SO/F. Reiner, Cleveland Orch/W. Furtwängler, J. Heifetz)

4509-96080-6 **4509-96080-3**
Carreras—A Tribute to Mario Lanza
Rodgers: Spring is Here (exc); *Brodszky:* Because you're

mine (exc); Student Prince (exc); Toast of New Orleans (exc); *Tosti:* Ultima canzone; Pour un baiser; Marechiare; *Califona:* Vieni sul mar'; *Mascagni:* Cavalleria rusticana (exc); *Gastaldon:* Musica proibita; *Donizetti:* Elisir d'amore (exc); *C. Palmer:* Mario Lanza Medley; *Romberg:* Student Prince (exc); *Cardillo:* Core 'ngrato; *De Curtis:* Tu, ca nun chiagne!; Torna a surriento; *Lara:* Granada; *Hardelot:* Because; *Schubert:* Ave Maria, D839. (J. Carreras, English Concert Chor, BBC Concert Orch/E. Ricci, D. Lowney, M. Lanza, orch)

4509-97869-3
The Last Night of the Proms 1994
Bach: Toccata and Fugue, BWV565; *Walton:* Belshazzar's Feast; *Kabalevsky:* Colas Breugnon (exc); *Creston:* Marimba concertino, Op. 21 (exc); *Miki:* Marimba spiritual; *Massenet:* Thaïs (exc); *Grainger:* Handel in the Strand; *Elgar:* Pomp and Circumstance Marches (exc); *Henry Wood:* Sea-Song Fantasia; *Arne:* Rule Britannia; *Parry:* Jerusalem. (B. Terfel, E. Glennie, BBC Sngrs, BBC Sym Chor, BBC SO/A. Davis, B. Large)

9031-71478-6 (3/92) **9031-71478-3** (3/92)
Teatro Comunale di Bologna production, December 1989
Verdi: Giovanna d'Arco (Cpte). (S. Dunn, V. La Scola, R. Bruson, P. Lefebre, P. Spagnoli, Parma Teatro Regio Chor, Bologna Teatro Comunale Chor, Bologna Teatro Comunale Orch/R. Chailly, W. Herzog)

9031-71482-6 (11/91) **9031-71482-3** (11/91)
Schwetzingen Festival production of Il Signor Bruschino
Rossini: Signor Bruschino (Cpte). (A. Corbelli, A. Rinaldi, A. Felle, D. Kuebler, C. Feller, J. Hall, V. Gobbi, O. di Credico, Stuttgart RSO/G. Gelmetti, M. Hampe)

9031-71486-6 (11/91) **9031-71486-3** (11/91)
Savolinna Opera Festival, Finland, July 1989
Wagner: Fliegende Holländer (Cpte). (F. Grundheber, H. Behrens, M. Salminen, R. Sirkiä, A. Välkki, J. Silvasti, Savonlinna Op Fest Chor, Savonlinna Op Fest Orch/L. Segerstam, I. Bäckmann)

9031-72674-3
The Winners' Gala Concert, International Tchaikovsky Comp. 1990
Tchaikovsky: Violin Concerto; Queen of Spades (exc); *Foster:* Beautiful Dreamer; *Tchaikovsky:* Rococo Variations; Queen of Spades (exc); *Leoncavallo:* Mattinata; *Tchaikovsky:* Piano Concerto 1. (A. Suwanai, D. Voigt, G. Rivinius, H. Choi, B. Berezovsky, Moscow PO/D. Kitaienko, A. Maslennikow)

9031-73827-6 (7/92) **9031-73827-3** (7/92)
Berlin deutsche Oper production of Salome
R. Strauss: Salome (Cpte). (C. Malfitano, S. Estes, H. Hiestermann, Leonie Rysanek, C. Bieber, C. Capasso, F. Molsberger, R. Lukas, W. Murray, B. Rundgren, K. Lang, A.E. Willis, Berlin Deutsche Op Orch/G. Sinopoli, P. Weigl, B. Large)

9031-73828-6 **9031-73828-3**
Rossini—La Scala di Seta
Rossini: Scala di seta (Cpte). (A. Corbelli, L. Serra, D. Kuebler, A. Rinaldi, J. Bunnell, D. Griffith, Stuttgart RSO/G. Gelmetti, M. Hampe)

9031-76372-6 **9031-76372-3**
Tchaikovsky —Women and Fate
Tchaikovsky: Storm (exc); Romeo and Juliet (exc); *Mozart:* Don Giovanni (exc); *Tchaikovsky:* Eugene Onegin (exc); Francesca da Rimini (exc); Liturgy (exc); Symphony 4 (exc); Symphony 5 (exc); Symphony 6 (exc); Manfred Symphony (exc); Piano Trio, Op. 50 (exc); Songs, Op. 73. (C. Bartha, H. Field, M. Silver, Swedish RSO/Vladimir Ashkenazy, P. Zukerman, J. Du Pré, D. Barenboim, Vladimir Ashkenazy, C. Nupen)

9031-77676-6 **9031-77676-3**
My World of Opera - Kiri Te Kanawa
R. Strauss: Rosenkavalier (exc); *Offenbach:* Contes d'Hoffmann (exc); *Verdi:* Ernani (exc); Nabucco (exc); Otello (exc); *Rossini:* Cenerentola (exc); *Gluck:* Orfeo ed Euridice (exc); *Giordano:* Andrea Chénier (exc); *Verdi:* Don Carlo (exc); *Puccini:* Bohème (exc); *J. Strauss II:* Fledermaus (exc). (K. Te Kanawa, A. Howells, B. Bonney, ROHO/G. Solti, P. Domingo/G. Prêtre, M. Freni, La Scala Orch/R. Muti, La Scala Chor, V. Atlantov, Verona Arena Orch/Z. Peskó, K. Kuhlmann, L. Dale, M. Taddei, L. Zannini, C. Desderi, R. Kennedy, A. Rinaldi, Glyndebourne Fest Orch/D. Renzetti, J. Baker/R. Leppard, J. Carreras/R. Chailly, R. Lloyd/B. Haitink, N. Shicoff, T. Allen, G. Howell, J. Rawnsley/L. Gardelli/P. Domingo, J. Meinrad, I. Cotrubas, K. Cheetham)

Video Artists International

VAI69079
Verdi—La Traviata
Verdi: Traviata (Cpte). (B. Sills, H. Price, R. Fredericks, F. Rakusin, E. Petros, N. Rosenshein, R. Orth, K. Kibler, R. Lucas, Wolf Trap Comp Chor, Filene Center Orch/J. Rudel, K. Browning)

VAI69100
Renata Tebaldi and Franco Corelli
Puccini: Madama Butterfly (exc); Bohème (exc); Tosca (exc); Turandot (exc); *Mascagni:* Cavalleria Rusticana (exc); *Wolf-Ferrari:* Gioielli della Madonna (exc); *Annibale:* 'O paese d' 'o sole; *Di Capua:* I' te vurria vasà. (R. Tebaldi, F. Corelli, orch/W. Pelletier)

VAI69101
Jussi Björling in Opera and Song Vol 1
Herbert: Princess Pat (exc); *Beach:* Browning Songs, Op.44 (exc); *Puccini:* Gianni Schicchi (exc); *Gounod:* Faust (exc); *Puccini:* Bohème (exc); *R. Strauss:* Lieder, Op. 17 (exc); *Leoncavallo:* Pagliacci (exc); *Brahms:* Hungarian Dances (exc); *Krenzer:* Prayer of Thanksgiving. (J. Björling, A-L. Björling, orch/H. Barlow)

VAI69102
Eleanor Steber in Opera and Song Vol 1
Rodgers: Oklahoma! (exc); *G. Charpentier:* Louise (exc); *Herbert:* Naughty Marietta (exc); *Speaks:* Morning; *Herbert:* Orange Blossoms (exc); *Weill:* Knickerbocker Holiday (exc); *Mozart:* Nozze di Figaro (exc); *N. Brown:* Kissing Bandit (exc); *Herbert:* Sweethearts (exc); *Verdi:* Forza del Destino (exc); *Geehl:* For you alone; *Porter:* Kiss Me, Kate (exc). (E. Steber, orch/H. Barlow)

VAI69103
Bidú Sayão in Opera and Song
Hahn: Si mes vers; *M. Sandoval:* They all dance the samba; *Massenet:* Manon (exc); *Bayly:* Long, long ago; *Padilla:* Violetera; Relicario; *Puccini:* Madama Butterfly (exc); Gianni Schicchi (exc); *M. Sandoval:* Slave Market; *Coward:* Conversation Piece (exc); *Wolf-Ferrari:* Gioielli della Madonna (exc); *Arditi:* Bacio. (B. Sayão, Orch/H. Barlow)

VAI69105
Leonard Warren in Opera and Song
E. Ball: Little bit of Heaven; *Tchaikovsky:* Songs, Op. 6 (exc); *Anon:* A Rovin'; *Bizet:* Carmen (exc); *Gounod:* Faust (exc); *Drake:* I believe; *Smetana:* Bartered Bride (exc); *Friml:* Three Musketeers (exc); *Sanderson:* Until; *Verdi:* Ballo in Maschera (exc); *Traditional:* Blow the man down; *Speaks:* On the road to Mandalay. (L. Warren, Orch/H. Barlow)

VAI69106
Risë Stevens in Opera and Song
Rodgers: Boys from Syracuse (exc); *Bizet:* Carmen (exc); *Friml:* Amour Toujours; *Schumann:* Myrthen, Op. 25 (exc); *Rodgers:* State Fair (exc); *Berlin:* Annie get your Gun (exc); *Kern:* Roberta (exc); *Bizet:* Carmen (exc); *Schubert:* Ave Maria, D839; *Lecuona:* Siboney. (R. Stevens, Orch/H. Barlow)

VAI69107
Lauritz Melchior in Opera and Song
Speaks: Morning; *R. Strauss:* Lieder, Op. 10 (exc); *Wagner:* Walküre (exc); Meistersinger (exc); *Tchaikovsky:* Songs, Op. 6 (exc); *Dvořák:* Slavonic Dances (exc); *Anon:* Vive l'Amour; *Hardelot:* Because; *Rodgers:* South Pacific (exc); *Geehl:* For you alone; *Wagner:* Fliegende Holländer (exc). (L. Melchior, Orch/H. Barlow)

VAI69108
Presenting Joan Sutherland
Arne: Artaxerxes (exc); *Rossini:* Semiramide (exc); *Donizetti:* Favorita (exc); *Puccini:* Bohème (exc); *Meyerbeer:* Huguenots (exc). (J. Sutherland, Orch/R. Bonynge)

VAI69109
Richard Tucker in Opera and Song
Moyer: Song of Songs; *Verdi:* Aida (exc); *Herbert:* Princess Pat (exc); *Romberg:* Student Prince (exc); *Luders:* Prince of Pilsen (exc); *Bizet:* Carmen (exc); *S. Ward:* America the Beautiful; *V. Young:* Around the World (exc); *Leoncavallo:* Pagliacci (exc); *Verdi:* Rigoletto (exc). (R. Tucker, Orch/H. Barlow/E. Buckley)

VAI69110
Leonard Warren in Opera and Song Vol 2
Speaks: On the road to Mandalay; *Puccini:* Tosca (exc); *Huhn:* Invictus; *O. Straus:* Tapfere Soldat (exc); *Rossini:* Barbiere di Siviglia (exc); *Wagner:* Tannhäuser; *Romberg:* Maytime (exc). (L. Warren, E. Steber, Orch/H. Barlow)

VAI69111
Jussi Björling in Opera and Song Vol 2
Krenzer: Prayer of Thanksgiving; *Schubert:* An Silvia, D891; *Glazunov:* Seasons (exc); *Bizet:* Carmen (exc); *Leoncavallo:* Mattinata; *Herbert:* Princess Pat (exc). (J. Björling, Chor, Orch/H. Barlow)

VAI69112
Eleanor Steber in Opera and Song Vol 2
F. Loesser: Where's Charley? (exc); *Verdi:* Ernani (exc); *O. Straus:* Tapfere Soldat (exc); *Gershwin:* Porgy and Bess (exc); *Puccini:* Madama Butterfly (exc); *Seitz:* World is waiting; *J. Strauss II:* Fledermaus (exc); *Verdi:* Rigoletto (exc); *Gounod:* Faust (exc); *Donizetti:* Lucia di Lammermoor (exc); *J.A. Bland:* Carry me back. (E. Steber, B. Sullivan, J. Hines, R. Rounseville, R. Stevens, T.L. Thomas, Orch/Anon)

VAI69114
Anna Moffo in Opera and Song
Puccini: Madama Butterfly (exc); Bohème (exc); *Gounod:* Faust (exc); *Rodgers:* South Pacific (exc); State Fair (exc); Sound of Music (exc); *Leoncavallo:* Pagliacci (exc); *N. Brown:* Kissing Bandit (exc). (A. Moffo, R. Merrill, Orch/H. Barlow/G. Osser/A. Fiedler)

VAI69116
Robert Merrill in Opera and Song
Weill: Knickerbocker Holiday (exc); *Bizet:* Carmen (exc); *Lehár:* Land des Lächelns (exc); *Rossini:* Barbiere di Siviglia (exc); *Leoncavallo:* Mattinata; *De Curtis:* Torna a Surriento; *Jurmann:* Cosi Cosà; *Speaks:* Sylvia; *Leoncavallo:* Pagliacci (exc); *Anon:* A rovin'; *A. Thomas:* Hamlet (exc); *Warren:* Dames (exc); *F. Loewe:* My Fair Lady (exc); *Verdi:* Trovatore (exc); *Herbert:* Red Mill (exc). (R. Merrill, Orch/H. Barlow)

VAI69117
Jan Peerce in Opera and Song
Herbert: Eileen (exc); *Bristol:* Laughter; *Leoncavallo:* Pagliacci (exc); *Rodgers:* South Pacific (exc); *Tchaikovsky:* Nutcracker Suite (exc); *Rossini:* Soirées musicales (exc). (J. Peerce, Orch/H. Barlow)

VAI69216
Puccini—Tosca
Puccini: Tosca (Cpte). (R. Tebaldi, E. Tobin, G. London, G. Grefe, H. Buchta, H. Cramer, S. Fischer-Sandt, W. Baur, C. Hellmann, Stuttgart Op Chor, Stuttgart Op Orch/F. Patanè)

Vision Video

VVD1138
Bellini—Norma
Bellini: Norma (Cpte). (J. Sutherland, M. Elkins, R. Stevens, C. Grant, T. Brown, E. Piha, Australian Op Chor, Sydney Eliz Orch/R. Bonynge, S. Sequi)

Wienerworld Classic

WNR2037
Desert Island Discs
Coates: By the Sleepy Lagoon; *Mozart:* Nozze di Figaro (exc); *Beethoven:* Symphony 6 (exc); *Tchaikovsky:* Swan Lake (exc); *Debussy:* Suite Bergamasque (exc); *Gounod:* Ave Maria; *Elgar:* Enigma Variations (exc); *Beethoven:* Symphony 9 (exc); *Vaughan Williams:* Greensleeves Fantasia; *Schubert:* String Quintet (exc); *Rachmaninov:* Paganini Rhapsody; *Bach:* 2-Violin Concerto (exc); *Handel:* Messiah (exc); *Elgar:* Pomp and Circumstance Marches (exc). (East England Orch/M. Nabarro, ASMF/N. Marriner, LSO/P. Monteux, Z. Kocsis, J. Carreras, Vienna SO/U.C. Harrer, RPO/Y. Menuhin, Leipzig Gewandhaus/K. Masur, Boston Pops/J.T. Williams, Guarneri Qt, B. Greenhouse, R. Orozco/E. de Waart, H. Szeryng, M. Hasson, LSC/Colin Davis/A. Previn)